The Library of Congress
Main Reading Room
Reference Collection
Subject Catalog

Compiled by Katherine Ann Gardner

Produced through the cooperation
of the MARC Development Office,
Processing Department,
and the General Reference and Bibliography Division,
Reference Department

Library of Congress   Washington   1975

Library of Congress Cataloging in Publication Data

United States.   Library of Congress.
  The Library of Congress Main Reading Room reference collection subject catalog.

  1. Reference books—Bibliography—Catalogs. 2. United States. Library of Congress. I. Gardner, Katherine Ann. II. Title.
Z1035.1.U526 1975   011'.02   75–619174
ISBN 0–8444–0167–6

For sale by the Superintendent of Documents, U.S. Government Printing Office
Washington, D.C. 20402 - Price $13
Stock Number 030–001–00067–2

Introduction

The collection of reference books available to users of the Main Reading Room of the Library of Congress contains about 14,000 titles, primarily in the humanities, social sciences, and bibliography. Of these more than 900 were published by the Library of Congress. Subject areas covered by the Library's specialized reading rooms, such as science and technology, music, law, Slavic studies, Oriental studies, American local history, and genealogy, are represented but not emphasized. Although some national bibliographies are available in the Main Reading Room, there are more extensive collections in the Descriptive and Shared Cataloging Divisions.

This catalog contains entries for approximately 11,000 monographs and 3,000 serials. Virtually all of the titles in the Main Reading Room on January 1, 1975, are included. In general, entries consist of author, short title, edition, place of publication, publisher, date of publication or beginning date for serials, paging, price, Dewey decimal number, card number, call number, and Main Reading Room location. The price is included only if it appears on the printed card; it is printed in brackets because some of the figures are given without currency symbols. Some Dewey numbers have slashes instead of primes.

The reference collection catalog project began in September 1967 as a joint effort of the General Reference and Bibliography Division and the Information Systems Office. There was then no catalog of the Main Reading Room reference collection. At the outset more than 6,000 volumes were weeded from the collection, and printed catalog cards were ordered from the Card Division for the remaining titles. In 1970 the Information Systems Office's share of the responsibility for the project was transferred to the MARC Development Office in the Processing Department. The latter was particularly interested because of the opportunities offered for conversion to machine-readable form of records for noncurrent monographs and serials.

Editing of the monographic titles not already in the MARC data base began in January 1970. The worksheet for each title was checked against the Library's Official Catalog, and all changes were noted. In the fall of 1971 the MARC serials staff started work on the Main Reading Room serials. Each serial piece was compared with its printed card. If there were changes in the entry or title, the item was forwarded to the Cataloging Section of the Serial Record Division for recataloging. If changes were found in the place of publication or frequency, the information was either updated or amalgamated with the existing printed card data. Thus, bibliographic data for some of the serials in this catalog differ from that found on the Library's printed cards. Over 900 serials were weeded from the reference collection.

Although several earlier Main Reading Room computer printouts are in use at the Library of Congress, this is the first catalog to be published for outside distribution. The Library plans to follow this subject catalog with a classified catalog arranged by call number.

Titles are entered alphabetically by subject heading and then by main entry. The subject headings are arranged word by word. A simple heading precedes its subdivisions or the same heading followed by qualifications or extensions of any kind. When the same word is used as the surname of a person, a place name, and the name of a thing, the subject entries are arranged in that order.

SCOPE

BACKGROUND

FILING ARRANGEMENT

WASHINGTON, GEORGE, PRES. U.S.
WASHINGTON, D.C.
WASHINGTON MONUMENT, WASHINGTON, D.C.
Subdivisions employing dashes are arranged in the following order:
   Chronological subdivisions arranged by date
   Form and topical subdivisions arranged alphabetically
   Geographical subdivisions arranged alphabetically
    EDUCATION, HIGHER
    EDUCATION, HIGHER—1965–
    EDUCATION, HIGHER—BIBLIOGRAPHY
    EDUCATION, HIGHER—HISTORY
    EDUCATION, HIGHER—UNITED STATES
    EDUCATION, HIGHER—UNITED STATES—DIRECTORIES
The various types of subject headings (each of which may have subdivisions) are
arranged in the following order:
   Direct entry subject headings
   Inverted headings
   Headings followed by qualifiers in parentheses
   Phrase headings
    COOKERY
    COOKERY—DICTIONARIES
    COOKERY—HISTORY
    COOKERY, AMERICAN
    COOKERY, FRENCH
    COOKERY (CHEESE)
    COOKERY (HERBS)
    COOKERY FOR THE SICK

    UNITED STATES
    UNITED STATES—BIBLIOGRAPHY
    UNITED STATES—HISTORY
    UNITED STATES—HISTORY—REVOLUTION, 1775–1783
    UNITED STATES—HISTORY—CIVIL WAR, 1861–1865
    UNITED STATES—HISTORY—1865–
    UNITED STATES—HISTORY—BIBLIOGRAPHY
    UNITED STATES—HISTORY—SOURCES
    UNITED STATES—HISTORY, LOCAL
    UNITED STATES—HISTORY, NAVAL
Geographic areas as subject precede subject entries for government agencies and
other corporate bodies, buildings, and uniform titles entered under place names.
    UNITED STATES
    UNITED STATES—HISTORY
    UNITED STATES—STATISTICS
    UNITED STATES. AIR FORCE
    UNITED STATES. CONGRESS
    UNITED STATES. CONSTITUTION
    UNITED STATES. DEPT. OF STATE
    UNITED STATES. TREATIES, ETC.

    WASHINGTON, D.C.—HISTORY
    WASHINGTON, D.C.—SOCIAL LIFE AND CUSTOMS
    WASHINGTON, D.C. CAPITOL
    WASHINGTON, D.C. WHITE HOUSE
Abbreviations, for example, "St." for *Saint,* are filed as abbreviated.
There are some unavoidable discrepancies in the arrangement of some headings

for serials which begin with the word THE. A few subject headings are alphabetized under THE, and occasionally THE WEST appears out of order in the geographic breakdown under a topical subject heading.

Subject headings continued from one page to the next are abridged to one line.

All of the subject headings appearing on the main entry card in the Library's Official Catalog are included in this catalog. Additional subject headings were supplied by General Reference and Bibliography Division staff to ensure that similar reference works would be listed together. Many titles in the Main Reading Room were cataloged years ago, and different headings would probably be assigned today. Also, the practice of assigning the most specific subject heading often means that reference works used in searching for the same bit of information may be listed under different subject headings. In other words, the subject control over a reference collection of 14,000 titles should and can be more precise than subject control over an enormous general collection of 16,000,000 volumes. Since the added subject headings also serve as a substitute for annotations, they may refer to special features such as appendixes or emphasize statistical and biographical information. Most of the headings added are established Library of Congress subject headings. Topical and geographic headings were added; for technical reasons, personal names or corporate bodies as subjects could not be added.

A few subject headings were invented, such as BOOKS IN PRINT, COMPANIES (used for directories giving more information than the address), DOCUMENT SOURCES (used for collections of historical documents), and GUIDES TO THE LITERATURE.

A special effort was made to add certain subject headings whenever appropriate. Among these were: ABBREVIATIONS; ACRONYMS; ASSOCIATIONS, INSTITUTIONS, ETC.; ATLASES; AUTHORS; BOOKS—REVIEWS—INDEXES; CHRONOLOGY, HISTORICAL; DRAMA—INDEXES; PERIODICALS—BIBLIOGRAPHY; PERIODICALS—DIRECTORIES; POETRY—INDEXES (used for concordances to the poems of individual poets), and QUOTATIONS.

Bilingual and polyglot dictionaries in special fields were given additional language headings such as FRENCH LANGUAGE—DICTIONARIES—ENGLISH. Bibliographies and indexes to government documents were given subject headings such as UNITED STATES—GOVERNMENT PUBLICATIONS—BIBLIOGRAPHY. Such headings are not usually assigned by the Subject Cataloging Division if the bibliography or index covers the publications of a single agency. The heading PERIODICALS—INDEXES was added to all periodical indexes and to bibliographies containing substantial numbers of periodical references. Statistical reference works were given additional subject headings under appropriate geographic areas such as GREAT BRITAIN—STATISTICS. Guides to hotels, restaurants, shopping, and museums were given headings such as SCOTLAND—DESCRIPTION AND TRAVEL—GUIDE-BOOKS. Subject headings such as UNITED STATES—BIOGRAPHY—DICTIONARIES were added to biographical works listing the members of a profession. Bibliographies useful in identifying the imprints of particular countries were given headings such as UNITED STATES—IMPRINTS.

For technical reasons the cross-references in this catalog were selected from those appearing in *Films and Other Materials for Projection*. Because the Main Reading Room catalog contains many subject headings which have not appeared in the film catalog, the cross-reference structure is quite incomplete. Users of this catalog should consult *Library of Congress Subject Headings* to locate all pertinent subject headings.

IDIOSYNCRASIES   A few peculiarities of this catalog should be explained. To save space, only the short title is printed. Whatever mark of punctuation appears at the end of the short title on the printed card appears in the subject catalog. The short title may end with a comma, a semicolon, a colon, or no punctuation. Since authors' birth and death dates are omitted, the author statement sometimes ends with a comma.

The abbreviation "mrr" before a card number means that there is no printed card for the work. Many of these titles are in the Loeb Classical Library series. Often the Library of Congress cataloged a slightly different edition, and cards were never printed for the edition in the Main Reading Room.

The symbols MRR Alc, MRR Ref Desk, MRR Biog, MRR Circ, and MRR Alc (Dk 33) indicate specific locations or collections of reference books in the Main Reading Room. For most of the collection, the symbol MRR Alc (Alcove) is used; MRR Ref Desk (Reference Desk) identifies the area where the reference librarians are located. A collection of biographical reference books is referred to by MRR Biog; MRR Circ (Circle) indicates the shelves near the issue or circulation desk in the center of the reading room. Deck 33 is a stack area adjacent to the reading room where various large library catalogs and congressional publications are kept.

Occasionally there is a blank line between the card number and the call number. The computer program calls for two blank spaces after the card number. Whenever there is not room for two blank spaces in the same line, a blank line results since the call number always begins a new line.

Although no attempt was made to indicate actual holdings of serials, a retention policy statement is included. "Latest edition" indicates that the Main Reading Room keeps only the latest edition received; superseded editions are returned to the general collections. "Latest edition*" means that the reading room should have the next-to-latest edition. "Partial set" indicates that the reading room has either the latest years of a serial or very incomplete holdings. "Full set" means that the reading room has all or almost all of the volumes.

ACKNOWLEDGMENTS   Special appreciation is due to the MARC Development Office for putting the Main Reading Room titles in machine-readable form, maintaining the data bases, and utilizing the programs to sort and print the catalog. The Library's serial descriptive catalogers spent many hours recataloging Main Reading Room serials. The Cataloging Distribution Service Division (formerly the Card Division) supplied thousands of printed cards. The Copyright Office and the Order Division sent out numerous inquiries to see if serials were still being published. Staff members from the Public Reference Section and several other sections of the General Reference and Bibliography Division assisted with the worksheets for monographs. Particular gratitude is owed to the Main Reading Room reference librarians who endured years of short-staffing while the compiler worked on the catalog project.

CONCLUSION   The Library hopes that this catalog will be a useful tool, especially for reference librarians. Any suggestions for improvement should be sent to the compiler in care of the General Reference and Bibliography Division, Reference Department, Library of Congress, Washington, D.C. 20540.

KATHERINE ANN GARDNER

AALBORG, DENMARK--DIRECTORIES.
Aalborg vejviser. Aalborg [Denmark]
W. Burmesters bogtrykkeri. 74-642174

DL291.A2 V4 MRR Alc Latest edition

ABBOTS
Beda Venerabilis, Baedae Opera
historica. London, W. Heinemann
ltd.; New York, G. P. Putnam's sons,
1930. 2 v.   274.2 31-26352
PA6156.B4 1930 MRR Alc.

ABBREVIATIONS.
see also Acronyms

see also Signs and symbols

Atlantic Refining Company.
Dictionary of abbreviations peculiar
to the oil industry. [Dallas, 1963]
62 p.   63-5675
TN865 .A75 1963 MRR Alc.

Bartholomew, Curtis Alford,
Epithetology. 1st ed. Red Bank,
N.J., Printed and distributed by the
Commercial Press [1948] 207 p.
378.2 48-2130
LB2381 .B28 MRR Alc.

Baudry, Hubert. "D.A.", dictionnaire
d'abreviations françaises et
étrangères. La Chapelle-Montligeon
(Orne) Éditions de Montligeon, 1951.
157 p.   53-24921
PC2693 .B3 MRR Alc.

Broderick, Robert C., Catholic
concise dictionary. Chicago,
Franciscan Herald Press [1966] xi,
330 p.   282.03 66-14726
BX841 .B7 1966 MRR Alc.

Business terms, phrases and
abbreviations. 13th ed.; London,
Pitman, 1966. [5], 232 p. [12/6]
650.03 67-72958
HF1002 .B9 1966 MRR Alc.

Buttress, F. A. World list of
abbreviations. 3rd ed. London,
Hill, 1966. vi, 186 p. [35/-]
060.148 66-71807
AS8 .B8 1966 MRR Alc.

Cassell's dictionary of
abbreviations. London, Cassell,
1966. vii, 220 p. [18/-]   423.1
66-77287
PE1693 .C3 MRR Alc.

A Catholic dictionary 3d ed. New
York, Macmillan, 1958. vii, 552 p.
282.03 58-5797
BX841 .C35 1958 MRR Alc.

Cherney, Richard A. Appraisal and
assessment dictionary. Englewood
Cliffs, N.J., Prentice-Hall [1960]
vii, 337 p.   333.332 60-11976
HD1387 .C45 MRR Alc.

Collins, Frederick Howard, Authors'
and printers' dictionary; 10th ed.,
rev. London, New York, Oxford
University Press, 1956. xiv, 442 p.
655.25 56-58185
Z254 .C76 1956 MRR Alc.

Dictionary of architectural
abbreviations, signs, and symbols.
New York, Odyssey Press [c1965]
xvii, 595 p.   720.3 65-18847
NA31 .D53 MRR Alc.

Dictionary of industrial engineering
abbreviations: New York, Odyssey
Press [1967] xviii, 898 p.
658.5/001/48 65-19183
T58 .D5 MRR Alc.

Dictionary of mechanical engineering
abbreviations: New York, Odyssey
Press [1967] xviii, 725 p.
621/.01/48 65-18844
TJ9 .D5 MRR Alc.

Dictionary of report series codes,
2d ed. New York, Special Libraries
Association, 1973. vi, 645 p.
029.9/6 72-87401
Z6945.A2 D5 1973 MRR Alc.

Dizionario Garzanti italiano-inglese,
inglese-italiano. Edizione minore,
Milano, Garzanti, 1968. 1067 p. [L
1900] 68-133578
PC1640 .D5 1968 MRR Alc.

Gale Research Company. Acronyms and
initialisms dictionary; 4th ed.
Detroit [1973] xv, 635 p.   423/.1
73-568
P365 .G3 1973 MRR Ref Desk.

Global Engineering Documentation
Services. Directory of engineering
document sources. Newport Beach,
Calif., Global Engineering
Documentation Services [1972] 1 v.
(unpaged) [$29.95]   029.9/62 72-
176333
Z5852 .G5 MRR Alc.

Greiser, Josef. Lexikon der
Abkürzungen; 2. Aufl. erganzt und
erweitert nach dem neuen Stande vom
1. Januar 1955. Oensbrück, A. Fromm
[1955] 271 p.   55-23756
PF3693 .G7 1955 MRR Alc.

International catalogue of scientific
literature. List of journals.
London, Harrison and sons; [etc.,
etc.] 1903. 2 p. l., v-xv, 312 p.
03-19593
Z7403 .I61 MRR Alc.

Jacobs, Horace. Missile and space
projects guide New York, Plenum
Press, 1962. x, 235 p.   629.403 62-
13473
TL788 .J3 MRR Alc.

Kettridge, Julius Ornan. French-
English and English-French dictionary
of commercial & financial terms,
phrases, & practice; London,
Routledge & Paul, 1957. xi, 647 p.
650.3 59-21494
HG151 .K42 1957 MRR Alc.

The Maryknoll Catholic dictionary.
[1st American ed. Wilkes-Barre, Pa.]
Dimension Books [1965] xvii, 710 p.
282.03 65-15436
BX841 .M36 1965 MRR Alc.

Medical abbreviations; 2d ed. [Ann
Arbor, Michigan Occupational Therapy
Association] 1967. vii, 165 p.
610/.1/48 67-66290
R121 .M49 1967 MRR Alc.

Moser, Reta C. Space-age acronyms;
2d ed., rev. and enl. New York,
IFI/Plenum, 1969. 534 p.
629.4/01/48 69-14416
TL788 .M6 1969 MRR Alc.

Paxton, John. Dictionary of
abbreviations. Totowa, N.J., Rowman
and Littlefield [1974] xiii, 384 p.
413 73-5881
P365 .P3 1974 MRR Ref Desk.

Shankle, George Earlie. Current
abbreviations New York, The H. W.
Wilson company, 1945. 207 p.   421.8
45-1051
PE1693 .S5 MRR Alc.

Spillner, Paul. World guide to
abbreviations. 2d ed. New York,
Bowker, 1970- v.   413 75-19811

P365 .S6 MRR Ref Desk.

Stufflebeam, George Teele, ed. The
traffic dictionary; 4th ed., enl.
and rev. New York, Simmons-Boardman
[1950] 292 p.   380.3 50-8273
HE141 .S8 1950 MRR Alc.

Symbols of American libraries. [1st]-
ed.; 1932- Washington, Library of
Congress. 018/.1 33-13797
Z663.79 .S9 MRR Alc MRR Alc
  Partial set

Tramonti, Nino. Dizionario delle
sigle e delle abbreviazioni. Busto
Arsizio, 1957. 330 p.   a 58-5061
Z52 .T68 MRR Alc.

Ulving, Tor. Periodica philologica
abbreviata; Stockholm, Almqvist &
Wiksell [1963] 137 p.   64-11932
Z6945.A2 U5513 MRR Alc.

United States. Joint Publications
Research Service. Abbreviations in
the African press. New York, CCM
Information Corp., 1972. ix, 108 p.
079.6/01/48 72-93345
P365 .U5 MRR Alc.

United States. Joint Publications
Research Service. Abbreviations in
the Latin American press. New York,
CCM Information Corp., 1972. ix, 172
p.   463/.1 72-93344
P365 .U53 MRR Alc.

United States. Library of Congress.
Technical Information Division. List
of abbreviations and symbols.
Washington, 1952. i, 14 l.   016.05
52-60047
Z663.49 .L48 MRR Alc.

Virtue's Catholic encyclopedia.
London, Virtue [1965] 3 v. (xv, 1136
p.)   282.03 66-92787
BX841 .V5 MRR Alc.

Wall, C. Edward. Periodical title
abbreviations. Detroit, Gale
Research Co., 1969. 210 p.   050 78-
86599
Z6945.A2 W34 MRR Ref Desk.

Walter, Frank Keller, Abbreviations
and technical terms used in book
catalogs and bibliographies, in eight
languages, 1917 handy edition.
Boston, The Boston book company
[1919?] 2 v. in 1.   27-13479
Z1006 .W261 1919 MRR Alc.

Walther, Rudolf, lexicographer.
Polytechnical dictionary, Oxford,
New York, Pergamon Press [1968,
c1967] 2 v.   603 67-25817
T10 .W3 1968 MRR Alc.

Whitlock, Carolyn, Abbreviations
used in the Department of agriculture
for titles of publications,
Washington, D.C. [U.S. Govt. print.
off., 1939] 278 p.   016.05 agr39-
503
Z6945.A2 W5 MRR Alc.

Who's who in Europe. éd. 1-
1964/65- Bruxelles, Éditions det
Feniks. 65-73851
D1070 .W48 MRR Biog Latest edition

ABBREVIATIONS, BULGARIAN.
United States. Library of Congress.
Slavic and Central European Division.
Bulgarian abbreviations;
Washington, 1961. 326 p.   491.8118
61-60056
Z663.47 .B8 MRR Alc.

ABBREVIATIONS, CZECH.
United States. Library of Congress.
Slavic and Central European Division.
Czech and Slovak abbreviations,
Washington, 1956. v, 164 p.
068.437 56-60067
Z663.47 .C9 MRR Alc.

ABBREVIATIONS, ENGLISH.
Aleshin, E. V. [Slovar' angliĭskikh
i amerikanskikh sokrashcheniĭ
(romanized form)] 1957. 767 p.   57-
36383
PE1693 .A38 1957 MRR Alc.

De Sola, Ralph, Abbreviations
dictionary: New international 4th
ed. New York, American Elsevier Pub.
Co. [1974] xiii, 428 p.   423/.1 73-
7687
PE1693 .D4 1974 MRR Ref Desk.

Eells, Walter Crosby, Academic
degrees; [Washington] U.S. Dept. of
Health, Education, and Welfare,
Office of Education [1960] vi, 324
p.   378.240973 hew61-6
LB2381 .E4 MRR Alc.

Fawcett, Frank Dubrez, ed.
Cyclopaedia of initials and
abbreviations, London, Business
Publications [1963] viii, 185 p.
421.8 64-3699
PE1693 .F37 MRR Ref Desk.

Funk & Wagnalls dictionary of
electronics. New York, Funk &
Wagnalls [1969] viii, 230 p. [6.95]
621.381/03 68-23735
TK7804 .F8 MRR Alc.

Gale Research Company. Reverse
acronyms and initialisms dictionary;
1st ed. Detroit, Gale Research Co.
[1972] x, 485 p.   423.1 71-165486
PE1693 .G3 1972 MRR Ref Desk.

Goldstein, Milton. Dictionary of
modern acronyms & abbreviations.
[1st ed.] Indianapolis, H. W. Sams
[1963] 158 p.   423 63-17022
PE1693 .G6 MRR Alc.

Hanson, John Lloyd. A dictionary of
economics and commerce, 3rd ed.
London, Macdonald & Evans, 1969. vi,
474 p. [42/-]   330/.03 77-437920
HB61 .H35 1969 MRR Alc.

Haycraft, Frank W. The degrees and
hoods of the world's universities and
colleges. [4th ed.] Cheshunt [Eng.]
Cheshunt Press, 1948. 159 p.
378.29 49-3552
LB2389 .H3 1948 MRR Alc.

Hughes, Leslie Ernest Charles.
Dictionary of electronics and
nucleonics New York, Barnes & Noble
[1970, c1969] viii, 443 p.
621.381/03 77-13060
TK7804 .H84 1970 MRR Alc.

Kleiner, Richard. Index of initials
and acronyms. Princeton, Auerbach
Publishers [1971] 145 p. [$7.95]
423.1 76-121868
PE1693 .K55 MRR Ref Desk.

Payton, Geoffrey. Payton's proper
names. London, New York, F. Warne,
1969. vii, 502 p. [45/-] 032 69-
20109
PE1660 .P3 MRR Alc.

Pugh, Eric. A dictionary of acronyms
& abbreviations; 2d, rev. and
expanded ed. [Hamden, Conn.] Archon
Books [1970] 389 p.   601/.48 72-
16645
T8 .P8 1970 MRR Alc.

Pugh, Eric. Second dictionary of
acronyms & abbreviations; [Hamden,
Conn.] Archon Books [1974] 410 p.
601/.48 74-4271
T8 .P82 MRR Alc.

ABBREVIATIONS, ENGLISH. (Cont.)
Rybicki, Stephen. Abbreviations;
1st ed. Ann Arbor, Mich., Pieran
Press, 1971. 334 p.   423/.1 74-
143239
  PE1693 .R94 MRR Ref Desk.

Shankle, George Earlie. Current
abbreviations New York, The H. W.
Wilson company, 1945. 207 p.   421.8
45-1051
  PE1693 .S5 MRR Alc.

Stephenson, Herbert John, Abbrevs.
(a dictionary of abbreviations) New
York, The Macmillan company, 1943.
vii p., 1 l., 126 p.   421.803 43-
14696
  PE1693 .S8 MRR Alc.

Taylor, Anna Marjorie. The language
of World War II: Rev. and enl. ed.
New York, H. W. Wilson Co., 1948.
265 p.   940.53014 48-8265
  PE3727.S7 T3 1948 MRR Alc.

Titles and forms of address: 14th
ed. London, Black, 1971. xi, 188 p.
[£1.25]   395/.4 72-170772
  CR3891 .T58 1971 MRR Alc.

Ultronic Systems Corporation. Stock
symbol guide: company to symbol,
symbol to company [New York] 1967.
80 p.   332.6/2/0148 75-31662
  HE7677.B2 U57 MRR Alc.

United States. Naval Oceanographic
Office. Navigation dictionary. 2d
ed. Washington, U.S. Govt. Print.
Off., 1969. iv, 282 p.   623.89/03
71-603652
  V23 .U557 1969 MRR Alc.

Wedertz, Bill. Dictionary of naval
abbreviations. 1970 ed. [Annapolis]
U.S. Naval Institute [1970] 249 p.
[3.50]   359/.001/48 72-96483
  V23 .W43 MRR Alc.

White, Donald P. J. A glossary of
acronyms, abbreviations, and symbols,
1st ed. Germantown, Md., Don White
Consultants [1971] ix, 235 p.
620/.001/48 72-138444
  T8 .W55 MRR Alc.

Wilkes, Ian H. British initials and
abbreviations 3d ed. London, Hill,
1971. 346 p. [£5.50 ($17.50 U.S.)]
060/.25/42 71-25205
  AS118 .W5 1971 MRR Alc.

ABBREVIATIONS, FRENCH.
Baudry, Hubert. "D.A.", dictionnaire
d'abreviations françaises et
étrangeres, La Chapelle-Montligeon
(Orne) Éditions de Montligeon, 1951.
157 p.   53-24921
  PC2693 .B3 MRR Alc.

Bilan du monde. [2. éd.] [Tournai]
Casterman, 1964. 2 v.   65-87638
  G122 .B442 MRR Alc.

Péron, Michel. Dictionnaire
français-anglais des affaires,
Paris, Larousse, 1968. 2 v. in 1.
(xvi, 230, xvi, 247 p.) [38 F] 68-
137592
  HF1002 .P418 MRR Alc.

ABBREVIATIONS, GERMAN.
Artschwager, Ernst Friedrich,
Dictionary of biological equivalents,
German-English, Baltimore, The
Williams & Wilkins company, 1930.
239 p. incl. 6 plates.   570.3 30-
18274
  QH13 .A7 MRR Alc.

Greiser, Josef. Lexikon der
Abkürzungen; 2. Aufl. ergänzt und
erweitert nach dem neuen Stande vom
1. Januar 1955. Osnabrück, A. Fromm
[1955] 271 p.   55-23756
  PF3693 .G7 1955 MRR Alc.

Gunston, C. A. Gunston & Corner's
German-English glossary of financial
and economic terms. 6th ed.; greatly
compressed, but in content much
amplified, Frankfurt am Main, F.
Knapp [1972] xxiii, 1203 p.
330/.03 72-188587
  HG151 .G85 1972 MRR Alc.

Mackensen, Lutz, ed. Deutsche
Rechtschreibung; [s. Aufl.
Gütersloh] C. Bertelsmann, 1954.
729 p.   54-32746
  PF3146 .M3 MRR Alc.

Spiller, Paul. Ullstein-
Abkürzungslexikon. (Frankfurt/M.,
Berlin, Ullstein, 1967). 407 p.
[DM4.80]   433.1 68-107367
  PF3693 .S63 MRR Alc.

ABBREVIATIONS, HEBREW.
Scharfstein, Zevi, [Milon leshonenu
(romanized form)] [New York, c1951]
304 p.   52-47510
  PJ4833 .S36 MRR Alc.

ABBREVIATIONS, HUNGARIAN.
United States. Library of Congress.
Slavic and Central European Division.
Hungarian abbreviations,
Washington, 1961. iv, 146 p.
494.51118 61-60004
  Z663.47 .H8 MRR Alc.

ABBREVIATIONS, ITALIAN.
Cappelli, Adriano. Lexicon
abbreviaturarum. 6. ed. Milano,
Hoepli, 1967. lxxiii, 531 p.   67-
122585
  Z111 .C24 1967 MRR Alc.

ABBREVIATIONS, LATIN.
Cappelli, Adriano. Lexicon
abbreviaturarum. 6. ed. Milano,
Hoepli, 1967. lxxiii, 531 p.   67-
122585
  Z111 .C24 1967 MRR Alc.

Martin, Charles Trice, The record
interpreter: 2d ed. London, Stevens
and sons, limited, 1910. xv, 464 p.
10-16320
  Z111 .M23 MRR Alc.

ABBREVIATIONS, MACEDONIAN.
Plamenatz, Ilija P. Yugoslav
abbreviations; 2d enl. ed.
Washington, Slavic and Central
European Division, Reference Dept.,
Library of Congress, 1962. iv, 198
p.   491.8218 62-60076
  Z663.47 .Y8 1962 MRR Alc.

ABBREVIATIONS, POLISH.
United States. Library of Congress.
Slavic and Central European Division.
Polish abbreviations; 2d ed., rev.
and enl. Washington, 1957. iv, 164
p.   491.8518 57-60055
  Z663.47 .P6 1957 MRR Alc.

ABBREVIATIONS, PORTUGUESE.
Houaiss, Antonio, ed. The new
Appleton dictionary of the English
and Portuguese languages. New York,
Appleton-Century-Crofts, 1964. xx,
636, 665 p.   469.32 64-25814
  PC5333 .H6 MRR Ref Desk.

ABBREVIATIONS, RUSSIAN.
Akademiia nauk SSSR. Institut
nauchnoĭ informatsii. Index of
abbreviated and full titles of
scientific and technical periodical
literature Wright-Patterson Air
Force Base, Ohio, 1960?] 247 l.   60-
60261
  Z6945.A2 A43 MRR Alc.

Institut zur Erforschung der UdSSR.
[Spisok russkikh sokrashchenii,
primen[a]emykh v SSSR (romanized
form)] 1954. 304 p.   54-41132
  PG2693 .I6 MRR Alc.

Russian-English aerospace dictionary.
Berlin, W. de Gruyter, 1965. xvi,
407 p.   65-73606
  TL509 .R83 MRR Alc.

United States. Library of Congress.
Aerospace Technology Division.
Glossary of Russian abbreviations and
acronyms. Washington, Library of
Congress; [for sale by the Supt. of
Docs., U.S. Govt. Print. Off.] 1967.
x, 806 p.   491.731 68-60006
  PG2693 .U47 MRR Alc.

United States. Library of Congress.
Aerospace Technology Division
Scientific research institutes of the
USSR. [Washington] 63-61636
  Began publication in Feb. 1960.
  Z663.23 .A27 MRR Alc MRR Alc
  Latest edition

United States. Library of Congress.
Reference Dept. Russian
abbreviations; 2d rev. and expanded
ed. Washington, 1957. ix, 513 p.
491.718 55-60063
  Z663.2 .R8 1957 MRR Alc.

Wheeler, Marcus. The Oxford Russian-
English dictionary, London,
Clarendon Press, 1972. xiii, 918 p.
[£5.00]   491.7/32/1 72-191016
  PG2640 .W5 MRR Ref Desk.

Zalucki, Henryk. Dictionary of
russian technical and scientific
abbreviations Amsterdam, New York
[etc.] Elsevier Pub. Co., 1968. 400
p.   601/.48 67-12784
  PG2693 .Z3 MRR Alc.

ABBREVIATIONS, SERBO-CROATIAN.
Plamenatz, Ilija P. Yugoslav
abbreviations; 2d enl. ed.
Washington, Slavic and Central
European Division, Reference Dept.,
Library of Congress, 1962. iv, 198
p.   491.8218 62-60076
  Z663.47 .Y8 1962 MRR Alc.

ABBREVIATIONS, SLOVAK.
United States. Library of Congress.
Slavic and Central European Division.
Czech and Slovak abbreviations,
Washington, 1956. v, 164 p.
068.437 56-60067
  Z663.47 .C9 MRR Alc.

ABBREVIATIONS, SLOVENIAN.
Plamenatz, Ilija P. Yugoslav
abbreviations; 2d enl. ed.
Washington, Slavic and Central
European Division, Reference Dept.,
Library of Congress, 1962. iv, 198
p.   491.8218 62-60076
  Z663.47 .Y8 1962 MRR Alc.

ABERDEEN, SCOT.--DIRECTORIES.
Post office Aberdeen directory.
Aberdeen [Scot.] 914.125 61-23122
  DA890.A2 P6 MRR Alc Latest edition

ABILITY.
see also Leadership

Garrison, Karl Claudius, The
psychology of exceptional children
4th ed. New York, Ronald Press Co.
[1965] vi, 571 p.   371.9 65-21809

  LC3965 .G3 1965 MRR Alc.

ABNORMAL CHILDREN
see Exceptional children

see Handicapped children

ABNORMAL PSYCHOLOGY
see Psychology, Pathological

ABORIGINES
see Ethnology

ABORTION--BIBLIOGRAPHY.
Driver, Edwin D. World population
policy; an annotated bibliography
Lexington, Mass. Lexington Books
[c1971] xxi, 1280 p.   016.30132 73-
184302
  Z7164.D3 D75 MRR Alc.

**ABORTION--UNITED STATES--STATISTICS--
PERIODICALS.**
Center for Disease Control. Abortion
surveillance. Atlanta. 301 74-
644021
  HQ767.5.U5 C45a MRR Alc Latest
  edition

ABSTRACT ART
see Art, Abstract

ABSTRACTING.
see also Indexing

ABSTRACTING--CHRONOLOGY.
California. University. University at
Los Angeles. School of Library
Service. The annals of abstracting,
1665-1970. Los Angeles, School of
Library Service & University Library,
University of California, 1971. v,
54 p.   011 76-29981
  Z695.9 .C34 MRR Alc.

ABSTRACTING AND INDEXING SERVICES.
France. Direction des bibliothèques
de France. Les bibliographies
internationales specialisees
courantes françaises ou a
participation française. Paris,
1958. 85 p.   60-21619
  Z1002 .F75 MRR Alc.

**ABSTRACTING AND INDEXING SERVICES--
BIBLIOGRAPHY.**
Bowker serials bibliography
supplement. 1972- New York, R. R.
Bowker Co. 011 72-2677
  Z6941 .U522 MRR Alc Latest edition
  / MRR Ref Desk Latest edition /
  Sci RR Latest edition

California. University. University at
Los Angeles. School of Library
Service. The annals of abstracting,
1665-1970. Los Angeles, School of
Library Service & University Library,
University of California, 1971. v,
54 p.   011 76-29981
  Z695.9 .C34 MRR Alc.

Index bibliographiens. [1st]- ed.;
1925- Le Haye Federation
Internationale de Documentation.
016.01 25-8351
  Z1002 .I38 MRR Alc Latest edition

Ulrich's international periodicals
directory. [1st]- ed.; [1932]-
New York, Bowker. 011 32-16320
  Z6941 .U5 Sci RR Latest edition /
  MRR Ref Desk Latest edition / MRR
  Ref Desk Latest edition

**ABSTRACTING AND INDEXING SERVICES--
DIRECTORIES.**
Chicorel, Marietta. Chicorel index
to abstracting and indexing services:
1st ed. New York, Chicorel Library
Pub. Corp. [1974] 2 v. (920 p.)
016.05 74-170424
  Z6293 .C54 MRR Ref Desk.

International Federation for
Documentation. Abstracting services.
[2d ed.] The Hague, 1969. 2 v.
029/.9/5 73-168592
  Z695.93 .I58 1969 MRR Ref Desk.

ABSTRACTION.
see also Concepts

ABSTRACTS--PERIODICALS.
Bulletin signalétique 519:
Philosophie, sciences religieuses.
v. 15-23; 1961-69. Paris, Centre de
documentation du C.N.R.S. 75-10205
Z7127 .F712 MRR Alc Full set

Rand Corporation. Selected Rand
abstracts. v. 1- 1963- Santa
Monica, Calif. 65-2088
AS36 .R284 MRR Alc Full set

ACADEMIC COSTUME.
Haycraft, Frank W. The degrees and
hoods of the world's universities and
colleges. [4th ed.] Cheshunt [Eng.]
Cheshunt Press, 1948. 159 p.
378.29 49-3552
LB2389 .H3 1948 MRR Alc.

Smith, Hugh. Academic dress and
insignia of the world; Cape Town, A.
A. Balkema, 1970. 3 v. (xiii, 1843
p.) 70-486324
LB2389 .S6 MRR Alc.

ACADEMIC ETIQUETTE.
Gunn, Mary Kemper. A guide to
academic protocol. New York,
Columbia University Press, 1969.
viii, 112 p. [5.95] 395 70-76250

LB2379 .G8 MRR Alc.

ACADEMY AWARDS (MOVING-PICTURES)
Fredrik, Nathalie. History of the
Academy award winners New York, Ace
Books, 1973. 217 p. [$1.50]
791.43/07/9 73-79788
PN1993.5.U6 F737 MRR Alc.

Likeness, George C. The Oscar
people; Mendota, Ill., Wayside Press
[1965] 415 p. 791.43079 65-17464

PN1993.5.U6 L5 MRR Alc.

Michael, Paul, comp. The Academy
awards: a pictorial history.
Indianapolis, Bobbs-Merrill [1964]
341 p. 791.43079 64-8653
PN1993.5.U6 M5 MRR Alc.

Osborne, Robert A. Academy awards
Oscar annual. La Habre, Calif., ESE
California. 791.43/079 74-640065
Began with vol. for 1971.
PN1993 .O8 MRR Alc Latest edition

Parish, James Robert. The MGM stock
company; New Rochelle, N.Y.,
Arlington House [1973] 862 p.
[$14.95] 791.43/028/0922 B 72-
91640
PN1998.A2 P394 MRR Alc.

Stambler, Irwin. Encyclopedia of
popular music. New York, St.
Martin's Press [1965] xiii, 350 p.
780.3 65-20817
ML102.J3 S8 MRR Alc.

ACCIDENTS.
see also Disasters

see also First aid in illness and
injury

see also Medical emergencies

ACCIDENTS--UNITED STATES--STATISTICS.
Accident facts. [Chicago, National
Safety Council] 28-14389
HA217 .A4 MRR Ref Desk Latest
edition / MRR Alc Latest edition

ACCIDENTS, AIRCRAFT
see Aeronautics--Accidents

ACCOUNTANTS.
Whiteside, Conon Doyle. Accountant's
guide to profitable management
advisory services Englewood Cliffs,
N.J., Prentice-Hall [1969] ix, 430
p. [29.95] 658.4/6 69-14584
HF5657 .W48 MRR Alc.

ACCOUNTANTS--UNITED STATES--DIRECTORIES.
American Institute of Certified
Public Accountants. List of
accounting firms and individual
practitioners. 1950- New York.
657.05873 51-1544
HF5601 .A8338 MRR Alc Latest
edition

American Institute of Certified
Public Accountants. List of members.
1942/44- New York. 657.06273 51-
16788
HF5601 .A834 MRR Alc Latest
edition

National Society of Public
Accountants. Membership directory.
Washington. 58-31623
HF5601 .N34 MRR Alc Latest edition

ACCOUNTING.
see also Bookkeeping

Accountants' handbook. 5th ed. New
York, Ronald Press Co. [1970] 1 v.
(various pagings) 657 72-110542
HF5621 .A22 1970 MRR Alc.

Casey, William J. Accounting desk
book; 3d ed. New York, Institute
for Business Planning [1972] vi,
410, A1-A62 p. 657/.02/02 72-
189426
HF5635 .C33 1972 MRR Alc.

Finney, Harry Anson, Finney and
Miller's Principles of accounting,
introductory. 7th ed. Englewood
Cliffs, N.J., Prentice-Hall [1970]
xiv, 688 p. 657/.042 79-113046
HF5635 .F537 1970 MRR Alc.

Finney, Harry Anson, Principles of
accounting, 6th ed. Englewood
Cliffs, N.J., Prentice-Hall [1965-71]
2 v. 657/.046 65-18498
HF5635 .F538 1965 MRR Alc.

Portfolio of accounting systems for
small and medium-sized businesses.
Englewood Cliffs, N.J., Prentice-Hall
[1968] 2 v. (1392 p.) [$35.00]
657.8/3 68-18738
HF5635 .P86 MRR Alc.

Wixon, Rufus, Principles of
accounting, 2d ed. New York, Ronald
Press Co. [1969] xii, 827 p. 657
69-14676
HF5635 .W844 1869 MRR Alc.

ACCOUNTING--ABSTRACTS.
Commerce Clearing House. Accounting
articles, 1967-1970; New York [1971]
1 v. (various pagings) 016.657 78-
26871
Z7164.C81 C782 MRR Alc.

ACCOUNTING--ADDRESSES, ESSAYS, LECTURES.
Handbook of modern accounting. New
York, McGraw-Hill [1970] 1 v.
(various pagings) 657 70-83264
HF5635 .H23 MRR Alc.

ACCOUNTING--BIBLIOGRAPHY.
American Institute of Certified
Public Accountants. Accountants'
index; [New York] American Institute
of Accountants, 1921. 1578 p. 21-
10690
Z7164.C81 A5 MRR Alc.

Bentley, Harry Clark, Bibliography
of works on accounting by American
authors, New York, A. M. Kelley,
1970. 2 v. in 1. 016.657 72-
115313
Z7164.C81 B5 1970 MRR Alc.

Commerce Clearing House. Accounting
articles, 1967-1970; New York [1971]
1 v. (various pagings) 016.657 78-
26871
Z7164.C81 C782 MRR Alc.

Demarest, Rosemary R. Accounting:
information sources Detroit, Gale
Research Co. [1970] 420 p. [$14.50]
016.657 70-120908
Z7164.C81 D28 MRR Alc.

Institute of Chartered Accountants in
England and Wales, London. Library.
Current accounting literature 1971;
London, Mansell [c1971] xii, 586 p.
016.657 72-182884
Z7164.C81 I43 1971 MRR Alc.

ACCOUNTING--CASE STUDIES.
Portfolio of accounting systems for
small and medium-sized businesses.
Englewood Cliffs, N.J., Prentice-Hall
[1968] 2 v. (1392 p.) [$35.00]
657.8/3 68-18738
HF5635 .P86 MRR Alc.

ACCOUNTING--DICTIONARIES.
Kohler, Eric Louis, A dictionary for
accountants 4th ed. Englewood
Cliffs, N.J., Prentice-Hall [1970]
vii, 456 p. [17.95] 657/.03 69-
10446
HF5621 .K6 1970 MRR Alc.

Prentice-Hall, inc. Industrial
accountant's encyclopedic dictionary,
Englewood Cliffs, N.J. [1964] 595
p. 657.03 64-13002
HF5621 .P73 MRR Alc.

ACCOUNTING--DICTIONARIES--POLYGLOT.
Union européenne des experts
comptables économiques et
financiers. Lexique U.E.C. Lexicon.
Dusseldorf, Verlagsbuchhandlung des
Instituts der Wirtschaftsprüfer,
1961. 1 v. (various pagings) 63-
31440
HF5621 .U5 MRR Alc.

ACCOUNTING--EXAMINATIONS, QUESTIONS, ETC.
American Institute of Certified
Public Accountants. Unofficial
answers to the Uniform certified
public accountants examination. May
1927/Nov. 1931- New York. 32-29514

HF5661 .A54 MRR Alc Latest edition

American Institute of Certified
Public Accountants. Board of
Examiners. Uniform certified public
accountant examinations. June
1917/Nov. 1927- New York. 657.076
28-10020
HF5661 .A53 MRR Alc Latest edition

Rhode, John Grant. CPA examination
review; Pacific Palisades, Calif.,
Goodyear Pub. Co. [1974] x, 604 p.
657/.61/076 73-80022
HF5661 .R44 MRR Alc.

ACCOUNTING--HISTORY--UNITED STATES.
Edwards, James Don. History of
public accounting in the United
States. East Lansing, Bureau of
Business and Economic Research,
Graduate School of Business
Administration, Michigan State
University [1960] 368 p. 657.60973
60-63369
HF5616.U5 E3 MRR Alc.

ACCOUNTING--PERIODICALS--INDEXES.
American Institute of Certified
Public Accountants. Accountants'
index: [New York] American Institute
of Accountants, 1921. 1578 p. 21-
10690
Z7164.C81 A5 MRR Alc.

Commerce Clearing House. Accounting
articles, 1967-1970; New York [1971]
1 v. (various pagings) 016.657 78-
26871
Z7164.C81 C782 MRR Alc.

ACCOUNTING--PROBLEMS, EXERCISES, ETC.
Finney, Harry Anson, Finney and
Miller's Principles of accounting,
introductory. 7th ed. Englewood
Cliffs, N.J., Prentice-Hall [1970]
xiv, 688 p. 657/.042 79-113046
HF5635 .F537 1970 MRR Alc.

Finney, Harry Anson, Principles of
accounting, 6th ed. Englewood
Cliffs, N.J., Prentice-Hall [1965-71]
2 v. 657/.046 65-18498
HF5635 .F538 1965 MRR Alc.

Lipkin, Lawrence. Accountant's
handbook of formulas and tables
Englewood Cliffs, N.J., Prentice-Hall
[c1963] 340 p. 63-18186
HF5661 .L53 MRR Alc.

ACHIEVEMENT TESTS
see Examinations

**ACKERMAN, CARL WILLIAM, 1890- --
MANUSCRIPTS--INDEXES.**
United States. Library of Congress.
Manuscript Division. Carl William
Ackerman: a register of his papers in
the Library of Congress. Washington,
Library of Congress, 1973. lii, 78
p. 016.070/92/4 73-4207
Z663.34 .A27 MRR Alc.

ACOUSTICAL ENGINEERING--DICTIONARIES--POLYGLOT.
Elsevier's dictionary of cinema,
sound, and music, in six languages:
Amsterdam, New York, Elsevier Pub.
Co., 1956. 948 p. 778.503 56-
13141
TR847 .E4 MRR Alc.

ACOUSTICS
see Sound

ACQUISITION OF AFRICAN PUBLICATIONS.
Witherell, Julian W. Africana
acquisitions; Washington, Library of
Congress, 1973. 122 p. 016.916/007
73-9620
Z663.285 .A74 MRR Alc.

ACQUISITION OF CUBAN PUBLICATIONS--CONGRESSES.
International Conference on Cuban
Acquisitions and Bibliography,
Library of Congress, 1970. Cuban
acquisitions and bibliography;
Washington, Library of Congress,
1970. viii, 164 p. 016.917291/03
76-609231
Z663.32 .C85 1970 MRR Alc.

ACQUISITION OF SERIAL PUBLICATIONS.
Neverman, F. John. International
directory of back issue vendors:
periodicals, newspapers, newspaper
indexes, documents. 2d enl. ed. New
York, Special Libraries Association
[c1968] vi, 95 p.
658.8/09/655572025 68-57264
Z286.P4 N4 1968 MRR Alc.

American Library Association. Joint
Committee to Revise List of
International Subscription Agents.
International subscription agents;
2d ed. Chicago, American Library
Association, 1969. vi, 87 p.
380.1/45/655572025 76-82255
Z282 .A44 1969 MRR Alc.

ACQUISITIONS (LIBRARIES)
Carter, Mary (Duncan) Building library collections, 3d ed. Metuchen, N.J., Scarecrow Press, 1969. xii, 319 p.   025.2/1 73-4902
    Z689 .C29 1969 MRR Alc.

Ford, Stephen. The acquisition of library materials. Chicago, American Library Association, 1973. xiii, 237 p.   025.2 73-9896
    Z689 .F74 MRR Alc.

Malia, Martin Edward. Report, to the Joint Committee on Slavic Studies and to the Library of Congress, on methods for improving Soviet book acquisitions by American research libraries, February-March, 1956. [Washington?] 1956. 2 l., 79 p.   63-61735
    Z663 .R394 MRR Alc.

ACQUISITIONS (LIBRARIES)--AUTOMATION.
United States. Library of Congress. MARC Development Office. Order Division automated system. Washington, 1972. 74 p.   025.2/3/02854 72-12530
    Z663.757 .O7 MRR Alc.

ACROGENS
see Ferns

ACRONYMS.
Angel, Juvenal Londoño. Directory of international agencies. 1st ed. New York, Simon & Schuster [1970] 447 p. [$25.00] 341/.24/025 70-121774
    AS8 .A5 MRR Alc.

Baudhuin, Fernand. Dictionnaire de l'économie contemporaine. (Verviers, Gérard et Co. 1968). 302 p. [80.00] 330/.03 78-409250
    HB61 .B36 MRR Alc.

Buttress, F. A. World list of abbreviations. 3rd ed. London, Hill, 1966. vi, 186 p. [35/-]
060.148 66-71807
    AS8 .B8 1966 MRR Alc.

De Sola, Ralph. Abbreviations dictionary: New international 4th ed. New York, American Elsevier Pub. Co. [1974] xiii, 428 p. 423/.1 73-7687
    PE1693 .D4 1974 MRR Ref Desk.

Directory of scientific research organizations in South Africa. 1971- Pretoria, South African Council for Scientific and Industrial Research. 507/.2068 72-621812
    Q180.A55 D53 MRR Alc Latest edition

Fawcett, Frank Dubrez, ed. Cyclopaedia of initials and abbreviations, London, Business Publications [1963] viii, 185 p. 421.8 64-3699
    PE1693 .F37 MRR Ref Desk.

Gale Research Company. Acronyms and initialisms dictionary; 4th ed. Detroit [1873] xv, 635 p. 423/.1 73-568
    P365 .G3 1973 MRR Ref Desk.

Gale Research Company. Reverse acronyms and initialisms dictionary; 1st ed. Detroit, Gale Research Co. [1972] x, 485 p. 423.1 71-165486

    PE1693 .G3 1972 MRR Ref Desk.

Global Engineering Documentation Services. Directory of engineering document sources. Newport Beach, Calif., Global Engineering Documentation Services [1972] 1 v. (unpaged) [$29.95] 029.9/62 72-176333
    Z5852 .G5 MRR Alc.

Goldstein, Milton. Dictionary of modern acronyms & abbreviations. [1st ed.] Indianapolis, H. W. Sams [1963] 158 p. 423 63-17022
    PE1693 .G6 MRR Alc.

Hanson, John Lloyd. A dictionary of economics and commerce, 3rd ed. London, Macdonald & Evans, 1969. vi, 474 p. [42/-] 330/.03 77-437920
    HB61 .H35 1969 MRR Alc.

International Chamber of Commerce. United States Council. International economic organizations & terms glossary. [New York, 1964] 48 p. 64-54675
    HB61 .I6 1964 MRR Alc.

International Council of Voluntary Agencies. Africa's NGOs. [Geneva,] Conseil international des agences bénévoles, 1968. iv, 299 p. [unpriced] 77-417459
    AS600 .I5AS5 MRR Alc.

Kleiner, Richard. Index of initials and acronyms. Princeton, Auerbach Publishers [1971] 145 p. [$7.95] 423.1 76-121868
    PE1693 .K55 MRR Ref Desk.

Marconi Company Limited. Glossary of abbreviations; [2d ed.] Great Baddow, Essex [1957] 38 p.   57-43854
    AS8 .M3 1957 MRR Alc.

Messenger, Elizabeth. The complete guide to etiquette London, Evans Bros., 1966. 206 p. [25/-]
395.0942 66-70820
    BJ1873 .M4 MRR Alc.

OECD-ICVA directory; Paris, OECD, 1967. 1378 p. [90.00] 309.2/062 68-82889
    HC60 .O2 TJ Rm.

Paxton, John. Dictionary of abbreviations. Totowa, N.J., Rowman and Littlefield [1974] xiii, 384 p. 413 73-5881
    P365 .P3 1974 MRR Ref Desk.

Polec. 2., verb. und erw. Aufl. Berlin, de Gruyter, 1967. xvi, 1037 p. with map. [DM 48.-] 330/.03 68-70864
    H40 .P6 1967 MRR Alc.

Pugh, Eric. A dictionary of acronyms & abbreviations; 2d, rev. and expanded ed. [Hamden, Conn.] Archon Books [1970] 389 p. 601/.48 72-16645
    T8 .P8 1970 MRR Alc.

Pugh, Eric. Second dictionary of acronyms & abbreviations; [Hamden, Conn.] Archon Books [1974] 410 p. 601/.48 74-4271
    T8 .P82 MRR Alc.

Ruppert, Fritz, writer on international organizations. Initials. München-Pullach, Verlag Dokumentation; Essen, Vulkan Verlag, 1966. 220 p. [DM 14.60] 060.25 67-71860
    JX1995 .R87 MRR Ref Desk.

Sippl, Charles J. Computer dictionary and handbook. [2d ed.] Indianapolis, H. W. Sams [1972] 778 p. [$16.95 ($22.25 Can)]
001.6/4/03 70-175572
    QA76.15 .S512 1972 MRR Alc.

Spillner, Paul. Ullstein-Abkürzungslexikon. (Frankfurt/M., Berlin, Ullstein, 1967). 407 p. [DM4.80] 433.1 68-107367
    PF3693 .S63 MRR Alc.

Spillner, Paul. World guide to abbreviations. 2d ed. New York, Bowker, 1970- v.   413 75-19811

    P365 .S6 MRR Ref Desk.

Symbols of American libraries. [1st]-ed.; 1932- Washington, Library of Congress. 018/.1 33-13797
    Z663.79 .S9 MRR Alc MRR Alc
    Partial set

Union of International Associations. International initialese; Enl. 2d ed. Bruxelles, 1963. 48 p.   63-42257
    AS8 .U4 1963 MRR Alc.

United States. Bureau of International Labor Affairs. Directory of labor organizations; Europe. Rev. ed. Washington, For sale by the Superintendent of Documents, U.S. Govt. Print. Off., 1965- 2 v. (loose-leaf)   l 65-81
    HD6656 .A5 1965 MRR Alc.

United States. Joint Publications Research Service. Abbreviations in the African press. New York, CCM Information Corp., 1972. ix, 108 p. 079.6/01/48 72-93345
    P365 .U5 MRR Alc.

United States. Joint Publications Research Service. Abbreviations in the Latin American press. New York, CCM Information Corp., 1972. ix, 172 p.   463/.1 72-93344
    P365 .U53 MRR Alc.

United States. Library of Congress. Aerospace Technology Division. Glossary of Russian abbreviations and acronyms. Washington, Library of Congress; [for sale by the Supt. of Docs., U.S. Govt. Print. Off.] 1967. x, 806 p.   491.731 68-60006
    PG2693 .U47 MRR Alc.

United States. Naval Oceanographic Office. Glossary of oceanographic terms. 2d ed. Washington, U.S. Naval Oceanographic Office, 1966. vi, 204 p.   551.4/6/003 66-62513
    GC9 .U5 1966 MRR Alc.

Versand, Kenneth. Polyglot's lexicon, 1943-1966. New York, Links [c1973] 468 p. [$12.50] 423 72-94094
    PE1630 .V4 MRR Alc.

White, Donald R. J. A glossary of acronyms, abbreviations, and symbols, 1st ed. Germantown, Md., Don White Consultants [1971] ix, 235 p. 620/.001/48 72-138444
    T8 .W55 MRR Alc.

Wilkes, Ian H. British initials and abbreviations 3d ed. London, Hill, 1971. 346 p. [£5.50 ($17.50 U.S.)] 060/.25/42 71-25205
    AS118 .W5 1971 MRR Alc.

ACTING.
see also Drama
see also Theater

Herman, Lewis Helmar. Foreign dialects; New York, Theatre Arts Books [1958? c1943] 415 p.   792.028 58-10332
    PN2071.F6 H4 1958 MRR Alc.

Strickland, Francis Cowles. The technique of acting. New York, McGraw-Hill, 1956. 306 p.   792.92 55-11573
    PN2061 .S76 MRR Alc.

Wilson, Garff B. A history of American acting, Bloomington, Indiana University Press [1966] x, 310 p.   792.0922 66-12736
    PN2226 .W5 MRR Alc.

ACTING--COSTUME
see Costume

ACTING--MAKE-UP
see Make-up, Theatrical

ACTING FOR TELEVISION.
Parish, James Robert. Actors' television credits, 1950-1972. Metuchen, N.J., Scarecrow Press, 1973. x, 869 p.   791.45/028/0922 73-9914
    PN1992.4.A2 P3 MRR Alc.

ACTION (SERVICE CORPS). PEACE CORPS
see United States. Peace Corps

ACTORS.
Coad, Oral Sumner. The American stage, New Haven, Yale university press; [etc., etc.] 1929. 3 p. l., 362 p.   29-22306
    E178.5 .P2 vol. 14 MRR Alc.

Geisinger, Marion. Plays, players, & playwrights; New York, Hart Pub. Co. [1971] 767 p. [$20.00] 792/.09 77-162054
    PN2101 .G4 MRR Alc.

May, Robin. A companion to the theatre; Guildford, Lutterworth Press, 1973. 304 p., [16] p. of plates. [£2.40] 792/.0942 74-164747
    PN2597 .M35 MRR Alc.

ACTORS--DICTIONARIES.
Dimmitt, Richard Bertrand. An actor guide to the talkies; Metuchen, N.J., Scarecrow Press, 1967-68. 2 v. (1555 p.) 791.43/8 67-12057
    PN1998 .D53 MRR Alc.

ACTORS--PORTRAITS.
National Portrait Gallery, Washington, D.C. Portraits of the American stage, 1771-1971; Washington, Smithsonian Institution Press; [for sale by the Supt. of Docs., U.S. Govt. Print. Off.] 1971. 203 p. [$4.50] 792/.0973 75-170284
    PN1583.A2 N3 MRR Biog.

ACTORS--PORTRAITS--CATALOGS.
Harvard university. Library. Theatre collection. Catalogue of dramatic portraits in the Theatre collection of the Harvard college library, Cambridge, Mass., Harvard university press, 1930- v.   927.92 30-13380
    PN2205 .H35 MRR Alc.

ACTORS--PORTRAITS--INDEXES.
Odell, George Clinton Densmore, Annals of the New York stage.   27-5965
    PN2277.N5 O4 Index MRR Alc.

ACTORS--UNITED STATES.
Parish, James Robert. Actors' television credits, 1950-1972. Metuchen, N.J., Scarecrow Press, 1973. x, 869 p.   791.45/028/0922 73-9914
    PN1992.4.A2 P3 MRR Alc.

ACTORS, AMERICAN.
Sherman, Robert Lowery, Drama cyclopedia, Chicago, The author [1944] 1 p. l., iii, 612 p.   792 44-40134
    PN2226 .S45 MRR Alc.

ACTORS, AMERICAN. (Cont.)
Who's who in the theatre; [1st]-
ed.; 1912- London, I. Pitman.
927.92 12-22402
PN2012 .W5 MRR Biog Latest edition

Wilson, Garff B. A history of
American acting. Bloomington,
Indiana University Press [1966] x,
310 p. 792.0922 66-12736
PN2226 .W5 MRR Alc.

ACTORS, AMERICAN--BIOGRAPHY.
Sherman, Robert Lowery. Actors and
authors. Chicago [1951] 433 p.
927.92 51-4020
PN2285 .S48 MRR Biog.

ACTORS, AMERICAN--DICTIONARIES.
Brown, Thomas Allston. History of
the American stage. New York, Blom
[1969] 6, 6-421 p. 792/.028/0922
72-81206
PN2285 .B75 1969 MRR Biog.

Rigdon, Walter, ed. The biographical
encyclopaedia & who's who of the
American theatre. [1st ed.] New
York, J. H. Heineman [1966, c1965]
xiv, 1101 p. 792.0922 B 65-19390
PN2285 .R5 MRR Biog.

Twomey, Alfred E. The versatiles;
South Brunswick [N.J.] A. S. Barnes
[1969] 304 p. [10.00]
791.43/028/0922 68-27218
PN1998 .A2 T9 MRR Biog.

ACTORS, AMERICAN--DIRECTORIES.
Players' guide ... 1st- ed.; Aug.
1944- [New York] 792.058 47-34214

PN2289 .P55 MRR Alc Latest edition

ACTORS, ENGLISH.
Arnott, James Fullarton. English
theatrical literature, 1559-1900:
London, Society for Theatre Research,
1970. xxii, 486 p. [£10/10/-]
016.792/0942 76-552584
Z2014.D7 A74 1970 MRR Alc.

Baker, David Erskine. Biographia
dramatica; London, Longman, Hurst,
Rees, Orme, and Brown [etc.] 1812. 3
v. in 4. 04-14124
Z2014.D7 B2 1812 MRR Alc.

Who's who in the theatre; [1st]-
ed.; 1912- London, I. Pitman.
927.92 12-22402
PN2012 .W5 MRR Biog Latest edition

ACTORS, ENGLISH--DICTIONARIES.
Nungezer, Edwin. A dictionary of
actors and other persons associated
with the public representation of
plays in England before 1642. New
York, Greenwood Press [1968, c1929]
437, [1] p. 792.028/0922 68-57633

PN2597 .N8 1968 MRR Biog.

ACTORS, FRENCH.
Annuaire du spectacle; [1]-
annee; 1942/43- Paris, Editions
Raoult [etc.] 45-27035
PN2620 .A67 MRR Alc Latest edition

ACTRESSES.
May, Robin. A companion to the
theatre; Guildford, Lutterworth
Press, 1973. 304 p., [16] p. of
plates. [£2.40] 792/.0942 74-
164747
PN2597 .M35 MRR Alc.

ACTUARIAL SCIENCE
see Insurance, Life

ADAMS, JOHN, PRES. U.S., 1735-1826.
Adams, Charles Francis. The life of
John Adams, Rev. and corr. New
York, Haskell House Publishers, 1968.
2 v. 973.4/4/0924 B 68-24969
E322 .A52 1968 MRR Alc.

Hawke, David Freeman. A transaction
of free men; New York, Scribner
[1964] 282 p. 973.313 64-13632
E221 .H26 MRR Alc.

Smith, Page. John Adams. [1st ed.]
Garden City, N.Y., Doubleday, 1962
[v. 2, c1963] (xx, 1170 p.)
923.173 63-7188
E322 .S64 MRR Alc.

ADAMS, JOHN QUINCY, PRES. U.S., 1767-
1848.
Bemis, Samuel Flagg. John Quincy
Adams and the foundations of American
foreign policy. [1st ed.] New York,
A. A. Knopf, 1949. xix, 588, xv p.
923.173 49-10664
E377 .B45 1949 MRR Alc.

Bemis, Samuel Flagg. John Quincy
Adams and the Union. [1st ed.] New
York, Knopf, 1956. xix, 546 p.
923.173 55-9271
E377 .B46 MRR Alc.

Hecht, Marie B. John Quincy Adams;
New York, Macmillan [1972] xiv, 682
p. [$12.95] 973.5/5/0924 B 72-
77279
E377 .H43 MRR Alc.

ADAPTATION (BIOLOGY)
see also Genetics

see also Man--Influence of environment

ADELAIDE--COMMERCE--DIRECTORIES.
Universal business directory for
Adelaide city & suburbs. Adelaide,
Universal Business Directories. 63-
2842
HF5308.A3 U5 MRR Alc Latest
edition

ADMINISTRATION
see Management

see Political science

ADMINISTRATION, PUBLIC
see Public administration

ADMINISTRATION OF CRIMINAL JUSTICE
see Criminal Justice, Administration
of

ADMINISTRATION OF JUSTICE
see Justice, Administration of

ADMINISTRATIVE AGENCIES--UNITED STATES.
Michael, James R. Working on the
system; New York, Basic Books [1974]
xxvi, 950 p. [$14.95] 353.09 73-
81135
KF5407 .M52 MRR Alc.

ADMINISTRATIVE COMMUNICATION
see Communication in management

ADMINISTRATIVE LAW--UNITED STATES.
United States. Federal register. v.
1- March 14, 1936- [Washington,
U.S. Govt. Print. off.] 353.005 36-
26246
J1 .A2 MRR Alc (Dk 33) Full set

ADMINISTRATIVE LAW--UNITED STATES--
BIBLIOGRAPHY.
Historical records survey. New
Jersey. List and index of
presidential executive orders,
Newark, N.J., Historical records
survey, Work projects administration
[1943] 1 p. l., xiv p., 1 l., 388,
[2] p. 016.353 43-13029
Z6455.A4 H5 MRR Alc.

ADMINISTRATIVE PROCEDURE--UNITED STATES.
Michael, James R. Working on the
system; New York, Basic Books [1974]
xxvi, 950 p. [$14.95] 353.09 73-
81135
KF5407 .M52 MRR Alc.

ADMINISTRATIVE RESPONSIBILITY.
see also Impeachments

ADMIRALS--UNITED STATES.
Generals of the Army and the Air
Force and admirals of the Navy. v. 1-
3; Feb. 1953-Jan. 1956. [Washington]
923.573 56-23963
U52 .G4 MRR Alc Full set

ADOLESCENCE.
see also Youth

ADOLESCENT PSYCHIATRY.
Child and adolescent psychiatry,
sociocultural and community
psychiatry. 2d ed. [Rev. and
expanded] New York, Basic Books
[1974] xi, 858 p. 616.8/9/008 s
616.8/9 72-89185
RC435 .A562 vol. 2 MRR Alc.

ADOLESCENT PSYCHOLOGY.
Cole, Luella, Psychology of
adolescence. 6th ed. New York,
Holt, Rinehart and Winston [1964]
xvi, 668 p. 136.7354 64-12918
BF724 .C55 1964 MRR Alc.

ADOLESCENT PSYCHOLOGY--ENCYCLOPEDIA--
POPULAR WORKS.
Levine, Milton Isra, The parents'
encyclopedia of infancy, childhood,
and adolescence New York, Crowell
[1973] 619 p. [$10.00] 649/.1/03
72-83769
RJ61 .L552 MRR Alc.

ADULT EDUCATION--BIBLIOGRAPHY.
Mezirow, Jack D. The literature of
liberal adult education, 1945-1957.
New York, Scarecrow Press, 1960. x,
308 p. 016.374 60-7264
Z5814.A24 M4 MRR Alc.

ADULT EDUCATION--DIRECTORIES.
White, Alex Sandri. Worldwide
register of adult education. [1st]-
ed.; 1960- Allenhurst, N.J. [etc.]
Aurea Publications. 374.4058 60-
2314
L900 .W45 MRR Alc Latest edition

ADULT EDUCATION--YEARBOOKS.
Public continuing and adult education
almanac. 1970- Washington, National
Association for Public Continuing &
Adult Education. [$10.00] 374/.003
73-643166
LC5201 .P8 MRR Alc Latest edition

ADULT EDUCATION--UNITED STATES--
CATALOGS.
Goodman, Steven E. National
directory of adult and continuing
education; Rochester, N.Y.,
Educational Training Association
[1968] x, 285 p. 374/.0025/73 68-
9819
LC5251 .G64 MRR Alc.

ADULT EDUCATION--UNITED STATES--
DIRECTORIES.
Adult Education Association.
Directory. Washington [etc.]
374.06273 57-41894
LC5201 .A427 MRR Alc Latest
edition

College Entrance Examination Board.
The New York Times guide to
continuing education in America.
[New York] Quadrangle Books [1972]
811 p. [$12.50] 374.8/73 74-
183190
L901 .C74 1972 MRR Ref Desk.

Handbook of adult education in the
United States. 1934- Chicago [etc.]
374.973 60-7359
LC5251 .H3 MRR Alc Latest edition

ADULT EDUCATION--UNITED STATES--
STATISTICS.
Public continuing and adult education
almanac. 1970- Washington, National
Association for Public Continuing &
Adult Education. [$10.00] 374/.003
73-643166
LC5201 .P8 MRR Alc Latest edition

ADULTHOOD.
see also Aged

see also Old age

ADVENTURE AND ADVENTURERS.
see also Explorers

ADVENTURE AND ADVENTURERS--BIBLIOGRAPHY.
Cox, Edward Godfrey, A reference
guide to the literature of travel,
Seattle, The University of
Washington, 1935-49. 3 v. 016.91
36-27679
Z6011 .C87 MRR Alc.

ADVENTURES AND ADVENTURERS.
see also Frontier and pioneer life

ADVERTISING.
see also Market surveys

see also Marketing

see also Public relations

see also Publicity

see also Sales promotion

see also Salesmen and salesmanship

Sunners, William, American slogans;
New York, Paebar Co., 1949. 345 p.
659.103 49-3280
HF5823 .S9 MRR Alc.

ADVERTISING--BIBLIOGRAPHY.
Sandeau, Georges. International
bibliography of marketing and
distribution. [Bruxelles, Presses
universitaires de Bruxelles]
Distributed exclusively in North
America and South America [by] R. R.
Bowker Co., New York, 1971. 1 v.
(various pagings) 016.6588 73-
159927
Z7164.M18 S2 1971b MRR Alc.

ADVERTISING--BIOGRAPHY.
Who's who in advertising. 1st-
ed.; 1963- New York. 926.591 63-
18786
HF5810.A2 W46 MRR Biog Latest
edition

ADVERTISING--DICTIONARIES.
Batten, Barton, Durstine and Osborn,
inc. Media Dept. One hundred basic
media terms defined; [New York]
1966. 44 p. 659.103 67-858
HF5803 .B3 MRR Alc.

Graham, Irvin, Encyclopedia of
advertising; 2d ed. New York,
Fairchild Publications [1969] xiii,
494 p. [20.00] 659.1703 68-14544

HF5803 .G68 1969 MRR Alc.

Grohmann, H. Victor, Advertising
terminology, New York, Priv. print.
[1952] 86 p. 659.103 52-28586
HF5803 .G7 MRR Alc.

ADVERTISING--DICTIONARIES. (Cont.)
Vigrolio, Tom. Marketing and
communications media dictionary,
[Norfolk, Mass., NBS Co., 1969]
xvii, 425 p.   658.8/003 76-80076
    HF5414 .V52 MRR Alc.

ADVERTISING--DICTIONARIES--POLYGLOT.
International Chamber of Commerce.
Dictionary of advertising and
distribution. Basel, Verlag für
Recht und Gesellschaft. 1954. 1 v.
(unpaged)   659.103 54-24644
    HF5803 .I58 1954 MRR Alc.

Townsend, Derek. Advertising and
public relations; London, A. Redman
[1964] xvi, 152 p.   65-6026
    HF5803 .T6 MRR Alc.

ADVERTISING--DIRECTORIES.
Media Scandinavia. 16.-   udg.; 1967-
København, Danske reklamebureauers
brancheforening.   72-623099
    Z6941 .M4 MRR Alc Latest edition

ADVERTISING--HANDBOOKS, MANUALS, ETC.
Stansfield, Richard H. The Dartnell
advertising manager's handbook,
Chicago, Dartnell Corp. [1969] 1503
p.   659.1 68-21480
    HF5823 .S78 MRR Alc.

ADVERTISING--HISTORY.
Wood, James Playsted, The story of
advertising. New York, Ronald Press
Co. [1958] 512 p.   659.109 58-8474

    HF5811 .W6 MRR Alc.

ADVERTISING--SOCIETIES.
International Advertising Association
(Founded 1938) Membership. [New
York]   59-28179
    HF5801 .I53 MRR Alc Latest edition

ADVERTISING--SPECIMENS.
Jones, Edgar Robert, Those were the
good old days: New York, Simon and
Schuster, 1959. 447 p. (chiefly
facsims.) 659.1084 59-13881
    HF5813.U6 J6 MRR Alc.

ADVERTISING--YEARBOOKS.
The Advertiser's annual with Empire
sections. London, Admark Directories
Ltd. [etc.] 659.1C58 49-14603
    HF5802 .A23 MRR Alc Latest edition

ADVERTISING--YEARBOOKS--STATISTICS.
National advertising investments.
Norwalk, Conn. [etc.] 659.1058 49-
23553
    HF5802 .N3 MRR Alc Latest edition

ADVERTISING--AFRICA--YEARBOOKS.
The Advertising & press annual of
Africa. Cape Town, National Pub. Co.
(Pty) Ltd. [etc.] 52-41681
    Z6959 .A65 MRR Alc Latest edition

ADVERTISING--CANADA--DIRECTORIES.
The National list of advertisers.
Toronto, Maclean-Hunter Pub. Co. 56-
46268
    HF5808.C2 N3 MRR Alc Latest
    edition

ADVERTISING--FRANCE--DIRECTORIES.
Annuaire Desechaliers ... Paris. 42-
34851
    "Fondé en 1895.
    Z308 .A75 MRR Alc Latest edition

ADVERTISING--FRANCE--YEARBOOKS.
Annuaire de la presse française et
étrangère. 1.- ed.; 1880-
Paris.   06-44929
    Z6956.F8 A6 MRR Alc Latest edition

ADVERTISING--GERMANY.
Der Leitfaden für Presse und
Werbung. Essen, W. Stamm. 073 51-
17269
    Z6956.G3 L4 MRR Alc Latest edition

ADVERTISING--GERMANY--DIRECTORIES.
Der Leitfaden für Presse und
Werbung. Essen, W. Stamm. 073 51-
17269
    Z6956.G3 L4 MRR Alc Latest edition

ADVERTISING--GREAT BRITAIN--DIRECTORIES.
The Advertiser's annual with Empire
sections. London, Admark Directories
Ltd. [etc.] 659.1C58 49-14603
    HF5802 .A23 MRR Alc Latest edition

The Newspaper press directory.
London, C. Mitchell [etc.] ca 07-6361
    Z6956.E5 M6 MRR Alc Latest edition

ADVERTISING--INDIA--YEARBOOKS.
I N F A press and advertisers year
book. 1962- New Delhi, INFA
Publications. sa 63-2244
    PN4709 .I2 MRR Alc Latest edition

ADVERTISING--NEW ENGLAND--DIRECTORIES.
The Book of names. Wellesley, Mass.,
New England Marketing Publications.
[$7.50] 380.1/025/74 74-644293
    HF5806.A11 B65 MRR Alc Latest
    edition

ADVERTISING--SPAIN--DIRECTORIES.
Anuario español de la publicidad.
1960- Madrid. 64-36955
    HF5808.S62 A7 MRR Alc Latest
    edition

ADVERTISING--UNITED STATES--DIRECTORIES.
The Advertising specialty register.
1950- ed. Trevose, Pa. [etc.]
Advertising Specialty Institute
[etc.] 659.114 50-54758
    HF6146.N7 A4 MRR Alc Latest
    edition

Consumer magazine and farm
publication rates and data. v. 38,
no. 10-   Oct. 1956- [Skokie, Ill.]
Standard Rate & Data Service, Inc.
659.l/025/73 72-622888
    HF5905 .S725 MRR Ref Desk Latest
    edition

Media records: v. 1-   1st quarter
1928- New York. 29-2345
    HF5903 .M45 MRR Alc Latest edition

Standard directory of advertisers.
Jan. 1916- Skokie, Ill. [etc.]
National Register Pub. Co.
659.102573 15-21147
    HF5805 .S7 MRR Alc Latest edition

Standard directory of advertisers.
Geographical index. Skokie, Ill.
[etc.] National Register Pub. Co.
659.102573 74-643538
    HF5805 .S712 MRR Alc Latest
    edition

Standard directory of advertising
agencies. Skokie, Ill. [etc.]
National Register Pub. Co. 66-6149
    HF5805 .S72 MRR Alc Latest edition

Standard Rate and Data Service, inc.
Business publication rates and data.
v.33- Jan. 1951- Skokie, Ill.
[etc.] 659.132058 53-36930
    HF5905 .S723 MRR Ref Desk Latest
    edition

Standard Rate and Data Service, inc.
Newspaper rates and data. v. 33-
Jan. 1951- Skokie, Ill.[etc.]
659.132058 53-36942
    HF5905 .S73 MRR Ref Desk Latest
    edition

Weekly newspaper rates and data. v.
48- Mar. 1966- [Skokie, Ill.]
Standard Rate & Data Service, Inc.
659.13/2 72-622887
    HF5905 .S72 MRR Ref Desk Latest
    edition

ADVERTISING--UNITED STATES--SOURCES.
Jones, Edgar Robert, Those were the
good old days: New York, Simon and
Schuster, 1959. 447 p. (chiefly
facsims.) 659.1084 59-13881
    HF5813.U6 J6 MRR Alc.

ADVERTISING--UNITED STATES--STATISTICS.
National advertising investments.
Norwalk, Conn. [etc.] 659.1058 49-
23553
    HF5802 .N3 MRR Alc Latest edition

ADVERTISING, ART IN
see Commercial art

ADVERTISING, DIRECT-MAIL.
see also Sales letters

ADVERTISING, MAGAZINE.
Bacon's publicity checker. 1933-
Chicago, R. H. Bacon. 659.111 34-
14702
    HD59 .B3 MRR Alc Latest edition

Consumer magazine and farm
publication rates and data. v. 38,
no. 10-   Oct. 1956- [Skokie, Ill.]
Standard Rate & Data Service, Inc.
659.l/025/73 72-622888
    HF5905 .S725 MRR Ref Desk Latest
    edition

Standard Rate and Data Service, inc.
Business publication rates and data.
v.33- Jan. 1951- Skokie, Ill.
[etc.] 659.132058 53-36930
    HF5905 .S723 MRR Ref Desk Latest
    edition

ADVERTISING, NEWSPAPER.
Media records: v. 1-   1st quarter
1928- New York. 29-2345
    HF5903 .M45 MRR Alc Latest edition

Standard Rate and Data Service, inc.
Newspaper rates and data. v. 33-
Jan. 1951- Skokie, Ill.[etc.]
659.132058 53-36942
    HF5905 .S73 MRR Ref Desk Latest
    edition

Weekly newspaper rates and data. v.
48- Mar. 1966- [Skokie, Ill.]
Standard Rate & Data Service, Inc.
659.13/2 72-622887
    HF5905 .S72 MRR Ref Desk Latest
    edition

ADVERTISING AGENCIES--DIRECTORIES.
Art directors handbook: Europe. v. 1-
1965- New York, P. Glenn
Publications. 659.112 65-1527
    HF5804 .A7 MRR Alc Latest edition

International reference handbook of
services, organizations, diplomatic
representation, marketing, and
advertising channels. 1954- New
York, World Trade Academy Press. a
55-1568
    HF54.U5 I52 MRR Alc Latest edition

Österreichs Presse, Werbung,
Graphik: Handbuch. 15.- Jahrg.;
1967- Wien, Verband
Österreichischer
Zeitungsherausgeber. 72-626652
    Z6905.A9 H3 MRR Alc Latest edition

Standard directory of advertising
agencies. Skokie, Ill. [etc.]
National Register Pub. Co. 66-6149
    HF5805 .S72 MRR Alc Latest edition

ADVERTISING CARDS.
Standard Rate and Data Service, inc.
Transit advertising rates and data.
[Skokie, Ill.] 380.1/45/6591344 72-
626448
    HF5905 .S75 MRR Ref Desk Latest
    edition

ADVERTISING CARDS--COLLECTORS AND
COLLECTING.
Burdick, Jefferson R. The American
card catalog; East Stroudsburg? Pa.,
1960] 240 p. 741.67 60-31578
    NC1280 .B87 1960 MRR Alc.

ADVERTISING SPECIALTIES--YEARBOOKS.
The Advertising specialty register.
1950- ed. Trevose, Pa [etc.]
Advertising Specialty Institute
[etc.] 659.114 50-54758
    HF6146.N7 A4 MRR Alc Latest
    edition

ADVOCATES
see Lawyers

AERIAL PHOTOGRAPH READING
see Photographic interpretation
(Military science)

AEROLOGY
see Meteorology

AERONAUTICAL CHARTS--BIBLIOGRAPHY.
United States. Library of Congress.
Map Division. Aviation cartography;
2d ed. rev. and enl. Washington,
1960. 245 p. 016.62913254 60-
61621
    Z663.35 .A8 1960 MRR Alc.

AERONAUTICAL CHARTS--HISTORY.
United States. Library of Congress.
Map Division. Aviation cartography;
2d ed. rev. and enl. Washington,
1960. 245 p. 016.62913254 60-
61621
    Z663.35 .A8 1960 MRR Alc.

AERONAUTICAL RESEARCH--UNITED STATES.
United States. Library of Congress.
Science Policy Research Division.
Policy planning for aeronautical
research and development.
Washington, U.S. Govt. Print. Off.,
1966. xiii, 279 p. 629.13/0072/073
66-61802
    Z663.6 .P58 MRR Alc.

AERONAUTICS.
see also Air lines

see also Airports

see also Astronautics

see also Helicopters

see also Private flying

see also Rocketry

see also Rockets (Aeronautics)

AERONAUTICS--ABBREVIATIONS.
Moser, Reta C. Space-age acronyms;
2d ed., rev. and enl. New York,
IFI/Plenum, 1969. 534 p.
629.4/01/48 69-14416
    TL788 .M6 1969 MRR Alc.

AERONAUTICS--ACCIDENTS.
Taylor, John William Ransom. The
Guiness book of air facts and feats.
[2nd ed.] Enfield, Guiness
Superlatives, 1973. 288 p. [£2.95]
629.13/09 74-168629
    TL515 .T352 1973 MRR Alc.

AERONAUTICS--ACRONYMS.
Moser, Reta C. Space-age acronyms;
2d ed., rev. and enl. New York,
IFI/Plenum, 1969. 534 p.
629.4/01/48 69-14416
    TL788 .M6 1969 MRR Alc.

AERONAUTICS--BIBLIOGRAPHY.
Dickson, Katherine Murphy. History
of aeronautics and astronautics;
Washington, National Aeronautics and
Space Administration, 1967. vi, 117
l. 016.01662913 67-61736
Z5063.A1 D5 MRR Alc.

AERONAUTICS--BIOGRAPHY.
Riverain, Jean, Dictionnaire des
aéronautes célèbres. Paris,
Larousse [1970] 159 p. 74-22366
TL539 .R56 MRR Biog.

Who's who in aviation. 1973- New
York, Harwood & Charles Pub. Co.
629.13/0092/2 B 73-88547
TL539 .W54 MRR Biog Latest edition
/ Sci RR Latest edition

AERONAUTICS--CHRONOLOGY.
Gurney, Gene. A chronology of world
aviation. New York, F. Watts [1965]
245 p. 387.709 65-11756
TL515 .G83 MRR Alc.

Payne, L. G. S., Air dates. New
York, Praeger [1958] 565 p.
629.1309 629.109* 57-12275
TL515 .P33 1958 MRR Alc.

AERONAUTICS--COMPETITIONS.
Friedlander, Mark P. Higher, faster,
and farther. New York, Morrow, 1973.
349 p. [$10.00] 629.13/09 73-
9377
TL515 .F755 MRR Alc.

AERONAUTICS--DICTIONARIES.
Aviation & space dictionary. 1st-
1940- Los Angeles [etc.] Aero
Publishers [etc.] 629.1303 54-28287

TL509 .A8 Sci RR Latest edition /
MRR Alc Latest edition

Beckford, Lawrence Leslie. An A.B.C.
of aeronautics. London, Cassell
[1957] 113 p. 629.1303 629.103*
57-13957
TL509 .B37 MRR Alc.

Cescotti, Roderich. Luftfahrt -
Wörterbuch; 2. verb. Aufl.
München, H. Reich [1957, c1954] 448
p. 629.1303 60-24363
TL509 .C4 1957 MRR Alc.

Marks, Robert W. The new dictionary
& handbook of aerospace. New York,
Praeger [1969] viii, 531 p. [10.00]
629.1/03 73-94221
TL509 .M35 MRR Alc.

Newlon, Clarke. The aerospace age
dictionary. New York, F. Watts
[1965] 282 p. 629.403 65-11382
TL788 .N4 MRR Alc.

Oppermann, Alfred. Wörterbuch der
modernen Technik. 3. Aufl. München-
Pullach, Verlag Dokumentation, 1972-
v. 603 72-306183
TL509 .O623 MRR Alc.

United States. National Aeronautics
and Space Administration.
Aeronautical dictionary. Washington,
U.S. Govt. Print. Off., 1959. vii,
199 p. 629.1305 60-60459
TL509 .U675 1959 MRR Alc.

AERONAUTICS--DICTIONARIES--GERMAN.
Cescotti, Roderich. Luftfahrt -
Wörterbuch; 2. verb. Aufl.
München, H. Reich [1957, c1954] 448
p. 629.1303 60-24363
TL509 .C4 1957 MRR Alc.

Leidecker, Kurt Friedrich, ed.
German-English technical dictionary
of aeronautics, rocketry, space
navigation ... New York, S. F. Vanni
[1950-51] 2 v. (968 p.) 629.1303
50-14702
TL509 .L4 MRR Alc.

Luftfahrttechnisches Wörterbuch,
Berlin, De Gruyter, 1960. xiv, 312
p. 62-33521
TL509 .L75 MRR Alc.

Oppermann, Alfred. Wörterbuch der
modernen Technik. 3. Aufl. München-
Pullach, Verlag Dokumentation, 1972-
v. 603 72-306183
TL509 .O623 MRR Alc.

AERONAUTICS--DICTIONARIES--POLYGLOT.
Elsevier's dictionary of aeronautics
in six languages: Amsterdam, New
York, Elsevier Pub. Co., 1964. 842
p. 629.1303 63-22063
TL509 .E4 MRR Alc.

AERONAUTICS--DICTIONARIES--RUSSIAN.
Konarski, Michael M. Russian-English
dictionary of modern terms in
aeronautics and rocketry. Oxford,
New York, Pergamon Press, 1962. xi,
515 p. 629.1303 62-16918
TL509 .K62 1962a MRR Alc.

Russian-English aerospace dictionary.
Berlin, W. de Gruyter, 1965. xvi,
407 p. 65-73606
TL509 .R83 MRR Alc.

AERONAUTICS--DIRECTORIES.
Interavia A B C. 1936- Geneve,
Interavia. 629.1305 36-22039
TL512 .I55 Sci RR Latest edition /
MRR Alc Latest edition

World aviation directory listing
companies and officials. v. 1-
(no. [1]-); spring 1940-
Washington, Ziff-Davis Pub. Co.,
Public Transportation and Travel
Division [etc.] 40-11496
TL512 .A63 MRR Alc Latest edition
/ Sci RR Latest edition

AERONAUTICS--FLIGHTS.
see also Space flight
Friedlander, Mark P. Higher, faster,
and farther. New York, Morrow, 1973.
349 p. [$10.00] 629.13/09 73-
9377
TL515 .F755 MRR Alc.

AERONAUTICS--HISTORY.
Friedlander, Mark P. Higher, faster,
and farther. New York, Morrow, 1973.
349 p. [$10.00] 629.13/09 73-
9377
TL515 .F755 MRR Alc.

Hildreth, Charles H. 1001 questions
answered about aviation history. New
York, Dodd, Mead [1969] xii, 419 p.
[8.50] 629.13/009 68-9453
TL515 .H56 MRR Alc.

Payne, L. G. S., Air dates. New
York, Praeger [1958] 565 p.
629.1309 629.109* 57-12275
TL515 .P33 1958 MRR Alc.

Taylor, John William Ransom. The
Guiness book of air facts and feats.
[2nd ed.] Enfield, Guiness
Superlatives, 1973. 288 p. [£2.95]
629.13/09 74-168629
TL515 .T352 1973 MRR Alc.

AERONAUTICS--LAWS AND REGULATIONS--
BIBLIOGRAPHY.
Heere, Wybo P. International
bibliography of air law 1900-1971.
Leiden, Sijthoff; Dobbs Ferry, N.Y.,
Oceana, 1972. xxvi, 569 p.
[fl78.00] 016.34146 72-86857
Z6464.A4 H43 MRR Alc.

AERONAUTICS--PERIODICALS--BIBLIOGRAPHY.
United States. Library of Congress.
Division of Aeronautics. A checklist
of aeronautical periodicals and
serials in the Library of Congress,
Washington, 1948. 129 p.
016.6291305 48-46903
Z663.22 .C45 MRR Alc.

United States. Library of Congress.
Science and Technology Division.
Aeronautical and space serial
publications; Washington, 1962. ix,
255 p. 61-60083
Z663.41 .A73 MRR Alc.

AERONAUTICS--STATISTICS.
Friedlander, Mark P. Higher, faster,
and farther. New York, Morrow, 1973.
349 p. [$10.00] 629.13/09 73-
9377
TL515 .F755 MRR Alc.

AERONAUTICS--YEARBOOKS.
Aerospace facts and figures. [1st]-
ed.; 1945- Fallbrook, Calif. [etc.]
Aero Publishers [etc.] 629.13058 46-
25007
TL501 .A818 Sci RR Latest edition
/ MRR Alc Latest edition

The Aerospace year book. [1st]-
1919- Washington [etc.] Books, inc.
[etc.] 629.13058 19-13828
TL501 .A563 Sci RR Latest edition
/ MRR Alc Latest edition

Jane's all the world's aircraft.
[1st]- issue; 1909- London [etc.]
S. Low, Marston & Co. 629.133058 10-
8268
TL501 .J3 MRR Alc Latest edition /
Sci RR Latest edition

World airline record. [1st]- ed.;
1950/51- Chicago, Roadcap Associates
[etc.] 387.72 51-3819
TL501 .W675 Sci RR Latest edition
/ MRR Alc Latest edition

AERONAUTICS--ASIA--DIRECTORIES.
Aviation directory of Asia. 1956-
Bombay, Aeronautical Publications of
India. 57-20446
TL512 .A846 MRR Alc Latest edition

AERONAUTICS--GREAT BRITAIN--DIRECTORIES.
"Flight" directory of British
aviation. 1970- Kingston upon
Thames, Kelly Directories Ltd.
629.13/0025/42 76-618594
TL512 .F48 Sci RR Latest edition /
MRR Alc Latest edition

AERONAUTICS--INDIA--DIRECTORIES.
Aviation directory of Asia. 1956-
Bombay, Aeronautical Publications of
India. 57-20446
TL512 .A846 MRR Alc Latest edition

AERONAUTICS--RUSSIA--BIBLIOGRAPHY.
United States. Library of Congress.
Reference Dept. Aeronautical
sciences and aviation in the Soviet
Union, Washington, 1955. xx, 274 p.
016.62913 55-60018
Z663.23 .A4 MRR Alc.

AERONAUTICS--UNITED STATES.
U.S. civil aircraft. v. 1- 1962-
Fallbrook, Calif. [etc.] Aero
Publishers. 629.13334 62-15967
TL670 .U15 MRR Alc Full set

AERONAUTICS--UNITED STATES--HISTORY.
Astronautics and aeronautics;
1915/60- Washington, Scientific and
Technical Information Division,
National Aeronautics and Space
Administration [etc.; for sale by the
Superintendent of Documents, U.S.
Govt. Print. Off.] 65-60008
TL521.3.A8 A3 MRR Alc Partial set

AERONAUTICS--UNITED STATES--STATISTICS.
Aerospace facts and figures. [1st]-
ed.; 1945- Fallbrook, Calif. [etc.]
Aero Publishers [etc.] 629.13058 46-
25007
TL501 .A818 Sci RR Latest edition
/ MRR Alc Latest edition

United States. Federal Aviation
Administration. F A A statistical
handbook of aviation. Washington,
For sale by the Supt. of Docs., U.S.
Govt. Print. Off. 387.7/0973 73-
609572
TL521 .A41612 Sci RR Latest
edition / MRR Alc Latest edition

AERONAUTICS--UNITED STATES--STATISTICS--
YEARBOOKS.
United States. Federal Aviation
Administration. F A A statistical
handbook of aviation. Washington,
For sale by the Supt. of Docs., U.S.
Govt. Print. Off. 387.7/0973 73-
609572
TL521 .A41612 Sci RR Latest
edition / MRR Alc Latest edition

AERONAUTICS, COMMERCIAL--CHARTERING.
Jurgen, Jens. Air travel and charter
flight handbook; Kings Park, N.Y.,
Travel Information Bureau [1973] 192
p. [$4.95] 387.7/42 73-168342
HE9787 .J87 MRR Alc.

AERONAUTICS, COMMERCIAL--UNITED STATES--
DIRECTORIES.
National highway and airway carriers
and routes. v. 1- Mar. 1942-
Chicago, National Highway Carriers
Directory. 388.3058 42-14688
HE5623.A45 N3 MRR Alc Latest
edition

AERONAUTICS, COMMERCIAL--UNITED STATES--
STATISTICS.
United States. Civil Aeronautics
Board. Handbook of airline
statistics; United States
certificated air carriers. 1938/42-
[Washington, U.S. Govt. Print. Off.]
44-40873
TL521 .A242 MRR Alc Latest edition

AERONAUTICS, MILITARY--DICTIONARIES.
United States. Aerospace Studies
Institute. The United States Air
Force dictionary. [Maxwell Air Force
Base? Ala.] Air University Press; for
sale by the Superintendent of
Documents, U.S. Govt. Print. Off.
1956. xi, 578 p. 358.403 56-61737

UG630 .U637 1956 MRR Alc.

AERONAUTICS, MILITARY--HISTORY.
Taylor, John William Ransom. The
Guiness book of air facts and feats.
[2nd ed.] Enfield, Guiness
Superlatives, 1973. 288 p. [£2.95]
629.13/09 74-168629
TL515 .T352 1973 MRR Alc.

AERONAUTICS, MILITARY--UNITED STATES.
Swanborough, Frederick Gordon.
United States military aircraft since
1908. Revised ed. London, Putnam,
1971 (i.e. 1972). xi, 675 p.
[£6.50] 623.74/6/0973 72-185449
TL685.3 .S95 1972 MRR Alc.

Swanborough, Frederick Gordon.
United States Navy aircraft since
1911. London, Putnam, 1968. x, 518
p. [84/-] 623.7/46 70-354248
VG93 .S92 MRR Alc.

United States. Bureau of Aeronautics
(Navy Dept.) A calendar of
significant events in the growth and
development of United States naval
aviation, 1898-1956. [Washington,
1956] 64 p. 623.74 629.13* 58-
60324
VG93 .A62 1956 MRR Alc.

AERONAUTICS, MILITARY--UNITED STATES--
HISTORY.
Glines, Carroll V., The compact
history of the United States Air
Force New and rev. ed. New York,
Hawthorn Books [1973]   366 p.
358.4/13/0973   72-11218
UG633 .G52 1973 MRR Alc.

Wagner, Ray. American combat planes.
New rev. ed. Garden City, N.Y.,
Doubleday, 1868.   442 p. [$12.95]
623.7/46   67-10351
TL685.3 .W17 1968 MRR Alc.

AERONAUTICS AND STATE--UNITED STATES.
United States. Library of Congress.
Science Policy Research Division.
Policy planning for aeronautical
research and development.
Washington, U.S. Govt. Print. Off.,
1966. xiii, 279 p.   629.13/0072/073
66-61802
Z663.6 .P58 MRR Alc.

AEROPLANE INDUSTRY AND TRADE--
DIRECTORIES.
Interavia A B C. 1936- Genève,
Interavia. 629.1305 36-22039
TL512 .I55 Sci RR Latest edition /
MRR Alc Latest edition

AEROPLANE INDUSTRY AND TRADE--ASIA--
DIRECTORIES.
Aviation directory of Asia. 1956-
Bombay, Aeronautical Publications of
India. 57-20446
TL512 .A846 MRR Alc Latest edition

AEROPLANE INDUSTRY AND TRADE--GREAT
BRITAIN--DIRECTORIES.
"Flight" directory of British
aviation. 1970- Kingston upon
Thames, Kelly Directories Ltd.
629.13/0025/42 76-618594
TL512 .F48 Sci RR Latest edition /
MRR Alc Latest edition

Sell's British aviation. London,
Sell's Publications Ltd. [etc.] 57-
22102
Began publication in 1947.
TL512 .S4 MRR Alc Latest edition

AEROPLANE INDUSTRY AND TRADE--UNITED
STATES.
U.S. civil aircraft. v. 1-   1962-
Fallbrook, Calif. [etc.] Aero
Publishers. 629.13334 62-15967
TL670 .U15 MRR Alc Full set

AEROPLANE INDUSTRY AND TRADE--UNITED
STATES--BIOGRAPHY.
Who's who in aviation. 1973- New
York, Harwood & Charles Pub. Co.
629.13/0092/2 B 73-88547
TL539 .W54 MRR Biog Latest edition
/ Sci RR Latest edition

AEROPLANE INDUSTRY AND TRADE--UNITED
STATES--DIRECTORIES.
World aviation directory listing
companies and officials. v. 1-
(no. [1]-   ); spring 1940-
Washington, Ziff-Davis Pub. Co.,
Public Transportation and Travel
Division [etc.] 40-11496
TL512 .A63 MRR Alc Latest edition
/ Sci RR Latest edition

AEROPLANES--HISTORY.
King, Horace Frederick, Milestones
of the air: New York, McGraw-Hill
[c1969] 157 p. [$10.00]
629.133/34 79-132100
TL670 .K52 MRR Alc.

Rolfe, Douglas. Airplanes of the
world, 1490-1969. Drawings and
descriptions of planes by Douglas
Rolfe. Historical introductions by
Alexis Dawydoff. Rev. by William
Winter, William Byshyn [and] Hank
Clark. [3d] rev. and enl. ed. New
York, Simon and Schuster [1969] 440
p. [7.50]   629.133/34/09 76-93904

TL670 .R58 1969 MRR Alc.

U.S. civil aircraft. v. 1-   1962-
Fallbrook, Calif. [etc.] Aero
Publishers. 629.13334 62-15967
TL670 .U15 MRR Alc Full set

AEROPLANES--IDENTIFICATION MARKS.
Wynn, Humphrey. World airline
insignia: London, Hamlyn, 1973. 159
p. [£0.50] 387.7/06/5 73-157590
TL603 .W96 MRR Alc.

AEROPLANES--MATERIALS.
United States. Library of Congress.
Science and Technology Division.
Materials research chronology, 1917-
1957. Dayton, Directorate of
Materials and Processes, Aeronautical
Systems Division, Wright Patterson
Air Force Base, 1962. viii, 59 p.
620.1 63-60204
Z663.41 .M33 MRR Alc.

AEROPLANES--MOTORS.
Wilkinson, Paul Howard, Aircraft
engines of the world. New York,
N.Y., P. H. Wilkinson [1941- v.
629.13435 41-13397
TL701 .W46 MRR Alc.

AEROPLANES--PILOTING.
America's flying book. New York,
Scribner [1972] xxvii, 365 p.
[$12.95] 629.132/5217 72-1213
TL721.4 .A4 MRR Alc.

AEROPLANES--RECOGNITION.
Green, William. The Macdonald
aircraft handbook. Garden City,
N.Y., Doubleday [1966, c1964] 596 p.
629.1333 66-21006
TL670 .G8835 1966 MRR Alc.

AEROPLANES--REGISTERS.
Registre aeronautique international.
[Paris?] 74-613237
HE9769.A3 R4 MRR Alc Latest
edition

Richardson, J. H. Fleet operators:
Europe. Brentwood, Air Britain
[1968] 56 p. [7/6] 387.7/33/4094
70-387656
HE9769.E9 R53 MRR Alc.

AEROPLANES--ROCKET ENGINES--
DICTIONARIES.
Herrick, John W., ed. Rocket
encyclopedia. Los Angeles, Aero
Publishers [1959] 607 p.
629.134354 59-8488
TL780.5 .H4 MRR Alc.

AEROPLANES--YEARBOOKS.
The Aerospace year book. [1st]-
1919- Washington [etc.] Books, inc.
[etc.] 629.13058 19-13828
TL501 .A563 Sci RR Latest edition
/ MRR Alc Latest edition

Jane's all the world's aircraft.
[1st]- issue; 1909- London [etc.]
S. Low, Marston & Co. 629.133058 10-
8268
TL501 .J3 MRR Alc Latest edition /
Sci RR Latest edition

AEROPLANES, GOVERNMENT
see Aeroplanes, Military

AEROPLANES, MILITARY.
Green, William. The world guide to
combat planes; London, Macdonald,
1966. 2 v. [25/- (each vol.)]
623.746 66-67853
TL685.3 .G735 MRR Alc.

King, Horace Frederick, Milestones
of the air: New York, McGraw-Hill
[c1969] 157 p. [$10.00]
629.133/34 79-132100
TL670 .K52 MRR Alc.

Larkins, William T., U.S. Navy
aircraft, 1921-1941. [1st ed.]
Concord, Calif., Aviation History
Publications, c1961. 391 p.
623.746 61-18083
VG93 .L32 MRR Alc.

Swanborough, Frederick Gordon.
United States military aircraft since
1908. Revised ed. London, Putnam,
1971 (i.e. 1972). xi, 675 p.
[£6.50] 623.74/6/0973 72-185449
TL685.3 .S95 1972 MRR Alc.

Taylor, John William Ransom. Combat
aircraft of the world; New York,
Putnam [1969] 647 p. [20.00]
623.7/46 68-25459
TL685.3 .T326 1969 MRR Alc.

Taylor, John William Ransom.
Military aircraft of the world New
York, Scribner [1971] 230 p.
[$5.95] 623.74/6 76-153657
TL685.3 .T3268 MRR Alc.

Taylor, John William Ransom.
Warplanes of the world New York,
Arco Pub. Co. [1966] 203, vii p.
623.746 66-23503
TL685.3 .T33 1966a MRR Alc.

Thetford, Owen Gordon, Aircraft of
the 1914-1918 war, Harleyford,
Marlow, Eng., Re-published under
licence by Harleyford Publications,
1954. v, 127 p. 623.746 629.133*
55-29424
TL685.3 .T44 1954 MRR Alc.

Thetford, Owen Gordon, British naval
aircraft since 1912. [2d ed.]
London, Putnam [1962] 430 p.
623.746 63-25486
VG95.G7 T48 1962 MRR Alc.

AEROPLANES, MILITARY--DICTIONARIES.
Quick, John, Dictionary of weapons
and military terms. New York, McGraw-
Hill [1973] xii, 515 p. 623/.03
73-8757
U24 .Q5 MRR Alc.

AEROPLANES, MILITARY--HISTORY.
Wagner, Ray. American combat planes.
New rev. ed. Garden City, N.Y.,
Doubleday, 1968. 442 p. [$12.95]
623.7/46 67-10351
TL685.3 .W17 1968 MRR Alc.

AEROPLANES, PRIVATE.
U.S. civil aircraft. v. 1-   1962-
Fallbrook, Calif. [etc.] Aero
Publishers. 629.13334 62-15967
TL670 .U15 MRR Alc Full set

AEROSPACE INDUSTRIES--DIRECTORIES.
World aviation directory listing
companies and officials. v. 1-
(no. [1]-   ); spring 1940-
Washington, Ziff-Davis Pub. Co.,
Public Transportation and Travel
Division [etc.] 40-11496
TL512 .A63 MRR Alc Latest edition
/ Sci RR Latest edition

AEROSPACE INDUSTRIES--UNITED STATES.
The Aerospace year book. [1st]-
1919- Washington [etc.] Books, inc.
[etc.] 629.13058 19-13828
TL501 .A563 Sci RR Latest edition
/ MRR Alc Latest edition

AEROSPACE MEDICINE
see Space medicine

AESCHYLUS--DICTIONARIES, INDEXES, ETC.
Dindorf, Wilhelm, Lexicon
Aeschyleum. Lipsiae, G. B. Teubner,
1876. vi, p., 1 l., 432 p. 09-
22327
PA3849.Z9D5 MRR Alc.

Italie, Gabriel, Index Aeschyleus.
Leiden, E. J. Brill, 1955 [i.e. 1954-
55] x, 336 p. a 55-1412
PA3849.Z9I8 MRR Alc.

AESTHETICS.
see also Art

see also Color

see also Painting

see also Sculpture

Sparshott, Francis Edward, The
structure of aesthetics. Toronto,
University of Toronto Press, 1963.
xiii, 471 p. 64-966
BH201 .S53 MRR Alc.

AESTHETICS--BIBLIOGRAPHY.
Borroni, Fabia. "Il Cicognara,"
Firenze, Sansoni, 1954- v. 55-
18980
Z2357 .B6 MRR Alc.

Hammond, William Alexander, A
bibliography of æsthetics and of the
philosophy of the fine arts from 1900
to 1932, Rev. and enl. ed. New
York, Longmans, Green, and company,
1934. x, 205 p. 016.701 34-13459

Z5870 .H22 1934 MRR Alc.

AESTHETICS--EARLY WORKS TO 1800.
Aristoteles. Aristotle: The poetics.
London, W. Heinemann, New York, G.
P. Putnam's sons, 1932. xx, 500 p.
808.1 mrr01-41
PA3612 .A8P5 1932d MRR Alc.

AESTHETICS--HISTORY.
Beardsley, Monroe C. Aesthetics from
classical Greece to the present;
[1st ed.] New York, Macmillan [1966]
414 p. 111.45 65-24765
BH81 .B4 1966 MRR Alc.

AFFORESTATION.
see also Forests and forestry

AFGHANISTAN.
Smith, Harvey Henry, Area handbook
for Afghanistan. 4th ed.
[Washington, For sale by the Supt. of
Docs., U.S. Govt. Print. Off.] 1973.
lvi, 453 p. [$4.35] 915.81/03/4
73-600084
DS352 .S55 1974 MRR Alc.

AFGHANISTAN--BIBLIOGRAPHY.
Wilber, Donald Newton. Annotated
bibliography of Afghanistan, 3d ed.
New Haven, Human Relations Area Files
Press, 1968. ix, 252 p. 016.91581
68-22209
Z3016 .W5 1968 MRR Alc.

AFGHANISTAN--DESCRIPTION AND TRAVEL--
GUIDE-BOOKS.
Fodor's Islamic Asia: Iran,
Afghanistan, Pakistan. 1973- New
York, D. McKay. [$12.95] 915 74-
641031
DS254 .F642 MRR Alc Latest edition

AFGHANISTAN--GAZETTEERS.
United States. Geographic Names
Division. Afghanistan: official
standard names Washington, 1971.
xvi, 170 p. 915.81/003 74-614522
DS351 .U55 MRR Alc.

AFGHANISTAN--HISTORY.
Fraser-Tytler, William Kerr, Sir,
Afghanistan: a study of political
developments in central and southern
Asia, 3rd ed., revised London, New
York [etc.] Oxford U.Pr., 1967. xvi,
362 p. [45/-] 958.1 67-88066
DS356 .F7 1967 MRR Alc.

AFGHANISTAN--HISTORY. (Cont.)
Gregorian, Vartan. The emergence of
modern Afghanistan; Stanford,
Calif., Stanford University Press,
1969. viii, 586 p. [17.50] 958.1
69-13178
  DS361 .G68 MRR Alc.

AFRICA.
Daggs, Elisa. All Africa; New York,
Hastings House [1970] viii, 824 p.
[30.00] 916/.03/3 67-15344
  DT3 .D3 1970 MRR Alc.

Legum, Colin, ed. Africa; a handbook
to the continent. Rev. and enl. ed.
New York, Praeger [1966] xii, 558 p.
916 66-12478
  DT5 .L35 1966a MRR Alc.

Mungai, Njoroge. The independent
nations of Africa. [Nairobi, Printed
by Acme Press, 1967] 352 p. [KSh
45/-] 916 67-105950
  DT5 .M8 MRR Alc.

Wallbank, Thomas Walter, ed.
Documents on modern Africa
Princeton, N.J., Van Nostrand [1964]
192 p. 960 64-4841
  DT20 .W25 MRR Alc.

AFRICA--BIBLIOGRAPHY.
The African experience. Evanston,
Northwestern University Press, 1970-
v. 916/.03/3 70-98466
  DT14 .A37 MRR Alc.

Aguolu, Christian Chukwunedu. Ghana
in the humanities and social
sciences, 1900-1971: a bibliography.
Metuchen, N.J., Scarecrow Press,
1973. xi, 469 p. 016.91667 73-
9519
  Z3785 .A65 MRR Alc.

American Universities Field Staff. A
select bibliography: Asia, Africa,
Eastern Europe, Latin America. New
York [1960] ix, 534 p. 016.9019
60-10482
  Z5579 .A5 MRR Alc.

Bratton, Michael. American doctoral
dissertations on Africa, 1886-1972.
Waltham, Mass. [African Studies
Association, Research, 1973] xx, 165
p. 016.916/03/3 73-168202
  Z3501 .B7 MRR Alc.

Brunn, Stanley D. Urbanization in
developing countries; East Lansing,
Latin American Studies Center,
Michigan State University, 1971.
xviii, 693 p. 016.30136/3/091724
79-172535
  Z7164.U7 B7 MRR Alc.

Cruger, Doris M. A list of American
doctoral dissertations on Africa,
Ann Arbor, Mich., Xerox, University
Microfilms Library Services, 1967.
36 p. 016.378/24 67-5644
  Z5055.U49 C75 MRR Alc.

Dinstel, Marion. List of French
doctoral dissertations on Africa,
1884-1961. Boston, G. K. Hall, 1966.
v, 336 p. 016.916 68-367
  Z3501 .D5 MRR Alc.

Duignan, Peter. Handbook of American
resources for African studies.
[Stanford, Calif.] Hoover Institution
on War, Revolution, and Peace,
Stanford University, 1967. xvii, 218
p. 016.916 66-20901
  Z3501 .D8 MRR Alc.

Fontán Lobé, Juan. Bibliografía
colonial. Madrid [Dirección general
de Marruecos y colonias] 1946. 669
p., 1 l. 47-3480
  Z3501 .F6 MRR Alc.

Fontvieille, Jean Roger. Guide
bibliographique du Monde noir.
Yaoundé, Direction des affaires
culturelles, 1970 [cover 1971- v.
72-205179
  Z5118.N4 F64 MRR Alc.

Halstead, John P. Modern European
imperialism; Boston, G. K. Hall,
1974. 2 v. 016.90908 73-19511
  Z6204 .H35 MRR Alc.

Harvard University. Library. African
history and literatures; Cambridge,
Mass.; distributed by Harvard
University Press, 1971. 600 p.
016.96 70-128716
  Z3509 .H37 MRR Alc.

Liniger-Goumaz, Max. Eurafrique:
bibliographie générale. Genève,
Editions du Temps, 1970. 160 p.
76-505812
  Z3508.R4 L5 MRR Alc.

Royal Commonwealth Society. Library.
Subject catalogue of the Library of
the Royal Empire Society, [1st ed.
reprinted] London, Dawsons for the
Royal Commonwealth Society, 1967. 4
v. [60/-/- per set (16/-/- per
vol.)] 016.942 68-70847
  Z7164.C7 R82 1967 MRR Alc.

United States. Library of Congress.
African Section. A list of American
doctoral dissertations on Africa.
Washington, General Reference and
Bibliography Division, Reference
Dept., Library of Congress; [for sale
by the Superintendent of Documents,
U.S. Govt. Print. Off.] 1962. 69 p.
62-60088
  Z663.285 .L5 MRR Alc.

United States. Library of Congress.
European Affairs Division.
Continuing sources for research on
Africa, [Washington] 1952. 21 p.
016.916 52-60041
  Z663.26 .C6 MRR Alc.

United States. Library of Congress.
European Affairs Division.
Introduction to Africa; Washington,
University Press of Washington [1952]
ix, 237 p. 016.96 52-60007
  Z663.26 .I5 MRR Alc.

United States. Library of Congress.
Reference Dept. Research and
information on Africa! Washington,
1954. vi, 70 p. 016.916 54-60024

  Z663.26 .C62 MRR Alc.

AFRICA--BIBLIOGRAPHY--CATALOGS.
Harvard University. Library. Africa:
classification schedule, Cambridge,
Published by the Harvard University
Library; distributed by the Harvard
University Press, 1965. 302, 204,
196 p. 016.91603 65-29301
  Z881 .H34035 MRR Alc.

Howard University, Washington, D.C.
Library. Moorland Foundation. A
catalogue of the African collection
in the Moorland Foundation, Howard
University Library. Washington,
Howard University Press, 1958. 398
p. 016.96 58-9338
  Z3509 .H75 MRR Alc.

Northwestern University, Evanston,
Ill. Library. Catalog of the African
collection. Boston, G.K. Hall, 1962.
2 v. a 64-262
  Z3509 .N6 MRR Alc.

Royal Commonwealth Society. Library.
Subject catalogue of the Royal
Commonwealth Society, London.
Boston, Mass., G. K. Hall, 1971. 7
v. 017.1 70-180198
  Z7164.C7 R83 MRR Alc (Dk 33)

AFRICA--BIBLIOGRAPHY--PERIODICALS.
African abstracts. v. 1- Jan. 1950-
[London] 960 55-18105
  DT1 .I553 MRR Alc Full set

AFRICA--BIOGRAPHY.
Melady, Thomas Patrick. Profiles of
African leaders. New York,
Macmillan, 1961. 186 p. 960.3 61-
5661
  DT30 .M4 MRR Biog.

Segal, Ronald, Political Africa;
London, Stevens, 1961. ix, 475 p.
920.06 62-1394
  DT18 .S4 1961a MRR Biog.

AFRICA--BIOGRAPHY--DICTIONARIES.
Dictionary of African biography. 1st
ed.: 1970- London, Melrose Press.
920.06 79-613005
  CT1920 .D52 MRR Biog Latest
edition

Les Élites africaines; "1re
édition 1970-71." Paris, Ediafric-
Service, 1971. 298 p. [180F] 77-
593637
  DT533.A2 E4 MRR Biog.

Herdeck, Donald E., African authors;
[1st ed.] Washington, Black Orpheus
Press, 1973- v. [$27.50 (v. 1)]
809/.89/6 B 73-172338
  PL8010 .H38 MRR Biog.

Répertoire de la diplomatie
africaine: 1. éd. Paris, Ediafric-
La Documentation africaine [1970]
369 p. 72-359872
  JX1861 .R44 1970 MRR Biog.

AFRICA--CENSUS--BIBLIOGRAPHY.
United States. Library of Congress.
Census Library Project. Population
censuses and other official
demographic statistics of Africa, not
including British Africa;
Washington, U.S. Govt. Print. Off.,
1950 [i.e.1951] v, 53 p. 016.312
52-60006
  Z7554.A34 U5 1950 MRR Alc.

United States. Library of Congress.
Census Library Project. Population
censuses and other official
demographic statistics of British
Africa; Washington, U.S. Govt.
Print. Off., 1950. v, 78 p.
016.312 50-60396
  Z7554.A35 U5 MRR Alc.

AFRICA--CIVILIZATION--ADDRESSES,
ESSAYS, LECTURES.
The African experience. Evanston,
Northwestern University Press, 1970-
v. 916/.03/3 70-98466
  DT14 .A37 MRR Alc.

AFRICA--CIVILIZATION--STUDY AND
TEACHING.
The African experience. Evanston,
Northwestern University Press, 1970-
v. 916/.03/3 70-98466
  DT14 .A37 MRR Alc.

AFRICA--CLIMATE.
Great Britain. Meteorological Office.
Tables of temperature, relative
humidity and precipitation for the
world. 2nd ed. London, H.M.S.O.,
1966- v. [1/5/- (pt. 3) 1/15/-
(pt. 4) 15/6 (pt. 5)] 551.5/021/2
76-385248
  QC982.5 .G732 MRR Alc.

AFRICA--COLONIZATION.
Hertslet, Edward, Sir, The map of
Africa by treaty, 3d ed.: London,
Printed for H.M. Stationery off., by
Harrison and sons, 1909. 3 v. and
portfolio of maps. 10-833
  JX1026 1886a MRR Alc.

AFRICA--COMMERCE--DIRECTORIES.
Annuaire des entreprises d'outre-mer.
Paris. 58-45147
  HC279 .A65 MRR Alc Latest edition

Anuário do ultramar português.
[Lisboa] Empresa Nacional de
Publicidade [etc.] 42-29
  Began publication 1935?
  JV4201 .A6 MRR Alc Latest edition

Bottin Afrique centrale, Algérie,
Maroc-Tunisie, etc. 1946- Paris,
Société Didot-Bottin [etc.] 48-
41815
  JV1801 .B6 MRR Alc Latest edition

Braby's commercial directory of
South, East and Central Africa.
Durban, A. C. Braby. 338.4/025/67
72-626695
  HF3893 .B7 MRR Alc Latest edition

Chico, Vicente V. International
importers & exporters: 1st ed.
Manila, Nationwide Business Agency
[1971] 1068 p. 382/.025 70-31299

  HF54.P6 C54 MRR Alc.

The Eastern trade directory. [Cairo]
ne 62-1365
  HF3760.8 .E25 MRR Alc Latest
edition

Owen's commerce and travel and
international register. London,
Owen's Commerce & Travel Ltd.
380.1/025 72-626541
  HF3872 .P3 MRR Alc Latest edition

Trado Asian African directory of
exporters-importers & manufacturers.
1959/60- New Delhi, Trado
Publications Private Ltd. [etc.]
338/.0025/5 72-622940
  HF3763 .T74 MRR Alc Latest edition

AFRICA--COMMERCE--YEARBOOKS.
Owen's commerce and travel and
international register. London,
Owen's Commerce & Travel Ltd.
380.1/025 72-626541
  HF3872 .P3 MRR Alc Latest edition

AFRICA--DESCRIPTION AND TRAVEL--1951-
Hance, William Adams, The geography
of modern Africa, New York, Columbia
University Press, 1964. xiv, 653 p.
916 64-14239
  DT12.2 .H28 MRR Alc.

Stamp, Laurence Dudley, Sir, Africa:
a study in tropical development 3rd
ed. New York, Wiley [1972] xi, 520
p. 916 75-178152
  DT12.2 .S66 1972 MRR Alc.

AFRICA--DESCRIPTION AND TRAVEL--1951- --
GUIDE-BOOKS.
Allen, Philip M. The traveler's
Africa; New York, Hopkinson and
Blake [1973] xix, 972 p. [$12.95]
916/.04/3 73-78904
  DT2 .A45 MRR Alc.

Kane, Robert S. Africa A to Z Rev.
ed. Garden City, N.Y., Doubleday
[1972] 430 p. [$8.95] 916/.04/3
75-175386
  DT2 .K35 1972 MRR Alc.

AFRICA--DESCRIPTION AND TRAVEL--GUIDE-
BOOKS.
Allen, Philip M. The traveler's
Africa; New York, Hopkinson and
Blake [1973] xix, 972 p. [$12.95]
916/.04/3 73-78904
    DT2 .A45 MRR Alc.

Automobile Association of South
Africa. Trans-African highways; 5th
ed., completely rev. Johannesburg,
1963. 352 p. 65-86771
    GV1025.A2 A84 1963 MRR Alc.

AFRICA--DICTIONARIES AND ENCYCLOPEDIAS.
African encyclopedia. London, Oxford
University Press, 1974. 3-554 p.
[£4.00] 032 74-169352
    DT2 .A3 MRR Alc.

AFRICA--DIPLOMATIC AND CONSULAR SERVICE-
-REGISTERS, LISTS, ETC.
Repertoire de la diplomatie
africaine: 1. ed. Paris, Ediafric-
La Documentation africaine [1970]
369 p. 72-359872
    JX1861 .R44 1970 MRR Biog.

AFRICA--DIRECTORIES.
Anuario do ultramar português.
[Lisboa] Empresa Nacional de
Publicidade [etc.] 42-29
Began publication 1935?
    JV4201 .A6 MRR Alc Latest edition

The Europa year book. 1959- London,
Europa Publications. 341.184 59-
2942
    JN1 .E85 Sci RR Latest edition /
    MRR Ref Desk Latest edition

AFRICA--ECONOMIC CONDITIONS--1945-
International Monetary Fund. Surveys
of African economies. Washington,
1968- v.   [5.00] 330.96 79-
3108
    HC502 .I57 MRR Alc.

Robson, Peter. The economies of
Africa. Evanston, [Ill.]
Northwestern University Press, 1969.
528 p. 330.96 72-7045
    HC502 .R63 1969b MRR Alc.

AFRICA--FILM CATALOGS.
Johnson, Harry Alleyn. Multimedia
materials for Afro-American studies;
New York, R. R. Bowker Co., 1971.
353 p. 016.9173/06/96073 75-126009

    LC2801 .J63 MRR Alc.

AFRICA--FOREIGN RELATIONS--TREATIES.
Hertslet, Edward, Sir, The map of
Africa by treaty, 3d ed.: London,
Printed for H.M. Stationery off., by
Harrison and sons, 1909. 3 v. and
portfolio of maps. 10-833
    JX1026 1896a MRR Alc.

AFRICA--GOVERNMENT PUBLICATIONS--
BIBLIOGRAPHY.
United States. Library of Congress.
African Section. Official
publications of French Equatorial
Africa, French Cameroons, and Togo,
Washington, General Reference and
Bibliography Division, Reference
Dept.; Library of Congress; [for sale
by the Superintendent of Documents,
U.S. Govt. Print. Off.] 1964. xi, 78
p. 64-60029
    Z663.285 .O32 MRR Alc.

AFRICA--GOVERNMENT PUBLICATIONS--
BIBLIOGRAPHY--CATALOGS.
Boston University. Libraries.
Catalog of African government
documents and African area index. 2d
ed., rev. and enl. Boston, G. K.
Hall, 1964. 471 p. 65-98838
    Z3508.O6 B6 1964 MRR Alc.

AFRICA--HANDBOOKS, MANUALS, ETC.
Black Africa; a comparative handbook
New York, Free Press [1972] xxviii,
483 p. 309.1/67 72-143505
    DT352.8 .B56 MRR Alc.

Worldmark encyclopedia of the
nations. [4th ed.] New York,
Worldmark Press, [1971] 5 v.
910/.3 76-152128
    G103 .W65 1971 MRR Ref Desk.

A Year book of the Commonwealth.
1969- London, H.M. Stationery Off.
320.9/171/242 79-7332
    JN248 .C5912 MRR Alc Latest
    edition

AFRICA--HISTORICAL GEOGRAPHY.
Hertslet, Edward, Sir, The map of
Africa by treaty, 3d ed.: London,
Printed for H.M. Stationery off., by
Harrison and sons, 1909. 3 v. and
portfolio of maps. 10-833
    JX1026 1896a MRR Alc.

AFRICA--HISTORY.
July, Robert William. A history of
the African people, 2d ed. New
York, Scribner [1974] xxiv, 731 p.
[$15.00] 960 73-1348
    DT20 .J8 1974 MRR Alc.

AFRICA--HISTORY--1884-1960.
Hallett, Robin. Africa since 1875 :
Ann Arbor : University of Michigan
Press, [1974] xi, 807, lix p. :
[$15.00] 960/.3 72-91505
    DT29 .H34 1974 MRR Alc.

AFRICA--HISTORY--1960-
Hallett, Robin. Africa since 1875 :
Ann Arbor : University of Michigan
Press, [1974] xi, 807, lix p. :
[$15.00] 960/.3 72-91505
    DT29 .H34 1974 MRR Alc.

AFRICA--HISTORY--BIBLIOGRAPHY--CATALOGS.
Harvard University. Library. African
history and literatures; Cambridge,
Mass.; distributed by Harvard
University Press, 1971. 600 p.
016.96 70-128716
    Z3509 .H37 MRR Alc.

AFRICA--HISTORY--CHRONOLOGY.
The African experience. Evanston,
Northwestern University Press, 1970-
v.   916/.03/3 70-98466
    DT14 .A37 MRR Alc.

AFRICA--HISTORY--SOURCES.
Hertslet, Edward, Sir, The map of
Africa by treaty, 3d ed.: London,
Printed for H.M. Stationery off., by
Harrison and sons, 1909. 3 v. and
portfolio of maps. 10-833
    JX1026 1896a MRR Alc.

AFRICA--HISTORY--SOURCES--BIBLIOGRAPHY.
Duignan, Peter. Handbook of American
resources for African studies.
[Stanford, Calif.] Hoover Institution
on War, Revolution, and Peace,
Stanford University, 1967. xvii, 218
p. 016.916 66-20901
    Z3501 .D8 MRR Alc.

AFRICA--LEARNED INSTITUTIONS AND
SOCIETIES--DIRECTORIES.
Museums in Africa; [Bonn, German
Africa Society] 1970. ix, 594 p.
[40.00] 069/.025/6 76-478923
    AM80.A2 M8 MRR Alc.

AFRICA--MANUFACTURES--DIRECTORIES.
Trade Asian African directory of
exporters-importers & manufacturers.
1959/60- New Delhi, Trade
Publications Private Ltd. [etc.]
338/.0025/5 72-622940
    HF3763 .T74 MRR Alc Latest edition

AFRICA--PERIODICALS--BIBLIOGRAPHY.
United States. Library of Congress.
African Section. Serials for African
studies, Washington, General
Reference and Bibliography Division,
Reference Dept.; Library of Congress,
1961. viii, 163 p. 016.916 61-
60072
    Z663.285 .S4 MRR Alc.

United States. Library of Congress.
Reference Dept. Periodicals on
Africa currently received in selected
American libraries. Washington,
1956. iv, 34 p. 56-60035
    Z663.2 .P4 MRR Alc.

United States. Library of Congress.
Reference Dept. Research and
information on Africa: Washington,
1954. vi, 70 p. 016.916 54-60024
    Z663.26 .C62 MRR Alc.

AFRICA--PERIODICALS--BIBLIOGRAPHY--
CATALOGS.
Michigan. State University, East
Lansing. Library. Research sources
for African studies; [East Lansing]
African Studies Center, Michigan
State University, 1969. vii, 384 p.
[3.00] 016.916/005 67-65352
    Z3503 .M52 MRR Alc.

AFRICA--PERIODICALS--INDEXES.
African abstracts. v. 1- Jan. 1950-
[London] 960 55-18105
    DT1 .I553 MRR Alc Full set

The African experience. Evanston,
Northwestern University Press, 1970-
v.   916/.03/3 70-98466
    DT14 .A37 MRR Alc.

Hess, Robert L. Semper ex Africa ...
[Stanford, Calif.] Hoover
Institution on War, Revolution, and
Peace, 1972] xxv, 800 p. 016.9167
71-185241
    Z3501 .H47 MRR Alc.

United States. Library of Congress.
African Section. Africa south of the
Sahara; index to periodical
literature, 1900-1970. Boston, G. K.
Hall, 1971. 4 v. 016/.9167/03 74-
170939
    Z3503 .U47 MRR Alc (Dk 33).

United States and Canadian
publications on Africa. 1960-
[Stanford, Calif., etc.] 016.9167
62-60021
    Z3501 .U59 MRR Alc Full set

AFRICA--POLITICS--1945-1960.
Mortimer, Edward. France and the
Africans, 1944-1960; New York,
Walker [1969] 390 p. [8.50]
325.344/096 68-13985
    DT33 .M65 1969b MRR Alc.

AFRICA--POLITICS--1960-
Segal, Ronald. Political Africa;
London, Stevens, 1961. ix, 475 p.
920.06 62-1384
    DT18 .S4 1961a MRR Biog.

AFRICA--POPULATION.
United States. Library of Congress.
Census Library Project. Population
censuses and other official
demographic statistics of Africa, not
including British Africa;
Washington, U.S. Govt. Print. Off.,
1950 [i.e.1951] v, 53 p. 016.312
52-60006
    Z7554.A34 U5 1950 MRR Alc.

United States. Library of Congress.
Census Library Project. Population
censuses and other official
demographic statistics of British
Africa; Washington, U.S. Govt.
Print. Off., 1950. v, 78 p.
016.312 50-60396
    Z7554.A35 U5 MRR Alc.

AFRICA--RELATIONS (GENERAL) WITH EUROPE-
-BIBLIOGRAPHY.
Liniger-Goumaz, Max. Eurafrique:
bibliographie générale. Geneve,
Editions du Temps, 1970. 160 p.
76-505812
    Z3508.R4 L5 MRR Alc.

AFRICA--SOCIETIES, ETC.--DIRECTORIES.
International Council of Voluntary
Agencies. Africa's NGOs. [Geneva,]
Conseil international des agences
benevoles, 1968. iv, 299 p.
[unpriced] 77-417459
    AS600 .I5A55 MRR Alc.

AFRICA--STATISTICS.
Africa. 1968- New York [etc.]
African Pub. Corp. [etc.] 915/.005
68-6810
    DT1 .A14 MRR Alc Latest edition

Africa Institute. Africa at a
glance; Pretoria, the Institute
[1968] [vi], 15, 16, [vi] p. [1.50]
316 70-386262
    DT5 .A52 1968 MRR Alc.

Black Africa; a comparative handbook
New York, Free Press [1972] xxviii,
483 p. 309.1/67 72-143505
    DT352.8 .B56 MRR Alc.

Deldycke, Tilo. La population active
et sa structure. Bruxelles, Centre
d'economie politique (de l'
Universite libre de Bruxelles,
(1968) viii, 236 p. [360.00]
331.1/12/0212 70-395436
    HD4826 .D34 MRR Alc.

Food and Agriculture Organization of
the United Nations. Trade yearbook.
v. 12- 1958- Rome. 338.14058 59-
3598
    HD9000.4 .F58 Sci RR Partial set /
    MRR Alc Latest edition

L'Industrie africaine. Paris,
Ediafric-La documentation africaine.
75-225548
    HC541 .I5 MRR Alc Latest edition

International Labor Office. Year
book of labour statistics. [1st]-
1935/36- Geneva. l 36-130
    HD4826 .I63 MRR Alc Latest edition

International Monetary Fund. Balance
of payments yearbook. 1946/47-
Washington. 382 49-6612
    HF1014 .I5 MRR Alc Latest edition

International Monetary Fund. Surveys
of African economies. Washington,
1968- v.   [5.00] 330.96 79-
3108
    HC502 .I57 MRR Alc.

Keyfitz, Nathan, Population: facts
and methods of demography San
Francisco, W. H. Freeman [1971] x,
613 p. [$13.50] 301.3/2/072 70-
141154
    HB885 .K43 MRR Alc.

Middle East and North Africa markets
review. [Epping, Eng.] Gower
Economic Publications. [£30.00]
330.9/56/04 74-640571
    HC410.7.A1 M48 MRR Alc Latest
    edition

Organization for Economic Cooperation
and Development. Foreign trade.
Commerce exterieur. Series C.
Commodity trade. Commerce par
produits. [Paris] 382/.021/2 72-
626755
    HF91 .O67 MRR Latest edition

AFRICA--STATISTICS. (Cont.)
Predicasts, inc. World food supply &
demand / Cleveland : Predicasts,
inc., 1974. v, 90 leaves ; 338.1/9
74-187853
HD9000.4 .P73 1974 MRR Alc

Showers, Victor, The world in
figures. New York, Wiley [1973]
xii, 585 p. 910/.21/2 73-9
G109 .S52 MRR Ref Desk

Stamp, Laurence Dudley, Sir, Africa:
a study in tropical development 3rd
ed. New York, Wiley [1972] xi, 520
p. 916 75-178152
DT12.2 .S66 1972 MRR Alc.

United Nations. Conference on Trade
and Development. Secretariat. Trade
prospects and capital needs of
developing countries; New York,
United Nations, 1968. ix, 614 p.
[8.00] 382/.09172/3 75-5913
HF1413 .U52 MRR Alc.

United Nations. Statistical Office.
The growth of world industry, 1938-
1961: New York, United Nations,
1963. xvi, 849 p. 338.4083 63-
25411
HC59 .U46 MRR Alc.

United Nations. Statistical Office.
Yearbook of international trade
statistics. 1st-   issue: 1950- New
York. 382.058 51-8987
JX1977 .A2   MRR Ref Desk Latest
edition

United States. Bureau of the Census.
U.S. foreign trade: general imports,
world area by commodity groupings.
1970- [Washington, For sale by the
Supt. of Docs., U.S. Govt. Print.
Off.] 382/.6/0973 78-649732
HF105 .C137172 MRR Alc Latest
edition

United States. Bureau of the Census.
U.S. foreign trade: exports, SIC-
based products. 1970- [Washington,
For sale by the Supt. of Docs., U.S.
Govt. Print. Off.] 382/.6/0973 71-
648606
HF105 .C137166 MRR Alc Latest
edition

United States. Bureau of the Census.
U.S. foreign trade: exports, world
area by commodity groupings. 1970-
[Washington, For sale by the Supt. of
Docs., U.S. Govt. Print. Off.]
382/.6/0873 79-648608
HF105 .C137132 MRR Alc Latest
edition

AFRICA--STATISTICS--BIBLIOGRAPHY.
Harvey, Joan M. Statistics Africa:
Beckenham (Kent), C.B.D. Research
Ltd, 1970. iii-xii, 175 p. [80/-]
016.316 72-479012
Z7554.A34 H37 MRR Alc.

Texas. University. Population
Research Center. International
population census bibliography.
Austin, Bureau of Business Research,
University of Texas, 1965-67. 6 v.
016.312 66-63578
Z7164.D3 T45 MRR Alc.

United States. Library of Congress.
Census Library Project. Population
censuses and other official
demographic statistics of Africa, not
including British Africa;
Washington, U.S. Govt. Print. Off.,
1950 [i.e.1951] v, 53 p. 016.312
52-60006
Z7554.A34 U5 1950 MRR Alc.

United States. Library of Congress.
Census Library Project. Population
censuses and other official
demographic statistics of British
Africa; Washington, U.S. Govt.
Print. Off., 1950. v, 78 p.
016.312 50-60396
Z7554.A35 U5 MRR Alc.

AFRICA--STUDY AND TEACHING.
Shapiro, Sandra. Directory of
financial aid in higher education;
Waltham, Mass., African Studies
Association, Research Liaison
Committee, Brandeis University [1973]
v, 166 p. 378.3/025/73 73-166271

LB2338 .S46 MRR Alc.

AFRICA--YEARBOOKS.
Africa. 1968- New York [etc.]
African Pub. Corp. [etc.] 915.005
68-6810
DT1 .A14 MRR Alc Latest edition

Bottin Afrique centrale, Algérie,
Maroc-Tunisie, etc. 1946- Paris,
Société Didot-Bottin [etc.] 48-
41815
JV1801 .B6 MRR Alc Latest edition

**AFRICA, BRITISH EAST--GOVERNMENT
PUBLICATIONS.**
United States. Library of Congress.
African Section. Official
publications of British East Africa,
Washington, General Reference and
Bibliography Division, Reference
Dept., Library of Congress, 1960-63.
4 v. 015.676 61-60009
Z663.285 .O3 MRR Alc.

AFRICA, CENTRAL--BIBLIOGRAPHY.
International African Institute.
South-east Central Africa and
Madagascar: general,
ethnography/sociology, linguistics,
London, 1961. v, 53 l. 016.91676
61-65578
Z3516 .I53 MRR Alc.

AFRICA, CENTRAL--COMMERCE--DIRECTORIES.
Braby's commercial directory of
South, East and Central Africa.
Durban, A. C. Braby. 338.4/025/67
72-626695
HF3893 .B7 MRR Alc Latest edition

AFRICA, EAST--BIBLIOGRAPHY.
International African Institute.
East Africa: general, ethnography,
sociology, linguistics, London,
1960. iii, 61 l. 60-44644
Z3516 .I47 MRR Alc.

International African Institute.
North-east Africa: general,
ethnography, sociology, linguistics,
London, 1959. iii, 51 l. 016.91676
60-34932
Z3516 .I5 MRR Alc.

International African Institute.
South-east Central Africa and
Madagascar: general,
ethnography/sociology, linguistics,
London, 1961. v, 53 l. 016.91676
61-65578
Z3516 .I53 MRR Alc.

AFRICA, EAST--BIOGRAPHY.
Pandit, Shanti, Asians in east and
central Africa. [Nairobi] Panco
Publications [1963?] 366 p. 79-
30824
DT429 .P27 MRR Biog.

Who's who in East Africa. 1963/64-
Nairobi, Marco Pub. (Africa) Ltd.
[etc.] 66-37949
DT433.A2 W5 MRR Biog Latest
edition

AFRICA, EAST--COMMERCE--DIRECTORIES.
Braby's commercial directory of
South, East and Central Africa.
Durban, A. C. Braby. 338.4/025/67
72-626695
HF3893 .B7 MRR Alc Latest edition

Trado Asian African directory of
exporters-importers & manufacturers.
1959/60- New Delhi, Trado
Publications Private Ltd. [etc.]
338/.0025/5 72-622940
HF3763 .T74 MRR Alc Latest edition

AFRICA, EAST--HISTORY.
History of East Africa, Oxford,
Clarendon Press, 1963- v. 967.6
63-4375
DT365 .H55 MRR Alc.

AFRICA, EAST--INDUSTRIES--DIRECTORIES.
Trado Asian African directory of
exporters-importers & manufacturers.
1959/60- New Delhi, Trado
Publications Private Ltd. [etc.]
338/.0025/5 72-622940
HF3763 .T74 MRR Alc Latest edition

AFRICA, EAST--LANGUAGES--BIBLIOGRAPHY.
International African Institute.
East Africa: general, ethnography,
sociology, linguistics, London,
1960. iii, 61 l. 60-44644
Z3516 .I47 MRR Alc.

AFRICA, EASTERN--BIBLIOGRAPHY.
United States. Library of Congress.
Library of Congress Office Nairobi.
Accessions list, Eastern Africa. v.
1-   Jan. 1968- Nairobi. 016.9167
76-607943
Z3516 .U52 MRR Alc Full set

AFRICA, EASTERN--COMMERCE--DIRECTORIES.
Kenya, Uganda, Tanzania, Zambia,
Malawi and Ethiopia directory; trade
and commercial index. 1968-
Nairobi, East African Directory Co.
380/.025/6 70-1157
HF3893 .K42 MRR Alc Latest edition

**AFRICA, EASTERN--DESCRIPTION AND TRAVEL--
GUIDE-BOOKS.**
Travellers' guide to East Africa:
[Revised ed.] London, Thornton Cox,
1968. 102 p. [12/6] 916.76/04/4
77-410746
DT365 .T7 1968 MRR Alc.

**AFRICA, FRENCH EQUATORIAL--BIOGRAPHY--
DICTIONARIES.**
Les élites africaines; "1re
édition 1970-71." Paris, Ediafric-
Service, 1971. 298 p. [180F] 77-
593637
DT533.A2 E4 MRR Biog.

**AFRICA, FRENCH-SPEAKING EQUATORIAL--
BIBLIOGRAPHY.**
United States. Library of Congress.
African Section. Official
publications of French Equatorial
Africa, French Cameroons, and Togo,
Washington, General Reference and
Bibliography Divison, Reference
Dept., Library of Congress; [for sale
by the Superintendent of Documents,
U.S. Govt. Print. Off.] 1964. xi, 78
p. 64-60029
Z663.285 .O32 MRR Alc.

**AFRICA, FRENCH-SPEAKING EQUATORIAL--
DESCRIPTION AND TRAVEL--GUIDE-BOOKS.**
Afrique centrale; les republiques
d'expression française. Paris,
Hachette, 1962. clxxxiii, 533 p.
62-47880
DT546 .A68 MRR Alc.

**AFRICA, FRENCH-SPEAKING EQUATORIAL--
DICTIONARIES AND ENCYCLOPEDIAS.**
L'Afrique noire de A à Z: Paris,
Ediafric, 1971. 317 p. 72-331085

DT523 .A68 MRR Alc.

**AFRICA, FRENCH-SPEAKING EQUATORIAL--
GOVERNMENT PUBLICATIONS--BIBLIOGRAPHY--
UNION LISTS.**
Witherell, Julian W. French-speaking
central Africa; Washington, General
Reference and Bibliography Division,
Library of Congress; [for sale by the
Supt. of Docs., U.S. Govt. Print.
Off.] 1973. xiv, 314 p. [$3.70]
015/.67 72-5766
Z663.285 .F7 MRR Alc.

**AFRICA, FRENCH-SPEAKING EQUATORIAL--
INDUSTRIES--PERIODICALS.**
L'Industrie africaine. Paris,
Ediafric-La documentation africaine.
75-225548
HC541 .I5 MRR Alc Latest edition

**AFRICA, FRENCH-SPEAKING EQUATORIAL--
DESCRIPTION AND TRAVEL--YEARBOOKS.**
Guid' ouest africain. Dakar, Agence
de distribution de presse. 51-36206

DT521 .G8 MRR Alc Latest edition

**AFRICA, FRENCH-SPEAKING WEST--
DICTIONARIES AND ENCYCLOPEDIAS.**
L'Afrique noire de A à Z: Paris,
Ediafric, 1971. 317 p. 72-331085

DT523 .A68 MRR Alc.

**AFRICA, FRENCH-SPEAKING WEST--
GOVERNMENT PUBLICATIONS--BIBLIOGRAPHY.**
United States. Library of Congress.
General Reference and Bibliography
Division. Official publications of
French West Africa, 1946-1958;
Washington, 1960. x, 88 p.
015.9661 60-60036
Z663.28 .O33 MRR Alc.

**AFRICA, FRENCH-SPEAKING WEST--
INDUSTRIES--PERIODICALS.**
L'Industrie africaine. Paris,
Ediafric-La documentation africaine.
75-225548
HC541 .I5 MRR Alc Latest edition

**AFRICA, FRENCH WEST--BIOGRAPHY--
DICTIONARIES.**
Les élites africaines; "1re
édition 1970-71." Paris, Ediafric-
Service, 1971. 298 p. [180F] 77-
593637
DT533.A2 E4 MRR Biog.

AFRICA, FRENCH WEST--DIRECTORIES.
Guid' ouest africain. Dakar, Agence
de distribution de presse. 51-36206

DT521 .G8 MRR Alc Latest edition

AFRICA, FRENCH WEST--POLITICS.
La Politique africaine en 1969: 2.
ed. Paris, Ediafric [1969?] 333 p.
70-459322
JQ3353 1969 .P6 MRR Alc.

AFRICA, NORTH.
Barbour, Nevill, ed. A survey of
North West Africa (the Maghrib) 2d
ed. London, New York, Oxford
University Press, 1962. xi, 411 p.
916.1 62-51256
DT185 .B3 1962 MRR Alc.

The Middle East and North Africa.
[1st]-   ed.; 1948- London, Europa
Publications. 48-3250
DS49 .M5 MRR Alc Latest edition

AFRICA, NORTH--BIBLIOGRAPHY.
Annuaire de l'Afrique du Nord. 1-
1962- [Paris] Centre national de la
recherche scientifique. 65-36969
DT181 .A74 MRR Alc Latest edition

AFRICA, NORTH--BIBLIOGRAPHY. (Cont.)
United States. Library of Congress.
General Reference and Bibliography
Division.   North and Northeast
Africa; Washington, 1957. v, 182 p.
016.96   57-60062
Z663.28 .N6 MRR Alc.

AFRICA, NORTH--BIOGRAPHY.
The Middle East and North Africa.
[1st]- ed:, 1948- London, Europa
Publications.   48-3250
DS49 .M5   MRR Alc Latest edition

AFRICA, NORTH--COMMERCE--DIRECTORIES.
The Middle East trade directory.
1961/62- Beirut, Y. S. Karam. ne 63-
729
HF3760.8 .M5 MRR Alc Latest
edition

AFRICA, NORTH--DESCRIPTION AND TRAVEL--
GUIDE-BOOKS.
Middle East, North Africa, Orient and
Pacific travel guide. [Washington,
D.C.] AAA World Wide Travel Dept.
910   72-622839
DS4 .M5 MRR Alc Latest edition

AFRICA, NORTH--ECONOMIC CONDITIONS.
Middle East and North Africa markets
review. [Epping, Eng.] Gower
Economic Publications. [£30.00]
330.9/56/04   74-640571
HC410.7.A1 M48 MRR Alc Latest
edition

The Middle East trade directory.
1961/62- Beirut, Y. S. Karam. ne 63-
729
HF3760.8 .M5 MRR Alc Latest
edition

AFRICA, NORTH--HISTORY.
Nickerson, Jane Soames. A short
history of North Africa, from pre-
Roman times to the present; New
York, Biblo and Tannen, 1968 [c1961]
252 p.   961 68-54233
DT194 .N5 1968 MRR Alc.

AFRICA, NORTH--HISTORY--CHRONOLOGY.
Annuaire de l'Afrique du Nord. 1-
1962- [Paris] Centre national de la
recherche scientifique. 65-36969
DT181 .A74 MRR Alc Latest edition

AFRICA, NORTH--PERIODICALS--
BIBLIOGRAPHY.
Ljunggren, Florence. Annotated guide
to journals dealing with the Middle
East and North Africa. Cairo,
American University in Cairo Press,
1964. viii, 105 p.   ne 65-2428
Z3013 .L655 MRR Alc.

AFRICA, NORTH--YEARBOOKS.
Annuaire de l'Afrique du Nord. 1-
1962- [Paris] Centre national de la
recherche scientifique. 65-36969
DT181 .A74 MRR Alc Latest edition

AFRICA, NORTHEAST--BIBLIOGRAPHY.
International African Institute.
North-east Africa: general,
ethnography, sociology, linguistics,
London, 1959. iii, 51 l. 016.91676
60-34932
Z3516 .I5 MRR Alc.

United States. Library of Congress.
General Reference and Bibliography
Division. North and Northeast
Africa; Washington, 1957. v, 182 p.
016.96   57-60062
Z663.28 .N6 MRR Alc.

AFRICA, SOUTH.
Kaplan, Irving. Area handbook for
the Republic of South Africa.
Washington, For sale by the Supt. of
Docs., U.S. Govt. Print. Off.] 1971.
xvi, 845 p. [$4.75] 916.8 75-
608712
DT753 .K3 MRR Alc.

AFRICA, SOUTH--BIBLIOGRAPHY.
Glazier, Kenneth M. Africa south of
the Sahara; a select and annotated
bibliography 1958-1963, [Stanford,
Calif.] Hoover Institution on War,
Revolution, and Peace, Stanford
University, 1964. iv, 65 p.
016.9167 64-20983
Z3501 .G5 MRR Alc.

Muller, C. F. J., ed. A select
bibliography of South African
history; Pretoria, University of
South Africa, 1966. xii, 215 p.
016.968 66-31478
Z3606 .M8 MRR Alc.

Musiker, Reuben. Guide to South
African reference books. 4th rev.
ed. Cape Town, A. A. Balkema, 1965.
x, 110 p. 015.68 66-8863
Z3601 .M8 1965 MRR Alc.

Musiker, Reuben. South African
bibliography; Hamden, Conn., Archon
Books [1970] 105 p. [5.50]
010/.968 73-16088
Z3601 .A1M9 MRR Alc.

AFRICA, SOUTH--BIOGRAPHY.
Rosenthal, Eric. Encyclopaedia of
southern Africa; 6th ed. London,
New York, Warne, 1973. ix, 662, [54]
p. [£4.00] 916.8/003 73-75028
DT729 .R65 1973 MRR Alc.

Rosenthal, Eric, comp. Southern
African dictionary of national
biography; London, Warne [1966]
xxxix, 430 p. [65/-] 920.06803 66-
15690
CT1923 .R6 MRR Biog.

Skota, Mweli T. D. The African who's
who; [Johannesburg] Distributed by
Central News Agency [196-] 373 p.
67-58880
DT913 .S55 1960z MRR Biog.

Who's who of southern Africa.
Johannesburg [etc.] Combined
Publishers (Pty.) Ltd. [etc.] 15-
10690
DT752 .S5 MRR Biog Latest Edition

AFRICA, SOUTH--COMMERCE--DIRECTORIES.
Braby's commercial directory of
South, East and Central Africa.
Durban, A. C. Braby. 338.4/025/67
72-626695
HF3893 .B7 MRR Alc Latest edition

AFRICA, SOUTH--DESCRIPTION AND TRAVEL--
GUIDE-BOOKS.
Guide to Southern Africa. 1893-
London, R. Hale [etc.] 02-9168
DT752 .Y4 MRR Alc Latest edition

AFRICA, SOUTH--ECONOMIC CONDITIONS.
Official South African municipal year
book. Pretoria, [etc.] S.A.
Association of Municipal Employees
(non political) [etc.] 14-9587
JS7531 .A5 MRR Alc Latest edition

AFRICA, SOUTH--ECONOMIC CONDITIONS--
YEARBOOKS.
State of South Africa. 1957-
Johannesburg [etc.] De Gama
Publishers [etc.] 57-40609
HC517.S7 S82 MRR Alc Latest
Edition

AFRICA, SOUTH--EXECUTIVE DEPARTMENTS--
DIRECTORIES.
Guide to state departments and
certain statutory bodies.
Johannesburg, H. MacCarthy
Publications. 354/.68/04 70-617389

JQ1902 .G83 MRR Alc Latest edition

AFRICA, SOUTH--GOVERNMENT PUBLICATIONS--
BIBLIOGRAPHY.
South African national bibliography.
1959- Pretoria, State Library. 72-
626530
Z3603 .P7 MRR Alc Full set

AFRICA, SOUTH--HISTORY.
Muller, C. F. J. Five hundred years;
3rd ed. Pretoria, Academica, 1973.
xiii, 467, [19] p. [R7.50] 968 73-
177403
DT766 .M9 1973 MRR Alc.

Wilson, Monica (Hunter) The Oxford
history of South Africa, New York,
Oxford University Press, 1969-71. 2
v. 968 74-77602
DT766 .W762 MRR Alc.

AFRICA, SOUTH--IMPRINTS.
S.A. katalogus. 4th- complete ed.;
1900/50- Johannesburg, Technical
Books & Careers (Pty) Ltd. 72-627425

Z3601 .S8 MRR Alc Partial set

S.A. katalogus. 4th- complete ed.;
1900/50- Johannesburg, Technical
Books & Careers (Pty) Ltd. 72-627425

Z3601 .S8 MRR Alc Partial set

AFRICA, SOUTH--IMPRINTS--PERIODICALS.
South African national bibliography.
1959- Pretoria, State Library. 72-
626530
Z3603 .P7 MRR Alc Full set

AFRICA, SOUTH--INDUSTRIES--DIRECTORIES.
The Business blue-book's national
trade index of South Africa &
Rhodesia. [Cape Town] National Pub.
Co.] 380.1/45/0002558 72-627239
HC517.S7 N22 MRR Alc Latest
edition

AFRICA, SOUTH--POLITICS AND GOVERNMENT--
1948-
Carter, Gwendolen Margaret. The
politics of inequality; [3d] rev.
ed. London, Thames and Hudson [1962,
c1958] 541 p. 65-84528
DT779.7 .C3 1962 MRR Alc.

AFRICA, SOUTH--SOCIAL CONDITIONS--
YEARBOOKS.
State of South Africa. 1957-
Johannesburg [etc.] De Gama
Publishers [etc.] 57-40609
HC517.S7 S82 MRR Alc Latest
Edition

AFRICA, SOUTH--STATISTICS.
Official South African municipal year
book. Pretoria, [etc.] S.A.
Association of Municipal Employees
(non political) [etc.] 14-9587
JS7531 .A5 MRR Alc Latest edition

State of South Africa. 1957-
Johannesburg [etc.] De Gama
Publishers [etc.] 57-40609
HC517.S7 S82 MRR Alc Latest
Edition

Suid-Afrikaanse statistieke.
Pretoria, Govt. Printer. 316.8 74-
644551
HA1991 .A232 MRR Alc Latest
edition

AFRICA, SOUTHERN--COMMERCE--DIRECTORIES.
Cape times directory of Southern
Africa. 23d- ed.; 1956- Cape
Town, Cape & Transvaal Print. and
Pub. Co. [etc.] 380.1/025/68 72-
622388
HF3873 .C35 MRR Alc Latest edition

AFRICA, SOUTHERN--DICTIONARIES AND
ENCYCLOPEDIAS.
Rosenthal, Eric. Encyclopaedia of
southern Africa; 6th ed. London,
New York, Warne, 1973. ix, 662, [54]
p. [£4.00] 916.8/003 73-75028
DT729 .R65 1973 MRR Alc.

AFRICA, SOUTHERN--DIRECTORIES.
The Rhodesia-Zambia-Malawi directory
(including Botswana and Mocambique).
Bulawayo, Publications (Central
Africa) [etc.] 916.89/0025 38-1460

"First published in 1910."
DT947 .R5 MRR Alc Latest edition

AFRICA, SOUTHERN--GAZETTEERS.
United States. Office of Geography.
South Africa; Washington, 1954. 2
v. (1081 p.) 916.8/003 73-10017
DT752 .U65 MRR Alc.

AFRICA, SOUTHWEST.
South Africa. Dept. of Foreign
Affairs. South West Africa survey,
1967. [Pretoria, Obtainable from the
Govt. Printer, 1967] 190 p.
916.8/8 67-8146
DT703 .A52 MRR Alc.

AFRICA, SPANISH WEST--GOVERNMENT
PUBLICATIONS--BIBLIOGRAPHY.
Rishworth, Susan Knoke. Spanish-
speaking Africa; Washington, Library
of Congress; for sale by the Supt. of
Docs., U.S. Govt. Print. Off., 1973.
xiii, 66 p. [$1.00] 015/.6 73-
10274
Z663.285 .S6 MRR Alc.

AFRICA, SUB-SAHARAN.
Africa South of the Sahara. 1971-
London, Europa Publications Ltd.
916.7 78-112271
DT351 .A37 MRR Alc Latest edition

Black Africa; a comparative handbook
New York, Free Press [1972] xxviii,
483 p. 309.1/67 72-143505
DT352.8 .B56 MRR Alc.

Kimble, George Herbert Tinley,
Tropical Africa. New York, Twentieth
Century Fund, 1960. 2 v. 916.7 60-
15160
DT352 .K48 MRR Alc.

The New Africans: London, Hamlyn,
1967. [1], 504 p. [45/-] 967 67-
107971
DT352.6 .N48 1967b MRR Alc.

AFRICA, SUB-SAHARAN--BIBLIOGRAPHY.
Duignan, Peter. Guide to research
and reference works on Sub-Saharan
Africa. Stanford, Calif., Hoover
Institution Press, Stanford
University [1971 or 2] xiii, 1102 p.
016.0169167/03 76-152424
Z3501 .D78 MRR Alc.

Glazier, Kenneth M. Africa south of
the Sahara; a select and annotated
bibliography, 1958-1963, [Stanford,
Calif.] Hoover Institution on War,
Revolution, and Peace, Stanford
University, 1964. iv, 65 p.
016.9167 64-20983
Z3501 .G5 MRR Alc.

Glazier, Kenneth M. Africa south of
the Sahara; a select and annotated
bibliography, 1964-1968, Stanford,
Calif., Hoover Institution Press
[c1969] vii, 139 p. [6.00]
016.9167 77-88767
Z3501 .G52 MRR Alc.

Hess, Robert L. Semper ex Africa ...
[Stanford, Calif., Hoover
Institution on War, Revolution, and
Peace, 1972] xxv, 800 p. 016.9167
71-185241
Z3501 .H47 MRR Alc.

AFRICA, SUB-SAHARAN-- (Cont.)
United States. Library of Congress.
African Section. Africa south of the
Sahara: Washington, General
Reference and Bibliography Division,
Reference Dept., Library of Congress,
1961. 7 p.   61-62137
Z663.285 .A35 MRR Alc.

United States. Library of Congress.
African Section. Africa south of the
Sahara: Washington, General
Reference and Bibliography Division,
Reference Dept., Library of Congress
[for sale by the Superintendent of
Documents, U.S. Govt. Print. Off.]
1963 [i.e. 1964] vi, 354 p.   63-
60087
Z663.285 .A7 MRR Alc.

United States. Library of Congress.
African Section. Africa south of the
Sahara; index to periodical
literature, 1900-1970. Boston, G. K.
Hall, 1971. 4 v.   016/.9167/03 74-
170939
Z3503 .U47 MRR Alc (Dk 33).

United States. Library of Congress.
General Reference and Bibliography
Division. Africa south of the
Sahara. Washington 1957. vii, 269
p.   016.96   57-60035
Z663.28 .A5 MRR Alc.

United States and Canadian
publications on Africa. 1960-
[Stanford, Calif., etc.]   016.9167
62-60021
Z3501 .U59   MRR Alc Full set

AFRICA, SUB-SAHARAN--BIOGRAPHY.
The New Africans: London, Hamlyn,
1967. [1], 504 p. [45/-] 967 67-
107971
DT352.6 .N48 1967b MRR Alc.

AFRICA, SUB-SAHARAN--DESCRIPTION AND
TRAVEL--BIBLIOGRAPHY.
Hess, Robert L. Semper ex Africa ...
[Stanford, Calif., Hoover
Institution on War, Revolution, and
Peace, 1972] xxv, 800 p.   016.9167
71-185241
Z3501 .H47 MRR Alc.

AFRICA, SUB-SAHARAN--HISTORY--SOURCES--
BIBLIOGRAPHY.
Hess, Robert L. Semper ex Africa ...
[Stanford, Calif., Hoover
Institution on War, Revolution, and
Peace, 1972] xxv, 800 p.   016.9167
71-185241
Z3501 .H47 MRR Alc.

AFRICA, SUB-SAHARAN--PERIODICALS--
BIBLIOGRAPHY.
United States. Library of Congress.
African Section. Sub-Saharan Africa:
a guide to serials. Washington,
Library of Congress; [for sale by the
Supt. of Docs., U.S. Govt. Print.
Off.] 1970. xx, 409 p. [$5.25]
016.9167/03 70-607392
Z663.285 .S9 MRR Alc.

AFRICA, SUB-SAHARAN--PERIODICALS--
DIRECTORIES.
Maison des sciences de l'homme,
Paris. Service d'échange
d'informations scientifiques.
Études africaines. Liste mondiale
des périodiques spécialisés. La
Haye, Mouton, 1970. 214 p. [25.50]
73-498025
Z3503 .M32 MRR Alc.

AFRICA, SUB-SAHARAN--PERIODICALS--
INDEXES.
United States. Library of Congress.
African Section. Africa south of the
Sahara; index to periodical
literature, 1900-1970. Boston, G. K.
Hall, 1971. 4 v.   016/.9167/03 74-
170939
Z3503 .U47 MRR Alc (Dk 33).

AFRICA, SUB-SAHARAN--POLITICS AND
GOVERNMENT--ADDRESSES, ESSAYS, LECTURES.
Coleman, James Smoot, ed. Political
parties and national integration in
tropical Africa. Berkeley,
University of California Press, 1964.
xiii, 730 p.   329.96   64-19636
DT352 .C56 MRR Alc.

AFRICA, SUB-SAHARAN--POPULATION.
Princeton University. Office of
Population Research. The demography
of tropical Africa Princeton, N.J.,
Princeton University Press, 1968.
xxix, 539 p.   312/.0967 67-21018
HB3661 .P7 MRR Alc.

AFRICA, WEST.
West Africa annual. 1962- Lagos
[etc.] John West Pubs. [etc.] 63-
39450
DT471 .W394 MRR Alc Latest edition

AFRICA, WEST--BIBLIOGRAPHY.
International African Institute.
West Africa: general, ethnography,
sociology, linguistics. London,
1958. v, 116 l. 016.9166 a 59-
4683
Z3516.5 .I5 MRR Alc.

AFRICA, WEST--BIOGRAPHY.
Personnalités publiques de l'Afrique
de l'ouest. Paris, Ediafric.
920.066 74-402066
DT475.5.A1 P46 MRR Biog Latest
edition

AFRICA, WEST--COMMERCE--DIRECTORIES.
West African directory. 1962-
London, T. Skinner.   63-39130
DT471 .W395 MRR Alc Latest edition

AFRICA, WEST--ECONOMIC CONDITIONS.
Hoepli, Nancy L., comp. West Africa
today. New York, H. W. Wilson Co.,
1971. 197 p.   309.1/66 76-149384
DT476.5 .H64 MRR Alc.

Morgan, William Basil. West Africa
London, Methuen, 1969. xxviii, 788
p. [6/-/-] 330.966 72-388281
HC503.W4 M6 MRR Alc.

AFRICA, WEST--HISTORY--SOURCES.
Carson, Patricia. Materials for West
African history in the archives of
Belgium and Holland. [London]
University of London, 1962. viii, 86
p.   016.966 62-6793
CD1000 .G8 no. 1 MRR Alc.

AFRICA, WEST--HISTORY--SOURCES--
BIBLIOGRAPHY.
Carson, Patricia. Materials for West
African history in French archives.
London, Athlone P.; distributed by
Constable, 1968. viii, 170 p. [42/-
] 016.9166 68-99964
CD2491.W4 C3 1968 MRR Alc.

AFRICA, WEST--POLITICS AND GOVERNMENT.
Hoepli, Nancy L., comp. West Africa
today. New York, H. W. Wilson Co.,
1971. 197 p.   309.1/66 76-149384
DT476.5 .H64 MRR Alc.

Price, Joseph Henry. Political
institutions of West Africa London,
Hutchinson, 1967. xii, 266 p. [35/-
] 320.9/66 67-97097
JQ2998.A91 P75 MRR Alc.

AFRICA, WEST--REGISTERS.
Personnalités publiques de l'Afrique
de l'ouest. Paris, Ediafric.
920.066 74-402066
DT475.5.A1 P46 MRR Biog Latest
edition

West African directory. 1962-
London, T. Skinner.   63-39130
DT471 .W395 MRR Alc Latest edition

AFRICA, WEST--STATISTICS.
West Africa annual. 1962- Lagos
[etc.] John West Pubs. [etc.] 63-
39450
DT471 .W394 MRR Alc Latest edition

AFRICA IN LITERATURE.
Tucker, Martin. Africa in modern
literature; New York, F. Ungar Pub.
Co. [1967] xii, 316 p.   820 66-
19472
PR9798 .T8 MRR Alc.

Wauthier, Claude, The literature and
thought of modern Africa; London,
Pall Mall P., 1966. 323 p. [45/-]
809.896 67-71993
DT21 .W313 1966 MRR Alc.

AFRICAN--AMERICANS
see Negroes

AFRICAN ART
see Art, African

AFRICAN LANGUAGES--ABSTRACTS.
African abstracts. v. 1- Jan. 1950-
[London] 960 55-18105
DT1 .I553 MRR Alc Full set

AFRICAN LANGUAGES--BIBLIOGRAPHY.
Murphy, John D., A bibliography of
African languages and linguistics,
Washington, Catholic University of
America Press, 1969. vii, 147 p.
016.496 71-98990
Z7106 .M8 MRR Alc.

AFRICAN LITERATURE--BIBLIOGRAPHY.
Jahn, Janheinz. A bibliography of
neo-African literature from Africa,
America, and the Caribbean. New
York, F. A. Praeger [1965] xxxv, 359
p.   016.8088917496 65-23927
Z3508.L5 J3 MRR Alc.

United States. Library of Congress.
African Section. Africa south of the
Sahara; index to periodical
literature, 1900-1970. Boston, G. K.
Hall, 1971. 4 v.   016/.8167/03 74-
170939
Z3503 .U47 MRR Alc (Dk 33).

Zell, Hans M. A reader's guide to
African literature. New York,
Africana Pub. Corp. [1971] xxi, 218
p.   809/.8967 76-83165
PR9798 .Z4 MRR Alc.

AFRICAN LITERATURE--BIBLIOGRAPHY--
CATALOGS
Harvard University. Library. African
history and literatures; Cambridge,
Mass.: distributed by Harvard
University Press, 1971. 600 p.
016.96 70-128716
Z3509 .H37 MRR Alc.

AFRICAN LITERATURE--BIO-BIBLIOGRAPHY.
Herdeck, Donald E., African authors;
[1st ed.] Washington, Black Orpheus
Press, 1973- v.   [$27.50 (v. 1)]
809/.89/6 B 73-172338
PL8010 .H38 MRR Biog.

The Penguin companion to classical,
Oriental & African literature. New
York, McGraw-Hill [1971, c1969] 359
p. [$9.95] 809 78-158064
PA31 .P4 1971 MRR Alc.

AFRICAN LITERATURE--HISTORY AND
CRITICISM.
Dathorne, O. R., The Black mind :
Minneapolis : University of Minnesota
Press, [1974] ix, 527 p. ;
809/.896 74-76744
PL8010 .D37 MRR Alc.

Jahn, Janheinz. Neo-African
literature; New York, Grove Press
[1969, c1968] 301 p. [7.50]
809/.8/91/7496 68-58154
PL8010 .J313 1969 MRR Alc.

Tucker, Martin. Africa in modern
literature; New York, F. Ungar Pub.
Co. [1967] xii, 316 p.   820 66-
19472
PR9798 .T8 MRR Alc.

Wauthier, Claude, The literature and
thought of modern Africa; London,
Pall Mall P., 1966. 323 p. [45/-]
809.896 67-71993
DT21 .W313 1966 MRR Alc.

AFRICAN LITERATURE (ENGLISH)--BIO-
BIBLIOGRAPHY.
Zell, Hans M. A reader's guide to
African literature. New York,
Africana Pub. Corp. [1971] xxi, 218
p.   809/.8967 76-83165
PR9798 .Z4 MRR Alc.

AFRICAN LITERATURE (ENGLISH)--HISTORY
AND CRITICISM--BIBLIOGRAPHY.
Zell, Hans M. A reader's guide to
African literature. New York,
Africana Pub. Corp. [1971] xxi, 218
p.   809/.8967 76-83165
PR9798 .Z4 MRR Alc.

AFRICAN NEWSPAPERS.
Ruth Sloan Associates, Washington,
D.C. The press in Africa.
Washington, 1956. 96 p.   079.6 57-
518
PN5450 .R8 MRR Alc.

AFRICAN NEWSPAPERS--BIBLIOGRAPHY--UNION
LISTS.
United States. Library of Congress.
Serial Division. African newspapers
in selected American libraries.
[1st]- ed.; 1956- Washington [For
sale by the Superintendent of
Documents, U.S. Govt. Print. Off.,
etc.] 62-60052
Z6663.44 .A46 MRR Alc MRR Alc
Latest edition

AFRICAN NEWSPAPERS--DIRECTORIES.
The Advertising & press annual of
Africa. Cape Town, National Pub. Co.
(Pty) Ltd. [etc.] 52-41681
Z6959 .A65 MRR Alc Latest edition

Feuereisen, Fritz. Die Presse in
Afrika; 2. Aufl. Pullach/München,
Verlag Dokumentation, 1973. 280 p.
079/.69/025 73-352494
Z6959 .F47 1973 MRR Alc.

AFRICAN PERIODICALS.
Ruth Sloan Associates, Washington,
D.C. The press in Africa.
Washington, 1956. 96 p.   079.6 57-
518
PN5450 .R8 MRR Alc.

AFRICAN PERIODICALS--BIBLIOGRAPHY.
Howard University, Washington, D.C.
Library. Moorland Foundation.
Dictionary catalog of the Jesse E.
Moorland Collection of Negro Life and
History, Howard University,
Washington, D.C. Boston, G. K. Hall,
1970. 9 v. 016.910/0396 72-195773

Z1361.N39 H82 MRR Alc (Dk 33)

Michigan. State University, East
Lansing. Library. Research sources
for African studies; [East Lansing]
African Studies Center, Michigan
State University, 1969. vii, 384 p.
[3.00] 016.916/005 67-65352
Z3503 .M52 MRR Alc.

United States. Library of Congress.
Library of Congress Office Nairobi.
Accessions list, Eastern Africa. v.
1- Jan. 1968- Nairobi. 016.9167
76-607943
Z3516 .U52 MRR Alc Full set

AFRICAN PERIODICALS--DIRECTORIES.
The Advertising & press annual of
Africa. Cape Town, National Pub. Co.
(Pty) Ltd. [etc.] 52-41681
Z6959 .A65 MRR Alc Latest edition

AFRICAN SCULPTURE
see Sculpture, African

AFRICAN STUDENTS IN THE UNITED STATES.
Shapiro, Sandra. Directory of
financial aid in higher education;
Waltham, Mass., African Studies
Association, Research Liaison
Committee, Brandeis University [1973]
v, 166 p.   378.3/025/73 73-166271

LB2338 .S46 MRR Alc.

AFRICAN STUDIES.
Shapiro, Sandra. Directory of
financial aid in higher education;
Waltham, Mass., African Studies
Association, Research Liaison
Committee, Brandeis University [1973]
v, 166 p.   378.3/025/73 73-166271

LB2338 .S46 MRR Alc.

AFRICAN STUDIES--BIBLIOGRAPHY.
Pearson, James Douglas, Oriental and
Asian bibliography; Hamden, Conn.,
Archon Books, 1966. xvi, 261 p.
016.915 66-1006
Z7046 .P4 MRR Alc.

AFRICAN STUDIES--BIO-BIBLIOGRAPHY.
United Nations Educational,
Scientific and Cultural Organization.
Secretariat. Social scientists
specializing in African studies;
[Paris, École pratique des hautes
etudes, 1963. 375 p.   64-4339
DT19.5 .U5 MRR Biog.

AFRICAN STUDIES--UNITED STATES--
DIRECTORIES.
African Studies Association. Research
Liaison Committee. Directory of
African studies in the United States,
1971-1972. Waltham, Mass., [1972?]
1 v. (unpaged)   916/.007/2073 73-
159527
DT19.9.U5 A64 MRR Alc.

AFRIKAANS LANGUAGE--DICTIONARIES.
Schoonees, Pieter Cornelis,
Woordeboek van die Afrikaanse taal.
Pretoria, Staatsdrukker, 1950- v.
52-29081
PF862 .S35 MRR Alc.

AFRIKAANS LANGUAGE--DICTIONARIES--
ENGLISH.
Bosman, Daniel Brink, Tweetalige
woordeboek 4., hersiene en sterk
verm. uitg. Kaapstad, Nasionale
Boekhandel, 1962. 2 v. (xvii, 1905
p.)   62-45246
PF862 .B618 MRR Alc.

AFRO-AMERICAN STUDIES--AUDIO-VISUAL
AIDS--BIBLIOGRAPHY.
Johnson, Harry Alleyn. Multimedia
materials for Afro-American studies;
New York, R. R. Bowker Co., 1971.
353 p.   016.9173/06/96073 75-126009

LC2801 .J63 MRR Alc.

AFRO-AMERICAN STUDIES--UNITED STATES.
Race Relations Information Center.
Directory of Afro-American resources.
New York, R. R. Bowker Co. [1970]
xv, 485 p.   917.3/06/96073 71-
126008
Z1361.N39 R3 MRR Alc.

AFRO-AMERICAN STUDIES--UNITED STATES--
DIRECTORIES.
African Studies Association. Research
Liaison Committee. Directory of
African studies in the United States,
1971-1972. Waltham, Mass., [1972?]
1 v. (unpaged)   916/.007/2073 73-
159527
DT19.9.U5 A64 MRR Alc.

AGE AND EMPLOYMENT.
Angel, Juvenal Londono, Occupations
for men and women after 45, 3d ed.,
rev. and enl. New York, World Trade
Academy Press; distributed by Regents
Pub. Co. [1964] 200 p.   331.7 64-
55030
HF5381 .A786 1964 MRR Alc.

AGE OF ROCKS
see Geology, Stratigraphic

AGED.
Burgess, Ernest Watson, ed. Aging in
Western societies. [Chicago]
University of Chicago Press [1960]
xvi, 492 p. 301.43594 60-5465
HQ1061 .B85 MRR Alc.

Williams, Richard Hays, ed.
Processes of aging; New York,
Atherton Press, 1963. 2 v.   301.435
63-13841
HQ1061 .W5 MRR Alc.

AGED--COLLECTIONS.
Tibbitts, Clark, ed. Handbook of
social gerontology; [Chicago]
University of Chicago Press [1960]
xix, 770 p.   301.435 60-5469
HQ1060 .T5 MRR Alc.

AGED--DWELLINGS.
Active Retirement Executives
Association. Retirement facilities
register. Los Angeles, 1964?] 224
p.   362.6105873 64-4960
HD7287.9 .A26 MRR Alc.

AGED--MEDICAL CARE--UNITED STATES.
[Newman, Joseph] Social security and
medicare simplified; [New York]
Collier Books [1970] 240 p. [2.95]
368.4/26/00973 73-129344
HD7125 .N45 1970 MRR Alc.

Schwartz, Jerome L. Medical plans
and health care; Springfield, Ill.,
Thomas [1968] xxxiii, 349 p.
658/.91/368382 67-12707
HG9396 .S3 MRR Alc.

AGED--STATISTICS.
Burgess, Ernest Watson, ed. Aging in
Western societies. [Chicago]
University of Chicago Press [1960]
xvi, 492 p. 301.43594 60-5465
HQ1061 .B85 MRR Alc.

AGED--EUROPE.
Burgess, Ernest Watson, ed. Aging in
Western societies. [Chicago]
University of Chicago Press [1960]
xvi, 492 p. 301.43594 60-5465
HQ1061 .B85 MRR Alc.

AGENCIES, EMPLOYMENT
see Employment agencies

AGGRESSIVENESS (PSYCHOLOGY)
see also Violence

AGING.
Williams, Richard Hays, ed.
Processes of aging; New York,
Atherton Press, 1963. 2 v. 301.435
63-13841
HQ1061 .W5 MRR Alc.

AGRICULTURAL BOTANY
see Botany, Economic

AGRICULTURAL CHEMICALS.
see also Pesticides

AGRICULTURAL CHEMISTRY.
see also Soils

AGRICULTURAL EDUCATION.
see also Forestry schools and
education

AGRICULTURAL ENGINEERING--SOCIETIES,
ETC.
Agricultural engineers yearbook. 1st
ed.; 1954- St. Joseph, Mich.,
American Society of Agricultural
Engineers. 54-14360
S671 .A32 MRR Alc Latest edition

AGRICULTURAL EXHIBITIONS--UNITED STATES-
-DIRECTORIES--PERIODICALS.
Cavalcade and directory of fairs.
[Cincinnati, Billboard Publications,
etc.]   791 72-624676
SF114 .D5 MRR Alc Latest edition

AGRICULTURAL EXTENSION WORK.
see also Community development

AGRICULTURAL EXTENSION WORK--
DIRECTORIES.
County agents directory. Flossmoor,
Ill. [etc.] C. L. Mast Jr. &
Associates [etc.] 630.717 agr46-228
S544 .C65 MRR Alc Latest edition

AGRICULTURAL LIBRARIES--DIRECTORIES.
International Association of
Agricultural Librarians and
Documentalists. World directory of
agricultural libraries &
documentation centres; Harpenden,
Herts, 1960. 280 p.   026.63 60-
3301
Z675.A8 I55 MRR Alc.

AGRICULTURAL MACHINERY--CATALOGS.
Official tractor and farm equipment
guide. St. Louis, NFEA
Publications, Inc. 52-44515
S677 .O35 MRR Alc Latest edition

AGRICULTURAL MACHINERY--TRADE AND
MANUFACTURE--UNITED STATES.
National farm tractor and implement
blue book. Chicago, National Market
Reports. 62-32340
Began publication in 1939.
HD9486.U3 N3 MRR Alc Latest
edition

AGRICULTURAL PRICE SUPPORTS--UNITED
STATES.
United States. Library of Congress.
Legislative Reference Service. Farm
program benefits and costs in recent
years; Washington, U.S. Govt. Print.
Off., 1964. iv, 6 p.   67-61367
Z663.6 .F3 MRR Alc.

AGRICULTURAL PRICES--STATISTICS.
Food and Agriculture Organization of
the United Nations. Production
yearbook. v. 12- 1958- Rome.
338.1058 59-3599
HD1421 .F585 Sci RR Partial set /
MRR Alc Latest edition

AGRICULTURAL PRODUCTS
see Farm produce

AGRICULTURAL RESEARCH.
United States. Dept. of Agriculture.
Crops in peace and war. Washington,
U.S. Govt. Print. Off. [1951] 942 p.
630.72 agr55-9
S21 .A35 1950-1951 MRR Alc.

United States. Dept. of Agriculture.
Science for better living.
[Washington, For sale by the Supt. of
Docs., U.S. Govt. Print. Off., 1968]
xlvi, 386 p. [3.00] 630/.72/073
agr68-301
S21 .A35 1968 MRR Alc.

AGRICULTURE.
see also Domestic animals

see also Field crops

see also Food industry and trade

see also Forests and forestry

see also Fruit-culture

see also Grasses

see also Insects, Injurious and
beneficial

see also Seeds

AGRICULTURE--BIBLIOGRAPHY.
Blanchard, Joy Richard, Literature
of agricultural research, Berkeley,
University of California Press, 1958.
x, 231 p.   016.63 57-12942
Z5071 .B5 MRR Alc.

Fundaburk, Emma Lila, Reference
materials and periodicals in
economics; Metuchen, N.J., Scarecrow
Press, 1971- v.   016.33 78-
142232
Z7164.E2 F83 MRR Alc.

AGRICULTURE--BIBLIOGRAPHY--CATALOGS.
United States. National Agricultural
Library. Dictionary catalog of the
National Agricultural Library, 1862-
1965. New York, Rowman and
Littlefield, 1967-70. 73 v.   016.63
67-12454
Z5076 .U63 MRR Alc (Dk 33).

AGRICULTURE--BIBLIOGRAPHY--CATALOGS--
PERIODICALS.
United States. National Agricultural
Library. Catalog. 1966/70- Totowa,
N.J., Rowman and Littlefield. 016.63
72-84831
Z5076 .U632b MRR Alc (DK 33) Full
set / Sci RR Full set

AGRICULTURE--BIBLIOGRAPHY--PERIODICALS.
Biological & agricultural index.
Jan. 1916- [Bronx, N.Y., etc.] H. W.
Wilson Co. 17-8906
Z5073 .A46 Sci RR Full set / MRR
Alc Full set

United States. National Agricultural
Library. Bibliography of
agriculture. v. 1- July 1942- New
York [etc.] CCM Information Corp.
[etc.] 63-24851
Z5073 .U572 Sci RR Partial set /
MRR Alc (Dk 33) Full set

AGRICULTURE--DICTIONARIES.
A Dictionary of agricultural and
allied terminology. [East Lansing]
Michigan State University Press,
1962. 905 p.   630.3 62-9169
S411 .D57 MRR Alc.

AGRICULTURE--DICTIONARIES--POLYGLOT.
Haensch, Günther. Wörterbuch der
Landwirtschaft: 3., uberarb. Aufl.
München, Bayerischer
Landwirtschaftverlag [1966] xxiv,
746 p.   630/.3 68-96091
S411 .H26 1966 MRR Alc.

AGRICULTURE--EARLY WORKS TO 1800.
Cato, Marcus Porcius, Censorius.
Marcus Porcius Cato, On agriculture;
Cambridge, Mass., Harvard university
press; London, W. Heinemann, ltd.,
1934. xxv, 542, [2] p.   630.945 35-
177
PA6156.C3 D4 1934 MRR Alc.

Columella, Lucius Junius Moderatus.
On agriculture, Cambridge, Harvard
University Press, 1941-55. 3 v.
878 a 42-3263
PA6156.C85 1941 MRR Alc.

AGRICULTURE--ECONOMIC ASPECTS--STUDY
AND TEACHING.
Graduate study in economics; 2d ed.
[Evanston? Ill., American Economic
Association] 1969. ix, 177 p.
[$2.50]   330/.071/173 74-28832
H62.5.U5 G7 1969 MRR Alc.

AGRICULTURE--ECONOMIC ASPECTS--AMERICA--
STATISTICS.
United States. Dept. of Agriculture.
Economic Research Service. Foreign
Regional Analysis Division. Indices
of agricultural production for the
Western Hemisphere excluding the
United States; Washington, 1969.
ii, 33 p.   338.1/0918/12 72-601512

HD1415 .U49 MRR Alc.

AGRICULTURE--ECONOMIC ASPECTS--UNITED
STATES.
Gates, Paul Wallace, The farmer's
age: agriculture, 1815-1860. New
York, Holt, Rinehart and Winston
[1960] xviii, 460 p. 338.10973 60-
5170
HC103 .E25 vol. 3 MRR Alc.

Shannon, Fred Albert, The farmer's
last frontier, agriculture, 1860-
1897. New York, Toronto, Farrar &
Rinehart, inc. [1945] xii, [2], 434
p. incl. front., plates, maps (1
fold.) diagrs. 338.1 45-35139
HC103 .E25 vol. 5 MRR Alc.

United States. Dept. of Agriculture.
Farmer's world. [Washington] U.S.
Govt. Print. Off. [1964] xiv, 592 p.
agr64-429
S21 .A35 1964 MRR Alc.

United States. Dept. of Agriculture.
A place to live. Washington [U.S.
Govt. Print. Off., 1963] xxiii, 854
p.   agr63-468
S21.A35 1963 MRR Alc.

AGRICULTURE--MAPS.
Van Royen, William, Atlas of the
world's resources. New York,
Published by Prentice-Hall for the
University of Maryland, 1952- v.
338 52-9034
G1046.G3 V3 1952 MRR Alc Atlas.

AGRICULTURE--PERIODICALS--INDEXES.
Biological & agricultural index.
Jan. 1916- [Bronx, N.Y., etc.] H. W.
Wilson Co.   17-8906
Z5073 .A46 Sci RR Full set / MRR
Alc Full set

United States. National Agricultural
Library. Bibliography of
agriculture. v. 1- July 1942- New
York [etc.] CCM Information Corp.
[etc.] 63-24851
Z5073 .U572 Sci RR Partial set /
MFR Alc (Dk 33) Full set

AGRICULTURE--STATISTICS.
Food and Agriculture Organization of
the United Nations. Trade yearbook.
v. 12- 1958- Rome. 338.14058 59-
3598
HD9000.4 .F58 Sci RR Partial set /
MRR Alc Latest edition

Gallatin Service. Gallatin
statistical indicators. [New York,
Copley International Corporation,
1967- v.   310   72-12086
HA42 .G32 MRR Alc.

Organization for Economic Cooperation
and Development. Agricultural and
food statistics, 1952-1963. Paris,
1965. 148 p. 66-33109
HD1421 .O67 MRR Alc.

United States. Dept. of Agriculture.
Economic Research Service. European
Economic Community; agricultural
trade statistics, 1961-67.
[Washington, 1969] 1 v. (unpaged)
382/.41/094 78-601937
HD9015.A3 U46 MRR Alc.

AGRICULTURE--STATISTICS--BIBLIOGRAPHY.
Ball, Joyce. Foreign statistical
documents; Stanford, Calif., Hoover
Institution in War, Revolution, and
Peace, Stanford University, 1967.
vii, 173 p.   016.3309 67-14234
Z7551 .B3 MRR Alc.

AGRICULTURE--STATISTICS--YEARBOOKS.
Food and Agriculture Organization of
the United Nations. Production
yearbook. v. 12- 1958- Rome.
338.1058 58-3599
HD1421 .F585 Sci RR Partial set /
MRR Alc Latest edition

AGRICULTURE--YEARBOOKS.
United States. Dept. of Agriculture.
Yearbook of agriculture. 1894-
[Washington, U.S. Govt. Print. Off.]
04-18127
S21 .A35 Sci RR Partial set / MRR
Alc Partial set

AGRICULTURE--AFRICA, SUB-SAHARAN--
BIBLIOGRAPHY.
United States. Library of Congress.
General Reference and Bibliography
Division. Agricultural development
schemes in sub-saharan Africa;
Washington [For sale by the
Superintendent of Documents, U.S.
Govt. Print. Off.] 1963. xii, 189 p.
63-60088
Z663.285 .A75 MRR Alc.

AGRICULTURE--EUROPE, EASTERN--
STATISTICS.
United States. Dept. of Agriculture.
Economic Research Service.
Agricultural statistics of Eastern
Europe and the Soviet Union, 1950-66.
[Washington, 1969] vi, 110 p.
338.1/094 70-601060
HD1916 .U65 MRR Alc.

AGRICULTURE--RUSSIA.
United States. Library of Congress.
Science and Technology Division.
Cold weather agriculture.
Washington, U.S. Govt. Print. Off.,
1960. v, 48 p.   631.0911 60-61031

Z663.41 .C6 MRR Alc.

AGRICULTURE--RUSSIA--STATISTICS.
United States. Dept. of Agriculture.
Economic Research Service.
Agricultural statistics of Eastern
Europe and the Soviet Union, 1950-66.
[Washington, 1969] vi, 110 p.
338.1/094 70-601060
HD1916 .U65 MRR Alc.

AGRICULTURE--SCANDINAVIA.
United States. Library of Congress.
Science and Technology Division.
Cold weather agriculture.
Washington, U.S. Govt. Print. Off.,
1960. v, 48 p.   631.0911 60-61031

Z663.41 .C6 MRR Alc.

AGRICULTURE--UNITED STATES.
United States. Dept. of Agriculture.
Contours of change. [Washington, For
sale by the Supt. of Docs.] 1970]
xl, 366 p. [$3.50] 338.1/0973 79-
609702
S21 .A35 1970 MRR Alc.

United States. Dept. of Agriculture.
Farmer's world. [Washington] U.S.
Govt. Print. Off. [1964] xiv, 592 p.
agr64-429
S21 .A35 1964 MRR Alc.

United States. Dept. of Agriculture.
Yearbook of agriculture. 1894-
[Washington, U.S. Govt. Print. Off.]
04-18127
S21 .A35 Sci RR Partial set / MRR
Alc Partial set

AGRICULTURE--UNITED STATES--
BIBLIOGRAPHY.
United States. National Agricultural
Library. Catalog. 1966/70- Totowa,
N.J., Rowman and Littlefield. 016.63
72-84831
Z5076 .U632b MRR Alc (DK 33) Full
set / Sci RR Full set

United States. National Agricultural
Library. Dictionary catalog of the
National Agricultural Library, 1862-
1965. New York, Rowman and
Littlefield, 1967-70. 73 v.   016.63
67-12454
Z5076 .U63 MRR Alc (Dk 33).

AGRICULTURE--UNITED STATES--HISTORY.
The Economic history of the United
States. New York, Toronto, Farrar &
Rinehart, inc. [19 - 330.973
45-7376
HC103 .E25 MRR Alc.

Gabriel, Ralph Henry, Toilers of
land and sea. New Haven, Yale
university press; [etc., etc.] 1926.
3 p. l., 340 p.   26-4275
E178.5 .P2 vol. 3 MRR Alc.

Gates, Paul Wallace, The farmer's
age: agriculture, 1815-1860. New
York, Holt, Rinehart and Winston
[1960] xviii, 460 p. 338.10973 60-
5170
HC103 .E25 vol. 3 MRR Alc.

Shannon, Fred Albert, The farmer's
last frontier, agriculture, 1860-
1897. New York, Toronto, Farrar &
Rinehart, inc. [1945] xii, [2], 434
p. incl. front., plates, maps (1
fold.) diagrs. 338.1 45-35139
HC103 .E25 vol. 5 MRR Alc.

AGRICULTURE--UNITED STATES--HISTORY--
BIBLIOGRAPHY.
Lovett, Robert Woodberry. American
economic and business history
information sources; Detroit, Gale
Research Co. [1971] 323 p. [$14.50]
016.330973 78-137573
Z7165.U5 L66 MRR Alc.

AGRICULTURE--UNITED STATES--STATISTICS.
The Almanac of the canning, freezing,
preserving industries. Westminster,
Md., E. E. Judge. 338.4/7/6640280973
72-622383
TX599 .C4 MRR Alc Latest edition

Commodity year book. 1st- ed.;
1939- New York, Commodity Research
Bureau, inc. 338.0973 39-11418
HF1041 .C56 MRR Alc Latest edition

United States. Dept. of Agriculture.
Agricultural statistics. 1936-
Washington, U.S. Govt. Print. Off.
338.10973 agr36-465
HD1751 .A43 MRR Ref Desk Latest
edition / MRR Alc Latest edition

AGRICULTURE, COOPERATIVE.
see also Collective farms

AGRICULTURE, COOPERATIVE--BIBLIOGRAPHY.
Year book of agricultural cooperation. [1925]- Oxford [etc.]
Basil Blackwell [etc.] 334.683
agr25-294
HD1491.A1 Y4 MRR Alc Latest
edition

AGRICULTURE, COOPERATIVE--YEARBOOKS.
Year book of agricultural cooperation. [1925]- Oxford [etc.]
Basil Blackwell [etc.] 334.683
agr25-294
HD1491.A1 Y4 MRR Alc Latest
edition

AGRICULTURE, COOPERATIVE--GREAT BRITAIN.
Year book of agricultural cooperation. [1925]- Oxford [etc.]
Basil Blackwell [etc.] 334.683
agr25-294
HD1491.A1 Y4 MRR Alc Latest
edition

AGRICULTURE AND STATE--UNITED STATES.
Benedict, Murray Reed, Farm policies
of the United States, 1790-1950: New
York, Octagon Books, 1966 [c1953]
xv, 548 p. 338.1/0973 66-28382
HD1761 .B37 1966 MRR Alc.

United States. Dept. of Agriculture.
A place to live. Washington [U.S.
Govt. Print. Off., 1963] xxiii, 854
p.   agr63-468
S21.A35 1963 MRR Alc.

AID TO UNDERDEVELOPED AREAS
see Economic assistance

see Technical assistance

AINU LANGUAGE--DICTIONARIES--ENGLISH.
Batchelor, John, An Ainu-English-
Japanese dictionary (3d ed.) ...
Tokyo, The Kyobunkan; London, K.
Paul, Trench, Trubner, co., 1926.
[823] p.   46-28350
PL495.Z5 B3 1926 MRR Alc.

AINU LANGUAGE--DICTIONARIES--JAPANESE.
Batchelor, John, An Ainu-English-
Japanese dictionary (3d ed.) ...
Tokyo, The Kyobunkan; London, K.
Paul, Trench, Trubner, co., 1926.
[823] p.   46-28350
PL495.Z5 B3 1926 MRR Alc.

AIR--POLLUTION.
see also Motor vehicles--Pollution
control devices

AIR--POLLUTION--BIBLIOGRAPHY.
The Air pollution bibliography. v. 1-
1957- Washington. 016.62853 57-
60050
Z663.49 .A4 MRR Alc   MRR Alc Full
set

AIR BASES--UNITED STATES--DIRECTORIES.
Air Force bases; [3d ed.]
Harrisburg, Pa., Stackpole Co. [1965]
224 p.   358.417058 65-13381
UG634.5.A1 A7 1965 MRR Alc.

AIR BASES, AMERICAN--DIRECTORIES.
Air Force bases; [3d ed.]
Harrisburg, Pa., Stackpole Co. [1965]
224 p.   358.417058 65-13381
UG634.5.A1 A7 1965 MRR Alc.

AIR CONDITIONING--CATALOGS.
D E catalog directory. 1923-
[Chicago, Medalist Publications,
etc.] 22-21100
TH6112 .D6 Sci RR Latest edition /
MRR Alc Latest edition

AIR CONDITIONING--HANDBOOKS, MANUALS,
ETC.
American Society of Heating,
Refrigerating and Air-Conditioning
Engineers. ASHRAE handbook & product
directory. 1973- New York. 697 73-
644272
TH7011 .A4 MRR Alc Latest edition
/ Sci RR Latest edition

AIR FORCE CHAPLAINS
see Chaplains, Military

AIR FORCES--STATISTICS.
The Military balance. London,
International Institute for Strategic
Studies. 355.03/32/05 79-617319
UA15 .L652 MRR Ref Desk Latest
edition

AIR LINES.
Wynn, Humphrey. World airline
insignia: London, Hamlyn, 1973. 159
p. [£0.50] 387.7/06/5 73-157590
TL603 .W86 MRR Alc.

AIR LINES--DIRECTORIES.
The Globe world directory for land,
sea and air traffic. 1st- ed.;
1948- Oslo, [etc.] Globe
Directories. 385.058 50-13703
HE9.A1 G5 MRR Alc Latest edition

Interavia A B C. 1936- Genève,
Interavia. 629.1305 36-22039
TL512 .I55 Sci RR Latest edition /
MRR Alc Latest edition

World airline record. [1st]- ed.;
1950/51- Chicago, Roadcap Associates
[etc.] 387.72 51-3819
TL501 .W675 Sci RR Latest edition
/ MRR Alc Latest edition

World aviation directory listing
companies and officials. v. 1-
(no. [1]-); spring 1940-
Washington, Ziff-Davis Pub. Co.,
Public Transportation and Travel
Division [etc.] 40-11496
TL512 .A63 MRR Alc Latest edition
/ Sci RR Latest edition

Wragg, David W. World's air fleets
2nd (revised) ed. London, Allan,
1969. 176 p. [25/-] 387.7/065 73-
432844
HE9768 .W7 1969 MRR Alc.

AIR LINES--RATES.
Jurgen, Jens. Air travel and charter
flight handbook; Kings Park, N.Y.,
Travel Information Bureau [1973] 192
p. [$4.95] 387.7/42 73-168342
HE9787 .J87 MRR Alc.

AIR LINES--YEARBOOKS.
World airline record. [1st]- ed.;
1950/51- Chicago, Roadcap Associates
[etc.] 387.72 51-3819
TL501 .W675 Sci RR Latest edition
/ MRR Alc Latest edition

AIR LINES--EUROPE--DIRECTORIES.
Richardson, J. H. Fleet operators:
Europe. Brentwood, Air Britain
[1968] 56 p. [7/6] 387.7/33/4094
70-387656
HE9769.E9 R53 MRR Alc.

AIR LINES--UNITED STATES.
Whitten, Charles A. Air-line
distances between cities in the
United States. Washington, U.S.
Govt. Print. Off., 1947. vi, 246 p.
387.7 47-46569
TL726.2 .W45 MRR Alc.

AIR LINES--UNITED STATES--STATISTICS.
United States. Civil Aeronautics
Board. Handbook of airline
statistics, United States
certificated air carriers. 1938/42-
[Washington, U.S. Govt. Print. Off.]
44-40873
TL521 .A242 MRR Alc Latest edition

AIR LINES--UNITED STATES--YEARBOOKS.
Moody's transportation manual:
American and foreign. 1954- New
York, Moody's Investors Service. 57-
15176
HG4971 .M74 MRR Alc Latest edition

AIR MAIL STAMPS--SOCIETIES, ETC.
American Air Mail Society.
Membership list. [Highland Park?
Ill., 1860?] 56 p. 63-47594
HE6188 .A56 MRR Alc.

AIR NAVIGATION
see Aeronautics

AIR-PILOT GUIDES--EUROPE.
Pryor, Louis R. Fly in Europe: your
guide to personal flying,
[Cleveland, Leisure Flying
Consultants] 1972. 235 p. [$5.95]
629.132/54/4 72-81620
TL726.15 .P78 MRR Alc.

AIR PILOTS.
see also Aeroplanes--Piloting

Robertson, Bruce, ed. Air aces of
the 1914-1918 war. Letchworth,
Herts. [Eng.] Harleyford
Publications, 1959. 211 p.
926.2913 58-13378
D600 .R6 MRR Alc.

AIR-SHIPS.
Clarke, Basil, The history of
airships. New York, St. Martin's
Press [1864, c1961] 194 p.
629.1332409 64-12336
TL650 .C55 1964 MRR Alc.

AIR-SHIPS--YEARBOOKS.
Jane's all the world's aircraft.
[1st]- issue; 1909- London [etc.]
S. Low, Marston & Co. 629.133058 10-
8268
TL501 .J3 MRR Alc Latest edition /
Sci RR Latest edition

AIR TRAVEL.
Jurgen, Jens. Air travel and charter
flight handbook; Kings Park, N.Y.,
Travel Information Bureau [1973] 192
p. [$4.95] 387.7/42 73-168342
HE9787 .J87 MRR Alc.

AIRCRAFT CARRIERS.
Polmar, Norman. Aircraft carriers;
[1st ed.] Garden City, N.Y.,
Doubleday, 1969. viii, 788 p.
[17.95] 359.32/55 69-12186
V874 .P6 MRR Alc.

AIRCRAFT PRODUCTION
see Aerospace industries

AIRLINES
see Air lines

AIRPLANES
see Aeroplanes

AIRPORTS--DIRECTORIES.
Hurren, Bernard John. Airports of
the world. London, Wolfe, 1970. 182
p. [30/-] 387.7/36/025 77-485929
HE9797 .H9 MRR Alc.

AIRPORTS--CANADA--DIRECTORIES--
YEARBOOKS.
Canadian aerodrome directory.
[Ottawa, R. Duhamel, Govt. Printer]
387.7/36/02571 72-626334
TL726.5C2 A36 MRR Alc Latest
edition

AIRPORTS--UNITED STATES--DIRECTORIES.
A O P A airport directory. 1962-
[Washington] Aircraft Owners and
Pilots Association. 387.736 62-
36518
TL726.2 .A558 MRR Alc Latest
edition

AKERSHUS, NORWAY--DIRECTORIES.
Akershus adressebok med
skatteligninger. Oslo. 60-22376
DL596.A59 A6 MRR Alc Latest
edition

ALABAMA.
Writers' program. Alabama. Alabama;
a guide to the deep South, New York,
R. R. Smith, 1941. xxii, 442 p.
917.61 41-52528
F326 .W7 MRR Ref Desk.

ALABAMA--BIBLIOGRAPHY.
Historical records survey. Alabama.
Check list of Alabama imprints, 1807-
1840. Birmingham, Ala., The Alabama
historical records survey project,
1939. xv, 159 p. 015.761 40-26269

Z1215 .H67 no. 8 MRR Alc.

ALABAMA--BIOGRAPHY.
Alabama. Dept. of Archives and
History. Alabama official and
statistical register. 1903-
Montgomery. 08-17761
JK4531 MRR Alc Latest edition

Alabama. Legislative Reference
Service. A manual for Alabama
legislators. [Montgomery, etc.]
328.7618 45-36936
First published in 1942.
JK4530 .A25 MRR Alc Latest edition

Who's who in Alabama. v. 1-
1939/40- [Birmingham, Ala., Sayers
Enterprises, etc.] 920.0761 41-
22943
F325 .W57 MRR Biog Latest edition

ALABAMA--DESCRIPTION AND TRAVEL--GUIDE-
BOOKS.
Writers' program. Alabama. Alabama;
a guide to the deep South, New York,
R. R. Smith, 1941. xxii, 442 p.
917.61 41-52528
F326 .W7 MRR Ref Desk.

ALABAMA--DIRECTORIES.
Alabama encyclopedia [and] book of
facts. v. 1- 1965- Northport
Ala., American Southern Pub. Co. 68-
200
F326 .A54 MRR Alc Latest edition

ALABAMA--EXECUTIVE DEPARTMENTS.
Alabama encyclopedia [and] book of
facts. v. 1- 1965- Northport
Ala., American Southern Pub. Co. 68-
200
F326 .A54 MRR Alc Latest edition

ALABAMA--EXECUTIVE DEPARTMENTS--
HANDBOOKS, MANUALS, ETC.
Alabama. University. Bureau of Public
Administration. Alabama government
manual. University, Ala., 1973.
xvi, 342 p. 320.4/761 73-166981
JK4531 1973 .A5 1973 MRR Alc.

ALABAMA--IMPRINTS.
Historical records survey. Alabama.
Check list of Alabama imprints, 1807-
1840. Birmingham, Ala., The Alabama
historical records survey project,
1939. xv, 159 p. 015.761 40-26269

Z1215 .H67 no. 8 MRR Alc.

ALABAMA--POLITICS AND GOVERNMENT.
Alabama. Dept. of Archives and
History. Alabama official and
statistical register. 1903-
Montgomery. 08-17761
JK4531 MRR Alc Latest edition

ALABAMA--POLITICS AND GOVERNMENT--
HANDBOOKS, MANUALS, ETC.
Alabama. University. Bureau of Public
Administration. Alabama government
manual. University, Ala., 1973.
xvi, 342 p. 320.4/761 73-166981
JK4531 1973 .A5 1973 MRR Alc.

ALABAMA--REGISTERS.
Alabama. Dept. of Archives and
History. Alabama official and
statistical register. 1903-
Montgomery. 08-17761
JK4531 MRR Alc Latest edition

Alabama encyclopedia [and] book of
facts. v. 1- 1965- Northport
Ala., American Southern Pub. Co. 68-
200
F326 .A54 MRR Alc Latest edition

ALABAMA--STATISTICS.
Alabama. Dept. of Archives and
History. Alabama official and
statistical register. 1903-
Montgomery. 08-17761
JK4531 MRR Alc Latest edition

Alabama encyclopedia [and] book of
facts. v. 1- 1965- Northport
Ala., American Southern Pub. Co. 68-
200
F326 .A54 MRR Alc Latest edition

ALABAMA. LEGISLATURE.
Alabama. Legislative Reference
Service. A manual for Alabama
legislators. [Montgomery, etc.]
328.7618 45-36936
First published in 1942.
JK4530 .A25 MRR Alc Latest edition

ALASKA.
The Alaska blue book. 1st- ed.;
1963- Anchorage, Alaska Press Club.
64-28838
F910 .A65 MRR Alc Latest edition

ALASKA--BIOGRAPHY.
The Alaska blue book. 1st- ed.;
1963- Anchorage, Alaska Press Club.
64-28838
F910 .A65 MRR Alc Latest edition

ALASKA--DESCRIPTION AND TRAVEL--1959-
Kursh, Harry. This is Alaska.
Englewood Cliffs, N.J., Prentice-Hall
[1961] 286 p. 917.98 60-7579
F910 .K8 MRR Alc.

ALASKA--DESCRIPTION AND TRAVEL--1959- --
GUIDE-BOOKS.
Cross, Cliff. Alaska. 1969-70 ed.
North Palm Springs, Calif. [1969]
170 p. [3.50] 917.98/04/5 78-
22107
F902.3 .C7 MRR Alc.

ALASKA--DESCRIPTION AND TRAVEL--GUIDE-
BOOKS.
Fodor, Eugene. Pacific States: 2d,
rev. ed. Litchfield, Conn.] Fodor's
Modern Guides; distributor: D. McKay
Co., New York [1967] 480 p.
917.9/04/3 67-20084
F851 .F6 1967 MRR Alc.

Hart, Robert G. McKay's guide to
Alaska. New York, D. McKay Co.
[1959] 330 p. 917.98 59-12261
F902.3 .H3 MRR Alc.

ALASKA--ECONOMIC CONDITIONS.
Alaska. Industrial Development
Division. Alaska statistical review.
[Juneau] 338/.09798 71-629375
HA231 .A33 MRR Alc Latest edition

ALASKA--EXECUTIVE DEPARTMENTS.
Alaska. Legislative Council.
Legislative handbook on Alaska State
government. 1960- Juneau. 342.798
61-62797
JK9530 .A274 MRR Alc Latest
edition

ALASKA--HISTORY.
Gruening, Ernest Henry, The State of
Alaska. New York, Random House
[1954] 606 p. 979.8 54-7799
F904 .G7 MRR Alc.

ALASKA--POLITICS AND GOVERNMENT--
HANDBOOKS, MANUALS, ETC.
Alaska. Legislative Council.
Legislative handbook on Alaska State
government. 1960- Juneau. 342.798
61-62797
JK9530 .A274 MRR Alc Latest
edition

ALASKA--STATISTICS--COLLECTIONS.
Alaska. Industrial Development
Division, Alaska statistical review.
[Juneau] 338/.09798 71-629375
HA231 .A33 MRR Alc Latest edition

ALAVA, SPAIN--DIRECTORIES.
Guía-anuario de Aragón, Rioja,
Navarra, Alava, Guipúzcoa y Vizcaya.
Zaragoza, E. Gallegos. 51-22040
DP11 .G78 MRR Alc Latest edition

ALBANIA.
Keefe, Eugene K. Area handbook for
Albania. Washington; For sale by the
Supt. of Docs., U.S. Govt. Print.
Off.] 1971. xiv, 223 p. [$2.50]
914.96/5 73-609651
DR701.S5 K36 MRR Alc.

ALBANIA--BIBLIOGRAPHY.
Horecky, Paul Louis. Southeastern
Europe; Chicago, University of
Chicago Press [1969] xxii, 755 p.
016.91496 73-110336
Z2831 .H67 MRR Alc.

ALBANIA--EXECUTIVE DEPARTMENTS--
DIRECOTIRES.
Directory of Albanian officials.
[n.p.] 1970. vii, 121 p.
354.496/5/002 79-13669
JN9684 .D55 MRR Alc.

ALBANIA--GAZETTEERS.
United States. Office of Geography.
Albania; 2d ed. Washington, U.S.
Govt. Print. Off., 1961. iii, 107 p.
914.965 61-60978
DR701.S495 U5 1961 MRR Alc.

ALBANIA--OFFICIALS AND EMPLOYEES--
DIRECTORIES.
Directory of Albanian officials.
[n.p.] 1970. vii, 121 p.
354.496/5/002 79-13669
JN9684 .D55 MRR Alc.

ALBANIA--REGISTERS.
Directory of Albanian officials.
[n.p.] 1970. vii, 121 p.
354.496/5/002 79-13669
JN9684 .D55 MRR Alc.

ALBANIAN LANGUAGE--CONVERSATION AND
PHRASE BOOKS--POLYGLOT.
Lyall, Archibald. A guide to 25
languages of Europe. Rev. ed.
[Harrisburg, Pa.] Stackpole Co.
[1966] viii, 407 p. 413 66-20847

PB73 .L85 1966 MRR Alc.

ALBANIAN LANGUAGE--DICTIONARIES--
ENGLISH.
Drizari, Nelo. Albanian-English and
English-Albanian dictionary. 2d,
enl. ed.; New York, F. Ungar Pub.
Co. [1957] vi, 320 p. 491.99132
57-9330
PG9591 .D7 1957 MRR Alc.

ALBANIAN LITERATURE--HISTORY AND
CRITCISM.
Mann, Stuart Edward, Albanian
literature; London, B. Quaritch,
1955. v, 121, [2] p. a 55-6613
PG9603 .M3 MRR Alc.

ALBERTA--REGISTERS.
The Alberta list of official
personnel in Federal, Provincial and
municipal governments in the Province
of Alberta. [n.p.] 58-31899
JL500.A8 A9 MRR Alc Latest edition

ALCOHOL--BIBLIOGRAPHY.
International bibliography of studies
on alcohol. New Brunswick, N.J.,
Publications Division, Rutgers Center
of Alcohol Studies [1966- v.
016.61381 60-14437
Z7721 .I5 MRR Alc.

ALCOHOL--TAXATION--UNITED STATES.
Distilled Spirits Institute, inc.,
Washington, D.C. Public revenue from
alcoholic beverages. [Washington]
336.27 38-17702
. HD9350.8.U5 A12 MRR Alc Latest
edition

ALCOHOLIC BEVERAGES.
see also Liquors

Bergeron, Victor Jules. Trader Vic's
bartender's guide, revised. Garden
City, N.Y., Doubleday, 1972. xii,
442 p. [$6.95] 641.8/74 72-76212

TX951 .B425 1972 MRR Alc.

Mario, Thomas. Playboy's host & bar
book. [1st ed. Chicago] Playboy
Press [c1971] vii, 339 p. [$12.95]
641.8/74 75-167615
TX951 .M266 MRR Alc.

Old Mr. Boston deluxe official
bartender's guide / New world wide
ed. Boston : Mr. Boston Distiller
Corp., 1974. 216 p. : [$2.50]
641.8/74 74-80666
TX951 .O4 1974 MRR Alc.

ALCOHOLISM--ABSTRACTS.
The Alcoholism digest annual. v. 1-
1972/73- Rockville, Md.,
Information Planning Associates.
362.2/92 74-644283
HV5001 .A34 MRR Alc Full set

ALCOHOLISM--ADDRESSES, ESSAYS, LECTURES.
The Alcoholism digest annual. v. 1-
1972/73- Rockville, Md.,
Information Planning Associates.
362.2/92 74-644283
HV5001 .A34 MRR Alc Full set

ALCOHOLISM--BIBLIOGRAPHY.
International bibliography of studies
on alcohol. New Brunswick, N.J.,
Publications Division, Rutgers Center
of Alcohol Studies [1966- v.
016.61381 60-14437
Z7721 .I5 MRR Alc.

ALCOHOLISM--DICTIONARIES.
Keller, Mark. A dictionary of words
about alcohol. New Brunswick, N.J.,
Publications Division, Rutgers Center
of Alcohol Studies [1968] xxviii,
236 p. [$7.50] 362.2/92/03 68-
64841
HV5017 .K42 MRR Alc.

ALCOHOLISM--STATISTICS.
Efron, Vera. Selected statistics on
consumption of alcohol (1850-1968)
and on alcoholism (1930-1968) New
Brunswick, N.J., Publications
Division, Rutgers Center of Alcohol
Studies [1970] 18 p. [$2.00]
362.2/92/0973 70-277380
HV5292 .E36 MRR Alc.

ALCOTT, LOUISA MAY, 1832-1888--
BIBLIOGRAPHY.
Ullom, Judith C. Louisa May Alcott:
a centennial for Little women;
Washington, Library of Congress; [for
sale by the Supt. of Docs., U.S.
Govt. Print. Off.] 1969. vii, 91 p.
[0.55] 016.813/4 76-600591
Z663.292 .U5 MRR Alc.

ALEXANDER THE GREAT, 356-323 B.C.
Arrianus, Flavius. Arrian, London,
W. Heinemann, ltd.; New York, G. P.
Putnam's sons, 1929-33. 2 v. 888.9
30-5835
PA3612 .A83 1929 MRR Alc.

Curtius Rufus, Quintus. Quintus
Curtius [History of Alexander]
Cambridge, Mass., Harvard Univ.
Press, 1946. 2 v. 878.8 48-41
PA6156.C9 1946 MRR Alc.

ALGEBRA.
see also Equations

see also Logarithms

ALGERIA.
American University, Washington, D.C.
Foreign Areas Studies Division. Area
handbook for Algeria. Washington,
For sale by the Superintendent of
Documents, U.S. Govt. Print. Off.,
1965. xii, 520 p. 65-62476
DT275 .A593 MRR Alc.

ALIENS.
see also Citizenship

ALIENS--JAPAN--DIRECTORIES.
The Japan times directory of foreign
residents, business firms &
organizations. Tokyo, Japan Times,
ltd. 915.2 72-627115
HE9463 .J3 MRR Alc Latest edition

ALIMENTATION
see Nutrition

ALL TERRAIN VEHICLE.
see also Snowmobiles

ALLEGORIES.
see also Fables

ALLEN, FREDERICK LEWIS, 1890-1954--
BIBLIOGRAPHY.
United States. Library of Congress.
Manuscript Division. Frederick Lewis
Allen: a register of his papers in
the Library of Congress. Washington,
1958. 7 l. 012 58-60049
Z663.34 .A4 MRR Alc.

ALLEN, HENRY TUREMAN, 1859-1930--
BIBLIOGRAPHY.
United States. Library of Congress.
Manuscript Division. Henry T. Allen;
a register of his papers in the
Library of Congress. Washington,
1958. 10 l. 012 58-60046
Z663.34 .A43 MRR Alc.

ALLERGY.
Dubos, René Jules, ed. Bacterial
and mycotic infections of man. 4th
ed. Philadelphia, Lippincott [1965]
xiii, 1025 p. 616.01 64-23602
RC115 .D75 1965 MRR Alc.

Rapaport, Howard G., The complete
allergy guide. New York, Simon and
Schuster [1971,c1970] 447 p.
[$9.95] 616.9/7 77-132775
RC584 .R36 MRR Alc.

ALLIANCES.
Treaties and alliances of the world;
[2d ed.] [Bristol] Keesing's
Publications; New York, Scribner
[1974] xv, 235 p. 341.3/7 73-
15927
JX4005 .T72 1974 MRR Alc.

ALLUSIONS.
Blumberg, Dorothy Rose. Whose what?
[1st ed.] New York, Holt, Rinehart
and Winston [1969] 184 p. [3.95]
031/.02 68-12199
AG105 .B72 MRR Alc.

Brewer, Ebenezer Cobham, Brewer's
dictionary of phrase and fable.
Centenary ed. (completely revised);
London, Cassell, 1970. xvi, 1175 p.,
plate. [60/-] 803 73-529591
PN43 .B65 1970 MRR Ref Desk.

Brewer, Ebenezer Cobham, The
reader's handbook of famous names in
fiction, A new ed., rev. throughout
and greatly enl. Detroit,
Republished by Gale Research Co.,
1966. 2 v. (viii, 1243 p.) 803 71-
134907
PN43 .B7 1965 MRR Alc.

Gerwig, Henrietta, ed. Crowell's
handbook for readers and writers;
New York, Thomas Y. Crowell company
[c1925] vi, 728 p. 25-20161
PN41 .G4 MRR Alc.

The Shakespere allusion-book;
London, H. Milford, Oxford university
press, 1932. 2 v. 822.33 32-31755

PR2959 .S5 1932 MRR Alc.

ALLUSIONS--DICTIONARIES.
Fulghum, Walter B. A dictionary of
Biblical allusions in English
literature New York, Holt, Rinehart
and Winston [1965] viii, 291 p.
820.93 65-19349
PR145 .F8 MRR Alc.

ALMAGRO FAMILY.
United States. Library of Congress.
Manuscript division. The Harkness
collection in the Library of
Congress. Washington, U.S. Govt.
print. off., 1936. xi, 253 p. 985
36-26004
Z663.34 .H29 MRR Alc.

ALMANACS, AMERICAN.
Arkansas almanac, the encyclopedia of
Arkansas. 1954/55- Little Rock,
Arkansas Almanac Co. 54-2919
F406 .A55 MRR Alc Latest edition

Assignment book and daily editorial
calendar; 1st- ed.] 1948- Santa
Monica, Calif. 529.43 48-13885
AY81.E35 A8 MRR Alc Latest edition

Associated Press. The official
Associated Press almanac. 1973- New
York, Almanac Pub. Co. 051 73-
643500
AY67.N5 T55 MRR Ref Desk Latest
edition

Buffalo evening news almanac and year
book. 1933- Buffalo, N.Y., Buffalo
evening news. 529.43 38-14967
AY67 .B9N4 MRR Alc Latest edition
/ MRR Alc Latest edition

The Bulletin ... almanac & year book.
1924- Philadelphia, The Evening and
Sunday bulletin. 352.0748 24-7750
AY286.P5 B9 MRR Alc Latest edition

The Hagerstown town and country
almanack. Hagerstown, Md., J.
Gruber. 01-21978
AY196.H2 H4 MRR Alc Latest edition

Information please almanac, atlas and
yearbook. [1st]- ed.: 1947- New
York [etc.] Simon and Schuster [etc.]
47-845
AY64 .I55 MRR Ref Desk Latest
edition / MRR Ref Desk Latest
edition / MRR Alc Latest edition
/ Sci RR Latest edition

Reader's digest almanac. 1st- ed.;
1966- Pleasantville, N.Y., Readers'
Digest Association. 031.02 66-14383

AY64 .R4 MRR Ref Desk Latest
edition

Vermont year book. Chester [etc.]
Vt., National Survey [etc.] 08-14736

Began publication in 1818.
JK3030 .Va MRR Alc Latest edition

Women's rights almanac. 1974-
Bethesda, Md., Elizabeth Cady Stanton
Pub. Co. [$4.95] 301.41/2/0973 74-
77527
HQ1406 .W65 MRR Ref Desk Latest
edition

ALMANACS, AMERICAN. (Cont.)
The World almanac and book of facts.
New York, Newspaper Enterprise
Association [etc.] 04-3781
AY67.N5 W7   Sci RR Latest edition
/ MRR Ref Desk Latest edition /
MRR Alc Latest edition / MRR Ref
Desk Latest edition / MRR Ref
Desk Latest edition

ALMANACS, AMERICAN--BIBLIOGRAPHY.
Drake, Milton. Almanacs of the
United States. New York, Scarecrow
Press, 1962. 2 v. (L, 1397 p.)
016.051 62-10127
Z1231.A6 D7 MRR Alc.

ALMANACS, AMERICAN--NEW ENGLAND.
The (Old) farmer's almanack, no. 1-
1793- Dublin, N.H. [etc.] Yankee,
inc. [etc.] 528.1 56-29681
AY81.F3 O6 MRR Alc Latest edition

ALMANACS, AMERICAN--OHIO.
Ohio almanac. 1st- ed.; 1968-
Lorain. 917.71/005 68-3162
AY271.L6 O5 MRR Alc Latest edition

ALMANACS, AMERICAN--TEXAS.
Texas almanac. 1857- [Dallas, etc.]
A. H. Belo Corp. [etc.] 10-3390
AY311.D3 T5 MRR Alc Latest edition

ALMANACS, CANADIAN.
Canadian almanac & directory. [1st]-
year; 1848- Vancouver [etc.] Copp
Clark Pub. Co. [etc.] 529.43 07-
24314
AY414 .C2 MRR Ref Desk Latest
edition

Corpus directory and almanac of
Canada. 7th- 1972- Toronto,
Corpus Publishers Services Ltd.
917.1 72-626058
F1004.7 .M3 Sci RR Latest Edition /
MRR Alc Latest edition

ALMANACS, ENGLISH.
An Almanack ... [1st]- annual
issue; 1869- London. 04-3780
AY754 .W5 MRR Ref Desk Latest
edition / MRR Alc Latest edition

The Daily mail year book. London,
Associated Newspaper Group Ltd.,
[etc.] 032/.02 74-642471
AY755 .L8D17 MRR Alc Latest
edition

Pears cyclopaedia. [London, etc.]
Pelham Books Ltd. [etc.] 032 a 34-
1196
AY756 .P4 MRR Alc Latest Edition

ALMANACS, ENGLISH--INDIA.
The World year book and current
affairs. Delhi, Malhotra Bros. 72-
627184
AY1057.E53 W6 MRR Alc Latest
edition

ALMANACS, ENGLISH--IRAN.
Iran almanac and book of facts. 1st-
ed.; 1961- Tehran, Echo of Iran.
62-50366
AY1185 .I7 MRR Alc Latest edition

ALMANACS, FINNISH.
Mita, missa, milloin. 1.-
vuosikerta; 1951- Helsinki,
Otava. 56-24850
AY1039.F5 M57 MRR Alc Latest
edition

ALMANACS, SPANISH.
Almanaque mundial; New York [etc.]
Editora Moderna, inc. [etc.] 55-
22432
AY514 .A52 MRR Alc Latest edition

ALMANACS, SWEDISH.
Nar-var-hur. 1.- årg.; 1945-
[Stockholm] Forum [etc.] 45-17468
AY982 .N3 MRR Alc Latest edition

Svenska kalendern; Uppsala,
Stockholm, Almqvist & Wiksells
boktryckeri. ca 13-812
AY983 .S7 MRR Alc Latest edition

Tidens kalender. Stockholm, Tidens
forlag. 529.43 46-36630
Publication began in 1922?
AY984 .T5 MRR Alc Latest edition

ALPHABET.
Diringer, David, The alphabet; 3d
ed. New York, Funk & Wagnalls [1968]
2 v. 411 68-22369
P211 .D53 1968b MRR Alc.

ALPHABETING.
see also Files and filing (Documents)

United States. Library of Congress.
Processing dept. Filing manual.
Washington, 1945- 1 v. 025.3 45-
35965
Z663.7 .F5 1945 MRR Alc.

United States. Library of Congress.
Processing Dept. Filing rules for
the dictionary catalogs of the
Library of Congress. [Rev. ed of the
1945 Filing manual] Washington,
1956. v, 187 p.   025.37 56-60026
Z663.7 .F5 1956 MRR Alc.

ALPHABETS.
Gleichen, Edward, Lord, Alphabets of
foreign languages, 2d ed. 1933
reprinted with incorporation of
supplement of 1938 London, The Royal
geographical society [etc.] 1944.
xvi, 82 p., 1 l. gs 46-161
P213 .G55 1944 MRR Alc.

Visual Graphics Corporation. The
world-famous photo typositor alphabet
library. New ed. [North Miami,
Fla.] c1973. xi, 270 p. 686.2/24
74-75693
Z250 .V67 1973 MRR Alc.

ALPS, BAVARIAN--DESCRIPTION AND TRAVEL--
GUIDE-BOOKS.
Clark, Sydney Aylmer, All the best
in Austria, 1973-1974 rev. ed. New
York, Dodd, Mead [1973] viii, 344 p.
[$9.95] 914.36/04/5 74-815
DB16 .C55 1973 MRR Alc.

AMATEUR THEATRICALS.
see also Children's plays

Downs, Harold, ed. Theatre and
stage; London, Pitman [1951] 2 v.
(x, 1181 p.) 792.03 a 53-2461
PN2035 .D6 1951 MRR Alc.

AMATEUR THEATRICALS--BIBLIOGRAPHY.
Ireland, Norma (Olin) An index to
skits and stunts. Boston, F. W.
Faxon Co., 1958. xxix, 348 p.
016.792 58-9930
Z5781 .I7 MRR Alc.

AMATEUR THEATRICALS--BIBLIOGRAPHY--
CATALOGS.
Dramatic Publishing Company, Chicago.
Catalog of plays. Chicago. 016.792
54-467
Z5785.Z9 D7 MRR Alc Latest edition

Plays and their plots. London, H. F.
W. Deane; Boston, W. H. Baker [1960?]
165 p.   016.82291 60-36283
Z2014.D7 P73 MRR Alc.

AMATEUR THEATRICALS--INDEXES.
Ireland, Norma (Olin) An index to
skits and stunts. Boston, F. W.
Faxon Co., 1958. xxix, 348 p.
016.792 58-9930
Z5781 .I7 MRR Alc.

AMBASSADORS.
United States. Dept. of State.
Historical Office. United States
Chiefs of Mission, 1778-1973
(complete to 31 March 1973)
[Washington] Dept. of State; [for
sale by the Supt. of Docs., U.S.
Govt. Print. Off.] 1973. v, 229 p.
[$2.70] 327/.2/0973 73-602788
JX1706.A59 U54 1973 MRR Ref Desk.

AMERICA--ANTIQUITIES.
Kelemen, Pal. Medieval American
art; New York, Macmillan, 1956.
xxii, 414, 33 p. 970.6571 57-335
E59.A7 K4 1956 MRR Alc.

Willey, Gordon Randolph, A history
of American archaeology San
Francisco, W. H. Freeman [1974] 252
p. 913/.031 73-17493
E61 .W67 1974b MRR Alc.

Willey, Gordon Randolph, An
introduction to American archaeology
Englewood Cliffs, N.J., Prentice-Hall
[1966-71] 2 v. [$24.00 (v. 2)]
970.1 66-10096
E61 .W68 MRR Alc.

Winsor, Justin, ed. Narrative and
critical history of America,
Standard library ed. [Boston, New
York, Houghton, Mifflin and company,
1923, c1884-89] 8 v. 23-16194
E18 .W77 MRR Alc.

AMERICA--ANTIQUITIES--ADDRESSES,
ESSAYS, LECTURES.
Deuel, Leo, comp. Conquistadors
without swords: New York, St.
Martin's Press, 1967. xix, 647 p.
970.1 67-22577
E61 .D46 MRR Alc.

Leone, Mark P., comp. Contemporary
archaeology; a guide to theory and
contributions. Carbondale, Southern
Illinois University Press [1972] xv,
460 p. [$15.00] 913/.031 79-
156779
GN739 .L46 MRR Alc.

William Marsh Rice University,
Houston, Tex. Prehistoric man in the
New World. Chicago] Published for
William Marsh Rice University by the
University of Chicago Press [1964]
x, 633 p. 913.7082 63-18852
E61 .W717 MRR Alc.

AMERICA--ANTIQUITIES--BIBLIOGRAPHY.
United States. Bureau of American
Ethnology. List of publications of
the Bureau of American Ethnology
1894- Washington, U.S. Govt. Print.
Off. 23-27414
E51 .U65 MRR Ref Desk Latest
edition

AMERICA--BIBLIOGRAPHY.
Baginsky, Paul Ben, German works
relating to America, 1493-1800; New
York, The New York public library,
1942. xv, 217 p. 016.9173 a 42-
1596
Z1207 .B2 MRR Alc.

Larned, Josephus Nelson, ed. The
literature of American history;
Columbus, Ohio, Long's College Book
Co., 1953 [c1902] ix, 588, 37 p.
016.973 55-45638
Z1236 .L3 1953 MRR Alc.

Livingston, Luther Samuel, Auction
prices of books; New York, Dodd,
Mead & company, 1905. 4 v. 05-9722

Z1000 .L65 MRR Alc.

Sabin, Joseph, A dictionary of books
relating to America, New York, 1868
[i.e. 1867]-1936. 29 v. 01-26958
Z1201 .S2 MRR Ref Desk.

Thompson, Lawrence Sidney, The new
Sabin; Troy, N.Y., Whitston Pub.
Co., 1974- v. 016.9173/03 73-
85960
Z1201 .T45 MRR Ref Desk (Alc 6)

Winsor, Justin, ed. Narrative and
critical history of America,
Standard library ed. [Boston, New
York, Houghton, Mifflin and company,
1923, c1884-89] 8 v. 23-16194
E18 .W77 MRR Alc.

AMERICA--BIBLIOGRAPHY--CATALOGS.
Church, Elihu Dwight, A catalogue of
books relating to the discovery and
early history of North and South
America, New York, P. Smith, 1951.
5 v. (vi, 2635 p.) 016.9731 51-
4055
Z1203 .C55 1951 MRR Ref Desk.

Field, Thomas Warren, An essay
towards an Indian bibliography;
Detroit, Gale Research Co., 1967.
iv, 430 p.   016.9701 67-14026
Z1209 .F45 1967 MRR Alc.

Newberry Library, Chicago. Edward E.
Ayer Collection. Dictionary catalog
of the Edward E. Ayer Collection of
Americana and American Indians in the
Newberry Library. Boston, G. K.
Hall, 1961. 16 v. (8062 p.) 76-
4986
Z1201 .N45 MRR Alc (Dk 33)

AMERICA--BIOGRAPHY--DICTIONARIES.
Appleton's cyclopaedia of American
biography. Detroit, Gale Research
Co., 1968. 7 v. [168.00] 920.07
67-14061
E176 .A666 MRR Biog.

The Cyclopedia of American biography.
New enl. ed. New York, The Press
association compilers, inc., 1915-
v.   15-15825
E176 .A665 MRR Biog.

AMERICA--CENSUS--BIBLIOGRAPHY.
United States. Library of Congress.
Census library project. General
censuses and vital statistics in the
Americas. Washington, U.S. Govt.
print. off., 1943. ix, 151 p.
016.312 44-40643
Z7553.C3 U45 MRR Alc.

AMERICA--DESCRIPTION AND TRAVEL.
Wright, Louis Booker, ed. The
Elizabethans' America; Cambridge,
Harvard University Press, 1965. xii,
295 p. 917.041 65-8877
E141 .W7 MRR Alc.

AMERICA--DICTIONARIES AND ENCYCLOPEDIAS.
Diccionario enciclopédico de las
Americas; [1. ed.] Buenos Aires,
Editorial Futuro [1947] 711 p.
970.03 a 48-2212
E14 .D5 MRR Alc.

AMERICA--DISCOVERY AND EXPLORATION.
Morison, Samuel Eliot, The European
discovery of America. New York,
Oxford University Press, 1971-1974.
2 v. [$15.00 (v. 1) $17.50 (v. 2)]
973.1/3 71-129637
E101 .M85 MRR Alc.

Winsor, Justin, ed. Narrative and
critical history of America,
Standard library ed. [Boston, New
York, Houghton, Mifflin and company,
1923, c1884-89] 8 v. 23-16194
E18 .W77 MRR Alc.

AMERICA--DISCOVERY AND (Cont.)
Wissler, Clark, Adventures in the
wilderness, New Haven, Yale
university press; [etc., etc.] 1925.
3 p. l., 369 p.   26-1142
E178.5 .P2 vol. 1 MRR Alc.

Wright, Louis Booker, ed. The
Elizabethans' America; Cambridge,
Harvard University Press, 1965. xii,
295 p.   917.041 65-8877
E141 .W7 MRR Alc.

AMERICA--DISCOVERY AND EXPLORATION--
BIBLIOGRAPHY.
Church, Elihu Dwight, A catalogue of
books relating to the discovery and
early history of North and South
America, New York, P. Smith, 1951.
5 v. (vi, 2635 p.) 016.9731 51-
4055
Z1203 .C55 1951 MRR Ref Desk.

AMERICA--DISCOVERY AND EXPLORATION--
BIBLIOGRAPHY--CATALOGS.
Newberry Library, Chicago. Edward E.
Ayer Collection. Dictionary catalog
of the Edward E. Ayer Collection of
Americana and American Indians in the
Newberry Library. Boston, G. K.
Hall, 1961. 16 v. (8062 p.) 76-
4986
Z1201 .N45 MRR Alc (Dk 33)

AMERICA--DISCOVERY AND EXPLORATION--
ENGLISH.
Burrage, Henry Sweetser, ed. Early
English and French voyages, chiefly
from Hakluyt, 1534-1648, New York,
C. Scribner's sons, 1906. xxii, 451
p.   06-44365
E187.C7 B85 MRR Alc.

AMERICA--DISCOVERY AND EXPLORATION--
FRENCH.
Burrage, Henry Sweetser, ed. Early
English and French voyages, chiefly
from Hakluyt, 1534-1648, New York,
C. Scribner's sons, 1906. xxii, 451
p.   06-44365
E187.C7 B85 MRR Alc.

Champlain, Samuel de, Voyages of
Samuel de Champlain, 1604-1618; New
York, C. Scribner's sons, 1907.
viii, 377 p.   07-22899
E187.C7 C5 MRR Alc.

Kellogg, Louise Phelps, ed. Early
narratives of the Northwest, 1634-
1699, New York, C. Scribner's sons,
1917. xiv, 382 p. [$3.00] 17-6235
E187.C7 K4 MRR Alc.

AMERICA--DISCOVERY AND EXPLORATION--
NORSE.
The Northmen, Columbus and Cabot, 985-
1503; New York, C. Scribner's sons,
1906. xv, 443 p.   973.1 06-36882
E187.C7 N6 MRR Alc.

AMERICA--DISCOVERY AND EXPLORATION--
SPANISH.
Bolton, Herbert Eugene, ed. Spanish
exploration in the Southwest, 1542-
1706, New York, C. Scribner's sons,
1916. xii p., 2 l., 3-487 p. 16-
6066
E187.C7 B6 MRR Alc.

Lowery, Woodbury, The Spanish
settlements within the present limits
of the United States, 1513-1561, New
York, London, G. P. Putnam's sons,
1901. xiii, 515 p.   973.16 01-
11942
E123 .L91 MRR Alc.

Morison, Samuel Eliot, Admiral of
the ocean sea; Boston, Little, Brown
and company, 1942. 2 v.   923.9 42-
5605
E111 .M86 1942 MRR Alc.

Spanish explorers in the southern
United States, 1528-1543; New York,
C. Scribner's sons, 1907. xx, 411 p.
07-10607
E187.C7 S7 MRR Alc.

AMERICA--EARLY ACCOUNTS TO 1600.
Wright, Louis Booker, ed. The
Elizabethans' America; Cambridge,
Harvard University Press, 1965. xii,
295 p.   917.041 65-8877
E141 .W7 MRR Alc.

AMERICA--HISTORY.
Winsor, Justin, ed. Narrative and
critical history of America,
Standard library ed. [Boston, New
York, Houghton, Mifflin and company,
1923, c1884-89] 8 v.   23-16194
E18 .W77 MRR Alc.

AMERICA--HISTORY--BIBLIOGRAPHY--
CATALOGS.
Michigan. University. William L.
Clements Library. Author/title
catalog of Americana, 1493-1860, in
the William L. Clements Library,
Boston, G. K. Hall, 1970. 7 v.
016.9173/03 73-156668
Z1236 .M53 MRR Alc (Dk 33)

New York. Public Library. Reference
Dept. Dictionary catalog of the
history of the Americas. Boston, G.
K. Hall, 1961. 28 v.   016.97 61-
4957
Z1201 .N4 MRR Alc (Dk 33).

AMERICA--HISTORY--FICTION--BIBLIOGRAPHY.
Hotchkiss, Jeanette. American
historical fiction and biography for
children and young people. Metuchen,
N.J., Scarecrow Press, 1973. 318 p.
016.9173/03 73-13715
Z1236 .H73 MRR Alc.

AMERICA--HISTORY--SOURCES--BIBLIOGRAPHY.
Leland, Waldo Gifford, Guide to
materials for American history in the
libraries and archives of Paris,
Washington, D.C., Carnegie
institution of Washington, 1932- v.
016.97 32-15616
CD1198.U6 L4 MRR Alc.

AMERICA--LEARNED INSTITUTIONS AND
SOCIETIES.
Handbook of learned societies and
institutions: America. Washington,
D.C., Carnegie institution of
Washington, 1908. viii, 592 p. 08-
21011
Z5055.U39 H2 MRR Alc.

AMERICA--MAPS--ADDRESSES, ESSAYS,
LECTURES.
Ristow, Walter William, comp. A la
carte; Washington, Library of
Congress [for sale by the Supt. of
Docs., U.S. Govt. Print. Off.] 1972.
x, 232 p. [$4.00] 912.73 75-
173026
Z663.35 .S42 MRR Alc.

AMERICA--MAPS--BIBLIOGRAPHY.
United States. Library of Congress.
Map Division. A list of maps of
America in the Library of Congress.
New York, B. Franklin [1967?] 2 v.
in 1 (1137 p.)   016.91273 67-7211
Z663.35 .L55 1967 MRR Alc.

AMERICA--MAPS, EARLY.
Winsor, Justin, ed. Narrative and
critical history of America,
Standard library ed. [Boston, New
York, Houghton, Mifflin and company,
1923, c1884-89] 8 v.   23-16194
E18 .W77 MRR Alc.

AMERICA--POLITICS.
Manning, William Ray, ed.
Arbitration treaties among the
American nations, to the close of the
year 1910, New York [etc.] Oxford
university press, 1924. xl, 472 p.
24-6749
JX1985 .M3 MRR Alc.

AMERICA--RELATIONS (GENERAL) WITH
GERMANY--BIBLIOGRAPHY.
Baginsky, Paul Ben, German works
relating to America, 1493-1800; New
York, The New York public library,
1942. xv, 217 p.   016.9173 a 42-
1596
Z1207 .B2 MRR Alc.

AMERICA--STATISTICS.
Statistical activities of the
American nations, 1940; Washington,
D.C., Inter American statistical
institute, 1941. xxxi, 842 p.
311.397 41-14318
HA175 .S75 MRR Alc.

AMERICA--STATISTICS--BIBLIOGRAPHY.
Harvey, Joan M. Statistics America:
sources for market research (North,
Central & South America), Beckenham,
CBD Research, 1973. xii, 225 p.
[£6.00 ($22.00 U.S.)]   016.317 73-
180742
Z7554.A5 H37 MRR Alc.

AMERICA--STATISTICS, VITAL--
BIBLIOGRAPHY.
United States. Library of Congress.
Census library project. General
censuses and vital statistics in the
Americas. Washington, U.S. Govt.
print. off., 1943. ix, 151 p.
016.312 44-40643
Z7553.C3 U45 MRR Alc.

AMERICA--LITERATURES--BIO-BIBLIOGRAPHY.
The Penguin companion to American
literature. New York, McGraw-Hill
[1971] 384 p. [$9.95] 809 70-
158062
PN843 .P4 MRR Alc.

AMERICAN ABORIGINES
see Indians

  see Indians of North America

  see Indians of South America

AMERICAN AIR BASES
see Air bases, American

AMERICAN ART
see Art, American

AMERICAN ART INDUSTRIES AND TRADE
see Art industries and trade, American

AMERICAN AUTHORS
see Authors, American

AMERICAN BALLADS
see Ballads, American

AMERICAN BALLADS AND SONGS.
Leach, MacEdward, ed. The ballad
book. New York, Harper, 1955. 842
p.   821.04 55-6778
PR1181 .L4 MRR Alc.

AMERICAN COMPOSERS
see Composers, American

AMERICAN COOKERY
see Cookery, American

AMERICAN CORPORATIONS
see Corporations, American

AMERICAN DIARIES--BIBLIOGRAPHY.
Edwards, Elza Ivan, The enduring
desert; [Los Angeles] W. Ritchie
Press, 1969. xiii, 306 p.
016.91794/09/154 68-8306
Z1251.S8 E32 MRR Alc.

Matthews, William, American diaries;
Boston, J. S. Canner 1959. xiv,
383 p.   016.920073 59-13345
Z5305.U5 M3 1959 MRR Biog.

Matthews, William, American diaries
in manuscript, 1580-1954; Athens,
University of Georgia Press [1974]
xvi, 176 p.   016.92/0073 73-76782
Z5305.U5 M32 MRR Alc.

AMERICAN DRAMA.
Gassner, John, comp. Best plays of
the early American theatre; New
York, Crown Publishers [1967]
xlviii, 716 p.   812/.008 67-6995
PS625 .G3 MRR Alc.

Quinn, Arthur Hodson, ed.
Representative American plays, from
1767 to the present day. 7th ed.,
rev. and enl. New York, Appleton-
Century-Crofts [1953] 1248 p.
812.082 53-5089
PS625 .Q8 1953 MRR Alc.

AMERICAN DRAMA--19TH CENTURY.
Clark, Barrett Harper, ed. Favorite
American plays of the nineteenth
century, Princeton, N.J., Princeton
university press, 1943. xxvii, 553
p.   812.3082 a 43-2497
PS632 .C58 MRR Alc.

AMERICAN DRAMA--19TH CENTURY--HISTORY
AND CRITICISM.
Nolan, Paul T., comp. Provincial
drama in America, 1870-1916;
Metuchen, N.J., Scarecrow Press,
1967. 234 p.   812/.4/09 67-12058
PS345 .N6 MRR Alc.

AMERICAN DRAMA--20TH CENTURY.
The Best plays. 1894/99- New York
[etc.] Dodd, Mead [etc.] 812.5082
20-21432
PN6112 .B45 MRR Alc Partial set

Cerf, Bennett Alfred, ed. Sixteen
famous American plays, New York,
Garden City publishing co., inc.
[1941] 13 p. l., 5-1049 p.
812.50822 41-5168
PS634 .C42 MRR Alc.

Cordell, Kathryn (Coe) ed. A new
edition of the Pulitzer prize plays,
New York, Random house [1940] 9 p.
l., 5-1091 p.   812.50822 40-34976
PS634 .C67 1940 MRR Alc.

Gassner, John, ed. Twenty-five best
plays of the modern American theatre.
New York, Crown Publishers [1949]
xxviii, 756 p.   812.5082 49-9571
PS634 .G32 MRR Alc.

Gaver, Jack, ed. Critics' choice;
[1st ed.] New York, Hawthorn Books
[1955] 661 p.   812.5082 55-10113
PS634 .G35 MRR Alc.

Toohey, John L. A history of the
Pulitzer Prize plays, [1st ed.] New
York, Citadel Press [1967] viii, 344
p.   792/.097/3 67-25654
PN2266 .T6 MRR Alc.

AMERICAN DRAMA--20TH CENTURY--BIO-
BIBLIOGRAPHY.
Vinson, James, Contemporary
dramatists; London, St. James Press;
New York, St. Martin's Press [1973]
xv, 926 p.   [£9.00 ($30.00 U.S.)]
822/.9/1409 B 73-80310
PR106 .V5 MRR Biog.

AMERICAN DRAMA--20TH CENTURY--HISTORY
AND CRITICISM.
Bonin, Jane F. Prize-winning
American drama: Metuchen, N.J.,
Scarecrow Press, 1973. xii, 222 p.
812/.5/09 73-3111
PS351 .B6 MRR Alc.

AMERICAN DRAMA--20TH CENTURY-- (Cont.)
Gould, Jean, Modern American
playwrights. New York, Dodd, Mead
[1966] x, 302 p.   812.509 66-18791

    PS351 .G6 MRR Alc.

Nolan, Paul T., comp. Provincial
drama in America, 1870-1916;
Metuchen, N.J., Scarecrow Press,
1967. 234 p.   812/.4/09 67-12058
    PS345 .N6 MRR Alc.

AMERICAN DRAMA--BIBLIOGRAPHY.
Bergquist, G. William, ed. Three
centuries of English and American
plays, New York, Hafner Pub. Co.,
1963. xii, 281 p.   016.821 63-
18015
    Z2014.D7 B45 MRR Alc.

Hatch, James Vernon, Black image on
the American stage; New York, DBS
Publications [1970] xiii, 162 p.
016.812/008 72-115695
    Z5784.N4 H35 MRR Alc.

Hill, Frank Pierce, American plays
printed 1714-1830; New York, B.
Blom, 1968. xi, 152 p.   016.812 68-
20229
    Z1231.D7 H6 1968 MRR Alc.

Patterson, Charlotte A. Plays in
periodicals; Boston, G. K. Hall,
1970. ix, 240 p.   016.22/9/108 76-
21033
    Z5781 .P3 MRR Alc.

Quinn, Arthur Hobson, A history of
the American drama, 2d ed. New
York, F. S. Crofts & co., 1943. xvi
p., 1 l., 530 p.   812.09 43-11974
    PS332 .Q5 1943 MRR Alc.

Roden, Robert F., Later American
plays, 1831-1900; New York, B.
Franklin [1969] 132 p.   016.812/3
71-6518
    Z1231.D7 W5 1969 MRR Alc.

Ryan, Pat M. American drama
bibliography; Fort Wayne, Ind., Fort
Wayne Public Library, 1969. 240 p.
016.812 77-11267
    Z1231.D7 R92 MRR Ref Desk.

Sherman, Robert Lowery, Drama
cyclopedia, Chicago, The author
[1944] 1 p. l., iii, 612 p.   792
44-40134
    PN2226 .S45 MRR Alc.

United States. Copyright office.
Dramatic compositions copyrighted in
the United States, 1870 to 1916.
Washington, Govt. print. off., 1918.
2 v.   18-26789
    Z663.8 .D7 MRR Alc.

Wegelin, Oscar, Early American
plays, 1714-1830; New York, B.
Franklin [1970] xxvi, 113 p.
016.8121 70-130101
    Z1231.D7 W4 1970 MRR Alc.

AMERICAN DRAMA--BIBLIOGRAPHY--CATALOGS.
Brown University. Library.
Dictionary catalog of the Harris
collection of American poetry and
plays, Brown University Library,
Providence, Rhode Island. Boston, G.
K. Hall, 1972. 13 v.   016.81 75-
184497
    Z1231.P7 B72 MRR Alc (Dk 33)

AMERICAN DRAMA--HISTORY AND CRITICISM.
Quinn, Arthur Hobson, A history of
the American drama, 2d ed. New
York, F. S. Crofts & co., 1943. xvi
p., 1 l., 530 p.   812.09 43-11974
    PS332 .Q5 1943 MRR Alc.

Wilson, Garff B. Three hundred years
of American drama and theatre, from
Ye bare and ye cubb to Hair
Englewood Cliffs, N.J., Prentice-Hall
[1973] viii, 536 p.   792/.0973 72-
3808
    PN2221 .W5 MRR Alc.

AMERICAN DRAMA--HISTORY AND CRITICISM--
BIBLIOGRAPHY.
Coleman, Arthur, Drama criticism
Denver, A. Swallow [1966-71] 2 v.
[$7.50 (v. 1) $12.50 (v. 2)]
016.809/2 66-30426
    Z5781 .C65 MRR Ref Desk.

Gohdes, Clarence Louis Frank,
Literature and theater of the States
and regions of the U.S.A.; Durham,
N.C., Duke University Press, 1967.
ix, 276 p.   016.8109 66-30584
    Z1225 .G63 MRR Alc.

Palmer, Helen H. American drama
criticism; Hamden, Conn., Shoe
String Press, 1967. 239 p.
016.792/0973 67-16009
    Z1231.D7 P3 MRR Ref Desk.

Ryan, Pat M. American drama
bibliography; Fort Wayne, Ind., Fort
Wayne Public Library, 1969. 240 p.
016.812 77-11267
    Z1231.D7 R92 MRR Ref Desk.

Salem, James M. A guide to critical
reviews, New York, Scarecrow Press,
1966- v.   [$4.50 (v. 1) varies]
016.8092 66-13733
    Z5782 .S34 MRR Ref Desk.

Salem, James M. A guide to critical
reviews, 2d ed. Metuchen, N.J.,
Scarecrow Press, 1973- v.
016.809/2 73-3120
    Z5782 .S342 MRR Ref Desk.

AMERICAN DRAMA--NEGRO AUTHORS.
Hatch, James V., comp. Black
theater, U.S.A.; forty-five plays by
black Americans, 1847-1974. New
York, Free Press [1974] x, 886 p.
[$19.95] 812/.008/0352 75-169234
    PS628.N4 H3 MRR Alc.

AMERICAN DRAMA--NEGRO AUTHORS--
BIBLIOGRAPHY.
Hatch, James Vernon, Black image on
the American stage; New York, DBS
Publications [1970] xiii, 162 p.
016.812/008 72-115695
    Z5784.N4 H35 MRR Alc.

AMERICAN DRAMA--STORIES, PLOTS, ETC.
Atkinson, Justin Brooks, The lively
years, 1920-1973 New York,
Association Press [1973] viii, 312
p. [$12.50] 792/.09747/1 73-14659
    PN2277.N5 A85 MRR Alc.

Bonin, Jane F. Prize-winning
American drama; Metuchen, N.J.,
Scarecrow Press, 1973. xii, 222 p.
812/.5/09 73-3111
    PS351 .B6 MRR Alc.

Lovell, John, Digests of great
American plays; New York, Crowell
[1961] 452 p.   812.0822 61-10482
    PS338.P5 L6 MRR Alc.

AMERICAN ECONOMIC ASSISTANCE
see Economic assistance, American

AMERICAN FEDERATION OF LABOR.
Taft, Philip, The A.F. of L. from
the death of Gompers to the merger.
New York, Octagon Books, 1970 [c1959]
xi, 499 p.   331.88/0973 75-96193
    HD8055 .A5T28 1970 MRR Alc.

Taft, Philip, The A.F. of L. in the
time of Gompers. New York, Octagon
Books, 1970 [c1957] xx, 508 p.
331.88/0973 71-96192
    HD8055 .A5T3 1970 MRR Alc.

AMERICAN FICTION.
see also Short stories, American

AMERICAN FICTION--19TH CENTURY--
BIBLIOGRAPHY.
Wright, Lyle Henry, American
fiction, 1851-1875; San Marino,
Calif., Huntington Library, 1965.
xviii, 438 p.   016.8133 65-20870
    Z1231.F4 W92 1965 MRR Alc.

Wright, Lyle Henry, American
fiction, 1876-1900; San Marino,
Calif., Huntington Library, 1966.
xix, 683 p.   016.8134 66-24112
    Z1231.F4 W93 MRR Alc.

AMERICAN FICTION--20TH CENTURY--
ADDRESSES, ESSAYS, LECTURES.
Bellow, Saul. Recent American
fiction; Washington, Reference
Dept., Library of Congress; [for sale
by the Superintendent of Documents,
U.S. Govt. Print. Off.] 1963. 12 p.
63-60073
    Z663.293 .R4 MRR Alc.

AMERICAN FICTION--20TH CENTURY--
BIBLIOGRAPHY.
Bufkin, E. C. The twentieth-century
novel in English; Athens, University
of Georgia Press [1967] vi, 138 p.
016.823/9/1208 67-27142
    Z2014.F5 B93 MRR Alc.

Deodene, Frank. Black American
fiction since 1952; Chatham, N.J.,
Chatham Bookseller, 1970. 25 p.
016.813/5/4 78-96384
    Z1361.N39 D45 MRR Alc.

AMERICAN FICTION--20TH CENTURY--HISTORY
AND CRITICISM.
Vinson, James, Contemporary
novelists. New York, St. Martin's
Press [1972] xvii, 1422 p. [$30.00]
823/.03 75-189694
    PR737 .V5 MRR Biog.

Warfel, Harry Redcay, American
novelists of today, New York,
American Book Co. [1951] vii, 478 p.
813.509 51-10144
    PS379 .W3 MRR Biog.

AMERICAN FICTION--20TH CENTURY--HISTORY
AND CRITICISM--BIBLIOGRAPHY.
Adelman, Irving. The contemporary
novel; Metuchen, N.J., Scarecrow
Press, 1972. 614 p.   016.823/03 72-
4451
    Z1231.F4 A34 MRR Ref Desk.

AMERICAN FICTION--BIBLIOGRAPHY.
Coan, Otis Welton. America in
fiction; 5th ed. Palo Alto, Calif.,
Pacific Books, 1967. viii, 232 p.
016.813/00803 66-28118
    Z1361.C6 C6 1966 MRR Alc.

Dickinson, A. T. American historical
fiction, 3d ed. Metuchen, N.J.,
Scarecrow Press, 1971. 380 p.
016.813/03 78-146503
    PS374.H5 D5 1971 MRR Alc.

Gardner, Frank M. Sequels, 5th ed.
London, Association of Assistant
Librarians, 1967. [4], vii-x,
215-291 p. [75/- 50/-(to L.A.
members)] 016.80883 67-89225
    Z5916 .G3 1967 MRR Alc.

Holman, Clarence Hugh, comp. The
American novel through Henry James,
New York, Appleton-Century-Crofts
[1966] ix, 102 p.   016.813 66-
24253
    Z1231.F4 H64 MRR Alc.

Johannsen, Albert, The House of
Beadle and Adams and its dime and
nickel novels; [1st ed.] Norman,
University of Oklahoma Press [1950-
62] 3 v.   655.4747 50-8158
    Z1231.F4 J68 MRR Alc.

Johnson, James Gibson, Southern
fiction prior to 1860: New York,
Phaeton Press, 1968. vii, 126 p.
016.813/2 67-30904
    Z1231.F4 J7 1968 MRR Alc.

Van Derhoof, Jack Warner. A
bibliography of novels related to
American frontier and colonial
history, Troy, N.Y., Whitston Pub.
Co., 1971. xii, 501 p.   016.813/03
70-150333
    Z1231.F4 V3 MRR Alc.

Wright, Lyle Henry, American
fiction, 1774-1850; 2d rev. ed. San
Marino, Calif., Huntington Library,
1969. xviii, 411 p. [$10.00]
016.813/2 68-29777
    Z1231.F4 W9 1969 MRR Alc.

AMERICAN FICTION--BIBLIOGRAPHY--FIRST
EDITIONS.
Deodene, Frank. Black American
fiction since 1952; Chatham, N.J.,
Chatham Bookseller, 1970. 25 p.
016.813/5/4 78-96384
    Z1361.N39 D45 MRR Alc.

AMERICAN FICTION--BOOK REVIEWS--
BIBLIOGRAPHY.
Eichelberger, Clayton L., A guide to
critical reviews of United States
fiction, 1870-1910, Metuchen, N.J.,
Scarecrow Press, 1971. 415 p.
016.813/4/09 77-149998
    Z1225 .E35 MRR Ref Desk.

AMERICAN FICTION--HISTORY AND CRITICISM.
Bone, Robert A. The Negro novel in
America [Rev. ed.] New Haven, Yale
University Press [1965] x, 289 p.
813.509 65-9819
    PS153.N5 B6 1965a MRR Alc.

Cowie, Alexander, The rise of the
American novel. New York, American
Book Co. [1951] xii, 877 p.   813.09
51-2714
    PS371 .C73 1951 MRR Alc.

Lass, Abraham Harold, Plot guide to
100 American and British novels;
Boston, The Writer [1971] xxi, 364,
364 p. [$8.95] 823/.03 73-138526

    PS373 .L28 MRR Alc.

Rubin, Louis Decimus, ed. The idea
of an American novel, New York,
Crowell [1961] 394 p.   813.09 61-
6174
    PS371 .R8 MRR Alc.

AMERICAN FICTION--HISTORY AND CRITICISM-
-BIBLIOGRAPHY.
Adelman, Irving. The contemporary
novel; Metuchen, N.J., Scarecrow
Press, 1972. 614 p.   016.823/03 72-
4451
    Z1231.F4 A34 MRR Ref Desk.

Cotton, Gerald Brooks. Fiction
guides; London, Bingley, 1967. 126
p. [25/-] 016.823/009 67-85300
    Z5916 .C77 1967a MRR Alc.

Eichelberger, Clayton L., A guide to
critical reviews of United States
fiction, 1870-1910, Metuchen, N.J.,
Scarecrow Press, 1971. 415 p.
016.813/4/09 77-149998
    Z1225 .E35 MRR Ref Desk.

Gerstenberger, Donna Lorine. The
American novel, 1789-1959; Denver,
A. Swallow [1961-70] 2 v.
016.813/03 61-9356
    Z1231.F4 G4 TJ Rm.

AMERICAN FICTION--HISTORY AND (Cont.)
Holman, Clarence Hugh, comp. The American novel through Henry James, New York, Appleton-Century-Crofts [1966] ix, 102 p. 016.813 66-24253
Z1231.F4 H64 MRR Alc

Thurston, Jarvis A. Short fiction criticism; Denver, A. Swallow [1960] 265 p. 016.80931 60-8070
Z5917.S5 T5 MRR Alc.

AMERICAN FICTION--NEGRO AUTHORS--BIBLIOGRAPHY.
Deodene, Frank. Black American fiction since 1952; Chatham, N.J., Chatham Bookseller, 1970. 25 p. 016.813/5/4 78-96384
Z1361.N39 D45 MRR Alc.

Whiteman, Maxwell. A century of fiction by American Negroes, 1853-1952; Philadelphia, 1955. 64 p. 016.8134 55-10876
Z1361.N39 W5 MRR Alc.

AMERICAN FICTION--STORIES, PLOTS, ETC.
Lass, Abraham Harold, Plot guide to 100 American and British novels; Boston, The Writer [1971] xxi, 364, 364 p. [$8.95] 823/.03 73-138526

PS373 .L28 MRR Alc.

AMERICAN FICTION--CALIFORNIA--BIBLIOGRAPHY.
Baird, Newton D. An annotated bibliography of California fiction, 1664-1970, Georgetown, Calif., Talisman Literary Research, 1971. xvi, 521 p. 016.813/008/0375 72-176607
Z1231.F4 B35 MRR Alc.

AMERICAN FICTION--SOUTHERN STATES--BIBLIOGRAPHY.
Johnson, James Gibson, Southern fiction prior to 1860: New York, Phaeton Press, 1968. vii, 126 p. 016.813/2 67-30904
Z1231.F4 J7 1968 MRR Alc.

AMERICAN FOLK MUSIC
see Folk music, American

AMERICAN FURNITURE
see Furniture, American

AMERICAN GUIDE SERIES--BIBLIOGRAPHY.
United States. Library of Congress. General reference and bibliography division. The American guide series: Washington, 1944. 1 p. l., 5 p. 016.9173 45-37859
Z1236 .U615 MRR Alc.

Writers' program. Catalogue, WPA Writers' program publications, the American guide series, the American life series; [Washington, U.S. Govt. print. off., 1942] 1 p. l., 54 p. 016.9173 42-37616
Z1236 .W75 MRR Alc.

AMERICAN HYMNS
see Hymns, English

AMERICAN INDIANS
see Indians

AMERICAN INSTITUTE OF PLANNERS--DIRECTORIES.
American Institute of Planners. Handbook & roster. [Washington, etc.] 711/.06/273 60-26104
NA9000 .A54 MRR Alc Latest edition

AMERICAN LIBRARY ASSOCIATION. COOPERATIVE CATALOGING COMMITTEE.
United States. Library of Congress. Cooperative cataloging and classification service. Cooperative work of Card division, Union catalog, Cooperative cataloging and classification service and A.L.A. Cooperative cataloging committee. Washington, 1938. v p., 26 numb. l.
cd 38-158
Z663.745.C63 MRR Alc.

AMERICAN LIBRARY ASSOCIATION. DIVISION OF CATALOGING AND CLASSIFICATION. A.L.A. CATALOGING RULES FOR AUTHOR AND TITLE ENTRIES.
Lubetzky, Seymour. Cataloging rules and principles; Washington, Processing Dept., Library of Congress, 1953. ix, 65 p. 025.32 53-60029
Z663.74 .C3 MRR Alc.

United States. Library of Congress. Descriptive Cataloging Division. Synoptic table of rules: [Washington] 1959. iii, 46 p. 025.32 59-64161
Z695 .U4737 MRR Alc.

AMERICAN LIFE SERIES--BIBLIOGRAPHY.
Writers' program. Catalogue, WPA Writers' program publications, the American guide series, the American life series; [Washington, U.S. Govt. print. off., 1942] 1 p. l., 54 p. 016.9173 42-37616
Z1236 .W75 MRR Alc.

AMERICAN LITERATURE.
Duyckinck, Evert Augustus, Cyclopædia of American literature, Detroit, Gale Research Co., Book Tower, 1965. 2 v. 66-31801
PS85 .D7 1965 MRR Biog.

Fadiman, Clifton, ed. The American treasury, 1455-1955, [1st ed.] New York, Harper [1955] 1108 p. 810.82 55-8019
PS509.H5 F3 MRR Ref Desk.

Macdonald, Dwight, ed. Parodies: New York, Random House [1960] 574 p. 827.082 60-12147
PN6231.P3 M3 MRR Alc.

The Speaker's desk book. New York, Grosset & Dunlap [1967] 613 p. 808.8 66-20654
PN4193.I5 S6 1967 MRR Alc.

AMERICAN LITERATURE--19TH CENTURY--BIBLIOGRAPHY.
Jones, Howard Mumford, Guide to American literature and its backgrounds since 1890 4th ed., rev. and enl. Cambridge, Mass., Harvard University Press, 1972. xii, 264 p. 016.81 72-85143
Z1225 .J65 1972 MRR Alc.

Rees, Robert A. Fifteen American authors before 1900; Madison, University of Wisconsin Press [1971] xvii, 442 p. [$12.50] 016.8109 77-157395
PS201 .R38 MRR Alc.

Schwartz, Jacob. 1100 obscure points: the bibliographies of 25 English and 21 American authors. [1st ed., reprinted]. Bristol, Chatford House Press, 1969. xiii, 95 p., 2 plates. [36/-] 016.820 70-465328
Z2013 .S38 1969 MRR Alc.

AMERICAN LITERATURE--19TH CENTURY--BIO-BIBLIOGRAPHY.
Stovall, Floyd, ed. Eight American authors: New York, Norton [1963] xii, 466 p. [1.95] 016.8109/003 70-8568
PS201 .S8 1963 MRR Alc.

AMERICAN LITERATURE--19TH CENTURY--HISTORY AND CRITICISM.
Rees, Robert A. Fifteen American authors before 1900; Madison, University of Wisconsin Press [1971] xvii, 442 p. [$12.50] 016.8109 77-157395
PS201 .R38 MRR Alc.

Stovall, Floyd, ed. Eight American authors: New York, Norton [1963] xii, 466 p. [1.95] 016.8109/003 70-8568
PS201 .S8 1963 MRR Alc.

AMERICAN LITERATURE--20TH CENTURY--BIBLIOGRAPHY.
Jones, Howard Mumford, Guide to American literature and its backgrounds since 1890 4th ed., rev. and enl. Cambridge, Mass., Harvard University Press, 1972. xii, 264 p. 016.81 72-85143
Z1225 .J65 1972 MRR Alc.

Schwartz, Jacob. 1100 obscure points: the bibliographies of 25 English and 21 American authors. [1st ed., reprinted]. Bristol, Chatford House Press, 1969. xiii, 95 p., 2 plates. [36/-] 016.820 70-465328
Z2013 .S38 1969 MRR Alc.

Vinson, James, Contemporary novelists. New York, St. Martin's Press [1972] xvii, 1422 p. [$30.00] 823/.03 75-189694
PR737 .V5 MRR Biog.

AMERICAN LITERATURE--20TH CENTURY--BIO-BIBLIOGRAPHY.
Phelps, Robert, The literary life; New York, Farrar, Straus and Giroux, 1968. 244 p. [$15.00] 016.8209/009/1 68-27533
Z2013 .P48 MRR Alc.

Shockley, Ann Allen. Living Black American authors: New York, R. R. Bowker Co., 1973. xv, 220 p. 810/.9/896073 73-17005
PS153.N5 S5 MRR Biog.

AMERICAN LITERATURE--20TH CENTURY--HISTORY AND CRITICISM.
Contemporary literary criticism. CLC 1- 1973- Detroit, Gale Research Co. 809/.04 76-38938
PN771 .C59 MRR Alc Full set

Curley, Dorothy Nyren, comp. Modern American literature. 4th enl. ed. New York, F. Ungar Pub. Co. [1969] 3 v. [45.00] 810.9/005 76-76599
PS221 .C8 1969 MRR Alc.

Heiney, Donald W., Recent American literature. Great Neck, N.Y., Barron's Educational Series, inc. [1958] 609 p. 810.904 58-59969
PS221 .H38 MRR Alc.

Sixteen modern American authors; [Rev. ed.] Durham, N.C., Duke University Press, 1974. xx, 673 p. [$10.00] 810/.9/0052 72-97454
PS221 .F45 1974 MRR Alc.

AMERICAN LITERATURE--BIBLIOGRAPHY.
The American catalogue ... New York, 1941. 8 v. in 13. 015.73 a 42-2938
Z1215 .A52 MRR Ref Desk.

American Studies Association. Committee on Microfilm Bibliography. Bibliography of American culture, 1493-1875. Ann Arbor, Mich., University Microfilms, 1957. xvi, 228 p. 016.9173 57-4827
Z1215 .A585 MRR Alc.

Blanck, Jacob Nathaniel, Bibliography of American literature, New Haven, Yale University Press, 1955- v. 016.81 54-5283
Z1225 .B55 MRR Alc.

Boyce, Richard Fyfe. American foreign service authors: Metuchen, N.J., Scarecrow Press, 1973. x, 321 p. 016.081 73-9780
Z1224 .B68 MRR Alc.

The Cambridge history of American literature, New York, G. P. Putnam's sons; [etc., etc.] 1917-21. 4 v. 17-30257
PS88 .C3 MRR Alc.

Gohdes, Clarence Louis Frank, Bibliographical guide to the study of the literature of the U.S.A. 3d ed., rev. and enl. Durham, N.C., Duke University Press, 1970. x, 134 p. [5.00] 016.81 79-110576
Z1225 .G6 1970 MRR Alc.

Havlice, Patricia Pate. Index to American author bibliographies. Metuchen, N.J., Scarecrow Press, 1971. 204 p. 016.01681 73-163870

Z1225 .H37 MRR Ref Desk

Historical records survey. American imprints inventory, Washington, D.C., [etc.] The Historical records survey, 1937- v. 015.73 38-6329
Z1215 .H67 MRR Alc.

Howes, Wright. U.S.-iana, 1650-1950; Rev. and enl. [i.e. 2d] ed. New York, Bowker for the Newberry Library, 1962. 652 p. 016.973 62-10988
Z1215 .H75 1962 MRR Alc.

Kirk, John Foster, A supplement to Allibone's critical dictionary of English literature and British and American authors. Detroit, Gale Research Co., 1965. 2 v. (x, 1562 p.) 820.3 67-296
Z1224 .A44 1891a MRR Biog.

Larrabee, Eric, ed. American panorama: [New York] New York University Press, 1957. 436 p. 016.9173 57-11743
Z1361.C6 L3 MRR Alc.

Literary history of the United States. 4th ed., rev. New York, Macmillan [1974] 2 v. 810/.9 73-14014
PS88 .L522 1974 MRR Alc.

O'Neill, Edward Hayes, Biography by Americans, 1658-1936; Philadelphia, University of Pennsylvania press; London, H. Milford, Oxford university press, 1939. x, 465 p. 016.92 39-30813
Z5301 .O58 MRR Alc.

Peet, Louis Harman, Who's the author? New York, T. Y. Crowell & co. [c1901] iv, 317 p. 01-23523
Z1225 .P37 MRR Alc.

Spargo, John Webster, A bibliographical manual for students of the language and literature of England and the United States; 3d ed. New York, Hendricks House, 1956. x, 285 p. 016.82 56-14402
Z2011 .S73 1956 MRR Alc.

Tanselle, George Thomas, Guide to the study of United States imprints Cambridge, Mass., Belknap Press of Harvard University Press 1971. 2 v. (lxiv, 1050 p.) 016.015/73 79-143232
Z1215.A2 T35 MRR Alc.

AMERICAN LITERATURE-- (Cont.)
United States. Library of Congress. General Reference and Bibliography Division. A guide to the study of the United States of America; Washington, 1960. xv, 1193 p. 016.9173 60-60009
 Z1215 .U53 MRR Alc.

The United States catalog; Minneapolis, H. W. Wilson [1900] 2 pt. in 1 v. 01-29127
 Z1215 .U58 MRR Ref Desk.

The United States catalog; 3d ed. Minneapolis, New York, The H. W. Wilson company, 1912. 3 p. l., 2837 p. 12-35572
 Z1215 .U6 1912a MRR Ref Desk (Alc. 6)

The United States catalog; books in print 1902. 2d ed. Minneapolis, The H. W. Wilson co., 1903. 2 p. l., 2150 p. 03-28279
 Z1215 .U6 1903 MRR Ref Desk.

Van Patten, Nathan, An index to bibliographies and bibliographical contributions relating to the work of American and British authors, 1923-1932. Stanford University, Calif., Stanford university press; London, H. Milford, Oxford university press, 1934. vii, 324 p. 016.82 34-5449

 Z1225.A1 V2 MRR Alc.

AMERICAN LITERATURE--BIBLIOGRAPHY--CATALOGS.
Harvard University. Library. English literature. Cambridge; Distributed by the Harvard University Press, 1971. 4 v. 016.82 74-128717
 Z2011 .H36 MRR Alc.

New York (City). Public Library. Berg Collection. Dictionary catalog of the Henry W. and Albert A. Berg Collection of English and American literature. Boston, G. K. Hall, 1969. 5 v. 016.82 75-21408
 Z2011 .N55 MRR Alc (Dk 33)

United States. Library of Congress. Library of Congress catalog; Books: authors. Jan. 1947-1955. Washington. 47-32682
 Z663.7 .L5 MRR Alc MRR Alc (DK 33) Full set

AMERICAN LITERATURE--BIBLIOGRAPHY--CONGRESSES.
A Catalog of books represented by Library of Congress printed cards issued to July 31, 1942. Ann Arbor, Mich., Edwards Bros., 1942-46. 167 v. 018.1 43-3338
 Z881.A1 C3 MRR Alc. (DK 33)

AMERICAN LITERATURE--BIBLIOGRAPHY--FIRST EDITIONS.
American Antiquarian Society, Worcester, Mass. Library. A dictionary catalog of American books pertaining to the 17th through 19th centuries. Westport, Conn. Greenwood Pub. Corp. [1971] 20 v. 015/.72 76-103820
 Z1215 .A264 MRR Alc (Dk 33)

Brussel, Isidore Rosenbaum, Anglo-American first editions. London, Constable & Co. ltd., New York, R. R. Bowker co., 1935-36. 2 v. 016.0944 016.82 35-19256
 Z2014.F5 B9 MRR Alc.

Foley, Patrick Kevin, American authors, 1795-1895; New York, Milford House, 1969. xvi, 350 p. 016.81 68-54462
 Z1231.F5 F65 1969 MRR Alc.

Johnson, Merle De Vore, Merle Johnson's American first editions. 4th ed. revised and enlarged New York, R. R. Bowker co., 1942. xviii, 553 p. 016.0944 016.81 42-11157
 Z1231.F5 J6 1942 MRR Alc.

AMERICAN LITERATURE--BIBLIOGRAPHY--PERIODICALS.
American literature; v. 1- Mar. 1929- [Durham, N.C. Duke University Press] 810.5 30-20216
 PS1 .A6 MRR Ref Desk Indexes only

Cumulative book index. 1898/99- New York [etc.] H. W. Wilson Co. 05-33604
 Z1219 .M78 MRR Circ Partial set

The United States quarterly book review. v. 1-12, no. 2; Mar. 1945-June 1956. [Denver etc.] Swallow Press [etc.] 015.73 48-46511
 Z663 .A6 MRR Alc MRR Alc Full set

AMERICAN LITERATURE--BIO-BIBLIOGRAPHY.
Adams, Oscar Fay, A dictionary of American authors. 5th ed. rev. and enl. Detroit, Gale Research Co., 1969. viii, 587 p. 810.9 68-21751

 Z1224 .A22 1969 MRR Biog.

Allibone, Samuel Austin, A critical dictionary of English literature and British and American authors, Detroit, Gale Research Co., 1965. 3 v. (3140 p.) 820.3 67-295
 Z1224 .A4317 MRR Biog.

American writers; New York, Scribner [1974- v. 810/.9 B 73-1759
 PS129 .A55 MRR Alc.

Browning, David Clayton, ed. Everyman's dictionary of literary biography, English & American, London, Dent; New York, Dutton [1958] x, 752 p. 928.2 a 58-2815
 PR19 .B7 MRR Biog.

Burke, William Jeremiah, American authors and books, 1640 to the present day 3d rev. ed. New York, Crown Publishers [c1972] 719 p. [$12.50] 015/.73 75-168332
 Z1224 .B87 1972 MRR Biog.

Curley, Dorothy Nyren, comp. Modern American literature. 4th enl. ed. New York, F. Ungar Pub. Co. [1969] 3 v. (45.00] 810.9/005 76-76599
 PS221 .C8 1969 MRR Alc.

Duyckinck, Evert Augustus, Cyclopædia of American literature, Detroit, Gale Research Co., Book Tower, 1965. 2 v. 66-31801
 PS85 .D7 1965 MRR Biog.

Hart, James David, The Oxford companion to American literature 4th ed. [rev. and enl.] New York, Oxford University Press, 1965. ix, 991 p. 810.3 65-22796
 PS21 .H3 1965 MRR Ref Desk.

Harvey, Paul, Sir, The Oxford companion to English literature; 4th ed. revised Oxford, Clarendon P., 1967. x, 961 p. [50/-] 820.3 67-111134
 PR19 .H3 1967 MRR Ref Desk.

Kunitz, Stanley Jasspon, ed. American authors, 1600-1900; New York, The H. W. Wilson company, 1938. vi, 846 p. 928.1 38-27938
 PS21 .K8 MRR Biog.

Moulton, Charles Wells, Library of literary criticism of English and American authors through the beginning of the twentieth century. New York, F. Ungar Pub. Co. [1966] 4 v. 820.9 65-16619
 PR83 .M73 1966 TJ Rm.

Myers, Robin, A dictionary of literature in the English language, from Chaucer to 1940, [1st ed.] Oxford, New York, Pergamon Press [1970] 2 v. 016.82 68-18529
 Z2010 .M9 MRR Alc.

The Penguin companion to American literature. New York, McGraw-Hill [1971] 384 p. [$9.95] 809 70-158062
 PN843 .P4 MRR Alc.

The Reader's encyclopedia of American literature, New York, Crowell [1962] x, 1280 p. 810.3 62-16546
 PS21 .R4 MRR Ref Desk.

Webster's new world companion to English and American literature. New York, World Pub. [1973] 850 p. [$15.00] 820/.9 72-12788
 PR19 .W4 1973 MRR Biog.

AMERICAN LITERATURE--DICTIONARIES.
Burke, William Jeremiah, American authors and books, 1640 to the present day 3d rev. ed. New York, Crown Publishers [c1972] 719 p. [$12.50] 015/.73 75-168332
 Z1224 .B87 1972 MRR Biog.

Chambers, Robert, Chambers's cyclopædia of English literature, London, Edinburgh, W. & R. Chambers, limited [1927-38] 3 v. 820.9 39-8587
 PR83 .C4 1927 MRR Alc.

Freeman, William, Dictionary of fictional characters. Boston, The Writer, inc. [1974, c1973] xi, 579 p. 820/.3 73-18065
 PR19 .F7 1974 MRR Ref Desk.

Hart, James David, The Oxford companion to American literature 4th ed. [rev. and enl.] New York, Oxford University Press, 1965. ix, 991 p. 810.3 65-22796
 PS21 .H3 1965 MRR Ref Desk.

Harvey, Paul, Sir, The Oxford companion to English literature; 4th ed. revised Oxford, Clarendon P., 1967. x, 961 p. [50/-] 820.3 67-111134
 PR19 .H3 1967 MRR Ref Desk.

The Reader's encyclopedia of American literature, New York, Crowell [1962] x, 1280 p. 810.3 62-16546
 PS21 .R4 MRR Ref Desk.

Webster's new world companion to English and American literature. New York, World Pub. [1973] 850 p. [$15.00] 820/.9 72-12788
 PR19 .W4 1973 MRR Biog.

AMERICAN LITERATURE--DISCOGRAPHY.
Roach, Helen Pauline, Spoken records, 3d ed. Metuchen, N.J., Scarecrow Press, 1970. 288 p. 016.82 77-10661
 Z2011 .R6 1970 MRR Alc.

United States. Library of Congress. General Reference and Bibliography Division. Archive of recorded poetry and literature; Washington, 1961. 132 p. 016.810847 61-60005
 Z1225 .U53 MRR Alc.

AMERICAN LITERATURE--HISTORY AND CRITICISM.
The Cambridge history of American literature, New York, G. P. Putnam's sons; [etc., etc.] 1917-21. 4 v. 17-30257
 PS88 .C3 MRR Alc.

The Critical temper; New York, Ungar [1969] 3 v. [45.00] 820.9 68-8116
 PR83 .C764 MRR Alc.

Hackett, Alice Payne, 70 years of best sellers, 1895-1965. New York, R. R. Bowker Co., 1967. xi, 280 p. 655.4/73 67-25025
 Z1033.B3 H34 MRR Ref Desk.

Literary history of the United States. 4th ed., rev. New York, Macmillan [1974] 2 v. 810/.9 73-14014
 PS88 .L522 1974 MRR Alc.

Moulton, Charles Wells, ed. The Library of literary criticism of English and American authors, New York, P. Smith, 1935. 8 v. 820.9 35-27242
 PR83 .M73 1935 MRR Alc.

Moulton, Charles Wells, Library of literary criticism of English and American authors through the beginning of the twentieth century. New York, F. Ungar Pub. Co. [1966] 4 v. 820.9 65-16619
 PR83 .M73 1966 TJ Rm.

Parrington, Vernon Louis, Main currents in American thought; [New York, Harcourt, Brace and company, 1927-30] 3 v. 27-8440
 PS88 .P3 MRR Alc.

Quinn, Arthur Hobson, ed. The literature of the American people, New York, Appleton-Century-Crofts [1951] xix, 1172 p. 810.9 51-10789
 PS88 .Q5 MRR Alc.

Thompson, Ralph, American literary annuals & gift books, 1825-1865. [Hamden, Conn.] Archon Books, 1967 [c1936] 190 p. 050 67-17791
 AY10 .T5 1967 MRR Alc.

Williams, Stanley Thomas, The American spirit in letters, New Haven, Yale university press; [etc., etc.] 1926. 3 p. l., 329 p. 26-12988
 E178.5 .P2 vol. 11 MRR Alc.

Williams, Stanley Thomas, The Spanish background of American literature. [Hamden, Conn.] Archon Books, 1968 [c1955] 2 v. 810.9 68-16337
 PS159.S7 W5 1968 MRR Alc.

AMERICAN LITERATURE--HISTORY AND CRITICISM--BIBLIOGRAPHY.
Altick, Richard Daniel, Selective bibliography for the study of English and American literature, 4th ed. New York, Macmillan [1971] xii, 164 p. [$2.95] 016.82 75-132867
 Z2011 .A4 1971 MRR Alc.

American writers; New York, Scribner [1974- v. 810/.9 B 73-1759
 PS129 .A55 MRR Alc.

Combs, Richard E. Authors: critical and biographical references; Metuchen, N.J., Scarecrow Press, 1971. 221 p. 016.809 73-167644
 PN524 .C58 MRR Alc.

Eichelberger, Clayton L., A guide to critical reviews of United States fiction, 1870-1910, Metuchen, N.J., Scarecrow Press, 1971. 415 p. 016.813/4/09 77-149998
 Z1225 .E35 MRR Ref Desk.

AMERICAN LITERATURE--HISTORY AND (Cont.)
English Association. The year's work
in English studies. v. [1]-
1919/20- New York [etc.] Humanities
Press [etc.] 22-10024
PE58 .E6 MRR Alc Full set

Gerstenberger, Donna Lorine. The
American novel, 1789-1959: Denver,
A. Swallow [1961-70] 2 v.
016.813/03   61-9356
Z1231.F4 G4 TJ Rm.

Gohdes, Clarence Louis Frank,
Literature and theater of the States
and regions of the U.S.A.: Durham,
N.C., Duke University Press, 1967.
ix, 276 p.   016.8109 66-30584
Z1225 .G63 MRR Alc.

Kennedy, Arthur Garfield, A concise
bibliography for students of English,
5th ed. Stanford, Calif., Stanford
University Press, 1972. xvi, 300 p.
016.82   77-183889
Z2011 .K35 1972 MRR Alc.

Leary, Lewis Gaston, Articles on
American literature, 1900-1950.
Durham, N.C., Duke University Press,
1954. 437 p.   016.81 54-5025
Z1225 .L49 MRR Ref Desk.

Leary, Lewis Gaston, Articles on
American literature, 1950-1967.
Durham, N.C., Duke University Press,
1970. xxi, 751 p.   016.8109 70-
132027
Z1225 .L492 MRR Ref Desk.

Literary history of the United
States. 4th ed., rev. New York,
Macmillan [1974] 2 v.   810/.9 73-
14014
PS88 .L522 1974 MRR Alc.

Marsh, John L., A student's
bibliography of American literature.
Dubuque, Iowa, Kendall/Hunt Pub. Co.
[1971] x, 109 p.   016.8109 78-
147255
Z1225 .M37 MRR Alc.

Modern Humanities Research
Association. Annual bibliography of
English Language and literature.
1920- [Leeds, Eng. etc.] 22-11861
Z2011 .M69 MRR Alc Full set

Modern Language Association of
America. MLA abstracts of articles
in scholarly journals. [New York]
408 72-624077
P1 .M64 MRR Alc Full set

Nilon, Charles H. Bibliography of
bibliographies in American
literature, New York, R. R. Bowker
Co., 1970. xi, 483 p.   016.01681
73-103542
Z1225 .A1N5 MRR Ref Desk.

The Romantic movement bibliography,
1936-1970: [Ann Arbor, Mich.]
Pierian Press, 1973. 7 v. (xiii,
3289 p.)   016.809/894   77-172773
Z6514.R6 R65 MRR Alc.

Rubin, Louis Decimus, A
bibliographical guide to the study of
Southern literature, Baton Rouge,
Louisiana State University Press
[1969] xxiv, 368 p. [10.00]
016.81   69-17627
Z1225 .R8 MRR Alc.

Sixteen modern American authors;
[Rev. ed.] Durham, N.C., Duke
University Press, 1974. xx, 673 p.
[$10.00]   810/.9/0052 72-97454
PS221 .F45 1974 MRR Alc.

Stovall, Floyd, ed. Eight American
authors: New York, Norton [1963]
xii, 466 p. [1.95]   016.8109/003
70-8568
PS201 .S8 1963 MRR Alc.

Turner, Darwin T., Afro-American
writers, New York, Appleton-Century-
Crofts, Educational Division [1970]
xvii, 117 p.   016.8108/091/7496 72-
79171
Z1361.N39 T78 MRR Alc.

Woodress, James Leslie.
Dissertations in American literature,
1891-1966 Durham, N.C., Duke
University Press, 1968. xii, 185 p.
016.8109 68-18961
Z1225 .W8 1968 MRR Ref Desk.

AMERICAN LITERATURE--HISTORY AND
CRITICISM--BIBLIOGRAPHY--YEARBOOKS.
American literary scholarship. 1963-
Durham, N.C., Duke University Press.
65-19450
PS3 .A47 MRR Alc Full set

AMERICAN LITERATURE--HISTORY AND
CRITICISM--DICTIONARIES.
The Explicator. The Explicator
cyclopedia. Chicago, Quadrangle
Books, 1966- v.   820.9 66-11875

PR401 .E9 MRR Alc.

AMERICAN LITERATURE--HISTORY AND
CRITICISM--PERIODICALS.
American literature; v. 1- Mar.
1929- [Durham, N.C. Duke University
Press] 810.5 30-20216
PS1 .A6 MRR Ref Desk Indexes only

The Explicator, v. 1- Oct. 1942-
Columbia [etc.] University of South
Carolina [etc.] 47-41241
PR1 .E9 MRR Alc Full set

AMERICAN LITERATURE--HISTORY AND
CRITICISM--PERIODICALS--INDEXES.
American literature; v. 1- Mar.
1929- [Durham, N.C. Duke University
Press] 810.5 30-20216
PS1 .A6 MRR Ref Desk Indexes only

AMERICAN LITERATURE--HISTORY AND
CRITICISM--YEARBOOKS.
American literary scholarship. 1963-
Durham, N.C., Duke University Press.
65-19450
PS3 .A47 MRR Alc Full set

AMERICAN LITERATURE--INDIAN AUTHORS.
Stensland, Anna Lee, Literature by
and about the American Indian;
[Urbana, Ill.] National Council of
Teachers of English [1973] x, 208 p.
[$3.95]   016.9701 73-83285
Z1209 .S73 MRR Alc.

AMERICAN LITERATURE--INDIAN AUTHORS--
BIBLIOGRAPHY.
Hirschfelder, Arlene B. American
Indian authors; New York,
Association on American Indian
Affairs [1970] 45 p. 016.81 78-
121863
Z7118 .H55 MRR Alc.

AMERICAN LITERATURE--MANUSCRIPTS.
Modern Language Association of
America. American Literature Group.
Committee on Manuscript Holdings.
American literary manuscripts;
Austin, University of Texas Press
[1961, c1960] xxviii, 421 p.
016.81 60-10356
Z6620.U5 M6 MRR Alc.

AMERICAN LITERATURE--NEGRO AUTHORS.
Patterson, Lindsay, comp. An
introduction to black literature in
America, [1st ed.] New York,
Publishers Co. [1968] xvii, 302 p.
810.8/091/7496 68-56838
PS508.N3 P3 MRR Alc.

United States. Library of Congress.
75 years of freedom; [Washington,
U.S. Govt. print. off. 1943] cover-
title, vi, 108 p.   325.260973 43-
52457
Z663 .S43 MRR Alc.

AMERICAN LITERATURE--NEGRO AUTHORS--
BIBLIOGRAPHY.
Loggins, Vernon, The Negro author,
his development in America to 1900.
Port Washington, N.Y., Kennikat Press
[1964, c1959] ix, 480 p. 810.9 64-
15540
PS153.N5 L65 1964 MRR Alc.

Stanford, Barbara Dodds. Negro
literature for high school students.
[Champaign, Ill.] National Council of
Teachers of English [1968] ix, 157
p. [$2.00]   016.810/9/9 68-7786
Z1361.N39 S75 MRR Alc.

Turner, Darwin T., Afro-American
writers, New York, Appleton-Century-
Crofts, Educational Division [1970]
xvii, 117 p.   016.8108/091/7496 72-
79171
Z1361.N39 T78 MRR Alc.

Whitlow, Roger. Black American
literature; Chicago, Nelson Hall
[1973] xv, 287 p. [$8.95]
810/.9/896073 73-75525
PS153.N5 W45 MRR Alc.

AMERICAN LITERATURE--NEGRO AUTHORS--BIO-
BIBLIOGRAPHY.
Bailey, Leaonead Pack. Broadside
authors and artists; [1st ed.]
Detroit, Mich., Broadside Press
[1974] 125 p. [$9.95] 811/.5/409
B 70-108887
Z1228.N39 B34 MRR Biog.

Shockley, Ann Allen. Living Black
American authors: New York, R. R.
Bowker Co., 1973. xv, 220 p.
810/.9/896073 73-17005
PS153.N5 S5 MRR Biog.

AMERICAN LITERATURE--NEGRO AUTHORS--
HISTORY AND CRITICISM.
Bone, Robert A. The Negro novel in
America [Rev. ed.] New Haven, Yale
University Press [1965] x, 289 p.
813.509 65-9819
PS153.N5 B6 1965a MRR Alc.

John, Janheinz. Neo-African
literature; New York, Grove Press
[1969, c1968] 301 p. [7.50]
809.8/91/7496 68-58154
PL8010 .J313 1969 MRR Alc.

Littlejohn, David, Black on white;
New York, Grossman, 1966. 180 p.
810.9 66-19523
PS153.N5 L5 MRR Alc.

Loggins, Vernon, The Negro author,
his development in America to 1900.
Port Washington, N.Y., Kennikat Press
[1964, c1959] ix, 480 p. 810.9 64-
15540
PS153.N5 L65 1964 MRR Alc.

Patterson, Lindsay, comp. An
introduction to black literature in
America, [1st ed.] New York,
Publishers Co. [1968] xvii, 302 p.
810.8/091/7496 68-56838
PS508.N3 P3 MRR Alc.

Stanford, Barbara Dodds. Negro
literature for high school students.
[Champaign, Ill.] National Council of
Teachers of English [1968] ix, 157
p. [$2.00]   016.810/9/9 68-7786
Z1361.N39 S75 MRR Alc.

Whitlow, Roger. Black American
literature; Chicago, Nelson Hall
[1973] xv, 287 p. [$8.95]
810/.9/896073 73-75525
PS153.N5 W45 MRR Alc.

AMERICAN LITERATURE--OUTLINES, SYLLABI,
ETC.
Holman, Clarence Hugh, A handbook to
literature, 3d ed. Indianapolis,
Odyssey Press [1972] viii, 646 p.
803 73-175226
PN41 .H6 1972 MRR Alc.

Whitcomb, Selden Lincoln,
Chronological outlines of American
literature, New York, London,
Macmillan and co., 1894. x, 286 p.
12-39940
PS94 .W4 MRR Alc.

AMERICAN LITERATURE--PERIODICALS--
INDEXES.
Index to American little magazines.
Troy, N.Y. [etc.] Whitston Pub. Co.
[etc.] 77-97476
AI3 .I54 MRR Alc Full set

AMERICAN LITERATURE--STUDY AND TEACHING-
-BIBLIOGRAPHY.
Altick, Richard Daniel, Selective
bibliography for the study of English
and American literature, 4th ed.
New York, Macmillan [1971] xii, 164
p. [$2.95]   016.82 75-132867
Z2011 .A4 1971 MRR Alc.

AMERICAN LITERATURE--TRANSLATIONS INTO
PORTUGUESE.
United States. Library of Congress.
Hispanic Foundation. Spanish and
Portuguese translations of United
States books, 1955-1962; Washington,
Library of Congress, 1963. xv, 506
p.   63-60091
Z663.32 .A5 no. 8 MRR Alc.

AMERICAN LITERATURE--TRANSLATIONS INTO
PORTUGUESE--BIBLIOGRAPHY.
United States. Library of Congress.
Hispanic Foundation. A provisional
bibliography of United States books
translated into Portuguese.
Washington, Library of Congress,
Reference Dept., 1957. vii, 182 p.
015.73 57-60009
Z663.32 .A5 no. 2 MRR Alc.

AMERICAN LITERATURE--TRANSLATIONS INTO
SPANISH--BIBLIOGRAPHY.
United States. Library of Congress.
Hispanic Foundation. A provisional
bibliography of United States books
translated into Spanish. Washington,
Library of Congress, Reference Dept.,
1957. ix, 471 p.   015.73 57-60028
Z663.32 .A5 no. 3 MRR Alc.

United States. Library of Congress.
Hispanic Foundation. Spanish and
Portuguese translations of United
States books, 1955-1962; Washington,
Library of Congress, 1963. xv, 506
p.   63-60091
Z663.32 .A5 no. 8 MRR Alc.

AMERICAN LITERATURE--ALABAMA--
BIBLIOGRAPHY.
Historical records survey. Alabama.
Check list of Alabama imprints, 1807-
1840. Birmingham, Ala., The Alabama
historical records survey project,
1939. xv, 159 p.   015.761 40-26269

Z1215 .H67 no. 8 MRR Alc.

AMERICAN LITERATURE--ARIZONA--
BIBLIOGRAPHY.
Historical records survey. ... A
check list of Arizona imprints, 1860-
1890. Chicago, The Historical
records survey, 1938. v, 81 p.
015.791 39-4907
Z1215 .H67 no. 3 MRR Alc.

AMERICAN LITERATURE--ARKANSAS--
BIBLIOGRAPHY.
Historical records survey. Arkansas.
A check list of Arkansas imprints,
1821-1876. Little Rock, Ark., The
Arkansas Historical records survey,
1942. 6 p. l., 139 numb. l., 2 l.
015.767   42-17366
    Z1215 .H67 no. 39 MRR Alc.

AMERICAN LITERATURE--CHICAGO--
BIBLIOGRAPHY.
Historical records survey. Check
list of Chicago ante-fire imprints,
1851-1871. Chicago, The Historical
records survey, 1938. 2 p. l., iii-
xvii, 727 p.   015.7731   39-4906
    Z1215 .H67 no. 4 MRR Alc.

AMERICAN LITERATURE--GEORGIA--
BIBLIOGRAPHY.
Bonner, John Wyatt. Bibliography of
Georgia authors, 1949-1965. Athens,
University of Georgia Press [c1966]
vii, 266 p.   013/.9758   66-23074
    Z1273 .B6 MRR Alc.

AMERICAN LITERATURE--IDAHO--
BIBLIOGRAPHY.
Historical records survey. A check
list of Idaho imprints, 1839-1890.
Chicago, The WPA Historical records
survey project, 1940. 66, 66a-66b,
67-74 numb. l.   015.796   41-50084
    Z1215 .H67 no. 13 MRR Alc.

AMERICAN LITERATURE--INDIANA--
BIBLIOGRAPHY.
Byrd, Cecil K. A bibliography of
Indiana imprints, 1804-1853,
Indianapolis, Indiana Historical
Bureau, 1955. xxi, 479 p.   015.772
55-4194
    Z1281 .B8 MRR Alc.

AMERICAN LITERATURE--IOWA--BIBLIOGRAPHY.
Historical records survey. A check
list of Iowa imprints 1838-1860,
Chicago, The WPA Historical records
survey project, 1940. 84 (i.e. 85)
numb. l.   015.777   42-17567
    Z1215 .H67 no. 15 MRR Alc.

AMERICAN LITERATURE--KANSAS--
BIBLIOGRAPHY.
Historical Records Survey. Check
list of Kansas imprints, 1854-1876.
Topeka, WPA Historical Records Survey
Project, 1939. xxxvii, 773 l.   40-
3090
    Z1215 .H67 no. 10 MRR Alc.

AMERICAN LITERATURE--KENTUCKY--
BIBLIOGRAPHY.
Historical records survey. Kentucky.
Supplemental check list of Kentucky
imprints, 1788-1820; Louisville,
Ky., Historical records survey,
Service division, Work projects
administration, 1942. 2 p. l., xii
(i.e. xiii) p., 1 l., 241 p. incl.
tables.   015.769   43-2549
    Z1215 .H67 no. 38 MRR Alc.

McMurtrie, Douglas Crawford, Check
list of Kentucky imprints, 1787-1810,
Louisville, The Historical records
survey, 1939. xxvii, 205 p.
015.769   39-4909
    Z1215 .H67 no. 5 MRR Alc.

AMERICAN LITERATURE--KENTUCKY--BIO-
BIBLIOGRAPHY.
Richey, Ish. Kentucky literature,
1784-1963. Tompkinsville, Ky.,
Printed by Monroe County Press, 1963.
236 p.   64-3008
    PS266.K4 R5 MRR Biog.

AMERICAN LITERATURE--MARYLAND--
BIBLIOGRAPHY.
Bristol, Roger Pattrell. Maryland
imprints, 1801-1810.
Charlottesville, Published by the
University of Virginia Press for the
Bibliographical Society of the
University of Virginia, 1953.
xxviii, 310 p.   015.752   53-7130
    Z1293 .B75 MRR Alc.

AMERICAN LITERATURE--MASSACHUSETTS--
BIBLIOGRAPHY.
American imprints inventory project.
Massachusetts. A check list of
Massachusetts imprints, 1801.
Boston, Mass., 1942. xxxiii, 157
numb. l., 5 l.   015.744   44-5151
    Z1215 .H67 no. 40 MRR Alc.

American imprints inventory project.
Massachusetts. A check list of
Massachusetts imprints, 1802.
Boston, Mass., 1942. xxxiii, 158
numb. l., 5 l.   015.744   43-444
    Z1215 .H67 no. 45 MRR Alc.

AMERICAN LITERATURE--MICHIGAN--
BIBLIOGRAPHY.
Historical records survey. Michigan.
Preliminary check list of Michigan
imprints, 1786-1850, Detroit, Mich.,
The Michigan Historical records
survey project, 1942. vii, 224 p., 4
numb. l.   015.774   44-41415
    Z1215 .H67 no. 52 MRR Alc.

AMERICAN LITERATURE--MISSOURI--
BIBLIOGRAPHY.
Historical records survey. ... A
preliminary check list of Missouri
imprints, 1808-1850. Washington,
D.C., The historical records survey,
1937. ix, 225 p.   015.778   39-4905

    Z1215 .H67 no. 1 MRR Alc.

AMERICAN LITERATURE--NEBRASKA--
BIBLIOGRAPHY.
Historical records survey. Nebraska.
A check list of Nebraska imprints,
1847-1876. Lincoln, Neb., 1942. 2
v.   015.782   42-16593
    Z1215 .H67 no. 26-27 MRR Alc.

AMERICAN LITERATURE--NEVADA--
BIBLIOGRAPHY.
Historical records survey. A check
list of Nevada imprints, 1859-1890.
Chicago, The Historical records
survey, 1939. xv, 127 numb. l.
015.793   39-29057
    Z1215 .H67 no. 7 MRR Alc.

AMERICAN LITERATURE--NEW MEXICO--
BIBLIOGRAPHY.
Historical records survey. Illinois.
Check list of New Mexico imprints and
publications, 1784-1876. [Detroit]
Michigan Historical records survey,
1942. 3 p. l., v-xiii, 115 p., 3 l.
015.798   43-5102
    Z1215 .H67 no. 25 MRR Alc.

AMERICAN LITERATURE--NORTHWEST, PACIFIC-
-BIBLIOGRAPHY.
Inland Empire Council of Teachers of
English. Northwest books, [2d ed.]
Portland, Or., Binfords & Mort [1942]
356 p.   016.81   42-21718
    Z1251.N7 I6 MRR Alc.

AMERICAN LITERATURE--NORTHWEST, PACIFIC-
-BIO-BIBLIOGRAPHY.
Who's who among Pacific Northwest
authors. 2d ed. [Missoula, Mont.?]
Pacific Northwest Library
Association, Reference Division, 1969
[c1970] 105 p.   810.9/979   74-16021

    Z1251.N7 W5 1970 MRR Biog.

AMERICAN LITERATURE--OHIO--BIBLIOGRAPHY.
Historical records survey. Ohio. A
check list of Ohio imprints, 1796-
1820. Columbus, O., Ohio Historical
records survey, 1941. 202 numb. l.
015.771   42-17565
    Z1215 .H67 no. 17 MRR Alc.

AMERICAN LITERATURE--OKLAHOMA--
BIBLIOGRAPHY.
Hargrett, Lester, Oklahoma imprints,
1835-1890. New York, Published for
the Bibliographical Society of
America [by] Bowker, 1951. xvii, 267
p.   015.766   51-3747
    Z1325 .H3 MRR Alc.

AMERICAN LITERATURE--SOUTHERN STATES--
BIBLIOGRAPHY.
Cantrell, Clyde Hull. Southern
literary culture; [University]
University of Alabama Press, 1955.
xiv, 124 p.   016.81   54-10880
    Z1251.S7 C3 MRR Alc.

Rubin, Louis Decimus, A
bibliographical guide to the study of
Southern literature, Baton Rouge,
Louisiana State University Press
[1969] xxiv, 368 p. [10.00]
016.81   68-17627
    Z1225 .R8 MRR Alc.

AMERICAN LITERATURE--SOUTHERN STATES--
HISTORY AND CRITICISM.
Hubbell, Jay Broadus, The South in
American literature, 1607-1900.
[Durham, N.C.] Duke University Press,
1954. xix, 987 p.   810.9   54-9434
    PS261 .H78 MRR Alc.

AMERICAN LITERATURE--TENNESSEE--
BIBLIOGRAPHY.
Historical records survey. Illinois.
A check list of Tennessee imprints,
1793-1840. Chicago, Ill., The
Illinois Historical records survey,
1942. xv, 285 p.   015.768   43-4097

    Z1215 .H67 no. 32 MRR Alc.

Historical records survey. Tennessee.
Check list of Tennessee imprints,
1841-1850. Nashville, Tenn., The
Tennessee Historical records survey,
1941. 1 p. l., iii-xiii, 138 numb.
l.   015.768   42-17566
    Z1215 .H67 no. 20 MRR Alc.

Historical records survey. Tennessee.
List of Tennessee imprints, 1793-
1840, in Tennessee libraries.
Nashville, Tenn., The Tennessee
Historical records survey, 1941.
viii, 97 numb. l.   015.768   41-52927

    Z1215 .H67 no. 16 MRR Alc.

Mitchell, Eleanor Drake. A
preliminary checklist of Tennessee
imprints, 1861-1866.
Charlottesville, Bibliographical
Society of the University of
Virginia, 1953. 98 l.   015.768   53-
7131
    Z1337 .M58 MRR Alc.

AMERICAN LITERATURE--TEXAS--
BIBLIOGRAPHY.
Streeter, Thomas Winthrop,
Bibliography of Texas, 1795-1845.
Cambridge, Harvard University Press,
1955-60. 3 pts. in 5 v.   016.9764
56-13552
    Z1339 .S8 MRR Alc.

AMERICAN LITERATURE--UTICA--
BIBLIOGRAPHY.
Historical records survey. Illinois.
A check list of Utica imprints, 1799-
1830, Chicago, Ill., Illinois
Historical records survey, Illinois
public records project, 1942. viii,
179 p.   015.747   43-5103
    Z1215 .H67 no. 36 MRR Alc.

AMERICAN LITERATURE--VIRGINIA--
BIBLIOGRAPHY.
Swem, Earl Gregg, A bibliography of
Virginia. Richmond, D. Bottom,
superintendent of public printing,
1916-55. 5 v.   16-4768
    Z1345 .S85 MRR Alc.

AMERICAN LITERATURE--WASHINGTON (STATE)-
-BIBLIOGRAPHY.
Historical records survey. Washington
(State) A check list of Washington
imprints, 1853-1876. Seattle, Wash.,
The Washington Historical records
survey, 1942. 89 p.   015.797   42-
21716
    Z1215 .H67 no. 44 MRR Alc.

AMERICAN LITERATURE--WEST VIRGINIA--
BIBLIOGRAPHY.
Historical records survey. A check
list of West Virginia imprints, 1791-
1830. Chicago, The WPA Historical
records survey project, 1940. 62
numb. l.   015.754   41-50571
    Z1215 .H67 no. 14 MRR Alc.

AMERICAN LITERATURE--WISCONSIN--
BIBLIOGRAPHY.
Historical Records Survey. Wisconsin.
A check list of Wisconsin imprints,
1833-1849[--1864-1869] Madison,
Wis., The Wisconsin Historical
Records Survey, 1942-53. 5 v.
015.775   42-16157
    Z1215 .H67 no. 23-24, 41-42 MRR
    Alc.

AMERICAN LITERATURE--WYOMING--
BIBLIOGRAPHY.
Historical records survey. Illinois.
A check list of Wyoming imprints,
1866-1890. Chicago, Ill., The
Illinois Historical records survey,
1941. 2 p. l., 3-69 (i.e. 70) numb.
l.   015.787   42-14492
    Z1215 .H67 no. 18 MRR Alc.

AMERICAN LOYALISTS.
Brown, Wallace, The king's friends;
Providence, Brown University Press,
1965. x, 411 p.   973.314   66-10179

    E277 .B82 MRR Alc.

AMERICAN LUTHERAN CHURCH (1961-)--
CLERGY--DIRECTORIES.
A Biographical directory of clergymen
of The American Lutheran Church.
Minneapolis, Augsburg Pub. House,
1972. ix, 1054 p.   284/.131/0922 B
72-80314
    BX8047.7 .B56 MRR Biog.

AMERICAN NATIONAL CHARACTERISTICS
see National characteristics, American

AMERICAN NATIONAL SONGS
see National songs, American

AMERICAN NEWSPAPERS.
Emery, Edwin. The press and America,
3d ed. Englewood Cliffs, N.J.,
Prentice-Hall [1972] xi, 788 p.
071.3   77-38634
    PN4855 .E6 1972 MRR Alc.

Mott, Frank Luther, American
journalism; 3d ed. New York,
Macmillan [1962] 901 p.   071.3   62-
7157
    PN4855 .M63 1962 MRR Alc.

AMERICAN NEWSPAPERS--BIBLIOGRAPHY.
American newspapers, 1821-1936; New
York, H. W. Wilson Co., 1937. xvi,
791 p.   37-12783
    Z6945 .A53 MRR Alc.

Arndt, Karl John Richard. German-
American newspapers and periodicals,
1732-1955; Heidelberg, Quelle &
Meyer, 1961. 794 p.   62-107
    Z6953.5.G3 A7 MRR Alc.

AMERICAN NEWSPAPERS-- (Cont.)
Brigham, Clarence Saunders, History
and bibliography of American
newspapers, 1690-1820. Worcester,
Mass., American Antiquarian Society,
1947. 2 v. (xvii, 1508 p.)   016.071
47-4111
    Z6951 .B86 MRR Alc.

Chicago Historical Society. Library.
A check list of the Kellogg
collection of "patent inside"
newspapers of 1876. Chicago, The WPA
Historical records survey project,
1939. ix, 99 numb. l.   016.071 39-
29378
    Z1215 .H67 no. 11 MRR Alc.

Directory of the college student
press in America. 1967/68- New York
[etc.] Oxbridge Pub. Co. [etc.]
378.1/98/9705 76-10981
    L901 .D52 MRR Ref Desk Latest
      edition

La Brie, Henry G. The Black
newspaper in America: 3d ed.
[Kennebunkport, Me., Mercer House
Press] 1973. 84 p.   [$5.00]
070/.02573 73-166319
    Z6944.N39 L3 1973 MRR Alc.

Lathem, Edward Connery.
Chronological tables of American
newspapers, 1690-1820; being a
tabular guide to holdings of
newspapers published in America
through the year 1820. [Worcester,
Mass.] American Antiquarian Society
[c1972] x, 131 p.   016.071/3 70-
185613
    Z6951 .L3 MRR Alc.

[Pride, Armistead Scott] Negro
newspapers on microfilm; Washington,
Library of Congress, Photoduplication
Service, 1953. 8 p.   016.071 53-
60015
    Z663.96 .N4 MRR Alc.

United States. Library of Congress.
Union Catalog Division. Selected
list of United States newspapers
recommended for preservation by the
ALA Committee on Cooperative
Microfilm Projects. Washington,
Library of Congress, 1953. xvii, 92
p.   016.071 53-60038
    Z663.79 .S4 MRR Alc.

AMERICAN NEWSPAPERS--BIBLIOGRAPHY--
CATALOGS.
New York. Public library. Checklist
of newspapers and official gazettes
in the New York public library; [New
York] The New York public library,
1915. iv, 579 p.   16-1688
    Z6945 .N6 MRR Alc.

Northwestern University, Evanston,
Ill. Library. Special Collections
Dept. Guide to underground
newspapers in the Special Collections
Department. Evanston, Northwestern
University Library, 1971. 60 p.
016.071/3 73-180306
    Z6951 .N9 1971 MRR Ref Desk.

United States. Library of Congress.
Periodicals Division. A check list
of American eighteenth century
newspapers in the Library of
Congress, New ed., rev. and enl.
New York, Greenwood Press [1968] vi,
401 p.   015/.73 68-55137
    Z6951 .U47 1968 MRR Alc.

United States. Library of Congress.
Periodicals division. A check list
of American eighteenth century
newspapers in the Library of
Congress, New ed., rev. and enl.
Washington, U.S. Govt. print.off.,
1936. vi, 401 p.   016.071 36-26003

    Z663.46 .C43 1936 MRR Alc.

United States. Library of Congress.
Periodicals division. A check list
of American newspapers in the Library
of Congress. Washington, Govt.
print. off., 1901. 9 p., 11-292
numb. l.   01-16621
    Z663.46 .C45 MRR Alc.

United States. Library of Congress.
Serial Division. Holdings of
American nineteenth and twentieth
century newspapers printed on wood
pulp paper. [Washington] 1950. 46
l.   016.071 51-62830
    Z663.44 .H6 MRR Alc.

AMERICAN NEWSPAPERS--BIBLIOGRAPHY--
UNION LISTS.
United States. Library of Congress.
Catalog Publication Division.
Newspapers in microform: United
States, 1948-1972. Washington,
Library of Congress, 1973. xxiii,
1056 p.   [$30.00] 016.071/3 73-
6936
    Z663.733 .N48 MRR Ref Desk.

AMERICAN NEWSPAPERS--CIRCULATION.
Audit Bureau of Circulations. A.B.C.
blue book, [Chicago?] 071 45-53615

    Z6951 .A67 MRR Alc Latest edition

Standard Rate and Data Service, inc.
S R D S newspaper circulation
analysis. Skokie, Ill. 67-6743
    HF5415.3 .S7 MRR Ref Desk Latest
      edition

AMERICAN NEWSPAPERS--CIRCULATION--
YEARBOOKS.
American Newspaper Markets, inc.,
Northfield, Ill. Circulation.
Northfield. 65-36529
    Began publication with 1962 volume.
    HF5905 .A57 MRR Alc Latest edition

AMERICAN NEWSPAPERS--DIRECTORIES.
Ahlers, Arvel W., Where and how to
sell your pictures. 4th ed. rev.
New York, American Photographic Book
Pub. Co.; book trade: Garden City
Books, Garden City, N.Y. [1959] 142
p.   770.69 59-4237
    TR820 .A35 1959 MRR Alc.

Audit Bureau of Circulations. A.B.C.
blue book, [Chicago?] 071 45-53615

    Z6951 .A67 MRR Alc Latest edition

Ayer directory of publications.
Philadelphia, Ayer Press. 071.3/025
73-640052
    Z6951 .A97 Sci RR Latest edition /
    MRR Ref Desk Latest edition / MRR
    Alc Latest edition

The Catholic press directory. 1923-
New York [etc.] Catholic Press Ass.
[etc.] 23-11774
    Z6951 .C36 MRR Alc Latest edition

Editor & publisher. Market guide.
v. [1]- 1924- New York. 658.8 45-
44873
    HF5905 .E38 MRR Ref Desk Latest
      edition

Media records; v. 1-   1st quarter
1928- New York. 29-2345
    HF5903 .M45 MRR Alc Latest edition

National directory of weekly
newspapers, including semi- and tri-
weekly newspapers. 1927/28- New
York, American Newspaper
Representatives, Inc. [etc.] 071 27-
19879
    Z6951 .C86 MRR Alc Latest edition

North, Simon Newton Dexter, History
and present condition of the
newspaper and periodical press of the
United States, [Elmsford, N.Y.,
Maxwell Reprint Co., 1971] vi, 446
p.   338/.0973 s 070.5/0973 73-
164452
    HC105 .A66 vol. 9 MRR Alc.

Standard Rate and Data Service, inc.
Newspaper rates and data. v. 33-
Jan. 1951- Skokie, Ill.[etc.]
659.132058 53-36942
    HF5905 .S73 MRR Ref Desk Latest
      edition

United States. Office of Minority
Business Enterprise. Directory of
minority media. [Washington]; for
sale by the Supt. of Docs., U.S.
Govt. Print. Off., 1973. ix, 89 p.
[$1.25]   301.16/1/02573 73-602286
    P88.8 .U55 MRR Alc.

Weekly newspaper rates and data. v.
48- Mar. 1966- [Skokie, Ill.]
Standard Rate & Data Service, Inc.
659.13/2 72-622887
    HF5905 .S72 MRR Ref Desk Latest
      edition

The Working press of the nation,
[1945]- Burlington, Iowa [etc.]
National Research Bureau [etc.]
071.47 46-7041
    Z6951 .W6 MRR Alc Latest edition

AMERICAN NEWSPAPERS--FOREIGN LANGUAGE
PRESS.
Wynar, Lubomyr Roman, Encyclopedic
directory of ethnic newspapers and
periodicals in the United States
Littleton, Colo., Libraries
Unlimited, 1972. 260 p. [$12.50]
070.4/84/02573 70-185344
    Z6944.E8 W94 MRR Ref Desk.

AMERICAN NEWSPAPERS--HISTORY.
Brigham, Clarence Saunders, History
and bibliography of American
newspapers, 1690-1820. Worcester,
Mass., American Antiquarian Society,
1947. 2 v. (xvii, 1508 p.)   016.071
47-4111
    Z6951 .B86 MRR Alc.

North, Simon Newton Dexter, History
and present condition of the
newspaper and periodical press of the
United States, [Elmsford, N.Y.,
Maxwell Reprint Co., 1971.] vi, 446
p.   338/.0973 s 070.5/0973 73-
164452
    HC105 .A66 vol. 9 MRR Alc.

Tebbel, John William, The compact
history of the American newspaper
New and rev. ed. New York, Hawthorn
Books [1969] 286 p. [6.95] 071/.3
69-20347
    PN4855 .T4 1969 MRR Alc.

Thomas, Isaiah, The history of
printing in America, Barre, Mass.,
Imprint Society, 1970. xxi, 650 p.
686.2/0973 75-100491
    Z205 .T56 1970 MRR Alc.

AMERICAN NEWSPAPERS--INDEXES.
The Christian Science monitor. Index.
[Boston, Mass.] Christian Science
Pub. Society. 051 74-644930
    AI21.C462 C45 MRR Alc Partial set

Christian Science monitor (Indexes)
Cumulated index of the Christian
Science monitor. 1960- [Corvallis,
Or., Christian Science Publishing Co.
64-1455
    AI21 .C46 MRR Alc Partial set

New York times. (Indexes) The New
York times index. New York,
Reprinted for the New York Times Co.
by R. R. Bowker Co. 66-41174
    AI21 .N452 MRR Circ Partial set

New York times. (Indexes) The New
York times index for the published
news. v. 1-   Jan./Mar. 1913- New
York. 13-13458
    AI21 .N45 MRR Circ Full set / MRR
    Circ Partial set

New York tribune. New-York daily
tribune index. 1875-1906. New York,
Tribune Association. 12-37148
    AI21 .N5 MRR Alc Full set

Wall Street journal. (Indexes)
Index. [New York] Dow Jones & Co.
59-35162
    HG1 .W26 MRR Alc Full set

AMERICAN NEWSPAPERS--INDEXES--
BIBLIOGRAPHY.
Brayer, Herbert Oliver. Preliminary
guide to indexed newspapers in the
United States, 1850-1900. [Cedar
Rapids? Ia., 1946?] 237-258 p.
016.071 48-12815
    Z6293 .B7 MRR Alc.

AMERICAN NEWSPAPERS--CALIFORNIA--
DIRECTORIES.
California publicity outlets. 1972-
Los Angeles, Unicorn Systems Co.,
Information Services Division.
658.2/025/794 76-181643
    HM263 .C2 MRR Alc Latest edition

AMERICAN NEWSPAPERS--NEW YORK (CITY)--
DIRECTORIES.
New York publicity outlets. New
York, Attention Inc. [etc.] 61-65657

    Z6953.N6 N6 MRR Alc Latest edition

AMERICAN NEWSPAPERS--NEW YORK (CITY)--
HISTORY.
The Working press of the nation,
[1945]- Burlington, Iowa [etc.]
National Research Bureau [etc.]
071.47 46-7041
    Z6951 .W6 MRR Alc Latest edition

AMERICAN NEWSPAPERS--VIRGINIA--
BIBLIOGRAPHY.
Cappon, Lester Jesse, Bibliography
of Virginia history since 1865,
University, Va., The Institute for
research in the social sciences,
1930. xviii, 900 p.   016.9755 30-
27506
    Z1345 .C25 MRR Alc.

AMERICAN ORATIONS.
Miller, Marion Mills, ed. Great
debates in American history, [The
national ed.] New York, Current
literature publishing company [c1913]
14 v.   13-23912
    E173 .M64 vol. 14 MRR Alc.

Hurd, Charles, ed. A treasury of
great American speeches. New and
rev. ed. New York, Hawthorn Books
[1970] 411 p. [10.00] 815/.01 77-
107901
    PS662 .H8 1970 MRR Alc.

Parrish, Wayland Maxfield, ed.
American speeches [1st ed.] New
York, Longmans, Green, 1954. 518 p.
815.082 54-10208
    PN6122 .P3 MRR Alc.

Wrage, Ernest J., ed. Contemporary
forum; New York, Harper [1962] 376
p.   815.5082 62-10074
    PS668 .W7 MRR Alc.

AMERICAN ORATIONS--20TH CENTURY.
Representative American speeches.
1937/38- New York, H. W. Wilson Co.
815.5082 38-27962
PS668 .B3 MRR Alc Full set

AMERICAN ORATIONS--INDEXES.
Sutton, Roberta (Briggs) Speech
index; 4th ed., rev. and enl. New
York, Scarecrow Press, 1966. vii,
947 p. 016.80885 66-13749
AI3 .S85 1966 MRR Ref Desk.

AMERICAN PAINTINGS
see Paintings, American

AMERICAN PERIODICALS.
Ford, James L. C. Magazines for
millions; Carbondale, Southern
Illinois University Press [c1969]
xvii, 320 p. [11.75] 051 79-76187

PN4877 .F6 MRR Alc.

AMERICAN PERIODICALS--BIBLIOGRAPHY.
Andriot, John L. Guide to U.S.
Government serials & periodicals,
1967 ed. McLean, Va., Documents
Index [c1967] 2 v. (1631 p.)
015/.73 68-3862
Z1223.Z7 A573 MRR Ref Desk.

Arndt, Karl John Richard. German-
American newspapers and periodicals,
1732-1955; Heidelberg, Quelle &
Meyer, 1961. 794 p. 62-107
Z6953.5.G3 A7 MRR Alc.

Birkos, Alexander S. East European
and Slavic studies. [Kent? Ohio]
Kent State University Press [1973]
572 p. [$7.50] 016.9147/03/05 73-
158303
Z2483 .B56 MRR Alc.

Birkos, Alexander S. Latin American
studies. [Kent, Ohio] Kent State
University Press [1971] 359 p.
808.02/5 70-160685
Z1601 .B54 MRR Alc.

Directory of business and financial
services. [1st]- ed.; 1824- New
York [etc.] Special Libraries
Association. 25-4599
HF5003 .H3 MRR Ref Desk Latest
edition / MRR Ref Desk Latest
edition

Directory of the college student
press in America. 1967/68- New York
[etc.] Oxbridge Pub. Co. [etc.]
378.1/98/8705 76-10981
L901 .D52 MRR Ref Desk Latest
edition

Educational Press Association of
America. America's education press;
[1st]- yearbook; 1925- Washington.
016.3705 41-9994
Z5813 .E24 MRR Alc Latest edition

Farber, Evan Ira. Classified list of
periodicals for the college library,
5th ed., rev. and enl. Westwood,
Mass., F. W. Faxon Co., 1972. xvii,
449 p. 016.05 72-76264
Z6941 .F25 1972 MRR Alc.

Goldwater, Walter. Radical
periodicals in America, 1890-1950;
New Haven, Yale University Library,
1964. xv, 51 p. 64-6244
Z7164.S67 .G57 MRR Alc.

Hernon, Peter. Library and library-
related publications: Littleton,
Colo., Libraries Unlimited, 1973.
216 p. [$10.00] 020/.5 73-84183
Z666 .H4 MRR Alc.

I L P A directory of member
publications. [1st]- 1957-
[Washington] International Labor
Press Association, AFL-CIO. 58-2503

PN4888.L3 L33 MRR Alc Latest
edition

International directory of little
magazines & small presses. 9th-
ed.; 1973/74- [Paradise, Calif.,
Dustbooks] [$3.50] 051/.025 73-
645432
Z6944.L5 D5 MRR Alc Latest edition

Katz, William Armstrong, Magazines
for libraries; 2d ed. New York, R.
R. Bowker, 1972. xviii, 822 p.
016.05 72-6607
Z6941 .K2 1972 MRR Alc.

Naas, Bernard G. American labor
union periodicals, Ithaca, Cornell
University [1956] xv, 175 p.
016.3318805 56-63004
Z7164.L1 N14 MRR Alc.

National directory of newsletters and
reporting services. 1st- ed.; 1966-
Detroit, Gale Research Co. 66-
15458
Z6941 .N3 MRR Ref Desk Latest
edition

Princeton University. Library.
American Indian periodicals in the
Princeton University Library;
Princeton, N.J., 1970. 78 p.
016.9701 76-26143
Z1209 .P75 MRR Alc.

Roorbach, Orville Augustus,
Bibliotheca americana. New York, P.
Smith, 1939. xi, 652 p. 015.73 39-
27504
Z1215 .A3 1939 MRR Ref Desk.

Roorbach, Orville Augustus,
Bibliotheca Americana: Metuchen,
N.J., Mini-Print Corp., 1967. 1 v.
(various pagings) 015.73 67-8332
Z1215 .A3 1967 MRR Alc.

Special Libraries Association. New
York Chapter. Advertising and
Marketing Group. Guide to special
issues and indexes of periodicals;
New York, Special Libraries
Association, 1962. vi, 125 p. 050
62-12644
Z6951 .S755 MRR Alc.

The Standard directory of
newsletters. 1st ed. New York,
Oxbridge Pub. Co. [1971, c1972] lvi,
210 p. [$20.00] 071/.025/73 71-
173896
Z6944.N44 S8 MRR Ref Desk.

Stratman, Carl Joseph, American
theatrical periodicals, 1798-1967;
Durham, N.C., Duke University Press,
1970. xxii, 133 p. 016.7902 72-
110577
Z6935 .S75 MRR Alc.

United States. Library of Congress.
Science and Technology Division.
Scientific and technical serial
publications, Washington, 1954.
viii, 238 p. 016.505 54-60022
Z663.41 .S33 MRR Alc.

United States Historical Documents
Institute. U.S. Government serial
titles, 1789-1970; Washington [1972]
xii, 527 p. 015.73 s 74-190737
Z1223.Z7 L45 vol. 4 MRR Ref Desk.

The Writer's handbook. [1936]-
Boston, Mass., The Writer, inc.
029.6 36-28596
PN137 .W73 MRR Ref Desk Latest
edition

The Writer's market. Cincinnati, O.,
Writer's digest. 051 [029.6] 31-
20772
PN161 .W83 MRR Ref Desk Latest
edition

AMERICAN PERIODICALS--BIBLIOGRAPHY--
YEARBOOKS.
The Standard periodical directory. 1-
ed.; 1964/65- New York, Oxbridge
Pub. Co. 016.051 64-7598
Z6951 .S78 Sci RR Latest edition /
MRR Ref desk Latest edition

AMERICAN PERIODICALS--DIRECTORIES.
An Advertiser's guide to scholarly
periodicals. New York, American
University Press Services. 659.132
65-9732
Began publication in 1958.
Z6944.S3 A25 MRR Alc Latest
edition

Ahlers, Arvel W., Where and how to
sell your pictures. 4th ed. rev.
New York, American Photographic Book
Pub. Co.: book trade: Garden City
Books, Garden City, N.Y. [1959] 142
p. 770.69 59-4237
TR820 .A35 1959 MRR Alc.

Ayer directory of publications.
Philadelphia, Ayer Press. 071.3/025
73-640052
Z6951 .A97 Sci RR Latest edition /
MRR Ref Desk Latest edition / MRR
Alc Latest edition

Bacon's publicity checker. 1933-
Chicago, R. H. Bacon. 659.111 34-
14702
HD59 .B3 MRR Alc Latest edition

Consumer magazine and farm
publication rates and data. v. 38,
no. 10- Oct. 1956- [Skokie, Ill.]
Standard Rate & Data Service, Inc.
659.1/025/73 72-622888
HF5905 .S725 MRR Ref Desk Latest
edition

Gebbie house magazine directory.
[Sioux City, Iowa, House Magazine
Pub. Co.] 016.0704/86 74-644438
Z7164.C81 N32 MRR Ref Desk Latest
edition

Media records; v. 1- 1st quarter
1928- New York. 29-2345
HF5903 .M45 MRR Alc Latest edition

Muller, Robert H. From radical left
to extreme right; 2d ed. rev. and
enl. Ann Arbor, Campus Publishers
[c1970- v. 79-126558
Z7165.U5 M82 MRR Ref Desk.

North, Simon Newton Dexter, History
and present condition of the
newspaper and periodical press of the
United States, [Elmsford, N.Y.,
Maxwell Reprint Co., 1971] vi, 446
p. 338/.0973 s 070.5/0973 73-
164452
HC105 .A66 vol. 9 MRR Alc.

Ross, Mary Bucher. Directory of
publishing opportunities: 2d ed.
Orange, N.J., Academic Media [1973]
x, 722 p. 808/.025 73-13565
Z479 .R67 1973 MRR Ref Desk.

Standard Rate and Data Service, inc.
Business publication rates and data.
v.33- Jan. 1951- Skokie, Ill.
[etc.] 659.132058 53-36930
HF5905 .S723 MRR Ref Desk Latest
edition

United States. Office of Minority
Business Enterprise. Directory of
minority media. [Washington]; for
sale by the Supt. of Docs., U.S.
Govt. Print. Off., 1973. ix, 89 p.
[$1.25] 301.16/1/02573 73-602686
P88.8 .U55 MRR Alc.

The Working press of the nation.
[1945]- Burlington, Iowa [etc.]
National Research Bureau [etc.]
071.47 46-7041
Z6951 .W6 MRR Alc Latest edition

AMERICAN PERIODICALS--FOREIGN LANGUAGE
PRESS.
Wynar, Lubomyr Roman, Encyclopedic
directory of ethnic newspapers and
periodicals in the United States
Littleton, Colo., Libraries
Unlimited, 1972. 260 p. [$12.50]
070.4/84/02573 70-185344
Z6944.E8 W94 MRR Ref Desk.

AMERICAN PERIODICALS--HISTORY.
The American radical press, 1880-
1960. Westport, Conn., Greenwood
Press [1974] 2 v. (xlv, 720 p.)
335/.00973 72-9825
HX1 .A49 MRR Alc.

Glessing, Robert J. The underground
press in America, Bloomington,
Indiana, University Press [1970]
xvi, 207 p. [6.50] 071/.3 71-
126209
PN4888.U5 G5 MRR Alc.

Mott, Frank Luther, A history of
American magazines. Cambridge,
Harvard University Press, 1938-68. 5
v. 051/.09 39-2823
PN4877 .M63 1938 MRR Alc.

North, Simon Newton Dexter, History
and present condition of the
newspaper and periodical press of the
United States, [Elmsford, N.Y.,
Maxwell Reprint Co., 1971] vi, 446
p. 338/.0973 s 070.5/0973 73-
164452
HC105 .A66 vol. 9 MRR Alc.

Peterson, Theodore Bernard,
Magazines in the twentieth century,
[2d ed.] Urbana, University of
Illinois Press, 1964. xi, 484 p.
051.09 64-18668
PN4877 .P4 1964 MRR Alc.

Tebbel, John William, The American
magazine; New York, Hawthorn Books
[1969 vii, 279 p. [6.95]
051/.09 73-87864
PN4832 .T4 1969 MRR Alc.

Wood, James Playsted, Magazines in
the United States. 3d ed. New York,
Ronald Press [1971] vi, 476 p. 051
78-112464
PN4877 .W6 1971 MRR Alc.

AMERICAN PERIODICALS--INDEXES.
Gephart, Ronald M. Periodical
literature on the American
Revolution: historical research and
changing interpretations; 1895-1970;
Washington, Library of Congress: [for
sale by the Supt. of Docs.: U.S.
Govt. Print. Off.] 1971. iv, 93 p.
[$1.00] 016.9733 74-609228
Z663.28 .P4 MRR Alc.

Index to periodical articles by and
about Negroes. v. 17- 1966-
Boston, G. K. Hall. 051 72-627261
AI3 .O4 MRR Alc Full set

Jaffe, Adrian H. Bibliography of
French literature in American
magazines in the 18th century. [East
Lansing] Michigan State College
Press, 1951. vii, 27 p. 016.84 51-
4374
Z2172 .J3 MRR Alc.

Ohio. Central State College,
Wilberforce. Library. Index to
selected periodicals. Mar. 1950-
Wilberforce. 50-62898
MRR Alc Full set

AMERICAN PERIODICALS--INDEXES--
PERIODICALS.
Index of American periodical verse.
1971- Metuchen, N.J., Scarecrow
Press. 016.811/5/4 73-3060
Z1231.P7 I47 MRR Alc Full set

AMERICAN PERIODICALS--CALIFORNIA--
DIRECTORIES.
California publicity outlets. 1972-
Los Angeles, Unicorn Systems Co.,
Information Services Division.
659.2/025/794 76-186163
HM263 .C2 MRR Alc Latest edition

AMERICAN PERIODICALS--NEW YORK (CITY)--
DIRECTORIES.
New York publicity outlets. New
York, Attention Inc. [etc.] 61-65657

Z6953.N6 N6 MRR Alc Latest edition

AMERICAN PERIODICALS--SOUTHERN STATES--
BIBLIOGRAPHY.
Gilmer, Gertrude Cordelia, Checklist
of southern periodicals to 1861,
Boston, The F. W. Faxon company,
1934. 128 p. 016.051 34-23493
Z6951 .G48 MRR Alc.

AMERICAN PERIODICALS--VIRGINIA--INDEXES.
Swem, Earl Gregg, comp. Virginia
historical index ... Roanoke, Va.,
Designed, printed, and bound by the
Stone printing and manufacturing
company, 1934-36. 2 v. 34-38514
F221 .S93 MRR Ref Desk.

AMERICAN POETRY.
Aldington, Richard, ed. The Viking
book of poetry of the English-
speaking world. Rev., Mid-century
ed. New York, Viking Press, 1958. 2
v. 821.082 58-8134
PR1175 .A64 1958 MRR Alc.

Allen, Gay Wilson, ed. American
poetry, New York, Harper & Row [1965]
xxxiv, 1274 p. 811.008 65-19490
PS583 .A5 MRR Alc.

Bronson, Bertrand Harris, ed. The
traditional tunes of the Child
ballads; Princeton, N.J., Princeton
University Press, 1959- v.
784.3 57-5468
ML3650 .B82 MRR Alc.

Brooks, Cleanth, ed. Understanding
poetry, 3d ed. New York, Holt,
Rinehart and Winston [1960] 584 p.
821.082 60-10578
PR1109 .B676 1960 MRR Alc.

Ernest, P. Edward, ed. The family
album of favorite poems. New York,
Grosset & Dunlap [1959] 538 p.
821.082 59-4502
PR1175 .E75 MRR Ref Desk.

Felleman, Hazel, comp. The best
loved poems of the American people.
Garden City, N.Y., Garden City Books
[1957, c1936] xxxiii, 670 p.
821.082 58-1240
PR1175 .F4 1957 MRR Ref Desk.

Gannett, Lewis Stiles, ed. The
family book of verse, [1st ed.] New
York, Harper [1961] 351 p. 821.082
61-9703
PR1175 .G25 MRR Ref Desk.

Legerman, David G., ed. The family
book of best loved poems, Garden
City, N.Y., Hanover House [1852] 485
p. 820.82 52-13663
PR1175 .L437 MRR Ref Desk.

The Oxford book of American verse;
New York, Oxford University Press,
1950. lvi, 1132 p. 811.082 50-
9826
PS583 .O82 MRR Alc.

Stevenson, Burton Egbert, comp. The
home book of verse, American and
English; 9th ed. New York, Holt
[1953] 2 v. (lxxxiv, 4013 p.)
821.982 53-3870
PR1175 .S76 1953 MRR Ref Desk.

Untermeyer, Louis, ed. A treasury of
great poems, English and American,
New York, Simon and Schuster, 1942.
lviii p., 1 l., 1288 p., 1 l. 42-
22424
PR1175 .U65 MRR Alc.

Wells, Carolyn, comp. The book of
humorous verse, Rev. and amplified
ed. Garden City, N.Y., Garden City
publishing co., inc. [c1936] 3 p.
l., v-xxv p., 1 l., 25-1011 p.
821.0822 827.0822 36-16566
PN6110.H8 W4 1936 MRR Alc.

Woods, Ralph Louis, Famous poems and
the little-known stories behind them.
[1st ed.] New York, Hawthorn Books
[1961] 336 p. 820.82 61-10821
PR1175 .W587 MRR Alc.

AMERICAN POETRY--19TH CENTURY.
Ellmann, Richard, comp. The Norton
anthology of modern poetry, [1st
ed.] New York, Norton [1973] xlvi,
1456 p. [$9.95 (pbk.)] 821/.008
73-6587
PS323.5 .E5 1973 MRR Alc.

Untermeyer, Louis, ed. Modern
American poetry. New and enl. ed.
New York, Harcourt, Brace & World
[c1969] xxvi, 710 p. 811/.008 69-
13702
PS611 .U6 1969 MRR Alc.

AMERICAN POETRY--19TH CENTURY--
BIBLIOGRAPHY.
United States. Library of Congress.
General Reference and Bibliography
Division. Sixty American poets, 1896-
1944. Rev ed. Washington, 1954.
xii, 155 p. 016.8115 54-60023
Z663.28 .S5 1954 MRR Alc.

AMERICAN POETRY--20TH CENTURY.
The biographical dictionary of
contemporary poets; New York, Avon
house, 1938. 4 p. l., 536 p. 928.1
38-23392
PS324 .B5 MRR Biog.

Brinnin, John Malcolm, comp.
Twentieth century poetry: American
and British (1900-1970); New York,
McGraw-Hill [1970] xx, 515 p.
[$8.95] 821./9/108 73-124305
PS613 .B7 1970b MRR Alc.

Cecil, David, Lord, ed. Modern verse
in English, 1900-1950. New York,
Macmillan [1958] 689 p. 821.91082
58-13621
PR1225 .C4 MRR Alc.

Ellmann, Richard, comp. The Norton
anthology of modern poetry, [1st
ed.] New York, Norton [1973] xlvi,
1456 p. [$9.95 (pbk.)] 821/.008
73-6587
PS323.5 .E5 1973 MRR Alc.

National Poetry Festival, Washington,
D.C., 1962. Proceedings.
Washington, General Reference and
Bibliography Division, Reference
Dept., Library of Congress [for sale
by the Superintendent of Documents,
U.S. Govt. Print. Off.] 1964. 367 p.
64-60048
Z663.28 .P77 MRR Alc.

Rosenthal, Macha Louis, ed. The new
modern poetry; New York, Macmillan
[1967] xxvii, 289 p. 821.91408 66-
17902
PR1225 .R68 MRR Alc.

Stevenson, Burton Egbert, comp. The
home book of modern verse, 2d ed.
New York, Holt [1953] 1124 p.
821.91082 53-3683
PR1175 .S762 1953 MRR Ref Desk.

Untermeyer, Louis, ed. Modern
American poetry. New and enl. ed.
New York, Harcourt, Brace & World
[c1969] xxvi, 710 p. 811/.008 69-
13702
PS611 .U6 1969 MRR Alc.

AMERICAN POETRY--20TH CENTURY--
ADDRESSES, ESSAYS, LECTURES.
Dickey, James. Spinning the crystal
ball; Washington, Library of
Congress; [for sale by the Supt. of
Docs., U.S. Govt. Print. Off.] 1967.
iii, 22 p. 811/.5/09 68-60008
Z663.293 .S685 MRR Alc.

United States. Library of Congress.
Gertrude Clarke Whittall Poetry and
Literature Fund. American poetry at
mid-century. Washington, Reference
Dept., Library of Congress, 1958. 49
p. 811.504 58-60074
Z663.293 .A5 MRR Alc.

AMERICAN POETRY--20TH CENTURY--
BIBLIOGRAPHY.
Deodene, Frank. Black American
poetry since 1944; Chatham, N.J.,
Chatham Bookseller, 1971. 41 p.
016.811/5/408 76-175303
Z1229.N39 D46 MRR Alc.

Irish, Wynot R. The modern American
muse; [Syracuse] Syracuse University
Press [1950] xii, 259 p. 016.8115
50-7785
Z1231.P7 I7 MRR Alc.

United States. Library of Congress.
General Reference and Bibliography
Division. Sixty American poets, 1896-
1944. Rev ed. Washington, 1954.
xii, 155 p. 016.8115 54-60023
Z663.28 .S5 1954 MRR Alc.

AMERICAN POETRY--20TH CENTURY--BIO-
BIBLIOGRAPHY.
Contemporary poets of the English
language. Chicago, St. James Press
[1970] xvii, 1243 p. [$25.00]
821/.9/109 79-23734
Z2014.P7 C63 MRR Biog.

The International who's who in
poetry. v. 1- 1958- London. 928
59-16302
PS324 .I5 MRR Biog Latest edition

AMERICAN POETRY--20TH CENTURY--
DISCOGRAPHY.
United States. Library of Congress.
Music Division. Twentieth century
poetry in English, Washington,
Reference Dept., Library of Congress,
1951. 18 p. 789.9 016.8115 51-
60323
Z663.37 .T9 1951 MRR Alc.

AMERICAN POETRY--20TH CENTURY--HISTORY
AND CRITICISM.
Gregory, Horace, A history of
American poetry, 1900-1940 New York,
Gordian Press, 1969 [c1946] xviii,
524 p. 811/.5/09 70-84695
PS324 .G7 1969 MRR Alc.

Malkoff, Karl. Crowell's handbook of
contemporary American poetry. New
York, Crowell [1973] ix, 338 p.
[$10.00] 811/.5/409 73-14787
PS323.5 .M3 MRR Biog.

Rosenthal, Macha Louis. The modern
poets: New York, Oxford University
Press, 1960. 228 p. 821.9109 60-
13204
PR601 .R6 MRR Alc.

AMERICAN POETRY--ADDRESSES, ESSAYS,
LECTURES.
Spender, Stephen, Chaos and control
in poetry; Washington, Reference
Dept., Library of Congress; [for sale
by the Supt. of Docs., U.S. Govt.
Print. Off.] 1966. 14 p. 821/.009
66-60054
Z663.293 .S67 MRR Alc.

AMERICAN POETRY--BIBLIOGRAPHY.
Wegelin, Oscar, Early American
poetry; 2d ed., rev. and enl. New
York, P. Smith, 1930. 2 v. in 1.
016.81 30-17830
Z1231.P7 W4 1930 MRR Alc.

AMERICAN POETRY--BIBLIOGRAPHY--CATALOGS.
Brown University. Library.
Dictionary catalog of the Harris
collection of American poetry and
plays, Brown University Library,
Providence, Rhode Island. Boston, G.
K. Hall, 1972. 13 v. 016.81 75-
184497
Z1231.P7 B72 MRR Alc (Dk 33)

AMERICAN POETRY--CONGRESSES.
National Poetry Festival, Washington,
D.C., 1962. Proceedings.
Washington, General Reference and
Bibliography Division, Reference
Dept., Library of Congress; [for sale
by the Superintendent of Documents,
U.S. Govt. Print. Off.] 1964. 367 p.
64-60048
Z663.28 .P77 MRR Alc.

AMERICAN POETRY--DICTIONARIES.
Spender, Stephen, ed. The concise
encyclopedia of English and American
poets and poetry, [1st ed.] New
York, Hawthorn Books [1963] 415 p.
821.003 63-8015
PR19 .S6 MRR Alc.

AMERICAN POETRY--DISCOGRAPHY.
United States. Library of Congress.
General Reference and Bibliography
Division. Archive of recorded poetry
and literature; Washington, 1961.
132 p. 016.810847 61-60005
Z1225 .U53 MRR Alc.

AMERICAN POETRY--EXPLICATION--
BIBLIOGRAPHY.
Kuntz, Joseph Marshall, Poetry
explication; Rev. ed. Denver, A.
Swallow, 1962. 331 p. 016.82109
62-12525
Z2014.P7 K8 MRR Alc.

AMERICAN POETRY--HISTORY AND CRITICISM.
Shaw, John MacKay. Childhood in
poetry; a catalogue, Detroit, Gale
Research Co. [1967-68, c1967] 5 v.
028.52 67-28092
Z1037 .S513 MRR Alc.

Stauffer, Donald Barlow, A short
history of American poetry. [1st
ed.] New York, Dutton, 1974. xvii,
459 p. [$11.95] 811/.009 69-13347

PS303 .S67 MRR Alc.

Two lectures: Leftovers: a care
package Washington, Library of
Congress; [for sale by the Supt. of
Docs., U.S. Govt. Print. Off.] 1973.
iii, 31 p. [$0.35] 811/.009 72-
13401
Z663.293 .T9 MRR Alc.

Untermeyer, Louis, Lives of the
poets; New York, Simon and Schuster,
1959. 757 p. 821.09 58-11205
PR502 .U5 MRR Biog.

AMERICAN POETRY--HISTORY AND (Cont.)
Waggoner, Hyatt Howe. American
poets. Boston, Houghton Mifflin
[1968] xxi, 740 p.   811/.009 66-
14759
    PS303 .W3 MRR Alc.

AMERICAN POETRY--HISTORY AND CRITICISM--
DICTIONARIES.
The Explicator. The Explicator
cyclopedia. Chicago, Quadrangle
Books, 1966- v.   820.9 66-11875
    PR401 .E9 MRR Alc.

AMERICAN POETRY--HISTORY AND CRITICISM--
INDEXES.
Cline, Gloria Stark. An index to
criticisms of British and American
poetry. Metuchen, N.J., Scarecrow
Press, 1973. x, 307 p.   821/.009
73-15542
    PR89 .C5 MRR Ref Desk.

AMERICAN POETRY--INDEXES.
Brewton, John Edmund. Index to
children's poetry; New York, Wilson,
1942. xxxii, 965 p.   821.0016 42-
20148
    PN1023 .B7 MRR Alc.

Brewton, John Edmund. Index to
poetry for children and young people,
1964-1969; New York, Wilson, 1972.
xxx, 575 p.   821/.001/6 71-161574
    PN1023 .B72 MRR Alc.

Chicorel, Marietta. Chicorel index
to poetry in collections in print, on
discs and tapes: 1st ed. New York,
Chicorel Library Pub. Corp., 1972.
443 p.   016.80882 73-160763
    PR1175.8 .C4 MRR Alc.

Cline, Gloria Stark. An index to
criticisms of British and American
poetry. Metuchen, N.J., Scarecrow
Press, 1973. x, 307 p.   821/.009
73-15542
    PR89 .C5 MRR Ref Desk.

Index of American periodical verse.
1971- Metuchen, N.J., Scarecrow
Press.   016.811/5/4 73-3060
    Z1231.P7 I47 MRR Alc Full set

Macpherson, Maud Russell. Children's
poetry index, Boston, The F. W.
Faxon company, 1938. xiii, 453 p.
808.81 38-8870
    PN1023 .M25 MRR Alc.

Morris, Helen (Soutar) Where's that
poem? Oxford, Blackwell, 1967.
xxxv, 300 p. [25/-] 016.821 67-
78385
    PN1023 .M6 MRR Alc.

AMERICAN POETRY--NEGRO AUTHORS--
BIBLIOGRAPHY.
Deodene, Frank. Black American
poetry since 1944; Chatham, N.J.,
Chatham Bookseller, 1971. 41 p.
016.811/5/408 76-175303
    Z1229.N39 D46 MRR Alc.

Porter, Dorothy (Burnett) North
American Negro poets, Hattiesburg,
Miss., The Book farm, 1945. 90 p.
016.811 45-4014
    Z1361.N39 P6 MRR Alc.

AMERICAN POETRY--NEGRO AUTHORS--HISTORY
AND CRITICISM.
Rollins, Charlemae Hill. Famous
American Negro poets, New York,
Dodd, Mead [1965] 95 p.   928.1 65-
11811
    PS153.N5 R6 MRR Biog.

AMERICAN POETRY--STUDY AND TEACHING.
Brooks, Cleanth, ed. Understanding
poetry. 3d ed. New York, Holt,
Rinehart and Winston [1960] 584 p.
821.082 60-10578
    PR1109 .B676 1960 MRR Alc.

AMERICAN POLITICAL SCIENCE ASSOCIATION--
DIRECTORIES.
American Political Science
Association. APSA directory of
members. Washington. 320/.06/273
74-646061
    JA28 .A562 MRR Biog Latest edition

AMERICAN POTTERY
see Pottery, American

AMERICAN PRINTS
see Prints, American

AMERICAN PROSE LITERATURE.
The Oxford book of American prose,
London, New York, Oxford university
press, 1932. 1 p. l., v-xxii, 662 p.
818.0822 32-32296
    PS645 .O8 MRR Alc.

AMERICAN PROSE LITERATURE--COLONIAL
PERIOD, CA. 1600-1775.
Dorson, Richard Mercer, ed. America
begins; [New York] Pantheon [1950]
x, 438 p.   810.82 50-8306
    PS531 .D6 MRR Alc.

AMERICAN PROSE LITERATURE--20TH CENTURY.
Hohenberg, John, ed. The Pulitzer
prize story; New York, Columbia
University Press, 1959. 375 p.
070.431 59-7702
    PS647.N4 H6 MRR Alc.

AMERICAN REPUBLICS
see America

AMERICAN SCULPTURE
see Sculpture, American

AMERICAN SINGERS
see Singers, American

AMERICAN STUDIES--BIBLIOGRAPHY.
American Studies Association.
Metropolitan New York Chapter.
Committee on Bibliography. Articles
in American studies, 1954-1968; Ann
Arbor, Mich., Pierian Press, 1972. 2
v. (x, 898 p.)   016.9173/03/45 71-
172769
    Z1361.C6 A44 MRR Alc.

AMERICAN TALES
see Tales, American

AMERICAN TEACHERS IN FOREIGN COUNTRIES--
EMPLOYMENT--DIRECTORIES.
Garraty, John Arthur. The new guide
to study abroad: 1974-1975 ed. New
York, Harper & Row [1974] xlii, 422
p. [$10.95] 370.19/6 72-9117
    LB2376 .G33 1974 MRR Ref Desk.

AMERICAN WIT AND HUMOR.
Botkin, Benjamin Albert, ed. A
treasury of American anecdotes; New
York, Random House [1957] 321 p.
817.082 57-10053
    PN6261 .B6 MRR Alc.

Braude, Jacob Morton, ed. Speaker's
encyclopedia of humor; Englewood
Cliffs, N.J., Prentice-Hall [1961]
387 p.   808.87 61-9710
    PN6162 .B69 MRR Alc.

Fell, Frederick Victor, comp. The
wit and wisdom of the Presidents,
New York, F. Fell [1966] 206 p.
973.0207 66-11923
    E176.1 .F4 MRR Alc.

Gingras, Angèle de T. "From bussing
to bugging"; Washington, Acropolis
Books [1973] 168 p. [$6.50]
320.9/73/0207 72-12394
    PN6231.P6 G54 MRR Alc.

Safian, Louis A., comp. 2,000
insults for all occasions; New York,
Citadel Press [1965] 224 p.   808.88
65-15489
    PN6162 .S23 MRR Alc.

Wells, Carolyn, comp. The book of
humorous verse, Rev. and amplified
ed. Garden City, N.Y., Garden City
publishing co., inc. [c1936] 3 p.
l., v-xxv p., 1 l., 25-1011 p.
821.0822 827.0822 36-16566
    PN6110.H8 W4 1936 MRR Alc.

Woods, Ralph Louis, comp. The modern
handbook of humor New York, McGraw-
Hill [1967] xxii, 618 p.   817/.008
67-19807
    PN6162 .W66 MRR Alc.

AMERICAN WIT AND HUMOR--HISTORY AND
CRITICISM.
Harris, Leon A. The fine art of
political wit; [1st ed.] New York,
Dutton, 1964. 288 p.   827.093 64-
19532
    PN6231.P6 H36 MRR Alc.

AMERICAN WIT AND HUMOR, PICTORIAL--
HISTORY.
Becker, Stephen D., Comic art in
America; New York, Simon and
Schuster, 1959. xi, 387 p.
741.5973 59-13140
    NC1420 .B4 MRR Alc.

AMERICANISMS.
Abbatt, William, comp. The
colloquial who's who; Tarrytown,
N.Y., W. Abbatt, 1924-25. 2 v. 24-
23254
    Z1045 .A12 MRR Alc.

Bartlett, John Russell, Dictionary
of Americanisms: 4th ed., greatly
improved and enl. Boston, Little,
Brown, and company, 1877. xlvi p., 1
l., 813 p.   11-7835
    PE2835 .B3 1877 MRR Alc.

Berrey, Lester V., The American
thesaurus of slang; 2d ed. New
York, Crowell [1953] xxxv, 1272 p.
427.09 427.9* 52-10837
    PE3729.A5 B4 1953 MRR Alc.

Bickerton, Anthea. American English,
English American: a two-way glossary
Bristol, The Abson Press [1971] [48]
p. [£0.25] 427/.9/73 70-576350
    PE2835 .B5 MRR Alc.

Bryant, Margaret M., ed. Current
American usage. New York, Funk &
Wagnalls [1962] 290 p.   428.3 62-
9735
    PE2835 .B67 MRR Ref Desk.

Clapin, Sylva. A new dictionary of
Americanisms; New York, L. Weiss &
co. [1902?] xii p., 2 l., 581 p.
03-17603
    PE2835 .C6 MRR Alc.

Craigie, William Alexander, Sir, ed.
A dictionary of American English on
historical principles, Chicago,
Ill., The University of Chicago press
[1938-44] 4 v.   427.9 39-8203
    PE2835 .C72 MRR Alc.

Current slang; Vermillion,
University of South Dakota, Dept. of
English, 1969] xvi, 103 p. [1.25]
427.09 78-13579
    PE3729.U5 C8 MRR Alc.

Deak, Étienne. Grand dictionnaire
d'américanismes, 4e édition
augmentée. Paris, Éditions du
Dauphin, 1966. xvi, 832 p. [49.50
F] 427/.9/73 68-104186
    PC2640 .D4 1966 MRR Alc.

A Dictionary of Americanisms on
historical principles; Chicago,
University of Chicago Press [1951] 2
v. (xvi, 1946 p.)   427.9 51-1957
    PE2835 .D5 MRR Alc.

Evans, Bergen, A dictionary of
contemporary American usage, New
York, Random House [1957] vii, 567
p.   427.09 427.9* 57-5379
    PE2835 .E84 MRR Alc.

Follett, Wilson, Modern American
usage; 1st ed.] New York, Hill &
Wang [1966] [xi], 436 p.   423.1 66-
18993
    PE2835 .F6 MRR Alc.

Horwill, Herbert William, A
dictionary of modern American usage,
Oxford, The Clarendon press, 1935.
ix, [2], 360 p.   427.9 35-27255
    PE2835 .H6 MRR Alc.

Maitland, James. The American slang
dictionary. Chicago [R. J. Kittredge
& co.] 1891. 308 p.   10-34825
    PE3729.A5 M3 MRR Alc.

Major, Clarence. Dictionary of Afro-
American slang. [1st ed.] New York,
International Publishers [1970] 127
p. [$5.95] 427.09 79-130863
    PE3727.N4 M3 MRR Alc.

Mathews, Mitford McLeod. American
words. [1st ed.] Cleveland, World
Pub. Co. [1959] 246 p.   427.97 59-
11541
    PE2831 .M3 MRR Alc.

Mencken, Henry Louis, The American
language; [1st abridged ed.] New
York, Knopf, 1963. xi, 777, cxxiv
p.   427.973 63-13628
    PE2808 .M43 MRR Alc.

Nicholson, Margaret. A dictionary of
American-English usage, New York,
Oxford University Press, 1957. xii,
671 p.   423 57-5560
    PE2835 .N5 MRR Ref Desk.

Norton, Charles Ledyard, Political
Americanisms; New York, London,
Longmans, Green & co., 1890. viii,
135 p.   10-31868
    PE2835 .N8 MRR Alc.

Partridge, Eric, A dictionary of
slang and unconventional English;
6th ed. New York, Macmillan [1967]
xiv, 1474 p.   427.09 67-30122
    PE3721 .P3 1967 MRR Ref Desk.

Ramsay, Robert Lee, A Mark Twain
lexicon, New York, Russell &
Russell, 1963. cxix, 278 p.   817.4
63-9325
    PS1345 .R3 1963 MRR Alc.

Schele De Vere, Maximilian,
Americanisms; the English of the New
world. New York, C. Scribner &
company, 1872. 685 p.   10-26369
    PE2835 .S4 MRR Alc.

Schmidt, Jacob Edward, English
idioms and Americanisms for foreign
students, professionals, physicians,
Springfield, Ill., C. C. Thomas
[1972] vi, 534 p.   428/.1 77-
177903
    PE1128 .S34 MRR Alc.

Schur, Norman W. British self-
taught: with comments in American,
New York, Macmillan [1973] xxxi, 438
p. [$6.95] 423/.1 70-127941
    PE1460 .S45 MRR Alc.

AMERICANISMS. (Cont.)
Thornton, Richard Hopwood, An
American glossary; New York, F.
Ungar Pub. Co. [1962] 3 v.   427.973
61-13641
PE2835 .T6 1962 MRR Alc.

Wentworth, Harold, Dictionary of
American slang, New York, Crowell
[1967] xviii, 718 p.   427.09 67-
3063
PE3729.U5 W4 1966 MRR Ref Desk.

Weseen, Maurice Harley, A dictionary
of American slang, New York, Thomas
Y. Crowell company [c1934] xiii, 543
p.   427.09 34-36774
PE3729.A5 W4 MRR Alc.

AMERICANISMS--DICTIONARIES.
Follett, Wilson, Modern American
usage; 1st ed.] New York, Hill &
Wang [1966] [xi], 436 p.   423.1 66-
18993
PE2835 .F6 MRR Alc.

Moss, Norman. What's the difference?
[1st ed.] New York, Harper & Row
[1973] 138 p.   [$6.95]   428/.1 72-
9140
PE2835 .M6 MRR Alc.

Whitford, Harold Crandall, A
dictionary of American homophones and
homographs, New York, Teachers
College Press, 1966. 83 p.   423.1
66-25461
PE2833 .W4 MRR Alc.

AMERICANS IN FOREIGN COUNTRIES.
Boyce, Richard Fyfe. The diplomat's
wife. [1st ed.] New York, Harper
[1956] 230 p.   341.7 56-6909
JX1706 .B74 MRR Alc.

Chamber of Commerce of the United
States of America. Foreign Commerce
Dept. Guide to foreign information
sources. [Rev. Washington] Chamber
of Commerce of the United States
[1960] 26 p.   327.73 61-25832
E744 .C46 1960 MRR Alc.

AMERICANS IN FOREIGN COUNTRIES--
EMPLOYMENT.
Angel, Juvenal Londono, Looking for
employment in foreign countries
reference handbook, 6th ed.; rev.
and enl. New York, World Trade
Academy Press; distributed by Simon &
Schuster [1972] 727 p.   [$25.00]
331.7/02 70-111351
HF5381 .A7847 1972 MRR Alc.

Angel, Juvenal Londono, Selective
guide to overseas employment [New
York] Regents Pub. Co. [1968] 217 p.
331.1/15 67-26550
HF5549.5.E45 A5 MRR Alc.

Winter, Elmer L. Your future in jobs
abroad [1st ed.] New York, R. Rosen
Press [1968] 191 p.   331.1/15 68-
13479
HF5548.5 .E45 W53 MRR Alc.

AMERICANS IN FOREIGN COUNTRIES--
EMPLOYMENT--DIRECTORIES.
Shaw, Ray. How to find those great
overseas jobs. New York, Award Books
[1973] 319 p.   [$1.50] 331.1/28
73-158782
HF5548.5.E45 S5 MRR Alc.

AMERICANS IN GREAT BRITAIN--HANDBOOKS,
MANUALS, ETC.
Cherry, Mary Spooner, Would you like
to live in England? [New York]
Quadrangle [1974] xii, 242 p.
914.2/04/85 74-77934
JV7674 1974 .C47 MRR Alc.

AMERICANS IN MEXICO.
Anglo-American directory of Mexico.
Mexico, D.F., Talleres tipograficos
de "Excelsior." 917.2 42-34594
F1204.5 .A4 MRR Alc Latest edition

AMHARIC LANGUAGE--DICTIONARIES--ENGLISH.
Armbruster, Carl Hubert, Initia
amharica; an introduction to spoken
Amharic, Cambridge, [Eng.] The
University press, 1908- pts. in v.
15-60
PJ9213 .A7 MRR Alc.

AMHARIC LANGUAGE--GRAMMAR.
Armbruster, Carl Hubert, Initia
amharica; an introduction to spoken
Amharic, Cambridge, [Eng.] The
University press, 1908- pts. in v.
15-60
PJ9213 .A7 MRR Alc.

AMISH
see Mennonites

AMMUNITION.
Hackley, F. W. History of modern
U.S. military small arms ammunition,
New York, Macmillan [1967- v.
623.4/55 67-10477
UF700 .H3 MRR Alc.

Johnson, Melvin Maynard, Ammunition;
New York, W. Morrow and co., 1943.
xii p.; 1 l., 374 p.   623.45532 43-
18535
UF740 .J6 MRR Alc.

AMPHIBIANS.
Grzimek, Bernhard. Grzimek's animal
life encyclopedia. New York, Van
Nostrand Reinhold Co. [1972- v. 13,
1972] v.   [$29.95 per vol.] 591
79-183178
QL3 .G7813 MRR Alc.

AMPHIBIANS--IDENTIFICATION.
Conant, Roger, A field guide to
reptiles and amphibians of the United
States and Canada east of the 100th
meridian, Boston, Houghton Mifflin,
1958. xv, 366 p.   597.6 58-6416
QL651 .C65 MRR Alc.

AMPHIBIANS--NORTH AMERICA.
Conant, Roger, A field guide to
reptiles and amphibians of the United
States and Canada east of the 100th
meridian. Boston, Houghton Mifflin,
1958. xv, 366 p.   597.6 58-6416
QL651 .C65 MRR Alc.

AMPHIBIOUS WARFARE.
Isely, Jeter Allen. The U.S. Marines
and amphibious war; Princeton,
Princeton University Press, 1951.
vii, 636 p.   940.545 51-9463
D769.45 .I7 MRR Alc.

AMUSEMENT PARKS--DIRECTORIES.
Griffin, Al. "Step right up, folks!"
Chicago, H. Regnery Co. [1974] xii,
257 p.   791/.068/73 73-19842
GV1851 .G74 1974 MRR Alc.

AMUSEMENT PARKS--HISTORY.
Griffin, Al. "Step right up, folks!"
Chicago, H. Regnery Co. [1974] xii,
257 p.   791/.068/73 73-19842
GV1851 .G74 1974 MRR Alc.

AMUSEMENTS.

see also Circus

see also Dancing

see also Games

see also Moving-pictures

see also Performing arts

see also Recreation

see also Theater

see also Toys

Depew, Arthur M. The Cokesbury party
book. Rev. ed. New York, Abingdon
Press [1959] 377 p.   793.2 59-
10358
GV1471 .D37 1959 MRR Alc.

AMUSEMENTS--UNITED STATES--DIRECTORIES--
PERIODICALS.
Cavalcade and directory of fairs.
[Cincinnati, Billboard Publications,
etc.] 791 72-624676
SF114 .D5 MRR Alc Latest edition

ANABAPTISTS.
see also Baptists

ANABAPTISTS--DICTIONARIES.
The Mennonite encyclopedia;
Hillsboro, Kan., Mennonite Brethren
Pub. House, 1955-59. 4 v.   289.703
55-4563
BX8106 .M37 MRR Alc.

ANALYSIS, MICROSCOPIC
see Microscope and microscopy

ANATOMY.
see also Physiology

De Coursey, Russell Myles, The human
organism. 4th ed. New York, McGraw-
Hill [1974] xi, 644 p.   612 73-
23016
QP34.5 .D38 1974 MRR Alc.

ANATOMY--TERMINOLOGY.
Lamela, Alberto. Handbook of medical
and anatomical terminology, [New
York? c1967] 240 p.   610/.1/4 68-
1195
R123 .L35 MRR Alc.

ANATOMY, COMPARATIVE.
see also Man--Origin

ANATOMY, HUMAN.
see also Heart

De Coursey, Russell Myles, The human
organism. 4th ed. New York, McGraw-
Hill [1974] xi, 644 p.   612 73-
23016
QP34.5 .D38 1974 MRR Alc.

Francis, Carl C,. Introduction to
human anatomy 6th ed. Saint Louis,
C. V. Mosby Co., 1973. xiii, 463 p.
611 72-90109
QM23.2 .F7 1973 MRR Alc.

Gray, Henry, Anatomy of the human
body, 29th American ed.,
Philadelphia, Lea & Febiger, 1973.
xvii, 1466 p.   611 73-170735
QM23.2 .G73 1973 MRR Alc.

Greisheimer, Esther Maud, Physiology
& anatomy 9th. ed. Philadelphia,
Lippincott [1972] xv, 678 p.
[$13.50] 612 73-101355
QP34 .G63 1972 MRR Alc.

Woodburne, Russell Thomas,
Essentials of human anatomy, 3d ed.
New York, Oxford University Press,
1965. xii, 673 p.   611 65-10004
QM23 .W9 1965 MRR Alc.

ANATOMY, HUMAN--ATLASES.
Grant, John Charles Boileau, An
atlas of anatomy, by regions ... 6th
ed. Baltimore, Williams & Wilkins,
1972. 1 v. (unpaged) 611/.0022/2
71-160140
QM25 .G7 1972 MRR Alc.

Schade, Johannes P. Introduction to
functional human anatomy;
Philadelphia, Saunders [1974, c1970]
189 p.   611 73-76188
QM25 .S3413 MRR Alc.

ANCIENT ART
see Art, Ancient

ANDERSEN, HANS CHRISTIAN, 1805-1875--
BIBLIOGRAPHY.
Bredsdorff, Elias. Danish literature
in English translation, Copenhagen,
E. Munksgaard, 1950. 198 p.
016.83981 51-4614
Z2574.T7 B7 MRR Alc.

United States. Library of Congress.
Catalog of the Jean Hersholt
collection of Hans Christian
Andersen; Washington, 1954. 97 p.
012 53-60043
Z663 .C3 MRR Alc.

ANDORRA--DESCRIPTION AND TRAVEL--GUIDE-
BOOKS.
Haggart, Stanley Mills. Spain on $5
a day, [New York, A. Frommer;
distributed by Simon and Schuster,
1968] 288 p.   914.6/04/82 68-4429

DP14 .H24 1968 MRR Alc.

ANDORRA--GAZETTEERS.
United States. Office of Geography.
Spain and Andorra; official standard
names approved by the United States
Board on Geographic Names.
Washington, 1961. ix, 651 p.   914.6
61-61785
DP12 .U6 MRR Alc.

ANDOVER, ENG.--DIRECTORIES.
Kelly's directory of Andover and
neighbourhood. Kingston upon Thames,
Surrey [etc.] Kelly's directories
Limited. 53-28317
DA690.A53 K4 MRR Alc Latest
edition

ANDROS, EDMUND, SIR, 1637-1714.
Andrews, Charles McLean, ed.
Narratives of the insurrections, 1675-
1690. New York, C. Scribner's sons,
1915. ix p., 2 l., 3-414 p.   973.2
15-4852
E187.07 A6 MRR Alc.

ANECDOTES.
Athenaeus. The Deipnosophists,
London, W. Heinemann; New York, G. P.
Putnam's sons, 1927-1941. 7 v.
mrr01-18
PA3612 .A87 1927d MRR Alc.

Bent, Samuel Arthur, comp. Familiar
short sayings of great men, with
historical and explanatory notes,
Rev. and enl. ed. Boston, New York,
Houghton Mifflin company [191-] xix,
665 p.   21-8813
PN6321 .B4 1910a MRR Alc.

Bombaugh, Charles Carroll, Gleanings
for the curious from the harvestfields of literature; Author's
unabridged ed. 1st ser. Detroit,
Gale Research Co., 1970. 864 p.
808.8 68-23465
PN43 .B62 1970 MRR Alc.

Botkin, Benjamin Albert, ed. A
treasury of American anecdotes; New
York, Random House [1957] 321 p.
817.082 57-10053
PN6261 .B6 MRR Alc.

Braude, Jacob Morton, comp. Braude's
source book for speakers and writers
Englewood Cliffs, N.J., Prentice-Hall
[1968] ix, 351 p.   [$7.95]
808.88/2 68-19973
PN4193.I5 B64 MRR Alc.

Braude, Jacob Morton, ed. The
complete speaker's index to selected
stories for every occasion Englewood
Cliffs, N.J., Prentice-Hall [1967,
c1966] x, 353 p.   808.5/1/0202 66-
18166
PN4193.I5 B66 MRR Alc.

ANECDOTES. (Cont.)
Braude, Jacob Morton, New treasury of stories for every speaking and writing occasion. Englewood Cliffs, N.J., Prentice-Hall [1959] 494 p. 808.88 59-13391
PN6261 .B73 MRR Alc.

Braude, Jacob Morton, ed. Second encyclopedia of stories, quotations, and anecdotes. Englewood Cliffs, N.J., Prentice-Hall, 1957. 468 p. 808.88* 57-5563
PN6081 .B67 MRR Alc.

Braude, Jacob Morton, Speaker's and toastmaster's handbook of anecdotes by and about famous personalities Englewood Cliffs, N.J., Prentice-Hall [1971] 303 p. 817./5/08 73-153947
PN4193.I5 B67 MRR Alc.

Bunting, Daniel George, ed. A book of anecdotes, 1st American ed. New York] Citadel Press, 1958 [c1957] 445 p. 808.8 58-14894
PN6261 .B78 1958 MRR Alc.

Copeland, Lewis, ed. 10,000 jokes, toasts & stories. Garden City, N.Y., Doubleday [c1965] xi, 1020 p. 66-737
PN6261 .C54 1965 MRR Alc.

Droke, Maxwell, ed. The Christian leader's golden treasury, Indianapolis, Droke House [1955] 620 p. 808.88* 55-11712
PN6083 .D7 MRR Alc.

Fogg, Walter. One thousand sayings of history presented as pictures in prose. Boston, Mass., The Beacon press, inc., 1929. vi, 919 p. 29-1093
PN6328.H5 F6 MRR Alc.

Hovey, E. Paul, comp. The treasury for special days and occasions: [Westwood, N.J.] Revell [1961] 317 p. 808.88 61-9238
PN6083 .H73 MRR Alc.

Hovey, E. Paul, comp. The treasury of inspirational anecdotes, quotations, and illustrations, [Westwood, N.J.] Revell [1959] 316 p. 808.88 59-8725
PN6083 .H75 MRR Alc.

Rosten, Leo Calvin, The joys of Yiddish: [1st ed.] New York, McGraw-Hill [1968] xxxix, 533 p. 492.49/3/2 68-29915
PN6231.J5 R67 MRR Alc.

The Speaker's desk book. New York, Grosset & Dunlap [1967] 613 p. 808.8 66-20654
PN4193.I5 S6 1967 MRR Alc.

ANECDOTES--GREAT BRITAIN.
Chambers, Robert, The book of days; Detroit, Gale Research Co., 1967. 2 v. 902/.02 67-13009
DA110 .C52 1967 MRR Alc.

ANECDOTES--WASHINGTON, D.C.
Boykin, Edward Carrington, Shrines of the Republic: Washington, Public Affairs Press [1953] 76 p. 975.3 52-12863
F195 .B6 MRR Alc.

ANGELS--DICTIONARIES.
Davidson, Gustav, A dictionary of angels, New York, Free Press [1967] xxxii, 387 p. 235/.3/03 66-19757
BL477 .D3 MRR Alc.

ANGLICAN COMMUNION.
Higgins, John Seville, bp., The expansion of the Anglican communion, Louisville, Ky., The Cloister press [1942] 248 p. 283 42-18899
BX5005 .H5 MRR Alc.

ANGLICAN COMMUNION--DICTIONARIES.
Malloch, James M., comp. A practical church dictionary, New York, Morehouse-Barlow [1964] xiv, 520 p. 203 64-23926
BR95 .M37 MRR Alc.

ANGLING
see Fishing

ANGLO-SAXON LANGUAGE--DICTIONARIES--ENGLISH.
Bosworth, Joseph, An Anglo-Saxon dictionary; London, Oxford University Press, 1972. [2], xiv, 1302 p. [£11.00] 73-152962
PE279 .B52 1972 MRR Alc.

Hall, John Richard Clark, A concise Anglo-Saxon dictionary, 4th ed. with supplement Cambridge [Eng.] University press, 1960 [i.e. 1961] xv, 432, [20] p. 429.32 61-1911
PE279 .H3 1961 MRR Alc.

ANGLO-SAXON LANGUAGE--GRAMMAR.
Campbell, Alistair, Old English grammar. Oxford, Clarendon Press, 1959. 423 p. 429.5 59-985
PE131 .C3 MRR Alc.

ANGLO-SAXON RACE--BIBLIOGRAPHY.
United States. Library of Congress. Division of bibliography. Select list of references on Anglo-Saxon interests. 2d issue, with additions. Washington, Gov't. print. off., 1906. 22 p. 06-35014
Z664.28 .S354 1906 MRR Alc.

ANGLO-SAXONS.
Stenton, Frank Merry, Sir, Anglo-Saxon England, Oxford, The Clarendon press, 1943. vii, [2], 748 [i.e. 747], [1] p. 942.01 a 44-638
DA152 .S74 MRR Alc.

ANGOLA.
Herrick, Allison Butler. Area handbook for Angola. Washington, For sale by the Supt. of Docs., U.S. Govt. Print. Off., 1967. xii, 439 p. 916.7/3 68-61155
DT611 .A47 MRR Alc.

ANGOLA--GAZETTEERS.
United States. Office of Geography. Angola; Washington, U.S. Govt. Print. Off., 1956. iii, 234 p. 916.73 56-62040
DT611 .U5 MRR Alc.

ANIMAL KINGDOM
see Zoology

ANIMAL LOCOMOTION.
Aristoteles. Parts of animals, Cambridge, Mass., Harvard university press; London, W. Heinemann, ltd., 1937. v, 555, [1] p. 888.5 38-4213
PA3612 .A8D3 1937 MRR Alc.

ANIMAL LORE.
see also Folk-lore

Garai, Jana. The book of symbols. [New York] Simon and Schuster [1974, c1973] 143 p. [$3.95] 398/.3 74-171892
GR950.S5 G37 1974 MRR Alc.

Rowland, Beryl. Animals with human faces; [1st ed. Knoxville] University of Tennessee Press [1973] xix, 192 p. [$10.75] 398/.369 70-173657
GR705 .R68 MRR Alc.

ANIMAL PARASITES
see Parasites

ANIMAL SOUNDS.
Murie, Olaus Johan, A field guide to animal tracks. Boston, Houghton Mifflin, 1954. xxii, 374 p. 591.5 54-9602
SK282 .M8 MRR Alc.

ANIMAL TRACKS.
Murie, Olaus Johan, A field guide to animal tracks. Boston, Houghton Mifflin, 1954. xxii, 374 p. 591.5 54-9602
SK282 .M8 MRR Alc.

ANIMALS, AQUATIC
see Marine fauna

ANIMALS, DISEASES OF
see Veterinary medicine

ANIMALS, DOMESTIC
see Domestic animals

ANIMALS, FOSSIL
see Paleontology

ANIMALS, HABITS AND BEHAVIOR OF.
see also Birds--Behavior

Breland, Osmond Philip, Animal facts and fallacies. London, Faber and Faber [1950] 245 p. 591.5 50-12802
QL50 .B84 1950 MRR Alc.

Murie, Olaus Johan, A field guide to animal tracks. Boston, Houghton Mifflin, 1954. xxii, 374 p. 591.5 54-9602
SK282 .M8 MRR Alc.

ANIMALS, LEGENDS AND STORIES OF.
see also Fables

ANIMALS, MOVEMENTS OF
see Animal locomotion

ANIMALS, MYTHICAL.
Borges, Jorge Luis, The book of imaginary beings. [1st ed.] New York, Dutton, 1969. 256 p. [6.95] 398.4/69 76-87180
GR825 .B613 MRR Alc.

Lum, Peter, Fabulous beasts. London, Thames and Hudson [1952?] 256 p. 398.4 52-36311
GR825 .L83 1952 MRR Alc.

ANIMALS, MYTHICAL--DICTIONARIES.
Barber, Richard W. A dictionary of fabulous beasts New York, Walker [1972, c1971] 167 p. 398/.469/03 70-188468
GR825 .B28 1972 MRR Alc.

ANIMALS, RARE
see Rare animals

ANIMALS IN THE BIBLE
see Bible--Natural history

ANNALS
see History

ANNIVERSARIES.
see also Festivals

see also Holidays

Hazeltine, Mary Emogene, Anniversaries and holidays, 2d ed., completely revised Chicago, American library association 1944. xix, 316 p. 394.26 44-53464
Z5710 .H42 1944 MRR Alc.

ANNIVERSARIES--DICTIONARIES.
Collison, Robert Lewis. Newnes Dictionary of dates: 2nd revised ed. London, Newnes, 1966. ix, 11-428 p. [35/-] 903 66-72492
D11.5 .C6 1966 MRR Alc.

Mirkin, Stanford M. What happened when; [New, rev. and enl. ed.] New York, I. Washburn [1966] v, 442 p. 902.02 66-10676
D11.5 .M57 1966 MRR Ref Desk.

ANNUALS (PLANTS)
Fogg, Harry George Witham. Dictionary of annual plants Newton Abbot, David and Charles, 1972. 184 p., leaf. [£2.25] 635.9/31 72-180908
SB422 .F63 MRR Alc.

Nehrling, Arno. The picture book of annuals, New York, Hearthside Press [1966] 288 p. 635.931 66-15785
SB422 .N44 MRR Alc.

ANONYMS AND PSEUDONYMS.
Force, Helen H. Who is who. Santa Ana, Calif., Professional Library Service [1967] 109 p. 929.4 67-21461
Z1045 .F6 MRR Biog.

Haynes, John Edward. Pseudonyms of authors; New York, 1882. 1 p. l., [iii]-vi, [7]-112 p. 04-4470
Z1041 .H42 MRR Alc.

Lectuur-repertorium, [2. en definitieve uitg. Antwerpen, Vlaamsche Boekcentrale, 1952-54] 3 v. 011 53-15682
Z1010 .L43 MRR Biog.

McGhan, Barry. Science fiction and fantasy pseudonyms. [Flint? Mich. c1971. iv, 34 p. [$1.00] 823/.009 72-176242
Z1041 .M28 MRR Alc.

Sharp, Harold S. Handbook of pseudonyms and personal nicknames, Metuchen, N.J., Scarecrow Press, 1972. 2 v. (1104 p.) 929.4 71-189886
Z1041 .S43 MRR Ref Desk.

Taylor, Archer, The bibliographical history of anonyma and pseudonyma, Chicago, Published for the Newberry Library by the University of Chicago Press, 1951. ix, 288 p. 014 51-4934
Z1041 .T3 MRR Alc.

Wheeler, William Adolphus, An explanatory and pronouncing dictionary of the noted names of fiction, Detroit, Gale Research Co., 1966. xxxii, 440 p. 803 66-25811
PN43 .W4 1966 MRR Alc.

ANONYMS AND PSEUDONYMS--BIBLIOGRAPHY.
Frattarolo, Renzo. Anonimi e pseudonimi; Caltanissetta, Sciascia [1955] 208 p. 56-28961
Z1070 .F7 MRR Alc.

Morris, Adah Vivian, Anonyms and pseudonyms Chicago, Ill., The University of Chicago press [1934] 2 p. l., 22 p. 016.014 34-3104
Z1041.A1 M8 MRR Alc.

Taylor, Archer, The bibliographical history of anonyma and pseudonyma, Chicago, Published for the Newberry Library by the University of Chicago Press, 1951. ix, 288 p. 014 51-4934
Z1041 .T3 MRR Alc.

ANONYMS AND PSEUDONYMS, AMERICAN.
Abbatt, William, comp. The colloquial who's who: Tarrytown, N.Y., W. Abbatt, 1924-25. 2 v. 24-23254
Z1045 .A12 MRR Alc.

ANONYMS AND PSEUDONYMS, (Cont.)
Cushing, William, Anonyms; Waltham,
Mass., Mark Press, 1963. 829 p. 65-
9520
  Z1045 .C98 1963 MRR Alc.

Cushing, William, Initials and
pseudonyms; Waltham, Mass., Mark
Press, 1963. 314 p. 66-38586
  Z1045 .C982 1963 MRR Alc.

Cushing, William, Initials and
pseudonyms; New York, T. Y. Crowell
& co., 1885. iv, 603 p. 01-26299
  Z1045 .C98I MRR Alc.

Foley, Patrick Kevin, American
authors, 1795-1895; New York,
Milford House, 1969. xvi, 350 p.
016.81 68-54462
  Z1231.F5 F65 1969 MRR Alc.

Gaines, Pierce Welch. Political
works of concealed authorship in the
United States, 1789-1810, Rev. and
enl. ed. Hamden, Conn., Shoe String
Press, 1965. 190 p. 014.1 65-
17720
  Z1045 .G3 1965 MRR Alc.

Gribbin, Lenore S. Who's whodunit;
Chapel Hill, University of North
Carolina Library, 1968. ix, 174 p.
823/.08/72 68-65305
  Z1065 .G73 MRR Alc.

Stonehill, Charles Archibald,
Anonyma and pseudonyma, 2d ed. New
York, Milford House, 1969. 4 v. in 2
(3448 columns) 014/.1 68-8311
  Z1065 .S882 MRR Alc.

ANONYMS AND PSEUDONYMS, CANADIAN.
Abbatt, William, comp. The
colloquial who's who; Tarrytown,
N.Y., W. Abbatt, 1924-25. 2 v. 24-
23254
  Z1045 .A12 MRR Alc.

ANONYMS AND PSEUDONYMS, CATALAN.
Rodergas i Calmell, Josep. Els
pseudonims usats a Catalunya.
Barcelona, Editorial Milla, 1951.
xv, 408 p. 52-35959
  Z1077 .R6 MRR Alc.

ANONYMS AND PSEUDONYMS, ENGLISH.
Abbatt, William, comp. The
colloquial who's who; Tarrytown,
N.Y., W. Abbatt, 1924-25. 2 v. 24-
23254
  Z1045 .A12 MRR Alc.

Cushing, William, Anonyms; Waltham,
Mass., Mark Press, 1963. 829 p. 65-
9520
  Z1045 .C98 1963 MRR Alc.

Cushing, William, Initials and
pseudonyms; New York, T. Y. Crowell
& co., 1885. iv, 603 p. 01-26299
  Z1045 .C98I MRR Alc.

Cushing, William, Initials and
pseudonyms; Waltham, Mass., Mark
Press, 1963. 314 p. 66-38586
  Z1045 .C982 1963 MRR Alc.

Gribbin, Lenore S. Who's whodunit;
Chapel Hill, University of North
Carolina Library, 1968. ix, 174 p.
823/.08/72 68-65305
  Z1065 .G73 MRR Alc.

Halkett, Samuel, Dictionary of
anonymous and pseudonymous English
literature New and enl. ed.
Edinburgh, Oliver and Boyd, 1926-[62]
9 v. 27-704
  Z1065 .H17 1926 MRR Alc.

Stonehill, Charles Archibald,
Anonyma and pseudonyma, 2d ed. New
York, Milford House, 1969. 4 v. in 2
(3448 columns) 014/.1 68-8311
  Z1065 .S882 MRR Alc.

Thomas, Ralph, Handbook of
fictitious names; Detroit, Gale
Research Co., 1969. xiv, 235 p.
929.4 70-90248
  Z1065 .T46 1969 MRR Alc.

Who's who in literature. 1924-34.
Liverpool, Literary Year Books Press.
26-26968
  Z2011 .L78 MRR Biog Latest edition

ANONYMS AND PSEUDONYMS, FRENCH.
Barbier, Antoine Alexandre,
Dictionnaire des ouvrages anonymes,
3. ed., rev. et augm. Paris, P.
Daffis, 1872-79. 4 v. 02-2815
  Z1067 .B23D3 MRR Alc.

Drevet, Marguerite L. Bibliographie
de la littérature française, 1940-
1949; Genève, Librairie E. Droz,
1954 [i.e. 1954-55] xvi, 644 p. 55-
949
  Z2171 .D73 MRR Alc.

Manne, Louis Charles Joseph de,
Nouveau dictionnaire des ouvrages
anonymes et pseudonymes, Nouv. ed.,
rev., cor. & tres-augm., Lyon, N.
Scheuring, 1862. vii, 406 p., 1 l.
06-44941
  Z1067 .M28 1862 MRR Alc.

Quérard, Joseph Marie, Les
supercheries littéraires
dévoilées, 2. éd.,
considérablement augmentée,
Hildesheim, Firmin Didot père et
fils, 1827-64. 1965. 3 v. [DM
252.00] 68-85826
  Z1067 .Q45 1965 MRR Alc.

ANONYMS AND PSEUDONYMS, GERMAN.
Holzmann, Michael, Deutsches
pseudonymen-lexikon. Wien,
Akademischer verlag, 1906. 3 p 1.,
[iii]-xxiv, 323 p. 06-23086
  Z1068 .H77 MRR Alc.

ANONYMS AND PSEUDONYMS, HEBREW.
Schwab, Moïse, Index of articles
relative to Jewish history and
literature published in periodicals,
from 1665 to 1900. Augmented ed.
New York, Ktav Pub. House [1971, i.e.
1972] xvi, 539, 409-613 p.
016.91/0039/24 74-114721
  Z6366 .S413 MRR Alc.

ANONYMS AND PSEUDONYMS, HUNGARIAN.
Gulyás, Pál, Magyar írói álnév
lexikon; Budapest, Akademiai
Kiado, 1956. 706 p. 57-25070
  Z1069.7 .G8 MRR Alc.

ANONYMS AND PSEUDONYMS, ITALIAN.
Frattarolo, Renzo. Anonimi e
pseudonimi; Caltanissetta, S.
Sciascia [1955] 208 p. 56-28961
  Z1070 .F7 MRR Alc.

Santi, Aldo, Dizionario pseudonimico
degli enigmografi italiani; Modena,
Edizioni della felce, 1956. 141 p.
57-35609
  Z1070 .S3 MRR Alc.

ANONYMS AND PSEUDONYMS, LATIN.
Barbier, Antoine Alexandre,
Dictionnaire des ouvrages anonymes,
3. ed., rev. et augm. Paris, P.
Daffis, 1872-79. 4 v. 02-2815
  Z1067 .B23D3 MRR Alc.

ANONYMS AND PSEUDONYMS, SPANISH
AMERICAN.
Beristain de Souza, José Mariano,
Biblioteca hispano americana
septentrional; [3. ed.] México,
Editorial Fuente Cultural [1947] 5
v. in 2. 015.72 48-9774
  Z1412 .B53 MRR Alc.

ANTARCTIC REGIONS--BIBLIOGRAPHY.
Antarctic bibliography. v. 1- 1965-
Washington, Library of Congress;
[For sale by the Supt. of Docs., U.S.
Govt. Print. Off.] 65-61825
  Z6005.41 .A24 MRR Alc.   Sci RR Full
  set / MRR Alc Full set

United States. Library of Congress.
Antarctic bibliography, 1951-1961.
Washington; [For sale by the Supt. of
Docs., U.S. Govt. Print. Off.] 1970.
vii, 349 p. [4.75] 016.509/99 74-
606139
  Z6005.41 .A76 MRR Alc.

ANTARCTIC REGIONS--GAZETTEERS.
United States. Geographic Names
Division. Antarctica; official name
decisions of the United States Board
on Geographic Names. 3d ed.
Washington, 1969. iii, 217 p.
919.9/003 75-604417
  G855 .U49 1969 MRR Alc.

ANTARCTIC REGIONS--MAPS.
United States. Library of Congress.
Map Division. Selected maps and
charts of Antarctica; Washington,
1959. vi, 193 p. 016.91299 59-
60051
  Z663.35 .S4 MRR Alc.

ANTEDILUVIAN ANIMALS
see Paleontology

ANTENNAS (ELECTRONICS)--DICTIONARIES--
POLYGLOT.
Elsevier's dictionary of television,
radar, and antennas, in six
languages: Amsterdam, New York,
Elsevier Pub Co., 1955. 760 p.
621.38803 55-6216
  TK6634 .E4 MRR Alc.

ANTHEMS, NATIONAL
see National songs

ANTHROPO-GEOGRAPHY.
see also Human ecology

Clarke, John Innes. Population
geography, [2d ed.] Oxford, New
York, Pergamon Press [1972] xi, 176
p. 301.32 70-183339
  HB1951 .C5 1972 MRR Alc.

James, Preston Everett, A geography
of man 3d ed. Waltham, Mass.,
Blaisdell Pub. Co. [1966] xvii, 581
p. 910 65-14575
  GB55 .J3 1966 MRR Alc.

ANTHROPOLOGISTS.
Davies, David Michael, A dictionary
of anthropology New York, Crane,
Russak [1973, c1972] 197 p.
[$10.50] 301.2/03 72-90702
  GN11 .D38 1972b MRR Alc.

Harvard University. Peabody Museum of
Archaeology and Ethnology. Library.
Catalogue: authors. Boston, G. K.
Hall, 1963. 26 v. 64-2646
  Z5119 .H35 MRR Alc (DK 33).

International directory of
anthropologists. 3d ed. Washington
[Division of Anthropology and
Psychology, National Research
Council] 1950. xiv, 210 p. 572.058
50-14305
  GN20 .I5 1950 MRR Biog.

ANTHROPOLOGY.
see also Archaeology

see also Ethnology

see also Man

Hoebel, Edward Adamson,
Anthropology: the study of man 4th
ed. New York, McGraw-Hill [1972] x,
756 p. 301.2 71-37097
  GN24 .H64 1972 MRR Alc.

Honigmann, John Joseph. The world of
man. New York, Harper [1959] 971 p.
572 58-13969
  GN24 .H68 MRR Alc.

Kroeber, Alfred Louis, Anthropology:
[New ed., rev.] New York, Harcourt,
Brace [1948] xii, 856, xxxix p.
572 48-6956
  GN24 .K7 1948 MRR Alc.

Linton, Ralph, The tree of culture.
[1st ed.] New York, Knopf, 1955.
692 p. 572 55-5173
  GN27 .L5 MRR Alc.

Murdock, George Peter, Social
structure. New York, Macmillan Co.,
1949. xvii, 387 p. 392 49-9317
  GN27 .M95 MRR Alc.

ANTHROPOLOGY--ABSTRACTS--PERIODICALS.
Abstracts in anthropology. v. 1-
Feb. 1970- Farmingdale, N.Y.,
Baywood Publishing Co. [etc.] 77-
20528
  GN1 .A15 MRR Alc Full set

ANTHROPOLOGY--BIBLIOGRAPHY.
Clapp, Jane. Museum publications.
New York, Scarecrow Press, 1962. 2
v. 016.0697 62-10120
  Z5051 .C5 MRR Alc.

Frantz, Charles. The student
anthropologist's handbook;
Cambridge, Mass., Schenkman Pub. Co.;
distributed by General Learning
Press, [Morristown, N.J., 1972] xi,
228 p. 301.2 77-170649
  GN42 .F7 MRR Alc.

Fürer-Haimendorf, Elizabeth von. An
anthropological bibliography of South
Asia, Paris, Mouton, 1958-70. 3 v.
[fl. 130.00 (v. 3)] a 59-1034
  Z5115 .F83 MRR Alc.

Mandelbaum, David Goodman, ed.
Resources for the teaching of
anthropology, Berkeley, University
of California Press, 1963. 316 p.
016.572 63-9935
  Z5111 .M3 MRR Alc.

ANTHROPOLOGY--BIBLIOGRAPHY--CATALOGS.
Biblioteca Nacional de Antropología
e Historia. Catalogos de la
Biblioteca Nacional de Antropología
e Historia. México. Boston, G. K.
Hall, 1972. 10 v. 74-225152
  Z885.A1 B5 1972 MRR Alc (Dk 33)

Harvard University. Peabody Museum of
Archaeology and Ethnology. Library.
Catalogue: authors. Boston, G. K.
Hall, 1963. 26 v. 64-2646
  Z5119 .H35 MRR Alc (DK 33).

Harvard University. Peabody Museum of
Archaeology and Ethnology. Library.
Catalogue: subjects. Boston, G. K.
Hall, 1963. 27 v. 016.1 64-2645
  Z5119 .H36 MRR Alc (Dk 33)

ANTHROPOLOGY--BIBLIOGRAPHY--YEARBOOKS.
Biennial review of anthropology. v.
1- 1959- Stanford, Calif.,
Stanford University Press.
016.572058 59-12726
  Z5112 .B56 MRR Alc Full set

ANTHROPOLOGY--COLLECTIONS.
Honigmann, John Joseph. Handbook of
social and cultural anthropology.
Chicago, Rand McNally Co. [c1973]
1295 p.   301.2   72-184062
GN315 .B642 MRR Alc

International Symposium on
Anthropology, New York, 1952.
Anthropology today; Chicago,
University of Chicago Press [1953]
xv, 966 p.   572.082   53-6171
GN4 .I52 MRR Alc.

ANTHROPOLOGY--DICTIONARIES.
Davies, David Michael, A dictionary
of anthropology New York, Crane,
Russak [1973, c1972] 197 p.
[$10.50]   301.2/03   72-90702
GN11 .D38 1972b MRR Alc.

Winick, Charles, Dictionary of
anthropology. New York,
Philosophical Library [1956] vii,
579 p.   572.03   56-14738
GN11 .W5 MRR Alc.

ANTHROPOLOGY--HISTORY.
Hays, Hoffman Reynolds. From ape to
angel; [1st ed.] New York, Knopf,
1958. xxii, 440, xv p.   572.09 58-
7713
GN405 .H34 MRR Alc.

One hundred years of anthropology.
Cambridge, Mass., Harvard University
Press, 1968. 276 p. [$5.95]
913.03 68-25606
GN17 .O5 MRR Alc.

Penniman, Thomas Kenneth, A hundred
years of anthropology, London,
Duckworth [1935] 400 p.   572.09 36-
9044
GN17 .P4 MRR Alc.

ANTHROPOLOGY--MAPS.
Spencer, Robert F. Atlas for
anthropology Dubuque, Iowa, W. C.
Brown Co., [1960] iii p., 52 l.
map61-161
G1406.E1 S7 1960 MRR Alc.

ANTHROPOLOGY--METHODOLOGY.
Human Relations Area Files, inc.
Outline of cultural materials 4th
rev. ed. New Haven, 1961. xxv, 164
p.   301.2 61-11509
H62 .E36 vol. 1, 1961 MRR Alc.

ANTHROPOLOGY--PERIODICALS.
Annual review of anthropology. v. 1-
1972- Palo Alto, Calif., Annual
Reviews Inc. 301.2/05 72-82136
GN1 .A623 MRR Alc Full set

ANTHROPOLOGY--PERIODICALS--BIBLIOGRAPHY.
Library-Anthropology Resource Group.
Serial publications in anthropology.
Chicago, University of Chicago Press
[1973] xi, 91 p. 016.3012/05 72-
91422
Z5112 .L53 1973 MRR Alc.

ANTHROPOLOGY--PERIODICALS--INDEXES.
Abstracts in anthropology. v. 1-
Feb. 1970- Farmingdale, N.Y.,
Baywood Publishing Co. [etc.] 77-
20528
GN1 .A15 MRR Alc Full set

International bibliography of social
and cultural anthropology. v. 1-
1955- London, Tavistock Pub.;
Chicago, Aldine Pub. Co. [etc.]
016.572 58-43266
Z7161 .I593 MRR Alc Full set

ANTHROPOLOGY--SOCIETIES, ETC.--DIRECTORIES.
The Archaeologists' year book. 1973-
[Park Ridge, N.J.] Noyes Press.
[$12.50] 913/.031/025 73-78778
CC120 .A67 MRR Alc Latest edition

Thomas, William Leroy, ed.
International directory of
anthropological institutions, New
York, Wenner-Gren Foundation for
Anthropological Research; distributed
by the American Anthropological
Association, 1953. xii, 468 p.
572.0621 53-3903
GN2 .T45 MRR Alc.

ANTHROPOLOGY--STUDY AND TEACHING.
Frantz, Charles. The student
anthropologist's handbook;
Cambridge, Mass., Schenkman Pub. Co.;
distributed by General Learning
Press, [Morristown, N.J., 1972] xi,
228 p.   301.2 77-170649
GN42 .F7 MRR Alc.

Mandelbaum, David Goodman, ed.
Resources for the teaching of
anthropology. Berkeley, University
of California Press, 1963. 316 p.
016.572 63-9935
Z5111 .M3 MRR Alc.

ANTI-COMMUNIST MOVEMENTS--DIRECTORIES.
First national directory of
"rightist" groups, publications, and
some individuals in the United States
and some foreign countries. 4th ed.
Sausalito, Calif., Distributed by the
Noontide Press, 1962. 36 p. 62-
2510
E743.5 .F48 1962 MRR Ref Desk

ANTI-COMMUNIST MOVEMENTS--UNITED STATES.
Forster, Arnold. Danger on the
Right, New York, Random House [1964]
xviii, 294 p. 320 64-7549
E743 .F68 MRR Alc.

ANTI-COMMUNIST MOVEMENTS--UNITED STATES--DIRECTORIES.
First national directory of
"rightist" groups, publications, and
some individuals in the United States
and some foreign countries. 4th ed.
Sausalito, Calif., Distributed by the
Noontide Press, 1962. 36 p. 62-
2510
E743.5 .F48 1962 MRR Ref Desk.

ANTI-NAZI MOVEMENT--HISTORY--SOURCES.
Remak, Joachim, comp. The Nazi
years; Englewood Cliffs, N.J.,
Prentice-Hall [1969] xi, 178 p.
[4.95]   943.086 69-11359
DD256.5 .R43 MRR Alc.

**ANTI-WAR MOVEMENTS (VIETNAMESE
CONFLICT, 1961-)**
see Vietnamese Conflict, 1961- --
Protest movements

ANTIQUARIAN BOOKSELLERS--DIRECTORIES.
Grose, B. Donald, The antiquarian
booktrade; Metuchen, N.J., Scarecrow
Press, 1972. p.   658.8/09/070573
72-6996
Z286.A55 G74 MRR Ref Desk.

International antiques yearbook,
encyclopaedia & directory. 1949/50-
Uxbridge, Middlesex [etc.] Antiques
Yearbook Ltd. [etc.] 705.8 49-53305

NK1125 .A315 MRR Alc Latest
edition

International directory of
antiquarian booksellers. 1951/52-
[Limoges] 655.5058 52-33958
Z282 .I58 MRR Alc Latest edition

ANTIQUARIAN BOOKSELLERS--PERIODICALS.
The A B bookman's yearbook. 1954-
Newark, N.J. 010.58 54-1676
Z990 .A18 MRR Alc Latest edition

ANTIQUARIAN BOOKSELLERS--EUROPE--DIRECTORIES.
European bookdealers. 1st- ed.;
1967/69- London, Sheppard Press.
658.8/09/65557025 71-208235
Z291.5 .E96 MRR Ref Desk Latest
edition

ANTIQUARIAN BOOKSELLERS--GREAT BRITAIN--DIRECTORIES.
Annual directory of booksellers in
the British Isles specialising in
antiquarian and out-of-print books.
1970- London, Clique Ltd.
380.1/45/070573 79-22674
Z327 .A6 MRR Alc Latest edition

The Complete booksellers directory
(mainly antiquarian) Wilbarston, G.
Coe, 1968. 62, 23 p. [unpriced]
658.89/6555/7302542 72-366726
Z327 .C64 MRR Alc.

A Directory of dealers in secondhand
and antiquarian books in the British
Isles. 1951/52- London, Sheppard
Press. 655.5 51-38118
Z327 .D57 MRR Alc Latest edition

ANTIQUARIAN BOOKSELLERS--UNITED STATES--DIRECTORIES.
Directory of American book
specialists; [New York, Continental
Pub. Co., 1972] 172 p.
380.1/45/07057302573 73-151032
Z286.A55 D57 MRR Ref Desk.

ANTIQUE DEALERS--GREAT BRITAIN--DIRECTORIES.
British Antique Dealers' Association.
List of members. London. 55-33242

NK1127 .B67 MRR Alc Latest edition

The British antiques yearbook.
London, Antiques yearbooks, etc.
745.1/0942 70-10915
Began with vol. for 1968/69.
N8630 .B7 MRR Alc Latest edition

ANTIQUE DEALERS--GREAT LAKES REGION--DIRECTORIES.
Great Lakes antique dealers
directory. Decatur, Ind., S. E.
Leonardson. 708.05] 57-48384
"Established 1944."
NK1127 .G7 MRR Alc Latest edition

ANTIQUE DEALERS--NEW YORK (CITY)--DIRECTORIES.
Brener, Carol. The underground
collector; New York, Simon and
Schuster [1970] 319 p. [2.95]
745.1/025/7471 72-107269
NK1127 .B64 MRR Alc.

ANTIQUITIES.
see also Archaeology

Charles-Picard, Gilbert. Larousse
encyclopedia of archaeology. New
York, Putnam [1972] 432 p. [$25.00]
913/.031 76-179972
CC165 .C4313 MRR Alc.

Watson, Vera, The British Museum;
London, Quartet Books Ltd., 1973.
271 p. [£3.50] 913/.031/07402142
74-175583
AM101.B87 W37 MRR Alc.

ANTIQUITIES, BIBLICAL
see Bible--Antiquities

ANTIQUITIES, PREHISTORIC
see Man, Prehistoric

ANTIQUITY OF MAN
see Man--Origin

ANVIL, A STUDENT SOCIALIST MAGAZINE--INDEXES.
Indexes to independent Socialist
periodicals. Berkeley, Calif.,
Independent Socialist Press [1969]
221 p. [9.75] 016.3091 77-16046
HX15 .I43 no. 4 MRR Alc.

APHORISMS AND APOTHEGMS.
Athenaeus. The Deipnosophists,
London, W. Heinemann; New York, G. P.
Putnam's sons, 1927-1941. 7 v.
mrr01-18
PA3612 .A87 1927d MRR Alc.

Auden, Wystan Hugh, ed. The Viking
book of aphorisms; New York, Viking
Press [1966] x, 431 p. 808.882 66-
3191
PN6271 .A85 1966 MRR Alc.

Braude, Jacob Morton, ed. Lifetime
speaker's encyclopedia. Englewood
Cliffs, N.J., Prentice-Hall [1962] 2
v. (xix, 1224 p.) 808.88 62-18248

PN6081 .B667 MRR Alc.

Braude, Jacob Morton, New treasury
of stories for every speaking and
writing occasion. Englewood Cliffs,
N.J., Prentice-Hall [1959] 494 p.
808.88 59-13391
PN6261 .B73 MRR Alc.

Braude, Jacob Morton, ed. Second
encyclopedia of stories, quotations,
and anecdotes. Englewood Cliffs,
N.J., Prentice-Hall, 1957. 468 p.
808.88* 57-5563
PN6081 .B67 MRR Alc.

Gilbert, Mark, ed. Wisdom of the
ages; London, Heinemann [1965] 431
p. 808.8 57-39679
PN6331 .G53 1956 MRR Alc.

Plotkin, David George, Dictionary of
American maxims, New York,
Philosophical Library [1955] 597 p.
398.9 55-13882
PN6271 .P6 MRR Ref Desk.

Prochnow, Herbert Victor, comp.
Speaker's handbook of epigrams and
witticisms. [1st ed.] New York,
Harper [c1955] 332 p. 808.88* 54-
12157
PN6271 .P7 MRR Alc.

APOCRYPHAL BOOKS (OLD TESTAMENT)
Comay, Joan. Who's who in the Old
Testament, [1st ed.] New York,
Holt, Rinehart and Winston [1971]
448 p. [$14.95] 221.92/2 B 79-
153655
BS570 .C64 MRR Alc.

APOCRYPHAL BOOKS (OLD TESTAMENT)--INTRODUCTIONS.
Eissfeldt, Otto, The Old Testament;
New York, Harper and Row [1965]
xxiv, 861 p. 221 65-15399
BS1140 .E583 MRR Alc.

APOLLO PROJECT
see Project Apollo

APOLLONIUS, OF TYANA.
Philostratus, Flavius. The life of
Apollonius of Tyana, the Epistles of
Apollonius and the Treatise of
Eusebius; London, W. Heinemann; New
York, The Macmillan co., 1912. 2 v.
921.9 13-5590
PA4272 .P4 1912 MRR Alc.

APOLOGETICS--EARLY CHURCH, CA. 30-600.
Augustinus, Aurelius, Saint, Bp. of
Hippo. The city of God against the
pagans. Cambridge, Harvard
University Press, 1957-72. 7 v.
239.3 239.1* a 57-8616
PA6156.A82 MRR Alc.

APOLOGETICS--EARLY CHURCH, CA. (Cont.)
Tertullianus, Quintus Septimus
Florens. Tertullian, Apology, De
spectaculis, London, W. Heinemann,
ltd; New York, G. P. Putnam's sons,
1931. xxvii, 445, [1] p. 239.1 31-
23025
PA6156.T45 1931 MRR Alc.

APOSTOLIC CHURCH
see Church history--Primitive and
early church

APPALACHIAN REGION--BIBLIOGRAPHY.
Munn, Robert F. The Southern
Appalachians; Morgantown, West
Virginia University Library, 1961.
iii, 106 p. 016.9755 a 62-9041
Z1251.A7 M8 MRR Alc.

APPALACHIAN TRAIL.
Appalachian Trail Conference. Guide
to the Appalachian trail in the
southern Appalachians. 4th ed.
Washington, D.C., 1960. 500 p.
mrr01-67
F106 .A62 no. 8 MRR Alc.

Potomac Appalachian Trail Club,
Washington, D.C. Guide to the
Appalachian Trail: 7th ed.
Washington, 1970. vii, 190 p.
917.5 75-14141
F217.B6 P83 1970 MRR Alc.

APPARATUS, ELECTRIC
see Electric apparatus and appliances

APPARATUS, MEDICAL
see Medical instruments and apparatus

APPLIANCES, ELECTRIC
see Electric apparatus and appliances

APPLICATIONS FOR POSITIONS.
Angel, Juvenal Londono, Specialized
resumes for executives and
professionals, [New York] Regents
Pub. Co. [1967] 160 p. 331.1/15
66-25832
HF5383 .A57 MRR Alc.

Angel, Juvenal Londoño, Why and how
to prepare an effective job resume;
5th ed.; rev. and enl. New York,
World Trade Academy Press,
distributed by Simon & Schuster
[1972] 506 p. 331.1/28 70-179618
HF5383 .A6 1972 MRR Ref Desk.

Brennan, Lawrence David, Résumés
for better jobs New York, Simon and
Schuster [1973] 187 p. [$2.95]
331.1/28 73-174889
HF5383 .B68 MRR Alc.

Jameson, Robert. The professional
job changing system; [3d ed.
Verona, N.J., Performance Dynamics,
1974] 280 p. 650/.14 73-82380
HF5383 .J28 1974 MRR Alc.

APPLIED SCIENCE
see Technology

APPRECIATION OF ART
see Art--Philosophy

see Art--Study and teaching

APPRECIATION OF MUSIC
see Music--Analysis, appreciation

AQUARIUM FISHES.
Schiøtz, Arne. A guide to aquarium
fishes and plants. Philadelphia,
Lippincott [1972] 223 p. [$6.95]
639/.34 75-38541
SF457 .S3313 MRR Alc.

AQUARIUM PLANTS.
Schiøtz, Arne. A guide to aquarium
fishes and plants. Philadelphia,
Lippincott [1972] 223 p. [$6.95]
639/.34 75-38541
SF457 .S3313 MRR Alc.

AQUARIUMS.
Axelrod, Herbert R. Exotic tropical
fishes Jersey City, T. F. H.
Publications, distributed by Sterling
Pub. Co. [c1962] 1 v. (unpaged)
639.34 63-4310
SH167.T8 A9 MRR Alc.

Innes, William Thornton, Exotic
aquarium fishes; 1st- ed.: 1935-
Norristown, Pa.[etc.] Aquarium Pub.
Co.[etc.] 35-8711
QL78 .I5 Sci RR Latest edition /
MRR Alc Latest edition

AQUARIUMS, PUBLIC--DIRECTORIES.
Tinker, Spencer Wilkie. Directory of
the public aquaria of the world,
Preliminary ed. Honolulu, Waikiki
Aquarium, University of Hawaii, 1962.
28 l. 62-63479
QL78 .T5 MRR Alc.

AQUARIUMS, PUBLIC--AMERICA--DIRECTORIES.
Gersh, Harry. The animals next door;
New York, Fleet Academic Editions
[1971] 170 p. [$6.95] 590/.744/7
71-104745
QL76 .G44 MRR Alc.

AQUARIUMS, PUBLIC--UNITED STATES--
DIRECTORIES.
Gersh, Harry. The animals next door;
New York, Fleet Academic Editions
[1971] 170 p. [$6.95] 590/.744/7
71-104745
QL76 .G44 MRR Alc.

AQUATIC BIOLOGY.
see also Marine biology

AQUATIC RESOURCES.
see also Fisheries

see also Marine resources

AQUATIC SPORTS.
see also Boats and boating

see also Fishing

see also Swimming

Gabrielsen, M. Alexander. Aquatics
handbook 2d ed. Englewood Cliffs,
N.J., Prentice-Hall [1968] xii, 256
p. 797 68-21590
GV775 .G3 1968 MRR Alc.

Liebers, Arthur, The complete book
of water sports. Rev. ed. New York,
Coward, McCann & Geoghegan [1972]
253 p. [$6.95] 797 75-189241
GV775 .L5 1972 MRR Alc.

ARAB COUNTRIES--BIBLIOGRAPHY.
American University of Beirut.
Economic Research Institute. A
selected and annotated bibliography
of economic literature on the Arab
countries of the Middle East, 1953-
1965. Beirut, 1967. xvii, 458 p.
016.3309174/927 ne 68-4814
Z7165.A67 A56 MRR Alc.

Selim, George Dimitri, American
doctoral dissertations on the Arab
world, 1883-1968. Washington,
Library of Congress; for sale by the
Supt. of Docs., U.S. Govt. Print.
Off., 1970. xvii, 103 p. [0.55]
016.91003/174/927 79-607590
Z663.387 A68 MRR Alc.

ARAB COUNTRIES--BIOGRAPHY.
The Encyclopaedia of Islam; Leyden,
E. J. Brill ltd.; London, Luzac & co,
1913- v. 26-26918
DS37 .E5 MRR Alc.

ARAB COUNTRIES--BIOGRAPHY--DICTIONARIES.
Heravi, Mehdi, Concise encyclopedia
of the Middle East. Washington,
Public Affairs Press [1973] 336 p.
[$12.00] 915.6/03/03 73-82012
DS43 .H47 MRR Alc.

Who's who in the Arab world. 1st-
ed.: 1965/66- Beirut, Publitec
Editions. 820.05 ne 67-1244
D198.3 .W5 MRR Blog Latest edition
/ MRR Alc Latest edition

ARAB COUNTRIES--COMMERCE--DIRECTORIES.
Guide du commerce mondial pour les
professions liberales. Beyrouth,
Mansour. ne 66-1383
HF3866 .G55 MRR Alc Latest edition

ARAB COUNTRIES--DESCRIPTION AND TRAVEL--
GUIDE-BOOKS.
Showker, Kay. Complete reference
guide to the Arab Middle East: [1st
ed. New York] Pan American Airways;
[trade distribution in the U.S. and
Canada by Simon and Schuster, 1967]
191 p. 915.6/04 67-19408
DS43 .S5 MRR Alc.

ARAB COUNTRIES--DICTIONARIES AND
ENCYCLOPEDIAS.
The Encyclopaedia of Islam; Leyden,
E. J. Brill ltd.; London, Luzac & co,
1913- v. 26-26918
DS37 .E5 MRR Alc.

ARAB COUNTRIES--ECONOMIC CONDITIONS--
BIBLIOGRAPHY.
American University of Beirut.
Economic Research Institute. A
selected and annotated bibliography
of economic literature on the Arab
countries of the Middle East, 1953-
1965. Beirut, 1967. xvii, 458 p.
016.3309174/927 ne 68-4814
Z7165.A67 A56 MRR Alc.

ARAB COUNTRIES--FOREIGN RELATIONS.
Mansoor, Menahem. Political and
diplomatic history of the Arab world,
1900-1967; [Washington] NCR
Microcard Editions, 1972. 7 v.
320.9/17/4927 72-184866
DS62.8 .M35 MRR Alc.

ARAB COUNTRIES--HISTORY.
Gabrieli, Francesco, The Arab
revival. London] Thames and Hudson
[1961] 178 p. 956 61-2298
DS38 .G243 MRR Alc.

ARAB COUNTRIES--HISTORY--CHRONOLOGY.
Mansoor, Menahem. Political and
diplomatic history of the Arab world,
1900-1967; [Washington] NCR
Microcard Editions, 1972. 7 v.
320.9/17/4927 72-184866
DS62.8 .M35 MRR Alc.

ARAB COUNTRIES--HISTORY--SOURCES.
Khalil, Muhammad, ed. The Arab
States and the Arab League; Beirut,
Khayats [1962] 2 v. ne 63-705
DS36.2 .K45 MRR Alc.

ARAB COUNTRIES--IMPRINTS.
United States Library of Congress.
American Libraries Book Procurement
Center, Cairo. Accessions list,
Middle East. v. 1- Jan. 1963-
Cairo. 63-24163
Z663.767.A1 A25 MRR Alc MRR Alc
Full set

ARAB COUNTRIES--PERIODICALS--INDEXES.
London. University. School of
Oriental and African Studies.
Library. Index Islamicus, 1906-1955;
Cambridge, Eng., W. Heffer [1958]
xxxvi, 897 p. 016.9156 59-23014
Z7835.M6 L6 MRR Alc.

ARAB COUNTRIES--POLITICS.
Kerr, Malcolm H. The Arab cold war:
Gamal 'Abd al-Nasir and his rivals,
1958-1970 3d ed. London, New York,
Published for the Royal Institute of
International Affairs by Oxford
University Press, 1971. viii, 166 p.
[$1.95 (U.S.)] 320.9/174/927 74-
171045
DS63.1 .K47 1971 MRR Alc.

Mansoor, Menahem. Political and
diplomatic history of the Arab world,
1900-1967; [Washington] NCR
Microcard Editions, 1972. 7 v.
320.9/17/4927 72-184866
DS62.8 .M35 MRR Alc.

ARAB COUNTRIES--STATISTICS.
Middle East and North Africa markets
review. [Epping, Eng.] Gower
Economic Publications. [£30.00]
330.9/56/04 74-640571
HC410.7.A1 M48 MRR Alc Latest
edition

ARAB COUNTRIES--COMMERCE.
Le Guide arabe pour le commerce,
l'industrie & les professions
liberales dans les pays arabes.
Beyrouth. 53-32838
Began publication with issue for
1945 in Arabic.
DS43 .G85 MRR Alc Latest edition

ARAB EMPIRE
see Islamic Empire

ARAB-JEWISH RELATIONS
see Jewish-Arab relations

ARABIA--BIBLIOGRAPHY.
Macro, Eric. Bibliography of the
Arabian Peninsula. Coral Gables,
Fla., University of Miami Press,
1958. xiv, 80 p. 016.9153 58-
12170
Z3026 .M25 MRR Alc.

United States. Library of Congress.
Near East Section. The Arabian
Peninsula; Washington, 1951. xi,
111 p. 016.9153 51-60030
Z663.387 .A7 MRR Alc.

ARABIA--GAZETTERS.
United States. Office of Geography.
Arabian Peninsula; Washington, U.S.
Govt. Print. Off., 1961. xiii, 458
p. 61-62196
DS203 .U5 MRR Alc.

ARABIC LANGUAGE--CONVERSATION AND
PHRASE BOOKS--POLYGLOT.
Lyall, Archibald, A guide to 25
languages of Europe. Rev. ed.
[Harrisburg, Pa.] Stackpole Co.
[1966] viii, 407 p. 413 66-20847
PB73 .L85 1966 MRR Alc.

ARABIC LANGUAGE--DICTIONARIES--ENGLISH.
Lewis, Bernard. A handbook of
diplomatic and political Arabic.
[London] Luzac, 1947. 72, [1] p.
492.732 49-6894
PJ6680 .L4 MRR Alc.

Wehr, Hans, A dictionary of modern
written Arabic. Ithaca, N.Y.,
Cornell University Press, 1961.
xvii, 1110 p. 492.732 61-3227
PJ6640 .W43 MRR Alc.

Wortabet, William Thomson.
Wortabet's Arabic-English dictionary.
4th ed. Beirut, Librairie du Liban,
1968. 802 p. 492.7/3/2 77-399717

PJ6640 .W6 1968 MRR Alc.

ARABIC LANGUAGE--GRAMMAR.
Caspari, Carl Paul, A grammar of the
Arabic language, 3d ed., revised
Cambridge [Eng.] The University
press, 1933. 2 v.   492.75 34-6522

    PJ6305 .C5 1933 MRR Alc

ARABIC LITERATURE--HISTORY AND
CRITICISM.
Huart, Clément Imbault, A history
of Arabic literature. Beirut,
Khayats, 1966. 478 p.   892.7/09 67-
7316
    PJ7510 .H83 1966 MRR Alc

ARABIC PERIODICALS--BIBLIOGRAPHY.
United States Library of Congress.
American Libraries Book Procurement
Center, Cairo. Accessions list,
Middle East. v. 1-   Jan. 1963-
Cairo.   63-24163
    Z663.767.A1 A25 MRR Alc   MRR Alc
    Full set

ARABS.
Hitti, Philip Khûri, History of the
Arabs from the earliest times to the
present 10th ed. [London]
Macmillan; [New York] St. Martin's
Press [1970] xxiv, 822 p. [$12.50]
953   74-102765
    DS37.7 .H58 1970 MRR Alc.

ARABS--HISTORY.
Glubb, John Bagot, Sir, A short
history of the Arab peoples New
York, Stein and Day [1969] 318 p.
909/.09/74927 69-16907
    DS223 .G56 1969b MRR Alc.

ARABS IN NORTH AFRICA.
Ronart, Stephan. Concise
encyclopaedia of Arabic civilization:
Amsterdam, Djambatan, 1966. vii,
413 p. [fl50.00]   910.03/174/927
67-93204
    DT185 .R6 1966 MRR Alc.

ARABS IN SPAIN.
Ronart, Stephan. Concise
encyclopaedia of Arabic civilization:
Amsterdam, Djambatan, 1966. vii,
413 p. [fl50.00]   910.03/174/927
67-93204
    DT185 .R6 1966 MRR Alc.

ARAGON--DIRECTORIES.
Guía-anuario de Aragón, Rioja,
Navarra, Alava, Guipúzcoa y Vizcaya.
Zaragoza, E. Gallegos. 51-22040
    DP11 .G78 MRR Alc Latest edition

ARAMAIC LANGUAGE--DICTIONARIES--ENGLISH.
Jastrow, Marcus, A dictionary of the
Targumim, the Talmud Babli and
Yerushalmi, and the Midrashic
literature. London, Luzac & co.; New
York, G. P. Putnam's sons, 1903. 2
v.   12-34766
    PJ5205 .J3 MRR Alc.

ARBITRATION, INDUSTRIAL--BIBLIOGRAPHY.
United States. Library of Congress.
Division of bibliography. Select
list of references on industrial
arbitration; Washington, Govt.
print. off., 1903. 15 p.   03-16888

    Z663.28 .S375 MRR Alc.

ARBITRATION, INTERNATIONAL.
Manning, William Ray, ed.
Arbitration treaties among the
American nations, to the close of the
year 1910. New York [etc.] Oxford
university press, 1924. xl, 472 p.
24-6749
    JX1985 .M3 MRR Alc.

Wainhouse, David Walter.
International peace observation.
Baltimore, Johns Hopkins Press, 1966.
xvii, 663 p.   341.11 66-14376
    JX1981.P7 W25 MRR Alc.

ARBITRATION, INTERNATIONAL--DIGESTS.
Stuyt, Alexander Marie. Survey of
international arbitrations, 1794-
1970. Leiden, A. W. Sijthoff; Dobbs
Ferry, N.Y., Oceana Publications,
1972. xv, 572 p.   341.5/2 72-79626

    JX1937 .S85 MRR Alc.

ARBITRATION AND AWARD--DICTIONARIES.
Seide, Katharine, comp. A dictionary
of arbitration and its terms; labor,
commercial, international; Dobbs
Ferry, N.Y., Published for the
Eastman Library of the American
Arbitration Association, by Oceana
Publications, 1970. xviii, 334 p.
[15.00]   331.15/5/03 70-94692
    KF9085 .A68S4 MRR Alc.

ARBITRATION AND AWARD--UNITED STATES--
DICTIONARIES.
Seide, Katharine, comp. A dictionary
of arbitration and its terms; labor,
commercial, international; Dobbs
Ferry, N.Y., Published for the
Eastman Library of the American
Arbitration Association, by Oceana
Publications, 1970. xviii, 334 p.
[15.00]   331.15/5/03 70-94692
    KF9085 .A68S4 MRR Alc.

ARBORETUMS.
    see also Botanical gardens

ARBORICULTURE.
    see also Forests and forestry

    see also Trees

ARCHAEOLOGISTS.
Bray, Warwick. A dictionary of
archaeology, London, Allen Lane,
1970. 288, [75] p.   [45/-]
913.03/1/03 76-586300
    CC70 .B73 MRR Alc.

ARCHAEOLOGICAL MUSEUMS AND COLLECTIONS--
DIRECTORIES.
Brennan, Louis A. Beginner's guide
to archaeology; [Harrisburg, Pa.]
Stackpole Books [1973] 318 p.
[$9.95]   913/.031 73-4193
    E77.9 .B73 MRR Alc.

ARCHAEOLOGICAL SOCIETIES--UNITED STATES.
Robbins, Maurice. The amateur
archaeologist's handbook 2d ed. New
York, Crowell [1973] xiv, 288 p.
[$7.95]   913/.031/028 73-245
    E77.9 .R6 1973 MRR Alc.

ARCHAEOLOGY.
    see also Costume

    see also Ethnology

    see also Funeral rites and ceremonies

    see also Man, Prehistoric

    see also Mythology

    see also Sculpture, Primitive

    see also Underwater archaeology

Charles-Picard, Gilbert. Larousse
encyclopedia of archaeology. New
York, Putnam [1972] 432 p. [$25.00]
913/.031 76-179972
    CC165 .C4313 MRR Alc.

Childe, Vere Gordon, The dawn of
European civilization. [6th ed.
rev. London, Routledge & Paul
[1957] xiii, 368 p.   901 58-872
    D65 .C5 1957 MRR Alc.

Hole, Frank. An introduction to
prehistoric archeology New York,
Holt, Rinehart and Winston [1965] x,
306 p.   571 65-11842
    CC165 .H64 MRR Alc.

Morgan, Jacques Jean Marie de,
Prehistoric man; London, K. Paul,
Trench, Trubner & co., ltd.; New
York; A. A. Knopf, 1924. xxiii, 304
p.   25-2564
    GN738 .M785 MRR Alc.

Wheeler, Margaret (Collingridge)
Lady, History was buried: [Rev.
Amer. ed.] New York, Hart Pub. Co.
[1967] 431 p.   913.03/1/08 67-
23615
    CC165 .W445 1967 MRR Alc.

ARCHAEOLOGY--ABSTRACTS.
Gettens, Rutherford John, comp.
Abstracts of technical studies in art
and archaeology, 1943-1952,
Washington, 1955. viii, 408 p.
016.7 55-61312
    N7428 .G44 MRR Alc.

ARCHAEOLOGY--ADDRESSES, ESSAYS,
LECTURES.
Leone, Mark P., comp. Contemporary
archaeology: a guide to theory and
contributions. Carbondale, Southern
Illinois University Press [1972] xv,
460 p. [$15.00]   913/.031 79-
156770
    GN739 .L46 MRR Alc.

ARCHAEOLOGY--BIBLIOGRAPHY.
Clapp, Jane. Museum publications.
New York, Scarecrow Press, 1962. 2
v.   016.0697 62-10120
    Z5051 .C5 MRR Alc.

Hammond, Philip C. Archaeological
techniques for amateurs. Princeton,
N.J., Van Nostrand [1963] 329 p.
913.018 63-4293
    CC75 .H3 MRR Alc.

Index of archæological papers
published 1891-1910, [1st]-20th
issue; 1892-1914. [London] 08-10988

    Z2027.A8 I7 MRR Alc Full set

ARCHAEOLOGY--BIBLIOGRAPHY--CATALOGS.
Biblioteca Nacional de Antropología
e Historia. Catalogos de la
Biblioteca Nacional de Antropología
e Historia. Mexico. Boston, G. K.
Hall, 1972. 10 v.   74-225152
    Z885.A1 B5 1972 MRR Alc (Dk 33)

Deutsches Archäologisches Institut.
Römische Abteilung. Bibliothek.
Kataloge der Bibliothek des Deutschen
Archaeologischen Instituts, Rom:
Autore- und Periodica Kataloge.
Boston, G. K. Hall, 1969. 7 v.
016.91337 73-202658
    Z5134 .R764 MRR Alc (Dk 33)

Deutsches Archäologisches Institut.
Römische Abteilung. Bibliothek.
Kataloge der Bibliothek des Deutschen
Archaeologischen Instituts Rom:
systematischer Katalog. Boston, G.
K. Hall, 1969. 3 v.   73-205023
    Z5134 .R76417 MRR Alc (Dk 33)

Harvard University. Peabody Museum of
Archaeology and Ethnology. Library.
Catalogue: authors. Boston, G. K.
Hall, 1963. 26 v.   64-2646
    Z5119 .H35 MRR Alc (Dk 33).

Harvard University. Peabody Museum of
Archaeology and Ethnology. Library.
Catalogue: subjects. Boston, G. K.
Hall, 1963. 27 v.   018.1 64-2645
    Z5119 .H36 MRR Alc (Dk 33)

ARCHAEOLOGY--BIBLIOGRAPHY--YEARBOOKS.
Istituto nazionale di archeologia e
storia dell'arte, Rome. Biblioteca.
Annuario bibliografico di
archeologia. anno 1-   1952-
Modena.   55-22588
    Z5132 .I782 MRR Alc Full set

ARCHAEOLOGY--DICTIONARIES.
Bray, Warwick. A dictionary of
archaeology. London, Allen Lane,
1970. 288, [75] p.   [45/-]
913.03/1/03 76-586300
    CC70 .B73 MRR Alc.

The Concise encyclopedia of
archaeology; 2nd ed. (revised in new
format). London, Hutchinson, 1970.
xxv, 430 p. [45/-]   913.03/1/03 77-
518566
    CC70 .C6 1970 MRR Alc.

Mollett, John William. An
illustrated dictionary of art and
archaeology. New York, American
Archives of World Art [1966] 350 p.
703 65-29110
    N33 .M6 1966 MRR Alc.

Palmer, Geoffrey. Archaeology A-Z: a
simplified guide and dictionary,
London, New York, Frederick Warne,
1968. xi, 225 p.   [25/-]
913.03/1/03 68-16851
    CC70 .P3 1968 MRR Alc.

Ville, Georges, Concise encyclopedia
of archaeology: from the Bronze Age;
Glasgow, Collins, 1971. 251 p.
[£1.25]   913/.031/03 73-331183
    CC70 .V513 MRR Alc.

ARCHAEOLOGY--DICTIONARIES--POLYGLOT.
Réau, Louis, Dictionnaire
polyglotte des termes d'art et
d'archéologie. [1. ed.] Paris,
Presses universitaires de France,
1953. viii, 247, [5] p.   703 a 53-
8484
    N33 .R42 MRR Alc.

ARCHAEOLOGY--HISTORY.
Daniel, Glyn Edmund. A hundred years
of archaeology. London, Duckworth
[1950] 343 p.   571.09 50-3526
    GN720 .D3 MRR Alc.

Marek, Kurt W. Gods, graves, and
scholars; 2d, rev. and substantially
enl. ed. New York, Knopf, 1967.
xvi, 441 p.   913.03/1 67-11119
    CC100 .M313 1967 MRR Alc.

Marek, Kurt W. The march of
archaeology, [1st American ed.] New
York, Knopf, 1958. xviii, 326, vi p.
913 58-10977
    CC100 .M323 MRR Alc.

Willey, Gordon Randolph, A history
of American archaeology San
Francisco, W. H. Freeman [1974] 252
p. 913/.031 73-17493
    E61 .W67 1974b MRR Alc.

ARCHAEOLOGY--INDEXES.
Gomme, George Laurence, Sir, Index
of archaeological papers, 1665-1890.
London, A. Constable & company, ltd.,
1907. xi, 910 p.   08-9803
    Z2027.A8 I6 MRR Alc.

ARCHAEOLOGY--INFORMATION SERVICES.
Brennan, Louis A. Beginner's guide
to archaeology; [Harrisburg, Pa.]
Stackpole Books [1973] 318 p.
[$9.95]   913/.031 73-4193
    E77.9 .B73 MRR Alc.

ARCHAEOLOGY--METHODOLOGY.
Atkinson, Richard John Copland,
Field archaeology. [2d ed., rev.]
London, Methuen [1953] 233 p.   913
54-36205
    CC75 .A8 1953 MRR Alc.

ARCHAEOLOGY--METHODOLOGY. (Cont.)
Brennan, Louis A. Beginner's guide
to archaeology; [Harrisburg, Pa.]
Stackpole Books [1973] 318 p.
[$9.95] 913/.031 73-4193
E77.9 .B73 MRR Alc.

Hammond, Philip C. Archaeological
techniques for amateurs. Princeton,
N.J., Van Nostrand [1963] 329 p.
913.018 63-4293
CC75 .H3 MRR Alc.

Heizer, Robert Fleming, A guide to
field methods in archaeology; [New
rev. ed.] Palo Alto, Calif.,
National Press [1967] ix, 274 p.
913 67-20072
CC75 .H45 1967 MRR Alc.

Kenyon, Kathleen Mary. Beginning in
archaeology. Rev. ed., New York,
Praeger [1961] 228 p. 571.018 61-
19626
CC75 .K4 1961 MRR Alc.

Robbins, Maurice. The amateur
archaeologist's handbook 2d ed. New
York, Crowell [1973] xiv, 288 p.
[$7.95] 913/.031/028 73-245
E77.9 .R6 1973 MRR Alc.

ARCHAEOLOGY--PERIODICALS--BIBLIOGRAPHY--
CATALOGS.
Deutsches Archäologisches Institut.
Römische Abteilung. Bibliothek.
Kataloge der Bibliothek des Deutschen
Archaeologischen Instituts, Rom:
Autore- und Periodica Kataloge.
Boston, G. K. Hall, 1969. 7 v.
016.91337 73-202658
Z5134 .R764 MRR Alc (Dk 33)

ARCHAEOLOGY--PERIODICALS--INDEXES.
Abstracts in anthropology. v. 1-
Feb. 1970- Farmingdale, N.Y.,
Baywood Publishing Co. [etc.] 77-
20528
GN1 .A15 MRR Alc Full set

British archaeological association.
The journal of the British
archaeological association. General
index to volumes I to XXX. London,
Printed for the Association, 1875.
225 p. 01-6360
DA20 .B83 Index MRR Alc.

Deutsches Archäologisches Institut.
Römische Abteilung. Bibliothek.
Kataloge der Bibliothek des Deutschen
Archaeologischen Instituts, Rom:
Zeitschriften--Autorenkatalog.
Boston, G. K. Hall, 1969. 3 v.
016.91337 73-202659
Z5134 .R7642 MRR Alc (Dk 33)

Gomme, George Laurence, Sir, Index
of archeological papers, 1665-1890.
London, A. Constable & company, ltd.,
1907. xl, 910 p. 08-8803
Z2027.A8 I6 MRR Alc.

Istituto nazionale di archeologia e
storia dell'arte, Rome. Biblioteca.
Annuario bibliografico di
archeologia. anno 1- 1952-
Modena. 55-22588
Z5132 .I782 MRR Alc Full set

ARCHAEOLOGY--SOCIETIES, ETC.--
DIRECTORIES.
The Archaeologists' year book. 1973-
[Park Ridge, N.J.] Noyes Press.
[$12.50] 913/.031/025 73-78778
CC120 .A67 MRR Alc Latest edition

ARCHAEOLOGY--STUDY AND TEACHING--
DIRECTORIES.
The Archaeologists' year book. 1973-
[Park Ridge, N.J.] Noyes Press.
[$12.50] 913/.031/025 73-78778
CC120 .A67 MRR Alc Latest edition

ARCHAEOLOGY, BIBLICAL
see Bible--Antiquities

ARCHAEOLOGY--BIBLIOGRAPHY.
Borroni, Fabia. "Il Cicognara,"
Firenze, Sansoni, 1954- v. 55-
18980
Z2357 .B6 MRR Alc.

ARCHERY--DICTIONARIES.
Hougham, Paul C., The encyclopedia
of archery. New York, Barnes [1958]
202 p. 799.32 57-9910
GV1185 .H68 MRR Alc.

ARCHITECTS.
Les Architectes célèbres. Paris]
L. Mazenod [c1958-59] 2 v. 720.9
60-24866
NA40 .A7 MRR Alc.

Forsee, Aylesa. Men of modern
architecture; Philadelphia, McCrae
Smith [1966] 223 p. 720.922 65-
24901
NA40 .F6 MRR Alc.

Studio dictionary of design &
decoration. Rev. and enl. ed.] New
York, Viking Press [1973] 538 p.
[$28.50] 745.4/03 73-1024
NK1165 .S78 1973 MRR Alc.

Sturgis, Russell, A dictionary of
architecture and building: Detroit,
Gale Research Co., 1966. 3 v.
720/.3 66-26997
NA31 .S84 1966 MRR Alc.

ARCHITECTS--BIBLIOGRAPHY.
Columbia University. Libraries. Avery
Architectural Library. Avery index
to architectural periodicals. 2d
ed.; rev. and enl. Boston, G. K.
Hall, 1973- v. 016.72 74-
152756
Z5945 .C653 1973 MRR Alc (Dk 33)

Columbia University. Libraries. Avery
Architectural Library. Avery
obituary index of architects and
artists. Boston, G. K. Hall, 1963.
338 p. 64-7017
Z5941 .C64 MRR Biog.

Sharp, Dennis. Sources of modern
architecture: London, published for
the Architectural Association by Lund
Humphries, 1967. 56 p. [30/-]
016.72 67-95916
Z5941 .S48 1967a MRR Biog.

ARCHITECTS--BIOGRAPHY.
International directory of behavior
and design research. 1974-
[Orangeburg, N.Y.] [$12.00] 300/.25
74-75207
H57 .I57 MRR Biog Latest edition /
Sci RR Latest edition

Sharp, Dennis. Sources of modern
architecture: London, published for
the Architectural Association by Lund
Humphries, 1967. 56 p. [30/-]
016.72 67-95916
Z5941 .S48 1967a MRR Biog.

ARCHITECTS--DICTIONARIES.
Koch, Willi August, Musisches
Lexikon: Künstler, Kunstwerke und
Motive aus Dichtung, Musik und
bildender Kunst, 2., veränderte und
ergeiterte Aufl. Stuttgart, A.,
Kröner [c1964] 1250 columns, xxxx
p. 65-69991
N31 .K57 1964 MRR Alc.

New international illustrated
encyclopedia of art. New York,
Greystone Press [1967- v. 703
67-24201
N31 .N4 MRR Alc.

ARCHITECTS--DICTIONARIES--FRENCH.
Oudin, Bernard. Dictionnaire des
architects. [Paris] Seghers [1970]
478, [2] p. [69.00] 76-513942
NA40 .O85 MRR Biog.

ARCHITECTS--DICTIONARIES--GERMAN.
Darmstaedter, Robert.
Künstlerlexikon: Bern, Francke
[1961] 527 p. 62-43121
N40 .D34 MRR Biog.

ARCHITECTS--FRANCE--DIRECTORIES.
Annuaire des architectes français.
Lyon, P. Saubiez. 720.58 46-17864
Publication began with issue for
1926?
NA60.F7 A5 MRR Alc Latest edition

Sageret; Paris. 53-28411
"Fondé en 1809."
TH12 .S25 MRR Alc Latest edition

ARCHITECTS--GREAT BRITAIN--BIOGRAPHY.
Ware, Dora. A short dictionary of
British architects: London, Allen &
Unwin, 1967. 3-312 p. [48/-]
720/.922 67-94834
NA996 .W3 MRR Biog.

ARCHITECTS--GREAT BRITAIN--DIRECTORIES.
The Register of architects. v. 27-
1960- London, Architects
Registration Council of the United
Kingdom. 720/.25/42 72-626697
NA60.G7 A7 MRR Alc Latest edition

ARCHITECTS--UNITED STATES--DIRECTORIES.
American architects directory. 1st
ed.: 1956- New York, Published
under the sponsorship of American
Institute of Architects by R. R.
Bowker. 720.69 55-12270
NA53 .A37 MRR Biog Latest edition

American Institute of Architects.
Membership list. Washington.
720.6273 53-27801
NA11 .A42 MRR Alc Latest edition

Sweet's industrial construction &
renovation file with plant
engineering extension market list.
1974- [New York, Sweet's Division,
McGraw-Hill Information Systems Co.]
338.4/7/69002573 74-645493
TH12 .S93 MRR Alc Latest edition /
Sci RR Latest edition

ARCHITECTS, AMERICAN--BIOGRAPHY--
DICTIONARIES.
Withey, Henry F. Biographical
dictionary of American architects
(deceased) Los Angeles, New Age Pub.
Co. [c1956] 678 p. 927.2 a 57-
1854
NA736 .W5 MRR Biog.

ARCHITECTS, BRITISH.
Colvin, Howard Montagu. A
biographical dictionary of English
architects, 1660-1840. [1st ed.]
London, J. Murray [1954] xiv, 821 p.
927.2 54-3859
NA996 .C6 1954 MRR Alc.

ARCHITECTURAL DESIGN--BIBLIOGRAPHY--
CATALOGS.
Harvard University. Graduate School
of Design. Library. Catalogue of the
Library of the Graduate School of
Design, Harvard University. Boston,
Mass., G. K. Hall, 1968. 44 v.
019/.1 73-169433
Z5945 .H28 1968 MRR Alc (Dk 33)

ARCHITECTURAL ENGINEERING
see Building

ARCHITECTURAL INSCRIPTIONS--WASHINGTON,
D.C.
Andriot, John L. Guide to the
building inscriptions of the Nation's
Capital. Arlington, Va., Jay-Way
Press, 1955. 57 p. 729 55-4977
NA4050.I5 A55 MRR Ref Desk.

ARCHITECTURE.
see also Buildings

ARCHITECTURE--BIBLIOGRAPHY.
Hamlin, Talbot Faulkner, Greek
revival architecture in America:
London, New York [etc.] Oxford
university press, 1944. xl, 439 p.
724.2735 44-865
NA707 .H32 MRR Alc.

Harvard University. Graduate School
of Design. Library. Catalogue of the
Library of the Graduate School of
Design, Harvard University. Boston,
Mass., G. K. Hall, 1968. 44 v.
019/.1 73-169433
Z5945 .H28 1968 MRR Alc (Dk 33)

Hitchcock, Henry Russell, American
architectural books: Minneapolis,
University of Minnesota Press [1962]
xii, 130 p. 016.72 62-11970
Z5941 .H67 1962 MRR Alc.

Smith, Denison Langley, How to find
out in architecture and building;
[1st ed.] Oxford, New York, Pergamon
Press [1967] xii, 232 p. 016.72
66-29605
Z5941 .S58 1967 MRR Alc.

Sturgis, Russell, A dictionary of
architecture and building: Detroit,
Gale Research Co., 1966. 3 v.
720/.3 66-26997
NA31 .S84 1966 MRR Alc.

ARCHITECTURE--BIBLIOGRAPHY--CATALOGS.
Columbia University. Libraries. Avery
Architectural Library. Catalog of
the Avery Memorial Architectural
Library of Columbia University.
Boston, Microphotography Co., 1958.
6 v. (11,534 p.) 55-4091
Z5945 .C652 MRR Alc (Dk 33).

ARCHITECTURE--CONSERVATION AND
RESTORATION.
Historic American Buildings Survey.
Preservation through documentation.
Washington, Library of Congress; [for
sale by the Supt. of Docs., Govt.
Print. Off., 1968] [16] p. [0.25]
720/.973 68-62342
Z663 .P73 MRR Alc.

ARCHITECTURE--DESIGNS AND PLANS.
De Chiara, Joseph, Time-saver
standards for building types. New
York, McGraw-Hill [1973] xiii, 1065
p. [$27.50] 729/.2 73-6663
NA2760 .D42 MRR Alc.

Historic American Buildings Survey.
Historic American Buildings Survey;
New York, B. Franklin [1971] vii,
470 p. 720.9/73 73-160016
NA707 .H45 MRR Alc.

ARCHITECTURE--DICTIONARIES.
Atkinson, Thomas Dinham, A glossary
of terms used in English
architecture. 7th ed. reprinted.
London, Methuen [1966] xxviii, 335
p. [10/6.] 720.942 66-73756
NA31 .A85 1966 MRR Alc.

Burke, Arthur Edward, Architectural
and building trades dictionary
Chicago, American Technical Society,
1955. xxxviii, 377 p. 690.3 56-
433
NA31 .B84 1955 MRR Alc.

Cowan, Henry J. Dictionary of
architectural science New York,
Wiley [1973] xi, 354 p. 721/.03
73-15839
NA31 .C64 MRR Alc.

Del Vecchio, Alfred. Dictionary of
mechanical engineering. New York,
Philosophical Library [1961] 346 p.
621.03 60-13664
TJ9 .D38 MRR Alc.

ARCHITECTURE--DICTIONARIES. (Cont.)
Dictionary of architectural
abbreviations, signs, and symbols.
New York, Odyssey Press [c1965]
xvii, 585 p.   720.3   65-18847
    NA31 .D53 MRR Alc.

Harris, John. Illustrated glossary
of architecture, 850-1830 New York,
C. N. Potter [c1966] xi, 78 p.
720/.3   67-22528
    NA31 .H34 1966a MRR Alc.

New international illustrated
encyclopedia of art. New York,
Greystone Press [1967- v.   703
67-24201
    N31 .N4 MRR Alc.

Osborne, Arthur Leslie. A dictionary
of English domestic architecture.
London, Country Life Limited [1954]
111 p.   728   54-29330
    NA31 .C8 MRR Alc.

Putnam, R. E. Architectural and
building trades dictionary 3d ed.
Chicago, American Technical Society
[1974]   510 p.   721/.03 74-75483
    TH9 .P82 1974 MRR Alc.

Studio dictionary of design &
decoration. Rev. and enl. ed.] New
York, Viking Press [1973]   538 p.
[$28.50]   745.4/03 73-1024
    NK1165 .S78 1973 MRR Alc.

Sturgis, Russell, A dictionary of
architecture and building: Detroit,
Gale Research Co., 1966. 3 v.
720/.3   66-26997
    NA31 .S84 1966 MRR Alc.

Walker, John Albert, Glossary of
art, architecture, and design since
1945. [Hamden, Conn.] Linnet Books
[1973] 240 p. [$10.50]   709/.04
73-3339
    N34 .W34 MRR Alc.

Ware, Dora. A short dictionary of
architecture, [3d ed., rev. and
enl.] London, Allen Unwin [1953]
xiv, 135 p.   720.3   54-16490
    NA31 .W27 1953 MRR Alc.

ARCHITECTURE--DICTIONARIES--GERMAN.
Koch, Wilhelm August, Musisches
Lexikon: Künstler. Kunstwerke und
Motive aus Dichtung, Musik und
bildender Kunst, 2., veränderte und
erweiterte Aufl. Stuttgart, A.,
Kröner [c1964] 1250 columns, xxxx
p.   65-69991
    N31 .K57 1964 MRR Alc.

Wasmuths lexikon der baukunst.
Berlin, E. Wasmuth, a.g. [c1929-c37]
5 v. 31-1582
    NA31 .W3 MRR Alc.

ARCHITECTURE--DICTIONARIES--POLYGLOT.
Vocabulaire international des termes
d'urbanisme et d'architecture. 1.
ed. Paris, Société de diffusion
des techniques du bâtiment et des
travaux publics, 1870- v.   [133F
(v. 1)]   70-860237
    NA31 .V6 MRR Alc.

Zboiński, A., ed. Dictionary of
architecture and building trades in
four languages: English, German,
Polish, Russian. Oxford, New York,
Pergamon Press; [distributed in the
Western Hemisphere by Macmillan, New
York, 1963] 491 p.   63-22975
    NA31 .Z34 MRR Alc.

ARCHITECTURE--EARLY WORKS TO 1800.
Vitruvius Pollio. On architecture,
London, W. Heinemann; New York, G. P.
Putnam's Sons, 1931-1934. 2 v.
mrr01-36
    PA6156.V5 1931d MRR Alc.

ARCHITECTURE--HISTORY.
Les Architectes celebres. Paris]
L. Mazenod [c1958-59] 2 v.   720.9
60-24966
    NA40 .A7 MRR Alc.

Fletcher, Banister Flight, Sir, A
history of architecture on the
comparative method. 17th ed., rev.
New York, Scribner, 1961. 1366 p.
720.9   61-65079
    NA200 .F63 1961 MRR Alc.

Gloag, John, Guide to Western
architecture. London, Allen and
Unwin [1958] xviii, 407 p.   720.9
58-2268
    NA200 .G6 1958a MRR Alc.

ARCHITECTURE--PERIODICALS--INDEXES.
The Architectural index. [Berkeley,
Calif., etc.] 016.7205 51-33537
    Z5941 .A66 MRR Alc Full set

Art index. v. 1- Jan. 1929/Sept.
1932- New York, H. W. Wilson. 016.7
31-7513
    Z5937 .A78 MRR Circ Full set

Columbia University. Libraries. Avery
Architectural Library. Avery index
to architectural periodicals. 2d
ed.; rev. and enl. Boston, G. K.
Hall, 1973- v.   016.72 74-
152756
    Z5945 .C653 1973 MRR Alc (Dk 33)

Harvard University. Graduate School
of Design. Library. Catalogue of the
Library of the Graduate School of
Design, Harvard University. Boston,
Mass., G. K. Hall, 1968. 44 v.
019/.1 73-169433
    Z5945 .H28 1968 MRR Alc (Dk 33)

ARCHITECTURE--ATHENS.
Traulos, Ioannes N., Pictorial
dictionary of Ancient Athens London,
Thames and Hudson, 1971. xvi, 590 p.
[£25.00]   720/.9/49512 72-178898
    NA280 .T68 1971 MRR Alc.

ARCHITECTURE--BALTIMORE.
Dorsey, John R., A guide to
Baltimore architecture, Cambridge,
Md., Tidewater Publishers, in
cooperation with the Peale Museum,
1973. L, 246 p. [$4.95]
917.52/2/043 73-12576
    NA735.B3 D67 MRR Alc.

ARCHITECTURE--BELGIUM--HISTORY.
Gerson, Horst. Art and architecture
in Belgium, 1600 to 1800 Baltimore,
Penguin Books [1960] xix, 236 p.
709.493 60-3193
    N6966 .G43 MRR Alc.

ARCHITECTURE--CHINA--HISTORY.
Sickman, Laurence C. S. The art and
architecture of China [Baltimore]
Penguin Books [1956] xxvi, 334 p.
709.51 56-1125
    N7340 .S46 MRR Alc.

ARCHITECTURE--EGYPT--HISTORY.
Smith, William Stevenson. The art
and architecture of ancient Egypt.
[Harmondsworth, Middlesex] Penguin
Books [1958] xxvii, 301 p.   709.32
58-3043
    N5350 .S5 MRR Alc.

ARCHITECTURE--ENGLAND--HISTORY.
Yarwood, Doreen. The architecture of
England: 2d ed. London, Batsford,
1967. xvi, 680 p. [£5/5/-]
720/.942 68-85154
    NA961 .Y3 1967 MRR Alc.

ARCHITECTURE--EUROPE--HISTORY.
Pevsner, Nikolaus, Sir, An outline
of European architecture. [6th,
Jubilee ed.] Baltimore, Penguin
Books [1960] 740 p.   720.94 60-
52016
    NA950 .P4 1960 MRR Alc.

Yarwood, Doreen. The architecture of
Europe. New York, Hastings House
[1974] 598 p.   720/.94 73-11105
    NA950 .Y37 MRR Alc.

ARCHITECTURE--FRANCE.
Blunt, Anthony, Sir, Art and
architecture in France, 1500 to 1700.
2nd ed. Harmondsworth, Penguin,
1970. xxii, 315 p., 193 plates.
[£7/10/-] 709/.44 70-521859
    N6844 .B6 1970 MRR Alc.

ARCHITECTURE--GREAT BRITAIN--HISTORY.
Nellist, John Bowman. British
architecture and its background
London, Macmillan; New York, St.
Martin's P.; 1967. xvii, 361 p.
[70/-] 720/.942 67-11466
    NA961 .N4 MRR Alc.

Summerson, John Newenham, Sir,
Architecture in Britain, 1530-1830
[Harmondsworth, Eng.] Penguin Books
[1970] 611 p. [($8.95 pbk.)]
720/.942 76-128006
    NA964 .S85 1970 MRR Alc.

Webb, Geoffrey Fairbank,
Architecture in Britain: the Middle
Ages. [Harmondsworth, Middlesex]
Penguin Books [1956] xxi, 234 p.
720.942 57-927
    NA963 .W4 MRR Alc.

ARCHITECTURE--JAPAN--HISTORY.
Paine, Robert Treat, The art and
architecture of Japan / 2d ed. /
Harmondsworth, Eng. ; Baltimore :
Penguin Books, 1974. xviii, 328 p.,
[87] leaves of plates : [$39.50
(U.S.)]   709/.52 74-186336
    N7350 .P3 1973 MRR Alc.

ARCHITECTURE--LATIN AMERICA--HISTORY.
Kubler, George, Art and architecture
in Spain and Portugal and their
American dominions, 1500 to 1800
[Harmondsworth, Middlesex] Penguin
Books [1959] xxviii, 445 p. 709.46
60-666
    N7104 .K8 1959b MRR Alc.

ARCHITECTURE--NEAR EAST.
Frankfort, Henri, The art and
architecture of the ancient Orient.
[Harmondsworth, Middlesex] Penguin
Books [1954] xxvi, 279 p.   709.3
55-12563
    N7265 .F7 MRR Alc.

ARCHITECTURE--NEW YORK (CITY)
American Institute of Architects. New
York Chapter. AIA guide to New York
City. New York, Macmillan [1968]
xii, 464 p. [$6.95] 917.47/2 68-
58489
    NA735.N5 A78 1968 MRR Alc.

ARCHITECTURE--PARIS--HISTORY.
Hulsman, Georges Maurice, Les
monuments de Paris [Paris] Hachette
[1966] 423 p.   66-80289
    NA1050 .H8 1966 MRR Alc.

ARCHITECTURE--PORTUGAL--HISTORY.
Kubler, George, Art and architecture
in Spain and Portugal and their
American dominions, 1500 to 1800
[Harmondsworth, Middlesex] Penguin
Books [1959] xxviii, 445 p.   709.46
60-666
    N7104 .K8 1959b MRR Alc.

ARCHITECTURE--RUSSIA--HISTORY.
Hamilton, George Heard. The art and
architecture of Russia. Baltimore,
Penguin Books [1954] xxi, 320 p.
709.47 a 55-4512
    N6981 .H34 MRR Alc.

ARCHITECTURE--SPAIN--HISTORY.
Kubler, George, Art and architecture
in Spain and Portugal and their
American dominions, 1500 to 1800
[Harmondsworth, Middlesex] Penguin
Books [1959] xxviii, 445 p.   709.46
60-666
    N7104 .K8 1959b MRR Alc.

ARCHITECTURE--UNITED STATES.
Andrews, Wayne. Architecture in
America: [1st ed.] New York,
Atheneum Publishers, 1960. 179 p.
720.973 60-7783
    NA705 .A53 MRR Alc.

Hamlin, Talbot Faulkner, The
American spirit in architecture, New
York, Yale university press; [etc.,
etc.] 1926. 3 p. l., 353 p. 26-
9196
    E178.5 .P2 vol. 13 MRR Alc.

Hamlin, Talbot Faulkner, Greek
revival architecture in America;
London, New York [etc.] Oxford
university press, 1944. xl, 439 p.
724.2735 44-865
    NA707 .H32 MRR Alc.

Historic American Buildings Survey.
Documenting a legacy; [Washington,
Library of Congress; 1973] 269-294
p. 720/.973 73-17422
    Z663 .D6 MRR Alc.

Hunter, Sam, American art of the
20th century: New York, H. N. Abrams
[1973] 583 p.   709/.73 73-10211
    N6512 .H78 1973 MRR Alc.

Tallmadge, Thomas Eddy, The story of
architecture in America, New, enl.
and rev. ed. New York, W. W. Norton
& company, inc. [c1936] xi p., 1 l.,
332 p.   720.973 36-23858
    NA705 .T3 1936 MRR Alc.

Whiffen, Marcus. American
architecture since 1780: Cambridge,
Mass., M.I.T. Press [1969] x, 313 p.
720/.973 69-10376
    NA705 .W47 MRR Alc.

ARCHITECTURE--UNITED STATES--
BIBLIOGRAPHY.
Hitchcock, Henry Russell, American
architectural books; Minneapolis,
University of Minnesota Press [1962]
xii, 130 p. 016.72 62-11970
    Z5941 .H67 1962 MRR Alc.

Roos, Frank John, Bibliography of
early American architecture; Urbana,
University of Illinois Press, 1968.
389 p. [12.50] 016.720/973 68-
24624
    Z5944.U5 R6 1968 MRR Alc.

ARCHITECTURE--UNITED STATES--
CONSERVATION AND RESTORATION.
Haas, Irvin. America's historic
houses and restorations. [1st ed.]
New York, Hawthorn Books [1967,
c1966] 271 p.   973 66-22320
    E159 .H12 MRR Alc.

Historic American Buildings Survey.
Historic American Buildings Survey;
New York, B. Franklin [1971] vii,
470 p.   720.9/73 73-160016
    NA707 .H45 MRR Alc.

ARCHITECTURE--UNITED STATES--HISTORY.
Kimball, Sidney Fiske, Domestic
architecture of the American colonies
and of the early Republic. New York,
Dover Publications [1966, c1922] xx,
314 p. 728/.0973 66-29154
   NA707 .K45 1966 MRR Alc.

ARCHITECTURE--VIRGINIA--GUIDE-BOOKS.
O'Neal, William Bainter.
Architecture in Virginia; 1st ed.
New York, Published for the Virginia
Museum by Walker, 1968. 192 p.
720.9/755 67-13230
   NA730.V8 O5 MRR Alc.

ARCHITECTURE--WASHINGTON, D.C.
Maddex, Diane. Historic buildings of
Washington, D.C. [1st ed.]
Pittsburgh, Ober Park Associates
[1973] 191 p. [$17.50] 720/.9753
72-92006
   NA735.W3 M32 MRR Alc.

ARCHITECTURE--WASHINGTON, D.C.--GUIDE-
BOOKS.
American Institute of Architects.
Washington-Metropolitan Chapter.
Washington architecture, 1791-1957,
New York, Reinhold [1957] 96 p.
720.9753 57-10358
   NA735.W3 A6 MRR Alc.

A Guide to the architecture of
Washington, D.C. [2d ed., rev. and
expanded] New York, McGraw-Hill
[1974] 246 p. 917.53/04/4 74-1336

   NA735.W3 G84 1974 MRR Alc.

ARCHITECTURE, ANCIENT.
see also Capitols

ARCHITECTURE, BAROQUE--HISTORY.
Hempel, Eberhard. Baroque art and
architecture in central Europe:
Baltimore, Penguin Books [1965]
xxiii, 370 p. 709.43 65-28970
   N6756 .H413 MRR Alc.

ARCHITECTURE, CHURCH
see Church architecture

ARCHITECTURE, COLONIAL--BIBLIOGRAPHY.
Roos, Frank John, Bibliography of
early American architecture; Urbana,
University of Illinois Press, 1968.
389 p. [12.50] 016.720/973 68-
24624
   Z5944.U5 R6 1968 MRR Alc.

ARCHITECTURE, COLONIAL--UNITED STATES.
Great Georgian houses of America.
New York, Printed by the Kalkhoff
Press, 1933-37. 2 v. (chiefly
illus., facsims., plans) 33-34801
   NA707 .G66 MRR Alc.

Kimball, Sidney Fiske, Domestic
architecture of the American colonies
and of the early Republic. New York,
Dover Publications [1966, c1922] xx,
314 p. 728/.0973 66-29154
   NA707 .K45 1966 MRR Alc.

Phipps, Frances, Colonial kitchens,
their furnishings, and their gardens,
New York, Hawthorn Books [1972]
xxii, 346 p. [$12.95] 643/.3/0974
78-158021
   TX653 .P48 1972 MRR Alc.

ARCHITECTURE, DOMESTIC--DESIGNS AND
PLANS.
Harmon, Allen Jackson, The guide to
home remodeling New York, Grosset &
Dunlap [1972] 255 p. [$7.95]
643/.7 72-185850
   TH4816 .H33 MRR Alc.

ARCHITECTURE, DOMESTIC--ENGLAND.
Osborne, Arthur Leslie. A dictionary
of English domestic architecture.
London, Country Life Limited [1954]
111 p. 728 54-29330
   NA31 .O8 MRR Alc.

ARCHITECTURE, DOMESTIC--UNITED STATES.
Album of American history. New York,
Scribner [1969- v.   973.022/2
74-91746
   E178.5 .A482 MRR Alc.

Carpenter, Ralph E. The fifty best
historic American houses, Colonial
and Federal, New York, Dutton, 1955.
112 p. 973 55-10288
   E159 .C3 MRR Alc.

Great Georgian houses of America.
New York, Printed by the Kalkhoff
Press, 1933-37. 2 v. (chiefly
illus., facsims., plans) 33-34801
   NA707 .G66 MRR Alc.

Kimball, Sidney Fiske, Domestic
architecture of the American colonies
and of the early Republic. New York,
Dover Publications [1966, c1922] xx,
314 p. 728/.0973 66-29154
   NA707 .K45 1966 MRR Alc.

Phipps, Frances, Colonial kitchens,
their furnishings, and their gardens,
New York, Hawthorn Books [1972]
xxii, 346 p. [$12.95] 643/.3/0974
78-158021
   TX653 .P48 1972 MRR Alc.

Williams, Henry Lionel. Great houses
of America, [1st ed.] New York,
Putnam [1966] 295 p. 728.80973 66-
19625
   E159 .W5 MRR Alc.

ARCHITECTURE, ENGLISH--DICTIONARIES.
Atkinson, Thomas Dinham, A glossary
of terms used in English
architecture. 7th ed. reprinted.
London, Methuen [1966] xxviii, 335
p. [10/6.] 720.942 66-73756
   NA31 .A85 1966 MRR Alc.

Osborne, Arthur Leslie. A dictionary
of English domestic architecture.
London, Country Life Limited [1954]
111 p. 728 54-29330
   NA31 .O8 MRR Alc.

ARCHITECTURE, GREEK--DICTIONARIES.
The New Century handbook of Greek art
and architecture. New York, Appleton-
Century-Crofts [1972] ix, 213 p.
709/.38 72-187738
   N5633 .N39 MRR Alc.

ARCHITECTURE, GREEK--HISTORY.
Lawrence, Arnold Walter, Greek
architecture. [Harmondsworth,
Middlesex] Penguin Books [1957]
xxxiv, 327 p. 722.8 722.6* 57-
59193
   NA270 .L36 MRR Alc.

ARCHITECTURE, GREEK--ATHENS.
Travlos, Ioannes N., Pictorial
dictionary of Ancient Athens London,
Thames and Hudson, 1971. xvi, 590 p.
[£25.00] 720/.9/49512 72-178898
   NA280 .T68 1971 MRR Alc.

ARCHITECTURE, INDIC.
Rowland, Benjamin, The art and
architecture of India: London,
Baltimore, Penguin Books [1953]
xvii, 288 p. 709.34 709.54* 53-
12998
   N7301 .R68 MRR Alc.

ARCHITECTURE, ITALIAN--HISTORY.
Wittkower, Rudolf. Art and
architecture in Italy, 1600 to 1750.
Baltimore, Penguin Books [1969,
c1958] xxiv, 462 p. [20.00]
709/.45 70-12230
   N6916 .W5 1969 MRR Alc.

ARCHITECTURE, LATIN AMERICAN.
United States. Library of Congress.
Prints and photographs division. The
colonial art of Latin America,
Washington, D.C., The Library of
Congress, 1945. xii, 43 p. 709.8
46-25650
   Z663.39 .C6 MRR Alc.

ARCHITECTURE, MEDIEVAL--GREAT BRITAIN--
HISTORY.
Webb, Geoffrey Fairbank,
Architecture in Britain: the Middle
Ages. [Harmondsworth, Middlesex]
Penguin Books [1956] xxi, 234 p.
720.942 57-927
   NA963 .W4 MRR Alc.

ARCHITECTURE, MODERN--19TH CENTURY.
Hitchcock, Henry Russell,
Architecture: nineteenth and
twentieth centuries. [Baltimore]
Penguin Books [1971] 682 p. [$8.95]
724 75-128606
   NA642 .H56 1971 MRR Alc.

ARCHITECTURE, MODERN--20TH CENTURY.
Forsee, Aylesa. Men of modern
architecture; Philadelphia, McCrae
Smith [1966] 223 p. 720.922 65-
24901
   NA40 .F6 MRR Alc.

Hitchcock, Henry Russell,
Architecture: nineteenth and
twentieth centuries. [Baltimore]
Penguin Books [1971] 682 p. [$8.95]
724 75-128606
   NA642 .H56 1971 MRR Alc.

ARCHITECTURE, MODERN--DICTIONARIES.
Encyclopedia of modern architecture,
New York, H. N. Abrams [1964] 336 p.
724.903 63-14758
   NA680 .E5 MRR Alc.

ARCHITECTURE, MODERN--FRANCE.
Blunt, Anthony, Sir, Art and
architecture in France, 1500 to 1700.
2nd ed. Harmondsworth, Penguin,
1970. xxii, 315 p. 193 plates.
[£7/10/-] 709/.44 70-521859
   N6844 .B6 1970 MRR Alc.

ARCHITECTURE, VICTORIAN--UNITED STATES.
Maass, John, The gingerbread age;
New York, Rinehart [1957] 212 p.
720.973 57-7370
   NA710 .M3 MRR Alc.

ARCHIVAL RESOURCES ON AFRICA--UNITED
STATES.
Duignan, Peter. Handbook of American
resources for African studies.
[Stanford, Calif.] Hoover Institution
on War, Revolution, and Peace,
Stanford University, 1967. xvii, 218
p. 016.916 66-20901
   Z3501 .D8 MRR Alc.

ARCHIVAL RESOURCES ON ASIA--GREAT
BRITAIN.
Wainwright, Mary Doreen. A guide to
Western manuscripts and documents in
the British Isles relating to South
and South East Asia. London, New
York, Oxford University Press, 1965.
xix, 532 p. 016.915 65-3147
   CD1048.A8 W3 MRR Alc.

ARCHIVAL RESOURCES ON WEST AFRICA--
FRANCE.
Carson, Patricia. Materials for West
African history in French archives.
London, Athlone P.; distributed by
Constable, 1968. viii, 170 p. [42/-
] 016.9166 68-99964
   CD2491.W4 C3 1968 MRR Alc.

ARCHIVES.
Langwell, William Herbert. The
conservation of books and documents.
London, I. Pitman [1957] 114 p.
025.7 57-3535
   Z701 .L3 MRR Alc.

Pine, Leslie Gilbert. The
genealogist's encyclopedia, New
York, Weybright and Talley [1969]
360 p. [12.50] 929.1/03 78-84622

   CS9 .P48 1969b MRR Alc.

Schellenberg, Theodore R., The
management of archives New York,
Columbia University Press, 1965.
xvi, 383 p. 025.171 65-14409
   CD950 .S29 MRR Alc.

Schellenberg, Theodore R., Modern
archives: [Chicago] University of
Chicago Press [1956] 247 p.
025.171 56-58525
   CD950 .S3 1956a MRR Alc.

ARCHIVES--BIBLIOGRAPHY.
International committee of historical
sciences. Archives committee.
Internationaler archivführer,
Zürich, Leipzig, Rascher [1936] 110
p., 1 l. 025.171 38-33255
   CD941 .I5 MRR Alc.

Oesterley, Hermann, Wegweiser durch
die literatur der urkundensammlungen,
Berlin, G. Reimer, 1885-86. 2 v.
03-7358
   CD995 .O3 MRR Alc.

United States. Library of Congress.
General Reference and Bibliography
Division. Safeguarding our cultural
heritage; a bibliography Washington,
1952. x, 117 p. 016.355232* 52-
60017
   Z663.28 .S3 MRR Alc.

ARCHIVES--DICTIONARIES.
Elsevier's lexicon of archive
terminology: Amsterdam, New York,
Elsevier Pub. Co., 1964. 83 p.
025.171014 64-56714
   CD945 .E4 MRR Alc.

Thompson, Edwin A. A glossary of
American historical and literary
manuscript terms. Washington, 1965.
ix, 183 l. 025 65-5693
   CD945 .T48 MRR Alc.

ARCHIVES--DIRECTORIES.
International committee of historical
sciences. Archives committee.
Internationaler archivführer,
Zürich, Leipzig, Rascher [1936] 110
p., 1 l. 025.171 38-33255
   CD941 .I5 MRR Alc.

ARCHIVES--AFRICA--BIBLIOGRAPHY.
United States. Library of Congress.
African Section. African libraries;
book production and activities:
Washington, General Reference and
Bibliography Division, Reference
Dept., Library of Congress, 1962.
vi, 64 p. 016.02096 62-64603
   Z663.285 .A73 MRR Alc.

ARCHIVES--AFRICA--DIRECTORIES.
Dadzie, E. W. Directory of archives,
libraries, and schools of
librarianship in Africa. [Paris]
UNESCO [1965] 112 p. 65-5420
   Z857.A1 D3 MRR Alc.

ARCHIVES--AUSTRIA--DIRECTORIES.
Handbuch der österreichischen
Wissenschaft. 1.- Bd.; 1947/48-
Wien, Österreichischer Bundesverlag
für Unterricht, Wissenschaft und
Kunst. 50-18117
   AS132 .J3 MRR Alc Latest edition

ARCHIVES--BELGIUM.
Carson, Patricia. Materials for West African history in the archives of Belgium and Holland. [London] University of London, 1962. viii, 86 p.   016.966   62-6793
   CD1000 .G8 no. 1 MRR Alc.

ARCHIVES--CANADA.
Burpee, Lawrence Johnstone, ed. Index and dictionary of Canadian history, Toronto, Morang & co., limited 1911. 2 p. l., vii-xvi, 446 p.   971   39-32912
   F1006 .E92 MRR Alc.

Society of American Archivists. Committee on State Archives. Guide to State and provincial archival agencies, 1961. Washington?] State Records Committee, Society of American Archivists, 1961. 87 l. 61-64344
   CD3021 .S63 MRR Alc.

ARCHIVES--CANADA--INVENTORIES, CALENDARS, ETC.
Union list of manuscripts in Canadian repositories. Ottawa [Queen's Printer] 1968. x, 734 p. [10.00] 091/.0971 74-410102
   CD3622 .U5 MRR Alc.

ARCHIVES--CONFEDERATE STATES OF AMERICA--INVENTORIES, CALENDARS, ETC.
Beers, Henry Putney, Guide to the archives of the Government of the Confederate States of America. Washington, National Archives, General Services Administration; [for sale by the Supt. of Docs., U.S. Govt. Print. Off.] 1968. ix, 536 p. [3.75] 016.97371/3 a 68-7603
   CD3047 .B4 MRR Alc.

ARCHIVES--ENGLAND.
Iredale, David. Enjoying archives: what they are, where to find them, how to use them. Newton Abbot, David and Charles, 1973. 264 p. [£3.85] 914.2   73-330085
   CD1041 .I73 MRR Alc.

ARCHIVES--ENGLAND--YORKSHIRE.
Society of Archivists. A brief guide to Yorkshire Record Offices; York, University of York (Borthwick Institute of Historical Research), 1968. [i], lv, 41 l. [5/-] 016.91427/4/03   70-455717
   CD1065.Y6 S6 MRR Alc.

ARCHIVES--EUROPE.
Thomas, Daniel H., ed. Guide to the diplomatic archives of Western Europe. Philadelphia, University of Pennsylvania Press [1959] xii, 389 p.   940.2   57-9123
   CD1001 .T4 MRR Alc.

ARCHIVES--EUROPE--INVENTORIES, CALENDARS, ETC.--BIBLIOGRAPHY.
United States. Library of Congress. Processing Dept. Unpublished bibliographical tools in certain archives and libraries of Europe; Washington, 1952. iv, 25 p.   016.01 52-6C036
   Z663.7 .U62 MRR Alc.

ARCHIVES--FRANCE--INVENTORIES, CALENDARS, ETC.
Carson, Patricia. Materials for West African history in French archives. London, Athlone P.; distributed by Constable, 1968. viii, 170 p. [42/-] 016.9166 68-99964
   CD2491.W4 C3 1968 MRR Alc.

ARCHIVES--FRANCE--PARIS.
Leland, Waldo Gifford, Guide to materials for American history in the libraries and archives of Paris, Washington, D.C., Carnegie institution of Washington, 1932- v.   016.97   32-15616
   CD1198.U6 L4 MRR Alc.

ARCHIVES--GERMANY.
United States. Dept. of State. Historical Office. A catalog of files and microfilms of the German Foreign Ministry archives, 1920-1945. Stanford, Calif., Hoover Institution, Stanford University, 1962- v.   016.943085   62-19204
   CD1261 .A65 MRR Alc.

ARCHIVES--GREAT BRITAIN.
Bond, Maurice Francis. Guide to the records of Parliament. London, H. M. Stationery Off., 1971. x, 352 p. [£3.25] 016.32842   72-176284
   CD1063 .B63 MRR Alc.

Galbraith, Vivian Hunter, An introduction to the use of the public records. [London] Oxford University Press [1952] 112 p. 025.171 57-38128
   CD1043 .G3 1952 MRR Alc.

Great Britain. Public Record Office. Guide to the contents of the Public Record Office. London, H.M. Stationery Off., 1963. 3 v. [27/6 ($4.95 U.S.) (v. 3)]   64-435
   CD1043 .A553 MRR Alc.

Hall, Hubert, A repertory of British archives, London, Offices of the Society, 1920- v.   22-19316
   CD1043 .H3 MRR Alc.

Hall, Hubert, Studies in English official historical documents, Cambridge, University press, 1908. xv, [1] p., 1 l., 404 p.   09-4071
   CD65 .H4 MRR Alc.

Marchant, Leslie Ronald. A guide to the archives and records of Protestant Christian missions Nedlands, W.A.: University of Western Australia Press [1966] xi, 134 p. [3.50]   016.2664 66-18025
   Z7817 .M3 MRR Alc.

ARCHIVES--GREAT BRITAIN--DIRECTORIES.
Joint Committee of the Historical Manuscripts Commission and the British Records Association. Record repositories in Great Britain; 3rd ed. London, H.M.S.O., 1968. xii, 53 p. [6/6] 026/.9142/03025 74-381933
   CD1041 .J6 1968 MRR Alc.

ARCHIVES--GREAT BRITAIN--INVENTORIES, CALENDARS, ETC.
Crick, Bernard R., ed. A guide to manuscripts relating to America in Great Britain and Ireland. [London] Published for the British Association for American Studies by the Oxford University Press, 1961. xxxvi, 667 p.   016.973   61-65029
   CD1048.U5 C7 MRR Alc.

Pugh, Ralph Bernard, The records of the Colonial and Dominions Offices London, H.M. Stationery Off., 1964. v, 118 p.   325.342 64-4582
   JV1011 .P8 MRR Alc.

Wainwright, Mary Doreen. A guide to Western manuscripts and documents in the British Isles relating to South and South East Asia. London, New York, Oxford University Press, 1965. xix, 532 p.   016.915   65-3147
   CD1048.A8 W3 MRR Alc.

ARCHIVES--ILLINOIS--INVENTORIES, CALENDARS, ETC.
Burton, William Lester, Descriptive bibliography of Civil War manuscripts in Illinois, [Evanston, Ill.] Published for the Civil War Centennial Commission of Illinois [Springfield] by Northwestern University Press [1966] xv, 393 p. 016.9737 65-24627
   Z1242 .B95 MRR Alc.

ARCHIVES--IRELAND--INVENTORIES, CALENDARS, ETC.
Crick, Bernard R., ed. A guide to manuscripts relating to America in Great Britain and Ireland. [London] Published for the British Association for American Studies by the Oxford University Press, 1961. xxxvi, 667 p.   016.973   61-65029
   CD1048.U5 C7 MRR Alc.

ARCHIVES--JAPAN--INVENTORIES, CALENDARS, ETC.
Uyehara, Cecil H., comp. Checklist of archives in the Japanese Ministry of Foreign Affairs, Tokyo, Japan, 1868-1945; Washington, Photoduplication Service, Library of Congress, 1954. xii, 262 p. 016.32752 53-60045
   Z663.96 .C5 MRR Alc.

ARCHIVES--LATIN AMERICA.
Hill, Roscoe R., The national archives of Latin America; Cambridge, Mass., Harvard university press, 1945. xx, 169 p.   980 a   46-1570
   CD3683 1945 .H5 MRR Alc.

ARCHIVES--NETHERLANDS.
Carson, Patricia. Materials for West African history in the archives of Belgium and Holland. [London] University of London, 1962. viii, 86 p.   016.966   62-6793
   CD1000 .G8 no. 1 MRR Alc.

ARCHIVES--RUSSIA.
Grimsted, Patricia Kennedy. Archives and manuscript repositories in the USSR, Moscow and Leningrad. Princeton, Princeton University Press [1972] xxx, 436 p. [$22.50] 947/.007 73-166375
   CD1711 .G7 MRR Alc.

ARCHIVES--RUSSIA--LENINGRAD--DIRECTORIES.
Grimsted, Patricia Kennedy. Archives and manuscript repositories in the USSR, Moscow and Leningrad. Princeton, Princeton University Press [1972] xxx, 436 p. [$22.50] 947/.007 73-166375
   CD1711 .G7 MRR Alc.

ARCHIVES--RUSSIA--MOSCOW--DIRECTORIES.
Grimsted, Patricia Kennedy. Archives and manuscript repositories in the USSR, Moscow and Leningrad. Princeton, Princeton University Press [1972] xxx, 436 p. [$22.50] 947/.007 73-166375
   CD1711 .G7 MRR Alc.

ARCHIVES--SCOTLAND.
Scotland. General registry office of births, deaths and marriages. A guide to the public records of Scotland deposited in H.M. General register house, Edinburgh; Edinburgh, H.M. General register house, 1905. xxvii, 233 p.   05-41700
   CD1072 .A3 MRR Alc.

ARCHIVES--SPAIN.
Robertson, James Alexander, List of documents in Spanish archives relating to the history of the United States, Washington, D.C, Carnegie institution of Washington, 1910. xv, 368 p.   10-16322
   CD1858.U6 R6 MRR Alc.

Spain. Archivo Histórico Nacional, Madrid. Guía del Archivo Histórico Nacional, [Madrid] 1958 [c1960] 235 p.   62-36977
   CD1853 .A52 MRR Alc.

ARCHIVES--SPAIN--BIBLIOGRAPHY.
Foulché-Delbosc, Raymond, Manuel de l'hispanisant. New York, G. P. Putnam's sons, 1920- v.   20-16867
   Z2681.A1 F7 MRR Alc.

Peña Cámara, José María de la. A list of Spanish residencias in the Archives of the Indies, 1516-1775; Washington, Library of Congress, Reference Dept., 1955. x, 109 p. 016.98 55-60017
   Z663.32.S7 MRR Alc.

ARCHIVES--SWEDEN.
Ottervik, Gosta, Libraries and archives in Sweden Stockholm, Swedish Institute, 1954. 216 p. 027.0485 55-14224
   Z827 .O8 MRR Alc.

ARCHIVES--UNITED STATES.
American Society of Genealogists. Genealogical research, methods and sources. Washington, 1960- v. 929/.1 60-819
   CS16 .A5 MRR Alc.

Kirkham, E. Kay. A survey of American church records; Salt Lake City, Deseret Book Co., 1959-60. 2 v.   929.3   59-65303
   CD3065 .K52 MRR Alc.

Society of American Archivists. Committee on State Archives. Guide to State and provincial archival agencies, 1961. Washington?] State Records Committee, Society of American Archivists, 1961. 87 l. 61-64344
   CD3021 .S63 MRR Alc.

United States. Dept. of state. The territorial papers of the United States. Washington, U.S. Govt. print. off., 1934- xv, 37 p. 973.082 35-26190
   E173 .U57 MRR Alc.

United States. Library of Congress. Legislative reference service. Documents illustrative of the formation of the union of the American states. Washington, Govt. print. off., 1927. x, 1115 p.   27-26258
   JK11 1927 MRR Alc.

United States. National Archives. Federal records of World War II. Washington [U.S. Govt. Print. Off.] 1950 [i.e. 1951] 2 v.   940.5373 a 51-9196
   D735.A1 U52 1950 MRR Alc.

United States. National Historical Publications Commission. A guide to archives and manuscripts in the United States. New Haven, Yale University Press, 1961. xxiii, 775 p.   025.171 61-6878
   CD3022 .A45 MRR Ref Desk.

Van Tyne, Claude Halstead, Guide to the archives of the government of the United States in Washington, 2d ed. rev. and enl. [Washington] Carnegie institution of Washington, 1907. xiii, 327 p.   08-9062
   CD3024 .V3 1907 MRR Alc.

ARCHIVES--UNITED STATES--BIBLIOGRAPHY.
United States. National Archives.
List of National Archives microfilm
publications. 1947-   Washington.
016.026873   a   61-9222
     CD3027 .W514 MRR Alc Latest
     edition

ARCHIVES--UNITED STATES--DIRECTORIES.
Directory of State and provincial
archivists and records
administrators. [n.p.] State Records
Committee, Society of American
Archivists. 61-64343
     CD3020 .D5 MRR Ref Desk Latest
     edition

Society of American Archivists.
Biographical directory. [n.p.] 58-
33262
     CD22 .S6A25 MRR Biog Latest
     edition

ARCHIVES--UNITED STATES--INVENTORIES,
CALENDARS, ETC.
Munden, Kenneth White. Guide to
Federal archives relating to the
Civil War, Washington, National
Archives, National Archives and
Records Service, General Services
Administration, 1962. x, 721 p.   a
62-9432
     CD3047 .M8 MRR Alc.

United States. National Archives.
Guide to the records in the National
Archives. Washington, U.S. Govt.
Print. Off., 1948. xvi, 684 p.   353
a 49-10088
     CD3023 .A46 1948 MRR Ref Desk.

United States. National Archives.
List of American-flag merchant
vessels that received certificates of
enrollment or registry at the Port of
New York, 1789-1867 Washington,
1968. 2 v. (vii, 804 p.)
387.2/097471 a 68-7106
     HE565.U5A43 MRR Alc.

United States. National Archives.
Population schedules, 1800-1870;
Washington, 1951. v, 217 p.
016.312 a 51-9540
     CD3039 .A53 MRR Alc.

United States. National Archives.
Preliminary inventory of the records
of the United States Senate.
Washington, 1950. x, 284 p.
016.32875 a 50-9249
     CD3026 .A32 no. 23 MRR Alc.

ARCHIVES--UNITED STATES--STATES.
Posner, Ernst. American State
archives. Chicago, University of
Chicago Press [1964] xiv, 397 p.
350 64-23425
     CD3050 .P67 MRR Alc.

ARCHIVES--WALES.
Iredale, David. Enjoying archives:
what they are, where to find them,
how to use them. Newton Abbot, David
and Charles, 1973. 264 p. [£3.95]
914.2 73-330885
     CD1041 .I73 MRR Alc.

ARCHIVES--WEST INDIES, BRITISH.
Bell, Herbert Clifford Francis,
Guide to British West Indian archive
materials, Washington, D.C.,
Carnegie institution of Washington,
1926. ix, 435 p.   26-10272
     CD1048.U5 B4 MRR Alc.

ARCHIVISTS--DIRECTORIES.
Directory of State and provincial
archivists and records
administrators. [n.p.] State Records
Committee, Society of American
Archivists. 61-64343
     CD3020 .D5 MRR Ref Desk Latest
     . edition

Society of American Archivists.
Biographical directory. [n.p.] 58-
33262
     CD22 .S6A25 MRR Biog Latest
     edition

ARCTIC REGIONS--BIBLIOGRAPHY.
Arctic bibliography. v.1- 1953-
Montreal [etc.] McGill-Queen's
University Press [etc.] 53-61783
     Z6005.P7 A72 Sci RR Full set / MRR
     Alc Full set

ARCTIC REGIONS--DICTIONARIES AND
ENCYCLOPEDIAS.
United States. Arctic, Desert and
Tropic Information Center. Glossary
of arctic and subarctic terms.
Maxwell Air Force Base, Ala., 1955.
viii, 90 p.   919.8 56-60228
     GB5 .U52 no. A-105 MRR Alc.

AREA STUDIES--BIBLIOGRAPHY.
Cruger, Doris M. A list of American
doctoral dissertations on Africa,
Ann Arbor, Mich., Xerox, University
Microfilms Library Services, 1967.
36 p.   016.378/24 67-5644
     Z5055.U49 C75 MRR Alc.

Foreign affairs bibliography;
1919/32-1952/62. New York, Published
for the Council on Foreign Relations
by R. R. Bowker [etc.] 016.327
[016.9] 33-7094
     Z6463 .F73 MRR Alc Full set

Halstead, John P. Modern European
imperialism; Boston, G. K. Hall,
1974. 2 v. 016.90908 73-19511
     Z6204 .H35 MRR Alc.

International Labor Office. Library.
International labour documentation:
cumulative edition. Boston, Mass.,
G. K. Hall. 72-625702
     H91 .I56 MRR Alc Full set

Krikler, Bernard. A reader's guide
to contemporary history. London,
Weidenfeld & Nicolson [1972] 259 p.
[£3.50] 016.90982 73-150568
     Z6204 .K7 MRR Alc.

Population index. v. 1-   Jan. 20,
1935- [Princeton, N.J., etc.]
016.312 39-10247
     Z7164.D3 P83 MRR Alc Partial set

AREA STUDIES--BIBLIOGRAPHY--CATALOGS.
Foreign Relations Library. Catalog
of the Foreign Relations Library.
Boston, G. K. Hall, 1969. 9 v.
016.327 75-6133
     Z6209 .F656 MRR Alc (Dk 33)

Great Britain. Foreign Office.
Library. Catalogue of the Foreign
Office Library, 1926-1968. Boston,
G. K. Hall, 1972. 8 v. 019/.1 73-
160726
     Z921 .G682 1972 MRR Alc (Dk 33)

Institut für Zeitgeschichte, Munich.
Bibliothek. Landerkatalog. Boston,
G. K. Hall, 1967. 2 v. 016.90908
72-191951
     Z6204 .I37 MRR Alc (Dk 33)

Kiel. Universität. Institut für
Weltwirtschaft. Bibliothek.
Personenkatalog. Boston, G. K. Hall,
1966. 30 v.   72-213362
     Z7164.E2 K55 MRR Alc. (Dk 33)

Kiel. Universität. Institut für
Weltwirtschaft. Bibliothek.
Regionenkatalog. Boston, G. K. Hall,
1967. 52 v. 017/.5 67-9425
     Z929 .K52 1967 MRR Alc. (Dk 33).

A London bibliography of the social
sciences. v. 1- 1929- London,
Mansell Information/Publishing Ltd.
[etc.] 016.3 31-9970
     Z7161 .L84 MRR Alc Full set

Princeton University. Office of
Population Research. Population
index bibliography, Boston, G. K.
Hall, 1971. 5 v. 016.312 79-30213

     Z7164.D3 P852 MRR Alc (Dk 33)

Royal Commonwealth Society. Library.
Subject catalogue of the Royal
Commonwealth Society, London.
Boston, Mass., G. K. Hall, 1971. 7
v.   017.1 70-180198
     Z7164.C7 R83 MRR Alc (Dk 33)

Stanford University. Hoover
Institution on War, Revolution, and
Peace. The library catalogs of the
Hoover Institution on War,
Revolution, and Peace, Stanford
University; Boston, G. K. Hall, 1969-
v.   017/.5 77-17709
     Z881.S785 1969e MRR Alc (Dk 33)

Washington, D.C. Joint Library of the
International Monetary Fund and the
International Bank for Reconstruction
and Development. Economics and
finance; index to periodical
articles, 1947-1971, Boston, G. K.
Hall, 1972. 4 v. 016.33 73-156075

     Z7164.E2 W34 MRR Alc (dk 33)

AREA STUDIES--DIRECTORIES.
International Council for Educational
Development. Area studies on U.S.
campuses: a directory. New York,
1971. vi, 71 p.   378.73 71-158546

     D16.25 .I55 MRR Ref Desk.

United States. Dept. of State. Office
of External Research. University
centers of foreign affairs research:
a selective directory. [Washington,
Dept. of State; for sale by the Supt.
of Docs., U.S. Govt. Print. Off.]
1968. xvi, 139 p.   327/.025/73 68-
60080
     JX1293.U6 A54 MRR Alc.

ARGENTINE LITERATURE--HISTORY AND
CRITICISM--BIBLIOGRAPHY.
Foster, David William. Research
guide to Argentine literature,
Metuchen, N.J., Scarecrow Press,
1970. 146 p. 016.86 70-9731
     Z1621 .F66 MRR Alc.

ARGENTINE REPUBLIC--BIOGRAPHY.
Quien es quien en la Argentina; año
1939- Buenos Aires, G. Kraft, ltda.
920.082 39-30109
     F2805 .Q55 MRR Biog Latest edition

ARGENTINE REPUBLIC--BIOGRAPHY--
DICTIONARIES.
Diccionario histórico argentino,
Buenos Aires, Ediciones Históricas
Argentinas [1953-54] 6 v.   54-24357
     F2804 .D5 MRR Alc.

ARGENTINE REPUBLIC--DICTIONARIES AND
ENCYCLOPEDIAS.
Gran enciclopedia argentina; Buenos
Aires, Ediar, 1956-64. 9 v.   56-
57422
     F2804 .G82 MRR Alc.

ARGENTINE REPUBLIC--GAZETTEERS.
United States. Office of Geography.
Argentina; Washington, 1968. viii,
699 p.   918.2/003 68-62101
     F2804 .U5 MRR Alc.

ARGENTINE REPUBLIC--HISTORY.
Levene, Ricardo, A history of
Argentina, Chapel Hill, The
University of North Carolina press,
1937. xii p., 2 l., 565 p.   982 37-
34878
     F2831 .L653 MRR Alc.

Scobie, James R., Argentina: a city
and a nation. New York, Oxford
University Press, 1964. vi, 294 p.
982 64-11238
     F2808 .S42 MRR Alc.

ARGENTINE REPUBLIC--HISTORY--
DICTIONARIES.
Diccionario histórico argentino,
Buenos Aires, Ediciones Históricas
Argentinas [1953-54] 6 v.   54-24357

     F2804 .D5 MRR Alc.

ARGONAUTS.
Valerius Flaccus, C. Valerius
Flaccus, Cambridge, Mass., Harvard
university press; London, W.
Heinemann, ltd., 1934. xxi, 458 p.,
1 l. 873.3 35-1932
     PA6156.V25 1934 MRR Alc.

ARGUMENTATION
see Debates and debating

ARID REGIONS.
see also Deserts

ARISTOPHANES--CONCORDANCES.
Dunbar, Henry, A complete
concordance to the comedies and
fragments of Aristophanes. New ed.
completely rev. and enl. Hildesheim,
New York, G. Olms, 1973. 372 p.   74-
313146
     PA3888.Z8 D8 1973 MRR Alc.

Todd, Otis Johnson. Index
Aristophaneus, Cantabrigiae, Ex
Universitatis Harvardianae prelis,
1932. ix, 275 p.   32-3739
     PA3888.Z8T6 MRR Alc.

ARISTOTELES--DICTIONARIES, INDEXES, ETC.
Aristoteles. Aristotle dictionary.
New York, Philosophical Library
[1962] 524 p.   185 61-10609
     PA3926.Z8 K53 1962 MRR Alc.

Organ, Troy Wilson. An index to
Aristotle in English translation.
Princeton, Princeton Univ. Press,
1949. vi, 181 p.   888.5 49-7450
     B401 .O7 MRR Alc.

ARITHMETIC.
see also Metric system

see also Multiplication

ARIZONA.
Writers' Program. Arizona. Arizona,
the Grand Canyon State; a State
guide. New York, Hastings House
[1956] xxv, 532 p.   917.91 56-446

     F811 .W87 1956 MRR Ref Desk.

ARIZONA--BIBLIOGRAPHY.
Historical records survey. ... A
check list of Arizona imprints, 1860-
1890. Chicago, The Historical
records survey, 1938. v, 81 p.
015.791 39-4907
     Z1215 .H67 no. 3 MRR Alc.

ARIZONA--DESCRIPTION AND TRAVEL--1951- -
-GUIDE-BOOKS.
All about Arizona. [1st]- ed.;
1957- Greenlawn, N.Y., Harian
Publications. 917.91 60-2020
     F809.3 .A55 MRR Alc Latest edition

Mobil travel guide: California and
the west. 1969- [Bloomfield, N.J.]
Simon and Schuster. 917.94/04/5 72-
623503
     F859.3 .M6 MRR Alc Latest edition

ARIZONA--DESCRIPTION AND TRAVEL--GUIDE-
BOOKS.
Writers' Program. Arizona. Arizona,
the Grand Canyon State; a State
guide. New York, Hastings House
[1956] xxv, 532 p. 917.91 56-446

F811 .W87 1956 MRR Ref Desk.

ARIZONA--MANUFACTURES--DIRECTORIES.
Arizona directory of manufacturers.
Phoenix. 55-36441
T12 .A72 Sci RR Latest edition /
MRR Alc Latest edition

ARIZONA--POLITICS AND GOVERNMENT.
Mason, Bruce Bonner. Constitutional
government in Arizona 2d ed.
[Tempe] Bureau of Government
Research, Arizona State University,
1965. 223 p. 320.9791 66-63732
JK8225 1965 .M3 MRR Alc.

ARIZONA--POLITICS AND GOVERNMENT--1951-
Arizona political almanac. 1956-
Phoenix, Sims Print. Co. 57-33262
JK8230 .A85 MRR Alc Latest edition

ARIZONA--REGISTERS.
Arizona political almanac. 1956-
Phoenix, Sims Print. Co. 57-33262
JK8230 .A85 MRR Alc Latest edition

League of Arizona Cities and Towns.
Directory of Arizona city and town
officials. Phoenix. 64-37719
JS451.A63 L4 MRR Alc Latest
edition

ARKANSAS.
Writers' program. Arkansas.
Arkansas: a guide to the state, New
York, Hastings house, 1941. xxvii,
447 p. 917.67 41-52931
F411 .W8 MRR Ref Desk.

ARKANSAS--BIBLIOGRAPHY.
Historical records survey. Arkansas.
A check list of Arkansas imprints,
1821-1876. Little Rock, Ark., The
Arkansas Historical records survey,
1942. 6 p. l., 139 numb. l., 2 l.
015.767 42-17366
Z1215 .H67 no. 39 MRR Alc.

ARKANSAS--BIOGRAPHY.
Who is who in Arkansas. v. 1- 1959-
Little Rock, Allard House [etc.]
920.0767 60-27733
F410 .W47 MRR Biog Latest edition

ARKANSAS--DESCRIPTION AND TRAVEL--GUIDE-
BOOKS.
Writers' program. Arkansas.
Arkansas: a guide to the state, New
York, Hastings house, 1941. xxvii,
447 p. 917.67 41-52931
F411 .W8 MRR Ref Desk.

ARKANSAS--DIRECTORIES.
Arkansas almanac, the encyclopedia of
Arkansas. 1954/55- Little Rock,
Arkansas Almanac Co. 54-2919
F406 .A55 MRR Alc Latest edition

ARKANSAS--IMPRINTS.
Historical records survey. Arkansas.
A check list of Arkansas imprints,
1821-1876. Little Rock, Ark., The
Arkansas Historical records survey,
1942. 6 p. l., 139 numb. l., 2 l.
015.767 42-17366
Z1215 .H67 no. 39 MRR Alc.

ARKANSAS--INDUSTRIES--DIRECTORIES.
Directory of Arkansas industries.
[Little Rock] 46-27479
"First ... published in 1945."
T12 .A73 Sci RR* Latest edition /
MRR Alc Latest edition

ARKANSAS--POLITICS AND GOVERNMENT.
Arkansas. Office of Secretary of
State. Historical report of the
secretary of state. 1958- [Little
Rock?] 320.9/767/05 68-64343
J87.A84a MRR Alc Latest edition

ARKANSAS--REGISTERS.
Arkansas. Office of Secretary of
State. Historical report of the
secretary of state. 1958- [Little
Rock?] 320.9/767/05 68-64343
J87.A84a MRR Alc Latest edition

Arkansas almanac, the encyclopedia of
Arkansas. 1954/55- Little Rock,
Arkansas Almanac Co. 54-2919
F406 .A55 MRR Alc Latest edition

ARLINGTON, VA. NATIONAL CEMETERY.
Hinkel, John Vincent, Arlington:
monument to heroes. New and enl. ed.
Englewood Cliffs, N.J., Prentice-
Hall [1970] x, 187 p. [5.95]
975.5/285 79-89542
F234.A7 H6 1970 MRR Alc.

ARMAMENTS.
Dupuy, Trevor Nevitt, The almanac of
world military power 2d ed. New
York, R. R. Bowker Co., 1972. xii,
373 p. 355.03/32/09047 72-2636
UA15 .D9 1972 MRR Ref Desk.

The Reference handbook of the armed
forces of the world. 1966- New York
[etc.] Praeger, [etc.] 66-17547
UA15 .R43 MRR Alc Latest edition

ARMAMENTS--YEARBOOKS.
International Institute for Peace and
Conflict Research. S I P R I
yearbook of world armaments and
disarmaments. 1968/69- New York,
Humanities Press. 341.6/7/05 76-
12210
UA10 .I55 MRR Alc Latest edition

ARMED FORCES.
Dupuy, Trevor Nevitt, The almanac of
world military power 2d ed. New
York, R. R. Bowker Co., 1972. xii,
373 p. 355.03/32/09047 72-2636
UA15 .D9 1972 MRR Ref Desk.

The Reference handbook of the armed
forces of the world. 1966- New York
[etc.] Praeger, [etc.] 66-17547
UA15 .R43 MRR Alc Latest edition

ARMED FORCES--ABBREVIATIONS.
Jacobs, Horace. Missile and space
projects guide New York, Plenum
Press, 1962. x, 235 p. 629.403 62-
13471
TL788 .J3 MRR Alc.

ARMED FORCES--INSIGNIA.
Bunkley, Joel William, Military and
naval recognition book; 2d ed. New
York, D. Van Nostrand company, inc.,
1942. xiv, 309 p. incl. col. front.,
illus. (part col.) 355.14 42-24855

UC530 .B8 1942a MRR Alc.

ARMED FORCES--PERIODICALS.
The Military balance. London,
International Institute for Strategic
Studies. 355.03/32/05 79-617319
UA15 .L652 MRR Ref Desk Latest
edition

ARMED FORCES--STATISTICS.
United States. Arms Control and
Disarmament Agency. Bureau of
Economic Affairs. World military
expenditures. 1970- [Washington,
For sale by the Supt. of Docs., U.S.
Govt. Print. Off.] 338.4/7/355005
70-649143
UA17 .U42 MRR Ref Desk Latest
edition

ARMED FORCES--YEARBOOKS.
Brassey's annual. 1st- year; 1886-
New York [etc.] Praeger [etc.]
359.058 12-30905
V10 .N3 MRR Alc Latest edition

ARMENIA--CIVILIZATION.
Der Nersessian, Sirarple, The
Armenians. London, Thames & Hudson,
1969. 216 p. [42/-] 913.39/55/03
75-467823
DS171 .D43 1969 MRR Alc.

ARMENIA--HISTORY.
Der Nersessian, Sirarple, The
Armenians. London, Thames & Hudson,
1969. 216 p. [42/-] 913.39/55/03
75-467823
DS171 .D43 1969 MRR Alc.

ARMENIA--HISTORY--1917-1921.
Hovannisian, Richard G. The Republic
of Armenia Berkeley, University of
California Press, 1971- v.
[$15.00 (v. 1)] 956.6/2 72-129613

DS195.5 .H56 MRR Alc.

ARMENIAN LANGUAGE--DICTIONARIES--
ENGLISH.
Kouyoumdjian, Mesrob G. A
comprehensive dictionary, Armenian-
English. Cairo, Sahag-Mesrob Press
[pref. 1950] 1150 p. 491.5432 53-
24821
PK8091 .K6 MRR Alc.

ARMIES.
see also Military service, Compulsory

Coggins, Jack. The fighting man;
[1st ed.] Garden City, N.Y.,
Doubleday [1966] xii, 372 p.
355.0009 66-20936
U750 .C6 MRR Alc.

Melegari, Vezio. The world's great
regiments. 1st American ed. New
York] Putnam [1969, c1968] 256 p.
[25.00] 355.3/5/09 69-15079
UA15 .M4413 1969b MRR Alc.

ARMIES--STATISTICS.
The Military balance. London,
International Institute for Strategic
Studies. 355.03/32/05 79-617319
UA15 .L652 MRR Ref Desk Latest
edition

ARMIES, COST OF--PERIODICALS.
United States. Arms Control and
Disarmament Agency. Bureau of
Economic Affairs. World military
expenditures. 1970- [Washington,
For sale by the Supt. of Docs., U.S.
Govt. Print. Off.] 338.4/7/355005
70-649143
UA17 .U42 MRR Ref Desk Latest
edition

ARMORED VEHICLES, MILITARY.
Crow, Duncan. American AFVs of World
War II, Windsor (Corburg House,
Sheet St., Windsor, Berks.), Profile
Publications Ltd., 1972. viii, 240,
63 p. [£6.00] 623.74/75/0973 73-
167485
UG446.5 .A694 Vol. 4 MRR Alc.

Crow, Duncan. British A.F.Vs, 1919-
40, Windsor, Profile Publications,
1970. viii, 176 p. [£3.75]
358/.18/0942 70-859341
UG446.5 .A694 vol. 2 MRR Alc.

Foss, Christopher F. Armoured
fighting vehicles of the world New
York, Scribner [1971] 192 p.
[$5.95] 623.74/75 73-162727
UG446.5 .F64 MRR Alc.

ARMORED VEHICLES, MILITARY--ADDRESSES,
ESSAYS, LECTURES.
Crow, Duncan. AFV's of World War
One, Windsor, Eng., Profile
Publications [1970] viii, 164 p.
358/.18/08 s 358/.18/09041 72-181764
UG446.5 .A694 vol. 1 MRR Alc.

ARMORED VESSELS.
see also Warships

ARMORERS.
Gardner, Robert Edward. Five
centuries of gunsmiths, swordsmiths
and armourers, 1400-1900. [Columbus,
Ohio, W. F. Heer] 1948. 244 p. 399
48-15654
U800 .G3 MRR Alc.

ARMORERS' MARKS.
Gyngell, Dudley Stuart Hawtrey.
Armourers marks, [1st ed.] London,
Thorsons Publishers [1959] xi, 131
p. 739.7 59-41997
NK6697 .G9 MRR Alc.

ARMS, COATS OF
see Heraldry

ARMS AND ARMOR.
see also Firearms

Neumann, George C. The history of
weapons of the American Revolution,
[1st ed.] New York, Harper & Row
[1967] viii, 373 p. 623.4/4 67-
20829
U815 .N4 MRR Alc.

ARMS AND ARMOR--COLLECTORS AND
COLLECTING.
Peterson, Harold Leslie, Arms and
armor in colonial America, 1526-1783.
Harrisburg, Pa., Stackpole Co.
[1956] 350 p. 399 56-11273
U818 .P4 MRR Alc.

ARMS AND ARMOR--DICTIONARIES.
Luttwak, Edward. A dictionary of
modern war. [1st U.S. ed.] New
York, Harper & Row [1971] 224 p.
[$7.95] 355/.003 77-159574
U24 .L93 1971 MRR Alc.

Puttock, A. G. A dictionary of
heraldry and related subjects,
Baltimore, Genealogical Pub. Co.,
1970. 256 p. [$10.00] 929.6/03
76-137421
CR13 .P8 1970b MRR Alc.

Quick, John, Dictionary of weapons
and military terms. New York, McGraw-
Hill [1973] xii, 515 p. 623/.03
73-8757
U24 .Q5 MRR Alc.

ARMS AND ARMOR--EXHIBITIONS.
Association of Museums of Arms and
Military History. Repertory of
museums of arms and military history.
Copenhagen, 1960. 158 p. 355.074
61-24144
U13.A1 A7 MRR Alc.

ARMS AND ARMOR--HISTORY.
Gardner, Robert Edward. Five
centuries of gunsmiths, swordsmiths
and armourers, 1400-1900. [Columbus,
Ohio, W. F. Heer] 1948. 244 p. 399
48-15654
U800 .G3 MRR Alc.

ARMS AND ARMOR, AMERICAN.
International Association of Chiefs
of Police. Police Weapons Center.
The Police Weapons Center data
service. Gaithersburg, Md.:
International Association of Chiefs
of Police, Research Services Section
[1972] 1 v. (loose leaf) [$30.00
per year.] 363.2/028 72-86295
HV7936.E7 I58 MRR Alc.

ARMS AND ARMOR, AMERICAN. (Cont.)
Peterson, Harold Leslie, Arms and armor in colonial America, 1526-1783. Harrisburg, Pa., Stackpole Co. [1956] 350 p. 399 56-11273
U818 .P4 MRR Alc.

ARMY
see Military art and science

ARNOLD, BENEDICT, 1741-1801.
Van Doren, Carl Clinton, Secret history of the American revolution. New York, The Viking press, 1941. 3 p. l., [v]-xiv p., 2 l., [3]-534 p. 41-24478
E277 .V23 1941 MRR Alc.

ARNOLD, HENRY HARLEY, 1886-1950.
United States. Library of Congress. The H. H. Arnold collection Washington, U.S. Govt. Print. Off., 1952] 11 p. 012 016.3584 52-60060

Z663.34 .H15 MRR Alc.

ARNOLD, MATTHEW, 1822-1888--CONCORDANCES.
Parrish, Stephen Maxfield. A concordance to the poems of Matthew Arnold. Ithaca, N.Y., Cornell University Press [1959] xxi, 965 p. 821.8 59-4899
PR4023.A3 P3 MRR Alc.

ART.
see also Archaeology

see also Architecture

see also Costume

see also Graphic arts

see also Painting

see also Performing arts

see also Primitivism in art

see also Sculpture

American Library Color Slide Company, inc., New York. The American Library compendium and index of world art; New York, American Archives of World Art [c1961] xv, 465 p. 016.704973 61-18783
N4040 .A45 MRR Alc.

ART--ABSTRACTS.
Gettens, Rutherford John, comp. Abstracts of technical studies in art and archaeology, 1943-1952. Washington, 1955. viii, 408 p. 016.7 55-61312
N7428 .G44 MRR Alc.

ART--ANALYSIS, INTERPRETATION, APPRECIATION
see Aesthetics

ART--BIBLIOGRAPHY.
Art index. v. 1- Jan. 1929/Sept. 1932- New York, H. W. Wilson. 016.7 31-7513
Z5937 .A78 MRR Circ Full set

Borroni, Fabia. "Il Cicognara," Firenze, Sansoni, 1954- v. 55-18980
Z2357 .B6 MRR Alc.

Carrick, Neville. How to find out about the arts; [1st ed.] Oxford, New York, Pergamon Press [1965] xi, 164 p. 016.7 65-19834
Z5931 .C3 1965 MRR Alc.

Chamberlin, Mary W. Guide to art reference books. Chicago, American Library Association, 1959. xiv, 418 p. 016.7 59-10457
Z5931 .C45 MRR Alc.

Clapp, Jane. Museum publications. New York, Scarecrow Press, 1962. 2 v. 016.0697 62-10120
Z5051 .C5 MRR Alc.

Dove, Jack. Fine arts. London, Bingley, 1966. 88 p. [16/-] 016.7 66-76603
Z5931 .D6 MRR Alc.

Istituto nazionale di archeologia e storia dell'arte, Rome. Biblioteca. Annuario bibliografico di storia dell'arte. anno 1- 1952- Modena. 55-58434
Z5931 .I73 MRR Alc Full set

Lucas, Edna Louise, Art books; Greenwich, Conn., New York Graphic Society [1968] 245 p. 016.7 68-12364
Z5931 .L92 MRR Alc.

Lucas, Edna Louise, The Harvard list of books on art. Cambridge, Harvard University Press, 1952. vi, 163 p. 016.7 52-5400
Z5931 .L93 1952 MRR Alc.

Rogers, A. Robert, The humanities; Littleton, Colo., Libraries Unlimited, 1974. 400 p. [$9.50] 016.0013 74-78393
Z5579 .R63 MRR Alc.

ART--BIBLIOGRAPHY--CATALOGS.
Columbia University. Libraries. Avery Architectural Library. Catalog of the Avery Memorial Architectural Library of Columbia University. Boston, Microphotography Co., 1958. 6 v. (11,534 p.) 016.72 58-4091
Z5945 .C652 MRR Alc (Dk 33).

ART--CATALOGS.
American Library Color Slide Company, inc., New York. The American Library compendium and index of world art; New York, American Archives of World Art [c1961] xv, 465 p. 016.704973 61-18783
N4040 .A45 MRR Alc.

Art-price annual. Munich [etc.] Kunst und Technik Verlag [etc.] 55-37582
N8670 .A68 MRR Alc Partial set

Clapp, Jane. Art reproductions. New York, Scarecrow Press, 1961. 350 p. 708.1 61-8714
N4000 .C5 MRR Ref Desk.

The Connoisseur art sales annual. London, The Connoisseur. 702/.9 74-24947
Began in 1969.
N8640 .C6 MRR Alc Full set

Janson, Horst Woldemar, ed. Key monuments of the history of art; Text ed. Englewood Cliffs, N.J., Prentice-Hall [1959] 1068 p. 709 59-6934
N5301 .J3 MRR Alc.

ART--CATALOGS--YEARBOOKS.
International auction records. v. [1]- 1967- [London, etc.] Editions E. M.-Publisol] 700/.29 78-2167
N8640 .I5 MRR Alc Full set

ART--CENSORSHIP--CHRONOLOGY.
Clapp, Jane. Art censorship; Metuchen, N.J., Scarecrow Press, 1972. 582 p. 700 76-172789
N8740 .C55 MRR Alc.

ART--COLLECTORS AND COLLECTING.
Drepperd, Carl William, A dictionary of American antiques. [1st ed.] Garden City, N.Y., Doubleday, 1952. vii, 404 p. 708.051 52-11623
N33 .D74 MRR Alc.

Hudson, William Norman. Antiques at auction South Brunswick, A. S. Barnes [1972] 403 p. [$20.00] 338.4/3745/10973 76-111646
N6507 .H82 MRR Alc.

Reitlinger, Gerald, The economics of taste. London, Barrie and Rockliff [1961-70] 3 v. [50/- (v. 1) varies] 069/.51 62-4300
N8675 .R44 MRR Alc.

ART--COLLECTORS AND COLLECTING--DIRECTORIES.
International directory of arts. [1st]- ed.; 1952/53- Berlin, Deutsche Zentraldruckerei AG [etc.] 55-28737
N50 .I6 MRR Alc Latest edition

ART--DICTIONARIES.
Adeline, Jules, The Adeline art dictionary, New York, F. Ungar Pub. Co. [1966] 459 p. 703 65-21727
N33 .A223 1966 MRR Alc.

Barron, John N. The language of painting; Cleveland, World Pub. Co. [1967] 207 p. 750/.3 67-21388
ND30 .B32 MRR Alc.

Benét, William Rose, ed. The reader's encyclopedia. 2d ed. New York, Crowell [1965] viii, 1118 p. 803 65-12510
PN41 .B4 1965 MRR Ref Desk.

Benét, William Rose, ed. The reader's encyclopedia. New York, T. Y. Crowell Co. [1955] vii, 1270 p. 803 55-10502
PN41 .B4 1955 MRR Alc.

The Book of art; New York, Grolier [c1965] 10 v. 709.4 65-10350
N31 .B6 MRR Alc.

Dictionary of modern painting. 3d ed., rev. and enl.] New York, Tudor Pub. Co. [1964] 416 p. 759.05 65-1420
ND30 .D515 1964 MRR Alc.

Drepperd, Carl William, A dictionary of American antiques. [1st ed.] Garden City, N.Y., Doubleday, 1952. vii, 404 p. 708.051 52-11623
N33 .D74 MRR Alc.

Encyclopaedia of the arts. New York, Meredith Press [1966] 966 p. 703 66-23883
N31 .E54 MRR Alc.

Encyclopedia of painting; New York, Crown Publishers, 1955. 511 p. 750.3 55-12456
ND30 .E5 MRR Alc.

Encyclopedia of world art. New York, McGraw-Hill [1959- v. 703 59-13433
N31 .E4833 MRR Alc.

Fairholt, Frederick William, A dictionary of terms in art. Detroit, Gale Research Co., 1969. vi, 474 p. 703 68-30630
N33 .F2 1969 MRR Alc.

Fernau, Joachim. The Praeger encyclopedia of old masters. New York, F. A. Praeger [1959] 334 p. 759.003 59-7456
ND30 .F413 MRR Alc.

Haggar, Reginald George, A dictionary of art terms; [1st ed.] New York, Hawthorn Books [1962] 416 p. 703 62-8288
N33 .H25 1962 MRR Alc.

Lemke, Antje B. Museum companion; [New York] Hippocrene [1974] vii, 211 p. [$6.95] 703 73-76577
N33 .L38 1974 MRR Alc.

Mayer, Ralph, A dictionary of art terms and techniques. New York, Crowell [1969] 447 p. [8.95] 703 69-15414
N33 .M36 MRR Alc.

McGraw-Hill dictionary of art. New York, McGraw-Hill [1969] 5 v. 703 68-26314
N33 .M23 MRR Alc.

Mollett, John William. An illustrated dictionary of art and archaeology, New York, American Archives of World Art [1966] 350 p. 703 65-29110
N33 .M6 1966 MRR Alc.

Murray, Peter. Dictionary of art and artists New York, Praeger [1966] 464 p. 703 65-20073
N31 .M8 1966 MRR Alc.

New international illustrated encyclopedia of art. New York, Greystone Press [1967- v. 703 67-24201
N31 .N4 MRR Alc.

The new standard encyclopedia of art; De luxe ed. New York, Garden City publishing co., inc. [1939] 2 v. in 1. 703 39-16979
N31 .H3 1939 MRR Alc.

The Oxford companion to art; Oxford, Clarendon P., 1970. xii, 1277 p., 2 plates. [6/-/-] 703 71-526168
N33 .O9 MRR Alc.

Praeger encyclopedia of art. New York, Praeger Publishers [1971] 5 v. (2139 p.) 703 75-122093
N33 .P68 MRR Alc.

The Praeger picture encyclopedia of art; New York, F. A. Praeger [1958] 584 p. 703 58-11404
N5300 .P773 MRR Alc.

Quick, John, Artists' and illustrators' encyclopedia. New York, McGraw-Hill [1969] xi, 273 p. 703 69-12774
N33 .Q5 MRR Alc.

Runes, Dagobert David, ed. Encyclopedia of the arts, New York, Philosophical library [1946] 6 p. l., 1064 p. 703 46-3185
N31 .R8 MRR Alc.

Savage, George, The art and antique restorers' handbook; [Rev. ed.] New York, Praeger [1967] 142 p. 708/.04/03 67-17963
N8560 .S38 1967a MRR Alc.

A Visual dictionary of art. Greenwich, Conn., New York Graphic Society [1974] 640 p. [$30.00] 703 73-76181
N33 .V56 1974 MRR Biog.

Waters, Clara (Erskine) Clement, A handbook of legendary and mythological art. [14th impression] Boston, New York, Houghton, Mifflin and company [189-?] xii, 575 p. 04-11646
N7760 .W33 MRR Alc.

Wolf, Martin L. Dictionary of painting, New York, Philosophical Library [1958] viii, 335 p. 750.3 58-1338
ND30 .W6 MRR Alc.

ART--DICTIONARIES. (Cont.)
Wolf, Martin L. Dictionary of the
arts; New York, Philosophical
Library [1951] xiii, 787 p.   703
51-13402
N33 .W6 MRR Alc.

ART--DICTIONARIES--FRENCH.
Cabanne, Pierre. Dictionnaire des
arts. Paris, Montreal, Bordas
[1971] i, 736 p. [110F]   73-177570
N33 .C32 MRR Alc.

Dictionnaire universel de l'art et
des artistes ou sont traites,
Paris, E. Hazan, 1967-68. 3 v.
[591.85]   703 68-70531
N33 .D48 MRR Alc.

ART--DICTIONARIES--GERMAN.
Koch, Willi August. Musisches
Lexikon: Künstler, Kunstwerke und
Motive aus Dichtung, Musik und
bildender Kunst. 2., veranderte und
erweiterte Aufl. Stuttgart, A.,
Kröner [c1964] 1250 columns, xxxx
p.   65-69891
N31 .K57 1964 MRR Alc.

Reallexikon zur deutschen
Kunstgeschichte. Stuttgart, J. B.
Metzler, 1937-   v.   38-25084
N6861 .R4 MRR Alc.

ART--DICTIONARIES--POLYGLOT.
Réau, Louis. Dictionnaire
polyglotte des termes d'art et
d'archeologie. [1. ed.] Paris,
Presses universitaires de France,
1953. viii, 247, [5] p.   703 a 53-
8484
N33 .R42 MRR Alc.

ART--DIRECTORIES.
International directory of arts.
[1st]-   ed.: 1952/53- Berlin,
Deutsche Zentraldruckerei AG [etc.]
55-28737
N50 .I6 MRR Alc Latest edition

ART--EXHIBITIONS.
Graves, Algernon. A dictionary of
artists who have exhibited works in
the principal London exhibitions from
1760 to 1893; 3d ed., with additions
and corrections. London, H. Graves
and co., Limited, 1901. xiv, 314 p.,
1 l.   02-25414
N5053 .G75 MRR Alc.

ART--GALLERIES AND MUSEUMS.
[Bilzer, Bert] ed. Paintings of the
world's great galleries; London,
Thames and Hudson [1961, c1960] 584
p.   759.074 62-6722
ND1170 .B513 1961a MRR Alc.

Cooper, Barbara. The world museums
guide; London, Threshold Books Ltd;
Sotheby Parke Bernet Publications
Ltd., 1973. 288 p. [£3.75]   708
74-174259
N405 .C66 MRR Alc.

ART--GALLERIES AND MUSEUMS--DIRECTORIES.
American art directory. v. [1]-
1898- New York, R. R. Bowker. 99-
1016
N50 .A54 MRR Ref Desk Latest
edition

International antiques yearbook,
encyclopaedia & directory. 1949/50-
Uxbridge, Middlesex [etc.] Antiques
Yearbook Ltd. [etc.] 705.8 49-53305

NK1125 .A315 MRR Alc Latest
edition

International directory of arts.
[1st]-   ed.: 1952/53- Berlin,
Deutsche Zentraldruckerei AG [etc.]
55-28737
N50 .I6 MRR Alc Latest edition

ART--HISTORY.
Canaday, John Edwin. The lives of
the painters [1st ed.] New York,
Norton [1969] 4 v.   759 B 67-17666
ND35 .C35 MRR Alc.

Gardner, Helen. Art through the
ages. 4th ed., rev. New York,
Harcourt, Brace [c1959] 840 p.   709
59-5510
N5300 .G25 1959 MRR Alc.

Hatje, Ursula, ed. The styles of
European art. London] Thames and
Hudson [1965] 468 p.   709.4 66-
6773
N5300 .H28813 MRR Alc.

Huyghe, René, ed. L'art et l'homme.
Paris, Larousse [1957-61] 3 v.   a
58-2942
N5300 .H95 MRR Alc.

Janson, Horst Woldemar, A basic
history of art Englewood Cliffs,
N.J., Prentice-Hall [1973, c1971]
412 p.   709 73-8718
N5300 .J28 1973 MRR Alc.

Janson, Horst Woldemar, History of
art; [Rev. and enl.] Englewood
Cliffs, N.J., Prentice-Hall [1969]
616 p.   709 73-91238
N5300 .J3 1969 MRR Alc.

Janson, Horst Woldemar, ed. Key
monuments of the history of art;
Text ed. Englewood Cliffs, N.J.,
Prentice-Hall [1959] 1068 p.   709
59-6934
N5301 .J3 MRR Alc.

The Praeger picture encyclopedia of
art; New York, F. A. Praeger [1958]
584 p.   703 58-11404
N5300 .P773 MRR Alc.

Robb, David Metheny, Art in the
Western World. 4th ed. New York,
Harper & Row [1963] 782 p.   709 63-
7032
N5300 .R56 1963 MRR Alc.

Tudor history of painting in 1000
color reproductions. New York, Tudor
Pub. Co. [1961] 325, [8] p.   759
61-17425
ND1170 .H513 MRR Alc.

ART--HISTORY--20TH CENTURY.
see also Art, Modern

Histoire de l'art contemporain;
Authorized reprint ed. in one volume.
New York, Arno Press [1968] 536 p.
68-9229
ND195 .H5 1968 MRR Alc.

ART--HISTORY--CHRONOLOGY.
Robb, David Metheny, Art in the
Western World. 4th ed. New York,
Harper & Row [1963] 782 p.   709 63-
7032
N5300 .R56 1963 MRR Alc.

ART--INDEXES.
Havlice, Patricia Pate. Art in Time.
Metuchen, N.J., Scarecrow Press,
1970. 350 p.   016.7 76-14885
N7225 .H38 MRR Alc.

Hewlett-Woodmere Public Library.
Index to art reproductions in books.
Metuchen, N.J., Scarecrow Press,
1974. xii, 178 p.   709 74-1286
N7525 .H48 1974 MRR Alc.

ART--MARKETING.
Chamberlain, Betty. The artist's
guide to his market. New York,
Watson-Guptill [1970] 128 p. [5.95]
658.8/09/7 70-87323
N8353 .C45 MRR Alc.

ART--OUTLINES, SYLLABI, ETC.
Shorewood Publishers, inc., New York.
The Shorewood art reference guide.
Rev. and enl. 3d ed. New York,
Shorewood Reproductions [1970]
xviii, 600 p.   759 70-110685
N5305 .S5 1970 MRR Alc.

ART--PERIODICALS--INDEXES.
Art index. v. 1- Jan. 1929/Sept.
1932- New York, H. W. Wilson. 016.7
31-7513
Z5937 .A78 MRR Circ Full set

Artbibliographies modern. Santa
Barbara, Calif., American
Bibliographical Center. 016.709/04
74-647780
Z5935 .L64 MRR Alc Full set

Chicago. Art Institute. Ryerson
Library. Index to art periodicals.
Boston, G. K. Hall, 1962. 11 v. (xi,
9635 p.)   016.7 62-6346
Z5937 .C55 MRR Alc (Dk 33)

Istituto nazionale di archeologia e
storia dell'arte, Rome. Biblioteca.
Annuario bibliografico di storia
dell'arte. anno 1- 1952- Modena.
55-58434
Z5931 .I73 MRR Alc Full set

Park, Esther Ailleen. Mural painters
in America. Pittsburg, Kansas State
Teachers College, 1949- pts.
016.75173 50-63160
ND236 .P3 MRR Biog.

ART--PHILOSOPHY.
McLanathan, Richard B. K. The
American tradition in the arts [1st
ed.] New York, Harcourt, Brace &
World [1968] xv, 492 p. [12.50]
709/.73 65-21032
N6505 .M28 MRR Alc.

Sparshott, Francis Edward, The
structure of aesthetics. Toronto,
University of Toronto Press, 1963.
xiii, 471 p.   64-966
BH201 .S53 MRR Alc.

ART--PHILOSOPHY--BIBLIOGRAPHY.
Hammond, William Alexander, A
bibliography of aesthetics and of the
philosophy of the fine arts from 1900
to 1932; Rev. and enl. ed. New
York, Longmans, Green, and company;
1934. x, 205 p.   016.701 34-13459

Z5870 .H22 1934 MRR Alc.

ART--PRICES.
Art-price annual. Munich [etc.]
Kunst und Technik Verlag [etc.] 55-
37582
N8670 .A68 MRR Alc Partial set

Art prices current. v. [1]-9,
1907/08-1915/16; new ser., v. 1-
1921/22-   704.938 09-23300
N8670 .A7 MRR Alc Partial set

Bérard, Michèle. Encyclopedia of
modern art auction prices. New York,
Arco Pub. Co. [1971] x, 417 p.
[$45.00] 338.4/3/7 79-161210
N6447 .B47 MRR Alc.

The Connoisseur art sales annual.
London, The Connoisseur. 702/.9 74-
24947
Began in 1969.
N8640 .C6 MRR Alc Full set

Hudson, William Norman. Antiques at
auction. South Brunswick, A. S.
Barnes [1972] 403 p. [$20.00]
338.4/3745/10973 76-111646
N6507 .H82 MRR Alc.

International auction records. v.
[1]- 1967- [London, etc.,
Editions E. M.-Publisol] 700/.29
78-21167
N8640 .I5 MRR Alc Full set

Kovel, Ralph M. The complete
antiques price list; 3d ed. New
York, Crown Publishers [1970] 616 p.
745.1/029 79-21772
NK1125 .K64 1970 MRR Alc.

Reitlinger, Gerald, The economics of
taste. London, Barrie and Rockliff
[1961-70] 3 v. [50/- (v. 1) varies]
069/.51 62-4300
N8675 .R44 MRR Alc.

Warman, Edwin G., Print price guide;
Uniontown, Pa., Warman Pub. Co.
[1955] 136 p.   763.085 56-521
NE2415.C7 W36 MRR Alc.

World collectors annuary. v. 1-
1946/49- Delft, Brouwer. 759.085
52-494
ND47 .W6 MRR Alc Full set

ART--STUDY AND TEACHING.
Shorewood Publishers, inc., New York.
The Shorewood art reference guide.
Rev. and enl. 3d ed. New York,
Shorewood Reproductions [1970]
xviii, 600 p.   759 70-110685
N5305 .S5 1970 MRR Alc.

ART--STUDY AND TEACHING--NEW YORK (CITY)
Scott, Thomas J. Greater New York
art directory. [New York, Center for
Urban Education, 1968] 314 p.
[1.00] 700/.25/747 68-56339
N6535.N5 S27 MRR Alc.

ART--TECHNIQUE--DICTIONAIRES.
Quick, John, Artists' and
illustrators' encyclopedia. New
York, McGraw-Hill [1969] xi, 273 p.
703 69-12774
N33 .Q5 MRR Alc.

ART--TERMINOLOGY.
Walker, John Albert, Glossary of
art, architecture, and design since
1945. [Hamden, Conn.] Linnet Books
[1973] 240 p. [$10.50] 709/.04
73-3339
N34 .W34 MRR Alc.

ART--THEMES, MOTIVES--DICTIONARIES.
Lemke, Antje B. Museum companion;
[New York] Hippocrene [1974] vii,
211 p. [$6.95] 703 73-76577
N33 .L38 1974 MRR Alc.

ART--YEARBOOKS.
International antiques yearbook,
encyclopaedia & directory. 1949/50-
Uxbridge, Middlesex [etc.] Antiques
Yearbook Ltd. [etc.] 705.8 49-53305

NK1125 .A315 MRR Alc Latest
edition

ART--ASIA, SOUTHEASTERN.
Rawson, Philip S. The art of
Southeast Asia; New York, F. A.
Praeger [1967] 288 p.   709/.54 67-
29398
N5877.A8 R3 1967 MRR Alc.

ART--BELGIUM--HISTORY.
Gerson, Horst. Art and architecture
in Belgium, 1600 to 1800 Baltimore,
Penguin Books [1960] xix, 236 p.
709.493 60-3193
N6966 .G43 MRR Alc.

ART--BUFFALO--CATALOGS.
Albright-Knox Art Gallery.
Contemporary art 1942-72. New York,
Praeger [1973, c1972] 479 p.
[$25.00] 709/.04/074014797 70-
189296
N6487.B83 A42 MRR Alc.

ART--CANADA--DIRECTORIES.
American art directory. v. [1]-
1898- New York, R. R. Bowker. 99-
1016
N50 .A54 MRR Ref Desk Latest
edition

ART--CHINA--HISTORY.
Sickman, Laurence C. S. The art and
architecture of China [Baltimore]
Penguin Books [1956] xxvi, 334 p.
709.51 56-1125
N7340 .S46 MRR Alc.

Sirén, Osvald. Chinese painting:
New York, Ronald Press [1956- v.
759.951 a 57-1105
ND1040 .S49 MRR Alc.

ART--EGYPT--HISTORY.
Smith, William Stevenson. The art
and architecture of ancient Egypt.
[Harmondsworth, Middlesex] Penguin
Books [1958] xxvii, 301 p. 709.32
58-3043
N5350 .S5 MRR Alc.

ART--ENGLAND.
Graves, Algernon. A dictionary of
artists who have exhibited works in
the principal London exhibitions from
1760 to 1893; 3d ed., with additions
and corrections. London, H. Graves
and co., limited, 1901. xiv, 314 p.,
1 l. 02-28414
N5053 .G75 MRR Alc.

ART--EUROPE.
Braider, Donald, Putnam's guide to
the art centers of Europe. New York,
Putnam [1965] ix, 542 p. 708 64-
18003
N6750 .B66 MRR Alc.

Norman, Jane. Traveler's guide to
Europe's art Rev. ed. New York,
Appleton-Century [1965] 426 p.
709.4 65-23426
N1010 .N6 1965 MRR Alc.

ART--EUROPE--GALLERIES AND MUSEUMS.
Braider, Donald, Putnam's guide to
the art centers of Europe. New York,
Putnam [1965] ix, 542 p. 708 64-
18003
N6750 .B66 MRR Alc.

Taubes, Frederic, The illustrated
guide to great art in Europe for
amateur artists: New York, Reinhold
Pub. Corp. [1966] xii, 307 p.
700.94 66-12167
N6750 .T3 MRR Alc.

ART--FLORENCE.
Molajoli, Bruno, Florence. [1st
ed.] New York, Holt, Rinehart and
Winston [1972] 288 p. [$9.95]
709/.45/51 72-155539
N6921.F7 M6413 1972 MRR Alc.

ART--FRANCE.
Blunt, Anthony, Sir, Art and
architecture in France 1500 to 1700.
2nd ed. Harmondsworth, Penguin,
1970. xiii, 315 p., 193 plates.
[£7/10/-] 709/.44 70-521859
N6844 .B6 1970 MRR Alc.

Guide artistique de la France.
[Paris,] Hachette, 1968. xviii, 1243
p. [57F] 709/.44 68-122321
N6841 .G78 MRR Alc.

ART--GREAT BRITAIN.
Hubbard, Eric Hesketh, A hundred
years of British painting, 1851-1951.
London, New York, Longmans, Green
[1951] xii, 325 p. 750.842 51-
14717
ND467 .H85 MRR Alc.

ART--GREAT BRITAIN--GALLERIES AND
MUSEUMS.
Directory of museums and art
galleries in the British Isles,
South Kensington. Museums Association
[1948] viii, 392 p. 069.0942 50-
395
AM41 .D52 1948 MRR Alc.

The Libraries, museums and art
galleries year book. 1897- London
[etc.] J. Clarke [etc.] 28-11281
Z791 .L7 MRR Alc Latest edition

Philip, Alexander John, An index to
the special collections in libraries,
museums and art galleries (public,
private and official) in Great
Britain and Ireland. London, Pub.
for the author by F. G. Brown [1949]
viii, 190 p. 016 49-48107
AM213 .P5 MRR Alc.

ART--GREAT BRITAIN--GALLERIES AND
MUSEUMS--DIRECTORIES.
Museums and galleries in Great
Britain and Ireland. London, Index
Publishers. 58-46843
Began publication with 1955 vol.
N1020 .M82 MRR Alc Latest edition

Museums Association. Museums
calendar. London. 64-36342
AM1 .M6734 MRR Alc Latest edition

ART--GREECE.
Baumeister, August, ed. Denkmäler
des klassischen altertums zur
erläuterung des lebens der Griechen
und Römer in religion, kunst und
sitte. München, Leipzig, R.
Oldenbourg, 1885-1888. 3 v. 04-
35149
DE5 .B34 MRR Alc.

Whibley, Leonard, ed. A companion to
Greek studies. 4th ed., rev. New
York, Hafner Pub. Co., 1963.
xxxviii, 790 p. 913.38 63-10743
DF77 .W5 1963 MRR Alc.

ART--HUNGARY.
Genthon, István. Magyarország
muemlékei. Budapest, Akademiai
Kiadó, 1951. 576 p. 55-32855
N6812 .G4 MRR Alc.

ART--IRELAND--GALLERIES AND MUSEUMS.
Philip, Alexander John, An index to
the special collections in libraries,
museums and art galleries (public,
private and official) in Great
Britain and Ireland. London, Pub.
for the author by F. G. Brown [1949]
viii, 190 p. 016 49-48107
AM213 .P5 MRR Alc.

ART--ITALY.
Horizon (New York, 1958-) The
Horizon book of the Renaissance, New
York, American Heritage Pub. Co.;
book trade distribution by Doubleday
[1961] 431 p. 945.05 61-11489
DG533 .H6 MRR Alc.

ART--ITALY--HISTORY.
Schmeckebier, Laurence Eli, A
handbook of Italian renaissance
painting, New York, G. P. Putnam's
sons [c1938] xl, 362 p. 759.5 38-
27574
N6615 .S38 MRR Alc.

Vasari, Giorgio, Lives of seventy of
the most eminent painters, sculptors
and architects, New York, C.
Scribner's sons, 1896. 4 v. 03-
16258
N6922 .V46 MRR Alc.

ART--JAPAN--HISTORY.
Paine, Robert Treat, The art and
architecture of Japan / 2d ed. /
Harmondsworth, Eng. ; Baltimore ;
Penguin Books, 1974. xvii, 328 p.,
[87] leaves of plates : [$39.50
(U.S.)] 709/.52 74-186336
N7350 .P3 1973 MRR Alc.

ART--LATIN AMERICA.
Kubler, George, The art and
architecture of ancient America;
Baltimore, Penguin Books [1962] xxv,
396 p. 970.67 62-5022
E59.A7 K8 MRR Alc.

ART--LATIN AMERICA--DIRECTORIES.
American art directory. v. [1]-
1898- New York, R. R. Bowker. 99-
1016
N50 .A54 MRR Ref Desk Latest
edition

ART--LATIN AMERICA--HISTORY.
Kubler, George, Art and architecture
in Spain and Portugal and their
American dominions, 1500 to 1800
[Harmondsworth, Middlesex] Penguin
Books [1959] xxviii, 445 p. 709.46
60-666
N7104 .K8 1959b MRR Alc.

ART--LONDON.
Brooke, Brian. Art in London.
London, Methuen, 1966. 223 p. [18/-
] 709.421 66-71544
N6770 .B7 MRR Alc.

Piper, David. London. [1st ed.]
New York, Holt, Rinehart and Winston
[1971] 288 p. [$9.95]
914.21/04/85 77-155540
N6770 .P5 MRR Alc.

ART--MEXICO.
Velázquez Chávez, Agustín.
Contemporary Mexican artists New
York, Covici-Friede [c1937] xvi p.,
1 l., 19-304 p. incl. front., plates.
759.972 927.5 37-15299
ND255 .V38 MRR Alc.

ART--NEAR EAST.
Frankfort, Henri, The art and
architecture of the ancient Orient.
[Harmondsworth, Middlesex] Penguin
Books [1954] xxvi, 279 p. 709.3
55-12563
N7265 .F7 MRR Alc.

ART--NEW ENGLAND--GALLERIES AND MUSEUMS.
Faison, Samson Lane, A guide to the
art museums of New England. [1st
ed.] New York, Harcourt, Brace
[1958] xvii, 270 p. 708.14 58-
8579
N510.5.N4 F2 MRR Alc.

Webster, Isabel Stevens. Antique
collectors' guide to New England;
New York, Grosset & Dunlap [1961]
165 p. 708.051 61-3263
NK1127 .W4 MRR Alc.

ART--NEW YORK (CITY)
Ashton, Dore. New York. [1st ed.]
New York, Holt, Rinehart and Winston
[1972] 288 p. [$9.95] 709/.747/1
70-155541
N6535.N5 A9 MRR Alc.

ART--NEW YORK (CITY)--GALLERIES AND
MUSEUMS.
Osman, Randolph E., Art centers of
the world; New York Cleveland, World
Pub. Co. [1968] 192 p. [$7.95]
708.1471 68-26017
N600 .O8 MRR Alc.

ART--NEW YORK METROPOLITAN AREA--
DIRECTORIES.
Scott, Thomas J. Greater New York
art directory [New York, Center for
Urban Education, 1968] 314 p.
[1.00] 700/.25/747 68-56339
N6535.N5 S27 MRR Alc.

ART--PORTUGAL--HISTORY.
Kubler, George, Art and architecture
in Spain and Portugal and their
American dominions, 1500 to 1800
[Harmondsworth, Middlesex] Penguin
Books [1959] xxviii, 445 p. 709.46
60-666
N7104 .K8 1959b MRR Alc.

ART--ROME.
Baumeister, August, ed. Denkmäler
des klassischen altertums zur
erläuterung des lebens der Griechen
und Römer in religion, kunst und
sitte. München, Leipzig, R.
Oldenbourg, 1885-1888. 3 v. 04-
35149
DE5 .B34 MRR Alc.

Thynne, Roger. The churches of Rome,
London, K. Paul, Trench, Trubner &
co., ltd.: New York, E. P. Dutton &
co., 1924. xxxii, 460 p. 25-3760
BX4634.R6 T5 MRR Alc.

ART--RUSSIA--HISTORY.
Hamilton, George Heard. The art and
architecture of Russia. Baltimore,
Penguin Books [1954] xxi, 320 p.
709.47 a 55-4512
N6981 .H34 MRR Alc.

ART--SPAIN--HISTORY.
Kubler, George, Art and architecture
in Spain and Portugal and their
American dominions, 1500 to 1800
[Harmondsworth, Middlesex] Penguin
Books [1959] xxviii, 445 p. 709.46
60-666
N7104 .K8 1959b MRR Alc.

ART--UNITED STATES.
Drepperd, Carl William, A dictionary
of American antiques. [1st ed.]
Garden City, N.Y., Doubleday, 1952.
vii, 404 p. 708.051 52-11623
N33 .D74 MRR Alc.

Illustrated guide to the treasures of
America. Pleasantville, N.Y.,
Reader's Digest Association [1974]
624 p. [$11.97] 917.3/03 73-83812

E159 .I44 MRR Alc.

Mather, Frank Jewett, The American
spirit in art, New Haven, Yale
university press; [etc., etc.] 1927.
3 p. l., 354 p. 27-5701
E178.5 .P2 vol. 12 MRR Alc.

ART--UNITED STATES--DIRECTORIES.
American art directory. v. [1]-
1898- New York, R. R. Bowker. 99-
1016
N50 .A54 MRR Ref Desk Latest
edition

ART--UNITED STATES--GALLERIES AND
MUSEUMS.
Christensen, Erwin Ottomar, A guide
to art museums in the United States
New York, Dodd, Mead [1968] xiii,
303 p. 708.13 67-26838
N510 .C5 MRR Alc.

Fundaburk, Emma Lila, Art at
educational institutions in the
United States; Metuchen, N.J.,
Scarecrow Press, 1974. xv, 670 p.
709/.73 74-3187
N510 .F86 MRR Alc.

Hilton, Ronald, ed. Handbook of
Hispanic source materials and
research organizations in the United
States. 2d ed. Stanford, Calif.,
Stanford University press, 1956.
xiv, 448 p. 980 56-6178
F1408.3 .H65 1956 MRR Alc.

Spaeth, Eloise, American art
museums: Rev. ed. New York, McGraw-
Hill [1969] xiii, 321 p. 708.13
68-55274
N510 .S6 1969 MRR Alc.

ART--UNITED STATES--GALLERIES AND
MUSEUMS--BIBLIOGRAPHY.
Wasserman, Paul. Museum media; 1st
ed. Detroit, Gale Research Co.,
1973. vii, 455 p.   011 73-16335
Z5052 .W35 MRR Alc.

ART--UNITED STATES--GALLERIES AND
MUSEUMS--DIRECTORIES.
Mastai, Boleslaw. Mastai's national
classified directory of American art
& antique dealers. 7th-   ed.; 1961-
New York, Mastai Pub. Co.   72-623808

N8630 .M3   MRR Alc Latest edition

ART--UNITED STATES--HISTORY.
Larkin, Oliver W. Art and life in
America. Rev. and enl. ed. New
York, Holt, Rinehart and Winston
[1960] xvii, 559 p.   709.73 60-
6491
N6505 .L37 1960 MRR Alc.

Pierson, William Harvey, ed. Arts of
the United States. New York, McGraw-
Hill [1960] x, 452 p.   709.73 60-
9855
N6505 .P55 MRR Alc.

ART--UNITED STATES--YEARBOOKS.
The Art collector's almanac. no. 1-
1965- Huntington Station [N.Y.] J.
E. Treisman.   65-15142
N9 .A38   MRR Alc Latest edition

ART--WASHINGTON, D.C.
Fairman, Charles Edwin. Art and
artists of the Capitol of the United
States of America. Washington, U.S.
Govt. print. off., 1927. xii, 526
p., 1 l. incl. illus., ports., plans,
facsims., tables.   28-26032
N853 .F4 MRR Ref Desk.

ART--WASHINGTON, D.C.--CATALOGS.
United States. Architect of the
Capitol. Compilation of works of art
and other objects in the United
States Capitol. Washington, U.S.
Govt. Print. Off., 1965. xxiv, 426
p.   708.153 66-60832
N853 .A52 1965 MRR Alc.

ART, ABSTRACT.
Berckelaers, Ferdinand Louis,
Dictionnaire de la peinture
abstraite, Paris, F. Hazan [1957]
305 p.   a 57-7206
ND35 .B4 MRR Alc.

ART, AFRICAN.
see also Negro art

ART, AFRICAN--BIBLIOGRAPHY.
Duignan, Peter. Handbook of American
resources for African studies.
[Stanford, Calif.] Hoover Institution
on War, Revolution, and Peace,
Stanford University, 1967. xvii, 218
p.   016.916 66-20901
Z3501 .D8 MRR Alc.

International African Institute. A
bibliography of African art; London,
International African Institute,
1965. x, 120 p. [50/-]   016.7096
66-70409
Z5938.A3 I5 MRR Alc.

ART, AMERICAN.
see also Negro art

The Arts in America: New York,
Scribner [1966] xvi, 368 p.   709.73
66-12921
N6507 .A7 MRR Alc.

Comstock, Helen, ed. The concise
encyclopedia of American antiques.
New York, Hawthorn Books [1965] 848
p.   745.10973 65-9391
NK805 .C65 1965 MRR Alc.

Hudson, William Norman. Antiques at
auction South Brunswick, A. S.
Barnes [1972] 403 p. [$20.00]
338.4/3745/10973 76-111646
N6507 .H82 MRR Alc.

Hunter, Sam. American art of the
20th century: New York, H. N. Abrams
[1973] 583 p.   709/.73 73-10211
N6512 .H78 1973 MRR Alc.

ART, AMERICAN--BIBLIOGRAPHY.
Whitehill, Walter Muir, The arts in
early American history: Chapel Hill,
Published for the Institute of Early
American History and Culture at
Williamsburg, Va., by the University
of North Carolina Press [1965] xv,
170 p.   016.70973 65-63132
Z5961.U5 W5 MRR Alc.

ART, AMERICAN--CATALOGS.
Pierson, William Harvey, ed. Arts of
the United States. New York, McGraw-
Hill [1960] x, 452 p.   709.73 60-
9855
N6505 .P55 MRR Alc.

ART, AMERICAN--HISTORY.
Christensen, Erwin Ottomar, The
Index of American Design. New York,
Macmillan 1950. xviii, 229 p.   745
50-10215
NK1403 .C5 MRR Alc.

Lipman, Jean (Herzberg) American
folk decoration. New York, Oxford
University Press, 1951. xii, 163 p.
745.3 51-11035
NK806 .L5 MRR Alc.

McLanathan, Richard B. K. The
American tradition in the arts [1st
ed.] New York, Harcourt, Brace &
World [1968] xv, 492 p. [12.50]
709/.73   65-21032
N6505 .M28 MRR Alc.

ART, AMERICAN--HISTORY--HISTORIOGRAPHY.
Whitehill, Walter Muir, The arts in
early American history; Chapel Hill,
Published for the Institute of Early
American History and Culture at
Williamsburg, Va., by the University
of North Carolina Press [1965] xv,
170 p.   016.70973 65-63132
Z5961.U5 W5 MRR Alc.

ART, AMERICAN--HISTORY--SOURCES--
BIBLIOGRAPHY.
McCoy, Garnett. Archives of American
art; New York, Bowker, 1972. ix,
163 p.   016.7/0973 72-5125
Z6611.A7 M3 MRR Alc.

ART, AMERICAN--PERIODICALS.
Artists U.S.A. 1970/71-
Philadelphia. 338.4/7/75913029 78-
134303
N6512 .A78 MRR Alc Latest edition

ART, ANCIENT.
Frankfort, Henri, The art and
architecture of the ancient Orient.
[Harmondsworth, Middlesex] Penguin
Books [1954] xxvi, 279 p.   709.3
55-12563
N7265 .F7 MRR Alc.

ART, ANCIENT--BIBLIOGRAPHY.
London. University. Warburg
Institute. Library. Catalogue. [2d
ed.] Boston, G. K. Hall, 1967. 12
v.   019/.2 68-4522
Z921 .L66 1967 MRR Alc (Dk 33)

ART, AUSTRALIAN--DICTIONARIES.
McCulloch, Alan. Encyclopedia of
Australian art. New York, Praeger
[1969, c1968] 668 p. [25.00]
709/.94 69-17079
N7400 .M27 1969 MRR Alc.

ART, AUSTRIAN--HISTORY.
Hempel, Eberhard, Baroque art and
architecture in central Europe:
Baltimore, Penguin Books [1965]
xxiii, 370 p.   709.43 65-28970
N6756 .H413 MRR Alc.

ART, BAROQUE--HISTORY.
Huyghe, René. Larousse encyclopedia
of Renaissance and Baroque art. New
York, Prometheus Press [1964] 444 p.
709.03 64-13787
N6350 .H813 MRR Alc.

ART, BAROQUE--EUROPE--HISTORY.
Hempel, Eberhard, Baroque art and
architecture in central Europe:
Baltimore, Penguin Books [1965]
xxiii, 370 p.   709.43 65-28970
N6756 .H413 MRR Alc.

ART, BRITISH--HISTORY.
The Connoisseur. The Connoisseur's
complete period guides to the houses,
decoration, furnishing and chattels
of the classic periods; London, The
Connoisseur. 1968. 1536 p. [84/-]
709/.42 70-369442
NK928 .C63 MRR Alc.

ART, CHINESE--TERMINOLOGY.
Hansford, S. Howard. A glossary of
Chinese art and archæology. London,
China Society, 1954. xi, 104 p.
709.51 55-24573
N7340 .H3 1954 MRR Alc.

ART, CHRISTIAN
see Christian art and symbolism

ART, COLONIAL--UNITED STATES.
Hudson, William Norman. Antiques at
auction South Brunswick, A. S.
Barnes [1972] 403 p. [$20.00]
338.4/3745/10973 76-111646
N6507 .H82 MRR Alc.

ART, COMMERCIAL
see Commercial art

ART, CZECH--HISTORY.
Hempel, Eberhard, Baroque art and
architecture in central Europe:
Baltimore, Penguin Books [1965]
xxiii, 370 p.   709.43 65-28970
N6756 .H413 MRR Alc.

ART, DECORATIVE.
see also Furniture

see also Illustration of books

see also Needlework.

ART, DECORATIVE--DICTIONARIES.
Clark, MaryJane. An illustrated
glossary of decorated antiques from
the late 17th century to the early
20th century. [1st ed.] Rutland,
Vt., C. E. Tuttle Co. [1972] 400 p.
[$8.75] 745.1 74-138080
NK30 .C43 MRR Alc.

ART, DUTCH--HISTORY.
Netherlands (Kingdom, 1815-)
Departement van Onderwijs, Kunsten en
Wetenschappen. Guide to Dutch art.
2d rev. ed. Hague, Govt. Print. and
Pub. Off., 1953. 152 p. 709.492
58-42372
N6941 .A48 1953 MRR Alc.

Osten, Gert von der. Painting and
sculpture in Germany and the
Netherlands, 1500 to 1600
Harmondsworth, Penguin, 1969. xxii,
403 p., 193 plates. [7/7/-] 759.3
79-514834
N6925 .O813 1969 MRR Alc.

Osten, Gert von der. Painting and
sculpture in Germany and the
Netherlands, 1500 to 1600 Baltimore,
Md., Penguin Books [1969] xxii, 403
p. [25.00] 709/.4 73-8246
N6925 .O813 MRR Alc.

ART, EGYPTIAN--CATALOGS.
Smith, William Stevenson. The art
and architecture of ancient Egypt.
[Harmondsworth, Middlesex] Penguin
Books [1958] xxvii, 301 p. 709.32
58-3043
N5350 .S5 MRR Alc.

ART, ENGLISH--HISTORY.
Halliday, Frank Ernest, An
illustrated cultural history of
England London, Thames & Hudson
[1967] 320 p. [42/-] 709/.42 67-
82640
DA110 .H315 MRR Alc.

ART, EUROPEAN.
Taubes, Frederic, The illustrated
guide to great art in Europe for
amateur artists: New York, Reinhold
Pub. Corp. [1966] xii, 307 p.
700.94 66-12167
N6750 .T3 MRR Alc.

ART, EUROPEAN--HISTORY.
Hamilton, George Heard. Painting and
sculpture in Europe, 1880-1940.
Baltimore, Penguin Books [1967]
xxiv, 443 p.   709.4 67-31947
ND457 .H3 MRR Alc.

Hatje, Ursula, ed. The styles of
European art. London Thames and
Hudson [1965] 468 p.   709.4 66-
6773
N5300 .H28813 MRR Alc.

Hempel, Eberhard, Baroque art and
architecture in central Europe:
Baltimore, Penguin Books [1965]
xxiii, 370 p.   709.43 65-28970
N6756 .H413 MRR Alc.

Novotny, Fritz, Painting and
sculpture in Europe, 1780 to 1880.
2nd ed. Harmondsworth, Penguin,
1970. xxii, 290, 192 p., leaf.
[£5.75] 759.94 74-149800
N6757 .N6813 1970 MRR Alc.

Robb, David Metheny, Art in the
Western World 4th ed. New York,
Harper & Row [1963] 782 p. 709 63-
7032
N5300 .R56 1963 MRR Alc.

ART, FLEMISH--HISTORY.
Osten, Gert von der. Painting and
sculpture in Germany and the
Netherlands, 1500 to 1600
Harmondsworth, Penguin, 1969. xxii,
403 p., 193 plates. [7/7/-] 759.3
79-514834
N6925 .O813 1969 MRR Alc.

Osten, Gert von der. Painting and
sculpture in Germany and the
Netherlands, 1500 to 1600 Baltimore,
Md., Penguin Books [1969] xxii, 403
p. [25.00] 709/.4 73-8246
N6925 .O813 MRR Alc.

Wilenski, Reginald Howard, Flemish
painters, 1430-1830. London, Faber
and Faber [1960] 2 v.   759.9493 60-
51134
ND672 .W5 1960a MRR Alc.

ART, FRENCH.
Bowness, Alan, ed. Impressionists
and post-impressionists. New York,
F. Watts [1965] 296 p. 709.034 65-
10269
ND1265 .B67 MRR Alc.

ART, GERMAN.
Bithell, Jethro, ed. Germany, a
companion to German studies. [5th
ed.; rev., enl.] London, Methuen
[1955] xii, 578 p.   914.3 55-3335
DD61 .B56 1955 MRR Alc.

ART, GERMAN--DICTIONARIES.
Reallexikon zur deutschen
Kunstgeschichte. Stuttgart, J. B.
Metzler, 1937-   v.   38-25084
N6861 .R4 MRR Alc.

ART, GERMAN--HISTORY.
Hempel, Eberhard, Baroque art and
architecture in central Europe:
Baltimore, Penguin Books [1965]
xxiii, 370 p.   709.43   65-28970
N6756 .H413 MRR Alc.

Osten, Gert von der. Painting and
sculpture in Germany and the
Netherlands, 1500 to 1600 Baltimore,
Md., Penguin Books [1969] xxii, 403
p. [25.00]   709/.4   73-8246
N6925 .O813 MRR Alc.

Osten, Gert von der. Painting and
sculpture in Germany and the
Netherlands, 1500 to 1600
Harmondsworth, Penguin, 1969. xxii,
403 p., 193 plates. [7/7/-]   759.3
79-514834
N6925 .O813 1969 MRR Alc.

ART, GREEK.
Bieber, Margarete, The history of
the Greek and Roman theater. [2d
ed., rev. and enl.] Princeton, N.J.,
Princeton University Press, 1961.
xiv, 343 p.   882.09   60-9367
PA3201 .B52 1961 MRR Alc.

Richter, Gisela Marie Augusta, A
handbook of Greek art. London,
Phaidon Press [1959] vi, 421 p.
709.38   59-4114
N5630 .R49 MRR Alc.

ART, GREEK--DICTIONARIES.
The New Century handbook of Greek art
and architecture. New York, Appleton-
Century-Crofts [1972] ix, 213 p.
709/.38   72-187738
N5633 .N39 MRR Alc.

ART, HUNGARIAN--HISTORY.
Hempel, Eberhard, Baroque art and
architecture in central Europe:
Baltimore, Penguin Books [1965]
xxiii, 370 p.   709.43   65-28970
N6756 .H413 MRR Alc.

ART, INDIC.
Rowland, Benjamin, The art and
architecture of India: London,
Baltimore, Penguin Books [1953]
xvii, 288 p.   709.34 709.54* 53-
12998
N7301 .R68 MRR Alc.

ART, ITALIAN.
Hartt, Frederick. History of Italian
Renaissance art: New York, H. N.
Abrams [1969] 636 p.   709/.45 74-
95193
N6915 .H37 MRR Alc.

ART, ITALIAN--BIBLIOGRAPHY.
Borroni, Fabia. "Il Cicognara,"
Firenze, Sansoni, 1954- v.   55-
18980
Z2357 .B6 MRR Alc.

ART, ITALIAN--HISTORY.
Wittkower, Rudolf. Art and
architecture in Italy, 1600 to 1750.
Baltimore, Penguin Books [1969,
c1958] xxiv, 462 p. [20.00]
709/.45   70-12230
N6916 .W5 1969 MRR Alc.

ART, JAPANESE--HISTORY.
Boger, H. Batterson. The traditional
arts of Japan, Garden City, N.Y.,
Doubleday, 1964. 351 p.   709.52 64-
11726
N7350 .B57 MRR Alc.

Paine, Robert Treat, The art and
architecture of Japan / 2d ed. /
Harmondsworth, Eng. : Baltimore :
Penguin Books, 1974. xviii, 328 p.,
[87] leaves of plates : [$39.50
(U.S.)]   709/.52 74-186336
N7350 .P3 1973 MRR Alc.

ART, LATIN AMERICAN.
United States. Library of Congress.
Prints and photographs division. The
colonial art of Latin America,
Washington, D.C., The Library of
Congress, 1945. xii, 43 p.   709.8
46-25650
Z663.39 .C6 MRR Alc.

ART, MODERN.
see also Neoclassicism (Art)

ART, MODERN--17TH-18TH CENTURIES--ITALY.
Wittkower, Rudolf. Art and
architecture in Italy 1600 to 1750.
Baltimore, Penguin Books [1969,
c1958] xxiv, 462 p. [20.00]
709/.45   70-12230
N6916 .W5 1969 MRR Alc.

ART, MODERN--19TH CENTURY.
Huyghe, René. Larousse encyclopedia
of modern art. London, P. Hamlyn
[1965] 444 p.   709.034 66-45473
N6450 .B813 1965 MRR Alc.

ART, MODERN--19TH CENTURY--CATALOGS.
Bérard, Michèle. Encyclopedia of
modern art auction prices. New York,
Arco Pub. Co. [1971] x, 417 p.
[$45.00]   338.4/3/7 79-161210
N6447 .B47 MRR Alc.

ART, MODERN--19TH CENTURY--EUROPE.
Novotny, Fritz, Painting and
sculpture in Europe, 1780 to 1880.
2nd ed. Harmondsworth, Penguin,
1970. xxii, 290, 192 p., leaf.
[£5.75]   759.94   74-149800
N6757 .N6813 1970 MRR Alc.

ART, MODERN--20TH CENTURY.
see also Expressionism (Art)

see also Impressionism (Art)

see also Post-impressionism (Art)

Cheney, Sheldon, A primer of modern
art. 14th rev. ed. New York,
Liveright Pub. Corp., 1966. xiii,
392 p.   709.04 66-24797
N6490 .C5 1966 MRR Alc.

Hughes, Graham. Modern jewelry:
Rev. ed. London, Studio Vista, 1968.
256 p. [70/-]   739.27/09/04 68-
97220
NK7310 .H8 1968 MRR Alc.

Huyghe, René. Larousse encyclopedia
of modern art. London, P. Hamlyn
[1965] 444 p.   709.034 66-45473
N6450 .H813 1965 MRR Alc.

Sylvester, David, ed. Modern art,
New York, F. Watts [1966, c1965] 296
p.   709.04 65-10270
N6490 .S9 MRR Alc.

ART, MODERN--20TH CENTURY--BIBLIOGRAPHY-
-PERIODICALS.
Artbibliographies modern. Santa
Barbara, Calif., American
Bibliographical Center.   016.709/04
74-647780
Z5935 .L64 MRR Alc Full set

ART, MODERN--20TH CENTURY--CATALOGS.
Albright-Knox Art Gallery.
Contemporary art, 1942-72: New York,
Praeger [1973, c1972] 479 p.
[$25.00]   709/.04/074014797 70-
189296
N6487.B83 A42 MRR Alc.

Bérard, Michèle. Encyclopedia of
modern art auction prices. New York,
Arco Pub. Co. [1971] x, 417 p.
[$45.00]   338.4/3/7 79-161210
N6447 .B47 MRR Alc.

ART, MODERN--20TH CENTURY--HISTORY.
Arnason, H. H. History of modern
art: New York, H. N. Abrams [1968]
663 p. [$25.00]   709.04 68-26863
N6490 .A713 MRR Alc.

ART, MODERN--20TH CENTURY--YEARBOOKS.
The Art collector's almanac, no. 1-
1965- Huntington Station [N.Y.] J.
E. Treisman.   65-15142
N9 .A38 MRR Alc Latest edition

ART, MODERN--20TH CENTURY--UNITED
STATES.
Artists U.S.A. 1970/71-
Philadelphia   338.4/7/75913029 78-
134303
N6512 .A78 MRR Alc Latest edition

Hunter, Sam, American art of the
20th century: New York, H. N. Abrams
[1973] 583 p.   709/.73 73-10211
N6512 .H78 1973 MRR Alc.

ART, MODERN--FRANCE.
Blunt, Anthony, Sir, Art and
architecture in France, 1500 to 1700.
2nd ed. Harmondsworth, Penguin,
1970. xxii, 315 p., 193 plates.
[£7/10/-]   709/.44 70-521859
N6844 .B6 1970 MRR Alc.

ART, ORIENTAL.
Frankfort, Henri, The art and
architecture of the ancient Orient.
[Harmondsworth, Middlesex] Penguin
Books [1954] xxvi, 279 p.   709.3
55-12563
N7265 .F7 MRR Alc.

ART, POLISH--HISTORY.
Hempel, Eberhard, Baroque art and
architecture in central Europe:
Baltimore, Penguin Books [1965]
xxiii, 370 p.   709.43   65-28970
N6756 .H413 MRR Alc.

ART, PRIMITIVE.
see also Sculpture, Primitive

ART, RENAISSANCE--HISTORY.
Huyghe, René. Larousse encyclopedia
of Renaissance and Baroque art. New
York, Prometheus Press [1964] 444 p.
709.03 64-13787
N6350 .H813 MRR Alc.

ART, RENAISSANCE--ITALY.
Hartt, Frederick. History of Italian
Renaissance art: New York, H. N.
Abrams [1969] 636 p.   709/.45 74-
95193
N6915 .H37 MRR Alc.

ART, ROMAN.
Bieber, Margarete, The history of
the Greek and Roman theater. [2d
ed., rev. and enl.] Princeton, N.J.,
Princeton University Press, 1961.
xiv, 343 p.   882.09 60-9367
PA3201 .B52 1961 MRR Alc.

ART, SPANISH.
Peers, Edgar Allison, ed. Spain:
5th ed., rev. and enl. London,
Methuen [1956] xii, 319 p.   914.6
56-58806
DP66 .P4 1956 MRR Alc.

ART, SWISS--HISTORY.
Hempel, Eberhard, Baroque art and
architecture in central Europe:
Baltimore, Penguin Books [1965]
xxiii, 370 p.   709.43   65-28970
N6756 .H413 MRR Alc.

ART AND MYTHOLOGY.
Hunger, Herbert, Lexikon der
griechischen und römischen
Mythologie. 6. erw. erg. Aufl.
Wien, Hollinek [1969], xi, p., 64 p.
of illus., 444 p. [260.00]   76-
495596
BL303 .H8 1969 MRR Alc.

Lemke, Antje B. Museum companion:
[New York] Hippocrene [1974] vii,
211 p. [$6.95]   703 73-76577
N33 .L38 1974 MRR Alc.

Whittlesey, Eunice S. Symbols and
legends in Western art; New York,
Scribner [1972] ix, 367 p. [$7.95]
704.94 71-162764
N7740 .W53 MRR Alc.

ART AND NATURE
see Nature (Aesthetics)

ART AND STATE--UNITED STATES--
DIRECTORIES.
Washington and the arts; New York]
Associated Councils of the Arts
[1971] vi, 176 p. [$6.50]
353.008/54/025753 79-163014
NX735 .W3 MRR Ref Desk.

ART AS A PROFESSION.
Holden, Donald. Art career guide;
3d ed., rev. and enl. [New York]
Watson-Guptill Publications [1973]
303 p. [$7.95]   702/.3 72-10192
N8350 .H6 1973 MRR Alc.

ART DEALERS--DIRECTORIES.
International directory of arts.
[1st]- ed.; 1952/53- Berlin,
Deutsche Zentraldruckerei AG [etc.]
55-28737
N50 .I6 MRR Alc Latest edition

Mastai, Boleslaw. Mastai's national
classified directory of American art
& antique dealers. 7th- ed.; 1961-
New York, Mastai Pub. Co. 72-623808

N8630 .M3 MRR Alc Latest edition

ART DEALERS--EUROPE--DIRECTORIES.
International antiques yearbook,
encyclopaedia & directory. 1949/50-
Uxbridge, Middlesex [etc.] Antiques
Yearbook Ltd. [etc.] 705.8 49-53305

NK1125 .A315 MRR Alc Latest
edition

ART DEALERS--NEW YORK (CITY)--
DIRECTORIES.
Gardner, Arron. Gardner's guide to
antiques and art buying in New York
City. Indianapolis, Bobbs-Merrill
[1969] xiii, 204 p. [5.95]
745.1/025/7471 69-13091
NK1127 .G3 MRR Alc.

ART DEALERS--UNITED STATES--DIRECTORIES.
The Antique trader directory of
antique dealers. Kewanee, Ill.,
Antique trader [etc.] 64-4643
NK1127 .A5 MRR Alc Latest edition

Eagle, Joanna. Buying art on a
budget; [1st ed.] New York,
Hawthorn Books [1968] vi, 442 p.
[$6.95]   706.5 67-24654
N8630 .E2 MRR Alc.

Great Lakes antique dealers
directory. Decatur, Ind., S. E.
Leonardson. 708.051 57-48384
"Established 1944."
NK1127 .G7 MRR Alc Latest edition

International antiques yearbook,
encyclopaedia & directory. 1949/50-
Uxbridge, Middlesex [etc.] Antiques
Yearbook Ltd. [etc.] 705.8 49-53305

NK1125 .A315 MRR Alc Latest
edition

ART DEALERS--UNITED STATES-- (Cont.)
Spaeth, Eloise. American art
museums; Rev. ed. New York, McGraw-
Hill [1969] xiii, 321 p.   708.13
68-55274
N510 .S6 1969 MRR Alc.

ART IN UNIVERSITIES AND COLLEGES--
UNITED STATES.
Fundaburk, Emma Lila. Art at
educational institutions in the
United States: Metuchen, N.J.,
Scarecrow Press, 1974. xv, 670 p.
709/.73   74-3187
N510 .F86 MRR Alc.

ART INDUSTRIES AND TRADE--DICTIONARIES.
Bernasconi, John R. The collectors'
glossary of antiques and fine arts,
[Rev. ed.] London, Estates Gazette,
ltd. [1963] xvi, 587 p.   66-48284
NK30 .B4 1963 MRR Alc.

Boger, Louise Ade. The dictionary of
antiques and the decorative arts:
New York, Scribner [1967] ix, 662 p.
703   67-18131
NK30 .B57 1967 MRR Alc.

Clark, MaryJane. An illustrated
glossary of decorated antiques from
the late 17th century to the early
20th century. [1st ed.] Rutland,
Vt., C. E. Tuttle Co. [1972] 400 p.
[$8.75]   745.1   74-138080
NK30 .C43 MRR Alc.

Comstock, Helen, ed. The concise
encyclopedia of American antiques.
New York, Hawthorn Books [1965] 848
p.   745.10973   65-9391
NK805 .C65 1965 MRR Alc.

Hayward, Helena, ed. The
Connoisseur's handbook of antique
collecting; New York, Hawthorn Books
[1960] 320 p.   703   60-8797
NK30 .H45 MRR Alc.

ART INDUSTRIES AND TRADE--GREAT BRITAIN.
Wood, Violet (Mackworth-Praed)
Victoriana, New York, Macmillan,
1961 [c1960] 175 p.   708.051   61-
65212
NK928 .W6 1961 MRR Alc.

ART INDUSTRIES AND TRADE--NEW ENGLAND--
DIRECTORIES.
Webster, Isabel Stevens. Antique
collectors' guide to New England:
New York, Grosset & Dunlap [1961]
165 p.   708.051   61-3263
NK1127 .W4 MRR Alc.

ART INDUSTRIES AND TRADE--UNITED STATES.
Christensen, Erwin Ottomar, The
Index of American Design. New York,
Macmillan, 1950. xviii, 229 p.   745
50-10215
NK1403 .C5 MRR Alc.

ART INDUSTRIES AND TRADE--UNITED STATES-
-DIRECTORIES.
American Crafts Council. Research &
Education Dept. Craft shops,
galleries, USA: [4th ed., New York]
American Crafts Council [1973] 214
p.   745.5/025/73   73-175467
NK805 .A67 1973 MRR Alc.

The Antique trader directory of
antique dealers, Kewanee, Ill.,
Antique trader [etc.]   64-4643
NK1127 .A5 MRR Alc Latest edition

Literary market place; [1st]- ed.;
1940- New York, Bowker.   655.473   41-
51571
PN161 .L5   Sci RR Partial set / MRR
Ref Desk Latest edition

ART INDUSTRIES AND TRADE, AMERICAN.
Comstock, Helen, ed. The concise
encyclopedia of American antiques.
New York, Hawthorn Books [1965] 848
p.   745.10973   65-9391
NK805 .C65 1965 MRR Alc.

Lantz, Louise K. Old American
kitchenware 1725-1925 Camden, T.
Nelson [1970] 289 p.   683/.82   75-
101527
NK806 .L29 MRR Alc.

ART INDUSTRIES AND TRADE, BRITISH--
HISTORY.
The Connoisseur. The Connoisseur's
complete period guides to the houses,
decoration, furnishing and chattels
of the classic periods: London, The
Connoisseur, 1968. 1536 p.   [84/-]
709/.42   70-369442
NK928 .C63 MRR Alc.

ART LIBRARIES.
Chamberlin, Mary W. Guide to art
reference books. Chicago, American
Library Association, 1959. xiv, 418
p.   016.7   59-10457
Z5931 .C45 MRR Alc.

ART METAL-WORK.
see also Jewelry

see also Silversmithing

ART METAL-WORK--HISTORY.
Aitchison, Leslie. A history of
metals. New York, Interscience
Publishers, 1960. 2 v. (xxi, 647 p.)
669.09   60-3041
TN615 .A5 MRR Alc.

ART NOUVEAU--COLLECTORS AND COLLECTING.
Mebane, John, The complete book of
collecting Art nouveau. New York,
Coward-McCann [1970]   256 p.   [$6.95]
709.03/4   76-132618
N6465.A7 M4 MRR alc.

ART OBJECTS.
see also Glassware

ART OBJECTS--CATALOGS.
Warman, Edwin G., Warman's antiques
and their current prices. [1st]-
1949- Uniontown, Pa., E. G. Warman
Pub. Co. [etc.]   56-2031
NK1133 .W33 MRR Alc Latest edition

ART OBJECTS--COLLECTORS AND COLLECTING.
Baker, Mary Gladys Steel, A
dictionary of antiques, Edinburgh,
W. & R. Chambers [1953]   263 p.
708.051   54-4571
NK1125 .B33 1953 MRR Alc.

Bedford, John, The collecting man.
London, Macdonald & Co., 1968. 256
p.   [55/-]   707/.5   68-114912
NK1125 .B38 MRR Alc.

Boger, Louise Ade. The dictionary of
antiques and the decorative arts;
New York, Scribner [1967] ix, 662 p.
703   67-18131
NK30 .B57 1967 MRR Alc.

Callahan, Claire (Wallis) How to
collect the new antiques; New York,
D. McKay Co. [1966] ix, 244 p.
745.1   66-14586
NK1125 .C262 MRR Alc.

Coysh, Arthur Wilfred. The antique
buyer's dictionary of names New
York, Praeger [1970]   278 p.
745.1/03   70-125355
N40 .C67 1970 MRR Alc.

Coysh, Arthur Wilfred. The buying
antiques reference book; Newton
Abbot, David & Charles, 1968.   232 p.
[45/-]   745.1/025   74-385636
NK1125 .C68 MRR Alc.

Dorn, Sylvia O'Neill. The insider's
guide to antiques, art, and
collectibles. [1st ed.] Garden
City, N.Y., Doubleday, 1974. xxii,
334 p.   [$7.95]   745.1/075   73-11701
NK1125 .D63 MRR Alc.

Kovel, Ralph M. The complete
antiques price list; 3d ed. New
York, Crown Publishers [1970]   616 p.
745.1/029   79-21772
NK1125 .K64 1970 MRR Alc.

Kovel, Ralph M. Know your antiques;
Rev. New York, Crown Publishers
[c1973] x, 343 p.   [$7.95]   745.1
74-160949
NK1125 .K65 1973 MRR Alc.

Mack, Jerry. What's it worth? [San
Angelo? Tex.] Educator Books, c1970.
94 p.   [$3.95]   380.1/025/73   74-
138825
HF5482 .M3 MRR Alc.

Mebane, John, New horizons in
collecting: South Brunswick [N.J.]
A. S. Barnes [1966]   280 p.   707.5
66-18199
NK1125 .M358 MRR Alc.

Phillips, Phoebe. The collectors'
encyclopedia of antiques. New York,
Crown Publishers [1973]   703 p.
[$20.00]   745.1   73-76934
NK28 .P494 1973 MRR Alc.

Phipps, Frances, The collector's
complete dictionary of American
antiques. [1st ed.] Garden City,
N.Y., Doubleday, 1974.   xv, 640 p.
[$25.00]   709/.73   72-97257
NK805 .P52 MRR Alc.

Reif, Rita. The antique collector's
guide to styles and prices. New
York, Hawthorn Books [1970] xii, 276
p.   [12.95]   749/.075   75-102019
NK1125 .R37 MRR Alc.

Rush, Richard H. Antiques as an
investment Englewood Cliffs, N.J.,
Prentice-Hall [1968] 536 p.
[$14.95]   749   68-10170
NK1125 .R86 MRR Alc.

Savage, George, The antique
collector's handbook; New revised
ed. Feltham, Spring Books, 1968.
304 p.   [25/-]   745.1   70-510278
NK1125 .S3 1968 MRR Alc.

ART OBJECTS--COLLECTORS AND COLLECTING--
DICTIONARIES.
The Connoisseur's concise
encyclopaedia of antiques; London,
Sphere, 1969. 2 v.   [15/- (per
vol.)]   745.1/03   71-519969
NK30 .C64 1969 MRR Alc.

The Random House encyclopedia of
antiques. [1st American ed.] New
York, Random House [1973] 400 p.
[$25.00]   745.1/075   73-3997
NK1125 .R35 1973 MRR Alc.

ART OBJECTS--COLLECTORS AND COLLECTING--
NEW YORK (CITY)
Brener, Carol. The underground
collector: New York, Simon and
Schuster [1970]   319 p.   [2.95]
745.1/025/7471   72-107269
NK1127 .B64 MRR Alc.

ART OBJECTS--COLLECTORS AND COLLECTING--
NEW YORK (CITY)--DIRECTORIES.
Gardner, Arron. Gardner's guide to
antiques and art buying in New York
city. Indianapolis, Bobbs-Merrill
[1969]   xiii, 204 p.   [5.95]
745.1/025/7471   69-13091
NK1127 .G3 MRR Alc.

ART OBJECTS--COLLECTORS AND COLLECTING--
UNITED STATES--DIRECTORIES.
Mastai, Boleslaw. Mastai's national
classified directory of American art
& antique dealers. 7th-   ed.; 1961-
New York, Mastai Pub. Co.   72-623808
N8630 .M3   MRR Alc Latest edition

National travel guide to antique
shops. [Casper, Wyo., Antique
Enterprises]   65-4691
NK1127 .N3   MRR Alc Latest edition

ART OBJECTS--CONSERVATION AND
RESTORATION.
Savage, George, The art and antique
restorers' handbook; [Rev. ed.] New
York, Praeger [1967]   142 p.
708/.04/03   67-17963
N8560 .S38 1967a MRR Alc.

ART OBJECTS--DICTIONARIES.
Bernasconi, John R. The collectors'
glossary of antiques and fine arts,
[Rev. ed.] London, Estates Gazette,
ltd. [1963] xvi, 587 p.   66-48284
NK30 .B4 1963 MRR Alc.

Boger, Louise Ade. The dictionary of
antiques and the decorative arts;
New York, Scribner [1967] ix, 662 p.
703   67-18131
NK30 .B57 1967 MRR Alc.

Clark, MaryJane. An illustrated
glossary of decorated antiques from
the late 17th century to the early
20th century. [1st ed.] Rutland,
Vt., C. E. Tuttle Co. [1972]   400 p.
[$8.75]   745.1   74-138080
NK30 .C43 MRR Alc.

Hayward, Helena, ed. The
Connoisseur's handbook of antique
collecting; New York, Hawthorn Books
[1960]   320 p.   703   60-8797
NK30 .H45 MRR Alc.

Pegler, Martin M. The dictionary of
interior design. London, Barker,
1967. [8], 500 p.   [55/-]   747/.03
67-110479
NK1165 .P4 1967 MRR Alc.

Phillips, Phoebe. The collectors'
encyclopedia of antiques. New York,
Crown Publishers [1973]   703 p.
[$20.00]   745.1   73-76934
NK28 .P494 1973 MRR Alc.

Ramsey, L. G. G., comp. The complete
encyclopedia of antiques. [1st ed.]
New York, Hawthorn Books [1962] 1472
p.   708   62-9526
NK30 .R33 MRR Alc.

The Random House encyclopedia of
antiques. [1st American ed.] New
York, Random House [1973] 400 p.
[$25.00]   745.1/075   73-3997
NK1125 .R35 1973 MRR Alc.

Savage, George, Dictionary of
antiques. New York, Praeger [1970]
ix, 534 p.   [14.95]   745.1/03   75-
107216
NK30 .S27 1970 MRR Alc.

Wood, Violet (Mackworth-Praed)
Victoriana, New York, Macmillan,
1961 [c1960] 175 p.   708.051   61-
65212
NK928 .W6 1961 MRR Alc.

ART OBJECTS--MISCELLANEA.
Boger, Louise Ade. House & garden's
antiques: questions & answers. New
York, Simon and Schuster [1973]
viii, 429 p.   [$9.95]   745.1   73-
180214
NK1125 .B56 MRR Alc.

ART OBJECTS--PRICES.
Art-price annual. Munich [etc.]
Kunst und Technik Verlag [etc.] 55-
37582
N8670 .A68 MRR Alc Partial set

Coysh, Arthur Wilfred. The buying
antiques reference book; Newton
Abbot, David & Charles, 1968. 232 p.
[45/-] 745.1/025 74-385636
NK1125 .C68 MRR Alc.

Kovel, Ralph M. The complete
antiques price list; 3d ed. New
York, Crown Publishers [1970] 616 p.
745.1/029 79-21772
NK1125 .K64 1970 MRR Alc.

Reif, Rita. The antique collector's
guide to styles and prices. New
York, Hawthorn Books [1970] xii, 276
p. [12.95] 749/.075 75-102019
NK1125 .R37 MRR Alc.

Reitlinger, Gerald. The economics of
taste. London, Barrie and Rockliff
[1961-70] 3 v. [50/- (v. 1) varies]
069/.51 62-4300
N8675 .R44 MRR Alc.

Warman, Edwin G., Warman's antiques
and their current prices. [1st]-
1949- Uniontown, Pa., E. G. Warman
Pub. Co. [etc.] 56-2031
NK1133 .W33 MRR Alc Latest edition

ART OBJECTS, AMERICAN.
Christensen, Erwin Ottomar, The
Index of American Design. New York,
Macmillan, 1950. xviii, 229 p. 745
50-10215
NK1403 .C5 MRR Alc.

Hudson, William Norman. Antiques at
auction South Brunswick, A. S.
Barnes [1872] 403 p. [$20.00]
338.4/3745/10973 76-111646
N6507 .B82 MRR Alc.

ART OBJECTS, AMERICAN--DICTIONARIES.
Phipps, Frances, The collector's
complete dictionary of American
antiques. [1st ed.] Garden City,
N.Y., Doubleday, 1974. xv, 640 p.
[$25.00] 709/.73 72-97257
NK805 .P52 MRR Alc.

ART OBJECTS, AMERICAN--HISTORY.
Davidson, Marshall B. The American
heritage history of American antiques
from the Revolution to the Civil War,
[New York] American Heritage Pub.
Co.; Distribution by Simon and
Schuster [1968] 416 p. [17.50]
709/.73 68-28301
NK806 .D37 MRR Alc.

Davidson, Marshall B. The American
heritage history of antiques from the
Civil War to World War I, [New York]
American Heritage Pub. Co. [1969]
415 p. [17.50] 745.1/0973 79-
80756
NK806 .D35 MRR Alc.

Davidson, Marshall B. The American
heritage history of colonial
antiques, [New York] American
Heritage Pub. Co.; book trade
distribution by Simon and Schuster
[1967] 384 p. 709/.73 67-23439
NK806 .D38 MRR Alc.

ART OBJECTS, ENGLISH--HISTORY.
The Connoisseur. The Connoisseur's
complete period guides to the houses,
decoration, furnishing and chattels
of the classic periods; London, The
Connoisseur 1968. 1536 p. [84/-]
709/.42 70-369442
NK928 .C63 MRR Alc.

ART OBJECTS AS AN INVESTMENT.
Rush, Richard H. Antiques as an
investment Englewood Cliffs, N.J.,
Prentice-Hall [1968] 536 p.
[$14.95] 749 68-10170
NK1125 .R86 MRR Alc.

ART SCHOOLS--DIRECTORIES.
American art directory. v. [1]-
1898- New York, R. R. Bowker. 99-
1016
N50 .A54 MRR Ref Desk Latest
edition

International directory of arts.
[1st]- ed.; 1952/53- Berlin,
Deutsche Zentraldruckerei AG [etc.]
55-28737
N50 .I6 MRR Alc Latest edition

ART SOCIETIES--DIRECTORIES.
American art directory. v. [1]-
1898- New York, R. R. Bowker. 99-
1016
N50 .A54 MRR Ref Desk Latest
edition

International directory of arts.
[1st]- ed.; 1952/53- Berlin,
Deutsche Zentraldruckerei AG [etc.]
55-28737
N50 .I6 MRR Alc Latest edition

ART TEACHERS--DIRECTORIES.
Scott, Thomas J. Greater New York
art directory. [New York, Center for
Urban Education, 1968] 314 p.
[1.00] 700/.25/747 68-56339
N6535.N5 S27 MRR Alc.

ARTHROPODA.
see also Insects

**ARTHUR, CHESTER ALAN, PRES. U.S. 1830-
1886.**
Howe, George Frederick. Chester A.
Arthur; New York, Dodd, Mead &
company, 1934. xi, 307 p. 923.173
34-38337
E692 .H67 MRR Alc.

**ARTIFICIAL SATELLITES--DICTIONARIES--
RUSSIAN.**
United States. Library of Congress.
Reference Dept. Russian-English
glossary of guided missile, rocket,
and satellite terms, Washington,
1958. vi, 352 p. 629.1333803
629.1435303* 58-60055
Z663.2 .R83 MRR Alc.

ARTIFICIAL SATELLITES--MOON.
see also Project Apollo

ARTIFICIAL WEATHER CONTROL
see Weather control

ARTILLERY--HISTORY.
Guns; Greenwich, Conn., New York
Graphic Society [1971] 216 p.
[$30.00] 358/.12/094 74-159805
UF15 .G85 MRR Alc.

ARTILLERY--UNITED STATES.
Ripley, Warren, Artillery and
ammunition of the Civil War. New
York, Van Nostrand Reinhold Co.
[1970] 384 p. 623.4 75-90331
UF23 .R56 1970 MRR Alc.

ARTISTIC PHOTOGRAPHY
see Photography, Artistic

ARTISTS.
see also Authors

see also Painters

see also Potters

Albright-Knox Art Gallery.
Contemporary art, 1942-72; New York,
Praeger [1973, c1972] 479 p.
[$25.00] 709/.04/074014797 70-
188296
N6487.B83 A42 MRR Alc.

Histoire de l'art contemporain;
Authorized reprint ed. in one volume.
New York, Arno Press [1968] 536 p.
68-9229
ND195 .H5 1968 MRR Alc.

Sylvester, David, ed. Modern art,
New York, F. Watts [1966, c1965] 296
p. 709.04 65-10270
N6490 .S9 MRR Alc.

ARTISTS--AUTOGRAPHS--FACSIMILES.
Édouard-Joseph, René. Dictionnaire
biographique des artistes
contemporains, 1910-1930. Paris, Art
& edition, 1930-34. 3 v. 927 30-
21197
N40 .E4 MRR Alc.

ARTISTS--BIBLIOGRAPHY.
Columbia University. Libraries. Avery
Architectural Library. Avery
obituary index of architects and
artists. Boston, G. K. Hall, 1963.
338 p. 64-7017
Z5941 .C64 MRR Biog.

The Index of twentieth century
artists. v. 1-4, no. 7; Oct 1933-
Apr. 1937. New York, College Art
Association. 705 016.7 36-30278
N1 .I5 MRR Alc Full set

Istituto nazionale di archeologia e
storia dell'arte, Rome. Biblioteca.
Annuario bibliografico di storia
dell'arte. anno 1- 1952- Modena.
55-58434
Z5931 .I73 MRR Alc Full set

Mallett, Daniel Trowbridge, Index of
artists, international-biographical;
New York, P. Smith., 1948 [c1935]
xxxiv, 493 p. 927 49-2699
N40 .M3 1948 MRR Alc.

ARTISTS--BIOGRAPHY.
Canaday, John Edwin, The lives of
the painters [1st ed.] New York,
Norton [1969] 4 v. 759 B 67-17666

ND35 .C35 MRR Alc.

Dawdy, Doris Ostrander. Artists of
the American West : 1st ed. Chicago
: Sage Books, [1974] viii, 275 p. :
[$12.50] 709/.2/2 72-91919
N6536 .D38 MRR Biog.

Who's who in art. 1st- ed.; 1927-
London, Art Trade Press. 27-14051
N40 .W6 MRR Biog Latest edition /
MRR Alc Latest edition

ARTISTS--BIOGRAPHY--DICTIONARIES.
A Visual dictionary of art.
Greenwich, Conn., New York Graphic
Society [1974] 640 p. [$30.00]
703 73-76181
N33 .V56 1974 MRR Biog.

ARTISTS--BIOGRAPHY--INDEXES.
Artbibliographies modern. Santa
Barbara, Calif., American
Bibliographical Center. 016.709/04
74-647780
Z5935 .L64 MRR Alc Full set

Havlice, Patricia Pate. Index to
artistic biography. Metuchen, N.J.,
Scarecrow Press, 1973. 2 v. (viii,
1362 p.) 709/.2/2 72-6412
N40 .H38 MRR Biog.

ARTISTS--DICTIONARIES.
The Art collector's almanac. no. 1-
1965- Huntington Station [N.Y.] J.
E. Treisman. 65-15142
N9 .A38 MRR Alc Latest edition

Atlantic brief lives: a biographical
companion to the arts. [1st ed.]
Boston, Little, Brown [1971] xxii,
900 p. [$15.00] 700/.922 B 73-
154960
NX90 .A73 1971 MRR Biog.

Bénézit, Emmanuel, Dictionnaire
critique et documentaire des
peintres, sculpteurs, dessinateurs et
graveurs de tous les temps et de tous
les pays, Nouv. éd. entièrement
refondue, rev. et corr. [Paris]
Gründ, 1948-55. 8 v. 927 49-
18054
N40 .B47 MRR Alc.

Bérard, Michèle. Encyclopedia of
modern art auction prices. New York,
Arco Pub. Co. [1971] x, 417 p.
[$45.00] 338.4/3/7 79-161210
N6447 .B47 MRR Alc.

Berckelaers, Ferdinand Louis,
Dictionnaire de la peinture
abstraite, Paris, F. Hazan [1957]
305 p. a 57-7206
ND35 .B4 MRR Alc.

Bernasconi, John R. The collectors'
glossary of antiques and fine arts,
[Rev. ed.] London, Estates Gazette,
ltd. [1965] xvi, 587 p. 66-48284
NK30 .B4 1963 MRR Alc.

The Book of art; New York, Grolier
[c1965] 10 v. 709.4 65-10350
N31 .B6 MRR Alc.

Bowness, Alan, ed. Impressionists
and post-impressionists. New York,
F. Watts [1965] 296 p. 709.034 65-
10269
ND1265 .B67 MRR Alc.

Bryan, Michael, Dictionary of
painters and engravers. New ed.,
rev. and enl. Port Washington,
N.Y., Kennikat Press [1964] 5 v.
927.5 64-15534
N40 .B945 MRR Alc.

Comstock, Helen, ed. The concise
encyclopedia of American antiques.
New York, Hawthorn Books [1965] 848
p. 745.10973 65-9391
NK805 .C65 1965 MRR Alc.

Coysh, Arthur Wilfred. The antique
buyer's dictionary of names New
York, Praeger [1970] 278 p.
745.1/03 70-125355
N40 .C67 1970 MRR Alc.

Dictionary of modern painting. 3d
ed., rev. and enl. New York, Tudor
Pub. Co. [1964] 416 p. 759.05 65-
1420
ND30 .D515 1964 MRR Alc.

Enciclopedia della pittura italiana
[Milano] Garzanti [1950] 2 v.
759.5 51-17931
ND622 .E5 MRR Alc.

Encyclopaedia of the arts. New York,
Meredith Press [1966] 966 p. 703
66-23883
N31 .E54 MRR Alc.

Encyclopedia of painting; New York,
Crown Publishers, 1955. 511 p.
750.3 55-12456
ND30 .E5 MRR Alc.

Encyclopedia of world art. New York,
McGraw-Hill [1959- v. 703 59-
13433
N31 .E4833 MRR Alc.

Fernau, Joachim. The Praeger
encyclopedia of old masters. New
York, F. A. Praeger [1959] 334 p.
759.003 59-7456
ND30 .F413 MRR Alc.

Foster, Joshua James, A dictionary
of painters of miniatures (1525-1850)
London, P. Allan & co., ltd., 1926.
xv, 330 p. 26-14138
N7616 .F72 MRR Alc.

ARTISTS--DICTIONARIES. (Cont.)
Goldstein, Franz. Monogramm-Lexikon;
Berlin, De Gruyter, 1964. 931 p.
65-47949
  N45 .G6 MRR Alc.

Grant, Maurice Harold, A dictionary
of British sculptors London,
Rockliff [1953] 317 p. 927.3 53-
30728
  NB496 .G7 1953 MRR Alc.

Hayward, Helena, ed. The
Connoisseur's handbook of antique
collecting; New York, Hawthorn Books
[1960] 320 p. 703 60-8787
  NK30 .H45 MRR Alc.

The Index of twentieth century
artists. v. 1-4, no. 7; Oct 1933-
Apr. 1937. New York, College Art
Association. 705 016.7 36-30278
  N1 .I5 MRR Alc Full set

Jakovsky, Anatole. Peintres naïfs;
New York, Universe Books [1967] 398
p. 758 67-15570
  ND35 .J28 MRR Alc.

The Lincoln library of the arts.
[1st ed.] Columbus, Ohio, Frontier
Press Co. [1973] 2 v. (846 p.)
700/.3 73-78393
  NX70 .L54 MRR Alc.

Mallett, Daniel Trowbridge, Index of
artists, international-biographical;
New York, P. Smith, 1948 [c1935]
xxxiv, 493 p. 927 49-2699
  N40 .M3 1948 MRR Alc.

Martin, Michael Rheta, The arts;
Indianapolis, Bobbs-Merrill [1965]
xxx, 423 p. 709 64-15664
  N5300 .M29 MRR Alc.

McGraw-Hill dictionary of art. New
York, McGraw-Hill [1969] 5 v. 703
68-26314
  N33 .M23 MRR Alc.

Muller, Joseph Émile. A dictionary
of Expressionism / London : Eyre
Methuen, 1973. 159 p. : [£1.50]
759.06   74-188205
  N6494.E9 M8413 MRR Alc.

Murray, Peter. Dictionary of art and
artists New York, Praeger [1966]
464 p. 703 65-20073
  N31 .M8 1966 MRR Alc.

New international illustrated
encyclopedia of art. New York,
Greystone Press [1967- v. 703
67-24201
  N31 .N4 MRR Alc.

The new standard encyclopedia of art:
De luxe ed. New York, Garden City
publishing co., inc. [1939] 2 v. in
1. 703 39-16979
  N31 .H3 1939 MRR Alc.

The Oxford companion to art; Oxford,
Clarendon P., 1970. xii, 1277 p., 2
plates. [6/-/-] 703 71-526168
  N33 .C9 MRR Alc.

Les Peintres célèbres. [2. éd.
Paris] L. Mazenod [1953-64] 3 v.
54-25077
  ND50 .P4 MRR Alc.

Praeger encyclopedia of art. New
York, Praeger Publishers [1971] 5 v.
(2139 p.) 703 75-122093
  N33 .P68 MRR Alc.

The Praeger picture encyclopedia of
art; New York, F. A. Praeger [1958]
584 p. 703 58-11404
  N5300 .P773 MRR Alc.

Pyke, E. J. A biographical
dictionary of wax modellers Oxford,
Clarendon Press, 1973. lxvi, 216,
[79] p. [£20.00] 736/.93/0922 73-
174552
  NK9580 .P94 MRR Biog.

Savage, George, Dictionary of
antiques. New York, Praeger [1970]
ix, 534 p. [14.95] 745.1/03 75-
107216
  NK30 .S27 1970 MRR Alc.

A Visual dictionary of art.
Greenwich, Conn., New York Graphic
Society [1974] 640 p. [$30.00]
703 73-76181
  N33 .V56 1974 MRR Alc.

Waters, Clara (Erskine) Clement,
Painters, sculptors, architects,
engravers, and their works. 7th ed.
Boston, J. R. Osgood and company,
1881. xlii, 1 l., 681 p. incl. 8
plates 08-21746
  N40 .W35 MRR Alc.

Who's who in graphic art. 1st-
ed.; 1962- Zurich, Amstutz & Herdeg
Graphis Press. 62-51802
  NC45 .W5 MRR Biog Latest edition

ARTISTS--DICTIONARIES--FRENCH.
Cabanne, Pierre. Dictionnaire des
arts. Paris, Montréal, Bordas
[1971] i, 736 p. [110F] 73-177570
  N33 .C32 MRR Alc.

Dictionnaire universel de l'art et
des artistes ou sont traites,
Paris, F. Hazan, 1967-68. 3 v.
[591.85] 703 68-70531
  N33 .D48 MRR Alc.

Édouard-JOseph, René. Dictionnaire
biographique des artistes
contemporains, 1910-1930. Paris, Art
& édition, 1930-34. 3 v. 927 30-
21197
  N40 .E4 MRR Alc.

ARTISTS--DICTIONARIES--GERMAN.
Darmstaedter, Robert.
Kunstlerlexikon: Bern, Francke
[1961] 527 p. 62-43121
  N40 .D34 MRR Biog.

Koch, Willi August, Musisches
Lexikon: Künstler, Kunstwerke und
Motive aus Dichtung, Musik und
bildender Kunst, 2., veranderte und
erweiterte Aufl. Stuttgart, A.
Kroner [c1964] 1250 columns, xxxx
p. 65-68991
  N31 .K57 1964 MRR Alc.

Kürschners Graphiker Handbuch: 2.
erw. Aufl. Berlin, De Gruyter [1967]
xi, 396 p., 188 p. of plates.
760/.0922 68-93136
  NC249 .K8 1967 MRR Biography.

Nagler, Georg Kaspar, Neues
allgemeines künstler-lexikon; 2.
aufl. Linz a. D., E. Mareis, 1904-
14. 25 v. 05-42072
  N40 .N2 MRR Alc.

Thieme, Ulrich, ed. Allgemeines
lexikon der bildenden kunstler von
der antike bis zur gegenwart:
Leipzig, W. Engelmann, 1907-50. 37
v. 08-5218
  N40 .T4 MRR Alc.

Vollmer, Hans, ed. Allgemeines
Lexikon der bildenden Kunstler des
XX. Jahrhunderts. Leipzig, E. A.
Seemann, 1953-62. 6 v. 927 54-
19064
  N40 .V6 MRR Alc.

ARTISTS--DICTIONARIES--ITALIAN.
Dizionario letterario Bompiani degli
autori di tutti i tempi e di tutte le
letterature. Milano, V. Bompiani,
1956-57. 3 v. 58-16111
  Z1010 .D5 MRR Biog.

ARTISTS--DIRECTORIES.
Director's Art Institute, New York.
Who's who in commercial art and
photography: [2d ed.] New York,
1964. 192 p. 66-235
  NC997 .D5 1964 MRR Biog.

International directory of arts.
[1st- ed.: 1952/53- Berlin,
Deutsche Zentraldruckerei AG [etc.]
55-28737
  N50 .I6 MRR Alc Latest edition

ARTISTS--CANADA--DICTIONARIES.
Creative Canada; [Toronto] Published
in association with McPherson
Library, University of Victoria, by
University of Toronto Press [1971-
v. [$15.00 (v. 1)] 790/.971 71-
151387
  NX513.A1 C7 MRR Biog.

ARTISTS--ENGLAND--DICTIONARIES.
Redgrave, Samuel, A dictionary of
artists of the English school from
the Middle Ages to the nineteenth
century: New and rev. ed.
Amsterdam, G. W. Hissink, 1970. xiv,
497 p. [72.00] 709/.22 78-493152

  N6796 .R4 1970b MRR Biog.

ARTISTS--FRANCE--DICTIONARIES.
Cogniat, Raymond, A dictionary of
Impressionism [with an introduction
by Jean Selz; London, Eyre Methuen,
1973. 168 p. [£1.50] 759.4 74-
180882
  N6847.I4 C6313 1973 MRR Alc.

ARTISTS--IRELAND--DICTIONARIES.
Strickland, Walter G., A dictionary
of Irish artists. New York, Hacker
Art Books [1969, c1968] 2 v.
709/.22 79-94898
  N6782 .S7 1969 MRR Biog.

ARTISTS--SWEDEN--DICTIONARIES.
Svenskt konstnärslexikon; Malmo,
Allhems forlag [1952-67] 5 v.
709/.22   a 52-10729
  N7092 .S94 MRR Alc.

ARTISTS--UNITED STATES--BIOGRAPHY.
Dawdy, Doris Ostrander. Artists of
the American West : 1st ed. Chicago
: Sage Books, [1974] viii, 275 p. :
[$12.50] 709/.2/2 72-91919
  N6536 .D38 MRR Biog.

ARTISTS--UNITED STATES--BIOGRAPHY--
DICTIONARIES.
Fielding, Mantle, Dictionary of
American painters, sculptors and
engravers / Enl. ed. with over 2,500
new listings of seventeenth,
eighteenth, and nineteenth century
American artists / Greens Farms,
Conn. : Modern Books and Crafts,
[1974] vi, 455 p. ; [$17.50]
709/.2/2 74-192539
  N6536 .F5 1974 MRR Biog.

ARTISTS, AMERICAN.
American Contemporary Art Gallery,
New York. 31 American contemporary
artists: New York [1959] unpaged.
759.13 59-4381
  N6512 .A59 MRR Alc.

Artists U.S.A. 1970/71-
Philadelphia. 338.4/7/75913029 78-
134303
  N6512 .A78 MRR Alc Latest edition

Belknap, Waldron Phoenix, American
colonial painting: Cambridge, Mass.,
Belknap Press of Harvard University
Press, 1959. xxi, 377 p. 759.13
59-10313
  ND1311 .B39 MRR Alc.

Fairman, Charles Edwin, Art and
artists of the Capitol of the United
States of America, Washington, U.S.
Govt. print. off., 1927. xii, 526
p., 1 l. incl. illus., ports., plans,
facsims., tables. 28-26032
  N853 .F4 MRR Ref Desk.

Fielding, Mantle, Dictionary of
American painters, sculptors and
engravers / Enl. ed. with over 2,500
new listings of seventeenth,
eighteenth, and nineteenth century
American artists / Greens Farms,
Conn. : Modern Books and Crafts,
[1974] vi, 455 p. ; [$17.50]
709/.2/2 74-192539
  N6536 .F5 1974 MRR Biog.

Illinois. University at Urbana-
Champaign. College of Fine and
Applied Arts. Contemporary American
painting and sculpture. Urbana.
759.13 74-642877
  ND212.A1 I4 MRR Alc Latest edition

The Index of twentieth century
artists. v. 1-4, no. 7; Oct 1933-
Apr. 1937. New York, College Art
Association. 705 016.7 36-30278
  N1 .I5 MRR Alc Full set

Lipman, Jean (Herzberg) comp.
Primitive painters in America, 1750-
1950; New York, Dodd, Mead [1950]
182 p. 759.13 50-58059
  ND236 .L7 MRR Alc.

McCoy, Garnett. Archives of American
art; New York, Bowker, 1972. ix,
163 p. 016.7/0973 72-5125
  Z6611.A7 M3 MRR Alc.

New York Historical Society.
Catalogue of American portraits in
the New York Historical Society. New
Haven : Published by the New York
Historical Society by Yale University
Press, 1974. 2 v. (ix, 964 p.) :
757/.9/0973 74-79974
  N7593 .N5 1974 MRR Alc.

Park, Esther Ailleen. Mural painters
in America. Pittsburg, Kansas State
Teachers College, 1949- pts.
016.75173 50-63160
  ND236 .P3 MRR Biog.

Princeton University. Library. Early
American book illustrators and wood
engravers, 1670-1870; Princeton,
N.J.; 1958. xlvii, 265 p. 761.2084
58-9784
  Z1023 .P9 1958 MRR Alc.

Smith, Ralph Clifton, A biographical
index of American artists,
Baltimore, The Williams & Wilkins
company, 1930. x, 102 p. 30-7664
  N6536 .S6 MRR Biog.

Taft, Robert, Artists and
illustrators of the Old West, 1850-
1900. New York, Scribner, 1953.
xvii, 400 p. 709.78 53-7577
  N6510 .T27 MRR Alc.

United States. Library of Congress.
Prints and Photographs Division.
American prints in the Library of
Congress; Baltimore, Published for
the Library of Congress by the Johns
Hopkins Press [1970] xxi, 568 p.
769/.973 73-106134
  NE505 .A47 MRR Alc.

Wehle, Harry Brandeis, American
miniatures, 1730-1850; Garden City,
N.Y., Garden City publishing company,
inc. [1937] xxv p., 1 l., 127 p.
757.0873 37-6103
  ND1337.U5 W4 1937 MRR Alc.

ARTISTS, AMERICAN--DICTIONARIES.
Cederholm, Theresa Dickason. Afro-
American artists; a bio-
bibliographical directory. [Boston]
Trustees of the Boston Public
Library, 1973. 348 p.   709/.73 73-
84951
   N6538.N5 C42 MRR Biog.

Collins, Jimmie Lee, Women artists
in America; [Chattanooga? Tenn.,
1973] 1 v. (unpaged) [$15.00]
709/.2/2 B 73-163882
   N43 .C64 MRR Biog.

Cummings, Paul. A dictionary of
contemporary American artists. 2d
ed. New York, St. Martin's Press
[1971] xv, 368 p. [$25.00]
709/.22 76-31377
   N6536 .C8 1971 MRR Biog.

Cummings, Paul. A dictionary of
contemporary American artists. New
York, St. Martin's Press [1966] xx,
331 p.   709.22 65-20815
   N6536 .C8 MRR Alc.

Dawdy, Doris Ostrander. Artists of
the American West : 1st ed. Chicago
: Sage Books, [1974] viii, 275 p. ;
[$12.50] 709/.2/2 72-91919
   N6536 .D38 MRR Biog.

Fielding, Mantle, Dictionary of
American painters, sculptors &
engravers, N.Y., P. A.
Struck, 1945. 4 p. l., 433 (i.e.
450) p. incl. front., illus.   927
45-3826
   N6536 .F5 1945 MRR Alc.

New York Historical Society.
Dictionary of artists in America,
1564-1860, New Haven, Yale
University Press, 1957. xxvii, 759
p.   927.5 57-6338
   N6536 .N4 MRR Alc.

Young, William, A dictionary of
American artists, sculptors and
engravers: Cambridge, Mass., W.
Young [1968] 515 p.   709/.73 68-
3733
   N6536 .Y7 MRR Biog.

ARTISTS, AMERICAN--WASHINGTON, D.C.--
DIRECTORIES.
Artists Equity Association. D.C.
Chapter. Washington artists;
[Washington, 1972] 123 p.   709/.2/2
72-189977
   N6535.W3 A68 MRR Biog.

ARTISTS, ARGENTINE.
Merlino, Adrián. Diccionario de
artistas plásticos de la Argentina,
[Buenos Aires, 1954] 433 p.   55-
20937
   N6638 .M4 MRR Alc.

ARTISTS, AUSTRALIAN.
McCulloch, Alan. Encyclopedia of
Australian art. New York, Praeger
[1969, c1968] 668 p.   [25.00]
709/.94 69-17079
   N7400 .M27 1969 MRR Alc.

ARTISTS, BRITISH.
Berea, T. B. Handbook of 17th, 18th,
and 19th century British landscape
painters & watercolorists
[Chattanooga? Tenn., 1970] 72 p.
758/.1/0942 78-13623
   ND496 .B4 MRR Biog.

Foskett, Daphne. A dictionary of
British miniature painters. New
York, Praeger Publishers [1972] 2 v.
[$135.00] 759.2 72-112634
   ND1337.G7 F463 1972 MRR Alc.

Grant, Maurice Harold, A dictionary
of British etchers. London,
Published for the author by Rockliff
[1952] 232 p.   767.2 52-3175
   NE2043 .G7 1952 MRR Alc.

Graves, Algernon. A dictionary of
artists who have exhibited works in
the principal London exhibitions from
1760 to 1893; 3d ed., with additions
and corrections. London, H. Graves
and co., limited, 1901. xiv, 314 p.,
1 l.   02-28414
   N5053 .G75 MRR Alc.

Who's who in art. 1st- ed.; 1927-
London, Art Trade Press.   27-14051
   N40 .W6 MRR Biog Latest edition /
   MRR Alc Latest edition

Wood, Christopher. Dictionary of
Victorian painters; [Woodbridge]
Antique Collectors' Club, 1971. v-
xvi, 435 p. [£8.00] 759.2 72-
188506
   ND35 .W6 MRR Biog.

ARTISTS, CATALAN.
Rafols, José F., ed. Diccionario
biografico de artistas de Cataluna
Barcelona, Editorial Millá, 1951-54.
3 v.   927 53-20793
   N7109.C3 R33 MRR Alc.

ARTISTS, CHINESE.
Siren, Osvald, Chinese painting;
New York, Ronald Press [1956- v.
759.951 A 57-1105
   ND1040 .S49 MRR Alc.

ARTISTS, DANISH.
Weilbach, Philip, Kunstnerleksikon;
[København] Aschehoug, 1947-52. 3 v.
50-24719
   N7022 .W44 MRR Alc.

ARTISTS, DUTCH.
Mander, Carel van, Dutch and Flemish
painters; New York, McFarlane,
Warde, McFarlane, 1936. lxix, 560 p.
759.9492 .36-25229
   ND625 .M24 MRR Alc.

ARTISTS, ENGLISH.
Rothenstein, John Knewstub Maurice,
Sir, Modern English painters.
London, Eyre & Spottiswoode, 1952-56.
2 v.   758.2 52-40976
   ND496 .R65 MRR Alc.

ARTISTS, FLEMISH.
Mander, Carel van, Dutch and Flemish
painters; New York, McFarlane,
Warde, McFarlane, 1936. lxix, 560 p.
759.9492 36-25229
   ND625 .M24 MRR Alc.

ARTISTS, FLEMISH--DICTIONARIES.
Wilenski, Reginald Howard, Flemish
painters, 1430-1830. London, Faber
and Faber [1960] 2 v.   759.8493 60-
51134
   ND672 .W5 1960a MRR Alc.

ARTISTS, FRENCH--DICTIONARIES.
Cogniat, Raymond, A dictionary of
Impressionism [with an introduction
by Jean Selz; London, Eyre Methuen,
1973. 168 p. [£1.50] 759.4 74-
180882
   N6847.I4 C6313 1973 MRR Alc.

Dictionnaire des peintres français.
[Paris, Seghers, 1961] 378 p.   62-
44444
   ND552 .D5 MRR Alc.

ARTISTS, GREEK.
The New Century handbook of Greek art
and architecture. New York, Appleton-
Century-Crofts [1972] ix, 213 p.
709/.38 72-187738
   N5633 .N39 MRR Alc.

ARTISTS, ITALIAN.
Enciclopedia della pittura italiana
[Milano] Garzanti [1950] 2 v.
759.5 51-17931
   ND622 .E5 MRR Alc.

Schmeckebier, Laurence Eli, A
handbook of Italian renaissance
painting. New York, G. P. Putnam's
sons [c1938] xi, 362 p.   759.5 38-
27574
   ND615 .S38 MRR Alc.

Vasari, Giorgio, Lives of seventy of
the most eminent painters, sculptors
and architects, New York, C.
Scribner's sons, 1896. 4 v.   03-
16258
   N6922 .V46 MRR Alc.

ARTISTS, MEXICAN.
Velazquez Chavez, Agustín.
Contemporary Mexican artists New
York, Covici-Friede [c1937] xvi p.,
1 l., 19-304 p. incl. front., plates.
759.972 927.5 37-15299
   ND255 .V38 MRR Alc.

ARTISTS, NEGRO
   see Negro artists

ARTISTS, NORWEGIAN--DICTIONARIES.
Illustrert norsk kunstnerleksikon;
Oslo, Broen bokhandel, 1956. 261 p.
a 57-5084
   N7072 .I55 MRR Alc.

ARTISTS, SPANISH.
Pintores españoles contemporáneos;
Madrid, Estiarte [1972] 250 p.
759.6 73-314037
   ND808 .P48 MRR Biog.

ARTISTS, WOMEN
   see Women artists

ARTISTS' MARKS.
Benezit, Emmanuel, Dictionnaire
critique et documentaire des
peintres, sculpteurs, dessinateurs et
graveurs de tous les temps et de tous
les pays, Nouv. ed. entièrement
refondue, rev. et corr. [Paris]
Grund, 1948-55. 8 v.   927 49-
18054
   N40 .B47 MRR Alc.

Goldstein, Franz. Monogramm-Lexikon;
Berlin, De Gruyter, 1964. 931 p.
65-47949
   N45 .G6 MRR Alc.

ARTISTS' MATERIALS.
Mayer, Ralph, The artist's handbook
of materials and techniques. 3d ed.,
rev. and expanded. New York, Viking
Press [1970] xv, 750 p. [$12.50]
751.4 75-18183
   ND1500 .M3 1970 MRR Alc.

ARTISTS' MATERIALS--DICTIONARIES.
Taubes, Frederic, The painter's
dictionary of materials and methods.
New York, Watson-Guptill Publications
[1971] 253 p. [$6.95] 703 71-
155142
   ND1505 .T38 MRR Alc.

ARTISTS' MATERIALS--FORMULAE, TABLES,
ETC.
Gettens, Rutherford John. Painting
materials; New York, Dover
Publications [1966] x, 333 p.   751
65-26655
   ND1500 .G4 1966 MRR Alc.

ARTS--ANECDOTES, FACETIAE, SATIRE, ETC.
Arvine, Kazlitt, The cyclopaedia of
anecdotes of literature and the fine
arts. Detroit, Gale Research co.,
1967. xxiv, 698 p.   700/.3 67-
14020
   PN6261 .A65 1967 MRR Alc.

ARTS--DICTIONARIES.
The Lincoln library of the arts.
[1st ed.] Columbus, Ohio, Frontier
Press Co. [1973] 2 v. (846 p.)
700/.3 73-78393
   NX70 .L54 MRR Alc.

Martin, Michael Rheta, The arts;
Indianapolis, Bobbs-Merrill [1965]
xxx, 423 p.   709 64-15664
   N5300 .M29 MRR Alc.

ARTS--SCHOLARSHIPS, FELLOWSHIPS, ETC.
Institute of International Education.
Directory of international
scholarships in the arts. New York,
1958. 120 p.   707.9 59-38191
   N347 .I5 MRR Alc.

ARTS--SCHOLARSHIPS, FELLOWSHIPS, ETC.--
NEW YORK (STATE)
New York (State). State University.
Washington Office. Support for the
arts; Washington] 1973. 164 p.
[$2.00] 338.4/7/7009747 73-176026

   NX705.5.U62 N77 1973 MRR Alc.

ARTS--SCHOLARSHIPS, FELLOWSHIPS, ETC.--
UNITED STATES.
National Endowment for the Arts.
Guide to programs:
architecture+environmental arts,
dance, education, expansion arts,
Federal-state partnership,
literature, museums, music, public
media, special projects, theatre,
visual arts. Washington, For sale by
the Supt. of Docs., U.S. Govt. Print.
Off. [1973] 60 p. [$0.95]
338.4/7/700973 73-603497
   NX398 .N37 1973 MRR alc.

ARTS--SCHOLARSHIPS, FELLOWSHIPS, ETC.--
UNITED STATES--DIRECTORIES.
Institute of International Education.
International awards in the arts;
[New York, 1969] 105 p.   707/.9 68-
57352
   NX398 .I5 MRR Ref Desk.

New York (State). State University.
Washington Office. Support for the
arts; Washington] 1973. 164 p.
[$2.00] 338.4/7/7009747 73-176026

   NX705.5.U62 N77 1973 MRR Alc.

Washington and the arts; New York]
Associated Councils of the Arts
[1971] vi, 176 p. [$6.50]
353.008/54/025753 79-163014
   NX735 .W3 MRR Ref Desk.

ARTS--UNITED STATES--SOCIETIES, ETC.--
DIRECTORIES.
Associated Councils of the Arts.
Directory of national arts
organizations. [New York] 1969. 76
p. [2.00 (pbk)] 700/.25/73 75-
77987
   NX22 .A823 MRR Alc.

ARTS, DECORATIVE
   see Decoration and ornament

   see Design, Decorative

   see Interior decoration

ARTS, USEFUL
   see Technology

ARTS AND CRAFTS MOVEMENT.
   see also Folk art

   see also Handicraft

   see also Metal-work

ARYAN LANGUAGES--ETYMOLOGY.
Buck, Carl Darling, A dictionary of
selected synonyms in the principal
Indo-European languages: Chicago,
University of Chicago Press [1949]
xix, 1515 p.   413   49-11769
P765 .B8 MRR Alc.

ARYAN LANGUAGES--GLOSSARIES,
VOCABULARIES, ETC.
Buck, Carl Darling, A dictionary of
selected synonyms in the principal
Indo-European languages: Chicago,
University of Chicago Press [1949]
xix, 1515 p.   413   49-11769
P765 .B8 MRR Alc.

ARYAN LANGUAGES--SEMANTICS.
Buck, Carl Darling, A dictionary of
selected synonms in the principal
Indo-European languages: Chicago,
University of Chicago Press [1949]
xix, 1515 p.   413   49-11769
P765 .B8 MRR Alc.

ASCETICISM--DICTIONARIES--FRENCH.
Dictionnaire de spiritualite
ascetique et mystique, Paris, G.
Beauchesne et ses fils, 1932- v.
282.03 38-24895
BX841 .D67 MRR Alc.

ASHANTI--HISTORY.
Ward, William Ernest Frank, A
history of Ghana. Revised 4th ed.
London, Allen & Unwin, 1967. 454 p.
[35/-] 966.7 68-101489
DT511 .W28 1967 MRR Alc.

ASIA.
Asia Society. Libraries in New York
City, New York, 1962. 23 p.   67-
46335
Z3001 .A8 MRR Alc.

Asian annual: [London, Eastern
world] 950 55-18104
DS4 .A8 MRR Alc Latest edition

Wint, Guy, ed. Asia; a handbook.
New York, Praeger [1966] xiii, 856
p.   915 65-13263
DS5 .W5 MRR Alc.

ASIA--BIBLIOGRAPHY.
American Universities Field Staff. A
select bibliography: Asia, Africa,
Eastern Europe, Latin America. New
York [1960] ix, 534 p.   016.9019
60-10482
Z5579 .A5 MRR Alc.

Asia Society. Asia: a guide to
paperbacks. Rev. ed. [New York]
1968. iii, 178 p.   016.915 68-4375
Z3001 .A79 1968 MRR Alc.

Brunn, Stanley D. Urbanization in
developing countries: East Lansing,
Latin American Studies Center,
Michigan State University, 1971.
xviii, 693 p.   016.30136/3/091724
79-172535
Z7164.U7 B7 MRR Alc.

Garde, P. K. Directory of reference
works published in Asia. [Paris]
UNESCO [1956] xxvii, 139 p.   016 a
57-2357
Z1035 .G27 MRR Alc.

Halstead, John P. Modern European
imperialism: Boston, G. K. Hall,
1974. 2 v.   016.90908 73-19511
Z6204 .H35 MRR Alc.

Nunn, Godfrey Raymond, Asia: a
selected and annotated guide to
reference workss. Cambridge, Mass.,
M.I.T. Press [1971] xiii, 223 p.
[$12.50] 016.016915 77-169004
Z3001 .N79 MRR Alc.

Pearson, James Douglas, Oriental and
Asian bibliography: Hamden, Conn.,
Archon Books, 1966. xvi, 261 p.
016.915 66-1006
Z7046 .P4 MRR Alc.

Quan, Lau-king, Introduction to
Asia; Washington, Library of
Congress, Reference Dept., 1955. x,
214 p.   016.915 54-60018
Z663.2 .I6 MRR Alc.

Royal Commonwealth Society. Library.
Subject catalogue of the Library of
the Royal Empire Society, [1st ed.
reprinted] London, Dawsons for the
Royal Commonwealth Society, 1967. 4
v.   [60/-/- per set (16/-/- per
vol.)] 016.942 68-70847
Z7164.C7 R82 1967 MRR Alc.

Stucki, Curtis W. American doctoral
dissertations on Asia, 1933-1962,
Ithaca, N.Y., Southeast Asia Program,
Dept. of Asian Studies, Cornell
University, 1963. 204 p.   016.915
64-2901
Z3001 .S72 MRR Alc.

Yang, Winston L. Y. Asian resources
in American libraries: New York
[Foreign Area Materials Center,
University of the State of New York]
1968. ix, 122 p.   016.915 68-16584
Z1009 .N54 no. 9 MRR Alc.

ASIA--BIBLIOGRAPHY--CATALOGS.
Royal Commonwealth Society. Library.
Subject catalogue of the Royal
Commonwealth Society, London.
Boston, Mass., G. K. Hall, 1971. 7
v.   017.1 70-180198
Z7164.C7 R83 MRR Alc (Dk 33)

ASIA--BIOGRAPHY.
The Far East and Australasia. 1st-
ed.: 1969- London, Europa
Publications. 915/.03/05 74-417170
DS1 .F3 MRR Alc Latest edition

ASIA--BIOGRAPHY--DICTIONARIES.
The Asia who's who. Hong Kong, Pan-
Asia Newspaper Alliance. 920.05 57-
35338
DS32 .A8 MRR Biog Latest edition

Who's who in U.A.R. and the Near
East. Cairo. 354.62 45-33763
DT44 .W47 MRR Biog Latest edition

ASIA--CLIMATE.
Great Britain. Meteorological Office.
Tables of temperature, relative
humidity and precipitation for the
world. 2nd ed. London, H.M.S.O.,
1966- v.   [1/5/- (pt. 3) 1/15-
(pt. 4) 15/6 (pt. 5)] 551.5/021/2
76-385248
QC982.5 .G732 MRR Alc.

ASIA--COMMERCE--DIRECTORIES.
A.A's Far East businessman's
directory. Hong Kong. 382/.025/5
79-237434
HF3763 .A65 MRR Alc Latest edition

Asian buyers' guide to Republic of
China, Hong Kong, Japan, Republic of
Singapore, and Thailand. 1st- ed.:
1968- Hong Kong, International Pub.
Co. 670 .25/5 68-7584
HF3763 .A82 MRR Alc Latest edition

Chico, Vicente V. International
importers & exporters; 1st ed.
Manila, Nationwide Business Agency
[1971] 1068 p.   382/.025 70-31299
HF54.P6 C54 MRR Alc.

The Eastern trade directory. [Cairo]
ne 62-1365
HF3760.8 .E25 MRR Alc Latest
edition

Owen's commerce and travel and
international register. London,
Owen's Commerce & Travel Ltd.
380.1/025 72-626541
HF3872 .P3 MRR Alc Latest edition

Trado Asian African directory of
exporters-importers & manufacturers.
1959/60- New Delhi, Trado
Publications Private Ltd. [etc.]
338/.0025/5 72-622940
HF3763 .T74 MRR Alc Latest edition

ASIA--COMMERCE--YEARBOOKS.
Owen's commerce and travel and
international register. London,
Owen's Commerce & Travel Ltd.
380.1/025 72-626541
HF3872 .P3 MRR Alc Latest edition

ASIA--COMMERCE--HAWAII--DIRECTORIES.
Hawaii overseas. 1968- [Honolulu]
Hawaii International Services Agency.
382/.025/969 73-626825
HF3161.H3 A3 MRR Alc Latest
edition

ASIA--DESCRIPTION AND TRAVEL--1951- --
GUIDE-BOOKS.
Adams, Stanley E. Oriental guide;
[1st ed.] New York, Pageant Press
[c1965] 551 p.   915/.04/42 64-8564
DS4 .A5 MRR Alc.

ASIA--DESCRIPTION AND TRAVEL--GUIDE-
BOOKS.
Middle East, North Africa, Orient and
Pacific travel guide. [Washington,
D.C.] AAA World Wide Travel Dept.
910 72-622839
DS4 .M5 MRR Alc Latest edition

ASIA--DIRECTORIES.
The Europa year book. 1959- London,
Europa Publications. 341.184 59-
2942
JN1 .E85 Sci RR Latest edition /
MRR Ref Desk Latest edition

ASIA--DISCOVERY AND EXPLORATION.
Pacific voyages. Garden City, N.Y.,
Doubleday [1973, c1971] 488 p.
[$14.95] 910/.09/1823 72-93388
DU19 .P3 1973 MRR Alc.

ASIA--ECONOMIC CONDITIONS--BIBLIOGRAPHY.
Kiel. Universitat. Institut fur
Weltwirtschaft. Bibliothek.
Regionenkatalog. Boston, G. K. Hall,
1967. 52 v.   017/.5 67-9425
Z929 .K52 1967 MRR Alc. (Dk 33).

ASIA--ECONOMIC CONDITIONS--YEARBOOKS.
Asia yearbook. 1974- [Hongkong]
330.9/5/042 74-641208
HC411 .F19 MRR Alc Latest edition

ASIA--FOREIGN RELATIONS--TREATIES.
Wint, Guy, ed. Asia; a handbook.
New York, Praeger [1966] xiii, 856
p.   915 65-13263
DS5 .W5 MRR Alc.

ASIA--GAZETTEERS.
United States. Geographic Names
Division. Asia: official standard
names approved by the United States
Board on Geographic Names.
Washington, 1972. iii, 137 p.
915/.03/42 72-602866
DS4 .U54 MRR Alc.

ASIA--HANDBOOKS, MANUALS, ETC.
Worldmark encyclopedia of the
nations. [4th ed.] New York,
Worldmark Press, [1971] 5 v.
910/.3 76-152128
G103 .W65 1971 MRR Ref Desk.

A Year book of the Commonwealth.
1969- London, H.M. Stationery Off.
320.9/171/242 79-7332
JN248 .C5912 MRR Alc Latest
edition

ASIA--HISTORY--CHRONOLOGY.
Asian recorder. v. 1- Jan. 1/7,
1955- [New Delhi, etc.] K. K. Thomas
[etc.] 950.05 58-24845
DS1 .A4747 MRR Alc Full set

Little, Charles Eugene, Cyclopedia
of classified dates with an
exhaustive index. Detroit, Gale
Research Co., 1967. vii, 1454 p.
902/.02 66-27839
D9 .L7 1967 MRR Alc.

ASIA--HISTORY--PERIODICALS.
Asian recorder. v. 1- Jan. 1/7,
1955- [New Delhi, etc.] K. K. Thomas
[etc.] 950.05 58-24845
DS1 .A4747 MRR Alc Full set

ASIA--HISTORY--SOURCES.
Higgins, Rosalyn. United Nations
peacekeeping, 1946-1967: London, New
York [etc.] issued under the auspices
of the Royal Institute of
International Affairs by Oxford U.P.,
1969- v.   [5/10- (v. 1)] 341.6
76-396893
JX1981.P7 H5 MRR Alc.

ASIA--HISTORY--SOURCES--BIBLIOGRAPHY.
Wainwright, Mary Doreen. A guide to
Western manuscripts and documents in
the British Isles relating to South
and South East Asia. London, New
York, Oxford University Press, 1965.
xix, 532 p.   016.915 65-3147
CD1048.A8 W3 MRR Alc.

ASIA--IMPRINTS.
United States. Library of Congress.
Orientalia Division. Southern Asia
accessions list. v. 1- Jan. 1952-
Washington. 016.95 52-60012
Z663.38 .S8 MRR Alc MRR Alc Full
set

ASIA--INDUSTRIES--DIRECTORIES.
Trado Asian African directory of
exporters-importers & manufacturers.
1959/60- New Delhi, Trado
Publications Private Ltd. [etc.]
338/.0025/5 72-622940
HF3763 .T74 MRR Alc Latest edition

ASIA--LEARNED INSTITUTIONS AND
SOCIETIES--DIRECTORIES.
United Nations Educational,
Scientific and Cultural Organization.
Regional Office for Education in
Asia, Bangkok. Directory of
educational research institutions in
the Asian region. [2d ed.] Bangkok,
1970. iv, 402 p.   77-279387
LB1028 .U42 1970 MRR Alc.

ASIA--MANUFACTURES--DIRECTORIES.
Asian buyers' guide to Republic of
China, Hong Kong, Japan, Republic of
Singapore, and Thailand. 1st- ed.:
1968- Hong Kong, International Pub.
Co. 670 .25/5 68-7584
HF3763 .A82 MRR Alc Latest edition

ASIA--PERIODICALS--INDEXES.
Cumulative bibliography of Asian
studies, 1941-1965: Boston, Mass.,
G. K. Hall, 1969 [i.e. 1970] 4 v.
016.915 79-12105
Z3001 .C93 MRR Alc.

ASIA--POLITICS--YEARBOOKS.
Asia yearbook. 1974- [Hongkong]
330.9/5/042 74-641208
HC411 .F19 MRR Alc Latest edition

ASIA--SOCIAL CONDITIONS--YEARBOOKS.
Asia yearbook. 1974- [Hongkong]
330.9/5/042 74-641208
HC411 .F19 MRR Alc Latest edition

ASIA--SOCIETIES, ETC.--DIRECTORIES.
Asia Society. American institutions
and organizations interested in Asia,
2d ed. New York, Taplinger Pub.
Co., 1961. xii, 581 p. 950.06273
61-11435
DS1 .C572 MRR Alc.

Technical Assistance Information
Clearing House. Far East technical
assistance programs of U.S. nonprofit
organizations, New York, 1966.
viii, 274 p. 309.2/23 67-60359
HC411 .T4 MRR Alc.

ASIA--STATISTICS.
Asian annual; [London, Eastern
world] 950 55-18104
DS4 .A8 MRR Alc Latest edition

Deldycke, Tilo. La population active
et sa structure. Bruxelles, Centre
d'économie politique (de l')
Université libre de Bruxelles,
(1968) viii, 236 p. [360.00]
331.1/12/0212 70-395436
HD4826 .D34 MRR Alc.

Food and Agriculture Organization of
the United Nations. Trade yearbook.
v. 12- 1958- Rome. 338.14058 59-
3598
HD9000.4 .F58 Sci FR Partial set /
MRR Alc Latest edition

International Labor Office. Year
book of labour statistics. [1st]-
1935/36- Geneva. l 36-130
HD4826 .I63 MRR Alc Latest edition

International Monetary Fund. Balance
of payments yearbook. 1946/47-
Washington. 382 49-6612
HF1014 .I5 MRR Alc Latest edition

Keyfitz, Nathan, Population: facts
and methods of demography San
Francisco, W. H. Freeman [1971] x,
613 p. [$13.50] 301.3/2/072 70-
141154
HB885 .K43 MRR Alc.

Organization for Economic Cooperation
and Development. Foreign trade.
Commerce extérieur. Series C.
Commodity trade. Commerce par
produits. [Paris] 382/.021/2 72-
626755
HF91 .O67 MRR Latest edition

Showers, Victor. The world in
figures. New York, Wiley [1973]
xii, 585 p. 910/.21/2 73-9
G109 .S52 MRR Ref Desk.

United Nations. Conference on Trade
and Development. Secretariat. Trade
prospects and capital needs of
developing countries; New York,
United Nations, 1968. ix, 614 p.
[8.00] 382/.09172/3 75-5913
HF1413 .U52 MRR Alc.

United Nations. Statistical Office.
The growth of world industry, 1938-
1961; New York, United Nations,
1963. xvi, 849 p. 338.4083 63-
25411
HC59 .U46 MRR Alc.

United Nations. Statistical Office.
Yearbook of international trade
statistics. 1st- issue; 1950- New
York. 382.058 51-8987
JX1977 .A2 MRR Ref Desk Latest
edition

United States. Bureau of the Census.
U.S. foreign trade: general imports,
world area by commodity groupings.
1970- [Washington, For sale by the
Supt. of Docs., U.S. Govt. Print.
Off.] 382/.5/0973 78-649732
HF105 .C137172 MRR Alc Latest
edition

United States. Bureau of the Census.
U.S. foreign trade: exports, SIC-
based products. 1970- [Washington,
For sale by the Supt. of Docs., U.S.
Govt. Print. Off.] 382/.6/0973 71-
648606
HF105 .C137166 MRR Alc Latest
edition

United States. Bureau of the Census.
U.S. foreign trade: exports, world
area by commodity groupings. 1970-
[Washington, For sale by the Supt. of
Docs., U.S. Govt. Print. Off.]
382/.6/0973 79-648608
HF105 .C137132 MRR Alc Latest
edition

United States. Dept. of Agriculture.
Economic Research Service. European
Economic Community: agricultural
trade statistics, 1961-67.
[Washington, 1969] 1 v. (unpaged)
382/.41/094 78-601937
HD9015.A3 U46 MRR Alc.

ASIA--STATISTICS--BIBLIOGRAPHY.
Texas. University. Population
Research Center. International
population census bibliography.
Austin, Bureau of Business Research,
University of Texas, 1965-67. 6 v.
016.312 66-63578
Z7164.D3 T45 MRR Alc.

ASIA--STATISTICS, VITAL.
Preston, Samuel H. Causes of death:
life tables for national population
New York, Seminar Press, 1972. xi,
787 p. 312/.2 72-80305
HB1321 .P73 MRR Alc.

ASIA--YEARBOOKS.
The Far East and Australasia. 1st-
ed.; 1969- London, Europa
Publications. 915/.03/05 74-417170
DS1 .F3 MRR Alc Latest edition

ASIA, SOUTHEASTERN--ANTIQUITIES.
Rawson, Philip S. The art of
Southeast Asia; New York, F. A.
Praeger [1967] 288 p. 709/.54 67-
29399
N5877.A8 R3 1967 MRR Alc.

ASIA, SOUTHEASTERN--BIBLIOGRAPHY.
Embree, John Fee, Bibliography of
the peoples and cultures of mainland
Southeast Asia, New Haven, Yale
University, Southeast Asia Studies,
1950. xxxiii, 821 p., xii l.
016.9159 50-14198
Z3001 .E5 MRR Alc.

Fürer-Haimendorf, Elizabeth von. An
anthropological bibliography of South
Asia, Paris, Mouton, 1958-70. 3 v.
[fl. 130.00 (v. 3)] a 59-1034
Z5115 .F83 MRR Alc.

Harvard University. Library.
Southern Asia: Cambridge;
Distributed by Harvard University
Press, 1968. iv, 543 p. 016.954
68-15927
Z3185 .H3 MRR Alc.

Hay, Stephen N. Southeast Asian
history; New York, Praeger [1962]
vii, 138 p. 016.959 62-20439
Z3221 .H36 MRR Alc.

Johnson, Donald Clay, A guide to
reference materials on Southeast
Asia, New Haven, Yale University
Press, 1970. xi, 160 p. [8.75]
016.9159 75-104616
Z3221 .J63 MRR Alc.

The, Lian. Treasures and trivia;
[Athens, Ohio] Ohio University,
Center for International Studies,
1968. xiv, 141 l. [3.25] 016.9159
68-66324
Z3221 .T5 MRR Alc.

Tregonning, K. G. Southeast Asia;
Tucson, University of Arizona Press
[1969] 103 p. 016.9159 68-9845
Z3221 .T7 MRR Alc.

United States. Library of Congress.
Orientalia Division. Southeast Asia:
Rev. and enl. Washington, [For sale
by the Superintendent of Documents,
U.S. Govt. Print. Off.] 1964. v, 180
p. 63-60089
Z663.389 .S6 1964 MRR Alc.

ASIA, SOUTHEASTERN--BIBLIOGRAPHY--
CATALOGS.
United States. Library of Congress.
Orientalia Division. Southeast Asia
subject catalog. Boston, G. K. Hall,
1972- v. 016.9159/03 72-5257
Z3221 .U525 MRR Alc (Dk 33)

United States. Library of Congress.
Orientalia Division. Southern Asia
accessions list. v. 1- Jan. 1952-
Washington. 016.95 52-60012
Z663.38 .S8 MRR Alc MRR Alc Full
set

ASIA, SOUTHEASTERN--BIOGRAPHY--
DICTIONARIES.
Tilman, Robert O. International
biographical directory of Southeast
Asia specialists [Ann Arbor, Mich.]
Interuniversity Southeast Asia
Committee, Association for Asian
Studies. [Distributed by Southeast
Asia Studies Center for International
Studies, Ohio University, Athens,
Ohio] 1969. xxxv, 337 p.
915.9/0072/022 76-631592
DS510.7 .T5 MRR Biog.

ASIA, SOUTHEASTERN--DESCRIPTION AND
TRAVEL.
Dobby, Ernest Henry George.
Southeast Asia 9th ed. London,
University of London P., [1966]. 415
p. [21/-] 915.9 67-85516
DS508 .D58 1966 MRR Alc.

ASIA, SOUTHEASTERN--DESCRIPTION AND
TRAVEL--GUIDE-BOOKS.
Caldwell, John Cope, John C.
Caldwell's Orient travel guide. New
York, John Day Co. [1970] 392 p.
[7.95] 915 75-101464
DS504 .C33 1970 MRR Alc.

ASIA, SOUTHEASTERN--DESCRIPTION AND
TRAVEL--GUIDE-BOOKS--PERIODICALS.
Fodor's Japan and East Asia. 1972-
New York, D. McKay. 915.2/04/4 72-
621341
DS805.2 F64 MRR Alc Latest edition

ASIA, SOUTHEASTERN--ECONOMIC CONDITIONS-
-ADDRESSES, ESSAYS, LECTURES.
Southeast Asia's economy in the
1970s. New York, Praeger Publishers
[1971], i.e. 1972] xxxii, 684 p.
[$28.50] 330.9/59 72-174242
HC412 .S596 MRR Alc.

ASIA, SOUTHEASTERN--HISTORY.
Hall, Daniel George Edward, A
history of South-east Asia, 3rd ed.
London, Melbourne [etc.] Macmillan;
New York, St. Martin's P., 1968.
xxiv, 1019 p. 959 68-15302
DS511 .H15 1968 MRR Alc.

ASIA, SOUTHEASTERN--PERIODICALS--
INDEXES.
United States. Library of Congress.
Orientalia Division. Southeast Asia
subject catalog. Boston, G. K. Hall,
1972- v. 016.9159/03 72-5257
Z3221 .U525 MRR Alc (Dk 33)

ASIA, SOUTHEASTERN--STATISTICS.
Southeast Asia's economy in the
1970s. New York, Praeger Publishers
[1971], i.e. 1972] xxxii, 684 p.
[$28.50] 330.9/59 72-174242
HC412 .S596 MRR Alc.

ASIA, WESTERN--DESCRIPTION AND TRAVEL--
GUIDE-BOOKS.
The Middle East, Lebanon, Syria,
Jordan, Iraq, Iran. Paris, Hachette
(impr. Brodard et Taupin], 1966.
1060 p. [37.95 F.] 915.6/04/3 68-
71419
DS43 .M6813 1966 MRR Alc.

ASIAN NEWSPAPERS--DIRECTORIES.
Feuereisen, Fritz. Die Presse in
Asien und Ozeanien; 1. Ausg.
Munchen-Pullach, Verlag
Dokumentation, 1968. 303 p.   79-
381760
Z6957 .F48 MRR Alc.

ASIAN PERIODICALS--BIBLIOGRAPHY.
United States. Library of Congress.
Library of Congress Office, Djakarta.
Accessions list, Indonesia,
Malaysia, Singapore, and Brunei. v.
1- July 1964- Djakarta. sa 66-444
Z663.767.I6 A25 MRR Alc MRR Alc
Full set

United States. Library of Congress.
Library of Congress Office, Djakarta.
Accessions list, Indonesia,
Malaysia, Singapore, and Brunei.
Cumulative list of serials. Jan.
1964/Sept. 1966-1964/68. Djakarta.
74-643581
Z663.767.I6 A252 MRR Alc MRR Alc
Full set

ASIAN PERIODICALS--INDEXES.
United States. Library of Congress.
Orientalia Division. Southern Asia
accessions list. v. 1- Jan. 1952-
Washington. 016.95 52-60012
Z663.38 .S8 MRR Alc MRR Alc Full
set

ASIANS IN THE UNITED STATES--BIOGRAPHY--
DICTIONARIES.
Lo, Samuel E. Asian who? in America.
[Roseland, N.J.] East-West Who?
[1971] 329 p. 920.0973 70-155285

E184.06 L6 MRR Biog.

ASSASSINATION.
see also Murder

McConnell, Brian. The history of
assassination. Nashville, Aurora
Publishers [1970] 359 p. [6.95]
364.15/24 78-114781
HV6278 .M1813 MRR Alc.

ASSASSINS.
Ray, Jo Anne. American assassins.
Minneapolis, Lerner Publications Co.
[1973, c1974] 127 p. [$5.95]
364.1/524/0922 B 920 72-8293
HV6785 .R38 MRR Alc.

ASSASSINS--UNITED STATES--BIOGRAPHY--
JUVENILE LITERATURE.
Ray, Jo Anne. American assassins.
Minneapolis, Lerner Publications Co.
[1973, c1974] 127 p. [$5.95]
364.1/524/0922 B 920 72-8293
HV6785 .R38 MRR Biog.

ASSESSMENT.
Keith, John H. Property tax
assessment practices: 1st ed.
Monterey Park, Calif. [Highland Pub.
Co.] 1966. xxiv, 544 p.
352.1310973 66-18555
  HJ3241 .K37 MRR Alc.

ASSESSMENTS, POLITICAL
see Campaign funds

ASSIGNMENT SPECIFICATIONS
see Job descriptions

ASSIMILATION (SOCIOLOGY)
see also Emigration and immigration

see also Minorities

see also Race problems

ASSISTANCE TO UNDERDEVELOPED AREAS
see Economic assistance

ASSOCIATION FOOTBALL
see Soccer

ASSOCIATIONS, INTERNATIONAL
see International agencies

ASSOCIATIONS, INSTITUTIONS, ETC.--
ABBREVIATIONS.
Buttress, F. A. World list of
abbreviations. 3rd ed. London,
Hill, 1966. vi, 186 p. [35/-]
060.148 66-71807
  AS8 .B8 1966 MRR Alc.

Marconi Company Limited. Glossary of
abbreviations; [2d ed.] Great
Baddow, Essex [1957] 38 p. 57-
43854
  AS8 .M3 1957 MRR Alc.

Union of International Associations.
International initialese: Enl. 2d
ed. Bruxelles, 1963. 48 p. 63-
42257
  AS8 .U4 1963 MRR Alc.

United States. Library of Congress.
Slavic and Central European Division.
Czech and Slovak abbreviations,
Washington, 1956. v, 164 p.
068.437 56-60067
  Z663.47 .C9 MRR Alc.

United States. Library of Congress.
Slavic and Central European Division.
Polish abbreviations; 2d ed.; rev.
and enl. Washington, 1957. iv, 164
p.   491.8518 57-60055
  Z663.47 .P6 1957 MRR Alc.

ASSOCIATIONS, INSTITUTIONS, ETC.--
DIRECTORIES.
American Council on Education.
Overseas Liaison Committee.
International directory for
educational liaison. Washington
[1972, c1973] xxii, 474 p.
378/.006/21 72-92152
  L900 .A47 1973 MRR Alc.

American University, Washington, D.C.
Bureau of Social Science Research.
Directory of organizations in
opinion, and related research outside
the United States. Washington,
c1956. 1 v. (various pagings) 57-
17609
  HM263 .A77 MRR Alc.

Anderson, Ian Gibson. Marketing &
management: Beckenham (Kent), C.B.D.
Research, 1869. iii-xii, 228 p.
[60/-] 658/.006 78-465981
  HF5415 .A616 MRR Alc.

Angel, Juvenal Londoño. Directory
of international agencies. 1st ed.
New York, Simon & Schuster [1970]
447 p. [$25.00] 341/.24/025 70-
121774
  AS8 .A5 MRR Alc.

Bedard Publications, Detroit.
Directory of worldwide philatelic
agencies. Detroit [1960] 16 l.
383.22058 60-3275
  HE6209 .B4 MRR Alc.

Bilan du monde. [2. éd.] [Tournai]
Casterman, 1964. 2 v. 65-87638
  G122 .B442 MRR Alc.

Center for Curriculum Design.
Somewhere else; [1st ed.] Chicago,
Swallow Press [1973] 213 p. [$6.00]
060/.25 72-91916
  AS8 .C4 1973 MRR Alc.

Directory of Soviet international
front organisations. [n.p.:, 1970] 1
v. (various pagings) 335.43/062/1
78-27355
  HX11 .D523 1970 MRR Alc.

Fang, Josephine R. Handbook of
national and international library
associations Prelim. ed. Chicago,
American Library Association, 1973.
xxvi, 326 p. [$8.50] 020/.6 73-
5619
  Z673.A1 F3 MRR Alc.

Fogle, Catherine. International
directory of population information
and library resources, 1st ed.
[Chapel Hill] Carolina Population
Center, 1972. xiii, 324 p.
301.32/025 79-190722
  HB850 .F6 MRR Alc.

Huenefeld, Irene Pennington.
International directory of historical
clothing. Metuchen, N.J., Scarecrow
Press, 1967. 175 p. 391/.0025 67-
10186
  NK4700 .H8 MRR Alc.

International Film and Television
Council. Le répertoire C.I.C.T. des
organisations internationales de
cinema et de télévision et de
leurs branches nationales. 1964-
[London] Film Centre. 65-71067
  PN1998 .I5 MRR Alc Latest edition

International Institute for
Educational Planning. Educational
Planning: a directory of training and
research institutions. 2d ed.
Paris, Unesco: International
Institute for Educational Planning,
1968. 239 p. [10.50 ($3.00)] 371
76-413666
  LB1026 .I5 MRR Alc.

International Trade Centre. World
directory of industry and trade
associations. [2d ed.] Geneva, 1970
viii, 370 p. [$5.00 (U.S.)]
338/.0062 70-590660
  HF294 .I87 1970 MRR Alc.

The Jewish year book. 1896- London,
Jewish Chronical Publications [etc.]
14-2382
  DS135.E5A3 MRR Alc Latest edition

Larson, Arthur D. National security
affairs: Detroit, Gale Research Co.,
[1973] 411 p. 016.35503/3/0973 70-
184013
  Z1215 .L37 MRR Alc.

Ljunggren, Florence, ed. An
international directory of institutes
and societies interested in the
Middle East. Amsterdam, Djambatan
[1962] 159 p. 060 63-36286
  DS41 .L5 MRR Alc.

The McGraw-Hill dictionary of modern
economics; 2d ed. New York, McGraw-
Hill [1973] xii, 792 p. 330/.03
72-11813
  HB61 .M16 1973 MRR Ref Desk.

Minerva: internationales Verzeichnis
wissenschaftlicher Institutionen.
Forschungsinstitute. 33.- Ausg.
(Jahrg.): 1972- Berlin, New York, W.
de Gruyter. 72-76041
  AS2 .M57 MRR Ref Desk Latest
  edition / MRR Alc Latest edition

Minerva: internationales Verzeichnis
wissenschaftlicher Institutionen.
Wissenschaftliche Gesellschaften.
33.-- Ausg. (Jahrg.); 1972- Berlin,
New York, de Gruyter. 060/.25 72-
624841
  AS2 .M58 MRR Ref Desk Latest
  edition / MRR Alc Latest edition

OECD-ICVA directory: Paris, OECD,
1967. 1378 p. [90.00] 309.2/062
68-82889
  HC60 .O2 TJ Rm.

Organization for Economic Cooperation and Development.
Development Centre. Catalogue of
social and economic development
training institutes and programmes.
Paris, O.E.C.D.; London, H.M.S.O.,
1968. [2], 344 p. [31/-]
309.2/23/0711 68-140061
  HD82 .O66 MRR Alc.

Organization for Economic Cooperation
and Development. International road
safety research directory. 2nd ed.
Paris, O.E.C.D., [London, H.M.S.O.,]
1966. 358 p. [44/-] 614.8/62/072
67-78356
  HE5614 .O73 1966 MRR Alc.

Organization for Economic Cooperation
and Development. Development Centre.
Catalogue of social and economic
development institutes and
programmes: research. Paris,
Development Centre of the
Organization for Economic Cooperation and Development, 1968. 413
p. [$4.50] 338.9/0072 75-417969
  HD82 .O656 MRR Alc.

Professional organisations in the
Commonwealth: London, Published for
The Commonwealth Foundation by
Hutchinson, 1970. 511 p. [90/-]
060 72-525242
  HD2421 .P73 MRR Alc.

Sable, Martin Howard. UFO guide:
1947-1967; 1st ed. Beverly Hills,
Calif.; Rainbow Press Co., 1967. 100
p. 016.001/9 67-30550
  Z5064.F5 S3 MRR Alc.

Technical Assistance Information
Clearing House. Far East technical
assistance programs of U.S. nonprofit
organizations, New York, 1966.
viii, 274 p. 309.2/23 67-60359
  HC411 .T4 MRR Alc.

Thomas, William Leroy, ed.
International directory of
anthropological institutions, New
York, Wenner-Gren Foundation for
Anthropological Research; distributed
by the American Anthropological
Association, 1953. xii, 468 p.
572.0621 53-3903
  GN2 .T45 MRR Alc.

Unesco handbook of international
exchanges. 1- 1965- [Paris]
Unesco. 65-5337
  AS8 .U35 MRR Alc Latest edition

United Nations Educational,
Scientific and Cultural Organization.
World index of social science
institutions. Paris, Unesco, 1970-
1 v. (loose-leaf) 300/.6 75-882769

  H10 .U53 MRR Alc.

United Nations Educational,
Scientific and Cultural Organization.
Mass Communication Techniques
Division. World film directory;
[Paris] UNESCO [1962] 66 p. 62-
4747
  PN1995.9.D6 U47 MRR Alc.

United States. Library of Congress.
International Organizations Section.
International scientific
organizations: Washington, General
Reference and Bibliography Division,
Reference Dept.,Library of Congress;
[for sale by the Superintendent of
Documents, U.S. Govt. Print. Off.]
1962 [i.e. 1963] xi, 794 p. 506
62-64648
  Z663.295 .I5 MRR Alc.

Verbände und Gesellschaften der
Wissenschaft: ein internat. Verz. 1
Ausg. [Pullach (Isartal)] Verlag
Dokumentation, 1974. xii, 481 p.
[DM98.00] 74-333569
  Q145 .V45 MRR Ref Desk.

White, Alex Sandri. The seeker's
guide to groups and societies.
Central Valley, N.Y., Aurea
Publications. 060.58 62-3443
  HS17 .W47 MRR Alc Latest edition

Wilson, William K. World directory
of environmental research centers,
2d ed. New York, Oryx Press;
distributed by R. R. Bowker Co.,
1974. xi, 330 p. 301.31/025 72-
87536
  HC79.E5 W54 1974 MRR Alc.

World guide to trade associations.
1st- ed.; 1973- New York, R. R.
Bowker Co. 380.1/06/2 74-644730
  HD2421 .W67 MRR Ref Desk Latest
  edition

World nuclear directory. 1st- ed.;
1961- London, Harrap Research
Publications [etc.] 62-52178
  QC770 .W65 Sci RR Latest edition /
  MRR Alc Latest edition

The World of learning. [1st]- 1947-
London, Europa Publications [etc.]
47-30172
  AS2 .W6 Sci RR Latest edition /
  MRR Ref Desk Latest edition

ASSOCIATIONS, INSTITUTIONS, ETC.--
AFRICA--DIRECTORIES.
International Council of Voluntary
Agencies. Africa's NGOs. [Geneva,]
Conseil international des agences
benevoles, 1968. iv, 299 p.
[unpriced] 77-417459
  AS600 .I5A55 MRR Alc.

United States. Bureau of
International Labor Affairs.
Directory of labor organizations:
Africa. Rev. ed. Washington, For
sale by the Superintendent of
Documents, U.S. Govt. Print. Off.,
1966- 2 v. (loose-leaf) 66-62771
  HD6856 .U63 MRR Alc.

World guide to trade associations.
1st- ed.; 1973- New York, R. R.
Bowker Co. 380.1/06/2 74-644730
  HD2421 .W67 MRR Ref Desk Latest
  edition

ASSOCIATIONS, INSTITUTIONS, ETC.--
AFRICA, SOUTH--DIRECTORIES.
Directory of scientific research
organizations in South Africa. 1971-
Pretoria, South African Council for
Scientific and Industrial Research.
507/.2068 72-621812
  Q180.A55 D53 MRR Alc Latest
  edition

ASSOCIATIONS, INSTITUTIONS, ETC.--ALBANIA--DIRECTORIES.
Directory of Albanian officials.
[n.p.] 1970. vii, 121 p.
354.496/5/002   79-13669
JN9684 .D55 MRR Alc.

ASSOCIATIONS, INSTITUTIONS, ETC.--ASIA.
Pearson, James Douglas. Oriental and
Asian bibliography; Hamden, Conn.,
Archon Books, 1966. xvi, 261 p.
016.915   66-1006
Z7046 .P4 MRR Alc.

ASSOCIATIONS, INSTITUTIONS, ETC.--ASIA--DIRECTORIES.
World guide to trade associations.
1st- ed.; 1973- New York, R. R.
Bowker Co.   380.1/06/2   74-644730
HD2421 .W67 MRR Ref Desk Latest
   edition

ASSOCIATIONS, INSTITUTIONS, ETC.--AUSTRIA--DIRECTORIES.
Who's who in Austria. 1954-
[Montreal, etc.] Intercontinental
Book and Pub. Co. [etc.] 920.0436 a
55-4612
DB36 .W45 MRR Biog Latest edition

ASSOCIATIONS, INSTITUTIONS, ETC.--BELGIUM--DIRECTORIES.
Belgium. Service des échanges
internationaux. Liste des sociétés
savantes et littéraires de Belgique.
Bruxelles, 1960. 141 p.   61-36159

AS238 .A5 MRR Alc.

Who's who in Belgium and Grand Duchy
of Luxembourg. [1st]- ed.; 1957/58-
Brussels, Intercontinental Book &
Pub. Co.   920.0493   59-3017
DH513 .W45 MRR Biog Latest edition

ASSOCIATIONS, INSTITUTIONS, ETC.--BULGARIA--DIRECTORIES.
Directory of Bulgarian officials.
[n.p.] 1965. vii, 167 p.
354.497/7/00025   73-10853
JN9604 .D53 MRR Alc.

ASSOCIATIONS, INSTITUTIONS, ETC.--CALIFORNIA--DIRECTORIES.
The California handbook. 1st- ed.;
1969- [Claremont] Center for
California Public Affairs. 917.94
75-171691
HC107.C2 C253 MRR Alc Latest
   edition

Yung, Judith. Directory of
California non-profit associations,
San Francisco, San Francisco Public
Library, 1970. iii, 217 p.   061.94
79-20791
HD2428.C3 Y84 MRR Alc.

ASSOCIATIONS, INSTITUTIONS, ETC.--CANADA--DIRECTORIES.
Canada. Dept. of the Secretary of
State. Directory of Canadian youth
organizations. Rev. ed. Ottawa,
[Queen's Printer] 1968. 213, 213 p.
[unpriced]   369.4/025/71   79-384222

HQ799.C2 A5 1968 MRR Alc.

Canadian Council for International Cooperation. Directory of Canadian non-
governmental organizations engaged in
international development assistance,
1970. Ottawa, 1970. 285 p. [$5.00]
309.2/233/7101724   79-855733
HC60 .C2877 1970a MRR Alc.

Corpus directory and almanac of
Canada. 7th- 1972- Toronto,
Corpus Publishers Services Ltd.
917.1   72-626058
F1004.7 .M3   Sci RR Latest edition
   / MRR Alc Latest edition

Directory of associations in Canada;
[Toronto, Buffalo] University of
Toronto Press [c1974] xlii, 393 p.
061.1   73-85085
AS40.A7 D57 MRR Alc.

Holmes, Jeffrey. Canadian
universities' guide to foundations
and granting agencies. [2d ed.]
Ottawa, Association of Universities
and Colleges of Canada, 1969. 110 p.
[$5.00]   361/.02/0257   75-454894
LB2339.C3 H6 1969 MRR Alc.

Scientific and technical societies of
Canada. 1968- Ottawa, National
Research Council of Canada.
506/.2/71   72-649212
AS40 .S34 Sci RR Latest edition /
   MRR Alc Latest edition

Universities and colleges of Canada.
1969- Ottawa, Association of
Universities and Colleges of Canada.
378.71   77-219268
L905 .C452 MRR Alc Latest edition

ASSOCIATIONS, INSTITUTIONS, ETC.--CARIBBEAN AREA--DIRECTORIES.
Vigo-Cepeda, Luisa C. Directory of
institutes and centers devoted to the
social and economic research in the
Caribbean. Rio Piedras, Institute of
Caribbean Studies, University of
Puerto Rico, 1968. 1 v. (various
pagings)   300/.72/0729   74-627100
H62 .V47 MRR Alc.

ASSOCIATIONS, INSTITUTIONS, ETC.--CHINA.
Perleberg, Max. Who's who in modern
China Hong Kong, Ye Olde Printerie,
1954. xii, 428 p.   920.051 54-
19583
DS734 .P4 1954 MRR Biog.

ASSOCIATIONS, INSTITUTIONS, ETC.--CHINA--DIRECTORIES.
United States. Library of Congress.
Science and Technology Division.
Mainland China organizations of
higher learning in science and
technology and their publications.
Washington, 1961. vi, 104 p.   61-
60070
Z663.41 .M2 MRR Alc.

ASSOCIATIONS, INSTITUTIONS, ETC.--CUBA--DIRECTORIES.
Directory of personalities of the
Cuban Government, official
organizations, and mass
organizations. [Washington] Central
Intelligence Agency, 1974. ix, 488
p.   354/.7291/002   74-601252
JL1007 .D57 1974 MRR Alc.

ASSOCIATIONS, INSTITUTIONS, ETC.--CZECHOSLOVAK REPUBLIC--DIRECTORIES.
Directory of Czechoslovak officials.
[n.p.] 1970. xi, 280 p.
354.437/002   74-16206
JN2217 .D5 1870 MRR Alc.

ASSOCIATIONS, INSTITUTIONS, ETC.--EUROPE.
United Nations Educational,
Scientific and Cultural Organization.
World directory of national science
policymaking bodies. Paris, Unesco;
Guernsey, Hodgson, 1966- [i.e. 1967-
v.   [65/- (v. 1)   506/.1 67-
78504
Q10 .U455 MRR Alc.

ASSOCIATIONS, INSTITUTIONS, ETC.--EUROPE--DIRECTORIES.
Annuaire du marketing européen.
[Amsterdam] ESOMAR 72-624633
HF5415.2 .A49 MRR Alc Latest
   edition

Directory of European associations.
1971- Beckenham, Eng., CBD Research
Ltd.; Detroit, Gale Research Co. 74-
175919
AS98 .D55   MRR Ref Desk Latest
   edition

European research index; 3d ed.
[St. Peter Port, Guernsey] Francis
Hodgson [1973] 2 v. (2293 p.)
507/.204 70-190255
Q180.E9 E9 1973 MRR Alc.

Fondazione Giovanni Agnelli. Guide
to European foundations. [Milano] F.
Angeli; distributed by Columbia
University Press, New York, 1973.
401 p. [$12.50]   361.7/6/0254 73-
163902
HV238.A2 F65 1973 MRR Alc.

United States. Bureau of
International Labor Affairs.
Directory of labor organizations;
Europe. Rev. ed. Washington, For
sale by the Superintendent of
Documents, U.S. Govt. Print. Off.,
1965- 2 v. (loose-leaf)   l 65-81
HD6656 .A5 1965 MRR Alc.

Williams, Colin H. Guide to European
sources of technical information. 3d
ed. [Guernsey] Francis Hodgson
[1970] 309 p. [$20.00 (U.S.)]   607
77-105217
T10.65.E8 W5 1970 MRR Alc.

World guide to trade associations.
1st- ed.; 1973- New York, R. R.
Bowker Co.   380.1/06/2   74-644730
HD2421 .W67 MRR Ref Desk Latest
   edition

ASSOCIATIONS, INSTITUTIONS, ETC.--EUROPE, EASTERN--DIRECTORIES.
Little (Arthur D.) inc. Directory of
selected research institutes in
Eastern Europe, New York, Columbia
University Press, 1967. x, 445 p.
507.204   66-20496
Q180.E9 L5 MRR Alc.

National Academy of Sciences,
Washington, D.C. Office of the
Foreign Secretary. The Eastern
European academies of sciences;
Washington, National Academy of
Sciences-National Research Council,
1963. 148 p.   067.058 63-60058
AS98 .N3 MRR Alc.

ASSOCIATIONS, INSTITUTIONS, ETC.--FRANCE--DIRECTORIES.
Conseil national du patronat
français. Annuaire. Paris, Union
française d'annuaire professionnels
[etc.] 62-25706
Began publication in 1949.
HD6683 .C6 MRR Alc Latest edition

ASSOCIATIONS, INSTITUTIONS, ETC.--FRIESLAND.
Provinciale almanak van Friesland.
Bolsward, A. J. Osinga.   51-17137
JN5999.F7 A4 MRR Alc Bind/Label

ASSOCIATIONS, INSTITUTIONS, ETC.--GERMANY--DIRECTORIES.
Domay, Friedrich. Handbuch der
deutschen wissenschaftlichen
Gesellschaften. Wiesbaden, F.
Steiner, 1964. x, 751 p.   65-34997

AS175 .D6 MRR Alc.

Vademecum deutscher Lehr- und
Forschungsstätten. [1.]- Ausg.;
1953- Essen [etc.] Stifterverband
für die Deutsche Wissenschaft [etc.]
58-26815
AS178 .V35 Sci RR Latest edition /
   MRR Alc Latest edition

Verbände, Behörden. 1950-
Darmstadt [etc.] Hoppenstedt. 51-
24746
HD2429.G3 W5 MRR Alc Latest
   edition

ASSOCIATIONS, INSTITUTIONS, ETC.--GERMANY (FEDERAL REPUBLIC, 1949-)
Who's who in Germany. 1956- Munich,
Intercontinental Book and Pub. Co.
920.043   56-3621
DD85 .W45 MRR Biog Latest edition

ASSOCIATIONS, INSTITUTIONS, ETC.--GREAT BRITAIN.
Anderson, Ian Gibson. Councils,
committees, & boards; 2d ed.
Beckenham, CBD Research Ltd., 1973.
iii-xiv, 327 p. [£7.50 ($25.00
U.S.)]   062   74-164686
AS118 .A5 1973 MRR Alc.

British Travel and Holidays
Association. Organisations in
Britain holding regular conferences.
[London, 1961] 92 p.   62-6159
AS118 .B7 MRR Alc.

Directory of British associations.
1965- Beckenham, Eng. [etc.] C.B.D.
Research Limited.   65-89384
AS118 .D56 MRR Alc Latest edition

Handbook of Commonwealth
organisations. London, Methuen
[1965] xvii, 236 p.   060.9171242
66-2744
AS118 .H3 MRR Alc.

A Year book of the Commonwealth.
1969- London, H.M. Stationery Off.
320.9/171/242   79-7332
JN248 .C5912 MRR Alc Latest
   edition

ASSOCIATIONS, INSTITUTIONS, ETC.--GREAT BRITAIN--ABBREVIATIONS.
Wilkes, Ian H. British initials and
abbreviations   3d ed. London, Hill,
1971. 346 p. [£5.50 ($17.50 U.S.)]
060/.25/42   71-25205
AS118 .W5 1971 MRR Alc.

ASSOCIATIONS, INSTITUTIONS, ETC.--GREAT BRITAIN--DIRECTORIES.
The British club year book and
directory. London. 68-1184
Began in 1961.
HS67 .B7 MRR Alc Latest edition

Construction Industry Research and
Information Association. CIRIA guide
to sources of information; London,
CIRIA, [1970]. 176 p.   690/.07 72-
194509
HD9715.G72 C65 MRR Alc.

Great Britain. Dept. of Education and
Science. Sources of information on
international and commonwealth
organisations. [London] Department
of Education and Science [1973] v,
45 p.   060/.25 74-164179
AS8 .G74 1973 MRR Alc.

Industrial research in Britain. 7th
ed. [St. Peter Port, Guernsey] F.
Hodgson [1972] 889 p.   607/.2/42
73-190253
T177.G7 I52 1972 MRR Alc.

Keeling, Guy Willing, comp. Trusts &
foundations; [Cambridge, Eng.] Bowes
& Bowes [1953] xi, 194 p.   068.42
53-3918
AS911.A2 K38 MRR Alc.

Millard, Patricia. Awards and   249
prizes. Havant, K. Mason, 1970.
p. [5/-/-]   001.4/4 70-498024
AS118 .M54 MRR Alc.

ASSOCIATIONS, INSTITUTIONS, (Cont.)
Millard, Patricia, ed. Trade
associations & professional bodies of
the United Kingdom. 3d ed., rev. and
enl. Oxford, New York, Pergamon
Press [1966] xiv, 372 p. 062.025
66-25839
  HD2429.G7 M5 1966 MRR Alc.

Scientific and learned societies of
Great Britain; 1st- ed.; 1884-
London, Allen & Unwin [etc.] 062 01-
15597
  AS115 .S313 MRR Ref Desk Latest
    edition

Wilkes, Ian H. British initials and
abbreviations 3d ed. London, Hill,
1971. 346 p. [£5.50 ($17.50 U.S.)]
060/.25/42 71-25205
  AS118 .W5 1971 MRR Alc.

The Year book of technical education
and careers in industry. 1st- 1957-
London, A. and C. Black. 607.42
57-2770
  T61 .Y4 Sci RR Latest edition /
    MRR Alc Latest edition

ASSOCIATIONS, INSTITUTIONS, ETC.--ITALY-
-DIRECTORIES.
Who's who in Italy. 1957/58-
Milano, Intercontinental Book & Pub.
920.045 60-3514
  DG578 .W5 MRR Biog Latest edition

ASSOCIATIONS, INSTITUTIONS, ETC.--JAPAN-
-DIRECTORIES.
J I T; Tokyo, [Kojunsha
International Publishers]
382/.025/52 68-51013
  HF54.J3 J2 MRR Alc Latest edition

Japan. Mombusho. Nihon Yunesuko
Kokunai Iinkai. Directory of
researchers and research institutes
on Oriental studies in Japan.
[Tokyo] Japanese National Commission
for UNESCO [1957] 50 p. 068.52 61-
32041
  AS548 .A543 MRR Alc.

ASSOCIATIONS, INSTITUTIONS, ETC.--LATIN
AMERICA--DIRECTORIES.
Sable, Martin Howard. Latin American
urbanization: Metuchen, N.J.,
Scarecrow Press, 1971. 1077 p.
016.3013/6/098 73-145643
  Z7165.L3 S28 MRR Alc.

Stromberg, Ann. Philanthropic
foundations in Latin America. New
York, Russell Sage Foundation, 1968.
viii, 215 p. [7.50] 361/.02/0258
68-54409
  HV110.5 .S87 MRR Alc.

World guide to trade associations.
1st- ed.; 1973- New York, R. R.
Bowker Co. 380.1/06/2 74-644730
  HD2421 .W67 MRR Ref Desk Latest
    edition

ASSOCIATIONS, INSTITUTIONS, ETC.--LOS
ANGELES--DIRECTORIES.
Gast, Monte. Getting the best of
L.A. [Los Angeles, Calif.] J. P.
Tarcher [1972] 208 p.
917.94/94/0025 73-189108
  F869.L83 G3 MRR Alc.

ASSOCIATIONS, INSTITUTIONS, ETC.--
MEXICO--DIRECTORIES.
Salas Ortega, Guadalupe, ed.
Directorio de asociaciones e
institutos científicos y culturales
de la Republica Mexicana. [1. ed.]
Mexico, Dirección General de
Publicaciones, 1959. 242 p. 60-
30892
  AS63.A7 S3 MRR Alc.

ASSOCIATIONS, INSTITUTIONS, ETC.--
NETHERLANDS.
Pyttersen's nederlandse almanak.
Zaltbommel, van de Garde. 46-18200
Began in 1800.
  JN5703 .N4 MRR Alc Latest edition*

ASSOCIATIONS, INSTITUTIONS, ETC.--
NETHERLANDS--DIRECTORIES.
Who's who in the Netherlands. 1st-
ed.; 1962/63- [Montreal]
Intercontinental Book and Pub. Co.
64-6538
  DJ289.A1 W5 MRR Biog Latest
    edition

ASSOCIATIONS, INSTITUTIONS, ETC.--NEW
YORK (CITY)--DIRECTORIES.
Directory of social and health
agencies of New York City. [1st]-
ed.; 1883- [New York] 360.58 12-
37275
  HV99.N59 N5 MRR Alc Latest edition

ASSOCIATIONS, INSTITUTIONS, ETC.--NEW
YORK (STATE)--DIRECTORIES.
Charitable organizations,
professional fund raisers, and
professional solicitors. [1st]-
ed.; 1955- Albany, N.Y.
361.7/3/025747 a 56-9301
  HV89 .N44 MRR Alc Latest edition

ASSOCIATIONS, INSTITUTIONS, ETC.--NORTH
AMERICA.
United Nations Educational,
Scientific and Cultural Organization.
World directory of national science
policymaking bodies. Paris, Unesco;
Guernsey, Hodgson, 1966- [i.e. 1967-
v.   [65/- (v. 1)]   506/.1 67-
78504
  Q10 .U455 MRR Alc.

ASSOCIATIONS, INSTITUTIONS, ETC.--
POLAND--DIRECTORIES.
Directory of Polish officials.
[n.p.] 1970. viii, 346 p.
354.438/002 74-11435
  JN6757 1970 .D56 MRR Alc.

ASSOCIATIONS, INSTITUTIONS, ETC.--
RUSSIA--DIRECTORIES.
Battelle Memorial Institute,
Columbus, Ohio. Directory of
selected scientific institutions in
the U.S.S.R. [Columbus, C. E.
Merrill Books] 1963. 1 v. (various
pagings) 506 63-24824
  Q60 .B36 MRR Alc.

A Guide to the Soviet academies.
Rev. [n.p.] 1961. 103 p.   63-61190

  AS258 .G82 MRR Alc.

United States. Central Intelligence
Agency. Directory of Soviet
officials. [Washington?] 1973- v.
354/.47/002 73-603419
  JN6521 .U55 1973 MRR Alc.

United States. Library of Congress.
Aerospace Technology Division.
Scientific institutes and
laboratories in Moscow. [Washington]
1963. ix, 133 p.   64-60333
  Z663.23 .S35 MRR Alc.

ASSOCIATIONS, INSTITUTIONS, ETC.--
SCANDINAVIA--DIRECTORIES.
Scandinavian Council for Applied
Research. Scandinavian research
guide. 2d rev. ed. Copenhagen,
Nordforsk [1965] 12, 438 p.
[77.00dkr] 507.2048 66-68485
  Q180.S3 S3 1965 MRR Alc.

ASSOCIATIONS, INSTITUTIONS, ETC.--SPAIN-
-DIRECTORIES.
Who's who in Spain. 1st- ed.; 1963-
[Montreal] Intercontinental Book
and Pub. Co. 64-841
  DP271.A2 W5 MRR Biog Latest
    edition

ASSOCIATIONS, INSTITUTIONS, ETC.--
SWEDEN--DIRECTORIES.
Sweden. Sveriges statskalender.
Uppsala, Stockholm, Almquist &
Wiksell Informations-industri AB. 07-
16334
  JN7724 MRR Alc Latest edition

ASSOCIATIONS, INSTITUTIONS, ETC.--
UNITED STATES.
Bates, Ralph Samuel. Scientific
societies in the United States 3d
ed. Cambridge, Mass., M.I.T. Press
[1965] 326 p. 506.273 65-8325
  Q11.A1 B3 1965 MRR Alc.

Forster, Arnold. Danger on the
Right, New York, Random House [1964]
xviii, 294 p.   320 64-7549
  E743 .F68 MRR Alc.

Kiger, Joseph Charles. American
learned societies. Washington,
Public Affairs Press [1963] 291 p.
061.3 63-16497
  AS25 .K5 MRR Alc.

Meisel, Max, A bibliography of
American natural history; Brooklyn,
N.Y., The Premier publishing co.,
1924-29. 3 v.   24-30970
  Z7408.U5 M5 MRR Alc.

United States. Congress. House.
Committee on Un-American Activities.
Guide to subversive organizations and
publications. 1951- Washington.
335.4 51-60585
  HX89.A28 MRR Alc Latest edition

Whitehill, Walter Muir, Independent
historical societies, [Boston] The
Boston Athenæum; distributed by
Harvard University Press, 1962.
xviii, 593 p. 973.06973 63-1190
  E172 .W5 MRR Alc.

ASSOCIATIONS, INSTITUTIONS, ETC.--
UNITED STATES--BIBLIOGRAPHY.
Bowker, Richard Rogers, Publications
of societies; New York, Office of
the Publishers' weekly, 1899. v, 181
p.   00-465
  Z5055.U39 B7 MRR Alc.

Wasserman, Paul. Museum media; 1st
ed. Detroit, Gale Research Co.,
1973. vii, 455 p.   011 73-16335
  Z5052 .W35 MRR alc.

ASSOCIATIONS, INSTITUTIONS, ETC.--
UNITED STATES--DIRECTORIES.
1971 directory of national
organizations concerned with land
pollution control. New York, Freed
Pub. Co. [1971] 36 p. [$7.00]
614/.776/02573 76-28602
  TD173.5 .N55 MRR Alc.

American Medical Association.
Directory. Chicago. 610.6906273 63-
6472
  R15 .A4385 MRR Alc Latest edition

Asia Society. American institutions
and organizations interested in Asia,
2d ed. New York, Taplinger Pub.
Co. 1961. xii, 581 p. 950.06273
61-11435
  DS1 .C572 MRR Alc.

Associated Councils of the Arts.
Directory of national arts
organizations. [New York] 1969. 76
p. [2.00 (pbk)] 700/.25/73 75-
77987
  NX22 .A823 MRR Alc.

Battelle Memorial Institute,
Columbus, Ohio. Dept. of Economics
and Information Research.
Specialized science information
services in the United States;
Washington, National Science
Foundation, Office of Science
Information Service, 1961. ix, 528
p.   505.873 61-64862
  AG521 .B3 MRR Alc.

Breitner, Ruby Church, ed. National
insurance organizations in the United
States and Canada. New York, Special
Libraries Association [c1957] vi, 65
p.   57-14850
  HG8525 .B7 MRR Alc.

Burke, Joan Martin. Civil rights;
2d ed. New York, Bowker, 1974. xi,
266 p. 323.4/025/73 74-4053
  JC599.U5 B85 1974 MRR Alc.

Clapp, Jane. Professional ethics and
insignia. Metuchen, N.J., Scarecrow
Press, 1974. xii, 851 p. 061/.3
74-10501
  HD6504 .A194 MRR Ref Desk.

Communication directory. 1973/74-
Silver Spring, Md., Council of
Communication Societies. [$8.00]
380.3/025/73 74-644695
  HE9.U5 D57 MRR Alc Latest edition
    / Sci RR Latest edition

Conservation directory. Washington,
National Wildlife Federation. 70-
10646
Began with 1956 vol.
  S920 .C64 Sci RR Latest edition /
    MRR Alc Latest edition

Council on foreign relations.
American agencies interested in
international affairs. 1931- New
York, [etc.] Frederick A. Praeger,
[etc.] 341.06 31-26874
  JX27 .C62 MRR Ref Desk Latest
    edition

Cushing, A. I. The international
"mystery schools" directory. New
1970 ed. Boston, A.C. Publications
[1970] 1 v. (unpaged) 133/.062 70-
16742
  BL35 .C86 MRR Alc.

De Bettencourt, F. G. The Catholic
guide to foundations 2d ed.
Washington, Guide Publishers [1973]
iii, 170 p. 361.7/6/02573 73-86563

  HV97.A3 D4 1973 MRR Alc.

Directory: National Black
organizations. 1972- Harlem, N. Y.,
Afram Associates. 301.45/19/607306
72-624646
  E185.5 .D5 MRR Ref Desk Latest
    edition

Directory of consumer protection and
environmental agencies. 1st ed.
Orange, N.J., Academic Media [1973]
xiii, 627 p.   381 72-75952
  HC110.C63 D55 MRR Ref Desk.

Directory of engineering societies
and related organizations. New York,
Engineers Joint Council. 620/.006
68-5491
Began in 1956.
  TA1 .D48 Sci RR Latest edition /
    MRR Alc Latest edition

Directory of historical societies and
agencies in the United States and
Canada. 1956- Nashville, Tenn.
[etc.] American Association for State
and Local History. 970.62 56-4164
  E172 .A538 MRR Ref Desk Latest
    edition / MRR Ref Desk Latest
    edition

ASSOCIATIONS, INSTITUTIONS. (Cont.)

Directory of national unions and employee associations. 1971- Washington, U.S. Bureau of Labor Statistics; For sale by the Supt. of Docs., U.S. Govt. Print. Off. [$2.00] 331.88/025/73 73-641250
   HD6504 .A15 MRR Ref Desk Latest edition

Directory of registered federal and state lobbyists. 1st- ed.; 1973- Orange, N.J., Academic Media. 328/.38/025/73 72-75953
   JK1118 .D56 MRR Ref Desk Latest edition

Environmental Resources, inc. Yell- [symbol for Earth] pages; [Washington] 1971. 240 p. 301.3/1/02573 72-27880
   HC110.E5 E499 MRR Alc.

Film Council of America. A guide to film services of national associations. Evanston, Ill. [1954] xlix, 146 p. 791.4058 792.93058* 54-3752
   PN1995.9.D6 F5 MRR Alc.

First national directory of "rightist" groups, publications, and some individuals in the United States and some foreign countries. 4th ed. Sausalito, Calif., Distributed by the Noontide Press, 1962. 36 p. 62-2510
   E743.5 .F48 1962 MRR Ref Desk.

The Foundation directory. 1st- ed.; 1960- New York, [Foundation Center] Distributed by Columbia University Press [etc.] 061 60-13807
   AS911 .A2F65 Sci RR Latest edition / MRR Alc Latest edition / MRR Ref Desk Latest edition

Foundation Research Service. Foundation research service. [Washington, Lawson & Williams Associates, 1972- 4 v. (loose-leaf) 507/.2073 72-184024
   Q180.U5 F68 MRR Alc.

Fraternal monitor. Combined statistics and consolidated chart of fraternal societies. 1958- Indianapolis. 58-45886
   HG9226 .F72 MRR Alc Latest edition

Gale Research Company. Encyclopedia of associations. 8th ed. Detroit, Mich. [1973- v.   [$45.00 (v. 1) $28.50 (v. 2)] 061/.3 73-7400
   HS17 .G334 1973 MRR Ref Desk.

Gannon, Francis Xavier. Biographical dictionary of the left, Boston, Western Islands [1969- v.   [8.00 (v. 1)] 920.73 76-12821
   E747 .G32 MRR Biog.

Governmental Research Association. Directory of organizations and individuals professionally engaged in governmental research and related activities. 1935- New York [etc.] 350.6273 35-16469
   JK3 .G627 MRR Alc Latest edition

Habenstein, Robert Wesley. Funeral customs the world over [1st ed.] Milwaukee, Bulfin Printers, 1960. 973 p.   393 60-53002
   GT3150 .H28 MRR Alc.

Halstead, Bruce W. A Golden guide to environmental organizations. New York, Golden Press [1972] 63 p. [$0.95] 301.31/06 72-79158
   GF5 .H34 MRR Alc.

Handbook of learned societies and institutions: America. Washington, D.C., Carnegie institution of Washington, 1908. viii, 592 p. 08-21011
   Z5055.U39 H2 MRR Alc.

Hartman, Joan E. Directory of United States standardization activities Washington [U.S. Dept. of Commerce, National Bureau of Standards]; for sale by the Supt. of Docs., U.S. Govt. Print. Off., 1967. v, 276 p. 389/.6/02573 67-60370
   QC100 .H33 MRR Alc.

Health organizations of the United States, Canada and internationally. [1st]- ed.; 1961- Ithaca, N.Y., Graduate School of Business and Public Administration, Cornell University. 610.62 61-3260
   R711 .H4 Sci RR Latest edition / MRR Alc Latest edition

The Hereditary register of the United States of America. 1972- Washington, United States Hereditary Register. 369/.1 76-184658
   E172.7 .H47 MRR Alc Latest edition

Hilton, Ronald, ed. Handbook of Hispanic source materials and research organizations in the United States. 2d ed. Stanford, Calif., Stanford University press, 1956. xiv, 448 p. 980 56-6178
   F1408.3 .H65 1956 MRR Alc.

Human Resources Network. Profiles of involvement. [Philadelphia, 1972] 3 v. (843 p.) [$50.00] 658.4/08 72-87222
   HD60.5.U5 H85 MRR Alc.

Latin America technical assistance programs of U.S. nonprofit organizations. New York, Technical Assistance Information Clearing House. 309.2/23 72-4820
   HC122 .L3 MRR Alc Latest edition

Literary market place; [1st]- ed.; 1940- New York, Bowker. 655.473 41-51571
   PN161 .L5 Sci RR Partial set / MRR Ref Desk Latest edition

Markotic, Vladimir. Biographical directory of Americans and Canadians of Croatian descent; 4th enl. and rev. ed. Calgary, Alta., Research Centre for Canadian Ethnic Studies, 1973. xiii, 204 p. 920/.071 74-176543
   E184.C93 M3713 1973 MRR Biog.

Miller, Roy. Lawyers' source book; New York, M. Bender, 1971- 2 v. (loose-leaf) 060 75-179681
   AS22 .M54 MRR alc.

National Association of Social Workers. Directory of agencies: U.S. voluntary, international voluntary, intergovernmental. Washington [1973] 96 p. 362/.025/73 73-83478
   HV89 .N223 1973 MRR Alc.

National Budget and Consultation Committee. Reports on national health and welfare agencies. New York. 63-47582
   HV88 .N13 MRR Alc Latest edition

National Council for Community Services to International Visitors. National directory of community organizations serving short-term international visitors. Washington. 64-55675
   Began publication in 1960.
   E744.5 .N35 MRR Alc Latest edition

National Council of Women of the United States. International directory of women's organizations. [75th anniversary souvenir ed., 1888-1963. New York, Research and Action Associates, 1963] 1 v. (various pagings) 63-25250
   HQ1883 .N3 MRR Alc.

National Social Welfare Assembly. Service directory of national organizations 1st- ed.; 1951- New York. 360.58 52-3715
   HV89 .N35 MRR Alc Latest edition

National trade and professional associations of the United States and labor unions. v. 7- 1972- Washington, D.C., Columbia Books, inc. [$15.00] 381/.06/273 74-647774
   HD2425 .D53 MRR Ref Desk Latest edition

Onyx Group, inc. Environment U.S.A.; New York, Bowker, 1974. xii, 451 p. 333.7/2/02573 73-20122
   TD171 .E58 MRR Alc.

Pan American associations in the United States: [1st]- ed.; 1955- Washington. pa 57-165
   F1401 .P263 MRR Alc Latest edition

Pinson, William M. Resource guide to current social issues; Waco, Tex., Word Books [1968] 272 p. 016.301 67-30735
   Z7164.S66 P47 MRR Alc.

Public administration organizations, a directory of unofficial organizations in the field of public administration in the United States and Canada. [1st]- ed.; 1932- Chicago, Public Administration Clearing House. 061 33-4186
   AS18 .P8 MRR Alc Latest edition

Research centers directory. 1st- ed.; 1960- Detroit, Gale Research Co. 60-14807
   AS25 .D5 Sci RR Latest edition / MRR Ref Desk Latest edition

Scientific and technical societies of the United States. 8th- ed.; 1968- Washington, National Academy of Sciences. 506 72-620448
   AS25 .S33 Sci RR Latest edition / MRR Ref Desk Latest edition / MRR Alc Latest edition

Shippers' Conference of Greater New York. List of non-profit shipper associations, New York [1970] 160 p. 380.5/025/73 70-21822
   HF5780.U6 S45 MRR Alc.

Solara, Ferdinand V. Key influences in the American right, Denver, Polifax Press [1972] xv, 68 p. [$4.95] 320.5/12/0973 72-189989
   E839.5 .S64 1972 MRR Ref Desk.

Sources of information and unusual services; New York, Informational Directory Co. 917.4741 53-4208
   AG521 .S6 MRR Ref Desk Latest edition

System Development Corporation. Directory of educational information resources. [Rev. and updated ed.] New York, CCM Information Corp., 1971. ix, 181 p. 370/.7 70-136093
   L901 .S95 1972 MRR Alc.

United States. Cabinet Committee on Opportunity for the Spanish Speaking. Directory of Spanish speaking organizations in the United States. Washington, 1970. x, 224 p. 061 77-608446
   E184.S75 A44 MRR Alc.

United States. Dept. of State. Office of External Research. University centers of foreign affairs research: a selective directory. [Washington, Dept. of State; for sale by the Supt. of Docs., U.S. Govt. Print. Off.] 1968. xvi, 139 p. 327/.025/73 68-60080
   JX1293.U6 A54 MRR Alc.

United States. Library of Congress. National Referral Center. A directory of information resources in the United States: biological sciences. Washington, Library of Congress; [for sale by the Supt. of Docs., U.S. Govt. Print. Off.] 1972. iv, 577 p. [$5.00] 570/.7 72-2659
   Z663.379 .D46 MRR Alc.

United States. Library of Congress. National Referral Center. A directory of information resources in the United States: physical sciences, engineering. Washington, Library of Congress; [for sale by the Supt. of Docs., U.S. Govt. Print. Off.] 1971. iv, 803 p. [$6.50] 500.2/07 78-611209
   Z663.379 .D5 1971 MRR Alc.

United States. Library of Congress. National Referral Center. A directory of information resources in the United States: social sciences. Rev. ed. Washington, Library of Congress; [for sale by the Supt. of Docs., U.S. Govt. Print. Off.] 1973. iv, 700 p. [$6.90] 300/.7 73-3297
   Z663.379 .D53 1973 MRR Alc.

United States. Library of Congress. National Referral Center for Science and Technology. A directory of information resources in the United States: general toxicology. Washington, Library of Congress; for sale by the Supt. of Docs., U.S. Govt. Print. Off.] 1969. v, 293 p. [3.00] 615.9/007 73-602563
   Z663.379 .D49 MRR Alc

United States. Office of Economic Opportunity. Community Action Programs. Community action agency atlas. [Washington] Office of Economic Opportunity, 1969. 2, 4, 362 p. 338.973 71-603810
   HC110.P63 A5543 MRR Alc.

United States. President's Council on Youth Opportunity. Youth resources manual for coordinators. Washington; For sale by the Supt. of Docs., U.S. Govt. Print. Off., 1971. iii l., 233 p. [$1.75] 301.43/15/0973 74-612177
   HQ796 .U62 MRR Alc.

United States trade associations. Loveland, Colo., Johnson Pub. Co. [$10.00] 338/.0025/73 74-642943
   HD2425 .H53 MRR Alc Latest edition

Urban Institute. A directory of university urban research centers. Washington [1969] 141 p. [3.50] 301.3/64/072073 72-112409
   HT110 .U7 MRR Alc.

Wasserman, Paul. Consumer sourcebook; Detroit, Gale Research Co. [1974] xi, 593 p. 381/.3 74-10494
   HC110.C63 W37 MRR Ref Desk.

ASSOCIATIONS, INSTITUTIONS, (Cont.)
Wheeler, Helen Rippier. Womanhood
media: current resources about women.
Metuchen, N.J., Scarecrow Press,
1972. 335 p. 016.30141/2 72-7396

   Z7961 .W48 MRR Alc.

Who's who in association management;
membership directory. Washington.
56-1087
   HD2425 .A573 MRR Alc Latest
   edition

Wolff, Garwood R. Environmental
information sources handbook. [New
York] Simon and Schuster [1974] 568
p. 301.31/07 73-3951
   GF503 .W64 MRR Alc.

Women's organizations & leaders
directory. 1973- Washington, D.C.,
Today Publications & News Service.
301.41/2/06273 72-86473
   HQ1883 .W64 MRR Ref Desk Latest
   edition

**ASSOCIATIONS, INSTITUTIONS, ETC.--
WASHINGTON, D.C.--DIRECTORIES.**
De Bettencourt, Margaret T. The
guide to Washington, D.C.
foundations. [Washington, Guide
Publishers, c1972] viii, 62 p.
[$8.00] 001.4/4 72-90810
   AS911.A2 D24 MRR Ref Desk.

Howard University, Washington, D.C.
Minority Economic Resource Center.
The District of Columbia directory of
inner city organizations active in
the field of minority business-
economic development. 3d ed.
Washington, 1972. iv, 20 p.
338/.04/025753 73-170762
   HD2346.U52 D54 1972 MRR Alc.

International Visitors Service
Council. Organizations serving
international visitors in the
National Capital area. [4th ed.]
Washington [1973] vii p., 15] l.,
155-191 p. 917.53/04/4025 72-96925
   F191 .I57 1973 MRR Alc.

Washington. 1966- Washington,
Potomac Books. 917.53/0025 s 66-
18579
   F192.5 .W3 MRR Ref Desk Latest
   edition / MRR Ref Desk Latest
   edition / Sci RR Latest edition

Washington. Supplement. Washington,
Potomac Books. 917.53/0025 s 74-
643552
   F192.5 .W32 MRR Ref Desk Latest
   edition / MRR Ref Desk Latest
   edition

Youth info digest. 1972-
[Washington] Washington Workshops
Press. 309.025/73 74-185964
   HN55 .Y68 MRR Alc Latest edition

**ASSOCIATIONS, INSTITUTIONS, ETC.--
YUGOSLAVIA--DIRECTORIES.**
Directory of Yugoslav officials.
[n.p.] 1970. ix, 216 p.
354.497/002 73-13670
   JN9667 .D55 MRR Alc.

Yugoslav scientific research
directory. 1964- Belgrad [Published
for the National Library of Medicine,
Washington, by the NOLIT Pub. House;
available from the National Technical
Information Service, etc.
Springfield, Va.] 64-64696
   Q180.Y8 Y8 Sci RR Latest edition /
   MRR Alc Latest edition

Yugoslav scientific research guide
1970 Belgrade, Nolit Pub. House,
1972. xii, 634 p. 507/.2/0497 73-
159775
   Q180.Y8 Y83 MRR Alc.

ASSYRIA--HISTORY.
Olmstead, Albert Ten Eyck. History
of Assyria. [Chicago] University of
Chicago Press [1960, c1951] 695 p.
935 60-51187
   DS71 .O6 1960 MRR Alc.

**ASSYRO-BABYLONIAN LANGUAGE--
DICTIONARIES.**
Muss-Arnolt, William. A concise
dictionary of the Assyrian languages.
Berlin, Reuther & Reichard; New
York, Lemcke & Büchner; [etc., etc.]
1905. 2 v. 12-37024
   PJ3525 .M7 MRR Alc.

**ASSYRO-BABYLONIAN LANGUAGE--
DICTIONARIES--ENGLISH.**
Muss-Arnolt, William. A concise
dictionary of the Assyrian languages.
Berlin, Reuther & Reichard; New
York, Lemcke & Büchner; [etc., etc.]
1905. 2 v. 12-37024
   PJ3525 .M7 MRR Alc.

**ASSYRO-BABYLONIAN LANGUAGE--
DICTIONARIES--GERMAN.**
Muss-Arnolt, William. A concise
dictionary of the Assyrian languages.
Berlin, Reuther & Reichard; New
York, Lemcke & Büchner; [etc., etc.]
1905. 2 v. 12-37024
   PJ3525 .M7 MRR Alc.

**ASSYRO-BABYLONIAN LANGUAGE--TERMS AND
PHRASES--BIBLIOGRAPHY.**
Muss-Arnolt, William. A concise
dictionary of the Assyrian languages.
Berlin, Reuther & Reichard; New
York, Lemcke & Büchner; [etc., etc.]
1905. 2 v. 12-37024
   PJ3525 .M7 MRR Alc.

ASTRODYNAMICS.
   see also Space flight

ASTROLOGY.
   see also Occult sciences

Hall, Manly Palmer, comp.
Astrological Keywords. New York,
Philosophical Library [c1959] 229 p.
133.5 59-61
   BF1701 .H25 1959 MRR Alc.

ASTROLOGY--DICTIONARIES.
De Vore, Nicholas. Encyclopedia of
astrology. New York, Philosophical
Library [1947] xii, 435 p. 133.5
47-31413
   BF1655 .D4 MRR Alc.

Lee, Dal. Dictionary of astrology.
New York, Coronet Communications
[1969, c1968] 250 p. [5.95]
133.5/03 77-14557
   BF1655 .L4 1969 MRR Alc.

ASTROLOGY--EARLY WORKS TO 1800.
Ptolemaeus, Claudius. Tetrabiblos;
Cambridge, Mass., Harvard university
press; London, W. Heinemann ltd.,
1940. xxiv, 466 p. 133.5 159.9615
a 41-4064
   PA3612 .M3 1940 MRR Alc.

ASTROLOGY--TABLES.
Ward, Craig. The 200 year ephemeris.
New York, Macoy Pub. Co., 1949. vi,
420 p. 133.5083 49-8975
   BF1715 .W3 MRR Alc.

ASTRONAUTICS.
   see also Artificial satellites

   see also Outer space

   see also Rocketry

   see also Space flight

   see also Space vehicles

Ley, Willy. Rockets, missiles, and
men in space. [Newly rev. and
expanded ed.] New York, Viking Press
[1968] xvii, 557 p. 629.4 67-
20676
   TL782 .L43 1968 MRR Alc.

ASTRONAUTICS--ABBREVIATIONS.
Jacobs, Horace. Missile and space
projects guide New York, Plenum
Press, 1962. x, 235 p. 629.403 62-
13473
   TL788 .J3 MRR Alc.

Moser, Reta C. Space-age acronyms;
2d ed.; rev. and enl. New York,
IFI/Plenum, 1969. 534 p.
629.4/01/48 69-14416
   TL788 .M6 1969 MRR Alc.

ASTRONAUTICS--ACRONYMS.
Moser, Reta C. Space-age acronyms;
2d ed.; rev. and enl. New York,
IFI/Plenum, 1969. 534 p.
629.4/01/48 69-14416
   TL788 .M6 1969 MRR Alc.

ASTRONAUTICS--BIBLIOGRAPHY.
Dickson, Katherine Murphy. History
of aeronautics and astronautics;
Washington, National Aeronautics and
Space Administration, 1967. vi, 117
l. 016.01662913 67-61736
   Z5063.A1 D5 MRR Alc.

United States. Library of Congress.
Science and Technology Division.
Space science and technology books,
1957-1961. Washington [For sale by
the Superintendent of Documents, U.S.
Govt. Print. Off.] 1962 [i.e. 1963]
iii, 133 p. 016.6294 62-60086
   Z663.41 .S65 MRR Alc.

ASTRONAUTICS--BIOGRAPHY.
Riverain, Jean. Dictionnaire des
aeronautes celebres. Paris,
Larousse [1970] 159 p. 74-22366
   TL539 .R56 MRR Biog.

Who's who in space. 1st- ed.;
1966/67- Washington, Space
Publications. 629.40922 65-28671
   TL789.85 .A1W5 Sci RR Full set /
   MRR Biog Latest edition

ASTRONAUTICS--CHRONOLOGY.
Gurney, Gene. A chronology of world
aviation. New York, F. Watts [1965]
245 p. 387.709 65-11756
   TL515 .G83 MRR Alc.

ASTRONAUTICS--DICTIONARIES.
Aviation & space dictionary. 1st-
1940- Los Angeles [etc.] Aero
Publishers [etc.] 629.1303 54-28287
   TL509 .A8 Sci RR Latest edition /
   MRR Alc Latest edition

Bergaust, Erik, ed. The new
illustrated space encyclopedia.
[Rev. ed.] New York, Putnam [1970]
190 p. 629.4/03 68-26072
   TL788 .B39 1970 MRR Alc.

Bergaust, Erik, ed. The new
illustrated space encyclopedia.
[Rev. ed.] New York, Putnam [1970]
190 p. 629.4/03 68-26072
   TL788 .B39 1970 MRR Alc.

Caidin, Martin. The man-in-space
dictionary, [1st ed.] New York,
Dutton, 1963. 224 p. 629.403 63-
14274
   TL788 .C3 MRR Alc.

Dictionary of guided missiles and
space flight. Princeton, N.J., Van
Nostrand [1959] vi, 688 p.
629.1388 59-10112
   TL788 .D5 MRR Alc.

Hyman, Charles J. German-English,
English-German astronautics
dictionary. New York, Consultants
Bureau, 1968. viii, 237 p.
629.4/03 65-20216
   TL788 .H8 MRR Alc.

Marks, Robert W. The new dictionary
& handbook of aerospace. New York,
Praeger [1969] viii, 531 p. [10.00]
629.1/03 73-94221
   TL509 .M35 MRR Alc.

McLaughlin, Charles. Space age
dictionary. 2d ed. Princeton, N.J.,
Van Nostrand [c1963] viii, 233 p.
629.403 63-22955
   TL788 .M3 1963 MRR Alc.

Nayler, Joseph Lawrence. Dictionary
of astronautics London, Newnes
[1964] v, 316 p. 65-36616
   TL788 .N3 MRR Alc.

The New space encyclopaedia; New,
rev. ed. New York, E. P. Dutton
[1973] 326 p. [$14.95] 520/.3 73-
12348
   QB14 .S66 1973 MRR Alc.

Newlon, Clarke. The aerospace age
dictionary. New York, F. Watts
[1965] 282 p. 629.403 65-11382
   TL788 .N4 MRR Alc.

Roes, Nicholas. The space-flight
encyclopedia Chicago, Follett Pub.
Co. [1968] ix, 213 p. [3.95]
629.4/03 68-18508
   TL788 .R6 MRR Alc.

Spitz, Armand N. Dictionary of
astronomy and astronautics New York,
Philosophical Library [1959] vi, 439
p. 520.3 59-16038
   QB14 .S73 MRR Alc.

Turnill, Reginald. The language of
space: London, Cassell, 1970.
xxxiv, 165 p. [42/-] 629.4/03 72-
571699
   TL788.3 .T87 MRR Alc.

ASTRONAUTICS--DICTIONARIES--GERMAN.
Hyman, Charles J. German-English,
English-German astronautics
dictionary. New York, Consultants
Bureau, 1968. viii, 237 p.
629.4/03 65-20216
   TL788 .H8 MRR Alc.

ASTRONAUTICS--DICTIONARIES--RUSSIAN.
Russian-English aerospace dictionary.
Berlin, W. de Gruyter, 1965. xvi,
407 p. 65-73606
   TL509 .R83 MRR Alc.

ASTRONAUTICS--HISTORY.
Von Braun, Wernher. History of
rocketry & space travel Rev. ed.
New York, Crowell [1969] xi, 276 p.
[17.50] 629.4/09 76-94786
   TK781 .V6 1969 MRR Alc.

ASTRONAUTICS--MISCELLANEA.
Newlon, Clarke. 1001 questions
answered about space. Rev. ed. New
York, Dodd, Mead, 1964. x, 356 p.
64-1372
   TL793 .N38 1964 MRR Alc.

ASTRONAUTICS--NOMENCLATURE.
Jacobs, Horace. Missile and space
projects guide New York, Plenum
Press, 1962. x, 235 p. 629.403 62-
13473
   TL788 .J3 MRR Alc.

ASTRONAUTICS--PERIODICALS--BIBLIOGRAPHY.
United States. Library of Congress.
Science and Technology Division.
Aeronautical and space serial
publications; Washington, 1962. ix,
255 p. 61-60083
Z663.41 .A73 MRR Alc

ASTRONAUTICS--YEARBOOKS.
Aerospace facts and figures. [1st]-
ed.; 1945- Fallbrook, Calif. [etc.]
Aero Publishers [etc.] 629.13058 46-
25007
TL501 .A818 Sci RR Latest edition
/ MRR Alc Latest edition

The Aerospace year book. [1st]-
1919- Washington [etc.] Books, inc.
[etc.] 629.13058 19-13828
TL501 .A563 Sci RR Latest edition
/ MRR Alc Latest edition

ASTRONAUTICS--UNITED STATES.
Bergaust, Erik, ed. The new
illustrated space encyclopedia.
[Rev. ed.] New York, Putnam [1970]
190 p. 629.4/03 68-26072
TL788 .E39 1970 MRR Alc.

ASTRONAUTICS--UNITED STATES--HISTORY.
Astronautics and aeronautics;
1915/60- Washington, Scientific and
Technical Information Division,
National Aeronautics and Space
Administration [etc.; for sale by the
Superintendent of Documents, U.S.
Govt. Print. Off.] 65-60308
TL521.3.A8 A3 MRR Alc Partial set

ASTRONAUTICS--UNITED STATES--STATISTICS.
Aerospace facts and figures. [1st]-
ed.; 1945- Fallbrook, Calif. [etc.]
Aero Publishers [etc.] 629.13058 46-
25007
TL501 .A818 Sci RR Latest edition
/ MRR Alc Latest edition

ASTRONAUTS.
Bergaust, Erik, ed. The new
illustrated space encyclopedia.
[Rev. ed.] New York, Putnam [1970]
190 p. 629.4/03 68-26072
TL788 .E39 1970 MRR Alc.

ASTRONOMICAL OBSERVATORIES--DIRECTORIES.
Moyer, Claire B. (Inch) Silver
domes; Denver, Big Mountain Press,
1955. 174 p. 522.1058 55-3846
QB81 .M7 MRR Alc.

ASTRONOMICAL SYMBOLS
see Abbreviations

ASTRONOMY.
see also Calendar

see also Comets

see also Constellations

see also Moon

see also Planets

see also Space sciences

see also Stars

see also Sun

Baker, Robert Horace, Astronomy 9th
ed. New York, Van Nostrand Reinhold
Co. [1971] xiv, 631 p. 520 74-
127649
QB45 .B15 1971 MRR Alc.

Flammarion, Camille, The Flammarion
book of astronomy. New York, Simon
and Schuster, 1964. 670 p. 523 64-
15354
QB44 .F5913 MRR Alc.

Jobes, Gertrude. Outer space; New
York, Scarecrow Press, 1964. 479 p.
291.212 64-11783
BL438 .J6 MRR Alc.

Olcott, William Tyler, Field book of
the skies. 4th ed. New York, Putnam
[1954] xi, 482 p. 523 54-8707
QB44 .C6 1954 MRR Alc.

Pickering, James Sayre. 1001
questions answered about astronomy,
Rev. ed. New York, Dodd, Mead, 1966.
xi, 420 p. 520.76 66-14989
QB44 .P63 1966 MRR Alc.

Rudaux, Lucien, Larousse
encyclopedia of astronomy, Revised
ed. London, Hamlyn, 1966. ix, 506
p. [30/-] 520 66-74769
QB44 .R883 1966 MRR Alc.

ASTRONOMY--CHARTS, DIAGRAMS, ETC.
Ernst, Bruno. Atlas of the universe
[London] Nelson, 1961. 226, [1] p.
523.1084 61-4868
QB65 .E713 MRR Alc.

ASTRONOMY--DICTIONARIES.
Fairbridge, Rhodes Whitmore, The
encyclopedia of atmospheric sciences
and astrogeology, New York, Reinhold
Pub. Corp. [1967] xv, 1200 p.
551.5/03 68-1126
QC854 .F34 MRR Alc.

Muller, Paul, Concise encyclopedia
of astronomy; Glasgow, London,
Collins; Chicago, Follet, 1968. vi,
281 p. [12/6] 520/.03 68-12313
QB14 .M8414 MRR Alc.

The New space encyclopaedia; New,
rev. ed. New York, E. P. Dutton
[1973] 326 p. [$14.95] 520/.3 73-
12348
QB14 .S66 1973 MRR Alc.

Spitz, Armand N. Dictionary of
astronomy and astronautics New York,
Philosophical Library [1959] vi, 439
p. 520.3 59-16038
QB14 .S73 MRR Alc.

Wallenquist, Åke, The Penguin
dictionary of astronomy;
Harmondsworth, Penguin, 1968. 238 p.
[7/6] 520/.3 68-94809
QB14 .W313 1968 MRR Alc.

Weigert, Alfred, A concise
encyclopedia of astronomy New York,
American Elsevier Pub. Co. [1968,
c1967] 368, 20 p. 520/.3 68-23260

QB14 .W413 1968 MRR Alc.

ASTRONOMY--DICTIONARIES--POLYGLOT.
Kleczek, Josip. Astronomical
dictionary. [Vyd. 1.] Praha, Nakl.
Československé akademie věd, 1961.
972 p. 62-25391
QB14 .K55 MRR Alc.

ASTRONOMY--HISTORY.
Vaucouleurs, Gérard Henri de,
Discovery of the universe; New York,
Macmillan [1957] 328 p. 520.9 57-
10015
QB15 .V353 1957a MRR Alc.

ASTRONOMY--OBSERVERS' MANUALS.
Muirden, James. The amateur
astronomer's handbook. Rev. expanded
ed. New York, Crowell [1974] 404 p.
520 74-5411
QB64 .M85 1974 MRR Alc.

Olcott, William Tyler, Field book of
the skies. 4th ed. New York, Putnam
[1954] xi, 482 p. 523 54-8707
QB44 .O6 1954 MRR Alc.

ASTRONOMY--YEARBOOKS.
Yearbook of astronomy. 1962- New
York, W. W. Norton. 523.058 62-1706

QB1 .Y4 Sci RR Partial set / MRR
Alc Latest edition

ASTRONOMY, GREEK.
Aristoteles. On the heavens,
Cambridge, Mass., Harvard University
Press; London, W. Heinemann, 1939.
378 p. mrr01-19
PA3612 .A8D4 1939d MRR Alc.

ASTRONOMY, SPHERICAL AND PRACTICAL.
see also Navigation

Children's Book Council, New York.
Children's books: awards & prizes.
[New York, 1969] [32] p. [$4.95]
028.52 78-24483
Z1037.A2 C52 MRR Alc.

ATATÜRK, KAMÂL, PRES. TURKEY, D. 1938-
--BIBLIOGRAPHY.
Bodurgil, Abraham. Atatürk and
Turkey: Washington. Library of
Congress; [for sale by the Supt. of
Docs., U.S. Govt. Print. Off.] 1974.
74 p. 016.9561 73-18313
Z663.387 .A8 MRR Alc.

ATHENS--ANTIQUITIES.
Travlos, Ioannes N., Pictorial
dictionary of Ancient Athens London,
Thames and Hudson, 1971. xvi, 590 p.
[£25.00] 720/.9/49512 72-178898
NA280 .T68 1971 MRR Alc.

ATHENS. CONSTITUTION.
Aristoteles. The Athenian
constitution; the Eudemian ethics;
London, W. Heinemann ltd.; Cambridge,
Mass, Harvard university press, 1935.
vii, 505, [1] p. 888.5 36-4460
PA3612.A8 A13 1935a MRR Alc.

ATHLETES.
Watman, Melvyn Francis. The
encyclopaedia of athletics, [3d ed.]
London, Hale [1973] 244 p. [£2.50]
796.4/03 73-178722
GV567 .W3 1973 MRR Alc.

Willoughby, David P. The super-
athletes; South Brunswick, A. S.
Barnes [1970] 665 p. [$15.00] 796
72-88302
GV741 .W54 MRR Alc.

ATHLETES--UNITED STATES--BIOGRAPHY--
DICTIONARIES.
Hickok, Ralph. Who was who in
American sports. New York, Hawthorn
Books [1971] xlii, 338 p. [$9.95]
796/.0922 72-158009
GV697.A1 H5 MRR Biog.

ATHLETES--UNITED STATES--BIOGRAPHY--
YEARBOOKS.
Outstanding college athletes of
America. 1969- Washington, D.C.
796 79-94524
GV697.A1 O86 MRR Biog Latest
edition

ATHLETES, AMERICAN--BIOGRAPHY.
Burrill, Bob. Who's who in boxing.
New Rochelle, N.Y., Arlington House
[1974] 208 p. [$7.95]
796.8/3/0922 73-13020
GV1131 .B87 MRR Biog.

Hanley, Reid M., Who's who in track
and field New Rochelle, N.Y.,
Arlington House [1973] 160 p.
[$6.95] 796.4/2/0922 B 73-11872
GV697.A1 H34 MRR Biog.

Karst, Gene, Who's who in
professional baseball New Rochelle,
N.Y., Arlington House [1973] 919 p.
796.357/64/0922 B 73-11870
GV865.A1 K37 MRR Biog.

Mendell, Ronald L., Who's who in
basketball New Rochelle, N.Y.,
Arlington House [1973] 248 p.
[$7.95] 796.32/3/0922 B 73-11871
GV884.A1 M46 MRR Biog.

ATHLETES, CANADIAN--BIOGRAPHY.
Kariher, Harry C., Who's who in
hockey New Rochelle, N.Y., Arlington
House [1973] 189 p. 796.9/62/0922
B 73-11868
GV848.5.A1 K37 MRR Biog.

ATHLETES, NEGRO
see Negro athletes

ATHLETIC CLUBS--GREAT BRITAIN--
DIRECTORIES.
The British club year book and
directory. London. 68-1184
Began in 1961.
HS67 .B7 MRR Alc Latest edition

ATHLETICS.
see also Boxing

see also Olympic games

see also Physical education and
training

see also Sports

see also Wrestling

The Blue book of college athletics.
[1931/32]- Cleveland [etc.] Rohrich
Corp. [etc.] 371.74 ca 31-721
GV741 .B5 MRR Alc Latest edition

ATHLETICS--GREECE.
Gardiner, Edward Norman, Athletics
of the ancient world, Oxford, The
Clarendon press, 1930. x, 246 p.
796.093 30-32919
GV21 .G25 MRR Alc.

ATHLETICS--ROME.
Gardiner, Edward Norman, Athletics
of the ancient world, Oxford, The
Clarendon press, 1930. x, 246 p.
796.093 30-32919
GV21 .G25 MRR Alc.

ATHOS (MONASTERIES) MSS.--CATALOGS.
United States. Library of Congress.
A descriptive checklist of selected
manuscripts in the monasteries of
Mount Athos Washington, Library of
Congress, Photoduplication Service,
1957. xlii, 36 p. 016.091 57-
60041
Z663.96 .D4 MRR Alc.

ATLANTIC STATES.
Gottmann, Jean. Megalopolis; the
urbanized northeastern seaboard of
the United States. New York,
Twentieth Century Fund, 1961. xi,
810 p. 301.36 61-17298
HT123.5.A12 G6 MRR Alc.

ATLANTIC STATES--DESCRIPTION AND TRAVEL-
-GUIDE-BOOKS.
American Automobile Association.
Mideastern tour book. Washington.
917.4 59-43016
F106 .A5 MRR Alc Latest edition

ATLANTIC STATES--INDUSTRIES--
DIRECTORIES.
Eastern manufacturers' & industrial
directory New York, Bell Directory
Publishers. 54-35021
Began publication in 1936.
HC107.A11 E2 MRR Alc Latest
edition

ATLASES.
Adams, James Truslow, ed. Atlas of
American history; New York, C.
Scribner's sons, 1943. xi, [1], 360
p. incl. maps. 911.73 map43-126
G1201.S1 A2 1943 MRR Ref Desk.

ATLASES. (Cont.)
American heritage. The American
heritage pictorial atlas of United
States history. New York, American
Heritage Pub. Co.; book trade
distribution by McGraw-Hill Book Co.
[1966] 424 p.   map66-29
  G1201.S1 A4 1966 MRR Alc.

Britannica atlas. Chicago,
Encyclopaedia Britannica [1974] xvi,
312, I:222 p.   912 74-170879
  G1019 .B766 1974 MRR Alc Atlas.

The Cambridge modern history. 2d ed.
New York, The Macmillan company,
1924. xix, 229 p., 141 maps (part
double)   28-6514
  D208 .C2 Atlas MRR Alc.

The Cambridge modern history, New
York, The Macmillan company; London,
Macmillan & co., ltd., 1902-12. 13
v. and atlas.   04-21616
  D208 .C17 MRR Alc.

The Century dictionary and
cyclopedia. [Rev. and enl. ed.] New
York, The Century co. [c1911] 12 v.
[$75.00]   11-31934
  PE1625 .C4 1911 MRR Alc.

Encyclopaedia Britannica. Chicago,
Encyclopaedia Britannica [1873] 24
v.   031 72-75874
  AE5 .E363 1873 MRR Alc.

Foster, Fred William. School and
library atlas of the world,
(Sycamore, Ill.] School and Library
Pub. Co.; distributed by Geographical
Pub. Co., Cleveland [1968] xxii, 324
p. map68-11
  G1019 .F62 1968 MRR Alc.

Generalstabens litografiska anstalt,
Stockholm. Svenska orter; Stockholm
[Generalstabens litografiska anstalt]
1932-   v. in   and atlas.   914.85
ac 34-2254
  DL605 .G4 MRR Alc.

Goode, John Paul. World atlas. 13th
ed. Chicago, Rand McNally, 1970.
xii, 315 p.   912 77-653844
  G1019 .G67 1970 MRR Ref Desk.

Grollenberg, Lucas Hendricus, Atlas
of the Bible. [London] Nelson, 1956.
165 p.   220.93 56-14320
  BS621 .G712 1956 MRR Alc.

Hammond Incorporated. Hammond
ambassador world atlas. Maplewood,
N.J. [1973] xvi p., 320 p. of col.
maps, [321] -462 p., 463-474 p. of
maps, 475-480 p.   912 72-14223
  G1019 .H265 1973 MRR Alc.

The International atlas. Chicago,
Rand McNally [1969] liv, 280, 223 p.
912 77-653339
  G1019 .I49 1969 MRR Alc Atlas.

Leahy's hotel-motel guide & travel
atlas of the United States, Canada
and Mexico. Chicago, American Hotel
Register Co.   647.84 09-20539
  TX907 .L5 MRR Alc Latest edition

Lord, Clifford Lee, Historical atlas
of the United States, Rev. ed. New
York, Holt [1953] xv, 238 p.   53-
10208
  G1201.S1 L6 1953 MRR Ref Desk.

May, Herbert Gordon, Oxford Bible
atlas. 2nd ed. / London ; New York
: Oxford University Press, 1974. 144
p. :   [£2.75 ($9.95 U.S.] 220.9
74-184843
  BS630 .M35 1974 MRR Alc.

The New York Times atlas of the
world. [New York] Quadrangle Books
[1972] 40, 143, I, 84 p. [$35.00]
912 72-650050
  G1019 .N4E8 1972 MRR Alc Atlas.

Oxford University Press. Oxford
economic atlas of the world; 4th
ed.; London, Oxford University
Press, 1972. viii, 239 p. [£5.75]
912/.1/33 72-169937
  G1046.G1 O82 1972 MRR Alc Atlas

Oxford University Press. United
States & Canada. Oxford, Clarendon
P., 1967. [12], [35] p. [75/- (35/-
pbk.)]   912.1/3308/73 map68-202
  G1201.G1 O9 1967 MRR Alc Atlas.

Paullin, Charles Oscar, Atlas of the
historical geography of the United
States, [Washington, D.C., New York]
Pub. jointly by Carnegie institution
of Washington and the American
geographical society of New York,
1932. 2 p. l., iii-xv p., 1 l., 162
p., 1 l., 688 maps (part col.) on 166
plates (part double) 911.73 map32-
54
  G1201.S1 P3 1932 MRR Alc Atlas.

Philip (George) and Son, ltd. The
mercantile marine atlas: 16th ed.
[rev.] London, 1959. xxvii, p., 41
plates (chiefly col. maps (part
fold.)), 23 p.   map59-990
  G1060 .P5 1959 MRR Alc Atlas.

Rand McNally and Company. The earth
and man. New York [1972] 439 p.
[$35.00]   912 70-654432
  G1019 .R26 1972 MRR Alc Atlas.

Rand McNally and Company. Rand
McNally cosmopolitan world atlas.
[Enl. "Planet Earth" ed.] Chicago
[1971] lxi, 252, 100X p. [$19.95]
912 72-654253
  G1019 .R24 1971 MRR Alc Atlas.

Rand McNally and Company. The World
book atlas. Chicago, Field
Enterprises Educational Corp. [1968]
xx, 392 p.   map68-1
  G1019 .R5285 1968 MRR Alc.

Shepherd, William Robert, Historical
atlas [by] William R. Shepherd.
[1st]-   ed.; 1911- New York, Barnes
& Noble. map64-26
  G1030 .S4 MRR Ref Desk Latest
  edition

Spencer, Robert F. Atlas for
anthropology Dubuque, Iowa, W. C.
Brown Co. [1960] iii p., 52 l.
map61-161
  G1406.E1 S7 1960 MRR Alc.

Spencer, Robert F. An ethno-atlas;
Dubuque, Iowa, W. C. Brown Co. [1958,
c1956] iii, 42 p. 572.084 56-
12496
  GN11 .S75 MRR Alc.

Steele, Matthew Forney, American
campaigns, Washington, B. S. Adams,
1909. viii p., 1 l., 731 p. and
atlas of xii p., 311 maps. war22-80
  E181 .S85 MRR Alc.

The Reader's digest. These United
States; Pleasantville, N.Y.,
Reader's Digest Association [1968]
236 p.   912.73 map68-2
  G1200 .R4 1968 MRR Alc Atlas.

United States. Military Academy, West
Point. Dept. of Military Art and
Engineering. A military history of
World War II; West Point, United
States Military Academy, 1953. 2 v.
and atlas ([3] l., 168 l. of col.
maps, 6 col. diagrs.) 940.542 53-
37497
  D743 .U465 MRR Alc.

United States. Military Academy, West
Point. Dept. of Military Art and
Engineering. The West Point atlas of
American Wars. New York, Praeger
[1959] 2 v.   912.73 59-7452
  G1201.S1 U5 1959 MRR Alc.

United States. Military Academy, West
Point. Dept. of Military Art and
Engineering. The West Point atlas of
the Civil War. New York, Praeger
[1962] 1 v. (various pagings)
973.79 map62-23
  G1201.S5 U58 1962 MRR Alc.

United States. War Dept. The
official atlas of the Civil War. New
York; T. Yoseloff [1958] [8] p.,
facsim.: 29 p., 175 plates (incl.
illus. (part col.) maps (part col.)
plans)   map58-3
  G1201.S5 U58 1958 MRR Alc.

Van Royen, William, Atlas of the
world's resources. New York,
Published by Prentice-Hall for the
University of Maryland, 1952- v.
338 52-8034
  G1046.G3 V3 1952 MRR Alc Atlas.

ATLASES--BIBLIOGRAPHY.
Alexander, Gerard L. Guide to
atlases: world, regional, national,
thematic; Metuchen, N.J.; Scarecrow
Press, 1971. 671 p.   016.912 70-
157728
  Z6021 .A43 MRR Alc.

International maps and atlases in
print. London, New York, Bowker
Publishing Co. [1974] 864 p.
[£15.00] 016.912 73-13336
  Z6021 .I596 MRR Alc.

United States. Library of Congress.
Map division. A list of atlases and
maps applicable to the world war;
Washington, Govt. print. off., 1918.
202 p.   18-26005
  Z663.35 .L54 MRR Alc.

United States Library of Congress.
Map Division. Noteworthy maps; no.
[1]-3; 1925/26-1927/28. Washington,
U.S. Govt. Print. Off. 27-26417
  Z663.35 .N6 MRR Alc MRR Alc
  Partial set

Walsh, James Patrick. Home reference
booker in print; New York, R. R.
Bowker Co., 1969. x, 284 p. [9.75]
011/.02 68-56427
  Z1035.1 .W35 MRR Alc.

ATLASES--BIBLIOGRAPHY--CATALOGS.
United States. Library of Congress.
Library of Congress catalog; Maps and
atlases. 1953-55. Washington.
016.912 53-60010
  Z663.35 .L45 MRR Alc MRR Alc Full
  set

United States. Library of Congress.
Map Division. A list of geographical
atlases in the Library of Congress,
Washington, Govt. Print. Off., 1909-
v.   016.912 09-35009
  Z663.35 .L5 MRR Alc.

United States. Library of Congress.
Map Division. United States atlases;
Washington, 1950- v.   016.91273
50-62950
  Z663.35 .U52 MRR Alc.

Walsh, James Patrick, comp. General
world atlases in print, 1972-1973;
[4th ed.; enl.] New York, Bowker,
1973. ix, 211 p. 016.912 72-13053
  Z6028 .W27 1973 MRR Ref Desk.

ATLASES--INDEXES.
Whyte, Fredrica Harriman. Whyte's
atlas guide. New York, Scarecrow
Press, 1962 [c1961] 172 p. 016.912
61-8723
  GA300 .W45 1962 MRR Alc Atlas.

ATLASES, BRAZILIAN.
Enciclopédia universal EPB; São
Paulo, Ed. Pedagógica Brasileira,
1969. 10 v. (3904, 226 p.) [500.00]
76-391018
  AE37 .E55 MRR Alc.

ATLASES, BRITISH.
Bartholomew (John) and Son, ltd. The
Times atlas of the world. [2d ed.,
rev.] London, Times Newspapers,
1968. xliii, 272 p. [15/15/-] 912
70-653400
  G1019 .B395 1968 MRR Alc Atlas.

Wright, George Ernest, The
Westminster historical atlas to the
Bible, Rev. [i.e. 5th British] ed.
London, SCM Press [1957, c1956] 130
p. map59-786
  G2230 .W7 1957 MRR Alc Atlas.

ATLASES, BRITISH--INDEXES.
Times, London. Index-gazetteer of
the world. London, Times Publishing
Co., 1965. xxxi, 964 p. [£10]
910.003 66-70286
  G103 .T5 MRR Alc Atlas.

ATLASES, GERMAN.
Das Grosse Duden-Lexikon in acht
Banden. Mannheim, Bibliographisches
Institut, 1946-69. 10 v. [33.00 (v.
3) varies] 033/.1 67-94115
  AE27 .G693 vol. 9-10 MRR Alc.

Mairs Geographischer Verlag,
Stuttgart. Der grosse Shell Atlas.
1.-   Aufl.; 1960- Stuttgart. map63-
200
  G1911.P2 M25 MRR Alc Atlas Latest
  edition

ATMOSPHERIC PRESSURE--STATISTICS.
World weather records. 1921/30-
Washington. 551.59083 59-65360
  QC982 .W6 MRR Alc Latest edition /
  Sci RR Full set

ATMOSPHERIC TEMPERATURE.
Great Britain. Meteorological Office.
Tables of temperature, relative
humidity and precipitation for the
world. 2nd ed. London, H&M.S.o;
1966- v.   [1/5/- (pt. 3) 1/15-
(pt. 4) 15/6 (pt. 5)] 551.5/021/2
76-385248
  QC982.5 .G732 MRR Alc.

ATMOSPHERIC TEMPERATURE--STATISTICS.
Conway, Hobart McKinley, ed. The
weather handbook ; Rev. ed. Atlanta
; Conway Research, 1974. 255 p. ;
[$25.00]   551.6/9/1732 74-187773
  QC982.5 .C6 1974 MRR Alc.

United States. National Oceanic and
Atmospheric Administration. Climates
of the States; [Port Washington,
N.Y., Water Information Center, 1974]
2 v. (975 p.) 551.6/9/73 73-93482
  QC983 .U58 1974 MRR Alc.

World weather records. 1921/30-
Washington. 551.59083 59-65360
  QC982 .W6 MRR Alc Latest edition /
  Sci RR Full set

ATOMIC ENERGY--BIBLIOGRAPHY.
Wang, Chi. Nuclear science in mainland China; [for sale by the Supt. of Docs., U.S. Govt. Print. Off.] 1968. vi, 70 p. [$0.70]
621.48/0951 68-62146
Z663.41 .W3 MRR Alc.

ATOMIC ENERGY--BIOGRAPHY.
Who's who in atoms. 1959- London, Harrap Research Publications [etc.]
925.3 59-2375
QC774 .A1W5 Sci RR Latest edition / MRR Alc Latest edition

ATOMIC ENERGY--DICTIONARIES.
Del Vecchio, Alfred, ed. Concise dictionary of atomics. New York, Philosophical Library [1964] ix, 262 p. 539./703 64-13028
QC772 .D4 MRR Alc.

United States of America Standards Institute. USA standard glossary of terms in nuclear science and technology. [New York, 1967] 111 p. 539/.03 74-3790
QC772 .U55 1967 MRR Alc.

ATOMIC ENERGY--DICTIONARIES--RUSSIAN.
Carpovich, Eugene A. Russian-English atomic dictionary. 2d rev. and enriched ed. New York, Technical Dictionaries Co., 1959. 317 p.
539.703 59-2755
QC772 .C3 1959 MRR Alc.

ATOMIC ENERGY--SOCIETIES, ETC.--DIRECTORIES.
World nuclear directory. 1st- ed.; 1961- London, Harrap Research Publications [etc.] 62-52178
QC770 .W65 Sci RR Latest edition / MRR Alc Latest edition

ATOMIC ENERGY INDUSTRIES--DIRECTORIES.
World nuclear directory. 1st- ed.; 1961- London, Harrap Research Publications [etc.] 62-52178
QC770 .W65 Sci RR Latest edition / MRR Alc Latest edition

ATOMS.
see also Nuclear physics

ATTICUS, TITUS POMPONIUS.
Cicero, Marcus Tullius. Cicero. Letters to Atticus; London, W. Heinemann; New York, G. P. Putnam's sons, 1925-1928. 3 v. mrr01-11
PA6156.C6 E6 1925d MRR Alc.

ATTITUDE (PSYCHOLOGY)
see also Public opinion

ATTORNEYS
see Lawyers

AUCKLAND, N.Z.--COMMERCE--DIRECTORIES.
Universal business directory for Auckland city and suburbs. Auckland, Universal Business Directories. 52-42130
HF5299.A83 U54 MRR Alc Latest edition

AUCKLAND, N.Z. (PROVINCIAL DISTRICT)--COMMERCE--DIRECTORIES.
Universal business directory for Auckland Province. Auckland, Universal Business Directories. 52-38581
HF5299.A83 U55 MRR Alc Latest edition

AUDIO-VISUAL EDUCATION.
see also Languages, Modern--Study and teaching--Audio-visual aids

see also Television in education

AUDIO-VISUAL EDUCATION--BIBLIOGRAPHY.
AVRG; audio-visual resource guide for use in religious education. [1st]-ed.; 1949- [New York, etc.]
016.268635 58-13297
BV1535 .A22 MRR Alc Latest edition

Educational Media Council. Educational media index. New York, McGraw-Hill [1964] 14 v. 016.37133 64-17810
Z5814.V8 E3 MRR Alc.

Limbacher, James L. A reference guide to audiovisual information, New York, Bowker, 1972. ix, 197 p. 016.00155/3 72-1737
Z5814.V8 L55 MRR Alc.

Rufsvold, Margaret Irene. Guides to newer educational media; 2d ed. Chicago, American Library Association, 1967. vi, 62 p. 016.37133 67-27792
Z5814.V8 R8 1967 MRR Alc.

AUDIO-VISUAL EDUCATION--UNITED STATES--CATALOGS.
American Film Institute. The American Film Institute guide to college courses in film and television. Washington, Acropolis Books [1973] xv, 309 p. [$5.95]
791.4/07/1173 72-12391
LB1043.Z9 A8 MRR Alc.

AUDIO-VISUAL EQUIPMENT--CATALOGS.
The Audio-visual equipment directory. Mar. 1953- Fairfax, Va. [etc.] National Audio-Visual Association. 778.55078 53-35264
TS2301.A7 A8 MRR Alc Latest edition

Audio visual market place. 1969-ed. New York, Bowker. 371.33/0973 69-18201
LB1043 .A817 MRR Alc Latest edition

AUDIO-VISUAL MATERIALS.
see also Filmstrips

see also Moving-pictures

AUDIO-VISUAL MATERIALS--BIBLIOGRAPHY.
The Elementary school library collection, phases 1-2-3: 8th ed. New Brunswick, N.J., Bro-Dart Foundation, 1973. xxviii, 780 p. 028.52 73-8819
Z1037 .E4 1973 MRR Alc.

Johnson, Harry Alleyn. Multimedia materials for Afro-American studies; New York, R. R. Bowker Co., 1971. 353 p. 016.9173/06/96073 75-126009
LC2801 .J63 MRR Alc.

Limbacher, James L. A reference guide to audiovisual information, New York, Bowker, 1972. ix, 197 p. 016.00155/3 72-1737
Z5814.V8 L55 MRR Alc.

Perkins, Flossie L. Book and non-book media; Urbana, Ill., National Council of Teachers of English [1972] ix, 298 p. 016.028 72-186931
Z1035.A1 P36 1972 MRR Alc.

Wasserman, Paul. Museum media; 1st ed. Detroit, Gale Research Co., 1973. vii, 455 p. 011 73-16335
Z5052 .W35 MRR alc.

AUDIO-VISUAL MATERIALS--CATALOGS.
National Information Center for Educational Media. Index to psychology: multimedia. 1st ed. [Los Angeles, University of Southern California] 1972. x, 461 p. 016.15 76-190637
BF77 .N37 1972 MRR Alc.

AUDIO-VISUAL MATERIALS--PERIODICALS.
Audio visual market place. 1969-ed. New York, Bowker. 371.33/0973 69-18201
LB1043 .A817 MRR Alc Latest edition

AUDIO-VISUAL MATERIALS--SOCIETIES, ETC.
National Audio-Visual Association. The N A V A membership list & trade directory. Fairfax, Va. [etc.] 52-21720
LB1043 .N32 MRR Alc Latest edition

AUDITING.
see also Accounting

Holmes, Arthur Wellington, Auditing: principles and procedure 7th ed. Homewood, Ill., R. D. Irwin, 1971. xv, 924 p. 657.4/5 76-105537
HF5667 .H63 1971 MRR Alc.

Holmes, Arthur Wellington, Basic auditing principles 4th ed. Homewood, Ill., R. D. Irwin, 1972. xii, 434 p. 657./45 79-185436
HF5667 .H64 1972 MRR Alc.

AUDITING--ADDRESSES, ESSAYS, LECTURES.
Prentice-Hall, inc. Encyclopedia of auditing techniques Englewood Cliffs, N.J. [1967, c1966] 2 v. (x, 1566 p.) 657.6 66-26236
HF5667 .P72 MRR Alc.

AUDITING--HANDBOOKS, MANUALS, ETC.
Handbook for auditors. New York, McGraw-Hill [1971] 1 v. (various pagings) [$29.50] 657.4/5 73-116660
HF5667 .H26 MRR Alc.

AUDITORIUMS.
see also Theaters

AUDITORIUMS--DIRECTORIES.
A A S G; [Cincinnati, Billboard Pub. Co] 725/.8/02573 72-626501
GV182 .A74 MRR Alc Latest edition

The National directory for the performing arts and civic centers. Dallas, Handel & Co. 790.2/0973 73-646635
PN2289 .N38 MRR Alc Latest edition

AUDITORS--UNITED STATES--DIRECTORIES.
Institute of Internal Auditors. Directory of membership and chapters. [New York?] 62-29251
HF5667 .I436 MRR Alc Latest edition

AUGSBURG--DIRECTORIES.
Adressbuch der Stadt Augsburg. Augsburg, Adressbuchverlag K. Arnold. 53-28350
DD901.A92 E35 MRR Alc Latest edition

AUST-AGDER, NORWAY--DIRECTORIES.
Aust-Agder fylkes adressebok med skattelikninger. Trondheim, H. G. Moe. 54-16870
DL576.A8 A8 MRR Alc Latest edition

AUSTRALASIA.
The World book encyclopedia. Chicago, Field Enterprises Educational Corp. [1973] 26 v. 031 74-189336
AE5 .W55 1973 MRR Alc.

AUSTRALASIA--DIRECTORIES.
The Europa year book. 1959- London, Europa Publications. 341.184 59-2942
JN1 .E85 Sci RR Latest edition / MRR Ref Desk Latest edition

AUSTRALASIA--MANUFACTURES--DIRECTORIES.
The Australasian manufacturers' directory. Sydney [etc.] Manufacturer Pub. Co. 23-10385
HD9738 .A2A8 MRR Alc Latest edition

AUSTRALIA.
Osborne, Charles, Australia, New Zealand, and the South Pacific; New York, Praeger [1970] xi, 580 p. [18.50] 919.4 69-12899
DU15 .O8 1970b MRR Alc.

AUSTRALIA--BIBLIOGRAPHY.
Borchardt, Dietrich Hans, Australian bibliography; [2d ed.] Melbourne, Canberra [etc.] Cheshire [1966] 96 p. [$3.00 Aust.] 016.9194 68-106257
Z4011 .B65 1966 MRR Alc.

Ferguson, John Alexander, Sir, Bibliography of Australia, Sydney, London, Angus and Robertson ltd., 1941- v. 016.994 a 42-1362
Z4011 .F47 MRR Alc.

Miller, Edmund Morris, Australian literature, [Rev. ed.] Sydney, Angus and Robertson [1956] vii, 503 p. 016.82 a 57-6327
Z4021 .M5 1956 MRR Alc.

Royal Commonwealth Society. Library. Subject catalogue of the Library of the Royal Empire Society, [1st ed. reprinted] London, Dawsons for the Royal Commonwealth Society, 1967. 4 v. (60/-/- per set (16/-/- per vol.)) 016.942 68-70847
Z7164.C7 R82 1967 MRR Alc.

AUSTRALIA--BIBLIOGRAPHY--CATALOGS.
Royal Commonwealth Society. Library. Subject catalogue of the Royal Commonwealth Society, London. Boston, Mass., G. K. Hall, 1971. 7 v. 017.1 70-180198
Z7164.C7 R83 MRR Alc (Dk 33)

AUSTRALIA--BIBLIOGRAPHY--PERIODICALS.
Australian public affairs information service: no. 1- July 1945-Canberra. 015.94 50-28427
Z7165.A8 A8 MRR Alc Partial set

AUSTRALIA--BIOGRAPHY.
The Far East and Australasia. 1st-ed.; 1969- London, Europa Publications. 915./03/05 74-417170
DS1 .F3 MRR Alc Latest edition

Learmonth, Andrew Thomas Amos, Encyclopaedia of Australia, [2d ed.] London, New York, F. Warne [c1973] viii, 606 p. 919.4/003 73-80243
DU90 .L4 1973 MRR Alc.

Parliamentary handbook of the Commonwealth of Australia. Canberra, Australia. Commonwealth Parliamentary Library. 328.94/07/3 72-626909
JQ4054 .C3 MRR Alc Latest edition

Serle, Percival, Dictionary of Australian biography. Sydney, Angus and Robertson [1949] 2 v. 920.094 49-6289
DU82 .S47 MRR Biog.

Whitington, Don. Ring the belle; Melbourne, Georgian House [1956] viii, 125 p. 342.94 320.94* 57-25049
JQ4005 .W5 MRR Alc.

Who's who in Australia. v. [1]-1922- Melbourne [etc.] Herald and Weekly Times Ltd. [etc.] 920.094 23-288
DU82 .W5 MRR Biog Latest edition

AUSTRALIA--BIOGRAPHY--DICTIONARIES.
Australian dictionary of biography.
Melbourne] Melbourne University
Press; London, New York, Cambridge
University Press [1966- v.
($12.00 (v. 1) varies)   920.094 66-
13723
    DU82 .A9 MRR Biog.

Kósa, Géza Attila. Who's who in
Australian libraries, Sydney,
Library Association of Australia,
1968. xiv, 181 p. [5.40]
021/.0025/94 75-398852
    Z720.A46A85 MRR Biog.

McCulloch, Alan. Encyclopedia of
Australian art. New York, Praeger
[1969, c1968] 668 p. [25.00]
709/.94 69-17079
    N7400 .M27 1969 MRR Alc.

AUSTRALIA--COMMERCE--DIRECTORIES.
Australian directory of exports.
1964/65- ed. Melbourne, P.
Isaacson Pty. 65-44637
    HF3943 .A84 MRR Alc Latest edition

The Business who's who of Australia.
1964- Sydney, R. G. Riddell. 64-
56752
    HF5292 .B785 MRR Alc Latest
    edition

Lloyd's Australian and New Zealand
trade register. Sydney. 57-47262
    HC602 .L55 MRR Alc Latest edition

AUSTRALIA--COMMERCE--YEARBOOKS.
The Business who's who of Australia.
1964- Sydney, R. G. Riddell. 64-
56752
    HF5292 .B785 MRR Alc Latest
    edition

**AUSTRALIA--DESCRIPTION AND TRAVEL--1951-
--GUIDE-BOOKS.**
White, Osmar. Guide to Australia.
New York, McGraw-Hill [1969 or 70,
c1968] 387 p. [8.95] 919.4/04/5
74-96245
    DU95 .W5 1969 MRR Alc.

**AUSTRALIA--DICTIONARIES AND
ENCYCLOPEDIAS.**
The Australian encyclopaedia.
Sydney, Angus and Robertson [1958]
10 v. 919.4 58-43303
    DU90 .A82 MRR Alc.

Learmonth, Andrew Thomas Amos.
Encyclopaedia of Australia, [2d ed.]
London, New York, F. Warne [c1973]
viii, 606 p. 919.4/003 73-80243
    DU90 .L4 1973 MRR Alc.

The Modern encyclopaedia of Australia
and New Zealand. Sydney, Horwitz-
Grahame [c1964] 1189 p. 65-2387
    DU90 .M6 MRR Alc.

AUSTRALIA--DISCOVERY AND EXPLORATION.
Pacific voyages. Garden City, N.Y.,
Doubleday [1973, c1971] 488 p.
[$14.95] 910/.09/1823 72-93388
    DU19 .P3 1973 MRR Alc.

**AUSTRALIA--ECONOMIC CONDITIONS--
BIBLIOGRAPHY.**
Australian public affairs information
service; no. 1-   July 1945-
Canberra. 015.94 50-28427
    Z7165.A8 A8 MRR Alc Partial set

AUSTRALIA--FOREIGN RELATIONS.
Australia in world affairs. 1950/55-
Melbourne, F. W. Cheshire. 327.94
58-206
    DU113 .A7 MRR Alc Full set

AUSTRALIA--GAZETTEERS.
United States. Office of Geography.
Australia; Washington, U.S. Govt.
Print. Off., 1957. iii, 750 p.
919.4 57-61579
    DU90 .U5 MRR Alc.

**AUSTRALIA--GOVERNMENT PUBLICATIONS--
BIBLIOGRAPHY.**
Australian national bibliography.
Jan. 1961- Canberra, National
Library of Australia. 63-33739
    Z4015 .A96 MRR Alc Full set

AUSTRALIA--HISTORY.
Turnbull, Clive. A concise history
of Australia. London, Thames and
Hudson [1965] 192 p. 66-54215
    DU112 .T9 1965a MRR Alc.

Younger, Ronald M. Australia and the
Australians: [Adelaide] Rigby [1970,
c1969] 869 p. [$10.95] 994 77-
538084
    DU110 .Y68 1970b MRR Alc.

AUSTRALIA--HISTORY--SOURCES.
Clark, Charles Manning Hope, ed.
Select documents in Australian
history. Sydney, Angus and Robertson
[1950- v.   994 51-2907
    DU80 .C58 MRR Alc.

AUSTRALIA--IMPRINTS.
Australian national bibliography.
Jan. 1961- Canberra, National
Library of Australia. 63-33739
    Z4015 .A96 MRR Alc Full set

Ferguson, John Alexander, Sir,
Bibliography of Australia. Sydney,
London, Angus and Robertson ltd.,
1941- v.   016.994 a 42-1362
    Z4011 .F47 MRR Alc.

Hubble, Gregory Valentine. The
Australian novel; Perth, Imperial
Instant Printing, 1970. 1 v.
(unpaged) 016.823 78-572128
    Z4024.F5 H8 MRR Alc.

Union list of higher degree theses in
Australian university libraries:
Hobart, University of Tasmania
Library, 1967. xxii, 568 p.
013.375 68-140995
    Z5055.A698 U5 MRR Alc.

AUSTRALIA--INDUSTRIES--DIRECTORIES.
Lloyd's Australian and New Zealand
trade register. Sydney. 57-47262
    HC602 .L55 MRR Alc Latest edition

Riddell's Australian purchasing year
book. 1st- ed.; 1967- [Sydney, R.
G. Riddell Pty. Ltd.] 602/.5/994 75-
612957
    T12.5.A8 R5 MRR Alc Latest edition

AUSTRALIA--MANUFACTURES.
Wheelwright, Edward Lawrence.
Anatomy of Australian manufacturing
industry; Sydney, Law Book Co.,
1967. xvii, 433 p. [$13.99 Aust.]
338.7/4/0994 67-95586
    HD2927 .W45 MRR Alc.

AUSTRALIA--MANUFACTURES--DIRECTORIES.
The Australasian manufacturers'
directory. Sydney [etc.]
Manufacturer Pub. Co. 23-10385
    HD9738 .A2A8 MRR Alc Latest
    edition

Riddell's Australian purchasing year
book. 1st- ed.; 1967- [Sydney, R.
G. Riddell Pty. Ltd.] 602/.5/994 75-
612957
    T12.5.A8 R5 MRR Alc Latest edition

**AUSTRALIA--POLITICS AND GOVERNMENT--
BIBLIOGRAPHY.**
Australian public affairs information
service; no. 1-   July 1945-
Canberra. 015.94 50-28427
    Z7165.A8 A8 MRR Alc Partial set

Liboiron, Albert A. Federalism and
intergovernmental relations in
Australia, Canada, the United States
and other countries; Kingston, Ont.,
Institute of Intergovernmental
Relations, Queen's University, 1967.
vi, 231 l. [$3.00 Can.] 016.351
68-110060
    Z7165.A8 L5 MRR Alc.

**AUSTRALIA--POLITICS AND GOVERNMENT--
DICTIONARIES.**
Whitington, Don. Ring the bells;
Melbourne, Georgian House [1956]
viii, 125 p. 342.94 320.94* 57-
25049
    JQ4005 .W5 MRR Alc.

AUSTRALIA--REGISTERS.
Parliamentary handbook of the
Commonwealth of Australia. Canberra,
Australia. Commonwealth Parliamentary
Library. 328.94/07/3 72-626909
    JQ4054 .C3 MRR Alc Latest edition

**AUSTRALIA--SOCIAL CONDITIONS--
BIBLIOGRAPHY.**
Australian public affairs information
service; no. 1-   July 1945-
Canberra. 015.94 50-28427
    Z7165.A8 A8 MRR ALc Partial set

AUSTRALIA--STATISTICS.
Organization for Economic Cooperation
and Development. National accounts
statistics, 1960-1971. [Paris, 1973]
471 p. [$7.50 (U.S.)] 339.3 74-
158206
    HC79.I5 O7 1973 MRR Alc.

AUSTRALIA--STATISTICS, VITAL.
Preston, Samuel H. Causes of death:
life tables for national population
New York, Seminar Press, 1972. xi,
787 p.; 312/.2 72-80305
    HB1321 .P73 MRR Alc.

AUSTRALIA--YEARBOOKS.
Australia handbook. Sidney,
Registered at G.P.O. Printed in
Australia by Halstead Press Pty, Ltd.
[etc.] 919.4/005 70-7283
    DU80 .A937 MRR Alc Latest edition

The Far East and Australasia. 1st-
ed.; 1969- London, Europa
Publications. 915/.03/05 74-417170

    DS1 .F3 MRR Alc Latest edition

AUSTRALIA. PARLIAMENT--BIOGRAPHY.
Parliamentary handbook of the
Commonwealth of Australia. Canberra,
Australia. Commonwealth Parliamentary
Library. 328.94/07/3 72-626909
    JQ4054 .C3 MRR Alc Latest edition

**AUSTRALIAN FICTION--20TH CENTURY--
BIBLIOGRAPHY.**
Hubble, Gregory Valentine. The
Australian novel; Perth, Imperial
Instant Printing, 1970. 1 v.
(unpaged) 016.823 78-572128
    Z4024.F5 H8 MRR Alc.

AUSTRALIAN LITERATURE--BIBLIOGRAPHY.
Miller, Edmund Morris, Australian
literature, [Rev. ed.] Sydney,
Angus and Robertson [1956] vii, 503
p. 016.82 a 57-6327
    Z4021 .M5 1956 MRR Alc.

**AUSTRALIAN LITERATURE--HISTORY AND
CRITICISM.**
Green, Henry Mackenzie, A history of
Australian literature, pure and
applied; [Sydney] Angus and
Robertson [1961] 2 v. (xxvii, 1469
p.) 820.9 62-38897
    PR9411 .G7 MRR Alc.

Miller, Edmund Morris, Australian
literature, [Rev. ed.] Sydney,
Angus and Robertson [1956] vii, 503
p. 016.82 a 57-6327
    Z4021 .M5 1956 MRR Alc.

AUSTRALIAN PERIODICALS--INDEXES.
Australian public affairs information
service; no. 1- July 1945-
Canberra. 015.94 50-28427
    Z7165.A8 A8 MRR ALc Partial set

AUSTRALIAN POETRY.
Murdoch, Walter, comp. A book of
Australian and New Zealand verse,
[4th ed.] London, Oxford University
Press [1950] 377 p. 821.082 53-
25334
    PR9551 .M9 1950 MRR Alc.

AUSTRALIAN POETRY--BIBLIOGRAPHY.
Cuthbert, Eleonora Isabel. Index of
Australian and New Zealand poetry.
New York, Scarecrow Press, 1963. 453
p. 016.821 63-7469
    Z4024.P7 C8 MRR Alc.

AUSTRALIAN POETRY--INDEXES.
Cuthbert, Eleonora Isabel. Index of
Australian and New Zealand poetry.
New York, Scarecrow Press, 1963. 453
p. 016.821 63-7469
    Z4024.P7 C8 MRR Alc.

AUSTRIA.
Österreichisches Jahrbuch. Wien,
Druck und Verlag der Österr.
Staatsdr. [etc.] 54-50667
    Began publication in 1919.
    DB1 .O4 MRR Alc Latest edition

Schulmeister, Otto, ed. Spectrum
Austriae, Wien, Herder [1957] 735
p. 57-58647
    DB4 .S3 MRR Alc.

AUSTRIA--BIO-BIBLIOGRAPHY.
Österreichisches biographisches
Lexikon 1815-1950. Graz, H. Bohlaus
Nachf., 1957 [i.e. 1954]- v.   63-
37408
    CT903 .O4 MRR Biog.

AUSTRIA--BIOGRAPHY.
Kosch, Wilhelm, Biographisches
Staatshandbuch; Bern, Francke [1963]
2 v. (1208 p.) 67-3923
    DD85 .K6 MRR Biog.

Kürschners biographisches Theater-
Handbuch: Berlin, W. de Gruyter,
1956. xii, 840 p. a 57-2818
    PN2657 .K8 MRR Biog.

Neue österreichische Biographie,
1815-1918. Wien, Amalthea-Verlag,
1923- v.   25-13674
    CT912 .N4 MRR Biog.

Österreichisches biographisches
Lexikon 1815-1950. Graz, H. Bohlaus
Nachf., 1957 [i.e. 1954]- v.   63-
37408
    CT903 .O4 MRR Biog.

Personen-Compass: [80.]-   Jahrg.;
1951- Wien, Compass-Verlag. 54-
17735
    HD2851 .P4 MRR Alc Latest edition

Ungar, Frederick, comp. Handbook of
Austrian literature. New York, F.
Ungar Pub. Co. [1973] xvi, 296 p.
830/.9/9436 71-125969
    PT155 .U5 MRR Biog.

Who's who in Austria. 1954-
[Montreal, etc.] Intercontinental
Book and Pub. Co. [etc.] 920.0436 a
55-4612
    DB36 .W45 MRR Biog Latest edition

AUSTRIA--BIOGRAPHY--DICTIONARIES.
Knaur, Oswald. Österreichs Männer
des öffentlichen Lebens von 1848 bis
heute. Wien, Manz, 1960. 128 p.   a
61-2171
   DB36 .K55 MRR Biog.

Wurzbach, Constantin, Ritter von
Tannenberg, Biographisches Lexikon
des Kaiserthums Oesterreich, New
York, Johnson Reprint Corp., [1966]
60 v.   79-235456
   CT903 .W82 MRR Biog.

AUSTRIA--BIOGRAPHY--INDEXES.
Stock, Karl Franz.
Personalbibliographien
österreichischer Dichter und
Schriftsteller; Pullach bei
München, Verlag Dokumentation, 1972.
xxiii, 703 p.   73-308989
   Z2111.A1 S76 MRR Biog.

AUSTRIA--COMMERCE--DIRECTORIES.
British & international buyers &
sellers guide. Manchester, Eng.
[etc.] C. G. Birn.   55-36686
   HF54.G7 B7 MRR Alc Latest edition

Export-Adressbuch von Österreich.
1950- Wien, Herold.   52-24158
   HF3543 .E9 MRR Alc Latest edition

Handels-Compass: 1946/47- Wien. 50-
20277
   HF5166 .H3 MRR Alc Latest edition

Herold Adressbuch von Österreich
für Industrie, Handel, Gewerbe.
1953- Wien, Herold. 72-626684
   HF3543 .A7 MRR Alc Latest edition

Industrie-Compass Österreich. Wien,
Compass-Verlag [etc.] 605.8 45-
33231
   HF5166 .I5 MRR Alc Latest edition

Made in Austria. Wien, Jupiter-
Verlag. 380/.025/436 68-77958
   HF3543 .M3 MRR Alc Latest edition

Österreichisches Telegramm-,
Fernschreiber-, Telex-Adressbuch.
[Salzburg, etc.] 53-28310
   HE8133 .O8 MRR Alc Latest edition

**AUSTRIA--DESCRIPTION AND TRAVEL--GUIDE-
BOOKS.**
Baedecker, Karl, firm. Austria. 2d
ed. Friburg, Karl Baedeker; New
York, Macmillan, 1970. 369 p.
[$9.95 (U.S.)] 914.36/04/5 74-
21961
   DB16 .B19 1970 MRR Alc.

Clark, Sydney Aylmer, All the best
in Austria, 1973-1974 rev. ed. New
York, Dodd, Mead [1973] viii, 344 p.
[$9.95] 914.36/04/5 74-815
   DB16 .C55 1973 MRR Alc.

Fodor's Austria. 1969- New York, D.
McKay. 914.36/04/5 72-622747
   DB16 .A8 MRR Alc Latest edition

Olson, Harvey Stuart, Olson's
complete motoring guide to Germany,
Austria & the Benelux countries,
[1st ed.] Philadelphia, Lippincott
[1968] xiv, 878 p. [$5.95] 914
68-24136
   GV1025.A2 O45 MRR Alc.

Pan American World Airways, inc.
Complete reference guide to Austria
and Switzerland, incl. Liechtenstein.
[2d rev. ed. New York, Trade
distribution by Simon & Schuster,
c1966] 128 p. 914.36/04/5 67-5271
   DB16 .P3 1967 MRR Alc.

AUSTRIA--DIRECTORIES.
Who's who in Austria. 1954-
[Montreal, etc.] Intercontinental
Book and Pub. Co. [etc.] 920.0436 a
55-4612
   DB36 .W45 MRR Biog Latest edition

AUSTRIA--ECONOMIC CONDITIONS--1945-
Heissenberger, Franz. The economic
reconstruction of Austria, 1945-1952;
Washington, Library of Congress,
Reference Dept., European Affairs
Division, 1953. xii, 153 p.
330.9436 53-60025
   Z663.26 .E35 MRR Alc.

AUSTRIA--FOREIGN RELATIONS--TREATIES.
Austria. Bundesministerium für
Unterricht. Österreich frei; Wien,
Österreichischer Bundesverlag für
Unterricht, Wissenschaft und Kunst
[1956] 159 p.   57-15203
   DB99.1 .A54 MRR Alc.

AUSTRIA--GAZETTEERS.
GOF-Verlag, Vienna. GOF-
Ortsverzeichnis von Österreich für
wirtschaft und Verkehr. 5.,
neubearb. erweiterte und verb. Aufl.
Wien, GOF-Verlag (1966) 296 p. [S
175.00 DM 28.50] 914.36/003 67-
82158
   DB14 .G2 1966 MRR Alc.

United States. Office of Geography.
Austria; Washington, U.S. Govt.
Print. Off., 1962. v, 391 p.   62-
62165
   DB14 .U5 MRR Alc.

AUSTRIA--HISTORY.
Hantsch, Hugo, Die Geschichte
Österreichs. Graz, Styria [1959-
v.   61-36214
   DB38 .H323 MRR Alc.

AUSTRIA--HISTORY--1789-1900.
Macartney, Carlile Aylmer, The
Habsburg Empire, 1790-1918 [1st
American ed.] New York, Macmillan
[1969] xiv, 886 p. 943.6/04 69-
12834
   DB80 .M3 1969 MRR Alc.

AUSTRIA--HISTORY--1867-1918.
Macartney, Carlile Aylmer, The
Habsburg Empire, 1790-1918 [1st
American ed.] New York, Macmillan
[1969] xiv, 886 p. 943.6/04 69-
12834
   DB80 .M3 1969 MRR Alc.

AUSTRIA--HISTORY--1918-1938.
Gulick, Charles Adams, Austria from
Habsburg to Hitler, Berkeley, Univ.
of California Press, 1948. 2 v.
943.6 48-1808
   DB96 .G8 MRR Alc.

**AUSTRIA--HISTORY--ALLIED OCCUPATION,
1945-1955.**
Austria. Bundesministerium für
Unterricht. Österreich frei; Wien,
Österreichischer Bundesverlag für
Unterricht, Wissenschaft und Kunst
[1956] 159 p.   57-15203
   DB99.1 .A54 MRR Alc.

Austria. Bundesministerium für
Unterricht. Österreich--Freies
Land, freies Volk; Wien,
Österreichischer Bundesverlag für
Unterricht, Wissenschaft und Kunst
[1957] 208 p.   59-19213
   DB99.1 .A544 MRR Alc.

Hiscocks, Richard. The rebirth of
Austria. London, New York, Oxford
University Press, 1953. 263 p.
943.6 53-4436
   DB99.1 .H5 MRR Alc.

AUSTRIA--HISTORY--SOURCES.
Austria. Bundesministerium für
Unterricht. Österreich--Freies
Land, freies Volk; Wien,
Österreichischer Bundesverlag für
Unterricht, Wissenschaft und Kunst
[1957] 208 p.   59-19213
   DB99.1 .A544 MRR Alc.

AUSTRIA--IMPRINTS.
British Museum. Dept. of Printed
Books. Short-title catalogue of
books printed in the German-speaking
countries London, Trustees of the
British Museum, 1962. viii, 1224 p.
63-24516
   Z2222 .B73 MRR Alc.

Deutsche Bibliographie; Jan./Juni
1951- Frankfurt a. M., Buchhändler-
Vereinigung. 52-39843
   Z2221 .F73 MRR Alc Full set

Deutsche Bibliographie; Fünfjahres-
Verzeichnis. 1945/50- Frankfurt a.
M., Buchhändler-Vereinigung. 53-
39084
   Z2221 .D47 MRR Alc Full set

Deutsches bücherverzeichnis: 1916-
[Leipzig] Börsenverein der deutschen
buchhandler zu Leipzig. 20-14984
   Z2221 .K25 MRR Alc Full set

Jahresverzeichnis des deutschen
Schrifttums. 1945/46- Leipzig,
Verlag des Börsenvereins der
Deutschen Buchhandler. 015.43 50-
38395
   Z2221 .J26 MRR Alc Full set

AUSTRIA--INDUSTRIES--DIRECTORIES.
Export-Adressbuch von Österreich.
1950- Wien, Herold. 52-24158
   HF3543 .E9 MRR Alc Latest edition

Industrie-Compass Österreich. Wien,
Compass-Verlag [etc.] 605.8 45-
33231
   HF5166 .I5 MRR Alc Latest edition

**AUSTRIA--LEARNED INSTITUTIONS AND
SOCIETIES.**
Handbuch der österreichischen
Wissenschaft. 1.- Bd.; 1947/48-
Wien, Österreichischer Bundesverlag
für Unterricht, Wissenschaft und
Kunst. 50-18117
   AS132 .J3 MRR Alc Latest edition

AUSTRIA--MANUFACTURES--DIRECTORIES.
Handels-Compass: 1946/47- Wien. 50-
20277
   HF5166 .H3 MRR Alc Latest edition

Industrie-Compass Österreich. Wien,
Compass-Verlag [etc.] 605.8 45-
33231
   HF5166 .I5 MRR Alc Latest edition

Made in Austria. Wien, Jupiter-
Verlag. 380/.025/436 68-77958
   HF3543 .M3 MRR Alc Latest edition

**AUSTRIA--POLITICS AND GOVERNMENT--1918-
1938.**
Gulick, Charles Adams, Austria from
Habsburg to Hitler, Berkeley, Univ.
of California Press, 1948. 2 v.
943.6 48-1808
   DB96 .G8 MRR Alc.

AUSTRIA--POPULATION.
Bodart, Gaston, Losses of life in
modern wars, Austria-Hungary; France,
Oxford, The Clarendon press; London,
New York [etc.] H. Milford, 1916. x,
207, 6 p. incl. tables. 16-20885
   D25.5 .B6 MRR Alc.

AUSTRIA--REGISTERS.
Österreichischer Amtskalender. 1-
Jahrg.; 1922- Wien, Österreichische
Staatsdruckerei. 68-128662
   JN1604 .A32 MRR Alc Latest edition

AUSTRIA--STATISTICS.
Austria. Statisches Zentralamt.
Statistisches Handbuch für die
Republik Österreich. 1.-17. Jahrg.,
1920-37; n. F., 1.- Jahrg., 1950-
Wien. 22-1159
   HA1171 .C3 MRR Alc Latest edition

AUSTRIA, LOWER--COMMERCE--DIRECTORIES.
Herold Adressbuch von
Niederösterreich für Industrie,
Handel, Gewerbe. Wien, Herold. 72-
622313
   HF3549.A7 A45 MRR Alc Latest
edition

AUSTRIA, UPPER--COMMERCE--DIRECTORIES.
Herold Adressbuch von Oberösterreich
für Industrie, Handel, Gewerbe.
Wien, Herold. 72-622321
   HF3549.A8 A45 MRR Alc Latest
edition

AUSTRIAN LITERATURE--BIO-BIBLIOGRAPHY.
Giebisch Hans, ed. Kleines
österreichisches Literaturlexikon,
Wien, Hollinek, 1948. viii, 550 p.
016.83 49-2882
   Z2110 .G5 MRR Biog.

Ungar, Frederick, comp. Handbook of
Austrian literature. New York, F.
Ungar Pub. Co. [1973] xvi, 296 p.
830/.9/9436 71-125969
   PT155 .U5 MRR Biog.

**AUSTRIAN LITERATURE--HISTORY AND
CRITICISM--BIBLIOGRAPHY.**
Stock, Karl Franz.
Personalbibliographien
österreichischer Dichter und
Schriftsteller; Pullach bei
München, Verlag Dokumentation, 1972.
xxiii, 703 p.   73-308989
   Z2111.A1 S76 MRR Biog.

**AUSTRIAN LITERATURE (GERMAN)--BIO-
BIBLIOGRAPHY.**
Giebisch, Hans, Bio-
bibliographisches Literaturlexikon
Österreichs, Wien, Brüder Hollinek
[1964] viii, 516 p.   64-56140
   Z2110 .G48 MRR Biog.

AUSTRIAN NEWSPAPERS--DIRECTORIES.
Österreichs Presse, Werbung,
Graphik; Handbuch. 15.- Jahrg.;
1967- Wien, Verband
Österreichischer
Zeitungsherausgeber. 72-626652
   Z6956.A9 H3 MRR Alc Latest edition

AUSTRIAN PERIODICALS--BIBLIOGRAPHY.
Deutschsprachige Zeitschriften.
Marbach am Neckar, Verlag der
Schillerbuchhandlung Hans Banger.
053.1/025 70-612760
   Z6956.G3 A55 MRR Alc Latest
edition

Handbuch der österreichischen
Wissengchaft. 1.- Bd.; 1947/48-
Wien, Österreichischer Bundesverlag
für Unterricht, Wissenschaft und
Kunst. 50-18117
   AS132 .J3 MRR Alc Latest edition

AUSTRIAN PERIODICALS--DIRECTORIES.
Österreichs Presse, Werbung,
Graphik; Handbuch. 15.- Jahrg.;
1967- Wien, Verband
Österreichischer
Zeitungsherausgeber. 72-626652
   Z6956.A9 H3 MRR Alc Latest edition

AUTHORS.
Atlantic brief lives: a biographical
companion to the arts. [1st ed.]
Boston, Little, Brown [1971] xxii,
900 p. [$15.00] 700/.922 B 73-
154960
   NX90 .A73 1971 MRR Biog.

Cassell's encyclopaedia of world
literature. Rev. and enl. New York,
Morrow, [1973] 3 v.   803 73-10405
   PN41 .C3 1972 MRR Biog.

AUTHORS. (Cont.)

The Concise encyclopedia of modern world literature. [2d ed.] New York, Hawthorn Books [1971, c1963] 430 p. [$12.85] 809/.04 B 76-29851
   PN771 .C58 1971 MRR Alc.

De Montreville, Doris. Third book of junior authors. New York, H. W. Wilson Co., 1972. 320 p. 809/.89282 75-149381
   PN1009.A1 D45 MRR Biog.

Dicionário biográfico universal de autores. [Lisboa?] Artis-Bompiani [1966- v. 70-209859
   CT183 .D55 MRR Biog.

Dictionnaire biographique des auteurs [2. ed.] Paris, Société d'édition de dictionnaires et encyclopedies [1964, c1956] 2 v. 66-98043
   PN41 .D48 1964 MRR Biog.

Dizionario biografico degli autori di tutti i tempi. Milano, Fabbri; Bompiani, [1970]. 4 v. 74-312802
   CT163 .D62 1970 MRR Biog.

Dizionario letterario Bompiani degli autori di tutti i tempi e di tutte le letterature. Milano, V. Bompiani, 1956-57. 3 v. 58-16111
   Z1010 .D5 MRR Biog.

Doyle, Brian. The who's who of children's literature. New York, Schocken Books [1968] xi, 380 p. [$10.00] 028.52 68-28904
   PN452 .D6 1968b MRR Biog.

Écrivains contemporains. Paris, Éditions d'art L. Mazenod [1965] 763 p. 67-45173
   PN773 .E3 MRR Biog.

Encyclopedia of world literature in the 20th century. New York, F. Ungar Pub. Co. [1967-71] 3 v. 803 67-13615
   PN774 .L433 MRR Alc.

Force, Helen H. Who is who. Santa Ana, Calif., Professional Library Service [1967] 109 p. 929.4 67-21461
   Z1045 .F6 MRR Biog.

Gidel, Charles Antoine, Dictionnaire-manuel-illustré des écrivains et des litteratures. Paris, A. Colin & cie 1898. 2 p. l., 908 p. f 01-3144
   Z1010 .G453 MRR Biog.

Harte, Barbara, comp. 200 contemporary authors. Detroit, Mich., Gale Research Co. [1969] 306 p. 809/.04 75-94113
   PN771 .H28 MRR Biog.

Heiney, Donald W. Essentials of contemporary literature. Great Neck, N.Y., Barron's Educational Series, inc. [1955, c1954] 555 p. 55-1318
   PN771 .H4 MRR Alc.

Hoehn, Matthew, ed. Catholic authors; Newark [N.J.] St. Mary's Abbey, 1948-52. 2 v. 928 48-2039
   PN485 .H6 MRR Biog.

Johnson, Rossiter, ed. Authors digest; Metuchen, N.J., Mini-Print Corp., 1970 [c1909] 21 v. in 5. 808.83 70-12099
   PN44 .J7 1970 MRR Alc.

Koch, Willi August, Musisches Lexikon: Künstler, Kunstwerke und Motive aus Dichtung, Musik und bildender Kunst. 2., veränderte und erweiterte Aufl. Stuttgart, A. Kröner [c1964] 1250 columns, xxxx p. 65-69991
   N31 .K57 1964 MRR Alc.

Kunitz, Stanley Jasspon, ed. The junior book of authors, New York, The H. W. Wilson company, 1934. xv, 400 p. 928 34-36776
   PN1009.A1 K8 MRR Biog.

Kunitz, Stanley Jasspon, ed. Twentieth century authors, New York, Wilson, 1942. vii, 1577 p. 928 920 43-51003
   PN771 .K86 MRR Alc.

Les écrivains célèbres ... 3e édition. Paris, L. Mazenod, 1966. 3 v. [130 F per vol.] 68-123034
   PN503 .E3 1966 MRR Alc.

Magill, Frank Northen, ed. Cyclopedia of world authors. Rev. ed. Englewood Cliffs, N.J., Salem Press [1974] 3 v. (vii, 1973, xi p.) 803 74-174980
   PN451 .M36 1974 MRR Biog.

Meyers Handbuch über die Literatur. 2., neu bearb. Aufl. Mannheim, Wien, Zürich, Bibliographisches Inst. (1970) 987 p. [36.00] 79-483796
   PN41 .M45 1970 MRR Biog.

The Reader's companion to world literature. 2d ed., rev. and updated New York, New American Library [1973] 577 p. [$1.95] 803 73-173311
   PN41 .R4 1973 MRR Alc.

Richardson, Kenneth Ridley. Twentieth century writing: London, New York [etc.] Newnes, 1969. viii, 751 p. [63/-] 809/.04 70-431735
   PN771 .R5 MRR Biog.

Something about the author. v. 1- [1971- Detroit, Gale Research. 028.52/0922 [B] [920] 72-27107
   PN451 .S6 MRR Biog Full set

Ward, Alfred Charles, Longman companion to twentieth century literature. Harlow, Longman, 1970. [6], 593 p. [65/-] 820.9/009/1 76-554609
   PN771 .W28 MRR Alc.

Warner, Charles Dudley, ed. Biographical dictionary and synopsis of books, ancient and modern. Detroit, Gale Research Co., 1965- [i.e. 1966- v. 803 66-4326
   PN41 .W3 MRR Biog.

Who's who among living authors of older nations, v. 1; 1931/32. Los Angeles, Calif., Golden Syndicate Pub. Co. 016.928 28-28492
   Z1010 .W62 MRR Alc Latest edition

AUTHORS--BIBLIOGRAPHY.

Combs, Richard E. Authors: critical and biographical references; Metuchen, N.J., Scarecrow Press, 1971. 221 p. 016.809 73-167644
   PN524 .C58 MRR Alc.

AUTHORS--BIOGRAPHY.

Frenz, Horst, comp. Literature 1901-1967; Amsterdam, New York, published for the Nobel Foundation by Elsevier Pub. Co., 1969. xxi, 640 p. [40.00] 808.9 68-20649
   PN771 .F74 MRR Alc.

AUTHORS--BIOGRAPHY--INDEXES.

Combs, Richard E. Authors: critical and biographical references; Metuchen, N.J., Scarecrow Press, 1971. 221 p. 016.809 73-167644
   PN524 .C58 MRR Alc.

AUTHORS, AFRICAN.

Herdeck, Donald E., African authors; [1st ed.] Washington, Black Orpheus Press, 1973- v. [$27.50 (v. 1)] 809/.89/6 B 73-172338
   PL8010 .H38 MRR Biog.

The Penguin companion to classical, Oriental & African literature. New York, McGraw-Hill [1971, c1969] 359 p. [$9.95] 809 78-158064
   PA31 .P4 1971 MRR Alc.

Zell, Hans M. A reader's guide to African literature. New York, Africana Pub. Corp. [1971] xxi, 218 p. 809/.8967 76-83165
   PR9798 .Z4 MRR Alc.

AUTHORS, AMERICAN.

Adams, Oscar Fay, A dictionary of American authors. 5th ed. rev. and enl. Detroit, Gale Research Co., 1969. viii, 587 p. 810.9 68-21751

   Z1224 .A22 1969 MRR Biog.

Allibone, Samuel Austin, A critical dictionary of English literature and British and American authors, Detroit, Gale Research Co., 1965. 3 v. (3140 p.) 820.3 67-295
   Z1224 .A4317 MRR Biog.

American writers; New York, Scribner [1974- v. 810/.9 B 73-1759
   PS129 .A55 MRR Alc.

Bailey, Leaonead Pack. Broadside authors and artists; [1st ed.] Detroit, Mich., Broadside Press [1974] 125 p. [$9.95] 811/.5/409 B 70-108887
   Z1229.N39 B34 MRR Biog.

Browning, David Clayton, ed. Everyman's dictionary of literary biography, English & American, London, Dent; New York, Dutton [1958] x, 752 p. 928.2 a 58-2815
   PR19 .B7 MRR Biog.

Burke, William Jeremiah, American authors and books, 1640 to the present day 3d rev. ed. New York, Crown Publishers [c1972] 719 p. [$12.50] 015/.73 75-168332
   Z1224 .B87 1972 MRR Biog.

Chambers, Robert, Chambers's cyclopaedia of English literature, London, Edinburgh, W. & R. Chambers, limited [1927-38] 3 v. 820.9 39-8587
   PR83 .C4 1927 MRR Alc.

The Critical temper; New York, Ungar [1969] 3 v. [45.00] 820.9 68-8116
   PR83 .C764 MRR Alc.

De Montreville, Doris. Third book of junior authors. New York, H. W. Wilson Co., 1972. 320 p. 809/.89282 75-149381
   PN1009.A1 D45 MRR Biog.

Duyckinck, Evert Augustus, Cyclopaedia of American literature, Detroit, Gale Research Co., Book Tower, 1965. 2 v. 66-31801
   PS85 .D7 1965 MRR Biog.

Higginson, Alexander Henry, British and American sporting authors, London, New York, Hutchinson, 1951. xvii, 443 p. 016.7992 53-18485
   Z7511 .H55 1951 MRR Biog.

Hopkins, Lee Bennett. Books are by people; New York, Citation Press, 1969. xv, 349 p. 028.5/0922 70-96312
   PN452 .H65 MRR Biog.

Kirk, John Foster, A supplement to Allibone's critical dictionary of English literature and British and American authors. Detroit, Gale Research Co., 1965. 2 v. (x, 1562 p.) 820.3 67-296
   Z1224 .A44 1891a MRR Biog.

Kunitz, Stanley Jasspon, ed. American authors, 1600-1900; New York, The H. W. Wilson company, 1938. vi, 846 p. 928.1 38-27938
   PS21 .K8 MRR Biog.

Lass, Abraham Harold, Plot guide to 100 American and British novels; Boston, The Writer [1971] xxi, 364, 364 p. [$8.95] 823/.03 73-138526

   PS373 .L28 MRR Alc.

Modern Language Association of America. American Literature Group. Committee on Manuscript Holdings. American literary manuscripts; Austin, University of Texas Press [1961, c1960] xxviii, 421 p. 016.81 60-10356
   Z6620.U5 M6 MRR Alc.

Myers, Robin, A dictionary of literature in the English language, from Chaucer to 1940, [1st ed.] Oxford, New York, Pergamon Press [1970] 2 v. 016.82 68-18529
   Z2010 .M9 MRR Alc.

The Penguin companion to American literature. New York, McGraw-Hill [1971] 384 p. [$9.95] 809 70-158062
   PN843 .P4 MRR Alc.

Shockley, Ann Allen. Living Black American authors: New York, R. R. Bowker Co., 1973. xv, 220 p. 810/.9/896073 73-17005
   PS153.N5 S5 MRR Biog.

Sixteen modern American authors; [Rev. ed.] Durham, N.C., Duke University Press, 1974. xx, 673 p. [$10.00] 810/.9/0052 72-97454
   PS221 .F45 1974 MRR Alc.

Tuck, Donald Henry. The encyclopedia of science fiction and fantasy through 1968: [1st ed.] Chicago, Advent: Publishers, 1974- v. 016.80883/876 73-91828
   Z5917.S36 T83 MRR Alc.

Vinson, James, Contemporary novelists. New York, St. Martin's Press [1972] xvii, 1422 p. [$30.00] 823/.03 75-189694
   PR737 .V5 MRR Alc.

Wallace, William Stewart, A dictionary of North American authors deceased before 1950. Toronto, Ryerson Press [1951] viii, 525 p. 928.1 51-7279
   PS128 .W3 MRR Biog.

Ward, Martha Eads. Authors of books for young people, 2d ed. Metuchen, N.J., Scarecrow Press, 1971. 579 p. 809.8/9282 B 70-157057
   PN452 .W35 1971 MRR Biog.

Webster's new world companion to English and American literature. New York, World Pub. [1973] 850 p. [$15.00] 820/.9 72-12788
   PR19 .W4 1973 MRR Biog.

Who's who among North American authors. [1921]- Los Angeles, Golden Syndicate Pub. Co. 22-1965
   Z1124 .W62 MRR Biog Latest edition

AUTHORS, AMERICAN--20TH CENTURY.
Contemporary authors; v. 1- 1962-
Detroit, Gale Research. 928.1 62-
52046
Z1224 .C6 MRR Biog Full set

AUTHORS, AMERICAN--20TH CENTURY--
BIOGRAPHY.
Contemporary authors; 1st revision.
Detroit, Gale Research Co. [1967- v.
810.9/005/2 67-9634
Z1224 .C59 MRR Biog.

AUTHORS, AMERICAN--BIBLIOGRAPHY.
Bonner, John Wyatt. Bibliography of
Georgia authors, 1849-1965. Athens,
University of Georgia Press [c1966]
vii, 266 p. 013/.9758 66-23074
Z1273 .B6 MRR Alc.

Havlice, Patricia Pate. Index to
American author bibliographies.
Metuchen, N.J., Scarecrow Press,
1971. 204 p. 016.01681 73-163870

Z1225 .H37 MRR Ref Desk.

Literary history of the United
States. 4th ed., rev. New York,
Macmillan [1974] 2 v. 810/.9 73-
14014
PS88 .L522 1974 MRR Alc.

Marsh, John L., A student's
bibliography of American literature.
Dubuque, Iowa, Kendall/Hunt Pub. Co.
[1971] x, 109 p. 016.8109 78-
147255
Z1225 .M37 MRR Alc.

Rees, Robert A. Fifteen American
authors before 1900; Madison,
University of Wisconsin Press [1971]
xvii, 442 p. [$12.50] 016.8109 77-
157395
PS201 .R38 MRR Alc.

Tanselle, George Thomas, Guide to
the study of United States imprints
Cambridge, Mass., Belknap Press of
Harvard University Press, 1971. 2 v.
(lxiv, 1050 p.) 016.015/73 79-
143232
Z1215.A2 T35 MRR Alc.

AUTHORS, AMERICAN--DIRECTORIES.
National Association of Science
Writers. Membership list. Sea
Cliff, N.Y. [etc.] 63-36780
T11 .N35 MRR Alc Latest edition

The Writers directory. 1971/73- New
York, St. Martin's Press. London, St.
James Press. 808 77-166289
PS1 .W73 MRR Biog Latest edition

AUTHORS, AMERICAN--KENTUCKY.
Richey, Ish. Kentucky literature,
1784-1963. Tompkinsville, Ky.,
Printed by Monroe County Press, 1963.
236 p. 64-3008
PS266.K4 R5 MRR Biog.

AUTHORS, AMERICAN--NORTHWEST, PACIFIC.
Who's who among Pacific Northwest
authors. 2d ed. [Missoula, Mont.?]
Pacific Northwest Library
Association, Reference Division, 1969
[c1970] 105 p. 810.9/979 74-16021

Z1251.N7 W5 1970 MRR Biog.

AUTHORS, AMERICAN--SOUTHERN STATES--
BIBLIOGRAPHY.
Rubin, Louis Decimus, A
bibliographical guide to the study of
Southern literature, Baton Rouge,
Louisiana State University Press
[1969] xxiv, 368 p. [10.00]
016.81 69-17627
Z1225 .R8 MRR Alc.

AUTHORS, AUSTRIAN.
Giebisch, Hans. Bio-
bibliographisches Literaturlexikon
Österreichs, Wien, Bruder Hollinek
[1964] viii, 516 p. 64-56140
Z2110 .G48 MRR Biog.

Giebisch Hans, ed. Kleines
österreichisches Literaturlexikon,
Wien, Hollinek, 1948. viii, 550 p.
016.83 49-2882
Z2110 .G5 MRR Biog.

Stock, Karl Franz.
Personalbibliographien
österreichischer Dichter und
Schriftsteller: Pullach bei
München, Verlag Dokumentation, 1972.
xxiii, 703 p. 73-308989
Z2111.A1 S76 MRR Biog.

Ungar, Frederick, comp. Handbook of
Austrian literature. New York, F.
Ungar Pub. Co. [1973] xvi, 296 p.
830/.9/9436 71-125969
PT155 .U5 MRR Biog.

AUTHORS, BRAZILIAN--RIO DE JANEIRO.
Ribeiro, Jogo de Souza. Dicionario
biobliografico de escritores
cariocas (1565-1965) Rio de Janeiro,
Livraria Brasiliana, 1965. 285 p.
66-51643
PQ9692.R5 R5 MRR Biog.

AUTHORS, CANADIAN.
Creative Canada: [Toronto] Published
in association with McPherson
Library, University of Victoria, by
University of Toronto Press [1971-
v. [$15.00 (v. 1)] 790?.971 71-
151387
NX513.A1 C7 MRR Biog.

Rhodenizer, Vernon Blair, comp.
Canadian literature in English.
[Montreal, Printed by Quality Press,
c1965] 1055 p. [10.00]
016.8108/0971 77-375203
Z1375 .R5 MRR Alc.

Société des écrivains canadiens,
Montreal. Repertoire bio-
bibliographique, 1954. Montréal
[1955] xviii, 248 p. 57-32232
PQ3900 .S68A3 MRR Biog.

Sylvestre, Guy. Canadian writers.
New ed. rev. and enl. Montreal,
Editions HMH [1966] xviii, 186 p.
[$9.50 Can.] 809.8/971 68-112492
PR9127 .S9 1966 MRR Biog.

Toye, William. Supplement to the
Oxford companion to Canadian history
and literature. Toronto, New York,
Oxford University Press, 1973. v,
318 p. [$9.50] 810/.9 74-180951
PR9180.2 .T6 1973 MRR Alc.

Wallace, William Stewart, A
dictionary of North American authors
deceased before 1950. Toronto,
Ryerson Press [1951] viii, 525 p.
928.1 51-7279
PS128 .W3 MRR Biog.

AUTHORS, CZECH.
Kunc, Jaroslav. Slovník soudobých
českých spisovatelu. Praha,
Orbis, 1945-46. 2 v. (1016 p.) a
49-479
Z2131 .K8 MRR Biog.

AUTHORS, DANISH.
Claudi, Jørgen, Contemporary Danish
authors, Copenhagen, Danske selskab,
1952. 163 p. 839.8109 52-14932
PT7760 .C55 MRR Biog.

Dansk skønlitterært
forfatterleksikon, 1900-1950.
København, Grønhold Pedersen, 1959-
64. 3 v. 60-20084
Z2573.3 .D3 MRR Alc.

AUTHORS, DUTCH.
Lectuur-repertorium, [2. en
definitieve uitg. Antwerpen,
Vlaamsche Boekcentrale, 1952-54] 3
v. 011 53-15682
Z1010 .L43 MRR Biog.

AUTHORS, DUTCH--PORTRAITS.
Wie is die ... Amsterdam, Em.
Querido, 1966 [1967] 160 p. with
illus. [fl 2.50] 67-95858
PT5104 .W5 MRR Biog.

AUTHORS, ENGLISH.
Allibone, Samuel Austin, A critical
dictionary of English literature and
British and American authors,
Detroit, Gale Research Co., 1965. 3
v. (3140 p.) 820.3 67-295
Z1224 .A4317 MRR Biog.

The Author's & writer's who's who.
[1934]- London, Burke's Peerage,
ltd. [etc.] 928.2 34-38025
Z2011 .A91 MRR Biog Latest edition

A Biographical dictionary of the
living authors of Great Britain and
Ireland; Detroit, Gale Research Co.,
1966. viii, 449 p. 013.82 66-
16419
Z2010 .B61 1966 MRR Biog.

Browning, David Clayton, ed.
Everyman's dictionary of literary
biography; English & American,
London, Dent; New York, Dutton [1958]
x, 752 p. 928.2 a 58-2815
PR19 .B7 MRR Biog.

Chambers, Robert, Chambers's
cyclopædia of English literature,
London, Edinburgh, W. & R. Chambers,
limited [1927-38] 3 v. 820.9 39-
8587
PR83 .C4 1927 MRR Alc.

The Critical temper; New York, Ungar
[1969] 3 v. [45.00] 820.9 68-
8116
PR83 .C764 MRR Alc.

Doyle, Brian. The who's who of
children's literature, New York,
Schocken Books [1968] xi, 380 p.
[$10.00] 028.52 68-28904
PN452 .D6 1968b MRR Biog.

Fredeman, William Evan, Pre-
Raphaelitism; a bibliocritical study
Cambridge, Harvard University Press,
1965. xix, 327 p. 016.70942 64-
21242
Z5948.P9 F7 MRR Alc.

Heiney, Donald W., British,
Woodbury, N.Y., Barron's Educational
Series [1973, c1974] x, 286 p.
[$2.95] 820/.9 74-158988
PR471 .H39 MRR Alc.

Higginson, Alexander Henry, British
and American sporting authors,
London, New York, Hutchinson, 1951.
xvii, 443 p. 016.7992 53-18485
Z7511 .H55 1951 MRR Biog.

Kirk, John Foster, A supplement to
Allibone's critical dictionary of
English literature and British and
American authors. Detroit, Gale
Research Co., 1965. 2 v. (x, 1562
p.) 820.3 67-296
Z1224 .A44 1891a MRR Alc.

Kunitz, Stanley Jasspon, ed. British
authors before 1800; New York,
Wilson, 1952. vi, 584 p. 928.2 52-
6758
PR105 .K9 MRR Alc.

Kunitz, Stanley Jasspon, ed. British
authors of the nineteenth century,
New York, The H. W. Wilson company,
1936. 3 p. l., 677 p. 928.2 36-
28581
PR451 .K8 1936 MRR Alc.

Lass, Abraham Harold, Plot guide to
100 American and British novels;
Boston, The Writer [1971] xxi, 364,
364 p. [$8.95] 823/.03 73-138526

PS373 .L28 MRR Alc.

Myers, Robin, A dictionary of
literature in the English language,
from Chaucer to 1940, [1st ed.]
Oxford, New York, Pergamon Press
[1970] 2 v. 016.82 68-18529
Z2010 .M9 MRR Alc.

The Penguin companion to English
literature. New York, McGraw-Hill
[1971] 575, [1] p. [$10.95] 820.9
B 77-158061
PN849.C5 P4 MRR Alc.

Thomas, Ralph, Handbook of
fictitious names; Detroit, Gale
Research Co., 1969. xiv, 235 p.
929.4 70-90248
Z1065 .T46 1969 MRR Alc.

Tod, Thomas Miller. A necrology of
literary celebrities, 1321-1943,
[Folcroft, Pa.] Folcroft Press [1969]
67, xiii p. 820/.9 B 72-195326
PN41 .T6 1969 MRR Biog.

Tuck, Donald Henry. The encyclopedia
of science fiction and fantasy
through 1968: [1st ed.] Chicago,
Advent: Publishers, 1974- v.
016.80883/876 73-91828
Z5917.S36 T83 MRR Alc.

Vinson, James, Contemporary
novelists. New York, St. Martin's
Press [1972] xvii, 1422 p. [$30.00]
823/.03 75-189694
PR737 .V5 MRR Biog.

Ward, Alfred Charles, Longman
companion to twentieth century
literature, Harlow, Longman, 1970.
[6], 593 p. [65/-] 820.9/009/1 76-
554609
PN771 .W28 MRR Alc.

Watt, Homer Andrew, A handbook of
English literature New York, Barnes
& Noble [1960, c1946] 430 p. 820.3
61-2985
PR19 .W3 1960 MRR Biog.

Webster's new world companion to
English and American literature. New
York, World Pub. [1973] 850 p.
[$15.00] 820/.9 72-12788
PR19 .W4 1973 MRR Biog.

Who's who in literature. 1924-34.
Liverpool, Literary Year Books Press.
26-26968
Z2011 .L78 MRR Biog Latest edition

AUTHORS, ENGLISH--18TH CENTURY--
BIBLIOGRAPHY.
Tobin, James Edward, Eighteenth
century English literature and its
cultural background; New York, Biblo
and Tannen, 1967. vii, 190 p.
016.8209/006 66-30405
Z2013 .T62 1967 MRR Alc.

AUTHORS, ENGLISH--19TH CENTURY--
BIBLIOGRAPHY.
Boyle, Andrew. An index to the
annuals. Worcester, A. Boyle, 1967-
v. [63/- (v. 1)] 820.8/007/05
67-101753
Z2013 .B65 MRR Alc.

AUTHORS, ENGLISH--20TH CENTURY-- BIBLIOGRAPHY.
Mellown, Elgin W. A descriptive catalogue of the bibliographies of 20th century British writers, Troy, N.Y., Whitston Pub. Co., 1972. xii, 446 p. [$17.50] 016.01682/08/0091 79-183301
Z2011 .A1M43 MRR Alc.

Temple, Ruth (Zabriskie) comp. Twentieth century British literature; New York, F. Ungar Pub. Co. [1968] x, 261 p. 016.8209/0091 67-13618
Z2013.3 .T4 MRR Alc.

AUTHORS, ENGLISH--BIBLIOGRAPHY.
Dick, Aliki Lafkidou. A student's guide to British literature; Littleton, Colo., Libraries Unlimited, 1972 [c1971] 285 p. 016.820/.8 77-189255
Z2011 .D53 MRR Alc.

Stratman, Carl Joseph, Restoration and eighteenth century theatre research; Carbondale, Southern Illinois University Press [1971] ix, 811 p. [$25.00] 016.822/5/09 71-112394
Z2014.D7 S854 MRR Alc.

AUTHORS, ENGLISH--BIOGRAPHY-- DICTIONARIES.
Hardwick, John Michael Drinkrow, A literary atlas & gazetteer of the British Isles Newton Abbot, David & Charles [1973] 216 p. [£4.95] 820/.3 73-181081
PR109 .H25 MRR Alc.

AUTHORS, ENGLISH--DICTIONARIES.
Lofts, William Oliver Gullement. The men behind boys' fiction London, Howard Baker, 1970. [5], 361 p. [84/-] 823/.009 70-564587
PR106 .L6 MRR Biog.

AUTHORS, ENGLISH--DIRECTORIES.
The Writers directory. 1971/73- New York, St. Martin's Press. London, St. James Press. 808 77-166289
PS1 .W73 MRR Biog Latest edition

AUTHORS, EUROPEAN.
Hargreaves-Mawdsley, W. N. Everyman's dictionary of European writers, London, Dent; New York, E. P. Dutton & Co., 1968. vi, 561 p. [38/-] 803 68-58559
PN451 .H3 MRR Biog.

The Penguin companion to European literature. New York, McGraw-Hill [1971, c1969] 907 p. [$11.95] 809.8/94 74-158063
PN41 .P43 1971 MRR Alc.

AUTHORS, EUROPEAN--BIOGRAPHY-- DICTIONARIES.
Kunitz, Stanley Jasspon, ed. European authors, 1000-1900; New York, Wilson, 1967. x, 1016 p. 920.04 67-13870
PN451 .K8 MRR Biog.

AUTHORS, FINNISH.
Litteraturen i Danmark og de øvrige nordiske lande. 4. udg. København, Politiken, 1967. 536 p. [21.45 dkr] 68-85482
PT7060 .L5 1967 MRR Alc.

AUTHORS, FRENCH.
Adam, Antoine. Littérature française ... Paris, Larousse, 1967-68. 2 v. 840.9 68-85663
PQ101 .A3 MRR Alc.

Girard, Marcel. Guide illustré de la littérature française moderne. Nouvelle édition mise à jour. Paris, Seghers, 1968. 408 p. [18.00] 71-397791
PQ305 .G5 1968b MRR Alc.

Le Sage, Laurent, Dictionnaire des critiques littéraires; University Park, Pennsylvania State University Press [c1969] 218 p. [6.50] 68-8181
PQ67.A2 L4 MRR Biog.

Lorenz, Otto Henri, Catalogue général de la librairie française. Paris, 1867-1945. 34 v. 02-7509
Z2161 .L86 MRR Alc.

Malignon, Jean, Dictionnaire des écrivains français. [Paris] Éditions du Seuil [1971] 552 p. [49.50F] 72-304186
PQ41 .M3 MRR Biog.

Quérard, Joseph Marie, La France littéraire, Paris, Firmin Didot père et Fils, 1827-64. 12 v. 02-3270
Z2161 .C4 MRR Alc.

Quérard, Joseph Marie, La littérature française contemporaine. Paris, Daguin frères, 1842-57. 6 v. 02-3271
Z2161 .Q41 MRR Alc.

Talvart, Hector. Bibliographie des auteurs modernes de langue française, Paris, Éditions de la Chronique des lettres françaises, 1928- v. 29-24892
Z2173 .T3 MRR Alc.

AUTHORS, FRENCH--BIBLIOGRAPHY.
Dreher, S. Bibliographie de la littérature française, 1930-1939, Lille, Giard, 1948- v. a 49-1233
Z2171 .D7 MRR Alc.

AUTHORS, FRENCH--DICTIONARIES.
Dictionnaire des auteurs français. [Paris, Seghers, 1961] 445 p. 62-44229
PQ146 .D5 MRR Biog.

AUTHORS, FRENCH-CANADIAN.
Sylvestre, Guy. Canadian writers. New ed. rev. and enl. Montreal, Éditions HMH [1966] xviii, 186 p. [$9.50 Can.] 809.8/971 68-112492
PR9127 .S9 1966 MRR Biog.

AUTHORS, GERMAN.
Albrecht, Günter. Lexikon deutschsprachiger Schriftsteller von den Anfängen bis zur Gegenwart. Leipzig, Bibliographisches Institut VEB, 1967- v. 830.9 68-108029

PT41 .A42 MRR Biog.

Frenzel, Herbert Alfred, Daten deutscher Dichtung. (Neubearb. Ausg.) (Köln, Berlin) Kiepenheuer u. Witsch (1971). 766 p. [DM36.00] 73-887412
PT103 .F72 1971 MRR Alc.

Germany (Democratic Republic, 1949-) Zentralinstitut für Bibliothekswesen. Schriftsteller der Deutschen Demokratischen Republik und ihre Werke; Leipzig, Verlag für Buch- und Bibliothekswesen [1955] 249 p. 56-29802
Z2244 .E38A52 MRR Biog.

Kosch, Wilhelm, Deutsches Literatur-Lexikon. Ausg. in einem Band Bern, Francke [1963] 511 p. 63-48267
Z2231 .K66 1963 MRR Alc.

Kosch, Wilhelm, Deutsches Literatur-Lexikon; 2., vollständig neubearb. und stark erweiterte Aufl. Bern, A. Francke, 1949 [i.e. 1947]-58. 4 v. a 48-4168
Z2230 .K862 MRR Biog.

Kürschners deutscher Gelehrten-Kalender. 1925- 1.- eng. Berlin, W. de Gruyter & Co. 25-15070

Z2230 .K93 MRR Biog Latest edition

Kürschners deutscher Literatur-kalender. 1.- Jahrg.; 1879- Berlin, Leipzig [etc.] 06-44921
Z2230 .K92 MRR Biog Latest edition

Kürschners Deutscher Literatur-Kalender; Berlin, New York, de Gruyter, 1973. xiv, 871 p. [DM220.00] 808 73-203144
Z2233.3 .K83 MRR Biog.

Lennartz, Franz. Dichter und Schriftsteller unserer Zeit; 7. Aufl. Stuttgart, A. Kröner [1957] vi, 672 p. 58-25924
PT401 .L35 1957 MRR Alc.

Stern, Desider. Bücher von Autoren jüdischer Herkunft in deutscher Sprache. Wien, 1967) 247 p. [S 30.00] 013/.2/96 67-101631
Z2241.J4 S8 MRR Alc.

Sternfeld, Wilhelm, Deutsche Exil-Literatur 1933-1945; 2., verb. und stark erw. Aufl. Heidelberg, L. Schneider, 1970. 606 p. 78-562446

Z2233 .S7 1970 MRR Alc.

AUTHORS, GREEK.
Fifty years (and twelve) of classical scholarship; [2d ed.] New York, Barnes & Noble, 1968. xiv, 523 p. 68-5952
PA3001 .F5 1968 MRR Alc.

Gwinup, Thomas. Greek and Roman authors; Metuchen, N.J., Scarecrow Press, 1973. x, 194 p. 016.88/009 72-10156
Z7016 .G9 MRR Alc.

Laloup, Jean. Dictionnaire de littérature grecque et latine. Paris, Éditions universitaires, 1969. 771 p. [39.90] 73-399862
PA31 .L3 MRR Alc.

The Penguin companion to classical, Oriental & African literature. New York, McGraw-Hill [1971, c1969] 359 p. [$9.95] 809 78-158064
PA31 .P4 1971 MRR Alc.

Tusculum-Lexikon griechischer und lateinischer Autoren des Altertums und des Mittelalters. München, Heimeran Verlag [1963] xvi, 544 p. 66-48071
PA31 .T8 1963 MRR Biog.

Tusculum-Lexikon griechischer und lateinischer Autoren des Altertums und des Mittelalters. München, Heimeran Verlag [1963] xvi, 544 p. 66-48071
PA31 .T8 1963 MRR Biog.

AUTHORS, INDIC.
Sahitya Akademi. Who's who of Indian writers. Honolulu, East-West Center Press [1964, c1961] 410 p. 928.914 64-7590
PK2903 .S3 1964 MRR Biog.

AUTHORS, ITALIAN.
Dizionario degli scrittori italiani d'oggi. Cosenza, Pellegrini, 1969. 269 p. [10000] 74-449684
Z2350 .D58 MRR Biog.

Ferrari, Luigi, Onomasticon; Milano, U. Hoepli, 1947. xlvi, 708 p. 015.45 48-17429
Z2350 .F4 1947 MRR Alc.

Fusco, Enrico M. Scrittori e idee; Torino, Società editrice internazionale [1956] xii, 626 p. 56-41593
PQ4006 .F8 MRR Biog.

Gubernatis, Angelo de, conte, Dictionnaire international des écrivains du monde latin, Rome, Chez l'auteur; [etc., etc.] 1905. xii, 1506 p. 06-46763
Z1010 .G93 MRR Biog.

Gubernatis, Angelo de, conte, Dizionario biografico degli scrittori contemporanei Firenze, Coi tipi dei successori Le Monier, 1879. xxxii, 1276 p. 02-2811
Z1010 .G92 MRR Biog.

Triggiani, Domenico. Dizionario degli scrittori. [1. ed.] Bari, Triggiani editore [1960] 221 p. 61-28580
PQ4057 .T7 MRR Biog.

AUTHORS, JAPANESE.
Japan. Mombusho. Nihon Yunesuko Kokunai Iinkai. Who's who among Japanese writers. [Tokyo, 1957] 140 p. 63-48768
PL723 .J3 MRR Biog.

AUTHORS, JEWISH.
Rosten, Leo Calvin, Leo Rosten's treasury of Jewish quotations. New York, McGraw-Hill [1972] xi, 716 p. [$10.95] 808.88/2 72-298
PN6095.J4 R6 MRR Ref Desk.

Stern, Desider. Bücher von Autoren jüdischer Herkunft in deutscher Sprache. Wien, 1967) 247 p. [S 30.00] 013/.2/96 67-101631
Z2241.J4 S8 MRR Alc.

AUTHORS, LATIN.
Fifty years (and twelve) of classical scholarship; [2d ed.] New York, Barnes & Noble, 1968. xiv, 523 p. 68-5952
PA3001 .F5 1968 MRR Alc.

Gwinup, Thomas. Greek and Roman authors; Metuchen, N.J., Scarecrow Press, 1973. x, 194 p. 016.88/009 72-10156
Z7016 .G9 MRR Alc.

Laloup, Jean. Dictionnaire de littérature grecque et latine. Paris, Éditions universitaires, 1969. 771 p. [39.90] 73-399862
PA31 .L3 MRR Alc.

Mantinband, James H. Dictionary of Latin literature. New York, Philosophical Library [1956] vi, 303 p. 870.3 56-14004
PA31 .M3 MRR Alc.

The Penguin companion to classical, Oriental & African literature. New York, McGraw-Hill [1971, c1969] 359 p. [$9.95] 809 78-158064
PA31 .P4 1971 MRR Alc.

Tusculum-Lexikon griechischer und lateinischer Autoren des Altertums und des Mittelalters. München, Heimeran Verlag [1963] xvi, 544 p. 66-48071
PA31 .T8 1963 MRR Biog.

AUTHORS, LATIN AMERICAN.
Beristain de Souza, José Mariano, Biblioteca hispano americana septentrional; [3. ed.] Mexico, Editorial Fuente Cultural [1947] 5 v. in 2. 015.72 48-9774
Z1412 .B53 MRR Alc.

Cejador y Frauca, Julio, Historia de la lengua y literature castellana ... Madrid, Imprenta Radio, 1916-30. 14 v. in 15. mrr01-65
PQ6032 .C3 1916 MRR Alc.

AUTHORS, LATIN AMERICAN. (Cont.)
Grismer, Raymond Leonard, A reference index to twelve thousand Spanish American authors; New York, The H. W. Wilson company, 1939. xvi p., 1 l., 150 p.   016.86 39-32334
Z1601 .G86 MRR Alc.

The Penguin companion to American literature. New York, McGraw-Hill [1971] 384 p. [$9.95] 809 70-158062
PN843 .P4 MRR Alc.

United States. Library of Congress. Latin American, Portuguese, and Spanish Division. The Archive of Hispanic Literature on Tape; Washington, Library of Congress; [for sale by the Supt. of Docs., U.S. Govt. Print. Off.] 1974. xii, 516 p. 016.86/008 73-19812
Z663.32 .A7 MRR Alc.

AUTHORS, MEXICAN.
Beristain de Souza, José Mariano, Biblioteca hispano americana septentrional; [3. ed.] Mexico, Editorial Fuente Cultural [1947] 5 v. in 2. 015.72 48-9774
Z1412 .B53 MRR Alc.

AUTHORS, ORIENTAL.
The Penguin companion to classical, Oriental & African literature. New York, McGraw-Hill [1971, c1969] 359 p. [$9.95] 809 78-158064
PA31 .P4 1971 MRR Alc.

AUTHORS, POLISH.
Korzeniewska Ewa, ed. Słownik współczesnych pisarzy polskich. Warszawa, Panstwowe Wydawn. Naukowe, 1963-1966. 4 v.   64-31836
Z2528.L5 K6 MRR Alc.

AUTHORS, RUSSIAN.
Dox, Georg. Die russische Sowjetliteratur; Berlin, De Gruyter, 1961. 184 p.   61-49174
PG3024 .D6 MRR Biog.

AUTHORS, SCANDINAVIAN.
Litteraturen i Danmark og de øvrige nordiske lande. 4. udg. København, Politiken, 1967. 536 p. [21.45 dkr] 68-85482
PT7060 .L5 1967 MRR Alc.

AUTHORS, SPANISH.
Amo, Julian, La obra impresa de los intelectuales españoles en América, 1936-1945; Stanford, Stanford University Press [1950] xiii, 145 p. 013.973046 50-9025
Z1609.R38 A7 MRR Alc.

Cejador y Frauca, Julio, Historia de la lengua y literatura castellana ... Madrid, Imprenta Radio, 1916-30. 14 v. in 15. mrr01-65
PQ6032 .C3 1916 MRR Alc.

San Vicente, Faustina. Diccionario de literatura española. Madrid, Ediciones Boris Bureba [1954] 212 p. 55-42212
Z2690 .S3 MRR Biog.

United States. Library of Congress. Latin American, Portuguese, and Spanish Division. The Archive of Hispanic Literature on Tape; Washington, Library of Congress; [for sale by the Supt. of Docs., U.S. Govt. Print. Off.] 1974. xii, 516 p. 016.86/008 73-19812
Z663.32 .A7 MRR Alc.

AUTHORS, SWEDISH.
Svenskt författarlexikon; 1900/40- Stockholm, Rabén & Sjögren. 53-34385
Z2630 .S92 MRR Alc Full set

AUTHORS, WOMEN
see Women authors

AUTHORSHIP.
  see also Journalism--Authorship
  see also Literature
  see also Report writing
  see also Short story

Nevins, Allan, The art of history; Washington, Published for the Library of Congress by the Gertrude Clarke Whittall Poetry and Literature Fund; [for sale by the Supt. of Docs., U.S. Govt. Print. Off.] 1967. v, 38 p. 907/.2 67-61610
Z663.293 .A7 MRR Alc.

Thomas, David St. John. Getting published, New York, Fleet Press Corp. [1973] 188 p. [$6.95] 808/.025 73-179016
PN147 .T37 1973 MRR Alc.

AUTHORSHIP--ADDRESSES, ESSAYS, LECTURES.
United States. Library of Congress. Gertrude Clarke Whittall Poetry and Literature Fund. The writer's experience; Washington, Published for the Library of Congress by the Gertrude Clarke Whittall Poetry and Literature Fund; [for sale by the Superintendent of Documents, U.S. Govt. Print. Off.] 1964. v, 32 p. 818.54 64-60086
Z663.293 .W7 MRR Alc.

AUTHORSHIP--HANDBOOKS, MANUALS, ETC.
Chicago. University. Press. A manual of style, [1st]- ed.; 1906- Chicago, 655.25 06-40582
Z253 .C57 MRR Ref Desk Latest edition

Collins, Frederick Howard, Authors' and printers' dictionary; 10th ed., rev. London, New York, Oxford University Press, 1956. xiv, 442 p. 655.25 56-58185
Z254 .C76 1956 MRR Alc.

Oleksy, Walter G., 1,000 tested money-making markets for writers West Nyack, N.Y., Parker Pub. Co. [1973] 225 p. 808/.025/0973 72-13005
PN161 .O5 MRR Alc.

Skillin, Marjorie E. Words into type. 3d ed., completely rev. Englewood Cliffs, N.J., Prentice-Hall [1974] xx, 585 p. 808/.02 73-21726
PN160 .S52 1974 MRR Ref Desk.

United States. Government Printing Office. Style manual. Rev. ed. Washington, 1973. viii, 548 p. [$4.25] 686.2/252 72-600382
Z253 .U58 1973 MRR Ref Desk.

The Writer's handbook. [1936]- Boston, Mass., The Writer, inc. 029.6 36-28596
PN137 .W73 MRR Ref Desk Latest edition

The Writer's market. Cincinnati, O., Writer's digest. 051 [029.6] 31-20772
PN161 .W83 MRR Ref Desk Latest edition

AUTHORSHIP--YEARBOOKS.
Literary market place: [1st]- ed.; 1940- New York, Bowker. 655.473 41-51571
PN161 .L5 Sci RR Partial set / MRR Ref Desk Latest edition

The Writers and artists' year book; [1st]- year; 1906- Boston [etc.] The Writer, inc. [etc.] 08-22320
PN12 .W8 MRR Ref Desk Latest edition

AUTOBIOGRAPHIES--BIBLIOGRAPHY.
Brignano, Russell Carl. Black Americans in autobiography; Durham, N.C., Duke University Press, 1974. ix, 118 p. [$5.75] 016.9173/06/96073022 B 73-92535
Z1361.N39 B67 MRR Alc.

Chicorel, Marietta. Chicorel index to biographies. 1st ed. New York, Chicorel Library Pub. Corp., 1974. 2 v. (898 p.) 016.92 74-175082
Z5301 .C54 MRR Biog.

Kaplan, Louis, A bibliography of American autobiographies, Madison, University of Wisconsin Press, 1961. xii, 372 p. 016.920073 61-5499
Z1224 .K3 MRR Alc.

Matthews, William, British autobiographies; Berkeley, University of California Press, 1955. xiv, 376 p. 016.920042 55-13593
Z2027.A9 M3 MRR Alc.

Matthews, William, Canadian diaries and autobiographies. Berkeley, University of California Press, 1950. 130 p. 016.920071 50-62732
Z5305.C3 M3 MRR Biog.

AUTOGIROS.
Lambermont, Paul Marcel. Helicopters and autogyros of the world Rev. ed. South Brunswick, Barnes [1970] xvi, 446 p. [15.00] 629.133/35 74-112289
TL714 .L3 1970 MRR Alc.

AUTOGRAPHS--COLLECTIONS.
United States. Library of Congress. Gertrude Clarke Whittall Foundation Collection. Autograph musical scores and autograph letters in the Whittall Foundation Collection, Rev. Washington, 1953. 18 p. 54-60005
Z663.375 .A8 1953 MRR Alc.

AUTOGRAPHS--COLLECTORS AND COLLECTING.
Benjamin, Mary A. Autographs: a key to collecting. New York, W. R. Benjamin Autographs, 1963. 313 p. 091.5 63-10776
Z41 .B4 1963 MRR Alc.

Hamilton, Charles, Collecting autographs and manuscripts. [1st ed.] Norman, University of Oklahoma Press [1961] xviii, 269 p. 091.5 61-9007
Z41 .H34 MRR Alc.

Patterson, Jerry E. Autographs: a collector's guide New York, Crown Publishers [1973] vii, 248 p. [$6.95] 929.8 73-82935
Z41 .P36 1973 MRR Alc.

Pelton, Robert W., The autograph collector; New York, Crown [1968] 240 p. [4.95] 652/.1/075 68-20470
Z41 .P45 MRR Alc.

AUTOGRAPHS--FACSIMILES.
Addis, Raymond E. Re-introducing our signers of the Declaration of independence, Holly, Mich., The Holly herald [c1940] 132 p. 978.313 40-36029
E221 .A45 MRR Alc.

AUTOGRAPHS--PRICES.
American book prices current. v. 1-1894/95- New York, Bancroft-Parkman [etc.] 018/.3 03-14557
Z1000 .A51 MRR Alc Partial set

AUTOMATIC COMPUTERS
see Computers

AUTOMATIC CONTROL--DICTIONARIES.
Bibbero, Robert J. Dictionary of automatic control. New York, Reinhold Pub. Corp. [1960] xii, 282 p. 629.803 60-14156
TJ212.5 .B5 MRR Alc.

Meetham, A. R. Encyclopaedia of linguistics, information, and control. [1st ed.] Oxford, New York, Pergamon Press [1969] xiv, 718 p. 001.5/39/03 68-18528
Q360 .M35 1969 MRR Alc.

AUTOMATIC CONTROL--DICTIONARIES--POLYGLOT.
Clason, W. E., Elsevier's dictionary of computers, automatic control and data processing. 2d rev. ed. of The dictionary of automation, computers, control and measuring. Amsterdam, New York, Elsevier Pub. Co., 1971. 484 p. [fl78.00] 001.6/4/03 73-151733
TJ212.5 .C55 1971 MRR Alc.

AUTOMATIC DATA PROCESSING
see Electronic data processing

AUTOMATIC DIGITAL COMPUTERS
see Electronic digital computers

AUTOMATION--DICTIONARIES--POLYGLOT.
Six-language dictionary of automation, electronics and scientific instruments; London, Iliffe Books; Englewood Cliffs, N.J., Prentice-Hall [1962] 732 p. 621.3803 63-5414
TK7804 .S5 1962 MRR Alc.

AUTOMOBILE DRIVERS' LICENSES--UNITED STATES--HANDBOOKS, MANUALS, ETC.
United States drivers license guide. [Redwood City, Calif., Drivers License Guide Co.] 343/.73/0946 70-612770
HE5623.A45 U54 MRR Alc Latest edition

AUTOMOBILE DRIVING--SAFETY MEASURES
see Traffic safety

AUTOMOBILE ENGINEERING--DICTIONARIES--POLYGLOT.
Elsevier's automobile dictionary in eight languages: Amsterdam, New York, Elsevier Pub. Co.; [distributed by Van Nostrand, Princeton, N.J.] 1960. 946 p. 629.203 59-8946
TL9 .E43 MRR Alc.

AUTOMOBILE ENGINEERING--HANDBOOKS, MANUALS, ETC.
Motor service's automotive encyclopedia. 1954- South Holland, Ill. [etc.] Goodheart-Willcox Co. 629.202 58-8645
TL151 .M658 Sci RR Latest edition / MRR Alc Latest edition

S.A.E. handbook. New York, Society of Automotive Engineers. 25-16527
TL151 .S62 Sci RR Latest edition / MRR Alc Latest edition

AUTOMOBILE EXHAUST GAS
see also Motor vehicles--Pollution control devices

AUTOMOBILE INDUSTRY AND TRADE--DIRECTORIES.
Motor/age who's who for the automotive service industry. Philadelphia, Chilton Company. 338.4/7/6292872202573 76-612602
HD9710.A2 M64 MRR Alc Latest edition

AUTOMOBILE INDUSTRY AND TRADE-- (Cont.)
Repertoire international de
l'industrie automobile. Paris,
Bureau permanent international des
constructeurs d'automobiles. 52-
38439
    TL12 .R46 MRR Alc Latest edition

AUTOMOBILE INDUSTRY AND TRADE--HISTORY.
Doyle, George Ralph. The world's
automobiles, 1880-1958: [3d ed.]
London, Temple Press [1959] 174 p.
629.209 59-34155
    TL15 .D67 1959 MRR Alc.

AUTOMOBILE INDUSTRY AND TRADE--
SOCIETIES, ETC.
Automobile facts and figures. 1920-
Detroit, Mich. [etc.] 338.4 36-
19542
    HD9710.U5 A8 MRR Alc Latest
    edition

AUTOMOBILE INDUSTRY AND TRADE--
STATISTICS.
Automobile facts and figures. 1920-
Detroit, Mich. [etc.] 338.4 36-
19542
    HD9710.U5 A8 MRR Alc Latest
    edition

Society of Motor Manufacturers and
Traders. Statistical Dept. The motor
industry of Great Britain. London.
338.4 38-34916
    HD9710.G7 S6 MRR Alc Latest
    edition

Ward's automotive year book. [1938]-
Detroit, Wards communications, inc.
[etc.] 338.4 40-33639
    HD9710.U5 W3 MRR Alc Latest
    edition

AUTOMOBILE INDUSTRY AND TRADE--
YEARBOOKS.
Trader handbook. London, IPC
Transport Press Ltd. [etc.] 629.2058
51-40281
    Began publication in 1906.
    HD9710.G7 T7 MRR Alc Latest
    edition

AUTOMOBILE INDUSTRY AND TRADE--GREAT
BRITAIN.
Society of Motor Manufacturers and
Traders. Statistical Dept. The motor
industry of Great Britain. London.
338.4 38-34916
    HD9710.G7 S6 MRR Alc Latest
    edition

Trader handbook. London, IPC
Transport Press Ltd. [etc.] 629.2058
51-40281
    Began publication in 1906.
    HD9710.G7 T7 MRR Alc Latest
    edition

AUTOMOBILE INDUSTRY AND TRADE--GREAT
BRITAIN--BIOGRAPHY.
Who's who in the motor and commercial
vehicle industries. Kingston upon
Thames, Surrey [etc.] Kelly's
Directories Ltd. [etc.] 56-19609
    Began publication with 1952 ed.
    HD9710.G7 W45 MRR Alc Latest
    edition

AUTOMOBILE INDUSTRY AND TRADE--GREAT
BRITAIN--DIRECTORIES.
The Directory of the motor inustry.
1st ed.: 1962- London, Society of
Motor Manufacturers and Traders. 66-
45007
    TL12 .D53 MRR Alc Latest edition

Who's who in the motor and commercial
vehicle industries. Kingston upon
Thames, Surrey [etc.] Kelly's
Directories Ltd. [etc.] 56-19609
    Began publication with 1952 ed.
    HD9710.G7 W45 MRR Alc Latest
    edition

AUTOMOBILE INDUSTRY AND TRADE--UNITED
STATES.
Automobile facts and figures. 1920-
Detroit, Mich. [etc.] 338.4 36-
19542
    HD9710.U5 A8 MRR Alc Latest
    edition

Motor Vehicle Manufacturers
Association of the United States.
Automobiles of America: milestones,
pioneers, roll call, highlights. 4th
ed., rev. Detroit, Wayne State
University Press, 1974. 301 p.
629.22/22/0973 73-19838
    TL23 .M63 1974 MRR Alc.

AUTOMOBILE INDUSTRY AND TRADE--UNITED
STATES--BIOGRAPHY.
Motor Vehicle Manufacturers
Association of the United States.
Automobiles of America: milestones,
pioneers, roll call, highlights. 4th
ed., rev. Detroit, Wayne State
University Press, 1974. 301 p.
629.22/22/0973 73-19838
    TL23 .M63 1974 MRR Alc.

AUTOMOBILE INDUSTRY AND TRADE--UNITED
STATES--DIRECTORIES.
Automotive aftermarket directory.
1960- Chicago, Irving-Cloud Pub. Co.
61-25770
    HD9710.U5 A83 MRR Alc Latest
    edition

National automotive directory.
[Atlanta, W. R. C. Smith] 65-9209
    TL12 .N34 Sci RR Latest edition /
    MRR Alc Latest edition

Ward's automotive year book. [1938]-
Detroit, Wards communications, inc.
[etc.] 338.4 40-33639
    HD9710.U5 W3 MRR Alc Latest
    edition

AUTOMOBILE INDUSTRY AND TRADE--UNITED
STATES--HISTORY.
Rae, John Bell, The American
automobile: Chicago, University of
Chicago Press [1965] xiv, 265 p.
338.476292 65-24981
    HD9710.U52 R29 MRR Alc.

AUTOMOBILE INDUSTRY AND TRADE--UNITED
STATES--STATISTICS.
Ward's automotive year book. [1938]-
Detroit, Wards communications, inc.
[etc.] 338.4 40-33639
    HD9710.U5 W3 MRR Alc Latest
    edition

AUTOMOBILE MAINTENANCE
see Automobiles--Maintenance and
repair

AUTOMOBILE RACING.
Walkerley, Rodney Lewis de Burgh,
Motor racing facts and figures.
Cambridge, Mass., R. Bentley, 1962.
196 p. 796.7202 62-2630
    GV1029 .W324 MRR Alc.

AUTOMOBILE RACING--BIOGRAPHY.
Cutter, Bob, The encyclopedia of
auto racing greats, Englewood
Cliffs N.J. Prentice-Hall [1973]
viii, 675 p. [$17.50] 796.7/2/0922
B 73-7541
    GV1032.A1 C87 MRR Biog.

The Encyclopedia of motor sport. New
York, Viking Press [1971] 656 p.
[$25.00] 796.7/2/03 73-162664
    GV1029 .E47 MRR Alc.

AUTOMOBILE RACING--DICTIONARIES.
The Encyclopedia of motor sport. New
York, Viking Press [1971] 656 p.
[$25.00] 796.7/2/03 73-162664
    GV1029 .E47 MRR Alc.

Pritchard, Anthony. The
encyclopaedia of motor racing;
London, Hale, 1969. 304 p. [45/-]
796.7/2/03 75-440630
    GV1029 .P74 1969 MRR Alc.

AUTOMOBILE RACING--YEARBOOKS.
Automobile year. no. 1- 1953/54-
Lausanne, Edita. 629.2058 55-17260

    TL5 .A58 MRR Alc Latest edition

AUTOMOBILE RACING--UNITED STATES.
Stone, William Sidney, A guide to
American sports car racing Rev., 3d
ed. Garden City, N.Y., Doubleday,
1967. 208 p. 796.72 66-23183
    GV1029 .S78 1967 MRR Alc.

AUTOMOBILES--AIR CONDITIONING--
HANDBOOKS, MANUALS, ETC.
Chilton Book Company. Automotive Book
Dept. Chilton's auto air
conditioning & wiring diagram manual.
Philadelphia, Chilton Book Co.
[1972] 1536 p. 629.2/77 72-182828

    TL271.5 .C45 1972 MRR Alc.

AUTOMOBILES--APPARATUS AND SUPPLIES--
CATALOGS.
National automotive directory.
[Atlanta, W. R. C. Smith] 65-9209
    TL12 .N34 Sci RR Latest edition /
    MRR Alc Latest edition

AUTOMOBILES--APPARATUS AND SUPPLIES--
DIRECTORIES.
Automotive aftermarket directory.
1960- Chicago, Irving-Cloud Pub. Co.
61-25770
    HD9710.U5 A83 MRR Alc Latest
    edition

Directory: home centers & hardware
chains, auto supply chains. 1974-
[New York, Business Guides, inc.]
[$59.00] 381/.45/629202573 74-
647308
    HD9745.U4 D485 MRR Alc Latest
    edition

AUTOMOBILES--BODIES--MAINTENANCE AND
REPAIR.
Toboldt, William King, Auto body
repairing and repainting: South
Holland, Ill., Goodheart-Willcox Co.
[1972] 232 p. 629.2/6 72-182233
    TL255 .T58 1972 MRR Alc.

AUTOMOBILES--COLLECTORS AND COLLECTING--
SOCIETIES, ETC.
Classic Car Club of America.
Handbook and directory. 1964-
[Madison, N.J. etc.) 629.22/22/06273
72-626908
    TL7 .C53 MRR Alc Latest edition

AUTOMOBILES--DICTIONARIES.
Georgano, G. N. The complete
encyclopedia of motorcars, 1885 to
the present. 2d ed.] New York,
Dutton [1973] 751 p. [$30.00]
629.22/22/09 73-174298
    TL15 .G39 1973 MRR Alc.

AUTOMOBILES--ELECTRIC EQUIPMENT.
Blanchard, Harold Frederick, Auto
engines and electrical systems, 5th
ed. New York, Motor [1970] 704 p.
629.2/5 79-15052
    TL210 .B52 1970 MRR Alc.

Crouse, William Harry, Automotive
electrical equipment: 6th ed. St.
Louis, Webster Division; McGraw-Hill
[1966] xiii, 530 p. 629.254 66-
8675
    TL272 .C73 1966 MRR Alc.

AUTOMOBILES--ELECTRIC WIRING--
HANDBOOKS, MANUALS, ETC.
Chilton Book Company. Automotive Book
Dept. Chilton's auto air
conditioning & wiring diagram manual.
Philadelphia, Chilton Book Co.
[1972] 1536 p. 629.2/77 72-182828

    TL271.5 .C45 1972 MRR Alc.

AUTOMOBILES--HANDBOOKS, MANUALS, ETC.
Motor service's automotive
encyclopedia. 1954- South Holland,
Ill. [etc.] Goodheart-Willcox Co.
629.202 58-8645
    TL151 .M658 Sci RR Latest edition
    / MRR Alc Latest edition

AUTOMOBILES--HISTORY.
1916-1939 vintage and post vintage
thoroughbred cars of the world:
Manchester, World Distributors, 1968.
5-124 p. [30/-] 629.22/22/09 74-
402240
    TL15 .N45 MRR Alc.

Collins, Herbert Ridgeway,
Presidents on wheels. Washington,
Acropolis Books [1971] 224 p.
[$15.00] 629.2/0973 75-146442
    TL23 .C597 MRR Alc.

Doyle, George Ralph. The world's
automobiles, 1880-1958: [3d ed.]
London, Temple Press [1959] 174 p.
629.209 59-34155
    TL15 .D67 1959 MRR Alc.

Georgano, G. N. The complete
encyclopedia of motorcars, 1885 to
the present. 2d ed.] New York,
Dutton [1973] 751 p. [$30.00]
629.22/22/09 73-174298
    TL15 .G39 1973 MRR Alc.

Harding, Anthony. Car facts and
feats: Enfield [Eng.] Guinness
Superlatives Ltd. [1971] 256 p.
[£2.00] 796.7/2/09 71-31381
    TL236 .H34 MRR Alc.

Matteucci, Marco. History of the
motor car. New York, Crown
Publishers [1971, c1970] 392 p.
[$17.50] 629.22/22/09 71-29405
    TL15 .M28 MRR Alc.

Wherry, Joseph H. Automobiles of the
world: [1st ed.] Philadelphia,
Chilton Book Co. [1968] xi, 713 p.
629.22/22/09 68-57510
    TL15 .W47 MRR Alc.

AUTOMOBILES--LAWS AND REGULATIONS--
ALASKA.
Automobole Club of Southern
California. License Dept. Summary of
motor vehicle acts ... United States
and provinces of Canada. (Los
Angeles] 388.30973 33-1709
    HE5623.A5 A8 MRR Ref Desk Latest
    edition

AUTOMOBILES--LAWS AND REGULATIONS--
CANADA.
Automobole Club of Southern
California. License Dept. Summary of
motor vehicle acts ... United States
and provinces of Canada. [Los
Angeles] 388.30973 33-1709
    HE5623.A5 A8 MRR Ref Desk Latest
    edition

AUTOMOBILES--LAWS AND REGULATIONS--
HAWAIIAN ISLANDS.
Automobole Club of Southern
California. License Dept. Summary of
motor vehicle acts ... United States
and provinces of Canada. [Los
Angeles] 388.30973 33-1709
    HE5623.A5 A8 MRR Ref Desk Latest
    edition

**AUTOMOBILES--LAWS AND REGULATIONS--
PANAMA CANAL.**
Automobole Club of Southern
California. License Dept. Summary of
motor vehicle acts ... United States
and provinces of Canada. [Los
Angeles] 388.30973 33-1709
    HE5623.A5 A8 MRR Ref Desk Latest
    edition

**AUTOMOBILES--LAWS AND REGULATIONS--
UNITED STATES.**
American Automobile Association.
Digest of motor laws. Washington.
343/.73/0944 74-642447
    KF2210.Z95 A39 MRR Alc Latest
    edition

Automobole Club of Southern
California. License Dept. Summary of
motor vehicle acts ... United States
and provinces of Canada. [Los
Angeles] 388.30973 33-1709
    HE5623.A5 A8 MRR Ref Desk Latest
    edition

AUTOMOBILES--MAINTENANCE AND REPAIR.
Chilton Book Company. Automotive
Editorial Dept. Chilton's motor/age
professional emission diagnostic and
safety manual / Radnor, Pa. :
Chilton Book Co., [1974] 1152 p. :
629.2/52 74-182330
    TL214.P6 C47 1974a MRR Alc.

Chilton's automobile repair manual.
1953- Philadelphia, Chilton Co.
629.28058 54-17274
    TL152 .C525 Sci RR Latest edition
    / MRR Alc Latest edition

Crouse, William Harry, The auto book
New York, McGraw-Hill [1974] 662 p.
629.28/7 73-22388
    TL152 .C68 MRR Alc.

Day, Richard, How to service and
repair your own car. New York,
Popular Science Pub. Co. [1973] xiv,
460 p. [$10.95] 629.28/8/22 72-
97173
    TL152 .D28 MRR Alc.

Motor (New York) Automobile trouble
shooter. 8th ed. [New York, Motor,
Book Dept., 1967] 252 p. 629.28/7
67-4752
    TL152 .M74 1967 MRR Alc.

Motor handbook. [New York, Motor]
629.28/7/05 74-644571
    TL152 .M73 MRR Alc Latest edition

Motor service's automotive
encyclopedia. 1954- South Holland,
Ill. [etc.] Goodheart-Willcox Co.
629.202 58-8645
    TL151 .M658 Sci RR Latest edition
    / MRR Alc Latest edition

Motor's auto repair manual. [1st]-
ed.; 1937- New York. 629.28 38-750
    TL152 .M815 Sci RR Latest edition
    / MRR Alc Latest edition

**AUTOMOBILES--MAINTENANCE AND REPAIR--
DIRECTORIES.**
Motor/age who's who for the
automotive service industry.
Philadelphia, Chilton Company.
338.4/7/6292872202573 76-612602
    HD9710.A2 M64 MRR Alc Latest
    edition

**AUTOMOBILES--MAINTENANCE AND REPAIR--
HANDBOOKS, MANUALS, ETC.**
Stockel, Martin W. Auto service and
repair; Homewood, Ill., Goodheart-
Willcox Co. [1969] 1 v. (various
pagings) 629.28/7 68-21030
    TL152 .S7745 MRR Alc.

**AUTOMOBILES--MAINTENANCE AND REPAIR--
RATES.**
Chilton's motor/age labor guide and
parts manual. [Philadelphia, Chilton
Co.] 338.4/3/629287 71-617211
    TL152 .C55 Sci RR Latest edition /
    MRR Alc Latest edition

Motor imported car crash estimating
guide. [New York, Hearst Corp.]
[$35.00] 338.4/3/629287220873 74-
645907
    TL152 .M714 MRR Alc Latest edition
    / Sci RR Latest edition

Motor's parts and time guide. 45th-
ed.; 1973- [New York, Motor]
658.8/16 73-640337
    TL152 .M82 Sci RR Latest edition /
    MRR Alc Latest edition

**AUTOMOBILES--MAINTENANCE AND REPAIR--
VOCATIONAL GUIDANCE.**
Crouse, William Harry, The auto book
New York, McGraw-Hill [1974] 662 p.
629.28/7 73-22388
    TL152 .C68 MRR Alc.

Crouse, William Harry, The auto book
New York, McGraw-Hill [1974] 662 p.
629.28/7 73-22388
    TL152 .C68 MRR Alc.

AUTOMOBILES--MOTORS.
Blanchard, Harold Frederick, Auto
engines and electrical systems, 5th
ed. New York, Motor [1970] 704 p.
629.2/5 79-15052
    TL210 .B52 1970 MRR Alc.

AUTOMOBILES--PAINTING.
Toboldt, William King, Auto body
repairing and repainting; South
Holland, Ill., Goodheart-Willcox Co.
[1972] 232 p. 629.2/6 72-182233
    TL255 .T58 1972 MRR Alc.

AUTOMOBILES--PARTS--CATALOGS.
Chilton's motor/age labor guide and
parts manual. [Philadelphia, Chilton
Co.] 338.4/3/629287 71-617211
    TL152 .C55 Sci RR Latest edition /
    MRR Alc Latest edition

Motor's parts and time guide. 45th-
ed.; 1973- [New York, Motor]
658.8/16 73-640337
    TL152 .M82 Sci RR Latest edition /
    MRR Alc Latest edition

AUTOMOBILES--PRICES.
Car fax. [New York, Fax
Publications] 338.5276292 56-38790
    HD9710.A1 C3 MRR Alc Latest
    edition

AUTOMOBILES--PRICES--UNITED STATES.
Red book official used car
valuations. [Chicago] National
Market Reports, inc. 381/.45/629222
72-626398
    HD9710.U5 N37 MRR Ref Desk Latest
    issue

**AUTOMOBILES--PRICES--UNITED STATES--
YEARBOOKS.**
Edmund's car prices. [New York]
Edmund Publications Corp.
629.22/2/029 70-158776
    HD9710.U5 E4 MRR Alc Latest
    edition

AUTOMOBILES--ROAD GUIDES--AFRICA.
Automobile Association of South
Africa. Trans-African highways; 5th
ed., completely rev. Johannesburg,
1963. 352 p. 65-86771
    GV1025.A2 A63 1963 MRR Alc.

AUTOMOBILES--ROAD GUIDES--ALASKA.
Cross, Cliff. Alaska. 1969-70 ed.
North Palm Springs, Calif. [1969]
170 p. [3.50] 917.98/04/5 78-
22107
    F902.3 .C7 MRR Alc.

**AUTOMOBILES--ROAD GUIDES--BENELUX
COUNTRIES.**
Benelux. Paris [etc.] Pneu Michelin,
Services de tourisme [etc.] 56-50955
    GV1025.B43 B4 MRR Alc Latest
    edition

AUTOMOBILES--ROAD GUIDES--BRITTANY.
Bretagne. Paris, Pneu Michelin
[etc.] 53-35559
    GV1025.F7 B7 MRR Alc Latest
    edition

AUTOMOBILES--ROAD GUIDES--BULGARIA.
Trans-Balkan Highway: Yugoslavia,
Bulgaria, Turkey. Beograd,
Turisticka Stampa; Sofia, Resorts
Magazine [1967] 175 p. [unpriced]
914.96/04 78-391387
    GV1025.A2 T7 MRR Alc.

AUTOMOBILES--ROAD GUIDES--CALIFORNIA.
American Automobile Association.
California-Nevada tour book,
Washington. 61-45102
    GV1024 .A2314 MRR Alc Latest
    edition

AUTOMOBILES--ROAD GUIDES--CANADA.
Eastern Canada. 1969/70-
[Washington, American Automobile
Association] 917.1/04/644 76-615935
    GV1025.C2 E172 MRR Alc Latest
    edition

North Central States. 1969/70-
[Washington] AAA. 917.7/04 72-
622646
    GV1024 .N82 MRR Alc Latest edition

**AUTOMOBILES--ROAD GUIDES--CENTRAL
AMERICA.**
Mexico and Central America;
Washington, American Automobile
Association. 917.2 35-8488
    GV1025.M4 A6 MRR Alc Latest
    edition

AUTOMOBILES--ROAD GUIDES--CONNECTICUT.
Federal writers' project.
Connecticut. Connecticut; a guide to
its roads, lore, and people, Boston,
Houghton Mifflin company, 1938.
xxxiii, 593 p. 917.46 38-27339
    F100 .F45 MRR Ref Desk.

AUTOMOBILES--ROAD GUIDES--EUROPE.
Continental handbook & guide to
Western Europe. London, Royal
Automobile Club. 914/.04/55 70-
216280
    GV1025.A2 C623 MRR Alc Latest
    edition

Dunn, William J. Enjoy Europe by car
[New ed.] New York, Scribner [1973]
xii, 284 p. [$4.95 (pbk.)]
914/.04/55 72-7940
    D909 .D8 1973 MRR Alc.

Europa touring. New York, [etc.] AAA
World Wide Travel, inc. [etc.] 32-
13844
    Began publication in 1928.
    GV1025.A2 E78 MRR Alc Latest
    edition

Guide pour l'auto international. 37.-
annee; 1966- [Paris, Editions
commerciales de France] 72-627080
    GV1025.F7 G84 MRR Alc Latest
    edition

Lippman, Paul. Camping guide to
Europe; [1st ed.] New York, Holt,
Rinehart and Winston [1968] x, 181
p. 914/.04/55 68-12211
    GV1025.E9 L5 MRR Alc.

Olson, Harvey Stuart, Olson's
complete motoring guide to Germany,
Austria & the Benelux countries,
[1st ed.] Philadelphia, Lippincott
[1968] xiv, 878 p. [$5.95] 914
68-24136
    GV1025.A2 O45 MRR Alc.

Townsend, Derek. The motorist's
holiday guide to Europe; London,
Collins, Glasgow, 1967. 160 p. [25/-]
914/.04/55 67-85314
    GV1025.E9 T6 MRR Alc.

Waldo, Myra. Travel and motoring
guide to Europe. 1968- [New York]
Macmillan. 914/.04/55 68-1456
    D922 .W312 MRR Alc Latest edition

AUTOMOBILES--ROAD GUIDES--FLORIDA.
Florida tour book. fall 1965-
[Washington] American Automobile
Association. 917.59/04/6 74-644579
    GV1024 .F56 MRR Alc Latest edition

AUTOMOBILES--ROAD GUIDES--FRANCE.
France. Paris Pneu Michelin,
Services de tourisme [etc.] 914.4
52-42664
    GV1025.F7 F68 MRR Alc Latest
    edition

Guide pour l'auto international. 37.-
annee; 1966- [Paris, Editions
commerciales de France] 72-627080
    GV1025.F7 G84 MRR Alc Latest
    edition

Olson, Harvey Stuart, Olson's
complete motoring guide to France,
Switzerland & Italy, [1st ed.]
Philadelphia, Lippincott [1967] xiv,
964 p. 914.4/04/83 66-16661
    GV1025.F7 O4 MRR Alc.

AUTOMOBILES--ROAD GUIDES--GERMANY.
Baedekers Autoführer-Verlag,
Stuttgart. Deutschland, die
Bundesrepublik. 10. Aufl.
Stuttgart, Baedekers Autoführer-
Verlag (1967) xx, 548 p.
914.3/04/87 68-80083
    GV1025.G3 B33 1967 MRR Alc.

AUTOMOBILES--ROAD GUIDES--GREAT BRITAIN.
Olson, Harvey Stuart, Olson's
complete motoring guide to the
British Isles, [1st ed.]
Philadelphia, Lippincott [1967] xiv,
861 p. 914.2/04/85 67-11310
    GV1025.G7 O4 MRR Alc.

Reader's Digest Association, ltd. AA
book of the road, incorporating the
Ordnance Survey four miles to the
inch series. [3d ed., 1st revise.
London, Published in collaboration
with the Automobile Association,
1972] 412 p. 914.2/04/85 73-
169037
    GV1025.G7 R4 1972 MRR Alc.

Royal Automobile Club, London. Guide
and handbook. London. 629.281 51-
34691
    GV1025.G7 R59 MRR Alc Latest
    edition

AUTOMOBILES--ROAD GUIDES--GUATEMALA.
Ford, Norman D. Mexico and Guatemala
by car; Greenlawn, N.Y., Harian
Publications; trade distributors:
Crown Publishers, 1963. 159 p.
917.2 63-5328
    GV1025.M4 F6 1963 MRR Alc.

AUTOMOBILES--ROAD GUIDES--ILLINOIS.
Federal writers' project. Illinois.
Illinois; a descriptive and
historical guide, Rev., Chicago, A.
C. McClurg & co. [1947] xxii, 707 p.
917.73 47-30173
    F546 .F45 1947 MRR Ref Desk.

AUTOMOBILES--ROAD GUIDES--IRELAND.
Automobile Association. Illustrated
road book of Ireland. [2d
illustrated ed. (rev.)] Dublin: [New
York, American Heritage Press] 1970.
285, v, 32 p. [$9.95] 914.15/04/9
75-25939
GV1025.I6 A82 1970 MRR Alc.

AUTOMOBILES--ROAD GUIDES--ITALY.
Olson, Harvey Stuart, Olson's
complete motoring guide to France,
Switzerland & Italy, [1st ed.]
Philadelphia, Lippincott [1967] xiv,
964 p. 914.4/04/83 66-16661
GV1025.F7 O4 MRR Alc.

AUTOMOBILES--ROAD GUIDES--LAKE STATES.
Great Lakes states. 1969/70-
[Washington, American Automobile
Association] 917.7/04/3 72-626760
GV1025 .G915 MRR Alc Latest
edition

AUTOMOBILES--ROAD GUIDES--MEXICO.
Ford, Norman D. Mexico and Guatemala
by car; Greenlawn, N.Y., Harian
Publications; trade distributors:
Crown Publishers, 1963. 159 p.
917.2 63-5328
GV1025.M4 F6 1963 MRR Alc.

Mexico and Central America;
Washington, American Automobile
Association. 917.2 35-8488
GV1025.M4 A6 MRR Alc Latest
edition

AUTOMOBILES--ROAD GUIDES--MISSISSIPPI.
Federal writers' project.
Mississippi. Mississippi; a guide to
the Magnolia state. New York, The
Viking press, 1938. 4 p. l., [vii]-
xxiv, 545 p. 917.62 38-12400
F341 .F45 MRR Ref Desk.

AUTOMOBILES--ROAD GUIDES--MONTANA.
Federal writers' project. Montana.
Montana, a state guide book. New
York, The Viking press, 1939. 2 p.
l., vii-xxiii, [1], 430, [12] p.
917.86 39-27792
F731 .F44 MRR Ref Desk.

AUTOMOBILES--ROAD GUIDES--NEBRASKA.
Federal writers' project. Nebraska.
Nebraska; a guide to the cornhusker
state. New York, The Viking press,
1939. xxiii, 424 p. 917.82 39-
27592
F666 .F46 MRR Ref Desk.

AUTOMOBILES--ROAD GUIDES--NEVADA.
American Automobile Association.
California-Nevada tour book,
Washington. 61-45102
GV1024 .A2314 MRR Alc Latest
edition

AUTOMOBILES--ROAD GUIDES--NEW JERSEY.
Federal writers' project. New Jersey.
New Jersey, a guide to its present
and past; New York, The Viking
Press, 1939. xxxii, 735 p. 917.49
39-20654
F139 .F45 MRR Ref Desk.

AUTOMOBILES--ROAD GUIDES--NORTH AMERICA.
Woodall's trailering parks and
campgrounds. 1st- ed.; 1967-
Highland Park, Ill., Woodall Pub. Co.
917.3/04/92 67-3869
GV1025.A2 W65 MRR Alc Latest
edition

AUTOMOBILES--ROAD GUIDES--NORTHEASTERN
STATES.
Northeastern States. 1969/70-
[Washington, American Automobile
Association] 917.4/04/4 76-615943
GV1024 .N84 MRR Alc Latest edition

Northeastern tour book. [Washington,
American Automobile Association]
917.4/04/4 74-644520
GV1024 .N84 MRR Alc Latest edition

AUTOMOBILES--ROAD GUIDES--NORTHWEST,
PACIFIC.
Northwestern tour book. [Falls
Church, Va., American Automobile
Association] 917.9 74-644286
GV1024 .N87 MRR Alc Latest edition

AUTOMOBILES--ROAD GUIDES--NORWAY.
Welle-Strand, Erling. Motoring in
Norway. Oslo] Norway Travel
Association, 1967. 127 p. [7.50
nkr] 914.81/04/4 67-89157
GV1025.N6 W383 MRR Alc.

AUTOMOBILES--ROAD GUIDES--PACIFIC COAST.
National Automobile Club. Touring
guide of the Pacific coast. San
Francisco. 629.281 53-31891
GV1024 .N325 MRR Alc Latest
edition

AUTOMOBILES--ROAD GUIDES--POLAND.
Bajcar, Adam. Poland; Warsaw,
Interpress Publishers, 1972. 226 p.
[zł42.00] 914.38/04/5 72-170457
DK403 .B3413 1972 MRR Alc.

AUTOMOBILES--ROAD GUIDES--RUSSIA.
Louis, Victor E. A motorist's guide
to the Soviet Union, [1st ed.]
Oxford, New York, Pergamon Press
[1967] x, 368 p. and portfolio (4
fold. maps (1 col.)) 914.7/04/85
65-16215
GV1025.R8 L6 1967 MRR Alc.

AUTOMOBILES--ROAD GUIDES--SOUTHERN
STATES.
American Automobile Association.
Southeastern tour book including the
West Indies. Washington. 629.281
53-40435
GV1024 .A215 MRR Alc Latest
edition

AUTOMOBILES--ROAD GUIDES--SPAIN.
Espagne. 1952/53- Paris, Pneu
Michelin, Services de tourisme [etc.]
629.281 53-38884
GV1025.S7 E77 MRR Alc Latest
edition

AUTOMOBILES--ROAD GUIDES--SWITZERLAND.
Baedekers Autoführer-Verlag,
Stuttgart. Switzerland: official
handbook of the Automobile Club of
Switzerland. 2nd ed. Freiburg,
Baedeker; New York, Macmillan [etc.]
1967. 355 p. [45/-] 914.94/04/7
67-101220
GV1025.S8 B32 1967 MRR Alc.

Olson, Harvey Stuart, Olson's
complete motoring guide to France,
Switzerland & Italy, [1st ed.]
Philadelphia, Lippincott [1967] xiv,
964 p. 914.4/04/83 66-16661
GV1025.F7 O4 MRR Alc.

AUTOMOBILES--ROAD GUIDES--TENNESSEE.
Federal writers' project. Tennessee.
Tennessee; a guide to the state. New
York, The Viking press, 1939. xxiv,
558 p. 917.68 39-28847
F436 .F45 MRR Ref Desk.

AUTOMOBILES--ROAD GUIDES--TEXAS.
Writers' Program. Texas. Texas; New
rev. ed. New York, Hastings House
[1969] xxxiv, 717 p. [8.95]
917.64/04/6 68-31690
F391 .W95 1969 MRR Ref Desk.

AUTOMOBILES--ROAD GUIDES--TURKEY.
Trans-Balkan Highway: Yugoslavia,
Bulgaria, Turkey. Beograd,
Turisticka Stampa; Sofia, Resorts
Magazine [1967] 175 p. [unpriced]
914.96/04 78-391387
GV1025.A2 T7 MRR Alc.

AUTOMOBILES--ROAD GUIDES--UNITED STATES.
America by car. Greenlawn, N.Y.,
Harian Publications; trade
distributor: Grosset & Dunlap [etc.,
New York] 917 58-16154
GV1024 .A198 MRR Alc Latest
edition

Hayes, Richard Lovejoy. Trailering
America's highways and byways,
[Beverly Hills, Calif., Trail-R-Club
of America, 1965-70. 2 v.
796.7/9/0973 66-1943
GV1024 .H38 MRR Alc.

North Central States. 1969/70-
[Washington] AAA. 917.7/04 72-
622646
GV1024 .N82 MRR Alc Latest edition

AUTOMOBILES--ROAD GUIDES--YUGOSLAVIA.
Trans-Balkan Highway: Yugoslavia,
Bulgaria, Turkey. Beograd,
Turisticka Stampa; Sofia, Resorts
Magazine [1967] 175 p. [unpriced]
914.96/04 78-391387
GV1025.A2 T7 MRR Alc.

AUTOMOBILES--SERVICE STATIONS--
DIRECTORIES.
L P-gas motor fuel station directory.
Chicago, Liquefied Petroleum Gas
Association. 58-39759
HD9579.P43U6 MRR Alc Latest
edition

AUTOMOBILES--SOCIAL ASPECTS.
see also Transportation, Automotive

AUTOMOBILES--STATISTICS.
Harding, Anthony. Car facts and
feats; Enfield [Eng.] Guinness
Superlatives Ltd. [1971] 256 p.
[£2.00] 796.7/2/09 71-31381
TL236 .H34 MRR Alc.

AUTOMOBILES--TESTING--YEARBOOKS.
Road & track's buyer's guide.
[Newport Beach, Calif.;
Bond/Parkhurst Publications] [$2.00]
629.22/22 74-645197
TL5 .R55 MRR Alc Latest edition

AUTOMOBILES--TRAILERS--DIRECTORIES.
The Mobile home and recreational
vehicle manufacturers of the United
States and Canada. Detroit
(Southfield) Mich., Automotive Credit
Service. 338.4/7/62922602573 75-
17387
HD9715.7.U6 M58 MRR Alc Latest
edition

AUTOMOBILES--YEARBOOKS.
Automobile year. no. 1- 1953/54-
Lausanne, Edita. 629.2058 55-17260

TL5 .A58 MRR Alc Latest edition

Motor trend world automotive
yearbook. [Los Angeles, Petersen
Pub. Co.] 629.22/2/05 72-212306
TL5 .C3 MRR Alc Latest edition

Road & track's buyer's guide.
[Newport Beach, Calif.,
Bond/Parkhurst Publications] [$2.00]
629.22/22 74-645197
TL5 .R55 MRR Alc Latest edition

Auto-universum. English ed. Zurich
[etc.] International Automobile
Parade Ltd. [etc.] 58-39061
Began publication in 1957.
TL5 .I57 MRR Alc Latest edition

AUTOMOBILES, AMERICAN.
Motor Vehicle Manufacturers
Association of the United States.
Automobiles of America: milestones,
pioneers, roll call, highlights. 4th
ed., rev. Detroit, Wayne State
University Press, 1974. 301 p.
629.22/22/0973 73-19838
TL23 .M63 1974 MRR Alc.

AUTOMOBILES, AMERICAN--DICTIONARIES.
Georgano, G. N. Encyclopedia of
American automobiles. New York,
Dutton [1971] 222 p. [$12.50]
629.22/22/0973 79-147885
TL23 .G46 MRR Alc.

AUTOMOBILES, AMERICAN--HISTORY.
The American car since 1775; 1st ed.
[New York?] L. S. Bailey, 1971. 504
p. [$17.95] 629.22/22/0973 76-
158590
TL23 .A48 MRR Alc.

Collins, Herbert Ridgeway,
Presidents on wheels. Washington,
Acropolis Books [1971] 224 p.
[$15.00] 629.2/0973 75-146442
TL23 .C597 MRR Alc.

Georgano, G. N. Encyclopedia of
American automobiles. New York,
Dutton [1971] 222 p. [$12.50]
629.22/22/0973 79-147885
TL23 .G46 MRR Alc.

Motor Vehicle Manufacturers
Association of the United States.
Automobiles of America: milestones,
pioneers, roll call, highlights. 4th
ed., rev. Detroit, Wayne State
University Press, 1974. 301 p.
629.22/22/0973 73-19838
TL23 .M63 1974 MRR Alc.

AUTOMOBILES, BRITISH.
Culshaw, David J. The complete
catalogue of British cars [London]
Macmillan [1974] 511 p. [£7.00]
629.22/22/0942 74-179880
TL57 .C78 MRR Alc.

AUTOMOBILES, FOREIGN.
Motor imported car crash estimating
guide. [New York, Hearst Corp.]
[$35.00] 338.4/3/629287220973 74-
645907
TL152 .M714 MRR Alc Latest edition
/ Sci RR Latest edition

Paulman, Henry. Foreign car shoppers
guide. [3d ed.] Chicago, Paulman
Publications, 1969. 159 p.
629.22/22 68-59619
TL55 .P3 1969 MRR Alc.

AUTOMOBILES, FOREIGN--MAINTENANCE AND
REPAIR.
Motor (New York) Motor's imported
car repair manual. 2d service trade
ed. New York, 1973. 1 v. (various
pagings) 629.28/7/22 73-158772
TL152 .M739 1973 MRR Alc.

AUTOMOBILES, FOREIGN--MAINTENANCE AND
REPAIR--PERIODICALS.
Chilton's foreign car repair manual.
German, Swedish, Italian cars
edition. 1971- Philadelphia,
Chilton Book Co. 629/.28/7/22094 73-
168562
TL152 .C528 Sci RR Latest edition
/ MRR Alc Latest edition

AUTOMOBILES, RACING.
Twite, M. L. The world's racing cars
4th ed., completely rev. Garden
City, N.Y., Doubleday [1971] viii,
190 p. [$3.95] 629.22/8 75-154706

TL236 .T9 1971 MRR Alc.

AUTOMOBILES, RACING--HISTORY.
Harding, Anthony. Car facts and
feats; Enfield [Eng.] Guinness
Superlatives Ltd. [1971] 256 p.
[£2.00] 796.7/2/09 71-31381
TL236 .H34 MRR Alc.

AUTOMOTIVE VEHICLES
see Motor vehicles

AUXILIARY SCIENCES OF HISTORY.
see also Archaeology

AVIATION
see Aeronautics

AVIATION ACCIDENTS
see Aeronautics--Accidents

AVIATION INDUSTRY
see Air lines

AVIATION MEDICINE--BIBLIOGRAPHY.
Aerospace medicine and biology; v.
[1]-11; 1952-1962/63. Washington.
016.61698021   56-60078
Z663.49 .A37 MRR Alc   MRR Alc
Partial set / Sci RR Full set

AVIATORS
see Air pilots

BABIES
see Infants

BACH, JOHANN SEBASTIAN, 1685-1750.
Geiringer, Karl, Symbolism in the
music of Bach; Washington, 1956.
iii, 16 p.   780.81   56-60068
Z663.37 .A5 1956 MRR Alc.

BACKPACKING.
Manning, Harvey. Backpacking one
step at a time. [1st ed.] Seattle,
REI Press [1972] xiv, 356 p.
[$7.95]   796.5   72-1473
G504.5 .M3 MRR Alc.

BACKWARD AREAS
see Underdeveloped areas

BACON'S REBELLION, 1676.
Andrews, Charles McLean, ed.
Narratives of the insurrections, 1675-
1690. New York, C. Scribner's sons,
1915. ix p., 2 l., 3-414 p.   973.2
15-4852
E187.C7 A6 MRR Alc.

BACTERIA--CLASSIFICATION.
Bergey's manual of determinative
bacteriology. 8th ed. Baltimore,
Williams & Wilkins Co. [1974] xxvi,
1246 p.   589.9/001/2   73-20173
QR81 .A5 1974 MRR Alc.

BACTERIA, PATHOGENIC.
Dubos, Rene Jules, ed. Bacterial
and mycotic infections of man. 4th
ed. Philadelphia, Lippincott [1965]
xlii, 1025 p.   616.01   64-23602
RC115 .D75 1965 MRR Alc.

BACTERIOLOGY.
Salle, Anthony Joseph, Fundamental
principles of bacteriology 6th ed.
New York, McGraw-Hill [1967] 822 p.
589.9   67-11211
QR41 .S3 1967 MRR Alc.

BACTERIOLOGY--BIBLIOGRAPHY.
Bergey's manual of determinative
bacteriology. 8th ed. Baltimore,
Williams & Wilkins Co. [1974] xxvi,
1246 p.   589.9/001/2   73-20173
QR81 .A5 1974 MRR Alc.

BACTERIOLOGY--CLASSIFICATION.
Bergey's manual of determinative
bacteriology. 8th ed. Baltimore,
Williams & Wilkins Co. [1974] xxvi,
1246 p.   589.9/001/2   73-20173
QR81 .A5 1974 MRR Alc.

BACTERIOLOGY--TERMINOLOGY.
Bergey's manual of determinative
bacteriology. 8th ed. Baltimore,
Williams & Wilkins Co. [1974] xxvi,
1246 p.   589.9/001/2   73-20173
QR81 .A5 1974 MRR Alc.

BACTERIOLOGY, MEDICAL.
Microbiology; including immunology
and molecular genetics 2d ed.
Hagerstown Md., Medical Dept.,
Harper & Row [1973] xv, 1562 p.
576   73-6349
QR41.2 .M49 1973 MRR Alc.

BADEN-WÜRTTEMBERG--DIRECTORIES.
Landesadressbuch Baden-Württemberg.
1-   1953- Karlsruhe, Bd.,
Adressbuchverlag G. Braun.   53-32454

DD801.B23 L3 MRR Alc Latest
edition

BADGES.
Kerrigan, Evans E. American badges
and insignia, New York, Viking Press
[1967] xvii, 286 p.   355.1/34 67-
13505
UC533 .K45 MRR Alc.

Weightman, Alfred Edwin. Heraldry in
the Royal Navy; Aldershot [Eng.]
Gale and Polden, 1957. xviii, 514 p.
623.825   60-36156
VB335.G7 W4 MRR Alc.

BAHAMAS.
Bahamas handbook and businessman's
annual. 1st- ed.; 1960- Nassau,
E. Dupuch, Jr., Publications. 61-
45647
F1650 .B3 MRR Alc Latest edition

BAHAMAS--BIOGRAPHY.
Who's who in Canada; Toronto,
International Press Limited. 17-
16282
Began publication in 1910.
F1033 .W62 Sci RR Latest edition /
MRR Biog Latest edition

**BAHAMAS--DESCRIPTION AND TRAVEL--GUIDE-
BOOKS.**
Fodor's guide to the Caribbean,
Bahamas and Bermuda; 1960- New
York, D. McKay. 917.29   60-908
F2171 .F65 MRR Alc Latest edition

**BAJA CALIFORNIA--DESCRIPTION AND TRAVEL--
GUIDE-BOOKS.**
Gerhard, Peter. Lower California
guidebook; 4th ed., with revision
notes. Glendale, Calif., A. H. Clark
Co., 1967. 243 p.   917.2/2/0482 67-
24413
F1246 .G4 1967 MRR Alc.

BAKERS AND BAKERIES--DIRECTORIES.
Biscuit & cracker baker blue book.
New York, American Trade Pub. Co.
338.4/7/66475202573 63-36580
HD9057 .A1B5 MRR Alc Latest
edition

BAKERS AND BAKERIES--UNITED STATES.
Bakers weekly. Selected directory of
bakers; 1929- New York, American
trade Pub. Co. ca 29-366
TX775 .B3 MRR Alc Latest edition

BALANCE OF NATURE
see Ecology

BALANCE OF PAYMENTS.
International Monetary Fund. Balance
of payments yearbook. 1946/47-
Washington. 382 49-6612
HF1014 .I5 MRR Alc Latest edition

BALANCE OF PAYMENTS--STATISTICS.
International Monetary Fund. Balance
of payments yearbook. 1946/47-
Washington. 382 49-6612
HF1014 .I5 MRR Alc Latest edition

Organization for Economic Cooperation
and Development. Statistics of
balance of payments, 1950-1961.
[Paris, 1964] 134 p.   65-50190
HG3881 .O65 MRR Alc.

BALKAN PENINSULA--BIBLIOGRAPHY.
Horecky, Paul Louis, Southeastern
Europe; Chicago, University of
Chicago Press [1969] xxii, 755 p.
016.91496 73-110336
Z2831 .H67 MRR Alc.

BALKAN PENINSULA--HISTORY.
Stavrianos, Leften Stavros. The
Balkans since 1453. New York,
Rinehart [1958] xxi, 970 p.   949.6
58-7242
DR36 .S83 MRR Alc.

**BALKAN PENINSULA--PERIODICALS--
BIBLIOGRAPHY.**
Birkos, Alexander S. East European
and Slavic studies. [Kent? Ohio]
Kent State University Press [1973]
572 p. [$7.50] 016.9147/03/05 73-
158303
Z2483 .B56 MRR Alc.

BALKAN STUDIES--UNITED STATES.
Language and area studies, East
Central and Southeastern Europe;
Chicago, University of Chicago Press
[1969] xix, 483 p.   914.7 72-81222

DR34.8 .L33 MRR Alc.

BALL LIGHTNING--BIBLIOGRAPHY.
United States. Library of Congress.
Science and Technology Division.
Ball lightning bibliography, 1950-
1960. Washington, 1961. 15 p.
106.55156 61-61409
Z663.41 .B2 MRR Alc.

BALLADS.
see also Folk-songs

BALLADS, AMERICAN.
Lomax, John Avery, comp. American
ballads and folk songs, New York,
The Macmillan company, 1935. xxxix,
625 p.   784.4973 38-9495
M1629 .L85A52 MRR Alc.

BALLADS, ENGLISH.
Bronson, Bertrand Harris, ed. The
traditional tunes of the Child
ballads; Princeton, N.J., Princeton
University Press, 1959- v.
784.3 57-5468
ML3650 .B82 MRR Alc.

Chappell, William, Old English
popular music. A new ed., New York,
J. Brussel [c1961] 2 v. in 1.
784.3 62-3231
M1740 .C52 1961 MRR Alc.

BALLADS, SCOTTISH.
Bronson, Bertrand Harris, ed. The
traditional tunes of the Child
ballads; Princeton, N.J., Princeton
University Press, 1959- v.
784.3 57-5468
ML3650 .B82 MRR Alc.

BALLET.
Maynard, Olga. The American ballet.
Philadelphia, Macrae Smith Co.
[c1959] 353 p.   792.80973 59-13260
GV1787 .M36 MRR Alc.

Terry, Walter. The ballet companion;
New York, Dodd, Mead [1968] xiii,
236 p.   792.8 67-26148
GV1787 .T323 MRR Alc.

BALLET--BIOGRAPHY--DICTIONARIES.
Wilson, George Buckley Laird. A
dictionary of ballet 3rd ed.
London, A. & C. Black, 1974. xi, 539
p., [8] p. of plates. [£6.00]
792.8/03 74-183304
GV1585 .W5 1974 MRR Alc.

BALLET--DICTIONARIES.
Crosland, Margaret, Ballet lovers'
dictionary. London, Arco
Publications, 1962. 181, [2] p.   62-
53205
GV1585 .C82 MRR Alc.

Dictionary of modern ballet. New
York, Tudor Pub. Co. [1959] 360 p.
792.803 59-16827
GV1787 .D513 MRR Alc.

Kersley, Leo. A dictionary of ballet
terms [2d ed., enl.] New York,
Pitman Pub. Corp. [1964] 112 p.
792.8203 64-6893
GV1585 .K45 1964 MRR Alc.

Sharp, Harold S., comp. Index to
characters in the performing arts,
New York, Scarecrow Press, 1966-73.
4 v. in 6. 808.8292703 66-13744
PN1579 .S45 MRR Alc.

Wilson, George Buckley Laird. A
dictionary of ballet 3rd ed.
London, A. & C. Black, 1974. xi, 539
p., [8] p. of plates. [£6.00]
792.8/03 74-183304
GV1585 .W5 1974 MRR Alc.

BALLET--DIRECTORIES.
The National directory for the
performing arts and civic centers.
Dallas, Handel & Co.   790.2/0973 73-
646635
PN2289 .N38 MRR Alc Latest edition

Pride, Leo Bryan, International
theatre directory; New York, Simon
and Schuster [1973] xviii, 577 p.
[$35.00]   792/.025 70-157681
PN2052 .P7 MRR Alc.

BALLET--HISTORY.
Lawson, Joan. A history of ballet
and its makers. London, Dance Books,
1973. xiii, 202, 32 p. [£4.00]
792.8/09 74-171336
GV1601 .L3 1973 MRR Alc.

BALLET--TERMINOLOGY.
Grant, Gail. Technical manual and
dictionary of classical ballet. 2d
rev. ed. New York, Dover
Publications [1967] xiv, 127 p.
792.8/01/4 67-26481
GV1787 .G68 1967 MRR Alc.

BALLETS--DISCOGRAPHY.
Balanchine, George. Balanchine's New
complete stories of the great
ballets; Garden City, N.Y.,
Doubleday [1968] xxi, 626 p. [8.95]
792.8/4 68-22606
MT95 .B3 1968 MRR Alc.

Drew, David, ed. The Decca book of
ballet. London, F. Muller [1958]
xxvii, 572 p.   792.84 59-1334
MT95 .D74 MRR Alc.

Lawrence, Robert, The Victor book of
ballets and ballet music. New York,
Simon and Schuster, 1950. xviii, 531
p.   792.8 50-11189
MT95 .L48 MRR Alc.

BALLETS--STORIES, PLOTS, ETC.
Balanchine, George. Balanchine's New
complete stories of the great
ballets. Garden City, N.Y.,
Doubleday [1968] xxi, 626 p. [8.95]
792.8/4 68-22606
MT95 .B3 1968 MRR Alc.

Drew, David, ed. The Decca book of
ballet. London, F. Muller [1958]
xxvii, 572 p.   792.84 59-1334
MT95 .D74 MRR Alc.

Lawrence, Robert, The Victor book of
ballets and ballet music. New York,
Simon and Schuster, 1950. xviii, 531
p.   792.8 50-11189
MT95 .L48 MRR Alc.

BALLOON ASCENSIONS--HISTORY.
Dollfus, Charles. The Orion book of
balloons. New York, Orion Press
[1961] 108 p. 629.13322 61-9303
TL616 .D613 MRR Alc

BALLOONS.
see also Aeronautics

BALLOONS--HISTORY.
Dollfus, Charles. The Orion book of
balloons. New York, Orion Press
[1961] 108 p. 629.13322 61-9303
TL616 .D613 MRR Alc

BALTIMORE--HISTORIC HOUSES, ETC.
Dorsey, John R. A guide to
Baltimore architecture, Cambridge,
Md., Tidewater Publishers, in
cooperation with the Peale Museum,
1973. l, 246 p. [$4.95]
917.52/2/043 73-12576
NA735.B3 D67 MRR Alc

**BALTIMORE METROPOLITAN AREA--
DESCRIPTION--GUIDE-BOOKS.**
Shosteck, Robert, Weekender's guide;
places of historic, scenic, and
recreational interest within 200
miles of the Washington-Baltimore
area. Washington, Potomac Books
[c1973] xiii, 400 p. [$2.90]
917.5 74-159051
F106 .S53 1973 MRR Alc.

BAND MUSIC--DISCOGRAPHY.
Smart, James Robert. The Sousa Band,
Washington, Library of Congress [For
sale by the Supt. of Docs., U.S.
Govt. Print. Off.] 1970. v, 123 p.
[1.50] 789.9/136/50671 70-604228
Z663.37 .S6 MRR Alc.

**BANGKOK, THAILAND--COMMERCE--
DIRECTORIES.**
Thai Chamber of Commerce. Directory.
[Bangkok] 52-18813
HF331 .T45 MRR Alc Latest edition

**BANGKOK, THAILAND--DESCRIPTION--GUIDE-
BOOKS.**
Wells, Margaretta B. Guide to
Bangkok, [Bangkok, Tiranasar Press]
sole distributors: Christian
Bookstore, 1965 [c1961] 165 p. 76-
270240
DS589.B2 W4 1965 MRR Alc.

BANGLADESH--IMPRINTS.
United States. Library of Congress.
American Libraries Book Procurement
Center, Delhi. Accessions list,
Bangladesh. v. 1- 1972- New
Delhi. 018/.1 73-902218
Z3186 .U55 MRR Alc Full set

BANGLADESH--YEARBOOKS.
East Pakistan annual. v. 1- 1961-
[Chittagong?] sa 63-638
DS485.B39 E18 MRR Alc Latest
edition

BANK-NOTES.
Sten, George J. Banknotes of the
world, 1368-1966: Menlo Park,
Calif., Shirjieh Publishers [1967-
v. 769/.55 67-7759
HG353 .S68 MRR Alc.

BANK STOCKS--UNITED STATES.
First Boston Corporation. Data on
selected commercial bank stocks. New
York. 332.6 58-44776
HG5123.B3 F5 MRR Alc Latest
edition

BANKERS--DIRECTORIES.
Who's who in banking. 1966- New
York, Business Press. 66-24372
HG2463.A1 W55 MRR Biog Latest
edition

BANKERS--CANADA--DIRECTORIES.
Rand McNally international bankers
directory. July 1876- Chicago, Rand
McNally. 99-3836
HG2441 .R3 MRR Ref Desk Latest
edition

BANKERS--UNITED STATES--DIRECTORIES.
Rand McNally international bankers
directory. July 1876- Chicago, Rand
McNally. 99-3836
HG2441 .R3 MRR Ref Desk Latest
edition

Who's who in banking. 1966- New
York, Business Press. 66-24372
HG2463.A1 W55 MRR Biog Latest
edition

BANKING LAW--DICTIONARIES.
Thomson, William, bank inspector.
Thomson's Dictionary of banking.
11th ed. London, Pitman [1965] ix,
641 p. 332.103 66-3511
HG1601 .T4 1965 MRR Alc.

BANKING LAW--UNITED STATES.
United States. Laws, statutes, etc.
Laws of the United States concerning
money, banking, and loans, 1778-1909;
Washington, Govt. print. off., 1910.
v. 267 p., 1 l., 269-812, xxii p.
10-36032
HG481 .A2 1910 MRR Alc.

BANKS AND BANKING.
see also Credit

see also Money

Bank Administration Institute.
Technical Division. Bank
administration manual. Park Ridge,
Ill. [c1970] xi, 932 p. [$20.00]
332.1/0973 71-134505
HG1601 .B13 MRR Alc.

Kent, Raymond P., Money and banking
6th ed. New York, Holt, Rinehart and
Winston [1972] xvi, 624 p. 332.1
73-183628
HG221 .K385 1972 MRR Alc.

BANKS AND BANKING--ACCOUNTING.
Bank Administration Institute.
Technical Division. Bank
administration manual. Park Ridge,
Ill. [c1970] xi, 932 p. [$20.00]
332.1/0973 71-134505
HG1601 .B13 MRR Alc.

BANKS AND BANKING--BIBLIOGRAPHY.
Burgess, Norman. How to find out
about banking and investment. [1st
ed.] Oxford, New York, Pergamon
Press [1969] xii, 300 p. 016.332
68-55021
Z7164.F5 B84 1969 MRR Alc.

United States. Library of Congress.
Division of bibliography. ... A list
of the more important books in the
Library of Congress on banks and
banking. Washington, Govt. print.
off., 1904. 55 p. 04-32519
Z663.28 .L586 MRR Alc.

BANKS AND BANKING--CALENDARS.
Donovan, John. The businessman's
international travel guide. New
York, Stein and Day [1971] ix, 253
p. [$7.95] 910/.202 76-163347
G153 .D6 1971 MRR Alc.

BANKS AND BANKING--DICTIONARIES.
Munn, Glenn Gaywaine. Glenn G.
Munn's Encyclopedia of banking and
finance. 7th ed. Boston, Bankers
Pub. Co. [1973] 953 p. 332/.03 73-
83395
HG151 .M8 1973 MRR Alc.

Skandinaviska banken, a.-b. Banking
terms: French, German, Italian,
Spanish, Swedish. Stockholm [1964]
65 p. 65-87814
HG151 .S46 MRR Alc.

Thomson, William, bank inspector.
Thomson's Dictionary of banking.
11th ed. London, Pitman [1965] ix,
641 p. 332.103 66-3511
HG1601 .T4 1965 MRR Alc.

**BANKS AND BANKING--DICTIONARIES--
POLYGLOT.**
Elsevier's banking dictionary in six
languages: Amsterdam, New York,
Elsevier Pub. Co., 1966. 302 p.
332.1003 65-20139
HG151 .E45 MRR Alc.

BANKS AND BANKING--DIRECTORIES.
The Bankers' almanac and year book.
Croydon, Eng. [etc.] Thomas Skinner
Directories [etc.] ca 20-372
HG2984 .B3 MRR Alc Latest edition

Nyhart, J. Daniel. A global
directory of development finance
institutions in developing countries
Paris, Development Centre of the
Organisation for Economic Cooperation and Development, 1967. x,
453 p. [30.00] 332.1/025/1724 76-
386919
HG4517 .N92 1967b MRR Alc.

Peterson cable address directory.
Bogota, N.J. [etc.] J. J. Ernau
[etc.] 26-3970
HE7677.B2 P45 MRR Alc Latest
edition

Polk's world bank directory:
international section. 1970-
Nashville, R. L. Polk & Co.
332.1/5/025 76-649946
HG1536 .P633 MRR Alc Latest
edition

Polk's world bank directory:
international section. 1970-
Nashville, R. L. Polk & Co.
332.1/5/025 71-617088
HG1536 .P633 MRR Alc Latest
edition

Rand McNally international bankers
directory. July 1876- Chicago, Rand
McNally. 99-3836
HG2441 .R3 MRR Ref Desk Latest
edition

**BANKS AND BANKING--HANDBOOKS, MANUALS,
ETC.**
International Finance Institute.
Handbook of world currency, banking
and foreign exchange. Washington
[1970] vii, 212 p. 332.1/02/02 70-
113538
HG219 .I53 MRR Ref Desk.

BANKS AND BANKING--HISTORY.
Auburn, H. W., ed. Comparative
banking 3rd ed. London, Waterlow,
1966. xiv, 218 p. [30/-] 332.1
66-70132
HG1572 .A85 1966 MRR Alc.

BANKS AND BANKING--YEARBOOKS.
Bank-aarbogen. [København] Danske
bankfunktionaerers landsforening.
332.1058 46-41146
Publication began with issue for
1926.
HG3143 .B3 MRR Alc Latest edition

**BANKS AND BANKING--ARKANSAS--
DIRECTORIES.**
Southwestern bank directory; Fort
Worth, Tex., Southwestern Banking
Publications [etc.] 332.1 41-18423

HG2441 .S64 MRR Alc Latest edition

BANKS AND BANKING--CANADA--DIRECTORIES.
Bank directory of Canada. Toronto,
Houston's Standard Publications. 53-
35488
HG2703 .B35 MRR Alc Latest edition

**BANKS AND BANKING--COMMONWEALTH OF
NATIONS.**
Crick, Wilfred Frank, ed.
Commonwealth banking systems,
Oxford, Clarendon Press, 1965. xi,
536 p. 66-460
HG1572 .C7 MRR Alc.

BANKS AND BANKING--DENMARK.
Bank-aarbogen. [København] Danske
bankfunktionaerers landsforening.
332.1058 46-41146
Publication began with issue for
1926.
HG3143 .B3 MRR Alc Latest edition

BANKS AND BANKING--FRANCE.
Annuaire Desfossés; Paris, Cote
Desfossés [etc.] 332.63 46-39086
HG5471 .A64 MRR Alc Latest edition

BANKS AND BANKING--GERMANY--DIRECTORIES.
Banken-Ortslexikon; [ ]. - Aufl.;
1950- Darmstadt [etc.] Spezial-
Archiv der Deutschen Wirtshaft,
Verlag Hoppenstedt. 53-32144
HG3045 .B33 MRR Alc Latest edition

BANKS AND BANKING--GREAT BRITAIN.
The Bankers' almanac and year book.
Croydon, Eng. [etc.] Thomas Skinner
Directories [etc.] ca 20-372
HG2984 .B3 MRR Alc Latest edition

Thomson, William, bank inspector.
Thomson's Dictionary of banking.
11th ed. London, Pitman [1965] ix,
641 p. 332.103 66-3511
HG1601 .T4 1965 MRR Alc.

**BANKS AND BANKING--GREAT BRITAIN--
DIRECTORIES.**
Who's who in British finance. 1972-
New York, R. R. Bowker Co.
332/.092/2 [B] 72-624453
HG71 .W44 MRR Biog Latest edition

**BANKS AND BANKING--LOUISIANA--
DIRECTORIES.**
Southwestern bank directory; Fort
Worth, Tex., Southwestern Banking
Publications [etc.] 332.1 41-18423

HG2441 .S64 MRR Alc Latest edition

BANKS AND BANKING--MEXICO--DIRECTORIES.
Anuario financero de México. v. 1-
1940- México, D. F., Editorial
Cultura. 332.0972 42-34567
HG69.M6 A6 MRR Alc Latest edition

BANKS AND BANKING--NEW ENGLAND.
National Shawmut Bank, Boston. Bank
directory of New England, Maine, New
Hampshire, Vermont, Massachusetts,
Rhode Island, Connecticut. Boston.
22-13977
HG2441 .N35 MRR Alc Latest edition

**BANKS AND BANKING--NEW MEXICO--
DIRECTORIES.**
Southwestern bank directory; Fort
Worth, Tex., Southwestern Banking
Publications [etc.] 332.1 41-18423

HG2441 .S64 MRR Alc Latest edition

**BANKS AND BANKING--NORTH AMERICA--
DIRECTORIES.**
Polk's world bank directory: North
American section. 154th- ed.;
Sept. 1971- Nashville, R. L. Polk &
Co. 332.1/0257 74-615562
HG1536 .P635 MRR Alc Latest
edition

BANKS AND BANKING--NORWAY.
Haandbok over norske obligationer og
aktier, Oslo. 24-10346
HG4207 .H3 MRR Alc Latest edition

**BANKS AND BANKING--OKLAHOMA--
DIRECTORIES.**
Southwestern bank directory; Fort
Worth, Tex., Southwestern Banking
Publications [etc.] 332.1 41-18423

HG2441 .S64 MRR Alc Latest edition

BANKS AND BANKING--SWEDEN.
Svenska aktiebolag. Stockholm, P. A.
Norstedt. 332.6309485   24-15054
HG4211.Z5 S8 MRR Alc Latest
edition

BANKS AND BANKING--TEXAS--DIRECTORIES.
Southwestern bank directory; Fort
Worth, Tex., Southwestern Banking
Publications [etc.] 332.1 41-18423

HG2441 .S64 MRR Alc Latest edition

BANKS AND BANKING--UNITED STATES.
Fischer, Gerald C. American banking
structure New York, Columbia
University Press, 1968. xii, 429 p.
332.1/0973 67-29292
HG2481 .F514 MRR Alc.

Munn, Glenn Gaywaine. Glenn G.
Munn's Encyclopedia of banking and
finance. 7th ed. Boston, Bankers
Pub. Co. [1973] 953 p.   332/.03 73-
83395
HG151 .M8 1973 MRR Alc.

Prather, Charles Lee. Money and
banking 9th ed. Homewood, Ill., R.
D. Irwin, 1969. xviii, 738 p.   332
69-15547
HG221 .P83 1969 MRR Alc.

BANKS AND BANKING--UNITED STATES--
DIRECTORIES.
American bank directory. Norcross,
Georgia, McFadden Business
Publications. 332.105873 61-33492
HG2441 .A56 MRR Alc Latest edition

Directory of the mutual savings banks
of the United States. New York,
National Association of Mutual
Savings Banks. [$17.00] 332.2/1 74-
640216
HG2441 .D5 MRR Alc Latest edition

Polk's world bank directory: North
American section. 154th- ed.:
Sept. 1971- Nashville, R. L. Polk &
Co. 332.1/0257 74-615562
HG1536 .F635 MRR Alc Latest
edition

Rand McNally international bankers
directory. July 1876- Chicago, Rand
McNally. 99-3836
HG2441 .R3 MRR Ref Desk Latest
edition

BANKS AND BANKING--UNITED STATES--
HISTORY.
Krooss, Herman Edward, comp.
Documentary history of banking and
currency in the United States. New
York, Chelsea House Publishers [1969]
4 v. (xlii, 3232 p.) 332/.0973 69-
16011
HG2461 .K76 MRR Alc.

BANKS AND BANKING--UNITED STATES--
PERIODICALS.
The Clearing house quarterly.
Minneapolis, Minn., Attorneys'
National Clearing House Co. 08-15550

KF195.C57 C4 MRR Alc Latest
edition

BANKS AND BANKING--UNITED STATES--
STATISTICS.
United States. Board of Governors of
the Federal Reserve System. All-bank
statistics, [Washington, 1959] vii,
1229 p. 332.10973 58-60050
HG2493 .A517 MRR Alc.

BANKS AND BANKING--UNITED STATES--
YEARBOOKS.
Moody's bank & finance manual:
American and foreign. New York,
Moody's Investors Service. 56-14722

HG4961 .M65 MRR Alc Latest edition

BANNERS
see Flags

BAPTISTS--BIOGRAPHY.
Cathcart, William, ed. The Baptist
encyclopædia; Philadelphia, L. H.
Everts, 1881. 1328 p. 286.03 41-
30966
BX6211 .C3 MRR Alc.

BAPTISTS--DICTIONARIES.
Cathcart, William, ed. The Baptist
encyclopædia; Philadelphia, L. H.
Everts, 1881. 1328 p. 286.03 41-
30966
BX6211 .C3 MRR Alc.

Encyclopedia of Southern Baptists.
Nashville, Broadman Press [1958-71]
3 v. (xxviii, 2064 p.) [$9.95 (v.
3)] 286.175 58-5417
BX6211 .E5 MRR Alc.

BAPTISTS--HISTORY.
Torbet, Robert George, A history of
the Baptists. Rev. Valley Forge,
Judson Press [1963] 553 p. 286.09
63-8225
BX6231 .T6 1963 MRR Alc.

BAPTISTS--HISTORY--SOURCES.
Sweet, William Warren, ed. The
Baptists, 1783-1830, New York, H.
Holt and company [c1931] ix, 652 p.
286.173 31-26855
BX6235 .S8 MRR Alc.

BAPTISTS--GREAT BRITAIN--YEARBOOKS.
The Baptist handbook. London,
Council of the Baptist Union of Great
Britain and Ireland. 16-1286
BX6213 .B35 MRR Alc Latest edition

BAPTISTS--KENTUCKY.
Historical records survey. Kentucky.
Supplemental check list of Kentucky
imprints, 1788-1820; Louisville,
Ky., Historical records survey,
Service division, Work projects
administration, 1942. 2 p. l., xii
(i.e. xiii) p., 1 l., 241 p. incl.
tables. 015.769 43-2549
Z1215 .H67 no. 38 MRR Alc.

BAPTISTS--UNITED STATES.
Sweet, William Warren, ed. The
Baptists, 1783-1830, New York, H.
Holt and company [c1931] ix, 652 p.
286.173 31-26855
BX6235 .S8 MRR Alc.

BARBADOS--BIOGRAPHY.
Who's who in Canada; Toronto,
International Press Limited. 17-
16282
Began publication in 1910.
F1033 .W62 Sci RR Latest edition /
MRR Biog Latest edition

BARBERS' SUPPLIES--DIRECTORIES.
Modern's market guide. 1967-
[Chicago] Modern beauty shop
magazine. 688/.5/0257 68-48983
HD9999.B253U5 MRR Alc Latest
edition

BAROMETER.
see also Atmospheric pressure

BAROQUE ARCHITECTURE
see Architecture, Baroque

BAROQUE ART
see Art, Baroque

BARRISTERS
see Lawyers

BAS-RELIEF.
see also Sculpture

BASEBALL.
Official baseball rules. [St. Louis]
Sporting news. 796.332022 60-3990
GV877 .O29 MRR Alc Latest edition

The Official National Collegiate
Athletic Association baseball guide.
Phoenix, Ariz. [etc.] College
Athletics Pub. Service [etc.]
796.357 30-11579
GV877 .O52 MRR Alc Latest edition

Turkin, Hy. The official
encyclopedia of baseball, [1st]-
ed.: 1951- South Brunswick [N.J.,
etc.] Barnes. 796.35703 63-9369
GV867 .T8 MRR Alc Latest edition

Who's who in baseball. 1912- New
York, N.Y., Baseball magazine
company. 12-4845
GV865.A1 W6 MRR Alc Latest edition

Zanger, Jack. Major league baseball.
1965- New York, Pocket Books.
796.3576/4 65-2163
GV877 .Z3 MRR Alc Latest edition

BASEBALL--BIOGRAPHY.
Baseball register. [St Louis]
Sporting news [etc.] 796.357058 41-
8772
GV862 .B43 MRR Alc Latest edition

Karst, Gene, Who's who in
professional baseball New Rochelle,
N.Y., Arlington House [1973] 919 p.
796.357/64/0922 B 73-11870
GV865.A1 K37 MRR Biog.

BASEBALL--DICTIONARIES.
Reichler, Joe. Ronald encyclopedia
of baseball. 2d ed. New York,
Ronald Press [1964] 1 v. (various
pagings) 796.35703 64-21882
GV877 .R4 1964 MRR Alc.

BASEBALL--HISTORY.
Danzig, Allison. The history of
baseball; Englewood Cliffs, N.J.,
Prentice-Hall [1959] 412 p.
796.357 59-14356
GV863 .D35 MRR Alc.

BASEBALL--HISTORY--UNITED STATES.
National Association of Professional
Baseball Leagues. The story of minor
league baseball; [1st ed. Columbus,
Ohio, 1953] xiii, 744 p. 796.357
53-1776
GV863 .N3 MRR Alc.

BASEBALL--RECORDS.
Official world series records. St.
Louis. 53-32918
GV877 .W67 MRR Alc Latest edition

BASEBALL--STATISTICS.
The Baseball encyclopedia; Rev. and
updated. New York, Macmillan [1974]
xl, 1532 p. [$17.95] 796.357/021/2
73-21291
GV877 .B27 1974 MRR Alc.

Baseball register. [St Louis]
Sporting news [etc.] 796.357058 41-
8772
GV862 .B43 MRR Alc Latest edition

The Book of baseball records. New
York. 796.357/021/2 72-622841
GV877 .B63 MRR Alc Latest edition

Reichler, Joe. Ronald encyclopedia
of baseball. 2d ed. New York,
Ronald Press [1964] 1 v. (various
pagings) 796.35703 64-21882
GV877 .R4 1964 MRR Alc.

BASEBALL--YEARBOOKS.
Baseball dope book. St. Louis, The
Sporting news. 796.357/021/2 72-
626340
GV877 .S767 MRR Alc Latest edition

Baseball register. [St Louis]
Sporting news [etc.] 796.357058 41-
8772
GV862 .B43 MRR Alc Latest edition

The Little red book of major league
baseball. 1926- New York [etc.]
Elias Sports Bureau, inc. [etc.]
796.357058 26-4174
GV877 .L5 MRR Alc Latest edition

Official baseball guide. 1940- St.
Louis [etc.] 40-9387
GV877 .B32 MRR Alc Latest edition

The Sporting news baseball record
book. 1972- ed. St. Louis,
Sporting News. 796.357/021/2 72-
622256
GV877 .O55 MRR Alc Latest edition

BASEBALL CLUBS.
Thompson, Sherley Clark, All-time
rosters of major league baseball
clubs. Rev. ed. South Brunswick, A.
S. Barnes [1973] 723 p. [$9.95]
796.357/64/0973 73-156
GV875.A1 T47 1973 MRR Alc.

BASEL--DIRECTORIES.
Basler Adressbuch. Basel, Schwabe.
53-32786
Began publication in 1854.
DQ389.2 .A64 MRR Alc Latest
edition

BASEL-LAND (CANTON)--DIRECTORIES.
Adressbuch und Firmenverzeichnis des
Kantons Baselland. [Basel etc.]
Lüdin AG Leestal. 53-28352
DQ364 .A37 MRR Alc Latest edition

BASIC ENGLISH.
Ogden, Charles Kay, The general
Basic English dictionary, New York,
W. W. Norton & company, inc. [1942]
x, 441 p. 428.25 423 42-36402
PE1073.5 .O372 1942 MRR Alc.

BASKETBALL.
The Official National Collegiate
Athletic Association basketball
guide. Phoenix, Ariz. [etc.] College
Athletics Pub. Service [etc.] 40-
6936
GV885.A1 O33 MRR Alc Latest
edition

BASKETBALL--BIOGRAPHY.
Mendell, Ronald L., Who's who in
basketball New Rochelle, N.Y.,
Arlington House [1973] 248 p.
[$7.95] 796.32/3/0922 B 73-11871
GV884.A1 M46 MRR Biog.

BASKETBALL--DICTIONARIES.
Hollander, Zander. The modern
encyclopedia of basketball. Rev. ed.
New York, Four Winds Press [1973]
xxi, 547 p. [$14.95] 796.32/3/0973
73-157043
GV883 .H6 1973 MRR Alc.

Mokray, William George, ed. Ronald
encyclopedia of basketball. New
York, Ronald Press Co. [1963] 1 v.
(various pagings) 796.32303 62-
21898
GV885 .M59 MRR Alc.

BASKETBALL--YEARBOOKS.
National Basketball Association.
Official guide. St. Louis, Sporting
news. 796.323 59-23107
GV885 .N26 MRR Alc Latest edition

BASQUE LANGUAGE.
Cejador y Frauca, Julio, Historia de
la lengua y literatura castellana ...
Madrid, Imprenta Radio, 1916-30. 14
v. in 15. mrr01-65
PQ6032 .C3 1916 MRR Alc.

Entwistle, William James, The
Spanish language, [2d ed.] London,
Faber & Faber [1962] vi, 367 p.
460 63-6431
PC4075 .E5 1962 MRR Alc.

BASQUE LITERATURE--BIBLIOGRAPHY.
Simón Díaz, José. ,Bibliografía
de literatura hispánica. 2. ed.
corr. y aumentada. Madrid, Consejo
Superior de Investigaciones
Científicas, Instituto "Miguel de
Cervantes" de Filología Hispánica,
1960-   v.   64-5767
Z2691 .S52 MRR Alc.

BASQUE PHILOLOGY--BIBLIOGRAPHY.
Golden, Herbert Hershel, Modern
Iberian language and literature;
Cambridge, Harvard University Press,
1958. x, 184 p. 016.46 58-12978
Z7031 .G6 MRR Alc.

BATRACHIA
see Amphibians

BATTLES.
Harbottle, Thomas Benfield,
Dictionary of battles. Revised [ed.]
London, Hart-Davis, 1971. 334 p.
[£2.95] 904/.7 70-855752
D25.A2 H2 1971b MRR Alc.

Oettinger, Eduard Maria, Moniteur
des dates. Leipzig, L. Denicke,
1869. 6 v. in 1.   02-3518
CT154 .O3 MRR Biog.

BATTLES--DICTIONARIES.
Brewer, Ebenezer Cobham, The
historic note-book: with an appendix
of battles. Detroit, Republished by
Gale Research Co., 1966. x, 997 p.
903 66-23191
D9 .B76 1966 MRR Alc.

Eggenberger, David. A dictionary of
battles. New York, Crowell [1967]
x, 526 p.   904/.7   67-12400
D25 .E35 MRR Alc.

BATTLES--EUROPE.
Chandler, David G. ed. A guide to
the battlefields of Europe,
Philadelphia, Chilton Books [1966,
c1965] 2 v.   904.7 66-17192
D25 .C47 MRR Alc.

BATTLES--GREAT BRITAIN.
Gordon, Lawrence L. British battles
and medals. 4th ed., rev. London,
Spink, 1971. xiv, 440 p.   355.1/34
72-180227
UB435.G8 G6 1971 MRR Alc.

BATTLES--UNITED STATES.
Boatner, Mark Mayo, Landmarks of the
American Revolution; [Harrisburg,
Pa.] Stackpole Books [1973] 608 p.
[$10.00] 917.3/03/3 73-6964
E159 .B67 MRR Alc.

Peters, Joseph P., comp. Indian
battles and skirmishes on the
American frontier, 1790-1898. New
York, Published for University
Microfilms, Ann Arbor, by Argonaut
Press, 1966. 26, 112, 65, 51 p.
970.5 66-28882
E81 .P4 MRR Alc.

Steele, Matthew Forney, American
campaigns, Washington, B. S. Adams,
1909. viii p., 1 l., 731 p. and
atlas of xii p., 311 maps. war22-80
E181 .S85 MRR Alc.

Strait, Newton Allen, comp.
Alphabetical list of battles, 1754-
1900; Washington, D.C., 1909. 1 p.
l., 252 p.   973.02 38-11790
E181 .S89 1909 MRR Ref Desk.

BATTLES--UNITED STATES--PICTORIAL WORKS.
United States. Library of Congress.
An album of American battle art, 1755-
1918. Washington, U.S. Govt. Print.
Off., 1947. xvi, 319 p. 769.49973
48-45628
Z663 .A8 MRR Alc.

BATTLESHIPS.
Breyer, Siegfried. Battleships and
battle cruisers, 1905-1970; Garden
City, N.Y., Doubleday [1973] 480 p.
[$25.00] 359.3/2/520904 72-84895
V765 .B6813 MRR Alc.

Pater, Alan Frederick. United States
battleships; [1st ed.] Beverly
Hills, Calif., Monitor Book Co.,
[1968] 279 p.   358.32/52/0973 68-
17423
VA58 .P3 MRR Alc.

BAVARIA--BIOGRAPHY.
Genealogisches Handbuch des in Bayern
immatrikulierten Adels. Bd. 1-
1950- Neustadt an der Aisch [etc.]
Degener 52-31795
CS644 .G4 MRR Biog Latest edition

BAVARIA--COMMERCE--DIRECTORIES.
Bayerisches Landes-Adressbuch für
Industrie, Handel und Gewerbe.
München,
Adressbuchverlagsgesellschaft Ruf.
53-30513
HC287.B3 B34 MRR Alc Latest
edition

Firmenhandbuch Bayern. Hannover,
Industrie- und Handelsverlag. 66-
40836
HF3569.B3 F53 MRR Alc Latest
edition

Handels- und Gewerbeadressbuch für
Bayern. München, Bayerischer
Adressbuchverlag A. & H. Kunze. 53-
29244
Began publication in 1947.
HC287.B3 H3 MRR Alc Latest edition

BAVARIA--GENEALOGY.
Genealogisches Handbuch des in Bayern
immatrikulierten Adels. Bd. 1-
1950- Neustadt an der Aisch [etc.]
Degener 52-31795
CS644 .G4 MRR Biog Latest edition

BAVARIA--INDUSTRIES--DIRECTORIES.
Bayerisches Landes-Adressbuch für
Industrie, Handel und Gewerbe.
München,
Adressbuchverlagsgesellschaft Ruf.
53-30513
HC287.B3 B34 MRR Alc Latest
edition

Handels- und Gewerbeadressbuch für
Bayern. München, Bayerischer
Adressbuchverlag A. & H. Kunze. 53-
29244
Began publication in 1947.
HC287.B3 H3 MRR Alc Latest edition

BAVARIA--MANUFACTURES--DIRECTORIES.
Firmenhandbuch Bayern. Hannover,
Industrie- und Handelsverlag. 66-
40836
HF3569.B3 F53 MRR Alc Latest
edition

BAVARIA--NOBILITY.
Genealogisches Handbuch des in Bayern
immatrikulierten Adels. Bd. 1-
1950- Neustadt an der Aisch [etc.]
Degener 52-31795
CS644 .G4 MRR Biog Latest edition

BEACHES.
Sunset. Sunset beachcombers' guide
to the Pacific coast. Menlo Park,
Calif., Lane Books [1966] 112 p.
917.90946 66-15333
F851 .S93 MRR Alc.

BEACONS.
see also Lighthouses

BEADLE AND ADAMS, FIRM.
Johannsen, Albert, The House of
Beadle and Adams and its dime and
nickel novels; [1st ed.] Norman,
University of Oklahoma Press [1950-
62] 3 v.   655.4747 50-8158
Z1231.F4 J68 MRR Alc.

BEASTS
see Domestic animals

BEAUTY
see Aesthetics

see Art--Philosophy

BEAUTY, PERSONAL.
see also Cosmetics

see also Costume

BEAUTY SHOPS--EQUIPMENT AND SUPPLIES--
DIRECTORIES.
Guide de la parfumerie. Paris,
Éditions publi-guid. 60-46355
TP383.A6 G8 MRR Alc Latest edition

Modern's market guide. 1967-
[Chicago] Modern beauty shop
magazine. 688/.5/0257 68-48983
HD9999.B253U5 MRR Alc Latest
edition

BEBOP MUSIC
see Jazz music

BEDDING--DIRECTORIES.
Bedding magazine annual buyers'
issue. [Washington, National
Association of Bedding Manufacturers]
338.4/7/6022573 72-621780
TT399 .B4 MRR Alc Latest edition

BEETLES.
Reitter, Ewald. Beetles. London, P.
Hamlyn [1961] 205 p. 595.76 62-
203
QL575 .R413 1961a MRR Alc.

BEETLES--CANADA.
Jaques, Harry Edwin, How to know the
beetles; 1st ed. Dubuque, W. C.
Brown Co. [1951] 372 p. 595.76 52-
4037
QL583 .J3 MRR Alc.

BEETLES--UNITED STATES.
Jaques, Harry Edwin, How to know the
beetles; 1st ed. Dubuque, W. C.
Brown Co. [1951] 372 p. 595.76 52-
4037
QL583 .J3 MRR Alc.

BEHAVIOR
see Conduct of life

see Etiquette

BEHAVIOR (PSYCHOLOGY)
see Animals, Habits and behavior of

BEHAVIOR THERAPY--BIBLIOGRAPHY.
Morrow, William R. Behavior therapy
bibliography, 1950-1969; Columbia,
University of Missouri Press [1971]
165 p. [$10.00] 016.61689/1 73-
633730
Z6664.N5 M67 MRR Alc.

BEHAVIORAL SCIENCES--DICTIONARY.
Wolman, Benjamin B. Dictionary of
behavioral science. New York, Van
Nostrand Reinhold Co. [1973] ix, 478
p. 150/.3 73-748
BF31 .W64 MRR Alc.

BELFAST--DIRECTORIES.
Belfast and Northern Ireland
directory. Belfast, Century
Newspaper Ltd. [etc.] 53-32016
"First published in May 1852."
DA995.B5 B45 MRR Alc Latest
edition

BELGIAN LITERATURE--HISTORY AND
CRITICISM.
Mallinson, Vernon. Modern Belgian
literature, 1830-1960. London,
Heinemann, 1966- [7], 205 p. [42/-]
809.889493 67-71833
PQ3814 .M25 1966a MRR Alc.

BELGIAN LITERATURE--HISTORY AND
CRITICISM--BIBLIOGRAPHY.
Culot, Jean Marie. Bibliographie des
écrivains français de Belgique,
1881- Bruxelles, Palais des
académies, 1958- v.   a 59-985
Z2413 .C8 MRR Alc.

BELGIAN PERIODICALS--BIBLIOGRAPHY.
Archives de la ville de Bruxelles.
Catalogue des journaux et
périodiques conserves aux Archives
de la Ville de Bruxelles. Bruxelles,
[Ville de Bruxelles], 1965. 3 v.
74-366082
Z6945 .A76 MRR Alc.

BELGIAN PERIODICALS--DIRECTORIES.
Maréchal, Yvon, Répertoire
pratique des périodiques belges
édites en langue française.
Louvain-Bruxelles, Vander, (1970).
[v], 128 p. [200F.] 74-564809
Z6956.B4 M27 MRR Alc.

BELGIUM.
Mallinson, Vernon. Belgium. New
York, Praeger [1970] 240 p. [7.00]
949.3 72-104772
DH418 .M25 1970 MRR Alc.

BELGIUM--BIBLIOGRAPHY--CATALOGS.
United States. Library of Congress.
Early printed books of the Low
Countries Washington, 1958. vi, 37
p. 016.09 58-60011
Z663.4 .E2 MRR Alc.

BELGIUM--BIOGRAPHY.
Le Livre bleu; 1950- Bruxelles, F.
Larcier. 52-19212
DH513 .L58 MRR Biog Latest edition

Who's who in Belgium and Grand Duchy
of Luxembourg. [1st] ed.; 1957/58-
Brussels, Intercontinental Book &
Pub. Co. 920.0493 59-3017
DH513 .W45 MRR Biog Latest edition

BELGIUM--COMMERCE--DIRECTORIES.
Annuaire du commerce et de
l'industrie de Belgique. Bruxelles,
A. Mertens. ca 11-1699
Began with 1849 vol.
HF5184 .A6 MRR Alc Latest edition

Annuaire général de la Belgique,
industrielle, commerciale, maritime.
Bruxelles. 53-34696
HC312. A55 MRR Alc Latest edition

Belgian American trade directory.
1946- New York, Chamber of Commerce
in the United States inc. [etc.]
382.058 46-17126
HF3603 .B4 MRR Alc Latest edition

Brussels. Chambre de commerce.
Annuaire officiel. Bruxelles, Impr.
Industrielle et financière [etc.]
380.1/06/24933 74-642351
HF314 .B85 MRR Alc Latest edition

Brussels. Chambre de commerce. New
directory of Belgian importers and
exporters. Bruxelles [1967] 119 p.
[225.00] 382.5/025493 72-465977
HF3603 .B68 MRR Alc.

BELGIUM--COMMERCE--YEARBOOKS.
Annuaire du commerce et de
l'industrie de Belgique. Bruxelles,
A. Mertens. ca 11-1699
Began with 1849 vol.
HF5184 .A6 MRR Alc Latest edition

Belgian American trade directory.
1946- New York, Chamber of Commerce
in the United States inc. [etc.]
382.058 46-17126
HF3603 .B4 MRR Alc Latest edition

BELGIUM--DESCRIPTION AND TRAVEL.
Gibson, Hugh, Belgium. New York,
Doubleday, Doran & company, inc.,
1939. xix, 347 p. 914.93 39-27653

DH433 .G5 MRR Alc.

BELGIUM--DESCRIPTION AND TRAVEL--
GAZETTEERS.
Houet, Albert. Dictionnaire moderne,
géographique, administratif,
statistique, des communes belges.
Bruxelles, Impr. F. van Muysewinkel
[1950] 621, [1] p. a 51-4145
DH414 .H6 MRR Alc.

BELGIUM--DESCRIPTION AND TRAVEL--GUIDE-
BOOKS.
Belgique, Luxembourg. [8. éd.]
Paris, Hachette, 1971. 730 p.
[46.00F] 74-24119
DH416 .B4 1971 MRR Alc.

Benelux. Paris [etc.] Pneu Michelin,
Services de tourisme [etc.] 56-50955

GV1025.B43 B4 MRR Alc Latest
edition

Fodor's Belgium and Luxembourg. 1969-
New York, D. McKay Co. 914.93/04/4
72-622746
DH416 .B43 MRR Alc Latest edition

BELGIUM--EXECUTIVE DEPARTMENTS.
Guide des ministères. 1951-
Bruxelles. 52-64591
JN6103 .G8 MRR Alc Latest edition

BELGIUM--GAZETTEERS.
United States. Office of Geography.
Belgium; Washington [U.S. Govt.
Print. Off.] 1963. v, 401 p. 63-
62497
DH414 .U5 MRR Alc.

BELGIUM--HISTORY.
Cammaerts, Émile. The keystone of
Europe; London, P. Davies [1939]
xvi, 393 p. 949.3 39-20271
DH620 .C3 1939 MRR Alc.

Mallinson, Vernon. Belgium. New
York, Praeger [1970] 240 p. [7.00]
949.3 72-104772
DH418 .M25 1970 MRR Alc.

BELGIUM--IMPRINTS.
British Museum. Dept. of Printed
Books. Short-title catalogue of
books printed in the Netherlands and
Belgium London, Trustees of the
British Museum, 1965. viii, 274 p.
66-4468
Z2402 .B7 MRR Alc.

Cockx-Indestege, Elly. Belgica
typographica 1541-1600. Nieuwkoop,
P. de Graaf, 1968- v. [180.00
(v. 1)] 68-14677
Z2402 .C6 MRR Alc.

Culot, Jean Marie. Bibliographie des
écrivains français de Belgique,
1881- Bruxelles, Palais des
académies, 1958- v. a 59-985
Z2413 .C8 MRR Alc.

Landwehr, John. Dutch emblem books;
a bibliography. Utrecht, Haentjens
Dekker & Gumbert [1962] xii, 98 p.
66-83333
Z2401 .L3 MRR Alc.

BELGIUM--INDUSTRIES--DIRECTORIES.
Annuaire général de la Belgique,
industrielle, commerciale, maritime.
Bruxelles. 53-34696
HC312 .A55 MRR Alc Latest edition

BELGIUM--INDUSTRIES--YEARBOOKS.
Annuaire du commerce et de
l'industrie de Belgique. Bruxelles,
A. Mertens. ca 11-1699
Began with 1849 vol.
HF5184 .A6 MRR Alc Latest edition

BELGIUM--LEARNED INSTITUTIONS AND
SOCIETIES.
Belgium. Service des échanges
internationaux. Liste des sociétés
savantes et littéraires de Belgique.
Bruxelles, 1960. 141 p. 61-36159

AS238 .A5 MRR Alc.

BELGIUM--MANUFACTURES--DIRECTORIES.
Belgian American trade directory.
1946- New York, Chamber of Commerce
in the United States inc. [etc.]
382.058 46-17126
HF3603 .B4 MRR Alc Latest edition

BELGIUM--REGISTERS.
Annuaire administratif et judiciaire
de Belgique. 94.- année; 1967/68-
Bruxelles, E. Bruylant. 72-627078
JN6105 .A6 MRR Alc Latest edition

Guide des ministères. 1951-
Bruxelles. 52-64591
JN6103 .G8 MRR Alc Latest edition

High-life de Belgique. Ixelles-
Bruxelles. Geeraerts ca 27-207
DH414 .H5 MRR Alc Latest edition

BELGIUM--SOCIAL REGISTERS.
High-life de Belgique. Ixelles-
Bruxelles, Geeraerts ca 27-207
DH414 .H5 MRR Alc Latest edition

BELGIUM--STATISTICS.
Annuaire statistique de la Belgique.
t. 81- 1960- [Bruxelles] Institut
national de statistique. 314.93 72-
622921
HA1393.A34 MRR Alc Latest edition

BELKNAP, GEORGE EUGENE, 1832-1903--
MANUSCRIPTS.
United States. Library of Congress.
Manuscript Division. George Eugene
Belknap, Reginald Rowan Belknap: a
register of their papers in the
Library of Congress. Washington,
Library of Congress, 1969. 5, 8 l.
016.3/31/0922 77-603257
Z663.34 .B38 MRR Alc.

BELKNAP, REGINALD ROWAN, 1871-1959--
MANUSCRIPTS.
United States. Library of Congress.
Manuscript Division. George Eugene
Belknap, Reginald Rowan Belknap: a
register of their papers in the
Library of Congress. Washington,
Library of Congress, 1969. 5, 8 l.
016.3/31/0922 77-603257
Z663.34 .B38 MRR Alc.

BELLES-LETTRES
see Literature

BENELUX COUNTRIES--DESCRIPTION AND
TRAVEL--GUIDE-BOOKS.
Olson, Harvey Stuart, Olson's
complete motoring guide to Germany,
Austria & the Benelux countries,
[1st ed.] Philadelphia, Lippincott
[1968] xiv, 878 p. [$5.95] 914
68-24136
GV1025.A2 O45 MRR Alc.

BENEVOLENT INSTITUTIONS
see Charities

BENGALI LANGUAGE--DICTIONARIES--ENGLISH.
Mitra, Subal Chandra. The student's
Bengali-English dictionary. 2d ed.
Calcutta, Sarat Chandra Mitra & Srish
Chandra Mitra, The New Bengal press
[1923] 1 p. l., ii, 1393, [1] p.
24-4364
PK1687 .M55 1923 MRR Alc.

BERGE, WENDELL, 1903-1955--BIBLIOGRAPHY.
United States. Library of Congress.
Manuscript Division. Wendell Berge:
a register of his papers in the
Library of Congress. Washington,
1958. 12 p. 012 58-60038
Z663.34 .B4 MRR Alc.

BERGEN, NORWAY--DIRECTORIES.
Adressebok for Hordaland fylke og
Bergen med skatteligninger. Oslo, S.
M. Bryde. 53-29091
DL576.H7 A7 MRR Alc Latest edition

Adressebok for Sogn og Fjordane fylke
og Bergen med skatteligninger. Oslo,
S. M. Bryde. 53-30568
DL596.B4 A6 MRR Alc Latest edition

BERLIN--DIRECTORIES.
Berliner Stadt Adressbuch. Berlin,
Berliner Adressbuch-Verlag. 53-30209

DD854 .B4 MRR Alc Latest edition

BERLIN--GAZETTEERS.
United States. Office of Geography.
Germany--Federal Republic and West
Berlin; Washington, 1960. 2 v.
914.3 60-62466
DD14 .U517 MRR Alc.

BERLIN--LIBRARIES--DIRECTORIES.
Berlin. Stadtbibliothek. Führer
durch die Bibliotheken und
Literaturstellen der Hauptstadt
Berlin. Leipzig, Verlag für Buch-
und Bibliothekswesen] 1963. 254 p.
63-41869
Z802 .B44B4 MRR Alc.

Lülies, Hildegard, Verzeichnis der
Bibliotheken in Berlin <West>
Berlin; Spitzing, 1966. 301 p. [DM
24.90] 027/.043/155 67-86023
Z801.B4 L8 MRR Alc.

BERLIN--POLITICS AND GOVERNMENT--1945- -
BIBLIOGRAPHY.
Price, Arnold Hereward, The Federal
Republic of Germany; Washington,
Library of Congress; [for sale by the
Supt. of Docs., U.S. Govt. Print.
Off.] 1972. ix, 63 p. 016.9143/03
72-677
Z663.47 .F43 MRR Alc.

BERLIN--STREETS.
Kauperts Strassenführer durch
Berlin. Berlin, Kaupert Verlag. 53-
30690
Began publication in 1945.
DD887 .K3 MRR Alc Latest edition

BERLIN QUESTION (1945-)
Deutsche Gesellschaft für
Auswärtige Politik.
Forschungsinstitut. Dokumente zur
Berlin-Frage, 1944-1959. München,
R. Oldenbourg, 1959. 434 p. 62-
25827
DD881 .D44 MRR Alc.

United States. Dept. of State.
Historical Office. Documents on
Germany, 1944-1961. Washington, U.S.
Govt. Print. Off., 1961. xv, 833 p.
62-60800
DD257 .U476 1961 MRR Alc.

BERMUDA ISLANDS--BIOGRAPHY.
Who's who in Canada; Toronto,
International Press Limited. 17-
16282
Began publication in 1910.
F1033 .W62 Sci RR Latest edition /
MRR Biog Latest edition

BERMUDA ISLANDS--DESCRIPTION AND TRAVEL-
-GUIDE-BOOKS.
Fodor's guide to the Caribbean,
Bahamas and Bermuda; 1960- New
York, D. McKay. 917.29 60-908
F2171 .F65 MRR Alc Latest edition

BERMUDA ISLANDS--GAZETTEERS.
United States. Office of Geography.
British West Indies and Bermuda;
Washington, U.S. Govt. Print. Off.,
1955. v, 157 p. 917.29 55-63708
F2131 .U52 MRR Alc.

BERN--DIRECTORIES.
Berner Adressbuch. Bern, Hallwag
[etc.] 42-31506
DQ409.2 .A4 MRR Alc Latest edition

BEST PLAYS--INDEXES.
Guernsey, Otis L., Directory of the
American theater, 1894-1971; New
York, Dodd, Mead [1971] vi, 343 p.
[$25.00] 812/.5/08 71-180734
PN6112 .B4524 MRR Alc.

BEST SELLERS.
Mott, Frank Luther, Golden
multitudes; New York, Macmillan Co.,
1947. xii, 357 p. 016 47-11742
Z1033.B3 M6 MRR Alc.

BEST SELLERS--BIBLIOGRAPHY.
Hackett, Alice Payne, 70 years of
best sellers, 1895-1965. New York,
R. R. Bowker Co., 1967. xi, 280 p.
655.4/73 67-25025
Z1033.B3 H34 MRR Ref Desk.

Kujoth, Jean Spealman. Best-selling
children's books. Metuchen, N.J.,
Scarecrow Press, 1973. 305 p.
028.52 72-11692
Z1037 .K83 MRR Alc.

Mott, Frank Luther, Golden
multitudes; New York, Macmillan Co.,
1947. xii, 357 p. 016 47-11742
Z1033.B3 M6 MRR Alc.

BETROTHAL.
see also Marriage

McCall's engagement and wedding
guide. New York, Saturday Review
Press [1972] xvi, 266 p. [$8.95]
395/.22 79-122130
BJ2051 .M27 MRR Alc.

BEVERAGES--BIBLIOGRAPHY.
Noling, A. W. Beverage literature:
Metuchen, N.J., Scarecrow Press,
1971. 865 p. 016.663 70-142238
Z5776.B4 N63 MRR Alc.

Vara, Albert C. Food and beverage
industries: a bibliography and
guidebook Detroit, Gale Research Co.
[1970] 215 p. [11.50]
016.3384/7/664 70-102058
Z7164.F7 V33 MRR Alc.

BEVERAGES--DIRECTORIES.
Noyes Data Corporation. Food and
beverage processing industries, 1971.
Park Ridge, N.J. [1971] iii, 169, 9
p. [$20.00] 338.4/7/664002573 70-
139403
HD9003 .N58 MRR Alc.

BHUTAN.
American University, Washington, D.C.
Foreign Areas Studies Divison. Area
handbook for Nepal (with Sikkim and
Bhutan). Washington, For sale by the
Supt. of Docs., U.S. Govt. Print.
Off., 1964. xv, 448 p. 67-115014
DS485.N4 A8 MRR Alc.

Harris, George Lawrence, Area
handbook for Nepal, Bhutan, and
Sikkim. 2d ed. [Washington; for
sale by the Supt. of Docs., U.S.
Govt. Print. Off.] 1973. lxxx, 431
p. [$6.85] 915.49/6/035 73-600139

DS493.4 .H37 1973 MRR Alc.

BHUTAN--GAZETTEERS.
United States. Office of Geography.
India; Washington, 1952. 2 v. 70-
10027
DS405 .U55 MRR Alc.

BIBLE--ANTIQUITIES.

Finegan, Jack, Light from the ancient past; [2d ed. Princeton, N.J.] Princeton University Press, 1959. xxxvii, 638 p. 220.93 59-11072
BS635 .F5 1959 MRR Alc.

Grollenberg, Lucas Hendricus, Atlas of the Bible. [London] Nelson, 1956. 165 p. 220.93 56-14320
BS621 .G712 1956 MRR Alc.

Lockyer, Herbert. All the trades and occupations of the Bible: Grand Rapids, Zondervan Pub. House [c1969] 327 p. [4.95] 220.8/33/7 70-95038

BS680.C3 L6 MRR Alc.

Young, Robert, Analytical concordance to the Bible 22d American ed., rev. New York, Funk & Wagnalls [1955] ix, 1090, 93, 23, 51 p. 220.2 55-5338
BS425 .Y7 1955 MRR Alc.

BIBLE--ANTIQUITIES--DICTIONARIES.

Corswant, Willy, A dictionary of life in Bible times. New York, Oxford University Press, 1960. 308, [1] p. 220.93 60-4719
BS621 .C653 1960 MRR Alc.

Negev, Avraham. Archaeological encyclopedia of the Holy Land. New York, Putnam [1972] 354 p. [$15.95] 913.33/03/03 71-190101
DS111.A2 N38 MRR Alc.

Pfeiffer, Charles F., ed. The Biblical world; Grand Rapids, Baker Book House [1966] 612 p. 220.9303 66-19312
BS622 .P4 MRR Alc.

BIBLE--ATLASES
see Bible--Geography--Maps

BIBLE--BIBLIOGRAPHY.

British and foreign Bible society. Library. Historical catalogue of the printed editions of Holy Scripture in the library of the British and foreign Bible society. London, The Bible house, 1903-11. 2 v. in 4. 07-20497
Z7770 .B73 MRR Alc.

BIBLE--BIOGRAPHY.

Deen, Edith. All of the women of the Bible. [1st ed.] New York, Harper [1955] xxii, 410 p. 220.92 55-8521
BS575 .D4 MRR Alc.

BIBLE--BIOGRAPHY--DICTIONARIES.

Barker, William Pierson. Everyone in the Bible Westwood, N.J., F. H. Revell Co. [1966] 370 p. 220.92 66-21894
BS570 .B3 MRR Alc.

Lockyer, Herbert. All the men of the Bible; Grand Rapids, Zondervan Pub. House [1958] 381 p. 220.92 58-4616
BS570 .L6 MRR Alc.

BIBLE--CHRONOLOGY.

Finegan, Jack, Handbook of Biblical chronology; Princeton, N.J., Princeton University Press, 1964. xxvi, 338 p. 220.9 63-18642
BS637.2 .F5 MRR Alc.

BIBLE--COMMENTARIES.

The Biblical expositor; [1st ed.] Philadelphia, A. J. Holman Co. [1960] 3 v. 220.7 60-5198
BS491.2 .B5 MRR Alc.

Black, Matthew, ed. Peake's commentary on the Bible. London, New York, T. Nelson, 1962. xv, 1126, 4 p. 220.7 62-6297
BS491 .B57 MRR Alc.

The Interpreter's Bible: New York, Abingdon-Cokesbury Press [1951-57, v. 1, 1952] 12 v. 220.7 51-12276
BS491.2 .I55 MRR Alc.

Orchard, Bernard, Father, ed. A Catholic commentary on Holy Scripture. London, New York, Nelson [1953] xvi, 1312 p. 220.7 53-1573
BS491 .O7 1953 MRR Alc.

BIBLE--CONCORDANCES, ENGLISH.

Cruden, Alexander, Complete concordance to the Old and New Testaments. Grand Rapids, Zondervan Pub. House [1955, c1949] vii, 800 p. 220.2 56-1384
BS425 .C8 1955 MRR Alc.

Hitchcock, Roswell Dwight, Hitchcock's Topical Bible and Cruden's Concordance. Grand Rapids, Baker Book House, 1959 [c1952] xxxvii, 685, 342 p. 220.2 56-12726

BS432 .H5 1959 MRR Alc.

Young, Robert, Analytical concordance to the Bible 22d American ed., rev. New York, Funk & Wagnalls [1955] ix, 1090, 93, 23, 51 p. 220.2 55-5338
BS425 .Y7 1955 MRR Alc.

BIBLE--CONCORDANCES, ENGLISH--MOFFATT.

Gant, William John. The Moffatt Bible concordance; New York, Harper [1950] 550 p. 220.2 50-12690
BS425 .G3 1950a MRR Alc.

BIBLE--CONCORDANCES, ENGLISH--REVISED STANDARD.

Ellison, John William, Nelson's complete concordance of the Revised standard version of the Bible. New York, Nelson [c1957] 2157 p. 220.2 57-7122
BS425 .E4 1957 MRR Ref Desk.

Metzger, Bruce Manning. The Oxford concise concordance to the Revised standard version of the Holy Bible. New York, Oxford University Press, 1962. 158 p. 62-52472
BS425 .M4 MRR Alc.

BIBLE--CONCORDANCES, ENGLISH--VERSIONS--DOUAI.

Thompson, Newton Wayland, Complete concordance to the Bible St. Louis, Mo., London, B. Herder book co., 1945. 2 p. l., 1914 p. 220.2 45-8426
BS425 .T45 1945 MRR Alc.

BIBLE--CONCORDANCES, LATIN.

Dutripon, François Pascal, Concordantiæ Bibliorum sacrorum Vulgatæ editionis, Parisiis, apud Belin-Mandar, 1838. 3 p. l., xxiii, [1], 1484 p. 10-717
BS423 .D8 MRR Alc.

BIBLE--DICTIONARIES.

Catholic Biblical encyclopedia New York, J. F. Wagner [1956, v. 2, c1950] 2 v. in 1. 220.3 58-33655

BS440 .C36 MRR Alc.

Cheyne, Thomas Kelly, Encyclopædia biblica: New York, The Macmillan company; [etc., etc.] 1899-1903. 4 v. 02-705
BS440 .C5 MRR Alc.

Cornfeld, Gaalyahu, ed. Pictorial Biblical encyclopedia; New York, Macmillan, 1964. 712 p. 220.3 65-12852
BS440 .C63 MRR Alc.

Douglas, James Dixon, ed. The new Bible dictionary. 1st ed.] London, Inter-varsity Fellowship [1962] xvi, 1375 p. 220.3 62-53521
BS440 .D6 1962a MRR Alc.

The Encyclopedia of the Bible. Englewood Cliffs, N.J., Prentice-Hall [1965] vi, 248 p. 220.3 64-23557
BS440 .E453 MRR Alc.

Gehman, Henry Snyder, The new Westminster dictionary of the Bible. Philadelphia, Westminster Press [1970] xi, 1027, 4 p. [10.95] 220/.3 69-10000
BS440 .G4 MRR Alc.

Hastings, James, ed. Dictionary of the apostolic church, New York, C. Scribner's sons; [etc., etc.] 1916-22. 2 v. 16-15591
BS440 .H4 MRR Alc.

Hastings, James, ed. Dictionary of the Bible. Rev. ed. New York, Scribner [1963] xxi, 1059 p. 220.3 62-21697
BS440 .H5 1963 MRR Alc.

The International standard Bible encyclopaedia; Chicago, The Howard Severance company, 1930. 5 v. 29-23505
BS440 .I6 1929 MRR Alc.

The Interpreter's dictionary of the Bible; New York, Abingdon Press [1962] 4 v. 220.3 62-9387
BS440 .I63 MRR Alc.

Léon-Dufour, Xavier. Dictionary of Biblical theology; London, Dublin [etc.] G. Chapman, 1967. xxix, 618 p. [63/-] 220.3 68-83461
BS543.A1 L413 MRR Alc.

Miller, Madeleine (Sweeny) Encyclopedia of Bible life. [Rev. ed.] London, A. and C. Black [1957] xvi, 493 p. 220.3 59-1815
BS440 .M5 1957 MRR Alc.

Miller, Madeleine (Sweeny) Harper's Bible dictionary, [7th ed.] New York, Harper [c1961] x, 854 p. 220.3 61-14623
BS440 .M52 1961 MRR Alc.

Neill, Stephen Charles, Bp., ed. The modern reader's dictionary of the Bible. New York, Association Press [1966] vi, 339 p. 220.3 65-25153
BS440 .N34 MRR Alc.

Smith, William, Sir, The new Smith's Bible dictionary. Garden City, N.Y., Doubleday, 1966. xi, 441 p. 220.3 66-20927
BS440 .S67 1966 MRR Alc.

Unger, Merrill Frederick, Unger's Bible dictionary, [3d ed., rev.] Chicago, Moody Press [c1966] vii, 1192 p. 220.3 67-1754
BS440 .U5 1966 MRR Alc.

Wilson, Walter Lewis, Wilson's dictionary of Bible types. Grand Rapids, Eerdmans [c1957] 519 p. 220.6 57-14495
BS477 .W53 MRR Alc.

The Zondervan pictorial Bible dictionary. Grand Rapids, Zondervan Pub. House, 1963. xiv, 927 p. 220.3 62-16808
BS440 .Z6 MRR Alc.

BIBLE--DICTIONARIES--FRENCH.

Vigouroux, Fulcran Grégoire, Dictionnaire de la Bible. Paris, Letouzey et Ané [1907]-12. 5 v. 10-20843
BS440 .V7 MRR Alc.

BIBLE--GEOGRAPHY.

Kraeling, Emil Gottlieb Heinrich, Rand McNally Bible atlas. Chicago, Rand McNally [1956] 487 p. 220.91 56-12823
BS630 .K7 MRR Alc.

May, Herbert Gordon, Oxford Bible atlas. 2nd ed. / London ; New York : Oxford University Press, 1974. 144 p. : [£2.75 ($9.95 U.S.)] 220.9 74-184843
BS630 .M35 1974 MRR Alc.

Pfeiffer, Charles F. Baker's Bible atlas. Grand Rapids, Baker Book House, 1961. 333 p. 220.91 60-15536
BS630 .P45 MRR Alc.

Wright, George Ernest, The Westminster historical atlas to the Bible, Rev. [i.e. 5th British] ed. London, SCM Press [1957, c1956] 130 p. map59-786
G2230 .W7 1957 MRR Alc Atlas.

BIBLE--GEOGRAPHY--DICTIONARIES.

Rowley, Harold Henry, Dictionary of Bible place names Old Tappan, N.J., F. H. Revell Co. [c1970] 173 p. [$3.95] 220.91/03 74-138743
BS630 .R645 MRR Alc.

BIBLE--GEOGRAPHY--MAPS.

Grollenberg, Lucas Hendricus, Atlas of the Bible. [London] Nelson, 1956. 165 p. 220.93 56-14320
BS621 .G712 1956 MRR Alc.

May, Herbert Gordon, Oxford Bible atlas. 2nd ed. / London ; New York : Oxford University Press, 1974. 144 p. : [£2.75 ($9.95 U.S.)] 220.9 74-184843
BS630 .M35 1974 MRR Alc.

Wright, George Ernest, The Westminster historical atlas to the Bible, Rev. [i.e. 5th British] ed. London, SCM Press [1957, c1956] 130 p. map59-786
G2230 .W7 1957 MRR Alc Atlas.

BIBLE--HANDBOOKS, MANUALS, ETC.

Bible handbook. Grand Rapids, Mich. [etc.] Zondervan Pub. House [etc.] 220.7 32-8057
First ed. published in 1924.
BS417 .B48 MRR Alc Latest issue

Leishman, Thomas Linton, The Bible handbook, [2d ed.] New York, T. Nelson [1965] 283 p. 220.02 65-15403
BS417 .L4 1965 MRR Alc.

Neil, William, ed. The Bible companion: London, Skeffington [1960] xii, 468 p. 220.02 60-40204
BS417 .N4 1960 MRR Alc.

BIBLE--HISTORY.

The Cambridge history of the Bible. Cambridge, University Press, 1963-70. [v. 1, 1970; v. 3, 1963] 3 v. 220/.09 63-24435
BS445 .C26 MRR Alc.

Kenyon, Frederic George, Sir, Our Bible and the ancient manuscripts. [5th ed., rev. and enl.] London, Eyre & Spottiswoode, 1958. 352 p. 220.4 58-2327
BS445 .K46 1958 MRR Alc.

BIBLE--HISTORY. (Cont.)
MacGregor, Geddes.   The Bible in the
making. London, Murray [1961, c1959]
310 p.   220.5   61-3682
BS445 .M28 1961 MRR Alc.

Reumann, John Henry Paul. The
romance of Bible scripts and
scholars: Englewood Cliffs, N.J.,
Prentice-Hall [1965] viii, 248 p.
220.409   65-21174
BS445 .R4 MRR Alc.

Wegener, Gunther S. 6000 years of
the Bible. London, Hodder and
Stoughton [1963] 352 p.   63-25103
BS445 .W373 MRR Alc.

BIBLE--HISTORY OF BIBLICAL EVENTS--
FICTION--BIBLIOGRAPHY.
Ehlert, Arnold D. The Biblical
novel. Anaheim, Calif., BCB
Publications [1960] 16 p.
016.22095 60-9759
Z5917.M6 E35 MRR Alc.

BIBLE--HISTORY OF CONTEMPORARY EVENTS,
ETC.
Finegan, Jack. Light from the
ancient past: [2d ed. Princeton,
N.J.] Princeton University Press,
1959. xxxvii, 638 p.   220.93 59-
11072
BS635 .F5 1959 MRR Alc.

BIBLE--INDEXES, TOPICAL.
Berrey, Lester V., ed. A treasury of
Biblical quotations. [1st ed.]
Garden City, N.Y., Doubleday, 1948.
viii, 240 p.   220.2   48-9181
BS432 .B4 MRR Alc.

Garland, George Frederick. Subject
guide to Bible stories. New York,
Greenwood Pub. Corp. [1969] x, 365
p. [12.00] 220.2 69-19012
BS432 .G258 1969 MRR Alc.

Hitchcock, Roswell Dwight.
Hitchcock's Topical Bible and
Cruden's Concordance. Grand Rapids,
Baker Book House, 1959 [c1952]
xxxvii, 685, 342 p.   220.2 56-12726

BS432 .H5 1959 MRR Alc.

Joy, Charles Rhind. Harper's topical
concordance. Rev. and enl. ed. New
York, Harper [1962] ix, 628 p.
220.2   62-11129
BS432 .J63 1962 MRR Alc.

The New World idea index to the Holy
Bible. New York, World Pub. [1972]
xxv, 907 p. [$14.95] 220.2 72-
77416
BS432 .N43 MRR Alc.

Stevenson, Burton Egbert, comp. The
home book of Bible quotations. New
York, Harper [1949] xxiv, 645 p.
220.2 49-11832
BS432 .S667 MRR Alc.

BIBLE--INTRODUCTIONS.
Parmelee, Alice. A guidebook to the
Bible. [1st ed.] New York, Harper
[1948] xi, 331 p.   220 48-9103
BS475 .P317 MRR Alc.

BIBLE--MUSIC.
Wellesz, Egon, ed. Ancient and
oriental music. London, New York,
Oxford University Press, 1957.
xxiii, 530 p.   781.8 780.93* 57-
4332
ML160 .N44 vol.1 MRR Alc.

BIBLE--NATURAL HISTORY.
Parmelee, Alice. All the birds of
the Bible. New York, Harper [1959]
279 p.   220.85982 59-14533
BS664 .P3 MRR Alc.

Walker, Winifred. All the plants of
the Bible. New York, Harper [1957]
244 p.   220.858 57-9886
BS665 .W3 MRR Alc.

BIBLE--PICTURES, ILLUSTRATIONS, ETC.
Reau, Louis. Iconographie de l'art
chretien. [1. ed.] Paris, Presses
universitaires de France, 1955-59. 3
v. in 6. a 56-1728
N7830 .R37 MRR Alc.

BIBLE--PUBLICATION AND DISTRIBUTION--
SOCIETIES, ETC.--DIRECTORIES.
Directory of Bible societies. 1965-
ed. London, United Bible Societies.
68-42087
BV2369 .D5 MRR Alc Latest edition

BIBLE--STUDY--BIBLIOGRAPHY.
Spurgeon, Charles Haddon. Commenting
and commentaries: Rev. ed. Grand
Rapids, Kregel Publications, 1954.
220 p.   016.2207 54-11448
BS482 .S6 1954 MRR Alc.

BIBLE--THEOLOGY.
Leon-Dufour, Xavier. Dictionary of
Biblical theology: London, Dublin
[etc.] G. Chapman, 1967. xxix, 618
p. [63/-] 220.3 68-83461
BS543.A1 L413 MRR Alc.

BIBLE--VERSIONS.
The Cambridge history of the Bible.
Cambridge, University Press, 1963-70.
[v. 1, 1970; v. 3, 1963] 3 v.
220/.09 63-24435
BS445 .C26 MRR Alc.

Kenyon, Frederic George, Sir, Our
Bible and the ancient manuscripts.
[5th ed., rev. and enl.] London,
Eyre & Spottiswoode, 1958. 352 p.
220.4 58-2327
BS445 .K46 1958 MRR Alc.

MacGregor, Geddes. The Bible in the
making. London, Murray [1961, c1959]
310 p.   220.5 61-3682
BS445 .M28 1961 MRR Alc.

Nida, Eugene Albert. The Book of a
thousand tongues. Rev. ed. [London]
United Bible Societies [1972] xviii,
536 p.   220.5 73-160367
P352.A2 N6 1972 MRR Alc.

Reumann, John Henry Paul. The
romance of Bible scripts and
scholars: Englewood Cliffs, N.J.,
Prentice-Hall [1965] viii, 248 p.
220.409 65-21174
BS445 .R4 MRR Alc.

BIBLE. GENESIS
see Bible. O.T. Genesis

BIBLE. ENGLISH--BIBLIOGRAPHY.
Norlie, Olaf Morgan. The Norlie
collection of English Bibles.
Northfield, Minn., Saint Olaf
college, 1944. 109 numb l.
016.22052 44-29016
Z7771.E5 N65 MRR Alc.

Pollard, Alfred William, ed. Records
of the English Bible. London, New
York [etc.] H. Frowde, 1911. xii,
387, [1] p.   11-13348
BS455 .P7 MRR Alc.

BIBLE. ENGLISH--GLOSSARIES,
VOCABULARIES, ETC.
Bridges, Ronald. The Bible word
book. New York, Nelson [1960] vii,
422 p.   220.52 60-6749
BS186 .B7 MRR Alc.

Elliott, Melvin E. The language of
the King James Bible: [1st ed.]
Garden City, N.Y., Doubleday, 1967.
x, 227 p.   220.52/03 67-11169
BS186 .E4 MRR Alc.

BIBLE. ENGLISH--HISTORY.
MacGregor, Geddes. A literary
history of the Bible: Nashville,
Abingdon Press [1968] 400 p.
220.5/09 68-11477
BS455 .M32 MRR Alc.

May, Herbert Gordon, Our English
Bible in the making; Rev. ed.
Philadelphia, Published for the
Cooperative Publication Association
by the Westminster Press [1965] 163
p.   220.52 65-4479
BS455 .M34 1965 MRR Alc.

Pollard, Alfred William, ed. Records
of the English Bible. London, New
York [etc.] H. Frowde, 1911. xii,
387, [1] p.   11-13348
BS455 .P7 MRR Alc.

Pope, Hugh, English versions of the
Bible. St. Louis, Herder, 1952. ix,
787 p.   220.52 52-10359
BS455 .P74 MRR Alc.

BIBLE. ENGLISH--VERSIONS.
Pope, Hugh, English versions of the
Bible. St. Louis, Herder, 1952. ix,
787 p.   220.52 52-10359
BS455 .P74 MRR Alc.

BIBLE. ENGLISH--VERSIONS--AUTHORIZED.
Bridges, Ronald. The Bible word
book. New York, Nelson [1960] vii,
422 p.   220.52 60-6749
BS186 .B7 MRR Alc.

Elliott, Melvin E. The language of
the King James Bible: [1st ed.]
Garden City, N.Y., Doubleday, 1967.
x, 227 p.   220.52/03 67-11169
BS186 .E4 MRR Alc.

BIBLE. ENGLISH--VERSIONS--REVISED
STANDARD.
Bridges, Ronald. The Bible word
book. New York, Nelson [1960] vii,
422 p.   220.52 60-6749
BS186 .B7 MRR Alc.

BIBLE. ENGLISH--VERSIONS, CATHOLIC.
Pope, Hugh. English versions of the
Bible. St. Louis, Herder, 1952. ix,
787 p.   220.52 52-10359
BS455 .P74 MRR Alc.

BIBLE. GREEK--TRANSLATIONS INTO ENGLISH.
Bible. O.T. English. 1960. Thomson.
The Septuagint Bible, 2d ed.
[Indian Hills, Colo.] Falcon's Wing
Press [c1960] xxvi, 1428 p.   221.48
59-14771
BS742.T42 1960 MRR Alc.

BIBLE IN LITERATURE--DICTIONARIES.
Fulghum, Walter B. A dictionary of
Biblical allusions in English
literature New York, Holt, Rinehart
and Winston [1965] viii, 291 p.
820.93 65-19349
PR145 .F8 MRR Alc.

BIBLE. MANUSCRIPTS.
Kenyon, Frederic George, Sir, Our
Bible and the ancient manuscripts.
[5th ed., rev. and enl.] London,
Eyre & Spottiswoode, 1958. 352 p.
220.4 58-2327
BS445 .K46 1958 MRR Alc.

MacGregor, Geddes. The Bible in the
making. London, Murray [1961, c1959]
310 p.   220.5 61-3682
BS445 .M28 1961 MRR Alc.

BIBLE. MANUSCRIPTS, LATIN. BIBLIA
LATINA. APRIL 4, 1452-JULY 9, 1453.
Miner, Dorothy Eugenia. The Giant
Bible of Mainz; [Philadelphia, 1952]
31 p.   220.47 52-60048
BS70.M3 M5 MRR Alc.

BIBLE. N.T.--BIBLIOGRAPHY.
Metzger, Bruce Manning. Index of
articles on the New Testament and the
early church published in
Festschriften. Philadelphia, Society
of Biblical Literature, 1951. xv,
182 p.   016.225 51-3190
Z7772.L1 M4 MRR Alc.

BIBLE. N.T.--BIOGRAPHY--DICTIONARIES.
Brownrigg, Ronald. Who's who in the
New Testament. [1st ed.] New York,
Holt, Rinehart and Winston [1971]
448 p. [$14.95] 225.92/2 B 75-
153654
BS2430 .B67 MRR Alc.

BIBLE. N.T.--COMMENTARIES.
Knox, Ronald Arbuthnott, A New
Testament commentary for English
readers. London, Burns, Oates and
Washbourne [1953-56] 3 v.   225.7
54-34236
BS2341 .K62 MRR Alc.

BIBLE. N.T.--CONCORDANCES, ENGLISH.
Bullinger, Ethelbert William, A
critical lexicon and concordance to
the English and Greek New Testament
[8th ed.] London, Lamp Press [1957]
999, xxxii p.   225.2 57-35622
BS2305 .B9 1957 MRR Alc.

BIBLE. N.T.--CONCORDANCES, ENGLISH--NEW
ENGLISH.
Elder, E. New English Bible, New
Testament: concordance. London,
Marshall, Morgan & Scott [1965,
c1964] 401 p.   65-4321
BS2305 .E4 1965 MRR Alc.

BIBLE. N.T.--CRITICISM, TEXTUAL.
Metzger, Bruce Manning. The text of
the New Testament: New York, Oxford
University Press, 1964. ix, 268 p.
225.4 64-2530
BS2325 .M4 MRR Alc.

BIBLE. N.T.--DICTIONARIES.
Guy, Harold A. Who's who in the
gospels London, Melbourne [etc.]
Macmillan; New York, St. Martin's P.,
1966. v, 152 p. [12/6 8/6 (school
ed.)]   225.3 66-15481
BS2312 .G8 1966 MRR Alc.

BIBLE. N.T.--HISTORY.
Metzger, Bruce Manning. The text of
the New Testament: New York, Oxford
University Press, 1964. ix, 268 p.
225.4 64-2530
BS2325 .K4 MRR Alc.

BIBLE. N.T.--HISTORY OF BIBLICAL EVENTS.
Kee, Howard Clark. Understanding the
New Testament 3d ed. Englewood
Cliffs, N.J., Prentice-Hall [1973]
xv, 446 p. [$9.95] 225.6/6 72-
13877
BS2407 .K37 1973 MRR Alc.

BIBLE. N.T.--HISTORY OF CONTEMPORARY
EVENTS, ETC.
Tenney, Merrill Chapin, New
Testament survey. [Rev. ed.] Grand
Rapids, Eerdmans [1961] 464 p.
225.6 61-10862
BS2330 .T4 1961 MRR Alc.

BIBLE. N.T.--INTRODUCTIONS.
Feine, Paul, Introduction to the New
Testament, 14th rev. ed. Nashville,
Abingdon Press [1966] 444 p. 225.6
66-11944
BS2330 .F413 MRR Alc.

Kee, Howard Clark. Understanding the
New Testament 3d ed. Englewood
Cliffs, N.J., Prentice-Hall [1973]
xv, 446 p. [$9.95] 225.6/6 72-
13877
BS2407 .K37 1973 MRR Alc.

Tenney, Merrill Chapin, New
Testament survey. [Rev. ed.] Grand
Rapids, Eerdmans [1961] 464 p.
225.6 61-10862
BS2330 .T4 1961 MRR Alc.

BIBLE. N.T.--STUDY.
Metzger, Bruce Manning. The New
Testament: New York, Abingdon Press
[1965] 288 p. 225 65-21981
   BS2535.2 .M4 MRR Alc.

BIBLE. N.T. 1 CORINTHIANS--COMMENTARIES.
Robertson, Archibald, bp. of Exeter,
A critical and exegetical commentary
on the First epistle of St. Paul to
the Corinthians, New York, C.
Scribner's sons, 1911. lxx, 424 p.
227.2 11-25460
   BS491 .I6 vol. 33 MRR Alc.

BIBLE. N.T. 2 CORINTHIANS--COMMENTARIES.
Plummer, Alfred, A critical and
exegetical commentary on the Second
epistle of St. Paul to the
Corinthians. New York, Scribner,
1915. lviii, 404 p. 227.3 16-915
   BS491 .I6 vol. 34 MRR Alc.

BIBLE. N.T. COLOSSIANS--COMMENTARIES.
Abbott, Thomas Kingsmill, A critical
and exegetical commentary on the
Epistles to the Ephesians and to the
Colossians, New York, C Scribner's
sons, 1909. lxv, 315 p. 20-5330
   BS491 .I6 vol. 36 MRR Alc.

BIBLE. N.T. ENGLISH--VERSIONS.
Bible. N.T. Greek. 1846? The English
hexapla, London, S. Bagster and sons
[1846?] 4 p. l., 168 (i.e. 120),
[1160] p. 225.48 32-79
   BS2025 1846 .E6 MRR Alc.

BIBLE. N.T. EPHESIANS--COMMENTARIES.
Abbott, Thomas Kingsmill, A critical
and exegetical commentary on the
Epistles to the Ephesians and to the
Colossians, New York, C Scribner's
sons, 1909. lxv, 315 p. 20-5330
   BS491 .I6 vol. 36 MRR Alc.

BIBLE. N.T. EPISTLES OF JOHN--
COMMENTARIES.
Brooke, Alan England, A critical and
exegetical commentary on the
Johannine epistles, New York, C.
Scribner's sons, 1912. vii-ix, xc,
242 p. 227.94 13-170
   BS491 .I6 vol. 43 MRR Alc.

BIBLE. N.T. GALATIANS--COMMENTARIES.
Burton, Ernest De Witt, A critical
and exegetical commentary on the
Epistle to the Galatians, New York,
C. Scribner's sons, 1920. lxxxix,
541 p. 227.4 20-21079
   BS491 .I6 vol. 35 MRR Alc.

BIBLE. N.T. HEBREWS--COMMENTARIES.
Moffatt, James, A critical and
exegetical commentary on the Epistle
to the Hebrews, Edinburgh, T. & T.
Clark, 1924. lxxvi, 264 p. 227.87
24-21703
   BS491 .I6 vol. 40 MRR Alc.

BIBLE. N.T. JAMES--COMMENTARIES.
Ropes, James Hardy, A critical and
exegetical commentary on the Epistle
of St. James, New York, C.
Scribner's sons, 1916. xiii, 319 p.
16-6543
   BS491 .I6 vol. 41 MRR Alc.

BIBLE. N.T. JOHN--COMMENTARIES.
Bernard, John Henry, abp. of Dublin,
A critical and exegetical commentary
on the Gospel according to St. John,
New York, C. Scribner's sons, 1929.
2 v. 226.5 29-17737
   BS491 .I6 vol. 29 MRR Alc.

BIBLE. N.T. JUDE--COMMENTARIES.
Bigg, Charles, A critical and
exegetical commentary on the Epistles
of St. Peter and St. Jude, New York,
C. Scribner's sons, 1901. 5 p. l., v-
xi, 353 p. 02-12311
   BS491 .I6 vol. 42 MRR Alc.

BIBLE. N.T. LUKE--COMMENTARIES.
Plummer, Alfred, A critical and
exegetical commentary on the Gospel
according to St. Luke, 5th ed. New
York, C. Scribner's sons, 1902. 5 p.
l., iii-lxxxviii, 590 p. 03-14726
   BS491 .I6 vol. 28 MRR Alc.

BIBLE. N.T. MARK--COMMENTARIES.
Gould, Ezra Palmer, A critical and
exegetical commentary on the Gospel
according to St. Mark, New York, C.
Scribner's sons, 1896. 5 p. l., v-
lvii, 317 p. 226.3 25-19356
   BS491 .I6 vol. 27 MRR Alc.

BIBLE. N.T. MATTHEW--COMMENTARIES.
Allen, Willoughby Charles, A
critical and exegetical commentary on
the gospel according to S. Matthew,
New York, C. Scribner's sons, 1907.
2 p. l., [iii]-iv, xcvi, 338 p.
226.2 07-25562
   BS491 .I6 vol. 26 MRR Alc.

BIBLE. N.T. PASTORAL EPISTLES--
COMMENTARIES.
Lock, Walter, A critical and
exegetical commentary on the Pastoral
epistles (I & II Timothy and Titus)
Edinburgh, T. & T. Clark, 1924. 3 p.
l., iii-xliv, 163 p. 227.83 24-
21704
   BS491 .I6 vol. 39 MRR Alc.

BIBLE. N.T. PETER--COMMENTARIES.
Bigg, Charles, A critical and
exegetical commentary on the Epistles
of St. Peter and St. Jude, New York,
C. Scribner's sons, 1901. 5 p. l., v-
xi, 353 p. 02-12311
   BS491 .I6 vol. 42 MRR Alc.

BIBLE. N.T. PHILEMON--COMMENTARIES.
Vincent, Marvin Richardson, A
critical and exegetical commentary on
the Epistles to the Philippians and
to Philemon, New York, C. Scribner's
sons, 1897. 4 p. l., v-xlv, 201 p.
227.6 04-1629
   BS491 .I6 vol. 37 MRR Alc.

BIBLE. N.T. PHILIPPIANS--COMMENTARIES.
Vincent, Marvin Richardson, A
critical and exegetical commentary on
the Epistles to the Philippians and
to Philemon, New York, C. Scribner's
sons, 1897. 4 p. l., v-xlv, 201 p.
227.6 04-1629
   BS491 .I6 vol. 37 MRR Alc.

BIBLE. N.T. REVELATION--COMMENTARIES.
Charles, Robert Henry, A critical
and exegetical commentary on the
Revelation of St. John, Edinburgh,
T. & T. Clark, 1920. 2 v. 21-5413
   BS491 .I6 vol. 44 MRR Alc.

BIBLE. N.T. ROMANS--COMMENTARIES.
Sanday, William, A critical and
exegetical commentary on the Epistle
to the Romans, 3d ed. New York, C.
Scribner's sons, 1897. 6 p. l., [v]-
cxii, 450 p. 227.1 25-13283
   BS491 .I6 vol. 32 MRR Alc.

BIBLE. N.T. THESSALONIANS--COMMENTARIES.
Frame, James Everett, A critical and
exegetical commentary on the Epistles
of St. Paul to the Thessalonians,
New York, C. Scribner's sons, 1912.
6 p. l., v-ix, 326 p. 227.81 12-
23430
   BS491 .I6 vol. 38 MRR Alc.

BIBLE. O.T.--ANTIQUITIES.
Heaton, Eric William. Everyday life
in Old Testament times: London, B.
T. Batsford [1956] 240 p. 221.93
56-3153
   BS620 .H4 1956 MRR Alc.

Unger, Merrill Frederick, Archeology
and the Old Testament. Grand Rapids,
Zondervan Pub. House [1954] 339 p.
221.93 55-136
   BS1180 .U6 MRR Alc.

BIBLE. O.T.--BIOGRAPHY--DICTIONARIES.
Comay, Joan. Who's who in the Old
Testament, [1st ed.] New York,
Holt, Rinehart and Winston [1971]
448 p. [$14.95] 221.92/2 B 79-
153655
   BS570 .C64 MRR Alc.

BIBLE. O.T.--CONCORDANCES, GREEK.
Hatch, Edwin, A concordance to the
Septuagint and the other Greek
versions of the Old Testament
(including the Apocryphal books)
Graz, Akademische Druck- u.
Verlagsanstalt, 1954. 2 v. (vi,
1504, 272 p.) 221.48 56-966
   BS1122 .H3 1954 MRR Alc.

BIBLE. O.T.--EVIDENCES, AUTHORITY, ETC.
Unger, Merrill Frederick, Archeology
and the Old Testament. Grand Rapids,
Zondervan Pub. House [1954] 339 p.
221.93 55-136
   BS1180 .U6 MRR Alc.

BIBLE. O.T.--HISTORY OF CONTEMPORARY
EVENTS, ETC.
Pritchard, James Bennett, ed.
Ancient Near Eastern texts relating
to the Old Testament. 2d ed., corr.
and enl. Princeton, Princeton
University Press, 1955. xxi, 544 p.
221.93 55-9033
   BS1180 .P83 1955 MRR Alc.

Unger, Merrill Frederick, Archeology
and the Old Testament. Grand Rapids,
Zondervan Pub. House [1954] 339 p.
221.93 55-136
   BS1180 .U6 MRR Alc.

BIBLE. O.T.--INTRODUCTIONS.
Eissfeldt, Otto, The Old Testament;
New York, Harper and Row [1965]
xxiv, 861 p. 221 65-15399
   BS1140 .E583 MRR Alc.

BIBLE. O.T.--STUDY--BIBLIOGRAPHY.
Rounds, Dorothy. Articles on
antiquity in Festschriften, an index:
Cambridge, Harvard University Press,
1962. 560 p. 62-7193
   Z6202 .R6 MRR Alc.

Society for Old Testament Study. A
decade of Bible bibliography;
Oxford, Blackwell, 1967. ix, 706 p.
[84/-] 016.221 68-103190
   Z7772.A1 S66 MRR Alc.

BIBLE. O.T.--THEOLOGY.
Jacob, Edmond. Theology of the Old
Testament. London, Hodder &
Stoughton [1958] 368 p. 221.6 58-
31962
   BS1192.5 .J313 1958 MRR Alc.

BIBLE. O.T. AMOS--COMMENTARIES.
Harper, William Rainey, A critical
and exegetical commentary on Amos and
Hosea, New York, C. Scribner's sons,
1905. 4 p. l., vii-clxxxi, 424 p.
05-7893
   BS491 .I6 vol. 23 MRR Alc.

BIBLE. O.T. APOCRYPHA--INTRODUCTIONS.
Eissfeldt, Otto, The Old Testament;
New York, Harper and Row [1965]
xxiv, 861 p. 221 65-15399
   BS1140 .E583 MRR Alc.

BIBLE. O.T. CHRONICLES--COMMENTARIES.
Curtis, Edward Lewis, A critical and
exegetical commentary on the books of
Chronicles, New York, C. Scribner's
sons, 1910. 5 p. l., vii-xxii, 534
p. 10-14958
   BS491 .I6 vol. 11 MRR Alc.

BIBLE. O.T. DANIEL--COMMENTARIES.
Montgomery, James Alan, A critical
and exegetical commentary on the book
of Daniel, New York, C. Scribner's
sons, 1927. xxxi, 488 p. 224.5 27-
14220
   BS491 .I6 vol. 22 MRR Alc.

BIBLE. O.T. DEUTERONOMY--COMMENTARIES.
Driver, Samuel Rolles, A critical
and exegetical commentary on
Deuteronomy. 3d ed. Edinburgh, T. &
T. Clark, 1902. 3 p. l., xi-xxviii,
xcv, 434 p. 222.15 02-25296
   BS491 .I6 vol. 5 MRR Alc.

BIBLE. O.T. ECCLESIASTES--COMMENTARIES.
Barton, George Aaron, A critical and
exegetical commentary on the book of
Ecclesiastes, New York, C.
Scribner's sons, 1908. 6 p. l., v-
xiv, 212 p. 223.8 08-15777
   BS491 .I6 vol. 17 MRR Alc.

BIBLE. O.T. ESTHER--COMMENTARIES.
Paton, Lewis Bayles, A critical and
exegetical commentary on the book of
Esther. New York, Scribner, 1908.
xvii, 339 p. 222.9 08-30156
   BS491 .I6 vol. 13 MRR Alc.

BIBLE. O.T. EZEKIEL--COMMENTARIES.
Cooke, George Albert, A critical and
exegetical commentary on the book of
Ezekiel, Edinburgh, T. & T. Clark,
1936. xlvii, 558 p. 224.4 38-
12281
   BS491 .I6 vol. 21 MRR Alc.

BIBLE. O.T. EZRA--COMMENTARIES.
Batten, Loring Woart, A critical and
exegetical commentary on the books of
Ezra and Nehemiah, New York, C.
Scribner's sons, 1913. 4 p. l., vii-
xv, 384 p. 222.7 13-21321
   BS491 .I6 vol. 12 MRR Alc.

BIBLE. O.T. GENESIS--COMMENTARIES.
Skinner, John, A critical and
exegetical commentary on Genesis.
New York, Scribner, 1910. xx, lxvii,
551 p. 10-20167
   BS491 .I6 vol. 1 MRR Alc.

BIBLE. O.T. GREEK--VERSIONS--SEPTUAGINT.
Bible. O.T. English. 1960. Thomson.
The Septuagint Bible, 2d ed.
[Indian Hills, Colo.] Falcon's Wing
Press [c1960] xxvi, 1428 p. 221.48
59-14771
   BS742.T42 1960 MRR Alc.

Hatch, Edwin, A concordance to the
Septuagint and the other Greek
versions of the Old Testament
(including the Apocryphal books)
Graz, Akademische Druck- u.
Verlagsanstalt, 1954. 2 v. (vi,
1504, 272 p.) 221.48 56-966
   BS1122 .H3 1954 MRR Alc.

BIBLE. O.T. HOSEA--COMMENTARIES.
Harper, William Rainey, A critical
and exegetical commentary on Amos and
Hosea, New York, C. Scribner's sons,
1905. 4 p. l., vii-clxxxi, 424 p.
05-7893
   BS491 .I6 vol. 23 MRR Alc.

BIBLE. O.T. ISAIAH--COMMENTARIES.
Gray, George Buchanan. A critical
and exegetical commentary on the book
of Isaiah, I-XXXIX, New York, C.
Scribner's sons, 1912. 6 p. l., v-ci
p., 1 l., 472 p. 12-16941
   BS491 .I6 vol. 18 MRR Alc.

BIBLE. O.T. JOB--COMMENTARIES.
Driver, Samuel Rolles, A critical
and exegetical commentary on the book
of Job, Edinburgh, T. & T. Clark,
1921. lxxix, 376, 360 p.   21-15647

BS491 .I6 vol. 14 MRR Alc.

BIBLE. O.T. JUDGES--COMMENTARIES.
Moore, George Foot, A critical and
exegetical commentary on Judges, New
York, C. Scribner's sons, 1895. 5 p.
l., v-L, 476 p.   222.3 25-19368
BS491 .I6 vol. 7 MRR Alc.

BIBLE. O.T. KINGS--COMMENTARIES.
Montgomery, James Alan, A critical
and exegetical commentary on the
Books of Kings, New York, Scribner,
1951. xlvi, 575 p.   222.5 52-8522

BS491 .I6 vol. 10 MRR Alc.

BIBLE. O.T. MINOR PROPHETS--
COMMENTARIES.
Mitchell, Hinckley Gilbert Thomas, A
critical and exegetical commentary on
Haggai, Zechariah, Malachi and Jonah,
New York, C. Scribner's sons, 1912.
7 p. l., vii-xxvi, 362, 88, 65 p.
[$3.00]   224.9 12-22008
BS491 .I6 vol. 25 MRR Alc.

Smith, John Merlin Powis, A critical
and exegetical commentary on Micah,
Zephaniah, Nahum, Habakkuk, Obadiah
and Joel, New York, C. Scribner's
sons, 1911. 5 p. l., iii-xix, 363,
28, 146 p.   224.9 11-31171
BS491 .I6 vol. 24 MRR Alc.

BIBLE. O.T. NEHEMIAH--COMMENTARIES.
Batten, Loring Woart, A critical and
exegetical commentary on the books of
Ezra and Nehemiah, New York, C.
Scribner's sons, 1913. 4 p. l., vii-
xv, 384 p.   222.7 13-21321
BS491 .I6 vol. 12 MRR Alc.

BIBLE. O.T. NUMBERS--COMMENTARIES.
Gray, George Buchanan, A critical
and exegetical commentary on Numbers,
Edinburgh, T. & T. Clark, 1903.
lii, 489 p.   222.14 03-31887
BS491 .I6 vol. 4 MRR Alc.

BIBLE. O.T. POETICAL BOOKS--CRITICISM,
INTERPRETATION, ETC.
Yoder, Sanford Calvin, Bp., Poetry
of the Old Testament, Scottdale,
Pa., Herald Press, 1948. xix, 426 p.
223   48-9854
BS1405 .Y6 MRR Alc.

BIBLE. O.T. PROVERBS--COMMENTARIES.
Toy, Crawford Howell, A critical and
exegetical commentary on the book of
Proverbs, New York, C. Scribner's
sons, 1899. 5 p. l., v-xxxvi, 554 p.
223.7 99-5903
BS491 .I6 vol. 16 MRR Alc.

BIBLE. O.T. PSALMS--COMMENTARIES.
Briggs, Charles Augustus, A critical
and exegetical commentary on the book
of Psalms, New York, C. Scribner's
sons, 1906-07. 2 v.   06-26084
BS491 .I6 vol. 15 MRR Alc.

BIBLE. O.T. SAMUEL--COMMENTARIES.
Smith, Henry Preserved, A critical
and exegetical commentary on the
books of Samuel. New York, C.
Scribner's sons, 1899. 6 p. l., vii-
xxxix, 421 p.   99-1608
BS491 .I6 vol. 9 MRR Alc.

BIBLIOGRAPHICAL CENTERS.
Berlin. Stadtbibliothek. Führer
durch die Bibliotheken und
Literaturstellen der Hauptstadt
Berlin. Leipzig, Verlag für Buch-
und Bibliothekswesen] 1963. 254 p.
63-41869
Z802 .B44B4 MRR Alc.

Horecky, Paul Louis, Libraries and
bibliographic centers in the Soviet
Union. [Bloomington, Indiana
University, 1959] xviii, 287 p.
027.047 59-63389
Z819 .H6 MRR Alc.

BIBLIOGRAPHICAL CENTERS--DIRECTORIES.
Brummel, Leendert, Guide des
catalogues collectifs et du prêt
international La Haye, M. Nijhoff,
1961. 89 p.   64-43892
Z685.83 .B68 MRR Ref Desk.

United Nations Educational,
Scientific and Cultural Organization.
Guide to national bibliographical
information centres. 3d rev. ed.
[Paris, 1970] 195 p.   [18F ($4.50
US)]   021.6/4 74-583949
Z674.5.A2 U52 1970 MRR Ref Desk.

BIBLIOGRAPHICAL EXHIBITIONS.
United States. Library of Congress.
Author, artist, and publisher: the
creation of notable books. [New
Haven] Printed for the American Book
Publishers Council at the Printing-
Office of the Yale University Press
[1965] 1 v. (unpaged)   65-60051
Z663 .A88 MRR Alc.

BIBLIOGRAPHICAL SERVICES.
Bibliographical services throughout
the world. 1st/2d-   1951/53-
Paris, UNESCO. 010 55-4898
Z1008 .U54 MRR Alc Partial set /
MRR Ref Desk Latest edition

BIBLIOGRAPHICAL SERVICES--DIRECTORIES.
Schneider, John Hoke, Survey of
commercially available computer-
readable bibliographic data bases.
[Washington] American Society for
Information Science [1973] 181 p.
029.7/53/02573 72-97793
Z699.22 .S35 MRR Alc.

BIBLIOGRAPHICAL SERVICES--WASHINGTON,
D.C.
United States. Library of Congress.
Technical Information Division.
Bibliographic services related to
Government sponsored research in the
Library of Congress. Washington,
1955. iv, 16 p.   010 55-60034
Z663.49 .B5 MRR Alc.

BIBLIOGRAPHICAL SOCIETY, LONDON--
BIBLIOGRAPHY.
Cole, George Watson, An index to
bibliographical papers published by
the Bibliographical society and the
Library association, London, 1877-
1932, Chicago, Ill., Pub. for the
Bibliographical society of America at
the University of Chicago press
[1933] ix, 262 p.   016.01 33-33065

Z1008 .B585 MRR Alc.

BIBLIOGRAPHY.
see also American literature

see also Books

see also Indexes

see also Indexing

see also Printing

Collier's encyclopedia, [New York]
Macmillan Educational Corp. [1974]
24 v.   031 73-13422
AE5 .C683 1974 MRR Alc.

Collison, Robert Lewis. Book
collecting; Fair Lawn, N.J.,
Essential Books, 1957. 244 p.   010
57-13673
Z987 .C6 MRR Alc.

Esdaile, Arundell James Kennedy,
Esdaile's manual of bibliography.
4th revised ed., London, Allen &
Unwin, 1967 [i.e. 1968] 336 p.   [50/-
]   010 68-114662
Z1001 .E75 1968 MRR Alc.

Malclès, Louise Noëlle. Les
sources du travail bibliographique.
Genève, E. Droz, 1950-58. 3 v. in
4.   016.01 51-17035
Z1002 .M4 MRR Ref Desk.

Mumey, Nolie, A study of rare books,
Denver, The Clason publishing
company, 1930. xvii p., 2 l., 3-572
p.   090 30-25438
Z1012 .M95 MRR Alc.

Schneider, Georg, Handbuch der
bibliographie, 4., ganzlich
veranderte und stark verm. aufl.
Leipzig, K. W. Hiersemann, 1930. ix,
674 p., 1 l.   010.2 31-10631
Z1001 .S35 1930 MRR Alc.

Van Hoesen, Henry Bartlett,
Bibliography, practical, enumerative,
historical; New York, London, C.
Scribner's sons, 1928. xiii p., 1
l., 519 p.   28-17678
Z1002 .V25 MRR Alc.

BIBLIOGRAPHY--BEST BOOKS.
American Library Association.
Children's Services Division. Book
Reevaluation Committee. Notable
children's books, 1940-1959.
Chicago, American Library
Association, 1966. vi, 39 p.
028.52 66-24177
Z1037 .A4885 MRR Alc.

Bertalan, Frank J. The junior
college library collection. 1970 ed.
Newark, N.J., Bro-Dart Foundation,
1970. xiv, 503, [129] p.   011 76-
122455
Z1035 .B443 1970 MRR Alc.

Books for college libraries;
Chicago, American Library
Association, 1967. ix, 1056 p.
016.028 66-30781
Z1035 .B72 MRR Alc.

British Museum. Dept. of Printed
Books. Subject index of the modern
works added to the British museum
library. [list]- 1901/05- London,
Trustees of the British Museum.
019.1 07-10319
Z1035 .B8613   MRR Alc (Dk33) Full
set

Eakin, Mary K. Good books for
children; 3d ed. Chicago,
University of Chicago Press [1966]
xv, 407 p.   028.52 66-23687
Z1035 .E15 1966 MRR Alc.

Enciclopedia de orientación
bibliográfica. Barcelona, J. Flors,
1964-65. 4 v.   65-53526
Z1035 .E5 MRR Alc.

Everyman's library. The reader's
Guide to Everyman's Library, Further
revised [ed.], London, Dent, 1971.
ix, 468 p. [£0.40] 015/.42 79-
595791
Z1035 .E91 1971 MRR Alc.

Good reading. 1933- New York [etc.]
New American Library [etc.] 016.028
33-10540
Z1035 .G6 MRR Alc Latest edition

Haines, Helen Elizabeth, Living with
books; 2d ed. New York, Columbia
University Press, 1950. xxiii, 610
p.   028 50-6478
Z1003 .H15 1950 MRR Alc.

Meyers Bücherlexikon: Mannheim,
Bibliographisches Institut [c1963]
ix, 785 p.   64-3402
Z1035.3 .M4 MRR Alc.

National Association of Independent
Schools. Library Committee. Books
for secondary school libraries. 4th
ed. New York, R. R. Bowker Co.,
1971. viii, 308 p.   028.52 71-
27321
Z1035 .N2 1971 MRR Alc.

Peddie, Robert Alexander, Subject
index of books published up to and
including 1880; London, Grafton &
co., 1935. xv, [1], 857, [1] p.   36-
890
Z1035 .P37 2d ser. MRR Alc.

Peddie, Robert Alexander, Subject
index of books published up to and
including 1880. London, Grafton,
1948. vii, 872 p.   016 a 48-8762
Z1035 .P38 MRR Alc.

Peddie, Robert Alexander, Subject
index of books published up to and
including 1880, A-Z, London, H.
Pordes, 1962. xv, 745 p.   64-46978

Z1035 .P37 1962 MRR Alc.

Pirie, James W., Books for Junior
college libraries; Chicago, American
Library Association, 1969. x, 452 p.
[35.00]   011 76-82133
Z1035 .P448 MRR Alc.

Public library catalog. 6th ed.,
1973. New York, H. W. Wilson Co.,
1974. x, 1543 p.   011 74-656
Z1035 .S83 1974 MRR Alc.

The Reader's adviser. [1st]- 1921-
New York, R. R. Bowker Co.   57-13277

Z1035 .B7 MRR Ref Desk Latest
edition / MRR Alc Latest edition

Senior high school library catalog.
10th ed. New York, H. W. Wilson Co.,
1972. xii, 1214 p.   028.52 72-3819

Z1035 .S42 1972 MRR Alc.

Spain. Junta de Intercambio y
Adquisición de Libros para
Bibliotecas Públicas. Catálogo
abreviado de una selección de libros
de consulta, referencia estudio y
ensenanza, Madrid, 1953. xxiii,
925 p.   66-33212
Z1035.7 .S68 MRR Alc.

Wheeler, Helen Rippier. A basic book
collection for the community college
library, [Hamden, Conn.] Shoe String
Press, 1968. x, 317 p.   011 67-
24193
Z1035 .W47 MRR Alc.

Wilson, H. W., firm, publishers.
Junior high school library catalog.
2d ed. New York, 1970. xii, 808 p.
[30.00] 028.52 75-126356
Z1037 .W765 1970 MRR Alc.

BIBLIOGRAPHY--BEST BOOKS--AMERICAN
LITERATURE.
The White House library; a short-
title list. Washington, White House
Historical Association, 1967. 219 p.
018/.2 67-5746
Z988 .W45 MRR Alc.

BIBLIOGRAPHY--BEST BOOKS--BUSINESS.
Johnson, Herbert Webster, How to use
the business library, 3d ed.
Cincinnati, South-western Pub. Co.
[c1964] v, 160 p.   016.65 63-21248

Z675.B8 J6 1964 MRR Alc.

BIBLIOGRAPHY--BEST BOOKS--CHEMISTRY.
Crane, Evan Jay, A guide to the
literature of chemistry 2d ed. New
York, Wiley [1957] 397 p. 016.54
57-8881
Z5521 .C89 1957 MRR Alc.

Mellon, Melvin Guy, Chemical
publications, 4th ed. New York,
McGraw-Hill [1965] xi, 324 p.
016.54 64-8418
Z5521 .M52 1965 MRR Alc.

**BIBLIOGRAPHY--BEST BOOKS--EARLY WORKS
TO 1800.**
Rosenwald, Lessing Julius, The 19th
book: Tesoro de poveri. [Washington]
Published for the Library of
Congress, 1961. 123 p. 62-60686
Z663.4 .N5 MRR Alc.

BIBLIOGRAPHY--BEST BOOKS--ECONOMICS.
Coman, Edwin Truman, Sources of
business information, Rev. ed.
Berkeley, University of California
Press, 1964. xii, 330 p. 016.65
64-18639
Z7164.C81 C75 1964 MRR Alc.

BIBLIOGRAPHY--BEST BOOKS--FICTION.
Wilson, H. W., firm, publishers.
Fiction catalog. 1908- New York
[etc.] 016.823 09-35044
Z5916 .W74 MRR Alc Latest edition

BIBLIOGRAPHY--BEST BOOKS--HISTORY.
American Historical Association.
Guide to historical literature. New
York, Macmillan, 1961. xxxv, 962 p.
016.9 61-7602
Z6201 .A55 MRR Alc.

**BIBLIOGRAPHY--BEST BOOKS--INDUSTRIAL
MANAGEMENT.**
Coman, Edwin Truman, Sources of
business information, Rev. ed.
Berkeley, University of California
Press, 1964. xii, 330 p. 016.65
64-18639
Z7164.C81 C75 1964 MRR Alc.

BIBLIOGRAPHY--BIBLIOGRAPHY.
American library association. Junior
members round table. Library
literature, 1921-1932; Chicago,
American library association, 1934.
x, [2], 450 p. 016.02 34-5185
Z666 .C21 1927 Suppl. MRR Alc.

Arnim, Max, Internationale
Personalbibliographie, 1800-1943.
2., verb. und stark verm. Aufl.
Leipzig, K. W. Hiersemann, 1944-52.
2 v. 016.012 45-22033
Z8001.A1 A72 MRR Biog.

Berkowitz, David Sandler,
Bibliographies for historical
researchers. Trial ed. Waltham,
Mass., 1969. 421 l. 016.016/9 76-
9931
Z6201 .B43 1969 MRR Alc.

Besterman, Theodore. A world
bibliography of bibliographies and of
bibliographical catalogues,
calendars, abstracts, digests,
indexes, and the like. 4th ed. rev.
and greatly enl. throughout.
Lausanne, Societas bibliographica
[1965-66] 5 v. (8425 columns)
016.01 71-7401
Z1002 .B5685 MRR Ref Desk.

Besterman, Theodore. Early printed
books to the end of the sixteenth
century; 2d ed., rev. and much enl.
Geneve, Societas Bibliographica,
1961. 344 p. 016.016093 62-2500
Z1002 .B562 1961 MRR Alc.

Bohatta, Hanns. Internationale
Bibliographie der Bibliographien;
Frankfurt am Main, V. Klostermann
[1950] 652 p. a 52-568
Z1002 .B682 MRR Alc.

Bond, Donald Frederic, A reference
guide to English studies. 2d ed.
Chicago, University of Chicago Press
[1971] x, 198 p. 016.0168 79-
130307
Z1002 .B72 1971 MRR Alc.

Brockett, Oscar Gross, A
bibliographical guide to research in
speech and dramatic art Chicago,
Scott, Foresman [1963] 118 p. 016
63-14554
Z1002 .B87 MRR Alc.

Cannons, Harry George Turner.
Bibliography of library economy;
Chicago, American library
association, 1927. 4 p. l., 11-680
p. 26-26801
Z666 .C21 1927 MRR Alc.

Caron, Pierre, ed. World list of
historical periodicals and
bibliographies. Oxford [Eng.]
International committee of historical
sciences, 1939 [i.e. 1940] xiv, [2],
391, [1] p. 016.905 41-4203
Z6201.A1 C3 MRR Alc.

Cole, George Watson, An index to
bibliographical papers published by
the Bibliographical society and the
Library association, London, 1877-
1932, Chicago, Ill., Pub. for the
Bibliographical society of America at
the University of Chicago press
[1933] ix, 262 p. 016.01 33-33065

Z1008 .B585 MRR Alc.

Courtney, William Prideaux, A
register of national bibliography,
New York, B. Franklin [1967] 3 v. in
2. 015 68-4438
Z1002 .C86 MRR Alc.

Downs, Robert Bingham, American
library resources; Chicago, American
Library Association, 1951. 428 p.
016.016 51-11156
Z1002 .D6 MRR Alc.

Downs, Robert Bingham, British
library resources; Chicago, American
Library Association, 1973 [i.e. 1974]
xvi, 332 p. 016.016 73-1598
Z1002 .D63 MRR Alc.

Five years' work in librarianship.
1951/55- London, Library
Association. 016.02 58-2169
Z666 .F5 MRR Alc Full set

France. Direction des bibliotheques
de France. Les bibliographies
internationales specialisees
courantes francaises ou a
participation francaise. Paris,
1958. 95 p. 60-21619
Z1002 .F75 MRR Alc.

Howard-Hill, Trevor Howard.
Bibliography of British literary
bibliographies Oxford, Clarendon P.,
1969. xxv, 570 p. [7/7/-]
016.01682 70-390421
Z2011 .H6 MRR Alc.

Index bibliographiens. [1st]- ed.;
1925- Le Haye Federation
Internationale de Documentation.
016.01 25-8351
Z1002 .I38 MRR Alc Latest edition

Istituto nazionale per le relazioni
culturali con l'estero. La
bibliografia italiana, 2. ed
interamente rifatta. Roma, 1946.
xxiv, 570 p. 016.01 48-15681
Z2341.A1 I8 1946 MRR Alc.

Library literature: 1933/35- New
York, H. W. Wilson Co. 016.02 36-
27468
Z666 .C211 MkR Alc Full set

Malcles, Louise Noëlle. Manuel de
bibliographie. [1. ed.] Paris,
Presses universitaires de France,
1963. viii, 328 p. 016.016 65-355

Z1002 .M28 MRR Alc.

Malcles, Louise Noëlle. Les
sources du travail bibliographique.
Geneve, E. Droz, 1950-58. 3 v. in
4. 016.01 51-17035
Z1002 .M4 MRR Ref Desk.

Perkins, Flossie L. Book and non-
book media; Urbana, Ill., National
Council of Teachers of English [1972]
ix, 298 p. 016.028 72-186931
Z1035.A1 P36 1972 MRR Alc.

Pinto, Olga, Le bibliografie
nazionali. 2. ed. riv., corr. ed
aggiornata. Firenze; L. S. Olschki,
1951. 94 p. 016.01 52-18924
Z1002.A2 P6 1951 MRR Alc.

Schneider, Georg, Handbuch der
bibliographie, 4., ganzlich
veranderte und stark verm. aufl.
Leipzig, K. W. Hiersemann, 1930. ix,
674 p., 1 l. 010.2 31-10631
Z1001 .S35 1930 MRR Alc.

Spargo, John Webster, A
bibliographical manual for students
of the language and literature of
England and the United States; 3d
ed. New York, Hendricks House, 1956.
x, 285 p. 016.82 56-14402
Z2011 .S73 1956 MRR Alc.

Taylor, Archer, Book catalogues:
their varieties and uses. Chicago,
Newberry Library, 1957. xii, 284 p.
010 56-12568
Z1001 .T34 MRR Alc.

Totok, Wilhelm. Handbuch der
bibliographischen Nachschlagewerke.
4., erw., vollig neu bearb. Aufl.
Frankfurt am Main, V. Klostermann
[c1972] xxxiv, 367 p. 72-371275
Z1002 .T68 1972 MRR Alc.

United States. Library of Congress.
General Reference and Bibliography
Division. Current national
bibliographies, Washington, 1955.
v, 132 p. 016.01 55-60025
Z663.28 .C8 MRR Alc.

United States. Library of Congress.
General Reference and Bibliography
Division. Current national
bibliographies. New York, Greenwood
Press [1968] iv, 132 p. 016.015
68-55128
Z1002 .U583 1968 MRR Ref Desk.

United States. Library of Congress.
General Reference and Bibliography
Division. A guide to bibliographic
tools for research in foreign
affairs, 2d ed. with suppl.
Washington, 1958. 145, 15 p.
016.341 58-60091
Z663.28 .G78 1958 MRR Alc.

United States. Library of Congress.
General Reference and Bibliography
Division. Guide to Soviet
bibliographies; Washington, 1950.
v, 158 p. 016.01547 50-62955
Z663.28 .G8 MRR Alc.

Van Hoesen, Henry Bartlett,
Bibliography, practical, enumerative,
historical; New York, London, C.
Scribner's sons, 1928. xiii p., 1
l., 519 p. 28-17678
Z1002 .V25 MRR Alc.

Virginia. University. Bibliographical
Society. Selective check lists of
bibliographical scholarship, 1949-
1955. Charlottesville, 1957 [c1958]
viii, 192 p. 016.01 58-10164
Z1002 .V59 MRR Alc.

White, Alex Sandri. Fact-finding
made easy; New, updated ed.
Allenhurst, N.J., Aurea Publications
[1967] 129 l. 016.016 67-3292
Z1002 .W45 1967 MRR Alc.

Williams, Cecil Brown, A research
manual for college studies and
papers. 3d ed. New York, Harper &
Row [1963] 212 p. 808.06 63-14052

LB2369 .W5 1963 MRR Alc.

BIBLIOGRAPHY--BIBLIOGRAPHY--AERONAUTICS.
Dickson, Katherine Murphy. History
of aeronautics and astronautics;
Washington, National Aeronautics and
Space Administration, 1967. vi, 117
l. 016.01662913 67-61736
Z5063.A1 D5 MRR Alc.

**BIBLIOGRAPHY--BIBLIOGRAPHY--AMERICAN
LITERATURE.**
Kennedy, Arthur Garfield, A concise
bibliography for students of English.
5th ed. Stanford, Calif., Stanford
University Press, 1972. xvi, 300 p.
016.82 77-183889
Z2011 .K35 1972 MRR Alc.

Nilon, Charles H. Bibliography of
bibliographies in American
literature, New York, R. R. Bowker
Co., 1970. xi, 483 p. 016.01681
73-103542
Z1225 .A1N5 MRR Ref Desk.

Van Patten, Nathan, An index to
bibliographies and bibliographical
contributions relating to the work of
American and British authors, 1923-
1932. Stanford University, Calif.,
Stanford university press; London, H.
Milford, Oxford university press,
1934. vii, 324 p. 016.82 34-5449

Z1225.A1 V2 MRR Alc.

BIBLIOGRAPHY--BIBLIOGRAPHY--ARCHEOLOGY.
Borroni, Fabia. "Il Cicognara,"
Firenze, Sansoni, 1954- v. 55-
18980
Z2357 .B6 MRR Alc.

BIBLIOGRAPHY--BIBLIOGRAPHY--ART.
Borroni, Fabia. "Il Cicognara,"
Firenze, Sansoni, 1954- v. 55-
18980
Z2357 .B6 MRR Alc.

**BIBLIOGRAPHY--BIBLIOGRAPHY--
ASTRONAUTICS.**
Dickson, Katherine Murphy. History
of aeronautics and astronautics;
Washington, National Aeronautics and
Space Administration, 1967. vi, 117
l. 016.01662913 67-61736
Z5063.A1 D5 MRR Alc.

**BIBLIOGRAPHY--BIBLIOGRAPHY--AUTHORS,
AMERICAN.**
Havlice, Patricia Pate. Index to
American author bibliographies.
Metuchen, N.J., Scarecrow Press,
1971. 204 p. 016.01681 73-163870

Z1225 .H37 MRR Ref Desk.

**BIBLIOGRAPHY--BIBLIOGRAPHY--AUTHORS,
ENGLISH.**
Mellown, Elgin W. A descriptive
catalogue of the bibliographies of
20th century British writers, Troy,
N.Y., Whitston Pub. Co., 1972. xii,
446 p. [$17.50] 016.01682/08/0091
79-183301
Z2011 .A1M43 MRR Alc.

BIBLIOGRAPHY--BIBLIOGRAPHY--CATALOGS.
Harvard University. Library.
Bibliography and bibliography
periodicals. Cambridge, Distributed
by the Harvard University Press,
1966. 1066 p.   017.1097444 66-
31367
  Z1002 .H26 MRR Alc.

BIBLIOGRAPHY--BIBLIOGRAPHY--CRIME AND
CRIMINALS.
Sellin, Johan Thorsten, A
bibliographical manual for the
student of criminology, [New York]
National Research and Information
Center on Crime and Delinquency
[1965] 1 v. (unpaged) 016.364 66-
862
  Z5118.C9 S4 1965 MRR Alc.

BIBLIOGRAPHY--BIBLIOGRAPHY--
DISSERTATIONS, ACADEMIC.
Palfrey, Thomas Rossman, Guide to
bibliographies of theses, United
States and Canada. Chicago, American
library association, 1936. 48 p.
016.016   36-29298
  Z5055.U49 A1P 1940 MRR Alc.

BIBLIOGRAPHY--BIBLIOGRAPHY--DRAMA.
Baker, Blanch (Merritt) Theatre and
allied arts; New York, Wilson, 1952.
xiii, 536 p.   016.792 52-6756
  Z5781 .B18 MRR Alc.

Brockett, Oscar Gross, A
bibliographical guide to research in
speech and dramatic art Chicago,
Scott, Foresman [1963] 118 p.   016
63-14554
  Z1002 .B87 MRR Alc.

BIBLIOGRAPHY--BIBLIOGRAPHY--ENGLISH
LITERATURE.
Bond, Donald Frederic, A reference
guide to English studies. 2d ed.
Chicago, University of Chicago Press
[1971] x, 198 p.   016.0168 79-
130307
  Z1002 .B72 1971 MRR Alc.

Dick, Aliki Lafkidou. A student's
guide to British literature;
Littleton, Colo., Libraries
Unlimited, 1972 [c1971] 285 p.
016.820/.8 77-189255
  Z2011 .D53 MRR Alc.

Howard-Hill, Trevor Howard.
Bibliography of British literary
bibliographies Oxford, Clarendon P.,
1969. xxv, 570 p.   [7/7/-]
016.01682 70-390421
  Z2011 .H6 MRR Alc.

Kennedy, Arthur Garfield, A concise
bibliography for students of English,
5th ed. Stanford, Calif., Stanford
University Press, 1972. xvi, 300 p.
016.82 77-183889
  Z2011 .K35 1972 MRR Alc.

Northup, Clark Sutherland, A
register of bibliographies of the
English language and literature, New
Haven, Yale university press; [etc.,
etc.] 1925. 6 p. l., 507 p.   25-
20533
  Z2011 .N87 MRR Alc.

Van Patten, Nathan, An index to
bibliographies and bibliographical
contributions relating to the work of
American and British authors, 1923-
1932. Stanford University, Calif.,
Stanford university press; London, H.
Milford, Oxford university press,
1934. vii, 324 p.   016.82 34-5449

  Z1225.A1 V2 MRR Alc.

BIBLIOGRAPHY--BIBLIOGRAPHY--ENGLISH
PHILOLOGY.
Northup, Clark Sutherland, A
register of bibliographies of the
English language and literature, New
Haven, Yale university press; [etc.,
etc.] 1925. 6 p. l., 507 p.   25-
20533
  Z2011 .N87 MRR Alc.

BIBLIOGRAPHY--BIBLIOGRAPHY--GEOGRAPHY.
Wright, John Kirtland, Aids to
geographical research:
bibliographies, periodicals, atlases,
gazetteers and other reference books,
2d ed., completely rev. New York,
Columbia University Press, 1947.
xii, 331 p.   016.91 47-30449
  Z6001.A1 W9 1947 MRR Alc.

BIBLIOGRAPHY--BIBLIOGRAPHY--GERMAN
IMPRINTS.
Bibliographie der deutschen
Bibliographien. Jahrg. 1-   1954-
Leipzig, Verlag für Buch- und
Bibliothekswesen.   59-43508
  Z1002 .B598 MRR Alc Full set

Leipzig. Deutsche Bücherei.
Bibliographie der versteckten
Bibliographien. Leipzig, Verlag für
Buch- und Bibliothekswesen [1956]
371 p.   56-42675
  Z1002 .L42 MRR Alc.

BIBLIOGRAPHY--BIBLIOGRAPHY--GERMAN
LITERATURE.
Stock, Karl Franz.
Personalbibliographien
österreichischer Dichter und
Schriftsteller; Pullach bei
München, Verlag Dokumentation, 1972.
xxiii, 703 p.   73-308989
  Z2111.A1 S76 MRR Biog.

BIBLIOGRAPHY--BIBLIOGRAPHY--GOVERNMENT
PUBLICATIONS.
International Committee for Social
Sciences Documentation. Etude des
bibliographies courantes des
publications officielles nationales;
[Paris] UNESCO [1958] 260 p.   58-
425
  Z7164.G7 I5 MRR Ref Desk.

Wynkoop, Sally. Subject guide to
government reference books.
Littleton, Colo., Libraries
Unlimited, 1972. 276 p.   015.73 72-
83382
  Z1223.Z7 W95 MRR Alc.

BIBLIOGRAPHY--BIBLIOGRAPHY--HISTORY.
Poulton, Helen J. The historian's
handbook; [1st ed.] Norman,
University of Oklahoma Press [1972]
xi, 304 p.   016.9 71-165774
  Z6201 .P65 MRR Alc.

Taylor, Archer, A history of
bibliographies of bibliographies.
New Brunswick, N. J., Scarecrow
Press, 1955. ix, 147 p.   016.01 55-
13727
  Z1002 .T32 MRR Alc.

BIBLIOGRAPHY--BIBLIOGRAPHY--INCUNABULA.
Berkowitz, David Sandler,
Bibliotheca bibliographica
incunabula; Waltham, Mass., 1967.
vi, 336 l.   016.016093 68-1209
  Z240.A1 B4 MRR Alc.

Peddie, Robert Alexander, Fifteenth-
century books; New York, B. Franklin
[1969] 89 p.   016.016/.093 73-
101990
  Z240.A1 P4 1969 MRR Alc.

BIBLIOGRAPHY--BIBLIOGRAPHY--INDEXES.
Havlice, Patricia Pate. Index to
American author bibliographies.
Metuchen, N.J., Scarecrow Press,
1971. 204 p.   016.01681 73-163870

  Z1225 .H37 MRR Ref Desk.

BIBLIOGRAPHY--BIBLIOGRAPHY--ITALIAN
LITERATURE.
Ferrari, Luigi, Onomasticon;
Milano, U. Hoepli, 1947. xlvi, 708
p.   015.45 49-17429
  Z2350 .F4 1947 MRR Alc.

BIBLIOGRAPHY--BIBLIOGRAPHY--JEWISH
LITERATURE.
Shunami, Shlomo. Bibliography of
Jewish bibliographies. 2d ed. enl.
Jerusalem, Magnes Press, Hebrew
University, 1965. xxiv, 992, xxiii
p.   he 65-1493
  Z7070.A1 S5 1965 MRR Alc.

BIBLIOGRAPHY--BIBLIOGRAPHY--JEWS.
Shunami, Shlomo. Bibliography of
Jewish bibliographies. 2d ed. enl.
Jerusalem, Magnes Press, Hebrew
University, 1965. xxiv, 992, xxiii
p.   he 65-1493
  Z7070.A1 S5 1965 MRR Alc.

BIBLIOGRAPHY--BIBLIOGRAPHY--LAW.
United States. Library of Congress.
Law library. Anglo-American legal
bibliographies, Washington, U.S.
Govt. print. off., 1944. xii, 166 p.
016.01634 44-41314
  Z663.5 .A5 MRR Alc.

United States. Library of Congress.
Law library. The bibliography of
international law and continental
law, Washington, Govt. print. off.,
1913. 93 p.   12-35015
  Z663.5 .B5 MRR Alc.

BIBLIOGRAPHY--BIBLIOGRAPHY--MASS MEDIA.
Brockett, Oscar Gross, A
bibliographical guide to research in
speech and dramatic art Chicago,
Scott, Foresman [1963] 118 p.   016
63-14554
  Z1002 .B87 MRR Alc.

BIBLIOGRAPHY--BIBLIOGRAPHY--MUSIC.
Davies, J. H. Musicalia; 2d ed.,
rev. and enl. Oxford, New York,
Pergamon Press [1969] xii, 184 p.
016.78 76-77013
  ML113.D383 M9 1969 MRR Alc.

Duckles, Vincent Harris, Music
reference and research materials; 2d
ed. New York, Free Press [1967]
xiii, 385 p.   016.78 67-17657
  ML113 .D83 1967 MRR Alc.

BIBLIOGRAPHY--BIBLIOGRAPHY--NATURAL
HISTORY.
Meisel, Max, A bibliography of
American natural history; Brooklyn,
N.Y., The Premier publishing co.,
1924-29. 3 v.   24-30970
  Z7408.U5 M5 MRR Alc.

BIBLIOGRAPHY--BIBLIOGRAPHY--NEWSPAPERS.
Duprat, Gabrielle. Bibliographie des
répertoires nationaux de
périodiques en cours London, IFLA,
1969. 141 p.   73-858215
  AS4.U8 A154 MRR Alc.

BIBLIOGRAPHY--BIBLIOGRAPHY--PERIODICALS.
Bibliographic index; v. 1-   1937/42-
[New York] H. W. Wilson Co.
016.016 46-41034
  Z1002 .B595 Sci RR Full set / MRR
       Ref Desk Full set

Crane, Evan Jay, A guide to the
literature of chemistry 2d ed. New
York, Wiley [1957] 397 p.   016.54
57-8881
  Z5521 .C89 1957 MRR Alc.

Duprat, Gabrielle. Bibliographie des
répertoires nationaux de
périodiques en cours London, IFLA,
1969. 141 p.   73-858215
  AS4.U8 A154 MRR Alc.

Fowler, Maureen J. Guides to
scientific periodicals: London,
Library Association [1966] xvi, 318
p. [84/- 63/- (to L.A. members)]
016.505 67-71339
  Z7403 .F6 MRR Alc.

France. Direction des bibliothèques
de France. Les bibliographies
internationales specialigees
courantes françaises ou à
participation française. Paris,
1958. 95 p.   60-21619
  Z1002 .F75 MRR Alc.

Gray, Richard A. Serial
bibliographies in the humanities and
social sciences. Ann Arbor, Mich.,
Pierian Press, 1969. xxiv, 345 p.
016.01605 68-58895
  Z1002 .G814 MRR Ref Desk.

BIBLIOGRAPHY--BIBLIOGRAPHY--POLITICAL
SCIENCE.
Harmon, Robert Bartlett, Political
science bibliographies, Metuchen,
N.J., Scarecrow Press, 1973- v.
016.01632 72-8849
  Z7161.A1 H35 MRR Alc.

Universal Reference System.
Bibliography of bibliographies in
political science; government, and
public policy; Princeton, N.J.,
Princeton Research Pub. Co. [1968]
xix, 927 p.   016.3 67-29647
  Z7161 .U64 vol. 3 MRR Alc.

BIBLIOGRAPHY--BIBLIOGRAPHY--READING.
Davis, Bonnie M. A guide to
information sources for reading.
Newark, Del., International Reading
Association, 1972. 158 p.
016.4284/.025 72-176095
  Z5814.R25 D37 MRR Alc.

BIBLIOGRAPHY--BIBLIOGRAPHY--SPANISH
LITERATURE.
Foulche-Delbosc, Raymond, Manuel de
l'hispanisant. New York, G. P.
Putnam's sons, 1920- v.   20-
16867
  Z2681.A1 F7 MRR Alc.

BIBLIOGRAPHY--BIBLIOGRAPHY--SPEECH.
Brockett, Oscar Gross, A
bibliographical guide to research in
speech and dramatic art Chicago,
Scott, Foresman [1963] 118 p.   016
63-14554
  Z1002 .B87 MRR Alc.

BIBLIOGRAPHY--BIBLIOGRAPHY--AFRICA,
SOUTH.
Musiker, Reuben. South African
bibliography; Hamden, Conn., Archon
Books [1970] 105 p.   [5.50]
010/.968 73-16088
  Z3601 .A1M9 MRR Alc.

BIBLIOGRAPHY--BIBLIOGRAPHY--AFRICA, SUB-
SAHARAN.
Duignan, Peter. Guide to research
and reference works on Sub-Saharan
Africa. Stanford, Calif., Hoover
Institution Press, Stanford
University [1971 or 2] xiii, 1102 p.
016.0169167/03 76-152424
  Z3501 .D78 MRR Alc.

BIBLIOGRAPHY--BIBLIOGRAPHY--ASIA.
Nunn, Godfrey Raymond, Asia: a
selected and annotated guide to
reference works Cambridge, Mass.,
M.I.T. Press [1971] xiii, 223 p.
[$12.50] 016.016915 77-169004
  Z3001 .N79 MRR Alc.

BIBLIOGRAPHY--BIBLIOGRAPHY--CANADA.
Lochhead, Douglas. Bibliography of
Canadian bibliographies. 2d ed. rev.
and enl. [Toronto] University of
Toronto, published in association
with the Bibliographical Society of
Canada [1972] xiv, 312 p. [$20.00]
016.01571 76-166933
Z1365.A1 L6 1972 MRR Alc.

BIBLIOGRAPHY--BIBLIOGRAPHY--DENMARK.
Munch-Petersen, Erland. A guide to
Danish bibliography. Copenhagen,
Royal School of Librarianship, 1965.
140 p. 016.9148903 66-6990
Z2561.A1 M8 MRR Alc.

BIBLIOGRAPHY--BIBLIOGRAPHY--GREAT
BRITAIN.
Berkowitz, David Sandler,
Bibliotheca bibliographica
Britannica. Waltham, Mass., 1963-
v. 63-3390
Z2016 .B45 MRR Alc.

Humphreys, Arthur Lee. A handbook to
county bibliography. London,
[Printed by Strangeways and sons]
1917. x, 501 p., 1 l. 17-14548
L2023.A1 H9 MRR Alc.

BIBLIOGRAPHY--BIBLIOGRAPHY--INDIA.
Jain, Sushil K. A bibliography of
Indian bibliographies relating to the
history & politcs [sic] of India;
Regina, Sask., 1966. 21 l. 67-4779

Z3201.A1 J3 MRR Alc.

BIBLIOGRAPHY--BIBLIOGRAPHY--IRELAND.
Eager, Alan R. A guide to Irish
bibliographical material. London,
Library Association, 1964. xiii, 392
p. 016.91415 65-2507
Z2031 .E16 MRR Alc.

BIBLIOGRAPHY--BIBLIOGRAPHY--ITALY.
Borroni, Fabia. "Il Cicognara,"
Firenze, Sansoni, 1954- v. 55-
18980
Z2357 .B6 MRR Alc.

Ottino, Giuseppe, Bibliotheca
bibliographica Italica; Graz,
Akademische Druck- u.
Verlangsanstalt, 1957. 6 v. in 1.
58-42417
Z2341.A1 O8 1957 MRR Alc.

BIBLIOGRAPHY--BIBLIOGRAPHY--KOREA.
Koh, Hesung Chun. Korea; an
analytical guide to bibliographies.
New Haven, Human Relations Area Files
Press, 1971. xviii, 334 p.
016.01691519 70-125119
Z3316.A1 K64 MRR Alc.

BIBLIOGRAPHY--BIBLIOGRAPHY--LATIN
AMERICA.
Groppo, Arthur Eric, A bibliography
of Latin American bibliographies.
Metuchen, N.J., Scarecrow Press,
1968. ix, 515 p. 016.01698 68-
9330
Z1601.A2 G76 1968 MRR Alc.

BIBLIOGRAPHY--BIBLIOGRAPHY--NETHERLANDS.
United States. Library of Congress.
Netherlands Studies Unit. A guide to
Dutch bibliographies. Washington,
1951. iii, 193 p. 015.492 51-
60014
Z2416 .U6 1951c MRR Alc.

BIBLIOGRAPHY--BIBLIOGRAPHY--NEW ZEALAND.
New Zealand Library Association. A
bibliography of New Zealand
bibliographies. Prelim. ed.
Wellington, 1967. 58 p. [10/- 7/6
(to members N.Z.)] 016.016/91931
68-88968
Z4101.A1 N4 MRR Alc.

BIBLIOGRAPHY--BIBLIOGRAPHY--PHILIPPINE
ISLANDS.
Bernardo, Gabriel Adriano,
Bibliography of Philippine
bibliographies, 1593-1961. Quezon
City, Ateneo University Press, 1968.
xiv, 192 p. 016.01691914/03 68-
17160
Z3291.A1 B45 MRR Alc.

BIBLIOGRAPHY--BIBLIOGRAPHY--POLAND.
Hahn, Wiktor, Bibliografia
bibliografij polskich. Wyd. 2.,
znacznje rozsz. Wrocław, Zakład im.
Ossolinskich, 1956. xxii, 645 p.
56-32462
Z2521.A1 H3 1956 MRR Alc.

BIBLIOGRAPHY--BIBLIOGRAPHY--RUSSIA.
Simmons, John Simon Gabriel. Russian
bibliography, libraries and archives:
Twickenham, Anthony C. Hall, 1973.
xviii, 76 p. [£1.00] 016.0169147
74-162047
Z2491.A1 S54 MRR Alc.

BIBLIOGRAPHY--BIBLIOGRAPHY--UNITED
STATES.
Beers, Henry Putney, Bibliographies
in American history; [Rev. ed.
Paterson] N.J., Pageant Books, 1959
[c1938] xv, 487 p. 016.016973 59-
14179
Z1236.A1 B4 1959 MRR Ref Desk.

Fingerhut, Eugene R. The Fingerhut
guide: sources in American history
Santa Barbara, Calif., American
Bibliographical Center - Clio Press
[1973] xii, 148 p. 016.0169173/03
72-95266
Z1215.A2 F55 MRR Alc.

Tanselle, George Thomas, Guide to
the study of United States imprints
Cambridge, Mass., Belknap Press of
Harvard University Press, 1971. 2 v.
(lxiv, 1050 p.) 016.015/73 79-
143232
Z1215.A2 T35 MRR Alc.

United States. Library of Congress.
General Reference and Bibliography
Division. American history and
civilization; a list of guides 2d
(rev.) ed. Washington, 1951. 18 p.
016.016973 51-60033
Z663.28 .A64 1951 MRR Alc.

BIBLIOGRAPHY--BIBLIOGRAPHY--URUGUAY.
Musso Ambrosi, Luis Alberto.
Bibliografía de bibliografías
uruguayas, Montevideo, 1964. vii,
102 p. 65-51822
Z1881.A1 M8 MRR Alc.

BIBLIOGRAPHY--BIBLIOGRAPHY--WEST.
Wallace, William Swilling.
Bibliography of published
bibliographies on the history of the
eleven Western States, 1941-1947;
Albuquerque, N.M., 1953 [i.e. 1954]
224-233 p. 016.016978 55-62545
Z1251.W5 W25 MRR Alc.

BIBLIOGRAPHY--BOOKS ISSUED IN SERIES.
The American catalogue ... New York,
1941. 8 v. in 13. 015.73 a 42-
2938
Z1215 .A52 MRR Ref Desk.

Andriot, John L. Checklist of major
U.S. Government series, McLean, Va.,
Documents Index, 1972- v.
015/.73 73-163950
Z1223.Z7 A544 MRR Alc.

Baer, Eleanora A. Titles in series;
2. ed. New York, Scarecrow Press,
1964. 2 v. (1530 p.) 011 64-11789

AI3 .B3 1964 MRR Alc.

Blum, Fred, Music monographs in
series; New York, Scarecrow Press,
1964. xiii, 197 p. 016.78 64-
11794
ML113 .B63 MRR Alc.

Catalog of reprints in series. [1st]-
ed.; 1940- Metuchen, N.J. [etc.]
Scarecrow Press [etc.] 011 61-8715

Z1033.S5 C3 MRR Alc Latest edition

Milne, Alexander Taylor. A centenary
guide to the publications of the
Royal Historical Society, 1868-1968,
London, Royal Historical Society,
1968. xi, 249 p. [unpriced]
016.942 77-436189
Z5055.G6 R66 MRR Alc.

Mullins, Edward Lindsay Carson.
Texts and calendars; London, Royal
Historical Society, 1958. xi, 674 p.
016.942 a 59-1596
Z2016 .M8 MRR Alc.

Otto Harrassowitz (Firm) German
series publications in the fields of
Germanic language & literature,
German history. Wiesbaden, 1967-69.
2 v. 015.43 67-85917
Z2235.A2 O8 1967 MRR Alc.

Rosenberg, Judith K. Young people's
literature in series: publishers' and
non-fiction series; Littleton,
Colo., Libraries Unlimited, 1973.
280 p. [$10.00] 028.52 73-75237
Z1037 .R7 MRR Alc.

BIBLIOGRAPHY--CHILDREN'S BOOKS ISSUED
IN SERIES.
Rosenberg, Judith K. Young people's
literature in series: publishers' and
non-fiction series; Littleton,
Colo., Libraries Unlimited, 1973.
280 p. [$10.00] 028.52 73-75237
Z1037 .R7 MRR Alc.

BIBLIOGRAPHY--DENTISTRY.
Index to dental literature. 1962-
Chicago, American Dental Association.
617.6/001/6 72-622063
Z6668 .I45 Sci RR Partial set /
MRR Alc Partial set

BIBLIOGRAPHY--DICTIONARIES.
American library association.
Editorial committee. Subcommittee on
library terminology. A.L.A. glossary
of library terms, Chicago, Ill.,
American library association, 1943.
viii, 159. [1] p. 020.3 43-51260
Z1006 .A5 MRR Ref Desk.

The Bookman's concise dictionary.
New York, Philosophical Library
[1956] 318 p. 010.3 57-678
Z1006 .B59 1956a MRR Ref Desk.

The Bookman's glossary. 4th ed.,
rev. and enl. New York, R. R. Bowker
[1961] viii, 212 p. 010.3 61-
13239
Z1006 .B6 1961 MRR Alc.

Carter, John, ABC for book-
collectors. [3d ed., rev.] London,
R. Hart-Davis [1961] 208 p. 62-
6733
Z1006 .C37 1961a MRR Alc.

Cowles, Barbara (Pehotsky)
Bibliographers' glossary of foreign
words and phrases; New York, R. R.
Bowker company, 1935. 3 p. l., 82
numb. l. 010.3 41-5736
Z1006 .C87 1935 MRR Alc.

Harrod, Leonard Montague, The
librarians glossary; [2d rev. ed.]
London, Grafton, 1959. 332 p.
010.3 59-2822
Z1006 .H32 1959 MRR Ref Desk.

Walter, Frank Keller, Abbreviations
and technical terms used in book
catalogs and bibliographies, in eight
languages, 1917 handy edition.
Boston, The Boston book company
[1919?] 2 v. in 1. 27-13479
Z1006 .W261 1919 MRR Alc.

BIBLIOGRAPHY--DICTIONARIES--GERMAN.
Lexikon des Buchwesens, Stuttgart,
Hiersemann, 1952-56. 4 v. 010.3
53-17416
Z118 .L65 MRR Alc.

Lexikon des gesamten Buchwesens.
Leipzig, K. W. Hiersemann, 1935 [i.e.
1934]-37. 3 v. 34-28790
Z118 .L67 MRR Alc.

BIBLIOGRAPHY--DICTIONARIES--POLYGLOT.
Lexikon des Bibliothekswesens.
Leipzig, VEB Verlag für Buch- und
Bibliothekswesen, 1969. xiii, 769 p.
[42.00] 70-423794
Z1006 .L46 MRR Alc.

Orne, Jerrold, The language of the
foreign book trade: 2d ed. Chicago,
American Library Association, 1962.
213 p. 010.3 61-12881
Z1006 .O7 1962 MRR Alc.

Pipics, Zoltán. Dictionarium
bibliothecarii practicum: ad usum
internationalem in XXII linguis. 6.,
rev. and enlarged ed. Pullach
(München) Verlag Dokumentation,
1974. 385 p. [DM98.00] 74-322719

Z1006 .P67 1974 MRR Ref Desk.

BIBLIOGRAPHY--EARLY PRINTED BOOKS.
British Museum. Dept. of Printed
Books. Short-title catalogue of
books printed in France and of French
books printed in other countries from
1470 to 1600 in the British Museum.
1st ed. reprinted. London, British
Museum [1966] viii, 491 p. [50/-]
015.44 67-73254
Z2162 .B86 1966 MRR Alc.

London. Guildhall Library. A list of
books printed in the British Isles
and of English books printed abroad
before 1701 in Guildhall Library.
London, Corporation of London, 1966-
67. 2 v. [40/- (v. 1)] 015/.42
68-77514
Z2002 .L62 MRR Alc.

Trienens, Roger J. Pioneer imprints
from fifty States, Washington,
Library of Congress; [for sale by the
Supt. of Docs., U.S. Govt. Print.
Off.] 1973. 87 p. [$4.25]
686.2/0973 72-10069
Z663 .P5 MRR Alc.

Welch, D'Alté Aldridge, A
bibliography of American children's
books printed prior to 1821. [Barre?
Mass.] American Antiquarian Society
and Barre Publishers, 1972. lxvi,
516 p. 081 s 028.52 73-162761
Z1232 .W44 1972b MRR Alc.

BIBLIOGRAPHY--EARLY PRINTED BOOKS--16TH
CENTURY.
Adams, Herbert Mayow, Catalogue of
books printed on the continent of
Europe, 1501-1600, in Cambridge
libraries; London, Cambridge U.P.,
1967. 2 v. [25/-/-] 018/.5 66-
10015
Z1014 .A38 MRR Alc.

Besterman, Theodore, Early printed
books to the end of the sixteenth
century; 2d ed., rev. and much enl.
Geneve, Societas Bibliographica,
1961. 344 p. 016.016093 62-2500
Z1002 .B562 1961 MRR Alc.

British Museum. Dept. of Printed
Books. Short-title catalogue of
books printed in the Netherlands and
Belgium London, Trustees of the
British Museum, 1965. viii, 274 p.
66-4468
Z2402 .B7 MRR Alc.

BIBLIOGRAPHY--EARLY PRINTED (Cont.)
Cockx-Indestege, Elly. Belgica typographica 1541-1600. Nieuwkoop, B. de Graaf, 1968- v.   [$180.00 (v. 1)] 68-14677
Z2402 .C6 MRR Alc.

Hispanic Society of America. Printed books, 1468-1700, in the Hispanic Society of America; New York, 1965. xlii, 614 p.   018.1 65-22528
Z1012 .H58 MRR Alc.

Index Aureliensis; Aureliae Aquensis, 1965- c1962- v.   66-44410
Z1014 .I5 MRR Alc.

United States. Library of Congress. Early printed books of the Low Countries Washington, 1958. vi, 37 p.   016.09 58-60011
Z663.4 .E2 MRR Alc.

BIBLIOGRAPHY--EARLY PRINTED BOOKS--16TH CENTURY--CATALOGS.
British Museum. Dept. of Printed Books. Short-title catalogue of books printed in Italy London Trustees of the British Museum, 1958. viii, 992 p.   015.45 a 60-1778
Z2342 .B7 MRR Alc.

Scotland. National Library, Edinburgh. A short-title catalogue of foreign books printed up to 1600; Edinburgh, H.M. Stationery Off., 1970. viii, 545 p.   [£17/-/-] 018/.1 77-579020
Z1014 .S35 MRR Alc.

BIBLIOGRAPHY--EARLY PRINTED BOOKS--17TH CENTURY.
Hispanic Society of America. Printed books, 1468-1700, in the Hispanic Society of America; New York, 1965. xlii, 614 p.   018.1 65-22528
Z1012 .H58 MRR Alc.

Michel, Suzanne P. Répertoire des ouvrages imprimés en langue italienne au XVIIe siècle Firenze, L. S. Olschki, 1970- v.   [L17500 (v. 1)] 70-558790
Z2342 .M52 MRR Alc.

Michel, Suzanne P. Répertoire des ouvrages imprimés en langue italienne au XVIIe siècle conservés dans les bibliothèques de France Paris, Éditions du Centre national de la recherche scientifique, 1967- v.   [38.00 (v. 1) varies] 015/.45 67-69528
Z2342 .M5 MRR Alc.

BIBLIOGRAPHY--EARLY PRINTED BOOKS--17TH CENTURY--CATALOGS.
British Museum. Dept. of Printed Books. A short title catalogue of French books, 1601-1700, Folkestone [Eng.] Dawsons, 1973. x, 690 p.   015/.44 73-176033
Z2162 .B87 1973 MRR Alc.

BIBLIOGRAPHY--EARLY PRINTED BOOKS--17TH CENTURY--UNION LISTS.
Wing, Donald Goddard. Short-title catalogue of books printed in England, Scotland, Ireland, Wales, and British America, and of English books printed in other countries, 1641-1700. New York, Index Society, 1945-51. 3 v.   015.42 45-8773
Z2002 .W5 MRR Alc.

Wing, Donald Goddard. Short-title catalogue of books printed in England, Scotland, Ireland, Wales, and British America, and of English books printed in other countries, 1641-1700. 2d ed.; rev. and enl. New York, Index Committee of the Modern Language Association of America, 1972- v.   015.42 70-185211
Z2002 .W52 MRR Alc.

BIBLIOGRAPHY--EARLY PRINTED BOOKS--CATALOGS.
American Antiquarian Society, Worcester, Mass. Library. A dictionary catalog of American books pertaining to the 17th through 19th centuries. Westport, Conn., Greenwood Pub. Corp. [1971] 20 v.   015/.73 76-103820
Z1215 .A264 MRR Alc (Dk 33)

Cambridge. University. Library. Early English printed books in the University library, Cambridge (1475 to 1640). Cambridge, The University press, 1900-07. 4 v.   01-15519
Z2002 .C17 MRR Alc.

BIBLIOGRAPHY--EARLY PRINTED BOOKS--UNION LISTS.
Aldis, Harry Gidney. A list of books printed in Scotland before 1700, [Edinburgh] Printed for the Edinburgh bibliographical society, 1904. xvi, 153 p.   05-9350
Z2051 .A55 MRR Alc.

Pollard, Alfred William. A short-title catalogue of books printed in England, Scotland, & Ireland and of English books printed abroad, 1475-1640, London, Bibliographical Society, 1946. xviii, 609 p.   015.42 47-20884
Z2002 .P77 1946 MRR Alc.

BIBLIOGRAPHY--EDITIONS.
Guide to reprints. 1967- Washington, Microcard Editions. 011 66-29279
Z1000-5 .G8 MRR Ref Desk Latest edition

Ostwald, Renate. Nachdruckverzeichnis von Einzelwerken, Serien und Zeitschriften Wiesbaden, G. Nobis, 1965- v.   66-31825
Z1011 .O78 MRR Alc.

BIBLIOGRAPHY--FIRST EDITIONS.
Boutell, Henry Sherman. First editions of today and how to tell them; 4th ed.; rev. and enl. Berkeley, Calif., Peacock Press, 1965 [c1964] 227 p.   094.4 64-10193
Z992 .B77 1965 MRR Alc.

Schwartz, Jacob. 1100 obscure points: the bibliographies of 25 English and 21 American authors. [1st ed., reprinted]. Bristol, Chatford House Press, 1969. xiii, 95 p., 2 plates.   [36/-] 016.820 70-465328
Z2013 .S38 1969 MRR Alc.

BIBLIOGRAPHY--HISTORY.
Malclès, Louise Noëlle. Bibliography; New York, Scarecrow Press, 1961. 152 p.   010.9 61-8721
Z1001.3 .M313 MRR Alc.

Malclès, Louise Noëlle. Manuel de bibliographie. [1. éd.] Paris, Presses universitaires de France, 1963. viii, 328 p.   016.016 65-355
Z1002 .M28 MRR Alc.

BIBLIOGRAPHY--PAPERBACK EDITIONS.
Andrews, David H. Latin America; a bibliography of paperback books, Washington, Hispanic Foundation, Reference Dept., Library of Congress; [for sale by the Superintendent of Documents, U.S. Govt. Print. Off.] 1964. v, 38 p.   64-60047
Z663.32 .A5 no. 9 MRR Alc.

Asia Society. Asia: a guide to paperbacks. Rev. ed. [New York] 1968. iii, 178 p.   016.915 68-4375
Z3001 .A79 1968 MRR Alc.

Dorn, Georgette M. Latin America; an annotated bibliography of paperback books, Washington, Library of Congress; [for sale by the Supt. of Docs., U.S. Govt. Print. Off.] 1967. 77 p.   016.918 67-60082
Z663.32 .A5 no. 11 MRR Alc.

Dorn, Georgette M. Latin America, Spain, and Portugal; an annotated bibliography of paperback books. Washington, Library of Congress, 1971. 180 p.   [$0.75] 016.918 71-37945
Z663.32 .A5 no. 12 MRR Alc.

Gillespie, John Thomas. Paperback books for young people; Chicago, American Library Association, 1972. viii, 177 p.   070.5/73 72-2390
Z479 .G55 MRR Alc.

Paperbacks in print. London, J. Whitaker. 66-8204
Began with May 1960 issue.
Z1033.P3 P28 MRR Alc Latest edition

Paperbound book guide for colleges. New York, R. R. Bowker. 016 60-3050
Z1033.P3 P3 MRR Alc Latest editions

Reginald, R. Cumulative paperback index, 1939-1959; Detroit, Gale Research Co. [1973] xxiv, 362 p.   018/.4 73-6866
Z1033.P3 R4 MRR Alc.

Schick, Frank Leopold. The paperbound book in America; New York, R. R. Bowker Co., 1958. xviii, 262 p.   655.473 58-10097
Z1033.P3 S35 MRR Alc.

Spector, Sherman David. Checklist of paperbound books on Russia, Albany, University of the State of New York, State Education Dept., 1964. iii, 63 p.   65-63612
Z2491 .S69 MRR Alc.

Wynar, Bohdan S. Reference books in paperback: an annotated guide. Littleton, Colo., Libraries Unlimited, 1972. 199 p.   [$4.75] 011.02 74-189257
Z1035.1 .W95 1972 MRR Alc.

BIBLIOGRAPHY--PAPERBACK EDITIONS--PERIODICALS.
Paperbound books in print. Mar. 1971- [New York, Bowker] 011 71-649559
Z1033.P3 P33 MRR Alc Latest edition / Sci RR Latest edition

BIBLIOGRAPHY--PERIODICALS.
American notes & queries. v. 1- Sept. 1962- [New Haven, Conn.] [$6.50] 031/.02 74-642751
Z1034 .A4 MRR Alc Full set

Biblio. 1934- Paris. 015.44 36-3965
Z2165 .B565 MRR Alc Latest edition

Book review digest. Annual cumulation. v. 1- 1905- New York [etc.] H. W. Wilson Co. 06-9994
Z1219 .C96 MRR Circ Full set

BIBLIOGRAPHY--PERIODICALS--INDEXES.
Ulrich, Carolyn Farquhar. Books and printing, Woodstock, Vt., W. E. Rudge; New York, The New York Public library, 1943. xi, [1], 244 p.   016.655 43-16214
Z1002 .U4 MRR Alc.

BIBLIOGRAPHY--RARE BOOKS.
American book prices current. v. 1- 1894/95- New York, Bancroft-Parkman [etc.] 018/.3 03-14557
Z1000 .A51 MRR Alc Partial set

Bradley, Van Allen. The book collector's handbook of values. New York, Putnam [1972] xvi, 569 p.   [$17.50] 016.09 75-136795
Z1029 .B7 MRR Alc.

Bradley, Van Allen. The new Gold in your attic. [2d ed.] New York, Fleet Press Corp. [1968] 280 p.   094/.4/0973 68-3458
Z1000 .B78 1968 MRR Alc.

Church, Elihu Dwight. A catalogue of books relating to the discovery and early history of North and South America. New York, P. Smith, 1951. 5 v. (vi, 2635 p.) 016.9731 51-4055
Z1203 .C55 1951 MRR Ref Desk.

Deschamps, Pierre Charles Ernest. Manuel du libraire et de l'amateur de livres. Paris, Firmin Didot et cie, 1878-80. 2 v. 02-2819
Z1011 .B9M5 MRR Alc.

Grässe, Johann Georg Theodor. Trésor de livres rares et précieux; Dresde, R. Kuntze [etc., etc.] 1859-69. 7 v. 02-3517
Z1011 .G73 MRR Alc.

Le Petit, Jules. Bibliographie des principales éditons originales d'écrivains français du XVe au XVIIIe siècle; Paris, Maison Quantin, 1888. 2 p. l., vii, [1], 383 (i.e. 583), [1] p.   04-15718
Z2174 .F5L5 MRR Alc.

Livingston, Luther Samuel. Auction prices of books; New York, Dodd, Mead & company, 1905. 4 v. 05-9722
Z1000 .L65 MRR Alc.

Mumey, Nolie. A study of rare books, Denver, The Clason publishing company, 1930. xvii p., 2 l., 3-572 p.   090 30-25438
Z1012 .M95 MRR Alc.

Palau y Dulcet, Antonio, 1867-1954. Manual del librero hispano-americano; 2. ed. corr. y aumentada por el autor. Barcelona, A. Palau, 1948- v.   015.46 48-2664
Z2681 .P16 MRR Alc.

United States. Library of Congress. The Rosenwald Collection; Washington, 1954. vi, 292 p.   016.09 54-60000
Z663.4 .R6 MRR Alc.

Wing, Donald Goddard. A gallery of ghosts; [New York] Index Committee, Modern Language Association of America, 1967. vi, 225 p.   015.42 67-9327
Z2002 .W48 MRR Alc.

BIBLIOGRAPHY--RARE BOOKS--CATALOGS.
United States. Library of Congress. A catalog of important recent additions to the Lessing J. Rosenwald Collection selected for exhibition at the Library of Congress, June 1947. [Washington, U.S. Govt. Print. Off., 1947] 52 p.   016.09 47-31900
Z663.4 .C3 1947 MRR Alc.

BIBLIOGRAPHY--RARE BOOKS--EXHIBITIONS.
United States. Library of Congress.
Treasures from the Lessing J.
Rosenwald Collection; Washington,
1973. [57] p.   mrr01-74
Z663.4 .T74 MRR Alc.

BIBLIOGRAPHY--RARE BOOKS--YEARBOOKS.
The A B bookman's yearbook. 1954-
Newark, N.J. 010.58   54-1676
Z990 .A18   MRR Alc Latest edition

BIBLIOGRAPHY--REFERENCE BOOKS
see Reference books

BIBLIOGRAPHY--THEORY, METHODS, ETC.
Bowers, Fredson Thayer. Principles
of bibliographical description, New
York, Russell & Russell, 1962 [c1949]
505 p.   010.1 62-13826
Z1001 .B78 1962 MRR Alc.

Gaskell, Philip. A new introduction
to bibliography. New York, Oxford
University Press, 1972. 438 p.
686.2/09 73-153680
Z116.A2 G27 1972b MRR Alc.

Hurt, Peyton. Bibliography and
footnotes; 3d ed., rev. and enl.
Berkeley, University of California
Press, 1968. xii, 163 p.   010 67-
26633
Z1001 .H95 1968 MRR Alc.

Pearce, M. J. A workbook of
analytical & descriptive
bibliography. London, Bingley, 1970.
110 p. [30/-] 025.3/2 70-530364

Z1001 .P34 1970 MRR Alc.

Taylor, Archer. Book catalogues:
their varieties and uses. Chicago,
Newberry Library, 1957. xii, 284 p.
010 56-12568
Z1001 .T34 MRR Alc.

United States. Library of Congress.
Committee on Bibliography and
Publications. Manual for
bibliographers in the Library of
Congress. Washington, 1944. iii, 28
p.   010.2 44-41691
Z663-13 .M2 MRR Alc.

United States. Library of Congress.
General Reference and Bibliography
Division. Bibliographical procedures
& style; Washington, 1954; reprinted
1966. vii, 133 p.   010.28 66-60057
Z663.28 .B5 1966 MRR Alc.

BIBLIOGRAPHY--UNIVERSAL CATALOGS.
British Museum. Dept. of Printed
Books. General catalogue of printed
books. Photolithographic edition to
1955. London, Trustees of the
British Museum, 1959-66. [v. 1, 1965]
263 p.   018/.1 66-2261
Z921 .B87 MRR Alc (Dk 33).

A Catalog of books represented by
Library of Congress printed cards
issued to July 31, 1942. Ann Arbor,
Mich., Edwards Bros., 1942-46. 167
v.   018.1 43-3338
Z881.A1 C3 MRR Alc. (DK 33)

Chicago. Center for Research
Libraries. The Center for Research
Libraries catalogue: monographs.
Chicago, 1969-70. 5 v. 018/.1 76-
13486
Z881 .C512 MRR Alc (DK 33)

Deschamps, Pierre Charles Ernest,
Manuel du libraire et de l'amateur de
livres. Paris, Firmin Didot et cie,
1878-80. 2 v.   02-2819
Z1011 .B9M5 MRR Alc.

Deutscher gesamtkatalog, Berlin,
Preussische druckerei- und verlags-
aktiengesellschaft, 1931- v.
019.1 32-9323
Z929 .A1D4 MRR Alc (Dk 33).

Ebert, Friedrich Adolf, A general
bibliographical dictionary, Oxford,
University press, 1837. 4 v.   02-
25780
Z1011 .E16E MRR Alc.

Grässe, Johann Georg Theodor,
Trésor de livres rares et précieux;
Dresde, R. Kuntze; [etc., etc.] 1859-
69. 7 v.   02-3517
Z1011 .G73 MRR Alc.

Library of Congress and National
union catalog author lists, 1942-
1962; Detroit, Gale Research Co.,
1969-71. 152 v. 018/.1/0973 73-
82135
Z881.A1 L63 MRR Alc (Dk 33)

London library. Catalogue of the
London library, London, 1913-14. 2
v.   14-5422
Z921 .L6 1913 MRR Alc (DK33).

The National union catalog, Totowa,
N.J., Rowman and Littlefield [1970-
v.   018/.1/0973 76-141020
Z881.A1U3742 MRR Alc (Dk 33)

Paris. Bibliothèque nationale.
Catalogue general des livres
imprimés; Paris, 1965- v.
018/.1 67-52152
Z927 .P1957 MRR Alc (Dk33)

Paris. Bibliothèque nationale.
Département des imprimés.
Catalogue general des livres
imprimés de la Bibliothèque
nationale. Paris, Imprimerie
nationale, 1897-19 v.   01-5989
Z927 .P2 MRR Alc (Dk 33)

Rome (City) Centro nazionale per il
catalogo unico delle biblioteche
italiane e per le informazioni
bibliografiche. Primo catalogo
collettivo delle biblioteche
italiane. Roma, 1962- v.   63-
50852
Z933 .A1R6 MRR Alc (Dk 33).

BIBLIOGRAPHY, NATIONAL.
Bibliographical services throughout
the world. 1st/2d- 1951/53-
Paris, UNESCO. 010 55-4898
Z1008 .U54 MRR Alc Partial set /
MRR Ref Desk Latest edition

BIBLIOGRAPHY, NATIONAL--BIBLIOGRAPHY.
Pinto, Olga. Le bibliografie
nazionali. 2. ed. riv., corr. ed
aggiornata. Firenze, L. S. Olschki,
1951. 94 p.   016.01 52-18924
Z1002.A2 P6 1951 MRR Alc.

United States. Library of Congress.
General Reference and Bibliography
Division. Current national
bibliographies. New York, Greenwood
Press [1968] iv, 132 p.   016.015
68-55128
Z1002 .U583 1968 MRR Ref Desk.

United States. Library of Congress.
General Reference and Bibliography
Division. Current national
bibliographies, Washington, 1955.
v, 132 p.   016.01 55-60025
Z663.28 .C8 MRR Alc.

BIBLIOGRAPHY, NATIONAL--DUTCH.
United States. Library of Congress.
Netherlands Studies Unit. A guide to
Dutch bibliographies, Washington,
1951. iii, 193 p.   015.492 51-
60014
Z2416 .U6 1951c MRR Alc.

BIBLIOGRAPHY, NATIONAL--HISTORY.
Linder, LeRoy Harold, The rise of
current complete national
bibliography. New York, Scarecrow
Press, 1959. 290 p.   015 59-6547
Z1001.3 .L5 MRR Alc.

BIBLIOGRAPHY, NATIONAL--AFRICA, SOUTH.
Musiker, Reuben. South African
bibliography; Hamden, Conn., Archon
Books [1970] 105 p. [$5.50]
010/.968 73-16088
Z3601 .A1M9 MRR Alc.

BIBLIOGRAPHY, NATIONAL--FRANCE.
Paris. Bibliothèque nationale.
Département des periodiques.
Répertoire national des annuaires
français, 1958-1968, Paris,
Bibliothèque nationale, Editions
Mercure, 1970. 811 p.   76-501237
Z2174.Y4 P29 MRR Alc.

BIBLIOGRAPHY, NATIONAL--UNITED STATES.
Rogers, Joseph William. U.S.
national bibliography and the
copyright law; New York, Bowker,
1960. xii, 115 p.   015.73 60-15545

Z1216 .R6 MRR Alc.

BIBLIOTECA NACIONAL DE ANTROPOLOGIA E
HISTORIA.
Biblioteca Nacional de Antropología
e Historia. Catalogos de la
Biblioteca Nacional de Antropología
e Historia. Mexico. Boston, G. K.
Hall, 1972. 10 v.   74-225152
Z885.A1 B5 1972 MRR Alc (Dk 33)

BICAMERALISM
see Legislative bodies

BICYCLES AND TRICYCLES.
Sloane, Eugene A. The new complete
book of bicycling, New York, Simon
and Schuster [1974] 531 p. [$12.50]
629.22/72 73-9362
GV1041 .S55 1974 MRR Alc.

BIG BUSINESS--GERMANY (FEDERAL
REPUBLIC, 1949-)
Die Grossen 500 [i.e. Fünfhundert]
1970- Dusseldorf, Droste Verlag.
70-612586
HD2859 .G7 MRR Alc Latest edition

BILINGUALISM--BIBLIOGRAPHY.
Mackey, William Francis.
Bibliographie internationale sur le
bilinguisme, Quebec, Presses de
l'Université Laval, 1972. xxviii,
337, 209, 203 p.   73-358929
Z7004.B5 M3 MRR Alc.

BILLS, LEGISLATIVE--UNITED STATES.
United States. Congress. Senate.
Library. Presidential vetoes;
Washington, U.S. Govt. Print. Off.,
1969 viii, 252 p. [1.00]
353/.032 70-602981
KF42.2 1969 MRR Ref Desk.

BILLS, LEGISLATIVE--UNITED STATES--
DIGESTS.
United States. Library of Congress.
Congressional Research Service.
Digest of public general bills and
resolutions. 92d- Congress; 1971-
[Washington, Library of Congress; for
sale by the Supt. of Docs., U.S.
Govt. Print. Off.] 348/.73/1 79-
611725
KF18 .L5 Sci RR Full set / MRR Alc
Full set

BIO-BIBLIOGRAPHY.
see also Authors

Chevalier, Cyr Ulysse Joseph,
Répertoire des sources historiques
du moyen âge, Paris, 1877-1903. 2
pt. in 3 v.   02-2025
Z6203 .C52 MRR Alc.

Gidel, Charles Antoine, Dictionnaire-
manuel-illustré des écrivains et
des littératures. Paris, A. Colin &
cie 1898. 2 p. l., 908 p. f 01-
3144
Z1010 .G453 MRR Biog.

Gubernatis, Angelo de, conte,
Dictionnaire international des
ecrivains du monde latin, Rome,
Chez l'auteur; [etc., etc.] 1905.
xii, 1506 p.   06-46763
Z1010 .G93 MRR Biog.

Gubernatis, Angelo de, conte,
Dizionario biografico degli scrittori
contemporanei. Firenze, Coi tipi dei
successori Le Monier, 1879. xxxii,
1276 p.   02-2811
Z1010 .G92 MRR Biog.

Jöcher, Christian Gottlieb,
Allgemeines gelehrten-lexicon ...
Leipzig, 1750-1897. 11 v.   06-3520
Z1010 .J63 MRR Biog.

Who's who among living authors of
older nations, v. 1; 1931/32. Los
Angeles, Calif., Golden Syndicate
Pub. Co. 016.928 28-28492
Z1010 .W62 MRR Alc Latest edition

BIO-BIBLIOGRAPHY--BIBLIOGRAPHY.
Arnim, Max, Internationale
Personalbibliographie, 1800-1943.
2., verb. und stark verm. Aufl.
Leipzig, K. W. Hiersemann, 1944-52.
2 v.   016.012 45-22033
Z8001.A1 A72 MRR Biog.

Oettinger, Eduard Maria,
Bibliographie biographique
universelle. Paris, A. Lacroix,
1866. 2 v. (iv, 2191 p.)   50-44257

Z5301 .O3 1866 MRR Biog.

BIO-BIBLIOGRAPHY--DICTIONARIES.
Vapereau, Gustave, Dictionnaire
universel des contemporains 6. ed.
entièrement refondue et
considérablement augm. Paris [etc.]
Hachette et cie, 1893. 2 p. l., iii,
[1], 1629 p., 1 l.   02-5034
CT148 .V3 1893 MRR Biog.

BIO-GEOGRAPHY
see Anthropo-geography

BIOASTRONAUTICS
see Space medicine

BIOETHICS--BIBLIOGRAPHY--PERIODICALS.
Bibliography of society, ethics and
the life sciences. Hastings-on-the
Hudson, N.Y., Institute of Society,
Ethics and the Life Sciences.
016.174/2 73-160650
Z5322.B5 B52 MRR Alc Full set /
Sci RR Full set

BIOGRAPHY.
Berühmte Köpfe; 3200 Männer und
Frauen im Bild. [1. Aufl.
Gütersloh] C. Bertelsmann [1959]
413 p.   920 60-26257
N7575 .B47 MRR Alc.

Clark, Barrett Harper, comp. Great
short biographies of the world, New
York, R. M. McBride, 1929. xiii,
1407 p.   920.02 30-24284
CT105 .C45 1929 MRR Biog.

De Ford, Miriam Allen, Who was when?
2d ed. New York, Wilson, 1950. 1
v. (unpaged) 902 51-796
CT103 .D4 1950 MRR Alc.

Nisenson, Samuel. The dictionary of
1001 famous people; [New York] Lion
Press [1966] 267 p. 920.02/03 920
71-4426
CT107 .N58 1966 MRR Biog.

BIOGRAPHY. (Cont.)
Stiles, Kent B. Postal saints and
sinners; Brooklyn, T. Gaus' Sons,
1964. ix, 295 p.   383.22 64-7712
   HE6215 .S7 MRR Alc.

Who did what; New York, Crown
Publishers [1974] 383 p. [$12.95]
920/.02 920 73-81194
   CT103 .W47 1974 MRR Biog.

BIOGRAPHY--MIDDLE AGES, 500-1500.
Fines, John. Who's who in the Middle
Ages. London, Blond, 1970. xii, 218
p.   940.1/0922 B 70-540350
   D115 .F5 1970 MRR Biog.

BIOGRAPHY--20TH CENTURY.
Celebrity register. 1959- New York,
Harper & Row [etc.] 920.02 59-15865

   CT120 .I46 MRR Biog Latest edition

Current biography yearbook. 1940-
New York, H. W. Wilson. 40-27432
   CT100 .C8 MRR Biog Full set

Elliott, Florence. A dictionary of
politics. 6th ed. Harmondsworth,
Penguin, 1971. 480 p. [10/-]
320/.03 72-186214
   D419 .E4 1971 MRR Alc.

Grant, Neil. World leaders of today.
London, New York, F. Watts, 1972.
[8], 310 p. [£2.75] 909.82/092/2 B
73-152399
   D412.6 .G68 MRR Biog.

The International year book and
statesmen's who's who. 1953-
London, Burke's Peerage. 305.8 53-
1425
   JA51 .I57 MRR Biog Latest edition

Lazić, Branko M. Biographical
dictionary of the Comintern.
Stanford, Calif., Hoover Institution
Press, 1973. xxxxii, 458 p.
[$15.00] 329/.072/0922 B 72-187265

   HX11.I5 L3378 MRR Biog.

Leaders of the communist world. New
York, Free Press [1971] xv, 632 p.
335.43/0922 B 74-84751
   HX23 .L4 MRR Biog.

Martell, Paul. World military
leaders / New York : Bowker, [1974]
268 p. ;   355/.0092/2 B 74-78392
   U51 .M35 MRR Biog.

The New York times biographical
edition. v. 1- Jan. 1, 1970- [New
York, New York times & Arno Press]
920.02 70-20206
   CT120 .N45 MRR Biog Partial set

Robinson, Donald B., The 100 most
important people in the world today
New York, Putnam [1970] 384 p.
[6.95] 920.02 75-81649
   CT120 .R6 1970 MRR Biog.

Tunney, Christopher, A biographical
dictionary of World War II. London,
Dent, 1972. viii, 216 p. [£3.50]
940.53/092/2 72-193297
   D736 .T78 MRR Biog.

BIOGRAPHY--20TH CENTURY--BIBLIOGRAPHY.
Johnson, Robert Owen. An index to
profiles in the New Yorker.
Metuchen, N.J., Scarecrow Press,
1972. vi, 190 p.   016.920/073 71-
186947
   Z5305.U5 J64 MRR Biog.

BIOGRAPHY--20TH CENTURY--DICTIONARIES.
The Blue book; leaders of the English-
speaking world. 1970- New York, St.
Martin's Press [etc.] 920.02 73-
13918
   CT120 .B55 MRR Biog Latest edition

Dictionary of international
biography. [1st]- ed.; 1963-
London. 920.02 64-1109
   CT101 .D5 MRR Biog Latest edition
   / MRR Ref Desk Latest edition /
   MRR Alc Latest edition

International who's who in community
service. 1973/74- ed. London,
Eddison Press. [12.50] 361/.0025
78-189467
   HV27 .I57 MRR Biog Latest edition

Laqueur, Walter Ze'ev, A dictionary
of politics / Rev. ed. New York :
Free Press, 1974, c1973. 565 p. ;
[$14.95] 320.9/04 74-9232
   D419 .L36 1974 MRR Alc.

National register of prominent
Americans and international notables.
Venice, Fla., National Register of
Prominent Americans and International
Notables Research Center. 920.02 74-
27338
   CT103 .N3 MRR Biog Latest edition

Royal blue book. Chicago [etc.] St.
James Press [etc.] 920/.0025 68-
6111
   CT103 .R64 MRR Biog Latest edition

Who's who in the world. 1st- ed.;
1971/72- Chicago, Marquis Who's Who,
inc. 920.02 78-139215
   CT120 .W5 MRR Biog Latest edition

BIOGRAPHY--BIBLIOGRAPHY.
Chicorel, Marietta. Chicorel index
to biographies. 1st ed. New York,
Chicorel Library Pub. Corp., 1974. 2
v. (898 p.)   016.92 74-175082
   Z5301 .C54 MRR Biog.

Gilbert, Judson Bennett, Disease and
destiny; London, Dawsons of Pall
Mall, 1962. 535 p.   016.92 62-4082

   Z6664.A1 G5 MRR Alc.

Hazeltine, Mary Emogene,
Anniversaries and holidays, 2d ed.,
completely revised Chicago, American
library association 1944. xix, 316
p.   394.26 44-53464
   Z5710 .H42 1944 MRR Alc.

Hefling, Helen. Hefling & Richards'
Index to contemporary biography and
criticism. A new ed. rev. and enl.
Boston, F. W. Faxon company, 1934. 3
p. l., 9-229 p.   016.92 34-28569
   Z5301 .H46 1934 MRR Biog.

Oettinger, Eduard Maria,
Bibliographie biographique
universelle. Paris, A. Lacroix,
1866. 2 v. (iv, 2191 p.)   50-44257

   Z5301 .O3 1866 MRR Biog.

O'Neill, Edward Hayes, Biography by
Americans, 1658-1936; Philadelphia,
University of Pennsylvania press;
London, H. Milford, Oxford university
press, 1939. x, 465 p.   016.92 39-
30813
   Z5301 .O58 MRR Alc.

Phillips, Lawrence Barnett, The
dictionary of biographical reference;
London, S. Low, son, & Marston,
1871. 1 p. l., x, [2], 1020 p.   02-
2800
   CT103 .P5 1871 MRR Biog.

Pittsburgh. Carnegie library. Men of
science and industry; Pittsburgh,
Carnegie library, 1915. 189, [3] p.
15-6134
   Z7404 .A1P6 MRR Biog.

Shaw, Thomas Shuler, Index to
profile sketches in New Yorker
magazine, Boston, The F. W. Faxon
company, 1946. 5 p. l., 100 p.
016.920073 47-450
   Z5305.U5 S5 1946 MRR Biog.

Slocum, Robert B. Biographical
dictionaries and related works;
Detroit, Gale Research Co. [1967]
xxiii, 1056 p.   016.92 67-27789
   Z5301 .S55 MRR Biog.

United States. Library of Congress.
General Reference and Bibliography
Division. Biographical sources for
the United States. Washington, 1961.
v, 58 p.   016.920073 61-60065
   Z663.28 .B53 MRR Alc.

BIOGRAPHY--BIBLIOGRAPHY--CATALOGS.
Institut für Zeitgeschichte, Munich.
Bibliothek. Biographischer Katalog.
Boston, G. K. Hall, 1967. viii, 764
p.   016.0920/02 72-217206
   Z5301 .I55 MRR Biog.

Royal Commonwealth Society. Library.
Biography catalogue of the Library of
the Royal Commonwealth Society.
London, Royal Commonwealth Society,
1961. xxiii, 511 p.   016.92002 61-
66062
   Z5301 .R6 MRR Biog.

Royal Commonwealth Society. Library.
Subject catalogue of the Royal
Commonwealth Society, London.
Boston, Mass., G. K. Hall, 1971. 7
v.   017.1 70-180198
   Z7164.C7 R83 MRR Alc (Dk 33)

BIOGRAPHY--BIBLIOGRAPHY--DICTIONARIES.
Nicholsen, Margaret E. People in
books; New York, H. W. Wilson Co.,
1969. xviii, 498 p. 016.92 69-
15811
   Z5301 .N53 MRR Biog.

BIOGRAPHY--DICTIONARIES.
Agramonte y Cortijo, Francisco,
Diccionario cronológico biográfico
universal; [2. ed. corr. y muy
aumentada] Madrid, Aguilar [1952]
1266 p.   57-18055
   CT183 .A4 1952 MRR Biog.

Atlantic brief lives: a biographical
companion to the arts. [1st ed.]
Boston, Little, Brown [1971] xxii,
900 p. [$15.00] 700/.922 B 73-
154960
   NX90 .A73 1971 MRR Biog.

Buckland, Charles Edward, Dictionary
of Indian biography. Detroit, Gale
Research Co., 1968. xii, 494 p.
920.054 68-23140
   DS434 .B8 1968 MRR Biog.

The Cadillac modern encyclopedia.
[1st ed.] New York, Cadillac Pub.
Co.; distributed by Derbibooks,
Secaucus, N.J. [1973] xiv, 1954 p.
[$24.95] 031 73-81377
   AG5 .C25 MRR Ref Desk.

Cassell's new biographical
dictionary, containing memoirs of the
most eminent men and women of all
ages and countries. New York,
Cassell publishing company [1893] 2
p. l., 741 p.   21-2554
   CT103 .C3 1893 MRR Biog.

The Century dictionary and
cyclopedia, [Rev. and enl. ed.] New
York, The Century co. [c1911] 12 v.
[$75.00]   11-31934
   PE1625 .C4 1911 MRR Alc.

Chambers's biographical dictionary.
Rev. ed. New York, St Martin's Press
[1969, c1968] vii, 1432 p. [17.50]
920.02/03 76-85529
   CT103 .C4 1969 MRR Biog.

Collison, Robert Lewis. Newnes
Dictionary of dates; 2nd revised ed.
London, Newnes, 1966. ix, 11-428 p.
[35/-] 903 66-72492
   D11.5 .C6 1966 MRR Alc.

Dictionary of world history; London,
Nelson, 1973. xxvii, 1720 p.
[£15.00] 903 74-174563
   D9 .D55 MRR Ref Desk.

Garollo, Gottardo, Dizionario
biografico universale. Milano, U.
Hoepli, 1907. 2 v.   08-25727
   CT163 .G3 MRR Biog.

The General biographical dictionary:
New ed., rev. and enl. London,
Printed for J. Nichols, 1812-1817.
32 v.   mrr01-32
   CT103 .G4 MRR Biog.

Grigson, Geoffrey, ed. People: a
volume of the good, bad, great &
eccentric New York, Hawthorn Books
[1956?] 469 p.   920.02 55-12436
   CT103 .G73 MRR Biog.

Herzfeld, Hans, ed. Biographisches
Lexikon zur Weltgeschichte.
[Überarb., erg. und illustrierte
Neuausg. Frankfurt am Main] S.
Fischer [1960] 1039 p.   70-494991
   CT153 .H4 1969 MRR Biog.

Hyamson, Albert Montefiore, A
dictionary of universal biography of
all ages and of all peoples. 2d ed.,
entirely rewritten. London,
Routledge and K. Paul [1951] xii,
679 p. 920.02 51-6367
   CT103 .H9 1951 MRR Biog.

The International who's who. [1st]-
ed.; [1935]- London, Europa
Publications ltd. 920.01 35-10257
   CT120 .I5 Sci RR Latest edition /
   MRR Biog Latest edition

Kunitz, Stanley Jasspon, ed. British
authors of the nineteenth century.
New York, The H. W. Wilson company,
1936. 3 p. l., 677 p.   928.2 36-
28581
   PR451 .K8 1936 MRR Alc.

Kunitz, Stanley Jasspon, ed. The
junior book of authors. New York,
The H. W. Wilson company, 1934. xv,
400 p.   928 34-36776
   PN1009.A1 K8 MRR Biog.

Launay, André Joseph. Dictionary of
contemporaries. Fontwell (Sx.),
Centaur P., 1967. 368 p. [45/-]
920/.003 67-86851
   D11.5 .L3 MRR Alc.

The McGraw-Hill encyclopedia of world
biography. New York, McGraw-Hill
[1973] 12 v. 920/.02 70-37402
   CT103 .M27 MRR Biog.

Meyers enzyklopädisches Lexikon.
9., völlig neu bearb. Aufl.
Mannheim, Wien, Zürich,
Bibliographisches Inst. (1971- v.
with illus. and maps. [DM89.00 per
vol.] 70-873556
   AE27 .M6 1971 MRR Alc.

Mourre, Michel, Dictionnaire
d'histoire universelle. Paris,
Éditions universitaires, 1968. 2 v.
(2368 p.) [175.00] 71-376184
   D9 .M89 MRR Alc.

The New Century cyclopedia of names.
New York, Appleton-Century-Crofts
[1954] 3 v. (xxviii, 4342 p.)
929.4 52-13878
   PE1625 .C43 1954 MRR Ref Desk.

BIOGRAPHY--DICTIONARIES. (Cont.)
The New Century Italian Renaissance
encyclopedia. New York, Appleton-
Century-Crofts [1972] xiii, 978 p.
914.5/03/503 76-181735
DG537.8.A1 N48 MRR Biog.

Nisenson, Samuel. The dictionary of
1001 famous people; [New York] Lion
Press [1966] 267 p. 920.02/03 920
71-4426
CT107 .N58 1966 MRR Biog.

Phillips, Lawrence Barnett, The
dictionary of biographical reference;
London, S. Low, son, & Marston,
1871. 1 p. l., x, [2], 1020 p. 02-
2800
CT103 .P5 1871 MRR Biog.

Rodale, Jerome Irving, The phrase
finder; Emmaus, Pa., Rodale Press
[c1953] 1325 p. 423 54-2348
PE1689 .R63 MRR Alc.

Thomas, Joseph, Universal
pronouncing dictionary of biography
and mythology, 5th ed.
Philadelphia, London, J. B.
Lippincott company [c1930] 2 p. l.,
iii-xi, [1] p., 1 l., 5-2550 p.
920.01 30-22946
CT103 .L7 1930 MRR Biog.

Webster's biographical dictionary.
Springfield, Mass., G. & C. Merriam
Co. [1974] xxxvi, 1697 p. [$12.95]
920/.02 73-14908
CT103 .W4 1974 MRR Ref Desk.

Webster's biographical dictionary.
Springfield, Mass., G & C. Merriam
Co. [1972] xxxvi, 1697 p. 920/.02
72-85
CT103 .W4 1972 MRR Biog.

Webster's biographical dictionary;
1st ed. Springfield, Mass., G & C.
Merriam Co. [1971] xxxvi, 1697 p.
920.02 77-23207
CT103 .W4 1971 MRR Alc.

Who did what; New York, Crown
Publishers [1974] 383 p. [$12.95]
920/.02 920 73-81194
CT103 .W47 1974 MRR Biog.

Who was who, v. [1]- ; 1897/1916-
London, A. & C. Black. 920.042 20-
14622
DA28 .W65 MRR Biog Full set

Who's who ; 1st- 1849- London,
A. and C. Black, [etc.] 04-16933
DA28 .W6 MRR Biog Latest edition /
MRR Biog Latest edition

BIOGRAPHY--DICTIONARIES--BIBLIOGRAPHY.
Royal Commonwealth Society. Library.
Biography catalogue of the Library of
the Royal Commonwealth Society,
London, Royal Commonwealth Society,
1961. xxiii, 511 p. 016.92002 61-
66062
Z5301 .R6 MRR Biog.

Slocum, Robert B. Biographical
dictionaries and related works;
Detroit, Gale Research Co. [1967]
xxiii, 1056 p. 016.92 67-27789
Z5301 .S55 MRR Biog.

BIOGRAPHY--DICTIONARIES--FRENCH.
Biographie universelle ancienne et
modern (Nouvelle ed.) Graz,
Akademische Druck- u. Verlagsanstalt,
1966- v. [1190.00 (v. 1) varies]
920/.003 68-105691
CT143 .M52 MRR Biog.

Grimal, Pierre, ed. Dictionnaire des
biographies. 1. ed.] Paris,
Presses universitaires de France,
1958. 2 v. (xii, 1563 p.) a 59-628
CT143 .G7 MRR Biog.

Mourre, Michel. Dictionnaire des
personnages historiques de tous les
temps. Paris, Bordas [1973] 715 p.
[42.00F] 420/.02/03 73-164812
CT143 .M68 MRR Biog.

Oettinger, Eduard Maria, Moniteur
des dates. Leipzig, L. Denicke,
1869. 6 v. in 1. 02-3518
CT154 .03 MRR Biog.

Vapereau, Gustave, Dictionnaire
universel des contemporains 6. ed.
entierement refondue et
considerablement augm. Paris [etc.]
Hachette et cie, 1893. 2 p. l., iii,
[1], 1629 p., 1 l. 02-5034
CT148 .V3 1893 MRR Biog.

BIOGRAPHY--DICTIONARIES--GERMAN.
Hirsching, Friedrich Karl Gottlob,
Historisch-literarisches handbuch
berühmter und denkwürdiger
personen, welche in dem 18.
Jahrhunderte gestorben sind;
Leipzig, Schwickert, 1794- v. in
920.01 32-19789
CT157 .H5 MRR Biog.

Jöcher, Christian Gottlieb,
Allgemeines gelehrten-lexicon ...
Leipzig, 1750-1897. 11 v. 06-3520

Z1010 .J63 MRR Biog.

Wer ist wer? [1]- Ausg.; 1905-
Berlin [etc.] Arani. 920.043 05-
32887
DD85 .W3 MRR Biog Latest edition

BIOGRAPHY--DICTIONARIES--ITALIAN.
Dizionario biografico degli autori di
tutti i tempi. Milano, Fabbri,
Bompiani, [1970]. 4 v. 74-312802
CT163 .D62 1970 MRR Biog.

BIOGRAPHY--DICTIONARIES--PORTUGUESE.
Dicionario biografico universal de
autores. [Lisboa?] Artis-Bompiani
[1966- v. 70-209859
CT183 .D55 MRR Biog.

BIOGRAPHY--DICTIONARIES--SPANISH.
Morales Diaz, Carlos. Quien es
quien en la nomenclatura de la
ciudad de Mexico; [Mexico] 1962.
ix, 582 p. 63-28910
F1386 .M74 MRR Biog.

BIOGRAPHY--FILM CATALOGS.
Sprecher, Daniel. Guide to films
(16mm) about famous people. [1st
ed.] Alexandria, Va., Serina Press
[1969] x, 206 p. 791.43/8 76-
110326
PN1998 .S694 MRR Alc.

BIOGRAPHY--INDEXES.
Arnim, Max, Internationale
Personalbibliographie, 1800-1943.
2., verb. und stark verm. Aufl.
Leipzig, K. W. Hiersemann, 1944-52.
2 v. 016.012 45-22033
Z8001.A1 A72 MRR Biog.

Barr, Ernest Scott, An index to
biographical fragments in
unspecialized scientific journals,
University, Ala., University of
Alabama Press [c1973] vii, 294 p.
016.5/092/2 B 73-13434
Q141 .B29 MRR Biog.

Biography index; v. 1- Jan.
1946/July 1949- New York, H. W.
Wilson Co. 016.92 47-6532
Z5301 .B5 MRR Biog Full set

Bull, Storm. Index to biographies of
contemporary composers. New York,
Scarecrow Press, 1964. 405 p.
016.9278 64-11781
ML105 .B9 MRR Biog.

Columbia University. Libraries. Avery
Architectural Library. Avery
obituary index of architects and
artists. Boston, G. K. Hall, 1963.
338 p. 64-7017
Z5941 .C64 MRR Biog.

Dargan, Marion. Guide to American
biography; Albuquerque, University
of New Mexico Press, 1949- v.
016.920073 49-48559
Z5305 .U5 D32 MRR Biog.

Havlice, Patricia Pate. Index to
artistic biography. Metuchen, N.J.,
Scarecrow Press, 1973. 2 v. (viii,
1362 p.) 709/.2/2 72-6412
N40 .H38 MRR Biog.

Hefling, Helen. Hefling & Richards'
Index to contemporary biography and
criticism. New ed. rev. and enl.
Boston, F. W. Faxon company, 1934. 3
p. l., 9-229 p. 016.92 34-28569
Z5301 .H46 1934 MRR Biog.

Historical Records Survey. District
of Columbia. Bio-bibliographical
index of musicians in the United
States of America since colonial
times. 2d ed. Washington, Music
Section, Pan American Union, 1956.
xxiii, 439 p. 016.78071 pa 57-4
ML106.U3 H6 1956 MRR Biog.

Howard University, Washington, D.C.
Library. Moorland Foundation.
Dictionary catalog of the Jesse E.
Moorland Collection of Negro Life and
History, Howard University,
Washington, D.C. Boston, G. K. Hall,
1970. 9 v. 016.910/0396 72-195773

Z1361.N39 H82 MRR Alc (Dk 33)

Hyamson, Albert Montefiore, A
dictionary of universal biography of
all ages and of all peoples. 2d ed.,
entirely rewritten. London,
Routledge and K. Paul [1951] xii,
679 p. 920.02 51-6367
CT103 .H9 1951 MRR Biog.

Institut für Zeitgeschichte, Munich.
Bibliothek. Biographischer Katalog.
Boston, G. K. Hall, 1967. viii, 764
p. 016.0920/02 72-217206
Z5301 .I55 MRR Biog.

Ireland, Norma (Olin) Index to
scientists of the world, from ancient
to modern times: Boston, F. W. Faxon
Co., 1962. xliii, 662 p. 016.925
62-13662
Z7404 .I7 MRR Biog.

Ireland, Norma (Olin) Index to women
of the world from ancient to modern
times; Westwood, Mass., F. W. Faxon
Co., 1970. xxcviii, 573 p.
016.92072 75-120841
Z7963.B6 I73 MRR Biog.

ISIS cumulative bibliography;
[London] Mansell, in conjunction with
the History of Science Society, 1971-
016.509 72-186272
Z7405.H6 I2 MRR Biog.

Johnson, Robert Owen. An index to
profiles in the New Yorker.
Metuchen, N.J., Scarecrow Press,
1972. vi, 190 p. 016.920/073 71-
186947
Z5305.U5 J64 MRR Biog.

Kiel. Universität. Institut für
Weltwirtschaft. Bibliothek.
Personenkatalog. Boston, G. K. Hall,
1966. 30 v. 72-213362
Z7164.E2 K55 MRR Alc. (Dk 33)

The New York times obituaries index,
1858-1968. New York, New York times,
1970. 1136 p. 929.3 72-113422
CT213 .N47 MRR Biog.

Nicholsen, Margaret E. People in
books; New York, H. W. Wilson Co.,
1969. xviii, 498 p. 016.92 69-
15811
Z5301 .N53 MRR Biog.

Park, Esther Ailleen. Mural painters
in America. Pittsburg, Kansas State
Teachers College, 1949- pts.
016.75173 50-63160
ND236 .P3 MRR Biog.

Pittsburgh. Carnegie library. Men of
science and industry; Pittsburgh,
Carnegie library, 1915. 189, [3] p.
15-6134
Z7404 .A1P6 MRR Biog.

Riches, Phyllis M. An analytical
bibliography of universal collected
biography, London, The Library
association, 1934. ix, 709, [1] p.
016.92 34-41786
Z5301 .R53 MRR Biog.

Royal Commonwealth Society. Library.
Biography catalogue of the Library of
the Royal Commonwealth Society,
London, Royal Commonwealth Society,
1961. xxiii, 511 p. 016.92002 61-
66062
Z5301 .R6 MRR Biog.

Schuster, Mel. Motion picture
directors; Metuchen, N.J., Scarecrow
Press, 1973. 418 p.
016.79143/0233/0922 73-780
Z5784.M9 S34 MRR Biog.

Schuster, Mel. Motion picture
performers; Metuchen, N.J., The
Scarecrow Press, 1971. 702 p.
016.79143/028/0922 70-154300
Z5784.M9 S35 MRR Biog.

Shaw, Thomas Shuler, Index to
profile sketches in New Yorker
magazine, Boston, The F. W. Faxon
company, 1946. 5 p. l., 100 p.
016.920073 47-450
Z5305.U5 S5 1946 MRR Biog.

Silverman, Judith, An index to young
readers' collective biographies; New
York, R. R. Bowker Co., 1970. ix,
282 p. 016.92003 73-126011
Z5301 .S523 MRR Biog.

Sousa, José Galante de, Indice de
biobibliografia brasileira Rio de
Janeiro] Instituto Nacional do Livro,
Ministerio da Educacao e Cultura
[1963] 440 p. 68-41350
Z1680 .S63 MRR Biog.

Spradling, Mary Mace, In black and
white: Afro-Americans in print;
Kalamazoo, Mich., Kalamazoo Library
System, 1971. ix, 127 p. [$3.00]
016.920073 77-31475
Z1361.N39 S653 MRR Biog.

Stanius, Ellen J. Index to short
biographies: for elementary and
junior high grades. Metuchen, N.J.,
Scarecrow Press, 1971. 348 p.
016.92002 70-149996
Z5301 .S7 MRR Biog.

Wallace, William Stewart, A
dictionary of North American authors
deceased before 1950. Toronto,
Ryerson Press [1951] viii, 525 p.
928.1 51-7279
PS128 .W3 MRR Biog.

BIOGRAPHY--JUVENILE LITERATURE.
Nisenson, Samuel. The dictionary of
1001 famous people: [New York] Lion
Press [1966] 267 p. 920.02/03 920
71-4426
CT107 .N58 1966 MRR Biog.

BIOGRAPHY--JUVENILE LITERATURE--
BIBLIOGRAPHY.
Hotchkiss, Jeanette. American
historical fiction and biography for
children and young people. Metuchen,
N.J., Scarecrow Press, 1973. 318 p.
016.9173/03 73-13715
Z1236 .H73 MRR Alc.

BIOGRAPHY--JUVENILE LITERATURE--INDEXES.
Silverman, Judith, An index to young
readers' collective biographies; New
York, R. R. Bowker Co., 1970. ix,
282 p. 016.92003 73-126011
Z5301 .S523 MRR Biog.

Stanius, Ellen J. Index to short
biographies: for elementary and
junior high grades. Metuchen, N.J.,
Scarecrow Press, 1971. 348 p.
016.92002 70-149996
Z5301 .S7 MRR Biog.

BIOGRAPHY--QUOTATIONS, MAXIMS, ETC.
Wale, William, ed. What great men
have said about great men; Detroit,
Gale Research Co., 1968. viii, 482
p. 808.88/2 68-17944
PN6084.G7 W2 1968 MRR Alc.

BIOLOGICAL CHEMISTRY.
Pritham, Gordon Herman, Anderson's
essentials of biochemistry St.
Louis, C. V. Mosby Co., 1968. xii,
710 p. 612/.015 68-21525
QP514 .P67 MRR Alc.

BIOLOGICAL CHEMISTRY--DICTIONARIES.
Williams, Roger John, The
encyclopedia of biochemistry, New
York, Reinhold [1967] xvii, 876 p.
574.1/92/03 67-15466
QP512 .W5 MRR Alc.

BIOLOGICAL PRODUCTS.
Physicians' desk reference to
pharmaceutical specialties and
biologicals. 1st- ed.; 1947-
Oradell [etc.] N.J., Medical
economics. 60-784
RS75 .P5 Sci RR latest edition /
MRR Ref Desk Latest edition

BIOLOGY.
see also Botany

see also Genetics

see also Marine biology

see also Microbiology

see also Microscope and microscopy

see also Physiology

see also Reproduction

see also Sex (Biology)

see also Space biology

Weisz, Paul B., The science of
biology 3d ed. New York, McGraw-
Hill [1967] xxiii, 886 p. 574 66-
23627
QH308 .W393 1967 MRR Alc.

BIOLOGY--BIBLIOGRAPHY.
Clapp, Jane. Museum publications.
New York, Scarecrow Press, 1962. 2
v. 016.0697 62-10120
Z5051 .C5 MRR Alc.

BIOLOGY--BIBLIOGRAPHY--PERIODICALS.
Biological & agricultural index.
Jan. 1916- [Bronx, N.Y., etc.] H. W.
Wilson Co. 17-8906
Z5073 .A46 Sci RR Full set / MRR
Alc Full set

BIOLOGY--DICTIONARIES.
Abercrombie, Michael. A dictionary
of biology 6th ed. [Harmondsworth,
Eng., Baltimore] Penguin Books [1973]
306 p. [$1.95 (U.S.)] £74/.03 73-
172135
QH13 .A25 1973 MRR Alc.

Artschwager, Ernst Friedrich,
Dictionary of biological equivalents,
German-English, Baltimore, The
Williams & Wilkins company, 1930.
239 p. incl. 6 plates. 570.3 30-
18274
QH13 .A7 MRR Alc.

Gray, Peter. The dictionary of the
biological sciences. New York,
Reinhold Pub. Corp. [1967] xx, 602
p. 574/.03 67-24690
QH13 .G68 MRR Alc.

Gray, Peter, ed. The encyclopedia of
the biological sciences. New York,
Reinhold Pub. Corp. [1961] xxi, 1119
p. 574.03 61-12385
QH13 .G7 MRR Alc.

Gray, Peter, Student dictionary of
biology, New York, Van Nostrand
Reinhold Co. [1973, c1972] vi, 194
p. 574/.03 73-742
QH13 .G73 MRR Alc.

Hanson, Herbert Christian,
Dictionary of ecology. New York,
Philosophical Library [1962] 382 p.
574.503 60-15954
QH541 .H25 MRR Alc.

Henderson, Isabella Ferguson. A
dictionary of biological terms,
Edinburgh [etc.] Oliver & Boyd [etc.]
574.03 61-383
QH13 .H38 Sci RR Latest edition /
MRR Alc Latest edition

Jaeger, Edmund Carroll, The
biologist's handbook of
pronunciations. Springfield, Ill.,
Thomas [1960] 317 p. 574.03 59-
14924
QH13 .J3 1960 MRR Alc.

Steen, Edwin Benzel, Dictionary of
biology New York, Barnes & Noble
[1971] vii, 630 p. [$3.95 ($4.50
Can)] 574/.03 70-156104
QH13 .S74 MRR Alc.

BIOLOGY--DICTIONARIES--FRENCH.
Lepine, Pierre. Dictionnaire
français-anglais, anglais-français,
des termes medicaux et biologiques;
Paris, Flammarion [1952] 829 p. 52-
3756
R121 .L39 MRR Alc.

BIOLOGY--DICTIONARIES--RUSSIAN.
Carpovich, Eugene A., Russian-
English biological & medical
dictionary. 1st ed. New York,
Technical Dictionaries Co., 1958.
400 p. 574.03 58-7915
QH13 .C37 1958 MRR Alc.

BIOLOGY--ECOLOGY
see Ecology

BIOLOGY--HISTORY.
Singer, Charles Joseph, A history of
biology to about the year 1900; 3d
and rev. ed. London and New York,
Abelard-Schuman [1959] 579 p.
574.09 58-6020
QH305 .S58 1959 MRR Alc.

BIOLOGY--INFORMATION SERVICES--
DIRECTORIES.
United States. Library of Congress.
National Referral Center. A
directory of information resources in
the United States: biological
sciences. Washington, Library of
Congress; [for sale by the Supt. of
Docs., U.S. Govt. Print. Off.] 1972.
iv, 577 p. [$5.00] 570/.7 72-2659

Z663.379 .D46 MRR Alc.

BIOLOGY--PERIODICALS--BIBLIOGRAPHY.
United States. Library of Congress.
Science and Technology Division.
Biological sciences serial
publications, Philadelphia,
Biological Abstracts, 1955. 269 p.
016.57405 55-60051
Z663.41 .B5 MRR Alc.

BIOLOGY--PERIODICALS--INDEXES.
Biological & agricultural index.
Jan. 1916- [Bronx, N.Y., etc.] H. W.
Wilson Co. 17-8906
Z5073 .A46 Sci RR Full set / MRR
Alc Full set

BIOLOGY--TABLES, ETC.
Spector, William S., ed. Handbook of
biological data. Philadelphia,
Saunders [1956] xxxvi, 584 p.
574.083 56-13410
QH310 .S6 MRR Alc.

BIOLOGY--TERMINOLOGY.
Jaeger, Edmund Carroll, A sourcebook of biological names and terms.
3d ed. Springfield, Ill., Thomas
[1955] xxxv, 317 p. 574.03 55-
8867
QH83 .J3 1955 MRR Alc.

BIOLOGY--UNITED STATES--INFORMATION
SERVICES--DIRECTORIES.
United States. Library of Congress.
National Referral Center. A
directory of information resources in
the United States: biological
sciences. Washington, Library of
Congress; [for sale by the Supt. of
Docs., U.S. Govt. Print. Off.] 1972.
iv, 577 p. [$5.00] 570/.7 72-2659

Z663.379 .D46 MRR Alc.

BIOLOGY, ECONOMIC.
see also Botany, Economic

BIOMEDICAL ENGINEERING.
see also Medical instruments and
apparatus

BIOMETRY.
see also Mathematical statistics

BIONOMICS
see Ecology

BIRD-SONG.
Wetmore, Alexander, Song and garden
birds of North America, Washington,
National Geographic Society [1964]
400 p. 598.2973 64-23367
QL681 .W46 MRR Alc.

BIRDS.
Austin, Oliver Luther, Birds of the
world; New York, Golden Press [1961]
316 p. 598.2 61-13290
QL673 .A88 MRR Alc.

Cruickshank, Allan D. 1001 questions
answered about birds, New York,
Dodd, Mead, 1958. 291 p. 598.2076
58-10784
QL673 .C7 MRR Alc.

Grzimek, Bernhard. Grzimek's animal
life encyclopedia. New York, Van
Nostrand Reinhold Co. [1972- v. 13,
1972] v. [$29.95 per vol.] 591
79-183178
QL3 .G7813 MRR Alc.

Welty, Joel Carl, The life of birds.
Philadelphia, W. B. Saunders co.,
1962. 546 p. 598.2 62-11639
QL673 .W38 MRR Alc.

BIRDS--PICTORIAL WORKS.
Audubon, John James, The birds of
America. New York, Dover
Publications [1967] 7 v. 598.2973
66-21183
QL674 .A9 1967 MRR Alc.

Hanzák, Jan. The pictorial
encyclopedia of birds London,
Hamlyn, 1967. 581 p. [30/-]
598.2/03 68-94508
QL674 .H23 1967b MRR Alc.

Reilly, Edgar M. The Audubon
illustrated handbook of American
birds New York, McGraw-Hill [1968]
xvii, 524 p. [$25.00 $19.95 (prior
to Jan. 1, 1969)] 598.297 68-22765

QL681 .R45 MRR Alc.

Wetmore, Alexander, Song and garden
birds of North America, Washington,
National Geographic Society [1964]
400 p. 598.2973 64-23367
QL681 .W46 MRR Alc.

BIRDS--AFRICA, EAST.
Williams, John George, A field guide
to the national parks of East Africa
London, Collins, 1967. 352 p. [45/-
] 591.967 68-76542
SB484.E3 W54 MRR Alc.

BIRDS--DISTRICT OF COLUMBIA.
Stewart, Robert E. Birds of Maryland
and the District of Columbia,
[Washington, U.S. Dept. of the
Interior, Fish and Wildlife Service,
1958] vi, 401 p. 598.29752 58-
61489
QL684.M3 S8 MRR Alc.

BIRDS--HAWAII.
Peterson, Roger Tory, A field guide
to western birds; 2d ed., rev. and
enl. Boston, Houghton Mifflin, 1961.
366 p. 598.2978 60-12250
QL683.W4 P4 1961 MRR Alc.

BIRDS--MARYLAND.
Stewart, Robert E. Birds of Maryland
and the District of Columbia,
[Washington, U.S. Dept. of the
Interior, Fish and Wildlife Service,
1958] vi, 401 p. 598.29752 58-
61489
QL684.M3 S8 MRR Alc.

BIRDS--NORTH AMERICA.
Audubon, John James, The birds of
America. New York, Dover
Publications [1967] 7 v. 598.2973
66-21183
QL674 .A9 1967 MRR Alc.

Chapman, Frank Michler, Handbook of
birds of eastern North America, 2d
rev. ed.] New York, Dover
Publications [1966] xxxvi, 581 p.
598.297 66-14553
QL681 .C46 1966 MRR Alc.

Elman, Robert. The hunter's field
guide to the game birds and animals
of North America. New York, Knopf;
[distributed by Random House] 1974.
655 p. 598.2/97 73-7289
SK40 .E45 1974 MRR Alc.

The New hunter's encyclopedia.
Updated new print. of 3d. ed. New
York : Galahad Books, [1974?] c1972.
xx, 1054 p. : [$24.95] 799.2/97
73-92819
SK33 .H945 1974 MRR Alc.

Palmer, Ralph Simon, ed. Handbook of
North American birds. New Haven,
Yale University Press, 1962- v.
598.297 62-8259
QL681 .P35 MRR Alc.

BIRDS--NORTH AMERICA. (Cont.)
Pough, Richard Hooper, Audubon
guides; [1st ed.] Garden City,
N.Y., Doubleday, 1953. xlii, 312,
xxviii, 352 p.   588.297 53-10998
    QL681 .P685 MRR Alc.

Reilly, Edgar M. The Audubon
illustrated handbook of American
birds New York, McGraw-Hill [1968]
xvii, 524 p. [$25.00 $19.95 (prior
to Jan. 1, 1969)] 598.297 68-22765

    QL681 .R45 MRR Alc.

Wetmore, Alexander, Song and garden
birds of North America, Washington,
National Geographic Society [1964]
400 p.   598.2973 64-23367
    QL681 .W46 MRR Alc.

BIRDS--NORTH AMERICA--NOMENCLATURE.
Gruson, Edward S. Words for birds;
[New York] Quadrangle Books [1972]
xiv, 305 p. [$8.95] 598.2/97 72-
77537
    QL677 .G78 1972 MRR Alc.

**BIRDS--NORTH AMERICA--NOMENCLATURE
(POPULAR)**
Gruson, Edward S. Words for birds;
[New York] Quadrangle Books [1972]
xiv, 305 p. [$8.95] 598.2/97 72-
77537
    QL677 .G78 1972 MRR Alc.

BIRDS--WEST.
Peterson, Roger Tory, A field guide
to western birds; 2d ed., rev. and
enl., Boston, Houghton Mifflin, 1961.
366 p.   558.2978 60-12250
    QL683.W4 P4 1961 MRR Alc.

BIRDS IN THE BIBLE
    see Bible--Natural history

BIRMINGHAM, ENG.--BIOGRAPHY.
The Birmingham post year book and
who's who. Birmingham, Birmingham
Post & Mail. 52-44929
    Began publication in 1949.
    DA690.B6 B5 MRR Alc Latest edition

BIRMINGHAM, ENG.--DIRECTORIES.
The Birmingham post year book and
who's who. Birmingham, Birmingham
Post & Mail. 52-44929
    Began publication in 1949.
    DA690.B6 B5 MRR Alc Latest edition

Kelly's directory of Birmingham
(including the suburbs and the
boroughs of Smethwick and Aston
Manor) Kingston upon Thames, Surrey
[etc.] Kelly's Directories. 15-2480

    DA690.B6 A4 MRR Alc Latest edition

BIRTH CONTROL.
    see also Abortion

Guttmacher, Alan Frank, Pregnancy,
birth, and family planning; New
York, Viking Press [1973] xv, 365 p.
[$10.00] 612.6/3 72-79006
    RG525 .G82 1973 MRR Alc.

BIRTH CONTROL--BIBLIOGRAPHY.
Driver, Edwin D. World population
policy: an annotated bibliography
Lexington, Mass., Lexington Books
[c1971] xxi, 1280 p. 016.30132 73-
184302
    Z7164.D3 D75 MRR Alc.

**BIRTH CONTROL--SOCIETIES, ETC.--
DIRECTORIES.**
Fogle, Catherine. International
directory of population information
and library resources, 1st ed.
[Chapel Hill] Carolina Population
Center, 1972. xiii, 324 p.
301.32/025 79-190722
    HB850 .F6 MRR Alc.

Women's rights almanac. 1974-
Bethesda, Md., Elizabeth Cady Stanton
Pub. Co. [$4.95] 301.41/2/0973 74-
77527
    HQ1406 .W65 MRR Ref Desk Latest
    edition

**BIRTH CONTROL--UNITED STATES--
STATISTICS.**
Planned Parenthood-World Population.
Center for Family Planning Program
Development. Need for subsidized
family planning services: United
States, each State and county, 1968.
[New York, 1969] viii, 255 p.
353.008/4 76-604306
    HQ766.5.U5 P56 MRR alc.

BIRTH-STONES.
Krythe, Maymie Richardson. All about
the months [1st ed.] New York,
Harper & Row [1966] 222 p.   529.2
66-18584
    GR930 .K7 MRR Alc.

BIRTH-STONES--JUVENILE LITERATURE.
Heaps, Willard Allison, Birthstones,
[1st ed.] New York, Meredith Press
[1969] 138 p. [4.95] 553/.8 78-
75692
    GR805 .H4 MRR Alc.

BIRTHDAYS.
Miller, Warren Hudson. Who shares
your birthday? 2d ed. New York,
Allwyn Press [1970] 187 p.   920.02
70-106046
    D11.5 .M56 1970 MRR Alc.

BIRTHSTONES.
Heaps, Willard Allison, Birthstones,
[1st ed.] New York, Meredith Press
[1969] 138 p. [4.95] 553/.8 78-
75692
    GR805 .H4 MRR Alc.

BISCUITS.
Biscuit & cracker baker blue book.
New York, American Trade Pub. Co.
338.4/7/66475202573 63-36580
    HD9057 .A1B5 MRR Alc Latest
    edition

BISCUITS, ENGLISH
    see Cookies

BISHOPS--GREAT BRITAIN.
Powicke, Frederick Maurice, Sir, ed.
Handbook of British chronology, 2d
ed. London, Offices of the Royal
Historical Society, 1961. xxxviii,
565 p.   942.002 62-3079
    DA34 .P6 1961 MRR Alc.

BISHOPS--UNITED STATES--DIRECTORIES.
Notable names in American history;
3d ed. of White's conspectus of
American biography. [Clifton, N.J.]
J. T. White, 1973. 725 p.   920/.073
73-6885
    E176 .N89 1973 MRR Biog.

BITUMINOUS COAL.
Bituminous coal facts. 1948-
Washington, National Coal
Association. 338.2724 49-816
    HD9544 .B47 MRR Alc Latest edition

BLACK AFRICA
    see Africa, Sub-Saharan

BLACK AMERICANS
    see Negroes

BLACK MASS
    see Satanism

BLAKE, WILLIAM, 1757-1827--CONCORDANCES.
Erdman, David V. A concordance to
the writings of William Blake,
Ithaca, N.Y., Cornell University
Press [1967] 2 v. (xxxvi, 2317 p.)
828/.7/09 66-18608
    PR4146 .A25 MRR Alc.

BLAZONRY
    see Heraldry

BLIND--EMPLOYMENT--BIBLIOGRAPHY.
United States. Library of Congress.
Division for the Blind. Reading for
profit; Rev. ed. Washington, 1963.
iii, 29 p.   63-60035
    Z663.25 .R4 1963 MRR Alc.

BLIND--PRINTING AND WRITING SYSTEMS.
Dorf, Maxine B. Instruction manual
for Braille transcribing, [1st]-
ed.; 1961- Washington, Division for
the Blind, Library of Congress. 61-
60007
    Z663.25 .A33 MRR Alc MRR Alc
    Latest edition

Dorf, Maxine B. Instruction manual
for Braille transcribing. Supplement:
Drills reproduced in Braille. 1961-
Washington, Division for the Blind,
Library of Congress. 74-643531
    Z663.25 .A332 MRR Alc MRR Alc
    Latest edition

United States. Library of Congress.
Division for the Blind. A Manual of
standard English braille for the
guidance of transcribers and other
embossers. [1st]- ed.; 1950-
Washington. 371.911 50-60999
    Z663.25 .M3 MRR Alc MRR Alc Latest
    edition

United States. Library of Congress.
Division for the Blind. Volunteer
Braille transcribing. Rev. ed.
Washington, 1961. 5 p. 655.38 61-
60015
    Z663.25 .V6 1961 MRR Alc.

United States. Library of Congress.
Divison for the Blind. Summary and
interpretation of changes in official
braille code. Washington, 1960. 18
p.   655.38 60-60045
    Z663.25 .S8 MRR Alc.

BLIND--REHABILITATION--BIBLIOGRAPHY.
United States. Library of Congress.
Division for the Blind. Counseling
and rehabilitation; Washington,
1962. iii, 9 p. 62-60018
    Z663.25 .C6 MRR Alc.

BLIND, BOOKS FOR THE.
United States. Library of Congress.
Division for the Blind. Books for
the blind. Washington [U.S. Govt.
Print. Off.] 655.38 789.912* 53-
60019
    Z663.25 .B6 MRR Alc   MRR Alc Latest
    edition

BLIND, BOOKS FOR THE--BIBLIOGRAPHY.
Joyce, Donald F., comp. The Civil
War; a list of one hundred books in
braille and on talking book records.
Washington, 1961. 7 p.   61-60075
    Z663.25 .C5 MRR Alc.

United States. Library of Congress.
Division for the blind. Books in
Braille, 1931-1938. Washington [U.S.
Govt. print. off.] 1939. viii, 95 p.
016.65538 39-26817
    Z663.25 .B63 MRR Alc.

United States. Library of Congress.
Division for the Blind. Books in
Braille placed in the distributing
libraries. 1931/32- Washington.
016.65538 43-44850
    Z5346.Z9. U442 MRR Alc Partial set

United States. Library of Congress.
Division for the Blind. Braille
books for juvenile readers;
Washington, 1960. 39 p.   016.028024
60-60059
    Z663.25 .B7 MRR Alc.

United States. Library of Congress.
Division for the Blind. Reading for
profit; Rev. ed. Washington, 1963.
iii, 29 p.   63-60035
    Z663.25 .R4 1963 MRR Alc.

United States. Library of Congress.
Division for the Blind. Union
catalog of hand-copied books in
braille. Washington, Library of
Congress, 1955. viii, 581 p.
016.028024 55-60022
    Z663.25 .U6 MRR Alc.

United States. Library of Congress.
Service for the blind. Moon type
books in the Room for the blind,
Library of Congress. July, 1921.
Washington, Govt. print. off.,
Library branch, 1921. 16 p.   21-
26006
    Z663.25 .M6 MRR Alc.

United States. Library of Congress.
Service for the blind. New York
point books in the Room for the
blind, Library of Congress. July,
1921. Washington, Govt. print. off.,
Library branch, 1921. 37 p.   21-
26007
    Z663.25 .N4 MRR Alc.

BLIND, BOOKS FOR THE--CONGRESSES.
Conference on Volunteer Activities in
Recording and Transcribing Books for
the Blind, Washington, D.C., 1952.
Proceedings. Washington, Library of
Congress, 1954. viii, 61 p.   54-
60014
    Z663.25 .P7 MRR Alc.

BLIND, BOOKS FOR THE--DIRECTORIES.
United States. Library of Congress.
Division for the Blind and Physically
Handicapped. Volunteers who produce
books: braille, large type, tape.
Washington, Division for the Blind
and Physically Handicapped, Library
of Congress, 1970 [i.e. 1971] xvii,
69 p.   362.4/1/02573 79-610882
    Z663.25 .V62 MRR Alc.

BLIND, LIBRARIES FOR THE--DIRECTORIES.
Directory of library resources for
the blind and physically handicapped.
Washington, Library of Congress,
Division for the Blind and Physically
Handicapped. 027.6/63/02573 70-
615605
    Z675.B6 D5 MRR Alc Latest edition

**BLIND, PERIODICALS FOR THE--
BIBLIOGRAPHY.**
United States. Library of Congress.
Division for the Blind and Physically
Handicapped. Magazines: braille and
recorded. Washington, 1968. 12 l.
016.05 68-60035
    Z663.25 .M28 MRR Alc.

**BLIND, WORKERS FOR THE--UNITED STATES--
DIRECTORIES.**
United States. Library of Congress.
Division for the Blind and Physically
Handicapped. Volunteers who produce
books: braille, large type, tape.
Washington, Division for the Blind
and Physically Handicapped, Library
of Congress, 1970 [i.e. 1971] xvii,
69 p.   362.4/1/02573 79-610882
    Z663.25 .V62 MRR Alc.

BLOCH, CLAUDE CHARLES, 1878-1967--
MANUSCRIPTS--CATALOGS.
United States. Library of Congress.
Manuscript Division. Claude Charles
Bloch, Julius Augustus Furer, John
Franklin Shafroth, William Harrison
Standley: a register of their papers
in the Library of Congress.
Washington, Library of Congress,
1973. iii, 6, 11, 6, 4, 11, p.
016.359   73-4374
Z663.34 .B55 MRR Alc.

BLOCK TRADING--DIRECTORIES.
Block trader directory. [New York,
Kennington Pub. Corp.] 332.6/2 68-
7218
HG4512 .B6 MRR Alc Latest edition

BLOOD--CIRCULATION.
see also Heart

BLUE RIDGE MOUNTAINS--DESCRIPTION AND
TRAVEL--GUIDE-BOOKS.
Potomac Appalachian Trail Club,
Washington, D.C. Guide to the
Appalachian Trail: 7th ed.
Washington, 1970. vii, 190 p.
917.5 75-14141
F217.B6 P83 1970 MRR Alc.

BLUES (SONGS, ETC.)--DISCOGRAPHY.
Whitburn, Joel. Top rhythm & blues
records, 1949-1971. Menomonee Falls,
Wis., Record Research, c1973. 184 p.
016.7899/12 73-78333
ML156.4.P6 W53 MRR Alc.

BLUNDERS
see Errors, Popular

BOARD OF TRADE--BELGIUM--BRUSSELS--
DIRECTORIES.
Brussels. Chambre de commerce.
Annuaire officiel. Bruxelles, Impr.
Industrielle et financière [etc.]
380.1/06/24933 74-642351
HF314 .B85 MRR Alc Latest edition

BOARDING SCHOOLS--CANADA--DIRECTORIES.
The Boarding school directory of the
United States and Canada. v. 3-
1969/72- Chicago, Educational
Bureau. 371/.02/0257 72-627132
L901 .B65 MRR Ref Desk Latest
edition

BOARDING SCHOOLS--UNITED STATES--
DIRECTORIES.
The Boarding school directory of the
United States and Canada. v.1-
1969/72- Chicago, Educational
Bureau. 371/.02/0257 72-627132
L901 .B65 MRR Ref Desk Latest
edition

BOARDS OF TRADE--DIRECTORIES.
Gale Research Company. Encyclopedia
of associations. 8th ed. Detroit,
Mich. [1973- v.   [$45.00 (v. 1)
$28.50 (v. 2)] 061/.3 73-7400
HS17 .G334 1973 MRR Ref Desk.

International Trade Centre. World
directory of industry and trade
associations. [2d ed.] Geneva, 1970
viii, 370 p.   [$5.00 (U.S.)]
338/.C062 70-590660
HF294 .I87 1970 MRR Alc.

BOARDS OF TRADE--NORTHERN IRELAND.
Northern Ireland Chamber of Commerce
and Industry. Yearbook. [Belfast]
380.1/025/415 74-615885
HF302 .N68 MRR Alc Latest edition

BOARDS OF TRADE--UNITED STATES--
DIRECTORIES.
American Chamber of Commerce
Executives. Membership directory.
[Washington] 56-36525
HF296 .A114 MRR Alc Latest edition

BOAT-BUILDING--DIRECTORIES.
B U C International Corporation.   B U
C's new boat directory. [Fort
Lauderdale, Fla.]
338.4/7/62382310973 72-620449
HD9999.B5 B2 MRR Alc Latest
edition

BOATING INDUSTRY--UNITED STATES--
DIRECTORIES.
B U C International Corporation.   B U
C's new boat directory. [Fort
Lauderdale, Fla.]
338.4/7/62382310973 72-620449
HD9999.B5 B2 MRR Alc Latest
edition

Used boat directory. [Fort
Lauderdale, Fla.] BUC International
Corp. 381/.45/62382310257/3 72-
627195
HD9999.B513 U58 MRR Alc Latest
edition

BOATS AND BOATING.
see also Aquatic sports

see also Ships

De Fontaine, Wade Hampton, 1001
questions answered about boats and
boating. New York, Dodd, Mead [1966]
xiv, 227 p.   797.1076 66-14988
GV775 .D4 MRR Alc.

United States. Coast Guard. Official
U.S. Coast Guard recreational boating
guide. New York, Grosset & Dunlap
[1967] 124 p.   623.88 67-3310
GV775 .U59 1967 MRR Alc.

BOATS AND BOATING--PRICES.
Blue book official outboard boat
trade-in guide. Kansas City, Mo.,
Abos Marine Publications Div.,
Intertect Pub. Corp. [etc.] [$4.95]
338.4/3/62382130973 74-644650
VM348 .B52 MRR Alc Latest edition

Used boat directory. [Fort
Lauderdale, Fla.] BUC International
Corp. 381/.45/62382310257/3 72-
627195
HD9999.B513 U58 MRR Alc Latest
edition

BOATS AND BOATING--MIDDLE STATES.
Waterway guide. Middle Atlantic
edition. no. 1- 1963- Chesapeake,
Va. [etc.] Waterway Guide Inc. [etc.]
64-2891
GV835 .W35 MRR Alc Latest edition

BOATS AND BOATING--NEW ENGLAND.
Waterway guide. Northern edition.
[Fort Lauderdale, Fla., Inland
Waterway Guide, inc.] 623.89/29/73
73-641441
VK994 .I55 MRR Alc Latest edition

BOATS AND BOATING--VIRGINIA.
Salt water sport fishing and boating
in Virginia. Alexandria, Va., 1971.
78 p.   [$5.00] 623.89 73-654615
G1291.L1 S2 1971 MRR Alc.

BODY, HUMAN.
see also Anatomy, Human

see also Physiology

BOGAN, LOUISE, 1897-1970.
Smith, William Jay. Louise Bogan: a
woman's words; Washington, Library
of Congress [for sale by the Supt. of
Docs., U.S. Govt. Print. Off.] 1971
[i.e. 1972] 81 p.   [$0.45]
811/.5/2 70-37000
Z663 .B6 MRR Alc.

BOGAN, LOUISE, 1897-1970--BIBLIOGRAPHY.
Smith, William Jay. Louise Bogan: a
woman's words; Washington, Library
of Congress [for sale by the Supt. of
Docs., U.S. Govt. Print. Off.] 1971
[i.e. 1972] 81 p.   [$0.45]
811/.5/2 70-37000
Z663 .B6 MRR Alc.

BOHEMIA--BIOGRAPHY.
Kosch, Wilhelm. Biographisches
Staatshandbuch; Bern, Francke [1963]
2 v. (1208 p.) 67-3923
DD85 .K6 MRR Biog.

BOHEMIA--HISTORY.
Thomson, Samuel Harrison,
Czechoslovakia in European history.
[2d ed., enl.] Princeton, Princeton
University Press, 1953. 485 p.
943.7 52-8780
DB205.1 .T48 1953 MRR Alc.

BOHEMIAN LITERATURE.
Chudoba, František. A short survey
of Czech literature, London, K.
Paul, Trench, Trubner & co., ltd.;
New York, E. P. Dutton & co., 1924.
vii, 280 p. 25-40
PG5001 .C5 MRR Alc.

BOHEMIANISM.
see also Hippies

BOLIVIA.
Weil, Thomas E. Area handbook for
Bolivia. 2d ed. [Washington; For
sale by the Supt. of Docs., U.S.
Govt. Print. Off.] 1974. xiv, 417 p.
918.4/03/5 73-600327
F3308 .W44 1974 MRR Alc.

BOLIVIA--BIOGRAPHY.
Heath, Dwight B. Historical
dictionary of Bolivia, Metuchen,
N.J., Scarecrow Press, 1972. vi, 324
p. 984/.003 73-172476
F3304 .H4 MRR Alc.

BOLIVIA--DICTIONARIES AND ENCYCLOPEDIAS.
Heath, Dwight B. Historical
dictionary of Bolivia, Metuchen,
N.J., Scarecrow Press, 1972. vi, 324
p. 984/.003 73-172476
F3304 .H4 MRR Alc.

BOLIVIA--GAZETTEERS.
United States. Office of Geography.
Bolivia; Washington, U.S. Govt.
Print. Off., 1955. v, 269 p. 55-
61876
F3304 .U52 MRR Alc.

BOLSHEVISM
see Communism

BONAPARTE, CHARLES JOSEPH, 1851-1921--
BIBLIOGRAPHY.
United States. Library of Congress.
Manuscript Division. Charles Joseph
Bonaparte: a register of his papers
in the Library of Congress.
Washington, 1958. 20 p.   012 58-
60036
Z663.34 .B6 MRR Alc.

BONDS.
see also Stocks

Econtel Research. World bond yields.
[London, Econtel Research, 1972] 20
p. 332.6/323 72-195436
HG4651 .E26 MRR Alc.

International bonds. [New York]
White, Weld & Co. 332.6/323 74-
642653
HG4507 .F64 MRR Alc Latest edition

Smythe, Roland Mulville. Valuable
extinct securities; New York, 1929.
v p., 1 l., 398 p.   30-1926
HG4927 .S63 MRR Alc.

Standard and Poor's Corporation.
Status of bonds under the federal
income and state taxes and coupon
directory. 1942- ed. New York.
332.630973 42-15584
HG4921 .S67 MRR Alc Latest edition

BONDS--YEARBOOKS.
Moody's municipal & government
manual: American and foreign. 1955-
New York, Moody's Investors Service.
57-29
HG4931 .M58 MRR Alc Latest edition

BONDS--CONFEDERATE STATES OF AMERICA.
Affleck, C. J. Confederate bonds and
certificates; [Winchester? Va.,
1960] 38 p.   60-44646
HG4941 .A54 MRR Alc.

BONDS--GREAT BRITAIN.
Pember and Boyle, London. British
Government securities in the
twentieth century; [2d ed. London,
1950] 596 p.   336.31 50-14274
HG5438 .P4 MRR Alc.

BONDS--ISRAEL.
Development Corporation for Israel.
Who's who, 1958 trustees of Israel;
New York, State of Israel Bond
Organization [1959] 215 p.
336.31095694 59-46141
HG5811.P3 D4 MRR Biog.

BONDS--NORWAY.
Haandbok over norske obligationer og
aktier, Oslo. 24-10346
HG4207 .H3 MRR Alc Latest edition

BONDS--UNITED STATES.
Corporate holdings of insurance
companies. 1st- ed.; 1948-
Morristown, N.J. [etc.] United
Statistical Associates. 332.63 49-
13782
HG8078 .C6 MRR Alc Latest edition

Dow, Jones & Co., New York. The Dow
Jones averages, 1885-1970. [New
York, 1972] 1 v. (unpaged)
332.6/322/0973 78-183053
HG4519 .D59 MRR Alc.

Dow, Jones & Co., New York. The Dow
Jones investor's handbook.
Princeton, N.J. [etc.] Dow Jones
Books [etc.] 332.67/8 66-17650
HG4921 .D66 MRR Alc Latest edition

First Boston Corporation. Handbook
of securities of the United States
government and federal agencies, 22d-
ed.; 1966- [New York] 332.6/323
72-622502
HG4936 .F5 MRR Alc Latest edition

Harris Trust and Savings Bank.
Investment Dept. Government Bond
Division. The U.S. Government
securities market. [Chicago, 1973]
106 p.   332.6/323 73-160711
HG4936 .H36 MRR Alc.

The U.S. news & world report guide to
stocks, bonds & mutual funds.
Washington, Books by U.S. News &
World Report [1972] 191 p. [$2.95]
332.6/78/0973 79-188880
HG4921 .U65 MRR Alc.

White, Wilson. White's tax exempt
bond market ratings. 1st- ed.;1954-
New York, Standard & Poor's
Corp.,[etc.] 65-47879
HG4537 .W5 MRR Alc Latest edition

BONDS--UNITED STATES--DIRECTORIES.
Standard and Poor's Corporation.
Standard and Poor's directory of bond
agents. 1974/75- ed. New York.
[$180.00] 332.6/7 74-645518
HG4907 .S7a MRR Alc Latest edition

BONDS--UNITED STATES--PERIODICALS.
The National monthly bond summary.
v. 80- July 1954- New York,
National Quotation Bureau.
332.6323/0973 72-624151
HG4905 .N3 MRR Alc Latest edition

BONDS--UNITED STATES--YEARBOOKS.
Best's market guide. 1st- ed.;
1970- Morristown, N.J., United
Statistical Associates. 332.67 79-
613273
HG4926.A3 B4 MRR Alc Latest
Edition

Financial daily called bond service.
Cumulative. no. 1- 1965- Jersey
City, Financial Information, inc. 68-
130193
HG4861 .F494 MRR Alc Latest
edition

Moody's municipal & government
manual: American and foreign. 1955-
New York, Moody's Investors Service.
57-29
HG4931 .M58 MRR Alc Latest edition

BONN--DIRECTORIES.
Adressbuch der Bundeshauptstadt Bonn.
Bonn, J. F. Carthaus. 53-38333
DD901.B6 A7 MRR Alc Latest edition

BONS MOTS
see Wit and humor

BOOK COLLECTING.
Boutell, Henry Sherman, First
editions of today and how to tell
them; 4th ed., rev. and enl.
Berkeley, Calif., Peacock Press, 1965
[c1964] 227 p. 094.4 64-10193
Z992 .B77 1965 MRR Alc.

Bradley, Van Allen, More gold in
your attic. New York, Fleet Pub.
Corp. [1961] 415 p. 016.094 61-
15017
Z1000 .B784 MRR Alc.

Collison, Robert Lewis. Book
collecting: Fair Lawn, N.J.,
Essential Books, 1957. 244 p. 010
57-13673
Z987 .C6 MRR Alc.

Private book collectors in the United
States and Canada. [3d] ed.; 1919-
New York, R. R. Bowker Co. 655.47
19-14681
Z988 .P83 MRR Alc Latest edition

Targ, William, ed. Bibliophile in
the nursery; [1st ed.] Cleveland,
World Pub. Co. [1957] 503 p. 028.5
57-9281
Z992 .T15 MRR Alc.

Winterich, John Tracy, A primer of
book collecting, 3d rev. ed. New
York, Crown Publishers [1966] ix,
228 p. 020.75 66-15129
Z992 .W78 1966 MRR Alc.

BOOK COLLECTORS.
British museum. Dept. of prints and
drawings. Franks bequest. London,
Printed by order of the Trustees,
1903-04. 3 v. 05-8688
Z994.E5 B8 MRR Alc.

BOOK COLLECTORS--DIRECTORIES.
Book collectors directory. 2nd ed.
Wilbarston (Leics.), Pilgrim
Publications, 1970. iii-xviii, 84 p.
[21/-] 020./75 73-164698
Z988 .B68 1970 MRR Alc.

BOOK COLLECTORS--CANADA.
Private book collectors in the United
States and Canada. [3d] ed.; 1919-
New York, R. R. Bowker Co. 655.47
19-14681
Z988 .P83 MRR Alc Latest edition

BOOK COLLECTORS--UNITED STATES.
American book trade directory. [1st]-
ed.; 1915- New York, R. R.
Bowker. 15-23627
Z475 .A5 Sci RR Latest edition /
MRR Ref Desk Latest edition

McKay, George Leslie, American book
auction catalogues, 1713-1934: New
York, The New York public library,
1937. xxxii, 540 p. 016.0173 37-
33888
Z999 .A1M2 MRR Alc.

Private book collectors in the United
States and Canada. [3d]- ed.; 1919-
New York, R. R. Bowker Co. 655.47
19-14681
Z988 .P83 MRR Alc Latest edition

BOOK DESIGN.
Williamson, Hugh Albert Fordyce,
Methods of book design: 2nd ed.
London, New York [etc.] Oxford U.P.,
1966. xvi, 433 p. [63/-] 655.53
66-73534
Z116.A3 W5 1966 MRR Alc.

BOOK INDUSTRIES AND TRADE.
see also Paper making and trade

see also Printing

Day, Kenneth, ed. Book typography,
1815-1965. London, Benn, 1966.
xxiii, 401 p. [5/5/-] 66-75818
Z116.A2 D313 MRR Alc.

Taubert, Sigfred. The book trade of
the world; Hamburg, Verlag für
Buchmarkt-Forschung; New York, R. R.
Bowker [1972- v. [$18.00 (v. 1)]
338.47/7/070573 72-142165
Z278 .T34 MRR Alc.

BOOK INDUSTRIES AND TRADE--BIBLIOGRAPHY.
Ulrich, Carolyn Farquhar, Books and
printing. Woodstock, Vt., W. E.
Rudge; New York, The New York Public
library, 1943. xi, [1], 244 p.
016.655 43-16214
Z1002 .U4 MRR Alc.

BOOK INDUSTRIES AND TRADE--DICTIONARIES.
The Bookman's glossary. 4th ed.,
rev. and enl. New York, R. R. Bowker
[1961] viii, 212 p. 010.3 61-
13239
Z1006 .B6 1961 MRR Alc.

Carter, John, ABC for book-
collectors. [3d ed., rev.] London,
R. Hart-Davis [1961] 208 p. 62-
6733
Z1006 .C37 1961a MRR Alc.

Cowles, Barbara (Pehotsky)
Bibliographers' glossary of foreign
words and phrases; New York, R. R.
Bowker company, 1935. 3 p. l., 82
numb. l. 010.3 41-5736
Z1006 .C87 1935 MRR Alc.

Elsevier's dictionary of the printing
and allied industries in four
languages; Amsterdam, New York,
[etc.] Elsevier Pub. Co., 1967. 596
p. [90.00] 655/.003 67-19851
Z118 .E5 MRR Alc.

Hiller, Helmut. Wörterbuch des
Buches. 3., durchgesehene und erw.
Aufl. Frankfurt a. M., Klostermann
(1967.) 341 p. [DM 18.50 (unb. DM
16.50)] 68-96779
Z118 .H55 1967 MRR Alc.

Walter, Frank Keller, Abbreviations
and technical terms used in book
catalogs and bibliographies, in eight
languages, 1917 handy edition.
Boston, The Boston book company
[1919?] 2 v. in 1. 27-13479
Z1006 .W261 1919 MRR Alc.

BOOK INDUSTRIES AND TRADE--DICTIONARIES-
-POLYGLOT.
Orne, Jerrold, The language of the
foreign book trade; 2d ed. Chicago,
American Library Association, 1962.
213 p. 010.3 61-12881
Z1006 .07 1962 MRR Alc.

BOOK INDUSTRIES AND TRADE--DIRECTORIES--
BIBLIOGRAPHY.
Internationales Bibliothek-Handbuch.
2.- Ausg.; 1968- München-Pullach,
Verlag Dokumentation. 72-627058
Z721 .I63 MRR Ref Desk Latest
edition

BOOK INDUSTRIES AND TRADE--AFRICA--
BIBLIOGRAPHY.
United States. Library of Congress.
African Section. African libraries,
book production, and archives;
Washington, General Reference and
Bibliography Division, Reference
Dept., Library of Congress, 1962.
vi, 64 p. 016.02096 62-64603
Z663.285 .A73 MRR Alc.

BOOK INDUSTRIES AND TRADE--AFRICA,
SOUTH--DIRECTORIES.
S.A. katalogus. 4th- complete ed.;
1900/50- Johannesburg, Technical
Books & Careers (Pty) Ltd. 72-627425

Z3601 .S8 MRR Alc Partial set

BOOK INDUSTRIES AND TRADE--ASIA--
DIRECTORIES.
Asian book trade directory. [Bombay]
Nirmala Sadanand Publishers.
655.5/73/0255 sa 68-13864
Began with 1964 vol.
Z448.5 A75 MRR Alc Latest edition

BOOK INDUSTRIES AND TRADE--BURMA--
DIRECTORIES.
New India directory of publishers &
booksellers. New Delhi, New Book
Society of India [1952?] 224 p.
655.454 52-40994
Z455 .N4 1952 MRR Alc.

BOOK INDUSTRIES AND TRADE--CEYLON--
DIRECTORIES.
New India directory of publishers &
booksellers. New Delhi, New Book
Society of India [1952?] 224 p.
655.454 52-40994
Z455 .N4 1952 MRR Alc.

BOOK INDUSTRIES AND TRADE--EUROPE--
DIRECTORIES.
Polygraph Adressbuch der graphischen
Industrie. 35.- Ausg.; 1969/70-
[Frankfurt am Main] 72-623129
Z291 .P6 MRR Alc Latest edition

BOOK INDUSTRIES AND TRADE--FRANCE--
DIRECTORIES.
Annuaire Deschaliers ... Paris. 42-
34851
"Fondé en 1895.
Z308 .A75 MRR Alc Latest edition

BOOK INDUSTRIES AND TRADE--GREAT
BRITAIN--BIOGRAPHY--DICTIONARIES.
Duff, Edward Gordon, A century of
the English book trade. London,
Printed for the Bibliographical
society, by Blades, East & Blades,
1905. xxxv, [1], 200 p. 06-595
Z151 .D86 MRR Alc.

Duff, Edward Gordon, A century of
the English book trade; [Folcroft,
Pa.] Folcroft Library Editions, 1972.
xxxv, 200 p. 686.2/092/2 72-
188912
Z151.2 .D83 1972 MRR Alc.

BOOK INDUSTRIES AND TRADE--GREAT
BRITAIN--DIRECTORIES.
Cassell's directory of publishing in
Great Britain, the Commwealth, and
Ireland. 1st- ed.; 1960/61-
London, Cassell. 655.442 60-52232
Z326 .C3 MRR Ref Desk Latest
edition

BOOK INDUSTRIES AND TRADE--GREAT
BRITAIN--HISTORY--SOURCES.
Greg, Walter Wilson, Sir, A
companion to Arber: Oxford,
Clarendon P., 1967. ix, 451 p.
[5/15/6] 655/.42 67-96150
Z151.3 .G68 1967 MRR Alc.

BOOK INDUSTRIES AND TRADE--INDIA--
DIRECTORIES.
Directory of Indian publishers. [1st
ed.] New Delhi, Federation of
Publishers & Booksellers Associations
in India; distributors: New Order
Book Co., Ahmedabad [1973] xv, 591
p. [Rs50.00] 070.5/025/54 74-
901329
Z455 .D494 MRR Alc.

New India directory of publishers &
booksellers. New Delhi, New Book
Society of India [1952?] 224 p.
655.454 52-40994
Z455 .N4 1952 MRR Alc.

BOOK INDUSTRIES AND TRADE--NETHERLANDS--
DIRECTORIES.
Sijthoff's adresboek voor den
Nederlandschen boekhandel Leiden, A.
W. Sijthoff. 26-11523
Z352 .S58 MRR Alc Latest edition

BOOK INDUSTRIES AND TRADE--NEW ENGLAND--
DIRECTORIES.
Printing trades blue book.
Northeastern edition. 1962/63- New
York, A. F. Lewis. 62-52220
Z475 .P78 MRR Alc Latest edition

BOOK INDUSTRIES AND TRADE--NEW JERSEY--
DIRECTORIES.
Printing trades blue book.
Metropolitan ed., Greater New York
and New Jersey. [no. 1]- 1916-
New York, A. F. Lewis. 16-1684
Z475 .P8N MRR Alc Latest edition

BOOK INDUSTRIES AND TRADE--NEW YORK
(CITY)--DIRECTORIES.
Printing trades blue book.
Metropolitan ed., Greater New York
and New Jersey. [no. 1]- 1916-
New York, A. F. Lewis. 16-1684
Z475 .P8N MRR Alc Latest edition

BOOK INDUSTRIES AND TRADE--NEW YORK
(STATE)--DIRECTORIES.
Printing trades blue book.
Northeastern edition. 1962/63- New
York, A. F. Lewis. 62-52220
Z475 .P78 MRR Alc Latest edition

BOOK INDUSTRIES AND TRADE--PAKISTAN--
DIRECTORIES.
New India directory of publishers &
booksellers. New Delhi, New Book
Society of India [1952?] 224 p.
655.454 52-40994
Z455 .N4 1952 MRR Alc.

BOOK INDUSTRIES AND TRADE--PENNSYLVANIA-
-DIRECTORIES.
Printing trades blue book.
Southeastern edition. 1961/62- New
York, A. F. Lewis. 62-52219
Z475 .P79 MRR Alc Latest edition

BOOK INDUSTRIES AND TRADE--RUSSIA.
Malia, Martin Edward. Report, to the
Joint Committee on Slavic Studies and
to the Library of Congress, on
methods for improving Soviet book
acquisitions by American research
libraries, February-March, 1956.
[Washington?] 1956. 2 l., 79 p. 63-
61735
Z663 .R394 MRR Alc.

BOOK INDUSTRIES AND TRADE--SOUTHERN
STATES--DIRECTORIES.
Printing trades blue book.
Southeastern edition. 1961/62- New
York, A. F. Lewis. 62-52219
Z475 .P79 MRR Alc Latest edition

BOOK INDUSTRIES AND TRADE--SPAIN.
Catalogo del papel, prensa y artes
graficas. 1957- [Barcelona,
Abarca] 58-26342
Z414 .C3 MRR Alc Latest edition

**BOOK INDUSTRIES AND TRADE--SPAIN--
DIRECTORIES.**
Instituto Nacional del Libro
Español. Guia de editores y
libreros. [1.]- ed.; 1950-
Madrid. 50-21236
Z413 .I533 MRR Alc Latest edition

**BOOK INDUSTRIES AND TRADE--UNITED
STATES.**
Mott, Frank Luther, Golden
multitudes; New York, Macmillan Co.,
1947. xii, 357 p. 016 47-11742
Z1033.E3 M6 MRR Alc.

**BOOK INDUSTRIES AND TRADE--UNITED
STATES--CREDIT GUIDES.**
Paper & Allied Trades Mercantile
Agency, inc., New York. P. A. T.
credit reference. New York. 27-9871

HF5585.P2 P3 MRR Alc Latest
edition

**BOOK INDUSTRIES AND TRADE--UNITED
STATES--DIRECTORIES.**
American book trade directory. [1st]-
ed.; 1915- New York, R. R.
Bowker. 15-23627
Z475 .A5 Sci RR Latest edition /
MRR Ref Desk Latest edition

Bestsellers who's who in independent
distribution. 1969- [Philadelphia,
North American Pub. Co.]
658.8/09/655572 70-15922
PN4889 .B45 MRR Alc Latest edition

Bristol, Roger Pattrell. Index of
printers, publishers, and booksellers
Charlottesville, Bibliographical
Society of the University of
Virginia, 1961. iv,172 p. 015.73
61-64087
Z1215 .E9233 MRR Ref Desk.

Literary market place; [1st]- ed.;
1940- New York, Bowker. 655.473 41-
51571
PN161 .L5 Sci RR Partial set / MRR
Ref Desk Latest edition

**BOOK INDUSTRIES AND TRADE--UNITED
STATES--YEARBOOKS.**
The Bowker annual of library and book
trade information. 1955/56- New
York, R. R. Bowker. 020.58 55-12434

Z731 .A47 Sci RR Latest edition /
MRR Alc Latest edition / MRR Ref
Desk Latest edition

BOOK NUMBERS
see Alphabeting

BOOK OF MORMON--CONCORDANCES.
Reynolds, George, A complete
concordance of the Book of Mormon.
Salt Lake City, Distributed by
Deseret Book Co. [1957] iv, 852 p.
289.3 57-59334
BX8627.A1 R4 1957 MRR Alc.

BOOK-PLATES, AMERICAN.
British museum. Dept. of prints and
drawings. Franks bequest. London,
Printed by order of the Trustees,
1903-04. 3 v. 05-8688
Z994.E5 B8 MRR Alc.

BOOK-PLATES, ENGLISH.
British museum. Dept. of prints and
drawings. Franks bequest. London,
Printed by order of the Trustees,
1903-04. 3 v. 05-8688
Z994.E5 B8 MRR Alc.

BOOK REVIEWING.
Drewry, John Eldridge, Writing book
reviews. Boston, The Writer [1966,
c1945] xv, 230 p. 808.066 66-
21115
PN98.B7 D7 1966 MRR Alc.

BOOK SELECTION.
Carter, Mary (Duncan) Building
library collections, 3d ed.
Metuchen, N.J., Scarecrow Press,
1969. xii, 319 p. 025.2/1 73-4902

Z689 .C29 1969 MRR Alc.

Haines, Helen Elizabeth, Living with
books; 2d ed. New York, Columbia
University Press, 1950. xxiii, 610
p. 028 50-4478
Z1003 .H15 1950 MRR Alc.

Perkins, Flossie L. Book and non-
book media; Urbana, Ill., National
Council of Teachers of English [1972]
ix, 298 p. 016.028 72-186931
Z1035.A1 P36 1972 MRR Alc.

**BOOK SELECTION--ADDRESSES, ESSAYS,
LECTURES.**
Moon, Eric, comp. Book selection and
censorship in the sixties. New York,
Bowker, 1969. xi, 421 p.
025.2/1/08 78-79423
Z689 .M56 MRR Alc.

BOOKBINDING.
Diehl, Edith. Bookbinding, its
background and technique, New York,
Toronto, Rinehart & company, inc.,
1946. 2 v. 686 47-938
Z266 .D5 MRR Alc.

Esdaile, Arundell James Kennedy,
Esdaile's manual of bibliography.
4th revised ed., London, Allen &
Unwin, 1967 [i.e. 1968] 336 p. [50/-
] 010 68-114662
Z1001 .E75 1968 MRR Alc.

Langwell, William Herbert. The
conservation of books and documents.
London, I. Pitman [1957] 114 p.
025.7 57-3535
Z701 .L3 MRR Alc.

BOOKBINDING--HANDBOOKS, MANUALS, ETC.
Robinson, Ivor. Introducing
bookbinding. London, Batsford; New
York, Watson-Guptill Pub., 1968. 112
p. [25/-] 655.7 68-18706
Z271 .R6 MRR Alc.

Town, Laurence. Bookbinding by hand,
London, Faber and Faber [1951] 281
p. 686 52-176
Z271 .T68 1951 MRR Alc.

BOOKBINDING--REPAIRING.
Lydenberg, Harry Miller, The care
and repair of books, [4th rev. ed.]
New York, Bowker, 1960. 122 p.
025.7 60-11980
Z701 .L98 1960 MRR Alc.

BOOKBINDING--UNITED STATES.
Lehmann-Haupt, Hellmut, Bookbinding
in America; New York, R. R. Bowker,
1967. xix, 293 p. 67-13796
Z270.U5 L4 1967 MRR Alc.

BOOKKEEPERS
see Accountants

BOOKKEEPING.
see also Accounting

BOOKKEEPING--BIBLIOGRAPHY.
Bentley, Harry Clark, Bibliography
of works on accounting by American
authors, New York, A. M. Kelley,
1970. 2 v. in 1. 016.657 72-
115313
Z7164.C81 B5 1970 MRR Alc.

BOOKS.
see also Illustration of books
Jennett, Seán. The making of books.
[New ed. London] Faber & Faber
[1956] 474 p. 655 57-28023
Z116.A2 J47 1956 MRR Alc.

BOOKS--BIBLIOGRAPHY.
Gaskell, Philip. A new introduction
to bibliography. New York, Oxford
University Press, 1972. 438 p.
686.2/09 73-153680
Z116.A2 G27 1972b MRR Alc.

BOOKS--CONSERVATION AND RESTORATION.
Langwell, William Herbert. The
conservation of books and documents.
London, I. Pitman [1957] 114 p.
025.7 57-3535
Z701 .L3 MRR Alc.

Lehmann-Haupt, Hellmut, Bookbinding
in America; New York, R. R. Bowker,
1967. xix, 293 p. 67-13796
Z270.U5 L4 1967 MRR Alc.

Lydenberg, Harry Miller, The care
and repair of books, [4th rev. ed.]
New York, Bowker, 1960. 122 p.
025.7 60-11980
Z701 .L98 1960 MRR Alc.

BOOKS--DICTIONARIES.
Glaister, Geoffrey Ashall. Glossary
of the book; London, G. Allen and
Unwin [1960] 484 p. 655.03 61-
2811
Z118 .G55 1960a MRR Alc.

BOOKS--DICTIONARIES--GERMAN.
Lexikon des Buchwesens. Stuttgart,
Hiersemann, 1952-56. 4 v. 010.3
53-17416
Z118 .L65 MRR Alc.

Lexikon des gesamten Buchwesens.
Leipzig, K. W. Hiersemann, 1935 [i.e.
1934]-37. 3 v. 34-28790
Z118 .L67 MRR Alc.

BOOKS--HISTORY.
Binns, Norman E. An introduction to
historical bibliography. 2d ed.,
rev. and enl. London, Association of
Assistant Librarians, 1962. 387 p.
63-25449
Z4 .B55 1962 MRR Alc.

Bland, David. A history of book
illustration; [1st ed.] Cleveland,
World Pub. Co. [1958] 448 p.
741.64 58-10061
NC960 .B62 MRR Alc.

Diringer, David, The illuminated
book; Rev. ed. New York, Praeger
[1967] 514 p. 745.6/7/09 66-12525
ND2920 .D55 1967 MRR Alc.

Esdaile, Arundell James Kennedy,
Esdaile's manual of bibliography.
4th revised ed., London, Allen &
Unwin, 1967 [i.e. 1968] 336 p. [50/-
] 010 68-114662
Z1001 .E75 1968 MRR Alc.

McMurtrie, Douglas Crawford, The
book; New York, London [etc.] Oxford
university press [1943] xxx p., 1
l., 676 p., 1 l. 002 43-4110
Z4 .M15 1943 MRR Alc.

Van Hoesen, Henry Bartlett,
Bibliography, practical, enumerative,
historical; New York, London, C.
Scribner's sons, 1928. xiii p., 1
l., 519 p. 28-17678
Z1002 .V25 MRR Alc.

BOOKS--HISTORY--1400-1600.
Pollard, Alfred William, Early
illustrated books; London, K. Paul,
Trench, Trübner & co., ltd., 1893.
xvi, 256 p. incl. illus., plates,
facsim. 02-8241
Z1023 .P77 MRR Alc.

BOOKS--HISTORY--BIBLIOGRAPHY.
Ulrich, Carolyn Farquhar, Books and
printing, Woodstock, Vt., W. E.
Rudge; New York, The New York Public
library, 1943. xi, [1], 244 p.
016.655 43-16214
Z1002 .U4 MRR Alc.

BOOKS--PRICES.
American book prices current. v. 1-
1894/95- New York, Bancroft-Parkman
[etc.] 018/.3 03-14557
Z1000 .A51 MRR Alc Partial set

Amtmann, Bernard. Contributions to a
short-title catalogue of Canadiana.
Montreal, 1971- v. 015/.71 73-
156377
Z1365 .A64 MRR Alc.

Book-auction records; v. 1- June
3, 1902- London, [etc.] Dawsons of
Pall Mall [etc.] 017.3 05-18641
Z1000 .B65 MRR Alc Full set

Bradford, Thomas Lindsley, The
bibliographer's manual of American
history, Philadelphia, S. V. Henkels
& co., 1907-10. 5 v. 07-23470
Z1250 .B85 MRR Alc.

Bradley, Van Allen, The book
collector's handbook of values. New
York, Putnam [1972] xvi, 569 p.
[$17.50] 016.09 75-136795
Z1029 .B7 MRR Alc.

Bradley, Van Allen, More gold in
your attic. New York, Fleet Pub.
Corp. [1961] 415 p. 016.094 61-
15017
Z1000 .B784 MRR Alc.

Bradley, Van Allen, The new Gold in
your attic. [2d ed.] New York,
Fleet Press Corp. [1968] 280 p.
094/.4/0973 68-3458
Z1000 .B78 1968 MRR Alc.

Heard, Joseph Norman, Bookman's
guide to Americana [5th ed.]
Metuchen, N.J., Scarecrow Press,
1969. ix, 472 p. 016.917 76-2468

Z998 .H42 1969 MRR Alc.

Jahrbuch der Auktionspreise für
Bücher und Autographen. Bd. 1-
1950- Hamburg, E. Hauswedell. 52-
30083
Z1000 .J235 MRR Alc Full set

Johnson, William T. Johnson's Civil
War book prices, Allegan, Mich.
[1962-65, pt. 3, 1965] 4 pts. 62-
1195
Z1242 .J6 MRR Alc.

Livingston, Luther Samuel, Auction
prices of books; New York, Dodd,
Mead & company, 1905. 4 v. 05-9722

Z1000 .L65 MRR Alc.

Mebane, John, Books relating to the
Civil War; New York, T. Yoseloff
[1963] 144 p. 016.9737 63-9375
Z1242 .M4 MRR Alc.

Palau y Dulcet, Antonio, 1867-1954.
Manual del librero hispano-americano;
2. ed. corr. y aumentada por el
autor. Barcelona, A. Palau, 1948-
v. 015.46 49-2664
Z2681 .P16 MRR Alc.

Roskie, Philip M. The bookman's
bible. Oakland, Calif., Roskie &
Wallace Bookstore, 1956- v. 56-
4782
Z1000 .R67 MRR Alc.

BOOKS--PRICES. (Cont.)
The Used book price guide. Kenmore, Wash., Price Guide Publishers. 63-24123
  Z1000 .U8 MRR Alc Full set

BOOKS--PRICES--BIBLIOGRAPHY.
McKay, George Leslie, American book auction catalogues, 1713-1934; New York, The New York public library, 1937. xxxii, 540 p. 016.0173 37-33888
  Z999 .A1M2 MRR Alc.

BOOKS--PRICES--PERIODICALS.
Bookman's price index. v. 1- 1964- Detroit, Gale Research Co. 018 64-8723
  Z1000 .B74 MRR Alc Full set

BOOKS--REVIEWS.
American literature; v. 1- Mar. 1929- [Durham, N.C. Duke University Press] 810.5 30-20216
  PS1 .A6 MRR Ref Desk Indexes only

American notes & queries. v. 1- Sept. 1962- [New Haven, Conn.] [$6.50] 031/.02 74-642751
  Z1034 .A4 MRR Alc Full set

American reference books annual. 1970- Littleton, Colo., Libraries Unlimited. 011/.02 75-120328
  Z1035.1 .A55 MRR Alc Full set

Bibliographie de la philosophie. (année) 1- Jan./mar. 1954- Paris, Librairie Philosophique J. Vrin. 58-31345
  Z7127 .B5 MRR Alc Full set

Bibliographie der Rezensionen, nach Titeln (alphabet der Verfasser) geordnetes Verzeichnis von Besprechungen deutscher und ausländischen Bücher und Karten, die ... in zumeist wissenschaftlichen und kritischen Zeitschriften, Zeitungen und Sammelwerken deutscher Zunge erschienen sind ... 1.- Supplementband; 1900- Leipzig [etc.] F. Dietrich. 01-15596
  AI9 .B6 MRR Alc Full set

Book review digest. Annual cumulation. v. 1- 1905- New York [etc.] H. W. Wilson Co. 06-9994
  Z1219 .C86 MRR Circ Full set

Child development abstracts and bibliography. v. 1- June/Sept./Dec. 1927- Chicago, Ill. [etc.] Univ. of Chicago Press [etc.] 016.6491 46-31872
  HQ750 .A1C47 MRR Alc Full set

Five years' work in librarianship. 1951/55- London, Library Association. 016.02 58-2169
  Z666 .F5 MRR Alc Full set

The Foreign affairs 50-year bibliography; New York, Published for the Council on Foreign Relations by R. R. Bowker Co., 1972. xxviii, 936 p. 016.327/09/04 75-163904
  Z6461 .F62 MRR Alc.

Journal of economic literature. v. 7- Mar. 1969- Menasha, Wis. American Economic Association] [$6.00] 330 73-646621
  HB1 .J6 MRR Alc Full set

Keller, Helen Rex, ed. The reader's digest of books, New and greatly enl. ed. New York, The Macmillan company, 1940. 3 p. l., 1447 p. 803 40-7463
  PN44 .K4 1940 MRR Alc.

Larrabee, Eric, ed. American panorama; [New York] New York University Press, 1957. 436 p. 016.9173 57-11743
  Z1361.C6 L3 MRR Alc.

The Library Journal book review. 1967- New York, R. R. Bowker Co. 028.1 68-58515
  Z1035 .A1L48 MRR Circ Full set

Magill, Frank Northen, Great events from history; modern European series. [1st ed.] Englewood Cliffs, N.J., Salem Press [1973] 3 v. (xxi, 1779 p.) 940 73-179232
  D209 .M29 MRR Alc.

Masterplots annual. 1954- New York, Salem Press. 55-41212
  Z1219 .M33 MRR Alc Latest edition

Notes and queries; v. 1- Nov. 3, 1849- London [etc.] Oxford Univ. Press [etc.] 12-25307
  AG305 .N7 MRR Alc Full set

Public library catalog. 6th ed., 1973. New York, H. W. Wilson Co., 1974. x, 1543 p. 011 74-656
  Z1035 .S83 1974 MRR Alc.

Recent publications in the social and behavioral sciences. 1966- [New York] The American behavioral scientist. 016.3 66-56737
  Z7161 .A42 MRR Alc Full set

Reference and subscription books reviews. 1968/70- Chicago, American Library Association. 028.1 73-159565
  Z1035.1 .S922 MRR Ref Desk Latest edition

Subscription books bulletin reviews. 1956/60-1968. Chicago, American Library Association. 028.7082 61-2636
  Z1035.1 .S92 MRR Ref Desk Full set

The United States quarterly book review. v. 1-12, no. 2; Mar. 1945-June 1956. [Denver etc.] Swallow Press] 015.73 48-46511
  Z663 .A6 MRR Alc MRR Alc Full set

Wilson, H. W., firm, publishers. Fiction catalog. 1908- New York [etc.] 016.823 09-35044
  Z5916 .W74 MRR Alc Latest edition

The Year book of world affairs. v. 1-1947- London, Stevens. 341.058 47-29156
  JX21 .Y4 MRR Alc Latest edition

BOOKS--REVIEWS--BIBLIOGRAPHY.
Gray, Richard A. A guide to book review citations; [Columbus] Ohio State University Press [1969, c1968] viii, 221 p. [7.00] 016.0281 67-63222
  Z1035.A1 G7 MRR Ref Desk.

BOOKS--REVIEWS--INDEXES.
The American historical review. v. 1- Oct. 1895- Washington [etc.] 973.05 05-18244
  E171 .A57 MRR Ref Desk Indexes only

American Theological Library Association. Index to religious periodical literature; 1949/52 [Chicago] a 54-6085
  Z7753 .A5 MRR Alc Full set

Bibliographie der Rezensionen, nach Titeln (alphabet der Verfasser) geordnetes Verzeichnis von Besprechungen deutscher und ausländischer Bücher und Karten, die ... in zumeist wissenschaftlichen und kritischen Zeitschriften, Zeitungen und Sammelwerken deutscher Zunge erschienen sind ... 1.- Supplementband; 1900- Leipzig [etc.] F. Dietrich. 01-15596
  AI9 .B6 MRR Alc Full set

Book review digest. Annual cumulation. v. 1- 1905- New York [etc.] H. W. Wilson Co. 06-9994
  Z1219 .C96 MRR Circ Full set

Buros, Oscar Krisen, Personality tests and reviews; Highland Park, N.J., Gryphon Press [1970] xxxi, 1659 p. 155.28 74-13192
  BF698.5 .B87 MRR Alc.

Canadian periodical index. v. 1- Jan. 1948- Ottawa. 49-2133
  AI3 .C242 MRR Alc Full set

The Catholic periodical and literature index. July/Aug. 1968-Haverford, Pa., Catholic Library Association. 011 70-649588
  AI3 .C32 MRR Alc Full set

The Catholic periodical index, 1930/33-May/June 1968. Haverford, Pa. [etc.] Catholic Library Association [etc.] 40-15160
  AI3 .C32 MRR Alc Full set

Cumulative index to a selected list of periodicals. v. -8; -June 1903. Cleveland, O., The Public library [etc.] ca 17-9
  AI3 .C8 MRR Alc Full set

Curley, Dorothy Nyren, comp. Modern Romance literatures, New York, F. Ungar Pub. Co. [1967] x, 510 p. 879.9/09 67-14053
  PN813 .C8 MRR Alc.

Dargan, Marion. Guide to American biography; Albuquerque, University of New Mexico Press, 1849- v. 016.920073 49-48559
  Z5305.U5 D32 MRR Biog.

Eichelberger, Clayton L., A guide to critical reviews of United States fiction, 1870-1910, Metuchen, N.J., Scarecrow Press, 1971. 415 p. 016.813/4/09 77-149998
  Z1225 .E35 MRR Ref Desk.

Glazier, Kenneth M. Africa south of the Sahara; a select and annotated bibliography, 1964-1968. Stanford, Calif., Hoover Institution Press [c1969] vii, 139 p. [6.00] 016.9167 77-88767
  Z3501 .G52 MRR Alc.

Index to American little magazines. Troy, N.Y. [etc.] Whitston Pub. Co. [etc.] 77-97476
  AI3 .I54 MRR Alc Full set

Index to South African periodicals. v. 1- 1940- Johannesburg [etc.] 052 41-26592
  AI3 .I65 MRR Alc Partial set

International bibliography of economics. v. 1- 1952- London, Tavistock Publications; Chicago, Aldine Pub. Co. 55-2317
  Z7164.E2 I58 MRR Alc Full set

Internationale Bibliographie der Rezensionen wissenschaftlicher Literatur. Jahrg. 1.- 1971- Osnabrück, F. Dietrich Verlag. 72-623124
  Z5051 .I64 MRR Alc Full set

Johnson, Robert Owen. An index to literature in the New Yorker, volumes I-XV, 1925-1940. Metuchen, N.J., Scarecrow Press, 1969-71. 3 v. 051 71-7740
  AP2 .N6764 MRR Alc.

Mental health book review index. v. [1]- (no. 1-); Jan./Feb. 1956- [New York] 66-9162
  Z6664.N5 M49 MRR Circ Full set

The Music index. v. 1- 1949- Detroit, Information Coordinators, inc.(etc.] 50-13627
  ML118 .M84 MRR Alc Full set

The Philosopher's index. Cumulative ed. 1967/68- Bowling Green, Ohio, Philosophy Documentation Center, Bowling Green University [etc.] 016.105 74-250928
  Z7127 .P47 MRR Alc Full set

Royal Historical Society, London. Writings on British history 1901-1933: London, Cape, 1968- v. [£5/5- (v. 1) 63/- (v.2) £5/5/- (v. 3)] 016.942 68-88411
  Z2016 .R85 MRR Alc.

Scientific American. v.1-14, Aug. 28, 1845-June 25, 1859; new ser., v.1-July 2, 1859- [New York] 505 04-17574
  T1 .S5 MRR Alc Indexes only / Sci RR Indexes only

Social sciences citation index. Philadelphia, Institute for Scientific Information. 016.3 73-85287
  Z7161 .S65 MRR Alc Full set

The New York review of books. Ten-year cumulative index, February 1963-January 1973. [New York] Arno Press, 1973. 90 p. mrr01-77
  ZP2 .N6552 MRR Circ.

BOOKS--REVIEWS--PERIODICALS.
The School library journal book review. 1968/69- New York. R. R. Bowker Co. 72-79427
  Z1037.A1 S3 MRR Alc Full set

BOOKS--WANT LISTS.
The A B bookman's yearbook. 1954- Newark, N.J. 010.58 54-1676
  Z990 .A18 MRR Alc Latest edition

United States. Library of Congress. Union Catalog Division. Select list of unlocated research books. no. 1-24; 1937-61. Washington. 37-10127
  Z663.79 S37 MRR Alc MRR Alc Partial set

BOOKS AND READING.
see also Literature

Haines, Helen Elizabeth, Living with books; 2d ed. New York, Columbia University Press, 1950. xxiii, 610 p. 028 50-4478
  Z1003 .H15 1950 MRR Alc.

Ogilvy, Jack David Angus. Books known to the English, 597-1066 Cambridge, Mass., Mediaeval Academy of America, 1967. xx, 300 p. 011 65-19630
  Z6602 .035 MRR Alc.

BOOKS AND READING--UNITED STATES.
Mott, Frank Luther, Golden multitudes; New York, Macmillan Co., 1947. xii, 357 p. 016 47-11742
  Z1033.B3 M6 MRR Alc.

BOOKS AND READING FOR CHILDREN--
BIBLIOGRAPHY.
Pellowski, Anne. The world of
children's literature. New York,
Bowker, 1968. x, 538 p. [$18.75
U.S. and Can. ($20.65 elsewhere)]
028.52 67-25022
Z1037 .P37 MRR Alc.

BOOKS FOR CHILDREN
see Children's literature

BOOKS IN PRINT.
International maps and atlases in
print. London, New York, Bowker
Publishing Co. [1974] 864 p.
[£15.00] 016.912 73-13336
Z6021 .I596 MRR Alc.

BOOKS IN PRINT--CANADA.
Butterfield, Rita. Canadian books in
print. [Toronto] Canadian Books in
Print Committee [1968] 2 v.
015/.71 68-31933
Z1365 .B962 MRR Ref Desk.

BOOKS IN PRINT--FRANCE.
Le Catalogue de l'édition
française. 1.- ed.; 1970-
[Paris] VPC livres, S.A.; [Port
Washington, N.Y.] Paris Publications,
Inc. 71-612834
Z2165 .C3 MRR Alc Latest edition

Répertoire des livres de langue
française disponibles. 1972-
[Paris] France-Expansion. 72-626991
Z2161 .R43 MRR Alc Latest edition

BOOKS IN PRINT--GERMANY.
Barsortiments-Lagerkatalog.
Stuttgart [etc.] Koehler & Volckmar
[etc.] 015.43 46-38153
Z2221 .B3 MRR Alc Latest edition

Bücher aus der DDR. 1972/73-
Leipzig, Deutscher Buch-Export und -
Import G.m.b.H. [20.00M] 73-642414

Z2250 .I4 MRR Alc Latest edition

Libri. Hamburg, G. Lingenbrink.
015/.43 78-2108
Z2225 .L5 MRR Alc Latest edition

Libri. Nachtrag. 1- 1971-
[Hamburg, G. Lingenbrink] 015/.43
74-643557
Z2225 .L5 Suppl 2 MRR Alc Latest
edition

Libri. Stich- und Schlagwortkatalog
mit Titel-Register. [Hamburg, G.
Lingenbrink] 015/.43 74-643558
Z2225 .L5 Suppl. MRR Alc Latest
edition

Literatur-Katalog. 1904/05- [Köln,
etc.] Koehler & Volckmar [etc.] 05-
10363
Z2221 .D5 MRR Alc Latest edition

Verzeichnis lieferbarer Bücher.
1971/72- Frankfurt am Main, Verlag
der Buchhändler-Vereinigung GmbH.
018.4 76-615229
Z2221 .V47 MRR Alc Latest edition

Verzeichnis lieferbarer Bücher.
Nachtrag. [Frankfurt am Main] 018.4
74-643578
Z2221 .V47 Suppl. MRR Alc Latest
edition

BOOKS IN PRINT--GREAT BRITAIN.
British books in print. 1874-
London, Whitaker; New York, Bowker
[etc.] 02-7486
Z2001 .R33 MRR Ref Desk Partial
set

Paperbacks in print. London, J.
Whitaker. 66-8204
Began with May 1960 issue.
Z1033.P3 P28 MRR Alc Latest
edition

Technical books in print; London,
Whitaker, 1966. viii, 313 p. 78-
982
Z7916 .T42 1966 MRR Alc.

BOOKS IN PRINT--INDIA.
Impex reference catalogue of Indian
books. 1st- ed.; Mar. 1960- New
Delhi, Indian Book Export and Import
Co. 62-4296
Z3201 .I57 MRR Alc Full set

Sher Singh. Indian books in print,
1955-67; Delhi, Indian Bureau of
Bibliographies [1969] 1116 p.
[100.00] 015/.54 78-104779
Z3201 .S47 MRR Alc.

BOOKS IN PRINT--ITALY.
Associazione italiana editori.
Catalogo dei libri italiani in
commercio. Milano, Associazione
italiana editori, 1970- v. 71-
19147
Z2341 .A833 MRR Alc.

BOOKS IN PRINT--LATIN AMERICA.
Libros en venta en Hispanoamérica y
España; [1. ed.] New York, R. R.
Bowker Co., 1964. 1891 p. 015.8
64-3492
Z1601 .L59 MRR Alc.

BOOKS IN PRINT--NEW ZEALAND.
New Zealand books in print.
Wellington [etc.] Published for the
Associated Booksellers of New Zealand
by Price Milburn [etc.] 62-44889
Began publication in 1957.
Z4101 .N56 MRR Alc Latest edition

BOOKS IN PRINT--SPAIN.
Libros en venta en Hispanoamérica y
España; [1. ed.] New York, R. R.
Bowker Co., 1964. 1891 p. 015.8
64-3492
Z1601 .L59 MRR Alc.

Libros españoles: catálogo ISBN.
1973- Madrid, Agencia Española del
International Standard Book Number
(ISBN) 74-644456
Z2681 .L53 MRR Alc Latest edition

BOOKS IN PRINT--UNITED STATES.
Books in print; 1948- New York, R.
R. Bowker Co. 015.73 74-643574
Z1215 .P972 Sci RR Latest edition
/ MRR Alc Latest edition / MRR
Ref Desk Latest edition

Books in print supplement; authors,
titles, subjects. 1972/73- New
York, R. R. Bowker Co. 015.73 74-
643521
Z1215 .P974 MRR Alc Latest edition
/ MRR Ref Desk Latest edition

Bowker's medical books in print.
1972- New York, R.R. Bowker Co.
016.61 78-37613
Z6658 .B65 MRR Alc Latest edition
/ Sci RR Latest edition

Business books in print: subject
index, author index, title index.
1973- New York, R. R. Bowker Co.
016.33 78-8590
Z7164.C81 B962 MRR Alc Latest
edition

Children's books in print. 1969-
New York, R. R. Bowker Co. 028.52
70-101705
Z1037.A1 C482 MRR Alc Latest
edition

El-Hi textbooks in print. [56th]-
[1927- New York, Bowker [etc.]
016.379/156 57-4667
Z5813 .A51 MRR Alc Latest edition

Guide to reprints. 1967-
Washington, Microcard Editions. 011
66-29279
Z1000.5 .G8 MRR Ref Desk Latest
edition

Kyed, James M., Scientific,
technical, and engineering societies
publications in print, New York, R.
R. Bowker Co., 1974. x, 223 p.
016.5 74-5094
Z7911 .K92 MRR Alc.

Landau, Robert A. Large type books
in print, New York, R. R. Bowker
Co., 1970. xxi, 193 p. 015/.73 74-
102773
Z5348 .L3 MRR Alc.

Paperbound books in print. Mar. 1971-
[New York, Bowker] 011 74-649559

Z1033.P3 P33 MRR Alc Latest
edition / Sci RR Latest edition

The Publishers' trade list annual.
[1st]- 1873- New York, R. R.
Bowker Co., Office of the Publisher's
Weekly [etc.] 015.73 04-12648
Z1215 .P97 MRR Ref Desk Latest
edition / Sci RR Latest edition

Schoolcraft, Ralph Newman.
Performing arts/books in print: an
annotated bibliography. [1st ed.]
New York, Drama Book Specialists
[1973] xiii, 761 p. 016.7902 72-
78909
Z6935 .S34 MRR Alc.

Scientific and technical books in
print. 1972- New York, R. R. Bowker
Co. 016.5 71-37614
Z7401 .S573 MRR Alc Latest edition
/ Sci RR Latest edition

Subject guide to Books in print;
1957- New York, R. R. Bowker Co.
015.73 74-643573
Z1215 .P973 MRR Alc Latest edition
/ MRR Ref Desk Latest edition /
Sci RR Latest edition

BOOKS OF KNOWLEDGE
see Encyclopedias and dictionaries

BOOKS ON MICROFILM.
United States. Library of Congress.
Photoduplication Service.
Specifications for the microfilming
of books and pamphlets in the Library
of Congress. Washington, Library of
Congress; [for sale by the Supt. of
Docs., U.S. Govt. Print. Off.] 1973.
iii, 16 p. [$0.40] 686.43 73-9756

Z663.96 .S68 MRR Alc.

BOOKS ON MICROFILM--BIBLIOGRAPHY.
Brown University. Library. List of
Latin American imprints before 1800,
Providence, 1952. iv, 140 p. 015.8
a 52-2246
Z1610 .B695 MRR Alc.

National register of microform
masters. Sept. 1965- Washington,
Library of Congress. 65-29419
Z663 .A43 MRR Alc MRR Alc Full set

Reichmann, Felix, Bibliographic
control of microforms, Westport,
Conn., Greenwood Press, Pub. Division
[1972] 256 p. 016.02517/9 72-2463

Z1033.M5 R43 MRR Alc.

BOOKS ON MICROFILM--BIBLIOGRAPHY--
CATALOGS.
Philadelphia Bibliographical Center
and Union Library Catalogue.
Committee on Microphotography. Union
list of microfilms; Ann Arbor,
Mich., J. W. Edwards, 1961. 2 v.
(xviii p., 2800 columns) 016.099
62-1343
Z1033.M5 P5 1961 MRR Alc.

BOOKS ON MICROFILM--INDEXES.
Early English books 1475-1640,
selected from Pollard and Redgrave's
short-title catalogue; cross index to
reels. 1- 1972- Ann Arbor,
University Microfilms. 015/.42 72-
627329
Z2002 .U574 MRR Alc Latest edition

BOOKSELLERS AND BOOKSELLING--
DICTIONARIES--POLYGLOT.
Dictionnaire à l'usage de la
librairie ancienne pour les langues:
française, anglaise, allemande,
suédoise, danoise, italienne,
espagnole, hollandaise, Paris, Ligue
internationale de la librairie
ancienne, 1956. 190 p. 655.403 57-
2275
Z282 .D5 MRR Alc.

BOOKSELLERS AND BOOKSELLING--
DIRECTORIES.
American Library Association. Joint
Committee to Revise List of
International Subscription Agents.
International subscription agents;
2d ed. Chicago, American Library
Association, 1969. vi, 87 p.
380.1/45/655572025 76-82255
Z282 .A44 1969 MRR Alc.

Grose, B. Donald, The antiquarian
booktrade; Metuchen, N.J., Scarecrow
Press, 1972. p. 658.8/09/00573
72-6996
Z286.A55 G74 MRR Ref Desk.

McNiff, Philip J. A list of book
dealers in underdeveloped countries,
[Chicago?] 1963. ii, 40 l. 63-
25235
Z282 .M25 MRR Alc.

Neverman, F. John. International
directory of back issue vendors:
periodicals, newspapers, newspaper
indexes, documents. 2d enl. ed. New
York, Special Libraries Association
[c1968] 95 p.
658.8/09/655572025 68-57264
Z286.P4 N4 1968 MRR Alc.

Publishers' international year book.
1st- ed.; 1960/6- London, A.P.
Wales. 655.5058 61-542
Z282 .P8 MRR Ref Desk Latest
edition

World directory of booksellers: an
international guide to booksellers,
1st ed. London, A. P. Wales, 1970.
xv, 911 p. 338.4/7/65809070573025
73-860901
Z282 .W6 MRR Alc.

BOOKSELLERS AND BOOKSELLING--AFRICA--
DIRECTORIES.
African book trade directory 1971,
München-Pullach, Verlag
Dokumentation; New York, Bowker,
1971. 319 p. 338.7/61/0705730256
73-142168
Z465.5 .A45 MRR Alc.

BOOKSELLERS AND BOOKSELLING--ASIA--
DIRECTORIES.
Asian book trade directory. [Bombay]
Nirmala Sadanand Publishers.
655.5/73/0255 sa 68-13864
Began with 1964 vol.
Z448.5 A75 MRR Alc Latest edition

BOOKSELLERS AND BOOKSELLING--EUROPE--DIRECTORIES.
Adressbuch des deutschsprachigen Buchhandels. 1954- Frankfurt am Main, Buchhändler-Vereinigung. 54-38005
  Z282 .A28 MRR Alc Latest edition

BOOKSELLERS AND BOOKSELLING--FRANCE--DIRECTORIES.
Cercle de la librairie, Paris. Répertoire des éditeurs et liste des collections. [Nouv. éd.] Paris [1963] 294 p. 64-48009
  Z307 .C4 1963 MRR Alc.

Répertoire international des librairies de langue française. Paris, Cercle de la librairie, 1971. xi, 347 p. 78-858018
  Z307 .R45 MRR Alc.

BOOKSELLERS AND BOOKSELLING--GREAT BRITAIN.
A dictionary of the printers and booksellers who were at work in England, Scotland and Ireland from 1726 to 1775; [Oxford] Printed for the Bibliographical society at the Oxford university press, 1932 (for 1930) xxi, 432 p. 655.142 32-23320
  Z151 .D54 MRR Alc.

Growoll, Adolf, Three centuries of English booktrade bibliography: New York, Pub. for the Dibdin club, by M. L. Greenhalgh, 1903. xv p., 1 l., 195 p., 1 l. incl 6 facsim. 03-13955
  Z2001.A1 G8 MRR Alc.

London. Stationers' Company. A transcript of the registers of the Company of Stationers of London, 1554-1640 A.D. [New York P. Smith, 1950] 5 v. 655.442 49-50201
  Z2002 .L64 MRR Alc.

London. Stationer's Company. A transcript of the registers of the worshipful Company of Stationers, from 1640-1708 A.D. [New York, P. Smith, 1950] 3 v. 655.442 50-37726
  Z2002 .L653 MRR Alc.

McKerrow, Ronald Brunlees, ed. A dictionary of printers and booksellers in England, Scotland and Ireland, and of foreign printers of English books 1557-1640. London, Printed for the Bibliographical society, by Blades, East & Blades, 1910. 2 p. l., [vii]-xxiii, 346 p. 11-5402
  Z151 .D51 MRR Alc.

Plomer, Henry Robert, A dictionary of the printers and booksellers who were at work in England, Scotland and Ireland from 1668 to 1725, [Oxford] Printed for the Bibliographical society, at the Oxford university press, 1922. 2 p. l., [vii]-xii, 342 p. 23-5
  Z151 .D53 MRR Alc.

Plomer, Henry Robert, A dictionary of the booksellers and printers who were at work in England, Scotland and Ireland from 1641 to 1667. London, Printed for the Bibliographical society, by Blades, East & Blades, 1907. 2 p. l., [vii]-xxiii, [1], 199 p. 08-16568
  Z151 .D52 MRR Alc.

Pollard, Alfred William, A short-title catalogue of books printed in England, Scotland, & Ireland and of English books printed abroad, 1475-1640, London, Bibliographical Society, 1946. xviii, 609 p. 015.42 47-20884
  Z2002 .P77 1946 MRR Alc.

Wing, Donald Goddard, Short-title catalogue of books printed in England, Scotland, Ireland, Wales, and British America, and of English books printed in other countries 1641-1700. New York, Index Society, 1945-51. 3 v. 015.42 45-8773
  Z2002 .W5 MRR Alc.

BOOKSELLERS AND BOOKSELLING--GREAT BRITAIN--DIRECTORIES.
Annual directory of booksellers in the British Isles specialising in antiquarian and out-of-print books. 1970- London, Clique Ltd. 380.1/45/070573 79-22674
  Z327 .A6 MRR Alc Latest edition

The Complete booksellers directory (mainly antiquarian) Wilbarston, G. Coe, 1968. 62, 23 p. [unpriced] 658.89/6555/7302542 72-366726
  Z327 .C64 MRR Alc.

BOOKSELLERS AND BOOKSELLING--INDIA--DIRECTORIES.
Directory of booksellers, publishers, libraries & librarians in India. 1st-ed.; 1968/69- New Delhi, Premier Publishers. 655.4/025/54 73-900620
  Z455 .D49 MRR Alc Latest edition

BOOKSELLERS AND BOOKSELLING--LONDON--DIRECTORIES.
Coe's guide to London bookshops. Market Harborough (Leics.), Gerald Coe Ltd., 1967. [86] p. [7/6] 658.8/09/655570254212 68-112509
  Z327 .C6 MRR Alc.

BOOKSELLERS AND BOOKSELLING--NORTH AMERICA.
Book dealers in North America; 1954/55- London, Sheppard Press. 655.47 55-435
  Z475 .B63 MRR Alc Latest edition / MRR Ref Desk Latest edition

BOOKSELLERS AND BOOKSELLING--PARIS.
Renouard, Philippe, Imprimeurs & librairies parisiens du XVIe siècle; Paris, 1964- v. 65-70946
  Z305 .R4 MRR Alc.

BOOKSELLERS AND BOOKSELLING--SPAIN--DIRECTORIES.
Instituto Nacional del Libro Español. Guía de editores y libreros. [1.]- ed.; 1950- Madrid. 50-21236
  Z413 .I533 MRR Alc Latest edition

BOOKSELLERS AND BOOKSELLING--UNITED STATES.
Book buyer's handbook. 1947/48- New York, American Booksellers' Assn. 655.473 48-512
  Z475 .B6 MRR Alc Latest edition

Burke, William Jeremiah, American authors and books, 1640 to the present day 3d rev. ed. New York, Crown Publishers [c1972] 719 p. [$12.50] 015/.73 75-168332
  Z1224 .B87 1972 MRR Biog.

Lehmann-Haupt, Hellmut, The book in America; 2d [rev. and enl. American] ed. New York, Bowker, 1951. xiv, 493 p. 655.473 51-11308
  Z473 .L522 1951 MRR Alc.

BOOKSELLERS AND BOOKSELLING--UNITED STATES--DIRECTORIES.
The A B bookman's yearbook. 1954- Newark, N.J. 010.58 54-1676
  Z990 .A18 MRR Alc Latest edition

American book trade directory. [1st]-ed.; 1915- New York, R. R. Bowker. 15-23627
  Z475 .A5 Sci RR Latest edition / MRR Ref Desk Latest edition

American Booksellers Association. A B A sidelines directory. 1957- New York. 57-3534
  Z477 .A614 MRR Alc Latest edition

Book dealers in North America; 1954/55- London, Sheppard Press. 655.47 55-435
  Z475 .B63 MRR Alc Latest edition / MRR Ref Desk Latest edition

Christian Booksellers Association. C B A suppliers directory. Colorado Springs [etc.] 070.5/94 72-622387
  Z479 .C5 MRR Alc Latest edition

Directory of American book specialists; [New York, Continental Pub. Co., 1972] 172 p. 380.1/45/07057302573 73-151032
  Z286.A55 D57 MRR Ref Desk.

McKay, George Leslie, American book auction catalogues, 1713-1934; New York, The New York public library, 1937. xxxii, 540 p. 016.0173 37-33888
  Z999 .A1M2 MRR Alc.

BOOTLE, ENG.--DIRECTORIES.
Kelly's (Gore's) directory of Liverpool, including Bootle, Birkenhead, Wallasey and environs. Kingston upon Thames, Surrey (etc.) Kelly's Directories Ltd. 35-15072
  DA690.L8 K4 MRR Alc Latest edition

BOOTS AND SHOES--HISTORY.
Wilcox, Ruth Turner, The mode in footwear. New York, C. Scribner's Sons, 1948. 190 p. 391.4 48-1300
  GT2130 .W5 MRR Alc.

BOOTS AND SHOES--MATERIALS.
Shoe factory buyers' guide. Boston, Mass., Shoe Trades Pub. Co. [etc.] 10-9844
  Began publication in 1909.
  TS945 .S5 MRR Alc Latest edition

BOOTS AND SHOES--TRADE AND MANUFACTURE--DIRECTORIES.
American shoemaking directory of shoe manufacturers ... in the United States and Canada. Boston, Shoe Traders Pub. Co. 09-4149
  Began with 1905 vol.
  TS945 .A6 MRR Alc Latest edition

Shoe factory buyers' guide. Boston, Mass., Shoe Trades Pub. Co. [etc.] 10-9844
  Began publication in 1909.
  TS945 .S5 MRR Alc Latest edition

BOOTS AND SHOES--TRADE AND MANUFACTURE--GREAT BRITAIN--DIRECTORIES.
The Shoe trades directory & diary. London, Shoe & leather news. 23 cm. 54-17271
  TS945 .S45 MRR Alc Latest edition

The Shoeman's guide. Leicester [Eng.] Halford Pub. Co. 53-29730
  HD9787.G7 S5 MRR Alc Latest edition

BOOTS AND SHOES--TRADE AND MANUFACTURE--IRELAND--DIRECTORIES.
The Shoeman's guide. Leicester [Eng.] Halford Pub. Co. 53-29730
  HD9787.G7 S5 MRR Alc Latest edition

BORDER LIFE
  see Frontier and pioneer life

BOSS RULE
  see Corruption (in politics)

BOSTON--COMMERCE--DIRECTORIES.
Directory of directors in the city of Boston and vicinity. 1905- Boston, Bankers Service Co. 05-8359
  HG4058.B7 MRR Alc Latest edition

BOSTON--DESCRIPTION--1951- --GUIDE-BOOKS.
Dimancescu, Dan, ed. This is Boston; Bicentennial ed. [Boston] Cities, inc. [1974] 95 p. 917.44/61/044 74-11306
  F73.18 .D55 MRR Alc.

Rubin, Jerome. Comprehensive guide to Boston; [Newton, Mass., Emporium Publications; distributed by A & A Distributors, Holbrook, Mass., 1972] 457 p. [$3.50] 917.44/61/044 72-81232
  F73.18 .R8 MRR Alc.

BOSTON--DESCRIPTION--GUIDE-BOOKS.
Dimancescu, Dan, ed. This is Boston; Bicentennial ed. [Boston] Cities, inc. [1974] 95 p. 917.44/61/044 74-11306
  F73.18 .D55 MRR Alc.

BOSTON--DIRECTORIES.
Rubin, Jerome. Comprehensive guide to Boston; [Newton, Mass., Emporium Publications; distributed by A & A Distributors, Holbrook, Mass., 1972] 457 p. [$3.50] 917.44/61/044 72-81232
  F73.18 .R8 MRR Alc.

BOTANICAL GARDENS.
Hyams, Edward S. Great botanical gardens of the world: London, Nelson, 1969. 288 p. [10/10/-] 580/.744 70-435497
  QK71 .H9 1969 MRR Alc.

BOTANY.
  see also Ferns

  see also Flowers

  see also House plants

  see also Microscope and microscopy

  see also Plants

  see also Poisonous plants

  see also Seeds

Manning, Stanley A. Systematic guide to flowering plants of the world, [1st American ed.] New York, Taplinger Pub. Co. [1965, c1964] 302 p. 582.13 65-17028
  QK97 .M3 1965 MRR Alc.

BOTANY--DICTIONARIES.
Chinery, Michael. A science dictionary of the plant world: New York, F. Watts [1969, c1966] 264 p. [4.95] 581/.03 68-17110
  QK9 .C46 1969 MRR Alc.

Healey, B. J. A gardener's guide to plant names New York, Scribner [1972] 284 p. [$7.95] 581/.01/4 72-1202
  QK11 .H4 MRR Alc.

Usher, George. A dictionary of botany, Princeton, N.J., Van Nostrand [1966] 404 p. 581.03 66-25447
  QK9 .U8 1966a MRR Alc.

BOTANY--DICTIONARIES--DUTCH.
Artschwager, Ernst Friedrich.
Dictionary of botanical equivalents,
Baltimore, The Williams & Wilkins
company, 1925. 5 p. l., 9-124 p.
25-11598
  QK9 .A7 1925 MRR Alc.

BOTANY--DICTIONARIES--FRENCH.
Artschwager, Ernst Friedrich.
Dictionary of botanical equivalents,
Baltimore, The Williams & Wilkins
company, 1925. 5 p. l., 9-124 p.
25-11598
  QK9 .A7 1925 MRR Alc.

BOTANY--DICTIONARIES--GERMAN.
Artschwager, Ernst Friedrich.
Dictionary of botanical equivalents,
Baltimore, The Williams & Wilkins
company, 1925. 5 p. l., 9-124 p.
25-11598
  QK9 .A7 1925 MRR Alc.

BOTANY--DICTIONARIES--ITALIAN.
Artschwager, Ernst Friedrich.
Dictionary of botanical equivalents,
Baltimore, The Williams & Wilkins
company, 1925. 5 p. l., 9-124 p.
25-11598
  QK9 .A7 1925 MRR Alc.

BOTANY--NOMENCLATORS.
Healey, B. J. A gardener's guide to
plant names New York, Scribner
[1972] 284 p. [$7.95]   581/.01/4
72-1202
  QK11 .H4 MRR Alc.

Little, Elbert Luther, Check list of
native and naturalized trees of the
United States (including Alaska)
Washington, Forest Service, 1953.
472 p.   582.16 581.973*   agr53-309
  QK481 .L5 MRR Alc.

Plowden, C. Chicheley. A manual of
plant names, London, Allen & Unwin,
1968. 260 p. [55/-] 581/.01/4 77-
384870
  QK96 .P57 MRR Alc.

BOTANY--NOMENCLATURE.
Plowden, C. Chicheley. A manual of
plant names, London, Allen & Unwin,
1968. 260 p. [55/-] 581/.01/4 77-
384870
  QK96 .P57 MRR Alc.

BOTANY--PICTORIAL WORKS.
Chinery, Michael. A science
dictionary of the plant world: New
York, F. Watts [1969, c1966] 264 p.
[4.95] 581/.03 68-17110
  QK9 .C46 1969 MRR Alc.

BOTANY--POPULAR WORKS.
Perry, Frances. Flowers of the
world. [New York] Crown [1972] 320
p. [$22.50]   582/.13 72-84313
  QK50 .P47 MRR Alc.

BOTANY--PRE-LINNEAN WORKS.
Theophrastus. Enquiry into plants
and minor works on odours and weather
signs, London, W. Heinemann; New
York, G. P. Putnam's sons, 1916. 2
v.   17-2706
  PA3612 .T4 1916 MRR Alc.

BOTANY--TERMINOLOGY.
Plowden, C. Chicheley. A manual of
plant names, London, Allen & Unwin,
1968. 260 p. [55/-] 581/.01/4 77-
384870
  QK96 .P57 MRR Alc.

BOTANY--CANADA.
Gleason, Henry Allan, The new
Britton and Brown illustrated flora
of the Northeastern United States and
adjacent Canada, [3d print.,
slightly rev.] New York, Published
for the New York Botanical Garden by
Hafner Pub. Co., 1963 [c1952] 3 v.
581.97 63-16478
  QK117 .G5 1963 MRR Alc.

BOTANY--NORTH AMERICA.
Walcott, Mary Morris (Vaux) Wild
flowers of America. New York, Crown
Publishers [1953] 71 p. 400 col.
plates. 581.97 53-9972
  QK112 .W35 MRR Alc.

BOTANY--NORTHEASTERN STATES.
Gleason, Henry Allan, The new
Britton and Brown illustrated flora
of the Northeastern United States and
adjacent Canada, [3d print.,
slightly rev.] New York, Published
for the New York Botanical Garden by
Hafner Pub. Co., 1963 [c1952] 3 v.
581.97 63-16478
  QK117 .G5 1963 MRR Alc.

BOTANY--UNITED STATES.
Gray, Asa, Manual of botany; 8th
(centennial) ed., illustrated.
Largely rewritten and expanded New
York, American Book Co. [1950] lxiv,
1632 p.   581.973 50-9007
  QK117 .G75 1950 MRR Alc.

BOTANY, ECONOMIC.
see also Grasses

see also Plants, Edible

BOTANY, ECONOMIC--DICTIONARIES.
Hocking, George Macdonald. A
dictionary of terms in pharmacognosy
and other divisions of economic
botany; Springfield, Ill., C. C.
Thomas [1955] xxv, 284 p.   581.603
55-7453
  QK99 .H69 1955 MRR Alc.

BOTANY, ECONOMIC--UNITED STATES.
Marx, David S. A modern American
herbal: useful trees and shrubs.
South Brunswick, A. S. Barnes [1973]
190 p.   582/.1609/73 71-86305
  QK482 .M43 MRR Alc.

BOTANY, MEDICAL.
Grieve, Maud. A modern herbal; New
York, Hafner Pub. Co., 1959. 2 v.
(xvi, 888 p.)   581.6303 59-15624
  QK9 .G7 1959 MRR Alc.

BOTSWANA--DIRECTORIES.
The Rhodesia-Zambia-Malawi directory
(including Botswana and Mocambique).
Bulawayo, Publications (Central
Africa) [etc.] 916.89/0025 38-1460

  "First published in 1910."
  DT947 .R5 MRR Alc Latest edition

BOTSWANA--GAZETTEERS.
United States. Office of Geography.
South Africa; Washington, 1954. 2
v. (1081 p.) 916.8/003 73-10017
  DT752 .U65 MRR Alc.

BOTSWANA--GOVERNMENT PUBLICATIONS--
BIBLIOGRAPHY--UNION LISTS.
Balima, Mildred Grimes. Botswana,
Lesotho, and Swaziland; a guide to
official publications, 1868-1968,
Washington, General Reference and
Bibliography Division, Library of
Congress; [for sale by the Supt. of
Docs., U.S. Govt. Print. Off.] 1971.
xvi, 84 p. [$1.00] 016.9168 74-
171029
  Z663.285 .B6 MRR Alc.

BOTTLES--COLLECTORS AND COLLECTING.
Munsey, Cecil. The illustrated guide
to collecting bottles. New York,
Hawthorn Books [1970] xi, 308 p.
[$9.95] 666/.19 75-122897
  NK5440.B6 M8 MRR Alc.

BOTTLES--COLLECTORS AND COLLECTING--
UNITED STATES.
Goodell, Donald. The American bottle
collector's price guide to historical
flasks, pontils, bitters, mineral
waters, inks & sodas. [1st ed.]
Rutland, Vt., C. E. Tuttle Co. [1973]
144 p. [$6.00] 666/.19 72-89738

  NK5440.B6 G6 MRR Alc.

BOTTLES--PRICES.
Cleveland, Hugh. Bottle pricing
guide. [Rev. ed. San Angelo, Tex.,
1972] 319 p. [$5.95] 666/.19 73-
153863
  NK5440.B6 C55 1972 MRR Alc.

Goodell, Donald. The American bottle
collector's price guide to historical
flasks, pontils, bitters, mineral
waters, inks & sodas. [1st ed.]
Rutland, Vt., C. E. Tuttle Co. [1973]
144 p. [$6.00] 666/.19 72-89738

  NK5440.B6 G6 MRR Alc.

Kovel, Ralph M. The official bottle
price list, 2d ed. New York, Crown
Publishers [1973] xxxvi, 219 p.
[$4.95] 666/.19 72-96660
  NK5440.B6 K6 1973 MRR Alc.

BOTTLES, AMERICAN.
Van Rensselaer, Stephen, Check list
of early American bottles and flasks.
Southampton, N.Y., Cracker Barrell
Press [1969? c1921] 109 p. [3.00]
748/.8 77-3756
  NK5440.B6 V3 1969 MRR Alc.

BOTTLES, AMERICAN--CATALOGS.
Goodell, Donald. The American bottle
collector's price guide to historical
flasks, pontils, bitters, mineral
waters, inks & sodas. [1st ed.]
Rutland, Vt., C. E. Tuttle Co. [1973]
144 p. [$6.00] 666/.19 72-89738

  NK5440.B6 G6 MRR Alc.

Kovel, Ralph M. The official bottle
price list, 2d ed. New York, Crown
Publishers [1973] xxxvi, 219 p.
[$4.95] 666/.19 72-96660
  NK5440.B6 K6 1973 MRR Alc.

BOTTLING--DIRECTORIES.
The United beverage bureau book.
Louisville, Ky. 663.065 28-11187
Began with 1922 vol.
  HF5585.B65 U5 MRR Alc Latest
edition

BOURNEMOUTH, ENG.--DIRECTORIES.
Kelly's directory of Bournemouth and
Poole. Kingston upon Thames [Eng.,
etc.] 53-28315
  DA690.B685 K4 MRR Alc Latest
edition

BOXING--BIOGRAPHY.
The Ring boxing encyclopedia and
record book. 1941- ed. New York
[etc] Ring Book Shop [etc.]
796.8/3/0212 64-1347
  GV1137 .R5 MRR Alc Latest edition

BOXING--BIOGRAPHY--DICTIONARIES.
Burrill, Bob. Who's who in boxing.
New Rochelle, N.Y., Arlington House
[1974] 208 p. [$7.95]
796.8/3/0922 73-13020
  GV1131 .B87 MRR Biog.

BOXING--DICTIONARIES.
Golesworthy, Maurice. The
encyclopedia of boxing. [New and
rev. ed.] London, R. Hale [1961]
240 p. 796.8303 62-6596
  GV1133 .G6 1961 MRR Alc.

BOXING--HISTORY.
Fleischer, Nathaniel S. The
heavyweight championship; Rev. ed.
New York, Putnam [1961] 318 p.
796.8309 61-5821
  GV1121 .F6 1961 MRR Alc.

BOXING--PICTORIAL WORKS.
Fleischer, Nathaniel S. A pictorial
history of boxing, Revised ed.
London, Spring Books, 1966. 352 p.
[17/6] 796.8/3/0222 67-82672
  GV1121 .F63 1966 MRR Alc.

BOXING--STATISTICS.
The Ring boxing encyclopedia and
record book. 1941- ed. New York
[etc] Ring Book Shop [etc.]
796.8/3/0212 64-1347
  GV1137 .R5 MRR Alc Latest edition

BOYCOTT--BIBLIOGRAPHY.
United States. Library of Congress.
Division of bibliography. ... Select
list of references on boycotts and
injunctions in labor disputes;
Washington, Govt. print. off., 1911.
iii, 3-69 p. 10-35010
  Z663.28 .S357 MRR Alc.

BRADY, MATHEW B., 1823 (CA.)-1896.
United States. Library of Congress.
Prints and Photographs Division.
Civil War photographs, 1861-1865;
Washington, Reference Dept., Library
of Congress, 1961. x, 74 p.
973.79085 61-60002
  Z663.39 .C5 MRR Alc.

BRAHMANISM.
see also Hinduism.

BRAILLE MUSIC--NOTATION.
De Garmo, Mary Turner. Introduction
to braille music transcription.
Washington, Division for the Blind
and Physically Handicapped, Library
of Congress, 1970. vi, 256 p.
781/.24 73-601990
  Z663.25 .I55 MRR Alc.

BRAIN.
see also Dreams

BRANDED MERCHANDISE--UNITED STATES--
HISTORY.
Franklin, Elizabeth. Why did they
name it ...? New York, Fleet Pub.
Corp. [1964] xv, 207 p. 608.87 64-
12968
  T223.V2 F7 MRR Alc.

BRAZIL--BIBLIOGRAPHY.
Ford, Jeremiah Denis Matthias, comp.
A tentative bibliography of Brazilian
belles-lettres, Cambridge, Mass.,
Harvard university press, 1931. vi,
201 p. 015.81 016.869 31-22233
  Z1681 .F71 MRR Alc.

Moraes, Rubens Borba de,
Bibliographia brasiliana; Amsterdam,
Colibris Editora [c1958] 2 v.
016.981 59-1097
  Z1671 .M6 MRR Alc.

Moraes, Rubens Borba de, ed. Manual
bibliografico de estudos
brasileiros, Rio de Janeiro,
Grafica Editora Souza, 1949. xi,
895 p. 015.81 50-26625
  Z1686 .M6 MRR Alc.

Topete, José Manuel. A working
bibliography of Brazilian literature.
Gainesville, University of Florida
Press, 1957. xii, 114 p. 016.869
57-12928
  Z1681 .T6 MRR Alc.

BRAZIL--BIO-BIBLIOGRAPHY--INDEXES.
Sousa, José Galante de, Indice de
biobibliografia brasileira Rio de
Janeiro] Instituto Nacional do Livro,
Ministerio da Educação e Cultura
[1963] 440 p. 68-41350
  Z1680 .S63 MRR Biog.

BRAZIL--BIOGRAPHY,
Verbo; enciclopédia luso-brasileira
de cultura. Lisboa, Editorial Verbo
[1963- v.   65-47647
AE37 .V4 MRR Alc.

BRAZIL--BIOGRAPHY--DICTIONARIES.
Quem é quem no Brasil. São Paulo,
Sociedade Brasileira de Expansão
Comercial Ltda. 55-27153
F2505 .Q4 MRR Biog Latest edition

BRAZIL--BIOGRAPHY--INDEXES.
Sousa, José Galante de, Índice de
biobibliografia brasileira Rio de
Janeiro] Instituto Nacional do Livro,
Ministério da Educação e Cultura
[1963] 440 p.   68-41350
Z1680 .S63 MRR Biog.

BRAZIL--COMMERCE--YEARBOOKS.
AIC; anuário da indústria e
comércio: Centro. [Rio de Janeiro,
S. S. Moreira] 338.4/025/815 74-
645596
HC189.R4 A18 MRR Alc Latest
edition

Brasil, sua indústria e exportação.
São Paulo [etc.] Cadastro Delta
[etc.] 53-19341
HC186 .B683 MRR Alc Latest edition

BRAZIL--GAZETTEERS.
United States. Office of Geography.
Brazil; Washington, 1963. v, 915 p.
63-62342
F2504 .U5 MRR Alc.

BRAZIL--HISTORY.
Poppino, Rollie E. Brazil: the land
and people 2d ed. New York, Oxford
University Press, 1973. viii, 385 p.
[$9.50] 918.1/03 73-82626
F2521 .P58 1973 MRR Alc.

BRAZIL--HISTORY--CHRONOLOGY.
Fitzgibbon, Russell Humke, Brazil: a
chronology and fact book, 1488-1973,
Dobbs Ferry, N.Y., Oceana
Publications, 1974. vi, 150 p.
[$7.50] 981 73-17058
F2521 .F55 MRR Alc.

BRAZIL--HISTORY--SOURCES.
Fitzgibbon, Russell Humke, Brazil: a
chronology and fact book, 1488-1973,
Dobbs Ferry, N.Y., Oceana
Publications, 1974. vi, 150 p.
[$7.50] 981 73-17058
F2521 .F55 MRR Alc.

BRAZIL--INDUSTRIES--YEARBOOKS.
Brasil, sua indústria e exportação.
São Paulo [etc.] Cadastro Delta
[etc.] 53-19341
HC186 .B683 MRR Alc Latest edition

BRAZIL--MANUFACTURES--DIRECTORIES.
Brasil, sua indústria e exportação.
São Paulo [etc.] Cadastro Delta
[etc.] 53-19341
HC186 .B683 MRR Alc Latest edition

BRAZIL--POPULATION.
Smith, Thomas Lynn, Brazil; people
and institutions 4th ed. Baton
Rouge, Louisiana State University
Press, 1972. xx, 778 p. [$15.00]
309.1/81 73-168396
HN283.5 .S58 1972 MRR Alc.

BRAZIL--SOCIAL CONDITIONS.
Smith, Thomas Lynn, Brazil; people
and institutions 4th ed. Baton
Rouge, Louisiana State University
Press, 1972. xx, 778 p. [$15.00]
309.1/81 73-168396
HN283.5 .S58 1972 MRR Alc.

BRAZIL--STATISTICS.
Anuário estatístico do Brasil. Rio
de Janeiro, Instituto Brasileiro de
Estatística. 73-642043
HA971 .A32 MRR Alc Latest edition

BRAZILIAN LITERATURE--BIBLIOGRAPHY.
Ford, Jeremiah Denis Matthias, comp.
A tentative bibliography of Brazilian
belles-lettres, Cambridge, Mass.,
Harvard university press, 1931. vi,
201 p. 015.81 016.869 31-22233
Z1681 .F71 MRR Alc.

Topete, José Manuel. A working
bibliography of Brazilian literature.
Gainesville, University of Florida
Press, 1957. xii, 114 p. 016.869
57-12928
Z1681 .T6 MRR Alc.

BRAZILIAN LITERATURE--RIO DE JANEIRO--
BIBLIOGRAPHY.
Ribeiro, João de Souza, Dicionário
biobibliográfico de escritores
cariocas (1565-1965) Rio de Janeiro,
Livraria Brasiliana, 1965. 285 p.
66-51643
PQ9692.R5 R5 MRR Biog.

BRAZILIAN NEWSPAPERS--BIBLIOGRAPHY--
UNION LISTS.
Latin American newspapers in United
States libraries; Austin, Published
for the Conference on Latin American
History by the University of Texas
Press [1969, c1968] xliv, 619 p.
[20.00] 016.07918 69-63004
Z6947 .C5 MRR Alc.

BRAZILIAN PERIODICALS--BIBLIOGRAPHY.
Ford, Jeremiah Denis Matthias, comp.
A tentative bibliography of Brazilian
belles-lettres, Cambridge, Mass.,
Harvard university press, 1931. vi,
201 p. 015.81 016.869 31-22233
Z1681 .F71 MRR Alc.

BREACH OF THE PEACE.
see also Riots

BREEDING.
see also Domestic animals

see also Genetics

BREEDS OF CATTLE
see Cattle breeds

BREEDS OF SHEEP
see Sheep breeds

BREEDS OF SWINE
see Swine breeds

BREMEN--COMMERCE--DIRECTORIES.
Firmenhandbuch Niedersachsen und Land
Bremen. Hannover, Industrie- und
Handelsverlag. 53-29246
HC287.S3 F5 MRR Alc Latest edition

BREMEN--DIRECTORIES.
Breger Adressbuch. Bremen, C.
Schünemann. 53-30963
DD901.B73 B7 MRR Alc Latest
edition

BREMERHAVEN, GERMANY--DIRECTORIES.
Adressbuch der Stadt Bremerhaven.
Bremen, Adressbuch- und
Anzeigenwerbegesellschaft. 53-28334

DD901.B82 A7 MRR Alc Latest
edition

BREWING INDUSTRY--DIRECTORIES.
Internationales Firmenregister der
Brauindustrie. Zürich, Verlag für
Internationale Wirtschaftsliteratur
[etc.] 338.476633 53-22138
TP572 .I57 MRR Alc Latest edition

BREWING INDUSTRY--AMERICA--DIRECTORIES.
Brewers digest. Annual buyers' guide
& directory. [1st]- 1947-
[Chicago, Siebel Pub. Co.] 663.3058
51-16022
TP572 .B78 MRR Alc Latest edition

BREWING INDUSTRY--EUROPE--DIRECTORIES.
Brauereien und Mälzereien in Europa.
51.- Aufl.; 1962/63- Darmstadt,
Hoppenstedt Wirtschaftsverlag.
338.4/7/66330254 72-626675
TP572 .B7 MRR Alc Latest edition

BREWING INDUSTRY--HAWAIIAN ISLANDS--
DIRECTORIES.
Brewers digest. Annual buyers' guide
& directory. [1st]- 1947-
[Chicago, Siebel Pub. Co.] 663.3058
51-16022
TP572 .B78 MRR Alc Latest edition

BREWING INDUSTRY--PUERTO RICO--
DIRECTORIES.
Brewers digest. Annual buyers' guide
& directory. [1st]- 1947-
[Chicago, Siebel Pub. Co.] 663.3058
51-16022
TP572 .B78 MRR Alc Latest edition

BREWING INDUSTRY--UNITED STATES.
Brewers' almanac. [Washington, etc.]
United States Brewers' Association.
338.476633 45-51432
Publication began in 1940?
HD9397.U5 B7 MRR Alc Latest
edition

Research Company of America, New
York. Brewing industry survey, New
York. 338.47663 42-4175
HD9397.U5 R4 MRR Alc Latest
edition

BREWING INDUSTRY--UNITED STATES--
DIRECTORIES.
Brewers digest. Annual buyers' guide
& directory. [1st]- 1947-
[Chicago, Siebel Pub. Co.] 663.3058
51-16022
TP572 .B78 MRR Alc Latest edition

Red book: encyclopaedic directory of
the wine and liquor industries. New
York, Schwartz Publications, inc.
[$19.50] 338.4/7/663102573 73-
646025
HD9373 .R43 MRR Alc Latest edition

BREWING INDUSTRY--UNITED STATES--
HISTORY.
Baron, Stanley Wade, Brewed in
America; [1st ed.] Boston, Little,
Brown [1962] 424 p. 338.476633 62-
9546
HD9397.U52 B3 MRR Alc.

BRIC-A-BRAC
see Art objects

BRICKLAYING.
Dezettel, Louis M. Masons and
builders library, Indianapolis, T.
Audel [1972] 2 v. 693 78-186134
TH5311 .D48 MRR Alc.

BRIDGES--HISTORY.
Smith, Hubert Shirley. The world's
great bridges, Rev. ed. New York,
Harper & Row [1965, c1964] x, 250 p.
624.209 65-21000
TG15 .S5 1965 MRR Alc.

BRIDGES--UNITED STATES.
United States. Army. Corps of
Engineers. Bridges over the
navigable waters of the United
States. [Washington] 1961- pts.
624.20973 61-61831
TG23 .A5 1961 MRR Alc.

BRIGHT CHILDREN
see Gifted children

BRIGHTON, ENG.--DIRECTORIES.
Kelly's directory of Brighton [and]
Hove. Kingston upon Thames, Surrey
[etc.] Kelly's Directories Limited
[etc.] 53-28330
DA690.B78 K36 MRR Alc Latest
edition

BRISBANE--COMMERCE--DIRECTORIES.
Universal business directory for
Brisbane city & suburbs. Brisbane,
Universal Business Directories. 57-
34435
HF5305.B7 U5 MRR Alc Latest
edition

BRITISH COLUMBIA--BIOGRAPHY.
Who's who in British Columbia; 1931-
Victoria, B.C., S. M. Carter. 31-
11351
F1086 .W65 MRR Biog Latest edition

BRITISH HONDURAS--DESCRIPTION AND
TRAVEL--GUIDE-BOOKS.
Aspinall, Algernon Edward, Sir, The
pocket guide to the West Indies and
British Guiana, British Honduras,
Bermuda, the Spanish Main, Surinam,
the Panama Canal, [10th ed.] rev.
London, Methuen [1960] xx, 474 p.
917.29 61-19408
F1609 .A84 1960 MRR Alc.

BRITISH HONDURAS--GAZETTEERS.
United States. Office of Geography.
British Honduras; Washington, 1956.
ii, 25 p. 917.282/003 75-10047
F1442 .U5 1956b MRR Alc.

BRITISH IN AMERICA.
Wright, Louis Booker, ed. The
Elizabethans' America; Cambridge,
Harvard University Press, 1965. xii,
295 p. 917.041 65-8877
E141 .W7 MRR Alc.

BRITISH IN INDIA--BIOGRAPHY--
DICTIONARIES.
Buckland, Charles Edward, Dictionary
of Indian biography. Detroit, Gale
Research Co., 1968. xii, 494 p.
920.054 68-23140
DS434 .B8 1968 MRR Biog.

BRITISH IN MEXICO.
Anglo-American directory of Mexico.
Mexico, D.F., Talleres tipográficos
de "Excélsior." 917.2 42-34594
F1204.5 .A4 MRR Alc Latest edition

BRITISH MUSEUM.
British Museum. Dept. of Printed
Books. A short title catalogue of
French books, 1601-1700, Folkestone
[Eng.] Dawsons, 1973. x, 690 p.
015/.44 73-176033
Z2162 .B87 1973 MRR Alc.

Watson, Vera, The British Museum;
London, Quartet Books Ltd., 1973.
271 p. [£3.50] 913/.031/07402142
74-175583
AM101.B87 W37 MRR Alc.

BRITISH MUSEUM--CATALOGS.
British Museum. The catalogues of
the British Museum. [London,
Trustees of the British Museum, 1951-
v. 1, 1952] v.   018.1 016* 53-
27893
Z695 .B85 MRR Alc.

BRITISH MUSEUM--HISTORY.
Miller, Edward, That noble cabinet :
London : Deutsch, 1973. 3-400 p.,
[16] p. of plates : [£4.80]
069/.09421/42 74-186524
AM101.B87 M63 1973 MRR Alc.

BRITISH POETRY
see English poetry

BRITTANY--DESCRIPTION AND TRAVEL--GUIDE-
BOOKS.
Pretagne. 1948- Paris, Hachette.
55-42610
DC611.B847 B67 MRR Alc Latest
edition

Pretagne. Paris, Pneu Michelin
[etc.] 53-35559
GV1025.F7 B7 MRR Alc Latest
edition

BROADSIDES--BIBLIOGRAPHY.
Edmond, John Philip, comp. Catalogue
of English broadsides, 1505-1897.
New York, B. Franklin [1968] xl, 526
p.   016.6552 71-6830
Z2027.P3 E2 1968 MRR Alc

United States. Library of Congress.
Manuscript division. Handbook of
manuscripts in the Library of
Congress. Washington, Govt. print.
off., 1918. xvi, 750 p.   17-26010
Z6621 .U55 MRR Alc.

BROADSIDES--BIBLIOGRAPHY--CATALOGS.
United States. Library of Congress.
Rare Book Division. Catalog of
broadsides in the Rare Book Division.
Boston, G. K. Hall 1972. 4 v.   011
72-6563
Z1231.B7 A5 MRR Alc (Dk 33)

BROKERS.
see also Stock-exchange

BROKERS--DIRECTORIES.
Security dealers of North America.
New York, Standard & Poor's Corp.
[etc.] 22-14045
HG4907 .S4 MRR Alc Latest edition

BROKERS--EUROPE--DIRECTORIES.
Esslen, Rainer. A guide to marketing
securities in Europe, 1971-1972. New
York, Wall Street Reports Pub. Corp.
[1971] viii, 215 p.   332.67/34/073
79-178914
HG4538 .E76 MRR Alc.

BROKERS--GREAT BRITAIN--DIRECTORIES.
The Times issuing house year book.
12th- ed; 1948- London, Times
Newspapers Ltd. [etc.] 332.6/32/0942
72-626344
HG5431 .I7 MRR Alc Latest edition

BROKERS--UNITED STATES--DIRECTORIES.
Broker-dealer directory.
[Washington] Securities and Exchange
Commission. 332.6/2/02573 74-644744

HG4907 .B74 MRR Alc Latest edition

Directory: municipal bond dealers of
the United States. New York, The
Bond buyer. 332.6/2/02573 74-642470

HG4907 .D5 MRR Alc Latest edition

Skinner & Co. Skinner's Directory of
security dealer name and address
changes (1965-1973) San Francisco
[1973] 82 p.   332.6/2 73-174234
HG4621 .S5 1973 MRR Alc.

Standard and Poor's Corporation.
Standard and Poor's directory of bond
agents. 1974/75- ed. New York.
[$180.00] 332.6/7 74-645518
HG4907 .S7a MRR Alc Latest edition

BROWNING, ROBERT, 1812-1889--
CONCORDANCES.
Molineux, Marie Ada. A phrase book
from the poetic and dramatic works of
Robert Browning. Ann Arbor, Mich.,
Gryphon Books, 1971. xiii, 520 p.
821/.8 71-145523
PR4230 .M6 1896ab MRR Alc.

BRUNEI, BORNEO (STATE)--IMPRINTS.
United States. Library of Congress.
Library of Congress Office, Djakarta.
Accessions list, Indonesia,
Malaysia, Singapore, and Brunei. v.
1- July 1964- Djakarta. sa 66-444
Z663.767.I6 A25 MRR Alc MRR Alc
Full set

United States. Library of Congress.
Library of Congress Office, Djakarta.
Accessions list, Indonesia,
Malaysia, Singapore, and Brunei.
Cumulative list of serials. Jan.
1964/Sept. 1966-1964/68. Djakarta.
74-643581
Z663.767.I6 A252 MRR Alc MRR Alc
Full set

BRUSSELS--COMMERCE--DIRECTORIES.
Annuaire du commerce et de
l'industrie de Belgique. Bruxelles,
A. Mertens. ca 11-1699
Began with 1849 vol.
HF5184 .A6 MRR Alc Latest edition

BRUSSELS--DIRECTORIES.
Annuaire du commerce et de
l'industrie de Belgique. Bruxelles,
A. Mertens. ca 11-1699
Began with 1849 vol.
HF5184 .A6 MRR Alc Latest edition

High-life de Belgique. Ixelles-
Bruxelles, Geeraerts ca 27-207
DB414 .H5 MRR Alc Latest edition

BRUSSELS. CHAMBRE DE COMMERCE.
Brussels. Chambre de commerce.
Annuaire officiel. Bruxelles, Impr.
Industrielle et financière [etc.]
380.1/06/24933 74-642351
HF314 .B85 MRR Alc Latest edition

BRYANT, DOUGLAS WALLACE, 1913-
MEMORANDUM ON THE SUBJECT OF THE
LIBRARY OF CONGRESS AND CONNECTED
LIBRARY MATTERS.
United States. Library of Congress.
Report of the Librarian of Congress
on the Bryant memorandum,
Washington, 1962. 54 l.   62-64798
Z663 .R39 MRR Alc.

BUCHANAN, JAMES, PRES. U.S., 1791-1868.
Buchanan, James, Pres. U.S., James
Buchanan, 1791-1868; Dobbs Ferry,
N.Y., Oceana Publications, 1968. v,
89 p. [$3.00] 973.6/8/08 68-21537

E436 .B88 MRR Alc.

Curtis, George Ticknor, Life of
James Buchanan, New York, Harper &
brothers, 1883. 2 v.   14-758
E437 .C98 MRR Alc.

Klein, Philip Shriver, President
James Buchanan, University Park,
Pennsylvania State University Press
[1962] xviii, 506 p.   923.173 62-
12623
E437 .K53 MRR Alc.

BUDAPEST--DIRECTORIES.
Kiraly, Elemer. Budapesti
utmutato, 1969. [Budapest]
Panorama, 1969. 730 p. [43.00]
74-10750
DB863 .K55 1969 MRR Alc.

BUDAPEST--STREETS.
Kiraly, Elemer. Budapesti
utmutato, 1969. [Budapest]
Panorama, 1969. 730 p. [43.00]
74-10750
DB863 .K55 1969 MRR Alc.

BUDDHA AND BUDDHISM.
see also Zen Buddhism

BUDDHA AND BUDDHISM--DICTIONARIES.
A Dictionary of Buddhism. New York,
Scribner [1972] x, 277 p. [$7.95]
294.3/03 72-37231
BQ130 .D5 MRR Alc.

Humphreys, Christmas, A popular
dictionary of Buddhism. [1st
American ed.] New York, Citadel
Press [1963] 223 p.   294.303 63-
16729
BL1403 .H8 1963 MRR Alc.

Nyanatiloka, bhikku. Buddhist
dictionary; [2d rev. ed.] Colombo,
Frewin, 1956. 197 p. sa 63-1754
BL1403 .N78 1956 MRR Alc.

BUDDHA AND BUDDHISM--SACRED BOOKS.
Goddard, Dwight, ed. A Buddhist
bible. Rev. and enl. New York,
Dutton, 1952. viii, 677 p.   294.32
52-7805
BL1410 .G6 1952 MRR Alc.

BUDDHA AND BUDDHISM--SACRED BOOKS--
QUOTATIONS.
Humphreys, Christmas, ed. The wisdom
of Buddhism. New York, Random House
[1961, c1960] 280 p.   294.3 61-
12139
BL1451.2 .H8 1961 MRR Alc.

BUDDHA AND BUDDHISM--UNITED STATES--
DIRECTORIES.
Buddhist Churches of America.
Directory. [San Francisco?] 66-
37500
BL1445.U6 B8 MRR Alc Latest
edition

BUDGET--BIBLIOGRAPHY.
United States. Library of Congress.
Division of bibliography. ... Select
list of references on the budget of
foreign countries. Washington, Govt.
print. off., 1904. 19 p.   04-32518

Z663.28 .S43 MRR Alc.

BUDGET--UNITED STATES.
Brown, William James, The Federal
budgeting and appropriations process,
New York, Dept. of Economics and
Research, American Bankers
Association [1967] xi, 50 p.
353.007/22 67-8435
HJ2050 .B7 MRR Alc.

United States. Congress.
Appropriations, budget estimates,
etc. Statements. Washington, U.S.
Govt. Print Off. 07-1777
HJ10.B6 MRR Alc Latest edition

United States. Treasury Dept. Bureau
of Accounts. Combined statement of
receipts, expenditures and balances
of the United States government.
1871/72- Washington. 10-11510
HJ10 .A6 MRR Alc Latest edition

BUDGET--UNITED STATES--PERIODICALS.
United States. Office of Management
and Budget. The budget of the United
States Government. 1971/72-
[Washington,For sale by the Supt. of
Docs., U.S. Govt. Print. Off.]
353.007/22 70-611049
HJ2051 .A59 MRR Ref Desk Latest
edition

United States. Office of Management
and Budget. The Budget of the United
States Government. Appendix. 1971/72-
[Washington, For sale by the Supt.
of Docs., U.S. Govt. Print. Off.]
353.007/22 74-643523
HJ2051 .A59 Suppl. MRR Ref Desk
Latest Edition

BUGANDA--POLITICS AND GOVERNMENT.
Apter, David Ernest, The political
kingdom in Uganda; [2d ed.]
Princeton, N.J., Princeton University
Press [1967] xxii, 498 p.
320.9/676/1 67-18831
DT434.U25 A6 1967 MRR Alc.

BUILDING.
see also Architecture

see also Engineering

Ulrey, Harry F. Carpenters and
builders library, [3d ed.]
Indianapolis, T. Audel [1970] 4 v.
694/.02/02 74-99760
TH5604 .U44 1970 MRR Alc.

BUILDING--BIBLIOGRAPHY.
Bentley, Howard B. Building
construction information sources.
Detroit, Gale Research Co. [1964]
181 p.   016.69 64-16502
Z7914.B9 B4 MRR Alc.

Smith, Denison Langley, How to find
out in architecture and building;
[1st ed.] Oxford, New York, Pergamon
Press [1967] xii, 232 p.   016.72
66-29605
Z5941 .S58 1967 MRR Alc.

BUILDING--CONTRACTS AND SPECIFICATIONS--
PERIODICALS.
Specification. Metric edition. 71st-
1970- [London, Architectural
Press] 692/.3/05 72-622381
TH425 .S65 MRR Alc Latest edition
/ Sci RR Latest edition*

BUILDING--DETAILS--DRAWINGS.
Ramsey, Charles George,
Architectural graphic standards 6th
ed. New York, J. Wiley [1970] 695
p.   692/.2 79-136970
TH2031 .R35 1970 MRR Alc.

BUILDING--DICTIONARIES.
Burke, Arthur Edward, Architectural
and building trades dictionary
Chicago, American Technical Society,
1955. xxxviii, 377 p.   690.3 56-
433
NA31 .B84 1955 MRR Alc.

Cowan, Henry J. Dictionary of
architectural science New York,
Wiley [1973] xi, 354 p.   721/.03
73-15839
NA31 .C64 MRR Alc.

National Association of Women in
Construction. Phoenix Chapter.
Construction dictionary; construction
terms & tables and an encyclopedia of
construction. Phoenix, Ariz. [1973]
viii, 599 p.   690/.03 73-83758
TH9 .N3 1973 MRR Alc.

Putnam, R. E. Architectural and
building trades dictionary 3d ed.
Chicago, American Technical Society
[1974] 510 p.   721/.03 74-75483
TH9 .P82 1974 MRR Alc.

Siegele, Herman Hugo, Building
trades dictionary; Chicago, F. J.
Drake [1959] 380 p.   690.3 59-
16934
TH9 .S5 1959 MRR Alc.

Ulrey, Harry F. Builders
encyclopedia, [1st ed.]
Indianapolis, T. Audel [1970] 593 p.
[$7.95 ($9.50 Can)] 690/.03 74-
128019
TH9 .U45 MRR alc.

BUILDING--DICTIONARIES--POLYGLOT.
Elsevier's dictionary of building
construction, Amsterdam, New York,
Elsevier Pub. Co., 1959. 471 p.
690.3 58-59508
TH9 .E47 MRR Alc.

333

3333

333

333

BUILDING--DICTIONARIES-- (Cont.)
Zboiński, A., ed. Dictionary of architecture and building trades in four languages: English, German, Polish, Russian. Oxford, New York, Pergamon Press; [distributed in the Western Hemisphere by Macmillan, New York, 1963] 491 p. 63-22975
NA31 .Z34 MRR Alc.

BUILDING--ESTIMATES.
Walker, Frank Rabold. The building estimator's reference book; [1st]-ed.; 1915- Chicago, F. R. Walker Co. [etc.] 692.5 15-23586
TH435 .W3 Sci RR Latest edition / MRR Alc Latest edition

BUILDING--FRANCE--DIRECTORIES.
Sageret; Paris. 53-28411
"Fondé en 1809."
TH12 .S25 MRR Alc Latest edition

BUILDING--UNITED STATES.
Condit, Carl W. American building art: the twentieth century. New York, Oxford University Press, 1961. 427 p. 624.10973 61-8369
TA23 .C57 MRR Alc.

BUILDING--UNITED STATES--DIRECTORIES.
Sweet's industrial construction & renovation file with plant engineering extension market list. 1974- [New York, Sweet's Division, McGraw-Hill Information Systems Co.] 338.4/7/69002573 74-645493
TH12 .S93 MRR Alc Latest edition / Sci RR Latest edition

BUILDING AND LOAN ASSOCIATIONS--BIOGRAPHY.
Building societies who's who. London, Franey & Co. 332.32058 53-29080
HG2123 .B8 MRR Alc Latest edition

BUILDING AND LOAN ASSOCIATIONS--GREAT BRITAIN.
Building societies year book. London. 332.3206242 39-31431
First issued in 1927.
HG2121 .B84 MRR Alc Latest edition

BUILDING AND LOAN ASSOCIATIONS--UNITED STATES--DIRECTORIES.
Directory of American savings and loan associations. 1st- ed.; 1955- Baltimore; T. K. Sanderson Organization. 55-41558
HG2441 .D53 MRR Alc Latest edition

National League of Insured Savings Associations. Membership directory. Washington. 332.3205873 60-21166
HG2151 .N3 MRR Alc Latest edition

United States Savings and Loan League. Directory of members. Chicago. 59-44374
HG2121 .U48 MRR Alc Latest edition / MRR Alc Latest edition

BUILDING AND LOAN ASSOCIATIONS--UNITED STATES--PERIODICALS.
Savings & loan fact book. 1974- Chicago, United States League of Savings Associations. 332.3/2/0973 74-647156
HG2151 .U55 MRR Alc Latest edition

BUILDING FITTINGS--CATALOGS.
Sweet's light construction catalog file. New York, Sweet's Division, McGraw-Hill Information Systems Co. 690 72-626784
TH455 .S85 MRR Alc Latest edition

BUILDING INDUSTRY
see Construction industry

BUILDING MATERIALS.
see also Concrete

BUILDING MATERIALS--CATALOGS.
Sweet's architectural catalog file. New York, Sweet's Division, McGraw-Hill Information Systems Co. 690 72-626781
TH455 .S8 MRR Alc Latest edition

Sweet's industrial construction and renovation file. 1974- New York, Sweet's Division, McGraw-Hill Information Systems Co. 338.4/7/624102573 74-640340
TA215 .S85 MRR Alc Latest edition

Sweet's light construction catalog file. New York, Sweet's Division, McGraw-Hill Information Systems Co. 690 72-626784
TH455 .S85 MRR Alc Latest edition

BUILDING MATERIALS--DICTIONARIES.
Hornbostel, Caleb. Materials for architecture; New York, Reinhold Pub. Corp. [1961] xi, 610 p. 691.03 61-13206
TA403 .H6 MRR Alc.

BUILDING MATERIALS--STANDARDS.
De Chiara, Joseph, Time-saver standards for building types. New York, McGraw-Hill [1973] xiii, 1065 p. [$27.50] 729/.2 73-6663
NA2760 .D42 MRR Alc.

BUILDING MATERIALS INDUSTRY--FRANCE--DIRECTORIES.
Sageret; Paris. 53-28411
"Fondé en 1809."
TH12 .S25 MRR Alc Latest edition

BUILDING MATERIALS INDUSTRY--GREAT BRITAIN--DIRECTORIES.
Construction Industry Research and Information Association. CIRIA guide to sources of information; London, CIRIA, [1970]. 176 p. 690/.07 72-194509
HD9715.G72 C65 MRR Alc.

Sell's building index. Epsom, Eng., Sell's Publications Ltd. [£4.50] 338.4/7/68002542 73-640925
HD9715.G7 S4 MRR Alc Latest edition

BUILDING MATERIALS INDUSTRY--SOUTHERN STATES--DIRECTORIES.
Southern wholesalers' guide. [Atlanta] W.R.C. Smith Pub. Co. 338.7/6/83 73-642885
HD9745.U4 S68 MRR Alc Latest edition

BUILDING MATERIALS INDUSTRY--SOUTHWEST, NEW--DIRECTORIES.
Southern wholesalers' guide. [Atlanta] W.R.C. Smith Pub. Co. 338.7/6/83 73-642885
HD9745.U4 S68 MRR Alc Latest edition

BUILDING MATERIALS INDUSTRY--UNITED STATES--DIRECTORIES.
Southern wholesalers' guide. [Atlanta] W.R.C. Smith Pub. Co. 338.7/6/83 73-642885
HD9745.U4 S68 MRR Alc Latest edition

BUILDING RESEARCH--UNITED STATES.
United States. Office of Science and Technology. Housing research and building technology activities of the Federal Government. Washington; [For sale by the Supt. of Docs., U.S. Govt. Print. Off.] 1970. 117 p. [1.25] 690/.072/073 75-608274
TH23 .A6 1970 MRR Alc.

BUILDINGS--MECHANICAL EQUIPMENT--CATALOGS.
M P C; Manhasset, N.Y., Hutton Pub. Co. 696/.00028 68-7522
Began with 1964 vol.
TH6010 .M2 MRR Alc Latest edition

BUILDINGS, PREFABRICATED--DIRECTORIES.
The Blue book of major homebuilders. [Crofton, Md.] CMR Associates. 338.4/7/690802573 72-621729
TH12.5 .B5 MRR Alc Latest edition

BUILDINGS, PUBLIC
see Public buildings

BULGARIA.
Rusinov, Spas. Bulgaria, a tourist handbook [Sofia] Sofia Press [1971?] 133 p. 914.97/7/043 74-867850
DR54 .R865 MRR Alc.

BULGARIA--BIBLIOGRAPHY.
Horecky, Paul Louis, Southeastern Europe; Chicago, University of Chicago Press [1969] xxii, 755 p. 016.91496 73-110336
Z2831 .H67 MRR Alc.

Pundeff, Marin V. Bulgaria; a bibliographic guide, Washington, Slavic and Central European Division, Reference Department, Library of Congress; [for sale by the Superintendent of Documents, U.S. Govt. Print. Off.] 1965. ix,98 p. 65-60006
Z663.47 .B77 MRR Alc.

BULGARIA--DESCRIPTION AND TRAVEL--1970---GUIDE-BOOKS.
Rusinov, Spas. Bulgaria, a tourist handbook [Sofia] Sofia Press [1971?] 133 p. 914.97/7/043 74-867850
DR54 .R865 MRR Alc.

BULGARIA--DESCRIPTION AND TRAVEL--GUIDE-BOOKS.
Bulgaria. Geneva, Paris, Munich, Nagel, (1968). 496 p. [$8.95] 914.97/7/043 78-439108
DR54 .B843 MRR Alc.

Trans-Balkan Highway: Yugoslavia, Bulgaria, Turkey. Beograd, Turisticka Stampa; Sofia, Resorts Magazine [1967] 175 p. [unpriced] 914.96/04 78-391387
GV1025.A2 T7 MRR Alc.

BULGARIA--EXECUTIVE DEPARTMENTS--DIRECTORIES.
Directory of Bulgarian officials. [n.p.] 1965. vii, 167 p. 354.497/7/00025 73-10853
JN9604 .D53 MRR Alc.

BULGARIA--GAZETTEERS.
United States. Office of Geography. Bulgaria; Washington, U.S. Govt. Print. Off., 1959. iii, 293 p. 914.977 59-61923
DR53 .U5 MRR Alc.

BULGARIA--OFFICIALS AND EMPLOYEES--DIRECTORIES.
Directory of Bulgarian officials. [n.p.] 1965. vii, 167 p. 354.497/7/00025 73-10853
JN9604 .D53 MRR Alc.

BULGARIA--REGISTERS.
Directory of Bulgarian officials. [n.p.] 1965. vii, 167 p. 354.497/7/00025 73-10853
JN9604 .D53 MRR Alc.

BULGARIA--STATISTICS.
Statisticheski godishnik na Narodna Republika Bulgaria. 19 -66. Sofia. 314.977 63-54446
HA1621 .A455 MRR Alc Latest edition

BULGARIAN LANGUAGE--DICTIONARIES--ENGLISH.
[Bulgaro-Angliiski rechnik (romanized form)] 1958. 700 p. 59-51449
PG979 .B8 MRR Alc.

BULGARIAN LANGUAGE--DICTIONARIES--FRENCH.
Ĭaranov, Atanas, [Bŭlgaro-frenski rechnik (romanized form)] [1949] vi, 774 p. 51-29019
PG981 .I17 MRR Alc.

BULGARIAN LITERATURE--HISTORY AND CRITICISM.
Manning, Clarence Augustus, The history of modern Bulgarian literature, New York, Bookman Associates [1960] 198 p. 891.8109 60-8549
PG1008 .M3 MRR Alc.

BUREAUCRACY.
see also Civil service

BUREAUCRACY--ANECDOTES, FACETIAE, SATIRE, ETC.
Martin, Thomas Lyle. Malice in Blunderland, New York, McGraw-Hill [1973] vii, 143 p. [$5.95] 658.4/002/07 73-4376
PN6231.M2 M3 MRR Ref Desk.

BUREAUCRACY--BIBLIOGRAPHY.
Universal Reference System. Administrative management: public and private bureaucracy; Princeton, N.J., Princeton Research Pub. Co. [1969] xx, 888 p. 011 68-57820
Z7161 .U64 vol. 4 MRR Alc.

BURGENLAND--COMMERCE--DIRECTORIES.
Herold Adressbuch von Burgenland für Industrie, Handel, Gewerbe. Wien, Herold. 72-622319
HF3549.B85 A45 MRR Alc Latest edition

BURIAL.
see also Funeral rites and ceremonies

BURIAL CUSTOMS
see Funeral rites and ceremonies

BURIED CITIES
see Cities and towns, Ruined, extinct, etc.

BURMA--BIBLIOGRAPHY.
United States. Library of Congress. Orientalia Division. Southeast Asia subject catalog. Boston, G. K. Hall, 1972- v. 016.9159/03 72-5257
Z3221 .U525 MRR Alc (Dk 33)

BURMA--BIOGRAPHY--DICTIONARIES.
Maring, Joel M. Historical and cultural dictionary of Burma. Metuchen, N.J., Scarecrow Press, 1973. vi, 290 p. 915.91/003 73-1477
DS485.B8 M37 MRR Alc.

BURMA--COMMERCE--DIRECTORIES.
Burma business directory and national trade register. Rangoon, Burma Publicity Services. 58-15883
HF3789.B8 B78 MRR Alc Latest edition

BURMA--COMMERCE--HANDBOOKS, MANUALS, ETC.
Burma business directory and national trade register. Rangoon, Burma Publicity Services. 58-15883
HF3789.B8 B78 MRR Alc Latest edition

BURMA--DICTIONARIES AND ENCYCLOPEDIAS.
Maring, Joel M. Historical and cultural dictionary of Burma. Metuchen, N.J., Scarecrow Press, 1973. vi, 290 p. 915.91/003 73-1477
DS485.B8 M37 MRR Alc.

BURMA--GAZETTEERS.
United States. Office of Geography.
Burma; Washington, 1966. v, 726 p.
915.91 66-61922
   DS485.B8 U52 1966 MRR Alc.

BURMA--HISTORY.
Cady, John Frank, A history of
modern Burma. Ithaca, N.Y., Cornell
University Press [1958] 682 p.
959.1 58-1545
   DS485.B86 C2 MRR Alc.

Trager, Frank N. Burma from kingdom
to republic; London, Pall Mall P.,
1966. xiii, 455 p. [70/-] 959.1
67-112228
   DS485.B86 T7 1966b MRR Alc.

BURMESE LANGUAGE--DICTIONARIES--ENGLISH.
Judson, Adoniram, Burmese-English
dictionary. Unabridged centenary ed.
Rangoon, Baptist Board of
Publications, 1953. 1123 p.
495.832 55-19092
   PL3957 .J834 1953 MRR Alc.

BURNS, ROBERT, 1759-1796.
United States. Library of Congress.
Gertrude Clarke Whittall Poetry and
Literature Fund. Anniversary
lectures, 1959. Washington,
Reference Dept., Library of Congress,
1959. iii, 56 p. 821.082 59-60090

   Z663.293 .A55 MRR Alc.

BURNS, ROBERT, 1759-1796--CONCORDANCES.
Reid, J. B. A complete word and
phrase concordance to the poems and
songs of Robert Burns. New York, B.
Franklin [1968] 568 p. 821/.6 68-
58477
   PR4345 .R4 1968 MRR Alc.

BURUNDI--GAZETTEERS.
United States. Office of Geography.
Burundi; Washington [U.S. Govt.
Print. Off.] 1964. ii, 44 p. 65-
60786
   DT449.B8 U5 MRR Alc.

BURUNDI--GOVERNMENT PUBLICATIONS--
BIBLIOGRAPHY--UNION LISTS.
Witherell, Julian W. French-speaking
central Africa; Washington, General
Reference and Bibliography Division,
Library of Congress; [for sale by the
Supt. of Docs., U.S. Govt. Print.
Off.] 1973. xiv, 314 p. [$3.70]
015/.67 72-5766
   Z663.285 .F7 MRR Alc.

BUS LINES
   see Motor bus lines

BUSH SURVIVAL
   see Wilderness survival

BUSINESS.
   see also Advertising

   see also Applications for positions

   see also Bookkeeping

   see also Commerce

   see also Credit

   see also Industrial management

   see also Manufactures

   see also Marketing

   see also Markets

   see also Occupations

   see also Real estate business

   see also Success

Kraus, Albert L. The New York times
guide to business and finance; [1st
ed.] New York, Harper & Row [1972]
viii, 280 p. [$8.95] 330.9/73/092
70-138745
   HG181 .K7 1972 MRR Alc.

Pitman's business man's guide. 14th
ed. London, Pitman, 1967. [5], 346
p. [32/-] 650/.03 68-92621
   HF1001 .S6 1967 MRR Alc.

BUSINESS--ANECDOTES, FACETIAE, SATIRE,
ETC.
Grizer, Leon, Wit and wisdom in
business; [1st ed.] New York,
Exposition Press [c1972] 509 p.
818/.02 75-146907
   HF5391 .G74 MRR Ref Desk.

BUSINESS--BIBLIOGRAPHY.
Bibliography of publications of
university bureaus of business and
economic research. [Boulder, Colo.,
etc.] Business Research Division,
University of Colorado.
016.33/007/2073 77-635614
   Z7165.U5 A8 MRR Alc Full set '

Business books in print: subject
index, author index, title index.
1973- New York, R. R. Bowker Co.
016.33 73-85950
   Z7164.C81 B962 MRR Alc Latest
   edition

Coman, Edwin Truman, Sources of
business information. Rev. ed.
Berkeley, University of California
Press, 1964. xii, 330 p. 016.65
64-18639
   Z7164.C81 C75 1964 MRR Alc.

Lovett, Robert Woodberry. American
economic and business history
information sources; Detroit, Gale
Research Co. [1971] 323 p. [$14.50]
016.330973 78-137573
   Z7165.U5 L66 MRR Alc.

BUSINESS--BIBLIOGRAPHY--CATALOGS.
Harvard University. Graduate School
of Business Administration. Baker
Library. Business reference sources;
[Boston] 1971. 108 p. [$3.00]
016.65/008 s 016.65/008 75-30038
   Z7164.C81 H273 no. 27 MRR Alc.

Harvard University. Graduate School
of Business Administration. Baker
Library. Subject catalog of the
Baker Library, Graduate School of
Business Administration. Harvard
University. Boston, G. K. Hall,
1971. 10 v. 016.33 70-170935
   Z7164.C81 H275 MRR Alc (Dk 33)

BUSINESS--DICTIONARIES.
Alexander Hamilton Institute, New
York. 2001 business terms and what
they mean; New York, Alexander
Hamilton Institute; book trade
distribution by Doubleday, Garden
City, N.Y. [1962] vii, 303 p.
650.3 62-21551
   HF1002 .A39 MRR Alc.

Benn, A. E. The management
dictionary; New York, Exposition
Press [1952] 381 p. 658.03 51-
11831
   HD19 .B4 MRR Alc.

Business terms, phrases and
abbreviations. 13th ed., London,
Pitman, 1966. [5], 232 p. [12/6]
650.03 67-72958
   HF1002 .B9 1966 MRR Alc.

Clark, Donald Thomas, Dictionary of
business and finance New York,
Crowell [1957] v, 409 p. 650.3 57-
14560
   HF1002 .C49 MRR Alc.

Davids, Lewis E. Instant business
dictionary, Mundelein, Ill., Career
Institute [1971] 320 p. 650/.03
78-150232
   HF1002 .D36 MRR Ref Desk.

Filkins, James H. Lexicon of
American business terms, New York,
Simon and Schuster [1973] 141 p.
[$1.95] 330/.03 73-175491
   HF1002 .F5 MRR Alc.

Hamburger, Edward. A business
dictionary of representative terms
used in accounting, advertising,
banking ... Englewood Cliffs, N.J.,
Prentice-Hall [1967] vii, 198 p.
650/.03 67-8253
   HF1002 .H27 MRR Alc.

Heyel, Carl, ed. The encyclopedia of
management. 2d ed. New York, Van
Nostrand Reinhold Co. [1973] xxvii,
1161 p. 658/.003 72-11784
   HD19 .H4 1973 MRR Alc.

Nanassy, Louis C. Business
dictionary Englewood Cliffs, N.J.,
Prentice-Hall [1960] vi, 263 p.
650.3 60-7410
   HF1002 .N3 MRR Alc.

Nemmers, Erwin Esser, Dictionary of
economics and business. [3rd ed.]
Totowa, N.J., Littlefield, Adams,
1974. 485 p. 330/.03 73-22090
   HB61 .N45 1974 MRR Alc.

Newnes encyclopaedia of business
management; London, Newnes, 1967.
637 p. [6/6/-] 650/.03 67-97096
   HD19 .N48 MRR Alc.

Osborn, Percy George. The concise
commercial dictionary, London, Sweet
& Maxwell, 1966. [4], 244 p. [45/-]
380/.03 67-73821
   HF1002 .O8 MRR Alc.

Péron, Michel. Dictionnaire
français-anglais des affaires,
Paris, Larousse, 1968. 2 v. in 1.
(xvi, 230, xvi, 247 p.) [38 F] 68-
137592
   HF1002 .P418 MRR Alc.

Prentice-Hall, inc. Encyclopedic
dictionary of business finance,
Englewood Cliffs, N.J. [1961, c1960]
vi, 658 p. 332.03 60-53430
   HG151 .P7 MRR Alc.

Prentice-Hall, inc. Encyclopedic
dictionary of systems and procedures,
Englewood Cliffs, N.J. [1966] 673
p. 658.5003 66-27954
   HD19 .P72 MRR Alc.

Private secretary's encyclopedic
dictionary. Englewood Cliffs, N.J.,
Prentice-Hall, 1958. v, 402 p.
651.03 58-11742
   HF1001 .P78 MRR Alc.

BUSINESS--DICTIONARIES--DUTCH.
Bons, A. Engels handelswoordenboek
(Nederlands-Engels) Deventer, Æ. E.
Kluwer [1957] 1170 p. 57-46259
   .HF1002 .B59 MRR Alc.

Bons, A. Engels handelswoordenboek
(Nederlands-Engels) Deventer, Æ. E.
Kluwer [1957] 1170 p. 57-56259
   HF1002 .B59 MRR Alc.

BUSINESS--DICTIONARIES--FRENCH.
Péron, Michel. Dictionnaire
français-anglais des affaires,
Paris, Larousse, 1968. 2 v. in 1.
(xvi, 230, xvi, 247 p.) [38 F] 68-
137592
   HF1002 .P418 MRR Alc.

BUSINESS--DICTIONARIES--GERMAN.
Sommer, Werner, Management
dictionary. 3., durchgesehene und
erw. Aufl. Berlin, De Gruyter, 1966-
68. 2 v. [DM 18.00 per vol.]
658.003 67-73661
   HF1002 .S622 MRR Alc.

BUSINESS--DICTIONARIES--ITALIAN.
Motta, Giuseppe, teacher of English.
Dizionario commerciale: inglese-
italiano, italiano-inglese. Milano,
C. Signorelli [1961] x, 1050 p. 61-
33500
   HF1002 .M6 MRR Alc.

BUSINESS--DICTIONARIES--POLYGLOT.
Servotte, Jozef V., 1903-
Dictionnaire commercial et financier;
2. ed., rev. et augm. Bruxelles,
Éditions Brepols [1960] ix, 955 p.
61-930
   HF1002 .S42 1960 MRR Alc.

BUSINESS--HANDBOOKS, MANUALS, ETC.
Executive handbook. Hauppauge, N.Y.
[International Evaluations, inc.,
1970] 256 p. 650/.02/02 79-14710

   HF5351 .E94 MRR Alc.

Financial handbook. [1st]- ed.;
1925- New York, Ronald Press. 658
25-21825
   HF5550 .F5 MRR Alc Latest edition

BUSINESS--HISTORY--BIBLIOGRAPHY.
Larson, Henrietta Melia. Guide to
business history; Cambridge, Harvard
University Press, 1948. xxvi, 1181
p. 650.9 48-7565
   Z7164.C81 L25 MRR Alc.

BUSINESS--INFORMATION SERVICES.
Cossman, E. Joseph. How to get
$50,000 worth of services free, each
year, from the U.S. Government; New
York, F. Fell [1965, c1964] 233 p.
658.02 64-8781
   HF5353 .C7 MRR Alc.

Directory of business and financial
services. [1st]- ed.; 1924- New
York [etc.] Special Libraries
Association. 25-4599
   HF5003 .H3 MRR Ref Desk Latest
   edition / MRR Ref Desk Latest
   edition

Encyclopedia of business information
sources; Detroit, Gale Research Co.,
1970. 2 v. (xxi, 689 p.) 016.33
79-127922
   HF5353 .E52 MRR Ref Desk.

Winser, Marian (Manley) Business
information, [1st ed.] New York,
Harper [1955] xvi, 265 p. 016.65
55-11399
   HF5353 .W56 MRR Alc.

BUSINESS--PERIODICALS--BIBLIOGRAPHY--
CATALOGS.
Harvard University. Graduate School
of Business Administration. Baker
Library. Current periodical
publications in Baker Library.
1971/72- [Boston] 016.33/005 72-
620452
   Z7164.C81 H266 MRR Alc Latest
   edition

BUSINESS--PERIODICALS--DIRECTORIES.
Standard Rate and Data Service, inc.
Business publication rates and data.
v.33- Jan. 1951- Skokie, Ill.
[etc.] 659.132058 53-36930
   HF5905 .S723 MRR Ref Desk Latest
   edition

BUSINESS--PERIODICALS--INDEXES.
Business periodicals index. v. 1-
Jan. 1958- New York, H. W. Wilson
Co. 016.6505 58-12645
   Z7164.C81 B983 MRR Circ Full set

BUSINESS--PERIODICALS--INDEXES. (Cont.)
F & S index international:
industries, countries, companies.
1st- ed.: 1968- Cleveland,
Predicasts. 016.338 74-644265
Z7164.C81 F13 MRR Alc Full set /
Sci RR Partial set

International bibliography of
economics. v. 1- 1952- London,
Tavistock Publications; Chicago,
Aldine Pub. Co. 55-2317
Z7164.E2 I58 MRR Alc Full set

Wall Street Journal. (Indexes)
Index. [New York] Dow Jones & Co.
59-35162
HG1 .W26 MRR Alc Full set

BUSINESS--SCHOLARSHIPS, FELLOWSHIPS,
ETC.--UNITED STATES--DIRECTORIES.
United States. Office of Minority
Business Enterprise. Higher
education aid for minority business;
Washington; [For sale by the Supt. of
Docs., U.S. Govt. Print. Off.] 1970.
viii, 103 p. [1.00] 650/.071/1 78-
607539
HF1131 .A55 MRR Alc

BUSINESS--SOCIAL ASPECTS
see Industry--Social aspects

BUSINESS--TERMS AND PHRASES.
Filkins, James H. Lexicon of
American business terms, New York,
Simon and Schuster [1973] 141 p.
[$1.95] 330/.03 73-175491
HF1002 .F5 MRR Alc.

Tver, David F. Dictionary of
business & scientific terms, 2d ed.
Houston, Tex., Gulf Pub. Co. [1968]
xi, 528 p. 503 68-6988
O123 .T85 1968 MRR Alc.

BUSINESS, CHOICE OF
see Vocational guidance

BUSINESS CONSULTANTS.
Angel, Juvenal Londoño,
International marketing guide for
technical, management and other
consultants. 1st ed. New York,
World Trade Academy Press;
distributed by Simon & Schuster
[1971] 600 p. [$25.00] 658.4/03
77-111350
HD69.C6 A676 MRR Alc.

Whiteside, Conon Doyle. Accountant's
guide to profitable management
advisory services Englewood Cliffs,
N.J., Prentice-Hall [1969] ix, 430
p. [29.95] 658.4/6 69-14584
HF5657 .W48 MRR Alc.

BUSINESS CONSULTANTS--DIRECTORIES.
American Management Association.
Directory of consultant members.
1956- New York. 57-27082
HD28 .A553 MRR Alc Latest edition

Association of Consulting Management
Engineers. Directory of membership
and services. New York. 658.06273
59-1437
HD28.A75 A6 MRR Alc Latest edition

Directory of consultant affiliates
and consultant services. 1970- New
York, National Retail Merchants
Association. 658.4/03 75-615636
HD69.C6 D5 MRR Ref Desk Latest
edition

Directory of consulting specialists.
Los Angeles, Stemm's Information
Systems and Indexes. 658.4/03 73-
641402
HD69.C6 D53 MRR Biog Latest
edition

United States. Office of Minority
Business Enterprise. National
roster: minority professional
consulting firms. Washington, 1973.
ix, 121 p. 658.4/03 73-601615
HD69.C6 U56 1973 MRR Alc.

Wasserman, Paul, ed. Consultants and
consulting organizations directory;
2d ed. Detroit, Gale Research Co.,
1973. 835 p. 658.4/03 72-14159
HD69.C6 W37 1973 MRR Ref Desk.

BUSINESS CONSULTANTS--DISTRICT OF
COLUMBIA--DIRECTORIES.
Howard University, Washington, D.C.
Minority Economic Resource Center.
The District of Columbia directory of
inner city organizations active in
the field of minority business-
economic development. 3d ed.
Washington, 1972. iv, 20 p.
338/.04/025753 73-170762
HD2346.U52 D54 1972 MRR Alc.

BUSINESS CONSULTANTS--UNITED STATES.
Dun and Bradstreet, inc. Business
Education Division. A guide to
management services. New York [1968]
260 p. [1.95] 658.4/6 73-92724
HD69.C6 D85 MRR Alc.

BUSINESS CONSULTANTS--UNITED STATES--
DIRECTORIES.
National Survey Information Co.
National service directory of
executive search consultants in the
United States. Executive service ed.
Lake Bluff, Ill., 1971. vi, 47 (i.e
95) p. [$17.50] 658.4/03 77-30076

HD69.C6 N4 MRR Alc.

United States. Office of Minority
Business Enterprise. Directory of
private programs assisting minority
business. Washington; For sale by
the Supt. of Docs., U.S. Govt. Print.
Off., 1970. iv, 364 p. [$2.50]
658.4/6/02573 72-602355
HD69.C6 U545 MRR Alc.

Who's who in consulting; 2d ed.
Detroit, Gale Research Co., 1973.
xvii, 1011 p. [$45.00] 658.4/03
73-16373
HD69.C6 W52 MRR Biog.

BUSINESS CORPORATIONS
see Corporations

BUSINESS CORRESPONDENCE
see Commercial correspondence

BUSINESS CYCLES.
Lee, Maurice Wentworth,
Macroeconomics; fluctuations, growth,
and stability 5th ed. Homewood,
Ill., R. D. Irwin, 1971. xix, 629 p.
338.54 74-141399
HB3711 .L55 1971 MRR Alc.

Moore, Geoffrey Hoyt, ed. Business
cycle indicators. Princeton [N.J.]
Princeton University Press, 1961. 2.
v. 338.540973 60-14062
HB3711 .M58 MRR Alc.

BUSINESS CYCLES--BIBLIOGRAPHY.
Wilson, Louise (Loeffler) Catalogue
of cycles, Pittsburgh, Foundation
for the Study of Cycles [c1964- v.
67-31862
Z7405.P66 W5 MRR Alc.

Woy, James B. Business trends and
forecasting: information sources;
Detroit, Gale Research Co. [1966,
c1965] 152 p. 016.33854 65-28351

Z7164.C81 W83 1966 MRR Alc.

BUSINESS EDUCATION.
see also Commercial law

BUSINESS EDUCATION--UNITED STATES--
DIRECTORIES.
Directory of accredited institutions.
1968/69- Detroit, Accrediting
Commission for Business Schools.
330/.07/1073 72-626693
HF1131 .A64 MRR Alc Latest edition

United Business Schools Association.
U B S A directory of business
schools. 1962/60- Washington. 65-
33750
HF1131 .U55 MRR Alc Latest edition

BUSINESS ENTERPRISES.
see also International business
enterprises

BUSINESS ENTERPRISES--PERIODICALS--
INDEXES.
F & S index international:
industries, countries, companies.
1st- ed.; 1968- Cleveland,
Predicasts. 016.338 74-644265
Z7164.C81 F13 MRR Alc Full set /
Sci RR Partial set

BUSINESS ENTERPRISES, FOREIGN.
see also Investments, Foreign

United States. Bureau of
International Commerce. Sources of
credit information on foreign firms
for United States firms trading,
investing or manufacturing abroad.
[Washington, For sale by the Supt. of
Docs., U.S. Govt. Print. Off.] 1967.
iv, 108 p. 658.88/025 67-62451
HF5571 .U63 MRR Alc.

BUSINESS ENTERPRISES, FOREIGN--UNITED
STATES--DIRECTORIES.
Angel, Juvenal Londoño, Directory
of foreign firms operating in the
United States. New York, Simon &
Schuster [1971] 385 p.
338.7/4/02573 72-150331
HG4057 .A155 MRR Alc.

BUSINESS ENTERPRISES, INTERNATIONAL
see International business enterprises

BUSINESS ETHICS--BIBLIOGRAPHY.
Christian, Portia, Ethics in
business conduct: Detroit, Gale
Research Co. [c1970] 156 p.
[$14.50] 016.174/4 77-127411
Z7164.C81 C524 MRR Alc.

BUSINESS ETIQUETTE.
Parker Publishing Company, West
Nyack, N.Y. Business etiquette
handbook. West Nyack [1965] xiii,
338 p. 395 64-7753
BJ2193 .P3 MRR Alc.

BUSINESS EXECUTIVES
see Executives

BUSINESS FORECASTING--BIBLIOGRAPHY.
Woy, James B. Business trends and
forecasting: information sources;
Detroit, Gale Research Co. [1966,
c1965] 152 p. 016.33854 65-28351

Z7164.C81 W83 1966 MRR Alc.

BUSINESS LIBRARIES.
Johnson, Herbert Webster, How to use
the business library, 3d ed.
Cincinnati, South-western Pub. Co.
[c1964] v, 160 p. 016.65 63-21248

Z675.B8 J6 1964 MRR Alc.

BUSINESS MATHEMATICS.
Grazda, Edward E., ed. Handbook of
applied mathematics, 4th ed.
Princeton, N.J., Van Nostrand [1966]
vi, 1119 p. 510.0202 66-9325
TA330 .G7 1966 MRR Alc.

Minrath, William R. Handbook of
business mathematics 2d ed.
Princeton, N.J., Van Nostrand [1967]
xii, 658 p. 511.8 67-18055
HF5691 .M562 1967 MRR Alc.

BUSINESS MATHEMATICS--TABLES, ETC.
Cox, Edwin Burk, Basic tables in
business and economics, New York,
McGraw-Hill [1967] xiv, 399 p.
511/.8 66-19284
HF5699 .C892 MRR Alc.

BUSINESS RESEARCH
see Economic research

BUSINESS TEACHERS--UNITED STATES--
DIRECTORIES.
American Association of Collegiate
Schools of Business. Faculty
personnel; a directory of the
instructional staffs of the member
schools. 1925- St. Louis, Missouri,
[etc.] 650.71173 29-24113
HF1101 .A53 MRR Biog Latest
edition

BUSINESSMEN.
see also Capitalists and financiers

Businessmen around the globe,
[Harrisburg, Pa.] Stackpole Books
[1967] xiv, 252 p. 650/.1/0922 67-
21669
HF5386 .B98 1967 MRR Biog.

BUSINESSMEN--BIOGRAPHY.
International businessmen's who's
who. 1st- ed.; 1967- London,
Burke's Peerage ltd. 650/.0922 68-
2468
HF5500 .I614 MRR Biog Latest
edition

BUSINESSMEN--UNITED STATES.
Harvard University. Graduate School
of Business Administration. Baker
Library. Studies in enterprise;
Boston. 1957. xiv, 169 p.
016.33874 57-11481
Z7164.C81 H26 1957 MRR Alc.

Who's who in finance and industry.
17th- ed.; 1972/73- Chicago,
Marquis Who's Who. 338/.00922 [B]
70-616550
HF3023.A2 W5 MRR Biog Latest
edition

BUSINESSMEN--UNITED STATES--BIOGRAPHY.
Dun and Bradstreet, inc. Dun's
reference book of corporate
managements. 1st- ed.; 1967- New
York. 658.1/145/02573 68-44776
HD2745 .D85 MRR Ref Desk Latest
edition

BUTTERFLIES--PICTORIAL WORKS.
Werner, Alfred, Butterflies and
moths [3rd] further revised &
enlarged ed. London, Deutsch, 1970.
138 p. [5/5/-] 595.78/022/2 77-
523008
QK543 .W47 1970 MRR Alc.

BUTTERFLIES--NORTH AMERICA--
IDENTIFICATION.
Holland, William Jacob, The
butterfly book; New and thoroughly
rev. ed. Garden City, N.Y.,
Doubleday, 1949 [c1931] xii, 424 p.
595.789 49-48043
QL549 .H732 1949 MRR Alc.

BUTTONS--COLLECTORS AND COLLECTING.
Albert, Alphaeus Homer, Record of
American uniform and historical
buttons, [Boyertown, Pa., Boyertown
Pub. Co.] 1973. 448, 28 p.
391/.45/0973 73-78488
NK3670 .A48 1973 MRR Alc.

BUTTONS--COLLECTORS AND (Cont.)
Albert, Lillian Smith. The button
sampler, New York, M. Barrows [1951]
185 p. 391.4 51-9881
NK3670 .A525 MRR Alc.

BUTTONS, AMERICAN.
Albert, Alphaeus Homer, Record of
American uniform and historical
buttons, [Boyertown, Pa., Boyertown
Pub. Co.] 1973. 448, 28 p.
391/.45/0973 73-78488
NK3670 .A48 1973 MRR Alc.

BUYERS' GUIDES
see Consumer education

see Shopping

BUYING
see Purchasing

BY-PRODUCTS
see Waste products

BYRON, GEORGE GORDON NOËL BYRON,
BARON, 1788-1824.
Young, Ione (Dodson) A concordance
to the poetry of Byron. Austin,
Tex., Pemberton Press, 1965. 4 v.
(xv, 1698 p.) 821.7 66-674
PR4395 .Y6 MRR Alc.

BYZANTINE EMPIRE--BIBLIOGRAPHY.
Rounds, Dorothy. Articles on
antiquity in Festschriften, an index;
Cambridge, Harvard University Press,
1962. 560 p. 62-7193
Z6202 .R6 MRR Alc.

BYZANTINE EMPIRE--HISTORY.
Bury, John Bagnell, History of the
later Roman Empire from the death of
Theodosius I. to the death of
Justinian. New York, Dover
Publications [1958] 2 v. 937.08
58-11273
DG311 .B98 1958 MRR Alc.

Gibbon, Edward, The decline and fall
of the Roman Empire. New York,
Modern Library [1932?] 3 v. 937 a
50-7554
DG311 .G5 1932a MRR Alc.

Vasiliev, Alexander Alexandrovich,
History of the Byzantine Empire, 324-
1453. 2d English ed., rev.]
Madison, University of Wisconsin
press, 1952. xi, 846 p. 949.5 52-
13951
DF552 .V3 1952 MRR Alc.

Woodhouse, Christopher Montague, The
story of modern Greece London,
Faber, 1968. 3-318 p. [36/-]
949.5 68-109407
DF757 .W6 MRR Alc.

BYZANTINE EMPIRE--HISTORY--JUSTINIAN I,
527-565.
Procopius, of Caesarea. Procopius,
Cambridge, Mass., Harvard University
Press; London, W. Heinemann, 1953-62
[v. 1, 1961] 7 v. 949.61 64-3759

PA3612 .P85 1953 MRR Alc.

BYZANTINE EMPIRE--HISTORY--CHRONOLOGY.
Muralt, Eduard von, Essai de
chronographie byzantine Paris,
Orient-Édition, 1963. xxxii, 858 p.
67-46639
DF553 .M9 1963 MRR Alc.

BYZANTINE LITERATURE--DICTIONARIES.
The Penguin companion to classical,
Oriental & African literature. New
York, McGraw-Hill [1971, c1969] 359
p. [$9.95] 809 78-158064
PA31 .P4 1971 MRR Alc.

BYZANTIUM.
see also Istanbul

CABINET OFFICERS.
Spuler, Bertold, Regenten und
Regierungen der Welt. Wurzburg, A.
G. Ploetz [196 v. 63-5493
D11 .S78 MRR Alc.

CABINET OFFICERS--DIRECTORIES.
Political handbook and atlas of the
world. Jan. 1, 1927- New York,
Simon and Schuster [etc., for Council
on Foreign Relations. 28-12165
JF37 .P6 MRR Ref Desk Latest
edition / MRR Alc Latest edition

CABINET OFFICERS--REGISTERS--
PERIODICALS.
United States. Central Intelligence
Agency. Chiefs of State and Cabinet
members of foreign governments.
[Washington] 354.0313/05 73-640502

JF37 .U5 MRR Ref Desk Latest
edition

CABINET OFFICERS--CANADA.
Canada. Privy Council. Guide to
Canadian ministries since
confederation, July 1, 1867-January
1, 1957. Ottawa, Public Archives of
Canada, 1957. 103 p. 57-3692
JL97.A53 MRR Alc.

CABINET OFFICERS--COMMONWEALTH OF
NATIONS--REGISTERS.
Bidwell, Robin Leonard. The British
Empire and successor states, 1900-
1972; London, F. Cass [1974] xi,
156 p. [£9.00 ($27.50 U.S.)]
351.2/09171/242 74-169172
JN248 .B52 1974 MRR Ref Desk.

CABINET OFFICERS--EUROPE--DIRECTORIES.
Bidwell, Robin Leonard. The major
powers and western Europe, 1900-1971;
[London] F. Cass, [1973] xi, 297 p.
354/.4/002 72-92958
JN12 .B5 MRR Ref Desk.

CABINET OFFICERS--UNITED STATES.
Bemis, Samuel Flagg, ed. The
American Secretaries of State and
their diplomacy, New York, Pageant
Book Co., 1958 (c1928] 10 v. in 5.
923.273 58-7201
E183.7 .B46 1958 MRR Alc.

Fenno, Richard F., The President's
Cabinet; Cambridge, Mass., Harvard
University Press, 1959. 327 p.
353.05 59-9272
JK611 .F4 MRR Alc.

Graebner, Norman A., ed. An
uncertain tradition; American
Secretaries of State in the twentieth
century. New York, McGraw-Hill,
1961. 341 p. 353.1 61-8654
E744 .G7 MRR Alc.

Horn, John Stephen. The Cabinet and
Congress. New York, Columbia
University Press, 1960. 310 p.
353.02 60-13237
JK616 .H6 MRR Alc.

Learned, Henry Barrett, The
President's cabinet; New York, B.
Franklin [1972] xii, 471 p.
321.8/043/0973 72-80393
JK611 .L5 1972 MRR Alc.

Mosher, Robert Brent, comp.
Executive register of the United
States, 1789-1902; Baltimore, Md.,
The Friedenwald company [1903] 1 p.
l., x, 351 p. 03-10230
JK661 1902 MRR Alc.

Roberts, Charles Wesley, LBJ's inner
circle, New York, Delacorte Press
[1965] 223 p. 973.9230922 65-
21935
E846 .R56 MRR Alc.

Smith, William Henry, History of the
cabinet of the United States of
America, from President Washington to
President Coolidge; Baltimore, Md.,
The Industrial printing company,
1925. 537 p. 25-9781
JK611 .S5 MRR Biog.

CABINET OFFICERS--UNITED STATES--
DIRECTORIES.
Notable names in American history;
3d ed. of White's conspectus of
American biography. [Clifton, N.J.]
J. T. White, 1973. 725 p. 920/.073
73-6885
E176 .N89 1973 MRR Biog.

Poore, Benjamin Perley, The
political register and congressional
directory; Boston, Houghton, Osgood
and company, 1878. vi p., 1 l., 716
p. 05-273
E176 .P82 MRR Alc.

CABINET OFFICERS--UNITED STATES--
REGISTERS.
United States. Congress.
Biographical directory of the
American Congress, 1774-1971,
[Washington] U.S. Govt. Print. Off.,
1971. 1972 p. [$15.75]
328.73/0822 B 79-616224
JK1010 .A5 MRR Biog.

CABINET-WORK.
see also Furniture making

see also Woodwork

Hinckley, F. Lewis. Directory of the
historic cabinet woods. New York,
Crown Publishers [1960] 186 p. 749
59-14030
NK2260 .H52 MRR Alc.

CABINET-WORKERS.
Honour, Hugh. Cabinet makers and
furniture designers. [1st American
ed.] New York, Putnam [1969] 320 p.
[22.50] 749.2 77-77548
NK2350 .H6 1969 MRR Alc.

CABINET-WORKERS--DICTIONARIES.
Bjerkoe, Ethel Hall. The
cabinetmakers of America, [1st ed.]
Garden City, N.Y., Doubleday, 1957.
xvii, 252 p. 749.211 57-7278
NK2406 .B55 MRR Alc.

CABINET-WORKERS--ENGLAND.
Edwards, Ralph, Georgian cabinet-
makers, c. 1700-1800, New and rev.
[i.e. 3d] ed. London, Country Life,
ltd., 1955. 247 p. 749.223 55-
13859
NK2529 .E3 1955 MRR Alc.

CABINET-WORKERS--LONDON.
Heal, Ambrose, Sir, The London
furniture makers, from the
Restoration to the Victorian Era,
1660-1840: London, Batsford [1953]
xx, 276 p. 749.222 54-503
NK2529 .H45 MRR Alc.

CABLE TV
see Community antenna television

CABOT, JOHN, D. 1498?
The Northmen, Columbus and Cabot, 985-
1503: New York, C. Scribner's sons,
1906. xv, 443 p. 973.1 06-36882
E187.O7 N6 MRR Alc.

CAIRO--LIBRARIES.
Jam'Iyat al-Maktabāt al-Miṣrīyah.
Directory of libraries in Cairo.
Cairo, 1950. 35 l. 027.062 51-
31798
Z857 .J3 MRR Alc.

CALABRIA--ECONOMIC CONDITIONS--
YEARBOOKS.
Guida economica della Sicilia,
Sardegna e Mezzogiorno d'Italia.
[1. ed.] 1946- Roma [etc.]
G.I.P.I. 49-17748
HC307.S5 G8 MRR Alc Latest edition

CALCULATING-MACHINES.
see also Computers

CALDECOTT MEDAL BOOKS.
Kingman, Lee, ed. Newbery and
Caldecott medal books: 1956-1965,
Boston, Horn Book, 1965. xix, 300 p.
028.5 65-26759
Z1037 .A2 K5 1965 MRR Alc.

Miller, Bertha E. (Mahony) ed.
Caldecott medal books, 1938-1957,
Boston, Horn Book, inc., 1957. xii,
329 p. 028.5 57-11582
Z1035.A2 M49 MRR Alc.

Smith, Irene, A history of the
Newbery and Caldecott medals. New
York, Viking Press [1957] 140 p.
028.5 57-4510
Z1037 .S648 MRR Alc.

CALENDAR.
The 20th century almanac;
Philadelphia, Allen, Lane & Scott.
23-10568
CE92 .T9 MRR Alc Latest edition

Fry, Edward Alexander. Almanacks for
students of English history. London,
Phillimore & co., ltd., 1915. vii,
138 p. 16-20586
CE61.G8 F8 MRR Alc.

Philip, Alexander. The calendar: its
history, structure and improvement,
Cambridge, University press, 1921.
xi, 104 p. 22-7432
CE73 .P45 MRR Alc.

Schram, Robert Gustav,
Kalendariographische und
chronologische tafeln, Leipzig, J.
C. Hinrichs, 1908. xxxvi, 368 p.
09-12404
CE11 .S3 MRR Alc.

Watkins, Harold. Time counts;
London, N. Spearman [1954] 274 p.
529.309 54-31937
CE73 .W3 1954a MRR Alc.

Wüstenfeld, Heinrich Ferdinand,
Vergleichungs-Tabellen zur
muslimischen und iranischen
Zeitrechnung mit Tafeln zur
Umrechnung orient-christlicher Ären.
3., verb. und erweiterte Aufl.
[Mainz] Deutsche Morgenländische
Gesellschaft; in Kommission bei F.
Steiner, Wiesbaden, 1961. 90 p. 62-
37955
CE15 .W8 1961 MRR Alc.

CALENDAR, CHINESE.
100 years Chinese-English calendar,
1864-1963. 1st ed. [Penang, Chee
Chin Chong, 1949?] 100 p. 57-47454

CE37 .O5 MRR Alc.

Welch, Windon Chandler. Chinese-
American calendar for the 102 Chinese
years commencing January 24, 1849,
and ending February 5, 1951.
Washington, U.S. Govt. Print. Off.,
1928. vii, 102 p. 1 28-36
CE37. W4 Suppl. 2 MRR Alc.

CALENDAR, GREGORIAN.
Burnaby, Sherrard Beaumont. Elements
of the Jewish and Muhammadan
calendars, London, G. Bell & sons,
1901. vi p., 1 l., vii-xv, 554 p.
02-12154
CE35 .B9 MRR Alc.

CALENDAR, ISLAMIC.
Freeman-Grenville, Greville Stewart Parker. The Muslim and Christian calendars. London, New York, Oxford University Press, 1963. vii, 87 p. 529.327   63-24830
    CE59 .F7 1963 MRR Alc.

Wüstenfeld, Heinrich Ferdinand, Vergleichungs-Tabellen zur muslimischen und iranischen Zeitrechnung mit Tafeln zur Umrechnung orient-christlicher Ären. 3., verb. und erweiterte Aufl. [Mainz] Deutsche Morgenländische Gesellschaft; in Kommission bei F. Steiner, Wiesbaden, 1961. 90 p. 62-37955
    CE15 .W8 1961 MRR Alc.

CALENDAR, JEWISH.
Burnaby, Sherrard Beaumont. Elements of the Jewish and Muhammadan calendars, London, G. Bell & sons, 1901. vi p., 1 l., vii-xv, 554 p. 02-12154
    CE35 .B9 MRR Alc.

Encyclopaedia Judaica. Jerusalem, Encyclopaedia Judaica: [New York] Macmillan [c1971-72, v. 1, c1972] 16 v. 296/.03 72-177492
    DS102.8 .E496 MRR Alc.

Spier, Arthur, The comprehensive Hebrew calendar; New York, Behrman House [1952] 228 p. 529.3   53-96
    CE35 .S6 MRR Alc.

CALENDAR, JULIAN.
Burnaby, Sherrard Beaumont. Elements of the Jewish and Muhammadan calendars, London, G. Bell & sons, 1901. vi p., 1 l., vii-xv, 554 p. 02-12154
    CE35 .B9 MRR Alc.

CALENDAR, MOHAMMEDAN.
Burnaby, Sherrard Beaumont. Elements of the Jewish and Muhammadan calendars, London, G. Bell & sons, 1901. vi p., 1 l., vii-xv, 554 p. 02-12154
    CE35 .B9 MRR Alc.

CALENDAR, PERPETUAL.
Benedict, Hugh C. 300 year calender, 1776-2075 Nampa, Idaho, Thorne Printing & Litho, 1964. 1 v. (unpaged)   65-4772
    CE92 .B47 MRR Ref Desk.

CALENDAR, TURKISH.
Wüstenfeld, Heinrich Ferdinand, Vergleichungs-Tabellen zur muslimischen und iranischen Zeitrechnung mit Tafeln zur Umrechnung orient-christlicher Ären. 3., verb. und erweiterter Aufl. [Mainz] Deutsche Morgenländische Gesellschaft; in Kommission bei F. Steiner, Wiesbaden, 1961. 90 p. 62-37955
    CE15 .W8 1961 MRR Alc.

CALENDARS.
Bowman, Robert Turnbull, Dateline: Canada Toronto, Holt, Rinehart and Winston of Canada [1973] 1 v. (unpaged)   971/.002 72-9493
    F1006 .B6 1973 MRR Alc.

Chases' calendar of annual events. 1958- Flint, Mich., Apple Tree Press.   57-14540
    GT4803 .C48 MRR Ref Desk Latest Edition

Collison, Robert Lewis. Newnes Dictionary of dates; 2nd revised ed. London, Newnes, 1966. ix, 11-428 p. [35/-]   903   66-72492
    D11.5 .C6 1966 MRR Alc.

Darling, William Young, Sir, A book of days: London, Richards Press [1951] 381 p. 902 52-67733
    D11.5 .D3 MRR Alc.

Hazeltine, Mary Emogene, Anniversaries and holidays, 2d ed., completely revised Chicago, American Library association 1944. xix, 316 p.   394.26   44-53464
    Z5710 .H42 1944 MRR Alc.

Mirkin, Stanford M. What happened when; [New, rev. and enl. ed.] New York, I. Washburn [1966] v, 442 p. 902.02   66-10676
    D11.5 .M57 1966 MRR Ref Desk.

CALENDARS--JUVENILE LITERATURE.
Hopkins, Lee Bennett. Important dates in Afro-American history. New York, F. Watts [1969] 188 p. 973/.09/7496 73-83648
    E185 .H6 MRR Alc.

CALIFORNIA.
California: Past, present, future. 1969- ed. Lakewood, Calif. [California Almanac Co.] 917.94/03/5 49-2266
    F856 .C255 MRR Alc Latest edition

CALIFORNIA--BIBLIOGRAPHY.
The California handbook. 1st- ed.; 1969- [Claremont] Center for California Public Affairs. 917.94 75-171691
    HC107.C2 C253 MRR Alc Latest edition

Edwards, Elza Ivan, The enduring desert; [Los Angeles] W. Ritchie Press, 1969. xiii, 306 p. 016.91794/09/154   68-8306
    Z1251.S8 E32 MRR Alc.

Hager, Anna Marie. The Historical Society of Southern California bibliography of all published works, 1884-1957, Los Angeles, Historical Society of Southern California, 1958. xix, 183 p.   016.9794 58-59890
    Z1261 .H22 MRR Alc.

United States. Library of Congress. California: the centennial of the Gold Rush and the first State Constitution: Washington, U.S. Govt. Print. Off., 1949. iv, 97 p. 016.9794   49-47128
    Z663.15.A6C2 1949 MRR Alc.

CALIFORNIA--BIOGRAPHY.
Bancroft, Hubert Howe, Register of pioneer inhabitants of California, 1542 to 1848, Los Angeles, Dawson's Book Shop, 1964. 683-795, 733-792, 688-786, 687-784 p.   920.0794 64-3538
    F861 .B21 1964 MRR Biog.

California. Legislature. List of members, officers, committees and rules of the two Houses. [Sacramento]   328.7945   10-14000
    JK8771 .A2 date MRR Alc Latest edition

California blue book. [Sacramento, Office of State Printing] 73-640050
    JK8730 .C37a MRR Alc Latest edition

California: Past, present, future. 1969- ed. Lakewood, Calif. [California Almanac Co.] 917.94/03/5 49-2266
    F856 .C255 MRR Alc Latest edition

Who's who executives in California. 1963- [Los Angeles] A. C. Armstrong. 63-49237
    F860 .W624 MRR Biog Latest edition

Who's who in California. 1955/56- [Los Angeles]   56-1715
    F860 .W628 MRR Biog Latest edition

CALIFORNIA--CENTENNIAL CELEBRATIONS, ETC.
United States. Library of Congress. California: the centennial of the Gold Rush and the first State Constitution; Washington, U.S. Govt. Print. Off., 1949. iv, 97 p. 016.9794   49-47128
    Z663.15.A6C2 1949 MRR Alc.

CALIFORNIA--COMMERCE--DIRECTORIES.
California international business directory. 1971- Los Angeles, Center for Advanced Studies in International Business. 338/.0025/794   71-146906
    HF5065.C2 C26 MRR Alc Latest edition

CALIFORNIA--DESCRIPTION AND TRAVEL--1951- --GUIDE-BOOKS.
Mobil travel guide: California and the west. 1969- [Bloomfield, N.J.] Simon and Schuster. 917.94/04/5 72-623503
    F859.3 .M6 MRR Alc Latest edition

CALIFORNIA--DESCRIPTION AND TRAVEL--GUIDE-BOOKS.
American Automobile Association. California-Nevada tour book, Washington.   61-45102
    GV1024 .A2314 MRR Alc Latest edition

Federal Writers' Project. California. California: a guide to the Golden State. New new rev. ed. New York, Hastings House [1967] xxxii, 733 p. 917.94/04/5   66-28958
    F859.3 .F4 1967 MRR Ref Desk.

CALIFORNIA--DIRECTORIES.
The California handbook. 1st- ed.; 1969- [Claremont] Center for California Public Affairs. 917.94 75-171691
    HC107.C2 C253 MRR Alc Latest edition

California publicity outlets. 1972- Los Angeles, Unicorn Systems Co., Information Services Division. 659.2/025/794 76-186163
    HM263 .C2 MRR Alc Latest edition

Yung, Judith. Directory of California non-profit associations, San Francisco, San Francisco Public Library, 1970. iii, 217 p.   061.94 79-20791
    HD2428.C3 Y84 MRR Alc.

CALIFORNIA--EXECUTIVE DEPARTMENTS.
California blue book. [Sacramento, Office of State Printing] 73-640050
    JK8730 .C37a MRR Alc Latest edition

Rosien, Barbara. Greater Los Angeles public service guide. 1972-73 ed. Los Angeles, Public Service Publications [1972] xvi, 688 p. [$10.95]   352.0794/93 72-184514
    JS1002.A2 R66 MRR Alc.

CALIFORNIA--GOVERNMENT PUBLICATIONS--BIBLIOGRAPHY.
California State publications. v. 1- July/Sept. 1947- [Sacramento, Printing Division, Documents Section] 015.794   52-19974
    Z1223.5.C2 C4 MRR Alc* Partial set

CALIFORNIA--HISTORY.
Beck, Warren A. California: a history of the Golden State [1st ed.] Garden City, N.Y., Doubleday, 1972. xiv, 552 p. [$11.95] 917.94/03   71-186005
    F861 .B43 MRR Alc.

Rolle, Andrew F. California; a history 2d ed. New York, Crowell [1969] xxiii, 739 p. 979.4 69-13261
    F861 .R78 1969 MRR Alc.

CALIFORNIA--HISTORY--BIBLIOGRAPHY.
California. University. Bancroft Library. Catalog of printed books. Boston, G. K. Hall, 1964. 22 v. 016.9178   67-52922
    Z881 .C1523 MRR Alc (DK33)

CALIFORNIA--HISTORY, LOCAL.
Rensch, Hero Eugene, Historic spots in California. 3d ed.; rev. Stanford, Calif., Stanford University Press, 1966. xiii, 642 p.   979.4 66-17562
    F868.A15 R43 MRR Alc.

CALIFORNIA--IMPRINTS.
California State publications. v. 1- July/Sept. 1947- [Sacramento, Printing Division, Documents Section] 015.794   52-19974
    Z1223.5.C2 C4 MRR Alc* Partial set

Historical records survey. California. A check list of California non-documentary imprints, 1833-1855. San Francisco, Calif., 1942. xvii, 109 numb. l.   015.794 44-8960
    Z1215 .H67 no. 31 MRR Alc.

CALIFORNIA--MANUFACTURES--DIRECTORIES.
California international business directory. 1971- Los Angeles, Center for Advanced Studies in International Business. 338/.0025/794   71-146906
    HF5065.C2 C26 MRR Alc Latest edition

California manufacturers annual register. 1948- Los Angeles, Times-Mirror Press. 670.58   48-3418
    T12 .D48 Sci RR Latest edition / MRR Alc Latest edition

CALIFORNIA--POLITICS AND GOVERNMENT.
California. Secretary of State. Roster: Federal, state, county, city, and township officials. 1958- [Sacramento] 353.9/794/002 72-622827
    JK8730.A27 MRR Alc Latest edition

California blue book. [Sacramento, Office of State Printing] 73-640050
    JK8730 .C37a MRR Alc Latest edition

CALIFORNIA--POLITICS AND GOVERNMENT--1951-
Owens, John Robert, California politics and parties [New York] Macmillan [1970] xiii, 338 p. 329/.009794   77-97764
    JK8725 1970 .O93 MRR Alc.

CALIFORNIA--REGISTERS.
California. Legislature. List of members, officers, committees and rules of the two Houses. [Sacramento]   328.7945   10-14000
    JK8771 .A2 date MRR Alc Latest edition

California. Secretary of State. Roster: Federal, state, county, city, and township officials. 1958- [Sacramento] 353.9/794/002 72-622827
    JK8730.A27 MRR Alc Latest edition

CALIFORNIA--REGISTERS. (Cont.)
California blue book. [Sacramento,
Office of State Printing] 73-640050

   JK8730 .C37a MRR Alc Latest
   edition

CALIFORNIA--STATISTICS.
California: Past, present, future.
1969- ed. Lakewood, Calif.
[California Almanac Co.] 917.94/03/5
49-2266
   F856 .C255 MRR Alc Latest edition

CALIFORNIA. LEGISLATURE--RULES AND
PRACTICE.
California. Legislature. List of
members, officers, committees and
rules of the two Houses.
[Sacramento] 328.7945 10-14000
   JK8771 .A2 date MRR Alc Latest
   edition

CALIFORNIA. UNIVERSITY. LIBRARY.
California. University. Library.
Author-title catalog. Boston, G. K.
Hall, 1963. 115 v. 018/.1 73-
153193
   Z881 .C1532 1963 MRR Alc (Dk 33)

California. University. Library.
University of California, Berkeley,
serials key word index. 1st- ed.;
1973- Berkeley. 016.05 73-645730
   Z6945 .C16a MRR Alc Latest edition

CALIFORNIA, SOUTHERN--COMMERCE--
DIRECTORIES.
Southern California business
directory and buyers guide. Los
Angeles, Los Angeles Area Chamber of
Commerce. 380.1/025/7949 74-641762

   HF5065.C2 S66 MRR Alc Latest
   edition

CALIFORNIA, SOUTHERN--DESCRIPTION AND
TRAVEL--GUIDE-BOOKS.
Hepburn, Andrew. Complete guide to
Southern California. New rev. ed.
Garden City, N.Y., Doubleday, 1962.
160 p. 917.949 62-7089
   F867 .H5 1962 MRR Alc.

CALIFORNIA, SOUTHERN--INDUSTRIES--
DIRECTORIES.
Southern California business
directory and buyers guide. Los
Angeles, Los Angeles Area Chamber of
Commerce. 380.1/025/7949 74-641762

   HF5065.C2 S66 MRR Alc Latest
   edition

CALIFORNIA IN LITERATURE--BIBLIOGRAPHY.
Baird, Newton D. An annotated
bibliography of California fiction,
1664-1970. Georgetown, Calif.,
Talisman Literary Research, 1971.
xvi, 521 p. 016.813/008/0375 72-
176607
   Z1231.F4 B35 MRR Alc.

CALLAN, JOHN LANSING, 1886-1958--
MANUSCRIPTS.
United States. Library of Congress.
Manuscript Division. John Lansing
Callan, John Crittenden Watson; a
register of their papers in the
Library of Congress. Washington,
Library of Congress, 1968. 6, 8 l.
973 68-67221
   Z663.34 .C29 MRR Alc.

CALLIGRAPHY.
Anderson, Donald M. The art of
written forms; New York, Holt,
Rinehart and Winston [1969] ix, 358
p. [10.95] 741 68-21782
   Z40 .A5 MRR Alc.

CALLISTHENICS.
see also Physical education and
training

CAMBODIA.
Munson, Frederick P. Area handbook
for Cambodia. Washington. For sale
by the Supt. of Docs., U.S. Govt.
Print. Off., 1968. xviii, 364 p.
[3.00] 915.96/03/4 72-600172
   DS557.C2 M94 1968 MRR Alc.

CAMBODIA--BIBLIOGRAPHY.
United States. Library of Congress.
Orientalia Division. Southeast Asia
subject catalog. Boston, G. K. Hall,
1972- v. 016.9159/03 72-5257
   Z3221 .U525 MRR Alc (Dk 33)

CAMBODIA--BIOGRAPHY.
Personalites du Cambodge. 1.-
ed.; 1963- Phnom-Penh [Cambodge]
Realites cambodgiennes. 63-39802
   DS557.C26A15 MRR Biog Latest
   edition

CAMBODIA--GAZETTEERS.
United States. Geographic Names
Division. Cambodia; official
standard names approved by the United
States board on Geographic Names. 2d
ed. Washington, 1971. xi, 392 p.
915.96/003 72-601295
   DS557.C22 U48 1971 MRR Alc.

CAMBRIDGE. UNIVERSITY--BIOGRAPHY.
Emden, Alfred Brotherston. A
biographical register of the
University of Cambridge to 1500.
Cambridge [Eng.] University Press,
1963. xl, 695 p. 378.42 63-24688

   LF113 .E4 MRR Biog.

CAMBRIDGE. UNIVERSITY--HANDBOOKS,
MANUALS, ETC.
Cambridge. University. Handbook.
57th- ed.: 1967/68- Cambridge
[Syndics of the Cambridge University
Press] 378.744/4 72-623016
   LF101 .C8 MRR Alc Latest edition

CAMBRIDGE. UNIVERSITY. KING'S COLLEGE--
BIOGRAPHY.
Cambridge. University. King's
College. A register of admissions to
King's College, Cambridge, 1919-1958.
London, 1963. vi, 462 p. 65-71149

   LF204 .A3 1963 MRR Biog.

CAMBRIDGE. UNIVERSITY LIBRARY.
Cambridge. University. Library.
Current serials available in the
University Library and in other
libraries connected with the
university. Cambridge. 016.05 74-
645183
Began in 1970.
   Z6945 .C175 MRR Alc Latest edition

CAMBRIDGE, MASS.--DESCRIPTION--GUIDE-
BOOKS.
Dimancescu, Dan, ed. This is Boston;
Bicentennial ed. [Boston] Cities,
inc. [1974] 95 p. 917.44/61/044
74-11306
   F73.18 .D55 MRR Alc.

CAMDEN SOCIETY, LONDON--BIBLIOGRAPHY.
Milne, Alexander Taylor. A centenary
guide to the publications of the
Royal Historical Society, 1868-1968.
London, Royal Historical Society,
1968. xi, 249 p. [unpriced]
016.942 77-436189
   Z5055.G6 R66 MRR Alc.

CAMEROON--BIBLIOGRAPHY.
Le Vine, Victor T. Historical
dictionary of Cameroon. Metuchen,
N.J., Scarecrow Press, 1974. xii,
198 p. 967/.11/003 74-901
   DT563 .L48 MRR Alc.

CAMEROON--BIOGRAPHY.
Le Vine, Victor T. Historical
dictionary of Cameroon. Metuchen,
N.J., Scarecrow Press, 1974. xii,
198 p. 967/.11/003 74-901
   DT563 .L48 MRR Alc.

CAMEROON--HISTORY--CHRONOLOGY.
Le Vine, Victor T. Historical
dictionary of Cameroon. Metuchen,
N.J., Scarecrow Press, 1974. xii,
198 p. 967/.11/003 74-901
   DT563 .L48 MRR Alc.

CAMEROON--HISTORY--DICTIONARIES.
Le Vine, Victor T. Historical
dictionary of Cameroon. Metuchen,
N.J., Scarecrow Press, 1974. xii,
198 p. 967/.11/003 74-901
   DT563 .L48 MRR Alc.

CAMEROUN--BIBLIOGRAPHY.
United States. Library of Congress.
African Section. Official
publications of French Equatorial
Africa, French Cameroons, and Togo,
Washington, General Reference and
Bibliography Divison, Reference
Dept., Library of Congress; [for sale
by the Superintendent of Documents,
U.S. Govt. Print. Off.] 1964. xi, 78
p. 64-60029
   Z6663.285 .032 MRR Alc.

CAMEROUN--GAZETTEERS.
United States. Office of Geography.
Cameroon; official standard names
approved by the United States Board
on Geographic Names. Washington,
U.S. Govt. Print. Off., 1962. iv,
255 p. 62-61562
   DT563 .U5 MRR Alc.

CAMP SITES, FACILITIES, ETC.--ATLANTIC
STATES.
Steinberg, Joseph L. Campers'
favorite campgrounds; New York, Dial
Press, 1974. ix, 262 p. 917.4/04/4
74-1006
   SK601.4.A85 S73 MRR Alc.

CAMP SITES, FACILITIES, ETC.--CANADA.
Rand McNally and Company. Campground
and trailer park guide. 1971- New
York. 917.3/04/924 78-613368
   SK601 .R285 MRR Alc Latest edition

CAMP SITES, FACILITIES, ETC.--CANADA--
DIRECTORIES.
Campground guide for tent or trailer
tourists, fishermen, hunters, etc.
Blue Rapids, Kan., Campgrounds
Unlimited. 796.54058 52-25678
Began publication in 1951.
   SK601 .C15 MRR Alc Latest edition

CAMP SITES, FACILITIES, ETC.--EUROPE.
Cope, Bob. European camping and
caravaning. New York, Drake
Publishers [1974] xi, 258 p.
914/.04/55 73-18222
   GV191.48.E8 C66 MRR Alc.

CAMP SITES, FACILITIES, ETC.--EUROPE--
DIRECTORIES.
Europa Camping+[i.e. und] Caravaning.
Stuttgart, Drei Brunner Verlag;
Distributed by Reise- und
Verkehrsverlag. 796.540584 61-23250

   SK601.A1 E8 MRR Alc Latest edition

Lippman, Paul. Camping guide to
Europe; [1st ed.] New York, Holt,
Rinehart and Winston [1968] x, 181
p. 914/.04/55 68-12211
   GV1025.E9 L5 MRR Alc.

CAMP SITES, FACILITIES, ETC.--NORTH
AMERICA--DIRECTORIES.
American Automobile Association.
Eastern campground directory: areas
in the Eastern United States and
Canada. [Washington, D.C.] 64-5093

   SK601.A1 A514 MRR Alc Latest
   edition

Western camping and trailering areas
in Western United States and Canada
including location maps. 1964-
[Washington] American Automobile
Association. 64-5094
   SK601 .W43 MRR Alc Latest edition

CAMP SITES, FACILITIES, ETC.--THE WEST.
Rand McNally western campground &
trailering guide. 1970- [New York,
Rand McNally] 917.9/04/3 79-23951
   SK601 .R29 MRR Alc Latest edition

CAMP SITES, FACILITIES, ETC.--UNITED
STATES.
Rand McNally and Company. Campground
and trailer park guide. 1971- New
York. 917.3/04/924 78-613368
   SK601 .R285 MRR Alc Latest edition

CAMP SITES, FACILITIES, ETC.--UNITED
STATES--
Cameron, Ben. The New York times
guide to outdoors U.S.A. [New York]
Quadrangle/New York Times Book Co.
1973- v. [$4.95 (v. 1) varies]
796.54/025/75 72-77535
   SK601.3 .C33 MRR Alc.

CAMP SITES, FACILITIES, ETC.--UNITED
STATES--DIRECTORIES.
American Automobile Association.
Eastern campground directory: areas
in the Eastern United States and
Canada. [Washington, D.C.] 64-5093

   SK601.A1 A514 MRR Alc Latest
   edition

Campground guide for tent or trailer
tourists, fishermen, hunters, etc.
Blue Rapids, Kan., Campgrounds
Unlimited. 796.54058 52-25678
Began publication in 1951.
   SK601 .C15 MRR Alc Latest edition

Let's go camping, let's go
trailering. [Beverly Hills, Calif.,
Trail-R-Club of America] 796.5405873
58-87
   SK601.A1 L4 MRR Alc Latest edition

Sloane, Howard N. The Goodyear guide
to State parks. New York, Crown
Publishers [1967- v.
352/.7/0974 66-26199
   SK601 .S6 MRR Alc.

Steinberg, Joseph L. Campers'
favorite campgrounds; New York, Dial
Press, 1974. ix, 262 p. 917.4/04/4
74-1006
   SK601.4.A85 S73 MRR Alc.

Western camping and trailering areas
in Western United States and Canada
including location maps. 1964-
[Washington] American Automobile
Association. 64-5094
   SK601 .W43 MRR Alc Latest edition

Woodall's trailering parks and
campgrounds directory. Eastern
edition. [Highland Park, Ill.,
Woodall Pub. Co.] 647/.9473 74-
644615
   GV191.35 .W66 MRR Alc Latest
   edition

CAMPAIGN FUNDS.
Runyon, John H. Source book of
American presidential campaign and
election statistics, 1948-1968. New
York, F. Ungar [1971] xiv, 380 p.
329/.023/0212 73-155093
   JK524 .R83 MRR Alc.

CAMPAIGN LITERATURE, 1940--REPUBLICAN.
Roosevelt, Franklin Delano, pres.
U.S. "Quotations" from Franklin
Delano Roosevelt. Washington, D.C.,
Republican national committee [c1940]
128 p. 973.917 40-32770
   E806 .R7495 1940 MRR Alc.

CAMPAIGN MANAGEMENT--DIRECTORIES.
Rosenbloom, David L. The political
marketplace. [New York] Quadrangle
Books [1972] xix, 948 p. [$25.00]
329/.0025/73 72-77926
JK2283 .R64 MRR Ref Desk.

CAMPAIGNS, PRESIDENTIAL
see Presidents--United States--
Election

CAMPERS AND COACHES, TRUCK--DIRECTORIES.
The Mobile home and recreational
vehicle manufacturers of the United
States and Canada. Detroit
(Southfield) Mich., Automotive Credit
Service. 338.4/7/62922602573 75-
17387
HD9715.7.U6 M58 MRR Alc Latest
edition

CAMPING.
see also Backpacking

Sparano, Vin T. Complete outdoors
encyclopedia, New York, Outdoor
Life, Harper & Row [1972] 622 p.
[$13.95] 789/.03 72-90934
SK33 .S646 MRR Alc.

CAMPING--OUTFITS, SUPPLIES, ETC.
Explorers Ltd. The Explorers Ltd.
source book. 1st ed. New York,
Harper & Row [c1973] 384 p. [$4.95]
790/.028 72-9115
GV187 .E95 1973 MRR Alc.

CAMPING--THE WEST--DIRECTORIES.
Rand McNally western campground &
trailering guide. 1970- [New York,
Rand McNally] 917.9/04/3 79-23951
SK601 .R29 MRR Alc Latest edition

CAMPS--WATER PROGRAMS
see Aquatic sports

CAMPS--EUROPE--DIRECTORIES.
Europa Camping+[i.e. und] Caravaning.
Stuttgart, Drei Brunner Verlag;
Distributed by Reise- und
Verkehrsverlag. 796.540584 61-23250

SK601.A1 E8 MRR Alc Latest edition

CAMPS--UNITED STATES--DIRECTORIES.
The Boarding school directory of the
United States and Canada. v. 3-
1969/72- Chicago, Educational
Bureau. 371/.02/0257 72-627132
L901 .B65 MRR Ref Desk Latest
edition

The Guide to summer camps and summer
schools. 1st- ed.; 1936- Boston,
P. Sargent. 37-4715
GV193 .G8 MRR Alc Latest edition

National directory of accredited
camps for boys and girls.
Martinsville, Ind., American Camping
Association. 796.54/22/02573 72-
612802
GV193 .N35 MRR Alc Latest edition

National directory of Jewish camps.
[Norfolk, Va., Camp Advisory Bureau]
796.5405873 60-28907
SK601.A1 N38 MRR Alc Latest
edition

CAMPS FOR THE HANDICAPPED--DIRECTORIES.
The Easter seal directory of resident
camps for persons with special health
needs. Chicago, National Easter Seal
Society for Crippled Children and
Adults. 796.54/22/02573 72-627459
GV197.H3 D5 MRR Alc Latest edition

CAMPSITES, FACILITIES, ETC.--NEW
ENGLAND--DIRECTORIES.
Parry, Don, Don Parry's guide to
Northeast camping areas. Rocky Hill,
Conn., Outdoor Publishers.
796.54/0974 72-623299
SK601.A1 T4 MRR Alc Latest edition

CAMPSITES, FACILITIES, ETC.--NEW YORK
(STATE)--DIRECTORIES.
Parry, Don, Don Parry's guide to
Northeast camping areas. Rocky Hill,
Conn., Outdoor Publishers.
796.54/0974 72-623299
SK601.A1 T4 MRR Alc Latest edition

CANADA.
Canada year book. [Ottawa]
Statistics Canada. [$6.00 (cloth-
bound)] 317.1 73-640929
HA744 .S81 MRR Alc Latest edition

Canadian Newspaper Service, ltd.
National reference book on Canadian
business personalities. [Montreal]
29-2668
F1001 .C277 MRR Biog Latest
edition

The Canadian pocket encyclopedia.
[Toronto, Quick Canadian Facts Ltd.]
[$3.00 (single issue)] 917.1/03/64
74-644527
F1009 .Q5 MRR Alc Latest edition

CANADA--1951- --DESCRIPTION AND TRAVEL--
GUIDE-BOOKS.
Off the beaten path. [1st]- ed.;
1957- 1957- Greenlawn, N.Y., Harian
Publications; trade distributor:
Crown Publishers [etc.] 917 59-
16155
E158 .O3 MRR Alc Latest edition

CANADA--ANTIQUITIES--BIBLIOGRAPHY.
Hammond, Philip C. Archaeological
techniques for amateurs. Princeton,
N.J., Van Nostrand [1963] 329 p.
913.018 63-4293
CC75 .H3 MRR Alc.

CANADA--BIBLIOGRAPHY.
Amtmann, Bernard. Contributions to a
short-title catalogue of Canadiana.
Montreal, 1971- v. 015/.71 73-
156377
Z1365 .A64 MRR Alc.

The Canadian catalogue of books
published in Canada, about Canada,
Consolidated English language reprint
ed., with cumulated author index.
[Toronto] Toronto Public Libraries,
1959. 2 v. 65-53618
Z1365 .C222 MRR Alc.

Canadiana. Jan. 15, 1951- [Ottawa]
015.71 53-35723
Z1365 .C23 MRR Alc Full set

Financial post. Directory of
directors [executives of Canada]
Toronto. 650.58 52-26909
HG4090.Z5 F5 MRR Alc Latest
edition

Haight, Willet Ricketson, Canadian
catalogue of books, 1791-1897;
London, H. Pordes, 1958. 130, 48, 57
p. 015.71 59-10
Z1365 .H16 MRR Alc.

Lochhead, Douglas. Bibliography of
Canadian bibliographies. 2d ed. rev.
and enl. [Toronto] University of
Toronto, published in association
with the Bibliographical Society of
Canada [1972] xiv, 312 p. [$20.00]
016.01571 76-166933
Z1365.A1 L6 1972 MRR Alc.

Peel, Bruce Braden, A bibliography
of the Prairie Provinces to 1953.
[Toronto] University of Toronto Press
[1956] xix, 680 p. 016.9712 56-
2717
Z1365 .P4 MRR Alc.

Royal Commonwealth Society. Library.
Subject catalogue of the Library of
the Royal Empire Society, [1st ed.
reprinted] London, Dawsons for the
Royal Commonwealth Society, 1967. 4
v. (60/-/- per set (16/-/- per
vol.)] 016.942 68-70847
Z7164.C7 R82 1967 MRR Alc.

Ryder, Dorothy E. Canadian reference
sources; Ottawa, Canadian Library
Association, 1973. x, 185 p.
011/.02/0971 73-169642
Z1365 .R8 MRR Alc.

Tod, Dorothea D. A check list of
Canadian imprints, 1900-1925,
Prelim. checking ed. Ottawa,
Canadian Bibliographic Centre, Public
Archives of Canada, 1950. 370 l.
015.71 50-12525
Z1365 .T6 MRR Alc.

Tremaine, Marie. A bibliography of
Canadian imprints, 1751-1800.
Toronto, University of Toronto Press,
1952. xxvii, 705 p. 015.71 52-
2955
Z1365 .T7 MRR Alc.

Watters, Reginald Eyre. A checklist
of Canadian literature and background
materials, 1628-1960, 2d ed., rev.
and enl. [Toronto, Buffalo]
University of Toronto Press [1972]
xxiv, 1085 p. [$30.00] 013/.971
72-80713
Z1375 .W3 1972 MRR Alc.

CANADA--BIBLIOGRAPHY--CATALOGS.
McGill University, Montreal. Library.
The Lawrence Lande collection of
Canadiana in the Redpath Library of
McGill University; Montreal,
Lawrence Lande Foundation for
Canadian Historical Research, 1965.
xxxv, 301 p. 65-18258
Z1365 .M14 MRR Alc.

Royal Commonwealth Society. Library.
Subject catalogue of the Royal
Commonwealth Society, London.
Boston, Mass., G. K. Hall, 1971. 7
v. 017.1 70-180198
Z7164.C7 R83 MRR Alc (Dk 33)

CANADA--BIOGRAPHY.
Canadian Newspaper Service, ltd.
National reference book on Canadian
business personalities, [Montreal]
29-2668
F1001 .C277 MRR Biog Latest
edition

The Canadian parliamentary guide.
Ottawa. 17-2753
JL5 .A4 MRR Alc Latest edition

The Canadian who's who. v. 1- 1910-
Toronto, Who's Who Canadian
Publications [etc.] 920.071 10-
17752
F1033 .C23 MRR Biog Latest edition
/ MRR Ref Desk Latest edition

Centennial Commission (Canada) The
founders and the guardians: fathers
of confederation, governors general,
prime ministers; [Ottawa, Queen's
Printer, 1968] ii, 147 p.
971.05/0922 B 71-381935
F1033 .C52 MRR Biog.

Charlesworth, Hector Willoughby, ed.
A cyclopedia of Canadian biography;
Toronto, The Hunter-Rose company,
limited, 1919. xii, 303 p. 21-
11183
F1005 .C47 MRR Biog.

Dictionary of Canadian biography. v.
1- 1000/1700- Toronto, University
of Toronto Press 920.07103 66-31909

F1005 .D49 MRR Biog Full set

Encyclopedia Canadiana. Toronto,
Grolier of Canada, c1972. 10 v.
[$109.50 (Schools and libraries)]
917.1/03/03 73-157945
F1006 .E625 1972 MRR Alc.

The Macmillan dictionary of Canadian
biography, 3d ed., rev and enl.
London, Macmillan; New York, St.
Martin's, 1963. 822 p. 920.071 64-
10158
F1005 .D5 1963 MRR Biog.

Ondaatje, Christopher. The Prime
Ministers of Canada, 1867-1968
Toronto, Pagurian Press, 1968. 191
p. [unpriced] 971 79-396883
F1033 .O56 1968 MRR Biog.

Peel, Bruce Braden, A bibliography
of the Prairie Provinces to 1953.
[Toronto] University of Toronto Press
[1956] xix, 680 p. 016.9712 56-
2717
Z1365 .P4 MRR Alc.

Rhodenizer, Vernon Blair, comp.
Canadian literature in English.
[Montreal, Printed by Quality Press,
c1965] 1055 p. [10.00]
016.8108/0971 77-375203
Z1375 .R5 MRR Alc.

Société des écrivains canadiens,
Montreal. Repertoire bio-
bibliographique, 1954. Montréal
[1955] xviii, 248 p. 57-32232
PQ3900 .S68A3 MRR Biog.

Story, Norah. The Oxford companion
to Canadian history and literature.
Toronto, New York [etc.] Oxford
University Press, 1967. xi, 935 p.
[$15.00 Can.] 810/.3 67-31959
PR9106 .S7 1967 MRR Alc.

Who's who in Canada; Toronto,
International Press Limited. 17-
16282
Began publication in 1910.
F1033 .W62 Sci RR Latest edition /
MRR Biog Latest edition

CANADA--BIOGRAPHY--BIBLIOGRAPHY.
Matthews, William, Canadian diaries
and autobiographies. Berkeley,
University of California Press, 1950.
130 p. 016.920071 50-62732
Z5305.C3 M3 MRR Biog.

CANADA--BIOGRAPHY--DICTIONARIES.
Burpee, Lawrence Johnstone, ed.
Index and dictionary of Canadian
history, Toronto, Morang & co.,
limited, 1911. 2 p. l., vii-xvi, 446
p. 971 39-32912
F1006 .B92 MRR Alc.

Creative Canada; [Toronto] Published
in association with McPherson
Library, University of Victoria, by
University of Toronto Press [1971-
v. [$15.00 (v. 1)] 790/.971 71-
151387
NX513.A1 C7 MRR Biog.

Sylvestre, Guy. Canadian writers.
New ed. rev. and enl. Montreal,
Editions HMH [1966] xviii, 186 p.
[$9.50 Can.] 809.8/971 68-112492
PR9127 .S9 1966 MRR Biog.

Toye, William. Supplement to the
Oxford companion to Canadian history
and literature. Toronto, New York,
Oxford University Press, 1973. v,
318 p. [$9.50] 810/.9 74-180951
PR9180.2 .T6 1973 MRR Alc.

Wallace, William Stewart, A
dictionary of North American authors
deceased before 1950. Toronto,
Ryerson Press [1951] viii, 525 p.
928.1 51-7279
PS128 .W3 MRR Biog.

CANADA--BIOGRAPHY--DICTIONARIES. (Cont.)
Who's who in finance and industry.
17th- ed.; 1972/73- Chicago,
Marquis Who's Who. 338/.00922 [B]
70-616550
HF3023.A2 W5 MRR Biog Latest
edition

Who's who in the East and Eastern
Canada. 1st- etc.; 1942/43-
Chicago [etc.] Marquis-Who's Who
[etc.] 920.07 43-18522
E176 .W643 MRR Biog Latest edition

Who's who in the Midwest and Central
Canada. 1st- ed.; 1947- Chicago,
Marquis-Who's Who [etc.] 920.07 50-
289
E176 .W644 MRR Biog Latest edition

Who's who in the West and Western
Canada. 1st- ed.; 1947- Chicago,
Marquis-Who's Who [etc.] 920.07 49-
48186
E176 .W646 MRR Biog Latest edition

CANADA--CIVILIZATION.
Careless, James Maurice Stockford,
The Canadians, 1867-1967, Toronto,
Macmillan of Canada, 1967. xix, 856
p. [$9.95 Can.] 917.1/03 67-93875

F1033 .C27 1967a MRR Alc.

CANADA--COMMERCE--HANDBOOKS, MANUALS,
ETC.
Newman, Dorothy M. Canadian business
handbook 2d ed. New York, MGraw-
Hill [1967] x, 681 p. 650/.02/02
67-8258
HF3227 .N4 1967 MRR Alc.

CANADA--COMMERCE--UNITED STATES--
BIBLIOGRAPHY.
United States. Library of Congress.
Division of bibliography. ... Select
list of books, with references to
periodicals, on reciprocity with
Canada. Washington, Govt. print.
off., 1907. 14 p. 07-35004
Z663.28 .S344 MRR Alc.

CANADA--CONSTITUTIONAL HISTORY.
Kennedy, William Paul McClure,
Statutes, treaties and documents of
the Canadian constitution, 1713-1929,
2d ed., rev. and enl. Toronto,
London, New York [etc.] Oxford
university press, 1930. xxviii, 752
p. 342.71 30-34203
JL11 .K45 1930 MRR Alc.

CANADA--CONSTITUTIONAL LAW.
Kennedy, William Paul McClure,
Statutes, treaties and documents of
the Canadian constitution, 1713-1929,
2d ed., rev. and enl. Toronto,
London, New York [etc.] Oxford
university press, 1930. xxviii, 752
p. 342.71 30-34203
JL11 .K45 1930 MRR Alc.

CANADA--DESCRIPTION AND TRAVEL.
White, Charles Langdon, Regional
geography of Anglo-America 4th ed.
Englewood Cliffs, N.J., Prentice-Hall
[1974] xv, 617 p. [$11.95] 917
73-3225
E169 .W54 1974 MRR Alc.

CANADA--DESCRIPTION AND TRAVEL--1951-
Kane, Robert S. Canada A to Z [1st
ed.] Garden City, N.Y., Doubleday
[1964] x, 348 p. 917.1 64-19234
F1016 .K28 MRR Alc.

Paterson, John Harris. North
America: a geography of Canada and
the United States 4th ed. London,
Oxford U.P., 1970. [16], 319 p., 16
plates. [50/-] 917 77-129101
E41 .P3 1870 MRR Alc.

Watson, James Wreford. North
America, its countries and regions,
[London] Longmans [1963] xxi, 854 p.
64-57181
E41 .W25 MRR Alc.

CANADA--DESCRIPTION AND TRAVEL--1951- --
GUIDE-BOOKS.
Cerbelaud Salagnac, Georges. Canada,
Alaska, Saint-Pierre and Miquelon,
the Bermudas, Paris, Librairie
Hachette, 1967. 1109 p.
917.1/04/64 68-85106
F1009 .C413 MRR Alc.

Reader's Digest Association (Canada)
Explore Canada; [Montreal, 1974]
476 p. [$19.95] 917.1/04/64 74-
161885
F1009 .R43 1974 MRR Alc.

CANADA--DESCRIPTION AND TRAVEL--GUIDE-
BOOKS.
Canadian museums and related
institutions, 1968. [Ottawa,
Canadian Museums Association, c1968]
xii, 138 p. [unpriced] 069/.025/71
77-430169
AM21.A2 C3 MRR Alc.

Eastern Canada. 1969/70-
[Washington, American Automobile
Association] 917.1/04/644 76-615935

GV1025.C2 E172 MRR Alc Latest
edition

Rand McNally vacation guide:
Chicago. 917.3 60-2943
E158 .R3 MRR Alc Latest edition

Reader's Digest Association (Canada)
Explore Canada; [Montreal, 1974]
476 p. [$19.95] 917.1/04/64 74-
161885
F1009 .R43 1974 MRR Alc.

CANADA--DESCRIPTION AND TRAVEL--
YEARBOOKS.
Canada. [Ottawa] Statistics Canada.
917.1 72-625370
HC115 .A425 MRR Alc Latest edition

CANADA--DICTIONARIES AND ENCYCLOPEDIAS.
Burpee, Lawrence Johnstone, ed.
Index and dictionary of Canadian
history, Toronto, Morang & co.,
limited, 1911. 2 p. l., vii-xvi, 446
p. 971 39-32912
F1006 .B92 MRR Alc.

Encyclopedia Canadiana. Toronto,
Grolier of Canada, c1972. 10 v.
[$109.50 (Schools and libraries)]
917.1/03/03 73-157945
F1006 .E625 1972 MRR Alc.

CANADA--DIRECTORIES.
Canadian almanac & directory. [1st]-
year; 1848- Vancouver [etc.] Copp
Clark Pub. Co. [etc.] 529.43 07-
24314
AY414 .C2 MRR Ref Desk Latest
edition

Corpus directory and almanac of
Canada. 7th- 1972- Toronto,
Corpus Publishers Services Ltd.
917.1 72-626058
F1004.7 .M3 Sci RR Latest edition
/ MRR Alc Latest edition

CANADA--ECONOMIC CONDITIONS--1968- --
YEARBOOKS.
Survey of markets and business year
book. Toronto, Maclean-Hunter Ltd.
330.9/71/0644 72-626543
HC111 .B8 MRR Alc Latest edition

CANADA--ECONOMIC CONDITIONS--MAPS.
Oxford University Press. United
States & Canada. Oxford, Clarendon
P., 1967. [2], [35] p. [75/- (35/-
pbk.)] 912.1/3309/73 map68-202
G1201.G1 O9 1967 MRR Alc Atlas.

CANADA--ECONOMIC CONDITIONS--YEARBOOKS.
Canada. [Ottawa] Statistics Canada.
917.1 72-625370
HC115 .A425 MRR Alc Latest edition

CANADA--EXECUTIVE DEPARTMENTS--
DIRECTORIES.
Corpus directory and almanac of
Canada. 7th- 1972- Toronto,
Corpus Publishers Services Ltd.
917.1 72-626058
F1004.7 .M3 Sci RR Latest edition
/ MRR Alc Latest edition

CANADA--GAZETTEERS.
Reader's Digest Association (Canada)
Explore Canada; [Montreal, 1974]
476 p. [$19.95] 917.1/04/64 74-
161885
F1009 .R43 1974 MRR Alc.

United States. Office of Geography.
Canada; Washington, Central
Intelligence Agency, 1953. 415 p.
917/.1/003 78-8049
F1004 .U5 MRR Alc.

CANADA--GENEALOGY--BIBLIOGRAPHY.
Stevenson, Noel C. Search and
research, the researcher's handbook;
Rev. ed. Salt Lake City, Deseret
Book Co., 1959. 364 p. 929.1072
59-11137
Z5313.U5 S8 1959 MRR Ref Desk.

CANADA--GOVERNMENT PUBLICATIONS.
Higgins, Marion Villiers, Canadian
government publication; Chicago,
American library association, 1935.
4 p. l., ix, 582 (i.e. 588) p.
015.71 35-27066
Z1373.C2 H6 MRR Alc.

CANADA--GOVERNMENT PUBLICATIONS--
BIBLIOGRAPHY.
Canada. Bureau of Statistics.
Library. Historical catalogue of
Dominion Bureau of Statistics
publications 1918-1960. Ottawa, DBS
Library [and] Canada Year Book
Division, 1966 [i.e. 1967] xiv, 298
p. [$2.50 Can.] 317.1 68-136228
Z7554.C2 A5 MRR Alc.

Canada. Dept. of Public Printing and
Stationery. Canadian Government
publications. Ottawa. 53-23554
Z1373 .C22 MRR Alc Partial set

Canada. Information Canada. Canadian
Government publications. Ottawa.
015.71 72-626335
Z1373 .C22 MRR Alc Full set

Canadiana. Jan. 15, 1951- [Ottawa]
015.71 53-35723
Z1365 .C23 MRR Alc Full set

Henderson, George Fletcher. Federal
royal commissions in Canada, 1867-
1966; [Toronto] University of
Toronto Press [1967] xvi, 212 p.
015/.71 68-91146
Z1373 .H4 MRR Alc.

Higgins, Marion Villiers, Canadian
government publication; Chicago,
American library association, 1935.
4 p. l., ix, 582 (i.e. 588) p.
015.71 35-27066
Z1373.C2 H6 MRR Alc.

CANADA--HISTORY.
Brebner, John Bartlet, Canada, a
modern history. Ann Arbor,
University of Michigan Press [1960]
553 p. 971 59-62500
F1026 .B84 MRR Alc.

CANADA--HISTORY--1763-1791--SOURCES.
Beers, Henry Putney, The French &
British in the Old Northwest;
Detroit, Wayne State University
Press, 1964. 297 p. 977 64-13305

F478.2 .B4 MRR Alc.

CANADA--HISTORY--1867- --ADDRESSES,
ESSAYS, LECTURES.
Careless, James Maurice Stockford,
The Canadians, 1867-1967, Toronto,
Macmillan of Canada, 1967. xix, 856
p. [$9.95 Can.] 917.1/03 67-93875

F1033 .C27 1967a MRR Alc.

CANADA--HISTORY--BIBLIOGRAPHY.
Griffin, Appleton Prentiss Clark,
Bibliography of American historical
societies 2d ed.; rev. and enl.
[Washington, Govt. print. off., 1907]
1374 p. 08-7356
Z1236 .G86 MRR Alc.

Thibault, Claude. Bibliographia
Canadiana. Don Mills, Ont., Longman
Canada, 1973. lxiv, 795 p. [$25.00]
917.1/03 74-163122
Z1382 .T47 MRR Alc.

CANADA--HISTORY--BIBLIOGRAPHY--CATALOGS.
Harvard University. Library.
Canadian history and literature;
Cambridge; Distributed by the Harvard
University Press, 1968. 411 p.
016.9171 68-22417
Z1365 .H3 MRR Alc.

CANADA--HISTORY--CHRONOLOGY.
Bowman, Robert Turnbull, Dateline:
Canada Toronto, Holt, Rinehart and
Winston of Canada [1973] 1 v.
(unpaged) 971/.002 72-9493
F1006 .B6 1973 MRR Alc.

Taplin, Glen W. Canadian chronology.
Metuchen, N.J., Scarecrow Press,
1970. xiv, 174 p. 971/.002 74-
9002
F1006 .T3 MRR Alc.

CANADA--HISTORY--PERIODICALS--INDEXES.
America, history and life. v. 1-
July 1964- [Santa Barbara, Calif.]
016.917 64-25630
Z1236 .A48 MRR Alc Full set

Thibault, Claude. Bibliographia
Canadiana. Don Mills, Ont., Longman
Canada, 1973. lxiv, 795 p. [$25.00]
917.1/03 74-163122
Z1382 .T47 MRR Alc.

CANADA--HISTORY--SOURCES.
Burpee, Lawrence Johnstone, ed.
Index and dictionary of Canadian
history, Toronto, Morang & co.,
limited, 1911. 2 p. l., vii-xvi, 446
p. 971 39-32912
F1006 .B92 MRR Alc.

Historical documents of Canada,
Toronto, Macmillan of Canada [1972-
v. 971.06 77-179356
F1003 .H5 MRR Alc.

Talman, James John, ed. Basic
documents in Canadian history.
Princeton, N.J., Van Nostrand [1959]
189 p. 971 59-9760
F1003 .T3 MRR Alc.

CANADA--HISTORY--SOURCES--BIBLIOGRAPHY.
Union list of manuscripts in Canadian
repositories. Ottawa [Queen's
Printer] 1968. x, 734 p. [10.00]
091/.0971 74-410102
CD3622 .U5 MRR Alc.

CANADA--HISTORY--TO 1763 (NEW FRANCE)--SOURCES.
Beers, Henry Putney, The French & British in the Old Northwest; Detroit, Wayne State University Press, 1964. 297 p. 977 64-13305
F478.2 .B4 MRR Alc.

CANADA--IMPRINTS.
Amtmann, Bernard. Contributions to a short-title catalogue of Canadiana. Montreal, 1871- v. 015/.71 73-156377
Z1365 .A64 MRR Alc

Butterfield, Rita. Canadian books in print. [Toronto] Canadian Books in Print Committee [1968] 2 v. 015/.71 68-31933
Z1365 .B962 MRR Ref Desk.

Canada. Dept. of Public Printing and Stationery. Canadian Government publications. Ottawa. 53-23554
Z1373 .C22 MRR Alc Partial set

Canada. Information Canada. Canadian Government publications. Ottawa. 015.71 72-626335
Z1373 .C22 MRR Alc Full set

Canadian books in print. 1967- [Toronto] University of Toronto Press. 015/.71 70-418272
Z1365 .C2196 MRR Ref Desk Latest edition

The Canadian catalogue of books published in Canada, about Canada, Consolidated English language reprint ed., with cumulated author index. [Toronto] Toronto Public Libraries, 1959. 2 v. 65-53618
Z1365 .C222 MRR Alc.

Canadiana. Jan. 15, 1951- [Ottawa] 015.71 53-35723
Z1365 .C23 MRR Alc Full set

Haight, Willet Ricketson, Canadian catalogue of books, 1791-1897; London, H. Pordes, 1958. 130, 48, 57 p. 015.71 59-10
Z1365 .H16 MRR Alc.

Peel, Bruce Braden, A bibliography of the Prairie Provinces to 1953. [Toronto] University of Toronto Press [1956] xix, 680 p. 016.9712 56-2717
Z1365 .P4 MRR Alc.

Rhodenizer, Vernon Blair, comp. Canadian literature in English. [Montreal], Printed by Quality Press, c1965] 1055 p. [10.00] 016.8108/0971 77-375203
Z1375 .R5 MRR Alc.

Tod, Dorothea D. A check list of Canadian imprints, 1900-1925, Prelim. checking ed. Ottawa, Canadian Bibliographic Centre, Public Archives of Canada, 1950. 370 l. 015.71 50-12525
Z1365 .T6 MRR Alc.

Tremaine, Marie. A bibliography of Canadian imprints, 1751-1800. Toronto, University of Toronto Press, 1952. xxvii, 705 p. 015.71 52-2955
Z1365 .T7 MRR Alc.

Watters, Reginald Eyre. A checklist of Canadian literature and background materials, 1628-1960, 2d ed., rev. and enl. [Toronto, Buffalo] University of Toronto Press [1972] xxiv, 1085 p. [$30.00] 013/.971 72-80713
Z1375 .W3 1972 MRR Alc.

CANADA--INDUSTRIES--HANDBOOKS, MANUALS, ETC.
Newman, Dorothy M. Canadian business handbook 2d ed. New York, McGraw-Hill [1967] x, 681 p. 650/.02/02 67-8258
HF3227 .N4 1967 MRR Alc.

CANADA--LEARNED INSTITUTIONS AND SOCIETIES.
Scientific and technical societies of Canada. 1968- Ottawa, National Research Council of Canada. 506/.2/71 72-649212
AS40 .S34 Sci RR Latest edition / MRR Alc Latest edition

CANADA--MANUFACTURES--DIRECTORIES.
Canadian trade index. [1900]- Toronto, Canadian Manufacturers' Association. 14-21699
HF3223 .C25 MRR Alc Latest edition

Chain drug stores buyers directory of variety merchandise. 1961- New York, Directory Division, Merchandiser Publications. 60-40115
T12 .C43 MRR Alc Latest edition

Fraser's Canadian trade directory. Montreal [etc.] Fraser publishing company. 670.58 39-5763
HF3223 .F7 MRR Alc Latest edition

Grocery supermarket non-food buyers directory. 1961- New York, Directory Division, Merchandiser Publications. 60-41591
T12 .G75 MRR Alc Latest edition

Manufacturers' Agent Publishing Company, New York. Verified directory of manufacturers' representatives (agents) 1957- New York. 57-17305
HD9723 .M33 MRR Alc Latest edition

CANADA--MAPS.
Oxford University Press. United States & Canada. Oxford, Clarendon P., 1967. [12], [35] p. [75/- (35/- pbk.)] 912.1/3309/73 map68-202
G1201.G1 09 1967 MRR Alc Atlas.

Rand, McNally and Company. Road atlas of the United States, Canada and Mexico. 1926- Chicago. 629.281 map26-19
G1201.P2 R35 MRR Ref Desk Latest edition / Sci RR Latest edition

CANADA--MAPS--BIBLIOGRAPHY.
Burpee, Lawrence Johnstone, ed. Index and dictionary of Canadian history, Toronto, Morang & co., limited, 1911. 2 p. l., vii-xvi, 446 p. 971 39-32912
F1006 .B92 MRR Alc.

CANADA--POLITICS AND GOVERNMENT.
Canada. Privy Council. Guide to Canadian ministries since confederation, July 1, 1867-January 1, 1957. Ottawa, Public Archives of Canada, 1957. 103 p. 57-3692
JL97.A53 MRR Alc.

Canadian Newspaper Service, ltd. National reference book on Canadian business personalities, [Montreal] 29-2668
F1001 .C277 MRR Blog Latest edition

Ondaatje, Christopher. The Prime Ministers of Canada, 1867-1968 Toronto, Pagurian Press, 1968. 191 p. [unpriced] 971 79-396883
F1033 .O56 1968 MRR Blog.

CANADA--POLITICS AND GOVERNMENT--1945-
Qualter, Terence H. The election process in Canada Toronto, New York, McGraw-Hill Co. of Canada [1970] xii, 203 p. 324/.71 75-127187
JL193 .Q34 MRR Alc.

CANADA--POLITICS AND GOVERNMENT--BIBLIOGRAPHY.
Liboiron, Albert A. Federalism and intergovernmental relations in Australia, Canada, the United States and other countries; Kingston, Ont., Institute of Intergovernmental Relations. Queen's University, 1967. vi, 231 l. [$3.00 Can.] 016.351 68-110060
Z7165.A8 L5 MRR Alc.

CANADA--POLITICS AND GOVERNMENT--HANDBOOKS, MANUALS, ETC.
Public administration organizations, a directory of unofficial organizations in the field of public administration in the United States and Canada. [1st]- ed.; 1932- Chicago, Public Administration Clearing House. 061 33-4186
AS18 .P8 MRR Alc Latest edition

CANADA--REGISTERS.
The Canadian parliamentary guide. Ottawa. 17-2753
JL5 .A4 MRR Alc Latest edition

Corpus directory and almanac of Canada. 7th- 1972- Toronto, Corpus Publishers Services Ltd. 917.1 72-626058
F1004.7 .M3 Sci RR Latest edition / MRR Alc Latest edition

CANADA--SOCIAL CONDITIONS.
Canadian society: sociological perspectives. New York] Free Press of Glencoe [1961] 622 p. 309.171 61-9160
HN103 .C3 MRR Alc.

Dhalla, Nariman K. These Canadians; Toronto, New York, McGraw-Hill Co. of Canada [1966] 749 p. 309.171 66-14580
HC115 .D54 MRR Alc.

CANADA--STATISTICS.
Canada. [Ottawa] Statistics Canada. 917.1 72-625370
HC115 .A425 MRR Alc Latest edition

The Canadian pocket encyclopedia. [Toronto, Quick Canadian Facts Ltd.] [$3.00 (single issue)] 917.1/03/64 74-644527
F1009 .Q5 MRR Alc Latest edition

Goeldner, Charles R. Travel trends in the United States and Canada, Boulder, Business Research Division, University of Colorado [1973] vi, 175 l. 338.4/7/9170453 73-166149
G155.U6 G6 1973 MRR Alc.

Mueller, Bernard. A statistical handbook of the North Atlantic area. New York, Twentieth Century Fund, 1965. 239 p. 301.91821 65-26294
HA1107 .M8 MRR Alc.

Organization for Economic Cooperation and Development. Basic statistics of energy, 1950-1964. Paris, O.E.C.D. [London, H.M.S.O.] 1966. 363 p. [24/-] 333.8 66-66031
HD9555.A4 O7 MRR Alc.

Organization for Economic Cooperation and Development. National accounts statistics 1950-1968. [Paris, 1970] 415 p. [$7.50 (U.S.)] 339.3 73-535302
HC79.I5 O674 MRR Alc.

Organization for Economic Cooperation and Development. National accounts statistics, 1960-1971. [Paris, 1973] 471 p. [$7.50 (U.S.)] 339.3 74-158206
HC79.I5 O7 1973 MRR Alc.

Organization for Economic Cooperation and Development. Statistics of balance of payments, 1950-1961. [Paris, 1964] 134 p. 65-50190
HG3881 .O65 MRR Alc.

Organization for European Economic Cooperation. Manpower population. Paris, 1959. vii, 20 p. 331.112 59-65495
HD5712 .O73 MRR Alc.

Statistical activities of the American nations, 1940; Washington, D.C., Inter American statistical institute, 1941. xxxi, 842 p. 311.397 41-14318
HA175 .S75 MRR Alc.

Survey of markets and business year book. Toronto, Maclean-Hunter Ltd. 330.9/71/0644 72-626543
HC111 .B8 MRR Alc Latest edition

United States. Dept. of Agriculture. Economic Research Service. Foreign Regional Analysis Division. Indices of agricultural production for the Western Hemisphere excluding the United States; Washington] 1969. ii, 33 p. 338.1/0918/12 72-601512

HD1415 .U49 MRR Alc.

Urquhart, M. C., ed. Historical statistics of Canada Cambridge [Eng.] University Press, 1965. xv, 672 p. 317.1 65-23641
HA746 .U7 MRR Alc.

CANADA--STATISTICS--BIBLIOGRAPHY.
Canada. Bureau of Statistics. Library. Historical catalogue of Dominion Bureau of Statistics publications, 1918-1960. Ottawa, DBS Library [and] Canada Year Book Division, 1966 [i.e. 1967] xiv, 298 p. [$2.50 Can.] 317.1 68-136228
Z7554.C2 A5 MRR Alc.

Harvey, Joan M. Statistics America: sources for market research (North, Central & South America), Beckenham, CBD Research, 1973. xii, 225 p. [£6.00 ($22.00 U.S.)] 016.317 73-180742
Z7554.A5 H37 MRR Alc.

Inter American Statistical Institute. Bibliography of selected statistical sources of the American nations. 1st ed. Washington, 1947. xvi, 689 p. 016.31 48-6568
Z7554.S75 I4 1947 MRR Alc.

CANADA--STATISTICS--YEARBOOKS.
Canada year book. [Ottawa] Statistics Canada. [$6.00 (cloth-bound)] 317.1 73-640929
HA744 .S81 MRR Alc Latest edition

CANADA. PARLIAMENT--BIOGRAPHY.
The Canadian parliamentary guide. Ottawa. 17-2753
JL5 .A4 MRR Alc Latest edition

CANADIAN DIARIES--BIBLIOGRAPHY.
Matthews, William, Canadian diaries and autobiographies. Berkeley, University of California Press, 1950. 130 p. 016.920071 50-62732
Z5305.C3 M3 MRR Biog.

CANADIAN FICTION--20TH CENTURY--INDEXES.
Wren, Sheila. Short story index compiled from the Canadian periodical index, 1938-1947. Ottawa, Canadian Library Association, 1967. 46 p. 813/.5/016 76-399974
Z1377.F4 W7 MRR Alc.

CANADIAN LITERATURE--BIBLIOGRAPHY.
The Canadian catalogue of books
published in Canada, about Canada,
Consolidated English language reprint
ed., with cumulated author index.
[Toronto] Toronto Public Libraries,
1959. 2 v.   65-53618
  Z1365 .C222 MRR Alc

Canadiana. Jan. 15, 1951- [Ottawa]
015.71 53-35723
  Z1365 .C23 MRR Alc Full set

Haight, Willet Ricketson, Canadian
catalogue of books, 1791-1897;
London, H. Pordes, 1958. 130, 48, 57
p.   015.71 59-10
  Z1365 .H16 MRR Alc

Peel, Bruce Braden, A bibliography
of the Prairie Provinces to 1953.
[Toronto] University of Toronto Press
[1956] xix, 680 p.   016.9712 56-
2717
  Z1365 .P4 MRR Alc

Rhodenizer, Vernon Blair, comp.
Canadian literature in English.
[Montreal, Printed by Quality Press,
c1965] 1055 p. [10.00]
016.8108/0971 77-375203
  Z1375 .R5 MRR Alc

Tod, Dorothea D. A check list of
Canadian imprints, 1900-1925,
Prelim. checking ed. Ottawa,
Canadian Bibliographic Centre, Public
Archives of Canada, 1950. 370 l.
015.71 50-12525
  Z1365 .T6 MRR Alc

Tremaine, Marie. A bibliography of
Canadian imprints, 1751-1800.
Toronto, University of Toronto Press,
1952. xxvii, 705 p.   015.71 52-
2955
  Z1365 .T7 MRR Alc

Watters, Reginald Eyre. A checklist
of Canadian literature and background
materials, 1628-1960, 2d ed., rev.
and enl. [Toronto, Buffalo]
University of Toronto Press [1972]
xxiv, 1085 p. [$30.00] 013/.971
72-80713
  Z1375 .W3 1972 MRR Alc.

**CANADIAN LITERATURE--BIBLIOGRAPHY--
CATALOGS.**
Brown University. Library.
Dictionary catalog of the Harris
collection of American poetry and
plays, Brown University Library,
Providence, Rhode Island. Boston, G.
K. Hall, 1972. 13 v.   016.81 75-
184497
  Z1231.P7 B72 MRR Alc (Dk 33)

Harvard University. Library.
Canadian history and literature;
Cambridge; Distributed by the Harvard
University Press, 1968. 411 p.
016.9171 68-22417
  Z1365 .H3 MRR Alc.

McGill University, Montreal. Library.
The Lawrence Lande collection of
Canadiana in the Redpath Library of
McGill University; Montreal,
Lawrence Lande Foundation for
Canadian Historical Research, 1965.
xxxv, 301 p.   65-18258
  Z1365 .M14 MRR Alc.

CANADIAN LITERATURE--BIO-BIBLIOGRAPHY.
Story, Norah. The Oxford companion
to Canadian history and literature.
Toronto, New York [etc.] Oxford
University Press, 1967. xi, 935 p.
[$15.00 Can.]   810/.3 67-31959
  PR9106 .S7 1967 MRR Alc.

Toye, William. Supplement to the
Oxford companion to Canadian history
and literature. Toronto, New York,
Oxford University Press, 1973. v,
318 p. [$9.50] 810/.9 74-180951
  PR9180.2 .T6 1973 MRR Alc.

CANADIAN LITERATURE--DICTIONARIES.
Toye, William. Supplement to the
Oxford companion to Canadian history
and literature. Toronto, New York,
Oxford University Press, 1973. v,
318 p. [$9.50] 810/.9 74-180951
  PR9180.2 .T6 1973 MRR Alc.

**CANADIAN LITERATURE--DICTIONARIES AND
ENCYCLOPEDIAS.**
Story, Norah. The Oxford companion
to Canadian history and literature.
Toronto, New York [etc.] Oxford
University Press, 1967. xi, 935 p.
[$15.00 Can.] 810/.3 67-31959
  PR9106 .S7 1967 MRR Alc.

**CANADIAN LITERATURE--HISTORY AND
CRITICISM.**
Klinck, Carl Frederick, ed. Literary
history of Canada; Toronto]
University of Toronto Press [1965]
xiv, 945 p.   65-1360
  PR9111 .K4 MRR Alc.

Pierce, Lorne Albert, An outline of
Canadian literature (French and
English) Toronto, The Ryerson press,
1927. 6 p. l., 251 p.   28-2647
  PR9112 .P5 MRR Alc.

Toye, William. Supplement to the
Oxford companion to Canadian history
and literature. Toronto, New York,
Oxford University Press, 1973. v,
318 p. [$9.50] 810/.9 74-180951
  PR9180.2 .T6 1973 MRR Alc.

**CANADIAN NEWSPAPERS--BIBLIOGRAPHY--
UNION LISTS.**
American newspapers, 1821-1936; New
York, H. W. Wilson Co., 1937. xvi,
791 p.   37-12783
  Z6945 .A53 MRR Alc.

CANADIAN NEWSPAPERS--DIRECTORIES.
Audit Bureau of Circulations. A.B.C.
blue book, [Chicago?] 071 45-53615

  Z6951 .A67 MRR Alc Latest edition

Ayer directory of publications.
Philadelphia, Ayer Press. 071.3/025
73-640052
  Z6951 .A97 Sci RR Latest edition /
  MRR Ref Desk Latest edition / MRR
  Alc Latest edition

CANADIAN PERIODICALS--BIBLIOGRAPHY.
Goggio, Emilio, A bibliography of
Canadian cultural periodicals
[Toronto] Dept. of Italian, Spanish
and Portuguese, University of
Toronto, 1955. 45 p.   016.051 55-
2983
  Z1369 .G6 MRR Alc.

**CANADIAN PERIODICALS--BIBLIOGRAPHY--
YEARBOOKS.**
The Standard periodical directory. 1-
ed.; 1964/65- New York, Oxbridge
Pub. Co.   016.051 64-7598
  Z6951 .S78 Sci RR Latest edition /
  MRR Ref desk Latest edition

CANADIAN PERIODICALS--DIRECTORIES.
Ayer directory of publications.
Philadelphia, Ayer Press. 071.3/025
73-640052
  Z6951 .A97 Sci RR Latest edition /
  MRR Ref Desk Latest edition / MRR
  Alc Latest edition

Canadian serials directory.
[Toronto, Buffalo] University of
Toronto Press. 016.051 73-643405
  Z6954.C2 C23 MRR Alc Latest
  edition

Directory of Canadian scientific and
technical periodicals. 1961-
Ottawa, National Research Council.
016.505 61-2342
  Z7403 .D5 MRR Alc Latest edition

CANADIAN PERIODICALS--INDEXES.
Canadian periodical index. 1938-May
1947. Toronto, Public Libraries
Branch, Ontario Department of
Education. 40-17273
  A13 .C262 MRR Alc Full set

Canadian periodical index. v. 1-
Jan. 1948- Ottawa. 49-2133
  AI3 .C242 MRR Alc Full set

CANADIAN POETRY.
Garvin, John William, ed. Canadian
poets, Toronto, McClelland &
Stewart, Limited [c1926] xi, 536 p.,
1 l.   27-26597
  PR9258 .G3 1926 MRR Alc.

Smith, Arthur James Marshall, ed.
The book of Canadian poetry, 3d ed.,
rev. and enl. Toronto, W. J. Gage
[c1957] xxv, 532 p.   811.082 59-
20696
  PR9250 .S58 1957 MRR Alc.

CANADIAN TECHNICAL ASSISTANCE
see Technical assistance, Canadian

**CANAL ZONE--DESCRIPTION AND TRAVEL--
GUIDE-BOOKS.**
Aspinall, Algernon Edward, Sir, The
pocket guide to the West Indies and
British Guiana, British Honduras,
Bermuda, the Spanish Main, Surinam,
the Panama Canal. [10th ed.] rev.
London, Methuen [1960] xx, 474 p.
917.29 61-19408
  F1609 .A84 1960 MRR Alc.

CANIDAE.
see also Dogs

**CANNING AND PRESERVING--INDUSTRY AND
TRADE--UNITED STATES--PERIODICALS.**
The Almanac of the canning, freezing,
preserving industries. Westminster,
Md., E. E. Judge. 338.4/7/6640280973
72-622383
  TX599 .C4 MRR Alc Latest edition

CANON LAW--DICTIONARIES.
Dictionnaire de droit canonique,
Paris, Letouzey et Ané, 1935- v.
25-20238
  BX1936 .D5 MRR Alc.

CANON LAW--DICTIONARIES--LATIN.
Palazzini, Pietro, Dictionarium
morale et canonicum. Romae, Officium
Libri Catholici, 1962-68. 4 v.   63-
34193
  BX1757 .A2P3 MRR Alc.

CANT--DICTIONARIES.
Dictionary of American underworld
lingo. New York, Twayne Publishers
[1950] 327 p.   427.9 50-58288
  PE3726 .D5 MRR Alc.

Tempest, Paul. Lag's lexicon;
London, Routledge & K. Paul [1950]
viii, 233 p.   427.09 51-5071
  PE3726 .T4 MRR Alc.

CANTERBURY, ENG.--DIRECTORIES.
Kelly's directory of Canterbury and
neighbourhood. Kingston upon Thames,
Surrey [etc.] Kelly's Directories
Limited 53-28329
  DA690.C3 K4 MRR Alc Latest edition

CANTERBURY, N.Z.--COMMERCE--DIRECTORIES.
Universal business directory for
Canterbury Province. Auckland,
Universal Business Directories. 52-
38736
  HF5299 .C35 MRR Alc Latest edition

CANVAS EMBROIDERY.
Lent, D. Geneva, Needle point as a
hobby. New York, London, Harper &
brothers, 1942. xiii p., 1 l., 180
p.   746 42-13832
  TT770 .L4 MRR Alc.

CAPE TOWN--DIRECTORIES.
Cape times Cape peninsula directory.
Cape Town, Cape & Transvaal Printers
[etc.] 53-30581
  DT848.C5 C285 MRR Alc Latest
  edition

CAPE VERDE ISLANDS--GAZETTEERS.
United States. Office of Geography.
Portugal and the Cape Verde Islands;
official standard names approved by
the United States Board on Geographic
Names. Washington, U.S. Govt. Print.
Off., 1961. v, 321 p.   914.69 61-
61738
  DP514 .U6 MRR Alc.

CAPITAL.
see also Capitalists and financiers

see also Saving and investment

United Nations. Statistical Office.
Yearbook of national accounts
statistics. 1957- New York. 58-
3719
  HC79.I5 U53 MRR Ref Desk Latest
  edition / MRR Alc Latest edition

CAPITAL--UNITED STATES--DIRECTORIES.
Rubel, Stanley M. Guide to venture
capital sources. 3d ed. [Chicago]
Capital Pub. Corp. [1974] 334 p.
332.1/025/73 74-75808
  HG65 .R8 1974 MRR Alc.

CAPITAL AND LABOR
see Industrial relations

CAPITAL EXPORTS
see Investments, Foreign

CAPITAL INVESTMENTS--UNITED STATES.
Venture capital. v. 1- 1970- [New
York, Technimetrics, inc.]
332.1/025/73 74-20999
  HG65 .V4 MRR Alc Latest edition

CAPITAL PUNISHMENT--BIBLIOGRAPHY.
United States. Library of Congress.
Division of bibliography. ... Select
list of references on capital
punishment. Washington, Govt. print.
off., 1912. 1 p. l., 45 p.   12-
35004
  Z663.28 .S359 MRR Alc.

CAPITAL PUNISHMENT--HISTORY.
Pritchard, John Laurence, A history
of capital punishment New York,
Citadel Press [1960] 230 p.   343.23
60-13927
  HV8694 .P7 1960 MRR Alc.

**CAPITAL PUNISHMENT--GREAT BRITAIN--
HISTORY.**
Pritchard, John Laurence, A history
of capital punishment New York,
Citadel Press [1960] 230 p.   343.23
60-13927
  HV8694 .P7 1960 MRR Alc.

**CAPITALISTS AND FINANCIERS--GREAT
BRITAIN--BIOGRAPHY.**
Who's who in British finance. 1972-
New York. R. R. Bowker Co.
332/.092/2 [B] 72-624453
  HG71 .W44 MRR Biog Latest edition

**CAPITALISTS AND FINANCIERS--ITALY--
DIRECTORIES.**
Il Chi e? nella finanza italiana.
1955- Milano, Casa Editrice Nuova
Mercurio, [etc.] 56-33152
  HG186.I8 C47 MRR Alc Latest
  edition

CAPITALISTS AND FINANCIERS--PITTSBURGH.
Official directors register of
Pittsburgh. 1st- annual ed.; 1935-
Pittsburgh, Pa., Directory Pub. Co.
[etc.]   332.0974886 36-387
   HG4058 .P64 MRR Alc Latest edition

**CAPITALISTS AND FINANCIERS--UNITED
STATES.**
Who's who in finance and industry.
17th- ed.; 1972/73- Chicago,
Marquis Who's Who. 338/.00922 [B]
70-616550
   HF3023.A2 W5 MRR Biog Latest
      edition

CAPITALIZATION (FINANCE)
see Securities

CAPITALS (CITIES)
Pollock, Paul W. The capital cities
of the United States. Phoenix,
Ariz., c1960. 206 p. 917.3 61-
22915
   E159 .P6 MRR Alc.

**CAPITALS (CITIES)--ADDRESSES, ESSAYS,
LECTURES.**
Rowat, Donald Cameron. The
government of federal capitals.
[Toronto] University of Toronto Press
[1973] xv, 377 p. [$15.00] 320.3
72-185733
   JF1900 .R68 MRR Alc.

CAPITOLS.
Daniel, Jean Houston. Executive
mansions and capitols of America.
Waukesha, Wis., Country Beautiful;
distributed by Putnam, New York
[1969] 290 p. [25.00] 725/.1 71-
77604
   E159 .D3 MRR Alc.

Franzen, Marilyn D. Capitol
capsules; Pierpont, S.D., Rushmore,
inc., 1964. 208 p. 973 64-2446
   E159 .F7 MRR Alc.

Lahde, Clarence William. Our
fourteen national capitols.
[Washington, 1952] 1 v. (unpaged)
917.3 53-15947
   E179 .L2 MRR Alc.

Pollock, Paul W. The capital cities
of the United States. Phoenix,
Ariz., c1960. 206 p. 917.3 61-
22915
   E159 .P6 MRR Alc.

Shankle, George Earlie. State names,
flags, seals, songs, birds, flowers,
and other symbols; Rev. ed. New
York, H. W. Wilson Co., 1941 [i.e.
1951, c1938] 524 p. 929.4 917.3*
52-52807
   E155 .S43 1951 MRR Alc.

CARBON.
see also Coal

CARD SYSTEM IN BUSINESS.
see also Files and filing (Documents)

CARDIAC DISEASES
see Heart--Diseases

CARDIOVASCULAR SYSTEM.
see also Heart

CARDIOVASCULAR SYSTEM--DISEASES.
Gould, Sylvester Emanuel, ed.
Pathology of the heart and blood
vessels; 3d ed. Springfield, Ill.,
Thomas [1968] xx, 1198 p. 616.1
67-16108
   RC681 .G68 1968 MRR Alc.

CARDS.
Foster, Robert Frederick. Foster's
complete Hoyle; Rev. and enl.
Philadelphia, Lippincott [1963]
xxiv, 697 p. 795 75-19113
   GV1243 .F77 1963 MRR Alc.

Frey, Richard L., ed. The new
complete Hoyle; [Rev. ed.] Garden
City, N.Y., Garden City Books [1956]
740 p. 795 55-11330
   GV1243 .F85 1956 MRR Alc.

Goren, Charles Henry. Goren's Hoyle
encyclopedia of games; New York,
Greystone Press [1961] 656 p.
795.03 61-7483
   GV1243 .G65 1961 MRR Alc.

Hervey, George F. The Hamlyn
illustrated book of card games
London, New York, Hamlyn [1973] 240
p. 785.4 74-160476
   GV1243 .H47 1973b MRR Alc.

Scarne, John. Scarne on cards.
Updated enl. ed. New York, Crown
Publishers [1974] viii, 535 p.
[$9.95] 795.4 73-91527
   GV1247 .S37 1974 MRR Alc.

Scarne, John. Scarne's encyclopedia
of games. [1st ed.] New York,
Harper & Row [1973] xii, 628 p.
[$13.95] 795/.03 72-79681
   GV1229 .S32 MRR Alc.

United States Playing Card Company.
The official rules of card games.
Cincinnati. 99-1251
   Began publication in 1887.
   GV1243 .U56 MRR Alc Latest edition

CARDS--COLLECTORS AND COLLECTING.
Burdick, Jefferson R. The American
card catalog; East Stroudsburg? Pa.,
1960] 240 p. 741.67 60-31578
   NC1280 .B87 1960 MRR Alc.

CARDS--DICTIONARIES.
Gibson, Walter Brown. Hoyle's modern
encyclopedia of card games; [1st
ed.] Garden City, N.Y., Dolphin
Books [1974] 398 p. [$3.95] 795.4
73-163085
   GV1243 .G49 MRR Alc.

CARDSHARPING.
Scarne, John. Scarne on cards.
Updated enl. ed. New York, Crown
Publishers [1974] viii, 535 p.
[$9.95] 795.4 73-91527
   GV1247 .S37 1974 MRR Alc.

CARE OF THE SICK.
see also Hospitals

   see also Nurses and nursing

CAREERS
see Vocational guidance

CARIBBEAN AREA.
Clark, Sydney Aylmer, All the best
in the Caribbean, New York, Dodd,
Mead [1969] xii, 461 p. [6.95]
917.29 70-76837
   F2171.2 .C55 1969 MRR Alc.

Véliz, Claudio. Latin America and
the Caribbean; New York, Praeger
[1968] xxiv, 840 p. 918/.03 68-
14143
   F1408 .V43 MRR Alc.

The West Indies and Caribbean year
book. 1st- year; 1926/27- London
[etc.] T. Skinner [etc.] 917.29 27-
21166
   F2131 .W47 MRR Alc Latest edition

CARIBBEAN AREA--BIBLIOGRAPHY.
Bayitch, S. A. Latin America and the
Caribbean; Coral Gables, Fla.,
University of Miami Press, 1967.
xxviii, 943 p. 016.918/03 67-28900

   Z1601 .B35 MRR Alc.

Comitas, Lambros. Caribbeana 1900-
1965, a topical bibliography.
Seattle, Published for Research
Institute for the Study of Man [by]
University of Washington Press [1968]
L, 909 p. 016.91729/03/5 68-14239

   Z1501 .C6 MRR Alc.

Mitchell, Harold Paton, Sir, bart.,
Caribbean patterns; 2d ed. New
York, Wiley [1972] xix, 583 p.
330.9/729/05 72-7741
   HC155 .M5 1972 MRR Alc.

United States. Dept. of the Army.
Latin America and the Caribbean;
Washington; [For sale by the Supt. of
Docs.], U.S. Govt. Print. Off.] 1969.
vii, 319 p. 016.918 76-603569
   Z1601 .U63 MRR Alc.

CARIBBEAN AREA--BIOGRAPHY.
The Caribbean who, what, why. 1st-
ed.; 1955/56- [n.p.] L. S. Smith.
972.9 56-4669
   F2131 .B85 MRR Biog Latest edition

Dictionary of Latin American and
Caribbean biography. 2d ed. London,
Melrose Press, 1971. 458 p. [£8.50
($20.00 U.S.)] 920.08 75-28705
   F1407 .D5 1971 MRR Biog.

Personalities Caribbean. Kingston,
Jamaica, Personalities Ltd.
920/.0729 72-62646
   F2175 .P4 MRR Biog Latest edition

**CARIBBEAN AREA--COMMERCIAL POLICY--
HANDBOOKS, MANUALS, ETC.**
Jonnard, Claude M. Caribbean
investment handbook Park Ridge,
N.J., Noyes Data Corporation, 1974.
xii, 306 p. [$24.00]
332.6/73/09729 74-75903
   HG5242 .J66 MRR Alc.

**CARIBBEAN AREA--DESCRIPTION AND TRAVEL--
1951- --GUIDE-BOOKS.**
Townsend, Derek. Caribbean guide;
London, Allen & Unwin, 1970. 232 p.
[48/-] 917.29/04/5 72-531098
   F2171.2 .T6 MRR Alc.

**CARIBBEAN AREA--DESCRIPTION AND TRAVEL--
GUIDE-BOOKS.**
Edson, Wesley. Terry's guide to the
Caribbean. [1st ed.] Garden City,
N.Y., Doubleday, 1970. xvii, 668 p.
[8.95] 917.29/04/5 73-78737
   F1609 .D36 1970 MRR Alc.

Fodor's guide to the Caribbean,
Bahamas and Bermuda; 1960- New
York, D. McKay. 917.29 60-908
   F2171 .F65 MRR Alc Latest edition

CARIBBEAN AREA--ECONOMIC CONDITIONS.
Jonnard, Claude M. Caribbean
investment handbook Park Ridge,
N.J., Noyes Data Corporation, 1974.
xii, 306 p. [$24.00]
332.6/73/09729 74-75903
   HG5242 .J66 MRR Alc.

Mitchell, Harold Paton, Sir, bart.,
Caribbean patterns; 2d ed. New
York, Wiley [1972] xix, 583 p.
330.9/729/05 72-7741
   HC155 .M5 1972 MRR Alc.

**CARIBBEAN AREA--LEARNED INSTITUTIONS
AND SOCIETIES--DIRECTORIES.**
Vigo-Cepeda, Luisa C. Directory of
institutes and centers devoted to the
social and economic research in the
Caribbean. Rio Piedras, Institute of
Caribbean Studies, University of
Puerto Rico, 1968. 1 v. (various
pagings) 300/.72/0729 74-627100
   H62 .V47 MRR Alc.

CARIBBEAN AREA--POLITICS AND GOVERNMENT.
Mitchell, Harold Paton, Sir, bart.,
Caribbean patterns; 2d ed. New
York, Wiley [1972] xix, 583 p.
330.9/729/05 72-7741
   HC155 .M5 1972 MRR Alc.

CARICATURE.
see also Wit and humor

CARICATURE--UNITED STATES--HISTORY.
Becker, Stephen D., Comic art in
America; New York, Simon and
Schuster, 1959. xi, 387 p.
741.5973 59-13140
   NC1420 .B4 MRR Alc.

**CARICATURES AND CARTOONS--MARKETING--
DIRECTORIES.**
Hagen, Natalie, comp. Cartoonist's
market. Cincinnati, Writer's digest
[1969] 80 p. [2.50] 741.5/025/73
70-76438
   NC1320 .H23 MRR Alc.

CARICATURES AND CARTOONS--UNITED STATES.
Hohenberg, John, ed. The Pulitzer
prize story; New York, Columbia
University Press, 1959. 375 p.
070.431 59-7702
   PS647.N4 H6 MRR Alc.

**CARICATURES AND CARTOONS--UNITED STATES-
-HISTORY.**
Becker, Stephen D., Comic art in
America; New York, Simon and
Schuster, 1959. xi, 387 p.
741.5973 59-13140
   NC1420 .B4 MRR Alc.

CARINTHIA--COMMERCE--DIRECTORIES.
Herold Adressbuch von Karnten und
Osttirol fur Industrie, Handel,
Gewerbe. Wien, Herold. 72-622315
   HF3549.C45 A45 MRR Alc Latest
      edition

CARINTHIA--DIRECTORIES.
Karntner Amts-und Adressbuch mit
Osttirol. Klagenfurt, F. Kleinmayr
[etc.] 914.36/6/0025 74-642466
   DB284.7 K33 MRR Alc Latest edition

**CARNEGIE, ANDREW, 1835-1919--
MANUSCRIPTS.**
United States. Library of Congress.
Manuscript Division. Andrew
Carnegie: a register of his papers in
the Library of Congress. Washington,
1964. 21 p. 64-65522
   Z663.34 .C32 MRR Alc.

CAROLINA.
Salley, Alexander Samuel, ed.
Narratives of early Carolina, 1650-
1708, New York, C. Scribner's sons,
1911. xi p., 2 l., 3-388 p. 11-
9548
   E187.07 S3 MRR Alc.

CAROLS.
The Oxford book of carols. London,
Oxford university press, H. Milford
[1931] xxix, 491, [1] p. 783.65
33-29080
   M2065 .O9 1931 MRR Alc.

CARPENTRY.
see also Woodwork

Mix, Floyd M., ed. Practical
carpentry. Chicago, Goodheart-
Willcox Co. [c1960] 448 p. 694 60-
6021
   TH5606 .M59 1960 MRR Alc.

Ulrey, Harry F. Carpenters and
builders library. [3d ed.]
Indianapolis, T. Audel [1970] 4 v.
694/.02/02 74-99760
   TH5604 .U44 1970 MRR Alc.

Wagner, Willis H. Modern carpentry;
Homewood, Ill., Goodheart-Wilcox
[1969] 480 p. 694 78-95711
   TH5604 .W34 MRR Alc.

CARPETBAG RULE
see Reconstruction

CARPETS.
Carpet annual. 1935- London,
Haymarket Pub. Ltd. [etc.] 677.64
35-15655
TS1772 .C33 MRR Alc Latest edition

CARRIAGES AND CARTS--HISTORY.
Collins, Herbert Ridgeway.
Presidents on wheels. Washington,
Acropolis Books [1971] 224 p.
[$15.00] 629.2/0973 75-146442
TL23 .C597 MRR Alc.

CARRIERS.
see also Freight and freightage

CARRIERS, AIRCRAFT
see Aircraft carriers

CARS (AUTOMOBILES)
see Automobiles

CARTOGRAPHERS.
Bonacker, Wilhelm. Kartenmacher
aller Länder und Zeiten. Stuttgart,
H. Hiersemann, 1966. 243 p.
[DM135.00] 016.526 67-89793
Z6021 .B69 MRR Alc.

CARTOGRAPHERS--DICTIONARIES.
Lister, Raymond. How to identify old
maps and globes, London, G. Bell
[1965] 256 p. 65-3799
GA201 .L56 1965a MRR Alc.

CARTOGRAPHY--BIBLIOGRAPHY.
United States. Library of Congress.
Map Division. A list of maps of
America in the Library of Congress.
New York, B. Franklin [1967?] 2 v.
in 1 (1137 p.) 016.91273 67-7211
Z663.35 .L55 1967 MRR Alc.

CARTOGRAPHY--BIBLIOGRAPHY--CATALOGS.
United States. Library of Congress.
Geography and Map Division. The
bibliography of cartography. Boston,
G. K. Hall, 1973. 5 v. 016.526 73-
12977
Z6028 .U49 1973 MRR Alc (Dk 33)

CARTOGRAPHY--DICTIONARIES.
United States. Army Topographic
Command. Glossary of mapping,
charting, and geodetic terms. 2d ed.
Washington, 1969. v, 281 p.
526.8/03 73-604750
GA102 .U53 1969 MRR Alc.

CARTOGRAPHY--HISTORY.
Bagrow, Leo. History of cartography.
London, C. A. Watts, 1964. 312 p.
526.809 64-56112
GA201 .E313 1964a MRR Alc.

Lister, Raymond. How to identify old
maps and globes, London, G. Bell
[1965] 256 p. 65-3799
GA201 .L56 1965a MRR Alc.

CARTOGRAPHY--HISTORY--BIBLIOGRAPHY.
Bonacker, Wilhelm. Kartenmacher
aller Länder und Zeiten. Stuttgart,
H. Hiersemann, 1966. 243 p.
[DM135.00] 016.526 67-89793
Z6021 .B69 MRR Alc.

Ristow, Walter William. Guide to the
history of cartography; Washington,
Geography and Map Division, Library
of Congress [for sale by the Supt. of
Docs., U.S. Govt. Print. Off.] 1973.
96 p. [$0.75] 016.5269/8 73-9776

Z663.35 .G82 MRR Alc.

United States. Library of Congress.
Map Division. A guide to historical
cartography; 2d ed., rev.
Washington, 1960. 18 p. 016.52698
60-60086
Z663.35 .G8 1960 MRR Alc.

CARTOGRAPHY--PERIODICALS--INDEXES.
United States. Library of Congress.
Geography and Map Division. The
bibliography of cartography. Boston,
G. K. Hall, 1973. 5 v. 016.526 73-
12977
Z6028 .U49 1973 MRR Alc (Dk 33)

CARTOGRAPHY--STUDY AND TEACHING.
Greenhood, David. Mapping. Chicago,
University of Chicago Press [1964]
xiii, 289 p. 526.8 63-20905
GA151 .G7 1964 MRR Alc.

CARTOGRAPHY--AMERICA.
Paullin, Charles Oscar, Atlas of the
historical geography of the United
States, [Washington, D.C., New York]
Pub. jointly by Carnegie institution
of Washington and the American
geographical society of New York,
1932. 2 p. l., iii-xv p., 1 l., 162
p., 1 l., 688 maps (part col.) on 166
plates (part double) 911.73 map32-
54
G1201.S1 P3 1932 MRR Alc Atlas.

Winsor, Justin, ed. Narrative and
critical history of America,
Standard library ed. [Boston, New
York, Houghton, Mifflin and company,
1923, c1884-89] 8 v. 23-16194
E18 .W77 MRR Alc.

CARTOGRAPHY--UNITED STATES--
BIBLIOGRAPHY.
Wheat, James Clements. Maps and
charts published in America before
1800; New Haven, Yale University
Press, 1969. xxii, 215 p. [30.00]
016.5268 69-15464
Z6027.A5 W68 MRR Alc.

CARTRIDGES.
Johnson, Melvin Maynard, Ammunition;
New York, W. Morrow and co., 1943.
xii p., 1 l., 374 p. 623.45532 43-
18535
UF740 .J6 MRR Alc.

Logan, Herschel C., Cartridges,
Harrisburg, Pa., Stackpole Co. [1959]
199 p. 623.455 59-2431
UF740 .L6 1959 MRR Alc.

Sharpe, Philip Burdette, The rifle
in America. 4th ed., New York, Funk
& Wagnalls [1958] 833 p. 623.442
58-4456
SK274 .S5 1958 MRR Alc.

Suydam, Charles R. The American
cartridge; Santa Ana, Calif., G. R.
Lawrence [1960] 184 p. 623.455 60-
14975
UF740 .S9 MRR Alc.

CASEY, SILAS, 1841-1913--MANUSCRIPTS.
United States. Library of Congress.
Manuscript Division. Silas Casey,
Stanford Caldwell Hooper; a register
of their papers in the Library of
Congress. Washington, Library of
Congress, 1968. 5, 9 l.
359.3/31/0922 68-61404
Z663.34 .C33 MRR Alc.

CASTILIAN LANGUAGE
see Spanish language

CASTLES--EUROPE.
Long, Robert P. Castle-hotels of
Europe; 4th ed. East Meadow, N.Y.;
distributor: Hastings House, New
York, 1973] 164 p. [$3.95]
647/.944 73-157418
TX907 .L6 1973 MRR Alc.

CASUALTY INSURANCE
see Insurance, Casualty

CAT
see Cats

CATALAN DRAMA--MICROCARD CATALOGS.
Thompson, Lawrence Sidney, A
bibliography of Spanish plays on
microcards; Hamden, Conn., Shoe
String Press, 1968. 490 p. 016.862
68-20280
Z2694.D7 T48 MRR Alc.

CATALAN LANGUAGE.
Entwistle, William James, The
Spanish language, [2d ed.] London,
Faber & Faber [1962] vi, 367 p.
460 63-6431
PC4075 .E5 1962 MRR Alc.

CATALAN LITERATURE--19TH-20TH CENTURIES-
-PHONOTAPE CATALOGS.
United States. Library of Congress.
Latin American, Portuguese, and
Spanish Division. The Archive of
Hispanic Literature on Tape;
Washington, Library of Congress; [for
sale by the Supt. of Docs., U.S.
Govt. Print. Off.] 1974. xii, 516 p.
016.86/008 73-19812
Z663.32 .A7 MRR Alc.

CATALAN LITERATURE--BIBLIOGRAPHY.
Simon Díaz, José. Bibliografía
de literatura hispánica. 2. ed
corr. y aumentada. Madrid, Consejo
Superior de Investigaciones
Científicas, Instituto "Miguel de
Cervantes" de Filología Hispánica,
1960- v. 64-5767
Z2691 .S52 MRR Alc.

CATALOGING.
see also Indexing

American Library Association.
Division of Cataloging and
Classification. Committee on
Descriptive Cataloging. Final report
on the Rules for descriptive
cataloging in the Library of Congress
Washington, Library of Congress,
1948. ii, 34 p. 025.32 48-47254
Z663.74 .R8 1948 MRR Alc.

Cataloging rules of the American
Library Association and the Library
of Congress. Washington, Library of
Congress, 1959. 76 p. 025.32 59-
61211
Z695 .C32 MRR Alc.

Eaton, Thelma, Cataloging and
classification, 3d ed. Champaign,
Ill., Distributed by the Illini Union
Bookstore [1963] 199 p. 025.3 63-
5885
Z695 .E171 1963 MRR Alc.

Mann, Margaret, Introduction to
cataloging and the classification of
books, 2d ed. Chicago, Ill.,
American library association, 1943.
ix, [1], 276 p., 1 l. 025.3 43-
51241
Z695 .M27 1943 MRR Alc.

Tauber, Maurice Falcolm, Cataloging
and classification, New Brunswick,
N.J., Graduate School of Library
Service, Rutgers, the State
University, 1960. 271, 92 p. 025.3
60-7278
Z695 .T25 MRR Alc.

United States. Library of Congress.
Card Division. Handbook of card
distribution. 1st- ed. 1902-
Washington. 025.3 02-21132
Z663.72 .H3 MRR Alc MRR Alc Latest
edition

United States. Library of Congress.
Card division. L.C. printed cards,
how to order and use them, 5th ed.
... Washington, Govt. print. off.,
1941. 38 p. 025.3 42-21943
Z663.72 .P7 1941 MRR Alc.

United States. Library of Congress.
Catalog division. Special rules on
cataloging, to supplement A.L.A.
rules--advance edition. 1-21.
Washington, Govt. print. off., 1906.
26 p. 06-35007
Z663.74.S8 MRR Alc.

United States. Library of Congress.
Descriptive Cataloging Division.
Reglas para la catalogación
descriptiva en The Library of
Congress Washington, 1953. vii, 174
p. 025.32 52-60037
Z663.74 .R815 MRR Alc.

United States. Library of Congress.
Descriptive Cataloging Division.
Regras de catalogaçao descritiva na
Library of Congress Washington,
1956. vii, 174 p. 025.32 56-60034

Z663.74 .R8116 MRR Alc.

United States. Library of Congress.
Descriptive Cataloging Division.
Rules for descriptive cataloging in
the Library of Congress. Prelim. ed.
Washington, U.S. Govt. Print. Off.,
1947. ix, 125 p. 025.3 47-31664
Z663.74 .R8 1947 MRR Alc.

United States. Library of Congress.
Descriptive Cataloging Division.
Rules for descriptive cataloging in
the Library of Congress Washington,
1949. vi, 141 p. 025.32 49-46964

Z695 .U4735 1949 MRR Alc.

United States. Library of Congress.
Descriptive Cataloging Division.
Synoptic table of rules:
[Washington] 1959. iii, 46 p.
025.32 59-64161
Z695 .U4737 MRR Alc.

Wynar, Bohdan S. Introduction to
cataloging and classification 4th
ed. Littleton, Colo., Libraries
Unlimited, 1971. 344 p. 025.3 77-
182404
Z693 .W94 1971 MRR Alc.

CATALOGING--ADDRESSES, ESSAYS, LECTURES.
Lubetzky, Seymour. Cataloging rules
and principles; Washington,
Processing Dept., Library of
Congress, 1953. ix, 65 p. 025.32
53-60029
Z663.74 .C3 MRR Alc.

CATALOGING--BOOKS FOR THE BLIND.
United States. Library of Congress.
Descriptive Cataloging Division.
Rules for descriptive cataloging in
the Library of Congress: books in
raised characters. Prelim. ed.
Washington, 1953. 2 p. 025.34 53-
60014
Z663.74 .R82 MRR Alc.

CATALOGING, COOPERATIVE.
United States. Library of Congress.
Cooperative cataloging and
classification service. Cooperative
work of Card division, Union catalog,
Cooperative cataloging and
classification service and A.L.A.
Cooperative cataloging committee.
Washington, 1938. v p., 26 numb. l.
cd 38-158
Z663.745.C63 MRR Alc.

CATALOGING, COOPERATIVE. (Cont.)
United States. Library of Congress.
Descriptive cataloging division.
Cooperative cataloging manual,
Washington, D.C., U.S. Govt. print.
off., 1944. 2 p. l., 104 p. incl.
forms.   025.3   44-41431
    Z663.745 .C6 MRR Alc.

CATALOGING IN PUBLICATION.
United States. Library of Congress.
Processing Dept. The cataloging-in-
source experiment; Washington,
Library of Congress, 1960. xxiv, 199
p.   025.3   60-60033
    Z663.7 .C38 MRR Alc.

CATALOGING OF EARLY PRINTED BOOKS--
HANDBOOKS, MANUALS, ETC.
Pearce, M. J. A workbook of
analytical & descriptive
bibliography, London, Bingley, 1970.
110 p. [30/-]   025.3/2 70-530364

    Z1001 .P34 1970 MRR Alc.

CATALOGING OF FILMSTRIPS.
United States. Library of Congress.
Descriptive Cataloging Division.
Reglas para la catalogacion
descriptiva en The Library of
Congress; peliculas animadas y
fijas. 2. ed. preliminar.
Washington, 1953. 19 p.   53-60007
    Z663.74 .R815 1953a MRR Alc.

United States. Library of Congress.
Descriptive Cataloging Division.
Regles de cataloguement descriptif
en usage ; The Library of Congress;
2. ed. preliminaire. Washington,
1953. 20 p.   53-60008
    Z663.74 .R813 1953a MRR Alc.

United States. Library of Congress.
Descriptive Cataloging Division.
Rules for descriptive cataloging in
the Library of Congress: motion
pictures and filmstrips. 1st ed.
Washington, 1965. 20 p.   025.3473
65-60011
    Z663.74 .R84 1965 MRR Alc.

CATALOGING OF GOVERNMENT PUBLICATIONS.
Childs, James Bennett. Author entry
for government publications,
Washington, U.S. Govt. print. off.,
1939. 38 p.   025.3 38-26001
    Z663.45 .A85 1939 MRR Alc.

United States. Library of Congress.
Union Catalog Division. United
States author headings, [2d printed
ed.] Ann Arbor, Mich., Edwards
Bros., 1946. 211 p.   025.3 47-5580

    Z663.79 .U5 1946 MRR Alc.

CATALOGING OF MANUSCRIPTS.
United States. Library of Congress.
Descriptive Cataloging Division.
Rules for descriptive cataloging in
the Library of Congress: manuscripts.
Prelim. ed. [Washington] 1954. 10
p.   025.31 55-60033
    Z663.74 .R83 1954 MRR Alc.

United States. Library of Congress.
Marc Development Office.
Manuscripts: a MARC format;
Washington, Library of Congress; for
sale by the Supt. of Docs., U.S.
Govt. Print. Off., 1973. v, 47 p.
[$0.80]   025.3/4/102854 72-13497
    Z663.757 .M36 MRR Alc.

CATALOGING OF MAPS.
Carrington, David K., Data
preparation manual for the conversion
of map cataloging records to machine-
readable form. Washington, Library
of Congress; [for sale by the Supt.
of Docs., U.S. Govt. Print. Off.]
1971. v, 317 p. [$2.75] 025.3/46
79-169093
    Z663.35 .D3 MRR Alc.

United States. Library of Congress.
Information Systems Office. Maps, a
MARC format: Washington; [For sale
by the Supt. of Docs., U.S. Govt.
Print. Off.] 1970. 45 p. [0.50]
526.8/018 77-607327
    Z663.172 .M27 MRR Alc.

CATALOGING OF MASONIC PUBLICATIONS.
United States. Library of Congress.
Catalog division. Guide to the
cataloguing of the serial
publications of societies and
institutions, 2d ed. Reprinted 1938.
Washington, U.S. Govt. print. off.,
1931 [i.e. 1938] x, 128 p.   mrr01-52
    Z663.74 G8 1938 MRR Alc.

CATALOGING OF MOVING-PICTURES.
United States. Library of Congress.
Descriptive Cataloging Division.
Reglas para la catalogacion
descriptiva en The Library of
Congress; peliculas animadas y
fijas. 2. ed. preliminar.
Washington, 1953. 19 p.   53-60007
    Z663.74 .R815 1953a MRR Alc.

United States. Library of Congress.
Descriptive Cataloging Division.
Regles de cataloguement descriptif
en usage § The Library of Congress;
2. ed. preliminaire. Washington,
1953. 20 p.   53-60008
    Z663.74 .R813 1953a MRR Alc.

United States. Library of Congress.
Descriptive Cataloging Division.
Rules for descriptive cataloging in
the Library of Congress: motion
pictures and filmstrips. 1st ed.
Washington, 1965. 20 p.   025.3473
65-60011
    Z663.74 .R84 1965 MRR Alc.

CATALOGING OF MUSIC.
Joint Committee on Music Cataloging.
Code for cataloging music and
phonorecords, Chicago, American
Library Association, 1958. iv, 88 p.
    025.348 57-13397
    ML111 .J6 MRR Alc.

CATALOGING OF NON-BOOK MATERIALS.
United States. Library of Congress.
Marc Development Office. Films: a
MARC format; Washington; [For sale
by the Supt. of Docs., U.S. Govt.
Print. Off.] 1970 [i.e. 1971] 65 p.
[$0.65]   025.3/4/7 77-611336
    Z663.757 .F5 MRR Alc.

CATALOGING OF PHONORECORDS.
Joint Committee on Music Cataloging.
Code for cataloging music and
phonorecords, Chicago, American
Library Association, 1958. iv, 88 p.
    025.348 57-13397
    ML111 .J6 MRR Alc.

United States. Library of Congress.
Descriptive Cataloging Division.
Rules for descriptive cataloging in
the Library of Congress:
phonorecords. 2d prelim. ed.
Washington, 1964. vi, 11 p.   63-
65387
    Z663.74 .R85 1964 MRR Alc.

CATALOGING OF PICTURES.
United States. Library of Congress.
Descriptive Cataloging Division.
Rules for descriptive cataloging in
the Library of Congress: pictures,
designs, and other two-dimensional
representations. Prelim. ed.
Washington, 1959. vii, 16 p.
025.347 59-60080
    Z663.74 .R86 1959 MRR Alc.

CATALOGING OF SERIAL PUBLICATIONS.
United States. Library of Congress.
Catalog division. Guide to the
cataloguing of periodicals. 3d ed.,
reprinted 1938. Washington, U.S.
Govt. print. off., 1925 [i.e. 1938]
3 p. l., 5-23 p.   025.3 44-49586
    Z663.74 .G78 1938 MRR Alc.

United States. Library of Congress.
Catalog division. Guide to the
cataloguing of the serial
publications of societies and
institutions, 2d ed. Reprinted 1938.
Washington, U.S. Govt. print. off.,
1931 [i.e. 1938] x, 128 p.   mrr01-52
    Z663.74 G8 1938 MRR Alc.

United States. Library of Congress.
Information Systems Office. Serials:
a MARC format. Preliminary ed.
Washington, Library of Congress; [for
sale by the Supt. of Docs., U.S.
Govt. Print. Off.] 1970. 72 p.
[$0.70]   025.3/4/3 73-606842
    Z663.172 .S4 MRR Alc.

United States. Library of Congress.
Marc Development Office. Serials: a
MARC format: 2d ed. Washington,
Library of Congress; [for sale by the
Supt. of Docs., U.S. Govt. Print.
Off.] 1974. 104 p.   025.3/4/3 74-
7176
    Z663.757 .S47 1974 MRR Alc.

United States. Library of Congress.
Serial Record Division. The
cataloging of serials at the Library
of Congress; Washington] 1956. 29
p.   025.3431 57-60026
    Z663.77 .C35 MRR Alc.

United States. Library of Congress.
Serial Record Division. Certain
proposals of numerical systems for
the control of serials evaluated for
their application at the Library of
Congress; [Washington] 1954. 22 p.
025.343 56-60282
    Z663.77 .C4 MRR Alc.

CATALOGING OF SOCIETY PUBLICATIONS.
United States. Library of Congress.
Catalog division. Guide to the
cataloguing of the serial
publications of societies and
institutions, 2d ed. Reprinted 1938.
Washington, U.S. Govt. print. off.,
1931 [i.e. 1938] x, 128 p.   mrr01-52
    Z663.74 G8 1938 MRR Alc.

CATALOGS--BIBLIOGRAPHY.
Tanselle, George Thomas, Guide to
the study of United States imprints
Cambridge, Mass., Belknap Press of
Harvard University Press, 1971. 2 v.
(lxiv, 1050 p.)   016.015/73 79-
143232
    Z1215.A2 T35 MRR Alc.

CATALOGS, BOOK.
Collison, Robert Lewis. Published
library catalogues: London, Mansell
Information Publishing, 1973. viii,
184 p. [£3.50]   016.01 74-177155
    Z695.87 .C6 MRR Alc.

Kingery, Robert Ernest, ed. Book
catalogs. New York, Scarecrow Press,
1963. viii, 330 p.   025.3 63-7470

    Z695.87 .K5 MRR Alc.

United States. Library of Congress.
Library of Congress catalogs in book
form and related publications.
[Washington, 1971] [21] p.
015/.753 72-612348
    Z663 .L452 MRR Alc.

CATALOGS, BOOK--BIBLIOGRAPHY.
Collison, Robert Lewis. Published
library catalogues: London, Mansell
Information Publishing, 1973. viii,
184 p. [£3.50]   016.01 74-177155
    Z695.87 .C6 MRR Alc.

Taylor, Archer, Book catalogues:
their varieties and uses. Chicago,
Newberry Library, 1957. xii, 284 p.
010 56-12568
    Z1001 .T34 MRR Alc.

CATALOGS, BOOKSELLERS'--INDEXES.
Bookman's price index. v. 1- 1964-
Detroit, Gale Research Co. 018 64-
8723
    Z1000 .B74 MRR Alc Full set

CATALOGS, BOOKSELLERS'--GERMANY
(DEMOCRATIC REPUBLIC, 1949-)
Leipziger Kommissions- und
Grossbuchhandel. L K G Lagerkatalog.
1962- [Leipzig] 72-626453
    Z1036 .L5 MRR Alc Latest edition

CATALOGS, BOOKSELLERS'--GREAT BRITAIN--
BIBLIOGRAPHY.
Growoll, Adolf, Three centuries of
English booktrade bibliography; New
York; Pub. for the Dibdin club, by M.
L. Greenhalgh, 1903. xv p., 1 l.,
195 p., 1 l. incl 6 facsim. 03-
13955
    Z2001.A1 G8 MRR Alc.

CATALOGS, BOOKSELLERS'--UNITED STATES--
BIBLIOGRAPHY.
McKay, George Leslie, American book
auction catalogues, 1713-1934: New
York, The New York public library,
1937. xxxii, 540 p.   016.0173 37-
33888
    Z999 .A1M2 MRR Alc.

CATALOGS, CARD.
United States. Library of Congress.
Card Division. Handbook of card
distribution. 1st- ed. 1902-
Washington.   025.3 02-21132
    Z663.72 .H3 MRR Alc MRR Alc Latest
edition

United States. Library of Congress.
Card division. L.C. printed cards,
how to order and use them, 5th ed.
... Washington, Govt. print. off.,
1941. 38 p.   025.3 42-21943
    Z663.72 .P7 1941 MRR Alc.

United States. Library of Congress.
Processing Dept. The card catalogs
of the Library of Congress;
Washington, 1955. v, 30 p.
027.5753 55-60020
    Z663.7 .C3 MRR Alc.

CATALOGS, CLASSIFIED (DEWEY DECIMAL)
American book publishing record. BPR
annual cumulative. 1960/64- New
York, Bowker. 015/.73 66-19741
    Z1201 .A52 MRR Ref Desk Full set

The British national bibliography
cumulated subject catalogue 1951/54-
London, Council of the British
National Bibliography. 015.42 59-
246
    Z2001 .B752 MRR Alc Full set

Harvard University. Library. Lamont
Library. Catalogue of the Lamont
Library, Harvard College. Cambridge,
Harvard University Press, 1953. ix,
562 p.   017.1 016* 53-12114
    Z881 .H348 MRR Alc (DK 33.)

Library Association. Library.
Catalogue. London, 1958. vii, 519
p.   017.1 58-40138
    Z921 .L323 MRR Alc.

New serial titles, classed subject
arrangement. Jan./May 1955-
[Washington, Library of Congress]
016.05 55-60037
    Z663.7 .A48 MRR Alc MRR Alc Full
set

CATALOGS, CLASSIFIED (DEWEY (Cont.)
Public library catalog. 6th ed.,
1973. New York, H. W. Wilson Co.,
1974. x, 1543 p.   011 74-656
  Z1035 .S83 1974 MRR Alc.

Senior high school library catalog.
10th ed. New York, H. W. Wilson Co.,
1972. xii, 1214 p.   028.52 72-3819

  Z1035 .S42 1972 MRR Alc.

CATALOGS, COMMERICAL.
Hart, Harold H., Catalog of the
unusual. New York, Hart Pub. Co.
[1973] 351 p. [$6.95]   380.1/025
73-80023
  HF1041 .H297 MRR Alc.

CATALOGS, COMMERCIAL--BIBLIOGRAPHY.
Romaine, Lawrence B., A guide to
American trade catalogs, 1744-1900.
New York, R. R. Bowker, 1960. xxiii,
422 p.   016.65085 60-16893
  Z7164.C8 R6 MRR Alc.

CATALOGS, DICTIONARY.
The American catalogue ... New York,
1941. 8 v. in 13.   015.73 a 42-
2938
  Z1215 .A52 MRR Ref Desk.

CATALOGS, LIBRARY
  see Library catalogs

CATALOGS, PUBLISHERS'--GREAT BRITAIN.
British books in print. 1874-
London, Whitaker; New York, Bowker
[etc.]   02-7496
  Z2001 .R33 MRR Ref Desk Partial
  set

CATALOGS, PUBLISHERS'--ITALY.
Associazione italiana editori.
Catalogo collettivo della libreria
italiana, 1959. Milano, Società
anonima per pubblicazioni
bibliografico-editoriali [1959?] 3
v. (11, dxxvii, 62, 3105 p.)   62-
45507
  Z2341 .A83 1959 MRR Alc.

CATALOGS, PUBLISHERS'--UNITED STATES.
The A B bookman's yearbook. 1954-
Newark, N.J.   010.58 54-1676
  Z990 .A18 MRR Alc Latest edition

The American catalogue ... New York,
1941. 8 v. in 13.   015.73 a 42-
2938
  Z1215 .A52 MRR Ref Desk.

Books in print; 1948- New York, R.
R. Bowker Co.   015.73 74-643574
  Z1215 .P972 Sci RR Latest edition
  / MRR Alc Latest edition / MRR
  Ref Desk Latest edition

CATALOG'S, PUBLISHERS'--UNITED STATES.
Books in print supplement; authors,
titles, subjects. 1972/73- New
York, R. R. Bowker Co.   015.73 74-
643521
  Z1215 .P974 MRR Alc Latest edition
  / MRR Ref Desk Latest edition

CATALOGS, PUBLISHERS'--UNITED STATES.
The Publishers' trade list annual.
[1st]- 1873- New York, R. R.
Bowker Co., Office of the Publisher's
Weekly [etc.]   015.73 04-12648
  Z1215 .P97 MRR Ref Desk Latest
  edition / Sci RR Latest edition

Subject guide to Books in print;
1957- New York, R. R. Bowker Co.
015.73 74-643573
  Z1215 .P973 MRR Alc Latest edition
  / MRR Ref Desk Latest edition /
  Sci RR Latest edition

CATALOGS, SUBJECT.
American book publishing record. BPR
annual cumulative. 1960/64- New
York, Bowker. 015/.73 66-19741
  Z1201 .A52 MRR Ref Desk Full set

British Museum. Dept. of Printed
Books. Subject index of the modern
works added to the British museum
library. [1st]- 1901/05- London,
Trustees of the British Museum.
019.1 07-10319
  Z1035 .B8613 MRR Alc (Dk33) Full
  set

Cambridge. University. Library.
Subject guide to class 'Ref' (current
reference books) in the University
Library Cambridge. Cambridge,
Cambridge University Library, 1968.
[6], 106 leaves. [5/-] 011/.02 72-
354270
  Z1035.1 .C35 MRR Alc.

Children's books in print. 1969-
New York, R. R. Bowker Co. 028.52
70-101705
  Z1037.A1 C482 MRR Alc Latest
  edition

Eakin, Mary K. Subject index to
books for intermediate grades. 3d
ed. Chicago, American Library
Association, 1963. vi, 308 p.
028.52 63-12951
  Z1037 .E16 1963 MRR Alc.

The English catalogue of books
London, Published for the Publishers'
Circular by S. Low, Marston, 1914.
655 p.   52-45201
  Z2001 .E517 MRR Alc.

Harvard University. Library. Lamont
Library. Catalogue of the Lamont
Library, Harvard College, Cambridge,
Harvard University Press, 1953. ix,
562 p.   017.1 016* 53-12114
  Z881 .H348 MRR Alc (DK 33).

Library Association. Library.
Catalogue. London, 1958. vii, 519
p.   017.1 58-40138
  Z921 .L323 MRR Alc.

A London bibliography of the social
sciences. v. 1- 1929- London,
Mansell Information/Publishing Ltd.
[etc.] 016.3 31-9970
  Z7161 .L84 MRR Alc Full set

Paperbound book guide for colleges.
New York, R. R. Bowker. 016 60-3050

  Z1033.P3 P3 MRR Alc Latest
  editions

Peabody institute, Baltimore.
Library. Catalogue of the library of
the Peabody institute of the city of
Baltimore ... Baltimore [I.
Friedenwald] 1883-92. 5 v. 02-5028

  Z881 .B2 MRR Alc (Dk33)

Peabody institute, Baltimore.
Library. Second catalogue of the
library of the Peabody institute of
the city of Baltimore, Baltimore,
1896-1905. 8 v.   02-5029
  Z881 .B21 MRR Alc (Dk33)

Peddie, Robert Alexander, Subject
index of books published up to and
including 1880. London, Grafton,
1948. vii, 872 p.   016 a 48-8762
  Z1035 .P38 MRR Alc.

Peddie, Robert Alexander, Subject
index of books published up to and
including 1880, A-Z, London, H.
Pordes, 1962. xv, 745 p.   64-46978

  Z1035 .P37 1962 MRR Alc.

Pirie, James W., Books for junior
college libraries; Chicago, American
Library Association, 1969. x, 452 p.
[35.00] 011 76-82133
  Z1035 .P448 MRR Alc.

Taylor, Archer, General subject-
indexes since 1548. Philadelphia,
University of Pennsylvania Press
[c1966] 336 p.   017 66-10221
  Z695 .T28 MRR Alc.

United States. Library of Congress.
Library of Congress catalog--Books:
subjects: Jan./Mar. 1950-
Washington.   017.1 50-60682
  Z663.7 .L52 MRR Alc (Dk 33) MRR
  Alc (Dk 33) Full set

The United States catalog; 3d ed.
Minneapolis, New York, The H. W.
Wilson company, 1912. 3 p. l., 2837
p.   12-35572
  Z1215 .U6 1912a MRR Ref Desk (Alc.
  6)

Watt, Robert, Bibliotheca
Britannica; New York, B. Franklin
[1965] 4 v. 011 77-6557
  Z2001 .W34 1965 MRR Alc.

CATALOGS, UNION.
Adams, Herbert Mayow, Catalogue of
books printed on the continent of
Europe, 1501-1600, in Cambridge
libraries; London, Cambridge U.P.,
1967. 2 v. [25/-/-] 018/.5 66-
10015
  Z1014 .A38 MRR Alc.

Bishop, William Warner, A checklist
of American copies "Short-title
catalogue" books. 2d ed. Ann Arbor,
University of Michigan Press, 1950.
xi, 203 p.   015.42 50-8677
  Z2002.P772 B5 1950 MRR Alc.

The British union-catalogue of early
music printed before the year 1801;
London, Butterworths Scientific
Publications, 1957. 2 v. (xx, 1178
p.) 781.97 58-526
  ML116 .B7 MRR Alc.

Brummel, Leendert, Guide des
catalogues collectifs et du prêt
international La Haye, M. Nijhoff,
1961. 89 p.   64-43892
  Z695.83 .B68 MRR Ref Desk.

A Catalog of books represented by
Library of Congress printed cards
issued to July 31, 1942. Ann Arbor,
Mich., Edwards Bros., 1942-46. 167
v. 018.1 43-3338
  Z881.A1 C3 MRR Alc. (DK 33)

Deutscher gesamtkatalog, Berlin,
Preussische druckerei- und verlags-
aktiengesellschaft, 1931- v.
019.1 32-9323
  Z929 .A1D4 MRR Alc (Dk 33).

Downs, Robert Bingham, ed. Union
catalogs in the United States,
Chicago, Ill., The American library
association, 1942. xxii, 409, [1] p.
incl. illus. (maps) diagrs., forms.
025.3 42-18942
  Z695.83 .D68 MRR Alc.

Goff, Frederick Richmond, ed.
Incunabula in American libraries;
New York, Bibliographical Society of
America, 1964. lxii, 798 p.
016.093 65-1485
  Z240 .G58 MRR Alc.

Hodgson, James Goodwin, comp. The
official publications of American
counties, Fort Collins, Col., 1937.
viii p., ix-xii numb. l., xiii-xxii,
594 p.   015.73 37-27440
  Z7164.L8 H72 MRR Alc.

Latin American newspapers in United
States libraries; Austin, Published
for the Conference on Latin American
History by the University of Texas
Press [1969, c1968] xiv, 619 p.
[20.00] 016.07918 69-63004
  Z6947 .C5 MRR Alc.

Library of Congress and National
union catalog author lists, 1942-
1962: Detroit, Gale Research Co.,
1969-71. 152 v. 018/.1/0973 73-
82135
  Z881.A1 L63 MRR Alc (Dk 33)

McKay, George Leslie, American book
auction catalogues, 1713-1934; New
York, The New York public library,
1937. xxxii, 540 p. 016.0173 37-
33888
  Z999 .A1M2 MRR Alc.

Pellechet, Marie Léontine Catherine,
Catalogue général des incunables
des bibliothèques publiques de
France. Paris, A. Picard et fils,
1897-1909. 3 v.   06-2931
  Z240 .P38 MRR Alc.

Polain, Louis, Catalogue des livres
imprimés au quinzième siècle des
bibliothèques de Belgique
Bruxelles, Pour la Société des
bibliophiles & iconophiles de
Belgique, 1932. 4 v. 016.093 33-
18424
  Z240 .P76 MRR Alc.

Ramage, David. A finding-list of
English books to 1640 in libraries in
the British Isles Durham [Eng.]
Council of the Durham Colleges, 1958.
xiv, 101 p. 015.42 a 60-1422
  Z2002.P772 R3 MRR Alc.

Ricci, Seymour de, Census of
medieval and renaissance manuscripts
in the United States and Canada, New
York, H. W. Wilson, 1935-40. 3 v.
35-31986
  Z6620.U5 R5 MRR Alc.

Rome (City) Centro nazionale per il
catalogo unico delle biblioteche
italiane e per le informazioni
bibliografiche. Primo catalogo
collettivo delle biblioteche
italiane. Roma, 1962- v.   63-
50852
  Z933 .A1R6 MRR Alc (Dk 33).

Sabin, Joseph, A dictionary of books
relating to America. New York, 1868
[i.e. 1867]-1936. 29 v. 01-26958
  Z1201 .S2 MRR Ref Desk.

Social Science Research Council.
Committee on Survey of Research on
Crime and Criminal Justice. A guide
to material on crime and criminal
justice. Montclair, N.J., Patterson
Smith, 1969 [c1929] 665 p.
016.364/9/73 69-16240
  Z5118.8.C9 S6 1969 MRR Alc.

United States. Library of Congress.
Library of Congress catalog: Books:
authors. Jan. 1947-1955.
Washington.   47-32682
  Z663.7 .L5 MRR Alc MRR Alc (DK 33)
  Full set

United States. Library of Congress.
Catalog Publication Division.
Newspapers in microform: foreign
countries, 1948-1972. Washington,
Library of Congress, 1973. xix, 269
p. [$10.00] 016.05 73-13554
  Z663.733 .N47 MRR Ref Desk.

United States. Library of Congress.
Catalog Publication Division.
Newspapers in microform: United
States, 1948-1972. Washington,
Library of Congress, 1973. xxiii,
1056 p. [$30.00] 016.071/3 73-
6936
  Z663.733 .N48 MRR Ref Desk.

CATALOGS, UNION--DIRECTORIES.
United Nations Educational,
Scientific and Cultural Organization.
Guide to national bibliographical
information centres. 3d rev. ed.
[Paris, 1970] 195 p. [18F ($4.50
US)] 021.6/4 74-583949
Z674.5.A2 U52 1970 MRR Ref Desk.

CATALOGS, UNION--CALIFORNIA.
California. University. Library.
University of California, Berkeley,
serials key word index. 1st- ed.;
1973- Berkeley. 016.05 73-645730
Z6945 .C16a MRR Alc Latest edition

CATALOGS, UNION--MIDDLE WEST.
Indiana. University. Library. Union
list of little magazines, Chicago,
Midwest Inter-Library Center, 1956.
iii, 98 l. a 57-2877
Z6944.L5 I53 MRR Alc.

CATALOGS, UNION--OHIO.
Swanson, Patricia. Union
bibliography of Ohio printed State
documents, 1803-1970. Columbus, Ohio
Historical Society, 1973. xiii, 750
p. 015.771 73-93700
Z1323 .S9 MRR Alc.

CATALOGS, UNION--UNITED STATES.
Balima, Mildred Grimes. Botswana,
Lesotho, and Swaziland; a guide to
official publications, 1868-1968,
Washington, General Reference and
Bibliography Division, Library of
Congress; [for sale by the Supt. of
Docs., U.S. Govt. Print. Off.] 1971.
xvi, 84 p. [$1.00] 016.9168 74-
171028
Z663.285 .B6 MRR Alc.

George Washington University,
Washington, D.C. Biological Sciences
Communication Project. A study of
resources and major subject holdings
available in U.S. Federal libraries
Washington, U.S. Office of Education,
Bureau of Research, 1970. ix, 670 p.
011 79-609579
Z881.A1 G4 1970b MRR Alc.

The National union catalog, Totowa,
N.J., Rowman and Littlefield [1970-
v. 018/.1/0973 76-141020
Z881.A1U3742 MRR Alc (Dk 33)

The National union catalog, 1952-1955
imprints; Ann Arbor, Mich., J. W.
Edwards, 1961. 30 v. 018.1 60-
53635
Z881.A1 U374 MRR Alc. (DK33)

The National union catalog, pre-1956
imprints; London, Mansell, 1968- v.
021.6/4 67-30001
Z663.7.L5115 MRR Alc (Dk 33)

Williams, Ethel L. Afro-American
religious studies: Metuchen, N.J.,
Scarecrow Press, 1972. 454 p.
016.301451/86073 78-166072
Z1361.N39 W55 MRR Alc.

Witherell, Julian W. French-speaking
central Africa; Washington, General
Reference and Bibliography Division,
Library of Congress; [for sale by the
Supt. of Docs., U.S. Govt. Print.
Off.] 1973. xiv, 314 p. [$3.70]
015/.67 72-5766
Z663.285 .F7 MRR Alc.

CATASTROPHES
see Disasters

CATHER, WILLA SIBERT, 1873-1947.
Edel, Leon, Willa Cather, the
paradox of success: Washington,
Reference Dept., Library of Congress,
1960. 17 p. 810.904 60-60031
Z663.293 .C3 MRR Alc.

CATHOLIC AUTHORS--BIOGRAPHY.
Hoehn, Matthew, ed. Catholic
authors; Newark [N.J.] St. Mary's
Abbey, 1948-52. 2 v. 928 48-2039
PN485 .H6 MRR Biog.

CATHOLIC CHURCH--BIBLIOGRAPHY.
Bernard, Jack F. A guide to Catholic
reading Garden City, N.Y., 1966.
vi, 392 p. 016.282 66-20941
Z7837 .B45 MRR Alc.

CATHOLIC CHURCH--BIOGRAPHY--
BIBLIOGRAPHY.
Brown, Stephen James Meredith,
International index of Catholic
biographies, 2d ed., rev. and
greatly enl. London, Burns, Oates
and Washbourne, 1935. 2 p. l., [vii]-
xix, 287 p. 016.9222 37-1357
Z7837 .B88 1935 MRR Biog.

CATHOLIC CHURCH--BIOGRAPHY--
DICTIONARIES.
Delaney, John J. Dictionary of
Catholic biography [1st ed.] Garden
City, N.Y., Doubleday [1961] xi,
1245 p. 922.2 62-7620
BX4651.2 .D4 MRR Biog.

CATHOLIC CHURCH--CEREMONIES AND
PRACTICES.
Fenner, Kay Toy. American Catholic
etiquette. Westminster, Md., Newman
Press, 1961. 402 p. 395 61-16569
BX1969 .F4 MRR Alc.

CATHOLIC CHURCH--CHARITIES--DIRECTORIES.
De Bettencourt, F. G. The Catholic
guide to foundations 2d ed.
Washington, Guide Publishers [1973]
iii, 170 p. 361.7/6/02573 73-86563
HV97.A3 D4 1973 MRR Alc.

CATHOLIC CHURCH--DICTIONARIES.
Bouyer, Louis, Dictionary of
theology. [New York, Desclee Co.,
c1965] xi, 470 p. 230.203 66-
13370
BR95 .B6413 MRR Alc.

Broderick, Robert C., Catholic
concise dictionary, Chicago,
Franciscan Herald Press [1966] xi,
330 p. 282.03 66-14726
BX841 .B7 1966 MRR Alc.

A Catholic dictionary 3d ed. New
York, Macmillan, 1958. vii, 552 p.
282.03 58-5797
BX841 .C35 1958 MRR Alc.

A Catholic dictionary of theology:
London, New York, Nelson [1962- v.
230.203 62-52257
BR95 .C27 MRR Alc.

The Maryknoll Catholic dictionary.
[1st American ed. Wilkes-Barre, Pa.]
Dimension Books [1965] xvii, 710 p.
282.03 65-15436
BX841 .M36 1965 MRR Alc.

New Catholic encyclopedia. New York,
McGraw-Hill [1967] 15 v. 282/.03
66-22292
BX841 .N44 1967 MRR Alc.

Parente, Pietro, Abp. Dictionary of
dogmatic theology 1st English ed.
Milwaukee, Bruce [1951] xxvi, 310 p.
203 51-7704
BR95 .P3 MRR Alc.

Virtue's Catholic encyclopedia.
London, Virtue [1965] 3 v. (xv, 1136
p.) 282.03 66-82787
BX841 .V5 MRR Alc.

CATHOLIC CHURCH--DICTIONARIES--FRENCH.
Barbieri, Pietro, Guide de l'Italie
catholique, 2. éd. Ed. française
rev, Paris, Éditions du Témoignage
chrétien, 1950. xii, 1338 p. 282
51-28419
BX842 .B314 1950 MRR Alc.

Dictionnaire de spiritualité
ascétique et mystique, Paris, G.
Beauchesne et ses fils, 1932- v.
282.03 38-24895
BX841 .D67 MRR Alc.

CATHOLIC CHURCH--DICTIONARIES--GERMAN.
Lexikon für Theologie und Kirche;
2., völlig neu bearb. Aufl.,
Freiburg, Herder, 1957-65. 10 v.
58-41506
BR95 .L48 MRR Alc.

CATHOLIC CHURCH--DICTIONARIES--ITALIAN.
Enciclopedia cattolica. Città del
Vaticano, Ente per l'Enciclopedia
cattolica e per il Libro cattolico
[1949-54] 12 v. a 50-1313
BX841 .E47 MRR Alc.

CATHOLIC CHURCH--DICTIONARIES--LATIN.
Palazzini, Pietro, Dictionarium
morale et canonicum. Romae, Officium
Libri Catholici, 1962-68. 4 v. 63-
34193
BX1757 .A2P3 MRR Alc.

CATHOLIC CHURCH--DIRECTORIES.
The Official Catholic directory.
1886- New York, P. J. Kenedy. 01-
30961
BX845 .C5 MRR Ref Desk Latest
edition

CATHOLIC CHURCH--DOCTRINAL AND
CONTROVERSIAL WORKS--PROTESTANT AUTHORS.
Wright, Charles Henry Hamilton, ed.
The Protestant dictionary, New ed.,
London, The Harrison trust [1933]
xix, 805, [1] p. 280.3 35-10289
BR95 .W7 1933 MRR Alc.

CATHOLIC CHURCH--HANDBOOKS, MANUALS,
ETC.
Barbieri, Pietro, Guide de l'Italie
catholique, 2. éd. Ed. française
rev, Paris, Éditions du Témoignage
chrétien, 1950. xii, 1338 p. 282
51-28419
BX842 .B314 1950 MRR Alc.

CATHOLIC CHURCH--HISTORY.
Eberhardt, Newman C. A summary of
Catholic history. St. Louis, Herder
[1961-62] 2 v. 282.09 61-8059
BX948 .E23 MRR Alc.

CATHOLIC CHURCH--HISTORY--PICTORIAL
WORKS.
Rice, Edward E., The church, a
pictorial history. New York, Farrar,
Straus & Cudahy [1961] 268 p.
282.084 61-6989
BX945.2 .R5 1961 MRR Alc.

CATHOLIC CHURCH--PERIODICALS--
BIBLIOGRAPHY.
The Catholic press directory. 1923-
New York [etc.] Catholic Press Ass.
[etc.] 23-11774
Z6951 .C36 MRR Alc Latest edition

CATHOLIC CHURCH--PERIODICALS--INDEXES.
The Catholic periodical and
literature index. July/Aug. 1968-
Haverford, Pa., Catholic Library
Association. 011 70-649588
AI3 .C32 MRR Alc Full set

The Catholic periodical index,
1930/33-May/June 1968. Haverford,
Pa. [etc.] Catholic Library
Association [etc.] 40-15160
AI3 .C32 MRR Alc Full set

CATHOLIC CHURCH--YEARBOOKS.
Annuario pontificio per l'anno
Città del Vaticano [etc.] Tipografia
poliglotta vaticana [etc.] 20-5316
BX845 .A75 MRR Alc Latest edition

Le Canada ecclésiastique. 1.-
année; 1887- Montréal, Librairie
Beauchemin limitée [etc.] 282.71
35-22140
BX1419 .C3 MRR Alc Latest edition

CATHOLIC CHURCH. LITURGY AND RITUAL.
PSALTER--GLOSSARIES, VOCABULARIES, ETC.
Britt, Matthew, ed. A dictionary of
the Psalter, New York, Cincinnati
[etc.] Benziger brothers, 1928.
xxxvi, 299 p. 29-1306
BX2033 .B7 MRR Alc.

CATHOLIC CHURCH. LITURGY AND RITUAL.
King, Archdale Arthur, Liturgies of
the religious orders. London, New
York, Longmans, Green [1955] xii,
431 p. 264.02 55-4576
BX2049.A1 K5 1955 MRR Alc.

CATHOLIC CHURCH. LITURGY AND RITUAL--
DICTIONARIES.
Podhradsky, Gerhard. New dictionary
of the liturgy. English ed. Staten
Island, N.Y., Alba House [1967,
c1966] 208 p. 264/.003 67-5547
BV173 .P613 1967 MRR Alc.

CATHOLIC CHURCH--BIBLIOGRAPHY.
McCabe, James Patrick. Critical
guide to Catholic reference books.
Littleton, Colo., Libraries
Unlimited, 1971. 287 p. 011/.02
78-144202
Z674 .R4 no. 2 MRR Alc.

CATHOLIC CHURCH IN CANADA--YEARBOOKS.
Le Canada ecclésiastique. 1.-
année; 1887- Montréal, Librairie
Beauchemin limitée [etc.] 282.71
35-22140
BX1419 .C3 MRR Alc Latest edition

CATHOLIC CHURCH IN ENGLAND--
BIBLIOGRAPHY.
Gillow, Joseph, A literary and
biographical history: New York, B.
Franklin [1968] 5 v. 914.2/03/0922
B 74-6323
Z2010 .G483 1968 MRR Biog.

CATHOLIC CHURCH IN FRANCE--DIRECTORIES.
Annuaire-agenda catholique; Paris,
P. Lethielleux. 57-36351
Began publication in 1938.
BX1528.A1 A4 MRR Alc Latest
edition

CATHOLIC CHURCH IN GREAT BRITAIN--
EDUCATION--DIRECTORIES.
Directory of independent and direct
grant Catholic schools and colleges.
London, Truman & Knightly [etc.]
377/.8/242 38-17003
Began in 1935.
LC506.G6 A15 MRR Alc Latest
edition

CATHOLIC CHURCH IN ITALY--DIRECTORIES.
Annuario cattolico d'Italia. Roma,
Editoriale italiana [etc.] 62-67073
BX1543 .A3A5 MRR Alc Latest
edition

CATHOLIC CHURCH IN ITALY.
Barbieri, Pietro, Guide de l'Italie
catholique, 2. éd. Ed. française
rev, Paris, Éditions du Témoignage
chrétien, 1950. xii, 1338 p. 282
51-28419
BX842 .B314 1950 MRR Alc.

CATHOLIC CHURCH IN SCOTLAND--
DIRECTORIES.
The Catholic directory for Scotland.
Glasgow, J. S. Burns. 282/.025/41
74-644568
BX1497.A3 C3 MRR Alc Latest
edition

CATHOLIC CHURCH IN THE UNITED STATES--
BIBLIOGRAPHY.
   The Catholic press directory. 1923-
   New York [etc.] Catholic Press Ass.
   [etc.] 23-11774
      Z6951 .C36 MRR Alc Latest edition

CATHOLIC CHURCH IN THE UNITED STATES--
EDUCATION.
   Catholic school guide. [New York]
   377.8273 52-25283
      LC461 .C346 MRR Alc Latest edition

CATHOLIC CHURCH IN THE UNITED STATES--
EDUCATION--DIRECTORIES.
   Catholic College Bureau, Chicago. A
   guide in the selection of a Catholic
   school. 1st- ed.; 1945- Chicago.
   377.82 50-31378
      LC501 .C345 MRR Alc Latest edition

CATHOLIC CHURCH IN THE UNITED STATES--
HISTORY--BIBLIOGRAPHY.
   Ellis, John Tracy, A guide to
   American Catholic history.
   Milwaukee, Bruce Pub. Co. [1959]
   viii, 147 p.   016.28273 59-13272
      Z7778.U6 E38 MRR Alc.

CATHOLIC CHURCH IN THE UNITED STATES--
HISTORY--SOURCES.
   Ellis, John Tracy, ed. Documents of
   American Catholic history. [2d ed.]
   Milwaukee, Bruce Pub. Co. [1962]
   xxii, 667 p.   282.73 62-12432
      BX1405 .E4 1962 MRR Alc.

CATHOLIC CHURCH IN THE UNITED STATES--
HISTORY--BIBLIOGRAPHY.
   Vollmar, Edward R. The Catholic
   Church in America: 2d ed. New York,
   Scarecrow Press, 1963. 399 p.
   016.28273 63-7466
      Z7778.U6 V6 1963 MRR Alc.

CATHOLIC CHURCH IN THE UNITED STATES
EDUCATION--DIRECTORIES.
   The Official guide to Catholic
   educational institutions and
   religious communities in the United
   States. 1936- New York [etc.]
   Catholic Institutional Directory Co.
   337.8273 38-4126
      LC501 .C35 MRR Alc Latest edition

CATHOLIC ENCYCLOPEDIA.
   The Catholic encyclopedia and its
   makers. New York, The Encyclopedia
   [!] press, inc. [c1917] viii, 192 p.
   [$2.00] 17-24118
      BX841 .C3 MRR Biog.

CATHOLIC INSTITUTIONS--UNITED STATES--
DIRECTORIES.
   De Bettencourt, F. G. The Catholic
   guide to foundations 2d ed.
   Washington, Guide Publishers [1973]
   iii, 170 p.   361.7/6/02573 73-86563

      HV97.A3 D4 1973 MRR Alc.

CATHOLIC LITERATURE--ABSTRACTS.
   Chapin, John, ed. The book of
   Catholic quotations: New York,
   Farrar, Straus and Cudahy [1956] x,
   1073 p.   808.8 56-11061
      PN6084.C2 C5 MRR Alc.

CATHOLIC LITERATURE--BIBLIOGRAPHY.
   Bernard, Jack F. A guide to Catholic
   reading Garden City, N.Y., 1966.
   vi, 392 p.   016.282 66-20941
      Z7837 .B45 MRR Alc.

   Brown, Stephen James Meredith,
   International index of Catholic
   biographies. 2d ed.; rev. and
   greatly enl. London, Burns, Oates
   and Washbourne, 1935. 2 p. l., [vii]-
   xix, 287 p.   016.9222 37-1357
      Z7837 .B88 1935 MRR Biog.

   McCabe, James Patrick. Critical
   guide to Catholic reference books.
   Littleton, Colo., Libraries
   Unlimited, 1971. 287 p.   011/.02
   78-144202
      Z674 .R4 no. 2 MRR Alc.

   Regis, Sister, ed. The Catholic
   bookman's guide; 1st ed.] New York,
   Hawthorn Books [1962] 638 p.
   016.80889 62-12956
      Z7837 .R37 MRR Alc.

CATHOLIC LITERATURE--BIO-BIBLIOGRAPHY.
   The Catholic periodical and
   literature index. July/Aug. 1968-
   Haverford, Pa., Catholic Library
   Association. 011 70-649588
      AI3 .C32 MRR Alc Full set

   Gillow, Joseph, A literary and
   biographical history: New York, B.
   Franklin [1968] 5 v.   914.2/03/0922
   B 74-6323
      Z2010 .G483 1968 MRR Biog.

CATHOLIC LITERATURE--HISTORY AND
CRITICISM.
   Brown, Stephen James Meredith, A
   survey of Catholic literature. [Rev.
   ed.] Milwaukee, Bruce Pub. Co.
   [1949] x, 281 p.   809 49-1416
      PN485 .B7 1949 MRR Alc.

Regis, Sister, ed. The Catholic
bookman's guide; 1st ed.] New York,
Hawthorn Books [1962] 638 p.
016.80889 62-12956
   Z7837 .R37 MRR Alc.

CATHOLIC UNIVERSITIES AND COLLEGES--
GREAT BRITAIN--DIRECTORIES.
   Directory of independent and direct
   grant Catholic schools and colleges.
   London, Truman & Knightly [etc.]
   377/.8/242 38-17003
   Began in 1935.
      LC506.G6 A15 MRR Alc Latest
      edition

CATHOLIC UNIVERSITIES AND COLLEGES--
UNITED STATES--DIRECTORIES.
   Catholic College Bureau, Chicago. A
   guide in the selection of a Catholic
   school. 1st- ed.; 1945- Chicago.
   377.82 50-31378
      LC501 .C345 MRR Alc Latest edition

   The Official guide to Catholic
   educational institutions and
   religious communities in the United
   States. 1936- New York [etc.]
   Catholic Institutional Directory Co.
   337.8273 38-4126
      LC501 .C35 MRR Alc Latest edition

CATHOLICS.
   The Catholic encyclopedia and its
   makers. New York, The Encyclopedia
   [!] press, inc. [c1917] viii, 192 p.
   [$2.00] 17-24119
      BX841 .C3 MRR Biog.

CATHOLICS IN GERMANY.
   Kosch, Wilhelm, Das katholische
   Deutschland, biographisch-
   bibliographisches lexikon, Augsburg,
   Haas & Grabherr, 1933- v.
   922.243 34-2159
      CT1055 .K6 MRR Biog.

CATHOLICS IN THE UNITED STATES.
   The American Catholic who's who.
   1911- Grosse Point, Mich. [etc.] W.
   Romig [etc.] 11-10944
      E184.C3 A6 MRR Biog Latest edition

CATHOLICS IN THE UNITED STATES--
BIOGRAPHY.
   American Catholic Philosophical
   Association. Directory of members.
   1- 1968- Washington. 106/.2/73
   78-5394
      B585 .A45 MRR Biog Latest edition

CATS.
   Carr, William H. A. The basic book
   of the cat. New York, Scribner
   [1963] 224 p.   636.808 62-20978
      SF447 .C3 MRR Alc.

   McCoy, Joseph J., The complete book
   of cat health and care. New York,
   Putnam [1968] xv, 237 p.   636.8 68-
   15514
      SF442 .M24 MRR Alc.

   Soderberg, Percy Measday, The care
   of your cat. 1st American ed.] New
   York, Harper [c1957] 302 p.
   636.808 57-8195
      SF447 .S66 1957a MRR Alc.

CATTELL, JAMES MCKEEN, 1860-1944--
BIBLIOGRAPHY.
   United States. Library of Congress.
   Manuscript Division. James McKeen
   Cattell; a register of his papers in
   the Library of Congress. Washington,
   1962. 24 p.   62-60057
      Z663.34 .C34 MRR Alc.

CATTLE BREEDS.
   Briggs, Hilton Marshall, Modern
   breeds of livestock. Rev. ed. New
   York, Macmillan [1958] 754 p.
   636.08 58-5049
      SF105 .B7 1958 MRR Alc.

   Mason, Ian Lauder. A world
   dictionary of livestock breeds, types
   and varieties, 2nd (revised) ed.
   Farnham Royal, Commonwealth
   Agricultural Bureaux, 1969. xviii,
   268 p. [70/-] 636/.003 75-454433

      SF21 .M3 1969 MRR Alc.

CATV
   see Community antenna television

CAUCASIAN RACE.
   Coon, Carleton Stevens, The races of
   Europe New York, The Macmillan
   company, 1939. xvi, 399 p., [29],
   400-739 p. incl. illus. (incl. maps)
   tables, diagrs. 572.94 39-10651
      GN575 .C6 MRR Alc.

CAVERSHAM, ENG.--DIRECTORIES.
   Kelly's directory of Reading,
   Caversham and neighbourhood.
   Kingston upon Thames, Surrey [etc.]
   Kelly's Directories Limited [etc.]
   53-30079
      DA690.R28 K4 MRR Alc Latest
      edition

CAVES--UNITED STATES--DIRECTORIES.
   Sloane, Howard N. Visiting American
   caves, New York, Crown Publishers
   [1966] x, 246 p.   917.309144 66-
   18457
      GB604 .S6 MRR Alc.

CELLS.
   see also Cytology

CELTIC LANGUAGE--BIBLIOGRAPHY.
   Bibliotheca celtica, 1909-1927/28;
   new ser., v. 1- 1929/33-
   Aberystwyth [National library of
   Wales] 11-5717
      Z2071 .B56 MRR Alc Partial set

CELTIC LITERATURE--BIBLIOGRAPHY.
   Bibliotheca celtica, 1909-1927/28;
   new ser., v. 1- 1929/33-
   Aberystwyth [National library of
   Wales] 11-5717
      Z2071 .B56 MRR Alc Partial set

CEMENT.
   see also Concrete

CEMETERIES--UNITED STATES--DIRECTORIES.
   National Association of Cemeteries.
   Official roster of membership.
   Washington. 57-19424
      RA626 .N322 MRR Alc Latest edition

CENSORSHIP.
   Downs, Robert Bingham, ed. The first
   freedom; Chicago, American Library
   Association, 1960. xiii, 469 p.
   323.445 59-13653
      Z657 .D76 MRR Alc.

CENSORSHIP--ADDRESSES, ESSAYS, LECTURES.
   Moon, Eric, comp. Book selection and
   censorship in the sixties. New York,
   Bowker, 1969. xi, 421 p.
   025.2/1/08 78-79423
      Z689 .M56 MRR Alc.

CENSORSHIP--BIBLIOGRAPHY.
   Schroeder, Theodore Albert, Free
   speech bibliography; New York, The
   H. W. Wilson company; London, Grafton
   & co., 1922. 4 p. l., 247 p.   22-
   8066
      Z657 .S383 MRR Alc.

CENSORSHIP--UNITED STATES.
   De Grazia, Edward. Censorship
   landmarks. New York, Bowker, 1969.
   xxxii, 657 p.   340 71-79424
      KF9444.A7 D4 MRR Alc.

CENSUS.
   Wolfenden, Hugh Herbert. Population
   statistics and their compilation.
   Rev. ed.: [Chicago] Published for
   the Society of Actuaries by the
   University of Chicago Press, 1954.
   258 p.   312 54-10735
      HB881 .W64 1954 MRR Alc.

CENSUS--BIBLIOGRAPHY.
   Texas. University. Population
   Research Center. International
   population census bibliography.
   Austin, Bureau of Business Research,
   University of Texas, 1965-67. 6 v.
   016.312 66-63578
      Z7164.D3 T45 MRR Alc.

   United States. Library of Congress.
   Census library project. General
   censuses and vital statistics in the
   Americas. Washington, U.S. Govt.
   print. off., 1943. ix, 151 p.
   016.312 44-40643
      Z7553.C3 U45 MRR Alc.

   United States. Library of Congress.
   Census Library Project. National
   censuses and vital statistics in
   Europe, 1918-1939: New York, B.
   Franklin [1969] vii, 215, v, 48 p.
   016.314 68-58214
      Z7553.C3 U46 1969 MRR Alc.

CENSUS--INFORMATION SERVICES--UNITED
STATES--DIRECTORIES.
   Clearinghouse and Laboratory for
   Census Data. Census processing
   center catalog. Rev. ed. Arlington,
   Va. [1974] 1 v. (unpaged)
   026/.312/0973 74-180379
      HA37.U55 C564 1974 MRR Alc.

CENTRAL AFRICAN REPUBLIC--GAZETTEERS.
   United States. Office of Geography.
   Central African Republic;
   Washington, U.S. Govt. Print. Off.,
   1962. iii, 220 p.   62-62080
      DT546.32 .U5 MRR Alc.

CENTRAL AMERICA--ANTIQUITIES--
BIBLIOGRAPHY.
   Bernal, Ignacio. Bibliografía de
   arqueología y etnografía: México,
   Instituto Nacional de Antropología e
   Historia, 1962. xvi, 634 p.   63-
   39894
      Z1209 .B45 MRR Alc.

CENTRAL AMERICA--CIVILIZATION--
BIBLIOGRAPHY.
   Rodríguez, Mario, A guide for the
   study of culture in Central America;
   Washington, Pan American Union, 1968.
   vii, 88 p.   pa 68-22
      Z1437 .R6 MRR Alc.

CENTRAL AMERICA--DESCRIPTION AND TRAVEL-
-1951-
Clark, Sydney Aylmer, All the best
in Central America New York, Dodd,
Mead [1970] xiii, 237 p. [6.95]
917.28/04/5 77-99182
F1433 .C5 1970 MRR Alc.

CENTRAL AMERICA--DESCRIPTION AND TRAVEL-
-GUIDE-BOOKS.
Mexico and Central America;
Washington, American Automobile
Association. 917.2 35-8488
GV1025.M4 A6 MRR Alc Latest
edition

CENTRAL AMERICA--STATISTICS--
BIBLIOGRAPHY.
Harvey, Joan M. Statistics America:
sources for market research (North,
Central & South America), Beckenham,
CBD Research, 1973. xii, 225 p.
[£6.00 ($22.00 U.S.)] 016.317 73-
180742
Z7554.A5 H37 MRR Alc.

CENTRAL EUROPE.
see also Europe, Eastern

CENTRAL EUROPE--BIBLIOGRAPHY.
Horna, Dagmar, ed. Current research
on central and eastern Europe. New
York, Mid-European Studies Center,
Free Europe Committee [1956] xviii,
251 p. 016.943 56-10866
Z2483 .H6 MRR Alc.

CENTRAL EUROPE--DESCRIPTION AND TRAVEL.
Mutton, Alice Florence Adelaide.
Central Europe; a regional and human
geography, 2nd ed. London,
Longmans, 1968. xxiv, 488 p. [65/-]
914 68-85425
D922 .M87 1968 MRR Alc.

CERAMIC INDUSTRIES.
see also Glass manufacture

CERAMIC INDUSTRIES--DICTIONARIES.
Searle, Alfred Broadhead, An
encyclopedia of the ceramic
industries, London, E. Benn,
limited, 1929-30. 3 v. 666.03 30-
8476
TP788 .S4 MRR Alc.

CERAMIC INDUSTRIES--EQUIPMENT AND
SUPPLIES.
Ceramic data book, 1st- ed.; 1922-
Chicago, Cahners Pub. Co. [etc.]
666.3058 22-15466
TP807 .C4 Sci RR Partial set / MRR
Alc Latest edition

CERAMICS.
see also Pottery

CERAMICS--DICTIONARIES.
Dodd, Arthur Edward. Dictionary of
ceramics: 2nd ed. London, Newnes,
1967. vi, 362 p. [42/-] 666/.03
67-114884
TP788 .D6 1967 MRR Alc.

Savage, George, An illustrated
dictionary of ceramics: New York,
Van Nostrand Reinhold Co. [1974] 319
p. [$18.95] 738/.03 73-17999
NK3770 .S38 1974b MRR Alc.

CERAMICS--PERIODICALS--INDEXES.
American Ceramic Society. Indexes to
publications of the American Ceramic
Society: Columbus, Ohio, 1957. 131
p. 666.05 a 58-237
TP785 .A643 MRR Alc.

CEREMONIES
see Rites and ceremonies

CERTIFIED PUBLIC ACCOUNTANTS
see Accountants

CERVANTES SAAVEDRA, MIGUEL DE, 1547-
1616--BIBLIOGRAPHY--CATALOGS.
United States. Library of Congress.
Works by Miguel de Cervantes Saavedra
in the Library of Congress.
Washington, Hispanic Foundation,
Reference Dept., Library of Congress,
1960. xliii, 120 p. 016.8633 60-
60060
Z663.32 .A5 no. 6 MRR Alc.

CEYLON.
Spate, Oskar Hermann Khristian.
India and Pakistan: 3d ed. revised
and completely reset. London,
Methuen, 1967. xxxiii, 877 p.
[£6/6/-] 915.4 68-86324
DS407 .S67 1967 MRR Alc.

CEYLON--COMMERCE--DIRECTORIES.
Ferguson's Ceylon directory. 1920/21-
Colombo, The Associated Newspapers
of Ceylon Ltd. [etc.] 915.49/3/0025
72-622384
DS488.9 .C4 MRR Alc Latest edition

CEYLON--DIRECTORIES.
Ferguson's Ceylon directory. 1920/21-
Colombo, The Associated Newspapers
of Ceylon Ltd. [etc.] 915.49/3/0025
72-622384
DS488.9 .C4 MRR Alc Latest edition

CEYLON--GAZETTEERS.
United States. Office of Geography.
Ceylon; Washington, U.S. Govt.
Print. Off., 1960. iii, 359 p.
915.489 60-62172
DS488.9 .U5 MRR Alc.

CEYLON--HISTORY.
Ludowyk, Evelyn Frederick Charles, A
short history of Ceylon New York,
Praeger [1967, c1962] 336 p.
954.9/3 67-21365
DS489.5 .L8 1967b MRR Alc.

Pakeman, Sidney Arnold, Ceylon. New
York, Praeger [1964] 256 p. 954.89
64-16684
DS489.5 .P3 MRR Alc.

CEYLON--IMPRINTS.
United States. Library of Congress.
American Libraries Book Procurement
Center, Delhi. Accessions list, Sri
Lanka. v. 7- Feb. 1973- New
Delhi. 015/.549/3 73-929618
Z3211 .U5 MRR Alc Full set

United States. Library of Congress.
American Libraries Book Procurement
Center, Delhi. Accessions list,
Ceylon. v. 1- Mar. 1967- New
Delhi. 015/.5493 sa 67-7489
Z663.767.C45 A25 MRR Alc MRR Alc
Full set

CHAD--GAZETTEERS.
United States. Office of Geography.
Chad; Washington, U.S. Govt. Print.
Off., 1962. v, 232 p. 62-62081
DT546.42 .U6 MRR Alc.

CHAIN STORES.
see also Supermarkets

CHAIN STORES--UNITED STATES.
Lebhar, Godfrey Montague, Chain
stores in America, 1859-1962. 3d ed.
New York, Chain Store Pub. Corp.
[1963] 430 p. 658.8730973 63-2856

HF5468 .L332 1963 MRR Alc.

CHAIN STORES--UNITED STATES--
DIRECTORIES.
Chain store guide; [New York,
Business Guides] 647.9505873 62-
4170
TX907 .C54 MRR Alc Latest edition

Chain store guide; directory of
leading chain stores in the United
States. 1959- [New York, Chain
Store Business Guide] 658.873058 58-
3958
HF5468 .C415 MRR Alc Latest
edition

Chain store guide directory: drug
store and health & beauty aids
chains. [New York, Business Guides,
inc.] 380.1/45/615102573 72-627445

HD9666.3 .C53 MRR Alc Latest
edition

Directory: General mdse., variety
and Jr. dept. store chains. 36th-
ed.; 1970- [New York, Business
Guides, inc.] 381 72-623621
HF5468.A1 C418 MRR Alc Latest
edition

Directory: home centers & hardware
chains, auto supply chains. 1974-
[New York, Business Guides, inc.]
[$59.00] 381/.45/629202573 74-
647308
HD9745.U4 D485 MRR Alc Latest
edition

Directory: Supermarket, grocery and
convenience store chains. 1956-
[New York, Business Guides, inc.]
381/.41/02573 72-623763
HD9321.3 .C43 MRR Alc Latest
edition

The Salesman's guide nationwide
directory of major mass market
merchandisers (exclusive of New York
metropolitan area) New York,
Salesman's Guide, inc. 380.1/025/73
73-640394
HF5468 .S27 MRR Alc Latest edition

Sheldon's retail directory of the
United States and Canada and Phelon's
resident buyers and merchandise
brokers. New York, Phelon, Sheldon &
Marsar. [$50.00] 381 74-644143
HF5429.3 .S52 MRR Alc Latest
edition

CHAIN STORES, VOLUNTARY--UNITED STATES--
DIRECTORIES.
Retailer owned cooperative chains,
wholesale grocers, and wholesaler
sponsored voluntary chains. [New
York, Business Guides, inc.]
658.87/00973 78-612833
HF5468.A1 D52 MRR Alc Latest
edition

CHAMBER MUSIC--DICTIONARIES.
Cobbett, Walter Willson, ed.
Cobbett's cyclopedic survey of
chamber music, London, Oxford
university press, H. Milford, 1929-
30. 2 v. 29-14486
ML1100 .C7 MRR Alc.

CHAMBERS, WASHINGTON IRVING--
MANUSCRIPTS.
United States. Library of Congress.
Manuscript Division. Washington
Irving Chambers; a register of his
papers in the Library of Congress.
Washington, Library of Congress,
1967. 15 l. 016.3593/32 67-60085

Z663.34 .C45 MRR Alc.

CHANGS, EDUCATIONAL
see Educational innovations

CHANGE, SOCIAL
see Social change

CHANNELS (HYDRAULIC ENGINEERING)
see also Harbors

CHAP-BOOKS--BIBLIOGRAPHY--CATALOGS.
Cleveland. Public Library. John G.
White Dept. Catalog of folklore and
folk songs. Boston, G. K. Hall,
1964. 2 v. 65-4290
Z5985 .C5 MRR Alc (Dk 33).

CHAPLAINS, MILITARY--UNITED STATES.
United States. Bureau of Naval
Personnel. The history of the
Chaplain Corps, United States Navy
[Washington, U.S. Govt. Print. Off.,
1948- v. 3, 1948] v. 359.34 48-
46297
VG23 .A45 MRR Biog.

CHARACTER.
see also Conduct of life

CHARACTER--BIBLIOGRAPHY.
Little, Lawrence Calvin, Researches
in personality, character and
religious education: [Pittsburgh]
University of Pittsburgh Press, 1962.
iv, 215 p. 013.3784886 62-12625
Z7849 .L54 MRR Alc.

CHARACTER TESTS.
see also Personality tests

Johnson, Orval G., Tests and
measurements in child development:
[1st ed.] San Francisco, Jossey-
Bass, 1971. xiii, 518 p. 155.41
78-110636
BF722 .J64 MRR Alc.

CHARACTER TESTS--BIBLIOGRAPHY.
Buros, Oscar Krisen, ed. The mental
measurements yearbook. [1st]- 1938-
Highland Park, N.J. [etc.] Gryphon
Press [etc.] 016.1512 016.159928 39-
3422
Z5814.P8 B932 MRR Alc Partial set

CHARACTERS AND CHARACTERISTICS.
Theophrastus. The characters of
Theophrastus, London, W. Heinemann,
ltd.; New York, G. P. Putnam's sons,
1929. vii, 132 p. 29-26911
PA3612 .T35 1929 MRR Alc.

CHARACTERS AND CHARACTERISTICS IN
LITERATURE.
Haycraft, Howard, Murder for
pleasure; Newly enl. ed. New York,
Biblo and Tannen, 1968 [c1941]
xviii, [14], 409 p. [10.00] 68-
25809
PN3448.D4 H3 1968 MRR Alc.

Magill, Frank Northen, ed.
Masterplots cyclopedia of literary
characters. New York, Salem Press
[1963] 2 v. 803 64-120
PN44 .M3 1963a MRR Alc.

CHARACTERS AND CHARACTERISTICS IN
LITERATURE--DICTIONARIES.
Brewer, Ebenezer Cobham, The
reader's handbook of famous names in
fiction, A new ed., rev. throughout
and greatly enl. Detroit,
Republished by Gale Research Co.,
1966. 2 v. (viii, 1243 p.) 803 71-
134907
PN43 .B7 1965 MRR Alc.

Broad, Lewis, Dictionary to the
plays and novels of Bernard Shaw,
New York, Haskell House, 1969. xi,
230 p. 822/.9/12 75-92947
PR5366 .A23 1969 MRR Alc.

Dizionario letterario Bompiani delle
opere e dei personaggi di tutti i
tempi e di tutte le letterature ...
[Milano] V. Bompiani, 1947 [c1946]-
50. 9 v. 803 47-20998
PN41 .D5 MRR Alc.

Freeman, William, Dictionary of
fictional characters. Boston, The
Writer, inc. [1974, c1973] xi, 579
p. 820/.3 73-18065
PR19 .F7 1974 MRR Ref Desk.

CHARACTERS AND CHARACTERISTICS (Cont.)
Gillespie, George T. A catalogue of persons named in German heroic literature (700-1600), including named animals and objects and ethnic names, Oxford, [Eng.] Clarendon Press, 1973. xxxvii, 166 p. [£10.50 ($33.75 U.S.)]   831/.009   73-173463

PT204 .G5 1973 MRR Alc.

Greaves, John. Who's who in Dickens. New York, Taplinger Pub. Co. [1973, c1972] 231 p. [$6.95]   823/.8   73-5335

PR4589 .G75 1973 MRR Alc.

Hagen, Ordean A. Who done it? New York, Bowker, 1969. xx, 834 p. 016.8C883/872   69-19209

Z5917.D5 H3 MRR Alc.

Hardwick, John Michael Drinkrow, The Charles Dickens companion London, J. Murray [1965] xiii, 250 p.   823.8   66-1009

PR4581 .H34 MRR Alc.

Hayward, Arthur Lawrence, The Dickens encyclopædia; London, G. Routledge and sons, ltd.; New York, E. P. Dutton & co., 1924. xii, 174 p., 1 l.   25-2059

PR4595 .H3 MRR Alc.

Irvine, Theodora Ursula. A pronouncing dictionary of Shakespearean proper names, New York, Barnes & Noble, inc., 1945. lviii, 387 p., incl. front. (facsim.) 822.33   46-104

PR3081 .I65 1945a MRR Alc.

Johnson, Rossiter, ed. Authors digest; Metuchen, N.J., Mini-Print Corp., 1970 [c1909] 21 v. in 5. 808.83   70-12099

PN44 .J7 1970 MRR Alc.

Litteraturen i Danmark og de øvrige nordiske lande. 4. udg. København, Politiken, 1967. 536 p. [21.45 dkr] 68-85482

PT7060 .L5 1967 MRR Alc.

Payton, Geoffrey. Payton's proper names. London, New York, F. Warne, 1969. vii, 502 p. [45/-]   032 69-20109

PE1660 .P3 MRR Alc.

Payton, Geoffrey. Webster's dictionary of proper names. Springfield, Mass., G. & C. Merriam Co. [c1970] 752 p.   423.1 72-22048

PE1660 .P34 MRR Ref Desk.

Quennell, Peter, Who's who in Shakespeare London, Weidenfeld and Nicolson [1973] 287 p. [£3.95] 822.3/3   73-177798

PR2989 .Q4 MRR Alc.

Rodale, Jerome Irving, The phrase finder; Emmaus, Pa., Rodale Press [c1953] 1325 p.   423 54-2348

PE1689 .R63 MRR Alc.

Sharp, Harold S., comp. Index to characters in the performing arts, New York, Scarecrow Press, 1966-73. 4 v. in 6.   808.8292703 66-13744

PN1579 .S45 MRR Alc.

Smith, Alfred Russell. A handbook index to those characters who have speaking parts assigned to them in the first folio of Shakespeare's plays 1623. London, A. R. Smith, 1904. 3 p. l., 133 p.   04-32201

PR2989 .S6 MRR Alc.

Stokes, Francis Griffin. A dictionary of the characters & proper names in the works of Shakespeare, Boston, New York, Houghton Mifflin company [pref. 1924] xv, 359, [1] p. incl. geneal. tables.   822.33 31-25861

PR2892 .S67 1924a MRR Alc.

Walsh, William Shepard, Heroes and heroines of fiction. Detroit, Republished by Gale Research Co., 1966. 2 v.   803 66-29782

PN43 .W33 1966 MRR Alc.

Wheeler, William Adolphus, An explanatory and pronouncing dictionary of the noted names of fiction, Detroit, Gale Research Co., 1966. xxxii, 440 p.   803 66-25811

PN43 .W4 1966 MRR Alc.

Young, William Arthur, A Kipling dictionary Revised ed. London, Melbourne [etc.] Macmillan; New York, St. Martin's P., 1967. x, 230 p. [50/-]   828/.8/09 67-11840

PR4856 .A28 1967 MRR Alc.

CHARACTERS AND CHARACTERISTICS IN LITERATURE--DICTIONARIES--FRENCH.
Dictionnaire des personnages littéraires et dramatiques de tous les temps et de tous les pays: 1. ed.] Paris, Société d'édition de dictionnaires et encyclopédies [1960] 668 p.   62-27565

PN41 .D485 MRR Alc.

CHARGING SYSTEMS (LIBRARIES)
Kirkwood, Leila H. Charging systems. New Brunswick, N.J., Graduate School of Library Service, Rutgers, the State University, 1961. 397 p. 025.6 60-16771

Z714 .K5 MRR Alc.

CHARITABLE USES, TRUSTS, AND FOUNDATIONS--LATIN AMERICA.
Stromberg, Ann. Philanthropic foundations in Latin America. New York, Russell Sage Foundation, 1968. viii, 215 p. [7.50]   361/.02/0258 68-54409

HV110.5 .S87 MRR Alc.

CHARITABLE USES, TRUSTS, AND FOUNDATIONS--UNITED STATES--DIRECTORIES.
De Bettencourt, F. G. The Catholic guide to foundations 2d ed. Washington, Guide Publishers [1973] ili, 170 p.   361.7/6/02573 73-86563

HV97.A3 D4 1973 MRR Alc.

CHARITABLE USES, TRUSTS, AND FOUNDATIONS--UNITED STATES--TAXATION.
United States. Congress. House. Select Committee on Small Business. Subcommittee No. 1. Tax-exempt foundations: their impact on small business. Washington, U.S. Govt. Print. Off., 1967 [i.e. 1968]-68. 2 v.   336.2/94 68-60557

KF27.5.S664 1967 vol. 2 MRR Alc.

CHARITIES.
see also Poor

CHARITIES--DIRECTORIES.
Technical Assistance Information Clearing House. Far East technical assistance programs of U.S. nonprofit organizations, New York, 1966. viii, 274 p.   309.2/23 67-60359

HC411 .T4 MRR Alc.

CHARITIES--CANADA--DIRECTORIES.
Canadian Council for International Co-operation. Directory of Canadian non-governmental organizations engaged in international development assistance, 1970. Ottawa, 1970. 285 p. [$5.00] 309.2/233/7101724 79-855733

HC60 .C2877 1970a MRR Alc.

CHARITIES--GREAT BRITAIN--DIRECTORIES.
Charities Aid Fund. Directory of grant-making trusts / 3rd compilation / Tonbridge, Kent : The Fund, 1973. 920 p. : £7.50] 001.4/4/02542 74-188784

AS911.A2 C45 1974 MRR Alc.

Charities digest. London. 361.7/6/02572 72-626402

HV245.A2 A3 MRR Alc Latest edition

CHARITIES--GREAT BRITAIN--YEARBOOKS.
Family Welfare Association, London. Guide to the social services. London, MacDonald & Evans, Ltd. [etc.] 362.8 55-33805

HV245.A2 F33 MRR Alc Latest edition

CHARITIES--NEW YORK (STATE)--DIRECTORIES.
Charitable organizations, professional fund raisers, and professional solicitors. [1st] ed.; 1955- Albany, N.Y. 361.7/3/025747 a 56-93011

HV89 .N44 MRR Alc Latest edition

CHARITIES--UNITED STATES.
Bruno, Frank John, Trends in social work, 1874-1956; [2d ed.] New York, Columbia University Press, 1957. xviii, 462 p.   360.973 57-9699

HV91 .B75 1957 MRR Alc.

National Budget and Consultation Committee. Reports on national health and welfare agencies. New York. 63-47582

HV88 .N13 MRR Alc Latest edition

CHARITIES--UNITED STATES--DIRECTORIES.
National Social Welfare Assembly. Service directory of national organizations 1st- ed.; 1951- New York. 360.58 52-3715

HV89 .N35 MRR Alc Latest edition

CHARITIES--UNITED STATES--HISTORY.
Bremner, Robert Hamlett, American philanthropy. [Chicago] University of Chicago Press [1960] 230 p. 361.973 60-7246

HV91 .B67 MRR Alc.

CHARITIES--UNITED STATES--YEARBOOKS.
Giving USA; a compilation of facts related to American philanthropy. New York, American Association of Fund-Raising Counsel. 361.705873 59-1874

HV89 .G5 MRR Ref Desk Latest edition

CHARMS.
Villiers, Elizabeth. The book of charms. [New York] Simon and Schuster [1974, c1973] 144 p. [$3.95]   133.4/4 74-171069

BF1561 .V5 1974 MRR Alc.

CHARTERS.
Kavenagh, W. Keith. Foundations of colonial America: New York, Chelsea House, 1973. 3 v. [$95.00] 325/.942/0873 72-80866

JK49 .K38 MRR Alc.

Thorpe, Francis Newton. comp. The Federal and State constitutions, colonial charters, and other organic laws of the state, territories, and colonies now or heretofore forming the United States of America. Washington, Govt. Print. Off., 1909. 7 v.   09-35371

KF4541 .T48 MRR Alc.

CHARTERS--BIBLIOGRAPHY.
United States. Library of Congress. Division of bibliography. ... List of cartularies (principally French) recently added to the Library of Congress, Washington, Govt. print. off., 1905- 30 p.   05-20009

Z663.28 .L567 MRR Alc.

CHASSIS-MOUNTED COACHES
see Campers and coaches, Truck

CHATHAM, ENG.--DIRECTORIES.
Kelly's directory of Medway towns. Kingston upon Thames. [-/27/6] 914.22/3/0025 73-642686

DA670.M4 K45 MRR Alc Latest edition

CHAUCER, GEOFFREY, D. 1400. CANTERBURY TALES.
Winter, Ezra Augustus, 1886- The Canterbury pilgrims, Washington [U.S. Govt. print. off.] 1946. folder ([6] p.)   751.73 46-27985

Z663 .C2 MRR Alc.

CHAUCER, GEOFFREY, D. 1400--CONCORDANCES.
Tatlock, John Strong Perry, A concordance to the complete works of Geoffrey Chaucer Washington, Carnegie institution of Washington, 1927. xiii, 1110 p., 1 l.   27-6088

PR1941 .T3 MRR Alc.

CHAUCER, GEOFFREY D. 1400--GLOSSARIES, ETC.
Skeat, Walter William, Glossarial index to the works of Geoffrey Chaucer, Oxford, Clarendon press, 1899. 2 p. l., 149, [1] p.   13-11604

PR1941 .S5 MRR Alc.

CHAUCER, GEOFFREY, D. 1400--LANGUAGE--GLOSSARIES, ETC.
Magoun, Francis Peabody, A Chaucer gazetteer. [Chicago] University of Chicago Press [1961] 173 p.   821.1 61-11293

PR1941 .M3 MRR Alc.

CHAUVINISM AND JINGOISM.
Roback, Abraham Aaron, A dictionary of international slurs (ethnophaulisms Cambridge, Mass., Sci-art publishers [1944] 394 p. 323.1 44-8328

HT1523 .R6 MRR Alc.

CHEESE.
Axler, Bruce H. The cheese handbook [New York] Hastings House [1969, c1968] 213 p. [5.95]   641.6/7/3 68-20555

TX382 .A9 MRR Alc.

Simon, André Louis, Cheeses of the world, [2d ed.] London, Faber and Faber [1965] 264 p.   67-5925

SF271 .S53 1965 MRR Alc.

CHEMICAL ADDITIVES IN FOOD
see Food additives

CHEMICAL ELEMENTS--DICTIONARIES.
Hampel, Clifford A. The encyclopedia of the chemical elements, New York, Reinhold Book Corp. [1968] viii, 849 p.   546/.11/03 68-29938

QD466 .H295 MRR Alc.

CHEMICAL ENGINEERING--APPARATUS AND SUPPLIES--CATALOGS.
Chemical engineering catalog. 1st ed.; 1916- Stamford, Conn. [etc.] Reinhold Pub. Corp. [etc.] 660.78 16-22887

TP157 .C4 MRR Alc Latest edition

CHEMICAL ENGINEERING--DICTIONARIES--
GERMAN.
Ernst, Richard. Dictionary of
chemistry, [3. Aufl.] Wiesbaden,
Brandstetter [1967-68, c1961-63] 2
v. 540/.3 76-390463
QD5 .E732 MRR Alc.

Ernst, Richard. Dictionary of
chemistry, [3. Aufl.] Wiesbaden,
Brandstetter [1967-68, c1961-63] 2
v. 540/.3 76-390463
QD5 .E732 MRR Alc.

CHEMICAL ENGINEERING--DICTIONARIES--
POLYGLOT.
Elsevier's dictionary of chemical
engineering. Amsterdam, New York,
1968. 2 v. [62.50 per vol.]
660/.2/03 68-54865
TP9 .E38 MRR Alc.

CHEMICAL ENGINEERING--DICTIONARIES--
RUSSIAN.
Carpovich, Eugene A., Russian-
English chemical dictionary: 2d
improved ed. New York, Technical
Dictionaries Co., 1963. 352 p.
660.2803 63-4199
TP9 .C33 1963 MRR Alc.

CHEMICAL EQUATIONS.
Gilman, Albert Franklin, ed. A
dictionary of chemical equations.
[9th ed.] Chicago, Eclectic
Publishers, 1961. 880 p.
541.390148 62-524
QD65 .G5 1961 MRR Alc.

CHEMICAL GEOLOGY
see Mineralogy, Determinative

CHEMICAL INDUSTRIES--COLLECTIONS.
Organization for Economic Cooperation
and Development. The chemical
industry. 1969/70- [Paris]
338.4/7/66 71-649804
HD9650.1 .074 MRR Alc Latest
edition

CHEMICAL INDUSTRIES--CANADA--
DIRECTORIES.
Chemical engineering catalog mailing
list. [Stamford, Conn., Reinhold
Pub. Corp.] 338.4/7/66002573 72-
623150
TP12 .C5 MRR Alc Latest edition

Chemical materials catalog mailing
list. [Stamford, Conn., Reinhold
Pub. Corp. 661/.0025/7 72-620095
TP12 .R43 Sci RR Latest edition /
MRR Alc Latest edition

Lloyd's Canadian chemical,
pharmaceutical, and product
directory. West Hill, Ont., Lloyd
Publications of Canada.
338.4/7/66002571 72-626360
HD9655.C2 W5 MRR Alc Latest
edition

CHEMICAL INDUSTRIES--EUROPE--
DIRECTORIES.
Chemical guide to Europe. [1st]-
ed.; 1961- Park Ridge, N.J. [etc.]
Noyes Data Corporation. 660/.025/4
68-55969
HD9656.A1 C18 Sci RR Latest
edition / MRR Alc Latest edition

CHEMICAL INDUSTRIES--GERMANY--
DIRECTORIES.
Firmenhandbuch chemische Industrie.
1.- Aufl.; 1952- Düsseldorf, Econ-
Verlag. 57-2640
TP12 .F5 MRR Alc Latest edition

CHEMICAL INDUSTRIES--UNITED STATES--
DIRECTORIES.
Belanger, Emil J. Modern
manufacturing formulary, New York,
Chemical Pub. Co., 1958. 399 p.
602 58-2072
T49 .B45 MRR Alc.

Chemical engineering catalog mailing
list. [Stamford, Conn., Reinhold
Pub. Corp.] 338.4/7/66002573 72-
623150
TP12 .C5 MRR Alc Latest edition

Chemical materials catalog mailing
list. [Stamford, Conn., Reinhold
Pub. Corp. 661/.0025/7 72-620095
TP12 .R43 Sci RR Latest edition /
MRR Alc Latest edition

Zimmerman, Oswald Theodore,
Industrial Research Service's
handbook of material trade names,
1953 ed. Dover, N.H., Industrial
Research Service, 1953. xvi, 794 p.
660.2 53-1074
TP151 .Z5 1953 MRR Alc.

CHEMICAL LITERATURE.
American Chemical Society. Division
of Chemical Literature. Searching
the chemical literature. Rev. and
enl. ed. Washington, American
Chemical Society, 1961. vi, 326 p.
016.54 61-11330
QD1 .A355 no. 30 MRR Alc.

Bottle, R. T. The use of chemical
literature, 2nd ed. London,
Butterworths, 1969. xii, 294 p., 2
plates. [65/-] 016.54 70-447638
QD8.5 .B6 1969b MRR Alc.

Mellon, Melvin Guy, Chemical
publications, 4th ed. New York,
McGraw-Hill [1965] xi, 324 p.
016.54 64-8418
Z5521 .M52 1965 MRR Alc.

CHEMICAL REACTIONS.
Gilman, Albert Franklin, ed. A
dictionary of chemical equations.
[9th ed.] Chicago, Eclectic
Publishers, 1961. 880 p.
541.390148 62-524
QD65 .G5 1961 MRR Alc.

CHEMICAL SYMBOLS
see Abbreviations

CHEMICAL TESTS AND REAGENTS--
SPECIFICATIONS.
Rosin, Joseph, Reagent chemicals and
standards, 5th ed. Princeton, N.J.,
Van Nostrand [1967] vii, 641 p.
543/.01 67-2886
QD77 .R63 1967 MRR Alc.

CHEMICALS--CATALOGS.
Chemical buyers directory. [1st]-
1913- New York, Schnell Pub. Co.
660/.025/73 13-6763
TP12 .O6 Sci RR Latest edition /
MRR Alc Latest edition

Chemical materials catalog and
directory of producers. 1st- ed.;
1949/50- New York, Reinhold Pub.
Corp. 660.838 50-2341
TP202 .C5 Sci RR Latest edition /
MRR Alc Latest edition

CHEMICALS--DICTIONARIES.
Gardner, William, Chemical synonyms
and trade names: 6th ed. revised and
enlarged London, Technical P., 1968.
[6], 635 p. [£5/-/-] 660/.003 68-
115161
TP9 .G28 1968 MRR Alc.

The Merck index: 8th ed. Rahway,
N.J., Merck, 1968. xii, 1713 p.
615/.1/03 68-12252
RS356 .M524 1968 MRR Alc.

Zimmerman, Oswald Theodore,
Industrial Research Service's
handbook of material trade names,
1953 ed. Dover, N.H., Industrial
Research Service, 1953. xvi, 794 p.
660.2 53-1074
TP151 .Z5 1953 MRR Alc.

CHEMICALS--MANUFACTURE AND INDUSTRY.
Snell, Foster Dee, Dictionary of
commercial chemicals 3d ed.
Princeton, N.J., Van Nostrand [1962]
viii, 714 p. 660.2 62-3474
TP200 .S55 1962 MRR Alc.

CHEMICALS--MANUFACTURE AND INDUSTRY--
COLLECTIONS.
Organization for Economic Cooperation
and Development. The chemical
industry. 1969/70- [Paris]
338.4/7/66 71-649804
HD9650.1 .074 MRR Alc Latest
edition

CHEMICALS--MANUFACTURE AND INDUSTRY--
DIRECTORIES.
Chemical industry directory & who's
who. 1923- London, Chemical age,
Benn Brothers. 23-4933
TP1 .C34 Sci RR Latest edition /
MRR Alc Latest edition

CHEMICALS--MANUFACTURE AND INDUSTRY--
CANADA--DIRECTORIES.
Chemical materials catalog mailing
list. [Stamford, Conn.] Reinhold
Pub. Corp. 661/.0025/7 72-620095
TP12 .R43 Sci RR Latest edition /
MRR Alc Latest edition

CHEMICALS--MANUFACTURE AND INDUSTRY--
EUROPE--DIRECTORIES.
Chemical guide to Europe. [1st]-
ed.; 1961- Park Ridge, N.J. [etc.]
Noyes Data Corporation. 660/.025/4
68-55969
HD9656.A1 C18 Sci RR Latest
edition / MRR Alc Latest edition

Noyes Development Corporation.
Chemical guide to Europe. [3d ed.]
Pearl River, N.Y., 1965. 137 p.
661.0584 65-13150
TP12 .N6 1965 MRR Alc.

CHEMICALS--MANUFACTURE AND INDUSTRY--
GERMANY--DIRECTORIES.
Firmenhandbuch chemische Industrie.
1.- Aufl.; 1952- Düsseldorf, Econ-
Verlag. 57-2640
TP12 .F5 MRR Alc Latest edition

CHEMICALS--MANUFACTURE AND INDUSTRY--
LATIN AMERICA.
Noyes Development Corporation. Latin
American chemical guide, 1964. Pearl
River, N.Y., 1964. 94 p. 338.47661
64-21638
HD9655.L3 N6 MRR Alc.

CHEMICALS--MANUFACTURE AND INDUSTRY--
LATIN AMERICA--DIRECTORIES.
Noyes Development Corporation. Latin
American chemical guide, 1964. Pearl
River, N.Y., 1964. 94 p. 338.47661
64-21638
HD9655.L3 N6 MRR Alc.

CHEMICALS--MANUFACTURE AND INDUSTRY--
UNITED STATES--DIRECTORIES.
Chemical buyers directory. [1st]-
1913- New York. Schnell Pub. Co.
660/.025/73 13-6763
TP12 .O6 Sci RR Latest edition /
MRR Alc Latest edition

Chemical engineering catalog mailing
list. [Stamford, Conn.] Reinhold
Pub. Corp.] 338.4/7/66002573 72-
623150
TP12 .C5 MRR Alc Latest edition

Chemical guide to the United States.
[1st]- ed.; 1962- Park Ridge, N.J.
[etc.] Noyes Data Corp. 660.5873 63-
5647
TP12 .C56 Sci RR Latest edition /
MRR Alc Latest edition

Chemical materials catalog mailing
list. [Stamford, Conn.] Reinhold
Pub. Corp. 661/.0025/7 72-620095
TP12 .R43 Sci RR Latest edition /
MRR Alc Latest edition

Directory of chemical producers:
United States of America. Menlo
Park, Chemical Information Services,
Stanford Research Institute.
338.4/7/66002573 73-644039
HD9651.3 .D57 MRR Alc Latest
edition / Sci RR Latest edition

CHEMICALS--PRICES--INDEXES.
Wasserman, Paul. Commodity prices:
Detroit, Gale Research Co. [1974]
xii, 200 p. [$15.00] 338.5/2/0973
73-19898
Z7164.P94 W33 MRR Alc.

CHEMICALS--TRADE-MARKS.
Gardner, William, Chemical synonyms
and trade names: 6th ed. revised and
enlarged London, Technical P., 1968.
[6], 635 p. [£5/-/-] 660/.003 68-
115161
TP9 .G28 1968 MRR Alc.

CHEMISTRY.
see also Biological chemistry

see also Color

CHEMISTRY--ABSTRACTS.
United States. Library of Congress.
European Affairs Division. Physics
and chemical sciences in Western
Germany: Washington, 1954. 123 p.
507.2 54-60012
Z663.26 .N3 1954 MRR Alc.

CHEMISTRY--BIBLIOGRAPHY.
Crane, Evan Jay, A guide to the
literature of chemistry 2d ed. New
York, Wiley [1957] 397 p. 016.54
57-8881
Z5521 .C89 1957 MRR Alc.

CHEMISTRY--DICTIONARIES.
Ballentyne, Denis William George. A
dictionary of named effects and laws
in chemistry, physics and mathematics
3rd ed. London, Chapman & Hall,
1970. iii-viii, 335 p. [£3.00]
500.2/03 71-552485
Q123 .B3 1970 MRR Alc.

Encyclopedia of chemical technology.
2d ed., completely rev. New York,
Interscience Publishers [1963-70] 22
v. 660/3 63-14348
TP9 .E685 MRR Alc.

The Encyclopedia of chemistry. 2d
ed. New York, Reinhold Pub. Corp.
[1966] xxi, 1144 p. 540.3 66-
22807
QD5 .E58 1966 MRR Alc.

Ernst, Richard. Dictionary of
chemistry, [3. Aufl.] Wiesbaden,
Brandstetter [1967-68, c1961-63] 2
v. 540/.3 76-390463
QD5 .E732 MRR Alc.

Flood, Walter Edgar. The origins of
chemical names London, Oldbourne
[1963] xxxi, 238 p. 68-2895
QD5 .F55 1963b MRR Alc.

CHEMISTRY--DICTIONARIES--GERMAN.
Ernst, Richard. Dictionary of
chemistry, [3. Aufl.] Wiesbaden,
Brandstetter [1967-68, c1961-63] 2
v. 540/.3 76-390463
QD5 .E732 MRR Alc.

Patterson, Austin McDowell, A German-
English dictionary for chemists. 3d
ed. New York, Wiley [1950] xviii,
541 p. 540.3 50-4541
QD5 .P3 1950 MRR Alc.

CHEMISTRY--DICTIONARIES--POLYGLOT.
Dictionary of chemistry and chemical
technology, in six languages: [Rev.
ed.] Oxford, New York, Pergamon
Press [1966] 1325 p.   540.3 65-
29008
    QD5 .D5 1966 MRR Alc.

International encyclopedia of
chemical science. Princeton, N.J.,
Van Nostrand [1964] 1331 p.   540.3
64-1619
    QD5 .I5 1964 MRR Alc.

CHEMISTRY--DICTIONARIES--RUSSIAN.
Carpovich, Eugene A., Russian-
English chemical dictionary: 2d
improved ed. New York, Technical
Dictionaries Co., 1963. 352 p.
660.2803 63-4199
    TP9 .C33 1963 MRR Alc.

Hoseh, Mordecai. Russian-English
dictionary of chemistry and chemical
technology New York, Reinhold Pub.
Corp. [1964] xiii, 522 p.   540.3
64-22149
    QD5 .H6 MRR Alc.

CHEMISTRY--HISTORY.
Farber, Eduard, ed. Great chemists.
New York, Interscience Publishers,
1961. 1642 p.   925.4 60-16809
    QD21 .F35 MRR Biog.

CHEMISTRY--NOMENCLATURE.
Flood, Walter Edgar. The origins of
chemical names London, Oldbourne
[1963] xxxi, 238 p.   68-2895
    QD5 .F55 1963b MRR Alc.

CHEMISTRY--PERIODICALS--BIBLIOGRAPHY.
Crane, Evan Jay, A guide to the
literature of chemistry 2d ed. New
York, Wiley [1957] 397 p.   016.54
57-8881
    Z5521 .C89 1957 MRR Alc.

CHEMISTRY--STUDY AND TEACHING.
Mellon, Melvin Guy, Chemical
publications, 4th ed. New York,
McGraw-Hill [1965] xi, 324 p.
016.54 64-8418
    Z5521 .M52 1965 MRR Alc.

CHEMISTRY--TABLES, ETC.
Handbook of chemistry and physics;
[1st] ed.; 1913- Cleveland,
Chemical Rubber Co. [etc.] 541.9 13-
11056
    QD65 .H3 Sci RR Latest edition /
    MRR Alc Latest edition

CHEMISTRY, ANALYTIC.
    see also Mineralogy, Determinative

CHEMISTRY, BIOLOGICAL
    see Biological chemistry

CHEMISTRY, FORENSIC.
    see also Poisons

CHEMISTRY, MEDICAL AND PHARMACEUTICAL.
    see also Drugs

CHEMISTRY, ORGANIC.
Morrison, Robert Thornton, Organic
chemistry 2d ed. Boston, Allyn and
Bacon, 1966. ix, 1204 p.   547 66-
25695
    QD251 .M72 1966 MRR Alc.

CHEMISTRY, PHYSICAL AND THEORETICAL.
    see also Nuclear physics

CHEMISTRY, TECHNICAL.
Snell, Foster Dee, Dictionary of
commercial chemicals 3d ed.
Princeton, N.J., Van Nostrand [1962]
viii, 714 p.   660.2 62-3474
    TP200 .S55 1962 MRR Alc.

Zimmerman, Oswald Theodore,
Industrial Research Service's
handbook of material trade names,
1953 ed. Dover, N.H., Industrial
Research Service, 1953. xvi, 794 p.
660.2 53-1074
    TP151 .Z5 1953 MRR Alc.

CHEMISTRY, TECHNICAL--DICTIONARIES.
Encyclopedia of chemical technology.
2d ed., completely rev. New York,
Interscience Publishers [1963-70] 22
v.   660/3 63-14348
    TP9 .E685 MRR Alc.

Stewart, Jeffrey R., An encyclopedia
of the chemical process industries,
New York, Chemical Pub. Co., 1956.
820 p.   660.3 56-2478
    TP9 .S68 MRR Alc.

CHEMISTRY, TECHNICAL--DICTIONARIES--
ITALIAN.
Aghina, Luisa. Dizionario tecnico
italiano-inglese, [Firenze]
Vallecchi [1961] 431 p.   a 61-3420
    TP9 .A35 MRR Alc.

CHEMISTRY, TECHNICAL--DICTIONARIES--
POLYGLOT.
Dictionary of chemistry and chemical
technology, in six languages: [Rev.
ed.] Oxford, New York, Pergamon
Press [1966] 1325 p.   540.3 65-
29008
    QD5 .D5 1966 MRR Alc.

CHEMISTRY, TECHNICAL--DICTIONARIES--
RUSSIAN.
Hoseh, Mordecai. Russian-English
dictionary of chemistry and chemical
technology New York, Reinhold Pub.
Corp. [1964] xiii, 522 p.   540.3
64-22149
    QD5 .H6 MRR Alc.

CHEMISTRY, TECHNICAL--FORMULAE,
RECEIPTS, PRESCRIPTIONS.
The Chemical formulary. v. 1-   1933-
New York [etc.] Chemical Pub. Co.
[etc.] 660.83 33-36898
    TP151 .C53 Sci RR Full set / MRR
    Alc Full set

CHEMISTRY, TECHNICAL--YEARBOOKS.
Chemical industry directory & who's
who. 1923- London, Chemical age,
Benn Brothers.   23-4933
    TP1 .C34   Sci RR Latest edition /
    MRR Alc Latest edition

CHEMISTRY OF FOOD
    see Food--Composition

CHEMISTS.
Farber, Eduard, ed. Great chemists.
New York, Interscience Publishers,
1961. 1642 p.   925.4 60-16809
    QD21 .F35 MRR Biog.

Farber, Eduard, Nobel prize winners
in chemistry, 1901-1961. Rev. ed.
London, New York, Abelard-Schuman
[1963] 341 p.   925.4 62-17263
    QD21 .F37 1963 MRR Biog.

CHEMISTS--GERMANY--DIRECTORIES.
Adressbuch deutscher Chemiker.
1950/51- Weinheim, Verlag Chemie.
52-24398
    QD23 .A4   MRR Biog Latest edition

CHEMISTS--GREAT BRITAIN--BIOGRAPHY.
Chemical industry directory & who's
who. 1923- London, Chemical age,
Benn Brothers.   23-4933
    TP1 .C34   Sci RR Latest edition /
    MRR Alc Latest edition

CHEMURGY.
United States. Dept. of Agriculture.
Crops in peace and war. Washington,
U.S. Govt. Print. Off. [1951] 942 p.
630.72   agr55-9
    S21 .A35 1950-1951 MRR Alc.

CHESAPEAKE BAY.
Blanchard, Fessenden Seaver, A
cruising guide to the Chesapeake;
Rev. ed. New York, Dodd, Mead, 1962.
235 p.   917.5 62-12579
    F187.C5 B55 1962 MRR Alc.

CHESS.
Sunnucks, Anne, The encyclopaedia of
chess. New York, St. Martin's Press
[1970] xv, 587 p. [10.00]   794.1
78-106371
    GV1445 .S88 MRR Alc.

CHESS--BIBLIOGRAPHY.
Betts, Douglas A. Chess; Boston, G.
K. Hall, 1974. xix, 659 p.
016.7941   73-15885
    Z5541 .B47 MRR Alc.

CHESS--BIOGRAPHY--DICTIONARIES.
A Catalog of chessplayers &
problemists. [1st]   ed.; 1969-
Philadelphia, J. Gaige.   794.1/092/2
70-24107
    GV1438 .C37   MRR Alc Latest edition

CHESS--DICTIONARIES.
Horton, Byrne Joseph, Dictionary of
modern chess. New York,
Philosophical Library [1959] xi, 224
p.   794.103 59-16259
    GV1447 .H67 MRR Alc.

CHESS--TOURNAMENTS.
Gligoric, Svetozar. The world chess
championship Updated. New York,
Harper & Row [c1972] 221 p. [$7.95]
794.1/57   72-10681
    GV1455 .G5513 1972c MRR Alc.

CHESS--TOURNAMENTS--HISTORY.
Horowitz, Israel Albert, The world
chess championship; New York,
Macmillan [1973] v, 291 p. [$6.95]
794.1/57   72-80175
    GV1455 .H66 MRR Alc.

CHEST.
    see also Heart

CHESTER, COLBY MITCHELL, 1844-1932--
MANUSCRIPTS.
United States. Library of Congress.
Manuscript Division. Colby Mitchell
Chester, William Freeland Fullam,
Samuel McGowan, Henry Croskey Mustin:
a register of their papers in the
Library of Congress. Washington,
Library of Congress, 1973. iii, 4,
6, 7, 5 p. 016.359 73-2939
    Z663.34 .C48 MRR Alc.

CHESTERTON, GILBERT KEITH, 1874-1936--
INDEXES.
Sprug, Joseph W., ed. An index to G.
K. Chesterton, Washington, Catholic
University of America Press [1966]
xx, 427 p.   828.91209 66-30169
    PR4453.C4 Z76 MRR Alc.

CHEVROLET AUTOMOBILE.
Fix your Chevrolet. South Holland,
Ill. [etc.] Goodheart-Willcox Co.
629.287 62-12426
    TL215.C5 F5 MRR Alc Latest edition

CHICAGO--BIBLIOGRAPHY.
Historical records survey. Check
list of Chicago ante-fire imprints,
1851-1871. Chicago The Historical
records survey, 1938. 2 p. l., iii-
xvii, 727 p.   015.7731 39-4906
    Z1215 .H67 no. 4 MRR Alc.

CHICAGO--BIOGRAPHY--DICTIONARIES.
Rather, Ernest R., Chicago Negro
almanac and reference book,
[Chicago, Chicago Negro Almanac Pub.
Co., c1972] viii, 256 p.
917.73/11/0696073025   72-81384
    F548.9.N3 R37 MRR Alc.

CHICAGO--DESCRIPTION--1951- --GUIDE-
BOOKS.
Graham, Jory, Chicago: an
extraordinary guide. Chicago, Rand
McNally [1968] xi, 499 p. [7.95]
917.73/11/044 68-28072
    F548.18 .G7 MRR Alc.

CHICAGO--LIBRARIES--DIRECTORIES.
Hamilton, Beth A. Libraries and
information centers in the Chicago
metropolitan area. Hinsdale,
Illinois Regional Library Council,
1973. 499 p.   021/.0025/77311 73-
89540
    Z732.12 H35 MRR Alc.

CHICANOS
    see Mexican Americans

CHIEF JUSTICES
    see Judges

CHILD DEVELOPMENT
    see Children--Growth

CHILD GUIDANCE--ENCYCLOPEDIA--POPULAR
WORKS.
Levine, Milton Isra, The parents'
encyclopedia of infancy, childhood,
and adolescence New York, Crowell
[1973] 619 p. [$10.00] 649/.1/03
72-83769
    RJ61 .L552 MRR Alc.

CHILD PSYCHIATRY.
Child and adolescent psychiatry,
sociocultural and community
psychiatry. 2d ed. [Rev. and
expanded] New York, Basic Books
[1974] xi, 858 p.   616.8/9/008 s
616.8/9 72-89185
    RC435 .A562 vol. 2 MRR Alc.

CHILD STUDY.
    see also Adolescence

    see also Education, Preschool

    see also Exceptional children

    see also Handicapped children

    see also Libraries, Children's

Bossard, James Herbert Siward, The
sociology of child development 3d
ed. New York, Harper [1960] 706 p.
301.431   60-7016
    HQ781 .B67 1960 MRR Alc.

Hurlock, Elizabeth Bergner, Child
development 5th ed. New York,
McGraw-Hill [1972] 494 p.   155.4
79-38613
    BF721 .H8 1972 MRR Alc.

Johnson, Ronald Charles. Child
psychology: behavior & development
2d ed. New York, Wiley [1969] xi,
677 p.   155.4 69-16125
    BF721 .J53 1969 MRR Alc.

CHILD STUDY--ABSTRACTS.
Child development abstracts and
bibliography. v. 1-
June/Sept./Dec. 1927- Chicago, Ill.
[etc.] Univ. of Chicago Press [etc.]
016.6491 46-31872
    HQ750 .A1C47 MRR Alc Full set

CHILD STUDY--ADDRESSES, ESSAYS,
LECTURES.
Review of child development research.
New York, Russell Sage Foundation,
1964- v.   155.4/1   64-20472
    HQ768.8 .R48 MRR Alc.

CHILD STUDY--BIBLIOGRAPHY.
Child development abstracts and
bibliography. v. 1-
June/Sept./Dec. 1927- Chicago, Ill.
[etc.] Univ. of Chicago Press [etc.]
016.6491   46-31872
    HQ750 .A1C47 MRR Alc Full set

CHILD STUDY--METHODOLOGY.
Johnson, Orval G., Tests and
measurements in child development:
[1st ed.] San Francisco, Jossey-
Bass, 1971. xiii, 518 p.   155.41
78-110636
    BF722 .J64 MRR Alc.

CHILD WELFARE--UNITED STATES--
DIRECTORIES.
Child Welfare League of America,
Directory of member agencies. [New
York] 61-65626
    HV741 .C523 MRR Alc Latest edition

CHILDBIRTH.
Boston. Children's Hospital Medical
Center. Pregnancy, birth & the
newborn baby [New York] Delacorte
Press [1972] 474 p. [$10.00] 613
71-175649
    RG525 .P645 MRR Alc.

Guttmacher, Alan Frank, Pregnancy,
birth, and family planning; New
York, Viking Press [1973] xv, 365 p.
[$10.00]   612.6/3   72-79006
    RG525 .G82 1973 MRR Alc.

CHILDREN.
see also Day nurseries

see also Infants

CHILDREN--ANECDOTES AND SAYINGS.
Baughman, Millard Dale, comp.
Educator's handbook of stories,
quotes and humor. Englewood Cliffs,
N.J., Prentice-Hall [c1963] xii, 340
p.   63-17504
    LB1785 .B28 MRR Alc.

CHILDREN--CARE AND HYGIENE.
see also Health education

see also Infants--Care and hygiene

Child development abstracts and
bibliography. v. 1-
June/Sept./Dec. 1927- Chicago, Ill.
[etc.] Univ. of Chicago Press [etc.]
016.6491   46-31872
    HQ750 .A1C47 MRR Alc Full set

Levine, Milton Isra, The parents'
encyclopedia of infancy, childhood,
and adolescence New York, Crowell
[1973] 619 p. [$10.00]   649/.1/03
72-83769
    RJ61 .L552 MRR Alc.

Newton, Niles, The family book of
child care. [1st ed.] New York,
Harper [1957] 477 p.   649.1 55-
8058
    RG525 .N43 MRR Alc.

Smith, Lendon H., The encyclopedia
of baby and child care, Englewood
Cliffs, N.J., Prentice-Hall [1972]
viii, 500 p.   618.92 70-180226
    RJ101 .S55 MRR Alc.

CHILDREN--COSTUME.
Moore, Doris (Langley-Levy) The
child in fashion. London, Batsford
[1953] 100 p.   391.3 54-1114
    GT1730 .M65 MRR Alc.

CHILDREN--DISEASES.
Barnett, Henry L. Pediatrics. 15th
ed. New York, Appleton-Century-
Crofts [1972] xxxi, 2070 p.
618.9/2 70-133170
    RJ45 .B35 1972 MRR Alc.

Hudson, Ian Donald. What to do until
the doctor comes Princeton, N.J.
[Auerbach, 1970, c1969] xvi, 269 p.
[$7.95]   614.8/8 79-124624
    RC81 .H9214 1970 MRR Alc.

Karelitz, Samuel. When your child is
ill; Completely rev., New York,
Random House [1969] xiv, 568 p.
[7.95]   618.92 69-16463
    RJ61 .K235 1969 MRR Alc.

Levine, Milton Isra, The parents'
encyclopedia of infancy, childhood,
and adolescence New York, Crowell
[1973] 619 p. [$10.00]   649/.1/03
72-83769
    RJ61 .L552 MRR Alc.

Smith, Lendon H., The encyclopedia
of baby and child care, Englewood
Cliffs, N.J., Prentice-Hall [1972]
viii, 500 p.   618.92 70-180226
    RJ101 .S55 MRR Alc.

CHILDREN--EMPLOYMENT--BIBLIOGRAPHY.
United States. Library of Congress.
Division of bibliography. List of
books (with references to
periodicals) relating to child labor.
Washington, Govt. print. off., 1906.
66 p.   06-35009
    Z663.28 .L564 1906 MRR Alc.

CHILDREN--LAW.
see also Juvenile delinquency

CHILDREN--MANAGEMENT--HANDBOOKS,
MANUALS, ETC.
Cava, Esther Laden. The complete
question-and-answer book of child
training. New York, Hawthorn Books
[1972] viii, 376 p.   [$8.95]
649/.1 79-179118
    HQ769 .C348 MRR Alc.

CHILDREN--PERIODICALS--INDEXES.
Child development abstracts and
bibliography. v. 1-
June/Sept./Dec. 1927- Chicago, Ill.
[etc.] Univ. of Chicago Press [etc.]
016.6491   46-31872
    HQ750 .A1C47 MRR Alc Full set

CHILDREN--POETRY--BIBLIOGRAPHY--
CATALOGS.
Shaw, John MacKay. Childhood in
poetry; a catalogue, Detroit, Gale
Research Co. [1967-68, c1967] 5 v.
028.52 67-28092
    Z1037 .S513 MRR Alc.

CHILDREN--RESEARCH.
Review of child development research.
New York, Russell Sage Foundation,
1964- v.   155.4/1 64-20472
    HQ768.8 .R48 MRR Alc.

CHILDREN, ABNORMAL AND BACKWARD
see Handicapped children

CHILDREN, ATYPICAL
see Exceptional children

CHILDREN, EXCEPTIONAL
see Exceptional children

CHILDREN IN LITERATURE.
see also Characters and
characteristics in literature

CHILDREN IN THE UNITED STATES.
Review of child development research.
New York, Russell Sage Foundation,
1964- v.   155.4/1 64-20472
    HQ768.8 .R48 MRR Alc.

CHILDREN'S ENCYCLOPEDIAS AND
DICTIONARIES.
Compton's encyclopedia and fact-
index. [Chicago] F. E. Compton Co.
[1974] 26 v.   031 73-84236
    AG5 .C73 1974 MRR Alc.

CHILDREN'S LIBRARIES
see School libraries

CHILDREN'S LITERATURE.
see also Books and reading for
children

see also Children's poetry

see also Fairy tales

Field, Carolyn W., Subject
collections in children's literature.
New York, Bowker, 1969. 142 p.
[6.50]   028.5 68-56955
    Z688.C47 F5 MRR Alc.

Johnson, Edna, comp. Anthology of
children's literature 2d ed.
[Boston] Houghton Mifflin Co. [1948]
xliv, 1114 p.   028.5 48-7250
    PN6110.C4 J64 1948 MRR Alc.

CHILDREN'S LITERATURE--BIBLIOGRAPHY.
see also School libraries

American Library Association.
Children's Services Division. Book
Reevaluation Committee. Notable
children's books, 1940-1959.
Chicago, American Library
Association, 1966. vi, 39 p.
028.52 66-24177
    Z1037 .A4885 MRR Alc.

American library association. Section
for library work with children.
International committee. Children's
books from foreign languages; New
York, The H. W. Wilson company, 1937.
148 p.   028.5 37-16044
    Z1037 .A4955 MRR Alc.

Best books for children; New York,
R. R. Bowker. 028.52 60-1536
    Z1037 .B545 MRR Alc Latest edition

Books for children. 1960/65-
Chicago, American Library
Association. 028.52 66-29507
    Z1037 .B723 MRR Alc Full set

Children's Book Council, New York.
Children's books: awards & prizes.
[New York, 1969] [32] p. [$4.95]
028.52 78-24483
    Z1037.A2 C52 MRR Alc.

Children's books in print. 1969-
New York, R. R. Bowker Co. 028.52
70-101705
    Z1037.A1 C482 MRR Alc Latest
    edition

Children's books in print. Subject
guide. 1970- New York, R. R. Bowker
Co. 028.52 74-643526
    Z1037.A1 C482 Suppl. MRR Alc
    Latest edition

Eakin, Mary K. Good books for
children; 3d ed. Chicago,
University of Chicago Press [1966]
xv, 407 p.   028.52 66-23687
    Z1037 .E15 1966 MRR Alc.

Eaton, Annie Thaxter. Treasure for
the taking; Rev. ed. New York,
Viking Press [1957] 322 p.   028.5
57-13407
    Z1037 .E2 1957 MRR Alc.

The Elementary school library
collection, phases 1-2-3; 8th ed.
New Brunswick, N.J., Bro-Dart
Foundation, 1973. xxviii, 780 p.
028.52 73-8819
    Z1037 .E4 1973 MRR Alc.

Ellis, Alec. How to find out about
children's literature. 2d ed.
Oxford, New York, Pergamon Press
[1968] xii, 242 p.   67-30614
    PN1009.A1 E43 1968 MRR Alc.

Georgiou, Constantine. Children and
their literature. Englewood Cliffs,
N.J., Prentice-Hall [1969] 501 p.
809.8/928/2 69-10223
    PN1009.A1 G4 MRR Alc.

Hodges, Elizabeth D., Books for
elementary school libraries:
Chicago, American Library
Association, 1969. xiii, 321 p.
[7.50 (pbk)]   028.52 76-77273
    Z1037 .H65 MRR Alc.

Hotchkiss, Jeanette. European
historical fiction and biography for
children and young people. 2d ed.
Metuchen, N.J., Scarecrow Press,
1972. 272 p.   028.52 72-1597
    Z5917.H6 H6 1972 MRR Alc.

Huus, Helen, Children's books to
enrich the social studies; Rev. ed.
Washington, National Council for the
Social Studies [c1966] xiii, 201 p.
016.3728/3 67-8284
    Z1037.9 .H8 1966 MRR Alc.

Keating, Charlotte Matthews.
Building bridges of understanding.
Tucson, Ariz., Palo Verde Pub. Co.,
1967. xvii, 134 p.   016.813/008/03
67-27778
    Z1037.A1 K4 MRR Alc.

Kircher, Clara J. Behavior patterns
in children's books; Washington,
Catholic University of America Press
[1966] v, 132 p.   016.6497 66-
18693
    Z1037 .K55 MRR Alc.

Kujoth, Jean Spealman. Best-selling
children's books. Metuchen, N.J.,
Scarecrow Press, 1973. 305 p.
028.52 72-11692
    Z1037 .K83 MRR Alc.

Lock, Clara Beatrice Muriel,
Reference material for young people.
[Hamden, Conn.] Archon Books [1967]
189 p.   028.7 67-41
    Z1037.1 .L8 MRR Alc.

Metzner, Seymour. American history
in juvenile books; New York, H. W.
Wilson Co., 1966. 329 p. 016.973
66-12299
    Z1037 .M32 MRR Alc.

Pellowski, Anne. The world of
children's literature. New York,
Bowker, 1968. x, 538 p. [$18.75
U.S. and Can. ($20.65 elsewhere)]
028.52 67-25022
    Z1037 .P37 MRR Alc.

Rosenberg, Judith K. Young people's
literature in series: publishers' and
non-fiction series; Littleton,
Colo., Libraries Unlimited, 1973.
280 p. [$10.00] 028.52 73-75237
    Z1037 .R7 MRR Alc.

Strang, Ruth May, Gateways to
readable books; [4th ed.] New York,
H. W. Wilson Co., 1966. 245 p.
028.52 65-24136
    Z1037 .S88 1966 MRR Alc.

United States. Library of Congress.
Division for the Blind. Braille
books for juvenile readers;
Washington, 1960. 39 p.   016.028024
60-60059
    Z663.25 .B7 MRR Alc.

CHILDREN'S LITERATURE-- (Cont.)
Wilson, H. W., firm, publishers.
Children's catalog. [1st]- ed.;
1909- New York, The H. W. Wilson
company;   028.5   10-4603
Z1037 .W76 MRR Alc Latest edition

CHILDREN'S LITERATURE--BIBLIOGRAPHY--
CATALOGS.
United States. Library of Congress.
Children's Book Section. The wide
world of children's books;
Washington [for sale by the Supt. of
Docs., U.S. Govt. Print. Off.] 1972.
iv, 84 p. [$0.50] 028.52 72-4848

Z663.292 .W5 MRR Alc.

CHILDREN'S LITERATURE--BIBLIOGRAPHY--
PERIODICALS.
The School library journal book
review. 1968/69- New York. R. R.
Bowker Co.   72-79427
Z1037.A1 S3 MRR Alc Full set

United States. Library of Congress.
Children's Book Section. Children's
books. 1964- Washington, Library of
Congress; [for sale by the
Superintendent of Documents, U.S.
Govt. Print. Off.] 65-60014
Z1037 .U7 MRR Alc Full set

CHILDREN'S LITERATURE--BIO-BIBLIOGRAPHY.
De Montreville, Doris. Third book of
junior authors. New York, H. W.
Wilson Co., 1972. 320 p.
809/.89282 75-149381
PN1009.A1 D45 MRR Biog.

Doyle, Brian. The who's who of
children's literature. New York,
Schocken Books [1968] xi, 380 p.
[$10.00] 028.52 68-28904
PN452 .D6 1968b MRR Biog.

Fuller, Muriel, ed. More junior
authors. New York, H. W. Wilson Co.,
1963. vi, 235 p. 928 63-11816
PN1009.A1 F8 MRR Biog.

Hopkins, Lee Bennett. Books are by
people; New York, Citation Press,
1969. xv, 349 p. 028.5/0922 70-
96312
PN452 .H65 MRR Biog.

Something about the author. v. 1-
[1971- Detroit, Gale Research.
028.52/0922 [B] [920] 72-27107
PN451 .S6 MRR Biog Full set

Ward, Martha Eads. Authors of books
for young people, 2d ed. Metuchen,
N.J., Scarecrow Press, 1971. 579 p.
809.8/9282 B 70-157057
PN452 .W35 1971 MRR Biog.

CHILDREN'S LITERATURE--HISTORY AND
CRITICISM.
Arbuthnot, May Hill, Children and
books 4th ed. Glenview, Ill.,
Scott, Foresman [1972] 836 p.
028.5 70-188618
PN1009.A1 A7 1972 MRR Alc.

Ellis, Alec. How to find out about
children's literature. 2d ed.
Oxford, New York, Pergamon Press
[1968] xli, 242 p.   67-30614
PN1009.A1 E43 MRR Alc.

Georgiou, Constantine. Children and
their literature. Englewood Cliffs,
N.J., Prentice-Hall [1969] 501 p.
809.8/928/2 69-10223
PN1009.A1 G4 MRR Alc.

Kunitz, Stanley Jasspon, ed. The
junior book of authors, New York,
The H. W. Wilson company, 1934. xv,
400 p. 928 34-36776
PN1009.A1 K8 MRR Biog.

Meigs, Cornelia Lynde, ed. A
critical history of children's
literature; Rev. ed. [New York]
Macmillan [1969] xxviii, 708 p.
028.5/09 73-7659
PN1009.A1 M4 1969 MRR Alc.

Targ, William, ed. Bibliophile in
the nursery; [1st ed.] Cleveland,
World Pub. Co. [1957] 503 p.   028.5
57-8281
Z992 .T15 MRR Alc.

CHILDREN'S LITERATURE--HISTORY AND
CRITICISM--BIBLIOGRAPHY.
Haviland, Virginia, Children's
literature; a guide to reference
sources. Washington, Library of
Congress; [for sale by the
Superintendent of Documents, U.S.
Govt. Print. Off.] 1966. x, 341 p.
016.8098/928/2 66-62734
Z663.292 .H35 MRR Alc.

CHILDREN'S LITERATURE--INDEXES.
Eakin, Mary K. Subject index to
books for intermediate grades. 3d
ed. Chicago, American Library
Association, 1963. vi, 308 p.
028.52 63-12951
Z1037 .E16 1963 MRR Alc.

Eakin, Mary K. Subject index to
books for primary grades. 3d ed.
Chicago, American Library
Association, 1967. viii, 113 p.
028.52 66-30062
Z1037 .E17 1967 MRR Alc.

CHILDREN'S LITERATURE--PUBLISHING--
UNITED STATES--DIRECTORIES.
Gillespie, John Thomas. Paperback
books for young people; Chicago,
American Library Association, 1972.
viii, 177 p.   070.5/73 72-2390
Z479 .G55 MRR Alc.

Welch, D'Alté Aldridge, A
bibliography of American children's
books printed prior to 1821. [Barre?
Mass.] American Antiquarian Society
and Barre Publishers, 1972. lxvi,
516 p.   081 s 028.52 73-162761
Z1232 .W44 1972b MRR Alc.

CHILDREN'S LITERATURE--BIO-BIBLIOGRAPHY.
Kunitz, Stanley Jasspon, ed. The
junior book of authors. 2d ed., rev.
New York, Wilson, 1951. vii, 309 p.
928 51-13057
PN1009.A1 K8 1951 MRR Biog.

CHILDREN'S LITERATURE, AMERICAN--
BIBLIOGRAPHY.
Welch, D'Alté Aldridge, A
bibliography of American children's
books printed prior to 1821. [Barre?
Mass.] American Antiquarian Society
and Barre Publishers, 1972. lxvi,
516 p.   081 s 028.52 73-162761
Z1232 .W44 1972b MRR Alc.

CHILDREN'S LITERATURE, ENGLISH--
BIBLIOGRAPHY.
Sloane, William. Children's books in
England & America in the seventeenth
century: New York, King's Crown
Press, Columbia University, 1955.
ix, 251 p.   028.5 54-9938
Z1037 .S62 MRR Alc.

CHILDREN'S LITERATURE, ENGLISH--HISTORY
AND CRITICISM.
Sloane, William. Children's books in
England & America in the seventeenth
century: New York, King's Crown
Press, Columbia University, 1955.
ix, 251 p.   028.5 54-9938
Z1037 .S62 MRR Alc.

CHILDREN'S PARAPHERNALIA.
see also Games

CHILDREN'S PERIODICALS--BIBLIOGRAPHY.
American Library Association.
Periodicals List Subcommittee.
Periodicals for school libraries;
Chicago, American Library
Association, 1969. xvii, 217 p.
016.051 70-80870
Z6944.S8 A4 MRR Alc.

CHILDREN'S PERIODICALS--DIRECTORIES.
Dobler, Lavinia G. The Dobler world
directory of youth periodicals, New
York, Schulte Pub. Co., 1966. xi, 37
p.   65-28886
Z6944.C5 D6 1966 MRR Alc.

CHILDREN'S PERIODICALS--INDEXES.
Subject index to children's
magazines. v. 2, no. 8-   Mar./Aug.
1950- Madison, Wis. 051 72-627331

Z6944.C5 W5 MRR Alc Full set

CHILDREN'S PLAYS--BIBLIOGRAPHY.
Chicorel, Marietta. Chicorel theater
index to plays for young people in
periodicals, anthologies, and
collections, 1st ed. New York,
Chicorel Library Pub. Corp., 1974.
489 p.   808/.82/016 74-173632
Z5784.C5 C55 MRR Alc.

Davis, Jed Horace. Children's
theatre; New York, Harper [1960]
416 p.   792.0226 60-15622
PN3157 .D3 MRR Alc.

CHILDREN'S PLAYS--INDEXES.
Kreider, Barbara. Index to
children's plays in collections.
Metuchen, N.J., Scarecrow Press,
1972. 138 p. 016.812/041 72-3008

PN1627 .K7 MRR Alc.

CHILDREN'S PLAYS--PRESENTATION, ETC.
Davis, Jed Horace. Children's
theatre; New York, Harper [1960]
416 p.   792.0226 60-15622
PN3157 .D3 MRR Alc.

CHILDREN'S POETRY.
see also Nursery rhymes

Cole, William, ed. Poems for seasons
and celebrations. [1st ed.]
Cleveland, World Pub. Co. [1961] 191
p.   808.81 (J) 61-12012
PS595.H6 C6 MRR Alc.

Ireson, Barbara, ed. The Barnes book
of nursery verse. New York, Barnes
[1960] 286 p.   808.81 59-14348
PN6110.C4 I7 MRR Alc.

Mother Goose. The annotated Mother
Goose, [1st ed.] New York, C. N.
Potter [c1962] 350 p.   398.8 62-
21606
PZ8.3.M85 Bar MRR Alc.

Opie, Iona (Archibald), comp. The
Oxford book of children's verse;
Oxford, Clarendon Press, 1973.
xxxii, 407 p. [£2.25] 821/.008 73-
172900
PN6110.C4 O529 1973b MRR Alc.

Sechrist, Elizabeth (Hough) One
thousand poems for children,
Philadelphia, Macrae-Smith-company,
1946. xiii p., 1 l., 601 p. 808.81
46-4924
PN6110.C4 S43 MRR Alc.

Stevenson, Burton Egbert, comp. The
home book of verse, American and
English; 9th ed. New York, Holt
[1953] 2 v. (lxxxiv, 4013 p.)
821.982 53-3870
PR1175 .S76 1953 MRR Ref Desk.

CHILDREN'S POETRY--BIBLIOGRAPHY.
American Library Association.
Subject index to poetry for children
and young people, Chicago, 1957.
582 p.   016.80881 57-8798
PN1023 .A5 MRR Alc.

Haviland, Virginia, Children &
poetry; Washington, Library of
Congress; [for sale by the Supt. of
Docs., U.S. Govt. Print. Off.] 1969.
x, 67 p. [0.75] 028.52 70-603744

Z663.292 .H34 MRR Alc.

CHILDREN'S POETRY--BIBLIOGRAPHY--
CATALOGS.
Shaw, John MacKay. Childhood in
poetry; a catalogue. Detroit, Gale
Research Co. [1967-68, c1967] 5 v.
028.52 67-28092
Z1037 .S513 MRR Alc.

CHILDREN'S POETRY--INDEXES.
American Library Association.
Subject index to poetry for children
and young people, Chicago, 1957.
582 p.   016.80881 57-8798
PN1023 .A5 MRR Alc.

Brewton, John Edmund, Index to
children's poetry; New York, Wilson,
1942. xxxii, 965 p.   821.0016 42-
20148
PN1023 .B7 MRR Alc.

Brewton, John Edmund, Index to
poetry for children and young people,
1964-1969; New York, Wilson, 1972.
xxx, 575 p.   821/.001/6 71-161574
PN1023 .B72 MRR Alc.

Macpherson, Maud Russell. Children's
poetry index, Boston, The F. W.
Faxon company, 1938. xiii, 453 p.
808.81 38-9870
PN1023 .M25 MRR Alc.

Morris, Helen (Soutar) Where's that
poem? Oxford, Blackwell, 1967.
xxxv, 300 p. [25/-] 016.821 67-
78385
PN1023 .M6 MRR Alc.

CHILDREN'S REFERENCE BOOKS.
Peterson, Carolyn Sue, Reference
books for elementary and junior high
school libraries. Metuchen, N.J.,
Scarecrow Press, 1970. 191 p.
028.52 72-8294
Z1037.1 .P4 MRR Alc.

CHILDREN'S STORIES--INDEXES.
American Library Association.
Subject and title index to short
stories for children. Chicago,
American Library Association, 1955.
vi, 333 p.   028.5 55-10208
Z1037 .A4924 MRR Alc.

CHILE--BIBLIOGRAPHY.
Briseno, Ramon, Estadística
bibliográfica de la literatura
chilena. Santiago de Chile, Imprenta
chilena, 1862-79. 2 v. 03-8013
Z1701 .B85 MRR Alc.

CHILE--BIOGRAPHY.
Diccionario biográfico de Chile.
[1.]- ed.; 1936- Santiago (Chile)
Soc. imp. y lit. Universo. 920.083
sd 40-12
F3055 .D45 MRR Biog Latest edition

CHILE--DIRECTORIES.
Guía de la administración pública
de Chile y de los principales
organismos del sector privado.
Santiago.   72-449697
JL2621 .G8 MRR Alc Latest edition

CHILE--GAZETTEERS.
United States. Office of Geography.
Chile; 2d ed. Washington, 1967.
vii, 591 p.   918.3 67-61143
F3054 .T52 1967 MRR Alc.

CHILE--IMPRINTS.
Briseño, Ramon, Estadística
bibliográfica de la literatura
chilena. Santiago de Chile, Imprenta
chilena, 1862-79. 2 v. 03-8013
Z1701 .B85 MRR Alc.

CHILE--REGISTERS.
Guía de la administración pública
de Chile y de los principales
organismos del sector privado.
Santiago. 72-449697
JL2621 .G8 MRR Alc Latest edition

CHILEAN FICTION--BIBLIOGRAPHY.
Castillo, Homero. Historia
bibliográfica de la novela chilena,
Charlottesville, Bibliographical
Society of the University of
Virginia, 1961. 214 p. 61-4723
Z1714.F4 C33 MRR Alc.

CHILEAN LITERATURE--BIBLIOGRAPHY.
Briseño, Ramon, Estadística
bibliográfica de la literatura
chilena. Santiago de Chile, Imprenta
chilena, 1862-79. 2 v. 03-8013
Z1701 .B85 MRR Alc.

CHINA.
China yearbook. 1937/43- Taipeh,
Taiwan [etc.] China Pub. Co. 43-
14605
DS777.53 .C459 MRR Alc Latest
edition

Whitaker, Donald P. Area handbook
for the People's Republic of China
Washington, For sale by the Supt. of
Docs., U.S. Govt. Print. Off.] 1972.
xvi, 729 p. [$4.75] 915.1/03/5 72-
600022
DS706 .W46 MRR Alc.

Wu, Yuan-li. China; New York,
Praeger [1973] 915 p. [$35.00]
915.1/03/5 72-101683
DS706 .W8 MRR Alc.

CHINA--ANTIQUITIES--TERMINOLOGY.
Hansford, S. Howard. A glossary of
Chinese art and archeology. London,
China Society, 1954. xi, 104 p.
709.51 55-24573
N7340 .H3 1954 MRR Alc.

CHINA--ARMED FORCES--STATISTICS.
United States. Dept. of the Army.
Communist China: a bibliographic
survey. Washington: [For sale by the
Supt. of Docs., U.S. Govt. Print.
Off.] 1971. x, 253 p.
016.9151/03/5 72-613755
Z3108.A5 U48 MRR Alc.

CHINA--BIBLIOGRAPHY.
Berton, Peter Alexander Menquez,
Contemporary China; Stanford,
Calif., Hoover Institution on War,
Revolution, and Peace 1967. xxix,
695 p. 016.9151/03/5 67-14235
Z3106 .B39 MRR Alc.

Kerner, Robert Joseph, Northeastern
Asia, a selected bibliography;
Berkeley, Calif., University of
California press, 1939. 2 v.
016.95 39-33136
Z3001 .K38 MRR Alc.

Lust, John. Index Sinicus:
Cambridge, Eng., W. Heffer [1964]
xxx, 663 p. 64-7164
Z3101 .L8 MRR Alc.

Nathan, Andrew James. Modern China,
1840-1972; Ann Arbor, Center for
Chinese Studies, University of
Michigan, 1973. vi, 95 p. [$2.00]
016.9151 74-167311
Z3106 .N32 MRR Alc.

United States. Dept. of the Army.
Communist China: a bibliographic
survey. Washington: [For sale by the
Supt. of Docs., U.S. Govt. Print.
Off.] 1971. x, 253 p.
016.9151/03/5 72-613755
Z3108.A5 U48 MRR Alc.

United States. Library of Congress.
Far Eastern languages catalog.
Boston, G. K. Hall, 1972. 22 v.
019.1/09753 72-5364
Z3009 .U56 MRR Alc (Dk 33)

United States. Library of Congress.
Division of bibliography.
Bibliography of China, Japan and the
Philippine Islands. [Concord, N.H.,
1925] 1. 214-246. 27-14560
Z663.28 .B52 MRR Alc.

Yüan, T'ung-li, China in Western
literature; New Haven, Far Eastern
Publications, Yale University, 1958.
xix, 802 p. 016.951 58-59833
Z3101 .Y8 MRR Alc.

Yüan, T'ung-li, Russian works on
China, 1918-1960. New Haven, Far
Eastern Publications, Yale
University, 1961. xiv, 162 p.
016.9151 61-16699
Z3106 .Y83 MRR Alc.

CHINA--BIBLIOGRAPHY--CATALOGS.
Harvard University. Library. China,
Japan, and Korea; classification
schedule, Cambridge, Distributed by
Harvard University Press, 1968. 494
p. 017/.1 68-14151
Z3109 .H3 MRR Alc.

CHINA--BIOGRAPHY.
Bartke, Wolfgang. Chinaköpfe.
Hannover, Verlag für Literatur und
Zeitgeschehen (1966) viii, 454 p.
[DM 54.00] 354.51/000922 67-76106
DS778.A1 B3 MRR Biog.

Biographical dictionary of Republican
China. New York, Columbia University
Press, 1967-71. 4 v. [$25.00 (v.
3)] 920.051 67-12006
DS778.A1 B5 MRR Biog.

Boorman, Howard L., ed. Men and
politics in modern China: New York,
Columbia University, 1960- v.
920.051 60-1816
DS778.A1 B6 MRR Biog.

Chinese Communist who's who. Taipei,
Institute of International Relations,
1970-71. 2 v. [$20.00 per vol.]
72-169537
DS778.A1 C4913 MRR Biog.

Klein, Donald W. Biographic
dictionary of Chinese communism, 1921-
1965 Cambridge, Mass., Harvard
University Press, 1971. 2 v. (1194
p.) [$30.00] 951.04/922 B 69-
12725
DS778.A1 K55 1971 MRR Biog.

Perleberg, Max, Who's who in modern
China. Hong Kong, Ye Olde Printerie,
1954. xii, 428 p. 920.051 54-
19583
DS734 .P4 1954 MRR Biog.

Surveys and Research Corporation,
Washington, D.C. Directory of
selected scientific institutions in
mainland China. Stanford, Calif.,
Published for the National Science
Foundation by the Hoover Institution
Press [c1970] xxii, 469 p. [$19.50]
502/.4/51 76-138410
Q72 .S9 MRR Alc.

United States. Central Intelligence
Agency. Chinese Communist Party
Central Committee members.
[Washington] 1972. iii, 76 p.
329.9/51 72-602398
JQ1519.AF U55 1972 MRR Biog.

United States. Library of Congress.
Orientalia division. Eminent Chinese
of the Ch'ing period (1644-1912)
Washington, U.S. Govt. print. off.,
1943-44. 2 v. 920.051 43-53640
Z663.382 .E5 MRR Alc.

Who's who in Communist China.
[Kowloon] Hong Kong, Union Research
Institute [1966] v, 754 p.
951.050922 66-4063
DS778.A1 W45 MRR Biog.

CHINA--BIOGRAPHY--BIBLIOGRAPHY.
Wu, Eugene Wen-chin, Leaders of
twentieth-century China; Stanford,
Calif., Stanford University Press,
1956- vi, 106 p. 016.920051 56-
13811
Z3106 .W8 MRR Biog.

**CHINA--CIVILIZATION--ADDRESSES, ESSAYS,
LECTURES.**
Meskill, John Thomas, An
introduction to Chinese civilization,
New York, Columbia University Press,
1973. 699 p. [$17.50] 915.1/03
72-9410
DS721 .M5 MRR Alc.

CHINA--COMMERCE--HISTORY.
Hsiao, Liang-lin, China's foreign
trade statistics, 1864-1949 /
Cambridge, Mass. : East Asian
Research Center, Harvard University :
distributed by Harvard University
Press, 1974. xvi, 297 p. ;
382/.0951 74-78789
HF3771 .H74 MRR Alc.

**CHINA--DESCRIPTION AND TRAVEL--1949- --
GUIDE-BOOKS.**
Felber, John Edward. The American's
tourist manual for the People's
Republic of China / [1st ed.].
Newark, N.J. : International
Intertrade Index, [1974] 224 p. :
915.1/04/5 73-93210
DS711 .F46 MRR Alc.

**CHINA--DESCRIPTION AND TRAVEL--GUIDE-
BOOKS.**
Felber, John Edward. The American's
tourist manual for the People's
Republic of China / [1st ed.].
Newark, N.J. : International
Intertrade Index, [1974] 224 p. :
915.1/04/5 73-93210
DS711 .F46 MRR Alc.

Nagel Publishers. China. Geneva,
Paris, [etc.] Nagel (1968). 1504, 32
p. 915.1/04/5 74-359710
DS705 .N313 MRR Alc.

**CHINA--EMIGRATION AND IMMIGRATION--
BIBLIOGRAPHY.**
United States. Library of Congress.
Division of bibliography. Select
list of references on Chinese
immigration. Washington, Govt.
Print. Off., 1904. 31 p. 04-5901
Z663.28 .S36 MRR Alc.

**CHINA--FOREIGN RELATIONS--1949- --
TREATIES.**
Johnston, Douglas M. Agreements of
the People's Republic of China, 1949-
1967: Cambridge, Harvard University
Press, 1968. xvii, 286 p. [$12.50]
341.2/51 68-28694
Z6464.T8 J63 MRR Alc.

CHINA--FOREIGN RELATIONS--INDIA.
Rowland, John, A history of Sino-
Indian relations: Princeton, N.J.,
Van Nostrand [1967] xv, 248 p.
327.51/054 66-29857
DS450.C5 R6 MRR Alc.

CHINA--FOREIGN RELATIONS--RUSSIA.
Gittings, John. Survey of the Sino-
Soviet dispute: London, New York
[etc.] issued under the auspices of
the Royal Institute of International
Affairs [by] Oxford U.P., 1968. xlix,
410 p. [84/-] 327.51/047 75-
356659
DS740.5.R8 G5 MRR Alc.

CHINA--FOREIGN RELATIONS--UNITED STATES.
United States. Dept. of State. The
China white paper, August 1949.
Stanford, Calif., Stanford University
Press [1967] xxii, 1079 p.
327.51/073 67-26650
E183.8.C5 U53 1967 MRR Alc.

United States. Dept. of State.
Historical Office. China, 1942-
Washington, U.S. Govt. Print. Off.,
1956- v. 327.73051 57-61196
JX1428.C6 A54 MRR Alc.

CHINA--GAZETTEERS.
United States. Geographic Names
Division. Mainland China: 2d ed.
Washington, Army Map Service, 1968-
v. 915.1/003 70-600383
DS705 .U482 MRR Alc.

CHINA--HISTORY.
Li, Dun Jen, The ageless Chinese,
New York, Scribner [1965] xvi, 586
p. 951 65-14034
DS735 .L43 MRR Alc.

Meskill, John Thomas, An
introduction to Chinese civilization,
New York, Columbia University Press,
1973. 699 p. [$17.50] 915.1/03
72-9410
DS721 .M5 MRR Alc.

Schurmann, Herbert Franz, comp. The
China reader, New York, Random House
[1967] 3 v. 951 66-21489
DS735 .S43 MRR Alc.

CHINA--HISTORY--1900-
Clubb, Oliver Edmund, 20th century
China, 2d ed. New York, Columbia
University Press, 1972. xiv, 526 p.
[$12.00] 951.04 78-187028
DS774 .C57 1972 MRR Alc.

CHINA--HISTORY--1949-
Hou, Fu-wu. A short history of
Chinese communism, completely updated
Englewood Cliffs, N.J., Prentice-
Hall [1973] x, 278 p. [$6.95]
915.1/03/5 73-9532
DS777.55 .H575 1973 MRR Alc.

CHINA--HISTORY--1949- --CHRONOLOGY.
Cheng, Peter, A chronology of the
People's Republic of China from
October 1, 1949. Totowa, N.J., Rowan
and Littlefield, 1972. xvii, 347 p.
951/.05 70-184667
DS777.55 .C44567 MRR Alc.

CHINA--HISTORY--CHRONOLOGY.
China yearbook. 1937/43- Taipeh,
Taiwan [etc.] China Pub. Co. 43-
14605
DS777.53 .C459 MRR Alc Latest
edition

Moule, Arthur Christopher, The
rulers of China, 221 B.C.-A.D. 1949;
London, Routledge and K Paul [1957]
xxiii, 131 p. 951.002 57-2823
DS733 .M6 1957 MRR Alc.

**CHINA--HISTORY, LOCAL--BIBLIOGRAPHY--
CATALOGS.**
United States. Library of Congress.
Orientalia Division. A catalog of
Chinese local histories in the
Library of Congress. Washington,
U.S. Govt. Print. Off., 1942. xi,
552, 21 p. c 66-3135
Z663.382 .C3 MRR Alc.

CHINA--IMPRINTS.
United States. Library of Congress.
Far Eastern languages catalog.
Boston, G. K. Hall, 1972. 22 v.
019.1/08753 72-5364
Z3009 .U56 MRR Alc (Dk 33)

United States. Library of Congress.
[Kuo hui t'u shu kuan ts'ang Chung-
kuo shan pên shu lu (romanized
form)] Washington, 1957. 2 v. (1306
p.) c 58-5001
Z663 .K8 MRR Alc.

CHINA--INTELLECTUAL LIFE--BIBLIOGRAPHY.
Liu, Chun-jo, Controversies in
modern Chinese intellectual history;
Cambridge. Published by the East
Asian Research Center, Harvard
University; distributed by Harvard
University Press, 1964. vii, 207 p.
64-56634
Z3108.A5 L5 MRR Alc.

CHINA--KINGS AND RULERS.
Moule, Arthur Christopher, The
rulers of China, 221 B.C.--A.D. 1949;
London, Routledge and K. Paul [1957]
xxiii, 131 p. 951.002 57-2823
DS733 .M6 1957 MRR Alc.

**CHINA--LEARNED INSTITUTIONS AND
SOCIETIES--DIRECTORIES.**
Surveys and Research Corporation,
Washington, D.C. Directory of
selected scientific institutions in
mainland China. Stanford, Calif.,
Published for the National Science
Foundation by the Hoover Institution
Press [c1970] xxii, 469 p. [$19.50]
502/.4/51 76-138410
Q72 .S9 MRR Alc.

United States. Library of Congress.
Science and Technology Division.
Mainland China organizations of
higher learning in science and
technology and their publications,
Washington, 1961. vi, 104 p. 61-
60070
Z663.41 .M2 MRR Alc.

CHINA--OFFICIALS AND EMPLOYEES.
Bartke, Wolfgang. Chinaköpfe.
Hannover, Verlag für Literatur und
Zeitgeschehen (1966) viii, 454 p.
[DM 54.00] 354.51/000922 67-76106
DS778.A1 B3 MRR Biog.

Who's who in Communist China.
[Kowloon] Hong Kong, Union Research
Institute [1966] v, 754 p.
951.050922 66-4063
DS778.A1 W45 MRR Biog.

**CHINA--OFFICIALS AND EMPLOYEES--
DIRECTORIES.**
Directory of Chinese Communist
officials. [n.p.] 1971. v, 434 p.
70-289477
JQ1507 .D52 1971 MRR Alc.

CHINA--POLITICS AND GOVERNMENT--1949-
Bartke, Wolfgang. Chinaköpfe.
Hannover, Verlag für Literatur und
Zeitgeschehen (1966) viii, 454 p.
[DM 54.00] 354.51/000922 67-76106
DS778.A1 B3 MRR Biog.

Perleberg, Max, Who's who in modern
China Hong Kong, Ye Olde Printerie,
1954. xii, 428 p. 920.051 54-
19583
DS734 .P4 1954 MRR Biog.

Who's who in Communist China.
[Kowloon] Hong Kong, Union Research
Institute [1966] v, 754 p.
951.050922 66-4063
DS778.A1 W45 MRR Biog.

CHINA--REGISTERS.
Bartke, Wolfgang. Chinaköpfe.
Hannover, Verlag für Literatur und
Zeitgeschehen (1966) viii, 454 p.
[DM 54.00] 354.51/000922 67-76106
DS778.A1 B3 MRR Biog.

Chinese Communist who's who. Taipei,
Institute of International Relations,
1970-71. 2 v. [$20.00 per vol.]
72-169537
DS778.A1 C4913 MRR Biog.

Directory of Chinese Communist
officials. [n.p.] 1971. v, 434 p.
70-289477
JQ1507 .D52 1971 MRR Alc.

United States. Central Intelligence
Agency. Chinese Communist Party
Central Committee members.
[Washington] 1972. iii, 76 p.
329.9/51 72-602398
JQ1519.A5 U55 1972 MRR Biog.

Who's who in Communist China.
[Kowloon] Hong Kong, Union Research
Institute [1966] v, 754 p.
951.050922 66-4063
DS778.A1 W45 MRR Biog.

CHINA--SOCIAL LIFE AND CUSTOMS.
Williams, Charles Alfred Speed,
Encyclopedia of Chinese symbolism and
art motives; New York, Julian Press,
1960 [i.e. 1961] xxi, 468 p.
398.30951 60-15987
GR335 .W53 1961 MRR Alc.

CHINA--STATISTICS.
Chen, Nai-ruenn, Chinese economic
statistics; Chicago, Aldine Pub. Co.
[1967] xxxi, 539 p. 315.1 66-
15200
HA1706 .C48 MRR Alc.

Hsiao, Liang-lin, China's foreign
trade statistics, 1864-1949 /
Cambridge, Mass. : East Asian
Research Center, Harvard University :
distributed by Harvard University
Press, 1974. xvi, 297 p. ;
382/.0951 74-78789
HF3771 .H74 MRR Alc.

Wu, Yuan-li. China; New York,
Praeger [1973] 915 p. [$35.00]
915.1/03/5 72-101683
DS706 .W8 MRR Alc.

**CHINA (PEOPLE'S REPUBLIC OF CHINA, 1949-
)--BIBLIOGRAPHY.**
Nathan, Andrew James. Modern China,
1840-1972; Ann Arbor, Center for
Chinese Studies, University of
Michigan, 1973. vi, 95 p. [$2.00]
016.9151 74-167311
Z3106 .N32 MRR Alc.

CHINAWARE
see Porcelain

CHINESE ART
see Art, Chinese

**CHINESE CHARACTERS--DICTIONARIES--
ENGLISH.**
Nelson, Andrew Nathaniel. The modern
reader's Japanese-English character
dictionary. 1st ed. Tokyo, Rutland,
Vt.; C. E. Tuttle Co. [1962] 1048 p.
495.632 61-11973
PL679 .N4 MRR Alc.

**CHINESE CHARACTERS--DICTIONARIES--
JAPANESE.**
Nelson, Andrew Nathaniel. The modern
reader's Japanese-English character
dictionary. 1st ed. Tokyo, Rutland,
Vt.; C. E. Tuttle Co. [1962] 1048 p.
495.632 61-11973
PL679 .N4 MRR Alc.

CHINESE IMPRINTS--CATALOGS.
United States. Library of Congress.
Far Eastern languages catalog.
Boston, G. K. Hall, 1972. 22 v.
019.1/08753 72-5364
Z3009 .U56 MRR Alc (Dk 33)

CHINESE IN THE UNITED STATES.
Kung, Shien-woo, Chinese in American
life: Seattle, University of
Washington Press, 1962. xv, 352 p.
325.2510973 62-9273
E184.C5 K8 MRR Alc.

Lee, Rose Hum. The Chinese in the
United States of America. [Hong
Kong] Hong Kong University Press,
1960. 465 p. 325.2510973 60-3959
E184.C5 L53 MRR Alc.

CHINESE LANGUAGE--DIALECTS--CANTON.
Chen, Janey. A practical English-
Chinese pronouncing dictionary; [1st
ed.] Rutland, Vt., C. E. Tuttle Co.
[1970] xxix, 601 p. [12.50]
495.1/3/2 78-77122
PL1455 .C579 MRR Alc.

Cowles, Roy T. The Cantonese
speaker's dictionary, [Hong Kong]
Hong Kong University Press;
[exclusive agents for all countries
except east of Burma: Oxford
University Press, London] 1965.
xvii, 1318, iv, 232 p. 66-808
PL1736 .C6 1965 MRR Alc.

CHINESE LANGUAGE--DICTIONARIES--ENGLISH.
Cowles, Roy T. The Cantonese
speaker's dictionary, [Hong Kong]
Hong Kong University Press;
[exclusive agents for all countries
except east of Burma: Oxford
University Press, London] 1965.
xvii, 1318, iv, 232 p. 66-808
PL1736 .C6 1965 MRR Alc.

Giles, Herbert Allen, A Chinese-
English dictionary, 2d ed., rev. &
enl. Shanghai [etc.] Kelly & Walsh,
limited; London, B. Quaritch, 1912.
2 v. 21-21489
PL1455 .G62 1912 MRR Alc.

Lin, Yutang, Chinese-English
dictionary of modern usage. [Hong
Kong] Chinese University of Hong Kong
[distributed by McGraw-Hill, New
York] 1972. lxvi, 1720 p.
495.1/3/21 72-3899
PL1455 .L67 MRR Alc.

MacGillivray, Donald, A Mandarin-
romanized dictionary of Chinese, 9th
ed. Shanghai, 1930. x, 1145, 43 p.
495.132 46-35796
PL1455 .M3 1930 MRR Alc.

Modern Chinese-English technical and
general dictionary. New York, McGraw-
Hill [1963] 3 v. 495.132 63-19880
PL1455 .M59 MRR Alc.

**CHINESE LANGUAGE--DICTIONARIES--
POLYGLOT.**
United States. Air Force. 6004th Air
Intelligence Service Squadron.
Dictionary of common oriental terms;
[n.p.] 1956. 1v. (various pagings)
495 57-60108
PL493 .U52 MRR Alc.

CHINESE LANGUAGE--TERMS AND PHRASES.
Lai, T'ien-ch'ang, ed. and tr.
[Ch'eng yü hsüan i (romanized
form)] [Hong Kong] University Book
Store, University of Hongkong, 1960.
191 p. 495.183 60-2495
PL1497 .L3 MRR Alc.

CHINESE LITERATURE--BIBLIOGRAPHY.
Yuan, T'ung-li, China in Western
literature; New Haven, Far Eastern
Publications, Yale University, 1958.
xix, 802 p. 016.951 58-59833
Z3101 .Y8 MRR Alc.

**CHINESE LITERATURE--BIBLIOGRAPHY--
CATALOGS.**
United States. Library of Congress.
[Kuo hui t'u shu kuan ts'ang Chung-
kuo shan pên shu lu (romanized
form)] Washington, 1957. 2 v. (1306
p.) c 58-5001
Z663 .K8 MRR Alc.

**CHINESE LITERATURE--HISTORY AND
CRITICISM.**
Ch'en, Shou-yi, Chinese literature,
New York, Ronald Press Co. [1961]
665 p. 895.109 61-9426
PL2265 .C45 MRR Alc.

Liu, Wu-chi, An introduction to
Chinese literature. Bloomington,
Indiana University Press, 1966. vii,
321 p. 895.109 66-12729
PL2265 .L5 MRR Alc.

CHINESE PERIODICALS--BIBLIOGRAPHY.
United States. Library of Congress.
Science and Technology Division.
Chinese scientific and technical
serial publications in the
collections of the Library of
Congress. Rev. ed. Washington,
1961. v, 107 p. 016.505 62-60011
Z663.41 .C45 1961 MRR Alc.

United States. Library of Congress.
Science and Technology Division.
Journals in science and technology
published in Japan and mainland
China; Washington, 1961. 47 p.
016.505 61-60647
Z663.41 .J6 MRR Alc.

CHIVALRY.
see also Civilization, Medieval

see also Heraldry

see also Knights and knighthood

CHIVALRY--DICTIONARIES.
Uden, Grant. A dictionary of
chivalry. New York, Crowell [1969,
c1968] 352 p. 394/.7/03 70-10564
CR13 .U3 1969 MRR Alc.

Uden, Grant. A dictionary of
chivalry. New York, Crowell [1969,
c1968] 352 p. 394/.7/03 70-10564
CR13 .U3 1969 MRR Alc.

CHOICE (PSYCHOLOGY)
see also Decision-making

CHOICE OF BOOKS
see Book selection

CHOICE OF PROFESSION
see Vocational guidance

CHOREOGRAPHY.
see also Ballet

CHRIST
see Jesus Christ

CHRISTIAN ANTIQUITIES.
Finegan, Jack, Light from the
ancient past; [2d ed. Princeton,
N.J.] Princeton University Press,
1959. xxxvii, 638 p. 220.93 59-
11072
BS635 .F5 1959 MRR Alc.

**CHRISTIAN ANTIQUITIES--DICTIONARIES--
FRENCH.**
Cabrol, Fernand, Dictionnaire
d'archéologie chrétienne et de
liturgie, Paris, Letouzey et Ané,
1907- v. 03-15097
BR95 .C2 MRR Alc.

CHRISTIAN ANTIQUITIES--ROME.
Thynne, Roger. The churches of Rome,
London, K. Paul, Trench, Trubner &
co., ltd.; New York, E. P. Dutton &
co., 1924. xxxii, 460 p.   25-3760
BX4634.R6 T5 MRR Alc.

CHRISTIAN ART AND SYMBOLISM.
see also Church architecture

Ferguson, George Wells, Signs &
symbols in Christian art. New York,
Oxford University Press [1954] xiii,
346 p.   704.9482 54-13072
N7830 .F37 MRR Alc.

Griffith, Helen Stuart. The sign
language of our faith; New York,
Morehouse-Gorham co. [1944] 3 p. l.,
9-92 p. incl. front., illus. 246.5
44-4303
BV150 .G7 1944 MRR Alc.

Post, Willard Ellwood. Saints,
signs, and symbols. New York,
Morehouse-Barlow Co. [1962] 80 p.
246 62-19257
BV150 .P6 MRR Alc.

Réau, Louis. Iconographie de l'art
chrétien. [1. éd.] Paris, Presses
universitaires de France, 1955-59. 3
v. in 6. a 56-1728
N7830 .R37 MRR Alc.

Waters, Clara (Erskine) Clement, A
handbook of legendary and
mythological art. [14th impression]
Boston, New York, Houghton, Mifflin
and company [189-?] xii, 575 p. 04-
11646
N7760 .W33 MRR Alc.

Webber, Frederick Roth, Church
symbolism; 2d ed., rev. Cleveland,
J. H. Jansen, 1938. 6 p. l., ix, 413
p. incl. front., illus., plates. 38-
33530
BV150 .W4 1938 MRR Alc.

Whittemore, Carroll Ernest. Symbols
of the church: [Boston, Whittemore
Associates, 1953] 14 p. 246 54-
9095
BV150 .W44 MRR Alc.

CHRISTIAN ART AND SYMBOLISM--
DICTIONARIES.
Appleton, LeRoy H. Symbolism in
liturgical art. New York, Scribner
[1959] 120 p. 704.948 59-7203
N7825 .A7 MRR Alc.

Lemke, Antje B. Museum companion;
[New York] Hippocrene [1974] vii,
211 p. [$6.95] 703 73-76577
N33 .L38 1974 MRR Alc.

Whittlesey, Eunice S. Symbols and
legends in Western art; New York,
Scribner [1972] ix, 367 p. [$7.95]
704.94 71-162764
N7740 .W53 MRR Alc.

CHRISTIAN BIOGRAPHY.
Barker, William Pierson. Who's who
in church history Old Tappan, N.J.,
F. H. Revell Co. [1969] 319 p.
[6.95] 209/.22 74-85306
BR1700.2 .B37 MRR Biog.

Corpus dictionary of Western
churches. Washington, Corpus
Publications [1970] xviii, 820 p.
[$25.00] 203 78-99501
BR95 .C67 MRR Alc.

Deen, Edith. Great women of the
Christian faith. [1st ed.] New
York, Harper [1959] 428 p.   922 59-
12821
BR1713 .D4 MRR Alc.

Lexikon für Theologie und Kirche;
2., völlig neu bearb. Aufl.,
Freiburg, Herder, 1957-65. 10 v.
58-41506
BR95 .L48 MRR Alc.

Moyer, Elgin Sylvester, ed. Who was
who in church history, Rev. ed.
Chicago, Moody Press [1968] vi, 466
p. 200/.922 67-14391
BR1700 .M64 1968 MRR Biog.

Neill, Stephen Charles, Bp. Concise
dictionary of the Christian world
mission. Nashville, Abingdon Press
[1971] xxi, 682 p. [$10.50]
266/.003 76-21888
BV2040 .N44 MRR Alc.

The Oxford dictionary of the
Christian Church, 2d ed., London,
New York, Oxford University Press,
1974. xxxi, 1518 p. [£13.50] 203
74-163871
BR95 .O8 1974 MRR Alc.

Payne, Pierre Stephen Robert, The
holy fire; [1st ed.] New York,
Harper [c1957] 313 p. 922.1 56-
12072
BR1705 .P3 MRR Alc.

Smith, William, Sir, A dictionary of
Christian biography, literature,
sects and doctrines; London, J.
Murray, 1877-87. 4 v.   12-3122
B895 .S65 1877 MRR Alc.

The Westminster dictionary of church
history. Philadelphia, Westminster
Press [1971] xii, 887 p. [$17.50]
270/.03 69-11071
BR95 .W496 MRR Alc.

CHRISTIAN EDUCATION
see Religious education

CHRISTIAN ETHICS--DICTIONARIES.
Macquarrie, John. Dictionary of
Christian ethics, Philadelphia,
Westminster Press [1967] viii, 366
p. 241/.03 67-17412
BJ63 .M3 MRR Alc.

CHRISTIAN ETHICS--DICTIONARIES--LATIN.
Palazzini, Pietro, Dictionarium
morale et canonicum. Romae, Officium
Libri Catholici, 1962-68. 4 v. 63-
34193
BX1757 .A2P3 MRR Alc.

CHRISTIAN LIFE.
see also Spiritual life

CHRISTIAN LIFE--CATHOLIC AUTHORS.
Fenner, Kay Toy. American Catholic
etiquette. Westminster, Md., Newman
Press, 1961. 402 p. 395 61-16569

BX1969 .F4 MRR Alc.

CHRISTIAN LITERATURE--PUBLICATION AND
DISTRIBUTION--DIRECTORIES.
Christian Booksellers Association. C
B A suppliers directory. Colorado
Springs [etc.] 070.5/94 72-622387
Z479 .C5 MRR Alc Latest edition

CHRISTIAN LITERATURE, EARLY.
Apostolic Fathers. The Apostolic
Fathers. [1st ed.] New York, Harper
[1950] xi, 321 p. 281.1082 50-
5878
BR60 .A62 MRR Alc.

Apostolic fathers. English & Greek.
The Apostolic fathers: London, W.
Heinemann; New York, G. P. Putnam's
sons, 1930. 2 v. mrr01-40
PA3611.A7 1930d MRR Alc.

CHRISTIAN LITERATURE, EARLY--HISTORY
AND CRITICISM.
Goodspeed, Edgar Johnson, A history
of early Christian literature.
[Chicago] University of Chicago Press
[1966] ix, 214 p. 281.1 66-13871

BR67 .G58 1966 MRR Alc.

Quasten, Johannes, Patrology.
Westminster, Md., Newman Press, 1950-
v. 281.1 51-622
BR67 .Q3 MRR Alc.

CHRISTIAN SAINTS--DICTIONARIES.
Holweck, Frederick George, A
biographical dictionary of the
saints, Detroit, Gale Research Co.,
1969. xxix, 1053 p. 282/.0922 68-
30625
BX4655 .H6 1969 MRR Biog.

CHRISTIAN SCIENCE--HISTORY.
Beasley, Norman. The cross and the
crown; [1st ed.] New York, Duell,
Sloan and Pearce [1952] xi, 664 p.
289.509 52-9086
BX6931 .B4 MRR Alc.

CHRISTIAN UNION--HISTORY--SOURCES.
Ward, Hiley H., ed. Documents of
dialogue Englewood Cliffs, N.J.,
Prentice-Hall [1966] xvi, 525 p.
262/.001 66-22100
BX6.5 .W3 MRR Alc.

CHRISTIANITY.
see also Jews

see also Missions

CHRISTIANITY--PHILOSOPHY--BIBLIOGRAPHY.
McLean, George H., comp. An
annotated bibliography of philosophy
in Catholic thought, 1900-1964, New
York, F. Ungar Pub. Co. [1967] xiv,
371 p. 016.201 67-24185
Z7821 .M25 MRR Alc.

CHRISTMAS.
Becker, May (Lamberton) ed. The home
book of Christmas, New York, Dodd,
Mead & company [c1941] xx p., 1 l.,
746 p. 394.268 41-52036
PN6071.C6 B4 MRR Alc.

Wernecke, Herbert Henry, Christmas
customs around the world.
Philadelphia, Westminster Press
[1959] 188 p. 394.268 59-9581
GT4985 .W44 MRR Alc.

CHRISTMAS--UNITED STATES.
Barnett, James Harwood. The American
Christmas; New York, Macmillan,
1954. 173 p. 394.268 54-12566
GT4985 .B3 MRR Alc.

CHRISTMAS CAROLS
see Carols

CHRISTMAS DECORATIONS--DICTIONARIES.
Stevenson, Violet W. The
encyclopedia of floristry New York,
Drake Publishers [1973] 160, 96 p.
[$9.95] 745.92/03 73-3102
SB449 .S716 1973 MRR Alc.

CHROMATICS
see Color

CHROMOSOMES.
see also Genetics

CHRONOLOGY, HISTORICAL.
Phelps, Robert, The literary life;
New York, Farrar, Straus and Giroux,
1968. 244 p. [$15.00]
016.8209/009/1 68-27533
Z2013 .P48 MRR Alc.

Williams, Neville, Chronology of the
modern world: London, Barrie &
Rockliffe, 1966. xiii, 923 p. [60/-
] 902.02 66-67189
D11.5 .W5 MRR Ref Desk.

CHRONOLOGY.
see also Calendar

see also Months

Schram, Robert Gustav,
Kalendariographische und
chronologische tafeln, Leipzig, J.
C. Hinrichs, 1908. xxxvi, 368 p.
09-12404
CE11 .S3 MRR Alc.

CHRONOLOGY, ECCLESIASTICAL.
Cheney, Christopher Robert, ed.
Handbook of dates for students of
English history, London, Office of
the Royal historical society, 1945.
xvii, 164 p. 942.002 a 46-270
DA34 .C5 MRR Alc.

CHRONOLOGY, HISTORICAL.
The 20th century almanac;
Philadelphia, Allen, Lane & Scott.
23-10568
CE92 .T9 MRR Alc Latest edition

Annals of English literature, 1475-
1950; 2d ed. Oxford, Clarendon
Press, 1961. vi, 380 p. 016.82 62-
16029
Z2011 .A5 1961 MRR Alc.

Asian recorder. v. 1- Jan. 1/7,
1955- [New Delhi, etc.] K. K. Thomas
[etc.] 950.05 58-24845
DS1 .A4747 MRR Alc Full set

Assignment book and daily editorial
calendar; 1st- ed.; 1948- Santa
Monica, Calif. 529.43 48-13885
AY81.E35 A8 MRR Alc Latest edition

Astronautics and aeronautics;
1915/60- Washington, Scientific and
Technical Information Division,
National Aeronautics and Space
Administration [etc.; for sale by the
Superintendent of Documents, U.S.
Govt. Print. Off.] 65-60308
TL521.3.A8 A3 MRR Alc Partial set

Bergman, Peter M. The chronological
history of the Negro in America,
[1st ed.] New York, Harper & Row
[1969] 698 p. [12.00]
973/.09/7496 68-27434
E185 .B46 MRR Ref Desk.

Bowman, Robert Turnbull, Dateline:
Canada Toronto, Holt, Rinehart and
Winston of Canada [1973] 1 v.
(unpaged) 971/.002 72-9493
F1006 .B6 1973 MRR Alc.

The Cadillac modern encyclopedia.
[1st ed.] New York, Cadillac Pub.
Co.; distributed by Derbibooks,
Secaucus, N.J. [1973] xiv, 1954 p.
[$24.95] 031 73-81377
AG5 .C25 MRR Ref Desk.

Carruth, Gorton. The encyclopedia of
American facts and dates. 6th ed.,
New York, Crowell [1972] vi, 922 p.
[$8.95] 973/.02 72-78262
E174.5 .C3 1972 MRR Ref Desk.

Chamberlin, Waldo, A chronology and
fact book of the United States, 1941-
1969 Dobbs Ferry, N.Y., Oceana
Publications, 1970. 234 p. 341/.23
73-127323
JX1977 .C4822 MRR alc.

Cheney, Christopher Robert, ed.
Handbook of dates for students of
English history, London, Office of
the Royal historical society, 1945.
xvii, 164 p. 942.002 a 46-270
DA34 .C5 MRR Alc.

Cheng, Peter, A chronology of the
People's Republic of China from
October 1, 1949. Totowa, N.J., Rowan
and Littlefield, 1972. xvii, 347 p.
951/.05 70-184667
DS777.55 .C44567 MRR Alc.

CHRONOLOGY, HISTORICAL. (Cont.)
Clair, Colin. A chronology of
printing. London, Cassell, 1969.
228 p. [70/-]   655.1   78-425147
Z124 .C6 MRR Alc.

Clapp, Jane. Art censorship;
Metuchen, N.J., Scarecrow Press,
1972. 582 p.   700   76-172789
N8740 .C55 MRR Alc.

Collison, Robert Lewis.
Encyclopaedias: their history
throughout the ages; 2d ed. New
York, Hafner Pub. Co., 1966. xvi,
334 p.   030.9   66-5463
AE1 .C6 1966 MRR Alc.

Collison, Robert Lewis. Newnes
Dictionary of dates; 2nd revised ed.
London, Newnes, 1966. ix, 11-428 p.
[35/-]   903   66-72492
D11.5 .C6 1966 MRR Alc.

Damon, Charles Ripley, comp. The
American dictionary of dates, 458-
1920; Boston, R. G. Badger [c1921]
3 v.   21-21758
E174.5 .D16 MRR Alc.

Dictionnaire des œvres de tous les
temps et de tous les pays; [1. ed.]
Paris, S.E.D.F. [1952-68] 5 v.   55-
15784
AE25 .D52 MRP Alc.

Dillon, Philip Robert, American
anniversaries; New York, The Philip
R. Dillon publishing company [c1918]
3 p. l., 349, xv p.   18-22970
E174.5 .D57 MRR Alc.

Dupuy, Richard Ernest, The
encyclopedia of military history;
[1st ed.] New York, Harper & Row
[1970] xiii, 1406 p. [20.00]
355/.0009   74-81871
D25.A2 D8 MPR Ref Desk.

Ecology USA 1971; New York, Special
Reports inc. [1972] xi, 610 p.
[$125.00]   333.7/2/0973   71-188164
QH541.145 .E26 MRR Alc.

Encyclopedia of Indians of the
Americas. St. Clair Shores, Mich.,
Scholarly Press [1974- v.
[$700.00 (set)]   970.1/03   74-5088
E54.5 .E52 MRR Alc.

Fetros, John G. This day in sports;
Novato, Calif., N. K. Gregg [1974]
264 p. [$5.95]   796/.09   74-75882
GV576 .F48 MRR Alc.

Garrison, Fielding Hudson, An
introduction to the history of
medicine, 4th ed., rev. and enl.
Philadelphia, London, W. B. Saunders
company, 1929. 996 p.   29-3665
R131 .G3 1929 MRR Alc.

Gassan, Arnold. A chronology of
photography; a critical survey of the
history of photography as a medium of
art. Athens, Ohio, Handbook Co.;
[distributed by Light Impressions,
Rochester, N.Y., 1972] 373 p.
770/.9   72-83426
TR15 .G33 MRR Alc.

Gurney, Gene. A chronology of world
aviation. New York, F. Watts [1965]
245 p.   387.709   65-11756
TL515 .G83 MRR Alc.

Hackett, Alice Payne, 70 years of
best sellers, 1895-1965. New York,
R. R. Bowker Co., 1967. xi. 280 p.
655.4/73   67-25025
Z1033.B3 H34 MRR Ref Desk.

Hall, Carl Mitchel. Chronicles in
world history : Baltimore : Gateway
Press, 1974. xvii, 709 p. :   909
73-79029
D11 .H19 MRR Alc.

Harper encyclopedia of the modern
world; [1st ed.] New York, Harper &
Row [1970] xxxii, 1271 p. [$17.50]
903   73-81879
D205 .H35 1970 MRR Ref Desk.

Harvard University. Library. English
literature. Cambridge; Distributed
by the Harvard University Press,
1971. 4 v.   016.82   74-128717
Z2011 .H36 MRR Alc.

Haydn, Joseph Timothy, Haydn's
dictionary of dates and universal
information relating to all ages and
nations, New York, Dover
Publications [1969] vi, 1605 p.
[25.00]   903   68-9154
D9 .H45 1969 MRR Alc.

Hazeltine, Mary Emogene,
Anniversaries and holidays, 2d ed.,
completely revised Chicago, American
library association 1944. xix, 316
p.   394.26   44-53464
Z5710 .H42 1944 MRR Alc.

Hornsby, Alton. The Black almanac.
Rev. and enl. Woodbury, N.Y.,
Barron's Educational Series, inc.
[1973] xxiv, 247 p. [$2.95]
917.3/06/96073   74-154291
E185 .H63 1973 MRR Alc.

Keller, Helen Rex. The dictionary of
dates, New York, The Macmillan
company, 1934. 2 v.   902   34-39180

D9 .K4 MRR Alc.

Kindermann, Heinz, Theatergeschichte
Europas. Salzburg, O. Müller [1957-
v.   59-37129
PN2570 .K55 MRR Alc.

King, Robert C. A dictionary of
genetics 2d ed. New York, Oxford
University Press, 1972. 337 p.
575.1/03   73-170262
QH431 .K518 1972 MRR Alc.

Krythe, Maymie Richardson. All about
the months [1st ed.] New York,
Harper & Row [1966] 222 p.   529.2
66-18584
GR930 .K7 MRR Alc.

Langer, William Leonard, An
encyclopedia of world history; 5th
ed., rev. and enl. Boston, Houghton
Mifflin, 1972. xxxix, 1569 p.
[$17.50]   902/.02   72-186219
D21 .L27 1972 MRR Ref Desk.

Launay, André Joseph. Dictionary of
contemporaries, Fontwell (Sx.),
Centaur P., 1967.   368 p. [45/-]
920/.003   67-86851
D11.5 .L3 MRR Alc.

Little, Charles Eugene, Cyclopedia
of classified dates with an
exhaustive index. Detroit, Gale
Research Co., 1967. vii, 1454 p.
902/.02   66-27839
D9 .L7 1967 MRR Alc.

Long, Everette B., The Civil War day
by day; [1st ed.] Garden City,
N.Y., Doubleday, 1971. xiii, 1135 p.
[$17.50]   973.7   73-163653
E468.3 .L6 MRR Alc.

Mansoor, Menahem. Political and
diplomatic history of the Arab world,
1900-1967; [Washington] NCR
Microcard Editions, 1972. 7 v.
320.9/17/4927   72-184866
DS62.8 .M35 MRR Alc.

Mattfeld, Julius, Variety music
cavalcade 1620-1961. Rev. ed.
Englewood Cliffs, N.J., Prentice-Hall
[1962] xxiii, 713 p.   781.97 62-
16317
ML128.V7 M4 1962 MRR Alc.

Miller, Warren Hudson. Who shares
your birthday? 2d ed. New York,
Allwyn Press [1970] 187 p.   920.02
70-106046
D11.5 .M56 1970 MRR Alc.

Mirkin, Stanford M. What happened
when; [New, rev. and enl. ed.] New
York, I. Washburn [1966] v, 442 p.
902.02   66-10676
D11.5 .M57 1966 MRR Ref Desk.

Morris, Richard Brandon, ed.
Encyclopedia of American history,
Updated and rev. New York, Harper &
Row [1965] xiv, 843 p.   973.03 65-
22859
E174.5 .M847 1965 MRR Alc.

Morris, Richard Brandon, ed.
Encyclopedia of American history.
Enl. and updated. New York, Harper &
Row [1970] xiv, 850 p. [$9.89]
973/.03   73-95647
E174.5 .M847 1970 MRR Ref Desk.

Motor Vehicle Manufacturers
Association of the United States.
Automobiles of America: milestones,
pioneers, roll call, highlights. 4th
ed., rev. Detroit, Wayne State
University Press, 1974. 301 p.
629.22/22/0973   73-19838
TL23 .M63 1974 MRR Alc.

Osborne, Robert A. When who did
what, [Los Angeles, Stationers
corporation, 1944] 207 p.   44-53427

E174.5 .O8 MRR Alc.

Pascoe, Lionel Craman. The teach
yourself encyclopaedia of dates and
events London, English Universities
P., 1968. [7], 776 p. [25/-]
901.9   70-368966
D11 .P3 MRR Alc.

Payne, L. G. S., Air dates. New
York, Praeger [1958] 565 p.
629.1309 629.109*   57-12275
TL515 .P33 1958 MRR Alc.

Rickmers, Christian Mabel (Duff) The
chronology of Indian history, from
the earliest times to the beginning
of the sixteenth century, Delhi,
Cosmo Publications, 1972. xi, 409 p.
[Rs65.00]   954.02   72-907831
DS433 .R5 1972 MRR Alc.

Robertson, John George, A history of
German literature, 6th ed.
Edinburgh, Blackwood, 1970. xxvii,
817 p. [60/-]   830.9   74-552609
PT91 .R7 1970 MRR Alc.

Saillot, Jacques. Chronologie
universelle des souverains et chefs
d'état. [Angers, H. Siraudeau,
1961] 41] p.   63-37133
D11 .S13 MRR Alc.

Schoyer's vital anniversaries. New
London, Conn. [etc.] W. Schoyer. 902
50-1815
Began publication with issue for
1948.
D11 .S36 MRR Alc Latest edition

Sharma, Jagdish Saran, India since
the advent of the British; [1st ed.]
Delhi, S. Chand, 1970. xxx, 817 p.
[60.00]   954/.02/02   78-121820
DS433 .S47 MRR Alc.

Slonimsky, Nicolas, Music since
1900. 4th ed. New York, C.
Scribner's Sons [1971] xvii, 1595 p.
[$49.50]   780/.904   70-114929
ML197 .S634 1971 MRR Alc.

Smith, Guy E. English literature;
Paterson, N.J., Littlefield, Adams,
1959. 2 v.   820.2   59-33833
PR87 .S65 1959 MRR Alc.

Storey, R. L. Chronology of the
medieval world: 800 to 1491 [1st
American ed.] New York, D. McKay Co.
[1973] xii, 705 p.   909.07 72-
90909
D118 .S855 1973b MRR Ref Desk.

Thornton, Willis. Almanac for
Americans New York, Greenberg
[c1941] 5 p. l., 3-418 p. incl.
front., illus.   973.02   41-23726
E174.5 .T5 MRR Alc.

The Times in review; New York, Arno
Press, 1970-73 [v. 1, 1973; v. 5,
1970] 5 v.   909.82   74-139439
D427 .T5 MRR Alc.

United States. Library of Congress.
Subject Cataloging Division. Period
subdivisions under names of places
Washington, U.S. Govt. Print. Off.,
1950. iv, 75 p.   025.33   50-62964
Z663.78 .P4 MRR Alc.

The United States in world affairs.
1931- New York, Simon & Schuster
[etc.]   32-26065
E744 .U66 MRR Alc Full set

Webster's guide to American history:
Springfield, Mass., G. & C. Merriam
Co. [1971] 1428 p.   973   76-24114
E174.5 .W4 MRR Ref Desk.

Williams, Neville, Chronology of the
expanding world, 1492-1762. [1st
American ed.] New York, McKay [1969]
x, 700 p. [12.50]   909.08/02/02
79-83695
D11.5 .W48 1969b MRR Ref Desk.

Wise, Leonard F. Kings, rulers, and
statesmen, New York, Sterling Pub.
Co. [1967] 446 p.   920.02   67-16020

D107 .W5 MRR Ref Desk.

Wyckoff, Peter. Wall Street and the
stock markets: [1st ed.]
Philadelphia, Chilton Book Co. [1972]
xlv, 304 p.   332.6/42/0973   72-8277

HG4572 .W87 MRR Alc.

CHRONOLOGY, HISTORICAL--CHARTS.
Ryland, Frederick, Chronological
outlines of English literature.
Detroit, Gale Research Co., 1968.
xii, 351 p.   820.9   68-30587
PR87 .R85 1968b MRR Alc.

Stephenson, Jim Bob, Chronological
chart of theatre history. Ann Arbor,
Ann Arbor Photo Lithographers, 1951.
ii, 57 p.   792.09   51-4984
PN2115 .S8 MRR Alc.

Whitcomb, Selden Lincoln,
Chronological outlines of American
literature. New York, London,
Macmillan and co., 1894. x, 286 p.
12-39940
PS94 .W4 MRR Alc.

Who did what; New York, Crown
Publishers [1974] 383 p. [$12.95]
920/.02 920   73-81194
CT103 .W47 1974 MRR Biog.

CHRONOLOGY, HISTORICAL--TABLES.
Balland, Robert, ed. Histoire
universelle Quillet: Paris, A.
Quillet, 1955. 2 v.   55-36261
D20 .E28 MRR Alc.

Bolton, Mary, Dictionary of dates,
London, New York, Foulsham [1958]
125 p.   902 59-20715
D11 .B649 MRR Alc.

De Ford, Miriam Allen, Who was when?
2d ed. New York, Wilson, 1950. 1
v. (unpaged)   902 51-796
CT103 .D4 1950 MRR Alc.

Dizionario universale della
letteratura contemporanea. 1. ed.
Milano] A. Mondadori [1959-63] 5 v.
60-644
PN41 .D53 MRR Alc.

Oettinger, Eduard Maria, Moniteur
des dates. Leipzig, L. Denicke,
1869. 6 v. in 1.   02-3518
CT154 .C3 MRR Biog.

Putnam, George Palmer, comp.
Putnam's handbook of universal
history; New York, London, G. P.
Putnam's sons [c1927] vi p., 1 l.,
592 p. incl. tables.   27-27820
D11 .P87 1927 MRR Alc.

Steinberg, Sigfrid Henry, Historical
tables, 58 B.C.--A.D. 1945 [i.e.
1955] 4th ed. London, Macmillan;
New York, St. Martin's Press, 1956.
x, 257 p.   902 56-43370
D11 .S83 1956 MRR Alc.

CHUNG-KUO KING CH'AN TANG. CHUNG YANG
WEI YÜAN HUI--BIOGRAPHY.
United States. Central Intelligence
Agency. Chinese Communist Party
Central Committee members.
[Washington] 1972. iii, 76 p.
329.9/51 72-602398
JQ1519.A5 U55 1972 MRR Biog.

CHUNG-KUO KUNG CH'AN TANG--HISTORY.
Brandt, Conrad. A documentary
history of Chinese communism,
London, Allen & Unwin [1952] 552 p.
951.04 52-67189
DS775 .B7 MRR Alc.

CHURCH--TEACHING OFFICE.
see also Religious education

CHURCH AND COLLEGE IN THE UNITED STATES.
Danforth Foundation, St. Louis.
Commission on Church Colleges and
Universities. Church-sponsored
higher education in the United
States; Washington, American Council
on Education [1966] xix, 309 p.
377.80973 66-28994
LC383 .D34 MRR Alc.

CHURCH AND EDUCATION IN THE UNITED
STATES--BIBLIOGRAPHY.
Little, Lawrence Calvin. Religion
and public education; 3d ed., rev.
and enl. Pittsburgh, University of
Pittsburgh Book Center, 1968. v, 214
p.   016.377/0973 68-1933
Z5814.C57 L5 1968 MRR Alc.

CHURCH AND SOCIAL PROBLEMS--
BIBLIOGRAPHY.
Pinson, William M. Resource guide to
current social issues, Waco, Tex.,
Word Books [1968] 272 p.   016.301
67-30735
Z7164.S66 P47 MRR Alc.

CHURCH AND STATE--BIBLIOGRAPHY.
LaNoue, George R. A bibliography of
doctoral dissertations undertaken in
American and Canadian universities,
1940-1962, [New York, Published for
the Dept. of Religious Liberty by the
Office of Publication and
Distribution, National Council of the
Churches of Christ in the U.S.A.,
1963] v, 49 p.   016.322 63-21606
Z7776.72 .L35 MRR Alc.

CHURCH AND STATE--DICTIONARIES--GERMAN.
Evangelisches Staatslexikon,
Stuttgart, Berlin, Kreuz-Verlag
[1966] lxiv, 2687 p. [DM 75.00]
203 66-67139
BR95 .E95 MRR Alc.

CHURCH AND STATE--HISTORY--SOURCES.
Ehler, Sidney Z., ed. and tr. Church
and state through the centuries; New
York, Biblo and Tannen, 1967. xii,
625 p.   261.7/08 66-30406
BV630.A1 E37 1967 MRR Alc.

CHURCH AND STATE IN GREAT BRITAIN.
Black, John Bennett, The reign of
Elizabeth, 1558-1603. 2d ed.
Oxford, Clarendon Press, 1959. xxvi,
539 p.   942.055 59-3629
DA355 .B65 1959 MRR Alc.

CHURCH AND STATE IN HUNGARY.
[Mid European Law Project] Hungary,
churches and religion. [Washington]
Library of Congress, Law Library
[1951] 74 l.   56-61358
Z663.55.D5H82 MRR Alc.

CHURCH AND STATE IN THE UNITED STATES.
Pfeffer, Leo, Church, state, and
freedom. Rev. ed. Boston, Beacon
Press [1967] xiii, 832 p.   261.7
66-23582
BR516 .P45 1967 MRR Alc.

Stokes, Anson Phelps, Church and
state in the United States ... [1st
ed.] New York, Harper [1950] 3 v.
261.7 50-7978
BR516 .S85 MRR Alc.

CHURCH AND THE WORLD.
see also Kingdom of God

CHURCH ARCHITECTURE--UNITED STATES.
Rose, Harold Wickliffe. The colonial
houses of worship in America; New
York, Hastings House [1964, c1963]
xiv, 574 p.   726.50973 63-19175
NA5207 .R6 MRR Alc.

CHURCH COLLEGES--UNITED STATES.
Danforth Foundation, St. Louis.
Commission on Church Colleges and
Universities. Church-sponsored
higher education in the United
States: Washington, American Council
on Education [1966] xix, 309 p.
377.80973 66-28994
LC383 .D34 MRR Alc.

CHURCH CONFERENCE CENTERS--CANADA--
DIRECTORIES.
Deemer, Philip. Ecumenical directory
of retreat and conference centers.
Boston, Jarrow Press [1974- v.
269/.6/02573 74-76974
BV1652 .D43 MRR Alc.

CHURCH CONFERENCE CENTERS--UNITED
STATES--DIRECTORIES.
Deemer, Philip. Ecumenical directory
of retreat and conference centers.
Boston, Jarrow Press [1974- v.
269/.6/02573 74-76974
BV1652 .D43 MRR Alc.

CHURCH DECORATION AND ORNAMENT.
see also Christian art and symbolism

CHURCH ETIQUETTE.
Fenner, Kay Toy. American Catholic
etiquette. Westminster, Md., Newman
Press, 1961. 402 p.   395 61-16569

BX1969 .F4 MRR Alc.

CHURCH HISTORY.
see also Missions

Guignebert, Charles Alfred Honoré,
Ancient, medieval, and modern
Christianity; New Hyde Park, N.Y.,
University Books [1961] 507 p.   270
61-15334
BR145 .G95 1961 MRR Alc.

Latourette, Kenneth Scott, A history
of Christianity. [1st ed.] New
York, Harper [1953] xxvii, 1516 p.
270 53-5004
BR145 .L28 MRR Alc.

Walker, Williston, A history of the
Christian church. New York, Scribner
[1959] 585 p.   270 58-12494
BR146 .W3 1959 MRR Alc.

CHURCH HISTORY--PRIMITIVE AND EARLY
CHURCH, CA. 30-600.
Carrington, Philip, Abp., The early
Christian church. Cambridge [Eng.]
University Press, 1957. 2 v.   270.1
a 58-589
BR165 .C33 MRR Alc.

Eusebius, Pamphili, bp. of Caesarea.
The ecclesiastical history, London,
W. Heinemann; New York, G. P.
Putnam's sons, 1926-32. 2 v.   27-
2020
P43612 .E85 1926 MRR Alc.

CHURCH HISTORY--PRIMITIVE AND EARLY
CHURCH, CA. 30-600--BIBLIOGRAPHY.
Metzger, Bruce Manning. Index of
articles on the New Testament and the
early church published in
Festschriften. Philadelphia, Society
of Biblical Literature, 1951. xv,
182 p.   016.225 51-3190
Z7772.L1 M4 MRR Alc.

CHURCH HISTORY--MIDDLE AGES, 600-1500.
Cannon, William Ragsdale, History of
Christianity in the Middle Ages; New
York, Abingdon Press [1960] 352 p.
270.2 60-6928
BR162.2 .C3 MRR Alc.

CHURCH HISTORY--REFORMATION, 1517-1648
see Reformation

CHURCH HISTORY--19TH CENTURY.
Latourette, Kenneth Scott,
Christianity in a revolutionary age;
[1st ed.] New York, Harper [1958-62]
5 v.   270.8 58-10370
BR475 .L32 MRR Alc.

CHURCH HISTORY--20TH CENTURY.
Latourette, Kenneth Scott,
Christianity in a revolutionary age;
[1st ed.] New York, Harper [1958-62]
5 v.   270.8 58-10370
BR475 .L32 MRR Alc.

CHURCH HISTORY--1945-
World Christian handbook. 1949-
London, World Dominion Press. 270.8
49-6861
BR481 .W6 MRR Alc Latest edition

CHURCH HISTORY--DICTIONARIES.
Corpus dictionary of Western
churches. Washington, Corpus
Publications [1970] xviii, 820 p.
[$25.00] 203 78-99501
BR95 .C67 MRR Alc.

The Oxford dictionary of the
Christian Church. 2d ed., London,
New York, Oxford University Press,
1974. xxxi, 1518 p. [£13.50] 203
74-163871
BR95 .08 1974 MRR Alc.

The Westminster dictionary of church
history. Philadelphia, Westminster
Press [1971] xii, 887 p. [$17.50]
270/.03 69-11071
BR95 .W496 MRR Alc.

CHURCH HISTORY--DICTIONARIES--FRENCH.
Baudrillart, Alfred, cardinal, ed.
Dictionnaire d'histoire et de
geographie ecclésiastiques, Paris,
Letouzey et Ané, 1912- v.   09-
26333
BR95 .B3 MRR Alc.

CHURCH HISTORY--OUTLINES, SYLLABI, ETC.
Bible handbook. Grand Rapids, Mich.
[etc.] Zandervan Pub. House [etc.]
220.7 32-8057
First ed. published in 1924.
BS417 .B48 MRR Alc Latest issue

CHURCH HISTORY--PHILOSOPHY.
Gay, Peter, A loss of mastery;
Berkeley, University of California
Press [1966] viii, 164 p.
974.02072 67-10969
E175.45 .G3 MRR Alc.

CHURCH HISTORY--PRIMITIVE AND EARLY
CHURCH.
Davies, John Gordon, The early
Christian church [1st ed.] New
York, Holt, Rinehart and Winston
[1965] xiii, 314 p.   281.1 65-
12074
BR165 .D37 1965 MRR Alc.

CHURCH HISTORY--SOURCES.
Bettenson, Henry Scowcroft, ed.
Documents of the Christian Church;
2nd ed. London, New York [etc.]
Oxford U. P., 1967. xvii, 343 p.
[12/6] 270 68-109402
BR141 .B4 1967 MRR Alc.

CHURCH MEMBERSHIP--STATISTICS.
National Council of the Churches of
Christ in the United States of
America. Bureau of Research and
Survey. Churches and church
membership in the United States; New
York, 1956-58. 80 no.   56-12497
BR526 .N3 MRR Alc.

CHURCH MUSIC--UNITED STATES.
Metcalf, Frank Johnson, American
writers and compilers of sacred
music, New York, Cincinnati, The
Abingdon press [c1925] 373 p.   25-
18155
ML106.U3 M3 MRR Biog.

CHURCH OF ENGLAND--DIRECTORIES.
Church of England. Year book. 80th-
1963- [Oxford?] Church Information
Office. 283/.05 72-622544
BX5015 .C45 MRR Alc Latest edition

CHURCH OF ENGLAND--GOVERNMENT.
Mayfield, Guy. The Church of
England: 2d ed. London, New York,
Oxford University Press, 1963. 211
p.   262 63-2421
BX5150 .M37 1963 MRR Alc.

CHURCH OF ENGLAND. BOOK OF COMMON
PRAYER.
Suter, John Wallace, The American
Book of common prayer; New York,
Oxford Univ. Press, 1949. vii, 85 p.
264.039 49-3873
BX5145 .S8 MRR Alc.

CHURCH OF ENGLAND. BOOK OF COMMON
PRAYER--HISTORY.
Procter, Francis, A new history of
the Book of common prayer, London,
Macmillan and co., limited; New York,
The Macmillan company, 1902. xxiv,
699 p.   03-2191
BX5145 .P8 MRR Alc.

CHURCH OF IRELAND--YEARBOOKS.
The Irish church directory and year-
book. Dublin, Church of Ireland
Printing and Publishing Co.   43-19761

BX5440 .I7 MRR Alc Latest edition

CHURCH OF JESUS CHRIST OF LATTER-DAY SAINTS--DIRECTORIES.
Church of Jesus Christ of Latter-Day Saints. Directory of the general authorities and officers. Salt Lake City. 289.3 48-37775
BX8606 .A3 MRR Alc Latest edition

CHURCH OF SCOTLAND--YEARBOOKS.
The Church of Scotland year-book. Edinburgh, Dept. of Publicity and Publication. 17-24381
BX9076 .A3 MRR Alc Latest copy

CHURCH STATISTICS.
World Christian handbook. 1949- London, World Dominion Press. 270.8 49-6861
BP481 .W6 MRR Alc Latest edition

CHURCH STATISTICS--UNITED STATES.
Johnson, Douglas W., Churches & church membership in the United States: Washington, Glenmary Research Center [1974] xiv, 237 p. [$15.00] 280/.0973 73-94224
BR526 .J64 MRR Alc.

National Council of the Churches of Christ in the United States of America. Bureau of Research and Survey. Churches and church membership in the United States; New York, 1956-58. 80 no. 56-12497
BR526 .N3 MRR Alc.

CHURCH UNITY
see Christian union

CHURCH YEAR.
see also Christmas

see also Easter

Denis-Boulet, Noële Maurice, The Christian calendar. [1st ed.] New York, Hawthorn Books [1960] 126 p. 264.021 60-13059
BV30 .D443 MRR Alc.

Weiser, Francis Xavier, Handbook of Christian feasts and customs; [1st ed.] New York, Harcourt, Brace [1958] 366 p. 264 58-10908
BV30 .W4 MRR Alc.

CHURCHES--DIRECTORIES.
World Christian handbook. 1949- London, World Dominion Press. 270.8 49-6861
BR481 .W6 MRR Alc Latest edition

CHURCHES--SCOTLAND.
The Church of Scotland year-book. Edinburgh, Dept. of Publicity and Publication. 17-24381
BX9076 .A3 MRR Alc Latest copy

CHURCHES--ENGLAND.
Betjeman, John, Sir, Collins pocket guide to English parish churches. London, Collins, 1968. 2 v. [30/- (per vol.)] 914.2 76-373482
NA5461 .B43 1968 MRR Alc.

CHURCHES--UNITED STATES.
Broderick, Robert C., Historic churches of the United States. New York, W. Funk [1958] 262 p. 726.5 58-7142
NA5205 .B7 MRR Alc.

Rose, Harold Wickliffe. The colonial houses of worship in America; New York, Hastings House [1964, c1963] xiv, 574 p. 726.50973 63-19175
NA5207 .R6 MRR Alc.

CHURCHES--UNITED STATES--BIBLIOGRAPHY.
Kirkham, E. Kay. A survey of American church records; Salt Lake City, Deseret Book Co., 1959-60. 2 v. 929.3 59-65303
CD3065 .K52 MRR Alc.

CHURCHES, ANGLICAN.
Betjeman, John, Sir, Collins pocket guide to English parish churches. London, Collins, 1968. 2 v. [30/- (per vol.)] 914.2 76-373482
NA5461 .B43 1968 MRR Alc.

CHURCHILL, WINSTON LEONARD SPENCER, SIR, 1874-1965.
Broad, Lewis, Winston Churchill, a biography. [1st ed.] New York, Hawthorne Books [1958-63] 2 v. 923.242 58-11830
DA566.9.C5 B69 MRR Alc.

Churchill, Randolph Spencer, Winston S. Churchill, London, Heinemann, 1966- v. in [63/- (v. 1) varies] 942.0820924 66-67264
DA566.9.C5 C472 MRR Alc.

Churchill, Winston Leonard Spencer, Sir, Winston S. Churchill: his complete speeches, 1897-1963. New York, Chelsea House Publishers, 1974. 8 v. (xvi, 8917 p.) [$185.00] 942.082/092/4 74-505
DA566.9.C5 A38 MRR Alc.

CICERO, MARCUS TULLIUS.
Merguet, Hugo, Handlexikon zu Cicero, Leipzig, Dieterich, 1905. 2 p. l., 816 p. 06-33549
PA6366 .M45 MRR Alc.

CINEMATOGRAPHY.
Quick, John, Handbook of film production New York, Macmillan [1972] xii, 304 p. [$12.95] 791.43/0232 72-151694
PN1995.9.P7 Q5 MRR Alc.

CINEMATOGRAPHY--DICTIONARIES.
The Focal encyclopedia of film & television techniques. [1st American ed.] New York, Hastings House [1969] xxiv, 1100 p. [37.50] 778.5/03 73-7135
TR847 .F62 1969 MRR Alc.

Levitan, Eli L. An alphabetical guide to motion picture, television, and videotape production New York, McGraw-Hill [1970] xvii, 797 p. 778.5/3/03 69-13610
TR847 .L47 MRR Alc.

CINEMATOGRAPHY--DICTIONARIES--POLYGLOT.
Dictionary of photography and cinematography: London, New York, Focal Press [1961] 1 v. (various pagings) 770.3 63-24356
TR9 .D5 MRR Alc.

Elsevier's dictionary of cinema, sound, and music, in six languages: Amsterdam, New York, Elsevier Pub. Co., 1956. 948 p. 778.503 56-13141
TR847 .E4 MRR Alc.

CIPHER AND TELEGRAPH CODES.
[Acme Code Company] Acme commodity and phrase code. [1971. viii, 902, 112 p. [NT$800.00] 72-837570
HE7676 .Z2 1971 MRR Alc.

CIPHER AND TELEGRAPH CODES--BANKERS AND BROKERS.
Ultronic Systems Corporation. Stock symbol guide: company to symbol, symbol to company. [New York] 1967. 80 p. 332.6/2/0148 75-31662
HE7677.B2 U57 MRR Alc.

CIRCLE.
Smoley, Constantine Kenneth, Segmental functions; Chautauqua, N.Y., C. K. Smoley, 1962. 255, 179, 193 p. 510.83 62-53086
QA342 .S65 1962 MRR Alc.

CIRCUS--BIBLIOGRAPHY.
Toole-Stott, Raymond. Circus and allied arts; Derby, Eng., Harpur, distributors [1958-71] 4 v. 016.7913 58-2986
Z7514.C6 T6 MRR Alc.

CIRCUS--DICTIONARIES.
The Language of show biz, Chicago, Dramatic Pub. Co. [1973] xliii, 251 p. 790/.03 73-173320
PN1579 .L3 MRR Alc.

O'Brien, Esse (Forrester) Circus; San Antonio, Naylor Co. [1959] 268 p. 791.309 59-9291
GV1801 .O2 MRR Alc.

CIRCUS--HISTORY.
O'Brien, Esse (Forrester) Circus; San Antonio, Naylor Co. [1959] 268 p. 791.309 59-9291
GV1801 .O2 MRR Alc.

CIRCUS--UNITED STATES--HISTORY.
Chindahl, George Leonard. A history of the circus in America. Caldwell, Idaho, Caxton Printers, 1959. 279 p. 791.30973 58-5336
GV1803 .C47 MRR Alc.

CITIES AND TOWNS.
see also Markets

see also Urbanization

Hope, Ronald, ed. The shoregoer's guide to world ports. London, Maritime Press [c1963] vi, 340 p. 910.2 64-5135
G140 .H6 MRR Alc.

Robson, William Alexander, ed. Great cities of the world; Beverly Hills, Calif., Sage Publications [1972] 2 v. (1114 p.) 352/.008 75-167875
HT151 .R585 1972b MRR Alc.

CITIES AND TOWNS--DICTIONARIES.
Abrams, Charles, The language of cities; a glossary of terms. New York, Viking Press [1971] ix, 365 p. [$10.00] 301.3/6/03 76-137500
HT108.5 .A24 MRR Alc.

CITIES AND TOWNS--GROWTH.
see also Metropolitan areas

Chandler, Tertius. 3000 years of urban growth New York, Academic Press [1974] ix, 431 p. 301.36/1 72-84378
HB2161 .C45 1974 MRR alc.

Gottmann, Jean. Megalopolis; the urbanized northeastern seaboard of the United States. New York, Twentieth Century Fund, 1961. xi, 810 p. 301.36 61-17298
HT123.5.A12 G6 MRR Alc.

CITIES AND TOWNS--HISTORY.
Chandler, Tertius. 3000 years of urban growth New York, Academic Press [1974] ix, 431 p. 301.36/1 72-84378
HB2161 .C45 1974 MRR alc.

Freri, Orlando, Dizionario storico italiano. Milano, Ceschina [1940] 4 p. l., [11]-399, [1] p. 945.003 44-45073
DG461 .F7 MRR Alc.

CITIES AND TOWNS--PLANNING.
see also Community development

see also Housing

see also Regional planning

see also Urban renewal

see also Urban transportation

Gallion, Arthur B. The urban pattern; 2d ed. Princeton, N.J., Van Nostrand [1963] x, 435 p. 711.4 63-24088
NA9031 .G3 1963 MRR Alc.

CITIES AND TOWNS--PLANNING--BIBLIOGRAPHY.
Branch, Melville Campbell, Comprehensive urban planning; a selective annotated bibliography Beverly Hills, Calif., Sage Publications [1970] 477 p. 016.711/4 73-92349
Z5942 .B7 MRR Alc.

Columbia University. Libraries. Avery Architectural Library. Avery index to architectural periodicals. 2d ed.; rev. and enl. Boston, G. K. Hall, 1973- v. 016.72 74-152756
Z5945 .C653 1973 MRR Alc (Dk 33)

Harvard University. Graduate School of Design. Library. Catalogue of the Library of the Graduate School of Design, Harvard University. Boston, Mass., G. K. Hall, 1968. 44 v. 019/.1 73-169433
Z5945 .H28 1968 MRR Alc (Dk 33)

United States. Dept. of Housing and Urban Development. New communities; Washington; For sale by the Supt. of Docs., U.S. Govt. Print. Off. [1970] iv, 84 p. [0.75] 016.3092/6 75-606174
Z5942 .U584 MRR Alc.

CITIES AND TOWNS--PLANNING--DICTIONARIES.
Encyclopedia of urban planning. New York, McGraw-Hill [1974] xxi, 1218 p. [$29.50] 309.2/62/03 73-19757
HT166 .E5 MRR Alc.

CITIES AND TOWNS--PLANNING--DICTIONARIES--POLYGLOT.
Vocabulaire international des termes d'urbanisme et d'architecture. 1. Paris, Société de diffusion des techniques du bâtiment et des travaux publics, 1970- v. [133F (v. 1)] 70-860237
NA31 .V6 MRR Alc.

CITIES AND TOWNS--PLANNING--EXHIBITIONS.
United States. Library of Congress. The grand design; Washington, 1967. 25 p. (chiefly plates (incl. maps, plans)) 711/.5 67-60041
.Z663.15.A6D52 MRR Alc.

CITIES AND TOWNS--PLANNING--UNITED STATES--BIBLIOGRAPHY.
Housing and planning references. new ser. no. 1- July/Aug. 1965- [Washington, U.S. Govt. Print. Off.] 016.3015/4 72-621364 -
Z7165.U5 A3 MRR Alc Full set

CITIES AND TOWNS--PLANNING--UNITED STATES--BIBLIOGRAPHY--CATALOGS.
United States. Dept. of Housing and Urban Development. Library and Information Division. The dictionary catalog of the United States Department of Housing and Urban Development, Library and Information Division. Boston, G. K. Hall, 1972. 19 v. 016.30154 73-152937
Z7164.H8 U4494 MRR Alc (Dk 33)

CITIES AND TOWNS--PLANNING--UNITED STATES--DIRECTORIES.
American Institute of Planners. Handbook & roster. [Washington, etc.] 711/.06/273 60-26104
NA9000 .A54 MRR Alc Latest edition

The Blue book of major homebuilders. [Crofton, Md.] CMR Associates. 338.4/7/690802573 72-621729
TH12.5 .B5 MRR Alc Latest edition

CITIES AND TOWNS--PLANNING--WASHINGTON,
D.C.
Peps, John William. Monumental
Washington; Princeton, N.J.,
Princeton University Press, 1967.
xv, 221 p.   711.4/09753 66-17708
NA9127.W2 R4 MRR Alc.

CITIES AND TOWNS--STATISTICS.
Chandler, Tertius. 3000 years of
urban growth New York, Academic
Press [1974] ix, 431 p.   301.36/1
72-84378
HB2161 .C45 1974 MRR alc.

International Union of Public
Transport. Statistiques des
transports publics urbains. (2e
ed.). Bruxelles, Union
internationale des transports
publics, (1968). 211 p.   388/.021/2
76-393796
HE4211 .I56 1968 MRR Alc.

Showers, Victor. The world in
figures. New York, Wiley [1973]
xii, 585 p.   910/.21/2 73-9
G109 .S52 MRR Ref Desk.

CITIES AND TOWNS--STATISTICS--YEARBOOKS.
Annuaire de statistique
internationale des grandes villes.
v. 1- 1961- La Haye. 66-88394
HA42 .A55 MRR Alc Latest edition

CITIES AND TOWNS--AFRICA, SOUTH.
Official South African municipal year
book. Pretoria, [etc.] S.A.
Association of Municipal Employees
(non political) [etc.] 14-9587
JS7531 .A5 MRR Alc Latest edition

CITIES AND TOWNS--ATLANTIC STATES.
Gottmann, Jean. Megalopolis; the
urbanized northeastern seaboard of
the United States. New York,
Twentieth Century Fund, 1961. xi,
810 p.   301.36 61-17298
HT123.5.A12 G6 MRR Alc.

CITIES AND TOWNS--CANADA--MAPS--
BIBLIOGRAPHY.
United States. Library of Congress.
Geography and Map Division.
Panoramic maps of Anglo-American
cities; Washington, Library of
Congress; [for sale by the Supt. of
Docs., U.S. Govt. Print. Off.] 1974.
v, 118 p.   016.912/7 73-18312
Z663.35 .P35 MRR Alc.

CITIES AND TOWNS--CONNECTICUT.
Bixby, William. Connecticut: a new
guide. New York, Scribner [1974]
ix, 386 p. [$10.00] 917.46/04/4
73-20261
F92.3 .B59 MRR Alc.

CITIES AND TOWNS--EUROPE.
Bottin Europe. 1959- Paris,
Société Didot-Bottin. 59-44496
HC240 .A1B6 Sci RR Latest edition
/ MRR Alc Latest edition

CITIES AND TOWNS--FRANCE--HISTORY--
BIBLIOGRAPHY.
Dollinger, Philippe. Bibliographie
d'histoire des villes de France,
Paris, C. Klincksieck, 1967. 756 p.
[60 F.] 015/.44 67-96161
Z2176 .D6 MRR Alc.

CITIES AND TOWNS--GERMANY.
Handbuch der historischen Stätten
Deutschlands. [Stuttgart, A.
Kröner, 1958- v.   59-52693
DD901.A1 H3 MRR Alc.

Müller, Friedrich, Grosses
deutsches Ortsbuch; 12.,
vollständig überarb. und erw.
Aufl., Wuppertal Barmen, 1958. iv,
1139 p.   59-19354
DD14 .M8 1958 MRR Alc.

Müller, Friedrich, Grosses
deutsches Ortsbuch; 15.,
vollständig überarb. und erw. Aufl.
Wuppertal-Barmen, 1965. v, 1225 p.
66-45490
DD14 .M8 1965 MRR Alc.

CITIES AND TOWNS--GERMANY--MAPS.
Mairs Geographischer Verlag,
Stuttgart. Der grosse Shell Atlas.
1.- Aufl.; 1960- Stuttgart. map63-
200
G1911.P2 M25 MRR Alc Atlas Latest
edition

CITIES AND TOWNS--GERMANY--STATISTICS.
Statistisches Jahrbuch deutscher
Gemeinden. 1- Jahrg.; [1890]-
[Braunschweig, etc.] Waisenhaus-
Buchdruckerei [etc.] 44-23595
HA1330 .A1S8 MRR Alc Latest
edition

CITIES AND TOWNS--GREAT BRITAIN.
Norton, Jane Elizabeth. Guide to the
national and provincial directories
of England and Wales, London,
Offices of the Royal Historical
Society, 1950. vii, 241 p.
016.9142 51-2465
Z5771 .N6 MRR Alc.

CITIES AND TOWNS--GREAT BRITAIN--
BIBLIOGRAPHY.
Humphreys, Arthur Lee, A handbook to
county bibliography, London,
[Printed by Strangeways and sons]
1917. x, 501 p.; 1 l.   17-14548
L2023.A1 H9 MRR Alc.

Martin, Geoffrey Haward. A
bibliography of British and Irish
municipal history Leicester,
Leicester University Press, 1972- v.
[£12.50 (v. 1)] 016.30136/0942
73-156398
Z2023 .M26 MRR Alc.

CITIES AND TOWNS--GREAT BRITAIN--
YEARBOOKS.
The Municipal year book and public
utilities directory. London,
Municipal Journal [etc.] 352.042 07-
24315
Began publication in 1897.
JS3003 .M8 MRR Alc Latest edition

CITIES AND TOWNS--IRELAND--BIBLIOGRAPHY.
Martin, Geoffrey Haward. A
bibliography of British and Irish
municipal history Leicester,
Leicester University Press, 1972- v.
[£12.50 (v. 1)] 016.30136/0942
73-156398
Z2023 .M26 MRR Alc.

CITIES AND TOWNS--ITALY--HISTORY.
Freri, Orlando, Dizionario storico
italiano. Milano, Ceschina [1940] 4
p. l., [11]-399, [1] p.   945.003 44-
45073
DG461 .F7 MRR Alc.

CITIES AND TOWNS--LATIN AMERICA--
BIBLIOGRAPHY.
Sable, Martin Howard. Latin American
urbanization: Metuchen, N.J.,
Scarecrow Press, 1971. 1077 p.
016.3013/6/098 74-145643
Z7165.L3 S28 MRR Alc.

CITIES AND TOWNS--MAINE.
Maine. Maine register, state year-
book and legislative manual. 1870-
Portland. 99-4262
JK2831 date MRR Alc Latest
edition

CITIES AND TOWNS--NEW HAMPSHIRE.
New Hampshire register, state year-
book and legislative manual. 1869-
Portland, Me. [etc.] F. L. Tower
Companies [etc.] 11-25112
JK2930 .N4 Sci RR Latest edition*
/ MRR Alc Latest edition

CITIES AND TOWNS--RUSSIA.
Telberg, Ina. Russian-English
geographical-encyclopedia. New York,
Telberg Book Co., c1960. x, 142 l.
914.7 60-9280
DK14 .T4 MRR Alc.

CITIES AND TOWNS--UNITED STATES.
Alexander, Gerald L. Nicknames of
American cities. New York, Special
Libraries Association [1951] 74 p.
929.4 51-8763
E155 .A5 MRR Alc.

Editor & publisher. Market guide.
v. [1]- 1924- New York. 658.8 45-
44873
HF5905 .E38 MRR Ref Desk Latest
edition

Franke, David. America's 50 safest
cities. New Rochelle, N.Y.,
Arlington House [1974] 301 p.
[$8.95] 301.36/3/0973 73-21890
HT123 .F72 MRR Alc.

The Hertz survival manual for
traveling businessmen. 1967- New
York, Renaissance Editions, inc.
917.3/04/923 67-14478
E158 .H57 MRR Alc Latest edition

Kane, Joseph Nathan, Nicknames and
sobriquets of U.S. cities and States,
2d ed. Methuchen, N.J., Scarecrow
Press, 1970. 456 p.   917.3/003 77-
103577
E155 .K24 1970 MRR Alc.

Pollock, Paul W. The capital cities
of the United States. Phoenix,
Ariz., c1960. 206 p.   917.3 61-
22915
E159 .P6 MRR Alc.

Schwartz, Alvin, America's exciting
cities; New York, Crowell [1966]
270 p.   917.304923 66-14944
E158 .S38 MRR Alc.

Spear, Dorothea N. Bibliography of
American directories through 1860.
Worcester, Mass., American
Antiquarian Society, 1961. 389 p.
016.9173 61-1054
Z5771 .S7 MRR Alc.

United States. Bureau of the Census.
County and city data book. 1949-
[Washington, U.S. Govt. Print. Off.]
317.3 52-4576
HA202 .A36 MRR Desk Latest edition
/ MRR Desk Latest edition / MRR
Alc Latest edition

United States. Bureau of the Census.
Directory of Federal statistics for
local areas, [Washington, For sale
by the Supt. of Docs., U.S. Govt.
Print. Off.] 1966. vi, 156 p. a
66-7475
HB2175 .A5 1966 TJ Rm.

CITIES AND TOWNS--UNITED STATES--
BIBLIOGRAPHY.
Government Affairs Foundation.
Metropolitan communities: Chicago,
Public Administration Service [1957,
c1956] xviii, 392 p.   016.352073
56-13382
Z7164.L8 G66 MRR Alc.

Public Affairs Information Service.
Bulletin ... annual cumulation. 1st-
1915- New York [etc.] 16-920
Z7163 .P9 MRR Circ Full set

United States. Dept. of Housing and
Urban Development. New communities;
Washington: For sale by the Supt. of
Docs., U.S. Govt. Print. Off. [1970]
iv, 84 p. [0.75] 016.3092/6 75-
606174
S942 .U584 MRR Alc.

United States. National Clearinghouse
for Mental Health Information.
Bibliography on the urban crisis;
Chevy Chase, Md., National Institute
of Mental Health [1968] iv, 158 p.
016.3091/73 77-600665
Z7164.S66 U57 MRR Alc.

CITIES AND TOWNS--UNITED STATES--
HISTORY.
Benagh, Christine L. 100 keys: names
across the land Nashville, Abingdon
Press [1973] 288 p. [$5.95]
917.3/003 70-186613
E180 .B45 MRR Alc.

CITIES AND TOWNS--UNITED STATES--
HISTORY--BIBLIOGRAPHY.
Bradford, Thomas Lindsley, The
bibliographer's manual of American
history, Philadelphia, S. V. Henkels
& co., 1907-10. 5 v.   07-23470
Z1250 .B85 MRR Alc.

CITIES AND TOWNS--UNITED STATES--
INDEXES--PERIODICALS.
Index to current urban documents. v.
1- July/Oct. 1972- Westport,
Conn., Greenwood Press. [$75.00]
016.30136/0973 73-641453
Z7165.U5 I654 MRR Alc Full set

CITIES AND TOWNS--UNITED STATES--MAPS--
BIBLIOGRAPHY.
United States. Library of Congress.
Geography and Map Division.
Panoramic maps of Anglo-American
cities; Washington, Library of
Congress; [for sale by the Supt. of
Docs., U.S. Govt. Print. Off.] 1974.
v, 118 p.   016.912/7 73-18312
Z663.35 .P35 MRR Alc.

CITIES AND TOWNS--UNITED STATES--
STATISTICS.
Ashby, Lowell De Witt. Growth
patterns in employment by county,
1940-1950 and 1950-1960.v
[Washington] U.S. Dept. of Commerce,
Office of Business Economics,
Regional Economics Division; [for
sale by the Superintendent of
Documents, U.S. Govt. Print. Off.,
1965-66] 8 v.   65-61774
HD5723 .A63 MRR Alc.

The Municipal year book; 1934-
Washington, D.C. [etc.] International
city manager's association. 34-27121
JS344.C5 A24 MRR Ref Desk Latest
edition / MRR Alc Latest edition

United States. Bureau of the Census.
1960 census of housing, [Washington,
1961-63] 6 v. in 66 pts. and 1 v. in
420 pts. a 61-9347
HD7293 .A4884 MRR Alc.

United States. Bureau of the Census.
1970 census of housing. [Washington]
For sale by the Supt. of Docs., U.S.
Govt. Print Off., 1972- v.
301.5/4/09791 72-600057
HD7293 .A512 1972 MRR Alc.

United States. Bureau of the Census.
1970 census of population and
housing. [Washington; For sale by
the Supt. of Docs., U.S. Govt. Print.
Off.] 1971- v. [$1.00 (v. 5)
varies] 312/.9/0973 73-186611
HA201 1970 .A542 MRR Alc.

CITIES AND TOWNS--UNITED STATES--
YEARBOOKS.
The Municipal year book; 1934-
Washington, D.C. [etc.] International
city manager's association. 34-27121

JS344.C5 A24 MRR Ref Desk Latest
edition / MRR Alc Latest edition

CITIES AND TOWNS--VERMONT.
Vermont year book. Chester [etc.]
Vt., National Survey [etc.] 08-14736

Began publication in 1818.
JK3030 .Va MRR Alc Latest edition

CITIES AND TOWNS, RUINED, EXTINCT, ETC.
Charles-Picard, Gilbert. Larousse
encyclopedia of archaeology. New
York, Putnam [1972] 432 p. [$25.00]
913/.031 76-179972
CC165 .C4313 MRR Alc.

CITIZENSHIP--UNITED STATES.
How to become a citizen of the United
States. New York, American Council
for Nationalities Service. 26-11021

JK1829 .C73 MRR Alc Latest edition

CITY AND TOWN LIFE--UNITED STATES.
Botkin, Benjamin Albert, ed.
Sidewalks of America; [1st ed.]
Indianapolis, Bobbs-Merrill [1954]
xxii, 605 p. 398 54-9485
GR105 .B57 MRR Alc.

CITY GOVERNMENT
see Municipal government

CITY TRANSPORTATION
see Urban transportation

CIVIC CENTERS.
see also Public buildings

CIVIC CENTERS--UNITED STATES--
DIRECTORIES.
The National directory for the
performing arts and civic centers.
Dallas, Handel & Co. 790.2/0973 73-
646635
PN2289 .N38 MRR Alc Latest edition

CIVICS.
see also Citizenship

CIVIL DEFENSE--BIBLIOGRAPHY.
United States. Library of Congress.
General Reference and Bibliography
Division. Safeguarding our cultural
heritage; a bibliography Washington,
1952. x, 117 p. 016.355232* 52-
60017
Z663.28 .S3 MRR Alc.

United States. Library of Congress.
Reference Dept. Civil defense, 1951;
a reading list of current material.
Washington [1951] [30] p.
016.35523 51-60028
Z663.2 .C5 MRR Alc.

CIVIL DISORDERS
see Riots

CIVIL ENGINEERING.
see also Mechanical engineering

CIVIL ENGINEERING--DICTIONARIES.
Bucksch, Herbert. Dictionary of
civil engineering and construction
machinery and equipment ... 2e
edition. Paris, Eyrolles, 1967. v.
624/.03 74-415882
TA9 .B892 MRR Alc.

Bucksch, Herbert. Dictionary of
civil engineering and construction
machinery and equipment, English-
French. Paris, Eyrolles 1960-62. 2
v. 624.03 62-6556
TA9 .B89 MRR Alc.

Bucksch, Herbert. Wörterbuch für
Bautechnik und Baumaschinen. 4.
wesentlich erw. Aufl. Wiesbaden,
Bauverlag, 1968- v.   [DM 140.-
(Bd. 1)] 624/.03 68-88879
TA9 .B924 MRR Alc.

Nelson, Archibald. Dictionary of
applied geology: mining and civil
engineering, London, Newnes, 1967.
vii, 421 p. [45/-] 550/.3 68-
86619
OE5 .N44 1967 MRR Alc.

Scott, John S., A dictionary of
civil engineering [2d ed., rev.
Harmondsworth, Eng.] Penguin Books
[1965, c1958] 347 p. 624/.03 67-
4197
TA9 .S35 1965 MRR Alc.

CIVIL ENGINEERING--DICTIONARIES--FRENCH.
Bucksch, Herbert. Dictionary of
civil engineering and construction
machinery and equipment ... 2e
édition. Paris, Eyrolles, 1967. v.
624/.03 74-415882
TA9 .B892 MRR Alc.

Bucksch, Herbert. Dictionary of
civil engineering and construction
machinery and equipment, English-
French. Paris, Eyrolles 1960-62. 2
v. 624.03 62-6556
TA9 .B89 MRR Alc.

CIVIL ENGINEERING--DICTIONARIES--GERMAN.
Bucksch, Herbert. Wörterbuch für
Bautechnik und Baumaschinen. 4.
wesentlich erw. Aufl. Wiesbaden,
Bauverlag, 1968- v.   [DM 140.-
(Bd. 1)] 624/.03 68-98879
TA9 .B924 MRR Alc.

CIVIL ENGINEERING--HANDBOOKS, MANUALS,
ETC.
Standard handbook for civil
engineers. New York, McGraw-Hill
[1968] 1 v. (various pagings) 624
67-12630
TA151 .S8 MRR Alc.

CIVIL ENGINEERING--UNITED STATES.
Condit, Carl W. American building
art: the twentieth century. New
York, Oxford University Press, 1961.
427 p. 624.10973 61-8369
TA23 .C57 MRR Alc.

CIVIL ENGINEERS--UNITED STATES--
BIOGRAPHY.
American Society of Civil Engineers.
Committee on History and Heritage of
American Civil Engineering. A
biographical dictionary of American
civil engineers. New York, 1972. x,
163 p. [$5.00] 624/.092/2 B 72-
194203
TA139 .A53 MRR Biog.

CIVIL ENGINEERS--UNITED STATES--
DIRECTORIES.
American Society of Civil Engineers.
Directory; New York. 58-20994
TA12 .A625 Sci RR Latest edition /
MRR Biog Latest edition

CIVIL GOVERNMENT
see Political science

CIVIL LIBERTY
see Liberty

CIVIL PLANNING
see Cities and towns--Planning

CIVIL RIGHTS.
see also Liberty

see also Negroes--Civil rights

CIVIL RIGHTS--YEARBOOKS.
Yearbook on human rights. 1946- New
York [etc.] United Nations. 323.4058
48-4455
JC571 .U4 MRR Ref Desk Latest
edition

CIVIL RIGHTS--UNITED STATES.
Longaker, Richard P. The Presidency
and individual liberties. Ithaca,
N.Y., Cornell University Press [1961]
239 p. 353.03 61-8206
JK518 .L6 MRR Alc.

Miller, Marion Mills, ed. Great
debates in American history, [The
national ed.] New York, Current
literature publishing company [c1913]
14 v. 13-23912
E173 .M64 vol. 14 MRR Alc.

CIVIL RIGHTS--UNITED STATES--HANDBOOKS,
MANUALS, ETC.
Burke, Joan Martin. Civil rights;
2d ed. New York, Bowker, 1974. xi,
266 p. 323.4/025/73 74-4053
JC599.U5 B85 1974 MRR Alc.

CIVIL RIGHTS--UNITED STATES--HISTORY.
Lewis, Anthony, Portrait of a
decade; New York, Random House
[1964] 322 p. 323.40973 64-14832

E185.61 .L52 1964 MRR Alc.

CIVIL RIGHTS--UNITED STATES--HISTORY--
SOURCES.
Friedman, Leon, comp. The civil
rights reader; New York, Walker
[1967] xxi, 348 p. 322.4/0973 67-
13235
E185.61 .F857 MRR Alc.

Ianniello, Lynne, ed. Milestones
along the march; New York, F. A.
Praeger [1965] xviii, 124 p.
323.408 65-24709
E185.61 .I2 MRR Alc.

CIVIL SERVICE.
see also Bureaucracy

CIVIL SERVICE--UNITED STATES.
Delap, Donald J. Civil service
manual; Fond du Lac, Wis., North
Central Consulting Press, 1965. x,
404 p. 353.004 65-18944
JK716 .D4 MRR Alc.

Federal employees' almanac. 1954-
[Washington] 351.1 351.3* 54-18878

JK671 .F385 MRR Ref Desk Latest
edition

Kilpatrick, Franklin Peirce, The
image of the Federal service
Washington, Brookings Institution
[1964] xvii, 301 p. 351.10973 64-
13789
JK691 .K44 MRR Alc.

United States. Civil Service
Commission. Minority group
employment in the Federal Government.
May 1970- Washington For sale by
the Supt. of Docs., U.S. Govt. Print.
Off. 331.1/33/0973 72-622550
JK639 .A42 subser MRR Alc Latest
edition

CIVIL SERVICE, MUNICIPAL
see Municipal officials and employees

CIVIL SERVICE POSITIONS--UNITED STATES.
Lukowski, Susan. Strategy and
tactics for getting a Government job,
Washington, Potomac Books [1972]
iii, 222 p. [$2.75] 331.1/28 72-
75155
JK716 .L9 MRR Alc.

Turner, David Reuben, Complete guide
to U.S. civil service jobs, [7th
ed.] New York, Arco [1971] 160 p.
[$1.00] 331.1/28 72-148867
JK716 .T833 1971 MRR Alc.

CIVIL SERVICE POSITIONS--UNITED STATES--
BIBLIOGRAPHY.
United States. Civil Service
Commission. Guide to Federal career
literature. [Washington: for sale by
the Supt. of Docs., U.S. Govt. Print.
off.] 1972] 34 p. [$0.45]
016.3317/95/0973 72-603286
Z1223 .A199 1972 MRR Ref Desk.

CIVILIZATION.
see also Anthropology

see also Archaeology

see also Art

see also Culture

see also Ethics

see also Ethnology.

see also Renaissance

see also Social problems

see also Social sciences

Wallbank, Thomas Walter,
Civilization past and present 5th
ed. Chicago, Scott, Foresman [1965]
2 v. 901.9 65-11902
CB57 .W372 MRR Alc.

CIVILIZATION--BIBLIOGRAPHY.
American Universities Field Staff. A
select bibliography: Asia, Africa,
Eastern Europe, Latin America. New
York [1960] ix, 534 p. 016.9019
60-10482
Z5579 .A5 MRR Alc.

CIVILIZATION--COLLECTED WORKS.
Dictionary of the history of ideas:
New York, Scribner [1973] 4 v.
[$35.00 (per vol.)] 901.9 72-7943
CB5 .D52 MRR Alc.

CIVILIZATION--HISTORY.
Bernal, John Desmond, Science in
history [3d ed.] New York, Hawthorn
Books [1965] xxviii, 1039 p. 901.9
65-22660
CB151 .B4 1965 MRR Alc.

Birket-Smith, Kaj, The paths of
culture; Madison, University of
Wisconsin Press, 1965. xi, 535 p.
301.2 64-8488
CB113.D3 B513 MRR Alc.

Bowle, John, ed. The concise
encyclopedia of world history. 1st
ed.] New York, Hawthorn Books [1958]
511 p. 901 58-10240
CB63 .B67 MRR Alc.

Breasted, James Henry, The conquest
of civilization, New York, London,
Harper & brothers, 1938. xii, 669 p.
930 38-27362
D59 .B78 1938 MRR Alc.

Brinton, Clarence Crane, A history
of civilization 2d ed. Englewood
Cliffs, N.J., Prentice-Hall, 1960. 2
v. 901.9 60-8503
CB53 .B754 MRR Alc.

Burns, Edward McNall, Western
civilizations, 6th ed. New York,
Norton [1963] 1083 p. 914 63-8026

CB57 .B8 1963 MRR Alc.

Columbia University. Columbia
College. Chapters in Western
civilization, 3d ed. New York,
Columbia University Press, 1961- v.
914 61-13862
CB245 .C632 MRR Alc.

CIVILIZATION--HISTORY. (Cont.)
King, Charles Harold, A history of
civilization: One-volume ed. New
York, Scribner [1969] xiv, 1089 p.
901.9 69-10385
  CB59 .K48 1969 MRR Alc.

Linton, Ralph, The tree of culture.
[1st ed.] New York, Knopf, 1955.
692 p.   572 55-5173
  GN27 .L5 MRR Alc.

Lips, Julius Ernst, The origin of
things; London, Harrap [1949] 420
p.   572 50-17122
  GN400 .L75 1949 MRR Alc.

Singer, Charles Joseph, ed. A
history of technology, Oxford,
Clarendon Press, 1954-1958. 5 v.   a
55-8645
  T15 .S53 MRR Alc.

CIVILIZATION--HISTORY--SOURCES.
Columbia University. Columbia
College. Introduction to
contemporary civilization in the
West; 3d ed. New York, Columbia
University Press, 1960-61. 2 v.
914 60-16650
  CB5 .C575 MRR Alc.

CIVILIZATION--JUVENILE LITERATURE--
BIBLIOGRAPHY.
Huus, Helen, Children's books to
enrich the social studies: Rev. ed.
Washington, National Council for the
Social Studies [c1966] xiii, 201 p.
016.3728/3 67-8284
  Z1037.9 .H8 1966 MRR Alc.

CIVILIZATION--OUTLINES, SYLLABI, ETC.
Bornecque, Pierre Henry, La France
et sa littérature, 3e édition
revue et corrigée. Lyon, A.
Desvigne, 1968. 896 p. [46F] 72-
367695
  PQ135 .B57 1968 MRR Alc.

Murdock, George Peter, Outline of
world cultures. [2d ed., rev.] New
Haven, HRAF Press, 1958. xi, 227 p.
025.469 58-5860
  H62 .B36 vol. 3 1958 MRR Alc.

CIVILIZATION--PHILOSOPHY.
Beard, Charles Austin, The American
spirit, New York, The Macmillan
company, 1942. vii , 2 l., 696 p.
917.3 42-50003
  E169.1 .B285 MRR Alc.

CIVILIZATION, AMERICAN
see United States--Civilization

CIVILIZATION, ANCIENT.
Bibby, Geoffrey. Four thousand years
ago; [1st ed.] New York, Knopf,
1961. 398 p.   901.91 61-14367
  CB311 .B5 MRR Alc.

Jones, Tom Bard, Ancient
civilization. Chicago, Rand McNally
[1960] 476 p.   901.91 60-5136
  CB311 .J59 MRR Alc.

Parkes, Henry Bamford, Gods and men;
[1st ed.] New York, Knopf, 1959.
489 p.   901.91 59-5425
  CB311 .P27 MRR Alc.

CIVILIZATION, ANCIENT--BIBLIOGRAPHY.
Marouzeau, Jules, Dix années de
bibliographie classique; New York,
B. Franklin [1969] 2 v. (xv, 1286
p.)   68-57915
  Z7016 .M35 1969 MRR Alc.

CIVILIZATION, ARAB.
Hitti, Philip Khuri, History of the
Arabs from the earliest times to the
present 10th ed. [London]
Macmillan; [New York] St. Martin's
Press [1970] xxiv, 822 p. [$12.50]
953 74-102765
  DS37.7 .H58 1970 MRR Alc.

CIVILIZATION, ARAB--DICTIONARIES AND
ENCYCLOPEDIAS.
Ronart, Stephan. Concise
encyclopaedia of Arabic civilization:
Amsterdam, Djambatan, 1966. vii,
413 p. [f150.00] 910.03/174/927
67-93204
  DT185 .R6 1966 MRR Alc.

CIVILIZATION, ARABIC.
Ronart, Stephan. Concise
encyclopaedia of Arabic civilization;
Amsterdam, Djambatan [1959] ix, 589
p.   915.3 59-46573
  DS215 .R6 MRR Alc.

CIVILIZATION, ASSYRO-BABYLONIAN.
Olmstead, Albert Ten Eyck, History
of Assyria. [Chicago] University of
Chicago Press [1960, c1951] 695 p.
935 60-51197
  DS71 .O6 1960 MRR Alc.

CIVILIZATION, GRECO-ROMAN--PICTORIAL
WORKS.
Heyden, A. A. M. van der, ed. Atlas
of the classical world. [London, New
York] Nelson, 1959 [i.e. 1960] 221
p.   911.38 60-1130
  DE29 .H463 MRR Alc.

CIVILIZATION, GREEK.
Andrewes, Antony, The Greeks.
London, Hutchinson, 1967. xxvi, 292
p. [50/-] 913.38/03 67-95763
  DF78 .A5 MRR Alc.

Mahaffy, John Pentland, Sir, The
social life of the Greeks. London,
New York, Macmillan, 1896-1907. 2 v.
mrr01-35
  DF77 .M218 MRR Alc.

CIVILIZATION, GREEK--DICTIONARIES.
The Praeger encyclopedia of ancient
Greek civilization New York, Praeger
[1967] 491 p. 913.3/8/0303 67-
25162
  DF16 .D513 1967c MRR Alc.

CIVILIZATION, HISPANIC.
Hilton, Ronald, ed. Handbook of
Hispanic source materials and
research organizations in the United
States. 2d ed. Stanford, Calif.,
Stanford University press, 1956.
xiv, 448 p.   980 56-6178
  F1408.3 .H65 1956 MRR Alc.

CIVILIZATION, HISPANIC--BIBLIOGRAPHY--
CATALOGS.
Hispanic Society of America. Library.
Catalogue of the library. Boston,
G. K. Hall, 1962. 10 v. (10048 p.)
62-52025
  Z881 .N639 MRR Alc (Dk33)

CIVILIZATION, ISLAMIC.
The Cambridge history of Islam;
Cambridge [Eng.] University Press,
1970. 2 v. [£13/-/- ($39.00 U.S.)]
910.03/176/7 73-77291
  DS35.6 .C3 MRR Alc.

CIVILIZATION, ISLAMIC--BIBLIOGRAPHY.
London. University. School of
Oriental and African Studies.
Library. Index Islamicus, 1906-1955;
Cambridge, Eng., W. Heffer [1958]
xxxvi, 897 p.   016.9156 59-23014
  Z7835.M6 L6 MRR Alc.

CIVILIZATION, MEDIEVAL.
see also Feudalism

Davies, Reginald Trevor, comp.
Documents illustrating the history of
civilization in medieval England,
1066-1500 New York, Barnes & Noble
[1969] x, 413 p.   914.2 74-4396
  DA170 .D3 1969 MRR Alc.

Heer, Friedrich, The medieval world:
Europe, 1100-1350. London,
Weidenfeld and Nicolson [1962] 365
p.   940.17 62-51871
  D200 .H413 1962a MRR Alc.

Hoyt, Robert Stuart. Europe in the
Middle Ages 2d ed. New York,
Harcourt, Brace & World [1966] xiv,
684 p.   940.1 66-16060
  CB351 .H6 1966 MRR Alc.

CIVILIZATION, MEDIEVAL--DICTIONARIES.
Kulturhistorisk leksikon for nordisk
middelalder fra vikingetid til
reformationstid. København,
Rosenkilde og Bagger, 1956- v.
56-58225
  DL30 .K8 MRR Alc.

CIVILIZATION, MODERN.
see also History, Modern

CIVILIZATION, MODERN--20TH CENTURY--
BIBLIOGRAPHY.
Universal Reference System.
Comparative government and cultures;
Princeton, N.J., Princeton Research
Pub. Co. [1969] xxi, 1255 p. 016.3
68-57826
  Z7161 .U64 vol. 10 MRR Alc.

CIVILIZATION, MODERN--20TH CENTURY--
HISTORY--SOURCES.
Wishy, Bernard W., ed. The Western
World in the twentieth century; New
York, Columbia University Press,
1961. 517 p.   901.94 61-8987
  CB425 .W57 MRR Alc.

CIVILIZATION, MODERN--HISTORY.
Brinton, Clarence Crane, Modern
civilization; 2d ed. Englewood
Cliffs, N.J., Prentice-Hall [1967]
xx, 961 p.   901.93 67-13122
  CB357 .B7 1967 MRR Alc.

CIVILIZATION, MYCENAEAN.
Palmer, Leonard Robert, Mycenaeans
and Minoans; 2d ed., substantially
rev. and enl. New York, Knopf, 1965.
369 p.   913.3918031 64-19093
  DF220 .P3 1965 MRR Alc.

CIVILIZATION, OCCIDENTAL.
Columbia University. Columbia
College. Chapters in Western
civilization, 3d ed. New York,
Columbia University Press, 1961- v.
914 61-13862
  CB245 .C632 MRR Alc.

Horton, Rod William, Backgrounds of
European literature: New York,
Appleton-Century-Crofts [1954] 462
p.   801 54-9623
  CB53 .H6 MRR Alc.

Lopez, Robert Sabatino, The birth of
Europe London, Phoenix House, 1967.
xxiii, 442 p. [84/-] 940.1 67-
76044
  CB245 .L613 MRR Alc.

CIVILIZATION, OCCIDENTAL--HISTORY.
Harrison, John Baugham. A short
history of Western civilization, 2d
ed. New York, A. A. Knopf, 1966.
xix, 729, xlii, p.   914 65-17483
  CB245 .H32 1966 MRR Alc.

Johnson, Edgar Nathaniel, An
introduction to the history of
Western tradition. Boston, Ginn
[1959] 2 v.   901.9 59-16066
  CB245 .J58 MRR Alc.

CIVILIZATION, OCCIDENTAL--HISTORY--
SOURCES.
Baumer, Franklin Le Van, ed. Main
currents of Western thought; 2d ed.,
rev. [and enl.] New York, Knopf,
1964. xviii, 746 p.   914 64-14416

  CB245 .B37 1964 MRR Alc.

Viorst, Milton. The great documents
of Western civilization. [1st ed.]
Philadelphia, Chilton Books [1965]
xv, 388 p.   914.0308 65-28123
  CB245 .V5 MRR Alc.

CIVILIZATION, ORIENTAL--HISTORY.
Reischauer, Edwin Oldfather. A
history of East Asian civilization
Boston, Houghton Mifflin [1960-65] 2
v.   915 60-4269
  CB253 .R4 MRR Alc.

CIVILIZATION AND SCIENCE
see Science and civilization

CLACKMANNANSHIRE, SCOT.--COMMERCE--
DIRECTORIES.
Fife and Kinross trades' directory,
including the counties of Stirling
and Clackmannan, Edinburgh, Town and
County Directories, Limited. 59-
31510
  HF5161 .F5 MRR Alc Latest edition

CLANS AND CLAN SYSTEM.
Bain, Robert. The clans and tartans
of Scotland. London, Collins [1954]
320 p.   941 55-1011
  DA880.H76 B3 1954 MRR Alc.

Innes, Thomas, Sir, The tartans of
the clans and families of Scotland.
5th ed. Edinburgh, W. & A. K.
Johnston, 1950. iv, 300 p. 929.2
51-3429
  DA880.H76 I5 1950 MRR Alc.

CLAPP, VERNER WARREN, 1901-1972.
Verner Warren Clapp, 1901-1972:
Washington, Library of Congress,
1973. 43 p. 020/.92/4 B 73-13555

  Z663 .V47 MRR Alc.

CLAPP, VERNER WARREN, 1901-1972--
BIBLIOGRAPHY.
Verner Warren Clapp, 1901-1972:
Washington, Library of Congress,
1973. 43 p. 020/.92/4 B 73-13555

  Z663 .V47 MRR Alc.

CLASS DISTINCTION
see Social classes

CLASSICAL ANTIQUITIES
see also Archaeology

CLASSICAL ANTIQUITIES--BIBLIOGRAPHY.
L'Année philologique; 1. année:
1924/26- Paris, Société d'édition
"Les Belles lettres." 29-9941
  Z7016 .M35A MRR Alc Full set

Borroni, Fabia. "Il Cicognara,"
Firenze, Sansoni, 1954- v.   55-
18980
  Z2357 .B6 MRR Alc.

London. University. Warburg
Institute. Library. Catalogue. [2d
ed.] Boston, G. K. Hall, 1967. 12
v.   019/.2 68-4522
  Z921 .L66 1967 MRR Alc (Dk 33)

Nairn, John Arbuthnot, Classical
hand-list; 3d ed., rev. and enl.
Oxford, 1953. viii, 164 p. 016.88
54-14555
  Z7016 .N17 1953 MRR Alc.

CLASSICAL ANTIQUITIES--BIBLIOGRAPHY--
CATALOGS.
Deutsches Archäologisches Institut.
Römische Abteilung. Bibliothek.
Kataloge der Bibliothek des Deutschen
Archaeologischen Instituts Rom;
systematischer Katalog. Boston, G.
K. Hall, 1969. 3 v.   73-205023
  Z5134 .F76417 MRR Alc (Dk 33)

CLASSICAL ANTIQUITIES--BIBLIOGRAPHY--
PERIODICALS.
International guide to classical
studies. v. 1- June 1961- Darien,
Conn., American Bibliographic
Service. 016.91338/03 64-6277
Z7016 .I5 MRR Alc Full set

CLASSICAL ANTIQUITIES--PERIODICALS--
BIBLIOGRAPHY.
Southan, Joyce F., comp. A survey of
classical periodicals; [London]
University of London, Institute of
Classical Studies, 1962. xii, 181 p.
65-9438
Z2260 .S67 MRR Alc.

CLASSICAL BIOGRAPHY.
Plutarchus. Plutarch's Lives,
London, Heinemann; New York, Putnam,
1915-1928. 11 v. mrr01-69
PA3612 .P7 1915d MRR Alc.

Radice, Betty. Who's who in the
ancient world; Revised [ed.]
Harmondsworth, Penguin, 1973. 336,
[32] p. [£0.60] 920/.038 74-
161490
DE7 .R33 1973 MRR Alc.

CLASSICAL DICTIONARIES.
Baumeister, August, ed. Denkmäler
des klassischen altertums zur
erläuterung des lebens der Griechen
und Römer in religion, kunst und
sitte. München, Leipzig, R.
Oldenbourg, 1885-1888. 3 v. 04-
35149
DE5 .B34 MRR Alc.

Croon, J. H. The Encyclopedia of the
classical world Englewood Cliffs,
N.J., Prentice-Hall [1965] viii, 239
p. 913.3/8/003 64-23565
DE5 .C713 MRR Alc.

Daremberg, Charles Victor,
Dictionnaire des antiquites grecques
et romaines Graz, Akademische Druck-
u. Verlagsanstalt, 1962-63. 6 v. in
10. 64-44287
DE5 .D22 MRR Alc.

Harvey, Paul, Sir, The Oxford
companion to classical literature.
Oxford, Clarendon Press [1966] xiv,
468 p. 880/.03 67-7951
DE5 .H3 1966 MRR Alc.

Der Kleine Pauly; Lexikon der Antike.
Stuttgart, A. Druckenmüller, 1964-
v. 66-780
DE5 .K5 MRR Alc.

Lempriere, John, Classical
dictionary of proper names mentioned
in ancient authors. New ed. rev.
with additions. New York, E. P.
Dutton, 1949. xxviii, 675 p.
913.38 49-9648
DE5 .L564 1949 MRR Alc.

The New Century classical handbook.
New York, Appleton-Century-Crofts
[1962] xiii, 1162 p. 913.3/8/003
62-10069
DE5 .N4 MRR Alc.

The Oxford classical dictionary, 2d
ed. Oxford [Eng.] Clarendon Press,
1970. xxii, 1176 p. 913.38003 73-
18819
DE5 .O9 1970 MRR Ref Desk.

Pauly, August Friedrich von, Paulys
real-encyclopädie der classischen
altertumswissenshaft; Stuttgart, J.
B. Metzler, 1894-19 v. in   g 01-
2869
DE5 .P33 MRR Alc.

The Praeger encyclopedia of ancient
Greek civilization New York, Praeger
[1967] 481 p. 913.3/8/0303 67-
25162
DF16 .D513 1967c MRR Alc.

Seyffert, Oskar, A dictionary of
classical antiquities, mythology,
religion, literature [and] art. New
York, Meridian Books, 1956. vi, 716
p. 913.38 56-10154
DE5 .S5 1956 MRR Alc.

Warrington, John. Everyman's
classical dictionary; London, Dent;
New York, Dutton [1961] xxxvii, 537
p. 913.38 61-65440
DE5 .W33 MRR Alc.

Whittlesey, Eunice S. Symbols and
legends in Western art; New York,
Scribner [1972] ix, 367 p. [$7.95]
704.94 71-162764
N7740 .W53 MRR Alc.

CLASSICAL DRAMA--HISTORY AND CRITICISM.
Harsh, Philip Whaley, A handbook of
classical drama, Stanford
University, Calif., Stanford
university press; London, H. Milford,
Oxford university press [1944] xii,
526 p. 882.082   a 44-4250
PA3024 .H3 MRR Alc.

Hathorn, Richmond Yancey, Crowell's
handbook of classical drama, New
York, Crowell [1967] 350 p.
882.003 67-12403
PA3024 .H35 TJ Rm.

CLASSICAL DRAMA--HISTORY AND CRITICISM--
BIBLIOGRAPHY.
Coleman, Arthur, Drama criticism
Denver, A. Swallow [1966-71] 2 v.
[$7.50 (v. 1) $12.50 (v. 2)]
016.809/2 66-30426
Z5781 .C65 MRR Ref Desk.

CLASSICAL EDUCATION.
see also Humanities

CLASSICAL GEOGRAPHY--DICTIONARIES.
The New Century handbook of classical
geography. New York, Appleton-
Century-Crofts [1972] v, 362 p.
913/.003 78-189006
DE25 .N48 MRR Alc.

Smith, William, Sir, A dictionary of
Greek and Roman geography, New York,
AMS Press, 1966. 2 v. 913.38/003
73-180902
DE25 .S664 MRR Alc.

CLASSICAL GEOGRAPHY--MAPS.
Heyden, A. A. M. van der, ed. Atlas
of the classical world. [London, New
York] Nelson, 1959 [i.e. 1960] 221
p. 911.38 60-1130
DE29 .H463 MRR Alc.

CLASSICAL LITERATURE--BIBLIOGRAPHY.
L'Annee philologique; 1.-   annee;
1924/26- Paris, Societé d'edition
"Les Belles Lettres." 29-9941
Z7016 .M35A MRR Alc Full set

Engelmann, Wilhelm, Bibliotheca
scriptorum classicorum, 8. aufl.
Leipzig [etc.] W. Engelmann, 1880-82.
2 v. 01-16689
Z7016 .E58 1880 MRR Alc.

Flodr, Miroslav. Incunabula
classicorum. Amsterdam, Adolf H.
Hakkert, 1973. xv, 530 p. 74-
310002
Z240.A1 F57 MRR Alc.

Lambrino, Scarlat. Bibliographie de
l'antiquite classique, 1896-1914.
Paris, Societé d'edition "Les
Belles Lettres," 1951- v.   a 52-
1454
Z7016 .L3 MRR Alc.

London. University. Warburg
Institute. Library. Catalogue. [2d
ed.] Boston, G. K. Hall, 1967. 12
v. 019/.2 68-4522
Z921 .L66 1967 MRR Alc (Dk 33)

Marouzeau, Jules, Dix années de
bibliographie classique, Paris,
Societé d'edition "Les belles
lettres," 1927-28. 2 v. 28-27582
Z7016 .M35 MRR Alc.

Marouzeau, Jules, Dix années de
bibliographie classique; New York,
B. Franklin [1969] 2 v. (xv, 1286
p.) 68-57915
Z7016 .M35 1969 MRR Alc.

Nairn, John Arbuthnot, Classical
hand-list; 3d ed., rev. and enl.
Oxford, 1953. viii, 164 p. 016.88
54-14555
Z7016 .N17 1953 MRR Alc.

CLASSICAL LITERATURE--BIO-BIBLIOGRAPHY.
Laloup, Jean. Dictionnaire de
litterature grecque et latine.
Paris, Éditions universitaires,
1969. 771 p. [39.90] 73-399862
PA31 .L3 MRR Alc.

The Penguin companion to classical,
Oriental & African literature. New
York, McGraw-Hill [1971, c1969] 359
p. [$9.95] 809 78-158064
PA31 .P4 1971 MRR Alc.

CLASSICAL LITERATURE--DICTIONARIES.
Feder, Lillian. Crowell's handbook
of classical literature. New York,
Crowell [1964] viii, 448 p. 880.3
64-18162
PA31 .F4 MRR Alc.

Tusculum-Lexikon griechischer und
lateinischer Autoren des Altertums
und des Mittelalters. München,
Heimeran Verlag [1963] xvi, 544 p.
66-48071
PA31 .T8 1963 MRR Biog.

CLASSICAL LITERATURE--HISTORY AND
CRITICISM.
Fifty years (and twelve) of classical
scholarship; [2d ed.] New York,
Barnes & Noble, 1968. xiv, 523 p.
68-5952
PA3001 .F5 1968 MRR Alc.

Rose, Herbert Jennings, Outlines of
classical literature for students of
English. London, Methuen [1959]
xiv, 303 p.   a 60-3062
PA3001 .R6 1959 MRR Alc.

CLASSICAL LITERATURE--HISTORY AND
CRITICISM--BIBLIOGRAPHY.
Gwinup, Thomas. Greek and Roman
authors; Metuchen, N.J., Scarecrow
Press, 1973. x, 194 p. 016.88/009
72-10156
Z7016 .G9 MRR Alc.

International guide to classical
studies. v. 1- June 1961- Darien,
Conn., American Bibliographic
Service. 016.91338/03 64-6277
Z7016 .I5 MRR Alc Full set

CLASSICAL LITERATURE--TRANSLATIONS INTO
ENGLISH--BIBLIOGRAPHY.
Smith, Frank Seymour. The classics
in translation; New York, B.
Franklin [1968] 307 p. 016.88 68-
57122
Z7018 .T7E87 1968 MRR Alc.

CLASSICAL PHILOLOGY--BIBLIOGRAPHY.
L'Annee philologique; 1.-   annee;
1924/26- Paris, Societé d'edition
"Les Belles Lettres." 29-9941
Z7016 .M35A MRR Alc Full set

Engelmann, Wilhelm, Bibliotheca
scriptorum classicorum, 8. aufl.
Leipzig [etc.] W. Engelmann, 1880-82.
2 v. 01-16689
Z7016 .E58 1880 MRR Alc.

Lambrino, Scarlat. Bibliographie de
l'antiquite classique, 1896-1914.
Paris, Societé d'edition "Les
Belles Lettres," 1951- v.   a 52-
1454
Z7016 .L3 MRR Alc.

Marouzeau, Jules, Dix années de
bibliographie classique; New York,
B. Franklin [1969] 2 v. (xv, 1286
p.) 68-57915
Z7016 .M35 1969 MRR Alc.

Marouzeau, Jules, Dix années de
bibliographie classique, Paris,
Societé d'edition "Les belles
lettres," 1927-28. 2 v. 28-27582
Z7016 .M35 MRR Alc.

McGuire, Martin Rawson Patrick,
Introduction to classical
scholarship, New and rev. ed.
Washington, Catholic University of
America Press, 1961. 257 p.
016.4891 61-66521
Z7016 .M25 1961 MRR Alc.

Thompson, Lawrence Sidney, A
bibliography of American doctoral
dissertations in classical studies
and related fields, [Hamden, Conn.]
Shoe String Press, 1968. xii, 250 p.
016.378/24/0973 67-24191
Z7016 .T48 MRR Alc.

CLASSICAL PHILOLOGY--BIBLIOGRAPHY--
PERIODICALS.
International guide to classical
studies. v. 1- June 1961- Darien,
Conn., American Bibliographic
Service. 016.91338/03 64-6277
Z7016 .I5 MRR Alc Full set

CLASSICAL PHILOLOGY--OUTLINES, SYLLABI,
ETC.
McGuire, Martin Rawson Patrick,
Introduction to classical
scholarship, New and rev. ed.
Washington, Catholic University of
America Press, 1961. 257 p.
016.4891 61-66521
Z7016 .M25 1961 MRR Alc.

CLASSICAL PHILOLOGY--STUDY AND TEACHING.
McGuire, Martin Rawson Patrick,
Introduction to classical
scholarship, New and rev. ed.
Washington, Catholic University of
America Press, 1961. 257 p.
016.4891 61-66521
Z7016 .M25 1961 MRR Alc.

CLASSICISM IN ART.
see also Neoclassicism (Art)

CLASSICISTS--CANADA--DIRECTORIES.
Carrubba, Robert W. Directory of
college and university classicists in
the United States and Canada.
[University Park] Pennsylvania State
University Press [1973] 221 p.
913.38 73-6882
PA83 .C3 MRR Biog.

CLASSICISTS--UNITED STATES--DIRECTORIES.
Carrubba, Robert W. Directory of
college and university classicists in
the United States and Canada.
[University Park] Pennsylvania State
University Press [1973] 221 p.
913.38 73-6882
PA83 .C3 MRR Biog.

CLASSIFICATION.
Foskett, Antony Charles. The subject
approach to information 2d ed., rev.
and enl. [Hamden, Conn.] Linnet
Books [1972, c1971] 429 p. 025.33
71-31243
Z695 .F66 1972 MRR Alc.

CLASSIFICATION. (Cont.)
Wynar, Bohdan S. Introduction to
cataloging and classification 4th
ed. Littleton, Colo., Libraries
Unlimited, 1971. 344 p. 025.3 77-
182404
Z693 .W94 1971 MRR Alc

CLASSIFICATION--BIBLIOGRAPHY.
Sayers, William Charles Berwick, A
manual of classification for
librarians and bibliographers. 3d
ed., rev. London, Grafton, 1955.
xviii, 346 p. 025.4 55-4554
Z696 .S2925 1955 MRR Alc.

Special Libraries Association. Guide
to the SLA loan collection of
classification schemes and subject
heading lists 5th ed. New York,
1961. 97 p. 016.02543 61-13157
Z696 .S8 1961 MRR Alc.

CLASSIFICATION--BOOKS.
Eaton, Thelma, Cataloging and
classification, 3d ed. Champaign,
Ill., Distributed by the Illini Union
Bookstore [1963] 199 p. 025.3 63-
5885
Z695 .E171 1963 MRR Alc.

LaMontagne, Leo E. American library
classification, Hamden, Conn., Shoe
String Press, 1961. x, 433 p.
025.4 61-15682
Z696 .L25 MRR Alc.

Mann, Margaret, Introduction to
cataloging and the classification of
books, 2d ed. Chicago, Ill.,
American library association, 1943.
ix, [1], 276 p., 1 l. 025.3 43-
51241
Z695 .M27 1943 MRR Alc.

Metcalfe, John Wallace, Subject
classifying and indexing of libraries
and literature. New York, Scarecrow
Press, 1959. 347 p. 025.4 59-
65011
Z696 .M59 MRR Alc.

Mills, Jack, A modern outline of
library classification. London,
Chapman & Hall, 1960. viii, 196 p.
025.4 60-4023
Z696 .M63 MRR Alc.

Tauber, Maurice Falcolm, Cataloging
and classification, New Brunswick,
N.J., Graduate School of Library
Service, Rutgers, the State
University, 1960. 271, 92 p. 025.3
60-7278
Z695 .T25 MRR Alc.

United States. Library of Congress.
Subject Cataloging Division. L.C.
classification--additions and
changes. List 1- Mar./May 1928-
[Washington] 025.4 40-31400
Z663.78 .A4 MRR Alc MRR Alc
Partial set

CLASSIFICATION--BOOKS--AFRIKAANS
LITERATURE.
United States. Library of Congress.
Subject Cataloging Division.
Classification. Class P, subclass PT,
part 2: Dutch and Scandinavian
literatures (with supplementary
pages) Washington [For sale by the
Superintendent of Documents, U.S.
Govt. Print. Off.] 1965. vii, 102,
27 p. 65-60061
Z663.78.C5 P95 1965 MRR Alc.

CLASSIFICATION--BOOKS--AGRICULTURE.
United States. Library of Congress.
Subject Cataloging Division.
Classification. Class S: Agriculture,
plant and animal industry, fish
culture and fisheries, hunting
sports. 3d ed. Washington, 1965.
101, 63 p. 65-60084
Z663.78.C5S 1965 MRR Alc.

CLASSIFICATION--BOOKS--AMERICAN
LITERATURE.
United States. Library of Congress.
Subject Cataloging Division.
Classification. Class P, subclasses
PN, PR, PS, PZ: Washington [For sale
by the Superintendent of Documents,
U.S. Govt. Print. Off.] 1964. 272,
277 p. 64-60069
Z663.78.C5P7 1964 MRR Alc.

CLASSIFICATION--BOOKS--ANIMAL INDUSTRY.
United States. Library of Congress.
Subject Cataloging Division.
Classification. Class S: Agriculture,
plant and animal industry, fish
culture and fisheries, hunting
sports. 3d ed. Washington, 1965.
101, 63 p. 65-60084
Z663.78.C5S 1965 MRR Alc.

CLASSIFICATION--BOOKS--ANTHROPOLOGY.
United States. Library of Congress.
Subject Cataloging Division.
Classification. Class G: Geography,
3d ed. Washington [For sale by the
Superintendent of Documents, U.S.
Govt. Print. Off.] 1954; reprinted
1966. xv, 502, 77 p. 025.4/6 66-
61847
Z663.78.C5G 1966 MRR Alc.

CLASSIFICATION--BOOKS--ARCHÆOLOGY.
Dgutsches Archaologisches Institut.
Römische Abteilung. Bibliothek.
Katalog der Bibliothek des Deutschen
Archaeologischen Instituts Rom;
systematischer Katalog. Boston, G.
K. Hall, 1969. 3 v. 73-205023
Z5134 .R76417 MRR Alc (Dk 33)

United States. Library of Congress.
Subject Cataloging Division.
Classification. Class C: Auxiliary
sciences of history. 2d ed.
Washington, 1948; reissued 1967.
vii, 167, 31 p. 025.4/6/9 67-61606

Z663.78.C5C 1967 MRR Alc.

CLASSIFICATION--BOOKS--ARCHIVES.
United States. Library of Congress.
Subject Cataloging Division.
Classification. Class C: Auxiliary
sciences of history. 2d ed.
Washington, 1948; reissued 1967.
vii, 167, 31 p. 025.4/6/9 67-61606

Z663.78.C5C 1967 MRR Alc.

CLASSIFICATION--BOOKS--ART.
United States. Library of Congress.
Subject Cataloging Division.
Classification. 4th ed. Washington;
[For sale by the Card Division,
Library of Congress] 1970. xi, 280
l. [3.00] 025.4/6/7 78-606523
Z663.78.C5N 1970 MRR Alc.

United States. Library of Congress.
Subject Cataloging Division.
Classification. Class N: Fine arts.
3d ed. Washington, 1922; reprinted
1962. 165, 77 p. 62-60073
Z663.78.C5N 1962 MRR Alc.

CLASSIFICATION--BOOKS--BIBLIOGRAPHY.
Case Western Reserve University.
Bibliographic Systems Center.
Selected materials in classification;
New York, Special Libraries
Association [c1968] 142 p.
016.0254 68-19707
Z696 .C3 MRR Alc.

Sayers, William Charles Berwick, A
manual of classification for
librarians and bibliographers. 3d
ed., rev. London, Grafton, 1955.
xviii, 346 p. 025.4 55-4554
Z696 .S2925 1955 MRR Alc.

United States. Library of Congress.
Subject Cataloging Division.
Classification. Class Z: Bibliography
and library science. 4th ed.,
Washington [For sale by the
Superintendent of Documents, U.S.
Govt. Print. Off.] 1965. ix, 226, 61
p. 65-60072
Z663.78.C5Z 1965 MRR Alc.

CLASSIFICATION--BOOKS--BIOGRAPHY.
United States. Library of Congress.
Subject Cataloging Division.
Classification. Class C: Auxiliary
sciences of history. 2d ed.
Washington, 1948; reissued 1967.
vii, 167, 31 p. 025.4/6/9 67-61606

Z663.78.C5C 1967 MRR Alc.

CLASSIFICATION--BOOKS--BYZANTINE
LITERATURE.
United States. Library of Congress.
Subject Cataloging Division.
Classification. Class P, subclass PA
supplement: Byzantine and modern
Greek literature, medieval and modern
Latin literature. Washington; [For
sale by the Card Division, Library of
Congress] 1968. v, 24, 1 p.
025.4/6/88 68-60095
Z663.78.C5P23 1968 MRR Alc.

CLASSIFICATION--BOOKS--CHRONOLOGY.
United States. Library of Congress.
Subject Cataloging Division.
Classification. Class C: Auxiliary
sciences of history. 2d ed.
Washington, 1948; reissued 1967.
vii, 167, 31 p. 025.4/6/9 67-61606

Z663.78.C5C 1967 MRR Alc.

CLASSIFICATION--BOOKS--CLASSICAL
PHILOLOGY.
United States. Library of Congress.
Subject Cataloging Division.
Classification. Class P, P-PA:
Philology, linguistics, classical
philology, classical literature
Washington [For sale by the Card
Division, Library of Congress] 1928;
reissued 1968. vii, 16, 447, 47 p.
025.4/6/4 67-61607
Z663.78.C5P2 1968 MRR Alc.

CLASSIFICATION--BOOKS--DENTISTRY.
Index to dental literature. 1962-
Chicago, American Dental Association.
617.6/001/6 72-622063
Z6668 .I45 Sci RR Partial set /
MRR Alc Partial set

CLASSIFICATION--BOOKS--DIPLOMATICS.
United States. Library of Congress.
Subject Cataloging Division.
Classification. Class C: Auxiliary
sciences of history. 2d ed.
Washington, 1948; reissued 1967.
vii, 167, 31 p. 025.4/6/9 67-61606

Z663.78.C5C 1967 MRR Alc.

CLASSIFICATION--BOOKS--DUTCH LITERATURE.
United States. Library of Congress.
Subject Cataloging Division.
Classification. Class P, subclass PT,
part 2: Dutch and Scandinavian
literatures (with supplementary
pages) Washington [For sale by the
Superintendent of Documents, U.S.
Govt. Print. Off.] 1965. vii, 102,
27 p. 65-60061
Z663.78.C5 P95 1965 MRR Alc.

CLASSIFICATION--BOOKS--EDUCATION.
United States. Library of Congress.
Subject Cataloging Division.
Classification. Class L: Education.
3d ed. Washington, 1951; reprinted,
1966. xi, 200, 69 p. 025.4/6/37
66-61846
Z663.78.C5L 1966 MRR Alc.

CLASSIFICATION--BOOKS--ENGLISH
LITERATURE.
United States. Library of Congress.
Subject Cataloging Division.
Classification. Class P, subclasses
PN, PR, PS, PZ: Washington [For sale
by the Superintendent of Documents,
U.S. Govt. Print. Off.] 1964. 272,
277 p. 64-60069
Z663.78.C5P7 1964 MRR Alc.

CLASSIFICATION--BOOKS--FISHERIES.
United States. Library of Congress.
Subject Cataloging Division.
Classification. Class S: Agriculture,
plant and animal industry, fish
culture and fisheries, hunting
sports. 3d ed., Washington, 1965.
101, 63 p. 65-60084
Z663.78.C5S 1965 MRR Alc.

CLASSIFICATION--BOOKS--FLEMISH
LITERATURE.
United States. Library of Congress.
Subject Cataloging Division.
Classification. Class P, subclass PT,
part 2: Dutch and Scandinavian
literatures (with supplementary
pages) Washington [For sale by the
Superintendent of Documents, U.S.
Govt. Print. Off.] 1965. vii, 102,
27 p. 65-60061
Z663.78.C5 P95 1965 MRR Alc.

CLASSIFICATION--BOOKS--FOLKLORE.
United States. Library of Congress.
Subject Cataloging Division.
Classification. Class G: Geography,
3d ed. Washington [For sale by the
Superintendent of Documents, U.S.
Govt. Print. Off.] 1954; reprinted
1966. xv, 502, 77 p. 025.4/6 66-
61847
Z663.78.C5G 1966 MRR Alc.

CLASSIFICATION--BOOKS--FRENCH
LITERATURE.
United States. Library of Congress.
Subject Cataloging Division.
Classification. Class P, subclass PQ,
part 1: French literature
Washington, 1963; reprinted 1966. v,
185, 17 p. 025.4/6/84 66-61874
Z663.78.C5P8 1966 MRR Alc.

CLASSIFICATION--BOOKS--GENEALOGY.
United States. Library of Congress.
Subject Cataloging Division.
Classification. Class C: Auxiliary
sciences of history. 2d ed.
Washington, 1948; reissued 1967.
vii, 167, 31 p. 025.4/6/9 67-61606

Z663.78.C5C 1967 MRR Alc.

CLASSIFICATION--BOOKS--GENERAL WORKS.
United States. Library of Congress.
Subject Cataloging Division.
Classification. 4th ed. Washington,
Library of Congress; [for sale by the
Card Division] 1973. v, 40 p.
[$5.00] 025.4/3 73-8530
Z663.78.C5 A 1973 MRR Alc.

CLASSIFICATION--BOOKS--GEOGRAPHY.
United States. Library of Congress.
Subject Cataloging Division.
Classification. Class G: Geography,
3d ed. Washington [For sale by the
Superintendent of Documents, U.S.
Govt. Print. Off.] 1954; reprinted
1966. xv, 502, 77 p. 025.4/6 66-
61847
Z663.78.C5G 1966 MRR Alc.

CLASSIFICATION--BOOKS--GERMAN
LITERATURE.
United States. Library of Congress.
Subject Cataloging Division.
Classification. Class P, subclass PT,
part 1: German literature, with
supplementary pages. Washington,
1938; reprinted 1966. v, 312, 17 p.
025.4683 66-60026
    Z663.78.C5 P9 1966 MRR Alc.

CLASSIFICATION--BOOKS--GOVERNMENT
PUBLICATIONS.
Poole, Mary Elizabeth, Documents
Office classification numbers for
cuttered documents, 1910-1924. Ann
Arbor, Mich., University Microfilms,
1960. 2 v. 025.4 61-3757
    Z697.G7 P6 1960 MRR Alc.

CLASSIFICATION--BOOKS--GREEK
LITERATURE, MODERN.
United States. Library of Congress.
Subject Cataloging Division.
Classification. Class P, subclass PA
supplement: Byzantine and modern
Greek literature, medieval and modern
Latin literature. Washington: [For
sale by the Card Division, Library of
Congress] 1968. v, 24, 1 p.
025.4/6/88 68-60095
    Z663.78.C5P23 1968 MRR Alc.

CLASSIFICATION--BOOKS--HERALDRY.
United States. Library of Congress.
Subject Cataloging Division.
Classification. Class C: Auxiliary
sciences of history. 2d ed.
Washington, 1948; reissued 1967.
vii, 167, 31 p. 025.4/6/9 67-61606

    Z663.78.C5C 1967 MRR Alc.

CLASSIFICATION--BOOKS--HISTORY.
United States. Library of Congress.
Subject Cataloging Division.
Classification. History: Class D,
General and Old World. 2d ed.
Washington, 1959; reprinted 1966.
xxxiv, 747, 55 p. 025.469 65-62173
    Z663.78.C5D 1966 MRR Alc.

CLASSIFICATION--BOOKS--HUNTING.
United States. Library of Congress.
Subject Cataloging Division.
Classification. Class S: Agriculture,
plant and animal industry, fish
culture and fisheries, hunting
sports. 3d ed., Washington, 1965.
101, 63 p. 65-60084
    Z663.78.C5S 1965 MRR Alc.

CLASSIFICATION--BOOKS--INDO-IRANIAN
PHILOLOGY.
United States. Library of Congress.
Subject Cataloging Division.
Classification. Class P, subclasses
PJ-PM: Languages and literatures of
Asia, Africa, Oceania, America, mixed
languages, artificial languages (with
supplementary pages) Washington,
1935; reprinted 1965. x, 246, 191 p.
65-60071
    Z663.78.C5 P5 1965 MRR Alc.

CLASSIFICATION--BOOKS--INSCRIPTIONS.
United States. Library of Congress.
Subject Cataloging Division.
Classification. Class C: Auxiliary
sciences of history. 2d ed.
Washington, 1948; reissued 1967.
vii, 167, 31 p. 025.4/6/9 67-61606

    Z663.78.C5C 1967 MRR Alc.

CLASSIFICATION--BOOKS--ITALIAN
LITERATURE.
United States. Library of Congress.
Subject Cataloging Division.
Classification. Class P, subclass PQ,
part 2: Italian, Spanish, and
Portuguese literatures Washington
[For sale by the Superintendent of
Documents, U.S. Govt. Print. Off.]
1965. viii, 223, 29 p. 65-60056
    Z663.78.C5P8 1965 MRR Alc.

CLASSIFICATION--BOOKS--LANGUAGE AND
LANGUAGES--INDEXES.
United States. Library of Congress.
Subject Cataloging Division.
Classification: Class P, subclasses P-
PM supplement: 2d ed., Washington,
1957; reprinted, 1965. iii, 71, 5 p.
65-61907
    Z663.78.C5 P6 1965 MRR Alc.

CLASSIFICATION--BOOKS--LANGUAGES,
MODERN.
United States. Library of Congress.
Subject Cataloging Division.
Classification. Class P, subclasses
PB-PH: modern European languages
(with supplementary pages)
Washington, 1933; reprinted, 1966.
vi, 226, 51 p. 65-62403
    Z663.78.C5 P3 1966 MRR Alc.

CLASSIFICATION--BOOKS--LATIN
LITERATURE, MEDIEVAL AND MODERN.
United States. Library of Congress.
Subject Cataloging Division.
Classification. Class P, subclass PA
supplement: Byzantine and modern
Greek literature, medieval and modern
Latin literature. Washington; [For
sale by the Card Division, Library of
Congress] 1968. v, 24, 1 p.
025.4/6/88 68-60095
    Z663.78.C5P23 1968 MRR Alc.

CLASSIFICATION--BOOKS--LAW.
Chicago. University. Law School.
Library. Classification: Class K,
Law. Washington, Library of
Congress, 1948. 172 p. 025.4634
49-45509
    Z663.78.C5 K 1948 MRR Alc.

United States. Library of Congress.
Subject Cataloging Division. Class
K: Law; working papers Washington,
1953- v. 025.4634 56-60073
    Z663.78.C5K 1953 MRR Alc.

United States. Library of Congress.
Subject Cataloging Division.
Classification. Washington, Library
of Congress; 1973. ix p., 114 l., 115-
163 p. [$5.75] 025.4/6/3400942 73-
8416
    Z663.78.C5 K 1973 MRR Alc.

CLASSIFICATION--BOOKS--LIBRARY SCIENCE.
Cannons, Harry George Turner.
Bibliography of library economy;
Chicago, American library
association, 1927. 4 p. l., 11-680
p. 26-26901
    Z666 .C21 1927 MRR Alc.

United States. Library of Congress.
Subject Cataloging Division.
Classification. Class Z: Bibliography
and library science. 4th ed.,
Washington [For sale by the
Superintendent of Documents, U.S.
Govt. Print. Off.] 1965. ix, 226, 61
p. 65-60072
    Z663.78.C5Z 1965 MRR Alc.

CLASSIFICATION--BOOKS--LITERATURE.
United States. Library of Congress.
Subject Cataloging Division.
Classification. Class P, subclasses
PN, PR, PS, PZ: Washington [For sale
by the Superintendent of Documents,
U.S. Govt. Print. Off.] 1964. 272,
277 p. 64-60069
    Z663.78.C5F7 1964 MRR Alc.

CLASSIFICATION--BOOKS--MANNERS AND
CUSTOMS.
United States. Library of Congress.
Subject Cataloging Division.
Classification. Class G: Geography,
3d ed. Washington [For sale by the
Superintendent of Documents, U.S.
Govt. Print. Off.] 1954; reprinted
1966. xv, 502, 77 p. 025.4/6 66-
61847
    Z663.78.C5G 1966 MRR Alc.

CLASSIFICATION--BOOKS--MEDICINE.
United States. Library of Congress.
Subject Cataloging Division.
Classification. Class R: Medicine.
3d ed., Washington, 1952; reprinted
1966. xiv, 240, 81 p. 025.4/6/61
66-61845
    Z663.78.C5R 1966 MRR Alc.

United States. National Library of
Medicine. Classification; 3d ed.
Bethesda, Md., 1964. xxi, 286 p.
64-61442
    Z697.M4 U5 1964 MRR Alc.

CLASSIFICATION--BOOKS--MILITARY ART AND
SCIENCE.
United States. Library of Congress.
Subject Cataloging Division.
Classification. Class U: Military
science. 3d ed., Washington, 1952;
reprinted 1966. v, 86, 21 p.
025.4/6/355 66-61848
    Z663.78.C5U 1966 MRR Alc.

CLASSIFICATION--BOOKS--MUSIC.
United States. Library of Congress.
Subject Cataloging Division.
Classification. Class M: Music and
books on music. 2d ed., Washington,
[For sale by the Card Division,
Library of Congress] 1917; reissued
1968. 157, 113 p. 025.4/6/78 68-
60011
    Z663.78.C5M 1968 MRR Alc.

CLASSIFICATION--BOOKS--NAVAL ART AND
SCIENCE.
United States. Library of Congress.
Subject Cataloging Division.
Classification. 2d ed. (with
supplementary pages) Washington,
[For sale by the Card Division,
Library of Congress] 1953; reprinted
1966 [i.e. 1968] v. 115, 39 p.
[1.50] 025.4/6/359 65-62543
    Z663.78 .C5V 1968 MRR Alc.

CLASSIFICATION--BOOKS--NUMISMATICS.
United States. Library of Congress.
Subject Cataloging Division.
Classification. Class C: Auxiliary
sciences of history. 2d ed.
Washington, 1948; reissued 1967.
vii, 167, 31 p. 025.4/6/9 67-61606
    Z663.78.C5C 1967 MRR Alc.

CLASSIFICATION--BOOKS--ORIENTAL
PHILOLOGY.
United States. Library of Congress.
Subject Cataloging Division.
Classification. Class P, subclasses
PJ-PM: Languages and literatures of
Asia, Africa, Oceania, America, mixed
languages, artificial languages (with
supplementary pages) Washington,
1935; reprinted 1965. x, 246, 191 p.
65-60071
    Z663.78.C5 P5 1965 MRR Alc.

CLASSIFICATION--BOOKS--PHILOLOGY.
United States. Library of Congress.
Subject Cataloging Division.
Classification. Class P, P-PA:
Philology, linguistics, classical
philology, classical literature
Washington [For sale by the Card
Division, Library of Congress] 1928;
reissued 1968. vii, 16, 447, 47 p.
025.4/6/4 67-61607
    Z663.78.C5P2 1968 MRR Alc.

United States. Library of Congress.
Subject Cataloging Division.
Classification. Class P, subclasses
PB-PH: modern European languages
(with supplementary pages)
Washington 1933; reprinted, 1966.
vii 226, 51 p. 65-62403
    Z663.78.C5 P3 1966 MRR Alc.

United States. Library of Congress.
Subject Cataloging Division.
Classification. Class P, subclasses
PJ-PM: Languages and literatures of
Asia, Africa, Oceania, America, mixed
languages, artificial languages (with
supplementary pages) Washington,
1935; reprinted 1965. x, 246, 191 p.
65-60071
    Z663.78.C5 P5 1965 MRR Alc.

CLASSIFICATION--BOOKS--PHILOSOPHY.
United States. Library of Congress.
Subject Cataloging Division.
Classification. Class B, part I, B-
BJ: Philosophy. 2d ed. Washington,
[For sale by the Card Division,
Library of Congress] 1950, reissued
1968. xi, 166, 101 p. 025.4/6/1
67-60098
    Z663.78.C5B1 1968 MRR Alc.

CLASSIFICATION--BOOKS--POLITICAL
SCIENCE.
United States. Library of Congress.
Subject Cataloging Division.
Classification. Class J: Political
science. 2d ed., Washington, 1924;
reprinted, 1966. 434, 161 p. 66-
60021
    Z663.78.C5J 1966 MRR Alc.

CLASSIFICATION--BOOKS--PORTUGUESE
LITERATURE.
United States. Library of Congress.
Subject Cataloging Division.
Classification. Class P, subclass PQ,
part 2: Italian, Spanish, and
Portuguese literatures Washington
[For sale by the Superintendent of
Documents, U.S. Govt. Print. Off.]
1965. viii, 223, 29 p. 65-60056
    Z663.78.C5P8 1965 MRR Alc.

CLASSIFICATION--BOOKS--RELIGION.
United States. Library of Congress.
Subject Cataloging Division.
Classification. Class B, part II, BL-
BX: Religion. 2d ed. Washington,
For sale by the Superintendent of
Documents, U.S. Govt. Print. Off.,
1962. xxii, 639 p. 025.462 62-
60072
    Z663.78.C5B2 1962 MRR Alc.

CLASSIFICATION--BOOKS--RUSSIAN
LITERATURE.
United States. Library of Congress.
Subject Cataloging Division.
Classification. Class P, subclass PG,
in part: Russian literature
Washington [For sale by the
Superintendent of Documents, U.S.
Govt. Print. Off.] 1965. v, 256, 15
p. 65-60025
    Z663.78.C5P4 1965 MRR Alc.

CLASSIFICATION--BOOKS--SCANDINAVIAN
LITERATURE.
United States. Library of Congress.
Subject Cataloging Division.
Classification. Class P, subclass PT,
part 2: Dutch and Scandinavian
literatures (with supplementary
pages) Washington [For sale by the
Superintendent of Documents, U.S.
Govt. Print. Off.] 1965. vii, 102,
27 p. 65-60061
    Z663.78.C5 P95 1965 MRR Alc.

CLASSIFICATION--BOOKS--SCIENCE.
Royal society of London. Catalogue
of scientific papers, 1800-1900.
Cambridge, University press, 1908-
v.   08-24586
  Z7403 .R8812 MRR Alc.

United States. Library of Congress.
Subject Cataloging Division.
Classification. 6th ed. Washington,
Library of Congress [for sale by the
Card Division] 1973. vii p., 282 l.,
283-415 p. [$9.00] 025.3/35 72-
10222
  Z663.78.C5 Q 1973 MRR Alc.

CLASSIFICATION--BOOKS--SOCIAL SCIENCES.
United States. Library of Congress.
Subject Cataloging Division.
Classification. Class H: Social
sciences. 3d ed., Washington, [For
sale by the Superintendent of
Documents, U.S. Govt. Print. Off.]
1965. xxxiv, 614, 173 p.   65-60024

  Z663.78.C5 H 1965 MRR Alc.

CLASSIFICATION--BOOKS--SPANISH
LITERATURE.
United States. Library of Congress.
Subject Cataloging Division.
Classification. Class P, subclass PQ,
part 2: Italian, Spanish, and
Portuguese literatures Washington
[For sale by the Superintendent of
Documents, U.S. Govt. Print. Off.]
1965. viii, 223, 29 p.   65-60056
  Z663.78.C5P8 1965 MRR Alc.

CLASSIFICATION--BOOKS--SPORTS.
United States. Library of Congress.
Subject Cataloging Division.
Classification. Class G: Geography,
3d ed. Washington [For sale by the
Superintendent of Documents, U.S.
Govt. Print. Off.] 1954: reprinted
1966. xv, 502, 77 p. 025.4/6 66-
61847
  Z663.78.C5G 1966 MRR Alc.

CLASSIFICATION--BOOKS--TECHNOLOGY.
United States. Library of Congress.
Subject Cataloging Division.
Classification. Class T: Technology.
5th ed. Washington, Library of
Congress, 1971. x p., 266 l., 267-
370 p. [$3.50] 025.4/66 76-611341

  Z663.78.C5T 1971 MRR Alc.

CLASSIFICATION--BOOKS--THEOLOGY.
United States. Library of Congress.
Subject Cataloging Division.
Classification. Class B, part II, BL-
BX: Religion. 2d ed. Washington,
For sale by the Superintendent of
Documents, U.S. Govt. Print. Off.,
1962. xxii, 639 p. 025.462 62-
60072
  Z663.78.C5B2 1962 MRR Alc.

CLASSIFICATION--BOOKS--AFRICA.
Harvard University. Library. Africa:
classification schedule, Cambridge,
Published by the Harvard University
Library; distributed by the Harvard
University Press, 1965. 302, 204,
196 p. 016.91603 65-29301
  Z881 .H34035 MRR Alc.

CLASSIFICATION--BOOKS--AMERICA.
United States. Library of Congress.
Subject Cataloging Division.
Classification. History: Class E-F,
America. 3d ed. Washington [For
sale by the Superintendent of
Documents, U.S. Govt. Print. Off.]
1965. xi, 607, 23 p.   65-60055
  Z663.78.C5E 1965 MRR Alc.

CLASSIFICATION--BOOKS--CANADA.
Harvard University. Library.
Canadian history and literature;
Cambridge; Distributed by the Harvard
University Press, 1968. 411 p.
016.9171 68-22417
  Z1365 .H3 MRR Alc.

CLASSIFICATION--BOOKS--GREAT BRITAIN.
Gross, Charles. The sources and
literature of English history from
the earliest times to about 1485, 2d
ed., rev. and enl. London, New York
[etc.] Longmans, Green, and co.,
1915. xxiii, 820 p. 15-16893
  Z2016 .G87 1915 MRR Alc.

CLASSIFICATION--MAPS.
United States. Library of Congress.
Subject Cataloging Division.
Classification. Class G: Geography,
3d ed. Washington [For sale by the
Superintendent of Documents, U.S.
Govt. Print. Off.] 1954: reprinted
1966. xv, 502, 77 p. 025.4/6 66-
61847
  Z663.78.C5G 1966 MRR Alc.

CLASSIFICATION--MUSIC.
United States. Library of Congress.
Subject Cataloging Division.
Classification. Class M: Music and
books on music. 2d ed. Washington,
[For sale by the Card Division,
Library of Congress] 1917; reissued
1968. 157, 113 p. 025.4/6/78 68-
60011
  Z663.78.C5M 1968 MRR Alc.

CLASSIFICATION, COLON.
Ranganathan, Shiyali Ramamrita, Rao
Sahib. Colon classification. [6th
ed. reprinted Bombay, New York, Asia
Pub. House [1963- pts. in v.
025.43 63-25965
  Z696 .R193 MRR Alc.

CLASSIFICATION, DECIMAL.
British Standards Institution. Guide
to the Universal decimal
classification (UDC) London, 1963.
128 p. 64-6080
  Z696.D6 B7 MRR Alc.

CLASSIFICATION, DEWEY DECIMAL.
Dewey, Melvil, Abridged Dewey
decimal classification and relative
index. Ed. 10. Lake Placid Club,
N.Y., Forest Press, 1971. vii, 529
p. 025.4/3 70-164427
  Z696 .D5129 1971 MRR Alc.

Dewey, Melvil, Dewey decimal
classification and relative index.
Ed. 18. Lake Placid Club, N.Y.,
Forest Press, 1971. 3 v. (viii, 2692
p.) 025.4/3 78-140002
  Z696 .D519 1971 MRR Alc.

United States. Library of Congress.
Decimal Classification Office. Guide
to use of Dewey decimal
classification, Lake Placid Club,
N.Y., Forest Press, 1962. 133 p.
025.43 61-16797
  Z696 .D5199 MRR Alc.

United States. Library of Congress.
Subject Cataloging Division. Decimal
classification, 14th and 15th
editions; Washington, Library of
Congress, Subject Cataloging
Division, Decimal Classification
Section, 1953. iv, 36 p. 025.4 53-
60013
  Z663.735 .D43 MRR Alc.

CLASSIFICATION, LIBRARY OF CONGRESS.
Immroth, John Phillip. A guide to
the Library of Congress
classification. 2d ed. Littleton,
Colo., Libraries Unlimited, 1971.
335 p. 025.4/3 75-178877
  Z696.U4 I5 1971 MRR Alc.

LaMontagne, Leo E. American library
classification, Hamden, Conn., Shoe
String Press, 1961. x, 433 p.
025.4 61-15682
  Z696 .L25 MRR Alc.

United States. Library of Congress.
Subject Cataloging Division.
Classification. 4th ed. Washington,
Library of Congress: [for sale by the
Card Division] 1973. iv, 40 p.
[$5.00] 025.4/3 73-8530
  Z663.78.C5 A 1973 MRR Alc.

United States. Library of Congress.
Subject Cataloging Division.
Classification. Washington, Library
of Congress; [for sale by the Card
Division] 1973. ix p., 114 l., 115-
163 p. [$5.75] 025.4/6/3400942 73-
8416
  Z663.78.C5 K 1973 MRR Alc.

United States. Library of Congress.
Subject Cataloging Division.
Classification. 4th ed. Washington;
[For sale by the Card Division,
Library of Congress] 1970. xi, 280
l. [3.00] 025.4/6/7 78-606523
  Z663.78.C5N 1970 MRR Alc.

United States. Library of Congress.
Subject Cataloging Division.
Classification. 6th ed. Washington,
Library of Congress: [for sale by the
Card Division] 1973. vii p., 282 l.,
283-415 p. [$9.00] 025.3/35 72-
10222
  Z663.78.C5 Q 1973 MRR Alc.

United States. Library of Congress.
Subject Cataloging Division.
Classification. 2d ed. (with
supplementary pages) Washington,
[For sale by the Card Division,
Library of Congress] 1953; reprinted
1966 i.e. 1968] v, 115, 39 p.
[1.50] 025.4/6/359 65-62543
  Z663.78 .C5V 1968 MRR Alc.

United States. Library of Congress.
Subject Cataloging Division.
Classification. Class B, part I, B-
BJ: Philosophy. 2d ed. Washington,
[For sale by the Card Division,
Library of Congress] 1950, reissued
1968. xxi, 166, 101 p. 025.4/6/1
67-60098
  Z663.78.C5B1 1968 MRR Alc.

United States. Library of Congress.
Subject Cataloging Division.
Classification. Class B, part II, BL-
BX: Religion. 2d ed. Washington,
For sale by the Superintendent of
Documents, U.S. Govt. Print. Off.,
1962. xxii, 639 p. 025.462 62-
60072
  Z663.78.C5B2 1962 MRR Alc.

United States. Library of Congress.
Subject Cataloging Division.
Classification. Class C: Auxiliary
sciences of history. 2d ed.
Washington, 1948; reissued 1967.
vii, 167, 31 p. 025.4/6/9 67-61606

  Z663.78.C5C 1967 MRR Alc.

United States. Library of Congress.
Subject Cataloging Division.
Classification. Class G: Geography,
3d ed. Washington [For sale by the
Superintendent of Documents, U.S.
Govt. Print. Off.] 1954: reprinted
1966. xv, 502, 77 p. 025.4/6 66-
61847
  Z663.78.C5G 1966 MRR Alc.

United States. Library of Congress.
Subject Cataloging Division.
Classification. Class H: Social
sciences. 3d ed., Washington, [For
sale by the Superintendent of
Documents, U.S. Govt. Print. Off.]
1965. xxxiv, 614, 173 p.   65-60024

  Z663.78.C5 H 1965 MRR Alc.

United States. Library of Congress.
Subject Cataloging Division.
Classification. Class J: Political
science. 2d ed., Washington, 1924;
reprinted, 1966. 434, 161 p.   66-
60021
  Z663.78.C5J 1966 MRR Alc.

United States. Library of Congress.
Subject Cataloging Division.
Classification. Class M: Music and
books on music. 2d ed. Washington,
[For sale by the Card Division,
Library of Congress] 1917; reissued
1968. 157, 113 p. 025.4/6/78 68-
60011
  Z663.78.C5M 1968 MRR Alc.

United States. Library of Congress.
Subject Cataloging Division.
Classification. Class N: Fine arts.
3d ed. Washington, 1922; reprinted
1962. 165, 77 p.   62-60073
  Z663.78.C5N 1962 MRR Alc.

United States. Library of Congress.
Subject Cataloging Division.
Classification. Class P, P-PA:
Philology, linguistics, classical
philology, classical literature
Washington [For sale by the Card
Division, Library of Congress] 1928;
reissued 1968. vii, 16, 447, 47 p.
025.4/6/4 67-61607
  Z663.78.C5P2 1968 MRR Alc.

United States. Library of Congress.
Subject Cataloging Division.
Classification. Class P, subclass PA
supplement: Byzantine and modern
Greek literature, medieval and modern
Latin literature. Washington: [For
sale by the Card Division, Library of
Congress] 1968. v, 24, 1 p.
025.4/6/88 68-60095
  Z663.78.C5P23 1968 MRR Alc.

United States. Library of Congress.
Subject Cataloging Division.
Classification. Class P, subclass PG,
in part: Russian literature
Washington [For sale by the
Superintendent of Documents, U.S.
Govt. Print. Off.] 1965. v, 256, 15
p. 65-60025
  Z663.78.C5P4 1965 MRR Alc.

United States. Library of Congress.
Subject Cataloging Division.
Classification. Class P, subclass PQ,
part 1: French literature
Washington, 1963; reprinted 1966. v,
185, 17 p. 025.4/6/844 66-61874
  Z663.78.C5P8 1966 MRR Alc.

United States. Library of Congress.
Subject Cataloging Division.
Classification. Class P, subclass PQ,
part 2: Italian, Spanish, and
Portuguese literatures Washington
[For sale by the Superintendent of
Documents, U.S. Govt. Print. Off.]
1965. viii, 223, 29 p.   65-60056
  Z663.78.C5P8 1965 MRR Alc.

United States. Library of Congress.
Subject Cataloging Division.
Classification. Class P, subclass PT,
part 1: German literature, with
supplementary pages. Washington,
1938; reprinted 1966. v, 312, 17 p.
025.4683 66-60026
  Z663.78.C5 P9 1966 MRR Alc.

CLASSIFICATION, LIBRARY OF (Cont.)
United States. Library of Congress.
Subject Cataloging Division.
Classification. Class P, subclass PT,
part 2: Dutch and Scandinavian
literatures (with supplementary
pages) Washington [For sale by the
Superintendent of Documents, U.S.
Govt. Print. Off.] 1965. vii, 102,
27 p.   65-60061
Z663.78.C5 P85 1965 MRR Alc

United States. Library of Congress.
Subject Cataloging Division.
Classification. Class P, subclasses
PN, PR, PS, PZ: Washington [For sale
by the Superintendent of Documents,
U.S. Govt. Print. Off.] 1964. 272,
277 p.   64-60069
Z663.78.C5P7 1964 MRR Alc.

United States. Library of Congress.
Subject Cataloging Division.
Classification. Class R: Medicine.
3d ed., Washington, 1952; reprinted
1966. xiv, 240, 81 p.   025.4/6/61
66-61845
Z663.78.C5R 1966 MRR Alc.

United States. Library of Congress.
Subject Cataloging Division.
Classification. Class S: Agriculture,
plant and animal industry, fish
culture and fisheries, hunting
sports. 3d ed., Washington, 1965.
101, 63 p.   65-60084
Z663.78.C5S 1965 MRR Alc.

United States. Library of Congress.
Subject Cataloging Division.
Classification. Class T: Technology.
5th ed. Washington, Library of
Congress, 1971. x p., 266 l., 267-
370 p. [$3.50]   025.4/66 76-611341

Z663.78.C5T 1971 MRR Alc.

United States. Library of Congress.
Subject Cataloging Division.
Classification. Class U: Military
science. 3d ed., Washington, 1952;
reprinted 1966. v, 86, 21 p.
025.4/6/355 66-61848
Z663.78.C5U 1966 MRR Alc.

United States. Library of Congress.
Subject Cataloging Division.
Classification. History: Class E-F,
America. 3d ed. Washington [For
sale by the Superintendent of
Documents, U.S. Govt. Print. Off.]
1965. xi, 607, 23 p.   65-60055
Z663.78.C5E 1965 MRR Alc.

United States. Library of Congress.
Subject Cataloging Division. L.C.
classification--additions and
changes. List 1- Mar./May 1928-
[Washington]   025.4 40-31400
Z663.78 .A4 MRR Alc MRR Alc
Partial set

United States. Library of Congress.
Subject Cataloging Division. Outline
of the Library of Congress
classification. 2d ed. Washington,
1970. 21 p.   025.4 76-607324
Z663.78 .C52 1970 MRR Alc.

Williams, James G. Classified
Library of Congress subject headings,
New York, M. Dekker, 1972. 2 v.
025.4 72-91323
Z695.U48 W55 MRR Alc.

CLASSIFICATION, UNIVERSAL DECIMAL.
British Standards Institution. Guide
to the Universal decimal
classification (UDC) London, 1963.
128 p.   64-6080
Z696.D6 B7 MRR Alc.

Mills, Jack, The Universal decimal
classification. New Brunswick, N.J.,
Graduate School of Library Service,
Rutgers, the State University, 1964.
132 p.   025.43 64-64955
Z696 .A1R8 no. 1 MRR Alc.

CLAY, HENRY, 1777-1852.
Mayo, Bernard, Henry Clay, spokesman
of the new West. [Unaltered and
unabridged] Hamden, Conn.] Archon
Books, 1966 [c1937] 570 p.
973.40924 66-25184
E340.C6 M2 1966 MRR Alc.

CLAY INDUSTRIES--DICTIONARIES.
Searle, Alfred Broadhead, An
encyclopedia of the ceramic
industries, London, E. Benn,
limited, 1929-30. 3 v.   666.03 30-
8476
TP788 .S4 MRR Alc.

CLAY INDUSTRIES--EQUIPMENT AND SUPPLIES.
Ceramic data book. 1st- ed.; 1922-
Chicago, Cahners Pub. Co. [etc.]
666.3058 22-15466
TP807 .C4 Sci RR Partial set / MRR
Alc Latest edition

CLAY INDUSTRIES--HANDBOOKS, MANUALS,
ETC.
Ceramic data book. 1st- ed.; 1922-
Chicago, Cahners Pub. Co. [etc.]
666.3058 22-15466
TP807 .C4 Sci RR Partial set / MRR
Alc Latest edition

CLEANING.
Moore, Alma (Chesnut) How to clean
everything; [Rev. ed.] New York,
Simon and Schuster, 1961. 203 p.
648 61-903
TP895 .M6 1961 MRR Alc.

CLEANLINESS
see Hygiene

CLEANNESS (MIDDLE ENGLISH POEM)--
CONCORDANCES.
Kottler, Barnet. A concordance to
five Middle English poems:
[Pittsburgh] University of Pittsburgh
Press [1966] xxxiii, 761 p.
821.1016 66-13311
PR265 .K6 MRR Alc.

CLEARY, CHARLES JOSEPH, 1891-1945.
United States. Library of Congress.
Science and Technology Division.
Charles J. Cleary awards for papers
on material sciences. [Washington]
Published for Directorate of
Materials and Processes, Aeronautical
Systems Division, Wright-Patterson
Air Force Base, Ohio, 1962. vii, 219
p.   620.1 63-60206
Z663.41 .C43 MRR Alc.

CLEMENS, SAMUEL LANGHORNE, 1835-1910--
DICTIONARIES, INDEXES, ETC.
Ramsay, Robert Lee, A Mark Twain
lexicon, New York, Russell &
Russell, 1963. cxix, 278 p.   817.4
63-9325
PS1345 .R3 1963 MRR Alc.

CLERGY--CANADA.
Le Canada ecclésiastique. 1.-
année; 1887- Montréal, Librairie
Beauchemin limitée [etc.] 282.71
35-22140
BX1419 .C3 MRR Alc Latest edition

CLERGY--UNITED STATES.
Sprague, William Buell, Annals of
the American pulpit; New York, R.
Carter and brothers, 1857-[69] 9 v.
03-17724
BR569 .S7 MRR Alc.

CLERGY--UNITED STATES--BIOGRAPHY.
A Biographical directory of clergymen
of The American Lutheran Church.
Minneapolis, Augsburg Pub. House,
1972. ix, 1054 p. 284/.131/0922 B
72-80314
BX8047.7 .B56 MRR Biog.

Who's who in the Protestant clergy.
Encino, Calif., Nygaard Associates
[1957] 264 p.   922 57-59372
BF569 .W5 MRR Biog.

CLERGY, NEGRO
see Negro clergy

CLERKS.
see also Office practice

CLEVELAND, GROVER, PRES. U.S., 1837-
1908.
Cleveland, Grover, Pres. U.S.,
Grover Cleveland, 1837-1908; Dobbs
Ferry, N.Y., Oceana Publications,
1968. 118 p.   973.8/5/08 68-21538

E696 .C617 1968 MRR Alc.

Nevins, Allan, Grover Cleveland; a
study in courage, New York, Dodd,
Mead & company, 1933. xiii p., 1 l.,
832 p.   923.173 33-23946
E697 .N465 MRR Alc.

Tugwell, Rexford Guy, Grover
Cleveland New York, Macmillan [1968]
xviii, 298 p.   973.8/5/0924 B 68-
12399
E697 .T8 MRR Alc.

CLIMATOLOGY.
see also Atmospheric pressure

see also Meteorology

see also Weather

Great Britain. Meteorological Office.
Tables of temperature, relative
humidity and precipitation for the
world. 2nd ed. London, H.M.S.O.,
1966- v.   [(1/5/- (pt. 3) 1/15-
(pt. 4) 15/6 (pt. 5)]   551.5/021/2
76-385248
QC982.5 .G732 MRR Alc.

Kendrew, Wilfrid George. The
climates of the continents. 5th ed.
Oxford, Clarendon Press, 1961. 608
p.   551.59 61-19753
QC981 .K4 1961 MRR Alc.

CLIMATOLOGY--TABLES, ETC.
Conway, Hobart McKinley, ed. The
weather handbook : Rev. ed. Atlanta
: Conway Research, 1974. 255 p. :
[$25.00]   551.6/9/1732 74-187773
QC982.5 .C6 1974 MRR Alc.

Showers, Victor, The world in
figures. New York, Wiley [1973]
xii, 585 p.   910/.21/2 73-9
G109 .S52 MRR Ref Desk.

CLIMATOLOGY, MEDICAL.
see also Hygiene

CLIMBING PLANTS.
Symonds, George Wellington
Dillingham. The shrub identification
book: New York, M. Barrows [1963]
379 p.   582.17 63-7388
QK482 .S89 MRR Alc.

CLIMBING PLANTS--NORTH AMERICA--
IDENTIFICATION.
Petrides, George A. A field guide to
trees and shrubs; 2d ed. Boston,
Houghton Mifflin, 1972. xxxii, 428
p. [$5.95]   582/.1609/7 76-157132

QK482 .P43 1972 MRR Alc.

CLINICAL ENDOCRINOLOGY.
Paschkis, Karl E. Clinical
endocrinology 3d ed. New York,
Hoeber Medical Division, Harper & Row
[1967] xxvi, 1060 p.   616.4 67-
2889
RC648 .P3 1967 MRR Alc.

CLINICAL MEDICINE
see Medicine, Clinical

CLINICAL PARASITOLOGY
see Medical parasitology

CLINICAL PSYCHOLOGY.
Wolman, Benjamin B., ed. Handbook of
clinical psychology, New York,
McGraw-Hill [1965] xv, 1596 p.
157.9 64-8976
RC467 .W6 MRR Alc.

CLINICS--UNITED STATES--DIRECTORIES.
American Association of Medical
Clinics. Directory. Alexandria, Va.
[etc.] 61-30176
Began publication with 1952 issue.
RA981.A2 A62 MRR Alc Latest
edition

CLIPPER-SHIPS.
Howe, Octavius Thorndike, American
clipper ships, 1833-1858, Salem,
Mass., Marine research society, 1926-
27. 2 v.   26-18490
VM23 .H6 MRR Alc.

CLOCK AND WATCH MAKERS.
Baillie, Granville Hugh. Watchmakers
and clockmakers of the world,
London, Methuen & co. ltd. [1929]
xiv p., 1 l., 415, [1] p.   29-11420

NK7486 .B26 MRR Alc.

Clutton, Cecil. Watches, 2nd ed.
London, Batsford, 1971. xvi, 159,
[84] p., 2 leaves. [£10.00]
681/.114/09 73-150917
NK7489 .C55 1971 MRR Alc.

CLOCK AND WATCH MAKERS--DIRECTORIES.
Britten, Frederick James, Britten's
old clocks and watches and their
makers; 8th ed. London, E. Methuen
in association with E. & F. Spon
[1973] xxiii, 532 p. [£15.00]
681/.11/09 73-174637
TS542 .B8 1973 MRR Alc.

CLOCK AND WATCH MAKERS--VIRGINIA.
Cutten, George Barton, The
silversmiths of Virginia, Richmond,
Dietz Press, 1952. xxiv, 259 p.
739.23 52-14077
NK7112 .C86 MRR Alc.

CLOCK AND WATCH MAKING--YEARBOOKS.
Annuaire de l'horlogerie suisse.
Genève, Chapalay & Mottier s.a.
681.105 46-34872
TS540 .A65 MRR Alc Latest edition

CLOCK AND WATCH MAKING--SWITZERLAND--
DIRECTORIES.
Annuaire de l'horlogerie suisse.
Genève, Chapalay & Mottier s.a.
681.105 46-34872
TS540 .A65 MRR Alc Latest edition

Indicateur suisse de l'horlogerie.
Bienne, L.C. Calame. 51-36795
TS543.S9 I5 MRR Alc Latest edition

CLOCKS AND WATCHES.
Britten, Frederick James, Watch &
clock makers' handbook; 15th ed.,
London, E. & F. N. Spon [1955] 598
p.   681.1 55-3052
TS545 .B87 1955 MRR Alc.

CLOCKS AND WATCHES--COLLECTORS AND
COLLECTING.
Palmer, Brooks. The book of American
clocks. New York, Macmillan, 1950.
viii, 318 p.   681.11 50-11068
NK7492 .P3 1950 MRR Alc.

CLOCKS AND WATCHES--COLLECTORS (Cont.)
Palmer, Brooks. A treasury of
American clocks. New York, Macmillan
[1967] xi, 371 p. 739.3/7/73 67-
28469
   NK7492 .P33 MRR Alc.

CLOCKS AND WATCHES--HISTORY.
Britten, Frederick James, Britten's
old clocks and watches and their
makers: 8th ed. London, E. Methuen
in association with E. & F. Spon
[1973] xxii, 532 p. [£15.00]
681/.11/09 73-174637
   TS542 .B8 1973 MRR Alc.

Clutton, Cecil. Watches, 2nd ed.
London, Batsford, 1971. xvi, 159,
[84] p., 2 leaves. [£10.00]
681/.114/09 73-150917
   NK7489 .C55 1971 MRR Alc.

Lloyd, Herbert Alan. Some
outstanding clocks over seven hundred
years, 1250-1950. London, L. Hill,
1958. xx, 160 p. 681.1109 58-4959

   TS542 .L5 MRR Alc.

**CLOCKS AND WATCHES--REPAIRING AND
ADJUSTING.**
Fried, Henry B., The watch
repairer's manual. 2d ed.
Princeton, N.J., Van Nostrand [1961]
310 p. 681.114 61-65042
   TS547 .F7 1961 MRR Alc.

CLOCKS AND WATCHES, AMERICAN.
Palmer, Brooks. The book of American
clocks. New York, Macmillan, 1950.
viii, 318 p. 681.11 50-11068
   NK7492 .P3 1950 MRR Alc.

Palmer, Brooks. A treasury of
American clocks. New York, Macmillan
[1967] xi, 371 p. 739.3/7/73 67-
28469
   NK7492 .P33 MRR Alc.

Thomson, Richard. Antique American
clocks & watches. Princeton [N.J.]
Van Nostrand [1968] 192 p. [$5.95]
739.3/7/73 68-29920
   NK7492 .T5 MRR Alc.

CLOTH
see Textile industry and fabrics

CLOTHING AND DRESS.
see also Costume

see also Fashion

see also Hats

CLOTHING AND DRESS--DICTIONARIES.
Ironside, Janey. A fashion alphabet;
London, Joseph, 1968. 262 p. [50/-
] 391/.2/03 68-141547
   TT503 .I7 MRR Alc.

Picken, Mary (Brooks) The fashion
dictionary; New York, Funk &
Wagnalls [1957] 397 p. 646.03 57-
10114
   TT503 .P49 MRR Alc.

CLOTHING TRADE--CANADA--DIRECTORIES.
Sheldon's retail directory of the
United States and Canada and Phelon's
resident buyers and merchandise
brokers. New York, Phelon, Sheldon &
Marsar. [$50.00] 381 74-644143
   HF5429.3 .S52 MRR Alc Latest
edition

CLOTHING TRADE--FRANCE--DIRECTORIES.
Annuaire de la bonneterie et mercerie
et de l'habillement; Paris, Horizons
de France s.a. 687.058 45-27349
   HD9940.F6 A6 MRR Alc Latest
edition

Annuaire de la chapellerie, de la
mode, et de la chemiserie. [Paris,
Éditions Louis Johanet, etc.] 61-
46407
   TT495 .A65 MRR Alc Latest edition

**CLOTHING TRADE--GREAT BRITAIN--
DIRECTORIES.**
Fabric & clothing trades index.
London. 55-58374
   TS1312 .F3 MRR Alc Latest edition

Skinner's British textile register.
1st- ed.; 1973- Croydon, Eng.;
Thomas Skinner Directories. [£10.50]
338.4/7/677002542 74-644855
   TS1312 .S55 MRR Alc Latest edition

**CLOTHING TRADE--NEW YORK (CITY)--
DIRECTORIES.**
G Q guide to fashion sources. New
York, Gentlemen's quarterly.
687/.11/02573 67-116689
   TT495 .G2 MRR Alc Latest edition

Phelon's resident buyers and
merchandise brokers of department
store merchandise, ready to wear,
millinery. New York, Phelon, Sheldon
& Marsar, inc. 380.1/45/68702573 72-
626495
   HD9940.U5 N736 MRR Alc Latest
edition

**CLOTHING TRADE--UNITED STATES--CREDIT
GUIDES.**
Apparel trades book. New York.
658.987 02-19199
   HF5585.C6 A7 MRR Alc Latest
edition

**CLOTHING TRADE--UNITED STATES--
DIRECTORIES.**
American Apparel Manufacturers
Association. Apparel, textile and
retail financial survey. 1st- ed.;
1971- Arlington, Va.
338.4/7/6870973 72-626946
   HD9940.U3 A567 MRR Alc Latest
edition

Apparel trades book. New York.
658.987 02-19199
   HF5585.C6 A7 MRR Alc Latest
edition

Davison's knit goods trade, "The
Standard." [Office ed.] Ridgewood,
N.J. [etc.] Davison Pub. Co. 08-
32658
   TT695 .D26 Sci RR Latest edition /
MRR Alc Latest edition

Phelon's resident buyers and
merchandise brokers of department
store merchandise, ready to wear,
millinery. New York, Phelon, Sheldon
& Marsar, inc. 380.1/45/68702573 72-
626495
   HD9940.U5 N736 MRR Alc Latest
edition

Phelon's women's specialty stores.
1st- ed.; 1963- New York, Phelon-
Sheldon & Marsar [etc.] 63-40375
   HD9940.U3 P5 MRR Alc Latest
edition

Salesman's Guide, inc., New York.
Nationwide directory, exclusive of
New York metropolitan area, [of]
men's and boys' wear buyers. New
York. 687.1105873 65-684
   HD9940.U4 S23 MRR Alc Latest
edition

The Salesman's guide nationwide
directory of major mass market
merchandisers (exclusive of New York
metropolitan area) New York,
Salesman's Guide, inc. 380.1/025/73
73-640394
   HF5468 .S27 MRR Alc Latest edition

Sheldon's jobbing and wholesale
trade. 87th- ed.; 1960- New York,
Phelon-Sheldon publications [etc.]
381 72-623015
   HF5421 .S5 MRR Alc Latest edition

Sheldon's retail directory of the
United States and Canada and Phelon's
resident buyers and merchandise
brokers. New York, Phelon, Sheldon &
Marsar. [$50.00] 381 74-644143
   HF5429.3 .S52 MRR Alc Latest
edition

**CLOTHING TRADE--UNITED STATES--
STATISTICS.**
American Apparel Manufacturers
Association. Apparel, textile and
retail financial survey. 1st- ed.;
1971- Arlington, Va.
338.4/7/6870973 72-626946
   HD9940.U3 A567 MRR Alc Latest
edition

CLOUD MODIFICATION
see Weather control

COACHES, TRUCK
see Campers and coaches, Truck

COACHES (ATHLETICS)--DIRECTORIES.
The Blue book of college athletics.
[1931/32]- Cleveland [etc.] Rohrich
Corp. [etc.] 371.74 ca 31-721
   GV741 .B5 MRR Alc Latest edition

COAL.
see also Bituminous coal

COAL--STATISTICS.
Darmstadter, Joel, Energy in the
world economy; Baltimore, Published
for Resources for the Future by the
Johns Hopkins Press [1971] x, 876 p.
[$22.50] 333.9 70-155848
   HD9540.4 D37 MRR Alc.

**COAL MINES AND MINING--GERMANY--
YEARBOOKS.**
Jahrbuch für Bergbau, Energie,
Mineralöl und Chemie. Essen,
Glückauf [etc.] 338.2/025 53-31420

Began in 1893.
   TN73 .J34 MRR Alc Latest edition

**COAL MINES AND MINING--GREAT BRITAIN--
DIRECTORIES.**
Guide to the coalfields. London
[etc.] Colliery guardian [etc.]
622.33 51-25790
   TN808.G6 G8 MRR Alc Latest edition

COAL MINES AND MINING--UNITED STATES.
Bituminous coal facts. 1948-
Washington, National Coal
Association. 338.2724 49-816
   HD9544 .B47 MRR Alc Latest edition

**COAL MINES AND MINING--UNITED STATES--
DIRECTORIES.**
Keystone coal industry manual. 1969-
New York, McGraw-Hill Mining
Publications, Mining Informational
Services. 338.2/7/20973 72-622648
   TN805.A4 K4 MRR Alc Latest edition

COAL-OIL
see Petroleum

COAL TRADE--GREAT BRITAIN--DIRECTORIES.
Coal trades directory. London, Coal
merchant and shipper [etc.] 47-44005

Began publication with vol. for
1922.
   HD9551.1 .C64 MRR Alc Latest
edition

COATS OF ARMS
see Heraldry

COCKTAILS.
Bergeron, Victor Jules. Trader Vic's
bartender's guide, revised, Garden
City, N.Y., Doubleday, 1972. xii,
442 p. [$6.95] 641.8/74 72-76212

   TX951 .B425 1972 MRR Alc.

Mario, Thomas. Playboy's host & bar
book. [1st ed. Chicago] Playboy
Press [c1971] vii, 339 p. [$12.95]
641.8/74 75-167615
   TX951 .M266 MRR Alc.

Old Mr. Boston deluxe official
bartender's guide / New world wide
ed. Boston : Mr. Boston Distiller
Corp., 1974. 216 p. : [$2.50]
641.8/74 74-80666
   TX951 .O4 1974 MRR Alc.

CODE NAMES.
see also Acronyms

Puffner, Frederick G., ed. Code
names dictionary; Detroit, Gale
Research Co. [1963] 555 p. 423 63-
21847
   PE1693 .R9 MRR Alc.

COIFFURE
see Hairdressing

COINAGE.
see also Mints

see also Money

COINAGE--HISTORY.
Burns, Arthur Robert, Money and
monetary policy in early times,
London, K. Paul, Trench, Trubner &
co., ltd.; New York, A. A. Knopf,
1927. xiii, 517 p. 27-21334
   HG237 .B86 MRR Alc.

COINAGE--AFRICA.
Davenport, John Stewart, The dollars
of Africa, Asia, & Oceania
Galesburg, Ill., 1969. 208 p.
737.4 76-7369
   CJ1529 .D3 MRR Alc.

COINAGE--ASIA.
Davenport, John Stewart, The dollars
of Africa, Asia, & Oceania
Galesburg, Ill., 1969. 208 p.
737.4 76-7369
   CJ1529 .D3 MRR Alc.

COINAGE--COMMONWEALTH OF NATIONS.
Linecar, Howard W. A. British
Commonwealth coinage. London, E.
Benn [1959] 291 p. 332.4942 59-
3878
   HG950.A3 L5 MRR Alc.

COINAGE--GREAT BRITAIN--COLONIES.
Linecar, Howard W. A. British
Commonwealth coinage. London, E.
Benn [1959] 291 p. 332.4942 59-
3878
   HG950.A3 L5 MRR Alc.

COINAGE--OCEANICA.
Davenport, John Stewart, The dollars
of Africa, Asia, & Oceania
Galesburg, Ill., 1969. 208 p.
737.4 76-7369
   CJ1529 .D3 MRR Alc.

COINAGE--ROME--HISTORY.
Sear, David R. Roman coins and their
values, Revised ed. London, Seaby,
1970. 376 p., 13 plates. [48/-]
737.49/37 77-538139
   CJ833 .S4 1970 MRR Alc.

COINAGE--UNITED STATES.
Reed, Fred Morton. Encyclopedia of
U.S. coins Completely rev. updated
ed. Chicago, Regnery [1972] xx, 303
p. 737.4/9/73 70-186778
   CJ1830 .R42 1972 MRR Alc.

COINAGE--UNITED STATES. (Cont.)
United States. Bureau of the Mint.
Domestic and foreign coins
manufactured by mints of the United
States, 1793-1970. [Washington, U.S.
Govt. Print. Off., 1972] vi, 138 p.
[$0.75] 338.47/7374973 72-603132
HG459 .U56 1972 MRR Alc.

United States. Laws, statutes, etc.
Laws of the United States concerning
money, banking, and loans, 1778-1909;
Washington, Govt. print. off., 1910.
v, 267 p., 1 l., 269-812, xxii p.
10-36032
HG481 .A2 1910 MRR Alc.

COINAGE--UNITED STATES--HISTORY.
Taxay, Don. The U.S. Mint and
coinage; New York, Arco Pub. Co.
[1966] xii, 400 p. 332.460973 66-
18413
HG459 .T3 MRR Alc.

COINAGE--UNITED STATES--STATISTICS.
United States. Bureau of the Mint.
Domestic and foreign coins
manufactured by mints of the United
States, 1793-1970. [Washington, U.S.
Govt. Print. Off., 1972] vi, 138 p.
[$0.75] 338.47/7374973 72-603132
HG459 .U56 1972 MRR Alc.

COINAGE OF WORDS
see Words, New

COINS.
see also Tokens

Andrews, Charles J. Fell's
international coin book. [1st]-
ed.; 1953- New York, Fell. 737.4
58-2154
CJ89 .A5 MRR Alc Latest edition

Carson, Robert Andrew Glindinning.
Coins ancient, mediaeval & modern
2nd (revised) ed. London,
Hutchinson, 1970. xiii, 642 p., 64
plates. [£6.00] 737.4/09 75-
862183
CJ75 .C3 1970 MRR Alc.

Craig, William D. Coins of the
world, 1750-1850, 2d ed. Racine,
Wis., Western Pub. Co. [1971] 448
p. [$10.00] 737.4 72-182612
CJ1751 .C7 1971 MRR Alc.

Krause, Chester L. Standard catalog
of world coins, [2d ed. Iola, Wis.,
Krause Publications, 1973] 864 p.
[$12.50] 737.4/021 73-88957
CJ1755 .K7 1973 MRR Ref Desk.

Lindleim, Leon, Facts & fictions
about coins. [1st ed.] Cleveland,
World Pub. Co. [1967] viii, 280 p.
737.4 66-25885
CJ36 .L5 MRR Alc.

Reinfeld, Fred, Catalogue of the
world's most popular coins. Enl. and
rev. ed., New York, President Coin
Corp. [1969] 416 p. [8.95]
737.4/075 77-7641
CJ63 .R4 1969 MRR Ref. Desk.

Reinfeld, Fred, Treasury of the
world's coins. [Rev. ed] New York,
Sterling Pub. Co. [1967] 221 p.
737.4 67-6175
CJ89 .R4 1967 MRR Alc.

Yeoman, Richard S. A catalog of
modern world coins. 1st- ed.; 1957-
Racine, Wis., Whitman Hobby
Division [etc.] 61-4597
CJ1753 .Y4 MRR Ref Desk Latest
edition

Yeoman, Richard S. Current coins of
the world, 4th ed. Racine, Wis.,
Western Pub. Co., Whitman Coin Supply
Division [1970] 256 p. 737.4 70-
21069
CJ1755 .Y4 1970 MRR Ref Desk.

Yeoman, Richard S. Current coins of
the world. 1st- ed.; 1966-
Racine, Wis., Western Pub. Co. 737.4
70-21069
CJ1755 .Y46 MRR Ref Desk Latest
edition

COINS--DICTIONARIES.
Chamberlain, Christopher Churchill.
Coin dictionary and guide New York,
Barnes & Noble [1961] 256 p.
737.4075 61-18192
CJ67 .C47 1961 MRR Alc.

Frey, Albert Romer, Dictionary of
numismatic names, [New York] Barnes
& Noble [1947] ix, 311, 94 p.
737.03 48-5357
CJ67 .F7 1947 MRR Alc.

Hobson, Burton. Illustrated
encyclopedia of world coins Garden
City, N.Y., Doubleday [1970] 512 p.
[$12.95] 737.4/03 76-81030
CJ67 .H6 1970 MRR Alc.

COINS--PRICES.
The Official black book of United
States coins; [Completely rev. 7th
ed.] New York, HC Publishers, 1970]
192 p. 737.49/73 78-253529
CJ1830 .O3 1970 MRR Alc.

Raymond, Wayte, ed. Coins of the
world, 5th ed. New York, W.
Raymond, inc. [1955] 326 p. 737.4
55-2551
CJ1755 .R3 1955 MRR Alc.

Taxay, Don. The comprehensive
catalogue and encyclopedia of United
States coins. 1st ed. New York,
Scott Pub. Co., 1971 [c1970] xiv,
397 p. [$15.00] 737.4/9/73 73-
176464
CJ1826 .T38 MRR Alc.

COINS--UNITED STATES.
The Official black book of United
States coins; [Completely rev. 7th
ed.] New York, HC Publishers, 1970]
192 p. 737.49/73 78-253529
CJ1830 .O3 1970 MRR Alc.

COINS, AMERICAN.
Andrews, Charles J. Fell's United
States coin book. [1st]- ed.; 1949-
New York, F. Fell. 58-2168
CJ1826 .A67 MRR Alc Latest edition

Appraising and selling your coins.
[1st]- ed.; 1960- New York, Coin
and Currency Institute. 66-18756
CJ1826 .A72 MRR Ref Desk Latest
edition

Bowers, Q. David. Coins and
collectors, [Johnson City, N.Y.,
Windsor Research Publications, 1964]
213 p. 737.4075 64-8501
CJ1830 .B6 MRR Alc.

Brown, Martin R. A guide to the
grading of United States coins, 5th
ed. Racine, Wis., Western Pub. Co.
[1969] 206 p. 737.49/73 70-13439

CJ1826 .B7 1969 MRR Alc.

Coin collectors' handbook. Garden
City, N.Y. [etc.] Doubleday [etc.]
737.4075 60-11003
CJ1830 .C65 MRR Ref Desk Latest
edition

Davis, Norman M., The complete book
of United States coin collecting New
York, Macmillan [1971] xii, 336 p.
[$7.95] 737.49/73 70-117963
CJ1830 .D36 MRR Alc.

French, Charles F. American guide to
U.S. Coins, 1971 ed. New York,
Cornerstone Library, 1971. 174 p.
[$1.25] 737.49/73 74-23225
CJ1830 .F7 1971 MRR Alc.

Green, Charles Elmore. Mint record
and type table, United States coins;
[Chicago, Printed by John S. Swift
co., inc., c1936] 3 p. l., [1], 252
p. 737.0973 37-1721
CJ1830 .G7 MRR Alc.

A Guide book of United States coins;
[1st]- ed.; 1947- Racine, Wis.,
Whitman Pub. Co.,Whitman Hobby
Division [etc.] 737.4 47-22284
CJ1826 .G785 MRR Ref Desk Latest
edition

Handbook of United States coins,
[1st]- ed.; 1942- Racine, Wis.,
Whitman Pub. Co., Whitman Coin Supply
Division [etc.] 737.0973 42-16475
CJ1826 .H3 MRR Alc Latest edition

Harris, Robert P. Gold coins of the
Americas; 1st ed. Florence, Ala.,
ANCO [1971] iv, 280 p. 737.4 75-
168568
CJ1808 .H37 MRR Alc.

Liebers, Arthur, United States
coins; New York, Putnam [1965] 212
p. 737.4973075 65-10857
CJ1826 .L5 MRR Alc.

The Official black book of United
States coins; [Completely rev. 7th
ed.] New York, HC Publishers, 1970]
192 p. 737.49/73 78-253529
CJ1830 .O3 1970 MRR Alc.

Reed, Fred Morton. Coins: an
investor's & collector's guide
Chicago, Regnery [1973] x, 403 p.
[$10.00] 737.4/973 72-11187
CJ1830 .R417 MRR Alc.

Reed, Fred Morton. Encyclopedia of
U.S. coins Completely rev., updated
ed. Chicago, Regnery [1972] xx, 303
p. 737.4/9/73 70-186778
CJ1830 .R42 1972 MRR Alc.

Ruby, Warren A. Commemorative coins
of the United States (gold and
silver) Lake Mills, Iowa, Graphic
Pub. Co. [1961] unpaged. 61-47618

CJ1839 .R8 MRR Alc.

Taxay, Don. The comprehensive
catalogue and encyclopedia of United
States coins. 1st ed. New York,
Scott Pub. Co., 1971 [c1970] xiv,
397 p. [$15.00] 737.4/9/73 73-
176464
CJ1826 .T38 MRR Alc.

Taxay, Don. An illustrated history
of U.S. commemorative coinage. New
York, Arco Pub. Co. [1967] viii, 256
p. 737.49/73 67-10696
CJ1839 .T3 MRR Alc.

Vlack, Robert A. Early American
coins; 2d ed. Johnson City, N.Y.,
Windsor Research Publications, 1965.
120 p. 737.4973 65-27408
CJ1842 .V5 1965 MRR Alc.

COINS, ANCIENT.
Burns, Arthur Robert, Money and
monetary policy in early times,
London, K. Paul, Trench, Trubner &
co., ltd.; New York, A. A. Knopf,
1927. xiii, 517 p. 27-21334
HG237 .B86 MRR Alc.

COINS, BRITISH.
Coin yearbook. [Brentwood, Eng.,
Numismatic Pub. Co.] [-/-/80]
737.4/9/42 74-644812
CJ2471 .C6 MRR Alc Latest edition

Seaby's standard catalogue: London,
B. A. Seaby. 737.4/9/42 72-626390
CJ2476 .S82 MRR Alc Latest edition

Wright, Laurence Victor Ward.
Colonial and Commonwealth coins;
London, G. G. Harrap [1959] 236 p.
737.4942 60-22696
CJ2560 .W7 MRR Alc.

COINS, CANADIAN.
Appraising and selling your coins.
[1st]- ed.; 1960- New York, Coin
and Currency Institute. 66-18756
CJ1826 .A72 MRR Ref Desk Latest
edition

Harris, Robert P. Gold coins of the
Americas; 1st ed. Florence, Ala.,
ANCO [1971] iv, 280 p. 737.4 75-
168568
CJ1808 .H37 MRR Alc.

Standard catalogue of Canadian coins,
tokens, and paper money. Racine,
Wis. [etc.] Whitman Hobby Division
[etc.] 737.4971 60-473
CJ1861 .S8 MRR Alc Latest edition

COINS, CENTRAL AMERICAN.
Wallace, Holland. Central American
coinage since 1821. [Weslaco? Tex.]
1966 [c1965] 123, [2] p. 737.49728
66-4669
CJ1916 .W3 1966 MRR Alc.

COINS, ENGLISH.
Bressett, Kenneth E. A guide book of
English coins, nineteenth and
twentieth centuries, 7th ed.
Racine, Wis., Western Pub. Co.
[c1968] 126 p. 737.49/42 71-9737

CJ2495 .B7 1968b MRR Alc.

Coin yearbook. [Brentwood, Eng.,
Numismatic Pub. Co.] [-/-/80]
737.4/9/42 74-644812
CJ2471 .C6 MRR Alc Latest edition

COINS, EUROPEAN.
Schlumberger, Hans. Gold coins of
Europe since 1800; New York,
Sterling Pub. Co. [1968] 352 p.
[$15.00] 737.4 68-18787
CJ1545 .S313 1968 MRR Alc.

COINS, GREEK.
Jenkins, G. Kenneth. Ancient Greek
coins, London, Barrie and Jenkins,
1972. 310 p. [£7.00] 737.4/9/38
73-160003
CJ335 .J45 1972b MRR Alc.

COINS, LATIN AMERICAN.
Harris, Robert P. Gold coins of the
Americas; 1st ed. Florence, Ala.,
ANCO [1971] iv, 280 p. 737.4 75-
168568
CJ1808 .H37 MRR Alc.

COINS, ROMAN.
Seaby, Herbert Allen. Roman coins
and their values. London, B. A.
Seaby, 1954. 133 p. 55-30103
CJ821 .S43 1954 MRR Alc.

Sear, David R. Roman coins and their
values, Revised ed. London, Seaby,
1970. 376 p., 13 plates. [48/-]
737.49/37 77-538139
CJ833 .S4 1970 MRR Alc.

Stevenson, Seth William, A
dictionary of Roman coins, London,
G. Bell and sons, 1889. viii, 929 p.
01-25230
CJ829 .S8 MRR Alc.

COINS AS AN INVESTMENT.
Reed, Fred Morton. Coins: an
investor's & collector's guide
Chicago, Regnery [1973] x, 403 p.
[$10.00]   737.4/973 72-11187
    CJ1830 .R417 MRR Alc.

COKE INDUSTRY.
see also Gas industry

COLCHESTER, ENG. UNIVERSITY OF ESSEX.
LIBRARY.
Colchester, Eng. University of Essex.
Library. Comparative and social
studies: Colchester, University of
Essex (Library), 1969. [4], xiv, 407
p.   017/.1 70-506935
    Z1035.1 .C63 1969 MRR Alc.

COLE, FAY-COOPER, 1881-
Griffin, James Bennett, ed.
Archeology of eastern United States.
[Chicago] University of Chicago Press
[1952] x, 392 p.   913.73 973.1* 52-
14698
    E53 .G7 MRR Alc.

COLEOPTERA
see Beetles

COLERIDGE, SAMUEL TAYLOR, 1772-1834--
CONCORDANCES.
Logan, Eugenia, sister. A
concordance to the poetry of Samuel
Taylor Coleridge, Saint Mary-of-the-
Woods, Ind. [Priv. print.] 1940.
xvi, 901 p.   821.72 40-5258
    PR4482 .L6 MRR Alc.

COLHOUN, EDMUND ROSS, 1821-1897--
BIBLIOGRAPHY.
United States. Library of Congress.
Manuscript Division. Edmund Ross
Colhoun; Charles O'Neil: a register
of their papers in the Library of
Congress. Washington, Library of
Congress, 1967. 8, 9 l.
016.3593/3/20922 68-60020
    Z663.34 .C57 MRR Alc.

COLLECTING OF ACCOUNTS.
Shultz, William John, Credit and
collection management   3d ed.
Englewood Cliffs, N.J., Prentice-
Hall, 1962. 637 p.   658.88 62-9584

    HF5566 .S5 1962 MRR Alc.

COLLECTING OF ACCOUNTS--PERIODICALS.
The Clearing house quarterly.
Minneapolis, Minn., Attorneys'
National Clearing House Co. 08-15550

    KF195.C57 C4 MRR Alc Latest
       edition

COLLECTION AGENCIES--DIRECTORIES.
The Regency international directory
of enquiry agents, private
detectives, debt collecting agencies,
the security services. Folkstone,
Eng., Regency International
Publications Limited. 363.2/3 68-
45751
    Began in 1967.
    HV8081 .R4 MRR Alc Latest edition

COLLECTION AGENCIES--UNITED STATES--
DIRECTORIES.
Allied Finance Adjusters Conference.
Directory. [Stockton, Calif.] 65-
42028
    HF5559.U5 A56 MRR Alc Latest
       edition

COLLECTIVE BARGAINING.
see also Trade-unions

COLLECTIVE FARMS--CZECHOSLOVAK REPUBLIC.
Mid-European Law Project. The
sovietization of Czechoslovak
farming; Washington [1953?] 42 p.
54-60587
    Z663.55 .S6 MRR Alc.

COLLECTIVE LABOR AGREEMENTS--UNITED
STATES--STATISTICS.
United States. Bureau of Labor
Statistics. Characteristics of
agreements covering 1,000 workers or
more. Washington, For sale by the
Supt. of Docs., U.S. Govt. Print.
Off. 331/.0973 s 331.89/0973 74-
600823
    HD8051 .A62 subser HD6501 MRR Alc
       Latest edition

COLLECTIVE SETTLEMENTS.
see also Collective farms

COLLECTIVE SETTLEMENTS--UNITED STATES.
Webber, Everett, Escape to Utopia;
New York, Hastings House Publishers
[1959] 444 p.   335.973 58-12525
    HX653 .W4 MRR Alc.

COLLECTIVISM.
see also Communism

COLLECTORS AND COLLECTING.
Callahan, Claire (Wallis) How to
collect the new antiques; New York,
D. McKay Co. [1966] ix, 244 p.
745.1 66-14586
    NK1125 .C262 MRR Alc.

Comstock, Helen, ed. The concise
encyclopedia of American antiques.
New York, Hawthorn Books [1965] 848
p.   745.10973 65-9391
    NK805 .C65 1965 MRR Alc.

Hayward, Helena, ed. The
Connoisseur's handbook of antique
collecting; New York, Hawthorn Books
[1960] 320 p.   703 60-8797
    NK30 .H45 MRR Alc.

Wood, Violet (Mackworth-Praed)
Victoriana, New York, Macmillan,
1961 [c1960] 175 p.   708.051 61-
65212
    NK928 .W6 1961 MRR Alc.

COLLECTORS AND COLLECTING--DICTIONARIES.
Baker, Mary Gladys Steel, A
dictionary of antiques, Edinburgh,
W. & R. Chambers [1953] 263 p.
708.051 54-4571
    NK1125 .B33 1953 MRR Alc.

Bernasconi, John R. The collectors'
glossary of antiques and fine arts,
[Rev. ed.] London, Estates Gazette,
ltd. [1963] xvi, 587 p.   66-48284
    NK30 .B4 1963 MRR Alc.

Boger, Louise Ade. The dictionary of
antiques and the decorative arts;
New York, Scribner [1967] ix, 662 p.
703 67-18131
    NK30 .B57 1967 MRR Alc.

COLLECTORS AND COLLECTING--DIRECTORIES.
The Antique trader directory of
antique dealers. Kewanee, Ill.,
Antique trader [etc.] 64-4643
    NK1127 .A5 MRR Alc Latest edition

British Antique Dealers' Association.
List of members. London. 55-33242

    NK1127 .B67 MRR Alc Latest edition

Byrns, John H. Europe's hidden flea
markets and budget antique shops,
[1st ed. New York, R. P. Long; trade
distributor: Hastings House, 1968]
112 p.   914/.04/55 68-2401
    HF5152 .B9 MRR Alc.

Great Lakes antique dealers
directory. Decatur, Ind., S. E.
Leonardson. 708.051 76-48384
    "Established 1944."
    NK1127 .G7 MRR Alc Latest edition

International antiques yearbook,
encyclopaedia & directory. 1949/50-
Uxbridge, Middlesex [etc.] Antiques
Yearbook Ltd. [etc.] 705.8 49-53305

    NK1125 .A315 MRR Alc Latest
       edition

Mack, Jerry. What's it worth? [San
Angelo? Tex.] Educator Books, c1970.
94 p. [$3.95]   380.1/025/73 74-
138825
    HF5482 .M3 MRR Alc.

National travel guide to antique
shops. [Casper, Wyo., Antique
Enterprises] 65-4691
    NK1127 .N3 MRR Alc Latest edition

Webster, Isabel Stevens. Antique
collectors' guide to New England;
New York, Grosset & Dunlap [1961]
165 p.   708.051 61-3263
    NK1127 .W4 MRR Alc.

COLLECTORS AND COLLECTING--YEARBOOKS.
International antiques yearbook,
encyclopaedia & directory. 1949/50-
Uxbridge, Middlesex [etc.] Antiques
Yearbook Ltd. [etc.] 705.8 49-53305

    NK1125 .A315 MRR Alc Latest
       edition

COLLEGE, CHOICE OF.
Handel, Lawrence. College
confidential; New York, Trident
Press [1969] 318 p. [5.95]   378.73
69-13514
    L901 .H32 MRR Ref Desk.

COLLEGE, CHOICE OF--HANDBOOKS, MANUALS,
ETC.
Mazel, Ella. The New York Times
guide to college selection. New
York, Quadrangle Books. 378.73 72-
178241
    LB2350.5 .M35 MRR Ref Desk Latest
       edition

COLLEGE ADMINISTRATORS--UNITED STATES--
BIOGRAPHY.
Who's who in American college and
university administration. 1970/71-
[New York?] Crowell-Collier
Educational Corp. 378.1/1/0922 79-
114035
    LA2311 .P72 MRR Biog Latest
       edition

COLLEGE AND SCHOOL JOURNALISM.
see also School yearbooks

COLLEGE AND SCHOOL PERIODICALS--
BIBLIOGRAPHY.
Ayer directory of publications.
Philadelphia, Ayer Press. 071.3/025
73-640052
    Z6951 .A97 Sci RR Latest edition /
       MRR Ref Desk Latest edition / MRR
       Alc Latest edition

COLLEGE AND SCHOOL PERIODICALS--
DIRECTORIES.
Directory of the college student
press in America. 1967/68- New York
[etc.] Oxbridge Pub. Co. [etc.]
378.1/98/9705 76-10981
    L901 .D52 MRR Ref Desk Latest
       edition

COLLEGE ATTENDANCE--NEW ENGLAND--
STATISTICS.
Facts about New England colleges and
universities. [Durham, N.H.] [etc.]
67-4398
    LC148 .F3 MRR Alc Latest edition

COLLEGE FACILITIES--EXTENDED USE--
CANADA--DIRECTORIES.
Mort. Mort's guide to low-cost
vacations & lodgings on college
campuses. 1974- Princeton, N.J.,
CMG Publications. 647/.9473 73-
94268
    TX907 .M854 MRR Alc Latest edition

COLLEGE FACILITIES--EXTENDED USE--
UNITED STATES--DIRECTORIES.
Mort. Mort's guide to low-cost
vacations & lodgings on college
campuses. 1974- Princeton, N.J.,
CMG Publications. 647/.9473 73-
94268
    TX907 .M854 MRR Alc Latest edition

COLLEGE GRADUATES--UNITED STATES.
Pierson, George Wilson, The
education of American leaders; New
York, Praeger [1969] xxxii, 261 p.
331.7/6 69-17173
    LA226 .P5 MRR Alc.

COLLEGE PRESIDENTS--BIOGRAPHY.
Who's who in American college and
university administration. 1970/71-
[New York?] Crowell-Collier
Educational Corp. 378.1/1/0922 79-
114035
    LA2311 .P72 MRR Biog Latest
       edition

COLLEGE SPORTS.
see also Football

see also Soccer

The Blue book of college athletics.
[1931/32]- Cleveland [etc.] Rohrich
Corp. [etc.] 371.74 ca 31-721
    GV741 .B5 MRR Alc Latest edition

COLLEGE SPORTS--DIRECTORIES.
National directory of college
athletics. 1968/69- Amarillo, R.
Franks. 796/.025/73 68-7776
    GV561 .N32 MRR Alc Latest edition

COLLEGE SPORTS--YEARBOOKS.
Outstanding college athletes of
America. 1969- Washington, D.C.
796 79-94524
    GV697.A1 O86 MRR Biog Latest
       edition

COLLEGE STORES--DIRECTORIES.
Klein (B.) and Company, New York.
Directory of college stores. New
York. 58-47005
    HF5483. K5 MRR Alc Latest edition

COLLEGE STUDENTS.
Lass, Abraham Harold, The college
student's handbook Rev. ed. New
York, D. White Co. [1970] xii, 201
p. [6.95]   378.1/98 71-113899
    LB3605 .L37 1970 MRR Alc.

COLLEGE STUDENTS--BIBLIOGRAPHY.
Altbach, Philip G. American
students: Lexington, Mass.,
Lexington Books [1973] xiv, 537 p.
016.3781/98/1 73-7992
    Z5814.S86 A55 1973 MRR Alc.

COLLEGE STUDENTS--UNITED STATES--
DIRECTORIES.
The National student register. 1st-
ed; 1969- Baton Rouge, La., Magna
Pub. Co. 378.1/98/02573 72-94671
    L901 .N35 MRR Biog Latest edition

Outstanding college athletes of
America. 1969- Washington, D.C.
796 79-94524
    GV697.A1 O86 MRR Biog Latest
       edition

Who's who among students in American
universities and colleges. v. 1-
1935- Washington [etc.] Randall Pub.
Co. [etc.] 35-8707
    LA2311 .W43 MRR Biog Latest
       edition

COLLEGE STUDENTS--UNITED STATES--
POLITICAL ACTIVITY--BIBLIOGRAPHY.
Altbach, Philip G. American
students: Lexington, Mass.,
Lexington Books [1973] xiv, 537 p.
016.3781/98/1 73-7992
Z5814.S86 A55 1973 MRR Alc.

COLLEGE STUDENTS--UNITED STATES--
STATISTICS.
Harris, Seymour Edwin, A statistical
portrait of higher education, New
York, McGraw-Hill [1972] xliv, 978
p. 378.73 72-38334
LA227.3 .H25 MRR Alc.

COLLEGE TEACHERS--DIRECTORIES.
Minerva; 1.- Jahrg.; 1891/92-
Berlin [etc.] W. de Gruyter [etc.]
06-13219
AS2 .M6 MRR Alc Latest edition /
MRR Ref Desk Latest edition

World guide to universities. 1st ed.
New York, R. R. Bowker Co., 1971-72.
4 v. (xxii, 3609 p.) 378/.0025 73-
172160
L900 .W53 MRR Alc.

COLLEGE TEACHERS--GERMANY--DIRECTORIES.
Deutsches Universitats-Handbuch.
1967- München, Consultverlag [etc.]
68-84305
L929 .D42 MRR Alc Latest edition

COLLEGE TEACHERS--GREAT BRITAIN--
DIRECTORIES.
The Academic who's who. 1973/74-
London, A. & C. Black; distributed in
U.S. by Bowker, New York. [$21.95]
001.3/092/2 73-641081
L915 .A658 MRR Biog Latest edition

COLLEGE TEACHERS--UNITED STATES--
BIOGRAPHY.
Directory of American scholars;
[1st]- ed.; 1942- New York [etc.]
Jaques Cattell Press [etc.] 57-9125

LA2311 .C32 Sci RR Latest edition
/ MRR Biog Latest edition

United States. Library of Congress.
Hispanic Foundation. National
directory of Latin Americanists; 2d
ed. Washington, Library of Congress;
[for sale by the Supt. of Docs., U.S.
Govt. Print. Off. 1971 [i.e. 1972]
684 p. [$4.25] 918/.03/072022 75-
37737
Z663.32 .A5 no. 12 MRR Alc.

COLLEGE TEACHERS--UNITED STATES--
DIRECTORIES.
American Association of Collegiate
Schools of Business. Faculty
personnel; a directory of the
instructional staffs of the member
schools. 1925- St. Louis, Missouri,
[etc.] 650.71173 29-24113
HF1101 .A53 MRR Biog Latest
edition

Carrubba, Robert W. Directory of
college and university classicists in
the United States and Canada.
[University Park] Pennsylvania State
University Press [1973] 221 p.
913.38 73-6882
PA83 .C3 MRR Biog.

The National faculty directory. 1970-
Detroit, Gale Research Co.
378.1/2/02573 76-114404
L901 .N34 MRR Biog Latest edition

COLLEGE THEATER--DIRECTORIES.
Directory of American college
theatre. 1st- ed.; 1960- Dallas,
Tex. [etc.] American Educational
Theatre Association. 792.0711 60-
4683
PN2078.U6 D5 MRR Alc Latest
edition

COLLINS, WILLIAM, 1721-1759--
CONCORDANCES.
Booth, Bradford Allen, comp. A
concordance to the poetical works of
William Collins. Berkeley, Calif.,
University of California press, 1939.
vi p., 1 l., 126 p. 821.57 40-344

PR3353.A3 B6 MRR Alc.

COLLISIONS--AIRCRAFT
see Aeronautics--Accidents

COLOGNE--DIRECTORIES.
Greven's Kölner Adressbuch. Köln.
54-17316
DD901.C73 G7 MRR Alc Latest
edition

COLOMBIA.
Weil, Thomas E. Area handbook for
Colombia. [Washington; For sale by
the Supt. of Docs., U.S. Govt. Print.
Off.] 1970. xiv, 595 p. [$3.75]
918.61/03/63 70-608487
F2258 .W43 MRR Alc.

COLOMBIA--BIBLIOGRAPHY.
Anuario bibliografico colombiano.
1951- Bogota [etc.] 015.861* 53-
28591
Z1731 .A58 MRR Alc Full set

COLOMBIA--BIBLIOGRAPHY--PERIODICALS.
Bibliografia colombiana. t. 1-
enero/jun. 1961- Coral Gables, Fla.
[etc.] 64-4610
Z1731 .B5 MRR Alc Full set

COLOMBIA--BIOGRAPHY.
Quién es quién en Colombia. 1944-
Bogota, Editorial ARGRA, Ltd. [etc.]
920.086 45-19818
F2255 .Q5 MRR Biog Latest edition

Quién es quién en Venezuela,
Panama, Ecuador, Columbia. Jun. 30,
1952- [Bogota] O. Perry. 920.086
54-19781
F2205 .Q54 MRR Biog Latest edition

COLOMBIA--GAZETTEERS.
United States. Office of Geography.
Colombia; Washington, 1965. vi, 396
p. 918.61/003 72-10030
F2254 .U5 MRR Alc.

COLOMBIA--IMPRINTS.
Anuario bibliografico colombiano.
1951- Bogota [etc.] 015.861* 53-
28591
Z1731 .A58 MRR Alc Full set

COLOMBIA--IMPRINTS--PERIODICALS.
Bibliografia colombiana. t. 1-
enero/jun. 1961- Coral Gables, Fla.
[etc.] 64-4610
Z1731 .B5 MRR Alc Full set

COLOMBIAN LITERATURE--BIBLIOGRAPHY.
Anuario bibliografico colombiano.
1951- Bogota [etc.] 015.861* 53-
28591
Z1731 .A58 MRR Alc Full set

COLOMBO, CRISTOFORO.
Morison, Samuel Eliot, Admiral of
the ocean sea; Boston, Little, Brown
and company, 1942. 2 v. 923.9 42-
5605
E111 .M86 1942 MRR Alc.

The Northmen, Columbus and Cabot, 985-
1503: New York, C. Scribner's sons,
1906. xv, 443 p. 973.1 06-36882
E187.07 N6 MRR Alc.

COLONIAL ARCHITECTURE
see Architecture, Colonial

COLONIAL ART
see Art, Colonial

COLONIES--BIBLIOGRAPHY.
Halstead, John P. Modern European
imperialism; Boston, G. K. Hall,
1974. 2 v. 016.90908 73-19511
Z6204 .H35 MRR Alc.

COLONIES--DICTIONARIES.
Bevel, Maurice Louis. Le
dictionnaire colonial (encyclopédie)
3. ed. Bruxelles, Impr. E. Guyot,
1955. 202 p., 26 p. 56-39556
DT643 .B45 1955 MRR Alc.

COLONIES--HISTORY.
Fieldhouse, David Kenneth, The
colonial empires; [1st American ed.]
New York, Delacorte Press [1967,
c1966] xiii, 450 p. 325.309 66-
23091
JV105 .F5 1967 MRR Alc.

COLONIZATION.
see also Emigration and immigration

see also Migration, Internal

COLOPHONS.
Mumey, Nolie, A study of rare books,
Denver, The Clason publishing
company, 1930. xvii p., 2 l., 3-572
p. 090 30-25438
Z1012 .M95 MRR Alc.

COLOR--TERMINOLOGY.
Kornerup, Andreas. Methuen handbook
of colour 2nd ed., revised. London,
Methuen, 1967. 243 p. 535.6 67-
91262
ND1285 .K613 1967 MRR Alc.

Kornerup, Andreas. Reinhold color
atlas, New York, Reinhold [1962,
c1961] 224 p. 752 62-8756
ND1285 .K6 1962 MRR Alc.

COLOR OF WOOD.
Hough, Romeyn Beck, Hough's
encyclopaedia of American woods,
[1st ed.] New York, R. Speller, 1957-
v. 634.98 57-10592
SD536 .H832 MRR Alc.

COLOR PRINTS--CATALOGS.
Bertran, Margaret. A guide to color
reproductions. 2d ed. Metuchen,
N.J., Scarecrow Press, 1971. 625 p.
338.4/7/76902573 74-142231
NE1850 .B3 1971 MRR Ref Desk.

Brooke, Milton. Guide to color
prints Washington, Scarecrow Press,
1953. xii, 257 p. 769.5 53-10394

NE1860.A2 B7 MRR Alc.

Clapp, Jane. Art reproductions. New
York, Scarecrow Press, 1961. 350 p.
708.1 61-8714
N4000 .C5 MRR Ref Desk.

Kass, Benjamin. The complete guide
to free prints. New York, Citadel
Press [1958] 112 p. 769.5 58-
10598
NE1860.A2 K3 MRR Alc.

New York Graphic Society. Fine art
reproductions of old & modern
masters; Greenwich, Conn. [1965]
540 p. (chiefly col. illus.)
750.216 65-9117
NE1860.N4 A3 1965 MRR Alc.

United Nations Educational,
Scientific and Cultural
Organization. Catalogue de
reproductions en couleurs de
peintures antérieures a 1860. [1]-
ed. [1950]- Paris. 759.0838 58-
21049
NE1860.A2 U5 MRR Ref Desk Latest
edition

COLORADO--BIBLIOGRAPHY.
Wilcox, Virginia Lee. Colorado: a
selected bibliography of its
literature, 1858-1952. Denver, Sage
Books [1954] 151 p. 016.9788 54-
35636
Z1263 .W5 MRR Alc.

COLORADO--BIBLIOGRAPHY--CATALOGS.
United States. Library of Congress.
Colorado, the diamond jubilee of
statehood; Washington, U.S. Govt.
Print. Off. 1951. iii, 75 p.
016.9788 51-60029
Z663.15.A6 C6 MRR Alc.

COLORADO--BIOGRAPHY.
Who's who in Colorado. Centennial
anniversary ed. [Denver] Who's Who
in Colorado, inc.; distributed by
Sage Books, 1958. 607 p. 920.0788
58-1659
F775 .W57 MRR Biog.

COLORADO--CENTENNIAL CELEBRATIONS, ETC.
United States. Library of Congress.
Colorado, the diamond jubilee of
statehood; Washington, U.S. Govt.
Print. Off. 1951. iii, 75 p.
016.9788 51-60029
Z663.15.A6 C6 MRR Alc.

COLORADO--DESCRIPTION AND TRAVEL--1951-
--GUIDE-BOOKS.
Colorado: a guide to the highest
state. New rev. ed. New York,
Hastings House [1970] xxxvi, 504 p.
[8.95] 917.88/04/3 75-132150
F781.2 .C64 1970 MRR Ref Desk.

COLORADO--ECONOMIC CONDITIONS.
Colorado. State Planning Commission.
Year book of the State of Colorado.
1918- Denver. 20-27280
HC107.C7 A27 MRR Alc Latest
edition

COLORADO--EXECUTIVE DEPARTMENTS.
Colorado. State Planning Commission.
Year book of the State of Colorado.
1918- Denver. 20-27280
HC107.C7 A27 MRR Alc Latest
edition

COLORADO--HISTORY--BIBLIOGRAPHY.
Wilcox, Virginia Lee. Colorado: a
selected bibliography of its
literature, 1858-1952. Denver, Sage
Books [1954] 151 p. 016.9788 54-
35636
Z1263 .W5 MRR Alc.

COLORADO--IMPRINTS.
Wilcox, Virginia Lee. Colorado: a
selected bibliography of its
literature, 1858-1952. Denver, Sage
Books [1954] 151 p. 016.9788 54-
35636
Z1263 .W5 MRR Alc.

COLORADO--POLITICS AND GOVERNMENT.
Colorado. State Planning Commission.
Year book of the State of Colorado.
1918- Denver. 20-27280
HC107.C7 A27 MRR Alc Latest
edition

COLORADO--STATISTICS.
Colorado. State Planning Commission.
Year book of the State of Colorado.
1918- Denver. 20-27280
HC107.C7 A27 MRR Alc Latest
edition

COLORED PEOPLE (UNITED STATES)
see Negroes

COLORS.
Kornerup, Andreas. Methuen handbook
of colour 2nd ed., revised. London,
Methuen, 1967. 243 p. 535.6 67-
91262
ND1285 .K613 1967 MRR Alc.

Kornerup, Andreas. Reinhold color
atlas, New York, Reinhold [1962,
c1961] 224 p. 752 62-8756
ND1285 .K6 1962 MRR Alc.

COLORS--DICTIONARIES.
Kornerup, Andreas. Methuen handbook
of colour 2nd ed., revised. London,
Methuen, 1967. 243 p. 535.6 67-
91262
    ND1285 .K613 1967 MRR Alc.

Kornerup, Andreas. Reinhold color
atlas. New York, Reinhold [1962,
c1961] 224 p. 752 62-8756
    ND1285 .K6 1962 MRR Alc.

COLORS (FLAGS)
see Flags

COLUMBIA UNIVERSITY. ORAL HISTORY
RESEARCH OFFICE.
Columbia University. Oral History
Research Office. The Oral History
Collection of Columbia University.
[3d ed.] New York: [Sold by
Microfilming Corp. of America, Glen
Rock, N.J.] 1973. xvii, 459 p.
016.9173/03 73-78480
    Z6621 .C725 1973 MRR Alc.

COLUMBUS, CHRISTOPHER
see Colombo, Cristoforo

COMBAT.
see also Battles

COMBINED OPERATIONS (MILITARY SCIENCE)
see Amphibious warfare

COMETS.
Middlehurst, Barbara M., ed. The
moon, meteorites, and comets,
Chicago, University of Chicago Press
[1963] xxii, 810 p. 523 62-18117

    QB501 .S6 vol. 4 MRR Alc.

COMIC BOOKS, STRIPS, ETC.--AMERICAN.
Daniels, Les. Comix: a history of
comic books in America. [New York]
Outerbridge & Dienstfrey; distributed
by E. P. Dutton [1971] x, 198 p.
741.59/73 75-169104
    NC1426 .D3 1971 MRR Alc.

COMIC BOOKS, STRIPS, ETC.--BIBLIOGRAPHY.
Kempkes, Wolfgang. Bibliographie der
internationalen Literatur über
Comics. München-Pullach, Verlag
Dokumentation, 1971. 213 p., [10] p.
of illus. 72-314525
    Z5956.C6 K45 1971b MRR Alc.

Overstreet, Robert M. The comic book
price guide, 1973; 3d ed.
Cleveland, Tenn. [1973] 399 p. (p.
377-399 advertisements) [$6.00]
381/.45/74159075 73-161590
    Z1000 .O9 1973 MRR Alc.

COMIC BOOKS, STRIPS, ETC.--PRICES.
Overstreet, Robert M. The comic book
price guide, 1973; 3d ed.
Cleveland, Tenn. [1973] 399 p. (p.
377-399 advertisements) [$6.00]
381/.45/74159075 73-161590
    Z1000 .O9 1973 MRR Alc.

COMIC OPERA
see Opera

COMMEMORATIVE COINS--UNITED STATES.
Bullowa, David M. The commemorative
coinage of the United States, 1892-
1938. New York, The American
numismatic society, 1938. 3 p. l., i-
ii, 192 p. 737.0973 39-6625
    CJ1839 .B8 MRR Alc.

Hibler, Harold E. So-called dollars:
[1st ed.] New York, Coin and
Currency Institute [c1963] xi, 156
p. 737.2085 63-11546
    CJ5806 .H5 MRR Alc.

Ruby, Warren A. Commemorative coins
of the United States (gold and
silver) Lake Mills, Iowa, Graphic
Pub. Co. [1961] unpaged. 61-47618

    CJ1839 .F8 MRR Alc.

Taxay, Don. An illustrated history
of U.S. commemorative coinage. New
York, Arco Pub. Co. [1967] viii, 256
p. 737.49/73 67-10696
    CJ1839 .T3 MRR Alc.

COMMEMORATIVE POSTAGE STAMPS--
COMMONWEALTH OF NATIONS.
Haverbeck, Harrison Donald Seaman.
The commemorative stamps of the
British Commonwealth. London, Faber
and Faber [1955] 239 p. 55-36219
    HE6185.G6 H36 1955a MRR Alc.

COMMEMORATIVE POSTAGE STAMPS--GREAT
BRITAIN.
Haverbeck, Harrison Donald Seaman.
The commemorative stamps of the
British Commonwealth. London, Faber
and Faber [1955] 239 p. 55-36219
    HE6185.G6 H36 1955a MRR Alc.

COMMERCE.
see also Business

see also Export marketing

see also Harbors

see also International business
enterprises

see also Markets

see also Money

see also Prices

see also Retail trade

see also Shipping

see also Transportation

see also Wholesale trade

Combs, Paul H. Handbook of
international purchasing, Boston,
Cahners Books [1971] viii, 168 p.
658.7/2 70-132670
    HF5437 .C585 MRR Alc.

COMMERCE--BIBLIOGRAPHY.
Foreign commerce handbook. 1922/1923-
[Washington, D.C.] Foreign commerce
department, Chamber of Commerce of
the United States. 22-23199
    HF3011 .F6 MRR Ref.Desk Latest
    edition / MRR Alc Latest edition

International Trade Centre.
Compendium of sources: international
trade statistics; Geneva, GATT
International Trade Centre, 1967.
150 p. [21.00] 016.382/021/2 73-
354490
    Z7164.C8 I64 MRR Alc.

Maltby, Arthur. Economics and
commerce; London, Bingley, 1968.
239 p. [48/-] 016.33 68-103704
    Z7164.E2 M38 1968b MRR Alc.

Wheeler, Lora Jeanne. International
business and foreign trade; Detroit,
Gale Research Co. [1968] 221 p.
[8.75] 016.6581/8 67-31263
    Z7164.C8 W5 MRR Alc.

COMMERCE--DICTIONARIES.
Greener, Michael. The Penguin
dictionary of commerce.
[Harmondsworth, Eng.] Penguin [1971]
350 p. [10/-] 330/.03 72-183816
    HF1002 .G73 1971 MRR Alc.

Hanson, John Lloyd. A dictionary of
economics and commerce, 2nd ed.
London, MacDonald & Evans, 1967.
[6], 432 p. [35/-] 330.03 67-
110693
    HB61 .H35 1967 MRR Alc.

Hanson, John Lloyd. A dictionary of
economics and commerce, 3rd ed.
London, Macdonald & Evans, 1969. vi,
474 p. [42/-] 330/.03 77-437920
    HB61 .H35 1969 MRR Alc.

Henderson, Harry William. Dictionary
of international agricultural trade.
Washington, U.S. Foreign Agricultural
Service: [for sale by the Supt. of
Docs., U.S. Govt. Print. Off.] 1971.
170 p. 382/.41/014 76-612219
    HF1002 .H38 1971 MRR Alc.

Kettridge, Julius Ornan. French-
English and English-French dictionary
of commercial & financial terms,
phrases, & practice; London,
Routledge & Paul, 1957. xi, 647 p.
650.3 59-21494
    HG151 .K42 1957 MRR Alc.

Motta, Giuseppe, teacher of English.
Dizionario commerciale: inglese-
italiano, italiano-inglese. Milano,
C. Signorelli [1961] x, 1050 p. 61-
33500
    HF1002 .M6 MRR Alc.

Nanassy, Louis C. Business
dictionary Englewood Cliffs, N.J.,
Prentice-Hall [1960] vi, 263 p.
650.3 60-7410
    HF1002 .N3 MRR Alc.

Osborn, Percy George. The concise
commercial dictionary, London, Sweet
& Maxwell, 1966. [4], 244 p. [45/-]
380/.03 67-7382]
    HF1002 .O8 MRR Alc.

Pitman's business man's guide; 14th
ed. London, Pitman, 1967. [5], 346
p. [32/-] 650/.03 68-92621
    HF1001 .S6 1967 MRR Alc.

COMMERCE--DICTIONARIES--DUTCH.
Bons, A. Engels handelswoordenboek
(Nederlands-Engels) Deventer, Æ. E.
Kluwer [1957] 1170 p. 57-56259
    HF1002 .B59 MRR Alc.

Bons, A. Engels handelswoordenboek
(Nederlands-Engels) Deventer, Æ. E.
Kluwer [1957] 1170 p. 57-46259
    HF1002 .B59 MRR Alc.

COMMERCE--DICTIONARIES--FRENCH.
Kettridge, Julius Ornan. French-
English and English-French dictionary
of commercial & financial terms,
phrases, & practice; London,
Routledge & Paul, 1957. xi, 647 p.
650.3 59-21494
    HG151 .K42 1957 MRR Alc.

Servotte, Jozef V., 1903-
Dictionnaire commercial et financier:
2. ed., rev. et augm. Bruxelles,
Éditions Brepols [1960] ix, 955 p.
61-930
    HF1002 .S42 1960 MRR Alc.

COMMERCE--DICTIONARIES--GERMAN.
Gunston, C. A. Gunston & Corner's
German-English glossary of financial
and economic terms. 6th ed., greatly
compressed, but in content much
amplified, Frankfurt am Main, F.
Knapp [1972] xxiii, 1203 p.
330/.03 72-188587
    HG151 .G85 1972 MRR Alc.

Závada, Dušan. Satzlexikon der
Handelskorrespondenz. Wiesbaden,
Brandstetter; London, Pitman, 1969.
xxi, 331 p. [20.00] 380/.03 79-
426305
    HF1002 .Z34 MRR Alc.

COMMERCE--DICTIONARIES--ITALIAN.
Motta, Giuseppe, teacher of English.
Dizionario commerciale: inglese-
italiano, italiano-inglese. Milano,
C. Signorelli [1961] x, 1050 p. 61-
33500
    HF1002 .M6 MRR Alc.

COMMERCE--DICTIONARIES--POLYGLOT.
Bari, G. Dizionario commerciale
italiano-inglese-francese-tedesco.
2. ed. Milano, L. di G. Pirolo,
1970. 865 p., leaf inserted. [8500]
70-488606
    HF1002 .B28 1970 MRR Alc.

Herbst, Robert. Dictionary of
commercial, financial, and legal
terms; 2d ed., Zug, Translegal
[1966- v. 330/.03 67-8369
    HB61 .H462 MRR Alc.

Horten, Hans Ernest. Export-import
correspondence in four languages
London, Gower Press Ltd., 1970. xi,
2-316 p. [80/-] 382/.03 76-495482

    HF1002 .H695 MRR Alc.

Servotte, Jozef V., 1903-
Dictionnaire commercial et financier:
2. ed., rev. et augm. Bruxelles,
Éditions Brepols [1960] ix, 955 p.
61-930
    HF1002 .S42 1960 MRR Alc.

COMMERCE--DIRECTORIES.
Bottin. Bottin international. 1947-
Paris, Société Didot-Bottin [etc.]
48-24844
    HF54.F8 B6 Sci RR Latest edition /
    MRR Alc Latest edition

Bottin. Paris, Société Didot-
Bottin [etc.] 50-49011
    HF53 .B6 MRR Alc Latest edition

British and international trades
index. 38th- ed.; 1969/70- Epsom,
Business Dictionaries.
380.1/025/171242 72-626689
    HF3503 .B75 MRR Alc Latest Edition

Cenypres trading register of the
United Nations countries. London,
Cenypres. 380.025 66-85954
    HF54.G7 C4 MRR Alc Latest edition

Chico, Vicente V. International
importers & exporters; 1st ed.
Manila, Nationwide Business Agency
[1971] 1068 p. 382/.025 70-31299

    HF54.P6 C54 MRR Alc.

The Globe world directory for land,
sea and air traffic. 1st- ed.;
1948- Oslo, [etc.] Globe
Directories. 385.058 50-13703
    HE9.A1 G5 MRR Alc Latest edition

Guide du commerce mondial pour les
professions liberales. Beyrouth,
Mansour. ne 66-1383
    HF3866 .G55 MRR Alc Latest edition

International reference handbook of
services, organizations, diplomatic
representation, marketing, and
advertising channels. 1954- New
York, World Trade Academy Press. a
55-1568
    HF54.U5 I52 MRR Alc Latest edition

The International telex book.
Americas edition. v. 1- 1974-
Atlanta, International Telex Corp.
384.1/4 74-645911
    HE7621 .I59 MRR Alc Latest edition

COMMERCE--DIRECTORIES. (Cont.)
International yellow pages. New York
[etc.] R. H. Donnelly Telephone
Directory Co. [etc.] 64-8064
     Began publication with 1963/64 vol.
     HE8721 .I67 MRR Alc Latest edition

J I T: Tokyo, [Kojunsha
International Publishers]
382/.025/52 68-51013
     HF54.J3 J2 MRR Alc Latest edition

Kelly's manufacturers and merchants
directory, 82d- ed.: 1968/69-
Kingston upon Thames, Kelly's
Directories. 380.1/025 72-622824
     HF54.G7 K4 MRR Alc Latest edition

The London directory & international
register of commerce. 1973- London.
338/.0025/421 73-642810
     D679 .A1315 MRR Alc Latest edition

Marconi's international register.
New York [etc.] 31-15824
     Began publication in 1917.
     HE7710 .I6 MRR Alc Latest edition

Owen's commerce and travel and
international register. London,
Owen's Commerce & Travel Ltd.
380.1/025 72-626541
     HF3872 .P3 MRR Alc Latest edition

Stores of the world. London, Newman
Books. 380.1025 66-9836
     Began publication in 1961.
     HF54.G7 S8 MRR Alc Latest edition

Stores, shops, supermarkets retail
directory. 21st- ed.: 1967-
London, Newman Books Ltd. 381 72-
623101
     HF5155 .S8 MRR Alc Latest edition

Trevor, John. Worldwide bargains
directory; Nottingham, Trade Guide
Publications, 1966. 256 p.
[unpriced] 338.7/6/025 68-141445
     HF54.G7 T7 1966 MRR Alc.

The Wenco international trade
directory. 1973/74- Portland, Or.,
Wenco Enterprises. [$125.00]
382/.025 73-646586
     HF54.U5 W45 MRR Alc Latest edition

Westminster directory of the world.
London, Tamar Publishing Co. Ltd.,
1968. 564 p. [unpriced] 380.1/025
73-403663
     HF54.G7 W46 MRR Alc.

World trade annual. 1963- New York,
Walker. 64-66238
     HF53 .W6 MRR Alc Latest edition

World trade annual. Supplement:
trade of the industrialized nations
with Eastern Europe and the
developing nations. 1964- New York,
Walker. 74-643539
     HF53 .W612 Suppl. MRR Alc Latest
     edition

COMMERCE--DIRECTORIES--BIBLIOGRAPHY.
International reference handbook of
services, organizations, diplomatic
representation, marketing, and
advertising channels. 1954- New
York, World Trade Academy Press. a
55-1568
     HF54.U5 I52 MRR Alc Latest edition

Smith, George Mayo. World wide
business publications directory, New
York, Simon and Schuster [1971] xvi,
593 p. 016.380/025 73-157682
     Z7164.C8 S55 MRR Ref Desk.

Trade directories of the world. 1st-
ed.: 1952- New York, Croner
Publications. 016.38 52-6569
     Z5771 .C7 MRR Alc Latest edition

COMMERCE--HANDBOOKS, MANUALS, ETC.
Angel, Juvenal Londono, The
handbook of international business
and investment facts and information
sources; New York, World Trade
Academy Press; distributed by Simon &
Schuster [1967] 565 p. 382 66-
28172
     HF1411 .A5 MRR Alc.

Angel, Juvenal Londoño,
International marketing guide for
technical, management and other
consultants. 1st ed. New York,
World Trade Academy Press;
distributed by Simon & Schuster
[1971] 600 p. [$25.00] 658.4/03
77-111350
     HD69.C6 A676 MRR Alc.

International reference handbook of
services, organizations, diplomatic
representation, marketing, and
advertising channels. 1954- New
York, World Trade Academy Press. a
55-1568
     HF54.U5 I52 MRR Alc Latest edition

Jonnard, Claude M. Exporter's
financial and marketing handbook
Park Ridge, N.J., Noyes Data Corp.,
1973. xii, 308 p. [$18.00] 658.8
72-96107
     HF1009.5 .J65 MRR Alc.

Naft, Stephen, International
conversion tables; New York, Duell,
Sloan and Pearce [1961] xii, 372 p.
389 61-10391
     HF5714 .N3 1961 MRR Alc.

The Economist (London) Guide to
weights and measures, [2d. ed.]
London [1962] 95 p. 65-87714
     HF5712 .E25 1962 MRR Alc.

COMMERCE--HISTORY.
Condliffe, John Bell, The commerce
of nations. London, Allen & Unwin
[1951] xi, 884 p. 380.9 51-7849
     HF352 .C68 1951 MRR Alc.

COMMERCE--INFORMATION SERVICES.
Angel, Juvenal Londono, The
handbook of international business
and investment facts and information
sources, New York, World Trade
Academy Press; distributed by Simon &
Schuster [1967] 565 p. 382 66-
28172
     HF1411 .A5 MRR Alc.

International reference handbook of
services, organizations, diplomatic
representation, marketing, and
advertising channels. 1954- New
York, World Trade Academy Press. a
55-1568
     HF54.U5 I52 MRR Alc Latest edition

COMMERCE--PERIODICALS--BIBLIOGRAPHY.
Internationale Bibliographie der
Fachzeitschriften für Technik und
Wirtschaft. München-Pullach, Verlag
Dokumentation [etc.] 67-118912
     Z7913 .I757 MRR Alc Latest edition

COMMERCE--PERIODICALS--INDEXES.
United States. Dept. of Commerce.
Library. Price sources; New York,
B. Franklin [1968] iv, 320 p.
016.33852 70-6381
     Z7164.P94 U56 1968 MRR Alc.

COMMERCE--TERMINOLOGY.
Business terms, phrases and
abbreviations. 13th ed., London,
Pitman, 1966. [5], 232 p. [12/6]
650.03 67-72958
     HF1002 .B9 1966 MRR Alc.

COMMERCE--YEARBOOKS.
Bottin. Bottin international, 1947-
Paris, Société Didot-Bottin [etc.]
48-24844
     HF54.F8 B6 Sci RR Latest edition /
     MRR Alc Latest edition

The Exporters year book - export
data. 55th- 1971- London, Benn
Bros. 382/.6/05 72-622714
     HF53 .S9 MRR Alc Latest edition

World trade annual. 1963- New York,
Walker. 64-66238
     HF53 .W6 MRR Alc Latest edition

World trade annual. Supplement:
trade of the industrialized nations
with Eastern Europe and the
developing nations. 1964- New York,
Walker. 74-643539
     HF53 .W612 Suppl. MRR Alc Latest
     edition

COMMERCIAL AERONAUTICS
see Aeronautics, Commercial

COMMERCIAL AGENTS--ISRAEL--DIRECTORIES.
Who represents whom in Israel and
abroad. 1st- ed.: 1968/69- Tel-
Aviv, A. L. Tanne. 382/.025/5694 78-
950757
     HF3861.P2 A37 MRR Alc Latest
     edition

COMMERCIAL AGENTS, FRENCH--DIRECTORIES.
Qui représente qui en France? 1.-
ed.: 1957- Paris, Société des
Annuaires "Qui represente qui",
[etc.] 60-20676
     HF3553 .Q5 MRR Alc Latest edition

COMMERCIAL ART--DIRECTORIES.
Director's Art Institute, New York.
Who's who in commercial art and
photography; [2d ed.] New York,
1964. 192 p. 66-235
     NC897 .D5 1964 MRR Biog.

COMMERCIAL CORRESPONDENCE.
see also Sales letters

Frailey, Lester Eugene, Handbook of
business letters, Rev. ed.
Englewood Cliffs, N.J., Prentice-Hall
[1965] x, 918 p. 651.75 64-15216

     HF5721 .F67 1965 MRR Alc.

Parkhurst, Charles Chandler,
Business communication for better
human relations, Englewood Cliffs,
N.J., Prentice-Hall, 1961. 579 p.
651.75 61-6605
     HF5721 .P368 MRR Alc.

Sheff, Alexander L. How to write
letters for all occasions. New ed.,
rev. Garden City, N.Y., Doubleday
[1961] 239 p. 651.75 61-10015
     HF5726 .S465 1961 MRR Ref Desk.

COMMERCIAL CREDIT
see Credit

COMMERCIAL ETHICS
see Business ethics

COMMERCIAL FINANCE COMPANIES--UNITED
STATES--DIRECTORIES.
National directory of finance
companies. 1951- Montpelier, Ohio,
Inter-state Service Co. 332.31
332.35* 52-18620
     HG2066 .N285 MRR Alc Latest
     edition

COMMERCIAL FINANCE COMPANIES--UNITED
STATES--YEARBOOKS.
Moody's bank & finance manual:
American and foreign. New York,
Moody's Investors Service. 56-14722
     HG4961 .M65 MRR Alc Latest edition

COMMERCIAL FISHING
see Fisheries

COMMERCIAL LAW.
see also Business enterprises

Pitman's business man's guide; 14th
ed. London, Pitman, 1967. [5], 346
p. [32/-] 650/.03 68-92621
     HF1001 .S6 1967 MRR Alc.

COMMERCIAL LAW--PERIODICALS.
The Clearing house quarterly.
Minneapolis, Minn., Attorneys'
National Clearing House Co. 08-15550

     KF195.C57 C4 MRR Alc Latest
     edition

COMMERCIAL LAW--UNITED STATES.
Credit manual of commercial laws.
New York. 11-31760
     KF889 .C74 MRR Alc Latest edition

COMMERCIAL POLICY.
Lary, Hal Buckner, Imports of
manufactures from less developed
countries New York, National Bureau
of Economic Research; distributed by
Columbia University Press, 1968.
xvii, 286 p. 382/.09172/401722 67-
28434
     HF1411 .L36 MRR Alc.

COMMERCIAL PRODUCTS.
see also Manufactures

see also Marine resources

Commodity year book. 1st- ed.;
1939- New York, Commodity Research
Bureau, inc. 338.0973 39-11418
     HF1041 .C56 MRR Alc Latest edition

United Nations. Statistical Office.
The growth of world industry. 1967
ed. New York, United Nations, 1968-
69 [v. 1, 1969] 2 v. 338 77-7739
     HC59 .U458 MRR Alc.

COMMERCIAL PRODUCTS--BIBLIOGRAPHY.
International Trade Centre.
Compendium of sources: Geneva, 1967.
232 p. [unpriced] 016.3824 74-
431255
     Z7164.C81 I58 MRR Alc.

International Trade Centre. Market
surveys by products and countries;
Geneva, 1969. ix, 203 p. $5.00
(U.S.)] 016.6588/3 72-186218
     Z7164.M18 I5 1969 MRR Alc.

United States. Dept. of Commerce.
Library. Price sources; New York,
B. Franklin [1968] iv, 320 p.
016.33852 70-6381
     Z7164.P94 U56 1968 MRR Alc.

COMMERCIAL PRODUCTS--CLASSIFICATION.
Marer, Paul. Soviet and East
European foreign trade, 1946-1969;
Bloomington, Indiana University Press
[1973, c1972] xviii, 408 p.
[$15.00] 382/.0947 72-76945
     HF3626.5 .M37 MRR Alc.

United States. Bureau of the Census.
U.S. foreign trade: general imports,
world area by commodity groupings.
1970- [Washington, For sale by the
Supt. of Docs., U.S. Govt. Print.
Off.] 382/.5/0973 78-649732
     HF105 .C137172 MRR Alc Latest
     edition

COMMERCIAL PRODUCTS-- (Cont.)
United States. Bureau of the Census.
U.S. foreign trade: exports, world
area by commodity groupings. 1970-
[Washington, For sale by the Supt. of
Docs., U.S. Govt. Print. Off.]
382/.6/0973 79-648608
    HF105 .C137132 MRR Alc Latest
    edition

COMMERCIAL PRODUCTS--CLASSIFICATION--
PERIODICALS.
United States. Bureau of the Census.
U.S. foreign trade: exports,
commodity groupings by world area.
1970- [Washington, For sale by the
Supt. of Docs., U.S. Govt. Print.
Off.] 382/.6/0973 70-616577
    HF105 .C137152 MRR Alc Latest
    edition

COMMERCIAL PRODUCTS--DICTIONARIES--
POLYGLOT.
Bari, G. Dizionario commerciale
italiano-inglese-francese-tedesco.
2. ed. Milano, L. di G. Pirolo,
1970. 865 p., leaf inserted. [8500]
70-488606
    HF1002 .B28 1970 MRR Alc.

COMMERCIAL PRODUCTS--DIRECTORIES.
Bottin. Bottin international. 1947-
Paris, Société Didot-Bottin [etc.]
48-24844
    HF54.F8 B6 Sci RR Latest edition /
    MRR Alc Latest edition

Westminster directory of the world.
London, Tamar Publishing Co. Ltd.,
1968. 564 p. [unpriced] 380.1/025
73-403663
    HF54.G7 W46 MRR Alc.

COMMERCIAL PRODUCTS--PERIODICALS--
INDEXES.
F & S index international:
industries, countries, companies.
1st- ed.; 1968- Cleveland,
Predicasts. 016.338 74-644265
Z7164.C81 F13 MRR Alc Full set /
    Sci RR Partial set

COMMERCIAL PRODUCTS--STATISTICS.
United States. Bureau of the Census.
U.S. foreign trade: general imports,
world area by commodity groupings.
1970- [Washington, For sale by the
Supt. of Docs., U.S. Govt. Print.
Off.] 382/.5/0973 78-649732
    HF105 .C137172 MRR Alc Latest
    edition

COMMERCIAL PRODUCTS--JAPAN--DIRECTORIES.
J I T: Tokyo, [Kojunsha
International Publishers]
382/.025/52 68-51013
    HF54.J3 J2 MRR Alc Latest edition

COMMERCIAL PRODUCTS--LOUISIANA--
CLASSIFICATION.
Louisiana. State University in New
Orleans. International Marketing
Institute. Louisiana international
trade directory. [1st ed.] New
Orleans [1973] 159 p. 382/.025/763
73-179263
    HF5065.L8 L66 1973 MRR Alc.

COMMERCIAL PRODUCTS--UNITED STATES.
Lechter, Max. U.S. exports and
imports classified by OBE end-use
commodity categories, 1923-1968;
[Washington] U.S. Office of Business
Economics, Balance of Payments
Division [for sale by the Supt. of
Docs., U.S. Govt. Print. Off.] 1970
[i.e. 1971] xxii, 411 p. [$4.00]
382.4/0973 75-611180
    HF3001 .L43 MRR Alc.

COMMERCIAL PRODUCTS--UNITED STATES--
CLASSIFICATION.
American import directory. New York,
Costa's Directories Co. 66-83670
    HF3012 .A65 MRR Alc Latest edition

United States. Bureau of the Census.
Alphabetic index of manufactured
products: [Washington, For sale by
the Supt. of Docs., U.S. Govt. Print.
Off., 1968] 192 p. [1.50]
338.4/7/6702573 70-601986
    HD9724 .A4 1967c MRR Alc.

United States. Bureau of the Census.
Numerical list of manufactured
products. [Washington, 1968] 165,
A141, B2 p. 338.4/0973 a 68-7403
    HD9724 .A4 1967 MRR Alc.

United States. Office of Management
and Budget. Statistical Policy
Division. Standard industrial
classification manual. [Washington;
For sale by the Supt. of Docs., U.S.
Govt. Print. Off.] 1972. 649 p.
[$6.75] 338/.02/0973 72-601529
    HF1042 .A55 1972 MRR Alc.

COMMERCIAL PRODUCTS--UNITED STATES--
DIRECTORIES.
Boe, John Oliver. Television
sponsors directory. Everglades,
Fla., Everglades Pub. Co.
659.14/3/02573 72-622327
    HF6146.T42 B6 MRR Alc Latest
    edition

The New product directory of New York
Stock Exchange listed companies.
Concord, Mass., Marketing
Development. 338/.0025/73 74-647304

    HD69.N4 N44 MRR Alc Latest edition

Plant and product directory. 1961-
[New York?] Market Research Dept. of
Fortune. 338.05873 61-12113
    HC102 .P59 MRR Alc Latest edition

Product design & development. PD&D
product encyclopedia; [Philadelphia,
1961] 253, 10, 10 p. 61-59873
    T12 .P8 MRR Alc.

Zimmerman, Oswald Theodore.
Industrial Research Service's
handbook of material trade names,
1953 ed. Dover, N.H., Industrial
Research Service, 1953. xvi, 794 p.
660.2 53-1074
    TP151 .Z5 1953 MRR Alc.

COMMERCIAL PRODUCTS--UNITED STATES--
PERIODICALS.
Consumer reports. v. 1- May 1936-
[Mount Vernon, N.Y., etc., Consumers
Union of United States] 43-33888
    TX335 .A1C6 MRR Ref Desk Buying
    guide issue only.

COMMERCIAL PRODUCTS--UNITED STATES--
STATISTICS.
Trade Relations Council of the United
States. General Counsel. Employment,
output, and foreign trade of U.S.
manufacturing industries.
Washington. 338/.0973 73-30363
    HC101 .T68 MRR Alc Latest edition

United States. Bureau of the Census.
1967 census of manufactures.
[Washington; For sale by the Supt. of
Docs., U.S. Govt. Print. Off.] 1971.
3 v. in 6 v. [$9.00 (varies)]
338.4/7/670973 74-609524
    HD9724 .A4445 MRR Alc.

United States. Bureau of the Census.
Annual survey of manufacturers.
1949/50- Washington, U.S. Govt.
Print. Off. 338.4 52-60884
    HD9724 .A211 MRR Alc Latest
    edition

United States. Bureau of the Census.
U.S. foreign trade: general imports,
commodity by world area.
[Washington, For sale by the Supt. of
Docs., U.S. Govt. Print. Off.]
382/.5/0973 75-648607
    HF105 .C137182 MRR Alc Latest
    edition

United States. Bureau of the Census.
U.S. foreign trade: imports SIC-based
products. [Washington, For sale by
Supt. of Docs., U.S. Govt. Print.
Off.] 382/.5/0973 72-626391
    HF105 .C1371663 MRR Alc Latest
    edition

United States. Bureau of the Census.
U.S. foreign trade: imports, TSUSA
commodity by country. 1970-
[Washington, For sale by the Supt. of
Docs., U.S. Govt. Print. Off.]
382/.5/0973 74-649695
    HF105 .C137232 MRR Alc Latest
    edition

United States. Bureau of the Census.
U.S. foreign trade: exports, SIC-
based products. 1970- [Washington,
For sale by the Supt. of Docs., U.S.
Govt. Print. Off.] 382/.6/0973 71-
648606
    HF105 .C137166 MRR Alc Latest
    edition

United States. Bureau of the Census.
U.S. foreign trade: exports, world
area by commodity groupings. 1970-
[Washington, For sale by the Supt. of
Docs., U.S. Govt. Print. Off.]
382/.6/0973 79-648608
    HF105 .C137132 MRR Alc Latest
    edition

COMMERCIAL PRODUCTS--UNITED STATES--
STATISTICS--BIBLIOGRAPHY.
Special Libraries Association.
Business and Finance Division.
Committee on Sources of Commodity
Prices. Sources of commodity prices.
New York, Special Libraries
Association, 1959 [c1960] 170 p.
338.505873 60-8102
    Z7164.P94 S6 MRR Alc.

COMMERCIAL PRODUCTS--UNITED STATES--
STATISTICS--PERIODICALS.
United States. Bureau of the Census.
U.S. foreign trade: exports,
commodity groupings by world area.
1970- [Washington, For sale by the
Supt. of Docs., U.S. Govt. Print.
Off.] 382/.6/0973 70-616577
    HF105 .C137152 MRR Alc Latest
    edition

COMMERCIAL PRODUCTS--UNITED STATES--
YEARBOOKS.
Price buying directory. [Chicago]
Consumers Digest. 77-789
    TX335.A1 P74 MRR Ref Desk Latest
    edition

COMMERCIAL STATISTICS.
Agence Havas. Keys to European
market. [Paris, Havas Conseil, 1969]
327 p. [206.25F] 330.9/4 72-
183572
    HC240 .A594 MRR Alc.

Commodity year book. 1st- ed.;
1939- New York, Commodity Research
Bureau, inc. 338.0973 39-11418
    HF1041 .C56 MRR Alc Latest edition

Gallatin Service. Gallatin
statistical indicators. [New York,
Copley International Corporation,
1967- v.   310 72-12086
    HA42 .G32 MRR Alc.

Mulhall, Michael George, The
dictionary of statistics. 4th ed.,
rev. to Nov., 1898. Detroit, Gale
Research Co., 1969. 853 p.   310/.3
68-18013
    HA17 .M8 1969 MRR Ref Desk.

Organization for Economic Cooperation
and Development. Foreign trade.
Commerce exterieur. Series C.
Commodity trade. Commerce par
produits. [Paris] 382/.021/2 72-
626755
    HF91 .O67 MRR Latest edition

Survey of current business. Business
statistics; 1951- Washington, U.S.
Govt. Print. Off. 330.5 74-643587
    HC101.A13122 MRR Alc Latest
    edition

Trade Relations Council of the United
States. General Counsel. Employment,
output, and foreign trade of U.S.
manufacturing industries.
Washington. 338/.0973 73-30363
    HC101 .T68 MRR Alc Latest edition

United Nations. Conference on Trade
and Development. Secretariat. Trade
prospects and capital needs of
developing countries; New York,
United Nations, 1968. ix, 614 p.
[8.00] 382/.09172/3 75-5913
    HF1413 .U52 MRR Alc.

United Nations. Statistical Office.
The growth of world industry. 1967
ed. New York, United Nations, 1968-
69 [v. 1, 1969] 2 v. 338 77-7739

    HC59 .U458 MRR Alc.

United Nations. Statistical Office.
The growth of world industry, 1938-
1961; New York, United Nations,
1963. xvi, 849 p. 338.4083 63-
25411
    HC59 .U46 MRR Alc.

United Nations. Statistical Office.
Patterns of industrial growth. New
York, United Nations, 1960. viii,
471 p. 338.019 60-50248
    HC58 .U5112 MRR Alc.

United Nations. Statistical Office.
Yearbook of international trade
statistics. 1st- issue; 1950- New
York. 382.058 51-8987
    JX1977 .A2 MRR Ref Desk Latest
    edition

United States. Bureau of the Census.
Foreign commerce and navigation of
the United States. 1865/66-
Washington, U.S. Govt. Print. Off.
07-19228
    HF105 .A2 MRR Alc Latest edition

United States. Bureau of the Census.
U.S. foreign trade: exports,
commodity groupings by world area.
1970- [Washington, For sale by the
Supt. of Docs., U.S. Govt. Print.
Off.] 382/.6/0973 70-616577
    HF105 .C137152 MRR Alc Latest
    edition

United States. Bureau of the Census.
U.S. foreign trade: general imports,
commodity by world area.
[Washington, For sale by the Supt. of
Docs., U.S. Govt. Print. Off.]
382/.5/0973 75-648607
    HF105 .C137182 MRR Alc Latest
    edition

United States. Bureau of the Census.
U.S. foreign trade: general imports,
world area by commodity groupings.
1970- [Washington, For sale by the
Supt. of Docs., U.S. Govt. Print.
Off.] 382/.5/0973 78-649732
    HF105 .C137172 MRR Alc Latest
    edition

COMMERCIAL STATISTICS. (Cont.)
United States. Bureau of the Census.
U.S. foreign trade: imports SIC-based
products. [Washington, For sale by
Supt. of Docs., U.S. Govt. Print.
Off.] 382/.5/0973 72-626391
HF105 .C1371663 MRR Alc Latest
edition

United States. Bureau of the Census.
U.S. foreign trade: imports, TSUSA
commodity by country. 1970-
[Washington, For sale by the Supt. of
Docs., U.S. Govt. Print. Off.]
382/.5/0973 74-649695
HF105 .C137232 MRR Alc Latest
edition

United States. Bureau of the Census.
U.S. foreign trade: exports, SIC-
based products. 1970- [Washington,
For sale by the Supt. of Docs., U.S.
Govt. Print. Off.] 382/.6/0973 71-
648606
HF105 .C137166 MRR Alc Latest
edition

United States. Bureau of the Census.
U.S. foreign trade: exports, world
area by commodity groupings. 1970-
[Washington, For sale by the Supt. of
Docs., U.S. Govt. Print. Off.]
382/.6/0973 78-649608
HF105 .C137132 MRR Alc Latest
edition

United States. Maritime
Administration. Essential United
States foreign trade routes. [1946]-
Washington, For sale by the
Superintendent of Documents, U.S.
Govt. Print. Off. [etc.] 60-62459
HE745 .A184 MRR Alc Latest edition

Webb, Augustus Duncan. The new
dictionary of statistics; London, G.
Routledge and sons, limited; New
York, E. P. Dutton and co., 1911.
xi, [1], 682 p. 11-10376
HA46 .W952 MRR Ref Desk.

COMMERCIAL STATISTICS--BIBLIOGRAPHY.
Ball, Joyce. Foreign statistical
documents; Stanford, Calif., Hoover
Institution on War, Revolution, and
Peace, Stanford University, 1967.
vii, 173 p. 016.3309 67-14234
Z7551 .B3 MRR Alc.

International Trade Centre.
Compendium of sources: Geneva, 1967.
232 p. [unpriced] 016.3824 74-
431255
Z7164.C81 I58 MRR Alc.

International Trade Centre.
Compendium of sources: international
trade statistics; Geneva, GATT
International Trade Centre, 1967.
150 p. [21.00] 016.382/021/2 73-
354490
Z7164.C8 I64 MRR Alc.

Statistics sources; Rev. 3d ed.
Detroit, Gale Research Co., 1971.
647 p. [$27.50] 016.31 72-127923
Z7551 .S84 1971 MRR Ref Desk.

Verwey, Gerlof, The economist's
handbook, Amsterdam, The economist's
handbook, 1934. viii, p., 1 l., 460
p. 016.31 35-4837
Z7553.E2 V6 MRR Alc.

COMMERCIAL TREATIES.
Mid-European Law Project. Economic
treaties and agreements of the Soviet
bloc in Eastern Europe, 1945-1951.
2d ed. New York, Mid-European
Studies Center, 1952. xliii, 138 p.
382 52-60057
Z663.55 .E3 MRR Alc.

COMMERICAL PRODUCTS.
Hart, Harold H., Catalog of the
unusual New York, Hart Pub. Co.
[1973] 351 p. [$6.95] 380.1/025
73-80023
HF1041 .H297 MRR Alc.

COMMISSIONS OF INQUIRY
see Governmental investigations

COMMODITY EXCHANGES.
see also Marketing

Kroll, Stanley. The commodity
futures market guide [1st ed.] New
York, Harper & Row [1972, c1973] ix,
370 p. [$15.00] 332.6/78 69-15315

HG6046 .K8 1973 MRR Alc.

Shaw, John E. B. A professional
guide to commodity speculation West
Nyack, N.Y., Parker Pub. Co. [1972]
172 p. 332.6/78 78-184452
HG6046 .S48 MRR Alc.

COMMODITY EXCHANGES--UNITED STATES.
Gold, Gerald. Modern commodity
futures trading. [4th rev. ed.] New
York, Commodity Research Bureau
[1966, c1959] 255 p. 332.64 66-
7166
HG6046 .G58 1966 MRR Alc.

Gould, Bruce G. Dow Jones-Irwin
guide to commodities trading
Homewood, Ill., Dow Jones-Irwin,
1973. xv, 357 p. 332.6/44/0973 72-
98126
HG6046 .G66 MRR Alc.

COMMONS (SOCIAL ORDER)
see Labor and laboring classes

COMMONWEALTH, THE
see Political science

COMMONWEALTH OF NATIONS.
Bradley, Kenneth, ed. The living
Commonwealth. London, Hutchinson
[1961] 543 p. 942 62-1087
DA16 .B66 MRR Alc.

COMMONWEALTH OF NATIONS--BIBLIOGRAPHY.
Royal Commonwealth Society. Library.
Subject catalogue of the Library of
the Royal Empire Society, [1st ed.
reprinted] London, Dawsons for the
Royal Commonwealth Society, 1967. 4
v. [60/-/- per set (16/-/- per
vol.)] 016.942 68-70847
Z7164.C7 R82 1967 MRR Alc.

COMMONWEALTH OF NATIONS--BIBLIOGRAPHY--CATALOGS.
Royal Commonwealth Society. Library.
Subject catalogue of the Royal
Commonwealth Society, London.
Boston, Mass., G. K. Hall. 1971. 7
v. 017.1 70-180198
Z7164.C7 R83 MRR Alc (Dk 33)

COMMONWEALTH OF NATIONS--COMMERCE--DIRECTORIES.
British and international trades
index. 38th- ed.; 1969/70- Epsom,
Business Dictionaries.
380.1/025/171242 72-626989
HF3503 .B75 MRR Alc Latest Edition

COMMONWEALTH OF NATIONS--DIRECTORIES--BIBLIOGRAPHY.
Current British directories. 1953-
Beckenham, Kent [etc.] CBD Research
Ltd. [etc.] 53-26894
Z5771 .C8 MRR Ref Desk Latest
edition

COMMONWEALTH OF NATIONS--HISTORY.
The Cambridge history of the British
Empire; New York, The Macmillan
company; Cambridge, Eng., The
University press, 1929- v. 942
29-14661
DA30 .C3 1929 MRR Alc.

Mansergh, Nicholas. The Commonwealth
experience. New York, Praeger [1969]
xix, 471 p. [12.50] 909/.09/71242
69-10570
DA16 .M248 1969b MRR Alc.

COMMONWEALTH OF NATIONS--LEARNED INSTITUTIONS AND SOCIETIES.
Handbook of Commonwealth
organisations. London, Methuen
[1965] xvii, 236 p. 060.9171242
66-2744
AS118 .H3 MRR Alc.

COMMONWEALTH OF NATIONS--LITERATURES--BIO-BIBLIOGRAPHY.
The Penguin companion to English
literature. New York, McGraw-Hill
[1971] 575, [1] p. [$10.95] 820.9
B 77-158061
PN849.C5 P4 MRR Alc.

COMMONWEALTH OF NATIONS--OFFICIALS, EMPLOYEES, ETC.--SALARIES, ALLOWANCES, ETC.
Wilding, Norman W. An encyclopaedia
of Parliament 4th ed., completely
rev. New York, St. Martin's Press
[1971] ix, 931 p. [$20.00]
328.42/003 72-162373
JN555 .W5 1971 MRR Alc.

COMMONWEALTH OF NATIONS--POLITICS.
Plaskitt, Harold, Government of
Britain and the Commonwealth, 9th
ed. London, University Tutorial P.,
1968. vii, 323 p. [13/- 11/6
(pbk.)] 320/.0942 68-135116
JN321 .P55 1968 MRR Alc.

COMMONWEALTH OF NATIONS--REGISTERS.
Bidwell, Robin Leonard. The British
Empire and successor states, 1900-
1972; London, F. Cass [1974] xi,
156 p. [£9.00 ($27.50 U.S.)]
351.2/09171/242 74-169172
JN248 .B52 1974 MRR Ref Desk.

COMMONWEALTH OF NATIONS--YEARBOOKS.
A Year book of the Commonwealth.
1969- London, H.M. Stationery Off.
320.9/171/242 79-7332
JN248 .C5912 MRR Alc Latest
edition

COMMONWEALTH OF NATIONS PERIODICALS--DIRECTORIES.
Commonwealth Secretariat.
Commonwealth directory of
periodicals: London, Commonwealth
Secretariat, Publications Section,
1973. ix, 157 p. [£2.50] 016.05
74-168502
Z6941 .C65 1973 MRR Alc.

COMMUNAL SETTLEMENTS
see Collective settlements

COMMUNICABLE DISEASES.
see also Bacteria, Pathogenic

see also Bacteriology

Dubos, René Jules, ed. Bacterial
and mycotic infections of man. 4th
ed. Philadelphia, Lippincott [1965]
xiii, 1025 p. 616.01 64-23602
RC115 .D75 1965 MRR Alc.

COMMUNICATION.
see also Oral communication

COMMUNICATION--BIBLIOGRAPHY.
Communication directory. 1973/74-
Silver Spring, Md., Council of
Communication Societies. [$8.00]
380.3/025/73 74-644695
HE9.U5 D57 MRR Alc Latest edition
/ Sci RR Latest edition

Handbook of communication. Chicago,
Rand McNally College Pub. Co. [c1973]
ix, 1011 p. 001.5/02/02 72-7851
P90 .H293 MRR Alc.

COMMUNICATION--DICTIONARIES.
Diamant, Lincoln. The broadcast
communications dictionary, New York,
Hastings House [1974] 128 p.
384.54/01/4 73-19610
P87.5 .D48 1974 MRR Alc.

COMMUNICATION--HANDBOOKS, MANUALS, ETC.
Handbook of communication. Chicago,
Rand McNally College Pub. Co. [c1973]
ix, 1011 p. 001.5/02/02 72-7851
P90 .H293 MRR Alc.

COMMUNICATION--SOCIAL ASPECTS--UNITED STATES--BIBLIOGRAPHY.
Kaid, Lynda Lee. Political campaign
communication: a bibliography and
guide to the literature. Metuchen,
N.J., Scarecrow Press, 1974. v, 206
p. 016.329/01/0973 73-22492
Z7165.U5 K34 MRR Alc.

COMMUNICATION--STUDY AND TEACHING--DIRECTORIES.
Communication directory. 1973/74-
Silver Spring, Md., Council of
Communication Societies. [$8.00]
380.3/025/73 74-644695
HE9.U5 D57 MRR Alc Latest edition
/ Sci RR Latest edition

COMMUNICATION--UNITED STATES--BIOGRAPHY.
Foremost women in communications;
New York, Foremost Americans Pub.
Corp. [1970] xvii, 788 p.
001.5/0922 79-125936
P92.5.A1 F6 MRR Biog.

COMMUNICATION--UNITED STATES--SOCIETIES, ETC.--DIRECTORIES.
Communication directory. 1973/74-
Silver Spring, Md., Council of
Communication Societies. [$8.00]
380.3/025/73 74-644695
HE9.U5 D57 MRR Alc Latest edition
/ Sci RR Latest edition

COMMUNICATION AND TRAFFIC.
see also Aeronautics

see also Mass media

COMMUNICATION AND TRAFFIC--RUSSIA--BIBLIOGRAPHY.
United States. Library of Congress.
Reference Dept. Soviet
transportation and communications;
Washington, 1952. xv, 330 p.
016.385 52-60024
Z663.28 .S6 MRR Alc.

COMMUNICATION IN MANAGEMENT--BIBLIOGRAPHY.
Carter, Robert M. Communication in
organizations; Detroit, Gale
Research Co. [1972] ix, 272 p.
[$14.50] 016.6584/5 73-161194
Z7164.C81 C27 MRR Alc.

COMMUNICATION IN MEDICINE.
see also Health education

COMMUNICATION THEORY
see Information theory

COMMUNICATIONS, MILITARY.
Marshall, Max L., ed. The story of
the U.S. Army Signal Corps, New
York, F. Watts [1965] xiv, 305 p.
358.240973 65-11938
UG573 .M35 MRR Alc.

COMMUNICATIONS RESEARCH.
Nafziger, Ralph O., ed. Introduction
to mass communications research.
[Rev. ed.] Baton Rouge, Louisiana
State University Press [1963] 281 p.
070.72 63-8223
PN4853 .J6 no. 6 1963 MRR Alc.

COMMUNISM--1945- --YEARBOOKS.
Yearbook on international communist
affairs. 1966- Stanford, Calif.,
Hoover Institution Press. 335.43/05
67-31024
HX1 .Y4 MRR Alc Latest edition

COMMUNISM--BIBLIOGRAPHY.
Delaney, Robert Finley. The
literature of communism in America;
Washington, Catholic University of
America Press, 1962. xii, 433 p.
016.33543   62-6923
Z7164.S67 D4 MRR Alc.

Hammond, Thomas Taylor. Soviet
foreign relations and world
communism; Princeton N.J.,
Princeton University Press, 1965.
xxiv, 1240 p.   016.32747 63-7069
Z2517.R4 H3 MRR Alc.

Spector, Sherman David, Checklist of
paperbound books on Russia, Albany,
University of the State of New York,
State Education Dept., 1964. iii, 63
p.   65-63612
Z2491 .S69 MRR Alc.

COMMUNISM--DICTIONARIES.
De Koster, Lester. Vocabulary of
communism: Grand Rapids, Eerdmans
[1964] 224 p.   335.4303 63-17784
HX17 .D4 MRR Alc.

Hyams, Edward S. A dictionary of
modern revolution New York,
Taplinger Pub. Co. [1973] 322 p.
[$9.95] 335.43/03 73-6175
HX17 .H9 1973 MRR Alc.

Marxism, Communism, and Western
society; [New York] Herder and
Herder [1972-73] 8 v. 300/.3 79-
176368
AE5 .M27 MRR Alc.

COMMUNISM--HISTORY.
Daniels, Robert Vincent, ed. A
documentary history of communism;
New York, Random House [1960] 321,
393 p.   335.4309 60-6380
HX40 .D3 MRR Alc.

Laidler, Harry Wellington, History
of socialism; [Updated and expanded
ed.] New York, Crowell [1968] xx,
970 p. [12.50] 335/.009 67-29698

HX21 .L37 1968 MRR Alc.

Seton-Watson, Hugh. From Lenin to
Khrushchev, New York, Praeger [1960]
432 p.   335.4309 60-6999
HX40 .S39 MRR Alc.

COMMUNISM--HISTORY--HANDBOOKS, MANUALS,
ETC.
Sworakowski, Witold S. World
communism; a handbook, 1918-1965,
Stanford, Calif., Hoover Institution
Press, 1973. xv, 576 p. [$25.00]
335.43/09 70-149798
HX40 .S89 MRR Alc.

COMMUNISM--HISTORY--SOURCES.
Communist International. The
Communist International, 1919-1943;
[London] F. Cass, 1971. 3 v.
[£23.00] 329/.072 72-182920
HX11.I5 A5314 1971 MRR Alc.

COMMUNISM--PERIODICALS--BIBLIOGRAPHY.
Goldwater, Walter. Radical
periodicals in America, 1890-1950;
New Haven, Yale University Library,
1964. xv, 51 p.   64-6244
Z7164.S67 .G57 MRR Alc.

COMMUNISM--PERIODICALS--HISTORY.
The American radical press, 1880-
1960. Westport, Conn., Greenwood
Press [1974] 2 v. (xiv, 720 p.)
335/.00973 72-9825
HX1 .A49 MRR Alc.

COMMUNISM--SOCIETIES, ETC.--
BIBLIOGRAPHY.
Sworakowski, Witold S. The Communist
International and its front
organizations; Stanford, Calif.,
Hoover Institution on War,
Revolution, and Peace, 1965. 493 p.
016.33544 65-12622
Z7164.S67 S86 MRR Alc.

COMMUNISM--SOCIETIES, ETC.--DIRECTORIES.
Directory of Soviet international
front organisations. [n.p., 1970] 1
v. (various pagings) 335.43/062/1
78-27355
HX11 .D523 1970 MRR Alc.

Phelps-Fetherston, Iain. Soviet
international front organizations,
New York, Praeger [1965] 178 p.
335.44 65-20503
HX11 .P5 MRR Alc.

COMMUNISM--CHINA.
Hou, Fu-wu. A short history of
Chinese communism, completely updated
Englewood Cliffs, N.J., Prentice-
Hall [1973] x, 278 p. [$6.95]
915.1/03/5 73-9532
DS777.55 .H575 1973 MRR Alc.

COMMUNISM--CHINA--HISTORY.
Brandt, Conrad. A documentary
history of Chinese communism,
London, Allen & Unwin [1952] 552 p.
951.04 52-67189
DS775 .B7 MRR Alc.

COMMUNISM--CZECHOSLOVAK REPUBLIC.
Taborsky, Edward. Communism in
Czechoslovakia, 1948-1960.
Princeton, N.J., Princeton University
Press, 1961. xii, 628 p.   943.704
61-7425
DB215.5 .T3 MRR Alc.

COMMUNISM--EUROPE.
Griffith, William E., ed. Communism
in Europe; Cambridge, Mass., M.I.T.
Press [1964-   v.   335.43/094 64-
21409
HX44 .G727 MRR Alc.

COMMUNISM--HUNGARY.
Vali, Ferenc Albert, Rift and
revolt in Hungary; Cambridge,
Harvard University Press, 1961.
xvii, 590 p.   943.9105 61-13745
DB956 .V3 MRR Alc.

COMMUNISM--RUSSIA.
Bauer, Raymond Augustine, How the
Soviet system works: Cambridge,
Harvard University Press, 1956. xiv,
274 p.   947.085* 56-8549
DK266 .B26 MRR Alc.

Daniels, Robert Vincent, ed. A
documentary history of communism;
New York, Random House [1960] 321,
393 p.   335.4309 60-6380
HX40 .D3 MRR Alc.

Kulski, Władysław Wszebór, Peaceful
co-existence; Chicago, H. Regnery
Co., 1959. xxi, 662 p.   59-13052
DK266 .K8 MRR Alc.

COMMUNISM--UNITED STATES.
Draper, Theodore, American communism
and Soviet Russia, New York, Viking
Press, 1960. 558 p.   335.430973 60-
7672
HX83 .D68 MRR Alc.

COMMUNISM--UNITED STATES--1917-
Howe, Irving. The American Communist
Party, Boston, Beacon Press [c1957]
x, 593 p.   329.8 58-6243
JK2391.C5 H68 MRR Alc.

United States. Congress. House.
Committee on Un-American Activities.
Guide to subversive organizations and
publications. 1951- Washington.
335.4 51-60395
HX89.A28 MRR Alc Latest edition

COMMUNISM--UNITED STATES--1917- --
BIBLIOGRAPHY.
Delaney, Robert Finley. The
literature of communism in America;
Washington, Catholic University of
America Press, 1962. xii, 433 p.
016.33543 62-6923
Z7164.S67 D4 MRR Alc.

Seidman, Joel Isaac, Communism in
the United States; Ithaca [N.Y.]
Cornell University Press [1969] xii,
526 p.   016.33543/0973 69-12427
Z7164.S67 S38 MRR Alc.

COMMUNISM--UNITED STATES--1917- --
INDEXES.
United States. Congress. Senate.
Committee on Government Operations.
Congressional investigations of
communism and subversive activities;
Washington, U.S. Govt. Print. Off.,
1956. xvi, 382 p.   56-62374
Z7164.S67 U5 MRR Alc.

COMMUNIST COUNTRIES.
Brzezinski, Zbigniew K., The Soviet
bloc, unity and conflict, Rev. and
enl. ed. Cambridge, Harvard
University Press, 1967. xviii, 599
p.   909.82 67-12531
D847 .B7 1967 MRR Alc.

COMMUNIST COUNTRIES--BIBLIOGRAPHY.
Hammond, Thomas Taylor. Soviet
foreign relations and world
communism; Princeton, N.J.,
Princeton University Press, 1965.
xxiv, 1240 p.   016.32747 63-7069
Z2517.R4 H3 MRR Alc.

COMMUNIST COUNTRIES--COMMERCE--
DIRECTORIES.
Black, Sam, Businessman's guide to
the centrally planned economy
countries: Albania, Bulgaria, China,
Cuba, Czechoslovakia, German
Democratic Republic, Hungary, Poland,
Romania, USSR, Yugoslavia; London,
Modino Press, 1972. 186 p. [£3.50
($9.00 U.S.)] 382/.09171/7 73-
157217
HF4050 .A2 MRR Alc.

COMMUNIST COUNTRIES--DICTIONARIES.
Slavonic encyclopaedia, New York,
Philosophical Library [1949] xi,
1445 p.   936.7 48-6489
D377 .S58 MRR Alc.

COMMUNIST INTERNATIONAL--BIBLIOGRAPHY.
Sworakowski, Witold S. The Communist
International and its front
organizations; Stanford, Calif.,
Hoover Institution on War,
Revolution, and Peace, 1965. 493 p.
016.33544 65-12622
Z7164.S67 S86 MRR Alc.

COMMUNIST INTERNATIONAL--BIOGRAPHY.
Lazic, Branko M. Biographical
dictionary of the Comintern,
Stanford, Calif., Hoover Institution
Press, 1973. xxxxii, 458 p.
[$15.00] 329/.072/0922 B 72-187265

HX11.I5 L3378 MRR Biog.

COMMUNIST PARTIES.
Griffith, William E., ed. Communism
in Europe; Cambridge, Mass., M.I.T.
Press [1964-   v.   335.43/094 64-
21409
HX44 .G727 MRR Alc.

United States. Dept. of State. Bureau
of Intelligence and Research. World
strength of the Communist Party
organizations; annual report.
[Washington] 329/.07 56-60986
HX40 .U626 MRR Alc Latest edition

COMMUNIST PARTIES--HISTORY--HANDBOOKS,
MANUALS, ETC.
Sworakowski, Witold S. World
communism; a handbook, 1918-1965,
Stanford, Calif., Hoover Institution
Press, 1973. xv, 576 p. [$25.00]
335.43/09 70-149798
HX40 .S89 MRR Alc.

COMMUNIST PARTIES--YEARBOOKS.
Yearbook on international communist
affairs. 1966- Stanford, Calif.,
Hoover Institution Press. 335.43/05
67-31024
HX1 .Y4 MRR Alc Latest edition

COMMUNIST PARTY OF THE UNITED STATES OF
AMERICA.
Howe, Irving. The American Communist
Party, Boston, Beacon Press [c1957]
x, 593 p.   329.8 58-6243
JK2391.C5 H68 MRR Alc.

COMMUNISTS.
Lazic, Branko M. Biographical
dictionary of the Comintern,
Stanford, Calif., Hoover Institution
Press, 1973. xxxii, 458 p.
[$15.00] 329/.072/0922 B 72-187265

HX11.I5 L3378 MRR Biog.

Leaders of the communist world. New
York, Free Press [1971] xv, 632 p.
335.43/0922 B 74-84751
HX23 .L4 MRR Biog.

COMMUNISTS--CHINA.
Chinese Communist who's who. Taipei,
Institute of International Relations,
1970-71. 2 v. [$20.00 per vol.]
72-169537
DS778.A1 C4913 MRR Biog.

Klein, Donald W. Biographic
dictionary of Chinese communism, 1921-
1965 Cambridge, Mass., Harvard
University Press, 1971. 2 v. (1194
p.) [$30.00] 951.04/922 B 69-
12725
DS778.A1 K55 1971 MRR Biog.

COMMUNITY ANTENNA TELEVISION.
35-mile CATV zone maps and full text
of FCC CATV inquiry; Washington,
Television Digest, Inc. [1969] 79 p.
[9.50] 384.55/4 78-80859
HE8700.8.U5 T45 MRR Alc.

COMMUNITY ANTENNA TELEVISION--UNITED
STATES--DIRECTORIES.
Broadcasting sourcebook C A T V.
[Washington] Broadcasting
Publications Inc.] 384.55/47 73-
615665
HE8700.7.C6 B75 MRR Ref Desk
Latest edition

COMMUNITY CENTERS.
see also Recreation

COMMUNITY CENTERS--DIRECTORIES.
National Federation of Settlements
and Neighborhood Centers. Directory
of member houses. New York.
361/.0025/7 68-47249
HV4193 .N3 MRR Alc Latest edition

COMMUNITY DEVELOPMENT.
see also Rehabilitation, Rural

COMMUNITY DEVELOPMENT--UNITED STATES.
Baker, John Austin, Guide to Federal
programs for rural development;
Washington, U.S. Govt. Print. Off.,
1971 [i.e. 1972] ii, 576 p. [$2.50
(paper cover)] 309.2/63/0973 72-
601448
HN90.C6 B352 MRR Alc.

COMMUNITY DEVELOPMENT--UNITED STATES--DIRECTORIES.
Community action agency atlas. 1969-
[Washington] 338.973 71-614540
HC110.P63 A28 MRR Alc Latest
edition

COMMUNITY MENTAL HEALTH SERVICES.
Child and adolescent psychiatry,
sociocultural and community
psychiatry. 2d ed. [Rev. and
expanded] New York, Basic Books
[1974] xi, 858 p. 616.8/9/008 s
616.8/9 72-89185
RC435 .A562 vol. 2 MRR Alc.

COMMUNITY NEWSPAPERS.
Byerly, Kenneth R. Community
Journalism. [1st ed.] Philadelphia,
Chilton Co., Book Division [1961]
435 p. 070.48 61-7188
PN4784.C73 B9 MRR Alc.

COMMUNITY ORGANIZATION.
see also Local government

COMMUNITY POWER--BIBLIOGRAPHY.
Leif, Irving P. Community power and
decision-making: Metuchen, N.J.,
Scarecrow Press, 1974. vi, 170 p.
016.30115/5 74-4171
Z7164.C842 L43 MRR Alc.

COMORO--GOVERNMENT PUBLICATIONS--BIBLIOGRAPHY.
United States. Library of Congress.
African Section. Madagascar and
adjacent islands; Washington,
General Reference and Bibliography
Division, Reference Department,
Library of Congress;[for sale by the
Superintendent of Documents, U.S.
Govt. Print. Off.] 1965. xiii, 58 p.
65-61703
Z663.285 .M3 MRR Alc.

COMPANIES.
American University, Washington, D.C.
Bureau of Social Science Research.
Directory of organizations in
opinion, and related research outside
the United States. Washington,
c1956. 1 v. (various pagings) 57-
17609
HM263 .A77 MRR Alc.

The Bulk carrier register, London,
H. Clarkson & Co. Ltd., 1969. xxii,
290 p. [10/-/-] 387.2/45/0216 71-
462684
HE566.F7 B8 MRR Alc.

The Directory of shipowners,
shipbuilders, and marine engineers.
London, Engineering, Chemical &
Marine Press [etc.] 25-4199
HE565.A3 D5 MRR Alc Latest edition

International petroleum register.
[1st]- ed.; 1917/18- New
York[etc.] Palmer Publications [etc.]
18-6917
TN867 .P4 Sci RR Latest edition /
MRR Alc Latest edition

Jane's world railways. 1st- ed.;
1950/51- London, B. P. C. Publishing
Ltd. [etc.] 385.05 51-29160
TF1 .J3 Sci RR Latest edition /
MRR Alc Latest edition

Mining year book. London, W. E.
Skinner [etc.] 338.2058 50-18583
"Established 1887."
TN13 .M7 MRR Alc Latest edition /
Sci RR Latest edition

Moody, Bert. Ocean ships [New ed.].
London, Allan 1967. vii, 359 p.
[25/-] 387.2/4 72-472168
HE565 .A5M6 1967 MRR Alc.

Non-ferrous metal works of the world.
1st- ed.; 1967- London, Metal
Bulletin Books. 68-39821
HD9539 .A1W62 MRR Alc Latest edition

The Oil and petroleum year book.
London ca 12-1196
HG4821 .O4 MRR Alc Latest edition

The Paper makers' & merchants'
directory of all nations. London,
Admark Directories Limited London
[etc.] 57-24181
TS1088 .P5 Sci RR Latest edition /
MRR Alc Latest edition

Phillips, S. C. & Co., London.
Phillips' paper trade directory of
the world. London. 338.4/7/6762025
74-642473
TS1088 .P8 MRR Alc Latest edition
/ Sci RR Latest edition

Répertoire international de
l'industrie automobile. Paris,
Bureau permanent international des
constructeurs d'automobiles. 52-
38439
TL12 .R46 MRR Alc Latest edition

Stores of the world. London, Newman
Books. 380.1025 66-9836
Began publication in 1961.
HF54.G7 S8 MRR Alc Latest edition

United Piece Dye Works. Guidebook to
man-made textile fibers and textured
yarns of the world 3d ed. New York,
[1969] 345 p. 677/.4 68-28677
TS1548.5 .U5 1969 MRR Alc.

Westminster directory of the world.
London, Tamar Publishing Co. Ltd.,
1968. 564 p. [unpriced] 380.1/025
73-403663
HF54.G7 W46 MRR Alc.

World airline record. [1st]- ed.;
1950/51- Chicago, Roadcap Associates
[etc.] 387.72 51-3819
TL501 .W675 Sci RR Latest edition
/ MRR Alc Latest edition

World nuclear directory. 1st- ed.;
1961- London, Harrap Research
Publications [etc.] 62-52178
QC770 .W65 Sci RR Latest edition /
MRR Alc Latest edition

Wragg, David W. World's air fleets
2nd (revised) ed. London, Allan,
1969. 176 p. [25/-] 387.7/065 73-
432844
HE9768 .W7 1969 MRR Alc.

COMPANIES--AFRICA, SOUTH.
Beerman's all mining year book.
Johannesburg [etc.] Combined
Publishers [etc.] 55-32931
HD9506.A5 R5 Sci RR Latest edition
/ MRR Alc Latest edition

Beerman's financial year book of
southern Africa; 1947/48-
Johannesburg [etc.] Combined
Publishers [etc.] 332.6/0968 48-
17050
HG5850.S6 S67 MRR Alc Latest
edition

Johannesburg. Stock Exchange. The
Stock Exchange handbook. 1967-
Johannesburg, Flesch Financial
Publications. 332.63/0968 68-130426

HG5841 .J63 MRR Alc Latest edition

South African mining and engineering
year book and directory.
Johannesburg. 622 gs 29-261
TN119.S7 A7 MRR Alc Latest edition

COMPANIES--ARIZONA.
Arizona directory of manufacturers.
Phoenix. 55-36441
T12 .A72 Sci RR Latest edition /
MRR Alc Latest edition

COMPANIES--ASIA.
Asian buyers' guide to Republic of
China, Hong Kong, Japan, Republic of
Singapore, and Thailand. 1st- ed.;
1968- Hong Kong, International Pub.
Co. 670 .25/5 68-7584
HF3763 .A82 MRR Alc Latest edition

COMPANIES--AUSTRALIA.
Australian directory of exports.
1964/65- ed. Melbourne, P.
Isaacson Pty. 65-44637
HF3943 .A84 MRR Alc Latest edition

The Business who's who of Australia.
1964- Sydney, R. G. Riddell. 64-
56752
HF5292 .B795 MRR Alc Latest
edition

The "Digest" year book of public
companies of Australia & New Zealand.
Sydney, N.S.W., Jobson's
publications pty. limited. 338.058
45-26276
Publication began in 1928.
HD2927 .D5 MRR Alc Latest edition

Jobson's mining year book. Sydney,
Jobson's Financial Services. 66-2200

HG5899.M4 J6 MRR Alc Latest
edition

Potter (Ian) & Company. Selected
Australian ordinary shares.
Melbourne. 66-99703
HG5894 .P6 MRR Alc Latest edition

Wheelwright, Edward Lawrence.
Anatomy of Australian manufacturing
industry; Sydney, Law Book Co.,
1967. xvii, 433 p. [$13.99 Aust.]
338.7/4/0994 67-95586
HD2927 .W45 MRR Alc.

COMPANIES--AUSTRIA.
Almanach der österreichischen
Aktiengesellschaften. Wien [Wiener
Borsen-Kurier, Verlag F. Brabec,
etc.] 62-27652
Began publication in 1927.
HG4007 .A6 MRR Alc Latest edition

Finanz-Compass: 79.- Jahrg.; 1950-
Wien, Compass-Verlag. 54-17734
HG5451 .F5 MRR Alc Latest edition

Handels-Compass: 1946/47- Wien. 50-
20277
HF5166 .H3 MRR Alc Latest edition

Made in Austria. Wien, Jupiter-
Verlag. 380/.025/436 68-77958
HF3543 .M3 MRR Alc Latest edition

COMPANIES--BELGIUM.
Le Recueil financier; Bruxelles, É.
Bruylant. 332.63 49-52017
Began publication in 1893.
HG5551 .R42 MRR Alc Latest edition

COMPANIES--BOSTON.
Directory of directors in the city of
Boston and vicinity. 1905- Boston,
Bankers Service Co. 05-8359
HG4058.B7 MRR Alc Latest edition

COMPANIES--BRAZIL.
Brasil, sua industria e exportação.
São Paulo [etc.] Cadastro Delta
[etc.] 53-19341
HC186 .B683 MRR Alc Latest edition

COMPANIES--CALIFORNIA.
California manufacturers annual
register. 1948- Los Angeles, Times-
Mirror Press. 670.58 48-3418
T12 .D48 Sci RR Latest edition /
MRR Alc Latest edition

Personnel directory of California oil
and gas producers. Los Angeles,
Conservation Committee of California
Oil Producers. 338.2/7/282025794 72-
622324
HD9567.C2 C6 MRR Alc Latest
edition

Southern California business
directory and buyers guide. Los
Angeles, Los Angeles Area Chamber of
Commerce. 380.1/025/7949 74-641762
HF5065.C2 S66 MRR Alc Latest
edition

COMPANIES--CANADA.
Canadian gas utilities directory.
Toronto, Canadian Gas Association.
338.4/7/3636302571 72-626910
TP714 .D5 MRR Alc Latest edition

Canadian mines handbook. 1935-
Toronto. 338.2065 35-19088
HG5159.M4C3 MRR Alc Latest edition

Canadian Newspaper Service, ltd.
National reference book on Canadian
business personalities, [Montreal]
29-2668
F1001 .C277 MRR Biog Latest
edition

Canadian trade index. [1900]-
Toronto, Canadian Manufacturers'
Association. 14-21699
HF3223 .C25 MRR Alc Latest edition

The Financial post survey of oils.
Montreal, New York, Maclean-Hunter
Pub. Co. 338.2728 52-31395
HD9574.C2 F5 MRR Alc Latest
edition

Financial times of Canada, Montreal.
A guide to 100 Canadian stocks; [2d
rev. ed., [Montreal] 1968. 61 p.
332.63/223/0971 71-499820
HG5158 .F53 1968 MRR Alc.

The National list of advertisers.
Toronto, Maclean-Hunter Pub. Co. 56-
46268
HF5808.C2 N3 MRR Alc Latest
edition

Northern Miner Press Limited,
Toronto. Canadian mines register of
dormant and defunct companies.
Toronto [1960] 419 p. 622.065 60-
23311
HD9506.C22 N6 1960 MRR Alc.

Noyes Development Corporation.
Pharmaceutical firms, 3d ed. Park
Ridge, N.J. [1965] 91 p.
615.1900257 65-21984
HD9666.3 .N6 1965 MRR Alc.

Oil directory of Canada. Tulsa,
Okla., C. L. Cooper. 57-49796
TN867 .O52 Sci RR Latest edition /
MRR Alc Latest edition

COMPANIES--CANADA--BIBLIOGRAPHY.
Harvard University. Graduate School
of Business Administration. Baker
Library. Studies in enterprise;
Boston, 1957. xiv, 169 p.
016.33874 57-11481
Z7164.C81 H26 1957 MRR Alc.

COMPANIES--DENMARK.
Kompas; 1- udg.; 1960- København,
Forlaget Kompas-Danmark [etc.] 63-
52026
HF3643 .K58 MRR Alc Latest edition

COMPANIES--EGYPT.
The Stock exchange year-book of
Egypt. Cairo, Egypt. 332.63 45-
33051
Publication began with issue for
1939?
HG5831 .S75 MRR Alc Latest edition

COMPANIES--EUROPE.
Brauereien und Mälzereien in Europa.
51.- Aufl.: 1962/63- Darmstadt,
Hoppenstedt Wirtschaftsverlag.
338.4/7/66330254 72-626675
    TP572 .B7 MRR Alc Latest edition

Chemical guide to Europe. [1st]-
ed.; 1961- Park Ridge, N.J. [etc.]
Noyes Data Corporation. 660/.025/4
68-55969
    HD8656.A1 C18 Sci RR Latest
    edition / MRR Alc Latest edition

European directory of economic and
corporate planning, 1973-74; Epping,
Gower Press, 1973. xvii, 442 p.
[£8.50] 309.2/12/0254 74-162022
    HD31 .E83 1973 MRR Alc.

European metals directory. [1st ed.]
London, Quin Press [1964] 375 p.
66-46321
    TS370 .E8 MRR Alc.

Henderson, G. P., ed. European
companies: 3rd ed. Beckenham, CBD
Research Ltd, 1972. iii-xiii, 224 p.
[£10.00 ($30.00 U.S.)]
016.3387/4/094 73-151246
    HC240 .H458 1972 MRR Ref Desk.

Jane's major companies of Europe.
1st- ed.:1965- London, S. Marston
& Co. [etc.] 65-2174
    HG5421 .J35 MRR Alc Latest edition

Noyes Data S.A. Key European
industrials 1970. Zug, Switzerland,
Noyes Data Corp.; Park Ridge, N.J.,
Noyes Data Corp. [c1970] 2 v.
[85.00DF per vol.] 338/.0025/4 78-
129041
    HD9720.3 .N65 MRR Alc.

Noyes Development Corporation.
Chemical guide to Europe. [3d ed.]
Pearl River, N.Y., 1965. 137 p.
661.0584 65-13150
    TP12 .N6 1965 MRR Alc.

Noyes Development Corporation.
European pharmaceutical firms, 1964.
Pearl River, N.Y., c1963. 84 p. 64-
397
    HD9665.3 .N6 MRR Alc.

Noyes Development Corporation. Food
guide to Europe. Park Ridge, N.J.,
1969. 130 p. [20.00] 338.1/9/4
70-75386
    HD9015.E82 N6 MRR Alc.

Who owns whom. Continental edition.
1st-   ed.; 1961/62- London, O. W.
Roskill. 63-24027
    HG4132.Z5 W5 MRR Alc Latest
    edition

COMPANIES--EUROPE, EASTERN.
Black, Sam, Businessman's guide to
the centrally planned economy
countries: Albania, Bulgaria, China,
Cuba, Czechoslovakia, German
Democratic Republic, Hungary, Poland,
Romania, USSR, Yugoslavia; London,
Modino Press, 1972. 186 p. [£3.50
($9.00 U.S.)] 382/.09171/7 73-
157217
    HF4050 .A2 MRR Alc.

COMPANIES--FINLAND.
Finnish foreign trade directory.
Helsinki, Finnish Foreign Trade
Association. 53-34818
    Began publication with issue for
1921.
    HF3631 .F5 MRR Alc Latest edition

COMPANIES--FLORIDA.
Florida. State Chamber of Commerce,
Jacksonville. Directory of Florida
industries. 1943/44- Jacksonville.
670.58 43-17176
    T12 .F6 Sci RR Latest edition /
    MRR Alc Latest edition

COMPANIES--FRANCE.
Annuaire-Chaix. Paris, Imprimerie
Chaix. ca 18-193
    HG5471 .A6 MRR Alc Latest edition

Annuaire Desfossés; Paris, Cote
Desfosses [etc.] 332.63 46-39086
    HG5471 .A64 MRR Alc Latest edition

Répertoire général alphabétique
des valeurs cotées en France et es
valeurs non cotées. Paris,
Éditions financières alphabétiques.
47-42094
    HG5471 .R4 MRR Alc Latest edition

COMPANIES--GERMANY.
Handbuch der deutschen Aktien-
Gesellschaften. Darmstadt [etc.]
Hoppenstedt [etc.] ca 15-275
    HG5491 .H4 MRR Alc Latest edition

Handbuch der Direktoren und
Aufsichtsräte. 1967/68- Berlin,
Finanz- und Korrespondenz-Verlag Dr.
G. Mossner. 72-626450
    HG4156 .H35 MRR Alc Latest edition

Handbuch der Grossunternehmen. [1.]-
Aufl.; 1941- Darmstadt [etc.]
Hoppenstedt [etc.] 338.058 47-37159
    HC281 .H28 MRR Alc Latest edition

Hiller, Helmut. Wörterbuch des
Buches. 3., durchgesehene und erw.
Aufl. Frankfurt a. M., Klostermann
(1967,) 341 p. [DM 18.50 (unb. DM
16.50)] 68-86779
    Z118 .H55 1967 MRR Alc.

Saling Aktienführer. Darmstadt,
Hoppenstedt. 57-40599
    Began publication with vol. for
1935/36;
    HG5501 .S3 MRR Alc Latest edition

Wer baut Maschinen. Darmstadt,
Hoppenstedt. 53-30932
    TJ1170 .W4 MRR Alc Latest edition

**COMPANIES--GERMANY (FEDERAL REPUBLIC,
1949-)**
Die Grossen 500 [i.e. Fünfhundert]
1970- Düsseldorf, Droste Verlag.
70-612586
    HD2859 .G7 MRR Alc Latest edition

COMPANIES--GREAT BRITAIN.
The British textile industry. 80th-
ed.; 1970/71- Croydon, Eng., T.
Skinner. 677/.0025/42 71-649662
    TS1312 .B76 MRR Alc Latest edition

Building societies year book.
London. 332.3206242 39-31431
    First issued in 1927.
    HG2121 .B84 MRR Alc Latest edition

The Consulting engineers who's who &
year book. London, Norwood
Industrial Publications Ltd.[etc.]
620.942 49-25787
    Began with vol. for 1947.
    TA1 .C774 Sci RR Latest edition /
    MRR Biog Latest edition

Dun & Bradstreet's guide to key
British enterprises. 1961- London.
62-41097
    HC252 .D8 MRR Alc Latest edition

European directory of economic and
corporate planning, 1973-74; Epping,
Gower Press, 1973. xvii, 442 p.
[£8.50] 309.2/12/0254 74-162022
    HD31 .E83 1973 MRR Alc.

"Flight" directory of British
aviation. 1970- Kingston upon
Thames, Kelly Directories Ltd.
629.13/0025/42 76-618594
    TL512 .F48 Sci RR Latest edition /
    MRR Alc Latest edition

Guide to British employers. London,
Cornmarket Press. 331.702/0942 72-
27261
    HF5382.5.G7 G8 MRR Alc Latest
    edition

Industrial research in Britain. 7th
ed. [St. Peter Port, Guernsey] F.
Hodgson [1972] 889 p. 607/.2/42
73-190253
    T177.G7 I52 1972 MRR Alc.

The Insurance directory & year book.
London [etc.] Buckley Press [etc.]
368.058 51-18382
    Began publication in 1840.
    HG8596 .I53 MRR Alc Latest edition

Kompass; 1st- ed.; 1962- Croydon,
Eng., Kompass Publishers [etc.] 63-
59135
    T12.5.G7 K6 MRR Alc Latest edition

Register of defunct and other
companies removed from the Stock
Exchange official year-book. 1946-
Croydon, Eng. [etc.] T. Skinner.
332.63 51-24150
    HG5431 .R44 MRR Alc Latest edition

Skinner's British textile register.
1st- ed.; 1973- Croydon, Eng.,
Thomas Skinner Directories [etc.] [£10.50]
338.4/7/677002542 74-644855
    TS1312 .S55 MRR Alc Latest edition

Skinner's hosiery and knit goods
directory. Croydon, Eng. [etc.] T.
Skinner. 338.4767766 51-18825
    TT679 .S5 MRR Alc Latest edition

The Stock exchange official yearbook. [1st]- 1934- Croydon, Eng.
[etc.] T. Skinner [etc.] 332.6305
34-16479
    HG5431 .S82 MRR Alc Latest edition

Who owns whom. U. K. edition.
London, O. W. Roskill. 59-52911
    Began publication in 1958.
    HG4135.Z5 W5 MRR Alc Latest
    edition

COMPANIES--GREECE, MODERN.
Oikonomikos hodegos ton en Helladi
anonymon hetaireion kai
hetaireion periorismenes
euthynes. 1964- Athens, ICAP
Hellas Ltd. 70-401893
    HF5175 .O4 MRR Alc Latest edition

COMPANIES--HAWAII.
State of Hawaii business directory.
1967- Honolulu, Kearney Co.
381/.45/00025969 66-18386
    HF5319.H3 S73 MRR Alc Latest
    edition

COMPANIES--HONGKONG.
Hong Kong dollar directory.
Hongkong, Local Property & Printing
Co. [etc.] 53-29957
    HF3789.H6 H64 MRR Alc Latest
    edition / MRR Alc Latest edition

Kompass; register of Hong Kong
industry and commerce. 2- ed.;
1972- Hong Kong, Kompass Asia.
338/.0025/5125 74-897962
    HC497.H6 K58 MRR Alc Latest
    edition

O. K. business directory. Hongkong
[O.K. Print Press] 53-30505
    HF3779.H65 O15 MRR Alc Latest
    edition

COMPANIES--IDAHO.
Idaho. Dept. of Commerce and
Development. Idaho directory of
manufacturers, 1967-1968. Boise
[1968] 83 p. [3.50] 338.4/09796
78-625584
    HD9727.I2 A35 MRR Alc.

Idaho manufacturers directory.
[Chicago, Manufacturers' News, inc.]
66-97800
    HC107.I2 I3 MRR Alc Latest edition

COMPANIES--ILLINOIS.
Where to buy, where to sell; 1941-
ed. Chicago, Manufacturers' news.
42-14309
    T12 .W5 Sci RR Latest edition /
    MRR Alc Latest edition

COMPANIES--INDIA.
Calcutta. Stock Exchange. Official
year book. Calcutta, Calcutta Stock
Exchange Assn. 332.6 49-39127
    HG5740 .C3 MRR Alc Latest edition

Kothari's economic and industrial
guide of India. 29th- ed.; 1971/72-
Madras, Kothari. [$25.00]
338/.0954 72-904460
    HG5731 .I57 MRR Alc Latest edition

COMPANIES--INDIANA.
The Indiana industrial directory.
Indianapolis, Ind., Indiana State
Chamber of Commerce. 670.9772 42-
6661
    T12 .I63 Sci RR Latest edition /
    MRR Alc Latest edition

COMPANIES--IRELAND.
Handbook of Irish securities, etc.
London, Straker Bros. ltd. 55-32941
    HG5443.I7 H3 MRR Alc Latest
    edition

COMPANIES--ITALY.
Associazione fra le società italiane
per azioni. Società italiane per
azioni; notizie statistiche. Roma.
54-44415
    HG4166 .A83 MRR Alc Latest edition

Kompass; repertorio generale
dell'economia italiana; register of
Italian industry and commerce.
Milano, ETAS-KOMPASS Edizioni per
l'informazione economica. 65-30593
    Began publication with 1962/63
edition.
    HF3583 .K6 MRR Alc Latest edition

COMPANIES--JAPAN.
1972 handbook of Japanese
financial/industrial combines; San
Francisco, Pacific Basin Reports
[1972] 83 l. [$25.00]
338.8/5/02552 73-150829
    HD2756.J3 N55 MRR Alc.

J I T; Tokyo, [Kojunsha
International Publishers]
382/.025/52 68-51013
    HF54.J3 J2 MRR Alc Latest edition

Japan company directory. 1957-
[Tokyo] Oriental economist. 62-29293
    HC161 .J35 MRR Alc Latest edition

Japan trade guide, with a
comprehensive mercantile directory.
1935- [Tokyo] JiJi Press [etc.]
338.0952 35-20033
    HF3823 .J35 MRR Alc Latest edition

The President directory. [Tokyo,
Diamond-Time Co.] [$8.00]
338.7/4/02552 73-645008
    Began in 1967.
    HC461 .P83 MRR Alc Latest edition

Standard trade index of Japan.
Tokyo, Japan Chamber of Commerce and
Industry. 55-36368
    HF3823 .S7 MRR Alc Latest edition

COMPANIES--JAPAN. (Cont.)
Tokyo news business directory. 1950-
Tokyo, Tokyo News Service.
338/.0025 51-14706
    HF5257.T6 T57 MRR Alc Latest
    edition

COMPANIES--KENTUCKY.
Kentucky directory of manufacturers.
1949- Frankfort. 602/.5/769 52-
62224
    T12 .K56 Sci RR Latest edition* /
    MRR Alc Latest edition

COMPANIES--LATIN AMERICA.
Noyes Development Corporation. Latin
American chemical guide, 1964. Pearl
River, N.Y., 1964. 94 p. 338.47661
64-21638
    HD9655.L3 N6 MRR Alc.

COMPANIES--MEXICO.
Noyes Development Corporation.
Pharmaceutical firms, 3d ed. Park
Ridge, N.J. [1965] 91 p.
615.1900257 65-21984
    HD9666.3 .N6 1965 MRR Alc.

COMPANIES--MICHIGAN.
The Directory of Michigan
manufacturers. Detroit, Mich.,
Manufacturer Pub. Co. 338.409774 41-
12489
    HD9723 .D43 Sci RR Latest edition
    / MRR Alc Latest edition

COMPANIES--MILAN (PROVINCE)
Annuario industriale della provincia
di Milano. [Milano, Associazione
industriale lombarda] a 52-7615
    HC307.M5 A5 MRR Alc Latest edition

COMPANIES--NETHERLANDS.
Kompass; informatiewerk over het
Nederlandse bedrijfsleven. Den Haag,
Kompass Nederland N.V. 72-620607
    Began with vol. for 1965/66.
    HF3613 .K58 MRR Alc Latest edition

Nederlands abc voor handel en
industrie. Haarlem, ABC voor Handel
en Industrie. 63-36606
    HF3613 .N4 MRR Alc Latest edition

Textiel adresboek van de Nederlandse
textiel-industrie en groothandel. 6.
geheel opnieuw bewerkte uitg.
Amsterdam, Diligentia [1967] 674 p.
[fl 35.-] 68-81684
    HD9865.N65 T4 1967 MRR Alc.

COMPANIES--NEW ENGLAND.
Directory of New England
manufacturers. Boston, Mass., G. D.
Hall, inc. 338.40974 34-5085
    HD9723 .D45 Sci RR Latest edition
    / MRR Alc Latest edition

COMPANIES--NEW HAMPSHIRE.
New Hampshire. Office of Industrial
Development. Made in New Hampshire;
[1st]- ed.; 1940- Concord. 54-
33797
    T12 .N4 MRR Alc Latest edition

COMPANIES--NEW JERSEY.
New Jersey State industrial
directory, New York [etc.] 13-33036
    Began publication with 1901 issue.
    HC107.N5 N45 Sci RR Latest edition
    / MRR Alc Latest edition

COMPANIES--NEW YORK (STATE)
Beverage media. Blue book. New
York. 178.4 51-38397
    HD9352 .B4 MRR Alc latest edition

New York State industrial directory.
New York. 64-39295
    HC107.N7 N45 Sci RR Latest
    edition* / MRR Alc Latest edition

COMPANIES--NEW ZEALAND.
The "Digest" year book of public
companies of Australia & New Zealand.
Sydney, N.S.W., Jobson's
publications pty. limited. 338.058
45-26276
    Publication began in 1928.
    HD2927 .D5 MRR Alc Latest edition

The New Zealand business who's who.
Wellington, L. T. Watkins, ltd. 338
51-32889
    Began in 1935.
    HC621 .N4 MRR Alc Latest edition

COMPANIES--NORWAY.
Haandbok over norske obligationer og
aktier, Oslo. 24-10346
    HG4207 .H3 MRR Alc Latest edition

COMPANIES--PENNSYLVANIA.
Industrial directory of the
Commonwealth of Pennsylvania. 1st-
1913- Harrisburg. 14-31832
    HC107.P4 A28 Sci RR Latest edition
    / MRR Alc Latest edition

COMPANIES--RHODE ISLAND.
Rhode Island directory of
manufacturers and list of commercial
establishments. Providence.
670.58745 59-62618
    HC107 .R4A158 Sci RR Latest
    edition / MRR Alc Latest edition

COMPANIES--SPAIN.
Anuario espanol de empresas.
Madrid, Editorial Financiera Alfa
Omega. 338/.0025/46 74-646231
    HG4216.Z5 A65 MRR Alc Latest
    edition

Anuario financiero. Bilbao, Spain.
31-28812
    "Founded in 1914."
    HG61 .A6 MRR Alc Latest edition

Anuario financiero y de sociedades
anonimas de Espana. Madrid,
Editorial Sopec. 74-642352
    Began with 1916.
    HG5631 .A47 MRR Alc Latest edition

Directorio de consejeros y
directores. ed. 1961/62- Madrid.
64-36554
    HC382 .D5 MRR Alc Latest edition

Kompass; manual de información de la
economía española. 1.- ed.; 1960-
Madrid, Kompass España, S.A. 62-
65190
    HF3683 .K6 MRR Alc Latest edition

COMPANIES--SWEDEN.
Some prominent Swedish companies.
Stockholm, P. A. Norstedt.
338.7/09485 78-276274
    HC372 .S64 MRR Alc Latest edition

Svensk industrikalender. Stockholm,
P. A. Norstedt [etc.] 74-642462
    HF3673 .S63 MRR Alc Latest edition

Svenska aktiebolag. Stockholm, P. A.
Norstedt. 332.6309485 24-15054
    HG4211.Z5 S8 MRR Alc Latest
    edition

Sveriges handelskalender. Stockholm,
A. Bonniers forlag. 74-642440
    Began in 1859.
    HF3673 .S8 MRR Alc Latest edition

Swedish export directory. 28th-
ed.; 1946- Stockholm, General Export
Association of Sweden. 72-623267
    HF3673 .S6 MRR Alc Latest edition

COMPANIES--SWITZERLAND.
Directory of Swiss manufacturers and
producers. 1917-   Zurich [etc.]
670.58 53-19872
    HF3703 .D5 MRR Alc Latest edition

Savoir. Genève [etc.] ATAR, S.A.
[etc.] 53-28495
    DQ444 .S3 MRR Alc Latest edition

COMPANIES--TAIWAN.
Business directory of Taiwan. 1961-
[Taipei, E. T. Tsu, etc.]
650.5851245 61-18919
    HF3829.F6 B8 MRR Alc Latest
    edition

COMPANIES--TEXAS.
Davis, James Walker. A money tree
grows in Texas; New York, Echo House
[1969] 352 p. [1.95]
338.7/4/09764 75-9616
    HG5128.T4 D37 MRR Alc.

The Texas life record; Dallas,
Record Pub. Co. 368.3 51-17253
    HG8961.T4 T4 MRR Alc Latest
    edition

COMPANIES--UNITED STATES.
A.S.T.A. manufacturers directory.
[Chicago] American Surgical Trade
Association. 617.078 60-25245
    RD76 .A2 Sci RR Latest edition* /
    MRR Alc Latest edition

The Aerospace year book. [1st]-
1919- Washington [etc.] Books, inc.
[etc.] 629.13058 19-13828
    TL501 .A563 Sci RR Latest edition
    / MRR Alc Latest edition

American Apparel Manufacturers
Association. Apparel, textile and
retail financial survey. 1st- ed.;
1971- Arlington, Va.
338.4/7/6870973 72-626946
    HD9940.U3 A567 MRR Alc Latest
    edition

American Council of Independent
Laboratories. Directory.
[Washington] 607.273 58-4459
    TA416 .A54 Sci RR Latest edition /
    MRR Alc Latest edition

American Institute of Management.
Manual of excellent managements. New
York. 658.02 56-14078
    HD2791 .A6 MRR Alc Latest edition

American Management Association.
Directory of consultant members.
1956- New York. 57-27082
    HD28 .A553 MRR Alc Latest edition

Annual directory of pipelines.
[Bayonne, N.J., Oildom Pub. Co.] 72-
626549
    TJ930 .P53 Sci RR Latest edition /
    MRR Alc Latest edition

Association of Consulting Management
Engineers. Directory of membership
and services. New York. 658.06273
59-1437
    HD28.A75 A6 MRR Alc Latest edition

Audio visual market place. 1969-
ed. New York, Bowker. 371.33/0973
69-18201
    LB1043 .A817 MRR Alc Latest
    edition

Best (A. M.) Company. Best's
insurance securities research
service; 2d ed.] Morristown, N.J.,
1969- 1 v. (loose-leaf) 332.63/2
70-11694
    HG5123.I6 B392 MRR Alc.

Best's insurance reports, life-
health. 1st- ed.; 1906/07-
Morristown, N.J. [etc.] A. M. Best
Co. [etc.] 368.3/2/0065 06-37901
    HG8943 .B3 MRR Alc Latest edition

Best's insurance reports, property-
liability. [1st]- ed.; 1899/1900-
Morristown, N.J. [etc.] A. M. Best
Co. 368.1/0065 00-3410
    HG9655 .B5 MRR Alc Latest edition

The Blue book of major homebuilders.
[Crofton, Md.] CMR Associates.
338.4/7/690802573 72-621729
    TH12.5 .B5 MRR Alc Latest edition

Bradford's directory of marketing
research agencies in the United
States and the world. [1st- ed.;
1944- Fairfax, Va. [etc.] 658.83058
44-5426
    HF5415.A2 B7 MRR Ref Desk Latest
    edition

Brewers digest. Annual buyers'
guide & directory. [1st]- 1947-
[Chicago, Siebel Pub. Co.] 663.3058
51-16022
    TP572 .B78 MRR Alc Latest edition

Brown's directory of North American
gas companies. 79th- ed.; 1964-
[Duluth] Harbrace. 338.4/7/665702573
72-620934
    TP714 .B8 Sci RR Latest edition /
    MRR Alc Latest edition

Chain store guide; [New York,
Business Guides] 647.9505873 62-
4170
    TX907 .C54 MRR Alc Latest edition

Chain store guide; directory of
leading chain stores in the United
States. 1959- [New York, Chain
Store Business Guide] 658.873058 58-
3958
    HF5468 .C415 MRR Alc Latest
    edition

Chemical guide to the United States.
[1st]- ed.; 1962- Park Ridge, N.J.
[etc.] Noyes Data Corp. 660.5873 63-
5647
    TP12 .C56 Sci RR Latest edition /
    MRR Alc Latest edition

College placement annual.
[Bethlehem, Pa.] College Placement
Council. 371.425 a 58-4606
    HF5382.5.U5 C6 MRR Ref Desk Latest
    edition

Council on Economic Priorities.
Guide to corporations; [1st ed.],
Chicago, Swallow Press [1974] iii,
393 p. [$4.95] 301.5/5 73-13212
    HD60.5.U5 C7 1974 MRR Alc.

Dairy Credit Bureau, Chicago. Dairy
credit book. Chicago. 637.116 41-
297
    HD9275 .A1D3 MRR Alc Latest
    edition

Davis, James Walker. A money tree
grows in Texas; New York, Echo House
[1969] 352 p. [1.95]
338.7/4/09764 75-9616
    HG5128.T4 D37 MRR Alc.

Davison's textile blue book. United
States and Canada. [Office ed.] 1st-
annual ed.; 1888- Ridgewood, N.J.
[etc.] Davison Pub. Co. [etc.] 99-
3738
    TS1312 .B6 MRR Alc Latest edition

Davison's textile directory for
executives and salesmen. [1st]-
ed.; 1911/12- Ridgewood, N.J. [etc.]
Davison Pub. Co. 677.058 11-19402
    TS1312 .D3 MRR Alc Latest edition

Directory: General mdse., variety
and jr. dept. store chains. 36th-
ed.; 1970- [New York, Business
Guides, inc.] 381 72-623621
    HF5468.A1 C418 MRR Alc Latest
    edition

Directory of American savings and
loan associations. 1st- ed.; 1955-
Baltimore, T. K. Sanderson
Organization. 55-41558
    HG2441 .D53 MRR Alc Latest edition

COMPANIES--UNITED STATES. (Cont.)
Directory of Central Atlantic States
manufacturers; 1.- ed.; 1950-
Baltimore, T. K. Sanderson
Organization. 670.58 50-2706
T12 .D485 Sci RR Latest edition /
MRR Alc Latest edition

Directory of chemical producers:
United States of America. Menlo
Park, Chemical Information Services,
Stanford Research Institute.
338.4/7/66002573 73-644039
HD9651.3 .D57 MRR Alc Latest
edition / Sci RR Latest edition

Directory of corporate affiliations
of major national advertisers.
Skokie, Ill., National Register Pub.
Co. 67-5728
HG4057 .A219 MRR Alc Latest
edition

Directory of department stores. 1955-
[New York, Department Store Guide]
55-39068
HF5465.U4 D47 MRR Alc Latest
edition / MRR Alc Latest edition

Directory of gas utility companies
and pipe line contractors. Tulsa,
Okla., Midwest oil register [etc.]
61-46648
TP714 .D55 MRR Alc Latest edition

Directory of industrial distributors.
New York. 650.58 53-40422
HF5035 .D485 MRR Alc Latest
edition

Directory [of] iron and steel plants.
Pittsburgh, Steel Publications
[etc.] 16-18550
TS301 .D35 Sci RR Latest edition /
MRR Alc Latest edition

Directory of movers. [Washington?]
American Movers Conference.
338.4/7/38832406273 74-4136
HE5623.A45 D572 MRR Alc Latest
edition

Directory of obsolete securities.
1970- [n.p.] Financial Information,
inc. 332.67 72-612940
HG4961 .D56 MRR Alc Latest edition

Directory of oil marketing and
wholesale distributors. Tulsa,
Okla., Midwest Oil Register. 63-
36095
HD9567.A3 D5 MRR Alc Latest
edition

Directory of producers and drilling
contractors: Louisiana, Mississippi,
Arkansas, Florida, Georgia. Tulsa,
Okla. Midwest oil register [etc.] 58-
17957
TN867 .D553 MRR Alc Latest edition

Directory of producers and drilling
contractors: Michigan, Indiana,
Illinois, Kentucky. Tulsa, Okla.,
Midwest oil register [etc.] 58-17949
TN867 .D555 MRR Alc Latest edition

Directory of United States importers.
New York, The Journal of commerce.
382.5/025/73 74-618556
HF3012 .D53 MRR Alc Latest edition

Directory of wholesale distributors
of frozen foods. New York, Quick
Frozen Foods. 664.85058 52-65843
HD9453 .D5 MRR Alc Latest edition

Dun and Bradstreet, inc. Dun's
reference book of corporate
managements. 1st- ed.; 1967- New
York. 658.1/145/02573 68-44776
HD2745 .D85 MRR Ref Desk Latest
edition

Dun and Bradstreet, inc.
Metalworking directory. New York.
62-533
Began publication with vol. for
1960.
TS203 .D8 MRR Alc Latest edition /
Sci RR Latest edition

Dun and Bradstreet, inc. Middle
market directory. 1964- New York.
64-275
HF5035 .D8 MRR Alc Latest edition

Dun and Bradstreet, inc. Million
dollar directory. 1959- New York.
338.0973 59-3033
HC102 .D8 MRR Ref Desk Latest
edition

Dun and Bradstreet, inc. Reference
book. v. [1]- 1859- New York 99-
819
HF5573 .D7 MRR Circ Latest edition

Dun and Bradstreet, inc. Reference
book: lumber and wood products
industries. [spring] 1968- New
York. 338.7/67/4002573 72-489
HD9753 .D85 MRR Alc Latest edition

Dun and Bradstreet, inc. Reference
book of manufacturers. Oct. 1965-
New York. 66-5210
HF5573 .D72 Sci RR Latest edition
/ MRR Circ Latest edition

Electrical world directory of
electric utilities. New York, McGraw-
Hill. 621.312/025/73 16-21431
TK1194 .M3 Sci RR Latest edition /
MRR Alc Latest edition

Electronic Industries Association.
Trade directory, membership list.
Washington, D.C. 338.4/7/62138106273
73-642784
TK7800 .E4383 MRR Alc Latest
edition

Electronic news financial fact book &
directory. 1st- ed.; 1962- New
York, Book Division, Fairchild
Publications. 31 cm. 62-19605
HD9696.A1 E5 MRR Alc Latest
edition

F & S index of corporate change.
Cleveland, Predicasts, inc.
338.8/3/02573 72-625662
HD2741 .F18 MRR Alc Full set

Fairchild's financial manual of
retail stores. New York, Fairchild
Publications. 658.8705873 59-4791
HG4961 .F3 MRR Alc Latest edition

Fenner, Terrence W. Inventor's
handbook New York, Chemical Pub.
Co., 1969. xi, 309 p. [7.50]
608.7 73-5567
T212 .F44 MRR Alc.

Financial world stock factographs.
38th- ed.; 1952- New York,
Guenther Publ. Corp. 332.6/78 72-
623291
HG4905 .S68 MRR Alc Latest edition

Forbes guide to common stock profits.
New York, Investors Advisory
Institute. 332.678 60-596
HG4905 .F793 MRR Alc Latest
edition

G Q guide to fashion sources. New
York, Gentlemen's quarterly.
687/.11/02573 67-116689
TT495 .G2 MRR Alc Latest edition

Gardner, Robert Edward. Five
centuries of gunsmiths, swordsmiths
and armourers, 1400-1900. [Columbus,
Ohio, W. F. Heer] 1948. 244 p. 399
48-15654
U800 .G3 MRR Alc.

Global directory of gas companies.
1973- [Houston, Tex., Editorial and
Research Staff of Gas Magazine]
[$90.00] 338.4/7/665702573 74-
645938
TP714 .G55 MRR Alc Latest edition
/ Sci RR Latest edition

Growth & acquisition guide yearbook.
1968- Cleveland, Predicasts. 72-
14099
HG4028.M4 G74 MRR Alc Full set

Hawken, William R. Copying methods
manual Chicago, Library Technology
Program, American Library Association
[1966] xv, 375 p. 655.3 66-25095
Z48 .H32 MRR Alc.

Hine's insurance counsel. Glen
Ellyn, Ill. [etc.] Hine's Legal
Directory [etc.] 07-28505
Began publication in 1907?
KF195.I5 H55 MRR Alc Latest
edition

Hudson's corporate mergers. New
York. 338.8/3/0973 74-644554
HG4915 .C67 MRR Alc Latest edition

Index of opportunity for engineers.
1968/69- New York, Macmillan.
620/.0025/73 76-1574
TA157 .I43 MRR Alc Latest edition

Industrial research laboratories of
the United States. [1st] ed.;
1920- Tempe, Ariz. [etc.] Jaques
Cattell Press [etc.] 21-26022
T176 .I65 Sci RR Latest edition /
MRR Ref Desk Latest edition

Institutional distribution's
marketing & purchasing guide.
Chicago. 338.1/0973 72-623464
HD9003 .I57 MRR Alc Latest edition

The Insurance almanac: who, what,
when and where in insurance; [1st]-
1913- New York, Underwriter Print.
and Pub. Co. 13-15895
HG8019 .I5 MRR Alc Latest edition

Investors Publishing Company, New
York. Pension funds, 1969. New
York, D. A. Campbell [c1969] xxxi,
930 p. 331.2/52 75-10552
HD7106.U5 I67 1969 MRR Alc.

The Journal of commerce
transportation telephone tickler.
[New York] 53-34476
HE9.U5 N7 MRR Alc Latest edition

Kelley, Etna M. The business
founding date directory. [1st ed.]
Scarsdale, N.Y., Morgan & Morgan
[1954] x, 228 p. 650.58 54-6999
HD2785 .K4 MRR Ref Desk.

Kelley, Richard E. The SBIC national
directory, [2d ed.] Los Angeles,
Keyfax Publications [1963] vii, 281
p. 332.672 76-12935
HG3729.U5 K38 1963 MRR Alc.

Life reports, financial and operating
results of life insurers.
[Cincinnati, National Underwriter
Company] 368.3/2/006573 72-624711
Began with vol. for 1971.
HG8955 .U5 MRR Alc Latest edition

Lockwood's directory of the paper and
allied trades. [1st]- ed.; [873/74-
New York, Lockwood Pub. Co. [etc.]
676.058 01-12840
TS1088 .L82 Sci RR Latest edition
/ MRR Alc Latest edition

MacRae's blue book. Western Springs,
Ill. [etc.] 56-36154
T12 .M3 Sci RR Latest edition /
MRR Alc Latest edition

Mahoney, Tom. The great merchants:
New and enl. ed. New York, Harper &
Row [1966] ix, 374 p. 658.8700973
67-11328
HF5429 .M288 1966 MRR Alc.

Marine Directory. [New York, Simmons-
Boardman Publ. Corp.]
338.4/7/6238025 72-623836
HE565.U5 S5 MRR Alc Latest edition

McKay, Ernest A. The Macmillan job
guide to American corporations for
college graduates, graduate students
and junior executives New York,
Macmillan [c1967] ix, 374 p.
331.115 66-20820
HF5382.5.U5 M3 MRR Alc.

The Medical and healthcare stock
market guide. 1972/73- ed.
Arcadia, Calif., International Biomedical Information Service.
332.6/7/22 72-84884
HG5123.M4 M44 MRR Alc Latest
edition

Moody's bank & finance manual:
American and foreign. New York,
Moody's Investors Service. 56-14722

HG4961 .M65 MRR Alc Latest edition

Moody's handbook of common stocks.
1965, 3d quarterly- ed. New York,
Moody's Investors Service, inc.
332.6/7 72-623694
HG4501 .M59 MRR Alc Latest edition

Moody's industrial manual: 1954-
New York, Moody's Investors Service.
56-14721
HG4961 .M67 MRR Alc Latest edition

Moody's OTC industrial manual. New
York, Moody's Investors Service.
332.67 77-649772
HG4961 .M7237 MRR Ref Desk Latest
edition

Moody's public utility manual. 1954-
New York, Moody's Investors Service.
56-3927
HG4961 .M7245 MRR Alc Latest
edition

Moody's transportation manual:
American and foreign. 1954- New
York, Moody's Investors Service. 57-
15176
HG4971 .M74 MRR Alc Latest edition

Motor/age who's who for the
automotive service industry.
Philadelphia, Chilton Company.
338.4/7/6292872202573 76-612602
HD9710.A2 M64 MRR Alc Latest
edition

National automotive directory.
[Atlanta, W. R. C. Smith] 65-9209
TL12 .N34 Sci RR Latest edition /
MRR Alc Latest edition

National directory of finance
companies. 1951- Montpelier, Ohio,
Inter-state Service Co. 332.31
332.35* 52-18620
HG2066 .N285 MRR Alc Latest
edition

National highway and airway carriers
and routes. v. 1- Mar. 1942-
Chicago, National Highway Carriers
Directory. 388.3058 42-14688
HE5623.A45 N3 MRR Alc Latest
edition

COMPANIES--UNITED STATES. (Cont.)
National Shawmut Bank, Boston. Bank directory of New England, Maine, New Hampshire, Vermont, Massachusetts, Rhode Island, Connecticut. Boston. 22-13977
    HG2441 .N35 MRR Alc Latest edition

National tank truck carrier directory. 1st- ed.; 1955-
Washington, National Tank Truck Carriers. 55-32635
    HE5623.A45 N33 MRR Alc Latest edition

New York. Stock Exchange. Listing statements of the New York Stock Exchange. New York, F. E. Fitch, inc., ca 24-283
    HG4501 .N4 MRR Alc Partial set

Noyes Development Corporation. Pharmaceutical firms, 3d ed. Park Ridge, N.J. [1965] 91 p. 615.1900257 65-21984
    HD9666.3 .N6 1965 MRR Alc.

The Optical industry and systems directory. no. 1- 1954- Pittsfield, Mass. [etc.] Optical Pub Co. a 54-6009
    HD9999.063U65 Sci RR Latest edition / MRR Alc Latest edition

P R blue book and supplement to the international Who's who in public relations. 1st- ed.; 1960-
Meriden, N.H., PR Pub. Co. 659.111 60-10969
    HM263 .P2 MRR Ref Desk Latest edition

Phelon's women's specialty stores. 1st- ed.; 1963- New York, Phelon-Sheldon & Marsar [etc.] 63-40375
    HD9940.U3 P5 MRR Alc Latest edition

Pit and quarry. Directory of the nonmetallic minerals industries. Chicago. 58-20992
    TN12 .P5 Sci RR Latest edition / MRR Alc Latest edition

Plant and product directory. 1961-
[New York?] Market Research Dept. of Fortune. 338.05873 61-12113
    HC102 .P59 MRR Alc Latest edition

The Pocket list of railroad officials. no. 1- 1895- New York, The Railway Equipment and Publication Co. 07-41367
    HE2723 .P7 MRR Alc Latest edition

Post's pulp & paper directory. San Francisco [etc.] M. Freeman Publications [etc.] 03-6150
    TS1088 .P85 Sci RR Latest edition / MRR Alc Latest edition

Progressive grocer's marketing guidebook. New York, Progressive grocer [etc.] 658.8/09/664002573 68-126162
    HD9321.3 .P75 MRR Alc Latest edition

Public Service Research, inc., Plainfield, N.J. American directory of water utilities, 1968-69. Plainfield, N.J. [c1968] 10 v. in 1. [95.00] 363.6/1/02573 68-55746
    HD4461 .P8 MRR Alc.

The Purchaser's guide to the music industries. 1897- New York, Music Trades Corp. [etc.] 99-2406
    ML18 .P9 MRR Alc Latest edition

Red book: encyclopaedic directory of the wine and liquor industries. New York, Schwartz Publications, inc. [$19.50] 338.4/7/663102573 73-646025
    HD9373 .R43 MRR Alc Latest edition

Resource Publications, inc. Computer industry guide. 1969-70 ed. Princeton, N.J. [1969] 1 v. (various pagings) [6.95] 331.7/61/6518 71-917780
    HD9696.C63 U57 MRR Alc.

Resource Publications, inc. Franchise guide; Princeton, N.J. [1969] 457 p. 658.87/0025/73 75-78653
    HF5429.3 .R46 MRR Alc.

Retailer owned cooperative chains, wholesale grocers, and wholesaler sponsored voluntary chains. [New York, Business Guides, inc.] 658.87/00873 78-612833
    HF5468.A1 D52 MRR Alc Latest edition

Society of the Plastics Industry. Directory. 1943/44- New York. 338.4/7/668402573 43-18308
    TP986.A1 S6 MRR Alc Latest edition

Standard and Poor's Corporation. Standard & Poor's stock market encyclopedia. New York 332.6/7 70-23142
    HG4921 .S68 MRR Ref Desk Latest edition

Standard and Poor's Corporation. Standard & Poor's stock market encyclopedia. 14th ed. New York [1971] 1 v. (unpaged) [$25.00] 332.67 70-23142
    HG4921 .S68 1971 MRR Ref Desk.

Standard and Poor's Corporation. Standard & Poor's stock reports: American Stock Exchange. Feb. 1973- New York. 332.6/7 70-183942
    HG4905 .S44 MRR Alc Latest edition

Standard and Poor's Corporation. Standard & Poor's stock reports: New York Stock Exchange. Jan. 1973- New York. 332.6/7 74-183943
    HG4905 .S443 MRR Alc Latest edition

Standard and Poor's Corporation. Standard & Poor's stock reports: over the counter. Mar. 1973- New York. 332.6/7 78-183944
    HG4905 .S444 MRR Alc Latest edition

Standard directory of advertisers. Jan. 1916- Skokie, Ill. [etc.] National Register Pub. Co. 659.102573 15-21147
    HF5805 .S7 MRR Alc Latest edition

Standard directory of advertising agencies. Skokie, Ill. [etc.] National Register Pub. Co. 66-6149
    HF5805 .S72 MRR Alc Latest edition

Stevenson, George A. Graphic arts encyclopedia New York, McGraw-Hill [1968] xv, 492 p. 655/.003 67-24445
    Z118 .S82 MRR Alc.

Tax Executives Institute. Foreign tax directory. [Kansas City, Mo.] 55-32647
    HD2753.U6 T27 MRR Alc Latest edition

Toys and novelties directory. 1961-
New York, Harbrace, etc. 338.4/7/6687202573 73-21279
    TS2301.T7 T632 MRR Alc Latest edition

Trinc's red book of the trucking industry. Washington, Trinc Associates. 64-28389
    HE5623.A1 T69 MRR Alc Latest edition

TTA Information Services Company. Guide to locating new products. San Mateo, Calif. [1971] 66 l. 338.4/7 71-153653
    HD69.N4 T15 MRR Alc.

U.S Labor-Management Services Administration. Register of retirement benefit plans, Washington, For sale by the Supt. of Docs., U.S. Govt. Print. Off. [1967] ix, 550 p. 331.2/52/02573 68-60198

    HD7106.U5 A539 MRR Alc.

U.S.A. oil industry directory. Tulsa, Petroleum Pub. Co. 338.2/7/2802573 72-621148
    HD9563 .U54 Sci RR Latest edition / MRR Alc Latest edition

United States. Office of Minority Business Enterprise. National roster: minority professional consulting firms. Washington, 1973. ix, 121 p. 658.4/03 73-601615
    HD69.C6 U56 1973 MRR Alc.

United States Savings and Loan League. Directory of members. Chicago. 59-44374
    HG2121 .U48 MRR Alc Latest edition / MRR Alc Latest edition

Venture capital. v. 1- 1970- [New York, Technimetrics, inc.] 332.1/025/73 74-20999
    HG65 .V4 MRR Alc Latest edition

Walker's manual of Western corporations & securities. 65th-ed.; 1973- San Francisco. 332.6/7/0978 74-640659
    HG5128.C2 W2 MRR Alc Latest edition

Wasserman, Paul, ed. Consultants and consulting organizations directory; 2d ed. Detroit, Gale Research Co., 1973. 835 p. 658.4/03 72-14159
    HD69.C6 W37 1973 MRR Ref Desk.

Weiner, Richard. Professional's guide to public relations services. 2d ed. Englewood Cliffs, N.J., Prentice-Hall [1971] 239 p. 659.2/025/73 71-136685
    HD59 .W38 1971 MRR Alc.

Worldwide directory of computer companies, 1973-1974. Orange, N.J., Academic Media [1973] viii, 633 p. 338.4/7/62138195025 77-114301
    HD8696.C62 W67 1973 MRR Alc.

COMPANIES--UNITED STATES--BIBLIOGRAPHY.
Harvard University. Graduate School of Business Administration. Baker Library. Studies in enterprise; Boston, 1957. xiv, 169 p. 016.33874 57-11481
    Z7164.C81 H26 1957 MRR Alc.

COMPANIES--VENEZUELA.
Diccionario biográfico de Venezuela. 1. ed. Madrid, Blass, 1953. li, 1558 p. pa 54-28
    F2305 .D5 MRR Biog.

COMPANIES--WISCONSIN.
Financial briefs of Wisconsin corporations. [Milwaukee] R. W. Baird. 332.63 51-6093
    HG4070.W5 F5 MRR Alc Latest edition

Wisconsin Manufacturers' Association. Classified directory of Wisconsin manufacturers. Milwaukee, Wis. [etc.] 670.58 42-21094
    TS24.W6 W7 Sci RR Latest edition* / MRR Alc Latest edition

COMPANIES--YUGOSLAVIA.
Privredni adresar S F R J. 1953-
Beograd, Privredni pregled [etc.] 54-39383
    HC407.Y6 P68 MRR Alc Latest edition

COMPANIES--ZÜRICH (CANTON)
Firmenverzeichnis des Kantons Zürich. Zürich, Orell Füssli. 54-29398
    HC398.Z8 F5 MRR Alc Latest edition

COMPARATIVE ECONOMICS.
Loucks, William Negele. Comparative economic systems 8th ed. New York, Harper & Row [1969] xiii, 582 p. 330.1 69-18489
    HB82 .L67 1969 MRR Alc.

COMPARATIVE EDUCATION.
Osborne, Gerald Stanley, Scottish and English schools, [Pittsburgh] University of Pittsburgh Press [1967, c1966] xv, 351 p. 370.19/5 67-10651
    LA651.8 .08 1967 MRR Alc.

Sharp, Theodore. The country index; North Hollywood, Calif., International Education Research Foundation [1971] xii, 217 p. 378.1/50/7 68-28836
    LB2805 .S576 MRR Alc.

Stout, Ralph E. Comparative education; Springfield, Mo., Elkins-Swyers Co. [1967] xviii, 392 p. 370.19/5 67-66373
    LA132 .S83 MRR Alc.

COMPARATIVE EDUCATION--BIBLIOGRAPHY.
Bristow, Thelma. Comparative education through the literature: London, Butterworths, 1968. ix, 181 p. [38/-] 016.37019/5 68-112254
    Z5814.C76 B7 1968b MRR Alc.

COMPARATIVE GOVERNMENT.
Beer, Samuel Hutchison, ed. Patterns of government; 3d ed. New York, Random House [1973] xv, 778 p. 320.3 72-681
    JN12 .B4 1973 MRR Alc.

Carter, Gwendolen Margaret. Major foreign powers 6th ed. New York, Harcourt Brace Jovanovich [1972] xvi, 743 p. 320.3 78-179411
    JF51 .C3 1972 MRR Alc.

Holt, Stephen. Six European states; New York, Taplinger Pub. Co. [1970] xi, 414 p. [$10.00] 320.3/094 78-127406
    JN94 .A3 1970 MRR Alc.

Jacobs, Walter Darnell. Modern governments 3d ed. Princeton, N.J., Van Nostrand [1966] xi, 756 p. 320.3 66-6003
    JF51 .J24 1966 MRR Alc.

Kantor, Harry. Patterns of politics and political systems in Latin America. Chicago, Rand McNally [1969] xiii, 742 p. 320.3/098 68-16840
    JF51 .K3 MRR Alc.

Macridis, Roy C., ed. Modern political systems. 2d ed. Englewood Cliffs, N.J., Prentice-Hall [1968-v. 320.3 68-16375
    JF51 .M33 1968 MRR Alc.

Wuest, John J., ed. New Source book in major European governments. Cleveland, World Pub. Co. [1966] xviii, 700 p. 320.308 66-13148
    JF51 .W8 MRR Alc.

COMPARATIVE GOVERNMENT--BIBLIOGRAPHY.
Universal Reference System.
Comparative government and cultures;
Princeton, N.J., Princeton Research
Pub. Co. [1969] xxi, 1255 p.   016.3
68-57826
    Z7161 .U64 vol. 10 MRR Alc

COMPARATIVE GOVERNMENT--HANDBOOKS,
MANUALS, ETC.
The World this year. 1971- New
York, Simon and Schuster. 320.9/046
76-649587
    JF37 .W65   MRR Ref Desk Latest
    edition

COMPARATIVE GRAMMAR
see Grammar, Comparative and general

COMPARATIVE RELIGION
see Religions

COMPENSATION
see Wages

COMPETITIVE EXAMINATIONS
see Examinations

COMPLAINTS (RETAIL TRADE)
Wasserman, Paul. Consumer
sourcebook; Detroit, Gale Research
Co. [1974] xi, 593 p.   381/.3   74-
10494
    HC110.C63 W37 MRR Ref Desk.

White, Jack M. The angry buyer's
complaint directory New York, P. H.
Wyden [1974] xxviii, 292 p. [$7.95]
381   73-86179
    HF5445.5 .W55 MRR Alc.

COMPOSER--EUROPE--BIOGRAPHY.
Ewen, David, ed. European composers
today, New York, Wilson, 1954. 200
p.   927.8   53-9024
    ML390 .E834 MRR Biog.

COMPOSERS.
Biancolli, Louis Leopold, ed. The
opera reader. New York, McGraw-Hill
Book Co. [1953] 678 p.   782.08   53-
9008
    ML1700 .B47 MRR Alc.

Ewen, David, The complete book of
classical music. Englewood Cliffs,
N.J., Prentice-Hall [1965] xx, 946
p.   780.9033 65-11033
    MT6 .E89 MRR Alc.

COMPOSERS--BIOGRAPHY.
Ewen, David, Great composers, 1300-
1900; New York, H. W. Wilson Co.,
1966. 429 p.   780.922 65-24585
    ML105 .E944 MRR Biog.

Ewen, David, The new book of modern
composers. 3d ed., rev. and enl.
New York, Knopf, 1961. 491 p.
927.8   61-15040
    ML390 .E83 1961 MRR Biog.

COMPOSERS--BIOGRAPHY--INDEXES.
Bull, Storm. Index to biographies of
contemporary composers. New York,
Scarecrow Press, 1964. 405 p.
016.9278 64-11781
    ML105 .B9 MRR Biog.

COMPOSERS--PORTRAITS.
Austin, William W. Music in the 20th
century, [1st ed.] New York, W. W.
Norton [1966] xx, 708 p.   780.904
65-18776
    ML197 .A9 MRR Alc.

COMPOSERS, AMERICAN.
American Society of Composers,
Authors and Publishers. The ASCAP
biographical dictionary of composers,
authors and publishers. [3d ed.]
New York, 1966. 845 p.   780.922 66-
20214
    ML106.U3 A5 1966 MRR Biog.

Green, Stanley. The world of musical
comedy; New York, Ziff-Davis Pub.
Co. [1960] xvi, 391 p.   782.810973
60-10522
    ML1711 .G74 MRR Alc.

Sonneck, Oscar George Theodore, A
bibliography of early secular
American music, 18th century. New
York, Da Capo Press, 1964. x, xvi,
616 p.   781.97 64-18992
    ML120.U5 S6 1964 MRR Alc.

Wolfe, Richard J. Secular music in
America, 1801-1825; [1st ed.] New
York, The New York Public Library,
1964. 3 v.   781.97 64-25006
    ML120.U5 W57 MRR Alc.

COMPOSERS, AMERICAN--BIO-BIBLIOGRAPHY.
Burton, Jack. The blue book of Tin
Pan Alley, [Expanded new ed.]
Watkins Glen, N.Y., Century House
[1962-65] 2 v.   784 62-16426
    ML390 .B963 MRR Alc.

COMPOSERS, AMERICAN--BIOGRAPHY.
Ewen, David, ed. American composers
today, New York, H. W. Wilson Co.,
1949. 265 p.   927.8   49-8927
    ML390 .E82 MRR Biog.

Ewen, David, Great men of American
popular song; Englewood Cliffs,
N.J., Prentice-Hall [1970]   x, 387 p.
[12.95]   784/.0922   79-110079
    ML3551 .E83 MRR Alc.

Goss, Madeleine (Binkley) Modern
music-makers, [1st ed.] New York,
Dutton, 1952. 499 p.   927.8   52-
5304
    ML390 .G69 MRR Biog.

Howard, John Tasker, Our
contemporary composers; New York,
Thomas Y. Crowell company, 1941. xv,
447 p.   780.973   41-6762
    ML390 .H8 MRR Biog.

Reis, Claire (Raphael) Composers in
America; Rev. and enl. ed. New
York, Macmillan Co., 1947. xvi, 399
p.   781.973   47-31210
    ML390 .R38 1947 MRR Biog.

COMPOSERS, GERMAN--BIOGRAPHY.
Mitteldeutsche Köpfe; Frankfurt am
Main, W. Weidlich, 1959 [c1958] 239
p.   62-35223
    CT1053 .M5 MRR Biog.

COMPOSITION (RHETORIC)
see Letter-writing

COMPULSORY MILITARY SERVICE
see Military service, Compulsory

COMPUTATION LABORATORIES--DIRECTORIES.
The International directory of
computer and information system
services. 1969- London, Europa
Publications. 651.8   70-5680
    QA74 .I65 Sci RR Latest edition /
    MRR Alc Latest edition

COMPUTER CONTROL
see Automation

COMPUTER INDUSTRY.
Lee, Wayne J. The international
computer industry. Washington,
Applied Library Resources [1971] v,
299 p.   338.4/7/62138195   75-157121
    HD9696.C62 L44 MRR Alc.

COMPUTER INDUSTRY--DIRECTORIES.
Computer Consultants Limited. Who is
related to whom in the computer
industry. 3d ed. Oxford, New York,
Pergamon Press [1969] 324 p.
338.4/7/62138195025   70-85766
    TK7885 .C6 1868 MRR Alc.

The International directory of
computer and information system
services. 1969- London, Europa
Publications. 651.8   70-5680
    QA74 .I65 Sci RR Latest edition /
    MRR Alc Latest edition

Worldwide directory of computer
companies, 1973-1974. Orange, N.J.,
Academic Media [1973]   viii, 633 p.
338.4/7/62138195025   77-114301
    HD9696.C62 W67 1973 MRR Alc.

COMPUTER INDUSTRY--VOCATIONAL GUIDANCE.
Resource Publications, inc. Computer
industry guide. 1969-70 ed.
Princeton, N.J. [1969] 1 v. (various
pagings) [6.95]   331.7/61/6518 71-
91780
    HD9696.C63 U57 MRR Alc.

COMPUTER INDUSTRY--UNITED STATES.
Resource Publications, inc. Computer
industry guide. 1969-70 ed.
Princeton, N.J. [1969] 1 v. (various
pagings) [6.95]   331.7/61/6518 71-
91780
    HD9696.C63 U57 MRR Alc.

COMPUTER INDUSTRY--UNITED STATES--
BIOGRAPHY.
Who's who in computers and data
processing. (Chicago) Quadrangle
Books.   001.6/4/0922 [B]   70-648600
    QA76.2 .A1W452 MRR Biog Latest
    edition / Sci RR Latest edition

COMPUTER INDUSTRY--UNITED STATES--
DIRECTORIES.
Computer industry annual. 1967/68-
[W. Concord, Mass.] 621.3819/5/05
68-5128
    QA76 .C565   MRR Alc Latest edition

Resource Publications, inc. Computer
industry guide. 1969-70 ed.
Princeton, N.J. [1969] 1 v. (various
pagings) [6.95]   331.7/61/6518 71-
91780
    HD9696.C63 U57 MRR Alc.

COMPUTERS.
see also Electronic data processing

see also Electronic digital computers

Booth, Andrew Donald. Automatic
digital calculators, 3rd ed.
London, Butterworths, 1965. xi, 263
p. [52/6]   621.381958 66-2364
    QA76.5 .B6 1965a MRR Alc.

Fahnestock, James D. Computers and
how they work. New York, Ziff-Davis
Pub. Co. [c1959] 228 p.   510.78 59-
15257
    QA76 .F3 MRR Alc.

COMPUTERS--BIBLIOGRAPHY.
Morrill, Chester. Computers and data
processing; information sources;
Detroit, Gale Research Co. [1969]
275 p. [8.75]   016.6518 70-85486
    Z6654.C17 M58 MRR Alc.

Pritchard, Alan. A guide to computer
literature; 2d ed., rev. and
expanded. [Hamden, Conn.] Linnet
Books [1972] 194 p.   [$7.50]
016.0016/4   72-197008
    Z6654.C17 P7 1972 MRR Alc.

COMPUTERS--DICTIONARIES.
Sippl, Charles J. Computer
dictionary, [2d ed.] Indianapolis,
H. W. Sams [1974] 488 p. [$8.95
($11.95 Can.)]   001.6/4/03   72-91729
    QA76.15 .S5 1974 MRR Alc.

Sippl, Charles J. Computer
dictionary and handbook, [2d ed.]
Indianapolis, H. W. Sams [1972] 778
p. [$16.95 ($22.25 Can)]
001.6/4/03   70-175572
    QA76.15 .S512 1972 MRR Alc.

Sondak, Norman E. The layman's
dictionary of computer terminology,
New York, Hawthorn Books [1973]
xvii, 203 p.   001.6/4/03   75-39269
    QA76.15 .S6 MRR Alc.

COMPUTERS--DICTIONARIES--POLYGLOT.
Burger, Erich. Technical dictionary
of data processing, computers, office
machines. [1st ed.] Oxford, New
York, Pergamon Press [1970] 1463 p.
651.8/03   75-81247
    QA76.15 .B46 1970 MRR Alc.

Clason, W. E., Elsevier's dictionary
of computers, automatic control and
data processing. 2d rev. ed. of The
dictionary of automation, computers,
control and measuring. Amsterdam,
New York, Elsevier Pub. Co., 1971.
484 p.   [fl78.00]   001.6/4/03   73-
151753
    TJ212.5 .C55 1971 MRR Alc.

COMPUTERS--PERIODICALS--BIBLIOGRAPHY.
A World list of computer periodicals.
Manchester, National Computing
Centre, 1970. [1], 102 p. [£3.00]
016.0016/4/05   78-586322
    Z6654.C17 W65 MRR Alc.

COMPUTERS--YEARBOOKS.
Computer industry annual. 1967/68-
[W. Concord, Mass.]   621.3819/5/05
68-5128
    QA76 .C565   MRR Alc Latest edition

COMPUTERS, ELECTRONIC DIGITAL
see Electronic digital computers

CONCEPTION--PREVENTION.
see also Population

CONCEPTS.
Laffal, Julius. A concept dictionary
of English. Essex, Conn., Gallery
Press [1973] xi, 305 p.   428/.1   72-
97297
    PE1691 .L3 MRR Alc.

CONCEPTS--DICTIONARIES.
Dictionary of the history of ideas;
New York, Scribner [1973] 4 v.
[$35.00 (per vol.)]   901.9   72-7943
    CB5 .D52 MRR Alc.

CONCEPTS--INDEXES.
Hart, Henry Harper. Conceptual index
to psychoanalytic technique and
training, [Croton-on-Hudson, N.Y.]
North River Press, 1972. 5 v. (xxxi,
1584 p.)   016.6168/917   72-77268
    Z7204.P8 H37 MRR Alc.

CONCHOLOGY
see Shells

CONCORDANCES.
see also Indexes

CONCRETE.
Dezettel, Louis M. Masons and
builders library, Indianapolis, T.
Audel [1972] 2 v.   693 78-186134
    TH5311 .D48 MRR Alc.

CONCRETE, ASPHALT
see Asphalt concrete

CONCRETE MUSIC.
see also Electronic music

CONDEMNED BOOKS--BIBLIOGRAPHY.
Haight, Anne (Lyon) Banned books:
2d ed. rev. and enl. New York, R. R.
Bowker, 1955. xvii, 172 p.   098.1
54-11650
    Z1019 .H15 1955 MRR Alc.

CONDEMNED BOOKS--BIBLIOGRAPHY. (Cont.)
Index librorum prohibitorum. Index
librorum prohibitorum. [In Civitate
Vaticana] Typis Polyglottis
Vaticanis, 1948. xxiv, 508 p.
098.11 a 52-648
Z1020 .I948 MRR Alc.

CONDUCT OF LIFE.
see also Ethics

see also Spiritual life

CONDUCT OF LIFE--QUOTATIONS, MAXIMS,
ETC.
Martin, Thomas Lyle. Malice in
Blunderland, New York, McGraw-Hill
[1973] vii, 143 p. [$5.95]
658.4/002/07 73-4376
PN6231.M2 M3 MRR Ref Desk.

Montapert, Alfred Armand, ed.
Distilled wisdom. Englewood Cliffs,
N.J., Prentice-Hall [1964] ix, 355
p. 808.88 64-8181
BJ1548 .M6 MRR Ref Desk.

CONFEDERATE STATES OF AMERICA.
Schwab, John Christopher, The
Confederate States of America, 1861-
1865; New York, B. Franklin [1968]
xi, 332 p. 330.975 68-56580
HC105.65 .S38 1968 MRR Alc.

CONFEDERATE STATES OF AMERICA--
BIOGRAPHY.
Hendrick, Burton Jesse, Statesmen of
the lost cause; Boston, Little,
Brown and company, 1939. xvii, 452
p. 923.273 39-28981
E487 .H47 MRR Alc.

Warner, Ezra J. Generals in gray;
[1st ed. Baton Rouge] Louisiana
State University Press [1959] xxvii,
420 p. 973.742 58-7551
E467 .W3 MRR Biog.

Wright, Marcus Joseph, comp. General
officers of the Confederate army,
New York, The Neale publishing
company, 1911. 188 p. [$1.50] 12-
144
E467 .W94 MRR Biog.

CONFEDERATE STATES OF AMERICA--FOREIGN
RELATIONS.
Owsley, Frank Lawrence, King Cotton
diplomacy; 2d ed., rev. [Chicago]
University of Chicago Press [1959]
xxiii, 614 p. 973.721 58-11952
E488 .O85 1959 MRR Alc.

CONFEDERATE STATES OF AMERICA--
GOVERNMENT PUBLICATIONS--BIBLIOGRAPHY.
Harwell, Richard Barksdale. More
Confederate imprints. Richmond,
Virginia State Library, 1957. 2 v.
(xxxvi, 345 p.) 015.75 a 57-9084
Z1242.5 .H33 MRR Alc.

CONFEDERATE STATES OF AMERICA--HISTORY.
Coulter, Ellis Merton, The
Confederate States of America, 1861-
1865. [Baton Rouge] Louisiana State
University Press, 1950. x, 644 p.
973.713 50-6319
E487 .C83 MRR Alc.

Eaton, Clement, A history of the
Southern Confederacy. New York,
Macmillan, 1954. 351 p. 973.713
54-8772
E487 .E15 MRR Alc.

CONFEDERATE STATES OF AMERICA--HISTORY--
SOURCES.
United States. War dept. The war of
the rebellion: a compilation of the
official records of the Union and
Confederate armies. Washington,
Govt. print. off., 1880-1901. 70 v.
in 128. 03-3452
E464 .U6 Index MRR Ref Desk.

CONFEDERATE STATES OF AMERICA--HISTORY--
SOURCES--BIBLIOGRAPHY.
Beers, Henry Putney, Guide to the
archives of the Government of the
Confederate States of America.
Washington, National Archives,
General Services Administration; [for
sale by the Supt. of Docs., U.S.
Govt. Print. Off.] 1968. ix, 536 p.
[3.75] 016.97371/3 a 68-7603
CD3047 .B4 MRR Alc.

Munden, Kenneth White. Guide to
Federal archives relating to the
Civil War, Washington, National
Archives, National Archives and
Records Service, General Services
Administration, 1962. x, 721 p. a
62-9432
CD3047 .M8 MRR Alc.

CONFEDERATE STATES OF AMERICA--IMPRINTS.
Alabama. University. Library.
Confederate imprints in the
University of Alabama Library.
University, Ala., 1961. iii, 156 l.
015.75 62-62614
Z1242.5 .A4 MRR Alc.

Crandall, Marjorie Lyle, Confederate
imprints; [Boston] Boston Athenæum,
1955. 2 v. (xxxv, 910 p.) 015.75
a 55-10799
Z1242.5 .C7 MRR Alc.

Harwell, Richard Barksdale. More
Confederate imprints. Richmond,
Virginia State Library, 1957. 2 v.
(xxxvi, 345 p.) 015.75 a 57-9084
Z1242.5 .H33 MRR Alc.

CONFEDERATE STATES OF AMERICA--POLITICS
AND GOVERNMENT.
Hendrick, Burton Jesse, Statesmen of
the lost cause; Boston, Little,
Brown and company, 1939. xvii, 452
p. 923.273 39-28981
E487 .H47 MRR Alc.

Yearns, Wilfred Buck, The
Confederate Congress. Athens,
University of Georgia Press [1960]
293 p. 973.713 60-9897
E487 .Y4 MRR Alc.

CONFEDERATE STATES OF AMERICA--
REGISTERS.
Wright, Marcus Joseph, comp. General
officers of the Confederate army,
New York, The Neale publishing
company, 1911. 188 p. [$1.50] 12-
144
E467 .W94 MRR Biog.

CONFEDERATE STATES OF AMERICA. ARMY.
Wiley, Bell Irvin, The common
soldier in the Civil War. New York,
Grosset & Dunlap [1958] 454, 444 p.
973.74 58-4364
E607 .W48 MRR Alc.

CONFEDERATE STATES OF AMERICA. ARMY--
EQUIPMENT.
Lord, Francis Alfred, Civil War
collector's encyclopedia; [1st ed.]
Harrisburg, Pa., Stackpole Co. [1963]
360 p. 355.80973 63-14636
UC23 1861-65 .L6 MRR Alc.

CONFEDERATE STATES OF AMERICA. ARMY--
FIREARMS.
Albaugh, William A., Confederate
arms, Harrisburg, Pa. [1957] xviii,
278 p. 623.4 57-13480
UD383.5 .A6 MRR Alc.

CONFEDERATE STATES OF AMERICA. ARMY--
ORDNANCE AND ORDNANCE STORES.
Ripley, Warren, Artillery and
ammunition of the Civil War. New
York, Van Nostrand Reinhold Co.
[1970] 384 p. 623.4 75-90331
UF23 .R56 1970 MRR Alc.

CONFEDERATE STATES OF AMERICA. ARMY--
REGISTERS.
Amann, William Frayne, ed. Personnel
of the Civil War. New York, T.
Yoseloff [1961] 2 v. 973.74 60-
9880
E494 .A5 MRR Alc.

CONFEDERATE STATES OF AMERICA. ARMY--
TRANSPORTATION.
Black, Robert C., The railroads of
the Confederacy. Chapel Hill,
University of North Carolina Press
[1952] xiv, 360 p. 973.7 52-3559
E545 .B55 MRR Alc.

CONFEDERATE STATES OF AMERICA. ARMY--
UNIFORMS.
Confederate States of America. War
Dept. Uniform and dress of the Army
and Navy of the Confederate States of
America. [Rev. ed.] Philadelphia,
R. Riling, 1960. [12] p., [4] p.
973.784 60-16421
UC483.5 .A223 MRR Alc.

CONFEDERATE STATES OF AMERICA. CONGRESS.
Yearns, Wilfred Buck, The
Confederate Congress. Athens,
University of Georgia Press [1960]
293 p. 973.713 60-9897
E487 .Y4 MRR Alc.

CONFEDERATE STATES OF AMERICA. NAVY--
UNIFORMS.
Confederate States of America. War
Dept. Uniform and dress of the Army
and Navy of the Confederate States of
America. [Rev. ed.] Philadelphia,
R. Riling, 1960. [12] p., [4] p.
973.784 60-16421
UC483.5 .A223 MRR Alc.

CONFERENCE ROOMS--UNITED STATES--
DIRECTORIES.
Auger, Bert Y. How to find better
business meeting places; St. Paul,
Business Services Press [1966] xvii,
637 p. 647.9473 66-24060
TX907 .A8 MRR Alc.

CONFORMITY.
see also Dissenters

CONFUCIUS AND CONFUCIANISM.
see also Buddha and Buddhism

CONGLOMERATE CORPORATIONS--JAPAN--
DIRECTORIES.
1972 handbook of Japanese
financial/industrial combines; San
Francisco Pacific Basin Reports
[1972] 83 l. [$25.00]
338.8/5/02552 73-150829
HD2756.J3 N55 MRR Alc.

CONGO (BRAZZAVILLE)--GAZETTEERS.
United States. Office of Geography.
Republic of Congo (Brazzaville);
official standard names approved by
the United States Board on Geographic
Names. Washington, 1962. iii, 109
p. 62-61686
DT546.22 .U6 MRR Alc.

CONGO (DEMOCRATIC REPUBLIC)
American University, Washington, D.C.
Foreign Areas Studies Division. Area
handbook for the Republic of the
Congo (Léopoldville) Washington,
1962. xii, 657 p. 67-115016
DT644 .A75 MRR Alc.

CONGO (LEOPOLDVILLE)--BIOGRAPHY.
Who's who in Belgium and Grand Duchy
of Luxembourg. [1st] ed.; 1957/58-
Brussels, Intercontinental Book &
Pub. Co. 920.0493 59-3017
DH513 .W45 MRR Biog Latest edition

CONGRESSES AND CONVENTIONS.
Association executives buyers' guide
and meeting planner. v. 1- 1973-
[Washington, Columbia Books] [$7.50]
658.4 72-92834
HD2743 .A75 MRR Alc Latest edition

CONGRESSES AND CONVENTIONS--
BIBLIOGRAPHY.
International congresses and
conferences, 1840-1937; New York,
The H. W. Wilson company, 1938. 3 p.
l., 229 p. 016.06 39-1264
Z5051 .I58 MRR Alc.

United States. Library of Congress.
International Organizations Section.
Documents of international meetings,
1953. Washington, General Reference
and Bibliography Division, Reference
Dept., Library of Congress, 1959.
iv, 210 p. 016.34111 59-60030
Z663.28 .D6 MRR Alc.

World list of scientific periodicals
published in the years 1900-1960.
4th ed. Washington, Butterworths,
1963-65. 3 v. (xxv, 1824 p.)
016.505 64-9729
Z7403 .W923 MRR Alc.

CONGRESSES AND CONVENTIONS--
BIBLIOGRAPHY--YEARBOOKS.
Yearbook of international congress
proceedings. 1st- ed.; 1960/67-
Brussels, Union of International
Associations. 060 70-21167
Z5051 .Y4 MRR Alc Full set

CONGRESSES AND CONVENTIONS--DIRECTORIES.
Directory of conventions.
Philadelphia, Sales meetings
magazine. 061.3 63-25787
AS8 .D48 MRR Ref Desk Latest
edition

Educator's world. 1970- ed.
Englewood, Colo., Fisher Pub. Co.
370/.6/273 73-646663
L901 .E45 MRR Ref Desk Latest
edition

International congress calendar.
1960/61- Brussels, Union of
International Associations. 060.58
60-1648
AS8 .I63 MRR Alc Latest edition

Sales meetings. Exhibits schedule.
Philadelphia. 600.74 63-23593
T391 .S3 Sci RR Latest edition /
MRR Alc Latest edition / MRR Alc
Latest edition (suppl.)

Washington Convention and Visitors
Bureau. Conventions and meetings,
Washington, D.C., 1972-1981.
Washington, 1972. 31 p. 061/.53
72-190130
AS8 .W37 MRR Ref Desk.

World list of future international
meetings. June 1959-Sept. 1969.
Washington, Reference Dept., Library
of Congress. 016.06 59-60061
Z663.295 .W6 MRR Alc MRR Alc Full
set

CONGRESSES AND CONVENTIONS--DIRECTORIES
--BIBLIOGRAPHY.
United States. Library of Congress.
International Organizations Section.
Future national and international
events; Washington, Reference Dept.,
Library of Congress, 1961. xxxiv p.
62-60291
Z663.295 .F85 1961 MRR Alc.

CONGRESSES AND CONVENTIONS--TERMINOLOGY.
Conference terminology, 2d ed., rev.
and augm. Amsterdam, New York,
Elsevier Pub. Co.; [sole distributors
for the U.S.: American Elsevier Pub.
Co., New York] 1962. 162 p.   413
63-8568
PB324.C6 C6 1962 MRR Alc.

CONGRESSES AND CONVENTIONS--GREAT
BRITAIN.
British Travel and Holidays
Association. Organisations in
Britain holding regular conferences.
[London, 1961] 92 p.   62-6159
AS118 .B7 MRR Alc.

CONGRESSES AND CONVENTIONS--WASHINGTON,
D.C.--DIRECTORIES.
Washington Convention and Visitors
Bureau. Conventions and meetings,
Washington, D.C., 1972-1981.
Washington, 1972. 31 p.   061/.53
72-190130
AS8 .W37 MRR Ref Desk.

CONIFERAE.
see also Evergreens

CONJURING.
see also Magic

Cyclopedia of magic Philadelphia, D.
McKay Co. [1949] 498 p.   793.8 49-
7321
GV1547 .C9 MRR Alc.

CONJURING--DICTIONARIES.
Dunninger, Joseph, Dunninger's
complete encyclopedia of magic. [New
York] L. Stuart [1967] 288 p.   66-
11851
GV1542.5 .D8 MRR Alc.

CONJURING--HISTORY.
Christopher, Milbourne. The
illustrated history of magic. New
York, Crowell [1973] 452 p.
[$14.95]   793.8 73-10390
GV1543 .C45 MRR Alc.

CONNALLY, THOMAS TERRY, 1877- --
BIBLIOGRAPHY.
United States. Library of Congress.
Manuscript Division. Tom Connally: a
register of his papers in the Library
of Congress. Washington, 1958. 31
p.   012 58-60048
Z663.34 .C6 MRR Alc.

CONNAUGHT, IRE.--COMMERCE--DIRECTORIES.
Dublin, Leinster and Connaught
trades directory, Edinburgh.
Trades' Directories.   57-36641
HF5164.D8 D8 MRR Alc Latest
edition

CONNECTICUT.
Federal writers' project.
Connecticut. Connecticut; a guide to
its roads, lore, and people, Boston,
Houghton Mifflin company, 1938.
xxxiii, 593 p.   917.46 38-27339
F100 .F45 MRR Ref Desk.

CONNECTICUT--COMMERCE--DIRECTORIES.
Classified business directory of the
State of Connecticut. Stamford,
Connecticut Directory Co. 63-35351
HF5065.C8 C55 MRR Alc Latest
edition

CONNECTICUT--DESCRIPTION AND TRAVEL--
1951- --GUIDE-BOOKS.
Bixby, William. Connecticut: a new
guide. New York, Scribner [1974]
ix, 386 p. [$10.00] 917.46/04/4
73-20261
F92.3 .B59 MRR Alc.

CONNECTICUT--DESCRIPTION AND TRAVEL--
GUIDE-BOOKS.
Bixby, William. Connecticut: a new
guide. New York, Scribner [1974]
ix, 386 p. [$10.00] 917.46/04/4
73-20261
F92.3 .B59 MRR Alc.

Federal writers' project.
Connecticut. Connecticut; a guide to
its roads, lore, and people, Boston,
Houghton Mifflin company, 1938.
xxxiii, 593 p.   917.46 38-27339
F100 .F45 MRR Ref Desk.

CONNECTICUT--DIRECTORIES.
Connecticut. Secretary of state.
Register and manual of the state of
Connecticut. 1887- Hartford. 10-
9548
JK3331 MRR Alc Latest edition

CONNECTICUT--EXECUTIVE DEPARTMENTS.
Connecticut. Dept. of Finance and
Control. Connecticut digest of
administrative reports to the
Governor. Hartford. 353.9/746 72-
622382
J87.C8 date α MRR Alc Latest
edition

CONNECTICUT--HISTORIC HOUSES, ETC.
Federal writers' project.
Connecticut. Connecticut; a guide to
its roads, lore, and people, Boston,
Houghton Mifflin company, 1938.
xxxiii, 593 p.   917.46 38-27339
F100 .F45 MRR Ref Desk.

CONNECTICUT--HISTORY.
Van Dusen, Albert Edward,
Connecticut. New York, Random House
[1961] x, 470 p.   974.6 61-6263
F94 .V3 MRR Alc.

CONNECTICUT--MANUFACTURES--DIRECTORIES.
Directory of New England
manufacturers. Boston, Mass., G. D.
Hall, inc. 338.40974 36-5085
HD9723 .D45 Sci RR Latest edition
/ MRR Alc Latest edition

CONNECTICUT--POLITICS AND GOVERNMENT.
Connecticut. Secretary of state.
Register and manual of the state of
Connecticut. 1887- Hartford. 10-
9548
JK3331 MRR Alc Latest edition

CONNECTICUT--POLITICS AND GOVERNMENT--
1951-
Connecticut. Dept. of Finance and
Control. Connecticut digest of
administrative reports to the
Governor. Hartford. 353.9/746 72-
622382
J87.C8 date q MRR Alc Latest
edition

CONNECTICUT--REGISTERS.
Connecticut. Secretary of state.
Register and manual of the state of
Connecticut. 1887- Hartford. 10-
9548
JK3331 MRR Alc Latest edition

CONSCRIPTION, MILITARY
see Military service, Compulsory

CONSENSUS (SOCIAL SCIENCES)
see also Decision-making

CONSERVATION OF NATURAL RESOURCES.
see also Human ecology

see also Nature conservation

Hilado, Carlos J., Handbook of
environmental management Westport,
Conn., Technomic Pub. Co. [1972- v.
301.31 74-174658
GF41 .H55 MRR Alc.

CONSERVATION OF NATURAL RESOURCES--
DIRECTORIES.
Conservation directory. Washington,
National Wildlife Federation. 70-
10646
Began with 1956 vol.
S920 .C64 Sci RR Latest edition /
MRR Alc Latest edition

CONSERVATION OF NATURAL RESOURCES--
SOCIETIES, ETC.--DIRECTORIES.
Halstead, Bruce W. A Golden guide to
environmental organizations. New
York, Golden Press [1972] 63 p.
[$0.95]   301.31/06 72-79158
GF5 .H34 MRR Alc.

CONSERVATION OF NATURAL RESOURCES--
UNITED STATES.
United States. Dept. of Agriculture.
Outdoors USA. [Washington, U.S.
Govt. Print. Off., 1967] xxxix, 408
p.   333.7/2/0973 agr67-359
S21.A35 1967 MRR Alc.

CONSERVATION OF NATURAL RESOURCES--
UNITED STATES--DIRECTORIES.
Onyx Group, inc. Environment U.S.A.;
New York, Bowker, 1974. xii, 451 p.
333.7/2/02573 73-20122
TD171 .E58 MRR Alc.

CONSERVATIONISTS--UNITED STATES.
Clepper, Henry Edward, comp. Leaders
of American conservation, New York,
Ronald Press Co. [1971] vii, 353 p.
333.7/2/0922 B 75-155206
S926.A2 C54 MRR Biog.

CONSERVATISM--UNITED STATES.
Forster, Arnold. Danger on the
Right, New York, Random House [1964]
xviii, 294 p.   320 64-7549
E743 .F68 MRR Alc.

CONSERVATISM--UNITED STATES--SOCIETIES,
ETC.
Solara, Ferdinand V. Key influences
in the American right, Denver,
Polifax Press [1972] xv, 68 p.
[$4.95]   320.5/12/0973 72-189989
E839.5 .S64 1972 MRR Ref Desk.

CONSOLIDATION AND MERGER OF
CORPORATIONS--UNITED STATES.
Hudson's corporate mergers. New
York. 338.8/3/0973 74-644554
HG4915 .C67 MRR Alc Latest edition

CONSOLIDATION AND MERGER OF
CORPORATIONS--UNITED STATES--
PERIODICALS.
F & S index of corporate change.
Cleveland, Predicasts, inc.
338.8/3/02573 72-625662
HD2741 .F18 MRR Alc Full set

CONSOLIDATION AND MERGER OF
CORPORATIONS--UNITED STATES--STATISTICS.
United States. Bureau of the Census.
Economic Statistics and Surveys
Division. Enterprise statistics:
1967. [Washington; For sale by the
Supt. of Docs., U.S. Govt. Print.
Off., Washington, 1971- [v. 1,
1972] v.   [$7.75 (v. 1)]
338/.0973 79-186224
HC106.6 .U55 1972 MRR Alc.

CONSOLIDATION AND MERGER OF
CORPORATIONS--UNITED STATES--YEARBOOKS.
Growth & acquisition guide yearbook.
1968- Cleveland, Predicasts. 72-
14099
HG4028.M4 G74 MRR Alc Full set

CONSTANTINOPLE
see Istanbul

CONSTELLATIONS.
Allen, Richard Hinckley, Star names,
their lore and meaning. New York,
Dover Publications [1963] xiv, 563
p.   523.89 63-21808
QB802 .A4 1963 MRR Alc.

CONSTITUTIONAL CONVENTIONS--
BIBLIOGRAPHY.
Chicago. University. Library.
Official publications relating to
American state constitutional
conventions, New York, The H. W.
Wilson company, 1936. 3 p. l., 91 p.
016.342732 37-4455
Z6457.A1 C5 MRR Alc.

CONSTITUTIONAL CONVENTIONS--ALABAMA--
BIBLIOGRAPHY.
Alabama. Dept. of Archives and
History. Alabama official and
statistical register. 1903-
Montgomery. 08-17761
JK4531 MRR Alc Latest edition

CONSTITUTIONAL CONVENTIONS--UNITED
STATES--STATES--BIBLIOGRAPHY.
Browne, Cynthia E. State
constitutional conventions from
independence to the completion of the
present Union, 1776-1959; Westport,
Conn., Greenwood Press [1973] xl,
250 p.   016.342/73/024 73-9327
KF4501 .B76 MRR Alc.

CONSTITUTIONAL HISTORY.
Palmer, Robert Roswell, The age of
the democratic revolution;
Princeton, N.J., Princeton University
Press, 1959-64. 2 v.   940.25 59-
10068
D295 .P3 MRR Alc.

CONSTITUTIONAL LAW.
see also Citizenship

see also Civil rights

see also Executive power

see also Federal government

see also Legislation

see also Legislative power

see also Separation of powers

CONSTITUTIONS, STATE--UNITED STATES.
Columbia University. Legislative
Drafting Research Fund.
Constitutions of the United States,
national and state. Dobbs Ferry,
N.Y., Oceana Publications [1962- 2
v. (loose-leaf)   342.73 61-18391
KF4530 .C6 MRR Alc.

Columbia University. Legislative
Drafting Research Fund. Index digest
of state constitutions. 2d ed. [New
York, 1959] xx, 1132 p.   342.738
59-15652
LAW MRR Alc.

Thorpe, Francis Newton. comp. The
Federal and State constitutions,
colonial charters, and other organic
laws of the state, territories, and
colonies now or heretofore forming
the United States of America.
Washington, Govt. Print. Off., 1909.
7 v.   09-35371
KF4541 .T48 MRR Alc.

CONSTITUTIONS, STATE--UNITED STATES--
BIBLIOGRAPHY.
Browne, Cynthia E. State
constitutional conventions from
independence to the completion of the
present Union, 1776-1959; Westport,
Conn., Greenwood Press [1973] xl,
250 p.   016.342/73/024 73-9327
KF4501 .B76 MRR Alc.

CONSTRUCTION
see Architecture

CONSTRUCTION (Cont.)
see Building

see Engineering

CONSTRUCTION EQUIPMENT--DICTIONARIES.
Bucksch, Herbert. Dictionary of
civil engineering and construction
machinery and equipment ... 2e
edition. Paris, Eyrolles, 1967. v.
    624/.03 74-415882
    TA9 .B892 MRR Alc.

Bucksch, Herbert. Dictionary of
civil engineering and construction
machinery and equipment, English-
French. Paris, Eyrolles 1960-62. 2
v. 624.03 62-6556
    TA9 .B89 MRR Alc.

Bucksch, Herbert. Wörterbuch für
Bautechnik und Baumaschinen. 4.
wesentlich erw. Aufl. Wiesbaden,
Bauverlag, 1968- v. [DM 140.-
(Bd. 1)] 624/.03 68-88879
    TA9 .B924 MRR Alc.

**CONSTRUCTION EQUIPMENT--DICTIONARIES--
FRENCH.**
Bucksch, Herbert. Dictionary of
civil engineering and construction
machinery and equipment ... 2e
edition. Paris, Eyrolles, 1967. v.
    624/.03 74-415882
    TA9 .B892 MRR Alc.

Bucksch, Herbert. Dictionary of
civil engineering and construction
machinery and equipment, English-
French. Paris, Eyrolles 1960-62. 2
v. 624.03 62-6556
    TA9 .B89 MRR Alc.

**CONSTRUCTION EQUIPMENT--DICTIONARIES--
GERMAN.**
Bucksch, Herbert. Wörterbuch für
Bautechnik und Baumaschinen. 4.
wesentlich erw. Aufl. Wiesbaden,
Bauverlag, 1968- v. [DM 140.-
(Bd. 1)] 624/.03 68-88879
    TA9 .B924 MRR Alc.

CONSTRUCTION INDUSTRY.
see also Building

CONSTRUCTION INDUSTRY--DICTIONARIES.
Cowan, Henry J. Dictionary of
architectural science New York,
Wiley [1973] xi, 354 p. 721/.03
73-15839
    NA31 .C64 MRR Alc.

Crispin, Frederic Swing, Dictionary
of technical terms. 11th ed., rev.
New York, Bruce Pub. Co. [1970] vi,
455 p. 603 73-104870
    T9 .C885 1970 MRR Alc.

National Association of Women in
Construction. Phoenix Chapter.
Construction dictionary; construction
terms & tables and an encyclopedia of
construction. Phoenix, Ariz. [1973]
viii, 599 p. 690/.03 73-83758
    TH9 .N3 1973 MRR Alc.

Putnam, R. E. Architectural and
building trades dictionary 3d ed.
Chicago, American Technical Society
[1974] 510 p. 721/.03 74-75483
    TH9 .P82 1974 MRR Alc.

CONSTRUCTION INDUSTRY--MANAGEMENT.
O'Brien, James Jerome. Contractor's
management handbook. New York,
McGraw-Hill [1971] 1 v. (various
pagings) [$24.50] 658/.92/4 76-
169190
    HD9715.A2 O23 MRR Alc.

**CONSTRUCTION INDUSTRY--FRANCE--
DIRECTORIES.**
Sageret; Paris. 53-28411
    "Fondé en 1809."
    TH12 .S25 MRR Alc Latest edition

**CONSTRUCTION INDUSTRY--GREAT BRITAIN--
DIRECTORIES.**
Construction Industry Research and
Information Association. CIRIA guide
to sources of information; London,
CIRIA, [1970]. 176 p. 690/.07 72-
194509
    HD9715.G72 C65 MRR Alc.

Sell's building index. Epsom, Eng.,
Sell's Publications Ltd. [£4.50]
338.4/7/69002542 73-640925
    HD9715.G7 S4 MRR Alc Latest
    edition

CONSTRUCTION INDUSTRY--UNITED STATES.
United States. Bureau of the Census.
Housing construction statistics, 1889
to 1964. Washington [For sale by the
Superintendent of Documents, U.S.
Govt. Print. Off., 1966] v, 805 p.
338.4/7/69080973 a 66-7417
    HD7293 .A5 1966d MRR Alc.

**CONSTRUCTION INDUSTRY--UNITED STATES--
BIBLIOGRAPHY.**
Lipsey, Robert E. Source book of
statistics relating to construction
New York, National Bureau of Economic
Research; distributed by Columbia
University Press, New York, 1966. x,
307 p. 338.476900973 66-22747
    HD9715.A2 L5 MRR Alc.

**CONSTRUCTION INDUSTRY--UNITED STATES--
DIRECTORIES.**
The Blue book of major homebuilders.
[Crofton, Md.] CMR Associates.
338.4/7/690802573 72-621729
    TH12.5 .B5 MRR Alc Latest edition

Contractors register. Elmsford, N.Y.
[etc.] Sub-contractors Register, inc.
[etc.] 620.58 31-33270
    "Established 1913."
    TA12 .C6 Sci RR Latest edition /
    MRR Alc Latest edition

**CONSTRUCTION INDUSTRY--UNITED STATES--
SEASONAL VARIATIONS.**
Lipsey, Robert E. Source book of
statistics relating to construction
New York, National Bureau of Economic
Research; distributed by Columbia
University Press, New York, 1966. x,
307 p. 338.476900973 66-22747
    HD9715.A2 L5 MRR Alc.

**CONSTRUCTION INDUSTRY--UNITED STATES--
STATISTICS.**
Lipsey, Robert E. Source book of
statistics relating to construction
New York, National Bureau of Economic
Research; distributed by Columbia
University Press, New York, 1966. x,
307 p. 338.476900973 66-22747
    HD9715.A2 L5 MRR Alc.

United States. Bureau of the Census.
1967 census of construction
industries. [Washington; For sale by
the Supt. of Docs., U.S. Govt. Print.
Off.] 1971. 2 v. [$5.00 (v. 1)
$6.50 (v. 2)] 338.4/7/624 79-
609528
    HD9715.U52 A57352 MRR Alc.

CONSULTING ENGINEERS--DIRECTORIES.
The Consulting engineers who's who &
year book. London, Norwood
Industrial Publications Ltd.[etc.]
620.942 49-25787
    Began with vol. for 1947.
    TA1 .C774 Sci RR Latest edition /
    MRR Biog Latest edition

**CONSULTING ENGINEERS--UNITED STATES--
DIRECTORIES.**
American Institute of Consulting
Engineers. Engineering consultants.
1952- New York. 620.58 53-8444
    TA12 .A62 MRR Biog Latest edition

CONSUMER ADVERTISING
see Advertising

CONSUMER EDUCATION.
see also Home economics

see also Shopping

Association of Better Business
Bureaus. Consumer's buying guide;
New York [1969] 205 p. [1.00]
640.73 68-15313
    TX335 .A87 MRR Alc.

Passell, Peter. The best New York,
Farrar, Straus and Giroux [1974] 169
p. 031/.02 73-87697
    TX335 .P35 1974 MRR Alc.

United States. Dept. of Agriculture.
Consumers all. [Washington, For sale
by the Superintendent of Documents,
U.S. Govt. Print. Off., 1965] xiv,
496 p. agr65-386
    S21. A35 1965 MRR Alc.

White, Jack M. The angry buyer's
complaint directory New York, P. H.
Wyden [1974] xxviii, 292 p. [$7.95]
381 73-86179
    HF5415.5 .W55 MRR Alc.

**CONSUMER EDUCATION--INFORMATION
SERVICES--UNITED STATES--DIRECTORIES.**
Wasserman, Paul. Consumer
sourcebook; Detroit, Gale Research
Co. [1974] xi, 593 p. 381/.3 74-
10494
    HC110.C63 W37 MRR Ref Desk.

CONSUMER EDUCATION--PERIODICALS.
Consumer reports. v. 1- May 1936-
[Mount Vernon, N.Y., etc., Consumers
Union of United States] 43-33888
    TX335 .A1C6 MRR Ref Desk Buying
    guide issue only.

CONSUMER EDUCATION--YEARBOOKS.
Price buying directory. [Chicago]
Consumers Digest. 77-789
    TX335.A1 P74 MRR Ref Desk Latest
    edition

**CONSUMER PROTECTION--INFORMATION
SERVICES--UNITED STATES--DIRECTORIES.**
Wasserman, Paul. Consumer
sourcebook; Detroit, Gale Research
Co. [1974] xi, 593 p. 381/.3 74-
10494
    HC110.C63 W37 MRR Ref Desk.

CONSUMER PROTECTION--UNITED STATES.
Rosenbloom, Joseph. Consumer
complaint guide, 1973. New York, CCM
Information Corp. [1972] iv, 476 p.
338.4/7/602573 73-154774
    T12 .R66 1972 MRR Alc.

**CONSUMER PROTECTION--UNITED STATES--
ADDRESSES, ESSAYS, LECTURES.**
McClellan, Grant S., comp. The
consuming public, New York, H. W.
Wilson Co., 1968. 219 p. 339.4 68-
17134
    HC110.C6 M22 MRR Alc.

**CONSUMER PROTECTION--UNITED STATES--
DIRECTORIES.**
Directory of consumer protection and
environmental agencies. 1st ed.
Orange, N.J., Academic Media [1973]
xiii, 627 p. 381 72-75952
    HC110.C63 D55 MRR Ref Desk.

Directory of Government agencies
safeguarding consumer and
environment. 1st- ed., 1968-
Alexandria, Va., Serina Press.
339.4/02573 68-20372
    HC110.C6 D5 MRR Alc Latest edition

White, Jack M. The angry buyer's
complaint directory New York, P. H.
Wyden [1974] xxviii, 292 p. [$7.95]
381 73-86179
    HF5415.5 .W55 MRR Alc.

CONSUMERS--UNITED STATES.
Surveys of consumers. 1971/72- [Ann
Arbor, Mich., Institute for Social
Research, University of Michigan]
658.8/3973 72-619718
    HC110.S3 A3 MRR Alc Latest edition

**CONSUMERS--UNITED STATES--ADDRESSES,
ESSAYS, LECTURES.**
McClellan, Grant S., comp. The
consuming public, New York, H. W.
Wilson Co., 1968. 219 p. 339.4 68-
17134
    HC110.C6 M22 MRR Alc.

CONSUMERS' GOODS
see Manufactures

CONSUMPTION (ECONOMICS)
see also Marketing

see also Prices

CONSUMPTION (ECONOMICS)--EUROPE.
A survey of Europe today; London,
Reader's Digest Association, 1970.
212 p. [£25/-] 339.4/094 73-
571754
    HD7022 .S86 MRR Alc.

CONSUMPTION (ECONOMICS)--UNITED STATES.
Surveys of consumers. 1971/72- [Ann
Arbor, Mich., Institute for Social
Research, University of Michigan]
658.8/3973 72-619718
    HC110.S3 A3 MRR Alc Latest edition

CONTAINER INDUSTRY--DIRECTORIES.
Jane's freight containers. 1st-
ed.; 1968/69- New York, McGraw-Hill
Book Co. 380.5/3 74-2497
    TA1215 .J34 Sci RR Latest edition
    / MRR Alc Latest edition

**CONTAINER INDUSTRY--UNITED STATES--
DIRECTORIES.**
Official container directory.
Chicago, Bittendorf Pub. [etc.]
658.78844058 53-16824
    TS2301.C8 O3 MRR Alc Latest
    edition

CONTAINERIZATION.
Jane's freight containers. 1st-
ed.; 1968/69- New York, McGraw-Hill
Book Co. 380.5/3 74-2497
    TA1215 .J34 Sci RR Latest edition
    / MRR Alc Latest edition

CONTAINERS.
see also Packaging

CONTAINERS--DIRECTORIES.
Official container directory.
Chicago, Bittendorf Pub. [etc.]
658.78844058 53-16824
    TS2301.C8 O3 MRR Alc Latest
    edition

CONTAMINATION (TECHNOLOGY)
see also Pollution

CONTEMPORARY ART
see Art, Modern--20th century

CONTRACEPTION
see Birth control

CONTRACT BRIDGE--BIOGRAPHY.
American Contract Bridge League. The official encyclopedia of bridge, New, rev. and expanded ed. New York, Crown Publishers [1971] 783 p. [$12.50] 795.4/15/03 73-108084
GV1282.3 .A44 1971 MRR Alc.

CONTRACT BRIDGE--DICTIONARIES.
American Contract Bridge League. The official encyclopedia of bridge, New, rev. and expanded ed. New York, Crown Publishers [1971] 783 p. [$12.50] 795.4/15/03 73-108084
GV1282.3 .A44 1971 MRR Alc.

Reese, Terence. Bridge player's dictionary. [New York] Sterling Pub. Co. [1959] 252 p. 795.415 59-65439
GV1282.3 .R34 MRR Alc.

CONTRACTIONS
see Abbreviations

CONTRACTORS--UNITED STATES--DIRECTORIES.
Contractors register. Elmsford, N.Y. [etc.] Sub-contractors Register, inc. [etc.] 620..58 31-33270
"Established 1913."
TA12 .C6 Sci RR Latest edition / MRR Alc Latest edition

CONTROL EQUIPMENT
see Automatic control

CONTROL OF PESTS
see Pest control

CONTROL THEORY--DICTIONARIES.
Meetham, A. R. Encyclopaedia of linguistics, information, and control. [1st ed.] Oxford, New York, Pergamon Press [1969] xiv, 718 p. 001.5/39/03 68-18528
Q360 .M35 1969 MRR Alc.

CONUNDRUMS
see Riddles

CONURBATIONS
see Metropolitan areas

CONVALESCENCE.
see also Nursing homes

CONVENTION FACILITIES--DIRECTORIES.
Official meeting facilities guide. spring 1974- [New York, Public Transportation & Travel Div., Ziff-Davis Publishing Co.] [$10.00]
647/94 74-644953
TX907 .O46 MRR Alc Latest edition

CONVERSATION.
see also Discussion

CONVICT LABOR--BIBLIOGRAPHY.
United States. Library of Congress. Division of bibliography. ... List of references on prison labor. Washington, Govt. print. off., 1915. 74 p. 14-30013
Z663.28 .L58 MRR Alc.

CONVICTS
see Prisoners

COOKERY.
see also Diet

see also Food

American Home Economics Association. Food and Nutrition Section. Terminology Committee. Handbook of food preparation. Washington, American Home Economics Association. 641.02 59-53013
Began publication with 1946 edition.
TX355 .A49 MRR Alc Latest edition

Pellaprat, Henri Paul. Modern French culinary art. Cleveland, World Pub. Co. [1966] xvi, 1171 p. 641.5944 65-25779
TX719 .P3813 1966 MRR Alc.

Quat, Helen. The wonderful world of freezer cooking. New York, Hearthside Press, 1964. 224 p. 641.5 64-19654
TX828 .Q3 MRR Alc.

United States. Dept. of Agriculture. Food for us all. [Washington: For sale by the Supt. of Docs., U.S. Govt. Print. Off., 1969] xxxix, 360 p. [3.50] 641.3 76-604428
S21 .A35 1969 MRR Alc.

COOKERY--BIBLIOGRAPHY.
Bitting, Katherine (Golden) Mrs., Gastronomic bibliography, San Francisco, Calif., 1939. 2 p. l., vii-xiii p., 1 l., 718 p. 016.641 39-15674
Z5776.G2 B6 MRR Alc.

Vicaire, Georges, Bibliographie gastronomique; [2d ed.] London, D. Verschoyle, Academic and Bibliographical Publications, 1954. [6] p., facsim.: xviii p., 972 columns. 54-6692
Z5776.G2 V5 1954 MRR Alc.

COOKERY--DICTIONARIES.
Funk & Wagnalls cook's and diner's dictionary. New York, Funk & Wagnalls [1969, c1968] xiv, 274 p. [$6.95] 641.3/003 68-21923
TX349 .F85 MRR Alc.

Senn, Charles Herman, Dictionary of foods and cookery terms [New ed.]; London, Ward Lock, 1972. [5], 164 p. [£2.25] 641.3/003 72-188538
TX349 .S46 1972 MRR Alc.

Shannon, Ellen C. The cook in the kitchen; South Brunswick, A. S. Barnes [1974, c1962] 204 p. [$8.95] 641.5/03 73-10527
TX349 .S49 1974 MRR Alc.

Simon, André Louis, A concise encyclopaedia of gastronomy; [1st American ed.] New York, Harcourt, Brace [1952] 816 p. 641.03 52-13763
TX631 .S53 1952a MRR Alc.

Simon, André Louis, A dictionary of gastronomy New York, McGraw-Hill [1970] 400 p. [$15.95] 641/.03 72-89318
TX349 .S53 1970 MRR Alc.

Smith, Henry, Classical recipes of the world, New York, Macmillan, 1955 [c1954] 631 p. 641.03 55-808
TX651 .S5 1955 MRR Alc.

Waldo, Myra. Dictionary of international food & cooking terms. New York, Macmillan Co. [1967] 648 p. 641/.03 67-27514
TX349 .W24 MRR Alc.

COOKERY--DICTIONARIES--FRENCH.
Montagné, Prosper, Larousse gastronomique; New York, Crown Publishers [1961] 1101 p. 641.03 61-15788
TX349 .M613 MRR Alc.

Smith, Henry, Classical recipes of the world, New York, Macmillan, 1955 [c1954] 631 p. 641.03 55-808
TX651 .S5 1955 MRR Alc.

COOKERY--DICTIONARIES--POLYGLOT.
Hering, Richard, writer on cookery. Dictionary of classical and modern cookery and practical reference manual for the hotel, restaurant, and catering trade. Translation of the 11th newly rev. ed. Giessen, Pfanneberg [1958] 852 p. 641.503 59-1834
TX349 .H543 MRR Alc.

COOKERY--HISTORY.
Hale, William Harlan, The Horizon cookbook and illustrated history of eating and drinking through the ages, [New York] American Heritage Pub. Co., book trade distribution by Doubleday [1968] 768 p. [16.50 12.95 (Pre-Christmas price)] 641 68-15655
TX631 .H3 MRR Alc.

Wason, Elizabeth, Cooks, gluttons & gourmets; [1st ed.] Garden City, N.Y., Doubleday, 1962. 381 p. 641.01 61-12598
TX631 .W3 MRR Alc.

COOKERY--INDEXES.
Forsman, John. Recipe index, 1970; Detroit, Gale Research Co. [1972] x, 772 p. 641.5/01/6 72-884
TX651 .F63 MRR Alc.

Forsman, John. Recipe index, 1971; Detroit, Gale Research Co. [c1973] viii, 764 p. 641.5/01/6 74-164317

TX651 .F633 MRR Alc.

Gaunt, Rezia. The food-finder; New Brunswick, N.J.; Scarecrow Press, 1956. 192 p. 641.5 56-8695
TX725 .G33 MRR Alc.

COOKERY--TERMINOLOGY.
Dale, Martin. How to read a French menu. [1st ed.] New York, Appleton-Century [1966] 95 p. 641.5944 65-26808
TX652.7 .D3 MRR Alc.

COOKERY, AMERICAN.
American heritage. The American heritage cookbook and illustrated history of American eating & drinking. [New York] American Heritage Pub. Co.; Distribution by Simon and Schuster [1964] 629 p. 641.5 64-21278
TX705 .A65 MRR Alc.

Beard, James Andrews, James Beard's American cookery. [1st ed.] Boston, Little, Brown [1972] 877 p. [$12.95] 641.5/973 70-165755
TX715 .B3715 MRR Alc.

Ervin, Janet Halliday, ed. The White House cookbook. Chicago, Follett Pub. Co., 1964. xvi, 510 p. 641.5 64-23612
TX715 .E715 MRR Alc.

Farmer, Fannie Merritt, The Fannie Farmer cookbook. 11th ed. Boston, Little, Brown [1965] xi, 624 p. 641.5 65-25022
TX715 .F234 1965 MRR Alc.

New York times. New York times cook book. [1st ed.] New York, Harper [1961] 717 p. 641.59 61-10840
TX725 .N46 MRR Alc.

Rombauer, Irma (von Starkloff) Joy of cooking [Rev. & enl.] Indianapolis, Bobbs-Merrill [1963] 849 p. 641.5 64-5436
TX715 .R75 1963 MRR Alc.

COOKERY, AMERICAN--BIBLIOGRAPHY.
Brown, Eleanor Parker. Culinary Americana; New York, Roving Eye Press [c1961] xiv, 417 p. 64-54658

Z5776.G2 B7 MRR Alc.

Lowenstein, Eleanor. Bibliography of American cookery books, 1742-1860. [3d ed.] Worcester [Mass.] American Antiquarian Society, 1972. xii, 132 p. 016.6415 72-81730
Z5776.G2 L68 1972 MRR Alc.

COOKERY, AMERICAN--HISTORY.
Phipps, Frances, Colonial kitchens, their furnishings, and their gardens, New York, Hawthorn Books [1972] xiii, 346 p. [$12.95] 643/.3/0974 78-158021
TX653 .P48 1972 MRR Alc.

COOKERY, CHINESE.
Miller, Gloria Bley. The thousand recipe Chinese cookbook. [1st ed.] New York, Atheneum, 1966. xiv, 926 p. 641.5/951 66-11398
TX724.5C5 M5 MRR Alc.

COOKERY, FRENCH.
Beck, Simone. Mastering the art of French cooking. [1st ed.] New York, Knopf, 1961-70. 2 v. [$12.50 (v. 2)] 641.5944 61-12313
TX719 .B388 MRR Alc.

Montagné, Prosper, Larousse gastronomique; New York, Crown Publishers [1961] 1101 p. 641.03 61-15788
TX349 .M613 MRR Alc.

Pellaprat, Henri Paul. Modern French culinary art. Cleveland, World Pub. Co. [1966] xvi, 1171 p. 641.5944 65-25779
TX719 .P3813 1966 MRR Alc.

COOKERY, INTERNATIONAL.
Hale, William Harlan, The Horizon cookbook and illustrated history of eating and drinking through the ages, [New York] American Heritage Pub. Co., book trade distribution by Doubleday [1968] 768 p. [16.50 12.95 (Pre-Christmas price)] 641 68-15655
TX631 .H3 MRR Alc.

New York times. New York times cook book. [1st ed.] New York, Harper [1961] 717 p. 641.59 61-10840
TX725 .N46 MRR Alc.

Rosengarten, Frederic. The book of spices. Wynnewood, Pa., Livingston Pub. Co., 1969. xiii, 489 p. [20.00] 641.6/3/83 69-18867
TX406 .R66 MRR Alc.

Smith, Henry, Classical recipes of the world, New York, Macmillan, 1955 [c1954] 631 p. 641.03 55-808
TX651 .S5 1955 MRR Alc.

Wason, Elizabeth, Cooks, gluttons & gourmets; [1st ed.] Garden City, N.Y., Doubleday, 1962. 381 p. 641.01 61-12598
TX631 .W3 MRR Alc.

COOKERY, SWEDISH.
The Great Scandinavian cook book: London, Allen & Unwin, 1966. 734 p. [£5/5/-] 641.59485 66-68078
TX722.S8 G68 MRR Alc.

COOKERY (CHEESE)
Axler, Bruce H. The cheese handbook [New York] Hastings House [1969, c1968] 213 p. [5.95] 641.6/7/3 68-20555
TX382 .A9 MRR Alc.

Simon, André Louis, Cheeses of the world, [2d ed.] London, Faber and Faber [1965] 264 p. 67-5925
SF271 .S53 1965 MRR Alc.

COOKERY (HERBS)
Loewenfeld, Claire. The complete book of herbs and spices / New York : Putnam, [1974] 313 p., [4] leaves of plates : [$14.95] 581.6/3 74-78005
SB351.H5 L67 MRR Alc

Loewenfeld, Claire. Herbs, health and cookery, [1st American ed.] New York, Hawthorn Books [1967] 320 p. 641.6 66-22312
TX819.H4 L6 1967 MRR Alc.

COOKERY (VEGETABLES)
Hawkes, Alex D., A world of vegetable cookery; New York, Simon and Schuster [1968] 274 p. [8.95] 641.6/5 68-25748
TX801 .H35 MRR Alc.

COOKERY FOR THE SICK.
Proudfit, Fairfax Throckmorton. Proudfit-Robinson's Normal and therapeutic nutrition. 13th ed. New York, Macmillan [1967] xiv, 891 p. 641.1 67-16055
RM216 .P83 1967 MRR Alc.

COOKIES.
Biscuit & cracker baker blue book. New York, American Trade Pub. Co. 338.4/7/66475202573 63-36580
HD9057 .A1B5 MRR Alc Latest edition

COOLING APPLIANCES
see Refrigeration and refrigerating machinery

COOPERATION, AGRICULTURAL
see Agriculture, Cooperative

COPENHAGEN--DIRECTORIES.
Krak. 199.- arg.; 1968-
København. 73-640519
HF3643 .K85 MRR Alc Latest edition

COPENHAGEN--STREETS.
Kraks lomme-vejviser for København. København, Kraks legat. 52-41852
DL276 .K67 MRR Alc Latest edition

COPPER AGE.
see also Archaeology

COPYING PROCESSES.
Hawken, William R. Copying methods manual Chicago, Library Technology Program, American Library Association [1966] xv, 375 p. 655.3 66-25095

Z48 .H32 MRR Alc.

COPYRIGHT.
United States. Copyright Office. Bulletin. no. 1- 1898- Washington, Govt. Print. Off. 05-8691
Z663.8 .A3 MRR Alc MRR Alc Partial set

United States. Copyright office. The Copyright bill: S. 6330; H.R. 19853 Fifty-ninth Congress, first session, compared with copyright statutes now in force and earlier United States copyright enactments ... Washington, Govt. print. off., 1906. 86 p. 06-46356
Z663.8 .A3 no. 12 1906 MRR Alc.

COPYRIGHT--BIBLIOGRAPHY.
United States. Copyright office. Report on copyright legislation, Washington, Govt. print. off., 1904. 159 p. 04-21057
Z663.8 .R4 MRR Alc.

COPYRIGHT--UNAUTHORIZED REPRINTS.
Brussel, Isidore Rosenbaum, Anglo-American first editions. London, Constable & co. ltd., New York, R. R. Bowker co., 1935-36. 2 v. 016.0944 016.82 35-18256
Z2014.F5 B9 MRR Alc.

COPYRIGHT--CANADA.
Solberg, Thorvald, comp. Copyright in Canada and Newfoundland. Washington, Govt print. off., 1903. 3 p. l., 5-126 p. 03-32910
Z663.8 .A3 no. 6 1903 MRR Alc.

COPYRIGHT--GREAT BRITAIN.
Great Britain. Laws, statutes, etc. Copyright in England. Washington, Govt. print. off., 1914. 1 p. l., 5-54 p. 14-30942
Z663.8 .A3 no. 16 1914 MRR Alc.

London. Stationers' company. Copyright office. Copyright in England. 2d ed Washington, Govt. print. off., 1902. 101 p. 03-33066

Z663.8 .A3 no. 5 1902 MRR Alc.

COPYRIGHT--JAPAN.
Japan. Laws, statutes, etc. Copyright in Japan. Washington, Govt. print. off., 1906. 3 p. l. 50 p. 06-38532
Z663.8 .A3 no. 11 1906 MRR Alc.

COPYRIGHT--PHILIPPINE ISLANDS.
Philippine Islands. Laws, statutes, etc. The copyright law of the Philippine Islands, March 6, 1924 ... Washington, U.S. Govt. Print. off., 1928. 11 p. 28-26672
Z663.8 .A3 no. 21 1928 MRR Alc.

COPYRIGHT--UNITED STATES.
Bentley, Harry Clark, Bibliography of works on accounting by American authors, New York, A. M. Kelley, 1970. 2 v. in 1. 016.657 72-115313
Z7164.C81 B5 1970 MRR Alc.

United States. Copyright Office. Bulletin. no. 1- 1898- Washington, Govt. Print. Off. 05-8691
Z663.8 .A3 MRR Alc MRR Alc Partial set

United States. Copyright office. Copyright in Congress, 1789-1904. Washington, Govt. print. off., 1905. 468 p. 06-604
Z663.8 .A3 no. 8 1905 MRR Alc.

United States. Copyright Office. Copyright law revision. Washington, U.S. Govt. Print. Off., 1961-[65] 6 v. 655.673 61-61901
Z663.8 .C58 1961 MRR Alc.

United States. Copyright office. Directions for securing copyrights. [2d ed.] Washington, Govt. print. off., 1899. 30 p. 06-20844
Z663.8 A3 no. 2 1899b MRR Alc.

United States. Copyright office. Report on copyright legislation, Washington, Govt. print. off., 1904. 159 p. 04-21057
Z663.8 .R4 MRR Alc.

United States. Laws, statutes, etc. Copyright enactments: Rev. Washington, Copyright Office, Library of Congress, 1963- 1 v. (loose-leaf) 63-60062
Z663.8 .A3 no. 3 1963 MRR Alc.

COPYRIGHT--UNITED STATES--ADDRESSES, ESSAYS, LECTURES.
Copyright: current viewpoints on history, laws, legislation. New York, Bowker, 1972. vii, 125 p. 346/.73/0482 72-774
KF2994.A2 C64 MRR Alc.

COPYRIGHT--UNITED STATES--CASES.
United States. Courts. Decisions of the United States courts involving copyright 1909/14- Washington, Copyright Office, Library of Congress [etc.] 655.673 15-26124
Z663.8 .A3 MRR Alc MRR Alc Partial set

COPYRIGHT--UNITED STATES--HISTORY.
United States. Copyright Office. The history of U.S.A. copyright law revision, 1901-1954. Washington [1955] 20 p. 655.673 55-61800
Z663.8 .H5 MRR Alc.

COPYRIGHT, INTERNATIONAL--ADDRESSES, ESSAYS, LECTURES.
Copyright: current viewpoints on history, laws, legislation. New York, Bowker, 1972. vii, 125 p. 346/.73/0482 72-774
KF2994.A2 C64 MRR Alc.

COREY, HERBERT, 1872-1954--BIBLIOGRAPHY.
United States. Library of Congress. Manuscript Division. Herbert Corey; a register of his papers in the Library of Congress. Washington, 1959. 7 l. 012 59-60029
Z663.34 .C63 MRR Alc.

CORK, IRELAND (COUNTY)--COMMERCE--DIRECTORIES.
Cork and Munster trades' directory. Edinburgh, Trades' Directories. 62-38597
HF5163.M8 C6 MRR Alc Latest edition

CORNISH LANGUAGE--DICTIONARIES--ENGLISH.
Nance, Robert Morton. A Cornish-English dictionary. Marazion, Printed for the Federation of Old Cornwall Societies by Worden, 1955. vii, 104 p. 62-50333
PB2537.E5 N33 1955 MRR Alc.

CORONATIONS--GREAT BRITAIN.
Jones, William, F.S.A. Crowns and coronations; New ed. Detroit, Singing Tree Press, 1968. xxx, 551 p. 394/.4 67-24356
DA112 .J8 1968 MRR Alc.

CORPORATE ENTRY (CATALOGING)
United States. Library of Congress. Catalog division. Guide to the cataloguing of the serial publications of societies and institutions, 2d ed. Reprinted 1938. Washington, U.S. Govt. print. off., 1931 [i.e. 1938] x, 128 p. mrr01-52
Z663.74 G8 1938 MRR Alc.

United States. Library of Congress. Technical Information Division. Corporate author headings; Washington, 1957. v, 348 p. 025.3 58-61093
Z663.49 .C64 MRR Alc.

CORPORATE MEETINGS.
Association executives buyers' guide and meeting planner. v. 1- 1973- [Washington, Columbia Books] [$7.50] 658.4 72-92834
HD2743 .A75 MRR Alc Latest edition

CORPORATION LAW.
see also Public utilities

CORPORATION LAW--UNITED STATES.
The Corporation manual; New York, United States Corporation Co. 21-4563
KF1415 .C63 MRR Alc Latest edition

CORPORATION REPORTS.
Bernstein, Leopold A. Understanding corporate reports! Homewood, Ill., Dow Jones-Irwin, 1974. xv, 596 p. [$12.95] 658.1/512 74-7869
HF5681.B2 B46 1974b MRR Alc.

Foster, Louis Omar, Understanding financial statements and corporate annual reports. [1st ed.] Philadelphia, Chilton Co., Book Division [1961] 135 p. 332.6 61-14509
HG4028.B2 F6 MRR Alc.

CORPORATION REPORTS--YEARBOOKS.
Accounting trends and techniques in published corporate annual reports. 1st- 1945/47- New York, American Institute of Accountants. 657 48-2517
HF5681.B2 A35 MRR Alc Latest edition

CORPORATION SECRETARIES--UNITED STATES.
American Society of Corporate Secretaries. Year book. New York. 658.16058 52-31396
HD2709 .A673 MRR Alc Latest edition

CORPORATIONS.
see also International business enterprises

see also Securities

CORPORATIONS--CHARITABLE CONTRIBUTIONS--UNITED STATES.
Aid-to-education programs of some leading business concerns. New York. 378.1 62-4102
LB2342 .C6744 MRR Alc Latest edition

CORPORATIONS--PERIODICALS--INDEXES.
F & S index international: industries, countries, companies. 1st- ed.; 1968- Cleveland, Predicasts. 016.338 74-644265
Z7164.C81 F13 MRR Alc Full set / Sci RR Partial set

CORPORATIONS--YEARBOOKS.
The "Digest" year book of public companies of Australia & New Zealand. Sydney, N.S.W., Jobson's publications pty. limited. 338.058 45-26276
Publication began in 1928.
HD2927 .D5 MRR Alc Latest edition

CORPORATIONS--AFRICA, SOUTH.
Beerman's financial year book of southern Africa; 1947/48- Johannesburg [etc.] Combined Publishers [etc.] 332.6/0968 48-17050
HG5850.S6 S67 MRR Alc Latest edition

Johannesburg. Stock Exchange. The Stock Exchange handbook. 1967- Johannesburg, Flesch Financial Publications. 332.63/0968 68-130426

HG5841 .J63 MRR Alc Latest edition

CORPORATIONS--ASIA--DIRECTORIES.
Asian buyers' guide to Republic of China, Hong Kong, Japan, Republic of Singapore, and Thailand. 1st- ed.; 1968- Hong Kong, International Pub. Co. 670 .25/5 68-7584
HF3763 .A82 MRR Alc Latest edition

CORPORATIONS--AUSTRALASIA--DIRECTORIES.
Who owns whom: Australasia and Far East. 1972- London, O. W. Roskill. 382/.025 74-642726
HD2927 .W48 MRR Alc Latest edition

CORPORATIONS--AUSTRALIA.
The "Digest" year book of public companies of Australia & New Zealand. Sydney, N.S.W., Jobson's publications pty. limited. 338.058 45-26276
Publication began in 1928.
HD2927 .D5 MRR Alc Latest edition

CORPORATIONS--AUSTRALIA. (Cont.)
Potter (Ian) & Company. Selected
Australian ordinary shares.
Melbourne. 66-99703
    HG5894 .P6 MRR Alc Latest edition

Wheelwright, Edward Lawrence.
Anatomy of Australian manufacturing
industry; Sydney, Law Book Co.,
1967. xvii, 433 p. [$13.99 Aust.]
338.7/4/0994 67-95586
    HD2927 .W45 MRR Alc.

CORPORATIONS--AUSTRALIA--DIRECTORIES.
The Business who's who of Australia.
1964- Sydney, R. G. Riddell. 64-
56752
    HF5292 .B795 MRR Alc Latest
    edition

CORPORATIONS--AUSTRIA--FINANCE--
YEARBOOKS.
Finanz-Compass: 79.- Jahrg.; 1950-
Wien, Compass-Verlag. 54-17734
    HG5451 .F5 MRR Alc Latest edition

CORPORATIONS--AUSTRIA--YEARBOOKS.
Almanach der österreichischen
Aktiengesellschaften. Wien [Wiener
Börsen-Kurier, Verlag F. Brabec,
etc.] 62-27652
    Began publication in 1927.
    HG4007 .A6 MRR Alc Latest edition

CORPORATIONS--BELGIUM.
Le Recueil financier; Bruxelles, É.
Bruylant. 332.63 49-52017
    Began publication in 1893.
    HG5551 .R42 MRR Alc Latest edition

CORPORATIONS--BOSTON--DIRECTORIES.
Directory of directors in the city of
Boston and vicinity. 1905- Boston,
Bankers Service Co. 05-8359
    HG4058.B7 MRR Alc Latest edition

CORPORATIONS--CANADA.
Canadian Newspaper Service, ltd.
National reference book on Canadian
business personalities, [Montreal]
29-2668
    F1001 .C277 MRR Biog Latest
    edition

Financial times of Canada, Montreal.
A guide to 100 Canadian stocks, [2d
rev. ed.; [Montreal] 1968. 61 p.
332.63/223/0971 71-489820
    HG5158 .F53 1968 MRR Alc.

CORPORATIONS--CANADA--BIBLIOGRAPHY.
Harvard University. Graduate School
of Business Administration. Baker
Library. Studies in enterprise;
Boston, 1957. xiv, 169 p.
016.33874 57-11481
    Z7164.C81 H26 1957 MRR Alc.

CORPORATIONS--CANADA--DIRECTORIES.
Financial post. Directory of
directors [executives of Canada]
Toronto. 650.58 52-26909
    HG4090.Z5 F5 MRR Alc Latest
    edition

The National list of advertisers.
Toronto, Maclean-Hunter Pub. Co. 56-
46268
    HF5808.C2 N3 MRR Alc Latest
    edition

Who owns whom. North American
edition. London, O. W. Roskill.
332.6/73/025 74-646353
    HG4538 .W423 MRR Alc Latest
    edition

CORPORATIONS--EAST (FAR EAST)--
DIRECTORIES.
Who owns whom: Australasia and Far
East. 1972- London, O. W. Roskill.
382/.025 74-642726
    HD2927 .W48 MRR Alc Latest edition

CORPORATIONS--EGYPT.
The Stock exchange year-book of
Egypt. Cairo, Egypt. 332.63 45-
33051
    Publication began with issue for
    1939?
    HG5831 .S75 MRR Alc Latest edition

CORPORATIONS--EUROPE.
Jane's major companies of Europe.
1st- ed.;1965- London, S. Marston
& Co. [etc.] 65-2174
    HG5421 .J35 MRR Alc Latest edition

CORPORATIONS--EUROPE--DIRECTORIES.
Noyes Data S.A. Key European
industrials 1970. Zug, Switzerland,
Noyes Data Corp.; Park Ridge, N.J.,
Noyes Data Corp. [c1970] 2 v.
[85.00F per vol.] 338/.0025/4 78-
129041
    HD9720.3 .N65 MRR Alc.

Who owns whom. Continental edition.
1st- ed.; 1961/62- London, O. W.
Roskill. 63-24027
    HG4132.Z5 W5 MRR Alc Latest
    edition

CORPORATIONS--EUROPE--DIRECTORIES--
BIBLIOGRAPHY.
Henderson, G. P., ed. European
companies: 3rd ed. Beckenham, CBD
Research Ltd., 1972. iii-xiii, 224 p.
[£10.00 ($30.00 U.S.)]
016.3387/4/094 73-151246
    HC240 .H458 1972 MRR Ref Desk.

CORPORATIONS--FRANCE.
Annuaire-Chaix. Paris, Imprimerie
Chaix. ca 18-193
    HG5471 .A6 MRR Alc Latest edition

Annuaire Desfossés; Paris, Cote
Desfossés [etc.] 332.63 46-39086
    HG5471 .A64 MRR Alc Latest edition

Répertoire général alphabétique
des valeurs cotées en France et es
valeurs non cotées. Paris,
Éditions financières alphabétiques.
47-42094
    HG5471 .R4 MRR Alc Latest edition

CORPORATIONS--FRANCE--DIRECTORIES.
Qui représente qui en France? 1.-
ed.; 1957- Paris, Société des
Annuaires "Qui représente qui",
[etc.] 60-20676
    HF3553 .Q5 MRR Alc Latest edition

CORPORATIONS--GERMANY.
Handbuch der deutschen Aktien-
Gesellschaften. Darmstadt [etc.]
Hoppenstedt [etc.] ca 15-275
    HG5491 .H4 MRR Alc Latest edition

Saling Aktienführer. Darmstadt,
Hoppenstedt. 57-40599
    Began publication with vol. for
    1935/36;
    HG5501 .S3 MRR Alc Latest edition

CORPORATIONS--GERMANY (FEDERAL
REPUBLIC, 1949-)
Die Grossen 500 [i.e. Fünfhundert]
1970- Düsseldorf, Droste Verlag.
70-612586
    HD2859 .G7 MRR Alc Latest edition

CORPORATIONS--GERMANY (FEDERAL
REPUBLIC, 1949-)--DIRECTORIES.
Handbuch der Direktoren und
Aufsichtsrate. 1967/68- Berlin,
Finanz- und Korrespondenz-Verlag Dr.
G. Mossner. 72-626450
    HG4156 .H35 MRR Alc Latest edition

CORPORATIONS--GREAT BRITAIN.
Guide to British employers. London,
Cornmarket Press. 331.702/0942 72-
27261
    HF5382.5.G7 G8 MRR Alc Latest
    edition

The Stock exchange official yearbook. [1st]- 1934- Croydon, Eng.
[etc.] T. Skinner [etc.] 332.6305
34-16479
    HG5431 .S82 MRR Alc Latest edition

The Times 1000. London, Times
Newspapers. 338.7/4/0942 72-617301

    HG4135 .T54 MRR Alc Latest edition

CORPORATIONS--GREAT BRITAIN--
DIRECTORIES.
Dun & Bradstreet's guide to key
British enterprises. 1961- London.
62-41097
    HC252 .D8 MRR Alc Latest edition

Register of defunct and other
companies removed from the Stock
Exchange official year-book. 1946-
Croydon, Eng. [etc.] T. Skinner.
332.63 51-24150
    HG5431 .R44 MRR Alc Latest edition

Who owns whom. U. K. edition.
London, O. W. Roskill. 59-52911
    Began publication in 1958.
    HG4135.Z5 W5 MRR Alc Latest
    edition

CORPORATIONS--GREAT BRITAIN--YEARBOOKS.
Moodies investment digest. 1966-
[London] Moodies Services. 332.67
68-119819
    HG5431 .M6 MRR Alc Latest edition
    / MRR Alc Latest edition

CORPORATIONS--INDIA--YEARBOOKS.
Calcutta. Stock Exchange. Official
year book. Calcutta, Calcutta Stock
Exchange Assn. 332.6 49-39127
    HG5740 .C3 MRR Alc Latest edition

Kothari's economic and industrial
guide of India. 29th- ed.; 1971/72-
Madras, Kothari. [$25.00]
338/.0954 72-904460
    HG5731 .I57 MRR Alc Latest edition

CORPORATIONS--IRELAND--YEARBOOKS.
Handbook of Irish securities, etc.
London, Straker Bros. ltd. 55-32941

    HG5443.I7 H3 MRR Alc Latest
    edition

CORPORATIONS--ITALY--STATISTICS.
Associazione fra le società italiane
per azioni. Società italiane per
azioni: notizie statistiche. Roma.
54-44415
    HG4166 .A83 MRR Alc Latest edition

CORPORATIONS--JAPAN.
Japan company directory. 1957-
[Tokyo] Oriental economist. 62-29293

    HC161 .J35 MRR Alc Latest edition

CORPORATIONS--JAPAN--DIRECTORIES.
1972 handbook of Japanese
financial/industrial combines; San
Francisco, Pacific Basin Reports
[1972] 83 l. [$25.00]
338.8/5/02552 73-150829
    HD2756.J3 N55 MRR Alc.

J I T; Tokyo, [Kojunsha
International Publishers]
382/.025/52 68-51013
    HF54.J3 J2 MRR Alc Latest edition

The President directory. [Tokyo,
Diamond-Time Co.] [$8.00]
338.7/4/02552 73-645008
    Began in 1967.
    HC461 .P83 MRR Alc Latest edition

CORPORATIONS--NEW YORK (CITY)--
DIRECTORIES.
Directory of directors in the city of
New York. [1898]- New York,
Directory of directors company,
[etc.] 00-1422
    HG4058.N55 MRR Alc Latest edition

CORPORATIONS--NEW ZEALAND.
The "Digest" year book of public
companies of Australia & New Zealand.
Sydney, N.S.W., Jobson's
publications pty. limited. 338.058
45-26276
    Publication began in 1928.
    HD2927 .D5 MRR Alc Latest edition

The New Zealand business who's who.
Wellington, L. T. Watkins, ltd. 338
51-32889
    Began in 1935.
    HC621 .N4 MRR Alc Latest edition

CORPORATIONS--SPAIN--DIRECTORIES--
PERIODICALS.
Anuario español de empresas.
Madrid, Editorial Financiera Alfa
Omega. 338/.0025/46 74-646231
    HG4216.Z5 A65 MRR Alc Latest
    edition

CORPORATIONS--SPAIN--FINANCE.
Anuario financiero y de sociedades
anónimas de España. Madrid,
Editorial Sopec. 74-642352
    Began with 1916.
    HG5631 .A47 MRR Alc Latest edition

CORPORATIONS--SPAIN--FINANCE--
PERIODICALS.
Anuario español de empresas.
Madrid, Editorial Financiera Alfa
Omega. 338/.0025/46 74-646231
    HG4216.Z5 A65 MRR Alc Latest
    edition

CORPORATIONS--SPAIN--YEARBOOKS.
Anuario financiero. Bilbao, Spain.
31-28812
    "Founded in 1914."
    HG61 .A6 MRR Alc Latest edition

CORPORATIONS--SWEDEN.
Svenska aktiebolag. Stockholm, P. A.
Norstedt. 332.6309485 24-15054
    HG4211.Z5 S8 MRR Alc Latest
    edition

CORPORATIONS--SWEDEN--DIRECTORIES.
Some prominent Swedish companies.
Stockholm, P. A. Norstedt.
338.7/09485 78-276274
    HC372 .S64 MRR Alc Latest edition

CORPORATIONS--TEXAS.
Davis, James Walker. A money tree
grows in Texas; New York, Echo House
[1969] 352 p. [1.95]
338.7/4/09764 75-9616
    HG5128.T4 D37 MRR Alc.

CORPORATIONS--THE WEST--YEARBOOKS.
Walker's manual of Western
corporations & securities. 65th-
ed.; 1973- San Francisco.
332.6/7/0978 74-640659
    HG5128.C2 W2 MRR Alc Latest
    edition

CORPORATIONS--UNITED STATES.
American Institute of Management.
Manual of excellent managements. New
York. 658.02 56-14078
    HD2791 .A6 MRR Alc Latest edition

Financial world stock factographs.
38th- ed.; 1952- New York,
Guenther Publ. Corp. 332.6/78 72-
623291
    HG4905 .S68 MRR Alc Latest edition

Index of opportunity for engineers.
1968/69- New York, Macmillan.
620/.0025/73 76-1574
    TA157 .I43 MRR Alc Latest edition

CORPORATIONS--UNITED STATES. (Cont.)
McKay, Ernest A. The Macmillan job
guide to American corporations for
college graduates, graduate students
and junior executives New York,
Macmillan [c1967] ix, 374 p.
331.115 66-20820
HF5382.5.U5 M3 MRR Alc.

Moody's handbook of common stocks.
1965, 3d quarterly- ed. New York,
Moody's Investors Service, inc.
332.6/7 72-623694
HG4501 .M59 MRR Alc Latest edition

New York. Stock Exchange. Listing
statements of the New York Stock
Exchange. New York, F. E. Fitch,
inc., ca 24-283
HG4501 .N4 MRR Alc Partial set

Robert D. Fisher manual of valuable &
worthless securities. v. 1- 1926-
New York, R. D. Fisher [etc.] 26-
5238
HG4055 .R6 MRR Alc Full set

Standard and Poor's Corporation.
Standard & Poor's stock market
encyclopedia. 14th ed. New York
[1971] 1 v. (unpaged) [$25.00]
332.67 70-23142
HG4921 .S68 1971 MRR Ref Desk.

Standard and Poor's Corporation.
Standard & Poor's stock market
encyclopedia. New York 332.6/7 70-
23142
HG4921 .S68 MRR Ref Desk Latest
edition

**CORPORATIONS--UNITED STATES--
BIBLIOGRAPHY.**
Harvard University. Graduate School
of Business Administration. Baker
Library. Studies in enterprise;
Boston, 1957. xiv, 169 p.
016.33874 57-11481
Z7164.C81 H26 1957 MRR Alc.

Wall Street Journal. (Indexes)
Index. [New York] Dow Jones & Co.
59-35162
HG1 .W26 MRR Alc Full set

**CORPORATIONS--UNITED STATES--CASE
STUDIES.**
Council on Economic Priorities.
Guide to corporations; [1st ed.]
Chicago, Swallow Press [1974] iii,
393 p. [$4.95] 301.5/5 73-13212
HD60.5.U5 C7 1974 MRR Alc.

**CORPORATIONS--UNITED STATES--
DIRECTORIES.**
Analyst contact directory. 1968-
[New York, Kennington Pub. Corp.]
658.2 73-246112
HD59 .A53 MRR Alc Latest edition

Directory of companies filing annual
reports with the Securities and
Exchange Commission under the
Securities Exchange Act. of 1934.
Washington, For sale by the Supt. of
Docs., U.S. Govt. Print. Off.
338.7/4/02573 72-620568
HG4556.U5 A39 MRR Alc Latest
edition

Directory of corporate affiliations
of major national advertisers.
Skokie, Ill., National Register Pub.
Co. 67-5728
HG4057 .A219 MRR Alc Latest
edition

Directory of obsolete securities.
1970- [n.p.] Financial Information,
inc. 332.67 72-612940
HG4961 .D56 MRR Alc Latest edition

Dun and Bradstreet, inc. Dun's
reference book of corporate
managements. 1st- ed.; 1967- New
York. 658.1/145/02573 68-44776
HD2745 .D85 MRR Ref Desk Latest
edition

Kelley, Etna M. The business
founding date directory. [1st ed.]
Scarsdale, N.Y., Morgan & Morgan
[1954] x, 228 p. 650.58 54-6999
HD2785 .K4 MRR Ref Desk.

Moody's OTC industrial manual. New
York, Moody's Investors Service.
332.67 77-649772
HG4961 .M7237 MRR Ref Desk Latest
edition

Plant and product directory. 1961-
[New York?] Market Research Dept. of
Fortune. 338.05873 61-12113
HC102 .P59 MRR Alc Latest edition

Standard and Poor's Corporation.
Standard & Poor's stock reports:
American Stock Exchange. Feb. 1973-
New York. 332.6/7 70-183942
HG4905 .S44 MRR Alc Latest edition

Standard and Poor's Corporation.
Standard & Poor's stock reports: New
York Stock Exchange. Jan. 1973- New
York. 332.6/7 74-183943
HG4905 .S443 MRR Alc Latest
edition

Standard and Poor's Corporation.
Standard & Poor's stock reports: over
the counter. Mar. 1973- New York.
332.6/7 78-183944
HG4905 .S444 MRR Alc Latest
edition

Standard directory of advertisers.
Jan. 1916- Skokie, Ill. [etc.]
National Register Pub. Co.
659.102573 15-21147
HF5805 .S7 MRR Alc Latest edition

Walker's manual of Western
corporations & securities. 65th-
ed.: 1973- San Francisco.
332.6/7/0978 74-640659
HG5128.C2 W2 MRR Alc Latest
edition

Wasserman, Paul. Consumer
sourcebook; Detroit, Gale Research
Co. [1974] xi, 593 p. 381/.3 74-
10494
HC110.C63 W37 MRR Ref Desk.

Who owns whom. North American
edition. London, O. W. Roskill.
332.6/73/025 74-646353
HG4538 .W423 MRR Alc Latest
edition

CORPORATIONS--UNITED STATES--FINANCE.
Hillstrom, Roger. 1960-1969, a
decade of corporate and international
finance. New York, IDD [1972] 381
p. 332 72-175335
HG4907 .H54 MRR Alc.

Hudson's corporate mergers. New
York. 338.8/3/0973 74-644554
HG4915 .C67 MRR Alc Latest edition

**CORPORATIONS--UNITED STATES--FINANCE--
STATISTICS.**
United States. Bureau of the Census.
Economic Statistics and Surveys
Division. Enterprise statistics:
1967. [Washington; For sale by the
Supt. of Docs., U.S. Govt. Print.
Off., Washington, 1971- [v. 1,
1972] v. [$7.75 (v. 1)]
338/.0973 79-186224
HC106.6 .U55 1972 MRR Alc.

CORPORATIONS--UNITED STATES--HISTORY.
Evans, George Heberton. Business
incorporations in the United States,
1800-1943. [New York] National
Bureau of Economic Research [1948]
viii, 184 p. 338.7 48-10514
HD2785 .E85 MRR Alc.

Kelley, Etna M. The business
founding date directory. [1st ed.]
Scarsdale, N.Y., Morgan & Morgan
[1954] x, 228 p. 650.58 54-6999
HD2785 .K4 MRR Ref Desk.

**CORPORATIONS--UNITED STATES--
PERIODICALS.**
F & S index of corporate change.
Cleveland, Predicasts, inc.
338.8/3/02573 72-625662
HD2741 .F18 MRR Alc Full set

Growth & acquisition guide yearbook.
1968- Cleveland, Predicasts. 72-
14099
HG4028.M4 G74 MRR Alc Full set

Moody's OTC industrial manual. New
York, Moody's Investors Service.
332.67 77-649772
HG4961 .M7237 MRR Ref Desk Latest
edition

CORPORATIONS--UNITED STATES--TAXATION.
Tax Executives Institute. Foreign
tax directory. [Kansas City, Mo.]
55-32647
HD2753.U6 T27 MRR Alc Latest
edition

Tax Executives Institute. Membership
list. Washington,D.C. [etc.] 55-
22247
HJ2360 .T248 MRR Alc Latest
edition

CORPORATIONS--UNITED STATES--VALUATION.
Badger, Ralph Eastman, The complete
guide to investment analysis New
York, McGraw-Hill [1967] viii, 504
p. 332.6 67-15850
HG4521 .B3432 MRR Alc.

Hudson's corporate mergers. New
York. 338.8/3/0973 74-644554
HG4915 .C67 MRR Alc Latest edition

CORPORATIONS--UNITED STATES--YEARBOOKS.
Moody's bank & finance manual:
American and foreign. New York,
Moody's Investors Service. 56-14722

HG4961 .M65 MRR Alc Latest edition

Moody's industrial manual: 1954-
New York, Moody's Investors Service.
56-14721
HG4961 .M67 MRR Alc Latest edition

Moody's public utility manual. 1954-
New York, Moody's Investors Service.
56-3927
HG4961 .M7245 MRR Alc Latest
edition

Moody's transportation manual:
American and foreign. 1954- New
York, Moody's Investors Service. 57-
15176
HG4971 .M74 MRR Alc Latest edition

CORPORATIONS, AMERICAN--WISCONSIN.
Financial briefs of Wisconsin
corporations. [Milwaukee] R. W.
Baird. 332.63 51-6093
HG4070.W5 F5 MRR Alc Latest
edition

CORPORATIONS, AMERICAN--DIRECTORIES.
Directory of American firms operating
in foreign countries. New York,
Simon & Schuster, Inc. [etc.] 55-
39067
HG4538.A1 D5 MRR Ref Desk Latest
edition

Shaw, Ray. How to find those great
overseas jobs. NewYork, Award Books
[1973] 319 p. [$1.50] 331.1/28
73-158782
HF5549.5.E45 S5 MRR Alc.

Who owns whom. North American
edition. London, O. W. Roskill.
332.6/73/025 74-646353
HG4538 .W423 MRR Alc Latest
edition

**CORPORATIONS, AMERICAN--FRANCE--
DIRECTORIES.**
American Chamber of Commerce in
France. Directory of American
business in France. Paris. 57-20161

HG4151.Z5 A5 MRR Alc Latest
edition

CORPORATIONS, CANADIAN--DIRECTORIES.
Who owns whom. North American
edition. London, O. W. Roskill.
332.6/73/025 74-646353
HG4538 .W423 MRR Alc Latest
edition

CORPORATIONS, FOREIGN.
United States. Bureau of
International Commerce. Sources of
credit information on foreign firms
for United States firms trading,
investing or manufacturing abroad.
[Washington, For sale by the Supt. of
Docs., U.S. Govt. Print. Off.] 1967.
iv, 108 p. 658.88/025 67-62451
HF5571 .U63 MRR Alc.

CORPORATIONS, FOREIGN--TAXATION.
Tax Executives Institute. Foreign
tax directory. [Kansas City, Mo.]
55-32647
HD2753.U6 T27 MRR Alc Latest
edition

**CORPORATIONS, FOREIGN--FRANCE--
DIRECTORIES.**
Qui represente qui en France? 1.-
ed.; 1957- Paris, Societe des
Annuaires "Qui represente qui",
[etc.] 60-20676
HF3553 .Q5 MRR Alc Latest edition

**CORPORATIONS, FOREIGN--UNITED STATES--
DIRECTORIES.**
Angel, Juvenal Londoño. Directory
of foreign firms operating in the
United States. New York, Simon &
Schuster [1971] 385 p.
338.7/4/02573 72-150331
HG4057 .A155 MRR Alc.

CORPORATIONS, INTERNATIONAL--STATISTICS.
Vaupel, James W. The world's
multinational enterprises; Boston,
Division of Research, Graduate School
of Business Administration, Harvard
University, 1973. xxxiii, 505 p.
[$25.00] 338.8/8 73-76600
HD69.I7 V36 MRR Alc.

CORRECTIONAL INSTITUTIONS.
see also Prisons

**CORRECTIONAL INSTITUTIONS--CANADA--
DIRECTORIES.**
Directory [of] correctional
institutions and agencies of the
United States of America, Canada, and
Great Britain. Washington, American
Correctional Association. 365/.9/7
74-5220
HV9463 .A84 MRR Alc Latest edition

**CORRECTIONAL INSTITUTIONS--GREAT
BRITAIN--DIRECTORIES.**
Directory [of] correctional
institutions and agencies of the
United States of America, Canada, and
Great Britain. Washington, American
Correctional Association. 365/.9/7
74-5220
HV9463 .A84 MRR Alc Latest edition

CORRECTIONAL INSTITUTIONS--UNITED
STATES--DIRECTORIES.
Directory [of] correctional
institutions and agencies of the
United States of America, Canada, and
Great Britain. Washington, American
Correctional Association. 365/.9/7
74-5220
    HV9463 .A84 MRR Alc Latest edition

CORRECTIONS--ADDRESSES, ESSAYS,
LECTURES.
Glaser, Daniel. Handbook of
criminology / Chicago : Rand McNally
College Pub. Co., [1974] xiii, 1180
p. :   364   74-241
    HV6028 .G5 MRR Alc.

CORRECTIONS--BIBLIOGRAPHY.
Wright, Martin. Use of criminology
literature. London, Butterworths
[1974] 242 p. [£5.50] 016.364 74-
174958
    Z5118.C9 W74 1974b MRR Alc.

CORRESPONDENCE
see Commercial correspondence

CORRESPONDENCE SCHOOLS AND COURSES.
The College blue book. [1st]- 1923-
New York [etc.] CCM Information
Corp. [etc.] 378.73 24-223
    LA226 .C685 MRR Ref Desk Latest
        edition

Wellman, Henry Q. The teenager and
home study; [1st ed.] New York, R.
Rosen Press [1970] 155 p. [4.00]
373   78-113611
    LC5951 .W4 MRR Alc.

CORRESPONDENCE SCHOOLS AND COURSES--
DIRECTORIES.
White, Alex Sandri. Extension
facilities guide; Allenhurst, N.J.,
Aurea Publications [1970] 44 l.
[7.00] 374.4/025/73 70-13124
    L900 .W44 MRR Alc.

White, Alex Sandri. Worldwide
register of adult education. [1st]-
ed.; 1960- Allenhurst, N.J. [etc.]
Aurea Publications. 374.4058 60-
2314
    L900 .W45 MRR Alc Latest edition

CORRESPONDENCE SCHOOLS AND COURSES--
UNITED STATES.
Pelton, Robert W., How to go to high
school or college by mail, New York,
F. Fell [1969, c1968] xii, 254 p.
[5.95] 374/.473 68-9264
    LC5951 .P44 MRR Ref Desk.

CORRESPONDENCE SCHOOLS AND COURSES--
UNITED STATES--DIRECTORIES.
College Entrance Examination Board.
The New York Times guide to
continuing education in America.
[New York] Quadrangle Books [1972]
811 p. [$12.50] 374.8/73 74-
183190
    L901 .C74 1972 MRR Ref Desk.

Wellman, Henry Q. The teenager and
home study; [1st ed.] New York, R.
Rosen Press [1970] 155 p. [4.00]
373   78-113611
    LC5951 .W4 MRR Alc.

CORRUPTION (IN POLITICS)
see also Campaign funds

see also Lobbying

CORRUPTION (IN POLITICS)--UNITED STATES.
Miller, Hope Ridings. Scandals in
the highest office; [1st ed.] New
York, Random House [1973] 280 p.
[$6.95] 973/.0892 B 73-5022
    E176.1 .M647 MRR Alc.

Sobel, Lester A., comp. Money &
politics : New York : Facts on File,
[1974] 204 p. ; [$7.95.]
329/.025/0973 74-81147
    JK1994 .S64 MRR Alc.

CORSICA--DESCRIPTION AND TRAVEL--GUIDE-
BOOKS.
Corse. Paris, Hachette [1973] 318
p. 914.4/945/0483 73-169071
    DC611.C81 C59 MRR Alc.

COSMETICS.
Bennett, Harry, The cosmetic
formulary; New York, Chemical
publishing co. of N.Y., inc., 1937-
v.   668   37-2793
    TP983 .B55 MRR Alc.

Gattefossé, René Maurice,
Formulary of perfumery and of
cosmetology. London: L. Hill, 1952.
252 p.   668.5   54-15112
    TP983 .G29 MRR Alc.

Greenberg, Leon Arnold, Handbook of
cosmetic materials: New York,
Interscience Publishers, 1954. ix,
455 p.   668.502 54-7989
    TP983 .G7 MRR Alc.

The Medicine show Rev. ed. New
York, Pantheon Books, 1974. 384 p.
610   74-10418
    RC81 .M496 1974 MRR Alc.

COSMETICS--BIBLIOGRAPHY.
Greenberg, Leon Arnold, Handbook of
cosmetic materials: New York,
Interscience Publishers, 1954. ix,
455 p.   668.502 54-7989
    TP983 .G7 MRR Alc.

COSMETICS--HISTORY.
Corson, Richard. Fashions in makeup;
New York, Universe Books [1972]
xxiv, 614 p. [$30.00] 391/.63/09
71-186143
    GT2340 .C67 MRR Alc.

COSMETICS INDUSTRY--FRANCE--DIRECTORIES.
Guide de la parfumerie. Paris,
Éditions publi-guid. 60-46355
    TP983.A6 G8 MRR Alc Latest edition

COSMETOLOGISTS
see Beauty shops

COSMOGRAPHY.
see also Geography

COSMOLOGY.
see also Astronomy

see also Earth

see also Life on other planets

see also Space sciences

COSMONAUTS
see Astronauts

COST.
see also Prices

COST ACCOUNTING--CASE STUDIES.
Prentice-Hall, inc. Encyclopedia of
cost accounting systems Englewood
Cliffs, N.J. [1965] 3 v. (viii, 1034
p.) 657.4203 65-25432
    HF5686.C8 P67 MRR Alc.

COST AND STANDARD OF LIVING.
see also Wages

COST AND STANDARD OF LIVING--
BIBLIOGRAPHY.
United States. Library of Congress.
Division of bibliography. Select
list of references on the cost of
living and prices; Washington, Govt.
print. off., 1910. v, 107 p. 10-
35008
    Z663.28 .S435 1910 MRR Alc.

COST AND STANDARD OF LIVING--EAST (FAR
EAST)
International Research Associates.
The new Far East; [Hong Kong]
Reader's Digest [Far East ltd.];
distributors: C.E. Tuttle Co.,
Rutland, Vt. [c1966] 159 p.
339.42/095 67-7110
    HD7049 .I53 MRR Alc.

COST AND STANDARD OF LIVING--EUROPE.
A survey of Europe today: London,
Reader's Digest Association, 1970.
212 p. [£25/-] 339.4/094 73-
571754
    HD7022 .S86 MRR Alc.

COST AND STANDARD OF LIVING--UNITED
STATES.
Douglas, Paul Howard, Real wages in
the United States, 1890-1926,
Boston, New York, Houghton Mifflin
company, 1930. xxviii, 682 p.
331.2973 30-12884
    HD4975 .D6 MRR Alc.

COSTA RICA--GAZETTEERS.
United States. Office of Geography.
Costa Rica; Washington, U.S. Govt.
Print. Off., 1956. ii, 48 p.
917.289 56-61443
    F1542 .U5 MRR Alc.

COSTUME.
see also Arms and armor

see also Clothing and dress

see also Wigs

Geen, Michael. Theatrical costume
and the amateur stage; London, Arco,
1968. 150 p. [36/-] 646.4 68-
122121
    GR1741 .G4 1968 MRR Alc.

Paterek, Josephine D. Costuming for
the theatre, New York, Crown
Publishers [1959] 159 p. 792.026
59-15827
    PN2067 .P3 MRR Alc.

Walkup, Fairfax (Proudfit) Dressing
the part; [Rev. ed.] New York
Appleton-Century Crofts, 1950. x,
423 p. 391 792 51-9016
    PN2067 .W3 1950 MRR Alc.

Wilcox, Ruth Turner, Folk and
festival costume of the world New
York, Scribner [1965] 1 v. (unpaged)
391   65-23986
    GT510 .W54 MRR Alc.

COSTUME--BIBLIOGRAPHY.
Baker, Blanch (Merritt) Theatre and
allied arts; New York, Wilson, 1952.
xiii, 536 p. 016.792 52-6756
    Z5781 .B18 MRR Alc.

Hiler, Hilaire, Bibliography of
costume; New York, B. Blom [1967]
xi, 911 p. 016.391 66-12285
    Z5691 .H64 1967 MRR Alc.

Monro, Isabel Stevenson, ed. Costume
index; New York, H. W. Wilson Co.,
1937. x, 338 p. 016.391 37-7142
    Z5691 .M75 MRR Alc.

COSTUME--DICTIONARIES.
Cunnington, Cecil Willett, A
dictionary of English costume,
London, A. & C. Black [1960] vi, 281
p. 391.0942 60-50250
    GT507 .C8 1960a MRR Alc.

Fairholt, Frederick William, Costume
in England; Detroit, Singing Tree
Press, 1968. 2 v. 391/.00942 68-
21769
    GT730 .F2 1968 MRR Alc.

Ironside, Janey. A fashion alphabet;
London, Joseph, 1968. 262 p. [50/-
] 391/.2/03 68-141547
    TT503 .I7 MRR Alc.

Picken, Mary (Brooks) The fashion
dictionary; New York, Funk &
Wagnalls [1957] 397 p. 646.03 57-
10114
    TT503 .P49 MRR Alc.

Schoeffler, O. E., Esquire's
encyclopedia of 20th century men's
fashions New York, McGraw-Hill
[1973] x, 709 p. [$35.00]
391/.07/10904 72-9811
    TT617 .S36 MRR Alc.

Wilcox, Ruth Turner, The dictionary
of costume New York, Scribner [1969]
406 p. [15.00] 391/.003 68-12503

    GT507 .W5 MRR Alc.

COSTUME--HISTORY.
Boucher, François León Louis,
20,000 years of fashion; New York,
H. N. Abrams [1967] 441 p.
746.9/09 66-12103
    GT510 .B6713 1967a MRR Alc.

Bradley, Carolyn Gertrude. Western
World costume, New York, Appleton-
Century-Crofts [1954] viii, 451 p.
391.09 53-7150
    GT510 .B69 MRR Alc.

Crawford, Morris De Camp, One world
of fashion. 3d ed. rev. and edited
New York, Fairchild Publications
[1967] 191 p. 391/.009 67-15747
    GT510 .C7 1967 MRR Alc.

Davenport, Millia. The book of
costume. New York, Crown Publishers
[1948] 2 v. (xii, 958 p.) 391.09
48-9980
    GT513 .D38 MRR Alc.

Evans, Mary, Costume throughout the
ages. [Rev. ed.] Philadelphia,
Lippincott [1950] xv, 360 p. 391
50-8475
    GT510 .E8 1950 MRR Alc.

Gorsline, Douglas W., What people
wore; New York, Viking Press, 1952.
xiii, 266 p. 391 52-12392
    GT513 .G6 MRR Alc.

Hansen, Henny Harald. Costume
cavalcade: 2nd ed. London, Eyre
Methuen Ltd., 1972. 160 p. [£1.95]
391/.009 72-187355
    GT510 .H33 1972 MRR Alc.

Kannik, Preben. Military uniforms in
colour; London, Blandford P., 1968.
278   [30/-] 355.1/4/09 68-
107828
    UC480 .K313 1968b MRR Alc.

Lister, Margot. Costume: an
illustrated survey from ancient times
to the twentieth century. London,
Jenkins, 1967. 347 p. [70/-]
391/.009 68-80448
    GT513 .L5 MRR Alc.

Payne, Blanche. History of costume,
New York, Harper & Row [1965] xiii,
607 p. 391.009 65-10419
    GT510 .P35 MRR Alc.

Walkup, Fairfax (Proudfit) Dressing
the part; [Rev. ed.] New York
Appleton-Century Crofts, 1950. x,
423 p. 391 792 51-9016
    PN2067 .W3 1950 MRR Alc.

Wilcox, Ruth Turner, The mode in
costume. New York, Scribner [1958]
xxvii, 463 p. 391.09 58-12732
    GT510 .W55 1958 MRR Alc.

COSTUME--HISTORY--16TH CENTURY.
Cunnington, Cecil Willett, Handbook
of English costume in the sixteenth
century, New & revised ed. London,
Faber, 1970. 3-244 p., plate. [55/-
] 391/.00942 79-509836
GT730 .C872 MRR Alc.

COSTUME--HISTORY--18TH CENTURY.
Bernstein, Aline (Frankau)
Masterpieces of women's costume of
the 18th and 19th centuries, New
York, Published under the auspices of
the American National Theatre and
Academy by Crown Publishers [1959]
xxii p., 83 plates (part col.)
391.20903 57-12831
GT595 .B45 MRR Alc.

COSTUME--HISTORY--19TH CENTURY.
Bernstein, Aline (Frankau)
Masterpieces of women's costume of
the 18th and 19th centuries, New
York, Published under the auspices of
the American National Theatre and
Academy by Crown Publishers [1959]
xxii p., 83 plates (part col.)
391.20903 57-12831
GT595 .B45 MRR Alc.

Cunnington, Cecil Willett, Handbook
of English costume in the nineteenth
century, [1st American ed.] Boston,
Plays, inc. [1971, c1970] 617 p.
[$14.95] 391/.00942 72-78805
GT737 .C814 1971 MRR Alc.

COSTUME--HISTORY--20TH CENTURY.
Bradshaw, Angela. World costumes.
London, A. and C. Black [1952] 191
p. 391 53-578
GT596 .B7 MRR Alc.

Schoeffler, O. E., Esquire's
encyclopedia of 20th century men's
fashions New York, McGraw-Hill
[1973] x, 709 p. [$35.00]
391/.07/10904 72-9811
TT617 .S36 MRR Alc.

COSTUME--HISTORY--PICTORIAL WORKS.
Bruhn, Wolfgang. A pictorial history
of costume; New York, Hasting House
Publishers [1973] 74 p., 200 p. of
illus. (part col.) 391/.009 73-
11745
GT513 .B763 1973 MRR Alc.

Kybalová, Ludmila. The pictorial
encyclopedia of fashion, Feltham,
Hamlyn, 1968. 608 p. [30/-]
391/.009 70-415002
GT513 .K813 MRR Alc.

COSTUME--INDEXES.
Monro, Isabel Stevenson, ed. Costume
index; New York, H. W. Wilson Co.,
1937. x, 338 p. 016.391 37-7142
Z5691 .M75 MRR Alc.

COSTUME--SOCIETIES, ETC.--DIRECTORIES.
Huenefeld, Irene Pennington.
International directory of historical
clothing. Metuchen, N.J., Scarecrow
Press, 1967. 175 p. 391/.0025 67-
10186
NK4700 .H8 MRR Alc.

COSTUME--AFRICA, SUB-SAHARAN--
BIBLIOGRAPHY.
Eicher, Joanne Bubolz. African
dress; [East Lansing] African
Studies Center, Michigan State
University, 1969. xi, 134 p.
[$4.00] 016.391/00967 73-631220
Z5694.A4 E53 MRR Alc.

COSTUME--GREAT BRITAIN.
Cunnington, Cecil Willett, A
dictionary of English costume,
London, A. & C. Black [1960] vi, 281
p. 391/.0942 60-50250
GT507 .C8 1960a MRR Alc.

Cunnington, Cecil Willett, Handbook
of English costume in the nineteenth
century, [1st American ed.] Boston,
Plays, inc. [1971, c1970] 617 p.
[$14.95] 391/.00942 72-78805
GT737 .C814 1971 MRR Alc.

Cunnington, Cecil Willett, Handbook
of English costume in the sixteenth
century, New & revised ed. London,
Faber, 1970. 3-244 p., plate. [55/-
] 391/.00942 79-509836
GT730 .C872 MRR Alc.

Cunnington, Cecil Willett, Handbook
of English costume in the sixteenth-
nineteenth century, London, Faber
and Faber [1954-59] 4 v. a 62-1155
GT730 .C87 MRR Alc.

Cunnington, Phillis Emily,
Occupational costume in England:
London, Black, 1967. 427 p. [63/-]
391/.04/0942 67-111119
GT730 .C88 MRR Alc.

Hill, Margot Hamilton. The evolution
of fashion: London, Batsford; New
York, Reinhold, 1967. xii, 225 p.
[25/-/-] 391/.009 68-10504
GT510 .H5 1967 MRR Alc.

Milton, Roger. The English
ceremonial book; Newton Abbot [Eng.]
David & Charles [1972] 216 p.
[£3.50] 391/.022/0942 72-185055
CR492 .M5 MRR Alc.

COSTUME--GREAT BRITAIN--HISTORY.
Cunnington, Cecil Willett, English
women's clothing in the nineteenth
century, London, Faber and Faber,
ltd. [1937] 2 p. l., vii-xx, 460 p.
391.2 38-33903
GT737 .C8 MRR Alc.

Fairholt, Frederick William, Costume
in England; Detroit, Singing Tree
Press, 1968. 2 v. 391/.00942 68-
21769
GT730 .F2 1968 MRR Alc.

COSTUME--UNITED STATES.
The History of American dress. New
York, B. Blom, 1965- v.
391.00973 65-20869
GT605 .H64 MRR Alc.

Klapthor, Margaret (Brown) The
dresses of the First Ladies of the
White House, Washington, Smithsonian
Institution, 1952. ix, 149 p.
391.2 52-61540
GT605 .K55 MRR Alc.

COSTUME DESIGNERS--BIOGRAPHY.
Schoeffler, O. E., Esquire's
encyclopedia of 20th century men's
fashions New York, McGraw-Hill
[1973] x, 709 p. [$35.00]
391/.07/10904 72-9811
TT617 .S36 MRR Alc.

Watkins, Josephine Jay. Who's who in
fashion. [New York] Office of
Community Resources, Fashion
Institute of Technology [1972] 150
l. 746.9/2/0922 B 72-190664
TT505.A1 W37 MRR Biog.

COTTAGES.
see also Architecture, Domestic

COTTON MANUFACTURE.
see also Textile industry and fabrics

COTTON MANUFACTURE--DIRECTORIES.
Skinner's cotton and man-made fibres
directory of the world. 1923-
Croydon, Eng. [etc.] T. Skinner
Directories [etc.] 26-3388
HD9870.3 .S5 MRR Alc Latest
edition

COTTON TRADE.
Owsley, Frank Lawrence, King Cotton
diplomacy; 2d ed., rev. [Chicago]
University of Chicago Press [1959]
xxiii, 614 p. 973.721 58-11952
E488 .O85 1959 MRR Alc.

COTTON TRADE--DIRECTORIES.
Skinner's cotton and man-made fibres
directory of the world. 1923-
Croydon, Eng. [etc.] T. Skinner
Directories [etc.] 26-3388
HD9870.3 .S5 MRR Alc Latest
edition

COUNCIL OF EUROPE.
Council of Europe. Secretariat.
Manual of the Council of Europe:
London, Stevens; South Hackensack,
N.J., Rothman, 1970. ix, 322 p.
[5/10/-] 341.18/4 75-106897
JN24 .C65 MRR Alc.

COUNSELING.
see also Marriage counseling

see also Personnel service in
education

see also Vocational guidance

Fullmer, Daniel W. Counseling:
content and process, Chicago,
Science Research Associates [1964]
ix, 278 p. 150.13 64-19639
BF637.C6 F8 MRR Alc.

COUNSELING--BIBLIOGRAPHY.
Freeman, Ruth (St. John) Counseling,
New York, Scarecrow Press, 1964.
986 p. 016.3613 64-11783
Z7204.A6 F7 MRR Alc.

COUNSELING--DICTIONARIES.
Hopke, William E. Dictionary of
personnel and guidance terms, [1st
ed.] Chicago, J. G. Ferguson Pub.
Co. [1968] xix, 464 p. 371.4/03
68-57491
LB15 .H66 MRR Alc.

COUNSELING--UNITED STATES--DIRECTORIES.
Directory of counseling services.
1970- [Washington, D.C.]
International Association of
Counseling Services. [$3.00]
362.8/5 73-642742
HF5381.A1 N4273 MRR Alc Latest
edition

COUNTERSTAMP (NUMISMATICS)
Davenport, John Stewart, The dollars
of Africa, Asia, & Oceania
Galesburg, Ill., 1969. 208 p.
737.4 76-7369
CJ1529 .D3 MRR Alc.

COUNTRY LIFE.
see also Outdoor life.

COUNTRY MUSIC--UNITED STATES--HISTORY
AND CRITICISM.
Gentry, Linnell. A history and
encyclopedia of country, western, and
gospel music. 2d ed., completely
rev. [Nashville, Tenn., Clairmont
Corp., 1969] xiv, 598 p.
784.4/9/73 70-7208
ML200 .G4 1969 MRR Biog.

COUNTY FINANCE
see Local finance

COUNTY GOVERNMENT--BIBLIOGRAPHY.
Hodgson, James Goodwin, comp. The
official publications of American
counties, Fort Collins, Col., 1937.
viii p., ix-xii numb. l., xiii-xxii,
594 p. 015.73 37-27440
Z7164.L8 H72 MRR Alc.

COUNTY GOVERNMENT--MAPS--BIBLIOGRAPHY--
CATALOGS.
United States. Library of Congress.
Geography and Map Division. Land
ownership maps; a checklist
Washington [For sale by the Supt. of
Docs. U.S. Govt. Print. Off.] 1967.
xxv, 86 p. 016.91273 67-60091
Z663.35 .L37 MRR Alc.

COUNTY GOVERNMENT--UNITED STATES.
Bollens, John Constantinus, American
country government, Beverly Hills,
Calif., Sage Publications [1969] 433
p. 016.352/0073/0973 69-20118
JS411 .B64 MRR Alc.

COURT CALENDARS--UNITED STATES.
Martindale-Hubbell law directory.
Summit, N.J. [etc.] 31-6356
KF190 .H813 MRR Biog Latest
edition

COURTESY.
see also Conduct of life

COURTS--OFFICIALS AND EMPLOYEES.
see also Judges

COURTS--UNITED STATES.
United States. Bureau of the Census.
National survey of court
organization. [Washington] U.S.
National Criminal Justice Information
and Statistics Service; [for sale by
the Supt. of Docs., U.S. Govt. Print.
Off.] 1973. 257 p. [$2.40]
347/.73/1 73-600321
KF8719 .A32 MRR Alc.

COURTS--UNITED STATES--DIRECTORIES.
Martindale-Hubbell law directory.
Summit, N.J. [etc.] 31-6356
KF190 .H813 MRR Biog Latest
edition

COURTS--UNITED STATES--STATES.
United States. Bureau of the Census.
National survey of court
organization. [Washington] U.S.
National Criminal Justice Information
and Statistics Service; [for sale by
the Supt. of Docs., U.S. Govt. Print.
Off.] 1973. 257 p. [$2.40]
347/.73/1 73-600321
KF8719 .A32 MRR Alc.

COURTSHIP.
see also Marriage

COVER PLANTS
see Ground cover plants

COVERS (PHILATELY)
see also Postage-stamps

Bartels, John Murray, Thorp-Bartels
Catalogue of the stamped envelopes
and wrappers of the United States;
6th (Century) ed. Netcong, N.J., H.
Thorp [1954] 597 p. 383.22 54-
37552
HE6185.U6 B32 1954 MRR Alc.

Dietz Confederate States catalog and
handbook of the postage stamps and
envelopes of the Confederate States
of America. 1931- Richmond, Dietz
Press [etc.] 31-20545
HE6185.U6 D5 MRR Alc Latest
edition

Simpson, Tracy Whittelsey. U.S.
postal markings 1851-61 and related
mail services, Berkeley, Calif.
[1959] 177 p. 383.22973 59-42054
HE6185.U5 S5 MRR Alc.

Thorp, Prescott Holden. Catalogue of
the 20th century stamped envelopes
and wrappers of the United States,
1st ed. Netcong, N.J. [1968] 205 p.
769/.569/73 68-2697
HE6185.U6 T46 MRR Alc.

COWPER, WILLIAM, 1731-1800--
CONCORDANCES.
Neve, John. A concordance to the
poetical works of William Cowper.
New York, B. Franklin [1969] viii,
504 p. 821/.6 68-58237
PR3383.A2 N4 1969 MRR Alc.

CRAFTS (HANDICRAFTS)
see Handicraft

CRANE, HART, 1899-1932--CONCORDANCES.
Landry, Hilton. A concordance to the
poems of Hart Crane. Metuchen, N.J.,
Scarecrow Press, 1973. viii, 379 p.
811/.5/2 72-10663
PS3505.R272 Z49 1973 MRR Alc.

CRANIOLOGY.
see also Man, Prehistoric

Koenigswald, Gustav Heinrich Ralph
von, Meeting prehistoric man. New
York, Harper [c1956] 216 p. 573.7
56-8769
GN75.A2 K63 1956a MRR Alc.

CREATION.
see also Geology

CREDIT--UNITED STATES.
Credit manual of commercial laws.
New York. 11-31760
KF889 .C74 MRR Alc Latest edition

Prather, Charles Lee, Money and
banking 9th ed. Homewood, Ill., R.
D. Irwin, 1969. xviii, 738 p. 332
69-15547
HG221 .P93 1969 MRR Alc.

CREDIT BUREAUS--DIRECTORIES.
United States. Bureau of
International Commerce. Sources of
credit information on foreign firms
for United States firms trading,
investing or manufacturing abroad.
[Washington, For sale by the Supt. of
Docs., U.S. Govt. Print. Off.] 1967.
iv, 108 p. 658.88/025 67-62451
HF5571 .U63 MRR Alc.

CREDIT GUIDES--CANADA.
Dun and Bradstreet, inc. Reference
book. v. [1]- 1859- New York 99-
819
HF5573 .D7 MRR Circ Latest edition

CREDIT GUIDES--EUROPE.
Dun and Bradstreet, inc.
International market guide;
continental Europe. v. 1- 1961-
New York. 658.880584 61-25822
HC240 .D8 MRR Alc Latest edition

CREDIT GUIDES--LATIN AMERICA.
Dun and Bradstreet, inc.
International market guide; v. 1-
1938- New York. 38-18610
HF54.U5 D8 MRR Alc Latest edition

CREDIT GUIDES--MEXICO.
Dun and Bradstreet, inc.
International market guide; Mexico.
New York. 380.1/025/72 72-621019
HC132 .D84 MRR Alc Latest edition

CREDIT GUIDES--PERU.
Dun and Bradstreet, inc.
International market guide; Peru.
New York. 380.1/025/85 72-621020
HC226 .D85 MRR Alc Latest edition

CREDIT GUIDES--PORTUGAL.
Dun and Bradstreet, inc.
International market guide; Portugal.
New York. 380.1/025/469 72-621021

HC391 .D84 MRR Alc Latest edition

CREDIT GUIDES--UNITED STATES.
Apparel trades book. New York.
658.987 02-19199
HF5585.C6 A7 MRR Alc Latest
edition

Dairy Credit Bureau, Chicago. Dairy
credit book. Chicago. 637.116 41-
297
HD9275 .A1D3 MRR Alc Latest
edition

Dun and Bradstreet, inc. Reference
book. v. [1]- 1859- New York 99-
819
HF5573 .D7 MRR Circ Latest edition

Dun and Bradstreet, inc. Reference
book: lumber and wood products
industries. [spring] 1968- New
York. 338.7/67/4002573 72-489
HD9753 .D85 MRR Alc Latest edition

Dun and Bradstreet, inc. Reference
book of manufacturers. Oct. 1965-
New York. 66-5210
HF5573 .D72 Sci RR Latest edition
/ MRR Circ Latest edition

Dun & Bradstreet reference book of
transportation. Washington, Trinc
Transportation Consultants.
380.5/2/02573 74-644693
HE5623.A45 D82 MRR Alc Latest
edition

Jewelers Board of Trade. Reference
book of the jewelry trade in the
United States. Mar. 1933-
Providence [etc.] 658.9173927 44-
14868
HF5585.J4 J37 MRR Alc Latest
edition

The Lumbermen's national red book
service reference book. Chicago,
Lumbermen's Credit Association.
338.47674 02-19114
"Established 1876."
HF5585.L8 L7 MRR Alc Latest
edition

Paper & Allied Trades Mercantile
Agency, inc., New York. P. A. T.
credit reference. New York. 27-9871

HF5585.P2 P3 MRR Alc Latest
edition

Produce Reporter Company's semi-
annual blue book. 1905- Wheaton,
Ill. [etc.] 338.7/63 53-55972
HF55.85.P7 P7 MRR Alc Latest
edition

Produce Reporter Company's semi-
annual blue book. Supplement.
Wheaton, Ill. [etc.] 338.7/63 74-
643555
HF5585.P7 P7 Suppl. MRR Alc
Partial set

CREDIT MANAGEMENT.
Shultz, William John, Credit and
collection management 3d ed.
Englewood Cliffs, N.J., Prentice-
Hall, 1962. 637 p. 658.88 62-9584

HF5566 .S5 1962 MRR Alc.

CREEDS--COMPARATIVE STUDIES.
Mayer, Frederick Emanuel. The
religious bodies of America. 4th
ed., rev. Saint Louis, Concordia
Pub. House, 1961. xiii, 598 p. 280
61-15535
BR516.5 .M3 1961 MRR Alc.

CREEDS--HISTORY AND CRITICISM.
Kelly, John Norman Davidson. Early
Christian creeds. [2d ed. London]
Longmans [1960] xi, 446 p. 238.1
60-51850
BT990 .K4 1960 MRR Alc.

CREMATION.
see also Funeral rites and ceremonies

CRESTS.
Fairbairn, James, comp. Fairbairn's
crests of the families of Great
Britain and Ireland, Rutland, Vt.,
C. E. Tuttle Co. [1968] 2 v. in 1
(ix, 644 p.) 929.8 68-25887
CR57.G7 F2 1968b MRR Alc.

Weightman, Alfred Edwin. Heraldry in
the Royal Navy; Aldershot [Eng.]
Gale and Polden, 1957. xviii, 514 p.
623.825 60-36156
VB335.G7 W4 MRR Alc.

CRETE--ANTIQUITIES.
Palmer, Leonard Robert, Mycenaeans
and Minoans; 2d ed., substantially
rev. and enl. New York, Knopf, 1965.
369 p. 913.3918031 64-19093
DF220 .P3 1965 MRR Alc.

CRETE--DESCRIPTION AND TRAVEL--GUIDE-
BOOKS.
Bowman, John Stewart, Crete;
travelers' guide, [Rev. and expanded
ed.] Indianapolis, Bobbs-Merrill Co.
[1969] 280 p. [5.50] 914.99/8/044
69-20310
DF901.C8 B59 1959 MRR Alc.

Bowman, John Stewart, A guide to
Crete. [1st American ed. New York]
Pantheon Books [1963, c1962] 200 p.
914.998 63-7351
DF901.C8 B6 1963 MRR Alc.

CRIME AND CRIMINALS.
see also Juvenile delinquency

see also Police

see also Prisons

Lunden, Walter Albin, Facts on
crimes and criminals. Ames, Iowa,
Art Press [1961] iii, 294 p. 62-
1421
HV6208 .L79 MRR Alc.

Reckless, Walter Cade. The crime
problem 5th ed. New York, Appleton-
Century-Crofts [1973] xiv, 718 p.
364 72-92703
HV6025 .R46 1973 MRR Alc.

CRIME AND CRIMINALS--ABSTRACTS.
Abstracts on criminology and
penology. Deventer. 364/.08 72-
626328
Began in 1969.
HV6001 .E9 MRR Alc Full set

Excerpta criminologica. v. 1-8; 1961-
68. Amsterdam. 63-59273
HV6001 .E9 MRR Alc Full set

CRIME AND CRIMINALS--ADDRESSES, ESSAYS,
LECTURES.
Glaser, Daniel. Handbook of
criminology / Chicago : Rand McNally
College Pub. Co., [1974] xiii, 1180
p. : 364 74-241
HV6028 .G5 MRR Alc.

CRIME AND CRIMINALS--BIBLIOGRAPHY.
Barzun, Jacques, A catalogue of
crime [1st ed.] New York, Harper &
Row [1971] xxxi, 831 p. [$18.95]
016.80883/872 75-123914
Z5917.D5 B37 1971 MRR Alc.

Crime and delinquency abstracts. v.
1- Jan. 1963- [Bethesda, Md.,
etc.] National Clearinghouse for
Mental Health Information [etc.] 66-
3911
Z5118.C9 I55 MRR Alc Full set

Glaser, Daniel. Handbook of
criminology / Chicago : Rand McNally
College Pub. Co., [1974] xiii, 1180
p. : 364 74-241
HV6028 .G5 MRR Alc.

Hewitt, William H. A bibliography of
police administration, public safety,
and criminology to July 1, 1965,
Springfield, Ill., Thomas [1967]
xiv, 242 p. 016.350/74 66-24629
Z7164.P76 H4 MRR Alc.

Sellin, Johan Thorsten, A
bibliographical manual for the
student of criminology. [New York]
National Research and Information
Center on Crime and Delinquency
[1965] 1 v. (unpaged) 016.364 66-
862
Z5118.C9 S4 1965 MRR Alc.

Wright, Martin. Use of criminology
literature. London, Butterworths
[1974] 242 p. [£5.50] 016.364 74-
174858
Z5118.C9 W74 1974b MRR Alc.

CRIME AND CRIMINALS--BIBLIOGRAPHY--
CATALOGS.
Los Angeles. Public Library.
Municipal Reference Library. Catalog
of the police library of the Los
Angeles Public Library; Boston, G.
K. Hall, 1972. 2 v. 016.3632 73-
158794
Z7164.P76 L58 MRR Alc (Dk 33)

CRIME AND CRIMINALS--BIOGRAPHY.
Wilson, Colin, Encyclopedia of
murder [1st American ed.] New York,
Putnam [1962, c1961] 576 p.
364.152 61-12748
HV6245 .W77 1962 MRR Alc.

CRIME AND CRIMINALS--DICTIONARIES.
Salottolo, A. Lawrence. Modern
police service encyclopedia; Rev.
ed. New York, Arco Pub. Co. [1970]
276 p. 363.2/03 70-125939
HV8133 .S2 1970 MRR Alc.

Scott, Harold Richard, Sir, ed. The
concise encyclopedia of crime and
criminals. 1st ed.] New York,
Hawthorn Books [1961] 351 p.
364.103 61-11624
HV6017 .S35 MRR Alc.

CRIME AND CRIMINALS--DICTIONARIES--
POLYGLOT.
Elsevier's dictionary of criminal
science, in eight languages:
Amsterdam, New York, Elsevier Pub.
Co.; [distributed by Van Nostrand,
Princeton, N.J.] 1960. xv, 1460 p.
364.03 59-12582
HV6017 .E4 MRR Alc.

CRIME AND CRIMINALS--HISTORY.
Symons, Julian, A pictorial history
of crime. New York, Crown Publishers
[1966] 288 p. 364.9 66-26186
HV6233 .S97 MRR Alc.

CRIME AND CRIMINALS--IDENTIFICATION.
Directory of identification bureaus
of the world. Chicago. 573.6 47-
26908
HV8073 .D5 MRR Alc Latest edition

CRIME AND CRIMINALS--PERIODICALS.
Abstracts on criminology and
penology. Deventer. 364/.08 72-
626328
Began in 1969.
HV6001 .E9 MRR Alc Full set

Excerpta criminologica. v. 1-8; 1961-
68. Amsterdam. 63-59273
HV6001 .E9 MRR Alc Full set

CRIME AND CRIMINALS--TERMINOLOGY.
Dictionary of American underworld
lingo. New York, Twayne Publishers
[1950] 327 p. 427.9 50-58288
PE3726 .D5 MRR Alc.

Tempest, Paul. Lag's lexicon;
London, Routledge & K. Paul [1950]
viii, 233 p. 427.09 51-5071
PE3726 .T4 MRR Alc.

CRIME AND CRIMINALS--GREAT BRITAIN--BIOGRAPHY.
Shew, Edward Spencer, A companion to murder; [1st American ed.] New York, Knopf, 1961. 303 p. 364.152 61-14626
HV6945 .S48 1961 MRR Alc.

CRIME AND CRIMINALS--UNITED STATES.
Bowen, Walter Scott. The United States Secret Service [1st ed.] Philadelphia, Chilton Co. [1960] 205 p. 351.742 60-6407
HV8138 .B6 MRR Alc.

Franke, David. America's 50 safest cities. New Rochelle, N.Y., Arlington House [1974] 301 p. [$8.95] 301.36/3/0973 73-21890
HT123 .F72 MRR Alc.

Glaser, Daniel. Handbook of criminology / Chicago : Rand McNally College Pub. Co., [1974] xiii, 1180 p. : 364 74-241
HV6028 .G5 MRR Alc.

United States. Library of Congress. Legislative Reference Service. Combating crime in the United States. Washington, U.S. Govt. Print.Off., 1967. v, 254 p. 353.007/5 67-62987
Z663.6 .C6 MRR Alc.

CRIME AND CRIMINALS--UNITED STATES--BIBLIOGRAPHY.
Social Science Research Council. Committee on Survey of Research on Crime and Criminal Justice. A guide to material on crime and criminal justice. Montclair, N.J., Patterson Smith, 1969 [c1929] 665 p. 016.364/9/73 69-16240
Z5118.8.C9 S6 1969 MRR Alc.

CRIME AND CRIMINALS--UNITED STATES--BIOGRAPHY.
Nash, Jay Robert. Bloodletters and badmen; New York, M. Evans; distributed in association with Lippincott, Philadelphia [1973] 640 p. [$16.95] 364/.092/2 B 72-95977

HV6785 .N37 MRR Biog.

CRIME AND CRIMINALS--WEST--BIBLIOGRAPHY.
Adams, Ramon Frederick, Six-guns and saddle leather; New ed., [Norman, University of Oklahoma Press, 1969] xxv, 808 p. [19.95] 016.3641 69-16728
Z1251.W5 A3 1969 MRR Alc.

CRIME PREVENTION--ADDRESSES, ESSAYS, LECTURES.
Glaser, Daniel. Handbook of criminology / Chicago : Rand McNally College Pub. Co., [1974] xiii, 1180 p. : 364 74-241
HV6028 .G5 MRR Alc.

CRIMES WITHOUT VICTIMS.
see also Drug abuse

CRIMINAL ANTHROPOLOGY--BIBLIOGRAPHY.
Sellin, Johan Thorsten, A bibliographical manual for the student of criminology, [New York] National Research and Information Center on Crime and Delinquency [1965] 1 v. (unpaged) 016.364 66-862
Z5118.C9 S4 1965 MRR Alc.

CRIMINAL INVESTIGATION--UNITED STATES.
United States. Library of Congress. Legislative Reference Service. Combating crime in the United States. Washington, U.S. Govt. Print.Off., 1967. v, 254 p. 353.007/5 67-62987
Z663.6 .C6 MRR Alc.

CRIMINAL INVESTIGATION--UNITED STATES--BIBLIOGRAPHY.
Hewitt, William H. A bibliography of police administration, public safety, and criminology to July 1, 1965; Springfield, Ill., Thomas [1967] xlv, 242 p. 016.350/74 66-24629
Z7164.P76 H4 MRR Alc.

Los Angeles. Public Library. Municipal Reference Library. Catalog of the police library of the Los Angeles Public Library; Boston, G. K. Hall, 1972. 2 v. 016.3632 73-158794
Z7164.P76 L58 MRR Alc (Dk 33)

CRIMINAL JURISDICTION--BIBLIOGRAPHY.
Schutter, Bart de. Bibliography on international criminal law. Leiden, Sijthoff, 1972. li, 423 p. [fl58.00] 016.34/77 72-80997
Z6464.C8 S38 MRR Alc.

CRIMINAL JUSTICE, ADMINISTRATION OF.
see also Impeachments.

CRIMINAL JUSTICE, ADMINISTRATION OF--ADDRESSES, ESSAYS, LECTURES.
Glaser, Daniel. Handbook of criminology / Chicago : Rand McNally College Pub. Co., [1974] xiii, 1180 p. : 364 74-241
HV6028 .G5 MRR Alc.

CRIMINAL JUSTICE, ADMINISTRATION OF--BIBLIOGRAPHY--CATALOGS.
Los Angeles. Public Library. Municipal Reference Library. Catalog of the police library of the Los Angeles Public Library; Boston, G. K. Hall, 1972. 2 v. 016.3632 73-158794
Z7164.P76 L58 MRR Alc (Dk 33)

CRIMINAL JUSTICE, ADMINISTRATION OF--UNITED STATES--BIBLIOGRAPHY.
Social Science Research Council. Committee on Survey of Research on Crime and Criminal Justice. A guide to material on crime and criminal justice. Montclair, N.J., Patterson Smith, 1969 [c1929] 665 p. 016.364/9/73 69-16240
Z5118.8.C9 S6 1969 MRR Alc.

CRIMINAL LAW.
see also Abortion

see also Capital punishment

see also Riots

CRIMINAL LAW--BIBLIOGRAPHY.
Crime and delinquency abstracts. v. 1- Jan. 1963- [Bethesda, Md., etc.] National Clearinghouse for Mental Health Information [etc.] 66-3911
Z5118.C9 I55 MRR Alc Full set

CRIMINAL LAW--UNITED STATES--BIBLIOGRAPHY.
Social Science Research Council. Committee on Survey of Research on Crime and Criminal Justice. A guide to material on crime and criminal justice. Montclair, N.J., Patterson Smith, 1969 [c1929] 665 p. 016.364/9/73 69-16240
Z5118.8.C9 S6 1969 MRR Alc.

CRIMINAL STATISTICS.
see also Violent deaths

Lunden, Walter Albin, Facts on crimes and criminals. Ames, Iowa, Art Press [1961] iii, 294 p. 62-1421
HV6208 .L79 MRR Alc.

CRIMINAL STATISTICS--UNITED STATES.
Franke, David. America's 50 safest cities. New Rochelle, N.Y., Arlington House [1974] 301 p. [$8.95] 301.36/3/0973 73-21890
HT123 .F72 MRR Alc.

CRIPPLES
see Physically handicapped

CRITICISM.
see also Aesthetics

see also Style, Literary

The Critical temper; New York, Ungar [1969] 3 v. [45.00] 820.9 68-8116
PR83 .C764 MRR Alc.

Moulton, Charles Wells, ed. The Library of literary criticism of English and American authors, New York, P. Smith, 1935. 8 v. 820.9 35-27242
PR83 .M73 1935 MRR Alc.

Moulton, Charles Wells, Library of literary criticism of English and American authors through the beginning of the twentieth century. New York, F. Ungar Pub. Co. [1966] 4 v. 820.9 65-16619
PR83 .M73 1966 TJ Rm.

CRITICISM--BIBLIOGRAPHY.
Hefling, Helen. Hefling & Richards' Index to contemporary biography and criticism. A new ed. rev. and enl. Boston, F. W. Faxon company, 1934. 3 p. l., 9-229 p. 016.92 34-28569
Z5301 .H46 1934 MRR Biog.

CRITICISM--DICTIONARIES.
Shipley, Joseph Twadell, Dictionary of world literary terms, forms, technique, criticism. Completely rev. and enl. ed. Boston, Writer [1970] xiii, 466 p. [12.95] 803 75-91879
PN41 .S5 1970 MRR Alc.

CRITICISM--HISTORY.
Wellek, Rene. A history of modern criticism: 1750-1950. New Haven, Yale University Press, 1955- v. 801 55-5989
PN86 .W4 MRR Alc.

Wimsatt, William Kurtz, Literary criticism; [1st ed.] New York, Knopf, 1957. 757 p. 801 57-5286
PN86 .W5 MRR Alc.

CRITICISM--FRANCE--BIO-BIBLIOGRAPHY.
Le Sage, Laurent, Dictionnaire des critiques litteraires; University Park, Pennsylvania State University Press [c1969] 218 p. [6.50] 68-8181
PQ67.A2 L4 MRR Biog.

CRITICISM--IRELAND.
Taylor, Estella Ruth. The modern Irish writers; Lawrence, University of Kansas Press, 1954. 176 p. 820.904 54-8406
PR8753 .T3 MRR Alc.

CRITICISM--UNITED STATES.
Curley, Dorothy Nyren, comp. Modern American literature. 4th enl. ed. New York, F. Ungar Pub. Co. [1969] 3 v. [45.00] 810.9/005 76-76599
PS221 .C8 1969 MRR Alc.

CRITTENDEN, JOHN JORDAN, 1787-1863--BIBLIOGRAPHY.
United States. Library of Congress. Manuscript Division. Calendar of the papers of John Jordan Crittenden. Washington, Govt. print. off., 1913. 355 p. 12-35010
Z6663.34 .C7 MRR Alc.

CROATIA.
Eterovich, Francis H., ed. Croatia: land, people, culture. [Toronto] Published for the Editorial Board by University of Toronto Press [1964- v. 914.394 65-2286
DB366 .E8 MRR Alc.

CROATIAN PERIODICALS--DIRECTORIES.
Markotic, Vladimir. Biographical directory of Americans and Canadians of Croatian descent; 4th enl. and rev. ed. Calgary, Alta., Research Centre for Canadian Ethnic Studies, 1973. xiii, 204 p. 920/.071 74-176543
E184.C93 M3713 1973 MRR Biog.

CROATS.
Eterovich, Francis H., ed. Croatia: land, people, culture. [Toronto] Published for the Editorial Board by University of Toronto Press [1964- v. 914.394 65-2286
DB366 .E8 MRR Alc.

CROATS IN CANADA--DIRECTORIES.
Markotic, Vladimir. Biographical directory of Americans and Canadians of Croatian descent; 4th enl. and rev. ed. Calgary, Alta., Research Centre for Canadian Ethnic Studies, 1973. xiii, 204 p. 920/.071 74-176543
E184.C93 M3713 1973 MRR Biog.

CROATS IN THE UNITED STATES--DIRECTORIES.
Markotic, Vladimir. Biographical directory of Americans and Canadians of Croatian descent; 4th enl. and rev. ed. Calgary, Alta., Research Centre for Canadian Ethnic Studies, 1973. xiii, 204 p. 920/.071 74-176543
E184.C93 M3713 1973 MRR Biog.

CROPS
see Agriculture

CROPS AND CLIMATE.
United States. Library of Congress. Science and Technology Division. Cold weather agriculture. Washington, U.S. Govt. Print. Off., 1960. v, 48 p. 631.0911 60-61031

Z6663.41 .C6 MRR Alc.

CROSBY (LANCASHIRE)--DIRECTORIES.
Kelly's (Gore's) directory of Liverpool, including Bootle, Birkenhead, Wallasey and environs. Kingston upon Thames, Surrey [etc.] Kelly's Directories Ltd. 35-15072
DA690.L8 K4 MRR Alc Latest edition

CROSS REFERENCES (CATALOGING)
Atkins, Thomas V. Cross-reference index: a subject heading guide; New York, R. R. Bowker Co., 1974. viii, 255 p. 025.3/3 73-23066
Z695 .A954 MRR Alc.

CROSSES.
see also Symbolism in art

CROSSWORD PUZZLES--GLOSSARIES, VOCABULARIES, ETC.
Cross word puzzle dictionary of the English language, Philadelphia, Winston, 1951. 1003 p. 423 51-6777
PE1628 .C8 MRR Alc.

The Dell crossword dictionary, [New York, Dell Pub. Co.]; distributed by the Dial Press, 1964 [c1960] 384 p. 793.732 64-11903
GV1507.C7 D39 1964 MRR Alc.

Elliott, Iris E., Instant word finder, Philadelphia, Lithographed by Braceland Bros. [1959] 352 p. 423 59-15222
PE1680 .E55 MRR Alc.

CROSSWORD PUZZLES--GLOSSARIES. (Cont.)
English word book of over 106,000
words; [Seattle, Pilot Press, 1963]
xx, 829 p.   65-3497
GV1507.W9 E5 MRR Alc.

Sisson, Albert Franklin, The
unabridged crossword puzzle word
finder. [1st ed.] Garden City,
N.Y., Doubleday, 1963. 526 p.
793.732   62-15910
GV1507.C7 S5 MRR Alc.

CROWDS.
see also Riots

CROWNS.
Jones, William, F.S.A. Crowns and
coronations; New ed. Detroit,
Singing Tree Press, 1968. xxx, 551
p. 394/.4   67-24356
DA112 .J8 1968 MRR Alc.

CRUISERS (WARSHIPS)
Breyer, Siegfried. Battleships and
battle cruisers, 1905-1970; Garden
City, N.Y., Doubleday [1973] 480 p.
[$25.00] 358.3/2/520904 72-84895
V765 .B6813 MRR Alc.

CRUSADES.
Runciman, Steven, Sir, A history of
the Crusades. [1st ed.] Cambridge
[Eng.] University Press, 1951-54. 3
v. 940.18 51-10801
D157 .R8 MRR Alc.

Setton, Kenneth Meyer, A history of
the Crusades. [Philadelphia]
University of Pennsylvania Press
[1955-62] 2 v. 940.18 55-2441
D157 .S48 MRR Alc.

CRYOGENICS
see Refrigeration and refrigerating
machinery

CRYPTOGAMS.
see also Ferns

CRYSTALLOGRAPHY.
see also Geology

see also Mineralogy

CUBA.
American University, Washington, D.C.
Foreign Areas Studies Division.
Special warfare area handbook for
Cuba. [Washington] 1961. x, 657 p.
mrr01-30
F1758 .A5 MRR Alc.

American University, Washington, D.C.
Foreign Areas Studies Division.
Special warfare area handbook for
Cuba. [Washington] 1961. x, 657 p.
mrr01-47
F1758 .A5 MRR Alc.

CUBA--BIBLIOGRAPHY.
International Conference on Cuban
Acquisitions and Bibliography,
Library of Congress, 1970. Cuban
acquisitions and bibliography;
Washington, Library of Congress,
1970. viii, 164 p. 016.817291/03
76-609231
Z663.32 .C85 1970 MRR Alc.

Valdés, Nelson P. The Cuban
revolution; [1st ed.] Albuquerque,
University of New Mexico Press [1971]
xii, 230 p. [$7.50] 016.972/91064
76-153937
Z1525 .V33 MRR Alc.

CUBA--BIOGRAPHY.
Directory of personalities of the
Cuban Government, official
organizations, and mass
organizations. [Washington] Central
Intelligence Agency, 1974. ix, 488
p. 354/.7291/002 74-601252
JL1007 .D57 1974 MRR Alc.

CUBA--BIOGRAPHY--DICTIONARIES.
Peraza Sarausa, Fermín, Diccionario
biográfico cubano. Habana,
Ediciones Anuario Bibliográfico
Cubano, 1951- v.   920.07291 52-
70
F1755 .P4 MRR Biog.

Peraza Sarausa, Fermín,
Personalidades cubanas. Habana,
Ediciones Anuario Bibliográfico
Cubano, 1957- v.   57-44896
F1755 .P45 MRR Biog.

CUBA--EXECUTIVE DEPARTMENTS--
DIRECTORIES.
Directory of personalities of the
Cuban Government, official
organizations, and mass
organizations. [Washington] Central
Intelligence Agency, 1974. ix, 488
p. 354/.7291/002 74-601252
JL1007 .D57 1974 MRR Alc.

CUBA--FOREIGN ECONOMIC RELATIONS--
UNITED STATES.
Smith, Robert Freeman, The United
States and Cuba: New York, Bookman
Associates [1961, c1960] 256 p.
327.7307291 60-53477
E183.8.C9 S6 MRR Alc.

CUBA--FOREIGN RELATIONS--UNITED STATES.
Smith, Robert Freeman, The United
States and Cuba: New York, Bookman
Associates [1961, c1960] 256 p.
327.7307291 60-53477
E183.8.C9 S6 MRR Alc.

CUBA--GAZETTEERS.
United States. Office of Geography.
Cuba; 2d ed. Washington, 1963. vi,
619 p.   63-65100
F1754 .U5 1963 MRR Alc.

CUBA--HISTORY.
Thomas, Hugh, Cuba; [1st U.S. ed.]
New York, Harper & Row [1971] xxiv,
1696 p. [$20.00] 972/.91 79-
162565
F1788 .T47 1971 MRR Alc.

CUBA--HISTORY--1959- --BIBLIOGRAPHY.
Valdés, Nelson P. The Cuban
revolution; [1st ed.] Albuquerque,
University of New Mexico Press [1971]
xii, 230 p. [$7.50] 016.972/91064
76-153937
Z1525 .V33 MRR Alc.

CUBA--OFFICIALS AND EMPLOYEES--
DIRECTORIES.
Directory of personalities of the
Cuban Government, official
organizations, and mass
organizations. [Washington] Central
Intelligence Agency, 1974. ix, 488
p. 354/.7291/002 74-601252
JL1007 .D57 1974 MRR Alc.

CUBA--REGISTERS.
Directory of personalities of the
Cuban Government, official
organizations, and mass
organizations. [Washington] Central
Intelligence Agency, 1974. ix, 488
p. 354/.7291/002 74-601252
JL1007 .D57 1974 MRR Alc.

CULBERTSON, WILLIAM SMITH, 1884- --
BIBLIOGRAPHY.
United States. Library of Congress.
Manuscript Division. William S.
Culbertson; a register of his papers
in the Library of Congress.
Washington, 1963. 12 l. 64-60018
Z663.34 .C8 MRR Alc.

CULTURAL ANTHROPOLOGY
see Ethnology

CULTURAL RELATIONS.
Unesco handbook of international
exchanges. 1- 1965- [Paris]
Unesco.   65-5337
AS8 .U35 MRR Alc Latest edition

CULTURALLY DEPRIVED CHILDREN
see Socially handicapped children

CULTURE--OUTLINES, SYLLABI, ETC.
Murdock, George Peter, Outline of
world cultures. [2d ed., rev.] New
Haven, HRAF Press, 1958. xi, 227 p.
025.469 58-4860
H62 .B36 vol. 3 1958 MRR Alc.

CULTURE CONFLICT.
see also Race problems

CUP PLATES.
Lee, Ruth Webb, American glass cup
plates; [1st ed.] Northborough,
Mass. [1948] xviii, 445 p.   748.8
49-250
NK5440.C8 L4 MRR Alc.

CUPS AND SAUCERS
see Porcelain

CURIOSA.
Walsh, William Shepard, Handy-book
of literary curiosities, Detroit,
Gale Research Co., 1966. 1104 p.
803 66-24370
PN43 .W3 1966 MRR Alc.

CURIOSITIES.
Passell, Peter. The best New York,
Farrar, Straus and Giroux [1974] 169
p. 031/.02 73-87697
TX335 .P35 1974 MRR Alc.

CURIOSITIES AND WONDERS.
Garrison, Webb B. How it started
Nashville, Abingdon Press [1972] 237
p. [$4.95] 390/.09 72-173951
GT75 .G3 MRR Alc.

The Guinness book of records. 1955-
[Enfield, Eng., etc., Guinness
Superlatives Ltd., etc.] [£1.20
(single issue)] 001.9/3 56-19118
AG243 .G86 MRR Ref Desk Latest
edition

Guinness book of world records. New
York, Sterling Pub. Co. [etc.] 032
64-4884
AG243 .G87 MRR Ref Desk Latest
edition

Meyer, Jerome Sydney, The book of
amazing facts; Cleveland, World Pub.
Co. [1950] 186 p.   031 51-243
AG243 .M4 MRR Alc.

CURIOSITIES AND WONDERS--DICTIONARIES.
Robertson, Patrick. The Shell book
of first / London : Ebury Press,
1974. 256 p. : [£3.50] 032/.02
74-190033
AG243 .R55 1974 MRR Ref Desk.

CURRENCY
see Money

CURRENCY QUESTION.
see also Finance

see also Finance, Public

see also Money

see also Paper money

CURRICULUM PLANNING--UNITED STATES.
Saylor, John Galen, Planning
curriculum for schools New York,
Holt, Rinehart and Winston [1974]
xi, 404 p.   375/.001 73-7843
LB1570 .S29 1974 MRR Alc.

CURRIER AND IVES
Conningham, Frederic Arthur, Currier
& Ives prints: [Rev. ed.] New York,
Crown Publishers [1970] xx, 300 p.
[12.50] 769/.02/9 77-105958
NE2415.C7 C62 1970 MRR Alc.

Warman, Edwin G., Print price guide;
Uniontown, Pa., Warman Pub. Co.
[1955] 136 p. 763.085 56-521
NE2415.C7 W36 MRR Alc.

CURVES, PLANE.
see also Circle

CUSTOMER SERVICE--DIRECTORIES.
White, Jack M. The angry buyer's
complaint directory New York, P. H.
Wyden [1974] xxviii, 292 p. [$7.95]
381 73-86179
HF5415.5 .W55 MRR Alc.

CUT GLASS.
Warman, Edwin G., American cut
glass; 1st ed. Uniontown, Pa.,
Warman Pub. Co. [1954] 115 p.
748.2 54-19848
NK5112 .W24 MRR Alc.

CUTTING
see Dressmaking

CYBERNETICS.
see also Computers

see also Information theory

CYCLES--BIBLIOGRAPHY.
Wilson, Louise (Loeffler) Catalogue
of cycles, Pittsburgh, Foundation
for the Study of Cycles [c1964- v.
67-31862
Z7405.P66 W5 MRR Alc.

CYCLES, MOTOR
see Motorcycles

CYCLING.
see also Motorcycling

Sloane, Eugene A. The new complete
book of bicycling, New York, Simon
and Schuster [1974] 531 p. [$12.50]
629.22/72 73-9362
GV1041 .S55 1974 MRR Alc.

CYCLING--WASHINGTON, D.C., REGION.
Berkowitz, Alan. Greater Washington
area bicycle atlas, Washington,
Potomac Area Council-American Youth
Hostels [1974] 128 p. [$2.00]
917.53/04/4 74-172742
F192.3 .B43 MRR Alc.

CYCLONES.
see also Storms

CYCLOPEDIAS
see Encyclopedias and dictionaries

CYPRUS.
American University, Washington, D.C.
Foreign Areas Studies Division. Area
handbook for Cyprus. Washington, For
sale by the Supt. of Docs., U.S.
Govt. Print. Off., 1964. xii, 441 p.
67-8503
D839.3 .A572 MRR Alc.

Purcell, Hugh Dominic, Cyprus, New
York, Praeger [1969, c1968] 416 p.
[9.00] 956.45 68-9731
DS54.5 .P8 1969b MRR Alc.

CYPRUS--DIRECTORIES.
The Diplomatic Press directory of the
Republic of Cyprus including trade
index and biographical section.
London, Diplomatic Press and Pub. Co.
63-1448
DS54.A2 D5 MRR Alc Latest edition

CYPRUS--HISTORY.
Maier, Franz Georg, Cyprus from
earliest time to the present day;
London, Elek, 1968. 176 p. [30/-]
956.45 68-119906
DS54.5 .M3613 MRR Alc.

CYRUS, THE GREAT, KING OF PERSIA, D.
B.C. 529.
Xenophon. Cyropaedia; London, W.
Heinemann; New York, G. P. Putnam's
sons, 1925-32. 2 v. 46-39509
PA3612 .X4 1925d MRR Alc.

CYTOLOGY.
Brachet, Jean, ed. The cell:
biochemistry, physiology, morphology.
New York, Academic Press, 1959-64.
6 v. 574.87082 59-7677
QH581 .B72 MRR Alc.

CZECH LANGUAGE--DICTIONARIES--ENGLISH.
Česko-anglický slovník středního
rozsahu. 3. vyd. Praha, SPN, 1968.
xxiv, 1236, [2] p. [48.00] 77-
390920
PG4640 .C43 1968 MRR Alc.

Česko-anglický technický slovník.
2., přeprac. a dopln. vyd. Praha,
SNTL, t. Tisk 2, Brno, 1972. 946,
[1] p. [Kčs85.00] 73-316042
T10 .C44 1972 MRR Alc.

Procházka, Jindřich, Slovník
anglicko-český a česko-anglický,
15. zcela přepracované vyd. Praha,
Orbis, 1952. 423, vii, 589 p.
491.8632 53-32256
PG4640 .P73 1952 MRR Alc.

CZECH LANGUAGE--DICTIONARIES--POLYGLOT.
Kleczek, Josip. Astronomical
dictionary. [Vyd. 1.] Praha, Nakl.
Československé akademie věd, 1961.
972 p. 62-25391
QB14 .K55 MRR Alc.

Orne, Jerrold, The language of the
foreign book trade: 2d ed. Chicago,
American Library Association, 1962.
213 p. 010.3 61-12881
Z1006 .C7 1962 MRR Alc.

CZECH LITERATURE--BIO-BIBLIOGRAPHY.
Kunc, Jaroslav. Slovník soudobých
českých spisovatelů. Praha,
Orbis, 1945-46. 2 v. (1016 p.) a
49-479
Z2131 .K8 MRR Biog.

CZECH LITERATURE--HISTORY AND CRITICISM.
Chudoba, František. A short survey
of Czech literature, London, K.
Paul, Trench, Trubner & co., ltd.;
New York, E. P. Dutton & co., 1924.
vii, 280 p. 25-40
PG5001 .C5 MRR Alc.

CZECHOSLOVAK REPUBLIC.
Busek, Vratislav, ed.
Czechoslovakia. New York, Published
for the Mid-European Studies Center
of the Free Europe Committee by
Praeger [1957] xvii, 520 p. 943.7
57-9333
DB215.5 .B83 MRR Alc.

Keefe, Eugene K. Area handbook for
Czechoslovakia. Washington, For sale
by the Supt. of Docs., U.S. Govt.
Print. Off.] 1972. xiv, 321 p.
[$3.00] 914.37 77-185481
DB196 .K4 MRR Alc.

CZECHOSLOVAK REPUBLIC--BIBLIOGRAPHY.
Horecky, Paul Louis, East Central
Europe; a guide to basic
publications. Chicago, University of
Chicago Press [1969] xxv, 956 p.
016.9143 70-79472
Z2483 .H56 MRR Alc.

Sturm, Rudolf. Czechoslovakia, a
bibliographic guide. Washington,
Library of Congress [for sale by the
Supt. of Docs., U.S. Govt. Print.
Off.] 1967 [i. e. 1968] xii, 157 p.
016.91437 68-60019
Z663.47 .C93 MRR Alc.

CZECHOSLOVAK REPUBLIC--DESCRIPTION AND
TRAVEL--GUIDE-BOOKS.
Nelson, Nina. Your guide to
Czechoslovakia. London, Redman,
1968. 219 p. [21/-] 914.3/7/044
68-140812
DB195 .N4 MRR Alc.

CZECHOSLOVAK REPUBLIC--EXECUTIVE
DEPARTMENTS--DIRECTORIES.
Directory of Czechoslovak officials.
[n.p.] 1970. xi, 280 p.
354.437/002 74-16206
JN2217 .D5 1970 MRR Alc.

CZECHOSLOVAK REPUBLIC--HISTORY.
Thomson, Samuel Harrison,
Czechoslovakia in European history.
[2d ed., enl.] Princeton, Princeton
University Press, 1953. 485 p.
943.7 52-8780
DB205.1 .T48 1953 MRR Alc.

CZECHOSLOVAK REPUBLIC--HISTORY--1918-
1938--SOURCES.
Jesina, Cestmir, comp. The birth of
Czechoslovakia. [Washington]
Czechoslovak National Council of
America, Washington, D.C. Chapter,
1968. ix, 110 p. [5.00] 74-18574

DB215.2 .J48 MRR Alc.

CZECHOSLOVAK REPUBLIC--OFFICIALS AND
EMPLOYEES--DIRECTORIES.
Directory of Czechoslovak officials.
[n.p.] 1970. xi, 280 p.
354.437/002 74-16206
JN2217 .D5 1970 MRR Alc.

CZECHOSLOVAK REPUBLIC--POLITICS AND
GOVERNMENT--1945-
Taborsky, Edward. Communism in
Czechoslovakia, 1948-1960.
Princeton, N.J., Princeton University
Press, 1961. xii, 628 p. 943.704
61-7425
DB215.5 .T3 MRR Alc.

CZECHOSLOVAK REPUBLIC--REGISTERS.
Directory of Czechoslovak officials.
[n.p.] 1970. xi, 280 p.
354.437/002 74-16206
JN2217 .D5 1970 MRR Alc.

CZECHOSLOVAK REPUBLIC--STATISTICS.
Císla pro každého; Praha,
Státní nakl. technické literatury.
62-34039
HA1191 .A8 MRR Alc Latest editon

Czechoslovakia: Statistical abstract.
1963- Prague, Orbis. [Kčs15.00]
914.37 74-644816
HA1195 .C9 MRR Alc Latest edition

Statistická ročenka
Československé socialistické
republiky. 1934- Praha, Státní
nakl. technické literatury. 38-
24080
HA1191 .A416 MRR Alc Latest
edition

CZECHS.
Thomson, Samuel Harrison,
Czechoslovakia in European history.
[2d ed., enl.] Princeton, Princeton
University Press, 1953. 485 p.
943.7 52-8780
DB205.1 .T48 1953 MRR Alc.

CZECHS IN THE UNITED STATES--
DIRECTORIES.
Czechoslovak Society of Arts and
Sciences in America. Directory of
the members. New York, 1969. v, 100
p. [6.00 (4.00 to members)] 060
68-58162
E184.B67 C982 1969 MRR Alc.

DAHOMEY--GAZETTEERS.
United States. Office of Geography.
Dahomey; Washington [U.S. Govt.
Print. Off.] 1965. iv, 89 p. 65-
62432
DT541.2 .U5 MRR Alc.

DAIRY PLANTS--UNITED STATES--
DIRECTORIES.
Dairy Credit Bureau, Chicago. Dairy
credit book. Chicago. 637.116 41-
297
HD9275 .A1D3 MRR Alc Latest
edition

DAIRYING.
see also Cheese

DAIRYING--UNITED STATES--CREDIT GUIDES.
Dairy Credit Bureau, Chicago. Dairy
credit book. Chicago. 637.116 41-
297
HD9275 .A1D3 MRR Alc Latest
edition

DAMS--DICTIONARIES--POLYGLOT.
International Commission on Large
Dams. Dictionnaire technique des
barrages. 2. ed. [Paris, 1960?]
380 p. 627.803 61-805
TC540 .I45 1860 MRR Alc.

DAMS--UNITED STATES.
International Commission on Large
Dams. United States Committee.
Committee on the Register of Dams.
Register of dams in the United
States, [Washington? United States
Committee on Large Dams, 1963] 1 v.
(various pagings) 627.8 63-5483
TC558.U6 I5 1963 MRR Alc.

DANCE, MODERN
see Modern dance

DANCE MUSIC, ENGLISH.
Chappell, William, Old English
popular music. A new ed., New York,
J. Brussel [c1961] 2 v. in 1.
784.3 62-3231
M1740 .C52 1961 MRR Alc.

DANCERS--DICTIONARIES.
Wilson, George Buckley Laird. A
dictionary of ballet 3rd ed.
London, A. & C. Black, 1974. xi, 539
p., [8] p. of plates. [£6.00]
792.8/03 74-183304
GV1585 .W5 1974 MRR Alc.

DANCING.
see also Ballet

see also Folk dancing

DANCING--BIBLIOGRAPHY.
American Association for Health,
Physical Education, and Recreation.
National Section on Dance.
Compilation of dance research, 1901-
1964. Washington, American
Association for Health, Physical
Education, and Recreation [1964] 52
p. 016.7933 64-56415
Z7514.D2 A48 MRR Alc.

Chicorel, Marietta. Chicorel
bibliography to the performing arts.
1st ed. New York, Chicorel Library
Pub. Corp. [1972] 498 p. 016.7902
73-155102
Z6935 .C45 MRR Alc.

Magriel, Paul David, Comp A
bibliography of dancing; New York,
The H. W. Wilson company, 1936. 229
p. 016.7933 37-842
Z7514.D2 M2 MRR Alc.

Schoolcraft, Ralph Newman.
Performing arts/books in print: an
annotated bibliography. [1st ed.]
New York, Drama Book Specialists
[1973] xiii, 761 p. 016.7902 72-
78909
Z6935 .S34 MRR Alc.

DANCING--DICTIONARIES.
Chujoy, Anatole, ed. The dance
encyclopedia, Rev. and enl. ed. New
York, Simon and Schuster [1967] xii,
992 p. 793.3/03 67-28038
GV1585 .C5 1967 MRR Alc.

Kersley, Leo. A dictionary of ballet
terms [2d ed., enl.] New York,
Pitman Pub. Corp. [1964] 112 p.
792.8203 64-6893
GV1585 .K45 1964 MRR Alc.

Raffé Walter George, Dictionary of
the dance, New York, A. S. Barnes
[1965, c1964] 583 p. 793.303 64-
21356
GV1585 .R3 1965 MRR Alc.

DANCING--HISTORY.
Kraus, Richard G. History of the
dance in art and education Englewood
Cliffs, N.J., Prentice-Hall [1969]
xii, 371 p. 793.3/09 69-13716
GV1601 .K7 MRR Alc.

DANCING--PERIODICALS--INDEXES.
Belknap, Sara (Yancey) Guide to the
musical arts; New York, Scarecrow
Press, 1957. 1 v. (unpaged) 016.78
57-6631
ML113 .B37 MRR Alc.

Guide to the performing arts. 1957-
Metuchen, N.J. [etc.] Scarecrow
Press. 016.78 60-7266
ML118 .G8 MRR Alc Full set

DANCING--YEARBOOKS.
Folk dance guide. New York.
793.31058 55-8175
Began in 1951.
GV1580 .F6 MRR Alc Latest edition

DANCING--AFRICA, SUB-SAHARAN--
BIBLIOGRAPHY.
International African Institute. A
select bibliography of music in
Africa, London, 1965. 83 p. 66-
36908
ML120.A35 I6 MRR Alc.

DANCING--ASIA.
Bowers, Faubion, Theatre in the
East; New York, T. Nelson [1956]
374 p. 792.095 56-8995
GV1689 .B6 MRR Alc.

DANCING--UNITED STATES.
Maynard, Olga. The American ballet.
Philadelphia, Macrae Smith Co.
[c1959] 353 p. 792.80973 59-13260

GV1787 .M36 MRR Alc.

DANCING--UNITED STATES--DIRECTORIES.
The National directory for the
performing arts and civic centers.
Dallas, Handel & Co. 790.2/0973 73-
646635
PN2289 .N38 MRR Alc Latest edition

DANGEROUS MATERIALS
see Hazardous substances

DANISH LANGUAGE--DICTIONARIES.
Nudansk ordbog. 4. revid. og
forøgede udg. København, Politikens
forlag, 1964. 2 v. (viii, 1162 p.)
66-47005
PD3625 .N8 1964 MRR Alc.

DANISH LANGUAGE--DICTIONARIES--ENGLISH.
Bolbjerg, Alfred Rovald, Dansk-
engelsk ordbog. 4. udg. København,
Berlingske forlag, 1963. 557 p. 64-
35775
PD3640 .B6 1963 MRR Alc.

DANISH LANGUAGE--DICTIONARIES-- (Cont.)
Moth, Axel Fredrik Carl Mathias,
Glossary of library terms, English,
Danish, Dutch, French, German,
Italian, Spanish, Swedish. Boston,
The Boston book company, 1915. 58 p.
15-3471
Z1006 .M72 MRR Alc.

Vinterberg, Hermann, Dansk-engelsk
ordbog København, Gyldendal, 1954-
56. 2 v.   55-256
PD3640 .V5 MRR Alc.

Vinterberg, Hermann, Dansk-engelsk
ordbog. 7. revid og forøgede udg.
København, Gyldendal, 1967. 8, 464
p. [23.00 dkr] 439.8/1/32 67-
82538
PD3640 .V48 1967 MRR Alc.

Warrern, Allan. Dansk-engelsk
teknisk ordbog. 2. stærkt øgede udg.
København, J. F. Clausen, 1957.
333p.   58-22125
T9 .W26 1957 MRR Alc.

Warrern, Allan. Dansk-engelsk
teknisk ordbog. 4. udg. København,
J. Fr. Clausen 1970. 368 p.
[kr88.50]   76-861852
T10 .W33 1970 MRR Alc.

DANISH LANGUAGE--DICTIONARIES--POLYGLOT.
Dictionnaire à l'usage de la
librairie ancienne pour les langues:
française, anglaise, allemande,
suédoise, danoise, italienne,
espagnole, hollandaise, Paris, Ligue
internationale de la librairie
ancienne, 1956. 190 p.   655.403 57-
2275
Z282 .D5 MRR Alc.

International insurance dictionary:
[n.p., European Conference of
Insurance Supervisory Services, 1959]
xxxi, 1083 p.   368.03 61-35675
HG8025 .I5 MRR Alc.

Nijdam, J. Tuinbouwkundig
woordenboek in acht talen. Herziene
en uitgebreide uitg. van de
Woordenlijst voor de tuinbouw in
zeven talen. ['s-Gravenhage,
Staatsdrukkerij- en
Uitgeverijbedrijf; voor alle anderen
landen: Interscience Publishers, New
York] 1961. 504 p.   62-52704
SB45 .N673 MRR Alc.

DANISH LANGUAGE--ETYMOLOGY--
DICTIONARIES.
Falk, Hjalmar Sejersted, Norwegisch-
dänisches etymologisches
Worterbuch, 2. Aufl. Oslo,
Universitetsforlaget, 1960. 2 v.
(1722 p.)   61-34051
PD2683 .F33 1960 MRR Alc.

DANISH LANGUAGE--SYNONYMS AND ANTONYMS.
Albeck, Ulla. Dansk synonymordbog.
5. revid. og forøgede udg.
København, Schultz, 1967. 301 p.
[34.65 dkr]   68-74485
PD3591 .A6 1967 MRR Alc.

DANISH LITERATURE--20TH CENTURY--BIO-
BIBLIOGRAPHY.
Dansk skønlitterært
forfatterleksikon, 1900-1950.
København, Grønholt Pedersen, 1959-
64. 3 v.   60-20084
Z2573.3 .D3 MRR Alc.

DANISH LITERATURE--BIBLIOGRAPHY.
Bredsdorff, Elias. Danish literature
in English translation, Copenhagen,
E. Munksgaard, 1950. 198 p.
016.83981 51-4614
Z2574.T7 B7 MRR Alc.

Dania polyglotta; 1.-24. année;
1945-1968. Copenhague, Bibliothèque
royale. 015.489 48-2634
Z2574.F6 D32 MRR Alc Partial set

Mitchell, Phillip Marshall, A
bibliographical guide to Danish
literature. Copenhagen, Munksgaard,
1951. 62 p.   016.83981 a 52-3783
Z2571 .M5 MRR Alc.

DANISH LITERATURE--HISTORY AND
CRITICISM.
Claudi, Jørgen, Contemporary Danish
authors, Copenhagen, Danske selskab,
1952. 163 p.   839.8109 52-14932
PT7760 .C55 MRR Biog.

Mitchell, Phillip Marshall, A
history of Danish literature, 2d.
augm. ed. New York, Kraus-Thomson
Organization, 1971. 339 p.
838.8/1/09 71-181092
PT7663 .M5 1871 MRR Alc.

DANISH LITERATURE--TRANSLATIONS INTO
ENGLISH--BIBLIOGRAPHY.
Bredsdorff, Elias. Danish literature
in English translation, Copenhagen,
E. Munksgaard, 1950. 198 p.
016.83981 51-4614
Z2574.T7 B7 MRR Alc.

Claudi, Jørgen, Contemporary Danish
authors, Copenhagen, Danske selskab,
1952. 163 p.   839.8109 52-14932
PT7760 .C55 MRR Biog.

DANISH NEWSPAPERS--INDEXES.
Minerva mikrofilm a/s, Copenhagen.
Fortegnelse over danske aviser 1648-
1967 med angivelse af de
mikrofilmede. København, [1967]. 35
p. [N.T.]   68-132074
AI13 .M52 MRR Alc.

DANISH PERIODICALS--INDEXES.
Dania polyglotta; 1.-24. année;
1945-1968. Copenhague, Bibliothèque
royale. 015.489 48-2634
Z2574.F6 D32 MRR Alc Partial set

Dania polyglotta. new ser., 1-
1969- Copenhagen [Royal Library] 72-
622671
Z2561 .D162 MRR Alc Full set

Dansk tidsskrift-index. København,
Udgivet af Bibliotekscentralen [etc.]
ca 18-1493
AI13. D3 MRR Alc Partial set

DANTE ALIGHIERI, 1265-1321. DIVINA
COMMEDIA.
Wilkins, Ernest Hatch, A concordance
to the Divine comedy of Dante
Alighieri. Cambridge, Belknap Press
of Harvard University Press, 1965.
ix, 636 p.   851.1 65-11195
PQ4464 .W5 MRR Alc.

DANTE ALIGHIERI, 1265-1321--ADDRESSES,
ESSAYS, LECTURES.
United States. Library of Congress.
Gertrude Clarke Whittall Poetry and
Literature Fund. Dante Alighieri:
three lectures. Washington,
Published for the Library of Congress
by the Gertrude Clarke Whittall
Poetry and Literature Fund; [for sale
by the Superintendent of Documents,
U.S. Govt. Print. Off.] 1965. vii,
53 p.   65-60093
Z663.293 .D3 MRR Alc.

DANTE ALIGHIERI, 1265-1321--
CONCORDANCES.
Wilkins, Ernest Hatch, A concordance
to the Divine comedy of Dante
Alighieri. Cambridge, Belknap Press
of Harvard University Press, 1965.
ix, 636 p.   851.1 65-11195
PQ4464 .W5 MRR Alc.

DANTE ALIGHIERI, 1265-1321--
DICTIONARIES, INDEXES, ETC.
Toynbee, Paget Jackson, A dictionary
of proper names and notable matters
in the works of Dante. [New ed.]
Oxford, Clarendon P., 1968 xxv, 722
p. [5/15/6] 851/.1 68-81646
PQ4333 .T7 1968 MRR Alc.

DARK AGES
see Middle Ages

DATA LIBRARIES--UNITED STATES--
DIRECTORIES.
Kruzas, Anthony Thomas. Encyclopedia
of information systems and services.
2d international ed. Ann Arbor,
Mich., A. T. Kruzas Associates; order
fulfillment by Edwards Bros. [1974]
xli, 1271 p.   028/.025/73 73-3732
Z674.3 .K78 1974 MRR Alc.

DATA PROCESSING
see Electronic data processing

see Punched card systems

DAVIS, JAMES JOHN, 1873-1947--
BIBLIOGRAPHY.
United States. Library of Congress.
Manuscript Division. James J. Davis;
a register of his papers in the
Library of Congress. Washington,
1958. 9 l.   012 58-60089
Z663.34 .D3 MRR Alc.

DAVIS, JEFFERSON, 1808-1889.
Hendrick, Burton Jesse, Statesmen of
the lost cause; Boston, Little,
Brown and company, 1939. xvii, 452
p.   923.273 39-28981
E487 .H47 MRR Alc.

DAY NURSERIES--UNITED STATES--
DIRECTORIES.
LaCrosse, E. Robert. Early childhood
education directory; 1st ed. New
York, R. R. Bowker Co., 1971. xiv,
455 p. [$19.50] 372.21/025/73 77-
126012
L901 .L3 MRR Ref Desk.

DAYS.
see also Festivals

see also Holidays

Chambers, Robert, The book of days;
Detroit, Gale Research Co., 1967. 2
v.   902/.02 67-13009
DA110 .C52 1967 MRR Alc.

Chases' calendar of annual events.
1958- Flint, Mich., Apple Tree
Press. 57-14540
GT4803 .C48 MRR Ref Desk Latest
Edition

Collison, Robert Lewis. Newnes
Dictionary of dates; 2nd revised ed.
London, Newnes, 1966. ix, 11-428 p.
[35/-] 903 66-72492
D11.5 .C6 1966 MRR Alc.

Darling, William Young, Sir, A book
of days: London, Richards Press
[1951] 381 p.   902 52-67733
D11.5 .D3 MRR Alc.

Douglas, George William, The
American book of days; New York, H.
W. Wilson Co., 1948. xxii, 697 p.
394.26973 48-28210
GT4803 .D6 1948 MRR Alc.

Harper, Howard V. Days and customs
of all faiths. New York, Fleet Pub.
Corp. [1957] 399 p.   264 57-14777

GR930 .H3 MRR Alc.

Hutchison, Ruth Shepherd, Every
day's a holiday [1st ed.] New York,
Harper [1951] xiv, 304 p.   394.26
51-9099
GT3930 .H85 MRR Alc.

Myers, Robert J. Celebrations; the
complete book of American holidays,
[1st ed.] Garden City, N.Y.,
Doubleday, 1972. x, 386 p.
394.2/6973 77-163086
GT4803.A2 M84 MRR Alc.

Thornton, Willis. Almanac for
Americans New York, Greenberg
[c1941] 5 p. l., 3-418 p. incl.
front., illus.   973.02 41-23726
E174.5 .T5 MRR Alc.

DEAD.
see also Funeral rites and ceremonies

DEAD SEA SCROLLS--HANDBOOKS, MANUALS,
ETC.
Mansoor, Menahem. The Dead Sea
scrolls; Leiden, E. J. Brill, 1964.
x, 210 p.   65-5955
BM487 .M27 1964a MRR Alc.

DEATH--CAUSES.
Elliot, Gil, Twentieth century book
of the dead. London, Allen Lane,
1972. viii, 242 p. [£2.75]
301.32/2 72-169396
D445 .E555 MRR Alc.

Preston, Samuel H. Causes of death:
life tables for national population
New York, Seminar Press, 1972. xi,
787 p.   312/.2 72-80305
HB1321 .P73 MRR Alc.

DEATH--PROOF AND CERTIFICATION--UNITED
STATES.
United States. Public Health Service.
Where to write for birth and death
records: United States and outlying
areas. [Washington, For sale by the
Supt. of Docs., U.S. Govt. Print.
Off.] 312/.1/072073 77-649981
HA38 .A232 MRR Ref Desk Latest
edition

DEATH PENALTY
see Capital punishment

DEBATES AND DEBATING.
see also Discussion

see also Public speaking

Debate index, New ed. rev. New
York, Wilson, 1939. 130 p.   016.3
39-27689
Z7161.5 .D28 1939 MRR Alc.

Kruger, Arthur N. Modern debate:
New York, McGraw-Hill, 1960. 448 p.
808.53 60-8032
PN4181 .K7 MRR Alc.

DEBATES AND DEBATING--BIBLIOGRAPHY.
Kruger, Arthur N. A classified
bibliography of argumentation and
debate. New York, Scarecrow Press,
1964. 400 p.   016.80853 64-11791
Z7161.5 .K75 MRR Alc.

DEBENTURES
see Bonds

DEBT.
see also Credit

DEBTS, PUBLIC--GREAT BRITAIN.
Pember and Boyle, London. British
Government securities in the
twentieth century; [2d ed. London,
1950] 596 p.   336.31 50-14274
HG5438 .P4 MRR Alc.

DEBTS, PUBLIC--UNITED STATES.
United States. Laws, statutes, etc.
Laws of the United States concerning
money, banking, and loans, 1778-1909;
Washington, Govt. print. off., 1910.
v, 267 p., 1 l., 269-812, xxii p.
10-36032
HG481 .A2 1910 MRR Alc.

DECENTRALIZATION IN GOVERNMENT.
see also Local government

DECISION-MAKING--BIBLIOGRAPHY.
Leif, Irving P., Community power and
decision-making; Metuchen, N.J.,
Scarecrow Press, 1974. vi, 170 p.
016.30115/5 74-4171
Z7164.C842 L43 MRR Alc.

Universal Reference System.
Legislative process, representation,
and decision-making; Princeton,
N.J., Princeton Research Pub. Co.
[c1967] xv, 749 p.   016.32 67-
29646
Z6461 .U64 vol. 2 MRR Alc.

DECORATION, INTERIOR
see Interior decoration

DECORATION AND ORNAMENT.
see also Art objects

see also Carpets

see also Furniture

see also Illustration of books

see also Interior decoration

see also Jewelry

see also Metal-work

see also Painting

see also Sculpture

Whiton, Augustus Sherrill, Interior
design and decoration. 4th ed.
Philadelphia, Lippincott [1974] vi,
699 p.   747 73-19987
NK2110 .W55 1974 MRR Alc.

DECORATION AND ORNAMENT--DICTIONARIES.
Clark, MaryJane. An illustrated
glossary of decorated antiques from
the late 17th century to the early
20th century. (1st ed.] Rutland,
Vt., C. E. Tuttle Co. [1972] 400 p.
[$8.75] 745.1 74-138080
NK30 .C43 MRR Alc.

Studio dictionary of design &
decoration. Rev. and enl. ed.] New
York, Viking Press [1973] 538 p.
[$28.50] 745.4/03 73-1024
NK1165 .S78 1973 MRR Alc.

DECORATION AND ORNAMENT--UNITED STATES.
Lipman, Jean (Herzberg) American
folk decoration. New York, Oxford
University Press, 1951. xii, 163 p.
745.3 51-11035
NK806 .L5 MRR Alc.

DECORATIONS OF HONOR.
Dorling, Henry Taprell, Ribbons and
medals; This ed. rev. under the
editorship of Francis K. Mason.
Garden City, N.Y., Doubleday, 1974.
359 p.   [$14.95] 355.1/34/09 73-
20952
UC530 .D63 1974 MRR Ref Desk.

Ducourtial, Claude. Ordres et
decorations ...   2e edition
augmentee et mise a jour. Paris,
Presses universitaires de France,
1968. 128 p. [3.30] 72-406717
CR4509 .D8 1968 MRR Alc.

Mericka, Vaclav. Orders and
decorations; London, Hamlyn, 1967.
316 p. [63/-] 929.7 68-78077
CR4509 .M4 MRR Alc.

Werlich, Robert. Orders and
decorations of all nations: ancient
and modern, civil and military. 2d
ed. [Washington, Quaker Press, 1974]
476 p.   928.8 74-177291
CR4509 .W4 1974 MRR Ref Desk.

Wyllie, Robert E., Orders,
decorations and insignia, military
and civil; New York, London, G. P.
Putnam's sons [c1921] 3 p. l., v-xxi
p., 1 l., 269 p.   21-4556
CR4509 .W9 MRR Alc.

DECORATIONS OF HONOR--DENMARK.
Forlaget Liber, Copenhagen. De
kongelige danske ridderordener og
medailler. København, Forlaget
liber, 1965. 611 p.   73-332590
CR5750 .F62 MRR Alc.

Forlaget Liber, Copenhagen. De
kongelige danske ridderordener og
medailler. [1964-1968.] København,
Liber, 1970. 591 p. [kr722.20] 72-
300129
CR5750 .F6 1970 MRR Alc.

DECORATIONS OF HONOR--EUROPE.
Hieronymussen, Poul Ohm. Orders,
medals and decorations of Britain and
Europe in colour, London, Blandford,
1967. 256 p. [35/-] 929.8 67-
96475
CR4515 .H513 1967b MRR Alc.

DECORATIONS OF HONOR--FRANCE.
Ducourtial, Claude. Ordres et
decorations ...   2e edition
augmentee et mise a jour. Paris,
Presses universitaires de France,
1968. 128 p. [3.30] 72-406717
CR4509 .D8 1968 MRR Alc.

France. Administration des monnaies
et medailles. Decorations
officielles françaises. Paris,
Impr. nationale [c1956] 291 p.   57-
24822
CR5085 .A53 MRR Alc.

DECORATIONS OF HONOR--GERMANY.
Doehle, Heinrich, Die Orden und
Ehrenzeichen des Grossdeutschen
Reichs. Berlin, Berliner Buch- und
Zeitschriften-Verlag, 1941. 128 p.
737.2 52-55855
CR5109 .D57 1941 MRR Alc.

DECORATIONS OF HONOR--GREAT BRITAIN.
Abbott, Peter Edward. British
gallantry awards Enfield, Guiness
Superlatives; London, Seaby, 1971.
359 p.; [£6.00] 355.1/34 72-
872853
CR4801 .A63 MRR Alc.

British orders and awards; 2nd
entirely revised ed. London, Kaye &
Ward, 1968. [5], 183 p. [30/-]
737/.2/0942 72-352008
CR4801 .B7 1968 MRR Alc.

Jocelyn, Arthur. Awards of honour;
London, A. and C. Black, 1956. xix,
276 p.   929.72 57-268
CR4529.G7 J6 MRR Alc.

Joslin, Edward C. The standard
catalogue of British orders,
decorations and medals 1969, London,
Spink, 1969. xiv, 114 p. chiefly
illus. [unpriced] 737.2 74-448443

CR4801 .J6 MRR Alc.

DECORATIONS OF HONOR--SWEDEN.
Ordenskalender. 1958/59- Stockholm.
Almqvist & Wiksell [etc.] 60-19478
CR5787 .O7 MRR Alc Latest edition

DECORATIONS OF HONOR--UNITED STATES.
Kerrigan, Evans E. American war
medals and decorations, Newly rev.
and expanded. New York, Viking Press
[1971] xiv, 173 p. [$8.50]
355.1/34 77-124322
CJ5805 .K4 1971 MRR Ref Desk.

DECORATIVE METAL-WORK
see Art metal-work

DEEP-SEA EXPLORATION
see Marine biology

see Marine fauna

DEFECTIVES
see Handicapped

DEFENSE CONTRACTS--UNITED STATES.
Council on Economic Priorities.
Guide to corporations; [1st ed.]
Chicago, Swallow Press [1974] iii,
393 p. [$4.95] 301.5/5 73-13212
HD60.5.U5 C7 1974 MRR Alc.

DEFICIENCY APPROPRIATION BILLS
see United States--Appropriations and
expenditures

DEFICIENCY DISEASES.
see also Nutrition

DEGENERATION.
Bodart, Gaston, Losses of life in
modern wars, Austria-Hungary; France,
Oxford, The Clarendon press; London,
New York [etc.] H. Milford, 1916. x,
207, 6 p. incl. tables. 16-20885
D25.5 .B6 MRR Alc.

DEGREES, ACADEMIC.
Bartholomew, Curtis Alford,
Epithetology. 1st ed. Red Bank,
N.J., Printed and distributed by the
Commercial Press [1948] 207 p.
378.2 48-2130
LB2381 .B28 MRR Alc.

Haycraft, Frank W. The degrees and
hoods of the world's universities and
colleges. [4th ed.] Cheshunt [Eng.]
Cheshunt Press, 1948. 159 p.
378.29 49-3552
LB2389 .H3 1948 MRR Alc.

DEGREES, ACADEMIC--ABBREVIATIONS.
Bartholomew, Curtis Alford,
Epithetology. 1st ed. Red Bank,
N.J., Printed and distributed by the
Commercial Press [1948] 207 p.
378.2 48-2130
LB2381 .B28 MRR Alc.

DEGREES, ACADEMIC--UNITED STATES.
American universities and colleges.
[1st]- ed.; 1928- Washington
[etc.] American Council on Education
[etc.] 378.73 28-5598
LA226 .A65 MRR Ref Desk Latest
edition / MRR Alc Latest edition

Cass, James. Comparative guide to
American colleges; 6th ed. New
York, Harper & Row [1973] xxxiii,
916 p. [$5.95] 378.73 73-4068
L901 .C33 1973 MRR Ref Desk.

The College blue book. [1st]- 1923-
New York [etc.] CCM Information
Corp. [etc.] 378.73 24-223
LA226 .C685 MRR Ref Desk Latest
edition

Eells, Walter Crosby, Academic
degrees; [Washington] U.S. Dept. of
Health, Education, and Welfare,
Office of Education [1960] vi, 324
p. 378.240973 hew61-6
LB2381 .E4 MRR Alc.

United States. Office of Education.
Earned degrees conferred by higher
educational institutions. 1947/48-
Washington, Federal Security Agency,
Office of Education. 378.2 e 48-19
L111 .A72 no. 247, etc. MRR Alc
Latest edition

**DEGREES, ACADEMIC--UNITED STATES--
STATISTICS.**
Reeves, Vernon H. Your college
degree; Chicago, Science Research
Associates [c1968] 221 p.
373.1/4/20202 77-12816
LB2381 .R4 MRR Alc.

DEGREES OF LATITUDE AND LONGITUDE
see Geodesy

DELAWARE.
Federal Writers' Project. Delaware.
Delaware, a guide to the first State.
New and rev. ed. New York, Hastings
House [1955] xxvi, 562 p. 917.51
55-14794
F164 .F45 1955 MRR Ref Desk.

DELAWARE--BIBLIOGRAPHY.
Reed, Henry Clay, A bibliography of
Delaware through 1960, Newark,
Published for the Institute of
Delaware History and Culture by the
University of Delaware Press, 1966.
vi, 196 p. 016.91751 66-18259
Z1267 .R4 MRR Alc.

United States. Library of Congress.
Old New Castle and modern Delaware,
Washington, U.S. Govt. Print. Off.,
1951. iv, 59 p. 016.9751 51-60024

Z663.15.A6D3 1951 MRR Alc.

DELAWARE--COMMERCE--DIRECTORIES.
Directory of commerce and industry,
State of Delaware. Wilmington,
Delaware State Chamber of Commerce.
[$10.00] 338/.0025/751 73-643193
HF3161.D3 D57 MRR Alc Latest
edition / Sci RR Latest edition

**DELAWARE--DESCRIPTION AND TRAVEL--GUIDE-
BOOKS.**
Federal Writers' Project. Delaware.
Delaware, a guide to the first State.
New and rev. ed. New York, Hastings
House [1955] xxvi, 562 p. 917.51
55-14794
F164 .F45 1955 MRR Ref Desk.

**DELAWARE--HISTORY--COLONIAL PERIOD, CA.
1600-1775--SOURCES.**
Myers, Albert Cook, ed. Narratives
of early Pennsylvania, West New
Jersey and Delaware, 1630-1707, New
York, C. Scribner's sons, 1912. xiv
p., 2 l., 3-476 p. 12-4611
E187.O7 M9 MRR Alc.

DELAWARE--INDUSTRIES--DIRECTORIES.
Directory of commerce and industry,
State of Delaware. Wilmington,
Delaware State Chamber of Commerce.
[$10.00] 338/.0025/751 73-643193
HF3161.D3 D57 MRR Alc Latest
edition / Sci RR Latest edition

DELAWARE--MANUFACTURES--DIRECTORIES.
Directory of Central Atlantic States
manufacturers; 1- ed.; 1950-
Baltimore, T. K. Sanderson
Organization. 670/.58 50-2706
T12 .D485 Sci RR Latest edition /
MRR Alc Latest edition

DELAWARE--POLITICS AND GOVERNMENT.
Delaware state manual. [Dover]
Secretary of State. 72-626413
JK3731 date MRR Alc Latest edition

DELAWARE--REGISTERS.
Delaware state manual. [Dover]
Secretary of State. 72-626413
JK3731 date MRR Alc Latest edition

DELAWARE--STATISTICS--PERIODICALS.
Delaware. State Planning Office.
Delaware, statistical abstract. 1973-
Dover. [$4.50] 317.51 74-646466
HA281 .S74a MRR Alc Latest edition

DELAWARE RIVER--HISTORY.
Myers, Albert Cook, ed. Narratives
of early Pennsylvania, West New
Jersey and Delaware, 1630-1707, New
York, C. Scribner's sons, 1912. xiv
p., 2 l. 3-476 p.   12-4611
E187.07 M9 MRR Alc.

DELEGATION OF POWERS.
see also Separation of powers

DELINQUENCY, JUVENILE
see Juvenile delinquency

DELINQUENTS.
see also Crime and criminals

see also Juvenile delinquency

DELUSIONS
see Errors, Popular

see Superstition

see Swindlers and swindling

DEMOCRATIC PARTY.
Brown, Stuart Gerry, The first
Republicans; [Syracuse] Syracuse
University Press, 1954. 186 p.
329.3 54-9917
JK2316 .B7 MRR Alc.

DEMOCRATIC PARTY--HISTORY.
Kent, Frank Richardson, The
Democratic party; a history New
York, London, The Century co. [1928]
xi, 568 p.   mrr01-29
JK2316 .K4 1928a MRR Alc.

Cunningham, Noble E., The
Jeffersonian Republicans; Chapel
Hill Published for the Institute of
Early American History and Culture at
Williamsburg by the University of
North Carolina Press [c1957] x, 279
p.   329.3 58-1263
JK2316 .C8 MRR Alc.

DEMOGRAPHY.
see also Population

Clark, Colin, Population growth and
land use. London, Melbourne [etc.]
Macmillan; New York, St. Martin's P.,
1967.   406 p. [70/-] 301.3/2 67-
15941
HB871 .C58 1967 MRR Alc.

Hauser, Philip Morris, ed. The study
of population: [Chicago] University
of Chicago Press [1959] 864 p.   312
58-11949
HB871 .H37 MRR Alc.

DEMOGRAPHY--BIBLIOGRAPHY.
Population index. v. 1-   Jan. 20,
1935-   [Princeton, N.J., etc.]
016.312 39-10247
Z7164.D3 P83 MRR Alc Partial set

Princeton University. Office of
Population Research. Population
index bibliography, Boston, G. K.
Hall, 1971. 4 v.   016.312 75-26979

Z7164.D3 P85 MRR Alc (Dk 33)

Princeton University. Office of
Population Research. Population
index bibliography, Boston, G. K.
Hall, 1971. 5 v.   016.312 79-30213

Z7164.D3 P852 MRR Alc (Dk 33)

DEMOGRAPHY--MATHEMATICAL MODELS.
Keyfitz, Nathan, Population: facts
and methods of demography San
Francisco, W. H. Freeman [1971] x,
613 p.   [$13.50]   301.3/2/072 70-
141154
HB885 .K43 MRR Alc.

DEMOGRAPHY--SOCIETIES, ETC.--
DIRECTORIES.
Fogle, Catherine. International
directory of population information
and library resources, 1st ed.
[Chapel Hill] Carolina Population
Center, 1972. xiii, 324 p.
301.32/025 79-190722
HB850 .F6 MRR Alc.

DEMONOLOGY.
see also Satanism

Summers, Montague, The geography of
witchcraft. Evanston [Ill.]
University Books [1958] 623 p.
133.4 58-8303
BF1566 .S82 1958 MRR Alc.

Summers, Montague, The history of
witchcraft and demonology. London,
Routledge & K. Paul [1965] xv, 353
p.   133.409 66-2254
BF1566 .S8 1965 MRR Alc.

DEMONOLOGY--DICTIONARIES.
Collin de Plancy, Jacques Albín
Simon, Dictionary of demonology.
New York, Philosophical Library
[1965] 177 p.   133.4 65-11952
BF1503 .C613 MRR Alc.

DEMONOLOGY--DICTIONARIES--ENGLISH.
Robbins, Rossell Hope, The
encyclopedia of witchcraft and
demonology. New York, Crown
Publishers [1959] 571 p.   133.403
59-9155
BF1503 .R6 MRR Alc.

DEMOUNTABLE BUILDINGS
see Buildings, Prefabricated

DENMARK.
Denmark. Udenrigsministeriet.
Denmark. 1924- Copenhagen. 24-
31213
HC355 .A3 MRR Alc Latest edition

Denmark. An official handbook. 14th
ed.] Copenhagen, Krak, 1970. 806 p.
[kr96.60] 914.89/03 73-564309
DL109 .D43 MRR Alc.

Facts about Denmark. 1946-
Copenhagen, Politiken Pub. House.
914.89 57-41466
DL111 .F3   MRR Alc Latest edition

DENMARK--BIBLIOGRAPHY.
Bruun, Henry. Dansk historisk
bibliografi 1913-1942. København,
Rosenkilde og Bagger, 1966- v.
[48.50 (v. 1)] 67-80149
Z2576 .B7 MRR Alc.

Copenhagen. Kongelige Bibliotek.
Denmark: literature, language,
history, society, education, arts; a
select bibliography København, The
Royal Library, 1966. 6, 151 p. [15.-
dkr] 016.91489/03 67-80750
Z2561 .C6 MRR Alc.

Dania polyglotta; 1.-24. année;
1945-1968. Copenhague, Bibliothèque
royale. 015.489 48-2634
Z2574.F6 D32 MRR Alc Partial set

Munch-Petersen, Erland. A guide to
Danish bibliography. Copenhagen,
Royal School of Librarianship, 1965.
140 p.   016.9148903 66-6990
Z2561.A1 M8 MRR Alc.

DENMARK--BIBLIOGRAPHY--YEARBOOKS.
Dania polyglotta. new ser., 1-
1969- Copenhagen [Royal Library] 72-
622671
Z2561 .D162 MRR Alc Full set

DENMARK--BIO-BIBLIOGRAPHY.
Krak[s] blå bog. Kjøbenhavn, Krak.
12-17961
DL144 .K7 MRR Biog Latest edition

DENMARK--BIOGRAPHY.
Bertelsen, Aage, ed. Store danske
personligheder. København,
Berlingske forlag, 1949. 2 v.   a
50-1267
DL144 .B4 MRR Biog.

Claudi, Jørgen, Contemporary Danish
authors. Copenhagen, Danske selskab,
1952. 163 p.   839.8109 52-14932
PT7760 .C55 MRR Biog.

Facts about Denmark. 1946-
Copenhagen, Politiken Pub. House.
914.89 57-41466
DL111 .F3   MRR Alc Latest edition

Forlaget Liber, Copenhagen. De
kongelige danske ridderordener og
medailler. København, Forlaget
liber, 1965. 611 p.   73-332590
CR5750 .F62 MRR Alc.

Forlaget Liber, Copenhagen. De
kongelige danske ridderordener og
medailler. [1964-1968] København,
Liber, 1970. 591 p. [kr722.20] 72-
300129
CR5750 .F6 1970 MRR Alc.

Nordisk konversationsleksikon,
København, 1960- v.   a 60-5895
AE41 .N83 MRR Alc.

DENMARK--BIOGRAPHY--BIBLIOGRAPHY.
Erichsen, Balder Vermund Aage, Dansk
historisk bibliografi, [Ny udg.]
København, I kommission hos G. E. C.
Gad, 1929. 3 v.   53-48097
Z2576 .E682 MRR Alc.

DENMARK--BIOGRAPHY--DICTIONARIES.
Bricka, Carl Frederik, Dansk
biografisk lexikon, Kjøbenhavn,
Gyldendal (F. Hegel & søn) 1887-1905.
19 v.   06-15106
CT1263 .B7 MRR Biog.

Dansk biografisk haandleksikon,
Kjøbenhavn, Kristiania, Gyldendal,
Nordisk forlag, 1920-26. 3 v.   21-
5224
CT1263 .D3 MRR Biog.

Dictionary of Scandinavian biography.
London, Melrose Press [1972] xxxv,
467 p.   [£10.50] 920/.048 B 73-
188270
DL1243 .D53 MRR Biog.

Krak[s] blå bog. Kjøbenhavn, Krak.
12-17961
DL144 .K7 MRR Biog Latest edition

DENMARK--COMMERCE--DIRECTORIES.
Denmark. Udenrigsministeriet.
Denmark. 1924- Copenhagen. 24-
31213
HC355 .A3 MRR Alc Latest edition

Export directory of Denmark. 1927-
Copenhagen, Kraks legat. 27-7552
HF3643. D3 MRR Alc Latest edition

Kompas; 1- udg.; 1960- København,
Forlaget Kompas-Danmark [etc.] 63-
52026
HF3643 .K58 MRR Alc Latest edition

Krak. 199.- årg.; 1968-
København. 73-640519
HF3643 .K85 MRR Alc Latest edition

Nordisk handelskalender, København,
H. P. Bov. 49-23912
Began with vol. for 1903.
HF5193 .N6 MRR Alc Latest edition

DENMARK--COMMERCE--DIRECTORIES--
YEARBOOKS.
Kongeriget Danmarks handels-kalender.
København. [75Kr.] 74-642463
Began in 1883.
HF3643 .K6 MRR Alc Latest edition

DENMARK--DESCRIPTION AND TRAVEL--GUIDE-
BOOKS.
Denmark. 2d ed. London, E. Benn;
[distributed in the U.S.A. by Rand
McNally, Chicago] 1965. lxxxii, 237
p.   65-79892
DL119 .D4 1965 MRR Alc.

Denmark. 4th ed.] Geneva, Paris
[etc.] Nagel Publishers [1968]. 120
p. [$4.95] 914.89/04/5 77-434377

DL107 .D4 1968 MRR Alc.

DENMARK--ECONOMIC CONDITIONS--1918-
Denmark. Udenrigsministeriet.
Denmark. 1924- Copenhagen. 24-
31213
HC355 .A3 MRR Alc Latest edition

DENMARK--GAZETTEERS.
United States. Office of Geography.
Denmark and the Faeroe Islands;
Washington, U.S. Govt. Print. Off.,
1961. viii, 239 p.   914.915 61-
62195
DL105 .U5 MRR Alc.

DENMARK--HISTORY.
Lauring, Palle. A history of the
kingdom of Denmark. 3rd. ed.
Copenhagen, Høst, 1968. 274 p.
[45.00dkr]   948/.9 68-118267
DL148 .L353 1968 MRR Alc.

Oakley, Stewart. A short history of
Denmark. New York, Praeger
Publishers [1972] 269 p. [$10.00]
948.9 72-78337
DL148 .O2 1972 MRR Alc.

DENMARK--HISTORY--BIBLIOGRAPHY.
Erichsen, Balder Vermund Aage, Dansk
historisk bibliografi, [Ny udg.]
København, I kommission hos G. E. C.
Gad, 1929. 3 v.   53-48097
Z2576 .E682 MRR Alc.

DENMARK--IMPRINTS.
Dania polyglotta; 1.-24. année;
1945-1968. Copenhague, Bibliothèque
royale. 015.489 48-2634
Z2574.F6 D32 MRR Alc Partial set

Dania polyglotta. new ser., 1-
1969- Copenhagen [Royal Library] 72-
622671
Z2561 .D162 MRR Alc Full set

Nyere dansk faglitteratur. 2. udg.
København, Bibliotekscentralen, 1969.
364 p. [72.70] 70-430490
Z2561 .N92 1969 MRR Alc.

DENMARK--INDUSTRIES--DIRECTORIES.
Dansk handels og industri kalender.
13.- årg.; 1965- [København]
Dansk handels og industri forlag. 72-
626757
T12.5.D4 D37 MRR Alc Latest
edition

Kompas; 1- udg.; 1960- København,
Forlaget Kompas-Danmark [etc.] 63-
52026
HF3643 .K58 MRR Alc Latest edition

DENMARK--MANUFACTURES--DIRECTORIES.
Dansk handels og industri kalender.
13.- årg.; 1965- [København]
Dansk handels og industri forlag. 72-
626757
T12.5.D4 D37 MRR Alc Latest
edition

Export directory of Denmark. 1927-
Copenhagen, Kraks legat. 27-7552
HF3643. D3 MRR Alc Latest edition

The Foreign trade directory for
Denmark. Copenhagen,
Udenrigshandelens informationsbureau.
338.4/7/6025489 72-626559
T12.5.D4 U5 MRR Alc Latest edition

DENMARK--POLITICS AND GOVERNMENT.
Denmark. Udenrigsministeriet.
Denmark. 1924- Copenhagen. 24-
31213
   HC355 .A3 MRR Alc Latest edition

DENMARK--REGISTERS.
Denmark. Kongelig dansk hof- og
statskalender. København, J. H.
Schultz. 08-4352
   JN7104 MRR Alc Latest Edition

DENMARK--SOCIAL CONDITIONS.
Denmark. Udenrigsministeriet.
Denmark. 1924- Copenhagen. 24-
31213
   HC355 .A3 MRR Alc Latest edition

DENMARK--STATISTICS.
Denmark. Statistiske departement.
Statistisk aarbog. 1896- København.
08-6112
   HA1477 MRR Alc Latest edition

DENOMINATIONS, RELIGIOUS
see Sects

DENTISTRY.
see also Mouth

DENTISTRY--BIBLIOGRAPHY.
Bowker's medical books in print.
1972- New York, R.R. Bowker Co.
016.61 78-37613
   Z6658 .B65 MRR Alc Latest edition
   / Sci RR Latest edition

Index to dental literature. 1962-
Chicago, American Dental Association.
617.6/001/6 72-622063
   Z6668 .I45 Sci RR Partial set /
   MRR Alc Partial set

DENTISTRY--PERIODICALS--INDEXES.
Index to dental literature. 1962-
Chicago, American Dental Association.
617.6/001/6 72-622063
   Z6668 .I45 Sci RR Partial set /
   MRR Alc Partial set

DENTISTS--GREAT BRITAIN--DIRECTORIES.
The Dentists register: London. ca
68-2960
   RK37 .D5 MRR Alc Latest edition

DENTISTS--UNITED STATES--BIOGRAPHY.
Who's who in American dentistry. Los
Angeles, Dale Dental Pub. Co.., 1963.
xi, 198 p. 927.6 62-13884
   RK41 .W6 MRR Biog.

DENTISTS--UNITED STATES--DIRECTORIES.
American dental directory. 1947-
[Chicago] American Dental
Association. med48-797
   RK37 .A25 MRR Alc Latest edition /
   Sci RR Latest edition

DENVER.
Barker, William J. Denver! [1st
ed.] Garden City, N.Y., Doubleday,
1972. 231 p. [$6.95] 917.88/83/04
77-175357
   F784.D4 B23 MRR Alc.

DEPARTMENT STORES.
Ferry, John William. A history of
the department store. New York,
Macmillan, 1960. 387 p. 658.871
60-10774
   HF5461 .F4 MRR Alc.

DEPARTMENT STORES--UNITED STATES.
National Retail Merchants
Association. Controllers' Congress.
Department and speciality store
merchandising and operating results.
44th- ed.; 1968- New York.
658.8/71 72-626565
   HF5465.U5 N28 MRR Alc Latest
   edition

**DEPARTMENT STORES--UNITED STATES--
DIRECTORIES.**
Directory: General mdse., variety
and Jr. dept. store chains. 36th-
ed.; 1970- [New York, Business
Guides, inc.] 381 72-623621
   HF5468.A1 C418 MRR Alc Latest
   edition

Directory of department stores. 1955-
[New York, Department Store Guide]
55-39068
   HF5465.U4 D47 MRR Alc Latest
   edition / MRR Alc Latest edition

Directory of discount centers. 1961-
[New York, Business Guides, inc.]
63-41082
   HF5035 .D46 MRR Alc Latest edition

Phelon's retail trade. 1st- ed.;
1960- New York, Phelon-Sheldon
Publications [etc.] 60-2106
   HF5465.U4 P5 MRR Alc Latest
   edition

Sheldon's retail directory of the
United States and Canada and Phelon's
resident buyers and merchandise
brokers. [$50.00] 381 74-644143
   HF5429.3 .S52 MRR Alc Latest
   edition

**DEPARTMENT STORES--UNITED STATES--
HISTORY.**
Mahoney, Tom. The great merchants;
New and enl. ed. New York, Harper &
Row [1966] ix, 374 p. 658.8700973
67-11328
   HF5429 .M288 1966 MRR Alc.

DERMATOLOGY.
Greenberg, Leon Arnold. Handbook of
cosmetic materials: New York,
Interscience Publishers, 1954. ix,
455 p. 668.502 54-7989
   TP983 .G7 MRR Alc.

Sauer, Gordon C. Manual of skin
diseases 3d ed. Philadelphia,
Lippincott [1973] xx, 357 p. 616.5
73-2568
   RL71 .S2 1973 MRR Alc.

DERMATOLOGY--TERMINOLOGY.
Leider, Morris. A dictionary of
dermatological words, terms, and
phrases New York, Blakiston
Division, McGraw-Hill [1968] xviii,
440 p. 616.5/003 67-27824
   RL39 .L44 MRR Alc.

DESCRIPTIVE CATALOGING.
American Library Association.
Division of Cataloging and
Classification. A.L.A. cataloging
rules for author and title entries.
2d ed., Chicago, American Library
Assn., 1949. xxi, 265 p. 025.32
48-9034
   Z695 .A52 1949 MRR Ref Desk.

Anglo-American cataloging rules,
North American text. Chicago,
American Library Association, 1967.
xxi, 400 p. 025.32 66-29239
   Z695 .A5215 MRR Alc.

Anglo-American cataloging rules.
Chicago, American Library
Association, 1974. vi, 122 p.
025.3/2 74-10946
   Z694 .A48 1974 MRR Ref Desk.

United States. Library of Congress.
Advisory committee on descriptive
cataloging. Report of the Advisory
committee on descriptive cataloging
to the librarian of Congress ...
Washington, The Library of Congress,
1946. x, 15 p. 025.3 46-27925
   Z663.99.A3 A55 MRR Alc.

United States. Library of Congress.
Descriptive Cataloging Division.
Reglas para la catalogacion
descriptiva en The Library of
Congress Washington, 1953. vii, 174
p. 025.32 52-60037
   Z663.74 .R815 MRR Alc.

United States. Library of Congress.
Descriptive Cataloging Division.
Rules for descriptive cataloging in
the Library of Congress Washington,
1949. vi, 141 p. 025.32 48-46964

   Z695 .U4735 1949 MRR Alc.

United States. Library of Congress.
Processing dept. Studies of
descriptive cataloging. Washington,
U.S. Govt. print. off., 1946. 2 p.
l., 48 p. incl. form, diagrs. 025.3
46-26314
   Z663.74 .S84 MRR Alc.

DESERTION, MILITARY--UNITED STATES.
Lonn, Ella. Desertion during the
Civil War. Gloucester, Mass., P.
Smith, 1966 [c1928] vii, 251 p.
973.74 66-31671
   E468 .L86 1966 MRR Alc.

DESERTS--UNITED STATES--BIBLIOGRAPHY.
Edwards, Elza Ivan. The enduring
desert; [Los Angeles] W. Ritchie
Press, 1969. xiii, 306 p.
016.91794/09/154 68-8306
   Z1251.S8 E32 MRR Alc.

DESIGN--DICTIONARIES.
Walker, John Albert. Glossary of
art, architecture, and design since
1945. [Hamden, Conn.] Linnet Books
[1973] 240 p. [$10.50] 709/.04
73-3339
   N34 .W34 MRR Alc.

DESIGN, DECORATIVE--DICTIONARIES.
Clark, MaryJane. An illustrated
glossary of decorated antiques from
the late 17th century to the early
20th century. [1st ed.] Rutland,
Vt., C. E. Tuttle Co. [1972] 400 p.
[$8.75] 745.1 74-138080
   NK30 .C43 MRR Alc.

Studio dictionary of design &
decoration. Rev. and enl. ed.] New
York, Viking Press [1973] 538 p.
[$28.50] 745.4/03 73-1024
   NK1165 .S78 1973 MRR Alc.

DESIGN, DECORATIVE--INDEXES.
Ellis, Jessie (Croft) Nature and its
applications; Boston, F. W. Faxon
Co., 1949. xii, 861 p. 016.745 49-
9331
   Z5956.D3 E53 MRR Alc.

Ellis, Jessie (Croft) comp. Nature
index; Boston, The F. W. Faxon
company, 1930. 4 p. l., 319 p.
016.745 30-20661
   Z5956.D3 E5 MRR Alc.

DESIGN, DECORATIVE--UNITED STATES.
Lipman, Jean (Herzberg) American
folk decoration. New York, Oxford
University Press, 1951. xii, 163 p.
745.3 51-11035
   NK806 .L5 MRR Alc.

DESIGN, INDUSTRIAL.
see also Environmental engineering

Product design & development. PD&D
product encyclopedia: [Philadelphia,
1961] 253, 10, 10 p. 61-59873
   T12 .P8 MRR Alc.

DESIGN (TYPOGRAPHY)
see Printing, Practical--Make-up

**DESIGN PROTECTION--UNITED STATES--
BIBLIOGRAPHY.**
United States. Copyright Office.
Bibliography on design protection,
Washington] 1955. vi, 70 p. 55-
61887
   Z663.84 .B5 MRR Alc.

DESPOTISM.
Beloff, Max. The age of absolutism:
1660-1815. London, Hutchinson, 1966.
190 p. [10/6] 940.22 66-67405
   D273 .B4 1966 MRR Alc.

DESTITUTION
see Poverty

DESTROYERS (WARSHIPS)
March, Edgar J. British destroyers;
London, Seeley Service [1967] xxxii,
539 p. [£10/10/-] 623.82/54 67-
74647
   V825.5.G7 M33 MRR Alc.

DETECTIVE AND MYSTERY STORIES.
see also Ghost stories

Gribbin, Lenore S. Who's whodunit;
Chapel Hill, University of North
Carolina Library, 1968. ix, 174 p.
823/.08/72 68-65305
   Z1045 .G73 MRR Alc.

**DETECTIVE AND MYSTERY STORIES--
BIBLIOGRAPHY.**
Barzun, Jacques. A catalogue of
crime [1st ed.] New York, Harper &
Row [1971] xxxi, 831 p. [$18.95]
016.80883/872 75-123914
   Z5917.D5 B37 1971 MRR Alc.

Hagen, Ordean A. Who done it? New
York, Bowker, 1969. xx, 834 p.
016.80883/872 69-19209
   Z5917.D5 H3 MRR Alc.

Haycraft, Howard. Murder for
pleasure; Newly enl. ed., New York,
Biblo and Tannen, 1968 [c1941]
xviii, [14], 409 p. [10.00] 68-
25809
   PN3448.D4 H3 1968 MRR Alc.

Mundell, E. H. A checklist of
detective short stories, Portage,
Ind. 1968. xii, 337 p.
016.80883/872 68-3329
   Z5917.D5 M8 MRR Alc.

**DETECTIVE AND MYSTERY STORIES--HISTORY
AND CRITICISM.**
Haycraft, Howard. Murder for
pleasure; Newly enl. ed. New York,
Biblo and Tannen, 1968 [c1941]
xviii, [14], 409 p. [10.00] 68-
25809
   PN3448.D4 H3 1968 MRR Alc.

**DETECTIVE AND MYSTERY STORIES, AMERICAN-
-BIBLIOGRAPHY.**
Mundell, E. H. The detective short
story : Manhattan : Kansas State
University Library, 1974. iv, 493 p.
; [$12.50] 016.823/.0872 74-
182860
   Z5917.D5 M82 MRR Alc.

**DETECTIVE AND MYSTERY STORIES, ENGLISH--
BIBLIOGRAPHY.**
Mundell, E. H. The detective short
story : Manhattan : Kansas State
University Library, 1974. iv, 493 p.
; [$12.50] 016.823/.0872 74-
182860
   Z5917.D5 M82 MRR Alc.

DETECTIVES.
see also Criminal investigation

see also Police

DETECTIVES--DIRECTORIES.
International directory of detective
agencies. Neosho, Mo., Inter-state
Service Co. 351.75 364.12* 53-24458

   HV8081 .I57 MRR Alc Latest edition

DETECTIVES--DIRECTORIES. (Cont.)
The Regency international directory
of enquiry agents, private
detectives, debt collecting agencies,
the security services. Folkstone,
Eng., Regency International
Publications Limited. 363.2/3 68-
45751
Began in 1967.
HV8081 .R4 MRR Alc Latest edition

DETECTIVES IN LITERATURE.
Haycraft, Howard, Murder for
pleasure; Newly enl. ed., New York,
Biblo and Tannen, 1968 [c1941]
xviii, [14], 409 p. [10.00] 68-
25809
PN3448.D4 H3 1968 MRR Alc.

Mundell, E. H. The detective short
story : Manhattan : Kansas State
University Library, 1974. iv, 493 p.
; [$12.50] 016.823/.0872 74-
182860
Z5917.D5 M82 MRR Alc.

DETECTIVES IN LITERATURE--DICTIONARIES.
Hagen, Ordean A. Who done it? New
York, Bowker, 1969. xx, 834 p.
016.80883/872 69-19209
Z5917.D5 H3 MRR Alc.

DETERMINATIVE MINERALOGY
see Mineralogy, Determinative

DETROIT--DESCRIPTION--GUIDE-BOOKS.
Fischhoff, Martin. Detroit guide;
4th ed. [Detroit] Speedball
Publications [1974, c1973] 330 p.
[$3.00] 917.74/34 74-178226
F574.D4 F57 1974 MRR Alc.

DETROIT--MAPS--BIBLIOGRAPHY.
Koerner, Alberta G. Auringer.
Detroit and vicinity before 1900;
Washington, Library of Congress; [for
sale by the Supt. of Docs., U.S.
Govt. Print. Off.] 1968. iv, 84 p.
[0.45] 016.912774/34 68-67060
Z663.35 .D4 MRR Alc.

DEVELOPING COUNTRIES
see Underdeveloped areas

DEVELOPMENT BANKS--DIRECTORIES.
Nyhart, J. Daniel. A global
directory of development finance
institutions in developing countries
Paris, Development Centre of the
Organisation for Economic Cooperation and Development, 1967. x,
453 p. [30.00] 332.1/025/1724 76-
386919
HG4517 .N92 1967b MRR Alc.

DEVELOPMENTAL PSYCHOLOGY.
Hurlock, Elizabeth Bergner.
Developmental psychology 3d ed. New
York, McGraw-Hill [1968] ix, 926 p.
155. 68-12265
BF701 .H87 1968 MRR Alc.

DEVICES.
see also Symbolism in art

DEVOTIONAL CALENDARS.
Butler, Alban, Lives of the saints.
Complete ed. [New York, Kenedy,
1962] 4 v. 922.22 62-51171
BX4654 .B8 1962 MRR Biog.

DEVOTIONAL EXERCISES.
see also Church music

DEWEY DECIMAL CLASSIFICATION
see Classification, Dewey decimal

DIAGNOSIS.
see also Medicine, Clinical

Gomez, Joan. Dictionary of symptoms:
Arundel (Sx.), Centaur P., 1967.
xxiv, 383 p. [45/-] 616.07/2/02
67-106674
RC82 .G6 MRR Alc.

Paschkis, Karl E. Clinical
endocrinology 3d ed. New York,
Hoeber Medical Division, Harper & Row
[1967] xxvi, 1060 p. 616.4 67-
2889
RC648 .P3 1967 MRR Alc.

Yater, Wallace Mason, Symptom
diagnosis 5th ed. New York,
Appleton-Century-Crofts [1961] 1035
p. 616.075 60-11757
RC71 .Y3 1961 MRR Alc.

DIALECTS
see Grammar, Comparative and general

DIALOGUES--INDEXES.
Ireland, Norma (Olin) An index to
monologs and dialogs. Rev. and enl.
ed. Boston, F. W. Faxon Co., 1949.
xxv, 171 p. 016.815 49-8379
PN4305.M6 164 1949 MRR Alc.

DIAMONDS.
see also Precious stones

Copeland, Lawrence L. Diamonds,
famous, notable and unique, [1st ed.
Los Angeles] Gemological Institute
of America [1966] ix, 188 p. 736.2
66-6158
TS753 .C6 MRR Alc.

DIAMONDS--DICTIONARIES.
Gemological Institute of America.
The diamond dictionary, 1st ed. Los
Angeles, 1960] 317 p. 736.2 60-
51947
TS753 .G4 MRR Alc.

DIARIES--BIBLIOGRAPHY.
Matthews, William, American diaries;
Boston, J. S. Canner, 1959. xiv,
383 p. 016.920073 59-13345
Z5305.U5 M3 1959 MRR Biog.

Matthews, William, British diaries;
Gloucester, Mass., P. Smith, 1967
[c1950] xxxiv, 339 p. 016.920042
67-6139
Z5305.G7 M3 1967 MRR Biog.

Matthews, William, Canadian diaries
and autobiographies. Berkeley,
University of California Press, 1950.
130 p. 016.920071 50-62732
Z5305.C3 M3 MRR Biog.

DICKENS, CHARLES, 1812-1870.
Hardwick, John Michael Drinkrow, The
Charles Dickens companion London, J.
Murray [1965] xiii, 250 p. 823.8
66-1009
PR4581 .H34 MRR Alc.

DICKENS, CHARLES, 1812-1870--CHARACTERS.
Greaves, John. Who's who in Dickens.
New York, Taplinger Pub. Co. [1973,
c1972] 231 p. [$6.95] 823/.8 73-
5335
PR4589 .G75 1973 MRR Alc.

**DICKENS, CHARLES, 1812-1870--
DICTIONARIES, INDEXES, ETC.**
Hayward, Arthur Lawrence, The
Dickens encyclopædia; London, G.
Routledge and sons, ltd.; New York,
E. P. Dutton & co., 1924. xii, 174
p., 1 l. 25-2059
PR4595 .H3 MRR Alc.

DICKENS, CHARLES, 1812-1870--CHARACTERS.
Hardwick, John Michael Drinkrow, The
Charles Dickens companion London, J.
Murray [1965] xiii, 250 p. 823.8
66-1009
PR4581 .H34 MRR Alc.

**DICKINSON, EMILY, 1830-1886--
CONCORDANCES.**
Rosenbaum, Stanford Patrick. A
concordance to the poems of Emily
Dickinson, Ithaca, N.Y., Cornell
University Press [1964] xxii, 899 p.
811.4 64-25335
PS1541.Z49 R6 MRR Alc.

DICTIONARIES
see Encyclopedias and dictionaries

DICTIONARIES, MEDICAL--GERMAN.
Lejeune, Fritz, Deutsch-Englisches,
Englisch-Deutsches Wörterbuch für
Ärzte. 2. völlig neubearb. Aufl.
Stuttgart, Thieme, 1968- v. [DM
64.00] 610/.3 68-69803
R121 .L372 MRR Alc.

DICTIONARIES, POLYGLOT.
Amelinckx, Frans. Lexicon
dendrologicum Antwerpen, De Sikkel,
1955. xvi, 508 p. 582.1603 56-
58034
SB435 .A6 MRR Alc.

Band-Kuzmany, Karin R. M. Glossary
of the theatre. Amsterdam, New York,
Elsevier Pub. Co., 1969. 140 p.
[31.20] 792/.03 68-57152
PN2035 .B3 MRR Alc.

Beeck, Peter. Fachausdrücke der
Presse. [3. Aufl.] Frankfurt am
Main, Polygraph Verlag, 1950. 174 p.
070.03 51-16343
PN4728 .B43 1950 MRR Alc.

Bergman, Peter M. The concise
dictionary of twenty-six languages in
simultaneous translations, New York,
Polyglot Library [1968] 406 p. 413
67-14284
P361 .B4 TJ Rm.

Bosch, Abraham ten, Viertalig
technisch woordenboek. Deventer, Æ.
E. Kluwer [1948-55] 4 v. 603 50-
18447
T10 .B72 MRR Alc.

Britannica world language dictionary,
[Chicago, 1958] 1483-2015 p. 413
58-4491
P361 .B7 1958 MRR Alc.

Byecken, Francisco J. Vocabulário
tecnico portugues-ingles-frances-
alemão. 4. ed. rev. [São Paulo]
Edições Melhoramentos [1961] 600
p. 603 62-3680
T10 .B82 1961 MRR Alc.

Bürger, Erich. Technical dictionary
of data processing, computers, office
machines. [1st ed.] Oxford, New
York, Pergamon Press [1970] 1463 p.
651.8/03 75-81247
QA76.15 .B46 1970 MRR Alc.

Capitol's concise dictionary.
Bologna, Capitol, 1972. 1051 (i.e.
1207] p. 413 72-172231
P361 .C3 MRR Alc.

Chalkiopoulos, Geórgios.
[Pentaglosson lexilogion technikōn
horōn (romanized form)] [1960]
1030 p. 61-31355
T10 .C46 1960 MRR Alc.

Clason, W. E., Elsevier's dictionary
of computers, automatic control and
data processing. 2d rev. ed. of The
dictionary of automation, computers,
control and measuring. Amsterdam,
New York, Elsevier Pub. Co., 1971.
484 p. [fl78.00] 001.6/4/03 73-
151733
TJ212.5 .C55 1971 MRR Alc.

Cowles, Barbara (Pehotsky)
Bibliographers' glossary of foreign
words and phrases; New York, R. R.
Bowker company, 1935. 3 p. l., 82
numb. l. 010.3 41-5736
Z1006 .C87 1935 MRR Alc.

Dictionar tehnic poliglot: Ediţia
a 2-a. Bucureşti, Editura Tehnica,
1967. xv, 1233 p. 603 68-2971
T10 .D54 1967 MRR Alc.

Dictionary of chemistry and chemical
technology, in six languages: [Rev.
ed.] Oxford, New York, Pergamon
Press [1966] 1325 p. 540.3 65-
29008
QD5 .D5 1966 MRR Alc.

Dictionary of photography and
cinematography: London, New York,
Focal Press [1961] 1 v. (various
pagings) 770.3 63-24356
TR9 .D5 MRR Alc.

Dictionnaire à l'usage de la
librairie ancienne pour les langues:
française, anglaise, allemande,
suédoise, danoise, italienne,
espagnole, hollandaise, Paris, Ligue
internationale de la librairie
ancienne, 1956. 190 p. 655.403 57-
2275
Z282 .D5 MRR Alc.

The Duden pictorial encyclopedia in
five languages: English, French,
German, Italian, Spanish. 2d, enl.
ed. New York, F. Ungar Pub. Co.
[1958] 2 v. 413 58-11093
P361 .D8 1958 MRR Alc.

Elektrotechnik und Elektrochemie.
München, R. Oldenbourg, 1955. xxiv,
1304 p. 57-18208
TK9 .E42 1955 MRR Alc.

Elsevier's banking dictionary in six
languages: Amsterdam, New York,
Elsevier Pub. Co., 1966. 302 p.
332.103 65-20139
HG151 .E45 MRR Alc.

Elsevier's dictionary of aeronautics
in six languages: Amsterdam, New
York, Elsevier Pub. Co., 1964. 842
p. 629.1303 63-22063
TL509 .E4 MRR Alc.

Elsevier's dictionary of chemical
engineering. Amsterdam, New York,
1968. 2 v. [62.50 per vol.]
660/.2/03 68-54865
TP9 .E38 MRR Alc.

Elsevier's dictionary of criminal
science, in eight languages:
Amsterdam, New York, Elsevier Pub.
Co.; [distributed by Van Nostrand,
Princeton, N.J.] 1960. xv, 1460 p.
364.03 59-12582
HV6017 .E4 MRR Alc.

Elsevier's dictionary of nuclear
science and technology. 2d rev. ed.
Amsterdam, New York, Elsevier Pub.
Co., 1970. 787 p. [85.00]
539.7/03 72-103357
QC772 .E4 1970 MRR Alc.

Elsevier's dictionary of photography
in three languages: Amsterdam, New
York, Elsevier Pub. Co.: distributed
by American Elsevier Pub. Co., New
York, 1965. 660 p. 770.3 63-16076
TR9 .E46 MRR Alc.

Elsevier's lexicon of stock-market
terms: Amsterdam, New York, Elsevier
Pub. Co., 1965. 131 p. 332.603 65-
13892
HG4513 .E4 MRR Alc.

Elsevier's wood dictionary in seven
languages: Amsterdam, New York,
Elsevier Pub. Co., 1964- v.
634.903 64-14178
SD431 .E4 MRR Alc.

DICTIONARIES, POLYGLOT. (Cont.)
Ernst, Richard. Wörterbuch der industriellen Technik. Wiesbaden, Brandstetter, 195 [c1948- v. 603 60-3617
   T10 .E75 Bd. 1-2 MRR Alc.

Ernst, Richard. Wörterbuch der industriellen Technik. Wiesbaden, Brandstetter [197]-[c1951]- v. 73-586747
   T10 .E76 MRR Alc.

Giteau, Cécile. Dictionnaire des arts du spectacle, français--anglais--allemand; Paris, Dunod, 1970. xxv, 429 p. [88.00] 79-499699
   PN1579 .G5 MRR Alc.

Great Britain. Naval intelligence division. A dictionary of naval equivalents covering English, French, Italian, Spanish, Russian, Swedish, Danish, Dutch, German. London, H.M. Stationery off., 1924. 2 v. 24-23792
   V24 .G7 MRR Alc.

Haensch, Günther. Dictionary of international relations and politics; Amsterdam, New York, Elsevier Pub. Co., 1965. xv, 638 p. 320.03 64-8710
   JX1226 .H26 MRR Alc.

Haensch, Günther. Wörterbuch der Landwirtschaft; 3. v. überarb. Aufl. München, Bayerischer Landwirtschaftverlag [1966] xxiv, 746 p. 630/.3 68-96091
   S411 .H26 1966 MRR Alc.

Horn, Stefan F., Glossary of financial terms. Amsterdam, New York, Elsevier Pub. Co., 1965. 271 p. 332.03 64-23405
   HG151 .H6 MRR Alc.

Horten, Hans Ernest. Export-import correspondence in four languages. London, Gower Press Ltd., 1970. xi, 2-316 p. [80/-] 382/.03 76-495482
   HF1002 .H695 MRR Alc.

International encyclopedia of chemical science. Princeton, N.J., Van Nostrand [1964] 1331 p. 540.3 64-1619
   QD5 .I5 1964 MRR Alc.

International insurance dictionary: [n.p., European Conference of Insurance Supervisory Services, 1959] xxxi, 1083 p. 368.03 61-35675
   HG8025 .I5 MRR Alc.

International Railway Documentation Bureau. Lexique général des termes ferroviaires, [2. ed. entièrement refondue et augm.] Amsterdam, J. H. De Bussy, 1965. 1357 p. 625.1003 66-87434
   TF9 .I46 1965 MRR Alc.

Jacks, Graham Vernon. Multilingual vocabulary of soil science. [2d ed., rev. Rome] Land & Water Division, Food and Agriculture Organization of the United Nations [1960] xxiii, 428 p. 631.403 60-50105
   S591 .J26 1960 MRR Alc.

Kerchove, René de, baron. International maritime dictionary; 2d ed. Princeton, N.J., Van Nostrand [1961] v, 1018 p. 623.803 61-16272
   V23 .K4 1961 MRR Alc.

Kleczek, Josip. Astronomical dictionary. [Vyd. 1.] Praha, Nakl. Československé akademie věd, 1961. 972 p. 62-25391
   QB14 .K55 MRR Alc.

Labarre, E. J. Dictionary and encyclopedia of paper and paper-making, 2d ed., rev. and enl. London, Oxford University Press, 1952. xxi, 488 p. 676.03 53-29414
   TS1085 .L3 1952a MRR Alc.

Lexicon opthalmologicum: Basel, New York, S. Karger, 1959. 223 p. 617.703 59-4669
   RE21 .L45 MRR Alc.

Nash, Rose. Multilingual lexicon of linguistics and philology: English, Russian, German, French. Coral Gables, Fla., University of Miami Press [1968] xxvi, 390 p. 413 68-31044
   P29 .N34 MRR Alc.

Nederlands Geologisch Mijnbouwkundig Genootschap. Geological nomenclature. Gorinchem, J. Noorduijn, 1959. xvi, 523 p. 550.3 a 60-3024
   QE5 .N413 MRR Alc.

Nøbel, Albert, Dictionnaire médical. 5. éd. rev. et augm. Paris, Masson, 1970 [c1969] xxii, 1329 p. [200.00] 77-93556
   R121 .N6 1970 MRR Alc.

Orne, Jerrold, The language of the foreign book trade: 2d ed. Chicago, American Library Association, 1962. 213 p. 010.3 61-12881
   Z1006 .O7 1962 MRR Alc.

Ouseg, H. L. 21-language dictionary. London, P. Owen [1962] xxxi, 333 p. 63-1285
   P361 .O85 1962 MRR Alc.

Pipics, Zoltán. Dictionarium bibliothecarii practicum: ad usum internationalem in XXII linguis. 6., rev. and enlarged ed. Pullach (München) Verlag Dokumentation, 1974. 385 p. [DM98.00] 74-322719
   Z1006 .P67 1974 MRR Ref Desk.

Pisant, Emmanuel. International dictionary. Paris, Editions Moderninter [1958] 373 p. 413 58-26075
   P361 .P5 MRR Alc.

Raaff, J. J. Index vocabulorum quadrilingius: verf en vernis, [Den Haag] Vereniging van Vernis- en Verffabrikanten in Nederland. Exportgroep Verf, 1958. 898 p. 667.603 58-27978
   TP934.3 .R2 MRR Alc.

Sachs, Wolfgang, ed. Lebensversicherungstechnisches Wörterbuch. Würzburg, K. Thiltsch, 1954. 308 p. 56-16246
   HG8759 .S3 MRR Alc.

Schloms, Irene. Fachwörterbuch für Programmierer, deutsch, englisch, französisch. Heidelberg, Hüthig (1966) 139, 139, 110 p. [DM 28.00] 651.8 67-91557
   QA76.15 .S35 MRR Alc.

Skandinaviska banken, a.-b. Banking terms: French, German, Italian, Spanish, Swedish. Stockholm [1964] 65 p. 65-87814
   HG151 .S46 MRR Alc.

Smith, William James, A dictionary of musical terms in four languages. London, Hutchinson [1961] 195 p. 61-65056
   ML108 .S64D5 MRR Alc.

Stowarzyszenie Geodetów Polskich. Słownik geodezyjny w 5 [i.e. pięciu] językach: polskim, rosyjskim, niemieckim, angielskim, francuskim. Warszawa, Państwowe Przedsiębiorstwo Wydawn. Kartograficznych, 1954. xv, 525 p. 55-34784
   QB279 .S8 MRR Alc.

Sube, Ralf. Kernphysik und Kerntechnik: Berlin, Verlag Technik [1962] 1606 p. 62-2924
   QC772 .S9 MRR Alc.

Sube, Ralf. Wörterbuch Physik; Zürich, H. Deutsch, 1973. 3 v. 74-320539
   QC5 .S9 MRR Alc.

2. uppl. Stockholm, Hedengren [1951] xix p., 1518 columns. 603 52-21624
   T10 .T358 1951 MRR Alc.

Thompson, Anthony. Vocabularium bibliothecarii. 2d ed. [Paris] UNESCO, 1962. 627 p. 63-5650
   Z1006 .T47 1962a MRR Alc.

Union européenne des experts comptables économiques et financiers. Lexique U.E.C. Lexicon. Düsseldorf, Verlagsbuchhandlung des Institute der Wirtschaftsprüfer, 1961. 1 v. (various pagings) 63-31440
   HF5621 .U5 MRR Alc.

Vocabulaire international des termes d'urbanisme et d'architecture. 1. éd. Paris, Société de diffusion des techniques du bâtiment et des travaux publics, 1970- v. [133F (v. 1)] 70-860237
   NA31 .V6 MRR Alc.

Wittfoht, Annemarie, Kunststofftechnisches Wörterbuch. München, C. Hanser, 1956- v. a 56-5235
   TP986 .A15W48 MRR Alc.

DICTIONARIES, POLYGLOT--BIBLIOGRAPHY.
Alston, R. C. Polyglot dictionaries and grammars; Bradford, printed for the author by Ernest Cummins [1967] xx, 311 p. 68-138251
   Z2015.A1 A4 vol. 2 MRR Alc.

Bibliography of interlingual scientific and technical dictionaries. [1st-] 1951- [Paris] UNESCO. 54-11648
   Z7405.D5 B5 Sci RR Latest edition / MRR Alc Latest edition

International bibliography of dictionaries. 5th, rev. ed. New York, R. R. Bowker Co., 1972. xxvi, 511 p. 016.03 72-214468
   Z7004.D5 I55 1972 MRR Alc.

Walford, Albert John. A guide to foreign language grammars and dictionaries. 2nd ed., revised and enlarged. London, Library Association, 1967. 240 p. [60/-] 016.415 68-86136
   Z7004.G7 W3 1967 MRR Alc.

Zaunmüller, Wolfram. Bibliographisches Handbuch der Sprachwörterbücher; Stuttgart, A. Hiersemann, 1958. xvi p., 496 columns. a 59-1510
   Z7004.D5 Z3 1958a MRR Alc.

DIESEL MOTOR.
Black, Perry O. Audels diesel engine manual, [3d ed.] Indianapolis, T. Audel [1966] 536 p. 621.436 66-30420
   TJ795 .B53 1966 MRR Alc.

DIESEL MOTOR--COLD WEATHER OPERATION--ABSTRACTS.
United States. Library of Congress. Technical Information Division. Cold weather operation of diesel engines; Washington, 1952-58. 2 v. 016.621436 53-60028
   Z663.49 .C6 MRR Alc.

DIESEL MOTOR--COLD WEATHER OPERATION--BIBLIOGRAPHY.
United States. Library of Congress. Technical Information Division. Cold weather operation of diesel engines; Washington, 1952-58. 2 v. 016.621436 53-60028
   Z663.49 .C6 MRR Alc.

DIESEL MOTOR--MAINTENANCE AND REPAIR--PERIODICALS.
Motor's truck & diesel repair manual. 24th ed.; 1971- [New York, Motor] 629.28/7/4 73-618596
   TL230.A1 M64 Sci RR Latest edition / MRR Alc Latest edition

DIET.
see also Cookery

see also Food

see also Nutrition

National Research Council. Food and Nutrition Board. Recommended dietary allowances. 8th rev. ed. Washington, National Academy of Sciences, 1974. v, 128 p. 641.1 74-5170
   TX551 .N39 1974 MRR Alc.

DIET--UNITED STATES.
United States. Dept. of Agriculture. Food. Washington [U.S. Govt. Print. Off., 1959] xii, 736 p. 641 agr59-296
   S21.A35 1959 MRR Alc.

DIET IN DISEASE.
see also Cookery for the sick

Proudfit, Fairfax Throckmorton. Proudfit-Robinson's Normal and therapeutic nutrition. 13th ed. New York, Macmillan [1967] xiv, 891 p. 641.1 67-16055
   RM216 .P83 1967 MRR Alc.

Williams, Sue Rodwell, Nutrition and diet therapy. 2d ed. Saint Louis, Mosby, 1973. xviii, 693 p. 641.1 72-88510
   RM216 .M684 1973 MRR Alc.

Wohl, Michael Gershon, ed. Modern nutrition in health and disease; 4th ed. Philadelphia, Lea & Febiger, 1968. xv, 1240 p. 615/.854 68-18869
   QP141 .W6 1968 MRR Alc.

DIGESTION.
see also Food

see also Nutrition

DIGITAL COMPUTERS, ELECTRONIC
see Electronic digital computers

DIME NOVELS.
Johannsen, Albert, The House of Beadle and Adams and its dime and nickel novels; [1st ed.] Norman, University of Oklahoma Press [1950-62] 3 v. 655.4747 50-8158
   Z1231.F4 J68 MRR Alc.

DIME NOVELS--BIBLIOGRAPHY.
Johannsen, Albert, The House of Beadle and Adams and its dime and nickel novels; [1st ed.] Norman, University of Oklahoma Press [1950-62] 3 v. 655.4747 50-8158
Z1231.F4 J68 MRR Alc.

DINNERS AND DINING.
see also Food

Tannahill, Reay. Food in history. New York, Stein and Day [1973] 448 p. [$15.00] 641.3/009 75-160342
GT2850 .T34 MRR Alc.

DIPLOMACY.
Harmon, Robert Bartlett, The art and practice of diplomacy: Metuchen, N.J., Scarecrow Press, 1971. xii, 355 p. 327/.2 75-142234
JX1662 .H273 MRR Alc.

DIPLOMACY--BIBLIOGRAPHY.
Harmon, Robert Bartlett, The art and practice of diplomacy: Metuchen, N.J., Scarecrow Press, 1971. xii, 355 p. 327/.2 75-142234
JX1662 .H273 MRR Alc.

DIPLOMACY--DICTIONARIES.
Gamboa, Melquiades Jereos, Elements of diplomatic and consular practice; Quezon City, Philippines, Central Lawbook Pub. Co.; [distributed by Central Book Supply, inc., Manila, 1966] xxxv, 489 p. 327.2/03 67-3357
JX1226 .G3 MRR Alc.

DIPLOMACY--DICTIONARIES--FRENCH.
Académie diplomatique internationale. Dictionnaire diplomatique, Paris [1933] 2 v. 341.03 33-36212
JX1226 .A312 vol. 3 MRR Biog.

DIPLOMATIC AND CONSULAR SERVICE-- BIBLIOGRAPHY.
Harmon, Robert Bartlett, The art and practice of diplomacy: Metuchen, N.J., Scarecrow Press, 1971. xii, 355 p. 327/.2 75-142234
JX1662 .H273 MRR Alc.

DIPLOMATIC AND CONSULAR SERVICE-- DICTIONARIES.
Gamboa, Melquiades Jereos, Elements of diplomatic and consular practice; Quezon City, Philippines, Central Lawbook Pub. Co.; [distributed by Central Book Supply, inc., Manila, 1966] xxxv, 489 p. 327.2/03 67-3357
JX1226 .G3 MRR Alc.

DIPLOMATIC AND CONSULAR SERVICE-- REGISTERS, LISTS, ETC.
The Diplomat's annual. London. 54-43085
Began publication in 1950.
JX1783 .A153 MRR Alc Latest edition

Political handbook and atlas of the world. Jan. 1, 1927- New York, Simon and Schuster [etc.] for Council on Foreign Relations. 28-12165
JF37 .P6 MRR Ref Desk Latest / MRR Alc Latest edition

Répertoire de la diplomatie africaine: 1. éd. Paris, Ediafric-La Documentation africaine [1970] 369 p. 72-359872
JX1861 .R44 1970 MRR Biog.

The Statesman's year-book; [1st]-1864- London, Macmillan; New York, St. Martin's Press [etc.] 04-3776
JA51 .S7 MRR Ref Desk Latest edition / MRR Ref Desk Latest edition

United Nations. Permanent missions to the United Nations. New York. 341.13 51-35159
JX1977.A2 MRR Ref Desk Latest edition

DIPLOMATIC AND CONSULAR SERVICE IN AFRICA.
Répertoire de la diplomatie africaine: 1. éd. Paris, Ediafric-La Documentation africaine [1970] 369 p. 72-359872
JX1861 .R44 1970 MRR Biog.

DIPLOMATIC AND CONSULAR SERVICE IN GREAT BRITAIN.
The Diplomat's annual. London. 54-43085
Began publication in 1950.
JX1783 .A153 MRR Alc Latest edition

DIPLOMATIC ETIQUETTE.
Radlovic, I. Monte, Etiquette & protocol; New York, Harcourt, Brace [1957] 240 p. 395 57-2649
BJ1858 .R3 1957 MRR Alc.

Wood, John R. Diplomatic ceremonial and protocol: New York, Colombia University Press, 1970. xviii, 378 p. [$25.00] 341.7 70-12844
JX1679 .W65 1970b MRR Alc.

DIPLOMATIC ETIQUETTE--UNITED STATES.
Lott, James E. Practical protocol; Houston, Tex., Gulf Pub. Co. [1973] x, 198 p. 341.3/3 73-75393
JX1679 .L67 MRR Alc.

DIPLOMATIC PRIVILEGES AND IMMUNITIES.
Wilson, Clifton E. Diplomatic privileges and immunities Tucson, University of Arizona Press [1967] ix, 300 p. 341.7 66-20660
JX1672 .W52 MRR Alc.

DIPLOMATICS.
Hall, Hubert, Studies in English official historical documents, Cambridge, University press, 1908. xv, [1] p., 1 l., 404 p. 09-4071
CD65 .H4 MRR Alc.

DIPLOMATICS--BIBLIOGRAPHY.
Oesterley, Hermann, Wegweiser durch die literatur der urkundensammlungen, Berlin, G. Reimer, 1885-86. 2 v. 03-7358
CD995 .O3 MRR Alc.

DIPLOMATICS--GREAT BRITAIN.
Hall, Hubert, comp. A formula book of English official historical documents. Cambridge, University press, 1908-09. 2 v. 09-4070
CD105 .H26 MRR Alc.

DIPLOMATS.
Académie diplomatique internationale. Dictionnaire diplomatique, Paris [1933] 2 v. 341.03 33-36212
JX1226 .A312 vol. 3 MRR Biog.

DIPLOMATS--UNITED STATES.
United States. Dept. of State. Historical Office. United States Chiefs of Mission, 1778-1973 (complete to 31 March 1973) [Washington] Dept. of State; [for sale by the Supt. of Docs., U.S. Govt. Print. Off.] 1973. v, 229 p. [$2.70] 327/.2/0973 73-602788
JX1706.A59 U54 1973 MRR Ref Desk.

DIPLOMATS, AFRICAN.
Répertoire de la diplomatie africaine: 1. éd. Paris, Ediafric-La Documentation africaine [1970] 369 p. 72-359872
JX1861 .R44 1970 MRR Biog.

DIPLOMATS, AMERICAN.
Boyce, Richard Fyfe. American foreign service authors: Metuchen, N.J., Scarecrow Press, 1973. x, 321 p. 016.081 73-9780
Z1224 .B68 MRR Alc.

DIPLOMATS' WIVES.
Boyce, Richard Fyfe. The diplomat's wife. [1st ed.] New York, Harper [1956] 230 p. 341.7 56-6909
JX1706 .B74 MRR Alc.

DIRECT TAXATION
see Income tax

DIRECTORIES--BIBLIOGRAPHY.
Association of North American directory publishers. Catalog and price list of city, county and state directories published in North America. New York. 43-47275
Z5771 .A7 MRR Alc Latest edition

British rate & data directories and annuals. [London, Maclean-Hunter Ltd. 3--/10/6] 016.05 73-645549
Z5771.4.C7 B75 MRR Alc Latest edition

Current British directories. 1953- Beckenham, Kent [etc.] CBD Research Ltd. [etc.] 53-26894
Z5771 .C8 MRR Alc Latest edition

Harvey, Anthony P. Directory of scientific directories; St. Peter Port, Guernsey, C.I., Francis Hodgson, 1969. 272 p. [unpriced] 016.5/025 68-8600
Z7405.D55 H37 MRR Ref Desk.

Hellström, Kajsa. Bibliography of directories of sources of information The Hague, International Federation for Documentation, 1960. 22 p. 016.06058 62-1923
Z5051 .H45 MRR Alc.

Henderson, G. P. Current European directories: Beckenham (Kent), C.B.D. Research Ltd., 1969. xvi, 222 p. [6/-/-] 016.914/0025 72-514512

Z5771 .H39 MRR Ref Desk.

Internationale Bibliographie der Fachadressbücher Wirtschaft, Wissenschaft, Technik. Began with 1962 edition. München-Pullach, Verlag Dokumentationen [etc.] 67-116857
Z7911 .I57 MRR Alc Latest edition

Internationale Bibliographie der Fachadressbücher Wirtschaft, Wissenschaft, Technik. Began with 1962 edition. München-Pullach, Verlag Dokumentationen [etc.] 67-116857
Z7911 .I57 MRR Alc Latest edition

Klein, Bernard. Guide to American scientific and technical directories. 1st ed. Rye, N.Y., B. Klein Publications [1972] v, 324 p. 016.3384/7/6702573 72-91671
Z7914.M3 K53 MRR Ref Desk.

Norton, Jane Elizabeth, Guide to the national and provincial directories of England and Wales, London, Offices of the Royal Historical Society, 1950. vii, 241 p. 016.9142 51-2465
Z5771 .N6 MRR Alc.

Prince, Martin. Commercial directories of the United States. [Cedarhurst] N.Y., WMD Publications, 1972, c1971] [44] 184, 28 p. 016.3801/025/73 71-185008
Z7165.U5 P73 MRR Alc.

Smith, George Mayo. World wide business publications directory, New York, Simon and Schuster [1971] xvi, 593 p. 016.380/025 75-157682
Z7164.C8 S55 MRR Ref Desk.

Spear, Dorothea N. Bibliography of American directories through 1860. Worcester, Mass., American Antiquarian Society, 1961. 389 p. 016.9173 61-1054
Z5771 .S7 MRR Alc.

Trade directories of the world. 1st-ed.; 1952- New York, Croner Publications. 016.38 52-6569
Z5771 .C7 MRR Alc Latest edition

United States. Library of Congress. Science and Technology Division. Directories in science and technology; Washington [For sale by the Superintendent of Documents, U.S. Govt. Print. Off.] 1963. vi, 65 p. 63-65164
Z663.41 .D5 MRR Alc.

DIRECTORS, MOVING-PICTURE
see Moving-picture producers and directors

DIRECTORS OF CORPORATIONS--AUSTRALIA.
The Business who's who of Australia. 1964- Sydney, R. G. Riddell. 64-56752
HF5292 .B795 MRR Alc Latest edition

DIRECTORS OF CORPORATIONS--AUSTRIA-- DIRECTORIES.
Personen-Compass: [80.]- Jahrg.; 1951- Wien, Compass-Verlag. 54-17735
HD2851 .P4 MRR Alc Latest edition

DIRECTORS OF CORPORATIONS--BOSTON-- DIRECTORIES.
Directory of directors in the city of Boston and vicinity. 1905- Boston, Bankers Service Co. 05-8359
HG4058.B7 MRR Alc Latest edition

DIRECTORS OF CORPORATIONS--CANADA-- DIRECTORIES.
Financial post. Directory of directors [executives of Canada] Toronto. 650.58 52-26909
HG4090.Z5 F5 MRR Alc Latest edition

Poor's register of corporations, directors and executive, United States and Canada. Supplement. Mar. 1935- New York, Standard and Poor's Corporation [etc.] 74-643528
HG4057.A42 MRR Ref Desk Partial set

Poor's register of corporations, directors and executives, United States and Canada. 1928- New York [etc.] 28-7849
HG4057.A4 MRR Ref Desk Latest edition / MRR Ref Desk Latest edition

Poor's register of corporations, directors and executives, United States and Canada. Geographical index. 1935- New York, Standard and Poor's Corporation [etc.] 74-643530

HG4057 .A41 MRR Ref Desk Latest edition / MRR Ref Desk Latest edition

DIRECTORS OF CORPORATIONS--FRANCE.
Annuaire Desfosses; Paris, Cote Desfosses [etc.] 332.63 46-39086
HG5471 .A64 MRR Alc Latest edition

DIRECTORS OF CORPORATIONS--GERMANY
(FEDERAL REPUBLIC, 1949-)--DIRECTORIES.
Handbuch der Direktoren und
Aufsichtsrate. 1967/68- Berlin,
Finanz- und Korrespondenz-Verlag Dr.
G. Mossner. 72-626450
HG4156 .H35 MRR Alc Latest edition

DIRECTORS OF CORPORATIONS--GREAT
BRITAIN--DIRECTORIES.
The Directory of directors; Croydon,
Eng. [etc.] T. Skinner Directories
[etc.] ca 48-3050
HG4135.Z5 D5 MRR Alc Latest
edition

DIRECTORS OF CORPORATIONS--NEW YORK
(CITY)--DIRECTORIES.
Directory of directors in the city of
New York. [1898]- New York,
Directory of directors company,
[etc.] 00-1422
HG4058.N55 MRR Alc Latest edition

DIRECTORS OF CORPORATIONS--PITTSBURGH.
Official directors register of
Pittsburgh. 1st- annual ed.; 1935-
Pittsburgh, Pa., Directory Pub. Co.
[etc.] 332.0974886 36-387
HG4058 .P64 MRR Alc Latest edition

DIRECTORS OF CORPORATIONS--SPAIN--
DIRECTORIES.
Directorio de consejeros y
directores. ed. 1961/62- Madrid.
64-36554
HC382 .D5 MRR Alc Latest edition

DIRECTORS OF CORPORATIONS--UNITED
STATES.
Dun and Bradstreet, inc. Million
dollar directory. 1959- New York.
338.0273 59-3033
HC102 .D8 MRR Ref Desk Latest
edition

DIRECTORS OF CORPORATIONS--UNITED
STATES--DIRECTORIES.
Dun and Bradstreet, inc. Dun's
reference book of corporate
managements. 1st- ed.; 1967- New
York. 658.1/145/02573 68-44776
HD2745 .D85 MRR Ref Desk Latest
edition

Poor's register of corporations,
directors and executive, United
States and Canada. Supplement. Mar.
1935- New York, Standard and Poor's
Corporation [etc.] 74-643528
HG4057.A42 MRR Ref Desk Partial
set

Poor's register of corporations,
directors and executives, United
States and Canada. 1928- New York
[etc.] 28-7849
HG4057.A4 MRR Ref Desk Latest
edition / MRR Ref Desk Latest
edition

Poor's register of corporations,
directors and executives, United
States and Canada. Geographical
index. 1935- New York, Standard and
Poor's Corporation [etc.] 74-643530
HG4057 .A41 MRR Ref Desk Latest
edition / MRR Ref Desk Latest
edition

DISABLED
see Handicapped

DISARMAMENT.
see also Peace

DISARMAMENT--BIBLIOGRAPHY.
Arms control & disarmament. v. 1-
winter 1964/65- [Washington, For
sale by the Superintendent of
Documents, U.S. Govt. Print. Off.]
64-62746
Z663.28 .A23 MRR Alc MRR Alc Full
set

Clemens, Walter C. Soviet
disarmament policy, 1917-1963;
[Stanford, Calif.] Hoover Institution
on War, Revolution and Peace,
Stanford University, 1965. xxvii,
151 p. 016-32747 65-12623
Z5517.R4 C4 MRR Alc

DISARMAMENT--YEARBOOKS.
International Institute for Peace and
Conflict Research. S I P R I
yearbook of world armaments and
disarmaments. 1968/69- New York,
Humanities Press. 341.6/7/05 76-
12210
UA10 .I55 MRR Alc Latest edition

DISASTERS.
Tufty, Barbara. 1001 questions
answered about natural land
disasters. New York, Dodd, Mead
[1969] xvi, 350 p. [$7.50] 551
68-29807
QE31 .T78 MRR Alc.

DISCIPLES OF CHRIST--YEARBOOKS.
Disciples of Christ. Year book of
Churches of Christ (Disciples)
Indianapolis [etc.] ca 18-56
BX730 .A3 MRR Alc Latest edition

DISCOUNT HOUSES (RETAIL TRADE)--UNITED
STATES.
Consumers digest guide to discount
buying. [Chicago, Consumers Digest,
inc.] [$4.95] 640.73 74-647121
HF5429.3 .C66 MRR Ref Desk Latest
edition

DISCOUNT HOUSES (RETAIL TRADE)--UNITED
STATES--DIRECTORIES.
Consumers digest guide to discount
buying. [Chicago, Consumers Digest,
inc.] [$4.95] 640.73 74-647121
HF5429.3 .C66 MRR Ref Desk Latest
edition

Directory of discount centers. 1961-
[New York, Business Guides, inc.]
63-41082
HF5035 .D46 MRR Alc Latest edition

Directory of discount houses and self-
service department stores. 1st-
ed.; 1961- Chicago, Directory
Division, National Research Bureau.
62-2505
HF5035 .D47 MRR Alc Latest edition

S.O.S. directory of factory outlet
stores in the entire United States
and Canada. [Dearborn, Mich., S.O.S.
Directory Inc.] [$4.95] 381 74-
75652
HF5421 .S2 MRR Alc Latest edition

DISCOVERIES (IN GEOGRAPHY)
see also Antarctic regions

see also Arctic regions

see also Explorers

see also Scientific expeditions

DISCOVERIES (IN GEOGRAPHY)--
DICTIONARIES.
Langnas, Izaak Abram, Dictionary of
discoveries New York, Philosophical
Library [1959] v, 201 p. 910.9 59-
16483
G200 .L3 MRR Biog.

Zavatti, Silvio. Dizionario degli
esploratori e delle scoperte
geografiche. Milano, Feltrinelli,
1967. vi, 360 p. [L800] 70-413209
G200 .Z3 MRR Biog.

Riverain, Jean, Concise encyclopedia
of explorations; London, Collins;
Chicago, Follet, 1969. [6], 279 p.
[12/6] 910/.922 79-514842
G200 .R5513 1969 MRR Biog.

DISCOVERIES (IN SCIENCE)
see Inventions

see Science

DISCRIMINATION.
see also Civil rights

see also Minorities

DISCRIMINATION--UNITED STATES.
Simpson, George Eaton, Racial and
cultural minorities; 4th ed. New
York, Harper & Row [1972] viii, 775
p. 301.45/1/042 72-76373
HT1521 .S53 1972 MRR Alc.

DISCRIMINATION IN EDUCATION.
see also Segregation in education

DISCRIMINATION IN EMPLOYMENT--UNITED
STATES.
Ross, Arthur Max, ed. Employment,
race, and poverty. [1st ed. New
York, Harcourt, Brace & World, 1967]
ix, 598 p. 331.1130973 65-23537
E185.8 .R6 MRR Alc.

United States. Civil Service
Commission. Minority group
employment in the Federal Government.
May 1970- Washington, For sale by
the Supt. of Docs., U.S. Govt. Print.
Off. 331.1/33/0973 72-622550
JK639 .A42 subser MRR Alc Latest
edition

DISCUSSION.
Crowell, Laura. Discussion, method
of democracy. Chicago, Scott,
Foresman [1963] 346 p. 374.24 63-
20555
BF637.D5 C7 MRR Alc.

DISEASE (PATHOLOGY)
see Pathology

DISEASE GERMS
see Bacteria, Pathogenic

DISEASES--CAUSES AND THEORIES OF
CAUSATION.
McCombs, Robert Pratt, Fundamentals
of internal medicine; 4th ed.
Chicago, Year Book Medical Publishers
[1971] xvi, 923 p. 616/.026 74-
115098
RC46 .M15 1971 MRR Alc.

DISEASES--CAUSES AND THEORIES OF
CAUSATIONS.
Harrison, Tinsley Randolph, ed.
Harrison's principles of internal
medicine. 7th ed. New York, McGraw-
Hill [1974] xxix, 2044, [87] p.
616/.026 73-18001
RC46 .H32 1974 MRR Alc.

DISEASES--DICTIONARIES.
Miller, Benjamin Frank, The family
book of preventive medicine; New
York, Simon and Schuster [1971] 704
p. [$12.95] 613 70-139644
RC81 .M664 MRR Alc.

DISEASES--NOMENCLATURE.
Jablonski, Stanley. Illustrated
dictionary of eponymic syndromes, and
diseases, and their synonyms.
Philadelphia, Saunders [1969] viii,
335 p. 610/.3 69-12884
R121 .J24 MRR Alc.

DISEASES, COMMUNICABLE
see Communicable diseases

DISEASES OF ANIMALS
see Veterinary medicine

DISPENSARIES.
see also Hospitals

DISPENSATORIES.
Pharmaceutical Society of Great
Britain, London. British
pharmaceutical codex, 1973, London,
Pharmaceutical Press [1973] xxxix,
983 p. [£10.50] 615/.12/42 73-
171134
RS151.3 .P54 1973 MRR Alc.

DISPENSATORIES--COLLECTED WORKS.
The United States dispensatory and
physicians' pharmacology. 26th-
ed.; 1967- Philadelphia, J. B.
Lippincott Co. 615/.12/73 67-17443
RS151.2 .D5 MRR Alc Latest edition

DISSENTERS.
Madison, Charles Allan. Critics &
crusaders; 2d ed. New York, Ungar
[1959] 662 p. 920.073 58-14283
E176 .M22 1959 MRR Alc.

DISSENTERS--UNITED STATES--BIBLIOGRAPHY.
Miller, Albert Jay. Confrontation,
conflict, and dissent: Metuchen,
N.J., Scarecrow Press, 1972. 567 p.
016.3091/73/092 78-189440
Z7165.U5 M53 MRR Alc.

DISSERTATIONS, ACADEMIC.
Allen, George Richard, The graduate
students' guide to theses and
dissertations; [1st ed.] San
Francisco, Jossey-Bass, 1973. xi,
108 p. 808/.02 73-3774
LB2369 .A595 MRR Alc.

Seeber, Edward Derbyshire, A style
manual for students, 2d ed., rev.
Bloomington, Indiana University Press
[1968, c1967] 94 p. [1.00] 808.02
67-11623
LB2369 .S4 1968 MRR Ref Desk.

Turabian, Kate L. Student's guide
for writing college papers. Chicago,
University of Chicago Press [1963]
vii, 172 p. 029.6 63-19753
LB2369 .T82 1963 MRR Ref Desk.

DISSERTATIONS, ACADEMIC--ABSTRACTS--
PERIODICALS.
Journalism abstracts. v. 1- 1963-
[Chapel Hill, N.C.] Association for
Education in Journalism. [$2.50]
070/.08 74-642577
PN4725 .J67 MRR Alc Full set

DISSERTATIONS, ACADEMIC--BIBLIOGRAPHY.
Altick, Richard Daniel, Guide to
doctoral dissertations in Victorian
literature, 1886-1958, Urbana,
University of Illinois Press, 1960.
vii, 119 p. 016.82/09/008 60-8339
Z2013 .A4 MRR Alc.

Bell, S. Peter. Dissertations on
British history, 1815-1914;
Metuchen, N.J.; Scarecrow Press,
1974. xii, 232 p. 016.9142/03 74-
16104
Z2016 .B43 MRR Alc.

Case, Margaret H. South Asian
history, 1750-1950: Princeton, N.J.,
Princeton University Press, 1968.
xiii, 561 p. 016.954 67-21019
Z3185 .C3 MRR Alc.

Dickson, Diane. World catalogue of
theses on the Pacific Islands,
Canberra, Australian National
University Press, 1970. xii, 123 p.
[$3.90] 016.919 70-128370
Z4501 .D52 MRR Alc.

DISSERTATIONS, ACADEMIC-- (Cont.)
Gillis, Frank, comp. Ethnomusicology
and folk music: [1st ed.]
Middletown, Conn., Published for the
Society for Ethnomusicology by the
Wesleyan University Press [1966] 148
p.   016.7817   66-23459
ML128.E8 G5 MRR Alc.

McNamee, Lawrence Francis.
Dissertations in English and American
literature: New York, Bowker, 1968.
xl, 1124 p.   [$17.50]   016.82 68-
27446
Z5053 .M32 MRR Alc.

United Nations Educational,
Scientific and Cultural Organization.
Thèses de sciences sociales:
[Paris, 1952] 236 p.   016.3 52-
4847
Z7161 .U4 MRR Alc.

Xerox University Microfilms.
Comprehensive dissertation index,
1861-1972. Ann Arbor, Mich., 1973.
37 v.   013/.379 73-89046
Z5053 .X47 1973 MRR Alc.

DISSERTATIONS, ACADEMIC--INDEXES.
Xerox University Microfilms.
Comprehensive dissertation index,
1861-1972. Ann Arbor, Mich., 1973.
37 v.   013/.379 73-89046
Z5053 .X47 1973 MRR Alc.

DISSERTATIONS, ACADEMIC--AUSTRALIA--
BIBLIOGRAPHY.
Union list of higher degree theses in
Australian university libraries:
Hobart, University of Tasmania
Library, 1967. xxii, 568 p.
013.375 68-140995
Z5055.A698 U5 MRR Alc.

DISSERTATIONS, ACADEMIC--CANADA--
BIBLIOGRAPHY.
Chronic, Byron John. Bibliography of
theses in geology, 1958-1963,
Washington, American Geological
Institute [c1964] 1 v. (unpaged)
016.55 65-19493
Z6034.U49 C44 MRR Alc.

Chronic, Byron John. Bibliography of
theses written for advanced degrees
in geology and related sciences at
universities and colleges in the
United States and Canada through
1957, Boulder, Colo., Pruett Press,
1958. 1 v. (unpaged) 016.55 a 59-
7426
Z6034.U49 C45 1958 MRR Alc.

LaNoue, George R. A bibliography of
doctoral dissertations undertaken in
American and Canadian universities,
1940-1962, [New York, Published for
the Dept. of Religious Liberty by the
Office of Publication and
Distribution, National Council of the
Churches of Christ in the U.S.A.,
1963] v, 49 p.   016.322 63-21606
Z7776.72 .L35 MRR Alc.

List of doctoral dissertations in
history now in progress at
universities in the United States.
Washington [etc.] 016.9 10-12162
Z5055.U49 L7 MRR Ref Desk Partial
set

Ottawa. National Library. Canadian
theses. 1952- Ottawa. 016 55-
31802
Z5055.C2 O883 MRR Alc Full set

Palfrey, Thomas Rossman, Guide to
bibliographies of theses, United
States and Canada, Chicago, American
library association, 1936. 48 p.
016.016 36-29298
Z5055.U49 A1P 1940 MRR Alc.

Ward, Dederick C. Bibliography of
theses in geology, 1967-1970.
[Boulder, Colo., Geological Society
of America, 1973] vii, 160, I-274 p.
016.55 73-78974
Z6034.U49 W32 MRR Alc.

DISSERTATIONS, ACADEMIC--FRANCE--
BIBLIOGRAPHY.
Dinstel, Marion. List of French
doctoral dissertations on Africa,
1884-1961. Boston, G. K. Hall, 1966.
v, 336 p.   016.916 68-367
Z3501 .D5 MRR Alc.

DISSERTATIONS, ACADEMIC--GERMANY--
BIBLIOGRAPHY--CATALOGS.
Pennsylvania. University. Library.
Catalog of the Programmschriften
collection. Boston, G. K. Hall,
1961. 117, 260 p.   61-66457
Z881 .P41 1961 MRR Alc (Dk33)

DISSERTATIONS, ACADEMIC--GREAT BRITAIN--
BIBLIOGRAPHY.
Index to theses accepted for higher
degrees by the universities of Great
Britain and Ireland. v. 18-
1967/68- London, Aslib.
013/.375/0942 72-626674
Z5055.G69 A84 MRR Alc Full set

DISSERTATIONS, ACADEMIC--NORTH AMERICA--
BIBLIOGRAPHY.
Chatham, James R., Dissertations in
Hispanic languages and literatures;
[Lexington] University Press of
Kentucky [1970] xiv, 120 p. [12.50]
016.46 70-80093
Z2695 .A2C46 MRR Alc.

Kuehl, Warren F., Dissertations in
history; [Lexington] University of
Kentucky Press, 1965-[72] 2 v.
016.9 65-11832
Z6201 .K8 MRR Ref Desk.

DISSERTATIONS, ACADEMIC--RUSSIA--
BIBLIOGRAPHY.
Magner, Thomas F. Soviet
dissertations for advanced degrees in
Russian literature and Slavic
linguistics, 1934-1962, University
Park, Dept. of Slavic Languages,
Pennsylvania State University, 1966.
iii, 100 p.   016.4918 68-66174
Z2505.A2 M3 MRR Alc.

DISSERTATIONS, ACADEMIC--UNITED STATES--
ABSTRACTS.
Schlachter, Gail A. Library science
dissertations, 1925-1972; Littleton,
Colo., Libraries Unlimited, 1974.
293 p.   020.8 s 016.02 73-90497
Z674 .R4 no. 12 MRR Alc.

DISSERTATIONS, ACADEMIC--UNITED STATES--
BIBLIOGRAPHY.
American doctoral dissertations.
1965/66- Ann Arbor, Mich. 73-20866
Z5055.U49 A62 MRR Alc Full set

Black, Dorothy M., comp. Guide to
lists of master's theses, Chicago,
American Library Association, 1965.
144 p.   016.011 65-24955
Z5055.U49 B55 MRR Ref Desk.

Bratton, Michael. American doctoral
dissertations on Africa, 1886-1972.
Waltham, Mass. [African Studies
Association, Research, 1973] xx, 165
p.   016.916/03/3 73-168202
Z3501 .B7 MRR Alc.

Cantrell, Clyde Hull. Southern
literary culture: [University]
University of Alabama Press, 1955.
xlv, 124 p.   016.81 54-10880
Z1251.S7 C3 MRR Alc.

Chatham, James R., Dissertations in
Hispanic languages and literatures;
[Lexington] University Press of
Kentucky [1970] xiv, 120 p. [12.50]
016.46 70-80093
Z2695 .A2C46 MRR Alc.

Chronic, Byron John. Bibliography of
theses in geology, 1958-1963,
Washington, American Geological
Institute [c1964] 1 v. (unpaged)
016.55 65-19493
Z6034.U49 C44 MRR Alc.

Chronic, Byron John. Bibliography of
theses written for advanced degrees
in geology and related sciences at
universities and colleges in the
United States and Canada through
1957, Boulder, Colo., Pruett Press,
1958. 1 v. (unpaged) 016.55 a 59-
7426
Z6034.U49 C45 1958 MRR Alc.

Cohen, Nathan Marshall, Library
science dissertations, 1925-60;
[Washington] U.S. Dept. of Health,
Education, and Welfare, Office of
Education; [for sale by the
Superintendent of Documents, U.S.
Govt. Print. Off., 1963] viii, 120
p.   hew63-119
Z666 .C67 MRR Alc.

Cordasco, Francesco, comp.
Educational sociology: New York,
Scarecrow Press, 1965. 226 p.
016.370193 65-22750
Z5055.U49 C6 MRR Alc.

Council on Graduate Studies in
Religion. Doctoral dissertations in
the field of religion, 1940-1952:
[New York] Columbia University Press
for the Council on Graduate Studies
in Religion in cooperation with the
National Council on Religion in
Higher Education [1954] iv, 194 p.
016.2 55-542
Z7751 .C7 MRR Alc.

Cruger, Doris M. A list of American
doctoral dissertations on Africa,
Ann Arbor, Mich., Xerox, University
Microfilms Library Services, 1967.
36 p.   016.378/24 67-5644
Z5055.U49 C75 MRR Alc.

Doctoral dissertations accepted by
American universities. no. 1-22;
1933/34-1954/55. New York, H. W.
Wilson. 34-40898
Z5055.U49 D6 MRR Alc Full set

Dossick, Jesse John, Doctoral
research on Russia and the Soviet
Union. [New York] New York
University Press, 1960. 248 p.
016.9147 60-14319
Z2491. D6 MRR Alc.

Eells, Walter Crosby, American
dissertations on foreign education;
Washington, Committee on
International Relations, National
Education Association of the United
States, 1959. xxxix, 300 p. 016.37
59-12819
Z5811 .E43 MRR Alc.

Fay, Leo Charles, Doctoral studies
in reading, 1919 through 1960,
[Bloomington] Bureau of Educational
Studies and Testing, School of
Education, Indiana University, 1964.
vi, 80 p.   016.37241 64-64749
Z5814.R25 F35 MRR Alc.

Industrial relations theses and
dissertations accepted at
universities. Berkeley, Institute of
Industrial Relations, University of
California.   016.331 52-62063
Z7914.A2 I53 MRR Alc Latest
edition

Joint Committee of the Music Teachers
National Association and the American
Musicological Society. Doctoral
dissertations in musicology. 4th ed.
Philadelphia, American Musicological
Society, 1965. 152 p.   016.78001
66-1684
ML128.M8 J6 1965 MRR Alc.

Journalism abstracts. v. 1- 1963-
[Chapel Hill, N.C.] Association for
Education in Journalism. [$2.50]
070/.08 74-642577
PN4725 .J67 MRR Alc Full set

Kuehl, Warren F., Dissertations in
history; [Lexington] University of
Kentucky Press, 1965-[72] 2 v.
016.9 65-11832
Z6201 .K8 MRR Ref Desk.

LaNoue, George R. A bibliography of
doctoral dissertations undertaken in
American and Canadian universities,
1940-1962, [New York, Published for
the Dept. of Religious Liberty by the
Office of Publication and
Distribution, National Council of the
Churches of Christ in the U.S.A.,
1963] v, 49 p.   016.322 63-21606
Z7776.72 .L35 MRR Alc.

List of doctoral dissertations in
history now in progress in
universities in the United States.
Washington [etc.] 016.9 10-12162
Z5055.U49 L7 MRR Ref Desk Partial
set

Little, Lawrence Calvin, Researches
in personality, character and
religious education; [Pittsburgh]
University of Pittsburgh Press, 1962.
iv, 215 p.   013.3784886 62-12625
Z7849 .L54 MRR Alc.

Litto, Fredric M., American
dissertations on the drama and the
theatre; [1st ed. Kent, Ohio] Kent
State University Press [1969] ix,
519 p.   016.8092 71-76761
Z5781 .L56 MRR Alc.

Lunday, G. Albert. Sociology
dissertations in American
universities, 1893-1966 Commerce,
East Texas State University, 1969.
x, 277 p.   016.301 74-630565
Z7164.S68 L9 MRR Alc.

Marckworth, M. Lois. Dissertations
in physics: Stanford, Calif.,
Stanford University Press, 1961.
xii, 803 p.   016.53 61-6530
Z7141 .M3 MRR Alc.

Master's theses in education.
1951/52- Cedar Falls, Iowa, Research
Publications. 016.37 53-62892
Z5816.I6 M3 MRR Alc Partial set

McNamee, Lawrence Francis.
Dissertations in English and American
literature: New York, Bowker, 1968.
xl, 1124 p.   [$17.50]   016.82 68-
27446
Z5053 .M32 MRR Alc.

Palfrey, Thomas Rossman, Guide to
bibliographies of theses, United
States and Canada, Chicago, American
library association, 1936. 48 p.
016.016 36-29298
Z5055.U49 A1P 1940 MRR Alc.

Research studies in education;
1941/51- Bloomington, Ind. [etc.]
Phi Delta Kappa [etc.] 016.37078 53-
3287
Z5811 .R4 MRR Alc Partial set

DISSERTATIONS, ACADEMIC--UNITED (Cont.)
Rutherford, Phillip R. A
bibliography of American doctoral
dissertations in linguistics, 1900-
1964. Washington, Center for Applied
Linguistics, 1968. iv, 139 p.
016.41   68-27431
Z7001 .R8 MRR Alc.

Selim, George Dimitri, American
doctoral dissertations on the Arab
world, 1883-1968. Washington,
Library of Congress; for sale by the
Supt. of Docs., U.S. Govt. Print.
Off., 1970. xvii, 103 p. [0.55]
016.91003/174/927 79-607590
Z663.387 A68 MRR Alc.

Stucki, Curtis W. American doctoral
dissertations on Asia, 1933-1962,
Ithaca, N.Y., Southeast Asia Program,
Dept. of Asian Studies, Cornell
University, 1963. 204 p. 016.915
64-2901
Z3001 .S72 MRR Alc.

The, Lian. Treasures and trivia;
[Athens, Ohio] Ohio University,
Center for International Studies,
1968. xiv, 141 l. [3.25] 016.9159
68-66324
Z3221 .T5 MRR Alc.

Thompson, Lawrence Sidney, A
bibliography of American doctoral
dissertations in classical studies
and related fields, [Hamden, Conn.]
Shoe String Press, 1968. xii, 250 p.
016.378/24/0973 67-24191
Z7016 .T48 MRR Alc.

United States. Cabinet Committee on
Opportunity for the Spanish Speaking.
The Spanish speaking in the United
States: a guide to materials.
Washington, 1971. iv, 175 p.
016.9173/06/68 75-614612
Z1361.S7 U54 MRR Alc.

United States. Library of Congress.
African Section. A list of American
doctoral dissertations on Africa.
Washington, General Reference and
Bibliography Division, Reference
Dept., Library of Congress; [for sale
by the Superintendent of Documents,
U.S. Govt. Print. Off.] 1962. 69 p.
62-60088
Z663.285 .L5 MRR Alc.

United States. Library of Congress.
Catalog division. A list of American
doctoral dissertations printed in
[1912]-1938. Received in the Catalog
division from [1912]-September 1939.
1913-1939. Washington, U.S. Govt.
Print. Off., 27 v. 13-35002
Z5055.U49 U5 MRR Alc Full set

United States and Canadian
publications on Africa. 1960-
[Stanford, Calif., 016.9167
62-60021
Z3501 .U59 MRR Alc Full set

Ward, Dederick C. Bibliography of
theses in geology, 1967-1970.
[Boulder, Colo., Geological Society
of America, 1973] vii, 160, I-274 p.
016.55 73-78974
Z6034.U49 W32 MRR Alc.

West, Earle H. A bibliography of
doctoral research on the Negro, 1933-
1966. [Washington] Xerox, 1969.
vii, 134 p. 016.301451/96/073 73-
76349
Z1361.N39 W44 MRR Alc.

Woodress, James Leslie.
Dissertations in American literature,
1891-1966 Durham, N.C., Duke
University Press, 1968. xii, 185 p.
016.8106 68-18961
Z1225 .W8 1968 MRR Ref Desk.

Zeigler, Earle F. Research in the
history, philosophy, and
international aspects of physical
education and sport: bibliographies
and techniques. Champaign, Ill.,
Stipes Pub. Co. [1971] vi, 350 p.
016.6137 76-26892
Z6121 .Z45 MRR Alc.

DISSERTATIONS, ACADEMIC--UNITED STATES--
INDEXES.
Xerox University Microfilms.
Comprehensive dissertation index,
1861-1972. Ann Arbor, Mich., 1973.
37 v. 013/.379 73-89046
Z5053 .X47 1973 MRR Alc.

DISTANCES--TABLES, ETC.
Reed's tables of distances between
ports and places in all parts of the
world. 12th ed. Sunderland [Eng.]
T. Reed [1953] 176 p. 656 387.52*
54-23940
G109 .R4 1953 MRR Alc.

DISTILLATION.
see also Alcohol

see also Liquors

DISTILLING INDUSTRIES--UNITED STATES--
DIRECTORIES.
Red book: encyclopaedic directory of
the wine and liquor industries. New
York, Schwartz Publications, inc.
[$19.50] 338.4/7/663102573 73-
646025
HD9373 .R43 MRR Alc Latest edition

DISTRIBUTION (ECONOMICS)
see Commerce

see Marketing

DISTRIBUTION OF WEALTH
see Wealth

DISTRICT OF COLUMBIA--BIBLIOGRAPHY.
Bryan, Wilhelmus Bogart,
Bibliography of the District of
Columbia, Washington, Govt. print.
off., 1900. v, 211 p. 016.9753 33-
21026
Z1269 .B92 MRR Alc.

DISTRICT OF COLUMBIA--BIBLIOGRAPHY--
CATALOGS.
United States. Library of Congress.
District of Columbia sesquicentennial
of the establishment of the permanent
seat of the Government, Washington,
U.S. Govt. Print. Off., 1950. iv, 89
p. 016.9753 51-60008
Z663.15.A6D5 MRR Alc.

DISTRICT OF COLUMBIA--CENTENNIAL
CELEBRATIONS, ETC.
United States. Library of Congress.
District of Columbia sesquicentennial
of the establishment of the permanent
seat of the Government, Washington,
U.S. Govt. Print. Off., 1950. iv, 89
p. 016.9753 51-60008
Z663.15.A6D5 MRR Alc.

DISTRICT OF COLUMBIA--POLITICS AND
GOVERNMENT.
League of Women Voters of
Metropolitan Washington.
Metropolitan Washington: District of
Columbia, Maryland, Virginia.
Washington, League of Women Voters
Education Fund [1970] 52 p. [$0.25]
320.4/753 77-27912
JK2725 1970 .L4 MRR Ref Desk.

DIVIDENDS--UNITED STATES.
Standard and Poor's Corporation.
Annual dividend record. New York.
332.63058 44-24425
HG4908 .S77 MRR Alc Latest edition

DIVINATION.
see also Dreams

see also Prophecies

Cicero, Marcus Tullius. De
senectute, De amicitia, De
divinatione, Cambridge, Mass.,
Harvard University Press; London, W.
Heinemann, 1938. vii, 567 p. mrr01-
1
PA6156.C5 A2 1938d MRR Alc.

Gibson, Walter Brown, The complete
illustrated book of divination and
prophecy, [1st ed.] Garden City,
N.Y., Doubleday, 1973. xii, 336 p.
[$7.95] 133.3 71-103748
BF1751 .G52 MRR Alc.

DIVING.
Amateur Athletic Union of the United
States. Rules for competitive and
synchronized swimming, diving ...
water polo. Indianapolis, Ind.
[etc.] A. A. U. House [etc.] 797.2
46-31932
Publication began in 1932.
GV837.A1 A45 MRR Alc Latest
edition

DIVING, SUBMARINE.
Fleming, Robert M. A primer of
shipwreck research and records for
skin divers, Milwaukee, Wis., Global
MFG. Corp. [1971] 73 p. [$2.75]
910.4/53 75-25624
VK1250 .F55 MRR Alc.

Potter, John Stauffer, The treasure
diver's guide Rev. ed. Garden City,
N.Y., Doubleday, 1972. xxvi, 567 p.
[$15.00] 910/.453 72-87681
G525 .P58 1972 MRR Alc.

DIVISION OF POWERS
see Federal government

see Separation of powers

DIVORCE--BIBLIOGRAPHY.
Israel, Stanley. A bibliography on
divorce, New York, Bloch Pub. Co.
[1974] xiv, 300 p. [$10.95]
016.30142/84 73-77287
Z7164.M2 I76 MRR Alc.

DIVORCE--UNITED STATES.
Jacobson, Paul Harold, American
marriage and divorce. New York,
Rinehart [1959] xviii, 188 p.
301.42 59-9748
HQ535 .J3 MRR Alc.

United States. Division of Vital
Statistics. Vital statistics of the
United States. 1937- [Washington,
U.S. Govt. Print. Off.] 40-26272
HA203 .A22 MRR Alc Latest edition

United States. National Vital
Statistics Division. Where to write
for divorce records. 1958-
[Washington] U.S. Dept. of Health,
Education, and Welfare, Public Health
Service [for sale by the Supt. of
Docs., U.S. Govt. Print. Off.] 59-
60669
HA38.A347 MRR Ref Desk Latest
edition

DIVORCE--UNITED STATES--STATISTICS.
Jacobson, Paul Harold, American
marriage and divorce. New York,
Rinehart [1959] xviii, 188 p.
301.42 59-9748
HQ535 .J3 MRR Alc.

Women's rights almanac. 1974-
Bethesda, Md., Elizabeth Cady Stanton
Pub. Co. [$4.95] 301.41/2/0973 74-
77527
HQ1406 .W65 MRR Ref Desk Latest
edition

DO-IT-YOURSELF WORK.
Lovell, Eleanor Cook, comp. Index to
handicrafts, modelmaking, and
workshop projects, Boston, Faxon,
1936. 476 p. 016.6 36-27324
Z7911 .L89 MRR Alc.

Popular mechanics do-it-yourself
encyclopedia. New York, Book
Division, Hearst Magazines [1968- v.
680/.2/02 68-3759
TT155 .P75 MRR Alc.

The Family handyman. America's
handyman book, New York, Scribner
[1961] 513 p. 643.7 61-7215
TT151 .F3 MRR Alc.

The Family handyman. America's
handyman book, Rev. ed. New York,
Scribner [1970] xiii, 529 p.
[$10.00] 643/.7 70-85277
TH4817 .F28 1970 MRR Alc.

DO-IT-YOURSELF WORK--BIBLIOGRAPHY.
Nueckel, Susan. Selected guide to
make-it, fix-it, do-it-yourself
books, New York, Fleet Press Corp.
[1973] 213 p. 016.643/7 72-82609
Z6151 .N83 MRR Alc.

DOCKS.
see also Harbors

DOCKS--DIRECTORIES.
Lloyd's register of shipping,
London, Wyman and sons [etc.] ca 08-
1387
"Founded 1760. Re-constituted
1834."
HE565.A3 L7 MRR Alc Latest edition

DOCTOR OF PHILOSOPHY DEGREE.
American Council on Education. A
guide to graduate study: 1st- ed.;
1957- Washington. 65-21729
LB2371 .A4 MRR Ref Desk Latest
edition

DOCTORS
see Physicians

DOCUMENT SOURCES.
Baumer, Franklin Le Van, ed. Main
currents of Western thought; 2d ed.,
rev. [and enl.] New York, Knopf,
1964. xviii, 746 p. 914 64-14416
CB245 .B37 1964 MRR Alc.

The Cadillac modern encyclopedia.
[1st ed.] New York, Cadillac Pub.
Co.; distributed by Derbibooks,
Secaucus, N.J. [1973] xiv, 1954 p.
[$24.95] 031 73-81377
AG5 .C25 MRR Ref Desk.

Cameron, Richard Morgan, comp. The
rise of Methodism, New York,
Philosophical Library [1954] xv, 397
p. 287.09 54-8668
BX8231 .C3 MRR Alc.

Carlen, Mary Claudia, Dictionary of
papal pronouncements, New York, P.
J. Kenedy [1958] 216 p. 262.82 58-
12095
BX873.7 .C3 MRR Alc.

Columbia University. Columbia
College. Introduction to
contemporary civilization in the
West; 3d ed. New York, Columbia
University Press, 1960-61. 2 v.
914 60-16650
CB5 .C575 MRR Alc.

Daniels, Robert Vincent, ed. A
documentary history of communism;
New York, Random House [1960] 321,
393 p. 335.4309 60-6380
HX40 .D3 MRR Alc.

DOCUMENT SOURCES. (Cont.)
Ehler, Sidney Z., ed. and tr. Church and state through the centuries; New York, Biblo and Tannen, 1967. xii, 625 p.　261.7/08　66-30406
　BV630.A1 E37 1967 MRR Alc.

Friedman, Leon, comp. The law of war; a documentary history. [1st ed.] New York, Random House [1972] 2 v. (xxv, 1764 p.)　341.6/026　72-765
　JX4505 .F7 MRR Alc.

Grenville, John Ashley Soames. The major international treaties, 1914-1973; New York, Stein and Day [1974] xxix, 575 p. [$25.00] 341/.026 75-163352
　JX171 .G74 MRR Alc.

Hartmann, Frederick H., ed. Basic documents of international relations. 1st ed. New York, McGraw-Hill, 1951. xv, 312 p.　341.082　51-9293

　JX68 .H35 MRR Alc.

Hudson, Manley Ottmer, ed. International legislation; Washington, Carnegie endowment for international peace, 1931-　v. 341.2　32-2876
　JX171 .H8 MRR Alc.

Hurst, Michael, comp. Key treaties for the great powers, 1814-1914. New York, St. Martin's Press [1972] 2 v. (xviii, 948 p.) [$31.50]　341/.026 72-188873
　JX151 .H87 1972b MRR Alc.

International organisation and integration. Deventer, Æ. E. Kluwer; Leiden, A. W. Sijthoff, 1968 [1969] xxvi, 1146 p. [67.30]　341.13 68-25399
　JX171 .I54 MRR Alc.

Israel, Fred L., comp. Major peace treaties of modern history, 1648-1967. New York, Chelsea House Publishers, 1967. 4 v. (xxix, 2880 p.)　341.2　67-27855
　JX121 .I8 MRR Alc.

Lawson, Ruth Catherine, International regional organizations: New York, Praeger [1962] xviii, 387 p.　341.18　62-13746
　JX1978 .L3 MRR Alc.

Lexikon für Theologie und Kirche; 2., völlig neu bearb. Aufl., Freiburg, Herder, 1957-61.　10 v. 58-41506
　BR95 .L48 MRR Alc.

Moore, John Bassett, A digest of international law Washington, Govt. print. off., 1906. 8 v.　30-10322
　JX237 .M7 1906a MRR Alc.

Peaslee, Amos Jenkins, ed. International governmental organizations: constitutional documents. Rev. 2d ed. [The Hague, M. Nijhoff, c1961] 2 v. (lviii, 1962 p.)　341.11　62-32304
　JX1995 .P4 1961 MRR Ref Desk.

Snyder, Louis Leo, ed. The imperialism reader: Princeton, N.J., Van Nostrand [1962] 619 p.　321.03 62-3115
　JC359 .S65 MRR Alc.

Trefousse, Hans Louis, ed. The cold war; a book of documents. New York, Putnam [1965] xxi, 296 p.　327.08 65-13298
　D839.3 .T67 MRR Alc.

Viorst, Milton. The great documents of Western civilization. [1st ed.] Philadelphia, Chilton Books [1965] xv, 388 p.　914.0308　65-28123
　CB245 .V5 MRR Alc.

Ward, Hiley H., ed. Documents of dialogue Englewood Cliffs, N.J., Prentice-Hall [1966] xvi, 525 p. 262/.001　66-22100
　BX6.5 .W3 MRR Alc.

Watkins, James Thomas, ed. General international organization, Princeton, Van Nostrand [1956] xi, 248 p.　341.11*　56-9730
　JX1937 .W3 MRR Alc.

Whiteman, Marjorie Millace. Digest of international law. [Washington, U.S. Dept. of State; for sale by the Superintendent of Documents, U.S. Govt. Print. Off., 1963-　v. [$6.25 (v. 14) varies]　341.02　63-62002
　JX237 .W55 MRR Alc.

Wishy, Bernard W., ed. The Western World in the twentieth century; New York, Columbia University Press, 1961. 517 p.　901.94　61-8987
　CB425 .W57 MRR Alc.

Yearbook on human rights. 1946- New York [etc.] United Nations.　323.4058 48-4455
　JC571 .U4　MRR Ref Desk Latest edition

DOCUMENT SOURCES--INDEXES.
Consolidated index to the Survey of international affairs, 1920-1938. London, Oxford U.P., 1967. [5], 272 p. [£5/-/-]　327　68-74749
　D442 .C6 MRR Alc.

DOCUMENT SOURCES--AFRICA.
Hertslet, Edward, Sir, The map of Africa by treaty, 3d ed.: London, Printed for H.M. Stationery off., by Harrison and sons, 1909. 3 v. and portfolio of maps.　10-833
　JX1026 1896a MRR Alc.

Legum, Colin. Pan-Africanism; New York, Praeger [1962] 296 p.　960 62-13489
　DT30 .L39 1962a MRR Alc.

Wallbank, Thomas Walter, ed. Documents on modern Africa Princeton, N.J., Van Nostrand [1964] 192 p.　960　64-4841
　DT20 .W25 MRR Alc.

DOCUMENT SOURCES--AFRICA, NORTH.
Annuaire de l'Afrique du Nord. 1-1962- [Paris] Centre national de la recherche scientifique.　65-36969
　DT181 .A74 MRR Alc Latest edition

DOCUMENT SOURCES--ARAB COUNTRIES.
Fisher, Carol Ann. Middle East in crisis; [Syracuse] Syracuse University Press [1959] 213 p.　956 59-9859
　DS63 .F5 MRR Alc.

Khalil, Muhammad, ed. The Arab States and the Arab League; Beirut, Khayats [1962] 2 v.　ne 63-705
　DS36.2 .K45 MRR Alc.

DOCUMENT SOURCES--ASIA.
Higgins, Rosalyn. United Nations peacekeeping, 1946-1967: London, New York [etc.] issued under the auspices of the Royal Institute of International Affairs by Oxford U.P., 1969-　v.　[5/10- (v. 1)]　341.6 76-396893
　JX1981.P7 H5 MRR Alc.

Wint, Guy, ed. Asia; a handbook. New York, Praeger [1966] xiii, 856 p.　915　65-13263
　DS5 .W5 MRR Alc.

DOCUMENT SOURCES--AUSTRALIA.
Clark, Charles Manning Hope, ed. Select documents in Australian history. Sydney, Angus and Robertson [1950-　v.　994　51-2907
　DU80 .C58 MRR Alc.

DOCUMENT SOURCES--AUSTRIA.
Austria. Bundesministerium für Unterricht. Österreich frei: Wien, Österreichischer Bundesverlag für Unterricht, Wissenschaft und Kunst [1956] 159 p.　57-15203
　DB99.1 .A54 MRR Alc.

Austria. Bundesministerium für Unterricht. Österreich--Freies Land, freies Volk; Wien, Österreichischer Bundesverlag für Unterricht, Wissenschaft und Kunst [1957] 208 p.　59-19213
　DB99.1 .A544 MRR Alc.

DOCUMENT SOURCES--BRAZIL.
Fitzgibbon, Russell Humke, Brazil: a chronology and fact book, 1488-1973, Dobbs Ferry, N.Y., Oceana Publications, 1974. vi, 150 p. [$7.50]　981　73-17058
　F2521 .F55 MRR Alc.

DOCUMENT SOURCES--CANADA.
Historical documents of Canada, Toronto, Macmillan of Canada [1972-　v.　971.06　77-179356
　F1003 .H5 MRR Alc.

Kennedy, William Paul McClure, Statutes, treaties and documents of the Canadian constitution, 1713-1929, 2d ed.; rev. and enl. Toronto, London, New York [etc.] Oxford university press, 1930. xxviii, 752 p.　342.71　30-34203
　JL11 .K45 1930 MRR Alc.

Talman, James John, ed. Basic documents in Canadian history. Princeton, N.J., Van Nostrand [1959] 189 p.　871　58-9760
　F1003 .T3 MRR Alc.

DOCUMENT SOURCES--CHINA.
Brandt, Conrad. A documentary history of Chinese communism, London, Allen & Unwin [1952] 552 p. 951.04　52-67189
　DS775 .B7 MRR Alc.

Gittings, John. Survey of the Sino-Soviet dispute: London, New York [etc.] issued under the auspices of the Royal Institute of International Affairs [by] Oxford U.P., 1968. xix, 410 p. [84/-]　327.51/047　75-356659
　DS740.5.R8 G5 MRR Alc.

United States. Dept. of State. The China white paper, August 1949. Stanford, Calif., Stanford University Press [1967] xli, 1079 p. 327.51/073　67-26650
　E183.8.C5 U53 1967 MRR Alc.

United States. Dept. of State. Historical Office. China, 1942-Washington, U.S. Govt. Print. Off., 1956-　v.　327.73051　57-61196
　JX1428.C6 A54 MRR Alc.

Wu, Yuan-li. China; New York, Praeger [1973]　915 p. [$35.00] 915.1/03/5　72-101683
　DS706 .W8 MRR Alc.

DOCUMENT SOURCES--CZECHOSLOVAK REPUBLIC.
Jesina, Cestmir, comp. The birth of Czechoslovakia. [Washington] Czechoslovak National Council of America, Washington, D.C. Chapter, 1968. ix, 110 p. [5.00]　74-18574
　DB215.2 .J48 MRR Alc.

DOCUMENT SOURCES--DELAWARE.
Myers, Albert Cook, ed. Narratives of early Pennsylvania, West New Jersey and Delaware, 1630-1707, New York C. Scribner's sons, 1912. xiv p., 2 l., 3-476 p.　12-4611
　E187.07 M9 MRR Alc.

DOCUMENT SOURCES--ETHIOPIA.
Perham, Margery Freda, Dame, The government of Ethiopia, 2nd ed. London, Faber, 1969. xviii, 531 p. [5/10/-]　320.9/63　78-394906
　JQ3754 .P4 1969 MRR Alc.

DOCUMENT SOURCES--EUROPE.
Allied and associated powers (1914-1920) Treaties, etc. The treaties of peace, 1919-1923. New York, Carnegie endowment for international peace, 1924. 2 v.　24-19994
　D643 .A2 1923 MRR Alc.

Annuaire européen. v. 1-　1955-La Haye, Nijhoff.　55-3837
　JN3 .A5　MRR Alc Latest edition

Baltzly, Alexander, Readings in twentieth-century European history, New York, Appleton-Century-Crofts [1950] xxv, 610 p.　940.5　50-6460

　D411 .B3 MRR Alc.

Bernard, Leon, ed. Readings in European history, New York, Macmillan [1958] 514 p.　940.082 58-5465
　D5.5 .B4 MRR Alc.

Bettenson, Henry Scowcroft, ed. Documents of the Christian Church: 2nd ed. London, New York [etc.] Oxford U. P., 1967. xvii, 343 p. [12/6]　270　68-109402
　BR141 .B4 1967 MRR Alc.

Catholic Church. Pope. The papal encyclicals in their historical context [New York] New American Library [1963] 448 p.　64-2656
　BX860 .A36 1963 MRR Alc.

Council of Europe. European conventions and agreements. Strasbourg, 1971-　v.　341.24/2 72-195347
　JX626 1971 .C68 MRR Alc.

Downs, Norton, ed. Basic documents in medieval history, Princeton, N.J., Van Nostrand [1959]　189 p. 940.1082　59-9758
　D113.5 .D6 MRR Alc.

Flower, Desmond, ed. The war, 1939-1945, London, Cassell [1960]　1120 p.　940.53　60-3389
　D743 .F55 MRR Alc.

Gantenbein, James Watson, ed. Documentary background of World War II, 1931-1941. New York, Columbia Univ. Press, 1948. xxxiii, 1122 p. 940.52　48-11573
　D735 .G25 MRR Alc.

Geiss, Imanuel. July 1914: the outbreak of the First World War: London, Batsford, 1967.　400 p. [50/-]　940.3/112/08　67-108481
　D505 .G2513 MRR Alc.

Hertslet, Edward, Sir, comp. The map of Europe by treaty; London, Butterworths [etc.] 1875-91. 4 v. 10-15038
　JX626 1875 MRR Alc.

DOCUMENT SOURCES--EUROPE. (Cont.)
Kertesz, G. A., comp. Documents in
the political history of the European
continent, 1815-1939; Oxford,
Clarendon P., 1968. xxvii, 507 p.
[70/-] 940 74-372140
D5 .K4 MRR Alc.

Langsam, Walter Consuelo, ed.
Documents and readings in the history
of Europe since 1918 Rev. and enl.
Philadelphia, Lippincott, c1951.
1190 p. 940.5 51-8285
D442 .L3 1951 MRR Alc.

Langsam, Walter Consuelo, ed.
Historic documents of World War II.
Princeton, N.J., Van Nostrand [1958]
192 p. 940.53082 58-14435
D735 .L3 MRR Alc.

Leiss, Amelia Catherine, ed.
European peace treaties after World
War II; [Boston] World Peace
Foundation [1954] xvi, 341 p.
940.53141 54-14902
D814 .L4 MRR Alc.

Mid-European Law Project. Economic
treaties and agreements of the Soviet
bloc in Eastern Europe, 1945-1951.
2d ed. New York, Mid-European
Studies Center, 1952. xliii, 138 p.
382 52-60057
Z663.55 .E3 MRR Alc.

Nations & empires; London,
Macmillan; New York, St. Martin's P.,
1969. 336 p. [50/-] 940.2 76-
85482
D5 .N3 MRR Alc.

Ogg, Frederic Austin, ed. A source
book of mediæval history; New York,
Cincinnati [etc.] American book
company [1908?] 504 p. 08-12576
D113 .O3 MRR Alc.

Pollard, Sidney, comp. Documents of
European economic history New York,
St. Martin's Press [1968- v.
[15.25 (v. 1)] 330.9/4 68-10751
HC240 .P5952 MRR Alc.

Postgate, Raymond William, ed.
Revolution from 1789 to 1906;
Gloucester, Mass., P. Smith, 1969.
xvi, 398 p. 940.2/7 70-10678
D351 .P86 1969 MRR Alc.

Pullan, Brian S., ed. Sources for
the history of medieval Europe from
the mid-eighth to the mid-thirteenth
century Oxford, Blackwell [1966] x,
277 p. [35/-] 940.14 66-75453
D113.5 .P8 MRR Alc.

Robertson, Arthur Henry. European
institutions: co-operation,
integration, unification, [3d ed.]
London, Stevens & Sons; New York,
Matthew Bender, 1973. xix, 478 p.
341.24/2 72-94556
JN15 .R58 1973 MRR Alc.

Routh, Charles Richard Nairne, comp.
They saw it happen in Europe; New
York, Barnes & Noble [1966, c1965]
xv, 514 p. 940.2 66-5348
D220 .R6 1966 MRR Alc.

Scott, James Brown, ed. Diplomatic
documents relating to the outbreak of
the European war, New York, Oxford
university press, American branch;
[etc., etc.] 1916. 2 v. 16-18046
D505 .S4 MRR Alc.

Stearns, Raymond Phineas, ed.
Pageant of Europe; Rev. ed. New
York, Harcourt, Brace & World [1961]
1072 p. 940.2082 61-10710
D5.5 .S8 1961 MRR Alc.

White, Donald A., ed. Medieval
history; Homewood, Ill., Dorsey
Press, 1965. ix, 575 p. 901.921
65-6954
D113.5 .W5 MRR Alc.

Wuest, John J., ed. New Source book
in major European governments,
Cleveland, World Pub. Co. [1966]
xviii, 700 p. 320.308 66-13148
JF51 .W8 MRR Alc.

DOCUMENT SOURCES--FRANCE.
Legg, Leopold George Wickham, ed.
Select documents illustrative of the
history of the French revolution.
Oxford, Clarendon press, 1905. 2 v.
05-18309
DC141.7 .L4 MRR Alc.

Stewart, John Hall, A documentary
survey of the French Revolution. New
York, Macmillan [1951] xxviii, 818
p. 944.04 51-10629
DC141.7 .S8 MRR Alc.

DOCUMENT SOURCES--GERMANY.
Remak, Joachim, comp. The Nazi
years; Englewood Cliffs, N.J.,
Prentice-Hall [1969] xi, 178 p.
[4.95] 943.086 69-11359
DD256.5 .R43 MRR Alc.

Snyder, Louis Leo, ed. Documents of
German history. New Brunswick, N.J.,
Rutgers University Press, 1958.
xxiii, 619 p. 943.0082 57-10968
DD3 .S55 MRR Alc.

Treue, Wolfgang, ed. Deutsche
Parteiprogramme seit 1861 [i. e.
achtzehnhunderteinundsechzig. 4.,
erw. Aufl.] Göttingen,
Musterschmidt-Verlag [1968, c1954]
506 p. 329.9/43 77-369618
JN3931 .T7 1968 MRR Alc.

United States. Dept. of State.
Historical Office. Documents on
Germany, 1944-1961. Washington, U.S.
Govt. Print. Off., 1961. xv, 833 p.
62-60800
DD257 .U476 1961 MRR Alc.

DOCUMENT SOURCES--GREAT BRITAIN.
American archives: consisting of a
collection of authentick records,
state papers, debates, and letters
and other notices of publick affairs,
[New York, Johnson Reprint Corp.,
1972] 9 v. 973.2/7 74-181484
E203 .A5 1972 MRR Alc.

Bettey, J. H. English historical
documents, 1906-1939; London,
Routledge & K. Paul, 1967. x, 198 p.
[21/- 12/6 (pbk.)] 942.083/08 67-
109889
DA576 .B45 MRR Alc.

Churchill, Winston Leonard Spencer,
Sir. The Second World War. Boston,
Published in association with the
Cooperation Pub. Co. [by] Houghton
Mifflin, 1948-53. 6 v. 940.53 48-
2880
D743 .C47 MRR Alc.

Cole, George Douglas Howard, comp.
British working class movements;
London, Macmillan, 1951. xxii, 628
p. 331.8 52-2264
HD8388 .C62 MRR Alc.

Craig, Fred W. S., comp. British
general election manifestos 1918-
1966. Chichester [Eng.] Political
Reference Publications, 1970. xii,
303 p. [75/- ($12.00 U.S.)]
329.9/42 70-77467
JN1121 .C73 MRR Alc.

Davies, Reginald Trevor, comp.
Documents illustrating the history of
civilization in medieval England,
1066-1500 New York, Barnes & Noble
[1969] x, 413 p. 914.2 74-4396
DA170 .D3 1969 MRR Alc.

English historical documents. [New
York, Oxford University Press, 195
v. 942 53-1506
DA26 .E55 MRR Alc.

Evans, Lloyd, comp. Contemporary
sources and opinions in modern
British history London, New York, F.
Warne, 1967. 2 v. [30/- (v. 1) 42/-
(v. 2)] 942.08/08 68-101076
DA530 .E9 1967 MRR Alc.

Ford, Percy, A breviate of
parliamentary papers, 1917-1939
Shannon, Ire., Irish University
Press, 1969. xlviii, 571 p.
320.9/42/082 76-27392
JN549 .F6 1969 MRR Alc.

Greg, Walter Wilson, Sir, A
companion to Arber; Oxford,
Clarendon P., 1967. ix, 451 p.
[5/15/6] 655/.42 67-96150
Z151.3 .G68 1967 MRR Alc.

Hall, Hubert, comp. A formula book
of English official historical
documents. Cambridge, University
press, 1908-09. 2 v. 09-4070
CD105 .H26 MRR Alc.

Hertslet's commercial treaties.
London, 1827-1925. 31 v. 01-4024
JX636 1827 Vol. 22 & 31 MRR Alc.

Pollard, Alfred William, ed. Records
of the English Bible. London, New
York [etc.] H. Frowde, 1911. xii,
387, [1] p. 11-13348
BS455 .P7 MRR Alc.

Stephenson, Carl, ed. and tr.
Sources of English constitutional
history; Rev. ed. New York, Harper
& Row [1972] 2 v. (xxvi, 953, xii
p.) 340/.73/024 72-84325
JN111 .S67 1972 MRR Alc.

Temperley, Harold William Vazeille,
ed. Foundations of British foreign
policy, New York, Barnes & Noble
[1966] xxx, 573 p. 327.42 66-3832

DA530 .T4 1966a MRR Alc.

DOCUMENT SOURCES--INDIA.
India (Dominion) India, 1947-50,
[London] Oxford University Press,
1959. 2 v. 954.04 60-1910
DS480.84 .A5 1959 MRR Alc.

DOCUMENT SOURCES--IRELAND.
Curtis, Edmund, ed. Irish historical
documents, 1172-1922, New York,
Barnes & Noble [1968] 331 p. [8.00]
941.5/08 68-6007
DA905 .C8 1968b MRR Alc.

DOCUMENT SOURCES--ISRAEL.
Khalil, Muhammad, ed. The Arab
States and the Arab League; Beirut,
Khayats [1962] 2 v. ne 63-705
DS36.2 .K45 MRR Alc.

Laqueur, Walter Ze'ev, comp. The
Israel-Arab reader; New York,
Citadel Press [1969] xi, 371 p.
[7.95] 956 68-25146
DS119.7 .L3 MRR Alc.

DOCUMENT SOURCES--LATIN AMERICA.
Gantenbein, James Watson, ed. The
evolution of our Latin-American
policy, New York, Columbia
University Press, 1950. xxvii, 979
p. 327.73098 49-50406
F1418 .G2 MRR Alc.

Manning, William Ray, ed.
Arbitration treaties among the
American nations, to the close of the
year 1910, New York [etc.] Oxford
university press, 1924. xl, 472 p.
24-6749
JX1985 .M3 MRR Alc.

Thomas, Norman F., comp. Selected
documents in the history of Latin
America. [Tacoma? Wash.] c1961. 174
p. 62-1117
F1410 .T5 MRR Alc.

DOCUMENT SOURCES--MARYLAND.
Hall, Clayton Colman, ed. Narratives
of early Maryland, 1633-1684, New
York, Charles Scribner's sons, 1910.
ix p., 2 l., 3-460 p. 10-23763
E187.O7 H3 MRR Alc.

DOCUMENT SOURCES--NEAR EAST.
Higgins, Rosalyn. United Nations
peacekeeping, 1946-1967: London, New
York [etc.] issued under the auspices
of the Royal Institute of
International Affairs by Oxford U.P.,
1969- v. [5/10- (v. 1)] 341.6
76-396893
JX1981.P7 H5 MRR Alc.

Hurewitz, Jacob Coleman, ed.
Diplomacy in the Near and Middle
East; New York, Octagon Books, 1972
[c1956] 2 v. 956 72-2494
DS42 .H782 MRR Alc.

Laqueur, Walter Ze'ev, comp. The
Israel-Arab reader; New York,
Citadel Press [1969] xi, 371 p.
[7.95] 956 68-25146
DS119.7 .L3 MRR Alc.

Magnus, Ralph H., comp. Documents on
the Middle East, Washington,
American Enterprise Institute for
Public Policy Research, 1969. viii,
232 p. [3.00] 327.56/073 75-93191

DS42 .M3 MRR Alc.

United States. Library of Congress.
Foreign Affairs Division. A select
chronology and background documents
relating to the Middle East. 1st
rev. ed. Washington, U.S. Govt.
Print. Off., 1969. vii, 287 p.
[1.25] 956/.002 76-602249
DS62.8 .U55 1969 MRR Alc.

DOCUMENT SOURCES--NEW JERSEY.
Myers, Albert Cook, ed. Narratives
of early Pennsylvania, West New
Jersey and Delaware, 1630-1707, New
York, C. Scribner's sons, 1912. xiv
p., 2 l., 3-476 p. 12-4611
E187.O7 M9 MRR Alc.

DOCUMENT SOURCES--NEW YORK (STATE).
New York state legislative annual.
1946- New York, New York Legislative
Service, inc. 328.747 47-20115
JK3401 .N48 MRR Alc Latest edition

DOCUMENT SOURCES--NORTH ATLANTIC TREATY
ORGANIZATION.
North Atlantic Treaty Organization.
NATO handbook. Brussels. 341.24/3
75-613327
JX1393 .N6122 MRR Alc Latest
edition

DOCUMENT SOURCES--NORTH CAROLINA.
Lefler, Hugh Talmage, ed. North
Carolina history told by
contemporaries. [4th ed., rev. and
enl.] Chapel Hill, University of
North Carolina Press [1965] xv, 580
p. 975.6 65-6351
F254 .L37 1965 MRR Alc.

Salley, Alexander Samuel, ed.
Narratives of early Carolina, 1650-
1708, New York, C. Scribner's sons,
1911. xi p., 2 l., 3-388 p. 11-
9548
E187.O7 S3 MRR Alc.

DOCUMENT SOURCES--PENNSYLVANIA.
Myers, Albert Cook, ed. Narratives
of early Pennsylvania, West New
Jersey and Delaware, 1630-1707, New
York, C. Scribner's sons, 1912. xiv
p., 2 l., 3-476 p.   12-4611
     E187.O7 M9 MRR Alc.

DOCUMENT SOURCES--PERU.
United States. Library of Congress.
Manuscript division. The Harkness
collection in the Library of
Congress. Washington, U.S. Govt.
print. off., 1936. xi, 253 p.   985
36-26004
     Z663.34 .H29 MRR Alc.

DOCUMENT SOURCES--PHILIPPINE ISLANDS.
Agoncillo, Teodoro A. History of the
Filipino people, [Rev. ed.] Quezon
City, Malaya Books, [1969, c1967]
xviii, 725 p.   991.4   76-10930
     DS668 .A32 1969 MRR Alc.

DOCUMENT SOURCES--POLAND.
Horak, Stephan M. Poland's
international affairs, 1919-1960;
Bloomington, Indiana University,
1964. xviii, 248 p.   341.2438   64-
63009
     JX760.P7 H6 MRR Alc.

DOCUMENT SOURCES--RUSSIA.
Communist International. The
Communist International, 1919-1943;
[London] F. Cass, 1971. 3 v.
[£23.00]   329/.072   72-182920
     HX11.I5 A5314 1971 MRR Alc.

Current digest of the Soviet press.
Current Soviet policies; 19th-
1952- New York, F. A. Praeger.
947.085*   53-6440
     JN6598 .K5 1952f   MRR Alc Full set

Degras, Jane (Tabrisky) ed. Soviet
documents on foreign policy. London,
New York, Oxford University Press,
1951-53. 3 v.   327.47   51-3107
     JX1555.A2 D4 MRR Alc.

Dmytryshyn, Basil, USSR: a concise
history. 2d ed. New York, Scribner
[1971] xv, 584 p.   [$12.50]
947.084   77-162787
     DK266 .D465 1971 MRR Alc.

Gittings, John. Survey of the Sino-
Soviet dispute: London, New York
[etc.] issued under the auspices of
the Royal Institute of International
Affairs [by] Oxford U.P., 1968. xix,
410 p.   [84/-]   327.51/047   75-
356659
     DS740.5.R8 G5 MRR Alc.

Jados, Stanley S., ed. Documents on
Russian-American relations,
Washington, Catholic University of
America Press [1965] viii, 416 p.
327.47073   65-12569
     E183.8.R9 J3 MRR Alc.

Khrushchev, Nikita Sergeevich,
Khrushchev speaks; Ann Arbor,
University of Michigan Press [1963]
466 p.   847.085   63-8075
     DK275.K5 A36 MRR Alc.

Lenin, Vladimir Il'ich, Lenin
reader, Chicago, H. Regnery Co.
[1966] xxxii, 528 p.   335.4308   65-
21487
     DK254.L3 A576 MRR Alc.

Rubinstein, Alvin Z., ed. The
foreign policy of the Soviet Union,
2d ed. New York, Random House [1966]
xx, 458 p.   327.47   66-15810
     DK63.3 .R8 1966 MRR Alc.

Russia (1917- R.S.F.S.R.) Treaties,
etc. Soviet treaty series;
Washington, Georgetown University
Press, 1950- v.   341.247   50-
2664
     JX756 1950 MRR Alc.

Slusser, Robert M. A calendar of
Soviet treaties, 1917-1957 Stanford,
Calif., Stanford University Press,
1959. xii, 530 p.   341.247   59-
10638
     JX756 1917 MRR Alc.

United States. Dept. of State. The
Soviet Union, 1933-1939. Washington,
U.S. Govt. Print. Off., 1952. cli,
1034 p.   327.730947   52-61069
     JX233.A6R93 MRR Alc.

DOCUMENT SOURCES--SCOTLAND.
Dickinson, William Croft, ed. A
source book of Scottish history, [2d
ed. rev. and enl.] London, T. Nelson
[1958-61] 3 v.   62-6746
     DA755 .D52 MRR Alc.

DOCUMENT SOURCES--SOUTH CAROLINA.
Salley, Alexander Samuel, ed.
Narratives of early Carolina, 1650-
1708, New York, C. Scribner's sons,
1911. xi p., 2 l., 3-388 p.   11-
9548
     E187.O7 S3 MRR Alc.

DOCUMENT SOURCES--SOUTHERN STATES.
Spanish explorers in the southern
United States, 1528-1543: New York,
C. Scribner's sons, 1907. xx, 411 p.
07-10607
     E187.O7 S7 MRR Alc.

DOCUMENT SOURCES--UNITED NATIONS.
Cordier, Andrew Wellington, comp.
Public papers of the Secretaries-
General of the United Nations. New
York, Columbia University Press, 1969-
v.   [12.50 (v. 1)]   341.13/08
68-8873
     JX1977 .C62 MRR Alc.

Harley, John Eugene, Documentary
textbook on the United Nations; 2d
ed., rev. and enl. Los Angeles,
Auspices of the Center for
International Understanding [1950]
xxvii, 1470 p.   341.1   50-10302
     JX1877 .H3 1950 MRR Alc.

Prosser, Michael H., comp. Sow the
wind, reap the whirlwind: New York,
Morrow, 1970. 2 v. (xviii, 1467 p.)
[$100.00]   341.1/08   73-118271
     JX1977 .P728 MRR Alc.

DOCUMENT SOURCES--UNITED STATES.
Adams, John, pres. U.S.   The works
of John Adams,   Boston, Little, Brown
and company [etc.] 1850-56 [v. 1,
'56] 10 v.   08-19755
     E302 .A26 MRR Alc.

Adams, John Quincy, Pres. U.S.,
Writings of John Quincy Adams. New
York, Greenwood Press [1968] 7 v.
973.4/0924   68-30993
     E337.8 .A22 MRR Alc.

American archives: consisting of a
collection of authentick records,
state papers, debates, and letters
and other notices of publick affairs,
[New York, Johnson Reprint Corp.,
1972] 9 v.   973.2/7   74-181484
     E203 .A5 1972 MRR Alc.

Andrews, Charles McLean, ed.
Narratives of the insurrections, 1675-
1690. New York, C. Scribner's sons,
1915. ix p., 2 l., 3-414 p.   973.2
15-4852
     E187.O7 A6 MRR Alc.

Angle, Paul McClelland, ed. By these
words; New York, Rand McNally [1954]
560 p.   973   54-10616
     E173 .A79 MRR Alc.

Bartlett, Ruhl Jacob, ed. The record
of American diplomacy; 4th ed. enl.
New York, Knopf, 1964. xxiv, 892,
xxii p.   327.73   64-23887
     E183.7 .B35 1964 MRR Alc.

Berrett, William Edwin, ed. Readings
in L.D.S. Church history from
original manuscripts, 1st ed. Salt
Lake City, Deseret Book Co., 1953-58.
3 v.   289.309   53-23418
     BX8611 .B346 MRR Alc.

Blakely, William Addison, ed.
American state papers and related
documents on freedom in religion.
4th rev. ed. Washington, Published
for the Religious Liberty Association
by the Review and Herald, 1949. 915
p.   263.8   50-206
     BV133 .B6 1949 MRR Alc.

Bolton, Herbert Eugene, ed. Spanish
exploration in the Southwest, 1542-
1706, New York, C. Scribner's sons,
1916. xii p., 2 l., 3-487 p.   16-
6066
     E187.O7 B6 MRR Alc.

Boorstin, Daniel Joseph, ed. An
American primer, Chicago, University
of Chicago Press [1966] 2 v. (xvii,
994 p.)   917.303   66-20576
     E173 .B7 MRR Alc.

Borden, Morton, ed. The
antifederalist papers. [East
Lansing, Mich.] Michigan State
University Press, 1965. xiv, 258 p.
342.7308   65-17929
     JK116 .B6 MRR Alc.

Boyd, Julian Parks, The Declaration
of independence; Princeton,
Princeton university press, 1945. 2
p. l., 46 p.   973.313   a   45-1832
     JK128 .B66 MRR Alc.

Buchanan, James, Pres. U.S., James
Buchanan, 1791-1868; Dobbs Ferry,
N.Y., Oceana Publications, 1968- v,
89 p.   [$3.00]   973.6/8/08   68-21537

     E436 .B88 MRR Alc.

Burnett, Edmund Cody, ed. Letters of
members of the Continental Congress.
Gloucester, Mass., P. Smith, 1963. 8
v.   973.31   64-2503
     JK1033 .B8 1963 MRR Alc.

Burr, George Lincoln, ed. Narratives
of the witchcraft cases, 1648-1706,
New York, C. Scribner's sons, 1914.
xviii, 467 p.   [3.00]   14-9773
     E187.O7 B8 MRR Alc.

Cain, Alfred E., ed. The winding
road to freedom: [1st ed.] Yonkers
[N.Y.] Educational Heritage [1965]
384 p.   973.097496   65-5735
     E185 .C14 MRR Alc.

Carter, Clarence Edwin, comp. The
territorial papers of the United
States. Washington, U.S. Govt.
Print. Off., 1934- v.   973.082
35-26191
     E173 .C3 MRR Alc.

Chamberlain, Neil W., ed. Sourcebook
on labor New York, McGraw-Hill Book
Co. [1964] x, 382 p.   331.1973   64-
21013
     HD8072 .C38 1964 MRR Alc.

Chambers, Bradford, comp. Chronicles
of Negro protest: New York, Parents'
Magazine Press [1968] 319 p.
[$4.50]   322/.4   68-16998
     E185.61 .C5 MRR Alc.

Cleveland, Grover, Pres. U.S.,
Grover Cleveland, 1837-1908: Dobbs
Ferry, N.Y., Oceana Publications,
1968. 118 p   973.8/5/08   68-21538

     E696 .C617 1968 MRR Alc.

Columbia University. Legislative
Drafting Research Fund.
Constitutions of the United States,
national and State. Dobbs Ferry,
N.Y., Oceana Publications [1962- 2
v. (loose-leaf)   342.73   61-18391
     KF4530 .C6 MRR Alc.

Commager, Henry Steele, ed.
Documents of American history. 9th
ed. New York, Appleton-Century-
Crofts [1973] xxiii, 815 p.
973/.08   73-11492
     E173 .C66 1973 MRR Ref Desk.

Commager, Henry Steele, ed. Living
ideas in America. New, enl. ed. New
York, Harper & Row [1964] xx, 872 p.
917.3   64-23898
     E173 .C67 1964 MRR Alc.

Commager, Henry Steele, ed. The
spirit of 'seventy-six; New York,
Harper & Row [1967] lii, 1348 p.
973.3/08   67-11325
     E203 .C69 1967 MRR Alc.

Dann, Martin E., comp. The Black
press, 1827-1890; New York, Putnam
[1971] 384 p.   [$.95]
301.451/96/073   72-127714
     E185.5 .D35 1971 MRR Alc.

Davenport, Frances Gardiner, ed.
European treaties bearing on the
history of the United States and its
dependencies. Washington, D.C.,
Carnegie institution of Washington,
1917-37. 4 v.   18-3383
     E173 .D24 MRR Alc.

De Grazia, Edward. Censorship
landmarks. New York, Bowker, 1969.
xxxii, 657 p.   340   71-79424
     KF9444.A7 D4 MRR Alc.

A Documentary history of American
life. New York, McGraw-Hill [1966-
v.   973.08   66-1167
     E173 .D58 MRR Alc.

Documentary history of the First
Federal Congress of the United States
of America, March 4, 1789-March 3,
1791. [Baltimore, Johns Hopkins
University Press, 1972- v.
328.73 s 328.73/01   73-155164
     JK1059 1st .D6 MRR Alc.

Documents on American foreign
relations. 1938/39- New York, Simon
and Schuster [etc.]   39-28987
     JX231 .D6 MRR Alc Full set

Donnan, Elizabeth, ed. Documents
illustrative of the history of the
slave trade to America. New York,
Octagon Books, 1965. 4 v.
326.10973   65-15753
     E441 .D69 MRR Alc.

Eisenhower, Dwight David, Pres. U.S.,
The papers of Dwight David
Eisenhower; the war years.
Baltimore, Johns Hopkins Press [1970]
5 v.   940.54/012   65-27672
     D735 .E37 MRR Alc.

Elliot, Jonathan, ed. The debates in
the several State conventions on the
adoption of the Federal Constitution
as recommended by the general
convention at Philadelphia in 1787
... 2d ed., with considerable
additions. Philadelphia, Lippincott,
1937. 5 v.   342.73/02   mrr01-64
     JK141 1937 MRR Alc.

DOCUMENT SOURCES--UNITED STATES. (Cont.)
Ellis, John Tracy, ed. Documents of
American Catholic history. [2d ed.]
Milwaukee, Bruce Pub. Co. [1962]
xxii, 667 p.   282.73 62-12432
   BX1405 .E4 1962 MRR Alc.

English historical documents. [New
York, Oxford University Press, 195
v.   842 53-1506
   DA26 .E55 MRR Alc.

Ewing, Cortez Arthur Milton, comp.
Documentary source book in American
government and politics. Boston, New
York [etc.] D.C. Heath and company
[c1931] xx, 823 p.   342.738 31-
24918
   JK11 1931 MRR Alc.

Federalist. The Federalist. [1st
ed.] Middletown, Conn., Wesleyan
University Press [1961] xxx, 672 p.
342.733 61-6971
   JK154 1961b MRR Alc.

Federalist. The Federalist.
Cambridge, Mass., Belknap Press of
Harvard University Press, 1961.
viii, 572 p.   342.733 61-6355
   JK154 1961a MRR Alc.

Filler, Louis, ed. The President
speaks: New York, Putnam [1964] 416
p.   973.082 64-13025
   E173 .F5 MRR Alc.

Fillmore, Millard, pres. U.S.,
Millard Fillmore papers. Buffalo,
N.Y., The Buffalo historical society,
1907. 2 v.   08-10420
   E427 .F48 MRR Alc.

Fleming, Walter Lynwood, ed.
Documentary history of
Reconstruction: Gloucester, Mass.,
P. Smith, 1960 [c1935] 2 v. in 1
973.81082 60-52262
   E668 .F58 1960 MRR Alc.

Franklin, Benjamin, The papers of
Benjamin Franklin. New Haven, Yale
University Press, 1959- v.   081
59-12697
   E302 .F82 1959 MRR Alc.

Franklin, Benjamin, The writings of
Benjamin Franklin: New York, The
Macmillan company; London, Macmillan
& co., ltd., 1905-07. 10 v. 05-
35396
   E302 .F82 1905 MRR Alc.

Friedman, Leon, comp. The civil
rights reader: New York, Walker
[1967] xxi, 348 p. 323.4/0973 67-
13235
   E185.61 .F857 MRR Alc.

Furer, Howard B., comp.   James A.
Garfield, 1831-1881: Chester A.
Arthur, 1830-1886: Dobbs Ferry,
N.Y., Oceana Publications, 1970. v,
148 p.   973.8/4/0922 74-111214
   E660.G25 F8 MRR Alc.

Gantenbein, James Watson, ed.
Documentary background of World War
II. 1931-1941. New York, Columbia
Univ. Press, 1948. xxxiii, 1122 p.
940.52 48-11573
   D735 .G25 MRR Alc.

Gantenbein, James Watson, ed. The
evolution of our Latin-American
policy, New York, Columbia
University Press, 1950. xxvii, 979
p. 327.73098 49-50406
   F1418 .G2 MRR Alc.

Grant, Ulysses Simpson, Pres. U.S.,
The papers of Ulysses S. Grant.
Carbondale, Southern Illinois
University Press [1967- v.
973.8/2/0924 67-10725
   E660 .G74 MRR Alc.

Grant, Ulysses Simpson, Pres. U.S.,
Ulysses S. Grant, 1822-1885: Dobbs
Ferry, N.Y., Oceana Publications,
1968. 114 p. [$4.00] 973.8/2/08
68-23568
   E671 .M8 MRR Alc.

Greene, Jack P., comp. Colonies to
nation, 1763-1789: New York, McGraw-
Hill [1967] xvii, 583 p.   973.3/08
67-24438
   E173 .D58 vol. 2 MRR Alc.

Greene, Jack P., ed. Settlements to
society: 1584-1763, New York, McGraw-
Hill [1966] xiv, 386 p.   973.2 66-
22295
   E173 .D58 vol. 1 MRR Alc.

Griffin, Bulkley S., comp. Offbeat
history: Cleveland, World Pub. Co.
[1967] xiii, 360 p.   973 67-5205
   E173 .G87 MRR Alc.

Hamilton, Alexander, The works of
Alexander Hamilton, [Federal ed.]
New York, London, G. P. Putnam's
sons, 1904. 12 v.   04-19021
   E302 .H24 MRR Alc.

Handlin, Oscar, ed.   Readings in
American history. 2d ed. New York,
Knopf [1970] 2 v.   973/.08 77-
107455
   E173 .H23 1970 MRR Alc.

Hayes, Rutherford Birchard, Pres.
U.S., Rutherford B. Hayes, 1822-
1893: Dobbs Ferry, N.Y., Oceana
Publications, 1969. 90 p. [3.00]
973.8/3/0924 69-15394
   E681 .B59 MRR Alc.

Historic documents. 1972-
[Washington] Congressional Quarterly,
inc. [$25.00] 917.3/03/9205 72-
97888
   E839.5 .H57 MRR Alc Full set

Hofstadter, Richard, ed. American
higher education. [Chicago]
University of Chicago Press [1961] 2
v. 378.73 61-15935
   LA226 .H53 1961 MRR Alc.

Hofstadter, Richard, comp. American
violence: [1st ed.] New York,
Knopf, 1970. xiv, 478, xiii p.
[$10.00]   973 73-111238
   E179 .H8 1970 MRR Alc.

Hollingsworth, Joseph Rogers, ed.
American democracy: New York,
Crowell [1961-62] 2 v. 973.082 61-
16899
   E173 .H77 MRR Alc.

Huszar, George Bernard de, ed. Basic
American documents. Ames, Iowa,
Littlefield, Adams [c1953] 365 p.
973 52-14779
   E173 .H95 MRR Alc.

Ianniello, Lynne, ed. Milestones
along the march: New York, F. A.
Praeger [1965] xviii, 124 p.
323.408 65-24709
   E185.61 .I2 MRR Alc.

Jacobs, Paul, The new radicals: New
York, Random House [1966] 333 p.
320.973 66-18328
   E839.5 .J3 MRR Alc.

Jados, Stanley S., ed. Documents on
Russian-American relations,
Washington, Catholic University of
America Press [1965] viii, 416 p.
327.47073 65-12569
   E183.8.R9 J3 MRR Alc.

Jameson, John Franklin, ed.
Narratives of New Netherland, 1609-
1664: New York, C. Scribner's sons,
1909. xx p., 2 l., 3-478 p. 09-
24463
   E187.O7 J3 MRR Alc.

Jefferson, Thomas, Pres. U.S.,
Papers. Princeton, Princeton
University Press 1950- v.
[$20.00 (v. 18)]   308.1 50-7486
   E302 .J463 MRR Alc.

Jefferson, Thomas, pres. U.S., The
writings of Thomas Jefferson.
Library ed., Washington, D.C.,
Issued under the auspices of the
Thomas Jefferson memorial association
of the United States, 1903-04. 20 v.
353.03 14-3171
   E302 .J469 MRR Alc.

Johannsen, Robert Walter, comp.
Democracy on trial, 1845-1877; New
York, McGraw-Hill [1966] x, 405 p.
973.7 66-14534
   E173 .D58 vol. 4 MRR Alc.

Johnson, Donald Bruce, comp.
National party platforms, 1840-1972.
[5th. ed.] Urbana, University of
Illinois Press [c1973] xii, 889 p.
329/.0213/0973 73-81566
   JK2255 .J64 1973 MRR Alc.

Johnson, Lyndon Baines, Pres. U.S.,
A time for action: [1st ed.] New
York, Atheneum Publishers, 1964. xv,
183 p.   308.1 64-16425
   E742.5 .J6 MRR Alc.

Kahn, Frank J., comp. Documents of
American broadcasting. 2d ed. New
York, Appleton-Century-Crofts [1973]
xv, 684 p. 343/.73/0994 72-12050
   KF2804 .K3 1973 MRR Alc.

Katz, William Loren, comp.
Eyewitness: New York, Pitman Pub.
Corp. [1967] xix, 554 p.
301.451/96/073 67-10838
   E185 .K28 MRR Alc.

Kavenagh, W. Keith. Foundations of
colonial America: New York, Chelsea
House, 1973. 3 v. [$95.00]
325/.342/0973 72-80866
   JK49 .K38 MRR Alc.

Kennedy, John Fitzgerald, Pres. U.S.,
Kennedy and the press: New York,
Crowell [1965] 555 p. 973.922 65-
12271
   E841 .K37 MRR Alc.

Kraditor, Aileen S., comp. Up from
the pedestal: Chicago, Quadrangle
Books [1968] 372 p. [$8.95]
301.41/2/0973 68-26443
   HQ1410 .K7 MRR Alc.

Krooss, Herman Edward, comp.
Documentary history of banking and
currency in the United States. New
York, Chelsea House Publishers [1969]
4 v. (xlii, 3232 p.) 332/.0973 69-
16011
   HG2461 .K76 MRR Alc.

Langsam, Walter Consuelo, ed.
Historic documents of World War II.
Princeton, N.J., Van Nostrand [1958]
192 p. 940.53082 58-14435
   D735 .L3 MRR Alc.

Leopold, Richard William, ed.
Problems in American history. 2d ed.
Englewood Cliffs, N.J., Prentice-
Hall, 1957. 706 p. 973 57-6544
   E178 .L5 1957 MRR Alc.

Letwin, William, ed. A documentary
history of American economic policy
since 1789. Chicago, Aldine Pub. Co.
(1964, c1961] 406 p. 338.973 62-
14752
   HC103 .L37 1964 MRR Alc.

Lincoln, Charles Henry, ed.
Narratives of the Indian wars, 1675-
1699: New York, C. Scribner's sons,
1913. xii p., 2 l., 3-316 p.
[$3.00]   13-24819
   E187.O7 L5 MRR Alc.

Madison, James, Pres. U.S., The
complete Madison: [1st ed.] New
York, Harper [1953] xi, 361 p.
308.1 53-5445
   E302 .M17 MRR Alc.

Madison, James, pres. U.S., Letters
and other writings of James Madison.
Philadelphia, J. B. Lippincott & co.,
1865. 4 v.   06-24330
   E302 .M18 MRR Alc.

Madison, James, Pres. U.S., Papers.
Chicago] University of Chicago Press
[1962- v.   923.173 62-9114
   E302 .M19 MRR Alc.

Manning, William Ray, ed.
Arbitration treaties among the
American nations, to the close of the
year 1910, New York [etc.] Oxford
university press, 1924. xl, 472 p.
24-6749
   JX1985 .M3 MRR Alc.

May, Ernest R., ed. Anxiety and
affluence: 1945-1965, New York,
McGraw-Hill [1966] xii, 404 p.
973.908 66-14810
   E173 .D58 vol. 8 MRR Alc.

McKee, Thomas Hudson. The national
conventions and platforms of all
political parties, 1789 to 1905; New
York, B. Franklin [1971] 414, 33 p.
329/.02 75-132682
   JK2255 .M2 1971 MRR Alc.

McPherson, Edward, The political
history of the United States of
America during the period of
reconstruction, (from April 15, 1865,
to July 15, 1870,) 2d ed.
Washington, Solomons & Chapman, 1875.
v, 6-9, 648 p.   04-7498
   E668 .M17 MRR Alc.

Mearns, David Chambers, The Lincoln
papers: [1st ed.] Garden City,
N.Y., Doubleday, 1948. 2 v. (xvii,
681 p.) 973.7 48-9019
   E457.92 1948 MRR Alc.

Miller, John Chester, ed. The
colonial image: New York, G.
Braziller, 1962. 500 p. 973.2 62-
8930
   E187.O7 M5 MRR Alc.

Mode, Peter George. Source book and
bibliographical guide for American
church history, Menasha, Wis.,
George Banta publishing company
[c1921] xxiv, 735 p. 22-3718
   BR514 .M6 MRR Alc.

Monroe, James, Pres. U.S., James
Monroe, 1758-1831: Dobbs Ferry,
N.Y., Oceana Publications, 1969. 86
p. [3.00] 973.5/4/0924 69-15393
   E371 .E4 MRR Alc.

Monroe, James, Pres. U.S., The
writings of James Monroe, including a
collection of his public and private
papers and correspondence, now for
the first time printed. New York,
AMS Press [1969] 7 v. 973.5/4 69-
18218
   E302 .M74 1969 MRR Alc.

Moore, Frank, comp. The diary of the
American Revolution, 1775-1781. New
York, Washington Square Press, 1967.
xxxiv, 605 p. 973.3 66-22119
   E203 .M68 1967 MRR Alc.

DOCUMENT SOURCES--UNITED STATES. (Cont.)
Moquin, Wayne, comp. A documentary
history of the Mexican Americans.
New York, Praeger [1971] xiv, 399 p.
[$13.50] 973.04/687/2 78-101671
   E184.M5 M63 1971 MRR Alc.

Morris, Richard Brandon, comp. The
American Revolution, 1763-1783; New
York, Harper & Row [1970] xix, 361
p. [$2.95] 973.3 70-20960
   E203 .M87 MRR Alc.

Morris, Richard Brandon, Great
Presidential decisions; New and enl.
ed. New York, Harper & Row [1973]
508 p. [$1.50] 973 73-176031
   E173 .M93 1973 MRR Alc.

The Negro in American History.
[Chicago] Encyclopaedia Britannica
Educational Corp. [1969] 3 v.
973/.0974/96 68-56369
   E185 .N4 MRR Alc.

Nixon, Richard Milhous, Nixon; the
fourth year of his Presidency.
Washington, Congressional Quarterly
[c1973] 46, 146 p. [$4.00]
320.9/73/0924 72-94077
   E855 .N494 MRR Alc.

Nixon, Richard Milhous, The White
House transcripts; New York, Viking
Press [1974] ix, 877 p. [$15.00]
364.1/32/0973 74-8869
   E860 .N57 1974c MRR Alc.

The Northmen, Columbus and Cabot, 985-
1503; New York, C. Scribner's sons,
1906. xv, 443 p. 973.1 06-36882
   E187.07 N6 MRR Alc.

Pierce, Franklin, Pres. U.S.,
Franklin Pierce, 1804-1869; Dobbs
Ferry, N.Y., Oceana Publications,
1968. v, 90 p. 973.6/6/08 68-
21539
   E415.6 .P6 1968 MRR Alc.

Platt, Anthony M., comp. The
politics of riot commissions, 1917-
1970; New York, Macmillan [1971] x,
534 p. 364.14/3 79-150069
   HV6477 .P5 MRR Alc.

Plischke, Elmer, Conduct of American
diplomacy. 3d ed. Princeton, N.J.,
Van Nostrand [1967] xvii, 677 p.
353.008/82 67-6536
   JX1407 .P58 1967 MRR Alc.

Ploski, Harry A. Afro USA; [New
York] Bellwether Pub. Co.;
distributed by Afro-American Press
[1971] 1110 p. 301.45/19/60730022
70-151238
   E185 .P55 1971 MRR Ref Desk.

Ploski, Harry A. The Negro almanac,
[1st ed.] New York, Bellwether Pub.
Co. [1967] xi, 1012 p. 973 66-
29721
   E185 .P55 MRR Ref Desk.

Presbyterian Church in the U.S.A.
General Assembly. A digest of the
acts and proceedings of the General
Assembly of the Presbyterian Church
in the United States, 1861-1965.
Atlanta, 1966. ix, 489 p. 262.9851
66-50073
   BX8956 .A5 1966a MRR Alc.

Ratner, Sidney, The tariff in
American history. New York, Van
Nostrand [c1972] viii, 214 p.
382.7/0973 72-7968
   HF1753 .R37 MRR Alc.

The Rebellion record; New York, G.
P. Putnam, 1861-63; D. Van Nostrand,
1864-68. 11 v. 02-9069
   E468 .R29 MRR Alc.

Rollins, Alfred Brooks, ed.
Depression, recovery, and war, 1929-
1945, New York, McGraw-Hill [1966]
xii, 404 p. 973.9108 66-14813
   E173 .D58 vol. 7 MRR Alc.

Romero, Patricia W., comp. I too am
America; [1st ed.] New York,
Publishers Co. [1968] xv, 304 p.
973 68-56836
   E185 .R76 MRR Alc.

Roosevelt, Franklin Delano, Pres.
U.S., The public papers and
addresses of Franklin D. Roosevelt,
New York, Random House, 1938-[50] 13
v. 973.917 38-11227
   E806 .R749 MRR Alc.

Schappes, Morris Urman, ed. A
documentary history of the Jews in
the United States, 1654-1875. 3d
ed.; [1st Schocken ed.] New York,
Schocken Books [1971] xxiv, 766 p.
917.3/06/824 72-122332
   E184.J5 S35 1971 MRR Alc.

Schlesinger, Arthur Meier, comp. The
dynamics of world power; New York,
Chelsea House Publishers, 1973- v.
[$149.00] 327.73 78-150208
   E744 .S395 MRR Alc.

Schlesinger, Arthur Meier, History
of American presidential elections,
1789-1968. New York, Chelsea House
[1971] 4 v. (xxxvii, 3959 p.)
329/.023/73 70-139269
   E183 .S28 MRR Alc.

Schlesinger, Arthur Meier, History
of U.S. political parties. New York,
Chelsea House Publishers, 1973. 4 v.
(liv, 3544 p.) 329/.02 72-8682
   JK2261 .S35 MRR Alc.

Schwartz, Bernard, comp. The Bill of
Rights: a documentary history. New
York, Chelsea House Publishers, 1971.
2 v. (xvii, 1234 p.) 342/.73/029
71-150209
   KF4744 1971 MRR Alc.

Seide, Katharine, comp. A dictionary
of arbitration and its terms; labor,
commercial, international; Dobbs
Ferry, N.Y., Published for the
Eastman Library of the American
Arbitration Association, by Oceana
Publications, 1970. xviii, 334 p.
[15.00] 331.15/5/03 70-94692
   KF9085 .A68S4 MRR Alc.

Shannon, David A., ed. Progressivism
and postwar disillusionment, 1898-
1928, New York, McGraw-Hill [1966]
383 p. 973.9108 65-26768
   E173 .D58 vol. 6 MRR Alc.

Smith, Hilrie Shelton, American
Christianity; New York, Scribner
[1960-63] 2 v. 277.3 60-8117
   BR514 .S55 MRR Alc.

State papers and publick documents of
the United States, from the accession
of George Washington to the
presidency, exhibiting a complete
view of our foreign relations since
that time. 3d ed. Boston, Printed
and published by Thomas B. Wait,
1819. 12 v. 27-5174
   J33 .W4 MRR Alc.

Teodori, Massimo, comp. The new
left; Indianapolis, Bobbs-Merrill
[1969] xiv, 501 p. [9.95]
301.15/3/0973 70-81291
   HN59 .T46 MRR Alc.

Thorpe, Francis Newton. comp. The
Federal and State constitutions,
colonial charters, and other organic
laws of the state, territories, and
colonies now or heretofore forming
the United States of America.
Washington, Govt. Print. Off., 1909.
7 v. 09-35371
   KF4541 .T48 MRR Alc.

Truman, Harry S., Pres. U.S., The
Truman administration, New York, New
York University Press, 1956. xii,
394 p. 973.918 56-7425
   E813 .T68 MRR Alc.

Tyler, Lyon Gardiner, The letters
and times of the Tylers. New York,
Da Capo Press, 1970 [c1884-86] 3 v.
973.5/8 71-75267
   E397 .T982 MRR Alc.

United States. Federal register. v.
1- March 14, 1936- [Washington,
U.S. Govt. Print. off.] 353.005 36-
26264
   J1 .A2 MRR Alc (Dk 33) Full set

United States. 1st Congress, 1789-
1791. Senate. Senate executive
Journal and related documents.
Baltimore, Johns Hopkins University
Press [1974] xvii, 574 p.
328.73/073 73-13443
   JK1059 1st .D6 vol. 2 MRR Alc.

United States. Bureau of rolls and
library. Documentary history of the
Constitution of the United States of
America, 1786-1870. Washington,
Department of state, 1894 [i.e. 1901]-
05. 5 v. 02-10164
   JK111 .A52 MRR Alc.

United States. Congress. American
state papers. Washington, Gales and
Seaton, 1832-61. 38 v. 09-33892
   J33 MRR Alc.

United States. Congress. House.
Committee on Foreign Affairs.
Collective defense treaties, with
maps, texts of treaties, a
chronology, status of forces
agreements, and comparative chart.
Rev.] Washington, U.S. Govt. Print.
Off., 1969. ix, 514 p. [2.50]
341.2 79-602271
   JX171 .U39 1969 MRR Alc.

United States. Congress. Senate.
Committee on Foreign Relations. A
decade of American foreign policy;
Washington, U.S. Govt. Print. Off.,
1950. xiv, 1381 p. 327.73 50-
60544
   JX1416 .A47 MRR Alc.

United States. Constitution
sesquicentennial commission. History
of the formation of the union under
the Constitution [Washington, U.S.
Govt. print. off., 1941] x, 885 p.
incl. front., illus. (1 col.; incl.
maps) ports., facsims., tables,
diagrs. 342.73 41-50348
   JK166 1941 MRR Alc.

United States. Constitutional
convention, 1787. The records of the
Federal convention of 1787; Rev. ed.
New Haven, Yale university press;
London, H. Milford, Oxford university
press, 1937. 4 v. 342.732 37-
25324
   KF4510 .F3 1937 MRR Alc.

United States. Continental congress.
Journals of the American congress:
from 1774 to 1788. Washington;
Printed and published by Way and
Gideon, 1823. 4 v. 17-23718
   J10 .A3 MRR Alc.

United States. Dept. of State. The
China white paper, August 1949.
Stanford, Calif., Stanford University
Press [1967] xli, 1079 p.
327.51/073 67-26650
   E183.8.C5 U53 1967 MRR Alc.

United States. Dept. of State.
Foreign relations of the United
States. [1861]- Washington, U.S.
Govt. Print. Off. 327.73 10-3793
   JX233 .A3 MRR Alc Full set

United States. Dept. of State. The
Soviet Union, 1933-1939. Washington,
U.S. Govt. Print. Off., 1952. cii,
1034 p. 327.730947 52-61069
   JX233.A6R93 MRR Alc.

United States. Dept. of State.
Historical Office. American foreign
policy; 1956- [Washington] 327.73
59-64042
   JX1417 .A33 MRR Alc Full set

United States. Dept. of State.
Historical Office. American foreign
policy, 1950-1955; Washington, U.S.
Govt. Print. Off., 1957.] 2 v. (lix,
3244, xxv p.) 327.73 sd 57-10
   JX1417 .A55 MRR Alc.

United States. Dept. of State.
Historical Office. China, 1942-
Washington, U.S. Govt. Print. Off.,
1956- v. 327.73051 57-61196
   JX1428.C6 A54 MRR Alc.

United States. Dept. of State.
Historical Office. Documents on
Germany, 1944-1961. Washington, U.S.
Govt. Print. Off., 1961. xv, 833 p.
62-60800
   DD257 .U476 1961 MRR Alc.

United States. Laws, statutes, etc.
Indian affairs. Laws and treaties.
Washington, Govt. print. off., 1903-
41. 5 v. 342/.73/087 03-13067
   KF8203 1903 MRR Alc.

United States. Laws, statutes, etc.
Laws of the United States concerning
money, banking, and loans, 1778-1909;
Washington, Govt. print. off., 1910.
v, 267 p., 1 l., 269-812, xxii p.
10-36032
   HG481 .A2 1910 MRR Alc.

United States. Laws, statutes, etc.
United States statutes at large,
containing the laws and concurrent
resolutions ... and reorganization
plan, amendment to the Constitution,
and proclamations. v. 1- 1789/1845-
Washington, U.S. Govt. Print. Off.
07-35353
   LAW MRR Alc (Dk 33) Full set

United States. Library of Congress.
Legislative reference service.
Documents illustrative of the
formation of the union of the
American states. Washington, Govt.
print. off., 1927. x, 1115 p. 27-
26258
   JK11 1927 MRR Alc.

United States. Library of Congress.
Manuscript Division. Naval records
of the American revolution, 1775-
1788. Washington, Govt. print. off.,
1906. 549 p. 06-35020
   Z1238 .U58 MRR Alc.

United States. Naval History
Division. Naval documents of the
American Revolution. Washington [For
sale by the Supt. of Docs., U.S.
Govt. Print. Off.] 1964- v. 64-
60087
   E271 .U583 MRR Alc.

United States. President. The Chief
Executive; New York, Crown
Publishers [1965] viii, 312 p.
353.035 65-24323
   J81 .C65 MRR Alc.

DOCUMENT SOURCES--UNITED STATES. (Cont.)
United States. President. A compilation of the messages and papers of the presidents. New York, Bureau of national literature, inc. [1917?] 20 v.   353.03   17-7545
J81 .B97a MRR Alc.

United States. President. The Presidents speak; the inaugural addresses of the American Presidents, from Washington to Nixon. [3d ed.] New York, Holt, Rinehart and Winston [1969]   xi, 308 p.   [10.00]   973   71-80344
J81 .C62 1969 MRR Alc.

United States. President. Public papers of the Presidents of the United States, containing the public messages, speeches, and statements of the President. Washington, U.S. Govt. Print. Off.   353.03   58-61050
J80 .A283 MRR Alc Full set

United States. President. The State of the Union messages of the Presidents, 1790-1966. New York, Chelsea House, 1966. 3 v. (xii, 3264 p.)   353.035   66-20309
J81 .C66 MRR Alc.

United States. President, 1901-1909 (Roosevelt) Theodore Roosevelt, 1858-1919; Dobbs Ferry, N.Y., Oceana Publications, 1968. 120 p. [4.00] 971.91/1/0924   69-15392
E756 .U68 MRR Alc.

United States. President, 1929-1933 (Hoover) Herbert Hoover : Washington : U.S. Govt. Print. Off., 1974. 2 v. (iii, 1566 p.) : [$24.55   353.03/5   74-602466
J82 .D5 1974 MRR Alc.

United States. Treaties, etc. Treaties and other international acts of the United States of America. Washington, U.S. Govt. Print. Off., 1931-   v.   341.273   31-28592
JX236 1931a MRR Alc.

United States. Treaties, etc. Treaties and other international agreements of the United States of America, 1776-1949. [Washington, Dept. of State; for sale by the Supt. of Docs., U.S. Govt. Print. Off.] 1968-   v.   [8.50 (v. 1) varies] 341/.0264/73   70-600742
JX236 1968 .A5 MRR Alc.

United States. Treaties, etc. Treaties, conventions, international acts, protocols and agreements between the United States of America and other powers ... Grosse Pointe, Mich., Scholarly Press [1970?] 4 v. (xxvi, 5755 p.)   341.2/73   78-121307

JX236 1910c MRR Alc.

United States. Treaties, etc. United States treaties and other international agreements. v. 1-1950-   [Washington] Dept. of State. 341.273   53-60242
JX231 .A34 MRR Alc Full set

Van Buren, Martin, Pres. U.S., Martin Van Buren, 1782-1862; Dobbs Ferry, N.Y., Oceana Publications, 1969. 116 p. [4.00]   973.5/7/0924   69-15391
E386 .S55 MRR Alc.

Washburn, Wilcomb E., comp. The American Indian and the United States; [1st ed.] New York, Random House [1973] 4 v. (xiv, 3119 p.) 970.5   72-10259
E93 .W27 MRR Alc.

Washington, George, Pres. U.S., The Washington papers; [1st ed.] New York, Harper [1955] 430 p.   308.1 54-12149
E312.72   1955 MRR Alc.

Washington, George, pres. U.S., The writings of George Washington from the original manuscript sources, 1745-1799; Washington, U.S. Govt. print. off. [1931-44] 39 v.   308   32-11075

E312.7 1931 MRR Alc.

Webster's guide to American history; Springfield, Mass., G. & C. Merriam Co. [1971] 1428 p.   973   76-24114
E174.5 .W4 MRR Ref Desk.

Weekly compilation of Presidential documents. v. 1-   Aug. 2, 1965-[Washington, Office of the Federal Register; distributed by Supt. of Docs., Govt. Print. Off.]   65-9929
J80 .A284 MRR Alc Partial set

Whitson, Robley Edward. Shaker theological sources; Bethlehem, Conn., United Institute, 1969. ix, 52 l.   230.9/8   77-13052
BX9771 .W53 MRR Alc.

Wilson, Thomas Williams. International environmental action; [New York] Dunellen [1971]   xviii, 364 p.   [$12.50]   301.3/1   73-168684

HC79.E5 W53 MRR Alc.

Wilson, Woodrow, Pres. U.S., 1856-1924. The papers of Woodrow Wilson. Princeton, N.J., Princeton University Press, 1966-   v.   [$20.00 per vol.]   973.91/3/0924   66-10880
E660 .W717 MRR Alc.

DOCUMENT SOURCES--VIETNAM.
Fall, Bernard B., The two Viet-Nams; 2d rev. ed. New York, Praeger [1967] xii, 507 p.   959.7   66-14505

DS557.A5 F34 1967 MRR Alc.

Raskin, Marcus G., ed. The Viet-Nam reader; New York, Random House [1965] xv, 415 p.   959.704   65-26331
DS557.A6 R3 MRR Alc.

DOCUMENT SOURCES--VIRGINIA.
Tyler, Lyon Gardiner, ed. Narratives of early Virginia, 1606-1625; New York, C. Scribner's sons, 1907. xv, 478 p.   07-33220
E187.O7 T9 MRR Alc.

Virginia company of London. The records of the Virginia company of London ... Washington, Govt. print. off., 1906-35. 4 v.   06-35006
Z663 .R38 MRR Alc.

DOCUMENT SOURCES--WEST INDIES, BRITISH.
Burns, Alan Cuthbert, Sir, History of the British West Indies [Rev. 2d ed.] London, Allen and Unwin [1965] 849 p.   66-174
F2131 .B96 1965 MRR Alc.

DOCUMENTATION.
see also Files and filing (Documents)

see also Indexing

see also Information services

Schweizerische Vereinigung für Dokumentation. Archiv, Bibliotheken und Dokumentationsstellen der Schweiz. 3. Aufl. Bern, 1958. xvi, 144 p.   59-45785
Z837 .S44 1958 MRR Alc.

DOCUMENTATION--BIBLIOGRAPHY.
Schutze, Gertrude. Documentation source book. New York, Scarecrow Press, 1965. 554 p.   016.02   65-13551
Z666 .S37 MRR Alc.

Western Reserve University, Cleveland. Center for Documentation and Communication Research. A selected bibliography of documentation & information retrieval. [Rev.] Cleveland, 1964. 10 l.   65-5680
Z699.2 .W4 1964 MRR Alc.

Zell, Hans M. An international bibliography of non-periodical literature on documentation & information. Oxford, R. Maxwell [1965] vi, 294 p.   016.0297   66-2713
Z699.2 .Z4 MRR Alc.

DOCUMENTATION--PERIODICALS.
Current research and development in scientific documentation. July 1957-1969. Washington.   010.78   58-2427
Z699.5.S3 C8 Sci RR Latest edition / MRR Alc Partial set

DOCUMENTATION--PERIODICALS--BIBLIOGRAPHY.
International Federation for Documentation. Library and documentation journals. 2d rev. ed. Hague, 1961. 30 p.   63-52506
Z666 .I55 1961 MRR Alc.

DOCUMENTATION--STUDY AND TEACHING.
United Nations Educational, Scientific and Cultural Organization. World guide to library schools and training courses in documentation. Paris, Unesco, London, Clive Bingley [1972] 245 p.   [3 British pounds] 020/./11   73-155165
Z668 .U56 MRR Alc.

DOCUMENTS LIBRARIANS--UNITED STATES--DIRECTORIES.
Shaw, Elizabeth Miller. Directory of documents librarians in the United States. Chicago, RSD/RTSD Interdivisional Committee on Public Documents, American Library Association, 1967. 93 p.   020/.922   78-23647
Z675.D4 S55 MRR Biog.

DOCUMENTS ON MICROFILM--BIBLIOGRAPHY.
Hale, Richard Walden, ed. Guide to photocopied historical materials in the United States and Canada. Ithaca, N.Y., published for the American Historical Association [by] Cornell University Press [1961] xxxiv, 241 p.   016.9   61-17269
Z6209 .H3 MRR Alc.

United States. Library of Congress. A guide to the microfilm collection of early state records, [Washington] Library of Congress, Photoduplication Service, 1950. 1 v. (various pagings)   016.01573   50-62956
Z663.96 .G8 MRR Alc.

DOCUMENTS ON MICROFILM--INDEXES.
Lester, Daniel W. Departmental keyword indexes to U.S. Government author-organizations, Washington, United States Historical Documents Institute, 1972. xxxiii, 959 p.   015.73 s   72-2109
Z1223.Z7 L45 vol. 3 MRR Ref Desk.

Lester, Daniel W. Master keyword index to the publication-issuing offices of the U.S. Government, 1789-1970, Washington, United States Historical Documents Institute, 1972. xxxiii, 855 p.   015.73 s   72-2110
Z1223.Z7 L45 vol. 5 MRR Ref Desk.

Lester, Daniel W. Superintendent of Documents classification number index of U.S. Government author-organization. Washington, United States Historical Documents Institute, 1972. xxxiii, 312 p. 015.73 s   72-2107
Z1223.Z7 L45 vol. 1 MRR Ref Desk.

United States Historical Documents Institute. U.S. Government author-organization index, 1789-1970. Washington [1972]   p.   015.73 s   72-2108
Z1223.Z7 L45 vol. 2 MRR Ref Desk.

United States Historical Documents Institute. 1789-1970; Washington [1972] xii, 527 p.   015.73 s   74-190737
Z1223.Z7 L45 vol. 4 MRR Ref Desk.

DOG BREEDS.
American Kennel Club. The complete dog book; New rev. ed. New York, Howell Book House [1972] 640 p. 636.7   72-88163
SF427 .A57 1972 MRR Alc.

Fiorone, Fiorenzo. The encyclopedia of dogs: the canine breeds. New York, Crowell [1973]   447 p. [$25.00]   636.7   73-6979
SF429.A1 F5413 MRR Alc.

Hamilton, Ferelith. The world encyclopedia of dogs. 1st American ed.] New York, World Pub. Co. [1971] 672 p.   [$20.00]   636.7/1   72-158530
SF429.A1 H28 1971 MRR Alc.

The New dog encyclopedia. Harrisburg, Pa., Stackpole Books [1970] 736 p.   [24.95]   636.7   78-102380
SF426 .N47 1970 MRR Alc.

DOGS.
American Kennel Club. The complete dog book; New rev. ed. New York, Howell Book House [1972] 640 p. 636.7   72-88163
SF427 .A57 1972 MRR Alc.

Bernstein, Susan. Dog digest. Northfield, Ill., Digest Books [1972] 320 p.   [$5.95]   636.7   72-189000
SF427 .B519 1972 MRR Alc.

The New dog encyclopedia. Harrisburg, Pa., Stackpole Books [1970] 736 p.   [24.95]   636.7   78-102380
SF426 .N47 1970 MRR Alc.

DOGS--DICTIONARIES.
Dangerfield, Stanley, The international encyclopedia of dogs. New York, McGraw-Hill [1971] 480 p. [$19.95]   636.7/003   70-161547
SF422 .D28 MRR Alc.

DOLL-HOUSES--HISTORY.
Jacobs, Flora Gill. A history of dolls' houses. New York, Scribner [1965] x, 342 p.   745.5923   65-24648
NK4894.A2 J3 1965 MRR Alc.

DOLLAR.
Nussbaum, Arthur, A history of the dollar. New York, Columbia University Press, 1957. 308 p. 332.4973   57-11693
HG501 .N8 MRR Alc.

DOLLMAKERS.
Coleman, Elizabeth A. Dolls: makers
and marks, [2d, rev. ed.]
Washington 1966- v.
745.59/22/09 66-25627
NK4894.A2 C62 MRR Alc.

DOLLS.
St. George, Eleanor. The dolls of
yesterday. New York, C. Scribner's
Sons, 1948. xvii, 204 p. 649.55
48-6042
GV1219 .S3 MRR Alc.

DOLLS--COLLECTORS AND COLLECTING.
Coleman, Dorothy S. The collector's
encyclopedia of dolls. New York,
Crown Publishers [1968] 697 p.
[25.00] 745.59/22/03 68-9101
NK4893 .C6 MRR Alc.

Smith, Patricia R. Modern
collector's dolls, 1st ed. Paducah,
Ky., Collector Books, c1973. iv, 309
p. [$17.95] 745.59/22 74-160943
NK4893 .S64 MRR Alc.

DOLLS--DICTIONARIES.
Coleman, Dorothy S. The collector's
encyclopedia of dolls. New York,
Crown Publishers [1968] 697 p.
[25.00] 745.59/22/03 68-9101
NK4893 .C6 MRR Alc.

DOLLS--HISTORY.
Coleman, Elizabeth A. Dolls: makers
and marks, [2d, rev. ed.]
Washington, 1966- v.
745.59/22/09 66-25627
NK4894.A2 C62 MRR Alc.

White, Gwen. European and American
dolls and their marks and patents.
London, Batsford, 1966. 3-274 p.
[£7/7/-] 745.592209 66-76549
NK4894.A2 W46 MRR Alc.

DOLLS--TRADE-MARKS.
Coleman, Elizabeth A. Dolls: makers
and marks, [2d, rev. ed.]
Washington, 1966- v.
745.59/22/09 66-25627
NK4894.A2 C62 MRR Alc.

White, Gwen. European and American
dolls and their marks and patents.
London, Batsford, 1966. 3-274 p.
[£7/7/-] 745.592209 66-76549
NK4894.A2 W46 MRR Alc.

DOMESTIC ANIMALS.
see also Cats

see also Dogs

see also Horses

see also Pets

DOMESTIC ANIMALS--DICTIONARIES.
Mason, Ian Lauder. A world
dictionary of livestock breeds, types
and varieties, 2nd (revised) ed.
Farnham Royal, Commonwealth
Agricultural Bureaux, 1969. xviii,
268 p. [70/-] 636/.003 75-454433
SF21 .M3 1969 MRR Alc.

DOMESTIC ANIMALS--DISEASES
see Veterinary medicine

DOMESTIC APPLIANCES
see Household appliances

DOMESTIC ARCHITECTURE
see Architecture, Domestic

DOMESTIC EDUCATION.
see also Children--Management

DOMESTIC ENGINEERING.
see also Plumbing

Household equipment 6th ed. New
York, Wiley [1970] xiv, 540 p.
643/.6 76-116772
TX298 .H68 1970 MRR Alc.

DOMESTIC ENGINEERING--DIRECTORIES.
D E catalog directory. 1923-
[Chicago, Medalist Publications,
etc.] 22-21100
TH6112 .D6 Sci RR Latest edition /
MRR Alc Latest edition

DOMESTIC RELATIONS.
see also Family

DOMESTIC SCIENCE
see Home economics

DOMINICAN REPUBLIC.
Wiarda, Howard J., The Dominican
Republic; New York, F. A. Praeger
[1969] viii, 249 p. [7.00]
917.293/03/5 69-12717
F1934 .W5 MRR Alc.

DOMINICAN REPUBLIC--POLITICS AND GOVERNMENT.
Operations and Policy Research, inc.,
Washington, D.C. Institute for the
Comparative Study of Political
Systems. Dominican Republic election
factbook, [Washington, 1966] 55 p.
324.2097293 66-23504
JL1138 .06 MRR Alc.

DOMINICANS--BIBLIOGRAPHY.
Daley, Charles Marie, Dominican
incunabula in the Library of
Congress, [New York, United States
Catholic historical society, 1932]
88 p. 016.093 33-476
Z240 .U58 1932 MRR Alc.

DONNE, JOHN, 1573-1631--CONCORDANCES.
Combs, Homer Carroll. A concordance
to the English poems of John Donne,
New York, Haskell House, 1969. ix,
418 p. 821/.3 74-92960
PR2248 .A3 1969 MRR Alc.

DORTMUND--DIRECTORIES.
Dortmunder Adressbuch. Dortmund, W.
Cruwell. 53-30689
DD901.D6 D6 MRR Alc Latest edition

DOVER, ENG.--DIRECTORIES.
Kelly's directory of Dover and
neighbourhood. Kingston upon Thames,
Surrey [etc.] Kelly's Directories
Limited. 53-28318
DA690.D7 K4 MRR Alc Latest edition

DOYLE, ARTHUR CONAN, SIR, 1859-1930--DICTIONARIES, INDEXES, ETC.
Christ, Jay Finley, An irregular
guide to Sherlock Holmes of Baker
Street. New York, Argus Books, 1947.
118 p. 823.91 48-3066
PR4623.A3 C5 MRR Alc.

DRAFT, MILITARY
see Military service, Compulsory

DRAGONS.
Fontenrose, Joseph Eddy, Python; a
study of Delphic myth and its
origins. Berkeley, University of
California Press, 1959. xviii, 616
p. 398.4 59-5144
GR830.D7 F6 MRR Alc.

DRAMA.
see also Characters and
characteristics in literature

see also Children's plays

see also English drama

see also Puppets and puppet-plays

see also Theater

Tennyson, G. B. An introduction to
drama New York, Holt, Rinehart and
Winston [c1967] viii, 134 p.
808.82 67-10599
PN1655 .T4 MRR Alc.

DRAMA--19TH CENTURY--DICTIONARIES.
Matlaw, Myron, Modern world drama;
[1st ed.] New York, Dutton, 1972.
xxi, 960 p. [$25.00] 809.2/34 71-
185032
PN1851 .M36 MRR Alc.

DRAMA--20TH CENTURY.
The Best plays. 1894/99- New York
[etc.] Dodd, Mead [etc.] 812.5082
20-21432
PN6112 .B45 MRR Alc Partial set

Kienzle, Siegfried, Modern world
theater; New York, Ungar [1970] v,
509 p. [12.50] 808.82 73-98342
PN6112.5 .K513 MRR Alc.

DRAMA--20TH CENTURY--DICTIONARIES.
Crowell's handbook of contemporary
drama, New York, Crowell [1971] vi,
505 p. [$10.00] 809.2/04 79-
158714
PN1861 .C7 MRR Alc.

Matlaw, Myron, Modern world drama;
[1st ed.] New York, Dutton, 1972.
xxi, 960 p. [$25.00] 809.2/34 71-
185032
PN1851 .M36 MRR Alc.

DRAMA--20TH CENTURY--HISTORY AND CRITICISM.
Atkinson, Justin Brooks, The lively
years, 1920-1973 New York,
Association Press [1973] viii, 312
p. [$12.50] 792/.09747/1 73-14659
PN2277.N5 A85 MRR Alc.

Clark, Barrett Harper, ed. A history
of modern drama. New York, D.
Appleton-Century Co. [1947] xii, 832
p. 809.2 47-11445
PN1861 .C55 MRR Alc.

Melchinger, Siegfried. The concise
encyclopedia of modern drama.
London, Vision P., 1966. 288 p.
[70/-] 792.03 66-73655
PN1861 .M4 1966 MRR Alc.

DRAMA--20TH CENTURY--HISTORY AND CRITICISM--BIBLIOGRAPHY.
Adelman, Irving, comp. Modern drama;
Metuchen, N.J., Scarecrow Press,
1967. xvii, 370 p. 016.808/2/04
67-10189
Z5781 .A35 MRR Ref Desk.

DRAMA--20TH CENTURY--HISTORY AND CRITICISM--INDEXES.
Breed, Paul Francis, Dramatic
criticism index; Detroit, Gale
Research Co. [1972] 1022 p.
016.8092/04 79-127598
Z5781 .B8 MRR Ref Desk.

DRAMA--20TH CENTURY--INDEXES.
Guernsey, Otis L., Directory of the
American theater, 1894-1971; New
York, Dodd, Mead [1871] vi, 343 p.
[$25.00] 812/.5708 71-180734
PN6112 .B4524 MRR Alc.

DRAMA--20TH CENTURY--STORIES, PLOTS, ETC.
Sprinchorn, Evert, ed. 20th-century
plays in synopsis. New York, T. Y.
Crowell Co. [1966, c1965] xii, 493
p. 808.8204 65-21412
PN6112.5 .S68 MRR Alc.

DRAMA--BIBLIOGRAPHY.
American Educational Theatre
Association. Theatre arts
publications available in the United
States, 1953-1957; Evanston? Ill.,
c1964] xiii, 188 p. 65-3361
Z5781 .A52 MRR Alc.

Baker, Blanch (Merritt) Theatre and
allied arts; New York, Wilson, 1952.
xiii, 536 p. 016.792 52-6756
Z5781 .B18 MRR Alc.

The Best plays. 1894/99- New York
[etc.] Dodd, Mead [etc.] 812.5082
20-21432
PN6112 .B45 MRR Alc Partial set

Brockett, Oscar Gross, A
bibliographical guide to research in
speech and dramatic art Chicago,
Scott, Foresman [1963] 118 p. 016
63-14554
Z1002 .B87 MRR Alc.

Chicorel, Marietta. Chicorel
bibliography to the performing arts.
1st ed. New York, Chicorel Library
Pub. Corp. [1972] 498 p. 016.7902
73-155102
Z6935 .C45 MRR Alc.

Chicorel, Marietta. Chicorel theater
index to plays in collections,
anthologies, periodicals, and discs
in England, 1st ed. New York,
Chicorel Library Pub. Corp. [1972]
466 p. 808/.82/016 73-174046
Z5781 .C486 MRR Alc.

Chicorel, Marietta. Chicorel theater
index to plays in periodicals. 1st
ed. New York, Chicorel Library Pub.
Corp., 1973. 500 p. 808/.82/016
73-174118
Z5781 .C487 MRR Alc.

Drury, Francis Keese Wynkoop,
Drury's Guide to best plays, 2d ed.
Metuchen, N.J., Scarecrow Press,
1969. 512 p. 016.80882 75-5006
Z5781 .D8 1969 MRR Alc.

Firkins, Ina Ten Eyck, comp. Index
to plays, 1800-1926, New York, The
H. W. Wilson company, 1927. 5 p. l.,
307 p. 016.8 27-27608
Z5781.A1 F5 MRR Alc.

Ireland, Norma (Olin) Index to full
length plays 1944 to 1964. Boston,
F. W. Faxon Co., 1965. xxxii, 296 p.
66-18982
Z5781 .T52 MRR Alc.

Keller, Dean H. Index to plays in
periodicals, Metuchen, N.J.,
Scarecrow Press, 1971. 558 p.
016.80882 72-142236
Z5781 .K43 MRR Alc.

McGraw-Hill encyclopedia of world
drama. New York, McGraw-Hill [1972]
4 v. 809.2 70-37382
PN1625 .M3 MRR Alc.

Melnitz, William W. Theatre arts
publications in the United States,
1947-1952; [Dubuque? Iowa, c1959]
xiii, 91 p. 016.792 60-882
Z5781 .M5 MRR Alc.

Ottemiller, John Henry, Ottemiller's
Index to plays in collections: 5th
ed., rev. and enl. Metuchen, N.J.,
Scarecrow Press, 1971. xiii, 452 p.
016.80882 71-166073
Z5781 .O8 1971 MRR Alc.

Samples, Gordon. The drama scholars'
index to plays and filmscripts:
Metuchen, N.J., Scarecrow Press
[1974] xii, 448 p. 016.80882 73-
22165
Z5781 .S17 MRR Alc.

DRAMA--BIBLIOGRAPHY. (Cont.)
Schoolcraft, Ralph Newman.
Performing arts/books in print: an
annotated bibliography. [1st ed.]
New York, Drama Book Specialists
[1973] xiii, 761 p. 016.7902 72-
78909
    Z6935 .S34 MRR Alc.

Schulz, Friedrich Ernst.
Dramenlexikon; ein Wegweiser zu etwa
10,000 urheberrechtlich geschützten
Bühnenwerken. Neu hrsg. Köln,
Kiepenheuer & Witsch [1958-62] 2 v.
61-34835
    Z2234.D7 S372 MRR Alc.

Sherman, Robert Lowery. Drama
cyclopedia. Chicago, The author
[1944] 1 p. l., iii, 612 p. 792
44-40134
    PN2226 .S45 MRR Alc.

Simon's directory of theatrical
materials, services & information.
1st ed.: 1955- New York, Package
Publicity Service [etc.] 792.058 55-
12448
    PN2289 .S5 MRR Ref Desk Latest
    edition

Thomson, Ruth Gibbons, Index to full
length plays. Boston, F. W. Faxon
co., 1946-56 [v. 1, 1956] 2 v.
016.8125 46-3756
    Z5781 .T5 MRR Alc.

United States. Copyright office.
Dramatic compositions copyrighted in
the United States, 1870 to 1916.
Washington, Govt. print. off., 1918.
2 v. 18-26789
    Z663.8 .D7 MRR Alc.

DRAMA--BIBLIOGRAPHY--CATALOGS.
British Drama League. Library. The
player's library; 1925- [London]
Faber and Faber [etc.] 016.822 26-
12434
    Z2014.D7 B8 MRR Alc Full set

British Drama League. Library. The
player's library; Supplement. 1st-
1951- [London] Faber and Faber
[etc.] 016.822 74-643566
    Z2014.D7 B8 Suppl. MRR Alc Full
    set

Dramatic Publishing Company, Chicago.
Catalog of plays. Chicago. 016.792
54-467
    Z5785.Z9 D7 MRR Alc Latest edition

Dramatists Play Service, New York.
Complete catalogue of plays. New
York. 016.812 63-289
    Z5785.Z9 D73 MRR Alc Latest
    edition

French, Samuel, firm, publishers.
The Samuel French basic catalog of
plays. New York. 28-485
    Z5785.Z9 F8 MRR Ref Desk Latest
    edition

New York (City). Public Library.
Research Libraries. Catalog of the
theatre and drama collections.
Boston, G. K. Hall, 1967. 21 v.
016.700 68-5330
    Z5785 .N56 MRR Alc. (DK 33).

Plays and their plots. London, H. F.
W. Deane; Boston, W. H. Baker [1960?]
165 p. 016.82291 60-36283
    Z2014.D7 P73 MRR Alc.

DRAMA--BIO-BIBLIOGRAPHY.
Kosch, Wilhelm, Deutsches Theater-
Lexikon; Klagenfurt, F. Kleinmayr,
1951- v. a 52-1902
    PN2035 .K6 MRR Alc.

DRAMA--COLLECTIONS.
Gilder, Rosamond. Theatre
collections in libraries and museums,
New York, Theatre arts inc. [c1936]
4 p. l., 182 p. 792.074 36-21492
    Z688.T6 G5 MRR Alc.

DRAMA--DICTIONARIES.
Bowman, Walter Parker, Theatre
language; New York, Theatre Arts
Books [1961] xii, 428 p. 792.03
60-10495
    PN2035 .B6 MRR Alc.

Collet, Paul, Theater A-Z
Antwerpen, Boekengilde Die Poorte
[1959] 2 v. 60-29346
    PN1625 .C6 MRR Alc.

Gassner, John, The reader's
encyclopedia of world drama, New
York, Crowell [1969] xi, 1030 p.
[15.00] 809.2 69-11830
    PN1625 .G3 1969 MRR Alc.

Melchinger, Siegfried. The concise
encyclopedia of modern drama;
London, Vision P., 1966. 288 p.
[70/-] 792.03 66-73655
    PN1861 .M4 1966 MRR Alc.

Sharp, Harold S., comp. Index to
characters in the performing arts,
New York, Scarecrow Press, 1966-73.
4 v. in 6. 808.8292703 66-13744
    PN1579 .S45 MRR Alc.

Sobel, Bernard, ed. The new theatre
handbook and digest of plays. [8th
ed., completely rev.] New York,
Crown Publishers, 1959. 749 p.
792.03 58-12876
    PN1625 .S6 1959 MRR Alc.

DRAMA--DISCOGRAPHY.
Chicorel, Marietta. Chicorel theater
index to plays in collections,
anthologies, periodicals, and discs
in England. 1st ed. New York,
Chicorel Library Pub. Corp. [1972]
466 p. 808/.82/016 73-174046
    Z5781 .C486 MRR Alc.

DRAMA--HISTORY AND CRITICISM.
Brockett, Oscar Gross, History of
the theatre [Boston, Allyn and
Bacon, 1968] viii, 741 p. 792/.09
68-18812
    PN2101 .B68 MRR Alc.

Gassner, John, Masters of the drama.
3d rev. and enl. ed. [New York]
Dover Publications [1954] xxi, 890
p. 809.2 54-12577
    PN1721 .G3 1954 MRR Alc.

Hewitt, Barnard Wolcott, Theatre
U.S.A., 1668 to 1957. New York,
McGraw-Hill, 1959. 528 p. 792.0973
58-11982
    PN2221 .H4 MRR Alc.

Kernodle, George Riley, Invitation
to the theatre New York, Harcourt,
Brace & World [1967] viii, 677 p.
792/.09 67-12523
    PN1655 .K4 MRR Alc.

Nicoll, Allardyce, World drama from
Æschylus to Anouilh. New York,
Harcourt, Brace [1950?] 1000 p.
809.2 50-6848
    PN2101 .N55 1950 MRR Alc.

Rowe, Kenneth Thorpe, A theater in
your head. New York, Funk & Wagnalls
[1960] 438 p. 808.2 60-7804
    PN1731 .R6 MRR Alc.

Shipley, Joseph Twadell, Guide to
great plays. Washington, Public
Affairs Press [1956] xi, 867 p.
808.2 56-6595
    PN6112.5 .S45 MRR Alc.

Slonim, Marc, Russian theater, [1st
ed.] Cleveland, World Pub. Co.
[1961] 354 p. 792.0947 61-15304
    PN2721 .S55 MRR Alc.

Whiting, Frank M. An introduction to
the theatre. Rev. ed. New York,
Harper [1961] 369 p. 792 61-5460
    PN2037 .W5 1961 MRR Alc.

**DRAMA--HISTORY AND CRITICISM--
BIBLIOGRAPHY.**
Adelman, Irving, comp. Modern drama;
Metuchen, N.J., Scarecrow Press,
1967. xvii, 370 p. 016.809/2/04
67-10189
    Z5781 .A35 MRR Ref Desk.

Baker, Blanch (Merritt) Dramatic
bibliography; New York, The H. W.
Wilson company, 1933. xvi, 320 p.
016.792 33-3167
    Z5781 .B16 MRR Alc.

Breed, Paul Francis, Dramatic
criticism index; Detroit, Gale
Research Co. [1972] 1022 p.
016.8092/04 79-127598
    Z5781 .B8 MRR Ref Desk.

Cheshire, David F. Theatre; history,
criticism and reference London,
Bingley, 1967. 131 p. [25/-]
016.792 67-92149
    Z5781 .C48 1967a MRR Alc.

Coleman, Arthur, Drama criticism
Denver, A. Swallow [1966-71] 2 v.
[$7.50 (v. 1) $12.50 (v. 2)]
016.809/2 66-30426
    Z5781 .C65 MRR Ref Desk.

Litto, Fredric M., American
dissertations on the drama and the
theatre; [1st ed. Kent, Ohio] Kent
State University Press [1969] ix,
519 p. 016.8092 71-76761
    Z5781 .L56 MRR Alc.

Palmer, Helen H. American drama
criticism; Hamden, Conn., Shoe
String Press, 1967. 239 p.
016.792/0973 67-16009
    Z1231.D7 P3 MRR Ref Desk.

Palmer, Helen H. European drama
criticism, Hamden, Conn., Shoe
String Press, 1968. 460 p.
016.809/2 67-24188
    Z5781 .P2 MRR Ref Desk.

Salem, James M. A guide to critical
reviews. New York, Scarecrow Press,
1966- v. [$4.50 (v. 1) varies]
016.8092 66-13733
    Z5782 .S34 MRR Ref Desk.

DRAMA--INDEXES.
American Educational Theatre
Association. Theatre arts
publications available in the United
States, 1953-1957; Evanston? Ill.,
c1964] xiii, 188 p. 65-3361
    Z5781 .A52 MRR Alc.

Chicorel, Marietta. Chicorel theater
index to plays for young people in
periodicals, anthologies, and
collections, 1st ed. New York,
Chicorel Library Pub. Corp., 1974.
489 p. 808/.82/016 74-173632
    Z5784.C5 C55 MRR Alc.

Chicorel, Marietta. Chicorel theater
index to plays in collections,
anthologies, periodicals, and discs
in England; 1st ed. New York,
Chicorel Library Pub. Corp. [1972]
466 p. 808/.82/016 73-174046
    Z5781 .C486 MRR Alc.

Chicorel, Marietta. Chicorel theater
index to plays in periodicals. 1st
ed. New York, Chicorel Library Pub.
Corp., 1973. 500 p. 808/.82/016
73-174118
    Z5781 .C487 MRR Alc.

Chicorel theater index to plays in
anthologies, periodicals, discs, and
tapes. v.1- 1970- New York,
Chicorel Library Pub. Co. 016.80882
71-106198
    Z5781 .C485 MRR Alc Full set

Cumulated Dramatic index, 1909-1949;
Boston, G. K. Hall, 1965. 2 v. 68-
4712
    Z5781 .C8 MRR Alc.

Davis, Jed Horace. Children's
theatre; New York, Harper [1960]
416 p. 792.0226 60-15622
    PN3157 .D3 MRR Alc.

Drury, Francis Keese Wynkoop,
Drury's Guide to best plays, 2d ed.
Metuchen, N.J., Scarecrow Press,
1969. 512 p. 016.80882 75-5006
    Z5781 .D8 1969 MRR Alc.

Ireland, Norma (Olin) Index to full
length plays 1944 to 1964. Boston,
F. W. Faxon Co., 1965. xxxii, 296 p.
66-18982
    Z5781 .T52 MRR Alc.

Keller, Dean H. Index to plays in
periodicals, Metuchen, N.J.,
Scarecrow Press, 1971. 558 p.
016.80882 72-142236
    Z5781 .K43 MRR Alc.

Kreider, Barbara. Index to
children's plays in collections.
Metuchen, N.J., Scarecrow Press,
1972. 138 p. 016.812/041 72-3008

    PN1627 .K7 MRR Alc.

Mersand, Joseph E., Index to plays,
New York, Scarecrow Press, 1966. 114
p. 016.80882 66-13745
    Z5781 .M575 MRR Alc.

Ottemiller, John Henry, Ottemiller's
Index to plays in collections; 5th
ed., rev. and enl. Metuchen, N.J.,
Scarecrow Press, 1971. xiii, 452 p.
016.80882 71-166073
    Z5781 .O8 1971 MRR Alc.

Patterson, Charlotte A. Plays in
periodicals; Boston, G. K. Hall,
1970. ix, 240 p. 016.22/9/108 76-
21033
    Z5781 .P3 MRR Alc.

Play index. 1949/52- New York, H.
W. Wilson Co. 64-1054
    Z5781 .P53 MRR Alc Full set

Samples, Gordon. The drama scholars'
index to plays and filmscripts;
Metuchen, N.J., Scarecrow Press
[1974] xii, 448 p. 016.80882 73-
22165
    Z5781 .S17 MRR Alc.

Thomson, Ruth Gibbons, Index to full
length plays. Boston, F. W. Faxon
co., 1946-56 [v. 1, 1956] 2 v.
016.8125 46-3756
    Z5781 .T5 MRR Alc.

DRAMA--STORIES, PLOTS, ETC.
Atkinson, Justin Brooks, The lively
years, 1920-1973 New York,
Association Press [1973] viii, 312
p. [$12.50] 792/.09747/1 73-14659

    PN2277.N5 A85 MRR Alc.

Bonin, Jane F. Prize-winning
American drama: Metuchen, N.J.,
Scarecrow Press, 1973. xii, 222 p.
812/.5/09 73-3111
    PS351 .B6 MRR Alc.

DRAMA--STORIES, PLOTS, ETC. (Cont.)
Broad, Lewis, Dictionary to the
plays and novels of Bernard Shaw,
New York, Haskell House, 1969. xi,
230 p.   822/.9/12 75-92947
PR5366 .A23 1969 MRR Alc.

Crowell's handbook of contemporary
drama, New York, Crowell [1971] vi,
505 p.   [$10.00] 809.2/04 79-
158714
PN1861 .C7 MRR Alc.

Dramatic Publishing Company, Chicago.
Catalog of plays. Chicago. 016.792
54-467
Z5785.Z9 D7 MRR Alc Latest edition

Dramatists Play Service, New York.
Complete catalogue of plays. New
York. 016.812 63-289
Z5785.Z9 D73 MRR Alc Latest
edition

Drury, Francis Keese Wynkoop,
Drury's Guide to best plays, 2d ed.
Metuchen, N.J., Scarecrow Press,
1969. 512 p. 016.80882 75-5006
Z5781 .D8 1969 MRR Alc.

French, Samuel, firm, publishers.
The guide to selecting plays.
London. 016.80882 55-26891
PN6112.5 .F7 MRR Alc Latest
edition

French, Samuel, firm, publishers.
The Samuel French basic catalog of
plays. New York. 28-485
Z5785.Z9 F8 MRR Ref Desk Latest
edition

Gassner, John, The reader's
encyclopedia of world drama, New
York, Crowell [1969] xi, 1030 p.
[15.00] 809.2 69-11830
PN1625 .G3 1969 MRR Alc.

Geisinger, Marion. Plays, players, &
playwrights; New York, Hart Pub. Co.
[1971] 767 p. [$20.00] 792/.09
77-162054
PN2101 .G4 MRR Alc.

Kienzle, Siegfried, Modern world
theater; New York, Ungar [1970] v,
509 p. [12.50] 808.82 73-98342
PN6112.5 .K513 MRR Alc.

Lovell, John, Digests of great
American plays; New York, Crowell
[1961] 452 p. 812.0822 61-10482
PS338.P5 L6 MRR Alc.

Magill, Frank Northen, Masterplots.
New York, Salem Press [1964] 6 v.
808.8 64-54679
PN44 .M32 MRR Alc.

Magill, Frank Northern, ed.
Masterplots; [Definitive ed.] New
York, Salem Press [1968] 8 v. (ix,
5795, xxii p.) 68-8171
PN44 .M33 MRR Alc.

Matlaw, Myron, Modern world drama;
[1st ed.] New York, Dutton, 1972.
xxi, 960 p. [$25.00] 809.2/34 71-
185032
PN1851 .M36 MRR Alc.

May, Robin. A companion to the
theatre; Guildford, Lutterworth
Press, 1973. 304 p. [16] p. of
plates. [£2.40] 792/.0542 74-
164747
PN2597 .M35 MRR Alc.

McGraw-Hill encyclopedia of world
drama. New York, McGraw-Hill [1972]
4 v. 809.2 70-37382
PN1625 .M3 MRR Alc.

Plays and their plots. London, H. F.
W. Deane; Boston, W. H. Baker [1960?]
165 p. 016.82291 60-36283
Z2014.D7 P73 MRR Alc.

Shank, Theodore Junior, ed. A digest
of 500 plays; New York, Collier
Books [1966, c1963] 475 p. 808.82
67-9505
PN6112.5 .S42 1966 MRR Alc.

Shipley, Joseph Twadell, Guide to
great plays. Washington, Public
Affairs Press [1956] xi, 867 p.
808.2 56-6585
PN6112.5 .S45 MRR Alc.

Sobel, Bernard, ed. The new theatre
handbook and digest of plays. [8th
ed., completely rev.] New York,
Crown Publishers, 1959. 749 p.
792.03 58-12876
PN1625 .S6 1959 MRR Alc.

DRAMA--STORIES, PLOTS, ETC.--INDEXES.
Koehmstedt, Carol L. Plot summary
index. Metuchen, N.J., Scarecrow
Press, 1973. 312 p. 809 72-13726

Z6514.P66 K63 MRR Ref Desk.

DRAMA--TECHNIQUE.
Busfield, Roger M. The playwright's
art; New York, Harper [1958] 260 p.
808.2 58-6918
PN1661 .B8 MRR Alc.

Niggli, Josephina. New pointers on
playwriting. Boston, The Writer,
inc. [1967] 166 p. 808.2 67-24454

PN1661 .N5 MRR Alc.

DRAMA--TRANSLATIONS INTO ENGLISH--
BIBLIOGRAPHY.
Patterson, Charlotte A. Plays in
periodicals; Boston, G. K. Hall,
1970. ix, 240 p. 016.22/9/108 76-
21033
Z5781 .P3 MRR Alc.

DRAMA, MEDIEVAL--BIBLIOGRAPHY.
Stratman, Carl Joseph, Bibliography
of medieval drama. 2d ed., rev. and
enl. New York, F. Unger [1972] 2 v.
xv, 1035 p.) [$35.00]
016.80882/02 78-163141
Z5782.A2 S8 1972 MRR Alc.

DRAMATIC MUSIC
see Opera

DRAMATISTS.
Collet, Paul, Theater A-Z
Antwerpen, Boekengilde Die Poorte
[1959] 2 v. 60-29346
PN1625 .C6 MRR Alc.

Crowell's handbook of contemporary
drama, New York, Crowell [1971] vi,
505 p.   [$10.00] 809.2/04 79-
158714
PN1861 .C7 MRR Alc.

Gassner, John, Masters of the drama.
3d rev. and enl. ed. [New York]
Dover Publications [1954] xxi, 890
p. 809.2 54-12577
PN1721 .G3 1954 MRR Alc.

Gassner, John, The reader's
encyclopedia of world drama, New
York, Crowell [1969] xi, 1030 p.
[15.00] 809.2 69-11830
PN1625 .G3 1969 MRR Alc.

Matlaw, Myron, Modern world drama;
[1st ed.] New York, Dutton, 1972.
xxi, 960 p. [$25.00] 809.2/34 71-
185032
PN1851 .M36 MRR Alc.

McGraw-Hill encyclopedia of world
drama. New York, McGraw-Hill [1972]
4 v. 809.2 70-37382
PN1625 .M3 MRR Alc.

Sherman, Robert Lowery, Actors and
authors. Chicago [1951] 433 p.
927.92 51-4020
PN2285 .S48 MRR Biog.

DRAMATISTS--BIO-BIBLIOGRAPHY.
Melchinger, Siegfried. The concise
encyclopedia of modern drama;
London, Vision P., 1966. 288 p.
[70/] 792.03 66-73655
PN1861 .M4 1966 MRR Alc.

DRAMATISTS--BIOGRAPHY--DICTIONARIES.
McGraw-Hill encyclopedia of world
drama. New York, McGraw-Hill [1972]
4 v. 809.2 70-37382
PN1625 .M3 MRR Alc.

DRAMATISTS, AMERICAN.
Bonin, Jane F. Prize-winning
American drama; Metuchen, N.J.,
Scarecrow Press, 1973. xii, 222 p.
812/.5/09 73-3111
PS351 .B6 MRR Alc.

Vinson, James, Contemporary
dramatists; London, St. James Press;
New York, St. Martin's Press [1973]
xv, 926 p. [£9.00 ($30.00 U.S.)]
822/.9/1409 B 73-80310
PR106 .V5 MRR Biog.

DRAMATISTS, CANADIAN.
Pierce, Lorne Albert, An outline of
Canadian literature (French and
English) Toronto, The Ryerson press,
1927. 6 p. l., 251 p. 28-2647
PR9112 .P5 MRR Alc.

DRAMATISTS, ENGLISH.
Baker, David Erskine, Biographia
dramatica; London, Longman, Hurst,
Rees, Orme, and Brown [etc.] 1812. 3
v. in 4. 04-14124
Z2014.D7 B2 1812 MRR Alc.

Vinson, James, Contemporary
dramatists; London, St. James Press;
New York, St. Martin's Press [1973]
xv, 926 p. [£9.00 ($30.00 U.S.)]
822/.9/1409 B 73-80310
PR106 .V5 MRR Biog.

DRAMATISTS, ENGLISH--BIBLIOGRAPHY.
Stratman, Carl Joseph, Restoration
and eighteenth century theatre
research; Carbondale, Southern
Illinois University Press [1971] ix,
811 p. [$25.00] 016.822/5/09 71-
112394
Z2014.D7 S854 MRR Alc.

DRAMATISTS, ITALIAN.
Kennard, Joseph Spencer, The Italian
theatre, New York, W. E. Rudge,
1932. 2 v. 852.09 792.0945 32-
13803
PQ4134 .K4 MRR Alc.

DRAMMEN, NORWAY--DIRECTORIES.
Adressebok for Vestfold fylke og
Drammen med skatteligninger. Oslo,
S. M. Bryde. 53-28837
DL576.V45 A7 MRR Alc Latest
edition

DRAWING.
see also Painting

DRAWING MATERIALS--CATALOGS.
see also Artists' materials

DRAWINGS--PRICES.
Art prices current. v. [1]-9,
1907/08-1915/16; new ser., v. 1-
1921/22- 704.938 09-23300
N8670 .A7 MRR Alc Partial set

International auction records. v.
[1]- 1967- [London, etc.]
Editions E. M.-Publisol] 700/.29
78-2167
N8640 .I5 MRR Alc Full set

DRAWINGS, AMERICAN.
Taft, Robert, Artists and
illustrators of the Old West; 1850-
1900. New York, Scribner, 1953.
xvii, 400 p. 709.78 53-7577
N6510 .T27 MRR Alc.

DREAMS.
King, Bruce. Zolar's encyclopedia
and dictionary of dreams, 1st ed.]
Garden City, N.Y., Doubleday, 1963.
xii, 417 p. 135.32 63-21071
BF1091 .K48 MRR Alc.

DRESS
see Clothing and dress

DRESSMAKING.
The Vogue sewing book. [1st ed.]
New York, Vogue Patterns;
distribution by Doubleday, Garden
City, N.Y. [1970] 416 p. 646.4/04
70-124559
TT515 .V63 MRR Alc.

DRINK QUESTION
see Liquor problem

DRINKING VESSELS.
Warman, Edwin G. The second Goblet
price guide; Uniontown, Pa., Warman
Pub. Co. [1953] 37 p. 748.8 54-
475
NK5112 .W25 1953 MRR Alc.

DRUG ABUSE.
see also Narcotic habit
Lingeman, Richard R. Drugs from A to
Z: Rev. & updated, 2d ed. New York,
McGraw-Hill [1974] xxii, 310 p.
613.8/3/03 74-13363
HV5804 .L54 1974 MRR Alc.

Maurer, David W. Narcotics and
narcotic addiction, 4th ed.
Springfield, Ill., Thomas [1973] xv,
473 p. 616.86/3 73-7879
RC566 .M3 1973 MRR Alc.

Maurer, David W. Narcotics and
narcotic addiction, 4th ed.
Springfield, Ill., Thomas [1973] xv,
473 p. 616.86/3 73-7879
RC566 .M3 1973 MRR Alc.

Wilder-Smith, A. E. The drug users;
[1st ed.] Wheaton, Ill., H. Shaw
[1969] 294, [10] p. [5.95]
615/.78 73-86528
RM315 .W55 MRR Alc.

DRUG ABUSE--BIBLIOGRAPHY.
Menditto, Joseph. Drugs of addiction
and non-addiction, their use and
abuse; Troy, N.Y., Whitston Pub.
Co., 1970. 315 p. 016.6138/3 79-
116588
Z7164.N17 M45 MRR Alc.

United States. National Clearinghouse
for Mental Health Information.
Bibliography on drug dependence and
abuse, 1928-1966. [Chevy Chase, Md.;
1969] 258 p. 016.6138/3 70-600726

Z7164.N17 U56 MRR Alc.

DRUG ABUSE--DICTIONARIES.
Lingeman, Richard R. Drugs from A to
Z: Rev. & updated, 2d ed. New York,
McGraw-Hill [1974] xxii, 310 p.
613.8/3/03 74-13363
HV5804 .L54 1974 MRR Alc.

DRUG ABUSE--TREATMENT--DIRECTORIES.
Andrews, Matthew, The parents' guide
to drugs. [1st ed.] Garden City,
N.Y., Doubleday, 1972. 186 p.
[$6.95] 362.2/93/0973 78-144245
HV5825 .A7 MRR Alc.

DRUG ABUSE--TREATMENT-- (Cont.)
Keville, Kathleen. Where to get help
for a drug problem. New York, Award
Books [1971] 237 p. [$1.25]
362.2/93/02573 71-31889
HV5815 .K44 MRR Alc.

DRUG ABUSE--UNITED STATES.
Andrews, Matthew. The parents' guide
to drugs. [1st ed.] Garden City,
N.Y., Doubleday, 1972. 186 p.
[$6.95] 362.2/93/0973 78-144245
HV5825 .A7 MRR Alc.

Brecher, Edward M. Licit and illicit
drugs; [1st ed.] Boston, Little,
Brown [1972] xv, 623 p. [$12.50]
362.2/9 75-186972
HV5825 .B72 MRR Alc.

DRUG ABUSE--UNITED STATES--DIRECTORIES.
Keville, Kathleen. Where to get help
for a drug problem. New York, Award
Books [1971] 237 p. [$1.25]
362.2/93/02573 71-31889
HV5815 .K44 MRR Alc.

DRUG ABUSE--UNITED STATES--INFORMATION
SERVICES--DIRECTORIES.
Student Association for the Study of
Hallucinogens. Directory of drug
information groups. Beloit, Wis.,
STASH Press [1970] 183 p.
613.8/3/0873 75-136212
HV5825 .S75 MRR Alc.

DRUG ADDICTION.
Brecher, Edward M. Licit and illicit
drugs; [1st ed.] Boston, Little,
Brown [1972] xv, 623 p. [$12.50]
362.2/9 75-186972
HV5825 .B72 MRR Alc.

Maurer, David W. Narcotics and
narcotic addiction. 4th ed.
Springfield, Ill., Thomas [1973] xv,
473 p. 616.86/3 73-7879
RC566 .M3 1973 MRR Alc.

DRUG ADDICTS
see Narcotic addicts--Rehabilitation

DRUG TRADE--DIRECTORIES.
Chemical buyers directory. [1st]-
1913- New York, Schnell Pub. Co.
660/.025/73 13-6763
TP12 .C6 Sci RR Latest edition /
MRR Alc Latest edition

Drug and cosmetic review. 1st-
ed.: 1931- New York, Drug and
cosmetic industry [etc.] 615.1 43-
43430
RS356 .D8 MRR Alc Latest edition

DRUG TRADE--YEARBOOKS.
Drug topics red book. 45th- year;
1941/42- New York, Topics Pub. Co.
338.476151 42-21682
HD9666.1 .D75 MRR Alc Latest
edition

DRUG TRADE--CANADA--DIRECTORIES.
Lloyd's Canadian chemical,
pharmaceutical, and product
directory. West Hill, Ont., Lloyd
Publications of Canada.
338.4/7/66002571 72-626360
HD9655.C2 W5 MRR Alc Latest
edition

Noyes Development Corporation.
Pharmaceutical firms, 3d ed. Park
Ridge, N.J. [1965] 91 p.
615.1900257 65-21984
HD9666.3 .N6 1965 MRR Alc.

DRUG TRADE--EUROPE--DIRECTORIES.
Noyes Development Corporation.
European pharmaceutical firms, 1964.
Pearl River, N.Y., c1963. 84 p. 64-
397
HD9665.3 .N6 MRR Alc.

DRUG TRADE--MEXICO--DIRECTORIES.
Noyes Development Corporation.
Pharmaceutical firms, 3d ed. Park
Ridge, N.J. [1965] 91 p.
615.1900257 65-21984
HD9666.3 .N6 1965 MRR Alc.

DRUG TRADE--UNITED STATES.
Drug topics red book. 45th- year;
1941/42- New York, Topics Pub. Co.
338.476151 42-21682
HD9666.1 .D75 MRR Alc Latest
edition

DRUG TRADE--UNITED STATES--DIRECTORIES.
Chain store guide directory: drug
store and health & beauty aids
chains. [New York, Business Guides,
inc.] 380.1/45/615102573 72-627445

HD9666.3 .C53 MRR Alc Latest
edition

Directory of chemical producers:
United States of America. Menlo
Park, Chemical Information Services,
Stanford Research Institute.
338.4/7/66002573 73-644039
HD9651.3 .D57 MRR Alc Latest
edition / Sci RR Latest edition

Drug topics buyers guide. Oradell,
N.J., Medical Economics Co.
381/.45/615102573 72-624938
HD9666.3 .L5 MRR Alc Latest
edition

Noyes Development Corporation.
Pharmaceutical firms, 3d ed. Park
Ridge, N.J. [1965] 91 p.
615.1900257 65-21984
HD9666.3 .N6 1965 MRR Alc.

DRUGS.
see also Pharmacology

Accepted dental therapeutics.
[Chicago, Council on Dental
Therapeutics of the American Dental
Association] 617.6/06/05 74-642043

RK701 .A3 MRR Alc Latest edition

American drug index. [1956]-
Philadelphia, Lippincott. 615 55-
6286
RS355 .A48 Sci RR Latest edition /
MRR Alc Latest edition

American Medical Association. Council
on Drugs. A M A drug evaluations.
1st- ed.; 1971- Chicago, American
Medical Association. 615/.1 75-
147249
RM300 .A553 MRR Alc Latest edition

Brecher, Edward M. Licit and illicit
drugs; [1st ed.] Boston, Little,
Brown [1972] xv, 623 p. [$12.50]
362.2/9 75-186972
HV5825 .B72 MRR Alc.

British pharmacopœia. London,
Published for the General Medical
Council by the Pharmaceutical Press
[etc.] 615.11 agr15-305
RS141.3 .B75 Sci RR Latest edition
/ MRR Alc Latest edition

Burack, Richard. The new handbook of
prescription drugs: official names,
prices, and sources for patient and
doctor. [Rev. ed.] New York,
Pantheon Books [1970] xiv, 362 p.
[7.95] 615/.1 76-15606
RS91 .B916 1970 MRR Alc.

Drugs of choice. St. Louis C. V.
Mosby Co. 615.1 58-6889
RM101 .D75 Sci RR Latest edition /
MRR Alc Latest edition

Goth, Andres. Medical pharmacology;
principles and concepts. 7th ed.
Saint Louis, Mosby, 1974. x, 753 p.
615/.7 73-20083
RM300 .G65 1974 MRR Alc.

Martindale, William, The extra
pharmacopoeia; incorporating Squire's
"Companion". 26th ed.; London,
Pharmaceutical Press, 1972. xxvi,
2320 p. [£14.00] 615/.11/42 72-
78897
RS141.3 .M4 1972 MRR Alc.

The Medicine show Rev. ed. New
York, Pantheon Books, 1974. 384 p.
610 74-10418
RC81 .M496 1974 MRR Alc.

The Merck index: 8th ed. Rahway,
N.J., Merck, 1968. xii, 1713 p.
615/.1/03 68-12252
RS356 .M524 1968 MRR Alc.

Modern drug encyclopedia and
therapeutic index. 1st- ed.; 1934-
New York, R. H. Donnelley [etc.] 34-
12823
RS153 .M57 Sci RR Latest edition /
MRR Alc Latest edition

National formulary. 1st- ed.; 1888-
Washington [etc.] American
Pharmaceutical Association [etc.]
615.1373 55-4116
RS141.2 N3 MRR Alc Latest edition

Pharmaceutical Society of Great
Britain, London. British
pharmaceutical codex, 1973. London,
Pharmaceutical Press [1973] xxxix,
983 p. [£10.50] 615/.12/42 73-
171134
RS151.3 .P54 1973 MRR Alc.

Veterinarians' blue book. [1st]-
ed.; 1953- [New York, R. H.
Donnelley, etc.] 53-24738
SF915 .V47 Sci RR Latest edition /
MRR Alc Latest edition

DRUGS--ABSTRACTS.
Ajami, Alfred M. Drugs: an annotated
bibliography and guide to the
literature, Boston, G. K. Hall,
1973. xxiv, 205 p. 615/.78 72-
13943
RM300 .A47 MRR Alc.

DRUGS--BIBLIOGRAPHY.
Ajami, Alfred M. Drugs: an annotated
bibliography and guide to the
literature, Boston, G. K. Hall,
1973. xxiv, 205 p. 615/.78 72-
13943
RM300 .A47 MRR Alc.

Menditto, Joseph. Drugs of addiction
and non-addiction, their use and
abuse; Troy, N.Y., Whitston Pub.
Co., 1970. 315 p. 016.6138/3 79-
116588
Z7164.N17 M45 MRR Alc.

United States. National Clearinghouse
for Mental Health Information.
Bibliography on drug dependence and
abuse, 1928-1966. [Chevy Chase, Md.,
1969] 258 p. 016.6138/3 70-600726

Z7164.N17 U56 MRR Alc.

DRUGS--CATALOGS.
Drug and cosmetic review. 1st-
ed.: 1931- New York, Drug and
cosmetic industry [etc.] 615.1 43-
43430
RS356 .D8 MRR Alc Latest edition

Physicians' desk reference to
pharmaceutical specialties and
biologicals. 1st- ed.; 1947-
Oradell [etc.] N.J., Medical
economics. 60-784
RS75 .P5 Sci RR Latest edition /
MRR Ref Desk Latest edition

DRUGS--DICTIONARIES.
Fisher, Richard B. A dictionary of
drugs; New York, Schocken Books
[1972, c1971] 252 p. [$6.95]
615/.1/03 72-80037
RS51 .F5 MRR Alc.

Lingeman, Richard R. Drugs from A to
Z: Rev. & updated, 2d ed. New York,
McGraw-Hill [1974] xxii, 310 p.
613.8/3/03 74-13363
HV5804 .L54 1974 MRR Alc.

DRUGS--PERIODICALS.
Drugs in current use and new drugs.
New York, Springer Pub. Co.
615/.1/05 72-622911
RS79 .D7 Sci RR Latest edition /
MRR Alc Latest edition

DRUGS--PHYSIOLOGICAL EFFECT.
Brecher, Edward M. Licit and illicit
drugs; [1st ed.] Boston, Little,
Brown [1972] xv, 623 p. [$12.50]
362.2/9 75-186972
HV5825 .B72 MRR Alc.

DRUGS--POPULAR WORKS.
The Medicine show Rev. ed. New
York, Pantheon Books, 1974. 384 p.
610 74-10418
RC81 .M496 1974 MRR Alc.

DRUGS--PRICES AND SALE.
Drug topics red book. 45th- year;
1941/42- New York, Topics Pub. Co.
338.476151 42-21682
HD9666.1 .D75 MRR Alc Latest
edition

DRUGS--YEARBOOKS.
Current drug handbook. 1958-
Philadelphia [etc.] W. B. Saunders
Co. 615.1 58-6390
RM300 .C8 Sci RR Latest edition /
MRR Alc Latest edition

DRUGS AND YOUTH--UNITED STATES.
Andrews, Matthew, The parents' guide
to drugs. [1st ed.] Garden City,
N.Y., Doubleday, 1972. 186 p.
[$6.95] 362.2/93/0973 78-144245
HV5825 .A7 MRR Alc.

DRUGSTORES--UNITED STATES--DIRECTORIES.
Chain store guide directory: drug
store and health & beauty aids
chains. [New York, Business Guides,
inc.] 380.1/45/615102573 72-627445

HD9666.3 .C53 MRR Alc Latest
edition

Directory of licensed pharmacies.
1st- ed.; July 1971- Chicago,
National Association of Boards of
Pharmacy. 380.1/45/615102573 79-
618245
HD9666.3 .D575 MRR Alc Latest
edition

Drug topics buyers guide. Oradell,
N.J., Medical Economics Co.
381/.45/615102573 72-624938
HD9666.3 .L5 MRR Alc Latest
edition

DRUNKENNESS
see Alcoholism

DRY-GOODS.
see also Textile industry and fabrics

DRY-GOODS--UNITED STATES--DIRECTORIES.
The Agent; [Chicago, Halper Pub.
Co.] 677.058 50-56303
TS1312 .A35 MRR Alc Latest edition

Chain drug stores buyers directory of
variety merchandise. 1961- New
York, Directory Division,
Merchandiser Publications. 60-40115

T12 .C43 MRR Alc Latest edition

DRY-GOODS--UNITED STATES-- (Cont.)
Phelon's retail trade, 1st- ed.;
1960- New York, Phelon-Sheldon
Publications [etc.] 60-2106
HF5465.U4 P5 MRR Alc Latest
edition

DRYDEN, JOHN, 1631-1700--CONCORDANCES.
Montgomery, Guy, comp. Concordance
to the poetical works of John Dryden,
New York, Russell & Russell [1967,
c1957] 722 p. 821/.4 66-27126
PR3422 .M6 1967 MRR Alc.

DUBLIN--COMMERCE--DIRECTORIES.
Dublin and district trades'
directory. Edinburgh, Town and
County Directories. 650.584183 60-
30162
HC258.D8 D8 MRR Alc Latest edition

Dublin, Leinster and Connaught
trades' directory, Edinburgh,
Trades' Directories. 57-36641
HF5164.D8 D8 MRR Alc Latest
edition

DUBLIN--INDUSTRIES--DIRECTORIES.
Dublin and district trades'
directory. Edinburgh, Town and
County Directories. 650.584183 60-
30162
HC258.D8 D8 MRR Alc Latest edition

DUBLIN (COUNTY)--DIRECTORIES.
Thom's directory: Dublin city,
county, and Bray. Dublin. 914.18/4
72-627089
DA990 .D8 T5 MRR Alc Latest
edition

DUDE RANCHES--CANADA--DIRECTORIES.
Farm and Ranch Vacations, inc. Farm,
ranch & countryside guide; [25th
anniversary ed.] New York; trade
distributor: Berkshire Traveller
Press, Stockbridge, Mass., 1974. 191
p. [$3.50] 917.3 74-174454
TX907 .F37 1974 MRR Alc.

DUDE RANCHES--UNITED STATES--
DIRECTORIES.
Farm and Ranch Vacations, inc. Farm,
ranch & countryside guide; [25th
anniversary ed.] New York; trade
distributor: Berkshire Traveller
Press, Stockbridge, Mass., 1974. 191
p. [$3.50] 917.3 74-174454
TX907 .F37 1974 MRR Alc.

DUISBURG--DIRECTORIES.
Adressbuch der Stadt Duisburg. Essen
[etc.] Beleke KG [etc.] 60-42040
DD901.D97 A4 MRR Alc Latest
edition

DULANY, BLADEN, 1792-1856--MANUSCRIPTS.
United States. Library of Congress.
Manuscript Division. Bladen Dulany,
Gustavus R. B. Horner, Daniel Todd
Patterson; a register of their papers
in the Library of Congress.
Washington, Library of Congress,
1970. 4, 8, 4 l. 016.3593/32/0922
78-606846
Z663.34 .D9 MRR Alc.

DUNDEE, SCOT.--DIRECTORIES.
The Dundee directory. Dundee, Burns
& Harris. 53-30545
DA890.D8 D8 MRR Alc Latest edition

DUPLICATE CONTRACT BRIDGE.
Kay, Norman. The complete book of
duplicate bridge New York, Putnam
[1965] xiii, 496 p. 795.415 65-
22224
GV1282.3 .K359 1965 MRR Alc.

DÜSSELDORF--DIRECTORIES.
Adressbuch der Landeshauptstadt
Düsseldorf. Düsseldorf,
Adressbuchverlag Schwann. 53-31493
DD901.D95 A3 MRR Alc Latest
edition

DUTCH IN THE UNITED STATES.
Lucas, Henry Stephen. Netherlanders
in America; Ann Arbor, University of
Michigan Press, 1955. xix, 744 p.
325.24920873 55-8647
E184.D9 L8 MRR Alc.

DUTCH LANGUAGE--DICTIONARIES.
Franck, Johannes. Franck's
Etymologisch woordenboek der
Nederlandsche taal. 2. druk 's-
Gravenhage, M. Nijhoff, 1912. xvi,
897 p. 11-22072
PF580 .F82 MRR Alc.

Hendriks, P. Nederlandse synoniemen;
Amsterdam, A. J. G. Strengholt
[1958] 256 p. 58-48788
PF591 .H4 MRR Alc.

DUTCH LANGUAGE--DICTIONARIES--ENGLISH.
Artschwager, Ernst Friedrich.
Dictionary of botanical equivalents,
Baltimore, The Williams & Wilkins
company, 1925. 5 p. l., 9-124 p.
25-11598
QK9 .A7 1925 MRR Alc.

Bons, A. Engels handelswoordenboek
(Nederlands-Engels) Deventer, Æ. E.
Kluwer [1957] 1170 p. 57-56259
HF1002 .B59 MRR Alc.

Bons, A. Engels handelswoordenboek
(Nederlands-Engels) Deventer, Æ. E.
Kluwer [1957] 1170 p. 57-46259
HF1002 .B59 MRR Alc.

Cassell's Dutch-English; English-
Dutch dictionary, New York, Funk &
Wagnalls [1967] 1354 p. 439.3/1/32
67-11998
PF640 .C375 1967b MRR Ref Desk.

Jansonius, Herman. Groot Nederlands-
Engels woordenboek voor studie en
praktijk. Leiden, Nederlandsche
Uitgeversmij., 1950. 2 v. (1837 p.)
a 51-4883
PF640 .J33 MRR Alc.

Kramers, Jacob. Kramers' woordenboek
Engels; 30. druk. Den Haag, Van
Goor [1970] [xlv], 615, 736 p. 76-
572768
PF640 .K7 1970 MRR Alc.

Moth, Axel Fredrik Carl Mathias.
Glossary of library terms, English,
Danish, Dutch, French, German,
Italian, Spanish, Swedish, Boston,
The Boston book company, 1915. 58 p.
15-3471
Z1006 .M72 MRR Alc.

Van Goor's Engels zakwoordenboek.
13. druk. Den Haag, Brussel, G. B.
van Goor, 1967. 684 p. [fl 6.90 bfr
120.-] 68-79147
PF640 .V28 1967 MRR Alc.

Walter, Frank Keller. Abbreviations
and technical terms used in book
catalogs and bibliographies, in eight
languages, 1917 handy edition.
Boston, The Boston book company
[1919?] 2 v. in 1. 27-13479
Z1006 .W261 1919 MRR Alc.

DUTCH LANGUAGE--DICTIONARIES--POLYGLOT.
Bosch, Abraham ten. Viertalig
technisch woordenboek. Deventer, Æ.
E. Kluwer [1948-55] 4 v. 603 50-
18447
T10 .B72 MRR Alc.

Capitol's concise dictionary.
Bologna, Capitol, 1972. 1051 (i.e.
1207) p. 413 72-172231
P361 .C3 MRR Alc.

Clason, W. E., Elsevier's dictionary
of computers, automatic control and
data processing. 2d rev. ed. of The
dictionary of automation, computers,
control and measuring. Amsterdam,
New York, Elsevier Pub. Co., 1971.
484 p. [fl78.00] 001.6/4/03 73-
151733
TJ212.5 .C55 1971 MRR Alc.

Clason, W. E., Supplement to the
Elsevier dictionaries of electronics,
nucleonics and telecommunication.
Amsterdam, New York, Elsevier Pub.
Co., 1963. 633 p. 603 63-11369
T10 .C55 MRR Alc.

Dictionnaire à l'usage de la
librairie ancienne pour les langues:
française, anglaise, allemande,
suédoise, danoise, italienne,
espagnole, hollandaise. Paris, Ligue
internationale de la librairie
ancienne, 1956. 190 p. 655.403 57-
2275
Z282 .D5 MRR Alc.

Elsevier's banking dictionary in six
languages: Amsterdam, New York,
Elsevier Pub. Co., 1966. 302 p.
332.103 65-20139
HG151 .E45 MRR Alc.

Elsevier's dictionary of building
construction, Amsterdam, New York,
Elsevier Pub. Co., 1959. 471 p.
690.3 58-59508
TH9 .E47 MRR Alc.

Elsevier's dictionary of chemical
engineering. Amsterdam, New York,
1968. 2 v. [62.50 per vol.]
660/.2/03 68-54865
TP9 .E38 MRR Alc.

Elsevier's dictionary of cinema,
sound, and music, in six languages:
Amsterdam, New York, Elsevier Pub.
Co., 1956. 948 p. 778.503 56-
13141
TR847 .E4 MRR Alc.

Elsevier's dictionary of criminal
science, in eight languages:
Amsterdam, New York, Elsevier Pub.
Co.: [distributed by Van Nostrand,
Princeton, N.J.] 1960. xv, 1460 p.
364.03 59-12582
HV6017 .E4 MRR Alc.

Elsevier's dictionary of electronics
and waveguides, 2d ed., rev. and
enl. Amsterdam, New York, Elsevier
Pub. Co., 1966 (i.e. 1965] 833 p.
621.38103 65-20142
TK7804 .E4 1965 MRR Alc.

Elsevier's dictionary of general
physics in six languages: Amsterdam,
New York, Elsevier Pub. Co., 1962.
859 p. 530.3 62-13015
QC5 .E46 MRR Alc.

Elsevier's dictionary of nuclear
science and technology. 2d rev. ed.
Amsterdam, New York, Elsevier Pub.
Co., 1970. 787 p. [85.00]
538.7/03 72-103357
QC772 .E4 1970 MRR Alc.

Elsevier's dictionary of television,
radar, and antennas, in six
languages: Amsterdam, New York,
Elsevier Pub. Co., 1955. 760 p.
621.38803 55-6216
TK6634 .E4 MRR Alc.

Elsevier's dictionary of the printing
and allied industries in four
languages, Amsterdam, New York,
[etc.] Elsevier Pub. Co., 1967. 596
p. [90.00] 655/.003 67-19851
Z118 .E5 MRR Alc.

Elsevier's lexicon of archive
terminology: Amsterdam, New York,
Elsevier Pub. Co., 1964. 83 p.
025.171014 64-56714
CD945 .E4 MRR Alc.

Elsevier's lexicon of stock-market
terms: Amsterdam, New York, Elsevier
Pub. Co., 1965. 131 p. 332.603 65-
13892
HG4513 .E4 MRR Alc.

Elsevier's wood dictionary in seven
languages: Amsterdam, New York,
Elsevier Pub. Co., 1964- v.
634.903 64-14178
SD431 .E4 MRR Alc.

Great Britain. Naval intelligence
division. A dictionary of naval
equivalents covering English, French,
Italian, Spanish, Russian, Swedish,
Danish, Dutch, German. London, H.M.
Stationery off., 1924. 2 v. 24-
23792
V24 .G7 MRR Alc.

International Chamber of Commerce.
Dictionary of advertising and
distribution, Basel, Verlag für
Recht und Gesellschaft, 1954. 1 v.
(unpaged) 659.103 54-24644
HF5803 .I58 1954 MRR Alc.

International insurance dictionary:
[n.p., European Conference of
Insurance Supervisory Services, 1959]
xxxi, 1083 p. 368.03 61-35675
HG8025 .I5 MRR Alc.

International Railway Documentation
Bureau. Lexique général des termes
ferroviaires, [2. éd. entièrement
refondue et augm.] Amsterdam, J. H.
De Bussy, 1965. 1357 p. 625.1003
66-87434
TF9 .I46 1965 MRR Alc.

Jacks, Graham Vernon. Multilingual
vocabulary of soil science. [2d ed.,
rev. Rome] Land & Water Division,
Food and Agriculture Organization of
the United Nations [1960] xxiii, 428
p. 631.403 60-50105
S591 .J26 1960 MRR Alc.

Labarre, E. J. Dictionary and
encyclopedia of paper and paper-
making, 2d ed., rev. and enl.
London, Oxford University Press,
1952. xxi, 488 p. 676.03 53-29414
TS1085 .L3 1952a MRR Alc.

Lana, Gabriella. Glossary of
geographical names in six languages:
Amsterdam, New York, Elsevier Pub.
Co., 1967. 184 p. 910/.003 66-
25762
G104.5 .L3 MRR Ref Desk.

Nijdam, J. Tuinbouwkundig
woordenboek in acht talen. Herziene
en uitgebreide uitg. van de
Woordenlijst voor de tuinbouw in
zeven talen. ['s-Gravenhage,
Staatsdrukkerij--
Uitgeverijbedrijf; voor alle anderen
landen: Interscience Publishers, New
York] 1961. 504 p. 62-52704
SB45 .N673 MRR Alc.

Raaff, J. J. Index vocabulorum
quadrilingius; verf en vernis, [Den
Haag] Vereniging van Vernis- en
Verffabrikanten in Nederland,
Exportgroep Verf, 1958. 898 p.
667.603 59-27978
TP934.3 .R2 MRR Alc.

DUTCH LANGUAGE--DICTIONARIES-- (Cont.)
Rae, Kenneth, ed. Lexique
international de termes techniques de
théatre Bruxelles, Elsevier [1959]
139 p.   60-26926
PN2035 .R3 MRR Alc.

Servotte, Jozef V., 1903-
Dictionnaire commercial et financier:
2. ed., rev. et augm. Bruxelles,
Éditions Brepols [1960] ix, 955 p.
61-930
HF1002 .S42 1960 MRR Alc.

Union européenne des experts
comptables économiques et
financiers. Lexique U.E.C. Lexicon.
Düsseldorf, Verlagsbuchhandlung des
Instituts der Wirtschaftsprüfer.
1961. 1 v. (various pagings) 63-
31440
HF5621 .U5 MRR Alc.

DUTCH LANGUAGE--ETYMOLOGY--DICTIONARIES.
Franck, Johannes, Franck's
Etymologisch woordenboek der
Nederlandsche taal. 2. druk 's-
Gravenhage, M. Nijhoff, 1912. xvi,
897 p.   11-22072
PF580 .F82 MRR Alc.

DUTCH LANGUAGE--SYNONYMS AND ANTONYMS.
Hendriks, P. Nederlandse synoniemen;
Amsterdam, A. J. G. Strengholt
[1958] 256 p.   58-48788
PF591 .H4 MRR Alc.

DUTCH LITERATURE--BIBLIOGRAPHY.
Brinkman's cumulatieve catalogus van
boeken, en verder in den boekhandel
voorkomende artikelen, die ... in
Nederland zijn uitgegeven of herdrukt
... voorts een alfabetische lijst van
nederlandsche boeken in Belgie
uitgegeven ... Leiden [etc.] A. W.
Sijthoff [etc.] 015.492 33-17363
Z2431 .A46 MRR Alc Partial set

DUTCH LITERATURE--BIO-BIBLIOGRAPHY.
Lectuur-repertorium, [2. en
definitieve uitg. Antwerpen,
Vlaamsche Boekcentrale, 1952-54] 3
v. 011 53-15682
Z1010 .L43 MRR Biog.

Wie is die ... Amsterdam, Em.
Querido, 1966 [1967] 160 p. with
illus. [fl 2.50]   67-95858
PT5104 .W5 MRR Biog.

DUTCH LITERATURE--TRANSLATIONS FROM
FOREIGN LITERATURE--BIBLIOGRAPHY.
Lectuur-repertorium, [2. en
definitieve uitg. Antwerpen,
Vlaamsche Boekcentrale, 1952-54] 3
v. 011 53-15682
Z1010 .L43 MRR Biog.

DUTCH NEWSPAPERS--DIRECTORIES.
Sijthoff's adresboek voor den
Nederlandschen boekhandel Leiden, A.
W. Sijthoff. 26-11523
Z352 .S58 MRR Alc Latest edition

DUTCH NEWSPAPERS--DIRECTORIES--
PERIODICALS.
Handboek van de Nederlandse pers.
Feb. 1964- Barendrecht, Publiciteit.
66-93771
Z6956.N45 H35 MRR Alc Latest
edition

DUTCH PAINTINGS
see Paintings, Dutch

DUTCH PERIODICALS--DIRECTORIES.
Sijthoff's adresboek voor den
Nederlandschen boekhandel Leiden, A.
W. Sijthoff. 26-11523
Z352 .S58 MRR Alc Latest edition

DUTCH PERIODICALS--DIRECTORIES--
PERIODICALS.
Handboek van de Nederlandse pers.
Feb. 1964- Barendrecht, Publiciteit.
66-93771
Z6956.N45 H35 MRR Alc Latest
edition

DUTY.
see also Conduct of life

see also Ethics

DWELLINGS--MAINTENANCE AND REPAIR.
Audels do-it-yourself encyclopedia;
Illustrated ed. N[ew] Y[ork] T.
Audel [1963-66, v. 1, c1960] 2 v.
(1020 p.) 643.7 66-3696
TT155 .A82 MRR Alc.

Better homes and gardens. Handyman's
book, [Des Moines, Meredith Corp.,
1970] 400 p. 690.8 73-10975
TX323 .B4 1970 MRR Alc.

Daniels, George Emery, The awful
handyman's book, [1st ed.] New
York, Harper & Row [1966] ix, 179 p.
643.7 66-20732
TX323 .D34 MRR Alc.

Gladstone, Bernard. The New York
times complete manual of home repair.
New York, Macmillan [1966] x, 438
p. 643.7 66-12347
TH4817 .G55 MRR Alc.

O'Neill, Barbara Powell. The unhandy
man's guide to home repairs; New
York, Macmillan [1966] xiii, 366 p.
643.7 66-21160
TH4817 .O5 MRR Alc.

The Family handyman. America's
handyman book, Rev. ed. New York,
Scribner [1970] xiii. 529 p.
[$10.00] 643.7 70-85277
TH4817 .F28 1970 MRR Alc.

The Family handyman. America's
handyman book, New York, Scribner
[1961] 513 p. 643.7 61-7215
TT151 .F3 MRR Alc.

DWELLINGS--REMODELING.
Audels do-it-yourself encyclopedia;
Illustrated ed. N[ew] Y[ork] T.
Audel [1963-66, v. 1, c1960] 2 v.
(1020 p.) 643.7 66-3696
TT155 .A82 MRR Alc.

Harmon, Allen Jackson, The guide to
home remodeling New York, Grosset &
Dunlap [1972] 255 p. [$7.95]
643/.7 72-185850
TH4816 .H33 MRR Alc.

O'Neill, Barbara Powell. The unhandy
man's guide to home repairs; New
York, Macmillan [1966] xiii, 366 p.
643.7 66-21160
TH4817 .O5 MRR Alc.

Stanforth, Deirdre. Buying and
renovating a house in the city; New
York, Knopf, 1972. xiv, 400, xiv p.
[$10.00] 643/.7 71-173774
TH4816 .S7 MRR Alc.

EARLY AMERICAN ART INDUSTRIES AND TRADE
see Art industries and trade, Early
American

EARTH.
see also Ocean

see also Oceanography

see also Climatology

see also Geography

see also Geology

Kuiper, Gerard Peter, ed. The earth
as a planet. Chicago, University of
Chicago Press [1954] xvii, 751 p.
525 61-45074
QB501 .S6 vol. 2 MRR Alc.

Kummel, Bernhard, History of the
earth; San Francisco, W. H. Freeman
[1961] 610 p. 551.7 61-6783
QE501 .K79 MRR Alc.

EARTH, EFFECT OF MAN ON
see Man--Influence on nature

EARTH SATELLITES
see Artificial satellites

EARTH SCIENCES.
Bertin, Léon, Larousse encyclopedia
of the earth. London, P. Hamlyn
[1961] 419 p. 550.3 61-66629
QE501 .B563 1961a MRR Alc.

Pearl, Richard Maxwell, 1001
questions answered about earth
science, Rev. ed. Illustrated with
photos. and drawings. New York,
Dodd, Mead, 1969. xvi, 327 p.
[6.50] 550 77-5935
QE840 .P4 1969 MRR Alc.

EARTH SCIENCES--POPULAR WORKS.
Tufty, Barbara. 1001 questions
answered about natural land
disasters. New York, Dodd, Mead
[1969] xvi, 350 p. [$7.50] 551
68-29807
QE31 .T78 MRR Alc.

EARTHENWARE
see Pottery

EARTHQUAKES.
Lane, Frank Walter. The elements
rage: Newton Abbot (Devon), David &
Charles [1966] xvi, 280 p. [50/-]
551 66-66261
QC866 .L3 1966 MRR Alc.

EAST (FAR EAST)
see also Asia, Southeastern

EAST (FAR EAST)--BIBLIOGRAPHY.
Cumulative bibliography of Asian
studies, 1941-1965: Boston, Mass.,
G. K. Hall, 1969 [i.e. 1970] 4 v.
016.95 79-12105
Z3001 .C93 MRR Alc.

Kerner, Robert Joseph, Northeastern
Asia, a selected bibliography;
Berkeley, Calif., University of
California press, 1939. 2 v.
016.95 39-33136
Z3001 .K38 MRR Alc.

United States. Library of Congress.
Division of bibliography. ... Select
list of books (with references to
periodicals) relating to the Far
East. Washington, Govt. print. off.,
1904. 74 p. 04-33374
Z663.28 .S353 MRR Alc.

EAST (FAR EAST)--BIO-BIBLIOGRAPHY.
Teng, Ssu-yu, Japanese studies on
Japan & the Far East; [Hong Kong]
Hong Kong University Press, 1961. x,
485 p. 016.915 61-66803
Z3306 .T4 MRR Alc.

EAST (FAR EAST)--COMMERCE--DIRECTORIES.
A.A's Far East businessman's
directory. Hong Kong. 382/.025/5
79-237434
HF3763 .A65 MRR Alc Latest edition

The Eastern trade directory. [Cairo]
ne 62-1365
HF3760.8 .E25 MRR Alc Latest
edition

EAST (FAR EAST)--DESCRIPTION AND TRAVEL.
Clark, Sydney Aylmer, All the best
in Japan and the Orient, New York,
Dodd, Mead [1967] x, 509 p. 915
67-22197
DS811 .C5 1967 MRR Alc.

EAST (FAR EAST)--DESCRIPTION AND TRAVEL
--GUIDE-BOOKS.
Caldwell, John Cope, John C.
Caldwell's Orient travel guide. New
York, John Day Co. [1970] 392 p.
[7.95] 915 75-101464
DS504 .C33 1970 MRR Alc.

Waldo, Myra. Travel guide to the
Orient and the Pacific, 1970-71.
[Rev. ed. New York] Macmillan [1970]
xxii, 712 p. 915/.04/42 70-93723
DS4 .W3 1970 MRR Alc.

EAST (FAR EAST)--DESCRIPTION AND TRAVEL
--GUIDE-BOOKS--PERIODICALS.
Fodor's Japan and East Asia. 1972-
New York, D. McKay. 915.2/04/4 72-
621341
DS805.2 F64 MRR Alc Latest edition

EAST (FAR EAST)--ECONOMIC CONDITIONS.
Kirby, E. Stuart. Economic
development in East Asia, London,
Allen & Unwin, 1967. 253 p. [50/-]
330.95 67-108267
HC412 .K48 1967b MRR Alc.

EAST (FAR EAST)--HISTORY.
Bain, Chester Arthur, The Far East,
5th ed. Totowa, N.J., Littlefield,
Adams, 1972. xiii, 335 p. [$2.95
(pbk.)] 950 72-171255
DS513 .B3 1972 MRR Alc.

Clyde, Paul Hibbert, The Far East;
5th ed. Englewood Cliffs, N.J.,
Prentice-Hall [1971] xxiii, 536 p.
950 72-144100
DS511 .C67 1971 MRR Alc.

Fairbank, John King, East Asia:
tradition and transformation Boston,
Houghton Mifflin [1973] xvi, 969 p.
915/.03 72-85909
DS511 .F28 MRR Alc.

Peffer, Nathaniel, The Far East; a
modern history. New ed., rev. and
enl. Ann Arbor, University of
Michigan Press [1968] vi, 559, xii
p. [$8.50] 950 68-29270
DS511 .P4 1968 MRR Alc.

EAST (FAR EAST)--STATISTICS.
International Research Associates.
The new Far East: [Hong Kong]
Reader's Digest [Far East ltd.];
distributors: C.E. Tuttle Co.,
Rutland, Vt. [c1966] 159 p.
339.42/095 67-7110
HD7049 .I53 MRR Alc.

EAST (NEAR EAST)
see Near East

EAST AFRICA
see Africa, East

EAST EUROPEAN STUDIES--UNITED STATES.
Language and area studies, East
Central and Southeastern Europe;
Chicago, University of Chicago Press
[1969] xix, 483 p. 914.7 72-81222
DR34.8 .L33 MRR Alc.

EAST INDIANS IN EAST AFRICA.
Pandit, Shanti, Asians in east and
central Africa. [Nairobi] Panco
Publications [1963?] 366 p. 79-
30824
DT429 .P27 MRR Biog.

EASTER.
Fry, Edward Alexander. Almanacks for
students of English history. London,
Phillimore & co., ltd., 1915. vii,
138 p. 16-20586
CE61.G8 F8 MRR Alc.

EASTER CAROLS
see Carols

EASTERN EUROPE
see Europe, Eastern

EASTERN QUESTION (BALKAN)
Miller, William, The Ottoman Empire
and its successors, 1801-1927: 3rd
ed., new impression. London, Cass,
1966. xv, 616 p. [90/-]   956.101
66-67163
DR557 .M6 1966 MRR Alc.

EASTERN QUESTION (CENTRAL ASIA)
Fraser-Tytler, William Kerr, Sir,
Afghanistan: a study of political
developments in central and southern
Asia, 3rd ed., revised London, New
York [etc.] Oxford U.P., 1967. xvi,
362 p. [45/-]   958.1 67-88066
DS356 .F7 1967 MRR Alc.

EASTERN QUESTION (FAR EAST)--
BIBLIOGRAPHY.
Kerner, Robert Joseph, Northeastern
Asia, a selected bibliography;
Berkeley, Calif., University of
California press, 1939. 2 v.
016.95   39-33136
Z3001 .K38 MRR Alc.

ECCLESIASTICAL GEOGRAPHY
see also Bible--Geography

ECCLESIASTICAL GEOGRAPHY--DICTIONARIES.
Baudrillart, Alfred, cardinal, ed.
Dictionnaire d'histoire et de
geographie ecclesiastiques, Paris,
Letouzey et Ane, 1912- v.   09-
26333
BR95 .B3 MRR Alc.

ECCLESIASTICAL GEOGRAPHY--UNITED STATES-
-MAPS.
Gaustad, Edwin Scott. Historical
atlas of religion in America. [1st
ed.] New York, Harper & Row, [1962]
179 p.   209.73084   map62-51
G1201.E4 G3 1962 MRR Alc Atlas.

ECCLESIASTICAL HISTORY
see Church history

ECCLESIASTICAL LAW--HUNGARY.
[Mid European Law Project] Hungary,
churches and religion. [Washington]
Library of Congress, Law Library
[1951] 74 l.   56-61358
Z663.55.D5H82 MRR Alc.

ECCLESIASTICAL LAW--UNITED STATES.
Blakely, William Addison, ed.
American state papers and related
documents on freedom in religion.
4th rev. ed. Washington, Published
for the Religious Liberty Association
by the Review and Herald, 1949. 915
p.   263.8   50-206
BV133 .B6 1949 MRR Alc.

ECOLOGY.
see also Conservation of natural
resources

see also Desert ecology

see also Human ecology

Odum, Eugene Pleasants, Fundamentals
of ecology 3d ed. Philadelphia,
Saunders, 1971. xiv, 574 p.   574.5
76-81826
QH541 .O3 1971 MRR Alc.

ECOLOGY--BIBLIOGRAPHY.
Woodrow Wilson International Center
for Scholars. The human environment.
Washington, 1972. 2 v. [$5.00 per
vol.]   016.30131 72-601602
Z5118.A5 W66 1972 MRR Alc.

ECOLOGY--DICTIONARIES.
Hanson, Herbert Christian,
Dictionary of ecology. New York,
Philosophical Library [1962] 382 p.
574.503   60-15954
QH541 .H25 MRR Alc.

ECOLOGY--PERIODICALS--BIBLIOGRAPHY.
Wilson, Thomas Williams.
International environmental action;
[New York] Dunellen [1971] xviii,
364 p. [$12.50]   301.3/1 73-168684

HC79.E5 W53 MRR Alc.

ECOLOGY--STATISTICS.
Hilado, Carlos J., Handbook of
environmental management Westport,
Conn., Technomic Pub. Co. [1972- v.
301.31   74-174658
GF41 .H55 MRR Alc.

ECOLOGY--UNITED STATES--DIRECTORIES.
Halstead, Bruce W. A Golden guide to
environmental organizations. New
York, Golden Press [1972] 63 p.
[$0.95]   301.31/06   72-79158
GF5 .H34 MRR Alc.

ECOLOGY--UNITED STATES--YEARBOOKS.
Ecology USA 1971; New York, Special
Reports inc. [1972] xi, 610 p.
[$125.00]   333.7/2/0973 71-188164
QH541.145 .E26 MRR Alc.

ECONOMIC ASSISTANCE.
see also Reconstruction (1939-1951)

ECONOMIC ASSISTANCE--SOCIETIES, ETC.
OECD-ICVA directory; Paris, OECD,
1967. 1378 p. [90.00] 309.2/062
68-82889
HC60 .O2 TJ Rm.

ECONOMIC ASSISTANCE--STATISTICS.
Gallatin Service. Gallatin
statistical indicators. [New York,
Copley International Corporation,
1967- v.   310 72-12086
HA42 .G32 MRR Alc.

Organization for Economic Cooperation
and Development. Geographical
distribution of financial flows to
less developed countries
(disbursement) 1960-1964. Paris,
O.E.C.D.; [London, H.M.S.O.] 1966.
xvi, 179 p. [24/-]   338.91 67-
78951
HC60 .O65 MRR Alc.

United States. Arms Control and
Disarmament Agency. Bureau of
Economic Affairs. World military
expenditures. 1970- [Washington,
For sale by the Supt. of Docs., U.S.
Govt. Print. Off.] 338.4/7/355005
70-649143
UA17 .U42   MRR Ref Desk Latest
edition

ECONOMIC ASSISTANCE, AMERICAN.
United States. Agency for
International Development. Office of
Statistics and Reports. U.S.
economic assistance programs
administered by the Agency for
International Development and
predecessor agencies, April 3, 1948-
June 30, 1970. [Washington, 1971]
1v, 78 p.   338.91/73 70-613871
HC60.U6 I48 1971 MRR Ref Desk.

ECONOMIC ASSISTANCE, AMERICAN--AUSTRIA.
Heissenberger, Franz. The economic
reconstruction of Austria, 1945-1952;
Washington, Library of Congress,
Reference Dept.; European Affairs
Division, 1953. xii, 153 p.
330.9436   53-60025
Z663.26 .E35 MRR Alc.

ECONOMIC ASSISTANCE, CANADIAN--
DIRECTORIES.
Canadian Council for International Cooperation. Directory of Canadian non-
governmental organizations engaged in
international development assistance,
1970. Ottawa, 1970. 285 p. [$5.00]
309.2/233/7101724 79-855733
HC60 .C2877 1970a MRR Alc.

ECONOMIC ASSISTANCE, DOMESTIC.
see also Community development

see also Subsidies

see also Unemployed

ECONOMIC ASSISTANCE, DOMESTIC--UNITED
STATES.
Baker, John Austin, Guide to Federal
programs for rural development;
Washington, U.S. Govt. Print. Off.,
1971 [i.e. 1972] ii, 576 p. [$2.50
(paper cover)]   309.2/63/0973 72-
601448
HN90.C6 B352 MRR Alc.

Cross, Theodore L., Black
capitalism; [1st ed.] New York,
Atheneum, 1969. xii, 274 p. [8.95]
658.42 72-80268
E185.8 .C9 MRR Alc.

The Encyclopedia of U.S. Government
benefits; [Union City, N.J.] W. H.
Wise, 1967. viii, 1011 p.   353.0003
67-6136
JK424 .E55 1967 MRR Alc.

Roth, William V., 1969 listing of
operating Federal assistance programs
compiled during the Roth study.
Washington, U.S. Govt. Print. Off.,
1969. x, 1132 p. [4.50]   338.973
73-605845
HJ275 .R6 1969 MRR Ref Desk.

Rowland, Howard S. The New York
times Guide to Federal aid for cities
and towns [New York] Quadrangle
Books [1972, c1971] xxxii, 1243 p.
336.1/85 72-78499
HJ275 .R64 MRR Ref Desk.

Toy, Henry, Federal dollars for
scholars [1st ed.] Washington, Nu-
Toy [1970] vii, 54 p., 292 columns.
378.3/0973 77-112985
LB2338 .T6 MRR Alc.

United States. Bureau of Outdoor
Recreation. Federal outdoor
recreation programs and recreation-
related environmental programs. [1st
revision. Washington; For sale by
the Supt. of Docs., U.S. Govt. Print.
Off.] 1970. 226 p. [2.75]
301.5/7/0973 70-607632
GV53 .A47 1970 MRR Alc.

United States. Dept. of Health,
Education, and Welfare. Center for
Community Planning. HEW cities
handbook. [Rev. Washington; For
sale by the Supt. of Docs., U.S.
Govt. Print. Off., 1969] 1 v.
(unpaged) [0.50]   353.84 76-604330

HV85 .A554 1969 MRR Alc.

United States. Office of Management
and Budget. 1973 catalog of Federal
domestic assistance. 7th ed.
Washington; [For sale by the Supt. of
Docs., U.S. Govt. Print. Off.] 1973-
1 v. (loose-leaf) [$7.00]   338.973
73-600118
HC110.P63 U55 1973 MRR Ref Desk.

ECONOMIC ASSISTANCE, DOMESTIC--UNITED
STATES--BIBLIOGRAPHY.
Tompkins, Dorothy Louise (Campbell)
Culver. Poverty in the United States
during the sixties; [Berkeley]
Institute of Governmental Studies,
University of California, 1970. ix,
542 p. [$10.00]   016.3625/0973 74-
632910
Z7165.U5 T62 MRR Alc.

ECONOMIC ASSISTANCE, DOMESTIC--UNITED
STATES--DIRECTORIES.
Community action agency atlas. 1969-
[Washington] 338.973 71-614540
HC110.P63 A28 MRR Alc Latest
edition

United States. Office of Economic
Opportunity. Community Action
Programs. Community action agency
atlas. [Washington] Office of
Economic Opportunity, 1969. 2, 4,
362 p.   338.973 71-603810
HC110.P63 A5543 MRR Alc.

United States. Office of Minority
Business Enterprise. Special catalog
of Federal programs assisting
minority enterprise. Washington; For
sale by the Supt. of Docs., U.S.
Govt. Print. Off., 1971. xiii, 89 p.
[$1.00]   338.973 77-614023
HC110.P63 A57 MRR Alc.

ECONOMIC BOTANY
see Botany, Economic

ECONOMIC DEVELOPMENT
see also Industrialization

see also Underdeveloped areas

Higgins, Benjamin Howard, Economic
development; Rev. ed. New York, W.
W. Norton [1968] xvi, 918 p.   338.9
67-11081
HD82 .H45 1968 MRR Alc.

ECONOMIC DEVELOPMENT--BIBLIOGRAPHY.
Brode, John. The process of
modernization; Cambridge, Mass.,
Harvard University Press, 1969. x,
378 p. [6.50]   016.3092 69-13765
Z7164.U5 B7 MRR Alc.

Geiger, H. Kent. National
development, 1776-1966: Metuchen,
N.J., Scarecrow Press, 1969. 247 p.
016.309 77-5813
Z7164.U5 G43 MRR Alc.

International Bank for Reconstruction
and Development. Development Services
Dept. List of national development
plans. 2d ed. Washington, 1968.
viii, 129 l.   016.3389 70-3493
Z7164.E15 I58 1968 MRR Alc.

ReQua, Eloise G. The developing
nations; Detroit, Gale Research Co.
[1965] 339 p.   016.33891 65-17576

Z7164.U5 R4 MRR Alc.

Spitz, Allan A. Developmental
change; an annotated bibliography,
Lexington, University Press of
Kentucky [1969] xi, 316 p. [12.50]
016.309 69-19766
Z7164.E15 S615 MRR Alc.

ECONOMIC DEVELOPMENT--RESEARCH.
Organization for Economic Cooperation
and Development. Development Centre.
Catalogue of social and economic
development institutes and
programmes: research. Paris,
Development Centre of the
Organization for Economic Cooperation and Development, 1968. 413
p. [$4.50]   338.9/0072 75-417969
HD82 .O656 MRR Alc.

ECONOMIC DEVELOPMENT--STUDY AND
TEACHING.
Organization for Economic Cooperation and Development.
Development Centre. Catalogue of
social and economic development
training institutes and programmes.
Paris, O.E.C.D.; London, H.M.S.O.,
1968. [2], 344 p. [31/-]
309.2/23/0711 68-140061
HD82 .O66 MRR Alc.

ECONOMIC DEVELOPMENT--STUDY AND (Cont.)
Organization for Economic Cooperation
and Development. Development Centre.
Catalogue of social and economic
development institutes and
programmes: research. Paris,
Development Centre of the
Organization for Economic Cooperation and Development, 1968. 413
p. [$4.50] 338.9/0072 75-417969
HD82 .O656 MRR Alc.

ECONOMIC ENTOMOLOGY
see Insects, Injurious and beneficial

ECONOMIC FORECASTING.
Ebasco Services Incorporated.
Business and economic charts.
Chicago. 59-44534
HD9685.U7 E3 MRR Alc Latest
edition

ECONOMIC FORECASTING--BIBLIOGRAPHY.
United States. Office of Regional
Development Planning. Guide to
economic projections and forecasts.
[Washington] U.S. Dept. of Commerce,
Economic Development Administration
[1968] iii, 113 p. 016.330973 77-
600326
Z7165.U5 A48 MRR Alc.

ECONOMIC FORECASTING--YEARBOOKS.
New York times. World economic
review and forecast. 1965-
Princeton, N.J. [etc.] Van Nostrand
[etc.] 65-17639
HC10 .N45 MRR Alc Latest edition

ECONOMIC HISTORY.
Clough, Shepard Bancroft, European
economic history; 2d ed. New York,
McGraw-Hill [c1968] xix, 623 p.
330.91821 68-11928
HC21 .C64 1968 MRR Alc.

ECONOMIC HISTORY--1918-1945.
United Nations. Statistical Office.
The growth of world industry, 1938-
1961; New York, United Nations,
1963. xvi, 849 p. 338.4083 63-
25411
HC59 .U46 MRR Alc.

ECONOMIC HISTORY--1918-
The United States in world affairs.
1931- New York, Simon & Schuster
[etc.] 32-26065
E744 .U66 MRR Alc Full set

ECONOMIC HISTORY--1945-
Econtel Research. World industrial
production. London, Econtel
Research, 1969. 20 p. [60/- ($8.00
U.S.)] 338/.09/045 79-557483
HA40.I6 E3 MRR Alc.

New geography. 1966/67- London, New
York, Abelard-Schuman. 330.9 67-
14202
HC59.A15 N4 MRR Alc Latest edition

United Nations. Statistical Office.
The growth of world industry. 1967
ed. New York, United Nations, 1968-
69 [v. 1, 1969] 2 v. 338 77-7739

HC59 .U458 MRR Alc.

United Nations. Statistical Office.
The growth of world industry, 1938-
1961; New York, United Nations,
1963. xvi, 849 p. 338.4083 63-
25411
HC59 .U46 MRR Alc.

ECONOMIC HISTORY--1945- --BIBLIOGRAPHY.
Allen, David E. comp. Business books
translated from English, 1950-1965,
Reading, Mass., Addison-Wesley Pub.
Co. [1966] xiv, 414 p. 016.33 66-
23644
Z7164.E2 A54 MRR Alc.

International Bank for Reconstruction
and Development. Development Services
Dept. List of national development
plans. 2d ed. Washington] 1968.
viii, 129 l. 016.3389 70-3493
Z7164.E15 I58 1968 MRR Alc.

ECONOMIC HISTORY--1945- --PERIODICALS.
Financial times yearbook: 1970- New
York, St. Martin's Press. 330/.05
76-95357
HC10 .F54 MRR Alc Latest edition

ECONOMIC HISTORY--1945- --STATISTICS.
Taylor, Charles Lewis. World
handbook of political and social
indicators, 2d ed. New Haven, Yale
University Press, 1972. xiv, 443 p.
[$15.00] 301/.01/8 70-179479
HN15 .T37 1972 MRR Alc.

ECONOMIC HISTORY--1945- --YEARBOOKS.
New York times. World economic
review and forecast. 1965-
Princeton, N.J. [etc.] Van Nostrand
[etc.] 65-17639
HC10 .N45 MRR Alc Latest edition

United Nations. Centre for
Development Planning, Projections,
and Policies. World economic survey.
New York. 300/.8 s [330.9/047] 72-
627143
JX1997 .A2 subser HC59 MRR Alc
Latest edition

ECONOMIC HISTORY--BIBLIOGRAPHY.
Ball, Joyce. Foreign statistical
documents; Stanford, Calif., Hoover
Institution in War, Revolution, and
Peace, Stanford University, 1967.
vii, 173 p. 016.3309 67-14234
Z7551 .B3 MRR Alc.

Foreign affairs bibliography;
1919/32-1952/62. New York, Published
for the Council on Foreign Relations
by R. R. Bowker [etc.] 016.327
[016.9] 33-7094
Z6463 .F73 MRR Alc Full set

Schleiffer, Hedwig, Index to
economic history essays in
Festschriften, 1900-1950 Cambridge,
A. H. Cole; distributed by Harvard
University Press, 1953. 68 p.
016.3304 53-11201
Z7164.E2 S36 MRR Alc.

United States. Library of Congress.
Reference Dept. International
economic and social development;
Washington, 1952. vi, 55 p.
016.3309 52-60016
Z663.28 .I5 MRR Alc.

ECONOMIC HISTORY--PERIODICALS--INDEXES.
Washington, D.C. Joint Library of the
International Monetary Fund and the
International Bank for Reconstruction
and Development. Economics and
finance; index to periodical
articles, 1947-1971. Boston, G. K.
Hall, 1972. 4 v. 016.33 73-156075

Z7164.E2 W34 MRR Alc (dk 33)

ECONOMIC HISTORY--YEARBOOKS.
The Economic almanac; 1940- New
York [etc.], Macmillan Co. [etc.]
330.58 40-30704
HC101 .E38 MRR Ref Desk Latest
edition

ECONOMIC INDICATORS--UNITED STATES.
United States. Bureau of Labor
Standards. State economic and social
indicators: wages, and family income,
educational attainment, projected
growth in labor force, 1970-80
Washington; For sale by the Supt. of
Docs., U.S. Govt. Print. Off.] 1970.
vii, 96 p. [$1.00] 330/.973 71-
610107
HA211 .A48 MRR Alc.

ECONOMIC POISONS
see Pesticides

ECONOMIC POLICY.
see also Agriculture and state

see also Labor supply

see also Regional planning

ECONOMIC POLICY--BIBLIOGRAPHY.
International Bank for Reconstruction
and Development. Development Services
Dept. List of national development
plans. 2d ed. Washington] 1968.
viii, 129 l. 016.3389 70-3493
Z7164.E15 I58 1968 MRR Alc.

ECONOMIC RESEARCH.
Berenson, Conrad. Research and
report writing for business and
economics [1st ed.] New York,
Random House [1971] x, 182 p.
808.06/6/65 75-126896
H62 .B42 MRR Alc.

ECONOMIC RESEARCH--BIBLIOGRAPHY.
Belson, William A. Bibliography on
methods of social and business
research London, London School of
Economics and Political Science;
Lockwood, 1973. viii, 300 p.
[£4.95] 016.3/001/8 73-155242
Z7161 .B44 MRR Alc.

ECONOMIC RESEARCH--UNITED STATES--
SOCIETIES, ETC.
United States. Office of Regional
Development Planning. Guide to
economic projections and forecasts.
[Washington] U.S. Dept. of Commerce,
Economic Development Administration
[1968] iii, 113 p. 016.330973 77-
600326
Z7165.U5 A48 MRR Alc.

ECONOMIC SECURITY.
see also Insurance, Social

ECONOMIC SECURITY--UNITED STATES.
Turnbull, John Gudert, Economic and
social security 4th ed. New York,
Ronald Press Co. [1973] v, 728 p.
368.4/00973 73-76680
HD7125 .T84 1973 MRR Alc.

ECONOMIC STATISTICS
see Statistics

ECONOMIC SURVEYS.
see also Market surveys

ECONOMIC SURVEYS--BIBLIOGRAPHY.
Belson, William A. Bibliography on
methods of social and business
research London, London School of
Economics and Political Science;
Lockwood, 1973. viii, 300 p.
[£4.95] 016.3/001/8 73-155242
Z7161 .B44 MRR Alc.

International Trade Centre. Market
surveys by products and countries;
Geneva, 1969. ix, 203 p. [$5.00
(U.S.)] 016.6588/3 72-186218
Z7164.M18 I5 1969 MRR Alc.

ECONOMICS.
see also Banks and banking

see also Business

see also Commerce

see also Consumption (Economics)

see also Credit

see also Finance

see also Finance, Public

see also Industry

see also Labor and laboring classes

see also Manufactures

see also Money

see also Prices

see also Saving and investment

see also Taxation

see also Transportation

Aristoteles. The Metaphysics ...
London, W. Heinemann, ltd.; New York,
G. P. Putnam's sons, 1933-35. 2 v.
33-17911
PA3612 .A8A13 1933 MRR Alc.

Harriss, Clement Lowell, The
American economy; 6th ed. Homewood,
Ill., R. D. Irwin, 1968. xv, 998 p.
330.973 68-14871
HC106.5 .H325 1968 MRR Alc.

ECONOMICS--ABSTRACTS--PERIODICALS.
Economic abstracts. v. 1- June 1,
1953- The Hague, Nijhoff. 56-41652

HB1.A1 E2 MRR Alc Full set

ECONOMICS--BIBLIOGRAPHY.
Allen, David E. comp. Business books
translated from English, 1950-1965,
Reading, Mass., Addison-Wesley Pub.
Co. [1966] xiv, 414 p. 016.33 66-
23644
Z7164.E2 A54 MRR Alc.

Bibliography of publications of
university bureaus of business and
economic research. [Boulder, Colo.,
etc.] Business Research Division,
University of Colorado.
016.33/007/2073 77-635614
Z7165.U5 A8 MRR Alc Full set

Business books in print: subject
index, author index, title index.
1973- New York, R. R. Bowker Co.
016.33 73-8590
Z7164.C81 B962 MRR Alc Latest
edition

Coman, Edwin Truman, Sources of
business information, Rev. ed.
Berkeley, University of California
Press, 1964. xii, 330 p. 016.65
64-18639
Z7164.C81 C75 1964 MRR Alc.

Fundaburk, Emma Lila, Development of
economic thought and analysis.
Metuchen, N.J.; Scarecrow Press,
1973. lvi, 875 p. 016.33/009's
016.33/009 72-13158
Z7164.E2 F82 vol. 1 MRR Alc.

Fundaburk, Emma Lila, Reference
materials and periodicals in
economics; Metuchen, N.J.; Scarecrow
Press, 1971- v. 016.33 78-
142232
Z7164.E2 F83 MRR Alc.

International bibliography of
economics v. 1- 1952- London,
Tavistock Publications; Chicago,
Aldine Pub. Co. 55-2317
Z7164.E2 I58 MRR Alc Full set

Journal of economic literature. v. 7-
Mar. 1969- Menasha, Wis. American
Economic Association] [$6.00] 330
73-646621
HB1 .J6 MRR Alc Full set

ECONOMICS--BIBLIOGRAPHY. (Cont.)
Lovett, Robert Woodberry. American
economic and business history
information sources; Detroit, Gale
Research Co. [1971] 323 p. [$14.50]
016.330973 78-137573
Z7165.U5 L66 MRR Alc.

Maltby, Arthur. Economics and
commerce; London, Bingley, 1968.
239 p. [48/-] 016.33 68-103704
Z7164.E2 M38 1968b MRR Alc.

Melnyk, Peter. Economics;
bibliographic guide to reference
books and information resources.
Littleton, Colo., Libraries
Unlimited, 1971. 263 p. 016.33 71-
144203
Z7164.E2 M45 MRR Alc.

Public Affairs Information Service.
Bulletin ... annual cumulation. 1st-
1915- New York [etc.] 16-920
Z7163 .P9 MRR Circ Full set

Public Affairs Information Service.
Foreign language index. 1968/71-
New York. 016.3 72-626907
Z7164.E2 P8 MRR Circ Full set

Reinhart, Bruce. The vocational-
technical library collection;
Williamsport, Pa., Bro-Dart Pub. Co.;
1970. xiv, 377 p. 016.6 70-122456

Z7911 .R45 MRR Alc.

Universal Reference System. Economic
regulation: business and government;
Princeton, N.J., Princeton Research
Pub. Co. [1869] xx, llll p. 016.33
68-57824
Z7161 .U64 vol. 8 MRR Alc.

Utz, Arthur Fridolin, Bibliographie
der Sozialethik. 1- 1956/59
Freiburg, New York, Herder. a 61-
2645
Z7161 .U83 MRR Alc Full set

Verwey, Gerlof. The economist's
handbook, Amsterdam, The economist's
handbook, 1934. viii, p., 1 l., 460
p. 016.31 35-4837
Z7553.E2 V6 MRR Alc.

ECONOMICS--BIBLIOGRAPHY--CATALOGS.
California. University. Institute of
Governmental Studies. Library.
Subject catalog of the Institute of
Governmental Studies Library,
University of California, Berkeley.
Boston, G. K. Hall, 1970 [pref. 1971]
26 v. 016.353 73-152341
Z7164.A2 C34 MRR Alc (Dk 33)

Harvard University. Graduate School
of Business Administration. Baker
Library. Subject catalog of the
Baker Library, Graduate School of
Business Administration, Harvard
University. Boston, G. K. Hall,
1971. 10 v. 016.33 70-170935
Z7164.C81 H275 MRR Alc (Dk 33)

Kiel. Universität. Institut für
Weltwirtschaft. Bibliothek.
Personenkatalog. Boston, G. K. Hall,
1966. 30 v. 72-213362
Z7164.E2 K55 MRR Alc. (Dk 33)

Kiel. Universität. Institut für
Weltwirtschaft. Bibliothek.
Regionenkatalog. Boston, G. K. Hall,
1967. 52 v. 017/.5 67-9425
Z929 .K52 1967 MRR Alc. (Dk 33).

ECONOMICS--BIBLIOGRAPHY--UNION LISTS.
Black, R. D. Collison. A catalogue
of pamphlets on economic subjects
published between 1750 and 1900 and
now housed in Irish libraries. New
York, A. M. Kelley, 1969. ix, 632 p.
016.33 79-81988
Z7164.E2 B6 MRR Alc.

ECONOMICS--BOOK REVIEWS--PERIODICALS.
Journal of economic literature. v. 7-
Mar. 1969- Menasha, Wis. American
Economic Association] [$6.00] 330
73-646621
HB1 .J6 MRR Alc Full set

ECONOMICS--COLLECTIONS.
Newman, Philip Charles, ed. Source
readings in economic thought; [1st
ed.] New York, Norton [1954] 762 p.
330.82 54-2375
HB34 .N46 MRR Alc.

ECONOMICS--DICTIONARIES.
Davis, William, The language of
money; [1st American ed.] Boston,
Houghton Mifflin, 1973. xiii, 267 p.
[$6.95] 330/.03 72-2281
HG151 .D37 MRR Alc.

The Economic almanac; 1940- New
York [etc.] Macmillan Co. [etc.]
330.58 40-30704
HC101 .E38 MRR Ref Desk Latest
edition

Economics: encyclopedia. 1973/74-
Guilford, Conn., Dushkin Pub. Group.
330/.03 72-90094
HB61 .E26 MRR Ref Desk Latest
edition

Eichborn, Reinhart von. Business
dictionary. Englewood Cliffs, N.J.,
Prentice-Hall [1962, v.2, c1961] 2
v. 330.3 62-13618
HB61 .E433 MRR Alc.

Gilpin, Alan. Dictionary of economic
terms. 3rd ed. London,
Butterworths, 1973. [8], 230 p.
[£4.00] 330/.03 74-165820
HB61 .G47 1973 MRR Alc.

Hanson, John Lloyd. A dictionary of
economics and commerce, 3rd ed.
London, Macdonald & Evans, 1969. vi,
474 p. [42/-] 330/.03 77-437920
HB61 .H35 1969 MRR Alc.

Hanson, John Lloyd. A dictionary of
economics and commerce, 2nd ed.
London, MacDonald & Evans, 1967.
[6], 432 p. [35/-] 330.03 67-
110693
HB61 .H35 1967 MRR Alc.

Hoof, Henri van. Economic
terminology English-French.
München, Hueber [1967]. 770 p.
[DM34.80] 330/.03 68-142981
HB61 .H57 MRR Alc.

Horton, Byrne Joseph, Dictionary of
modern economics, Washington, Public
Affairs Press [1948] ix, 365 p.
330.3 48-10684
HB61 .H585 MRR Alc.

International Chamber of Commerce.
United States Council. International
economic organizations & terms
glossary. [New York, 1964] 48 p.
64-54675
HB61 .I6 1964 MRR Alc.

Lazarus, Harold. American business
dictionary. New York, Philosophical
Library [1957] xvi, 522 p. 650.3
57-867
HB61 .L3 MRR Alc.

Marxism, Communism, and Western
society; [New York] Herder and
Herder [1972-73] 8 v. 300/.3 79-
176368
AE5 .M27 MRR Alc.

The McGraw-Hill dictionary of modern
economics; 2d ed. New York, McGraw-
Hill [1973] xii, 792 p. 330/.03
72-11813
HB61 .M16 1973 MRR Ref Desk.

Nemmers, Erwin Esser, Dictionary of
economics and business. [3rd ed.]
Totowa, N.J., Littlefield, Adams,
1974. 485 p. 330/.03 73-22090
HB61 .N45 1974 MRR Alc.

Palgrave, Robert Harry Inglis, Sir,
ed. Palgrave's Dictionary of
political economy, London, Macmillan
and co., limited, 1925-26. 3 v.
mrr01-31
HB61 .P17 1925a MRR Alc.

Paradis, Adrian A. The economics
reference book [1st ed.]
Philadelphia, Chilton Book Co.
[c1970] 191 p. 330/.03 77-131881

HB61 .P34 MRR Alc.

Pitman's business man's guide: 14th
ed. London, Pitman, 1967. [5], 346
p. [32/-] 650/.03 68-92621
HF1001 .S6 1967 MRR Alc.

Renner, Rüdiger. Deutsch-englische
Wirtschaftssprache; München, M.
Hueber, 1965. 556 p. 65-79732
HB61 .R38 MRR Alc.

Schwartz, Robert J. The dictionary
of business and industry. New York,
B. C. Forbes and Sons Pub. Co. [1954]
xlvi, 561 p. 603 54-3133
T9 .S38 MRR Alc.

Seldon, Arthur, ed. Everyman's
dictionary of economics; London, J.
M. Dent [1965] xxix, 449 p. 65-
5820
HB61 .S39 MRR Alc.

Sloan, Harold Stephenson, A
dictionary of economics, 4th ed.
rev. [and enl.] N[ew] Y[ork], Barnes
& Noble [1964] xii, 371 p. 330.3
64-18785
HB61 .S54 1964 MRR Alc.

Taylor, Philip A. S. A new
dictionary of economics, London,
Routledge & K. Paul, 1966. vii, 304
p. [25/-] 330.03 66-2665
HB61 .T38 MRR Alc.

ECONOMICS--DICTIONARIES--DUTCH.
Bons, A. Engels handelswoordenboek
(Nederlands-Engels) Deventer, Æ. E.
Kluwer [1957] 1170 p. 57-46259
HF1002 .B59 MRR Alc.

Bons, A. Engels handelswoordenboek
(Nederlands-Engels) Deventer, Æ. E.
Kluwer [1957] 1170 p. 57-56259
HF1002 .B59 MRR Alc.

ECONOMICS--DICTIONARIES--FRENCH.
Baudhuin, Fernand, Dictionnaire de
l'économie contemporaine.
(Verviers, Gérard et Co, 1968). 302
p. [80.00] 330/.03 78-409250
HB61 .B36 MRR Alc.

ECONOMICS--DICTIONARIES--GERMAN.
Eichborn, Reinhart von. Business
dictionary. Englewood Cliffs, N.J.,
Prentice-Hall [1962, v.2, c1961] 2
v. 330.3 62-13618
HB61 .E433 MRR Alc.

Gunston, C. A. Gunston & Corner's
German-English glossary of financial
and economic terms. 6th ed., greatly
compressed, but in content much
amplified, Frankfurt am Main, F.
Knapp [1972] xxiii, 1203 p.
330/.03 72-188587
HG151 .G85 1972 MRR Alc.

Handwörterbuch der
Sozialwissenschaften. Stuttgart, G.
Fisher, 1952- v. a 53-7990
H45 .H18 MRR Alc.

Renner, Rüdiger. Deutsch-englische
Wirtschaftssprache; München, M.
Hueber, 1965. 556 p. 65-79732
HB61 .R38 MRR Alc.

ECONOMICS--DICTIONARIES--POLYGLOT.
Herbst, Robert. Dictionary of
commercial, financial, and legal
terms; 2d ed., Zug, Translegal
[1966- v. 330/.03 67-8369
HB61 .H462 MRR Alc.

Herbst, Robert. Dictionary of
commercial, financial, and legal
terms 3rd ed. rev. Zug, Translegal
[1968- v. [unpriced] 330/.03
76-410368
HB61 .H463 MRR Alc.

Polec. 2., verb. und erw. Aufl.
Berlin, de Gruyter, 1967. xvi, 1037
p. with map. [DM 48.-] 330/.03 68-
70864
H40 .P6 1967 MRR Alc.

Zahn, Hans E. Euro-Wirtschafts-
Worterbuch; Frankfurt am Main, F.
Knapp [c1973] xiii, 702 p. 73-
318519
HB61 .Z34 MRR Alc.

ECONOMICS--DICTIONARIES--SPANISH.
Sell, Lewis L. Español-ingles
diccionario para especialistas en
seguros, finanzas, derecho, trabajo,
politica, comercio; New York, D.
McKay Co. [1957] 650 p. 330.3 57-
3078
HB61 .S4 MRR Alc.

ECONOMICS--HISTORY.
Bell, John Fred, A history of
economic thought; 2d ed. New York,
Ronald Press [1967] iii, 745 p.
330/.01/09 67-11583
HB75 .B4 1967 MRR Alc.

Blaug, Mark. Economic theory in
retrospect. Rev. ed. Homewood,
Ill., R. D. Irwin, 1968. xxiv, 710
p. 330.1/09 67-21000
HB75 .B664 1968 MRR Alc.

ECONOMICS--HISTORY--BIBLIOGRAPHY.
Fundaburk, Emma Lila, Development of
economic thought and analysis.
Metuchen, N.J., Scarecrow Press,
1973. lvi, 875 p. 016.33/009 s
016.33/009 72-13158
Z7164.E2 F82 vol. 1 MRR Alc.

Schleiffer, Hedwig, Index to
economic history essays in
Festschriften, 1900-1950 Cambridge,
A. H. Cole; distributed by Harvard
University Press, 1953. 68 p.
016.3304 53-11201
Z7164.E2 S36 MRR Alc.

ECONOMICS--HISTORY--CHRONOLOGY.
Baudhuin, Fernand, Dictionnaire de
l'économie contemporaine.
(Verviers, Gérard et Co, 1968). 302
p. [80.00] 330/.03 78-409250
HB61 .B36 MRR Alc.

ECONOMICS--HISTORY--SWEDEN.
Landgren, Karl Gustav, Economics in
modern Sweden. Washington, Reference
Dept., Library of Congress, 1957.
ix, 117 p. 330.1 57-60010
Z663.2.E33 MRR Alc.

ECONOMICS--HISTORY--UNITED STATES.
Dorfman, Joseph. The economic mind
in American civilization. New York,
Viking Press, 1946-59. 5 v.
330.973   45-11318
   HB119.A2 D6 MRR Alc.

Wilhite, Virgle Glenn. Founders of
American economic thought and policy.
New York, Bookman Associates [1958]
442 p.   330.973   58-2334
   HB119.A2 W5 MRR Alc.

ECONOMICS--PERIODICALS.
Journal of economic literature. v. 7-
Mar. 1969- Menasha, Wis. American
Economic Association] [$6.00]   330
73-646621
   HB1 .J6   MRR Alc Full set

ECONOMICS--PERIODICALS--BIBLIOGRAPHY.
Committee on Latin America. Latin
American economic & social serials:
London, Published on behalf of CQLA
by Bingley, 1969. 189 p. [50/-]
016.3091/8 74-382598
   Z7165.L3 C65 MRR Alc.

Harvard University. Graduate School
of Business Administration. Baker
Library. Current periodical
publications in Baker Library.
1971/72- [Boston] 016.33/005 72-
620452
   Z7164.C81 H266 MRR Alc Latest
   edition

ECONOMICS--PERIODICALS--INDEXES.
Business periodicals index. v. 1-
Jan. 1958- New York, H. W. Wilson
Co. 016.6505 58-12645
   Z7164.C81 B983 MRR Circ Full set

F & S index international:
industries, countries, companies.
1st- ed.: 1968- Cleveland,
Predicasts. 016.338   74-644265
   Z7164.C81 F13 MRR Alc Full set /
   Sci RR Partial set

Fondation nationale des sciences
politiques. Bibliographie courante
d'articles de périodiques
postérieurs à 1944 sur les
problèmes politiques, économiques,
et sociaux. Boston, G. K. Hall,
1968. 17 v.   70-409780
   AI7 .F6 MRR Alc. (Dk 33).

Index of economic articles. v. 7-A:
1964/65. Homewood, Ill., R. D.
Irwin. 73-14217
   Z7164.E2 I45 MRR Alc Full set

Index of economic articles in
journals and collective volumes. v.
8- 1966- Homewood, Ill., R. D.
Irwin. 016.33 72-622847
   Z7164.E2 I4812 MRR Alc Latest
   edition

Index of economic journals. v. 1-7:
1886/1924-1964/65. Homewood, Ill.,
R. D. Irwin. 61-8020
   Z7164.E2 I48 MRR Alc Full set

International bibliography of
economics. v. 1- 1952- London,
Tavistock Publications; Chicago,
Aldine Pub. Co. 55-2317
   Z7164.E2 I58 MRR Alc Full set

International Labor Office. Library.
International labour documentation:
cumulative edition. Boston, Mass.,
G. K. Hall. 72-625702
   H91 .I56 MRR Alc Full set

International Labor Office. Library.
Subject index to International labour
documentation, 1957-1964. Boston, G.
K. Hall, 1968. 2 v.   mrr01-76
   Z7164.L1 I646 MRR Alc.

Journal of economic literature. v. 7-
Mar. 1969- Menasha, Wis. American
Economic Association] [$6.00]   330
73-646621
   HB1 .J6 MRR Alc Full set

Kiel. Universität. Institut für
Weltwirtschaft. Bibliothek.
Personenkatalog. Boston, G. K. Hall,
1966. 30 v.   72-213362
   Z7164.E2 K55 MRR Alc. (Dk 33)

Public Affairs Information Service.
Bulletin ... annual cumulation. 1st-
1915- New York [etc.] 16-820
   Z7163 .P9 MRR Circ Full set

Public Affairs Information Service.
Foreign language index. 1968/71-
New York. 016.3 72-626907
   Z7164.E2 P8 MRR Circ Full set

United States. Dept. of Commerce.
Library. Price sources; New York,
B. Franklin [1968] iv, 320 p.
016.33852 70-6381
   Z7164.P94 U56 1968 MRR Alc.

Wall Street Journal. (Indexes)
Index. [New York] Dow Jones & Co.
59-35162
   HG1 .W26 MRR Alc Full set

Washington, D.C. Joint Library of the
International Monetary Fund and the
International Bank for Reconstruction
and Development. Economics and
finance; index to periodical
articles, 1947-1971. Boston, G. K.
Hall, 1972. 4 v.   016.33 73-156075

   Z7164.E2 W34 MRR Alc (dk 33)

**ECONOMICS--SOCIETIES, ETC.--
DICTIONARIES.**
The McGraw-Hill dictionary of modern
economics; 2d ed. New York, McGraw-
Hill [1973] xii, 792 p.   330/.03
72-11813
   HB61 .M16 1973 MRR Ref Desk.

**ECONOMICS--STUDY AND TEACHING--CANADA--
DIRECTORIES.**
Graduate study in economics; 2d ed.
[Evanston? Ill., American Economic
Association] 1969. ix, 177 p.
[$2.50]   330/.071/173 74-28832
   H62.5.U5 G7 1969 MRR Alc.

**ECONOMICS--STUDY AND TEACHING--UNITED
STATES--DIRECTORIES.**
Graduate study in economics; 2d ed.
[Evanston? Ill., American Economic
Association] 1969. ix, 177 p.
[$2.50]   330/.071/173 74-28832
   H62.5.U5 G7 1969 MRR Alc.

ECONOMICS--TERMINOLOGY.
Howell, James M. Dictionary of
economic and statistical terms
Washington] U.S. Dept. of Commerce;
[for sale by the Supt. of Docs., U.S.
Govt. Print. Off.] 1969. 73 p.
[1.25]   330/.01/4 70-605347
   HB61 .H68 MRR Alc.

Moreno Pacheco, Miguel. Economic
terminology English-Spanish.
München, Hueber (1967)   480 p. [DM
24.80]   330/.01/4 68-82025
   HB61 .M6 MRR Alc.

ECONOMICS, COMPARATIVE
see Comparative economics

ECONOMISTS.
Economics: encyclopedia. 1973/74-
Guilford, Conn., Dushkin Pub. Group.
330/.03 72-90094
   HB61 .E26 MRR Ref Desk Latest
   edition

ECONOMISTS--UNITED STATES--BIOGRAPHY.
American men and women of science;
economics. 1st- 1974- New York,
R. R. Bowker. 330/.092/2[B] 74-
645741
   HB119.A3 A43 MRR Biog Latest
   edition

ECONOMISTS, AMERICAN.
American economic association. Hand
book of the American economic
association. 1890/91, 1894-99, 1906-
[New York, etc.] 330.6273 08-25517

   HB1 .A585 MRR Biog Latest edition

ECUADOR.
Linke, Lilo. Ecuador; country of
contrasts. London, New York, Royal
Institute of International Affairs
[1954] ix, 173 p. 918.66* a 54-
8960
   F3708 .L5 MRR Alc.

Weil, Thomas E. Area handbook for
Ecuador. [Washington, For sale by
the Supt. of Docs., U.S. Govt. Print.
Off.] 1973. xiii, 403 p. [$4.10]
918.66/03 73-601644
   F3708 .W44 MRR Alc.

ECUADOR--BIOGRAPHY.
Quien es quién en Venezuela,
Panamá, Ecuador, Columbia. Jun. 30,
1952- [Bogota] O. Perry. 920.086
54-19781
   F2205 .Q54 MRR Biog Latest edition

ECUADOR--EXECUTIVE DEPARTMENTS.
Quito. Universidad Central. Instituto
de Estudios Administrativos. Manual
de gobierno, República del Ecuador
[Quito, Editorial Universitaria,
1965] 445 p.   67-41051
   JL3031 .Q5 1965 MRR Alc.

ECUADOR--GAZETTEERS.
United States. Office of Geography.
Ecuador; Washington, U.S. Govt.
Print. Off., 1957. iii, 189 p.   57-
60472
   F3704 .U5 MRR Alc.

**ECUADOR--POLITICS AND GOVERNMENT--
HANDBOOKS, MANUALS, ETC.**
Quito. Universidad Central. Instituto
de Estudios Administrativos. Manual
de gobierno, República del Ecuador
[Quito, Editorial Universitaria,
1965] 445 p.   67-41051
   JL3031 .Q5 1965 MRR Alc.

ECUMENICAL MOVEMENT.
see also Christian union

ECUMENICAL MOVEMENT--HISTORY.
Rouse, Ruth, ed. A history of the
ecumenical movement, 1517-1948,
London, Published on behalf of the
Ecumenical Institute by S.P.C.K.,
1954. xxiv, 822 p.   280.1* 54-3125

   BX6.5 .R6 1954a MRR Alc.

EDIBLE OILS AND FATS
see Oils and fats, Edible

EDIBLE PLANTS
see Plants, Edible

EDINBURGH--DIRECTORIES.
Edinburgh & Leith post office
directory. Edinburgh, Meill [etc.]
34-38962
   DA890.E3 E15 MRR Alc Latest
   edition

EDUCATION.
see also Adult education

see also Child study

see also Examinations

see also Moving-pictures in education

see also Physical education and
training

see also Public schools

see also Schools

see also Students

see also Teaching

see also Youth

Guilford, Joy Paul, Fundamental
statistics in psychology and
education 5th ed. New York, McGraw-
Hill [1973] xii, 546 p.   519.5 72-
6960
   HA29 .G9 1973 MRR Alc.

EDUCATION--BIBLIOGRAPHY.
Burke, Arvid James, Documentation in
education New York, Teachers College
Press, Teachers College, Columbia
University [1967] xiv, 413 p.
028.7 67-17818
   Z711 .B93 1967 MRR Alc.

Complete guide and index to ERIC
reports: Englewood Cliffs, N.J.,
Prentice-Hall [1970] 1338 p.
370/.78 79-123091
   Z5814.R4 C6 MRR Ref Desk.

Education index. Jan. 1929- New
York, H. W. Wilson Co. 016.3705 30-
23807
   Z5813 .E23 MRR Circ Full set

Eells, Walter Crosby, American
dissertations on foreign education;
Washington, Committee on
International Relations, National
Education Association of the United
States, 1959. xxxix, 300 p. 016.37
59-12819
   Z5811 .E43 MRR Alc.

El-Hi textbooks in print. [56th]-
[1927- New York, Bowker [etc.]
016.379/156 57-4667
   Z5813 .A51 MRR Alc Latest edition

Encyclopedia of educational research;
4th ed. [New York] Macmillan [1969]
xliv, 1522 p.   370/.78 75-4932
   LB15 .E48 1969 MRR Ref Desk.

Manheim, Theodore, Sources in
educational research; Detroit, Wayne
State University Press, 1969- v.
016.37 68-64690
   Z5811 .M252 MRR Alc.

Master's theses in education.
1951/52- Cedar Falls, Iowa, Research
Publications. 016.37 53-62892
   Z5816.I6 M3 MRR Alc Partial set

Paulston, Rolland G. Non-formal
education; New York, Praeger [1972]
xxi, 332 p.   016.37 72-186197
   Z5811 .P27 MRR Alc.

Research studies in education;
1941/51- Bloomington, Ind. [etc.]
Phi Delta Kappa [etc.] 016.37078 53-
3287
   Z5811 .R4 MRR Alc Partial set

Review of educational research. v. 1-
Jan. 1931- [Washington, American
Educational Research Association]
370.5 33-19994
   L11 .R35 MRR Alc Partial set

United Nations Educational,
Scientific and Cultural Organization.
International guide to educational
documentation, 1955-1960. [Paris,
1963] 700 p.   64-734
   Z5811 .U32 MRR Alc.

EDUCATION--BIBLIOGRAPHY. (Cont.)
United Nations Educational,
Scientific and Cultural Organization.
International guide to educational
documentation, 1960-1965. 2d ed.
Paris, Unesco, 1971. 575 p. [$20.00
(U.S.)] 060/.8 s 016.37 72-179108

    AS4.U8 A15 ED70/D54/AFS MRR Alc.

United States. Educational Research
Information Center. Office of
Education research reports, 1956-65,
ED 002 747-ED 003 960. [Washington,
U.S. Govt. Print. Ofr., 1967] 2 v.
016.370/78 hew67-155
    Z5814.R4 U5 MRR Ref Desk.

EDUCATION--BIBLIOGRAPHY--CATALOGS.
Harvard University. Library.
Education and education periodicals.
Cambridge; Distributed by Harvard
University Press, 1968. 2 v.
016.370/5 68-15925
    Z5817 .H33 MRR Alc.

EDUCATION--BIOGRAPHY.
International who's who in community
service. 1973/74-   ed. London,
Eddison Press. [12.50] 361/.0025
78-189467
    HV27 .I57 MRR Biog Latest edition

EDUCATION--CURRICULA--BIBLIOGRAPHY.
Association for Supervision and
Curriculum Development. Curriculum
materials. Washington. 016.375 50-
1296
    Z5814.C9 A8 MRR Alc Latest edition

EDUCATION--DICTIONARIES.
Dewey, John, Dictionary of
education. New York, Philosophical
Library [1959] x, 150 p.   370.3 59-
4783
    LB875 .D37 MRR Alc.

Encyclopedia of education. New York,
Philosophical Library [1970] xi, 882
p.   370/.3 72-13749
    LB15 .B56 1970 MRR Alc.

The Encyclopedia of education. [New
York] Macmillan [19   v.   370/.3
70-133143
    LB15 .E47 MRR Alc.

Encyclopedia of educational research;
4th ed. (New York) Macmillan [1969]
xliv, 1522 p.   370/.78 75-4932
    LB15 .E48 1969 MRR Ref Desk.

Good, Carter Victor, ed. Dictionary
of education; 3d ed. New York,
McGraw-Hill [1973] xix, 681 p.
370/.3 73-4784
    LB15 .G6 1973 MRR Alc.

Hopke, William E. Dictionary of
personnel and guidance terms, [1st
ed.] Chicago, J. G. Ferguson Pub.
Co. [1968] xix, 464 p.   371.4/03
68-57491
    LB15 .H66 MRR Alc.

International federation of
university women. Lexique
international des termes
universitaires. [Paris] Fédération
internationale des femmes diplomées
des universites, 1939. xvii, 755,
[1] p.   378.03 40-30813
    LB2331 .I6 MRR Alc.

Monroe, Paul, ed. A cyclopedia of
education. New York, The Macmillan
company, 1911-13. 5 v. [$5.00 per
vol.]   11-1511
    LB15 .M6 MRR Alc.

EDUCATION--DIRECTORIES.
Chambers, Merritt Madison, ed.
Universities of the world outside
U.S.A. 1st ed. Washington, American
Council on Education, 1950. xvii,
924 p.   378.058 50-5321
    LA183 .C48 MRR Ref Desk.

International federation of
university women. Lexique
international des termes
universitaires. [Paris] Fédération
internationale des femmes diplomées
des universites, 1939. xvii, 755,
[1] p.   378.03 40-30813
    LB2331 .I6 MRR Alc.

Schools abroad of interest to
Americans. 2d ed. Boston, P.
Sargent, 1967. 350 p.   371/.02/025
67-18844
    L900 .S3 1967 MRR Alc.

EDUCATION--DIRECTORIES--BIBLIOGRAPHY.
Guide to American educational
directories. 1st- ed.:1963- New
York, B. Klein. 016.3705873 63-
14270
    Z5813 .G8 MRR Ref Desk Latest
        edition

EDUCATION--ECONOMIC ASPECTS--UNITED
STATES.
Angel, Juvenal Londoño, Students'
guide to occupational opportunities
and their lifetime earnings, New
York, World Trade Academy Press;
distributed by Simon & Schuster
[1967] 312 p.   331.702/0973 67-
25270
    HF5382 .A57 MRR Alc.

EDUCATION--ECONOMIC ASPECTS--UNITED
STATES--STATISTICS.
Harris, Seymour Edwin, A statistical
portrait of higher education, New
York, McGraw-Hill [1972] xliv, 978
p.   378.73 72-38334
    LA227.3 .H25 MRR Alc.

EDUCATION--EXPERIMENTAL METHODS--
DIRECTORIES.
Center for Curriculum Design.
Somewhere else; [1st ed.] Chicago,
Swallow Press [1973] 213 p. [$6.00]
060/.25 72-91916
    AS8 .C4 1973 MRR Alc.

EDUCATION--INFORMATION SERVICES.
International Institute for
Educational Planning. Educational
Planning: a directory of training and
research institutions. 2d ed.
Paris, Unesco: International
Institute for Educational Planning,
1968. 239 p. [10.50 ($3.00)] 371
76-413666
    LB1026 .I5 MRR Alc.

United Nations Educational,
Scientific and Cultural Organization.
International guide to educational
documentation, 1955-1960. [Paris,
1963] 700 p.   64-734
    Z5811 .U32 MRR Alc.

EDUCATION--PERIODICALS.
Davis, Sheldon Emmor, Educational
periodicals during the nineteenth
century. Metuchen, N.J., Scarecrow
Reprint Corp., 1970. 125 p. 370/.5
79-18630
    Z5811 .D36 1970 MRR Alc.

Review of educational research. v. 1-
Jan. 1931- [Washington, American
Educational Research Association]
370.5 33-19994
    L11 .R35 MRR Alc Partial set

EDUCATION--PERIODICALS--BIBLIOGRAPHY.
Camp, William L. Guide to
periodicals in education. Metuchen,
N.J., Scarecrow Press, 1968. 419 p.
016.370/5 68-12625
    Z5813 .C28 MRR Alc.

Educational Press Association of
America. America's education press;
[1st]- yearbook; 1925- Washington.
016.3705 41-9994
    Z5813 .E24 MRR Alc Latest edition

Educator's world. 1970-   ed.
Englewood, Colo., Fisher Pub. Co.
370/.6/273 73-646663
    L901 .E45 MRR Ref Desk Latest
        edition

United Nations Educational,
Scientific and Cultural Organization.
Educational periodicals. [Paris?]
64-6395
    Began publication with 1957 issue.
    Z5813 .U52 MRR Alc Latest edition

EDUCATION--PERIODICALS--CATALOGS.
Harvard University. Library.
Education and education periodicals.
Cambridge; Distributed by Harvard
University Press, 1968. 2 v.
016.370/5 68-15925
    Z5817 .H33 MRR Alc.

EDUCATION--PERIODICALS--INDEXES.
British education index. v. 1-
Aug. 1954/Nov. 1958- London, Library
Association. 61-45718
    Z5813 .B7 MRR Alc Full set

Current index to journals in
education. v. 1- 1969- New York,
CCM Information Corp. 016.370/5 75-
7532
    Z5813 .C8 MRR Circ Full set

Education index. Jan. 1929- New
York, H. W. Wilson Co. 016.3705 30-
23807
    Z5813 .E23 MRR Circ Full set

National Center for Educational
Communication. Educational Reference
Center. Educational finance: [New
York, CCM Information Corp., 1972]
x, 438 p.   016.37/0973 72-77543
    Z5815.U5 N2 MRR Alc.

EDUCATION--PERSONNEL SERVICE
see Personnel service in education

EDUCATION--PHILOSOPHY.
Mayer, Frederick, The great
teachers. [1st ed.] New York,
Citadel Press [1967] 384 p.   920.02
67-18085
    LA2303 .M35 MRR Alc.

EDUCATION--QUOTATIONS, MAXIMS, ETC.
Baughman, Millard Dale, comp.
Educator's handbook of stories,
quotes and humor. Englewood Cliffs,
N.J., Prentice-Hall [c1963] xii, 340
p. 63-17504
    LB1785 .B28 MRR Alc.

Kerber, August, comp. Quotable
quotes on education. Detroit, Wayne
State University Press, 1968. ix,
382 p.   370 67-26384
    LB41 .K42 1968 MRR Alc.

EDUCATION--SEGREGATION
see Segregation in education

EDUCATION--STATISTICS.
International yearbook of education.
10th-   1948- Geneva. 370.58 49-
48323
    L10 .I6952 MRR Alc Latest edition

United Nations Educational,
Scientific and Cultural Organization.
Statistical yearbook. 1963-
[Paris] 65-3517
    AZ361 .U45 MRR Ref Desk Latest
        edition

United Nations Educational,
Scientific and Cultural Organization.
Statistics on special education.
[Paris, 1960] 154 p. 371.9083 60-
50763
    LA132 .U53 MRR Alc.

World survey of education. v. [1]-
1955- [Paris] UNESCO. 371.2 59-
1913
    L900 .W56 MRR Alc Full set

EDUCATION--TERMINOLOGY.
Hopke, William E. Dictionary of
personnel and guidance terms, [1st
ed.] Chicago, J. G. Ferguson Pub.
Co. [1968] xix, 464 p.   371.4/03
68-57491
    LB15 .H66 MRR Alc.

EDUCATION--UNITED STATES--STATISTICS.
Harris, Seymour Edwin, A statistical
portrait of higher education, New
York, McGraw-Hill [1972] xliv, 978
p.   378.73 72-38334
    LA227.3 .H25 MRR Alc.

EDUCATION--YEARBOOKS.
Den Danske skolehaandbog. København,
Finn Suenson Forlag [etc.] 370.9489
46-29024
    LA870 .D3 MRR Alc Latest edition

The Girl's school year book (public
schools) London, Adam & Charles
Black, [etc.] ca 08-3162
    LC2055 .A3 MRR Alc Latest edition

International yearbook of education.
10th-   1948- Geneva. 370.58 49-
48323
    L10 .I6952 MRR Alc Latest edition

Patterson's American education. v.
[1]-   1904- Mount Prospect, Ill.
Educational Directories [etc.] 04-
12953
    L901 .P3 MRR Ref Desk Latest
        edition

Die Schweiz; Dübendorf, ZH., [etc.]
E. Rohner. 379.494 51-24537
    L101.S9 S28 MRR Alc Latest edition

The World year book of education.
1932- London, Evans Bros. 32-18413
    L101.G8 YA MRR Alc Latest edition

EDUCATION--AFRICA--CURRICULA.
Sasnett, Martena Tenney. Educational
systems of Africa; Berkeley,
University of California Press [1967,
c1966] xliv, 1550 p. 370/.25/6 66-
27654
    L971.A2 S3 MRR Alc.

EDUCATION--AFRICA--DIRECTORIES.
Sasnett, Martena Tenney. Educational
systems of Africa; Berkeley,
University of California Press [1967,
c1966] xliv, 1550 p.   370/.25/6 66-
27654
    L971.A2 S3 MRR Alc.

EDUCATION--ARAB COUNTRIES.
Qubain, Fahim Issa, Education and
science in the Arab world. Baltimore,
Johns Hopkins Press [1966] xxii, 539
p. 378.00917165 65-26182
    LA1101 .Q3 MRR Alc.

EDUCATION--DENMARK.
Den Danske skolehaandbog. København,
Finn Suenson Forlag [etc.] 370.9489
46-29024
    LA870 .D3 MRR Alc Latest edition

EDUCATION--ENGLAND.
Paton's list of schools and tutors.
London, J. & J. Paton. ca 14-333
    L915 .P3 MRR Alc Latest edition

EDUCATION--EUROPE--DIRECTORIES.
Herman, Shirley Yvonne. Guide to
study in Europe; New York, Four
Winds Press [1969] 288 p. [8.50]
378.4 68-27281
   L914.5 .H4 MRR Alc.

Leitfaden der höheren Lehranstalten.
4. Ausg. München-Pasing,
Wirtschaftsverlag Klug (1967). 245
p. [28.00] 78-433478
   L914.5 .L4 1967 MRR Alc.

EDUCATION--EUROPE--HANDBOOKS, MANUALS,
ETC.
Schools in Europe. Weinheim, Berlin,
Beltz (1968-70) 3 v. in 6 370/.94
74-371683
   LA621.82 .S33 MRR Alc.

EDUCATION--EUROPE--STATISTICS.
Schools in Europe. Weinheim, Berlin,
Beltz (1968-70) 3 v. in 6 370/.94
74-371683
   LA621.82 .S33 MRR Alc.

EDUCATION--FRANCE--DIRECTORIES.
Dran, Pierre. Le guide pratique de
l'enseignement en France. Verviers,
Gérard et Cie; Paris, l'Inter, 1965.
346 p. [7,30 F.] 370.2544 66-
72289
   L927 .D7 MRR Alc.

France. Ministère de l'éducation
nationale. Annuaire de l'éducation
nationale. 1945/46- Paris. 370.58
47-17849
   L927 .A25 MRR Alc Latest edition

EDUCATION--GERMANY--1945-
Wenke, Hans, Education in Western
Germany; Washington, Library of
Congress, Reference Dept., European
Affairs Division, 1953. 102 p.
370.943 53-60003
   Z663.26 .E37 MRR Alc.

EDUCATION--GREAT BRITAIN.
The Girl's school year book (public
schools) London, Adam & Charles
Black, [etc.] ca 08-3162
   LC2055 .A3 MRR Alc Latest edition

EDUCATION--GREAT BRITAIN--DIRECTORIES.
The Education authorities directory
and annual. Merstham, Surrey [etc.]
School Government Pub. Co. [etc.] 54-
31801
   L915 .E3 MRR Alc Latest edition

The Public and preparatory schools
year book. 1935- London, Adam &
Charles Black [etc.] 373.2/22/02542
72-626709
   L915 .P9 MRR Alc Latest edition

Schools; London, Truman & Knightley,
ltd. 370.942 [370.58] 34-29857
   L915 .S43 MRR Alc Latest edition

The Schools of England, Wales,
Scotland and northern Ireland with
particulars of recommended schools on
the continent of Europe and tutors'
announcements; Cheltenham, Glos.
[etc.] Burrow's Scholastic Bureau. e
11-1602
   L915 .S44 MRR Alc latest edition

EDUCATION--GREAT BRITAIN--HISTORY.
Osborne, Gerald Stanley, Scottish
and English schools, [Pittsburgh]
University of Pittsburgh Press [1967,
c1966] xv, 351 p. 370.19/5 67-
10651
   LA651.8 .08 1967 MRR Alc.

EDUCATION--GREAT BRITAIN--HISTORY--
BIBLIOGRAPHY.
Bell, S. Peter. Dissertations on
British history, 1815-1914;
Metuchen, N.J.; Scarecrow Press,
1974. xii, 232 p. 016.9142/03 74-
16104
   Z2016 .B43 MRR Alc.

EDUCATION--IRELAND--HISTORY--
BIBLIOGRAPHY.
Bell, S. Peter. Dissertations on
British history, 1815-1914;
Metuchen, N.J.; Scarecrow Press,
1974. xii, 232 p. 016.9142/03 74-
16104
   Z2016 .B43 MRR Alc.

EDUCATION--NEW JERSEY--1965- --
DIRECTORIES.
New Jersey public school directory.
1967/68- [Trenton, Dept. of
Education] 371/.01/025749 72-623504

   L903.N5A3 MRR Alc Latest edition

EDUCATION--SCOTLAND--HISTORY.
Osborne, Gerald Stanley, Scottish
and English schools, [Pittsburgh]
University of Pittsburgh Press [1967,
c1966] xv, 351 p. 370.19/5 67-
10651
   LA651.8 .08 1967 MRR Alc.

EDUCATION--SWEDEN--DIRECTORIES.
Sverige-Amerika stiftelsen. Travel,
study and research in Sweden. 6. ed.
Stockholm, Sverige-Amerika stift.
[Nord. bokh. (distr.)] 1965 [i. e.
1966] xi, 277, [2] p. [15.00] 67-
79953
   L947 .S858 1965 MRR Alc.

EDUCATION--SWITZERLAND.
Die Schweiz; Dübendorf, ZH., [etc.]
E. Rohner. 379.494 51-24537
   L101.S9 S28 MRR Alc Latest edition

EDUCATION--TRANSVAAL.
Skota, Mweli T. D. The African who's
who; [Johannesburg] Distributed by
Central News Agency [196-] 373 p.
67-58880
   DT913 .S55 1960z MRR Biog.

EDUCATION--UNITED STATES.
Congressional Quarterly, inc.
Education for a nation. Washington
[1972] 103 p. [$4.00] 370/.973
72-87225
   LA205 .C56 MRR Ref Desk.

Review of educational research. v. 1-
Jan. 1931- [Washington, American
Educational Research Association]
370.5 33-19994
   L11 .R35 MRR Alc Partial set

EDUCATION--UNITED STATES--1945-
De Young, Chris Anthony, American
education 7th ed. New York, McGraw-
Hill [1972] 501 p. 370/.973 75-
39293
   LA210 .D45 1972 MRR Alc.

EDUCATION--UNITED STATES--BIBLIOGRAPHY.
Dressel, Paul Leroy. The world of
higher education [1st ed.] San
Francisco, Jossey-Bass, 1971. xv,
238 p. 016.378 71-158562
   Z5814.U7 D65 MRR Alc.

United States. Office of Education.
Bibliography of publications of the
United States Office of Education,
1867-1959. Totowa, N.J.; Rowman and
Littlefield, 1971. xiv, 57, x, 158,
v, 157 p. 016.37 73-28324
   Z5815.U5 U5354 MRR Alc.

EDUCATION--UNITED STATES--CONGRESSES--
DIRECTORIES.
Educator's world. 1970- ed.
Englewood, Colo., Fisher Pub. Co.
370/.6/273 73-646663
   L901 .E45 MRR Ref Desk Latest
   edition

EDUCATION--UNITED STATES--DIRECTORIES.
American universities and colleges.
[1st]- ed.; 1928- Washington
[etc.] American Council on Education
[etc.] 378.73 28-5598
   LA226 .A65 MRR Ref Desk Latest
   edition / MRR Alc Latest edition

Axford, Lavonne B. A directory of
educational programs for the gifted,
Metuchen, N.J.; Scarecrow Press,
1971. 282 p. 371.95/025/73 70-
142230
   L901 .A95 MRR Alc.

Catholic school guide. [New York]
377.8273 52-25283
   LC461 .C346 MRR Alc Latest edition

Standard education almanac. 1968-
Los Angeles, Academic Media. 370/.5
68-3442
   L101 .U6S7 MRR Ref Desk Latest
   edition

System Development Corporation.
Directory of educational information
resources. [Rev. and updated ed.]
New York, CCM Information Corp.,
1971. ix, 181 p. 370/.7 70-136093

   L901 .S95 1972 MRR Alc.

EDUCATION--UNITED STATES--FINANCE--
BIBLIOGRAPHY.
Education Services Press, St. Paul.
Guide to support programs for
education. St. Paul [1966] 160 p.
371 66-18553
   Z5814.F5 E18 MRR Alc.

National Center for Educational
Communication. Educational Reference
Center. Educational finance; [New
York, CCM Information Corp., 1972]
x, 438 p. 016.37/0973 72-77543
   Z5815.U5 N2 MRR Alc.

EDUCATION--UNITED STATES--HISTORY.
Council of Chief State School
Officers. Education in the States;
Washington, National Education
Association of the United States
[1969] 2 v. 370/.973 70-81973
   LA205 .C58 MRR Alc.

Edwards, Newton, The school in the
American social order 2d. ed.
Boston, Houghton Mifflin [1963] 694
p. 370.973 63-4262
   LA205 .E3 1963 MRR Alc.

Folger, John K. Education of the
American population, [Washington]
U.S. Dept. of Commerce, Bureau of the
Census; [for sale by the Supt. of
Docs., U.S. Govt. Print. Off., 1967]
ix, 290 p. [2.25] 370/.973 a 66-
7677
   LA205 .F6 MRR Alc.

Good, Harry Gehman, A history of
American education 3d. ed. New
York, Macmillan [1973] ix, 570 p.
370/.973 72-86503
   LA209 .G58 1973 MRR Alc.

Thayer, Vivian Trow, Formative ideas
in American education, New York,
Dodd, Mead, 1965. xii, 394 p.
370.10973 65-12348
   LA212 .T45 MRR Alc.

Weigle, Luther Allan, American
idealism, New Haven, Yale university
press; [etc., etc.] 1928. 3 p. l.,
356 p. 28-25825
   E178.5 .P2 vol. 10 MRR Alc.

EDUCATION--UNITED STATES--INFORMATION
SERVICES.
System Development Corporation.
Directory of educational information
resources. [Rev. and updated ed.]
New York, CCM Information Corp.,
1971. ix, 181 p. 370/.7 70-136093

   L901 .S95 1972 MRR Alc.

EDUCATION--UNITED STATES--PERIODICALS.
Educator's world. 1970- ed.
Englewood, Colo., Fisher Pub. Co.
370/.6/273 73-646663
   L901 .E45 MRR Ref Desk Latest
   edition

EDUCATION--UNITED STATES--STATISTICS.
Congressional Quarterly, inc.
Education for a nation. Washington
[1972] 103 p. [$4.00] 370/.973
72-87225
   LA205 .C56 MRR Ref Desk.

Digest of educational statistics.
1962- ed. [Washington] U.S. Dept.
of Health, Education, and Welfare,
Office of Education; [for sale by the
Superintendent of Documents, U.S.
Govt. Print. Off.] hew62-154
   L111 .A6 MRR Alc Latest edition

Folger, John K. Education of the
American population, [Washington]
U.S. Dept. of Commerce, Bureau of the
Census; [for sale by the Supt. of
Docs., U.S. Govt. Print. Off., 1967]
ix, 290 p. [2.25] 370/.973 a 66-
7677
   LA205 .F6 MRR Alc.

Gertler, Diane (Bochner) Directory:
public elementary and secondary
schools in large school districts
with enrollment and instructional
staff, by race: fall 1967,
[Washington] U.S. National Center for
Educational Statistics; [for sale by
the Supt. of Docs., U.S. Govt. Print.
Off., 1969] v, 840 p. [7.25]
371//01/02573 72-604076
   L901 .G38 MRR Alc.

Pennsylvania. Dept. of Public
Instruction. Bureau of Statistics.
Rankings of universities in the
United States. Harrisburg, 1966.
iv, 32 p. 378.73 73-628460
   LA226 .P36 MRR Alc.

Pierson, George Wilson, The
education of American leaders; New
York, Praeger [1969] xxxii, 261 p.
331.7/6 69-17173.
   LA226 .P5 MRR Alc.

Reeves, Vernon H. Your college
degree; Chicago, Science Research
Associates [c1968] 221 p.
373.1/4/20202 77-12816
   LB2381 .R4 MRR Alc.

Standard education almanac. 1968-
Los Angeles, Academic Media. 370/.5
68-3442
   L101 .U6S7 MRR Ref Desk Latest
   edition

United States. Bureau of the Census.
1967 census of governments.
[Washington, For sale by the Supt. of
Docs., U.S. Govt. Print. Off., 1968-
v. in 353.000021/2 a 68-7201
   JS3.A257 MRR Alc.

United States. Office of Education.
Earned degrees conferred by higher
educational institutions. 1947/48-
Washington, Federal Security Agency,
Office of Education. 378.2 e 49-19
   L111 .A72 no. 247, etc. MRR Alc
   Latest edition

Yearbook of higher education. 1969-
Los Angeles, Academic Media. 378.73
69-18308
   LB2300 .Y4 MRR Ref Desk Latest
   edition

EDUCATION--UNITED STATES--YEARBOOKS.
Standard education almanac. 1968-
Los Angeles, Academic Media. 370/.5
68-3442
   L101 .U6S7 MRR Ref Desk Latest
   edition

EDUCATION, ART
see Art--Study and teaching

EDUCATION, COMMUNIST
see Communist education

EDUCATION, COMPARATIVE
see Comparative education

EDUCATION, COOPERATIVE--UNITED STATES--
DIRECTORIES.
A Directory of cooperative education.
Philadelphia, Cooperative Education
Association. [$6.00] 331.2/5922 73-
645562
   First vol. published in 1968.
   L901 .D48 MRR Alc Latest edition

Lewchuk, Ross C., National register
of internships and experiential
education. Washington, Acropolis
Books [1973] 175 p.   [$3.95]
378.1/03/02573 73-6911
   L901 .L45 MRR Alc.

EDUCATION, ELEMENTARY.
World survey of education. v. [1]-
1955- [Paris] UNESCO. 371.2 59-
1913
   L900 .W56 MRR Alc Full set

EDUCATION, HIGHER.
Brubacher, John Seiler, Higher
education in transition; Rev. and
enl. New York, Harper & Row [1968]
vii, 529 p. [$12.00] 378.73 68-
17041
   LA226 .B75 1968 MRR Alc.

Burn, Barbara B. Higher education in
nine countries; New York, McGraw-
Hill [1971] viii, 387 p. 378 79-
132352
   LB2322 .B85 MRR Alc.

Higher education in the United
Kingdom. London, Longmans & Green.
378.42 58-15421
   "First published 1936."
   LA637.7 H5 MRR Alc Latest edition

World survey of education. v. [1]-
1955- [Paris] UNESCO. 371.2 59-
1913
   L900 .W56 MRR Alc Full set

EDUCATION, HIGHER--1965-
Heckman, Dale M. Inventory of
current research on higher education.
1968 New York, McGraw-Hill [1968]
xxvi, 198 p. [2.75] 370/.78 71-
3638
   LB2322 .H4 MRR Alc.

EDUCATION, HIGHER--ADDRESSES, ESSAYS,
LECTURES.
Hofstadter, Richard, ed. American
higher education [Chicago]
University of Chicago Press [1961] 2
v.   378.73 61-15935
   LA226 .H53 1961 MRR Alc.

EDUCATION, HIGHER--DIRECTORIES.
American Council on Education.
Overseas Liaison Committee.
International directory for
educational liaison. Washington
[1972, c1973] xxii, 474 p.
378/.006/21 72-92152
   L900 .A47 1973 MRR Alc.

EDUCATION, HIGHER--HISTORY.
Pierson, George Wilson, The
education of American leaders; New
York, Praeger [1969] xxxii, 261 p.
331.7/6 69-17173
   LA226 .P5 MRR Alc.

EDUCATION, HIGHER--PERIODICALS.
Yearbook of higher education. 1969-
Los Angeles, Academic Media. 378.73
69-18308
   LB2300 .Y4 MRR Ref Desk Latest
   edition

EDUCATION, HIGHER--UNITED STATES--1965-
--STATISTICS.
Harris, Seymour Edwin, A statistical
portrait of higher education, New
York, McGraw-Hill [1972] xliv, 978
p. 378.73 72-38334
   LA227.3 .H25 MRR Alc.

EDUCATION, HIGHER--UNITED STATES--
BIBLIOGRAPHY.
Willingham, Warren W. The source
book for higher education; New York,
College Entrance Examination Board,
1973. xxii, 481 p. [$15.00]
016.37873 72-97458
   Z5814.U7 S55 MRR Alc.

EDUCATION, HIGHER--UNITED STATES--
DIRECTORIES.
College Entrance Examination Board.
The New York Times guide to
continuing education in America,
[New York] Quadrangle Books [1972]
811 p. [$12.50] 374.8/73 74-
183190
   L901 .C74 1972 MRR Ref Desk.

Lewchuk, Ross C., National register
of internships and experiential
education. Washington, Acropolis
Books [1973] 175 p.   [$3.95]
378.1/03/02573 73-6911
   L901 .L45 MRR Alc.

EDUCATION, HUMANISTIC.
Hutchins, Robert Maynard, The great
conversation; Chicago, Encyclopedia
Britannica [1955, c1952] xxvii, 131
p. 028.3 55-10312
   AC1 .G72 vol. 1 MRR Alc.

EDUCATION, PHYSICAL
see Physical education and training

EDUCATION, PRESCHOOL--UNITED STATES--
DIRECTORIES.
LaCrosse, E. Robert. Early childhood
education directory; 1st ed. New
York, R. R. Bowker Co., 1971. xiv,
455 p. [$19.50] 372.21/025/73 77-
126012
   L901 .L3 MRR Ref Desk.

EDUCATION, RELIGIOUS
see Religious education

EDUCATION, SECONDARY.
The Girl's school year book (public
schools) London, Adam & Charles
Black, [etc.] ca 08-3162
   LC2055 .A3 MRR Alc Latest edition

World survey of education. v. [1]-
1955- [Paris] UNESCO. 371.2 59-
1913
   L900 .W56 MRR Alc Full set

EDUCATION, VOCATIONAL
see Vocational education

EDUCATION AND STATE--UNITED STATES.
United States. Library of Congress.
Legislative Reference Service.
Federal educational policies,
programs and proposals; Washington,
U.S. Govt. Print. Off., 1968. 3 v.
[0.75 (v. 1) varies] 379/.0973 76-
600437
   LC71 .U5332 MRR Alc.

EDUCATION OF ADULTS
see Adult education

EDUCATION OF WOMEN.
The Girl's school year book (public
schools) London, Adam & Charles
Black, [etc.] ca 08-3162
   LC2055 .A3 MRR Alc Latest edition

EDUCATION OF WOMEN--BIBLIOGRAPHY.
Astin, Helen S., Women; Washington,
Human Service Press [1971] v, 243 p.
[$5.95] 016.3314 76-30266
   Z7963.E7 A86 MRR Alc.

EDUCATIONAL ADMINISTRATION
see School management and organization

EDUCATIONAL ASSOCIATIONS.
The Encyclopedia of education. [New
York] Macmillan [19 v.   370/.3
70-133143
   LB15 .E47 MRR Alc.

Universities and colleges of Canada.
1969- Ottawa, Association of
Universities and Colleges of Canada.
378.71 77-219268
   L905 .C452 MRR Alc Latest edition

Yearbook of higher education. 1969-
Los Angeles, Academic Media. 378.73
69-18308
   LB2300 .Y4 MRR Ref Desk Latest
   edition

EDUCATIONAL ASSOCIATIONS--DIRECTORIES.
American Council on Education.
Overseas Liaison Committee.
International directory for
educational liaison. Washington
[1972, c1973] xxii, 474 p.
378/.006/21 72-92152
   L900 .A47 1973 MRR Alc.

The College blue book. [1st]- 1923-
New York [etc.] CCM Information
Corp. [etc.] 378.73 24-223
   LA226 .C685 MRR Ref Desk Latest
   edition

Gale Research Company. Encyclopedia
of associations. 8th ed. Detroit,
Mich. [1973- v.   [$45.00 (v. 1)
$28.50 (v. 2)] 061/.3 73-7400
   HS17 .G334 1973 MRR Ref Desk.

International federation of
university women. Lexique
international des termes
universitaires. [Paris] Fédération
internationale des femmes diplomées
des universités, 1939. xvii, 755,
[1] p. 378.03 40-30813
   LB2331 .I6 MRR Alc.

International Institute for
Educational Planning. Educational
Planning: a directory of training and
research institutions. 2d ed.
Paris, Unesco: International
Institute for Educational Planning,
1968. 239 p. [10.50 ($3.00)] 371
76-413666
   LB1026 .I5 MRR Alc.

Liste mondiale. Paris, International
Association of Universities. a 55-
6642
   Began in 1952.
   L900 .I57 MRR Alc Latest edition

Minerva; 1.- Jahrg.; 1891/92-
Berlin [etc.] W. de Gruyter [etc.]
06-13219
   AS2 .M6 MRR Alc Latest edition /
   MRR Ref Desk Latest edition

National Council of Teachers of
English. Directory of officers,
committees, and affiliates.
Champaign, Ill. 65-5403
   PE11 .N317 MRR Alc Latest edition

National Education Association of the
United States. N E A handbook. 1st-
ed.; 1945/46- Washington.
370.6273 45-8313
   L13 .N4625 MRR Alc Latest edition

System Development Corporation.
Directory of educational information
resources. [Rev. and updated ed.]
New York, CCM Information Corp.,
1971. ix, 181 p. 370/.7 70-136093
   L901 .S95 1972 MRR Alc.

United Nations Educational,
Scientific and Cultural Organization.
International guide to educational
documentation, 1960-1965. 2d ed.
Paris, Unesco, 1971. 575 p. [$20.00
(U.S.)] 060/.8 s 016.37 72-179108
   AS4.U8 A15 ED70/D54/AFS MRR Alc.

Willingham, Warren W. The source
book for higher education; New York,
College Entrance Examination Board,
1973. xxii, 481 p. [$15.00]
016.37873 72-97458
   Z5814.U7 S55 MRR Alc.

EDUCATIONAL ASSOCIATIONS--UNITED STATES-
-DIRECTORIES.
Educator's world. 1970- ed.
Englewood, Colo., Fisher Pub. Co.
370/.6/273 73-646663
   L901 .E45 MRR Ref Desk Latest
   edition

EDUCATIONAL BROADCASTING.
National Association of Educational
Broadcasters. N A E B directory of
members. Urbana, Ill. 61-22844
   LB1044.5.A1 N316 MRR Alc Latest
   edition

EDUCATIONAL EXCHANGES.
International Association for the
Exchange of Students for Technical
Experience. Report. [London] 378.3
52-65801
   Began publication in 1948.
   LB2376 .I57 MRR Alc Latest edition

Johnson, Walter, The Fulbright
program; Chicago, University of
Chicago Press [1965] xv, 380 p.
378.1791 65-24978
   LB2283 .J6 MRR Alc.

Study abroad. v. 1- 1948- [Paris]
UNESCO. 378.3 49-2511
   LB2338 .S86 MRR Ref Desk Latest
   edition / MRR Alc Latest edition

Unesco handbook of international
exchanges. 1- 1965- [Paris]
Unesco. 65-5337
   AS8 .U35 MRR Alc Latest edition

Vacation study abroad. [Paris,
United Nations Educational,
Scientific and Cultural Organization]
370.19/62 72-627046
   LB2338 .V3 MRR Ref Desk Latest
   edition

EDUCATIONAL EXCHANGES--UNITED STATES.
Institute of International Education.
Open doors; foreign students,
foreign doctors, foreign faculty
members in the United States, U.S.
students, U.S. faculty members
abroad. [New York?] 378.3 55-4594
   LB2283 .I615 MRR Alc Latest
   edition

EDUCATIONAL EXCHANGES--UNITED (Cont.)
Institute of Research on Overseas
Programs. The international programs
of American universities; 2d ed.
Honolulu, Institute of Advanced
Projects, East-West Center, in
cooperation with International
Programs, Michigan State University
[East Lansing] 1966. x, 466 p.
378.3/5/0973 67-63980
LB2285.U6 I53 1966 TJ Rm.

United States. Bureau of Educational
and Cultural Affairs. International
exchange. [Washington, For sale by
the Supt. of Docs., U.S. Govt. Print.
Off.] 370.19/6/0973 72-626994
LB2283 .U438 MRR Alc Latest
edition

EDUCATIONAL GAMES--BIBLIOGRAPHY.
Belch, Jean. Contemporary games;
Detroit, Gale Research Co. [1973- v.
371.3/078 72-6353
LB1029.G3 B44 MRR Alc.

EDUCATIONAL GAMES--DIRECTORIES.
Belch, Jean. Contemporary games;
Detroit, Gale Research Co. [1973- v.
371.3/078 72-6353
LB1029.G3 B44 MRR Alc.

**EDUCATIONAL INNOVATIONS--UNITED STATES--
DIRECTORIES.**
Center for Curriculum Design.
Somewhere else; [1st ed.] Chicago,
Swallow Press [1973] 213 p. [$6.00]
060/.25 72-91916
AS8 .C4 1973 MRR Alc.

**EDUCATIONAL LAW AND LEGISLATION--UNITED
STATES.**
Congressional Quarterly, inc.
Education for a nation. Washington
[1972] 103 p. [$4.00] 370/.973
72-87225
LA205 .C56 MRR Ref Desk.

Elliott, Edward Charles, ed.
Charters and basic laws of selected
American universities and colleges,
New York city, The Carnegie
foundation for the advancement of
teaching, 1934. 2 p. l., iii-vii p.,
1 l., 640 379.1473 378.73 34-
3109
LB2525 .E55 MRR Alc.

EDUCATIONAL PLANNING.
International Institute for
Educational Planning. Educational
Planning: a directory of training and
research institutions. 2d ed.
Paris, Unesco: International
Institute for Educational Planning,
1968. 239 p. [10.50 ($3.00)] 371
76-413666
LB1026 .I5 MRR Alc.

EDUCATIONAL PLANNING--DIRECTORIES.
International Institute for
Educational Planning. Educational
Planning: a directory of training and
research institutions. 2d ed.
Paris, Unesco: International
Institute for Educational Planning,
1968. 239 p. [10.50 ($3.00)] 371
76-413666
LB1026 .I5 MRR Alc.

EDUCATIONAL PSYCHOLOGY.
see also Child study

Garrison, Karl Claudius, The
psychology of exceptional children
4th ed. New York, Ronald Press Co.
[1965] vi, 571 p. 371.9 65-21809

LC3965 .G3 1965 MRR Alc.

Klausmeier, Herbert John, Learning
and human abilities; 3d ed. New
York, Harper & Row [1971] xxii, 810
p. 370.15 73-132660
LB1051 .K67 1971 MRR Alc.

Lindgren, Henry Clay, Educational
psychology in the classroom. 4th ed.
New York, Wiley [1971, c1972] xvi,
516 p. 370.15 75-168647
LB1051 .L67 1972 MRR Alc.

EDUCATIONAL PSYCHOLOGY--TERMINOLOGY.
Topetzes, Nick J. Definitions of
professional terms in educational
psychology, Dubuque, Iowa, Wm. C.
Brown Co. [c1958] 116 p. 370.15014
59-1307
LB1055 .T6 MRR Alc.

EDUCATIONAL RESEARCH.
Good, Carter Victor, Introduction to
educational research: 2d ed. New
York, Appleton-Century-Crofts [1963]
542 p. 370.78 62-17505
LB1028 .G615 1963 MRR Alc.

Heckman, Dale M. Inventory of
current research on higher education,
1968 New York, McGraw-Hill [1968]
xxvi, 198 p. [2.75] 370/.78 71-
3638
LB2322 .H4 MRR Alc.

EDUCATIONAL RESEARCH--BIBLIOGRAPHY.
Complete guide and index to ERIC
reports: Englewood Cliffs, N.J.,
Prentice-Hall [1970] 1338 p.
370/.78 79-123091
Z5814.R4 C6 MRR Ref Desk.

Encyclopedia of educational research;
4th ed. [New York] Macmillan [1969]
xliv, 1522 p. 370/.78 75-4932
LB15 .E48 1969 MRR Ref Desk.

Manheim, Theodore, Sources in
educational research; Detroit, Wayne
State University Press, 1969- v.
016.37 68-64690
Z5811 .M252 MRR Alc.

Research studies in education;
1941/51- Bloomington, Ind. [etc.]
Phi Delta Kappa [etc.] 016.37078 53-
3287
Z5811 .R4 MRR Alc Partial set

United States. Educational Research
Information Center. Office of
Education research reports, 1956-65,
ED 002 747-ED 003 960. [Washington,
U.S. Govt. Print. Off., 1967] 2 v.
016.370/78 hew67-155
Z5814.R4 U5 MRR Alc.

EDUCATIONAL RESEARCH--DIRECTORIES.
American Council on Education.
Overseas Liaison Committee.
International directory for
educational liaison. Washington
[1972, c1973] xxii, 474 p.
378/.006/21 72-92152
L900 .A47 1973 MRR Alc.

International Institute for
Educational Planning. Educational
Planning: a directory of training and
research institutions. 2d ed.
Paris, Unesco: International
Institute for Educational Planning,
1968. 239 p. [10.50 ($3.00)] 371
76-413666
LB1026 .I5 MRR Alc.

EDUCATIONAL RESEARCH--PERIODICALS.
Review of educational research. v. 1-
Jan. 1931- [Washington, American
Educational Research Association]
370.5 33-19994
L11 .R35 MRR Alc Partial set

EDUCATIONAL RESEARCH--ASIA--DIRECTORIES.
United Nations Educational,
Scientific and Cultural Organization.
Regional Office for Education in
Asia, Bangkok. Directory of
educational research institutions in
the Asian region. [2d ed.] Bangkok,
1970. iv, 402 p. 77-279387
LB1028 .U42 1970 MRR Alc.

EDUCATIONAL RESEARCH--UNITED STATES.
Gage, Nathaniel Lees, ed. Handbook
of research on teaching; Chicago,
Rand McNally [1963] 1218 p. 371
63-7142
LB1028 .G3 MRR Alc.

**EDUCATIONAL RESEARCH--UNITED STATES--
DIRECTORIES.**
National register of educational
researchers. 1966- Bloomington,
Ind., Phi Delta Kappa. 370.780922
65-29124
LB1028 .N32 MRR Alc Latest edition

System Development Corporation.
Directory of educational information
resources. [Rev. and updated ed.]
New York, CCM Information Corp.,
1971. v, 181 p. 370/.7 70-136093

L901 .S95 1972 MRR Alc.

**EDUCATIONAL RESOURCES INFORMATION
CENTER--BIBLIOGRAPHY.**
National Center for Educational
Communication. Educational Reference
Center. Educational finance; [New
York, CCM Information Corp., 1972]
x, 438 p. 016.37/0973 72-77543
Z5815.U5 N2 MRR Alc.

EDUCATIONAL SOCIOLOGY--BIBLIOGRAPHY.
Cordasco, Francesco, comp.
Educational sociology: New York,
Scarecrow Press, 1965. 226 p.
016.370193 65-22750
Z5055.U49 C6 MRR Alc.

EDUCATIONAL STATISTICS.
Guilford, Joy Paul, Fundamental
statistics in psychology and
education 5th ed. New York, McGraw-
Hill [1973] xii, 546 p. 519.5 72-
6960
HA29 .G9 1973 MRR Alc.

EDUCATIONAL SURVEYS.
Gourman, Jack. The Gourman report;
1967-68 ed. Phoenix, Continuing
Education Institute [1967] xxviii,
1187 p. 378.1/001/8 67-6498
LB2341 .G62 MRR Alc.

EDUCATIONAL TECHNOLOGY.
see also Audio-visual education

EDUCATIONAL TELEVISION
see Television in education

**EDUCATIONAL TESTS AND MEASUREMENTS--
BIBLIOGRAPHY.**
Buros, Oscar Krisen, ed. The mental
measurements yearbook. [1st]- 1938-
Highland Park, N.J. [etc.] Gryphon
Press [etc.] 016.1512 016.159928 39-
3422
Z5814.P8 B902 MRR Alc Partial set

Buros, Oscar Krisen, ed. Tests in
print; Highland Park, N.J., Gryphon
Press [1961] xxix, 479 p.
016.37126 61-16302
Z5814.E9 B8 MRR Alc.

EDUCATIONAL TRANSPARENCIES
see Transparencies in education

EDUCATORS.
see also Teachers

EDUCATORS--UNITED STATES.
Leaders in education; 1st- ed.;
1932- Lancaster, Pa. [etc.] Science
Press. 923.773 32-10194
LA2311 .L4 MRR Biog Latest edition

EDUCATORS--UNITED STATES--BIOGRAPHY.
Outstanding educators of America.
1970- [Chicago] 370/.92/2 [B] 74-
148050
LA2311 .O9 MRR Biog Latest edition

EDUCATORS, AMERICAN.
The Encyclopedia of education. [New
York] Macmillan [19   v.   370/.3
70-133143
LB15 .E47 MRR Alc.

National register of educational
researchers. 1966- Bloomington,
Ind., Phi Delta Kappa. 370.780922
65-29124
LB1028 .N32 MRR Alc Latest edition

Who's who in American college and
university administration. 1970/71-
[New York?] Crowell-Collier
Educational Corp. 378.1/1/0922 79-
114035
LA2311 .P72 MRR Biog Latest
edition

Who's who in American education. v.
1-24; 1928-1967/68. Hattiesburg,
Miss. [etc.] 29-2351
LA2311 .W45 MRR Biog Latest
edition

EFFICIENCY, INDUSTRIAL.
see also Labor productivity

EGG TRADE--UNITED STATES.
Who's who in the egg and poultry
industries. Mt. Morris, Ill. [etc.]
Watt Pub. Co. [etc.] 28-14796
HD9284.U4 W5 MRR Alc Latest
edition

EGYPT.
American University, Washington, D.C.
Foreign Areas Studies Division. Area
handbook for the United Arab Republic
(Egypt) Washington, For sale by the
Superintendent of Documents, U.S.
Govt. Print. Off., 1964. ix, 441 p.
65-61849
DT107.83 .A745 MRR Alc.

EGYPT--BIBLIOGRAPHY.
United States. Library of Congress.
European Affairs Division. Egypt and
the Anglo-Egyptian Sudan, a selective
guide to background reading.
Washington, University Press of
Washington [1952] 26 p. 016.9162
52-60008
Z663.26 .E4 MRR Alc.

EGYPT--BIOGRAPHY.
Who's who in U.A.R. and the Near
East. Cairo. 354.62 45-33763
DT44 .W47 MRR Biog Latest edition

EGYPT--COMMERCE--DIRECTORIES.
Commercial directory of Egypt.
Cairo, Modern Pub. Co. 56-46432
HF3883 .C6 MRR Alc Latest edition

**EGYPT--DESCRIPTION AND TRAVEL--GUIDE-
BOOKS.**
Abdallah, Hassan. The handbook of
Egypt. [Cairo, National Publication
and Print. House, 1966] 293 p.
[£E1.00] 916.2/04/5 ne 67-1355
DT45 .A62 MRR Alc.

EGYPT--GAZETTEERS.
United States. Office of Geography.
Egypt and the Gaza Strip;
Washington, U.S. Govt. Print. Off.,
1959. vi, 415 p. 916.2 59-62055
DT45 .U5 MRR Alc.

EGYPT--HISTORY--TO 332 B.C.
Gardiner, Alan Henderson, Sir, Egypt
of the Pharaohs. Oxford, Clarendon
Press, 1961. 461 p. 932.01 61-
1371
DT83 .G2 MRR Alc.

EGYPT--HISTORY--1798-
Little, Tom. Modern Egypt. London,
Benn, 1967. xv, 300 p. [42/-]
916.2/03 67-101233
DT107 .L5 1967 MRR Alc.

EGYPT--INDUSTRIES--DIRECTORIES.
Commercial directory of Egypt.
Cairo, Modern Pub. Co. 56-46432
HF3883 .C6 MRR Alc Latest edition

EGYPTIAN ART
see Art, Egyptian

EGYPTOLOGY.
Bratton, Fred Gladstone, A history
of Egyptian archaeology London,
Hale, 1967. 315 p. [35/-] 913/32
67-90828
DT60 .B7 1967 MRR Alc

EGYPTOLOGY--BIOGRAPHY--DICTIONARIES.
Dawson, Warren Royal, Who was who in
Egyptology. London, Egypt
Exploration Society, 1951. x, 172 p.
920.02 52-27063
DT58 .D3 MRR Biog.

EIGHT-HOUR MOVEMENT--BIBLIOGRAPHY.
United States. Library of Congress.
Division of bibliography. ... List
of books, with references to
periodicals, relating to the eight-
hour working day and to limitation of
working hours in general.
Washington, Gov't. print. off., 1908.
24 p.   07-35012
Z663.28 .L566 MRR Alc.

EIGHTEENTH CENTURY.
Hirsching, Friedrich Karl Gottlob,
Historisch-literarisches handbuch
berühmter und denkwürdiger
personen, welche in dem 18.
Jahrhunderte gestorben sind:
Leipzig, Schwickert, 1784- v. in
920.01 32-19789
CT157 .H5 MRR Biog.

EISENHOWER, DWIGHT DAVID, PRES. U.S.,
1890- --DICTIONARIES, INDEXES, ETC.
Shoemaker, Ralph Joseph, The
Presidents words, an index.
Louisville, Ky., E. De G. Shoemaker
and R. J. Shoemaker [1954- v.
973.92* 54-44837
E835 .S5 MRR Alc.

EISENHOWER, DWIGHT DAVID, PRES. U.S.,
1890-1969--BIBLIOGRAPHY.
Stapleton, Margaret L. The Truman
and Eisenhower years: 1945-1960:
Metuchen, N.J., Scarecrow Press,
1973. vii, 221 p. 016.973918 73-
1791
Z1245 .S7 MRR Alc.

ELECTION DISTRICTS--UNITED STATES.
Barone, Michael. The almanac of
American politics: [2d ed.] Boston,
Gambit [c1973] xxiii, 1240 p.
[$15.00]   328.73 72-96875
JK271 .B343 1974 MRR Ref Desk.

Congressional Quarterly, inc.
Congressional districts in the 1970s.
Washington [1973] 236 p. [$10.00]
328.73/07/345 73-2311
JK1341 .C66 MRR Ref Desk.

ELECTION DISTRICTS--UNITED STATES--MAPS.
Clements, John. Taylor's
encyclopedia of Government officials,
Federal and State. v. 1- 1967/68-
Dallas, Political Research, inc. 67-
22269
JK6 .T36 Sci RR Latest edition /
MRR Alc Latest edition

Republican Congressional Committee.
1972 congressional vote statistics,
93rd Congress: [Washington, 1973] 1
v. (various pagings) 324/.2 73-
168210
JK1868 1972 .R46 1973 MRR Alc.

United States. Bureau of the Census.
Congressional district atlas
(districts of the 93d Congress).
[Washington, For sale by the Supt. of
Docs., U.S. Govt. Print. Off., 1973]
1 v. (unpaged) [$3.70 $3.25 (GPO
bookstore)] 912/.1/3287307345 72-
600344
G1201.F7 U45 1973 MRR Alc.

ELECTION DISTRICTS--UNITED STATES--
STATISTICS.
United States. Bureau of the Census.
Congressional district data book: 93d
Congress: [Washington: For sale by
the Supt. of Docs., U.S. Govt. Print.
Off., 1973] xvii, 550 p. [$8.30]
312/.0973 74-601251
HA205 .B87 1973 MRR Ref Desk.

ELECTION DISTRICTS--VIRGINIA.
Tayloe Murphy Institute. The
Virginia constituency: election
district data-1970.
[Charlottesville] Tayloe Murphy
Institute and the Institute of
Government, University of Virginia,
1973. v, 315 p. 328/.755/07345 73-
620026
JK3968 .T38 1973 MRR Alc.

ELECTION LAW--UNITED STATES.
United States. Congress. Senate.
Library. Nomination and election of
the President and Vice President of
the United States, including the
manner of selecting delegates to
national political conventions,
Washington, U.S. Govt. Print. Off.,
1972. v, 273 p. [$1.50]
329/.0221/0973 72-600557
JK2063 .A513 1972 MRR Ref Desk.

ELECTIONEERING--UNITED STATES.
Weisbord, Marvin Ross. Campaigning
for president; [Rev. and expanded
ed.] New York, Washington Square
Press [1966] xv, 447 p. 329.023
67-519
E183 .W4 1966 MRR Alc.

ELECTIONEERING--UNITED STATES--
BIBLIOGRAPHY.
Kaid, Lynda Lee. Political campaign
communication: a bibliography and
guide to the literature. Metuchen,
N.J., Scarecrow Press, 1974. v, 206
p. 016.329/01/0973 73-22492
Z7165.U5 K34 MRR Alc.

ELECTIONEERING--UNITED STATES--
DIRECTORIES.
Rosenbloom, David L. The political
marketplace. [New York] Quadrangle
Books [1972] xix, 948 p. [$25.00]
328/.0025/73 72-77826
JK2283 .R64 MRR Ref Desk.

ELECTIONS.
see also Campaign management

see also Negroes--Politics and
suffrage

see also Voting

see also Woman--Suffrage

Institute of Electoral Research.
Parliaments and electoral systems,
[London] 1962. 128 p. 64-53190
JF511 .I555 MRR Alc.

Lakeman, Enid. How democracies vote:
3rd ed., London, Faber, 1970. 3-
318 p. [45/-] 324/.21 73-481393
JF1001 .L27 1970 MRR Alc.

ELECTIONS--STATISTICS.
International guide to electoral
statistics: The Hague, Mouton [c1969-
v. [$16.50 (v. 1)] 324/.2/021
73-101067
JF1001 .I55 MRR Alc.

United States. Dept. of State. Bureau
of Intelligence and Research. World
strength of the Communist Party
organizations; annual report.
[Washington] 329/.07 56-60986
HX40 .U626 MRR Alc Latest edition

ELECTIONS--STATISTICS--BIBLIOGRAPHY.
International guide to electoral
statistics: The Hague, Mouton [c1969-
v. [$16.50 (v. 1)] 324/.2/021
73-101067
JF1001 .I55 MRR Alc.

ELECTIONS--ALABAMA--STATISTICS.
Alabama. Dept. of Archives and
History. Alabama official and
statistical register. 1903-
Montgomery. 08-17761
JK4531 MRR Alc Latest edition

ELECTIONS--ARIZONA--STATISTICS.
Arizona political almanac. 1956-
Phoenix, Sims Print. Co. 57-33262
JK8230 .A85 MRR Alc Latest edition

ELECTIONS--AUSTRALIA.
Parliamentary handbook of the
Commonwealth of Australia. Canberra,
Australia. Commonwealth Parliamentary
Library. 328.94/07/3 72-626909
JQ4054 .C3 MRR Alc Latest edition

ELECTIONS--CALIFORNIA.
Lee, Eugene C. California votes,
1928-1960, Berkeley, Institute of
Governmental Studies, University of
California, 1963. xiv, 91, 218 p.
324.209794 64-1225
JK8793 1963 .L4 MRR Alc.

ELECTIONS--CALIFORNIA--STATISTICS.
California. Legislature. List of
members, officers, committees and
rules of the two Houses.
[Sacramento] 328.7945 10-14000
JK8771 .A2 date MRR Alc Latest
edition

ELECTIONS--CANADA.
Qualter, Terence H. The election
process in Canada Toronto, New York,
McGraw-Hill Co. of Canada [1970]
xii, 203 p. 324/.71 75-127187
JL193 .Q34 MRR Alc.

ELECTIONS--CANADA--STATISTICS.
The Canadian parliamentary guide.
Ottawa. 17-2753
JL5 .A4 MRR Alc Latest edition

ELECTIONS--CONNECTICUT--STATISTICS.
Connecticut. Secretary of state.
Register and manual of the state of
Connecticut. 1887- Hartford. 10-
9548
JK3331 MRR Alc Latest edition

ELECTIONS--DOMINICAN REPUBLIC.
Operations and Policy Research, inc.,
Washington, D.C. Institute for the
Comparative Study of Political
Systems. Dominican Republic election
factbook, [Washington, 1966] 55 p.
324.2097293 66-23504
JL1138 .O6 MRR Alc.

ELECTIONS--FLORIDA--STATISTICS.
The Florida handbook. 1947/48-
Tallahassee, Peninsular Pub. Co.
917.59 49-53676
F306 .F597 MRR Alc Latest edition

ELECTIONS--FRANCE.
Mourre, Michel, Dictionnaire
d'histoire universelle. Paris,
Éditions universitaires, 1968. 2 v.
(2368 p.) [175.00] 71-376184
D9 .M89 MRR Alc.

ELECTIONS--FRANCE--STATISTICS.
L'Année politique économique,
sociale et diplomatique en France.
1963- Paris, Presses Universitaires
de France. 72-626951
DC398 .A6 MRR Alc Latest edition

ELECTIONS--GEORGIA--STATISTICS.
Georgia. Dept. of Archives and
History. Georgia's official and
statistical register. 1969/70-
Atlanta. 353.9/758 73-640860
JK4330 .A3 MRR Alc Last edition

ELECTIONS--GERMANY--STATISTICS.
Germany (Federal Republic, 1949-).
Bundestag. Amtliches Handbuch des
Deutschen Bundestages.,1.- 1953-
[Darmstadt] Neue Darmstädter
Verlagsanstalt. 55-23929
JN3971 .A7A35 MRR Alc Latest
edition

ELECTIONS--GREAT BRITAIN.
Butler, David E. British political
facts, 1900-1968, 3rd ed. London,
Macmillan; New York, St Martin's P.,
1969. xix, 314 p. [70/-] 320.9/42
74-82434
JN231 .B8 1969 MRR Alc

Dod's parliamentary companion.
Epsom, Surrey, [etc.] Sell's
publications Ltd. [etc.] 06-7438
JN500 .D7 MRR Biog Latest edition

Guide to the House of Commons. 1970-
London, Times Newspapers Ltd.
328.42/0922 76-20856
JN956 .G9 MRR Alc Latest edition

Leonard, Richard Lawrence. Elections
in Britain London, Princeton, N.J.
[etc.] Van Nostrand, 1968. vi, 192
27865 [35/- 12/6 (pbk.)] 324/.42 67-
27865
JN955 .L45 1968 MRR Alc.

ELECTIONS--GREAT BRITAIN--HISTORY.
Craig, Fred W. S., comp. British
general election manifestos 1918-
1966, Chichester [Eng.] Political
Reference Publications, 1970. xii,
303 p. [75/- ($12.00 U.S.)]
329.9/42 70-77467
JN1121 .C73 MRR Alc.

ELECTIONS--GREAT BRITAIN--STATISTICS.
Craig, Fred W. S. British
parliamentary election results, 1950-
1970, Chichester, Political
Reference Publications, 1971, xviii,
780 p. [£9.50 ($28.00 U.S.)]
329/.023/42085 70-157739
JN1037 .C7142 MRR Alc.

Craig, Fred W. S. British
parliamentary election statistics,
1918-1970. 2nd ed. Chichester,
Political Reference Publications,
1971. xvi, 127 p. [£3.75 ($12.00
U.S.)] 329/.023/4208 79-131304
JN1037 .C72 1971 MRR Alc.

ELECTIONS--ILLINOIS--STATISTICS.
Gove, Samuel Kimball. Illinois
votes, 1900-1958; [Urbana] Institute
of Government and Public Affairs,
University of Illinois, 1959. ix p.,
185 p. of tables. 324.773 a 59-
9928
JK5792 .G6 MRR Alc.

ELECTIONS--INDIA--STATISTICS.
India; a statistical outline.
Calcutta, Oxford & IBH Publishing Co.
[etc.] 70-912219
HA1724 .I49 MRR Alc Latest edition

ELECTIONS--INDIANA.
Francis, Wayne L. Indiana votes:
Bloomington, Bureau of Government
Research, Indiana University, 1962.
115 p. 324.209772 63-63185
JK5693 1962 .F7 MRR Alc.

ELECTIONS--INDIANA. (Cont.)
Pitchell, Robert J., ed. Indiana
votes; Bloomington, Bureau of
Government Research, Indiana
University, 1960. 103 p.
324.209772 62-62552
JK5693 1960 .P5 MRR Alc.

ELECTIONS--INDIANA--STATISTICS.
Indiana almanac and government guide.
1st- ed.; 1961- [Indianapolis,
Republican Citizens' Finance
Committee of Indiana] 64-32364
JK5630 .I5 MRR Alc Latest edition

ELECTIONS--IOWA--STATISTICS.
Iowa. Secretary of State. Official
register. 1886- Des Moines [etc.]
10-11583
JK6331 MRR Alc Latest edition

ELECTIONS--KANSAS.
Cabe, June G. Kansas votes;
[Lawrence] Governmental Research
Center, University of Kansas, 1957.
v, 215 p. (chiefly tables) 324.781
58-63006
JK6892 .C3 MRR Alc.

Hein, Clarence Jacob. Kansas votes;
[Lawrence] Governmental Research
Center, University of Kansas, 1958.
103 p. (chiefly tables) 324.781 59-
62811
JK6853.E6 H4 MRR Alc.

ELECTIONS--LOUISIANA--STATISTICS.
Louisiana almanac and fact book.
1949- New Orleans. a 50-7997
F375 .L9435 MRR Alc Latest edition

ELECTIONS--MARYLAND--STATISTICS.
Maryland manual. [Baltimore, etc.]
10-6200
JK3831 MRR Alc Latest edition

ELECTIONS--MICHIGAN--STATISTICS.
Michigan manual. 1959/60-
[Lansing?] 353.9/774/0202 72-623543

JK5830 .A32 MRR Alc Latest edition

ELECTIONS--MINNESOTA--STATISTICS.
The Minnesota legislative manual.
1967/68- [St. Paul] 328/.776/05 72-
623459
JK6130.A36 MRR Alc Latest edition

ELECTIONS--MISSISSIPPI--STATISTICS.
Abney, F. Glenn. Mississippi
election statistics, 1900-1967,
University, Miss. [Bureau of
Governmental Research, 1968] vi, 480
p. 324/.2021/762 68-66456
JK4693 1968.A62 MRR Alc.

ELECTIONS--MISSOURI--STATISTICS.
Missouri. State Dept. Official
manual. 1878- [Jefferson City,
etc.] 353.9/778 54-47364
JK5431 date MRR Alc Latest
edition

Missouri. State Dept. Roster of
State, district and county officers
of the State of Missouri. [Jefferson
City] 43-30785
Began publication in 1893.
JK5430.A33 MRR Alc Latest edition

ELECTIONS--MONTANA.
Waldron, Ellis L., comp. Montana
politics since 1864; [Missoula]
Montana State University Press [1958]
x, 428 p. 324.786 58-45388
JK7392 .W3 MRR Alc.

ELECTIONS--MONTANA--STATISTICS.
Montana directory of public affairs.
1864/1955- [Hamilton? Mont.] 56-
62504
JK7330 .M65 MRR Alc Latest edition

ELECTIONS--NEBRASKA--STATISTICS.
Nebraska blue book. Lincoln, Neb.
353.9782 99-1456
JK6630 .N4 MRR Alc Latest edition

ELECTIONS--NEVADA.
Nevada. Secretary of State.
Political history of Nevada. 5th ed.
Carson City, S[tate] P[rint.] O[ff.]
1965. 213 p. 67-64717
JK8516 .A5 1965 MRR Alc.

ELECTIONS--NEW HAMPSHIRE--STATISTICS.
New Hampshire. Secretary of State.
Manual for the General court. no.
[1]- 1889- Concord N.H. [etc.] 13-
33250
JK2931 date e MRR Alc Latest
edition

ELECTIONS--NEW JERSEY--STATISTICS.
Manual of the Legislature of New
Jersey. Trenton, N.J. [etc.] 05-
11203
JK3531 MRR Alc Latest edition

ELECTIONS--NORTH CAROLINA.
North Carolina. University. Political
Studies Program. North Carolina
votes; Chapel Hill, University of
North Carolina Press [1962] x, 315
p. 324.2 63-62870
JK4192 .N6 MRR Alc.

ELECTIONS--OKLAHOMA--STATISTICS.
Oklahoma. University. Bureau of
Government Research. Oklahoma votes,
1907-1962. Norman, 1964. vi, 147 p.
a 64-7348
JK7193 1964 .O5 MRR Alc.

ELECTIONS--OKLAHOMA--STATISTICS--
PERIODICALS.
Directory of Oklahoma. 1973-
[Oklahoma City] State Election Board.
353.9 766/002 74-647993
JK7192 .A36 MRR Alc Latest edition

ELECTIONS--OREGON.
Onstine, Burton W. Oregon votes;
1858-1972, election returns,
Portland] Oregon Historical Society,
1973. vi, 395 p. 324/.2021/795
73-88980
JK9092 .O55 MRR Alc.

ELECTIONS--PENNSYLVANIA--STATISTICS.
The Pennsylvania manual. 1923/24-
Harrisburg. 25-4346
JK3630 .P4 MRR Alc Latest edition

ELECTIONS--RHODE ISLAND--STATISTICS.
Rhode Island. Dept. of State.
Manual, with rules and orders, for
the use of the General Assembly of
the state of Rhode Island. 1867/68-
Providence. 328.7455 09-34249
JK3230 .A25 MRR Alc Latest edition

ELECTIONS--RHODESIA, SOUTHERN.
Passmore, Gloria C. Source book of
parliamentary elections and referenda
in Southern Rhodesia, 1898-1962.
[Salisbury] Dept. of Government,
University College of Rhodesia and
Nyasaland, 1963. ii, 255 p. 64-
53188
JQ2921 .A23 no. 1 MRR Alc.

ELECTIONS--SCOTLAND.
The Year book for Scotland and
Scottish parliamentary election
manual. Edinburgh. 58-24072
JN1371.U5 Y4 MRR Alc Latest
edition

ELECTIONS--SOUTH DAKOTA--STATISTICS.
South Dakota. Legislature. South
Dakota legislative manual. [Pierre,
State Pub. Co.] ca 10-1009
JK6531. MRR Alc Latest edition

ELECTIONS--TENNESSEE.
Tennessee blue book. Nashville.
353.9768 28-11250
JK5230 .T4 MRR Alc Latest edition

ELECTIONS--TEXAS.
Politics, inc. Texas precinct votes
'66; [Austin, Tex., 1968, c1967]
ix, 173 p. 324/.24/09764 67-29303

JK4893 1966 .P65 MRR Alc.

ELECTIONS--UNITED STATES.
Bain, Richard C. Convention
decisions and voting records 2d ed.
Washington, Brookings Institution
[1973] x, 350, [120] p. [$14.95]
329/.0221 73-1082
JK2255 .B3 1973 MRR Alc.

Bean, Louis Hyman, How America votes
in presidential elections, Metuchen,
N.J., Scarecrow Press, 1968. 152 p.
324/.2/0973 68-12641
JK1967 .B42 MRR Alc.

Johnson, Donald Bruce, comp.
National party platforms, 1840-1972.
[5th. ed.] Urbana, University of
Illinois Press [c1973] xii, 889 p.
329/.0213/0973 73-81566
JK2255 .J64 1973 MRR Alc.

Lorant, Stefan, The Presidency; New
York, Macmillan, 1951. 775 p. 973
51-12817
E183 .L65 MRR Alc.

Michigan. University. Survey Research
Center. The American voter New
York, Wiley [1960] viii, 573 p.
324.73 60-11615
JK1976 .M5 MRR Alc.

Stone, Irving, They also ran;
Garden City,N.Y., Doubleday [1966]
xi, 434 p. 973 66-21914
E176 .S87 1966 MRR Alc.

ELECTIONS--UNITED STATES--ABSTRACTS.
Smith, Dwight La Vern. The American
political process; selected abstracts
of periodical literature, 1954-1971.
Santa Barbara, Calif., ABC-CLIO
[1972] xvi, 630 p. 016.329/00973
72-77549
JK2261 .S73 MRR Alc.

ELECTIONS--UNITED STATES--CAMPAIGN
FUNDS.
Alexander, Herbert E. Financing the
1968 election Lexington, Mass.,
Heath Lexington Books [1971] xv, 355
p. 329/.025/0973 76-151790
JK1991 .A683 1971 MRR Alc.

Common Cause (U.S.). Campaign Finance
Monitoring Project. 1972 Federal
campaign finances, interest groups,
and political parties. Washington,
Common Cause [1974] 3 v.
329/.025/0973 74-77718
JK1991 .C655 1974 MRR Alc.

Sobel, Lester A., comp. Money &
politics : New York : Facts on File,
[1974] 204 p. ; [$7.95.]
329/.025/0973 74-81147
JK1994 .S64 MRR Alc.

United States. Office of Federal
Elections. Federal election campaign
act of 1971 (Public law 92-225):
alphabetical listing of 1972
presidential campaign receipts.
[Washington: For sale by the Supt. of
Docs., U.S. Govt. Print. Off., 1974]
2 v. [$17.40 per set]
329/.025/0973 74-601308
JK1991 .U54 1974 MRR Alc.

ELECTIONS--UNITED STATES--STATISTICS.
America votes; 1- <1956- >
Washington. 324.73 56-10132
JK1967 .A8 MRR Alc Full set

Barone, Michael. The almanac of
American politics: [2d ed.] Boston,
Gambit [c1973] xxiii, 1240 p.
[$15.00] 328.73 72-96875
JK271 .B343 1974 MRR Ref Desk.

Burnham, Walter Dean. Presidential
ballots, 1836-1892. Baltimore, Johns
Hopkins Press [1955] xix, 956 p.
324.73 55-8428
JK524 .B8 MRR Alc.

Governmental Affairs Institute,
Washington, D.C. Elections Research
Center. America at the polls:
Pittsburgh, University of Pittsburgh
Press, 1965. 521 p. 324.202173 65-
27801
JK524 .G6 MRR Alc.

McKee, Thomas Hudson. The national
conventions and platforms of all
political parties, 1789 to 1905; New
York, B. Franklin [1971] 414, 33 p.
329/.02 75-132682
JK2255 .M2 1971 MRR Alc.

Petersen, Svend, A statistical
history of the American presidential
elections. New York, Ungar [1963]
xxiii, 247 p. 324.73 62-21786
JK1967 .P4 1963 MRR Alc.

Republican Congressional Committee.
1970 congressional vote statistics.
[Washington, 1971] i v. (various
pagings) 328.73/077 78-25665
JK1968 1970 .R46 MRR Alc.

Republican Congressional Committee.
1972 congressional vote statistics,
93rd Congress; [Washington, 1973] 1
v. (various pagings) 324/.2 73-
168210
JK1968 1972 .R46 1973 MRR Alc.

Runyon, John H. Source book of
American presidential campaign and
election statistics, 1948-1968. New
York, F. Ungar [1971] xiv, 380 p.
329/.023/0212 73-155093
JK524 .R83 MRR Alc.

United States. Bureau of the Census.
Elections. Washington, Govt. Print.
Off. 56-33149
Began publication in 1942.
JK1967 .A35 MRR Alc Latest edition

United States. Congress. House.
Statistics of the presidential and
congressional election of November 2,
1920- Showing the highest vote for
presidential electors, and the vote
cast for each nominee for United
states senator, representative,
delegate, and resident commissioner
to the Sixty-seventh- Congress,
together with a recapitulation
thereof, including the electoral
vote. 1921- Washington, U.S. Govt.
Print Off. 324.73 21-26389
JK1967 .A3 MRR Alc Partial set

United States. Congress. Senate.
Library. Nomination and election of
the President and Vice President of
the United States, including the
manner of selecting delegates to
national political conventions,
Washington, U.S. Govt. Print. Off.,
1972. v, 273 p. [$1.50]
329/.0221/0973 72-600557
JK2063 .A513 1972 MRR Ref Desk.

Walton, Hanes, Black political
parties; New York, Free Press [1972]
xi, 276 p. 329/.894 76-143514
JK2261 .W33 MRR Alc.

ELECTIONS--UNITED STATES--STATISTICS--
BIBLIOGRAPHY.
Press, Charles. State manuals, blue
books, and election results,
Berkeley, Institute of Governmental
Studies, University of California,
1962. i, 101 p.   016.3539 63-63225

Z7165.U5 P7 MRR Ref Desk.

ELECTIONS--UNITED STATES--YEARBOOKS.
Clements, John. Taylor's
encyclopedia of Government officials,
Federal and State. v. 1- 1967/68-
Dallas, Political Research, inc. 67-
22269
    JK6 .T36 Sci RR Latest edition /
    MRR Alc Latest edition

ELECTIONS--VERMONT--STATISTICS.
Vermont. Secretary of state. Vermont
legislative directory. 1867-
Montpelier [etc.] 09-34113
    JK3031 MRR Alc Latest edition

ELECTIONS--VIRGINIA.
Eisenberg, Ralph, Virginia votes.
[Charlottesville] Governmental and
Administrative Research Division,
University of Virginia, 1971- v.
329/.023/755 72-32113
    JK3993 1924 .E57 MRR Alc.

ELECTIONS--WEST VIRGINIA--YEARBOOKS.
The West Virginia political almanac.
1956- [Charleston] 324.754 57-1342

    JK4092 .W4 MRR Alc Latest edition

ELECTIONS--WISCONSIN.
Wisconsin. University. Institute of
Governmental Affairs. How Wisconsin
voted, 1848-1960 Madison, 1962. 115
p.   62-63755
    JK6092 .W512 MRR Alc.

ELECTIONS--WYOMING.
Wyoming. Secretary of State. Wyoming
official directory and election
returns. [Cheyenne, etc.] 10-11585

    First published for 1902.
    JK7630 .A33 MRR Alc Latest edition

ELECTORAL COLLEGE
    see Presidents--United States--
    Election

ELECTRIC APPARATUS AND APPLIANCES.
Bibliographisches Institut A.G.,
Mannheim. The way things work, New
York, Simon and Schuster [1967] 590
p.   600 67-27972
    T47 .B552 MRR Alc.

Graf, Rudolf F. How it works,
illustrated: everyday devices and
mechanisms, New York, Popular
science [1974] viii, 184 p.
[$10.95] 620 73-80716
    TK298 .G68 MRR Alc.

ELECTRIC APPARATUS AND APPLIANCES--
MAINTENANCE AND REPAIR.
Anderson, Edwin P., Audels home
appliance service guide, [2d ed.]
Indianapolis, T. Audel [1965] 600 p.
683.83 65-18185
    TK7019 .A5 1965 MRR Alc.

ELECTRIC APPARATUS AND APPLIANCES,
DOMESTIC
    see Household appliances, Electric

ELECTRIC COMMUNICATION
    see Telecommunication

ELECTRIC ENGINEERING--DICTIONARIES.
Coyne Electrical School, Chicago.
Coyne technical dictionary of 4000
terms used in television, radio,
electricity [and] electronics,
Chicago, 1955. 152 p.   621.303 55-
14738
    TK9 .C63 MRR Alc.

Manly, Harold Phillips, Drake's
radio-television electronic
dictionary. Chicago, F. J. Drake Co.
[1960] 1 v. (unpaged) 621.3803 60-
4753
    TK6544 .M33 1960 MRR Alc.

Oldfield, Ruth L. The practical
dictionary of electricity and
electronics. Chicago, American
Technical Society, 1959. 216 p.
631.303 58-59540
    TK9 .O4 MRR Alc.

ELECTRIC ENGINEERING--DICTIONARIES--
POLYGLOT.
Elektrotechnik und Elektrochemie.
München, R. Oldenbourg, 1955. xxiv,
1304 p.   57-18208
    TK9 .E42 1955 MRR Alc.

ELECTRIC ENGINEERING--HANDBOOKS,
MANUALS, ETC.
The Electrical engineer's reference
book. [1st]- ed.; 1945- London,
G. Newnes. 621.302 45-8496
    TK151 .E44 Sci RR Latest edition /
    MRR Alc Latest edition

Oldfield, Ruth L. The practical
dictionary of electricity and
electronics. Chicago, American
Technical Society, 1959. 216 p.
631.303 58-59540
    TK9 .O4 MRR Alc.

Standard handbook for electrical
engineers. [1st]- ed.; 1908- New
York, McGraw-Hill. 56-6964
    TK151 .S8 Sci RR Latest edition /
    MRR Alc Latest edition

ELECTRIC ENGINEERING--INSURANCE
REQUIREMENTS.
N F P A handbook of the National
electrical code. 1932- New York,
McGraw-Hill. 621.30202 66-20008
    TK260 .N2 Sci RR Latest edition /
    MRR Alc Latest edition

ELECTRIC ENGINEERING--GREAT BRITAIN--
DIRECTORIES.
The Electrical contractors' year book
and reference book. London,
Electrical Contractors' Association.
621.3/025/42 72-622846
    TK12 .E3873 MRR Alc Latest edition

ELECTRIC ENGINEERS--GREAT BRITAIN--
DIRECTORIES.
Electrical who's who. 1950- London,
Iliffe Books Ltd.[etc.] 926.213 51-
23486
    TK12 .E388 Sci RR Latest edition /
    MRR Biog Latest edition

ELECTRIC ENGINEERS--UNITED STATES--
BIOGRAPHY.
Who's who in the electronics
industry. 1961/62- New York, SETI
Publishers. 621.38058 61-15101
    TA139 .W56 Sci RR Full set / MRR
    Biog Latest edition

ELECTRIC ENGINEERS--UNITED STATES--
DIRECTORIES.
Institute of Electrical and
Electronics Engineers. I E E E
membership directory. [New York] 66-
83668
    TK1 .A1I47 Sci RR Latest edition /
    MRR Biog Latest edition

ELECTRIC INDUSTRIES--GERMANY (FEDERAL
REPUBLIC, 1949-)--DIRECTORIES.
Jahresschau der deutschen Industrie.
[Darmstadt, Industrieschau-
Verlagsgesellschaft] 60-36839
    TK13 .J37 MRR Alc Latest edition

ELECTRIC INDUSTRIES--GERMANY (FEDERAL
REPUBLIC, 1949-)--YEARBOOKS.
Jahresschau der deutschen Industrie.
[Darmstadt, Industrieschau-
Verlagsgesellschaft] 60-36839
    TK13 .J37 MRR Alc Latest edition

ELECTRIC INDUSTRIES--GREAT BRITAIN--
DIRECTORIES.
Electrical and electronics trades
directory. 86th- ed.; 1968-
London, Benn Bros. 381/.45/621302542
76-618342
    TK12 .E4 MRR Alc Latest edition /
    Sci RR Latest edition

ELECTRIC INDUSTRIES--UNITED STATES--
YEARBOOKS.
Moody's public utility manual. 1954-
New York, Moody's Investors Service.
56-3927
    HG4961 .M7245 MRR Alc Latest
    edition

ELECTRIC POWER--STATISTICS.
Darmstadter, Joel, Energy in the
world economy; Baltimore, Published
for Resources for the Future by the
Johns Hopkins Press [1971] x, 876 p.
[$22.50] 333.9 70-155848
    HD9540.4 D37 MRR Alc.

Guyol, Nathaniel B., The world
electric power industry Berkeley,
University of California Press, 1969.
xviii, 366 p. [20.00]
363.6/2/0212 68-54567
    HD9685.A2 G8 MRR Alc.

ELECTRIC POWER-PLANTS--UNITED STATES--
DIRECTORIES.
Electrical world directory of
electric utilities. New York, McGraw-
Hill. 621.312/025/73 16-21431
    TK1194 .M3 Sci RR Latest edition /
    MRR Alc Latest edition

ELECTRIC RAILROADS--CARS.
Middleton, William D., The time of
the trolley, [Milwaukee, Kalmbach
Pub. Co., 1967] 436 p.
388.4/6/0973 67-20155
    TF723 .M5 MRR Alc.

ELECTRIC RAILROADS--CARS--DIRECTORIES.
Arnold, Ian. Locomotive, trolley,
and rail car builders, [Los Angeles,
Trans-Anglo Books, 1965] 64 p.
625.202573 65-17586
    TF355 .A7 MRR Alc.

ELECTRIC STREET-RAILROADS
    see Street-railroads

ELECTRIC UTILITIES--STATISTICS.
Guyol, Nathaniel B., The world
electric power industry Berkeley,
University of California Press, 1969.
xviii, 366 p. [20.00]
363.6/2/0212 68-54567
    HD9685.A2 G8 MRR Alc.

ELECTRIC UTILITIES--RUSSIA--
BIBLIOGRAPHY.
United States. Library of Congress.
Reference Dept. Electric power
industry of the U.S.S.R.;
Washington 1952. xi, 154 p.
016.6213 52-60044
    Z663.47 .E4 MRR Alc.

ELECTRIC UTILITIES--UNITED STATES.
Ebasco Services Incorporated.
Business and economic charts.
Chicago. 59-44534
    HD9685.U7 E3 MRR Alc Latest
    edition

Turner, Clarence A. Financial
statistics, public utilities.
1938/43- Chicago, Ill. 621.3002 44-
47562
    HD9685.U5 T8 MRR Alc Latest
    edition

ELECTRIC UTILITIES--UNITED STATES--
DIRECTORIES.
Electrical world directory of
electric utilities. New York, McGraw-
Hill. 621.312/025/73 16-21431
    TK1194 .M3 Sci RR Latest edition /
    MRR Alc Latest edition

ELECTRIC UTILITIES--UNITED STATES--
RATES.
E.E.I. rate book. New York, Edison
Electric Institute, Rate Research
Committee. 38-17113
    HD9685.U4 E3 MRR Alc Latest
    edition

ELECTRIC UTILITIES--UNITED STATES--
STATISTICS.
United States. Federal Power
Commission. Statistics of privately
owned electric utilities in the
United States; classes A and B
companies. Washington, For sale by
the Supt. of Docs., U.S. Govt. Print.
Off. 338.4/7/621310973 72-626949
    HD9685.U4 A452 MRR Alc Latest
    edition

United States. Federal Power
Commission. Statistics of publicly
owned electric utilities in the
United States. Washington, For sale
by the Supt. of Docs., U.S. Govt.
Print. Off. 338.4/7/621310973 72-
626948
    HD9685.U4 A4523 MRR Alc Latest
    edition

ELECTRIC WIRING, INTERIOR.
Richter, Herbert P. Practical
electrical wiring, 7th ed. New
York, McGraw-Hill [1967] viii, 594
p.   621.319/2 66-15839
    TK3271 .R8 1967 MRR Alc.

ELECTRICITY IN TRANSPORTATION.
    see also Automobiles--Electric
    equipment

ELECTROCHEMISTRY--DICTIONARIES--
POLYGLOT.
Elektrotechnik und Elektrochemie.
München, R. Oldenbourg, 1955. xxiv,
1304 p.   57-18208
    TK9 .E42 1955 MRR Alc.

ELECTRONIC ANALOG COMPUTERS.
Truitt, Thomas D. Basics of analog
computers New York, J. F. Rider
[c1960] 124, 160, 94 p. 510.7824
60-11049
    QA76.4 .T7 MRR Alc.

ELECTRONIC APPARATUS AND APPLIANCES.
    see also Antennas (Electronics)

ELECTRONIC APPARATUS AND APPLIANCES--
CATALOGS.
The Radio-electronic master. New
York, United Technical Publications
[etc.] 621.384085 39-15586
    TK6560.Z5 R35 Sci RR Latest
    edition / MRR Alc Latest edition

ELECTRONIC CALCULATING-MACHINES--
DIRECTORIES.
Computer yearbook and directory. 1st-
ed.; 1966- [Detroit, American
Data Processing] 651.8 66-25748
    QA76 .C576 Sci RR Partial set /
    MRR Alc Latest edition

ELECTRONIC CALCULATING-MACHINES--
YEARBOOKS.
Computer yearbook and directory. 1st-
ed.; 1966- [Detroit, American
Data Processing] 651.8 66-25748
    QA76 .C576 Sci RR Partial set /
    MRR Alc Latest edition

ELECTRONIC DATA PROCESSING.
Lee, Wayne J. The international
computer industry. Washington,
Applied Library Resources [1971] v,
299 p. 338.4/7/62138195 75-157121

HD9696.C62 L44 MRR Alc.

Lott, Richard W. Basic data
processing 2d ed. Englewood Cliffs,
N.J., Prentice-Hall [1971] xii, 290
p. [$8.95] 001.6/4 79-151512
HF5548.2 .L6 1971 MRR Alc.

Sippl, Charles J. Computer
dictionary and handbook, [2d ed.]
Indianapolis, H. W. Sams [1972] 778
p. [$16.95 ($22.25 Can)]
001.6/4/03 70-175572
QA76.15 .S512 1972 MRR Alc.

ELECTRONIC DATA PROCESSING--
BIBLIOGRAPHY.
Computer education directory. South
Pasadena, Calif., Data Processing
Horizons, inc. 651.8/025 68-58845
QA76.25 .C55 MRR Alc Latest
edition

Computer yearbook and directory. 1st-
ed.; 1966- [Detroit, American
Data Processing] 651.8 66-25748
QA76 .C576 Sci RR Partial set /
MRR Alc Latest edition

Morrill, Chester. Computers and data
processing: information sources;
Detroit, Gale Research Co. [1969]
275 p. [8.75] 016.6518 70-85486
Z6654.C17 M58 MRR Alc.

Pritchard, Alan. A guide to computer
literature; 2d ed., rev. and
expanded. [Hamden, Conn.] Linnet
Books [1972] 194 p. [$7.50]
016.0016/4 72-197008
Z6654.C17 P7 1972 MRR Alc.

ELECTRONIC DATA PROCESSING--BIOGRAPHY.
Who's who in computers and data
processing. [Chicago] Quadrangle
Books. 001.6/4/0922 [B] 70-648600
QA76.2 .A1W452 MRR Biog Latest
edition / Sci RR Latest edition

ELECTRONIC DATA PROCESSING--BUSINESS--
BIBLIOGRAPHY.
Morrill, Chester. Systems &
procedures including office
management: information sources;
Detroit, Gale Research Co. [1967]
375 p. 016.658 67-31261
Z7914.A2 M65 MRR Alc.

ELECTRONIC DATA PROCESSING--
DICTIONARIES.
Casey, Florence, Compilation of
terms in information sciences
technology. [Springfield, Va.]
National Technical Information
Service, 1970. 470 l. on [240] p.
001.5/03 77-612498
Z1006 .C38 MRR Alc.

Sippl, Charles J. Computer
dictionary, [2d ed.] Indianapolis,
H. W. Sams [1974] 488 p. [$8.95
($11.95 Can.)] 001.6/4/03 72-91729

QA76.15 .S5 1974 MRR Alc.

Sippl, Charles J. Computer
dictionary and handbook, [2d ed.]
Indianapolis, H. W. Sams [1972] 778
p. [$16.95 ($22.25 Can)]
001.6/4/03 70-175572
QA76.15 .S512 1972 MRR Alc.

Sondak, Norman E. The layman's
dictionary of computer terminology.
New York, Hawthorn Books [1973]
xvii, 203 p. 001.6/4/03 75-39269
QA76.15 .S6 MRR Alc.

Thompson, Dana L. Glossary of STINFO
terminology. [Washington, Office of
Aerospace Research, U.S. Air Force,
1963] vii, 154 p. 63-65366
Z699 .T5 MRR Alc.

Weik, Martin H. Standard dictionary
of computers and information
processing New York, Hayden Book Co.
[1969] vii, 326 p. [$10.95] 651.8
72-80828
QA76.15 .W4 MRR Alc.

ELECTRONIC DATA PROCESSING--
DICTIONARIES--POLYGLOT.
Burger, Erich. Technical dictionary
of data processing, computers, office
machines. [1st ed.] Oxford, New
York, Pergamon Press [1970] 1463 p.
651.8/03 75-81247
QA76.15 .B46 1970 MRR Alc.

Clason, W. E., Elsevier's dictionary
of computers, automatic control and
data processing. 2d rev. ed. of The
dictionary of automation, computers,
control and measuring. Amsterdam,
New York, Elsevier Pub. Co., 1971.
484 p. [f178.00] 001.6/4/03 73-
151733
TJ212.5 .C55 1971 MRR Alc.

Schloms, Irene. Fachwörterbuch für
Programmierer, deutsch, englisch,
französisch. Heidelberg, Hüthig
(1966) 139, 139, 110 p. [DM 28.00]
651.8 67-91557
QA76.15 .S35 MRR Alc.

Trollhann, Lilian, comp. Dictionary
of data processing. Amsterdam, New
York, Elsevier Pub. Co., 1964. 300
p. 651 64-8676
QA76.15 .T7 MRR Alc.

ELECTRONIC DATA PROCESSING--DIRECTORIES.
Association for Computing Machinery.
Roster of members. 1959- New York.
510.78 59-42107
QA76 .A775 MRR Alc Latest edition

Computer Consultants Limited. Who is
related to whom in the computer
industry. 3d ed. Oxford, New York,
Pergamon Press [1969] 324 p.
338.4/7/62138195025 70-85766
TK7885 .C6 1968 MRR Alc.

Computer yearbook and directory. 1st-
ed.; 1966- [Detroit, American
Data Processing] 651.8 66-25748
QA76 .C576 Sci RR Partial set /
MRR Alc Latest edition

The International directory of
computer and information system
services. 1969- London, Europa
Publications. 651.8 70-5680
QA74 .I65 Sci RR Latest edition /
MRR Alc Latest edition

ELECTRONIC DATA PROCESSING--INFORMATION
SERVICES.
D-U-N-S code book: New York, Dun &
Bradstreet. 64-5833
HC102 .D22 MRR Alc Latest edition

ELECTRONIC DATA PROCESSING--PERIODICALS-
-BIBLIOGRAPHY--UNION LISTS.
A World list of computer periodicals.
Manchester, National Computing
Centre, 1970. [1], 102 p. [£3.00]
016.0016/4/05 78-586322
Z6654.C17 W65 MRR Alc.

ELECTRONIC DATA PROCESSING--PUBLIC
ADMINISTRATION.
Herner, Saul. Selected Federal
computer-based information systems,
Washington, Information Resources
Press, 1972. ix, 215 p. 027.5 72-
85016
Z699 .H47 MRR Alc.

ELECTRONIC DATA PROCESSING--STUDY AND
TEACHING--DIRECTORIES.
Computer education directory. South
Pasadena, Calif., Data Processing
Horizons, inc. 651.8/025 68-58845
QA76.25 .C55 MRR Alc Latest
edition

ELECTRONIC DATA PROCESSING--VOCATIONAL
GUIDANCE--DIRECTORIES.
Computer education directory. South
Pasadena, Calif., Data Processing
Horizons, inc. 651.8/025 68-58845
QA76.25 .C55 MRR Alc Latest
edition

ELECTRONIC DATA PROCESSING--YEARBOOKS.
Computer yearbook and directory. 1st-
ed.; 1966- [Detroit, American
Data Processing] 651.8 66-25748
QA76 .C576 Sci RR Partial set /
MRR Alc Latest edition

ELECTRONIC DIGITAL COMPUTERS.
Benrey, Ronald. Understanding
digital computers. New York, J. F.
Rider [c1964] viii, 166 p. 510.783
63-20782
QA76.5 .B4 MRR Alc.

Ledley, Robert Steven. Digital
computer and control engineering.
New York, McGraw-Hill, 1960. 835 p.
510.7834 59-15055
QA76.5 .L4 MRR Alc.

ELECTRONIC DIGITAL COMPUTERS--
BIBLIOGRAPHY.
Pritchard, Alan. A guide to computer
literature; 2d ed., rev. and
expanded. [Hamden, Conn.] Linnet
Books [1972] 194 p. [$7.50]
016.0016/4 72-197008
Z6654.C17 P7 1972 MRR Alc.

ELECTRONIC DIGITAL COMPUTERS--
DICTIONARIES.
Weik, Martin H. Standard dictionary
of computers and information
processing New York, Hayden Book Co.
[1969] vii, 326 p. [$10.95] 651.8
72-80828
QA76.15 .W4 MRR Alc.

ELECTRONIC DIGITAL COMPUTERS--
PERIODICALS--BIBLIOGRAPHY--UNION LISTS.
A World list of computer periodicals.
Manchester, National Computing
Centre, 1970. [1], 102 p. [£3.00]
016.0016/4/05 78-586322
Z6654.C17 W65 MRR Alc.

ELECTRONIC DIGITAL COMPUTERS--
PROGRAMMING.
Leeds, Herbert D. Computer
programming fundamentals 2d ed. New
York, McGraw-Hill [1966] xvi, 459 p.
001.424 65-21588
QA76.5 .L42 1966 MRR Alc.

ELECTRONIC INDUSTRIES--DIRECTORIES.
Who's who in the electronics
industry. 1961/62- New York, SETI
Publishers. 621-38058 61-15101
TA139 .W56 Sci RR Full set / MRR
Biog Latest edition

ELECTRONIC INDUSTRIES--YEARBOOKS.
Computer industry annual. 1967/68-
[W. Concord, Mass.] 621.3819/5/05
68-5128
QA76 .C565 MRR Alc Latest edition

ELECTRONIC INDUSTRIES--GREAT BRITAIN--
DIRECTORIES.
Electrical and electronics trades
directory. 86th- ed.; 1968-
London, Benn Bros. 381/.45/621302542
76-618342
TK12 .E4 MRR Alc Latest edition /
Sci RR Latest edition

ELECTRONIC INDUSTRIES--UNITED STATES.
Census of the electronic market in
the U.S.A.; Philadelphia, Electronic
engineer, a Chilton Publication
[1968] c1967. 1 v. (unpaged)
338.4/7/6213810973 67-31315
HD9696.A1 C4 MRR Alc.

ELECTRONIC INDUSTRIES--UNITED STATES--
DIRECTORIES.
EITD: electronic industry telephone
directory. [Cleveland, Harris Pub.
Co.] [$10.00] 384.6 74-645053
HD9696.A3 U513 MRR Alc Latest
edition

Electronic Industries Association.
Trade directory, membership list.
Washington, D.C. 338.4/7/62138106273
73-642784
TK7800 .E4383 MRR Alc Latest
edition

Electronic marketing directory. 1959-
New York, National Credit Office.
621.3805873 60-3916
HD9696.A1 E48 MRR Alc Latest
edition

Electronic news financial fact book &
directory. 1st- ed.; 1962- New
York, Book Division, Fairchild
Publications. 31 cm. 62-19605
HD9696.A1 E5 MRR Alc Latest
edition

Electronic specifying & purchasing.
Cleveland, Electronic Periodicals
[etc.] 621.381 53-23113
HD9697.U4 E38 Sci RR Latest
edition / MRR Alc Latest edition

ELECTRONIC MUSIC--BIBLIOGRAPHY.
Cross, Lowell M., comp. A
bibliography of electronic music.
[Toronto] University of Toronto Press
[1967] ix, 126 p. 016.7899 67-
2573
ML128.E4 C76 MRR Alc.

ELECTRONIC OFFICE MACHINES.
see also Computers

ELECTRONIC OFFICE MACHINES--
DICTIONARIES--POLYGLOT.
Burger, Erich. Technical dictionary
of data processing, computers, office
machines. [1st ed.] Oxford, New
York, Pergamon Press [1970] 1463 p.
651.8/03 75-81247
QA76.15 .B46 1970 MRR Alc.

ELECTRONIC OFFICE MACHINES--DIRECTORIES.
Geyer's "who makes it" directory.
[New York, Geyer-McAllister
Publications] 338.4/7/651202573 74-
647065
TS1088 .W7 MRR Alc Latest edition

ELECTRONICS--BIBLIOGRAPHY.
Randle, Gretchen R. Electronic
industries; information sources
Detroit, Gale Research Co. [1968]
227 p. 016.621381 67-31262
Z5836 .R3 MRR Alc.

ELECTRONICS--DICTIONARIES.
Coyne Electrical School, Chicago.
Coyne technical dictionary of 4000
terms used in television, radio,
electricity [and] electronics,
Chicago, 1955. 152 p. 621.303 55-
14738
TK9 .C63 MRR Alc.

Funk & Wagnalls dictionary of
electronics. New York, Funk &
Wagnalls [1969] viii, 230 p. [6.95]
621.381/03 68-23735
TK7804 .F8 MRR Alc.

Hughes, Leslie Ernest Charles.
Dictionary of electronics and
nucleonics New York, Barnes & Noble
[1970, c1969] viii, 443 p.
621.381/03 77-13060
TK7804 .H84 1970 MRR Alc.

ELECTRONICS--DICTIONARIES. (Cont.)
The International dictionary of
physics and electronics. 2d ed.
Princeton, N.J., Van Nostrand [1961]
1355 p.   530.3 61-2485
    QC5 .I5 1961 MRR Alc.

Manly, Harold Phillips, Drake's
radio-television electronic
dictionary. Chicago, F. J. Drake Co.
[1960] 1 v. (unpaged) 621.3803 60-
4753
    TK6544 .M33 1960 MRR Alc.

Modern dictionary of electronics
[4th ed.] Indianapolis, H. W. Sams
[1972] 688 p. 621.381/03 76-
175571
    TK7804 .H6 1972 MRR Alc.

National Radio Institute, Washington,
D.C. Radio-television-electronics
dictionary. New York, J. F. Rider
[1962] 190 p. 621.38403 62-21929

    TK6544 .N3 1962 MRR Alc.

Oldfield, Ruth L. The practical
dictionary of electricity and
electronics. Chicago, American
Technical Society, 1959. 216 p.
631.303 58-59540
    TK9 .O4 MRR Alc.

Sarbacher, Robert Irving.
Encyclopedic dictionary of
electronics and nuclear engineering.
Englewood Cliffs, N.J., Prentice-
Hall, 1959. 1417 p. 621.4803 59-
11990
    TK7804 .S3 MRR Alc.

Susskind, Charles. The encyclopedia
of electronics. New York, Reinhold
Pub. Corp. [1962] xxi, 974 p.
621.38103 62-13258
    TK804 .S9 MRR Alc.

ELECTRONICS--DICTIONARIES--POLYGLOT.
Clason, W. E., Supplement to the
Elsevier dictionaries of electronics,
nucleonics and telecommunication.
Amsterdam, New York, Elsevier Pub.
Co., 1963. 633 p. 603 63-11369
    T10 .C55 MRR Alc.

Elsevier's dictionary of electronics
and waveguides. 2d ed., rev. and
enl. Amsterdam, New York, Elsevier
Pub. Co., 1966 [i.e. 1965] 833 p.
621.38103 65-20142
    TK7804 .E4 1965 MRR Alc.

Six-language dictionary of
automation, electronics and
scientific instruments; London,
Iliffe Books; Englewood Cliffs, N.J.,
Prentice-Hall [1962] 732 p.
621.3803 63-5414
    TK7804 .S5 1962 MRR Alc.

ELECTROPLATING.
Metal finishing guidebook-directory.
Westwood, N.J. [etc.] Metals and
Plastics Publications [etc.] 41-
10188
    Began publication in 1930.
    TS670 .A47 Sci RR Latest edition /
    MRR Alc Latest edition

ELEMENTARY EDUCATION
see Education, Elementary

ELEMENTARY SCHOOLS--UNITED STATES--
DIRECTORIES.
Gertler, Diane (Bochner) Directory:
public elementary and secondary day
schools, 1968-69, [Washington] U.S.
National Center for Educational
Statistics; [for sale by the Supt. of
Docs., U.S. Govt. Print. Off., 1970-
v.   [2.00] 371/.01/02573 70-
607482
    L901 .G39 MRR Alc.

ELIZABETH II, QUEEN OF GREAT BRITAIN,
1926-
Cathcart, Helen. Her Majesty the
Queen; Rev. ed. New York, Dodd,
Mead, 1966. 215 p. 942.085/0924
66-24275
    DA590 .C3 1966 MRR Alc.

ELOCUTION.
see also Debates and debating

EMANCIPATION OF SLAVES
see Slavery in the United States--
Emancipation

EMANCIPATION OF WOMEN
see Woman--Rights of women

EMBLEMS.
see also Symbolism in art

Clapp, Jane. Professional ethics and
insignia. Metuchen, N.J., Scarecrow
Press, 1974. xii, 851 p. 061/.3
74-10501
    HD6504 .A194 MRR Ref Desk.

EMBLEMS--BIBLIOGRAPHY.
Landwehr, John. Dutch emblem books;
a bibliography. Utrecht, Haentjens
Dekker & Gumbert [1962] xii, 98 p.
66-83333
    Z2401 .L3 MR Alc.

EMBLEMS, NATIONAL.
see also Flags

Great Britain. Admiralty. Flags of
all nations. [Rev. ed.] London,
H.M.Stationery Off., 1955- v.
929.9 56-41972
    V300 .G72 MRR Alc.

Hope, A. Guy. Symbols of the
nations. Washington, Public Affairs
Press [1973] 348 p. [$10.00]
929.8 73-82015
    JC345 .H66 MRR Alc.

EMBLEMS, NATIONAL--UNITED STATES.
Lehner, Ernst, comp. American
symbols; New York, W. Penn Pub. Co.
[1957] 95 p. 973.084 57-14579
    E178.5 .L4 MRR Alc.

EMBROIDERY--UNITED STATES--HISTORY.
Harbeson, Georgiana (Brown) Mrs.,
American needlework; New York,
Coward-McCann, inc., 1938. xxxviii,
232 p. 746 38-29098
    NK9212 .H3 MRR Alc.

EMBRYOLOGY.
see also Genetics

see also Reproduction

EMERGENCIES, MEDICAL
see First aid in illness and injury

see Medical emergencies

EMERSON, RALPH WALDO, 1803-1882--
CONCORDANCES.
Hubbell, George Shelton. A
concordance to the poems of Ralph
Waldo Emerson; New York, Russell &
Russell [1967] x, 478 p. 811/.3
67-18293
    PS1645 .H8 1967 MRR Alc.

EMIGRATION AND IMMIGRATION.
see also Anthropo-geography

see also Migration, Internal

EMIGRATION AND IMMIGRATION--
BIBLIOGRAPHY.
Mangalam, J. J. Human migration;
Lexington, University of Kentucky
Press, 1968. 194 p. [15.00]
016.3013/2 67-23777
    Z7164.D3 M36 MRR Alc.

EMISSION CONTROL DEVICES (MOTOR
VEHICLES)
see Motor vehicles--Pollution control
devices

EMPIRE, ISLAMIC
see Islamic Empire

EMPLOYEE COMMUNICATION
see Communication in management

EMPLOYEE TRAINING DIRECTORS--UNITED
STATES--DIRECTORIES.
Who's who in training and
development. 1970- Madison, Wis.,
American Society for Training and
Development. [$25.00]
658.31/24/02573 73-647735
    HF5549.5.T7 A58 MRR Alc Latest
    edition

EMPLOYEES, TRAINING OF.
see also Executives, Training of

EMPLOYER-EMPLOYEE RELATIONS
see Industrial relations

EMPLOYERS' ASSOCIATIONS--FRANCE--
DIRECTORIES.
Conseil national du patronat
français. Annuaire. Paris, Union
française d'annuaire professionnels
[etc.] 62-25706
    Began publication in 1949.
    HD6683 .C6 MRR Alc Latest edition

EMPLOYERS' LIABILITY--BIBLIOGRAPHY.
United States. Library of Congress.
Division of bibliography. ... Select
list of works relating to employers
liability. Washington, Govt. print.
off., 1906. 25 p. 06-35013
    Z663.28 .S46 MRR Alc.

EMPLOYMENT (ECONOMIC THEORY)
see also Labor supply

EMPLOYMENT AGENCIES--DIRECTORIES.
Zimmerman, Oswald Theodore, College
placement directory, 4th ed. Dover,
N.H., Industrial Research Service,
1965. vii, 643 p. 331.11502573 66-
919
    LB2343.5 .Z5 1965 MRR Alc.

EMPLOYMENT AGENCIES--UNITED STATES--
DIRECTORIES.
Jameson, Robert, The professional
job changing system; [3d ed.]
Verona, N.J., Performance Dynamics,
1974] 280 p. 650/.14 73-92380
    HF5383 .J28 1974 MRR Alc.

United States. Bureau of
Apprenticeship and Training.
Directory for reaching minority
groups. [Washington: For sale by the
Supt. of Docs., U.S. Govt. Print.
Off.] 1973. 214 p. [$2.85] 331.6
73-602280
    HD6305 .M5 U53 1973 MRR alc.

EMPLOYMENT DISCRIMINATION
see Discrimination in employment

EMPLOYMENT OF WOMEN
see Woman--Employment

ENAMEL PAINTS
see Paint

ENCYCLICALS, PAPAL.
Catholic Church. Pope. The papal
encyclicals in their historical
context [New York] New American
Library [1963] 448 p. 64-2656
    BX860 .A36 1963 MRR Alc.

ENCYCLICALS, PAPAL--BIBLIOGRAPHY.
Carlen, Mary Claudia, A guide to the
encyclicals of the Roman pontiffs
from Leo XIII to the present day
(1878-1937) New York, The H. W.
Wilson company, 1939. 247 p.
016.2628 39-13091
    Z7838.E5 C3 MRR Alc.

ENCYCLOPEDIAS AND DICTIONARIES.
Ackermann, Alfred Seabold Eli,
Popular fallacies: 4th ed. London,
Old Westminster Press; sole
distributors, S. Marshall, 1950. xv,
843 p. 133.7 50-32195
    AZ999 .A3 1950 MRR Alc.

Blumberg, Dorothy Rose. Whose what?
[1st ed.] New York, Holt, Rinehart
and Winston [1969] 184 p. [3.95]
031/.02 68-12199
    AG105 .B72 MRR Alc.

Britannica book of the year. 1938-
Chicago, Encyclopaedia Britannica,
inc. 032 38-12082
    AE5 .E364 MRR Alc Latest edition

Bumpus, John Skelton, A dictionary
of ecclesiastical terms; London, T.
W. Laurie [1910] 2 p. l., 323 [1] p.
11-21155
    BR95 .B8 MRR Alc.

The Cadillac modern encyclopedia.
[1st ed.] New York, Cadillac Pub.
Co.; distributed by Derbibooks,
Secaucus, N.J. [1973] xiv, 1954 p.
[$24.95] 031 73-81377
    AG5 .C25 MRR Ref Desk.

The Century dictionary and
cyclopedia, [Rev. and enl. ed.] New
York, The Century co. [c1911] [2 v.
[$75.00] 11-31934
    PE1625 .C4 1911 MRR Alc.

Chambers's encyclopaedia. New rev.
ed. Oxford, New York, Pergamon Press
[1967, c1966] 15 v. 032 66-19618

    AE5 .C443 1967 MRR Alc.

Collier's encyclopedia, [New York]
Macmillan Educational Corp. [1974]
24 v. 031 73-13422
    AE5 .C683 1974 MRR Alc.

The Columbia encyclopedia, 3d ed.
New York, Columbia University Press,
1963. 2388 p. 031 63-20205
    AG5 .C725 1963 MRR Alc.

Compton's encyclopedia and fact-
index, [Chicago] F. E. Compton Co.
[1974] 26 v. 031 73-84236
    AG5 .C73 1974 MRR Alc.

Compton's encyclopedia and fact-
index, [Chicago] F. E. Compton Co.
[1974] 26 v. 031 73-84236
    AG5 .C73 1974 MRR Alc.

Cowles volume library. 1968- New
York, Cowles Book Co. [etc.] 031/.02
77-7030
    AG5 .V62 MRR Alc Latest edition

Dictionary of the history of ideas;
New York, Scribner [1973] 4 v.
[$35.00 (per vol.)] 901.9 72-7943

    CB5 .D52 MRR Alc.

Encyclopaedia Britannica. Chicago,
Encyclopaedia Britannica [1973] 24
v. 031 72-75874
    AE5 .E363 1973 MRR Alc.

The Encyclopædia britannica; 11th
ed. ... New York, The Encyclopædia
britannica company, 1910-11. 29 v.
agr16-592
    AE5 .E399 MRR Alc.

ENCYCLOPEDIAS AND DICTIONARIES. (Cont.)
The Encyclopedia Americana.
International ed. New York,
Americana Corp. [1974] 30 v.   031
73-8981
   AE5 .E333 1974 MRR Alc.

Encyclopedia Canadiana. Toronto,
Grolier of Canada, c1972. 10 v.
[$109.50 (Schools and libraries)]
917.1/03/03 73-157945
   F1006 .E625 1972 MRR Alc.

Everyman's encyclopaedia. 5th ed.
London, Dent, 1967. 12 v. [28/-/-]
031 78-390426
   AE5 .E85 1967 MRR Alc.

Garrison, Webb B. How it started
Nashville, Abingdon Press [1972] 237
p. [$4.95] 390/.09 72-173951
   GT75 .G3 MRR Alc.

Garrison, Webb B. The ignorance
book. New York, Morrow, 1971. 250
p. [$6.95] 031/.02 70-135148
   AG106 .G3 MRR Alc.

Kane, Joseph Nathan, Famous first
facts; 3d ed. New York, H. W.
Wilson, 1964. 1165 p.   031 63-
14893
   AG5 .K315 1964 MRR Ref Desk.

Latham, Edward. A dictionary of
names, nicknames, and surnames of
persons, places and things. Detroit,
Republished by Gale Research Co.,
1966. vii, 334 p. 031.02 66-22674
   AG5 .L35 1966 MRR Alc.

Laughlin, William H. Laughlin's fact
finder; West Nyack, N.Y., Parker
Pub. Co. [1969] viii, 30, 701 p.
[12.95] 031/.02 69-11218
   AG5 .L38 1969 MRR Alc.

The Lincoln library of essential
information; [1st] ed.; 1924-
Columbus, Ohio [etc.] Frontier Press.
031 24-14708
   AG105 .L55 MRR Ref Desk Latest
edition

Marxism, Communism, and Western
society; [New York] Herder and
Herder [1972-73] 8 v. 300/.3 79-
176368
   AE5 .M27 MRR Alc.

McWhirter, Norris Dewar. Dunlop
illustrated encyclopedia of facts,
Garden City, N.Y., Doubleday [1969]
864 p. [8.95] 031/.02 68-59630
   AG6 .M34 MRR Ref Desk.

The New Encyclopaedia Britannica.
15th ed. Chicago, Encyclopaedia
Britannica [1974] 30 v. 031 73-
81025
   AE5 .E363 1974 MRR Alc.

Origin of things familiar;
Cincinnati, O., United book
corporation [c1934] 4 p. l., 280 p.
031 35-2154
   AG5 .O7 MRR Alc.

Pears cyclopaedia. [London, etc.]
Pelham Books Ltd. [etc.] 032 a 34-
1196
   AY756 .P4 MRR Alc Latest Edition

Phyfe, William Henry Pinkney, 5000
facts and fancies; Rev. and corr.
ed. Detroit, Gale Research Co.,
1966. vii, 816 p. 031 66-24369
   AG5 .P6 1901a MRR Alc.

Stimpson, George William, A book
about a thousand things, New York,
London, Harper & brothers [1946] x
p., 1 l., 552 p. 031 46-4143
   AG5 .S84 MRR Ref Desk.

Stimpson, George William,
Information roundup. [1st ed.] New
York, Harper [1948] x, 587 p. 031
48-6728
   AG5 .S85 MRR Alc.

Stimpson, George William, Nuggets of
knowledge, New York, G. Sully and
company [c1928] viii p., 1 l., 427
p. 28-24287
   AG105 .S85 MRR Ref Desk.

Stimpson, George William, Popular
questions answered, Detroit, Gale
Research Co., 1970. viii, 426 p.
031 74-109601
   AG195 .S74 1970 MRR Ref Desk.

Stimpson, George William, Uncommon
knowledge, Indianapolis, New York,
The Bobbs-Merrill company [c1936]
368 p. 031 36-17991
   AG105 .S855 MRR Ref Desk.

Thorne, Robert, ed. Fugitive facts.
2d ed. New York, A. L. Burt, 1890.
10-5531
   AG105 .T48 1890 MRR Alc.

The Webster encyclopedic dictionary
of the English language and
compendium of usable knowledge.
Chicago, Consolidated Book Publishers
[c1965] 1 v. (various pagings) 423
66-615
   PE1628 .W5515 MRR Alc.

Weideman, Hugh, comp. The rapid fact
finder; New York, Crowell [1958]
xiv, 495 p. 031 58-6207
   AG5 .W44 MRR Ref Desk.

The World book encyclopedia.
Chicago, Field Enterprises
Educational Corp. [1973] 26 v. 031
74-189336
   AE5 .W55 1973 MRR Alc.

**ENCYCLOPEDIAS AND DICTIONARIES--
BIBLIOGRAPHY.**
Collison, Robert Lewis. Dictionaries
of English and foreign languages; 2d
ed. [New York] Hafner Pub. Co.,
1971. xvii, 303 p. 016.403 78-
130513
   Z7004.D5 C6 1971 MRR Alc.

International bibliography of
dictionaries. 5th, rev. ed. New
York, R. R. Bowker Co., 1972. xxvi,
511 p. 016.03 72-214468
   Z7004.D5 I55 1972 MRR Alc.

Mathews, Mitford McLeod, A survey of
English dictionaries, New York,
Russell & Russell, 1966. 119 p.
016.423 65-17912
   Z2015.D6 M4 1966 MRR Alc.

Turnbull, William R. Scientific and
technical dictionaries; San
Bernardino, Calif., Bibliothek Press,
1966- v. 016.503 67-25830
   Z7401 .T8 MRR Alc.

United States. Library of Congress.
General Reference and Bibliography
Division. Foreign language-English
dictionaries. Washington, 1955. 2
v. 016.413 55-60042
   Z663.28 .F58 MRR Alc.

Walford, Albert John. A guide to
foreign language grammars and
dictionaries, 2nd ed., revised and
enlarged. London, Library
Association, 1967. 240 p. [60/-]
016.415 68-86136
   Z7004.G7 W3 1967 MRR Alc.

Walsh, James Patrick. Anglo-American
general encyclopedias; New York,
Bowker, 1968. xix, 270 p. 016.031
67-25023
   Z5849.E5 W3 MRR Alc.

Walsh, James Patrick. General
encyclopedias in print. 1963- New
York [etc.] Bowker [etc.] 63-24124
   Z1035 .W267 MRR Ref Desk Latest
edition

Whittaker, Kenneth. Dictionaries.
London, Bingley, 1966. 88 p. [16/-]
016.03 66-72684
   Z7004.D5 W5 MRR Alc.

Zaunmüller, Wolfram.
Bibliographisches Handbuch der
Sprachwörterbücher; Stuttgart, A.
Hiersemann, 1958. xvi p., 496
columns. a 59-1510
   Z7004.D5 Z3 1958a MRR Alc.

Zischka, Gert A. Index lexicorum;
Wien, Verlag Brüder Hollinek [1959]
xliii, 290 p. 59-34653
   Z1035 .Z5 MRR Alc.

**ENCYCLOPEDIAS AND DICTIONARIES--HISTORY
AND CRITICISM.**
Collison, Robert Lewis. Dictionaries
of English and foreign languages; 2d
ed. [New York] Hafner Pub. Co.,
1971. xvii, 303 p. 016.403 78-
130513
   Z7004.D5 C6 1971 MRR Alc.

Collison, Robert Lewis.
Encyclopaedias: their history
throughout the ages; 2d ed. New
York, Hafner Pub. Co., 1966. xvi,
334 p. 030.9 66-5463
   AE1 .C6 1966 MRR Alc.

Walsh, James Patrick. General
encyclopedias in print. 1963- New
York [etc.] Bowker [etc.] 63-24124
   Z1035 .W267 MRR Ref Desk Latest
edition

ENCYCLOPEDIAS AND DICTIONARIES, DANISH.
Nordisk konversationsleksikon.
København, 1960- v. a 60-5895
   AE41 .N83 MRR Alc.

ENCYCLOPEDIAS AND DICTIONARIES, DUTCH.
Grote Winkler Prins. [7e geheel
nieuwe druk] Amsterdam, Brussel,
Elsevier, 1966- v. [49.50 (v. 1)
varies] 68-112964
   AE19 .W5262 MRR Alc.

Winkler Prins encyclopaedie. [6.
geheel nieuwe druk] Amsterdam,
Elsevier, 1947- v. a 48-2479
   AE19 .W526 MRR Alc.

ENCYCLOPEDIAS AND DICTIONARIES, FINNISH.
Otavan iso tietosanakirja. Helsinki,
Otava [1965-67] 10 v. 68-46948
   AE21 .O84 MRR Alc.

ENCYCLOPEDIAS AND DICTIONARIES, FRENCH.
Dictionnaire des œuvres
contemporaines de tous les pays.
Paris, Société d'édition de
dictionnaires et encyclopédies,
1967. viii, 767 p. [155 F] 703
68-119409
   AE25 .D552 MRR Alc.

Dictionnaire des œvres de tous les
temps et de tous les pays; [1. ed.]
Paris, S.E.D.E. [1952-68] 5 v. 55-
15784
   AE25 .D52 MRR Alc.

Encyclopédie générale Larousse.
Paris, Larousse, 1967-68. 3 v.
[162.00 (v. 1)] 034/.1 68-83508
   AG25 .E66 MRR Alc.

Grand Larousse encyclopédique en dix
volumes. Paris, Librairie Larousse
[1960-64] 10 v. 60-50563
   AE25 .G64 MRR Alc.

La Grande encyclopédie ... Paris,
Larousse, 1971- v. [39.00F (v.
1)] 034/.1 72-334017
   AE25 .G69 MRR Alc.

La Grande encyclopédie, Paris, H.
Lamirault et cie [1886-1902] 31 v.
01-14506
   AE25 .G7 MRR Alc.

Larousse trois volumes en couleurs.
Paris, Larousse, 1965-1966. 3 v.
[145 F. (v. 1) 168 F. (v. 2) 180 F.
(v. 3)] 034/.1 67-77658
   AG25 .L26 MRR Alc.

Petit Larousse illustré, 1973.
Paris, Larousse [1972] 1092, xvi,
[1093]-1790 p. 73-364482
   AG25 .N75 1972 MRR Alc.

ENCYCLOPEDIAS AND DICTIONARIES, GERMAN.
Das Bertelsmann Lexikon in zehn
Banden. [Gütersloh] Bertelsmann
Lexikon-Verlag [c1972- v. 73-
300258
   AE27 .B424 MRR Alc.

Brockhaus Enzyklopädie in zwanzig
Banden. Siebzehnte völlig neu
bearb. Aufl. des Grossen Brockhaus.
Wiesbaden, Brockhaus, 1966- v.
[DM79.- (v. 1)] 033.1 66-68667
   AE27 .O672 MRR Alc.

Das Grosse Duden-Lexikon in acht
Banden. Mannheim, Bibliographisches
Institut, 1946-69. 10 v. [33.00 (v.
3) varies] 033/.1 67-94115
   AE27 .G693 vol. 9-10 MRR Alc.

Der Grosse Herder; 5., neubearb.
Aufl. von Herders
Konversationslexikon. Freiburg,
Herder, 1952- v. 033 53-18624

   AE27 .H5 1952 MRR Alc.

Meyers enzyklopädisches Lexikon.
9., völlig neu bearb. Aufl.
Mannheim, Wien, Zürich,
Bibliographisches Inst. (1971- v.
with illus. and maps. [DM89.00 per
vol.] 70-873556
   AE27 .M6 1971 MRR Alc.

Meyers konversations-lexikon. Meyers
grosses konversations-lexikon. 6.
ganzlich neubearb. und verm. aufl.
... Neuer abdruck. Leipzig, Wien,
Bibliographisches Institut, 1909-13.
24 v. mrr01-63
   AE27 .M6 1909 MRR Alc.

Der Neue Herder. Freiburg (i. Br.),
Basel Wien, Herder (1970- v.
[75.00 per vol.] 79-551463
   AG27 .N394 MRR Alc.

Schweizer lexikon. Zürich,
Encyclios-verlag a. g. [1945-48] 7
v. 033 a 46-3754
   AE69 .S35 MRR Alc.

**ENCYCLOPEDIAS AND DICTIONARIES,
HUNGARIAN.**
Révai nagy lexikona; Budapest,
Révai Testverek, 1911-35. 21 v.
039.94511 36-4433
   AE31 .R4 MRR Alc.

Új magyar lexikon. Budapest,
Akadémiai Kiadó [1959- 7 v. 65-
77054
   AE31 .U44 MRR Alc.

ENCYCLOPEDIAS AND DICTIONARIES, ITALIAN.
Dizionario enciclopedico italiano.
Roma, Istituto della Enciclopedia
italiana [1955-61] 12 v. 55-36452

   AE35 .D516 MRR Alc.

ENCYCLOPEDIAS AND DICTIONARIES, (Cont.)
Enciclopedia italiana di scienze, lettere ed arti ... [Roma] Istituto Giovanni Treccani, 1929-39. 36 v. 035   29-20675
    AE35 .E5 MRR Alc.

Enciclopedia Sansoni illustrata. Firenze, Sansoni, 1968. 4 v. [48000]   73-390457
    AE35 .E53 MRR Alc.

Modernissimo dizionario illustrato ... Novara, Istituto geografico De Agostini, 1968. 2 v. [9000]   77-436091
    PC1625 .M6 MRR Alc.

Nuova enciclopedia universale Curcio delle lettere, delle scienze, delle arti. [Roma] A. Curcio, 1968-69. 8 v.   035/.1   68-143026
    AE35 .N95 MRR Alc.

ENCYCLOPEDIAS AND DICTIONARIES, NORWEGIAN.
Aschehougs konversasjons leksikon. 4. utg. Oslo, Aschehoug, 1954-61. 18 v.   62-59870
    AE43 .I33 MRR Alc.

Gyldendals ett-binds konversasjonsleksikon. 5. utg. Oslo, Gyldendal [1967]   4221 columns. [198.00 nkr]   038/.8/2   67-105339
    AG43 .G85 1967 MRR Alc.

ENCYCLOPEDIAS AND DICTIONARIES, POLISH.
Wielka encyklopedia powszechna PWN. Wyd. 1.] Warszawa, Panstwowe Wydawn. Naukowe [1962]-[70] 13 v. 039/.918/5   63-37817
    AE53 .W44 MRR Alc.

ENCYCLOPEDIAS AND DICTIONARIES, PORTUGUESE.
Enciclopédia Delta Larousse. 2. ed. rev. e atual. Rio de Janeiro, Ed. Delta [1967] 15 v.   036/.9   68-117581
    AE37 .E48 1967 MRR Alc.

Enciclopédia universal EPB; São Paulo, Ed. Pedagogica Brasileira, 1969. 10 v. (3904, 226 p.) [500.00] 76-391018
    AE37 .E55 MRR Alc.

Grande enciclopédia portuguesa e brasileira. Lisboa, Rio de Janeiro, Editorial Enciclopedia, limitada [1936-60] 40 v.   036.9   36-32193
    AE37 .G7 MRR Alc.

Verbo; enciclopédia luso-brasileira de cultura. Lisboa, Editorial Verbo [1963-   v.   65-47647
    AE37 .V4 MRR Alc.

ENCYCLOPEDIAS AND DICTIONARIES, RUSSIAN.
[Bol'shaia sovetskaia entsiklopediia (romanized form)] [1950]-58. 51 v.   50-38716
    AE55 .B62 MRR Alc.

ENCYCLOPEDIAS AND DICTIONARIES, SPANISH.
Diccionario enciclopédico abreviado, 7. ed. Madrid, Espasa-Calpe, 1957 [c1954-55] 7 v.   71-205627
    AE61 .D45 1957 MRR Alc.

Diccionario enciclopédico Salvat. 11. ed. Barcelona, Salvat Editores [1964] 12 v.   68-124541
    AE61 .D62 1964 MRR Alc.

Diccionario enciclopédico Salvat universal Barcelona, etc. [Salvat, 1970-   v.   72-883776
    AE61 .D64 MRR Alc.

Diccionario enciclopédico U.T.E.H.A. [1. ed.] México, Unión Tipografica Editorial Hispano Americana [1951-52, c1950-52] 10 v. 036   51-35243
    AE65 .D47 MRR Alc.

Enciclopedia universal Sopena; Barcelona, R. Sopena [1963-   v. 64-49331
    PC4625 .E62 MRR Alc.

Enciclopedia vniversal ilvstrada evropeo-americana; Barcelona, J. Espasa [1907?-30] 70 v. in 72.   036 32-1302
    AE61 .E6 MRR Alc.

Gran enciclopedia del mundo. [1, ed.] Bilbao, Durvan; distribucion general: Editorial Marin, Barcelona [1961-   v.   62-67391
    AE61 .G7 MRR Alc.

ENCYCLOPEDIAS AND DICTIONARIES, SWEDISH.
Svensk uppslagsbok. 2. omarb. och utvidgade uppl. Malmö, Förlagshuset Norden [1947-   v. 52-26563
    AE45 .S82 MRR Alc.

ENDANGERED SPECIES
see Rare animals

ENDOWED CHARITIES
see Charities

ENDOWMENT OF RESEARCH.
see also Science and state

Handbook of learned societies and institutions: America. Washington, D.C., Carnegie institution of Washington, 1908. viii, 592 p.   08-21011
    Z5055.U39 H2 MRR Alc.

ENDOWMENTS--DIRECTORIES.
Annual register of grant support. 1969-   Orange, N.J. [etc.] Academic Media.   001.4/4   69-18307
    AS911 .A2A67 Sci RR Latest edition / MRR Ref Desk Latest edition

The Foundation directory. 1st-ed.; 1960-   New York, [Foundation Center] Distributed by Columbia University Press [etc.]   061   60-13807
    AS911 .A2F65 Sci RR Latest edition / MRR Alc Latest edition / MRR Ref Desk Latest edition

The Foundation grants index. New York, Distributed by Columbia University Press.   001.4/4   72-76018
    AS911.A2 F66   MRR Alc Latest edition

Foundation Research Service. Foundation research service. [Washington, Lawson & Williams Associates, 1972-   4 v. (loose-leaf) 507/.2073   72-184024
    Q180.U5 F68 MRR Alc.

Technical Assistance Information Clearing House. Far East technical assistance programs of U.S. nonprofit organizations, New York, 1966. viii, 274 p.   309.2/23   67-60359
    HC411 .T4 MRR Alc.

United States. Congress. House. Select Committee on Small Business. Subcommittee No. 1. Tax-exempt foundations: their impact on small business. Washington, U.S. Govt. Print. Off., 1967 [i.e. 1968]-68. 2 v.   336.2/94   68-60557
    KF27.5.S664 1967 vol. 2 MRR Alc.

ENDOWMENTS--CANADA--DIRECTORIES.
Holmes, Jeffrey. Canadian universities' guide to foundations and granting agencies. [2d ed.] Ottawa, Association of Universities and Colleges of Canada, 1969. 110 p. [5.00]   361/.02/0257 75-454894
    LB2339.C3 H6 1969 MRR Alc.

ENDOWMENTS--EUROPE--DIRECTORIES.
Fondazione Giovanni Agnelli. Guide to European foundations, [Milano] F. Angeli; distributed by Columbia University Press, New York, 1973. 401 p.   [$12.50]   361.7/6/0254 73-163802
    HV238.A2 F65 1973 MRR Alc.

ENDOWMENTS--GREAT BRITAIN--DIRECTORIES.
Charities Aid Fund. Directory of grant-making trusts / 3rd compilation / Tonbridge, Kent : The Fund, 1973. 920 p. : [£7.50] 001.4/4/02542   74-188784
    AS911.A2 C45 1974 MRR Alc.

Holmes, Jeffrey. Canadian universities' guide to foundations and granting agencies. [2d ed.] Ottawa, Association of Universities and Colleges of Canada, 1969. 110 p. [5.00]   361/.02/0257 75-454894
    LB2339.C3 H6 1969 MRR Alc.

Keeling, Guy Willing, comp. Trusts & foundations; [Cambridge, Eng.] Bowes & Bowes [1953] x1, 194 p.   068.42 53-3918
    AS911.A2 K38 MRR Alc.

ENDOWMENTS--LATIN AMERICA--DIRECTORIES.
Stromberg, Ann. Philanthropic foundations in Latin America. New York, Russell Sage Foundation, 1968. viii, 215 p.   [7.50]   361/.02/0258 68-54409
    HV110.5 .S87 MRR Alc.

ENDOWMENTS--UNITED STATES.
Dermer, Joseph. How to raise funds from foundations. New York, Public Service Materials Center [1968] 55 p.   361.7/3   68-5018
    AS911.A2 D4 MRR Alc.

Shapiro, Sandra. Directory of financial aid in higher education; Waltham, Mass., African Studies Association, Research Liaison Committee, Brandeis University [1973] v, 166 p.   378.3/025/73   73-166271
    LB2338 .S46 MRR Alc.

ENDOWMENTS--UNITED STATES--DIRECTORIES.
De Bettencourt, F. G. The Catholic guide to foundations 2d ed. Washington, Guide Publishers [1973] iii, 170 p.   361.7/6/02573 73-86563
    HV97.A3 D4 1973 MRR Alc.

Holmes, Jeffrey. Canadian universities' guide to foundations and granting agencies. Ottawa, Association of Universities and Colleges of Canada, 1969. 110 p. [5.00]   361/.02/0257 75-454894
    LB2339.C3 H6 1969 MRR Alc.

Latin America technical assistance programs of U.S. nonprofit organizations. New York, Technical Assistance Information Clearing House.   309.2/23   72-4820
    HC122 .L3   MRR Alc Latest edition

ENDOWMENTS--UNITED STATES--STATISTICS.
Giving USA; a compilation of facts related to American philanthropy. New York, American Association of Fund-Raising Counsel.   361.705873   59-1874
    HV89 .G5   MRR Ref Desk Latest edition

ENDOWMENTS--WASHINGTON, D.C.--DIRECTORIES.
De Bettencourt, Margaret T. The guide to Washington, D.C. foundations, [Washington, Guide Publishers, c1972] viii, 62 p. [$8.00]   001.4/4   72-90810
    AS911.A2 D24 MRR Ref Desk.

ENERGY RESOURCES
see Power resources

ENFORCEMENT OF LAW
see Law enforcement

ENGAGEMENT
see Betrothal

ENGINEERING.
see also Architecture

see also Civil engineering

see also Environmental engineering

see also Industrial engineering

see also Machinery

ENGINEERING--AUTHORSHIP
see Technical writing

ENGINEERING--BIOGRAPHY--BIBLIOGRAPHY.
Pittsburgh. Carnegie library. Men of science and industry; Pittsburgh, Carnegie library, 1915. 189, [3] p. 15-6134
    Z7404 .A1P6 MRR Biog.

ENGINEERING--DICTIONARIES.
De Vries, Louis, English-German technical and engineering dictionary, 2d ed., completely rev. and enl. New York, McGraw-Hill [c1967] 1154 p.   603   68-2779
    T9 .D47 1967 MRR Alc.

Jones, Franklin Day, ed. Engineering encyclopedia; 3d ed. New York, Industrial Press [1963] 1431 p. 620.3   63-10415
    TA9 .J65 1963 MRR Alc.

Malgorn, Guy Marie, Lexique technique anglais-français: 4. éd. rev. et corr. Paris, Gauthier-Villars, 1956. xxxiv, 493 p.   57-155
    T9 .M16 1956 MRR Alc.

ENGINEERING--DICTIONARIES--GERMAN.
De Vries, Louis, German-English technical and engineering dictionary, 2d ed., completely rev. and enl. New York, McGraw-Hill [1965, c1966] 1178 p.   603   65-23218
    T9 .D48 1966 MRR Alc.

Leidecker, Kurt Friedrich, ed. German-English technical dictionary of aeronautics, rocketry, space navigation ... New York, S. F. Vanni [1950-51] 2 v. (968 p.)   629.1303 50-14702
    TL509 .L4 MRR Alc.

ENGINEERING--DICTIONARIES--POLYGLOT.
Bosch, Abraham ten, Viertalig technisch woordenboek. Deventer, Æ. E. Kluwer [1948-55] 4 v.   603   50-18447
    T10 .B72 MRR Alc.

The International dictionary of applied mathematics. Princeton, N.J., Van Nostrand [1960] 1173 p. 510.3   60-16931
    QA5 .I5 MRR Alc.

ENGINEERING--HANDBOOKS, MANUALS, ETC.
Kempe's engineer's year-book. West Wickham, Kent [etc.], Morgan-Grampian Books Ltd. [etc.]   57-33039
    Began publication in 1894.
    TA151 .A1E6   MRR Alc Latest edition

Potter, James Harry. Handbook of the engineering sciences. Princeton, N.J., Van Nostrand [1967] 2 v.   620 67-4632
    TA151 .P79 MRR Alc.

ENGINEERING--HISTORY.
Poirier, René. The fifteen wonders
of the world. London, V. Gollancz,
1960. 400 p. 620.9 61-65848
TA15 .P633 1960 MRR Alc

ENGINEERING--INDEXES.
Scientific and technical books in
print. 1972- New York, R. R. Bowker
Co. 016.5 71-37614
Z7401 .S573 MRR Alc Latest edition
/ Sci RR Latest edition

United States. Army. Corps of
engineers. Analytical and topical
index to the reports of the chief of
engineers and officers of the Corps
of engineers, United States Army,1866-
1900 ... Washington, Govt. print.
off., 1903. 3 v. 03-27940
TC23 .A3 1866-1900 MRR Alc.

ENGINEERING--MATERIALS
see Materials

ENGINEERING--PERIODICALS--BIBLIOGRAPHY.
Global Engineering Documentation
Services. Directory of engineering
document sources. Newport Beach,
Calif., Global Engineering
Documentation Services [1972] 1 v.
(unpaged) [$29.95] 029.9/62 72-
176333
Z5852 .G5 MRR Alc.

ENGINEERING--PERIODICALS--INDEXES.
American Society of Mechanical
Engineers. Seventy-seven year index:
technical papers, 1880-1956. New
York [1957] 382 p. 621.06273 57-
59509
TJ1 .A774 MRR Alc.

Applied science & technology index.
v. 1- Feb. 1913- [Bronx, N.Y.,
etc.] H. W. Wilson [etc.] 016.6 14-
5408
Z7913 .I7 MRR Circ Partial set /
Sci RR Partial set

Engineering index. 1906- New York
[etc.] 07-38575
Z5851 .E62 Sci RR Full set / MRR
Alc (Dk 33) Partial set

ENGINEERING--SUPPLIES--CATALOGS.
Plant engineering catalog file. New
York, Sweet's Division, McGraw-Hill
Information Systems Co.
338.4/7/69028 72-626783
TA215 .S8 MRR Alc Latest edition

Sweet's industrial construction and
renovation file. 1974- New York,
Sweet's Division, McGraw-Hill
Information Systems Co.
338.4/7/624102573 74-640340
TA215 .S85 MRR Alc Latest edition

ENGINEERING--SUPPLIES--DIRECTORIES.
Product design & development. PD&D
product encyclopedia; [Philadelphia,
1961] 253, 10, 10 p. 61-59873
T12 .P8 MRR Alc.

ENGINEERING--TABLES, CALCULATIONS, ETC.
Smoley, Constantine Kenneth,
Smoley's four combined tables for
engineers, architects, and students,
Chautauqua, N.Y., C. K. Smoley &
Sons, 1956. 1 v. (various pagings)
510.835 56-14448
TA332 .S56 1956 MRR Alc.

ENGINEERING--GREAT BRITAIN--YEARBOOKS.
The Consulting engineers who's who &
year book. London, Norwood
Industrial Publications Ltd.[etc.]
620.942 49-25787
Began with vol. for 1947.
TA1 .C774 Sci RR Latest edition /
MRR Biog Latest edition

ENGINEERING--UNITED STATES--COLLECTED
WORKS.
Index of opportunity for engineers.
1968/69- New York, Macmillan.
620/.0025/73 76-1574
TA157 .I43 MRR Alc Latest edition

ENGINEERING--UNITED STATES--DIRECTORIES.
Index of opportunity for engineers.
1968/69- New York, Macmillan.
620/.0025/73 76-1574
TA157 .I43 MRR Alc Latest edition

ENGINEERING, ARCHITECTURAL
see Building

ENGINEERING, CHEMICAL
see Chemical engineering

ENGINEERING, MECHANICAL
see Mechanical engineering

ENGINEERING, TRAFFIC
see Traffic engineering

ENGINEERING AS A PROFESSION--COLLECTED
WORKS.
Index of opportunity for engineers.
1968/69- New York, Macmillan.
620/.0025/73 76-1574
TA157 .I43 MRR Alc Latest edition

ENGINEERING CYBERNETICS
see Automation

ENGINEERING DESIGN--BIBLIOGRAPHY--
CATALOGS.
Harvard University. Graduate School
of Design. Library. Catalogue of the
Library of the Graduate School of
Design, Harvard University. Boston,
Mass., G. K. Hall, 1968. 44 v.
019/.i 73-169433
Z5945 .H28 1968 MRR Alc (Dk 33)

ENGINEERING LIBRARIES.
Johns, Ada Winifred. Special
libraries: development of the
concept, their organizations, and
their services. Metuchen, N.J.,
Scarecrow Press, 1968. 245 p. 026
68-12628
Z675.A2 J57 MRR Alc.

ENGINEERING MATHEMATICS.
Grazda, Edward E., ed. Handbook of
applied mathematics, 4th ed.
Princeton, N.J., D. Van Nostrand [1966]
vi, 1119 p. 510.0202 66-9325
TA330 .G7 1966 MRR Alc.

ENGINEERING METEOROLOGY.
see also Environmental engineering

ENGINEERING SOCIETIES--DIRECTORIES.
Directory of engineering societies
and related organizations. New York,
Engineers Joint Council. 620/.006
68-5491
Began in 1956.
TA1 .D48 Sci RR Latest edition /
MRR Alc Latest edition

Engineers Joint Council. Engineers
of distinction, 1st ed. New York
[1970] xx, 457 p. 620/.00922 B 75-
21290
TA139 .E37 MRR Biog.

ENGINEERS.
Rolt, Lionel Thomas Caswell, Great
engineers. New York, St Martin's
Press [1963, c1962] xii, 244 p.
926.2 63-17259
TA139 .R6 1963 MRR Biog.

Who's who in the electronics
industry. 1961/62- New York, SETI
Publishers. 621.38058 61-15101
TA139 .W56 Sci RR Full set / MRR
Biog Latest edition

ENGINEERS--BIBLIOGRAPHY.
United States. Library of Congress.
Science and Technology Division.
Scientific personnel, a bibliography.
Washington, 1950. vii, 164 p.
016.5069 50-61484
Z663.49 .S35 MRR Alc.

ENGINEERS--BIOGRAPHY--INDEXES.
Pittsburgh. Carnegie library. Men of
science and industry; Pittsburgh,
Carnegie library, 1915. 189, [3] p.
15-6134
Z7404 .A1P6 MRR Biog.

ENGINEERS--GREAT BRITAIN--DIRECTORIES.
Electrical who's who. 1950- London,
Iliffe Books Ltd.[etc.] 926.213 51-
23486
TK12 .E388 Sci RR Latest edition /
MRR Biog Latest edition

Who's who of British engineers. 1966-
London, Maclaren. 620/.0025/42 66-
76317
TA12 .W54 Sci RR Latest edition /
MRR Biog Latest edition

ENGINEERS--GREAT BRITAIN--DIRECTORY.
The Consulting engineers who's who &
year book. London, Norwood
Industrial Publications Ltd.[etc.]
620.942 49-25787
Began with vol. for 1947.
TA1 .C774 Sci RR Latest edition /
MRR Biog Latest edition

ENGINEERS--UNITED STATES--BIOGRAPHY.
Who's who in the electronics
industry. 1961/62- New York, SETI
Publishers. 621.38058 61-15101
TA139 .W56 Sci RR Full set / MRR
Biog Latest edition

ENGINEERS--UNITED STATES--BIOGRAPHY--
DICTIONARIES.
Engineers Joint Council. Engineers
of distinction, 1st ed. New York
[1970] xx, 457 p. 620/.00922 B 75-
21290
TA139 .E37 MRR Biog.

ENGINEERS--UNITED STATES--DIRECTORIES.
American Institute of Consulting
Engineers. Engineering consultants.
1952- New York. 620.58 53-8444
TA12 .A62 MRR Biog Latest edition

American Society of Civil Engineers.
Directory; New York. 58-20994
TA12 .A625 Sci RR Latest edition /
MRR Biog Latest edition

Institute of Electrical and
Electronics Engineers. I E E E
membership directory. [New York] 66-
83668
TK1 .A1I47 Sci RR Latest edition /
MRR Biog Latest edition

Who's who in engineering; [1st]-
ed.; 1922/23- New York, Lewis
Historical Pub. Co. [etc.] 22-14132
TA139 .W4 Sci RR Latest edition /
MRR Biog Latest edition

ENGINES.
see also Gas and oil engines

ENGINES--JUVENILE LITERATURE.
Boumphrey, Geoffrey Maxwell, Engines
and how they work. New York, F.
Watts [1967] 256 p. 67-5972
TJ147 .B68 1967 MRR Alc.

ENGINES--MAINTENANCE AND REPAIR.
Small engines service manual. Kansas
City, Mo. 621.43 59-65139
TJ789 .S5 MRR Alc Latest edition

ENGLAND--ANTIQUITIES--DICTIONARIES.
Thomas, Nicholas, A guide to
prehistoric England. London,
Batsford [1960] 268 p. 913.42 60-
4121
GN805 .T5 MRR Alc.

ENGLAND--CIVILIZATION.
Smith, Egerton. A guide to English
traditions and public life. London,
New York, Oxford University Press,
1953. 334 p. 914.2 54-688
DA110 .S6 MRR Alc.

ENGLAND--CIVILIZATION--MEDIEVAL PERIOD,
1066-1485.
Poole, Austin Lane, ed. Medieval
England. A new ed. rewritten and
rev. Oxford, Clarendon Press, 1958.
2 v. (xxviii, 661 p.) 942 58-4429

DA130 .P65 1958 MRR Alc.

ENGLAND--CIVILIZATION--HISTORY.
Gillie, Christopher. Longman
companion to English literature.
[London] Longman, 1972. xiv, 881 p.
[£2.80] 820/.9 73-150591
PR85 .G45 MRR Alc.

ENGLAND--COMMERCE--DIRECTORIES.
Macdonald's English directory and
gazetteer. Edinburgh [etc.] W.
Macdonald. ca 08-3137
HF5158 .M2 MRR Alc Latest edition

North-western counties of England
trades' directory. Edinburgh,
Trades' Directories. 60-38503
HF5158 .N63 MRR Alc Latest edition

South-western counties of England
trades' directory. Manchester,
Trades' Directories. 55-57170
HF5158 .S6 MRR Alc Latest edition

ENGLAND--DESCRIPTION AND TRAVEL--1946-
1970.
Clark, Sydney Aylmer, All the best
in Britain: New York, Dodd, Mead
[1969] x, 526 p. 914.2/04/85 71-
76840
DA630 .C57 1969 MRR Alc.

ENGLAND--DESCRIPTION AND TRAVEL--1946-
Shears, William Sydney, The face of
England: London, Spring Books [1959]
631 p. 914.2 61-65326
DA600 .S46 1959 MRR Alc.

ENGLAND--DESCRIPTION AND TRAVEL--1946--
-GUIDE-BOOKS.
Betjeman, John, Sir, Collins pocket
guide to English parish churches.
London, Collins, 1968. 2 v. [30/-
(per vol.)] 914.2 76-373482
NA5461 .B43 1968 MRR Alc.

Muirhead, Litellus Russell, ed.
England. 7th ed. London, E. Benn,
1965. lxx, 665 p. 66-42077
DA650 .M86 1965 MRR Alc.

The Shell guide to England, London,
Joseph, 1970. 921 p., 16 plates.
[50/-] 914.2/04/85 72-127111
DA650 .S55 MRR Alc.

ENGLAND--DESCRIPTION AND TRAVEL--1971--
-GUIDE-BOOKS.
Rossiter, Stuart. England; 6th ed.
London, Benn, 1972. 703, [6] p.
[£3.50] 914.2/04/85 72-94560
DA650 .R67 1972 MRR Alc.

ENGLAND--DESCRIPTION AND TRAVEL--GUIDE-
BOOKS.
Thomas, Nicholas, A guide to
prehistoric England. London,
Batsford [1960] 268 p. 913.42 60-
4121
GN805 .T5 MRR Alc.

ENGLAND--DESCRIPTION AND TRAVEL--TOURS.
Gibbons annual index of daily sight-
seeing tours: Rome, Paris, Florence,
London. [Los Angeles] 914 72-80819

D909 .G5 MRR Alc Latest edition

ENGLAND--DIRECTORIES--BIBLIOGRAPHY.
Norton, Jane Elizabeth, Guide to the
national and provincial directories
of England and Wales, London,
Offices of the Royal Historical
Society, 1950. vii, 241 p.
016.9142 51-2465
Z5771 .N6 MRR Alc.

ENGLAND--GAZETTEERS.
Macdonald's English directory and
gazetteer. Edinburgh [etc.] W.
Macdonald. ca 08-3137
HF5158 .M2 MRR Alc Latest edition

Smith, Frank, A genealogical
gazetteer of England; Baltimore,
Genealogical Pub. Co., 1968. xv, 599
p. 914.2/003 68-23458
DA640 .S6 MRR Alc.

ENGLAND--SOCIAL LIFE AND CUSTOMS.
Quennell, Marjorie (Courtney) A
history of everyday things in
England, London, Batsford, 1937-[68,
v. 1, 1938] 5 v. 914.2 40-3988
DA110 .Q43 MRR Alc.

ENGLAND--SOCIAL LIFE AND CUSTOMS--16TH
CENTURY.
Pearson, Lu Emily (Hess)
Elizabethans at home. Stanford,
Calif., Stanford University Press,
1957. 630 p. 942.055 57-9305
DA320 .P4 MRR Alc.

ENGLAND--SOCIAL LIFE AND CUSTOMS--
JUVENILE LITERATURE.
Bagley, John J., Life in medieval
England. London, Batsford [1960]
175 p. 914.2 60-51677
DA185 .B2 1960 MRR Alc.

ENGLISH BALLADS AND SONGS.
see also Ballads, English

Bronson, Bertrand Harris, ed. The
traditional tunes of the Child
ballads; Princeton, N.J., Princeton
University Press, 1959- v.
784.3 57-5468
ML3650 .B82 MRR Alc.

Leach, MacEdward, ed. The ballad
book. New York, Harper, 1955. 842
p. 821.04 55-6778
PR1181 .L4 MRR Alc.

The Oxford book of ballads, Oxford,
The Clarendon press, 1920. xxiii,
[1], 871, [1] p. 23-6784
PR1181 .O8 1920 MRR Alc.

ENGLISH DIARIES--BIBLIOGRAPHY.
Matthews, William, British diaries;
Gloucester, Mass., P. Smith, 1967
[c1950] xxxiv, 339 p. 016.920042
67-6139
Z5305.G7 M3 1967 MRR Biog.

ENGLISH DRAMA--TO 1500--HISTORY AND
CRITICISM.
Williams, Arnold, The drama of
medieval England. [East Lansing]
Michigan State University Press,
1961. 186 p. 822.109 60-16415
PR641 .W55 MRR Alc.

Wilson, Frank Percy, The English
drama, 1485-1585, Oxford, Clarendon
P., 1969. [7], 244 p. [27/6]
822/.2/09 70-386045
PR641 .W58 1969b MRR Alc.

ENGLISH DRAMA--EARLY MODERN AND
ELIZABETHAN, 1500-1600--DICTIONARIES.
Halliday, Frank Ernest. A
Shakespeare companion, 1564-1964
[Rev. ed.] New York, Schocken Books
[1964] 569 p. 822.33 64-14774
PR2892 .H3 1964a MRR Alc.

ENGLISH DRAMA--EARLY MODERN AND
ELIZABETHAN, 1500-1600--HISTORY AND
CRITICISM.
Wilson, Frank Percy, The English
drama, 1485-1585, Oxford, Clarendon
P., 1969. [7], 244 p. [27/6]
822/.2/09 70-386045
PR641 .W58 1969b MRR Alc.

ENGLISH DRAMA--EARLY MODERN AND
ELIZABETHAN, 1500-1600--HISTORY AND
CRITICISM--BIBLIOGRAPHY.
Ribner, Irving. Tudor and Stuart
drama. New York, Appleton-Century-
Crofts [1966] viii, 72 p. 016.8223
66-26656
Z2014.D7 R5 MRR Alc.

ENGLISH DRAMA--RESTORATION, 1660-1700--
BIBLIOGRAPHY.
Summers, Montague, A bibliography of
the restoration drama. New York,
Russell & Russell [1970] 143 p.
016.822/4 70-81479
Z2014.D7 S9 1970 MRR Alc.

ENGLISH DRAMA--RESTORATION, 1660-1700--
HISTORY AND CRITICISM--BIBLIOGRAPHY.
Stratman, Carl Joseph, Restoration
and eighteenth century theatre
research; Carbondale, Southern
Illinois University Press [1971] ix,
811 p. [$25.00] 016.822/5/09 71-
112394
Z2014.D7 S854 MRR Alc.

ENGLISH DRAMA--18TH CENTURY--HISTORY
AND CRITICISM--BIBLIOGRAPHY.
Stratman, Carl Joseph, Restoration
and eighteenth century theatre
research; Carbondale, Southern
Illinois University Press [1971] ix,
811 p. [$25.00] 016.822/5/09 71-
112394
Z2014.D7 S854 MRR Alc.

ENGLISH DRAMA--20TH CENTURY--
BIBLIOGRAPHY.
Plays and their plots. London, H. F.
W. Deane; Boston, W. H. Baker [1960?]
165 p. 016.82291 60-36283
Z2014.D7 P73 MRR Alc.

ENGLISH DRAMA--20TH CENTURY--BIO-
BIBLIOGRAPHY.
Vinson, James, Contemporary
dramatists; London, St. James Press;
New York, St. Martin's Press [1973]
xv, 926 p. [£9.00 ($30.00 U.S.)]
822/.9/1409 B 73-80310
PR106 .V5 MRR Biog.

ENGLISH DRAMA--BIBLIOGRAPHY.
Bergquist, G. William, ed. Three
centuries of English and American
plays, New York, Hafner Pub. Co.,
1963. xii, 281 p. 016.821 63-
18015
Z2014.D7 B45 MRR Alc.

Eldredge, H. J., comp. "The Stage"
cyclopaedia; London, "The Stage,"
1909. 503, [1] p. 016.822 10-9325
Z2014.D7 E4 MRR Alc.

Halliwell-Phillips, James Orchard, A
dictionary of old English plays,
existing either in print or in
manuscript, from the earliest times
to the close of the seventeenth
century; Naarden, [Turfpoortstraat
11] Anton W. van Bekhoven, 1968.
viii, 296 p. [65.00] 74-375761
Z2014.D7 H12 1968 MRR Alc.

Nicoll, Allardyce, A history of
English drama, 1660-1900. Cambridge
[Eng.] University Press, 1952-59. 6
v. 822.09 52-14525
PR625 .N52 1952 MRR Alc.

Patterson, Charlotte A. Plays in
periodicals; Boston, G. K. Hall,
1970. ix, 240 p. 016.22/9/108 76-
21033
Z5781 .P3 MRR Alc.

ENGLISH DRAMA--BIBLIOGRAPHY--CATALOGS.
British Drama League. Library. The
player's library, 1925- [London]
Faber and Faber [etc.] 016.822 26-
12434
Z2014.D7 B8 MRR Alc Full set

British Drama League. Library. The
player's library; Supplement. 1st-
1951- [London] Faber and Faber
[etc.] 016.822 74-643566
Z2014.D7 B8 Suppl. MRR Alc Full
set

ENGLISH DRAMA--BIO-BIBLIOGRAPHY.
Baker, David Erskine, Biographia
dramatica; London, Longman, Hurst,
Rees, Orme, and Brown [etc.] 1812. 3
v. in 4. 04-14124
Z2014.D7 B2 1812 MRR Alc.

ENGLISH DRAMA--DICTIONARIES.
Baker, David Erskine, Biographia
dramatica; London, Longman, Hurst,
Rees, Orme, and Brown [etc.] 1812. 3
v. in 4. 04-14124
Z2014.D7 B2 1812 MRR Alc.

ENGLISH DRAMA--HISTORY AND CRITICISM.
Nicoll, Allardyce, A history of
English drama, 1660-1900. Cambridge
[Eng.] University Press, 1952-59. 6
v. 822.09 52-14525
PR625 .N52 1952 MRR Alc.

ENGLISH DRAMA--HISTORY AND CRITICISM--
BIBLIOGRAPHY.
Coleman, Arthur, Drama criticism
Denver, A. Swallow [1966-71] 2 v.
[$7.50 (v. 1) $12.50 (v. 2)]
016.809/2 66-30426
Z5781 .C65 MRR Ref Desk.

Salem, James M. A guide to critical
reviews. New York, Scarecrow Press,
1966- v. [$4.50 (v. 1) varies]
016.8092 66-13733
Z5782 .S34 MRR Ref Desk.

ENGLISH DRAMA--STORIES, PLOTS, ETC.
Houle, Peter J. The English morality
and related drama; [Hamden, Conn.]
Archon Books, 1972. xviii, 195 p.
822/.051 70-38714
PR643.M7 H6 MRR Alc.

ENGLISH DRAMA--TRANSLATIONS FROM
FOREIGN LITERATURE--BIBLIOGRAPHY.
Patterson, Charlotte A. Plays in
periodicals; Boston, G. K. Hall,
1970. ix, 240 p. 016.22/9/108 76-
21033
Z5781 .P3 MRR Alc.

ENGLISH DRAMA--TRANSLATIONS FROM GREEK.
Oates, Whitney Jennings, ed. The
complete Greek drama; New York,
Random house [c1938] 2 v. 882.0822
38-17746
PA3626.A2 O2 MRR Alc.

ENGLISH DRAMA (TRAGEDY)--BIBLIOGRAPHY.
Stratman, Carl Joseph, ed.
Bibliography of English printed
tragedy, 1565-1900, Carbondale,
Southern Illinois University Press
[1966] xx, 843 p. 016.822051 66-
19720
Z2014.D7 S83 MRR Alc.

ENGLISH ESSAYS--19TH CENTURY--HISTORY
AND CRITICISM.
Houtchens, Carolyn Washburn, ed. The
English Romantic poets & essayists;
Rev. ed. [New York] Published for
the Modern Language Association of
America by New York University Press,
1966. xviii, 395 p. 820.9007 66-
12599
PR590 .H6 1966 MRR Alc.

ENGLISH FICTION--EARLY MODERN, 1500-
1700--BIBLIOGRAPHY.
Bonheim, Helmut W., The English
novel before Richardson; Metuchen,
N.J., Scarecrow Press, 1971. vi, 145
p. 016.823/03 75-19590
Z2014.F4 B65 MRR Alc.

ENGLISH FICTION--EARLY MODERN, 1500-
1700--HISTORY AND CRITICISM--
BIBLIOGRAPHY.
Bonheim, Helmut W., The English
novel before Richardson; Metuchen,
N.J., Scarecrow Press, 1971. vi, 145
p. 016.823/03 75-19590
Z2014.F4 B65 MRR Alc.

ENGLISH FICTION--18TH CENTURY--
BIBLIOGRAPHY.
Beasley, Jerry C. A check list of
prose fiction published in England,
1740-1749. Charlottesville,
Published for the Bibliographical
Society of the University of Virginia
by the University Press of Virginia
[1972] xiv, 213 p. [$7.50]
016.823/5/08 72-75044
Z2014.F4 B37 MRR Alc.

Block, Andrew, The English novel,
1740-1850: [New and rev., i.e. 2d
ed.] London, Dawsons of Pall Mall,
1961. xv, 349 p. 016.8236 61-3325
Z2014.F4 B6 1961 MRR Alc.

McBurney, William Harlin. A check
list of English prose fiction, 1700-
1739. Cambridge, Harvard University
Press, 1960. 154 p. 016.8235 60-
13292
Z2014.F4 M3 MRR Alc.

Summers, Montague, A Gothic
bibliography. London, Fortune P.
[1969] iii-xx, 621 p. 22 plates.
[6/15/-] 016.823/6 78-442345
Z2014.F4 S9 1969 MRR Alc.

ENGLISH FICTION--19TH CENTURY--
ADDRESSES, ESSAYS, LECTURES.
Stevenson, Lionel, ed. Victorian
fiction; Cambridge, Harvard
University Press, 1964. vi, 440 p.
823.809 64-21246
PR873 .S8 MRR Alc.

ENGLISH FICTION--19TH CENTURY--
BIBLIOGRAPHY.
Block, Andrew, The English novel,
1740-1850: [New and rev., i.e. 2d
ed.] London, Dawsons of Pall Mall,
1961. xv, 349 p. 016.8236 61-3325
Z2014.F4 B6 1961 MRR Alc.

Stevenson, Lionel, ed. Victorian
fiction; Cambridge, Harvard
University Press, 1964. vi, 440 p.
823.809 64-21246
PR873 .S8 MRR Alc.

Summers, Montague, A Gothic
bibliography. London, Fortune P.
[1969] iii-xx, 621 p. 22 plates.
[6/15/-] 016.823/6 78-442345
Z2014.F4 S9 1969 MRR Alc.

ENGLISH FICTION--20TH CENTURY--
BIBLIOGRAPHY.
Bufkin, E. C. The twentieth-century
novel in English; Athens, University
of Georgia Press [1967] vi, 138 p.
016.823/9/1208 67-27142
Z2014.F4 B93 MRR Alc.

ENGLISH FICTION--20TH CENTURY--HISTORY
AND CRITICISM.
Vinson, James, Contemporary
novelists. New York, St. Martin's
Press [1972] xvii, 1422 p. [$30.00]
823/.03 75-189694
PR737 .V5 MRR Biog.

ENGLISH FICTION--20TH CENTURY--HISTORY AND CRITICISM--BIBLIOGRAPHY.
Adelman, Irving. The contemporary novel. Metuchen, N.J., Scarecrow Press, 1972. 614 p. 016.823/03 72-4451
Z1231.F4 A34 MRR Ref Desk.

ENGLISH FICTION--BIBLIOGRAPHY.
Fiction index. [1945/52]- London, Association of Assistant Librarians. 016.80883 53-7788
Z5916 .F52 MRR Alc Full set

Gardner, Frank M. Sequels. 5th ed. London, Association of Assistant Librarians, 1967. [4], 214, vii-x, 215-291 p. [75/- 50/-(to L.A. members)] 016.80883 67-89225
Z5916 .G3 1967 MRR Alc.

Leclaire, Lucien, A general analytical bibliography of the regional novelists of the British Isles, 1800-1950. Clermont-Ferrand, Impr. G. de Bussac [1954] 399 p. 016.823 54-32919
Z2014.F4 L4 1954 MRR Alc.

Wagenknecht, Edward Charles, Cavalcade of the English novel. 1954 ed., New York, Holt [1954] 686 p. 823.09 54-2094
PR821 .W25 1954 MRR Alc.

Wilson, H. W., firm, publishers. Fiction catalog. 1908- New York [etc.] 016.823 09-35044
Z5916 .W74 MRR Alc Latest edition

ENGLISH FICTION--HISTORY AND CRITICISM.
Lass, Abraham Harold, Plot guide to 100 American and British novels; Boston, The Writer [1971] xxi, 364, 364 p. [$8.95] 823/.03 73-138526
PS373 .L28 MRR Alc.

Stevenson, Lionel, The English novel. Boston, Houghton Mifflin [1960] 539 p. 823.09 60-16142
PR821 .S7 MRR Alc.

Wagenknecht, Edward Charles, Cavalcade of the English novel. 1954 ed., New York, Holt [1954] 686 p. 823.09 54-2094
PR821 .W25 1954 MRR Alc.

ENGLISH FICTION--HISTORY AND CRITICISM--BIBLIOGRAPHY.
Adelman, Irving. The contemporary novel. Metuchen, N.J., Scarecrow Press, 1972. 614 p. 016.823/03 72-4451
Z1231.F4 A34 MRR Ref Desk.

Bell, Inglis Freeman, The English novel, 1578-1956; Denver, A. Swallow [1959] xii, 169 p. 016.82309 59-8212
Z2014.F4 B4 MRR Alc.

Cotton, Gerald Brooke. Fiction guides; London, Bingley, 1967. 126 p. [25/-] 016.823/009 67-85300
Z5916 .C77 1967a MRR Alc.

Thurston, Jarvis A. Short fiction criticism; Denver, A. Swallow [1960] 265 p. 016.80931 60-8070
Z5917.S5 T5 MRR Alc.

ENGLISH FICTION--IRISH AUTHORS--BIBLIOGRAPHY.
Brown, Stephen James Meredith, Ireland in fiction; New ed. Dublin, London, Maunsel and company, limited, 1919. xx, 362 p. 20-4278
Z2039.F4 B8 1919 MRR Alc.

ENGLISH FICTION--STORIES, PLOTS, ETC.
Heiney, Donald W., British, Woodbury, N.Y., Barron's Educational Series [1973, c1974] x, 286 p. [$2.95] 820/.9 74-158988
PR471 .H39 MRR Alc.

Lass, Abraham Harold, Plot guide to 100 American and British novels; Boston, The Writer [1971] xxi, 364, 364 p. [$8.95] 823/.03 73-138526
PS373 .L28 MRR Alc.

ENGLISH FICTION--TRANSLATIONS FROM FOREIGN LITERATURE--BIBLIOGRAPHY.
Beasley, Jerry C. A check list of prose fiction published in England, 1740-1749. Charlottesville, Published for the Bibliographical Society of the University of Virginia [by] the University Press of Virginia [1972] xiv, 213 p. [$7.50] 016.823/5/08 72-75044
Z2014.F4 B37 MRR Alc.

Block, Andrew, The English novel, 1740-1850; [New and rev., i.e. 2d ed.] London, Dawsons of Pall Mall, 1961. xv, 349 p. 016.8236 61-3325

Z2014.F4 B6 1961 MRR Alc.

McBurney, William Harlin. A check list of English prose fiction, 1700-1739. Cambridge, Harvard University Press, 1960. 154 p. 016.8235 60-13292
Z2014.F4 M3 MRR Alc.

ENGLISH IMPRINTS.
Cumulative index to English translations, 1948-1968. Boston, G. K. Hall, 1973. 2 v. 016.011 74-167325
Z6514.T7 C8 MRR Alc.

English, 1948-1964. 2d rev. ed. Gottingen, Vandenhoeck & Ruprecht, 1968. 509 p. 016.9143/03 72-590351
Z2221 .T73 no. 1 MRR Alc.

London. Guildhall Library. A list of books printed in the British Isles and of English books printed abroad before 1701 in Guildhall Library. London, Corporation of London, 1966-67 v. [40/- (v. 1)] 015/.42 68-77514
Z2002 .L62 MRR Alc.

Pollard, Alfred William, A short-title catalogue of books printed in England, Scotland, & Ireland and of English books printed abroad, 1475-1640, London, Bibliographical Society, 1946. xviii, 609 p. 015.42 47-20884
Z2002 .P77 1946 MRR Alc.

Wing, Donald Goddard, A gallery of ghosts; [New York] Index Committee, Modern Language Association of America, 1967. vi, 225 p. 015.42 67-9327
Z2002 .W48 MRR Alc.

Wing, Donald Goddard, Short-title catalogue of books printed in England, Scotland, Ireland, Wales, and British America, and of English books printed in other countries, 1641-1700. New York, Index Society, 1945-51. 3 v. 015.42 45-8773
Z2002 .W5 MRR Alc.

ENGLISH IMPRINTS--BIBLIOGRAPHY.
Cumulative book index. 1898/99- New York [etc.] H. W. Wilson Co. 05-33604
Z1219 .M78 MRR Circ Partial set

ENGLISH IMPRINTS--CATALOGS.
British Museum. Dept. of Printed Books. General catalogue of printed books. Photolithographic edition to 1955. London, Trustees of the British Museum, 1959-66 [v. 1, 1965] 263 p. 018/.1 66-2261
Z921 .B87 MRR Alc (Dk 33).

Cambridge. University. Library. Early English printed books in the University library, Cambridge (1475 to 1640). Cambridge, The University press, 1900-07. 4 v. 01-15519
Z2002 .C17 MRR Alc.

United States. Library of Congress. English language books by title: Detroit, Gale Research Co., 1971. 20 v. 018/.1 75-165487
Z881.A1 C34 MRR Alc (Dk 33)

ENGLISH IMPRINTS--UNION LISTS.
Pollard, Alfred William, A short-title catalogue of books printed in England, Scotland, & Ireland and of English books printed abroad, 1475-1640. London, Bibliographical Society, 1946. xviii, 609 p. 015.42 47-20884
Z2002 .P77 1946 MRR Alc.

Wing, Donald Goddard, Short-title catalogue of books printed in England, Scotland, Ireland, Wales, and British America, and of English books printed in other countries, 1641-1700. New York, Index Society, 1945-51. 3 v. 015.42 45-8773
Z2002 .W5 MRR Alc.

Wing, Donald Goddard, Short-title catalogue of books printed in England, Scotland, Ireland, Wales, and British America, and of English books printed in other countries, 1641-1700. 2d ed., rev. and enl. New York, Index Committee of the Modern Language Association of America, 1972- v. 015.42 70-185211
Z2002 .W52 MRR Alc.

ENGLISH IMPRINTS--INDIA.
Sher Singh, Indian books in print, 1955-67: Delhi, Indian Bureau of Bibliographies [1969] 1116 p. [100.00] 015/.54 78-104779
Z3201 .S47 MRR Alc.

ENGLISH LANGUAGE.
Fowler, Henry Watson, A dictionary of modern English usage, 2d ed., rev. Oxford, Clarendon Press, 1965. xx, 725 p. 423 65-2840
PE1628 .F65 1965 MRR Ref Desk.

ENGLISH LANGUAGE--MIDDLE ENGLISH, 1100-1500--DICTIONARIES.
Middle English dictionary. Ann Arbor, University of Michigan Press [1952- pts. 427.02* 53-62158
PE679 .M54 MRR Alc.

Stratmann, Franz Heinrich. A Middle-English dictionary, A new ed., re-arranged, rev., and enl. Oxford, The Clarendon press, 1891. xxiii, 708 p. 01-2659
PE679 .S7 1891 MRR Alc.

ENGLISH LANGUAGE--MIDDLE ENGLISH, 1100-1500--ETYMOLOGY--DICTIONARIES.
Stratmann, Franz Heinrich. A Middle-English dictionary, A new ed., re-arranged, rev., and enl. Oxford, The Clarendon press, 1891. xxiii, 708 p. 01-2659
PE679 .S7 1891 MRR Alc.

ENGLISH LANGUAGE--EARLY MODERN, 1500-1700--GLOSSARIES, VOCABULARIES, ETC.
Skeat, Walter William, A glossary of Tudor and Stuart words, Oxford, The Clarendon press, 1914. xviii, p., 1 l., 461, [1] p. 14-7721
PE1667 .S5 MRR Alc.

ENGLISH LANGUAGE--ACRONYMS
see Acronyms

ENGLISH LANGUAGE--BUSINESS ENGLISH.
Mansat, André. Vocabulaire d'anglais commercial. Nouvelle édition, augmentée, d'un index, Paris, Didier, 1966. 210 p. [10 F.] 67-80658
PE1115 .M26 1966 MRR Alc.

Parkhurst, Charles Chandler, Business communication for better human relations. Englewood Cliffs, N.J., Prentice-Hall, 1961. 579 p. 651.75 61-6605
HF5721 .P368 MRR Alc.

Schutte, William M. Communication in business and industry New York, Holt, Rinehart and Winston [1960] 393 p. 651.7 60-6403
PE1408 .S34 MRR Alc.

ENGLISH LANGUAGE--COMPOSITION AND EXERCISES.
Perrin, Porter Gale, Writer's guide and index to English. 5th ed., rev. Glenview, Ill., Scott, Foresman [1972] 765 p. 808/.042 70-184064

PE1411 .P4 1972 MRR alc.

Shaw, Harry, McGraw-Hill handbook of English. 2d ed. New York, McGraw-Hill [1960] 500 p. 808 59-10723
PE1111 .S413 1960 MRR Ref Desk.

Shaw, Harry, McGraw-Hill handbook of English. 3d ed. St. Louis, McGraw-Hill [1969] 598 p. 808.04/2 69-19306
PE1112 .S5 1969 MRR Ref Desk.

Walsh, James Martyn, Plain English handbook; Rev.ed. Wichita, Kan., McCormick-Mathers Pub. Co. [1959] 159 p. 425 59-2547
PE1111 .W3546 1959 MRR Alc.

Warriner, John E. English grammar and composition; New York, Harcourt, Brace [1957] 692 p. 808 57-1729
PE1111 .W36857 MRR Ref Desk.

ENGLISH LANGUAGE--COMPOUND WORDS.
Ball, Alice Morton. The compounding and hyphenation of English words. New York, Funk & Wagnalls [1951] ix, 246 p. 425.1 51-9951
PE1175 .B29 MRR Alc.

ENGLISH LANGUAGE--CONVERSATION AND PHRASE BOOKS--POLYGLOT.
DeLand, Graydon S. American traveler's companion; New York, Fielding Publications [1966] 287 p. 413 66-17187
PE1131 .D4 1966 MRR Alc.

Dony, Yvonne P. de. Léxico del lenguaje figurado, comparado, Buenos Aires, Ediciones Desclee, De Brouwer [1951] 804 p. 52-21901
PB331 .D6 MRR Alc.

Lyall, Archibald, A guide to 25 languages of Europe. Rev. ed. [Harrisburg, Pa.] Stackpole Co. [1966] viii, 407 p. 413 66-20847

PB73 .L85 1966 MRR Alc.

ENGLISH LANGUAGE--DIALECTS.
Herman, Lewis Helmar, Foreign dialects; New York, Theatre Arts Books [1958? c1943] 415 p. 792.028 58-10332
PN2071.F6 H4 1958 MRR Alc.

Wright, Joseph, ed. The English dialect dictionary, New York, Reprinted by Hacker Art Books, 1962. 6 v. 427 65-5677
PE1766 .W8 1962 MRR Alc.

ENGLISH LANGUAGE--DIALECTS--SCOTCH.
Jamieson, John, Jamieson's
Dictionary of the Scottish language,
Paisley, A. Gardner, 1910. 2 v. in
1.   10-14987
    PE2106 .J36 MRR Alc.

The Scottish national dictionary,
Edinburgh, The Scottish national
dictionary association limited [1931-
v.   427.9   36-20042
    PE2106 .S4 MRR Alc.

Warrack, Alexander, comp. A Scots
dialect dictionary, London [etc.] W.
& R. Chambers, limited, 1911. xxiii,
[1], 717, [1] p.   11-11559
    PE2106 .W2 MRR Alc.

ENGLISH LANGUAGE--DIALECTS--SCOTCH--
GLOSSARIES, VOCABULARIES, ETC.
Reid, J. B. A complete word and
phrase concordance to the poems and
songs of Robert Burns, New York, B.
Franklin [1968] 568 p.   821/.6 68-
58477
    PR4345 .R4 1968 MRR Alc.

ENGLISH LANGUAGE--DIALECTS--AUSTRALIA.
Baker, Sidney John, Australia
speaks; Sydney, New York,
Shakespeare Head Press [1953] 836 p.
427.9 54-20332
    PE3601 .B28 MRR Alc.

ENGLISH LANGUAGE--DICTIONARIES.
The American college dictionary. New
York, Random House, [c1966] xxviii,
1444 p.   423 66-13581
    PE1628 .A55 1966 MRR Ref Desk.

The American Heritage dictionary of
the English language. [New York]
American Heritage Pub. Co. [1973] l,
1550 p.   423 73-163370
    PE1625 .A54 1973 MRR Ref Desk.

Australian national quick reference
dictionary and encyclopaedia;
Melbourne, Age Publications [1969]
320 p.   423 73-563415
    PE1628 .A87 MRR Alc.

The Barnhart dictionary of new
English since 1963. [1st ed.]
Bronxville, N.Y., Barnhart/Harper &
Row [1973] 512 p.   423 73-712
    PE1630 .B3 MRR Ref Desk.

The Century dictionary and
cyclopedia, [Rev. and enl. ed.] New
York, The Century co. [c1911] 12 v.
[$75.00]   11-31934
    PE1625 .C4 1911 MRR Alc.

Chambers twentieth century
dictionary. New ed.; Edinburgh, W.
and R. Chambers, 1972. xii, 1651 p.;
[£2.50]   423 72-197407
    PE1628 .C43 1972 MRR Ref Desk.

Chambers's shorter English
dictionary. New ed. with suppl.
Edinburgh, W. & R. Chambers, 1963
[c1948] xlvii, 784 p.   64-28317
    PE1628 .C42 1963 MRR Alc.

The Compact edition of the Oxford
English dictionary: complete text
reproduced micrographically. Oxford,
Clarendon Press, 1971. 2 v. (xii,
4116 p.) [£28.00]   423 72-177361
    PE1625 .N53 1971 MRR Ref Desk.

Cross word puzzle dictionary of the
English language, Philadelphia,
Winston, 1951. 1003 p.   423 51-
6777
    PE1628 .C8 MRR Alc.

D. U. W. ... Dictionary of unusual
words. Leigh-on-sea, Essex, The
Thames bank publishing company
limited, 1946- v.   423 47-8357

    PE1628 .D85 MRR Alc.

A Dictionary of Canadianisms on
historical principles; Toronto, W.
J. Gage, ltd., 1967. xxiii, 926, [1]
p.   427/.9/71 78-5962
    PE3243 .D5 MRR Alc.

A dictionary of difficult words.
[5th impression, rev.] London,
Hutchinson, 1969. 368 p.   [25/-]
423.1 70-448336
    PE1628 .J3 1969 MRR Alc.

Dossor, Howard F. Terms of thought;
Melbourne, Hawthorn Press, 1970. 61
p. [$1.20]   423 71-568187
    PE1680 .D6 MFR Alc.

Fennell, Charles Augustus Maude, ed.
The Stanford dictionary of anglicised
words and phrases; Cambridge [Eng.],
University press, 1892. xv, [1], 826
p.   03-7772
    PE1670 .F3 MRR Alc.

Fowler, Henry Watson, The concise
Oxford dictionary of current English,
5th ed.; rev. Oxford, Clarendon
Press, 1964. xvi, 1558 p.   423 64-
1941
    PE1628 .F6 1964 MRR Alc.

Funk & Wagnalls new Desk Standard
dictionary, Em'-pha-type ed. New
York, Funk & Wagnalls [c1959] xvi,
949 p.   423 60-1852
    PE1628 .S6 1959 MRR Alc.

Funk & Wagnalls new practical
Standard dictionary of the English
language. Em'-pha-type ed. New
York, Funk & wagnalls [1961] xvii,
1574 p.   423 61-3443
    PE1628 .S585 1961 MRR Alc.

Funk & Wagnalls new Standard
dictionary of the English language.
New York, Funk & Wagnalls, 1963.
lxx, 2816 p.   64-99
    PE1625 .S7 1963 MRR Circ.

Funk & Wagnalls Standard college
dictionary. New York, Funk &
Wagnalls [1968] xxvi, 1606 p. [6.50
7.50 (thumb-indexed)]   423 70-826
    PE1628 .F82 1968 MRR Alc.

Funk & Wagnalls Standard college
dictionary. New York, Funk &
Wagnalls [1966] xxvi, 1606 p.   423
66-21606
    PE1628 .S586 1966 MRR Ref Desk.

Funk & Wagnalls standard dictionary
of the English language.
International ed. New York, Funk &
Wagnalls [1969] 2 v. (xx, 1505 p.)
423 69-11209
    PE1625 .S713 1969 MRR Alc.

Funk & Wagnalls Standard encyclopedic
dictionary. Chicago, J. G. Ferguson
Pub. Co. [1970] xii, 1138 p.   423
72-10720
    PE1625 .F8 1970 MRR Ref Desk.

Jamieson, John, Jamieson's
Dictionary of the Scottish language,
Paisley, A. Gardner, 1910. 2 v. in
1.   10-14987
    PE2106 .J36 MRR Alc.

Laffal, Julius. A concept dictionary
of English. Essex, Conn., Gallery
Press [1973] xi, 305 p.   428/.1 72-
97927
    PE1691 .L3 MRR Alc.

Lewis, Norman, The comprehensive
word guide. [1st ed.] Garden City,
N.Y., Doubleday [1958] xxiii, 912 p.
423 58-11514
    PE1591 .L4 MRR Ref Desk.

Little, William, The shorter Oxford
English dictionary on historical
principles; 3rd. ed.; Oxford,
Clarendon Press, 1973. xxix, 2672 p.
[£10.00]   423 74-174806
    PE1625 .L53 1973 MRR Alc.

March, Francis Andrew, March's
thesaurus and dictionary of the
English language Garden City, N.Y.,
Doubleday [1968] vii, 1240 p.   68-
24820
    PE1625 .M3 1968 MRR Alc.

Moss, Norman. What's the difference?
[1st ed.] New York, Harper & Row
[1973] 138 p. [$6.95]   428/.1 72-
9140
    PE2835 .M6 MRR Alc.

The New Elizabethan reference
dictionary; London, Newnes [1956]
xiii, 1874 p.   423 57-41986
    PE1628 .N42 MRR Alc.

The New Zealand contemporary
dictionary; Christchurch, Auckland
[etc.] Whitcombe & Tombs, 1966. 640
p.   423 68-112228
    PE1628 .N47 MMR Alc.

Odhams dictionary of the English
language ... London, Odhams Books
[1965] x, 1334 p.   65-66209
    PE1628 .O3 1965 MRR Alc.

The Oxford English dictionary;
Oxford, At the Clarendon press, 1933.
13 v.   423 a 33-3399
    PE1625 .N53 1933 MRR Alc.

Oxford illustrated dictionary.
Oxford, Clarendon Press, 1962. xvi,
974 p.   423 62-51929
    PE1628 .O9 MRR Alc.

Partridge, Eric, Usage and abusage:
a guide to good English. 6th ed.
(revised and slightly englarged).
London, H. Hamilton, 1965. 392 p.
[21/-]   423.1 66-70200
    PE1460 .P17 1965a MRR Ref Desk.

Pei, Mario Andrew, ed. Language of
the specialists; [New York] Funk &
Wagnalls [1966] xii, 388 p.   423.1
66-22843
    PE1680 .P4 MRR Alc.

The Pitman dictionary of the English
language. London, I. Pitman, 1949.
xxi, 733 p.   423 49-6362
    PE1628 .P63 MRR Alc.

The Random House college dictionary.
[New York, Random House, 1973]
xxxii, 1568 p. [$7.95]   423 73-
175504
    PE1625 .R29 MRR Ref Desk.

The Random House dictionary of the
English language / Unabridged ed.
New York : Random House, c1973.
xxxii, 2059 p. :   423 74-186424
    PE1625 .R3 1973 MRR Ref Desk.

Schur, Norman W. British self-
taught: with comments in American,
New York, Macmillan [1973] xxxi, 438
p. [$6.95]   423/.1 70-127941
    PE1460 .S45 MRR Alc.

Scott, George Ryley, Swan's Anglo-
American dictionary, New York,
Library Publishers [1952] 1514 p.
423 52-12036
    PE1628 .S35 1952 MRR Alc.

The Scottish national dictionary,
Edinburgh, The Scottish national
dictionary association limited [1931-
v.   427.9   36-20042
    PE2106 .S4 MRR Alc.

Skeat, Walter William, An
etymological dictionary of the
English language, New ed., rev. and
enl. ... Oxford, The Clarendon
press, 1910. xliv, 780 p.   11-35447

    PE1580 .S5 1910 MRR Alc.

The Reader's digest. The Reader's
digest great encyclopedic dictionary,
Pleasantville, N.Y., Reader's Digest
Association [1966] xviii, 2094 p.
413 66-8737
    PE1625 .R4 MRR Alc.

Thorndike-Barnhart comprehensive desk
dictionary, Garden City, N.Y.,
Doubleday [1967] xiii, 896 p.   423
67-18142
    PE1628 .T55 1967 MRR Alc.

Urdang, Laurence. The New York times
everyday reader's dictionary of
misunderstood, misused, mispronounced
words. [New York] Quadrangle Books
[1972] 377 p. [$7.95]   423 74-
184644
    PE1680 .U7 MRR Ref Desk.

Versand, Kenneth. Polyglot's
lexicon, 1943-1966. New York, Links
[c1973] 468 p. [$12.50]   423 72-
94094
    PE1630 .V4 MRR Alc.

Virtue's English dictionary.
Encyclopedic ed., illustrated.
London, Virtue, 1964. xviii, 1050 p.
65-56182
    PE1625 .V5 MRR Alc.

Warrack, Alexander, comp. A Scots
dialect dictionary, London [etc.] W.
& R. Chambers, limited, 1911. xxiii,
[1], 717, [1] p.   11-11559
    PE2106 .W2 MRR Alc.

The Webster encyclopedic dictionary
of the English language and
compendium of usable knowledge.
Chicago, Consolidated Book Publishers
[c1965] 1 v. (various pagings)   423
66-615
    PE1625 .W5515 MRR Alc.

Webster's new collegiate dictionary.
Springfield, Mass., G. & C. Merriam
Co. [1973] 32, 1536 p.   423 72-
10966
    PE1628.W4 M4 1973 MRR Ref Desk.

Webster's new international
dictionary of the English language.
2d ed., unabridged. Springfield,
Mass., G. & C. Merriam Co., 1957.
cxxxvi, 3194 p.   423 57-697
    PE1625 .W3 1957 MRR Circ.

Webster's new international
dictionary of the English language.
2d ed., unabridged ... Springfield,
Mass., G. & C. Merriam Co., 1953.
cxxxii, 3194 p.   423 53-369
    PE1625 .W3 1953 MRR Ref Desk.

Webster's new twentieth century
dictionary of the English language,
unabridged, 2d ed. Cleveland, World
Pub. Co., [c] 1964. xiv, 2129, 160
p.   64-2398
    PE1625 .W4 1964 MRR Circ.

Webster's New World dictionary of the
American language. 2d college ed.
New York, World Pub. Co. [1970]
xxxvi, 1692 p. and phonodisc (2 s. 7
in. 33 1/3 rpm. microgroove) [8.95]
423 70-105348
    PE1625 .W33 1970 MRR Ref Desk.

Webster's New World dictionary of the
American language. Concise ed.
Cleveland, World Pub. Co. [c1964]
xiv, 882 p.   423 64-12966
    PE1628 .W5633 1964 MRR Alc.

ENGLISH LANGUAGE--DICTIONARIES. (Cont.)
Webster's New World dictionary of the
American language. Everyday
encyclopedic ed., enl. from the
Concise ed. Nashville, Southwestern
Co., 1965. xiii, 1202 p.   423 65-
6891
  PE1628 .W5635 1965 MRR Alc.

Webster's third new international
dictionary of the English language,
unabridged. Springfield, Mass., G. &
C. Merriam Co. [1971] 72a, 2662 p.
423 76-29598
  PE1625 .W36 1971 MRR Circ.

Webster's third new international
dictionary of the English language,
unabridged. Springfield, Mass., G. &
C. Merriam Co., 1966. 64a, 2662 p.
423 66-27646
  PE1625 .W36 1966 MRR Ref Desk.

The World book dictionary. Chicago,
Published exclusively for Field
Enterprises Educational Corp. [1974]
2 v.   423 73-15081
  PE1625 .W73 1974 MRR Alc.

Wright, Joseph, ed. The English
dialect dictionary. New York,
Reprinted by Hacker Art Books, 1962.
6 v.   427 65-5677
  PE1766 .W8 1962 MRR Alc.

Wyld, Henry Cecil Kennedy, ed. The
universal dictionary of the English
language; London, Routledge & Paul
[1952] xix, 1447 p.   423 53-17846
  PE1625 .W9 1952 MRR Alc.

Yule, Henry, Sir, Hobson-Jobson: a
glossary of colloquial Anglo-Indian
words and phrases. New ed. London,
Routledge & K. Paul, 1968. xlviii,
1021 p. [£6/6/-]   422/.4/91 68-
96009
  PE3501 .Y78 1968 MRR Alc.

Żytka, Romuald. Geological
dictionary Warszawa, Wydawnictwa
Geologiczne, 1970. 1439 p.
[zł1250.00]   550/.3 72-31794
  QE5 .Z9 MRR Alc.

**ENGLISH LANGUAGE--DICTIONARIES--
AFRIKAANS.**
Bosman, Daniël Brink, Tweetalige
woordeboek 4., hersiene en sterk
verm. uitg. Kaapstad, Nasionale
Boekhandel, 1962. 2 v. (xvii, 1905
p.)   62-45246
  PF862 .B618 MRR Alc.

ENGLISH LANGUAGE--DICTIONARIES--AINU.
Batchelor, John, An Ainu-English-
Japanese dictionary (3d ed.) ...
Tokyo, The Kyobunkan; London, K.
Paul, Trench, Trubner, co., 1926.
[823] p.   46-28350
  PL495.Z5 B3 1926 MRR Alc.

**ENGLISH LANGUAGE--DICTIONARIES--
ALBANIAN.**
Drizari, Nelo, Albanian-English and
English-Albanian dictionary. 2d,
enl. ed.; New York, F. Ungar Pub.
Co. [1957] vi, 320 p.   491.99132
57-9330
  PG9591 .D7 1957 MRR Alc.

ENGLISH LANGUAGE--DICTIONARIES--AMHARIC.
Armbruster, Carl Hubert, Initia
amharica; an introduction to spoken
Amharic. Cambridge, [Eng.] The
University press, 1908-   pts. in   v.
15-60
  PJ9213 .A7 MRR Alc.

ENGLISH LANGUAGE--DICTIONARIES--ARABIC.
Lewis, Bernard. A handbook of
diplomatic and political Arabic.
[London] Luzac, 1947. 72, [1] p.
492.732 49-6894
  PJ6680 .L4 MRR Alc.

The Oxford English-Arabic dictionary
of current usage: Oxford, Clarendon
Press, 1972. xii, 1392 p. [£12.00]
492.7/3/21 73-151265
  PJ6640 .O93 MRR Alc.

Wortabet, William Thomson.
Wortabet's Arabic-English dictionary.
4th ed.   Beirut, Librairie du Liban,
1968. 802 p.   492.7/3/2 77-399717
  PJ6640 .W6 1968 MRR Alc.

**ENGLISH LANGUAGE--DICTIONARIES--
ASSAMESE.**
Sarman, Giridhar. Anglo-Assamese
dictionary. [1st ed.] Shillong,
Chapala Book Stall [1950] 799 p.
52-40636
  PK1556 .S3 MRR Alc.

**ENGLISH LANGUAGE--DICTIONARIES--
BIBLIOGRAPHY.**
Alston, R. C. The English dictionary
Leeds, Printed for the author by E.
J. Arnold, c1966. xxvi, 195 p. 68-
70119
  Z2015.A1 A4 vol. 5 MRR Alc.

Alston, R. C. Old English, Middle
English, early modern English,
miscellaneous works, vocabulary.
Menston [Eng.], Printed for the
author by Scolar Press, [1970-   v.
016.42 s 016.42 72-176678
  Z2015.A1 A4 vol. 3, pt. 1 MRR Alc.

Mathews, Mitford McLeod, A survey of
English dictionaries. New York,
Russell & Russell, 1966. 119 p.
016.423 65-17912
  Z2015.D6 M4 1966 MRR Alc.

Walsh, James Patrick. Home reference
books in print; New York, R. R.
Bowker Co., 1969. x, 284 p. [9.75]
011/.02 68-56427
  Z1035.1 .W35 MRR Alc.

**ENGLISH LANGUAGE--DICTIONARIES--
BULGARIAN.**
[Angliĭsko-bŭlgarski rechnik
(romanized form)] 1966. 2 v.   67-
48011
  PG979 .A48 MRR Alc.

ENGLISH LANGUAGE--DICTIONARIES--BURMESE.
Judson, Adoniram, English and
Burmese dictionary.   3d ed. Rangoon,
W. H. Sloan, American mission press,
1877. 3 p. l., [9]-862 p.   46-36492
  PL3957 .J82 1877 MRR Alc.

ENGLISH LANGUAGE--DICTIONARIES--CHINESE.
Chen, Janey. A practical English-
Chinese pronouncing dictionary; [1st
ed.] Rutland, Vt., C. E. Tuttle Co.
[1970] xxix, 601 p. [12.50]
495.1/3/2 78-77122
  PL1455 .C579 MRR Alc.

Cheng, I-li. [Tsui hsin hsiang chich
Ying Hua ta tz'u tien. (romanized
form)] [Peking] Sheng Huo, Tu Shu,
Hsin Chih, San lien shu tien [1953]
2143 p.   55-31039
  PL1455 .C585 1953 MRR Alc.

Cowles, Roy T. The Cantonese
speaker's dictionary, [Hong Kong]
Hong Kong University Press;
[exclusive agents for all countries
except east of Burma: Oxford
University Press, London] 1965.
xvii, 1318, iv, 232 p.   66-808
  PL1736 .C6 1965 MRR Alc.

International dictionary, English-
Chinese. 1968. [29], 1872, 39 p.
[40 Hongkong dollars]   78-835321
  PL1455 .W25 1968 MRR Alc.

ENGLISH LANGUAGE--DICTIONARIES--CZECH.
Procházka, Jindřich, Slovník
anglicko-český a česko-anglický,
15. zcela přepracované vyd. Praha,
Orbis, 1952.   423 vii, 589 p.
491.8632 53-32256
  PG4640 .P73 1952 MRR Alc.

ENGLISH LANGUAGE--DICTIONARIES--DANISH.
Haislund, Niels. Engelsk-Dansk
ordbog. 3., stærkt forøgede udg.
København, Berlingske forlag, 1964.
563 p.   65-54753
  PD3640 .H3 1964 MRR Alc.

ENGLISH LANGUAGE--DICTIONARIES--DUTCH.
Bosch, Abraham ten, Viertalig
technisch woordenboek. Deventer, Æ.
E. Kluwer [1948-55] 4 v.   603 50-
18447
  T10 .B72 MRR Alc.

Cassell's Dutch-English; English-
Dutch dictionary. New York, Funk &
Wagnalls [1967] 1354 p.   439.3/1/32
67-11998
  PF640 .C375 1967b MRR Ref Desk.

Kramers, Jacob, Kramers' woordenboek
Engels, 30. druk, Den Haag, Van
Goor [1970] [xiv], 615, 736 p. 76-
572768
  PF640 .K7 1970 MRR Alc.

Van Goor's Engels zakwoordenboek.
13. druk. Den Haag, Brussel, G. B.
van Goor, 1967. 684 p. [fl 6.90 bfr
120.-]   68-79147
  PF640 .V8 1967 MRR Alc.

Wevers, B. J. Standaard groot Engels-
Nederlands woordenboek. Antwerpen,
Standaard, [1971]. 933 p. [fl42.50]
74-341940
  PF640 .W47 MRR Alc.

**ENGLISH LANGUAGE--DICTIONARIES--
ESPERANTO.**
Connor, George Alan. Esperanto, the
world interlanguage, New rev. ed.
New York, T. Yoseloff [1959] 245 p.
408.92 59-10560
  PM8213 .C6 1959 MRR Alc.

Fulcher, Fleming. English-Esperanto
dictionary, 2d ed. ... London, E.
Marlborough & co., ltd, [1925] 3 p.
l., viii, [2], 346, [6] p. 46-29444
  PM8237 .F8 1925 MRR Alc.

**ENGLISH LANGUAGE--DICTIONARIES--
ESTONIAN.**
Silvet, J. Inglise-eesti
sõnaraamat. Vadstena, Eesti
Kirjastus Orto [1949] 1205 p.
494.54532 49-49174
  PH625 .S5 MRR Alc.

ENGLISH LANGUAGE--DICTIONARIES--FINNISH.
Hurme, Raija. Englantilais-
suomalainen suursanakirja. [Porvoo],
Söderström, 1973. xi, 1182 (1) p.
494/.541/321 74-300993
  PH279 .H8 MRR Alc.

Lampén, Lea. Kuololaisen
pgrusšanakirja. Helsinki, W.
Söderström, 1972. (6) 724 p.
[Fmk40.00]   73-333264
  PH278 .L3 1964 MRR Alc.

Swan, Carl Gustaf. English and
Finnish dictionary, [Helsingissä,
Suomal. kirjallis. seuran kirjapainon
osakeyhtiö, 1904] ix, 1218 p.   09-
27858
  PH279 .S8 MRR Alc.

Vuolle, Aino, Englantilais-
suomalainen koulusanakirja. 11.,
täysin uus. p. Porvoo, W.
Söderström, 1969. x, 535 (1) p.
[7.20]   76-441606
  PH279 .V78 1969 MRR Alc.

ENGLISH LANGUAGE--DICTIONARIES--FRENCH.
Archambeaud, Pierre. Dictionnaire
anglais-français, français-anglais
des industries graphiques Paris,
Compagnie française d'editions,
[1968?] 200 p. [15.00]   77-550452
  Z118 .A7 MRR Alc.

Bucksch, Herbert. Dictionary of
civil engineering and construction
machinery and equipment ... 2e
édition. Paris, Eyrolles, 1967. v.
624/.03 74-415882
  TA9 .B892 MRR Alc.

Bucksch, Herbert. Dictionary of
civil engineering and construction
machinery and equipment, English-
French. Paris, Eyrolles 1960-62. 2
v.   624.03 62-6556
  TA9 .B89 MRR Alc.

Cassell's compact French-English,
English-French dictionary: London,
Cassell, 1968. xiv, 658 p. [18/-]
443/.2 72-353833
  PC2640 .C28 MRR Ref Desk.

Cassell's French-English, English-
French dictionary, New ed.
completely revised New York, Funk &
Wagnalls [1951] xxiv, 727, 557 p.
443.2 52-39
  PC2640 .C3 1951 MRR Ref Desk.

Cassell's new French-English, English-
French dictionary. London, Cassell
[1962] xvi, 762, 655 p.   443.2 62-
5157
  PC2640 .C3 1962a MRR Ref Desk.

Castonguay, Jacques. Dictionary of
psychology and related sciences:
English-French. St.-Hyacinthe,
Québec, Edisem; Paris, Maloine, 1973
[i.e. 1972]. 153, 162 p. [$14.50]
150/.3 74-179864
  BF31 .C34 MRR Alc.

Clifton, C. Ebenezer. A new French-
English and English-French dictionary
A new rev. ed. Paris, Garnier
[1961] 2 v. in 1.   443.2 62-6395
  PC2640 .C63 1961 MRR Alc.

Deak, Étienne. Grand dictionnaire
d'américanismes, 4e édition
augmentée. Paris, Éditions du
Dauphin, 1966. xvi, 832 p. [49.50
F]   427/.9/73 68-104186
  PC2640 .D4 1966 MRR Alc.

Dictionnaire canadien, français-
anglais, anglais-français. Ed.
abrégée. [Toronto] McClelland and
Stewart [1962] xxxiv, 861 p.   62-
48993
  PC2640 .D44 MRR Alc.

Dictionnaire moderne français-
anglais, [anglais-français] Paris,
Larousse [1960] xii, 768, xii, 751
p.   a 61-4733
  PC2640 .D56 MRR Ref Desk.

France. Armée. Direction technique
des armes et de l'instruction.
Lexique militaire moderne français-
anglais. Paris, Charles-Lavauzelle
et Cie, 1968. 544 p. [25 F]
355/.0003 68-118881
  U25 .F66 MRR Alc.

Harrap's standard French and English
dictionary. New York, Scribner
[1970] 2 v. [$27.50 (v. 1)]
443/.21 76-182803
  PC2640 .H317 1970 MRR Alc.

ENGLISH LANGUAGE--DICTIONARIES-- (Cont.)
Hoof, Henri van. Economic
tgrminology English-French.
München, Hueber (1967). 770 p.
[DM34.80]   330/.03 68-142981
   HB61 .H57 MRR Alc.

Kettridge, Julius Ornan. French-
English and English-French dictionary
of commercial & financial terms,
phrases, & practice; London,
Routledge & Paul, 1957. xi, 647 p.
650.3 59-21484
   HG151 .K42 1957 MRR Alc.

Larousse modern French-English,
[English-French] dictionary, New
York, McGraw-Hill [1964, c1960] xvi,
768, xvi, 751 p.   66-504
   PC2640 .L33 1964 MRR Alc.

Leitner, Moses Jonathan, ed.
Dictionary of French and American
slang. New York, Crown Publishers
[1965] xix, 272 p.   447.0903 64-
23818
   PC3741 .L58 MRR Alc.

Lépine, Pierre. Dictionnaire
français-anglais, anglais-français,
des termes médicaux et biologiques;
Paris, Flammarion [1952] 829 p.   52-
3756
   R121 .L39 MRR Alc.

Malgorn, Guy Marie, Lexique
technique anglais-français: 4. éd.
rev. et corr. Paris, Gauthier-
Villars, 1956. xxxiv, 493 p.   57-
155
   T9 .M16 1956 MRR Alc.

Mansat, André. Vocabulaire
d'anglais commercial. Nouvelle
edition, augmentee, d'un index,
Paris, Didier, 1966. 210 p. [10 F.]
67-80658
   PE1115 .M26 1966 MRR Alc.

Nixon, James William. Glossary of
terms in official statistics, English-
French, French-English. Edinburgh,
Published for the International
Statistical Institute by Oliver &
Boyd [1964] xiv, 106 p.   65-50152
   HA17 .N5 MRR Alc.

Péron, Michel. Dictionnaire
français-anglais des affaires,
Paris, Larousse, 1968. 2 v. in 1.
(xvi, 230, xvi, 247 p.) [38 F] 68-
137592
   HF1002 .P418 MRR Alc.

Petit, Charles. Dictionnaire
classique, anglais-français et
français-anglais Paris, Hachette,
1967. xxi, 664, 719 p. [30.70]
443/.2 76-380727
   PC2640 .P45 MRR Alc.

Rueil-Malmaison, France. Institut
français du pétrole. Dictionnaire
technique des termes utilisés dans
l'industrie du pétrole, anglais-
français, français-anglais. Paris,
Éditions Technip, 1963. xvi, 385 p.
64-56844
   TN865 .R82 MRR Alc.

Smith, Henry, Classical recipes of
the world, New York, Macmillan, 1955
[c1954] 631 p.   641.03 55-808
   TX651 .S5 1955 MRR Alc.

Urwin, Kenneth. Dictionnaire
pratique français-anglais, anglais-
français .,. Paris, Larousse, 1968.
1216 p. [26.50]   75-374590
   PC2640 .U7 MRR Ref Desk.

Urwin, Kenneth. Langenscheidt
standard dictionary of the French and
English languages, [New York] McGraw-
Hill [1969, c1968] 1216 p. [5.95]
443/.2 78-15234
   PC2640 .U73 1969 MRR Alc.

ENGLISH LANGUAGE--DICTIONARIES--GAELIC.
M'Alpine, Neil, A pronouncing Gaelic-
English dictionary, Glasgow, A.
MacLaren & sons [1842, '36] 2 v. in
1.   491.6332 43-12346
   PB1591 .M25 1942 MRR Alc.

ENGLISH LANGUAGE--DICTIONARIES--GERMAN.
Betteridge, Harold T. Cassell's
German & English dictionary; 10th
ed. London, Cassell, 1965. 629, 619
p. [36/-]   67-94525
   PF3640 .B45 1965a MRR Ref Desk.

Betteridge, Harold T., ed. Cassell's
German & English dictionary; 12th
ed.; completely revised & re-edited
London, Cassell, 1968. xx, 630 [4],
619 p. [45/-]   433/.2 79-540689
   PF3640 .B45 1968 MRR Alc.

Betteridge, Harold T., ed. The new
Cassell's German dictionary; New
York, Funk & Wagnalls [c1971] xx,
646, 632 p. [$8.95 (thumb-indexed)]
433/.21 73-157904
   PF3640 .B45 1971 MRR Ref Desk.

Breuer, Karl. Technisch-
wissenschaftliches
Taschenwörterbuch. 6., völlig
uberarb. u. erg. Aufl. Berlin,
Bielefeld, Siemens (1971). 405 p.
[DM38.00]   75-597125
   T10 .B77 1971 MRR Alc.

Breul, Karl Herman, Heath's German
and English dictionary, Boston, New
York [etc.] D.C. Heath & co. [pref.
1909] 797, 545, [1] p.   26-366
   PF3640 .B8 1909 MRR Alc.

Breul, Karl Hermann, Cassell's new
German and English dictionary, Rev.
and enl. New York, Funk and Wagnalls
company [1939] xix 2 1 l., 813,
687 p.   433.2 42-1037
   PF3640 .B84 1939a MRR Alc.

Brockhaus illustrated German-English,
English-German dictionary. New York,
McGraw-Hill [c1959-60: v. 1, 1960] 2
v. in 1.   433.2 61-17213
   PF3640 .B867 MRR Alc.

Bucksch, Herbert. Wörterbuch für
Bautechnik und Baumaschinen. 4.
wesentlich erw. Aufl. Wiesbaden,
Bauverlag, 1968- v.   [DM 140.-
(Bd. 1)]   624/.03 68-98879
   TA9 .B924 MRR Alc.

Cescotti, Roderich. Luftfahrt -
Wörterbuch; 2. verb. Aufl.
München, H. Reich [1957, c1954] 448
p.   629.1303 60-24363
   TL509 .C4 1957 MRR Alc.

De Vries, Louis, English-German
technical and engineering dictionary,
2d ed., completely rev. and enl.
New York, McGraw-Hill [c1967] 1154
p.   603 68-2779
   T9 .D47 1967 MRR Alc.

De Vries, Louis, Wörterbuch der
Textilindustrie. Wiesbaden,
Brandstetter [1959-60] 2 v.   677.03
59-42656
   TS1309 .D43 MRR Alc.

Dictionary of physics and allied
sciences. London, P. Owen [1958-62]
2 v.   530.3 58-35180
   QC5 .D52 MRR Alc.

Eggeling, Hans F. A dictionary of
modern German prose usage. Oxford,
Clarendon Press, 1961. xii, 418 p.
433.2 61-2526
   PF3640 .E38 MRR Alc.

Eichborn, Reinhart von. Business
dictionary. Englewood Cliffs, N.J.,
Prentice-Hall [1962] v.2, c1961] 2
v.   330.3 62-13618
   HB61 .E433 MRR Alc.

Engeroff, Karl Wilhelm, An English-
German Dictionary of idioms. (2.,
erw. Aufl.) München, Hueber (1967),
313 p. [DM19.80]   433.1 68-74488
   PF3640 .E48 1967 MRR Alc.

Ernst, Richard. Dictionary of
chemistry, [3. Aufl.] Wiesbaden,
Brandstetter [1967-68, c1961-63] 2
v.   540/.3 76-390463
   QD5 .E732 MRR Alc.

Ernst, Richard. Wörterbuch der
industriellen Technik, Wiesbaden,
Brandstetter [197]-[c1951]- v.
73-586747
   T10 .E76 MRR Alc.

Ernst, Richard. Wörterbuch der
industriellen Technik, Wiesbaden,
Brandstetter, 195 [c1948]- v.
603 60-3617
   T10 .E75 Bd. 1-2 MRR Alc.

Freeman, Henry George, Wörterbuch
Werkzeuge; 2. Aufl. Essen, W.
Girardet [1960] 658 p.   621.7503
61-1734
   TJ9 .F72 1960 MRR Alc.

Harrap's standard German and English
dictionary, London, Harrap, [1963-
v.   433.2 64-6113
   PF3640 .H3 MRR Ref Desk.

Herland, Leo Joseph. Dictionary of
mathematical sciences. New York, F.
Ungar Pub. Co. [1951-54] 2 v.
510.3 51-13545
   QA5 .H4 MRR Alc.

Herland, Leo Joseph. Dictionary of
mathematical sciences 2d ed., rev.
and enl. New York, F. Ungar Pub. Co.
[1965- v.   510.3 65-16622
   QA5 .H42 MRR Alc.

Hyman, Charles J. German-English,
English-German astronautics
dictionary, New York, Consultants
Bureau, 1968. viii, 237 p.
629.4/03 65-20216
   TL788 .H8 MRR Alc.

Köhler, Eduard Ludwig, English-
German and German-English dictionary
for the iron and steel industry,
Vienna, Springer, 1955. xii, 168,
162 p.   a 55-6643
   TN609 .K6 MRR Alc.

Langenscheidt concise German
dictionary. [New York] McGraw-Hill
[1969, c1964] 2 v. in 1. [9.50]
433/.2 76-3544
   PF3640 .L22 MRR Ref. Desk.

Langenscheidt's concise German
dictionary. New York, Barnes & Noble
[1964: v. 2, c1961] 2 v. in 1.
433.2 64-56958
   PF3640 .L243 MRR Alc.

Langenscheidt's new Muret-Sanders
encyclopedic dictionary of the
English and German languages. [1st
ed.] New York, Barnes & Noble [1962-
v. in   62-6984
   PF3640 .L257 MRR Alc.

Lejeune, Fritz, Deutsch-Englisches,
Englisch-Deutsches Wörterbuch für
Ärzte. 2. völlig neubearb. Aufl.
Stuttgart, Thieme, 1968- v. [DM
64.00]   610/.3 68-69803
   R121 .L372 MRR Alc.

Merz, Otto, Deutsch-englisches und
englisch-deutsches Fachwörterbuch
für Farbausdrücke aus dem Lack- und
Farbengebiet. 2., neubearb. und
erweiterte Aufl. Stuttgart,
Wissenschaftliche Verlagsgesellschaft, 1954. 351 p.   55-
22330
   TP935 .M45 1954 MRR Alc.

Messinger, Heinz. Langenscheidts
Grosswörterbuch Englisch-Deutsch.
[1. Aufl.] Berlin, Langenscheidt
[1972] 1104 p.   72-316942
   PF3640 .M54 MRR Alc.

Muret, Eduard, Muret-Sanders
Enzyklopädisches englisch-deutsches
und deutsch-englisches wörterbuch,
Grosse ausg. Durchgesehene und verb.
stereotyp-aufl. Berlin-Schöneberg,
Langenscheidt [1922?] v.   mrr01-
71
   PF3640 .M8 1922 MRR Alc.

Oppermann, Alfred. Wörterbuch der
modernen Technik. 3. Aufl. München-
Pullach, Verlag Dokumentation, 1972-
v.   603 72-306183
   TL509 .O623 MRR Alc.

Polygraph dictionary der graphischen
Techniken und der verwandten Gebiete.
2., durch die Polygraph-Redaktion
überarb. erg. und erw. Aufl.
Frankfurt am Main, Polygraph Verlag
[1967] 330 p.   68-123818
   Z118 .P63 1967 MRR Alc.

Renner, Rüdiger. Deutsch-englische
Wirtschaftssprache; München, M.
Hueber, 1965. 556 p.   65-79732
   HB61 .R38 MRR Alc.

Sattler, Wilhelm Ferdinand. Deutsch-
englisches sachwörterbuch. Leipzig,
Renger, 1904. xx, 1035 p.   05-16230

   PF3640 .S3 MRR Alc.

Schöffler, Herbert, The new
Schöffler-Weis compact German and
English dictionary: English-German,
German-English, London, Harrap,
1969. 562, 495 [19] p. [50/-]
433/.2 71-504148
   PF3640 .S435 1969 MRR Ref Desk.

Sommer, Werner, Management
dictionary. 3., durchgesehene und
erw. Aufl. Berlin, De Gruyter, 1966-
68. 2 v. [DM 18.00 per vol.]
658.003 67-73661
   HF1002 .S622 MRR Alc.

Walther, Rudolf, lexicographer.
Polytechnical dictionary, Oxford,
New York, Pergamon Press [1968,
c1967] 2 v.   603 67-25817
   T10 .W3 1968 MRR Alc.

Wildhagen, Karl, Englisch-deutsches,
deutsch-englisches Wörterbuch:
Wiesbaden, Brandstetter-Verlag [1952]-
2 v.   64-28884
   PF3640 .W544 MRR Alc.

Wildhagen, Karl, Englisch-Deutsches,
deutsch-englisches Wörterbuch: 2.,
vollkommen überarbeitete und erw.
Aufl. Wiesbaden: Brandstetter;
London: Allen and Unwin, 19 v.
433/.2/1 72-349225
   PF3640 .W544 1972 MRR Alc.

Wittfoht, Annemarie,
Kunststofftechnisches Wörterbuch.
München, C. Hanser, 1956- v.   a
56-5235
   TP986 .A15W48 MRR Alc.

ENGLISH LANGUAGE--DICTIONARIES--GREEK.
Woodhouse, Sidney Chawner, English-
Greek dictionary; London, G.
Routledge & sons, limited, 1910.
viii, 1029, [1] p.   11-11560
    PA445.E5 W6 MRR Alc.

ENGLISH LANGUAGE--DICTIONARIES--GREEK,
MODERN.
Argyropoulou-Mpenekou, Ourania.
[Anglo-Helleno-Anglikon lexikon
(romanized form)] [195-]   672 p.
54-44611
    PA1139.E5 A67 MRR Alc.

Divry, George Constantopoulos,
Divry's modern English-Greek and
Greek-English desk dictionary. New
York, D. C. Divry, 1974.   767 p.
489.3/3/21   74-220350
    PA1139.E5 D46 1974 MRR Ref Desk.

Divry, George Constantopoulos,
Modern English-Greek and Greek-
English desk dictionary. New York,
D. C. Divry [1961]   767 p.   489.332
62-25241
    PA1139.E5 D46 MRR Alc.

Mega Anglo-Hellēnikon lexikon
(romanized form)] [1959?] 4 v.   72-
208549
    PA1139.E5 M4 MRR Alc.

Swanson, Donald Carl Eugene,
Vocabulary of modern spoken Greek.
Minneapolis, University of Minnesota
Press, 1959. 408 p. 489.332 59-
16514
    PA1139.E5 S9 1959a MRR Alc.

ENGLISH LANGUAGE--DICTIONARIES--
HAWAIIAN.
Pukui, Mary (Wiggin) Hawaiian
dictionary; Honolulu, University of
Hawaii Press, 1971. xxxix, 402, x,
188 p. [$15.00]   499/.4 70-142751

    PL6446 .P785 MRR Alc.

ENGLISH LANGUAGE--DICTIONARIES--HEBREW.
Alcalay, Reuben, 1907- [Milon angli-
ivri shalem (romanized form)]
[1965] 2 v. (4270 columns) 492.432
he 66-1229
    PJ4833 .A4 1965 MRR Alc.

Brown, Francis, A Hebrew and English
lexicon of the Old Testament,
[Reprinted with corrections] Oxford,
Clarendon Press [1962] xix,1127 p.
66-33161
    PJ4833 .B68 1962 MRR Alc.

Harkavy, Alexander, [Ozar leshon
hamikra (romanized form)] New York,
Hebrew publishing company, 1914. vi,
786, [2], 102 p. 14-11012
    PJ4833 .H3 MRR Alc.

ENGLISH LANGUAGE--DICTIONARIES--HEBREW,
POST-BIBLICAL.
Harkavy, Alexander, [Ozar leshon
hamikra (romanized form)] New York,
Hebrew publishing company, 1914. vi,
786, [2], 102 p. 14-11012
    PJ4833 .H3 MRR Alc.

ENGLISH LANGUAGE--DICTIONARIES--HINDI.
Nalanda students' dictionary, Delhi,
New Imperial Book Depot [195-] ii,
1144 p.   491.4332 58-43867
    PK1936 .N33 MRR Alc.

Raghu Vira. A comprehensive English-
Hindi dictionary of governmental &
educational words & phrases ...
[Nagpur, Lokesh Chandra,
International Academy of Indian
Culture, 1955] 189, 1579 p.
491.4332 56-19893
    PK1937 .R3 MRR Alc.

ENGLISH LANGUAGE--DICTIONARIES--
HUNGARIAN.
Bizonfy, Ferencz, Angol-magyar
szótár, 6., bov. kiad.
[Cleveland, O.] "Szabadság" [1938?]
2 v. in 1.   42-33903
    PH2640 .B6 1938 MRR Alc.

Országh, László. Angol-magyar
szótár. 3. kiad. Budapest,
Akademiai Kiado, 1970. 2 v. (xiii,
2344 p.) [460.00 Ft]   494/.511/32
72-19001
    PH2640 .O67 1970b MRR Alc.

ENGLISH LANGUAGE--DICTIONARIES--
ICELANDIC AND OLD NORSE.
Zoëga, Geir Tomasson, A concise
dictionary of old Icelandic, Oxford,
The Clarendon press, 1926. vii, 551,
[1] p.   46-29683
    PD2379 .Z6 1926 MRR Alc.

ENGLISH LANGUAGE--DICTIONARIES--
ICELANDIC, MODERN.
Zoëga, Geir Tomasson, Íslenzk-
ensk orðabók, 3. útg. Reykjavík,
S. Kristjánssonar, 1942. 631, [1]
p.   439.632 46-28351
    PD2437 .Z7 1942 MRR Alc.

ENGLISH LANGUAGE--DICTIONARIES--IDO.
Dyer, Luther H., English-Ido
dictionary, London, The
International language (Ido) society
of Great Britain, 1924. 3 p. l.,
[ix]-xi, [1], 392 p.   42-41232
    PM8393 .D9 MRR Alc.

ENGLISH LANGUAGE--DICTIONARIES--
INDONESIAN.
Van Goor's kamus Inggeris ketjil.
Rutland, Vt., C. E. Tuttle Co. [1966]
359 p.   499.22132 66-23535
    PL5125 .V28 1966 MRR Alc.

Wittermans-Pino, Elizabeth. Kamus
inggeris, 3rd ed. Groningen, J. B.
Wolters, 1963. 2 v. 499.22132 65-
6750
    PL5076 .W5 1963 MRR Alc.

ENGLISH LANGUAGE--DICTIONARIES--IRISH.
Dinneen, Patrick Stephen, [Foclóir
Gaedhilge agus Béarla (romanized
form)] New ed., rev. and greatly
enl. Dublin [etc.] Pub. for the
Irish texts society by the
Educational company of Ireland, ltd.,
1927. 4 p. l., [vii]-xxx, 1340 p.
28-14495
    PB1291 .D5 1927 MRR Alc.

Fournier d'Albe, Edmund Edward, An
English-Irish dictionary and phrase
book, Dublin, The Celtic
association, 1903. viii p., 1 l.,
338 p.   28-12337
    PB1291 .F65 MRR Alc.

Ó Siochfhradha, Micheál, Irish-
English, English-Irish dictionary.
[New ed. Dublin, Talbot Press, 1972]
131, x, 190 p. [£1.70]
491.6/2/321 73-171932
    PB1291 .O83 MRR Alc.

O'Reilly, Edward, An Irish-English
dictionary, A new ed., carefully
rev. and cor. Dublin, J. Duffy and
co., limited [191-] 3 p. l., 5-724,
[2] p.   14-11541
    PB1291 .O8 MRR Alc.

ENGLISH LANGUAGE--DICTIONARIES--ITALIAN.
Cassell's Italian dictionary: Italian-
English, English-Italian. New York,
Funk & Wagnalls [1959, c1958] xxi,
1079 p.   453.2 59-12386
    PC1640 .C33 1959 MRR Ref Desk.

Cassell's Italian-English, English-
Italian dictionary; 7th ed. London,
Cassell, 1967. xxi, 1096 p. [42/-]
453/.2 70-392670
    PC1640 .C33 1967 MRR Ref Desk.

Cassell's Italian-English, English-
Italian dictionary. London, Cassell
[1958] xxi, 1079 p.   453.2 58-4262

    PC1640 .C33 MRR Ref Desk.

Dizionario Garzanti italiano-inglese,
inglese-italiano. Edizione minore.
Milano, Garzanti, 1968. 1067 p. [L
1900] 68-133578
    PC1640 .D5 1968 MRR Alc.

Hazon, Mario, Grande dizionario
inglese-italiano, italiano-inglese.
Milano, Garzanti, 1969. x, 2100 p.
[7800] 76-508865
    PC1640 .H35 1969 MRR Alc.

Hoare, Alfred, A short Italian
dictionary. [New York] Cambridge
University Press, 1957. xxxii, 443,
v, 421 p.   453.2 58-2938
    PC1640 .H63 1957 MRR Alc.

Lysle, Andrea de Roever, called A. de
R., Nuovo dizionario moderno delle
lingue italiana e inglese. Ed. riv.
e aggiornata, con aggiunta di un
supplemento commerciale Torino, F.
Casanova, 1951. 2 v.   56-29687
    PC1640 .L8 1951 MRR Alc.

Marolli, Giorgio. Dizionario tecnico
inglese-italiano, italiano-inglese
... 9. edizione riveduta e ampliata.
Firenze, F. Le Monnier, 1968. xxii,
1841 p. [16000] 603 70-378230
    T9 .M18 1968 MRR Alc.

Motta, Giuseppe, teacher of English.
Dizionario commerciale: inglese-
italiano, italiano-inglese. Milano,
C. Signorelli [1961] x, 1050 p. 61-
33500
    HF1002 .M6 MRR Alc.

Orlandi, Giuseppe, Dizionario
italiano-inglese, inglese-italiano;
3. ed. riv., corr. e interamente
ricomposta. Milano, C. Signorelli
[1957] xiv, 2130 p.   57-24559
    PC1640 .O7 1957 MRR Ref Desk.

Ragazzini, Giuseppe. Dizionario
inglese e italiano. Concise edition
Bologna, Zanichelli: [London]
Longman, [1972] xiii, 1200 p.
[L2700] 73-307395
    PC1640 .R26 1972 MRR Alc.

Reynolds, Barbara. The Cambridge
Italian dictionary. Cambridge,
University Press, 1962- v.
453.2 62-2528
    PC1640 .R4 MRR Ref Desk.

Spinelli, Nicola, Dizionario
italiano-inglese, inglese-italiano.
3. ed. interamente rifatta. Torino,
Società editrice internazionale
[1955] 2 v. a 55-8274
    PC1640 .S7 1955 MRR Alc.

ENGLISH LANGUAGE--DICTIONARIES--
JAPANESE.
Iwanami Ei-Wa daijiten. 1970. 2124
p. [3200] 495.6/32 72-814290
    PL679 .I9 MRR Alc.

Nyū wārudo Ei-Wa jiten. 1969 1557
p. [2300] 76-811998
    PL679 .N9 1969b MRR Alc.

ENGLISH LANGUAGE--DICTIONARIES--KOREAN.
Yu, Hyong-gi, ed. New Life English-
Korean dictionary, American ed.
Washington, Educational Services,
1952. viii, 1301 p. 495.732 52-
3246
    PL937.E5 Y8 1952 MRR Alc.

ENGLISH LANGUAGE--DICTIONARIES--LAO.
Marcus, Russell. English-Lao, Lao-
English dictionary. Rutland, Vt., C.
E. Tuttle Co. [1970] 416 p. [5.00]
495/.919 77-116487
    PL4251.L34 M3 1970 MRR Alc.

ENGLISH LANGUAGE--DICTIONARIES--LATIN.
Cassell's Latin dictionary, Latin-
English and English-Latin. New York,
Funk & Wagnalls [1957] xiv, 927 p.
473.2 58-1875
    PA2365.E5 C3 1957 MRR Ref Desk.

Cassell's new Latin dictionary. New
York, Funk & Wagnalls [1960, c1959]
xvii, 883 p.   473.2 60-7805
    PA2365.L3 C3 1960 MRR Alc.

Cassell's new Latin-English, English-
Latin dictionary, London, Cassell
[1959] xvii, 883 p.   473.2 59-
65014
    PA2365.L3 C3 MRR Ref Desk.

Levine, Edwin B. Follett world-wide
Latin dictionary; Chicago, Follett
Pub. Co., 1967. 767 p.   473/.2 67-
15559
    PA2365.E5 L65 MRR Alc.

ENGLISH LANGUAGE--DICTIONARIES--LATVIAN.
Anglu-latviesu vardnica. Riga,
Latvijas valsts izdevnieciba, 1962.
720 p.   63-58176
    PG8979 .A48 MRR Alc.

ENGLISH LANGUAGE--DICTIONARIES--
LITHUANIAN.
Lalis, Anthony, Lietuviškos ir
angliškos kalbu žodynas. 3.,
išnaujo taisytas ir gausiai
papildytas, spaudimas. Chicago,
Ill., Turtu ir spauda "Lietuvos,"
1915. 2 pt. in 1 v.   20-5148
    PG8679 .L33 1915 MRR Alc.

ENGLISH LANGUAGE--DICTIONARIES--MALAY.
Winstedt, Richard Olof, Sir, A
practical modern English-Malay
dictionary. Singapore, Kelly & Walsh
[1952?] 387 p.   499.22132 53-26600

    PL5125 .W68 MRR Alc.

ENGLISH LANGUAGE--DICTIONARIES--
MALAYALAM.
Gundert, Hermann, A Malayalam and
English dictionary, Mangalore, C.
Stolz; London, Trübner & co.; [etc.,
etc.] 1872. xviii, 1116 p.   03-
18077
    PL4716 .G8 MRR Alc.

Raman Menon, K. The V. V. English
Malayalam dictionary. 1st ed.
Quilon, S. India, S. T. Reddiar, V.
V. Press, 1951. 675 p. 494.81232
52-40313
    PL4716 .R3 MRR Alc.

ENGLISH LANGUAGE--DICTIONARIES--
MONGOLIAN.
Boberg, Folke. Mongolian-English
dictionary. Stockholm, Forlaget
Filadelfia [1954-55] 3 v.   494.2
55-36672
    PL406 .B6 MRR Alc.

ENGLISH LANGUAGE--DICTIONARIES--
NORWEGIAN.
Brynildsen, John, Norsk-engelsk
ordbok. 3. omarb. utg. Oslo, H.
Aschehoug & co. (W. Nygaard) 1927. 4
p. l., 1228 p.   28-8395
    PD2691 .B8 1927 MRR Alc.

Gyldendal's English-Norwegian and
Norwegian-English dictionary. New
York, McKay [1951] 2 v. in 1.
439.8232 a 51-7382
    PD2691 .G9 1951 MRR Alc.

ENGLISH LANGUAGE--DICTIONARIES--
ORIENTAL.
United States. Air Force. 6004th Air
Intelligence Service Squadron.
Dictionary of common oriental terms;
[n. p.] 1956. 1v. (various pagings)
495   57-60108
     PL493 .U52 MRR Alc.

ENGLISH LANGUAGE--DICTIONARIES--
PANGASINAN.
Enriquez, Pablo Jacobo. Pocket
dictionary, Manila, Philippine Book
Co. [c1952] 249 p.   499.2 54-22065
     PL5525 .E6 MRR Alc.

ENGLISH LANGUAGE--DICTIONARIES--PERSIAN.
Hayyīm, Sulaymān. One-volume
English-Persian dictionary,
Teheran, Beroukhim, 1952. 1465,
11 p.   491.5532   54-15132
     PK6379 .H33 MRR Alc.

ENGLISH LANGUAGE--DICTIONARIES--
PHILIPPINE.
Enriquez, Pablo Jacobo. Pocket
dictionary, Manila, Philippine Book
Co. [c1952] 249 p.   499.2 54-22065
     PL5525 .E6 MRR Alc.

ENGLISH LANGUAGE--DICTIONARIES--POLISH.
The Kosciuszko Foundation
dictionary: New York, 1960-62. 2 v.
     491.8532   60-1190
     PG6640 .K652 MRR Alc.

ENGLISH LANGUAGE--DICTIONARIES--
POLYGLOT.
Associazione industriale lombarda.
Glossario del lavoro: italiano,
francese, inglese, tedesco. Milano,
1964. 1335 p.   67-43249
     HD4839 .A78 MRR Alc.

Band-Kuzmany, Karin R. M. Glossary
of the theatre. Amsterdam, New York,
Elsevier Pub. Co., 1969. 140 p.
[31.20]   792/.03 68-57152
     PN2035 .B3 MRR Alc.

Beeck, Peter. Fachausdrücke der
Presse. [3. Aufl.] Frankfurt am
Main, Polygraph Verlag, 1950. 174 p.
     070.03 51-16343
     PN4728 .B43 1950 MRR Alc.

Bergman, Peter M. The concise
dictionary of twenty-six languages in
simultaneous translations, New York,
Polyglot Library [1968] 406 p.   413
67-14284
     P361 .B4 TJ Rm.

Britannica world language dictionary,
[Chicago, 1958] 1483-2015 p.   413
58-4491
     P361 .B7 1958 MRR Alc.

Buck, Carl Darling. A dictionary of
selected synonyms in the principal
Indo-European languages; Chicago,
University of Chicago Press [1949]
xix, 1515 p.   413 49-11769
     P765 .B8 MRR Alc.

Lyecken, Francisco J. Vocabulário
tecnico portuguès-inglês-francès-
alemão. 4. ed. rev. [Sao Paulo]
Edições Melhoramentos [1961] 600
p.   603 62-3680
     T10 .B82 1961 MRR Alc.

Bürger, Erich. Technical dictionary
of data processing, computers, office
machines. [1st ed.] Oxford, New
York, Pergamon Press [1970] 1463 p.
651.8/03   75-81247
     QA76.15 .B46 1970 MRR Alc.

Capitol's concise dictionary.
Bologna, Capitol, 1972. 1051 (i.e.
1207) p.   413 72-172231
     P361 .C3 MRR Alc.

Chalkiopoulos, Georgios.
[Pentaglosson lexilogion technikōn
horōn (romanized form)] [1960]
1030 p.   61-31355
     T10 .C46 1960 MRR Alc.

Clason, W. E., Elsevier's dictionary
of computers, automatic control and
data processing. 2d rev. ed. of The
dictionary of automation, computers,
control and measuring. Amsterdam,
New York, Elsevier Pub. Co., 1971.
484 p. [fl78.00]   001.6/4/03 73-
151733
     TJ212.5 .C55 1971 MRR Alc.

Clason, W. E., Supplement to the
Elsevier dictionaries of electronics,
nucleonics and telecommunication.
Amsterdam, New York, Elsevier Pub.
Co., 1963. 633 p.   603 63-11369
     T10 .C55 MRR Alc.

Conference terminology, 2d ed., rev.
and augm. Amsterdam, New York,
Elsevier Pub. Co.: [sole distributors
for the U.S.: American Elsevier Pub.
Co., New York] 1962. 162 p.   413
63-8568
     PB324.C6 C6 1962 MRR Alc.

Cooper, S. A. Concise international
dictionary of mechanics & geology;
New York, Philosophical Library
[1958] viii, 400 p.   621.03 58-
3594
     TJ9 .C6 1958 MRR Alc.

DeLand, Graydon S. American
traveler's companion: New York,
Fielding Publications [1966] 297 p.
413   66-17187
     PE1131 .D4 1966 MRR Alc.

Dictionar tehnic poliglot: Ediția
a 2-a. București, Editura Tehnica,
1967. xv, 1233 p.   603 68-2971
     T10 .D54 1967 MRR Alc.

Dictionary of chemistry and chemical
technology, in six languages: [Rev.
ed.] Oxford, New York, Pergamon
Press [1966] 1325 p.   540.3 65-
29008
     QD5 .D5 1966 MRR Alc.

Dictionary of photography and
cinematography: London, New York,
Focal Press [1961] 1 v. (various
pagings)   770.3 63-24356
     TR9 .D5 MRR Alc.

Dictionnaire à l'usage de la
librairie ancienne pour les langues:
française, anglaise, allemande,
suédoise, danoise, italienne,
espagnole, hollandaise. Paris, Ligue
internationale de la librairie
ancienne, 1956. 190 p.   655.403 57-
2275
     Z282 .D5 MRR Alc.

The Duden pictorial encyclopedia in
five languages: English, French,
German, Italian, Spanish. 2d, enl.
ed. New York, F. Ungar Pub. Co.
[1958] 2 v.   413 58-11093
     P361 .D8 1958 MRR Alc.

Elektrotechnik und Elektrochemie.
München, R. Oldenbourg, 1955. xxiv,
1304 p.   57-18208
     TK9 .E42 1955 MRR Alc.

Elsevier's automobile dictionary in
eight languages: Amsterdam, New
York, Elsevier Pub. Co.; [distributed
by Van Nostrand, Princeton, N.J.]
1960. 946 p.   629.203 59-8946
     TL9 .E43 MRR Alc.

Elsevier's banking dictionary in six
languages: Amsterdam, New York,
Elsevier Pub. Co., 1966. 302 p.
332.103   65-20139
     HG151 .E45 MRR Alc.

Elsevier's dictionary of aeronautics
in six languages: Amsterdam, New
York, Elsevier Pub. Co., 1964. 842
p.   629.1303 63-22063
     TL509 .E4 MRR Alc.

Elsevier's dictionary of building
construction, Amsterdam, New York,
Elsevier Pub. Co., 1959. 471 p.
690.3   58-59508
     TH9 .E47 MRR Alc.

Elsevier's dictionary of chemical
engineering. Amsterdam, New York,
1968. 2 v. [62.50 per vol.]
660/.3   63-54865
     TP9 .E38 MRR Alc.

Elsevier's dictionary of cinema,
sound, and music, in six languages:
Amsterdam, New York, Elsevier Pub.
Co., 1956. 948 p.   778.503 56-
13141
     TR847 .E4 MRR Alc.

Elsevier's dictionary of criminal
science, in eight languages:
Amsterdam, New York, Elsevier Pub.
Co.; [distributed by Van Nostrand,
Princeton N.J.] 1960. xv, 1460 p.
364.03   59-12582
     HV6017 .E4 MRR Alc.

Elsevier's dictionary of electronics
and waveguides, 2d ed., rev. and
enl. Amsterdam, New York, Elsevier
Pub. Co., 1966 [i.e. 1965] 833 p.
621.38103   65-20142
     TK7804 .E4 1965 MRR Alc.

Elsevier's dictionary of general
physics in six languages: Amsterdam,
New York, Elsevier Pub. Co., 1962.
859 p.   530.3 62-13015
     QC5 .E46 MRR Alc.

Elsevier's dictionary of nuclear
science and technology. 2d rev. ed.
Amsterdam, New York, Elsevier Pub.
Co., 1970. 787 p.   [85.00]
539.7/03   72-103557
     QC772 .E4 1970 MRR Alc.

Elsevier's dictionary of photography
in three languages: Amsterdam, New
York, Elsevier Pub. Co.: distributed
by American Elsevier Pub. Co., New
York, 1965. 660 p.   770.3 63-16076
     TR9 .E46 MRR Alc.

Elsevier's dictionary of television,
radar, and antennas, in six
languages: Amsterdam, New York,
Elsevier Pub. Co., 1955. 760 p.
621.38803   55-6216
     TK6634 .E4 MRR Alc.

Elsevier's dictionary of the printing
and allied industries in four
languages, Amsterdam, New York,
[etc.] Elsevier Pub. Co., 1967. 596
p. [90.00]   655/.003 67-19851
     Z118 .E5 MRR Alc.

Elsevier's lexicon of archive
terminology: Amsterdam, New York,
Elsevier Pub. Co., 1964. 83 p.
025.171014   64-56714
     CD945 .E4 MRR Alc.

Elsevier's lexicon of international
and national units; Amsterdam, New
York, Elsevier Pub. Co., 1964. 75 p.
389.103   63-11366
     QC82 .E37 MRR Alc.

Elsevier's lexicon of stock-market
terms: Amsterdam, New York, Elsevier
Pub. Co., 1965. 131 p.   332.603 65-
13892
     HG4513 .E4 MRR Alc.

Elsevier's medical dictionary in five
languages: Amsterdam, New York,
Elsevier Pub. Co., 1964. 1588 p.
610.3   62-13022
     R121 .E5 1964 MRR Alc.

Elsevier's wood dictionary in seven
languages: Amsterdam, New York,
Elsevier Pub. Co., 1964- v.
634.903   64-14178
     SD431 .E4 MRR Alc.

Fabierkiewicz, Wacław. Podręczny
słownik włókienniczy w 5 językach:
[Wyd. 1] [Warszawa] Państwowe
Wydawn. Techniczne [1955] xlvii, 305
p.   55-38912
     TS1309 .F3 MRR Alc.

Frey, Albert Romer, Dictionary of
numismatic names. [New York] Barnes
& Noble [1947] ix, 311, 94 p.
737.03   48-5357
     CJ67 .F7 1947 MRR Alc.

Giteau, Cécile. Dictionnaire des
arts du spectacle, français--anglais-
-allemand; Paris, Dunod, 1970. xxv,
429 p. [88.00]   79-499699
     PN1579 .G5 MRR Alc.

Great Britain. Naval intelligence
division. A dictionary of naval
equivalents covering English, French,
Italian, Spanish, Russian, Swedish,
Danish, Dutch, German. London, H.M.
Stationery off., 1924. 2 v.   24-
23792
     V24 .G7 MRR Alc.

Haensch, Günther. Dictionary of
international relations and politics;
Amsterdam, New York, Elsevier Pub.
Co., 1965. xv, 638 p.   320.03 64-
8710
     JX1226 .H26 MRR Alc.

Haensch, Günther. Wörterbuch der
Landwirtschaft: 3., überarb. Aufl.
München, Bayerischer
Landwirtschaftverlag [1966] xxiv,
746 p.   630/.3 68-96091
     S411 .H26 1966 MRR Alc.

Herbst, Robert. Dictionary of
commercial, financial, and legal
terms; 2d ed., Zug, Translegal
[1966- v.   330/.03 67-8369
     HB61 .H462 MRR Alc.

Herbst, Robert. Dictionary of
commercial, financial, and legal
terms 3rd ed. rev. Zug, Translegal
[1968- v. [unpriced]   330/.03
76-410368
     HB61 .H463 MRR Alc.

Hering, Richard, writer on cookery.
Dictionary of classical and modern
cookery and practical reference
manual for the hotel, restaurant, and
catering trade. Translation of the
11th newly rev. ed. Giessen,
Pfanneberg [1958] 852 p.   641.503
59-1834
     TX349 .H543 MRR Alc.

Hétnyelvü sportszótár: Budapest,
Terra, 1960- v.   61-21333
     GV567 .H45 MRR Alc.

Horn, Stefan F., Glossary of
financial terms, Amsterdam, New
York, Elsevier Pub. Co., 1965. 271
p.   332.03 64-23405
     HG151 .H6 MRR Alc.

Horten, Hans Ernest. Export-import
correspondence in four languages
London, Gower Press Ltd., 1970. xi,
2-316 p. [80/-]   382/.03 76-495482
     HF1002 .H695 MRR Alc.

ENGLISH LANGUAGE--DICTIONARIES-- (Cont.)
Inter-American Statistical Institute.
Statistical vocabulary. 2d ed.
Washington, Pan American Union, 1960.
xi, 83 p.   310.3 pa 60-56
HA17 .I6 1960 MRR Alc.

Intergovernmental Maritime
Consultative Organization. Glossary
of maritime technical terms. London
[c1963] 118 p.   64-56993
V24 .I5 MRR Alc.

International Chamber of Commerce.
Dictionary of advertising and
distribution. Basel, Verlag für
Recht und Gesellschaft, 1954. 1 v.
(unpaged) 659.103 54-24644
HF5803 .I58 1954 MRR Alc.

International Commission on Large
Dams. Dictionnaire technique des
barrages. 2. ed. [Paris, 1960?]
380 p.   627.803 61-805
TC540 .I45 1960 MRR Alc.

International insurance dictionary:
[n.p., European Conference of
Insurance Supervisory Services, 1959]
xxxi, 1083 p.   368.03 61-35675
HG8025 .I5 MRR Alc.

International Railway Documentation
Bureau. Lexique général des termes
ferroviaires, [2. éd. entièrement
refondue et augm.] Amsterdam, J. H.
De Bussy, 1965. 1357 p.   625.1003
66-87434
TF9 .I46 1965 MRR Alc.

Jacks, Graham Vernon. Multilingual
vocabulary of soil science. [2d ed.,
rev. Rome] Land & Water Division,
Food and Agriculture Organization of
the United Nations [1960] xxiii, 428
p.   631.403 60-50105
S591 .J26 1960 MRR Alc.

Kerchove, René de, baron.
International maritime dictionary:
2d ed. Princeton, N.J., Van Nostrand
[1961] v, 1018 p.   623.803 61-
16272
V23 .K4 1961 MRR Alc.

Kleczek, Josip. Astronomical
dictionary. [Vyd. 1.] Praha, Nakl.
Československé akademie věd, 1961.
972 p.   62-25391
QB14 .K55 MRR Alc.

Lana, Gabriella. Glossary of
geographical names in six languages:
Amsterdam, New York, Elsevier Pub.
Co., 1967. 184 p.   910/.003 66-
28762
G104.5 .L3 MRR Ref Desk.

Lessere, Samuel E. Harian's foreign
language speak-easy. [3d ed.]
Greenlawn, N.Y., Harian Publications
[1957] 106 p.   418.24 57-14033
PE1635 .L4 1957 MRR Alc.

Lexicon opthalmologicum: Basel, New
York, S. Karger, 1959. 223 p.
617.703 59-4669
RE21 .L45 MRR Alc.

Lexikon des Bibliothekswesens.
Leipzig, VEB Verlag für Buch- und
Bibliothekswesen, 1969. xiii, 769 p.
[42.00] 70-423794
Z1006 .L46 MRR Alc.

Nash, Rose. Multilingual lexicon of
linguistics and philology: English,
Russian, German, French. Coral
Gables, Fla., University of Miami
Press [1968] xxvi, 390 p.   413 68-
31044
P29 .N34 MRR Alc.

Nederlands Geologisch Mijnbouwkundig
Genootschap. Geological
nomenclature. Gorinchem, J.
Noorduijn, 1959. xvi, 523 p.   550.3
a 60-3024
QE5 .N413 MRR Alc.

Nijdam, J. Tuinbouwkundig
woordenboek in acht talen. Herziene
en uitgebreide uitg. van de
Woordenlijst voor de tuinbouw in
zeven talen. ['s-Gravenhage,
Staatsdrukkerij- en
Uitgeverijbedrijf; voor alle anderen
landen: Interscience Publishers, New
York] 1961. 504 p.   62-52704
SB45 .N673 MRR Alc.

Nobel, Albert, Dictionnaire
médical. 5. éd. rev. et augm.
Paris, Masson, 1970 [c1969] xxii,
1329 p. [200.00] 77-93556
R121 .N6 1970 MRR Alc.

Ouseg, H. L. 21-language dictionary.
London, P. Owen [1962] xxxi, 333 p.
63-1285
P361 .O85 1962 MRR Alc.

Pipics, Zoltán. Dictionarium
bibliothecarii practicum: ad usum
internationalem in XXII linguis. 6.,
rev. and enlarged ed. Pullach
(München) Verlag Dokumentation
1974. 385 p. [DM98.00] 74-322718
Z1006 .P67 1974 MRR Ref Desk.

Pisant, Emmanuel. International
dictionary. Paris, Editions
Moderninter [1958] 373 p.   413 58-
26075
P361 .P5 MRR Alc.

Polec. 2., verb. und erw. Aufl.
Berlin, de Gruyter, 1967. xvi, 1037
p. with map. [DM 48.-] 330/.03 68-
70864
H40 .P6 1967 MRR Alc.

Raaff, J. J. Index vocabulorum
quadrilingius; verf en vernis, [Den
Haag] Vereniging van Vernis- en
Verffabrikanten in Nederland,
Exportgroep Verf, 1958. 898 p.
667.603 59-27978
TP934.3 .R2 MRR Alc.

Rae, Kenneth, ed. Lexique
international de termes techniques de
theatre Bruxelles, Elsevier [1959]
139 p.   60-26926
PN2035 .R3 MRR Alc.

Sachs, Wolfgang, ed.
Lgbensversicherungstechnisches
Wörterbuch. Würzburg, K. Thiltsch,
1954. 308 p.   56-16246
HG8759 .S3 MRR Alc.

Schloms, Irene. Fachwörterbuch für
Programmierer, deutsch, englisch,
französisch. Heidelberg, Hüthig
(1966) 139, 139, 110 p. [DM 28.00]
651.8 67-91557
QA76.15 .S35 MRR Alc.

Schulz, Ernst, lexicographer.
Wörterbuch der Optik und
Feinmechanik. Wiesbaden,
Brandstetter [1960-61] 3 v.   a 61-
3700
QC351.2 .S34 MRR Alc.

Servotte, Jozef V., 1903-
Dictionnaire commercial et financier:
2. ed., rev. et augm. Bruxelles,
Éditions Brepols [1960] ix, 955 p.
61-930
HF1002 .S42 1960 MRR Alc.

Six-language dictionary of
automation, electronics and
scientific instruments: London,
Iliffe Books; Englewood Cliffs, N.J.,
Prentice-Hall [1962] 732 p.
621.3803 63-5414
TK7804 .S5 1962 MRR Alc.

Skandinaviska banken, a.-b. Banking
terms: French, German, Italian,
Spanish, Swedish. Stockholm [1964]
65 p.   65-87814
HG151 .S46 MRR Alc.

Smith, William James, A dictionary
of musical terms in four languages.
London, Hutchinson [1961] 195 p.
61-65056
ML108 .S64D5 MRR Alc.

Stowarzyszenie Geodetów Polskich.
Slownik geodezyjny w 5 [i.e. pięciu]
językach: polskim, rosyjskim,
niemieckim, angielskim, francuskim.
Warszawa, Państwowe
Przedsiębiorstwo Wydawn.
Kartograficznych, 1954. xv, 525 p.
55-34784
QB279 .S8 MRR Alc.

Sube, Ralf. Kernphysik und
Kerntechnik: Berlin, Verlag Technik
[1962] 1606 p.   62-2924
QC772 .S9 MRR Alc.

Sube, Ralf. Wörterbuch Physik:
Zürich, H. Deutsch, 1973. 3 v.   74-
320539
QC5 .S9 MRR Alc.

Thompson, Anthony. Vocabularium
bibliothecarii. 2d ed. [Paris]
UNESCO, 1962. 627 p.   63-5650
Z1006 .T47 1962a MRR Alc.

Townsend, Derek. Advertising and
public relations; London, A. Redman
[1964] xvi, 152 p.   65-6026
HF5803 .T6 MRR Alc.

Trollhann, Lilian, comp. Dictionary
of data processing. Amsterdam, New
York, Elsevier Pub. Co., 1964. 300
p.   651 64-8676
QA76.15 .T7 MRR Alc.

Union européenne des experts
comptables économiques et
financiers. Lexique U.E.C. Lexicon.
Düsseldorf, Verlagsbuchhandlung des
Instituts der Wirtschaftsprüfer,
1961. 1 v. (various pagings). 63-
31440
HF5621 .U5 MRR Alc.

Vocabulaire international des termes
d'urbanisme et d'architecture. 1.
ed. Paris, Société de diffusion
des techniques du bâtiment et des
travaux publics, 1970- v.   [133F
(v. 1)] 70-860237
NA31 .V6 MRR Alc.

Walter, Frank Keller. Abbreviations
and technical terms used in book
catalogs and bibliographies, in eight
languages, 1917 handy edition.
Boston, The Boston book company
[1919?] 2 v. in 1.   27-13479
Z1006 .W261 1919 MRR Alc.

Zboiński, A., ed. Dictionary of
architecture and building trades in
four languages: English, German,
Polish, Russian. Oxford, New York,
Pergamon Press; [distributed in the
Western Hemisphere by Macmillan, New
York, 1963] 491 p.   63-22975
NA31 .Z34 MRR Alc.

Żytka, Romuald. Geological
dictionary Warszawa, Wydawnictwa
Geologiczne, 1970. 1439 p.
[zł1250.00] 550/.3 72-31794
QE5 .Z9 MRR Alc.

ENGLISH LANGUAGE--DICTIONARIES--
POLYGLOT--BIBLIOGRAPHY.
Alston, R. C. Polyglot dictionaries
and grammars: Bradford, printed for
the author by Ernest Cummins [1967]
xx, 311 p.   68-138251
Z2015.A1 A4 vol. 2 MRR Alc.

ENGLISH LANGUAGE--DICTIONARIES--
PORTUGUESE.
Grande dicionário português-
inglês, inglês-português. São
Paulo, Li-Bra [1968] 4 v.   79-
357089
PC5333 .G7 MRR Alc.

Houaiss, Antonio, ed. The new
Appleton dictionary of the English
and Portuguese languages. New York,
Appleton-Century-Crofts, 1964. xx,
636, 665 p.   469.32 64-25814
PC5333 .H6 MRR Ref Desk.

The New Barsa dictionary of the
English and Portuguese languages.
New York, Appleton-Century-Crofts,
1967. 2 v.   469.3/2 67-8024
PC5333 .N4 1967 MRR Alc.

Novo Michaelis, dicionário
ilustrado. São Paulo, Edições
Melhoramentos [c1958-] 2 v.   59-
39106
PC5333 .N6 1958 MRR Alc.

Valladro, Leonel. Dicionário
inglês-português; Rio de Janeiro,
Editôra Globo [1954] 1135 p.   54-
44677
PC5333 .V3 MRR Alc.

ENGLISH LANGUAGE--DICTIONARIES--
ROMANIAN.
Levitchi, Leon. Dicționar englez-
român, București, Editura
științifică, 1971. 1071 p. with
errata. [lei 80.00] 72-312170
PC779 .L39 MRR Alc.

ENGLISH LANGUAGE--DICTIONARIES--RUSSIAN.
Aleshin, E. V. [Slovar angliiskikh
i amerikanskikh sokrashchenii
(romanized form)] 1957. 767 p.   57-
36383
PE1693 .A38 1957 MRR Alc.

[Anglo-russkii fizicheskii slovar'
(romanized form)] 1968. 848 p.
[3.13] 70-382641
QC5 .A55 MRR Alc.

Langenscheidt's Russian-English,
English-Russian dictionary. [1st
ed.] Berlin, Langenscheidt [1964]
505 p.   491.732 64-56693
PG2640 .L3 1964 MRR Alc.

Müller, Vladimir Karlovich, [Anglo-
russkii slovar (romanized form)]
1965. 912 p.   65-57325
PG2640 .M8 1965 MRR Alc.

Segal, Louis, New complete Russian-
English dictionary (new orthography)
[Pocket ed.] New York, Praeger
[1959] 2 v. in 1.   491.732 59-8959
PG2640 .S42 MRR Alc.

ENGLISH LANGUAGE--DICTIONARIES--
SANSKRIT.
Monier-Williams, Monier, Sir, A
dictionary of English and Sanskrit,
Delhi, Motilal Banarsidass [1964]
xii, 859 p.   491/.2/32 73-495007
PK933 .M5 1964 MRR Alc.

ENGLISH LANGUAGE--DICTIONARIES--SERBO-
CROATIAN.
Bogadek, Francis Aloysius, New
English-Croatian and Croatian-English
dictionary. 3d ed., enl. and corr.
New York, Hafner Pub. Co., 1949
[c1944] 2 v. in 1.   491.8332 50-
2223
PG1377 .B72 1949 MRR Alc.

ENGLISH LANGUAGE--DICTIONARIES-- (Cont.)
Cahen, Louis. Dzepni srpsko-
engleski i englesko-srpski recnik,
[4th impression] London, K. Paul,
Trench, Trubner & co., ltd., 1920.
iv, 268 p.   22-13793
    PG1376 .C3 1920 MRR Alc.

Drvodelić, Milan. Englesko-hrvatski
ili srpski rječnik / 4. izd.
Zagreb : "Skolska knjiga," 1973.
[8], 1161, [1] p.   74-970911
    PG1377 .D77 1973 MRR Alc.

Drvodelić, Milan. Englesko-
hrvatskogrpski rječnik. 3. izd.
Zagreb, Skolska knjiga, 1970. 1198
p. [60.00] 79-974853
    PG1377 .D77 1970 MRR Alc.

ENGLISH LANGUAGE--DICTIONARIES--SLOVAK.
Hrobak, Philip Anthony. Hrobak's
English-Slovak dictionary; [Rev. 2d
ed.] New York, R. Speller [1965]
xxxii, 702 p.   491.87 65-25765
    PG5379 .H7 1965 MRR Alc.

ENGLISH LANGUAGE--DICTIONARIES--
SLOVENIAN.
Škerlj, Ružena. Angleško-
slovenski slovar. 4., izpopolnjena
izdaja. Ljubljana, Državna zalozba
Slovenije, 1957. viii, 773 p.   60-
28644
    PG1891 .S48 1957 MRR Alc.

ENGLISH LANGUAGE--DICTIONARIES--SOMALI.
Abraham, Roy Clive. English-Somali
dictionary, London, University of
London P. [1967] [7] 208 p. [22/6]
493/.5 67-112860
    PJ2533 .A18 MRR Alc.

ENGLISH LANGUAGE--DICTIONARIES--SPANISH.
Cassell's Spanish-English, English-
Spanish dictionary; 6th ed. London,
Cassell, 1968. xv, 1477 p. [42/-]
463/.2 71-386569
    PC4640 .C35 1968 MRR Ref Desk.

Castilla's Spanish and English
technical dictionary. London,
Routledge & Paul [1958] 2 v.   603
58-2320
    T9 .C34 MRR Alc.

Corona Bustamante, Francisco. A new
dictionary of the Spanish-English and
English-Spanish languages. New ed.,
Baltimore, Ottenheimer Publishers,
c1959. 664, 536 p.   463.2 60-20298

    PC4640 .C58 1959 MRR Alc.

Cuyás, Arturo, Appleton's new
Cuyás English-Spanish and Spanish-
English dictionary. 5th ed.; rev.
New York, Appleton-Century-Crofts,
1972. 2 v. in 1. [$7.95] 463/.21
75-182137
    PC4640 .C8 1972 MRR Alc.

Cuyás, Arturo, Appleton's new
Cuyás English-Spanish and Spanish-
English dictionary. 5th ed. New
York, Appleton-Century-Crofts, 1966.
2 v. in 1. 463/.21 66-22193
    PC4640 .C8 1966 MRR Alc.

Diccionario moderno Langenscheidt de
los idiomas ingles y espanol.
Berlin, Munich, Zurich,
Langenscheidt, (1966). 568, 503 p.
[17.00] 79-390437
    PC4640 .D564 MRR Alc.

Enríquez, Pablo Jacobo. Pocket
dictionary, Manila, Philippine Book
Co. [c1952] 249 p.   499.2 54-22065

    PL5525 .E6 MRR Alc.

Moreno Pacheco, Miguel. Economic
terminology English-Spanish.
München, Hueber (1967). 480 p. [DM
24.80] 330/.01/4 68-82025
    HB61 .M6 MRR Alc.

The New World Spanish-English and
English-Spanish dictionary. New
York, World Pub. Co. [1969] xvi,
257, 311 p. [$5.95 $6.95 (thumb
indexed)] 463.2 68-17418
    PC4640 .N4 MRR Ref Desk.

Nuevo diccionario general inglés-
español, [español-ingles] Madrid,
P.D.& F. Ediciones-Distribuciones
[1966] 2 v. 67-51963
    PC4640 .N82 MRR Alc.

Pepper, William M. Dictionary of
newspaper and printing terms; New
York, Columbia University Press
[1959] 344 p. 070.03 59-16345
    PN4728 .P4 MRR Alc.

Rodríguez, César. Bilingual
dictionary of the graphic arts; New
and complete ed., rev. and enl.
Farmingdale, N.Y., G. A. Humphrey
[1966] 448 p. 655.03 66-27570
    Z118 .R6 1966 MRR Alc.

Simon and Schuster's international
dictionary. New York, Simon and
Schuster [1973] xviii, 1605 p.
[$12.95 (thumb-indexed)] 463/.21
71-180718
    PC4640 .S48 MRR Ref Desk.

Velázquez de la Cadena, Mariano,
New revised Velázquez Spanish and
English dictionary, Chicago, Follett
Pub. Co. [1974] 698, 788 p.
463/.21 74-78935
    PC4640 .V5 1974 MRR Ref Desk.

Vox modern college Spanish and
English dictionary. 2d ed. New
York, Scribner [1972, c1970] xxxi,
1417 p. [$9.95] 463/.21 75-38123

    PC4640 .V6813 1972 MRR Alc.

Williams, Edwin Bucher, The Williams
Spanish & English dictionary;
Expanded ed. New York, Scribner
[1973, c1963] xvi, 623, lxiv, 620 p.
[$9.95] 463/.21 72-11299
    PC4640 .W55 1973 MRR Ref Desk.

ENGLISH LANGUAGE--DICTIONARIES--SWEDISH.
Freudenthal, Fritiof. English-
Swedish dictionary. 2d rev ed.
London, Allen & Unwin [1956] 348 p.
439.732 56-40994
    PD5640 .F72 1956 MRR Alc.

Kärre, Karl, Engelsk-svensk ordbok,
skolupplaga, 3. omarb. uppl.
Stockholm, Svenska bokförlaget,
Norstedt [1953] xvi, 973 p.
439.732 a 53-6763
    PD5640 .K3 1953 MRR Alc.

Modern engelsk-svensk ordbok. 5
uppl. Stockholm, Prisma; [Solna,
Seelig,] 1970. (11), 395, (1) p.
[kr17.80] 79-579077
    PD5640 .M56 1970 MRR Alc.

Nöjd, Ruben, McKay's modern English-
Swedish and Swedish-English
dictionary. New York, D. McKay Co.
[1954] x, 248, 220 p.   439.732 53-
11359
    PD5640 .N613 MRR Alc.

ENGLISH LANGUAGE--DICTIONARIES--TAGALOG.
Enríquez, Pablo Jacobo. Pocket
dictionary, Manila, Philippine Book
Co. [c1952] 249 p.   499.2 54-22065

    PL5525 .E6 MRR Alc.

ENGLISH LANGUAGE--DICTIONARIES--TAMIL.
Percival, Peter. A dictionary,
English and Tamil, Rev. ed. Madras,
The Madras school book and literature
society, 1935. 441 p. 494.81132
36-16388
    PL4756 .P47 1935 MRR Alc.

Visvanātha Pillai, V. A
dictionary, Tamil and English, 4th
ed.--3,000 copies. Madras, The
Madras school book and literature
society, 1921. 1 p. l., 653 p. 24-
1034
    PL4756 .V6 1921 MRR Alc.

ENGLISH LANGUAGE--DICTIONARIES--THAI.
Photchananukrom 'Angkrit-Thai
[romanized form] [2511 i.e. 1968]
2 v. (2737 p.) [80.00] 75-261090
    PL4116 .P5 MRR Alc.

ENGLISH LANGUAGE--DICTIONARIES--TIBETAN.
Zla-ba-Bsam-'grub, Kazi, An
English-Tibetan dictionary,
Calcutta, The University, 1919. xiv,
989 p.   24-1029
    PL3637 .Z6 MRR Alc.

ENGLISH LANGUAGE--DICTIONARIES--TONGA.
Churchward, Clerk Maxwell. Tongan
dictionary; London, Oxford
University Press, 1959. xiv, 836 p.
499.4 59-3277
    PL6531 .C48 MRR Alc.

ENGLISH LANGUAGE--DICTIONARIES--TURKISH.
İz, Fahir. An English-Turkish
dictionary, Oxford, Clarendon Press,
1952. x, 510 p. 494.3532 52-14083

    PL137 .I9 MRR Alc.

Redhouse yeni Türkçe-İngilizce
sozluk. [1. baski.] İstanbul,
Redhouse Yayınevi, 1968.] xxxii, 1292
p. 494/.35/32 ne 68-3786
    PL191 .R55 1968 MRR Alc.

ENGLISH LANGUAGE--DICTIONARIES--
VIETNAMESE.
Le-ba-Khanh. Standard pronouncing
Vietnamese-English and English-
Vietnamese dictionary. [New York, F.
Ungar Pub. Co.,] 1955] 2 v. in 1.
495.9232 55-12581
    PL4376 .L48 MRR Alc.

ENGLISH LANGUAGE--DICTIONARIES--WELSH.
Evans, Harold Meurig. Y geiriadur
mawr, the complete Welsh-English,
English-Welsh dictionary [1st ed.]
Llandybie, Llyfrau'r Dryw [1958]
470, 342 p. 491.6632 59-44325
    PB2191 .E685 MRR Alc.

ENGLISH LANGUAGE--DICTIONARIES--YIDDISH.
Harkavy, Alexander, [English-
yidisher werterbuch (romanized form)]
22d ed. New York, Hebrew publishing
co. [19--] 1 p. l., vii [1], 759 p.;
v p., 1 l., [vii]-xv, [1], 364 p.
46-39199
    PJ5117 .H5 1940z MRR Alc.

Kogos, Fred. A dictionary of Yiddish
slang & idioms. [1st ed.] New York,
Citadel Press [1968, c1967] 167 p.
67-18084
    PJ5117 .K58 MRR Alc.

Weinreich, Uriel. Modern English-
Yiddish, Yiddish-English dictionary.
New York, Yivo Institute for Jewish
Research [1968. xliii, 789, [1], 16
p. 492.49/3/2 67-23848
    PJ5117 .W4 MRR Alc.

ENGLISH LANGUAGE--DICTIONARIES,
SUPPLEMENTARY.
Wall, C. Edward. Words and phrases
index; Ann Arbor, Mich., Pierian
Press, 1969- v. [17.95 (v. 1)]
016.423 68-58894
    PE1689 .W3 MRR Alc.

ENGLISH LANGUAGE--EPONYMS.
Severn, William. People words, New
York, Washburn [1966] 184 p.
422.09 66-8757
    PE1574 .S4 MRR Alc.

ENGLISH LANGUAGE--EPONYMS--DICTIONARIES.
Hendrickson, Robert, Human words;
[1st ed.] Philadelphia, Chilton Book
Co. [1972] 342 p. [$9.95] 423/.1
72-6492
    PE1596 .H4 MRR Alc.

ENGLISH LANGUAGE--ETYMOLOGY.
Bridges, Ronald. The Bible word
book, New York, Nelson [1960] vii,
422 p. 220.52 60-6749
    BS186 .B7 MRR Alc.

Elliott, Melvin E. The language of
the King James Bible; [1st ed.]
Garden City, N.Y., Doubleday, 1967.
x, 227 p. 220.52/03 67-11169
    BS186 .E4 MRR Alc.

Ernst, Margaret (Samuels) More about
words. [1st ed.] New York, Knopf,
1951. vi, 233, xii p. 422 51-2800

    PE1574 .E72 MRR Alc.

Funk, Charles Earle, Horsefeathers,
and other curious words, New York,
Harper [1958] 240 p. 422 58-8870

    PE1574 .F76 MRR Alc.

Funk, Charles Earle, Thereby hangs a
tale; New York, Harper [1950] xii,
303 p. 422 50-6750
    PE1574 .F78 MRR Alc.

Garrison, Webb B. What's in a word?
New York, Abingdon Press [1965] 351
p. 422 65-20368
    PE1574 .G29 MRR Alc.

Gause, John Taylor. The complete
word hunter. New York, Crowell
[1965] viii, 497 p. 423 55-11106

    PE1449 .G345 MRR Alc.

Mathews, Mitford McLeod. American
words. [1st ed.] Cleveland, World
Pub. Co. [1959] 246 p. 427.97 59-
11541
    PE2831 .M3 MRR Alc.

Origin of things familiar;
Cincinnati, O., United book
corporation [c1934] 4 p. l., 280 p.
031 35-2154
    AG5 .07 MRR Alc.

Pei, Mario Andrew, Words in sheep's
clothing [1st ed.] New York,
Hawthorn Books [1969] 248 p. [6.95]
422 69-20348
    PE1585 .P4 1969 MRR Alc.

Radford, Edwin, To coin a phrase;
Revised ed.; London, Hutchinson,
1973. 128 p. [£1.95] 422/.03 73-
162277
    PE1580 .R3 1973b MRR Alc.

Serjeantson, Mary Sidney, A history
of foreign words in English· New
York, Barnes & Noble [1961] ix, 354
p. 422.4 61-3807
    PE1582.A3 S4 1961 MRR Alc.

Severn, William, Place words New
York, Washburn [1969] 148 p. [3.95]
422.4 75-82646
    PE1574 .S42 MRR Alc.

Shipley, Joseph Twadell, Dictionary
of early English. New York,
Philosophical Library [1955] xiii,
753 p. 427 55-4892
    PE1667 .S48 MRR Alc.

ENGLISH LANGUAGE--ETYMOLOGY--
DICTIONARIES.
Brown, Roland Wilbur. Composition of
scientific words; [Rev. ed.
Washington, 1956] 882 p.   422.03
56-56233
   PE1580 .B7 1956 MRR Alc.

Fennell, Charles Augustus Maude, ed.
The Stanford dictionary of anglicised
words and phrases; Cambridge [Eng.],
University press, 1892. xv, [1], 826
p.   03-7772
   PE1580 .F3 MRR Alc.

Hargrave, Basil. Origins and
meanings of popular phrases and
names. [Rev. ed.] London, T. W.
Laurie [1948] vi, 350 p.   423 49-
1451
   AG5 .H18 1948 MRR Ref Desk.

Holt, Alfred Hubbard, Phrase
origins; New York, Thomas Y. Crowell
company [c1936] vii, [1], 328 p.
428.3 422 36-10206
   PE1580 .H55 1936 MRR Alc.

Klein, Ernest. A comprehensive
etymological dictionary of the
English language. Amsterdam, New
York [etc.] Elsevier, 1966- v.
[f190.- (v. 1)]   422/.03 65-13229
   PE1580 .K47 MRR Alc.

Morris, William, Dictionary of word
and phrase origins, [1st ed.] New
York, Harper & Row [1962- v.
422.03 61-10842
   PE1580 .M6 MRR Alc.

Onions, Charles Talbut, ed. The
Oxford dictionary of English
etymology; Oxford, Clarendon P.,
1966. xvi, 1025 p. [70/-] 422.03
66-71621
   PE1580 .O5 MRR Ref Desk.

The Oxford English dictionary;
Oxford, At the Clarendon press, 1933.
13 v. 423 a 33-3399
   PE1625 .N53 1933 MRR Alc.

Palmer, Abram Smythe. Folk-
etymology; New York, Greenwood Press
[1969] xxviii, 664 p.   427.09 68-
57636
   PE1584 .P3 1969b MRR Alc.

Partridge, Eric, Name into word;
[2d ed., rev. and enl.] New York,
Macmillan, 1950. xv, 648 p.   422
53-31511
   PE1583 .P35 1950a MRR Alc.

Partridge, Eric, Origins: a short
etymological dictionary of modern
English. 4th ed. (with numerous
revisions and some substantial
additions). London, Routledge & K.
Paul, 1966. xix, 972 p. [90/-]
422.03 66-72884
   PE1580 .P3 1966 MRR Ref Desk.

Shipley, Joseph Twadell, Dictionary
of word origins, 2d ed. New York,
Greenwood Press [1969, c1945] x, 430
p.   422 68-14079
   PE1580 .S45 1969 MRR Alc.

Skeat, Walter William, An
etymological dictionary of the
English language, New ed., rev. and
enl. ... Oxford, The Clarendon
press, 1910. xliv, 780 p.   11-35447

   PE1580 .S5 1910 MRR Alc.

Skinner, Henry Alan. The origin of
medical terms. 2d ed. Baltimore,
Williams & Wilkins, 1961. x, 438 p.
610.14 61-10562
   R123 .S54 1961 MRR Alc.

Weekley, Ernest, An etymological
dictionary of modern English. New
York, Dover Publications [1967] 2 v.
(xx p., 1660 columns) 422/.03 67-
26968
   PE1580 .W5 1967 MRR Alc.

Whiting, Bartlett Jere, Proverbs,
sentences, and proverbial phrases;
Cambridge, Mass., Belknap Press of
Harvard University Press, 1968. li,
733 p. [$25.00]   808.88/2 67-22874

   PN6083 .W45 MRR Alc.

ENGLISH LANGUAGE--ETYMOLOGY--INDEXES.
Wall, C. Edward. Words and phrases
index; Ann Arbor, Mich., Pierian
Press, 1969- v.   [17.95 (v. 1)]
016.423 68-58894
   PE1689 .W3 MRR Alc.

ENGLISH LANGUAGE--ETYMOLOGY--NAMES.
Ekwall, Eilert, The concise Oxford
dictionary of English place-names.
4th ed. Oxford, Clarendon Press,
1960. L, 546 p.   914.2 60-2031
   DA645 .E38 1960 MRR Alc.

ENGLISH LANGUAGE--FIGURES OF SPEECH
   see Figures of speech

ENGLISH LANGUAGE--FOREIGN ELEMENTS.
Serjeantson, Mary Sidney, A history
of foreign words in English. New
York, Barnes & Noble [1961] ix, 354
p. 422.4 61-3807
   PE1582.A3 S4 1961 MRR Alc.

ENGLISH LANGUAGE--FOREIGN WORDS AND
PHRASES.
Schmidt, Jacob Edward, 1000 elegant
phrases, Springfield, Ill., C. C.
Thomas [1965] x, 223 p.   423.1 65-
12384
   PE1670 .S3 MRR Alc.

Serjeantson, Mary Sidney, A history
of foreign words in English. New
York, Barnes & Noble [1961] ix, 354
p. 422.4 61-3807
   PE1582.A3 S4 1961 MRR Alc.

ENGLISH LANGUAGE--FOREIGN WORDS AND
PHRASES--DICTIONARIES.
Bliss, Alan Joseph. A dictionary of
foreign words and phrases in current
English London, Routledge & K. Paul,
1966. ix, 389 p. [40/-] 422.4 66-
75485
   PE1670 .B55 MRR Ref Desk.

Carroll, David, The dictionary of
foreign terms in the English
language. New York, Hawthorn Books
[1973] ix, 212 p. [$9.95] 422/.4
70-39281
   PE1670 .C3 1973 MRR Alc.

Fennell, Charles Augustus Maude, ed.
The Stanford dictionary of anglicised
words and phrases; Cambridge [Eng.],
University press, 1892. xv, [1], 826
p.   03-7772
   PE1580 .F3 MRR Alc.

Guinagh, Kevin, comp. Dictionary of
foreign phrases and abbreviations.
[2d ed.] New York, H. W. Wilson Co.,
1972. xiv, 352 p.   418 72-149383
   PE1670 .G8 1972 MRR Ref Desk.

Newmark, Maxim. Dictionary of
foreign words. Paterson, N.J.,
Littlefield, Adams, 1962. 245 p.
65-6424
   PE1670 .N4 1962 MRR Ref Desk.

Newmark, Maxim. Dictionary of
foreign words and phrases; New York,
Greenwood Press [1969] 245 p.   413
70-88915
   PE1582.A3 N4 1969 MRR alc.

ENGLISH LANGUAGE--FOREIGN WORDS AND
PHRASES--INDIC.
Yule, Henry, Sir, Hobson-Jobson: a
glossary of colloquial Anglo-Indian
words and phrases, New ed. London,
Routledge & K. Paul, 1968. xlviii,
1021 p. [£6/6/-] 422/.4/91 68-
96009
   PE3501 .Y78 1968 MRR Alc.

ENGLISH LANGUAGE--FOREIGN WORDS AND
PHRASES--MAORI.
Morris, Edward Ellis, Austral
English; London, Macmillan and co.,
limited; New York, The Macmillan
company, 1898. 3 p. l., [ix]-xxiv,
525, [1] p.   01-5504
   PE3601 .M8 MRR Alc.

ENGLISH LANGUAGE--FOREIGN WORDS AND
PHRASES--SPANISH.
Bentley, Harold Woodmansee, A
dictionary of Spanish terms in
English, New York, Octagon Books,
1973 [c1932] x, 243 p.   422/.4/61
73-11936
   PE2962 .B4 1973 MRR Alc.

ENGLISH LANGUAGE--FOREIGN WORDS AND
PHRASES--YIDDISH.
Rosten, Leo Calvin, The joys of
Yiddish; [1st ed.] New York, McGraw-
Hill [1968] xxxix, 533 p.
492.49/3/2 68-29915
   PN6231.J5 R67 MRR Alc.

ENGLISH LANGUAGE--GLOSSARIES,
VOCABULARIES, ETC.
Bickerton, Anthea. American English,
English American: a two-way glossary
Bristol, The Abson Press [1971] [48]
p. [£0.25] 427.9/73 70-576350
   PE2835 .B5 MRR Alc.

A Dictionary of contemporary and
colloquial usage. [1st ed.]
Chicago, English-Language Institute
of America [1972] 32 p.   427.09 77-
38007
   PE3721 .D5 MRR Alc.

Dossor, Howard F. Terms of thought;
Melbourne, Hawthorn Press, 1970. 61
p. [$1.20] 423 71-568187
   PE1680 .D6 MRR Alc.

Elliott, Iris E. Instant word
finder, Philadelphia, Lithographed
by Braceland Bros. [1959] 352 p.
423 59-15222
   PE1680 .E55 MRR Alc.

Finkenstaedt, Thomas, A
chronological English dictionary.
Heidelberg, C. Winter, 1970. xvi,
1395 p. [DM92.00] 422 79-575516
   PE1680 .F5 MRR Alc.

Lewis, Norman, The comprehensive
word guide. [1st ed.] Garden City,
N.Y., Doubleday [1958] xxiii, 912 p.
423 58-11514
   PE1591 .L4 MRR Alc.

Nares, Robert, A glossary of words,
phrases, names, and allusions in the
works of English authors New ed.,
Detroit, Republished by Gale Research
Co., 1966. ix, 981 p.   423.1 66-
25635
   PE1667 .N32 MRR Alc.

O'Connor, Johnson, English
vocabulary builder. Boston, Human
Engineering Laboratory, 1948-51. 2
v.   423 48-11371
   PE1691 .O32 MRR Alc.

Ogden, Charles Kay, The general
Basic English dictionary. New York,
W. W. Norton & company, inc. [1942]
x, 441 p.   428.25 423 42-36402
   PE1073.5 .O372 1942 MRR Alc.

Opdycke, John Baker, Don't say it!
New York, London, Funk & Wagnalls
company [1943] vii, 850 p.   428.3
43-3547
   PE1680 .O6 1943 MRR Ref Desk.

Rodale, Jerome Irving, ed. The word
finder; Allentown, Rodale Press,
1947. xxxii, 1317 p.   423 47-11408

   PE1680 .R63 1947 MRR Alc.

Sheffield, Eng. Free Public Libraries
and Museum. "Isms: a dictionary of
words ending in -ism, -ology, and -
phobia, 2nd ed. Sheffield,
Corporation of Sheffield; Wakefield,
EP Publishing Ltd, 1972. 100 p.
[£1.50] 423/.1 73-159938
   PE1680 .S37 1972b MRR Ref Desk.

Young, Kenn W. Naz's underground
dictionary; Vancouver, Wash. [Naz
Enterprises, 1973] vi, 67 p.
[$2.00] 427/.9/73 74-156957
   PE3727.N3 Y6 MRR Alc.

ENGLISH LANGUAGE--GRAMMAR--1870-
Walsh, James Martyn, Plain English
handbook; Rev.ed. Wichita, Kan.,
McCormick-Mathers Pub. Co. [1959]
159 p.   425 59-2547
   PE1111 .W3546 1959 MRR Alc.

ENGLISH LANGUAGE--GRAMMAR--1950-
Crews, Frederick C. The Random House
handbook. [1st ed.] New York, Random
House [1974] xviii, 409 p. [$6.95]
808/.042 73-13640
   PE1408 .C715 MRR Ref Desk.

Hook, Julius Nicholas, Guide to good
writing; New York, Ronald Press Co.
[1962] 515 p.   808 61-15346
   PE1408 .H678 MRR Alc.

Hook, Julius Nicholas, Modern
American grammar and usage New York,
Ronald Press Co. [1956] 475 p.   425
56-6265
   PE1111 .H638 MRR Alc.

Hutchinson, Lois Irene. Standard
handbook for secretaries 8th ed.
[New York] McGraw-Hill, 1969. x, 638
p.   650 69-19201
   HF5547 .H77 1969 MRR Ref Desk.

Ives, Sumner. A new handbook for
writers. [1st ed.] New York, Knopf,
1960. 372 p.   808 60-8283
   PE1111 .I9 MRR Alc.

Jones, Rhodri. English language
reference book. London, Blackie,
1970. xi, 243 p. [13/9] 428/.003
70-566676
   PE1460 .J6 MRR Alc.

Lewis, Norman, Better English. New
York, Crowell [1956] 356 p.   425
56-11370
   PE1111 .L455 MRR Alc.

Marckwardt, Albert Henry, Scribner
handbook of English [4th ed.] New
York, Scribner [1967] xii, 554 p.
808.04/2 67-18132
   PE1408 .M384 1967 MRR Alc.

Partridge, Eric, Usage and abusage:
a guide to good English. 6th ed.
(revised and slightly englarged).
London, H. Hamilton, 1965. 392 p.
[21/-] 423.1 66-70200
   PE1460 .P17 1965a MRR Ref Desk.

Perrin, Porter Gale, Writer's guide
and index to English 5th ed., rev.
Glenview, Ill., Scott, Foresman
[1972] 765 p.   808/.042 70-184064

   PE1411 .P4 1972 MRR alc.

ENGLISH LANGUAGE--GRAMMAR--1950- (Cont.)
Quirk, Randolph. A concise grammar
of contemporary English New York,
Harcourt Brace Jovanovich [c1973]
xi, 484 p. [$8.95] 425 73-8062
PE1112 .Q5 1973 MRR Alc.

Shaw, Harry, McGraw-Hill handbook of
English 2d ed. New York, McGraw-
Hill [1960] 500 p. 808 59-10723
PE1111 .S413 1960 MRR Ref Desk.

Shaw, Harry, McGraw-Hill handbook of
English. 3d ed. St. Louis, McGraw-
Hill [1969] 598 p. 808.04/2 69-
19306
PE1112 .S5 1969 MRR Ref Desk.

Taintor, Sarah Augusta. The
secretary's handbook; 9th ed. fully
rev. [New York] Macmillan [1969]
xi, 530 p. 651.7/402 69-10466
HF5547 .T25 1969 MRR Alc.

Warriner, John E. English grammar
and composition; New York, Harcourt,
Brace [1957] 692 p. 808 57-1729
PE1111 .W36857 MRR Ref Desk.

ENGLISH LANGUAGE--GRAMMAR--BIBLIOGRAPHY.
Alston, R. C. English grammars
written in English and English
grammars written in Latin by native
speakers Leeds [Eng.] Printed for
the author by E. J. Arnold [1965]
xxvii, 118 p. 66-38400
Z2015.A1 A4 vol. 1 MRR Alc.

ENGLISH LANGUAGE--GRAMMAR--DICTIONARIES.
Gerson, Stanley. A glossary of
grammatical terms; [St. Lucia, Q.]
University of Queensland Press [1969]
73 p. 415/.03 78-497971
P29 .G4 MRR Alc.

Lazarus, Arnold Leslie. Modern
English; New York, Grosset & Dunlap
[1971] 462 p. [$10.00] 423 78-
86706
PE31 .L3 MRR Ref Desk.

ENGLISH LANGUAGE--HISTORY.
Nist, John A. A structural history
of English New York, St. Martin's
Press [1966] xvii, 426 p. 420.09
66-12685
PE1075 .N5 MRR Alc.

Pei, Mario Andrew, The story of the
English language, [New ed.] London,
Allen & Unwin, 1968. viii, 430 p.
[45/-] 420.9 73-381547
PE1075 .P4 1968 MRR Alc.

ENGLISH LANGUAGE--HOMONYMS--
DICTIONARIES.
Franklyn, Julian. Which witch?
London, H. Hamilton, 1966. xxvi, 198
p. [21/-] 423.1 66-77648
PE1595 .F7 1966a MRR Alc.

Whitford, Harold Crandall, A
dictionary of American homophones and
homographs, New York, Teachers
College Press, 1966. 83 p. 423.1
66-25461
PE2833 .W4 MRR Alc.

ENGLISH LANGUAGE--IDIOMS, CORRECTIONS,
ERRORS.
Bernstein, Theodore Menline, Watch
your language; Great Neck, N.Y.,
Channel Press [1958] 276 p. 428.3
58-12309
PE1460 .B463 MRR Alc.

Collins, Vere Henry. A book of
English idioms, London, New York,
Longmans, Green [1956] xiii, 258 p.
423.1 56-1804
PE1460 .C59 1956 MRR Alc.

Copperud, Roy H., A dictionary of
usage and style; [1st ed.] New
York, Hawthorn Books [1964] 452 p.
428 64-19207
PE1460 .C66 MRR Alc.

Engeroff, Karl Wilhelm, An English-
German Dictionary of idioms. (2.,
erw. Aufl.) München, Hueber [1967].
313 p. [DM19.80] 433.1 68-74488

PF3640 .E48 1967 MRR Alc.

Evans, Bergen, Comfortable words.
New York, Random House [1962] 379 p.
422.03 62-10775
PE1460 .E9 MRR Alc.

Flesch, Rudolf Franz, The ABC of
style; [1st ed.] New York, Harper &
Row [1964] x, 303 p. 808 64-25139

PE1421 .F55 MRR Alc.

Fowler, Henry Watson, A dictionary
of modern English usage, 2d ed.,
rev. Oxford, Clarendon Press, 1965.
xx, 725 p. 423 65-2840
PE1628 .F65 1965 MRR Ref Desk.

Freeman, William, A concise
dictionary of English idioms.
London, English Universities Press
[1951] 300 p. 423.1 51-2718
PE1460 .F66 1951 MRR Alc.

Henderson, Bernard Lionel Kinghorn,
A dictionary of English idioms.
London, J. Blackwood [1947-50?] 2 v.
423.1 51-1250
PE1460 .H452 MRR Alc.

Jones, Rhodri. English language
reference book. London, Blackie,
1970. xi, 243 p. [13/9] 428/.003
70-566676
PE1460 .J6 MRR Alc.

Lewis, Norman, Better English. New
York, Crowell [1956] 356 p. 425
56-13170
PE1111 .L455 MRR Alc.

Partridge, Eric, Usage and abusage:
a guide to good English. 6th ed.
(revised and slightly enlarged)
London, H. Hamilton, 1965. 392 p.
[21/-] 423.1 66-70200
PE1460 .P17 1965a MRR Ref Desk.

Schmidt, Jacob Edward, English
idioms and Americanisms for foreign
students, professionals, physicians,
Springfield, Ill., C. C. Thomas
[1972] vi, 534 p. 428/.1 77-
177903
PE1128 .S34 MRR Alc.

Schur, Norman W. British self-
taught: with comments in American,
New York, Macmillan [1973] xxxi, 438
p. [$6.95] 423/.1 70-127941
PE1460 .S45 MRR Alc.

Taylor, Ronald Jack, A German-
English dictionary of idioms;
München, M. Hueber, 1960. 597 p.
a 61-2669
PF3460 .T3 MRR Alc.

Wood, Frederick Thomas, English
colloquial idioms, London,
Macmillan, 1969. [5], 306 p. [35/-]
423.1 69-17406
PE1460 .W662 1969 MRR Alc.

Wood, Frederick Thomas, English
prepositional idioms, London,
Melbourne [etc.] Macmillan; New York,
St. Martin's P., 1967. vii, 562 p.
[30/-] 425 67-10579
PE1335 .W6 1967 MRR Alc.

ENGLISH LANGUAGE--LEXICOGRAPHY.
Hulbert, James Root, Dictionaries,
British and American. [London] A.
Deutsch [1955] 107 p. 423.09 55-
3172
PE1611 .H8 MRR Alc.

Starnes, De Witt Talmage, The
English dictionary from Cawdrey to
Johnson, 1604-1755, Chapel Hill, The
University of North Carolina press,
1946. x p., 1 l., 299 p. 423 46-
5776
PE1611 .S68 MRR Alc.

ENGLISH LANGUAGE--OBSOLETE WORDS.
Halliwell-Phillipps, James Orchard,
A dictionary of archaic and
provincial words, obsolete phrases,
proverbs, and ancient customs, from
the XIV century: 6th ed. London, G.
Routledge and sons, limited; New
York, E. P. Dutton & co., 1904.
xxxvi, 960 p. 05-30078
PE1667 .H3 1904 MRR Alc.

Nares, Robert, A glossary of words,
phrases, names, and allusions in the
works of English authors New ed.,
Detroit, Republished by Gale Research
Co., 1966. ix, 981 p. 423.1 66-
25635
PE1667 .N32 MRR Alc.

Shipley, Joseph Twadell, Dictionary
of early English. New York,
Philosophical Library [1955] xiii,
753 p. 427 55-4892
PE1667 .S48 MRR Alc.

Skeat, Walter William, A glossary of
Tudor and Stuart words, Oxford, The
Clarendon press, 1914. xviii, p., 1
l., 461, [1] p. 14-7721
PE1667 .S5 MRR Alc.

Wright, Thomas, Dictionary of
obsolete and provincial English,
Detroit, Gale Research Co., 1967. 2
v. (vii, 1039 p.) 427 67-14062
PE1667 .W7 1967 MRR Alc.

ENGLISH LANGUAGE--ORTHOGRAPHY AND
SPELLING.
Collins, Frederick Howard, Authors'
and printers' dictionary: 10th ed.,
rev. London, New York, Oxford
University Press, 1956. xiv, 442 p.
655.25 56-58185
Z254 .C76 1956 MRR Alc.

Lewis, Norman, Dictionary of correct
spelling, [1st ed. New York] Harper
& Row [1962] xi, 206 p. 428.1 62-
9901
PE1143 .L45 MRR Alc.

Opdycke, John Baker, Don't say it:
New York, London, Funk & Wagnalls
company [1943] vii, 850 p. 428.3
43-3547
PE1680 .O6 1943 MRR Ref Desk.

ENGLISH LANGUAGE--PHONETICS.
Herman, Lewis Helmar, Foreign
dialects; New York, Theatre Arts
Books [1958? c1943] 415 p. 792.028
58-10332
PN2071.F6 H4 1958 MRR Alc.

West, Robert William, Phonetics;
Rev. ed. New York, Harper [1960]
433 p. 421.5 60-7010
PE1135 .W4 1960 MRR Alc.

ENGLISH LANGUAGE--PREPOSITIONS.
Wood, Frederick Thomas, English
prepositional idioms, London,
Melbourne [etc.] Macmillan; New York,
St. Martin's P., 1967. vii, 562 p.
[30/-] 425 67-10579
PE1335 .W6 1967 MRR Alc.

ENGLISH LANGUAGE--PRONUNCIATION.
Bender, James Frederick, NBC
handbook of pronunciation. 3d ed.
rev. New York, Crowell [1964] xii,
418 p. 421.5 63-9205
PE1137 .B573 1964 MRR Alc.

Bronstein, Arthur J. The
pronunciation of American English;
New York, Appleton-Century-Crofts
[1960] 320 p. 421.5 60-6750
PE1137 .B77 MRR Alc.

Colby, Frank O., ed. The American
pronouncing dictionary of troublesome
words. New York, Crowell [1950] 399
p. 421.5 50-10743
PE1137 .C56 MRR Alc.

Greet, William Cabell, World words,
2d ed., rev. and enl. New York,
Columbia Univ. Press, 1948. liii,
608 p. 411.5 48-6140
PE1660 .G7 1948 MRR Alc.

Mackey, Mary Stuart. The
pronunciation of 10,000 proper names,
New ed., New York, Dodd, Mead and
company, 1922. xiii, 329 p. 22-
22423
PE1137 .M5 1922 MRR Alc.

Noory, Samuel, Dictionary of
pronunciation. 2d ed. South
Brunswick, A. S. Barnes [1971]
xliii, 525 p. [$7.95] 428/.1 76-
151120
PE1137 .N65 1971 MRR Alc.

Opdycke, John Baker, Don't say it:
New York, London, Funk & Wagnalls
company [1943] vii, 850 p. 428.3
43-3547
PE1680 .O6 1943 MRR Ref Desk.

Vizetelly, Francis Horace, A desk-
book of twenty-five thousand words
frequently mispronounced, 4th ed.
New York, London, Funk & Wagnalls
company [c1929] xxxvi, 906 p. 29-
23343
PE1137 .V5 1929 MRR Alc.

ENGLISH LANGUAGE--PRONUNCIATION BY
FOREIGNERS.
Herman, Lewis Helmar, Foreign
dialects; New York, Theatre Arts
Books [1958? c1943] 415 p. 792.028
58-10332
PN2071.F6 H4 1958 MRR Alc.

ENGLISH LANGUAGE--PROVINCIALISMS.
Halliwell-Phillipps, James Orchard,
A dictionary of archaic and
provincial words, obsolete phrases,
proverbs, and ancient customs, from
the XIV century: 6th ed. London, G.
Routledge and sons, limited; New
York, E. P. Dutton & co., 1904.
xxxvi, 960 p. 05-30078
PE1667 .H3 1904 MRR Alc.

Palmer, Abram Smythe. Folk-
etymology; New York, Greenwood Press
[1969] xxviii, 664 p. 427.09 68-
57636
PE1584 .P3 1969b MRR Alc.

Wright, Thomas, Dictionary of
obsolete and provincial English,
Detroit, Gale Research Co., 1967. 2
v. (vii, 1039 p.) 427 67-14062
PE1667 .W7 1967 MRR Alc.

ENGLISH LANGUAGE--PROVINCIALISMS--
AUSTRALASIA.
Morris, Edward Ellis, Austral
English; London, Macmillan and co.,
limited; New York, The Macmillan
company, 1898. 3 p. l., [ix]-xxiv,
525, [1] p. 01-5504
PE3601 .M8 MRR Alc.

ENGLISH LANGUAGE--PROVINCIALISMS--
CANADA.
A Dictionary of Canadianisms on
historical principles; Toronto, W,
J. Gage, ltd., 1967. xxiii, 926, [1]
p. 427.9/71 78-5962
PE3243 .D5 MRR Alc.

ENGLISH LANGUAGE--PROVINCIALISMS--INDIA.
Yule, Henry, Sir, Hobson-Jobson: a
glossary of colloquial Anglo-Indian
words and phrases, New ed. London,
Routledge & K. Paul, 1968. xlviii,
1021 p. [£6/6/-] 422/.4/81 68-
96009
PE3501 .Y78 1968 MRR Alc.

ENGLISH LANGUAGE--PROVINCIALISMS--WEST.
Adams, Ramon Frederick, Western
words; New ed., rev. and enl.
Norman, University of Oklahoma Press
[1968] xviii, 355 p. 427.9/78 68-
31369
PE2970.W4 A3 1968 MRR Alc.

ENGLISH LANGUAGE--REVERSE INDEXES.
Gale Research Company. Reverse
acronyms and initialisms dictionary;
1st ed. Detroit, Gale Research Co.
[1972] x, 485 p. 423.1 71-165486

PE1693 .G3 1972 MRR Ref Desk.

Rybicki, Stephen. Abbreviations;
1st ed. Ann Arbor, Mich., Pieran
Press, 1971. 334 p. 423/.1 74-
143239
PE1693 .R94 MRR Ref Desk.

ENGLISH LANGUAGE--RHETORIC.
Copperud, Roy H., A dictionary of
usage and style; [1st ed.] New
York, Hawthorn Books [1964] 452 p.
428 64-19207
PE1460 .C66 MRR Alc.

Crews, Frederick C. The Random House
handbook [1st ed.] New York, Random
House [1974] xviii, 409 p. [$6.95]
808/.042 73-13640
PE1408 .C715 MRR Ref Desk.

Fowler, Henry Watson, A dictionary
of modern English usage, 2d ed.,
rev. Oxford, Clarendon Press, 1965.
xx, 725 p. 423 65-2840
PE1628 .F65 1965 MRR Ref Desk.

Graves, Harold Frank, Report writing
4th ed. Englewood Cliffs, N.J.,
Prentice-Hall [1965] viii, 286 p.
808.066 65-11494
PE1478 .G7 MRR Alc.

Hook, Julius Nicholas, Guide to good
writing; New York, Ronald Press Co.
[1962] 515 p. 808 61-15346
PE1408 .H678 MRR Alc.

Hutchinson, Lois Irene. Standard
handbook for secretaries 8th ed.
[New York] McGraw-Hill, 1969. x, 638
p. 650 69-19201
HF5547 .H77 1969 MRR Ref Desk.

Ives, Sumner. A new handbook for
writers. [1st ed.] New York, Knopf,
1960. 372 p. 808 60-8283
PE1111 .I9 MRR Alc.

Lanham, Richard A. A handlist of
rhetorical terms; Berkeley,
University of California Press, 1968.
148 p. [6.50] 423.1 68-31636
PE1445.A2 L3 MRR Alc.

Leggett, Glenn H., Prentice-Hall
handbook for writers 5th ed.
Englewood Cliffs, N.J., Prentice-Hall
[1970] xxiv, 484 p. [4.95] 428.2
72-102045
PE1408 .L38 1970 MRR Alc.

Marckwardt, Albert Henry, Scribner
handbook of English [4th ed.] New
York, Scribner [1967] xii, 554 p.
808.04/2 67-18132
PE1408 .M384 1967 MRR Alc.

Nicholson, Margaret. A dictionary of
American-English usage, New York,
Oxford University Press, 1957. xii,
671 p. 423 57-5560
PE2835 .N5 MRR Ref Desk.

Perrin, Porter Gale, Writer's guide
and index to English 5th ed., rev.
Glenview, Ill. Scott, Foresman
[1972] 765 p. 808/.042 70-184064

PE1411 .P4 1972 MRR Alc.

Rodale, Jerome Irving, ed. The word
finder; Allentown, Rodale Press,
1947. xxxii, 1317 p. 423 47-11408
PE1680 .R63 1947 MRR Alc.

Schutte, William M. Communication in
business and industry New York,
Holt, Rinehart and Winston [1960]
393 p. 651.7 60-6403
PE1408 .S34 MRR Alc.

Skillin, Marjorie E. Words into
type. 3d ed., completely rev.
Englewood Cliffs, N.J., Prentice-Hall
[1974] xx, 585 p. 808/.02 73-
21726
PN160 .S52 1974 MRR Ref Desk.

Whitford, Robert Calvin, Concise
dictionary of American grammar and
usage, New York, Philosophical
Library [c1955] viii, 168 p. 423
54-13498
PE1680 .W49 MRR Alc.

ENGLISH LANGUAGE--RHETORIC--
BIBLIOGRAPHY.
Alston, R. C. Rhetoric, style,
elecution, prosody, rhyme,
pronunciation, spelling reform.
Bradford, Printed for the author by
Ernest Cummins [1969] 202 p. mrr01-
75
Z2015.A1 A4 vol. 6 MRR Alc.

ENGLISH LANGUAGE--RIME--DICTIONARIES.
Holofcener, Lawrence. A practical
dictionary of rhymes, New York,
Crown Publishers [1960] 211 p.
426.03 59-14023
PE1519 .H6 MRR Alc.

Johnson Burges, New rhyming
dictionary and poets' handbook. Rev.
ed. New York, Harper [1957] x, 464
p. 426.603 808.1* 57-9585
PE1519 .J6 1957 MRR Alc.

National High School Poetry
Association. Rhyming dictionary,
Los Angeles [c1949] 224 p. 426.603
808.1* 55-23773
PE1519 .N3 MRR Alc.

Redfield, Bessie Gordon, Aid to
rhyme, 3d ed., rev. and enl. New
York, G. P. Putnam's sons, 1938.
viii, 625 p. 426.603 38-28229
PE1519 .R4 1938 MRR Alc.

Reed, Langford, The writer's rhyming
dictionary. Boston, The Writer
[1961] xii, 244 p. 426.03 61-
16086
PE1519 .R46 MRR Alc.

Stillman, Frances. The poet's manual
and rhyming dictionary. London,
Thames & Hudson [1966] xviv, 363 p.
[42/-] 66-69064
PE1505 .S8 1966 MRR Alc.

Whitfield, Jane Shaw. The improved
rhyming dictionary; New York,
Crowell [1951] xx, 283 p. 426.603
52-125
PE1519 .W49 MRR Alc.

ENGLISH LANGUAGE--SEMANTICS.
Evans, Bergen, Comfortable words.
New York, Random House [1962] 379 p.
422.03 62-10775
PE1460 .E9 MRR Alc.

Funk, Charles Earle, Horsefeathers,
and other curious words, New York,
Harper [1958] 240 p. 422 58-8870

PE1574 .F76 MRR Alc.

Pei, Mario Andrew, Double-speak in
America, New York, Hawthorn Books
[1973] 216 p. [$6.95] 422 78-
39894
PE1585 .P38 MRR Alc.

Pei, Mario Andrew, Words in sheep's
clothing [1st ed.] New York,
Hawthorn Books [1969] 248 p. [6.95]
422 69-20348
PE1585 .P4 1969 MRR Alc.

ENGLISH LANGUAGE--SLANG.
Berrey, Lester V., The American
thesaurus of slang; 2d ed. New
York, Crowell [1953] xxxv, 1272 p.
427.09 427.9* 52-10837
PE3729.A5 B4 1953 MRR Alc.

Clapin, Sylva, A new dictionary of
Americanisms; New York, L. Weiss &
co. [1902?] xii p., 2 l., 581 p.
03-17603
PE2835 .C6 MRR Alc.

Partridge, Eric, Slang to-day and
yesterday, 2d ed., carefully rev.;
London, G. Routledge & sons, ltd.;
1935. ix, 476 p. 427.09 36-6938
PE3711 .P3 1935 MRR Alc.

ENGLISH LANGUAGE--SLANG--DICTIONARIES.
Current slang; Vermillion,
University of South Dakota, Dept. of
English, 1969. xvi, 103 p. [1.25]
427.09 78-13579
PE3729.U5 C8 MRR Alc.

Dictionary of American underworld
lingo, New York, Twayne Publishers
[1950] 327 p. 427.9 50-58288
PE3726 .D5 MRR Alc.

A Dictionary of contemporary and
colloquial usage. [1st ed.]
Chicago, English-Language Institute
of America [1972] 32 p. 427.09 77-
38007
PE3721 .D5 MRR Alc.

Farmer, John Stephen, Dictionary of
slang & its analogues, past &
present; Rev. ed. New Hyde Park,
N.Y., University Books [1966- v.
427.09 65-24476
PE3721 .F32 MRR Alc.

Farmer, John Stephen, Slang and its
analogues [New York] Arno Press
[1970] 7 v. in 1. [8.95] 427.09
77-109023
PE3721 .F4 1970 MRR Alc.

Franklyn, Julian, A dictionary of
rhyming slang. London, Routledge and
Paul [1960] xi, 180 p. 427.09 60-
2861
PE3727.R5 F7 MRR Alc.

Fraser, Edward, comp. Soldier and
sailor words and phrases; London, G.
Routledge and sons, ltd., 1925. vii,
372 p. 25-9719
PE3727.S7 F7 MRR Alc.

Freeman, William, A concise
dictionary of English slang. London,
English Universities Press [1956]
268 p. 427.03 56-25547
PE3721 .F7 1956 MRR Alc.

Grose, Francis, A classical
dictionary of the vulgar tongue. New
York, Barnes & Noble [1963] ix, 396
p. 427.09 63-6024
PE3721 .G7 1963 MRR Alc.

Landy, Eugene E. The underground
dictionary, New York, Simon and
Schuster [1971] 206 p. [$5.95]
427.09 73-139637
PE3721 .L3 MRR Alc.

Leitner, Moses Jonathan, ed.
Dictionary of French and American
slang, New York, Crown Publishers
[1965] xix, 272 p. 447.0903 64-
23818
PC3741 .L58 MRR Alc.

Maitland, James. The American slang
dictionary, Chicago [R. J. Kittredge
& co.] 1891. 308 p. 10-34825
PE3729.A5 M3 MRR Alc.

McCulloch, Walter Fraser. Woods
words; [Portland] Oregon Historical
Society, 1958. vi, 219 p. 427.9
58-63667
PE3727.L8 M3 MRR Alc.

Morris, William, Dictionary of word
and phrase origins, [1st ed.] New
York, Harper & Row [1962- v.
422.03 61-10842
PE1580 .M6 MRR Alc.

Partridge, Eric, A dictionary of
Forces' slang, 1939-1945, Freeport,
N.Y., Books for Libraries Press
[1970] xi, 212 p. 427.09 75-
117899
PE3727.S7 P25 1970 MRR Alc.

Partridge, Eric, A dictionary of
slang and unconventional English;
6th ed. New York, Macmillan [1967]
xiv, 1474 p. 427.09 67-30122
PE3721 .P3 1967 MRR Ref Desk.

Partridge, Eric, The Routledge
dictionary of historical slang /
Abridged [ed.] / London : Routledge
and Kegan Paul, 1973. 1065 p. ;
[£10.50] 427/.09 74-188972
PE3721 .P3 1973 MRR Alc.

Schmidt, Jacob Edward, Cyclopedic
lexicon of sex; [2d ed.] New York,
Brussel & Brussel, 1967. viii, 389
p. [$10.00] 301.41/7/03 74-152205

HQ9 .S28 1967 MRR Alc.

Tak, Montie. Truck talk; [1st ed.]
Philadelphia, Chilton Book Co. [1971]
xiv, 191 p. [$5.95] 388.3/24/014
72-169583
PE3727.H5 T3 MRR Alc.

Taylor, Anna Marjorie, The language
of World War II; Rev. and enl. ed.
New York, H. W. Wilson Co., 1948.
265 p. 940.53014 48-8265
PE3727.S7 T3 1948 MRR Alc.

Ware, James Redding. Passing English
of the Victorian era, Wakefield, EP
Publishing, 1972. [5], iii-viii, 217
p. [£2.50] 427/.09 73-175927
PE3721 .W3 1972 MRR Alc.

Wilson, Robert Anton, Playboy's book
of forbidden words; [1st ed.
Chicago, Playboy Press; distributed
by Simon & Schuster, New York, c1972]
xi, 302 p. [$8.95] 72-81109
HQ9 .W54 MRR Alc.

Young, Kenn W. Naz's underground
dictionary; Vancouver, Wash. [Naz
Enterprises, 1973] vi, 67 p.
[$2.00] 427/.9/73 74-156957
PE3727.N3 Y6 MRR Alc.

ENGLISH LANGUAGE--SPELLING
see English language--Orthography and spelling

ENGLISH LANGUAGE--STUDY AND TEACHING--BIBLIOGRAPHY.
Centre for Information on Language Teaching. A language-teaching bibliography, 2d ed. Cambridge [Eng.] University Press, 1972. x, 242 p. 016.407 76-152633
Z5814.L26 C45 1972 MRR Alc.

Ohannessian, Sirarpi, ed. Reference list of materials for English as a second language. Washington, Center for Applied Linguistics, 1964-69. 3 v. [5.00 (v. 3)] 016.42824 64-8917
Z5814.E59 O35 MRR Alc.

ENGLISH LANGUAGE--STUDY AND TEACHING--SOCIETIES, ETC.
National Council of Teachers of English. Directory of officers, committees, and affiliates. Champaign, Ill. 65-5403
PE11 .N317 MRR Alc Latest edition

ENGLISH LANGUAGE--STYLE.
Copperud, Roy H., A dictionary of usage and style; [1st ed.] New York, Hawthorn Books [1964] 452 p. 428 64-19207
PE1460 .C66 MRR Alc.

Flesch, Rudolf Franz, The ABC of style; [1st ed.] New York, Harper & Row [1964] x, 303 p. 808 64-25139

PE1421 .F55 MRR Alc.

Leggett, Glenn H., Prentice-Hall handbook for writers 5th ed. Englewood Cliffs, N.J., Prentice-Hall [1970] xxiv, 484 p. [4.95] 428.2 72-102045
PE1408 .L39 1970 MRR Alc.

ENGLISH LANGUAGE--SYLLABICATION.
Collins, Frederick Howard, Authors' and printers' dictionary; 10th ed., rev. London, New York, Oxford University Press, 1956. xiv, 442 p. 655.25 56-58185
Z254 .C76 1956 MRR Alc.

ENGLISH LANGUAGE--SYNONYMS AND ANTONYMS.
Berrey, Lester V., The American thesaurus of slang; 2d ed. New York, Crowell [1953] xxxv, 1272 p. 427.09 427.9* 52-10837
PE3729.A5 B4 1953 MRR Alc.

Funk & Wagnalls modern guide to synonyms and related words; New York, Funk & Wagnalls [1968] x, 726 p. 67-26446
PE1591 .F8 1968 MRR Ref Desk.

Gause, John Taylor. The complete word hunter. New York, Crowell [1965] viii, 497 p. 423 55-11106

PE1449 .G345 MRR Alc.

Hartman, Dennis, The new alphabetical thesaurus and word-finder; Los Angeles, National Poetry Association [1954?] 179 p. 55-20540
PE1591 .H34 MRR Alc.

Laffal, Julius. A concept dictionary of English. Essex, Conn., Gallery Press [1973] xi, 305 p. 428/.1 72-97927
PE1691 .L3 MRR Alc.

Laird, Charlton Grant, Laird's promptory; New York, H. Holt [1948] 957 p. 424.03 48-2345
PE1591 .L26 MRR Ref Desk.

Lewis, Norman, The comprehensive word guide. [1st ed.] Garden City, N.Y., Doubleday [1958] xxiii, 912 p. 423 58-11514
PE1591 .L4 MRR Ref Desk.

Lewis, Norman, ed. The new Roget's Thesaurus of the English language in dictionary form. Rev., greatly enl. ed. Garden City, N.Y., Garden City Books [1961] 552 p. 424 61-5978
PE1591 .L43 1961 MRR Ref Desk.

March, Francis Andrew, March's thesaurus and dictionary of the English language Garden City, N.Y., Doubleday [1968] vii, 1240 p. 68-24820
PE1625 .M3 1968 MRR Alc.

Opdycke, John Baker, The Opdycke lexicon of word selection. New York, Funk & Wagnalls, 1950. xix, 492 p. 423 51-379
PE1591 .O76 MRR Alc.

Rodale, Jerome Irving, The phrase finder; Emmaus, Pa., Rodale Press [c1953] 1325 p. 423 54-2348
PE1689 .R63 MRR Alc.

Rodale, Jerome Irving, ed. The synonym finder. Emmaus, Pa., Rodale Books, 1961. 1388 p. 424 61-2540

PE1591 .R64 MRR Alc.

Roget, Peter Mark, Thesaurus of English words and phrases. New ed., completely rev. and modernized New York, St. Martin's Press [1964, c1962] lii, 1309 p. 424 64-23442

PE1591 .R7 1964 MRR Ref Desk.

Roget's international thesaurus. [1st]- [1911]- New York, Crowell. 62-12806
PE1591 .R73 MRR Ref Desk Latest edition / MRR Alc Latest edition

Sattler, Wilhelm Ferdinand. Deutsch-englisches sachwörterbuch. Leipzig, Renger, 1904. xx, 1035 p. 05-16230

PF3640 .S3 MRR Alc.

Sheffield, Eng. Free Public Libraries and Museum. 'Isms: a dictionary of words ending in -ism, -ology, and -phobia, 2nd ed. Sheffield, Corporation of Sheffield; Wakefield, EP Publishing Ltd, 1972. 100 p. [£1.50] 423/.1 73-158938
PE1680 .S37 1972b MRR Ref Desk.

Sisson, Albert Franklin, Sisson's synonyms; West Nyack, N.Y., Parker Pub. Co. [1969] xi, 691 p. 423.1 74-77314
PE1591 .S5 MRR Alc.

Sisson, Albert Franklin, The unabridged crossword puzzle word finder. [1st ed.] Garden City, N.Y., Doubleday, 1963. 526 p. 793.732 62-15910
GV1507.C7 S5 MRR Alc.

Soule, Richard, A dictionary of English synonyms & synonymous expressions, Boston, Little, Brown [1959] xiv, 614 p. 424 59-7990
PE1591 .S7 1959 MRR Ref Desk.

Starr, Marion Marjorie, Synonyms; a "right" name finder for objects or arrangements thereof, identifiable by sight, picture, or diagram. [1st ed.] Kensington, Md. [1955] 188 p. 424 55-18845
PE1591 .S78 MRR Alc.

Webster's new dictionary of synonyms; Springfield, Mass., Merriam [1973] 31a, 909 p. [$7.95] 423/.1 73-180866
PE1591 .W4 1973 MRR Ref Desk.

ENGLISH LANGUAGE--TERMS AND PHRASES.
American notes & queries; v. 1-8; Apr. 1941-Mar. 1950. [New York] 051 43-6120
AG305 .A48 MRR Alc Full set

Brewer, Ebenezer Cobham, Brewer's dictionary of phrase and fable. Centenary ed. (completely revised); London, Cassell, 1870. xvi, 1175 p., plate. [60/-] 803 73-529591
PN43 .B65 1870 MRR Ref Desk.

Colcord, Joanna Carver, Sea language comes ashore New York, Cornell maritime press [1945] ix, 213 p. 427.9 45-966
PE1689 .C65 MRR Alc.

Fairchild, Henry Pratt, ed. Dictionary of sociology, New York city, Philosophical library [1944] 4 p. l., 342 p. 303 44-4755
HM17 .F3 MRR Alc.

Hargrave, Basil. Origins and meanings of popular phrases and names. [Rev. ed.] London, T. W. Laurie [1948] vi, 350 p. 423 49-1451
AG5 .H18 1948 MRR Ref Desk.

Henderson, Bernard Lionel Kinghorn, A dictionary of English idioms. London, J. Blackwood [1947-50?] 2 v. 423.1 51-1250
PE1460 .H452 MRR Alc.

Hendrickson, Robert, Human words; [1st ed.] Philadelphia, Chilton Book Co. [1972] 342 p. [$9.95] 423/.1 72-6492
PE1596 .H4 MRR Alc.

Holt, Alfred Hubbard, Phrase origins; New York, Thomas Y. Crowell company [c1936] vii, [1], 328 p. 428.3 422 36-10206
PE1580 .H55 1936 MRR Alc.

Hyamson, Albert Montefiore, A dictionary of English phrases; London, G. Routledge & sons, ltd.; New York, E. P. Dutton & co., 1922. 3 p. l., ix-xvi, 365 p. 22-8430
PE1689 .H9 MRR Alc.

Lewis, Norman, The comprehensive word guide. [1st ed.] Garden City, N.Y., Doubleday [1958] xxiii, 912 p. 423 58-11514
PE1591 .L4 MRR Ref Desk.

Lipton, James. An exaltation of larks; [New York] Grossman Publishers [1968] 118 p. [4.95] 427.09 68-30774
PE1689 .L5 MRR Alc.

Morgan, Robert L. Why we say ... New York, Sterling Pub. Co. [c1953] 128 p. 428.2 53-13405
PE1689 .M6 MRR Alc.

Morris, William, Dictionary of word and phrase origins, [1st ed.] New York Harper & Row [1962- v. 422.03 61-10842
PE1580 .M6 MRR Alc.

Origin of things familiar; Cincinnati, O., United book corporation [c1934] 4 p. l., 280 p. 031 35-2154
AG5 .O7 MRR Alc.

Partridge, Eric, A dictionary of cliches, [4th ed.] London, Routledge & Paul [1950] ix, 259 p. 428.3 51-1735
PE1689 .P3 1950 MRR Alc.

Pei, Mario Andrew, Double-speak in America. New York, Hawthorn Books [1973] 216 p. [$6.95] 422 78-39894
PE1585 .P38 MRR Alc.

Pei, Mario Andrew, Words in sheep's clothing [1st ed.] New York, Hawthorn Books [1969] 248 p. [6.95] 422 69-20348
PE1585 .P4 1969 MRR Alc.

Radford, Edwin, To coin a phrase: Revised ed.; London, Hutchinson, 1973. 128 p. [£1.95] 422/.03 73-162277
PE1580 .R3 1973b MRR Alc.

Rodale, Jerome Irving, The phrase finder; Emmaus, Pa., Rodale Press [c1953] 1325 p. 423 54-2348
PE1689 .R63 MRR Alc.

Safire, William L. The new language of politics; New York, Random House [1968] xvi, 528 p. 320/.03 68-14508
JK9 .S2 MRR Ref Desk.

Sheffield, Eng. Free Public Libraries and Museum. 'Isms: a dictionary of words ending in -ism, -ology, and -phobia, 2nd ed. Sheffield, Corporation of Sheffield; Wakefield, EP Publishing Ltd, 1972. 100 p. [£1.50] 423/.1 73-158938
PE1680 .S37 1972b MRR Ref Desk.

Taylor, Anna Marjorie, The language of World War II; Rev. and enl. ed. New York, H. W. Wilson Co., 1948. 265 p. 940.53014 48-8265
PE3727.S7 T3 1948 MRR Alc.

Ware, James Redding. Passing English of the Victorian era. Wakefield, EP Publishing, 1972. [5], iii-viii, 217 p. [£2.50] 427/.09 73-175927
PE3721 .W3 1972 MRR Alc.

Whiting, Bartlett Jere, Proverbs, sentences, and proverbial phrases; Cambridge, Mass., Belknap Press of Harvard University Press, 1968. li, 733 p. [$25.00] 808.88/2 67-22874

PN6083 .W45 MRR Alc.

ENGLISH LANGUAGE--TERMS AND PHRASES--INDEXES.
Notes and queries: v. 1- Nov. 3, 1849- London [etc.] Oxford Univ. Press [etc.] 12-25307
AG305 .N7 MRR Alc Full set

Wall, C. Edward. Words and phrases index; Ann Arbor, Mich., Pierian Press, 1969- v. [17.95 (v. 1)] 016.423 68-58894
PE1689 .W3 MRR Alc.

ENGLISH LANGUAGE--TEXT-BOOKS FOR FOREIGNERS.
Schmidt, Jacob Edward, English idioms and Americanisms for foreign students, professionals, physicians, Springfield, Ill., C. C. Thomas [1972] vi, 534 p. 428/.1 77-177903
PE1128 .S34 MRR Alc.

ENGLISH LANGUAGE--TEXT-BOOKS FOR FOREIGNERS--BIBLIOGRAPHY.
Alston, R. C. Polyglot dictionaries and grammars; Bradford, printed for the author by Ernest Cummins [1967] xx, 311 p. 68-138251
Z2015.A1 A4 vol. 2 MRR Alc.

ENGLISH LANGUAGE--TEXT-BOOKS FOR (Cont.)
Ohannessian, Sirarpi, ed. Reference
list of materials for English as a
second language. Washington, Center
for Applied Linguistics, 1964-69. 3
v. [5.00 (v. 3)] 016.42824 64-
8917
   Z5814.E59 O35 MRR Alc.

ENGLISH LANGUAGE--TEXT-BOOKS FOR
FOREIGNERS--NORWEGIAN.
Follestad, Sverre. Engelske idiomer;
[Oslo] Fabritius [1962] 512 p.   63-
28474
   PD2691 .F6 MRR Alc.

ENGLISH LANGUAGE--USAGE.
Berry, Thomas Elliott. The most
common mistakes in English usage.
[1st ed.] Philadelphia, Chilton Co.,
Book Division [1961] 146 p.   428.3
61-15418
   PE1460 .B4635 MRR Alc.

Hook, Julius Nicholas. Guide to good
writing. New York, Ronald Press Co.
[1962] 515 p.   808 61-15346
   PE1408 .H678 MRR Alc.

ENGLISH LANGUAGE--USAGE--DICTIONARIES.
Evans, Bergen. A dictionary of
contemporary American usage. New
York, Random House [1957] vii, 567
p.   427.09 427.9* 57-5379
   PE2835 .E84 MRR Alc.

ENGLISH LANGUAGE--VERB.
Henderson, Bernard Lionel Kinghorn.
A dictionary of English idioms.
London, J. Blackwood [1947-50?] 2 v.
423.1 51-1250
   PE1460 .H452 MRR Alc.

ENGLISH LANGUAGE--VERSIFICATION.
Johnson Burgess. New rhyming
dictionary and poets' handbook. Rev.
ed. New York, Harper [1957] x, 464
p.   426.603 808.1* 57-9585
   PE1519 .J6 1957 MRR Alc.

Malof, Joseph. A manual of English
meters. Bloomington, Indiana
University Press [1970] xvi, 236 p.
[8.50] 426 70-98979
   PE1505 .M3 1970 MRR Alc.

Shapiro, Karl Jay. A prosody
handbook. New York, Harper & Row
[1965] x, 214 p.   416 64-24535
   PN1042 .S57 MRR Alc.

Stillman, Frances. The poet's manual
and rhyming dictionary. London,
Thames & Hudson [1966] xviv, 363 p.
[42/-] 66-69064
   PE1505 .S8 1966 MRR Alc.

ENGLISH LANGUAGE--WORD FORMATION.
Brown, Roland Wilbur. Composition of
scientific words. [Rev. ed.]
Washington, 1956] 882 p.   422.03
56-56233
   PE1580 .B7 1956 MRR Alc.

ENGLISH LANGUAGE--WORDS--HANDBOOKS,
MANUALS, ETC.
The Dell crossword dictionary. [New
York, Dell Pub. Co.]; distributed by
the Dial Press, 1964 [c1960] 384 p.
793.732 64-11903
   GV1507.C7 D39 1964 MRR Alc.

English word book of over 106,000
words. [Seattle, Pilot Press, 1963]
xx, 829 p.   65-3497
   GV1507.W9 E5 MRR Alc.

ENGLISH LANGUAGE--WORDS--HISTORY.
The Compact edition of the Oxford
English dictionary: complete text
reproduced micrographically. Oxford,
Clarendon Press, 1971. 2 v. (xii,
4116 p.) [£28.00] 423 72-177361
   PE1625 .N53 1971 MRR Ref Desk.

Morris, William. Dictionary of word
and phrase origins. [1st ed.] New
York, Harper & Row [1962- v.
422.03 61-10842
   PE1580 .M6 MRR Alc.

The Oxford English dictionary.
Oxford, At the Clarendon press, 1933.
13 v.   423   a 33-3399
   PE1625 .N53 1933 MRR Alc.

Pei, Mario Andrew. Double-speak in
America. New York, Hawthorn Books
[1973] 216 p. [$6.95] 422 78-
39894
   PE1585 .P38 MRR Alc.

Pei, Mario Andrew. Words in sheep's
clothing. [1st ed.] New York,
Hawthorn Books [1969] 248 p. [6.95]
422 69-20348
   PE1585 .P4 1969 MRR Alc.

Shipley, Joseph Twadell. Dictionary
of early English. New York,
Philosophical Library [1955] xiii,
753 p.   427 55-4892
   PE1667 .S48 MRR Alc.

ENGLISH LANGUAGE--SYNONYMS AND ANTONYMS.
Guide to the use of Roget's
international thesaurus. New York,
Crowell. 74-643593
   PE1591 .R732 MRR Ref Desk Latest
edition / MRR Alc Latest edition

ENGLISH LANGUAGE IN AUSTRALIA--
DICTIONARIES.
Australian national quick reference
dictionary and encyclopaedia;
Melbourne, Age Publications [1969]
320 p.   423 73-563415
   PE1628 .A87 MRR Alc.

ENGLISH LANGUAGE IN CANADA--
BIBLIOGRAPHY.
Avis, Walter Spencer. A bibliography
of writings on Canadian English (1857-
1965) Toronto, W. J. Gage [c1965]
17 p. [$1.25 Can.] 68-103809
   Z1379 .A85 MRR Alc.

ENGLISH LANGUAGE IN CANADA--
DICTIONARIES.
A Dictionary of Canadianisms on
historical principles; Toronto, W.
J. Gage, ltd., 1967. xxiii, 926, [1]
p.   427/.9/71 78-5962
   PE3243 .D5 MRR Alc.

ENGLISH LANGUAGE IN GREAT BRITAIN--
DICTIONARIES.
Moss, Norman. What's the difference?
[1st ed.] New York, Harper & Row
[1973] 138 p. [$6.95] 428/.1 72-
9140
   PE2835 .M6 MRR Alc.

ENGLISH LANGUAGE IN THE UNITED STATES.
Mallery, Richard Davis. Our American
language. [1st ed.] Garden City,
N.Y., Halcyon House [1947] xii, 276
p.   427.9 47-11747
   PE2808 .M27 MRR Alc.

Mencken, Henry Louis. The American
language; [1st abridged ed.] New
York, Knopf, 1963. xxv, 777, cxxiv
p.   427.873 63-13628
   PE2808 .M43 MRR Alc.

Mencken, Henry Louis. The American
language; New York, A. A. Knopf,
1936. xi, 769, xxix, [1] p.   427.9
36-27236
   PE2808 .M4 1936 MRR Alc.

ENGLISH LANGUAGE IN THE UNITED STATES--
BIBLIOGRAPHY.
Brenni, Vito Joseph. American
English, a bibliography,
Philadelphia, University of
Pennsylvania Press [1964] 221 p.
016.427973 63-15008
   Z1231.D5 B7 MRR Alc.

ENGLISH LANGUAGE IN THE UNITED STATES--
DIALECTS.
Herman, Lewis Helmar. American
dialects; New York, Theatre Arts
Books [1959] 328 p.   427.9 59-
13238
   PE2841 .H4 1959 MRR Alc.

Wentworth, Harold. American dialect
dictionary. New York, Thomas Y.
Crowell company, 1944. xv, 747 p.
427.9 44-6209
   PE2835 .W4 MRR Alc.

ENGLISH LANGUAGE IN THE UNITED STATES--
DIALECTS--ALASKA.
Bowen, Robert O. An Alaskan
dictionary. Spenard, Alaska,
Nooshnik Press [1965] 35 p.   66-
6594
   PE3101.A4 B6 MRRAlc.

ENGLISH LANGUAGE IN THE UNITED STATES--
DIALECTS--SOUTHERN STATES--BIBLIOGRAPHY.
McMillan, James B. Annotated
bibliography of Southern American
English. Coral Gables, Fla.,
University of Miami Press [1971] 173
p.   016.427/9/75 70-129666
   Z1234.D5 M32 MRR Alc.

ENGLISH LANGUAGE IN THE UNITED STATES--
DICTIONARIES.
Adams, Ramon Frederick. Western
words; New ed., rev. and enl.
Norman, University of Oklahoma Press
[1968] xviii, 355 p.   427.9/78 68-
31369
   PE2970.W4 A3 1968 MRR Alc.

Bartlett, John Russell. Dictionary
of Americanisms; 4th ed., greatly
improved and enl. Boston, Little,
Brown, and company, 1877. xlvi p., 1
l., 813 p.   11-7835
   PE2835 .B3 1877 MRR Alc.

Bryant, Margaret M., ed. Current
American usage. New York, Funk &
Wagnalls [1962] 290 p.   428.3 62-
9735
   PE2835 .B67 MRR Ref Desk.

Craigie, William Alexander, Sir, ed.
A dictionary of American English on
historical principles. Chicago,
Ill., The University of Chicago press
[1938-44] 4 v.   427.9 39-8203
   PE2835 .C72 MRR Alc.

A Dictionary of Americanisms on
historical principles; Chicago,
University of Chicago Press [1951] 2
v. (xvi, 1946 p.) 427.9 51-1957
   PE2835 .D5 MRR Alc.

Moss, Norman. What's the difference?
[1st ed.] New York, Harper & Row
[1973] 138 p. [$6.95] 428/.1 72-
9140
   PE2835 .M6 MRR Alc.

Nicholson, Margaret. A dictionary of
American-English usage. New York,
Oxford University Press, 1957. xii,
671 p.   423 57-5560
   PE2835 .N5 MRR Ref Desk.

ENGLISH LANGUAGE IN THE UNITED STATES--
GLOSSARIES, VOCABULARIES, ETC.
Whitford, Robert Calvin. Concise
dictionary of American grammar and
usage. New York, Philosophical
Library [c1955] viii, 168 p.   423
54-13498
   PE1680 .W49 MRR Alc.

ENGLISH LANGUAGE IN THE UNITED STATES--
GRAMMAR--1870-
Hook, Julius Nicholas. Modern
American grammar and usage. New York,
Ronald Press Co. [1956] 475 p.   425
56-6265
   PE1111 .H638 MRR Alc.

ENGLISH LANGUAGE IN THE UNITED STATES--
HOMONYMS--DICTIONARIES.
Whitford, Harold Crandall. A
dictionary of American homophones and
homographs. New York, Teachers
College Press, 1966. 83 p.   423.1
66-25461
   PE2833 .W4 MRR Alc.

ENGLISH LANGUAGE IN THE UNITED STATES--
IDIOMS, CORRECTIONS, ERRORS.
Horwill, Herbert William. A
dictionary of modern American usage.
Oxford, The Clarendon press, 1935.
ix, [2], 360 p.   427.9 35-27255
   PE2835 .H6 MRR Alc.

ENGLISH LANGUAGE IN THE UNITED STATES--
IDIOMS, CORRECTIONS, ERRORS--
DICTIONARIES.
Whitford, Harold Crandall. Handbook
of American idioms and idiomatic
usage. New York, Regents Pub. Co.
[1953] 155 p.   423.1 53-7695
   PE1460 .W56 MRR Alc.

ENGLISH LANGUAGE IN THE UNITED STATES--
PRONUNCIATION.
Bender, James Frederick. NBC
handbook of pronunciation. 3d ed.
rev. New York, Crowell [1964] xii,
418 p.   421.5 63-9205
   PE1137 .B573 1964 MRR Alc.

Bronstein, Arthur J. The
pronunciation of American English;
New York, Appleton-Century-Crofts
[1960] 320 p.   421.5 60-6750
   PE1137 .B77 MRR Alc.

Colby, Frank O., ed. The American
pronouncing dictionary of troublesome
words. New York, Crowell [1950] 399
p.   421.5 50-10743
   PE1137 .C56 MRR Alc.

Kenyon, John Samuel, ed. A
pronouncing dictionary of American
English. Springfield, Mass., G. & C.
Merriam Co. [c1953] lvi, 484 p.
421.5 53-1416
   PE1137 .K37 1953 MRR Alc.

ENGLISH LANGUAGE IN THE UNITED STATES--
PROVINCIALISMS.
Wentworth, Harold. American dialect
dictionary. New York, Thomas Y.
Crowell company, 1944. xv, 747 p.
427.9 44-6209
   PE2835 .W4 MRR Alc.

ENGLISH LANGUAGE IN THE UNITED STATES--
PROVINCIALISMS--SOUTHWEST, NEW.
Bentley, Harold Woodmansee. A
dictionary of Spanish terms in
English. New York, Octagon Books,
1973 [c1932] x, 243 p.   422/.4/61
73-1936
   PE2962 .B4 1973 MRR Alc.

ENGLISH LANGUAGE IN THE UNITED STATES--
PROVINCIALISMS--WEST.
Adams, Ramon Frederick. Western
words; New ed., rev. and enl.
Norman, University of Oklahoma Press
[1968] xviii, 355 p.   427.9/78 68-
31369
   PE2970.W4 A3 1968 MRR Alc.

ENGLISH LANGUAGE IN THE UNITED STATES--
SLANG--DICTIONARIES.
Major, Clarence. Dictionary of Afro-
American slang. [1st ed.] New York,
International Publishers [1970] 127
p. [$5.95] 427.09 79-130863
   PE3727.N4 M3 MRR Alc.

Wentworth, Harold. Dictionary of
American slang. New York, Crowell
[1967] xviii, 718 p.   427.09 67-
3063
   PE3729.U5 W4 1966 MRR Ref Desk.

ENGLISH LANGUAGE IN THE UNITED (Cont.)
Weseen, Maurice Harley, A dictionary
of American slang. New York, Thomas
Y. Crowell company, [c1934] xiii, 543
p.   427.09   34-36774
   PE3729.A5 W4 MRR Alc.

ENGLISH LANGUAGE IN THE UNITED STATES--
SYNONYMS AND ANTONYMS.
Hogan, Homer. Dictionary of American
synonyms. New York, Philosophical
Library [1956] ix, 388 p.   424 56-
14013
   PE1591 .H6 MRR Alc.

ENGLISH LANGUAGE IN THE UNITED STATES--
TERMS AND PHRASES--DICTIONARIES.
Schmidt, Jacob Edward, English
idioms and Americanisms for foreign
students, professionals, physicians,
Springfield, Ill., C. C. Thomas
[1972] vi, 534 p.   428/.1 77-
177903
   PE1128 .S34 MRR Alc.

ENGLISH LANGUAGE IN THE UNITED STATES--
USAGE.
Follett, Wilson, Modern American
usage; 1st ed.]. New York, Hill &
Wang [1966] [xi], 436 p.   423.1 66-
18993
   PE2835 .F6 MRR Alc.

ENGLISH LANGUAGE IN THE UNITED STATES--
USAGE--DICTIONARIES.
Whitford, Harold Crandall, Handbook
of American idioms and idiomatic
usage. New York, Regents Pub. Co.
[1953] 155 p.   423.1 53-7695
   PE1460 .W56 MRR Alc.

ENGLISH LITERATURE.
Kermode, John Frank, comp. The
Oxford anthology of English
literature. New York, Oxford
University Press, 1973. 2 v.
820/.8 72-92355
   PR1105 .K4 MRR Alc.

Macdonald, Dwight, ed. Parodies:
New York, Random House [1960] 574 p.
827.082 60-12147
   PN6231.P3 M3 MRR Alc.

The Speaker's desk book. New York,
Grosset & Dunlap [1967] 613 p.
808.8 66-20654
   PN4193.I5 S6 1967 MRR Alc.

ENGLISH LITERATURE--MIDDLE ENGLISH,
1100-1500--BIBLIOGRAPHY.
A Manual of the writings in Middle
English, 1050-1500. New Haven,
Connecticut Academy of Arts and
Sciences [order from: Archon Books,
Hamden, Conn.] 1967- v.
016.820/9/001 67-7687
   PR255 .M3 MRR Alc.

ENGLISH LITERATURE--MIDDLE ENGLISH,
1100-1500--HISTORY AND CRITICISM.
A Manual of the writings in Middle
English, 1050-1500. New Haven,
Connecticut Academy of Arts and
Sciences [order from: Archon Books,
Hamden, Conn.] 1967- v.
016.820/9/001 67-7687
   PR255 .M3 MRR Alc.

ENGLISH LITERATURE--EARLY MODERN, 1500-
1700.
Gray, George John, A general index
to Hazlitt's Handbook and his
Bibliographical collections (1867-
1889) New York, B. Franklin, 1961.
866 p.   016.82 78-7293
   Z2012 .G8 1961 MRR Alc.

ENGLISH LITERATURE--EARLY MODERN, 1500-
1700--BIBLIOGRAPHY.
Bush, Douglas, English literature in
the earlier seventeenth century, 1600-
1660. 2d ed., rev. Oxford,
Clarendon Press, 1962. viii, 680 p.
820.903 62-51930
   PR431 .B8 1962 MRR Alc.

Ebisch, Walther. A Shakespeare
bibliography. Oxford, The Clarendon
press, 1931. xviii, 294 p., 1 l.
012 822.33 31-26966
   Z8811 .E18 MRR Alc.

Hazlitt, William Carew, Collections
and notes, 1867-1876. New York, B.
Franklin, 1961. xi, 498 p.   016.82
79-7446
   Z2012 .H31 1961 MRR Alc.

Hazlitt, William Carew, Handbook to
the popular, poetical, and dramatic
literature of Great Britain. New
York, B. Franklin, 1961. xii, 701 p.
016.82 75-7445
   Z2012 .H3 1961 MRR Alc.

Lewis, Clive Staples, English
literature in the sixteenth century,
Oxford, Clarendon Press, 1954. vi,
696 p.   820.903 54-4883
   PR411 .L4 MRR Alc.

Livingston, Luther Samuel, Auction
prices of books; New York, Dodd,
Mead & company, 1905. 4 v. 05-9722

   Z1000 .L65 MRR Alc.

London. Guildhall Library. A list of
books printed in the British Isles
and of English books printed abroad
before 1701 in Guildhall Library.
London, Corporation of London, 1966-
67. v.   [40/- (v. 1) 015/.42
68-77514
   Z2002 .L62 MRR Alc.

London. Stationers' Company. A
transcript of the registers of the
Company of Stationers of London, 1554-
1640 A.D. [New York P. Smith, 1950]
5 v.   655.442 49-50201
   Z2002 .L64 MRR Alc.

London. Stationer's Company. A
transcript of the registers of the
worshipful Company of Stationers,
from 1640-1708 A.D. [New York, P.
Smith, 1950] 3 v.   655.442 50-
37726
   Z2002 .L653 MRR Alc.

Oxford. University. Christ Church.
Library. The Christ Church
supplement to Wing's Short-title
catalogue, 1641-1700. Oxford,
Printed for Christ Church at the
Holywell Press, 1956. 47 p.   015.42
57-624
   Z2002.W5 O9 MRR Alc.

Sutherland, James Runcieman, English
literature of the late seventeenth
century, Oxford, Clarendon P., 1969.
ix, 589 p. [55/-] 820.9/004 79-
391852
   PR437 .S9 1969 MRR Alc.

The Term catalogues, 1668-1709 A.D.;
London, 1903-06. 3 v.   05-8720
   Z2002 .A31 MRR Alc.

Wing, Donald Goddard, A gallery of
ghosts; [New York] Index Committee,
Modern Language Association of
America, 1967. vi, 225 p.   015.42
67-9327
   Z2002 .W48 MRR Alc.

ENGLISH LITERATURE--EARLY MODERN, 1500-
1700--HISTORY AND CRITICISM.
Bush, Douglas, English literature in
the earlier seventeenth century, 1600-
1660. 2d ed., rev. Oxford,
Clarendon Press, 1962. viii, 680 p.
820.903 62-51930
   PR431 .B8 1962 MRR Alc.

Lewis, Clive Staples, English
literature in the sixteenth century,
Oxford, Clarendon Press, 1954. vi,
696 p.   820.903 54-4883
   PR411 .L4 MRR Alc.

Sutherland, James Runcieman, English
literature of the late seventeenth
century, Oxford, Clarendon P., 1969.
ix, 589 p. [55/-] 820.9/004 79-
391852
   PR437 .S9 1969 MRR Alc.

ENGLISH LITERATURE--18TH CENTURY--
BIBLIOGRAPHY.
Dobrée, Bonamy, English literature
in the early eighteenth century, 1700-
1740. Oxford, Clarendon Press, 1959.
xii, 701 p.   820.903 60-95
   PR445 .D6 MRR Alc.

London. Stationer's Company. A
transcript of the registers of the
worshipful Company of Stationers,
from 1640-1708 A.D. [New York, P.
Smith, 1950] 3 v.   655.442 50-
37726
   Z2002 .L653 MRR Alc.

The Monthly catalogues from 'The
London Magazine,' 1732-66; London,
Gregg P.; Archive P., 1966 [i.e.
1967]. [740] p. [£12/10/-] 015.42
67-86316
   Z2002 .M64 MRR Alc.

The Term catalogues, 1668-1709 A.D.;
London, 1903-06. 3 v.   05-8720
   Z2002 .A31 MRR Alc.

Tobin, James Edward, Eighteenth
century English literature and its
cultural background; New York, Biblo
and Tannen, 1967. vii, 190 p.
016.8209/006 66-30405
   Z2013 .T62 1967 MRR Alc.

ENGLISH LITERATURE--18TH CENTURY--
HISTORY AND CRITICISM.
Bernbaum, Ernest, Guide through the
romantic movement. 2d ed., rev. and
enl. New York, Ronald Press [1949]
xi, 351 p.   820.903 49-8022
   PR447 .B55 1949 MRR Alc.

Dobrée, Bonamy, English literature
in the early eighteenth century, 1700-
1740. Oxford, Clarendon Press, 1959.
xii, 701 p.   820.903 60-95
   PR445 .D6 MRR Alc.

Renwick, William Lindsay, English
literature, 1789-1815. Oxford,
Clarendon Press, 1963. 293 p.
820.903 63-3139
   PR447 .R4 1963 MRR Alc.

ENGLISH LITERATURE--19TH CENTURY--
BIBLIOGRAPHY.
Bibliographies of studies in
Victorian literature for the ten
years 1955-1964. Urbana, University
of Illinois Press, 1967. xvi, 461 p.
016.8209/008 67-20150
   Z2013 .B59 MRR Alc.

Boyle, Andrew. An index to the
annuals. Worcester, A. Boyle, 1967-
v.   [63/- (v. 1) 820.8/007/05
67-101753
   Z2013 .B65 MRR Alc.

Brussel, Isidore Rosenbaum, Anglo-
American first editions. London,
Constable & co. ltd., New York, R. R.
Bowker co., 1935-36. 2 v.   016.0944
016.82 35-19256
   Z2014.F5 B9 MRR Alc.

Cutler, Bradley Dwayne, comp. Modern
British authors, their first
editions, New York, Greenberg
[c1930] xi, 171 p.   016.82 30-
20445
   Z2014.F55 C8 1930 MRR Alc.

Fogle, Richard Harter. Romantic
poets and prose writers. New York,
Appleton-Century-Crofts [1967] viii,
87 p.   016.8208008 66-29743
   Z2013. F6 MRR Alc.

Jack, Ian Robert James. English
literature, 1815-1832. Oxford,
Clarendon Press, 1963. xii, 643 p.
820.903 63-25209
   PR457 .J24 MRR Alc.

Parrott, Thomas Marc, A companion to
Victorian literature New York,
Scribner [1955] 308 p.   820.903 55-
7295
   PR461 .P3 MRR Alc.

Schwartz, Jacob. 1100 obscure
points: the bibliographies of 25
English and 21 American authors.
[1st ed. reprinted]. Bristol,
Chatford House Press, 1969. xiii, 95
p., 2 plates. [36/-] 820.9 70-
465328
   Z2013 .S38 1969 MRR Alc.

ENGLISH LITERATURE--19TH CENTURY--BIO-
BIBLIOGRAPHY.
Heiney, Donald W., British,
Woodbury, N.Y., Barron's Educational
Series [1973, c1974] x, 286 p.
[$2.95] 820/.9 74-158988
   PR471 .H39 MRR Alc.

ENGLISH LITERATURE--19TH CENTURY--
HISTORY AND CRITICISM.
Bernbaum, Ernest, Guide through the
romantic movement. 2d ed., rev. and
enl. New York, Ronald Press [1949]
xi, 351 p.   820.903 49-8022
   PR447 .B55 1949 MRR Alc.

Heiney, Donald W., British,
Woodbury, N.Y., Barron's Educational
Series [1973, c1974] x, 286 p.
[$2.95] 820/.9 74-158988
   PR471 .H39 MRR Alc.

Jack, Ian Robert James. English
literature, 1815-1832. Oxford,
Clarendon Press, 1963. xii, 643 p.
820.903 63-25209
   PR457 .J24 MRR Alc.

Parrott, Thomas Marc, A companion to
Victorian literature New York,
Scribner [1955] 308 p.   820.903 55-
7295
   PR461 .P3 MRR Alc.

Renwick, William Lindsay, English
literature, 1789-1815. Oxford,
Clarendon Press, 1963. 293 p.
820.903 63-3139
   PR447 .R4 1963 MRR Alc.

ENGLISH LITERATURE--19TH CENTURY--
HISTORY AND CRITICISM--BIBLIOGRAPHY.
Altick, Richard Daniel, Guide to
doctoral dissertations in Victorian
literature, 1886-1958. Urbana,
University of Illinois Press, 1960.
vii, 119 p.   016.82/09/008 60-8339

   Z2013 .A4 MRR Alc.

Bibliographies of studies in
Victorian literature for the ten
years 1945-1954. Urbana, University
of Illinois Press, 1956. 310 p.   56-
5687
   Z2013 .B5892 MRR Alc.

Bibliographies of studies in
Victorian literature for the thirteen
years 1932-1944. Urbana, University
of Illinois Press, 1945. ix, 450 p.
46-77
   Z2013 .B589 MRR Alc.

DeLaura, David J. Victorian prose;
New York, Modern Language Association
of America, 1973. xvi, 560 p.
[$12.00] 820/.9/008 73-80586
   PR785 .D4 MRR Alc.

ENGLISH LITERATURE--19TH (Cont.)
Fredeman, William Evan, Pre-
Raphaelitism: a bibliocritical study
Cambridge, Harvard University Press,
1965. xix, 327 p. 016.70942 64-
21242
Z5948.P9 F7 MRR Alc.

ENGLISH LITERATURE--20TH CENTURY--
BIBLIOGRAPHY.
Cutler, Bradley Dwyane, comp. Modern
British authors, their first
editions. New York, Greenberg
[c1930] xi, 171 p. 016.82 30-
20445
Z2014.F55 C8 1930 MRR Alc.

Daiches, David, The present age in
British literature. [1st American
ed.] Bloomington, Indiana University
Press [1958] x, 376 p. 820.904 58-
6954
PR471 .D3 MRR Alc.

Mellown, Elgin W. A descriptive
catalogue of the bibliographies of
20th century British writers. Troy,
N.Y., Whitston Pub. Co., 1972. xii,
446 p. [$17.50] 016.01682/08/0091
79-183301
Z2011 .A1M43 MRR Alc.

Schwartz, Jacob. 1100 obscure
points: the bibliographies of 25
English and 21 American authors.
[1st ed., reprinted]. Bristol,
Chatford House Press, 1969. xiii, 95
p. 2 plates. [36/-] 016.820 70-
465328
Z2013 .S38 1969 MRR Alc.

Temple, Ruth (Zabriskie) comp.
Modern British literature, New York,
F. Ungar Pub. Co. [1966] 3 v.
820.90091 65-16618
PR473 .T4 MRR Alc.

Temple, Ruth (Zabriskie) comp.
Twentieth century British literature;
New York, F. Ungar Pub. Co. [1968]
x, 261 p. 016.8209/0091 67-13618
Z2013.3 .T4 MRR Alc.

Vinson, James, Contemporary
novelists. New York, St. Martin's
Press [1972] xvii, 1422 p. [$30.00]
823/.03 75-189694
PR737 .V5 MRR Biog.

ENGLISH LITERATURE--20TH CENTURY--BIO-
BIBLIOGRAPHY.
Heiney, Donald W., British,
Woodbury, N.Y., Barron's Educational
Series [1973, c1974] x, 286 p.
[$2.95] 820/.9 74-158988
PR471 .H39 MRR Alc.

Phelps, Robert, The literary life;
New York, Farrar, Straus and Giroux,
1968. 244 p. [$15.00]
016.8209/009/1 68-27533
Z2013 .P48 MRR Alc.

ENGLISH LITERATURE--20TH CENTURY--
HISTORY AND CRITICISM.
Daiches, David, The present age in
British literature. [1st American
ed.] Bloomington, Indiana University
Press [1958] x, 376 p. 820.904 58-
6954
PR471 .D3 MRR Alc.

Heiney, Donald W., British,
Woodbury, N.Y., Barron's Educational
Series [1973, c1974] x, 286 p.
[$2.95] 820/.9 74-158988
PR471 .H39 MRR Alc.

Temple, Ruth (Zabriskie) comp.
Modern British literature, New York,
F. Ungar Pub. Co. [1966] 3 v.
820.90091 65-16618
PR473 .T4 MRR Alc.

ENGLISH LITERATURE--20TH CENTURY--
HISTORY AND CRITICISM--BIBLIOGRAPHY.
Temple, Ruth (Zabriskie) comp.
Twentieth century British literature;
New York, F. Ungar Pub. Co. [1968]
x, 261 p. 016.8209/0091 67-13618
Z2013.3 .T4 MRR Alc.

ENGLISH LITERATURE--AFRICAN AUTHORS.
Tucker, Martin. Africa in modern
literature; New York, F. Ungar Pub.
Co. [1967] xii, 316 p. 820 66-
19472
PR9798 .T8 MRR Alc.

ENGLISH LITERATURE--AFRICAN AUTHORS--
BIBLIOGRAPHY.
Abrash, Barbara. Black African
literature in English since 1952;
New York, Johnson Reprint Corp.,
1967. xiv, 92 p. 016.82 67-29100

Z3508.L5 A25 MRR Alc.

ENGLISH LITERATURE--BIBLIOGRAPHY.
Annals of English literature, 1475-
1950; 2d ed. Oxford, Clarendon
Press, 1961. vi, 380 p. 016.82 62-
16029
Z2011 .A5 1961 MRR Alc.

Bateson, Frederick Wilse, The
Cambridge bibliography of English
literature, New York, The Macmillan
company; Cambridge, Eng., The
University press, 1941. 4 v.
015.42 41-4948
Z2011 .B3 1941 MRR Alc.

Bateson, Frederick Wilse, The
Cambridge bibliography of English
literature, Cambridge [Eng.] The
University press, 1940-57. 5 v.
016.82 41-2592
Z2011 .B28 vol. 5 MRR Alc.

Bateson, Frederick Wilse, A guide to
English literature, 2d ed. Garden
City, N.Y., Anchor Books, 1968. xi,
261 p. 016.82 68-12039
Z2011 .B32 1968 MRR Alc.

Baugh, Albert Croll, ed. A literary
history of England; 2nd. ed.
London, Routledge & K. Paul, 1967.
xv, 1796, lxxx p. [80/-] 820.9 68-
140788
PR83 .B3 1967b MRR Alc.

The Cambridge history of English
literature, New York, London, G. P.
Putnam's sons, 1907-17. 14 v. 07-
40854
PR83 .C22 MRR Alc.

Dick, Aliki Lafkidou. A student's
guide to British literature;
Littleton, Colo., Libraries
Unlimited, 1972 [c1971] 285 p.
016.820/.6 77-189255
Z2011 .D53 MRR Alc.

English Association. The year's work
in English studies. v. [1]-
1919/20- New York [etc.] Humanities
Press [etc.] 22-10024
PE58 .E6 MRR Alc Full set

The English catalogue of books
London, Published for the Publishers'
Circular by S. Low, Marston, 1914.
655 p. 52-45201
Z2001 .E517 MRR Alc.

The English catalogue of books
[annual] London, Publishers'
Circular Ltd. [etc.] 06-44930
Began publication in 1864.
Z2001 .E53 MRR Alc Partial set

English literature, 1660-1800;
Princeton, Princeton University
Press, 1950- v. 016.82 a 51-
6808
Z2011 .E6 MRR Alc.

Howard-Hill, Trevor Howard.
Bibliography of British literary
bibliographies Oxford, Clarendon P.,
1969. xxv, 570 p. [7/7/-]
016.01682 70-390421
Z2011 .H6 MRR Alc.

Howard-Hill, Trevor Howard.
Shakespearian bibliography and
textual criticism: Oxford, Clarendon
Press, 1971. 322 p. [£4.25]
016.8223/3 79-858175
Z8811 .H67 MRR Alc.

Kirk, John Foster, A supplement to
Allibone's critical dictionary of
English literature and British and
American authors. Detroit, Gale
Research Co., 1965. 2 v. (x, 1562
p.) 820.3 67-296
Z1224 .A44 1891a MRR Biog.

Lancaster, Joan Cadogan, comp.
Bibliography of historical works
issued in the United Kingdom, 1946-
1956, [London] University of London,
Institute of Historical Research,
1957. xxii, 388 p. 016.9 a 58-
2313
Z2016 .L3 MRR Alc.

The London catalogue of books,
London, W. Bent, 1822. 2 p. l., 239,
[1] p. 02-7516
Z2001 .E5 1822 MRR Alc.

The London catalogue of books,
London, Printed for W. Bent, 1811.
239 p. 06-10976
Z2001 .E5 1811 MRR Alc.

The London catalogue of books
published in Great Britain. London,
T. Hodgson, 1855. vi, 583 p. 02-
7489
Z2001 .E5 1855 MRR Alc.

Lowndes, William Thomas. The
bibliographer's manual of English
literature New ed. rev., cor. and
enl. London, H. G. Bohn, 1857-61;
Bell & Daldy, 1864-65. 10 v.
015.42 35-36008
Z2001 .L92 1857-65 MRR Alc.

Modern Humanities Research
Association. Annual bibliography of
English Language and literature.
1920- [Leeds, Eng. etc.] 22-11861
Z2011 .M69 MRR Alc Full set

The New Cambridge bibliography of
English literature, Cambridge [Eng.]
University Press, 1969- v. [10/-
/- $28.50 (U.S.) (v. 3)] 016.82 69-
10199
Z2011 .N45 MRR Alc.

Northup, Clark Sutherland, A
register of bibliographies of the
English language and literature, New
Haven, Yale university press; [etc.,
etc.] 1925. 6 p. l., 507 p. 25-
20533
Z2011 .N87 MRR Alc.

Spargo, John Webster, A
bibliographical manual for students
of the language and literature of
England and the United States; 3d
ed. New York, Hendricks House, 1956.
x, 285 p. 016.82 56-14402
Z2011 .S73 1956 MRR Alc.

Van Patten, Nathan, An index to
bibliographies and bibliographical
contributions relating to the work of
American and British authors, 1923-
1932. Stanford University, Calif.,
Stanford university press; London, H.
Milford, Oxford university press,
1934. vii, 324 p. 016.82 34-5449

Z1225.A1 V2 MRR Alc.

Watson, George, ed. The concise
Cambridge bibliography of English
literature, 600-1950. 2d ed.
Cambridge [Eng.] University Press,
1965. xi, 269 p. 65-14341
Z2011 .W3 1965 MRR Alc.

Watt, Robert, Bibliotheca
Britannica; New York, B. Franklin
[1965] 4 v. 011 77-6557
Z2001 .W34 1965 MRR Alc.

Whitaker's cumulative book list.
1924- London, J. Whitaker. 25-4576

Z2005 .W57 MRR Alc Partial set

ENGLISH LITERATURE--BIBLIOGRAPHY--
CATALOGS.
The British national bibliography
cumulated subject catalogue 1951/54-
London, Council of the British
National Bibliography. 015.42 59-
246
Z2001 .B752 MRR Alc Full set

Harvard University. Library. English
literature. Cambridge; Distributed
by the Harvard University Press,
1971. 4 v. 016.82 74-128717
Z2011 .H36 MRR Alc.

New York (City). Public Library. Berg
Collection. Dictionary catalog of
the Henry W. and Albert A. Berg
Collection of English and American
literature. Boston, G. K. Hall,
1969. 5 v. 016.82 75-21408
Z2011 .N55 MRR Alc (Dk 33)

ENGLISH LITERATURE--BIBLIOGRAPHY--FIRST
EDITIONS.
Brussel, Isidore Rosenbaum, Anglo-
American first editions. London,
Constable & co. ltd.; New York, R. R.
Bowker co., 1935-36. 2 v. 016.0944
016.82 35-19256
Z2014.F5 B9 MRR Alc.

Cutler, Bradley Dwyane, comp. Modern
British authors, their first
editions. New York, Greenberg
[c1930] xi, 171 p. 016.82 30-
20445
Z2014.F55 C8 1930 MRR Alc.

ENGLISH LITERATURE--BIBLIOGRAPHY--
PERIODICALS.
Cumulative book index. 1898/99- New
York [etc.] H. W. Wilson Co. 05-
33604
Z1219 .M78 MRR Circ Partial set

ENGLISH LITERATURE--BIO-BIBLIOGRAPHY.
Allibone, Samuel Austin, A critical
dictionary of English literature and
British and American authors,
Detroit, Gale Research Co., 1965. 3
v. (3140 p.) 820.3 67-295
Z1224 .A4317 MRR Biog.

A Biographical dictionary of the
living authors of Great Britain and
Ireland; Detroit, Gale Research Co.,
1966. viii, 449 p. 013.82 66-
16419
Z2010 .B61 1966 MRR Biog.

Browning, David Clayton, ed.
Everyman's dictionary of literary
biography, English & American,
London, Dent; New York, Dutton [1958]
x, 752 p. 928.2 a 58-2815
PR19 .B7 MRR Biog.

Gillow, Joseph, A literary and
biographical history; New York, B.
Franklin [1968] 5 v. 914.2/03/0922
a 74-6323
Z2010 .G483 1968 MRR Biog.

ENGLISH LITERATURE--BIO- (Cont.)
Harvey, Paul, Sir, The Oxford
companion to English literature; 4th
ed. revised Oxford, Clarendon P.,
1967. x, 961 p. [50/-] 820.3 67-
111134
  PR19 .H3 1967 MRR Ref Desk.

Moulton, Charles Wells, Library of
literary criticism of English and
American authors through the
beginning of the twentieth century.
New York, F. Ungar Pub. Co. [1966] 4
v. 820.9 65-16619
  PR83 .M73 1966 TJ Rm.

Myers, Robin, A dictionary of
literature in the English language,
from Chaucer to 1940, [1st ed.]
Oxford, New York, Pergamon Press
[1970] 2 v. 016.82 68-18529
  Z2010 .M9 MRR Alc.

The New Century handbook of English
literature, Rev. ed. New York,
Appleton-Century-Crofts [1967] vii,
1167 p. 820.3 67-12396
  PR19 .N4 1967 MRR Ref Desk.

The Penguin companion to English
literature. New York, McGraw-Hill
[1971] 575, [1] p. [$10.95] 820.9
B   77-158061
  PN849.C5 P4 MRR Alc.

Webster's new world companion to
English and American literature. New
York, World Pub. [1973] 850 p.
[$15.00] 820/.9 72-12788
  PR19 .W4 1973 MRR Biog.

**ENGLISH LITERATURE--CATHOLIC AUTHORS--
BIBLIOGRAPHY.**
Gillow, Joseph, A literary and
biographical history: New York, B.
Franklin [1968] 5 v. 914.2/03/0922
B   74-6323
  Z2010 .G483 1968 MRR Biog.

ENGLISH LITERATURE--DICTIONARIES.
Adams, William Davenport, Dictionary
of English literature, 2d ed.
Detroit, Republished by Gale Research
Co., 1966. iv, 708 p. 820.3 66-
25162
  PR19 .A38 1966 MRR Alc.

Chambers, Robert, Chambers's
cyclopedia of English literature,
London, Edinburgh, W. & R. Chambers,
limited [1927-38] 3 v. 820.9 39-
8587
  PR83 .C4 1927 MRR Alc.

Freeman, William, Dictionary of
fictional characters. Boston, The
Writer, inc. [1974, c1973] xi, 579
p. 820/.3 73-18065
  PR19 .F7 1974 MRR Ref Desk.

Gillie, Christopher. Longman
companion to English literature.
[London] Longman, 1972. xiv, 881 p.
[£2.80] 820/.9 73-150591
  PR85 .G45 MRR Alc.

Harvey, Paul, Sir, The Oxford
companion to English literature; 4th
ed. revised Oxford, Clarendon P.,
1967. x, 961 p. [50/-] 820.3 67-
111134
  PR19 .H3 1967 MRR Ref Desk.

The New Century handbook of English
literature, Rev. ed. New York,
Appleton-Century-Crofts [1967] vii,
1167 p. 820.3 67-12396
  PR19 .N4 1967 MRR Ref Desk.

Watt, Homer Andrew, A handbook of
English literature New York, Barnes
& Noble [1960, c1946] 430 p. 820.3
61-2985
  PR19 .W3 1960 MRR Biog.

Webster's new world companion to
English and American literature. New
York, World Pub. [1973] 850 p.
[$15.00] 820/.9 72-12788
  PR19 .W4 1973 MRR Biog.

ENGLISH LITERATURE--DISCOGRAPHY.
Roach, Helen Pauline, Spoken
records, 3d ed. Metuchen, N.J.,
Scarecrow Press, 1970. 288 p.
016.82 77-10661
  Z2011 .R6 1970 MRR Alc.

**ENGLISH LITERATURE--EXAMINATIONS,
QUESTIONS, ETC.**
Notes and queries; v. 1- Nov. 3,
1849- London [etc.] Oxford Univ.
Press [etc.] 12-25307
  AG305 .N7 MRR Alc Full set

**ENGLISH LITERATURE--HISTORY AND
CRITICISM.**
Baugh, Albert Croll, ed. A literary
history of England; 2nd. ed.
London, Routledge & K. Paul, 1967.
xv, 1796, lxxx p. [80/-] 820.9 68-
140788
  PR83 .B3 1967b MRR Alc.

The Cambridge history of English
literature, New York, London, G. P.
Putnam's sons, 1907-17. 14 v. 07-
40854
  PR83 .C22 MRR Alc.

The Critical temper; New York, Ungar
[1969] 3 v. [45.00] 820.9 68-
8116
  PR83 .C764 MRR Alc.

Daiches, David, A critical history
of English literature. 2d ed. New
York, Ronald Press Co. [1970] 2 v.
(1178 p.) 820.9 70-112497
  PR83 .D29 1970 MRR Alc.

Disraeli, Isaac, Curiosities of
literature, New York, London, D.
Appleton and company, 1932. xx p., 1
l., 312 p. 828.7 32-28946
  PN43 .D5 1932 MRR Alc.

English Association. The year's work
in English studies. v. [1]
1919/20- New York [etc.] Humanities
Press [etc.] 22-10024
  PE58 .E6 MRR Alc Full set

Ford, Boris, ed. The Pelican guide
to English literature.
[Harmondsworth, Middlesex] Penguin
Books [1957-62; v. 1, 1959] 7 v.
820.9 60-4556
  PR85 .F66 MRR Alc.

Fulghum, Walter B. A dictionary of
Biblical allusions in English
literature New York, Holt, Rinehart
and Winston [1965] viii, 291 p.
820.93 65-19349
  PR145 .F8 MRR Alc.

Gillie, Christopher. Longman
companion to English literature.
[London] Longman, 1972. xiv, 881 p.
[£2.80] 820/.9 73-150591
  PR85 .G45 MRR Alc.

Legouis, Émile Hyacinthe, A history
of English literature; Rev. ed. New
York, Macmillan [1957] xxiii, 1427
p. 820.9 57-13898
  PR93 .L43 1957 MRR Alc.

Moulton, Charles Wells, ed. The
Library of literary criticism of
English and American authors, New
York, P. Smith, 1935. 8 v. 820.9
35-27242
  PR83 .M73 1935 MRR Alc.

Moulton, Charles Wells, Library of
literary criticism of English and
American authors through the
beginning of the twentieth century.
New York, F. Ungar Pub. Co. [1966] 4
v. 820.9 65-16619
  PR83 .M73 1966 TJ Rm.

Ryland, Frederick, Chronological
outlines of English literature.
Detroit, Gale Research Co., 1968.
xii, 351 p. 820.9 68-30587
  PR87 .R85 1968b MRR Alc.

Sampson, George, The concise
Cambridge history of English
literature. 3rd ed., London,
Cambridge U.P., 1970. xiii, 876 p.
[65/-] 820.9 69-16287
  PR85 .S34 1970 MRR Alc.

Stowell, Helen Elizabeth. An
introduction to English literature
London, Longmans, 1966. xi, 192 p.
[14/-] 820/.9 67-74066
  PR83 .S7 MRR Alc.

Ward, Alfred Charles, Illustrated
history of English literature.
London, New York, Longmans, Green
[1953-55] 3 v. 820.9 54-76
  PR83 .W35 MRR Alc.

**ENGLISH LITERATURE--HISTORY AND
CRITICISM--BIBLIOGRAPHY.**
Altick, Richard Daniel, Selective
bibliography for the study of English
and American literature, 4th ed.
New York, Macmillan [1971] xii, 164
p. [$2.95] 016.82 75-132867
  Z2011 .A4 1971 MRR Alc.

Bateson, Frederick Wilse, The
Cambridge bibliography of English
literature, New York, The Macmillan
company; Cambridge, Eng., The
University press, 1941. 4 v.
015.42 41-4948
  Z2011 .B3 1941 MRR Alc.

Bateson, Frederick Wilse, The
Cambridge bibliography of English
literature, Cambridge [Eng.] The
University press, 1940-57. 5 v.
016.82 41-2592
  Z2011 .B28 vol. 5 MRR Alc.

Bond, Donald Frederic, A reference
guide to English studies. 2d ed.
Chicago, University of Chicago Press
[1971] x, 198 p. 016.0168 79-
130307
  Z1002 .B72 1971 MRR Alc.

Bonheim, Helmut W., The English
novel before Richardson: Metuchen,
N.J., Scarecrow Press, 1971. vi, 145
p. 016.823/03 75-19590
  Z2014.F4 B65 MRR Alc.

Combs, Richard E. Authors: critical
and biographical references:
Metuchen, N.J., Scarecrow Press,
1971. 221 p. 016.809 73-167644
  PN524 .C58 MRR Alc.

Dick, Aliki Lafkidou. A student's
guide to British literature;
Littleton, Colo., Libraries
Unlimited, 1972 [c1971] 285 p.
016.820/.8 77-189255
  Z2011 .D53 MRR Alc.

English literature, 1660-1800;
Princeton, Princeton University
Press, 1950- v. 016.82 a 51-
6808
  Z2011 .E6 MRR Alc.

Modern Humanities Research
Association. Annual bibliography of
English Language and literature.
1920- [Leeds, Eng. etc.] 22-11861
  Z2011 .M69 MRR Alc Full set

Modern Language Association of
America. MLA abstracts of articles
in scholarly journals. [New York]
408 72-624077
  P1 .M64 MRR Alc Full set

The New Cambridge bibliography of
English literature. Cambridge [Eng.]
University Press, 1969- v. [10/-
/- $28.50 (U.S.) (v. 3) 016.82 69-
10199
  Z2011 .N45 MRR Alc.

The Romantic movement bibliography,
1936-1970; [Ann Arbor, Mich.]
Pierian Press, 1973. 7 v. (xiii,
3289 p.) 016.809/894 77-172773
  Z6514.R6 R65 MRR Alc.

Stratman, Carl Joseph, Restoration
and eighteenth century theatre
research; Carbondale, Southern
Illinois University Press [1971] ix,
811 p. [$25.00] 016.822/5/09 71-
112394
  Z2014.D7 S854 MRR Alc.

**ENGLISH LITERATURE--HISTORY AND
CRITICISM--DICTIONARIES.**
The Explicator. The Explicator
cyclopedia. Chicago, Quadrangle
Books, 1966-. v. 820.9 66-11875
  PR401 .E9 MRR Alc.

**ENGLISH LITERATURE--HISTORY AND
CRITICISM--PERIODICALS.**
The Explicator. v. 1- Oct. 1942-
Columbia [etc.] University of South
Carolina [etc.] 47-41241
  PR1 .E9 MRR Alc Full set

**ENGLISH LITERATURE--IRISH AUTHORS--
HISTORY AND CRITICISM.**
Howarth, Herbert. The Irish writers,
1880-1940; London, Rockliff [1958]
x, 318 p. 820.903 a 59-4779
  PR8753 .H6 MRR Alc.

Taylor, Estella Ruth. The modern
Irish writers; Lawrence, University
of Kansas Press, 1954. 176 p.
820.904 54-8406
  PR8753 .T3 MRR Alc.

**ENGLISH LITERATURE--OUTLINES, SYLLABI,
ETC.**
Holman, Clarence Hugh, A handbook to
literature; 3d ed. Indianapolis,
Odyssey Press [1972] viii, 646 p.
803 73-175226
  PN41 .H6 1972 MRR Alc.

Lass, Abraham Harold, ed. A
student's guide to 50 British novels,
New York, Washington Square Press
[1966] xix, 364 p. 823.00202 66-
2898
  PR825 .L3 MRR Alc.

Ryland, Frederick, Chronological
outlines of English literature.
Detroit, Gale Research Co., 1968.
xii, 351 p. 820.9 68-30587
  PR87 .R85 1868b MRR Alc.

Smith, Guy E. English literature;
Paterson, N.J., Littlefield, Adams,
1959. 2 v. 820.2 59-33833
  PR87 .S65 1959 MRR Alc.

ENGLISH LITERATURE--PERIODICALS.
American notes & queries. v. 1-
Sept. 1962- [New Haven, Conn.]
[$6.50] 031/.02 74-642751
  Z1034 .A4 MRR Alc Full set

Notes and queries; v. 1- Nov. 3,
1849- London [etc.] Oxford Univ.
Press [etc.] 12-25307
  AG305 .N7 MRR Alc Full set

ENGLISH LITERATURE--STUDY AND TEACHING--
BIBLIOGRAPHY.
Altick, Richard Daniel, Selective
bibliography for the study of English
and American literature, 4th ed.
New York, Macmillan [1971] xii, 164
p. [$2.95] 016.82 75-132867
Z2011 .A4 1971 MRR Alc.

ENGLISH LITERATURE--TRANSLATIONS FROM
CLASSICAL LITERATURE--BIBLIOGRAPHY.
Smith, Frank Seymour. The classics
in translation. New York, B.
Franklin [1968] 307 p. 016.88 68-
57122
Z7018.T7E87 1968 MRR Alc.

ENGLISH LITERATURE--TRANSLATIONS FROM
DANISH--BIBLIOGRAPHY.
Bredsdorff, Elias. Danish literature
in English translation. Copenhagen,
E. Munksgaard, 1950. 198 p.
016.83981 51-4614
Z2574.T7 B7 MRR Alc.

Claudi, Jørgen, Contemporary Danish
authors. Copenhagen, Danske selskab,
1952. 163 p. 838.8109 52-14932
PT7760 .C55 MRR Biog.

ENGLISH LITERATURE--TRANSLATIONS FROM
FOREIGN LITERATURE--BIBLIOGRAPHY.
American library association. Section
for library work with children.
International committee. Children's
books from foreign languages; New
York, The H. W. Wilson company, 1937.
148 p. 028.5 37-16044
Z1037 .A4955 MRR Alc.

Farrar, Clarissa Palmer.
Bibliography of English translations
from medieval sources. New York,
Columbia university press, 1946.
xiii, 534 p. 016.8 a 46-1541
Z6517 .F3 MRR Alc.

Ferguson, Mary Anne. Bibliography of
English translations from medieval
sources, 1943-1967. New York,
Columbia University Press, 1974. x,
274 p. 016.08 73-7751
Z6517 .F47 MRR Alc.

ENGLISH LITERATURE--TRANSLATIONS FROM
GERMAN.
Ramage, Craufurd Tait, comp.
Beautiful thoughts from German and
Spanish authors. New rev. ed.
London, New York, G. Routledge and
sons, 1884. 3 p. l., [ix]-xvi, 559
p. 15-9871
PN6080 .R32 1884 MRR Alc.

ENGLISH LITERATURE--TRANSLATIONS FROM
GERMAN--BIBLIOGRAPHY.
English, 1948-1964. 2d rev. ed.
Gottingen, Vandenhoeck & Ruprecht,
1968. 509 p. 016.9143/03 72-
590351
Z2221 .T73 no. 1 MRR Alc.

Morgan, Bayard Quincy, A critical
bibliography of German literature in
English translation, 1481-1927. 2d
ed., completely rev. and greatly
augm. New York, Scarecrow Press,
1965 [c1938] 690 p. 016.83 65-
13549
Z2234.T7 M8 1965 MRR Alc.

Rose, Ernst, A history of German
literature. [New York] New York
University Press, 1960. 353 p.
830.9 60-9405
PT91 .R75 MRR Alc.

Smith, Murray F., A selected
bibliography of German literature in
English translation, 1956-1960.
Metuchen, N.J., Scarecrow Press,
1972. v, 398 p. 016.83 76-157727

Z2234.T7 S6 MRR Alc.

ENGLISH LITERATURE--TRANSLATIONS FROM
GREEK.
Page, Denys Lionel, comp. Greek
literary papyri in two volumes. I.
Cambridge, Harvard University Press,
1942. xlix, 617 p. a 42-4500
PA3611.A22 1942 MRR Alc.

ENGLISH LITERATURE--TRANSLATIONS FROM
NORWEGIAN--BIBLIOGRAPHY.
Nordiska kulturkommissionen.
Oversettelse til engelsk av nordisk
skjønnlitteratur; [Oslo, 1960] 143
p. 66-84821
Z2604.T7 N58 MRR Alc.

ENGLISH LITERATURE--TRANSLATIONS FROM
ORIENTAL LITERATURE.
Pritchard, James Bennett, ed.
Ancient Near Eastern texts relating
to the Old Testament. 2d ed., corr.
and enl. Princeton, Princeton
University Press, 1955. xxi, 544 p.
221.93 55-9033
BS1180 .P83 1955 MRR Alc.

ENGLISH LITERATURE--TRANSLATIONS FROM
PERSIAN.
Browne, Edward Granville, A literary
history of Persia ... Cambridge
[Eng.] The University press, 1928-
1930. 4 v. mrr01-34
PK6097 .B73 MRR Alc.

ENGLISH LITERATURE--TRANSLATIONS FROM
PORTUGUESE--BIBLIOGRAPHY.
Levine, Suzanne Jill. Latin America
fiction & poetry in translation. New
York, Center for Inter-American
Relations [1970] 71 p. [1.25]
016.8608 75-121376
Z1609.T7 L45 MRR Alc.

ENGLISH LITERATURE--TRANSLATIONS FROM
ROMANCE LITERATURE--BIBLIOGRAPHY.
Parks, George Bruner, The Romance
literatures. New York, F. Ungar Pub.
Co. [1970] 2 v. [$45.00]
016.84009 70-98341
Z7033.T7E65 MRR Alc.

ENGLISH LITERATURE--TRANSLATIONS FROM
RUSSIAN--BIBLIOGRAPHY.
Bibliography of Russian literature in
English translation to 1945. Totowa,
N.J., Rowman and Littlefield [1972]
74, 96 p. 016.8917/08 72-180612
Z2504.T8 B53 MRR Alc.

ENGLISH LITERATURE--TRANSLATIONS FROM
SLAVIC LITERATURE--BIBLIOGRAPHY.
Lewanski, Richard Casimir, The
Slavic literatures. New York, New
York Public Library, and F. Ungar
Pub. Co. [1967] xiii, 630 p.
016.8917 65-23122
Z7041 .L59 MRR Alc.

ENGLISH LITERATURE--TRANSLATIONS FROM
SPANISH.
Ramage, Craufurd Tait, comp.
Beautiful thoughts from German and
Spanish authors. New rev. ed.
London, New York, G. Routledge and
sons, 1884. 3 p. l., [ix]-xvi, 559
p. 15-9871
PN6080 .R32 1884 MRR Alc.

ENGLISH LITERATURE--TRANSLATIONS FROM
SPANISH--BIBLIOGRAPHY.
Granier, James Albert, Latin
American belles-lettres in English
translation; [2d rev. ed.]
Washington, 1943. ii, 33 p. 016.86
44-40918
Z663.32 .A5 no. 1 1943 MRR Alc.

Levine, Suzanne Jill. Latin America
fiction & poetry in translation. New
York, Center for Inter-American
Relations [1970] 71 p. [1.25]
016.8608 75-121376
Z1609.T7 L45 MRR Alc.

Pane, Remigio Ugo. English
translations from the Spanish, 1484-
1943. New Brunswick, Rutgers
university press, 1944. vi, 218 p.
016.86 44-12659
Z2694.T7 P2 MRR Alc.

ENGLISH LITERATURE--TRANSLATIONS FROM
YIDDISH--BIBLIOGRAPHY.
Abramowicz, Dina. Yiddish literature
in English translation; 2d ed., New
York, Yivo Institute for Jewish
Research, 1968 [c1969] 39 p. [2.00]
016.89249/08 71-5871
Z7070 .A2 1969 MRR Alc.

ENGLISH LITERATURE--HISTORY AND
CRITICISM--BIBLIOGRAPHY.
Kennedy, Arthur Garfield, A concise
bibliography for students of English,
5th ed. Stanford, Calif., Stanford
University Press, 1972. xvi, 300 p.
016.82 77-183889
Z2011 .K35 1972 MRR Alc.

ENGLISH NEWSPAPERS--BIBLIOGRAPHY.
Crane, Ronald Salmon, A census of
British newspapers and periodicals,
1620-1800, London, Holland P., 1966.
205 p. 016.072 67-112604
Z6956.E5 C8 1966 MRR Alc.

Hewitt, Arthur R. Union list of
Commonwealth newspapers in London,
Oxford, and Cambridge. [London]
Published for the Institute of
Commonwealth Studies [by] the Athlone
Press, University of London, 1960.
ix, 101 p. 016.072 60-51452
Z6945 .H55 1960 MRR Alc.

The New Cambridge bibliography of
English literature. Cambridge [Eng.]
University Press, 1969- v. [10/-
/- $28.50 (U.S.) (v. 3)] 016.82 69-
10199
Z2011 .N45 MRR Alc.

The Times, London. Tercentenary
handlist of English & Welsh
newspapers, magazines & reviews ...
London, The Times, 1920. 212 p., 1
l., L p., 1 l., [215]-324, xxxv p.
21-6520
Z6956.E5 T5 MRR Alc.

ENGLISH NEWSPAPERS--DIRECTORIES.
Directory of newspaper and magazine
personnel and data. London,
Haymarket Publishing Group, [etc.]
072.058 59-18302
Z6956.E5 D5 MRR Alc Latest edition

The Newspaper press directory.
London, C. Mitchell [etc.] ca 07-6361
Z6956.E5 M6 MRR Alc Latest edition

Who's who in journalism. 1969-
[London] 070/.025/42 71-11173
Z6956.G6 W5 MRR Alc Latest edition

Willing's press guide. London, J.
Willing, Ltd. [etc.] 53-36485
Began publication with issue for
1874.
Z6956.E5 W5 MRR Alc Latest edition

ENGLISH NEWSPAPERS--HISTORY.
Frank, Joseph, The beginnings of the
English newspaper; 1620-1660.
Cambridge, Harvard University Press,
1961. x, 384 p. 072 61-13735
PN5115 .F7 1961 MRR Alc.

ENGLISH NEWSPAPERS IN FOREIGN COUNTRIES--
DIRECTORIES.
Wilcox, Dennis L. English language
newspapers abroad; Detroit, Gale
Research Co. [1967] 243 p.
017/.025 67-25558
Z6941 .W5 MRR Alc.

ENGLISH PERIODICALS--BIBLIOGRAPHY.
The Advertiser's annual with Empire
sections. London, Admark Directories
Ltd. [etc.] 659.1058 49-14603
HF5802 .A23 MRR Alc Latest edition

British house journals. 1956-
[London] British Association of
Industrial Editors. 57-39809
Z7164.C81 B83 MRR Alc Latest
edition

British union-catalogue of
periodicals; London, Butterworths
Scientific Publications, 1955-58. 4
v. 016.05 56-1295
Z6945 .B87 MRR Alc.

Crane, Ronald Salmon, A census of
British newspapers and periodicals,
1620-1800, London, Holland P., 1966.
205 p. 016.072 67-112604
Z6956.E5 C8 1966 MRR Alc.

The New Cambridge bibliography of
English literature, Cambridge [Eng.]
University Press, 1969- v. [10/-
/- $28.50 (U.S.) (v. 3)] 016.82 69-
10199
Z2011 .N45 MRR Alc.

Stratman, Carl Joseph, Britain's
theatrical periodicals, 1720-1967,
New York, New York Public Library,
1972. xxiv, 160 p. 016.792/0942
72-134260
Z6935 .S76 1972 MRR Alc.

The Times, London. Tercentenary
handlist of English & Welsh
newspapers, magazines & reviews ...
London, The Times, 1920. 212 p., 1
l., L p., 1 l., [215]-324, xxxv p.
21-6520
Z6956.E5 T5 MRR Alc.

Ward, William Smith, Index and
finding list of serials published in
the British Isles, 1789-1832.
Lexington, University of Kentucky
Press [1953] xv, 180 p. 016.052
53-5521
Z6956.E5 W27 MRR Alc.

ENGLISH PERIODICALS--DIRECTORIES.
Directory of newspaper and magazine
personnel and data. London,
Haymarket Publishing Group, [etc.]
072.058 59-18302
Z6956.E5 D5 MRR Alc Latest edition

The Newspaper press directory.
London, C. Mitchell [etc.] ca 07-6361
Z6956.E5 M6 MRR Alc Latest edition

Who's who in journalism. 1969-
[London] 070/.025/42 71-11173
Z6956.G6 W5 MRR Alc Latest edition

Willing's press guide. London, J.
Willing, Ltd. [etc.] 53-36485
Began publication with issue for
1874.
Z6956.E5 W5 MRR Alc Latest edition

Woodworth, David. Guide to current
British journals; 2nd ed. London,
Library Association, 1973. 2 v.
[£8.50 (v. 1) £4.50 (v. 2)] 016.052
74-159014
Z6956.G6 W66 1973 MRR Alc.

The Writers and artists' year book;
[1st] year: 1906- Boston [etc.]
The Writer, inc. [etc.] 08-22320
PN12 .W8 MRR Ref Desk Latest
edition

ENGLISH PERIODICALS--HISTORY.
Graham, Walter James, English
literary periodicals. New York, T.
Nelson & sons, 1930. 424 p. incl.
front., plates, ports., facsims.
052   31-2432
     PN5124.P4 G73 MRR Alc.

ENGLISH PERIODICALS--INDEXES.
Bibliotheca celtica. 1909-1927/28;
new ser., v. 1- 1929/33-
Aberystwyth [National library of
Wales] 11-5717
     Z2071 .B56 MRR Alc Partial set

Index to Commonwealth little
magazines. 1964/65- Troy, N.Y.
[etc.] Whitston Pub. Co. [etc.] 66-
28796
     AI3 .I48 MRR Alc Latest edition

The Subject index to periodicals.
1915/16-1961. London, Library
Association. 28-19815
     AI3.A72 MRR Alc Full set

The Wellesley index to Victorian
periodicals, 1824-1900. [Toronto]
University of Toronto Press; [London]
Routledge & K. Paul [c1966- v.
[$75.00 Can. (v. 1)]   052 67-79381

     AI3 .W45 MRR Alc.

ENGLISH PHILOLOGY--BIBLIOGRAPHY.
Alston, R. C. A bibliography of the
English language from the invention
of printing to the year 1800; Leeds
[Eng.] Printed for the author by E.
J. Arnold, 1965- v.   66-38399
     Z2015.A1 A4 MRR Alc.

Alston, R. C. Old English, Middle
English, early modern English,
miscellaneous works, vocabulary.
Menston [Eng.], Printed for the
author by Scolar Press, [1970- v.
016.42 s 016.42 72-176678
     Z2015.A1 A4 vol. 3, pt. 1 MRR Alc.

Bond, Donald Frederic, A reference
guide to English studies. 2d ed.
Chicago, University of Chicago Press
[1971] x, 188 p. 016.0168 79-
130307
     Z1002 .B72 1971 MRR Alc.

English Association. The year's work
in English studies. v. [1]-
1919/20- New York [etc.] Humanities
Press [etc.] 22-10024
     PE58 .E6 MRR Alc Full set

Kennedy, Arthur Garfield, A
bibliography of writings on the
English language New York, Hafner
Pub. Co., 1961 [c1927] xvii, 517 p.
016.42 61-8940
     Z2015.A1 K3 1961 MRR Alc.

Kennedy, Arthur Garfield, A concise
bibliography for students of English.
5th ed. Stanford, Calif., Stanford
University Press, 1972. xvi, 300 p.
016.82 77-183889
     Z2011 .K35 1972 MRR Alc.

McNamee, Lawrence Francis.
Dissertations in English and American
literature; New York, Bowker, 1968.
xi, 1124 p. [$17.50] 016.82 68-
27446
     Z5053 .M32 MRR Alc.

Modern Humanities Research
Association. Annual bibliography of
English Language and literature.
1920- [Leeds, Eng. etc.] 22-11861
     Z2011 .M69 MRR Alc Full set

Northup, Clark Sutherland, A
register of bibliographies of the
English language and literature, New
Haven, Yale university press; [etc.,
etc.] 1925. 6 p. l., 507 p. 25-
20533
     Z2011 .N87 MRR Alc.

ENGLISH PHILOLOGY--DICTIONARIES.
Lazarus, Arnold Leslie. Modern
English; New York, Grosset & Dunlap
[1971] 462 p. [$10.00]   423 78-
86706
     PE31 .L3 MRR Ref Desk.

ENGLISH PHILOLOGY--HISTORY.
English Association. The year's work
in English studies. v. [1]-
1919/20- New York [etc.] Humanities
Press [etc.] 22-10024
     PE58 .E6 MRR Alc Full set

ENGLISH PHILOLOGY--PERIODICALS--
DIRECTORIES.
Directory of periodicals publishing
articles on English and American
literature and language. [1st]-
[1960- Chicago [etc.] Swallow Press.
016.42/05 65-9218
     Z2015.P4 .D56 MRR Alc Latest
          edition / MRR Ref Desk Latest
          edition

ENGLISH PHILOLOGY--SOCIETIES, ETC.--
DIRECTORIES.
National Council of Teachers of
English. Directory of officers,
committees, and affiliates.
Champaign, Ill. 65-5403
     PE11 .N317 MRR Alc Latest edition

ENGLISH POETRY.
Aldington, Richard, ed. The Viking
book of poetry of the English-
speaking world. Rev., Mid-century
ed. New York, Viking Press, 1958. 2
v.   821.082 58-8134
     PR1175 .A64 1958 MRR Alc.

Bronson, Bertrand Harris, ed. The
traditional tunes of the Child
ballads; Princeton, N.J., Princeton
University Press, 1959- v.
784.3 57-5468
     ML3650 .B82 MRR Alc.

Brooks, Cleanth, ed. Understanding
poetry, 3d ed. New York, Holt,
Rinehart and Winston [1960] 584 p.
821.082 60-10578
     PR1109 .B676 1960 MRR Alc.

Ernest, P. Edward, ed. The family
album of favorite poems. New York,
Grosset & Dunlap [1959] 538 p.
821.082 59-4502
     PR1175 .E75 MRR Ref Desk.

Felleman, Hazel, comp. The best
loved poems of the American people.
Garden City, N.Y., Garden City Books
[1957, c1936] xxxiii, 670 p.
821.082 58-1240
     PR1175 .F4 1957 MRR Ref Desk.

Gannett, Lewis Stiles, ed. The
family book of verse, [1st ed.] New
York, Harper [1961] 351 p. 821.082
61-9703
     PR1175 .G25 MRR Ref Desk.

Legerman, David G., ed. The family
book of best loved poems, Garden
City, N.Y., Hanover House [1952] 485
p. 820.82 52-13663
     PR1175 .L437 MRR Ref Desk.

Stevenson, Burton Egbert, comp. The
home book of verse, American and
English; 9th ed. New York, Holt
[1953] 2 v. (lxxxiv, 4013 p.)
821.982 53-3870
     PR1175 .S76 1953 MRR Ref Desk.

Untermeyer, Louis, ed. A treasury of
great poems, English and American,
New York, Simon and Schuster, 1942.
lviii p., 1 l., 1288 p., 1 l. 42-
22424
     PR1175 .U65 MRR Alc.

Wells, Carolyn, comp. The book of
humorous verse, Rev. and amplified
ed. Garden City, N.Y., Garden City
publishing co., inc. [c1936] 3 p.
l., v-xxv p., 1 l., 25-1011 p.
821.0822 827.0822 36-16566
     PN6110.H8 W4 1936 MRR Alc.

Woods, Ralph Louis, Famous poems and
the little-known stories behind them.
[1st ed.] New York, Hawthorn Books
[1961] 336 p. 820.82 61-10821
     PR1175 .W587 MRR Alc.

ENGLISH POETRY--MIDDLE ENGLISH, 1100-
1500--INDEXES.
Brown, Carleton Fairchild, The index
of Middle English verse. New York,
Printed for the Index Society by
Columbia University Press, 1943.
xix, 785 p. 016.821/1 43-16653
     Z2012 .B86 MRR Alc.

ENGLISH POETRY--EARLY MODERN, 1500-1700.
The Oxford book of seventeenth
century verse, Oxford, Clarendon
Press [1951] 974 p. 821.082 57-
25248
     PR1209 .O8 1951 MRR Alc.

ENGLISH POETRY--EARLY MODERN, 1500-1700-
-INDEXES.
First-line index of English poetry,
1500-1800, in manuscripts of the
Bodleian Library, Oxford; Oxford,
Clarendon P., 1969. 2 v. (xi, 1257
p.) [11/5/-] 821/.0016 72-397656

     Z2014.P7 F5 MRR Alc.

ENGLISH POETRY--18TH CENTURY.
The Oxford book of eighteenth century
verse, Oxford, The Clarendon Press,
1926. xii, 727 p.   mrr01-39
     PR1215 .O85 1926a MRR Alc.

ENGLISH POETRY--18TH CENTURY--INDEXES.
First-line index of English poetry,
1500-1800, in manuscripts of the
Bodleian Library, Oxford; Oxford,
Clarendon P., 1969. 2 v. (xi, 1257
p.) [11/5/-] 821/.0016 72-397656

     Z2014.P7 F5 MRR Alc.

ENGLISH POETRY--19TH CENTURY.
Ellmann, Richard, comp. The Norton
anthology of modern poetry, [1st
ed.] New York, Norton [1973] xlvi,
1456 p. [$9.95 (pbk.)] 821/.008
73-6587
     PS323.5 .E5 1973 MRR Alc.

The Oxford book of English verse of
the Romantic period, 1798-1837.
Oxford, Clarendon Press [1958] 887
p. 821.7082 60-44641
     PR1221 .O8 1958 MRR Alc.

The Oxford book of modern verse, 1892-
1935, New York, Oxford university
press, 1936. xiv, 454 p.
821.910822 36-28578
     PR1225 .O9 1936 MRR Alc.

The Oxford book of Victorian verse,
Oxford, The Clarendon press, 1925.
xv, 1023, [1] p. 821.80822 33-
28868
     PR1223 .O8 1925 MRR Alc.

Taylor, Geoffrey, ed. Irish poets of
the nineteenth century. London,
Routledge and Paul [1951] viii, 406
p. 821.7082 51-2435
     PR8857 .T3 1951 MRR Alc.

Untermeyer, Louis, ed. Modern
British poetry. New and enl. ed.
New York, Harcourt, Brace & World
[c1969] xxiii, 548 p. 821/.9/109
69-13703
     PR1224 .U6 1969 MRR Alc.

ENGLISH POETRY--19TH CENTURY--
BIBLIOGRAPHY.
Faverty, Frederic Everett, ed. The
Victorian poets, 2d ed. Cambridge,
Harvard University Press, 1968. 433
p. 821/.8/09 68-15636
     PR593 .F3 1968 MRR Alc.

ENGLISH POETRY--19TH CENTURY--HISTORY
AND CRITICISM.
Faverty, Frederic Everett, ed. The
Victorian poets, 2d ed. Cambridge,
Harvard University Press, 1968. 433
p. 821/.8/09 68-15636
     PR593 .F3 1968 MRR Alc.

Houtchens, Carolyn Washburn, ed. The
English Romantic poets & essayists;
Rev. ed. [New York] Published for
the Modern Language Association of
America by New York University Press,
1966. xviii, 395 p. 820.9007 66-
12599
     PR590 .H6 1966 MRR Alc.

Raysor, Thomas Middleton, ed. The
English romantic poets; Rev. [i.e.
2d] ed. New York, Modern Language
Association of America, 1956. 307 p.
016.8217 57-4146
     PR590 .R3 1956 MRR Alc.

ENGLISH POETRY--20TH CENTURY.
Brinnin, John Malcolm, comp.
Twentieth century poetry: American
and British (1900-1970): New York,
McGraw-Hill [1970] xx, 515 p.
[$8.95] 821/.9/108 73-124305
     PS613 .B7 1970b MRR Alc.

Cecil, David, Lord, ed. Modern verse
in English, 1900-1950. New York,
Macmillan [1958] 689 p. 821.91082
58-13621
     PR1225 .C4 MRR Alc.

Ellmann, Richard, comp. The Norton
anthology of modern poetry, [1st
ed.] New York, Norton [1973] xlvi,
1456 p. [$9.95 (pbk.)] 821/.008
73-6587
     PS323.5 .E5 1973 MRR Alc.

Heath-Stubbs, John Francis Alexander,
ed. The Faber book of twentieth
century verse, Rev. [i.e., 2d] ed.
London, Faber and Faber [1965] 366
p. 67-4365
     PR1225 .H4 1965 MRR Alc.

Larkin, Philip, comp. The Oxford
book of twentieth-century English
verse; Oxford, Clarendon Press,
1973. l, 641 p. [£3.00]
821/.9/108 73-159943
     PR1225 .L3 MRR Alc.

The Oxford book of modern verse, 1892-
1935, New York, Oxford university
press, 1936. xiv, 454 p.
821.910822 36-28578
     PR1225 .O9 1936 MRR Alc.

Rosenthal, Macha Louis, ed. The new
modern poetry; New York, Macmillan
[1967] xxvii, 289 p. 821.91408 66-
17902
     PR1225 .R68 MRR Alc.

Stevenson, Burton Egbert, comp. The
home book of modern verse, 2d ed.
New York, Holt [1953] 1124 p.
821.91082 53-3683
     PR1175 .S762 1953 MRR Ref Desk.

ENGLISH POETRY--20TH CENTURY. (Cont.)
Untermeyer, Louis, ed. Modern
British poetry. New and enl. ed.
New York, Harcourt, Brace & World
[c1969] xxiii, 548 p.   821/.9/109
69-13703
   PR1224 .U6 1969 MRR Alc.

ENGLISH POETRY--20TH CENTURY--BIO-
BIBLIOGRAPHY.
Contemporary poets of the English
language. Chicago, St. James Press
[1970] xvii, 1243 p.   [$25.00]
821/.9/109   79-23734
   Z2014.P7 C63 MRR Biog.

The International who's who in
poetry. v. 1-   1958- London.   928
59-16302
   PS324 .I5 MRR Biog Latest edition

ENGLISH POETRY--20TH CENTURY--HISTORY
AND CRITICISM.
Rosenthal, Macha Louis. The modern
poets. New York, Oxford University
Press, 1960. 228 p.   821.9109 60-
13204
   PR601 .R6 MRR Alc.

ENGLISH POETRY--20TH CENTURY--
TRANSLATIONS FROM FRENCH.
Fowlie, Wallace, ed. and tr. Mid-
century French poets. New York,
Twayne [1955] 273 p.   841.91082 55-
830
   PQ1184 .F6 MRR Alc.

ENGLISH POETRY--ADDRESSES, ESSAYS,
LECTURES.
Spender, Stephen. Chaos and control
in poetry; Washington, Reference
Dept., Library of Congress; [for sale
by the Supt. of Docs., U.S. Govt.
Print. Off.] 1966. 14 p.   821/.009
66-60054
   Z663.293 .S67 MRR Alc.

United States. Library of Congress.
Gertrude Clarke Whittall Poetry and
Literature Fund. American poetry at
mid-century. Washington, Reference
Dept., Library of Congress, 1958. 49
p.   811.504 58-60074
   Z663.293 .A5 MRR Alc.

ENGLISH POETRY--BIO-BIBLIOGRAPHY.
Who's who in English speaking poets.
Los Angeles, National Poetry
Association [1958] 140 p.   016.821
58-38323
   Z2014.P7 W5 MRR Biog.

ENGLISH POETRY--DICTIONARIES.
Spender, Stephen, ed. The concise
encyclopedia of English and American
poets and poetry. [1st ed.] New
York, Hawthorn Books [1963] 415 p.
821.003 63-8015
   PR19 .S6 MRR Alc.

ENGLISH POETRY--EXPLICATION--
BIBLIOGRAPHY.
Kuntz, Joseph Marshall. Poetry
explication; Rev. ed. Denver, A.
Swallow 1962. 331 p.   016.82109
62-12525
   Z2014.P7 K8 MRR Alc.

ENGLISH POETRY--HISTORY AND CRITICISM.
Malof, Joseph. A manual of English
meters. Bloomington, Indiana
University Press [1970] xvi, 236 p.
[8.50]   426 70-98979
   PE1505 .M3 1970 MRR Alc.

Reeves, James. A short history of
English poetry, 1340-1940. [1st]
American ed. New York, Dutton, 1962.
234 p.   821.09 62-7817
   PR502 .R45 1962 MRR Alc.

Shaw, John MacKey. Childhood in
poetry; a catalogue. Detroit, Gale
Research Co. [1967-68, c1967] 5 v.
028.52   67-28092
   Z1037 .S513 MRR Alc.

Untermeyer, Louis. Lives of the
poets; New York, Simon and Schuster,
1959. 757 p.   821.09 59-11205
   PR502 .U5 MRR Biog.

ENGLISH POETRY--HISTORY AND CRITICISM--
DICTIONARIES.
The Explicator. The Explicator
cyclopedia. Chicago, Quadrangle
Books, 1966- v.   820.9 66-11875

   PR401 .E9 MRR Alc.

ENGLISH POETRY--HISTORY AND CRITICISM--
INDEXES.
Cline, Gloria Stark. An index to
criticisms of British and American
poetry. Metuchen, N.J., Scarecrow
Press, 1973. x, 307 p.   821/.009
73-15542
   PR89 .C5 MRR Ref Desk.

ENGLISH POETRY--INDEXES.
Brewton, John Edmund. Index to
children's poetry; New York, Wilson,
1942. xxxii, 965 p.   821.0016 42-
20148
   PN1023 .B7 MRR Alc.

Brewton, John Edmund. Index to
poetry for children and young people,
1964-1969; New York, Wilson, 1972.
xxx, 575 p.   821/.001/6   71-161574
   PN1023 .B72 MRR Alc.

Chicorel, Marietta. Chicorel index
to poetry in collections in print, on
discs and tapes: 1st ed. New York,
Chicorel Library Pub. Corp., 1972.
443 p.   016.80882 73-160763
   PR1175.8 .C4 MRR Alc.

Cline, Gloria Stark. An index to
criticisms of British and American
poetry. Metuchen, N.J., Scarecrow
Press, 1973. x, 307 p.   821/.009
73-15542
   PR89 .C5 MRR Ref Desk.

Granger, Edith. Granger's index to
poetry. 6th ed., completely rev. and
enl., indexing anthologies published
through December 31, 1970. New York,
Columbia University Press, 1973.
xxxvii, 2223 p.   [$80.00]
808.81/0016 73-4186
   PN1022 .G7 1973 MRR Ref Desk.

Granger, Edith. Granger's index to
poetry. 5th ed., completely rev. and
enl., New York, Columbia University
Press, 1962. xxxix, 2123 p.   808.81
62-3885
   PN1021 .G7 1962 MRR Ref Desk.

Granger, Edith. Granger's index to
poetry and recitations; 3d ed.,
completely rev. and enl., Chicago,
A. C. McClurg & co. [c1940] 2 p. l.,
vii-xxiv p., 1 l., 1525 p.   808.8
40-5254
   PN4321 .G8 1940 MRR Ref Desk.

Granger, Edith. Index to poetry.
4th ed., completely rev. & enl., New
York, Columbia University Press,
1953. xxxvii, 1832 p.   808.81 53-
987
   PN4321 .G8 1953 MRR Ref Desk.

Granger, Edith. An index to poetry
and recitations, Rev. and enl. ed.
Chicago, A. C. McClurg & co., 1927.
3 p. l., [v]-xv, 1059 p.   28-3385
   PN4321 .G8 1927 MRR Ref Desk.

Granger, Edith. An index to poetry
and recitations, Rev. and enl. ed.
Chicago, A. C. McClurg & company,
1918. xiv p., 1 l., 1059 p.
[$10.00]   18-23538
   PN4321 .G8 1918 MRR Ref Desk.

Granger, Edith. An index to poetry
and recitations; Chicago, A. C.
McClurg & company, 1904. 970 p.   04-
24547
   PN4321 .G8 MRR Ref Desk.

Macpherson, Maud Russell. Children's
poetry index, Boston, The F. W.
Faxon company, 1938. xiii, 453 p.
808.81   38-9870
   PN1023 .M25 MRR Alc.

Morris, Helen (Soutar) Where's that
poem? Oxford, Blackwell, 1967.
xxxv, 300 p.   [25/-]   016.821 67-
78385
   PN1023 .M6 MRR Alc.

ENGLISH POETRY--IRISH AUTHORS.
Cooke, John, M.A., ed. The Dublin
book of Irish verse, 1728-1909.
Dublin, Hodges, Figgis & co., ltd.;
London, H. Frowde, Oxford university
press, 1915. 4 p. l., 803, [1] p.
19-13564
   PR8851 .C6 1915 MRR Alc.

Taylor, Geoffrey, ed. Irish poets of
the nineteenth century. London,
Routledge and Paul [1951] viii, 406
p.   821.7082 51-2435
   PR8857 .T3 1951 MRR Alc.

ENGLISH POETRY--IRISH AUTHORS--
BIBLIOGRAPHY.
O'Donoghue, David James. The poets
of Ireland; Dublin, Hodges, Figgis &
co., ltd.; [etc.] 1912. 3 p.
l., iv, 504 p.   12-24411
   PR8706 .O3 MRR Biog.

ENGLISH POETRY--STUDY AND TEACHING.
Brooks, Cleanth, ed. Understanding
poetry, 3d ed. New York, Holt,
Rinehart and Winston [1960]   584 p.
821.082 60-10578
   PR1109 .B676 1960 MRR Alc.

ENGLISH POETRY--TRANSLATIONS FROM
FRENCH.
Conder, Alan, comp. and tr.
Cassell's anthology of French poetry.
London, Cassell [1950] 388 p.
841.082 51-7414
   PQ1170.E6 C6 1950 MRR Alc.

Flores, Angel, ed. An anthology of
French poetry from Nerval to Valéry
in English translation; New rev. ed.
Garden City, N.Y., Doubleday, 1962.
456 p.   841.7082 62-10456
   PQ1170.E6 F5 1962 MRR Alc.

ENGLISH POETRY--TRANSLATIONS FROM
GAELIC.
Dixon, William Macneile, ed. The
Edinburgh book of Scottish verse,
1300-1900. London, Meiklejohn and
Holden, 1910. xx, 938 p.   a 11-1394
   PR8651 .D5 MRR Alc.

ENGLISH POETRY--TRANSLATIONS FROM GREEK.
Anthologia graeca. The Greek
anthology. London, W. Heinemann; New
York, G. P. Putnam's sons, 1925-1927.
5 v.   881/.008   mrr01-22
   PA3611.A2 1925d MRR Alc.

Edmonds, John Maxwell, ed. and tr.
Elegy and iambus, London, W.
Heinemann, ltd.; New York, G. P.
Putnam's sons, 1931. 2 v.   881.08
mrr01-26
   PA3611.A14 1931d MRR Alc.

Edmonds, John Maxwell, ed. and tr.
Lyra graeca; London, W. Heinemann;
Cambridge, Mass., Harvard University
Press, 1927-1934 [v. 1, 1934] 3 v.
mrr01-23
   PA3611.A15 1927d MRR Alc.

Theocritus. The Greek bucolic poets,
London, W. Heinemann, New York, G.
P. Putnam's sons, 1916. xxviii, 527,
[1] p.   19-6715.
   PA3611 .A3 1916 MRR Alc.

ENGLISH POETRY--TRANSLATIONS FROM
ITALIAN.
Golino, Carlo Luigi, ed.
Contemporary Italian poetry;
Berkeley, University of California
Press, 1962. 223 p.   851.91082 62-
7436
   PQ4214 .G6 MRR Alc.

ENGLISH POETRY--TRANSLATIONS FROM LATIN.
Duff, John Wight, ed. and tr. Minor
Latin poets; Cambridge, Mass.,
Harvard university press; London, W.
Heinemann, ltd., 1934. xii, 838 p.,
1 l.   871.0822 35-178
   PA6156.A2 1934 MRR Alc.

ENGLISH POETRY--TRANSLATIONS FROM
RUSSIAN.
Yarmolinsky, Avrahm, ed. Two
centuries of Russian verse; New
York, Random House [1966] lxxv, 322
p.   891.71008   66-10992
   PG3237.E5 Y3 1966 MRR Alc.

ENGLISH POETRY--TRANSLATIONS FROM
SPANISH.
Flakoll, Darwin J., ed. and tr. New
voices of Hispanic America, Boston,
Beacon Press [1962] 226 p.   860.82
62-7248
   PQ7087.E5 F55 MRR Alc.

Turnbull, Eleanor Laurelle, ed. Ten
centuries of Spanish poetry;
Baltimore, Johns Hopkins Press [1955]
452 p.   861.082 55-8424
   PQ6267.E2 1955 MRR Alc.

ENGLISH PROSE LITERATURE--19TH CENTURY--
BIO-BIBLIOGRAPHY.
DeLaura, David J. Victorian prose;
New York, Modern Language Association
of America, 1973. xvi, 560 p.
[$12.00]   820/.9/008 73-80586
   PR785 .D4 MRR Alc.

ENGLISH WIT AND HUMOR.
Wells, Carolyn, comp. The book of
humorous verse, Rev. and amplified
ed. Garden City, N.Y., Garden City
publishing co., inc. [c1936] 3 p.
l., v-xxv p., 1 l., 25-1011 p.
821.0822 827.0822 36-16566
   PN6110.H8 W4 1936 MRR Alc.

ENGLISH WIT AND HUMOR--HISTORY AND
CRITICISM.
Harris, Leon A. The fine art of
political wit; [1st ed.] New York,
Dutton, 1964. 288 p.   827.093 64-
19532
   PN6231.P6 H36 MRR Alc.

ENGRAVERS--DICTIONARIES.
Bryan, Michael. Dictionary of
painters and engravers. New ed.,
rev. and enl., Port Washington,
N.Y., Kennikat Press [1964] 5 v.
927.5 64-15534
   N40 .B945 MRR Alc.

ENGRAVERS, AMERICAN.
Fielding, Mantle. Dictionary of
American painters, sculptors and
engravers / Enl. ed. with over 2,500
new listings of seventeenth,
eighteenth, and nineteenth century
American artists / Greens Farms,
Conn.: Modern Books and Crafts,
[1974] vi, 455 p. ; [$17.50]
709/.2/2 74-192539
   N6536 .F5 1974 MRR Biog.

United States. Library of Congress.
Prints and Photographs Division.
American prints in the Library of
Congress; Baltimore, Published for
the Library of Congress by the Johns
Hopkins Press [1970] xxi, 568 p.
769/.973 73-106134
   NE505 .A47 MRR Alc.

ENGRAVERS, AMERICAN--DICTIONARIES.
Young, William, A dictionary of
American artists, sculptors and
engravers: Cambridge, Mass., W.
Young [1868] 515 p. 709/.73 68-
3733
   N6536 .Y7 MRR Biog.

ENGRAVING.
see also Lithography

ENGRAVING--DICTIONARIES.
Zigrosser, Carl, A guide to the
collecting and care of original
prints, New York, Crown Publishers
[1967, c1965] vi, 120 p. 769/.1
68-115
   NE885 .Z5 1967 MRR Alc.

ENGRAVING--TECHNIQUE.
Peterdi, Gabor. Printmaking: methods
old and new. Rev. ed. New York,
Macmillan [1971] xxxix, 342 p.
[$15.00] 760/.28 79-130950
   NE850 .P4 1971 MRR Alc.

ENGRAVING--GREAT BRITAIN.
Ames, Joseph, Typographical
antiquities; London, W. Miller, 1810-
19. 4 v. 02-2021
   Z151 .A512 MRR Alc.

ENGRAVINGS.
see also Color prints

ENGRAVINGS--CATALOGS.
United States. Library of Congress.
Prints and photographs division.
Catalog of the Gardiner Greene
Hubbard collection of engravings,
presented to the Library of Congress
by Mrs. Gardiner Greene Hubbard,
Washington, Govt. print. off., 1905.
xxiii, 517 p. 05-20002
   Z663.39 .C28 MRR Alc.

ENGRAVINGS--PRICES.
Art prices current. v. [1]-9,
1907/08-1915/16; new ser., v. 1-
1921/22- 704.938 09-23300
   N8670 .A7 MRR Alc Partial set

International auction records. v.
[1]- 1967- [London, etc.,
Editions E. M.-Publisol] 700/.29
78-2167
   N8640 .I5 MRR Alc Full set

ENGRAVINGS--CAMBRIDGE, MASS.--CATALOGS.
Harvard university. Library. Theatre
collection. Catalogue of dramatic
portraits in the Theatre collection
of the Harvard college library,
Cambridge, Mass., Harvard university
press, 1930- v. 927.92 30-
13380
   PN2205 .H35 MRR Alc.

ENGRAVINGS, AMERICAN.
United States. Library of Congress.
An album of American battle art, 1755-
1918. Washington, U.S. Govt. Print.
Off., 1947. xvi, 319 p. 769.49973
48-45628
   Z663 .A8 MRR Alc.

ENIGMAS
see Riddles

ENSIGNS
see Flags

ENTERPRISES
see Business enterprises

ENTERTAINERS--DIRECTORIES.
Who's who in show business; 1967/68-
New York. 790.2/0922 72-220578
   PN1583.A2 W5 MRR Alc Latest
   edition

ENTERTAINERS--PORTRAITS.
National Portrait Gallery,
Washington, D.C. Portraits of the
American stage, 1771-1971:
Washington, Smithsonian Institution
Press: [for sale by the Supt. of
Docs., U.S. Govt. Print. Off.] 1971.
203 p. [$4.50] 792/.0973 75-
170284
   PN1583.A2 N3 MRR Biog.

ENTERTAINERS--UNITED STATES.
Hughes, Langston, Black magic;
Englewood Cliffs, N.J., Prentice-Hall
[1967] 375 p. 790.2/09174/96 67-
22993
   PN2286 .H75 MRR Alc.

ENTERTAINING.
see also Games

Depew, Arthur M. The Cokesbury party
book. Rev. ed. New York, Abingdon
Press [1959] 377 p. 793.2 59-
10358
   GV1471 .D37 1959 MRR Alc.

ENTOMOLOGY.
see also Insects

Borror, Donald Joyce, An
introduction to the study of insects
3d ed. New York, Holt, Rinehart and
Winston [1971] xiii, 812 p. 595.7
73-86139
   QL463 .B69 1971 MRR Alc.

Little, Van Allen, General and
applied entomology 3d ed. New York,
Harper & Row [1972] xi, 527 p.
595.7 79-181540
   QL463 .L5 1972 MRR Alc.

ENTOMOLOGY--DICTIONARIES.
De la Torre-Bueno, José Rollin, A
glossary of entomology: Lancaster,
Penna., Printed by the Science press
printing co., 1937. ix, 336 p.
595.703 38-8454
   QL462.3 .D4 MRR Alc.

ENTOMOLOGY, ECONOMIC
see Insects, Injurious and beneficial

ENTREPRENEUR.
see also Business enterprises

ENVIRONMENT
see Anthropo-geography

see Ecology

see Human ecology

see Man--Influence of environment

see Man--Influence on nature

ENVIRONMENT, COLLEGE
see College environment

ENVIRONMENTAL ENGINEERING--DIRECTORIES.
International directory of behavior
and design research, 1974-
[Orangeburg, N.Y.] [$12.00] 300/.25
74-75207
   H57 .I57 MRR Biog Latest edition /
   Sci RR Latest edition

ENVIRONMENTAL ENGINEERING--SOCIETIES,
ETC.--DIRECTORIES.
Halstead, Bruce W. A Golden guide to
environmental organizations. New
York, Golden Press [1972] 63 p.
[$0.95] 301.31/06 72-79158
   GF5 .H34 MRR Alc.

ENVIRONMENTAL ENGINEERING (BUILDINGS)
see also Interior decoration

ENVIRONMENTAL POLICY.
see also Conservation of natural
resources

see also Human ecology

see also Man--Influence on nature

Wilson, Thomas Williams.
International environmental action:
[New York] Dunellen [1971] xviii,
364 p. [$12.50] 301.3/1 73-168684
   HC79.E5 W53 MRR Alc.

ENVIRONMENTAL POLICY--BIBLIOGRAPHY.
Wilson, Thomas Williams.
International environmental action:
[New York] Dunellen [1971] xviii,
364 p. [$12.50] 301.3/1 73-168684
   HC79.E5 W53 MRR Alc.

ENVIRONMENTAL POLICY--UNITED STATES--
BIBLIOGRAPHY.
Meshenberg, Michael J. Environmental
planning: [Chicago, American Society
of Planning Officials, c1970] ii, 78
p. [$6.00] 016.3337/0973 70-22732

   Z7165.U5 M42 MRR Alc.

ENVIRONMENTAL POLICY--UNITED STATES--
DIRECTORIES.
Annual directory of environmental
information sources. 1971- Boston,
National Foundation for Environmental
Control. 301.3/1/0973 78-158971
   HC110.E5 A7 MRR Alc Latest edition
   / Sci RR Latest edition

Environmental Resources, inc. Yell-
[symbol for Earth] pages:
[Washington] 1971. 240 p.
301.3/1/02573 72-27880
   HC110.E5 E499 MRR Alc.

ENVIRONMENTAL POLICY--UNITED STATES--
PERIODICALS.
Your government and the environment.
v. 1- 1971- Arlington, Va., Output
Systems Corp. 301.3/1 77-166183
   HC110.E5 Y6 Sci RR Latest edition
   / MRR Alc Latest edition

ENVIRONMENTAL POLICY RESEARCH--
DIRECTORIES.
Wilson, William K. World directory
of environmental research centers,
2d ed. New York, Oryx Press:
distributed by R. R. Bowker Co.,
1974. xi, 330 p. 301.31/025 72-
87536
   HC79.E5 W54 1974 MRR Alc.

ENVIRONMENTAL POLLUTION
see Pollution

ENVIRONMENTAL PROTECTION--BIBLIOGRAPHY.
Morrison, Denton E. Environment:
Washington, Office of Research and
Monitoring, U.S. Environmental
Protection Agency; for sale by the
Supt. of Docs., U.S. Govt. Print.
Off., 1974, c1973. vii, 860 p.
[$7.45] 016.3 74-601576
   Z7161 .M56 1974 MRR Alc.

ENVIRONMENTAL PROTECTION--INFORMATION
SERVICES.
Wolff, Garwood R. Environmental
information sources handbook. [New
York] Simon and Schuster [1974] 568
p. 301.31/07 73-3951
   GF503 .W64 MRR Alc.

ENVIRONMENTAL PROTECTION--STUDY AND
TEACHING--DIRECTORIES.
International Institute for
Environmental Affairs. World
directory of environmental education
programs: New York, R. R. Bowker
Co., 1973. xiii, 289 p.
301.31/07/11 73-14872
   GF26 .I57 1973 MRR Alc.

ENVIRONMENTAL PROTECTION--UNITED STATES-
-BIBLIOGRAPHY.
Wolff, Garwood R. Environmental
information sources handbook. [New
York] Simon and Schuster [1974] 568
p. 301.31/07 73-3951
   GF503 .W64 MRR Alc.

ENVIRONMENTAL PROTECTION--UNITED STATES-
-DIRECTORIES.
Conservation directory. Washington,
National Wildlife Federation. 70-
10646
   S920 .C64 Sci RR Latest edition /
   MRR Alc Latest edition
   Began with 1956 vol.

Directory of consumer protection and
environmental agencies. 1st ed.
Orange, N.J., Academic Media [1973]
xiii, 627 p. 381 72-75952
   HC110.C63 D55 MRR Ref Desk.

Onyx Group, inc. Environment U.S.A.:
New York, Bowker, 1974. xii, 451 p.
333.7/2/02573 73-20122
   TD171 .E58 MRR Alc.

ENVIRONMENTAL PROTECTION--UNITED STATES-
-SOCIETIES, ETC.--DIRECTORIES.
Wolff, Garwood R. Environmental
information sources handbook. [New
York] Simon and Schuster [1974] 568
p. 301.31/07 73-3951
   GF503 .W64 MRR Alc.

EPHEMERIDES.
Stahlman, William D. Solar and
planetary longitudes for years--2500
to +2000 by 10-day intervals.
Madison, University of Wisconsin
Press, 1963. 566 p. 528.1 63-
10534
   QB7 .S73 MRR Alc.

Ward, Craig, The 200 year ephemeris:
New York, Macoy Pub. Co., 1949. vi,
420 p. 133.5083 49-8975
   BF1715 .W3 MRR Alc.

EPIC LITERATURE, GERMAN--DICTIONARIES.
Gillespie, George T. A catalogue of
persons named in German heroic
literature (700-1600), including
named animals and objects and ethnic
names. Oxford, [Eng.] Clarendon
Press, 1973. xxxvii, 166 p. [£10.50
($33.75 U.S.)] 831/.009 73-173463

   PT204 .G5 1973 MRR Alc.

EPIC POETRY.
Rabb, Kate (Milner) National epics.
Freeport, N.Y., Books for Libraries
Press [1969] 398 p. 808.81/3 76-
84355
   PN1323 .R3 1969 MRR Alc.

EPIDEMICS.
see also Communicable diseases

EPIDEMIOLOGY--STATISTICS--YEARBOOKS.
World health statistics annual. 1962-
Geneve, World Health Organization.
312/.2/05 72-624373
   RA651.A485 MRR Alc Latest edition
   / Sci RR Latest edition

EPIGRAMS.
Fuller, Edmund, ed. Thesaurus of
epigrams. Garden City, N.Y., Garden
City Pub. Co. [1948] 382 p. 808.8
48-5656
   PN6281 .F8 1948 MRR Alc.

Martialis, Marcus Valerius.
Epigrams, London, W. Heinemann; New
York, G. P. Putnam's sons, 1930. 2
v. mrr01-9
   PA6156.M3 1930d MRR Alc.

Prochnow, Herbert Victor, comp.
Speaker's handbook of epigrams and
witticisms. [1st ed.] New York,
Harper [c1955] 332 p. 808.88* 54-
12157
   PN6271 .P7 MRR Alc.

EPIGRAMS. (Cont.)
The Speaker's desk book. New York,
Grosset & Dunlap [1967] 613 p.
808.8 66-20654
PN4193.I5 S6 1967 MRR Alc.

EPIZOA
see Parasites

EPONYMS.
Hendrickson, Robert, Human words;
[1st ed.] Philadelphia, Chilton Book
Co. [1972] 342 p. [$9.95] 423/.1
72-6492
PE1596 .H4 MRR Alc.

EQUATIONS, CHEMICAL
see Chemical equations

EQUATIONS, CUBIC.
Salzer, Herbert Ellis, Table for the
solution of cubic equations New
York, McGraw-Hill, 1958. 161 p.
512.82 57-12910
QA215 .S3 MRR Alc.

EQUATORIAL GUINEA--DESCRIPTION AND
TRAVEL--GAZETTEERS.
United States. Office of Geography,
Rio Muni, Fernando Po, and Sao Tome
e Principe; official standard names
approved by the United States Board
on Geographic Names. Washington,
U.S. Govt. Print. Off., 1962. iv, 95
p.   62-62087
DT619 .U47 MRR Alc.

EQUESTRIANISM
see Horsemanship

EQUUS.
see also Horses

ERITREA--BIBLIOGRAPHY.
United States. Library of Congress.
General Reference and Bibliography
Division. North and Northeast
Africa; Washington, 1957. v, 182 p.
016.96 57-60062
Z663.28 .N6 MRR Alc.

ERITREA--GAZETTEERS.
United States. Office of Geography.
Ethiopia, Eritrea, and the
Somalilands; Washington, 1950. 498
p.   73-10041
DT378.2 .U5 MRR Alc.

ERKENWALD, SAINT. LEGEND--CONCORDANCES.
Kottler, Barnet. A concordance to
five Middle English poems;
[Pittsburgh] University of Pittsburgh
Press [1966] xxxiii, 761 p.
821.1016 66-13311
PR265 .K6 MRR Alc.

EROSION.
see also Geomorphology

ERRORS, POPULAR.
Ackermann, Alfred Seabold Eli,
Popular fallacies: 4th ed. London,
Old Westminster Press; sole
distributors, S. Marshall, 1950. xv,
843 p.   133.7 50-32195
AZ999 .A3 1950 MRR Alc.

Kominsky, Morris. The hoaxers: plain
liars, fancy liars, and damned liars.
Boston, Branden Press [1970] 735 p.
[$12.50] 909 76-109134
E839.8 .K6 MRR Alc.

ESCHATOLOGY.
see also Kingdom of God

ESKIMOS--ECONOMIC CONDITIONS--
BIBLIOGRAPHY.
Snodgrass, Marjorie P. Economic
development of American Indians and
Eskimos, 1930 through 1967;
[Washington, U.S. Bureau of Indian
Affairs; for sale by the Supt. of
Docs., U.S. Govt. Print. Off.] 1968
[i.e. 1969] v, 263 p. [2.00]
330.9 79-601798
Z1209 .S56 MRR Alc.

ESPERANTO.
Connor, George Alan. Esperanto, the
world interlanguage. New rev. ed.
New York, T. Yoseloff [1959] 245 p.
408.92 59-10560
PM8213 .C6 1959 MRR Alc.

ESPERANTO--CONVERSATION AND PHRASE
BOOKS--POLYGLOT.
Lyall, Archibald, A guide to 25
languages of Europe. Rev. ed.
[Harrisburg, Pa.] Stackpole Co.
[1966] viii, 407 p. 413 66-20847

PB73 .L85 1966 MRR Alc.

ESPERANTO--DICTIONARIES--ENGLISH.
Butler, Montagu C. Esperanto-English
dictionary, London, British
Esperanto Association, 1967. 450 p.
[25/-] 499.9/92/32 68-78904
PM8237 .B8 MRR Alc.

Connor, George Alan. Esperanto, the
world interlanguage, New rev. ed.
New York, T. Yoseloff [1959] 245 p.
408.92 59-10560
PM8213 .C6 1959 MRR Alc.

ESPERANTO--DICTIONARIES--POLYGLOT.
Bergman, Peter M. The concise
dictionary of twenty-six languages in
simultaneous translations, New York,
Polyglot Library [1968] 406 p.   413
67-14284
P361 .B4 TJ Rm.

ESPIONAGE--DICTIONARIES.
Seth, Ronald. Encyclopedia of
espionage. Garden City, N.Y.,
Doubleday [1974, c1972] 718 p.
[$10.00] 327/.12/03 76-131105
UB270 .S4385 1974 MRR Biog.

ESSAYS--INDEXES.
Essay and general literature index;
v. 1- 1930/33- New York, H. W.
Wilson Co. 016 34-14581
AI3 .E752 MRR Alc Full set

Index to the contemporary scene. v.
1- 1973- Detroit, Gale Research
Co. [$14.00] 016.3 73-645955
Z7161 .I52 MRR Alc Full set

ESSEN--DIRECTORIES.
Essener Adressbuch. Essen,
Hoppenstedt Wirtschaftsverlag. 53-
30698
DD901.E75 E8 MRR Alc Latest
edition

ESTATE PLANNING.
see also Insurance

see also Investments

ESTATES (SOCIAL ORDERS)
see also Feudalism

see also Legislative bodies

ESTHETICS
see Aesthetics

ESTONIA--BIBLIOGRAPHY.
United States. Library of Congress.
Slavic and Central European Division.
Estonia: a selected bibliography.
Washington, 1958. iv, 74 p.
016.94741* 58-60040
Z663.47 .E8 MRR Alc.

ESTONIAN LANGUAGE--DICTIONARIES--
ENGLISH.
Vares, Maria. Eesti-inglise
taskusõnaraamat. Wadstena, Sverige,
Eesti Kirjastus Orto [1946] xv, 584
p. 52-64244
PH625 .V3 MRR Alc.

ETCHERS, BRITISH.
Grant, Maurice Harold, A dictionary
of British etchers. London,
Published for the author by Rockliff
[1952] 232 p. 767.2 52-3175
NE2043 .G7 1952 MRR Alc.

ETHICS.
see also Conduct of life

see also Good and evil

see also Social problems

see also Spiritual life

Aristoteles. The Athenian
constitution; the Eudemian ethics;
London, W. Heinemann ltd.; Cambridge,
Mass, Harvard university press, 1935.
vii, 505, [1] p. 888.5 36-4460
PA3612.A8 A13 1935a MRR Alc.

Aristoteles. The Metaphysics ...
London, W. Heinemann, ltd.; New York,
G. P. Putnam's sons, 1933-35. 2 v.
33-17911
PA3612 .A8A13 1933 MRR Alc.

Aristoteles. The Nicomachean ethics,
Cambridge, Harvard University Press;
London, H. Heinemann, 1934. 649 p.
170 mrr01-42
PA3612 .A8E6 1934d MRR Alc.

ETHICS--DICTIONARIES.
Encyclopædie of religion and ethics,
Edinburgh, T. & T. Clark; New York,
C. Scribner's sons, 1908-26. 13 v.
08-35833
BL31 .E4 MRR Alc.

Ferm, Vergilius Ture Anselm, ed.
Encyclopedia of morals. New York,
Philosophical Library [1956] x, 682
p.   170.3 56-58813
BJ63 .F4 MRR Alc.

Macquarrie, John. Dictionary of
Christian ethics, Philadelphia,
Westminster Press [1967] viii, 366
p. 241/.03 67-17412
BJ63 .M3 MRR Alc.

Mathews, Shailer, ed. A dictionary
of religion and ethics, New York,
The Macmillan company, 1923. 2 p.
l., iii-vii, 513 p. 203 31-24963
BL31 .M3 1923 MRR Alc.

ETHICS--HISTORY.
Brinton, Clarence Crane, A history
of Western morals. [1st ed.] New
York, Harcourt, Brace [1959] 502 p.
170.9 59-6426
BJ71 .B68 MRR Alc.

ETHICS, COMMERCIAL
see Business ethics

ETHICS, POLITICAL
see Political ethics

ETHICS, PRACTICAL
see Conduct of life

ETHICS, SOCIAL
see Social ethics

ETHIOPIA.
American University, Washington, D.C.
Foreign Areas Studies Division. Area
handbook for Ethiopia. 2d ed.
Washington [Dept. of the Army] for
sale by the Superintendent of
Documents, U.S. Govt. Print. Office,
1964. xi, 621 p. 65-60683
DT387.9 .A65 1964 MRR Alc.

Lipsky, George Arthur, Ethiopia: its
people, its society, its culture New
Haven, HRAF Press [1962] 376 p.
916.3 62-13515
DT373 .L56 MRR Alc.

ETHIOPIA--BIBLIOGRAPHY.
United States. Library of Congress.
General Reference and Bibliography
Division. North and Northeast
Africa; Washington, 1957. v, 182 p.
016.96 57-60062
Z663.28 .N6 MRR Alc.

ETHIOPIA--GAZETTEERS.
United States. Office of Geography.
Ethiopia, Eritrea, and the
Somalilands; Washington, 1950. 498
p. 73-10041
DT378.2 .U5 MRR Alc.

ETHIOPIA--HISTORY.
Greenfield, Richard. Ethiopia: a new
political history. African paperback
ed. London, Pall Mall P., 1969. ix,
515 p. [25/-] 963 76-444971
DT381 .G7 1969 MRR Alc.

Pankhurst, Estelle Sylvia, Ethiopia,
a cultural history. Essex [Eng.]
Lalibela House [1955] xxxviii, 747
p. 963 56-22371
DT381 .P35 MRR Alc.

ETHIOPIA--HISTORY--CHRONOLOGY.
Perham, Margery Freda, Dame, The
government of Ethiopia, 2nd ed.
London, Faber, 1969. xcii, 531 p.
[5/10/-] 320.9/63 78-394906
JQ3754 .P4 1969 MRR Alc.

ETHIOPIA--POLITICS AND GOVERNMENT.
Perham, Margery Freda, Dame, The
government of Ethiopia, 2nd ed.
London, Faber, 1969. xcii, 531 p.
[5/10/-] 320.9/63 78-394906
JQ3754 .P4 1969 MRR Alc.

ETHNIC GROUPS
see Minorities

ETHNIC PRESS--UNITED STATES--
DIRECTORIES.
United States. Office of Minority
Business Enterprise. Directory of
minority media. [Washington]: for
sale by the Supt. of Docs., U.S.
Govt. Print. Off., 1973. ix, 89 p.
[$1.25] 301.16/1/02573 73-602686
P88.8 .U55 MRR Alc.

Wynar, Lubomyr Roman, Encyclopedic
directory of ethnic newspapers and
periodicals in the United States
Littleton, Colo., Libraries
Unlimited, 1972. 260 p. [$12.50]
070.4/84/02573 70-185344
Z6944.E8 W94 MRR Ref Desk.

ETHNIC TYPES.
see also Race

ETHNOLOGY.
see also Anthropo-geography

see also Anthropology

see also Archaeology

see also Civilization

see also Costume

see also Folk-lore

see also Indians

see also Man, Prehistoric

see also Negroes

see also Religion, Primitive

Birket-Smith, Kaj, The paths of
culture: Madison, University of
Wisconsin Press, 1965. xi, 535 p.
301.2 64-8488
CB113.D3 B513 MRR Alc.

ETHNOLOGY. (Cont.)
Herskovits, Melville Jean, Cultural anthropology. New York, Knopf, 1955. 569 p.   572 55-5171
GN400 .H588 MRR Alc.

Honigmann, John Joseph. Handbook of social and cultural anthropology, Chicago, Rand McNally Co. [c1973] 1295 p.   301.2 72-184062
GN315 .H642 MRR Alc.

ETHNOLOGY--BIBLIOGRAPHY.
United States. Immigration Commission, 1907-1910. Dictionary of races or peoples. Detroit, Gale Research Co., 1969. vii, 150 p. 572/.03 68-30665
GN11 .U6 1969 MRR Alc.

ETHNOLOGY--BIBLIOGRAPHY--CATALOGS.
Harvard University. Peabody Museum of Archaeology and Ethnology. Library. Catalogue: authors. Boston, G. K. Hall, 1963. 26 v.   64-2646
Z5119 .H35 MRR Alc (DK 33).

Harvard University. Peabody Museum of Archaeology and Ethnology. Library. Catalogue: subjects. Boston, G. K. Hall, 1963. 27 v.   018.1 64-2645
Z5119 .H36 MRR Alc (Dk 33).

ETHNOLOGY--CLASSIFICATION.
Murdock, George Peter, Outline of world cultures. [2d ed., rev.] New Haven, HRAF Press, 1958. xi, 227 p. 025.469 58-4860
H62 .B36 vol. 3 1958 MRR Alc.

ETHNOLOGY--DICTIONARIES.
Leyburn, James Graham. Handbook of ethnography, New Haven, Yale university press; London, H. Milford, Oxford university press, 1931. vii, [2], 323 p.   572.03 31-14940
GN11 .L4 MRR Alc.

Spencer, Robert F. An ethno-atlas; Dubuque, Iowa, W. C. Brown Co. [1958, c1956] iii, 42 p.   572.084 56-12496
GN11 .S75 MRR Alc.

Textor, Robert B., comp. A cross-cultural summary, New Haven, HRAF Press [1967] 1 v. (various pagings) 390 67-18560
GN307 .T4 MRR Alc.

United States. Immigration Commission, 1907-1910. Dictionary of races or peoples. Detroit, Gale Research Co., 1969. vii, 150 p. 572/.03 68-30665
GN11 .U6 1969 MRR Alc.

ETHNOLOGY--HISTORY.
Lowie, Robert Harry, The history of ethnological theory, New York, Farrar & Rinehart, inc. [c1937] xiii, 296 p.   572.01 38-2861
GN17 .L6 MRR Alc.

ETHNOLOGY--MAPS.
Spencer, Robert F. An ethno-atlas; Dubuque, Iowa, W. C. Brown Co. [1958, c1956] iii, 42 p.   572.084 56-12496
GN11 .S75 MRR Alc.

ETHNOLOGY--PERIODICALS--INDEXES.
International bibliography of social and cultural anthropology. v. 1-1955- London, Tavistock Pub.; Chicago, Aldine Pub. Co. [etc.] 016.572 58-43266
Z7161 .I593 MRR Alc Full set

ETHNOLOGY--AFRICA--ABSTRACTS.
African abstracts. v. 1-   Jan. 1950- [London] 960 55-18105
DT1 .I553 MRR Alc Full set

ETHNOLOGY--AFRICA--BIBLIOGRAPHY.
Fontvieille, Jean Roger. Guide bibliographique du Monde noir. Yaounde, Direction des affaires culturelles, 1970 [cover 1971- v. 72-205179
Z5118.N4 F64 MRR Alc.

ETHNOLOGY--AFRICA, EAST--BIBLIOGRAPHY.
International African Institute. East Africa: general, ethnography, sociology, linguistics, London, 1960. iii, 61 l.   60-44644
Z3516 .I47 MRR Alc.

ETHNOLOGY--AMERICA--BIBLIOGRAPHY.
United States. Bureau of American Ethnology. List of publications of the Bureau of American Ethnology 1894- Washington, U.S. Govt. Print. Off.   23-27414
E51 .U65 MRR Ref Desk Latest edition

ETHNOLOGY--AMERICA--INDEXES.
United States. Bureau of American Ethnology. Bulletin. (Indexes) Index to Bulletins 1-100 of the Bureau of American Ethnology; Washington, U.S. Govt. Print. Off., 1963. vi, 726 p. 64-60461
Z1209 .U49 MRR Alc.

ETHNOLOGY--ASIA, SOUTHEASTERN--BIBLIOGRAPHY.
Furer-Haimendorf, Elizabeth von. An anthropological bibliography of South Asia, Paris, Mouton, 1958-70. 3 v. [fl. 130.00 (v. 3)]   a 59-1034
Z5115 .F83 MRR Alc.

ETHNOLOGY--EUROPE.
Coon, Carleton Stevens, The races of Europe New York, The Macmillan company, 1939. xvi, 398 p., [29], 400-739 p. incl. illus. (incl. maps) tables, diagrs. 572.94 39-10651
GN575 .C6 MRR Alc.

ETHNOLOGY--EUROPE--BIBLIOGRAPHY.
Theodoratus, Robert J., Europe: a selected ethnographic bibliography, New Haven, Conn., Human Relations Area Files, 1969. xi, 544 p. 016.30129/4 75-87851
Z5117 .T5 MRR Alc.

ETHNOLOGY--ISLANDS OF THE PACIFIC--BIBLIOGRAPHY.
Taylor, Clyde Romer Hughes, A Pacific bibliography; 2nd ed. Oxford, Clarendon Press, 1965. xxx, 692 p.   016.919 66-1568
Z4501 .T3 1965 MRR Alc.

ETHNOLOGY--LATIN AMERICA.
Murdock, George Peter, Outline of South American cultures. New Haven, Human Relations Area Files, 1951. 148 p.   a 52-972
H62 .B36 vol. 2, 1951 MRR Alc.

ETHNOLOGY--NEW ZEALAND--BIBLIOGRAPHY.
Taylor, Clyde Romer Hughes, A Pacific bibliography; 2nd ed. Oxford, Clarendon Press, 1965. xxx, 692 p.   016.919 66-1568
Z4501 .T3 1965 MRR Alc.

ETHNOLOGY--NORTH AMERICA--BIBLIOGRAPHY.
Murdock, George Peter, Ethnographic bibliography of North America. 3d ed. New Haven, Human Relations Area Files, 1960. xxiii, 393 p. 016.9701 60-16689
Z1209 .M8 1960 MRR Alc.

ETHNOLOGY--SAHARA.
Briggs, Lloyd Cabot, Tribes of the Sahara. Cambridge, Harvard University Press, 1960. xx, 295 p. 572.96611 60-7988
DT337 .B7 MRR Alc.

ETHNOLOGY--SOUTH AMERICA--BIBLIOGRAPHY.
O'Leary, Timothy J. Ethnographic bibliography of South America. New Haven, Human Relations Area Files, 1963. xxiv, 387 p. 016.57298 63-20695
Z5114 .O4 MRR Alc.

ETHNOMUSICOLOGY--BIBLIOGRAPHY.
Gillis, Frank, comp. Ethnomusicology and folk music: [ist ed.] Middletown, Conn., Published for the Society for Ethnomusicology by the Wesleyan University Press [1966] 148 p.   016.7817 66-23459
ML128.E8 G5 MRR Alc.

Nettl, Bruno, Reference materials in ethnomusicology; [Detroit, Information Service, 1961] 46 p. 62-2237
ML128.E8 N5 MRR Alc.

ETHNOPSYCHOLOGY.
see also Negroes--Race identity

see also Social psychology

ETHOLOGY
see Ethics

ETIQUETTE.
Fenner, Kay Toy. American Catholic etiquette. Westminster, Md., Newman Press, 1961. 402 p.   395 61-16569

BX1969 .F4 MRR Alc.

Free, Anne R. Social usage [2d ed.] New York, Appleton-Century-Crofts [1969] vii, 255 p.   395 69-11706
BJ1853 .F7 1969 MRR Alc.

Post, Emily (Price) Etiquette. 12th rev. ed. New York, Funk & Wagnalls [1968, c1969] xi, 721 p. [6.95] 395 68-55996
BJ1853 .P6 1969b MRR Ref Desk.

Roosevelt, Eleanor (Roosevelt) Book of common sense etiquette. New York, Macmillan [1962] 591 p.   395 62-19667
BJ1853 .R65 MRR Alc.

Vanderbilt, Amy. Etiquette. [New rev. ed.] Garden City, N.Y., Doubleday [1972] xxiii, 929 p. [8.95] 395 78-171326
BJ1853 .V27 1972 MRR Ref Desk.

Vogue's book of etiquette and good manners. New York, Conde Nast Publications, 1969. xvii, 749 p. [12.95 (de luxe binding)] 395 69-11100
BJ1853 .V6 1969 MRR Alc.

Watson, Lillian (Eichler) The customs of mankind. De luxe ed. Garden City, N.Y., Garden City publishing company, inc. [1937] xvii, [2], 753 p.   390 37-15874
GT75 .W35 1937 MRR Alc.

Wood, John R. Diplomatic ceremonial and protocol; New York, Colombia University Press, 1970. xviii, 378 p. [25.00] 341.7 70-12944
JX1679 .W65 1970b MRR Alc.

ETIQUETTE--DICTIONARIES.
Miller, Llewellyn. The encyclopedia of etiquette: New York, Crown Publishers [1967] xvi, 640 p. 395/.03 67-27041
BJ1815 .M5 MRR Alc.

ETIQUETTE--STATIONERY.
Crane and Company, inc., Dalton, Mass. Approved forms for engraved stationery. Dalton [c1958] 119 p. 395 58-33248
BJ2081 .C7 1958 MRR Alc.

ETIQUETTE--ENGLAND.
Messenger, Elizabeth. The complete guide to etiquette London, Evans Bros., 1966. 206 p. [25/-] 395.0942 66-70820
BJ1873 .M4 MRR Alc.

ETIQUETTE--UNITED STATES.
McCandless, Bruce. Service etiquette; 2d ed. Annapolis, Md., United States Naval Institute [1963] 447 p.   355.13 63-13586
U766 .M2 1963 MRR Alc.

ETIQUETTE--WASHINGTON, D.C.
Radlovic, I. Monte, Etiquette & protocol; New York, Harcourt, Brace [1957] 240 p.   395 57-2649
BJ1858 .R3 1957 MRR Alc.

ETIQUETTE FOR CHILDREN AND YOUTH.
Post, Elizabeth L. The Emily Post book of etiquette for young people, New York, Funk & Wagnalls [1967] viii, 238 p. 395/.1/23 67-25416
BJ1857.C5 P6 MRR Alc.

ETIQUETTE FOR MEN.
Esquire. Esquire's guide to modern etiquette, Philadelphia, Lippincott [1969] xii, 427 p. [7.95] 395/.1/42 79-85109
BJ1855 .E82 MRR Alc.

ETIQUETTE FOR WOMEN.
The Cosmo girl's guide to the new etiquette. New York, Cosmopolitan Books [1971] xiv, 269 p. [$5.95] 395/.1/233 72-165584
BJ1856 .C67 MRR Alc.

ETRUSCANS.
Bloch, Raymond, The Etruscans. New York, Praeger [1958] 260 p. 937.5 58-8176
DG223 .B513 MRR Alc.

EUGENICS.
see also Birth control

see also Genetics

Bodart, Gaston, Losses of life in modern wars, Austria-Hungary; France, Oxford, The Clarendon press; London, New York [etc.] H. Milford, 1916. x, 207, 6 p. incl. tables. 16-20885
D25.5 .B6 MRR Alc.

EURIPIDES--CONCORDANCES.
Allen, James Turney, A concordance to Euripides, Berkeley, University of California Press, 1954. xi, 686 p.   882.3 a 55-8636
PA3992 .Z8 1954 MRR Alc.

EUROPE--ANTIQUITIES--DICTIONARIES.
Filip, Jan. Enzyklopädisches Handbuch zur Ur- und Frühgeschichte Europas. Prag, Academia, Verlag der Tschechoslowakischen Akademie der Wissenschaften, 1966- v. with illus. [DM 94.00(v. 1)] 914.03/1/03 67-77896
GN803 .F49 MRR Alc.

EUROPE--BIBLIOGRAPHY.
European Cultural Centre. The European bibliography. Leyden, A. W. Sijthoff, 1965. viii, 472 p. 65-14836
Z2000 .E8 MRR Alc.

Horecky, Paul Louis, Southeastern Europe; Chicago, University of Chicago Press [1969] xxii, 755 p. 016.91496 73-110336
Z2831 .H67 MRR Alc.

EUROPE--BIBLIOGRAPHY. (Cont.)
Theodoratus, Robert J., Europe: a
selected ethnographic bibliography.
New Haven, Conn., Human Relations
Area Files, 1969. xi, 544 p.
016.30129/4 75-87851
Z5117 .T5 MRR Alc.

United States. Library of Congress.
European Affairs Division.
Introduction to Europe: Washington,
1950. v, 201 p. 016.94 50-62973
Z663.26 .I6 MRR Alc.

EUROPE--BIOGRAPHY.
Routh, Charles Richard Nairne, comp.
They saw it happen in Europe; New
York, Barnes & Noble [1966, c1965]
xv, 514 p. 940.2 66-5348
D220 .R6 1966 MRR Alc.

Who's who in Europe. éd. 1-
1964/65- Bruxelles, Éditions det
Feniks. 65-73851
D1070 .W48 MRR Biog Latest edition

EUROPE--BIOGRAPHY--DICTIONARIES.
Pedley, Avril J. M., comp. They
looked like this (Europe); New York,
Barnes & Noble [1967] xliii, 265 p.
920.04 68-463
D226 .P4 1967 MRR Biog.

Pedley, Avril J. M., comp. They
looked like this (Europe): Oxford,
Blackwell [1966] xiii, 265 p.
[32/6] 920.04 68-85817
D226 .P4 1966 MRR Alc.

Who's who in science in Europe:
Guernsey, F. Hodgson, 1967. 3 v.
[£10/-/- (v. 1-2) unpriced (v. 3)]
502/.5/4 67-27363
Q145 .W5 MRR Biog.

Zischka, Gert A. Allgemeines
Gelehrten-Lexikon: Stuttgart, A.
Kröner [1961] viii, 710 p. 62-
31158
CT3990.A2 Z5 MRR Biog.

EUROPE--CENSUS--BIBLIOGRAPHY.
United States. Library of Congress.
Census Library Project. National
censuses and vital statistics in
Europe, 1918-1939; New York, B.
Franklin [1969] vii, 215, v, 48 p.
016.314 68-58214
Z7553.C3 U46 1969 MRR Alc.

EUROPE--CENSUS, 1960--DIRECTORIES.
Blake, Judith. Western European
censuses, 1960; Berkeley, Institute
of International Studies, University
of California [1971] v, 421 p.
[$3.25] 016.312/094 77-634274
HA37.E93 B5 MRR Alc.

EUROPE--CIVILIZATION--HISTORY.
Burns, Edward McNall, Western
civilizations, 6th ed. New York,
Norton [1963] 1083 p. 914 63-8026

CB57 .B8 1963 MRR Alc.

Childe, Vere Gordon, The dawn of
European civilization. [6th ed.
rev.] London, Routledge & Paul
[1957] xiii, 368 p. 901 58-872
D65 .C5 1957 MRR Alc.

EUROPE--CLIMATE.
Great Britain. Meteorological Office.
Tables of temperature, relative
humidity and precipitation for the
world. 2nd ed. London, H.M.S.O.,
1966- v. [1/5/- (pt. 3) 1/15-
(pt. 4) 15/6 (pt. 5)] 551.5/021/2
76-385248
QC982.5 .G732 MRR Alc.

Powers, Edward. Fair weather travel
in western Europe, New York, Mason &
Lipscomb [1974] xiv, 434 p.
551.6/9/4 74-5227
QC989.A1 P68 MRR Alc.

EUROPE--COMMERCE.
Director's guide to Europe; 3rd ed.
Epping, Directors Bookshelf, 1973.
x, 782 p. [£7.50] 914/.04/55 74-
175459
HC240 .I55 1973 MRR Alc.

Finney, Paul B. Business week's The
businessman's guide to Europe New
York, McGraw-Hill [1965] xiv, 625 p.
914 65-17052
D909 .F47 MRR Alc.

EUROPE--COMMERCE--DIRECTORIES.
Bottin, Europe. 1959- Paris,
Société Didot-Bottin. 59-44496
HC240 .A1B6 Sci RR Latest edition
/ MRR Alc Latest edition

Chico, Vicente V. International
importers & exporters; 1st ed.
Manila, Nationwide Business Agency
[1971] 1068 p. 382/.025 70-31299

HF54.P6 C54 MRR Alc.

Dun and Bradstreet, inc.
International market guide:
continental Europe. v. 1- 1961-
New York. 658.880584 61-25822
HC240 .D8 MRR Alc Latest edition

The Eastern trade directory. [Cairo]
ne 62-1365
HF3760.8 .E25 MRR Alc Latest
edition

Jaeger's Europa-Register; Teleurope.
Darmstadt, Deutscher Adressbuch-
Verlag. 338/.0025/4 74-643010
HC240 .J34 MRR Alc Latest edition

Kelly's manufacturers and merchants
directory, 82d- ed.; 1968/69-
Kingston upon Thames, Kelly's
Directories. 380.1/025 72-622824
HF54.G7 K4 MRR Alc Latest edition

Made in Europe. Frankfurt, H. E.
Reisner Publication. 58-34827
HF3493 .M3 MRR Alc Latest edition

Slog Europa. 21.- éd.; 1968-
[Paris, Slog S. A.] 382/.025/4 72-
623278
HF3493 .S5 MRR Alc Latest edition

EUROPE--COMMERCE--INFORMATION SERVICES.
Henderson, G. P., ed. European
companies: 3rd ed. Beckenham, CBD
Research Ltd, 1972. iii-xiii, 224 p.
[£10.00 ($30.00 U.S.)]
016.3387/4/094 73-151246
HC240 .H458 1972 MRR Ref Desk.

EUROPE--DESCRIPTION AND TRAVEL.
Gottmann, Jean. A geography of
Europe. 4th ed. New York, Holt,
Rinehart and Winston [1969] xii, 866
p. 914 69-20455
D907 .G6 1969 MRR Alc.

Pounds, Norman John Greville. Europe
and the Soviet Union 2d ed. New
York, McGraw-Hill [1966] 528 p.
914 65-24529
D921 .P6835 1966 MRR Alc.

EUROPE--DESCRIPTION AND TRAVEL--1945-
Martin, Lawrence, Europe: the grand
tour; New York, McGraw-Hill [1967]
x, 512 p. 914/.04/55 67-15038
D922 .M288 MRR Alc.

Monkhouse, Francis John. A regional
geography of Western Europe 4th ed.
[Harlow] Longmans, 1974. iii-xxi,
704 p. [£6.25] 914.4 74-165365
D967 .M693 1974 MRR Alc.

Temple Fieldings' selective shopping
guide to Europe. 1957/58- ed. New
York, Fielding Publications [etc.]
658.87058 57-9112
HF5341 .T4 MRR Alc Latest edition

Townsend, Derek. The photographer's
holiday guide to Europe: London,
Collins, Glasgow, 1967. 176 p. [25/-
] 914/.04/55 67-85313
D922 .T67 MRR Alc.

EUROPE--DESCRIPTION AND TRAVEL--1945- --
GUIDE-BOOKS.
Aboard and abroad. 1954-
Philadelphia [etc.] Lippincott [etc.]
914 58-5848
D909 .A2 MRR Alc Latest edition

American overseas guide. [New York]
American Overseas Tourist-Service of
New York. 910.2 56-43375
HF5341 .A65 MRR Alc Latest edition

Braider, Donald, Putnam's guide to
the art centers of Europe. New York,
Putnam [1965] ix, 542 p. 708 64-
18003
N6750 .B66 MRR Alc.

Clark, Sydney Aylmer, All the best
in Europe New York, Dodd, Mead
[1967] ix, 667 p. 914/.04/55 67-
18227
D909 .C55 1967 MRR Alc.

Dunn, William J. Enjoy Europe by
train New York, Scribner [1974]
viii, 255 p. 914/.04/55 73-19289
TF55 .D8 1974 MRR Alc.

Europe. 3rd. ed.] Geneva, Paris
[etc.] Nagel Publishers [1968]
xxxiii, 1019 p. [$8.95] 914/.04/55
72-435886
D909 .E8 1968 MRR Alc.

Farquhar, William Gordon. Enjoy
Europe by rail; London, I. Allan
[1965] 222 p. 914.04 66-7033
TF55 .F3 MRR Alc.

Fielding, Temple Hornaday,
Fielding's super-economy guide to
Europe. 1967/68- New York, Fielding
Publications Inc. in association with
William Morrow & Co. Inc. [etc.]
914/.04/55 67-4403
D909 .F44 MRR Alc Latest edition

Fielding's travel guide to Europe.
1948- ed. New York, W. Sloane
Associates. 914 59-7408
D909 .F45 MRR Alc Latest edition

Finney, Paul B. Business week's The
businessman's guide to Europe New
York, McGraw-Hill [1965] xiv, 625 p.
914 65-17052
D909 .F47 MRR Alc.

Fodor's Europe on a budget. 1972-
New York, D. McKay Co. 914/.04/55
72-76243
D909 .F632 MRR Alc Latest edition

Fodor's Europe under 25. 1972- New
York, D. McKay. 914/.04/55 72-95992

D909 .F633 MRR Alc Latest edition

Lanier, Alison Raymond. Living in
Europe. New York, Scribner [1973]
xiv, 402 p. [$8.95] 914/.04/55 72-
1182
D909 .L25 MRR Alc.

Newman, Harold. The open road guide
to Europe. 1968- South Brunswick
[N.J.] A.S. Barnes. 914/.04 68-
14395
D909 .N46 MRR Alc Latest edition

Norman, Jane. Traveler's guide to
Europe's art Rev. ed. New York,
Appleton-Century [1965] 426 p.
709.4 65-23426
N1010 .N6 1965 MRR Alc.

Petry, Diana. The Shell guide to
Europe London, Joseph; London,
Rainbird, 1968. 448 p. [40/-]
914/.04/55 68-114623
D909 .P4 MRR Alc.

Powers, Edward. Fair weather travel
in western Europe, New York, Mason &
Lipscomb [1974] xiv, 434 p.
551.6/9/4 74-5227
QC989.A1 P68 MRR Alc.

Rand McNally and Company. The book
of Europe; Chicago [1973] 256 p.
[$19.95] 914/.04/55 73-3723
D909 .R322 1973 MRR Alc.

Stein, Howard, The budget guide to
Europe, Princeton, N.J., Van
Nostrand [c1962] 980 p. 910.2 62-
905
D909 .S82 1962 MRR Alc.

Taubes, Frederic, The illustrated
guide to great art in Europe for
amateur artists: New York, Reinhold
Pub. Corp. [1966] xii, 307 p.
700.94 66-12167
N6750 .T3 MRR Alc.

Waldo, Myra. Travel and motoring
guide to Europe. 1968- [New York]
Macmillan. 914/.04/55 68-1456
D922 .W312 MRR Alc Latest edition

EUROPE--DESCRIPTION AND TRAVEL--1971-
Director's guide to Europe; 3rd ed.
Epping, Directors Bookshelf, 1973.
x, 782 p. [£7.50] 914/.04/55 74-
175459
HC240 .I55 1973 MRR Alc.

EUROPE--DESCRIPTION AND TRAVEL--1971- --
GUIDE-BOOKS.
The Book of Europe, your guide to the
best things to see and do, London,
Mitchell Beazley, 1973. 256 p.
[£4.95] 74-177110
D909 .B665 MRR Alc.

Dunn, William J. Enjoy Europe by car
[New ed.] New York, Scribner [1973]
xii, 284 p. [$4.95 (pbk.)]
914/.04/55 72-7940
D909 .D8 1973 MRR Alc.

Hadley, Leila. Fielding's guide to
traveling with children in Europe.
New York, Fielding Publications
[1972] 470 p. [$7.95] 914/.04/55
73-166359
D909 .H24 MRR Alc.

A Horizon guide: great historic
places of Europe, New York, American
Heritage Pub. Co.; book trade
distribution by McGraw-Hill [1974]
384 p. 914/.03/55 74-10941
D909 .H73 MRR Alc.

Youth Hostels Association (England
and Wales) Youth hosteler's guide to
Europe. New York, Collier Books
[1973] iii, 491 p. [$2.95]
914/.04/55 72-89051
D909 .Y68 1973 MRR Alc.

EUROPE--DESCRIPTION AND TRAVEL--
BIBLIOGRAPHY.
United States. Library of Congress.
European Affairs Division. Travel in
Europe: Washington [1950] 90 p.
016.914 51-60289
Z663.26 .T7 MRR Alc.

EUROPE--DESCRIPTION AND TRAVEL--GUIDE-
BOOKS.
The Book of Europe, your guide to the
best things to see and do, London,
Mitchell Beazley, 1973. 256 p.
[£4.95] 74-177110
    D909 .B665 MRR Alc.

Continental handbook & guide to
Western Europe. London, Royal
Automobile Club. 914/.04/55 70-
216280
    GV1025.A2 C623 MRR Alc Latest
    edition

Cope, Bob. European camping and
caravaning, New York, Drake
Publishers [1974] xi, 258 p.
914/.04/55 73-18222
    GV191.48.E8 C66 MRR Alc.

Crosland, Margaret, A guide to
literary Europe. Philadelphia,
Chilton Books [1966] 3 v. in 1.
914/.04/55 66-22874
    PN164 .C7 MRR Alc.

Director's guide to Europe; 3rd ed.
Epping, Directors Bookshelf, 1973.
x, 782 p. [£7.50] 914/.04/55 74-
175042
    HC240 .I55 1973 MRR Alc.

Dunn, William J. Enjoy Europe by car
[New ed.] New York, Scribner [1973]
xii, 284 p. [$4.95 (pbk.)]
914/.04/55 72-7940
    D909 .D8 1973 MRR Alc.

Dunn, William J. Enjoy Europe by
train New York, Scribner [1974]
viii, 255 p. 914/.04/55 73-19289
    TF55 .D8 1974 MRR Alc.

Europa touring. New York, [etc.] AAA
World Wide Travel, inc. [etc.] 32-
13844
    Began publication in 1928.
    GV1025.A2 E78 MRR Alc Latest
    edition

Fielding, Dodge Temple. Fielding's
selected favorites: hotels & inns,
Europe. 1972- New York. [$3.95]
647/.944 72-188897
    TX910.A1 F47 MRR Alc Latest
    edition

Fodor's Europe. New York, D. McKay.
914/.04/55 72-622713
    D909 .F63 MRR Alc Latest edition

Fodor's Europe on a budget. 1972-
New York, D. McKay Co. 914/.04/55
72-76243
    D909 .F632 MRR Alc Latest edition

Fodor's Europe under 25. 1972- New
York, D. McKay. 914/.04/55 72-95992
    D909 .F633 MRR Alc Latest edition

Galin, Saul. Skiing in Europe; [1st
ed.] New York, Hawthorn Books [1967]
318 p. 796.9/3/094 67-27331
    GV854.8.E9 G34 MRR Alc.

Guide pour l'auto international. 37.-
année; 1966- [Paris, Editions
commerciales de France] 72-627080
    GV1025.F7 G84 MRR Alc Latest
    edition

Hudson, Kenneth. A guide to the
industrial archaeology of Europe.
[1st American ed.] Madison [N.J.]
Fairleigh Dickinson University Press
[1971] xi, 186 p. [$15.00] 609/.4
76-160459
    T26.A1 H8 1971b MRR Alc.

Lippman, Paul. Camping guide to
Europe; [1st ed.] New York, Holt,
Rinehart and Winston [1968] x, 181
p. 914/.04/55 68-12211
    GV1025.E9 L5 MRR Alc.

Powers, Edward. Fair weather travel
in western Europe, New York, Mason &
Lipscomb [1974] xiv, 434 p.
551.6/9/4 74-5227
    QC989.A1 P68 MRR Alc.

Pryor, Louis R. Fly in Europe: your
guide to personal flying,
[Cleveland, Leisure Flying
Consultants] 1972. 235 p. [$5.95]
629.132/54/4 72-81620
    TL726.15 .P78 MRR Alc.

Rand McNally and Company. The book
of Europe; Chicago [1973] 256 p.
[$19.95] 914/.04/55 73-3723
    D909 .R322 1973 MRR Alc.

Townsend, Derek. The motorist's
holiday guide to Europe; London,
Collins, Glasgow, 1967. 160 p. [25/-
] 914/.04/55 67-85314
    GV1025.E9 T6 MRR Alc.

Youth Hostels Association (England
and Wales) Youth hosteler's guide to
Europe. New York, Collier Books
[1973] iii, 491 p. [$2.95]
914/.04/55 72-89051
    D909 .Y68 1973 MRR Alc.

EUROPE--DESCRIPTION AND TRAVEL--
GUIDEBOOKS.
Fodor's Europe under 25. 1972- New
York, D. McKay. 914/.04/55 72-95992

    D909 .F633 MRR Alc Latest edition

EUROPE--DESCRIPTION AND TRAVEL--GUIDE-
BOOKS.
A Horizon guide: great historic
places of Europe, New York, American
Heritage Pub. Co.; book trade
distribution by McGraw-Hill [1974]
384 p. 914/.03/55 74-10941
    D909 .H73 MRR Alc.

EUROPE--DIRECTORIES.
Art directors handbook: Europe. v. 1-
1965- New York, P. Glenn
Publications. 659.112 65-1527
    HF5804 .A7 MRR Alc Latest edition

Fondazione Giovanni Agnelli. Guide
to European foundations, [Milano] F.
Angeli; distributed by Columbia
University Press, New York, 1973.
401 p. [$12.50] 361.7/6/0254 73-
163902
    HV238.A2 F65 1973 MRR Alc.

EUROPE--DIRECTORIES--BIBLIOGRAPHY.
Henderson, G. P. Current European
directories: Beckenham (Kent),
C.B.D. Research Ltd., 1969. xvi, 222
p. [6/-/-] 016.914/0025 72-514512

    Z5771 .H39 MRR Ref Desk.

Henderson, G. P., ed. European
companies: 3rd ed. Beckenham, CBD
Research Ltd, 1972. iii-xiii, 224 p.
[£10.00 ($30.00 U.S.)]
016.3387/4/094 73-151246
    HC240 .H458 1972 MRR Ref Desk.

EUROPE--ECONOMIC CONDITIONS.
The Cambridge economic history of
Europe; 2nd ed. Cambridge,
Cambridge U. P., 1966- v. [75/-
(v. 1)] 330.94 66-66029
    HC240 .C312 MRR Alc.

The Cambridge economic history of
Europe from the decline of the Roman
empire, Cambridge [Eng.] The
University press, 1941- v.
330.94 a 41-3509
    HC240 .C3 MRR Alc.

Clough, Shepard Bancroft, European
economic history; 2d ed. New York,
McGraw-Hill [c1968] xix, 623 p.
330.91821 68-11928
    HC21 .C64 1968 MRR Alc.

Dillard, Dudley D. Economic
development of the North Atlantic
community; Englewood Cliffs, N.J.,
Prentice-Hall [1967] viii, 747 p.
330/.0918/21 67-15169
    HC21 .D5 MRR Alc.

Thompson, James Westfall, Economic
and social history of the Middle
Ages, 300-1300. New York, Ungar
[1959] 2 v. (ix, 900 p.) 940.1 59-
10886
    D117 .T5 1959 MRR Alc.

Tuma, Elias H. European economic
history: tenth century to the
present; New York, Harper & Row
[1971] x, 384 p. [$12.95] 330.94
70-137796
    HC240 .T8 MRR Alc.

EUROPE--ECONOMIC CONDITIONS--1945-
Agence Havas. Keys to European
market. [Paris, Havas Conseil, 1969]
327 p. [206.25F] 330.9/4 72-
183572
    HC240 .A594 MRR Alc.

Director's guide to Europe; 3rd ed.
Epping, Directors Bookshelf, 1973.
x, 782 p. [£7.50] 914/.04/55 74-
175042
    HC240 .I55 1973 MRR Alc.

Taschenbuch für den Gemeinsamen
Markt EWG, EURATOM, Montan-Union.
Recklinghausen, Kommunal-Verlag
[etc.] 60-26020
    HC240 .T32 MRR Alc Latest edition

EUROPE--ECONOMIC CONDITIONS--
BIBLIOGRAPHY.
Kiel. Universität. Institut für
Weltwirtschaft. Bibliothek.
Regionenkatalog. Boston, G. K. Hall,
1967. 52 v. 017/.5 67-9425
    Z929 .K52 1967 MRR Alc. (Dk 33).

EUROPE--ECONOMIC CONDITIONS--SOURCES.
Pollard, Sidney, comp. Documents of
European economic history New York,
St. Martin's Press [1968- v.
[15.25 (v. 1)] 330.9/4 68-10751
    HC240 .P5952 MRR Alc.

EUROPE--ECONOMIC CONDITIONS--YEARBOOKS.
Bottin, Europe. 1959- Paris,
Société Didot-Bottin. 59-44496
    HC240 .A186 Sci RR Latest edition
    / MRR Alc Latest edition

EUROPE--ECONOMIC POLICY.
Organization for Economic Cooperation
and Development. The industrial
policies of 14 member countries.
[Paris, 1971] 385 p. [$5.75 (U.S.)]
338.94 74-882853
    HD3616.E83 073 MRR Alc.

EUROPE--FOREIGN RELATIONS--SOURCES.
Nations & empires: London,
Macmillan; New York, St. Martin's P.,
1969. 336 p. [50/-] 940.2 76-
85482
    D5 .N3 MRR Alc.

EUROPE--FOREIGN RELATIONS--TREATIES.
Council of Europe. European
conventions and agreements.
Strasbourg, 1971- v. 341.24/2
72-195347
    JX626 1971 .C68 MRR Alc.

Hertslet, Edward, Sir, comp. The map
of Europe by treaty; London,
Butterworths [etc.] 1875-91. 4 v.
10-15038
    JX626 1875 MRR Alc.

EUROPE--GAZETTEERS.
United States. Geographic Names
Division. Europe and U.S.S.R.:
official standard names Washington,
1971. iii, 151 p. 914/.003 70-
30251
    D904 .U5 MRR Alc.

EUROPE--GAZETTEERS--BIBLIOGRAPHY.
Meynen, Emil, Amtliche und private
Ortsnamenverzeichnisse des
Grossdeutschen Reiches Leipzig, S.
Hirzel [1942] 162 p. 54-47213
    Z2247.G4 M4 MRR Alc.

EUROPE--HANDBOOKS, MANUALS, ETC.
Calmann, John. Western Europe; a
handbook. New York, Praeger [1967]
xxii, 697 p. 914/.03/55 67-23393
    D967 .C154 1967 MRR Alc.

Worldmark encyclopedia of the
nations. [4th ed.] New York,
Worldmark Press, [1971] 5 v.
.910/.3 76-152128
    G103 .W65 1971 MRR Ref Desk.

EUROPE--HISTORIC HOUSES, ETC.
Long, Robert P. Castle-hotels of
Europe; 4th ed. East Meadow, N.Y.:
distributor: Hastings House, New
York, 1973] 164 p. [$3.95]
647/.944 73-157418
    TX907 .L6 1973 MRR Alc.

EUROPE--HISTORICAL GEOGRAPHY.
Hertslet, Edward, Sir, comp. The map
of Europe by treaty; London,
Butterworths [etc.] 1875-91. 4 v.
10-15038
    JX626 1875 MRR Alc.

EUROPE--HISTORY.
The Cambridge economic history of
Europe; 2nd ed. Cambridge,
Cambridge U. P., 1966- v. [75/-
(v. 1)] 330.94 66-66029
    HC240 .C312 MRR Alc.

The Cambridge economic history of
Europe from the decline of the Roman
empire, Cambridge [Eng.] The
University press, 1941- v.
330.94 a 41-3509
    HC240 .C3 MRR Alc.

Ergang, Robert Reinhold, Europe from
the Renaissance to Waterloo, 3d ed.
Boston, Heath [1966, c1967] xvii,
753, lviii p. 940.2 67-14922
    D208 .E7 1967 MRR Alc.

Hayes, Carlton Joseph Huntley,
History of Western civilization 2d
ed. New York, Macmillan [1967]
xviii, 940 p. 940 67-13596
    D103 .H39 1967 MRR Alc.

Magill, Frank Northen, Great events
from history: modern European series.
[1st ed.] Englewood Cliffs, N.J.,
Salem Press [1973] 3 v. (xxi, 1779
p.) 940 73-179232
    D209 .M29 MRR Alc.

EUROPE--HISTORY--476-1492.
Bloch, Marc Léopold Benjamin,
Feudal society. [Chicago] University
of Chicago Press [1961] xxi, 498 p.
940.14 61-4322
    D131 .B513 1961 MRR Alc.

Hoyt, Robert Stuart. Europe in the
Middle Ages 2d ed. New York,
Harcourt, Brace & World [1966] xiv,
684 p. 940.1 66-16060
    CB351 .H6 1966 MRR Alc.

EUROPE--HISTORY--1492-1648.
Blum, Jerome, The emergence of the
European world Boston, Little, Brown
[1966] xvi, 539 p. 940.2 66-13545

    D220 .B4 MRR Alc.

EUROPE--HISTORY--1492-1648--SOURCES.
Routh, Charles Richard Nairne, comp.
They saw it happen in Europe; New
York, Barnes & Noble [1966, c1965]
xv, 514 p.   940.2 66-5348
    D220 .R6 1966 MRR Alc.

EUROPE--HISTORY--1492-
Gottschalk, Louis Reichenthal,
Europe and the modern world Chicago,
Scott, Foresman [1951-54] 2 v.
940.2 51-10670
    D208 .G6 MRR Alc.

EUROPE--HISTORY--1492- --SOURCES.
Nations & empires: London,
Macmillan; New York, St. Martin's P.,
1969. 336 p. [50/-]   940.2 76-
85482
    D5 .N3 MRR Alc.

EUROPE--HISTORY--1648-1789.
Beloff, Max, The age of absolutism:
1660-1815. London, Hutchinson, 1966.
190 p. [10/6]   940.22 66-67405
    D273 .B4 1966 MRR Alc.

Blum, Jerome, The emergence of the
European world Boston, Little, Brown
[1966] xvi, 539 p.   940.2 66-13545
    D220 .B4 MRR Alc.

EUROPE--HISTORY--1789-1815.
Beloff, Max, The age of absolutism:
1660-1815. London, Hutchinson, 1966.
190 p. [10/6]   940.22 66-67405
    D273 .B4 1966 MRR Alc.

EUROPE--HISTORY--1789-1900.
Albrecht-Carrie, Rene, A
diplomatic history of Europe since
the Congress of Vienna. New York,
Harper [1958] 736 p.   940.28 58-
6131
    D363 .A58 MRR Alc.

Ergang, Robert Reinhold, Europe
since Waterloo 3d ed., Boston,
Heath [1966, c1967] xviii, 952 p.
940.2 67-12299
    D359 .E7 1967 MRR Alc.

Rayner, Robert Macey, A concise
history of modern Europe, 1789-1914,
[New ed.] London, New York,
Longmans, Green [1958] 425 p.
940.2 59-1354
    D299 .R3 1958 MRR Alc.

Thomson, David, Europe since
Napoleon. Newly revised ed.
Harmondsworth, Penguin, 1966. 1004
p. [15/-]   940.28 66-70236
    D299 .T53 1966 MRR Alc.

EUROPE--HISTORY--1789-1900--SOURCES.
Kertesz, G. A., comp. Documents in
the political history of the European
continent, 1815-1939; Oxford,
Clarendon P., 1968. xxvii, 507 p.
[70/-]   940 74-372140
    D5 .K4 MRR Alc.

Postgate, Raymond William, ed.
Revolution from 1789 to 1906;
Gloucester, Mass., P. Smith, 1969.
xvi, 398 p.   940.2/7 70-10678
    D351 .P86 1969 MRR Alc.

EUROPE--HISTORY--1871-1918.
Benns, Frank Lee, Europe, 1870-1914,
New York, Appleton-Century-Crofts,
Division of Meredith Pub. Co. [1965]
xi, 393 p.   940.287 65-13128
    D395 .B39 MRR Alc.

Roberts, John Morris, Europe, 1880-
1945 London, Longmans, 1967. xv,
575 p. [42/-]   940.2 67-108854
    D424 .R6 MRR Alc.

EUROPE--HISTORY--1871-
Gooch, George Peabody, History of
modern Europe, 1878-1919, London,
New York [etc.] Cassell and company,
ltd., 1923. vi p., 1 l., 728 p. 23-
12189
    D395 .G6 1923 MRR Alc.

EUROPE--HISTORY--20TH CENTURY.
Albrecht-Carrie, Rene, A
diplomatic history of Europe since
the Congress of Vienna. New York,
Harper [1958] 736 p.   940.28 58-
6131
    D363 .A58 MRR Alc.

Black, Cyril Edwin, Twentieth
century Europe; 3d ed. New York,
Knopf [1966] xxii, 939, xxiv p.
940.5 66-19304
    D424 .B58 1966 MRR Alc.

Ergang, Robert Reinhold, Europe
since Waterloo 3d ed., Boston,
Heath [1966, c1967] xviii, 952 p.
940.2 67-12299
    D359 .E7 1967 MRR Alc.

Kertesz, G. A., comp. Documents in
the political history of the European
continent, 1815-1939; Oxford,
Clarendon P., 1968. xxvii, 507 p.
[70/-]   940 74-372140
    D5 .K4 MRR Alc.

Rayner, Robert Macey, A concise
history of modern Europe, 1789-1914,
[New ed.] London, New York,
Longmans, Green [1958] 425 p.
940.2 59-1354
    D299 .R3 1958 MRR Alc.

Thomson, David, Europe since
Napoleon. Newly revised ed.
Harmondsworth, Penguin, 1966. 1004
p. [15/-]   940.28 66-70236
    D299 .T53 1966 MRR Alc.

EUROPE--HISTORY--20TH CENTURY--SOURCES.
Baltzly, Alexander, Readings in
twentieth-century European history,
New York, Appleton-Century-Crofts
[1950] xxv, 610 p.   940.5 50-6460

    D411 .B3 MRR Alc.

EUROPE--HISTORY--1918-1945.
Benns, Frank Lee, Europe, 1914-1939,
New York, Appleton-Century-Crofts
[1965] xiii, 521 p.   940.5 65-
10297
    D720 .B4 MRR Alc.

Roberts, John Morris, Europe, 1880-
1945 London, Longmans, 1967. xv,
575 p. [42/-]   940.2 67-108854
    D424 .R6 MRR Alc.

EUROPE--HISTORY--1918-1945--SOURCES.
Langsam, Walter Consuelo, ed.
Documents and readings in the history
of Europe since 1918 Rev. and enl.
Philadelphia, Lippincott, c1951.
1190 p.   940.5 51-8285
    D442 .L3 1951 MRR Alc.

EUROPE--HISTORY--1945-
Benns, Frank Lee, Europe, 1939 to
the present Rev. ed. New York,
Appleton-Century-Crofts [1971] xi,
552 p.   940.55 71-152376
    D1051 .B4 1971 MRR Alc.

EUROPE--HISTORY--BIBLIOGRAPHY.
Stuttgart. Bibliothek für
Zeitgeschichte. Bibliothek für
Zeitgeschichte--Weltkriegsbücherei,
Stuttgart; systematischer Katalog.
Boston, G. K. Hall, 1968. 20 v. 74-
225445
    Z6204 .S8 1968 MRR Alc (Dk 33)

EUROPE--HISTORY--CHRONOLOGY.
Little, Charles Eugene, Cyclopedia
of classified dates with an
exhaustive index. Detroit, Gale
Research Co., 1967. vii, 1454 p.
902/.02 66-27839
    D9 .L7 1967 MRR Alc.

EUROPE--HISTORY--JUVENILE LITERATURE--
BIBLIOGRAPHY.
Hotchkiss, Jeanette. European
historical fiction and biography for
children and young people. 2d ed.
Metuchen, N.J., Scarecrow Press,
1972. 272 p.   028.52 72-1587
    Z5917.H6 H6 1972 MRR Alc.

EUROPE--HISTORY--SOURCES.
Bernard, Leon, ed. Readings in
European history, New York,
Macmillan [1958] 514 p.   940.082
58-5465
    D5.5 .B4 MRR Alc.

Pollard, Sidney, comp. Documents of
European economic history New York,
St. Martin's Press [1968-   v.
[15.25 (v. 1)]   330.9/4 68-10751
    HC240 .P5952 MRR Alc.

Stearns, Raymond Phineas, ed.
Pageant of Europe; Rev. ed. New
York, Harcourt, Brace & World [1961]
1072 p.   940.2082 61-10710
    D5.5 .S8 1961 MRR Alc.

EUROPE--IMPRINTS.
Adams, Herbert Mayow, Catalogue of
books printed on the continent of
Europe, 1501-1600, in Cambridge
libraries; London, Cambridge U.P.;
1967. 2 v. [25/-/-]   018/.5 66-
10015
    Z1014 .A38 MRR Alc.

Streeter, Thomas Winthrop,
Bibliography of Texas, 1795-1845.
Cambridge, Harvard University Press,
1955-60. 3 pts. in 5 v.   016.9764
56-13552
    Z1339 .S8 MRR Alc.

EUROPE--INDUSTRIES.
Organization for Economic Cooperation
and Development. Industrial
production. [Paris,] Organisation
for Economic Co-operation and
Development, 1968. 308 p. [14.00]
338/.09 76-422848
    HC240 .O693 MRR Alc.

Organization for Economic Cooperation
and Development. Industrial
statistics. Paris. 56-1623
    HC240.A1 O6916 MRR Alc Latest
edition

EUROPE--INDUSTRIES--DIRECTORIES.
Bottin, Europe. 1959- Paris,
Société Didot-Bottin. 59-44496
    HC240 .A1B6 Sci RR Latest edition
    / MRR Alc Latest edition

Dun and Bradstreet, inc.
International market guide;
continental Europe. v. 1- 1961-
New York. 658.880584 61-25822
    HC240 .D8 MRR Alc Latest edition

Jaeger's Europa-Register; Teleurope.
Darmstadt, Deutscher Adressbuch-
Verlag. 338/.0025/4 74-643010
    HC240 .J34 MRR Alc Latest edition

Noyes Data Corporation. Europe's
largest companies, 1972. Park Ridge,
N.J. [1972] v, 104 p. [$20.00]
338.6/44/0254 72-75232
    HC240 .N69 MRR Alc.

EUROPE--INDUSTRIES--INFORMATION
SERVICES.
Henderson, G. P., ed. European
companies: 3rd ed. Beckenham, CBD
Research Ltd, 1972. iii-xiii, 224 p.
[£10.00 ($30.00 U.S.)]
016.3387/4/094 73-151246
    HC240 .H458 1972 MRR Ref Desk.

EUROPE--KINGS AND RULERS.
Curley, Walter J. P. Monarchs-in-
waiting New York, Dodd, Mead [1973]
xv, 238 p. [$7.95]   929.7/094 73-
11549
    D412.7 .C87 MRR Alc.

Isenburg, Wilhelm Karl von, Prinz,
Stammtafeln zur Geschichte der
europäischen Staaten. [2. verb.
Aufl., Marburg, J. A. Stargardt,
1953. 2 v. in 1.   54-15926
    CS616 .I72 1953 MRR Alc.

EUROPE--LEARNED INSTITUTIONS AND
SOCIETIES--DIRECTORIES.
European research index; 3d ed.
[St. Peter Port, Guernsey] Francis
Hodgson [1973] 2 v. (2293 p.)
507/.204 70-190255
    Q180.E9 E9 1973 MRR Alc.

Williams, Colin H. Guide to European
sources of technical information. 3d
ed. [Guernsey] Francis Hodgson
[1970] 309 p. [$20.00 (U.S.)] 607
77-105217
    T10.65.E8 W5 1970 MRR Alc.

EUROPE--MANUFACTURES--DIRECTORIES.
Bottin, Europe. 1959- Paris,
Société Didot-Bottin. 59-44496
    HC240 .A1B6 Sci RR Latest edition
    / MRR Alc Latest edition

Dun and Bradstreet, inc.
International market guide;
continental Europe. v. 1- 1961-
New York. 658.880584 61-25822
    HC240 .D8 MRR Alc Latest edition

Europ production. Darmstadt, Europ
Export Edition GMBH. 382/.025/4 72-
623764
    T12.5.E8 A2 Sci RR Latest edition
    / MRR Alc Latest edition

Jaeger's Europa-Register; Teleurope.
Darmstadt, Deutscher Adressbuch-
Verlag. 338/.0025/4 74-643010
    HC240 .J34 MRR Alc Latest edition

Made in Europe. Frankfurt, H. E.
Reisner Publication. 58-34827
    HF3493 .M3 MRR Alc Latest edition

Noyes Data Corporation. Europe's
largest companies, 1972. Park Ridge,
N.J. [1972] v, 104 p. [$20.00]
338.6/44/0254 72-75232
    HC240 .N69 MRR Alc.

Noyes Data S.A. Key European
industrials 1970. Zug, Switzerland,
Noyes Data Corp.; Park Ridge, N.J.,
Noyes Data Corp. [c1970] 2 v.
[85.00F per vol.]   338/.0025/4 78-
129041
    HD9720.3 .N65 MRR Alc.

EUROPE--NOBILITY.
The Royalty, peerage and aristocracy
of the world. London, Annuaire de
France. 929.7 74-644555
    CS404 .R68 MRR Alc Latest edition

EUROPE--POLITICS.
Davenport, Frances Gardiner, ed.
European treaties bearing on the
history of the United States and its
dependencies, Washington, D.C.,
Carnegie institution of Washington,
1917-37. 4 v.   18-3383
    E173 .D24 MRR Alc.

Holt, Stephen. Six European states;
New York, Taplinger Pub. Co. [1970]
xi, 414 p. [$10.00] 320.3/094 78-
127406
    JN94 .A3 1970 MRR Alc.

EUROPE--POLITICS. (Cont.)
Mowat, Robert Balmain. A history of
European diplomacy, 1451-1789; New
York, Longmans, Green & co.; London,
E. Arnold & co., 1928. viii, 311 p.
29-8126
    D217 .M65 MRR Alc.

Wuest, John J., ed. New Source book
in major European governments;
Cleveland, World Pub. Co. [1966]
xviii, 700 p.   320.308 65-13148
    JF51 .W8 MRR Alc.

EUROPE--POLITICS--18TH CENTURY.
Morris, Richard Brandon. The
peacemakers; [1st ed.] New York,
Harper & Row [1965] xviii, 572 p.
973.317 65-20435
    E249 .M68 MRR Alc.

Palmer, Robert Roswell. The age of
the democratic revolution;
Princeton, N.J., Princeton University
Press, 1959-64. 2 v.   940.25 59-
10068
    D295 .P3 MRR Alc.

EUROPE--POLITICS--1789-1900.
Hertslet, Edward, Sir, comp. The map
of Europe by treaty; London,
Butterworths [etc.] 1875-91. 4 v.
10-15038
    JX626 1875 MRR Alc.

EUROPE--POLITICS--1871-1918.
Albertini, Luigi. The origins of the
war of 1914. London, New York,
Oxford University Press, 1952-57. 3
v.   940.311 52-12126
    D511 .A574 MRR Alc.

Schmitt, Bernadotte Everly. The
coming of the war, 1914. New York,
H. Fertig, 1966 [c1958] 2 v.
940.3112 66-24353
    D511 .S275 1966 MRR Alc.

EUROPE--POLITICS--20TH CENTURY.
Rogger, Hans, ed. The European
right: Berkeley, University of
California Press, 1965. vi, 589 p.
320.52094 65-18562
    JN12 .R6 MRR Alc.

EUROPE--POLITICS--1945-
Beer, Samuel Hutchison, ed. Patterns
of government; 3d ed. New York,
Random House [1973] xv, 778 p.
320.3 72-681
    JN12 .B4 1973 MRR Alc.

European political parties; New
York, Praeger [1970, c1969] 565 p.
[13.50]   329.9/4 76-97185
    JN94.A979 E85 1970 MRR Alc.

Political and Economic Planning.
European unity: [Revised ed.]
London, Political and Economic
Planning; Allen & Unwin, 1968. 3-519
p. [63/-]   068/.4 68-111444
    JN94 .P6 1968 MRR Alc.

Robertson, Arthur Henry. European
institutions: co-operation,
integration, unification, [3d ed.]
London, Stevens & Sons; New York,
Matthew Bender, 1973. xix, 478 p.
341.24/2 72-94556
    JN15 .R58 1973 MRR Alc.

EUROPE--POLITICS--YEARBOOKS.
The Europa year book. 1959- London,
Europa Publications. 341.184 59-
2942
    JN1 .E85 Sci RR Latest edition /
    MRR Ref Desk Latest edition

EUROPE--POPULATION.
Berelson, Bernard. Population policy
in developed countries. New York,
McGraw-Hill [1974] xiii, 783 p.
301.32 73-18368
    HB851 .B45 MRR Alc.

EUROPE--REGISTERS.
Bidwell, Robin Leonard. The major
powers and western Europe, 1900-1971:
[London] F. Cass, [1973] xi, 297 p.
354/.4/002 72-92958
    JN12 .B5 MRR Ref Desk.

EUROPE--RELATIONS (GENERAL) WITH AFRICA-
-BIBLIOGRAPHY.
Liniger-Goumaz, Max. Eurafrique:
bibliographie générale. Genève,
Editions du Temps, 1970. 160 p.
76-505812
    Z3508.P4 L5 MRR Alc.

EUROPE--ROAD MAPS.
Mairs Geographischer Verlag,
Stuttgart. Der grosse Shell Atlas.
1.- Aufl.; 1960- Stuttgart. map63-
200
    G1911.P2 M25 MRR Alc Atlas Latest
    edition

EUROPE--SOCIAL CONDITIONS.
Thompson, James Westfall. Economic
and social history of the Middle
Ages, 300-1300. New York, Ungar
[1959] 2 v. (ix, 900 p.) 940.1 59-
10886
    D117 .T5 1959 MRR Alc.

EUROPE--SOCIAL LIFE AND CUSTOMS.
Lanier, Alison Raymond. Living in
Europe. New York, Scribner [1973]
xiv, 402 p. [$8.95] 914/.04/55 72-
1182
    D909 .L25 MRR Alc.

EUROPE--STATISTICAL SERVICES.
Blake, Judith. Western European
censuses, 1960: Berkeley, Institute
of International Studies, University
of California [1971] v, 421 p.
[$3.25]   016.312/094 77-634274
    HA37.E93 B5 MRR Alc.

Harvey, Joan M. Statistics Europe:
sources for market research, 2nd
ed.; revised and enlarged. Beckenham
(154 High St., Beckenham, Kent):
C.B.D. Research Ltd., 1972. 255 p.
[£5.00 ($18.00 U.S.)] 016.314 72-
195848
    Z7554.E8 H35 1972 MRR Ref Desk.

EUROPE--STATISTICS.
Agence Havas. Keys to European
market. [Paris, Havas Conseil, 1969]
327 p. [206.25F]   330.9/4 72-
183572
    HC240 .A594 MRR Alc.

Deldycke, Tilo. La population active
et sa structure. Bruxelles, Centre
d'économie politique (de l')
Université libre de Bruxelles
(1968) viii, 236 p. [360.00]
331.1/12/0212 70-395436
    HD4826 .D34 MRR Alc.

European marketing data and
statistics. v. 1- 1962- London,
European Research Consultants.
338.09/4 67-118045
    HA1107 .E87 MRR Alc Latest edition

Food and Agriculture Organization of
the United Nations. Trade yearbook.
v. 12- 1958- Rome. 338.14058 59-
3598
    HD9000.4 .F58 Sci RR Partial set /
    MRR Alc Latest edition

International Labor Office. Year
book of labour statistics. [1st]-
1935/36- Geneva. l 36-130
    HD4826 .I63 MRR Alc Latest edition

International Monetary Fund. Balance
of payments yearbook. 1946/47-
Washington. 382 49-6612
    HF1014 .I5 MRR Alc Latest edition

Keyfitz, Nathan. Population: facts
and methods of demography San
Francisco, W. H. Freeman [1971] x,
613 p. [$13.50] 301.3/2/072 70-
141154
    HB885 .K43 MRR Alc.

Mueller, Bernard. A statistical
handbook of the North Atlantic area.
New York, Twentieth Century Fund,
1965. 238 p. 301.91821 65-26294
    HA1107 .M8 MRR Alc.

Organization for Economic Cooperation
and Development. Agricultural and
food statistics, 1952-1963. Paris,
1965. 148 p.   66-33109
    HD1421 .067 MRR Alc.

Organization for Economic Cooperation
and Development. Basic statistics of
energy, 1950-1964. Paris, O.E.C.D.
[London, H.M.S.O.] 1966. 363 p.
[24/-]   333.8 66-66031
    HD9555.A4 O7 MRR Alc.

Organization for Economic Cooperation
and Development. Foreign trade.
Commerce extérieur. Series C.
Commodity trade. Commerce par
produits. [Paris] 382/.021/2 72-
626755
    HF91 .067 MRR Latest edition

Organization for Economic Cooperation
and Development. Industrial
production. [Paris.] Organisation
for Economic Co-operation and
Development, 1968. 308 p. [14.00]
338/.09 76-422848
    HC240 .0693 MRR Alc.

Organization for Economic Cooperation
and Development. Manpower
statistics. 1950/60-1954/64. Paris.
66-202
    HD5764.A6 059 MRR Alc Latest
    edition

Organization for Economic Cooperation
and Development. National accounts
statistics 1950-1968. [Paris, 1970]
415 p. [$7.50 (U.S.)]   339.3 73-
535302
    HC79.I5 0674 MRR Alc.

Organization for Economic Cooperation
and Development. National accounts
statistics, 1960-1971. [Paris, 1973]
471 p. [$7.50 (U.S.)]   339.3 74-
158206
    HC79.I5 O7 1973 MRR Alc.

Organization for Economic Cooperation
and Development. Statistics of
balance of payments, 1950-1961.
[Paris, 1964] 134 p.   65-50190
    HG3881 .065 MRR Alc.

Organization for Economic Cooperation
and Development. Statistics of
energy, 1953-1967. Paris, 1969. 265
p. 333.8 71-459605
    HD9540.4 .073 1969 MRR Alc.

Organization for European Economic
Cooperation. Manpower population.
Paris, 1959. vii, 20 p. 331.112
59-65495
    HD5712 .073 MRR Alc.

Organization for European Economic
Cooperation. Statistics of sources
and uses of finance, 1948-1958.
Paris [1960] 195 p. (chiefly tables)
332.094 60-51684
    HG186 .A1074 MRR Alc.

Prag, Derek. Businessman's guide to
the Common Market London, Pall Mall
Press, 1973. x, 462 p. [£5.95]
382/.9142 73-166685
    HC241.2 .P657 MRR Alc.

Predicasts, inc. World food supply &
demand / Cleveland : Predicasts,
inc., 1974. v, 90 leaves ; 338.1/9
74-187853
    HD9000.4 .P73 1974 MRR Alc.

Schools in Europe. Weinheim, Berlin,
Beltz (1968-70) 3 v. 370/.94
74-371683
    LA621.82 .S33 MRR Alc.

Showers, Victor. The world in
figures. New York, Wiley [1973]
xii, 585 p.   910/.21/2 73-9
    G109 .S52 MRR Ref Desk.

Statistical Office of the European
Communities. Basic statistics of the
community; 8th ed. [Brussels, 1967]
218 p. [unpriced] 314 75-386707

    HA1107 .S7 1967 MRR Alc.

Statistical Office of the European
Communities. The Common Market ten
years on: tables 1958-1967.
[Brussels, Luxembourg, 1968] 109 p.
[unpriced]   330.94 74-415168
    HA1107 .S73 MRR Alc.

A survey of Europe today: London,
Reader's Digest Association, 1970.
212 p. [£25/-]   339.4/094 73-
571754
    HD7022 .S86 MRR Alc.

United Nations. Economic Commission
for Europe. Annual bulletin of
transport statistics. 1st- year;
1949- Geneva. 385 51-1244
    HE242 .U5 MRR Alc Latest edition

United Nations. Statistical Office.
The growth of world industry, 1938-
1961; New York, United Nations,
1963. xvi, 849 p. 338.4083 63-
25411
    HC59 .U46 MRR Alc.

United Nations. Statistical Office.
Yearbook of international trade
statistics. 1st- issue; 1950- New
York. 382.058 51-8987
    JX1977 .A2 MRR Ref Desk Latest
    edition

United States. Bureau of the Census.
U.S. foreign trade: general imports,
world area by commodity groupings.
1970- [Washington, For sale by the
Supt. of Docs., U.S. Govt. Print.
Off.] 382/.5/0973 78-649732
    HF105 .C137172 MRR Alc Latest
    edition

United States. Bureau of the Census.
U.S. foreign trade: exports, SIC-
based products. 1970- [Washington,
For sale by the Supt. of Docs., U.S.
Govt. Print. Off.] 382/.6/0973 71-
648606
    HF105 .C137166 MRR Alc Latest
    edition

United States. Bureau of the Census.
U.S. foreign trade: exports, world
area by commodity groupings. 1970-
[Washington, For sale by the Supt. of
Docs., U.S. Govt. Print. Off.]
382/.6/0973 79-648608
    HF105 .C137132 MRR Alc Latest
    edition

United States. Dept. of Agriculture.
Economic Research Service. European
Economic Community; agricultural
trade statistics, 1961-67.
[Washington, 1969] 1 v. (unpaged)
382/.41/094 78-601937
    HD9015.A3 U46 MRR Alc.

EUROPE--STATISTICS--BIBLIOGRAPHY.
Blake, Judith. Western European
censuses, 1960; Berkeley, Institute
of International Studies, University
of California [1971] v, 421 p.
[$3.25]   016.312/094   77-634274
HA37.E93 B5 MRR Alc.

Harvey, Joan M. Statistics Europe:
sources for market research, 2nd
ed.; revised and enlarged. Beckenham
(154 High St., Beckenham, Kent):
C.B.D. Research Ltd, 1972. 255 p.
[£5.00 ($18.00 U.S.)]   016.314 72-
195848
Z7554.E8 B35 1972 MRR Ref Desk.

International guide to electoral
statistics; The Hague, Mouton [c1969-
v.   [$16.50 (v. 1)]   324/.2/021
73-101067
JF1001 .I55 MRR Alc.

Texas. University. Population
Research Center. International
population census bibliography.
Austin, Bureau of Business Research,
University of Texas, 1965-67. 6 v.
016.312 66-63578
Z7164.D3 T45 MRR Alc.

Verwey, Gerlof, The economist's
handbook, Amsterdam, The economist's
handbook, 1834. viii, p., 1 l., 460
p.   016.31 35-4837
Z7553.E2 V6 MRR Alc.

EUROPE--STATISTICS, VITAL.
Preston, Samuel H. Causes of death:
life tables for national population
New York, Seminar Press, 1972. xi,
787 p.   312/.2 72-80305
HB1321 .P73 MRR Alc.

EUROPE--STATISTICS, VITAL--BIBLIOGRAPHY.
United States. Library of Congress.
Census Library Project. National
censuses and vital statistics in
Europe, 1918-1939; New York, B.
Franklin [1969] vii, 215, v, 48 p.
016.314 68-58214
Z7553.C3 U46 1969 MRR Alc.

EUROPE--YEARBOOKS.
Annuaire europeen. v. 1-   1955-
La Haye, Nijhoff. 55-3837
JN3 .A5 MRR Alc Latest edition

EUROPE, EASTERN.
Language and area studies, East
Central and Southeastern Europe;
Chicago, University of Chicago Press
[1969] xix, 483 p.   914.7 72-81222
DR34.8 .L33 MRR Alc.

Pounds, Norman John Greville.
Eastern Europe Chicago, Aldine Pub.
Co. [1969] xx, 912 p.   914.7 69-
16902
HC244 .P68 1969b MRR Alc.

The Soviet Union and Eastern Europe;
New York, Praeger [1970] xii, 614 p.
[$25.00] 914.7 70-100941
DK17 .S64 1970b MRR Alc.

EUROPE, EASTERN--BIBLIOGRAPHY.
American Universities Field Staff. A
select bibliography: Asia, Africa,
Eastern Europe, Latin America. New
York [1960] ix, 534 p.   016.9019
60-10482
Z5579 .A5 MRR Alc.

Horak, Stephan M., Junior Slavica;
Rochester, N.Y., Libraries Unlimited,
1968. 244 p. [$7.85]   016.9147 68-
26959
Z2491 .H58 MRR Alc.

Horecky, Paul Louis, East Central
Europe; a guide to basic
publications. Chicago, University of
Chicago Press [1969] xxv, 956 p.
016.9143 70-79472
Z2483 .H56 MRR Alc.

Horna, Dagmar, ed. Current research
on central and eastern Europe. New
York, Mid-European Studies Center,
Free Europe Committee [1956] xviii,
251 p.   016.943 56-10866
Z2483 .H6 MRR Alc.

United States. Dept. of the Army.
Communist Eastern Europe; analytical
survey of literature. Washington;
[For sale by the Supt. of Docs., U.S.
Govt. Print. Off.] 1971. xi, 367 p.
016.9147 78-611513
Z2483 .U48 MRR Alc.

EUROPE, EASTERN--BIBLIOGRAPHY--CATALOGS.
East European accessions index. v. 1-
Sept./Oct. 1951- Washington [U.S.
Govt. Print. Off.] 016.94 51-60032
Z663.7 .A3 MRR Alc MRR Alc Full
set

Johann Gottfried Herder-Institut,
Marburg. Bibliothek. Bibliothek des
Johann Gottfried Herder-Instituts,
Marburg/Lahn, Germany; alphabetischer
Katalog. Boston, G. K. Hall, 1964.
5 v.   65-85879
Z2483 .J6 MRR Alc. (Dk 33)

EUROPE, EASTERN--BIOGRAPHY.
Kleine slavische Biographie.
Wiesbaden, O. Harrassowitz, 1958.
832 p.   59-21195
CT205 .K53 MRR Biog.

National Academy of Sciences,
Washington, D.C. Office of the
Foreign Secretary. The Eastern
European academies of sciences;
Washington, National Academy of
Sciences-National Research Council,
1963. 148 p.   067.058 63-60058
AS98 .N3 MRR Alc.

Who's who in Eastern Europe. [n.p.,
1962?- 2 v. (loose-leaf)   64-1325
DR33 .W5 MRR Biog.

EUROPE, EASTERN--COMMERCE.
Marer, Paul. Soviet and East
European foreign trade, 1946-1969;
Bloomington, Indiana University Press
[1973, c1972] xviii, 408 p.
[$15.00] 382/.0947 72-76945
HF3626.5 .M37 MRR Alc.

Mid-European Law Project. Economic
treaties and agreements of the Soviet
bloc in Eastern Europe, 1945-1951.
2d ed. New York, Mid-European
Studies Center, 1952. xliii, 138 p.
382 52-60057
Z663.55 .E3 MRR Alc.

EUROPE, EASTERN--COMMERCE--DIRECTORIES.
Black, Sam, Businessman's guide to
the centrally planned economy
countries: Albania, Bulgaria, China,
Cuba, Czechoslovakia, German
Democratic Republic, Hungary, Poland,
Romania, USSR, Yugoslavia; London,
Modino Press, 1972. 186 p. [£3.50
($9.00 U.S.)] 382/.09171/7 73-
157217
HF4050 .A2 MRR Alc.

International Trade Centre. Foreign
trade enterprises in Eastern Europe.
[Revised ed.] Geneva [1968] 98 p.
76-503842
HF3493 .I5 MRR Alc.

**EUROPE, EASTERN--COMMERCE--HANDBOOKS,
MANUALS, ETC.**
Trade handbook for East Europe and
Scandinavia. 1971- [Copenhagen]
Wilkenschildt Publishers. 72-626883

HF3497 .T73 MRR Alc Latest edition

**EUROPE, EASTERN--COMMERCE--GREAT
BRITAIN.**
Zentner, Peter. East-West trade:
London, Parrish [1967]. 300 p. [45/-
] 658.8 67-111075
HF3508.E19 Z4 MRR Alc.

EUROPE, EASTERN--DESCRIPTION AND TRAVEL.
Osborne, Richard Horsley. East-
Central Europe: a geographical
introduction to seven socialist
states, London, Chatto & Windus,
1967. 384 p. [35/-] 914 67-88612

HC244 .O67 MRR Alc.

**EUROPE, EASTERN--DESCRIPTION AND TRAVEL-
-GUIDE-BOOKS.**
Ekvall, David H. Complete guide to
Eastern Europe New York, Hart Pub.
Co. [1970] 562 p. [9.95] 914.3
69-18898
DR7 .E37 MRR Alc.

Kane, Robert S. Eastern Europe, A to
Z; [1st ed.] Garden City, N.Y.,
Doubleday [1968] x, 348 p.   914.7
67-19081
DR7 .K3 MRR Alc.

EUROPE, EASTERN--ECONOMIC CONDITIONS.
Osborne, Richard Horsley. East-
Central Europe: a geographical
introduction to seven socialist
states, London, Chatto & Windus,
1967. 384 p. [35/-] 914 67-88612

HC244 .O67 MRR Alc.

EUROPE, EASTERN--EXECUTIVE DEPARTMENTS.
Black, Sam, Businessman's guide to
the centrally planned economy
countries: Albania, Bulgaria, China,
Cuba, Czechoslovakia, German
Democratic Republic, Hungary, Poland,
Romania, USSR, Yugoslavia; London,
Modino Press, 1972. 186 p. [£3.50
($9.00 U.S.)] 382/.09171/7 73-
157217
HF4050 .A2 MRR Alc.

**EUROPE, EASTERN--FOREIGN RELATIONS--
TREATIES.**
Mid-European Law Project. Economic
treaties and agreements of the Soviet
bloc in Eastern Europe, 1945-1951.
2d ed. New York, Mid-European
Studies Center, 1952. xliii, 138 p.
382 52-60057
Z663.55 .E3 MRR Alc.

**EUROPE, EASTERN--HISTORICAL GEOGRAPHY--
MAPS.**
Adams, Arthur E. An atlas of Russian
and East European history New York,
Praeger [1967, c1966] 204 p.   map67-
61
G2111.S1 A2 1967 MRR Alc.

EUROPE, EASTERN--IMPRINTS.
East European accessions index. v. 1-
Sept./Oct. 1951- Washington [U.S.
Govt. Print. Off.] 016.94 51-60032

Z663.7 .A3 MRR Alc MRR Alc Full
set

**EUROPE, EASTERN--LEARNED INSTITUTIONS
AND SOCIETIES.**
National Academy of Sciences,
Washington, D.C. Office of the
Foreign Secretary. The Eastern
European academies of sciences;
Washington, National Academy of
Sciences-National Research Council,
1963. 148 p.   067.058 63-60058
AS98 .N3 MRR Alc.

**EUROPE, EASTERN--LEARNED INSTITUTIONS
AND SOCIETIES--DIRECTORIES.**
Little (Arthur D.) inc. Directory of
selected research institutes in
Eastern Europe, New York, Columbia
University Press, 1967. x, 445 p.
507.204 66-20496
Q180.E9 L5 MRR Alc.

EUROPE, EASTERN--MAPS.
Adams, Arthur E. An atlas of Russian
and East European history New York,
Praeger [1967, c1966] 204 p.   map67-
61
G2111.S1 A2 1967 MRR Alc.

**EUROPE, EASTERN--PERIODICALS--
BIBLIOGRAPHY.**
Birkos, Alexander S. East European
and Slavic studies. [Kent? Ohio]
Kent State University Press [1973]
572 p. [$7.50] 016.9147/03/05 73-
158303
Z2483 .B56 MRR Alc.

East European accessions index. v. 1-
Sept./Oct. 1951- Washington [U.S.
Govt. Print. Off.] 016.94 51-60032

Z663.7 .A3 MRR Alc MRR Alc Full
set

United States. Library of Congress.
Slavic and Central European Division.
East and East Central Europe:
periodicals Washington, 1958. v,
126p.   016.943 58-60065
Z663.47 .E2 MRR Alc.

United States. Library of Congress.
Slavic and Central European Division.
The USSR and Eastern Europe; 3d ed.
rev. and enl. Washington, Library of
Congress; [for sale by the Supt. of
Docs., U.S. Govt. Print. Off.] 1967.
89 p.   016.05 68-60045
Z663.47 .U22 1967 MRR Alc.

EUROPE, EASTERN--POLITICS.
United States. Dept. of the Army.
Communist Eastern Europe; analytical
survey of literature. Washington;
[For sale by the Supt. of Docs., U.S.
Govt. Print. Off.] 1971. xi, 367 p.
016.9147 78-611513
Z2483 .U48 MRR Alc.

EUROPE, EASTERN--STATISTICS.
Marer, Paul. Soviet and East
European foreign trade, 1946-1969;
Bloomington, Indiana University Press
[1973, c1972] xviii, 408 p.
[$15.00] 382/.0947 72-76945
HF3626.5 .M37 MRR Alc.

Trade handbook for East Europe and
Scandinavia. 1971- [Copenhagen]
Wilkenschildt Publishers. 72-626883

HF3497 .T73 MRR Alc Latest edition

United States. Dept. of Agriculture.
Economic Research Service.
Agricultural statistics of Eastern
Europe and the Soviet Union, 1950-66.
[Washington, 1969] vi, 110 p.
338.1/094 70-601060
HD1916 .U65 MRR Alc.

EUROPEAN COMMON MARKET (1955-)
see European Economic Community

EUROPEAN ECONOMIC COMMUNITY.
Broad, Roger. Community Europe today
[Revised and enlarged ed.] London,
Oswald Wolff [1972] 255 p. [£1.50]
309.1/4/055 72-185333
HC241.2 .B68 1972 MRR Alc.

EUROPEAN ECONOMIC COMMUNITY. (Cont.)
Prag, Derek. Businessman's guide to
the Common Market London, Pall Mall
Press, 1973. x, 462 p. [£5.95]
382/.9142 73-166685
   HC241.2 .P657 MRR Alc.

Taschenbuch für den Gemeinsamen
Markt EWG, EURATOM, Montan-Union.
Recklinghausen, Komminal-Verlag
[etc.] 60-26020
   HC240 .T32 MRR Alc Latest edition

EUROPEAN ECONOMIC COMMUNITY--YEARBOOKS.
Bottin, Europe. 1959- Paris,
Société Didot-Bottin. 59-44496
   HC240 .A1B6 Sci RR Latest edition
   / MRR Alc Latest edition

EUROPEAN ECONOMIC COMMUNITY COUNTRIES--
COMMERCE--HANDBOOKS, MANUALS, ETC.
Prag, Derek. Businessman's guide to
the Common Market London, Pall Mall
Press, 1973. x, 462 p. [£5.95]
382/.9142 73-166685
   HC241.2 .P657 MRR Alc.

EUROPEAN ECONOMIC COMMUNITY COUNTRIES--
POLITICS AND GOVERNMENT.
Holt, Stephen. Six European states;
New York, Taplinger Pub. Co. [1970]
xi, 414 p. [$10.00] 320.3/094 78-
127406
   JN94 .A3 1970 MRR Alc.

EUROPEAN ECONOMIC COMMUNITY COUNTRIES--
STATISTICS.
Statistical Office of the European
Communities. The Common Market ten
years on: tables 1958-1967.
[Brussels, Luxembourg, 1968] 109 p.
[unpriced] 330.94 74-415168
   HA1107 .S73 MRR Alc.

EUROPEAN FEDERATION.
Political and Economic Planning.
European unity: [Revised ed.]
London, Political and Economic
Planning; Allen & Unwin, 1968. 3-519
p. [63/-] 068/.4 68-111444
   JN94 .P6 1968 MRR Alc.

Robertson, Arthur Henry. European
institutions: co-operation,
integration, unification, [3d ed.]
London, Stevens & Sons; New York,
Matthew Bender, 1973. xix, 478 p.
341.24/2 72-94556
   JN15 .R58 1973 MRR Alc.

Zurcher, Arnold John. The struggle
to unite Europe, 1940-1958; [New
York] New York University Press,
1958. 254 p. 940.55 58-6825
   D1060 .Z8 MRR Alc.

EUROPEAN FEDERATION--YEARBOOKS.
Annuaire européen. v. 1- 1955-
La Haye, Nijhoff. 55-3837
   JN3 .A5 MRR Alc Latest edition

The Europa year book. 1959- London,
Europa Publications. 341.184 59-
2942
   JN1 .E85 Sci RR Latest edition /
   MRR Ref Desk Latest edition

EUROPEAN NEWSPAPERS.
United States. Library of Congress.
European Affairs Division. The
European press today. Washington,
1949. 152 p. 016.07 49-46986
   Z663.26 .E84 MRR Alc.

EUROPEAN NEWSPAPERS--BIBLIOGRAPHY.
United States. Library of Congress.
European Affairs Division. Reference
notes on the press in European
countries participating in the
European recovery program;
[Washington] 1948. 39 p. 338.942
49-45627
   Z663.26 .E4 MRR Alc.

EUROPEAN NEWSPAPERS--BIBLIOGRAPHY--
CATALOGS.
United States. Library of Congress.
Slavic and Central European Division.
Newspapers of east central and
southeastern Europe in the Library of
Congress. Washington, 1965. vii,
204 p. 65-60088
   Z663.47 .N37 MRR Alc.

EUROPEAN PERIODICALS.
United States. Library of Congress.
European Affairs Division. The
European press today. Washington,
1949. 152 p. 016.07 49-46986
   Z663.26 .E84 MRR Alc.

EUROPEAN PERIODICALS--BIBLIOGRAPHY.
United States. Library of Congress.
European Affairs Division. Reference
notes on the press in European
countries participating in the
European recovery program;
[Washington] 1948. 39 p. 338.942
49-45627
   Z663.26 .R4 MRR Alc.

Vesenyi, Paul E., European
periodical literature in the social
sciences and the humanities.
Metuchen, N.J., Scarecrow Press,
1969. 226 p. 016.052 79-7052
   Z6955 .Z9V45 MRR Alc.

EUROPEAN PERIODICALS--BIBLIOGRAPHY--
CATALOGS.
United States. Library of Congress.
Slavic and Central European Division.
East and East Central Europe:
periodicals Washington, 1958. v,
126p. 016.943 58-60065
   Z663.47 .E2 MRR Alc.

United States. Library of Congress.
Slavic and Central European Division.
The USSR and Eastern Europe; 3d ed.
rev. and enl. Washington, Library of
Congress; [for sale by the Supt. of
Docs., U.S. Govt. Print. Off.] 1967.
89 p. 016.05 68-60045
   Z663.47 .U22 1967 MRR Alc.

EUROPEAN WAR, 1914-1918.
Falls, Cyril Bentham, The Great War.
New York, Putnam [1959] 447 p.
940.3 59-7851
   D521 .F25 MRR Alc.

The History of the First World War.
Commemorative ed. New York, Grolier
[1965] 4 v. (1360, x p.) 65-27999
   D521 .H47 MRR Alc.

Liddell Hart, Basil Henry, Sir,
History of the First World War.
[Enlarged ed.] London, Cassell,
1970. 635 p. [84/-] 940.4 70-
557411
   D521 .L48 1970 MRR Alc.

EUROPEAN WAR, 1914-1918--AERIAL
OPERATIONS.
Robertson, Bruce, ed. Air aces of
the 1914-1918 war. Letchworth,
Herts. [Eng.] Harleyford
Publications, 1959. 211 p.
926.2913 59-13378
   D600 .R6 MRR Alc.

Thetford, Owen Gordon, Aircraft of
the 1914-1918 war, Harleyford,
Marlow, Eng., Re-published under
licence by Harleyford Publications,
1954. v, 127 p. 623.746 629.133*
55-29424
   TL685.3 .T44 1954 MRR Alc.

EUROPEAN WAR, 1914-1918--BIBLIOGRAPHY.
The Two world wars; selective
bibliography. Oxford, New York,
Pergamon Press [1965, c1964] 246 p.
016.9403 65-6499
   Z6207.E8 T85 1965 MRR Alc.

EUROPEAN WAR, 1914-1918--BIBLIOGRAPHY--
CATALOGS.
British Museum. Dept. of Printed
Books. Subject index of the modern
works added to the British museum
library. [1st]- 1901/05- London,
Trustees of the British Museum.
019.1 07-10319
   Z1035 .B8613 MRR Alc (Dk33) Full
   set

Stuttgart. Bibliothek für
Zeitgeschichte. Bibliothek für
Zeitgeschichte--Weltkriegsbücherei,
Stuttgart:alphabetischer Katalog.
Boston, G. K. Hall, 1968. 11 v. 74-
223544
   Z6209 .S85 1968 MRR Alc (Dk 33)

Stuttgart. Bibliothek für
Zeitgeschichte. Bibliothek für
Zeitgeschichte--Weltkriegsbücherei,
Stuttgart; systematischer Katalog.
Boston, G. K. Hall, 1968. 20 v. 74-
225445
   Z6204 .S8 1968 MRR Alc (Dk 33)

EUROPEAN WAR, 1914-1918--CAMPAIGNS.
McEntee, Girard Lindsley, Military
history of the world war, New York,
C. Scribner's sons, 1943. xxii p., 1
l., 583 p. 940.4 43-4740
   D521 .M14 1943 MRR Alc.

EUROPEAN WAR, 1914-1918--CAUSES.
Albertini, Luigi, The origins of the
war of 1914. London, New York,
Oxford University Press, 1952-57. 3
v. 940.311 52-12126
   D511 .A574 MRR Alc.

Schmitt, Bernadotte Everly, The
coming of the war, 1914, New York,
H. Fertig, 1966 [c1958] 2 v.
940.3112 66-24353
   D511 .S275 1966 MRR Alc.

EUROPEAN WAR, 1914-1918--DIPLOMATIC
HISTORY.
Albertini, Luigi, The origins of the
war of 1914. London, New York,
Oxford University Press, 1952-57. 3
v. 940.311 52-12126
   D511 .A574 MRR Alc.

Geiss, Imanuel. July 1914: the
outbreak of the First World War:
London, Batsford, 1967. 400 p. [50/-
] 940.3/112/08 67-108481
   D505 .G2513 MRR Alc.

Scott, James Brown, ed. Diplomatic
documents relating to the outbreak of
the European war, New York, Oxford
university press, American branch;
[etc., etc.] 1916. 2 v. 16-18046
   D505 .S4 MRR Alc.

EUROPEAN WAR, 1914-1918--LANGUAGE (NEW
WORDS, SLANG, ETC.).
Abbatt, William, comp. The
colloquial who's who; Tarrytown,
N.Y., W. Abbatt, 1924-25. 2 v. 24-
23254
   Z1045 .A12 MRR Alc.

EUROPEAN WAR, 1914-1918--LANGUAGE (NEW
WORDS, SLANG, ETC.)
Fraser, Edward, comp. Soldier and
sailor words and phrases; London, G.
Routledge and sons, ltd., 1925. vii,
372 p. 25-9719
   PE3727.S7 F7 MRR Alc.

Hargrave, Basil. Origins and
meanings of popular phrases and
names. [Rev. ed.] London, T. W.
Laurie [1948] vi, 350 p. 423 49-
1451
   AG5 .H18 1948 MRR Ref Desk.

EUROPEAN WAR, 1914-1918--MAPS.
McEntee, Girard Lindsley, Military
history of the world war, New York,
C. Scribner's sons, 1943. xxii p., 1
l., 583 p. 940.4 43-4740
   D521 .M14 1943 MRR Alc.

EUROPEAN WAR, 1914-1918--MAPS--
BIBLIOGRAPHY.
United States. Library of Congress.
Map division. A list of atlases and
maps applicable to the world war;
Washington, Govt. print. off., 1918.
202 p. 18-26005
   Z663.35 .L54 MRR Alc.

EUROPEAN WAR, 1914-1918--NAVAL
OPERATIONS.
Frothingham, Thomas Goddard, The
naval history of the world war
Cambridge, Harvard university press,
1924-26. 3 v. 24-14384
   D580 .F75 MRR Alc.

EUROPEAN WAR, 1914-1918--NEGROES.
Scott, Emmett Jay, Scott's official
history of the American Negro in the
World War. New York, Arno Press,
1969. 511 p. 940.4/03 69-18556
   D639.N4 S3 1969 MRR Alc.

EUROPEAN WAR, 1914-1918--PEACE.
Allied and associated powers (1914-
1920) Treaties, etc. The treaties of
peace, 1919-1923. New York, Carnegie
endowment for international peace,
1924. 2 v. 24-19994
   D643 .A2 1923 MRR Alc.

EUROPEAN WAR, 1914-1918--REGIMENTAL
HISTORIES--GREAT BRITAIN.
Lewis, Peter M. H. Squadron
histories: R.F.C., R.N.A.S. and
R.A.F., since 1912 2nd ed. London,
Putnam, 1968. 224 p. [50/-]
358.41/3/50942 68-133976
   UG635.G7 L47 1968 MRR Alc.

EUROPEAN WAR, 1914-1918--REGIMENTAL
HISTORIES--UNITED STATES.
Stubbs, Mary Lee. Armor-cavalry,
Washington, Office of the Chief of
Military History, U.S. Army; [for
sale by the Supt. of Docs., U.S.
Govt. Print. Off., 1969- v.
[6.75] 357/.0973 69-60002
   UA30 .S8 MRR Alc.

United States. Dept. of the Army.
Office of Military History. The Army
lineage book. Washington, U.S. Govt.
Print. Off., 1953- v. 355.309
54-61235
   UA25 .A516 MRR Alc.

EUROPEAN WAR, 1914-1918--REGIMENTAL
HISTORIES--UNITED STATES--BIBLIOGRAPHY.
Dornbusch, Charles Emil, Histories,
personal narratives: United States
Army; Cornwallville, N.Y., Hope Farm
Press, 1967. [15]-399 p. 016.355
67-5273
   Z1249.M5 D6 1967 MRR Ref Desk.

EUROPEAN WAR, 1914-1918--SOURCES--
BIBLIOGRAPHY.
United States. Library of Congress.
Manuscript Division. Charles Pelot
Summerall: a register of his papers
in the Library of Congress.
Washington, 1958. 9 l. 012 58-
60068
   Z663.34 .S8 MRR Alc.

EUROPEAN WAR, 1914-1918--SUPPLIES--
ADDRESSES, ESSAYS, LECTURES.
Crow, Duncan. AFV's of World War
One, Windsor, Eng., Profile
Publications [1970] viii, 164 p.
358/.18/08 s 358/.18/09041 72-181764
   UG446.5 .A694 vol. 1 MRR Alc.

EUROPEAN WAR, 1914-1918--TERRITORIAL
QUESTIONS.
Allied and associated powers (1914-
1920) Treaties, etc. The treaties of
peace, 1919-1923. New York, Carnegie
endowment for international peace,
1924. 2 v.   24-19994
D643 .A2 1923 MRR Alc.

EUROPEAN WAR, 1914-1918--TREATIES.
Allied and associated powers (1914-
1920) Treaties, etc. The treaties of
peace, 1919-1923. New York, Carnegie
endowment for international peace,
1924. 2 v.   24-19994
D643 .A2 1923 MRR Alc.

Hertslet's commercial treaties.
London, 1827-1925. 31 v.   01-4024
JX636 1827 Vol. 22 & 31 MRR Alc.

EUROPEAN WAR, 1914-1918--UNITED STATES.
Baker, Ray Stannard, Woodrow Wilson;
life and letters ... Garden City,
N.Y., Doubleday, Page & co., 1927-39.
8 v.   27-25411
E767 .B16 MRR Alc.

Sullivan, Mark, Our Times; the
United States, 1900-1925 ... New
York [etc.] C. Scribner's sons, 1927-
35. 6 v.   mrr01-51
E741 .S92 MRR Alc.

United States. Army War College.
Historical Section. Order of battle
of the United States land forces in
the World War. Washington, U.S.
Govt. Print. Off., 1931-49. 3 v. in
4.   940.41273 31-27280
D570 .A353 MRR Alc.

United States. National archives.
Handbook of federal world war
agencies and their records, 1917-
1921. Washington, U.S. Govt. print.
off., 1943. xiii, 666 p.   353 43-
50551
JK464.1963 .A52 MRR Alc.

Wood, William Charles Henry, In
defense of liberty, New Haven, Yale
university press; [etc., etc.] 1928.
3 p. l., 370 p.   28-25826
E178.5 .P2 vol. VII MRR Alc.

EUROPEAN WAR, 1939-1945
see World War, 1939-1945

EVANGELICAL FREE CHURCH OF AMERICA--
HISTORY.
The Diamond Jubilee story of the
Evangelical Free Church of America,
Minneapolis, Free Church Publications
[1959] 335 p.   289.9 59-10976
BX7548.A4 D5 MRR Alc.

EVANGELISCHE KIRCHE IN DEUTSCHLAND--
DIRECTORIES.
Taschenbuch der evangelischen Kirchen
in Deutschland. 1955- Stuttgart,
Evangelisches Verlagswerk.   60-30113

RX8020 .A1T3 MRR Alc Latest editon

EVANS, CHARLES, 1850-1935. AMERICAN
BIBLIOGRAPHY.
Shipton, Clifford Kenyon, National
index of American imprints through
1800; [Worcester, Mass.] American
Antiquarian Society, 1969. 2 v.
(xxv, 1028 p.) 015/.73 69-11248
Z1215 .S495 MRR Ref Desk.

EVANS, LUTHER HARRIS, 1902- --
BIBLIOGRAPHY.
United States. Library of Congress.
Writings and addresses of Luther
Harris Evans, Washington, 1953. 92
p.   012 53-60039
Z663 .W7 MRR Alc.

EVANSTON, ILL. TRANSPORTATION CENTER AT
NORTHWESTERN UNIVERSITY. LIBRARY.
Evanston, Ill. Transportation Center
at Northwestern University. Library.
Catalog. Boston, G. K. Hall, 1972.
12 v.   016.3805 74-171017
Z7164.T8 E83 1972 MRR Alc (Dk 33)

EVENING AND CONTINUATION SCHOOLS--
UNITED STATES--DIRECTORIES.
College Entrance Examination Board.
The New York Times guide to
continuing education in America,
[New York] Quadrangle Books [1972]
811 p. [$12.50]   374.8/73 74-
183190
L901 .C74 1972 MRR Ref Desk.

EVERGREENS.
Beale, James H. The evergreens.
[1st ed.] Garden City,N.Y.,
Doubleday, 1960. 285 p.   635.977
59-12024
SB435 .B36 MRR Alc.

EVIL SPIRITS
see Demonology

EVOLUTION.
see also Biology

see also Genetics

see also Man--Origin

EX-SERVICE MEN
see Veterans

EXAMINATIONS.
see also Educational tests and
measurements

EXAMINATIONS--BIBLIOGRAPHY.
Buros, Oscar Krisen, ed. The mental
measurements yearbook. [1st]- 1938-
Highland Park, N.J. [etc.] Gryphon
Press [etc.] 016.1512 016.159928 39-
3422
Z5814.P8 B932 MRR Alc Partial set

Buros, Oscar Krisen, ed. Tests in
print; Highland Park, N.J., Gryphon
Press [1961] xxix, 479 p.
016.37126 61-16302
Z5814.E9 B8 MRR Alc.

EXAMINATIONS--UNITED STATES.
College Entrance Examination Board.
A description of the College Board
achievement tests. 1956-
[Princeton, N.J.] 371.26 59-4353
LB2367 .C6 MRR Alc Latest edition

EXAMINATIONS, MEDICAL
see Diagnosis

EXCAVATION (ARCHAEOLOGY)
see also Archaeology

EXCAVATIONS (ARCHAEOLOGY)
Atkinson, Richard John Copland,
Field archaeology. [2d ed., rev.]
London, Methuen [1953] 233 p.   913
54-36205
CC75 .A8 1953 MRR Alc.

EXCAVATIONS (ARCHAEOLOGY)--AMERICA--
ADDRESSES, ESSAYS, LECTURES.
Deuel, Leo, comp. Conquistadors
without swords; New York, St.
Martin's Press, 1967. xix, 647 p.
970.1 67-22577
E61 .D46 MRR Alc.

EXCAVATIONS (ARCHAEOLOGY)--NORTH
AMERICA.
Robbins, Maurice. The amateur
archaeologist's handbook 2d ed. New
York, Crowell [1973] xiv, 288 p.
[$7.95] 913/.031/028 73-245
E77.9 .R6 1973 MRR Alc.

EXCAVATIONS (ARCHAEOLOGY)--UNITED
STATES.
Brennan, Louis A. Beginner's guide
to archaeology; [Harrisburg, Pa.]
Stackpole Books [1973] 318 p.
[$9.95] 913/.031 73-4193
E77.9 .B73 MRR Alc.

EXCEPTIONAL CHILDREN.
see also Gifted children

see also Handicapped children

Garrison, Karl Claudius, The
psychology of exceptional children
4th ed. New York, Ronald Press Co.
[1965] vi, 571 p.   371.9 65-21809
LC3965 .G3 1965 MRR Alc.

EXCEPTIONAL CHILDREN--DIRECTORIES.
Directory for exceptional children;
[1st]- ed.; 1954- Boston, P.
Sargent. 371.92058 54-4975
LC4007 .D5 MRR Alc Latest edition

EXCEPTIONAL CHILDREN--EDUCATION.
Cruickshank, William M., ed.
Education of exceptional children and
youth. 2d ed. Englewood Cliffs, N.
J., Prentice-Hall [1967] xvii, 730
p. 371.9 67-10116
LC3951 .C7 1967 MRR Alc.

EXCEPTIONAL CHILDREN--EDUCATION--
DIRECTORIES.
Directory for exceptional children;
[1st]- ed.; 1954- Boston, P.
Sargent. 371.92058 54-4975
LC4007 .D5 MRR Alc Latest edition

United Nations Educational,
Scientific, and Cultural
Organization. Special education.
[Paris, 1969] 142 p. [$3.50]
371.9/025 78-9239
L900 .U56 MRR Alc.

EXCEPTIONAL CHILDREN--EDUCATION--UNITED
STATES--DIRECTORIES.
Leib, Robert J. U.S. private schools
classified; Los Angeles, Sherbourne
Press [1968] 192 p.   371/.02/02573
68-14283
L901 .L4 MRR Alc.

EXCHANGE.
see also Commerce

see also Money

EXCHANGE OF PERSONS PROGRAMS.
see also Visitors, Foreign

Unesco handbook of international
exchanges. 1- 1965- [Paris]
Unesco. 65-5337
AS8 .U35 MRR Alc Latest edition

EXCHANGES, COMMODITY
see Commodity exchanges

EXCHANGES, LITERARY AND SCIENTIFIC.
Malia, Martin Edward. Report, to the
Joint Committee on Slavic Studies and
to the Library of Congress, on
methods for improving Soviet book
acquisitions by American research
libraries, February-March, 1956.
[Washington?] 1956. 2 l., 79 p.   63-
61735
Z663 .R394 MRR Alc.

Unesco handbook of international
exchanges. 1- 1965- [Paris]
Unesco. 65-5337
AS8 .U35 MRR Alc Latest edition

United Nations Educational,
Scientific and Cultural Organization.
Handbook on the international
exchange of publications. 3d ed.,
edited and rev. [Paris, 1964] 767
p. 64-33470
Z690 .U454 1964 MRR Alc.

United States. Library of Congress.
Processing Dept. The role of the
Library of Congress in the
international exchange of official
publications; Washington, 1953. 85
p. 021.852 53-60020
Z663.7 .R6 MRR Alc.

EXECUTIONS AND EXECUTIONERS.
see also Capital punishment

EXECUTIONS AND EXECUTIONERS--GREAT
BRITAIN.
Pritchard, John Laurence, A history
of capital punishment New York,
Citadel Press [1960] 230 p.   343.23
60-13927
HV8694 .P7 1960 MRR Alc.

EXECUTIVE ABILITY
see also Leadership

see also Management

EXECUTIVE ADVISORY BODIES--GREAT
BRITAIN.
Anderson, Ian Gibson. Councils,
committees, & boards; 2d ed.
Beckenham, CBD Research Ltd. 1973.
iii-xiv, 327 p. [£7.50 ($25.00
U.S.)] 062 74-164686
AS118 .A5 1973 MRR Alc.

EXECUTIVE INVESTIGATIONS
see Governmental investigations

EXECUTIVE ORDERS--UNITED STATES.
Historical records survey. New York
(City) Presidential executive
orders. New York, Books, inc.,
distributed by Archives publishing
company, a division of Hastings house
[1944] 2 v.   353.03 44-2050
J80.A72 MRR Alc.

United States. Federal register. v.
1- March 14, 1936- [Washington,
U.S. Govt. Print. off.] 353.005 36-
26246
J1 .A2 MRR Alc (Dk 33) Full set

United States. President, 1929-1933
(Hoover) Herbert Hoover :
Washington : U.S. Govt. Print. Off.,
1974. 2 v. (iii, 1566 p.) : [$24.55
] 353.03/5 74-602466
J82 .D5 1974 MRR Alc.

EXECUTIVE ORDERS--UNITED STATES--
INDEXES.
Historical records survey. New
Jersey. List and index of
presidential executive orders,
Newark, N.J., Historical records
survey, Work projects administration
[1943] 1 p. l., xiv p., 1 l., 388,
[2] p. 016.353 43-13029
Z6455.A4 H5 MRR Alc.

United States. Library of Congress.
Legislative Reference Service. Table
of Executive orders appearing in the
Federal register and the Code of
Federal regulations. Washington,
Reference Dept., Library of Congress,
1955. 76 p. 016.353 55-60053
Z663.2 .T3 MRR Alc.

EXECUTIVE POWER.
see also Presidents

see also Separation of powers

EXECUTIVE POWER--UNITED STATES.
Corwin, Edward Samuel, The
President, office and powers, 1787-
1948; [3d ed., rev.] New York, New
York Univ. Press [1948] xvii, 552 p.
353.03 48-7474
JK516 .C63 1948 MRR Alc.

Fisher, Louis. President and
Congress; New York, Free Press
[1972] xvi, 347 p. 353.03/72 78-
142362
JK305 .F55 MRR Alc.

EXECUTIVE POWER--UNITED STATES. (Cont.)
Horn, John Stephen. The Cabinet and
Congress. New York, Columbia
University Press, 1960. 310 p.
353.02 60-13237
JK616 .H6 MRR Alc.

Jackson, Carlton. Presidential
vetoes, 1792-1945. Athens,
University of Georgia Press [1967]
x, 264 p. 353/.032 67-17405
JK586 .J3 MRR Alc.

Longaker, Richard P. The Presidency
and individual liberties. Ithaca,
N.Y., Cornell University Press [1961]
239 p. 353.03 61-8206
JK518 .L6 MRR Alc.

McCoy, Charles Allan, Polk and the
Presidency. Austin, University of
Texas Press [c1960] 238 p. 973.61
60-9515
E417 .M15 MRR Alc.

Smith, John Malcolm. Powers of the
President during crises, Washington,
Public Affairs Press [1960] viii,
184 p. 353.032 59-14964
JK516 .S66 MRR Alc.

Tugwell, Rexford Guy, The
enlargement of the Presidency. [1st
ed.] Garden City, N.Y., Doubleday,
1960. 508 p. 353.03 60-11391
JK516 .T8 MRR Alc.

EXECUTIVES--RECRUITING.
Jameson, Robert, The professional
job changing system; [3d ed.]
Verona, N.J., Performance Dynamics,
1974] 280 p. 650/.14 73-92380
HF5383 .J28 1974 MRR Alc.

EXECUTIVES--CALIFORNIA--BIOGRAPHY.
Who's who executives in California.
1963- [Los Angeles] A. C. Armstrong.
63-49837
F860 .W624 MRR Biog Latest edition

EXECUTIVES--GERMANY.
Leitende Manner der Wirtschaft.
1951- Darmstadt [etc.] Hoppenstedt,
[etc.] 52-16904
HF3564.5 .L4 MRR Alc Latest
edition

EXECUTIVES--GREAT BRITAIN--BIOGRAPHY.
Who's who in British finance. 1872-
New York. R. R. Bowker Co.
332/.092/2 [B] 72-624453
HG71 .W44 MRR Biog Latest edition

EXECUTIVES--UNITED STATES--DIRECTORIES.
Dun and Bradstreet, inc. Dun's
reference book of corporate
managements. 1st- ed.; 1867- New
York. 658.1/145/02573 68-44776
HD2745 .D85 MRR Ref Desk Latest
edition

Notable names in American history;
3d ed. of White's conspectus of
American biography. [Clifton, N.J.]
J. T. White, 1973. 725 p. 920/.073
73-6885
E176 .N89 1973 MRR Biog.

Who's who in risk management.
Englewood, N.J. [etc.] Underwriter
Printing and Pub. Co. 368/.81/002573
70-648918
HG8059.B8 W5 MRR Biog Latest
edition

EXECUTIVES--UNITED STATES--RECRUITING.
McKay, Ernest A. The Macmillan job
guide to American corporations for
college graduates, graduate students
and junior executives New York,
Macmillan [c1967] ix, 374 p.
331.115 66-20820
HF5382.5.U5 M3 MRR Alc.

National Survey Information Co.
National service directory of
executive search consultants in the
United States. Executive service ed.
Lake Bluff, Ill., 1971. vi, 47 (i.e
95) p. [$17.50] 658.4/03 77-30076

HD69.C6 N4 MRR Alc.

EXECUTIVES, TRAINING OF--DIRECTORIES.
McNulty, Nancy G. Training managers;
[1st ed.] New York, Harper & Row
[1969] x, 572 p. [12.95]
658.4/0071/5 70-83612
HD20 .M253 MRR Alc.

EXECUTIVES, TRAINING OF--UNITED STATES--
DIRECTORIES.
Bricker, George W. Bricker's
directory of university-sponsored
executive development programs. 1970-
Wilton, Conn. 658.4/0071/173 73-
110249
HD20.15.U5 B7 MRR Alc Latest
edition

EXEMPTION FROM MILITARY SERVICE
see Military service, Compulsory

EXERCISE.
see also Physical education and
training

EXHAUST CONTROL DEVICES (MOTOR VEHICLES)
see Motor vehicles--Pollution control
devices

EXHIBITIONS.
see also Fairs

EXHIBITIONS--DIRECTORIES.
Directory of conventions.
Philadelphia, Sales meetings
magazine. 063.3 63-25787
AS8 .D48 MRR Ref Desk Latest
edition

World exhibits. 3d- ; 1966-
Athens, Maecenas Publications [etc.]
607/.34 72-622650
HF5470 .I64 MRR Alc Latest edition

EXHIBITIONS--YEARBOOKS.
Sales meetings. Exhibits schedule.
Philadelphia. 600.74 63-23593
T391 .S3 Sci RR Latest edition /
MRR Alc Latest edition / MRR Alc
Latest edition (suppl.)

EXISTENTIALISM--DICTIONARIES.
Nauman, St. Elmo. The new dictionary
of existentialism. New York,
Philosophical Library [1971] 166 p.
[$10.00] 142/.7 78-118311
B819 .N28 MRR Alc.

EXORCISM.
see also Demonology

EXPANSION (UNITED STATES POLITICS)
see Imperialism

see United States--Colonial question

EXPEDITIONS, ANTARCTIC
see Antarctic regions

EXPEDITIONS, ARCTIC
see Arctic regions

EXPEDITIONS, SCIENTIFIC
see Scientific expeditions

EXPERIMENTAL PSYCHOLOGY
see Psychology, Physiological

EXPLORERS.
Langnas, Izaak Abram, Dictionary of
discoveries New York, Philosophical
Library [1959] v, 201 p. 910.9 59-
16483
G200 .L3 MRR Biog.

Riverain, Jean, Concise encyclopedia
of explorations; London, Collins;
Chicago, Follet, 1969. [6], 279 p.
[12/6] 910/.922 79-514842
G200 .R5513 1969 MRR Biog.

Zavatti, Silvio. Dizionario degli
exploratori e delle scoperte
geografiche. Milano, Feltrinelli,
1967. vi, 360 p. [L800] 70-413209

G200 .Z3 MRR Biog.

EXPORT CREDIT--UNITED STATES.
Jonnard, Claude M. Exporter's
financial and marketing handbook
Park Ridge, N.J., Noyes Data Corp.,
1973. xii, 308 p. [$18.00] 658.8
72-96107
HF1009.5 .J65 MRR Alc.

EXPORT MARKETING.
Dun & Bradstreet exporters'
encyclopaedia. New York, Dun and
Bradstreet International. 382/.6 72-
622175
HF3011 .E9 MRR Alc Latest edition

Jonnard, Claude M. Exporter's
financial and marketing handbook
Park Ridge, N.J., Noyes Data Corp.,
1973. xii, 308 p. [$18.00] 658.8
72-96107
HF1009.5 .J65 MRR Alc.

EXPORT SALES--HANDBOOKS, MANUALS, ETC.
Dun & Bradstreet exporters'
encyclopaedia. New York, Dun and
Bradstreet International. 382/.6 72-
622175
HF3011 .E9 MRR Alc Latest edition

EXPORT SALES--UNITED STATES.
Jonnard, Claude M. Exporter's
financial and marketing handbook
Park Ridge, N.J., Noyes Data Corp.,
1973. xii, 308 p. [$18.00] 658.8
72-96107
HF1009.5 .J65 MRR Alc.

EXPORTS
see Commerce

EXPRESSIONISM (ART)--DICTIONARIES.
Muller, Joseph Émile. A dictionary
of Expressionism / London : Eyre
Methuen, 1973. 159 p. : [£1.50]
759.06 74-188205
N6494.E9 M8413 MRR Alc.

EXTENDED CARE FACILITIES.
see also Nursing homes

EXTENDED RANGE FORECASTS
see Long-range weather forecasting

EXTERMINATION
see Pest control

EXTINCT ANIMALS.
see also Paleontology

see also Rare animals

EXTINCT CITIES
see Cities and towns, Ruined,
extinct, etc.

FABLES.
see also Animals, Legends and stories
of

see also Folk-lore

FABLES--BIBLIOGRAPHY--CATALOGS.
Cleveland. Public Library. John G.
White Dept. Catalog of folklore and
folk songs. Boston, G. K. Hall,
1964. 2 v. 65-4280
Z5985 .C5 MRR Alc (Dk 33).

FABLES--JUVENILE LITERATURE--
BIBLIOGRAPHY.
Quinnam, Barbara. Fables from
incunabula to modern picture books;
Washington, General Reference and
Bibliography Division, Reference
Dept., Library of Congress; [for sale
by the Superintendent of Documents,
U.S. Govt. Print. Off.] 1966. viii,
85 p. 016.3982 66-60012
Z663.292 .F3 MRR Alc.

FABLES, GREEK.
Babrius. Babrius and Phaedrus.
London. W. Heinemann; Cambridge,
Harvard University Press, 1965. cii,
634 p. 881.01 65-29002
PA3611 .A26 MRR Alc.

FABRIC SHOPS--UNITED STATES--
DIRECTORIES.
Marsar's fabric shop list. 1st-
ed.; 1972- New York, Phelon, Sheldon
& Marsar. 380.1/45/677002573 71-
616616
HD9869.F33 U55 MRR Alc Latest
edition

FACETIAE
see Wit and humor

FACTOR ANALYSIS.
Cattell, Raymond Bernard, Factor
analysis: New York, Harper [1952]
462 p. 311.23 51-11893
BF39 .C3 MRR Alc.

FACTORIES--EQUIPMENT AND SUPPLIES--
CATALOGS.
Plant engineering catalog file. New
York, Sweet's Division, McGraw-Hill
Information Systems Co.
338.4/7/67028 72-626783
TA215 .S8 MRR Alc Latest edition

Sweet's industrial construction and
renovation file. 1974- New York,
Sweet's Division, McGraw-Hill
Information Systems Co.
338.4/7/624102573 74-640340
TA215 .S85 MRR Alc Latest edition

FACTORIES--FIRES AND FIRE PREVENTION.
Factory Mutual Engineering
Corporation. Handbook of industrial
loss prevention; 2d ed. New York,
McGraw-Hill [1967] 1 v. (various
paging) 628/.92 66-23623
TH9445.M4 F3 1967 MRR Alc.

FACTORIES--PROTECTION.
Factory Mutual Engineering
Corporation. Handbook of industrial
loss prevention; 2d ed. New York,
McGraw-Hill [1967] 1 v. (various
paging) 628/.92 66-23623
TH9445.M4 F3 1967 MRR Alc.

FACTORIES--UNITED STATES--DIRECTORIES.
Marketing economics key plants. 1973-
New York, Marketing Economics
Institute. 338.4/025/73 73-642154
HC102 .M25 MRR Alc Latest edition

Plant and product directory. 1961-
[New York?] Market Research Dept. of
Fortune. 338.05873 61-12113
HC102 .P59 MRR Alc Latest edition

Sweet's industrial construction &
renovation file with plant
engineering extension market list.
1974- [New York, Sweet's Division,
McGraw-Hill Information Systems Co.]
338.4/7/69002573 74-645493
TH12 .S93 MRR Alc Latest edition /
Sci RR Latest edition

FACTORIES--UNITED STATES--STATISTICS.
McGraw-Hill Publishing Company, inc.
America's manufacturing plants; New
York, [1960] 118 p. 338.476 60-
3420
HD9724 .M2 MRR Alc.

FACTORY AND TRADE WASTE.
see also Pollution

FACTORY MANAGEMENT.
see also Industrial engineering

FACULTY (EDUCATION)
  see Educators

FAIR EMPLOYMENT PRACTICE
  see Discrimination in employment

FAIRS.
  see also Markets

FAIRS--DIRECTORIES.
  Sales meetings. Exhibits schedule.
  Philadelphia. 600.74 63-23593
  T391 .S3 Sci RR Latest edition /
    MRR Alc Latest edition / MRR Alc
    Latest edition (suppl.)

  World exhibits. 3d-   ; 1966-
  Athens, Maecenas Publications [etc.]
  607/.34 72-622650
  HF5470 .I64 MRR Alc Latest edition

FAIRY TALES.
  see also Folk-lore

FAIRY TALES--BIBLIOGRAPHY.
  Eastman, Mary Huse. Index to fairy
  tales, myths, and legends. 2d ed.,
  rev. and enl. Boston, F. W. Faxon
  Co., 1926. ix, 610 p. 016.398 26-
  11491
  Z5883.F17 E2 1926 MRR Alc.

FAIRY TALES--INDEXES.
  Eastman, Mary Huse. Index to fairy
  tales, myths, and legends. 2d ed.,
  rev. and enl. Boston, F. W. Faxon
  Co., 1926. ix, 610 p. 016.398 26-
  11491
  Z5883.F17 E2 1926 MRR Alc.

  Ireland, Norma (Olin) Index to fairy
  tales, 1949-1972; Westwood, Mass.,
  F. W. Faxon Co., 1973. xxxviii, 741
  p. 398.2/01/6 73-173454
  Z5883.F17 I73 MRR Alc.

FALCONRY--DICTIONARIES.
  Brander, Michael. A dictionary of
  sporting terms. London, Black, 1968.
  224 p. [35/-] 798 77-353522
  SK11 .B66 MRR Alc.

FAMILY.
  see also Marriage

  Byrd, Oliver Erasmus. Family life
  sourcebook. Stanford, Stanford
  University Press [1956] ix, 371 p.
  392 301.42* 56-7270
  HQ728 .B9 MRR Alc.

  Kirkpatrick, Clifford, The family as
  process and institution. 2d ed. New
  York, Ronald Press Co. [1963] 705 p.
  301.42 63-10429
  HQ728 .K48 1963 MRR Alc.

  Murdock, George Peter, Social
  structure. New York, Macmillan Co.,
  1949. xvii, 387 p. 392 49-9317
  GN27 .M95 MRR Alc.

FAMILY--BIBLIOGRAPHY.
  Aldous, Joan. International
  bibliography of research in marriage
  and the family, 1900-1964
  [Minneapolis] Distributed by the
  University of Minnesota Press for the
  Minnesota Family Study Center and the
  Institute of Life Insurance [1967]
  508 p. 016.30142 67-63014
  Z7164.M2 A48 MRR Alc.

  Mogey, John M. Sociology of marriage
  and family behaviour 1957-1968; The
  Hague, Mouton [1971] 364 p.
  016.30142 78-28387
  Z7164.M2 M64 MRR Alc.

FAMILY--UNITED STATES.
  Cavan, Ruth (Shonle) The American
  family. 4th ed. New York, Crowell
  [1969] xi, 556 p. 301.42/0973 69-
  13254
  HQ535 .C33 1969 MRR Alc.

  Glick, Paul C. American families,
  New York, Wiley [1957] xiv, 240 p.
  392 301.42* 57-5910
  HQ535 .G6 MRR Alc.

FAMILY LIFE EDUCATION.
  see also Counseling

  see also Finance, Personal

FAMILY PLANNING
  see Birth control

FAMILY SIZE.
  see also Birth control

FANCY DRESS
  see Costume

FANTASTIC FICTION.
  see also Science fiction

FANTASTIC FICTION--BIBLIOGRAPHY.
  Bleiler, Everett Franklin, ed. The
  checklist of fantastic literature;
  [1st ed.] Chicago, Shasta
  Publishers, 1948. xix, 455 p.
  016.8083 48-6709
  Z5917.F3 B55 MRR Alc.

Day, Bradford M. The supplemental
  checklist of fantastic literature.
  Denver, N.Y., Science-Fiction &
  Fantasy Publications [1963] 155 p.
  64-46968
  Z5917.F3 D35 MRR Alc.

Tuck, Donald Henry. The encyclopedia
  of science fiction and fantasy
  through 1968: [1st ed.] Chicago,
  Advent: Publishers, 1974- v.
  016.80883/876 73-91828
  Z5917.S36 T83 MRR Alc.

FANTASTIC FILMS--CATALOGS.
  Lee, Walt. Reference guide to
  fantastic films; Los Angeles,
  Chelsea-Lee Books, 1972- v.
  016.79143 72-88775
  PN1995.9.F36 L4 MRR Alc.

FARM ANIMALS
  see Domestic animals

FARM BUILDINGS.
  see also Architecture, Domestic

FARM INCOME--UNITED STATES.
  United States. Library of Congress.
  Legislative Reference Service. Farm
  program benefits and costs in recent
  years; Washington, U.S. Govt. Print.
  Off., 1964. iv, 6 p. 67-61367
  Z663.6 .F3 MRR Alc.

FARM MACHINERY
  see Agricultural machinery

FARM PRODUCE.
  see also Food industry and trade

  United States. Dept. of Agriculture.
  Crops in peace and war. Washington,
  U.S. Govt. Print. Off. [1951] 942 p.
  630.72 agr55-9
  S21 .A35 1950-1951 MRR Alc.

FARM PRODUCE--MARKETING.
  United States. Dept. of Agriculture.
  Marketing. [Washington, U.S. Govt.
  Print. Off., 1954] xiv, 506 p.
  631.18 agr55-4
  S21.A35 1954 MRR Alc.

FARM PRODUCE--MARKETING--UNITED STATES.
  United States. Dept. of Agriculture.
  Marketing. [Washington, U.S. Govt.
  Print. Off., 1954] xiv, 506 p.
  631.18 agr55-4
  S21.A35 1954 MRR Alc.

FARM PRODUCE--UNITED STATES--STATISTICS.
  United States. Dept. of Agriculture.
  Agricultural statistics. 1936-
  Washington, U.S. Govt. Print. Off.
  338.10973 agr36-465
  HD1751 .A43 MRR Ref Desk Latest
    edition / MRR Alc Latest edition

FARMERS' COOPERATIVES
  see Agriculture, Cooperative

FARMING
  see Agriculture

FARMINGTON PLAN.
  Williams, Edwin Everitt, Farmington
  plan handbook. [Ithaca, N.Y.]
  Association of Research Libraries,
  1961. 141 p. 025.22 61-17125
  Z689 .W6 1961 MRR Alc.

FARMS--RECREATIONAL USE--CANADA--
DIRECTORIES.
  Farm and Ranch Vacations, inc. Farm,
  ranch & countryside guide; [25th
  anniversary ed.] New York; trade
  distributor: Berkshire Traveller
  Press, Stockbridge, Mass., 1974. 191
  p. [$3.50] 917.3 74-174454
  TX907 .F37 1974 MRR Alc.

FARMS--RECREATIONAL USE--UNITED STATES--
DIRECTORIES.
  Farm and Ranch Vacations, inc. Farm,
  ranch & countryside guide; [25th
  anniversary ed.] New York; trade
  distributor: Berkshire Traveller
  Press, Stockbridge, Mass., 1974. 191
  p. [$3.50] 917.3 74-174454
  TX907 .F37 1974 MRR Alc.

FAROE ISLANDS--GAZETTEERS.
  United States. Office of Geography.
  Denmark and the Faeroe Islands;
  Washington, U.S. Govt. Print. Off.,
  1961. viii, 239 p. 914.915 61-
  62195
  DL105 .U5 MRR Alc.

FASHION.
  see also Clothing and dress

  see also Costume

FASHION--DICTIONARIES.
  Ironside, Janey. A fashion alphabet;
  London, Joseph, 1968. 262 p. [50/-
  ] 391/.2/03 68-141547
  TT503 .I7 MRR Alc.

  Picken, Mary (Brooks) The fashion
  dictionary; New York, Funk &
  Wagnalls [1957] 397 p. 646.03 57-
  10114
  TT503 .P49 MRR Alc.

FASHION--HISTORY.
  Crawford, Morris De Camp, One world
  of fashion. 3d ed. rev. and edited
  New York, Fairchild Publications
  [1967] 191 p. 391/.009 67-15747
  GT510 .C7 1967 MRR Alc.

  Hansen, Henny Harald. Costume
  cavalcade: 2nd ed. London, Eyre
  Methuen Ltd., 1972. 160 p. [£1.95]
  391/.009 72-187355
  GT510 .H33 1972 MRR Alc.

  Hill, Margot Hamilton. The evolution
  of fashion: London, Batsford; New
  York, Reinhold, 1967. xii, 225 p.
  [£5/-/-] 391/.009 68-10504
  GT510 .H5 1967 MRR Alc.

FASHION--PERIODICALS--BIBLIOGRAPHY.
  Hiler, Hilaire, Bibliography of
  costume; New York, B. Blom [1967]
  xi, 911 p. 016.391 66-12285
  Z5691 .H64 1967 MRR Alc.

FASTENINGS--DIRECTORIES--PERIODICALS.
  Assembly engineering master catalog.
  [Wheaton, Ill., Hitchcock Pub. Co.]
  338.4/7/62188025 72-622720
  TJ1320 .H5 MRR Alc Latest edition
    / Sci RR Latest edition

FASTS AND FEASTS.
  see also Christmas

  see also Church year

  see also Easter

  see also Festivals

  see also Holidays

  Chambers, Robert, The book of days;
  Detroit, Gale Research Co., 1967. 2
  v. 902/.02 67-13009
  DA110 .C52 1967 MRR Alc.

  Douglas, George William, The
  American book of days; New York, H.
  W. Wilson Co., 1948. xxii, 697 p.
  394.26973 48-28210
  GT4803 .D6 1948 MRR Alc.

  Foulds, Elfrida Vipont (Brown) Some
  Christian festivals; New York, Roy
  Publishers [1964, c1963] 194 p.
  264 64-22187
  BV30 .F63 1964 MRR Alc.

  Ickis, Marguerite, The book of
  religious holidays and celebrations.
  New York, Dodd, Mead [1966] 161 p.
  394.26 66-26665
  GT3930 .I27 MRR Alc.

  Weiser, Francis Xavier, Handbook of
  Christian feasts and customs: [1st
  ed.] New York, Harcourt, Brace
  [1958] 366 p. 264 58-10908
  BV30 .W4 MRR Alc.

FASTS AND FEASTS--JUDAISM.
  Gaster, Theodor Herzl, Festivals of
  the Jewish year; New York, Sloane
  [1953] 308 p. 296.4* 53-9341
  BM690 .G33 MRR Alc.

  Schauss, Hayyim, Guide to Jewish
  holy days; New York, Schocken Books
  [1962, c1938] 316 p. 296.43 62-
  13140
  BM690 .S32 1962 MRR Alc.

FASTS AND FEASTS--GREAT BRITAIN.
  Hazlitt, William Carew, Faiths and
  folklore of the British Isles; [New
  York] B. Blom [1965] 2 v. (x, 672
  p.) 914.2 64-18758
  DA110 .H38 1965 MRR Alc.

FASTS AND FEASTS--ITALY.
  Monaco, Franco. What's on in Italian
  folklore. [Roma], Automobile club
  d'Italia L'editrice dell'automobile,
  1967. 163 p. 398.3/3 68-117406
  GT4852.A2 M613 MRR Alc.

FATHERS OF THE CHURCH--DICTIONARIES.
  Smith, William, Sir, A dictionary of
  Christian biography, literature,
  sects and doctrines; London, J.
  Murray, 1877-87. 4 v.   12-3122
  BR95 .S65 1877 MRR Alc.

FATHERS OF THE CHURCH, GREEK.
  Payne, Pierre Stephen Robert, The
  holy fire; [1st ed.] New York,
  Harper [c1957] 313 p. 922.1 56-
  12072
  BR1705 .P3 MRR Alc.

FAUNA, PREHISTORIC
  see Paleontology

FEAR.
  see also Phobias

FEATURE FILMS.
  see also Fantastic films

FEDERAL AID TO EDUCATION.
United States. Library of Congress.
Legislative Reference Service.
Federal educational policies,
programs and proposals; Washington,
U.S. Govt. Print. Off., 1968. 3 v.
[0.75 (v. 1) varies]   379/.0973 76-
600437
   LC71 .U5332 MRR Alc.

FEDERAL AID TO EDUCATION--UNITED STATES.
Yearbook of higher education. 1969-
Los Angeles, Academic Media. 378.73
69-18308
   LB2300 .Y4 MRR Ref Desk Latest
      edition

Cooperative Program for Educational
Opportunity. Financial aid for
higher education. [Washington] U.S.
Office of Education; [for sale by the
Supt. of Docs., U.S. Govt. Print.
Off., 1965] iv, 110 p. [1.00]
379/.12142/0973 76-601803
   LB2338 .C66 MRR Ref Desk.

Rowland, Howard S. Federal aid for
schools, 1967-1968 guide; New York,
Macmillan [1967] xv, 396 p.
379/.121/0973 67-19680
   LB2825 .R64 MRR Alc.

FEDERAL AID TO EDUCATION--UNITED STATES-
-BIBLIOGRAPHY.
Education Services Press, St. Paul.
Guide to support programs for
education. St. Paul [1966] 160 p.
371 66-18553
   Z5814.F5 E18 MRR Alc.

FEDERAL AID TO HIGHER EDUCATION--UNITED
STATES.
Toy, Henry, Federal dollars for
scholars [1st ed.] Washington, Nu-
Toy [1970] vii, 54 p., 292 columns.
378.3/0973 77-112985
   LB2338 .T6 MRR Alc.

FEDERAL AID TO OUTDOOR RECREATION.
United States. Bureau of Outdoor
Recreation. Federal outdoor
recreation programs and recreation-
related environmental programs. [1st
revision. Washington; For sale by
the Supt. of Docs., U.S. Govt. Print.
Off.] 1970. 226 p. [2.75]
301.5/7/0973 70-607632
   GV53 .A47 1970 MRR Alc.

FEDERAL AID TO THE ARTS--NEW YORK
(STATE)
New York (State). State University.
Washington Office. Support for the
arts; Washington] 1973. 164 p.
[$2.00]   338.4/7/7009747 73-176026

   NX705.5.U62 N77 1973 MRR Alc.

FEDERAL AID TO THE ARTS--UNITED STATES.
National Endowment for the Arts.
Guide to programs:
architecture+environmental arts,
dance; education; expansion arts,
Federal-state partnership,
literature, museums, music, public
media, special projects, theatre,
visual arts. Washington, For sale by
the Supt. of Docs., U.S. Govt. Print.
Off. [1973] 60 p. [$0.95]
338.4/7/700973 73-603497
   NX398 .N37 1973 MRR Alc.

New York (State). State University.
Washington Office. Support for the
arts; Washington] 1973. 164 p.
[$2.00]   338.4/7/7009747 73-176026

   NX705.5.U62 N77 1973 MRR Alc.

Washington and the arts; New York]
Associated Councils of the Arts
[1971] vi, 176 p. [$6.50]
353.008/54/025753 79-163014
   NX735 .W3 MRR Ref Desk.

FEDERAL GOVERNMENT.
see also Legislative power

see also State governments

FEDERAL GOVERNMENT--ADDRESSES, ESSAYS,
LECTURES.
Rowat, Donald Cameron. The
government of federal capitals,
[Toronto] University of Toronto Press
[1973] xv, 377 p. [$15.00]   320.3
72-185733
   JF1900 .R68 MRR Alc.

FEDERAL GOVERNMENT--AUSTRALIA--
BIBLIOGRAPHY.
Liboiron, Albert A. Federalism and
intergovernmental relations in
Australia, Canada, the United States
and other countries; Kingston, Ont.,
Institute of Intergovernmental
Relations, Queen's University, 1967.
vi, 231 l. [$3.00 Can.]   016.351
68-110060
   Z7165.A8 L5 MRR Alc.

FEDERAL GOVERNMENT--CANADA--
BIBLIOGRAPHY.
Liboiron, Albert A. Federalism and
intergovernmental relations in
Australia, Canada, the United States
and other countries; Kingston, Ont.,
Institute of Intergovernmental
Relations, Queen's University, 1967.
vi, 231 l. [$3.00 Can.]   016.351
68-110060
   Z7165.A8 L5 MRR Alc.

FEDERAL GOVERNMENT--UNITED STATES--
BIBLIOGRAPHY.
Liboiron, Albert A. Federalism and
intergovernmental relations in
Australia, Canada, the United States
and other countries; Kingston, Ont.,
Institute of Intergovernmental
Relations, Queen's University, 1967.
vi, 231 l. [$3.00 Can.]   016.351
68-110060
   Z7165.A8 L5 MRR Alc.

United States. Library of Congress.
Legislative Reference Service.
Intergovernmental relations in the
United States; Washington, 1953. 73
p.   55-60203
   Z663.6 .I6 MRR Alc.

FEDERAL PARTY.
Fischer, David Hackett, The
revolution of American conservatism;
[1st ed.] New York, Harper & Row
[1965] xx, 455 p. 973.4 65-14680

   E331 .F5 MRR Alc.

FEDERAL RESERVE BANKS.
Prochnow, Herbert Victor, ed. The
Federal Reserve System. New York,
Harper [1960] 393 p. 332.110973
60-6767
   HG2563 .P7 MRR Alc.

FEDERAL WRITERS' PROJECT.
Mangione, Jerre Gerlando, The dream
and the deal; [1st ed.] Boston,
Little, Brown [1972] xvi, 416 p.
917.3/006/173 75-187787
   E175.4.W9 M3 MRR Ref Desk.

FEEBLE-MINDED
see Mentally handicapped

FEEBLEMINDEDNESS
see Mental deficiency

FELIDAE.
see also Cats

FELONY
see Criminal law

FEMALE
see Woman

FENDERICH, CHARLES.
United States. Library of Congress.
Prints and Photographs Division.
Charles Fenderich, lithographer of
American statesmen: Washington,
1959. ii, 64 p. 769.973 59-60089

   Z663.39 .F4 MRR Alc.

FERMENTATION.
see also Wine and wine making

FERNANDO PO, SPANISH GUINEA--
DESCRIPTION AND TRAVEL--GAZETTEERS.
United States. Office of Geography,
Rio Muni, Fernando Po, and Sao Tom
e Príncipe; official standard names
approved by the United States Board
on Geographic Names. Washington,
U.S. Govt. Print. Off., 1962. iv, 95
p.   62-62087
   DT619 .U47 MRR Alc.

FERNS--CANADA.
Cobb, Boughton. A field guide to the
ferns and their related families of
northeastern and central North
America Boston, Houghton Mifflin,
1956. xviii, 281 p. 587.3 55-
10024
   QK525 .C75 MRR Alc.

FERNS--DELAWARE.
Reed, Clyde Franklin, The ferns and
fern-allies of Maryland and Delaware,
including District of Columbia.
Baltimore, Reed Herbarium, 1953.
xviii, 286 p. 587.3 53-37165
   QK525.5.M3 R4 MRR Alc.

FERNS--DISTRICT OF COLUMBIA.
Reed, Clyde Franklin, The ferns and
fern-allies of Maryland and Delaware,
including District of Columbia.
Baltimore, Reed Herbarium, 1953.
xviii, 286 p. 587.3 53-37165
   QK525.5.M3 R4 MRR Alc.

FERNS--MARYLAND.
Reed, Clyde Franklin, The ferns and
fern-allies of Maryland and Delaware,
including District of Columbia.
Baltimore, Reed Herbarium, 1953.
xviii, 286 p. 587.3 53-37165
   QK525.5.M3 R4 MRR Alc.

FERNS--NORTH AMERICA--IDENTIFICATION.
Cobb, Boughton. A field guide to the
ferns and their related families of
northeastern and central North
America Boston, Houghton Mifflin,
1956. xviii, 281 p. 587.3 55-
10024
   QK525 .C75 MRR Alc.

FERNS--UNITED STATES.
Cobb, Boughton. A field guide to the
ferns and their related families of
northeastern and central North
America Boston, Houghton Mifflin,
1956. xviii, 281 p. 587.3 55-
10024
   QK525 .C75 MRR Alc.

FERROUS METAL INDUSTRIES
see Iron industry and trade

FERTILE CRESCENT
see Asia, Western

FERTILIZER INDUSTRY--CANADA--YEARBOOKS.
Commercial fertilizer year book.
[Atlanta, W. W. Brown Pub. Co.]
668/.62/05 72-622386
   TP963 .A1C6 MRR Alc Latest edition

FERTILIZER INDUSTRY--UNITED STATES--
DIRECTORIES.
Commercial fertilizer year book.
[Atlanta, W. W. Brown Pub. Co.]
668/.62/05 72-622386
   TP963 .A1C6 MRR Alc Latest edition

FERTILIZER INDUSTRY--UNITED STATES--
YEARBOOKS.
Commercial fertilizer year book.
[Atlanta, W. W. Brown Pub. Co.]
668/.62/05 72-622386
   TP963 .A1C6 MRR Alc Latest edition

FESTIVALS.
see also Holidays

Ickis, Marguerite, The book of
festivals and holidays the world
over. New York, Dodd, Mead [1970]
ix, 164 p. [$5.00] 394.2 70-
129957
   GT3932 .I27 MRR Alc.

Spicer, Dorothy Gladys. The book of
festivals, New York, N.Y., The
Woman's press, 1937. xiv, 429 p.
394.269 37-23629
   GT3930 .S58 MRR Alc.

FESTIVALS--HISTORY.
James, Edwin Oliver, Seasonal feasts
and festivals. New York, Barnes &
Noble [1961] 336 p. 394.2 61-3828

   GT3930 .J3 1961 MRR Alc.

FESTIVALS--JUVENILE LITERATURE.
Ickis, Marguerite, The book of
festivals and holidays the world
over. New York, Dodd, Mead [1970]
ix, 164 p. [$5.00] 394.2 70-
129957
   GT3932 .I27 MRR Alc.

FESTIVALS--CANADA.
Meyer, Robert Eugene, Festivals
U.S.A. & Canada New York, I.
Washburn [1967] viii, 280 p.   394.2
67-22014
   GT4002 .M4 MRR Alc.

FESTIVALS--CHINA.
Eberhard, Wolfram, Chinese
festivals. New York, H. Schuman
[1952] 152 p. 398.33 52-3720
   GT4883.A2 E2 MRR Alc.

FESTIVALS--ENGLAND.
Spicer, Dorothy Gladys. Yearbook of
English festivals. New York, H. W.
Wilson Co., 1954. xxv, 298 p.
398.33 54-7724
   GT4843 .S6 MRR Alc.

FESTIVALS--EUROPE.
Cooper, Gordon. Festivals of Europe.
London, P. Marshall; [stamped: New
York, British Book Centre] 1961 [i.e.
1962] 172 p. 791.6094 62-4156
   GT4842 .C6 MRR Alc.

Spicer, Dorothy Gladys. Festivals of
Western Europe. New York, H. W.
Wilson Co., 1958. 275 p. 398.33
58-7291
   GT4842 .S6 MRR Alc.

FESTIVALS--GREAT BRITAIN.
Trent, Christopher. The B P book of
festivals and events In Britain.
London, Phoenix House, 1966. 160 p.
[25/-]   394.20942 66-74114
   GT4843 .T7 MRR Alc.

FESTIVALS--SPAIN.
Epton, Nina Consuelo. Spanish
fiestas: London, Cassell, 1968.
xix, 250 p. [42/-] 394.2/0946 68-
132014
   GT4062.A2 E6 MRR Alc.

FESTIVALS--UNITED STATES.
Douglas, George William, The
American book of days; New York, H.
W. Wilson Co., 1948. xxii, 697 p.
394.26973 48-28210
GT4803 .D6 1948 MRR Alc.

Meyer, Robert Eugene, Festivals
U.S.A.; New York, Washburn [1950]
438 p.   394.26973 50-11439
GT4803 .M48 MRR Alc.

Meyer, Robert Eugene, Festivals
U.S.A. & Canada New York, I.
Washburn [1967] viii, 280 p.   394.2
67-22014
GT4002 .M4 MRR Alc.

Myers, Robert J. Celebrations; the
complete book of American holidays,
[1st ed.] Garden City, N.Y.,
Doubleday, 1972. x, 386 p.
394.2/6973 77-163086
GT4803.A2 M84 MRR Alc.

FESTSCHRIFTEN--BIBLIOGRAPHY.
Golden, Herbert Hershel, Modern
Iberian language and literature;
Cambridge, Harvard University Press,
1958. x, 184 p. 016.46 58-12978
Z7031 .G6 MRR Alc.

Metzger, Bruce Manning. Index of
articles on the New Testament and the
early church published in
Festschriften. Philadelphia, Society
of Biblical Literature, 1951. xv,
182 p.   016.225 51-3190
Z7772.L1 M4 MRR Alc.

Rounds, Dorothy. Articles on
antiquity in Festschriften, an index;
Cambridge, Harvard University Press,
1962. 560 p.   62-7193
Z6202 .R6 MRR Alc.

Schleiffer, Hedwig, Index to
economic history essays in
Festschriften, 1900-1950 Cambridge,
A. H. Cole; distributed by Harvard
University Press, 1953. 68 p.
016.3304 53-11201
Z7164.E2 S36 MRR Alc.

Williams, Harry Franklin, An index
of mediaeval studies published in
Festschriften, 1865-1946, Berkeley,
University of California Press, 1951.
x, 165 p. 016.9401 51-62136
Z6203 .W5 MRR Alc.

FESTSCHRIFTEN--INDEXES.
Danton, J. Periam, Index to
Festschriften in librarianship New
York, R. R. Bowker Co., 1970. xi,
461 p.   016.02 75-88796
Z666 .D35 MRR Alc.

Golden, Herbert Hershel, Modern
Italian language and literature;
Cambridge, Harvard University Press,
1959. x, 207 p. 016.4504 59-14742

Z2355.A2 G6 MRR Alc.

Rounds, Dorothy. Articles on
antiquity in Festschriften, an index;
Cambridge, Harvard University Press,
1962. 560 p.   62-7193
Z6202 .R6 MRR Alc.

FETUS, DEATH OF.
see also Abortion

FEUDALISM.
Bloch, Marc Léopold Benjamin,
Feudal society. [Chicago] University
of Chicago Press [1961] xxi, 498 p.
940.14 61-4322
D131 .B513 1961 MRR Alc.

FICTION.
see also Children's stories

see also English fiction

see also Folk-lore

see also Short stories

FICTION--20TH CENTURY--HISTORY AND
CRITICISM.
Wilson, John Anthony Burgess, The
novel now; New York, Norton [1967]
224 p.   823/.9/1409 67-24015
PN3503 .W5 1967b MRR Alc.

FICTION--ADDRESSES, ESSAYS, LECTURES.
United States. Library of Congress.
Gertrude Clarke Whittall Poetry and
Literature Fund. Three views of the
novel; Washington, Reference Dept.,
Library of Congress, 1957. 41 p.
808.3 57-60059
Z663.293 .T5 MRR Alc.

FICTION--BIBLIOGRAPHY.
Baker, Ernest Albert, A guide to the
best fiction, English and American,
New and enlarged ed. reissued.
London, Routledge & K. Paul, 1967.
viii, 634 p. [6/6/-] 016.80883 68-
71150
Z5916 .B18 1967 MRR Alc.

Brown, Stephen James Meredith,
Ireland in fiction; New ed. Dublin,
London, Maunsel and company, limited,
1919. xx, 362 p.   20-4278
Z2039.F4 B8 1919 MRR Alc.

Dixson, Zella (Allen) The
comprehensive subject index to
universal prose fiction; New York,
Dodd, Mead & co., 1897. ix, 421 p.
03-19072
Z5916 .D62 MRR Alc.

Fiction index. [1945/52]- London,
Association of Assistant Librarians.
016.80883 53-7788
Z5916 .F52 MRR Alc Full set

Kerr, Elizabeth Margaret,
Bibliography of the sequence novel.
Minneapolis, University of Minnesota
Press [1950] v, 126 p.   016.80883/3
50-6957
Z5917.S45 K4 MRR Alc.

FICTION--DICTIONARIES.
Brewer, Ebenezer Cobham, The
reader's handbook of famous names in
fiction, A new ed., rev. throughout
and greatly enl. Detroit,
Republished by Gale Research Co.,
1966. 2 v. (viii, 1243 p.) 803 71-
134907
PN43 .B7 1965 MRR Alc.

Frey, Albert Romer, Sobriquets and
nicknames, Detroit, Republished by
Gale Research Co., 1966. iii, 482 p.
929.403 66-22671
CT108 .F7 1966 MRR Alc.

Walsh, William Shepard, Heroes and
heroines of fiction. Detroit,
Republished by Gale Research Co.,
1966. 2 v.   803 66-29782
PN43 .W33 1966 MRR Alc.

Wheeler, William Adolphus, An
explanatory and pronouncing
dictionary of the noted names of
fiction, Detroit, Gale Research Co.,
1966. xxxii, 440 p.   803 66-25811

PN43 .W4 1966 MRR Alc.

FICTION--HISTORY AND CRITICISM.
Uzzell, Thomas H., The technique of
the novel; [Rev. ed.] New York,
Citadel Press [1959] 350 p. 808.3
59-13061
PN3365 .U9 1959 MRR Alc.

FICTION--HISTORY AND CRITICISM--
BIBLIOGRAPHY.
Cotton, Gerald Brooks. Fiction
guides; London, Bingley, 1967. 126
p. [25/-] 016.823/009 67-85300
Z5916 .C77 1967a MRR Alc.

Kearney, E. I. The continental
novel; Metuchen, N.J., Scarecrow
Press, 1968. xiv, 460 p.
016.8093/3 68-12626
Z5916 .K4 MRR Ref Desk.

Thurston, Jarvis A. Short fiction
criticism; Denver, A. Swallow [1960]
265 p.   016.80931 60-8070
Z5917.S5 T5 MRR Alc.

Walker, Warren S. Twentieth-century
short story explication; 2d ed.
[Hamden, Conn.] Shoe String Press,
1967 vi, 697 p.   016.8093/1 67-
24192
Z5917.S5 W33 MRR Ref Desk.

FICTION--STORIES, PLOTS, ETC.
Barzun, Jacques, A catalogue of
crime [1st ed.] New York, Harper &
Row [1971] xxxi, 831 p. [$18.95]
016.80883/872 75-123914
Z5917.D5 B37 1971 MRR Alc.

Brown, Stephen James Meredith,
Ireland in fiction; New ed. Dublin,
London, Maunsel and company, limited,
1919. xx, 362 p.   20-4278
Z2039.F4 B8 1919 MRR Alc.

Cohen, Sam D., ed. The digest of the
world's great classics. [New York?]
Daily Compass, 1950. 833 p.   808.83
51-8653
PN44 .C6 MRR Alc.

Lass, Abraham Harold, Plot guide to
100 American and British novels;
Boston, The Writer [1971] xxi, 364,
364 p. [$8.95]   823/.03 73-138526

PS373 .L28 MRR Alc.

Lass, Abraham Harold, ed. A
student's guide to 50 British novels,
New York, Washington Square Press
[1966] xix, 364 p.   823.00202 66-
2898
PR825 .L3 MRR Alc.

Magill, Frank Northen, Masterplots.
New York, Salem Press [1964] 6 v.
808.8 64-54679
PN44 .M32 MRR Alc.

Magill, Frank Northen, comp. Survey
of contemporary literature; New
York, Salem Press [1971] 7 v. (xlv,
5194, xviii p.) 809/.04 75-25876
PN44 .M34 MRR Alc.

Magill, Frank Northern, ed.
Masterplots; [Definitive ed.] New
York, Salem Press [1968] 8 v. (ix,
5795, xxii p.)   68-8171
PN44 .M33 MRR Alc.

Masterplots annual. 1954- New York,
Salem Press.   55-41212
Z1219 .M33 MRR Alc Latest edition

Olfson, Lewy, ed. Plot outlines of
100 famous novels; the second
hundred. [1st ed.] Garden City,
N.Y., Dolphin Books, 1966. xii, 507
p.   808.833 66-21023
PN3326 .O5 MRR Alc.

Der Romanführer. 2., neu bearb. und
veränderte Aufl. Stuttgart, A.
Hiersemann, 1960- v.   62-40309
PN3326 .R62 MRR Alc.

Vinson, James, Contemporary
novelists. New York, St. Martin's
Press [1972] xvii, 1422 p. [$30.00]
823/.03 75-189694
PR737 .V5 MRR Biog.

Ward, Alfred Charles, Longman
companion to twentieth century
literature, Harlow, Longman, 1970.
[6], 593 p. [65/-] 820.9/009/1 76-
554609
PN771 .W28 MRR Alc.

FICTION--STORIES, PLOTS, ETC.--INDEXES.
Koehmstedt, Carol L. Plot summary
index, Metuchen, N.J., Scarecrow
Press, 1973. 312 p.   809 72-13726

Z6514.P66 K63 MRR Ref Desk.

FICTION--TECHNIQUE.
Uzzell, Thomas H., The technique of
the novel; [Rev. ed.] New York,
Citadel Press [1959] 350 p. 808.3
59-13061
PN3365 .U9 1959 MRR Alc.

FICTION--TRANSLATIONS INTO ENGLISH--
BIBLIOGRAPHY.
Beasley, Jerry C. A check list of
prose fiction published in England,
1740-1749. Charlottesville,
Published for the Bibliographical
Society of the University of Virginia
[by] the University Press of Virginia
[1972] xiv, 213 p. [$7.50]
016.823/5/08 72-75044
Z2014.F4 B37 MRR Alc.

FICTION, HISTORICAL
see Historical fiction

FIDDLE
see Violin

FIEFS
see Feudalism

FIELD CROPS--STATISTICS.
Food and Agriculture Organization of
the United Nations. Production
yearbook. v. 12- 1958- Rome.
338 .1058 59-3599
HD1421 .F585 Sci RR Partial set /
MRR Alc Latest edition

FIELD SPORTS
see Hunting

FIFE, SCOT.--COMMERCE--DIRECTORIES.
Fife and Kinross trades' directory,
including the counties of Stirling
and Clackmannan, Edinburgh, Town and
County Directories, Limited. 59-
31510
HF5161 .F5 MRR Alc Latest edition

FIGHTING
see Battles

see Boxing

see War

FIGURES OF SPEECH.
Lanham, Richard A. A handlist of
rhetorical terms; Berkeley,
University of California Press, 1968.
148 p. [6.50] 423.1 68-31636
PE1445.A2 L3 MRR Alc.

Lipton, James. An exaltation of
larks; [New York] Grossman
Publishers [1968] 118 p. [4.95]
427.09 68-30774
PE1689 .L5 MRR Alc.

FIGURINES
see Dolls

FILES AND FILING (DOCUMENTS)
see also Alphabeting

see also Indexing

FILES AND FILING (DOCUMENTS) (Cont.)
Kahn, Gilbert, Progressive filing
8th ed. New York, Gregg Division
[1969] ix, 118 p.   651/.5   68-15469

  HF5736 .K28 1969 MRR Alc.

United States. Library of Congress.
Technical Information Division. A
filing manual for TIP cards.
Washington, Documentation Research
Section, Technical Information
Division, Library of Congress, 1952.
12 p.   025.37   53-60016
  Z663.49 .F47 MRR Alc.

Vertical file index. v. [1]-
1932/34- New York, H. W. Wilson.
016   45-40505
  Z1231.P2 V48   MRR Alc Full set

FILICINAE
  see Ferns

FILIPINOS IN THE UNITED STATES--
BIOGRAPHY.
Nicanor, Precioso M. Profiles of
notable Filipinos in the U.S.A. ...
[1st ed.] New York, Pre-Mer Pub. Co.
[c1963- v.   920.0914   63-22694
  E184.F4 N5 MRR Biog.

FILLING STATIONS
  see Automobiles--Service stations

FILLMORE, MILLARD, PRES. U.S., 1800-
1874.
Griffis, William Elliot, Millard
Fillmore, constructive statesman,
defender of the Constitution,
president of the United States,
Ithaca, N.Y., Andrus & Church [c1915]
ix, 159 p.   15-5696
  E427 .G85 MRR Alc.

FILLMORE, MILLARD, PRES. U.S., 1800-
1874--BIBLIOGRAPHY.
Fillmore, Millard, pres. U.S.,
Millard Fillmore papers. Buffalo,
N.Y., The Buffalo historical society,
1907. 2 v.   08-10420
  E427 .F48 MRR Alc.

FILM ADAPTATIONS--BIBLIOGRAPHY.
Dimmitt, Richard Bertrand. A title
guide to the talkies; New York,
Scarecrow Press, 1965. 2 v. (2133
p.)   791.438   65-13556
  PN1998 .D55 MRR Alc.

Enser, A. G. S. Filmed books and
plays; Revised ed.; London,
Deutsch, 1971. 509 p. [£4.20]
016.79143   74-585261
  Z5784.M9 E55 1971 MRR Alc.

FILM AUTHORSHIP
  see Moving-picture plays

FILM EDITING (CINEMATOGRAPHY)
  see Moving-pictures--Editing

FILM MUSIC
  see Moving-picture music

FILMSTRIPS.
  see also Lantern slides

FILMSTRIPS--CATALOGS.
Educators' guide to free filmstrips.
1st- 1949- Randolph, Wis.,
Educators' Progress Service.
371.3352   50-11650
  LB1043.8 .E4   MRR Alc Latest
  edition

National Information Center for
Educational Media. Index to 35mm
educational filmstrips. 4th ed. Los
Angeles, 1973. 2 v.
371.33/522/0216   70-190630
  LB1043.8.Z9 N37 1973 MRR Alc.

National Information Center for
Educational Media. Index to
psychology: multimedia. 1st ed.
[Los Angeles, University of Southern
California] 1972. x, 461 p.   016.15
76-190637
  BF77 .N37 1972 MRR Alc.

United States. Library of Congress.
Library of Congress catalog; Motion
pictures and filmstrips; 1953-
Washington. 53-60011
  Z663.7 .L54 MRR Alc   MRR Alc Full
  set

United States. Library of Congress.
Stack and Reader Division. Libraries
and library services on film; 2d ed.
Washington, Reference Dept., Library
of Congress, 1957. 19 p.   020.84
57-60043
  Z663.48 .L5 1957 MRR Alc.

FINANCE.
  see also Capitalists and financiers

  see also Commerce

  see also Credit

  see also Insurance

  see also Money

  see also Prices

  see also Saving and investment

  see also Securities

FINANCE--BIBLIOGRAPHY.
Burgess, Norman. How to find out
about banking and investment. [1st
ed.] Oxford, New York, Pergamon
Press [1969] xii, 300 p.   016.332
68-55021
  Z7164.F5 B84 1969 MRR Alc.

FINANCE--DICTIONARIES.
Blahut, Robert. The A to Z of
finance, [Hackensack? N.J., 1962] 1
v. (unpaged)   332.03   62-36848
  HG151 .B5 MRR Alc.

Clark, Donald Thomas, Dictionary of
business and finance New York,
Crowell [1957] v, 409 p.   650.3   57-
14560
  HF1002 .C49 MRR Alc.

Davids, Lewis E. Instant business
dictionary, Mundelein, Ill., Career
Institute [1971] 320 p.   650/.03
78-150232
  HF1002 .D36 MRR Ref Desk.

Davis, William, The language of
money; [1st American ed.] Boston,
Houghton Mifflin, 1973. xiii, 267 p.
[$6.95]   330/.03   72-2281
  HG151 .D37 MRR Alc.

Kettridge, Julius Ornan. French-
English and English-French dictionary
of commercial & financial terms,
phrases, & practice; London,
Routledge & Paul, 1957. xi, 647 p.
650.3   59-21494
  HG151 .K42 1957 MRR Alc.

Munn, Glenn Gaywaine. Glenn G.
Munn's Encyclopedia of banking and
finance. 7th ed. Boston, Bankers
Pub. Co. [1973] 953 p.   332/.03   73-
83395
  HG151 .M8 1973 MRR Alc.

Prentice-Hall, inc. Encyclopedic
dictionary of business finance,
Englewood Cliffs, N.J. [1961, c1960]
vi, 658 p.   332.03   60-53430
  HG151 .P7 MRR Alc.

FINANCE--DICTIONARIES--FRENCH.
Kettridge, Julius Ornan. French-
English and English-French dictionary
of commercial & financial terms,
phrases, & practice; London,
Routledge & Paul, 1957. xi, 647 p.
650.3   59-21494
  HG151 .K42 1957 MRR Alc.

FINANCE--DICTIONARIES--GERMAN.
Gunston, C. A. Gunston & Corner's
German-English glossary of financial
and economic terms. 6th ed., greatly
compressed, but in content much
amplified, Frankfurt am Main, F.
Knapp [1972] xxiii, 1203 p.
330/.03   72-188587
  HG151 .G85 1972 MRR Alc.

FINANCE--DICTIONARIES--POLYGLOT.
Bari, G. Dizionario commerciale
italiano-inglese-francese-tedesco.
2. ed. Milano, L. di G. Pirolo,
1970. 865 p., leaf inserted. [8500]
70-488606
  HF1002 .B28 1970 MRR Alc.

Horn, Stefan F., Glossary of
financial terms, Amsterdam, New
York, Elsevier Pub. Co., 1965. 271
p.   332.03   64-23405
  HG151 .H6 MRR Alc.

FINANCE--HANDBOOKS, MANUALS, ETC.
Financial handbook. [1st]- ed.;
1925- New York, Ronald Press. 658
25-21825
  HF5550 .F5 MRR Alc Latest edition

FINANCE--PERIODICALS--BIBLIOGRAPHY.
Directory of business and financial
services. [1st]- ed.; 1924- New
York [etc.] Special Libraries
Association. 25-4599
  HF5003 .H3   MRR Ref Desk Latest
  edition / MRR Ref Desk Latest
  edition

FINANCE--PERIODICALS--INDEXES.
Washington, D.C. Joint Library of the
International Monetary Fund and the
International Bank for Reconstruction
and Development. Economics and
finance; index to periodical
articles, 1947-1971, Boston, G. K.
Hall, 1972. 4 v.   016.33   73-156075

  Z7164.E2 W34 MRR Alc (dk 33)

FINANCE--STATISTICS--BIBLIOGRAPHY.
Woy, James B. Investment
information: Detroit, Gale Research
Co. [1970] 231 p.   [$11.50]
016.33267   79-118791
  Z7164.F5 W93 MRR Ref Desk.

FINANCE--CONFEDERATE STATES OF AMERICA.
Schwab, John Christopher, The
Confederate States of America, 1861-
1865; New York, B. Franklin [1968]
xi, 332 p.   330.975   68-56580
  HC105.65 .S38 1968 MRR Alc.

FINANCE--EUROPE--STATISTICS.
Organization for European Economic
Cooperation. Statistics of sources
and uses of finance, 1948-1958.
Paris [1960] 195 p. (chiefly tables)
332.094   60-51684
  HG186 .A1O74 MRR Alc.

FINANCE--GREAT BRITAIN--DIRECTORIES.
Who's who in British finance. 1972-
New York, R. R. Bowker Co.
332/.092/2 [B]   72-624453
  HG71 .W44 MRR Biog Latest edition

FINANCE--[ITALY--BIOGRAPHY.
Il Chi è? nella finanza italiana.
1955- Milano, Casa Editrice Nuova
Mercurio, [etc.]   56-33152
  HG186.I8 C47   MRR Alc Latest
  edition

FINANCE--MEXICO.
Anuario financiero de México. v. 1-
1940- México, D. F., Editorial
Cultura.   332.0972   42-34567
  HG68.M6 A6   MRR Alc Latest edition

FINANCE--UNITED STATES.
Badger, Ralph Eastman, The complete
guide to investment analysis New
York, McGraw-Hill [1967] viii, 504
p.   332.6   67-15850
  HG4521 .B3432 MRR Alc.

Financial daily card service; Jersey
City, N.J. Financial Information. 74-
642472
  HG4905 .F45   MRR Alc Latest edition

Kraus, Albert L. The New York times
guide to business and finance; [1st
ed.] New York, Harper & Row [1972]
viii, 280 p. [$8.95]   330.9/73/092
70-138745
  HG181 .K7 1972 MRR Alc.

FINANCE--UNITED STATES--DIRECTORIES.
Goodman, Steven E. Financial market
place; New York, Bowker, 1972. x,
363 p.   332/.025/73   72-1736
  HG65 .G62 MRR Ref Desk.

FINANCE--UNITED STATES--HISTORY.
Studenski, Paul, Financial history
of the United States: 2d ed. New
York, McGraw-Hill [1963] 605 p.
332.0973   62-21575
  HG181 .S83 1963 MRR Alc.

FINANCE--UNITED STATES--STATISTICS.
Friedman, Milton, Monetary
statistics of the United States:
estimates, sources, methods New
York, National Bureau of Economic
Research, 1970. xx, 629 p.   [15.00]
332.4/9/73   78-85410
  HG538 .F863 MRR Alc.

FINANCE--UNITED STATES--YEARBOOKS.
Moody's bank & finance manual;
American and foreign. New York,
Moody's Investors Service.   56-14722

  HG4961 .M65   MRR Alc Latest edition

FINANCE, LOCAL
  see Local finance

FINANCE, PERSONAL--YEARBOOKS.
Surveys of consumers. 1971/72- [Ann
Arbor, Mich., Institute for Social
Research, University of Michigan]
658.8/3973   72-619718
  HC110.S3 A3 MRR Alc Latest edition

FINANCE, PUBLIC.
  see also Bonds

FINANCE, PUBLIC--ACCOUNTING.
Mikesell, Rufus Merrill,
Governmental accounting. 4th ed.
Homewood, Ill., R. D. Irwin, 1969.
xiv, 758 p.   657.8/35   69-11390
  HJ9733 .M5 1969 MRR Alc.

FINANCE, PUBLIC--BIBLIOGRAPHY.
Knox, Vera H. Public finance:
information sources Detroit, Gale
Research Co. [1964] 142 p.   016.336
64-16503
  Z7164.F5 K65 MRR Alc.

FINANCE, PUBLIC--UNITED STATES.
Schultz, William John, American
public finance 8th ed. Englewood
Cliffs, N.J., Prentice-Hall [1965]
x, 565 p.   336.73   65-13570
  HJ241 .S3 1965 MRR Alc.

United States. Treasury Dept. Bureau
of Accounts. Combined statement of
receipts, expenditures and balances
of the United States government.
1871/72- Washington. 10-11510
  HJ10 .A6   MRR Alc Latest edition

FINANCE, PUBLIC--UNITED STATES--1789-
1800.
Hamilton, Alexander, The works of
Alexander Hamilton, [Federal ed.]
New York, London, G. P. Putnam's
sons, 1904. 12 v. 04-19021
E302 .H24 MRR Alc.

FINANCE, PUBLIC--UNITED STATES--1933-
Tax Foundation, New York. Facts and
figures on government finance. 1941-
New York. 336.73 44-7109
HJ257 .T25 MRR Alc Latest edition
/ MRR Ref Desk Latest edition

FINANCE, PUBLIC--UNITED STATES--
BIBLIOGRAPHY.
Knox, Vera H. Public finance:
information sources Detroit, Gale
Research Co. [1964] 142 p. 016.336
64-16503
Z7164.F5 K65 MRR Alc.

FINANCE, PUBLIC--UNITED STATES--
SPEECHES IN CONGRESS.
Miller, Marion Mills, ed. Great
debates in American history, [The
national ed.] New York, Current
literature publishing company [c1913]
14 v. 13-23912
E173 .M64 vol. 14 MRR Alc.

FINANCE, PUBLIC--UNITED STATES--
STATISTICS.
United States. Bureau of the Census.
1967 census of governments.
[Washington, For sale by the Supt. of
Docs., U.S. Govt. Print. Off., 1968-
v. in 353.000021/2 a 68-7201
JS3.A257 MRR Alc.

FINANCIAL INSTITUTIONS
see also Banks and banking

FINANCIAL INSTITUTIONS.
Financial institutions 4th ed.
Homewood, Ill., R. D. Irwin, 1966.
xvii, 768 p. 332 66-24588
HG173 .F5 1966 MRR Alc.

FINANCIAL INSTITUTIONS--UNITED STATES.
Financial institutions 4th ed.
Homewood, Ill., R. D. Irwin, 1966.
xvii, 768 p. 332 66-24588
HG173 .F5 1966 MRR Alc.

FINANCIAL INSTITUTIONS--UNITED STATES--
DIRECTORIES.
Goodman, Steven E. Financial market
place: New York, Bowker, 1972. x,
363 p. 332/.025/73 72-1736
HG65 .G62 MRR Ref Desk.

Rubel, Stanley M. Guide to venture
capital sources, 3d ed. [Chicago]
Capital Pub. Corp. [1974] 334 p.
332.1/025/73 74-75808
HG65 .R8 1974 MRR Alc.

FINANCIAL INSTITUTIONS--UNITED STATES--
DIRECTORIES--COLLECTIONS.
Venture capital. v. 1- 1970- [New
York, Technimetrics, inc.]
332.1/025/73 74-20999
HG65 .V4 MRR Alc Latest edition

FINANCIAL STATEMENTS.
Bernstein, Leopold A. Understanding
corporate reports: Homewood, Ill.,
Dow Jones-Irwin, 1974. xv, 596 p.
[$12.95] 658.1/512 74-7869
HF5681.B2 B46 1974b MRR Alc.

Foster, Louis Omar, Understanding
financial statements and corporate
annual reports. [1st ed.]
Philadelphia, Chilton Co., Book
Division [1961] 135 p. 332.6 61-
14508
HG4028.B2 F6 MRR Alc.

Myer, John Nicholas, What the
investor should know about corporate
financial statements, 2d ed.
Larchmont, N.Y., American Research
Council [1965] v, 120 p. 332.6 65-
28333
HF5681.B2 M92 1965 MRR Alc.

FINANCIAL STATEMENTS--YEARBOOKS.
Accounting trends and techniques in
published corporate annual reports.
1st- 1945/47- New York, American
Institute of Accountants. 657 48-
2517
HF5681.F2 A35 MRR Alc Latest
edition

Robert Morris Associates. Annual
statement studies. [Philadelphia]
338/.0973 72-626355
HF5681.B2 R6 MRR Alc Latest
edition

FINANCIAL STATEMENTS--UNITED STATES.
Robert Morris Associates. Annual
statement studies. [Philadelphia]
338/.0973 72-626355
HF5681.B2 R6 MRR Alc Latest
edition

FINANCIERS
see Capitalists and financiers

FINE ARTS
see Art

see Arts

FINLAND.
Sømme, Axel Christian Zetlitz, The
geography of Norden: London,
Heinemann [1961] 363 p. 914.8 62-
5819
DL5 .S6 1961a MRR Alc.

Stoddard, Theodore Lothrop, Area
handbook for Finland. 1st ed.
[Washington; For sale by the Supt. of
Docs., U.S. Govt. Print. Off.] 1974.
xiv, 259 p. 914.71/03/3 73-600338

DK449 .S83 MRR Alc.

FINLAND--ADDRESSES, ESSAYS, LECTURES.
Nickels, Sylvie. Finland; an
introduction, New York, Praeger
[1973] 377 p. [$12.00]
914.71/03/08 72-89453
DK449 .N53 1973 MRR Alc.

FINLAND--BIO-BIBLIOGRAPHY.
Kuka kukin on. [1920]-
Helsingissa, Kustannusosakeyhtio
Otava [etc.] 52-41608
CT1220 .K8 MRR Biog Latest edition

FINLAND--BIOGRAPHY.
Finlands ridderskaps och adels
kalender. Helsingfors, Frenckellska
trycheri aktiebolagets forlag [etc.]
08-21285
CS884 .F5 MRR Biog Latest edition

FINLAND--BIOGRAPHY--DICTIONARIES.
Dictionary of Scandinavian biography.
London, Melrose Press [1972] xxxv,
467 p. [£10.50] 920/.048 B 73-
189270
CT1243 .D53 MRR Biog.

Finsk biografisk handbok,
Helsingfors, G. W. Edlunds förlag,
1903. 2 v. 06-44362
CT1220 .F5 MRR Biog.

Heikinheimo, Ilmari, ed. Suomen
elamakergasto. Helsinki, W.
Söderström [1955] vii, 855 p. 57-
33968
DK448 .H4 MRR Biog.

Kuka kukin on. [1920]-
Helsingissa, Kustannusosakeyhtio
Otava [etc.] 52-41608
CT1220 .K8 MRR Biog Latest edition

FINLAND--COMMERCE--DIRECTORIES.
Finnish foreign trade directory.
Helsinki, Finnish Foreign Trade
Association. 53-34818
Began publication with issue for
1921.
HF3631 .F5 MRR Alc Latest edition

Nordisk handelskalender, København,
H. P. Bov. 49-23912
Began with vol. for 1903.
HF5193 .N6 MRR Alc Latest edition

FINLAND--DESCRIPTION AND TRAVEL--GUIDE-
BOOKS.
Finland. [3d ed.] Geneva, Paris
[etc.] Nagel Publishers [1968] 255
p. [$6.95] 914.7/1/043 79-438915

DK450 .F52 1968 MRR Alc.

Nickels, Sylvie. Finland: a travel
guide. New York, Harper & Row [1966,
c1965] 232 p. 914.71043 66-19357

DK450.2 .N5 1966 MRR Alc.

FINLAND--ECONOMIC CONDITIONS--
BIBLIOGRAPHY.
United States. Library of Congress.
European Affairs Division.
Political, economic and social
writings in postwar Finland;
[Washington, 1952] vi, 41 p. 016.3
52-60040
Z663.26 .P58 MRR Alc.

FINLAND--GAZETTEERS.
United States. Office of Geography.
Finland: Washington, 1962. vi, 556
p. 62-61796
DK448.3 .U6 MRR Alc.

FINLAND--GENEALOGY.
Finlands ridderskaps och adels
kalender. Helsingfors, Frenckellska
trycheri aktiebolagets forlag [etc.]
08-21285
CS884 .F5 MRR Biog Latest edition

FINLAND--HISTORY.
Jutikkala, Eino Kaarlo Ilmari, A
history of Finland Rev. ed. New
York, Praeger Publishers [1974] ix,
293 p. [$10.00] 947.1 72-94339
DK451 .J78613 1974 MRR Alc.

FINLAND--INDUSTRIES--DIRECTORIES.
Finnish foreign trade directory.
Helsinki, Finnish Foreign Trade
Association. 53-34818
Began publication with issue for
1921.
HF3631 .F5 MRR Alc Latest edition

Sininen Kirja. Helsinki. 49-12970
T12.5 .F5S5 MRR Alc Latest edition

FINLAND--NOBILITY.
Finlands ridderskaps och adels
kalender. Helsingfors, Frenckellska
trycheri aktiebolagets forlag [etc.]
08-21285
CS884 .F5 MRR Biog Latest edition

FINLAND--POLITICS AND GOVERNMENT.
Finlands statskalender. Helsingfors.
19-41213
JN6707 date MRR Alc Latest
edition

FINLAND--SOCIAL CONDITIONS--
BIBLIOGRAPHY.
United States. Library of Congress.
European Affairs Division.
Political, economic and social
writings in postwar Finland;
[Washington, 1952] vi, 41 p. 016.3
52-60040
Z663.26 .P58 MRR Alc.

FINLAND--REGISTERS.
Finlands statskalender. Helsingfors.
19-41213
JN6707 date MRR Alc Latest
edition

FINMARK, NORWAY--DIRECTORIES.
Adressebok for Finmark fylke med
skatteligninger. Oslo, S. M. Bryde.
53-29104
DL576.F5 A7 MRR Alc Latest edition

FINNISH LANGUAGE--DICTIONARIES--ENGLISH.
Alanne, Vieno Severi, Suomalais-
englantilainen sanakirja. Superior,
Wis., Finnish kustannusyhtion
kustannuksella, 1919. viii, 957 p.
26-8806
PH279 .A6 1919a MRR Alc.

Halme, P. E. Suomalais-
englantilainen sanakirja. Helsinki,
Suomalaisen Kirjallisuuden Seura,
1957. 632 p. 58-44492
PH279 .H27 MRR Alc.

Lampén, Lea. Kuolulaisen
perussanakirja. Helsinki, W.
Söderström, 1972. (6) 724 p.
[Fmk40.00] 73-333264
PH278 .L3 MRR Alc.

Swan, Carl Gustaf. English and
Finnish dictionary, [Helsingissä,
Suomal. kirjallis. seuran kirjapainon
osakeyhtio, 1904] ix, 1218 p. 09-
27858
PH279 .S8 MRR Alc.

FINNISH LANGUAGE--DICTIONARIES--
POLYGLOT.
International insurance dictionary:
[n.p., European Conference of
Insurance Supervisory Services, 1959]
xxxi, 1083 p. 368.03 61-35675
HG8025 .I5 MRR Alc.

Lampén, Lea. Kuolulaisen
perussanakirja. Helsinki, W.
Söderström, 1972. (6) 724 p.
[Fmk40.00] 73-333264
PH278 .L3 MRR Alc.

FINNISH LANGUAGE--FOREIGN WORDS AND
PHRASES--DICTIONARIES.
Nykysuomen laitos. Nykysuomen
sivistyssanakirja. [Helsinki], W.
Söderström, 1973. xvi, 462 p.
[Fmk57.00] 74-306465
PH284 .N9 MRR Alc.

FINNISH LITERATURE--HISTORY AND
CRITICISM.
Litteraturen i Danmark og de øvrige
nordiske lande. 4. udg. København,
Politiken, 1967. 536 p. [21.45 dkr]
68-85482
PT7060 .L5 1967 MRR Alc.

FINNO-UGRIAN LANGUAGES.
Collinder, Björn, An introduction
to the Uralic languages. Berkeley,
University of California Press, 1965.
xii, 167 p. 494.4 65-21136
PH14. C58 MRR Alc.

FINNO-UGRIAN LANGUAGES--CONVERSATION
AND PHRASE BOOKS--POLYGLOT.
Lyall, Archibald, A guide to 25
languages of Europe. Rev. ed.
[Harrisburg, Pa.] Stackpole Co.
[1966] viii, 407 p. 413 66-20847

PB73 .L85 1966 MRR Alc.

FINNO-UGRIAN LANGUAGES--DICTIONARIES--
POLYGLOT.
Bergmann, Peter M. The concise
dictionary of twenty-six languages in
simultaneous translations, New York,
Polyglot Library [1968] 406 p. 413
67-14284
P361 .B4 TJ Rm.

Ouseg, H. L. 21-language dictionary.
London, P. Owen [1962] xxxi, 333 p.
63-1285
P361 .O85 1962 MRR Alc.

FIRE-DEPARTMENTS--DIRECTORIES.
International security directory.
London, Security Gazette, ltd.
363.2/025 75-20715
HV7900 .I63 MRR Alc Bind/Label

FIRE EXTINCTION.
Meidl, James H. Hazardous materials
handbook Beverly Hills, Calif.,
Glencoe Press [1972] xviii, 349 p.
604/.7/0202 72-177437
THS446.I47 M44 MRR Alc.

FIRE EXTINCTION--PERIODICALS.
National Fire Protection Association.
National fire codes. 1938- Boston,
614.8/41/0873 38-27236
TH9111 .N375a MRR Alc Latest
edition

The Visiting fireman. [Detroit,
Mich., A. J. Burch] 628.9/2/05 72-
627326
TH9111 .V55 MRR Alc Latest edition

FIRE INSURANCE
see Insurance, Fire

FIRE-MARKS.
Bulau, Alwin E. Footprints of
assurance. New York, Macmillan,
1953. xiii, 319 p. 368.109 53-
1691
HG9660 .B8 MRR Alc.

FIRE PREVENTION.
Lincoln, Walter Osborn. Insurance
inspection and underwriting; 8th
ed., rev., condensed. Philadelphia,
The Spectator [c1965] xiv, 1290 p.
65-24092
HG9715 .L5 1965 MRR Alc.

FIRE PREVENTION--PERIODICALS.
The Visiting fireman. [Detroit,
Mich., A. J. Burch] 628.9/2/05 72-
627326
TH9111 .V55 MRR Alc Latest edition

FIRE PREVENTION--UNITED STATES--
PERIODICALS.
National Fire Protection Association.
National fire codes. 1938- Boston,
614.8/41/0873 38-27236
TH9111 .N375a MRR Alc Latest
edition

FIREARMS.
Hayward, John Forrest, The art of
the gunmaker. London, Barrie and
Rockliff [1962- v.   62-38883
TS535 .H34 MRR Alc.

Johnson, George B. International
armament; [1st ed.] Cologne,
Germany, International Small Arms
Publishers [c1965] 2 v. 739.7/4
64-24567
UD380 .J56 MRR Alc.

Johnson, Melvin Maynard. Automatic
arms, New York, W. Morrow and co.,
1941. xv, 344 p. 623.4225 42-
36006
UF520 .J6 MRR Alc.

Moyer, Frank A. Foreign weapons
handbook, Boulder, Colo., Panther
Publications [1970] vi, 326 p.
[$12.95] 623.4/4 70-93554
UD380 .M67 MRR Alc.

Small arms in profile. Windsor,
Berkshire, Eng., Profile Publications
[1973- v.   [£6.00 (v. 1)]
623.4/4 74-171635
UD380 .S57 MRR Alc.

Smith, Joseph Edward, Small arms of
the world; 9th ed. completely rev.
Harrisburg, Pa., Stackpole Books
[1969] 768 p. [17.95] 683/.4 72-
90881
UD380 .S58 1969 MRR Alc.

Sparano, Vin T. Complete outdoors
encyclopedia, New York, Outdoor
Life, Harper & Row [1972] 622 p.
[$13.95] 799/.03 72-90934
SK33 .S646 MRR Alc.

Van Rensselaer, Stephen, American
firearms; Watkins Glen, N.Y.,
Century House [1947] 288 p.   683
48-1408
TS535 .V3 MRR Alc.

FIREARMS--CATALOGS.
Chapel, Charles Edward, The gun
collector's handbook of values. 10th
rev. ed., New York, Coward, McCann &
Geoghegan [c1972] xiii, 398 p.
[$12.50] 623.4/4/075 72-86474
TS532.4 .C47 1972 MRR Alc.

Guns illustrated. 1st- ed.: 1969-
Chicago, Follett Pub. Co. [etc.]
338.4/7/68340029 69-11342
TS534.7 G8 MRR Alc Latest edition

Wahl, Paul Francis, Shooter's bible:
gun trader's guide [5th rev. ed.
South Hackensack, N.J., Shooter's
Bible, inc.] distributed by Stoeger
Arms Corp. [1968] 220 p. [3.95]
623.4/4/029 68-58113
TS535 .W2 1968 MRR Alc.

FIREARMS--COLLECTORS AND COLLECTING.
Chapel, Charles Edward. The gun
collector's handbook of values. 10th
rev. ed., New York, Coward, McCann &
Geoghegan [c1972] xiii, 398 p.
[$12.50] 623.4/4/075 72-86474
TS532.4 .C47 1972 MRR Alc.

FIREARMS--DICTIONARIES.
Mueller, Chester, Shooter's bible
small arms lexicon and concise
encyclopedia, 1st ed. South
Hackensack, N.J., Shooter's Bible,
inc.; distributed by Stoeger Arms
Corp., 1968. vii, 309 p. 683.4/003
67-30798
TS535 .M83 MRR Alc.

Nonte, George C. Firearms
encyclopedia, New York, Harper & Row
[1973] viii, 341 p. [$11.95]
683/.4/003 73-80712
TS532.15 .N66 MRR Alc.

Quick, John, Dictionary of weapons
and military terms. New York, McGraw-
Hill [1973] xii, 515 p.   623/.03
73-8757
U24 .Q5 MRR Alc.

Steindler, R. A. The firearms
dictionary [Harrisburg, Pa.]
Stackpole Books [1970] 288 p.
[7.95] 683/.4/003 75-107957
TS534.5 .S74 MRR Alc.

FIREARMS--HISTORY.
Johnson, Melvin Maynard, Ammunition;
New York, W. Morrow and co., 1943.
xii p., 1 l., 374 p. 623.45532 43-
18535
UF740 .J6 MRR Alc.

Pollard, Hugh Bertie Campbell, A
history of firearms. London, G.
Bles, 1936. x, p., 1 l., 320 p.
623.4409 39-44791
U884 .P6 1936 MRR Alc.

FIREARMS--LAWS AND REGULATIONS--UNITED
STATES.
United States. Library of Congress.
Legislative Reference Service.
Combating crime in the United States.
Washington, U.S. Govt. Print.Off.,
1967. v, 254 p. 353.007/5 67-
62987
Z663.6 .C6 MRR Alc.

FIREARMS--YEARBOOKS.
Gun digest. [1st]- ed.; 1944-
Northfield, Ill. [etc.] 623.44 44-
32588
GV1174 .G8 MRR Alc Latest edition

Sports afield gun annual. 1953-
[New York, Hearst Corp.] 683.058 54-
19452
TS519 .S66 MRR Alc Latest edition

FIREARMS, AMERICAN.
Albaugh, William A., Confederate
arms, Harrisburg, Pa. [1957] xviii,
278 p. 623.4 57-13480
UD383.5 .A6 MRR Alc.

Gluckman, Arcadi, Identifying old
U.S. muskets, rifles & carbines.
Harrisburg, Pa., Stackpole Books
[1965] 487 p. 623.4425 65-20534
UD383 .G5 1965 MRR Alc.

International Association of Chiefs
of Police. Police Weapons Center.
The Police Weapons Center data
service. Gaithersburg, Md.,
International Association of Chiefs
of Police, Research Services Section
[1972] 1 v. (loose leaf) $30.00
per year. 363.2/028 72-86295
HV7936.E7 I58 MRR Alc.

Neumann, George C. The history of
weapons of the American Revolution,
[1st ed.] New York, Harper & Row
[1967] viii, 373 p. 623.4/4 67-
20829
U815 .N4 MRR Alc.

Ripley, Warren, Artillery and
ammunition of the Civil War. New
York, Van Nostrand Reinhold Co.
[1970] 384 p. 623.4 75-90331
UF23 .R56 1970 MRR Alc.

FIREARMS INDUSTRY AND TRADE--
CONFEDERATE STATES OF AMERICA.
Albaugh, William A., Confederate
arms, Harrisburg, Pa. [1957] xviii,
278 p. 623.4 57-13480
UD383.5 .A6 MRR Alc.

FIREARMS INDUSTRY AND TRADE--UNITED
STATES--DIRECTORIES.
Van Rensselaer, Stephen, American
firearms; Watkins Glen, N.Y.,
Century House [1947] 288 p.   683
48-1408
TS535 .V3 MRR Alc.

FIRMS
see Business enterprises

FIRST AID IN ILLNESS AND INJURY.
see also Medical emergencies

Cole, Warren Henry, ed. First aid,
diagnosis and management 5th ed.
New York, Appleton-Century-Crofts
[1960] 420 p. 614.88 60-5249
RD131 .C62 1960 MRR Alc.

Hudson, Ian Donald. What to do until
the doctor comes Princeton, N.J.
[Auerbach, 1970, c1969] xvi, 269 p.
[$7.95] 614.8/8 79-124624
RC81 .H9214 1970 MRR Alc.

FISH PROTEIN CONCENTRATE--BIBLIOGRAPHY.
United States. Library of Congress.
Science and Technology Division.
Special Bibliographies Section. Fish
protein concentrate; Washington,
Library of Congress; [available from
the Clearinghouse for Federal
Scientific and Technical Information,
Springfield, Va.] 1970. v, 77 p.
[3.00] 016.664/94 79-606672
Z663.41 .F5 MRR Alc.

FISHER, WALTER LOWRIE, 1862-1935--
BIBLIOGRAPHY.
United States. Library of Congress.
Manuscript Division. Walter L.
Fisher: a register of his papers in
the Library of Congress. Washington,
1960. 9 l.   012 60-60041
Z6663.34 .F5 MRR Alc.

FISHERIES.
Hardy, Alister Clavering, Sir. The
open sea: London, Fontana, 1970-71.
2 v. [15/- (v. 1)]   574.92 75-
857351
QH91 .H293 MRR Alc.

FISHERIES--DICTIONARIES.
Firth, Frank E. The encyclopedia of
marine resources. New York, Van
Nostrand Reinhold Co. [1969] xi, 740
p. 551.4/6/003 70-78014
SH201 .F56 1969 MRR Alc.

FISHERIES--DIRECTORIES--PERIODICALS.
Fishing industry index international
London, Haymarket. 338.3/72/7025 77-
649338
SH203 .F55 MRR Alc Latest edition

FISHERIES--RESEARCH--BIBLIOGRAPHY.
Selected references to literature on
marine expeditions, 1700-1960.
Boston, G. K. Hall, 1972. iv, 517 p.
016.5514/6 72-6452
Z5971 .S4 MRR Alc.

FISHERIES--STATISTICS.
Yearbook of fishery statistics. v.
[1]- 1947- Rome, [etc.] Food and
Agriculture Organization of the
United Nations. 49-27366
SH1 .Y4 MRR Alc Latest edition

FISHERIES--EUROPE--YEARBOOKS.
Scandinavian fishing year-book; 1955-
Copenhagen, Jørgen Frimodt [etc.]
56-15740
SH1 .S35 MRR Alc Latest edition

FISHERIES--SCANDINAVIA--YEARBOOKS.
Scandinavian fishing year-book; 1955-
Copenhagen, Jørgen Frimodt [etc.]
56-15740
SH1 .S35 MRR Alc Latest edition

FISHERIES--UNITED STATES.
Gabriel, Ralph Henry, Toilers of
land and sea, New Haven, Yale
university press; [etc., etc.] 1926.
3 p. l., 340 p.   26-4275
E178.5 .P2 vol. 3 MRR Alc.

FISHERY LAW AND LEGISLATION--CANADA.
Brooks, Joseph W., Complete guide to
fishing across North America; New
York, Outdoor Life [1966] 613 p.
799.12097 66-10660
SH462 .B76 MRR Alc.

FISHERY LAW AND LEGISLATION--UNITED
STATES.
Brooks, Joseph W., Complete guide to
fishing across North America; New
York, Outdoor Life [1966] 613 p.
799.12097 66-10660
SH462 .B76 MRR Alc.

FISHES.
see also Aquariums

Dalrymple, Byron W., Sportsman's
guide to game fish, New York, World
Pub. Co. [1968] xvi, 480 p. [$6.95]
799.1 68-31228
QL617 .D34 MRR Alc.

Grzimek, Bernhard. Grzimek's animal
life encyclopedia. New York, Van
Nostrand Reinhold Co. [1972- v. 13,
1972] v.   [$29.95 per vol.]   591
79-183178
QL3 .G7813 MRR Alc.

Hardy, Alister Clavering, Sir. The
open sea: London, Fontana, 1970-71.
2 v. [15/- (v. 1)]   574.92 75-
857351
QH91 .H293 MRR Alc.

FISHES--NOMENCLATURE.
American Fisheries Society. Committee
on Names of Fishes. A list of common
and scientific names of fishes from
the United States and Canada. 2d ed.
Ann Arbor, Mich., 1960. 102 p.
597.097 60-50217
QL618 .A48 1960 MRR Alc.

FISHES--NORTH AMERICA.
American Fisheries Society. Committee
on Names of Fishes. A list of common
and scientific names of fishes from
the United States and Canada. 2d ed.
Ann Arbor, Mich., 1960. 102 p.
597.097 60-50217
QL618 .A48 1960 MRR Alc.

FISHES, FRESH-WATER--IDENTIFICATION.
Eddy, Samuel. How to know the
freshwater fishes. 2d ed. Dubuque,
Iowa, W. C. Brown Co. [1969] x, 286
p.   597/.09/2973 75-89533
QL627 .E4 1969 MRR Alc.

FISHES, FRESH-WATER--UNITED STATES.
Eddy, Samuel. How to know the
freshwater fishes. 2d ed. Dubuque,
Iowa, W. C. Brown Co. [1969] x, 286
p.   597/.09/2973 75-89533
QL627 .E4 1969 MRR Alc.

FISHING.
Dalrymple, Byron W., Sportsman's
guide to game fish, New York, World
Pub. Co. [1968] xvi, 480 p. [$6.95]
QL617 .D34 MRR Alc.

Herter, George Leonard, Professional
guide's manual, [1st ed. Waseca,
Minn.] Herter's [1960] 207 p.   799
60-21551
SK601 .H497 MRR Alc.

Oppianus. Oppian, Colluthus,
Tryphiodorus, London, W. Heinemann,
ltd.; New York, G. P. Putnam's sons,
1928. lxxx, 635, [1] p.   29-2710
PA3612 .O5 1928 MRR Alc.

Sparano, Vin T. Complete outdoors
encyclopedia, New York, Outdoor
Life, Harper & Row [1972] 622 p.
[$13.95]   799/.03 72-90934
SK33 .S646 MRR Alc.

FISHING--DICTIONARIES.
Brander, Michael. A dictionary of
sporting terms. London, Black, 1968.
224 p. [35/-] 798 77-353522
SK11 .B66 MRR Alc.

McClane, Albert Jules, ed. McClane's
standard fishing encyclopedia and
international angling guide, [1st
ed.] New York, Holt, Rinehart and
Winston [1965] 1057 p.   799.103 65-
22460
SH411 .M18 MRR Alc.

FISHING--BAHAMAS.
Brooks, Joseph W., Complete guide to
fishing across North America; New
York, Outdoor Life [1966] 613 p.
799.12097 66-10660
SH462 .B76 MRR Alc.

FISHING--BERMUDA ISLANDS.
Brooks, Joseph W., Complete guide to
fishing across North America; New
York, Outdoor Life [1966] 613 p.
799.12097 66-10660
SH462 .B76 MRR Alc.

FISHING--NORTH AMERICA.
Brooks, Joseph W., Complete guide to
fishing across North America; New
York, Outdoor Life [1966] 613 p.
799.12097 66-10660
SH462 .B76 MRR Alc.

FISHING--UNITED STATES.
Farquhar, Carley. The sportsman's
almanac, [1st ed.] New York, Harper
& Row [1965] xiii, 493 p.
799.05873 64-25143
SK41 .F3 MRR Alc.

FISKE, MINNIE MADDERN (DAVEY) 1865-1932-
-BIBLIOGRAPHY.
United States. Library of Congress.
Manuscript Division. Minnie Maddern
Fiske; a register of her papers in
the Library of Congress. Washington,
1962. 16 p.   62-60071
Z663.34 .F53 MRR Alc.

FLAGS.
see also Emblems, National

Campbell, Gordon, The book of flags
5th ed. London, Oxford University
Press, 1965. xi, 124 p. 929.9 65-
8503
CR101 .C3 1965 MRR Alc.

Elting, Mary, Flags of all nations
and the people who live under them,
New York, Grosset & Dunlap [1969]
157 p. [4.95] 929.9 71-86695
CR109 .E4 1969 MRR Alc.

Flags of the world. London, New
York, F. Warne [1965] x, 325 p.
929.9 65-8875
CR101 .F55 1965 MRR Alc.

Gordon, William John. A manual of
flags; London, F. Warne and co.,
ltd.; New York, F. Warne and co.,
inc. [c1933] x, 294 p. 929.9 34-
13218
CR101 .G72 MRR Alc.

Great Britain. Admiralty. Flags of
all nations. [Rev. ed.] London,
H.M.Stationery Off., 1955- v.
929.9 56-41972
V300 .G72 MRR Alc.

Hope, A. Guy. Symbols of the
nations. Washington, Public Affairs
Press [1973] 348 p. [$10.00]
929.8 73-82015
JC345 .H66 MRR Alc.

Pedersen, Christian Fogd. The
international flag book in color.
New York, Morrow [1971] 237 p.
[$5.95] 929.9 73-136268
CR109 .P413 1971 MRR Alc.

Preble, George Henry, Origin and
history of the American flag and of
the naval and yacht-club signals,
seals and arms, and principal
national songs of the United States,
New ed. in two volumes.
Philadelphia, N. L. Brown, 1917. 2
v.   17-21758
CR113 .P7 1917 MRR Alc.

Smith, Cleveland Henry, Flags of all
nations, New York, Crowell [1950]
168 p.   929.9 50-12740
CR109 .S6 1950 MRR Alc.

FLAGS--BIBLIOGRAPHY.
Smith, Whitney. The bibliography of
flags of foreign nations. Boston, G.
K. Hall, 1965. viii, 169 p.
016.9299 66-894
Z5980 .S55 MRR Alc.

FLAGS--JUVENILE LITERATURE.
Elting, Mary, Flags of all nations
and the people who live under them,
New York, Grosset & Dunlap [1969]
157 p. [4.95] 929.9 71-86695
CR109 .E4 1969 MRR Alc.

FLAGS--GREAT BRITAIN.
Perrin, William Gordon, British
flags, their early history, and their
development at sea; Cambridge, The
University press, 1922. xii, 207,
[1] p.   22-11380
CR115.G7 P4 MRR Alc.

FLAGS--UNITED STATES.
Blakeney, Jane, Heroes, U.S. Marine
Corps, 1861-1955; [1st ed.
Washington, 1957] xviii, 621 p.
359.96 57-13185
VE23 .B56 MRR Biog.

Brown, James LaSalle, The flag of
the United States, its use in
commerce, Washington, U.S. Govt.
print. off., 1941. iv, 51 p.
929.90973 41-50088
CR113 .B845 MRR Alc.

Eggenberger, David. Flags of the
U.S.A. Enl. ed. New York, Crowell
[1964] 222 p.   929.90973 64-12115

CR113 .E35 1964 MRR Alc.

Harrison, Peleg Dennis, The stars
and stripes and other American flags,
Boston, Little, Brown, and company,
1918. 2 p. l., [vii]-xii, p., 2 l.,
431 p.   929.90973 31-5082
CR113 .H32 1918 MRR Alc.

Mahn, Herbert A. Flags and their
history, New York, Carlton Press
[1966] 264 p.   929.9 66-5267
CR113 .M24 MRR Alc.

Moss, James Alfred, The flag of the
United States; (3d ed.) Washington,
D.C., The United States flag
association [1941] xii, 272 p.
929.90973 41-20691
CR113 .M56 1941 MRR Alc.

Moss, James Alfred, Origin and
significance of military customs,
including military miscellany of
interest to soldiers and civilians,
Menasha Wis., George Banta
publishing company [c1917] 78 p.
18-509
U766 .M6 MRR Alc.

Preble, George Henry, Origin and
history of the American flag and of
the naval and yacht-club signals,
seals and arms, and principal
national songs of the United States,
New ed. in two volumes.
Philadelphia, N. L. Brown, 1917. 2
v.   17-21758
CR113 .P7 1917 MRR Alc.

Quaife, Milo Milton, The history of
the United States flag, [1st ed.]
New York, Harper [1961] 182 p.
929.90973 61-6428
CR113 .Q32 MRR Alc.

Shankle, George Earlie. State names,
flags, seals, songs, birds, flowers,
and other symbols; Rev. ed. New
York, H. W. Wilson Co., 1941 [i.e.
1951, c1938] 524 p.   929.4 917.3*
52-52807
E155 .S43 1951 MRR Alc.

Smith, Whitney. The flag book of the
United States. New York, Morrow
[1970] xiii, 306 p. [12.95]
929.8/0973 78-86879
JC346.Z3 S63 MRR Alc.

FLAGS--UNITED STATES--EXHIBITIONS.
United States. Library of Congress.
American Revolution Bicentennial
Office. Twelve flags of the American
Revolution. Washington, Library of
Congress, 1974. [16] p.   973.3/6
73-10402
Z663.115 .T93 MRR Alc.

FLAGS--UNITED STATES--HISTORY.
Mastai, Boleslaw. The Stars and the
Stripes; [1st ed.] New York, Knopf,
1973. 238 p. [$25.00] 929.9/0973
73-7276
JC346.Z3 M37 1973 MRR Alc.

FLAGS--UNITED STATES--STATES.
Gebhart, John Robert, Your State
flag, Philadelphia, Franklin Pub.
Co. [1973] xxi, 242 p. [$9.95]
929.9 73-79747
CR113.2 .G4 MRR Alc.

FLIGHT.
see also Aeronautics

FLIGHT CREWS.
see also Air pilots

FLIGHT TRAINING.
see also Aeroplanes--Piloting

FLOOR COVERINGS.
see also Carpets

FLORA
see Botany

FLORENCE--DESCRIPTION.
MoleJoli, Bruno, Florence. [1st
ed.] New York, Holt, Rinehart and
Winston [1972] 288 p. [$9.95]
709/.45/51 72-155539
N6921.F7 M6413 1972 MRR Alc.

FLORENCE--DESCRIPTION--GUIDE-BOOKS.
Borsook, Eve. The companion guide to
Florence. 2nd ed. London, Collins,
1973. 448, [24] p. [£3.00]
914.5/51 74-167897
DG732 .B6 1973 MRR Alc.

FLORENCE--DESCRIPTION--TOURS.
Gibbons annual index of daily sight-
seeing tours: Rome, Paris, Florence
London. [Los Angeles] 914 72-80819

D909 .G5 MRR Alc Latest edition

FLORICULTURE.
see also Flowers

see also House plants

see also Plants, Ornamental

FLORICULTURE--DIRECTORIES--PERIODICALS.
Who's who in floriculture.
[Washington] 635.9/025/73 68-4796
SB404.U5 W45 MRR Alc Latest
edition

FLORIDA.
Federal writers' project. Florida.
Florida; a guide to the southernmost
state. New York, Oxford university
press [1944] xxiv, 600 p. 917.59
45-2317
F316 .F44 1944 MRR Ref Desk.

The Florida handbook. 1947/48-
Tallahassee, Peninsular Pub. Co.
917.59 49-53676
F306 .F597 MRR Alc Latest edition

Norman Ford's Florida; 1953-
Greenlawn, N.Y., Harian Publications.
917.59 56-1848
F306 .N6 MRR Alc Latest edition

FLORIDA--BIBLIOGRAPHY--CATALOGS.
United States. Library of Congress.
Florida's centennial, Washington,
U.S. Govt. Print. Off., 1946. 36 p.
975.9 46-26780
Z663.15.A6F6 1946 MRR Alc.

FLORIDA--BIOGRAPHY.
The Florida handbook. 1947/48-
Tallahassee, Peninsular Pub. Co.
917.59 49-53676
F306 .F597 MRR Alc Latest edition

Tebeau, Charlton W. Florida from
Indian trail to space age; Delray
Beach, Fla., Southern Pub. Co., 1965.
3 v.   67-4792
F311 .T4 MRR Alc.

FLORIDA--BIOGRAPHY--DICTIONARIES.
Who's who in Florida. 1st- ed.;
1973/74- Lexington, Ky., Names of
Distinction, inc. 920/.0759[B] 73-
87147
CT229 .W5 MRR Biog Latest edition

FLORIDA--CENTENNIAL CELEBRATIONS, ETC.
United States. Library of Congress.
Florida's centennial, Washington,
U.S. Govt. Print. Off., 1946. 36 p.
975.9 46-26780
Z663.15.A6F6 1946 MRR Alc.

FLORIDA--DESCRIPTION AND TRAVEL--1951-
Morris, Allen Covington, Your
Florida government, Gainesville,
University of Florida Press, 1965.
142 p. 320.9759 64-8897
JK4425 1965 .M6 MRR Alc.

FLORIDA--DESCRIPTION AND TRAVEL--1951- -
GUIDE-BOOKS.
Hepburn, Andrew. Complete guide to
Florida. New rev. ed. Garden City,
N.Y., Doubleday, 1961. 160 p.
917.59 61-7606
F309.3 .H4 1961 MRR Alc.

Rand McNally and Company. Guide to
Florida. Chicago [1972] vi, 154 p.
[$3.95] 917.59/04/6 72-7999
F316.2 .R33 MRR Alc.

FLORIDA--DESCRIPTION AND TRAVEL--GUIDE-
BOOKS.
Federal writers' project. Florida.
Florida; a guide to the southernmost
state. New York, Oxford university
press [1944] xxiv, 600 p. 917.59
45-2317
F316 .F44 1944 MRR Ref Desk.

Florida tour book. fall 1965-
[Washington] American Automobile
Association. 917.59/04/6 74-644579

GV1024 .F56 MRR Alc Latest edition

Rand McNally and Company. Guide to
Florida. Chicago [1972] vi, 154 p.
[$3.95] 917.59/04/6 72-7999
F316.2 .R33 MRR Alc.

FLORIDA--ECONOMIC CONDITIONS--YEARBOOKS.
Florida statistical abstract. 1st-
ed.; 1967- Gainesville, Bureau of
Economic and Business Research,
University of Florida. 317.59 a 67-
7393
HA311 .F55 MRR Alc Latest edition

FLORIDA--EXECUTIVE DEPARTMENTS.
The Florida handbook. 1947/48-
Tallahassee, Peninsular Pub. Co.
917.59 49-53676
F306 .F597 MRR Alc Latest edition

FLORIDA--HISTORY.
Tebeau, Charlton W. Florida from
Indian trail to space age; Delray
Beach, Fla., Southern Pub. Co., 1965.
3 v. 67-4792
F311 .T4 MRR Alc.

Tebeau, Charlton W. A history of
Florida, Coral Gables, Fla.,
University of Miami Press [1971]
xiv, 502 p. [$12.50] 975.9 76-
109098
F311 .T42 MRR Alc.

FLORIDA--HISTORY--TO 1565.
Spanish explorers in the southern
United States, 1528-1543; New York,
C. Scribner's sons, 1907. xx, 411 p.
07-10607
E187.O7 S7 MRR Alc.

FLORIDA--HISTORY--HUGUENOT COLONY, 1562-
1565.
Lowery, Woodbury, The Spanish
settlements within the present limits
of the United States. Florida 1562-
1574, New York, London, G. P.
Putnam's sons, 1905. xxi, 500 p.
05-32489
E123 .L92 MRR Alc.

FLORIDA--HISTORY--SPANISH COLONY, 1565-
1763.
Lowery, Woodbury, The Spanish
settlements within the present limits
of the United States. Florida 1562-
1574, New York, London, G. P.
Putnam's sons, 1905. xxi, 500 p.
05-32489
E123 .L92 MRR Alc.

FLORIDA--INDUSTRIES--DIRECTORIES.
Florida. State Chamber of Commerce,
Jacksonville. Directory of Florida
industries. 1943/44- Jacksonville.
670.58 43-17176
T12 .F6 Sci RR Latest edition /
MRR Alc Latest edition

FLORIDA--MANUFACTURES--DIRECTORIES.
Florida. State Chamber of Commerce,
Jacksonville. Directory of Florida
industries. 1943/44- Jacksonville.
670.58 43-17176
T12 .F6 Sci RR Latest edition /
MRR Alc Latest edition

FLORIDA--POLITICS AND GOVERNMENT--1951-
Morris, Allen Covington, Your
Florida government, Gainesville,
University of Florida Press, 1965.
142 p. 320.9759 64-8897
JK4425 1965 .M6 MRR Alc.

FLORIDA--STATISTICS.
The Florida handbook. 1947/48-
Tallahassee, Peninsular Pub. Co.
917.59 49-53676
F306 .F597 MRR Alc Latest edition

FLORIDA--STATISTICS--YEARBOOKS.
Florida statistical abstract. 1st-
ed.; 1967- Gainesville, Bureau of
Economic and Business Research,
University of Florida. 317.59 a 67-
7393
HA311 .F55 MRR Alc Latest edition

FLORISTS--DIRECTORIES.
Who's who in floriculture.
[Washington] 635.9/025/73 68-4796
SB404.U5 W45 MRR Alc Latest
edition

FLORISTS--GREAT BRITAIN--DIRECTORIES.
Castle's guide to the fruit, flower,
vegetable, & allied trades. London,
Castle Pub. Co. 61-26296
HD9251.3 .C3 MRR Alc Latest
edition

FLORISTS--UNITED STATES--DIRECTORIES.
National florist directory.
Leachville, Ark. 56-35043
SB404.U5 N3 MRR Alc Latest edition

FLOWER ARRANGEMENT--DICTIONARIES.
Stevenson, Violet W. The
encyclopedia of floristry New York,
Drake Publishers [1973] 160, 96 p.
[$9.95] 745.92/03 73-3102
SB449 .S716 1973 MRR Alc.

FLOWER LANGUAGE.
Lehner, Ernst, Folklore and
symbolism of flowers, plants and
trees, New York, Tudor Pub. Co.
[1960] 128 p. 581.508 60-15038
QK83 .L4 MRR Alc.

Moulton, Mary K. A floral
dictionary; [Wayne Countryside
Garden Club ed.] St. Charles, Ill.,
c1961. [14] p. 62-459
QK84 .M68 MRR Alc.

FLOWERS.
see also Annuals (Plants)

see also Roses

Krythe, Maymie Richardson. All about
the months [1st ed.] New York,
Harper & Row [1966] 222 p. 529.2
66-18584
GR930 .K7 MRR Alc.

Limburg, Peter R. What's in the
names of flowers, New York, Coward,
McCann & Geoghegan [1974] 189 p.
[$4.64 (lib. bdg.)] 582/.13 73-
88535
QK13 .L5 1974

Perry, Frances. Flowers of the
world. [New York] Crown [1972] 320
p. [$22.50] 582/.13 72-84313
QK50 .P47 MRR Alc.

Taylor, Norman, 1001 questions
answered about flowers. New York,
Dodd, Mead [1963] 335 p. 635.9 63-
14006
QK83 .T34 MRR Alc.

FLOWERS--HISTORY.
Coats, Alice M. Flowers and their
histories, [New ed.] London, Black,
1968. xiii, 346 p. [42/-]
635.9/09 68-119595
SB404.5 .C6 1968 MRR Alc.

FLOWERS--JUVENILE LITERATURE.
Limburg, Peter R. What's in the
names of flowers, New York, Coward,
McCann & Geoghegan [1974] 189 p.
[$4.64 (lib. bdg.)] 582/.13 73-
88535
QK13 .L5 1974

FLOWERS, WILD
see Wild flowers

FLUID POWER TECHNOLOGY.
Fluid power handbook & directory.
Cleveland, Industrial Pub. Corp. 58-
30725
TJ950 .F5 MRR Alc Latest edition

FLUTE--CATALOGS.
United States. Library of Congress.
Music Division. The Dayton C. Miller
flute collection: Washington, 1961.
vi, 115 p. .61-60077
Z663.37 .D3 MRR Alc.

FLYING SAUCERS.
Colorado. University. Final report
of the scientific study of
unidentified flying objects. New
York, Dutton, 1969. xxiv, 967 p.
[12.95] 001/.94 73-77914
TL789 .C658 1969 MRR Alc.

FLYING SAUCERS--BIBLIOGRAPHY.
Sable, Martin Howard. UFO guide:
1947-1967; 1st ed. Beverly Hills,
Calif. Rainbow Press Co., 1967. 100
p. 016.001/9 67-30550
Z5064.F5 S3 MRR Alc.

FLYING SAUCERS--SOCIETIES, ETC.--
DIRECTORIES.
Sable, Martin Howard. UFO guide:
1947-1967; 1st ed. Beverly Hills,
Calif. Rainbow Press Co., 1967. 100
p. 016.001/9 67-30550
Z5064.F5 S3 MRR Alc.

FOG-SIGNALS.
The Lights and tides of the world,
including a description of all the
fog-signals. London, Imray, Laurie,
Norie & Wilson, ltd. ca 08-3141
VK1150 .L7 MRR Alc Latest edition

FOLIAGE PLANTS.
see also Ferns

FOLK ART--UNITED STATES.
Christensen, Erwin Ottomar, The
Index of American Design. New York,
Macmillan, 1950. xviii, 229 p. 745
50-10215
NK1403 .C5 MRR Alc.

Guilland, Harold F. Early American
folk pottery [1st ed.]
Philadelphia, Chilton Book Co. [1971]
xii, 321 p. 738.3/0973 70-159513

NK4006 .G8 1971 MRR Alc.

Lipman, Jean (Herzberg) American
folk decoration, New York, Oxford
University Press, 1951. xii, 163 p.
745.3 51-11035
NK806 .L5 MRR Alc.

FOLK COSTUME
see Costume

FOLK DANCING--YEARBOOKS.
Folk dance guide. New York.
793.31058 55-8175
Began in 1951.
GV1580 .F6 MRR Alc Latest edition

FOLK LITERATURE--BIBLIOGRAPHY.
Thompson, Stith, Motif-index of folk-
literature; Rev. and enl. ed.
Copenhagen, Rosenkilde and Bagger
[1955-58] 6 v. 398.012 56-14401
GR67 .T53 MRR Alc.

FOLK LITERATURE--THEMES, MOTIVES.
Baughman, Ernest Warren, Type and
motif-index of the folktales of
England and North America. The
Hague, Mouton & Co. 1966 [1967]
lxxvii, 607 p. [il. 58.-]
016.3982 64-64495
GR67 .B3 MRR Alc.

Thompson, Stith, Motif-index of folk-
literature; Rev. and enl. ed.
Copenhagen, Rosenkilde and Bagger
[1955-58] 6 v. 398.012 56-14401
GR67 .T53 MRR Alc.

FOLK-LORE.
see also Animals, Legends and stories
of

see also Mythology

see also Nursery rhymes

see also Superstition

Larousse encyclopedia of mythology.
London, Batchworth Press [1959]
viii, 500 p. 59-4844
BL310 .L453 1959 MRR Alc.

New Larousse encyclopedia of
mythology. New ed. New York] Putnam
[1968, c1959] xi, 500 p. [17.95]
200.4/03 68-57758
BL311 .N43 1968 MRR Alc.

Origin of things familiar;
Cincinnati, O., United book
corporation [c1934] 4 p. l., 280 p.
031 35-2154
AG5 .O7 MRR Alc.

Weiser, Francis Xavier, Handbook of
Christian feasts and customs; [1st
ed.] New York, Harcourt, Brace
[1958] 366 p. 264 58-10908
BV30 .W4 MRR Alc.

FOLK-LORE--BIBLIOGRAPHY.
Diehl, Katharine Smith. Religions,
mythologies, folklores: an annotated
bibliography. 2d ed. New York,
Scarecrow Press, 1962. 573 p.
016.2 62-16003
Z7751 .D54 1962 MRR Alc.

Modern Language Association of
America. MLA abstracts of articles
in scholarly journals. [New York]
408 72-624077
P1 .M64 MRR Alc Full set

FOLK-LORE--BIBLIOGRAPHY--CATALOGS.
Cleveland. Public Library. John G.
White Dept. Catalog of folklore and
folk songs. Boston, G. K. Hall,
1964. 2 v.   65-4290
   Z5985 .C5 MRR Alc (Dk 33).

FOLK-LORE--BIBLIOGRAPHY--PERIODICALS.
Internationale volkskundliche
Bibliographie. 1939/41- Bonn [etc.]
R. Habelt [etc.] 53-24243
   Z5982 .I523 MRR Alc Full set

FOLK-LORE--CLASSIFICATION.
Baughman, Ernest Warren. Type and
motif-index of the folktales of
England and North America. The
Hague, Mouton & Co., 1966 [1967]
lxxvii, 607 p.   [fl. 58.-]
016.3982 64-64495
   GR67 .B3 MRR Alc.

Thompson, Stith. Motif-index of folk-
literature; Rev. and enl ed.
Copenhagen, Rosenkilde and Bagger
[1955-58] 6 v. 398.012 56-14401
   GR67 .T53 MRR Alc.

FOLK-LORE--DICTIONARIES.
Bonnerjea, Biren. A dictionary of
superstitions and mythology. London,
Folk Press, Detroit, Singing Tree
Press, 1969. 314 p. 291/.13/03 69-
17755
   BL303 .B6 1969 MRR Alc.

Edwardes, Marian. A dictionary of
non-classical mythology, London, J.
M. Dent & sons, ltd.; New York, E. P.
Dutton & co. [1912] xii, 214 p.; 1
l. incl. front., plates. 290.3 13-
8773
   BL303 .E25 MRR Alc.

Funk & Wagnalls standard dictionary
of folklore, mythology and legend.
New York, Funk & Wagnalls Co., 1949-
[50] 2 v. 398.03 49-48675
   GR35 .F8 MRR Alc.

Jobes, Gertrude. Dictionary of
mythology, folklore and symbols. New
York, Scarecrow Press, 1961. 2 v.
(1758 p.) 398.03 61-860
   GR35 .J6 MRR Alc.

Radford, Edwin. Encyclopaedia of
superstitions Chester Springs [Pa.]
Dufour Editions [1969, c1961] 384 p.
[8.95] 398.3/7/03 69-20013
   BF1775 .R3 1969 MRR Alc.

FOLK-LORE--DICTIONARIES--FRENCH.
Chevalier, Jean. Dictionnaire des
symboles: [Paris] R. Laffont [1969]
xxxii, 844 p. [140.00] 79-463013
   GR35 .C47 MRR Alc.

FOLK-LORE--INDEXES.
Ireland, Norma (Olin) Index to fairy
tales, 1949-1972; Westwood, Mass.,
F. W. Faxon Co., 1973. xxxviii, 741
p. 398.2/01/6 73-173454
   Z5983.F17 I73 MRR Alc.

FOLK-LORE--PERIODICALS--INDEXES.
Internationale volkskundliche
Bibliographie. 1939/41- Bonn [etc.]
R. Habelt [etc.] 53-24243
   Z5982 .I523 MRR Alc Full set

**FOLK-LORE--ASIA, SOUTHEASTERN--
BIBLIOGRAPHY.**
Furer-Haimendorf, Elizabeth von. An
anthropological bibliography of South
Asia. Paris, Mouton, 1958-70. 3 v.
[fl. 130.00 (v. 3)] a 59-1034
   Z5115 .F83 MRR Alc.

FOLK-LORE--GREAT BRITAIN.
Folklore, myths and legends of
Britain. [1st ed. London] Reader's
Digest Association [1973] 552 p.
390/.0942 73-177007
   GR141 .F65 MRR Alc.

Hazlitt, William Carew. Faiths and
folklore of the British Isles; [New
York] B. Blom [1965] 2 v. (x, 672
p.) 914.2 64-18758
   DA110 .H38 1965 MRR Alc.

FOLK-LORE--GREECE.
Fontenrose, Joseph Eddy. Python; a
study of Delphic myth and its
origins. Berkeley, University of
California Press, 1959. xviii, 616
p. 398.4 59-5144
   GR830.D7 F6 MRR Alc.

FOLK-LORE--MISSISSIPPI VALLEY.
Botkin, Benjamin Albert, ed. A
treasury of Mississippi River
folklore; New York, Crown Publishers
[1955] xx, 620 p. 398 55-10172
   GR109 .B58 MRR Alc.

FOLK-LORE--NEW ENGLAND.
Botkin, Benjamin Albert, ed. A
treasury of New England folklore;
Rev. ed. New York, Crown Publishers
[1965] xxii, 618 p. 398 64-17848

   GR106 .B6 1965 MRR Alc.

FOLK-LORE--SOUTHERN STATES.
Botkin, Benjamin Albert, ed. A
treasury of southern folklore; New
York, Crown Publishers [1949] xxiv,
776 p. 398 49-11786
   GR108 .B6 MRR Alc.

FOLK-LORE--UNITED STATES.
Botkin, Benjamin Albert, ed.
Sidewalks of America; [1st ed.]
Indianapolis, Bobbs-Merrill [1954]
xxii, 605 p. 398 54-9485
   GR105 .B57 MRR Alc.

Botkin, Benjamin Albert, ed. A
treasury of American folklore; New
York, Crown publishers [1944] xxvii,
[1], 932 p. 398 44-4275
   GR105 .B58 MRR Alc.

Emrich, Duncan. Folklore on the
American land. [1st ed.] Boston,
Little, Brown [1972] xxviii, 707 p.
[$15.00] 398/.0973 72-161865
   GR105 .E47 MRR Alc.

Lys, Claudia de. A treasury of
American superstitions. New York,
Philosophical Library [1948] xxii,
494 p. 398.3 48-6722
   BF1775 .L9 MRR Alc.

FOLK-LORE--UNITED STATES--BIBLIOGRAPHY.
Haywood, Charles. A bibliography of
North American folklore and folksong.
2d rev. ed. New York, Dover
Publications [1961] 2 v. (xxx, 1301
p.) 016.398 62-3483
   Z5984.U5 H32 MRR Alc.

FOLK-LORE, AMERICAN.
Botkin, Benjamin Albert, ed. A
treasury of American folklore; New
York, Crown publishers [1944] xxvii,
[1], 932 p. 398 44-4275
   GR105 .B58 MRR Alc.

Shay, Frank. A sailor's treasury;
[1st ed.] New York, Norton [1951]
196 p. 910.4 51-7454
   GR910 .S36 MRR Alc.

FOLK-LORE, CHINESE.
Williams, Charles Alfred Speed.
Encyclopedia of Chinese symbolism and
art motives: New York, Julian Press,
1960 [i.e. 1961] xxi, 468 p.
398.30951 60-15987
   GR335 .W53 1961 MRR Alc.

FOLK-LORE, ENGLISH.
Baughman, Ernest Warren. Type and
motif-index of the folktales of
England and North America. The
Hague, Mouton & Co., 1966 [1967]
lxxvii, 607 p. [fl. 58.-]
016.3982 64-64495
   GR67 .B3 MRR Alc.

FOLK-LORE, INDIAN--BIBLIOGRAPHY.
Haywood, Charles. A bibliography of
North American folklore and folksong.
2d rev. ed. New York, Dover
Publications [1961] 2 v. (xxx, 1301
p.) 016.398 62-3483
   Z5984.U5 H32 MRR Alc.

**FOLK-LORE, INDIAN--JUVENILE LITERATURE--
BIBLIOGRAPHY.**
Ullom, Judith C. Folklore of the
North American Indians; Washington,
Library of Congress; [for sale by the
Supt. of Docs., U.S. Govt. Print.
Off.] 1969. x, 126 p. [2.25]
398/.0973 70-601462
   Z663.292 .U48 MRR Alc.

FOLK-LORE, IRISH.
Colum, Padraic, ed. A treasury of
Irish folklore: Rev. ed. New York,
Crown Publishers [1962] xx, 620 p.
398 62-10297
   GR147 .C5 1962 MRR Alc.

FOLK-LORE, NEGRO.
Hughes, Langston, ed. The book of
Negro folklore, New York, Dodd,
Mead, 1958. 624 p. 398 58-13097
   GR103 .H74 MRR Alc.

FOLK-LORE, NEGRO--BIBLIOGRAPHY.
Haywood, Charles. A bibliography of
North American folklore and folksong.
2d rev. ed. New York, Dover
Publications [1961] 2 v. (xxx, 1301
p.) 016.398 62-3483
   Z5984.U5 H32 MRR Alc.

FOLK-LORE OF RAILROADS.
Botkin, Benjamin Albert, ed. A
treasury of railroad folklore; New
York, Crown Publishers [1953] xiv,
530 p. 398 53-9973
   GR920.R3 B6 MRR Alc.

FOLK-LORE OF THE SEA.
Dorling, Henry Taprell. Salt water
quiz London] Hodder and Stoughton
[1952] 157 p. 387.076 53-6532
   V21 .D65 MRR Alc.

Shay, Frank. A sailor's treasury;
[1st ed.] New York, Norton [1951]
196 p. 910.4 51-7454
   GR910 .S36 MRR Alc.

FOLK-LORE OF TREES.
Lehner, Ernst. Folklore and
symbolism of flowers, plants and
trees, New York, Tudor Pub. Co.
[1960] 128 p. 581.508 60-15038
   QK83 .L4 MRR Alc.

FOLK MEDICINE--UNITED STATES.
Meyer, Clarence, comp. American folk
medicine, New York, Crowell [1973]
296 p. [$8.95] 615/.882/0973 73-
4300
   R152 .M49 MRR Alc.

FOLK MUSIC--BIBLIOGRAPHY.
Gillis, Frank, comp. Ethnomusicology
and folk music: [1st ed.]
Middletown, Conn., Published for the
Society for Ethnomusicology by the
Wesleyan University Press [1966] 148
p. 016.7817 66-23459
   ML128.E8 G5 MRR Alc.

FOLK MUSIC--AMERICA--DISCOGRAPHY.
United States. Library of Congress.
Archive of American Folk Song. Folk
music: 1943- [Washington, For sale
by the Superintendent of Documents,
U.S. Govt. Print. Off.] 789.913 58-
60095
   Z663.378 .F6 MRR Alc MRR Alc
   Latest edition

FOLK-SONGS.
see also Ballads

see also National songs

FOLK-SONGS--BIBLIOGRAPHY--CATALOGS.
Cleveland. Public Library. John G.
White Dept. Catalog of folklore and
folk songs. Boston, G. K. Hall,
1964. 2 v.   65-4290
   Z5985 .C5 MRR Alc (Dk 33).

FOLK-SONGS--UNITED STATES.
Lomax, John Avery, comp. American
ballads and folk songs, New York,
The Macmillan company, 1935. xxxix,
625 p. 784.4973 38-9495
   M1629 .L85A52 MRR Alc.

FOLK-SONGS--UNITED STATES--BIBLIOGRAPHY.
Haywood, Charles. A bibliography of
North American folklore and folksong.
2d rev. ed. New York, Dover
Publications [1961] 2 v. (xxx, 1301
p.) 016.398 62-3483
   Z5984.U5 H32 MRR Alc.

FOLK-SONGS, AMERICAN.
see also Ballads, American

Emrich, Duncan. Folklore on the
American land. [1st ed.] Boston,
Little, Brown [1972] xxviii, 707 p.
[$15.00] 398/.0973 72-161865
   GR105 .E47 MRR Alc.

Lomax, Alan, ed. The folk songs of
North America, in the English
language. London, Cassell [1960]
xxx, 623 p. 784.4973 m 60-2860
   M1629 .L83F6 MRR Alc.

FOLK-SONGS, AMERICAN--BIBLIOGRAPHY.
Lawless, Ray McKinley. Folksingers
and folksongs in America; New rev.
ed. New York, Duell, Sloan and
Pearce [1965] xviii, 750 p.
784.4973 65-21677
   ML3550 .L4 1965 MRR Alc.

FOLK-SONGS, AMERICAN--DISCOGRAPHY.
Lawless, Ray McKinley. Folksingers
and folksongs in America; New rev.
ed. New York, Duell, Sloan and
Pearce [1965] xviii, 750 p.
784.4973 65-21677
   ML3550 .L4 1965 MRR Alc.

Lomax, Alan, ed. The folk songs of
North America, in the English
language. London, Cassell [1960]
xxx, 623 p. 784.4973 m 60-2860
   M1629 .L83F6 MRR Alc.

United States. Library of Congress.
Archive of American Folk Song. A
list of American folksongs currently
available on records. Washington,
Library of Congress, 1953. 176 p.
789.9/13 53-60046
   Z663.373 .L5 MRR Alc.

FOLK-SONGS, ENGLISH.
see also Ballads, English

Chappell, William. Old English
popular music. A new ed. New York,
J. Brussel [c1961] 2 v. in 1.
784.3 62-3231
   M1740 .C52 1961 MRR Alc.

FOLK-SONGS, IRISH.
Colum, Padraic, ed. A treasury of
Irish folklore: Rev. ed. New York,
Crown Publishers [1962] xx, 620 p.
398 62-10297
   GR147 .C5 1962 MRR Alc.

FOLK-TALES
see Legends

see Tales

FOLKLORE.
Meyer, Clarence, comp. American folk medicine. New York, Crowell [1973] 296 p. [$8.95] 615/.882/0973 73-4300
  R152 .M49 MRR Alc.

FOLKLORE--HISTORY.
Meyer, Clarence, comp. American folk medicine. New York, Crowell [1973] 296 p. [$8.95] 615/.882/0973 73-4300
  R152 .M49 MRR Alc.

FOOD.
  see also Cookery

  see also Farm produce

  see also Nutrition

American Home Economics Association. Food and Nutrition Section. Terminology Committee. Handbook of food preparation. Washington, American Home Economics Association. 641.02 59-53013
  Began publication with 1946 edition.
  TX355 .A49 MRR Alc Latest edition

Food industries manual: [1st]-ed.: [1931]- London, L. Hill, ltd. 664.058 a 33-456
  TX353 .F65 Sci RR Latest edition / MRR Alc Latest edition

Margolius, Sidney K. Health foods: facts and fakes New York, Walker [1973] 293 p. [$6.95] 641.3 75-186187
  TX355 .M35 1973 MRR Alc.

Trager, James. The enriched, fortified, concentrated, country-fresh, lip-smacking, finger-licking, international, unexpurgated foodbook. New York, Grossman Publishers, 1970. xv, 578 p. [$15.00] 641.3 76-114944
  TX355 .T7 1970 MRR Alc.

United States. Dept. of Agriculture. Food. Washington [U.S. Govt. Print. Off., 1959] xii, 736 p. 641 agr59-296
  S21.A35 1959 MRR Alc.

United States. Dept. of Agriculture. Food for us all. [Washington: For sale by the Supt. of Docs., U.S. Govt. Print. Off., 1969] xxxix, 360 p. [3.50] 641.3 76-604428
  S21 .A35 1969 MRR Alc.

FOOD--COMPOSITION.
Jacobson, Michael F. Eater's digest; [1st ed.] Garden City, N.Y., Doubleday, 1972. xviii, 260 p. [$5.95] 664/.06 75-186030
  TX553.A3 J23 MRR Alc.

FOOD--DICTIONARIES.
Bender, Arnold E. Dictionary of nutrition and food technology 3rd ed. London, Butterworths, 1968. viii, 228 p. [50/-] 641/.03 79-451065
  TX349 .B4 1968b MRR Alc.

Food industries manual: [1st]-ed.: [1931]- London, L. Hill, ltd. 664.058 a 33-456
  TX353 .F65 Sci RR Latest edition / MRR Alc Latest edition

Funk & Wagnalls cook's and diner's dictionary: New York, Funk & Wagnalls [1969, c1968] xiv, 274 p. [$6.95] 641.3/003 68-21923
  TX349 .F85 MRR Alc.

Senn, Charles Herman, Dictionary of foods and cookery terms [New ed.]: London, Ward Lock, 1972. [5], 164 p. [£2.25] 641.3/003 72-188538
  TX349 .S46 1972 MRR Alc.

Simon, André Louis, A dictionary of gastronomy New York, McGraw-Hill [1970] 400 p. [$15.95] 641/.03 72-89318
  TX349 .S53 1970 MRR Alc.

Waldo, Myra. Dictionary of international food & cooking terms. New York, Macmillan Co. [1967] 648 p. 641/.03 67-27514
  TX349 .W24 MRR Alc.

FOOD--DICTIONARIES--FRENCH.
Montagne, Prosper. Larousse gastronomique: New York, Crown Publishers [1961] 1101 p. 641.03 61-15788
  TX349 .M613 MRR Alc.

FOOD--HISTORY.
Tannahill, Reay. Food in history. New York, Stein and Day [1973] 448 p. [$15.00] 641.3/009 75-160342
  GT2850 .T34 MRR Alc.

FOOD--PACKAGING--DIRECTORIES.
Lloyd's Canadian food and packaging directory. [Scarborough, Ont., etc., Lloyd Publications of Canada, etc.] 664/.0025/71 52-22816
  HD9014.C2 L54 MRR Alc Latest edition

FOOD--PRESERVATION.
  see also Canning and preserving

FOOD--TABLES, CALCULATIONS, ETC.
Bogert, Lotta Jean, Nutrition and physical fitness 9th ed. Philadelphia, Saunders, 1973. xi, 598 p. 641.1 76-188385
  TX354 .B6 1973 MRR Alc.

Bowes, Anna De Planter. Food values of portions commonly served, 1st-ed.; 1937- Philadelphia, J. B. Lippincott [etc.] 641.1083 40-7159
  TX551 .B64 MRR Alc Latest edition

FOOD, FROZEN.
The Almanac of the canning, freezing, preserving industries. Westminster, Md., E. E. Judge. 338.4/7/6640280973 72-622383
  TX599 .C4 MRR Alc Latest edition

Quat, Helen. The wonderful world of freezer cooking, New York, Hearthside Press, 1964. 224 p. 641.5 64-19654
  TX828 .Q3 MRR Alc.

FOOD, FROZEN--DIRECTORIES.
Directory of frozen food processors of fruits, vegetables, seafoods, meats, poultry, concentrates and prepared foods, New York, E. W. Williams [etc.] 55-40318
  TP493.5 .A1D5 MRR Alc Latest edition

FOOD, FROZEN--STATISTICS.
Frozen food pack statistics. Washington, American Frozen Food Institute. 338.4/7/6640 72-626490
  HD9004 .N28 MRR Alc Latest edition

FOOD, FROZEN--YEARBOOKS.
Frozen food factbook and directory. [New York] 664.85058 58-27616
  HD9001 .F7 MRR Alc Latest Edition

FOOD ADDITIVES.
Jacobson, Michael F. Eater's digest; [1st ed.] Garden City, N.Y., Doubleday, 1972. xviii, 260 p. [$5.95] 664/.06 75-186030
  TX553.A3 J23 MRR Alc.

FOOD ADDITIVES--ANALYSIS.
National Research Council. Committee on Specifications of the Food Chemicals Codex., Food chemicals codex. 2d ed. Washington, National Academy of Sciences, 1972. xvi, 1039 p. 664/.06 72-193763
  TP455 .N37 1972 MRR Alc.

FOOD ADDITIVES--DICTIONARIES.
Winter, Ruth, A consumer's dictionary of food additives. New York, Crown Publishers [1972] 235 p. [$5.95] 664/.06/03 79-185093
  TX553.A3 W55 1972 MRR Alc.

FOOD ADDITIVES--HANDBOOKS, MANUALS, ETC.
CRC handbook of food additives. 2d ed. Cleveland, CRC Press [c1972] xi, 998 p. 664/.06 73-153870
  TX553.A3 C2 1972 MRR Alc.

FOOD ADDITIVES--STANDARDS--UNITED STATES.
National Research Council. Committee on Specifications of the Food Chemicals Codex. Food chemicals codex. 2d ed. Washington, National Academy of Sciences, 1972. xvi, 1039 p. 664/.06 72-193763
  TP455 .N37 1972 MRR Alc.

FOOD FOR INVALIDS
  see Cookery for the sick

FOOD INDUSTRY AND TRADE.
  see also Cheese

FOOD INDUSTRY AND TRADE--BIBLIOGRAPHY.
Vara, Albert C. Food and beverage industries: a bibliography and guidebook Detroit, Gale Research Co. [1970] 215 p. [11.50] 016.3384/7/664 70-102058
  Z7164.F7 V33 MRR Alc.

FOOD INDUSTRY AND TRADE--DICTIONARIES.
Bender, Arnold E. Dictionary of nutrition and food technology 3rd ed. London, Butterworths 1968. viii, 228 p. [50/-] 641/.03 79-451065
  TX349 .B4 1968b MRR Alc.

FOOD INDUSTRY AND TRADE--DIRECTORIES.
Directory of frozen food processors of fruits, vegetables, seafoods, meats, poultry, concentrates and prepared foods. New York, E. W. Williams [etc.] 55-40318
  TP493.5 .A1D5 MRR Alc Latest edition

Food trades directory [and] food buyer's yearbook. London, Newman Books. 66-83910
  Began publication in 1958.
  HD9011.3 .F6 MRR Alc Latest edition

FOOD INDUSTRY AND TRADE--STANDARDS--UNITED STATES.
Jacobson, Michael F. Eater's digest; [1st ed.] Garden City, N.Y., Doubleday, 1972. xviii, 260 p. [$5.95] 664/.06 75-186030
  TX553.A3 J23 MRR Alc.

FOOD INDUSTRY AND TRADE--CALIFORNIA--DIRECTORIES.
Grocery bulletin buying guide and reference issue. [Los Angeles, Grocery bulletin, etc.] 44-34611
  HD9007.C2 G7 MRR Alc Latest edition

FOOD INDUSTRY AND TRADE--CANADA--DIRECTORIES.
Lloyd's Canadian food and packaging directory. [Scarborough, Ont., etc., Lloyd Publications of Canada, etc.] 664/.0025/71 52-22816
  HD9014.C2 L54 MRR Alc Latest edition

FOOD INDUSTRY AND TRADE--EUROPE--DIRECTORIES.
Noyes Development Corporation. Food guide to Europe, Park Ridge, N.J., 1969. 130 p. [20.00] 338.1/9/4 70-75386
  HD9015.E82 N6 MRR Alc.

FOOD INDUSTRY AND TRADE--FRANCE--DIRECTORIES.
Toute l'alimentation. Paris. 52-16897
  HD9012.3 .C67 MRR Alc Latest edition

FOOD INDUSTRY AND TRADE--GREAT BRITAIN--DIRECTORIES.
Food processing & packaging directory. [1st] ed.; 1954-London, NTP Business Journals Ltd. [etc.] 55-39270
  TP373 .F53 MRR Alc Latest edition

Food trades directory [and] food buyer's yearbook. London, Newman Books. 66-83910
  Began publication in 1958.
  HD9011.3 .F6 MRR Alc Latest edition

FOOD INDUSTRY AND TRADE--NEW ENGLAND--DIRECTORIES.
Grocery industry directory of New England. 1st- ed.; 1952/53-Wakefield, Mass [etc.] New England Wholesale Food Distributors Association. 658.9414 53-17865
  HD9321.3 .G695 MRR Alc Latest editions

FOOD INDUSTRY AND TRADE--UNITED STATES.
Margolius, Sidney K. Health foods: facts and fakes New York, Walker [1973] 293 p. [$6.95] 641.3 75-186187
  TX355 .M35 1973 MRR Alc.

United States. Dept. of Agriculture. Marketing. [Washington, U.S. Govt. Print. Off., 1954] xiv, 506 p. 631.18 agr55-4
  S21.A35 1954 MRR Alc.

United States. Dept. of Agriculture. Protecting our food. [Washington] U.S. Govt. Print. Off. [1966] xiii, 386 p. 641.3 agr66-345
  S21 .A35 1966 MRR Alc.

FOOD INDUSTRY AND TRADE--UNITED STATES--DIRECTORIES.
Chain store guide directory: 1973- [New York, Business Guides] [$49.00] 658.8/7k 73-645662
  HD9321.3 .D53 MRR Alc Latest edition

Institutional distribution's marketing & purchasing guide. Chicago. 338.1/0973 72-623464
  HD9003 .I57 MRR Alc Latest edition

Noyes Data Corporation. Food and beverage processing industries, 1971. Park Ridge, N.J. [1971] iii, 169, 9 p. [$20.00] 338.4/7/664002573 70-139403
  HD9003 .N58 MRR Alc.

The Organic directory, [Completely rev. ed.] Emmaus, Pa., Rodale Press [1974] 229 p. [$2.95] 641.3/1 74-166399
  TX356 .O69 1974 MRR Alc.

FOOD INDUSTRY AND TRADE--UNITED (Cont.)
Thomas grocery register. 68th-
ed.; 1966- New York, Thomas Publ.
Co. 381/.45/664097 72-623125
HD9321.3 T5 MRR Alc Latest edition

FOOD LAW AND LEGISLATION--UNITED STATES.
The Almanac of the canning, freezing,
preserving industries. Westminster,
Md., E. E. Judge. 338.4/7/6640280973
72-622383
TX599 .C4 MRR Alc Latest edition

FOOD RELIEF--UNITED STATES--STATISTICS.
United States. Congress. Senate.
Select Committee on Nutrition and
Human Needs. Poverty, malnutrition,
and Federal food assistance programs:
Washington, U.S. Govt. Print. Off.,
1969. v, 56 p. 338.1/9/73 78-
603619
HD9006 .A5256 1969 MRR Alc.

FOOD SERVICE--DIRECTORIES.
Who's who in food service in America.
Chicago, National Restaurant
Association. 72-626563
TX907 .N35 MRR Alc Latest edition

FOOD SUPPLY--STATISTICS.
Organization for Economic Cooperation
and Development. Agricultural and
food statistics, 1952-1963. Paris,
1965. 148 p. 66-33109
HD1421 .O67 MRR Alc.

Predicasts, inc. World food supply &
demand / Cleveland : Predicasts,
inc., 1974. v, 90 leaves : 338.1/9
74-187853
HD9000.4 .P73 1974 MRR Alc.

FOOD SUPPLY--UNITED STATES.
American heritage. The American
heritage cookbook and illustrated
history of American eating &
drinking. [New York] American
Heritage Pub. Co.; Distribution by
Simon and Schuster [1964] 629 p.
641.5 64-21278
TX705 .A65 MRR Alc.

United States. Dept. of Agriculture.
Protecting our food. [Washington]
U.S. Govt. Print. Off. [1966] xiii,
386 p. 641.3 agr66-345
S21 .A35 1966 MRR Alc.

FOOTBALL.
see also Soccer
Treat, Roger L. The encyclopedia of
football / 12th rev. ed. / South
Brunswick [N.J.] : A. S. Barnes,
[1974] 723 p. : [$13.95]
796.33/264/0873 73-22593
GV954 .T7 1974 MRR Alc.

FOOTBALL--BIOGRAPHY.
Football register. 1st- ed.; 1966-
St. Louis, The Sporting news.
796.332640212 66-8708
GV955 .F64 MRR Alc Latest edition

McCallum, John Dennis, College
football U.S.A., 1869 ... 1972;
[Greenwich, Conn.] Hall of Fame Pub.
[1972] 564 p. [$25.00]
796.33/263/0873 73-168805
GV950 .M32 MRR Alc.

FOOTBALL--HISTORY.
Classen, Harold, ed. Ronald
encyclopedia of football. 3d ed,
New York, Ronald Press Co. [1963] 1
v. (various pagings) 796.33209 63-
18863
GV951 .C56 1963 MRR Alc.

Danzig, Allison. The history of
American football: Englewood Cliffs,
N.J., Prentice-Hall, 1956. xii, 525
p. 796.33 56-9844
GV938 .D35 MRR Alc.

McCallum, John Dennis, College
football U.S.A., 1869 ... 1972;
[Greenwich, Conn.] Hall of Fame Pub.
[1972] 564 p. [$25.00]
796.33/263/0873 73-168805
GV950 .M32 MRR Alc.

FOOTBALL--RULES.
National Collegiate Athletic
Association. The Official National
Collegiate Athletic Association
football rules interpretations which
supplements the NCAA official
football rules. Shawnee Mission,
Kan., NCAA Publishing Service.
796.33/202022 74-645430
GV956.8 .N36a MRR Alc Latest
edition

FOOTBALL--STATISTICS.
Boda, Steve, College football all-
time record book, 1869-1969. New
York, [National Collegiate Athletic
Association] 1969. 176 p. [4.95]
796.332/63/0973 72-269547
GV955 .B6 MRR Alc.

Football register. 1st- ed.; 1966-
St. Louis, The Sporting news.
796.332640212 66-8708
GV955 .F64 MRR Alc Latest edition

National Football League. Official
record manual. New York.
796.33/264/0973 72-626572
GV955 .N328 MRR Alc Latest edition

FOOTBALL--YEARBOOKS.
National Football League. Official
record manual. New York.
796.33/264/0973 72-626572
GV955 .N328 MRR Alc Latest edition

The Official National Collegiate
Athletic Association football guide.
Phoenix, Ariz. [etc., National
Collegiate Athletic Association,
etc.] 08-27124
GV955 .S72 MRR Alc Latest edition

Pro football. 1959- New York,
Pocket Books. 796.33264 60-51813
GV937 .P7 MRR Alc Latest edition

FOOTPATHS
see Trails

FOOTWEAR
see Boots and shoes

FORAGE PLANTS.
see also Grasses

FORCED LABOR.
see also Convict labor

FORD AUTOMOBILE.
Fix your Ford, V8's and 6's. South
Holland, Ill. [etc.] Goodheart-
Willcox Co. 629.287 61-9347
TL215.F7 F5 MRR Alc Latest edition

FORECASTS, LONG-RANGE WEATHER
see Long-range weather forecasting

FOREIGN AID PROGRAM
see Economic assistance

FOREIGN CORRESPONDENTS, AMERICAN--
BIOGRAPHY.
Overseas Press Club of America.
Directory [of the] Overseas Press
Club of America and American
correspondents overseas. 1966- [New
York] 070.4/3/02573 66-18719
PN4871 O882 MRR Alc Latest edition

FOREIGN CORRESPONDENTS, AMERICAN--
DIRECTORIES.
Overseas Press Club of America.
Directory [of the] Overseas Press
Club of America and American
correspondents overseas. 1966- [New
York] 070.4/3/02573 66-18719
PN4871 O882 MRR Alc Latest edition

FOREIGN EXCHANGE.
see also Balance of payments

American International Investment
Corporation, San Francisco. World
currency charts. [5th ed.] San
Francisco [1970] 77 fold. l.
332.4/5 74-285254
HG3863 .A652 1970 MRR Alc.

Bidwell, Robin Leonard. Currency
conversion tables: London, Rex
Collings Ltd., 1970. v, 66 p. [20/-
] 385/.15 78-489912
HG219 .B5 MRR Ref Desk.

Money converter and tipping guide for
European travel. [1st]- ed.; 1953-
[New York] Dover Publications.
332.4083 58-4482
HG219 .M58 MRR Alc Latest edition

Perera's official illustrated foreign
money guide. New York, Random House
[1970] 1 v. (unpaged) [1.95]
332.4/021/2 75-102307
HG219 .P46 MRR Ref Desk.

Pick's currency yearbook. 1955- New
York, Pick Pub. Corp. [etc.]
332.4058 55-11013
HG219 .P5 MRR Ref Desk Latest
edition

Richard Joseph's world wide money
converter and tipping guide. 1953-
Garden City, N.Y., Doubleday. 332.45
52-13383
HG219 .R5 MRR Ref Desk Latest
edition

FOREIGN INVESTMENTS
see Investments, Foreign

FOREIGN POPULATION
see Emigration and immigration

FOREIGN RELATIONS
see International relations

FOREIGN STUDY.
The College blue book. [1st]- 1923-
New York [etc.] CCM Information
Corp. [etc.] 378.73 24-223
LA226 .C685 MRR Ref Desk Latest
edition

Garraty, John Arthur, The new guide
to study abroad; 1974-1975 ed. New
York, Harper & Row [1974] xiii, 422
p. [$10.95] 370.19/6 72-9117
LB2376 .G33 1974 MRR Ref Desk.

Handbook on international study.
1955- [New York] Institute of
International Education. 55-8482
LB2376 .H3 MRR Ref Desk Latest
edition

Herman, Shirley Yvonne. Guide to
study in Europe. New York, Four
Winds Press [1969] 288 p. [8.50]
378.4 68-27281
L914.5 .H4 MRR Alc.

Institute of International Education.
Undergraduate study abroad; [2d ed.
New York, 1966] 132 p. 370.196
66-8922
LB2376 .I53 1966 MRR Alc.

Study abroad. v. 1- 1948- [Paris]
UNESCO. 378.3 49-2511
LB2338 .S86 MRR Ref Desk Latest
edition / MRR Alc Latest edition

United States National Student
Association. The student traveler
abroad; work, study, travel. New
York, Grosset & Dunlap. 370.19/62
72-626265
LB2376 .U7 MRR Ref Desk Latest
edition

Vacation study abroad. [Paris,
United Nations Educational,
Scientific and Cultural Organization]
370.19/62 72-627046
LB2338 .V3 MRR Ref Desk Latest
edition

FOREIGN STUDY--DIRECTORIES.
Institute of Research on Overseas
Programs. The international programs
of American universities; 2d ed.
Honolulu, Institute of Advanced
Projects, East-West Center in
cooperation with International
Programs, Michigan State University
[East Lansing] 1966. x, 466 p.
378.3/5/0973 67-63980
LB2285.U6 I53 1966 TJ Rm.

Summer study abroad. New York,
Institute of International Education.
370.19/6/025 73-78423
LB2375 .S8 MRR Alc Latest edition

FOREIGN STUDY--HANDBOOKS, MANUALS, ETC.
Whole world handbook. 1972- [New
York, Frommer/Pasmantier Pub. Co.]
370.19/6 72-622559
LB2376 .W48 MRR Alc Latest edition

FOREIGN TRADE
see Commerce

FOREIGN TRADE PROMOTION--GREAT BRITAIN--
DIRECTORIES.
Directory of British export houses.
1st- ed.; 1971- Croydon, IPC
Business Press Information Services.
382/.6/02542 71-616998
HF3503 .D58 MRR Alc Latest edition

FOREIGN TRADE PROMOTION--RUSSIA--
DIRECTORIES.
United States. Central Intelligence
Agency. Directory of USSR foreign
trade organizations and officials.
[Washington] 1974. v, 71 p.
354/.47/00827025 74-600845
HF3623 .U53 1974 MRR Alc.

FOREIGN TRADE PROMOTION--UNITED STATES.
Jonnard, Claude M. Exporter's
financial and marketing handbook
Park Ridge, N.J., Noyes Data Corp.,
1973. xii, 308 p. [$18.00] 658.8
72-96107
HF1009.5 .J65 MRR Alc.

FOREIGN VISITORS
see Visitors, Foreign

FORENSIC MEDICINE
see Medical jurisprudence

FORENSIC ORATIONS.
Mead, Leon, comp. Manual of forensic
quotations. New York, J. F. Taylor &
company, 1903. xiv, 207 p. 03-
10774
LAW MRR Alc.

FOREST PRODUCTS.
see also Lumber trade

see also Rubber

FOREST PRODUCTS--STATISTICS.
Yearbook of forest products
statistics. 1947- Rome, [etc.] Food
and Agriculture Organization of the
United Nations. 338.17498 48-28149
HD9750.4 .Y4 MRR Alc Latest
edition

FOREST PRODUCTS--YEARBOOKS.
Yearbook of forest products
statistics. 1947- Rome, [etc.] Food
and Agriculture Organization of the
United Nations. 338.17498 48-28149
HD9750.4 .Y4 MRR Alc Latest
edition

FOREST RESERVES.
see also National parks and reserves

FOREST RESERVES. (Cont.)
see also Wilderness areas

FOREST RESERVES--UNITED STATES.
Farquhar, Carley. The sportsman's
almanac. [1st ed.] New York, Harper
& Row [1965] xiii, 493 p.
799.05873 64-25143
SK41 .F3 MRR Alc.

FORESTS AND FORESTRY.
see also Lumbering

see also Timber

see also Trees

see also Wood

FORESTS AND FORESTRY--UNITED STATES.
United States. Dept. of Agriculture.
Trees. Washington, U.S. Govt. Print.
Off. [1949] xiv, 944 p. 634.90973
agr55-2
S21 .A35 1949 MRR Alc.

FORESTS AND FORESTRY--UNITED STATES--
DIRECTORIES.
United States. Dept. of Agriculture.
Trees. Washington, U.S. Govt. Print.
Off. [1949] xiv, 944 p. 634.90973
agr55-2
S21 .A35 1949 MRR Alc.

FORMAL GARDENS
see Gardens

FORMS (LAW)--UNITED STATES.
The Corporation manual; New York,
United States Corporation Co. 21-
4563
KF1415 .C63 MRR Alc Latest edition

FORMS OF ADDRESS.
Broderick, Robert C., Catholic
concise dictionary. Chicago,
Franciscan Herald Press [1966] xi,
330 p. 282.03 66-14726
BX841 .B7 1966 MRR Alc.

A Catholic dictionary 3d ed. New
York, Macmillan, 1958. vii, 552 p.
282.03 58-5797
BX841 .C35 1958 MRR Alc.

Fenner, Kay Toy. American Catholic
etiquette. Westminster, Md., Newman
Press, 1961. 402 p. 395 61-16569
BX1969 .F4 MRR Alc.

Heywood, Valentine, British titles;
2d ed. London, A. and C. Black
[1953] 188 p. 929.7 53-32018
CR3891 .H4 1953 MRR Alc.

The Maryknoll Catholic dictionary.
[1st American ed. Wilkes-Barre, Pa.]
Dimension Books [1965] xvii, 710 p.
282.03 65-15436
BX841 .M36 1965 MRR Alc.

Measures, Howard, Styles of address;
3d ed. New York, St. Martin's Press
[1970, c1969] vii, 161 p. [5.95]
395 72-85142
CR3515 .M4 1970 MRR Ref Desk.

Titles and forms of address: 14th
ed. London, Black, 1971. xi, 188 p.
[£1.25] 395/.4 72-170772
CR3891 .T58 1971 MRR Alc.

Virtue's Catholic encyclopedia.
London, Virtue [1965] 3 v. (xv, 1136
p.) 282.03 66-92787
BX841 .V5 MRR Alc.

Whittemore, Carroll Ernest. Symbols
of the church; [Boston, Whittemore
Associates, 1953] 14 p. 246 54-
9095
BV150 .W44 MRR Alc.

FORTIFICATION--NORTH AMERICA.
Hammond, John Martin, Quaint and
historic forts of North America,
Philadelphia, London, J. B.
Lippincott company, 1915. xiii, [1]
p., 1 l., 308, [1] p. 16-645
E159 .H22 MRR Alc.

FORTIFICATION--UNITED STATES.
Hammond, John Martin, Quaint and
historic forts of North America,
Philadelphia, London, J. B.
Lippincott company, 1915. xiii, [1]
p., 1 l., 308, [1] p. 16-645
E159 .H22 MRR Alc.

FORTUNE-TELLING.
see also Dreams

Holzer, Hans W., The directory of
the occult Chicago, H. Regnery Co.
[1974] x, 201 p. 133/.025/73 74-
6895
BF1409 .H6 MRR Alc.

FORTUNES
see Wealth

FORWARDING MERCHANTS--DIRECTORIES.
The Globe world directory for land,
sea and air traffic. 1st-   ed.;
1948- Oslo, [etc.] Globe
Directories. 385.058 50-13703
HE9.A1 G5 MRR Alc Latest edition

FORWARDING MERCHANTS--UNITED STATES--
YEARBOOKS.
Shippers' Conference of Greater New
York. List of non-profit shipper
associations. New York [1970] 160
p. 380.5/025/73 70-21822
HF5780.U6 S45 MRR Alc.

FOSSILS
see Paleontology

FOSTER, STEPHEN COLLINS, 1826-1864--
BIBLIOGRAPHY.
United States. Library of Congress.
Music division. Catalogue of first
editions of Stephen C. Foster (1826-
1864) Washington, Govt. print. off.,
1915. 79 p. 14-30011
Z663.37 .F6 MRR Alc.

FOSTER DAY CARE.
see also Day nurseries

FOUNDING--DIRECTORIES.
Penton's foundry list. Cleveland,
Penton Pub. Co. 08-20029
TS229 .P5 MRR Alc Latest edition /
Sci RR Latest edition

FOUNDRIES--UNITED STATES--DIRECTORIES.
Penton's foundry list. Cleveland,
Penton Pub. Co. 08-20029
TS229 .P5 MRR Alc Latest edition /
Sci RR Latest edition

FOWLING.
Oppianus. Oppian, Colluthus,
Tryphiodorus, London, W. Heinemann,
ltd.; New York, G. P. Putnam's sons,
1928. lxxx, 635, [1] p. 29-2710
PA3612 .O5 1928 MRR Alc.

FOX-HUNTING--BIBLIOGRAPHY.
Higginson, Alexander Henry, British
and American sporting authors,
London, New York, Hutchinson, 1951.
xvii, 443 p. 016.7992 53-18485
Z7511 .H55 1951 MRR Biog.

FPC
see Fish protein concentrate

FRANCE--BIBLIOGRAPHY.
Cruger, Doris M. A list of American
doctoral dissertations on Africa,
Ann Arbor, Mich., Xerox, University
Microfilms Library Services. 1967.
36 p. 016.378/24 67-5644
Z5055.U49 C75 MRR Alc.

La Librairie française; les livres
de l'année. 1933/45- Paris, Cercle
de la librairie. 48-11426
Z2161 .L695 MRR Alc.

Pemberton, John E. How to find out
about France; [1st ed.] Oxford, New
York, Pergamon Press [1966] xvi, 199
p. 016.914403 66-19080
Z2161 .P4 1966 MRR Alc.

FRANCE--BIO-BIBLIOGRAPHY.
Glaeser, Ernest, Biographie
nationale des contemporains, Paris,
Glaeser et cie, 1878. 1 p. l., 4,
834 p. 03-7355
Z2170 .G54 MRR Biog.

Lorenz, Otto Henri, Catalogue
général de la librairie française.
Paris, 1867-1945. 34 v. 02-7509
Z2161 .L86 MRR Alc.

Quérard, Joseph Marie, La France
littéraire, Paris, Firmin Didot
père et Fils, 1827-64. 12 v. 02-
3270
Z2161 .Q4 MRR Alc.

Quérard, Joseph Marie, La
littérature française contemporaine.
Paris, Daguin frères, 1842-57. 6
v. 02-3271
Z2161 .Q41 MRR Alc.

FRANCE--BIOGRAPHY.
Annuaire diplomatique et consulaire
de la République française ... 18
- Paris, Imprimerie Nationale. 08-
31436
JX1793 .A2 MRR Alc Latest edition

Biographie nouvelle des
contemporains, Paris, Librairie
historique, 1820-25. 20 v. 06-
46326
CT148 .B54 MRR Biog.

Centre français du théâtre.
Dictionnaire des hommes de théâtre
français contemporains, Paris,
Librairie théâtrale [1957- v.
59-35428
PN2635 .C4 MRR Biog.

Dictionnaire biographique français
contemporain. [2. ed.] Paris,
Pharos; agent pour les États-Unis:
Stechert-Hafner, New York [1954] 708
p. 54-4253
DC406 .D5 1954 MRR Biog.

Dictionnaire national des
contemporains, Paris, Les Éditions
Lajeunesse, 1936- v. 920.044
37-8680
CT1013 .D52 MRR Biog.

Dictionnaire national des
contemporains, Paris, Office
général d'édition [1899-1905] 5
v. 10-8136
CT1013 .D5 MRR Biog.

Girard, Marcel. Guide illustré de
la littérature française moderne.
Nouvelle édition mise à jour.
Paris, Seghers, 1968. 408 p.
[18.00] 71-397791
PQ305 .G5 1968b MRR Alc.

Grimal, Pierre, ed. Dictionnaire des
biographies. 1. ed.] Paris,
Presses universitaires de France,
1958. 2 v. (xii, 1563 p.) a 59-628
CT143 .G7 MRR Biog.

Noël, Bernard. Dictionnaire de la
Commune. Paris, F. Hazan [1971]
365, [2] p. [78.00F] 71-595371
DC317 .N6 MRR Alc.

Schurr, Gérald. 1820 [i.e. Dix-huit
cent vingt]-1920 [i.e. dix-neuf cent
vingt], les petits maîtres de la
peinture; [Paris, Éditions de la
Gazette, c1969] 159 p. [120.00]
77-466202
ND547 .S473 MRR Alc.

Vapereau, Gustave, Dictionnaire
universel des contemporains 6. éd.
entièrement refondue et
considérablement augm. Paris [etc.]
Hachette et cie, 1893. 2 p. l., iii,
[1], 1629 p., 1 l. 02-5034
CT148 .V3 1893 MRR Biog.

FRANCE--BIOGRAPHY--DICTIONARIES.
Biographie universelle ancienne et
moderne (Nouvelle éd.) Graz,
Akademische Druck- u. Verlagsanstalt,
1966- v. [1190.00 (v. 1) varies]
920/.003 68-105681
CT143 .M52 MRR Biog.

Braun, Sidney David, ed. Dictionary
of French literature. New York,
Philosophical Library [1958] xiii,
362 p. 840.3 58-59407
PQ41 .B7 MRR Alc.

Coston, Henry. Dictionnaire de la
politique française. Paris,
Publications H. Coston [Diffusion: la
Librairie française] 1967- v.
[90.00F (v. 1) varies] 320.9/44 67-
99935
DC55 .C72 MRR Alc.

Dictionnaire des personnages
historiques français. [Paris,
Éditions Seghers, 1922] 381 p. 63-
51474
DC36 .D5 MRR Biog.

Dictionnaire de biographie
française, Paris, Letouzey et Ané,
1933- v. 920.044 33-10965
CT143 .D5 MRR Biog.

Dictionnaire des auteurs français.
[Paris, Seghers, 1961] 445 p. 62-
44229
PQ146 .D5 MRR Biog.

Dictionnaire des parlementaires
français; [1. ed.] Paris, Presses
universitaires de France, 1960- v.
62-34030
JN2785 .D5 MRR Biog.

Glaeser, Ernest, Biographie
nationale des contemporains, Paris,
Glaeser et cie, 1878. 1 p. l., 4,
834 p. 03-7355
Z2170 .G54 MRR Biog.

Hayes, Richard. Biographical
dictionary of Irishmen in France.
Dublin, M. H. Gill, 1949. 332 p.
325.24150944 50-17250
DC34.5.I7 H3 MRR Biog.

Jal, Auguste, Dictionnaire critique
de biographie et d'histoire; 2. éd.
cor. et augm. d'articles nonveaux et
renfermant 218 fac-similé
d'autographes. Paris, H. Plon, 1872.
2 p. l., iv, 1357 p. 05-35970
DC35 .J26 MRR Biog.

Kuscínski, August. Dictionnaire
des conventionnels. Paris, Société
de l'histoire de la Révolution
française, 1917 [cover 1919] iv,
615 p. 54-51011
DC145 .K82 MRR Biog.

FRANCE--BIOGRAPHY--DICTIONARIES. (Cont.)
Le Sage, Laurent, Dictionnaire des
critiques littéraires; University
Park, Pennsylvania State University
Press [c1969] 218 p. [6.50] 68-
8181
PQ67.A2 L4 MRR Biog.

Maitron, Jean, ed. Dictionnaire
biographique du mouvement ouvrier
français. Paris, Éditions
ouvrières [1964- v. 65-30024
HD8433.A1 M3 MRR Biog.

Nouveau dictionnaire national des
contemporains. t. [1]- 1961/62-
Paris. 63-41423
DC412 .N58 MRR Alc Full set

Pierrard, Pierre. Dictionnaire de la
IIIe République. Paris, Larousse,
1968. 256 p. [9.90 F] 76-362125
DC337 .P5 MRR Alc.

Rousselot, Jean, Dictionnaire de la
poésie française contemporaine.
Paris, Larousse, 1968. 256 p.
[9.90F] 841/.9/103 68-106149
PQ41 .R6 MRR Biog.

Who's who in France. 1.- éd.;
1953/54- Paris, J. Lafitte. 920.044
54-17054
DC705.A1 W46 MRR Biog Latest
edition

FRANCE--CIVILIZATION.
Duby, Georges. A history of French
civilization New York, Random House
[1964] xvi, 626 p. 914.4 64-14834

DC33 .D793 MRR Alc.

**FRANCE--CIVILIZATION--1830-1900--
BIBLIOGRAPHY.**
Thieme, Hugo Paul, Bibliographie de
la littérature française de 1800 à
1930. Paris, E. Droz, 1933. 3 v.
015.44 33-11487
Z2171 .T43 1933 MRR Alc.

**FRANCE--CIVILIZATION--OUTLINES,
SYLLABI, ETC.**
Bornecque, Pierre Henry, La France
et sa littérature. 3e édition
revue et corrigée. Lyon, A.
Desvigne, 1968. 896 p. [46F] 72-
367685
PQ135 .B57 1968 MRR Alc.

FRANCE--COLONIES--BIBLIOGRAPHY.
Halstead, John P. Modern European
imperialism; Boston, G. K. Hall,
1974. 2 v. 016.90908 73-19511
Z6204 .H35 MRR Alc.

FRANCE--COLONIES--GAZETTEERS.
Dictionnaire des communes; 32. éd.
Paris, Berger-Levrault, 1970. ix,
956 p. [58.00] 70-531850
DC14 .D6 1970 MRR Alc.

**FRANCE--COLONIES--INDUSTRIES--
DIRECTORIES.**
Annuaire des entreprises d'outre-mer.
Paris. 58-45147
HC279 .A65 MRR Alc Latest edition

FRANCE--COLONIES--YEARBOOKS.
Bottin Afrique centrale, Algérie,
Maroc-Tunisie, etc. 1946- Paris,
Société Didot-Bottin [etc.]. 48-
41815
JV1801 .B6 MRR Alc Latest edition

FRANCE--COLONIES--AFRICA.
Mortimer, Edward. France and the
Africans, 1944-1960; New York,
Walker [1969] 390 p. [8.50]
325.344/096 68-13985
DT33 .M65 1969b MRR Alc.

FRANCE--COLONIES--AFRICA, WEST.
Carson, Patricia. Materials for West
African history in French archives.
London, Athlone P.; distributed by
Constable, 1968. viii, 170 p. [42/-
.016.9166 68-99964
CD2491.W4 C3 1968 MRR Alc.

FRANCE--COMMERCE--DIRECTORIES.
American Chamber of Commerce in
France. Directory of American
business in France. Paris. 57-20161

HG4151.Z5 A5 MRR Alc Latest
edition

Annuaire Desfossés; Paris, Cote
Desfossés [etc.] 332.63 46-39086
HG5471 .A64 MRR Alc Latest edition

Annuaire officiel français des
adresses télégraphiques [Paris]
Ministère des postes et
télécommunications. 72-622826
HF3553 .A77 MRR Alc Latest edition

Bottin. Paris, Société Didot-
Bottin [etc.]. 50-49011
HF53 .B6 MRR Alc Latest edition

Qui représente qui en France? 1.-
éd.; 1957- Paris, Société des
Annuaires "Qui représente qui",
[etc.] 60-20676
HF3553 .Q5 MRR Alc Latest edition

Répertoire français du commerce
extérieur. 1961- Paris, Union
française d'annuaire professionnels.
72-627076
HC272 .R4 MRR Alc Latest edition

FRANCE--COMMERCE--YEARBOOKS.
Bottin. Paris, Société Didot-
Bottin [etc.]. 50-49011
HF53 .B6 MRR Alc Latest edition

FRANCE--CONSTITUTIONAL HISTORY.
Wallace-Hadrill, John Michael, ed.
France: government and society; 2nd
ed. London, Methuen, 1970. vii, 275
p. [$2.10] 944/.008 76-579489
JN2325 .W3 1970 MRR Alc.

FRANCE--DESCRIPTION AND TRAVEL.
La France, géographie-tourisme.
Paris, Librairie Larousse [1951-52]
2 v. 52-27084
DC29 .F7 MRR Alc.

**FRANCE--DESCRIPTION AND TRAVEL--1945- --
GUIDE-BOOKS.**
France 5th ed.] Geneva, Paris
[etc.] Nagel Publishers [1968] xxvi,
821 p. [$6.95] 914.4/04/83 78-
432166
DC16 .F76 1968 MRR Alc.

Guide artistique de la France.
[Paris,] Hachette, 1968. xviii, 1243
p. [57F] 709/.44 68-122321
N6841 .G78 MRR Alc.

Guide bleu France: [Paris] Hachette.
914.4/04/8305 73-643708
DC16 .F69 MRR Alc Latest edition

Pan American World Airways, inc.
Complete reference guide to France,
and Monaco. [2d rev. ed. New York,
Trade distribution by Simon &
Schuster, 1966] 159 p. 914.4/04
67-3753
DC16 .P3 1966 MRR Alc.

Stern, Lillian. Beyond Paris; [1st
ed.] New York, Norton [1967] 533 p.
914.4/04/83 65-13032
DC16 .S77 MRR Alc.

**FRANCE--DESCRIPTION AND TRAVEL--GUIDE-
BOOKS.**
Fodor's France. New York, D. McKay.
914.4/04/83 72-622335
DC16 .F75 MRR Alc Latest edition

Guide bleu France. [Paris] Hachette.
914.4/04/8305 73-643708
DC16 .F69 MRR Alc Latest edition

Guide pour l'auto international. 37.-
année; 1966- [Paris, Editions
commerciales de France] 72-627080
GV1025.F7 G84 MRR Alc Latest
edition

Guide religieux de la France,
[Paris,] Hachette, 1967. xvi, 1240
p. [48.63 F.] 274.4 67-113748
BR843 .G8 MRR Alc.

Olson, Harvey Stuart, Olson's
complete motoring guide to France,
Switzerland & Italy, [1st ed.]
Philadelphia, Lippincott [1967] xiv,
964 p. 914.4/04/83 66-16661
GV1025.F7 O4 MRR Alc.

FRANCE--DESCRIPTION AND TRAVEL--TOURS.
Gibbons annual index of daily sight-
seeing tours: Rome; Paris, Florence;
London. [Los Angeles] 914 72-80819

D909 .G5 MRR Alc Latest edition

FRANCE--DIPLOMATIC AND CONSULAR SERVICE.
Annuaire diplomatique et consulaire
de la République française ... 18
- Paris, Imprimerie Nationale. 08-
31436
JX1793 .A2 MRR Alc Latest edition

**FRANCE--DIPLOMATIC AND CONSULAR SERVICE--
UNITED STATES.**
France. Archives nationales. French
consuls in the United States:
Washington, Library of Congress; [for
sale by the Supt. of Docs., U.S.
Govt. Print. Off.] 1967. xi, 605 p.
327.73044 67-62310
E183.8.F8 A45 MRR Alc.

FRANCE--ECONOMIC CONDITIONS--1945-
Annuaire économique. 1962- Paris
[Éditions P. Waltz et M. Puget] 64-
27671
HC271 .A68 MRR Alc Latest edition

FRANCE--ECONOMIC POLICY--1945-
Annuaire économique. 1962- Paris
[Éditions P. Waltz et M. Puget] 64-
27671
HC271 .A68 MRR Alc Latest edition

**FRANCE--EXECUTIVE DEPARTMENTS--
DIRECTORIES.**
Bottin administratif et documentaire.
1942- Paris, Société Didot-Bottin
[etc.] 66-43255
JN2303 .B6 MRR Alc Latest edition

**FRANCE--FOREIGN RELATIONS--CONFEDERATE
STATES OF AMERICA.**
Owsley, Frank Lawrence, King Cotton
diplomacy; 2d ed., rev. [Chicago]
University of Chicago Press [1959]
xxiii, 614 p. 973.721 58-11952
E488 .O85 1959 MRR Alc.

**FRANCE--FOREIGN RELATIONS--UNITED
STATES.**
De Conde, Alexander. The quasi-war;
New York, Scribner [1966] xiv, 498
p. 973.45 66-24482
E323 .D4 MRR Alc.

France. Archives nationales. French
consuls in the United States:
Washington, Library of Congress; [for
sale by the Supt. of Docs., U.S.
Govt. Print. Off.] 1967. xi, 605 p.
327.73044 67-62310
E183.8.F8 A45 MRR Alc.

FRANCE--GAZETTEERS.
Dictionnaire des communes; 32. éd.
Paris, Berger-Levrault, 1970. ix,
956 p. [59.00] 70-531850
DC14 .D6 1970 MRR Alc.

Joanne, Paul Bénigne, ed.
Dictionnaire géographique et
administratif de la France; Paris,
Hachette et cie, 1890-1905. 7 v.
108 05-24019
DC14 .J63 MRR Alc.

Meyrat, J., Dictionnaire national
des communes de France: 19. éd.
entièrement refondue; mise à jour
au 1er jan. 1970 et conforme au
recensement de 1968. Paris, A.
Michel [1970] lxi, 1346 p. [49.00]
77-528796
DC14 .M57 1970 MRR Alc.

United States. Office of Geography.
France; Washington, 1964. 2 v. (ix,
1381 p.) 65-60643
DC14 .U56 MRR Alc.

FRANCE--HISTORY.
Cobban, Alfred. A history of modern
France. [New ed. rev. and enl.] New
York, Braziller [1965] 3 v. in 1.
944 65-14605
DC110 .C57 1965 MRR Alc.

Guérard, Albert Léon, France; a
modern history. New ed. rev. and
enl. Ann Arbor, University of
Michigan Press [1969] xxiv, 578,
xxvii p. [8.75] 944 69-19782
DC38 .G85 1969 MRR Alc.

Maurois, André, A history of
France. New York, Farrar, Straus and
Cudahy [1957, c1956] 598 p. 944
57-10003
DC39 .M372 1957 MRR Alc.

Reinhard, Marcel R., ed. Histoire de
France. Paris, Librairie Larousse
[1954] 2 v. 55-28038
DC38 .R43 MRR Alc.

Wallace-Hadrill, John Michael, ed.
France: government and society; 2nd
ed. London, Methuen, 1970. vii, 275
p. [$2.10] 944/.008 76-579489
JN2325 .W3 1970 MRR Alc.

**FRANCE--HISTORY--16TH CENTURY--
BIBLIOGRAPHY.**
Cioranescu, Alexandre. Bibliographie
de la littérature française du
seizième siècle. Paris, C.
Klincksieck, 1959. xiv, 745 p. a
60-3660
Z2172 .C5 MRR Alc.

**FRANCE--HISTORY--17TH CENTURY--
BIBLIOGRAPHY.**
Cioranescu, Alexandre. Bibliographie
de la littérature française du dix-
septième siècle. Paris, Editions
du Centre national de la recherche
scientifique, 1965-66. 3 v. (2283
p.) [80 F (v. 1) 110 F (v. 2) 100 F
(v. 3)] 011 66-71677
Z2172 .C52 MRR Alc.

**FRANCE--HISTORY--18TH CENTURY--
BIBLIOGRAPHY.**
Cioranescu, Alexandre. Bibliographie
de la littérature française du dix-
huitième siècle ... Paris,
Editions du Centre national de la
recherche scientifique, 1969- v.
[120.00 (v. 1)] 70-453192
Z2172 .C48 MRR Alc.

FRANCE--HISTORY--REVOLUTION, 1789-1794.
Thompson, James Matthew, The French
Revolution. [5th ed.] Oxford, B.
Blackwell, 1955. xvi, 544 p.
944.04 56-3363
DC161 .T47 1955 MRR Alc.

FRANCE--HISTORY--REVOLUTION, 1789-1799.
Furet, François, French Revolution.
London, Weidenfeld & Nicolson, 1970.
416 p. [70/-] 944.04 76-477201
DC148 .F8713 MRR Alc.

FRANCE--HISTORY--REVOLUTION, 1789-1799--
BIOGRAPHY.
Kuscinski, August. Dictionnaire
des conventionnels. Paris, Société
de l'historie de la Revolution
française, 1917 [cover 1919] iv,
615 p.   54-51011
   DC145 .K82 MRR Biog.

FRANCE--HISTORY--REVOLUTION, 1789-1799--
SOURCES.
Legg, Leopold George Wickham, ed.
Select documents illustrative of the
history of the French revolution.
Oxford, Clarendon press, 1905. 2 v.
05-18309
   DC141.7 .L4 MRR Alc.

Stewart, John Hall, A documentary
survey of the French Revolution. New
York, Macmillan [1951] xxviii, 818
p.   944.04   51-10629
   DC141.7 .S8 MRR Alc.

FRANCE--HISTORY--19TH CENTURY.
Zeldin, Theodore, France, 1848-1945,
Oxford, Clarendon Press, 1973- v.
[£6.00 (v. 1)] 914.4/03/81 73-
180595
   DC330 .Z44 MRR Alc.

FRANCE--HISTORY--THIRD REPUBLIC, 1870-
1940.
Brogan, Denis William, Sir, The
development of modern France, 1870-
1939, New and revised ed. London,
H. Hamilton, 1967. xxii, 775 p.
[63/-]   944.08   68-73213
   DC335 .B75 1967 MRR Alc.

FRANCE--HISTORY--THIRD REPUBLIC, 1870-
1940--DICTIONARIES.
Pierrard, Pierre. Dictionnaire de la
IIIe République. Paris, Larousse,
1968.   256 p. [9.90 F] 76-362125
   DC337 .P5 MRR Alc.

FRANCE--HISTORY--20TH CENTURY.
Zeldin, Theodore, France, 1848-1945,
Oxford, Clarendon Press, 1973- v.
[£6.00 (v. 1)] 914.4/03/81 73-
180595
   DC330 .Z44 MRR Alc.

FRANCE--HISTORY--GERMAN OCCUPATION,
1940-1945.
Werth, Alexander, France, 1940-1955.
London, R. Hale [1956] 764 p.   56-
3622
   DC400 .W4 MRR Alc.

FRANCE--HISTORY--1945-
L'Année politique economique,
sociale et diplomatique en France.
1963- Paris, Presses Universitaires
de France. 72-626951
   DC398 .A6 MRR Alc Latest edition

Werth, Alexander, France, 1940-1955.
London, R. Hale [1956] 764 p.   56-
3622
   DC400 .W4 MRR Alc.

FRANCE--HISTORY--CHRONOLOGY.
Dujarric, Gaston, Précis
chronologique d'histoire de France,
Nouvelle édition revue et mise a
Jour Paris, A. Michel [1966] 246 p.
[4.50 F.]   944   67-87567
   DC35 .D8 1966 MRR Alc.

FRANCE--HISTORY--DICTIONARIES.
Jal, Auguste, Dictionnaire critique
de biographie et d'histoire; 2. ed.
cor. et augm. d'articles nonveaux et
renfermant 218 fac-simile
d'autographes. Paris, H. Plon, 1872.
2 p. l., iv, 1357 p.   05-35970
   DC35 .J26 MRR Biog.

FRANCE--HISTORY--OUTLINES, SYLLABI, ETC.
Kunstler, Charles, Rois, empereurs
et presidents de la France. [Paris]
Hachette [1960] 255 p.   61-29004
   DC36.6 .K8 MRR Alc.

FRANCE--IMPRINTS.
Biblio. 1934- Paris. 015.44 36-
3965
   Z2165 .B565 MRR Alc Latest edition

British Museum. Dept. of Printed
Books. Short-title catalogue of
books printed in France and of French
books printed in other countries from
1470 to 1600 in the British Museum.
1st ed. reprinted. London, British
Museum [1966] viii, 491 p. [50/-]
015.44 67-73254
   Z2162 .B86 1966 MRR Alc.

British Museum. Dept. of Printed
Books. A short title catalogue of
French books 1601-1700, Folkestone
[Eng.] Dawsons 1973. x, 690 p.
015/.44 73-176033
   Z2162 .B87 1973 MRR Alc.

A Catalog of books represented by
Library of Congress printed cards
issued to July 31, 1942. Ann Arbor,
Mich., Edwards Bros., 1942-46. 167
v.   018.1 43-3338
   Z881.A1 C3 MRR Alc. (DK 33)

Le Catalogue de l'édition
française. 1.- ed.; 1970-
[Paris] VPC livres, S.A.; [Port
Washington, N.Y.] Paris Publications,
Inc.   71-612834
   Z2165 .C3 MRR Alc Latest edition

La Librairie française; les livres
de l'année. 1933/45- Paris, Cercle
de la librairie. 48-11426
   Z2161 .L695 MRR Alc Full set

Library of Congress and National
union catalog author lists, 1942-
1962. Detroit, Gale Research Co.,
1969-71. 152 v. 018/.1/0973 73-
82135
   Z881.A1 L63 MRR Alc (Dk 33)

Lindsay, Robert O. French political
pamphlets, 1547-1648; Madison,
University of Wisconsin Press, 1969.
xii, 510 p. 016.944/.03 78-84953
   Z2177.5 .L54 MRR Alc.

Les Livres de l'année-Biblio. 1971-
Paris, Cercle de la librairie. 011
73-647755
   Z2161 .L6952 MRR Alc Full set

Lorenz, Otto Henri, Catalogue
général de la librairie française.
Paris, 1867-1945. 34 v.   02-7509
   Z2161 .L86 MRR Alc.

The National union catalog. Totowa,
N.J., Rowman and Littlefield [1970-
v.   018/.1/0973 76-141020
   Z881.A1U3742 MRR Alc (Dk 33)

The National union catalog, pre-1956
imprints; London, Mansell, 1968- v.
021.6/4 67-30001
   Z663.7.L5115 MRR Alc (Dk 33)

Paris. Bibliothèque nationale.
Catalogue général des livres
imprimes; Paris, 1965- v.
018/.1 67-52152
   Z927 .P1957 MRR Alc (Dk33)

Paris. Bibliothèque nationale.
Département des imprimes.
Catalogue général des livres
imprimes de la Bibliothèque
nationale. Paris Imprimerie
nationale, 1897-19 v.   01-5989
   Z927 .P2 MRR Alc (Dk 33)

Paris. Bibliothèque nationale.
Département des périodiques.
Repertoire national des annuaires
français, 1958-1968, Paris,
Bibliothèque nationale, Éditions
Mercure, 1970. 811 p.   76-501237
   Z2174.Y4 P29 MRR Alc.

Quérard, Joseph Marie, La
litterature française contemporaine.
Paris, Daguin freres, 1842-57. 6
v.   02-3271
   Z2161 .Q41 MRR Alc.

Répertoire des livres de langue
française disponibles. 1972-
[Paris] France-Expansion. 72-626991

   Z2161 .R43   MRR Alc Latest edition

United States. Library of Congress.
Acquisitions Dept. European Imprints
for the war years Washington, 1945-
46. 3 v.   015.4 45-37835
   Z663.76 .E8 MRR Alc.

Vicaire, Georges, Manuel de
l'amateur de livres du XIXe siecle,
1801-1893. New York, B. Franklin
[1973] 8 v.   015/.44 79-144832
   Z2161 .V62 1973 MRR Alc.

FRANCE--INDUSTRIES--DIRECTORIES.
Repertoire français du commerce
exterieur. 1961- Paris, Union
française d'annuaire professionnels.
72-627076
   HC272 .R4 MRR Alc Latest edition

FRANCE--INTELLECTUAL LIFE--BIBLIOGRAPHY.
Osburn, Charles B. Research and
reference guide to French studies,
Metuchen, N. J., Scarecrow Press,
1968. 517 p. [$11.50] 016.44 68-
12638
   Z2175.A2 O8 MRR Ref Desk.

FRANCE--KINGS AND RULERS.
Kunstler, Charles, Rois, empereurs
et presidents de la France. [Paris]
Hachette [1960] 255 p.   61-29004
   DC36.6 .K8 MRR Alc.

FRANCE--MANUFACTURES--DIRECTORIES.
Repertoire français du commerce
exterieur. 1961- Paris, Union
française d'annuaire professionnels.
72-627076
   HC272 .R4 MRR Alc Latest edition

FRANCE--OFFICIALS AND EMPLOYEES--
DIRECTORIES.
France. Archives nationales. French
consuls in the United States:
Washington, Library of Congress: [for
sale by the Supt. of Docs., U.S.
Govt. Print. Off. 1967. xi, 605 p.
327.73044 67-62310
   E183.8.F8 A45 MRR Alc.

FRANCE--POLITICS AND GOVERNMENT.
Beer, Samuel Hutchison, ed. Patterns
of government; 3d ed. New York,
Random House [1973] xv, 778 p.
320.3 72-681
   JN12 .B4 1973 MRR Alc.

Blondel, Jean, The government of
France. 4th ed. New York, Crowell
[1974] xii, 307 p. 320.4/44 73-
6854
   JN2594.2 .B53 1974 MRR Alc.

Carter, Gwendolen Margaret, Major
foreign powers 6th ed. New York,
Harcourt Brace Jovanovich [1972]
xvi, 743 p. 320.3 78-179411
   JF51 .C3 1972 MRR Alc.

FRANCE--POLITICS AND GOVERNMENT--16TH
CENTURY--BIBLIOGRAPHY.
Lindsay, Robert O. French political
pamphlets, 1547-1648; Madison,
University of Wisconsin Press, 1969.
xii, 510 p. 016.944/.03 78-84953
   Z2177.5 .L54 MRR Alc.

FRANCE--POLITICS AND GOVERNMENT--17TH
CENTURY--BIBLIOGRAPHY.
Lindsay, Robert O. French political
pamphlets, 1547-1648; Madison,
University of Wisconsin Press, 1969.
xii, 510 p. 016.944/.03 78-84953
   Z2177.5 .L54 MRR Alc.

FRANCE--POLITICS AND GOVERNMENT--1870-
1940.
Brogan, Denis William, Sir, The
development of modern France, 1870-
1939, New and revised ed. London,
H. Hamilton, 1967. xxii 775 p.
[63/-] 944.08 68-73213
   DC335 .B75 1967 MRR Alc.

FRANCE--POLITICS AND GOVERNMENT--1945-
Bottin administratif et documentaire.
1942- Paris, Société Didot-Bottin
[etc.] 66-43255
   JN2303 .B6 MRR Alc Latest edition

FRANCE--POLITICS AND GOVERNMENT--1958-
Blondel, Jean, The government of
France. 4th ed. New York, Crowell
[1974] xii, 307 p. 320.4/44 73-
6854
   JN2594.2 .B53 1974 MRR Alc.

FRANCE--POLITICS AND GOVERNMENT--1958- -
-BIBLIOGRAPHY--CATALOGS.
Heinz, Grete. The French Fifth
Republic; establishment and
consolidation (1958-1965); Stanford,
Calif., Hoover Institution Press
[1970] xiii, 170 p. [9.00]
016.3209/44 70-92497
   Z2180.3 .H45 MRR Alc.

FRANCE--POLITICS AND GOVERNMENT--1958- -
-PERIODICALS.
L'Année politique economique,
sociale et diplomatique en France.
1963- Paris, Presses Universitaires
de France. 72-626951
   DC398 .A6 MRR Alc Latest edition

FRANCE--POLITICS AND GOVERNMENT--
DICTIONARIES.
Coston, Henry. Dictionnaire de la
politique française, Paris,
Publications H. Coston (Diffusion: la
Librairie française) 1967- v.
[90.00F (v. 1) varies] 320.9/44 67-
99935
   DC55 .C72 MRR Alc.

FRANCE--POPULATION.
Bodart, Gaston, Losses of life in
modern wars, Austria-Hungary; France,
Oxford, The Clarendon press; London,
New York [etc.] H. Milford, 1916. x,
207, 6 p. incl. tables.   16-20885
   D25.5 .B6 MRR Alc.

FRANCE--PRESIDENTS.
Kunstler, Charles, Rois, empereurs
et presidents de la France. [Paris]
Hachette [1960] 255 p.   61-29004
   DC36.6 .K8 MRR Alc.

FRANCE--PUBLIC WORKS--DIRECTORIES.
Sageret; Paris. 53-28411
"Fonde en 1809."
   TH12 .S25   MRR Alc Latest edition

FRANCE--REGISTERS.
Bottin administratif et documentaire.
1942- Paris, Société Didot-Bottin
[etc.] 66-43255
   JN2303 .B6 MRR Alc Latest edition

Coston, Henry. Dictionnaire de la
politique française, Paris,
Publications H. Coston (Diffusion: la
Librairie française) 1967- v.
[90.00F (v. 1) varies] 320.9/44 67-
99935
   DC55 .C72 MRR Alc.

FRANCE--REGISTERS. (Cont.)
Dictionnaire des parlementaires français; [1. ed.] Paris, Presses universitaires de France, 1960- v. 62-34030
JN2785 .D5 MRR Biog.

FRANCE--RELIGION.
Guide religieux de la France, [Paris,] Hachette, 1967. xvi, 1240 p. [48.63 F.] 274.4 67-113748
BR843 .G8 MRR Alc.

FRANCE--STATISTICS.
France. Institut national de la statistique et des etudes economiques. Annuaire statistique de la France. v. 1-   1878- Paris [etc.] 07-39079
HA1213 .A4 MRR Alc Latest edition

FRANCE--STATISTICS--BIBLIOGRAPHY.
Cormier, Reine. Les Sources des statistiques actuelles. Paris, Gauthier-Villars, 1969. 287 p. [48.00] 016.3144 75-423353
Z7551 .C65 MRR Alc.

FRANCE. ASSEMBLÉE NATIONALE, 1871-1942--BIOGRAPHY.
Dictionnaire des parlementaires français; [1. ed.] Paris, Presses universitaires de France, 1960- v. 62-34030
JN2785 .D5 MRR Biog.

FRANCE. ASSEMBLÉE NATIONALE CONSTITUANTE, 1789-1791.
Legg, Leopold George Wickham, ed. Select documents illustrative of the history of the French revolution. Oxford, Clarendon press, 1905. 2 v. 05-18309
DC141.7 .L4 MRR Alc.

FRENCH CANADIAN DIALECT--DICTIONARIES.
Bélisle, Louis Alexandre. Dictionnaire général de la langue française au Canada. 2. ed. Québec, Bélisle [1971] 1390 p. [112.50F (France)] 72-343538
PC3637 .B4 1971 MRR Alc.

FRANCHISE
see Elections

FRANCHISES (RETAIL TRADE)--UNITED STATES.
Directory of franchising organizations and a guide to franchising. New York, Pilot Industries, inc. 62-39831
HF5429 .D5 MRR Alc Latest edition

FRANCHISES (RETAIL TRADE)--UNITED STATES--DIRECTORIES.
Resource Publications, inc. Franchise guide; Princeton, N.J. [1969] 457 p. 658.87/0025/73 75-78653
HF5429.3 .R46 MRR Alc.

FRANKFURT AM MAIN--COMMERCE--DIRECTORIES.
Frankfurter Geschäfts-Adressbuch. Darmstadt, Almanach Verlags Gesellschaft Otto Schaffer [etc.] 54-36620
HF5173.F7 F73 MRR Alc Latest edition

FRANKFURT AM MAIN--DIRECTORIES.
Adressbuch der Stadt Frankfurt a.M. Frankfurt am Main, W. Dorn Verlag [etc.] 53-29184
DD901.F73 A6 MRR Alc Latest edition

FRANKFURTER, FELIX, 1882-1965--BIBLIOGRAPHY.
United States. Library of Congress. Manuscript Division. Felix Frankfurter: a register of his papers in the Library of Congress. Washington, Library of Congress, 1971. 70   016.347/7326/34 76-609869
Z6633.34 .F68 MRR Alc.

FRANKLIN, BENJAMIN, 1706-1790.
Van Doren, Carl Clinton. Benjamin Franklin. New York, The Viking press, 1938. xix p., 2 l., [3]-845 p. 923.273 38-31193
E302.6.F8 V32 MRR Alc.

FRANKLIN, BENJAMIN, 1706-1790--ANNIVERSARIES, ETC.
United States. Library of Congress. Benjamin Franklin, the two hundred and fiftieth anniversary of his birth, 1706-1956; Philadelphia, American Philosophical Society, 1956. vi, 31 p. 923.273 56-60066
Z6633.2 .B4 MRR Alc.

FRANKLIN, BENJAMIN, 1706-1790--MANUSCRIPTS.
United States. Library of Congress. Manuscript division. List of the Benjamin Franklin papers in the Library of Congress. Washington, Govt. print. off., 1905. 322 p. 05-20007
Z6633.34 .L5 MRR Alc.

FRANKLIN, BENJAMIN, 1706-1790--MANUSCRIPTS--CATALOGS.
United States. Library of Congress. Manuscript Division. Benjamin Franklin: a register and index of his papers in the Library of Congress. Washington, Library of Congress, 1973. iii, 27 p. 016.9733/2/0924 73-4185
Z6633.34 .F69 MRR Alc.

FREE MATERIAL.
Aubrey, Ruth H., ed. Selected free materials for classroom teachers 3d ed. Palo Alto, Calif., Fearon Publishers [1969] 124 p. [2.00] 016.3713/078 77-91551
Z5817.2 .A85 1969 MRR Alc.

Dever, Esther. Sources of free and inexpensive educational materials. 4th ed. Grafton, W. Va., [1970] iii, 538 p. [$6.30] 016.3713/078 70-21751
AG600 .D45 1970 MRR Alc.

Educators grade guide to free teaching aids. 1955- Randolph, Wis., Educators Progress Service. 016.3713 56-2444
AG600 .E3 MRR Alc Latest edition

Educators' guide to free films. Randolph, Wis., Educators' Progress Service. 371.335230838 45-412 Began with 1941 vol.
LB1044 .E3 MRR Alc Latest edition

Educators' guide to free filmstrips. 1st- 1949- Randolph, Wis., Educators' Progress Service. 371.3352 50-11650
LB1043.8 .E4 MRR Alc Latest edition

Educators guide to free guidance materials. 1st- ed.; 1962- Randolph, Wis., Educators Progress Service. 016.37142 62-18761
HF5381.A1 E3 MRR Alc Latest edition

Educators guide to free health, physical education and recreation materials. 1st- ed.; 1968- Randolph, Wis., Educators Progress Service. 011 68-57948
Z6121 .E38 MRR Alc Latest edition

Educators guide to free science materials. 1st- ed.;1960- Randolph, Wis., Educators Progress Service. 507 61-919
Q181.A1 E3 MRR Alc Latest edition

Educators guide to free social studies materials. 1st- ed.; 1961- Randolph, Wis., Educators Progress Service. 307 61-65910
AG600 .E315 MRR Alc Latest edition

Educators guide to free tapes, scripts and transcriptions. 1st- ed.; Jan. 1955- Randolph, Wis., Educators' Progress Service. 789.913* 55-2784
LB1044.2 .E3 MRR Alc Latest edition

Elementary teachers' guide for free curriculum materials. 1st- ed.; Sept. 1944- Randolph, Wis., Educators' Progress Service. 016.372 44-52255
Z5817.2 .E45 MRR Alc Latest edition

Field Enterprises Educational Corporation. Sources of free and inexpensive educational materials. Chicago [1958] 192 p. 58-1432
Z5817.2 .F42 1958 MRR Alc.

O'Hara, Frederic J., Over 2000 free publications, New York, New American Library [1968] 352 p. [0.95] 015/.73 71-3122
Z1223.Z7 O5 MRR Alc.

Pepe, Thomas J. Free and inexpensive educational aids, 4th rev. ed. New York, Dover Publications [1970] xi, 173 p. [$2.00] 016.3713/078 70-18964
AG600 .P45 1970 MRR Alc.

Weisinger, Mort, 1001 valuable things you can get free. 7th ed. New York, Bantam Books [1970] viii, 168 p. [$0.75] 031/.02 72-21292
AG600 .W4 1970 MRR Alc.

FREE SCHOOLS--UNITED STATES--DIRECTORIES.
Center for Curriculum Design. Somewhere else; [1st ed.] Chicago, Swallow Press [1973] 213 p. [$6.00] 060/.25 72-91916
AS8 .C4 1973 MRR Alc.

FREEDMEN.
see also Negroes

Litwack, Leon F. North of slavery; [Chicago] University of Chicago Press [1961] 318 p. 326.973 61-10869
E185.9 .L5 MRR Alc.

FREEDOM
see Liberty

FREEDOM OF INFORMATION--BIBLIOGRAPHY.
United States. Library of Congress. European Affairs Division. Freedom of information; Washington [1952]. v, 40 p. 016.32344 52-60051
Z663.26 .F72 MRR Alc.

United States. Library of Congress. European Affairs Division. Freedom of information; Washington, 1949. 153 p. 016.32344 49-45997
Z663.26 .F7 MRR Alc.

FREEMAN, DOUGLAS SOUTHALL, 1886-1953--BIBLIOGRAPHY.
United States. Library of Congress. Manuscript Division. Douglas Southall Freeman; a register of his papers in the Library of Congress. Washington, 1960. 14 l. 012 60-60054
Z663.34 .F7 MRR Alc.

FREEMASONS. UNITED STATES--DIRECTORIES.
List of regular lodges, masonic. [1929]- Bloomington, Ill., Pantagraph printing & stationery Co. 29-11910
HS383 .L5 MRR Alc Latest edition

FREEMASONS.
Waite, Arthur Edward, A new encyclopaedia of Freemasonry (Ars magna latomorum) and of cognate instituted mysteries: their rites, literature, and history. New and rev. ed. New Hyde Park, N.Y., University Books [1970] 2 v. [$35.00] 366/.103 70-19282
HS375 .W3 1970 MRR Alc.

FREEMASONS--DICTIONARIES.
Beha, Ernest. A comprehensive dictionary of Freemasonry. [1st American ed.] New York, Citadel Press [1963] 207 p. 366.1 63-16731
HS375 .B4 1963 MRR Alc.

Coil, Henry Wilson. Coil's Masonic encyclopedia. New York, Macoy Pub. & Masonic Supply Co. [1961] 731 p. 366.103 60-53289
HS375 .C6 MRR Alc.

Mackey, Albert Gallatin, Encyclopedia of freemasonry, Chicago, Ill., The Masonic history company [1946] 3 v. 366.1 47-17640
HS375 .M25 1946 MRR Alc.

FREEMASONS--DIRECTORIES.
List of regular lodges, masonic. [1929]- Bloomington, Ill., Pantagraph printing & stationery Co. 29-11910
HS383 .L5 MRR Alc Latest edition

FREEZING
see Refrigeration and refrigerating machinery

FREIBURG I. B.--DIRECTORIES.
Einwohnerbuch der Stadt Freiburg im Breisgau. Freiburg im Breisgau, Adressbuchverlag Rombach. 53-31494
DD901.F87 A25 MRR Alc Latest edition

FREIGHT AND FREIGHTAGE.
Leonard's guide, parcel post, express, freight rates and routing. 1st- ed.; 1923- Northbrook, Ill. [etc.] G. R. Leonard. 383.1 23-6413
HE9.U5 L46 MRR Alc Latest edition

FREIGHT AND FREIGHTAGE--DICTIONARIES.
American association of port authorities. Committee on standardization and special research. A port dictionary of technical terms, New Orleans, La., The American association of port authorities, 1940. 2 p. l., 7-208 p. 656 40-33335
V23 .A48 MRR Alc.

FREIGHT AND FREIGHTAGE--DIRECTORIES.
The Globe world directory for land, sea and air traffic. 1st- ed.; 1948- Oslo, [etc.] Globe Directories. 385.058 50-13703
HE9.A1 G5 MRR Alc Latest edition

FREIGHT AND FREIGHTAGE--YEARBOOKS.
Jane's freight containers. 1st- ed.; 1968/69- New York, McGraw-Hill Book Co. 380.5/3 74-2497
TA1215 .J34 Sci RR Latest edition / MRR Alc Latest edition

FREIGHT AND FREIGHTAGE--UNITED STATES--DIRECTORIES.
Dun & Bradstreet reference book of transportation. Washington, Trinc Transportation Consultants. 380.5/2/02573 74-644693
HE5623.A45 D82 MRR Alc Latest edition

FREIGHT AND FREIGHTAGE--UNITED (Cont.)
Dun & Bradstreet reference book of transportation. Washington, Trinc Transportation Consultants. 380.5/2/02573   74-644693
    HE5623.A45 D82   MRR Alc Latest edition

FREIGHT AND FREIGHTAGE--UNITED STATES--STATISTICS.
United States. Interstate Commerce Commission. Bureau of Accounts. Transport statistics in the United States. Washington. 380.5/0973   72-627360
    HE2708 .I73   MRR Alc Latest edition

FREIGHT FORWARDERS.
Murr, Alfred, Export/import traffic management and forwarding. New rev. ed.   Cambridge, Md., Cornell Maritime Press, 1967.   ix, 595 p. 658/.91/387   67-18222
    HE5999.A3 M8 1967 MRR Alc.

FREIGHT FORWARDERS--DIRECTORIES.
Offizielles Spediteur-Adressbuch. Hamburg, [etc.] Deutscher Verkehrs-Verlag.   52-23000
    HE5999.27 G3   MRR Alc Latest edition

FREIGHT FORWARDERS--GERMANY--DIRECTORIES.
Offizielles Spediteur-Adressbuch. Hamburg, [etc.] Deutscher Verkehrs-Verlag.   52-23000
    HE5999.27 G3   MRR Alc Latest edition

FREIGHTERS--PASSENGER TRAFFIC.
Ford's freighter travel guide. 19th-rev. ed.; summer 1962- [Woodland Hills, Calif., etc.] 387.5/42/05   72-622651
    HE566.F7 F6   MRR Alc Latest edition

Freighter days. Greenlawn, N.Y., Hadrian Publications; trade distributor: Grosset & Dunlap [etc., New York] 910.2   61-16001
    G550 .F73   MRR Alc Latest edition / MRR Alc Latest edition

Harian's today's outstanding buys in freighter travel. 1959- Greenlawn, N.Y., Harian Publications; trade distributor: Grosset & Dunlap [etc., New York] 910.2   61-1539
    HE566.F7 H3   MRR Alc Latest edition

Travel routes around the world. Greenlawn, N.Y. [etc.] Harian Publications.   42-44894
    G153 .T75   MRR Alc Latest edition

FREIGHTERS--REGISTERS.
The Bulk carrier register. London, H. Clarkson & Co.   387.2/45   70-618134
    HE566.F7 B79   MRR Alc Latest edition

The Bulk carrier register, London, H. Clarkson & Co. Ltd., 1969.   xxii, 290 p.   [10/-/-]   387.2/45/0216 71-462684
    HE566.F7 B8 MRR Alc.

Moody, Bert. Ocean ships   [New ed.]. London, Allan 1967.   vii, 359 p. [25/-]   387.2/4   72-472168
    HE565 .A5M6 1967 MRR Alc.

FREIGHTERS--STATISTICS.
The Bulk carrier register, London, H. Clarkson & Co. Ltd., 1969.   xxii, 290 p.   [10/-/-]   387.2/45/0216 71-462684
    HE566.F7 B8 MRR Alc.

FREIGHTERS--UNITED STATES--HISTORY.
Sawyer, Leonard Arthur. Victory ships and tankers;   Cambridge, Md., Cornell Maritime Press [1974] 230 p. 387.2/45/0973   73-22561
    VM391 .S39 1974 MRR Alc.

FRENCH-CANADIAN DIALECT--DICTIONARIES.
Dictionnaire Beauchemin canadien. Montréal, Librairie Beauchemin [1968] 1080 p.   [7.50]   72-404475
    PC3637 .D47 MRR Alc.

FRENCH-CANADIAN LITERATURE--BIBLIOGRAPHY.
Tod, Dorothea D. A check list of Canadian imprints, 1900-1925, Prelim. checking ed. Ottawa, Canadian Bibliographic Centre, Public Archives of Canada, 1950. 370 l. 015.71   50-12525
    Z1365 .T6 MRR Alc.

FRENCH-CANADIAN LITERATURE--BIO-BIBLIOGRAPHY.
Société des écrivains canadiens, Montréal. Répertoire bio-bibliographique, 1954. Montréal [1955] xviii, 248 p.   57-32232
    PQ3900 .S68A3 MRR Biog.

Toye, William. Supplement to the Oxford companion to Canadian history and literature. Toronto, New York, Oxford University Press, 1973.   v, 318 p.   [$9.50]   810/.9   74-180951
    PR9180.2 .T6 1973 MRR Alc.

FRENCH-CANADIAN LITERATURE--DICTIONARIES.
Toye, William. Supplement to the Oxford companion to Canadian history and literature. Toronto, New York, Oxford University Press, 1973.   v, 318 p.   [$9.50]   810/.9   74-180951
    PR9180.2 .T6 1973 MRR Alc.

FRENCH-CANADIAN LITERATURE--HISTORY AND CRITICISM.
Pierce, Lorne Albert, An outline of Canadian literature (French and English) Toronto, The Ryerson press, 1927.   6 p. l., 251 p.   28-2647
    PR9112 .P5 MRR Alc.

Tougas, Gérard. History of French-Canadian literature. 2d ed. Toronto, Ryerson Press [c1966]   ix, 301 p.   [$10.00]   840   67-76652
    PQ3901 .R613 1966 MRR Alc.

FRENCH COMMUNITY--YEARBOOKS.
Bottin Afrique centrale, Algérie, Maroc-Tunisie, etc.   1946- Paris, Société Didot-Bottin [etc.]   48-41815
    JV1801 .B6   MRR Alc Latest edition

FRENCH DRAMA--18TH CENTURY--BIBLIOGRAPHY.
Brenner, Clarence Dietz, A bibliographical list of plays in the French language, 1700-1789. Berkeley, Calif., 1947.   iv, 229 p. 016.8424   48-1262
    Z2174.D7 B7 MRR Alc.

FRENCH DRAMA--20TH CENTURY--HISTORY AND CRITICISM.
Fowlie, Wallace, Dionysus in Paris; New York, Meridian Books [1960] 314 p.   842.91082   60-6740
    PQ556 .F6 MRR Alc.

FRENCH DRAMA--BIBLIOGRAPHY.
Thompson, Lawrence Sidney, A bibliography of French plays on microcards, Hamden, Conn., Shoe String Press, 1967.   vii, 689 p. 016.842   67-13750
    Z2174.D7 T48 MRR Alc.

FRENCH DRAMA--MICROCARD EDITIONS.
Thompson, Lawrence Sidney, A bibliography of French plays on microcards, Hamden, Conn., Shoe String Press, 1967.   vii, 689 p. 016.842   67-13750
    Z2174.D7 T48 MRR Alc.

FRENCH FICTION--18TH CENTURY--BIBLIOGRAPHY.
Jones, Silas Paul, A list of French prose fiction from 1700 to 1750, New York, The H. W. Wilson company, 1939. xxxii p., 1 l., 150 p.   016.8435 39-27135
    Z2174.F7 J7 MRR Alc.

FRENCH GUIANA--GAZETTEERS.
United States. Office of Geography. The Guianas;   Washington, 1954. 234 p.   918.8   78-10045
    F2364 .U5 MRR Alc.

FRENCH IMPRINTS.
Les Livres de l'année-Biblio. 1971- Paris, Cercle de la librairie. 011 73-647755
    Z2161 .L6952   MRR Alc Full set

Répertoire des livres de langue française disponibles. 1972- [Paris] France-Expansion.   72-626991
    Z2161 .R43   MRR Alc Latest edition

FRENCH IMPRINTS--BIBLIOGRAPHY.
Biblio. 1934-   Paris.   015.44   36-3965
    Z2165 .B565   MRR Alc Latest edition

FRENCH IMPRINTS--BOOKSELLING--DIRECTORIES.
Repertoire international des librairies de langue française. Paris, Cercle de la librairie, 1971. xi, 347 p.   78-858018
    Z307 .R45 MRR Alc.

FRENCH IMPRINTS--CATALOGS.
British Museum. Dept. of Printed Books. A short title catalogue of French books, 1601-1700, Folkestone [Eng.] Dawsons, 1973.   x, 690 p. 015/.44   73-176033
    Z2162 .B87 1973 MRR Alc.

FRENCH IMPRINTS--PERIODICALS.
Le Catalogue de l'édition française. 1.-   ed.; 1970- [Paris] VPC Livres, S.A.; [Port Washington, N.Y.] Paris Publications, Inc.   71-612834
    Z2165 .C3   MRR Alc Latest edition

FRENCH IMPRINTS--PUBLISHING--DIRECTORIES.
Cercle de la librairie, Paris. Le Livre de langue française, Paris, Cercle de la librairie, 1967.   213 p. 655.4/025   68-116457
    Z282 .C42 MRR Alc.

Répertoire international des éditeurs de langue française. Paris, Cercle de la librairie, 1971. xliv, 315 p.   [51.66F]   070.5/025 72-857877
    Z282 .R44 MRR Alc.

FRENCH IN NORTH AMERICA--HISTORY--SOURCES--BIBLIOGRAPHY.
Beers, Henry Putney, The French in North America;   Baton Rouge, Louisiana State University Press [1957]   xi, 413 p.   016.97   57-11541
    Z1361.F8 B4 MRR Alc.

FRENCH LANGUAGE--EARLY MODERN, 1500-1700.
Huguet, Edmond Eugène August, Dictionnaire de la langue française du seizième siècle ... Paris, E. Champion, 1925-35.   2 v. and 2 pt. 26-5837
    PC2650 .H7 MRR Alc.

FRENCH LANGUAGE--EARLY MODERN, 1500-1700--DICTIONARIES.
Dubois, Jean, grammarian. Dictionnaire du français classique, Paris, Larousse [1971] xxxi, 564 p. [39.00F]   71-884265
    PC2650 .D83 MRR Alc.

FRENCH LANGUAGE--BIBLIOGRAPHY.
Osburn, Charles B. Research and reference guide to French studies, Metuchen, N. J., Scarecrow Press, 1968.   517 p.   [$11.50]   016.44   68-12638
    Z2175.A2 O8 MRR Ref Desk.

FRENCH LANGUAGE--CONVERSATION AND PHRASE BOOKS.
Levieux, Michel. Beyond the dictionary in French, London, Cassell, 1967.   156 p.   [15/-]   443 67-94064
    PC2680 .L4 MRR Alc.

FRENCH LANGUAGE--CONVERSATION AND PHRASE BOOKS--POLYGLOT.
Dony, Yvonne P. de. Léxico del lenguaje figurado, comparado, Buenos Aires, Ediciones Desclee, De Brouwer [1951]   804 p.   52-21901
    PB331 .D6 MRR Alc.

FRENCH LANGUAGE--DICTIONARIES.
Académie française, Paris. Dictionnaire de l'Académie française. 8. éd.   [Paris] Hachette, 1932-35.   2 v.   443   32-15754
    PC2625 .A3 1932 MRR Alc.

Dictionnaire du français contemporain Éd. rev. et corr. Paris, Larousse [1973] xxii, 1224 p. [48.00F]   443   73-76513
    PC2625 .D46 1973 MRR Alc.

Dictionnaire Quillet de la langue française; Paris, Librairie A. Quillet [1956]   3 v. (clxiii, 2110 p.)   57-18802
    PC2625 .D5 1956 MRR Alc.

Grand Larousse de la langue française en six volumes. Paris, Larousse [1971-   v.   [99.50F per vol.]   71-854777
    PC2625 .G7 MRR Alc.

Huguet, Edmond Eugène August, Dictionnaire de la langue française du seizième siècle ... Paris, E. Champion, 1925-35.   2 v. and 2 pt. 26-5837
    PC2650 .H7 MRR Alc.

Imbs, Paul. Trésor de la langue française; Paris, Éditions du Centre national de la recherche scientifique, 1971-   v.   [200F (v. 1)]   72-327996
    PC2625 .I4 MRR Alc.

Littré, Émile, Dictionnaire de la langue française. Éd. intégrale. [Paris] J. J. Pauvert, 1956-58.   7 v. 56-44528
    PC2625 .L63 MRR Alc.

Petit Larousse illustré, 1973. Paris, Larousse [1972] 1092, xvi, [1093]-1790 p.   73-364482
    AG25 .N75 1972 MRR Alc.

Rémy, Maurice. Dictionnaire usuel du français moderne. Montréal, Mame, Hatier, Lidec, c1967.   770, lxii p.   [$5.50 Can.]   443   68-138535
    PC2625 .R4 MRR Alc.

Rheims, Maurice. Dictionnaire des mots sauvages Paris, Larousse, 1969. 605 p.   [45.00]   443   79-413814
    PC2460 .R45 MRR Alc.

FRENCH LANGUAGE--DICTIONARIES. (Cont.)
Robert, Paul, Dictionnaire
alphabetique et analogique de la
langue française, Paris, Société
du nouveau Littré, 1968. xxxii,
1972 p. [80.00] 70-402432
PC2625 .R554 MRR Alc.

Robert, Paul, Dictionnaire
alphabétique et analogique de la
langue française, Paris, Société
du Nouveau Littré, 1970. 6 v. 70-
559630
PC2625 .R552 1970 MRR Alc.

Thomas, Adolphe V. Dictionnaire des
difficultes de la langue française.
Paris, Larousse [1956] xi, [1], 435
p. a 57-1436
PC2460 .T46 MRR Alc.

FRENCH LANGUAGE--DICTIONARIES--DUTCH.
Bosch, Abraham ten, Viertalig
technisch woordenboek. Deventer, Æ.
E. Kluwer [1948-55] 4 v. 603 50-
18447
T10 .B72 MRR Alc.

FRENCH LANGUAGE--DICTIONARIES--ENGLISH.
Archambeaud, Pierre. Dictionnaire
anglais-français, français-anglais
des industries graphiques Paris,
Compagnie française d'editions,
[1968?] 200 p. [15.00] 77-550452
Z118 .A7 MRR Alc.

Artschwager, Ernst Friedrich,
Dictionary of botanical equivalents,
Baltimore, The Williams & Wilkins
company, 1925. 5 p. l., 9-124 p.
25-11598
QK9 .A7 1925 MRR Alc.

Bucksch, Herbert. Dictionary of
civil engineering and construction
machinery and equipment ... 2e
edition. Paris, Eyrolles, 1967. v.
624/.03 74-415882
TA9 .B882 MRR Alc.

Bucksch, Herbert. Dictionary of
civil engineering and construction
machinery and equipment, English-
French. Paris, Eyrolles 1960-62. 2
v. 624.03 62-6556
TA9 .B89 MRR Alc.

Cassell's compact French-English,
English-French dictionary: London,
Cassell, 1968. xiv, 658 p. [18/-]
443/.2 72-353833
PC2640 .C28 MRR Ref Desk.

Cassell's French-English, English-
French dictionary, New ed.
completely revised New York, Funk &
Wagnalls [1951] xxiv, 727, 557 p.
443.2 52-39
PC2640 .C3 1951 MRR Ref Desk.

Cassell's new French-English, English-
French dictionary. London, Cassell
[1962] xvi, 762, 655 p. 443.2 62-
5157
PC2640 .C3 1962a MRR Ref Desk.

Castonguay, Jacques. Dictionary of
psychology and related sciences:
English-French. St-Hyacinthe,
Quebec, Edisem; Paris, Maloine, 1973
[i.e. 1972]. 153, 162 p. [$14.50]
150/.3 74-179864
BF31 .C34 MRR Alc.

Clifton, C. Ebenezer. A new French-
English and English-French dictionary
A new rev. ed. Paris, Garnier
[1961] 2 v. in 1. 443.2 62-6395
PC2640 .C63 1961 MRR Alc.

De Vries, Louis, French-English
science dictionary for students in
agricultural, biological, and
physical sciences, 3d ed. New York,
McGraw-Hill [1962] 655 p. 503 61-
17943
Q123 .D37 1962 MRR Alc.

Deak, Étienne. A dictionary of
colorful French slanguage and
colloquialisms, New York, Dutton
[1961, c1959] 209 p. 447.09 61-
16214
PC3741 .D35 1961 MRR Alc.

Dictionnaire canadien, français-
anglais, anglais-français. Ed.
abrégée. [Toronto] McClelland and
Stewart [1962] xxxiv, 861 p. 62-
48993
PC2640 .D44 MRR Alc.

Dictionnaire français-anglais de
locutions et expressions verbales,
Paris, Larousse [1973] viii, 386 p.
443/.21 74-158187
PC2684 .D48 MRR Alc.

Dictionnaire moderne français-
anglais, [anglais-français] Paris,
Larousse [1960] xii, 768, xii, 751
p. a 61-4733
PC2640 .D56 MRR Ref Desk.

Farmer, John Stephen, Dictionary of
slang & its analogues, past &
present; Rev. ed. New Hyde Park,
N.Y., University Books [1966- v.
427.09 65-24476
PE3721 .F32 MRR Alc.

France. Armée. Direction technique
des armes et de l'instruction.
Lexique militaire moderne français-
anglais, Paris, Charles-Lavauzelle
et Cie, 1968. 544 p. [25 F]
355/.0003 68-118881
U25 .F66 MRR Alc.

Harrap's new standard French and
English dictionary [Completely rev.
and enl. ed.] New York, Scribner
[1972] 2 v. [$39.50 ($25.00 per
vol.)] 443/.21 72-2297
PC2640 .H32 1972b MRR Alc.

Harrap's new standard French and
English dictionary; Completely
revised and enlarged ed.; London,
Harrap, 1972- v. in [£6.00 per
vol.] 443/.21 73-163555
PC2640 .H317 1972 MRR Ref Desk.

Harrap's standard French and English
dictionary. New York, Scribner
[1970] 2 v. [$27.50 (v. 1)]
443/.21 76-182803
PC2640 .H317 1970 MRR Alc.

Hoof, Henri van. Economic
terminology English-French.
München, Hueber (1967). 770 p.
[DM34.80] 330/.03 68-142981
HB61 .H57 MRR Alc.

International encyclopedia of
chemical science. Princeton, N.J.,
Van Nostrand [1964] 1331 p. 540.3
64-1619
QD5 .I5 1964 MRR Alc.

Kettridge, Julius Ornan. French-
English and English-French dictionary
of commercial & financial terms,
phrases, & practice; London,
Routledge & Paul, 1957. xi, 647 p.
650.3 59-21494
HG151 .K42 1957 MRR Alc.

Larousse modern French-English,
[English-French] dictionary, New
York, McGraw-Hill [1964, c1960] xvi,
768, xvi, 751 p. 66-504
PC2640 .L33 1964 MRR Alc.

Leitner, Moses Jonathan, ed.
Dictionary of French and American
slang, New York, Crown Publishers
[1965] xix, 272 p. 447.0903 64-
23818
PC3741 .L58 MRR Alc.

Lépine, Pierre. Dictionnaire
français-anglais, anglais-français,
des termes medicaux et biologiques:
Paris, Flammarion [1952] 829 p. 52-
3756
R121 .L39 MRR Alc.

Malgorn, Guy Marie, Lexique
technique français-anglais: Paris,
Gauthier-Villars, 1956. xxviii, 475
p. 57-156
T9 .M163 MRR Alc.

Marks, Joseph. Harrap's French-
English dictionary of slang and
colloquialisms; London, Harrap,
1970. 255 p. [50/-] 447/.09/03
78-578889
PC3741 .M33 MRR Alc.

Moth, Axel Fredrik Carl Mathias,
Glossary of library terms, English,
Danish, Dutch, French, German,
Italian, Spanish, Swedish, Boston,
The Boston book company, 1915. 58 p.
15-3471
Z1006 .M72 MRR Alc.

Nixon, James William. Glossary of
terms in official statistics, English-
French, French-English. Edinburgh,
Published for the International
Statistical Institute by Oliver &
Boyd [1964] xiv, 106 p. 65-50152
HA17 .N5 MRR Alc.

Péron, Michel. Dictionnaire
français-anglais des affaires
Paris, Larousse, 1968. 2 v. in 1.
(xvi, 230, xvi, 247 p.) [38 F] 68-
137592
HF1002 .P418 MRR Alc.

Petit, Charles, Dictionnaire
classique, anglais-français et
français-anglais Paris, Hachette,
1967. xxi, 664, 719 p. [30.70]
443/.2 76-390727
PC2640 .P45 MRR Alc.

La Psychologie moderne de A à Z
Paris, Centre d'etude et de
promotion de la lecture, 1971] 544
p. [45.25F] 74-501160
BF31 .P75 1971 MRR Alc.

Rueil-Malmaison, France. Institut
français du petrole. Dictionnaire
technique des termes utilises dans
l'industrie du petrole, anglais-
français, français-anglais. Paris,
Editions Technip, 1963. xvi, 385 p.
64-56944
TN865 .R82 MRR Alc.

Smith, Henry, Classical recipes of
the world, New York, Macmillan, 1955
[c1954] 631 p. 641.03 55-808
TX651 .S5 1955 MRR Alc.

Urwin, Kenneth. Dictionnaire
pratique français-anglais, anglais-
français ... Paris, Larousse, 1968.
1216 p. [26.50] 75-374590
PC2640 .U7 MRR Alc.

Urwin, Kenneth. Langenscheidt
standard dictionary of the French and
English languages. [New York] McGraw-
Hill [1969, c1968] 1216 p. [5.95]
443/.2 78-15234
PC2640 .U73 1969 MRR Alc.

Walter, Frank Keller, Abbreviations
and technical terms used in book
catalogs and bibliographies, in eight
languages. 1917 handy edition.
Boston, The Boston book company
[1919?] 2 v. in 1. 27-13479
Z1006 .W261 1919 MRR Alc.

FRENCH LANGUAGE--DICTIONARIES--POLYGLOT.
Associazione industriale lombarda.
Glossario del lavoro: italiano,
francese, inglese, tedesco. Milano,
1964. 1335 p. 67-43249
HD4839 .A78 MRR Alc.

Band-Kuzmany, Karin R. M. Glossary
of the theatre. Amsterdam, New York,
Elsevier Pub. Co., 1969. 140 p.
[31.20] 792/.03 68-57152
PN2035 .B3 MRR Alc.

Beeck, Peter. Fachausdrücke der
Presse. [3. Aufl.] Frankfurt am
Main, Polygraph Verlag, 1950. 174 p.
070.03 51-16343
PN4728 .B43 1950 MRR Alc.

Britannica world language dictionary,
[Chicago, 1958] 1483-2015 p. 413
58-4491
P361 .B7 1958 MRR Alc.

Buecken, Francisco J. Vocabulário
tecnico portugues-inglês-frances-
alemão. 4. ed. rev. [São Paulo]
Edições Melhoramentos [1961] 600
p. 603 62-3680
T10 .B82 1961 MRR Alc.

Bürger, Erich. Technical dictionary
of data processing, computers, office
machines. [1st ed.] Oxford, New
York, Pergamon Press [1970] 1463 p.
651.8/03 75-81247
QA76.15 .B46 1970 MRR Alc.

Capitol's concise dictionary.
Bologna, Capitol, 1972. 1051 (i.e.
1207) p. 413 72-172231
P361 .C3 MRR Alc.

Chalkiopoulos, Georgios.
[Pentaglosson lexilogion technikōn
horōn (romanized form)] [1960]
1030 p. 61-31355
T10 .C46 1960 MRR Alc.

Clason, W. E., Elsevier's dictionary
of computers, automatic control and
data processing. 2d rev. ed. of The
dictionary of automation, computers,
control and measuring. Amsterdam,
New York, Elsevier Pub. Co., 1971.
484 p. [fl78.00] 001.6/4/03 73-
151733
TJ212.5 .C55 1971 MRR Alc.

Clason, W. E., Supplement to the
Elsevier dictionaries of electronics,
nucleonics and telecommunication.
Amsterdam, New York, Elsevier Pub.
Co., 1963. 633 p. 603 63-11369
T10 .C55 MRR Alc.

Conference terminology, 2d ed., rev.
and augm. Amsterdam, New York,
Elsevier Pub. Co.; [sole distributors
for the U.S.: American Elsevier Pub.
Co., New York] 1962. 162 p. 413
63-8568
PB324.C6 C6 1962 MRR Alc.

Cooper, S. A. Concise international
dictionary of mechanics & geology;
New York, Philosophical Library
[1958] viii, 400 p. 621.03 58-
3594
TJ9 .C6 1958 MRR Alc.

Dictionar tehnic poliglot: Ediţia
a 2-a. Bucureşti, Editura Tehnica,
1967. xv, 1233 p. 603 68-2971
T10 .D54 1967 MRR Alc.

Dictionary of chemistry and chemical
technology, in six languages: [Rev.
ed.] Oxford, New York, Pergamon
Press [1966] 1325 p. 540.3 65-
29008
QD5 .D5 1966 MRR Alc.

FRENCH LANGUAGE--DICTIONARIES-- (Cont.)
Dictionary of photography and
cinematography: London, New York,
Focal Press [1961] 1 v. (various
pagings)   770.3   63-24356
   TR9 .D5 MRR Alc.

Dictionnaire à l'usage de la
librairie ancienne pour les langues:
française, anglaise, allemande,
suedoise, danoise, italienne,
espagnole, hollandaise, Paris, Ligue
internationale de la librairie
ancienne, 1956. 190 p.   655.403 57-
2275
   Z282 .D5 MRR Alc.

The Duden pictorial encyclopedia in
five languages: English, French,
German, Italian, Spanish. 2d, enl.
ed. New York, F. Ungar Pub. Co.
[1958] 2 v.   413   58-11093
   P361 .D8 1958 MRR Alc.

Elektrotechnik und Elektrochemie.
München, R. Oldenbourg, 1955. xxiv,
1304 p.   57-18208
   TK9 .E42 1955 MRR Alc.

Elsevier's automobile dictionary in
eight languages: Amsterdam, New
York, Elsevier Pub. Co.: [distributed
by Van Nostrand, Princeton, N.J.]
1960. 946 p.   629.203 59-8946
   TL9 .E43 MRR Alc.

Elsevier's banking dictionary in six
languages: Amsterdam, New York,
Elsevier Pub. Co., 1966. 302 p.
332.103 65-20139
   HG151 .E45 MRR Alc.

Elsevier's dictionary of aeronautics
in six languages: Amsterdam, New
York, Elsevier Pub. Co., 1964. 842
p.   629.1303 63-22063
   TL509 .E4 MRR Alc.

Elsevier's dictionary of building
construction, Amsterdam, New York,
Elsevier Pub. Co., 1959. 471 p.
690.3 58-59508
   TH9 .E47 MRR Alc.

Elsevier's dictionary of chemical
engineering. Amsterdam, New York,
1968. 2 v.   [$2.50 per vol.]
660/.2/03 68-54865
   TP9 .E38 MRR Alc.

Elsevier's dictionary of cinema,
sound, and music, in six languages:
Amsterdam, New York, Elsevier Pub.
Co., 1956. 948 p.   778.503 56-
13141
   TR847 .E4 MRR Alc.

Elsevier's dictionary of criminal
science, in eight languages:
Amsterdam, New York, Elsevier Pub.
Co.; [distributed by Van Nostrand,
Princeton, N.J.] 1960. xv, 1460 p.
364.03 59-12582
   HV6017 .E4 MRR Alc.

Elsevier's dictionary of electronics
and waveguides, 2d ed., rev. and
enl. Amsterdam, New York, Elsevier
Pub. Co., 1966 [i.e. 1965] 833 p.
621.38103 65-20142
   TK7804 .E4 1965 MRR Alc.

Elsevier's dictionary of general
physics in six languages: Amsterdam,
New York, Elsevier Pub. Co., 1962.
859 p.   530.3 62-13015
   QC5 .E46 MRR Alc.

Elsevier's dictionary of nuclear
science and technology. 2d rev. ed.
Amsterdam, New York, Elsevier Pub.
Co., 1970. 787 p.   [$85.00]
539.7/03 72-100357
   QC772 .E4 1970 MRR Alc.

Elsevier's dictionary of photography
in three languages: Amsterdam, New
York, Elsevier Pub. Co.: distributed
by American Elsevier Pub. Co., New
York, 1965. 660 p.   770.3 63-16076

   TR9 .E46 MRR Alc.

Elsevier's dictionary of television,
radar, and antennas, in six
languages: Amsterdam, New York,
Elsevier Pub. Co., 1955. 760 p.
621.38803 55-6216
   TK6634 .E4 MRR Alc.

Elsevier's dictionary of the printing
and allied industries in four
languages, Amsterdam, New York,
[etc.] Elsevier Pub. Co., 1967. 596
p. [$90.00] 655/.003 67-19851
   Z118 .E5 MRR Alc.

Elsevier's lexicon of archive
terminology: Amsterdam, New York,
Elsevier Pub. Co., 1964. 83 p.
025.171014 64-56714
   CD945 .E4 MRR Alc.

Elsevier's lexicon of stock-market
terms: Amsterdam, New York, Elsevier
Pub. Co., 1965. 131 p.   332.603 65-
13882
   HG4513 .E4 MRR Alc.

Elsevier's medical dictionary in five
languages: Amsterdam, New York,
Elsevier Pub. Co., 1964. 1588 p.
610.3 62-13022
   R121 .E5 1964 MRR Alc.

Elsevier's wood dictionary in seven
languages: Amsterdam, New York,
Elsevier Pub. Co., 1964- v.
634.903 64-14178
   SD431 .E4 MRR Alc.

Fabierkiewicz, Wacław. Podręczny
słownik włókienniczy w 5 językach:
[Wyd. 1] [Warszawa] Państwowe
Wydawn. Techniczne [1955] xlvii, 305
p.   55-38912
   TS1309 .F3 MRR Alc.

Frey, Albert Romer. Dictionary of
numismatic names, [New York] Barnes
& Noble [1947] ix, 311, 94 p.
737.03 48-5357
   CJ67 .F7 1947 MRR Alc.

Giteau, Cécile. Dictionnaire des
arts du spectacle, français--anglais-
-allemand: Paris, Dunod, 1970. xxv,
429 p. [88.00]   79-489689
   PN1579 .G5 MRR Alc.

Great Britain. Naval intelligence
division. A dictionary of naval
equivalents covering English, French,
Italian, Spanish, Russian, Swedish,
Danish, Dutch, German. London, H.M.
Stationery off., 1924. 2 v.   24-
23792
   V24 .G7 MRR Alc.

Haensch, Günther. Dictionary of
international relations and politics:
Amsterdam, New York, Elsevier Pub.
Co., 1965. xv, 638 p.   320.03 64-
8710
   JX1226 .H26 MRR Alc.

Haensch, Günther. Wörterbuch der
Landwirtschaft: 3., überarb. Aufl.
München, Bayerischer
Landwirtschaftverlag [1966] xxiv,
746 p.   630/.3 68-96091
   S411 .H26 1966 MRR Alc.

Herbst, Robert. Dictionary of
commercial, financial, and legal
terms; 2d ed., Zug, Translegal
[1966- v.   330/.03 67-8369
   HB61 .H442 MRR Alc.

Herbst, Robert. Dictionary of
commercial, financial, and legal
terms 3rd ed. rev. Zug, Translegal
[1968- v.   [unpriced]   330/.03
76-410368.
   HB61 .H463 MRR Alc.

Hétnyelvü sportszótár: Budapest,
Terra, 1960- v.   61-21333
   GV567 .H45 MRR Alc.

Horn, Stefan F., Glossary of
financial terms, Amsterdam, New
York, Elsevier Pub. Co., 1965. 271
p.   332.03 64-23405
   HG151 .H6 MRR Alc.

Horten,Hans Ernest. Export-import
correspondence in four languages
London, Gower Press Ltd. 1970. xi,
2-316 p. [80/-]   382/.03 76-495482

   HF1002 .H695 MRR Alc.

Inter-American Statistical Institute.
Statistical vocabulary. 2d ed.
Washington, Pan American Union, 1960.
xi, 83 p.   310.3 pa 60-56
   HA17 .I6 1960 MRR Alc.

Intergovernmental Maritime
Consultative Organization. Glossary
of maritime technical terms. London
[c1963] 118 p.   64-56993
   V24 .I5 MRR Alc.

International Chamber of Commerce.
Dictionary of advertising and
distribution, Basel, Verlag für
Recht und Gesellschaft, 1954. 1 v.
(unpaged) 659.103 54-24644
   HF5803 .I58 1954 MRR Alc.

International Commission on Large
Dams. Dictionnaire technique des
barrages. 2. ed. [Paris, 1960?]
380 p.   627.803 61-805
   TC540 .I45 1960 MRR Alc.

International insurance dictionary:
n.p.: European Conference of
Insurance Supervisory Services, 1959]
xxxi, 1083 p.   368.03 61-35675
   HG8025 .I5 MRR Alc.

International Railway Documentation
Bureau. Lexique général des termes
ferroviaires, [2. ed. entièrement
refondue et augm.] Amsterdam, J. H.
De Bussy, 1965. 1357 p.   625.1003
66-87434
   TF9 .I46 1965 MRR Alc.

Jacks, Graham Vernon. Multilingual
vocabulary of soil science. [2d ed.,
rev. Rome] Land & Water Division,
Food and Agriculture Organization of
the United Nations [1960] xxiii, 428
p.   631.403 60-50105
   S591 .J26 1960 MRR Alc.

James, Glenn, ed. Mathematics
dictionary, Multilingual ed.
Princeton, N.J., Van Nostrand [1959]
546 p.   510.3 59-8656
   QA5 .J32 1959 MRR Alc.

Kerchove, René de, baron,
International maritime dictionary:
2d ed. Princeton, N.J., Van Nostrand
[1961] v, 1018 p.   623.803 61-
16272
   V23 .K4 1961 MRR Alc.

Kleczek, Josip. Astronomical
dictionary. [Vyd. 1.] Praha, Nakl.
Československé akademie ved, 1961.
972 p.   62-25391
   QB14 .K55 MRR Alc.

Labarre, E. J. Dictionary and
encyclopedia of paper and paper-
making, 2d ed., rev. and enl.
London, Oxford University Press,
1952. xxi, 488 p.   676.03 53-29414

   TS1085 .L3 1952a MRR Alc.

Lana, Gabriella. Glossary of
geographical names in six languages:
Amsterdam, New York, Elsevier Pub.
Co., 1967. 184 p.   910/.003 66-
25762
   G104.5 .L3 MRR Ref Desk.

Lexicon opthalmologicum; Basel, New
York, S. Karger, 1959. 223 p.
617.703 59-4669
   RE21 .L45 MRR Alc.

Lexikon des Bibliothekswesens.
Leipzig, VEB Verlag für Buch- und
Bibliothekswesen, 1969. xiii, 769 p.
[42.00]   70-423794
   Z1006 .L46 MRR Alc.

Nash, Rose. Multilingual lexicon of
linguistics and philology: English,
Russian, German, French. Coral
Gables, Fla., University of Miami
Press [1968] xxvi, 390 p.   413 68-
31044
   P29 .N34 MRR Alc.

Nijdam, J. Tuinbouwkundig
woordenboek in acht talen. Herziene
en uitgebreide uitg. van de
Woordenlijst voor de tuinbouw in
zeven talen. ['s-Gravenhage,
Staatsdrukkerij- en
Uitgeverijbedrijf; voor alle anderen
landen: Interscience Publishers, New
York] 1961. 504 p.   62-52704
   SB45 .N673 MRR Alc.

Nobel, Albert, Dictionnaire
medical. 5. ed. rev. et augm.
Paris, Masson, 1970 [c1969] xxii,
1328 p. [200.00] 77-93556
   R121 .N6 1970 MRR Alc.

Pisant, Emmanuel. International
dictionary. Paris, Editions
Moderninter [1958] 373 p.   413 58-
26075
   P361 .P5 MRR Alc.

Polec. 2., verb. und erw. Aufl.
Berlin, de Gruyter, 1967. xvi, 1037
p. with map. [DM 48.-]   330/.03 68-
70864
   H40 .P6 1967 MRR Alc.

Raaff, J. J. Index vocabulorum
quadrilingius: verf en vernis, [Den
Haag] Vereniging van Vernis- en
Verffabrikanten in Nederland,
Exportgroep Verf, 1958. 898 p.
667.603 59-27978
   TP934.3 .R2 MRR Alc.

Rae, Kenneth, ed. Lexique
international de termes techniques de
théatre Bruxelles, Elsevier [1959]
139 p.   60-26926
   PN2035 .R3 MRR Alc.

Réau, Louis, Dictionnaire
polyglotte des termes d'art et
d'archeologie. [1. ed.] Paris,
Presses universitaires de France,
1953. viii, 247, [5] p.   703 a 53-
8484
   N33 .R42 MRR Alc.

Sachs, Wolfgang, ed.
Lebensversichegungstechnisches
Worterbuch. Würzburg, K. Thiltsch,
1954. 308 p.   56-16246
   HG8759 .S3 MRR Alc.

FRENCH LANGUAGE--DICTIONARIES-- (Cont.)
Schloms, Irene. Fachwörterbuch für
Programmierer, deutsch, englisch,
französisch. Heidelberg, Hüthig
[1966] 139, 139, 110 p. [DM 28.00]
651.8 67-91557
QA76.15 .S35 MRR Alc.

Schulz, Ernst, lexicographer.
Wörterbuch der Optik und
Feinmechanik. Wiesbaden,
Brandstetter [1960-61] 3 v. a 61-
3700
QC351.2 .S34 MRR Alc.

Servotte, Jozef V., 1903-
Dictionnaire commercial et financier;
2. éd., rev. et augm. Bruxelles,
Éditions Brepols [1960] ix, 955 p.
61-930
HF1002 .S42 1960 MRR Alc.

Six-language dictionary of
automation, electronics and
scientific instruments; London,
Iliffe Books; Englewood Cliffs, N.J.,
Prentice-Hall [1962] 732 p.
621.3803 63-5414
TK7804 .S5 1962 MRR Alc.

Skandinaviska banken, a.-b. Banking
terms: French, German, Italian,
Spanish, Swedish. Stockholm [1964]
65 p. 65-87814
HG151 .S46 MRR Alc.

Smith, William James, A dictionary
of musical terms in four languages.
London, Hutchinson [1961] 195 p.
61-65056
ML108 .S64D5 MRR Alc.

Stowarzyszenie Geodetów Polskich.
Słownik geodezyjny w 5 [i.e. pięciu]
językach: polskim, rosyjskim,
niemieckim, angielskim, francuskim.
Warszawa, Państwowe
Przedsiębiorstwo Wydawn.
Kartograficznych, 1954. xv, 525 p.
55-34784
QB279 .S8 MRR Alc.

Sube, Ralf. Kernphysik und
Kerntechnik; Berlin, Verlag Technik
[1962] 1606 p. 62-2924
QC772 .S9 MRR Alc.

Sube, Ralf. Wörterbuch Physik;
Zürich, H. Deutsch, 1973. 3 v. 74-
320539
QC5 .S9 MRR Alc.

Thompson, Anthony. Vocabularium
bibliothecarii. 2d ed. [Paris]
UNESCO, 1962. 627 p. 63-5650
Z1006 .T47 1962a MRR Alc.

Townsend, Derek. Advertising and
public relations; London, A. Redman
[1964] xvi, 152 p. 65-6026
HF5803 .T6 MRR Alc.

Trollhann, Lilian, comp. Dictionary
of data processing. Amsterdam, New
York, Elsevier Pub. Co., 1964. 300
p. 651 64-8676
QA76.15 .T7 MRR Alc.

Union européenne des experts
comptables économiques et
financiers. Lexique U.E.C. Lexicon.
Dusseldorf, Verlagsbuchhandlung des
Instituts der Wirtschaftsprüfer,
1961. 1 v. (various pagings) 63-
31440
HF5621 .U5 MRR Alc.

Vocabulaire international des termes
d'urbanisme et d'architecture. 1.
éd. Paris, Société de diffusion
des techniques du bâtiment et des
travaux publics, 1970- v. [133F
(v. 1)] 70-860237
NA31 .V6 MRR Alc.

Żytka, Romuald. Geological
dictionary Warszawa, Wydawnictwa
Geologiczne, 1970. 1439 p.
[zł1250.00] 550/.3 72-31794
QE5 .Z9 MRR Alc.

FRENCH LANGUAGE--DICTIONARIES--
PROVENÇAL, MODERN.
Mistral, Frédéric, Lou tresor dóu
Felibrige Reimpression de
l'édition 1879-1886. Osnabrück,
Biblio-Verlag, 1966. 2 v. [DM
360.00] 67-84128
PC3376 .M72 MRR Alc.

FRENCH LANGUAGE--ETYMOLOGY.
Rheims, Maurice. Dictionnaire des
mots sauvages Paris, Larousse, 1969.
605 p. [45.00] 443 79-413814
PC2460 .R45 MRR Alc.

FRENCH LANGUAGE--ETYMOLOGY--
DICTIONARIES.
Bloch, Oscar, Dictionnaire
étymologique de la langue française
5e édition revue et augmentée
Paris, Presses universitaires de
France, 1968. xxxvi, 683 p. [60F]
79-363198
PC2580 .B55 1968 MRR Alc.

Dauzat, Albert, Dictionnaire
étymologique de la langue
française; Paris, Larousse [c1938]
xxxvii, 762 p. 442.03 ac 38-3992
PC2580 .D3 MRR Alc.

Dupré, P. Encyclopédie du bon
français dans l'usage contemporain;
Paris, Éditions de Trévise [1972]
3 v. (2716 p.) [140F (v. 3)] 72-
339663
PC2460 .D88 MRR Alc.

Imbs, Paul. Trésor de la langue
française; Paris, Éditions du
Centre national de la recherche
scientifique, 1971- v. [200F (v.
1)] 72-327996
PC2625 .I4 MRR Alc.

FRENCH LANGUAGE--ETYMOLOGY--NAMES.
Dauzat, Albert, Dictionnaire
étymologique des noms de lieux en
France, Paris, Librairie Larousse
[1963] xii, 738 p. 65-33799
DC14 .D28 MRR Alc.

FRENCH LANGUAGE--GLOSSARIES,
VOCABULARIES, ETC.
Dale, Martin. How to read a French
menu. [1st ed.] New York, Appleton-
Century [1966] 95 p. 641.5944 65-
26808
TX652.7 .D3 MRR Alc.

Levieux, Michel. Beyond the
dictionary in French, London
Cassell, 1967. 156 p. [15/-] 443
67-94064
PC2680 .L4 MRR Alc.

FRENCH LANGUAGE--GLOSSARIES,
VOCABULARIES, ETC.--POLYGLOT.
Lessere, Samuel E. Harlan's foreign
language speak-easy, [3d ed.]
Greenlawn, N.Y., Harlan Publications
[1957] 106 p. 418.24 57-14033
PE1635 .L4 1957 MRR Alc.

FRENCH LANGUAGE--IDIOMS, CORRECTIONS,
ERRORS.
Deak, Étienne. A dictionary of
colorful French slanguage and
colloquialisms, New York, Dutton
[1961, c1959] 209 p. 447.09 61-
16214
PC3741 .D35 1961 MRR Alc.

Thomas, Adolphe V. Dictionnaire des
difficultés de la langue française.
Paris, Larousse [1956] xi, [1], 435
p. a 57-1436
PC2460 .T46 MRR Alc.

FRENCH LANGUAGE--OLD FRENCH--
DICTIONARIES.
Du Cange, Charles Du Fresne, sieur,
Glossarium mediæ et infimæ
latinitatis, Editio nova, aucta
pluribus verbis aliorum scriptorum
Paris, Librairie des sciences et des
arts, 1937-38. 10 v. in 11. 40-
3397
PA2889 .D8 1937 Mrr Alc.

Godefroy, Frédéric Eugène,
Dictionnaire de l'ancienne langue
française, Paris, F. Vieweg, 1881-
1902. 10 v. 03-21764
PC2889 .G6 MRR Alc.

Greimas, Algirdas Julien.
Dictionnaire de l'ancien français
jusqu'au milieu du XIVe siècle,
Paris, Larousse, 1968. xvi, 676 p.
[35.00] 72-403305
PC2889 .G76 MRR Alc.

FRENCH LANGUAGE--SLANG--DICTIONARIES.
Deak, Étienne. A dictionary of
colorful French slanguage and
colloquialisms, New York, Dutton
[1961, c1959] 209 p. 447.09 61-
16214
PC3741 .D35 1961 MRR Alc.

Farmer, John Stephen, Dictionary of
slang & its analogues, past &
present; Rev. ed. New Hyde Park,
N.Y., University Books [1966- v.
427.09 65-24476
PE3721 .F32 MRR Alc.

Leitner, Moses Jonathan, ed.
Dictionary of French and American
slang, New York, Crown Publishers
[1965] xix, 272 p. 447.0903 64-
23818
PC3741 .L58 MRR Alc.

Marks, Joseph. Harrap's French-
English dictionary of slang and
colloquialisms; London, Harrap,
1970. 255 p. [50/-] 447./09/03
78-578889
PC3741 .M33 MRR Alc.

Sandry, Géo. Dictionnaire de
l'argot moderne 9e édition revue,
augmentée et mise à jour. Paris,
Éditions du Dauphin, 1967. 431 p.
[15.00] 74-462536
PC3741 .S35 1967 MRR Alc.

FRENCH LANGUAGE--SPOKEN FRENCH.
Levieux, Michel. Beyond the
dictionary in French, London,
Cassell, 1967. 156 p. [15/-] 443
67-94064
PC2680 .L4 MRR Alc.

FRENCH LANGUAGE--SYNONYMS AND ANTONYMS.
Bénac, Henri, Dictionnaire des
synonymes, Paris, Hachette [1956]
1026 p. a 57-1839
PC2591 .B4 MRR Alc.

FRENCH LANGUAGE--TERMS AND PHRASES.
Dictionnaire français-anglais de
locutions et expressions verbales,
Paris, Larousse [1973] viii, 386 p.
443/.21 74-158187
PC2684 .D48 MRR Alc.

FRENCH LANGUAGE--USAGE.
Dupré, P. Encyclopédie du bon
français dans l'usage contemporain;
Paris, Éditions de Trévise [1972]
3 v. (2716 p.) [140F (v. 3)] 72-
339663
PC2460 .D88 MRR Alc.

FRENCH LANGUAGE--VERB--TABLES, LISTS,
ETC.
Caput, Josette. Dictionnaire des
verbes français, Paris, Larousse
[1969] xvi, 589 p. [37.00] 78-
467900
PC2271 .C28 MRR Alc.

FRENCH LANGUAGE--WORDS--HISTORY.
Dupré, P. Encyclopédie du bon
français dans l'usage contemporain;
Paris, Éditions de Trévise [1972]
3 v. (2716 p.) [140F (v. 3)] 72-
339663
PC2460 .D88 MRR Alc.

Imbs, Paul. Trésor de la langue
française; Paris, Éditions de la
Centre national de la recherche
scientifique, 1971- v. [200F (v.
1)] 72-327996
PC2625 .I4 MRR Alc.

FRENCH LANGUAGE IN CANADA--DICTIONARIES.
Bélisle, Louis Alexandre,
Dictionnaire général de la langue
française au Canada. 2. éd.
Québec, Bélisle [1971] 1390 p.
[112.50F (France)] 72-343538
PC3637 .B4 1971 MRR Alc.

Dictionnaire canadien, français-
anglais, anglais-français. Ed.
abrégée. [Toronto] McClelland and
Stewart [1962] xxxiv, 861 p. 62-
48993
PC2640 .D44 MRR Alc.

FRENCH LITERATURE.
Pingaud, Bernard, ed. Écrivains
d'aujourd'hui, 1940-1960; Paris, B.
Grasset [1960] 535 p. 61-2755
PQ305 .P5 MRR Alc.

FRENCH LITERATURE--16TH CENTURY--
BIBLIOGRAPHY.
Cioranescu, Alexandre. Bibliographie
de la littérature française du
seizième siècle. Paris, C.
Klincksieck, 1959. xiv, 745 p. a
60-3660
Z2172 .C5 MRR Alc.

FRENCH LITERATURE--17TH CENTURY--
BIBLIOGRAPHY.
Cioranescu, Alexandre. Bibliographie
de la littérature française du dix-
septième siècle. Paris, Éditions
du Centre national de la recherche
scientifique, 1965-66. 3 v. (2283
p.) [80 F (v. 1) 110 F (v. 2) 100 F
(v. 3)] 011 66-71677
Z2172 .C52 MRR Alc.

FRENCH LITERATURE--17TH CENTURY--
HISTORY AND CRITICISM--BIBLIOGRAPHY.
Modern Language Association of
America. French III. Bibliography of
French seventeenth century studies;
no. 1- 1952/53- n.p.
Z2172 .M6 MRR Alc Full set 54-35632

FRENCH LITERATURE--18TH CENTURY--
BIBLIOGRAPHY.
Cioranescu, Alexandre. Bibliographie
de la littérature française du dix-
huitième siècle ... Paris,
Éditions du Centre national de la
recherche scientifique, 1969- v.
[120.00 (v. 1)] 70-453192
Z2172 .C48 MRR Alc.

FRENCH LITERATURE--19TH CENTURY--
BIBLIOGRAPHY.
Talvart, Hector. Bibliographie des
auteurs modernes de langue
française, Paris, Éditions de la
Chronique des lettres françaises,
1928- v. 29-24892
Z2173 .T3 MRR Alc.

FRENCH LITERATURE--19TH CENTURY--BIO-
BIBLIOGRAPHY.
Dreher, S. Bibliographie de la
littérature française, 1930-1939,
Lille, Giard, 1948- v. a 49-
1233
Z2171 .D7 MRR Alc.

FRENCH LITERATURE--19TH CENTURY-- (Cont.)
Drevet, Marguerite L. Bibliographie
de la littérature française, 1940-
1949: Genève, Libraire E. Droz,
1954 [i.e. 1954-55] xvi, 644 p.   55-
949
Z2171 .D73 MRR Alc.

FRENCH LITERATURE--20TH CENTURY--
BIBLIOGRAPHY.
Talvart, Hector. Bibliographie des
auteurs modernes de langue
française, Paris, Éditions de la
Chronique des lettres françaises,
1928-   v.   29-24892
Z2173 .T3 MRR Alc.

United States. Library of Congress.
Acquisitions Dept. European imprints
for the war years Washington, 1945-
46. 3 v.   015.4 45-37835
Z663.76 .E8 MRR Alc.

FRENCH LITERATURE--20TH CENTURY--BIO-
BIBLIOGRAPHY.
Dictionnaire national des
contemporains, Paris, Les Éditions
Lajeunesse, 1936- v.   920.044
37-8680
CT1013 .D52 MRR Biog.

Dreher, S. Bibliographie de la
littérature française, 1930-1939,
Lille, Giard, 1948- v.   a 49-
1233
Z2171 .D7 MRR Alc.

Drevet, Marguerite L. Bibliographie
de la littérature française, 1940-
1949: Genève, Libraire E. Droz,
1954 [i.e. 1954-55] xvi, 644 p.   55-
949
Z2171 .D73 MRR Alc.

Pingaud, Bernard, ed. Écrivains
d'aujourd'hui, 1940-1960; Paris, B.
Grasset [1960] 535 p.   61-2755
PQ305 .P5 MRR Alc.

FRENCH LITERATURE--20TH CENTURY--
HISTORY AND CRITICISM.
Boisdeffre, Pierre de. Une Histoire
vivante de la littérature
d'aujourd'hui ... 7 editon
entièrement refondue et mise à
jour, Paris, Librairie Académique
Perrin, 1968. 1104 p. [35 F]
840.9/008/1 68-107002
PQ305 .B56 1968 MRR Alc.

Girard, Marcel. Guide illustré de
la littérature française moderne.
Nouvelle édition mise à jour.
Paris, Seghers, 1968. 408 p.
[18.00]   71-397781
PQ305 .G5 1968b MRR Alc.

FRENCH LITERATURE--20TH CENTURY--
HISTORY AND CRITICISM--BIBLIOGRAPHY.
French VII bibliography; v. [1]-
(1-   ); 1949- New York, French
Institute [etc.] 49-3084
Z2173 .F7 MRR Alc Full set

French XX bibliography. v. 5-   (no.
21-   ); 1969- New York, French
Institute. 016.8409 77-648803
Z2171 .F7 MRR Alc Full set

FRENCH LITERATURE--ADDRESSES, ESSAYS,
LECTURES.
United States. Library of Congress.
Gertrude Clarke Whittall Poetry and
Literature Fund. French and German
letters today; Washington, Reference
Dept., Library of Congress, 1960. v,
53 p.   840.9   60-60062
Z663.293 .F7 MRR Alc.

FRENCH LITERATURE--AFRICAN AUTHORS--BIO-
BIBLIOGRAPHY.
Zell, Hans M. A reader's guide to
African literature, New York,
Africana Pub. Corp. [1971] xxi, 218
p.   809/.8867 76-83165
PR9798 .Z4 MRR Alc.

FRENCH LITERATURE--AFRICAN AUTHORS--
HISTORY AND CRITICISM--BIBLIOGRAPHY.
Zell, Hans M. A reader's guide to
African literature, New York,
Africana Pub. Corp. [1971] xxi, 218
p.   809/.8867 76-83165
PR9798 .Z4 MRR Alc.

FRENCH LITERATURE--BELGIAN AUTHORS--
BIBLIOGRAPHY.
Culot, Jean Marie. Bibliographie des
écrivains français de Belgique,
1881- Bruxelles, Palais des
académies, 1958- v.   a 59-985
Z2413 .C8 MRR Alc.

FRENCH LITERATURE--BIBLIOGRAPHY.
Cabeen, David Clark, ed. A critical
bibliography of French literature.
[Syracuse, N.Y.] Syracuse university
press, 1847- v.   016.84 47-3282

Z2171 .C3 MRR Alc.

Giraud, Jeanne. Manuel de
bibliographie littéraire pour les
XVIe, XVIIe et XVIIIe siècles
français, 1936-1945. Paris, Nizer,
1956. xiii, 270 p.   a 57-1834
Z2171 .G5 MRR Alc.

Langlois, Pierre, of Paris. Guide
bibliographique des études
littéraires Paris, Hachette [1958]
255 p.   016.84 59-41738
Z2171 .L17 MRR Alc.

Lanson, Gustave, Manuel
bibliographique de la littérature
française moderne, Nouv. ed. rev.
et cor. Paris, Hachette, 1931.
xxxii, 1820 p.   016.84 39-30135
Z2171 .L22 1931 MRR Alc.

La Librairie française: les livres
de l'année. 1933/45- Paris, Cercle
de la librairie. 48-11426
Z2161 .L695 MRR Alc Full set

Lorenz, Otto Henri, Catalogue
général de la librairie française.
Paris, 1867-1945. 34 v.   02-7509
Z2161 .L86 MRR Alc.

Quérard, Joseph Marie, La France
littéraire, Paris, Firmin Didot
père et Fils, 1827-64. 12 v.   02-
3270
Z2161 .Q4 MRR Alc.

Quérard, Joseph Marie, La
littérature française contemporaine.
Paris, Daguin frères, 1842-57. 6
v. 02-3271
Z2161 .Q41 MRR Alc.

Talvart, Hector. Bibliographie des
auteurs modernes de langue
française, Paris, Éditions de la
Chronique des lettres françaises,
1928- v.   29-24892
Z2173 .T3 MRR Alc.

FRENCH LITERATURE--BIBLIOGRAPHY--
CATALOGS.
Paris. Bibliothèque nationale.
Departement des imprimes.
Catalogue général des livres
imprimes de la Bibliothèque
nationale. Paris, Imprimerie
nationale, 1897-19 v.   01-5989
Z927 .P2 MRR Alc (Dk 33)

FRENCH LITERATURE--BIBLIOGRAPHY--EARLY.
Jaffe, Adrian H. Bibliography of
French literature in American
magazines in the 18th century. [East
Lansing] Michigan State College
Press, 1951. vii, 27 p.   016.84 51-
4374
Z2172 .J3 MRR Alc.

FRENCH LITERATURE--BIBLIOGRAPHY--FIRST
EDITIONS.
Le Petit, Jules, Bibliographie des
principales editons originales
d'écrivains français du XVe au
XVIIIe siècle; Paris, Maison
Quantin, 1888. 2 p. l., vii, [1],
383 (i.e. 583), [1]p.   04-15718
Z2174 .F5L5 MRR Alc.

FRENCH LITERATURE--BIBLIOGRAPHY--
PERIODICALS.
Biblio. 1934- Paris. 015.44 36-
3965
Z2165 .B565   MRR Alc Latest edition

Bibliographie de la littérature
française moderne (16.-20.
siècles). Paris, Librairie A.
Colin. 67-40990
  Began publication in 1962.
Z2171 .B55 MRR Alc Full set

FRENCH LITERATURE--BIO-BIBLIOGRAPHY.
Dictionnaire des lettres françaises.
Paris, A. Fayard, 1951- [v. 1, 1964]
v.   840.3 52-2304
PQ41 .D53 MRR Alc.

Girard, Marcel. Guide illustré de
la littérature française moderne.
Nouvelle édition mise à jour.
Paris, Seghers, 1968. 408 p.
[18.00]   71-397781
PQ305 .G5 1968b MRR Alc.

Harvey, Paul, Sir, ed. The Oxford
companion to French literature.
Oxford, Clarendon Press, 1959. x,
771 p.   840.3 58-2367
PQ41 .H3 MRR Alc.

Malignon, Jean, Dictionnaire des
écrivains français, [Paris]
Editions du Seuil [1971] 552 p.
[49.50F]   72-304186
PQ41 .M3 MRR Biog.

Thieme, Hugo Paul, Bibliographie de
la littérature française de 1800 à
1930, Paris, E. Droz, 1933. 3 v.
015.44 33-11487
Z2171 .T43 1933 MRR Alc.

FRENCH LITERATURE--DICTIONARIES.
Braun, Sidney David, ed. Dictionary
of French literature. New York,
Philosophical Library [1958] xiii,
362 p.   840.3 58-59407
PQ41 .B7 MRR Alc.

Dictionnaire des lettres françaises.
Paris, A. Fayard, 1951- [v. 1, 1964]
v.   840.3 52-2304
PQ41 .D53 MRR Alc.

Harvey, Paul, Sir, ed. The Oxford
companion to French literature.
Oxford, Clarendon Press, 1959. x,
771 p.   840.3 59-2367
PQ41 .H3 MRR Alc.

FRENCH LITERATURE--HAITIAN AUTHORS--
BIBLIOGRAPHY.
Bissainthe, Max. Dictionnaire de
bibliographie haïtienne.
Washington, Scarecrow Press, 1951.
x, 1052 p.   51-12164
Z1531 .B5 MRR Alc.

FRENCH LITERATURE--HISTORY AND
CRITICISM.
Adam, Antoine. Littérature
française ... Paris, Larousse, 1967-
68. 2 v.   840.9 68-85663
PQ101 .A3 MRR Alc.

A Literary history of France.
London, Benn; New York, Barnes &
Noble, 1967-   v.   [63/- (v. 2) 70/-
(v. 3) 63/- (v. 4) 50/- (v. 5)] 67-
87148
PQ103 .L5 MRR Alc.

Mason, Germaine. A concise survey of
French literature. New York,
Philosophical Library [1959] 344 p.
840.9 59-2218
PQ119 .M3 MRR Alc.

FRENCH LITERATURE--HISTORY AND
CRITICISM--BIBLIOGRAPHY.
Bibliographie de la littérature
française moderne (16.-20.
siècles). Paris, Librairie A.
Colin. 67-40990
  Began publication in 1962.
Z2171 .B55 MRR Alc Full set

Bibliographie der französischen
Literaturwissenschaft. Bd. 1-
1956/58- Frankfurt am Main, V.
Klostermann. 60-43852
Z2171 .B56 MRR Alc Full set

Cioranescu, Alexandre. Bibliographie
de la littérature française du dix-
huitième siècle ... Paris,
Éditions du Centre national de la
recherche scientifique, 1969- v.
[120.00 (v. 1)]   70-453182
Z2172 .C48 MRR Alc.

Dreher, S. Bibliographie de la
littérature française, 1930-1939,
Lille, Giard, 1948- v.   a 49-
1233
Z2171 .D7 MRR Alc.

Drevet, Marguerite L. Bibliographie
de la littérature française, 1940-
1949: Genève, Libraire E. Droz,
1954 [i.e. 1954-55] xvi, 644 p.   55-
949
Z2171 .D73 MRR Alc.

Lanson, Gustave, Manuel
bibliographique de la littérature
française moderne, Nouv. ed. rev.
et cor. Paris, Hachette, 1931.
xxxii, 1820 p.   016.84 39-30135
Z2171 .L22 1931 MRR Alc.

Osburn, Charles B. Research and
reference guide to French studies,
Metuchen, N. J., Scarecrow Press,
1968. 517 p. [$11.50] 016.44 68-
12638
Z2175.A2 O8 MRR Ref Desk.

Osburn, Charles B., comp. The
present state of French studies: a
collection of research reviews.
Metuchen, N.J., Scarecrow Press,
1971. 995 p.   840.8 78-149990
PQ51 .O8 MRR Alc.

The Romantic movement bibliography,
1936-1970: [Ann Arbor, Mich.]
Pierian Press, 1973. 7 v. (xiii,
3289 p.) 016.809/894 77-172773
Z6514.R6 R65 MRR Alc.

Talvart, Hector. Bibliographie des
auteurs modernes de langue
française, Paris, Éditions de la
Chronique des lettres françaises,
1928- v.   29-24892
Z2173 .T3 MRR Alc.

Thieme, Hugo Paul, Bibliographie de
la littérature française de 1800 à
1930, Paris, E. Droz, 1933. 3 v.
015.44 33-11487
Z2171 .T43 1933 MRR Alc.

FRENCH LITERATURE--OLD FRENCH--
BIBLIOGRAPHY.
Bossuat, Robert, Manuel
bibliographique de la littérature
française du Moyen Age. Melun,
Librairie d'Argences, 1951. xxxiv,
638 p. 016.84 51-5797
Z2172 .B7 MRR Alc.

FRENCH LITERATURE--OLD FRENCH--HISTORY
AND CRITICISM--BIBLIOGRAPHY.
Bossuat, Robert, Manuel
bibliographique de la littérature
française du Moyen Age. Melun,
Librairie d'Argences, 1951. xxxiv,
638 p. 016.84 51-5797
Z2172 .B7 MRR Alc.

FRENCH LITERATURE--OUTLINES, SYLLABI, ETC.
Bornecque, Pierre Henry. La France et sa littérature, 3e édition revue et corrigée. Lyon, A. Desvigne, 1968. 896 p. [46F] 72-367695
    PQ135 .B57 1968 MRR Alc.

FRENCH LITERATURE--STUDY AND TEACHING--ADDRESSES, ESSAYS, LECTURES.
Osburn, Charles B., ed. The present state of French studies: a collection of research reviews. Metuchen, N.J., Scarecrow Press, 1971. 885 p. 840.8 78-149990
    PQ51 .O8 MRR Alc.

FRENCH LITERATURE--TRANSLATIONS INTO ENGLISH--BIBLIOGRAPHY.
Parks, George Bruner. The Romance literatures. New York, F. Ungar Pub. Co. [1970] 2 v. [$45.00] 016.84009 70-98341
    Z7033.T7E65 MRR Alc.

FRENCH LITERATURE--TRANSLATIONS INTO GERMAN--BIBLIOGRAPHY.
Fromm, Hans. Bibliographie deutscher Übersetzungen aus dem Französischen, 1700-1948. Baden-Baden, Verlag für Kunst und Wissenschaft, 1950- v. 51-24434
    Z2174.T7 F7 MRR Alc.

FRENCH NEWSPAPERS--BIBLIOGRAPHY.
Répertoire de la presse et des publications périodiques françaises. [1.]- ed.; 1957- Paris, La Documentation française. a 58-3274
    Z6956.F8 R39 MRR Alc Latest edition

FRENCH NEWSPAPERS--DIRECTORIES.
La Presse française; 1965- [Paris, Hachette] 65-80951
    Z6956.F8 P7 MRR Alc Latest edition

FRENCH NEWSPAPERS--INDEXES.
Paris. Université. Institut français de presse. Section d'histoire. Tables du Journal Le Temps. Paris, Éditions du Centre national de la recherche scientifique, 1966- v. 074.43/6 67-42357
    AI21 .T375 MRR Alc.

FRENCH PAINTING
see Painting, French

FRENCH PERIODICALS.
Coston, Henry. Dictionnaire de la politique française. Paris, Publications H. Coston (Diffusion: la Librairie française) 1967- v. [90.00F (v. 1) varies] 320.9/44 67-99935
    DC55 .C72 MRR Alc.

FRENCH PERIODICALS--BIBLIOGRAPHY.
Paris. Bibliothèque nationale. Département des périodiques. Répertoire national des annuaires français, 1958-1968, Paris, Bibliothèque nationale, Éditions Mercure, 1970. 811 p. 76-501237
    Z2174.Y4 P29 MRR Alc.

Répertoire de la presse et des publications périodiques françaises. [1.]- ed.; 1957- Paris, La Documentation française. a 58-3274
    Z6956.F8 R39 MRR Alc Latest edition

FRENCH PERIODICALS--DIRECTORIES.
Annuaire de la presse française et étrangère. 1.- ed.; 1880- Paris. 06-44929
    Z6956.F8 A6 MRR Alc Latest edition

Association des universités entièrement ou partiellement de langue française. Catalogue des publications périodiques universitaires de langue française. [2. ed. Montréal, 1969] viii, 150 p. 77-478508
    Z6944.S3 A7 1969 MRR Alc.

La Presse française; 1965- [Paris, Hachette] 65-80951
    Z6956.F8 P7 MRR Alc Latest edition

FRENCH PERIODICALS--INDEXES.
Talvart, Hector. Bibliographie des auteurs modernes de langue française, Paris, Éditions de la Chronique des lettres françaises, 1928- v. 29-24892
    Z2173 .T3 MRR Alc.

FRENCH PHILOLOGY--BIBLIOGRAPHY.
Osburn, Charles B. Research and reference guide to French studies, Metuchen, N.J., Scarecrow Press, 1968. 517 p. [$11.50] 016.44 68-12638
    Z2175.A2 O8 MRR Ref Desk.

FRENCH POETRY.
The Oxford book of French verse. 2d ed., Oxford, Clarendon Press, 1957. 641 p. 57-13844
    PQ1165 .O84 1957 MRR Alc.

Pompidou, Georges Jean Raymond, ed. Anthologie de la poésie française. Paris, Le Livre de poche, 1968. 541 p. [3.60] 73-452259
    PQ1165 .P78 1968 MRR Alc.

FRENCH POETRY--19TH CENTURY.
Flores, Angel, ed. An anthology of French poetry from Nerval to Valéry in English translation; New rev. ed. Garden City, N.Y., Doubleday, 1962. 456 p. 841.7082 62-10456
    PQ1170.E6 F5 1962 MRR Alc.

FRENCH POETRY--20TH CENTURY.
Flores, Angel, ed. An anthology of French poetry from Nerval to Valéry in English translation; New rev. ed. Garden City, N.Y., Doubleday, 1962. 456 p. 841.7082 62-10456
    PQ1170.E6 F5 1962 MRR Alc.

Fowlie, Wallace, ed. and tr. Mid-century French poets; New York, Twayne [1955] 273 p. 841.91082 55-830
    PQ1184 .F6 MRR Alc.

FRENCH POETRY--20TH CENTURY--DICTIONARIES.
Rousselot, Jean, Dictionnaire de la poésie française contemporaine. Paris, Larousse, 1968. 256 p. [9.90F] 841.9/103 68-106149
    PQ41 .R6 MRR Biog.

FRENCH POETRY--HISTORY AND CRITICISM.
Brereton, Geoffrey. An introduction to the French poets: Villon to the present day. 2nd ed. London, Methuen, 1973. xii, 320 p. [£3.80] 841/.009 73-162190
    PQ401 .B7 1973 MRR Alc.

FRENCH POETRY--TRANSLATIONS INTO ENGLISH.
Conder, Alan, comp. and tr. Cassell's anthology of French poetry. London, Cassell [1950] 388 p. 841.082 51-7414
    PQ1170.E6 C6 1950 MRR Alc.

Flores, Angel, ed. An anthology of French poetry from Nerval to Valéry in English translation; New rev. ed. Garden City, N.Y., Doubleday, 1962. 456 p. 841.7082 62-10456
    PQ1170.E6 F5 1962 MRR Alc.

FRESH-WATER FAUNA.
see also Aquariums

FRESHMEN, COLLEGE
see College freshmen

FREUD, SIGMUND, 1856-1939.
Freud, Sigmund, Abstracts of The standard edition of the complete psychological works of Sigmund Freud. New York, J. Aronson [c1973] 315 p. [$15.00] 150/.19/52 mrr01-78
    BF173 .F6253 Suppl. 3 MRR Alc.

Laplanche, Jean. The language of psycho-analysis, New York, Norton [1974, c1973] xv, 510 p. [$14.95] 616.8/917/03 73-18418
    RC437 .L313 1974 MRR Alc.

FRIARS.
see also Monasticism and religious orders

FRIENDLY SOCIETIES--UNITED STATES--DIRECTORIES.
Fraternal monitor. Combined statistics and consolidated chart of fraternal societies. 1958- Indianapolis. 58-45886
    HG9226 .F72 MRR Alc Latest edition

FRIENDSHIP.
Cicero, Marcus Tullius. De senectute, De amicitia, De divinatione, Cambridge, Mass., Harvard University Press; London, W. Heinemann, 1938. vii, 567 p. mrr01-1
    PA6156.C5 A2 1938d MRR Alc.

FRIESLAND--REGISTERS.
Provinciale almanak van Friesland. Bolsward, A. J. Osinga. 51-11137
    JN5999.F7 A4 MRR Alc Bind/Label

FRONTIER AND PIONEER LIFE.
see also Pioneers

FRONTIER AND PIONEER LIFE--BIBLIOGRAPHY.
Rader, Jesse Lee, South of forty, [1st ed.] Norman, Univ. of Oklahoma Press, 1947. xi, 336 p. 016.976 47-5360
    Z1251.S83 R3 MRR Alc.

FRONTIER AND PIONEER LIFE--UNITED STATES.
Billington, Ray Allen, America's frontier heritage. [New York, Holt, Rinehart and Winston [1966] xiv, 302 p. 917.303 66-13289
    E179.5 .B62 MRR Alc.

Billington, Ray Allen, ed. The frontier thesis: valid interpretation of American history? New York, Holt, Rinehart and Winston [1966] 122 p. 973.01 66-21640
    E179.5 .B625 MRR Alc.

Dunbar, Seymour. A history of travel in America, New York, Tudor publishing company, 1937. L p., 2 l., 1530, [1] p. 385.0973 38-7081
    HE203 .D77 1937 MRR Alc.

Gabriel, Ralph Henry, The lure of the frontier; New Haven, Yale university press; [etc., etc.] 1929. 3 p. l., 327 p. 29-22308
    E178.5 .P2 vol. 2 MRR Alc.

Gabriel, Ralph Henry, Toilers of land and sea, New Haven, Yale university press; [etc., etc.] 1926. 3 p. l., 340 p. 26-4275
    E178.5 .P2 vol. 3 MRR Alc.

Klose, Nelson, A concise study guide to the American frontier. Lincoln, University of Nebraska Press, 1964. xi, 269 p. 973 64-15180
    E179.5 .K55 MRR Alc.

Sweet, William Warren, ed. The Baptists, 1783-1830, New York, H. Holt and company [c1931] ix, 652 p. 286.173 31-26855
    BX6235 .S8 MRR Alc.

FRONTIER AND PIONEER LIFE--UNITED STATES--BIBLIOGRAPHY.
Vail, Robert William Glenroi, The voice of the old frontier. Philadelphia, University of Pennsylvania Press, 1949. xii, 492 p. 016.9173 49-50000
    Z1249.F9 V3 MRR Alc.

Van Derhoof, Jack Warner. A bibliography of novels related to American frontier and colonial history, Troy, N.Y., Whitston Pub. Co., 1971. xii, 501 p. 016.813/03 70-150333
    Z1231.F4 V3 MRR Alc.

FRONTIER AND PIONEER LIFE--WEST--BIBLIOGRAPHY.
Adams, Ramon Frederick, Six-guns and saddle leather; New ed., [Norman, University of Oklahoma Press, 1969] xxv, 808 p. [19.95] 016.3641 69-16729
    Z1251.W5 A3 1969 MRR Alc.

Soliday, George W., A descriptive check list, together with short title index, describing almost 7500 items of western Americana: [Reprinted with corrections] New York, Antiquarian Press, 1960. 1 v. (various pagings) 016.97 61-45337
    Z1251.W5 S62 MRR Alc.

Wagner, Henry Raup, The Plains and the Rockies; 3d ed. Columbus, Ohio, Long's College Book Co., 1953. 601 p. 016.9178 53-2473
    Z1251.W5 W2 1953 MRR Alc.

Wallace, William Swilling. Bibliography of published bibliographies on the history of the eleven Western States, 1941-1947; Albuquerque, N.M., 1953 [i.e. 1954] 224-233 p. 016.016978 55-62545
    Z1251.W5 W25 MRR Alc.

FRONTIER THESIS.
Billington, Ray Allen, ed. The frontier thesis: valid interpretation of American history? New York, Holt, Rinehart and Winston [1966] 122 p. 973.01 66-21640
    E179.5 .B625 MRR Alc.

FROST, ROBERT, 1874-1963.
Untermeyer, Louis, Robert Frost: a backward look. Washington, Reference Dept., Library of Congress; [for sale by the Superintendent of Documents, U.S. Govt. Print. Off.] 1964. v, 40 p. 64-60031
    Z663.293 .F74 MRR Alc.

FROST, ROBERT, 1874-1963--CONCORDANCES.
Lathem, Edward Connery. A concordance to The poetry of Robert Frost. New York, Holt Information Systems [1971] x, 640 p. [$30.00] 811/.5/2 75-177494
    PS3511.R94 Z49 1971 MRR Alc.

FROST.
see also Ice

FROZEN FOOD
see Food, Frozen

FROZEN FOODS INDUSTRY--UNITED STATES--DIRECTORIES.
Directory of wholesale distributors of frozen foods. New York, Quick Frozen Foods. 664.85058 52-65843
HD9453 .D5 MRR Alc Latest edition

FRUIT CULTURE--CANADA.
Shoemaker, James Sheldon, Small-fruit culture; 3d ed. New York, McGraw-Hill [1955] 447 p. 634.7 54-11318
SB355 .S58 1958 MRR Alc.

FRUIT-CULTURE--UNITED STATES.
Shoemaker, James Sheldon, Small-fruit culture; 3d ed. New York, McGraw-Hill [1955] 447 p. 634.7 54-11318
SB355 .S58 1958 MRR Alc.

FRUIT JUICES.
Tressler, Donald Kiteley, Fruit and vegetable juice processing technology, 2d ed. Westport, Conn., Avi Pub. Co., 1971. xi, 486 p. 663/.63 75-138801
TP562 .T72 1971 MRR Alc.

FRUIT TRADE--DIRECTORIES.
Fruit trades world directory. London, Haymarket. 338.1/7/4025 75-648560
HD9240.3 .F76 MRR Alc Latest edition

FRUIT TRADE--GREAT BRITAIN--DIRECTORIES.
Castle's guide to the fruit, flower, vegetable, & allied trades. London, Castle Pub. Co. 61-26296
HD9251.3 .C3 MRR Alc Latest edition

FRUIT WINES.
see also Wine and wine making

FUEL--STATISTICS.
Darmstadter, Joel, Energy in the world economy; Baltimore, Published for Resources for the Future by the Johns Hopkins Press [1971] x, 876 p. [$22.50] 333.9 70-155848
HD9540.4 D37 MRR Alc.

FUEL TRADE.
see also Coal trade

FUEL TRADE--STATISTICS.
Organization for Economic Cooperation and Development. Statistics of energy, 1953-1967. Paris, 1969. 265 p. 333.8 71-459605
HD9540.4 .O73 1969 MRR Alc.

FULL EMPLOYMENT POLICIES.
see also Employment agencies

see also Labor supply

see also Unemployed

FULLAM, WILLIAM FREELAND, 1855-1926--MANUSCRIPTS.
United States. Library of Congress. Manuscript Division. Colby Mitchell Chester, William Freeland Fullam, Samuel McGowan, Henry Croskey Mustin: a register of their papers in the Library of Congress. Washington, Library of Congress, 1973. iii, 4, 6, 7, 5 p. 016.359 73-2939
Z663.34 .C48 MRR Alc.

FUND RAISING.
Dermer, Joseph. How to raise funds from foundations. New York, Public Service Materials Center [1968] 55 p. 361.7/3 68-5018
AS911.A2 D4 MRR alc.

Grantsmanship; money and how to get it. Orange, N.J., Academic Media [1973] 27 p. [$5.00] 001.4/4 72-13214
HG174 .G72 MRR Alc.

Leibert, Edwin Reisinger, Handbook of special events for nonprofit organizations. New York, Association Press [1972] 224 p. [$12.95] 361.7/3 75-129437
HV41 .L415 MRR Alc.

Pritchard, J. Harris. Complete fund-earning guide; [New York, A.J.L. Pub. Co; distributed by Grosset & Dunlap, 1967] 416 p. 361.7/3 67-24202
HV41 .P7 MRR Alc.

FUND RAISING--NEW YORK (STATE)--DIRECTORIES.
Charitable organizations, professional fund raisers, and professional solicitors. [1st]-ed.; 1955- Albany, N.Y. 361.7/3/025747 a 56-9301
HV89 .N44 MRR Alc Latest edition

FUNDAMENTAL EDUCATION (COMMUNITY DEVELOPMENT)
see Community development

FUNDAMENTALISM.
Gasper, Louis. The fundamentalist movement. The Hague, Mouton [1963] vii, 181 p. 230 63-24282
BT82.2 .G3 MRR Alc.

FUNDS
see Finance

FUNERAL RITES AND CEREMONIES.
Habenstein, Robert Wesley, Funeral customs the world over [1st ed.] Milwaukee, Bulfin Printers, 1960. 973 p. 393 60-53002
GT3150 .H28 MRR Alc.

FUNERAL RITES AND CEREMONIES--UNITED STATES.
Mossman, B. C. The last salute: civil and military funerals, 1921-1969. Washington, Dept. of the Army; [for sale by the Supt. of Docs., U.S. Govt. Print. Off.] 1971 [i.e. 1972] xxii, 428 p. [$5.75] 393/.0973 77-606843
GT3203 .M67 MRR Alc.

FUNGOUS DISEASES
see Medical mycology

FURER, JULIUS AUGUSTUS--MANUSCRIPTS--CATALOGS.
United States. Library of Congress. Manuscript Division. Claude Charles Bloch, Julius Augustus Furer, John Franklin Shafroth, William Harrison Standley: a register of their papers in the Library of Congress. Washington, Library of Congress, 1973. iii, 6, 10, 4, 11, p. 016.359 73-4374
Z663.34 .B55 MRR Alc.

FURNITURE.
see also Art objects

Boger, Louise Ade. House & garden's antiques: questions & answers. New York, Simon and Schuster [1973] viii, 429 p. [$9.95] 745.1 73-180214
NK1125 .B56 MRR Alc.

Hinckley, F. Lewis. A directory of antique furniture: New York, Crown Publishers [1953] xxxiv p., 355 p. of illus. 749 52-10776
NK2260 .H5 MRR Alc.

Hinckley, F. Lewis. Directory of the historic cabinet woods. New York, Crown Publishers [1960] 186 p. 749 59-14030
NK2260 .H52 MRR Alc.

FURNITURE--COLLECTORS AND COLLECTING.
Baker, Mary Gladys Steel, A dictionary of antiques. Edinburgh, W. & R. Chambers [1953] 263 p. 708.051 54-4571
NK1125 .B33 1953 MRR Alc.

Ormsbee, Thomas Hamilton, Field guide to American Victorian furniture. [1st ed.] Boston, Little, Brown [1952] 428 p. 749.212 52-9095
NK2407 .O7 MRR Alc.

Reif, Rita. The antique collector's guide to styles and prices. New York, Hawthorn Books [1970] xii, 276 p. [12.95] 749/.075 75-102019
NK1125 .R37 MRR Alc.

FURNITURE--DICTIONARIES.
Aronson, Joseph, The new encyclopedia of furniture. New York, Crown Publishers [1967] ix, 484 p. 749/.03 67-9815
NK2205 .A7 1967 MRR Alc.

Gloag, John, A short dictionary of furniture. Revised and enlarged ed. London, Allen & Unwin, 1969. 813 p. [6/6/-] 749/.03 79-389777
NK2205 .G55 1969 MRR Alc.

Studio dictionary of design & decoration. Rev. and enl. ed.] New York, Viking Press [1973] 538 p. [$28.50] 745.4/03 73-1024
NK1165 .S78 1973 MRR Alc.

FURNITURE--DIRECTORIES.
Furnishing trade directory and buyer's guide. London, Trade Chronicles Limited [etc.] 58-29799
TS842 .F68 MRR Alc Latest edition

FURNITURE--HISTORY.
Boger, Louise Ade. The complete guide to furniture styles. Enl. ed. New York, Scribner [1969] xii, 500 p. [17.50] 749.2 73-85267
NK2270 .B63 1969 MRR Alc.

Boger, Louise Ade. Furniture past & present; [1st ed.] Garden City, N.Y., Doubleday, 1966. 520 p. 749.2 66-20938
NK2270 .B64 MRR Alc.

Hayward, Helena, ed. World furniture; London, Hamlyn, 1969. 320 p. [£3.45] 749.2 74-171438
NK2270 .H3 1969 MRR Alc.

Molesworth, Hender Delves, Three centuries of furniture in color New York, Viking Press [1972] 328 p. [$19.95] 749.2/03 72-81670
NK2350 .M64 1972 MRR Alc.

Schmitz, Hermann, The encyclopaedia of furniture; London, A. Zwemmer, 1956. liii, 320 p. of illus. 749.09 57-1862
NK2270 .S363 1956 MRR Alc.

Wanscher, Ole. The art of furniture: London, Allen & Unwin, 1968. 420 p. (chiefly illus. (incl. 12 col.), coat of arms, facsims., plans, ports). [£6/-/-] 749.2 68-101488
NK2270 .W313 1968 MRR Alc.

FURNITURE, AMERICAN.
Bjerkoe, Ethel Hall. The cabinetmakers of America, [1st ed.] Garden City, N.Y., Doubleday, 1957. xvii, 252 p. 749.211 57-7278
NK2406 .B55 MRR Alc.

Hudson, William Norman. Antiques at auction. South Brunswick, A. S. Barnes [1972] 403 p. [$20.00] 338.4/3745/109973 76-111646
N6507 .H82 MRR Alc.

Kirk, John T. Early American furniture: how to recognize, evaluate, buy & care for the most beautiful pieces--high-style, country, primitive & rustic; [1st pbk. ed.] [New York] Knopf; [distributed by Random House] 1974 [c1970] x, 208 p. 749.2/13 73-21822
NK2406 .K56 1974 MRR Alc.

Ormsbee, Thomas Hamilton, Field guide to American Victorian furniture. [1st ed.] Boston, Little, Brown [1952] 428 p. 749.212 52-9095
NK2407 .O7 MRR Alc.

FURNITURE, ENGLISH.
Edwards, Ralph, Georgian cabinet-makers, c. 1700-1800, New and rev. (i.e. 3d) ed. London, Country Life ltd., 1955. 247 p. 749.223 55-13858
NK2529 .E3 1955 MRR Alc.

Heal, Ambrose, Sir, The London furniture makers, from the Restoration to the Victorian Era, 1660-1840; London, Batsford [1953] xx, 276 p. 749.222 54-503
NK2529 .H45 MRR Alc.

FURNITURE, ENGLISH--DICTIONARIES.
Macquoid, Percy, The dictionary of English furniture. [2d ed.] rev. and enl. London, Country Life Limited [1954] 3 v. 54-3800
NK2529 .M32 MRR Alc.

FURNITURE DESIGN--HISTORY.
Honour, Hugh. Cabinet makers and furniture designers. [1st American ed.] New York, Putnam [1969] 320 p. [22.50] 749.2 77-77548
NK2350 .H6 1969 MRR Alc.

FURNITURE FINISHING.
Pattou, Albert Brace. Furniture; furniture finishing, decoration and patching. Wilmette, Ill., F. J. Drake [1955] 551 p. 645.4 55-895
TS880 .P3 1955 MRR Alc.

FURNITURE INDUSTRY AND TRADE--FRANCE--DIRECTORIES.
Annuaire de l'ameublement. Paris, L. Johaner. 50-55059
HD9773.F8 A6 MRR Alc Latest edition

FURNITURE INDUSTRY AND TRADE--GREAT BRITAIN--DIRECTORIES.
Directory to the furnishing trade. London, Benn Bros. 59-26520
Began in 1957.
HD9773.G7 C3 MRR Alc Latest edition

Furnishing trade directory and buyer's guide. London, Trade Chronicles Limited [etc.] 58-29799
TS842 .F68 MRR Alc Latest edition

FURNITURE INDUSTRY AND TRADE--UNITED STATES--DIRECTORIES.
Lumber requirements of factory consumers in the United States & Canada. 10th- ed.; 1959- Memphis, Lumber Requirements Co. 338.1/7/490973 72-622539
HD9752.L8 MRR Alc Latest edition

FURNITURE MAKING.
Joyce, Ernest. Encyclopedia of furniture making. [New York] Drake Publications [1970] 484 p. 684.1 73-24132
TS880 .J68 MRR Alc.

FURNITURE WORKERS.
Honour, Hugh. Cabinet makers and
furniture designers. [1st American
ed.] New York, Putnam [1969] 320 p.
[$22.50] 749.2 77-77548
NK2350 .H6 1969 MRR Alc.

FURNITURE WORKERS--DICTIONARIES.
Gloag, John, A short dictionary of
furniture. Revised and enlarged ed.
London, Allen & Unwin, 1969. 813 p.
[6/6/-] 749/.03 79-389777
NK2205 .G55 1969 MRR Alc.

FUTUH
see Islamic Empire

FUTURES
see Commodity exchanges

GABON--GAZETTEERS.
United States. Office of Geography.
Gabon; Washington, For sale by the
Superintendent of Documents, U.S.
Govt. Print. Off., 1962. iv, 113 p.
916.721 62-61408
DT546.12 .U5 MRR Alc.

GAELIC LANGUAGE--DICTIONARIES--ENGLISH.
Dwelly, Edward, comp. The
illustrated Gaelic-English
dictionary; containing every Gaelic
word and meaning given in all
previously published dictionaries and
a great number never in print before,
to which is prefixed a concise Gaelic
grammar; 7th ed. Glasgow, Gairm
Publications, 1971. [2], xiv, 1034
p. [£5.50] 491.6/3/321 72-191085

PB1591 .D8 1971 MRR Alc.

M'Alpine, Neil, A pronouncing Gaelic-
English dictionary, Glasgow, A.
MacLaren & sons [1842, '36] 2 v. in
1. 491.6332 43-12346
PB1591 .M25 1842 MRR Alc.

**GAELIC LANGUAGE--ETYMOLOGY--
DICTIONARIES.**
Macbain, Alexander, An etymological
dictionary of the Gaelic language,
Stirling, E. Mackay, 1911. xvi,
xxxvii. A-D p., 1 l., 412 p. 12-642

PB1583 .M33 MRR Alc.

**GAELIC POETRY--TRANSLATIONS INTO
ENGLISH.**
Dixon, William Macneile, ed. The
Edinburgh book of Scottish verse,
1300-1900. London, Meiklejohn and
Holden, 1910. xx, 938 p. a 11-1394
PR8651 .D5 MRR Alc.

GALES
see Storms

GALLEGAN LITERATURE--BIBLIOGRAPHY.
Simón Díaz, José. Bibliografía
de literatura hispánica. 2. ed.
corr. y aumentada. Madrid, Consejo
Superior de Investigaciones
Científicas, Instituto "Miguel de
Cervantes" de Filología Hispánica,
1960- v. 64-5767
Z2691 .S52 MRR Alc.

GALLERIES (ART)
see Art--Galleries and museums

GAMBIA--GAZETTEERS.
United States. Geographic Names
Division. Gambia; official standard
names approved by the United States
Board on Geographic Names.
Washington, 1968. ii, 35 p. 68-
62723
DT509.2 .U55 MRR Alc.

**GAMBIA--GOVERNMENT PUBLICATIONS--
BIBLIOGRAPHY.**
United States. Library of Congress.
African Section. Official
publications of Sierra Leone and
Gambia. Washington, General
Reference and Bibliography Division,
Reference Department, Library of
Congress [for sale by the
Superintendent of Documents, U.S.
Govt. Print. Off.] 1963. xii, 92 p.
63-60090
Z663.285 .O34 MRR Alc.

GAMBIA--HISTORY.
Gray, John Milner, Sir, A history of
the Gambia New York, Barnes & Noble
[1966] x, 508 p. 966.51 66-31474

DT509 .G7 1966 MRR Alc.

GAMBLING--DICTIONARIES.
Salak, John S. Dictionary of
gambling, New York, Philosophical
Library [1963] 284 p. 795 62-
15034
GV1301 .S2 MRR Alc.

GAME AND GAME-BIRDS.
see also Hunting

see also Trapping

GAME AND GAME-BIRDS--NORTH AMERICA.
Boone and Crockett Club. Committee on
Records of North American Big Game.
Records of North American big game;
New York, Holt, Rinehart and Winston,
1964. 398 p. 799.2973 64-21933
SK40 .B63 1964 MRR Alc.

Elman, Robert. The hunter's field
guide to the game birds and animals
of North America. New York, Knopf;
[distributed by Random House] 1974.
655 p. 598.2/97 73-7289
SK40 .E45 1974 MRR Alc.

The New hunter's encyclopedia.
Updated new print. of 3d. ed. New
York : Galahad Books, [1974?] c1972.
xx, 1054 p. : [$24.95] 799.2/97
73-92819
SK33 .H945 1974 MRR Alc.

Rue, Leonard Lee. Sportsman's guide
to game animals; New York, Outdoor
Life Books [1968] 655 p. 599/.097
68-12140
QL715 .R83 MRR Alc.

GAME-LAWS--UNITED STATES.
Farquhar, Carley. The sportsman's
almanac; [1st ed.] New York, Harper
& Row [1965] xiii, 493 p.
799.05873 64-25143
SK41 .F3 MRR Alc.

GAME THEORY.
see also Decision-making

GAMES.
see also Cards

see also Educational games

see also Geographical recreations

see also Tennis

Belch, Jean. Contemporary games;
Detroit, Gale Research Co. [1973- v.
371.3/078 72-6353
LB1029.G3 B44 MRR Alc.

Depew, Arthur M. The Cokesbury game
book. Rev. ed. New York, Abingdon
Press [1960] 319 p. 790 60-14771

GV1201 .D38 1960 MRR Alc.

Depew, Arthur M. The Cokesbury party
book. Rev. ed. New York, Abingdon
Press [1959] 377 p. 793.2 59-
10358
GV1471 .D37 1959 MRR Alc.

Frankel, Lillian Berson. Giant book
of games, New York, Sterling Pub.
Co., 1956] 1 v. 793 56-1637
GV1201 .F78 MRR Alc.

Hunt, Sarah Ethridge. Games and
sports the world around. 3d ed. New
York, Ronald Press Co. [1964] xii,
271 p. 793.4 64-18466
GV1201 .H9 1964 MRR Alc.

Mulac, Margaret Elizabeth, Fun and
games, New York, Harper [1956] 329
p. 793 56-6038
GV1201 .M8 MRR Alc.

Scarne, John. Scarne's encyclopedia
of games. [1st ed.] New York,
Harper & Row [1973] xii, 628 p.
[$13.95] 795/.03 72-79691
GV1229 .S32 MRR Alc.

GAMES--BIBLIOGRAPHY.
Nueckel, Susan. Selected guide to
sports and recreation books. New
York, Fleet Press Corp. [1974] 168
p. 016.7901 73-3735
Z7511 .N83 MRR Alc.

GAMES, OLYMPIC
see Olympic games

GARAGES.
see also Automobiles--Service stations

GARDENING.
see also Insects, Injurious and
beneficial

see also Plants, Ornamental

Rockwell, Frederick Frye, ed. 10,000
garden questions answered by 20
experts. New rev. ed. Garden City,
N.Y., Doubleday [1959] 1390 p. 635
59-7582
SB453 .R66 1959 MRR Alc.

The Reader's digest. Reader's digest
complete book of the garden.
Pleasantville, N.Y., Reader's Digest
Association [1966] 896 p. 635 66-
15517
SB453 .R35 MRR Alc.

GARDENING--DICTIONARIES.
Dictionary of gardening; Oxford,
Clarendon Press, 1951. 4 v. (xvi,
2316 p.) 635/.03 52-7366
SB45 .D63 MRR Alc.

The New illustrated encyclopedia of
gardening (unabridged). [New and
rev. ed.] New York, Greystone Press
[1972-73] 26 v. (4206 p.) 635/.03
72-192032
SB45 .N424 MRR Alc.

GARDENING--MARYLAND.
Youngman, Wilbur Hughes, The
Washington star garden book.
[Washington, Washington star etc.]
61-461
Began publication in 1944.
SB453.2.M5 Y6 MRR Alc Latest
edition

GARDENING--UNITED STATES--HISTORY.
Phipps, Frances, Colonial kitchens,
their furnishings, and their gardens,
New York, Hawthorn Books [1972]
xxii, 346 p. [$12.95] 643/.3/0974
78-158021
TX653 .P48 1972 MRR Alc.

GARDENING--VIRGINIA.
Youngman, Wilbur Hughes, The
Washington star garden book.
[Washington, Washington star etc.]
61-461
Began publication in 1944.
SB453.2.M5 Y6 MRR Alc Latest
edition

GARDENING--WASHINGTON, D.C.
Youngman, Wilbur Hughes, The
Washington star garden book.
[Washington, Washington star etc.]
61-461
Began publication in 1944.
SB453.2.M5 Y6 MRR Alc Latest
edition

GARDENS--NORTH AMERICA.
Logan, Harry Britton, A traveler's
guide to North American gardens. New
York, Scribner [1974] vii, 253 p.
917/.04/53 73-1103
SB446.U6 L63 MRR Alc.

GARDENS--UNITED STATES.
Frohman, Louis H. A pictorial guide
to American gardens, New York, Crown
Publishers [1960] xv, 364 p.
712.0973 60-8622
SB466.U6 F7 MRR Alc.

Logan, Harry Britton, A traveler's
guide to North American gardens. New
York, Scribner [1974] vii, 253 p.
917/.04/53 73-1103
SB446.U6 L63 MRR Alc.

The New illustrated encyclopedia of
gardening (unabridged). [New and
rev. ed.] New York, Greystone Press
[1972-73] 26 v. (4206 p.) 635/.03
72-192032
SB45 .N424 MRR Alc.

**GARFIELD, JAMES ABRAM, PRES. U.S., 1831-
1881.**
Smith, Theodore Clarke, The life and
letters of James Abram Garfield, New
Haven, Yale university press; [etc.,
etc.] 1925. 2 v. 25-19753
E687 .S66 MRR Alc.

**GARFIELD, JAMES ABRAM, PRES. U.S., 1831-
1881--MANUSCRIPTS--INDEXES.**
Garfield, James Abram, Pres. U.S.,
James A. Garfield papers.
Washington, Library of Congress,
1970- 177 reels. 016.9738/4/0924
73-9594
Z663.34 .G34 MRR Alc.

GARRETT, JOHN WORK, 1872-1942.
Baer, Elizabeth. Seventeenth century
Maryland; Baltimore, John Work
Garrett Library, 1949. xxix, 219 p.
016.9752 49-6516
Z1293 .B3 MRR Alc.

**GARRISON, FIELDING HUDSON, 1870-1935. A
MEDICAL BIBLIOGRAPHY.**
Ash, Lee, Serial publications
containing medical classics; New
Haven, Antiquarium, 1961. xxiv, 147
p. 016.61 61-8290
Z6658 .G26 MRR Alc.

GAS.
see also Petroleum

GAS, NATURAL.
see also Oil fields

International petroleum register.
[1st- ed.; 1917/18- New
York[etc.] Palmer Publications [etc.]
18-6917
TN867 .P4 Sci RR Latest edition /
MRR Alc Latest edition

GAS, NATURAL--BIBLIOGRAPHY.
Special Libraries Association.
Petroleum Section. Committee on U.S.
Sources of Petroleum and Natural Gas
Statistics. U.S. sources of
petroleum and natural gas statistics,
New York, Special Libraries
Association, 1961. vii, 94 p.
016.6655 61-15740
Z6972 .S65 MRR Alc.

GAS, NATURAL--DIRECTORIES--PERIODICALS.
The Oil & gas directory: worldwide
exploration, drilling, producing
coverage. [Houston, Tex.]
338.2/7/28025 72-623151
TN867 .O4953 MRR Alc Latest
edition

GAS, NATURAL--STATISTICS.
Darmstadter, Joel. Energy in the
world economy. Baltimore, Published
for Resources for the Future by the
Johns Hopkins Press [1971] x, 876 p.
[$22.50] 333.9 70-155848
HD9540.4 D37 MRR Alc.

GAS, NATURAL--CANADA.
The Financial post survey of oils.
Montreal, New York, Maclean-Hunter
Pub. Co. 338.2728 52-31395
HD9574.C2 F5 MRR Alc Latest
edition

GAS, NATURAL--UNITED STATES.
United States. Federal Power
Commission. Statistics for
interstate natural gas pipeline
companies. 1942- Washington, For
sale by the Superintendent of
Documents, U.S. Govt. Print. Off. 44-
40870
TN880 .U58 MRR Alc Latest edition

GAS, NATURAL--UNITED STATES--
BIBLIOGRAPHY.
Special Libraries Association.
Petroleum Section. Committee on U.S.
Sources of Petroleum and Natural Gas
Statistics. U.S. sources of
petroleum and natural gas statistics.
New York, Special Libraries
Association, 1961. vii, 94 p.
016.6655 61-15740
Z6972 .S65 MRR Alc.

GAS AND OIL ENGINES.
The Motor ship reference book.
London, Temple press ltd. 25-22579
VM315 .A2 MRR Alc Latest edition

GAS AND OIL ENGINES--MAINTENANCE AND
REPAIR.
Small engines service manual. Kansas
City, Mo. 621.43 59-65139
TJ789 .S5 MRR Alc Latest edition

GAS AND OIL ENGINES--MAINTENANCE AND
REPAIR--PERIODICALS.
Motor handbook. [New York, Motor]
629.28/7/05 74-644571
TL152 .M73 MRR Alc Latest edition

GAS COMPANIES--DIRECTORIES.
Global directory of gas companies.
1973- [Houston, Tex., Editorial and
Research Staff of Gas Magazine]
[$90.00] 338.4/7/665702573 74-
645938
TP714 .G55 MRR Alc Latest edition
/ Sci RR Latest edition

International petroleum register.
[1st] ed.; 1917/18- New
York[etc.] Palmer Publications [etc.]
18-5917
TN867 .P4 Sci RR Latest edition /
MRR Alc Latest edition

GAS COMPANIES--CANADA--DIRECTORIES.
Brown's directory of North American
gas companies. 79th- ed.; 1964-
[Duluth] Harbrace. 338.4/7/665702573
72-620934
TP714 .B8 Sci RR Latest edition /
MRR Alc Latest edition

Canadian gas utilities directory.
Toronto, Canadian Gas Association.
338.4/7/3636302571 72-626910
TP714 .D5 MRR Alc Latest edition

GAS COMPANIES--UNITED STATES.
Turner, Clarence A. Financial
statistics, public utilities.
1938/43- Chicago, Ill. 621.3002 44-
47562
HD9685.U5 T8 MRR Alc Latest
edition

United States. Federal Power
Commission. Statistics for
interstate natural gas pipeline
companies. 1942- Washington, For
sale by the Superintendent of
Documents, U.S. Govt. Print. Off. 44-
40870
TN880 .U58 MRR Alc Latest edition

GAS COMPANIES--UNITED STATES--
DIRECTORIES.
Brown's directory of North American
gas companies. 79th- ed.; 1964-
[Duluth] Harbrace. 338.4/7/665702573
72-620934
TP714 .B8 Sci RR Latest edition /
MRR Alc Latest edition

Directory of gas utility companies
and pipe line contractors. Tulsa,
Okla., Midwest oil register [etc.]
61-46648
TP714 .D55 MRR Alc Latest edition

Global directory of gas companies.
1973- [Houston, Tex., Editorial and
Research Staff of Gas Magazine]
[$90.00] 338.4/7/665702573 74-
645938
TP714 .G55 MRR Alc Latest edition
/ Sci RR Latest edition

GAS COMPANIES--UNITED STATES--YEARBOOKS.
Moody's public utility manual. 1954-
New York, Moody's Investors Service.
56-3927
HG4961 .M7245 MRR Alc Latest
edition

GAS INDUSTRY--DIRECTORIES.
Gas industry directory and
undertakings of the world. [1st]-
year; 1898- London, Benn Brothers
[etc.] 338.2/7/28505 78-214205
TP700 .G3 MRR Alc Latest edition

Global directory of gas companies.
1973- [Houston, Tex., Editorial and
Research Staff of Gas Magazine]
[$90.00] 338.4/7/665702573 74-
645938
TP714 .G55 MRR Alc Latest edition
/ Sci RR Latest edition

GAS INDUSTRY--YEARBOOKS.
Gas industry directory and
undertakings of the world. [1st]-
year; 1898- London, Benn Brothers
[etc.] 338.2/7/28505 78-214205
TP700 .G3 MRR Alc Latest edition

GAS INDUSTRY--CANADA--STATISTICS.
American Gas Association. Bureau of
Statistics. Historical statistics of
the gas industry. 1956- New York.
338.476657 57-302
TP722 .A6 MRR Alc Latest edition

GAS INDUSTRY--CANADA--STATISTICS--
PERIODICALS.
American Gas Association. Dept. of
Statistics. Gas facts. 1967-
Arlington, Va. [etc.]
338.4/7/6657097 72-622849
TP722 .A59 MRR Alc Latest edition

GAS INDUSTRY--UNITED STATES--STATISTICS.
American Gas Association. Bureau of
Statistics. Historical statistics of
the gas industry. 1956- New York.
338.476657 57-302
TP722 .A6 MRR Alc Latest edition

American Gas Association. Bureau of
Statistics. Survey of residential
gas service by county. 1949- New
York. 58-33327
TP723 .A68 MRR Alc Latest edition

United States. Federal Power
Commission. Statistics for
interstate natural gas pipeline
companies. 1942- Washington, For
sale by the Superintendent of
Documents, U.S. Govt. Print. Off. 44-
40870
TN880 .U58 MRR Alc Latest edition

GAS INDUSTRY--UNITED STATES--STATISTICS-
-PERIODICALS.
American Gas Association. Dept. of
Statistics. Gas facts. 1967-
Arlington, Va. [etc.]
338.4/7/6657097 72-622849
TP722 .A59 MRR Alc Latest edition

GAS STATIONS
see Automobiles--Service stations

GASOLINE.
American Petroleum Institute.
Petroleum facts and figures. [1st]-
ed.; [1928]- New York. 338.2 41-
10749
HD9561 .A7 MRR Alc Latest edition

GASOLINE AUTOMOBILES
see Automobiles

GASTRONOMY.
see also Cookery

see also Food

American heritage. The American
heritage cookbook and illustrated
history of American eating &
drinking. [New York] American
Heritage Pub. Co.; Distribution by
Simon and Schuster [1964] 629 p.
641.5 64-21278
TX705 .A65 MRR Alc.

Athenaeus. The Deipnosophists.
London, W. Heinemann; New York, G. P.
Putnam's sons, 1927-1941. 7 v.
mrr01-18
PA3612 .A87 1927d MRR Alc.

Simon, André Louis, A concise
encyclopaedia of gastronomy; [1st
American ed.] New York, Harcourt,
Brace [1952] 816 p. 641.03 52-
13763
TX631 .S53 1952a MRR Alc.

Wason, Elizabeth, Cooks, gluttons &
gourmets; [1st ed.] Garden City,
N.Y., Doubleday, 1962. 381 p.
641.01 61-12598
TX631 .W3 MRR Alc.

GASTRONOMY--BIBLIOGRAPHY.
Bitting, Katherine (Golden) Mrs.,
Gastronomic bibliography, San
Francisco, Calif., 1939. 2 p. l.,
vii-xiii p., 1 l., 718 p. 016.641
39-15674
Z5776.G2 B6 MRR Alc.

Vicaire, Georges, Bibliographie
gastronomique; [2d ed.] London, D.
Verschoyle, Academic and
Bibliographical Publications, 1954.
[6] p., facsim.: xviii p., 972
columns. 54-6692
Z5776.G2 V5 1954 MRR Alc.

GASTRONOMY--DICTIONARIES.
Simon, André Louis, A dictionary of
gastronomy New York, McGraw-Hill
[1970] 400 p. [$15.95] 641/.03
72-89318
TX349 .S53 1970 MRR Alc.

GASTRONOMY--HISTORY.
Hale, William Harlan, The Horizon
cookbook and illustrated history of
eating and drinking through the ages.
[New York] American Heritage Pub.
Co., book trade distribution by
Doubleday [1968] 768 p. [16.50
12.95 (Pre-Christmas price)] 641
68-15655
TX631 .H3 MRR Alc.

GAWAIN AND THE GRENE KNIGHT--
CONCORDANCES.
Kottler, Barnet. A concordance to
five Middle English poems:
[Pittsburgh] University of Pittsburgh
Press [1966] xxxiii, 761 p.
821.1016 66-13311
PR265 .K6 MRR Alc.

GAZA STRIP.
United States. Office of Geography.
Egypt and the Gaza Strip;
Washington, U.S. Govt. Print. Off.,
1959. vi, 415 p. 916.2 59-62055
DT45 .U5 MRR Alc.

GAZETTEERS.
Webster's New geographical
dictionary. Springfield, Mass., G. &
C. Merriam Co. [1972] xxix, 1370 p.
[14.95] 910/.3 72-6103
G103 .W45 1972 MRR Ref Desk.

GEMS.
see also Precious stones

GEMS--CATALOGS.
Sinkankas, John. Van Nostrand's
standard catalog of gems. Princeton,
N.J., Van Nostrand [1968] xiii, 286
p. 553/.8 68-19369
TS752 .S53 1968 MRR Alc.

GENEALOGY.
see also Biography

American Society of Genealogists.
Genealogical research, methods and
sources. Washington, 1960- v.
929/.1 60-919
CS16 .A5 MRR Alc.

Colket, Meredith Bright, Guide to
genealogical records in the National
Archives. Washington, National
Archives, National Archives and
Records Service, General Services
Administration; [for sale by the
Superintendent of Documents, U.S.
Govt. Print. Off.] 1964. x, 145 p.
a 64-7048
CS15 .C6 MRR Alc.

Doane, Gilbert Harry, Searching for
your ancestors; [3d ed.]
Minneapolis, University of Minnesota
Press [1960] 198 p. 929.1 60-
12200
CS16 .D6 1960 MRR Alc.

Everton, George B. The handy book
for genealogists, 4th ed., rev. and
enl. Logan, Utah, Everton Publishers
[1962] x, 226 p. 929.1 62-15376
CS16 .E85 1962 MRR Alc.

Kirkham, E. Kay. Research in
American genealogy; [Salt Lake City,
1956] xii, 447 p. 929.1072 56-
58780
CS16 .K53 MRR Alc.

Pine, Leslie Gilbert. American
origins. [1st ed.] Garden City,
N.Y., Doubleday, 1960. 357 p.
929.1 60-10679
CS16 .P55 MRR Alc.

Pine, Leslie Gilbert. The
genealogist's encyclopedia. New
York, Weybright and Talley [1969]
360 p. [12.50] 929.1/03 78-84622
CS9 .P48 1969b MRR Alc.

GENEALOGY--BIBLIOGRAPHY.
Doane, Gilbert Harry, Searching for
your ancestors; [3d ed.]
Minneapolis, University of Minnesota
Press [1960] 198 p. 929.1 60-
12200
CS16 .D6 1960 MRR Alc.

GENEALOGY--BIBLIOGRAPHY. (Cont.)
United States. Library of Congress.
American and English genealogies in
the Library of Congress. 2d ed.
Washington, Govt. print. off., 1919.
iv, 1332 p. 19-26004
Z663.74 .A5 1919 MRR Alc.

GENEALOGY--DICTIONARIES.
Puttock, A. G. A dictionary of
heraldry and related subjects.
Baltimore, Genealogical Pub. Co.,
1970. 256 p. [$10.00] 929.6/03
76-137421
CR13 .P8 1970b MRR Alc.

GENEALOGY--RESEARCH.
American Society of Genealogists.
Genealogical research, methods and
sources. Washington, 1960- v.
929/.1 60-919
CS16 .A5 MRR Alc.

GENERALS.
Martell, Paul. World military
leaders / New York : Bowker, [1974]
268 p. ; 355/.0092/2 B 74-78392
U51 .M35 MRR Biog.

GENERALS--CONFEDERATE STATES OF AMERICA.
Warner, Ezra J. Generals in gray:
[1st ed. Baton Rouge] Louisiana
State University Press [1959] xxvii,
420 p. 973.742 58-7551
E467 .W3 MRR Biog.

GENERALS--UNITED STATES.
Billias, George Athan, ed. George
Washington's generals. New York, W.
Morrow, 1964. xvii, 327 p. 973.33
64-12038
E206 .B5 MRR Biog.

Generals of the Army and the Air
Force and admirals of the Navy. v. 1-
3; Feb. 1953-Jan. 1956. [Washington]
923.573 56-23963
U52 .G4 MRR Alc Full set

Warner, Ezra J. Generals in blue;
lives of the Union commanders.
[Baton Rouge] Louisiana State
University Press [1964] xxiv, 679,
[1] p. 973.741 64-21593
E467 .W29 MRR Biog.

GENERATION
see Reproduction

GENERATIVE ORGANS.
see also Reproduction

GENESIS (BOOK OF THE OLD TESTAMENT)
see Bible. O.T. Genesis

GENETIC COUNSELING--DIRECTORIES.
Levine, Milton Isra, The parents'
encyclopedia of infancy, childhood,
and adolescence New York, Crowell
[1973] 619 p. [$10.00] 649/.1/03
72-83769
RJ61 .L552 MRR Alc.

GENETIC PSYCHOLOGY.
see also Child study

GENETICS.
see also Biology

GENETICS--DICTIONARIES.
King, Robert C. A dictionary of
genetics 2d ed. New York, Oxford
University Press, 1972. 337 p.
575.1/03 73-170262
QH431 .K518 1972 MRR Alc.

GENEVA--DIRECTORIES.
Annuaire genevois; Genève, Chapalay
& Mottier [etc.] 60-29961
Began publication in 1878.
DQ444 .A5 MRR Alc Latest edition

GENEVA. LEAGUE OF NATIONS
see League of Nations

GENEVA (CANTON)--DIRECTORIES.
Savoir. Genève [etc.] ATAR, S.A.
[etc.] 53-28495
DQ444 .S3 MRR Alc Latest edition

GENIUS.
see also Gifted children

GENOA--COMMERCE--DIRECTORIES.
Annuario genovese. Genova, Editrice
Euroitalia [etc.] 380.1/025/45182
74-642350
Began in 1814.
DG631.6 A6 MRR Alc Latest edition

GENOA--COMMERCE--DIRECTORIES--YEARBOOKS.
Annuario genovese. Genova, Editrice
Euroitalia [etc.] 380.1/025/45182
74-642350
Began in 1814.
DG631.6 A6 MRR Alc Latest edition

GENOA--POLITICS AND GOVERNMENT--
YEARBOOKS.
Annuario genovese. Genova, Editrice
Euroitalia [etc.] 380.1/025/45182
74-642350
Began in 1814.
DG631.6 A6 MRR Alc Latest edition

GEOCHEMISTRY.
see also Mineralogy, Determinative

GEODESY--DICTIONARIES.
United States. Army Topographic
Command. Glossary of mapping,
charting, and geodetic terms. 2d ed.
Washington, 1969. v, 281 p.
526.8/03 73-604750
GA102 .U53 1969 MRR Alc.

GEODESY--DICTIONARIES--POLYGLOT.
Stowarzyszenie Geodetów Polskich.
Słownik geodezyjny w 5 [i.e. pięciu]
językach: polskim, rosyjskim,
niemieckim, angielskim, francuskim.
Warszawa, Państwowe
Przedsiębiorstwo Wydawn.
Kartograficznych, 1954. xv, 525 p.
55-34784
QB279 .S8 MRR Alc.

GEOGRAPHERS.
Freeman, Thomas Walter. A hundred
years of geography. [1st ed.]
reprinted with revisions. London,
Duckworth, 1971. 335 p. [£1.00]
910/.9/034 72-181348
G99 .F7 1971 MRR Alc.

Orbis geographicus. 1952-
Wiesbaden, F. Steiner. 923.9 53-
36007
G64 .O7 MRR Alc Latest edition

GEOGRAPHERS, AMERICAN.
James, Preston Everett, ed. American
geography: [Syracuse, N.Y.]
Published for the Association of
American Geographers by Syracuse
University Press, 1954. xii, 590 p.
910.7 54-9225
G76.5.U5 J3 MRR Alc.

GEOGRAPHICAL DISTRIBUTION OF MAN
see Ethnology

GEOGRAPHICAL NAMES
see Names, Geographical

GEOGRAPHICAL RECREATIONS.
Hunt, Sarah Ethridge. Games and
sports the world around. 3d ed. New
York, Ronald Press Co. [1964] xii,
271 p. 793.4 64-18466
GV1201 .H9 1964 MRR Alc.

GEOGRAPHICAL RESEARCH.
Durrenberger, Robert W. Geographical
research and writing New York,
Crowell [1971] ix, 246 p.
808.06/6/91 77-136033
G73 .D97 MRR Alc.

GEOGRAPHICAL SOCIETIES--DIRECTORIES.
Orbis geographicus. 1952-
Wiesbaden, F. Steiner. 923.9 53-
36007
G64 .O7 MRR Alc Latest edition

GEOGRAPHY.
see also Anthropo-geography

see also Ethnology

see also Maps

Bilan du monde. [2. éd.] [Tournai]
Casterman, 1964. 2 v. 65-87638
G122 .B442 MRR Alc.

Elting, Mary, Flags of all nations
and the people who live under them,
New York, Grosset & Dunlap [1969]
157 p. [4.95] 929.9 71-86695
CR109 .E4 1969 MRR Alc.

Larousse encyclopedia of world
geography. New York, Odyssey Press
[1965] 736 p. 910.003 65-6905
G115 .G5535 MRR Alc.

The McGraw-Hill illustrated world
geography. [1st ed.] New York,
McGraw-Hill [1960] xvi, 519 p. 910
60-7030
G122 .M24 MRR Alc.

GEOGRAPHY--BIBLIOGRAPHY.
American Geographical Society of New
York. Current geographical
publications; v. 1- Jan. 1938-
New York. 016.91 41-27154
Z6009 .A47 MRR Alc Partial set*

Bibliographie géographique
internationale. [1.]— 1891-
Paris, Centre national de la
recherche scientifique [etc.] 25-
1167
Z6001 .B57 MRR Alc Partial set

Brewer, James Gordon. The literature
of geography; [Hamden, Conn.] Linnet
Books [1973] 208 p. [$10.50]
016.91 73-10088
Z6001 .B74 1973 MRR Alc.

Church, Martha. A basic geographical
library; Washington, Association of
American Geographers [1966] xi, 153
p. 016.91 66-18595
Z6001 .C48 MRR Alc.

Durrenberger, Robert W. Geographical
research and writing New York,
Crowell [1971] ix, 246 p.
808.06/6/91 77-136033
G73 .D97 MRR Alc.

Lock, Clara Beatrice Muriel,
Geography; [Hamden, Conn.] Archon
Books [1968] 179 p. 016.91 68-
1008
Z6001 .L58 MRR Alc.

Vinge, Clarence L. U.S. Government
publications for research and
teaching in geography, Totowa, N.J.,
Littlefield, Adams, 1967. xiv, 360
p. 016.910/7 67-8345
Z6001 .V5 1967 MRR Alc.

Wright, John Kirtland, Aids to
geographical research:
bibliographies, periodicals, atlases,
gazetteers and other reference books,
2d ed.; completely rev. New York,
Columbia University Press, 1947.
xii, 331 p. 016.91 47-30449
Z6001.A1 W9 1947 MRR Alc.

GEOGRAPHY--DICTIONARIES.
Académie diplomatique
internationale. Dictionnaire
diplomatique, Paris [1933] 2 v.
341.03 33-36212
JX1226 .A312 vol. 3 MRR Biog.

Angel, Juvenal Londoño,
International marketing guide for
technical, management and other
consultants. 1st ed. New York,
World Trade Academy Press;
distributed by Simon & Schuster
[1971] 600 p. [$25.00] 658.4/03
77-111350
HD69.C6 A676 MRR Alc.

Angel, Juvenal Londoño, Looking for
employment in foreign countries
reference handbook, 6th ed., rev.
and enl. New York, World Trade
Academy Press; distributed by Simon &
Schuster [1972] 727 p. [$25.00]
331.7/02 70-111351
HF5381 .A7847 1972 MRR Alc.

Chambers's world gazetteer and
geographical dictionary; Revised
ed., reprinted Edinburgh, London,
Chambers, 1965. viii, 806 p. [37/6]
910.003 66-70419
G103 .C47 1965 MRR Alc.

The Columbia Lippincott gazetteer of
the world. Morningside Heights, New
York, Columbia University Press
[1962] x, 2148, 22 p. 910.3 62-
4711
G103 .L7 1962 MRR Ref Desk.

Dun & Bradstreet exporters'
encyclopaedia. New York, Dun and
Bradstreet International. 382/.6 72-
622175
HF3011 .E9 MRR Alc Latest edition

Elliott, Florence. A dictionary of
politics. 6th ed. Harmondsworth,
Penguin, 1971. 480 p. [10/-]
320/.03 72-186214
D419 .E4 1971 MRR Alc.

International Christian Broadcasters.
World directory of religious radio
and television broadcasting. South
Pasadena, Calif. William Carey
Library [1973] 808 p. 791.45/5 73-
8853
BV656 .I53 MRR Alc.

International Telecommunication
Union. General Secretariat. Official
list of telegraph offices opened for
international traffic. Geneva.
384.1 13-16092
HE7621 .I55 MRR Alc Latest edition

The International year book and
statesmen's who's who. 1953-
London, Burke's Peerage. 305.8 53-
1425
JA51 .I57 MRR Biog Latest edition

Knox, Alexander, Glossary of
geographical and topographical terms
London, E. Stanford, 1904. xl, 432
p. 05-4475
G103 .K72 MRR Alc.

Lock, Clara Beatrice Muriel,
Geography; [Hamden, Conn.] Archon
Books [1968] 179 p. 016.91 68-
1008
Z6001 .L58 MRR Alc.

Longmans dictionary of geography;
London, Longmans, 1966. xv, 482 p.
[65/-] 910.3 66-71574
G103 .L8 MRR Alc.

Monkhouse, Francis John. A
dictionary of geography, 2d ed.
Chicago, Aldine Pub. Co. [1970] v,
378 p. 910/.003 76-115841
G108.E5 M6 1970 MRR Alc.

Moore, Wilfred George, The Penguin
encyclopedia of places
Harmondsworth, Penguin, 1971. 835 p.
[£1.00] 910/.3 72-179950
G103 .M66 MRR Alc.

GEOGRAPHY--DICTIONARIES. (Cont.)
The New Century cyclopedia of names,
New York, Appleton-Century-Crofts
[1954] 3 v. (xxviii, 4342 p.)
929.4 52-13879
   PE1625 .C43 1954 MRR Ref Desk.

Novissima enciclopedia Ceschina.
Milano, Ceschina. [1968?] 1552 p.
[L 12000] 910/.003 68-107668
   G103 .N58 MRR Alc.

Room, Adrian. Place names of the
world. Newton Abbot, David & Charles
[1974] 216 p. [£3.50] 910/.3 74-
155897
   G103 .R7 MRR Alc.

Smith, William, Sir, A dictionary of
Greek and Roman geography, New York,
AMS Press, 1966. 2 v. 913.38/003
73-180902
   DE25 .S664 MRR Alc.

Times, London. Index-gazetteer of
the world. London, Times Publishing
Co., 1965. xxxi, 964 p. [£10]
910.003 66-70286
   G103 .T5 MRR Alc Atlas.

The World this year. 1971- New
York, Simon and Schuster. 320.9/046
76-648587
   JF37 .W65 MRR Ref Desk Latest
     edition

Worldmark encyclopedia of the
nations. [4th ed.] New York,
Worldmark Press, [1971] 5 v.
910/.3 76-152128
   G103 .W65 1971 MRR Ref Desk.

Zaroubi, Nasri. Geographical
encyclopaedia of the world. 1st ed.
Beirut, Printed by Dagher Press,
1968. xxxi, 1216 p. 910/.3 76-
5723
   G103 .Z3 MRR Alc.

GEOGRAPHY--DICTIONARIES--BIBLIOGRAPHY.
Meynen, Emil, Amtliche und private
Ortsnamenverzeichnisse des
Grossdeutschen Reiches Leipzig, S.
Hirzel [1942] 162 p. 54-47213
   Z2247.G4 M4 MRR Alc.

GEOGRAPHY--DICTIONARIES--POLYGLOT.
Lana, Gabriella. Glossary of
geographical names in six languages:
Amsterdam, New York, Elsevier Pub.
Co., 1967. 184 p. 910/.003 66-
25762
   G104.5 .L3 MRR Ref Desk.

GEOGRAPHY--EXHIBITIONS.
International Geographical Congress.
17th, Washington, D.C., 1952.
Catalog of national exhibits,
Washington, 1952. 81 p. 910.74 52-
60053
   Z663.35 .C3 MRR Alc.

GEOGRAPHY--HISTORY.
Freeman, Thomas Walter. A hundred
years of geography, [1st ed.]
reprinted with revisions. London,
Duckworth, 1971. 335 p. [£1.00]
910/.9/034 72-181348
   G99 .F7 1971 MRR Alc.

GEOGRAPHY--INFORMATION SERVICES.
Kaplan, Stuart R., ed. A guide to
information sources in mining,
minerals, and geosciences. New York,
Interscience Publishers [1965] xiv,
599 p. 016.622 65-24304
   Z7401 .G83 vol. 2 MRR Alc.

GEOGRAPHY--JUVENILE LITERATURE.
Elting, Mary, Flags of all nations
and the people who live under them,
New York, Grosset & Dunlap [1969]
157 p. [4.85] 929.9 71-86695
   CR109 .E4 1969 MRR Alc.

GEOGRAPHY--METHODOLOGY.
Brewer, James Gordon. The literature
of geography; [Hamden, Conn.] Linnet
Books [1973] 208 p. [$10.50]
016.91 73-10088
   Z6001 .B74 1973 MRR Alc.

GEOGRAPHY--PERIODICALS--BIBLIOGRAPHY.
Wright, John Kirtland, Aids to
geographical research:
bibliographies, periodicals, atlases,
gazetteers and other reference books,
2d ed., completely rev. New York,
Columbia University Press, 1947.
xii, 331 p. 016.91 47-30449
   Z6001.A1 W8 1947 MRR Alc.

GEOGRAPHY--PERIODICALS--BIBLIOGRAPHY--
UNION LISTS.
Harris, Chauncy Dennison,
International list of geographical
serials. 2d ed., rev., expanded, and
updated. (Chicago) University of
Chicago, Dept. of Geography, 1971.
xxvi, 267 p. [$4.50] 016.91/05 79-
163720
   H31 .C514 no. 138 MRR Alc.

GEOGRAPHY--PERIODICALS--INDEXES.
American Geographical Society of New
York. Current geographical
publications; v. 1- Jan. 1938-
New York. 016.91 41-27154
   Z6009 .A47 MRR Alc Partial set*

Bibliographie géographique
internationale. [1.]- 1891-
Paris, Centre national de la
recherche scientifique [etc.] 25-
1167
   Z6001 .B57 MRR Alc Partial set

United States. Library of Congress.
Geography and Map Division. The
bibliography of cartography. Boston,
G. K. Hall, 1973. 5 v. 016.526 73-
12977
   Z6028 .U49 1973 MRR Alc (Dk 33)

GEOGRAPHY--PICTORIAL WORKS--
BIBLIOGRAPHY.
Ellis, Jessie (Croft) Travel through
pictures; Boston, The F. W. Faxon
company, 1935. xi, 699 p. 016.91
35-27172
   Z6020 .E47 MRR Alc.

GEOGRAPHY--STUDY AND TEACHING.
James, Preston Everett, ed. American
geography; [Syracuse, N.Y.]
Published for the Association of
American Geographers by Syracuse
University Press, 1954. xii, 590 p.
910.7 54-9225
   G76.5.U5 J3 MRR Alc.

GEOGRAPHY--STUDY AND TEACHING (HIGHER)--
DIRECTORIES.
Orbis geographicus. 1952-
Wiesbaden, F. Steiner. 923.9 53-
36007
   G64 .O7 MRR Alc Latest edition

GEOGRAPHY--TABLES, ETC.
Showers, Victor, The world in
figures. New York, Wiley [1973]
xii, 585 p. 910/.21/2 73-9
   G109 .S52 MRR Ref Desk.

GEOGRAPHY--TERMINOLOGY.
British Association for the
Advancement of Science. Research
Committee. A glossary of
geographical terms; 2nd ed. London,
Longmans, 1966. xxxii, 539 p. [75/-
] 910.003 66-77972
   G108.A2 B7 1966 MRR Alc.

A Dictionary of basic geography
Boston, Allyn and Bacon [1970] xii,
299 p. 910/.003 74-94338
   G108.A2 D5 MRR Alc.

Swayne, James Colin. A concise
glossary of geographical terms, 2d
ed.; [reprint with amendments]
London, G. Philip [1962, c1958] 164
p. 910/.3 74-156601
   G108.A2 S9 1962 MRR Alc.

GEOGRAPHY--YEARBOOKS.
The Book of the world. 1971- New
York, Collier Books [etc.] 910/.5
77-617076
   G1 .B65 MRR Ref Desk Latest
     edition

Calendario-atlante di Agostini
Novara. ca 15-282
   G1 .C2 MRR Alc Latest edition

GEOGRAPHY, ANCIENT.
Strabo. The geography of Strabo,
London, W. Heinemann; New York, G. P.
Putnam's sons, 1917-33. 8 v. 17-
13967
   PA3612 .S8 1917 MRR Alc.

GEOGRAPHY, ANCIENT--DICTIONARIES.
Besnier, Maurice, Lexique de
géographie ancienne, Paris, C.
Klincksieck, 1914. xx, 893 p. 14-
14721
   DE25 .B4 MRR Alc.

The New Century handbook of classical
geography. New York, Appleton-
Century-Crofts [1972] v, 362 p.
913/.003 78-189006
   DE25 .N48 MRR Alc.

GEOGRAPHY, BIBLICAL
see Bible--Geography

GEOGRAPHY, COMMERCIAL.
New geography. 1966/67- London, New
York, Abelard-Schuman. 330.9 67-
14202
   HC59.A15 N4 MRR Alc Latest edition

Pitman's business man's guide: 14th
ed. London, Pitman, 1967. [5], 346
p. [32/-] 650/.03 68-92621
   HF1001 .S6 1967 MRR Alc.

GEOGRAPHY, ECONOMIC.
Bengtson, Nels August, Fundamentals
of economic geography; 5th ed.
Englewood Cliffs, N.J., Prentice-Hall
[1964] xviii, 613 p. 330.9 64-
14983
   HF1025 .B43 1964 MRR Alc.

New geography. 1966/67- London, New
York, Abelard-Schuman. 330.9 67-
14202
   HC59.A15 N4 MRR Alc Latest edition

GEOGRAPHY, ECONOMIC--MAPS.
Oxford University Press. Oxford
economic atlas of the world; 4th
ed.; London, Oxford University
Press, 1972. viii, 239 p. [£5.75]
912/.1/33 72-169337
   G1046.G1 O92 1972 MRR Alc Atlas

Van Royen, William, Atlas of the
world's resources. New York,
Published by Prentice-Hall for the
University of Maryland, 1952- v.
338 52-9034
   G1046.G3 V3 1952 MRR Alc Atlas.

GEOGRAPHY, HISTORICAL.
Hertslet, Edward, Sir, comp. The map
of Europe by treaty; London,
Butterworths [etc.] 1875-91. 4 v.
10-15038
   JX626 1875 MRR Alc.

Paullin, Charles Oscar, Atlas of the
historical geography of the United
States, [Washington, D.C., New York]
Pub. Jointly by Carnegie institution
of Washington and the American
geographical society of New York,
1932. 2 p. l., iii-xv p., 1 l., 162
p., 1 l., 688 maps (part col.) on 166
plates (part double) 911.73 map32-
54
   G1201.S1 P3 1932 MRR Alc Atlas.

GEOGRAPHY, HISTORICAL--MAPS.
Shepherd, William Robert, Historical
atlas [by] William R. Shepherd.
[1st] ed.; 1911- New York, Barnes
& Noble. map64-26
   G1030 .S4 MRR Ref Desk Latest
     edition

GEOGRAPHY, MATHEMATICAL.
see also Cartography

GEOGRAPHY, MEDIEVAL--DICTIONARIES.
Grasse, Johann Georg Theodor, Orbis
latinus; 2. aufl., Berlin, R. C.
Schmidt & co.; New York, E. Steiger &
co.; [etc., etc.] 1909. 4 p. l., 348
p. 10-4247
   G107 .G8 MRR Ref Desk.

Grasse, Johann Georg Theodor, Orbis
Latinus; Grossausgabe,
Braunschweig, Klinkhardt & Biermann
[c1972] 3 v. 72-345986
   G107 .G8 1972 MRR Alc.

GEOGRAPHY, PHYSICAL
see Physical geography

GEOGRAPHY, POLITICAL.
see also Cities and towns

GEOLOGICAL SOCIETIES--DIRECTORIES.
Kaplan, Stuart R., ed. A guide to
information sources in mining,
minerals, and geosciences, New York,
Interscience Publishers [1965] xiv,
599 p. 016.622 65-24304
   Z7401 .G83 vol. 2 MRR Alc.

GEOLOGICAL SURVEYS--BIBLIOGRAPHY.
Corbin, John Boyd, comp. An index of
state geological survey publications
issued in series. New York,
Scarecrow Press. 1965. xi, 667 p.
016.5573 65-13555
   Z6031 .C6 MRR Alc.

GEOLOGY.
see also Mountains

see also Oceanography

see also Paleontology

see also Petrology

see also Rocks

see also Volcanoes

GEOLOGY--BIBLIOGRAPHY.
Chronic, Byron John. Bibliography of
theses written for advanced degrees
in geology and related sciences at
universities and colleges in the
United States and Canada through
1957, Boulder, Colo., Pruett Press,
1958. 1 v. (unpaged) 016.55 a 59-
7426
   Z6034.U49 C45 1958 MRR Alc.

Ward, Dederick C. Geologic reference
sources; Metuchen, N.J., Scarecrow
Press, 1972. 453 p. 016.55 71-
190223
   Z6031 .W35 1972 MRR Alc.

GEOLOGY--DICTIONARIES.
Challinor, John. A dictionary of
geology. 3rd ed. Cardiff, Wales
U.P., 1967. xv, 298 p. [42/-]
550/.3 67-87723
   QE5 .C45 1967 MRR Alc.

GEOLOGY--DICTIONARIES. (Cont.)
Gary, Margaret. Glossary of geology.
Washington, American Geological
Institute [1973, c1972] xiv, 805, 52
p. 550/.3 72-87856
QE5 .G37 MRR Alc

Nelson, Archibald. Dictionary of
applied geology: mining and civil
engineering. London, Newnes, 1967.
viii, 421 p. [45/-] 550/.3 68-
86619
QE5 .N44 1967 MRR Alc.

GEOLOGY--DICTIONARIES--POLYGLOT.
Cooper, S. A. Concise international
dictionary of mechanics & geology;
New York, Philosophical Library
[1958] viii, 400 p. 621.03 58-
3594
TJ9 .C6 1958 MRR Alc.

Nederlands Geologisch Mijnbouwkundig
Genootschap. Geological
nomenclature. Gorinchem, J.
Noorduijn, 1959. xvi, 523 p. 550.3
a 60-3024
QE5 .N413 MRR Alc.

Żytka, Romuald. Geological
dictionary Warszawa, Wydawnictwa
Geologiczne, 1970. 1439 p.
[zł1250.00] 550/.3 72-31794
QE5 .Z9 MRR Alc.

GEOLOGY--EXAMINATIONS, QUESTIONS, ETC.
Pearl, Richard Maxwell, 1001
questions answered about earth
science, Rev. ed. Illustrated with
photos. and drawings. New York,
Dodd, Mead, 1969. xvi, 327 p.
[6.50] 550 77-5935
QE40 .P4 1969 MRR Alc.

GEOLOGY--INDEXES.
Corbin, John Boyd, comp. An index of
state geological survey publications
issued in series. New York,
Scarecrow Press, 1965. xi, 667 p.
016.5573 65-13555
Z6031 .C6 MRR Alc.

GEOLOGY--INFORMATION SERVICES.
Kaplan, Stuart R., ed. A guide to
information sources in mining,
minerals, and geosciences. New York,
Interscience Publishers [1965] xiv,
599 p. 016.622 65-24304
Z7401 .G83 vol. 2 MRR Alc.

GEOLOGY--TERMINOLOGY.
Nederlands Geologisch Mijnbouwkundig
Genootschap. Geological
nomenclature. Gorinchem, J.
Noorduijn, 1959. xvi, 523 p. 550.3
a 60-3024
QE5 .N413 MRR Alc.

GEOLOGY--CANADA--BIBLIOGRAPHY.
Chronic, Byron John. Bibliography of
theses in geology, 1958-1963,
Washington, American Geological
Institute [c1964] 1 v. (unpaged)
016.55 65-19493
Z6034.U49 C44 MRR Alc.

Ward, Dederick C. Bibliography of
theses in geology, 1967-1970.
[Boulder, Colo., Geological Society
of America, 1973] vii, 160, I-274 p.
016.55 73-78974
Z6034.U49 W32 MRR Alc.

GEOLOGY--NORTH AMERICA--BIBLIOGRAPHY.
Darton, Nelson Horatio, Catalogue
and index of contributions to North
American geology, 1732-1891,
Washington, Govt. print. off., 1896.
1045 p. gs 05-696
Z6034.U49 D21 MRR Alc.

United States. Geological Survey.
Bibliography of North American
geology. 1785/1918-1950/59.
Washington, U.S. Govt. Print. Off.
016.557 gs 24-38
Z6034.U49 U45 Sci RR Sci RR
Partial set / MRR Alc Partial set

United States. Geological Survey.
Bibliography of North American
geology. 1906- Washington, U.S.
Govt. Print. Off. 016.557 gs 09-427
QE75 .B9 MRR Alc Partial set / Sci
RR Partial set

GEOLOGY--UNITED STATES--BIBLIOGRAPHY.
Chronic, Byron John. Bibliography of
theses in geology, 1958-1963,
Washington, American Geological
Institute [c1964] 1 v. (unpaged)
016.55 65-19493
Z6034.U49 C44 MRR Alc.

Chronic, Byron John. Bibliography of
theses written for advanced degrees
in geology and related sciences at
universities and colleges in the
United States and Canada through
1957, Boulder, Colo., Pruett Press,
1958. 1 v. (unpaged) 016.55 a 59-
7426
Z6034.U49 C45 1958 MRR Alc.

Ward, Dederick C. Bibliography of
theses in geology, 1967-1970.
[Boulder, Colo., Geological Society
of America, 1973] vii, 160, I-274 p.
016.55 73-78974
Z6034.U49 W32 MRR Alc.

GEOLOGY--UNITED STATES--GUIDE-BOOKS.
Matthews, William Henry, A guide to
the national parks; Garden City,
N.Y., Doubleday, 1973. xx, 529 p.
[$5.95] 551.4/0973 72-89824
GB427.5 .M37 1973 MRR Alc.

GEOLOGY--UNITED STATES--NOMENCLATURE.
Wilmarth, Mary Grace, Lexicon of
geologic names of the United States
(including Alaska) Washington, U.S.
Govt. print off., 1938. 2 v. gs 38-
279
QE5 .W5 MRR Alc.

GEOLOGY--UNITED STATES--SURVEYS--
BIBLIOGRAPHY.
Corbin, John Boyd, comp. An index of
state geological survey publications
issued in series. New York,
Scarecrow Press, 1965. xi, 667 p.
016.5573 65-13555
Z6031 .C6 MRR Alc.

GEOLOGY, CHEMICAL
see Mineralogy, Determinative

GEOLOGY, ECONOMIC.
see also Gas, Natural

see also Mines and mineral resources

see also Petroleum

GEOLOGY, STRATIGRAPHIC.
Kummel, Bernhard, History of the
earth; San Francisco, W. H. Freeman
[1961] 610 p. 551.7 61-6783
QE501 .K79 MRR Alc.

GEOMETRICAL DRAWING.
see also Design

GEOMETRY.
see also Trigonometry

GEOMETRY, PLANE.
see also Circle

GEOMORPHOLOGY--DICTIONARIES.
Fairbridge, Rhodes Whitmore, The
encyclopedia of geomorphology, New
York, Reinhold Book Corp. [c1968]
xvi, 1295 p. 551.4/03 68-58342
GB10 .F3 MRR Alc.

GEOMORPHOLOGY--UNITED STATES--GUIDE-
BOOKS.
Matthews, William Henry, A guide to
the national parks; Garden City,
N.Y., Doubleday, 1973. xx, 529 p.
[$5.95] 551.4/0973 72-89824
GB427.5 .M37 1973 MRR Alc.

GEORGIA.
Writers' Program. Georgia. Georgia,
a guide to its towns and countryside.
Atlanta, Tupper & Love [1954] xxii,
457 p. 917.58 54-10344
F291 .W94 1954 MRR Ref Desk.

GEORGIA--BIBLIOGRAPHY--CATALOGS.
United States. Library of Congress.
An exhibition commemorating the
settlement of Georgia, 1733-1948,
Washington, U.S. Govt. Print. Off.,
1948. iii, 92 p. 016.9758 48-
47033
Z663.15.A6 G4 1948 MRR Alc.

GEORGIA--BIOGRAPHY.
Georgia. Dept. of Archives and
History. Georgia's official and
statistical register. 1969/70-
Atlanta. 353.8/758 73-640860
JK4330 .A3 MRR Alc Last edition

GEORGIA--BIOGRAPHY--DICTIONARIES.
Who's who in Georgia. 1st- ed.;
1973- Atlanta, United States Public
Relations Service. 920/.0758 73-
85871
CT230 .W47 MRR Biog Latest edition

GEORGIA--CENTENNIAL CELEBRATIONS, ETC.
United States. Library of Congress.
An exhibition commemorating the
settlement of Georgia, 1733-1948,
Washington, U.S. Govt. Print. Off.,
1948. iii, 92 p. 016.9758 48-
47033
Z663.15.A6 G4 1948 MRR Alc.

GEORGIA--DESCRIPTION AND TRAVEL--GUIDE-
BOOKS.
Writers' Program. Georgia. Georgia,
a guide to its towns and countryside.
Atlanta, Tupper & Love [1954] xxii,
457 p. 917.58 54-10344
F291 .W94 1954 MRR Ref Desk.

GEORGIA--EXECUTIVE DEPARTMENTS.
Georgia. Dept. of Archives and
History. Georgia's official and
statistical register. 1969/70-
Atlanta. 353.8/758 73-640860
JK4330 .A3 MRR Alc Last edition

GEORGIA--HISTORY.
Coulter, Ellis Merton, Georgia, a
short history. Rev. and enl. ed.
Chapel Hill, University of North
Carolina Press [1960] 537 p. 975.8
60-16233
F286 .C78 1960 MRR Alc.

GEORGIA--POLITICS AND GOVERNMENT--1951-
--HANDBOOKS, MANUALS, ETC.
Georgia. Dept. of Archives and
History. Georgia's official and
statistical register. 1969/70-
Atlanta. 353.8/758 73-640860
JK4330 .A3 MRR Alc Last edition

GEORGIA--REGISTERS.
Georgia. Dept. of Archives and
History. Georgia's official and
statistical register. 1969/70-
Atlanta. 353.8/758 73-640860
JK4330 .A3 MRR Alc Last edition

GEORGIA--STATISTICS.
Georgia. University. Bureau of
Business and Economic Research.
Georgia statistical abstract. 1951-
Athens. 52-62944
HA321 .G4 MRR Alc Latest edition

GEORGIA. GENERAL ASSEMBLY--HANDBOOKS,
MANUALS, ETC.
Georgia. Secretary of State.
Handbook of the General Assembly of
the State of Georgia. [Atlanta] 10-
12138
JK4330 .A33 MRR Alc Latest edition

GEORGIA. GENERAL ASSEMBLY--REGISTERS.
Georgia. Secretary of State. Members
of General Assembly, State Senate and
House of Representatives. Atlanta.
57-23044
JK4330 .A335 MRR Alc Latest
edition

GEORGIAN LANGUAGE--DICTIONARIES--
ENGLISH.
Cherkesi, E. Georgian-English
dictionary. [Oxford] Printed for the
trustees of the Marjory Wardrop Fund,
University of Oxford, 1950. 275 p.
494.7 494.8* 52-32066
PK9125 .C47 MRR Alc.

GEOSCIENCE
see Earth sciences

GEREFORMEERDE KERKEN IN NEDERLAND--
YEARBOOKS.
Gereformeerde Kerken in Nederland.
Jaarboek. Goes, Oostermaan & Le
Cointre. 52-67670
BX9470 .G47 MRR Alc Latest edition

GERM THEORY OF DISEASE.
see also Bacteria, Pathogenic

see also Diseases--Causes and
theories of causation

GERMAN-AMERICAN NEWSPAPERS--
BIBLIOGRAPHY.
Arndt, Karl John Richard. German-
American newspapers and periodicals,
1732-1955; Heidelberg, Quelle &
Meyer, 1961. 794 p. 62-107
Z6953.5.G3 A7 MRR Alc.

GERMAN-AMERICAN PERIODICALS--
BIBLIOGRAPHY.
Arndt, Karl John Richard. German-
American newspapers and periodicals,
1732-1955; Heidelberg, Quelle &
Meyer, 1961. 794 p. 62-107
Z6953.5.G3 A7 MRR Alc.

GERMAN DRAMA--19TH CENTURY--
BIBLIOGRAPHY.
Johns Hopkins university. Library.
Fifty years of German drama;
Baltimore, The Johns Hopkins press,
1941. ix, 111 p. 016.8328 41-
11617
Z2234.D7 J6 MRR Alc.

GERMAN DRAMA--20TH CENTURY--
BIBLIOGRAPHY.
Johns Hopkins university. Library.
Fifty years of German drama;
Baltimore, The Johns Hopkins press,
1941. ix, 111 p. 016.8328 41-
11617
Z2234.D7 J6 MRR Alc.

GERMAN DRAMA--BIBLIOGRAPHY.
Binger, Norman. A bibliography of
German plays on microcards. Hamden,
Conn., Shoe String Press, 1970. 224
p. 016.832 78-117199
Z2234.D7 B55 MRR Alc.

Schulz, Friedrich Ernst.
Dramenlexikon: ein Wegweiser zu etwa
10,000 urheberrechtlich geschützten
Bühnenwerken. Neu hrsg. Köln,
Kiepenheuer & Witsch [1958-62] 2 v.
61-34835
Z2234.D7 S372 MRR Alc.

GERMAN DRAMA--MICROCARD CATALOGS.
Binger, Norman. A bibliography of
German plays on microcards. Hamden,
Conn., Shoe String Press, 1970. 224
p. 016.832 78-117199
Z2234.D7 B55 MRR Alc.

GERMAN DRAMA--TRANSLATIONS FROM FOREIGN
LITERATURE--BIBLIOGRAPHY.
  Schulz, Friedrich Ernst.
    Dramenlexikon; ein Wegweiser zu etwa
    10,000 urheberrechtlich geschützten
    Bühnenwerken. Neu hrsg. Köln,
    Kiepenheuer & Witsch [1958-62] 2 v.
    61-34835
      Z2224.D7 S372 MRR Alc.

GERMAN FICTION--BIBLIOGRAPHY.
  Luther, Arthur. Land und Leute in
    deutscher Erzählung; 3. gänzlich
    veränderte und ergänzte Aufl.
    Stuttgart, Hiersemann, 1954. 555 p.
    55-19035
      Z5917.H6 L87 1954 MRR Alc.

  Der Romanführer. 2., neu bearb. und
    veränderte Aufl. Stuttgart, A.
    Hiersemann, 1960-   62-40309
      PN3326 .R62 MRR Alc.

GERMAN IMPRINTS.
  Verzeichnis lieferbarer Bücher.
    1971/72- Frankfurt am Main, Verlag
    der Buchhändler-Vereinigung GmbH.
    018.4 76-615229
      Z2221 .V47 MRR Alc Latest edition

  Verzeichnis lieferbarer Bücher.
    Nachtrag. [Frankfurt am Main] 018.4
    74-643578
      Z2221 .V47 Suppl. MRR Alc Latest
        edition

GERMAN IMPRINTS--CATALOGS.
  Leipziger Kommissions- und
    Grossbuchhandel. L K G Lagerkatalog.
    1962- [Leipzig] 72-626453
      Z1036 .L5 MRR Alc Latest edition

GERMAN IMPRINTS--PERIODICALS.
  Jahresverzeichnis der
    Verlagsschriften und einer Auswahl
    der ausserhalb des Buchhandels
    erschienenen Veröffentlichungen der
    DDR, der BDR und Westberlins sowie
    der deutschsprachigen Werke anderer
    Länder. Leipzig, VEB Verlag für
    Buch- und Bibliothekswesen. 73-
    640585
      Z2221 .J26 MRR Alc Partial set

GERMAN LANGUAGE--BIBLIOGRAPHY.
  Bibliographie der deutschen Sprach-
    und Literaturwissenschaft. Bd. 9-
    1969- Frankfurt am Main, V.
    Klostermann. 72-612758
      Z2231 .B5 MRR Alc Full set

  Otto Harrassowitz (Firm) German
    series publications in the fields of
    Germanic language & literature,
    German history. Wiesbaden, 1967-69.
    2 v. 015.43 67-85917
      Z2235.A2 O8 1967 MRR Alc.

GERMAN LANGUAGE--CONVERSATION AND
PHRASE BOOKS.
  Anderson, Beatrix. Cassell's Beyond
    the dictionary in German. New York,
    Funk & Wagnalls [1968, c1968] 171 p.
    [2.95]   433/.2 74-80701
      PF3640 .A5 1969 MRR Alc.

GERMAN LANGUAGE--CONVERSATION AND
PHRASE BOOKS--POLYGLOT.
  Dony, Yvonne P. de. Léxico del
    lenguaje figurado, comparado, Buenos
    Aires, Ediciones Desclée, De Brouwer
    [1951] 804 p. 52-21901
      PB331 .D6 MRR Alc.

GERMAN LANGUAGE--DICTIONARIES.
  Grimm, Jakob Ludwig Karl, Deutsches
    wörterbuch Leipzig, S. Hirzel, 1854-
    19 v. in   g 01-2349
      PF3625 .G7 MRR Alc.

  Heyne, Moriz, Deutsches Wörterbuch.
    (Reprogr. Nachdr. d. 2. Aufl.
    Leipzig 1905-1906) Stuttgart,
    Hirzel, 1970. 3 v. [DM248.00] 75-
    881501
      PF3625 .H4 1970 MRR Alc.

  Mackensen, Lutz, ed. Deutsche
    Rechtschreibung; [8. Aufl.]
    Gütersloh] C. Bertelsmann, 1954.
    729 p. 54-32746
      PF3146 .M3 MRR Alc.

  Mackensen, Lutz, Deutsches
    Wörterbuch. (6., verb. u. erw.
    Aufl.) München, Südwest-Verl.
    (1970) xliii, 1064 p. [DM24.00]
    72-863935
      PF3625 .M25 1970 MRR Alc.

GERMAN LANGUAGE--DICTIONARIES--DUTCH.
  Bosch, Abraham ten, Viertalig
    technisch woordenboek. Deventer, Æ.
    E. Kluwer [1948-55] 4 v. 603 50-
    18447
      T10 .B72 MRR Alc.

GERMAN LANGUAGE--DICTIONARIES--ENGLISH.
  Artschwager, Ernst Friedrich,
    Dictionary of biological equivalents,
    German-English, Baltimore, The
    Williams & Wilkins company, 1930.
    239 p. incl. 6 plates. 570.3 30-
    18274
      QH13 .A7 MRR Alc.

  Artschwager, Ernst Friedrich,
    Dictionary of botanical equivalents,
    Baltimore, The Williams & Wilkins
    company, 1925. 5 p. l., 9-124 p.
    25-11598
      QK9 .A7 1925 MRR Alc.

  Beigel, Hugo G. Dictionary of
    psychology and related fields: German-
    English. New York, F. Ungar Pub. Co.
    [1971] 256 p. [$9.00] 150/.3 74-
    115063
      BF31 .B27 MRR Alc.

  Bein, Gerhard. Wörterbuch des
    internationalen Verkehrs. Leipzig,
    Verlag Enzyklopädie VEB (1968). 232
    p. [18.00]   380.5/03 71-410715
      HE141 .B44 MRR Alc.

  Betteridge, Harold T. Cassell's
    German & English dictionary; 10th
    ed. London, Cassell, 1965. 629, 619
    p. [36/-]   67-94525
      PF3640 .B45 1965a MRR Ref Desk.

  Betteridge, Harold T., ed. Cassell's
    German & English dictionary; 12th
    ed.; completely revised & re-edited
    London, Cassell, 1968. xx, 630 [4],
    619 p. [45/-] 433/.2 78-540689
      PF3640 .B45 1968 MRR Alc.

  Betteridge, Harold T., ed. The new
    Cassell's German dictionary; New
    York, Funk & Wagnalls [c1971] xx,
    646, 632 p. [$9.95 (thumb-indexed)]
    433/.21 73-157904
      PF3640 .B45 1971 MRR Ref Desk.

  Breuer, Karl. Technisch-
    wissenschaftliches
    Taschenwörterbuch. 6., völlig
    überarb. u. erg. Aufl. Berlin,
    Bielefeld, Siemens (1971). 405 p.
    [DM38.00]   75-597125
      T10 .B77 1971 MRR Alc.

  Breul, Karl Herman, Heath's German
    and English dictionary, Boston, New
    York [etc.] D.C. Heath & co. [pref.
    1909] xii, 797, 545, [1] p. 26-366

      PF3640 .B8 1909 MRR Alc.

  Breul, Karl Hermann, Cassell's new
    German and English dictionary, Rev.
    and enl. New York, Funk and Wagnalls
    company [1939] xix p; 1 l., 813,
    687 p. 433.2 42-1037
      PF3640 .B84 1939a MRR Alc.

  Brockhaus illustrated German-English,
    English-German dictionary. New York,
    McGraw-Hill [c1959-60; v. 1, 1960] 2
    v. in 1. 433.2 61-17213
      PF3640 .B867 MRR Alc.

  Bucksch, Herbert. Wörterbuch für
    Bautechnik und Baumaschinen. 4.
    wesentlich erw. Aufl. Wiesbaden,
    Bauverlag, 1968- v.   [DM 140.-
    (Bd. 1)]   624/.03 68-98879
      TA9 .B924 MRR Alc.

  Cescotti, Roderich. Luftfahrt -
    Wörterbuch; 2. verb. Aufl.
    München, H. Reich [1957, c1954] 448
    p. 629.1303 60-24363
      TL509 .C4 1957 MRR Alc.

  De Vries, Louis, German-English
    science dictionary for students in
    chemistry, physics, biology,
    agriculture, and related sciences 3d
    ed.; xlii, 592 p.   503 59-9412
      Q123 .D4 1959 MRR Alc.

  De Vries, Louis, German-English
    technical and engineering dictionary,
    2d ed., completely rev. and enl.
    New York, McGraw-Hill [1965, c1966]
    1178 p.   603 65-23218
      T9 .D48 1966 MRR Alc.

  De Vries, Louis, Wörterbuch der
    Textilindustrie. Wiesbaden,
    Brandstetter [1959-60] 2 v.   677.03
    59-42656
      TS1309 .D43 MRR Alc.

  Dictionary of physics and allied
    sciences. London, P. Owen [1958-62]
    2 v. 530.3 58-35180
      QC5 .D52 MRR Alc.

  Eggeling, Hans F. A dictionary of
    modern German prose usage. Oxford,
    Clarendon Press, 1961. xii, 418 p.
    433.2 61-2526
      PF3640 .E38 MRR Alc.

  Eichborn, Reinhart von. Business
    dictionary. Englewood Cliffs, N.J.,
    Prentice-Hall [1962, v.2, c1961] 2
    v. 330.3 62-13618
      HB61 .E433 MRR Alc.

  Ernst, Richard. Dictionary of
    chemistry, [3. Aufl.] Wiesbaden,
    Brandstetter [1967-68] [c1961-63] 2
    v. 540/.3 76-390463
      QD5 .E732 MRR Alc.

  Ernst, Richard. Wörterbuch der
    industriellen Technik, Wiesbaden,
    Brandstetter, 195 [c1948- v.
    603 60-3617
      T10 .E75 Bd. 1-2 MRR Alc.

  Freeman, Henry George, Wörterbuch
    Werkzeuge; 2. Aufl. Essen, W.
    Girardet [1960] 658 p. 621.7503
    61-1734
      TJ9 .F72 1960 MRR Alc.

  Goulden, William Owen. German-
    English medical dictionary. London,
    J. & A. Churchill, 1955. VI, 513 p.
    610.3 56-2079
      R121 .G73 1955 MRR Alc.

  Gunston, C. A. Gunston & Corner's
    German-English glossary of financial
    and economic terms. 6th ed., greatly
    compressed, but in content much
    amplified, Frankfurt am Main, F.
    Knapp [1972] xxiii, 1203 p.
    330/.03 72-188587
      HG151 .G85 1972 MRR Alc.

  Harrap's standard German and English
    dictionary. London, Harrap, [1963-
    v.   433.2 64-6113
      PF3640 .H3 MRR Ref Desk.

  Herland, Leo Joseph. Dictionary of
    mathematical sciences. New York, F.
    Ungar Pub. Co. [1951-54] 2 v.
    510.3 51-13545
      QA5 .H4 MRR Alc.

  Herland, Leo Joseph. Dictionary of
    mathematical sciences 2d ed., rev.
    and enl. New York, F. Ungar Pub. Co.
    [1965- v.   510.3 65-16622
      QA5 .H42 MRR Alc.

  Hyman, Charles J. German-English,
    English-German astronautics
    dictionary, New York, Consultants
    Bureau, 1968. viii, 237 p.
    629.4/03 65-20216
      TL788 .H8 MRR Alc.

  International encyclopedia of
    chemical science. Princeton, N.J.,
    Van Nostrand [1964] 1331 p.   540.3
    64-1619
      QD5 .I5 1964 MRR Alc.

  Köhler, Eduard Ludwig, English-
    German and German-English dictionary
    for the iron and steel industry,
    Vienna, Springer, 1955. xii, 168,
    162 p.   55-6643
      TN609 .K6 MRR Alc.

  Langenscheidt concise German
    dictionary. [New York] McGraw-Hill
    [1969, c1964] 2 v. in 1. [9.50]
    433/.2 76-3544
      PF3640 .L22 MRR Ref. Desk.

  Langenscheidt's concise German
    dictionary. New York, Barnes & Noble
    [1964] v. 2, c1961] 2 v. in 1.
    433.2 64-56958
      PF3640 .L243 MRR Alc.

  Langenscheidts Handwörterbuch.
    Deutsch-Englisch, [3. Aufl.] Berlin-
    Schöneberg, Langenscheidt [1961]
    672 p. 63-49805
      PF3640 .L25 1961a MRR Alc.

  Langenscheidt's new Muret-Sanders
    encyclopedic dictionary of the
    English and German languages, [1st
    ed.] New York, Barnes & Noble [1962-
    v. in   62-6984
      PF3640 .L257 MRR Alc.

  Leidecker, Kurt Friedrich, ed.
    German-English technical dictionary
    of aeronautics, rocketry, space
    navigation ... New York, S. F. Vanni
    [1950-51] v. (968 p.) 629.1303
    50-14702
      TL509 .L4 MRR Alc.

  Lejeune, Fritz, Deutsch-Englisches,
    Englisch-Deutsches Wörterbuch für
    Ärzte. 2. völlig neubearb. Aufl.
    Stuttgart, Thieme, 1968- v. [DM
    64.00] 610/.3 68-69803
      R121 .L372 MRR Alc.

  Luftfahrttechnisches Wörterbuch,
    Berlin, De Gruyter, 1960. xiv, 312
    p. 62-33521
      TL509 .L75 MRR Alc.

  Merz, Otto, Deutsch-englisches und
    englisch-deutsches Fachwörterbuch
    für Fachausdrücke aus dem Lack- und
    Farbengebiet. 2., neubearb. und
    erweiterte Aufl. Stuttgart,
    Wissenschaftliche Verlags-
    gesellschaft, 1954. 351 p.   55-
    22330
      TP935 .M45 1954 MRR Alc.

  Moth, Axel Fredrik Carl Mathias,
    Glossary of library terms, English,
    Danish, Dutch, French, German,
    Italian, Spanish, Swedish, Boston,
    The Boston book company, 1915. 58 p.
    15-3471
      Z1006 .M72 MRR Alc.

GERMAN LANGUAGE--DICTIONARIES-- (Cont.)
Muret, Eduard, Muret-Sanders
Enzyklopädisches englisch-deutsches
und deutsch-englisches wörterbuch,
Grosse ausg. Durchgesehene und verb.
stereotyp-aufl. Berlin-Schöneberg,
Langenscheidt [1922?] v.   mrr01-
71
    PF3640 .M8 1922 MRR Alc.

Oppermann, Alfred. Wörterbuch der
modernen Technik. 3. Aufl. München-
Pullach, Verlag Dokumentation, 1972-
v.   603   72-306183
    TL509 .O623 MRR Alc.

Pattermann, Wilhelm. Deutsch-
englisches Wörter- und Phrasenbuch
mit Berücksichtigung des
amerikanischen Englisch. 3.,
durchgesehene Aufl. München, G.
Freytag, 1959. 1452 p.   59-38388
    PF3640 .P27 1959 MRR Ref Desk.

Patterson, Austin McDowell, A German-
English dictionary for chemists. 3d
ed. New York, Wiley [1950] xviii,
541 p.   540.3   50-4541
    QD5 .P3 1950 MRR Alc.

Polygraph dictionary der graphischen
Techniken und der verwandten Gebiete.
.2., durch die Polygraph-Redaktion
überarb., erg. und erw. Aufl.
Frankfurt am Main, Polygraph Verlag
[1967] 330 p.   68-123918
    Z118 .P63 1967 MRR Alc.

Sattler, Wilhelm Ferdinand. Deutsch-
englisches sachwörterbuch. Leipzig,
Renger, 1904. xx, 1035 p.   05-16230

    PF3640 .S3 MRR Alc.

Schöffler, Herbert, The new
Schöffler-Weis compact German and
English dictionary: English-German,
German-English, London, Harrap,
1969. 562, 495 [19] p. [50/-]
433/.2 71-504148
    PF3640 .S435 1969 MRR Ref Desk.

Sommer, Werner, Management
dictionary. 3., durchgesehene und
erw. Aufl. Berlin, De Gruyter, 1966-
68. 2 v. [DM 18.00 per vol.]
658.003 67-73661
    HF1002 .S622 MRR Alc.

Sommer, Werner, Management
dictionary. 3., durchgesehene und
erw. Aufl. Berlin, De Gruyter, 1966-
68. 2 v. [DM 18.00 per vol.]
658.003 67-73661
    HF1002 .S622 MRR Alc.

Taylor, Ronald Jack, A German-
English dictionary of idioms;
München, M. Hueber, 1960. 597 p.
a   61-2669
    PF3460 .T3 MRR Alc.

Walter, Frank Keller, Abbreviations
and technical terms used in book
catalogs and bibliographies, in eight
languages, 1817 handy edition
Boston, The Boston book company
[1919?] 2 v. in 1.   27-13479
    Z1006 .W261 1919 MRR Alc.

Walther, Rudolf, lexicographer.
Polytechnical dictionary, Oxford,
New York, Pergamon Press [1968,
c1967] 2 v.   603 67-25817
    T10 .W3 1868 MRR Alc.

Wildhagen, Karl, Englisch-deutsches,
deutsch-englisches Wörterbuch;
Wiesbaden, Brandstetter-Verlag [1952]-
2 v. 64-28884
    PF3640 .W544 MRR Alc.

Wildhagen, Karl, Englisch-Deutsches,
deutsch-englisches Wörterbuch: 2.,
vollkommen überarbeitete und erw.
Aufl. Wiesbaden: Brandstetter;
London: Allen and Unwin, 19 v.
433/.2/1 72-349225
    PF3640 .W544 1972 MRR Alc.

Wittfoht, Annemarie,
Kunststofftechnisches Wörterbuch.
München, C. Hanser, 1956- v.   a
56-5235
    TP886 .A15W48 MRR Alc.

Závada, Dušan, Satzlexikon der
Handelskorrespondenz. Wiesbaden,
Brandstetter; London, Pitman, 1969.
xxi, 331 p. [20.00]   380/.03 79-
426305
    HF1002 .Z34 MRR Alc.

GERMAN LANGUAGE--DICTIONARIES--LATIN.
Merguet, Hugo, Handlexikon zu
Cicero, Leipzig, Dieterich, 1905. 2
p. l., 816 p.   06-33549
    PA6366 .M45 MRR Alc.

GERMAN LANGUAGE--DICTIONARIES--POLYGLOT.
Associazione industriale lombarda.
Glossario del lavoro: italiano,
francese, inglese, tedesco. Milano,
1964. 1335 p.   67-43249
    HD4839 .A78 MRR Alc.

Band-Kuzmany, Karin R. M. Glossary
of the theatre. Amsterdam, New York,
Elsevier Pub. Co., 1969. 140 p.
[31.20]   792/.03 68-57152
    PN2035 .B3 MRR Alc.

Beeck, Peter. Fachausdrücke der
Presse. [3. Aufl.] Frankfurt am
Main, Polygraph Verlag, 1950. 174 p.
070.03 51-16343
    PN4728 .B43 1950 MRR Alc.

Britannica world language dictionary,
[Chicago, 1958] 1483-2015 p.   413
58-4491
    P361 .B7 1958 MRR Alc.

Buecken, Francisco J. Vocabulário
tecnico portuguez-inglês-francês-
alemão. 4. ed. rev. [São Paulo]
Edições Melhoramentos [1961] 600
p.   603 62-3680
    T10 .B82 1961 MRR Alc.

Bürger, Erich. Technical dictionary
of data processing, computers, office
machines. [1st ed.] Oxford, New
York, Pergamon Press [1970] 1463 p.
651.8/03 75-81247
    QA76.15 .B46 1970 MRR Alc.

Capitol's concise dictionary.
Bologna, Capitol, 1972.   1051 (i.e.
1207) p.   413 72-172231
    P361 .C3 MRR Alc.

Chalkiopoulos, Geórgios.
[Pentaglosson lexilogion technikōn
horon (romanized form)] [1960]
1030 p.   61-31355
    T10 .C46 1960 MRR Alc.

Clason, W. E., Elsevier's dictionary
of computers, automatic control and
data processing. 2d rev. ed. of The
dictionary of automation, computers,
control and measuring. Amsterdam,
New York, Elsevier Pub. Co., 1971.
484 p.   [fl78.00] 001.6/4/03 73-
151733
    TJ212.5 .C55 1971 MRR Alc.

Clason, W. E., Supplement to the
Elsevier dictionaries of electronics,
nucleonics and telecommunication.
Amsterdam, New York, Elsevier Pub.
Co., 1963. 633 p.   603 63-11369
    T10 .C55 MRR Alc.

Conference terminology, 2d ed., rev.
and augm. Amsterdam, New York,
Elsevier Pub. Co.; [sole distributors
for the U.S.: American Elsevier Pub.
Co., New York] 1962. 162 p.   413
63-8568
    PB324.C6 C6 1962 MRR Alc.

Cooper, S. A. Concise international
dictionary of mechanics & geology;
New York, Philosophical Library
[1958] viii, 400 p.   621.03 58-
3594
    TJ9 .C6 1958 MRR Alc.

Dictionar tehnic poliglot: Ediția
a 2-a. București, Editura Tehnica,
1967. xv, 1233 p.   603 68-2971
    T10 .D54 1967 MRR Alc.

Dictionary of chemistry and chemical
technology, in six languages: [Rev.
ed.] Oxford, New York, Pergamon
Press [1966] 1325 p.   540.3 65-
29008
    QD5 .D5 1966 MRR Alc.

Dictionary of photography and
cinematography: London, New York,
Focal Press [1961] 1 v. (various
pagings) 770.3 63-24356
    TR9 .D5 MRR Alc.

Dictionnaire à l'usage de la
librairie ancienne pour les langues:
française, anglaise, allemande,
suédoise, danoise, italienne,
espagnole, hollandaise, Paris, Ligue
internationale de la librairie
ancienne, 1956. 190 p.   655.403 57-
2275
    Z282 .D5 MRR Alc.

The Duden pictorial encyclopedia in
five languages: English, French,
German, Italian, Spanish. 2d, enl.
ed. New York, F. Ungar Pub. Co.
[1958] 2 v.   413 58-11093
    P361 .D8 1958 MRR Alc.

Elektrotechnik und Elektrochemie.
München, R. Oldenbourg, 1955. xxiv,
1304 p.   57-18208
    TK9 .E42 1955 MRR Alc.

Elsevier's automobile dictionary in
eight languages: Amsterdam, New
York, Elsevier Pub. Co.; [distributed
by Van Nostrand, Princeton, N.J.]
1960. 946 p.   629.203 59-8946
    TL9 .E43 MRR Alc.

Elsevier's banking dictionary in six
languages: Amsterdam, New York,
Elsevier Pub. Co., 1966. 302 p.
332.103 65-20139
    HG151 .E45 MRR Alc.

Elsevier's dictionary of aeronautics
in six languages: Amsterdam, New
York, Elsevier Pub. Co., 1964. 842
p.   629.1303 63-22063
    TL509 .E4 MRR Alc.

Elsevier's dictionary of building
construction, Amsterdam, New York,
Elsevier Pub. Co., 1959. 471 p.
690.3 58-59508
    TH9 .E47 MRR Alc.

Elsevier's dictionary of chemical
engineering. Amsterdam, New York,
1968. 2 v. [62.50 per vol.]
660/.2/03 68-54865
    TP9 .E38 MRR Alc.

Elsevier's dictionary of cinema,
sound, and music, in six languages:
Amsterdam, New York, Elsevier Pub.
Co., 1956. 948 p.   778.503 56-
13141
    TR847 .E4 MRR Alc.

Elsevier's dictionary of criminal
science, in eight languages:
Amsterdam, New York, Elsevier Pub.
Co.; [distributed by Van Nostrand,
Princeton, N.J.] 1960. xv, 1460 p.
364.03 59-12582
    HV6017 .E4 MRR Alc.

Elsevier's dictionary of electronics
and waveguides, 2d ed., rev. and
enl. Amsterdam, New York, Elsevier
Pub. Co., 1966 [i.e. 1965] 833 p.
621.38103 65-20142
    TK7804 .E4 1965 MRR Alc.

Elsevier's dictionary of general
physics in six languages: Amsterdam,
New York, Elsevier Pub. Co., 1962.
859 p.   530.3 62-13015
    QC5 .E46 MRR Alc.

Elsevier's dictionary of nuclear
science and technology. 2d rev. ed.
Amsterdam, New York, Elsevier Pub.
Co., 1970. 787 p. [85.00]
539.7/03 72-103357
    QC772 .E4 1970 MRR Alc.

Elsevier's dictionary of photography
in three languages: Amsterdam, New
York, Elsevier Pub. Co.: distributed
by American Elsevier Pub. Co., New
York, 1965. 660 p.   770.3 63-16076
    TR9 .E46 MRR Alc.

Elsevier's dictionary of television,
radar, and antennas, in six
languages: Amsterdam, New York,
Elsevier Pub. Co., 1955. 760 p.
621.38803 55-6216
    TK6634 .E4 MRR Alc.

Elsevier's dictionary of the printing
and allied industries in four
languages, Amsterdam, New York,
[etc.] Elsevier Pub. Co., 1967. 596
p. [90.00]   655/.003 67-19851
    Z118 .E5 MRR Alc.

Elsevier's lexicon of archive
terminology: Amsterdam, New York,
Elsevier Pub. Co., 1964. 83 p.
025.171014 64-56714
    CD945 .E4 MRR Alc.

Elsevier's lexicon of stock-market
terms: Amsterdam, New York, Elsevier
Pub. Co., 1965. 131 p.   332.603 65-
13892
    HG4513 .E4 MRR Alc.

Elsevier's medical dictionary in five
languages: Amsterdam, New York,
Elsevier Pub. Co., 1964. 1588 p.
610.3 62-13022
    R121 .E5 1964 MRR Alc.

Elsevier's wood dictionary in seven
languages: Amsterdam, New York,
Elsevier Pub. Co., 1964- v.
634.903 64-14178
    SD431 .E4 MRR Alc.

Fabierkiewicz, Wacław. Podręczny
słownik włókienniczy w 5 językach:
[Wyd. 1] [Warszawa] Państwowe
Wydawn. Techniczne [1955] xlvii, 305
p.   55-38912
    TS1309 .F3 MRR Alc.

Frey, Albert Romer, Dictionary of
numismatic names, [New York] Barnes
& Noble [1947] ix, 311, 94 p.
737.03 48-5357
    CJ67 .F7 1947 MRR Alc.

Giteau, Cécile. Dictionnaire des
arts du spectacle, français--anglais
--allemand; Paris, Dunod, 1970. xxv,
429 p. [88.00] 79-499699
    PN1579 .G5 MRR Alc.

Great Britain. Naval intelligence
division. A dictionary of naval
equivalents covering English, French,
Italian, Spanish, Russian, Swedish,
Danish, Dutch, German. London, H.M.
Stationery off., 1924. 2 v.   24-
23782
    V24 .G7 MRR Alc.

GERMAN LANGUAGE--DICTIONARIES-- (Cont.)
Haensch, Günther. Dictionary of international relations and politics; Amsterdam, New York, Elsevier Pub. Co., 1965. xv, 638 p. 320.03 64-8710
   JX1226 .H26 MRR Alc.

Haensch, Günther. Wörterbuch der Landwirtschaft: 3., überarb. Aufl. München, Bayerischer Landwirtschaftverlag [1966] xxiv, 746 p. 630/.3 68-96091
   S411 .H26 1966 MRR Alc.

Herbst, Robert. Dictionary of commercial, financial, and legal terms; 2d ed., Zug, Translegal [1966- v. 330/.03 67-8369
   HB61 .H462 MRR Alc.

Herbst, Robert. Dictionary of commercial, financial, and legal terms 3rd ed. rev. Zug, Translegal [1968- v. [unpriced] 330/.03 76-410368
   HB61 .H463 MRR Alc.

Hétnyelvű sportszótár: Budapest, Terra, 1960- v. 61-21333
   GV567 .H45 MRR Alc.

Horn, Stefan F., Glossary of financial terms, Amsterdam, New York, Elsevier Pub. Co., 1965. 271 p. 332.03 64-23405
   HG151 .H6 MRR Alc.

Horten, Hans Ernest. Export-import correspondence in four languages London, Gower Press Ltd., 1970. xi, 2-316 p. [80/-] 382/.03 76-495482
   HF1002 .H695 MRR Alc.

International Chamber of Commerce. Dictionary of advertising and distribution, Basel, Verlag für Recht und Gesellschaft, 1954. 1 v. (unpaged) 659.103 54-24644
   HF5803 .I58 1954 MRR Alc.

International Commission on Large Dams. Dictionnaire technique des barrages. 2. ed. [Paris, 1960?] 380 p. 627.803 61-805
   TC540 .I45 1960 MRR Alc.

International insurance dictionary: [n.p., European Conference of Insurance Supervisory Services, 1959] xxxi, 1083 p. 368.03 61-35675
   HG8025 .I5 MRR Alc.

International Railway Documentation Bureau. Lexique général des termes ferroviaires, [2. ed. entièrement refondue et augm.] Amsterdam, J. H. De Bussy, 1865. 1357 p. 625.1003 66-87434
   TF9 .I46 1965 MRR Alc.

Jacks, Graham Vernon. Multilingual vocabulary of soil science. [2d ed., rev. Rome] Land & Water Division, Food and Agriculture Organization of the United Nations [1960] xxiii, 428 p. 631.403 60-50105
   S591 .J26 1960 MRR Alc.

James, Glenn, ed. Mathematics dictionary, Multilingual ed. Princeton, N.J., Van Nostrand [1959] 546 p. 510.3 59-8656
   QA5 .J32 1959 MRR Alc.

Kerchove, René de, baron, International maritime dictionary: 2d ed. Princeton, N.J., Van Nostrand [1961] v, 1018 p. 623.803 61-16272
   V23 .K4 1961 MRR Alc.

Kleczek, Josip. Astronomical dictionary. [Vyd. 1.] Praha, Nakl. Československé akademie věd, 1961. 972 p. 62-25391
   QB14 .K55 MRR Alc.

Labarre, E. J. Dictionary and encyclopaedia of paper and paper-making, 2d ed., rev. and enl. London, Oxford University Press, 1952. xxi, 488 p. 676.03 53-29414

   TS1085 .L3 1952a MRR Alc.

Lana, Gabriella. Glossary of geographical names in six languages: Amsterdam, New York, Elsevier Pub. Co., 1967. 184 p. 910/.003 66-25762
   G104.5 .L3 MRR Ref Desk.

Lexicon opthalmologicum; Basel, New York, S. Karger, 1959. 223 p. 617.703 58-4669
   RE21 .L45 MRR Alc.

Lexikon des Bibliothekswesens. Leipzig, VEB Verlag für Buch- und Bibliothekswesen, 1969. xiii, 769 p. [42.00] 70-423794
   Z1006 .L46 MRR Alc.

Nash, Rose. Multilingual lexicon of linguistics and philology: English, Russian, German, French. Coral Gables, Fla., University of Miami Press [1968] xxvi, 390 p. 413 68-31044
   P29 .N34 MRR Alc.

Nijdam, J. Tuinbouwkundig woordenboek in acht talen. Herziene en uitgebreide uitg. van de Woordenlijst voor de tuinbouw in zeven talen. ['s-Gravenhage, Staatsdrukkerij- en Uitgeverijbedrijf; voor alle anderen landen: Interscience Publishers, New York] 1961. 504 p. 62-52704
   SB45 .N673 MRR Alc.

Nobel, Albert, Dictionnaire medical. 5. ed. rev. et augm. Paris, Masson, 1970 [c1969] xxii, 1329 p. [200.00] 77-93556
   R121 .N6 1970 MRR Alc.

Pisant, Emmanuel. International dictionary. Paris, Editions Moderninter [1958] 373 p. 413 58-26075
   P361 .P5 MRR Alc.

Polec. 2., verb. und erw. Aufl. Berlin, de Gruyter, 1967. xvi, 1037 p. with map. [DM 48.-] 330/.03 68-70864
   H40 .P6 1967 MRR Alc.

Raaff, J. J. Index vocabulorum quadrilingius; verf en vernis, [Den Haag] Vereniging van Vernis- en Verffabrikanten in Nederland, Exportgroep Verf, 1958. 898 p. 667.603 59-27978
   TP934.3 .R2 MRR Alc.

Rae, Kenneth, ed. Lexique international de termes techniques de theatre Bruxelles, Elsevier [1959] 139 p. 60-26926
   PN2035 .R3 MRR Alc.

Sachs, Wolfgang, ed. Lebensversicherungstechnisches Wörterbuch. Würzburg, K. Thiltsch, 1954. 308 p. 56-16246
   HG8759 .S3 MRR Alc.

Schloms, Irene. Fachwörterbuch für Programmierer, deutsch, englisch, französisch. Heidelberg, Hüthig [1966] 139, 139, 110 p. [DM 28.00] 651.8 67-91557
   QA76.15 .S35 MRR Alc.

Schulz, Ernst, lexicographer. Wörterbuch der Optik und Feinmechanik. Wiesbaden, Brandstetter [1960-61] 3 v. a 61-3700
   QC351.2 .S34 MRR Alc.

Servotte, Jozef V., 1903- Dictionnaire commercial et financier: 2. ed., rev. et augm. Bruxelles, Éditions Brepols [1960] ix, 955 p. 61-930
   HF1002 .S42 1960 MRR Alc.

Six-language dictionary of automation, electronics and scientific instruments; London, Iliffe Books; Englewood Cliffs, N.J., Prentice-Hall [1962] 732 p. 621.3803 63-5414
   TK7804 .S5 1962 MRR Alc.

Skandinaviska banken, a.-b. Banking terms: French, German, Italian, Spanish, Swedish. Stockholm [1964] 65 p. 65-87814
   HG151 .S46 MRR Alc.

Smith, William James, A dictionary of musical terms in four languages. London, Hutchinson [1961] 195 p. 61-65056
   ML108 .S64D5 MRR Alc.

Stowarzyszenie Geodetów Polskich. Słownik geodezyjny w 5 [i.e. pięciu] językach: polskim, rosyjskim, niemieckim, angielskim, francuskim. Warszawa, Państwowe Przedsiębiorstwo Wydawn. Kartograficznych, 1954. xv, 525 p. 55-34784
   QB279 .S8 MRR Alc.

Sube, Ralf. Kernphysik und Kerntechnik: Berlin, Verlag Technik [1962] 1606 p. 62-2924
   QC772 .S9 MRR Alc.

Sube, Ralf. Wörterbuch Physik; Zürich, H. Deutsch, 1973. 3 v. 74-320593
   QC5 .S9 MRR Alc.

   2. uppl. Stockholm, Hedengren [1951] xix p., 1518 columns. 603 52-21624
   T10 .T358 1951 MRR Alc.

Thompson, Anthony. Vocabularium bibliothecarii. 2d ed. [Paris] UNESCO, 1962. 627 p. 63-5650
   Z1006 .T47 1962a MRR Alc.

Townsend, Derek. Advertising and public relations; London, A. Redman [1964] xvi, 152 p. 65-6026
   HF5803 .T6 MRR Alc.

Trollhann, Lilian, comp. Dictionary of data processing. Amsterdam, New York, Elsevier Pub. Co., 1964. 300 p. 651 64-8676
   QA76.15 .T7 MRR Alc.

Union européenne des experts comptables économiques et financiers. Lexique U.E.C. Lexicon. Düsseldorf, Verlagsbuchhandlung des Instituts der Wirtschaftsprüfer, 1961. 1 v. (various pagings) 63-31440
   HF5621 .U5 MRR Alc.

Vocabulaire international des termes d'urbanisme et d'architecture. 1. ed. Paris, Société de diffusion des techniques du bâtiment et des travaux publics, 1970- v. [133F (v. 1)] 70-860237
   NA31 .V6 MRR Alc.

Zahn, Hans E. Euro-Wirtschafts-Wörterbuch; Frankfurt am Main, F. Knapp [c1973] xiii, 702 p. 73-318519
   HB61 .Z34 MRR Alc.

Zboiński, A., ed. Dictionary of architecture and building trades in four languages: English, German, Polish, Russian. Oxford, New York, Pergamon Press; [distributed in the Western Hemisphere by Macmillan, New York, 1963] 491 p. 63-22975
   NA31 .Z34 MRR Alc.

Żytka, Romuald. Geological dictionary Warszawa, Wydawnictwa Geologiczne, 1970. 1439 p. [zł1250.00] 550/.3 72-31794
   QE5 .Z9 MRR Alc.

GERMAN LANGUAGE--ETYMOLOGY--DICTIONARIES.
Kluge, Friedrich, Etymologisches Wörterbuch der deutschen Sprache. 19. Aufl. Berlin, De Gruyter, 1963. xvi, 917 p. 64-29768
   PF3580 .K5 1963 MRR Alc.

Walshe, Maurice O'Connell. A concise German etymological dictionary. London, Routledge & K. Paul [1952] xxiv, 275 p. 432.03 52-3114
   PF3580 .W3 MRR Alc.

GERMAN LANGUAGE--ETYMOLOGY--NAMES.
Gottschald, Max. Deutsche Namenkunde, 3., verm. Aufl. Berlin, W. de Gruyter, 1954. 630 p. 54-4252
   CS2545 .G6 1954 MRR Alc.

GERMAN LANGUAGE--FOREIGN WORDS AND PHRASES--DICTIONARIES.
Fischer, Paul, Goethe-Wortschatz; Leipzig, E. Rohmkopf, 1929. xi, 905 p. 31-16505
   PT2239 .F5 1929 MRR Alc.

GERMAN LANGUAGE--GLOSSARIES, VOCABULARIES, ETC.
Anderson, Beatrix. Cassell's Beyond the dictionary in German, New York, Funk & Wagnalls [1969, c1968] 171 p. [2.95] 433/.2 74-80701
   PF3640 .A5 1969 MRR Alc.

Dornseiff, Franz, Der deutsche Wortschatz nach Sachgruppen. 7., unveränd. Aufl. Berlin, de Gruyter, 1970. 166, 922 p. [DM38.00] 73-588410
   PF3591 .D6 1970 MRR Alc.

GERMAN LANGUAGE--GLOSSARIES, VOCABULARIES, ETC.--POLYGLOT.
Lessere, Samuel E. Harlan's foreign language speak-easy, [3d ed.] Greenlawn, N.Y., Harlan Publications [1957] 106 p. 418.24 57-14033
   PE1635 .L4 1957 MRR Alc.

GERMAN LANGUAGE--GRAMMAR--1950-
Eggeling, Hans F. A dictionary of modern German prose usage. Oxford, Clarendon Press, 1961. xii, 418 p. 433.2 61-2526
   PF3640 .E38 MRR Alc.

Lederer, Herbert, Reference grammar of the German language. American ed. New York, Scribner [1969] xx, 709 p. 438/.2/42 69-17352
   PF3105 .L43 MRR Alc.

GERMAN LANGUAGE--IDIOMS, CORRECTIONS, ERRORS.
Drosdowski, Günther, Duden. Hauptschwierigkeiten der deutschen Sprache. Mannheim, Bibliographisches Institut (1967). 759 p. [17.00] 71-432700
   PF3460 .D7 MRR Alc.

GERMAN LANGUAGE--IDIOMS, (Cont.)
Engeroff, Karl Wilhelm, An English-German Dictionary of idioms. (2.,
erw. Aufl.) München, Hueber (1967).
313 p. [DM19.80] 433.1 68-74488

PF3640 .E48 1967 MRR Alc.

Friederich, Wolf. Moderne deutsche
Idiomatik. München, Hueber (1966)
823 p. [DM 34.80] 67-74707
PF3689 .F7 MRR Alc.

Pattermann, Wilhelm. Deutsch-englisches Wörter- und Phrasenbuch
mit Berücksichtigung des
amerikanischen Englisch. 3.,
durchgesehene Aufl. München, G.
Freytag, 1959. 1452 p. 58-38388
PF3640 .P27 1959 MRR Ref Desk.

Taylor, Ronald Jack, A German-English dictionary of idioms;
München, M. Hueber, 1960. 597 p.
a 61-2668
PF3460 .T3 MRR Alc.

GERMAN LANGUAGE--IDIOMS, CORRECTIONS,
ERRORS--DICTIONARIES.
Rohrich, Lutz. Lexikon der
sprichwörtlichen Redensarten.
Freiburg, Herder [1973] 2 v. (1255
p.) 73-364707
PF689 .R6 MRR Alc.

GERMAN LANGUAGE--MIDDLE HIGH GERMAN--
DICTIONARIES.
Lexer, Matthias von,
Mittelhochdeutsches handwörterbuch
Leipzig, S. Hirzel, 1872-78. 3 v.
03-27592
PF4327 .L4 MRR Alc.

Müller, Wilhelm,
Mittelhochdeutsches wörterbuch;
Leipzig, S. Hirzel, 1854-66. 3 v. in
4. 03-27590
PF4327 .M8 MRR Alc.

GERMAN LANGUAGE--MIDDLE HIGH GERMAN--
ETYMOLOGY--DICTIONARIES.
Walshe, Maurice O'Connell. A concise
German etymological dictionary.
London, Routledge & K. Paul [1952]
xxiv, 275 p. 432.03 52-3114
PF3580 .W3 MRR Alc.

GERMAN LANGUAGE--ORTHOGRAPHY AND
SPELLING.
Mackensen, Lutz, ed. Deutsche
Rechtschreibung; [s. Aufl.
Gütersloh] C. Bertelsmann, 1954.
729 p. 54-32746
PF3146 .M3 MRR Alc.

GERMAN LANGUAGE--PRONUNCIATION--
DICTIONARIES.
Duden Aussprachewörterbuch.
Mannheim, Dudenverlag des
Bibliographischen Instituts [c1962]
827 p. 63-2233
PF3137 .D8 MRR Alc.

GERMAN LANGUAGE--SPOKEN GERMAN.
Anderson, Beatrix. Cassell's Beyond
the dictionary in German, New York,
Funk & Wagnalls [1969, c1968] 171 p.
[2.95] 433/.2 74-80701
PF3640 .A5 1969 MRR Alc.

GERMAN LANGUAGE--STUDY AND TEACHING--
BIBLIOGRAPHY.
Centre for Information on Language
Teaching. A language-teaching
bibliography. 2d ed. Cambridge
[Eng.] University Press, 1972. x,
242 p. 016.407 76-152633
Z5814.L26 C45 1972 MRR Alc.

GERMAN LANGUAGE--SYNONYMS AND ANTONYMS.
Dornseiff, Franz, Der deutsche
Wortschatz nach Sachgruppen. 7.,
unveränd. Aufl. Berlin, de Gruyter,
1970. 166, 822 p. [DM38.00] 73-588410
PF3591 .D6 1970 MRR Alc.

Eberhard, Johann August, Johann
August Eberhards Synonymisches
handwörterbuch der deutschen
sprache. 16. aufl. Leipzig, T.
Grieben's verlag (L. Fernau) 1904.
xliv, 1131, [1] p. 08-26849
PF3591 .E3 1904 MRR Alc.

Peltzer, Karl. Das treffende Wort;
5., verb. Aufl. Thun, Ott Verlag
[1959] 582, [1] p. 60-42987
PF3591 .P4 1959 MRR Alc.

GERMAN LANGUAGE--TERMS AND PHRASES.
Friederich, Wolf. Moderne deutsche
Idiomatik. München, Hueber (1966)
823 p. [DM 34.80] 67-74707
PF3689 .F7 MRR Alc.

Pattermann, Wilhelm. Deutsch-englisches Wörter- und Phrasenbuch
mit Berücksichtigung des
amerikanischen Englisch. 3.,
durchgesehene Aufl. München, G.
Freytag, 1959. 1452 p. 59-38388
PF3640 .P27 1959 MRR Ref Desk.

GERMAN LANGUAGE--TERMS AND PHRASES--
DICTIONARIES.
Rohrich, Lutz. Lexikon der
sprichwörtlichen Redensarten.
Freiburg, Herder [1973] 2 v. (1255
p.) 73-364707
PF689 .R6 MRR Alc.

GERMAN LITERATURE--19TH CENTURY--
ADDRESSES, ESSAYS, LECTURES.
Hatfield, Henry Caraway, Modern
German literature: London, Edward
Arnold, 1966. viii, 167 p. [30/-]
830.8 67-70627
PT403 .H3 MRR Alc.

GERMAN LITERATURE--20TH CENTURY--
ADDRESSES, ESSAYS, LECTURES.
Hatfield, Henry Caraway, Modern
German literature: London, Edward
Arnold, 1966. viii, 167 p. [30/-]
830.8 67-70627
PT403 .H3 MRR Alc.

GERMAN LITERATURE--20TH CENTURY--
BIBLIOGRAPHY.
United States. Library of Congress.
Acquisitions Dept. European imprints
for the war years Washington, 1945-
46. 3 v. 015.4 45-37835
Z663.76 .E8 MRR Alc.

GERMAN LITERATURE--20TH CENTURY--BIO-
BIBLIOGRAPHY.
Kürschners Deutscher Literatur-
Kalender; Berlin, New York, de
Gruyter, 1973. xiv, 871 p.
[DM220.00] 808 73-203144
Z2233.3 .K83 MRR Biog.

Lennartz, Franz. Dichter und
Schriftsteller unserer Zeit; 7.
Aufl. Stuttgart, A. Kröner [1957]
vi, 672 p. 58-25924
PT401 .L35 1957 MRR Biog.

Ungar, Frederick, comp. Handbook of
Austrian literature. New York, F.
Ungar Pub. Co. [1973] xvi, 296 p.
830/.9/9436 71-125969
PT155 .U5 MRR Biog.

GERMAN LITERATURE--20TH CENTURY--
HISTORY AND CRITICISM.
Domandi, Agnes Körner, comp. Modern
German literature. New York, Unger
[1972] 2 v. [$30.00] 830/.9/0091
70-160436
PT401 .D6 MRR Alc.

Lennartz, Franz. Dichter und
Schriftsteller unserer Zeit; 7.
Aufl. Stuttgart, A. Kröner [1957]
vi, 672 p. 58-25924
PT401 .L35 1957 MRR Biog.

Moore, Harry Thornton. Twentieth-
century German literature New York,
Basic Books [1967] 224 p.
830.9/0091 67-16887
PT401 .M6 MRR Alc.

United States. Library of Congress.
Gertrude Clarke Whittall Poetry and
Literature Fund. French and German
letters today; Washington, Reference
Dept., Library of Congress, 1960. v,
53 p. 840.9 60-60062
Z663.293 .F7 MRR Alc.

GERMAN LITERATURE--AUSTRIAN AUTHORS--
BIBLIOGRAPHY.
Stock, Karl Franz.
Personalbibliographien
österreichischer Dichter und
Schriftsteller; Pullach bei
München, Verlag Dokumentation, 1972.
xxiii, 703 p. 73-308989
Z2111.A1 S76 MRR Biog.

GERMAN LITERATURE--AUSTRIAN AUTHORS--
BIO-BIBLIOGRAPHY.
Giebisch, Hans, Bio-
bibliographisches Literaturlexikon
Österreichs, Wien, Brüder Hollinek
[1964] viii, 516 p. 64-56140
Z2110 .G48 MRR Biog.

Ungar, Frederick, comp. Handbook of
Austrian literature. New York, F.
Ungar Pub. Co. [1973] xvi, 296 p.
830/.9/9436 71-125969
PT155 .U5 MRR Biog.

GERMAN LITERATURE--BIBLIOGRAPHY.
Ahnert, Heinz Jörg. Deutsches
Titelbuch 2. Berlin, Haude &
Spenersche Verlagsbuchhandlung (1966)
xii, 636 p. [DM 85.00]
016.83/090091 67-75457
Z2231 .A55 MRR Alc.

Albrecht, Günter. Internationale
Bibliographie zur Geschichte der
deutschen Literatur von den Anfangen
bis zur Gegenwart, [1. Aufl.]
Berlin, Volk und Wissen, 1969- v.
76-430568
Z2231 .A4 MRR Alc.

Bibliographie der deutschen
Literaturwissenschaft. Bd. [1]-8;
1945/53-1967/68. Frankfurt am Main,
V. Klostermann. a 57-5262
Z2231 .B5 MRR Alc Full set

Bibliographie der deutschen Sprach-
und Literaturwissenschaft. Bd. 9-
1969- Frankfurt am Main, V.
Klostermann. 72-612758
Z2231 .B5 MRR Alc Full set

Deutsche Bibliographie: Fünfjahres-
Verzeichnis. 1945/50- Frankfurt a.
M., Buchhändler-Vereinigung. 53-
39084
Z2221 .D47 MRR Alc Full set

Deutscher gesamtkatalog, Berlin,
Preussische druckerei- und verlags-
aktiengesellschaft, 1931- v.
019.1 32-9323
Z929 .A1D4 MRR Alc (Dk 33.)

Deutsches bücherverzeichnis: 1916-
[Leipzig] Börsenverein der deutschen
buchhändler zu Leipzig. 20-14984
Z2221 .K25 MRR Alc Full set

Hansel, Johannes. Bücherkunde für
Germanisten. [Berlin] E. Schmidt
[1959] 233 p. a 60-1097
Z2235.A2 H3 MRR Alc.

Hansel, Johannes. Bücherkunde für
Germanisten. Studienausg. 4., verm.
Aufl. (Berlin) E. Schmidt (1967)
163 p. [DM 9.80] 016.43 67-103467

Z2235.A2 H3 1967 MRR Alc.

Jahresverzeichnis des deutschen
Schrifttums. 1945/46- Leipzig,
Verlag des Börsenvereins der
Deutschen Buchhändler. 015.43 50-
38395
Z2221 .J26 MRR Alc Full set

Körner, Josef, Bibliographisches
Handbuch des deutschen Schrifttums.
3. völlig umgearb. und wesentlich
verm. Aufl. Bern, A. Francke, 1949.
644 p. 016.83 a 50-664
Z2231 .K6 1949 MRR Alc.

Otto Harrassowitz (Firm) German
series publications in the fields of
Germanic language & literature,
German history. Wiesbaden, 1967-69.
2 v. 015.43 67-85917
Z2235.A2 O8 1967 MRR Alc.

GERMAN LITERATURE--BIBLIOGRAPHY--
CATALOGS.
Literatur-Katalog. 1904/05- [Köln,
etc.] Koehler & Volckmar [etc.] 05-
10363
Z2221 .D5 MRR Alc Latest edition

GERMAN LITERATURE--BIBLIOGRAPHY--
PERIODICALS.
Barsortiments-Lagerkatalog.
Stuttgart [etc.] Koehler & Volckmar
[etc.] 015.43 46-38153
Z2221 .B3 MRR Alc Latest edition

Deutsche Bibliographie; Jan./Juni
1951- Frankfurt a. M., Buchhändler-
Vereinigung. 52-39843
Z2221 .F73 MRR Alc Full set

GERMAN LITERATURE--BIO-BIBLIOGRAPHY.
Albrecht, Günter. Lexikon
deutschsprachiger Schriftsteller von
den Anfangen bis zur Gegenwart
Leipzig, Bibliographisches Institut
VEB, 1967- v. 830.9 68-108029

PT41 .A42 MRR Biog.

Kosch, Wilhelm, Deutsches Literatur-
Lexikon. Ausg. in einem Band Bern,
Francke [1963] 511 p. 63-48267
Z2231 .K66 1963 MRR Alc.

Kosch, Wilhelm, Deutsches Literatur-
Lexikon; 2., vollständig neubearb.
und stark erweiterte Aufl. Bern, A.
Francke, 1949 [i.e. 1947]-58. 4 v.
a 48-4168
Z2230 .K862 MRR Biog.

Kürschners deutscher Gelehrten-
Kalender. 1925- 1.- eng.
Berlin, W. de Gruyter & Co. 25-15070

Z2230 .K93 MRR Biog Latest edition

Kürschners deutscher Literatur-
kalender. 1.- Jahrg.; 1879-
Berlin, Leipzig [etc.] 06-44921
Z2230 .K92 MRR Biog Latest edition

Stern, Desider. Bücher von Autoren
jüdischer Herkunft in deutscher
Sprache. Wien, 1967) 247 p. [s
30.00] 013/.2/96 67-101631
Z2241.J4 S8 MRR Alc.

GERMAN LITERATURE--CHRONOLOGY.
Frenzel, Herbert Alfred, Daten
deutscher Dichtung. (Neubearb.
Ausg.) (Köln, Berlin) Kiepenheuer
u. Witsch (1971). 766 p. [DM36.00]
73-887412
PT103 .F72 1971 MRR Alc.

GERMAN LITERATURE--DICTIONARIES.
Gillespie, George T. A catalogue of
persons named in German heroic
literature (700-1600), including
named animals and objects and ethnic
names. Oxford, [Eng.] Clarendon
Press, 1973. xxxviii, 166 p. [£10.50
($33.75 U.S.)]   831/.009 73-173463

   PT204 .G5 1973 MRR Alc.

Reallexikon der deutschen
Literaturgeschichte. 2. Aufl.
Berlin, De Gruyter, 1958 [i.e. 1955-
v.   a 56-1120
   PT41 .R42 MRR Alc.

Reallexikon der dutschen
literaturgeschichte, Berlin, W. de
Gruyter & co., 1925-31. 4 v.   830.3
                              30-23017
   PT41 .R4 MRR Alc.

GERMAN LITERATURE--HISTORY AND
CRITICISM.
Bithell, Jethro, ed. Germany, a
companion to German studies. [5th
ed., rev., enl.] London, Methuen
[1955] xii, 578 p.   914.3 55-3335

   DD61 .B56 1955 MRR Alc.

Fechter, Paul, Dichtung der
Deutschen, Berlin, Deutsche buchgemeinschaft, g.m.b.h. [c1932] 815,
[1] p.   830.9 33-9660
   PT85 .F4 MRR Alc.

Reallexikon der deutschen
Literaturgeschichte. 2. Aufl.
Berlin, De Gruyter, 1958 [i.e. 1955-
v.   a 56-1120
   PT41 .R42 MRR Alc.

Reallexikon der dutschen
literaturgeschichte, Berlin, W. de
Gruyter & co., 1925-31. 4 v.   830.3
                              30-23017
   PT41 .R4 MRR Alc.

Robertson, John George, A history of
German literature, 6th ed.
Edinburgh, Blackwood, 1970. xxvii,
817 p. [60/-]   830.9 74-552609
   PT91 .R7 1970 MRR Alc.

Rose, Ernst, A history of German
literature. [New York] New York
University Press, 1960. 353 p.
                        830.9 60-9405
   PT91 .R75 MRR Alc.

GERMAN LITERATURE--HISTORY AND
CRITICISM--BIBLIOGRAPHY.
Albrecht, Günter. Internationale
Bibliographie zur Geschichte der
deutschen Literatur von den Anfängen
bis zur Gegenwart, [1. Aufl.]
Berlin, Volk und Wissen, 1969- v.
                              76-430568
   Z2231 .A4 MRR Alc.

Bibliographie der deutschen
Literaturwissenschaft. Bd. [1]-8;
1945/53-1967/68. Frankfurt am Main,
V. Klostermann.   a 57-5262
   Z2231 .B5 MRR Alc Full set

Bibliographie der deutschen Sprach-
und Literaturwissenschaft. Bd. 9-
1969- Frankfurt am Main, V.
Klostermann.   72-612758
   Z2231 .B5 MRR Alc Full set

Reallexikon der deutschen
Literaturgeschichte. 2. Aufl.
Berlin, De Gruyter, 1958 [i.e. 1955-
v.   a 56-1120
   PT41 .R42 MRR Alc.

Reallexikon der dutschen
literaturgeschichte, Berlin, W. de
Gruyter & co., 1925-31. 4 v.   830.3
                              30-23017
   PT41 .R4 MRR Alc.

The Romantic movement bibliography,
1936-1970; [Ann Arbor, Mich.]
Pierian Press, 1973. 7 v. (xiii,
3289 p.) 016.809/894 77-172773
   Z6514.R6 R65 MRR Alc.

Schmitt, Franz Anselm. Stoff- und
Motivgeschichte der deutschen
Literatur: 2. neubearb. und stark
erweiterte Aufl. [Berlin] De
Gruyter, 1965. xvi, 332 p.
016.8309 66-9736
   Z2231 .S35 1965 MRR Alc.

GERMAN LITERATURE--INDEXES.
Ahnert, Heinz Jörg. Deutsches
Titelbuch 2. Berlin, Haude &
Spenersche Verlagsbuchhandlung (1966)
xii, 636 p. [DM 85.00]
016.83/090091 67-75457
   Z2231 .A55 MRR Alc.

GERMAN LITERATURE--JEWISH AUTHORS--
BIBLIOGRAPHY--CATALOGS.
Stern, Desider. Bücher von Autoren
jüdischer Herkunft in deutscher
Sprache. Wien, 1967) 247 p. [s
30.00] 013/.2/96 67-101631
   Z2241.J4 S8 MRR Alc.

GERMAN LITERATURE--OUTLINES, SYLLABI,
ETC.
Frenzel, Herbert Alfred, Daten
deutscher Dichtung. (Neubearb.
Ausg.) (Köln, Berlin) Kiepenheuer
u. Witsch (1971). 766 p. [DM36.00]
                        73-887412
   PT103 .F72 1971 MRR Alc.

GERMAN LITERATURE--TRANSLATIONS FROM
FRENCH--BIBLIOGRAPHY.
Fromm, Hans. Bibliographie deutscher
Übersetzungen aus dem
Französischen, 1700-1948. Baden-
Baden, Verlag für Kunst und
Wissenschaft, 1950- v.   51-24434

   Z2174.T7 F7 MRR Alc.

GERMAN LITERATURE--TRANSLATIONS INTO
ENGLISH.
Ramage, Craufurd Tait, comp.
Beautiful thoughts from German and
Spanish authors, New rev. ed.
London, New York, G. Routledge and
sons, 1884. 3 p. l., [ix]-xvi, 559
p.   15-9871
   PN6080 .R32 1884 MRR Alc.

GERMAN LITERATURE--TRANSLATIONS INTO
ENGLISH--BIBLIOGRAPHY.
English, 1948-1964. 2d rev. ed.
Gottingen, Vandenhoeck & Ruprecht,
1968. 509 p. 016.9143/03 72-
590351
   Z2221 .T73 no. 1 MRR Alc.

Morgan, Bayard Quincy, A critical
bibliography of German literature in
English translation, 1481-1927. 2d
ed., completely rev. and greatly
augm. New York, Scarecrow Press,
1965 [c1938] 690 p. 016.83 65-
13549
   Z2234.T7 M8 1965 MRR Alc.

Rose, Ernst, A history of German
literature. [New York] New York
University Press, 1960. 353 p.
830.9 60-9405
   PT91 .R75 MRR Alc.

Smith, Murray F., A selected
bibliography of German literature in
English translation, 1956-1960,
Metuchen, N.J., Scarecrow Press,
1972. v, 398 p. 016.83 76-157727

   Z2234.T7 S6 MRR Alc.

GERMAN LITERATURE--TRANSLATIONS INTO
FOREIGN LANGUAGES--BIBLIOGRAPHY.
Translations from the German;
Gottingen, Vandenhoeck & Ruprecht,
1968- v. 76-590301
   Z2221 .T73 MRR Alc.

GERMAN LITERATURE IN FOREIGN COUNTRIES--
BIO-BIBLIOGRAPHY.
Sternfeld, Wilhelm, Deutsche Exil-
Literatur 1933-1945; 2., verb. und
stark erw. Aufl. Heidelberg, L.
Schneider, 1970. 606 p. 78-562446

   Z2233 .S7 1970 MRR Alc.

GERMAN NEWSPAPERS.
Kosch, Wilhelm, Biographisches
Staatshandbuch; Bern, Francke [1963]
2 v. (1208 p.) 67-3923
   DD85 .K6 MRR Biog.

GERMAN NEWSPAPERS--BIBLIOGRAPHY.
Die Deutsche Presse; 1954- Berlin,
Duncker & Humbolt. 54-38930
   Z6956.G3 D43 MRR Alc Latest
   edition

GERMAN NEWSPAPERS--BIBLIOGRAPHY--
CATALOGS.
United States. Library of Congress.
Serial Division. Postwar German
newspapers in the Library of
Congress. [Washington] Reference
Dept., European Affairs Division,
1950. 29 l. 016.073 51-61784
   Z663.44 .P63 MRR Alc.

GERMAN NEWSPAPERS--BIBLIOGRAPHY--UNION
LISTS.
Berlin. Institut für
zeitungswissenschaft.
Standortskatalog wichtiger
zeitungsbestande in deutschen
bibliotheken, Leipzig, K. W.
Hiersemann, 1933. xxxi, 254 p., 1 l.
016.073 33-24972
   Z6945 .B46 MRR Alc.

GERMAN NEWSPAPERS--DIRECTORIES.
Der Leitfaden für Presse und
Werbung. Essen, W. Stamm. 073 51-
17269
   Z6956.G3 L4 MRR Alc Latest edition

GERMAN PERIODICALS--BIBLIOGRAPHY.
Die Deutsche Presse; 1954- Berlin,
Duncker & Humbolt. 54-38930
   Z6956.G3 D43 MRR Alc Latest
   edition

Deutschsprachige Zeitschriften.
Marbach am Neckar, Verlag der
Schillerbuchhandlung Hans Banger.
053.1/025 70-612760
   Z6956.G3 A55 MRR Alc Latest
   edition

Kürschners deutscher Gelehrten-
Kalender. 1925- 1.- eng.
Berlin, W. de Gruyter & Co. 25-15070

   Z2230 .K93 MRR Biog Latest edition

Ueberreiter, Kurt, A statistical
postwar survey on the natural
sciences and German universities.
[Washington] Library of Congress,
European Affairs Division [1950] 31
p. 507.2 50-61523
   Z663.26 .S7 MRR Alc.

Verzeichnis deutscher
wissenschaftlicher Zeitschriften.
[1.]- Aufl.; 1939/52- Wiesbaden
[etc.] F. Steiner [etc.] 54-30714
   Z6956.G3 V45 MRR Alc Latest
   edition

GERMAN PERIODICALS--BIBLIOGRAPHY--
CATALOGS.
Stanford University. Libraries.
German periodical publications;
Stanford, Calif., Hoover Institution
on War, Revolution, and Peace,
Stanford University, 1967. viii, 175
p. 016.053/1 66-28530
   Z6956.G3 S78 MRR Alc.

GERMAN PERIODICALS--DIRECTORIES.
Deutschsprachige Zeitschriften.
Marbach am Neckar, Verlag der
Schillerbuchhandlung Hans Banger.
053.1/025 70-612760
   Z6956.G3 A55 MRR Alc Latest
   edition

Der Leitfaden für Presse und
Werbung. Essen, W. Stamm. 073 51-
17269
   Z6956.G3 L4 MRR Alc Latest edition

GERMAN PERIODICALS--INDEXES.
Bibliographie der Rezensionen, nach
Titeln (alphabet der Verfasser)
geordnetes Verzeichnis von
Besprechungen dgutscher und
ausländischer Bücher und Karten,
die ... in zumeist wissenschaftlichen
und kritischen Zeitschriften,
Zeitungen und Sammelwerken deutscher
Zunge erschienen sind ... 1.-
Supplementband; 1900- Leipzig [etc.]
F. Dietrich. 01-15596
   AI9 .B6 MRR Alc Full set

Internationale Bibliographie der
Zeitschriften-literatur aus allen
Gebieten des Wissens. Jahrg. 1-
1965- Osnabrück, F. Dietrich. 67-
1836
   AI9 .I5 MRR Alc Full set

GERMAN PHILOLOGY--BIBLIOGRAPHY.
Hansel, Johannes. Bücherkunde für
Germanisten. [Berlin] E. Schmidt
[1959] 233 p. a 60-1097
   Z2235.A2 H3 MRR Alc.

Hansel, Johannes. Bücherkunde für
Germanisten. Studienausg. 4., verm.
Aufl. (Berlin) E. Schmidt (1967)
163 p. [DM 9.80] 016.43 67-103467

   Z2235.A2 H3 1967 MRR Alc.

GERMAN PHILOLOGY--COLLECTIONS--
BIBLIOGRAPHY.
Otto Harrassowitz (Firm) German
series publications in the fields of
Germanic language & literature,
German history. Wiesbaden, 1967-69.
2 v. 015.43 67-85917
   Z2235.A2 O8 1967 MRR Alc.

GERMAN POETRY.
Closs, August, ed. The Harrap
anthology of German poetry, London,
Harrap [1957] 562 p. 831.082 58-
3715
   PT1155 .C55 MRR Alc.

Das Oxforder buch deutscher dichtung
vom 12ten bis zum 20sten Jahrhundert,
Oxford, Universitäts-verlag, 1927.
xii, 647 p. 28-26460
   PT1155 .O8 1927 MRR Alc.

GERMANIC LANGUAGES.
see also English language

GERMANIC LANGUAGES--CONVERSATION AND
PHRASE BOOKS--POLYGLOT.
Lyall, Archibald, A guide to 25
languages of Europe. Rev. ed.
[Harrisburg, Pa.] Stackpole Co.
[1966] viii, 407 p. 413 66-20847

   PB73 .L85 1966 MRR Alc.

GERMANIC LANGUAGES--DICTIONARIES--
POLYGLOT.
Bergman, Peter M. The concise
dictionary of twenty-six languages in
simultaneous translations, New York,
Polyglot Library [1968] 406 p. 413
67-14284
   P361 .B4 TJ Rm.

Orne, Jerrold, The language of the
foreign book trade: 2d ed. Chicago,
American Library Association, 1962.
213 p. 010.3 61-12881
   Z1006 .O7 1962 MRR Alc.

GERMANIC LANGUAGES-- (Cont.)
Ouseg, H. L. 21-language dictionary.
London. P. Owen [1962] xxxi, 333 p.
63-1285
P361 .O85 1962 MRR Alc.

GERMANIC LANGUAGES--ETYMOLOGY--NAMES--
DICTIONARIES.
Gillespie, George T. A catalogue of
persons named in German heroic
literature (700-1600), including
named animals and objects and ethnic
names. Oxford, [Eng.] Clarendon
Press, 1973. xxxvii, 166 p. [£10.50
($33.75 U.S.)] 831/.009 73-173463
PT204 .G5 1973 MRR Alc.

GERMANIC LITERATURE--BIBLIOGRAPHY.
The Year's work in modern language
studies. 1929/30- [Leeds, Eng.,
etc.] Modern Humanities Research
Association [etc.] 405.8 31-32540
PB1 .Y45 MRR Alc Full set

GERMANIC PHILOLOGY--PERIODICALS--
BIBLIOGRAPHY.
London. University. Institute of
Germanic Studies. Union list of
periodicals dealing with Germanic
languages and literatures London,
1956. 58 p. (p. 56-58 blank for
"Additions") 57-39974
Z7036 .L6 MRR Alc.

GERMANS IN THE UNITED STATES--
BIBLIOGRAPHY.
Meynen, Emil. Bibliographie des
deutschtums der kolonialzeitlichen
einwanderung in Nordamerika.
Leipzig, O. Harrassowitz, 1937.
xxxvi, 636 p. 016.3252430873 38-
7457
Z1361.G37 M6 MRR Alc.

Pochmann, Henry August. Bibliography
of German culture in America to 1940;
Madison, University of Wisconsin
Press, 1953. xxxii, 483 p.
016.3252430973 53-12539
Z1361.G37 P6 MRR Alc.

United States. Library of Congress.
Division of bibliography. ... A list
of works relating to the Germans in
the United States. Washington, Govt.
print. off., 1904. 32 p. 04-21051
Z663.28 .L59 MRR Alc.

GERMANY.
Arntz, Helmut. Facts about Germany.
7th ed., completely revised. [Bonn]
Press and Information Office of the
Federal Government [1968] 359 p.
[10.90] 914.3/03/87 78-431134
DD259 .A8 1968 MRR Alc.

Great Britain. Naval Intelligence
Division. Germany. [Oxford?] 1944-
45. 4 v. 65-57470
DD17 .G73 MRR Alc.

GERMANY--BIBLIOGRAPHY.
Bithell, Jethro, ed. Germany, a
companion to German studies. [5th
ed., rev., enl.] London, Methuen
[1955] xii, 578 p. 914.3 55-3335
DD61 .B56 1955 MRR Alc.

Deutsches bücherverzeichnis: 1916-
[Leipzig] Börsenverein der deutschen
buchhandler zu Leipzig. 20-14984
Z2221 .K25 MRR Alc Full set

English, 1948-1964. 2d rev. ed.
Gottingen, Vandenhoeck & Ruprecht,
1968. 509 p. 016.9143/03 72-
590351
Z2221 .T73 no. 1 MRR Alc.

Luther, Arthur. Land und Leute in
deutscher Erzählung; 3. gänzlich
veranderte und erganzte Aufl.
Stuttgart, Hiersemann, 1954. 555 p.
55-18035
Z5917.H6 L87 1954 MRR Alc.

Translations from the German;
Gottingen, Vandenhoeck & Ruprecht,
1968- v. 76-590301
Z2221 .T73 MRR Alc.

Wiener Library, London. After Hitler
Germany, 1945-1963. London,
Vallentine, Mitchell, 1963. x, 261
p. 016.9143 64-7078
Z2240.3 .W5 MRR Alc.

GERMANY--BIO-BIBLIOGRAPHY.
Kosch, Wilhelm. Das katholische
Deutschland, biographisch-
bibliographisches lexikon. Augsburg,
Haas & Grabherr, 1933- v.
922.243 34-2159
CT1055 .K6 MRR Biog.

Kürschners deutscher Gelehrten-
Kalender. 1925- 1.- eng.
Berlin, W. de Gruyter & Co. 25-15070
Z2230 .K93 MRR Biog Latest edition

Kürschners deutscher Literatur-
kalender. 1.- Jahrg.; 1879-
Berlin, Leipzig [etc.] 06-44921
Z2230 .K92 MRR Biog Latest edition

GERMANY--BIOGRAPHY.
Allgemeine deutsche biographie.
Leipzig, Duncker & Humblot, 1875-
1912. 56 v. 920.043 01-13117
CT1053 .A5 MRR Biog.

Biographisches Lexikon zur deutschen
Geschichte; 2. Druckquote] Berlin,
Deutscher Verlag der Wissenschaften,
1971. 770 p. 70-555370
DD85 .B5 1971 MRR Biog.

Germany (Federal Republic, 1949-).
Bundestag. Amtliches Handbuch des
Deutschen Bundestages. 1.- 1953-
[Darmstadt] Neue Darmstädter
Verlagsanstalt. 55-23929
JN3971 .A7A35 MRR Alc Latest
edition

Die Grossen Deutschen; Berlin,
Propyläen-Verlag [c1935-37] 5 v.
36-3488
CT1054 .G7 MRR Biog.

Die Grossen Deutschen; Berlin,
Propyläen-Verlag [1956-57] 5 v.
56-38290
CT1054 .G72 MRR Biog.

Hirsching, Friedrich Karl Gottlob.
Historisch-literarisches handbuch
berühmter und denkwürdiger
personen, welche in dem 18.
Jahrhunderte gestorben sind;
Leipzig, Schwickert, 1794- v. in
920.01 32-19789
CT157 .H5 MRR Biog.

Jahrbuch der deutschen Bibliotheken.
1.- Jahrg.; 1902- Wiesbaden [etc.]
O. Harrassowitz. 02-17084
Z801 .J2 MRR Alc Latest edition

Konstantin, Prince of Bavaria. Die
grossen Namen; München, Kindler
[1956] 503 p. a 57-4150
CT1063 .K6 MRR Biog.

Kosch, Wilhelm. Biographisches
Staatshandbuch; Bern, Francke [1963]
2 v. (1208 p.) 67-3923
DD85 .K6 MRR Biog.

Kürschners biographisches Theater-
Handbuch: Berlin, W. de Gruyter,
1956. xii, 840 p. a 57-2818
PN2657 .K8 MRR Biog.

Mitteldeutsche Köpfe; Frankfurt am
Main, W. Weidlich, 1959 [c1958] 239
p. 62-35223
CT1053 .M5 MRR Biog.

Oettinger, Eduard Maria. Moniteur
des dates. Leipzig, L. Denicke,
1869. 6 v. in 1. 02-3518
CT154 .O3 MRR Biog.

GERMANY--BIOGRAPHY--DICTIONARIES.
Adressbuch deutscher Chemiker.
1950/51- Weinheim, Verlag Chemie.
52-24398
QD23 .A4 MRR Biog Latest edition

Handbuch der Direktoren und
Aufsichtsrate. 1967/68- Berlin,
Finanz- und Korrespondenz-Verlag Dr.
G. Mossner. 72-626450
HG4156 .H35 MRR Alc Latest edition

Jöcher, Christian Gottlieb.
Allgemeines gelehrten-lexicon ...
Leipzig, 1750-1897. 11 v. 06-3520

Z1010 .J63 MRR Biog.

Kosch, Wilhelm. Das katholische
Deutschland, biographisch-
bibliographisches lexikon. Augsburg,
Haas & Grabherr, 1933- v.
822.243 34-2159
CT1055 .K6 MRR Biog.

Kosch, Wilhelm. Deutsches Literatur-
Lexikon; 2., vollständig neubearb.
und stark erweiterte Aufl. Bern, A.
Francke, 1949 [i.e. 1947]-58. 4 v.
a 48-4168
Z2230 .K862 MRR Biog.

Kosch, Wilhelm. Deutsches Theater-
Lexikon; Klagenfurt, F. Kleinmayr,
1951- v. a 52-1902
PN2035 .K6 MRR Alc.

Kürschners deutscher Gelehrten-
Kalender. 1925- 1.- eng.
Berlin, W. de Gruyter & Co. 25-15070

Z2230 .K93 MRR Biog Latest edition

Kürschners deutscher Literatur-
kalender. 1.- Jahrg.; 1879-
Berlin, Leipzig [etc.] 06-44821
Z2230 .K92 MRR Biog Latest edition

Neue deutsch Biographie. Berlin,
Duncker & Humblot [1953]- v. a
54-1573
CT1053 .N4 MRR Biog.

Wer ist wer? [1]- Ausg.; 1905-
Berlin [etc.] Arani. 920.043 05-
32887
DD85 .W3 MRR Biog Latest edition

GERMANY--CIVILIZATION.
American University, Washington, D.C.
Foreign Areas Studies Division. Area
handbook for Germany. 2d ed.
[Washington] Headquarters, Dept. of
the Army, 1964. xi, 955 p. 309.143
64-62639
DD61 .A495 1964 MRR Alc.

GERMANY--CIVILIZATION--HISTORY.
Bithell, Jethro, ed. Germany, a
companion to German studies. [5th
ed., rev., enl.] London, Methuen
[1955] xii, 578 p. 914.3 55-3335

DD61 .B56 1955 MRR Alc.

GERMANY--COMMERCE--DIRECTORIES.
Biedermann, C. Ed., firm, Hamburg.
Export-Handbuch für Handel und
Industrie. Hamburg. 53-35489
HF3563 .B54 MRR Alc Latest edition

Handbuch der Grossunternehmen. [1.]-
Aufl.; 1941- Darmstadt [etc.]
Hoppenstedt [etc.] 338.058 47-37159

HC281 .H28 MRR Alc Latest edition

GERMANY--DESCRIPTION AND TRAVEL--1945-
Ernst, Rudolf. Deutschland 1961.
[München, 1960] 106 p. 61-34868
DD43 .E7 MRR Alc.

GERMANY--DESCRIPTION AND TRAVEL--GUIDE-
BOOKS.
Baedekers Autoführer-Verlag,
Stuttgart. Deutschland, die
Bundesrepublik. 10. Aufl.
Stuttgart: Baedekers Autoführer-
Verlag (1967) xx, 548 p.
914.3/04/87 68-80083
GV1025.G3 B33 1967 MRR Alc.

Fodor's Germany. 1969- New York, D.
McKay. 914.3/04/87 76-648504
DD16 .F6 MRR Alc Latest edition

Olson, Harvey Stuart. Olson's
complete motoring guide to Germany,
Austria & the Benelux countries.
[1st ed.] Philadelphia, Lippincott
[1968] xiv, 878 p. [$5.95] 914
68-24136
GV1025.A2 O45 MRR Alc.

Varta-Führer. Stuttgart, Mairs
Geographischer Verlag. 647/.944 74-
644633
TX910.G4 V3 MRR Alc Latest edition

GERMANY--ECONOMIC CONDITIONS--1902-
Stolper, Gustav. The German economy,
1870 to the present. New York,
Harcourt, Brace & World [1967] xiv,
353 p. 330.943 67-13682
HC285 .S84 1967 MRR Alc.

GERMANY--ECONOMIC CONDITIONS--
BIBLIOGRAPHY.
Kiel. Universität. Institut für
Weltwirtschaft. Bibliothek.
Regionenkatalog. Boston, G. K. Hall,
1967. 52 v. 017/.5 67-9425
Z929 .K52 1967 MRR Alc. (Dk 33).

GERMANY--ECONOMIC POLICY.
Stolper, Gustav. The German economy,
1870 to the present. New York,
Harcourt, Brace & World [1967] xiv,
353 p. 330.943 67-13682
HC285 .S84 1967 MRR Alc.

GERMANY--GAZETTEERS.
Müller, Friedrich. Grosses
deutsches Ortsbuch; 15.,
vollständig überarb. und erw. Aufl.
Wuppertal-Barmen, 1965. v. 1225 p.
66-45490
DD14 .M8 1965 MRR Alc.

Müller, Friedrich. Grosses
deutsches Ortsbuch; 12.,
vollständig überarb. und erw.
Aufl. Wuppertal Barmen, 1958. iv,
1139 p. 59-19354
DD14 .M8 1958 MRR Alc.

GERMANY--GAZETTEERS--BIBLIOGRAPHY.
Meynen, Emil. Amtliche und private
Ortsnamenverzeichnisse des
Grossdeutschen Reiches Leipzig, S.
Hirzel [1942] 162 p. 54-47213
Z2247.O4 M4 MRR Alc.

GERMANY--GEOGRAPHY--DICTIONARIES.
Leitende Manner der Wirtschaft.
1951- Darmstadt [etc.] Hoppenstedt,
[etc.] 52-16904
HF3564.5 .L4 MRR Alc Latest
edition

GERMANY--HISTORY.
Bithell, Jethro, ed. Germany, a
companion to German studies. [5th
ed., rev., enl.] London, Methuen
[1955] xii, 578 p. 914.3 55-3335

DD61 .B56 1955 MRR Alc.

GERMANY--HISTORY. (Cont.)
Flenley, Ralph. Modern German
history; 4th ed. revised. London,
Dent; New York, Dutton, 1968. xii,
503 p. [50/-] 943 74-374512
   DD175 .F5 1968 MRR Alc.

Gebhardt, Bruno. Handbuch der
deutschen Geschichte. 9., neu bearb.
Aufl. Stuttgart, Union Verlag, 1970-
v. [DM68.00 (v. 1)] 78-533119

   DD90 .G322 MRR Alc.

Handbuch der deutschen Geschichte.
Neu hrsg. Konstanz, Akademische
Verlagsgesellschaft Athenaion [c1956-
v. 1, c1957] v. 64-50340
   DD89 .H313 MRR Alc.

Handbuch der historischen Stätten
Deutschlands. [Stuttgart, A.
Kröner, 1958- v. 59-52693
   DD901.A1 H3 MRR Alc.

Holborn, Hajo. A history of modern
Germany. [1st ed.] New York, A. A.
Knopf, 1959-69. 3 v. 943 59-5991

   DD175 .H62 MRR Alc.

GERMANY--HISTORY--1789-1900.
Pinson, Koppel Shub. Modern Germany;
2d ed. New York, Macmillan [1966]
xv, 682 p. 943.08 66-16925
   DD203 .P5 1966 MRR Alc.

GERMANY--HISTORY--20TH CENTURY.
Pinson, Koppel Shub. Modern Germany;
2d ed. New York, Macmillan [1966]
xv, 682 p. 943.08 66-16925
   DD203 .P5 1966 MRR Alc.

GERMANY--HISTORY--1918-1933.
Eyck, Erich. A history of the Weimar
Republic. Cambridge, Harvard
University Press, 1962-63. 2 v.
943.085 62-17219
   DD237 .E913 MRR Alc.

GERMANY--HISTORY--1933-1945.
Shirer, William Lawrence. The rise
and fall of the Third Reich. New
York, Simon and Schuster, 1960. 1245
p. 943.086 60-6729
   DD256.5 .S48 MRR Alc.

Zentner, Kurt. Illustrierte
Geschichte des Dritten Reiches.
Wien, Buchgemeinschaft Donauland
[1966] 623 p. [S 125.00] 943.086
68-86744
   DD256.5 .Z43 1966 MRR Alc.

**GERMANY--HISTORY--1933-1945--SOURCES--
BIBLIOGRAPHY.**
Heinz, Grete. NSDAP Hauptarchiv;
[Stanford, Calif.] Hoover Institution
on War, Revolution, and Peace,
Stanford University, 1964. xii, 175
p. 016.329943 64-17344
   DD256.5 .H364 MRR Alc.

**GERMANY--HISTORY--ALLIED OCCUPATION,
1945-**
United States. Dept. of State.
Historical Office. Documents on
Germany, 1944-1961. Washington, U.S.
Govt. Print. Off., 1961. xv, 833 p.
62-60800
   DD257 .U476 1961 MRR Alc.

**GERMANY--HISTORY--ALLIED OCCUPATION,
1945- --BIBLIOGRAPHY.**
Wiener Library, London. After Hitler
Germany, 1945-1963. London,
Vallentine, Mitchell, 1963. x, 261
p. 016.9143 64-7078
   Z2240.3 .W5 MRR Alc.

**GERMANY--HISTORY--ALLIED OCCUPATION,
1945- --CHRONOLOGY.**
Germany (Federal Republic, 1949-)
Bundesministerium für Gesamtdeutsche
Fragen. SBZ von 1945 bis 1954. [1.
Aufl.] Bonn [Auslieferung für den
Buchhandel: Deutscher Bundes-Verlag]
1956. 361 p. 56-43247
   DD261 .G46 1956 MRR Alc.

GERMANY--HISTORY--BIBLIOGRAPHY.
Dahlmann, Friedrich Christoph.
Dahlmann-Waitz. Quellenkunde der
deutschen geschichte. 9. aufl.
Leipzig, K. F. Koehler, 1931. xl,
992 p. 016.943 32-9099
   Z2236 .D14 1931 MRR Alc.

Franz, Günther. Bücherkunde zur
deutschen Geschichte.
[Studentenausgabe] München, R.
Oldenbourg, 1951. 279 p. 016.943
51-30743
   Z2236 .F7 1951 MRR Alc.

**GERMANY--HISTORY--COLLECTIONS--
BIBLIOGRAPHY.**
Otto Harrassowitz (Firm) German
series publications in the fields of
Germanic language & literature,
German history. Wiesbaden, 1967-69.
2 v. 015.43 67-85917
   Z2235.A2 O8 1967 MRR Alc.

GERMANY--HISTORY--DICTIONARIES.
Rössler, Hellmuth. Sachwörterbuch
zur deutschen Geschichte München,
R. Oldenbourg, 1958. xl, 1472 p.
59-54622
   DD84 .R6 MRR Alc.

GERMANY--HISTORY--FICTION--BIBLIOGRAPHY.
Luther, Arthur. Land und Leute in
deutscher Erzählung; 3. gänzlich
veränderte und ergänzte Aufl.
Stuttgart, Hiersemann, 1954. 555 p.
55-19035
   Z5917.H6 L97 1954 MRR Alc.

GERMANY--HISTORY--SOURCES.
Snyder, Louis Leo, ed. Documents of
German history. New Brunswick, N.J.,
Rutgers University Press, 1958.
xxiii, 619 p. 943.0082 57-10968
   DD3 .S55 MRR Alc.

GERMANY--IMPRINTS.
Ahnert, Heinz Jörg. Deutsches
Titelbuch 2. Berlin, Haude &
Spenersche Verlagsbuchhandlung (1966)
xii, 636 p. [DM 85.00]
016.83/090091 67-75457
   Z2231 .A55 MRR Alc.

Barsortiments-Lagerkatalog.
Stuttgart [etc.] Koehler & Volckmar
[etc.] 015.43 46-38153
   Z2221 .B3 MRR Alc Latest edition

British Museum. Dept. of Printed
Books. Short-title catalogue of
books printed in the German-speaking
countries London, Trustees of the
British Museum, 1962. viii, 1224 p.
63-24516
   Z2222 .B73 MRR Alc.

Bücher aus der DDR. 1972/73-
Leipzig, Deutscher Buch-Export und -
Import G.m.b.H. [20.00M] 73-642414

   Z2250 .L4 MRR Alc Latest edition

A Catalog of books represented by
Library of Congress printed cards
issued to July 31, 1942. Ann Arbor,
Mich., Edwards Bros., 1942-46. 167
v. 018.1 43-3338
   Z881.A1 C3 MRR Alc. (DK 33)

Deutsche Bibliographie: Fünfjahres-
Verzeichnis. 1945/50- Frankfurt a.
M., Buchhändler-Vereinigung. 53-
39084
   Z2221 .D47 MRR Alc Full set

Deutscher gesamtkatalog, Berlin,
Preussische druckerei- und verlags-
aktiengesellschaft, 1931- v.
019.1 32-9323
   Z929 .A1D4 MRR Alc (Dk 33).

Deutsches bücherverzeichnis: 1916-
[Leipzig] Börsenverein der deutschen
buchhändler zu Leipzig. 20-14984
   Z2221 .K25 MRR Alc Full set

Hersch, Gisela. A bibliography of
German studies, 1945-1971;
Bloomington, Indiana University Press
[1972] xvi, 603 p. 016.9143/03/87
72-79903
   Z2221 .H48 MRR Alc.

Jahresverzeichnis der
Verlagsschriften und einer Auswahl
der ausserhalb des Buchhandels
erschienenen Veröffentlichungen der
DDR, der BDR und Westberlins sowie
der deutschsprachigen Werke anderer
Länder. Leipzig, VEB Verlag für
Buch- und Bibliothekswesen. 73-
640585
   Z2221 .J26 MRR Alc Partial set

Jahresverzeichnis des deutschen
Schrifttums. 1945/46- Leipzig,
Verlag des Börsenvereins der
Deutschen Buchhändler. 015.43 50-
38395
   Z2221 .J26 MRR Alc Full set

Leipziger Kommissions- und
Grossbuchhandel. L K G Lagerkatalog.
1962- [Leipzig] 72-626453
   Z1036 .L5 MRR Alc Latest edition

Library of Congress and National
union catalog author lists, 1942-
1962: Detroit, Gale Research Co.,
1969-71. 152 v. 018/.1/0973 73-
82135
   Z881.A1 L63 MRR Alc (Dk 33)

Libri. Hamburg, G. Lingenbrink.
015/.43 78-2108
   Z2225 .L5 MRR Alc Latest edition

Libri. Nachtrag. 1- 1971-
[Hamburg, G. Lingenbrink] 015/.43
74-643557
   Z2225 .L5 Suppl 2 MRR Alc Latest
   edition

Libri. Stich- und Schlagwortkatalog
mit Titel-Register. [Hamburg, G.
Lingenbrink] 015/.43 74-643558
   Z2225 .L5 Suppl. MRR Alc Latest
   edition

Literatur-Katalog. 1904/05- [Köln,
etc.] Koehler & Volckmar [etc.] 05-
10363
   Z2221 .D5 MRR Alc Latest edition

The National union catalog, Totowa,
N.J., Rowman and Littlefield [1970-
v. 018/.1/0973 76-141020
   Z881.A1U3742 MRR Alc (Dk 33)

The National union catalog, pre-1956
imprints; London, Mansell, 1968- v.
021.6/4 67-30001
   Z663.7.L5115 MRR Alc (Dk 33)

Ostwald, Renate.
Nachdruckverzeichnis von
Einzelwerken, Serien und
Zeitschriften Wiesbaden, G. Nobis,
1965- v. 66-31825
   Z1011 .O78 MRR Alc.

Stuttgart. Bibliothek für
Zeitgeschichte. Bibliothek für
Zeitgeschichte--Weltkriegsbücherei,
Stuttgart:alphabetischer Katalog.
Boston, G. K. Hall, 1968. 11 v. 74-
223544
   Z6209 .S85 1968 MRR Alc (Dk 33)

United States. Library of Congress.
Acquisitions Dept. European imprints
for the war years Washington, 1945-
46. 3 v. 015.4 45-37835
   Z663.76 .E8 MRR Alc.

Verzeichnis lieferbarer Bücher.
1971/72- Frankfurt am Main, Verlag
der Buchhändler-Vereinigung GmbH.
018.4 76-615229
   Z2221 .V47 MRR Alc Latest edition

Verzeichnis lieferbarer Bücher.
Nachtrag. [Frankfurt am Main] 018.4
74-643578
   Z2221 .V47 Suppl. MRR Alc Latest
   edition

GERMANY--IMPRINTS--PERIODICALS.
Deutsche Bibliographie: Jan./Juni
1951- Frankfurt a. M., Buchhändler-
Vereinigung. 52-39843
   Z2221 .F73 MRR Alc Full set

GERMANY--INDUSTRIES--DIRECTORIES.
A B C der deutschen Wirtschaft. 1949-
Darmstadt. 52-30587
   HC282 .A2 MRR Alc Latest edition

Biedermann, C. Ed., firm, Hamburg.
Export-Handbuch für Handel und
Industrie. Hamburg. 53-35489
   HF3563 .B54 MRR Alc Latest edition

Handbuch der Grossunternehmen. [1.]-
Aufl.; 1941- Darmstadt [etc.]
Hoppenstedt [etc.] 338.058 47-37159

   HC281 .H28 MRR Alc Latest edition

Seibt export directory of German
industries. Muenchen, Business
Dictionaries Ltd. 338.4/7/602543 72-
622306
   T12.5.G3 E98 MRR Alc Latest
   edition

Seibt Industriekatalog. München
[etc.] Seibt-Verlag [etc.] 53-38052

   Began publication in 1922.
   T12.5.G3 B45 MRR Alc Latest
   edition

Wer liefert was? 23.- Ausg.; 1960-
Leipzig, Leipziger Messeamt. 72-
626685
   T12.5.G3 O68 MRR Alc Latest
   edition

GERMANY--KINGS AND RULERS.
Isenburg, Wilhelm Karl von, Prinz.
Stammtafeln zur Geschichte der
europäischen Staaten. [2. verb.
Aufl.] Marburg, J. A. Stargardt,
1953. 2 v. in 1. 54-15926
   CS616 .I72 1953 MRR Alc.

**GERMANY--LEARNED INSTITUTIONS AND
SOCIETIES.**
Domay, Friedrich. Handbuch der
deutschen wissenschaftlichen
Gesellschaften, Wiesbaden, F.
Steiner, 1964. x, 751 p. 65-34997

   AS175 .D6 MRR Alc.

**GERMANY--LEARNED INSTITUTIONS AND
SOCIETIES--DIRECTORIES.**
Vademecum deutscher Lehr- und
Forschungsstätten. [1.- Ausg.;
1853- Essen [etc.] Stifterverband
für die Deutsche Wissenschaft [etc.]
58-26815
   AS178 .V35 Sci RR Latest edition /
   MRR Alc Latest edition

GERMANY--MANUFACTURES--DIRECTORIES.
A B C der deutschen Wirtschaft. 1949-
Darmstadt. 52-30587
   HC282 .A2 MRR Alc Latest edition

Biedermann, C. Ed., firm, Hamburg.
Export-Handbuch für Handel und
Industrie. Hamburg. 53-35489
   HF3563 .B54 MRR Alc Latest edition

GERMANY--MANUFACTURES--(Cont.)
Rademacher Handbuch für Industrie
und Export. [Hamburg, K. Rademacher]
72-626903
HF3563 .R44 MRR Alc Latest edition

Seibt export directory of German
industries. Muenchen, Business
Dictionaries Ltd. 338.4/7/602543 72-
622306
T12.5.G3 E98 MRR Alc Latest
edition

Seibt Industriekatalog. München
[etc.] Seibt-Verlag [etc.] 53-38052
Began publication in 1922.
T12.5.G3 B45 MRR Alc Latest
edition

Wer baut Maschinen. Darmstadt,
Hoppenstedt. 53-30932
TJ1170 .W4 MRR Alc Latest edition

Wer liefert was? 23.- Ausg.; 1960-
Leipzig, Leipziger Messeamt. 72-
626685
T12.5.G3 068 MRR Alc Latest
edition

GERMANY--POLITICS AND GOVERNMENT.
Beer, Samuel Hutchison, ed. Patterns
of government. 3d ed. New York,
Random House [1973] xv, 778 p.
320.3 72-681
JN12 .B4 1973 MRR Alc.

Carter, Gwendolen Margaret, Major
foreign powers 6th ed. New York,
Harcourt Brace Jovanovich [1972]
xvi, 743 p. 320.3 78-179411
JF51 .C3 1972 MRR Alc.

GERMANY--POLITICS AND GOVERNMENT--1789-
1900.
Ramm, Agatha. Germany, 1789-1919: a
political history. London, Methuen;
New York, distributed by Barnes &
Noble, 1967. [10], 517 p. [84/-]
320.9/43 67-111047
DD204 .R3 MRR Alc.

GERMANY--POLITICS AND GOVERNMENT--1871-
1918.
Ramm, Agatha. Germany, 1789-1919: a
political history. London, Methuen;
New York, distributed by Barnes &
Noble, 1967. [10], 517 p. [84/-]
320.9/43 67-111047
DD204 .R3 MRR Alc.

GERMANY--POLITICS AND GOVERNMENT--1871-
1918.
Treue, Wolfgang, ed. Deutsche
Parteiprogramme seit 1861 [i. e.
achtzehnhundertundsechzig. 4.,
erw. Aufl.] Göttingen,
Musterschmidt-Verlag [1968, c1954]
506 p. 329.9/43 77-369618
JN3931 .T7 1968 MRR Alc.

GERMANY--POLITICS AND GOVERNMENT--1933-
1945.
Remak, Joachim, comp. The Nazi
years: Englewood Cliffs, N.J.,
Prentice-Hall [1969] xi, 178 p.
[4.95] 943.086 69-11359
DD256.5 .R43 MRR Alc.

GERMANY--POLITICS AND GOVERNMENT--1945-
Sozialdemokratische Partei
Deutschlands. Jahrbuch. 1947-
[Göttingen] 51-24620
JN3946.S8 J3 MRR Alc Latest
edition

GERMANY--RELATIONS (GENERAL) WITH
AMERICA--BIBLIOGRAPHY.
Baginsky, Paul Ben, German works
relating to America, 1493-1800; New
York, The New York public library,
1942. xv, 217 p. 016.9173 a 42-
1596
Z1207 .B2 MRR Alc.

GERMANY--ROAD MAPS.
Mairs Geographischer Verlag,
Stuttgart. Der grosse Shell Atlas.
1.- Aufl.; 1960- Stuttgart. map63-
200
G1911.P2 M25 MRR Alc Atlas Latest
edition

GERMANY--STATISTICS.
Statistisches Jahrbuch deutscher
Gemeinden. 1- Jahrg.; [1890]-
[Braunschweig, etc.] Waisenhaus-
Buchdruckerei [etc.] 44-23595
HA1330 .A1S8 MRR Alc Latest
edition

GERMANY. KRIEGSMARINE.
Taylor, John Charles. German
warships of World War II Garden
City, N.Y., Doubleday [1968, c1966]
168 p. 623.82/5/0943 68-10550
VA513 .T39 1968 MRR Alc.

GERMANY (DEMOCRATIC REPUBLIC, 1949-)
American University, Washington, D.C.
Foreign Areas Studies Division. Area
handbook for Germany. 2d ed.
[Washington] Headquarters, Dept. of
the Army, 1964. xi, 955 p. 309.143
64-62639
DD61 .A495 1964 MRR Alc.

Childs, David. East Germany. New
York, Praeger [1969] 286 p. [7.50]
309.1/431 73-76976
DD261 .C45 1969b MRR Alc.

GDR; 300 questions, 300 answers.
Dresden, Zeit im Bild [1968]. 317 p.
with illus.; 8 l. of illus. 1 l.
[5.60] 943/.1087 72-412771
DD261 .G24 MRR Alc.

Germany (Federal Republic, 1949-)
Bundesministerium für Gesamtdeutsche
Fragen. SBZ von 1945 bis 1954. [1.
Aufl.] Bonn [Auslieferung für den
Buchhandel: Deutscher Bundes-Verlag]
1956. 361 p. 56-43247
DD261 .G46 1956 MRR Alc.

Keefe, Eugene K. Area handbook for
East Germany. Washington; For sale
by the Supt. of Docs., U.S. Govt.
Print. Off.] 1972. xiv, 329 p.
[$3.00] 914.31/087 72-600041
DD261 .K4 MRR Alc.

GERMANY (DEMOCRATIC REPUBLIC, 1949-)--
BIBLIOGRAPHY.
Hersch, Gisela. A bibliography of
German studies, 1945-1971;
Bloomington, Indiana University Press
[1972] xvi, 603 p. 016.9143/03/87
72-79903
Z2221 .H48 MRR Alc.

Horecky, Paul Louis, East Central
Europe; a guide to basic
publications. Chicago, University of
Chicago Press [1969] xxv, 956 p.
016.9143 70-79472
Z2483 .H56 MRR Alc.

Price, Arnold Hereward, East
Germany, a selected bibliography;
Washington, Library of Congress; [for
sale by the Supt. of Docs., U.S.
Govt. Print. Off.] 1967. viii, 133
p. 016.9143/1 67-61608
Z663.47 .P74 MRR Alc.

GERMANY (DEMOCRATIC REPUBLIC, 1949-)--
BIO-BIBLIOGRAPHY.
Germany (Democratic Republic, 1949-)
Zentralinstitut für
Bibliothekswesen. Schriftsteller der
Deutschen Demokratischen Republik und
ihre Werke; Leipzig, Verlag für
Buch- und Bibliothekswesen [1955]
249 p. 56-29802
Z2244 .E38A52 MRR Alc.

GERMANY (DEMOCRATIC REPUBLIC, 1949-)--
BIOGRAPHY.
A bis Z. 11.- Aufl.; 1969- Bonn,
Deutscher Bundes-Verlag. 72-626880
DD261 .S15 MRR Alc Latest edition

Buch, Günther. Namen und Daten;
Berlin, J. H. W. Dietz [c1973] xv,
332 p. 920/.043/1 74-316647
DD261.6 .B8 MRR Biog.

Wer ist wer in der SBZ? Berlin-
Zehlendorf, Verlag für
Internationalen Kulturaustausch
[1958] 307 p. 58-11317
DD261.6 .W4 MRR Biog.

GERMANY (DEMOCRATIC REPUBLIC, 1949- --
DESCRIPTION AND TRAVEL--GUIDE-BOOKS.
Reiseführer Deutsche Demokratische
Republik. (Leipzig) Edition Leipzig,
1966. 415 p. 68-84637
DD43 .R4 1966 MRR Alc.

GERMANY (DEMOCRATIC REPUBLIC, 1949-)--
DICTIONARIES AND ENCYCLOPEDIAS.
A bis Z. 11.- Aufl.; 1969- Bonn,
Deutscher Bundes-Verlag. 72-626880
DD261 .S15 MRR Alc Latest edition

GERMANY (DEMOCRATIC REPUBLIC, 1949-)--
EXECUTIVE DEPARTMENTS.
Childs, James Bennett, German
Democratic Republic official
publications. Washington, Library of
Congress; Reference Dept.; Serial
Division, 1960- v. 015.43087
60-61800
Z663.44 .G39 MRR Alc.

GERMANY (DEMOCRATIC REPUBLIC, 1949-)--
GAZETTEERS.
Krupkat, Werner Günther, ed.
Ortslexikon der Deutschen
Demokratischen Republik. [2. Aufl.]
Ausg. 1957. Berlin, Deutscher
Zentralverlag, 1958. 385 p. 58-
33703
DD14 .K7 1958 MRR Alc.

United States. Office of Geography.
Germany--Soviet Zone and East Berlin;
Washington, U.S. Govt. Print. Off.,
1959. v, 487 p. 914.31 59-61922
DD14 .U52 MRR Alc.

GERMANY (DEMOCRATIC REPUBLIC, 1949-)--
GOVERNMENT PUBLICATIONS--BIBLIOGRAPHY.
Childs, James Bennett, German
Democratic Republic official
publications. Washington, Library of
Congress; Reference Dept.; Serial
Division, 1960- v. 015.43087
60-61800
Z663.44 .G39 MRR Alc.

GERMANY (DEMOCRATIC REPUBLIC, 1949-)--
IMPRINTS--CATALOGS.
Bücher aus der DDR. 1972/73-
Leipzig, Deutscher Buch-Export und -
Import G.m.b.H. [20.00M] 73-642414

Z2250 .L4 MRR Alc Latest edition

GERMANY (DEMOCRATIC REPUBLIC, 1949-)--
STATISTICS.
Germany (Democratic Republic, 1949-
). Staatliche Zentralverwaltung für
Statistik. Statistisches Jahrbuch
der Deutschen Demokratischen
Republik. 1.- Jahrg.; 1955-
Berlin, Staatsverlag der deutschen
demokratischen Republik [etc.] 57-
34426
HA1248 .A2A33 MRR Alc Latest
edition

GERMANY (FEDERAL REPUBLIC, 1949-)
American University, Washington, D.C.
Foreign Areas Studies Division. Area
handbook for Germany. 2d ed.
[Washington] Headquarters, Dept. of
the Army, 1964. xi, 955 p. 309.143
64-62639
DD61 .A495 1964 MRR Alc.

Germany (Federal Republic, 1949-).
Presse- und Informationsamt. Germany
Reports. 4th, completely revised ed.
(Wiesbaden, Steiner, 1966.] 1015 p.
[36.00] 914.3/03/87 79-351629
DD259 .A5183 1968 MRR Alc.

GERMANY (FEDERAL REPUBLIC, 1949-)--
BIBLIOGRAPHY.
Hersch, Gisela. A bibliography of
German studies, 1945-1971;
[1972] xvi, 603 p. 016.9143/03/87
72-79903
Z2221 .H48 MRR Alc.

Price, Arnold Hereward, The Federal
Republic of Germany; Washington,
Library of Congress; [for sale by the
Supt. of Docs., U.S. Govt. Print.
Off.] 1972. ix, 63 p. 016.9143/03
72-677
Z663.47 .F43 MRR Alc.

GERMANY (FEDERAL REPUBLIC, 1949-)--
BIOGRAPHY.
Saur, Karl Otto. Who's who in German
politics; New York, R. R. Bowker
Co., 1971. x, 342 p. 329/.00922 B
72-204749
DD259.63 .S28 MRR Biog.

GERMANY (FEDERAL REPUBLIC, 1949-)--
BIOGRAPHY--DICTIONARIES.
Who's who in Germany. 1956- Munich,
Intercontinental Book and Pub. Co.
920/.043 56-3621
DD85 .W45 MRR Biog Latest edition

GERMANY (FEDERAL REPUBLIC, 1949-)--
COMMERCE--DIRECTORIES.
British & international buyers &
sellers guide. Manchester, Eng.
[etc.] C. G. Birn. 55-36686
HF54.G7 B7 MRR Alc Latest edition

Bundesfirmenregister. Hannover, W.
Dorn. 62-28754
Began publication with issue for
1951/53.
HF3563 .B78 MRR Alc Latest edition

Das Deutsche Firmen-Alphabet.
Darmstadt, Deutscher Adressbuch-
Verlag. 66-41702
HF3563 .D34 MRR Alc Latest edition

Der Grosse Hartmann. Bonn,
Adressbuch-Verlag G. Hartmann. 62-
28727
HF3563 .G7 MRR Alc Latest edition

Rademacher Handbuch für Industrie
und Export. [Hamburg, K. Rademacher]
72-626903
HF3563 .R44 MRR Alc Latest edition

Wer liefert was? Hamburg. 59-51341
HF3563 .W44 MRR Alc Latest edition

GERMANY (FEDERAL REPUBLIC, 1949-)--
COMMERCE--YEARBOOKS.
Buyer's guide to imported German
products. 1957- New York, Nordeman
Pub. Co. 57-33277
HF3563 .B8 MRR Alc Latest edition

GERMANY (FEDERAL REPUBLIC, 1949-)--
COMMERCE--UNITED STATES.
Baudler, Paul G. Directory of
American business in Germany. 4th
ed. Munich, Seibt-Verlag [1971]
xviii, 533 p. 338/.0025/43 72-
178863
HF3099 .B3 1971 MRR Alc.

GERMANY (FEDERAL REPUBLIC, 1949-)--
DESCRIPTION AND TRAVEL--GUIDE-BOOKS.
Germany, 3d ed.] Geneva, Paris
[etc.] Nagel Publishers [1968] 863,
xxxv p. [$8.95] 914.3/04/87 76-
434374
DD16 .G413 1968 MRR Alc.

GERMANY (FEDERAL REPUBLIC, 1949-)--
DIRECTORIES.
Taschenbuch des öffentlichen Lebens.
[1.]- Jahrg.; 1850- Bonn,
Festland Verlag [etc.] 52-38676
DD15.5 .T38 MRR Alc Latest edition

GERMANY (FEDERAL REPUBLIC, 1949-)--
GAZETTEERS.
United States. Office of Geography.
Germany--Federal Republic and West
Berlin; Washington, 1960. 2 v.
914.3 60-62466
DD14 .U517 MRR Alc.

GERMANY (FEDERAL REPUBLIC, 1949-)--
GOVERNMENT PUBLICATIONS--BIBLIOGRAPHY.
Childs, James Bennett. German
Federal Republic official
publications, 1949-1957, Washington,
Library of Congress, Reference Dept.,
Serial Division, 1958. 2 v. in 1
(vii, 887 p.) 015.43 58-61090
Z2229 .C45 MRR Alc.

GERMANY (FEDERAL REPUBLIC, 1949-)--
INDUSTRIES--DIRECTORIES.
Deutsches Bundes-Adressbuch der
Firmen aus Industrie, Handel und
Verkehr. Darmstadt, Deutscher
Adressbuch-Verlag. 57-22884
Began publication with 1953 ed.
HC282 .D4 MRR Alc Latest edition

GERMANY (FEDERAL REPUBLIC, 1949-)--
MANUFACTURES--DIRECTORIES.
Baudler, Paul G. Directory of
American business in Germany. 4th
ed. Munich, Seibt-Verlag [1971]
xviii, 533 p.   338/.0025/43 72-
178863
HF3099 .B3 1971 MRR Alc.

Buyer's guide to imported German
products. 1957- New York, Nordeman
Pub. Co. 57-33277
HF3563 .B8 MRR Alc Latest edition

Das Deutsche Firmen-Alphabet.
Darmstadt, Deutscher Adressbuch-
Verlag. 66-41702
HF3563 .D34 MRR Alc Latest edition

Deutsches Bundes-Adressbuch der
Firmen aus Industrie, Handel und
Verkehr. Darmstadt, Deutscher
Adressbuch-Verlag. 57-22884
Began publication with 1953 ed.
HC282 .D4 MRR Alc Latest edition

Deutschland liefert. Darmstadt,
Gemeinschaftsverlag Deutsches
Exportadressbuch. 57-18208
T12.5.G3 D43 MRR Alc Latest
edition

Der Grosse Hartmann. Bonn,
Adressbuch-Verlag G. Hartmann. 62-
28727
HF3563 .G7 MRR Alc Latest edition

GERMANY (FEDERAL REPUBLIC, 1949-)--
POLITICS AND GOVERNMENT--1945-
Gurland, Arcadius Rudolph Lang.
Political science in Western Germany;
Washington, Library of Congress,
Reference Dept., European Affairs
Division, 1952. 118 p. 320.943 52-
60058
Z663.26 .P6 MRR Alc.

GERMANY (FEDERAL REPUBLIC, 1949-)--
REGISTERS.
Verbände, Behörden. 1950-
Darmstadt [etc.] Hoppenstedt. 51-
24746
HD2429.G3 W5 MRR Alc Latest
edition

GERMANY (FEDERAL REPUBLIC, 1949-)--
STATISTICS.
Germany (Federal Republic, 1949-).
Statistisches Bundesamt.
Statistisches Jahrbuch für die
Bundesrepublik Deutschland. 1.-
1952- Stuttgart, W. Kohlhammer. 52-
43575
HA1232 .A45 MRR Alc Latest edition

GERMANY (FEDERAL REPUBLIC, 1949-)--
BUNDESTAG--HANDBOOKS, MANUALS, ETC.
Germany (Federal Republic, 1949-).
Bundestag. Amtliches Handbuch des
Deutschen Bundestages. 1.- 1953-
[Darmstadt] Neue Darmstädter
Verlagsanstalt. 55-23209
JN3971 .A7A35 MRR Alc Latest
edition

GERMANY (TERRITORY UNDER ALLIED
OCCUPATION, 1945-1955)--BIBLIOGRAPHY.
Hersch, Gisela. A bibliography of
German studies, 1945-1971;
Bloomington, Indiana University Press
[1972] xvi, 603 p. 016.9143/03/87
72-79903
Z2221 .H48 MRR Alc.

GERMANY (TERRITORY UNDER ALLIED
OCCUPATION, 1945- RUSSIAN ZONE)
Germany (Federal Republic, 1949-)
Bundesministerium für Gesamtdeutsche
Fragen. SBZ von 1945 bis 1954. [1.
Aufl.] Bonn [Auslieferung für den
Buchhandel: Deutscher Bundes-Verlag]
1956. 361 p.   56-43247
DD261 .G46 1956 MRR Alc.

GERMANY, EASTERN.
Göttinger Arbeitskreis. Eastern
Germany; a handbook. Wuerzburg,
Holzner-Verlag, 1960- [v. 1, 1961]
v.   943.1087 60-13392
DD801.O35 G59 MRR Alc.

GERMANY, EASTERN--BIBLIOGRAPHY.
United States. Library of Congress.
Slavic and Central European Division.
East Germany: a selected
bibliography, Washington, 1959.
vii, 55 p.   016.9431 59-60084
Z663.47 .E24 MRR Alc.

GERMS
see Bacteria

see Bacteriology

GERONTOLOGY
see Aged

see Old age

GESTATION
see Pregnancy

GHANA.
American University, Washington, D.C.
Foreign Areas Studies Division.
Special warfare area handbook for
Ghana. [Washington, U.S. Govt.
Print. Off., 1962. xii, 533 p.
mrr01-45
DT512 .A75 MRR Alc.

The Diplomatic Press Ghana trade
directory. [1st]- 1959- London,
Diplomatic Press and Pub. Co.
380.1/025/667 59-16943
DT512 .D5 MRR Alc Latest edition

Ghana year book. [Accra Graphic
Corp., etc.] 55-42476
Began publication in 1953.
DT511 .A17 MRR Alc Latest edition

GHANA--BIBLIOGRAPHY.
Aguolu, Christian Chukwunedu, Ghana
in the humanities and social
sciences, 1900-1971: a bibliography.
Metuchen, N.J., Scarecrow Press,
1973. xi, 469 p. 016.91667 73-
9519
Z3785 .A65 MRR Alc.

Johnson, Albert Frederick. A
bibliography of Ghana, 1930-1961,
[Evanston, Ill.] Published for the
Ghana Library Board by Northwestern
University Press, 1964. xiii, 210 p.
016.91667 64-17304
Z3785 .J58 MRR Alc.

Witherell, Julian W. Ghana; a guide
to official publications, 1872-1968.
Washington, General Reference and
Bibliography Division, Library of
Congress; [for sale by the Supt. of
Docs., U.S. Govt. Print. Off.] 1969.
xi, 110 p.   015/.667 74-601680
Z663.285 .W52 MRR Alc.

GHANA--BIOGRAPHY.
The Diplomatic Press Ghana trade
directory. [1st]- 1959- London,
Diplomatic Press and Pub. Co.
380.1/025/667 59-16943
DT512 .D5 MRR Alc Latest edition

Ghana year book. [Accra Graphic
Corp., etc.] 55-42476
Began publication in 1953.
DT511 .A17 MRR Alc Latest edition

GHANA--COMMERCE--DIRECTORIES.
The Diplomatic Press Ghana trade
directory. [1st]- 1959- London,
Diplomatic Press and Pub. Co.
380.1/025/667 59-16943
DT512 .D5 MRR Alc Latest edition

GHANA--COMMERCE--HANDBOOKS, MANUALS,
ETC.
Ghana, handbook of commerce and
industry. 1st- issue; 1957-
[Accra] 382/.09667 58-38378
HF3899.G6 A25 MRR Alc Latest
edition

GHANA--DEFENSES.
American University, Washington, D.C.
Foreign Areas Studies Division.
Special warfare area handbook for
Ghana. [Washington, U.S. Govt.
Print. Off., 1962. xii, 533 p.
mrr01-45
DT512 .A75 MRR Alc.

GHANA--DIRECTORIES.
Ghana year book. [Accra Graphic
Corp., etc.] 55-42476
Began publication in 1953.
DT511 .A17 MRR Alc Latest edition

GHANA--ECONOMIC CONDITIONS.
American University, Washington, D.C.
Foreign Areas Studies Division.
Special warfare area handbook for
Ghana. [Washington, U.S. Govt.
Print. Off., 1962. xii, 533 p.
mrr01-45
DT512 .A75 MRR Alc.

GHANA--GAZETTEERS.
United States. Office of Geography.
Ghana; Washington, 1967. iii, 282
p. 916.67/003 68-60134
DT510.2 .U5 MRR Alc.

GHANA--GOVERNMENT PUBLICATIONS--
BIBLIOGRAPHY.
Witherell, Julian W. Ghana; a guide
to official publications, 1872-1968.
Washington, General Reference and
Bibliography Division, Library of
Congress; [for sale by the Supt. of
Docs., U.S. Govt. Print. Off.] 1969.
xi, 110 p.   015/.667 74-601680
Z663.285 .W52 MRR Alc.

GHANA--HISTORY.
Bourret, F. M. Ghana, the road to
independence, 1919-1957. [Rev. ed.]
Stanford, Calif., Stanford University
Press, 1960. 246 p.   966.7 60-
13872
DT511 .B68 1960 MRR Alc.

Ward, William Ernest Frank. A
history of Ghana, Revised 4th ed.
London, Allen & Unwin, 1967. 454 p.
[35/-] 966.7 68-101489
DT511 .W28 1967 MRR Alc.

GHANA--POLITICS AND GOVERNMENT--1957-
American University, Washington, D.C.
Foreign Areas Studies Division.
Special warfare area handbook for
Ghana. [Washington, U.S. Govt.
Print. Off., 1962. xii, 533 p.
mrr01-45
DT512 .A75 MRR Alc.

GHOST STORIES--BIBLIOGRAPHY.
Barzun, Jacques. A catalogue of
crime [1st ed.] New York, Harper &
Row [1971] xxxi, 831 p. [$18.95]
016.80883/872 75-123914
Z5917.D5 B37 1971 MRR Alc.

GHOST STORIES--INDEXES.
Siemon, Fred. Ghost story index:
San Jose, Calif., Library Research
Associates, 1967. 141 p.
016.80883/872 67-30345
Z6514.G5 S5 MRR Alc.

GHOST TOWNS
see Cities and towns, Ruined,
extinct, etc.

GHOSTS.
see also Psychical research

GIFT-BOOKS (ANNUALS, ETC.)--
BIBLIOGRAPHY.
Boyle, Andrew. An index to the
annuals. Worcester, A. Boyle, 1967-
v.   [63/- (v. 1)] 820.8/007/05
67-101753
Z2013 .B65 MRR Alc.

British rate & data directories and
annuals. [London, Maclean-Hunter
Ltd.] [-/10/6] 016.05 73-645549
Z5771.4.G7 B75 MRR Alc Latest
edition

Faxon, Frederick Winthrop, Literary
annuals and gift books : [1st ed.]
reprinted / Pinner (Ravelston,
Southview Rd, Pinner, Middx) :
Private Libraries Association, 1973.
352 p. in various pagings ; [£6.00]
015/.42 74-186776
Z6520.G4 F3 1973 MRR Alc.

Paris. Bibliothèque nationale.
Département des périodiques.
Répertoire national des annuaires
français, 1958-1968, Paris,
Bibliothèque nationale, Éditions
Mercure, 1970. 811 p. 76-501237
Z2174.Y4 P29 MRR Alc.

Thompson, Ralph, American literary
annuals & gift books, 1825-1865.
[Hamden, Conn.] Archon Books, 1967
[c1936] 190 p.   050 67-17791
AY10 .T5 1967 MRR Alc.

GIFT-BOOKS (ANNUALS, ETC.)--HISTORY.
Thompson, Ralph, American literary
annuals & gift books, 1825-1865.
[Hamden, Conn.] Archon Books, 1967
[c1936] 190 p.   050 67-17791
AY10 .T5 1967 MRR Alc.

GIFTED CHILDREN--EDUCATION--UNITED
STATES--DIRECTORIES.
Axford, Lavonne B. A directory of
educational programs for the gifted,
Metuchen, N.J., Scarecrow Press,
1971. 282 p.   371.95/025/73 70-
142230
L901 .A95 MRR Alc.

GIFTWARES.
Hart, Harold H., Catalog of the
unusual New York, Hart Pub. Co.
[1973] 351 p. [$6.95] 380.1/025
73-80023
HF1041 .H297 MRR Alc.

GIFTWARES--UNITED STATES--DIRECTORIES.
The Gift and decorative accessory
buyers directory. [New York, Geyer-
McAllister Publications]
338.4/7/745502573 74-644351
T12 .G46 MRR Alc Latest edition

GILDING.
see also Electroplating

GILDS.
see also Trade-unions

GILLINGHAM, ENG.--DIRECTORIES.
Kelly's directory of Medway towns.
Kingston upon Thames. [-/27/6]
914.22/3/0025 73-642686
    DA670.M4 K45 MRR Alc Latest
    edition

GIPSIES.
Esty, Katharine. The gypsies; [1st
ed.] New York, Meredith Press [1969]
vii, 152 p. [3.95]
390/.09/1748149 69-19050
    DX115 .E8 MRR Alc.

GIPSIES--DICTIONARIES AND ENCYCLOPEDIAS.
Wedeck, Harry Ezekiel, Dictionary of
gypsy life and lore New York,
Philosophical Library [1973] vi, 518
p. [$20.00] 910/.03/91487 72-
75317
    DX115 .W4 MRR Alc.

GIRLS--EMPLOYMENT
see Woman--Employment

GLASGOW--COMMERCE--DIRECTORIES.
Glasgow and west of Scotland trades'
directory including the counties of
Argyll, Ayr, Bute, Dunbarton,
Dumfries, Kirkcudbright, Lanark,
Renfrew and Wigtown, accompanied with
a gazetteer of Scotland. Edinburgh,
Trades' Directories [etc.] 57-44904

    HF5162.G6 G6 MRR Alc Latest
    edition

GLASGOW--DIRECTORIES.
Kelly's directory of Glasgow.
Kingston upon Thames [Eng., etc.] 34-
33226
    DA890.G49 K4 MRR Alc Latest
    edition

Post office Glasgow directory.
Glasgow, Printed by Bell, Aird &
Coghill [etc.] 15-2477
    DA890.G49 P7 MRR Alc Latest
    edition

GLASS BLOWING AND WORKING.
McKearin, Helen. Two hundred years
of American blown glass New York,
Crown Publishers [1966, c1950] xvi,
382 p. 748.2913 66-5563
    NK5112 .M28 1966 MRR Alc.

GLASS MANUFACTURE--GREAT BRITAIN--
DIRECTORIES.
Pottery gazette and glass trade
review reference book and directory.
London, S. Greenwood. 666.6058
666.3058* 47-41231
    TP785 .P83 MRR Alc Latest edition

GLASS MANUFACTURE--UNITED STATES.
McKearin, Helen. Two hundred years
of American blown glass New York,
Crown Publishers [1966, c1950] xvi,
382 p. 748.2913 66-5563
    NK5112 .M28 1966 MRR Alc.

GLASSWARE--COLLECTORS AND COLLECTING.
Elville, E. M. The collector's
dictionary of glass. London, Country
Life, ltd. [1961] 194 p. 748.203
62-2440
    NK5104 .E4 MRR Alc.

Lee, Ruth Webb, American glass cup
plates; [1st ed.] Northborough,
Mass. [1948] xviii, 445 p. 748.8
49-250
    NK5440.C8 L4 MRR Alc.

Lee, Ruth Webb, Early American
pressed glass. Enl. and rev.
Northboro, Mass., The author [1946]
xxix, 666 p. 748.2 46-2536
    NK5112 .L4 1946 MRR Alc.

Lee, Ruth Webb, Victorian glass;
Northboro, Mass., The author [1944]
xxix, 608 p. incl. front., illus.
748.8 45-171
    NK5112 .L46 MRR Alc.

Lindsey, Bessie M. Lore of our land
pictured in glass. [n.p.] 1948- v.
748.8 48-3817
    NK5112 .L53 MRR Alc.

Warman, Edwin G., American cut
glass; 1st ed. Uniontown, Pa.,
Warman Pub. Co. [1954] 115 p.
748.2 54-19848
    NK5112 .W24 MRR Alc.

Warman, Edwin G., The second Goblet
price guide; Uniontown, Pa., Warman
Pub. Co. [1953] 37 p. 748.8 54-
475
    NK5112 .W25 1953 MRR Alc.

GLASSWARE--DICTIONARIES.
Drepperd, Carl William, ABC's of old
glass. [1st ed.] Garden City, N.Y.,
Doubleday, 1949. 282 p. 748.8 49-
8384
    NK5104 .D7 MRR Alc.

Elville, E. M. The collector's
dictionary of glass. London, Country
Life, ltd. [1961] 194 p. 748.203
62-2440
    NK5104 .E4 MRR Alc.

GLASSWARE--HISTORY.
Wilkinson, O. N. Old glass: London,
Benn, 1968. 200 p. [45/-] 748.2/9
68-106932
    NK5106 .W5 MRR Alc.

GLASSWARE--PRICES.
Lee, Ruth Webb, Current values of
antique glass: Victorian glass,
Sandwich glass, art glass, cup
plates; Rev. ed. Wellesley Hills,
Mass., Lee Publications [1969] 339
p. 748.2/913 79-26606
    NK5112 .L39 1969 MRR Alc.

Lee, Ruth Webb, The revised price
guide to pattern glass. 3d ed. New
York, M. Barrows, 1963. 331 p.
748.2085 63-17698
    NK5104 .L35 1963 MRR Alc.

Warman, Edwin G., The second Goblet
price guide; Uniontown, Pa., Warman
Pub. Co. [1953] 37 p. 748.8 54-
475
    NK5112 .W25 1953 MRR Alc.

GLASSWARE--GREAT BRITAIN--DIRECTORIES.
Pottery gazette and glass trade
review reference book and directory.
London, S. Greenwood. 666.6058
666.3058* 47-41231
    TP785 .P83 MRR Alc Latest edition

GLASSWARE--UNITED STATES.
Doubles, Malcolm Ray, Pattern glass
checklist. Richmond, 1959. 100 p.
748.2973 58-3293
    NK5112 .D64 MRR Alc.

Lee, Ruth Webb, American glass cup
plates; [1st ed.] Northborough,
Mass. [1948] xviii, 445 p. 748.8
49-250
    NK5440.C8 L4 MRR Alc.

Lee, Ruth Webb, Victorian glass;
Northboro, Mass., The author [1944]
xxix, 608 p. incl. front., illus.
748.8 45-171
    NK5112 .L46 MRR Alc.

McKearin, Helen. Two hundred years
of American blown glass New York,
Crown Publishers [1966, c1950] xvi,
382 p. 748.2913 66-5563
    NK5112 .M28 1966 MRR Alc.

Van Rensselaer, Stephen, Check list
of early American bottles and flasks.
Southampton, N.Y., Cracker Barrell
Press [1969? c1921] 109 p. [3.00]
748/.8 77-71635
    NK5440.B6 V3 1969 MRR Alc.

Warman, Edwin G., American cut
glass; 1st ed. Uniontown, Pa.,
Warman Pub. Co. [1954] 115 p.
748.2 54-19848
    NK5112 .W24 MRR Alc.

Warman, Edwin G., The second Goblet
price guide; Uniontown, Pa., Warman
Pub. Co. [1953] 37 p. 748.8 54-
475
    NK5112 .W25 1953 MRR Alc.

GLASSWARE--UNITED STATES--DICTIONARIES.
Kamm, Minnie Elizabeth (Watson) The
Kamm-Wood encyclopedia of antique
pattern glass. Watkins Glen, N.Y.,
Century House, c1961. 2 v.
748.2913 61-5439
    NK5112 .K284 MRR Alc.

GLASSWARE, AMERICAN.
Kamm, Minnie Elizabeth (Watson) The
Kamm-Wood encyclopedia of antique
pattern glass. Watkins Glen, N.Y.,
Century House, c1961. 2 v.
748.2913 61-5439
    NK5112 .K284 MRR Alc.

Lee, Ruth Webb, Current values of
antique glass: Victorian glass,
Sandwich glass, art glass, cup
plates; Rev. ed. Wellesley Hills,
Mass., Lee Publications [1969] 339
p. 748.2/913 79-26606
    NK5112 .L39 1969 MRR Alc.

Lee, Ruth Webb, Early American
pressed glass. Enl. and rev.
Northboro, Mass., The author [1946]
xxix, 666 p. 748.2 46-2536
    NK5112 .L4 1946 MRR Alc.

Lindsey, Bessie M. Lore of our land
pictured in glass. [n.p.] 1948- v.
748.8 48-3817
    NK5112 .L53 MRR Alc.

GLEAVES, ALBERT, 1858-1937--MANUSCRIPTS.
United States. Library of Congress.
Manuscript Division. Albert Gleaves;
a register of his papers in the
Library of Congress. Washington,
Library of Congress, 1968. 12 l.
359.3/31/0924 68-61413
    Z6633.34 .G5 MRR Alc.

GLOVE INDUSTRY--UNITED STATES--
DIRECTORIES.
Gloves directory, New York [etc.]
Haire Pub. Co. [etc.] 42-13130
    HD9947.U6 G5 MRR Alc Latest
    edition

GOATS.
Briggs, Hilton Marshall, Modern
breeds of livestock. Rev. ed. New
York, Macmillan [1958] 754 p.
636.08 58-5049
    SF105 .B7 1958 MRR Alc.

GOD, KINGDOM OF
see Kingdom of God

GODS.
see also Mythology

GOETHE, JOHANN WOLFGANG VON, 1749-1832--
DICTIONARIES, INDEXES, ETC.
Fischer, Paul, Goethe-Wortschatz;
Leipzig, E. Rohmkopf, 1929. xi, 905
p. 31-16505
    PT2239 .F5 1929 MRR Alc.

GOLD.
see also Money

GOLD--UNITED STATES.
Koschmann, Albert Herbert, Principal
gold-producing districts of the
United States, Washington, U.S.
Dept. of the Interior, 1968. v, 283
p. [4.75] 553/.41/0973 gs 68-342
    TN423.A5 K6 MRR Alc.

GOLD COINS.
Friedberg, Robert, Gold coins of the
world, 2d ed., rev. New York, Coin
and Currency Institute [1965] 415 p.
737.40216 65-27635
    CJ113 .F7 1965 MRR Alc.

Harris, Robert P. Gold coins of the
Americas; 1st ed. Florence, Ala.,
ANCO [1971] iv, 280 p. 737.4 75-
168568
    CJ1808 .H37 MRR Alc.

Hobson, Burton. Historic gold coins
of the world. Garden City, N.Y.,
Doubleday [1971] 192 p. [$25.00]
737.4 70-28263
    CJ113 .H6 MRR Alc.

Schlumberger, Hans. Gold coins of
Europe since 1800; New York,
Sterling Pub. Co. [1968] 352 p.
[$15.00] 737.4 68-18787
    CJ1545 .S313 1968 MRR Alc.

GOLD MINES AND MINING--UNITED STATES.
Koschmann, Albert Herbert, Principal
gold-producing districts of the
United States, Washington, U.S.
Dept. of the Interior, 1968. v, 283
p. [4.75] 553/.41/0973 gs 68-342
    TN423.A5 K6 MRR Alc.

GOLDSMITH, OLIVER, 1728-1774--
CONCORDANCES.
Paden, William Doremus, ed. A
concordance to the poems of Oliver
Goldsmith, Gloucester, Mass., P.
Smith, 1966 [c1940] xii, 180 p.
821.6 66-9077
    PR3492 .P3 1966 MRR Alc.

GOLDSMITHING.
see also Jewelry making

GOLDSMITHING--GREAT BRITAIN--
DICTIONARIES.
Clayton, Michael. The collector's
dictionary of the silver and gold of
Great Britain and North America.
[1st Amer. ed.] New York, World Pub.
Co. [1971] 350 p. [$35.00]
739.2/0942 73-149055
    NK7143 .C55 1971 MRR Alc.

GOLDSMITHING--SCHLESWIG-HOLSTEIN.
Stierling, Hubert, Der Silberschmuck
der Nordseeküste hauptsächlich in
Schleswig-Holstein. Neumünster, K.
Wachholtz, 1935-55. v.   56-41823

    NK7150 .S68 MRR Alc.

GOLDSMITHING--UNITED STATES--
DICTIONARIES.
Clayton, Michael. The collector's
dictionary of the silver and gold of
Great Britain and North America.
[1st Amer. ed.] New York, World Pub.
Co. [1971] 350 p. [$35.00]
739.2/0942 73-149055
    NK7143 .C55 1971 MRR Alc.

GOLDSMITHS, BRITISH.
Jackson, Charles James, Sir, English
goldsmiths and their marks; 2d ed.,
rev. and enl. New York, Dover
Publications [1964, c1921] xvi, 747
p. 739.22742 64-18852
    NK7143 .J15 1964 MRR Alc.

GOLF.
Golf guide. New York, Snibbe Sports
Publishers [etc.] 63-24740
    GV971 .G53 MRR Alc Latest edition

GOLF. (Cont.)
Golf magazine's encyclopedia of golf.
Updated [ed.] New York, Harper &
Row [1973] vi, 424 p. [$13.95]
796.352 73-173401
GV965 .G5455 1973 MRR Alc.

GOLF--BIOGRAPHY.
Evans, Webster. Encyclopedia of
golf. [New ed.] New York, St.
Martin's Press [1974] 320 p.
[$10.95] 796.352/03 73-88040
GV965 .E84 1974 MRR Alc.

Golf magazine's encyclopedia of golf.
Updated [ed.] New York, Harper &
Row [1973] vi, 424 p. [$13.95]
796.352 73-173401
GV965 .G5455 1973 MRR Alc.

GOLF--DICTIONARIES.
Evans, Webster. Encyclopaedia of
golf. [New ed.] New York, St.
Martin's Press [1974] 320 p.
[$10.95] 796.352/03 73-88040
GV965 .E84 1974 MRR Alc.

GOLF--HISTORY.
Gibson, Nevin H. The encyclopedia of
golf. Rev. ed. New York, A. S.
Barnes [1964] viii, 310 p. 796.352
64-7785
GV963 .G5 1964a MRR Alc.

Grimsley, Will. Golf; its history,
people & events. Englewood Cliffs,
N.J., Prentice-Hall [1966] xiv, 331
p. 796.35209 66-12565
GV963 .G7 MRR Alc.

GOLF--STATISTICS.
Golf guide. New York, Snibbe Sports
Publishers [etc.] 63-24740
GV871 .G53 MRR Alc Latest edition

McCormack, Mark H. The wonderful
world of professional golf [1st ed.]
New York, Atheneum, 1973. xii, 467
p. [$20.00] 796.352/74 72-94251
GV970 .M32 1973 MRR Alc.

McCormack, Mark H The world of
professional golf. 1967- ed.
Cleveland [etc.] World Pub. Co.
[etc.] 796.352/64/05 68-13716
GV961 .M3 MRR Alc Latest edition

GOLF--TOURNAMENTS--HISTORY.
McCormack, Mark H. The wonderful
world of professional golf [1st ed.]
New York, Atheneum, 1973. xii, 467
p. [$20.00] 796.352/74 72-94251
GV970 .M32 1973 MRR Alc.

GOLF--YEARBOOKS.
The Golfer's handbook. Glasgow
[etc.] 796.352058 51-18000
Began publication in 1898.
GV961 .G75 MRR Alc Latest edition

McCormack, Mark H The world of
professional golf. 1967- ed.
Cleveland [etc.] World Pub. Co.
[etc.] 796.352/64/05 68-13716
GV961 .M3 MRR Alc Latest edition

GOLF-LINKS--EUROPE.
Galin, Saul. Golf in Europe; [1st
ed.] New York, Hawthorn Books [1967]
281 p. 796.352/094 67-14858
GV875 .G3 MRR Alc.

GOLF-LINKS--UNITED STATES.
Baron, Harry, Golf resorts of the
U.S.A. [New York] New American
Library [1967] xvi, 335 p.
796.352/06 67-26237
GV875 .B33 MRR Alc.

GOOD AND EVIL.
Fontenrose, Joseph Eddy, Python; a
study of Delphic myth and its
origins. Berkeley, University of
California Press, 1959. xviii, 616
p. 398.4 59-5144
GR830.D7 F6 MRR Alc.

**GOSFORTH, ENG. (NORTHUMBERLAND)--
DIRECTORIES.**
Kelly's (incorporating "Ward's")
directory of the city of Newcastle
upon Tyne and Gosforth. Kingston
upon Thames, Surrey [etc.] Kelly's
Directories Ltd. 53-28852
DA690.N6 K4 MRR Alc Latest edition

**GOTHIC REVIVAL (LITERATURE)--
BIBLIOGRAPHY.**
Summers, Montague, A Gothic
bibliography. London, Fortune P.
[1969] iii-xx, 621 p. 22 plates.
[6/15/-] 016.823/6 78-442345
Z2014.F4 S9 1969 MRR Alc.

GOVERNMENT
see Political science

GOVERNMENT, RESISTANCE TO.
see also Revolutions

see also Vietnamese Conflict, 1961- --
Protest movements

GOVERNMENT AND THE PRESS--UNITED STATES.
Blanchard, Robert O., comp. Congress
and the news media. New York,
Hastings House [1974] xiv, 506 p.
[$14.95] 323.44/5 74-1091
PN4738 .B5 MRR Alc.

Pollard, James Edward, The
presidents and the press. New York,
The Macmillan company, 1947. xiii,
866 p. 071 47-1213
PN4888.P7 P6 MRR Alc.

GOVERNMENT BUILDINGS
see Public buildings

**GOVERNMENT CONSULTANTS--UNITED STATES--
DIRECTORIES.**
Who's who in consulting; 2d ed.
Detroit, Gale Research Co., 1973.
xvii, 1011 p. [$45.00] 658.4/03
73-16373
HD69.C6 W52 MRR Biog.

GOVERNMENT EMPLOYEES
see Civil service

GOVERNMENT INFORMATION--UNITED STATES.
Kerbec, Matthew J., comp. Legally
available U.S. Government information
as a result of the Public Information
Act. [1st ed.] Arlington, Va.,
Output Systems Corp. [1970] 2 v.
353/.0007 70-108181
KF5753 .A33 1970 MRR Alc.

GOVERNMENT JOBS
see Civil service positions

**GOVERNMENT LENDING--UNITED STATES--
DIRECTORIES.**
Levy, Robert S. Directory of State
and Federal funds for business
development. [New York] Pilot Books
[1968] 64 p. 332.7/42 68-55429
HG3729.U5 L4 MRR Alc.

GOVERNMENT PLANNING
see Regional planning

GOVERNMENT PUBLICATIONS.
Childs, James Bennett, Government
publications. 016.011 73-208222
Z7164.G7 C53 MRR Ref Desk.

United States. Library of Congress.
Processing Dept. The role of the
Library of Congress in the
international exchange of official
publications; Washington, 1953. 85
p. 021.852 53-60020
Z663.7 .R6 MRR Alc.

GOVERNMENT PUBLICATIONS--BIBLIOGRAPHY.
International Committee for Social
Sciences Documentation. Etude des
bibliographies courantes des
publications officielles nationales;
[Paris] UNESCO [1958] 260 p. 58-
428
Z7164.G7 I5 MRR Ref Desk.

List of the serial publications of
foreign governments, 1815-1931,
Millwood, N.Y., Kraus Reprint Co.,
1973. 720 p. 016.05 73-9866
Z7164.G7 L7 1973 MRR Alc.

New York. Public library. Checklist
of newspapers and official gazettes
in the New York public library; [New
York] The New York public library,
1915. iv, 579 p. 16-1688
Z6945 .N6 MRR Alc.

Wynar, Lubomyr Roman, Guide to
reference materials in political
science; Denver, Colorado
Bibliographic Institute, 1966-68. 2
v. 016.32 66-1321
Z7161 .W9 MRR Alc.

**GOVERNMENT PUBLICATIONS--BIBLIOGRAPHY--
CATALOGS.**
Foreign Relations Library. Catalog
of the Foreign Relations Library.
Boston, G. K. Hall, 1969. 9 v.
016.327 75-6133
Z6209 .F656 MRR Alc (Dk 33)

New York (City). Public Library.
Research Libraries. Catalog of
Government publications in the
Research Libraries: Boston, G. K.
Hall, 1972. 40 v. 011 74-171015
Z7164.G7 N54 1972 MRR Alc (Dk 33)

**GOVERNMENT PUBLICATIONS--BIBLIOGRAPHY--
PERIODICALS.**
Government publications guide.
Boston, G. K. Hall. 011 73-19397
Z7164.G7 G68 MRR Ref Desk Partial
set

GOVERNMENT PURCHASING--UNITED STATES.
Guide to governmental purchasing;
[Minneapolis, Lakewood Publications,
1973?] 449 p. [$22.50] 353.007/12
78-153400
JK1673 .G84 MRR Alc.

GOVERNMENT RECORDS
see Public records

GOVERNMENT REGULATION OF COMMERCE
see Industry and state

GOVERNMENTAL INVESTIGATIONS.
see also Criminal investigation

see also Police

**GOVERNMENTAL INVESTIGATIONS--CANADA--
BIBLIOGRAPHY.**
Henderson, George Fletcher. Federal
royal commissions in Canada, 1867-
1966; [Toronto] University of
Toronto Press [1967] xvi, 212 p.
015/.71 68-91146
Z1373 .H4 MRR Alc.

**GOVERNMENTAL INVESTIGATIONS--GREAT
BRITAIN.**
Anderson, Ian Gibson. Councils,
committees, & boards; 2d ed.
Beckenham, CBD Research Ltd, 1973.
iii-xiv, 327 p. [£7.50 ($25.00
U.S.)] 062 74-164686
AS118 .A5 1973 MRR Alc.

Butler, David E. British political
facts, 1900-1968, 3rd ed. London,
Macmillan; New York, St Martin's P.,
1969. xix, 314 p. [70/-] 320.9/42
74-82434
JN231 .B8 1969 MRR Alc.

**GOVERNMENTAL INVESTIGATIONS--GREAT
BRITAIN--BIBLIOGRAPHY.**
Cole, Arthur Harrison, ed. A finding-
list of British royal commission
reports; 1860 to 1935, Cambridge,
Mass., Harvard university press,
1935. 3 p. l., 5-66 p. 015.42 35-
11452
Z2009 .C68 MRR Alc.

Cole, Arthur Harrison, ed. A finding-
list of British royal commission
reports: 1860 to 1935, Cambridge,
Mass., Harvard university press,
1935. 3 p. l., 5-66 p. 015.42 35-
11452
Z2009 .C68 MRR Alc.

**GOVERNMENTAL INVESTIGATIONS--SWEDEN--
BIBLIOGRAPHY.**
Sweden. Riksdagen. Biblioteket.
Forteckning över statliga
utredningar 1904-1945. Norrköping,
Östergötlands dagblads tryckeri,
1953. vi, 1405 p. 54-20125
Z2629 .S943 MRR Alc.

**GOVERNMENTAL INVESTIGATIONS--UNITED
STATES--HISTORY.**
Platt, Anthony M., comp. The
politics of riot commissions, 1917-
1970: New York, Macmillan [1971] x,
534 p. 364.14/3 79-150069
HV6477 .P5 MRR Alc.

**GOVERNMENTAL INVESTIGATIONS--UNITED
STATES--INDEXES.**
United States. Congress. Senate.
Committee on Government Operations.
Congressional investigations of
communism and subversive activities;
Washington, U.S. Govt. Print. Off.,
1956. xvi, 382 p. 56-62374
Z7164.S67 U5 MRR Alc.

GOVERNORS--UNITED STATES.
Daniel, Jean Houston. Executive
mansions and capitols of America.
Waukesha, Wis., Country Beautiful;
distributed by Putnam, New York
[1969] 290 p. [25.00] 725/.1 71-
77604
E159 .D3 MRR Alc.

Hunt, William Welch, comp. The book
of governors. (2d ed.) Los Angeles,
Calif., Printed by Washington
typographers [c1935] 84 p. 973.02
36-764
E174.5 .H862 MRR Ref Desk.

Kallenbach, Joseph Ernest, The
American Chief Executive; New York,
Harper & Row [1966] xii, 622 p.
353.032 66-10838
JK516 .K3 MRR Alc.

Peterson, Clarence Stewart, First
governors of the forty-eight States.
New York, Hobson Book Press, 1947.
xviii, 110 p. 923.273 48-5475
E176 .P49 MRR Biog.

[United States. Library of Congress.
Legislative Reference Service] The
Governors of the States, 1900-1966.
Chicago, Council of State
Governments, 1966. [56] p. 72-
175683
JS308 .C6 no. 377, 1966 MRR Ref
Desk.

GOVERNORS--UNITED STATES--DIRECTORIES.
Notable names in American history;
3d ed. of White's conspectus of
American biography. [Clifton, N.J.]
J. T. White, 1973. 725 p. 920/.073
73-6885
E176 .N89 1973 MRR Biog.

GRADING.
see also Standardization

GRADING AND MARKING (STUDENTS)
Sharp, Theodore. The country index;
North Hollywood, Calif.,
International Education Research
Foundation [1971] xii, 217 p.
378.1/50/7 68-28836
LB2805 .S576 MRR Alc.

GRAFF, EVERETT DWIGHT, 1885-1964--
LIBRARY.
Newberry Library, Chicago. A
catalogue of the Everett D. Graff
collection of Western Americana.
Chicago, Published for the Newberry
Library by the University of Chicago
Press, 1968. xxv, 854 p. 016.978
66-20577
Z1251.W5 N43 MRR Alc.

GRAFT (IN POLITICS)
see Corruption (in politics)

GRAIN TRADE.
Broomhall, George J. S. Broomhall's
corn trade year book. Liverpool
[etc.] Northern Pub. Co. [etc.] 13-
13438
HD9030.2 B8 MRR Alc Latest edition

GRAMMAR, COMPARATIVE AND GENERAL.
Pei, Mario Andrew. The world's chief
languages; 3d ed. London, G. Allen
& Unwin [1848] 663 p. 410 49-
28175
P121 .P36 1949 MRR Ref Desk.

GRAMMAR, COMPARATIVE AND GENERAL--
DICTIONARIES.
Gerson, Stanley. A glossary of
grammatical terms; [St. Lucia, Q.]
University of Queensland Press [1969]
73 p. 415/.03 78-497971
P29 .G4 MRR Alc.

GRAMMAR, COMPARATIVE AND GENERAL--
TERMINOLOGY.
Pei, Mario Andrew. Glossary of
linguistic terminology Garden City,
N.Y., Anchor Books, 1966. xvi, 299
p. 410.3 66-21013
P29 .P39 MRR Alc.

GRAND TETON NATIONAL PARK.
Scharff, Robert, ed. Yellowstone and
Grand Teton National Parks, New
York, D. McKay Co. [1966] xi, 209 p.
917.875 66-17872
F722 .S3 MRR Alc.

GRANT, ULYSSES SIMPSON, PRES. U.S.,
1822-1885.
Hesseltine, William Best. Ulysses S.
Grant, politician, New York, Dodd,
Mead & company, 1935. xiii, 480 p.
923.173 35-17052
E672 .H46 MRR Alc.

GRANT, ULYSSES SIMPSON, PRES. U.S.,
1822-1885--CHRONOLOGY.
Simon, John Y. Ulysses S. Grant
chronology. [n.p. A publication of
the Ohio Historical Society for
Ulysses S. Grant Association and Ohio
Civil War Centenial Commission, 1963]
39 p. 63-63828
E672 .S59 MRR Alc.

GRANTS
see Subsidies

GRANTS-IN-AID--UNITED STATES.
Roth, William V. 1969 listing of
operating Federal assistance programs
compiled during the Roth study.
Washington, U.S. Govt. Print. Off.,
1968. x, 1132 p. [4.50] 338.973
73-605845
HJ275 .R6 1969 MRR Ref Desk.

Rowland, Howard S. The New York
times Guide to Federal aid for cities
and towns [New York] Quadrangle
Books [1972, c1971] xxxii, 1243 p.
336.1/85 72-78499
HJ275 .R64 MRR Ref Desk.

United States. Office of Minority
Business Enterprise. Special catalog
of Federal programs assisting
minority enterprise. Washington; For
sale by the Supt. of Docs., U.S.
Govt. Print. Off. 1971. xiii, 89 p.
[$1.00] 338.973 77-614023
HC110.P63 A57 MRR Alc.

GRANTS-IN-AID--UNITED STATES--
BIBLIOGRAPHY.
United States. Library of Congress.
Legislative Reference Service.
Intergovernmental relations in the
United States; Washington, 1953. 73
p. 55-60203
Z663.6 .I6 MRR Alc.

GRANTS-IN-AID--UNITED STATES--
DIRECTORIES.
Rowland, Howard S. The New York
times Guide to Federal aid for cities
and towns [New York] Quadrangle
Books [1972, c1971] xxxii, 1243 p.
336.1/85 72-78499
HJ275 .R64 MRR Ref Desk.

United States. Office of Management
and Budget. 1973 catalog of Federal
domestic assistance. 7th ed.
Washington; [For sale by the Supt. of
Docs., U.S. Govt. Print. Off.] 1973-
1 v. (loose-leaf) [$7.00] 338.973
73-600118
HC110.P63 U55 1973 MRR Ref Desk.

GRANTS-IN-AID--UNITED STATES--
STATISTICS.
United States. Division of Government
Financial Operations. Federal aid to
States. [Washington?] 338.973 72-
618404
HJ275 .A36 MRR Ref Desk Latest
edition

GRAPES.
see also Wine and wine making

GRAPHIC ARTS.
see also Painting

see also Printing

see also Prints

Who's who in graphic art. 1st ed.;
1962- Zurich, Amstutz & Herdeg
Graphis Press. 62-51802
NC45 .W5 MRR Biog Latest edition

GRAPHIC ARTS--DICTIONARIES.
Aldag, Keith A. Modern graphics
terminology [Hurstbridge, Vic.,
Hyphen Publishing, 1969] 350 p.
[8.40] 760.3 76-459625
Z118 .A53 MRR Alc.

Rodríguez, César. Bilingual
dictionary of the graphic arts; New
and complete ed., rev. and enl.
Farmingdale, N.Y., G. A. Humphrey
[1966] 448 p. 655.03 66-27570
Z118 .R6 1966 MRR Alc.

Stevenson, George A. Graphic arts
encyclopedia New York, McGraw-Hill
[1968] xv, 492 p. 655/.003 67-
24445
Z118 .S82 MRR Alc.

Vigrolio, Tom. Marketing and
communications media dictionary,
[Norfolk, Mass., NBS Co., 1969]
xvii, 425 p. 658.8/003 76-80076
HF5414 .V52 MRR Alc.

GRAPHIC ARTS--DICTIONARIES--GERMAN.
Polygraph dictionary der graphischen
Techniken und der verwandten Gebiete.
2., durch die Polygraph-Redaktion
überarb., erg. und erw. Aufl.
Frankfurt am Main, Polygraph Verlag
[1967] 330 p. 68-123818
Z118 .P63 1967 MRR Alc.

GRAPHIC ARTS--DIRECTORIES.
Director's Art Institute, New York.
Who's who in commercial art and
photography; [2d ed.] New York,
1964. 192 p. 66-235
NC997 .D5 1964 MRR Biog.

GRAPHIC ARTS--SPAIN--DIRECTORIES.
Catalogo del papel, prensa y artes
graficas. 1957- [Barcelona,
Abarca] 58-26342
Z414 .C3 MRR Alc Latest edition

GRAPHIC ARTS, AUSTRIAN--BIOGRAPHY.
Kürschners Graphiker Handbuch: 2.
erw. Aufl. Berlin, De Gruyter [1967]
xi, 396 p., 188 p. of plates.
760/.0922 68-93136
NC249 .K8 1967 MRR Biography.

GRAPHIC ARTS, GERMAN--BIOGRAPHY.
Kürschners Graphiker Handbuch: 2.
erw. Aufl. Berlin, De Gruyter [1967]
xi, 396 p., 188 p. of plates.
760/.0922 68-93136
NC249 .K8 1967 MRR Biography.

GRAPHIC ARTS, SWISS--BIOGRAPHY.
Kürschners Graphiker Handbuch: 2.
erw. Aufl. Berlin, De Gruyter [1967]
xi, 396 p., 188 p. of plates.
760/.0922 68-93136
NC249 .K8 1967 MRR Biography.

GRAPHIC METHODS.
Lockwood, Arthur. Diagrams: London,
Studio Vista; New York, Watson-
Guptill, 1969. 144 p. [84/-]
311/.26 77-82136
HA31 .L58 1969 MRR Alc.

GRAPHOLOGY.
Golson, K. K. Presidents are people
New York, Carlton Press [1964] 270
p. 923.173 64-56026
E176.1 .G637 MRR Alc.

GRAPHOLOGY--DICTIONARIES.
Roman, Klara Goldzieher.
Encyclopedia of the written word;
New York, F. Ungar Pub. Co. [1968]
xviii, 550 p. [$12.50] 155.28/2/03
68-12124
BF889.5 .R6 MRR Alc.

GRASSES--UNITED STATES.
United States. Dept. of Agriculture.
Grass. Washington, U.S. Govt. Print.
Off.; 1948. xiv, 892 p. 633.2
agr55-8
S21 .A35 1948 MRR Alc.

GRAVES
see Funeral rites and ceremonies

GRAY, THOMAS, 1716-1771--CONCORDANCES.
Cook, Albert Stanburrough. A
concordance to the English poems of
Thomas Gray. Gloucester, Mass., P.
Smith, 1967 [c1908] x, 160 p.
821/.6 67-8967
PR3504 .C6 1967 MRR Alc.

GRAZ--DIRECTORIES.
Amts- und Geschäfts-Adressbuch der
steirischen Landeshauptstadt Graz.
68.- Jahrg.; 1952/53- Graz, Verlag
U. Moser. 72-626831
DB879.G8 A3 MRR Alc Latest edition

GREAT BOOKS OF THE WESTERN WORLD.
The Great ideas; Chicago,
Encyclopedia Britannica [1955, c1952]
2 v. 028.3 55-10313
AC1 .G72 vol. 2-3 MRR Alc.

Hutchins, Robert Marynard. The great
conversation; Chicago, Encyclopedia
Britannica [1955, c1952] xxvii, 131
p. 028.3 55-10312
AC1 .G72 vol. 1 MRR Alc.

GREAT BRITAIN.
The World book encyclopedia.
Chicago, Field Enterprises
Educational Corp. [1973] 26 v. 031
74-189336
AE5 .W55 1973 MRR Alc.

GREAT BRITAIN--ANTIQUITIES.
Chambers, Robert. The book of days;
Detroit, Gale Research Co., 1967. 2
v. 902/.02 67-13009
DA110 .C52 1967 MRR Alc.

Wood, Eric Stuart. Collins field
guide to archaeology 3rd ed.
London, Collins, 1972. 384 p., 32 p.
of plates. [£2.25] 913.362 74-
179596
DA90 .W6 1972 MRR Alc.

Wood, Eric Stuart. Collins field
guide to archaeology 2nd ed. revised
and reset. London Collins, 1968.
384 p. [30/-] 913.3/6 68-119612
DA90 .W6 1968 MRR Alc.

GREAT BRITAIN--ANTIQUITIES--
BIBLIOGRAPHY.
Gomme, George Laurence, Sir. Index
of archaeological papers, 1665-1890.
London, A. Constable & company, ltd.,
1907. xi, 910 p. 08-9803
Z2027.A8 I6 MRR Alc.

Index of archaeological papers
published 1891-1910. [1st]-20th
issue; 1892-1914. [London] 08-10988

Z2027.A8 I7 MRR Alc Full set

Mullins, Edward Lindsay Carson. A
guide to the historical and
archaeological publications of
societies in England and Wales, 1901-
1933; London, Athlone P., 1968.
xiii, 850 p. [10/10/-] 016.9142
79-367032
Z5055.G6 M8 MRR Alc.

GREAT BRITAIN--ANTIQUITIES, ROMAN.
British Museum. Dept. of British and
Mediæval Antiquities. Guide to the
antiquities of Roman Britain. [3d
ed.] London, Trustees of the British
Museum, 1964. 86 p. 66-33323
DA145 .B89 1964 MRR Alc.

GREAT BRITAIN--ARMED FORCES--
BIBLIOGRAPHY.
Higham, Robin D. S. A guide to the
sources of British military history.
Berkeley, University of California
Press, 1971. xii, 630 p.
016.355/00942 74-104108
Z2021.M5 H54 MRR Alc.

GREAT BRITAIN--ARMED FORCES--MEDALS,
BADGES, DECORATIONS, ETC.
Dorling, Henry Taprell. Ribbons and
medals; This ed. rev. under the
editorship of Francis K. Mason.
Garden City, N.Y., Doubleday, 1974.
359 p. [$14.95] 355.1/34/09 73-
20952
UC530 .D63 1974 MRR Ref Desk.

Gordon, Lawrence L. British battles
and medals. 4th ed., rev. London,
Spink, 1971. xiv, 440 p. 355.1/34
72-180227
UB435.G8 G6 1971 MRR Alc.

GREAT BRITAIN--BARONETAGE.
Debrett's peerage, baronetage,
knightage, and companionage...
Kingston upon Thames, Surrey, Kelly's
Directories [etc.] 929.72 42-17925

CS420 .D32 MRR Biog Latest edition

GREAT BRITAIN--BIBLIOGRAPHY.
Anderson, John Parker. The book of
British topography. London, W.
Satchell & co., 1881. xvi, 472 p.
03-32393
     Z2023 .A54 MRR Alc

Berkowitz, David Sandler.
Bibliotheca bibliographica
Britannica [Waltham, Mass., 1963-
v.   63-3390
     Z2016 .B45 MRR Alc.

Bibliotheca celtica, 1909-1927/28;
new ser., v. 1- 1929/33-
Aberystwyth [National library of
Wales] 11-5717
     Z2071 .B56 MRR Alc Partial set

The English catalogue of books
London, Published for the Publishers'
Circular by S. Low, Marston, 1914.
655 p.   52-45201
     Z2001 .E517 MRR Alc.

The English catalogue of books
(annual] London, Publishers'
Circular Ltd. [etc.] 06-44930
Began publication in 1864.
     Z2001 .E53 MRR Alc Partial set

Humphreys, Arthur Lee, A handbook to
county bibliography, London,
[Printed by Strangeways and sons]
1917. x, 501 p., 1 l.   17-14548
     L2023.A1 H9 MRR Alc.

Lancaster, Joan Cadogan, comp.
Bibliography of historical works
issued in the United Kingdom, 1946-
1956. [London] University of London,
Institute of Historical Research,
1957. xxii, 388 p.   016.9 a   58-
2313
     Z2016 .L3 MRR Alc.

Oxford. University. Christ Church.
Library. The Christ Church
supplement to Wing's Short-title
catalogue, 1641-1700, Oxford,
Printed for Christ Church at the
Holywell Press, 1956.   47 p. 015.42
57-624
     Z2002.W5 O9 MRR Alc.

Royal Historical Society, London.
Writings on British history 1901-
1933: London, Cape, 1968- v.
[£5/5- (v. 1) 63/- (v.2) £5/5/- (v.
3)]   016.942 68-88411
     Z2016 .R85 MRR Alc.

Writings on British history. 1901/33-
New York, Barnes & Noble. 61-2932

     Z2016 .R88 MRR Alc Full set

GREAT BRITAIN--BIBLIOGRAPHY--CATALOGS.
The British national bibliography
cumulated subject catalogue 1951/54-
London, Council of the British
National Bibliography. 015.42 59-
246
     Z2001 .B752 MRR Alc Full set

GREAT BRITAIN--BIO-BIBLIOGRAPHY.
The Dictionary of national biography,
The concise dictionary. London,
Oxford University Press [1953]-61. 2
v.   58-26259
     DA28 .D56 MRR Ref Desk.

The dictionary of national biography,
London, Oxford university press
[1921-27] 24 v.   920.042 30-29308

     DA28 .D45 1921 MRR Biog.

Fredeman, William Evan, Pre-
Raphaelitism; a bibliocritical study
Cambridge, Harvard University Press,
1965. xix, 327 p. 016.70942 64-
21242
     Z5948.P9 F7 MRR Alc.

Kirk, John Foster, A supplement to
Allibone's critical dictionary of
English literature and British and
American authors. Detroit, Gale
Research Co., 1965. 2 v. (x, 1562
p.)   820.3 67-296
     Z1224 .A44 1891a MRR Biog.

GREAT BRITAIN--BIOGRAPHY.
Arnott, James Fullarton, English
theatrical literature, 1558-1900:
London, Society for Theatre Research,
1970. xxii, 486 p.   [£10/10/-]
016.792/0942 76-552584
     Z2014.D7 A74 1970 MRR Alc.

The Birmingham post year book and
who's who. Birmingham, Birmingham
Post & Mail. 52-44829
Began publication in 1948.
     DA690.B6 B5 MRR Alc Latest edition

British film and television year
book. [1st]- ed: 1946- [London,
British and American Film Press,
etc.] 791.4058 792.93058* 46-4765
     PN1993.3 .B7 MRR Biog Latest
     edition

Burke's genealogical and heraldic
history of the peerage, baronetage
and knightage. London, Burke's
Peerage Ltd. [etc.]   35-32046
Began publication in 1826.
     CS420 .B85 MRR Biog Latest edition

Butler, David E. British political
facts, 1900-1968.   3rd ed. London,
Macmillan; New York, St Martin's P.,
1969. xlix, 314 p. [70/-] 320.9/42
74-82434
     JN231 .B8 1969 MRR Alc.

Cambridge. University. King's
College. A register of admissions to
King's College, Cambridge, 1919-1958.
London, 1963. vi, 462 p.   65-71149

     LF204 .A3 1963 MRR Biog.

City of London directory and diary
and livery companies guide. London,
City Press [etc.] 53-29778
     DA679 .A12 MRR Biog Latest edition

Debrett's peerage, baronetage,
knightage, and companionage ...
Kingston upon Thames, Surrey, Kelly's
Directories [etc.] 929.72 42-17925

     CS420 .D32 MRR Biog Latest edition

The dictionary of national biography,
London, Oxford university press
[1921-27] 24 v.   920.042 30-29308

     DA28 .D45 1921 MRR Biog.

The Dictionary of national biography,
The concise dictionary. London,
Oxford University Press [1953]-61. 2
v.   58-26259
     DA28 .D56 MRR Ref Desk.

The Diplomatic Service list. 1966-
London, H. M. Stationery Off.
354.42061 66-4595
     JX1783 .A22 MRR Biog Latest
     edition

The Directory of directors; Croydon,
Eng. [etc.] T. Skinner Directories
[etc.] ca 48-3050
     HG4135.Z5 D5 MRR Alc Latest
     edition

Dod's parliamentary companion.
Epsom, Surrey, [etc.] Sell's
publications Ltd. [etc.] 06-7438
     JN500 .D7 MRR Biog Latest edition

Flegon, Alec Who's who in
translating and interpreting;
London, Flegon P. [1967] 190 p.
418/.02/0922 68-71375
     PN241 .F55 MRR Biog.

"Flight" directory of British
aviation. 1970- Kingston upon
Thames, Kelly Directories Ltd.
629.13/0025/42 76-618594
     TL512 .F48 Sci RR Latest edition /
     MRR Alc Latest edition

The Foreign office list and
diplomatic and consular year book.
London, Harrison and sons. 07-21419

     JX1783 .A2 MRR ALc Latest edition

Guide to the House of Commons. 1970-
London, Times Newspapers Ltd.
328.42/0922 76-20856
     JN956 .G9 MRR Alc Latest edition

Higginson, Alexander Henry, British
and American sporting authors,
London, New York, Hutchinson, 1951.
xvii, 443 p.   016.7992 53-18485
     Z7511 .H55 1951 MRR Biog.

The Jewish year book. 1896- London,
Jewish Chronical Publications [etc.]
14-2382
     DS135.E5A3 MRR Alc Latest edition

London. University. Institute of
Historical Research. Corrections and
additions to the Dictionary of
national biography. Boston, G. K.
Hall, 1966. iv, 212 p. 920.04203
67-3481
     DA28 .L65 MRR Biog.

The Medical directory. London, J. &
A. Churchill ltd. 35-7636
     R713.29 .M4 MRR Biog Latest
     edition

Namier, Lewis Bernstein, Sir, The
House of Commons, 1754-1790 New
York, Published for the History of
Parliament Trust by Oxford University
Press, 1964. 3 v.   328.42 64-3513

     JN672 .N2 MRR Alc.

Pike, Edgar Royston, Britain's Prime
Ministers from Walpole to Wilson
Feltham, Odhams, 1968. 487 p. [30/-
]   942.07/0922 B 79-435231
     DA28.4 .P48 MRR Alc.

Sedgwick, Romney, The House of
Commons, 1715-1754; New York,
Published for the History of
Parliament Trust, by Oxford
University Press, 1970. 2 v.
[$70.00]   328.42/07/32 75-21905
     JN675 1715 .S4 MRR Alc.

Uden, Grant, comp. They looked like
this; New York, Barnes & Noble
[1966] viii, 306 p.   920.042 66-
7971
     CT775 .U3 MRR Alc.

Untermeyer, Louis, Lives of the
poets; New York, Simon and Schuster,
1959.   757 p.   821.09 59-11205
     PR502 .U5 MRR Biog.

Valentine, Alan Chester, The British
establishment, 1760-1784; [1st ed.]
Norman, University of Oklahoma Press
[1970] 2 v. (xii, 960 p.) 920.042
69-16734
     CT781 .V3 MRR Biog.

Who was who, v. [1]- : 1897/1916-
London, A. & C. Black. 920.042 20-
14622
     DA28 .W65 MRR Biog Full set

Who's who ... 1st- 1849- London,
A. and C. Black, [etc.] 04-16933
     DA28 .W6 MRR Biog Latest edition /
     MRR Biog Latest edition

Who's who in history. Oxford,
Blackwell, 1960- v.   920.042 61-
66758
     DA28 .W618 MRR Biog.

Who's who in the motor and commercial
vehicle industries. Kingston upon
Thames, Surrey [etc.] Kelly's
Directories Ltd. [etc.] 56-19609
Began publication with 1952 ed.
     HD9710.G7 W45 MRR Alc Latest
     edition

GREAT BRITAIN--BIOGRAPHY--BIBLIOGRAPHY.
Farrar, Robert Henry. An index to
the biographical and obituary notices
in the Gentleman's magazine, 1731-
1780. London, 1891 [i.e. 1886-91]
677 p.   10-20807
     AI3 .I4 vol. 15 MRR Alc.

Matthews, William, British
autobiographies; Berkeley,
University of California Press, 1955.
xiv, 376 p.   016.920042 55-13593
     Z2027.A9 M3 MRR Alc.

Matthews, William, British diaries;
Gloucester, Mass., P. Smith, 1967
[c1950] xxxiv, 339 p. 016.920042
67-6139
     Z5305.G7 M3 1967 MRR Biog.

GREAT BRITAIN--BIOGRAPHY--DICTIONAIRIES.
Who's who of British scientists.
1969/70- [London] Longman. 509/.22
71-10910
     Q145 .D52 Sci RR Latest edition /
     MRR Biog Latest edition

GREAT BRITAIN--BIOGRAPHY--DICTIONARIES.
The Academic who's who. 1973/74-
London, A. & C. Black; distributed in
U.S. by Bowker, New York. [$21.95]
001.3/092/2 73-641081
     L915 .A658 MRR Biog Latest edition

Allibone, Samuel Austin, A critical
dictionary of English literature and
British and American authors,
Detroit, Gale Research Co., 1965. 3
v. (3140 p.)   820.3 67-295
     Z1224 .A4317 MRR Biog.

The Author's & writer's who's who.
[1934]- London, Burke's Peerage,
ltd. [etc.] 928.2 34-38025
     Z2011 .A91 MRR Biog Latest edition

Bellamy, Joyce M. Dictionary of
labour biography [Clifton] N.J., A.
M. Kelley, 1972- v.   331/.092/2
B 78-185417
     HD8393.A1 B44 MRR Biog.

A Biographical dictionary of the
living authors of Great Britain and
Ireland; Detroit, Gale Research Co.,
1966. viii, 449 p.   013.82 66-
16419
     Z2010 .B61 1966 MRR Biog.

Boase, Frederic, Modern English
biography: Truro, Netherton and
Worth, 1892-1921. 6 v.   01-5198
     CT773 .B612 MRR Biog.

Browning, David Clayton, ed.
Everyman's dictionary of literary
biography, English & American,
London, Dent; New York, Dutton [1958]
x, 752 p.   928.2 a 58-2815
     PR19 .B7 MRR Biog.

Buckland, Charles Edward, Dictionary
of Indian biography. Detroit, Gale
Research Co., 1968. xii, 494 p.
920.054 68-23140
     DS434 .B8 1968 MRR Biog.

GREAT BRITAIN--BIOGRAPHY-- (Cont.)
The Consulting engineers who's who &
year book. London, Norwood
Industrial Publications Ltd.[etc.]
620.942   49-25787
Began with vol. for 1947.
TA1 .C774 Sci RR Latest edition /
MRR Biog Latest edition

The dictionary of national biography,
London, Oxford university press
[1921-27] 24 v. 920.042 30-29308

DA28 .D45 1921 MRR Biog.

Duff, Edward Gordon, A century of
the English book trade; [Folcroft,
Pa.] Folcroft Library Editions, 1972.
xxxv, 200 p. 686.2/092/2 72-
188912
Z151.2 .D83 1972 MRR Alc.

Electrical who's who. 1950- London,
Iliffe Books Ltd.[etc.] 926.213 51-
23486
TK12 .E388 Sci RR Latest edition /
MRR Biog Latest edition

Emden, Alfred Brotherston, A
biographical register of the
University of Cambridge to 1500.
Cambridge [Eng.] University Press,
1963. xl, 695 p. 378.42 63-24688

LF113 .E4 MRR Biog.

Foskett, Daphne. A dictionary of
British miniature painters. New
York, Praeger Publishers [1972] 2 v.
[$135.00] 759.2 72-112634
ND1337.G7 F463 1972 MRR Alc.

The General biographical dictionary;
New ed.; rev. and enl. London,
Printed for J. Nichols, 1812-1817.
32 v.   mrr01-32
CT103 .G4 MRR Biog.

Gillow, Joseph, A literary and
biographical history; New York, B.
Franklin [1968] 5 v. 914.2/03/0922
B 74-6323
Z2010 .G483 1968 MRR Biog.

Gunnis, Rupert. Dictionary of
British sculptors, 1660-1851. New
revised ed. London, [Murrays Book
Sales], 1968. 515 p. [30/-]
730/.922 78-381295
NB496 .G85 1968 MRR Biog.

International businessmen's who's
who. 1st- ed.; 1967- London,
Burke's Peerage ltd. 650/.0922 68-
2468
HF5500 .I614 MRR Biog Latest
edition

International who's who in community
service. 1973/74- ed. London,
Eddison Press. [12.50] 361/.0025
78-189467
HV27 .I57 MRR Biog Latest edition

Kelly's handbook to the titled,
landed & official classes. 1875-
London, Kelly's Directories, Ltd.
[etc.] 08-5253
CS419 .K5 MRR Biog Latest edition*

Kirk, John Foster, A supplement to
Allibone's critical dictionary of
English literature and British and
American authors. Detroit, Gale
Research Co., 1965. 2 v. (x, 1562
p.) 820.3 67-296
Z1224 .A44 1891a MRR Biog.

Landau, Thomas. Who's who in
librarianship and information
science; 2nd ed. London, New York,
Abelard-Schuman, 1972. v, 311 p.
[25.50] 020/.92/2 70-184398
Z720.A46 G75 1972 MRR Alc.

Lofts, William Oliver Gullement. The
men behind boys' fiction London,
Howard Baker, 1970. [5], 361 p.
[84/-] 823/.009 70-564587
PR106 .L6 MRR Biog.

May, Robin. A companion to the
theatre; Guildford, Lutterworth
Press, 1973. 304 p., [16] p. of
plates. [£2.40] 792/.0942 74-
164747
PN2597 .M35 MRR Alc.

Nungezer, Edwin, A dictionary of
actors and other persons associated
with the public representation of
plays in England before 1642. New
York, Greenwood Press [1968, c1929]
437, [1] p. 792.028/0922 68-57633

PN2597 .N8 1968 MRR Biog.

The Penguin companion to English
literature. New York, McGraw-Hill
[1971] 575, [1] p. [$10.95] 820.9
B 77-158061
PN849.C5 P4 MRR Alc.

Redgrave, Samuel, A dictionary of
artists of the English school from
the Middle Ages to the nineteenth
century; New and rev. ed.
Amsterdam, G. W. Hissink, 1970. xiv,
497 p. [72.00] 709/.22 78-493152

N6796 .R4 1970b MRR Biog.

Spender, Stephen, ed. The concise
encyclopedia of English and American
poets and poetry, [1st ed.] New
York, Hawthorn Books [1963] 415 p.
821.003 63-8015
PR19 .S6 MRR Biog.

Vinson, James, Contemporary
dramatists; London, St. James Press;
New York, St. Martin's Press [1973]
xv, 926 p. [£9.00 ($30.00 U.S.)]
822/.9/1409 B 73-80310
PR106 .V5 MRR Biog.

Ware, Dora. A short dictionary of
British architects; London, Allen &
Unwin, 1967. 3-312 p. [48/-]
720/.922 67-94834
NA996 .W3 MRR Biog.

Watt, Homer Andrew, A handbook of
English literature New York, Barnes
& Noble [1960, c1946] 430 p. 820.3
61-2985
PR19 .W3 1960 MRR Biog.

Who's who in art. 1st- ed.; 1927-
London, Art Trade Press. 27-14051
N40 .W6 MRR Biog Latest edition /
MRR Alc Latest edition

Who's who in British finance. 1972-
New York, R. R. Bowker Co.
332/.092/2 [B] 72-624453
HG71 .W44 MRR Biog Latest edition

Who's who in literature. 1924-34.
Liverpool, Literary Year Books Press.
26-26968
Z2011 .L78 MRR Biog Latest edition

Who's who in the theatre; [1st]-
ed.; 1912- London, I. Pitman.
927.92 12-22402
PN2012 .W5 MRR Biog Latest edition

Who's who of British engineers. 1966-
London, Maclaren. 620/.0025/42 66-
76317
TA12 .W54 Sci RR Latest edition /
MRR Biog Latest edition

Wood, Christopher. Dictionary of
Victorian painters; [Woodbridge]
Antique Collectors' Club, 1971. v-
xvi, 435 p. [£8.00] 759.2 72-
188506
ND35 .W6 MRR Biog.

The Writers directory. 1971/73- New
York, St. Martin's Press. London, St.
James Press. 808 77-166289
PS1 .W73 MRR Biog Latest edition

GREAT BRITAIN--BIOGRAPHY--DIRECTORIES.
Building societies who's who.
London, Franey & Co. 332.32058 53-
29080
HG2123 .B8 MRR Alc Latest edition

Crockford's clerical directory
London, [etc.] Oxford University
Press. 07-24317
BX5031 .C8 MRR Alc Latest edition

GREAT BRITAIN--CHURCH HISTORY--ANGLO-
SAXON PERIOD, 449-1066.
Beda Venerabilis, Baedae Opera
historica, London, W. Heinemann
ltd.; New York, G. P. Putnam's sons,
1930. 2 v. 274.2 31-26352
PA6156.B4 1930 MRR Alc.

GREAT BRITAIN--CIVILIZATION.
Sattler, Wilhelm Ferdinand. Deutsch-
englisches sachwörterbuch. Leipzig,
Renger, 1904. xx, 1035 p. 05-16230

PF3640 .S3 MRR Alc.

Traill, Henry Duff, ed. Social
England; [New illustrated ed.]
London, New York [etc.] Cassell and
company, limited, 1901-04. 6 v. 04-
17441
DA30 .T77 1901 MRR Alc.

GREAT BRITAIN--CIVILIZATION--TO 1066.
Quennell, Marjorie (Courtney)
Everyday life in Roman and Anglo-
Saxon times, [Rev. ed.] London,
Batsford [1959] 235 p. 913.42 60-
1047
DA130 .Q4 1959 MRR Alc.

GREAT BRITAIN--CIVILIZATION--16TH
CENTURY.
Black, John Bennett, The reign of
Elizabeth, 1558-1603. 2d ed.
Oxford, Clarendon Press, 1959. xxvi,
539 p. 942.055 59-3629
DA355 .B65 1959 MRR Alc.

GREAT BRITAIN--CIVILIZATION--1945-
Sampson, Anthony. The new anatomy of
Britain. New York, Stein and Day
[1972, c1971] xviii, 773 p.
309.1/42/085 78-186150
DA592 .S23 1972 MRR Alc.

GREAT BRITAIN--CIVILIZATION--
BIBLIOGRAPHY.
Berkowitz, David Sandler,
Bibliotheca bibliographica
Britannica; Waltham, Mass., 1963-
v.   63-3390
Z2016 .B45 MRR Alc.

GREAT BRITAIN--CIVILIZATION--HISTORY.
The Connoisseur. The Connoisseur's
complete period guides to the houses,
decoration, furnishing and chattels
of the classic periods; London, The
Connoisseur, 1968. 1536 p. [84/-]
709/.42 70-369442
NK928 .C63 MRR Alc.

GREAT BRITAIN--CIVILIZATION--HISTORY--
SOURCES.
Davies, Reginald Trevor, comp.
Documents illustrating the history of
civilization in medieval England,
1066-1500 New York, Barnes & Noble
[1969] x, 413 p. 914.2 74-4396
DA170 .D3 1968 MRR Alc.

GREAT BRITAIN--CLUBS--DIRECTORIES.
The British club year book and
directory. London. 68-1184
Began in 1961.
HS67 .B7 MRR Alc Latest edition

GREAT BRITAIN--COLONIES--ADMINISTRATION.
Pugh, Ralph Bernard, The records of
the Colonial and Dominions Offices
London, H.M. Stationery Off., 1964.
v, 118 p. 325.342 64-4582
JV1011 .P8 MRR Alc.

GREAT BRITAIN--COLONIES--BIBLIOGRAPHY.
Berkowitz, David Sandler,
Bibliotheca bibliographica
Britannica; Waltham, Mass., 1963-
v.   63-3390
Z2016 .B45 MRR Alc.

Halstead, John P. Modern European
imperialism; Boston, G. K. Hall,
1974. 2 v. 016.90908 73-19511
Z6204 .H35 MRR Alc.

Parker, John, Books to build an
empire; Amsterdam, N. Israel, 1965.
viii, 290 p. 67-1417
Z2021.C7 P35 MRR Alc.

Royal Commonwealth Society. Library.
Subject catalogue of the Library of
the Royal Empire Society, [1st ed.
reprinted] London, Dawsons for the
Royal Commonwealth Society, 1967. 4
v. [60/-/- per set (16/-/- per
vol.)] 016.942 68-70847
Z7164.C7 R82 1967 MRR Alc.

GREAT BRITAIN--COLONIES--BIBLIOGRAPHY--
CATALOGS.
Royal Commonwealth Society. Library.
Subject catalogue of the Royal
Commonwealth Society, London.
Boston, Mass., G. K. Hall, 1971. 7
v. 017.1 70-180198
Z7164.C7 R83 MRR Alc (Dk 33)

GREAT BRITAIN--COLONIES--HISTORY.
The Cambridge history of the British
Empire; New York, The Macmillan
company; Cambridge, Eng., The
University press, 1929- v.   942
29-14661
DA30 .C3 1929 MRR Alc.

The Cambridge history of the British
Empire. [2d ed.] Cambridge [Eng.]
University Press, 1963- v.   942
63-24285
DA16 .C252 MRR Alc.

GREAT BRITAIN--COLONIES--HISTORY--
CHRONOLOGY.
Williamson, James Alexander, A
notebook of Commonwealth history. 2d
ed. London, MacMillan; New York, St.
Martin's Press, 1960. 307 p.
942.002 61-212
DA16 .W73 1960 MRR Alc.

GREAT BRITAIN--COLONIES--HISTORY--
SOURCES.
Pugh, Ralph Bernard, The records of
the Colonial and Dominions Offices
London, H.M. Stationery Off., 1964.
v, 118 p. 325.342 64-4582
JV1011 .P8 MRR Alc.

GREAT BRITAIN--COLONIES--NUMISMATICS.
Wright, Laurence Victor Ward.
Colonial and Commonwealth coins;
London, G. G. Harrap [1959] 236 p.
737.4942 60-22696
CJ2560 .W7 MRR Alc.

GREAT BRITAIN--COLONIES--AFRICA--CENSUS-
-BIBLIOGRAPHY.
United States. Library of Congress.
Census Library Project. Population
censuses and other official
demographic statistics of British
Africa; Washington, U.S. Govt.
Print. Off., 1950. v, 78 p.
016.312 50-60396
Z7554.A35 U5 MRR Alc.

GREAT BRITAIN--COLONIES--AMERICA.
Andrews, Charles McLean, The
colonial background of the American
Revolution; New Haven, Yale
University Press [1961, c1958] 220
p. 973.311 61-19714
E210 .A55 1961 MRR Alc.

Andrews, Charles McLean, The
colonial period of American history,
New Haven, Yale University Press
[1964] 4 v. 973.2 64-54917
E188 .A5745 MRR Alc.

Gipson, Lawrence Henry, The British
Empire before the American
Revolution. Caldwell, Id., Caxton
Printers, 1936-70. 15 v. 942.07/2
36-20870
DA500 .G5 MRR Alc.

Gipson, Lawrence Henry, The British
Empire before the American
Revolution. [Completely rev.] New
York, Knopf, 1958- v. 942.072
58-9670
DA500 .G52 MRR Alc.

Osgood, Herbert Levi, The American
colonies in the eighteenth century,
New York, Columbia university press,
1924. 4 v. 973.2 24-3889
E195 .082 MRR Alc.

GREAT BRITAIN--COLONIES--AMERICA--
ADMINISTRATION.
Sosin, Jack M. Agents and merchants;
Lincoln, University of Nebraska
Press, 1965. xvi, 267 p. 973.3112
65-13913
E210 .S73 MRR Alc.

GREAT BRITAIN--COLONIES--AMERICA--
BIBLIOGRAPHY.
Gipson, Lawrence Henry, The British
Empire before the American
Revolution. Caldwell, Id., Caxton
Printers, 1936-70. 15 v. 942.07/2
36-20870
DA500 .G5 MRR Alc.

GREAT BRITAIN--COLONIES--AMERICA--
COMMERCE.
Dickerson, Oliver Morton, The
navigation acts and the American
Revolution. Philadelphia, University
of Pennsylvania Press, 1951. xv, 344
p. 973.3112 51-13206
E215.1 .D53 MRR Alc.

GREAT BRITAIN--COLONIES--AMERICA--
POPULATION.
Greene, Evarts Boutell, American
population before the federal census
of 1790, New York, Columbia
university press, 1932. xxii p., 2
l., [3]-228 p., 1 l. 312.0873 33-
718
HB3505 .G7 MRR Alc.

GREAT BRITAIN--COLONIES--ASIA,
SOUTHEASTERN.
Wainwright, Mary Doreen. A guide to
Western manuscripts and documents in
the British Isles relating to South
and South East Asia. London, New
York, Oxford University Press, 1965.
xix, 532 p. 016.915 65-3147
CD1048.A8 W3 MRR Alc.

GREAT BRITAIN--COLONIES--NORTH AMERICA.
Osgood, Herbert Levi, The American
colonies in the seventeenth century,
New York, The Macmillan company;
London, Macmillan & co., ltd. 1904-
07. 3 v. 04-14597
E191 .082 MRR Alc.

GREAT BRITAIN--COMMERCE.
Wills, Gordon, comp. Sources of U.K.
marketing information; London,
Nelson, 1969. xiii, 304 p. [60/-]
658.83/8/42 70-412725
HF5415.12.G7 W5 MRR Alc.

GREAT BRITAIN--COMMERCE--DIRECTORIES.
Anglo-American trade directory. 1913-
London. 62-51858
HF54.G7 A7 MRR Alc Latest edition

British & international buyers &
sellers guide. Manchester, Eng.
[etc.] C. G. Birn. 55-36686
HF54.G7 B7 MRR Alc Latest edition

British and international trades
index. 38th- ed.; 1969/70- Epsom,
Business Dictionaries.
380.1/025/171242 72-626989
HF3503 .B75 MRR Alc Latest Edition

British exports. 1st- London,
Croydon [Eng.] Kompass Publishers.
382/.6/02542 75-219439
HF3503 .B79 MRR Alc Latest edition

British industries trade register
London, Industries Trade
Publications. 338.4/025/42 75-
206136
Began in 1964.
HC252 .B7 MRR Alc Latest edition

Castle's town & county trades
directory. London, United Publicity
Services. 380.1/025/42 70-615352
HF5155 .C37 MRR Alc Latest edition

Cenypres trading register of the
United Nations countries. London,
Cenypres. 380.025 66-85954
HF54.G7 C4 MRR Alc Latest edition

Directory of British export houses.
1st- ed.; 1971- Croydon, IPC
Business Press Information Services.
382/.6/02542 71-616998
HF3503 .D58 MRR Alc Latest edition

Dun & Bradstreet's guide to key
British enterprises. 1961- London.
62-41097
HC252 .D8 MRR Alc Latest edition

International town & country business
guide. London, County Advertising
and Pub. Co. 380.1/025/42 70-616534
HF3503 .I56 MRR Alc Latest edition

Kelly's manufacturers and merchants
directory, 82d- ed.; 1968/69-
Kingston upon Thames, Kelly's
Directories. 380.1/025 72-622824
HF54.G7 K4 MRR Alc Latest edition

Kemp's directory, London, Kemp's
Directory, Ltd. [etc.] 55-43556
HF3503 .K4 MRR Alc Latest edition

The London directory & international
register of commerce. 1973- London.
338/.0025/421 73-642810
D679 .A1315 MRR Alc Latest edition

North-western counties of England
trades' directory. Edinburgh,
Trades' Directories. 60-38503
HF5158 .N63 MRR Alc Latest edition

Sell's British exporters' register &
national directory. London, Business
Dictionaries. 48-25925
Began publication in 1916.
HF3503 .S4 MRR Alc Latest edition

Sell's directory of products &
services. 87th- 1972- Epsom,
Eng., Sell's Publications Ltd.
338/.0025/42 73-640793
HC252 .S44 MRR Alc Latest edition

South-eastern counties of England
trades' directory, including London,
London surburbs, Brighton and
Reading. Edinburgh, Trades'
Directories. 55-26292
HF5159.L6 S6 MRR Alc Latest
Edition

Stores, shops, supermarkets retail
directory. 21st- ed.; 1967-
London, Newman Books Ltd. 381 72-
623101
HF5155 .S8 MRR Alc Latest edition

Stubbs' directory [of] manufacturers,
merchant shippers, and professional;
London. 53-30509
HF3503 .S7 MRR Alc Latest edition

United Kingdom telex directory.
London, General Post Office. 56-
26931
HE7742.G7 U55 MRR Alc Latest
edition

GREAT BRITAIN--COMMERCE--HANDBOOKS,
MANUALS, ETC.
Netherlands-British trade directory.
London, Netherlands Chamber of
Commerce in the United Kingdom.
382/.0942 73-645767
HF302 .N37 MRR Alc Latest edition

GREAT BRITAIN--COMMERCE--HISTORY.
Page, William, ed. Commerce and
industry; London, Constable and
company, ltd., 1919. 2 v. 19-18954

HC255 .P3 MRR Alc.

Schumpeter, Elizabeth (Boody)
English overseas trade statistics,
1697-1808. Oxford, Clarendon Press,
1960 [i.e. 1961] vii, 72 p.
382.0942 61-1155
HF3501 .S35 MRR Alc.

GREAT BRITAIN--COMMERCE--INFORMATION
SERVICES.
Davinson, Donald Edward. Commercial
information; [1st ed.] Oxford, New
York, Pergamon Press [1965] vii, 164
p. 380.0942 65-22918
HF3507 .D3 1965 MRR Alc.

GREAT BRITAIN--COMMERCE--EUROPE,
EASTERN.
Zentner, Peter. East-West trade;
London, Parrish [1967]. 300 p. [45/-
] 658.8 67-111075
HF3508.E19 Z4 MRR Alc.

GREAT BRITAIN--COMMERCIAL TREATIES.
Hertslet's commercial treaties.
London, 1827-1925. 31 v. 01-4024
JX636 1827 Vol. 22 & 31 MRR Alc.

GREAT BRITAIN--CONSTITUTIONAL HISTORY--
SOURCES.
Stephenson, Carl, ed. and tr.
Sources of English constitutional
history; Rev. ed. New York, Harper
& Row [1972] 2 v. (xxvi, 953, xii
p.) 340/.73/024 72-84325
JN111 .S67 1972 MRR Alc.

GREAT BRITAIN--DESCRIPTION AND TRAVEL--
1946- --GUIDE-BOOKS.
Newby, Eric. Wonders of Britain:
London, Hodder & Stoughton, 1968.
xviii, 200 p. [30/-] 914.9/04/85
68-135721
DA650 .N4 MRR Alc.

GREAT BRITAIN--DESCRIPTION AND TRAVEL--
1971-
Rees, Henry, The British Isles: a
regional geography. 2nd ed., revised
and metricated. London, Harrap,
1972. xii, 404 p. [£2.30] 914.2
73-150498
DA631 .R4 1972 MRR Alc.

GREAT BRITAIN--DESCRIPTION AND TRAVEL--
GUIDE-BOOKS.
Automobile Association. AA guide to
hotels & restaurants in Great Britain
and Ireland. [Basingstoke, Eng.;
Distributed in the U.S.A. by Harper &
Row, New York, 1974] 671, 48 p.
[£1.95 ($7.95 U.S.)] 647/.9442 74-
167286
TX910.G7 A8 1974 MRR Alc.

Automobile Association. Treasures of
Britain and treasures of Ireland.
[2d American ed.] New York, Norton
[1972] 680 p. [$17.50] 914.2 72-
193038
DA650 .A92 1972 MRR Alc.

Baedeker, Karl, firm. Great
Britain; handbook for travellers.
10th ed. Freiburg, Baedecker;
London, Allen & Unwin; New York,
Macmillan (N.Y.) 1966- v. [35/-
(v. 1)] 914.20485 66-30829
DA650 .B2 1966 MRR Alc.

Baxter, Robert G. Baxter's Britrail
pass travel guide, [1972-73 ed.]
Alexandria, Va., Rail-Europe, 1972]
162 p. [$2.95] 914.2/04/4 72-
83184
HE3014 .B38 1972 MRR Alc.

Boumphrey, Geoffrey Maxwell, ed. The
Shell guide to Britain [2d ed.]
New York, Dutton [1969] xxxii, 808
p. [8.95] 914.2/04/85 69-10871
DA650 .B68 1969 MRR Alc.

Cherry, Mary Spooner, Would you like
to live in England? [New York]
Quadrangle [1974] xii, 242 p.
914.2/04/85 74-77934
JV7674 1974 .C47 MRR Alc.

Courtenay, Ashley. Let's halt awhile
in Great Britain. [London
Distributed in the United States by
Hastings House Publishers. 647/.9442
73-642063
TX910.G7 A67 MRR Alc Latest
edition

Coysh, Arthur Wilfred. The buying
antiques reference book; Newton
Abbot, David & Charles, 1968. 232 p.
[45/-] 745.1/025 74-385636
NK1125 .C68 MRR Alc.

Fedden, Henry Romilly, The National
Trust guide; London, Cape, 1973.
688 p. [£4.50] 914.2/04/85 73-
177113
DA660 .F33 MRR Alc.

Fodor's Great Britain. New York, D.
McKay. 914.2/04/85 72-622645
DA650 .G68 MRR Alc Latest edition

Hotels and restaurants in the British
Isles. 1951- London, British Travel
and Holidays Association. 647.9442
52-21171
TX910.G7 H64 MRR Alc Latest
edition

Museums and galleries in Great
Britain and Ireland. London, Index
Publishers. 58-46943
Began publication with 1955 vol.
N1020 .M82 MRR Alc Latest edition

Olson, Harvey Stuart, Olson's
complete motoring guide to the
British Isles, [1st ed.]
Philadelphia, Lippincott [1967] xiv,
861 p. 914.2/04/85 67-11310
GV1025.G7 O4 MRR Alc.

GREAT BRITAIN--DESCRIPTION AND (Cont.)
Reader's Digest Association, ltd. AA
book of the road, incorporating the
Ordnance Survey four miles to the
inch series [3d ed., 1st revise.
London, Published in collaboration
with the Automobile Association,
1972] 412 p.   914.2/04/85 73-
169037
  GV1025.G7 R4 1972 MRR Alc.

Royal Automobile Club, London. Guide
and handbook. London. 629.281 51-
34691
  GV1025.G7 R59 MRR Alc Latest
    edition

GREAT BRITAIN--DIPLOMATIC AND CONSULAR
SERVICE.
The Foreign office list and
diplomatic and consular year book.
London, Harrison and sons. 07-21419
  JX1783 .A2 MRR Alc Latest edition

GREAT BRITAIN--DIPLOMATIC AND CONSULAR
SERVICE--REGISTERS.
The Diplomatic Service list. 1966-
London, H. M. Stationery Off.
354.42061 66-4595
  JX1783 .A22 MRR Biog Latest
    edition

GREAT BRITAIN--DIRECTORIES.
Anderson, Ian Gibson. Councils,
committees, & boards; 2d ed.
Beckenham, CBD Research Ltd. 1973.
iii-xiv, 327 p.   [£7.50 ($25.00
U.S.)]   062 74-164686
  AS118 .A5 1973 MRR Alc.

Directory of British associations.
1965- Beckenham, Eng. [etc.] C.B.D.
Research Limited.   65-89384
  AS118 .D56 MRR Alc Latest edition

Industrial research in Britain. 7th
ed. [St. Peter Port, Guernsey] F.
Hodgson [1972] 889 p.   607/.2/42
73-180253
  T177.G7 I52 1972 MRR Alc.

GREAT BRITAIN--DIRECTORIES--
BIBLIOGRAPHY.
British rate & data directories and
annuals. [London, Maclean-Hunter
Ltd. [-/10/6]   016.05   73-645548
  Z5771.4.G7 B75 MRR Alc Latest
    edition

Current British directories. 1953-
Beckenham, Kent [etc.] CBD Research
Ltd. [etc.] 53-26894
  Z5771 .C8 MRR Ref Desk Latest
    edition

The Newspaper press directory.
London, C. Mitchell [etc.] ca 07-6361
  Z6956.E5 N6 MRR Alc Latest edition

Norton, Jane Elizabeth. Guide to the
national and provincial directories
of England and Wales. London,
Offices of the Royal Historical
Society, 1950. vii, 241 p.
016.9142 51-2465
  Z5771 .N6 MRR Alc.

GREAT BRITAIN--DESCRIPTION AND TRAVEL--
GUIDE-BOOKS.
Hardwick, John Michael Drinkrow, A
literary atlas & gazetteer of the
British Isles Newton Abbot, David &
Charles [1973] 216 p. [£4.95]
820/.3 73-181081
  PR109 .H25 MRR Alc.

GREAT BRITAIN--ECONOMIC CONDITIONS.
Gayler, J. L. A sketch-map economic
history of Britain, 4th ed. revised.
London, Harrap, 1966. 3-266 p.
[15/-]   330.942 67-78007
  HC253 .G3 1966 MRR Alc.

Gregg, Pauline. Modern Britain: 5th
ed., rev. New York, Pegasus [1967,
c1965] 615 p.   309.142 67-25498
  HN385 .G7 1967 MRR Alc.

Lipson, Ephraim, The economic
history of England. London, A. and
C. Black [1960-64] 3 v. 330.942
60-23691
  HC253 .L5535 MRR Alc.

Murphy, Brian. A history of the
British economy, 1086-1970.
[London], Longman, 1973. 819, xlii
p. [£4.50] 330.9/42 73-165914
  HC253 .M85 MRR Alc.

Page, William, ed. Commerce and
industry; London, Constable and
company, ltd., 1919. 2 v. 19-18954
  HC255 .P3 MRR Alc.

Stamp, Laurence Dudley, Sir, The
British Isles: a geographic and
economic survey 6th ed. London,
Longman, 1971. ix, 881 p. [£7.00]
914.2   72-170778
  HC253 .S67 1971b MRR Alc.

GREAT BRITAIN--ECONOMIC CONDITIONS--
1945-
Stamp, Laurence Dudley, Sir, The
British Isles: a geographic and
economic survey 6th ed. London,
Longman, 1971. ix, 881 p. [£7.00]
914.2 72-170778
  HC253 .S67 1971b MRR Alc.

GREAT BRITAIN--ECONOMIC CONDITIONS--
1945- --PERIODICALS.
Financial times yearbook: 1970- New
York, St. Martin's Press. 330/.05
76-85357
  HC10 .F54 MRR Alc Latest edition

GREAT BRITAIN--ECONOMIC CONDITIONS--
BIBLIOGRAPHY.
Kiel. Universität. Institut für
Weltwirtschaft. Bibliothek.
Regionenkatalog. Boston, G. K. Hall,
1967. 52 v.   017/.5 67-9425
  Z929 .K52 1967 MRR Alc. (Dk 33).

GREAT BRITAIN--ECONOMIC CONDITIONS--
MAPS.
Gayler, J. L. A sketch-map economic
history of Britain, 4th ed. revised.
London, Harrap, 1966. 3-266 p.
[15/-]   330.942 67-78007
  HC253 .G3 1966 MRR Alc.

GREAT BRITAIN--EMIGRATION AND
IMMIGRATION--HANDBOOKS, MANUALS, ETC.
Cherry, Mary Spooner. Would you like
to live in England? [New York]
Quadrangle [1974] xii, 242 p.
914.2/04/85 74-77934
  JV7674 1974 .C47 MRR Alc.

GREAT BRITAIN--EXECUTIVE DEPARTMENTS.
Dod's parliamentary companion.
Epsom, Surrey, [etc.] Sell's
publications Ltd. [etc.] 06-7438
  JN500 .D7 MRR Biog Latest edition

Industrial research in Britain. 7th
ed. [St. Peter Port, Guernsey] F.
Hodgson [1972] 889 p.   607/.2/42
73-180253
  T177.G7 I52 1972 MRR Alc.

GREAT BRITAIN--EXECUTIVE DEPARTMENTS--
DIRECTORIES.
The Civil service year book. 1974-
London, H.M. Stationery Off. [£1.60]
354/.42 74-643279
  JN106 .B8 MRR Alc Latest edition

GREAT BRITAIN--FOREIGN RELATIONS--1789-
1820.
Temperley, Harold William Vazeille,
ed. Foundations of British foreign
policy, New York, Barnes & Noble
[1966] xxx, 573 p. 327.42 66-3832
  DA530 .T4 1966a MRR Alc.

GREAT BRITAIN--FOREIGN RELATIONS--19TH
CENTURY.
Temperley, Harold William Vazeille,
ed. Foundations of British foreign
policy, New York, Barnes & Noble
[1966] xxx, 573 p. 327.42 66-3832
  DA530 .T4 1966a MRR Alc.

GREAT BRITAIN--FOREIGN RELATIONS--
BIBLIOGRAPHY.
Great Britain. Foreign Office.
Library. Catalogue of the Foreign
Office Library, 1926-1968. Boston,
G. K. Hall, 1972. 8 v.   019/.1 73-
160726
  Z921 .G682 1972 MRR Alc. (Dk 33)

Temperley, Harold William Vazeille,
ed. A century of diplomatic blue
books, 1814-1914; London, Cass,
1966. xviii, 600 p. [84/-]
016.32742 66-70453
  Z2009 .T28 1966 MRR Alc.

Vogel, Robert. A breviate of British
diplomatic blue books, 1919-1939.
Montreal, McGill University Press,
1963. xxxv, 474 p.   a 64-408
  Z2009 .V6 MRR Alc.

GREAT BRITAIN--FOREIGN RELATIONS--
TREATIES.
Hertslet's commercial treaties.
London, 1827-1925.   31 v   01-4024
  JX636 1827 Vol. 22 & 31 MRR Alc.

GREAT BRITAIN--FOREIGN RELATIONS--
TREATIES--INDEXES.
Parry, Clive. An index of British
treaties, 1101-1968, London,
H.M.S.O., 1970. 1 v. in 3
341/.0264/42 75-873903
  JX636 1970 .P37 MRR Alc.

GREAT BRITAIN--FOREIGN RELATIONS--
CONFEDERATE STATES OF AMERICA.
Owsley, Frank Lawrence. King Cotton
diplomacy; 2d ed., rev. [Chicago]
University of Chicago Press [1959]
xxiii, 614 p.   973.721 58-11952
  E488 .085 1959 MRR Alc.

GREAT BRITAIN--FOREIGN RELATIONS--
UNITED STATES.
Allen, Harry Cranbrook. Great
Britain and the United States; New
York, St. Martin's Press, 1955. 1024
p.   327.730942 55-7753
  E183.8.G7 A47 1955 MRR Alc.

GREAT BRITAIN--GAZETTEERS.
Automobile Association. Treasures of
Britain and treasures of Ireland.
[2d American ed.] New York, Norton
[1972] 680 p. [$17.50] 914.2 72-
193038
  DA650 .A92 1972 MRR Alc.

Bartholomew, John George, Gazetteer
of the British Isles. 9th ed.,
reprinted. Edinburgh, J.
Bartholomew, 1963. xxxii, 748 p.
65-53267
  DA640 .B23 1963 MRR Alc.

The Railway & commercial gazetteer of
England, Scotland & Wales. 21st ed.
London, McCorquodale [1965] vi, 716
p.   385/.31 70-219483
  HE3014 .R14 1965 MRR Alc.

United States. Office of Geography.
United Kingdom; Washington, 1950.
733 p.   914.2/003 76-10015
  DA640 .U5 MRR Alc.

GREAT BRITAIN--GENEALOGY--BIBLIOGRAPHY.
Filby, P. William, American &
British genealogy & heraldry; a
selected list of books. Chicago,
American Library Association, 1970.
xix, 184 p. [10.00] 016.9291/097
75-106200
  Z5311 .F55 MRR Alc.

Whitmore, John Beach. A genealogical
guide; London, Sold by Walford
Bros., 1953. xxxvii, 658 p.
016.9291 55-24360
  Z5313.G69 W45 1953 MRR Alc.

GREAT BRITAIN--GENEALOGY--BIBLIOGRAPHY--
CATALOGS.
United States. Library of Congress.
American and English genealogies in
the Library of Congress, 2d ed.
Washington, Govt. print. off., 1919.
iv, 1332 p.   19-26004
  Z663.74 .A5 1919 MRR Alc.

United States. Library of Congress.
Genealogies in the Library of
Congress; Baltimore, Md., Magna
Carta Book Co., 1972. 2 v.
016.929/1 74-187078
  Z5319 .U53 MRR Alc.

GREAT BRITAIN--GENTRY.
Debrett's peerage, baronetage,
knightage, and companionage.
Kingston upon Thames, Surrey, Kelly's
Directories [etc.] 929.72 42-17925
  CS420 .D32 MRR Biog Latest edition

GREAT BRITAIN--GOVERNMENT PUBLICATIONS.
Ford, Percy, A guide to
parliamentary papers; 3d ed.
Totowa, N.J., Rowman and Littlefield,
1972. xiii, 87 p. [$8.50] 015.42
72-171410
  Z2009.A1 F6 1972 MRR Ref Desk.

Horrocks, Sidney. The State as
publisher; London, Library
Association, 1952. 32 p.   655.142
53-3314
  Z232.G8735 H6 MRR Ref Desk.

Ollé, James Gordon Herbert. An
introduction to British government
publications, London, Association of
Assistant Librarians, 1965. 128 p.
67-103334
  Z2009 .O4 MRR Alc.

Staveley, Ronald. Government
information and the research worker.
2nd revised ed. London, Library
Association, 1965. 267 p. [56/- 42/-
(to members)] 015.42 66-2624
  Z2009 .S7 1965 MRR Alc.

GREAT BRITAIN--GOVERNMENT PUBLICATIONS--
BIBLIOGRAPHY.
Cole, Arthur Harrison, ed. A finding-
list of British royal commission
reports: 1860 to 1935, Cambridge,
Mass., Harvard university press,
1935. 3 p. l., 5-66 p. 015.42 35-
11452
  Z2009 .C68 MRR Alc.

Ford, Percy, A breviate of
parliamentary papers, 1900-1916
Oxford, Blackwell, 1957. xlix, 470
p.   342.42 58-1414
  JN549 .F59 MRR Alc.

Ford, Percy, A breviate of
parliamentary papers, 1917-1939
Shannon, Ire., Irish University
Press, 1969. xlviii, 571 p.
320.9/42/082 76-27392
  JN549 .F6 1969 MRR Alc.

GREAT BRITAIN--GOVERNMENT (Cont.)
Ford, Percy, A breviate of
parliamentary papers, 1940-1954:
Oxford, Blackwell, 1961. l, 515 p.
63-205
JN549 .F62 MRR Alc.

Great Britain. Parliament. House of
Commons. Hansard's Catalogue and
breviate of parliamentary papers,
1696-1834. Oxford, Blackwell, 1953.
xv p., facsim.: viii, 220 p.
328.4204 53-12375
J301 .K62 1953 MRR Alc.

Great Britain. Parliament. House of
Commons. Library. A bibliography of
parliamentary debates of Great
Britain. London, H.M. Stationery
Off., 1956. 62 p. 57-32205
Z2009 .G7 MRR Alc.

Great Britain. Stationery Office.
Government publications. Jan. 1936-
[London] 015.42 36-13303
Z2009 .G822 MRR Alc Full set

New York (City). Public Library.
Research Libraries. Catalog of
Government publications in the
Research Libraries: Boston, G. K.
Hall, 1972. 40 v. 011 74-171015
Z7164.G7 N54 1972 MRR Alc (Dk 33)

Pemberton, John E. British official
publications 2d rev. ed. Oxford,
New York, Pergamon Press [1973] xiv,
328 p. 015/.42 73-16231
Z2009 .P45 1973 MRR Ref Desk.

Temperley, Harold William Vazeille,
ed. A century of diplomatic blue
books, 1814-1914; London, Cass,
1966. xviii, 600 p. [84/-]
016.32742 66-70453
Z2009 .T28 1966 MRR Alc.

Vogel, Robert. A breviate of British
diplomatic blue books, 1919-1939.
Montreal, McGill University Press,
1963. xxxv, 474 p. a 64-408
Z2009 .V6 MRR Alc.

GREAT BRITAIN--GOVERNMENT PUBLICATIONS--
BIBLIOGRAPHY--CATALOGS.
King (P. S.) & son, ltd., London.
Catalogue of parliamentary papers,
1801-1900, London, P. S. King & son
[1904] vii, [1], 317 p. 04-14268
Z2009 .K55 MRR Alc.

GREAT BRITAIN--GOVERNMENT PUBLICATIONS--
INDEXES.
Di Roma, Edward, A numerical finding
list of British command papers
published 1833-1961/62, [New York]
New York Public Library, 1967. 148
p. 015/.42 67-56501
Z2009 .D5 MRR Ref Desk.

Ford, Percy, Select list of British
parliamentary papers, 1833-1899
[Rev. ed.] Shannon, Irish University
Press, 1969. xxii, 165 p.
328.42/04 72-29483
J301 .M3 1869 MRR Alc.

Great Britain. Parliament. House of
commons. General index to the
Accounts and papers, Reports of
commissioners, Estimates, &c., &c.
London, H.M. Stationery off. [printed
by P. Lund, Humphries & co., ltd.]
1938. 2 v. l., 1, 3-1080 p.
328.4204 39-10063
J301 .M3 1801-1852a MRR Ref Desk.

Great Britain. Parliament. House of
Commons. Library. General index to
the Bills, Reports and papers printed
by order of the House of Commons
London, H.M. Stationery Off., 1960.
viii, 893 p. 328.4204 61-3087
LAW MRR Ref Desk.

Irish University Press. Checklist of
British parliamentary papers in the
Irish University Press 1000-volume
series, 1801-1899. Shannon, Ireland
[1972] xii, 218 p. 015.42 73-
150718
Z2019 .I73 MRR Ref Desk.

Irish University Press series of
British parliamentary papers.
Shannon, Irish University Press
[1968] 8 v. 016.32842/01 77-
456705
Z2019 .I74 MRR Alc.

Morgan, Annie Mary. British
government publications: London,
Library Association, Reference,
Special and Information Section,
1973. [3], 198 p. [£3.75] 015/.42
73-595554
Z2009 .M64 1973 MRR Ref Desk.

Rodgers, Frank, Serial publications
in the British Parliamentary papers,
1900-1968: Chicago, American Library
Association, 1971. xix, 146 p.
015/.42 74-117628
Z2009 .R63 MRR Alc.

GREAT BRITAIN--HISTORIC HOUSES, ETC.
Automobile Association. Treasures of
Britain and treasures of Ireland.
[2d American ed.] New York, Norton
[1972] 680 p. [$17.50] 914.2 72-
193038
DA650 .A92 1972 MRR Alc.

Fedden, Henry Romilly, The National
Trust guide; London, Cape, 1973.
688 p. [£4.50] 914.2/04/85 73-
177113
DA660 .F33 MRR Alc.

The Libraries, museums and art
galleries year book. 1897- London
[etc.] J. Clarke [etc.] 28-11281
Z791 .L7 MRR Alc Latest edition

GREAT BRITAIN--HISTORY.
Ashley, Maurice Percy. Great Britain
to 1688, Ann Arbor, University of
Michigan Press [1961] xi, 444, xxii
p. 942 61-8033
DA130 .A8 MRR Alc.

The Cambridge history of the British
Empire. [2d ed.] Cambridge [Eng.]
University Press, 1963- v. 942
63-24285
DA16 .C252 MRR Alc.

The Cambridge history of the British
Empire: New York, The Macmillan
company; Cambridge, Eng., The
University press, 1929- v. 942
29-14661
DA30 .C3 1929 MRR Alc.

Shears, William Sydney, The face of
England; London, Spring Books [1959]
631 p. 914.2 61-65326
DA600 .S46 1959 MRR Alc.

Traill, Henry Duff, ed. Social
England; [New illustrated ed.]
London, New York [etc.] Cassell and
company, limited, 1901-04. 6 v. 04-
17441
DA30 .T77 1901 MRR Alc.

GREAT BRITAIN--HISTORY--TO 1066--
BIBLIOGRAPHY.
Bonser, Wilfrid, An Anglo-Saxon and
Celtic bibliography, 450-1087.
Oxford, Blackwell, 1957. 2 v.
016.94201 a 58-1987
Z2017 .B6 MRR Alc.

GREAT BRITAIN--HISTORY--ROMAN PERIOD,
55 B.C.-449 A.D.
Collingwood, Robin George, Roman
Britain and the English settlements,
2d ed. Oxford, The Clarendon press,
1937. xxv, [1], 515, [1] p. 942.01
38-2347
DA145 .C583 1937 MRR Alc.

GREAT BRITAIN--HISTORY--ANGLO-SAXON
PERIOD, 449-1066.
Collingwood, Robin George, Roman
Britain and the English settlements,
2d ed. Oxford, The Clarendon press,
1937. xxv, [1], 515, [1] p. 942.01
38-2347
DA145 .C583 1937 MRR Alc.

Stenton, Frank Merry, Sir, Anglo-
Saxon England, Oxford, The Clarendon
press, 1943. vii, [2], 748 [i.e.
747], [1] p. 942.01 a 44-638
DA152 .S74 MRR Alc.

GREAT BRITAIN--HISTORY--WILLIAM I, 1066-
1087--BIBLIOGRAPHY.
Bonser, Wilfrid, An Anglo-Saxon and
Celtic bibliography, 450-1087.
Oxford, Blackwell, 1957. 2 v.
016.94201 a 58-1987
Z2017 .B6 MRR Alc.

GREAT BRITAIN--HISTORY--MEDIEVAL
PERIOD, 1066-1485.
Poole, Austin Lane, From Domesday
book to Magna Carta, 1087-1216. 2d
ed. Oxford, Clarendon Press, 1955.
xv, 541 p. 942.02 56-13761
DA175 .P6 1955 MRR Alc.

GREAT BRITAIN--HISTORY--MEDIEVAL
PERIOD, 1066-1485--SOURCES.
Davies, Reginald Trevor, comp.
Documents illustrating the history of
civilization in medieval England,
1066-1500 New York, Barnes & Noble
[1969] x, 413 p. 914.2 74-4396
DA170 .D3 1969 MRR Alc.

GREAT BRITAIN--HISTORY--13TH CENTURY.
Powicke, Frederick Maurice, Sir, The
thirteenth century, 1216-1307. 2d
ed. Oxford, Clarendon Press, 1962.
xiv, 829 p. 942.034 62-6745
DA225 .P65 1962 MRR Alc.

GREAT BRITAIN--HISTORY--14TH CENTURY.
McKisack, May. The fourteenth
century, 1307-1399. Oxford,
Clarendon Press, 1959. xix, 598 p.
942.037 59-16710
DA230 .M25 MRR Alc.

GREAT BRITAIN--HISTORY--LANCASTER AND
YORK, 1399-1485.
Jacob, Ernest Fraser, The fifteenth
century, 1399-1485. Oxford,
Clarendon Press, 1961. xvi, 775 p.
942.04 61-66708
DA245 .J3 MRR Alc.

GREAT BRITAIN--HISTORY--TUDORS, 1485-
1603.
Mackie, John Duncan, The earlier
Tudors, 1485-1558. Oxford, Clarendon
Press, 1952. xxi, 699 p. 942.05
52-4641
DA325 .M3 MRR Alc.

GREAT BRITAIN--HISTORY--TUDORS, 1485-
1603--BIBLIOGRAPHY.
Levine, Mortimer. Tudor England 1485-
1603. London, Cambridge U.P. for the
Conference on British Studies, 1968.
xii, 115 p. 016.942/05 68-12060
Z2017.5 .L4 MRR Alc.

Read, Conyers, ed. Bibliography of
British history; Tudor period, 1485-
1603; 2d ed. Oxford, Clarendon
Press, 1959. xxviii, 624 p.
016.94205 59-3413
Z2018 .R28 1959 MRR Alc.

GREAT BRITAIN--HISTORY--EARLY
STUARTS, 1603-1649.
Davies, Godfrey, The early Stuarts,
1603-1660. 2d ed. Oxford, Clarendon
Press, 1959. xxiii, 458 p. 942.06
59-1862
DA390 .D3 1959 MRR Alc.

GREAT BRITAIN--HISTORY--STUARTS, 1603-
1714.
Clark, George Norman, Sir, The later
Stuarts, 1660-1714. 2d ed.
[reprinted with corrections] Oxford,
Clarendon Press [1961] xxiii, 479 p.
68-105542
DA435 .C55 1961 MRR Alc.

GREAT BRITAIN--HISTORY--STUARTS, 1603-
1714--BIBLIOGRAPHY.
Davies, Godfrey, ed. Bibliography of
British history, Stuart period, 1603-
1714: Oxford, At the Clarendon
press, 1928. x, 459, [1] p. 28-
27579
Z2018 .D25 MRR Alc.

GREAT BRITAIN--HISTORY--STUARTS, 1603-
1714--SOURCES.
Upton, Eleanor Stuart, Guide to
sources of English history from 1603
to 1660 2d ed. New York, Scarecrow
Press, 1964. 258 p. 016.94206 64-
11782
DA25.M1 U6 1964 MRR Alc.

GREAT BRITAIN--HISTORY--COMMONWEALTH
AND PROTECTORATE, 1649-1660.
Davies, Godfrey, The early Stuarts,
1603-1660. 2d ed. Oxford, Clarendon
Press, 1959. xxiii, 458 p. 942.06
59-1862
DA390 .D3 1959 MRR Alc.

GREAT BRITAIN--HISTORY--18TH CENTURY.
Gipson, Lawrence Henry, The British
Empire before the American
Revolution. [Completely rev.] New
York, Knopf, 1958- v. 942.072
58-9670
DA500 .G52 MRR Alc.

Gipson, Lawrence Henry, The British
Empire before the American
Revolution. Caldwell, Id., Caxton
Printers 1936-70. 15 v. 942.07/2
36-20870
DA500 .G5 MRR Alc.

Valentine, Alan Chester, The British
establishment, 1760-1784: [1st ed.]
Norman, University of Oklahoma Press
[1970] 2 v. (xii, 960 p.) 920.042
69-16734
CT781 .V3 MRR Biog.

GREAT BRITAIN--HISTORY--18TH CENTURY--
BIBLIOGRAPHY.
Morgan, William Thomas, A
bibliography of British history (1700-
1715) Bloomington, Ind., 1934-42. 5
v. 016.942069 35-27707
Z2019 .M85 1934 MRR Alc.

Pargellis, Stanley McCrory,
Bibliography of British history:
Oxford, Clarendon Press, 1951. xxvi,
642 p. 016.94207 51-4275
Z2019 .P3 MRR Alc.

GREAT BRITAIN--HISTORY--18TH CENTURY--
SOURCES--BIBLIOGRAPHY.
Morgan, William Thomas, A
bibliography of British history (1700-
1715) Bloomington, Ind., 1934-42. 5
v. 016.942069 35-27707
Z2019 .M85 1934 MRR Alc.

GREAT BRITAIN--HISTORY--ANNE, 1702-1714-
-BIBLIOGRAPHY.
Morgan, William Thomas, A
bibliography of British history (1700-
1715) Bloomington, Ind., 1934-42. 5
v. 016.942069 35-27707
Z2019 .M85 1934 MRR Alc.

GREAT BRITAIN--HISTORY--ANNE, 1702-1714-
-PAMPHLETS--BIBLIOGRAPHY.
Morgan, William Thomas, A
bibliography of British history (1700-
1715) Bloomington, Ind., 1934-42. 5
v.   016.942069   35-27707
Z2019 .M85 1934 MRR Alc.

GREAT BRITAIN--HISTORY--ANNE, 1702-1714-
-SOURCES--BIBLIOGRAPHY.
Morgan, William Thomas, A
bibliography of British history (1700-
1715) Bloomington, Ind., 1934-42. 5
v.   016.942069   35-27707
Z2019 .M85 1934 MRR Alc.

GREAT BRITAIN--HISTORY--GEORGE I-II,
1714-1760.
Williams, Basil, The Whig supremacy,
1714-1760. 2d ed. rev. Oxford,
Clarendon Press, 1962. xix, 504 p.
942.071 62-2655
DA498 .W5 1962 MRR Alc.

GREAT BRITAIN--HISTORY--GEORGE III,
1760-1820.
Watson, John Steven. The reign of
George III, 1760-1815. Oxford,
Clarendon Press, 1960. xviii, 637 p.
942.073 60-50916
DA505 .W38 MRR Alc.

GREAT BRITAIN--HISTORY--1789-1820--
SOURCES.
Temperley, Harold William Vazeille,
ed. Foundations of British foreign
policy, New York, Barnes & Noble
[1966] xxx, 573 p.   327.42 66-3832

DA530 .T4 1966a MRR Alc.

GREAT BRITAIN--HISTORY--19TH CENTURY.
Woodward, Ernest Llewellyn Sir, The
age of reform, 1815-1870. 2d ed.
Oxford, Clarendon Press, 1962. xix,
681 p.   942.07 62-4675
DA530 .W6 1962 MRR Alc.

GREAT BRITAIN--HISTORY--19TH CENTURY--
SOURCES.
Evans, Lloyd, comp. Contemporary
sources and opinions in modern
British history London, New York, F.
Warne, 1967. 2 v. [30/- (v. 1) 42/-
(v. 2)]   942.08/08 68-101076
DA530 .E9 1967 MRR Alc.

Temperley, Harold William Vazeille,
ed. Foundations of British foreign
policy, New York, Barnes & Noble
[1966] xxx, 573 p.   327.42 66-3832

DA530 .T4 1966a MRR Alc.

GREAT BRITAIN--HISTORY--VICTORIA, 1837-
1901.
Ensor, Robert Charles Kirkwood,
England, 1870-1914. Oxford, The
Clarendon press [1936] xxiii, 634
p., 1 l.   mrr01-24
DA560 .E6 1936a MRR Alc.

Parrott, Thomas Marc, A companion to
Victorian literature New York,
Scribner [1955] 308 p.   820.903 55-
7295
PR461 .P3 MRR Alc.

GREAT BRITAIN--HISTORY--20TH CENTURY.
Ensor, Robert Charles Kirkwood,
England, 1870-1914. Oxford, The
Clarendon press [1936] xxiii, 634
p., 1 l.   mrr01-24
DA560 .E6 1936a MRR Alc.

Havighurst, Alfred F. Twentieth-
century Britain 2d ed. New York,
Harper & Row [1966] xiv, 572 p.
942.082 66-12556
DA566 .H37 1966 MRR Alc.

Marwick, Arthur, Britain in the
century of total war: London, Sydney
[etc.] Bodley Head, 1968. 511 p.
[63/-]   942.082 68-110065
DA566 .M34 MRR Alc.

Medlicott, William Norton,
Contemporary England, 1914-1964,
London, Longmans, 1967. [13], 614 p.
[42/-]   942.082 67-104863
DA566 .M38 MRR Alc.

Taylor, Alan John Percivale, English
history, 1914-1945 New York, Oxford
University Press, 1965. xxvii, 708
p.   942.083 65-27513
DA566 .T38 MRR Alc.

GREAT BRITAIN--HISTORY--20TH CENTURY--
SOURCES.
Bettey, J. H. English historical
documents, 1906-1939: London,
Routledge & K. Paul, 1967. x, 198 p.
[21/- 12/6 (pbk.)]   942.083/08 67-
109889
DA576 .B45 MRR Alc.

Evans, Lloyd, comp. Contemporary
sources and opinions in modern
British history London, New York, F.
Warne, 1967. 2 v. [30/- (v. 1) 42/-
(v. 2)]   942.08/08 68-101076
DA530 .E9 1967 MRR Alc.

GREAT BRITAIN--HISTORY--BIBLIOGRAPHY.
Bell, S. Peter. Dissertations on
British history, 1815-1914:
Metuchen, N.J., Scarecrow Press,
1974. xii, 232 p.   016.9142/03 74-
16104
Z2016 .B43 MRR Alc.

Berkowitz, David Sandler,
Bibliotheca bibliographica
Britannica: Waltham, Mass., 1963-
v.   63-3390
Z2016 .B45 MRR Alc.

Lancaster, Joan Cadogan, comp.
Bibliography of historical works
issued in the United Kingdom, 1946-
1956, [London] University of London,
Institute of Historical Research,
1957. xxii, 388 p.   016.9 a 58-
2313
Z2016 .L3 MRR Alc.

Milne, Alexander Taylor. A centenary
guide to the publications of the
Royal Historical Society, 1868-1968,
London, Royal Historical Society,
1968. xi, 249 p. [unpriced]
016.942 77-436189
Z5055.G6 R66 MRR Alc.

Mullins, Edward Lindsay Carson. A
guide to the historical and
archaeological publications of
societies in England and Wales, 1901-
1933: London, Athlone P., 1968.
xiii, 850 p. [10/10/-] 016.9142
79-367032
Z5055.G6 M8 MRR Alc.

New York. Union theological seminary.
Library. Catalogue of the McAlpin
collection of British history and
theology, New York, 1927-30. 5 v.
29-29688
Z7757.E5 N5 MRR Alc.

Royal Historical Society, London.
Writings on British history 1901-
1933: London, Cape, 1968- v.
[£5/5- (v. 1) 63/- (v.2) £5/5/- (v.
3)]   016.942 68-88411
Z2016 .R85 MRR Alc.

Writings on British history. 1901/33-
New York, Barnes & Noble. 61-2932

Z2016 .R88 MRR Alc Full set

GREAT BRITAIN--HISTORY--CHRONOLOGY.
Cheney, Christopher Robert, ed.
Handbook of dates for students of
English history, London, Office of
the Royal historical society, 1945.
xvii, 164 p.   942.002 a 46-270
DA34 .C5 MRR Alc.

Fry, Edward Alexander. Almanacks for
students of English history, London,
Phillimore & co., ltd., 1915. vii,
138 p.   16-20586
CE61.G8 F8 MRR Alc.

Phelps, Robert, The literary life:
New York, Farrar, Straus and Giroux,
1968. 244 p. [$15.00]
016.8209/009/1 68-27533
Z2013 .P48 MRR Alc.

Powicke, Frederick Maurice, Sir, ed.
Handbook of British chronology, 2d
ed. London, Offices of the Royal
Historical Society, 1961. xxxviii,
565 p.   942.002 62-3079
DA34 .P6 1961 MRR Alc.

Who's who in history. Oxford,
Blackwell, 1960- v.   920.042 61-
66758
DA28 .W618 MRR Biog.

GREAT BRITAIN--HISTORY--DICTIONARIES.
Brendon, John Adams, ed. A
dictionary of British history, New
York, Longmans, Green & co.; London,
E. Arnold & co., 1937. vii, 603 p.
842.003 37-28742
DA34 .B68 MRR Alc.

Haydn, Joseph Timothy, Haydn's
dictionary of dates and universal
information relating to all ages and
nations, New York, Dover
Publications [1969] vi, 1605 p.
[25.00]   903 68-8154
D9 .H45 1969 MRR Alc.

Low, Sidney James Mark, Sir, ed. The
dictionary of English history, New
ed., rev. and enl. London, New York
[etc.] Cassell and company, limited
[1928] x, 154 (i.e. 1154) p.   29-
1323
DA34 .L9 1928 MRR Alc.

Steinberg, Sigfrid Henry, ed.
Steinberg's dictionary of British
history. 2nd ed.: London, Edward
Arnold, 1970. vii, 421 p. [50/-]
942/.003 70-586955
DA34 .S7 1970 MRR Alc.

GREAT BRITAIN--HISTORY--FICTION--
BIBLIOGRAPHY.
Buckley, John Anthony. A guide to
British historical fiction, London,
G. G. Harrap & company, 1912. vi, 7-
182 p.   13-2128
Z5917.H6 B85 MRR Alc.

GREAT BRITAIN--HISTORY--SOURCES.
English historical documents. [New
York, Oxford University Press, 195
v.   942 53-1506
DA26 .E55 MRR Alc.

Gross, Charles, The sources and
literature of English history from
the earliest times to about 1485, 2d
ed., rev. and enl. London, New York
[etc.] Longmans, Green, and co.,
1915. xxiii, 820 p.   15-16893
Z2016 .G87 1915 MRR Alc.

Hall, Hubert, comp. A formula book
of English official historical
documents. Cambridge, University
press, 1908-09. 2 v.   09-4070
CD105 .H26 MRR Alc.

Hall, Hubert, Studies in English
official historical documents,
Cambridge, University press, 1908.
xv, [1] p., 1 l., 404 p.   09-4071
CD65 .H4 MRR Alc.

Stephenson, Carl, ed. and tr.
Sources of English constitutional
history, Rev. ed. New York, Harper
& Row [1972] 2. [xxvi, 953, xii
p.]   340/.73/024 72-84325
JN111 .S67 1972 MRR Alc.

United States. Library of Congress.
Processing Dept. British manuscripts
project: New York, Greenwood Press
[1968] xvii, 179 p. 016.02517/1
68-55138
Z6620.G7 U5 1968 MRR Alc.

United States. Library of Congress.
Processing Dept. British manuscripts
project: Washington, Library of
Congress, 1955. xvii, 179 p.
016.025179 55-60041
Z663.7 .B7 MRR Alc.

GREAT BRITAIN--HISTORY--SOURCES--
BIBLIOGRAPHY.
Great Britain. Historical Manuscripts
Commission. Guide to the reports of
the Royal Commission on Historical
Manuscripts, 1911-1957. London,
H.M.S.O., 1966- v.   [£10/10/-
(pt. 2)]   942.082/08 67-31924
DA25 .M252 MRR Alc.

Great Britain. Historical Manuscripts
Commission. A guide to the reports
on collections of manuscripts of
private families, corporations and
institutions in Great Britain and
Ireland London, H.M. Stationery
Off., 1914-38. 2 pts. in 3. 15-
7434
DA25 .M25 MRR Alc.

King (P. S.) & son, ltd., London.
Catalogue of parliamentary papers,
1801-1900, London, P. S. King & son
[1904] vii, [1], 317 p.   04-14268
Z2009 .K55 MRR Alc.

Mullins, Edward Lindsay Carson.
Texts and calendars: London, Royal
Historical Society, 1958. xi, 674 p.
016.942 a 59-1596
Z2016 .M8 MRR Alc.

GREAT BRITAIN--HISTORY--SOURCES--
INDEXES.
Irish University Press. Checklist of
British parliamentary papers in the
Irish University Press 1000-volume
series, 1801-1899. Shannon, Ireland
[1972] xii, 218 p.   015.42 73-
150718
Z2019 .I73 MRR Ref Desk.

Irish University Press series of
British parliamentary papers.
Shannon, Irish University Press
[1968] 8 v.   016.32842/01 77-
456705
Z2019 .I74 MRR Alc.

GREAT BRITAIN--HISTORY, LOCAL--
BIBLIOGRAPHY.
Anderson, John Parker, The book of
British topography. London, W.
Satchell & co., 1881. xvi, 472 p.
03-32393
Z2023 .A54 MRR Alc.

Dillon's University Bookshop, London.
British local history: London,
1964. 80 p.   67-52451
Z2023 .D5 MRR Alc.

Humphreys, Arthur Lee, A handbook to
county bibliography, London,
[Printed by Strangeways and sons]
1917. x, 501 p., 1 l.   17-14548
L2023.A1 H9 MRR Alc.

GREAT BRITAIN--HISTORY, LOCAL-- (Cont.)
Martin, Geoffrey Haward. A
bibliography of British and Irish
municipal history Leicester,
Leicester University Press, 1972- v.
[£12.50 (v. 1)]   016.30136/0942
73-156398
Z2023 .M26 MRR Alc.

GREAT BRITAIN--HISTORY, MILITARY.
Barnett, Correlli. Britain and her
army, 1509-1970; New York, W.
Morrow, 1970. xx, 529 p. [15.00]
355/.00942 74-116805
DA65 .B283 1970 MRR Alc.

Gordon, Lawrence L. British battles
and medals. 4th ed., rev. London,
Spink, 1971. xiv, 440 p. 355.1/34
72-180227
UB435.G8 G6 1971 MRR Alc.

Young, Peter. The British army,
London, Kimber, 1967. 286 p. [70/-]
355/.00942 67-109907
UA649 .Y6 MRR Alc.

GREAT BRITAIN--HISTORY, MILITARY--
BIBLIOGRAPHY.
Higham, Robin D. S. A guide to the
sources of British military history.
Berkeley, University of California
Press, 1971. xxi, 630 p.
016.355/00942 74-104108
Z2021.M5 H54 MRR Alc.

White, Arthur Sharpin. A
bibliography of regimental histories
of the British Army, [London]
Society for Army Historical Research,
1965. viii, 265 p. 66-54213
Z2021.M5 W5 MRR Alc.

GREAT BRITAIN--IMPRINTS.
Alston, R. C. A bibliography of the
English language from the invention
of printing to the year 1800; Leeds
[Eng.] Printed for the author by E.
J. Arnold, 1965- v. 66-38399
Z2015.A1 A4 MRR Alc.

Ames, Joseph, Typographical
antiquities; London, W. Miller, 1810-
19. 4 v. 02-2021
Z151 .A512 MRR Alc.

Annals of English literature, 1475-
1950; 2d ed. Oxford, Clarendon
Press, 1961. v, 380 p. 016.82 62-
16029
Z2011 .A5 1961 MRR Alc.

Beasley, Jerry C. A check list of
prose fiction published in England,
1740-1749. Charlottesville,
Published for the Bibliographical
Society of the University of Virginia
[by] the University Press of Virginia
[1972] xiv, 213 p. [$7.50]
016.823/5/08 72-75044
Z2014.F4 E37 MRR Alc.

Black, R. D. Collison. A catalogue
of pamphlets on economic subjects
published between 1750 and 1900 and
now housed in Irish libraries, New
York, A. M. Kelley, 1969. ix, 632 p.
016.33 79-81989
Z7164.E2 B6 MRR Alc.

British books in print. 1874-
London, Whitaker; New York, Bowker
[etc.] 02-7496
Z2001 .R33 MRR Ref Desk Partial
set

British Museum. Dept. of Printed
Books. General catalogue of printed
books. Photolithographic edition to
1955. London, Trustees of the
British Museum 1959-66 [v. 1, 1965]
263 p. 018/.1 66-2261
Z921 .B87 MRR Alc (Dk 33).

Cambridge. University. Library.
Early English printed books in the
University library, Cambridge (1475
to 1640). Cambridge, The University
press, 1900-07. 4 v. 01-15519
Z2002 .C17 MRR Alc.

A Catalog of books represented by
Library of Congress printed cards
issued to July 31, 1942. Ann Arbor,
Mich., Edwards Bros., 1942-46. 167
v. 018/.1 43-3338
Z881.A1 C3 MRR Alc. (DK 33)

Church, Elihu Dwight, A catalogue of
books relating to the discovery and
early history of North and South
America, New York, P. Smith, 1951.
5 v. (vi, 2635 p.) 016.9731 51-
4055
Z1203 .C55 1951 MRR Ref Desk.

Cumulative book index. 1898/99- New
York [etc.] H. W. Wilson Co. 05-
33604
Z1219 .M78 MRR Circ Partial set

Edmond, John Philip, comp. Catalogue
of English broadsides, 1505-1897,
New York, B. Franklin [1968] xl, 526
p. 016.6552 71-6830
Z2027.P3 E2 1968 MRR Alc.

The English catalogue of books
London, Published for the Publishers'
Circular by S. Low, Marston, 1914.
655 p. 52-45201
Z2001 .E517 MRR Alc.

The English catalogue of books
[annual] London, Publishers'
Circular Ltd. [etc.] 06-44930
Began publication in 1864.
Z2001 .E53 MRR Alc Partial set

Faxon, Frederick Winthrop, Literary
annuals and gift books : [1st ed.]
reprinted / Pinner (Ravelston,
Southview Rd, Pinner, Middx) :
Private Libraries Association, 1973.
352 p. in various pagings ; [£6.00]
015/.42 74-186776
Z6520.G4 F3 1973 MRR Alc.

Gray, George John, A general index
to Hazlitt's Handbook and his
Bibliographical collections (1867-
1889) New York, B. Franklin, 1961.
866 p. 016.82 78-7293
Z2012 .G8 1961 MRR Alc.

Great Britain. Stationery Office.
Government publications. Jan. 1936-
[London] 015.42 36-13303
Z2009 .G822 MRR Alc Full set

Halliwell-Phillips, James Orchard, A
dictionary of old English plays,
existing either in print or in
manuscript, from the earliest times
to the close of the seventeenth
century; Naarden, [Turfpoortstraat
11] Anton W. van Bekhoven, 1968.
viii, 296 p. [65.00] 74-375761
Z2014.D7 H12 1968 MRR Alc.

Harvard University. Library. English
literature. Cambridge; Distributed
by the Harvard University Press,
1971. 4 v. 016.82 74-128717
Z2011 .H36 MRR Alc.

Hazlitt, William Carew, Collections
and notes, 1867-1876. New York, B.
Franklin, 1961. xi, 498 p. 016.82
79-7446
Z2012 .H31 1961 MRR Alc.

Hazlitt, William Carew, Handbook to
the popular, poetical, and dramatic
literature of Great Britain, New
York, B. Franklin, 1961. xii, 701 p.
016.82 75-7445
Z2012 .H3 1961 MRR Alc.

Lancaster, Joan Cadogan, comp.
Bibliography of historical works
issued in the United Kingdom, 1946-
1956, (London) University of London,
Institute of Historical Research,
1957. xxii, 388 p. 016.9 a 58-
2313
Z2016 .L3 MRR Alc.

Library of Congress and National
union catalog author lists, 1942-
1962; Detroit, Gale Research Co.,
1969-71. 152 v. 018/.1/0973 73-
82135
Z881.A1 L63 MRR Alc (Dk 33)

London. Guildhall Library. A list of
books printed in the British Isles
and of English books printed abroad
before 1701 in Guildhall Library.
London, Corporation of London, 1966-
67. 2 v. [40/- (v. 1)] 015/.42
68-77514
Z2002 .L62 MRR Alc.

London. Stationers' Company. A
transcript of the registers of the
Company of Stationers of London, 1554-
1640 A.D. [New York P. Smith, 1950]
5 v. 655.442 49-50201
Z2002 .L64 MRR Alc.

London. Stationer's Company. A
transcript of the registers of the
worshipful Company of Stationers,
from 1640-1708 A.D. [New York, P.
Smith, 1950] 3 v. 655.442 50-
37726
Z2002 .L653 MRR Alc.

The London catalogue of books,
London, Printed for W. Bent, 1811.
239 p. 06-10976
Z2001 .E5 1811 MRR Alc.

The London catalogue of books,
London, W. Bent, 1822. 2 p. l., 239,
[1] p. 02-7516
Z2001 .E5 1822 MRR Alc.

The London catalogue of books
published in Great Britain. London,
T. Hodgson, 1855. vi, 583 p. 02-
7489
Z2001 .E5 1855 MRR Alc.

Lowndes, William Thomas, The
bibliographer's manual of English
literature New ed., rev., cor. and
enl., London, H. G. Bohn, 1857-61;
Bell & Daldy, 1864-65. 10 v.
015.42 35-36009
Z2001 .L92 1857-65 MRR Alc.

The Monthly catalogues from 'The
London Magazine,' 1732-66: London,
Gregg P.; Archive P., 1966 [i.e.
1967]. [740] [£12/10/-] 015.42
67-86316
Z2002 .M64 MRR Alc.

Mullins, Edward Lindsay Carson. A
guide to the historical and
archaeological publications of
societies in England and Wales, 1901-
1933; London, Athlone P., 1968.
xiii, 850 p. [10/10/-] 016.9142
79-367032
Z5055.G6 M8 MRR Alc.

The National union catalog, Totowa,
N.J., Rowman and Littlefield [1970-
v. 018/.1/0973 76-141020
Z881.A1U3742 MRR Alc (Dk 33)

The National union catalog, pre-1956
imprints; London, Mansell, 1968- v.
021.6/4 67-30001
Z663.7.L5115 MRR Alc (Dk 33)

New York. Union theological seminary.
Library. Catalogue of the McAlpin
collection of British history and
theology; New York, 1927-30. 5 v.
29-29688
Z7757.E5 N5 MRR Alc.

New York (City). Public Library. Berg
Collection. Dictionary catalog of
the Henry W. and Albert A. Berg
Collection of English and American
literature. Boston, G. K. Hall,
1969. 5 v. 016.82 75-21408
Z2011 .N55 MRR Alc (Dk 33)

Oxford. University. Christ Church.
Library. The Christ Church
supplement to Wing's Short-title
catalogue, 1641-1700, Oxford,
Printed for Christ Church at the
Holywell Press, 1956. 47 p. 015.42
57-624
Z2002.W5 O9 MRR Alc.

Paperbacks in print. London, J.
Whitaker. 66-8204
Began with May 1960 issue.
Z1033.P3 P28 MRR Alc Latest
edition

Pollard, Alfred William, A short-
title catalogue of books printed in
England, Scotland, & Ireland and of
English books printed abroad, 1475-
1640, London, Bibliographical
Society, 1946. xviii, 609 p.
015.42 47-20884
Z2002 .P77 1946 MRR Alc.

Ransom, Will, Selective check list
of press books; New York, P. C.
Duschnes, 1945- pts. 015 46-
583
Z1028 .R3 MRR Alc.

Ridler, William. British modern
press books: London, Covent Garden
Press, 1971. iii-xvi, 310 p.
[£5.25] 015/.42 72-179701
Z231.5.P7 R54 MRR Alc.

Sloane, William. Children's books in
England & America in the seventeenth
century: New York, King's Crown
Press, Columbia University, 1955.
ix, 251 p. 028.5 54-9938
Z1037 .S62 MRR Alc.

Summers, Montague, A bibliography of
the restoration drama. New York,
Russell & Russell [1970] 143 p.
016.822/4 70-81479
Z2014.D7 S9 1970 MRR Alc.

Summers, Montague, A Gothic
bibliography. London, Fortune P.
[1969] iii-xx, 621 p. 22 plates.
[6/15/-] 016.823/6 78-442345
Z2014.F4 S9 1969 MRR Alc.

The Term catalogues, 1668-1709 A.D.;
London, 1903-06. 3 v. 05-8720
Z2002 .A31 MRR Alc.

United States. Library of Congress.
English language books by title;
Detroit, Gale Research Co., 1971. 20
v. 018/.1 75-165487
Z881.A1 C34 MRR Alc (Dk 33)

United States. Library of Congress.
Jefferson Collection. Catalogue of
the library of Thomas Jefferson.
Washington, Library of Congress, 1952-
59. 5 v. 017.1 52-60000
Z663.4 .C4 MRR Alc.

United States. National Library of
Medicine. Index-catalogue of the
Library of the Surgeon-General's
Office, United States Army: authors
and subjects. Washington, Govt.
Print. Off., 1880-1961. 61 v.
016.61 01-2344
Z6676 .U6 MRR Alc (DK 33).

Watt, Robert, Bibliotheca
Britannica; New York, B. Franklin
[1965] 4 v. 011 77-6557
Z2001 .W34 1965 MRR Alc.

GREAT BRITAIN--IMPRINTS. (Cont.)
Whitaker's cumulative book list.
1924- London, J. Whitaker. 25-4576

Z2005 .W57 MRR Alc Partial set

Wing, Donald Goddard, A gallery of
ghosts; [New York] Index Committee,
Modern Language Association of
America, 1967. vi, 225 p. 015.42
67-9327
Z2002 .W48 MRR Alc.

Wing, Donald Goddard, Short-title
catalogue of books printed in
England, Scotland, Ireland, Wales,
and British America, and of English
books printed in other countries,
1641-1700. 2d ed.; rev. and enl.
New York, Index Committee of the
Modern Language Association of
America, 1972- v. 015.42 70-
185211
Z2002 .W52 MRR Alc.

Wing, Donald Goddard, Short-title
catalogue of books printed in
England, Scotland, Ireland, Wales,
and British America, and of English
books printed in other countries,
1641-1700. New York, Index Society,
1945-51. 3 v. 015.42 45-8773
Z2002 .W5 MRR Alc.

GREAT BRITAIN--INDEXES.
Gomme, George Laurence, Sir, Index
of archæological papers, 1665-1890.
London, A. Constable & company, ltd.,
1907. xi, 910 p. 08-8803
Z2027.A8 I6 MRR Alc.

GREAT BRITAIN--INDUSTRIES.
Great Britain. Dept. of Employment
and Productivity. British labour
statistics; London, H.M. Stationery
Off., 1871. 436 p. [£7.00]
331/.0942 75-860907
HD8388 .A5 MRR Alc.

Stamp, Laurence Dudley, Sir, The
British Isles: a geographic and
economic survey 6th ed. London,
Longman, 1971. ix, 881 p. [£7.00]
914.2 72-170778
HC253 .S67 1971b MRR Alc.

GREAT BRITAIN--INDUSTRIES--DIRECTORIES.
British industrial and professional
register. London, Lloyd's Commercial
Publications. 338.7/4/02542 72-
200729
T12.5.G7 B73 MRR Alc Latest
edition

British industries trade register
London, Industries Trade
Publications. 338.4/025/42 75-
206136
Began in 1964.
HC252 .B7 MRR Alc Latest edition

Dun & Bradstreet's guide to key
British enterprises. 1961- London.
62-41097
HC252 .D8 MRR Alc Latest edition

Kompass; 1st- ed.; 1962- Croydon,
Eng., Kompass Publishers [etc.] 63-
59135
T12.5.G7 K6 MRR Alc Latest edition

The Manufacturers manual. 1954-
Worcester [Eng.] Littlebury. 54-
39506
TS1 .N34 MRR Alc Latest edition

Sell's directory of products &
services. 87th- 1972- Epsom,
Eng., Sell's Publications Ltd.
338/.0025/42 73-640793
HC252 .S44 MRR Alc Latest edition

South-eastern counties of England
trades' directory, including London,
London surburbs, Brighton and
Reading. Edinburgh, Trades'
Directories. 55-26292
HF5159.16 S6 MRR Alc Latest
Edition

South-western counties of England
trades' directory. Manchester,
Trades' Directories. 55-57170
HF5158 .S6 MRR Alc Latest edition

GREAT BRITAIN--INDUSTRIES--HISTORY.
Page, William, ed. Commerce and
industry; London, Constable and
company, ltd., 1919. 2 v. 19-18954

HC255 .P3 MRR Alc.

GREAT BRITAIN--INDUSTRIES--PERIODICALS.
Guide to British employers. London,
Cornmarket Press. 331.702/0942 72-
27261
HF5382.5.G7 G8 MRR Alc Latest
edition

GREAT BRITAIN--INTELLECTUAL LIFE.
Halliday, Frank Ernest, An
illustrated cultural history of
England London, Thames & Hudson
[1967] 320 p. [42/-] 709/.42 67-
82640
DA110 .H315 MRR Alc.

GREAT BRITAIN--KINGS AND RULERS.
Powicke, Frederick Maurice, Sir, ed.
Handbook of British chronology, 2d
ed. London, Offices of the Royal
Historical Society, 1961. xxxviii,
565 p. 942.002 62-3079
DA34 .P6 1961 MRR Alc.

GREAT BRITAIN--LEARNED INSTITUTIONS AND
SOCIETIES.
British Travel and Holidays
Association. Organisations in
Britain holding regular conferences.
[London, 1961] 92 p. 62-6159
AS118 .B7 MRR Alc.

Scientific and learned societies of
Great Britain; 1st- ed.; 1884-
London, Allen & Unwin [etc.] 062 01-
15597
AS115 .S313 MRR Ref Desk Latest
edition

GREAT BRITAIN--LEARNED INSTITUTIONS AND
SOCIETIES--BIBLIOGRAPHY.
The English catalogue of books
[annual] London, Publishers'
Circular Ltd. [etc.] 06-44930
Began publication in 1864.
Z2001 .E53 MRR Alc Partial set

Lowndes, William Thomas, The
bibliographer's manual of English
literature New ed.; rev., cor. and
enl., London, H. G. Bohn, 1857-61;
Bell & Daldy, 1864-65. 10 v.
015.42 35-36009
Z2001 .L92 1857-65 MRR Alc.

Mullins, Edward Lindsay Carson.
Texts and calendars; London, Royal
Historical Society, 1958. xi, 674 p.
016.942 a 59-1596
Z2016 .M8 MRR Alc.

GREAT BRITAIN--MANUFACTURES--
DIRECTORIES.
British exports. 1st- 1969-
Croydon [Eng.] Kompass Publishers.
382/.6/02542 75-219438
HF3503 .B79 MRR Alc Latest edition

British industrial and professional
register. London, Lloyd's Commercial
Publications. 338.7/4/02542 72-
200729
T12.5.G7 B73 MRR Alc Latest
edition

Castle's town & county trades
directory. London, United Publicity
Services. 380.1/025/42 70-615352
HF5155 .C37 MRR Alc Latest edition

International town & country business
guide. London, County Advertising
and Pub. Co. 380.1/025/42 70-616534

HF3503 .I56 MRR Alc Latest edition

Kemp's directory. London, Kemp's
Directory, Ltd. [etc.] 55-43556
HF3503 .K4 MRR Alc Latest edition

Kompass; 1st- ed.; 1962- Croydon,
Eng., Kompass Publishers [etc.] 63-
59135
T12.5.G7 K6 MRR Alc Latest edition

Macdonald's English directory and
gazetteer. Edinburgh [etc.] W.
Macdonald. ca 08-3137
HF5158 .M2 MRR Alc Latest edition

Mechanical engineering directory and
buyers guide. 1965/66- London,
British Mechanical Engineering
Federation. 621.8/025/42 74-201520

TJ1170 .M39 Sci RR Latest edition
/ MRR Alc Latest edition

Sell's British exporters' register &
national directory. London, Business
Dictionaries. 48-25925
Began publication in 1916.
HF3503 .S4 MRR Alc Latest edition

Skinner's British textile register.
1st- ed.; 1973- Croydon, Eng.,
Thomas Skinner Directories. [£10.50]
338.4/7/677002542 74-644855
TS1312 .S55 MRR Alc Latest edition

Stubbs' directory [of] manufacturers,
merchant shippers, and professional;
London. 53-30509
HF3503 .S7 MRR Alc Latest edition

GREAT BRITAIN--MANUFACTURES--SOCIETIES,
ETC.
The Manufacturers manual. 1954-
Worcester [Eng.] Littlebury. 54-
39506
TS1 .N34 MRR Alc Latest edition

GREAT BRITAIN--MANUFACTURES--STATISTICS.
Great Britain. Dept. of Employment
and Productivity. British labour
statistics; London, H.M. Stationery
Off., 1971. 436 p. [£7.00]
331/.0942 75-860907
HD8388 .A5 MRR Alc.

GREAT BRITAIN--MAPS.
Briscoe, John D'Auby. A mapbook of
English literature, New York, H.
Holt and company [1936] 47 p.
820.9 36-18473
PR109 .B7 MRR Alc.

GREAT BRITAIN--NOBILITY.
Burke's genealogical and heraldic
history of the peerage, baronetage
and knightage, London, Burke's
Peerage Ltd. [etc.] 35-32046
Began publication in 1826.
CS420 .B85 MRR Biog Latest edition

Kelly's handbook to the titled,
landed & official classes. 1875-
London, Kelly's Directories, Ltd.
[etc.] 08-5253
CS419 .K5 MRR Biog Latest edition*

Powicke, Frederick Maurice, Sir, ed.
Handbook of British chronology, 2d
ed. London, Offices of the Royal
Historical Society, 1961. xxxviii,
565 p. 942.002 62-3079
DA34 .P6 1961 MRR Alc.

GREAT BRITAIN--OCCUPATIONS--PERIODICALS.
Guide to British employers. London,
Cornmarket Press. 331.702/0942 72-
27261
HF5382.5.G7 G8 MRR Alc Latest
edition

GREAT BRITAIN--OFFICIALS AND EMPLOYEES.
Butler, David E. British political
facts, 1900-1968. 3rd ed. London,
Macmillan; New York, St Martin's P.,
1969. xix, 314 p. [70/-] 320.9/42
74-82434
JN231 .B8 1969 MRR Alc.

The Civil service year book. 1974-
London, H.M. Stationery Off. [£1.60]
354/.42 74-643279
JN106 .B8 MRR Alc Latest edition

GREAT BRITAIN--OFFICIALS AND EMPLOYEES--
DIRECTORIES.
Haydn, Joseph Timothy, The book of
dignities, containing lists of the
official personages of the British
empire ... from the earliest periods
to the present time; 3d ed. London,
W. H. Allen & co., limited, 1894. 2
p. 1., [iii]-xxviii, 1170 p. 09-
6387
DA34 .H32 MRR Alc.

GREAT BRITAIN--PEERAGE.
Burke's genealogical and heraldic
history of the peerage, baronetage
and knightage, London, Burke's
Peerage Ltd. [etc.] 35-32046
Began publication in 1826.
CS420 .B85 MRR Biog Latest edition

Debrett's peerage, baronetage,
knightage, and companionage ...
Kingston upon Thames, Surrey, Kelly's
Directories [etc.] 929.72 42-17925

CS420 .D32 MRR Biog Latest edition

Kelly's handbook to the titled,
landed & official classes. 1875-
London, Kelly's Directories, Ltd.
[etc.] 08-5253
CS419 .K5 MRR Biog Latest edition*

Titles and forms of address: 14th
ed. London, Black, 1971. xi, 188 p.
[£1.25] 395/.4 72-170772
CR3891 .T58 1971 MRR Alc.

GREAT BRITAIN--POLITICS AND GOVERNMENT.
Beer, Samuel Hutchison, ed. Patterns
of government; 3d ed. New York,
Random House [1973] xv, 778 p.
320.3 72-681
JN12 .B4 1973 MRR Alc.

Carter, Gwendolen Margaret, Major
foreign powers 6th ed. New York,
Harcourt Brace Jovanovich [1972]
xvi, 743 p. 320.3 78-179411
JF51 .C3 1972 MRR Alc.

Jennings, William Ivor, Sir,
Parliament. 2d ed. Cambridge [Eng.]
University Press, 1957. xi, 573 p.
328.42 57-14459
JN550 1957 .J4 MRR Alc.

Page, William, ed. Commerce and
industry; London, Constable and
company, ltd., 1919. 2 v. 19-18954

HC255 .P3 MRR Alc.

Pike, Edgar Royston, Britain's Prime
Ministers from Walpole to Wilson
Feltham, Odhams, 1968. 487 p. [30/-]
942.07/0922 B 79-435231
DA28.4 .P48 MRR Alc.

GREAT BRITAIN--POLITICS AND GOVERNMENT--
1714-1760.
Sedgwick, Romney, The House of
Commons, 1715-1754; New York,
Published for the History of
Parliament Trust, by Oxford
University Press, 1970. 2 v.
[$70.00] 328.42/07/32 75-21905
JN675 1715 .S4 MRR Alc.

GREAT BRITAIN--POLITICS AND (Cont.)
Williams, Basil. The Whig supremacy,
1714-1760. 2d ed. rev. Oxford,
Clarendon Press. 1962. xix, 504 p.
842.071   62-2655
DA498 .W5 1962 MRR Alc.

GREAT BRITAIN--POLITICS AND GOVERNMENT--
19TH CENTURY.
Woodward, Ernest Llewellyn, Sir, The
age of reform, 1815-1870. 2d ed.
Oxford, Clarendon Press. 1962. xix,
681 p.   842.07 62-4675
DA530 .W6 1962 MRR Alc.

GREAT BRITAIN--POLITICS AND GOVERNMENT--
20TH CENTURY.
Cole, George Douglas Howard, A
history of the Labour Party from
1914. New York, A. M. Kelley [1969]
x, 517 p.   329.9/42 73-90407
JN1129.L32 C6 1969b MRR Alc.

GREAT BRITAIN--POLITICS AND GOVERNMENT--
20TH CENTURY--COLLECTED WORKS.
Churchill, Winston Leonard Spencer,
Sir, Winston S. Churchill: his
complete speeches, 1897-1963. New
York, Chelsea House Publishers, 1974.
8 v. (xvi, 8817 p.) [$185.00]
842.082/092/4 74-505
DA566.9.C5 A38 MRR Alc.

GREAT BRITAIN--POLITICS AND GOVERNMENT--
20TH CENTURY--HANDBOOKS, MANUALS, ETC.
Butler, David E. British political
facts, 1900-1968. 3rd ed. London,
Macmillan; New York, St Martin's P.,
1969. xix, 314 p. [70/-] 320.9/42
74-82434
JN231 .B8 1969 MRR Alc.

GREAT BRITAIN--POLITICS AND GOVERNMENT--
20TH CENTURY--SOURCES.
Craig, Fred W. S., comp. British
general election manifestos 1918-
1966. Chichester [Eng.] Political
Reference Publications. 1970. xii,
303 p. [75/- ($12.00 U.S.)]
329.8/42 70-77467
JN1121 .C73 MRR Alc.

GREAT BRITAIN--POLITICS AND GOVERNMENT--
1901-1936.
Ford, Percy, A breviate of
parliamentary papers, 1900-1916
Oxford, Blackwell. 1957. xlix, 470
p.   342.42 58-1414
JN549 .F59 MRR Alc.

GREAT BRITAIN--POLITICS AND GOVERNMENT--
1910-1936.
Ford, Percy, A breviate of
parliamentary papers, 1917-1939
Shannon, Ire., Irish University
Press, 1969. xlviii, 571 p.
320.9/42/082 76-27392
JN549 .F6 1969 MRR Alc.

GREAT BRITAIN--POLITICS AND GOVERNMENT--
1936-1945.
Ford, Percy, A breviate of
parliamentary papers, 1917-1939
Shannon, Ire., Irish University
Press, 1969. xlviii, 571 p.
320.9/42/082 76-27392
JN549 .F6 1969 MRR Alc.

Ford, Percy, A breviate of
parliamentary papers, 1940-1954:
Oxford, Blackwell, 1961. l, 515 p.
63-205
JN549 .F62 MRR Alc.

GREAT BRITAIN--POLITICS AND GOVERNMENT--
1945-1864.
Ford, Percy, A breviate of
parliamentary papers, 1940-1954:
Oxford, Blackwell, 1961. l, 515 p.
63-205
JN549 .F62 MRR Alc.

GREAT BRITAIN--POLITICS AND GOVERNMENT--
1945-
Stacey, Frank A. The government of
modern Britain, Oxford, Clarendon
P., 1968. xii, 419 p. [45/-]
320/.0942 68-103797
JN234 1868 .S7 MRR Alc.

GREAT BRITAIN--POLITICS AND GOVERNMENT--
1964-
Sampson, Anthony. The new anatomy of
Britain. New York, Stein and Day
[1972, c1971] xviii, 773 p.
309.1/42/085 78-186150
DA592 .S23 1972 MRR Alc.

GREAT BRITAIN--POLITICS AND GOVERNMENT--
ANECDOTES, FACETIAE, SATIRE, ETC.
Harris, Leon A. The fine art of
political wit; [1st ed.] New York,
Dutton, 1964. 288 p. 827.093 64-
19532
PN6231.P6 H36 MRR Alc.

GREAT BRITAIN--POLITICS AND GOVERNMENT--
BIBLIOGRAPHY.
Temperley, Harold William Vazeille,
ed. A century of diplomatic blue
books, 1814-1914; London, Cass,
1966. xviii, 600 p. [84/-]
016.32742 66-70453
Z2009 .T28 1966 MRR Alc.

Vogel, Robert. A breviate of British
diplomatic blue books, 1919-1939.
Montreal, McGill University Press,
1963. xxxv, 474 p. a 64-408
Z2009 .V6 MRR Alc.

GREAT BRITAIN--POLITICS AND GOVERNMENT--
DICTIONARIES.
Montgomery, Hugh. A dictionary of
political phrases and allusions with
a short bibliography, London, S.
Sonnenschein & co. ltd., 1906. 3 p.
l., 406 p. w 07-84
JN114 .M7 MRR Alc.

Spaull, Hebe, The new ABC of civics;
New and enl. ed. London, Barrie and
Rockliff [1963] 136 p. 64-32552
JA61 .S63 1963 MRR Alc.

Wilding, Norman W. An encyclopaedia
of Parliament 4th ed., completely
rev. New York, St. Martin's Press
[1971] ix, 931 p. [$20.00]
328.42/003 72-162373
JN555 .W5 1971 MRR Alc.

GREAT BRITAIN--POLITICS AND GOVERNMENT--
HANDBOOKS, MANUALS, ETC.
Plaskitt, Harold, Government of
Britain and the Commonwealth. 9th
ed. London, University Tutorial P.,
1968. vii, 323 p. [13/-11/6
(pbk.)] 320/.0942 68-135116
JN321 .P55 1968 MRR Alc.

GREAT BRITAIN--REGISTERS.
The Civil service year book. 1974-
London, H.M. Stationery Off. [£1.60]
354/.42 74-643279
JN106 .B8 MRR Alc Latest edition

The Diplomatic Service list. 1966-
London, H. M. Stationery Off.
354.42061 66-4595
JX1783 .A22 MRR Blog Latest
edition

Haydn, Joseph Timothy, The book of
dignities, containing lists of the
official personages of the British
empire ... from the earliest periods
to the present time; 3d ed. London,
W. H. Allen & co., limited, 1894. 2
p. l., [iii]-xxviii, 1170 p. 09-
6387
DA34 .H32 MRR Alc.

Powicke, Frederick Maurice, Sir, ed.
Handbook of British chronology, 2d
ed. London, Offices of the Royal
Historical Society, 1961. xxxviii,
565 p. 942.002 62-3079
DA34 .P6 1961 MRR Alc.

Wilding, Norman W. An encyclopaedia
of Parliament 4th ed., completely
rev. New York, St. Martin's Press
[1971] ix, 931 p. [$20.00]
328.42/003 72-162373
JN555 .W5 1971 MRR Alc.

GREAT BRITAIN--REGISTERS--BIBLIOGRAPHY.
British rate & data directories and
annuals. [London, Maclean-Hunter
Ltd.] [-/10/6] 016.05 73-645549
Z5771.4.G7 B75 MRR Alc Latest
edition

GREAT BRITAIN--RELATIONS (GENERAL) WITH
FOREIGN COUNTRIES--BIBLIOGRAPHY.
Parker, John. Books to build an
empire; Amsterdam, N. Israel, 1965.
viii, 290 p. 67-1417
Z2021.C7 P35 MRR Alc.

GREAT BRITAIN--SOCIAL CONDITIONS.
Gregg, Pauline. Modern Britain: 5th
ed., rev. New York, Pegasus [1967,
c1965] 615 p. 309.142 67-25498
HN385 .G7 1967 MRR Alc.

Traill, Henry Duff, ed. Social
England; [New illustrated ed.]
London, New York [etc.] Cassell and
company, limited, 1901-04. 6 v. 04-
17441
DA30 .T77 1901 MRR Alc.

Williams, Basil, The Whig supremacy,
1714-1760. 2d ed. rev. Oxford,
Clarendon Press, 1962. xix, 504 p.
942.071 62-2655
DA498 .W5 1962 MRR Alc.

Woodward, Ernest Llewellyn, Sir, The
age of reform, 1815-1870. 2d ed.
Oxford, Clarendon Press, 1962. xix,
681 p. 942.07 62-4675
DA530 .W6 1962 MRR Alc.

GREAT BRITAIN--SOCIAL CONDITIONS--
DICTIONARIES.
Cowie, Leonard W. A dictionary of
British social history, London,
Bell, 1973. vi, 326 p. [£5.00]
914.2/03/03 73-174596
DA110 .C75984 MRR Alc.

GREAT BRITAIN--SOCIAL LIFE AND CUSTOMS.
Brand, John, Observations on the
popular antiquities of Great Britain:
Arranged, rev., and greatly enl.,
London, G. Bell and sons, 1900-02. 3
v. 04-11295
DA110 .B83 MRR Alc.

Folklore, myths and legends of
Britain. [1st ed. London] Reader's
Digest Association [1973] 552 p.
390/.0942 73-177007
GR141 .F65 MRR Alc.

Hazlitt, William Carew, Faiths and
folklore of the British Isles; [New
York] B. Blom [1965] 2 v. (x, 672
p.) 914.2 64-18758
DA110 .H38 1965 MRR Alc.

The Connoisseur. The Connoisseur's
complete period guides to the houses,
decoration, furnishing and chattels
of the classic periods; London, The
Connoisseur, 1968. 1536 p. [84/-]
708/.42 70-369442
NK928 .C63 MRR Alc.

GREAT BRITAIN--SOCIAL LIFE AND CUSTOMS--
DICTIONARIES.
Cowie, Leonard W. A dictionary of
British social history, London,
Bell, 1973. vi, 326 p. [£5.00]
914.2/03/03 73-174596
DA110 .C75984 MRR Alc.

GREAT BRITAIN--STATISTICS.
Beveridge, William Henry Beveridge,
baron, Prices and wages in England
from the twelfth to the nineteenth
century London, New York [etc.]
Longmans, Green and co. [1939- v.
338.50942 39-16200
HB235.G7 B4 MRR Alc.

Britain; an official handbook.
London, H.M. Stationery Off. 914.2
72-626487
DA630 .A17 MRR Ref Desk Latest
edition / MRR Alc Latest edition

Butler, David E. British political
facts, 1900-1968. 3rd ed. London,
Macmillan; New York, St Martin's P.,
1969. xix, 314 p. [70/-] 320.9/42
74-82434
JN231 .B8 1969 MRR Alc.

Craig, Fred W. S. British
parliamentary election statistics,
1918-1970, 2nd ed. Chichester,
Political Reference Publications,
1971. xvi, 127 p. [£3.75 ($12.00
U.S.)] 329/.023/4208 79-131304
JN1037 .C72 1971 MRR Alc.

Great Britain Central Statistical
Office. Annual abstract of
statistics. no. [1]- 1840/53-
London. 314.2 07-25340
HA1122 .A33 MRR Alc Latest
edition

Great Britain. Central Statistical
Office. National accounts
statistics: London, H.M.S.O., 1968.
vii, 502 p. [45/-] 339.2/0942 79-
356609
HC260.I5 A45 MRR Alc.

Great Britain. Dept. of Employment
and Productivity. British labour
statistics: London, H.M. Stationery
Off., 1971. 436 p. [£7.00]
331/.0942 75-860907
HD8388 .A5 MRR Alc.

Kendall, Maurice George, ed. The
sources and nature of the statistics
of the United Kingdom; London,
Published for the Royal Statistical
Society by Oliver and Boyd, 1952-57.
2 v. 314.2 52-3168
HA37.G7 K4 MRR Alc.

London and Cambridge Economic
Service. The British economy: key
statistics, 1900-1966. London,
published for the London & Cambridge
Economic Service by Times Newspapers
[1967]. 28 p. [10/6] 314.2 68-
106297
HA1137 .L62 MRR Alc.

Mitchell, Brian R. Abstract of
British historical statistics.
Cambridge [Eng.] University Press,
1962. xlv, 513 p. 314.2 63-44
HA1135 .M5 MRR Alc.

Mitchell, Brian R. Second abstract
of British historical statistics,
Cambridge [Eng.] University Press,
1971. vii, 227 p. 314.2 72-128502

HA1135 .M52 MRR Alc.

Page, William, ed. Commerce and
industry; London, Constable and
company, ltd., 1919. 2 v. 19-18954

HC255 .P3 MRR Alc.

Schumpeter, Elizabeth (Boody)
English overseas trade statistics,
1697-1808. Oxford, Clarendon Press,
1960 [i.e. 1961] vii, 72 p.
382.0942 61-1155
HF3501 .S35 MRR Alc.

GREAT BRITAIN--STATISTICS--BIBLIOGRAPHY.
Harvey, Joan M. Sources of statistics [Hamden, Conn.] Archon Books [1969] 100 p. [4.00] 016.31 74-4258
    Z7554.G7 H3 1969b MRR Alc.

GREAT BRITAIN. ARMY--HISTORY.
Young, Peter. The British army,
London, Kimber, 1967. 286 p. [70/-] 355/.00942 67-109907
    UA649 .Y6 MRR Alc.

GREAT BRITAIN. ARMY--HISTORY--BIBLIOGRAPHY.
White, Arthur Sharpin. A bibliography of regimental histories of the British Army, [London] Society for Army Historical Research, 1965. viii, 265 p. 66-54213
    Z2021.M5 W5 MRR Alc.

GREAT BRITAIN. ARMY--MEDALS, BADGES, DECORATIONS, ETC.
Fraser, Edward, comp. Soldier and sailor words and phrases; London, G. Routledge and sons, ltd., 1925. vii, 372 p. 25-8719
    PE3727.S7 F7 MRR Alc.

GREAT BRITAIN. ARMY--UNIFORMS.
Carman, W. Y. British military uniforms from contemporary pictures: Henry VII to the present day [1st ed. reprinted]. Feltham, Spring Books, 1968. iii-xix, 168 p. [35/-] 355.1/4/0942 75-386810
    UC485.G7 C3 1968 MRR Alc.

GREAT BRITAIN. FOREIGN OFFICE. LIBRARY.
Great Britain. Foreign Office. Library. Catalogue of the Foreign Office Library, 1926-1968. Boston, G. K. Hall, 1972. 8 v. 019/.1 73-160726
    Z921 .G682 1972 MRR Alc (Dk 33)

GREAT BRITAIN. NAVY.
All about ships & shipping; 11th ed., rev. and brought up to date. London, Faber & Faber [1964] xii, 723 p. 387.5 64-56470
    VK155 .A6 1964 MRR Alc.

Parkes, Oscar. British battleships, 'Warrior' 1860 to 'Vanguard' 1950: New and revised ed. London, Seeley Service [1966] xv, 701 p. [£8/8/-] 623.82520942 67-72751
    VA454 .P28 1966 MRR Alc.

GREAT BRITAIN. NAVY--AVIATION.
Thetford, Owen Gordon, British naval aircraft since 1912. [2d ed.] London, Putnam [1962] 430 p. 623.746 63-25486
    VG95.G7 T48 1962 MRR Alc.

GREAT BRITAIN. NAVY--HISTORY.
Kemp, Peter Kemp, History of the Royal Navy, London, Barker, 1969. 304 p. [63/-] 359/.00942 74-444156
    VA454 .K42 1969b MRR Alc.

GREAT BRITAIN. NAVY--LISTS OF VESSELS.
Colledge, J. J. Ships of the Royal Navy; New York, A. M. Kelley, 1969- v. 358.32/0942 69-10859
    VA456 .C66 MRR Alc.

Manning, Thomas Davys, British warship names London, Putnam; [label: Cambridge, Md., Cornell Maritime Press, 1959] 498 p. 359.32 59-13450
    VA456 .M27 MRR Alc.

Weightman, Alfred Edwin. Heraldry in the Royal Navy; Aldershot [Eng.] Gale and Polden, 1957. xviii, 514 p. 623.825 60-36156
    VB335.G7 W4 MRR Alc.

GREAT BRITAIN. NAVY--MEDALS, BADGES, DECORATIONS.
Weightman, Alfred Edwin. Heraldry in the Royal Navy; Aldershot [Eng.] Gale and Polden, 1957. xviii, 514 p. 623.825 60-36156
    VB335.G7 W4 MRR Alc.

GREAT BRITAIN. NAVY. FLEET AIR ARM.
Thetford, Owen Gordon, British naval aircraft since 1912. [2d ed.] London, Putnam [1962] 430 p. 623.746 63-25486
    VG95.G7 T48 1962 MRR Alc.

GREAT BRITAIN. PARLIAMENT.
Bradshaw, Kenneth. Parliament & Congress Austin, University of Texas Press [1972] 426 p. [$10.00] 328.42 78-37857
    JN508 .B7 MRR Alc.

Jennings, William Ivor, Sir, Parliament. 2d ed. Cambridge [Eng.] University Press, 1957. xi, 573 p. 328.42 57-14459
    JN550 1957 .J4 MRR Alc.

Margach, James D. How Parliament works London, Tom Stacey Ltd., 1972. 143, [8] p.; [£1.90] 328.42 72-185828
    JN511 .M28 MRR Alc.

GREAT BRITAIN. PARLIAMENT--ARCHIVES.
Bond, Maurice Francis. Guide to the records of Parliament London, H. M. Stationery Off., 1971. x, 352 p. [£3.25] 016.32842 72-176284
    CD1063 .B63 MRR Alc.

GREAT BRITAIN. PARLIAMENT--BIBLIOGRAPHY.
Great Britain. Parliament. House of Commons. Library. A bibliography of parliamentary debates of Great Britain. London, H.M. Stationery Off., 1956. 62 p. 57-32205
    Z2009 .G7 MRR Alc.

GREAT BRITAIN. PARLIAMENT--DICTIONARIES.
Wilding, Norman W. An encyclopaedia of Parliament 4th ed., completely rev. New York, St. Martin's Press [1971] ix, 931 p. [$20.00] 328.42/003 72-162373
    JN555 .W5 1971 MRR Alc.

GREAT BRITAIN. PARLIAMENT--ELECTIONS.
Craig, Fred W. S. British parliamentary election results, 1950-1970. Chichester, Political Reference Publications, 1971. xviii, 780 p. [£9.50 ($28.00 U.S.)] 329/.023/42085 70-157739
    JN1037 .C7142 MRR Alc.

GREAT BRITAIN. PARLIAMENT--ELECTIONS--STATISTICS.
Craig, Fred W. S. British parliamentary election statistics, 1918-1970, 2nd ed. Chichester, Political Reference Publications, 1971. xvi, 127 p. [£3.75 ($12.00 U.S.)] 328/.023/4208 79-131304
    JN1037 .C72 1971 MRR Alc.

GREAT BRITAIN. PARLIAMENT--ELECTIONS, 1970.
Guide to the House of Commons. 1970- London, Times Newspapers Ltd. 328.42/0922 76-20856
    JN956 .G9 MRR Alc Latest edition

GREAT BRITAIN. PARLIAMENT--REGISTERS.
Dod's parliamentary companion. Epsom, Surrey, [etc.] Sell's publications Ltd. [etc.] 06-7438
    JN500 .D7 MRR Blog Latest edition

GREAT BRITAIN. PARLIAMENT--RULES AND PRACTICE--DICTIONARIES.
Abraham, Louis Arnold. A parliamentary dictionary, 2d ed. London, Butterworths, 1964. viii, 241 p. 65-1879
    JN594 .A7 1964 MRR Alc.

GREAT BRITAIN. PARLIAMENT. HOUSE OF COMMONS. JOURNALS.
Menhennet, David. The Journal of the House of Commons; London, H. M. Stationery Off., 1971. viii, 96 p. [£0.65] 328/.42/01 72-194495
    JN673 .M45 MRR Alc.

GREAT BRITAIN. PARLIAMENT. HOUSE OF COMMONS. SESSIONAL PAPERS--INDEXES.
Rodgers, Frank, Serial publications in the British Parliamentary papers, 1900-1968: Chicago, American Library Association, 1971. xix, 146 p. 015/.42 74-117628
    Z2009 .R63 MRR Alc.

GREAT BRITAIN. PARLIAMENT. HOUSE OF COMMONS--BIBLIOGRAPHY.
Great Britain. Parliament. House of Commons. Hansard's Catalogue and breviate of parliamentary papers, 1696-1834. Oxford, Blackwell, 1953. xv p., facsim.: viii, 220 p. 328.4204 53-12375
    J301 .K62 1953 MRR Alc.

GREAT BRITAIN. PARLIAMENT. HOUSE OF COMMONS--BIOGRAPHY.
Guide to the House of Commons. 1970- London, Times Newspapers Ltd. 328.42/0922 76-20856
    JN956 .G9 MRR Alc Latest edition

Namier, Lewis Bernstein, Sir, The House of Commons, 1754-1790 New York, Published for the History of Parliament Trust by Oxford University Press, 1964. 3 v. 328.42 64-3513

    JN672 .N2 MRR Alc.

GREAT BRITAIN. PARLIAMENT. HOUSE OF COMMONS--HISTORY.
Sedgwick, Romney, The House of Commons, 1715-1754; New York, Published for the History of Parliament Trust, by Oxford University Press, 1970. 2 v. [$70.00] 328.42/07/32 75-21905
    JN675 1715 .S4 MRR Alc.

GREAT BRITAIN. PUBLIC RECORD OFFICE.
Galbraith, Vivian Hunter, An introduction to the use of the public records. [London] Oxford University Press [1952] 112 p. 025.171 57-38128
    CD1043 .G3 1952 MRR Alc.

GREAT BRITAIN. ROYAL AIR FORCE--HISTORY.
Lewis, Peter M. H. Squadron histories: R.F.C., R.N.A.S. and R.A.F., since 1912 2nd ed. London, Putnam, 1968. 224 p. [50/-] 358.41/3/50942 68-133976
    UG635.G7 L47 1968 MRR Alc.

GREAT BRITAIN. ROYAL FLYING CORPS--HISTORY.
Lewis, Peter M. H. Squadron histories: R.F.C., R.N.A.S. and R.A.F., since 1912 2nd ed. London, Putnam, 1968. 224 p. [50/-] 358.41/3/50942 68-133976
    UG635.G7 L47 1968 MRR Alc.

GREAT BRITAIN. STATIONERY OFFICE.
Horrocks, Sidney. The State as publisher; London, Library Association, 1952. 32 p. 655.142 53-3314
    Z232.G8735 H6 MRR Ref Desk.

GREAT BRITAIN IN LITERATURE--BIBLIOGRAPHY.
Leclaire, Lucien, A general analytical bibliography of the regional novelists of the British Isles, 1800-1950. Clermont-Ferrand, Impr. G. de Bussac [1954] 399 p. 016.823 54-32919
    Z2014.F4 L4 1954 MRR Alc.

GREAT LAKES REGION--DESCRIPTION AND TRAVEL--GUIDE-BOOKS.
Mobil travel guide: Great Lakes area. 1961- New York, Simon and Schuster. 917.7 61-9604
    F551 .M64 MRR Alc Latest edition

GREAT PLAINS.
Peirce, Neal R. The Great Plains States of America: people, politics, and power in the nine Great Plains States [1st ed.] New York, Norton [1973] 402 p. 917.8 72-13928
    F595.2 .P44 MRR Alc.

GREAT PLAINS--DESCRIPTION AND TRAVEL--GUIDE-BOOKS.
Fodor, Eugene. Rockies and plains: 2d, rev. ed. Litchfield, Conn.: Fodor's Modern Guides; distributor: D. McKay Co., New York [1967] 432 p. 917.8/04/3 67-20083
    F721 .F6 1967 MRR Alc.

Mobil travel guide: Northwest and Great Plains States; good food, lodging and sightseeing. 1962/63- New York, Simon and Schuster. 917.8 62-12969
    F587 .M7 MRR Alc Latest edition

GREECE--ANTIQUITIES.
Baumeister, August, ed. Denkmäler des klassischen altertums zur erläuterung des lebens der Griechen und Römer in religion, kunst und sitte. München, Leipzig, R. Oldenbourg, 1885-1888. 3 v. 04-35149
    DE5 .B34 MRR Alc.

Daremberg, Charles Victor; Dictionnaire des antiquités grecques et romaines Graz, Akademische Druck- u. Verlagsanstalt, 1962-63. 6 v. in 10. 64-44287
    DE5 .D22 MRR Alc.

Pausanias. Pausanias Description of Greece, London, W. Heinemann; New York, G. P. Putnam's sons, 1918-35. 5 v. 888.9 19-6903
    PA3612 .P3 1918 MRR Alc.

Whibley, Leonard, ed. A companion to Greek studies. 4th ed., rev. New York, Hafner Pub. Co., 1963. xxxviii, 790 p. 913.38 63-10743
    DF77 .W5 1963 MRR Alc.

GREECE--BIBLIOGRAPHY.
Rounds, Dorothy. Articles on antiquity in Festschriften, an index; Cambridge, Harvard University Press, 1962. 560 p. 62-7193
    Z6202 .R6 MRR Alc.

GREECE--BIOGRAPHY.
Plutarchus. Plutarch's Lives, London, Heinemann; New York, Putnam, 1915-1928. 11 v. mrr01-69
    PA3612 .P7 1915d MRR Alc.

GREECE--BIOGRAPHY--DICTIONARIES.
The Praeger encyclopedia of ancient Greek civilization New York, Praeger [1967] 491 p. 913.3/8/0303 67-25162
    DF16 .D513 1967c MRR Alc.

Radice, Betty. Who's who in the ancient world; Revised [ed.] Harmondsworth, Penguin, 1973. 336, [32] p. [£0.60] 920/.038 74-161490
    DE7 .R33 1973 MRR Alc.

GREECE--CIVILIZATION
see Civilization, Greek

GREECE--DESCRIPTION, GEOGRAPHY.
Pausanias. Pausanias Description of
Greece, London, W. Heinemann; New
York, G. P. Putnam's sons, 1918-35.
5 v.   888.9 19-6903
    PA3612 .P3 1918 MRR Alc.

Whibley, Leonard, ed. A companion to
Greek studies. 4th ed., rev. New
York, Hafner Pub. Co., 1963.
xxxviii, 790 p.   913.38 63-10743
    DF77 .W5 1963 MRR Alc.

GREECE--ECONOMIC CONDITIONS.
Rostovtsev, Mikhail Ivanovich, The
social & economic history of the
Hellenistic world, Oxford, The
Clarendon press, 1941. 3 v.   938.08
    a 41-4669
    DF235.3 .R6 MRR Alc.

GREECE--HISTORY.
Botsford, George Willis, Hellenic
history, New York, The Macmillan
company, 1922. 8 p. l., 520 p.   22-
6185
    DF215 .B74 MRR Alc.

Hammond, Nicholas Geoffrey
Lempriere. A history of Greece to
322 B.C., 2nd ed. Oxford, Clarendon
P., 1967. xxiv, 691 p.   838 67-
91674
    DF214 .H28 1967 MRR Alc.

Herodotus. Herodotus, London, W.
Heinemann; New York, G. P. Putnam's
sons, 1921-24. 4 v.   21-6980
    PA3612 .H5 1921 MRR Alc.

Polybius. The histories, London, W.
Heinemann; New York, G. P. Putnam's
sons, 1922-27. 6 v.   23-2839
    PA3612 .P8 1922 MRR Alc.

Rostovtsev, Mikhail Ivanovich, The
social & economic history of the
Hellenistic world, Oxford, The
Clarendon press, 1941. 3 v.   938.08
    a 41-4669
    DF235.3 .R6 MRR Alc.

Xenophon. Xenophon, London, W.
Heinemann; New York, G. P. Putnam,
1930-38. 4 v.   mrr01-72
    PA3612 .X3 1930d MRR Alc.

GREECE--HISTORY--PELOPONNESIAN WAR, 431-
404 B.C.
Thucydides. Thucydides, London, W.
Heinemann; Cambridge, Harvard
University Press, 1930-35. 4 v.
mrr01-68
    PA3612.T5 1930d MRR Alc.

GREECE--HISTORY--DICTIONARIES.
The Oxford classical dictionary, 2d
ed. Oxford [Eng.] Clarendon Press,
1970. xxii, 1176 p.   913.38003 73-
18819
    DE5 .09 1970 MRR Ref Desk.

GREECE--SOCIAL CONDITIONS.
Rostovtsev, Mikhail Ivanovich, The
social & economic history of the
Hellenistic world, Oxford, The
Clarendon press, 1941. 3 v.   938.08
    a 41-4669
    DF235.3 .R6 MRR Alc.

GREECE--SOCIAL LIFE AND CUSTOMS.
Mahaffy, John Pentland, Sir, The
social life of the Greeks. London,
New York, Macmillan, 1896-1907. 2 v.
mrr01-35
    DF77 .M218 MRR Alc.

GREECE, MODERN--BIBLIOGRAPHY.
Dimaras, C. Th., Modern Greek
culture; [Enl. ed.] Thessaloniki,
Institute for Balkan Studies, 1968.
viii, 137 p.   016.91495/03 74-6784

    Z2281 .D55 1968 MRR Alc.

Horecky, Paul Louis, Southeastern
Europe; Chicago, University of
Chicago Press [1969] xxii, 755 p.
016.91496 73-110336
    Z2831 .H67 MRR Alc.

GREECE, MODERN--BIOGRAPHY.
[Mega Hellenikon biographikon
lexikon (romanized form)] [1958- v.
59-34268
    DF750 .M4 MRR Biog.

GREECE, MODERN--COMMERCE--DIRECTORIES.
American-Hellenic Chamber of
Commerce. Business directory [of]
the members of American-Hellenic
Chamber of Commerce, Athens, Greece.
1959- [Athens, Transorient
Publications] 65-67894
    T12.5.G73 A75 MRR Alc Latest
    edition

Oikonomikos hodegos ton en Helladi
anonymon hetaireion kai
hetaireion periorismenes
euthynes. 1964- Athens, ICAP
Hellas Ltd. 70-401893
    HF5175 .04 MRR Alc Latest edition

GREECE, MODERN--DESCRIPTION AND TRAVEL--
1951- --GUIDE-BOOKS.
Brockway, Lucile. Greece; a
classical tour with extras, [1st
ed.] New York, Knopf, 1966. xiv,
260 p.   914.95047 66-19371
    DF727 .B76 MRR Alc.

GREECE, MODERN--DESCRIPTION AND TRAVEL--
GUIDE-BOOKS.
Fodor's Greece. 1969- New York, D.
McKay. 914.95/04/7 71-613011
    DF716 G742 MRR Alc Latest edition

Greece. 3d ed.] Geneva, Paris
[etc.] Nagel Publishers [1968] xxii,
869 p. [9.95] 914.95/04/7 74-
435471
    DF716 .G713 1968 MRR Alc.

Pan American World Airways, inc.
Complete reference guide to Greece,
Turkey, and Yugoslavia. [1st ed.
New York, Trade distribution in the
U.S. and Canada by Simon and
Schuster, 1967] 159 p.   914.9 67-
19409
    DF716 .P3 MRR Alc.

Rossiter, Stuart. Greece. London,
Benn; Chicago, Rand McNally, 1967.
lxiv, 765 p. [70/-] 914.95/047 67-
85934
    DF716 .R6 MRR Alc.

GREECE, MODERN--ECONOMIC CONDITIONS--
1918-
Sweet-Escott, Bickham. Greece; a
political and economic survey, 1939-
1953. London, New York, Royal
Institute of International Affairs
[1954] vii, 206 p.   949.507 a 54-
3352
    DF849 .S85 MRR Alc.

GREECE, MODERN--GAZETTEERS.
United States. Office of Geography.
Greece; official standard names
approved by the U.S. Board on
Geographic Names. Washington,
Central Intelligence Agency, 1960.
viii, 454 p.   914.95 74-180964
    DF714 .U52 1960 MRR Alc.

GREECE, MODERN--HISTORY.
Campbell, John Kennedy. Modern
Greece, New York, Praeger [1968]
426 p. [$9.00] 914.95/0376 68-
55984
    DF802 .C28 1968b MRR Alc.

Woodhouse, Christopher Montague, The
story of modern Greece London,
Faber, 1968. 3-318 p. [36/-]
949.5 68-109407
    DF757 .W6 MRR Alc.

GREECE, MODERN--HISTORY--1821-
Mavrogordato, John, Modern Greece, a
chronicle and a survey, 1800-1931,
London, Macmillan and co., limited,
1931. xi, 251 p.   949.506 32-7788

    DF802 .M3 MRR Alc.

GREECE, MODERN--HISTORY--1944-1949.
United States. Library of Congress.
European Affairs Division. War and
postwar Greece; Washington, 1952.
xv, 175 p.   949.507 52-60049
    Z663.26 .W3 MRR Alc.

GREECE, MODERN--INDUSTRIES--DIRECTORIES.
Oikonomikos hodegos ton en Helladi
anonymon_hetaireion kai
hetaireion periorismenes
euthynes. 1964- Athens, ICAP
Hellas Ltd. 70-401893
    HF5175 .04 MRR Alc Latest edition

GREECE, MODERN--MANUFACTURES--
DIRECTORIES.
American-Hellenic Chamber of
Commerce. Business directory [of]
the members of American-Hellenic
Chamber of Commerce. Athens, Greece.
1959- [Athens, Transorient
Publications] 65-67894
    T12.5.G73 A75 MRR Alc Latest
    edition

GREECE, MODERN--POLITICS AND GOVERNMENT-
-1935--1935-1967.
Sweet-Escott, Bickham. Greece; a
political and economic survey, 1939-
1953. London, New York, Royal
Institute of International Affairs
[1954] vii, 206 p.   949.507 a 54-
3352
    DF849 .S85 MRR Alc.

GREECE, MODERN--SOCIAL CONDITIONS.
Campbell, John Kennedy. Modern
Greece, New York, Praeger [1968]
426 p. [$9.00] 914.95/0376 68-
55984
    DF802 .C28 1968b MRR Alc.

GREEK ARCHITECTURE
see Architecture, Greek

GREEK ART
see Art, Greek

GREEK CHURCH--DICTIONARIES.
Langford-James, Richard Lloyd. A
dictionary of the Eastern orthodox
church. London, The Faith press,
ltd. [1923] xiv, 144 p.   24-4538
    BX230 .L3 MRR Alc.

GREEK DRAMA--HISTORY AND CRITICISM.
Bieber, Margarete, The history of
the Greek and Roman theater. [2d
ed., rev. and enl.] Princeton, N.J.,
Princeton University Press, 1961.
xiv, 343 p.   882.09 60-9367
    PA3201 .B52 1961 MRR Alc.

Harsh, Philip Whaley, A handbook of
classical drama, Stanford
University, Calif., Stanford
university press; London, H. Milford,
Oxford universi ty press [1944] xii,
526 p.   882.082 a 44-4250
    PA3024 .H3 MRR Alc.

Hathorn, Richmond Yancey, Crowell's
handbook of classical drama, New
York, Crowell [1967] 350 p.
882.003 67-12403
    PA3024 .H35 TJ Rm.

GREEK DRAMA--TRANSLATIONS INTO ENGLISH.
Oates, Whitney Jennings, ed. The
complete Greek drama; New York,
Random house [c1938] 2 v.   882.0822
38-17746
    PA3626.A2 O2 MRR Alc.

GREEK LANGUAGE--CONVERSATION AND PHRASE
BOOKS--POLYGLOT.
Lyall, Archibald, A guide to 25
languages of Europe. Rev. ed.
[Harrisburg, Pa.] Stackpole Co.
[1966] vii, 407 p.   413 66-20847

    PB73 .L85 1966 MRR Alc.

GREEK LANGUAGE--DICTIONARIES.
[Demetrakou mega lexikon tes
Hellenikes glosses (romanized
form] 1936-[50] 9 v. (35, 8056 p.)
40-36940
    PA441 .D4 MRR Alc.

GREEK LANGUAGE--DICTIONARIES--ENGLISH.
Liddell, Henry George, A Greek-
English lexicon, Rev. and augm.
throughout Oxford, Clarendon Press
[1968] xlv, 2042, xi, 153 p.
483/.2 71-2271
    PA445.E5 L6 1968 MRR Alc.

GREEK LANGUAGE--DICTIONARIES--FRENCH.
Boisacq, Émile, Dictionnaire
étymologique de la langue grecque,
4. éd., augm. Heidelberg, C.
Winter, 1950. xxxii, 1256 p.
482.03 a 51-2358
    PA421 .B6 1950 MRR Alc.

GREEK LANGUAGE--DICTIONARIES--LATIN.
Estienne, Henri, [Thesaurus tes
Hellenikes glosses (Romanized
form)] Post editionem anglicam novis
additamentis auctum, ordineque
alphabetico digestum Parisiis,
excudebat A. Firmin Didot [1831-65]
8 v. in 9.   06-39594
    PA442 .E8 MRR Alc.

GREEK LANGUAGE--DICTIONARIES--POLYGLOT.
Bergman, Peter M. The concise
dictionary of twenty-six languages in
simultaneous translations. New York,
Polyglot Library [1968] 406 p.   413
67-14284
    P361 .B4 TJ Rm.

Chalkiopoulos, Georgios.
[Pentaglosson lexilogion technikon
horon (romanized form)] [1960]
1030 p.   61-31355
    T10 .C46 1960 MRR Alc.

GREEK LANGUAGE--ETYMOLOGY--DICTIONARIES.
Boisacq, Émile, Dictionnaire
étymologique de la langue grecque,
4. éd., augm. Heidelberg, C.
Winter, 1950. xxxii, 1256 p.
482.03 a 51-2358
    PA421 .B6 1950 MRR Alc.

GREEK LANGUAGE--SEMANTICS.
Burton, Ernest De Witt, A critical
and exegetical commentary on the
Epistle to the Galatians, New York,
C. Scribner's sons, 1920. lxxxix,
541 p.   227.4 20-21079
    BS491 .I6 vol. 35 MRR Alc.

GREEK LANGUAGE--TERMS AND PHRASES.
Peters, Francis E. Greek
philosophical terms; New York, New
York University Press, 1967. xii,
234 p.   103 67-25043
    B49 .P4 MRR Alc.

GREEK LANGUAGE, BIBLICAL--DICTIONARIES--
ENGLISH.
Bauer, Walter, A Greek-English
lexicon of the New Testament, and
other early Christian literature;
Chicago, University of Chicago Press
[1957] xxxvi, 909 p.   487.383
487.04* 56-5028
    PA881 .B38 TJ Rm.

GREEK LANGUAGE, BIBLICAL-- (Cont.)
Bullinger, Ethelbert William, A
critical lexicon and concordance to
the English and Greek New Testament.
[8th ed.] London, Lamp Press [1957]
999, xxxii p. 225.2 57-35622
BS2305 .B9 1957 MRR Alc.

Young, Robert, Analytical
concordance to the Bible 22d
American ed., rev. New York, Funk &
Wagnalls [1955] ix, 1090, 93, 23, 51
p. 220.2 55-5338
BS425 .Y7 1955 MRR Alc.

GREEK LANGUAGE, BIBLICAL--DICTIONARIES--
HEBREW.
Hatch, Edwin, A concordance to the
Septuagint and the other Greek
versions of the Old Testament
(including the Apocryphal books)
Graz, Akademische Druck- u.
Verlagsanstalt, 1954. 2 v. (vi,
1504, 272 p.) 221.48 56-866
BS1122 .H3 1954 MRR Alc.

GREEK LANGUAGE, BIBLICAL--GLOSSARIES,
VOCABULARIES, ETC.
Moulton, James Hope, The vocabulary
of the Greek Testament, London,
Hodder and Stoughton, Limited, 1930.
xxxii, 705 p. 487.33 31-21018
PA881 .M7 1930 MRR Alc.

GREEK LANGUAGE, BIBLICAL--SEMANTICS.
Burton, Ernest De Witt, A critical
and exegetical commentary on the
Epistle to the Galatians, New York,
C. Scribner's sons, 1920. lxxxix,
541 p. 227.4 20-21079
BS491 .I6 vol. 35 MRR Alc.

GREEK LANGUAGE, MEDIEVAL AND LATE--
DICTIONARIES.
Du Cange, Charles du Fresne, sieur,
Glossarium ad scriptores mediæ &
infimæ Græcitatis ... [Graz,
1958] 2 v. in 1 (xl, p., 1793, 214,
101, 316 columns) 60-21441
PA1125 .D8 1688a MRR Alc.

GREEK LANGUAGE, MODERN--DICTIONARIES.
[Demetrakou mega lexikon tes
Hellenikes glosses (romanized
form)] 1836-[50] 9 v. (35, 8056 p.)
40-36940
PA441 .D4 MRR Alc.

GREEK LANGUAGE, MODERN--DICTIONARIES--
ENGLISH.
Crighton, William. [Mega Helleno-
Anglikon lexikon (romanized form)]
[pref. 1960] 1681 p. 70-274042
PA1139.E5 C7 MRR Alc.

Divry, George Constantopoulos,
Divry's modern English-Greek and
Greek-English desk dictionary. New
York, D. C. Divry, 1974. 767 p.
489.3/3/21 74-220350
PA1139.E5 D46 1974 MRR Ref Desk.

Divry, George Constantopoulos,
Modern English-Greek and Greek-
English desk dictionary. New York,
D. C. Divry [1961] 767 p. 489.332
62-25241
PA1139.E5 D46 MRR Alc.

Mega Anglo-Hellenikon lexikon
(romanized form)] [1959?] 4 v. 72-
208549
PA1139.E5 M4 MRR Alc.

Pring, Julian Talbot, comp. The
Oxford dictionary of modern Greek
(Greek-English) Oxford, Clarendon
Press, 1965. xiv, 219 p. 489.332
65-9620
PA1139.E5 P76 MRR Ref Desk.

Swanson, Donald Carl Eugene,
Vocabulary of modern spoken Greek.
Minneapolis, University of Minnesota
Press, 1959. 408 p. 489.332 59-
16514
PA1139.E5 S9 1959a MRR Alc.

GREEK LETTER SOCIETIES.
Baird's manual of American college
fraternities. [1st] ed.; 1879-
Menasha, Wis. [etc.] G. Banta Co.
[etc.] 371.85 49-4194
LJ31 .B2 MRR Ref Desk Latest
edition

United States. Bureau of
Apprenticeship and Training.
Directory for reaching minority
groups. [Washington; For sale by the
Supt. of Docs., U.S. Govt. Print.
Off.] 1973. 214 p. [$2.85] 331.6
73-602280
HD6305.M5 U53 1973 MRR Alc.

GREEK LETTER SOCIETIES--YEARBOOKS.
Leland's annual; [Saint Paul, Leland
Publishers] 371.85058 57-1334
LJ3 .L4 MRR Ref Desk Latest
edition

GREEK LETTERS.
Alciphron. The letters of Alciphron,
Aelian and Philostratus; Cambridge,
Harvard University Press, 1949. xi,
587 p. 886.2 50-2151
PA3612 .A45 MRR Alc.

GREEK LITERATURE.
Page, Denys Lionel, comp. Greek
literary papyri in two volumes. I.
Cambridge, Harvard University Press,
1942. xix, 617 p. a 42-4500
PA3611.A22 1942 MRR Alc.

Ramage, Craufurd Tait, comp.
Familiar quotations from Greek
authors. Detroit, Gale Research Co.,
1968. 589 p. 888/.002 68-22044
PN6080 .R33 1968 MRR Alc.

GREEK LITERATURE--BIBLIOGRAPHY.
Engelmann, Wilhelm, Bibliotheca
scriptorum classicorum, 8. aufl.
Leipzig [etc.] W. Engelmann, 1880-82.
2 v. 01-16689
Z7016 .E58 1880 MRR Alc.

Lambrino, Scarlat. Bibliographie de
l'antiquité classique, 1896-1914.
Paris, Société d'édition "Les
Belles Lettres," 1951- v. a 52-
1454
Z7016 .L3 MRR Alc.

Marouzeau, Jules, Dix années de
bibliographie classique, Paris,
Société d'édition "Les belles
lettres," 1927-28. 2 v. 28-27582
Z7016 .M35 MRR Alc.

Nairn, John Arbuthnot, Classical
hand-list; 3d ed., rev. and enl.
Oxford, 1953. viii, 164 p. 016.88
54-14555
Z7016 .N17 1953 MRR Alc.

GREEK LITERATURE--DICTIONARIES.
Mantinband, James H. Concise
dictionary of Greek literature. New
York, Philosophical Library [1962]
409 p. 880.3 62-9769
PA31 .M29 MRR Alc.

GREEK LITERATURE--HISTORY AND CRITICISM.
Lesky, Albin, A history of Greek
literature. New York, Crowell [1966]
xviii, 921 p. 880.9001 65-25033
PA3057 .L413 1966 MRR Alc.

Rose, Herbert Jennings, A handbook
of Greek literature from Homer to the
age of Lucian. [4th ed., rev.]
London, Methuen [1950] 454 p.
880.9 52-188
PA3052 .R6 1950 MRR Alc.

Whibley, Leonard, ed. A companion to
Greek studies. 4th ed., rev. New
York, Hafner Pub. Co., 1963.
xxxviii, 790 p. 913.38 63-10743
DF77 .W5 1963 MRR Alc.

GREEK LITERATURE--HISTORY AND CRITICISM-
-BIBLIOGRAPHY.
L'Année philologique; 1.- année;
1924/26- Paris, Société d'édition
"Les Belles Lettres." 29-9941
Z7016 .M35A MRR Alc Full set

Fifty years (and twelve) of classical
scholarship; [2d ed.] New York,
Barnes & Noble, 1968. xiv, 523 p.
68-5952
PA3001 .F5 1968 MRR Alc.

Gwinup, Thomas. Greek and Roman
authors; Metuchen, N.J.; Scarecrow
Press, 1973. x, 194 p. 016.88/009
72-10156
Z7016 .G9 MRR Alc.

Marouzeau, Jules, Dix années de
bibliographie classique; New York,
B. Franklin [1969] 2 v. (xv, 1286
p.) 68-57915
Z7016 .M35 1969 MRR Alc.

GREEK LITERATURE--TRANSLATIONS INTO
ENGLISH.
Page, Denys Lionel, comp. Greek
literary papyri in two volumes. I.
Cambridge, Harvard University Press,
1942. xix, 617 p. a 42-4500
PA3611.A22 1942 MRR Alc.

GREEK LITERATURE, MODERN--BIBLIOGRAPHY.
Dimaras, C. Th., Modern Greek
culture; [Enl. ed.] Thessaloniki,
Institute for Balkan Studies, 1968.
viii, 137 p. 016.91495/03 74-6784

Z2281 .D55 1968 MRR Alc.

GREEK MYTHOLOGY
see Mythology, Greek

GREEK ORATIONS.
Minor Attic orators. Cambridge,
Harvard University Press, 1941-54. 2
v. 41-2546
PA3611.A93 1941 MRR Alc.

GREEK PHILOLOGY--HANDBOOKS, MANUALS,
ETC.
Whibley, Leonard, ed. A companion to
Greek studies. 4th ed., rev. New
York, Hafner Pub. Co., 1963.
xxxviii, 790 p. 913.38 63-10743
DF77 .W5 1963 MRR Alc.

GREEK POETRY.
Edmonds, John Maxwell, ed. and tr.
Elegy and iambus, London, W.
Heinemann, ltd.; New York, G. P.
Putnam's sons, 1931. 2 v. 881.08
mrr01-26
PA3611.A14 1931d MRR Alc.

Edmonds, John Maxwell, ed. and tr.
Lyra graeca; London, W. Heinemann;
Cambridge, Mass., Harvard University
Press, 1927-1934 [v. 1, 1934] 3 v.
mrr01-23
PA3611.A15 1927d MRR Alc.

GREEK POETRY--HISTORY AND CRITICISM.
Edmonds, John Maxwell, ed. and tr.
Elegy and iambus, London, W.
Heinemann, ltd.; New York, G. P.
Putnam's sons, 1931. 2 v. 881.08
mrr01-26
PA3611.A14 1931d MRR Alc.

Edmonds, John Maxwell, ed. and tr.
Lyra graeca; London, W. Heinemann;
Cambridge, Mass., Harvard University
Press, 1927-1934 [v. 1, 1934] 3 v.
mrr01-23
PA3611.A15 1927d MRR Alc.

GREEK POETRY--TRANSLATIONS INTO ENGLISH.
Anthologia graeca. The Greek
anthology. London, W. Heinemann; New
York, G. P. Putnam's sons, 1925-1927.
5 v. 881/.008 mrr01-22
PA3611.A2 1925d MRR Alc.

Edmonds, John Maxwell, ed. and tr.
Elegy and iambus, London, W.
Heinemann, ltd.; New York, G. P.
Putnam's sons, 1931. 2 v. 881.08
mrr01-26
PA3611.A14 1931d MRR Alc.

Edmonds, John Maxwell, ed. and tr.
Lyra graeca; London, W. Heinemann;
Cambridge, Mass., Harvard University
Press, 1927-1934 [v. 1, 1934] 3 v.
mrr01-23
PA3611.A15 1927d MRR Alc.

Theocritus. The Greek bucolic poets,
London, W. Heinemann, New York, G.
P. Putnam's sons, 1916. xxviii, 527,
[1] p. 19-6715
PA3611 .A3 1916 MRR Alc.

GREEK REVIVAL (ARCHITECTURE)--UNITED
STATES.
Hamlin, Talbot Faulkner, Greek
revival architecture in America;
London, New York [etc.] Oxford
university press, 1944. xl, 439 p.
724.2735 44-865
NA707 .H32 MRR Alc.

GREEKS IN THE UNITED STATES.
Saloutos, Theodore. The Greeks in
the United States. Cambridge,
Harvard University Press, 1964. xiv,
445 p. 64-13428
E184.G7 S29 MRR Alc.

GREENHOUSE MANAGEMENT.
Preston, F. G., ed. The greenhouse;
New York, Abelard-Schuman [1958] 640
p. 635.982 58-3807
SB415 .P7 MRR Alc.

GREENHOUSE PLANTS.
Preston, F. G., ed. The greenhouse;
New York, Abelard-Schuman [1958] 640
p. 635.982 58-3807
SB415 .P7 MRR Alc.

GREENLAND.
Denmark. Udenrigsministeriet.
Denmark. 1924- Copenhagen. 24-
31213
HC355 .A3 MRR Alc Latest edition

GREENLAND--GAZETTEERS.
United States. Office of Geography.
Greenland; Washington, Central
Intelligence Agency, 1950. 106 p.
919.8/2 72-8775
G743 .U65 MRR Alc.

GREETING CARDS.
Chase, Ernest Dudley, The romance of
greeting cards; [Rev. ed.] [Dedham,
Mass., Rust Craft, 1956] x, 252 p.
741.68 741.67* a 57-3053
NC1860 .C5 1956 MRR Alc.

GROCERY TRADE.
see also Supermarkets

GROCERY TRADE--CANADA--DIRECTORIES.
Thomas grocery register. 68th-
ed.; 1966- New York, Thomas Publ.
Co. 381/.45/664097 72-623125
HD9321.3 T5 MRR Alc Latest edition

GROCERY TRADE—GREAT BRITAIN—DIRECTORIES.
Food trades directory [and] food buyer's yearbook. London, Newman Books. 66-83910
Began publication in 1958.
HD9011.3 .F6 MRR Alc Latest edition

GROCERY TRADE—NEW ENGLAND—DIRECTORIES.
Grocery industry directory of New England. 1st ed.; 1952/53- Wakefield, Mass [etc.] New England Wholesale Food Distributors Association. 658.9414 53-17865
HD9321.3 .G695 MRR Alc Latest editions

GROCERY TRADE—UNITED STATES—DIRECTORIES.
Chain store guide directory: 1973- [New York, Business Guides] [$49.00] 658.8/6 73-645662
HD9321.3 .D53 MRR Alc Latest edition

Directory of wholesale distributors of frozen foods. New York, Quick Frozen Foods. 664.85058 52-65843
HD9453 .D5 MRR Alc Latest edition

Directory: Supermarket, grocery and convenience store chains. 1956- [New York, Business Guides, inc.] 381/.41/02573 72-623763
HD9321.3 .C43 MRR Alc Latest edition

Grocery supermarket non-food buyers directory. 1961- New York, Directory Division, Merchandiser Publications. 60-41591
T12 .G75 MRR Alc Latest edition

Progressive grocer's marketing guidebook. New York, Progressive grocer [etc.] 658.8/09/664002573 68-126162
HD9321.3 .P75 MRR Alc Latest edition

Retailer owned cooperative chains, wholesale grocers, and wholesaler sponsored voluntary chains. [New York, Business Guides, inc.] 658.87/00873 78-612833
HF5466.A1 D52 MRR Alc Latest edition

Thomas grocery register. 68th ed.; 1966- New York, Thomas Publ. Co. 381/.45/664097 72-623125
HD9321.3 T5 MRR Alc Latest edition

GRONINGEN (PROVINCE)—DICTIONARIES.
Laan, Kornelis ter, Groninger encyclopedie. Groningen, Spiering, 1954-55. 2 v. 55-32966
DJ401.G462 L32 MRR Alc.

GROSS NATIONAL PRODUCT.
see also Income

United Nations. Statistical Office. Yearbook of national accounts statistics. 1957- New York. 58-3719
HC79.I5 U53 MRR Ref Desk Latest edition / MRR Alc Latest edition

United States. Arms Control and Disarmament Agency. Bureau of Economic Affairs. World military expenditures. 1970- [Washington, For sale by the Supt. of Docs., U.S. Govt. Print. Off.] 338.4/7/355005 70-649143
UA17 .U42 MRR Ref Desk Latest edition

GROSS NATIONAL PRODUCT—CANADA.
Organization for Economic Cooperation and Development. National accounts statistics 1950-1968. [Paris, 1970] 415 p. [$7.50 (U.S.)] 339.3 73-535302
HC79.I5 O674 MRR Alc.

GROSS NATIONAL PRODUCT—EUROPE.
Organization for Economic Cooperation and Development. National accounts statistics 1950-1968. [Paris, 1970] 415 p. [$7.50 (U.S.)] 339.3 73-535302
HC79.I5 O674 MRR Alc.

GROSS NATIONAL PRODUCT—JAPAN.
Organization for Economic Cooperation and Development. National accounts statistics 1950-1968. [Paris, 1970] 415 p. [$7.50 (U.S.)] 339.3 73-535302
HC79.I5 O674 MRR Alc.

GROSS NATIONAL PRODUCT—ORGANIZATION FOR ECONOMIC COOPERATION AND DEVELOPMENT COUNTRIES—STATISTICS.
Organization for Economic Cooperation and Development. National accounts statistics. 1960-1971. [Paris, 1973] 471 p. [$7.50 (U.S.)] 339.3 74-158206
HC79.I5 O7 1973 MRR Alc.

GROSS NATIONAL PRODUCT—UNITED STATES.
Organization for Economic Cooperation and Development. National accounts statistics 1950-1968. [Paris, 1970] 415 p. [$7.50 (U.S.)] 339.3 73-535302
HC79.I5 O674 MRR Alc.

GROTTOES
see Caves

GROUND COVER PLANTS.
Symonds, George Wellington Dillingham. The shrub identification book: New York, M. Barrows [1963] 379 p. 582.17 63-7388
QK482 .S89 MRR Alc.

GROUP DISCUSSION
see Discussion

GROUP DYNAMICS
see Social groups

GROUP GUIDANCE IN EDUCATION.
Hoppock, Robert, Occupational information; 3d ed. New York, McGraw-Hill [1967] xiv, 598 p. 371.42/5 67-14672
HF5381 .H582 1967 MRR Alc.

GROWTH.
see also Children—Growth

GRYPHONS
see Heraldry

GUATEMALA—BIOGRAPHY.
Quién; diccionario biográfico. Guatemala, 1966- v. 920.07281 67-88702
F1462.7 .Q5 MRR Biog.

GUATEMALA—BIOGRAPHY—DICTIONARIES.
Moore, Richard E., Historical dictionary of Guatemala, Rev. ed. Metuchen, N.J., Scarecrow Press, 1973. 285 p. 917.281/03/03 73-2828
F1462 .M6 1973 MRR Alc.

GUATEMALA—DESCRIPTION AND TRAVEL—GUIDE-BOOKS.
Ford, Norman D. Mexico and Guatemala by car; Greenlawn, N.Y., Harian Publications; trade distributors: Crown Publishers, 1963. 159 p. 917.2 63-5328
GV1025.M4 F6 1963 MRR Alc.

GUATEMALA—DICTIONARIES AND ENCYCLOPEDIAS.
Moore, Richard E., Historical dictionary of Guatemala, Rev. ed. Metuchen, N.J., Scarecrow Press, 1973. 285 p. 917.281/03/03 73-2828
F1462 .M6 1973 MRR Alc.

GUATEMALA—GAZETTEERS.
United States. Office of Geography. Guatemala; Washington [U.S. Govt. Print. Off.] 1965. v, 213 p. 66-60162
F1462 .U5 MRR Alc.

GUATEMALA—HISTORY—DICTIONARIES.
Moore, Richard E., Historical dictionary of Guatemala, Rev. ed. Metuchen, N.J., Scarecrow Press, 1973. 285 p. 917.281/03/03 73-2828
F1462 .M6 1973 MRR Alc.

GUELFS AND GHIBELLINES.
Toynbee, Paget Jackson, A dictionary of proper names and notable matters in the works of Dante. [New ed.] Oxford, Clarendon P., 1968 xxv, 722 p. [5/15/6] 851/.1 68-81646
PQ4333 .T7 1968 MRR Alc.

GUESTS
see Entertaining

GUIANA—BIBLIOGRAPHY.
Comitas, Lambros. Caribbeana 1900-1965, a topical bibliography. Seattle, Published for Research Institute for the Study of Man [by] University of Washington Press [1968] L, 909 p. 016.81729/03/5 68-14239
Z1501 .C6 MRR Alc.

GUIDANCE, STUDENT
see Personnel service in education

GUIDANCE, VOCATIONAL
see Vocational guidance

GUIDED MISSILES.
Bowman, Norman John, The handbook of rockets and guided missiles. 2d ed. Newtown Square, Pa., Perastadion Press, 1963. 1008 p. 629.13338 63-3212
TL782 .B6 1963 MRR Alc.

Ordway, Frederick Ira, International missile and spacecraft guide New York, McGraw-Hill, 1960. 1 v. (various pagings) 623.4513 59-14463
UG630 .O67 MRR Alc.

United States. Air Force. Air Training Command. Fundamentals of guided missiles. Los Angeles, Aero Publishers, 1960. 575 p. 623.4/519 59-14965
UG632 .U5 1960 MRR Alc.

GUIDED MISSILES—DICTIONARIES.
Dictionary of guided missiles and space flight. Princeton, N.J., Van Nostrand [1959] vi, 688 p. 629.1388 59-10112
TL788 .D5 MRR Alc.

Jacobs, Horace. Missile and space projects guide New York, Plenum Press, 1962. x, 235 p. 629.403 62-13473
TL788 .J3 MRR Alc.

GUIDED MISSILES—DICTIONARIES—RUSSIAN.
United States. Library of Congress. Reference Dept. Russian-English glossary of guided missile, rocket, and satellite terms, Washington, 1958. vi, 352 p. 629.1333803 629.1435303* 58-60055
Z663.2 .R83 MRR Alc.

GUIDED MISSILES—YEARBOOKS.
Jane's all the world's aircraft. [1st]- issue: 1909- London [etc.] S. Low, Marston & Co. 629.133058 10-8268
TL501 .J3 MRR Alc Latest edition / Sci RR Latest edition

Jane's weapon systems. 1st ed.; 1969/70- New York, McGraw-Hill. 623.4/05 79-12909
U104 .J35 Sci RR Latest edition / MRR Alc Latest edition

GUIDES TO THE LITERATURE.
France. Direction des bibliothèques de France. Les bibliographies internationales specialisées courantes françaises ou a participation française. Paris, 1958. 95 p. 60-21619
Z1002 .F75 MRR Alc.

Malclès, Louise Noëlle. Cours de bibliographie à l'intention des étudiants de l'université et des candidats aux examens de bibliothécaire. Genève, E. Droz, 1954. xii, 350 p. a 55-2888
Z1035 .M117 MRR Alc.

The Reader's adviser. [1st]- 1921- New York, R. R. Bowker Co. 57-13277
Z1035 .B7 MRR Ref Desk Latest edition / MRR Alc Latest edition

GUIDES TO THE LITERATURE—AMERICAN LITERATURE.
Altick, Richard Daniel, Selective bibliography for the study of English and American literature, 4th ed. New York, Macmillan [1971] xii, 164 p. [$2.95] 016.82 75-132867
Z2011 .A4 1971 MRR Alc.

Gohdes, Clarence Louis Frank, Bibliographical guide to the study of the literature of the U.S.A. 3d ed., rev. and enl. Durham, N.C., Duke University Press, 1970. x, 134 p. [5.00] 016.81 79-110576
Z1225 .G6 1970 MRR Alc.

Kennedy, Arthur Garfield, A concise bibliography for students of English, 5th ed. Stanford, Calif., Stanford University Press, 1972. xvi, 300 p. 016.82 77-183889
Z2011 .K35 1972 MRR Alc.

GUIDES TO THE LITERATURE—ANTHROPOLOGY.
Frantz, Charles. The student anthropologist's handbook; Cambridge, Mass., Schenkman Pub. Co.; distributed by General Learning Press, [Morristown, N.J., 1972] xi, 228 p. 301.2 77-170649
GN42 .F7 MRR Alc.

GUIDES TO THE LITERATURE—ARCHITECTURE.
Smith, Denison Langley, How to find out in architecture and building; [1st ed.] Oxford, New York, Pergamon Press [1967] xii, 232 p. 016.72 66-29605
Z5941 .S58 1967 MRR Alc.

GUIDES TO THE LITERATURE—ART.
Carrick, Neville. How to find out about the arts; [1st ed.] Oxford, New York, Pergamon Press [1965] xi, 164 p. 016.7 65-19834
Z5931 .C3 1965 MRR Alc.

Chamberlin, Mary W. Guide to art reference books. Chicago, American Library Association, 1959. xiv, 418 p. 016.7 59-10457
Z5931 .C45 MRR Alc.

Dove, Jack. Fine arts. London, Bingley, 1966. 88 p. [16/-] 016.7 66-76603
Z5931 .D6 MRR Alc.

GUIDES TO THE LITERATURE--BANKS AND
BANKING.
Burgess, Norman. How to find out
about banking and investment. [1st
ed.] Oxford, New York, Pergamon
Press [1969] xii, 300 p. 016.332
68-55021
Z7164.F5 B84 1969 MRR Alc.

GUIDES TO THE LITERATURE--BIOGRAPHY.
Slocum, Robert B. Biographical
dictionaries and related works;
Detroit, Gale Research Co. [1967]
xxiii, 1056 p.   016.92 67-27789
Z5301 .S55 MRR Biog.

GUIDES TO THE LITERATURE--BUILDING.
Bentley, Howard B. Building
construction information sources;
Detroit, Gale Research Co. [1964]
181 p.   016.69 64-16502
Z7914.B9 B4 MRR Alc.

Smith, Denison Langley. How to find
out in architecture and building;
[1st ed.] Oxford, New York, Pergamon
Press [1967] xii, 232 p.   016.72
66-29605
Z5941 .S58 1967 MRR Alc.

GUIDES TO THE LITERATURE--BUSINESS.
Coman, Edwin Truman, Sources of
business information, Rev. ed.
Berkeley, University of California
Press, 1964. xii, 330 p.   016.65
64-18639
Z7164.C81 C75 1964 MRR Alc.

Encyclopedia of business information
sources; Detroit, Gale Research Co.,
1970. 2 v. (xxi, 689 p.)   016.33
79-127922
HF5353 .E52 MRR Ref Desk.

Frank, Nathalie D., Data sources for
business and market analysis. 2d ed.
Metuchen, N.J., Scarecrow Press,
1969. 361 p.   016.65883/8/73 73-
5855
HF5415.1 .F7 1969 MRR Alc.

Harvard University. Graduate School
of Business Administration. Baker
Library. Business reference sources;
[Boston] 1971. 108 p.   [$3.00]
016.65/008 s 016.65/008 75-30038
Z7164.C81 E273 no. 27 MRR Alc.

Johnson, Herbert Webster, How to use
the business library, 3d ed.
Cincinnati, South-western Pub. Co.
[c1964] v, 160 p.   016.65 63-21248

Z675.B8 J6 1964 MRR Alc.

Winser, Marian (Manley) Business
information, [1st ed.] New York,
Harper [1955] xvi, 265 p.   016.65
55-11399
HF5353 .W56 MRR Alc.

Woy, James B. Business trends and
forecasting: information sources;
Detroit, Gale Research Co. [1966,
c1965] 152 p.   016.33854 65-28351

Z7164.C81 W83 1966 MRR Alc.

GUIDES TO THE LITERATURE--CANADA.
Ryder, Dorothy E. Canadian reference
sources; Ottawa, Canadian Library
Association, 1973. x, 185 p.
011/.02/0971 73-169642
Z1365 .R8 MRR Alc.

GUIDES TO THE LITERATURE--CATHOLIC
LITERATURE.
McCabe, James Patrick. Critical
guide to Catholic reference books.
Littleton, Colo., Libraries
Unlimited, 1971. 287 p.   011/.02
78-144202
Z674 .R4 no. 2 MRR Alc.

GUIDES TO THE LITERATURE--CHEMISTRY.
American Chemical Society. Division
of Chemical Literature. Searching
the chemical literature. Rev. and
enl. ed. Washington, American
Chemical Society, 1961. vi, 326 p.
016.54 61-11330
QD1 .A355 no. 30 MRR Alc.

Bottle, R. T. The use of chemical
literature, 2nd ed. London,
Butterworths, 1969. xii, 294 p., 2
plates. (65/-] 016.54 70-447638
QD8.5 .B6 1969b MRR Alc.

Crane, Evan Jay, A guide to the
literature of chemistry 2d ed. New
York, Wiley [1957] 397 p.   016.54
57-8881
Z5521 .C89 1957 MRR Alc.

Mellon, Melvin Guy, Chemical
publications. 4th ed. New York,
McGraw-Hill [1965] xi, 324 p.
016.54 64-8418
Z5521 .M52 1965 MRR Alc.

GUIDES TO THE LITERATURE--CHILDREN'S
LITERATURE.
Ellis, Alec. How to find out about
children's literature. 2d ed.
Oxford, New York, Pergamon Press
[1968] xii, 242 p.   67-30614
PN1009.A1 E43 1968 MRR Alc.

GUIDES TO THE LITERATURE--COMMERCE.
Foreign commerce handbook. 1922/1923-
[Washington, D.C.] Foreign commerce
department, Chamber of Commerce of
the United States. 22-23199
HF3011 .F6 MRR Ref Desk Latest
edition / MRR Alc Latest edition

Maltby, Arthur. Economics and
commerce; London, Bingley, 1968.
239 p. [48/-]   016.33 68-103704
Z7164.E2 M38 1968b MRR Alc.

GUIDES TO THE LITERATURE--CRIMINOLOGY.
Sellin, Johan Thorsten, A
bibliographical manual for the
student of criminology, [New York]
National Research and Information
Center on Crime and Delinquency
[1965] 1 v. (unpaged)   016.364 66-
862
Z5118.C9 S4 1965 MRR Alc.

GUIDES TO THE LITERATURE--ECONOMICS.
Fundaburk, Emma Lila, Reference
materials and periodicals in
economics; Metuchen, N.J., Scarecrow
Press, 1971- v.   016.33 78-
142232
Z7164.E2 F83 MRR Alc.

Maltby, Arthur. Economics and
commerce; London, Bingley, 1968.
239 p. [48/-]   016.33 68-103704
Z7164.E2 M38 1968b MRR Alc.

Melnyk, Peter. Economics;
bibliographic guide to reference
books and information resources.
Littleton, Colo., Libraries
Unlimited, 1971. 263 p.   016.33 71-
144203
Z7164.E2 M45 MRR Alc.

GUIDES TO THE LITERATURE--EDUCATION.
Burke, Arvid James, Documentation in
education New York, Teachers College
Press, Teachers College, Columbia
University [1967] xiv, 413 p.
028.7 67-17818
Z711 .B93 1967 MRR Alc.

Manheim, Theodore, Sources in
educational research; Detroit, Wayne
State University Press, 1969- v.
016.37 68-64690
Z5811 .M252 MRR Alc.

United Nations Educational,
Scientific and Cultural Organization.
International guide to educational
documentation, 1955-1960. [Paris,
1963] 700 p.   64-734
Z5811 .U32 MRR Alc.

United Nations Educational,
Scientific and Cultural Organization.
International guide to educational
documentation, 1960-1965. 2d ed.
Paris, Unesco, 1971. 575 p.   [$20.00
(U.S.)]   060/.8 s 016.37 72-179108

AS4.U8 A15 ED70/D54/AFS MRR Alc.

GUIDES TO THE LITERATURE--ELECTIONS.
International guide to electoral
statistics; The Hague, Mouton [c1969-
v.   [$16.50 (v. 1)]   324/.2/021
73-101067
JF1001 .I55 MRR Alc.

GUIDES TO THE LITERATURE--ELECTRONIC
DATA PROCESSING.
Morrill, Chester. Computers and data
processing: information sources
Detroit, Gale Research Co. [1969]
275 p. [8.75]   016.6518 70-85486
Z6654.C17 M58 MRR Alc.

Pritchard, Alan. A guide to computer
literature; 2d ed., rev. and
expanded. [Hamden, Conn.] Linnet
Books [1972] 194 p. [$7.50]
016.0016/4 72-197008
Z6654.C17 P7 1972 MRR Alc.

GUIDES TO THE LITERATURE--ELECTRONICS.
Randle, Gretchen R. Electronic
industries, information sources
Detroit, Gale Research Co. [1968]
227 p.   016.621381 67-31262
Z5836 .R3 MRR Alc.

GUIDES TO THE LITERATURE--ENGLISH
LITERATURE.
Altick, Richard Daniel, Selective
bibliography for the study of English
and American literature, 4th ed.
New York, Macmillan [1971] xii, 164
p. [$2.95]   016.82 75-132867
Z2011 .A4 1971 MRR Alc.

Bond, Donald Frederic, A reference
guide to English studies. 2d ed.
Chicago, University of Chicago Press
[1971] x, 198 p.   016.0168 79-
130307
Z1002 .B72 1971 MRR Alc.

Kennedy, Arthur Garfield, A concise
bibliography for students of English,
5th ed. Stanford, Calif., Stanford
University Press, 1972. xvi, 300 p.
016.82 77-183889
Z2011 .K35 1972 MRR Alc.

GUIDES TO THE LITERATURE--FINANCE.
Burgess, Norman. How to find out
about banking and investment. [1st
ed.] Oxford, New York, Pergamon
Press [1969] xii, 300 p.   016.332
68-55021
Z7164.F5 B84 1969 MRR Alc.

GUIDES TO THE LITERATURE--FRENCH
LITERATURE.
Osburn, Charles B. Research and
reference guide to French studies.
Metuchen, N. J. Scarecrow Press,
1968. 517 p. [$11.50] 016.44 68-
12638
Z2175.A2 O8 MRR Ref Desk.

GUIDES TO THE LITERATURE--GENEALOGY.
American Society of Genealogists.
Genealogical research, methods and
sources. Washington, 1960- v.
929/.1 60-819
CS16 .A5 MRR Alc.

Doane, Gilbert Harry, Searching for
your ancestors; [3d ed.]
Minneapolis, University of Minnesota
Press [1960] 198 p.   929.1 60-
12200
CS16 .D6 1960 MRR Alc.

Everton, George B. The handy book
for genealogists, 4th ed., rev. and
enl. Logan, Utah, Everton Publishers
[1962] x, 226 p.   929.1 62-15376
CS16 .E85 1962 MRR Alc.

Kirkham, E. Kay. Research in
American genealogy; [Salt Lake City,
1956] xii, 447 p.   929.1072 56-
58780
CS16 .K53 MRR Alc.

Stevenson, Noel C. Search and
research, the researcher's handbook;
Rev. ed. Salt Lake City, Deseret
Book Co., 1959. 364 p.   929.1072
59-11137
Z5313.US S8 1959 MRR Ref Desk.

GUIDES TO THE LITERATURE--GEOGRAPHY.
Brewer, James Gordon. The literature
of geography; [Hamden, Conn.] Linnet
Books [1973] 208 p. [$10.50]
016.91 73-10088
Z6001 .B74 1973 MRR Alc.

Durrenberger, Robert W. Geographical
research and writing New York,
Crowell [1971] ix, 246 p.
808.06/6/91 77-136033
G73 .D97 MRR Alc.

Wright, John Kirtland, Aids to
geographical research:
bibliographies, periodicals, atlases,
gazetteers and other reference books,
2d ed., completely rev. New York,
Columbia University Press, 1947.
xii, 331 p.   016.91 47-30449
Z6001.A1 W9 1947 MRR Alc.

GUIDES TO THE LITERATURE--GOVERNMENT
PUBLICATIONS.
Wynkoop, Sally. Subject guide to
government reference books.
Littleton, Colo., Libraries
Unlimited, 1972. 276 p.   015.73 72-
83382
Z1223.Z7 W95 MRR Alc.

GUIDES TO THE LITERATURE--GUIDE-BOOKS.
Neal, Jack A., comp. Reference guide
for travellers. New York, Bowker,
1969. xi, 674 p. [17.50] 016.910
69-16399
Z6011 .N4 MRR Alc.

GUIDES TO THE LITERATURE--HISTORY.
American Historical Association.
Guide to historical literature. New
York, Macmillan, 1961. xxxv, 962 p.
016.9 61-7602
Z6201 .A55 MRR Alc.

Handbook for history teachers. 2nd
ed., rewritten and enlarged. London,
Methuen Educational, 1970. iii-xv,
716 p. [£2.00] 907 72-186140
D16.2 .H23 1970 MRR Alc.

Hepworth, Philip. How to find out in
history; [1st ed.] Oxford, New York
[etc.] Pergamon, 1966. xiv, 242 p.
[30/- (20/- lp.]   016.9 65-29063
D16.2 .H4 1966 MRR Alc.

Kitson Clark, George Sidney Roberts,
Guide for research students working
on historical subjects, 2nd ed.
London, Cambridge U.P., 1968. 63 p.
[7/6 ($1.75]   907/.2 75-403504
D16 .K58 1968 MRR Alc.

Poulton, Helen J. The historian's
handbook; [1st ed.] Norman,
University of Oklahoma Press [1972]
xi, 304 p.   016.9 71-165774
Z6201 .P65 MRR Alc.

GUIDES TO THE LITERATURE--HUMANITIES.
Rogers, A. Robert, The humanities;
Littleton, Colo., Libraries
Unlimited, 1974. 400 p. [$9.50]
016.0013 74-78393
Z5579 .R63 MRR Alc.

Stevens, Rolland Elwell, Reference
books in the social sciences and
humanities 3d ed. Champaign, Ill.,
Distributed by Illini Union Bookstore
[1971] v, 188 p.   016.3 74-151299

Z1035.1 .S85 1971 MRR Ref Desk.

GUIDES TO THE LITERATURE--INSURANCE.
Thomas, Roy Edwin, comp. Insurance
information sources. Detroit, Mich.,
Gale Research Co. [1971] 332 p.
[$14.50] 016.368/9/73 75-137575
Z7164.I7 T48 MRR Alc.

GUIDES TO THE LITERATURE--INVESTMENTS.
Burgess, Norman. How to find out
about banking and investment. [1st
ed.] Oxford, New York, Pergamon
Press [1969] xii, 300 p. 016.332
68-55021
Z7164.F5 B84 1969 MRR Alc.

Woy, James B. Investment
information: Detroit, Gale Research
Co. [1970] 231 p. [$11.50]
016.33267 78-118791
Z7164.F5 W83 MRR Ref Desk.

GUIDES TO THE LITERATURE--LIBRARIES.
Harris, Michael H. A guide to
research in American library history,
Metuchen, N.J., Scarecrow Press,
1968. 186 p. 016.021/009 67-12068

Z731 .H3 MRR Alc.

GUIDES TO THE LITERATURE--MANAGEMENT.
Bakewell, K. G. B. How to find out:
management and productivity; 2d ed.
Oxford, New York, Pergamon Press
[1970] x, 389 p. 016.6585 78-
89775
Z7164.O7 B2 1970 MRR Alc.

GUIDES TO THE LITERATURE--MARKETING.
Frank, Nathalie D., Data sources for
business and market analysis, 2d ed.
Metuchen, N.J., Scarecrow Press,
1969. 361 p. 016.65883/9/73 73-
5855
HF5415.1 .F7 1969 MRR Alc.

Frank, Nathalie D., Market analysis:
a handbook of current data sources,
New York, Scarecrow Press, 1964. 268
p. 658.83 64-21869
HF5415 .F686 MRR Alc.

Wills, Gordon, comp. Sources of U.K.
marketing information; London,
Nelson 1969. xiii, 304 p. [60/-]
658.83/9/42 70-412725
HF5415.12.G7 W5 MRR Alc.

GUIDES TO THE LITERATURE--MEDICINE.
Medical Library Association.
Handbook of medical library practice,
2d ed., rev. and enl. Chicago,
American Library Association, 1956.
xv, 601 p. 026.61 55-6481
Z675.M4 M45 1956 MRR Alc.

GUIDES TO THE LITERATURE--MIDDLE AGES,
500-1500.
Rouse, Richard H. Serial
bibliographies for medieval studies
Berkeley, University of California
Press 1969. xiii, 150 p.
016.016914/03/1 68-31637
Z6203 .R66 MRR Alc.

GUIDES TO THE LITERATURE--MONEY.
Burgess, Norman. How to find out
about banking and investment. [1st
ed.] Oxford, New York, Pergamon
Press [1969] xii, 300 p. 016.332
68-55021
Z7164.F5 B84 1969 MRR Alc.

GUIDES TO THE LITERATURE--MUSIC.
Davies, J. H. Musicalia; 2d ed.,
rev. and enl. Oxford, New York,
Pergamon Press [1969] xii, 184 p.
016.78 76-77013
ML113 .D383 M9 1969 MRR Alc.

Duckles, Vincent Harris, Music
reference and research materials; 2d
ed. New York, Free Press [1967]
xiii, 385 p. 016.78 67-17657
ML113 .D83 1967 MRR Alc.

GUIDES TO THE LITERATURE--NEGROES.
Porter, Dorothy (Burnett), The Negro
in the United States; Washington,
Library of Congress; [for sale by the
Supt. of Docs., U.S. Govt. Print.
Off.] 1970. x, 313 p. [3.25]
016.9173/09/7496 78-606085
Z1361.N39 P59 MRR Alc.

Welsch, Erwin K. The Negro in the
United States; Bloomington, Indiana
University Press, 1965. xiii, 142 p.
016.30145196073 65-23085
Z1361.N38 W4 1965 MRR Alc.

GUIDES TO THE LITERATURE--PERIODICALS.
Fowler, Maureen J. Guides to
scientific periodicals: London,
Library Association [1966] xvi, 318
p. [84/- 63/- (to L.A. members)]
016.505 67-71339
Z7403 .F6 MRR Alc.

GUIDES TO THE LITERATURE--PHILOSOPHY.
Borchardt, Dietrich Hans, How to
find out in philosophy and
psychology, [1st ed.] Oxford, New
York, Pergamon Press [1968] vii, 97
p. 016.1 67-28659
Z7125 .B65 1968 MRR Alc.

Koren, Henry J. Research in
philosophy; Pittsburgh, Duquesne
University Press [1966] 203 p.
016.1 66-28340
Z7125 .K65 MRR Alc.

GUIDES TO THE LITERATURE--PHYSICS.
Whitford, Robert H. Physics
literature; 2d ed. Metuchen, N.J.,
Scarecrow Press, 1968. 272 p.
016.53 68-12636
Z7141 .W47 1968 MRR Alc.

Yates, Bryan, How to find out about
physics; [1st ed.] Oxford, New
York, Pergamon Press [1965] x, 175
p. 016.53 65-25338
Z7141 .Y3 1965 MRR Alc.

GUIDES TO THE LITERATURE--POLITICAL
PARTIES--UNITED STATES.
Wynar, Lubomyr Roman, American
political parties; Littleton, Colo.,
Libraries Unlimited, 1969. 427 p.
016.329/02/0973 75-96954
Z7166.U5 W88 MRR Alc.

GUIDES TO THE LITERATURE--POLITICAL
SCIENCE.
Brock, Clifton. The literature of
political science; New York, Bowker,
1969. xii, 232 p. 016.32 79-79426

Z7161 .B83 MRR Alc.

GUIDES TO THE LITERATURE--PSYCHIATRY.
Ennis, Bernice, Guide to the
literature in psychiatry. Los
Angeles, Partridge Press, 1971. xi,
127 p. 016.61689 76-150718
Z6664.N5 E6 MRR Alc.

GUIDES TO THE LITERATURE--PSYCHOLOGY.
Borchardt, Dietrich Hans, How to
find out in philosophy and
psychology, [1st ed.] Oxford, New
York, Pergamon Press [1968] vii, 97
p. 016.1 67-28659
Z7125 .B65 1968 MRR Alc.

GUIDES TO THE LITERATURE--READING.
Davis, Bonnie M. A guide to
information sources for reading.
Newark, Del., International Reading
Association, 1972. 158 p.
016.4284/.025 72-176095
Z5814.R25 D37 MRR Alc.

GUIDES TO THE LITERATURE--SCIENCE.
Jenkins, Frances Briggs, Science
reference sources. 5th ed.
Cambridge, Mass., M.I.T. Press [1969]
xvi, 231 p. 016.5 73-95001
Z7401 .J4 1969 MRR Alc.

Jenkins, Frances Briggs, Science
reference sources. 4th ed.
Champaign, Ill., Distributed by
Illini Union Bookstore [c1965] xvi,
143 p. 016.5 66-966
Z7401 .J4 1965 MRR Alc.

GUIDES TO THE LITERATURE--SCIENCE--
HISTORY.
Sarton, George, A guide to the
history of science; Waltham, Mass.,
Chronica Botanica Co., 1952. xvii,
316 p. 509 52-10902
Q125 .S24 MRR Alc.

Sarton, George, Introduction to the
history of science ... Baltimore,
Pub. for the Carnegie institution of
Washington by the Williams & Wilkins
company [c1927- v. 27-11418
Q125 .S32 MRR Alc.

GUIDES TO THE LITERATURE--SOCIAL
SCIENCES.
Freides, Thelma. Literature and
bibliography of the social sciences.
Los Angeles, Melville Pub. Co. [1973]
xviii, 284 p. 300/.1/8 73-10111
H61 .F635 MRR Alc.

Frykholm, Lars. Översikt över
samhällsvetenskapliga bibliografiska
hjälpmedel: [Stockholm, I
distribution: C. E. Fritzes Kungl.
Hovbokhandel, 1960] 160 p. 65-
54908
Z7161 .F78 MRR Alc.

Hoselitz, Berthold Frank, ed. A
reader's guide to the social
sciences. Rev. ed. New York, Free
Press [1970] xiv, 425 p. 016.3 71-
15373
H61 .H69 1970 MRR Alc.

Lewis, Peter R. The literature of
the social sciences; London, Library
Association, 1960. 222 p. 016.3
60-3467
Z7161 .L45 MRR Alc.

Mason, John Brown, Research
resources; Santa Barbara, Calif.,
ABC-Clio, 1968- v. [3.00]
016.327/.09/04 68-9685
Z7161 .M36 MRR Ref Desk.

Stevens, Rolland Elwell, Reference
books in the social sciences and
humanities 3d ed. Champaign, Ill.,
Distributed by Illini Union Bookstore
[1971] v, 188 p. 016.3 74-151299

Z1035.1 .S85 1971 MRR Ref Desk.

White, Carl Milton, Sources of
information in the social sciences, a
guide to the literature 2d ed.
Chicago, American Library
Association, 1973. xviii, 702 p.
016.3 73-9825
Z7161 .W49 1973 MRR Ref Desk.

GUIDES TO THE LITERATURE--SOCIOLOGY.
Odum, Howard Washington, American
sociology; [1st ed.] New York,
Longmans, Green, 1951. vi, 501 p.
301 51-12390
HM22.U5 O4 1951 MRR Alc.

GUIDES TO THE LITERATURE--STATISTICS.
Cormier, Reine. Les Sources des
statistiques actuelles, Paris,
Gauthier-Villars, 1969. 287 p.
[48.00] 016.3144 75-423353
Z7551 .C65 MRR Alc.

GUIDES TO THE LITERATURE--STATISTICS--
GREAT BRITAIN.
Kendall, Maurice George, ed. The
sources and nature of the statistics
of the United Kingdom; London,
Published for the Royal Statistical
Society by Oliver and Boyd, 1952-57.
2 v. 314.2 52-3168
HA37.G7 K4 MRR Alc.

GUIDES TO THE LITERATURE--STATISTICS--
LATIN AMERICA.
Statistical activities of the
American nations, 1940: Washington,
D.C., Inter American statistical
institute, 1941. xxxi, 842 p.
311.397 41-14318
HA175 .S75 MRR Alc.

GUIDES TO THE LITERATURE--STATISTICS--
UNITED STATES.
Hauser, Philip Morris, ed.
Government statistics for business
use, 2d ed. New York, Wiley [1956]
xx, 440 p. 311.3973 310.61* 56-
5054
HA37.U55 H3 1956 MRR Alc.

United States. Bureau of Labor
Statistics. Guide to employment
statistics of BLS; [Washington]
1961. i, 134 p. l 62-75
HD8064 .A52 1961 MRR Alc.

United States. Bureau of the Census.
Directory of Federal statistics for
local areas, [Washington, For sale
by the Supt. of Docs., U.S. Govt.
Print. Off.] 1966. vi, 156 p. a
66-7475
HB2175 .A5 1966 TJ Rm.

GUIDES TO THE LITERATURE--STATISTICS--
UNITED STATES--STATES.
United States. Bureau of Labor
Statistics. Guide to area employment
statistics; [Washington] 1960. iii,
227 p. l 60-70
HD8064 .A52 1960b MRR Alc.

GUIDES TO THE LITERATURE--TECHNOLOGY.
Ferguson, Eugene S. Bibliography of
the history of technology Cambridge,
Mass., Society for the History of
Technology [1968] xx, 347 p.
016.609 68-21559
Z7914.H5 F4 MRR Alc.

GUIDES TO THE LITERATURE--TECHNOLOGY--
RUSSIA.
Tolpin, Jacob Gerschon, Searching
the Russian technical literature.
[n. p., 1960] 81 l. 016.60947 60-
23665
Z7915.R9 T73 MRR Alc.

GUIDES TO THE LITERATURE--
TRANSPORTATION.
Flood, Kenneth U. Research in
transportation: legal/legislative and
economic sources and procedure
Detroit, Gale Research Co. [c1970]
126 p. [$11.50] 016.3805 72-
118792
Z7164.T8 F55 MRR Alc.

GUIDES TO THE LITERATURE--UNITED
NATIONS.
Brimmer, Brenda. A guide to the use
of United Nations documents Dobbs
Ferry, N.Y., Oceana Publications,
1962. xv, 272 p. 025.173 63-3667

Z674 .B7 1962a MRR Alc.

GUIDES TO THE LITERATURE--ZOOLOGY.
Smith, Roger Cletus. Guide to the literature of the zoological sciences. 7th ed. Minneapolis, Burgess Pub. Co. [1967] xiv, 238 p.
016.591 66-23383
Z7991 .S5 1967 MRR Alc.

GUIDES TO THE LITERATURE--AFRICA, SOUTH.
Musiker, Reuben. Guide to South African reference books. 4th rev. ed. Cape Town, A. A. Balkema, 1965. x, 110 p. 015.68 66-8863
Z3601 .M8 1965 MRR Alc.

Musiker, Reuben. South African bibliography; Hamden, Conn., Archon Books [1970] 105 p. [5.50]
010/.968 73-16088
Z3601 .A1M9 MRR Alc.

GUIDES TO THE LITERATURE--AFRICA, SUB-SAHARAN.
Duignan, Peter. Guide to research and reference works on Sub-Saharan Africa. Stanford, Calif., Hoover Institution Press, Stanford University [1971 or 2] xiii, 1102 p.
016.0169167/03 76-152424
Z3501 .D78 MRR Alc.

GUIDES TO THE LITERATURE--ASIA.
Garde, P. K. Directory of reference works published in Asia. [Paris] UNESCO [1956] xxvii, 139 p. 016 a 57-2357
Z3035 .G27 MRR Alc.

Nunn, Godfrey Raymond. Asia: a selected and annotated guide to reference works. Cambridge, Mass., M.I.T. Press [1971] xiii, 223 p. [$12.50] 016.016915 77-169004
Z3001 .N79 MRR Alc.

Pearson, James Douglas. Oriental and Asian bibliography; Hamden, Conn., Archon Books, 1966. xvi, 261 p.
016.915 66-1006
Z7046 .P4 MRR Alc.

GUIDES TO THE LITERATURE--AUSTRALIA.
Borchardt, Dietrich Hans. Australian bibliography; [2d ed.] Melbourne, Canberra [etc.] Cheshire [1966] 96 p. [$3.00 Aust.] 016.9194 68-106257
Z4011 .B65 1966 MRR Alc.

GUIDES TO THE LITERATURE--CHINA.
Berton, Peter Alexander Menquez. Contemporary China; Stanford, Calif., Hoover Institution on War, Revolution, and Peace, 1967. xxix, 695 p. 016.9151/03/5 67-14235
Z3106 .B39 MRR Alc.

Nathan, Andrew James. Modern China, 1840-1972; Ann Arbor, Center for Chinese Studies, University of Michigan, 1973. vi, 95 p. [$2.00]
016.9151 74-167311
Z3106 .N32 MRR Alc.

GUIDES TO THE LITERATURE--COMMONWEALTH OF NATIONS.
National Book League, London. Commonwealth reference books and bibliographical guide. London, 1965. 54 p. 011.02 66-85951
Z1035 .N29 MRR Alc.

GUIDES TO THE LITERATURE--DENMARK.
Munch-Petersen, Erland. A guide to Danish bibliography. Copenhagen, Royal School of Librarianship, 1965. 140 p. 016.9148903 66-6980
Z2561.A1 M8 MRR Alc.

GUIDES TO THE LITERATURE--EUROPE, SOUTHEASTERN.
Horecky, Paul Louis. Southeastern Europe; Chicago, University of Chicago Press [1969] xxii, 755 p.
016.91486 73-110336
Z2831 .H67 MRR Alc.

GUIDES TO THE LITERATURE--FRANCE.
Malcles, Louise Noelle. Les sources du travail bibliographique. Geneve, E. Droz, 1950-58. 3 v. in 4. 016.01 51-17035
Z1002 .M4 MRR Ref Desk.

Pemberton, John E. How to find out about France; [1st ed.] Oxford, New York, Pergamon Press [1966] xvi, 199 p. 016.914403 66-19080
Z2161 .P4 1966 MRR Alc.

GUIDES TO THE LITERATURE--GERMANY.
Bithell, Jethro, ed. Germany, a companion to German studies. [5th ed., rev., enl.] London, Methuen [1955] xii, 578 p. 914.3 55-3335

DD61 .B56 1955 MRR Alc.

GUIDES TO THE LITERATURE--GREAT BRITAIN.
Bagley, William Alfred. Facts and how to find them; 7th ed. London, Pitman [1964] xii, 148 p. 65-68024

Z1035.1 .E3 1964 MRR Alc.

Berkowitz, David Sandler. Bibliotheca bibliographica Britannica; Waltham, Mass., 1963-v. 63-3390
Z2016 .B45 MRR Alc.

Cambridge. University. Library. Subject guide to class 'Ref' (current reference books) in the University Library Cambridge. Cambridge, Cambridge University Library, 1968. [6], 106 leaves. [5/-] 011/.02 72-354270
Z1035.1 .C35 MRR Alc.

Chandler, George. How to find out: 2nd ed. Oxford, New York [etc.] Pergamon, 1966. xiv, 198 p. [17/6]
016.0287 66-76421
Z1035 .C44 1966 MRR Alc.

Colchester, Eng. University of Essex. Library. Comparative and social studies: Colchester, University of Essex (Library), 1969. [4], xiv, 407 p. 017/.1 70-506935
Z1035.1 .C63 1969 MRR Alc.

Library Association. Reference, Special and Information Section. Basic stock for the reference library. 2d ed. London, Library Association (Reference, Special and Information Section), 1967 [i.e. 1968]. 24 p. [1/6] 011/.02 68-105269
Z1035.1 .L6 1968 MRR Alc.

Walford, Albert John, ed. Guide to reference material. 2nd ed. London, Library Association, 1966-1970. 3 v. [£15/-/-] 011/.02 66-71608
Z1035 .W252 MRR Alc.

Walford, Albert John, ed. Guide to reference material. 3d ed. [London] Library Association, 1973- v.
011/.02 73-174024
Z1035.1 .W33 MRR Ref Desk.

GUIDES TO THE LITERATURE--HUNGARY.
Bako, Elemer. Guide to Hungarian studies. Stanford, Calif., Hoover Institution Press [1973] 2 v. (xv, 1218 p.) 016.91438 79-152422
Z2146 .B3 MRR Alc.

Szentmihályi, János. Útmutató a tudományos munka magyar es nemezetkozi irodalmahoz. Budapest, Gondolat, 1963. 730 p. 65-84718
Z1035.1 .S97 MRR Alc.

GUIDES TO THE LITERATURE--ISLAMIC COUNTRIES.
Sauvaget, Jean. Introduction to the history of the Muslim East: Berkeley, University of California Press, 1965. xxi, 252 p. 64-25271

Z3013 .S314 MRR Alc.

GUIDES TO THE LITERATURE--JAPAN.
Nihon no Sanko Tosho Henshu Iinkai. Guide to Japanese reference books. Chicago, American Library Association, 1966. 303 p. 66-23396

Z3306 .N5 1966 MRR Alc.

GUIDES TO THE LITERATURE--LATIN AMERICA.
Griffin, Charles Carroll. Latin America: a guide to the historical literature. Austin, Published for the Conference on Latin American History by the University of Texas Press [c1971] xxx, 700 p. [$25.00]
016.98 71-165916
Z1601 .G75 MRR Alc.

GUIDES TO THE LITERATURE--PAKISTAN.
Siddiqui, Akhtar H. A guide to reference books published in Pakistan Karachi, Pakistan Reference Publications, 1966. 41 p. 015.549 sa 66-7465
Z1035.9 .S5 MRR Alc.

GUIDES TO THE LITERATURE--RUSSIA.
Maichel, Karol. Guide to Russian reference books. [Stanford, Calif.] Hoover Institution on War, Revolution, and Peace, Stanford University, 1962- v. 016.9147 62-14067
Z2491 .M25 MRR Alc.

Neiswender, Rosemary. Guide to Russian reference and language aids. New York, Special Libraries Association, 1962. iv, 92 p.
016.4917 62-21081
Z2505 .N4 1962 MRR Alc.

GUIDES TO THE LITERATURE--RUSSIA--HISTORY.
Morley, Charles. Guide to research in Russian history. [Syracuse] Syracuse University Press [1951] xiii, 227 p. 016.947 51-12526
Z2506 .M85 MRR Alc.

GUIDES TO THE LITERATURE--UNITED STATES.
American Library Association. Ad Hoc Reference Books Review Committee. Reference books for small and medium-sized libraries. 2d ed., rev. Chicago, American Library Association, 1973. xii, 146 p.
011/.02 73-8306
Z1035.1 .A47 1973 MRR Alc.

American reference books annual. 1970- Littleton, Colo., Libraries Unlimited. 011/.02 75-120328
Z1035.1 .A55 MRR Alc Full set

Brockett, Oscar Gross. A bibliographical guide to research in speech and dramatic art. Chicago, Scott, Foresman [1963] 118 p. 016 63-14554
Z1002 .B87 MRR Alc.

Encyclopedia of business information sources; Detroit, Gale Research Co., 1970. 2 v. (xxi, 689 p.) 016.33 79-127922
HF5353 .E52 MRR Ref Desk.

Enoch Pratt Free Library, Baltimore. Reference books; [1st]- ed.; 1947-Baltimore. 016 54-4633
Z1035.1 .E5 MRR Ref Desk Latest edition / MRR Alc Latest edition

Galin, Saul. Reference books: New York, Random House [1969] xxi, 312 p. [7.95] 011/.02 69-16443
Z1035.1 .G3 MRR Alc.

Gates, Jean Key. Guide to the use of books and libraries. 3d ed. New York, McGraw-Hill [1974] xii, 308 p. 028.7 73-9502
Z710 .G27 1974 MRR Alc.

Gohdes, Clarence Louis Frank. Bibliographical guide to the study of the literature of the U.S.A. 3d ed., rev. and enl. Durham, N.C., Duke University Press, 1970. x, 134 p. [5.00] 016.81 79-110576
Z1225 .G6 1970 MRR Alc.

Harvard University. Library. Reference collections shelved in the Reading Room and Acquisitions Department. Cambridge, Distributed by the Harvard University Press, 1966. 187 p. 011.02 66-31368
Z1035.1 .H27 MRR Ref Desk.

Katz, William Armstrong. Introduction to reference work. New York, McGraw-Hill [1969] 2 v.
011/.02 69-13223
Z711 .K32 MRR Alc.

Perkins, Ralph. The new concept guide to reference books; [n.p., 1965] 68 l. 011.02 65-6500
Z1035 .P4 MRR Alc.

Poulton, Helen J. The historian's handbook; [1st ed.] Norman, University of Oklahoma Press [1972] xi, 304 p. 016.9 71-165774
Z6201 .P65 MRR Alc.

Shores, Louis. Basic reference sources; Chicago, American Library Association, 1954. ix, 378 p.
028.7 53-7487
Z1035 .S49 1954 MRR Alc.

Wisconsin. University. Library School. Reference syllabus for use in advanced reference classes. 2d ed. Madison, College Print. and Typing Co. [1965] 273 p. 028.7 65-6718
Z1035 .W864 1965 MRR Alc.

Wynar, Christine L. Guide to reference books for school media centers. Littleton, Colo., Libraries Unlimited, 1973. xviii, 473 p. [$17.50] 011/.02 73-87523
Z1035.1 .W97 MRR Alc.

Wynar, Lubomyr Roman. Guide to reference materials in political science; Denver, Colorado Bibliographic Institute, 1966-68. 2 v. 016.32 66-1321
Z7161 .W9 MRR Alc.

Ziskind, Sylvia. Reference readiness; [Hamden, Conn.] Linnet Books, 1971. xiii, 310 p. [$10.00]
011/.02 72-134871
Z1035.1 .Z56 MRR Alc.

GUIDES TO THE LITERATURE--UNITED STATES--GENEALOGY.
Stevenson, Noel C. Search and research, the researcher's handbook; Rev. ed. Salt Lake City, Deseret Book Co., 1959. 364 p. 929.1072 59-11137
Z5313.U5 S8 1959 MRR Ref Desk.

**GUIDES TO THE LITERATURE--UNITED STATES-
-HISTORY.**
Freidel, Frank Burt. Harvard guide
to American history. Rev. ed.
Cambridge, Mass., Belknap Press of
Harvard University Press, 1974. 2 v.
(xxx, 1290 p.)   016.9173/03   72-
81272
     Z1236 .F77 1974 MRR Ref Desk.

Handlin, Oscar, Harvard guide to
American history Cambridge, Mass.,
Belknap Press, 1954. xxiv, 689 p.
016.973   53-5066
     Z2136 .H27 TJ Rm.

United States. Library of Congress.
General Reference and Bibliography
Division. A guide to the study of
the United States of America;
Washington, 1960.   xv, 1193 p.
016.9173   60-60009
     Z1215 .U53 MRR Alc.

**GUIDES TO THE LITERATURE--UNITED STATES-
-POLITICS AND GOVERNMENT.**
Brock, Clifton. The literature of
political science; New York, Bowker,
1969. xii, 232 p.   016.32   70-79426

     Z7161 .B83 MRR Alc.

Wynar, Lubomyr Roman, American
political parties; Littleton, Colo.,
Libraries Unlimited, 1969.   427 p.
016.329/02/0973   75-96954
     Z7166.U5 W88 MRR Alc.

**GUIDES TO THE LITERATURE--UNITED STATES-
-STATES.**
Parish, David W. State government
reference publications : Littleton,
Colo. : Libraries Unlimited, 1974.
237 p. ;   [$11.50]   015/.73   74-
81322
     Z1223.5.A1 P37 MRR Alc.

GUINEA.
American University, Washington, D.C.
Foreign Areas Studies Division.
Special warfare: area handbook for
Guinea. [Washington, U.S. Govt.
Print. Off.] 1961 [i.e. 1962] xii,
534 p.   mrr01-46
     DT543.8 .A63 MRR Alc.

GUINEA--BIOGRAPHY.
American University, Washington, D.C.
Foreign Areas Studies Division.
Special warfare: area handbook for
Guinea. [Washington, U.S. Govt.
Print. Off.] 1961 [i.e. 1962] xii,
534 p.   mrr01-46
     DT543.8 .A63 MRR Alc.

GUINEA--ECONOMIC CONDITIONS.
American University, Washington, D.C.
Foreign Areas Studies Division.
Special warfare: area handbook for
Guinea. [Washington, U.S. Govt.
Print. Off.] 1961 [i.e. 1962] xii,
534 p.   mrr01-46
     DT543.8 .A63 MRR Alc.

GUINEA--GAZETTEERS.
United States. Office of Geography.
Guinea; Washington [U.S. Govt.
Print. Off.] 1965. iv, 175 p.   65-
61815
     DT543.2 .U54 MRR Alc.

GUINEA--POLITICS AND GOVERNMENT.
American University, Washington, D.C.
Foreign Areas Studies Division.
Special warfare: area handbook for
Guinea. [Washington, U.S. Govt.
Print. Off.] 1961 [i.e. 1962] xii,
534 p.   mrr01-46
     DT543.8 .A63 MRR Alc.

GUINEA, PORTUGUESE--GAZETTEERS.
United States. Geographic Names
Division. Portuguese Guinea;
Washington, 1968. iii, 122 p.
916.6/57/003   68-62349
     DT613.2 .U5 MRR Alc.

GUIPUZCOA, SPAIN--DIRECTORIES.
Guia-anuario de Aragon, Rioja,
Navarra, Alava, Guipuzcoa y Vizcaya.
Zaragoza, E. Gallegos.   51-22040
     DP11 .G78   MRR Alc Latest edition

GUN
see Firearms

GUNSMITHS.
Gardner, Robert Edward. Five
centuries of gunsmiths, swordsmiths
and armourers, 1400-1900. [Columbus,
Ohio, W. F. Beer] 1948. 244 p.   399
48-15654
     U800 .G3 MRR Alc.

Pollard, Hugh Bertie Campbell, A
history of firearms, London, G.
Bles, 1936. x p., 1 l., 320 p.
623.4409   39-4478
     U884 .P6 1936 MRR Alc.

GUNSMITHS, AMERICAN.
Albaugh, William A., Confederate
arms, Harrisburg, Pa. [1957] xviii,
278 p.   623.4   57-13480
     UD383.5 .A6 MRR Alc.

Gluckman, Arcadi, United States
martial pistols and revolvers.
Harrisburg, Pa., Stackpole Co., 1956.
249, xxxvii, [1] p.   623.443   56-
3215
     UD413 .G5 1956 MRR Alc.

Van Rensselaer, Stephen, American
firearms; Watkins Glen, N.Y.,
Century House [1947] 288 p.   683
48-1408
     TS535 .V3 MRR Alc.

GUYANA.
Johnson Research Associates. Area
handbook for Guyana. Washington, For
sale by the Supt. of Docs., U.S.
Govt. Print. Off.] 1969. xiv, 378 p.
[3.25]   918.8/1   79-606159
     F2368 .J6 MRR Alc.

GUYANA--BIOGRAPHY.
Who's who in Canada; Toronto,
International Press Limited. 17-
16282
     Began publication in 1910.
     F1033 .V62 Sci RR Latest edition /
     MRR Biog Latest edition

**GUYANA--DESCRIPTION AND TRAVEL--GUIDE-
BOOKS.**
Aspinall, Algernon Edward, Sir, The
pocket guide to the West Indies and
British Guiana, British Honduras,
Bermuda, the Spanish Main, Surinam,
the Panama Canal, [10th ed.] rev.
London, Methuen [1960] xx, 474 p.
917.29   61-19408
     F1609 .A84 1960 MRR Alc.

GUYANA--GAZETTEERS.
United States. Office of Geography.
The Guianas; Washington, 1954. 234
p.   918.8   78-10045
     F2364 .U5 MRR Alc.

GYMNASTICS.
see also Physical education and
training

**GYNECOLOGISTS--UNITED STATES--
DIRECTORIES.**
American directory of obstetricians
and gynecologists. 1st-   ed.;
1954/55-   Knoxville, Tenn., Joe T.
Smith.   614.24   55-27820
     RG32 .A5 Sci RR Latest edition /
     MRR Biog Latest edition

HABITS OF ANIMALS
see Animals, Habits and behavior of

HAIRDRESSING.
see also Costume

Keyes, Jean. A history of women's
hairstyles, 1500-1965. London,
Methuen, 1967. 86 p.   [22/6 13/6
(non-net)]   391/.5   67-111706
     GT2290 .K45 MRR Alc.

HAIRDRESSING--DICTIONARIES.
Cox, James Stevens. An illustrated
dictionary of hairdressing and
wigmaking; London, Hairdressers'
Technical Council, 1966. xxiii, 359
p. [42/-]   646.72403   67-73133
     TT951 .C6 MRR Alc.

HAIRDRESSING--HISTORY.
Corson, Richard. Fashions in hair;
New York, Hilary House, 1969 [i.e.
1970, c1965] 701 p.   391/.5   78-
8334
     GT2290 .C6 1970 MRR Alc.

**HAIRDRESSING--UNITED STATES--
DIRECTORIES.**
Modern's market guide. 1967-
[Chicago] Modern beauty shop
magazine. 688/.5/0257   68-48983
     HD9999.B253U5 MRR Alc Latest
     edition

HAITI--BIBLIOGRAPHY.
Bissainthe, Max. Dictionnaire de
bibliographie haitienne.
Washington, Scarecrow Press, 1951.
x, 1052 p.   51-12164
     Z1531 .B5 MRR Alc.

HAITI--GAZETTEERS.
United States. Office of Geography.
Haiti; Washington, U.S. Govt. Print.
Off., 1956. iii, 41 p.   917.294   57-
60174
     F1913 .U5 MRR Alc.

HALL-MARKS.
Bradbury, Frederick, British and
Irish silver assay office marks, 1544-
1968. 12th ed. Sheffield, Northend,
1968. 93 p.   [24/-]   739.2/3/0278
78-391328
     NK7210 .B74 1968 MRR Alc.

Cutten, George Barton, The
silversmiths of Virginia, Richmond,
Dietz Press, 1952. xxiv, 259 p.
739.23   52-14077
     NK7112 .C86 MRR Alc.

Ensko, Stephen Guernsey Cook,
American silversmiths and their
marks. New York, Priv. print., 1927-
v.   739   27-13408
     NK7112 .E65 MRR Alc.

Jackson, Charles James, Sir, English
goldsmiths and their marks; 2d ed.,
rev. and enl. New York, Dover
Publications [1964, c1921] xvi, 747
p.   739.22742   64-18852
     NK7143 .J15 1964 MRR Alc.

Jacobs, Carl. Guide to American
pewter. New York, McBride, 1957.
216 p.   739.53388   56-12017
     NK8412 .J3 MRR Alc.

Kovel, Ralph M. A directory of
American silver, pewter, and silver
plate. New York, Crown Publishers
[1961]   352 p.   739.205873   60-8620

     NK7112 .K66 MRR Alc.

Laughlin, Ledlie Irwin. Pewter in
America. Boston, Houghton Mifflin
company, 1940. 2 v.   739   41-1939
     NK8412 .L3 MRR Alc.

Laughlin, Ledlie Irwin. Pewter in
America: its makers and their marks.
Barre, Mass., Barre Publishers, 1969-
71. 3 v. [27.50 per vol.]
739/.533/0973   77-86912
     NK8412 .L33 MRR Alc.

Macdonald-Taylor, Margaret Stephens,
ed. A dictionary of marks:
metalwork, furniture, ceramics.
London, Connoisseur [c1962] 318 p.
63-1876
     NK7210 .M25 1962a MRR Alc.

New York. Metropolitan Museum of Art.
Three centuries of French domestic
silver: New York, 1960. 2 v.
739.23744   60-9288
     NK7149 .N42 MRR Alc.

Stierling, Hubert, Der Silberschmuck
der Nordseekuste hauptsachlich in
Schleswig-Holstein. Neumunster, K.
Wachholtz, 1935-55. v.   56-41823

     NK7150 .S68 MRR Alc.

Thorn, C. Jordan. Handbook of
American silver and pewter marks;
New York, Tudor Pub. Co. [1949] xii,
289 p.   739.23   50-5385
     NK7210 .T5 MRR Alc.

Wyler, Seymour B. The book of old
silver, English, American, foreign,
New York, Crown publishers [c1937] x
p., 1 l., 447 p. incl. illus.,
plates.   739   37-24775
     NK7230 .W9 MRR Alc.

HALLUCINATIONS AND ILLUSIONS.
Mackay, Charles, Extraordinary
popular delusions and the madness of
crowds. London, G. G. Harrap [1956]
xxiv, 724 p.   301.15 133.7   57-1736
     AZ999 .M2 1956 MRR Alc.

HALLUCINOGENS--DICTIONARIES.
Lingeman, Richard R. Drugs from A to
Z: Rev. & updated, 2d ed. New York,
McGraw-Hill [1974] xxii, 310 p.
613.8/3/03   74-13363
     HV5804 .L54 1974 MRR Alc.

HAMBURG--COMMERCE--DIRECTORIES.
Hamburger Firmenhandbuch und
offizielles Borsenfirmenverzeichnis.
Hamburg, Hamburger Adressbuch-Verlag
Dumrath & Fassnacht Komm.-Ges.   54-
43648
     HF5173.H35 H3   MRR Alc Latest
     edition

HAMBURG--DIRECTORIES.
Hamburger Adressbuch. Hamburg. 53-
28343
     "Gegründet 1786."
     DD901.H23 H3 MRR Alc Latest
     edition

HAMBURG--INDUSTRIES--DIRECTORIES.
Hamburger Firmenhandbuch und
offizielles Borsenfirmenverzeichnis.
Hamburg, Hamburger Adressbuch-Verlag
Dumrath & Fassnacht Komm.-Ges.   54-
43648
     HF5173.H35 H3   MRR Alc Latest
     edition

HAMILTON, ALEXANDER, 1757-1804.
Mitchell, Broadus, Alexander
Hamilton: the revolutionary years.
New York, Crowell [1970] viii, 386
p. [10.00]   973.3/0924   B   70-106586

     E302.6.H2 M62 MRR Alc.

HAMILTON, ONT.--DIRECTORIES.
Vernon's city of Hamilton; Hamilton,
Ont., Vernon Directories Ltd.   54-
23489
     F1059.5.H2 V47   MRR Alc Latest
     edition

HAMPTON ROADS.
Hampton Roads Maritime Association,
Norfolk, Va. The ports of Greater
Hampton Roads annual. 1925-
Norfolk, Va.   28-31191
     HE554.H3 A25   MRR Alc Latest
     edition

HANDBOOKS, VADE-MECUMS, ETC.
see also Text-books

Ackermann, Alfred Seabold Eli,
Popular fallacies; 4th ed. London,
Old Westminster Press; sole
distributors, S. Marshall, 1950. xv,
843 p.   133.7 50-32195
   AZ999 .A3 1950 MRR Alc.

The Cadillac modern encyclopedia.
[1st ed.] New York, Cadillac Pub.
Co.; distributed by Derbibooks,
Secaucus, N.J. [1973] xiv, 1854 p.
[$24.95] 031 73-81377
   AG5 .C25 MRR Ref Desk.

Cowles volume library. 1968- New
York, Cowles Book Co. [etc.] 031/.02
77-7030
   AG5 .V62 MRR Alc Latest edition

Garrison, Webb B. How it started
Nashville, Abingdon Press [1972] 237
p. [$4.85] 390/.09 72-173951
   GT75 .G3 MRR Alc.

Garrison, Webb B. The ignorance
book, New York, Morrow, 1971. 250
p. [$6.85] 031/.02 70-135148
   AG106 .G3 MRR Alc.

The Guinness book of records. 1955-
[Enfield, Eng., etc., Guinness
Superlatives Ltd., etc.] £1.20
(single issue) 001.9/3 56-19118
   AG243 .G86 MRR Ref Desk Latest
   edition

Guinness book of world records. New
York, Sterling Pub. Co. [etc.] 032
64-4884
   AG243 .G87 MRR Ref Desk Latest
   edition

Laughlin, William H. Laughlin's fact
finder; West Nyack, N.Y., Parker
Pub. Co. [1969] viii, 30, 701 p.
[12.95] 031/.02 69-11218
   AG5 .L38 1969 MRR Alc.

The Lincoln library of essential
information; [1st]- ed.; 1924-
Columbus, Ohio [etc.] Frontier Press.
031 24-14708
   AG105 .L55 MRR Ref Desk Latest
   edition

McWhirter, Norris Dewar. Dunlop
illustrated encyclopedia of facts,
Garden City, N.Y., Doubleday [1969]
864 p. [8.95] 031/.02 68-59630
   AG6 .M34 MRR Ref Desk.

Stimpson, George William, Popular
questions answered, Detroit, Gale
Research Co., 1970. viii, 426 p.
031 74-109601
   AG195 .S74 1970 MRR Ref Desk.

HANDICAPPED.
see also Mentally handicapped

see also Physically handicapped

**HANDICAPPED--EDUCATION--CANADA--
DIRECTORIES.**
Ellingson, Careth. Directory of
facilities for the learning-disabled
and handicapped [1st ed.] New York,
Harper & Row [1972] xii, 624 p.
[$15.00] 371.9/045/0257 77-95952
   L901 .E5 1972 MRR Alc.

**HANDICAPPED--EDUCATION--UNITED STATES--
DIRECTORIES.**
Ellingson, Careth. Directory of
facilities for the learning-disabled
and handicapped [1st ed.] New York,
Harper & Row [1972] xii, 624 p.
[$15.00] 371.9/045/0257 77-95952
   L901 .E5 1972 MRR Alc.

HANDICAPPED--EMPLOYMENT--UNITED STATES.
Angel, Juvenal Londono, Employment
opportunities for the handicapped,
New York, World Trade Academy Press;
distributed by Simon & Schuster
[1969] 411 p. 331.5/9 67-22382
   HV3018 .A67 MRR Alc.

Arthur, Julietta K. Employment for
the handicapped; Nashville, Abingdon
Press [1967] 272 p. 331.590973 67-
11009
   HD7256.U5 A77 MRR Alc.

**HANDICAPPED--EMPLOYMENT--UNITED STATES--
BIBLIOGRAPHY.**
Wright, George Nelson.
Rehabilitation counselor functions:
annotated references Madison,
University of Wisconsin, Regional
Rehabilitation Research Institute,
1968. viii, 451 p. 016.3628/5 68-
63360
   HF7256.U6 W56 ser. 1, vol. 1 MRR
   Alc.

HANDICAPPED CHILDREN.
see also Socially handicapped children

**HANDICAPPED CHILDREN--EDUCATION--
BIBLIOGRAPHY.**
Goldberg, Icchok Ignacy, Selected
bibliography of special education
[New York, Teachers College, Columbia
University, 1967] vi, 126 p.
016.3719 67-19388
   Z5814.C52 G62 MRR Alc.

**HANDICAPPED CHILDREN--EDUCATION--
DIRECTORIES.**
Directory for exceptional children;
[1st]- ed.; 1954- Boston, P.
Sargent. 371.92058 54-4975
   LC4007 .D5 MRR Alc Latest edition

Ellingson, Careth. Directory of
facilities for the learning-disabled
and handicapped [1st ed.] New York,
Harper & Row [1972] xii, 624 p.
[$15.00] 371.9/045/0257 77-95952
   L901 .E5 1972 MRR Alc.

**HANDICAPPED CHILDREN--EDUCATION--
STATISTICS.**
United Nations Educational,
Scientific and Cultural Organization.
Statistics on special education.
[Paris, 1960] 154 p. 371.9083 60-
50763
   LA132 .U53 MRR Alc.

HANDICRAFT.
see also Jewelry making

see also Occupations

Audels do-it-yourself encyclopedia;
Illustrated ed. N[ew] Y[ork] T.
Audel [1963-66, v. 1, c1960] 2 v.
(1020 p.) 643.7 66-3696
   TT155 .A82 MRR Alc.

Popular mechanics do-it-yourself
encyclopedia. New York, Book
Division, Hearst Magazines [1968- v.
680/.2/02 68-3759
   TT155 .P75 MRR Alc.

HANDICRAFT--BIBLIOGRAPHY.
Harwell, Rolly M. Crafts for today:
ceramics, glasscrafting,
leatherworking, candlemaking, and
other popular crafts Littleton,
Colo., Libraries Unlimited, 1974.
211 p. 016.7455 73-92979
   Z6151 .H37 MRR Alc.

How-to-do-it books; 3d ed. rev. New
York, R. R. Bowker Co., 1963. xxi,
265 p. 016 63-15626
   Z7911 .H6 1963 MRR Alc.

Nueckel, Susan. Selected guide to
make-it, fix-it, do-it-yourself
books. New York, Fleet Press Corp.
[1973] 213 p. 016.643/7 72-82609

   Z6151 .N83 MRR Alc.

Smith, Frank Seymour. Know-how
books; London, Thames and Hudson
[1956] xi, 306 p. 028 57-17217
   Z1035.9 .S6 1956 MRR Alc.

HANDICRAFT--DICTIONARIES.
Practical encyclopedia of crafts.
New York, Sterling Pub. Co. [1970]
544 p. [$20.00] 745.5 71-126844
   TT155 .P88 MRR Alc.

HANDICRAFT--HANDBOOKS, MANUALS, ETC.
Swezey, Kenneth M. Formulas,
methods, tips, and data for home and
workshop, New York, Popular Science
Pub. Co. [1969] xvii, 691 p. [7.95]
745.5/02/02 68-54377
   TT153 .S88 MRR Alc.

HANDICRAFT--INDEXES.
Lovell, Eleanor Cook, comp. Index to
handicrafts, modelmaking, and
workshop projects, Boston, Faxon,
1936. 476 p. 016.6 36-27324
   Z7911 .L89 MRR Alc.

HANDICRAFT--UNITED STATES--DIRECTORIES.
American Crafts Council. Research &
Education Dept. Craft shops,
galleries, USA; [4th ed. New York]
American Crafts Council [1973] 214
p. 745.5/025/73 73-175467
   NK805 .A67 1973 MRR Alc.

HANDWRITING
see Writing

HANOVER--DIRECTORIES.
Adressbuch der Landeshauptstadt
Hannover. Hannover, W. Dorn Verlag.
72-622920
   DD901.H43 A7 MRR Alc Latest
   edition

HARBORS.
Hope, Ronald, ed. The shoregoer's
guide to world ports. London,
Maritime Press [c1963] vi, 340 p.
910.2 64-5135
   G140 .H6 MRR Alc.

Ports, dues, charges and
accommodation throughout the world.
London [etc.] G. Philip [etc.] 62-
5407
   Began publication in 1869.
   HE552 .P58 MRR Alc Latest edition

United States. Naval Oceanographic
Office. World port index. 1st-
ed.; 1953- Washington, For sale by
the Supt. of Docs., U.S. govt. Print.
Off. 58-60168
   HE552 .U49 MRR Alc Latest edition

HARBORS--DIRECTORIES.
Pielow, Colin L. Guide to port
entry; London, Shipping Guides
[c1971] xi, 590 p. 387.1/025 73-
168261
   HE551 .P5 MRR Alc.

HARBORS--YEARBOOKS.
Jane's freight containers. 1st-
ed.; 1968/69- New York, McGraw-Hill
Book Co. 380.5/3 74-2497
   TA1215 .J34 Sci RR Latest edition
   / MRR Alc Latest edition

Navis; annuaire de la marine
marchande, de la construction navale
et des ports maritimes. Paris, R.
Moreux. 56-27553
   HE730 .N35 MRR Alc Latest edition

Ports of the world. 1st- ed.; 1946-
London, Benn Bros, (Marine
Publications) Ltd. [etc.] 387.1058
48-3083
   HE552 .P6 MRR Alc Latest edition

HARBORS--CANADA--DIRECTORIES.
Canadian ports and seaway directory,
including United States ports on the
Great Lakes. [1st]- ed.; 1934-
Gardenvale, Quebec, National Business
Publications. 36-1220
   HE553 .C32 MRR Alc Latest edition

HARBORS--GREAT LAKES--DIRECTORIES.
Canadian ports and seaway directory,
including United States ports on the
Great Lakes. [1st]- ed.; 1934-
Gardenvale, Quebec, National Business
Publications. 36-1220
   HE553 .C32 MRR Alc Latest edition

HARBORS--ILLINOIS.
Interstate port handbook. [Chicago]
368.2 44-33741
   HE554.A5 I5 MRR Alc Latest edition

HARBORS--INDIANA.
Interstate port handbook. [Chicago]
368.2 44-33741
   HE554.A5 I5 MRR Alc Latest edition

HARBORS--UNITED STATES.
Custom house guide. New York. 99-
1545
   HE554.N5 C8 MRR Alc Latest edition

Interstate port handbook. [Chicago]
368.2 44-33741
   HE554.A5 I5 MRR Alc Latest edition

**HARDING, WARREN GAMALIEL, PRES. U.S.,
1865-1923.**
Sinclair, Andrew. The available man;
New York, Macmillan [1965] viii,
344 p. 923.173 65-14332
   E786 .S5 MRR Alc.

HARDWARE.
see also Tools

HARDWARE--CATALOGS.
Assembly engineering master catalog.
[Wheaton, Ill., Hitchcock Pub. Co.]
338.4/7/62188025 72-622720
   TJ1320 .H5 MRR Alc Latest edition
   / Sci RR Latest edition

HARDWARE--DIRECTORIES.
Hardware age. Verified list of
hardware wholesalers and other
related lists. New York. 20-13874
   TS403 .H3 MRR Alc Latest edition

HARDWARE--GREAT BRITAIN--DIRECTORIES.
Benn Brothers Limited, London.
Benn's hardware directory. London.
338.4/7/68302542 79-5145
   Began with vol. for 1963.
   TS403 .B4 MRR Alc Latest edition

HARDWARE--SOUTHERN STATES--DIRECTORIES.
Southern wholesalers' guide.
[Atlanta] W.R.C. Smith Pub. Co.
338.7/6/83 73-642885
   HD9745.U4 S68 MRR Alc Latest
   edition

HARDWARE--SOUTHWEST, NEW--DIRECTORIES.
Southern wholesalers' guide.
[Atlanta] W.R.C. Smith Pub. Co.
338.7/6/83 73-642885
   HD9745.U4 S68 MRR Alc Latest
   edition

HARDWARE--UNITED STATES--DIRECTORIES.
Southern wholesalers' guide.
[Atlanta] W.R.C. Smith Pub. Co.
338.7/6/83 73-642885
   HD9745.U4 S68 MRR Alc Latest
   edition

HARDWARE STORES--UNITED STATES--
DIRECTORIES.
Directory: home centers & hardware
chains, auto supply chains. 1974-
[New York, Business Guides, inc.]
[$59.00] 381/.45/629202573 74-
647308
HD9745.U4 D485 MRR Alc Latest
edition

HARDWOODS.
Hinckley, F. Lewis. Directory of the
historic cabinet woods. New York,
Crown Publishers [1960] 186 p. 749
59-14030
NK2260 .H52 MRR Alc.

HARPENDEN, ENG.--DIRECTORIES.
Kelly's directory of St. Albans.
Kingston upon Thames, Surrey [etc.]
53-28203
DA690.S13 K4 MRR Alc Latest
edition

HARRIMAN, FLORENCE JAFFRAY (HURST) 1870-
--BIBLIOGRAPHY.
United States. Library of Congress.
Manuscript Division. Florence
Jaffray Harriman; a register of her
papers in the Library of Congress.
Washington, 1958. 10 l. 012 58-
60045
Z663.34 .H3 MRR Alc.

HARRISON, BENJAMIN, PRES. U.S., 1833-
1901.
Sievers, Harry Joseph, Benjamin
Harrison. Chicago, H. Regnery Co.,
1952-[68] 3 v. 973.8/6/0924 B 67-
27226
E702 .S54 MRR Alc.

HARRISON, WILLIAM HENRY, PRES. U.S.,
1773-1841.
Green, James Albert, William Henry
Harrison, his life and times.
Richmond, Va., Garrett and Massie,
incorporated [c1941] xii p., 1 l.,
536 p. 923.173 41-25076
E392 .G8 MRR Alc.

HARROW ON THE HILL, ENG.--DIRECTORIES.
Kemps Harrow and district local
directory. London, Kemp's Printing &
Pub. Co. [etc.] 54-19437
DA690.H327 K4 MRR Alc Latest
edition

HARVARD UNIVERSITY--DIRECTORIES.
Harvard University. Directory of
faculty, professional and
administrative staff, and students.
1972/73- Cambridge. 378/.744/4 73-
640782
LD2123 .A43 MRR Alc Latest edition

HARVARD UNIVERSITY--REGISTERS.
Harvard alumni directory. 1910-
Cambridge [etc.] Harvard University
[etc.] 55-4974
LD2138 .H3 MRR Alc Latest edition

HARVARD UNIVERSITY. GRADUATE SCHOOL OF
DESIGN. LIBRARY.
Harvard University. Graduate School
of Design. Library. Catalogue of the
Library of the Graduate School of
Design, Harvard University. Boston,
Mass., G. K. Hall, 1968. 44 v.
019/.1 73-169433
Z5945 .H28 1968 MRR Alc (Dk 33)

HATFIELD, ENG.--DIRECTORIES.
Kelly's directory of St. Albans.
Kingston upon Thames, Surrey [etc.]
53-28203
DA690.S13 K4 MRR Alc Latest
edition

HATS.
Wilcox, Ruth Turner, The mode in
hats and headdress. New York,
Scribner [1959] xiii, 348 p. 391.4
59-14064
GT2110 .W5 1959 MRR Alc.

HAVILAND CHINA.
Schleiger, Arlene, Two hundred
patterns of Haviland china. [3d rev.
ed. Omaha, 1967- v. 738.2/7
67-6751
NK4399.H4 S34 MRR Alc.

HAWAII.
All about Hawaii. 1st- ed; 1875-
Honolulu, Honolulu star-bulletin
[etc.] 02-1171
DU621.T5 MRR Alc Latest Edition

HAWAII--BIOGRAPHY.
Men and women of Hawaii. [Honolulu]
Honolulu Star-Bulletin, Inc. [etc.]
820.0969 55-32260
DU624.9 .M38 MRR Biog Latest
edition

HAWAII--COMMERCE--DIRECTORIES.
Industrial buyer's guide. 1963-
[Honolulu] Hawaii Business and
Industry. 63-32442
HF5319.H3 I5 MRR Alc Latest
edition

State of Hawaii business directory.
1967- Honolulu, Kearney Co.
381/.45/00025969 66-18386
HF5319.H3 S73 MRR Alc Latest
edition

HAWAII--COMMERCE--ASIA--DIRECTORIES.
Hawaii overseas. 1968- [Honolulu]
Hawaii International Services Agency.
382/.025/969 73-626825
HF3161.H3 A3 MRR Alc Latest
edition

HAWAII--DESCRIPTION AND TRAVEL--1951- --
GUIDE-BOOKS.
American Automobile Association.
Southwestern tour book. Washington.
917.9 58-48032
F787 .A6 MRR Alc Latest edition

Fodor's Hawaii. 1969- New York, D.
McKay Co. 919.69/04/4 72-626454
DU622 .H33 MRR Alc Latest edition

Sutton, Horace. Aloha, Hawaii; [1st
ed.] Garden City, N.Y., Doubleday,
1967. x, 276 p. 919.69/04/4 67-
28639
DU622 .S97 MRR Alc.

HAWAII--DESCRIPTION AND TRAVEL--GUIDE-
BOOKS.
What to see, where to stay, where to
dine in Hawaii. [Washington] AAA.
919.69/04/4 72-622641
DU622 .A65 MRR Alc Latest edition

Younger, Ronald M. All the best in
Hawaii, New York, Dodd, Mead [1972]
vii, 333 p. [$7.95] 919.69/04/4
72-2341
DU622 .Y68 MRR Alc.

HAWAII--EXECUTIVE DEPARTMENTS--
DIRECTORIES.
Directory of State, county, and
Federal officials. 1973- Honolulu,
Legislative Reference Bureau. [$1.50]
353.9/969/002 74-644932
JK9330 .H38a MRR Alc Latest
edition

HAWAII--HISTORY.
Kuykendall, Ralph Simpson, Hawaii: a
history, Rev. ed. Englewood Cliffs,
N.J., Prentice-Hall [1961] 331 p.
996.9 61-8894
DU625 .K778 1961 MRR Alc.

HAWAII--MANUFACTURES--DIRECTORIES.
Industrial buyer's guide. 1963-
[Honolulu] Hawaii Business and
Industry. 63-32442
HF5319.H3 I5 MRR Alc Latest
edition

HAWAII--OFFICIALS AND EMPLOYEES--
DIRECTORIES.
Directory of State, county, and
Federal officials. 1973- Honolulu,
Legislative Reference Bureau. [$1.50]
353.9/969/002 74-644932
JK9330 .H38a MRR Alc Latest
edition

HAWAII--POLITICS AND GOVERNMENT.
Guide to government in Hawaii. 1st-
ed.; 1961- Honolulu, Legislative
Reference Bureau, University of
Hawaii. 353.9 62-62866
JQ6121 .G8 MRR Alc Latest edition

HAWAII--REGISTERS.
Directory of State, county, and
Federal officials. 1973- Honolulu,
Legislative Reference Bureau. [$1.50]
353.9/969/002 74-644932
JK9330 .H38a MRR Alc Latest
edition

Guide to government in Hawaii. 1st-
ed.; 1961- Honolulu, Legislative
Reference Bureau, University of
Hawaii. 353.9 62-62866
JQ6121 .G8 MRR Alc Latest edition

HAWAII--STATISTICS.
Hawaii. Dept. of Planning and
Economic Development. The State of
Hawaii data book; Honolulu, 1967.
63 p. 319.69 68-66724
HA329.1 .A5 MRR Alc.

HAWAIIAN ISLANDS--GAZETTEERS.
United States. Office of Geography.
Hawaiian Islands; Washington, U.S.
Govt. Print. Off., 1956. iii, 89 p.
919.69 56-63927
DU622 .U6 MRR Alc.

HAWAIIAN LANGUAGE--DICTIONARIES--
ENGLISH.
Pukui, Mary (Wiggin) Hawaiian
dictionary; Honolulu, University of
Hawaii Press, 1971. xxxix, 402, x,
188 p. [$15.00] 499/.4 70-142751
PL6446 .P795 MRR Alc.

HAWAIIAN NEWSPAPERS--HONOLULU.
Audit Bureau of Circulations. A.B.C.
blue book, [Chicago?] 071 45-53615

Z6951 .A67 MRR Alc Latest edition

HAWKES BAY, N.Z. (PROVINCIAL DISTRICT)--
COMMERCE--DIRECTORIES.
Universal business directory for
Hawkes Bay-East coast. Auckland,
Universal Business Directories. 51-
38052
HF5299 .H38 MRR Alc Latest edition

HAWTHORNE, NATHANIEL, 1804-1864--
DICTIONARIES, INDEXES, ETC.
O'Connor, Evangeline Maria (Johnson)
An analytical index to the works of
Nathaniel Hawthorne, Detroit, Gale
Research Co., Book Tower, 1967. 294
p. 813/.3/016 66-27844
PS1880 .O4 1967 MRR Alc.

HAYDN, JOSEPH, 1732-1809.
Hoboken, Anthony van, Discrepancies
in Haydn biographies; Washington,
Library of Congress, 1962. iii, 23
p. 62-64846
Z663.37 .A5 1962 MRR Alc.

HAYES, RUTHERFORD BIRCHARD, PRES. U.S.,
1822-1893.
Barnard, Harry, Rutherford B. Hayes,
and his America. [1st ed.]
Indianapolis, Bobbs-Merrill [1954]
606 p. 923.173 54-11942
E682 .B3 MRR Alc.

Williams, Charles Richard, The life
of Rutherford Birchard Hayes,
Boston, New York, Houghton Mifflin
company, 1914. 2 v. [$7.50] 14-
18560
E682 .W7 MRR Alc.

HAZARDOUS SUBSTANCES.
Meidl, James H. Hazardous materials
handbook Beverly Hills, Calif.,
Glencoe Press [1972] xviii, 349 p.
604/.7/0202 72-177437
TH9446.I47 M44 MRR Alc.

HEAD.
see also Mouth

HEAD-GEAR.
see also Costume

see also Hats

HEADS OF STATE.
Bidwell, Robin Leonard. The British
Empire and successor states, 1900-
1972; London, F. Cass [1974] xi,
156 p. [29.00 ($27.50 U.S.)]
351.2/09171/242 74-169172
JN248 .B52 1974 MRR Ref Desk.

Bidwell, Robin Leonard. The major
powers and western Europe, 1900-1971;
[London] F. Cass, [1973] xi, 297 p.
354/.4/002 72-92958
JN12 .B5 MRR Ref Desk.

Prosser, Michael H., comp. Sow the
wind, reap the whirlwind; New York,
Morrow, 1970. 2 v. (xviii, 1467 p.)
[$100.00] 341.1/08 73-118271
JX1977 .P728 MRR Alc.

Webster's biographical dictionary.
Springfield, Mass., G. & C. Merriam
Co. [1974] xxxvi, 1697 p. [$12.95]
920/.02 73-14908
CT103 .W4 1974 MRR Ref Desk.

HEADS OF STATE--BIOGRAPHY.
Spuler, Bertold, Regenten und
Regierungen der Welt. Wurzburg, A.
G. Ploetz [196- v. 63-5493
D11 .S78 MRR Alc.

HEADS OF STATE--REGISTERS.
The Cadillac modern encyclopedia.
[1st ed.] New York, Cadillac Pub.
Co.; distributed by Derbibooks,
Secaucus, N.J. [1973] xiv, 1954 p.
[$24.95] 031 73-81377
AG5 .C25 MRR Ref Desk.

HEADS OF STATE--REGISTERS--PERIODICALS.
United States. Central Intelligence
Agency. Chiefs of State and Cabinet
members of foreign governments.
[Washington] 354.0313/05 73-640502

JF37 .U5 MRR Ref Desk Latest
edition

HEALTH
see Hygiene

HEALTH BOARDS--UNITED STATES--
DIRECTORIES.
U. S. medical directory. Miami,
Fla., U.S. Directory Service.
610/.25/73 77-23067
R712.A1 U5 MRR Alc Latest edition
/ Sci RR Latest edition

HEALTH CARE
see Medical care

HEALTH EDUCATION--BIBLIOGRAPHY.
Educators guide to free health,
physical education and recreation
materials. 1st- ed.; 1968-
Randolph, Wis., Educators Progress
Service. 011 68-57948
Z6121 .E38 MRR Alc Latest edition

HEALTH FACILITIES.
see also Hospitals

HEALTH FACILITIES--UNITED STATES--DIRECTORIES.
U. S. medical directory. Miami, Fla., U.S. Directory Service. 610/.25/73   77-23057
R712.A1 U5 MRR Alc Latest edition / Sci RR Latest edition

HEALTH OF CHILDREN
see Children--Care and hygiene

HEALTH OF WORKERS
see Industrial hygiene

HEART--DISEASES.
Gould, Sylvester Emanuel, ed. Pathology of the heart and blood vessels, 3d ed. Springfield, Ill., Thomas [1968] xx, 1198 p.   616.1 67-16108
RC681 .G68 1968 MRR Alc.

HEAT ENGINEERING--HANDBOOKS, MANUALS, ETC.
American Society of Heating, Refrigerating and Air-Conditioning Engineers. ASHRAE handbook & product directory. 1973- New York. 697 73-644272
TH7011 .A4 MRR Alc Latest edition / Sci RR Latest edition

HEAT-ENGINES.
see also Gas and oil engines

HEATING--CATALOGS.
D E catalog directory. 1923- [Chicago, Medalist Publications, etc.]   22-21100
TH6112 .D6 Sci RR Latest edition / MRR Alc Latest edition

HEATING--EQUIPMENT AND SUPPLIES--CATALOGS.
M P C; Manhasset, N.Y., Hutton Pub. Co. 696/.00028 68-7522
Began with 1964 vol.
TH6010 .M2 MRR Alc Latest edition

HEBREW IMPRINTS--CATALOGS.
Paris. Bibliothèque nationale. Catalogue général des livres imprimés: Paris, 1965- v.   018/.1 67-52152
Z927 .P1857 MRR Alc (Dk33)

HEBREW LANGUAGE--DICTIONARIES--ENGLISH.
Brown, Francis, A Hebrew and English lexicon of the Old Testament, [Reprinted with corrections] Oxford, Clarendon Press [1962] xix, 1127 p.   66-33161
PJ4833 .B68 1962 MRR Alc.

Harkavy, Alexander, [Ozar leshon hamikra (romanized form)] New York, Hebrew publishing company, 1914. vi, 786, [2], 102 p.   14-11012
PJ4833 .H3 MRR Alc.

Jastrow, Marcus, A dictionary of the Targumim, the Talmud Babli and Yerushalmi, and the Midrashic literature, London, Luzac & co.; New York, G. P. Putnam's sons, 1903. 2 v.   12-34766
PJ5205 .J3 MRR Alc.

Rybak, Benjamin, Milon makif 'ivri-angli 1973- v.   73-952688
PJ4833 .R9 MRR Alc.

Scharfstein, Zevi, [Milon leshonenu (romanized form)] [New York, c1951] 304 p.   52-47510
PJ4833 .S36 MRR Alc.

Young, Robert, Analytical concordance to the Bible 22d American ed., rev. New York, Funk & Wagnalls [1955] ix, 1090, 93, 23, 51 p.   220.2 55-53398
BS425 .Y7 1955 MRR Alc.

HEBREW LANGUAGE--GLOSSARIES, VOCABULARIES, ETC.
Rosten, Leo Calvin, Leo Rosten's treasury of Jewish quotations. New York, McGraw-Hill [1972] xi, 716 p.   [$10.95]   808.88/2 72-298
PN6095.J4 R6 MRR Ref Desk.

HEBREW LANGUAGE, POST-BIBLICAL--DICTIONARIES--ENGLISH.
Harkavy, Alexander, [Ozar leshon hamikra (romanized form)] New York, Hebrew publishing company, 1914. vi, 786, [2], 102 p.   14-11012
PJ4833 .H3 MRR Alc.

Scharfstein, Zevi, [Milon leshonenu (romanized form)] [New York, c1951] 304 p.   52-47510
PJ4833 .S36 MRR Alc.

HEBREW LITERATURE.
see also Bible

HEBREW LITERATURE--BIBLIOGRAPHY.
Schwab, Moïse, Index of articles relative to Jewish history and literature published in periodicals, from 1665 to 1900. Augmented ed., New York, Ktav Pub. House [1971, i.e. 1972] xvi, 539, 409-613 p.   016.91/0039/24 74-114721
Z6366 .S413 MRR Alc.

HEBREW LITERATURE--HISTORY AND CRITICISM.
Waxman, Meyer, A history of Jewish literature. New York, T. Yoseloff [c1960] 5 v. in 6.   892.409 61-1793
PJ5008 .W323 MRR Alc.

HEBREW NEWSPAPERS--DIRECTORIES.
Encyclopaedia Judaica. [Jerusalem, Encyclopaedia Judaica; New York] Macmillan [c1971-72, v. 1, c1972] 16 v.   296/.03 72-177492
DS102.8 .E496 MRR Alc.

HEBREW PERIODICALS--DIRECTORIES.
Encyclopaedia Judaica. [Jerusalem, Encyclopaedia Judaica; New York] Macmillan [c1971-72, v. 1, c1972] 16 v.   296/.03 72-177492
DS102.8 .E496 MRR Alc.

HEBREW POETRY--HISTORY AND CRITICISM.
Yoder, Sanford Calvin, Bp., Poetry of the Old Testament. Scottdale, Pa., Herald Press, 1948. xix, 426 p.   223 48-9854
BS1405 .Y6 MRR Alc.

HEBREWS
see Jews

HEIDELBERG--DIRECTORIES.
Adressbuch der Stadt Heidelberg. Heidelberg, J. Hörning. 53-30583
DD901.H56 A7 MRR Alc Latest edition

HELDENSAGE--CONCORDANCES.
Gillespie, George T. A catalogue of persons named in German heroic literature (700-1600), including named animals and objects and ethnic names, Oxford, [Eng.] Clarendon Press, 1973. xxxvii, 166 p.   [£10.50 ($33.75 U.S.)]   831/.009 73-173463
PT204 .G5 1973 MRR Alc.

HELICOPTERS.
Lambermont, Paul Marcel. Helicopters and autogyros of the world Rev. ed. South Brunswick, Barnes [1970] xvi, 446 p.   [15.00]   629.133/35 74-112289
TL714 .L3 1970 MRR Alc.

HELLENISM.
Mahaffy, John Pentland, Sir, The social life of the Greeks. London, New York, Macmillan, 1896-1907. 2 v. mrr01-35
DF77 .M218 MRR Alc.

HELSINKI--STATISTICS.
Helsinki. Tilastotoimisto. Tilastollinen vuosikirja. 59- 1967- Helsinki. 72-626523
HA1449.H4 A3 MRR Alc Latest edition

HERALDRY.
see also Emblems, National

see also Knights and knighthood

Boutell, Charles, Boutell's heraldry. [Rev. ed.] London, New York, F. Warne [1973] xii, 355 p.   [£4.95 ($20.00 U.S.)]   929.6/0942 73-75030
CR21 .B7 1973 MRR Alc.

Hope, A. Guy. Symbols of the nations, Washington, Public Affairs Press [1973] 348 p.   [$10.00]   929.8 73-82015
JC345 .H66 MRR Alc.

Lynch-Robinson, Christopher Henry, Sir, bart., Intelligible heraldry; London, Macdonald [1948] 205 p.   929.6 49-2435
CR21 .L9 MRR Alc.

Pine, Leslie Gilbert. The genealogist's encyclopedia, New York, Weybright and Talley [1969] 360 p.   [12.50]   929.1/03 78-84622
CS9 .P48 1969b MRR Alc.

Pine, Leslie Gilbert. International heraldry, [1st ed.] Rutland, Vt., C. E. Tuttle Co. [1970] 244 p.   [6.00]   929.6 72-109405
CR191 .P55 1970b MRR Alc.

Volborth, Carl Alexander von. Heraldry of the world, 1st English ed.] London, Blandford Press, 1973. 251 p.   [£2.40]   929.6 74-164622
CR23 .V6313 MRR Alc.

HERALDRY--DICTIONARIES.
Franklyn, Julian. An encyclopaedic dictionary of heraldry, [1st ed.] Oxford, New York, Pergamon Press [1969] xv, 367 p.   929.6/03 69-19596
CR13 .F7 1969 MRR Alc.

Gough, Henry, A glossary of terms used in heraldry New ed. [Detroit] Gale Research Co., 1966. xxviii, 659 p.   929.6/03 66-28259
CR1618 .G6 1966 MRR Alc.

Puttock, A. G. A dictionary of heraldry and related subjects, Baltimore, Genealogical Pub. Co., 1970. 256 p.   [$10.00]   929.6/03 76-137421
CR13 .P8 1970b MRR Alc.

HERALDRY--GREAT BRITAIN.
The Armorial who is who. 1st- ed.; 1961/62- Edinburgh, The Armorial. 63-34814
CR1619 .A7 MRR Alc Latest edition

Boutell, Charles, Boutell's heraldry. [Rev. ed.] London, New York, F. Warne [1973] xii, 355 p.   [£4.95 ($20.00 U.S.)]   929.6/0942 73-75030
CR21 .B7 1973 MRR Alc.

Burke's genealogical and heraldic history of the peerage, baronetage and knightage. London, Burke's Peerage Ltd. [etc.] 35-32046
Began publication in 1826.
CS420 .B85 MRR Biog Latest edition

Debrett's peerage, baronetage, knightage, and companionage ... Kingston upon Thames, Surrey, Kelly's Directories [etc.] 929.72 42-17925
CS420 .D32 MRR Biog Latest edition

Fairbairn, James, comp. Fairbairn's crests of the families of Great Britain and Ireland, Rutland, Vt., C. E. Tuttle Co. [1968] 2 v. in 1 (ix, 644 p.)   929.8 68-25887
CR57.G7 F2 1968b MRR Alc.

Gough, Henry, A glossary of terms used in heraldry New ed. [Detroit] Gale Research Co., 1966. xxviii, 659 p.   929.6/03 66-28259
CR1618 .G6 1966 MRR Alc.

Milton, Roger. The English ceremonial book; Newton Abbot [Eng.] David & Charles [1972] 216 p.   [£3.50]   391/.022/0942 72-185055
CR492 .M5 MRR Alc.

Weightman, Alfred Edwin. Heraldry in the Royal Navy; Aldershot [Eng.] Gale and Polden, 1957. xviii, 514 p.   623.825 60-36156
VB335.G7 W4 MRR Alc.

HERALDRY--GREAT BRITAIN--BIBLIOGRAPHY.
Filby, P. William, American & British genealogy & heraldry; a selected list of books. Chicago, American Library Association, 1970. xix, 184 p.   [10.00]   016.9291/097 75-106200
Z5311 .F55 MRR Alc.

HERALDRY--IRELAND.
Fairbairn, James, comp. Fairbairn's crests of the families of Great Britain and Ireland, Rutland, Vt., C. E. Tuttle Co. [1968] 2 v. in 1 (ix, 644 p.)   929.8 68-25887
CR57.G7 F2 1968b MRR Alc.

HERALDRY--SCOTLAND.
Anderson, William, The Scottish nation; Edinburgh [etc.] A. Fullarton & co. [1859]-63. 3 v. in 9.   27-11180
CT813 .A6 MRR Biog.

HERALDRY--UNITED STATES.
Crozier, William Armstrong, ed. Crozier's general armory; Baltimore, Genealogical Pub. Co., 1966. 155 p.   929.8 66-22143
CR1209 .C82 1966 MRR Alc.

HERALDRY--UNITED STATES--BIBLIOGRAPHY.
Filby, P. William, American & British genealogy & heraldry; a selected list of books. Chicago, American Library Association, 1970. xix, 184 p.   [10.00]   016.9291/097 75-106200
Z5311 .F55 MRR Alc.

HERB GARDENING.
Loewenfeld, Claire. The complete book of herbs and spices / New York : Putnam, [1974] 313 p., [4] leaves of plates :   [$14.95]   581.6/3 74-78005
SB351.H5 L67 MRR Alc.

HERBS.
Grieve, Maud. A modern herbal; New York, Hafner Pub. Co., 1959. 2 v. (xvi, 888 p.)   581.6303 59-15624
QK9 .G7 1959 MRR Alc.

Loewenfeld, Claire. The complete book of herbs and spices / New York : Putnam, [1974] 313 p., [4] leaves of plates :   [$14.95]   581.6/3 74-78005
SB351.H5 L67 MRR Alc.

Loewenfeld, Claire. Herbs, health and cookery, [1st American ed.] New York, Hawthorn Books [1967] 320 p.   641.6 66-22312
TX819.H4 L6 1967 MRR Alc.

HERBS--HISTORY.
Coats, Alice M. Flowers and their
histories. [New ed.] London, Black,
1968. xiii, 346 p. [42/-]
635.9/09 68-119585
SB404.5 .C6 1968 MRR Alc.

HERBS--THERAPEUTIC USE
see Botany, Medical

HEREDITY.
see also Genetics

HERESIES AND HERETICS--MODERN PERIOD,
1500-
see Sects

HERODOTUS--DICTIONARIES, INDEXES, ETC.
Powell, John Enoch, A lexicon to
Herodotus 2d ed. Hildesheim, Georg
Olms, 1966. x, 392 p. [DM18.50]
938/.03 68-100081
PA4007 .Z8 1966 MRR Alc.

HEROES.
see also Mythology

HEROES IN LITERATURE--DICTIONARIES.
Gillespie, George T. A catalogue of
persons named in German heroic
literature (700-1600), including
named animals and objects and ethnic
names. Oxford, [Eng.] Clarendon
Press, 1973. xxxvii, 166 p. [£10.50
($33.75 U.S.)] 831/.009 73-173463
PT204 .G5 1973 MRR Alc.

HERPETOLOGY.
see also Reptiles

HERRICK, ROBERT, 1591-1674--
CONCORDANCES.
MacLeod, Malcolm Lorimer, A
concordance to the poems of Robert
Herrick. New York, Oxford university
press, 1936. xviii p., 1 l., 299 p.
821.43 36-24656
PR3513.A3 M2 1936 MRR Alc.

HERTFORDSHIRE, ENG.--DIRECTORIES.
Kelly's directory of Watford.
Kingston upon Thames, Surrey [etc.]
Kelly's Directories Limited. 53-
28498
DA670.H5 K45 MRR Alc Latest
edition

HESSE--COMMERCE--DIRECTORIES.
Landes-Adressbuch Hessen für
Industrie, Handel, Handwerk und
Gewerbe. Wiesbaden [etc.] Hessische
Adressbuch-GMBH. 53-29245
Began publication in 1948.
HC287.H4 L3 MRR Alc Latest edition

HESSE--INDUSTRIES--DIRECTORIES.
Landes-Adressbuch Hessen für
Industrie, Handel, Handwerk und
Gewerbe. Wiesbaden [etc.] Hessische
Adressbuch-GMBH. 53-29245
Began publication in 1948.
HC287.H4 L3 MRR Alc Latest edition

HEXAPODA
see Insects

HIBERNATION.
see also Animals, Habits and behavior
of

HIEROCLES, SOSSIANUS, PROCONSUL OF
BITHYNIA, FL. 293-303 A.D.
Philostratus, Flavius. The life of
Apollonius of Tyana, the Epistles of
Apollonius and the Treatise of
Eusebius; London, W. Heinemann; New
York, The Macmillan co., 1912. 2 v.
921.9 13-5590
PA3612 .P4 1912 MRR Alc.

HIEROGLYPHICS.
see also Alphabet

see also Picture-writing

HIGH-FIDELITY SOUND SYSTEMS--
PERIODICALS.
Stereo directory & buying guide.
[New York, Ziff-Davis Pub. Co.]
[$1.50] 338.4/7/621393302573 73-
641957
TK7881.8 .S73 MRR Alc Latest
edition

HIGH SCHOOL STUDENTS--UNITED STATES--
DIRECTORIES.
Merit's who's who among American high
school students. v. 1- 1966/67-
[Chicago, Merit Pub. Co.]
373.1/8/02573 68-43796
LA2311 .M4 MRR Biog Latest edition

HIGH SCHOOLS.
see also Education, Secondary

HIGH SCHOOLS--EUROPE--DIRECTORIES.
Leitfaden der höheren Lehranstalten.
4. Ausg. München-Pasing,
Wirtschaftsverlag Klug (1967). 245
p. [28.00] 78-433478
L914.5 .L4 1967 MRR Alc.

HIGH SCHOOLS--UNITED STATES--
DIRECTORIES.
The College blue book. [1st]- 1923-
New York [etc.] CCM Information
Corp. [etc.] 378.73 24-223
LA226 .C685 MRR Ref Desk Latest
edition

Gertler, Diane (Bochner) Directory:
public elementary and secondary day
schools, 1968-69, [Washington] U.S.
National Center for Educational
Statistics; [for sale by the Supt. of
Docs., U.S. Govt. Print. Off., 1970-
v. [2.00] 371/.01/02573 70-
607482
L901 .G39 MRR Alc.

HIGHER EDUCATION
see Education, Higher

HIGHLANDS OF SCOTLAND--DESCRIPTION AND
TRAVEL--GUIDE-BOOKS.
Murray, William Hutchison. The
companion guide to the West Highlands
of Scotland; [5th ed.] London,
Collins [1973, c1968] 415 p.
[£2.75] 914.11/04/81 73-178899
DA880.H7 M95 MRR Alc.

Ward, Lock and Company, ltd. The
Highlands of Scotland, 13th ed.
London [1961] 191 p. 914.1 62-
41052
DA880.H7 W34 1961 MRR Alc.

HIGHWAY DEPARTMENTS--UNITED STATES--
DIRECTORIES.
American Association of State Highway
Officials. A A S H O reference book
of member department personnel and
committees. Washington.
625.7/06/273 72-626460
TE1 .A623 MRR Alc Latest edition

HIGHWAY SAFETY
see Traffic safety

HIGHWAY TRANSPORT WORKERS--LANGUAGE
(NEW WORDS, SLANG, ETC.)
Tak, Montie. Truck talk; [1st ed.]
Philadelphia, Chilton Book Co. [1971]
xiv, 191 p. [$5.95] 388.3/24/014
72-169583
PE3727.H5 T3 MRR Alc.

HIGHWAYS
see Roads

HIKING.
see also Backpacking

see also Trails

Colwell, Robert. Introduction to
foot trails in America. [Harrisburg,
Pa.] Stackpole Books [1972] 221 p.
[$5.95] 917.3/04/924 74-178603
E158 .C76 MRR Alc.

HILDESHEIM--DIRECTORIES.
Einwohnerbuch der kreisfreien Stadt
Hildesheim. Hildesheim,
Adressbuchverlag A. Lax. 72-626705
DD901.H66 E5 MRR Alc Latest
edition

HINDUISM.
see also Buddha and Buddhism

HINDUISM--DICTIONARIES.
Walker, George Benjamin, The Hindu
world; New York, Praeger [1968] 2
v. [$35.00] 294.5/03 68-26182
BL1105 .W34 1968 MRR Alc.

HINDUSTANI LANGUAGE--DICTIONARIES--
ENGLISH.
Fallon, S. W., A new Hindustani-
English dictionary. Banaras, E. J.
Lazarus and co.; London, Trubner and
co., 1879. 3 p. l., xxiv p., 2 l.,
1216. ix p. 06-18861
PK1986 .F3 MRR Alc.

The Student's practical dictionary,
12th ed., thoroughly rev. and
improved. Allahabad, R. N. Lal,
1956. 667 p. 73-289068
PK1986 .S7 1956 MRR Alc.

HIPPIES--UNITED STATES.
Acton, Jay. Mug shots: who's who in
the new earth. New York, World Pub.
[1972] 244 p. [$8.95] 920/.073
77-174672
CT220 .A27 1972 MRR Biog.

HISPANOS
see Mexican Americans

HISTOLOGY.
see also Microscope and microscopy

Ham, Arthur Worth, Histology 6th
ed. Philadelphia, Lippincott [1969]
xviii, 1037 p. 611/.018 69-14855
QM551 .H147 1969 MRR Alc.

HISTORIANS.
Bowman, Francis John. A handbook of
historians and history writing.
Dubuque, Iowa, W. C. Brown Co., 1951.
110 p. 907 51-8249
D13 .B57 MRR Alc.

HISTORIANS, AMERICAN.
Cline, Howard Francis, comp.
Historians of Latin America in the
United States, 1965; Durham, N.C.,
Published for the Conference on Latin
American History [by] Duke University
Press, 1966. xiv, 105 p.
980.0720922 66-22489
F1409.8.A2 C55 MRR Biog.

Gay, Peter, A loss of mastery;
Berkeley, University of California
Press [1966] viii, 164 p.
974.02072 67-10869
E175.45 .G3 MRR Alc.

Skotheim, Robert Allen. American
intellectual histories and
historians. Princeton, N.J.,
Princeton University Press, 1966.
xi, 326 p. 973.072 66-11960
E175.45 .S5 MRR Alc.

Wish, Harvey, The American
historian; New York, Oxford
University Press, 1960. 366 p.
973.072 60-13202
E175 .W5 MRR Alc.

HISTORIANS, ARGENTINE.
Cutolo, Vicente Osvaldo.
Historiadores argentinos y
americanos, 1963-65. Buenos Aires,
Casa Pardo, 1966. xxiii, 447 p. 66-
93008
F1409.8.A2 C8 MRR Biog.

HISTORIANS, LATIN AMERICAN.
Cutolo, Vicente Osvaldo.
Historiadores argentinos y
americanos, 1963-65. Buenos Aires,
Casa Pardo, 1966. xxiii, 447 p. 66-
93008
F1409.8.A2 C8 MRR Biog.

HISTORIC AMERICAN BUILDINGS SURVEY.
Historic American Buildings Survey.
Documenting a legacy; [Washington,
Library of Congress, 1973] 269-294
p. 720/.973 73-17422
Z663 .D6 MRR Alc.

HISTORIC BUILDINGS--UNITED STATES.
Daniel, Jean Houston. Executive
mansions and capitols of America.
Waukesha, Wis., Country Beautiful;
distributed by Putnam, New York
[1969] 290 p. [25.00] 725/.1 71-
77604
E159 .D3 MRR Alc.

Historic American Buildings Survey.
Historic American Buildings Survey;
New York, B. Franklin [1971] vii,
470 p. 720.9/73 73-160016
NA707 .H45 MRR Alc.

Historic houses of America, New
York, American Heritage Pub. Co.
[1971] 320 p. [$6.95]
917.3/03/924 78-149725
E159 .H7 MRR Alc.

United States. Library of Congress.
Subject Cataloging Division. Outline
of the Library of Congress
classification. 2d ed. Washington,
1970. 21 p. 025.4 76-607324
Z663.78 .C52 1970 MRR Alc.

United States. Office of Archeology
and Historic Preservation. Advisory
list to the National register of
historic places, 1969. Washington,
U.S. National Park Service [1970]
vii, 311 p. 917.3/03 77-607631
E159 .U555 MRR Alc.

HISTORIC SITES--EUROPE--GUIDE-BOOKS.
A Horizon guide: great historic
places of Europe; New York, American
Heritage Pub. Co.; book trade
distribution by McGraw-Hill [1974]
384 p. 914/.03/55 74-10941
D909 .H73 MRR Alc.

HISTORIC SITES--GREAT BRITAIN.
Fedden, Henry Romilly, The National
Trust guide; London, Cape, 1973.
688 p. [£4.50] 914.2/04/85 73-
177113
DA660 .F33 MRR Alc.

HISTORIC SITES--UNITED STATES.
Boatner, Mark Mayo, Landmarks of the
American Revolution; [Harrisburg,
Pa.] Stackpole Books [1973] 608 p.
[$10.00] 917.3/03/3 73-6964
E159 .B67 MRR Alc.

Illustrated guide to the treasures of
America. Pleasantville, N.Y.,
Reader's Digest Association [1974]
624 p. [$11.97] 917.3/03 73-83812

E159 .I44 MRR Alc.

National parks & monuments; New 1973
revision. Menlo Park, Calif., 1973.
140 p. [$1.95] 917.3/04/92 73-
163780
E160 .N26 MRR Alc.

HISTORICAL DRAMA.
see also English drama--Early modern
and Elizabethan, 1500-1600

HISTORICAL FICTION.
Kaye, James Ross, Historical fiction
chronologically and historically
related. Chicago, Ill., Snowden
publishing company, 1920. x, [2],
747 p. 20-15352
    PN3441 .K3 MRR Alc.

HISTORICAL FICTION--BIBLIOGRAPHY.
Buckley, John Anthony. A guide to
British historical fiction. London,
G. G. Harrap & company, 1912. vi, 7-
182 p. 13-2128
    Z5917.H6 B85 MRR Alc.

Hotchkiss, Jeanette. American
historical fiction and biography for
children and young people. Metuchen,
N.J., Scarecrow Press. 1973. 318 p.
016.813/73/03 73-13715
    Z1236 .H73 MRR Alc.

Hotchkiss, Jeanette. European
historical fiction and biography for
children and young people. 2d ed.
Metuchen, N.J., Scarecrow Press,
1972. 272 p. 028.52 72-1597
    Z5917.H6 H6 1972 MRR Alc.

Irwin, Leonard Bertram, A guide to
historical fiction for the use of
schools, libraries, and the general
reader. 10th ed., new and rev.
Brooklawn, N.J., McKinley Pub. Co.,
1971. vii, 255 p. [$10.00]
016.823/081 70-31631
    Z5917.H6 I7 1971 MRR Alc.

Luther, Arthur, Land und Leute in
deutscher Erzählung; 3. ganzlich
veranderte und erganzte Aufl.
Stuttgart, Hiersemann, 1954. 555 p.
55-19035
    Z5917.H6 L97 1954 MRR Alc.

Nield, Jonathan, A guide to the best
historical novels and tales. London,
E. Mathews & Marrot, 1929. xxvi,
[2], 424 p. 29-16250
    Z5917.H6 N6 1929 MRR Alc.

HISTORICAL FICTION--INDEXES.
McGarry, Daniel D. World historical
fiction guide: an annotated
chronological, geographical and
topical list of selected historical
novels, 2d ed. Metuchen, N.J.,
Scarecrow Press, 1973. xxi, 629 p.
016.80983/081 73-4367
    Z5917.H6 M3 1973 MRR Alc.

HISTORICAL FICTION, AMERICAN.
Dickinson, A. T. American historical
fiction, 3d ed. Metuchen, N.J.,
Scarecrow Press, 1971. 380 p.
016.813/03 78-146503
    PS374.H5 D5 1971 MRR Alc.

HISTORICAL FICTION, AMERICAN--
BIBLIOGRAPHY.
Coan, Otis Welton. America in
fiction; 5th ed. Palo Alto, Calif.,
Pacific Books, 1967. viii, 232 p.
016.813/00803 66-28118
    Z1361.C6 C6 1966 MRR Alc.

Dickinson, A. T. American historical
fiction, 3d ed. Metuchen, N.J.,
Scarecrow Press, 1971. 380 p.
016.813/03 78-146503
    PS374.H5 D5 1971 MRR Alc.

Van Derhoof, Jack Warner. A
bibliography of novels related to
American frontier and colonial
history. Troy, N.Y., Whitston Pub.
Co., 1971. xii, 501 p. 016.813/03
70-150333
    Z1231.F4 V3 MRR Alc.

HISTORICAL FICTION, ENGLISH--
BIBLIOGRAPHY.
Van Derhoof, Jack Warner. A
bibliography of novels related to
American frontier and colonial
history. Troy, N.Y., Whitston Pub.
Co., 1971. xii, 501 p. 016.813/03
70-150333
    Z1231.F4 V3 MRR Alc.

HISTORICAL RECORDS SURVEY--BIBLIOGRAPHY.
Child, Sargent Burrage, Check list
of Historical Records Survey
publications; Baltimore,
Genealogical Pub. Co., 1969. vi, 110
p. 016.973/08 79-17126
    Z1223.Z7 C52 MRR Alc.

HISTORICAL RESEARCH.
Gray, Wood, Historian's handbook,
2d ed. Boston, Houghton Mifflin
[1964] vii, 88 p. 907.2 64-2075
    D13 .G78 1964 MRR Alc.

Hockett, Homer Carey, The critical
method in historical research and
writing. New York, Macmillan [1955]
330 p. 973.072 55-13664
    E175.7 .H6446 MRR Alc.

Kitson Clark, George Sidney Roberts,
Guide for research students working
on historical subjects, 2nd ed.
London, Cambridge U.P., 1968. 63 p.
[7/6 ($1.75)] 907/.2 75-403504
    D16 .K58 1968 MRR Alc.

Kitson Clark, George Sidney Roberts,
Guide to research facilities in
history in the universities of Great
Britain and Ireland. 2d ed.
Cambridge [Eng.] University Press,
1965. 54 p. 65-24953
    D16.4.G7 K5 1965 MRR Alc.

Poulton, Helen J. The historian's
handbook: [1st ed.] Norman,
University of Oklahoma Press [1972]
xi, 304 p. 016.9 71-165774
    Z6201 .P65 MRR Alc.

HISTORICAL SOCIETIES--CANADA--
DIRECTORIES.
Directory of historical societies and
agencies in the United States and
Canada. 1956- Nashville, Tenn.
[etc.] American Association for State
and Local History. 970.62 56-4164
    E172 .A538 MRR Ref Desk Latest
    edition / MRR Ref Desk Latest
    edition

HISTORICAL SOCIETIES--GREAT BRITAIN--
BIBLIOGRAPHY.
Mullins, Edward Lindsay Carson. A
guide to the historical and
archaeological publications of
societies in England and Wales, 1901-
1933; London, Athlone P., 1968.
xiii, 850 p. [10/10/-] 016.9142
79-367032
    Z5055.G6 M8 MRR Alc.

Mullins, Edward Lindsay Carson.
Texts and calendars; London, Royal
Historical Society, 1958. xi, 674 p.
016.942 a 59-1596
    Z2016 .M8 MRR Alc.

HISTORICAL SOCIETIES--SCOTLAND--
BIBLIOGRAPHY.
Matheson, Cyril, A catalogue of the
publications of Scottish historical
and kindred clubs and societies,
Aberdeen, Milne and Hutchinson, 1928.
viii, 232 p. 28-23797
    Z2061 .T34 MRR Alc.

Terry, Charles Sanford, A catalogue
of the publications of Scottish
historical and kindred clubs and
societies, Glasgow, J. MacLehose and
sons, 1909. xiii, 253 p. 10-1995
    Z2061 .T32 MRR Alc.

HISTORICAL SOCIETIES--UNITED STATES.
Whitehill, Walter Muir, Independent
historical societies, [Boston] The
Boston Athenaeum; distributed by
Harvard University Press, 1962.
xviii, 593 p. 973.06973 63-1190
    E172 .W5 MRR Alc.

HISTORICAL SOCIETIES--UNITED STATES--
BIBLIOGRAPHY.
Griffin, Appleton Prentiss Clark,
Bibliography of American historical
societies 2d ed., rev. and enl.
[Washington, Govt. print. off., 1907]
1374 p. 08-7356
    Z1236 .G86 MRR Alc.

Wasserman, Paul. Museum media; 1st
ed. Detroit, Gale Research Co.,
1973. vii, 455 p. 011 73-16335
    Z5052 .W35 MRR alc.

HISTORICAL SOCIETIES--UNITED STATES--
DIRECTORIES.
Directory of historical societies and
agencies in the United States and
Canada. 1956- Nashville, Tenn.
[etc.] American Association for State
and Local History. 970.62 56-4164
    E172 .A538 MRR Ref Desk Latest
    edition / MRR Ref Desk Latest
    edition

HISTORICAL SOCIETY OF SOUTHERN
CALIFORNIA--BIBLIOGRAPHY.
Hager, Anna Marie. The Historical
Society of Southern California
bibliography of all published works,
1884-1957; Los Angeles, Historical
Society of Southern California, 1958.
xix, 183 p. 016.9794 58-59890
    Z1261 .H22 MRR Alc.

HISTORICAL SOCIOLOGY.
    see also Culture

HISTORIOGRAPHY.
Barnes, Harry Elmer, A history of
historical writing, Norman,
University of Oklahoma press, 1937.
x [-, 3 l., [3]-434 p., 1 l. 907
37-30365
    D13 .B32 MRR Alc.

Barzun, Jacques, The modern
researcher Rev. ed. New York,
Harcourt, Brace & World [1970] xvii,
430 p. [8.50] 907.2 72-115861
    D13 .B334 1970 MRR Alc.

Bowman, Francis John. A handbook of
historians and history writing.
Dubuque, Iowa, W. C. Brown Co., 1951.
110 p. 907 51-8249
    D13 .B57 MRR Alc.

Fitzsimons, Matthew A., ed. The
development of historiography, Port
Washington, N.Y., Kennikat Press
[1967, c1954] 471 p. 907 66-25913
    D13 .F53 1967 MRR Alc.

Nevins, Allan, The art of history;
Washington, Published for the Library
of Congress by the Gertrude Clarke
Whittall Poetry and Literature Fund;
[for sale by the Supt. of Docs., U.S.
Govt. Print. Off.] 1967. v, 38 p.
907/.2 67-61610
    Z663.293 .A7 MRR Alc.

HISTORIOGRAPHY--HANDBOOKS, MANUALS, ETC.
Gray, Wood, Historian's handbook,
2d ed. Boston, Houghton Mifflin
[1964] vii, 88 p. 907.2 64-2075
    D13 .G78 1964 MRR Alc.

HISTORY.
    see also Anthropo-geography

    see also Ethnology

    see also Riots

    see also World history

HISTORY--BIBLIOGRAPHY.
American Historical Association.
Guide to historical literature. New
York, Macmillan, 1961. xxxv, 962 p.
016.9 61-7602
    Z6201 .A55 MRR Alc.

Berkowitz, David Sandler,
Bibliographies for historical
researchers. Trial ed. Waltham,
Mass., 1969. 421 l. 016.016/9 76-
9931
    Z6201 .B43 1969 MRR Alc.

Bibliografia storica nazionale. Bari
[etc.] Gius. Laterza & Figli. 52-
23151
    Began publication in 1939.
    Z6201 .B54 MRR Alc Full set

Boehm, Inge P. Reference works:
history and related fields, Santa
Barbara, Calif., ABC-Clio Press,
1967. vi, 58 p. 016.0287 67-20730
    Z1035 .B655 MRR Alc.

The Foreign affairs 50-year
bibliography; New York, Published
for the Council on Foreign Relations
by R. R. Bowker Co., 1972. xxviii,
936 p. 016.327/09/04 75-163904
    Z6461 .F62 MRR Alc.

Handbook for history teachers. 2nd
ed., rewritten and enlarged. London,
Methuen Educational, 1970. iii-xv,
716 p. [£2.00] 907 72-186140
    D16.2 .H23 1970 MRR Alc.

Hepworth, Philip. How to find out in
history: [1st ed.] Oxford, New York
[etc.] Pergamon, 1966. xiv, 242 p.
[30/- (20/- lp.)] 016.9 65-29063
    D16.2 .H4 1966 MRR Alc.

International bibliography of
historical sciences. 1st- year;
1926- Paris, A. Colin [etc.] 016.9
31-15829
    Z6205 .I61 MRR Alc Full set

Irwin, Leonard Bertram, A guide to
historical reading: non-fiction; 9th
rev. ed. Brooklawn, N.J., McKinley
Pub. Co., 1970. vii, 276 p. 016.9
77-16961
    Z6201 .I7 1970 MRR Alc.

Kuehl, Warren F., Dissertations in
history; [Lexington] University of
Kentucky Press, 1965-[72] 2 v.
016.9 65-11832
    Z6201 .K8 MRR Ref Desk.

Lancaster, Joan Cadogan, comp.
Bibliography of historical works
issued in the United Kingdom, 1946-
1956, [London] University of London,
Institute of Historical Research,
1957. xxii, 388 p. 016.9 a 58-
2313
    Z2016 .L3 MRR Alc.

List of doctoral dissertations in
history now in progress at
universities in the United States.
Washington [etc.] 016.9 10-12162
    Z5055.U49 L7 MRR Ref Desk Partial
    set

Mason, John Brown, Research
resources; Santa Barbara, Calif.,
ABC-Clio, 1968- v. [3.00]
016.327/.09/04 68-9685
    Z7161 .M36 MRR Ref Desk.

Poulton, Helen J. The historian's
handbook; [1st ed.] Norman,
University of Oklahoma Press [1972]
xi, 304 p. 016.9 71-165774
    Z6201 .P65 MRR Alc.

HISTORY--BIBLIOGRAPHY. (Cont.)
Scott, Franklin Daniel, Guide to the
American historical review, 1895-
1945;   46-25831
    E172 .A60 1944, vol. 1 MRR Ref
    Desk.

HISTORY--BIBLIOGRAPHY--CATALOGS.
Biblioteca Nacional de Antropología
e Historia. Catálogos de la
Biblioteca Nacional de Antropología
e Historia. Mexico. Boston, G. K.
Hall, 1972. 10 v.   74-225152
    Z885.A1 B5 1972 MRR Alc (Dk 33)

Great Britain. Foreign Office.
Library. Catalogue of the Foreign
Office Library, 1926-1968. Boston,
G. K. Hall, 1972. 8 v.   019/.1 73-
160726
    Z921 .G682 1972 MRR Alc (Dk 33)

HISTORY--BIOGRAPHY
see Biography

HISTORY--BOOK REVIEWS.
Magill, Frank Northen, Great events
from history; modern European series.
[1st ed.] Englewood Cliffs, N.J.,
Salem Press [1973] 3 v. (xxi, 1779
p.)   940   73-179232
    D209 .M29 MRR Alc.

HISTORY--COLLECTIONS.
Snyder, Louis Leo, ed. The
imperialism reader; Princeton, N.J.,
Van Nostrand [1962] 619 p.   321.03
62-3115
    JC359 .S65 MRR Alc.

HISTORY--DICTIONARIES.
Bolton, Mary, Dictionary of dates,
London, New York, Foulsham [1958]
125 p.   902   59-20715
    D11 .B649 MRR Alc.

Brewer, Ebenezer Cobham, The
historic note-book: with an appendix
of battles. Detroit, Republished by
Gale Research Co., 1966. x, 997 p.
903   66-23191
    D9 .B76 1966 MRR Alc.

Canning, John, ed. 100 great events
that changed the world, New York,
Hawthorn Books [1966, c1965] 672 p.
902.02   66-25543
    D9 .C3 1966a MRR Alc.

Dictionary of world history; London,
Nelson, 1973. xxvii, 1720 p.
[£15.00]   903   74-174563
    D9 .D55 MRR Ref Desk.

Dunner, Joseph. Handbook of world
history; New York, Philosophical
Library [1967] 1011 p.   909/.003
66-10222
    D9 .D88 MRR Alc.

Everyman's dictionary of dates. 6th
ed. London, Dent; New York, Dutton,
1971. viii, 518 p. [£1.60]   903
73-177861
    D9 .D5 1971 MRR Alc.

Harbottle, Thomas Benfield,
Dictionary of historical allusions,
[2d ed.] London, S. Sonnenschein &
co., ltd.; New York, E. P. Dutton &
co., 1904. 2 p. l., 306 p.   05-1641

    D9 .H26 MRR Alc.

Haydn, Joseph Timothy, Haydn's
dictionary of dates and universal
information relating to all ages and
nations, New York, Dover
Publications [1969] vi, 1605 p.
[25.00]   903   68-9154
    D9 .H45 1969 MRR Alc.

Keller, Helen Rex. The dictionary of
dates, New York, The Macmillan
company, 1934. 2 v.   902 34-39180

    D9 .K4 MRR Alc.

Mourre, Michel, Dictionnaire
d'histoire universelle. Paris,
Éditions universitaires, 1968. 2 v.
(2368 p.) [175.00]   71-376184
    D9 .M89 MRR Alc.

Worldmark encyclopedia of the
nations. [4th ed.] New York,
Worldmark Press, [1971] 5 v.
910/.3   76-152128
    G103 .W65 1971 MRR Ref Desk.

HISTORY--DICTIONARIES--GERMAN.
Haberkern, Eugen, Hilfswörterbuch
für Historiker; 2., neubearb. und
erweiterte Aufl. Bern, Francke,
1964. 678 p.   66-39385
    D9 .H2 1964 MRR Alc.

HISTORY--ERRORS, INVENTIONS, ETC.
Thornton, Willis. Fable, fact and
history. New York, Greenberg [1957]
242 p.   804   57-5807
    D10 .T45 MRR Alc.

HISTORY--JUVENILE LITERATURE--
BIBLIOGRAPHY.
Handbook for history teachers. 2nd
ed., rewritten and enlarged. London,
Methuen Educational, 1970. iii-xv,
716 p. [£2.00]   907   72-186140
    D16.2 .H23 1970 MRR Alc.

HISTORY--OUTLINES, SYLLABI, ETC.
Dupuy, Richard Ernest, The
encyclopedia of military history;
[1st ed.] New York, Harper & Row
[1970] xiii, 1406 p. [20.00]
355/.0009   74-81871
    D25.A2 D8 MRR Ref Desk.

Langer, William Leonard, An
encyclopedia of world history; 5th
ed., rev. and enl. Boston, Houghton
Mifflin, 1972. xxxix, 1569 p.
[$17.50]   902/.02 72-186219
    D21 .L27 1972 MRR Ref Desk.

HISTORY--PERIODICALS.
The American historical review. v. 1-
Oct. 1895-   Washington [etc.]
973.05   05-18244
    E171 .A57 MRR Ref Desk Indexes
    only

HISTORY--PERIODICALS--BIBLIOGRAPHY.
Boehm, Eric H., Historical
periodicals; Santa Barbara, Calif.,
Clio Press, 1961. xviii, 618 p.
016.905   59-8783
    Z6205 .B6 MRR Alc.

Caron, Pierre, ed. World list of
historical periodicals and
bibliographies. Oxford [Eng.]
International committee of historical
sciences, 1939 [i.e. 1940] xiv, [2],
391, [1] p.   016.905   41-4203
    Z6201.A1 C3 MRR Alc.

Kirby, John Lavan. A guide to
historical periodicals in the English
language, [London] Historical
Association, 1970. 48 p. [6/-]
016.91003   70-22365
    Z6205 .K55 MRR Alc.

HISTORY--PERIODICALS--INDEXES.
Historical abstracts. v. 1-   Mar.
1955-   [Santa Barbara, Calif., etc.]
909.8082   56-56304
    D299 .H5 MRR Alc Full set

International bibliography of
historical sciences. 1st-   year;
1926-   Paris, A. Colin [etc.] 016.9
31-15829
    Z6205 .I61 MRR Alc Full set

HISTORY--PHILOSOPHY.
Gay, Peter, A loss of mastery;
Berkeley, University of California
Press [1966] viii, 164 p.
974.02072   67-10969
    E175.45 .G3 MRR Alc.

HISTORY--SOCIETIES, ETC.
American Historical Association.
Annual report. 1889-   Washington,
Smithsonian Institution Press [etc.]
04-18261
    E172 .A60 MRR Ref Desk Partial set

HISTORY--SOURCES--BIBLIOGRAPHY.
Hale, Richard Walden, ed. Guide to
photocopied historical materials in
the United States and Canada.
Ithaca, N.Y., published for the
American Historical Association [by]
Cornell University Press [1961]
xxxiv, 241 p.   016.9   61-17269
    Z6209 .H3 MRR Alc.

Oesterley, Hermann, Wegweiser durch
die literatur der urkundensammlungen,
Berlin, G. Reimer, 1885-86. 2 v.
03-7358
    CD995 .O3 MRR Alc.

HISTORY--STUDY AND TEACHING.
Cantor, Norman F. How to study
history New York, Crowell [1967] x,
274 p.   807   67-14303
    D16.2 .C32 MRR Alc.

Handbook for history teachers. 2nd
ed., rewritten and enlarged. London,
Methuen Educational, 1970. iii-xv,
716 p. [£2.00]   907   72-186140
    D16.2 .H23 1970 MRR Alc.

Hepworth, Philip. How to find out in
history: [1st ed.] Oxford, New York
[etc.] Pergamon, 1966. xiv, 242 p.
[30/- (20/- lp.)]   016.9   65-29063
    D16.2 .H4 1966 MRR Alc.

HISTORY--STUDY AND TEACHING--AUDIO-
VISUAL AIDS.
Handbook for history teachers. 2nd
ed., rewritten and enlarged. London,
Methuen Educational, 1970. iii-xv,
716 p. [£2.00]   907   72-186140
    D16.2 .H23 1970 MRR Alc.

HISTORY--STUDY AND TEACHING (HIGHER)--
GREAT BRITAIN.
Kitson Clark, George Sidney Roberts,
Guide to research facilities in
history in the universities of Great
Britain and Ireland. 2d ed.,
Cambridge [Eng.] University Press,
1965. 54 p.   65-24953
    D16.4.G7 K5 1965 MRR Alc.

HISTORY--YEARBOOKS.
The Americana annual; 1923-   New
York, Chicago, Americana Corporation
[etc.]   031   23-10041
    AE5 .A55 MRR Alc Full set

The Annual register of world events;
1758-   [London] Longman [etc.] 04-
17979
    D2 .A7 MRR Alc Latest edition

Britannica book of the year. 1938-
Chicago, Encyclopaedia Britannica,
inc.   032   38-12082
    AE5 .E364 MRR Alc Latest edition

Current events year book and world
gazetteer. Dehra Dun, EBD Pub. &
Distributing Co. [etc.]   sa 63-1073
Began in 1958.
    D410 .C75 MRR Alc Latest edition

Enciclopedia vniversal ilvstrada
evropeo-americana; Barcelona, J.
Espasa [1907?-30] 70 v. in 72.   036
32-1302
    AE61 .E6 MRR Alc.

Encyclopedia year book; 1947-   [New
York] Grolier Society. 909.82   48-
171
    D410 .S83 MRR Alc Latest edition

Le Livre de l'année. Montréal,
Grolier Limitée [etc.]   52-20762
    AP21 .L53 MRR Alc Latest edition

The New international year book;
1907-   New York [etc.] Funk &
Wagnalls Co.   08-19148
    AE5 .I64 MRR Alc Full set

News dictionary. 1964-   New York,
Facts on File.   65-17649
    D410 .N44 MRR Alc Latest edition

What they said. 1969-   [Beverly
Hills, Calif.] Monitor Book Co.
901.9/4   74-111080
    D410 .W46 MRR Ref Desk Full set

The World year book and current
affairs. Delhi, Malhotra Bros.   72-
627184
    AY1057.E53 W6   MRR Alc Latest
    edition

The Year book. London, Grolier
Society, ltd.   901.9/4   72-9618
    D410 .Y43 MRR Alc Latest edition

HISTORY, ANCIENT.
see also Archaeology

see also Bible

see also Civilization, Ancient

Breasted, James Henry, The conquest
of civilization, New York, London,
Harper & brothers, 1938. xii, 669 p.
930   38-27362
    D59 .B78 1938 MRR Alc.

The Cambridge ancient history. 3rd
ed. London, Cambridge University
Press, 1970-   v.   [£6.00 (v. 1,
pt. 1) ($19.50 U.S.)]   913   75-85719

    D57 .C252 MRR Alc.

The Cambridge ancient history ...
Cambridge [Eng.] The University
press, 1923-39. 12 v.   23-11667
    D57 .C25 MRR Alc.

Finegan, Jack, Light from the
ancient past; [2d ed. Princeton,
N.J.] Princeton University Press,
1959. xxxvii, 638 p.   220.93 59-
11072
    BS635 .F5 1959 MRR Alc.

Herodotus. Herodotus, London, W.
Heinemann; New York, G. P. Putnam's
sons, 1921-24. 4 v.   21-6980
    PA3612 .H5 1921 MRR Alc.

Larousse encyclopedia of ancient and
medieval history. London, P. Hamlyn
[1963] 413 p.   64-363
    D59 .H553 1963a MRR Alc.

Polybius. The histories, London, W.
Heinemann; New York, G. P. Putnam's
sons, 1922-27. 6 v.   23-2839
    PA3612 .P8 1922 MRR Alc.

HISTORY, ANCIENT--BIBLIOGRAPHY.
Bengtson, Hermann, Introduction to
ancient history. Berkeley,
University of California Press, 1970.
viii, 213 p. [$7.50]   016.93 78-
118685
    Z6202 .B413 MRR Alc.

HISTORY, ANCIENT--BIBLIOGRAPHY. (Cont.)
Rounds, Dorothy. Articles on
antiquity in Festschriften, an index;
Cambridge, Harvard University Press,
1962. 560 p.   62-7193
    Z6202 .R6 MRR Alc.

HISTORY, ANCIENT--CHRONOLOGY.
Bickerman, Elias Joseph, Chronology
of the ancient world London, Thames
& Hudson, 1968. 253 p. [57/6]
529/.32 68-78121
    D54.5 .B5 MRR Alc.

Ehrich, Robert W., ed. Chronologies
in Old World archaeology. Chicago,
University of Chicago Press [1965]
xii, 557 p. 930.02 65-17296
    D54.5 .E4 1965 MRR Alc.

HISTORY, ANCIENT--DICTIONARIES.
Lexikon der alten Welt. Zurich,
Stuttgart, Artemis Verlag (1965) xv
p., 3524 columns with maps. [DM
280.00 Subscription price DM 245.00]
930/.03 67-105898
    D54 .L48 MRR Alc.

HISTORY, CHURCH
see Church history

HISTORY, ECONOMIC
see Economic history

HISTORY, MODERN.
see also Civilization, Modern

see also Renaissance

The Cambridge modern history. New
York, The Macmillan company; London,
Macmillan & co., ltd., 1902-12. 13
v. and atlas. 04-21616
    D208 .C17 MRR Alc.

Larousse encyclopedia of modern
history. [1st ed.] New York, Harper
& Row [1964] 405 p. 909 64-14384

    D209 .H5153 MRR Alc.

Magill, Frank Northen, Great events
from history: modern European series.
[1st ed.] Englewood Cliffs, N.J.,
Salem Press [1973] 3 v. (xxi, 1779
p.) 940 73-178232
    D209 .M29 MRR Alc.

The New Cambridge modern history.
Cambridge [Eng.] University Press,
1957-   v. 940.2 57-14935
    D208 .N4 MRR Alc.

Palmer, Robert Roswell, A history of
the modern world, 3d ed. New York,
Knopf, 1965. xiv, 996, xxxv p. 909
65-11962
    D209 .P26 1965 MRR Alc.

**HISTORY, MODERN--19TH CENTURY--
BIBLIOGRAPHY.**
Halstead, John P. Modern European
imperialism; Boston, G. K. Hall,
1974. 2 v. 016.90908 73-19511
    Z6204 .H35 MRR Alc.

**HISTORY, MODERN--19TH CENTURY--
BIBLIOGRAPHY--CATALOGS.**
Institut für Zeitgeschichte, Munich.
Bibliothek. Landerkatalog. Boston,
G. K. Hall, 1967. 2 v. 016.90908
72-191851
    Z6204 .I37 MRR Alc (Dk 33)

**HISTORY, MODERN--19TH CENTURY--FILM
CATALOGS.**
London. National Film Archive.
Catalogue. London, British Film
Institute, 1951- v. 792.93
791.4085 52-4264
    PN1998 .L58 MRR Alc.

HISTORY, MODERN--20TH CENTURY.
see also World War, 1939-1945

Emerson, Edwin, Hoover and his
times: Garden City, N.Y., Garden
City publishing company, inc., 1932.
xvi p., 1 l., 632 p. 923.173 32-
25411
    E801 .E75 MRR Alc.

Fontaine, André. History of the
Cold War. [1st American ed.] New
York, Pantheon Books [1968-69] 2 v.
327.1/09/04 67-19180
    D421 .F613 MRR Alc.

Quigley, Carroll. Tragedy and hope:
New York, Macmillan [c1966] xi, 1348
p. 309.104 65-13589
    D421 .Q5 MRR Alc.

United States. Library of Congress.
Legislative reference service.
Abstracts of postwar literature.
[Washington] Library of Congress,
Legislative reference service, 1943-
v. 910.53144 44-6264
    Z663.6 .A73 MRR Alc.

United States. Library of Congress.
Legislative reference service.
Postwar abstracts, July 1942 to June,
1943. [Washington] Legislative
reference service, Library of
Congress, 1943. 3 v. 940.53114 43-
16029
    Z663.6 .P6 MRR Alc.

**HISTORY, MODERN--20TH CENTURY--
BIBLIOGRAPHY.**
Halstead, John P. Modern European
imperialism; Boston, G. K. Hall,
1974. 2 v. 016.90908 73-19511
    Z6204 .H35 MRR Alc.

**HISTORY, MODERN--20TH CENTURY--
BIBLIOGRAPHY--CATALOGS.**
Institut für Zeitgeschichte, Munich.
Bibliothek. Landerkatalog. Boston,
G. K. Hall, 1967. 2 v. 016.90908
72-191851
    Z6204 .I37 MRR Alc (Dk 33)

Stuttgart. Bibliothek für
Zeitgeschichte. Bibliothek für
Zeitgeschichte--Weltkriegsbücherei,
Stuttgart:alphabetischer Katalog.
Boston, G. K. Hall, 1968. 11 v. 74-
223544
    Z6209 .S85 1968 MRR Alc (Dk 33)

Stuttgart. Bibliothek für
Zeitgeschichte. Bibliothek für
Zeitgeschichte--Weltkriegsbücherei,
Stuttgart: systematischer Katalog.
Boston, G. K. Hall, 1968. 20 v. 74-
225445
    Z6204 .S8 1968 MRR Alc (Dk 33)

**HISTORY, MODERN--20TH CENTURY--
CHRONOLOGY.**
The Times in review; New York, Arno
Press, 1970-73 [v. 1, 1973; v. 5,
1970] 5 v. 909.82 74-139439
    D427 .T5 MRR Alc.

**HISTORY, MODERN--20TH CENTURY--
DICTIONARIES.**
Burickson, Sherwin, comp. Concise
dictionary of contemporary history.
New York, Philosophical Library
[1959] viii, 216 p. 909.82 59-997

    D419 .B8 MRR Alc.

Laqueur, Walter Ze'ev, A dictionary
of politics / Rev. ed. New York :
Free Press, 1974, c1973. 565 p. ;
[$14.95] 320.9/04 74-9232
    D419 .L36 1974 MRR Alc.

**HISTORY, MODERN--20TH CENTURY--FILM
CATALOGS.**
London. National Film Archive.
Catalogue. London, British Film
Institute, 1951- v. 792.93
791.4085 52-4264
    PN1998 .L58 MRR Alc.

HISTORY, MODERN--1945-
The Times history of our times:
London, Weidenfeld and Nicolson
[1971] 416 p. [£6.00] 909.82 78-
882862
    D840 .L57 1971b MRR Alc.

HISTORY, MODERN--1945- --BIBLIOGRAPHY.
Krikler, Bernard. A reader's guide
to contemporary history. London,
Weidenfeld & Nicolson [1972] 259 p.
[£3.50] 016.90982 73-150568
    Z6204 .K7 MRR Alc.

Universal Reference System. Current
events and problems of modern
society; Princeton, N.J., Princeton
Research Pub. Co. [1969] xx, 935 p.
016.90982 68-57821
    Z7161 .U64 vol. 5 MRR Alc.

**HISTORY, MODERN--1945- --PICTORIAL
WORKS.**
Whitney, David C. The trials and
triumphs of two dynamic decades,
Chicago, J. G. Ferguson Pub. Co.;
distributed by Doubleday [1968] 320
p. 909.82/022/2 68-17666
    D840 .W45 MRR Alc.

HISTORY, MODERN--1945- --SOURCES.
Trefousse, Hans Louis, ed. The cold
war: a book of documents. New York,
Putnam [1965] xxi, 296 p. 327.08
65-13298
    D839.3 .T67 MRR Alc.

HISTORY, MODERN--ABSTRACTS.
Historical abstracts. v. 1-   Mar.
1955-   [Santa Barbara, Calif., etc.]
909.8082 56-56304
    D299 .H5 MRR Alc Full set

HISTORY, MODERN--BIBLIOGRAPHY.
Roach, John Peter Charles. A
bibliography of modern history;
London, Cambridge U.P., 1968. xxiv,
388 p. [30/-] 016.9402 67-11528
    Z6204 .R62 MRR Alc.

HISTORY, MODERN--DICTIONARIES.
Harper encyclopedia of the modern
world; [1st ed.] New York, Harper &
Row [1970] xxxii, 1271 p. [$17.50]
903 73-81879
    D205 .H35 1970 MRR Ref Desk.

Hyams, Edward S. A dictionary of
modern revolution New York,
Taplinger Pub. Co. [1973] 322 p.
[$9.95] 335.43/03 73-6175
    HX17 .H9 1973 MRR Alc.

Palmer, Alan Warwick. A dictionary
of modern history, 1789-1945,
Philadelphia, Dufour Editions, 1964.
vii, 314 p. 909.003 64-18500
    D299 .P32 1964 MRR Alc.

HISTORY, MODERN--SOURCES.
Stearns, Raymond Phineas, ed.
Pageant of Europe: Rev. ed. New
York, Harcourt, Brace & World [1961]
1072 p. 940.2082 61-10710
    D5.5 .S8 1961 MRR Alc.

HISTORY, NATURAL
see Natural history

HISTORY AND SCIENCE
see Science and civilization

HISTORY IN ART.
Taft, Robert, Artists and
illustrators of the Old West, 1850-
1900. New York, Scribner, 1953.
xviii, 400 p. 709.78 53-7577
    N6510 .T27 MRR Alc.

HITLER, ADOLF, 1889-1945.
Bullock, Alan Louis Charles. Hitler,
a study in tyranny. [4th impression,
with revisions] London, Odhams Press
[1959] 776 p. 923.143 60-51960
    DD247.H5 B85 1959 MRR Alc.

HOBBIES.
Newgold, Bill. Guide to modern
hobbies: arts, and crafts. New York,
D. McKay Co. [1960] 289 p. 790.2
60-9564
    GV1201 .N42 MRR Alc.

HOBBIES--BIBLIOGRAPHY.
How-to-do-it books: 3d ed. rev. New
York, R. R. Bowker Co., 1963. xxi,
265 p. 016 63-15626
    Z7911 .H6 1963 MRR Alc.

Lovell, Eleanor Cook, comp. Index to
handicrafts, modelmaking, and
workshop projects. Boston, Faxon,
1936. 476 p. 016.6 36-27324
    Z7911 .L89 MRR Alc.

Smith, Frank Seymour. Know-how
books: London, Thames and Hudson
[1956] xl, 306 p. 028 57-17217
    Z1035.9 .S6 1956 MRR Alc.

HOCKEY.
Hollander, Zander. The complete
encyclopedia of ice hockey : Rev.
ed. Englewood Cliffs, N.J. :
Prentice-Hall [1974] xi, 702 p. :
[$14.95] 796.9/62/03 73-15019
    GV847.8.N3 H6 1974 MRR Alc.

Ronberg, Gary. The hockey
encyclopedia / New York : Macmillan,
1974. 392 p. : [$14.95]
796.9/62/03 73-21287
    GV847 .R62 MRR Alc.

Styer, Robert A. The encyclopedia of
hockey. New and rev. ed. South
Brunswick, A. S. Barnes [1973] 412
p. [$12.50] 796.9/62/03 72-5182
    GV847 .S76 1973 MRR Alc.

HOCKEY--BIOGRAPHY.
Kariher, Harry C., Who's who in
hockey New Rochelle, N.Y., Arlington
House [1973] 189 p. 796.9/62/0922
B 73-11868
    GV848.5.A1 K37 MRR Biog.

Pro and senior hockey guide. St.
Louis, Sporting news. 796.9/62 68-
44188
    GV848.S3 P7 MRR Alc Latest edition

HOCKEY--STATISTICS.
Styer, Robert A. The encyclopedia of
hockey. New and rev. ed. South
Brunswick, A. S. Barnes [1973] 412
p. [$12.50] 796.9/62/03 72-5182
    GV847 .S76 1973 MRR alc.

HOCKEY CLUBS.
Pro and senior hockey guide. St.
Louis, Sporting news. 796.9/62 68-
44188
    GV848.S3 P7 MRR Alc Latest edition

HOLDING COMPANIES--EUROPE--DIRECTORIES.
Who owns whom. Continental edition.
1st-   ed.; 1961/62- London, O. W.
Roskill. 63-24027
    HG4132.Z5 W5 MRR Alc Latest
    edition

**HOLDING COMPANIES--GREAT BRITAIN--
DIRECTORIES.**
Who owns whom. U. K. edition.
London, O. W. Roskill. 59-52911
    Began publication in 1958.
    HG4135.Z5 W5 MRR Alc Latest
    edition

HOLDING COMPANIES--UNITED STATES--DIRECTORIES.
Directory of corporate affiliations of major national advertisers. Skokie, Ill., National Register Pub. Co. 67-5728
HG4057 .A219   MRR Alc Latest edition

HOLIDAY DECORATIONS.
see also Christmas decorations

HOLIDAY DECORATIONS--DICTIONARIES.
Stevenson, Violet W. The encyclopedia of floristry New York, Drake Publishers [1973] 160, 96 p. [$9.95]   745.92/03 73-3102
SB449 .S716 1973 MRR Alc.

HOLIDAYS.
see also Christmas

Brand, John. Observations on the popular antiquities of Great Britain: Arranged, rev., and greatly enl., London, G. Bell and sons, 1900-02. 3 v.   04-11295
DA110 .B83 MRR Alc.

Chambers, Robert, The book of days; Detroit, Gale Research Co., 1967. 2 v.   902/.02 67-13009
DA110 .C52 1967 MRR Alc.

Dobler, Lavinia G. National holidays around the world. New York, Fleet Press Corp. [1968] 234 p. [5.95]   394.26 66-16525
GT3930 .D64 MRR Alc.

Donovan, John. The businessman's international travel guide. New York, Stein and Day [1971] ix, 253 p. [$7.85] 910/.202 76-163347
G153 .D6 1971 MRR Alc.

Douglas, George William, The American book of days; New York, H. W. Wilson Co., 1948. xxii, 697 p.   394.26973 48-28210
GT4803 .D6 1948 MRR Alc.

Gaer, Joseph, Holidays around the world. [1st ed.] Boston, Little, Brown [1953] 212 p.   394.26 52-12639
GT3930 .G2 MRR Alc.

Hazeltine, Mary Emogene, Anniversaries and holidays, 2d ed., completely revised Chicago, American library association 1944. xix, 316 p.   394.26 44-53464
Z5710 .H42 1944 MRR Alc.

Hovey, E. Paul, comp. The treasury for special days and occasions; [Westwood, N.J.] Revell [1961] 317 p.   808.88 61-9238
PN6083 .H73 MRR Alc.

Hutchison, Ruth Shepherd, Every day's a holiday [1st ed.] New York, Harper [1951] xiv, 304 p.   394.26 51-9099
GT3930 .H85 MRR Alc.

Morgan Guaranty Trust Company of New York. Bank and public holidays throughout the world. New York. 72-626359
GT3930 .G8 MRR Ref Desk Latest edition

Schoyer's vital anniversaries. New London, Conn. [etc.] W. Schoyer. 902 50-1815
Began publication with issue for 1948.
D11 .S36 MRR Alc Latest edition

Spicer, Dorothy Gladys. The book of festivals, New York, N.Y., The Woman's press, 1937. xiv, 429 p.   394.269 37-23629
GT3930 .S58 MRR Alc.

Van Buren, Maud, Quotations for special occasions, New York, The H. W. Wilson company, 1938. 201 p.   808.8 38-27833
PN6084.C3 V3 MRR Alc.

HOLIDAYS--BIBLIOGRAPHY.
Hazeltine, Mary Emogene, Anniversaries and holidays, 2d ed., completely revised Chicago, American library association 1944. xix, 316 p.   394.26 44-53464
Z5710 .H42 1944 MRR Alc.

HOLIDAYS--JUVENILE LITERATURE.
Ickis, Marguerite, The book of festivals and holidays the world over. New York, Dodd, Mead [1970] ix, 164 p. [$5.00] 394.2 70-129957
GT3932 .I27 MRR Alc.

HOLIDAYS--POETRY.
Cole, William, ed. Poems for seasons and celebrations. [1st ed.] Cleveland, World Pub. Co. [1961] 191 p.   808.81 (J) 61-12012
PS595.H6 C6 MRR Alc.

HOLIDAYS--SONGS AND MUSIC.
The Oxford book of carols, London, Oxford university press, H. Milford [1931] xxix, 491, [1] p.   783.65 33-29080
M2065 .O9 1931 MRR Alc.

HOLIDAYS--UNITED STATES.
Chases' calendar of annual events. 1958- Flint, Mich., Apple Tree Press. 57-14540
GT4803 .C48 MRR Ref Desk Latest Edition

Krythe, Maymie Richardson. All about American holidays. [1st ed.] New York, Harper [1962] 275 p.   394.26973 61-6450
GT4803 .K75 MRR Alc.

Myers, Robert J. Celebrations; the complete book of American holidays, [1st ed.] Garden City, N.Y., Doubleday, 1972. x, 386 p.   394.2/6973 77-163086
GT4803.A2 M84 MRR Alc.

HOLLAND, SOUTH (PROVINCE)--REGISTERS.
Provinciale almanak voor Zuid-Holland. Alphen aan den Rijn, N.Samsom n.v. 46-40227
Publication began with issue for 1889?
JN5999.H6 A4 MRR Alc Latest edition

HOLOCAUST, JEWISH--BIBLIOGRAPHY.
Robinson, Jacob, Guide to Jewish history under Nazi impact. New York [Yivo Institute for Jewish Research] 1960. xxxi, 425 p.   016.940535693 61-65976
Z6207.W8 R56 MRR Alc.

HOLY SCRIPTURES
see Bible

HOME.
see also Family
see also Marriage

HOME ECONOMICS.
see also Consumer education
see also Cookery
see also Food
see also Food service
see also Furniture
see also Household appliances

Cruse, Heloise. Heloise's housekeeping hints, Englewood Cliffs, N.J., Prentice-Hall [1962] 208 p.   640 62-20632
TX158 .C79 MRR Alc.

HOME ECONOMICS--BIBLIOGRAPHY.
Vicaire, Georges, Bibliographie gastronomique; [2d ed.] London, D. Verschoyle, Academic and Bibliographical Publications, 1954. [6] p., facsim.: xviii p., 972 columns.   54-6692
Z5776.G2 V5 1954 MRR Alc.

HOME ECONOMICS--EQUIPMENT AND SUPPLIES.
Household equipment 6th ed. New York, Wiley [1970] xiv, 540 p.   643/.6 76-116772
TX298 .H68 1970 MRR Alc.

HOME ECONOMICS--HANDBOOKS, MANUALS, ETC.
United States. Dept. of Agriculture. Consumers all. [Washington, For sale by the Superintendent of Documents, U.S. Govt. Print. Off., 1965] xiv, 496 p.   agr65-386
S21. A35 1965 MRR Alc.

HOME PURCHASE
see House buying

HOME STUDY COURSES
see Correspondence schools and courses

HOMERUS. ILIAS--CONCORDANCES.
Prendergast, Guy Lushington. A complete concordance to the Iliad of Homer. London, Longmans, Green, and co., 1875. 3 p. l., 416 p.   03-15393
PA4209 .P7 MRR Alc.

HOMERUS--CONCORDANCES.
Dunbar, Henry, comp. A complete concordance to the Odyssey and Hymns of Homer. Oxford, Clarendon press, 1880. iv, 419 p.   01-3069
PA4209 .D7 MRR Alc.

HOMERUS--LANGUAGE--GLOSSARIES, ETC.
Autenrieth, Georg Gottlieb Philipp, A Homeric dictionary for schools and colleges; [New ed.] Norman, University of Oklahoma Press [1958] xvi, 297 p.   883.1 58-7776
PA4209.Z5 A9 1958 MRR Alc.

HOMES (INSTITUTIONS)
see Charities

HOMES FOR THE AGED
see Old age homes

HOMESTEADING
see Frontier and pioneer life

HOMICIDE.
see also Murder

HOMILETICAL ILLUSTRATIONS.
Hovey, E. Paul, comp. The treasury for special days and occasions: [Westwood, N.J.] Revell [1961] 317 p.   808.88 61-9238
PN6083 .H73 MRR Alc.

HOMOSEXUALITY--BIBLIOGRAPHY.
Parker, William. Homosexuality: a selective bibliography of over 3,000 items. Metuchen, N.J., Scarecrow Press, 1971. viii, 323 p.   016.30141/57 71-163430
Z7164.S42 P35 MRR Alc.

Weinberg, Martin S. Homosexuality; an annotated bibliography. [1st ed.] New York, Harper & Row [1972] xiii, 550 p. [$15.00] 016.30141/57 70-160653
Z7164.S42 S425 MRR Alc.

HONDURAS--GAZETTEERS.
United States. Office of Geography. Honduras; Washington, U.S. Govt. Print. Off., 1956. ii, 235 p.   917.283 56-60091
F1502 .U5 MRR Alc.

HONGKONG--BIOGRAPHY.
Hong Kong who's who. 1958/60- Hong Kong, R. Luzzatto. 920.05125 59-4033
DS796.H7 H68 MRR Biog Latest edition

HONGKONG--BIOGRAPHY--YEARBOOKS.
Hongkong album. 1st- ed.; 1960- [Hongkong] 920.05125 61-210
DS796.H7 H623 MRR Biog Latest edition

HONGKONG--COMMERCE--DIRECTORIES.
Hong Kong dollar directory. Hongkong, Local Property & Printing Co. [etc.] 53-29957
HF3789.H6 H64 MRR Alc Latest edition / MRR Alc Latest edition

Kompass; register of Hong Kong industry and commerce. 2- ed.; 1972- Hong Kong, Kompass Asia. 338/.0025/5125 74-897962
HC497.H6 K58 MRR Alc Latest edition

O. K. business directory. Hongkong [O.K. Print Press] 53-30505
HF3779.H65 O15 MRR Alc Latest edition

HONGKONG--DIRECTORIES.
Hong Kong who's who. 1958/60- Hong Kong, R. Luzzatto. 920.05125 59-4033
DS796.H7 H68 MRR Biog Latest edition

HONGKONG--ECONOMIC CONDITIONS.
Hongkong. Report on Hong Kong. Hong Kong. 951.25 51-30035
HC428.H6 A3 MRR Alc Latest Edition

HONGKONG--INDUSTRIES--DIRECTORIES.
Kompass; register of Hong Kong industry and commerce. 2- ed.; 1972- Hong Kong, Kompass Asia. 338/.0025/5125 74-897962
HC497.H6 K58 MRR Alc Latest edition

HONGKONG--MANUFACTURES--DIRECTORIES.
Guide to Hong Kong products. [Hong Kong, International Pub. Co.] 63-38363
T12.5.H6 G8 MRR Alc Latest edition

Hong Kong dollar directory. Hongkong, Local Property & Printing Co. [etc.] 53-29957
HF3789.H6 H64 MRR Alc Latest edition / MRR Alc Latest edition

Kompass; register of Hong Kong industry and commerce. 2- ed.; 1972- Hong Kong, Kompass Asia. 338/.0025/5125 74-897962
HC497.H6 K58 MRR Alc Latest edition

HONGKONG--POLITICS AND GOVERNMENT.
Hongkong. Report on Hong Kong. Hong Kong. 951.25 51-30035
HC428.H6 A3 MRR Alc Latest Edition

HONGKONG--REGISTERS.
O. K. business directory. Hongkong [O.K. Print Press] 53-30505
HF3779.H65 O15 MRR Alc Latest edition

HONGKONG--STATISTICS.
Hongkong. Hong Kong; report. 1960- Hong Kong, Govt. Press 354/.51/25 78-220558
DS796.H7 A33 MRR Alc Latest edition

HONGKONG--YEARBOOKS.
Hong Kong; report. 1960-
Hong Kong, Govt. Press 354/.51/25
78-220558
DS796.H7 A33 MRR Alc Latest
edition

HOOPER, STANFORD CALDWELL, 1884-1955--
MANUSCRIPTS.
United States. Library of Congress.
Manuscript Division. Silas Casey,
Stanford Caldwell Hooper; a register
of their papers in the Library of
Congress. Washington, Library of
Congress, 1968. 5, 9 l.
359.3/31/0922 68-61404
Z663.34 .C33 MRR Alc.

HOOVER, HERBERT CLARK, PRES. U.S., 1874-
1964.
Emerson, Edwin, Hoover and his
times; Garden City, N.Y., Garden
City publishing company, inc., 1932.
xvi p., 1 l., 632 p. 923.173 32-
25411
E801 .E75 MRR Alc.

Lyons, Eugene. Herbert Hoover, a
biography. [1st ed.] Garden City,
N.Y., Doubleday, 1964. xii, 444 p.
923.173 64-15934
E802 .L82 MRR Alc.

HOPKINS, GERARD MANLEY, 1844-1889--
CONCORDANCES.
Dilligan, Robert J. A concordance to
the English poetry of Gerard Manley
Hopkins, Madison, University of
Wisconsin Press, 1970. xx, 321 p.
[10.00] 821/.8 70-101504
PR4803.H44 Z49 1970 MRR Alc.

HORATIUS FLACCUS, QUINTUS--CONCORDANCES.
Cooper, Lane, ed. A concordance of
the works of Horace. Washington, The
Carnegie Institution of Washington,
1916. ix, [1], 593 p. 16-20920
PA6444 .C6 MRR Alc.

HORDALAND, NORWAY--DIRECTORIES.
Adressebok for Hordaland fylke og
Bergen med skatteligninger. Oslo, S.
M. Bryde. 53-29091
DL576.H7 A7 MRR Alc Latest edition

HORNER, GUSTAVUS R. B.--MANUSCRIPTS.
United States. Library of Congress.
Manuscript Division. Bladen Dulany,
Gustavus R. B. Horner, Daniel Todd
Patterson: a register of their papers
in the Library of Congress.
Washington, Library of Congress,
1970. 4, 8, 4 l. 016.3593/32/0922
78-606846
Z663.34 .D9 MRR Alc.

HORROR FILMS--CATALOGS.
Willis, Donald C. Horror and science
fiction films: Metuchen, N.J.,
Scarecrow Press, 1972. x, 612 p.
791.43/0909/16 72-3682
PN1995.9.H6 W5 MRR Alc.

HORROR TALES.
see also Ghost stories

HORSE BREEDS.
Briggs, Hilton Marshall, Modern
breeds of livestock. Rev. ed. New
York, Macmillan [1958] 754 p.
636.08 58-5049
SF105 .B7 1958 MRR Alc.

Mason, Ian Lauder. A world
dictionary of livestock breeds, types
and varieties, 2nd (revised) ed.
Farnham Royal, Commonwealth
Agricultural Bureaux, 1969. xviii,
268 p. [70/-] 636/.003 75-454433

SF21 .M3 1969 MRR Alc.

HORSE-RACING--DICTIONARIES.
Mortimer, Roger, comp. The
encyclopaedia of flat racing.
London, Hale, 1971. [8], 444 p., 16
plates. [£3.50] 798/.43/03 71-
568712
SF321.5 .M67 1971 MRR Alc.

HORSE-RACING--HISTORY.
Longrigg, Roger, The history of
horse racing. [London] Macmillan
[1972] 320 p. [£6.50] 798/.4/009
72-172027
SF335.A1 L66 1972b MRR Alc.

HORSE-RACING--CALIFORNIA.
California turf directory and
stallion register. 1959- San Mateo,
Calif.: N. Rayden [etc.] 636.10822
59-42113
SF321 .C3 MRR Alc Latest edition

HORSE-RACING--UNITED STATES.
The American racing manual. 1906-
Chicago, Daily Racing Form. 06-3772

SF325 .A5 Sci RR Latest edition /
MRR Alc Latest edition

Who's who in thoroughbred racing.
1st-   ed.: 1946- Washington, D.C.,
Who's who in thoroughbred racing,
inc. 798.4 agr46-284
SF321 .W45 MRR Alc Latest edition

HORSE-RAILROADS
see Street-railroads

HORSE-SHOWS--YEARBOOKS.
Horse and hound year book. London,
Odhams Press [etc.] 799.25 50-22666

Began publication in 1947.
SK7 .H6 MRR Alc Latest edition

HORSE TRAILS
see Trails

HORSEMANSHIP--DICTIONARIES.
Brander, Michael. A dictionary of
sporting terms. London, Black, 1968.
224 p. [35/-] 798 77-353522
SK11 .B66 MRR Alc.

Summerhays, Reginald Sherriff,
Summerhays' encyclopaedia for
horsemen, [5th rev. ed.] London,
New York, F. Warne [1970] xvi, 385
p. [$6.95 (U.S.)] 636.1/003 79-
114792
SF278 .S8 1970 MRR Alc.

Taylor, Louis. Harper's encyclopedia
for horsemen: [1st ed.] New York,
Harper & Row [1973] xi, 558 p.
[$15.00] 636.1/003 72-79697
SF278 .T39 1973 MRR Alc.

HORSEMEN.
Mortimer, Roger, comp. The
encyclopaedia of flat racing.
London, Hale, 1971. [8], 444 p., 16
plates. [£3.50] 798/.43/03 71-
568712
SF321.5 .M67 1971 MRR Alc.

Who's who in horsedom. v. [1]-
1948- Louisville, Ky. [etc.]
798.058 56-47235
SF31 .W45 MRR Alc Latest edition

Who's who in thoroughbred racing.
1st-   ed.: 1946- Washington, D.C.,
Who's who in thoroughbred racing,
inc. 798.4 agr46-284
SF321 .W45 MRR Alc Latest edition

HORSES.
Ensminger, M. Eugene. Horses and
horsemanship [4th ed.] Danville,
Ill., Interstate Printers &
Publishers [1969] xiv, 907 p.
636.1 68-24651
SF285 .E53 1969 MRR Alc.

Gianoli, Luigi. Horses and
horsemanship through the ages New
York, Crown Publishers [1969, c1967]
441 p. 636.1 68-9102
SF285 .G463 1969 MRR Alc.

Who's who in horsedom. v. [1]-
1948- Louisville, Ky. [etc.]
798.058 56-47235
SF31 .W45 MRR Alc Latest edition

HORSES--DICTIONARIES.
Summerhays, Reginald Sherriff,
Summerhays' encyclopaedia for
horsemen, [5th rev. ed.] London,
New York, F. Warne [1970] xvi, 385
p. [$6.95 (U.S.)] 636.1/003 79-
114792
SF278 .S8 1970 MRR Alc.

Taylor, Louis. Harper's encyclopedia
for horsemen: [1st ed.] New York,
Harper & Row [1973] xi, 558 p.
[$15.00] 636.1/003 72-79697
SF278 .T39 1973 MRR Alc.

HORSES RACING--DIRECTORIES.
United States Trotting Association.
Racing farm and stable names.
[Columbus, Ohio] 59-42692
SF321 .U52 MRR Alc Latest edition

HORTICULTURE.
see also Fruit-culture

see also Gardening

see also Insects, Injurious and
beneficial

HORTICULTURE--DICTIONARIES.
Dictionary of gardening: Oxford,
Clarendon Press, 1951. 4 v. (xvi,
2316 p.) 635/.03 52-7366
SB45 .D63 MRR Alc.

HORTICULTURE--DICTIONARIES--POLYGLOT.
Nijdam, J. Tuinbouwkundig
woordenboek in acht talen. Herziene
en uitgebreide uitg. van de
Woordenlijst voor de tuinbouw in
zeven talen. ['s-Gravenhage,
Staatsdrukkerij- en
Uitgeverijbedrijf; voor alle anderen
landen: Interscience Publishers, New
York] 1961. 504 p. 62-52704
SB45 .N673 MRR Alc.

HOSIERY INDUSTRY--CANADA--DIRECTORIES.
Davison's knit goods trade, "The
Standard." [Office ed.] Ridgewood,
N.J. [etc.] Davison Pub. Co. 08-
32658
TT695 .D26 Sci RR Latest edition /
MRR Alc Latest edition

HOSIERY INDUSTRY--GREAT BRITAIN--
DIRECTORIES.
Skinner's hosiery and knit goods
directory. Croydon, Eng. [etc.] T.
Skinner. 338.4767766 51-18825
TT679 .S5 MRR Alc Latest edition

HOSIERY INDUSTRY--UNITED STATES--
DIRECTORIES.
Davison's knit goods trade, "The
Standard." [Office ed.] Ridgewood,
N.J. [etc.] Davison Pub. Co. 08-
32658
TT695 .D26 Sci RR Latest edition /
MRR Alc Latest edition

HOSPITAL ADMINISTRATORS--UNITED STATES--
BIOGRAPHY.
American College of Hospital
Administrators. Directory. 1938-
Chicago. 362.06273 39-2135
RA977 .A57 Sci RR Latest edition /
MRR Biog Latest edition

HOSPITALS.
see also Medicine, Clinical

see also Nurses and nursing

see also Nursing homes

HOSPITALS--ADMINISTRATION.
see also Hospital administrators

HOSPITALS--FURNITURE, EQUIPMENT, ETC.
The Hospital purchasing file. 1st
ed.: 1919- New York [etc.] McGraw-
Hill [etc.] 362.1085 19-5366
RA968 .H6 MRR Alc Latest edition

HOSPITALS--INDEXES.
American Hospital Association.
Library. Asa S. Bacon Memorial.
Cumulative index of hospital
literature. Chicago. 016.3621 50-
11277
Z6675.H7 A5 MRR Alc Partial set /
Sci RR Full set

HOSPITALS--NURSES
see Nurses and nursing

HOSPITALS--CANADA--DIRECTORIES.
Canadian hospital directory.
Toronto, Canadian Hospital
Association. 56-35632
RA977 .C33 MRR Alc Latest edition

Began publication in 1953.

The Modern hospital directory of
hospitals in the United States, U.S.
territories, and Canada. 1958-
[Chicago, Modern Hospital]
362.1/1/0257 72-623523
RA977 .M6 Sci RR Latest edition /
MRR Ref Desk Latest edition

HOSPITALS--FRANCE--DIRECTORIES.
Guide médical et pharmaceutique
Rosenwald. Paris, L'Expansion
scientifique française [etc.]
610.58 46-33196
Publication began with the guide
for 1887.
R713.43 .A6G8 MRR Alc Latest
edition

HOSPITALS--GREAT BRITAIN--DIRECTORIES--
YEARBOOKS.
The Hospitals yearbook and directory
of hospital suppliers. 1968-
London. 362.1/1/02542 72-622672
RA986.A1 H6 MRR Alc Latest edition

HOSPITALS--UNITED STATES.
American College of Hospital
Administrators. Directory. 1938-
Chicago. 362.06273 39-2135
RA977 .A57 Sci RR Latest edition /
MRR Biog Latest edition

HOSPITALS--UNITED STATES--DIRECTORIES.
The Modern hospital directory of
hospitals in the United States, U.S.
territories, and Canada. 1958-
[Chicago, Modern Hospital]
362.1/1/0257 72-623523
RA977 .M6 Sci RR Latest edition /
MRR Ref Desk Latest edition

HOSTILITIES
see War

HOTEL MANAGEMENT--UNITED STATES--
BIOGRAPHY.
Who's who among innkeepers 1st ed.,
1974-1975. [New York, Rating
Publications, 1974] 210 p.
647/.94/0922 73-89548
TX910.3 .W48 MRR Biog.

HOTELS, TAVERNS, ETC.
Hotels and restaurants in the British
Isles. 1951- London, British Travel
and Holidays Association. 647.9442
52-21171
TX910.G7 H64 MRR Alc Latest
edition

HOTELS, TAVERNS, ETC.--DIRECTORIES.
ABC hotel guide. [Dunstable, Eng.,
ABC Travel Guides Ltd] 647/.94 72-
627196
TX907 .A14 MRR Ref Desk Latest
edition

HOTELS, TAVERNS, ETC.-- (Cont.)
Directory of hotel & motel systems.
New York, American Hotel Association
Directory Corp. 44-29752
	TX907 .D5 MRR Alc Latest edition

Guide international des hôtels.
Paris, Association internationale de
l'hôtellerie. 647.94058 52-16324
	TX907 .G83 MRR Alc Latest edition

Hotel & motel red book. 1886- New
York, American Hotel Association
Directory Corp. 98-295
	TX907 .045 Sci RR Latest edition /
	MRR Ref Desk Latest edition

OAG travel planner & hotel/motel
guide. [Oak Brook, Ill. R.H.
Donnelley Corp.] [$20.00] 910/.202
73-640442
	G153 .018 MRR Ref Desk Latest
	edition

Official meeting facilities guide.
spring 1974- [New York, Public
Transportation & Travel Div., Ziff-
Davis Publishing Co.] [$10.00]
647/.94 74-644953
	TX907 .046 MRR Alc Latest edition

Travel industry personnel directory.
[New York, Travel Agent Magazine]
338.4/7/81009025 72-622913
	G155 .A1T655 MRR Alc Latest
	edition

Women's Rest Tour Association,
Boston. Foreign lodging list.
Boston. 647.94094 ca 35-238
	D910 .W82 MRR Alc Latest edition

World Association of Travel Agencies.
National tourist information and
general tariff. Geneva. 61-65430
Began in 1953.
	G155.A1 G4 MRR Alc Latest edition

HOTELS, TAVERNS, ETC.--AFRICA, SOUTH--
DIRECTORIES.
Guide to the hotels and other
accommodation establishments of South
Africa and adjacent territories.
[Johannesburg, South African Tourist
Corporation] 647/.9468 72-622670
	TX910.A37 G63 MRR Alc Latest
	edition

HOTELS, TAVERNS, ETC.--AFRICA, SOUTHERN-
-DIRECTORIES.
Guide to the hotels and other
accommodation establishments of South
Africa and adjacent territories.
[Johannesburg, South African Tourist
Corporation] 647/.9468 72-622670
	TX810.A37 G63 MRR Alc Latest
	edition

HOTELS, TAVERNS, ETC.--ASIA--
DIRECTORIES.
Pacific hotel directory and travel
guide. [San Francisco, Pacific
travel news] 63-49077
	TX907 .P2 MRR Alc Latest edition

HOTELS, TAVERNS, ETC.--CANADA--
DIRECTORIES.
Mort. Mort's guide to low-cost
vacations & lodgings on college
campuses. 1974- Princeton, N.J.,
CMG Publications. 647/.9473 73-
94258
	TX907 .M854 MRR Alc Latest edition

Wrigley's hotel directory. Vancouver
[B.C., etc.] Wrigley Directories Ltd.
[etc.] 16-24253
	TX907 .W7 MRR Alc Latest edition

HOTELS, TAVERNS, ETC.--EUROPE--
DIRECTORIES.
Fielding, Dodge Temple. Fielding's
selected favorites: hotels & inns,
Europe. 1972- New York. [$3.95]
647/.944 72-188897
	TX910.A1 F47 MRR Alc Latest
	edition

Hotel- u. Städte-Adressbuch für
Deutschland mit Saar. Konstanz
[etc.] Poppe & Neumann. 51-39392
"Gegründet 1895."
	TX907 .H58 MRR Alc Latest edition

Long, Robert P. Castle-hotels of
Europe; 4th ed. East Meadow, N.Y.;
distributor: Hastings House, New
York, 1973] 164 p. [$3.95]
647/.944 73-157418
	TX907 .L6 1973 MRR Alc.

HOTELS, TAVERNS, ETC.--FRANCE--
DIRECTORIES.
Guide bleu France. [Paris] Hachette.
914.4/04/8305 73-643708
	DC16 .F69 MRR Alc Latest edition

Guide Kléber: France. 1969-
[Neuilly-sur-Seine] 647/.9444 72-
622708
	TX910.F8 G822 MRR Alc Latest
	edition

HOTELS, TAVERNS, ETC.--GERMANY--
DIRECTORIES.
Hotel- u. Städte-Adressbuch für
Deutschland mit Saar. Konstanz
[etc.] Poppe & Neumann. 51-39392
"Gegründet 1895."
	TX907 .H58 MRR Alc Latest edition

HOTELS, TAVERNS, ETC.--GERMANY (FEDERAL
REPUBLIC, 1949-)--DIRECTORIES.
Varta-Führer. Stuttgart, Mairs
Geographischer Verlag. 647/.944 74-
644633
	TX910.G4 V3 MRR Alc Latest edition

HOTELS, TAVERNS, ETC.--GREAT BRITAIN.
Hotels and restaurants in the British
Isles. 1951- London, British Travel
and Holidays Association. 647.9442
52-21171
	TX910.G7 H64 MRR Alc Latest
	edition

HOTELS, TAVERNS, ETC.--GREAT BRITAIN--
DIRECTORIES.
Automobile Association. AA guide to
hotels & restaurants in Great Britain
and Ireland. [Basingstoke, Eng.;
Distributed in the U.S.A. by Harper &
Row, New York, 1974] 671, 48 p.
[£1.95 ($7.95 U.S.)] 647/.9442 74-
167286
	TX910.G7 A8 1974 MRR Alc.

Courtenay, Ashley. Let's halt awhile
in Great Britain. [London]
Distributed in the United States by
Hastings House Publishers. 647/.9442
73-642063
	TX910.G7 A67 MRR Alc Latest
	edition

Royal Automobile Club, London. Guide
and handbook. London. 629.281 51-
34691
	GV1025.G7 R59 MRR Alc Latest
	edition

HOTELS, TAVERNS, ETC.--IRELAND--
DIRECTORIES.
Automobile Association. AA guide to
hotels & restaurants in Great Britain
and Ireland. [Basingstoke, Eng.;
Distributed in the U.S.A. by Harper &
Row, New York, 1974] 671, 48 p.
[£1.95 ($7.95 U.S.)] 647/.9442 74-
167286
	TX910.G7 A8 1974 MRR Alc.

Courtenay, Ashley. Let's halt awhile
in Great Britain. [London]
Distributed in the United States by
Hastings House Publishers. 647/.9442
73-642063
	TX910.G7 A67 MRR Alc Latest
	edition

Where to stay in Ireland. [Dublin,
Irish Tourist Board] 70-230381
	TX910.I7 W46 MRR Alc Latest
	edition

HOTELS, TAVERNS, ETC.--ITALY--
DIRECTORIES.
Touring club italiano. Vademecum del
turista. [Milano] 57-48011
	DG413 .T6 MRR Alc Latest edition

HOTELS, TAVERNS, ETC.--NETHERLANDS--
DIRECTORIES.
Lasschuit's officieel adresboek:
Bilthoven, J. G. Lasschuit. 67-37932

Began publication with vol. for
1908.
	TX910.N4 L3 MRR Alc Latest edition

HOTELS, TAVERNS, ETC.--NORTH AMERICA--
DIRECTORIES.
Leahy's hotel-motel guide & travel
atlas of the United States, Canada
and Mexico. Chicago, American Hotel
Register Co. 647.94 09-20539
	TX907 .L5 MRR Alc Latest edition

HOTELS, TAVERNS, ETC.--PACIFIC AREA--
DIRECTORIES.
Pacific hotel directory and travel
guide. [San Francisco, Pacific
travel news] 63-49077
	TX907 .P2 MRR Alc Latest edition

HOTELS, TAVERNS, ETC.--UNITED STATES.
Harris, Kerr, Forster and Company.
Trends in the hotel-motel business.
Atlanta [etc.] a 40-3316
Began publication with 1936 issue?
	TX909.A1 H3 MRR Alc Latest edition

HOTELS, TAVERNS, ETC.--UNITED STATES--
DIRECTORIES.
Hotel & motel red book. 1886- New
York, American Hotel Association
Directory Corp. 98-295
	TX907 .045 Sci RR Latest edition /
	MRR Ref Desk Latest edition

Leahy's hotel-motel guide & travel
atlas of the United States, Canada
and Mexico. Chicago, American Hotel
Register Co. 647.94 09-20539
	TX907 .L5 MRR Alc Latest edition

Mort. Mort's guide to low-cost
vacations & lodgings on college
campuses. 1974- Princeton, N.J.,
CMG Publications. 647/.9473 73-
94258
	TX907 .M854 MRR Alc Latest edition

Wrigley's hotel directory. Vancouver
[B.C., etc.] Wrigley Directories Ltd.
[etc.] 16-24253
	TX907 .W7 MRR Alc Latest edition

HOTELS, TAVERNS, ETC.--WEST--
DIRECTORIES.
TravelVision. Humble vacation guide
U.S.A.; favorite West Central
recreation regions. Houston, Tex.,
Humble Travel Club [1970] 224 p.
647/.9478 77-17741
	TX907 .T8526 1970 MRR Alc.

HOTELS, TAVERNS, ETC.--UNITED STATES--
DIRECTORIES.
Auger, Bert Y. How to find better
business meeting places; St. Paul,
Business Services Press [1966] xvii,
637 p. 647/.9473 66-24060
	TX907 .A8 MRR Alc.

HOURS OF LABOR--BIBLIOGRAPHY.
United States. Library of Congress.
Division of bibliography. ...List
of books, with references to
periodicals, relating to the eight-
hour working day and to limitation of
working hours in general.
Washington, Gov't. print. off., 1908.
24 p. 07-35012
	Z663.28 .L566 MRR Alc.

HOUSE BUYING.
Stanforth, Deirdre. Buying and
renovating a house in the city; New
York, Knopf, 1972. xiv, 400, xiv p.
[$10.00] 643/.7 71-173774
	TH4816 .S7 MRR Alc.

HOUSE CONSTRUCTION--UNITED STATES--
DIRECTORIES.
The Blue book of major homebuilders.
[Crofton, Md.] CMR Associates.
338.4/7/690802573 72-621729
	TH12.5 .B5 MRR Alc Latest edition

HOUSE DECORATION--UNITED STATES--
DIRECTORIES.
The Interior decorators' handbook,
New York, Clifford & Lawton. 44-
15433
	NK1127 .I5 MRR Alc Latest edition

HOUSE DRAINAGE
see Plumbing

HOUSE FURNISHINGS.
see also Furniture

	see also Glassware

HOUSE FURNISHINGS--DICTIONARIES.
Studio dictionary of design &
decoration. Rev. and enl. ed.] New
York, Viking Press [1973] 538 p.
[$28.50] 745.4/03 73-1024
	NK1165 .S78 1973 MRR Alc.

HOUSE FURNISHINGS INDUSTRY AND TRADE--
UNITED STATES--DIRECTORIES.
The Gift and decorative accessory
buyers directory. [New York, Geyer-
McAllister Publications]
338.4/7/745502573 74-644351
	T12 .G46 MRR Alc Latest edition

The Interior decorators' handbook,
New York, Clifford & Lawton. 44-
15433
	NK1127 .I5 MRR Alc Latest edition

HOUSE ORGANS--DIRECTORIES.
British house journals. 1956-
[London] British Association of
Industrial Editors. 57-39809
	Z7164.C81 B83 MRR Alc Latest
	edition

HOUSE ORGANS--UNITED STATES--
DIRECTORIES.
Gebbie house magazine directory.
[Sioux City, Iowa, House Magazine
Pub. Co.] 016.0704/86 74-644438
	Z7164.C81 N32 MRR Ref Desk Latest
	edition

HOUSE PAINTING.
Goodheart-Willcox's painting and
decorating encyclopedia; Homewood,
Ill., Goodheart-Willcox Co. [1964]
288 p. 698 64-22379
	TT320 .G6 1964 MRR Alc.

HOUSE PLANTS.
Schuler, Stanley. 1001 house plant
questions answered. Princeton, N.J.,
Van Nostrand [1963] 278 p. 635.965
63-1730
	SB419 .S37 MRR Alc.

HOUSE PLANTS--PICTORIAL WORKS.
Graf, Alfred Byrd. Exotica, series
3; 6th ed. E. Rutherford, N.J.,
Roehrs Co. [1973] 1834 p. 635.9/65
72-90669
	SB407 .G7 1973 MRR Alc.

HOUSEHOLD APPLIANCES.
Graf, Rudolf F. How it works,
illustrated: everyday devices and
mechanisms. New York, Popular
science [1974] viii, 184 p.
[$10.95]   620   73-80716
TX298 .G68 MRR Alc.

HOUSEHOLD APPLIANCES--TERMINOLOGY.
American Home Economics Association.
Home Economists in Business Section.
Housing, Furnishings, and Equipment
Committee. Handbook of household
equipment terminology. 3d ed.
Washington, American Home Economics
Association [1970] v, 50 p.
643/.6/014   76-129097
TX298 .A6 1970 MRR Alc.

HOUSEHOLD APPLIANCES, ELECTRIC.
Anderson, Edwin P., Audels home
appliance service guide, [2d ed.]
Indianapolis, T. Audel [1965] 600 p.
683.83   65-18185
TK7019 .A5 1965 MRR Alc.

Official home appliance trade-in blue
book. Madison, Wis., Select Pub. Co.
338.4/7/6838   72-626358
HD9697.U4 N33 MRR Alc Latest
edition

HOUSEHOLD APPLIANCES, ELECTRIC--
MAINTENANCE AND REPAIR.
Powell, Evan. Complete guide to home
appliance repair / New York :
Popular Science, [1974] vii, 464 p.
: [$11.95]   643/.6   73-92403
TK7018 .P69 MRR Alc.

HOUSEHOLD PESTS--CONTROL.
Mallis, Arnold. Handbook of pest
control; 5th ed. New York, MacNair-
Dorland Co. [1969] 1158 p.   648/.7
79-10395
TX325 .M3 1969 MRR Alc.

HOUSEMAN, ALFRED EDWARD, 1859-1936--
CONCORDANCES.
Hyder, Clyde Kenneth, ed. A
concordance to the poems of A. E.
Housman. Gloucester, Mass., P.
Smith, 1966 [c1940] vii, 133 p.
821.912   66-8388
PR4809.H15 H9 1966 MRR Alc.

HOUSES
see Dwellings

HOUSES, PREFABRICATED
see Buildings, Prefabricated

HOUSING--BIBLIOGRAPHY.
Columbia University. Libraries. Avery
Architectural Library. Avery index
to architectural periodicals. 2d
ed.; rev. and enl. Boston, G. K.
Hall, 1973- v.   016.72   74-
152756
Z5945 .C653 1973 MRR Alc (Dk 33)

HOUSING--DICTIONARIES.
Abrams, Charles, The language of
cities; a glossary of terms. New
York, Viking Press [1971] ix, 365 p.
[$10.00]   301.3/6/03   76-137500
HT108.5 .A24 MRR Alc.

HOUSING--PERIODICALS--INDEXES.
Paulus, Virginia, Housing: New
York, AMS Press [1974] xii, 339 p.
016.3015/4/0973   73-15863
Z7164.H8 P38 MRR Alc.

HOUSING--UNITED STATES.
United States. Bureau of the Census.
1960 census of housing, [Washington,
1961-63] 6 v. in 66 pts. and 1 v. in
420 pts.   a   61-9347
HD7293 .A4884 MRR Alc.

HOUSING--UNITED STATES--BIBLIOGRAPHY.
Housing and planning references. new
ser. no 1- July/Aug. 1965-
[Washington, U.S. Govt. Print. Off.]
016.3015/4   72-621364
Z7165.U5 A3 MRR Alc Full set

Paulus, Virginia. Housing: New
York, AMS Press [1974] xii, 339 p.
016.3015/4/0973   73-15863
Z7164.H8 P38 MRR Alc.

HOUSING--UNITED STATES--BIBLIOGRAPHY--
CATALOGS.
United States. Dept. of Housing and
Urban Development. Library and
Information Division. The dictionary
catalog of the United States
Department of Housing and Urban
Development, Library and Information
Division, Boston, G. K. Hall, 1972.
19 v.   016.30154   73-152937
Z7164.H8 U4484 MRR Alc (Dk 33)

HOUSING--UNITED STATES--DIRECTORIES.
Active Retirement Executives
Association. Retirement facilities
register. Los Angeles, 1964?] 224
p.   362.6105873   64-4960
HD7287.9 .A26 MRR Alc.

National Association of Housing and
Redevelopment Officials. NAHRO
renewal agency directory. 1969-
Washington. 309.2/62/02573 73-
641791
HD7293.A1 N235 MRR Alc Latest
edition

HOUSING--UNITED STATES--STATISTICS.
United States. Bureau of the Census.
1960 census of housing, [Washington,
1961-63] 6 v. in 66 pts. and 1 v. in
420 pts.   a   61-9347
HD7293 .A4884 MRR Alc.

United States. Bureau of the Census.
1970 census of housing. [Washington;
For sale by the Supt. of Docs., U.S.
Govt. Print Off., 1972- v.
301.5/4/09791   72-600057
HD7293 .A512 1972 MRR Alc.

United States. Bureau of the Census.
1970 census of population and
housing. [Washington; For sale by
the Supt. of Docs., U.S. Govt. Print.
Off.] 1971- v.   [$1.00 (v. 5)
varies]   312/.9/0973   73-186611
HA201 1870 .A542 MRR Alc.

United States. Bureau of the Census.
Housing construction statistics, 1889
to 1964. Washington [For sale by the
Superintendent of Documents, U.S.
Govt. Print. Off., 1966] v, 805 p.
338.4/7/69080973   a 66-7417
HD7293 .A5 1966d MRR Alc.

United States. Bureau of the Census.
New one-family homes sold and for
sale: 1963 to 1967. [Washington]
U.S. Dept. of Commerce; [for sale by
the Supt. of Docs., U.S. Govt. Print.
Off., 1869] iii, 293 p.   [4.75]
333.3/33/0973   76-601125
HD7293 .A5 1969c MRR Alc.

United States. Dept. of Housing and
Urban Development. Statistical
yearbook. 1966- Washington, For
sale by the Supt. of Docs., U.S.
Govt. Print. Off.   301.5/4/0212   68-
62733
HD7293.A49H67 MRR Ref Desk Full
set

Urban Growth Patterns Research Group.
Demographic profiles of the United
States. Oak Ridge, Tenn., Oak Ridge
National Laboratory, 1971-72. 8 v.
[$3.00 (v. 1) varies]   312/.0973   76-
616120
HA215 .U73 MRR Alc.

HOUSING AUTHORITIES--UNITED STATES--
DIRECTORIES.
National Association of Housing and
Redevelopment Officials. N A H R O
housing directory. [Washington]
301.5/4/02573   72-626673
HD7293.A1 N23 MRR Alc Latest
edition

HOUSING RESEARCH.
United States. Office of Science and
Technology. Housing research and
building technology activities of the
Federal Government. Washington; [For
sale by the Supt. of Docs., U.S.
Govt. Print. Off.] 1970. 117 p.
[1.25]   690/.072/073   75-608274
TH23 .A6 1970 MRR Alc.

HOUSING RESEARCH--BIBLIOGRAPHY.
United States. Dept. of Housing and
Urban Development. Library and
Information Division. The dictionary
catalog of the United States
Department of Housing and Urban
Development, Library and Information
Division, Boston, G. K. Hall, 1972.
19 v.   016.30154   73-152937
Z7164.H8 U4484 MRR Alc (Dk 33)

HOUSMAN, ALFRED EDWARD, 1859-1936.
United States. Library of Congress.
Gertrude Clarke Whittall Poetry and
Literature Fund. Anniversary
lectures, 1959. Washington,
Reference Dept., Library of Congress,
1959. iii, 56 p.   821.082   59-60090

Z663.293 .A55 MRR Alc.

HOUSTON, TEX.--DESCRIPTION--GUIDE-BOOKS.
Coates, Felicia. Texas monthly's
Guide to Houston [Austin] Texas
monthly, 1973 382 p. $2.95]
917.64/1411/046   73-179186
F394.H8 C63 MRR Alc.

HOVE, ENG.--DIRECTORIES.
Kelly's directory of Brighton [and]
Hove. Kingston upon Thames, Surrey
[etc.] Kelly's Directories Limited
[etc.]   53-28330
DA690.B78 K36 MRR Alc Latest
edition

HOW TO USE THE LIBRARY
see Libraries and readers

HUMAN BIOLOGY.
see also Anatomy, Human

see also Medicine

see also Physiology

see also Psychology

HUMAN ECOLOGY.
see also Conservation of natural
resources

see also Environmental policy

see also Man--Influence on nature

see also Social psychology

see also Sociology

Hilado, Carlos J., Handbook of
environmental management Westport,
Conn., Technomic Pub. Co. [1972- v.
301.31   74-174658
GF41 .H55 MRR Alc.

Nobile, Philip, comp. The complete
ecology fact book. [1st ed.] Garden
City, N.Y., Doubleday, 1972. xx, 472
p.   [$10.00]   301.31   73-175364
TD174 .N6 MRR Alc.

Rand McNally and Company. The earth
and man. New York [1972] 439 p.
[$35.00]   912   70-654432
G1019 .R26 1972 MRR Alc Atlas.

HUMAN ECOLOGY--ADDRESSES, ESSAYS,
LECTURES.
Woodrow Wilson International Center
for Scholars. The human environment.
Washington, 1972. 2 v.   [$5.00 per
vol.]   016.30131   72-601602
Z5118.A5 W66 1972 MRR Alc.

HUMAN ECOLOGY--BIBLIOGRAPHY.
Morrison, Denton E. Environment:
Washington, Office of Research and
Monitoring, U.S. Environmental
Protection Agency; for sale by the
Supt. of Docs., U.S. Govt. Print.
Off., 1974, c1973. vii, 860 p.
[$7.45]   016.3   74-601576
Z7161 .M56 1974 MRR Alc.

Woodrow Wilson International Center
for Scholars. The human environment.
Washington, 1972. 2 v.   [$5.00 per
vol.]   016.30131   72-601602
Z5118.A5 W66 1972 MRR Alc.

HUMAN ECOLOGY--DIRECTORIES.
Directory of Government agencies
safeguarding consumer and
environment. 1st- ed.; 1968-
Alexandria, Va., Serina Press.
339.4/7/02573   68-20372
HC110.C6 D5 MRR Alc Latest edition

International directory of behavior
and design research. 1974-
[Orangeburg, N.Y.] [$12.00]   300/.25
74-75207
H57 .I57 MRR Blog Latest edition /
Sci RR Latest edition

HUMAN ECOLOGY--SOCIETIES, ETC.--
DIRECTORIES.
Halstead, Bruce W. A Golden guide to
environmental organizations. New
York, Golden Press [1972] 63 p.
[$0.95]   301.31/06   72-79158
GF5 .H34 MRR Alc.

HUMAN ECOLOGY--STUDY AND TEACHING
(HIGHER)--DIRECTORIES.
International Institute for
Environmental Affairs. World
directory of environmental education
programs; New York, R. R. Bowker
Co., 1973. xiii, 289 p.
301.31/07/11   73-14872
GF26 .I57 1973 MRR Alc.

HUMAN ECOLOGY--UNITED STATES--
BIBLIOGRAPHY.
Wolff, Garwood R. Environmental
information sources handbook. [New
York] Simon and Schuster [1974] 568
p.   301.31/07   73-3951
GF503 .W64 MRR Alc.

HUMAN ECOLOGY--UNITED STATES--
SOCIETIES, ETC.--DIRECTORIES.
Wolff, Garwood R. Environmental
information sources handbook. [New
York] Simon and Schuster [1974] 568
p.   301.31/07   73-3951
GF503 .W64 MRR Alc.

HUMAN ENGINEERING--BIBLIOGRAPHY.
[United States. Library of Congress.
Technical Information Division]
Human engineering; Washington, 1953.
v p., 35 l. (incl. cover)   016.15
54-61809
Z663.49 .H8 1953 MRR Alc.

HUMAN EVOLUTION.
Brace, C. Loring. The stages of
human evolution; Englewood Cliffs,
N.J., Prentice-Hall [1967] xi, 116
p.   573/.8   67-22426
GN741 .B68 MRR Alc.

Mellersh, H. E. L. The story of
early man; New York, Viking Press,
1960 [c1959] 256 p.   573.3   60-5837

GN743 .M4 1960 MRR Alc.

HUMAN GENETICS.
Scheinfeld, Amram, Heredity in
humans. Philadelphia, Lippincott,
1972 [c1971] xiv, 303 p.   573.2/1
70-159730
    QH431 .S335 1972 MRR Alc.

HUMAN GEOGRAPHY
    see Anthropo-geography

HUMAN PARASITOLOGY
    see Medical parasitology

HUMAN PHYSIOLOGY.
De Coursey, Russell Myles, The human
organism. 4th ed. New York, McGraw-
Hill [1874] xi, 644 p.   612 73-
23016
    QP34.5 .D38 1974 MRR Alc.

Greisheimer, Esther Maud, Physiology
& anatomy 9th ed. Philadelphia,
Lippincott [1972] xv, 678 p.
[$13.50] 612 73-101355
    QP34 .G63 1972 MRR Alc.

HUMAN REPRODUCTION.
Smith, Anthony, The body. New York,
Walker [1968] xiii, 524 p.   612 68-
13972
    QP38 .S67 1968b MRR Alc.

HUMAN RIGHTS
    see Civil rights

HUMANE SOCIETIES
    see Child welfare

HUMANISM.
    see also Renaissance

HUMANISM--BIO-BIBLIOGRAPHY.
Cosenza, Mario Emilio, Biographical
and bibliographical dictionary of the
Italian humanists [2d ed., rev. and
enl. Boston, G. K. Hall, 1962]-67.
6 v.   820.045 62-13227
    Z7128.H8 C6 MRR Alc.

HUMANITIES.
Asheim, Lester Eugene, The
humanities and the library; Chicago,
American Library Association, 1957.
xix, 278 p.   020 56-12395
    Z665 .A727 MRR Alc.

HUMANITIES--ABSTRACTING AND INDEXING.
International Federation for
Documentation. Abstracting services.
[2d ed.] The Hague, 1969. 2 v.
029/.9/5 73-168592
    Z695.93 .I58 1969 MRR Ref Desk.

HUMANITIES--BIBLIOGRAPHY.
Gray, Richard A. Serial
bibliographies in the humanities and
social sciences. Ann Arbor, Mich.,
Pierian Press, 1969. xxiv, 345 p.
016.01605 68-58895
    Z1002 .G814 MRR Ref Desk.

Rogers, A. Robert, The humanities;
Littleton, Colo., Libraries
Unlimited, 1974. 400 p. [$9.50]
016.0013 74-78393
    Z5579 .R63 MRR Alc.

Stevens, Rolland Elwell, Reference
books in the social sciences and
humanities 3d ed. Champaign, Ill.,
Distributed by Illini Union Bookstore
[1971] v, 188 p. 016.3 74-151299

    Z1035.1 .S85 1971 MRR Ref Desk.

HUMANITIES--BIBLIOGRAPHY--PERIODICALS.
Bulletin signalétique: Philosophie,
sciences humaines. v. 1-14; 1947-60.
Paris, Centre de documentation du C.
N. R. S. 51-30077
    Z7127 .F7 MRR Alc Full set

HUMANITIES--DICTIONARIES.
Dictionary of the history of ideas;
New York, Scribner [1973] 4 v.
[$35.00 (per vol.)]   901.9 72-7943
    CB5 .D52 MRR Alc.

Pei, Mario Andrew, ed. Language of
the specialists; [New York] Funk &
Wagnalls [1966] xii, 388 p.   423.1
66-22943
    PE1680 .P4 MRR Alc.

HUMANITIES--PERIODICALS--BIBLIOGRAPHY.
Paoletti, Odette. Périodiques et
publications en série concernant les
sciences sociales et humaines,
Paris, Maison des sciences de
l'homme, Service bibliothèque-
documentation, 1966. 2 v. (xxiv, 684
p.) [80.00F] 016.07 67-100583
    Z6941 .P3 MRR Alc.

Zimmerman, Irene, A guide to current
Latin American periodicals: [1st
ed.] Gainesville, Fla., Kallman Pub.
Co., 1961. x, 357 p.   61-15751
    Z6854.S8 Z5 MRR Alc.

HUMANITIES--PERIODICALS--BIBLIOGRAPHY--
UNION LISTS.
Ottawa National Library.
Periodicals in the social sciences
and humanities currently received by
Canadian libraries. [Ottawa, Queen's
Printer] 1968. 2 v. [unpriced]
016.300/5 68-105183
    Z6945 .O895 MRR Alc.

HUMANITIES--PERIODICALS--INDEXES.
British humanities index. 1962-
London, Library Association. 63-
24940
    AI3 .B7 MRR Alc Full set

Bulletin signalétique 519:
Philosophie, sciences religieuses.
v. 15-23; 1961-69. Paris, Centre de
documentation du C.N.R.S. 75-10205
    Z7127 .F712 MRR Alc Full set

Social sciences & humanities index.
v. 1- 1907/15- New York [etc.] H.
W. Wilson Co. 17-4969
    AI3 .R49 MRR Circ Partial set /
    MRR Circ Partial set

HUMANITIES--PERIODICALS--INDEXES--
BIBLIOGRAPHY.
Vesenyi, Paul E., European
periodical literature in the social
sciences and the humanities,
Metuchen, N.J., Scarecrow Press,
1969. 226 p. 016.052 79-7052
    Z6955 .Z9V45 MRR Alc.

HUMANITIES--STUDY AND TEACHING--UNITED
STATES--DIRECTORIES.
The Annual guides to graduate study.
1966/67- Princeton, N.J.] Peterson's
Guides Inc. 378.73 68-1823
    L901 .P46 MRR Alc Latest edition

HUMBUG
    see Swindlers and swindling

HUMOR
    see Wit and humor

HUMPHREY, HUBERT HORATIO, 1911-
Griffith, Winthrop. Humphrey, a
candid biography. New York, Morrow,
1965. xii, 337 p. 65-14953
    E748.H945 G7 MRR Alc.

HUNGARIAN LANGUAGE--DICTIONARIES--
ENGLISH.
Bizonfy, Ferencz, Angol-magyar
szotar, 6., bov. kiad.
(Cleveland, O.) "Szabadság" [1938?]
2 v. in 1.   42-33903
    PH2640 .B6 1938 MRR Alc.

Magyar-angol müszaki szótár.
Budapest, Akadémiai Kiadó, 1957.
viii, 752 p. 57-49792
    T9 .M14 MRR Alc.

Országh, László. Magyar-angol
kéziszótár. 2, bov. kiad.
Budapest, Akadémiai Kiadó, 1959.
xvi, 1167 p. 59-38406
    PH2640 .O725 1959 MRR Alc.

Országh, László. Magyar-angol
szótár. 2. teljesen átdolg. es
bov. kiad. Budapest, Akadémiai
Kiadó, 1963. xv, 2144 p. 64-48702

    PH2640 .O73 1963 MRR Alc.

HUNGARIAN LANGUAGE--DICTIONARIES--
POLYGLOT.
Hétnyelvü sportszótár: Budapest,
Terra, 1960-   v. 61-21333
    GV567 .H45 MRR Alc.

HUNGARIAN LANGUAGE--GRAMMAR.
Wojatsek, Charles. Hungarian:
textbook and grammar, Boulder,
Colo., Pruett Press [1962] 265 p.
494.5115 62-20830
    PH2111 .W6 MRR Alc.

HUNGARIAN LITERATURE--BIBLIOGRAPHY.
Tezla, Albert. An introductory
bibliography to the study of
Hungarian literature. Cambridge,
Harvard University Press, 1964.
xxvi, 290 p. 64-19586
    Z2148.L5 T4 MRR Alc.

HUNGARIAN LITERATURE--BIBLIOGRAPHY--
EARLY.
Szabó, Károly, Régi magyar
könyvtár ... Budapest, A. M. Tud.
Akademia Konyvkiado Hivatala, 1879-
98. 3 v. in 4.   04-32267
    Z2142 .S98 MRR Alc.

HUNGARIAN LITERATURE--HISTORY AND
CRITICISM.
Remenyi, Joseph. Hungarian writers
and literature. New Brunswick, N.
J., Rutgers University Press [1964]
xv, 512 p. 894.51109 63-16305
    PH3012 .R4 MRR Alc.

HUNGARIAN PERIODICALS--BIBLIOGRAPHY.
Bako, Elemer. Guide to Hungarian
studies. Stanford, Calif., Hoover
Institution Press [1973] 2 v. (xv,
1218 p.) 016.91439 79-152422
    Z2146 .B3 MRR Alc.

HUNGARIANS IN ROMANIA--BIBLIOGRAPHY--
CATALOGS.
United States. Library of Congress.
Hungarians in Rumania and
Transylvania; Washington, U.S. Govt.
Print. Off., 1969. vii, 192 p.
016.30145/19/451104984 71-603017
    Z2928.H8 U54 MRR Alc.

HUNGARIANS IN THE UNITED STATES--
BIOGRAPHY.
Szy, Tibor, ed. Hungarians in
America; New York, Kossuth
Foundation [c1966] viii, 488 p.
920.00917494511 66-29798
    E184.H95 S9 1966 MRR Biog.

HUNGARIANS IN TRANSYLVANIA--
BIBLIOGRAPHY--CATALOGS.
United States. Library of Congress.
Hungarians in Rumania and
Transylvania; Washington, U.S. Govt.
Print. Off., 1969. vii, 192 p.
016.30145/19/451104984 71-603017
    Z2928.H8 U54 MRR Alc.

HUNGARY.
Halasz, Zoltán, ed. Hungary,
Budapest] Corvina Press [1966] 456
p. 943.9105 66-31623
    DB906 .H28 MRR Alc.

HUNGARY--BIBLIOGRAPHY.
Bako, Elemer. Guide to Hungarian
studies. Stanford, Calif., Hoover
Institution Press [1973] 2 v. (xv,
1218 p.) 016.91439 79-152422
    Z2146 .B3 MRR Alc.

Horecky, Paul Louis, East Central
Europe; a guide to basic
publications. Chicago, University of
Chicago Press [1969] xxv, 956 p.
016.9143 70-79472
    Z2483 .H56 MRR Alc.

Szabó, Károly, Régi magyar
könyvtár ... Budapest, A. M. Tud.
Akademia Konyvkiado Hivatala, 1879-
98. 3 v. in 4.   04-32267
    Z2142 .S98 MRR Alc.

HUNGARY--BIOGRAPHY.
Kosch, Wilhelm, Biographisches
Staatshandbuch; Bern, Francke [1963]
2 v. (1208 p.) 67-3923
    DD85 .K6 MRR Biog.

Magyar életrajzi lexikon. Budapest,
Akadémiai Kiadó, 1967-69. 2 v.
68-82545
    DB822 .M25 MRR Biog.

HUNGARY--DESCRIPTION AND TRAVEL--GUIDE-
BOOKS.
Hungary; 6th rev. ed. Budapest]
Corvina Press [1969] 384 p.
914.39/1/045 72-6947
    DB905 .H8 1969 MRR Alc.

HUNGARY--DIRECTORIES.
Magyarorszag cimtara. Budapest,
Kozgazdasagi es Jogi Konyvkiado,
1961. 632 p. 62-25526
    DB904 .M32 MRR Alc.

HUNGARY--GAZETEERS.
Hungary. Kozponti Statisztikai
Hivatal. Magyarorszag
helysegnevtara. Budapest,
Statisztikai Kiado [etc.] 52-56146

    DB904 .A3 MRR Alc Latest edition

HUNGARY--GAZETTEERS.
United States. Office of Geography.
Hungary; Washington, U.S. Govt.
Print. Off., 1961. iv, 301 p. 61-
62094
    DB904 .U5 MRR Alc.

HUNGARY--HISTORY.
Ignotus, Paul, Hungary. London,
Benn, 1972. 333 p. [£3.00]
943.9/05 72-178402
    DB947 .I34 MRR Alc.

Sinor, Denis. History of Hungary.
London, Allen & Unwin [1959] 310 p.
a 60-1085
    DB925 .S28 MRR Alc.

HUNGARY--HISTORY--20TH CENTURY.
Ignotus, Paul, Hungary. London,
Benn, 1972. 333 p. [£3.00]
943.9/05 72-178402
    DB947 .I34 MRR Alc.

HUNGARY--HISTORY--CHRONOLOGY.
Bako, Elemer. Guide to Hungarian
studies. Stanford, Calif., Hoover
Institution Press [1973] 2 v. (xv,
1218 p.) 016.91439 79-152422
    Z2146 .B3 MRR Alc.

HUNGARY--IMPRINTS.
Szabó, Károly, Régi magyar
könyvtár ... Budapest, A. M. Tud.
Akademia Konyvkiado Hivatala, 1879-
98. 3 v. in 4.   04-32267
    Z2142 .S98 MRR Alc.

HUNGARY--PERIODICALS--INDEXES.
Bako, Elemer. Guide to Hungarian
studies. Stanford, Calif., Hoover
Institution Press [1973] 2 v. (xv,
1218 p.) 016.91439 79-152422
Z2146 .B3 MRR Alc.

HUNGARY--POLITICS AND GOVERNMENT--1945-
Vali, Ferenc Albert, Rift and
revolt in Hungary; Cambridge,
Harvard University Press, 1961.
xvii, 590 p. 943.9105 61-13745
DB956 .V3 MRR Alc.

HUNGARY--RELIGION.
[Mid European Law Project] Hungary,
churches and religion. [Washington]
Library of Congress, Law Library
[1951] 74 l. 56-61358
Z663.55.D5582 MRR Alc.

HUNGARY--STATISTICS.
Hungary. Kozponti Statisztikai
Hivatal. Statistical pocket book of
Hungary. Budapest, Statistical Pub.
House [etc.] 312.094391 59-40142
HA1201 .A4 MRR Alc Latest edition

Hungary. Kozponti Statisztikai
Hivatal. Statistical yearbook.
Budapest. 60-29637
HA1201 .A523 MRR Alc Latest
Edition

Hungary. Kozponti Statisztikai
Hivatal. Statisztikai evkonyv.
Budapest. 58-16707
HA1201 .A52 MRR Alc Latest edition

HUNTING.
see also Trapping

Herter, George Leonard, Professional
guide's manual, [1st ed. Waseca,
Minn.] Herter's [1960] 207 p.   799
60-21551
SK601 .H487 MRR Alc.

Oppianus. Oppian, Colluthus,
Tryphiodorus, London, W. Heinemann,
ltd.; New York, G. P. Putnam's sons,
1928. lxxx, 635, [1] p.   29-2710
PA3612 .O5 1928 MRR Alc.

Sparano, Vin T. Complete outdoors
encyclopedia. New York, Outdoor
Life, Harper & Row [1972] 622 p.
[$13.95] 799/.03 72-90934
SK33 .S646 MRR Alc.

HUNTING--DICTIONARIES.
Brander, Michael. A dictionary of
sporting terms. London, Black, 1968.
224 p. [35/-] 798 77-353522
SK11 .B66 MRR Alc.

The New hunter's encyclopedia.
Updated new print. of 3d. ed. New
York : Galahad Books, [1974?] c1972.
xx, 1054 p. : [$24.95] 799.2/97
73-92819
SK33 .H945 1974 MRR Alc.

HUNTING--YEARBOOKS.
Horse and hound year book. London,
Odhams Press [etc.] 799.25 50-22666

Began publication in 1947.
SK7 .B6 MRR Alc Latest edition

Sports afield gun annual. 1953-
[New York, Hearst Corp.] 683.058 54-
19452
TS519 .S66 MRR Alc Latest edition

HUNTING--GREAT BRITAIN.
Horse and hound year book. London,
Odhams Press [etc.] 799.25 50-22666

Began publication in 1947.
SK7 .H6 MRR Alc Latest edition

HUNTING--NORTH AMERICA.
Elman, Robert. The hunter's field
guide to the game birds and animals
of North America. New York, Knopf;
[distributed by Random House] 1974.
655 p.   598.2/97 73-7289
SK40 .E45 1974 MRR Alc.

The New hunter's encyclopedia.
Updated new print. of 3d. ed. New
York : Galahad Books, [1974?] c1972.
xx, 1054 p. : [$24.95] 799.2/97
73-92819
SK33 .H945 1974 MRR Alc.

HUNTING--UNITED STATES.
Farquhar, Carley. The sportsman's
almanac; [1st ed.] New York, Harper
& Row [1965] xiii, 493 p.
799.05873 64-25143
SK41 .F3 MRR Alc.

HUNTING DOGS.
The New hunter's encyclopedia.
Updated new print. of 3d. ed. New
York : Galahad Books, [1974?] c1972.
xx, 1054 p. : [$24.95] 799.2/97
73-92819
SK33 .H945 1974 MRR Alc.

HUNTING RIFLES.
Sharpe, Philip Burdette, The rifle
in America. 4th ed., New York, Funk
& Wagnalls [1958] 833 p.   623.442
58-4456
SK274 .S5 1958 MRR Alc.

HUNTING TROPHIES.
Boone and Crockett Club. Committee on
Records of North American Big Game.
Records of North American big game;
New York, Holt, Rinehart and Winston,
1964. 398 p.   799.2873 64-21933
SK40 .B63 1964 MRR Alc.

HURRICANES.
see also Storms

Dunn, Gordon E. Atlantic hurricanes
[Rev. ed. Baton Rouge] Louisiana
State University Press [1964] xx,
377 p. 551.552 64-21598
QC945 .D8 1964 MRR Alc.

Tannehill, Ivan Ray, Hurricanes,
their nature and history, [1st-
ed.] Princeton, Princeton University
Press, 1938- v.   551.55 38-
27260
QC945 .T32 MRR Alc.

HUSBANDRY
see Agriculture

HYBRID COMPUTERS.
see also Electronic digital computers

HYBRIDIZATION.
see also Genetics

HYDROBIOLOGY
see Marine biology

HYDROGRAPHY.
see also Lakes

see also Navigation

see also Rivers

HYDROLOGY.
see also Oceanography

see also Water

HYGIENE.
see also Air

see also Children--Care and hygiene

see also Food

see also Physical education and
training

see also Physiology

Miller, Benjamin Frank, The family
book of preventive medicine; New
York, Simon and Schuster [1971] 704
p. [$12.95] 613 70-139644
RC81 .M664 MRR Alc.

HYGIENE--STUDY AND TEACHING
see Health education

HYGIENE, INDUSTRIAL
see Industrial hygiene

HYGIENE, MENTAL
see Mental hygiene

HYGIENE, PUBLIC.
see also Hospitals

see also Medical care

see also Pollution

HYGIENE, PUBLIC--BIBLIOGRAPHY.
World Health Organization.
Publications; 1947/57- Geneva. 58-
4871
Z6660 .W57 MRR Alc Full set

HYGIENE, PUBLIC--DIRECTORIES.
American Public Health Association.
Membership directory. New York
[etc.] 614.06273 52-42786
RA421 .A557 MRR Alc Latest edition

HYGIENE, PUBLIC--RESEARCH GRANTS--
UNITED STATES.
United States. National Institutes of
Health. Division of Research Grants.
Research grants index. 1961-
Bethesda, Md. [etc.; For sale by the
Supt. of Docs., U.S. Govt. Print.
Off., Washington] 614 61-64708
RA440.6 .U47 Sci RR Latest edition
/ MRR Alc Latest edition

HYGIENE, PUBLIC--SOCIETIES, ETC.--
DIRECTORIES.
Health organizations of the United
States, Canada and internationally.
[1st]- ed.; 1961- Ithaca, N.Y.,
Graduate School of Business and
Public Administration, Cornell
University. 610.62 61-3260
R711 .H4 Sci RR Latest edition /
MRR Alc Latest edition

HYGIENE, PUBLIC--UNITED STATES--
DIRECTORIES.
American Public Health Association.
Membership directory. New York
[etc.] 614.06273 52-42786
RA421 .A557 MRR Alc Latest edition

HYGIENE, SEXUAL.
see also Birth control

McCary, James Leslie. Human
sexuality; physiological,
psychological, and sociological
factors. 2d ed. New York, Van
Nostrand [1973] xiii, 542 p.   612.6
72-7809
HQ21 .M115 1973 MRR Alc.

HYMNS--DICTIONARIES.
Julian, John, A dictionary of
hymnology, New York, Dover
Publications [1957] 2 v. (xviii,
1768 p.) 245.03 58-416
BV305 .J8 1957 MRR Alc.

HYMNS--INDEXES.
Julian, John, A dictionary of
hymnology, New York, Dover
Publications [1957] 2 v. (xviii,
1768 p.) 245.03 58-416
BV305 .J8 1957 MRR Alc.

HYMNS, ENGLISH.
Protestant Episcopal Church in the
U.S.A. Hymnal. The hymnal of the
Protestant Episcopal Church in the
United States of America. Greenwich,
Conn., Seabury Press [1953, c1943]
673 p.   65-6189
BX5943.A1 1953 MRR Alc.

HYMNS, ENGLISH--HISTORY AND CRITICISM.
Metcalf, Frank Johnson, American
writers and compilers of sacred
music, New York, Cincinnati, The
Abingdon press [c1925] 373 p.   25-
18159
ML106.U3 M3 MRR Biog.

HYMNS, ENGLISH--INDEXES.
McDormand, Thomas Bruce. Judson
concordance to hymns Valley Forge,
Judson Press [1965] 375 p.   245.203
65-15009
BV305 .M3 MRR Alc.

HYPNOTISM.
Volgyesi, Ferenc Andras, Hypnosis
of man and animals, 2d ed., rev.
Baltimore, Williams & Wilkins Co.
[c1966] xiv, 216 p.   154.7 67-2798
BF1148.H8 V63 1966a MRR Alc.

HYPNOTISM--DICTIONARIES.
Winn, Ralph Bubrich, Dictionary of
hypnosis, New York, Philosophical
Library [1965] 124 p.   134.03 65-
10663
BF1141 .W717 MRR Alc.

ICE--CLASSIFICATION.
United States. Library of Congress.
Reference Dept. Russian-English
glossary and Soviet classification of
ice found at sea, Washington, 1959.
vi, 30 p.   551.3403 59-60067
Z663.2 .R825 MRR Alc.

ICE HOCKEY
see Hockey

ICELAND.
Nordal, Johannes, Iceland 1966;
Reykjavik, Central Bank of Iceland,
1967. xi, 390 p.   914.81/2/03 73-
8309
DL313 .T52 MRR Alc.

ICELAND--BIOGRAPHY.
Pall Eggert Olason, Islenzkar
eviskrar fra landnamstimum til
arsloka 1940. Reykjavik, Birt a
kostnad hins islenzka
bokmenntafelags, 1948- v.   50-
28079
CT1280 .P34 MRR Biog.

ICELAND--BIOGRAPHY--DICTIONARIES.
Dictionary of Scandinavian biography.
London, Melrose Press [1972] xxxv,
467 p. [£10.50] 920/.048 B 73-
189270
CT1243 .D53 MRR Biog.

ICELAND--COMMERCE--DIRECTORIES.
Nordisk handelskalender, Kobenhavn,
H. P. Bov. 49-23912
Began with vol. for 1903.
HF5193 .N6 MRR Alc Latest edition

Vidskiptaskrain; atvinnu- og
kaupsysluskra Islands.
Reykjavik, Steindorsprent h.f.
650.58 45-22755
HF5199 .V5 MRR Alc Latest edition

ICELAND--DESCRIPTION AND TRAVEL--GUIDE-
BOOKS.
Iceland. 2d ed. New York, McGraw-
Hill [1965] 111 p.   914.912044 65-
8612
DL304 .I2 1965 MRR Alc.

ICELAND--DESCRIPTION AND TRAVEL- (Cont.)
Karlsson, Petur Kidson, Iceland in
a nutshell; [3d ed.] Reykjavik,
Iceland Travel Books, 1971. 240 p.
914.91/2/044 72-181175
DL304 .K37 1971 MRR Alc.

ICELAND--GAZETTEERS.
United States. Office of Geography.
Iceland; Washington, U.S. Govt.
Print. Off., 1961. ix, 231 p. 62-
60600
DL304 .U5 MRR Alc.

ICELAND--INDUSTRIES--DIRECTORIES.
Vidskiptaskráin; atvinnu- og
kaupsýsluskra Íslands.
Reykjavik, Steindorsprent h.f.
650.58 45-22755
HF5199 .V5 MRR Alc Latest edition

ICELANDIC AND OLD NORSE LANGUAGES--
BIBLIOGRAPHY--PERIODICALS.
Bibliography of Old Norse-Icelandic
studies. Copenhagen, Munksgaard.
016.91003/175/396 68-45376
Began in 1963.
Z2556 .B5 MRR Alc Full set

ICELANDIC AND OLD NORSE LANGUAGES--
DICTIONARIES--ENGLISH.
Cleasby, Richard, An Icelandic-
English dictionary, 2d ed. Oxford,
Clarendon Press, 1957. xiv, 833 p.
439.6 57-4901
PD2379 .C5 1957 MRR Alc.

Zoëga, Geir Tómasson, A concise
dictionary of old Icelandic, Oxford,
The Clarendon press, 1926. vii, 551,
[1] p. 46-28683
PD2379 .Z6 1926 MRR Alc.

ICELANDIC AND OLD NORSE LITERATURE--
BIBLIOGRAPHY--PERIODICALS.
Bibliography of Old Norse-Icelandic
studies. Copenhagen, Munksgaard.
016.91003/175/396 68-45376
Began in 1963.
Z2556 .B5 MRR Alc Full set

ICELANDIC AND OLD NORSE LITERATURE--
HISTORY AND CRITICISM.
Einarsson, Stefán, A history of
Icelandic literature. New York,
Johns Hopkins Press for the American-
Scandinavian Foundation, 1957. xii,
409 p. 839.609 57-9519
PT7150 .E4 MRR Alc.

ICELANDIC LANGUAGE, MODERN--
DICTIONARIES--ENGLISH.
Arngrímur Sigurdsson, Íslenzk-ensk
ordabók. Reykjavík, Prentsmidjan
Leiftur [1970] 925 p. 73-263432
PD2437 .A7 MRR Alc.

Zoëga, Geir Tómasson, Íslenzk-
ensk ordabók, 3. utg. Reykjavík,
S. Kristjánssonar, 1942. 631, [1]
p. 438.632 46-28351
PD2437 .Z7 1942 MRR Alc.

ICELANDIC LITERATURE, MODERN--HISTORY
AND CRITICISM.
Einarsson, Stefán, A history of
Icelandic literature. New York,
Johns Hopkins Press for the American-
Scandinavian Foundation, 1957. xii,
409 p. 839.609 57-9519
PT7150 .E4 MRR Alc.

ICHTHYOLOGY.
see also Fishes

ICONOGRAPHY
see Art

see Portraits

IDAHO.
Federal Writers' Project. Idaho.
Idaho, a guide in word and picture.
[2d ed. rev.] New York, Oxford
University Press, 1950. xiv, 300 p.
917.96 50-13175
F746 .F453 MRR Ref Desk.

Federal writers' project. Idaho. The
Idaho encyclopedia, Caldwell, Id.,
The Caxton printers, ltd., 1938. 4
p. l., [7]-452 p. 917.96 38-27097

F746 .F46 MRR Alc.

IDAHO--BIBLIOGRAPHY.
Historical records survey. A check
list of Idaho imprints, 1839-1890.
Chicago, The WPA Historical records
survey project, 1940. 66, 66a-66b,
67-74 numb. l. 015.796 41-50084
Z1215 .H67 no. 13 MRR Alc.

IDAHO--DESCRIPTION AND TRAVEL--GUIDE-
BOOKS.
Federal Writers' Project. Idaho.
Idaho, a guide in word and picture.
[2d ed. rev.] New York, Oxford
University Press, 1950. xiv, 300 p.
917.96 50-13175
F746 .F453 MRR Ref Desk.

IDAHO--IMPRINTS.
Historical records survey. A check
list of Idaho imprints, 1839-1890.
Chicago, The WPA Historical records
survey project, 1940. 66, 66a-66b,
67-74 numb. l. 015.796 41-50084
Z1215 .H67 no. 13 MRR Alc.

IDAHO--INDUSTRIES--DIRECTORIES.
Idaho manufacturers directory.
[Chicago, Manufacturers' News, inc.]
66-97800
HC107.I2 I3 MRR Alc Latest edition

IDAHO--MANUFACTURES--DIRECTORIES.
Idaho. Dept. of Commerce and
Development. Idaho directory of
manufacturers, 1967-1968. Boise
[1968] 83 p. [3.50] 338.4/09796
78-625584
HD9727.I2 A35 MRR Alc.

IDAHO--POLITICS AND GOVERNMENT.
Idaho. Secretary of State. Report.
Boise [etc.] 53-25888
J87. I24a MRR Alc Latest edition

IDAHO--REGISTERS.
Idaho. Secretary of State. Report.
Boise [etc.] 53-25888
J87. I24a MRR Alc Latest edition

IDEA (PHILOSOPHY)--DICTIONARIES.
Dictionary of the history of ideas;
New York, Scribner [1973] 4 v.
[$35.00 (per vol.)] 901.9 72-7943

CB5 .D52 MRR Alc.

IDEAL STATES
see Utopias

IDENTIFICATION.
Directory of identification bureaus
of the world. Chicago. 573.6 47-
26908
HV8073 .D5 MRR Alc Latest edition

IDENTIFICATION OF ROCKS
see Rocks--Identification

IDEOGRAPHY
see Picture-writing

IDOLS AND IMAGES.
see also Dolls

ILE DE FRANCE (PROVINCE)--DESCRIPTION
AND TRAVEL--GUIDE-BOOKS.
Ile de France, environs de Paris.
Paris, Hachette, 1958. lxxii, 758 p.
58-48587
DC768 .E52 MRR Alc.

ILLINOIS--BIBLIOGRAPHY--CATALOGS.
United States. Library of Congress
Illinois: the sesquicentennial of
statehood; Washington; [For sale by
the Supt. of Docs., U.S. Govt. Print.
Off.] 1968. viii, 58 p. [$0.70]
977.3 68-67013
Z663.15.A6 I5 MRR Alc.

ILLINOIS--BIOGRAPHY.
Illinois blue book. [Springfield]
10-13132
JK5730 .A25 MRR Alc Latest edition

ILLINOIS--CENTENNIAL CELEBRATIONS, ETC.
United States. Library of Congress
Illinois: the sesquicentennial of
statehood; Washington; [For sale by
the Supt. of Docs., U.S. Govt. Print.
Off.] 1968. viii, 58 p. [$0.70]
977.3 68-67013
Z663.15.A6 I5 MRR Alc.

ILLINOIS--DESCRIPTION AND TRAVEL--GUIDE-
BOOKS.
Federal writers' project. Illinois.
Illinois; a descriptive and
historical guide, Rev, Chicago, A.
C. McClurg & co. [1947] xxii, 707 p.
917.73 47-30173
F546 .F45 1947 MRR Ref Desk.

ILLINOIS--DICTIONARIES AND
ENCYCLOPEDIAS.
Clayton, John, The Illinois fact
book and historical almanac, 1673-
1968. Carbondale, Southern Illinois
University Press [1970] vii, 568 p.
[3.25] 977.3/003 68-21417
F539 .C55 MRR Alc.

ILLINOIS--EXECUTIVE DEPARTMENTS.
Illinois. Office of Planning and
Analysis. State of Illinois
statistical report. 1972-
[Springfield] 317.73 73-641048
HA341 .A38 MRR Alc Latest edition

ILLINOIS--HISTORY.
Federal writers' project. Illinois.
Illinois; a descriptive and
historical guide, Rev, Chicago, A.
C. McClurg & co. [1947] xxii, 707 p.
917.73 47-30173
F546 .F45 1947 MRR Ref Desk.

Howard, Robert P. Illinois; a
history of the Prairie State, Grand
Rapids, Mich., W. B. Eerdmans Pub.
Co. [1972] xxiv, 626 p. [$10.95]
977.3 72-77179
F541 .H68 MRR Alc.

Pease, Theodore Calvin; The story of
Illinois. 3d ed., rev. Chicago,
University of Chicago Press [1965]
xvi, 331 p. 977.3 65-17299
F541 .P36 1965 MRR Alc.

ILLINOIS--HISTORY--DICTIONARIES.
Clayton, John, The Illinois fact
book and historical almanac, 1673-
1968. Carbondale, Southern Illinois
University Press [1970] vii, 568 p.
[3.25] 977.3/003 68-21417
F539 .C55 MRR Alc.

ILLINOIS--IMPRINTS.
Byrd, Cecil K. A bibliography of
Illinois imprints, 1814-58, Chicago,
University of Chicago Press [1966]
xxv, 601 p. 015.773 65-24423
Z1277 .B9 MRR Alc.

ILLINOIS--INDUSTRIES--CLASSIFICATION.
Illinois services directory. 1974-
Chicago, Manufacturers' News, inc.
[$49.95] 338/.0025/773 73-647474
HC107.I3 I62 MRR Alc Latest
edition

ILLINOIS--INDUSTRIES--DIRECTORIES.
Illinois services directory. 1974-
Chicago, Manufacturers' News, inc.
[$49.95] 338/.0025/773 73-647474
HC107.I3 I62 MRR Alc Latest
edition

ILLINOIS--MANUFACTURES--DIRECTORIES.
Midwest manufacturers and industrial
directory buyers guide. [Detroit,
Industrial Directory Publishers]
338.4/0977 72-626483
HC107.A15 M5 MRR Alc Latest
edition

Where to buy, where to sell; 1941-
ed. Chicago, Manufacturers' news.
42-14309
T12 .W5 Sci RR Latest edition /
MRR Alc Latest edition

ILLINOIS--POLITICS AND GOVERNMENT--
YEARBOOKS.
Illinois blue book. [Springfield]
10-13132
JK5730 .A25 MRR Alc Latest edition

ILLINOIS--REGISTERS.
Illinois. Secretary of State.
Directory of Illinois State officers.
1942- [Springfield] a 57-9172
JK5730 .A23 MRR Alc Latest edition

Illinois blue book. [Springfield]
10-13132
JK5730 .A25 MRR Alc Latest edition

ILLINOIS--STATISTICS.
Clayton, John, The Illinois fact
book and historical almanac, 1673-
1968. Carbondale, Southern Illinois
University Press [1970] vii, 568 p.
[3.25] 977.3/003 68-21417
F539 .C55 MRR Alc.

Illinois. Office of Planning and
Analysis. State of Illinois
statistical report. 1972-
[Springfield] 317.73 73-641048
HA341 .A38 MRR Alc Latest edition

Illinois State and regional economic
data book. 1972- [Springfield,
Dept. of Business and Economic
Development] 330.9/773 74-644521
HA343 .A3 MRR Alc Latest edition

ILLINOIS--STATISTICS--PERIODICALS.
Illinois. Bureau of the Budget.
State of Illinois statistical
abstract. [Springfield] 317.73 74-
645555
HA341 .B85a MRR Alc Latest edition

ILLUMINATION OF BOOKS AND MANUSCRIPTS--
HISTORY.
Bland, David. A history of book
illustration: [1st ed.] Cleveland,
World Pub. Co. [1958] 448 p.
741.64 58-10061
NC960 .B62 MRR Alc.

Diringer, David, The illuminated
book; Rev. ed. New York, Praeger
[1967] 514 p. 745.6/7/09 66-12525

ND2920 .D55 1967 MRR Alc.

ILLUMINATION OF BOOKS AND MANUSCRIPTS--
SPECIMENS, REPRODUCTIONS, ETC.
Browne, Edward Granville, A literary
history of Persia ... Cambridge
[Eng.] The University press, 1828-
1930. 4 v. mrr01-34
PK6097 .B73 MRR Alc.

ILLUSTRATED BOOKS--15TH AND 16TH
CENTURY.
Pollard, Alfred William, Early
illustrated books; London, K. Paul,
Trench, Trübner & co., ltd., 1893.
xvi, 256 p. incl. illus., plates,
facsim. 02-8241
Z1023 .P77 MRR Alc.

ILLUSTRATED BOOKS--BIBLIOGRAPHY.
Bolton, Theodore, American book
illustrators; New York, R. R. Bowker
company, 1938. xii p., 1 l., 290 p.
016.0961 38-6154
Z1023 .B71 MRR Alc.

Latimer, Louise Payson,
Illustrators, a finding list,
Boston, The F. W. Faxon company,
1929. 2 p. l., 3-29, [1], 30-47 p.
016.74 29-27458
NC960 .L3 1929 MRR Alc.

ILLUSTRATED BOOKS--BIBLIOGRAPHY--
CATALOGS.
Princeton University. Library. Early
American book illustrators and wood
engravers, 1670-1870; Princeton,
N.J., 1958. xlvii, 265 p. 761.2084
58-9784
Z1023 .P9 1958 MRR Alc.

ILLUSTRATED BOOKS--INDEXES.
Clapp, Jane. Sculpture index.
Metuchen, N.J., Scarecrow Press, 1970
[c1970-71] 2 v. in 3. 730/.16 79-
9538
NB36 .C55 MRR Alc.

Ellis, Jessie Croft, comp. General
index to illustrations; Boston, The
F. W. Faxon company, 1931. 4 p. l.,
467 p. 016.74 31-28562
NC996 .E6 MRR Ref Desk.

Ellis, Jessie (Croft) Index to
illustrations. Boston, F. W. Faxon
Co., 1966 [c1967] xi, 682 p.
741.6/01/6 66-11619
NC996 .E62 MRR Ref Desk.

Ellis, Jessie (Croft) Nature and its
applications; Boston, F. W. Faxon
Co., 1949. xii, 861 p. 016.745 49-
9331
Z5956.D3 E53 MRR Alc.

Ellis, Jessie (Croft) comp. Nature
index; Boston, The F. W. Faxon
company, 1930. 4 p. l., 319 p.
016.745 30-20661
Z5956.D3 E5 MRR Alc.

Ellis, Jessie (Croft) Travel through
pictures; Boston, The F. W. Faxon
company, 1935. xi, 699 p. 016.91
35-27172
Z6020 .E47 MRR Alc.

Hewlett-Woodmere Public Library.
Index to art reproductions in books.
Metuchen, N.J., Scarecrow Press,
1974. xii, 178 p. 709 74-1286
N7525 .H48 1974 MRR Alc.

Monro, Isabel Stevenson, ed. Costume
index; New York, H. W. Wilson Co.,
1937. x, 338 p. 016.391 37-7142
Z5691 .M75 MRR Alc.

Monro, Isabel Stevenson. Index to
reproductions of American paintings;
New York, H. W. Wilson Co., 1948.
731 p. 759.13 48-8663
ND205 .M57 MRR Ref Desk.

Monro, Isabel Stevenson. Index to
reproductions of European paintings;
New York, Wilson, 1956. 668 p.
016.759 55-6803
ND45 .M6 M44 Ref Desk.

Shepard, Frederick Job, comp. Index
to illustrations, Preliminary ed.
Chicago, American library
association, 1924. 89 p. 24-26753
NC996 .S5 MRR Ref Desk.

Vance, Lucile E. Illustration index,
2d ed. New York, Scarecrow Press,
1966. 527 p. 011 65-13558
N7525 .V3 1966 MRR Ref Desk.

ILLUSTRATED BOOKS, CHILDREN'S--
BIBLIOGRAPHY.
Children's books in print. 1969-
New York, R. R. Bowker Co. 028.52
70-101705
Z1037.A1 C482 MRR Alc Latest
edition

Kingman, Lee, comp. Illustrators of
children's books, 1957-1966, Boston,
Horn Book, 1968. xvii, 295 p.
[20.00] 016.7416/42/0922 76-4001
NC965 .K54 MRR Alc.

Miller, Bertha E. (Mahony)
Illustrators of children's books,
1744-1945, [1st ed.] Boston, Horn
Book, 1947. xvi, 527 p. 741.642
47-31264
NC965 .M59 MRR Alc.

Viguers, Ruth Hill, comp.
Illustrators of children's books,
1946-1956, Boston, Horn Book, 1958.
xvii, 299 p. 741.6/42/0922 79-4034
NC965 .V5 MRR Alc.

ILLUSTRATED PERIODICALS--INDEXES.
Ellis, Jessie Croft, comp. General
index to illustrations; Boston, The
F. W. Faxon company, 1931. 4 p. l.,
467 p. 016.74 31-28562
NC996 .E6 MRR Ref Desk.

Ellis, Jessie (Croft) Index to
illustrations. Boston, F. W. Faxon
Co., 1966 [c1967] xi, 682 p.
741.6/01/6 66-11619
NC996 .E62 MRR Ref Desk.

Ellis, Jessie (Croft) Nature and its
applications; Boston, F. W. Faxon
Co., 1949. xii, 861 p. 016.745 49-
9331
Z5956.D3 E53 MRR Alc.

Ellis, Jessie (Croft) comp. Nature
index; Boston, The F. W. Faxon
company, 1930. 4 p. l., 319 p.
016.745 30-20661
Z5956.D3 E5 MRR Alc.

Ellis, Jessie (Croft) Travel through
pictures; Boston, The F. W. Faxon
company, 1935. xi, 699 p. 016.91
35-27172
Z6020 .E47 MRR Alc.

Greer, Roger C., Illustration index,
3d ed. Metuchen, N.J., Scarecrow
Press, 1973. 164 p. 011 72-10918

N7525 .G72 1973 MRR Ref Desk.

Havlice, Patricia Pate. Art in Time.
Metuchen, N.J., Scarecrow Press,
1970. 350 p. 016.7 76-14885
N7225 .H38 MRR Alc.

Shepard, Frederick Job, comp. Index
to illustrations, Preliminary ed.
Chicago, American library
association, 1924. 89 p. 24-26753

NC996 .S5 MRR Ref Desk.

Vance, Lucile E. Illustration index,
2d ed. New York, Scarecrow Press,
1966. 527 p. 011 65-13558
N7525 .V3 1966 MRR Ref Desk.

ILLUSTRATION OF BOOKS--HISTORY.
Bland, David. A history of book
illustration; [1st ed.] Cleveland,
World Pub. Co. [1958] 448 p.
741.64 58-10061
NC960 .B62 MRR Alc.

Bland, David. The illustration of
books. [2d ed.; rev.] London, Faber
and Faber [1953] 164 p. 741.64 54-
24772
Z1023 .B63 1953 MRR Alc.

ILLUSTRATION OF BOOKS--UNITED STATES.
Reed, Walt, ed. The illustrator in
America, 1900-1960's, New York,
Reinhold Pub. Corp. [1967, c1966]
271, [1] p. 741.60973 66-24545
NC975 .R4 MRR Alc.

ILLUSTRATION OF BOOKS--UNITED STATES--
HISTORY.
Princeton University. Library. Early
American book illustrators and wood
engravers, 1670-1870; Princeton,
N.J., 1958. xlvii, 265 p. 761.2084
58-9784
Z1023 .P9 1958 MRR Alc.

ILLUSTRATORS.
De Montreville, Doris. Third book of
junior authors. New York, H. W.
Wilson Co., 1972. 320 p.
809/.89282 75-149381
PN1009.A1 D45 MRR Biog.

Doyle, Brian. The who's who of
children's literature, New York,
Schocken Books [1968] xi, 380 p.
[$10.00] 028.52 68-28904
PN452 .D6 1968b MRR Biog.

Hopkins, Lee Bennett. Books are by
people; New York, Citation Press,
1969. xv, 349 p. 028.5/0922 70-
86312
PN452 .H65 MRR Biog.

Kingman, Lee, comp. Illustrators of
children's books, 1957-1966, Boston,
Horn Book, 1968. xvii, 295 p.
[20.00] 016.7416/42/0922 76-4001
NC965 .K54 MRR Alc.

Kunitz, Stanley Jasspon, ed. The
junior book of authors, New York,
The H. W. Wilson company, 1934. xv,
400 p. 928 34-36776
PN1009.A1 K8 MRR Biog.

Latimer, Louise Payson,
Illustrators, a finding list,
Boston, The F. W. Faxon company,
1929. 2 p. l., 3-29, [1], 30-47 p.
016.74 29-27458
NC960 .L3 1929 MRR Alc.

Miller, Bertha E. (Mahony)
Illustrators of children's books,
1744-1945, [1st ed.] Boston, Horn
Book, 1947. xvi, 527 p. 741.642
47-31264
NC965 .M59 MRR Alc.

Viguers, Ruth Hill, comp.
Illustrators of children's books,
1946-1956, Boston, Horn Book, 1958.
xvii, 299 p. 741.6/42/0922 79-4034

NC965 .V5 MRR Alc.

Who's who in graphic art. 1st-
ed.; 1962- Zurich, Amstutz & Herdeg
Graphis Press. 62-51802
NC45 .W5 MRR Biog Latest edition

ILLUSTRATORS--UNITED STATES.
Bolton, Theodore, American book
illustrators; New York, R. R. Bowker
company, 1938. xii p., 1 l., 290 p.
016.0961 38-6154
Z1023 .B71 MRR Alc.

Reed, Walt, ed. The illustrator in
America, 1900-1960's, New York,
Reinhold Pub. Corp. [1967, c1966]
271, [1] p. 741.60973 66-24545
NC975 .R4 MRR Alc.

Taft, Robert, Artists and
illustrators of the Old West, 1850-
1900. New York, Scribner, 1953.
xvii, 400 p. 709.78 53-7577
N6510 .T27 MRR Alc.

ILLUSTRATORS, AMERICAN--BIBLIOGRAPHY.
Children's books in print. 1969-
New York, R. R. Bowker Co. 028.52
70-101705
Z1037.A1 C482 MRR Alc Latest
edition

Princeton University. Library. Early
American book illustrators and wood
engravers, 1670-1870; Princeton,
N.J., 1958. xlvii, 265 p. 761.2084
58-9784
Z1023 .P9 1958 MRR Alc.

IMAGINARY WARS AND BATTLES.
see also Prophecies

IMBECILITY
see Mentally handicapped

IMMIGRATION
see Emigration and immigration

IMMUNOPATHOLOGY.
see also Allergy

IMPEACHMENTS--UNITED STATES.
Congressional Quarterly, inc.
Impeachment and the U.S. Congress.
Washington, 1974. 60 p.
342/.73/062 74-5285
KF4985 .C65 MRR Ref Desk.

IMPEACHMENTS--UNITED STATES--
BIBLIOGRAPHY.
United States. Library of Congress.
Division of bibliography ... Select
list of references on impeachment.
2d ed. with additions, Washington,
Govt. print. off., 1912. 38 p. 12-
35011
Z663.28 .S37 1912 MRR Alc.

IMPERIAL FEDERATION.
Williamson, James Alexander, A
notebook of Commonwealth history. 2d
ed. London, MacMillan; New York, St.
Martin's Press, 1960. 307 p.
942.002 61-212
DA16 .W73 1960 MRR Alc.

IMPERIALISM--BIBLIOGRAPHY.
Halstead, John P. Modern European
imperialism; Boston, G. K. Hall,
1974. 2 v. 016.90908 73-19511
Z6204 .H35 MRR Alc.

IMPERIALISM--COLLECTIONS.
Snyder, Louis Leo, ed. The
imperialism reader; Princeton, N.J.,
Van Nostrand [1962] 619 p. 321.03
62-3115
JC359 .S65 MRR Alc.

IMPLEMENTS, UTENSILS, ETC.
see also Agricultural machinery

see also Tools

IMPLEMENTS, UTENSILS, ETC.--COLLECTORS
AND COLLECTING.
Lantz, Louise K. Old American
kitchenware 1725-1925 Camden, T.
Nelson [1970] 289 p. 683/.82 75-
101527
NK806 .L28 MRR Alc.

IMPLIED POWERS (CONSITIONAL LAW)
see also Legislative power

IMPORTS
see Commerce

IMPOSTORS AND IMPOSTURE.
Mackay, Charles, Extraordinary
popular delusions and the madness of
crowds. London, G. G. Harrap [1956]
xxiv, 724 p. 301.15 133.7 57-1736

AZ999 .M2 1956 MRR Alc.

McBride, Robert Medill, ed. Great
hoaxes of all time. [1st ed.] New
York, R. M. McBride Co. [1956] 282
p. 133.7 56-13433
CT9980 .M2 MRR Alc.

300 MAIN READING ROOM REFERENCE COLLECTION SUBJECT CATALOG

IMPRESSIONISM (ART)
Bowness, Alan, ed. Impressionists and post-impressionists. New York, F. Watts [1965] 296 p. 709.034 65-10269
ND1265 .B67 MRR Alc.

Rewald, John. The history of impressionism. Rev. and enl. ed. New York, Museum of Modern Art [1961] 662 p. 759.05 61-7684
ND1265 .R4 1961 MRR Alc.

IMPRESSIONISM (ART)--FRANCE--DICTIONARIES.
Cogniat, Raymond, A dictionary of Impressionism [with an introduction by Jean Selz; London, Eyre Methuen, 1973. 168 p. [£1.50] 759.4 74-180882
N6847.I4 C6313 1973 MRR Alc.

IMPRINTS (IN BOOKS)
Grasse, Johann Georg Theodor, Orbis Latinus; Grossausgabe, Braunschweig, Klinkhardt & Biermann [c1972] 3 v. 72-345986
G107 .G8 1972 MRR Alc.

Peddie, Robert Alexander, Place names in imprints; London, Grafton & co., 1932. vii, [1] p., 1 l., 61 numb. l., 1 l. 929.4 32-11548
Z125 .P37 MRR Ref Desk.

IMPRINTS (IN BOOKS), FICTITIOUS.
Parenti, Marino, Dizionario dei luoghi di stampa falsi, inventati o supposti in opere di autori e traduttori italiani, Firenze, Sansoni, 1951. 311 p. a 52-649
Z125 .P3 MRR Alc.

IMPRISONMENT.
see also Prisons

INCANTATIONS.
Ovidius Naso, Publius. Ovid; the Art of love, and other poems, London, W. Heinemann; New York, G. P. Putnam's sons, 1929. xiv, 381 [1] p. mrr01-57
PA6156.082 1929d MRR Alc.

INCOME.
Organization for Economic Cooperation and Development. National accounts statistics 1950-1968. [Paris, 1970] 415 p. [$7.50 (U.S.)] 339.3 73-535302
HC79.I5 0674 MRR Alc.

Organization for Economic Cooperation and Development. National accounts statistics, 1960-1971. [Paris, 1973] 471 p. [$7.50 (U.S.)] 339.3 74-158206
HC79.I5 07 1973 MRR Alc.

United Nations. Statistical Office. The growth of world industry, 1938-1961; New York, United Nations, 1963. xvi, 849 p. 338.4083 63-25411
HC59 .U46 MRR Alc.

United Nations. Statistical Office. Yearbook of national accounts statistics. 1957- New York. 58-3719
HC79.I5 U53 MRR Ref Desk Latest edition / MRR Alc Latest edition

INCOME--UNITED STATES.
Surveys of consumers. 1971/72- [Ann Arbor, Mich., Institute for Social Research, University of Michigan] 658.8/3973 72-619718
HC110.S3 A3 MRR Alc Latest edition

Swinton, David H. Aggregate personal income of the Black population in the U.S.A.: 1947-1980, [New York, Black Economic Research Center, c1973] viii, 75 p. [$3.00] 339.4/1/0973 74-157912
E185.8 .S98 MRR Alc.

United States. Office of Business Economics. Personal income, by States, since 1929; New York, Greenwood Press [1969] iv, 229 p. 339.41/0973 79-92310
HC110.I5 A55 1969 MRR Alc.

INCOME--UNITED STATES--STATISTICS.
Henson, Mary F. Trends in the income of families and persons in the United States, 1947-1964, [Washington] U.S. Dept. of Commerce, Bureau of the Census [1967] vi, 294 p. 339.2/1/0973 a 67-7508
HC110.I5 H4 MRR Alc.

INCOME TAX--UNITED STATES.
Standard and Poor's Corporation. Status of bonds under the federal income and state taxes and coupon directory. 1942- ed. New York. 332.630973 42-15584
HG4921 .S67 MRR Alc Latest edition

INCOME TAX--UNITED STATES--LAW.
J. K. Lasser's your income tax. New York, Simon and Schuster. 39-27140 Began publication with 1936 issue.
KF6369.6 .J18 MRR Ref Desk Latest edition

Prentice-Hall, inc. Federal tax handbook. 1947- Englewood Cliffs, N.J. [etc.] 336.2 47-5117
KF6289.A1 P73 MRR Alc Latest edition

INCUNABULA.
Hain, Ludwig Friedrich Theodor, Repertorium bibliographicum, Milano, Gorlich [1948] 2 v. in 4. 016.093 49-5506
Z240 .H15 1948 MRR Alc.

Peddie, Robert Alexander, Fifteenth-century books: New York, B. Franklin [1969] 89 p. 016.016/.093 73-101990
Z240.A1 P4 1969 MRR Alc.

Pollard, Alfred William, Early illustrated books; London, K. Paul, Trench, Trubner & co., ltd. 1893. xvi, 256 p. incl. illus., plates, facsim. 02-8241
Z1023 .P77 MRR Alc.

INCUNABULA--BIBLIOGRAPHY.
Besterman, Theodore, Early printed books to the end of the sixteenth century; 2d ed., rev. and much enl. Geneve, Societas Bibliographica, 1961. 344 p. 016.016093 62-2500
Z1002 .B562 1961 MRR Alc.

British Museum. Dept. of Printed Books. Short-title catalogue of books printed in the Netherlands and Belgium London, Trustees of the British Museum, 1965. viii, 274 p. 66-4468
Z2402 .B7 MRR Alc.

Copinger, Walter Arthur, Supplement to Hain's Repertorium bibliographicum; Milano, Gorlich [1950] 2 pts. in 3 v. 016.093 50-4684
Z240.H15 S 1950 MRR Alc.

Daley, Charles Marie, Dominican incunabula in the Library of Congress, [New York, United States Catholic historical society, 1932] 88 p. 016.093 33-476
Z240 .U58 1932 MRR Alc.

Flodr, Miroslav. Incunabula classicorum. Amsterdam, Adolf H. Hakkert, 1973. xv, 530 p. 74-310002
Z240.A1 F57 MRR Alc.

Gesamtkatalog der wiegendrucke, herausgegeben von der Kommission für den Gesamtkatalog der wiegendrucke ... Leipzig, K. W. Hiersemann, 1925- v. 25-23783
Z240 .G39 MRR Alc.

Hain, Ludwig Friedrich Theodor, Repertorium bibliographicum, Milano, Gorlich [1948] 2 v. in 4. 016.093 49-5506
Z240 .H15 1948 MRR Alc.

Mumey, Nolie, A study of rare books, Denver, The Clason publishing company, 1930. xvii p., 2 l., 3-572 p. 090 30-25438
Z1012 .M95 MRR Alc.

Polain, Louis, Catalogue des livres imprimes au quinzieme siecle des bibliotheques de Belgique. Bruxelles, Pour la Societé des bibliophiles & iconophiles de Belgique, 1932. 4 v. 016.093 33-18424
Z240 .P76 MRR Alc.

Reichling, Dietrich, Appendices ad Hainii-Copingeri Repertorivm bibliographicvm; Monachii, svmptibvs R. Rosenthal, 1905-11. 7 v. 05-10368
Z240.H15 S2 MRR Alc.

United States. Library of Congress. Rare Book Division. Fifteenth century books in the Library of Congress; Washington, U.S. Govt. Print. Off., 1950. 82 p. 016.093 50-62960
Z663.4 .F4 MRR Alc.

INCUNABULA--BIBLIOGRAPHY--CATALOGS.
British Museum. Dept. of Printed Books. Catalogue of books printed in the XVth century now in the British Museum. London, Printed by order of the trustees; sold at the British Museum, 1908- v. in 016.093 09-22616
Z240 .B85 MRR Alc (Dk 33).

British Museum. Dept. of Printed Books. Short-title catalogue of books printed in Italy London, Trustees of the British Museum, 1958. viii, 992 p. 015.45 a 60-1778
Z2342 .B7 MRR Alc.

British Museum. Dept. of Printed Books. Short-title catalogue of books printed in the German-speaking countries London, Trustees of the British Museum, 1962. viii, 1224 p. 63-24516
Z2222 .B73 MRR Alc.

Cambridge. University. Library. Early English printed books in the University library, Cambridge (1475 to 1640). Cambridge, The University press, 1900-07. 4 v. 01-15519
Z2002 .C17 MRR Alc.

Goff, Frederick Richmond, ed. Incunabula in American libraries; New York, Bibliographical Society of America, 1964. [xii], 798 p. 016.093 65-1485
Z240 .G58 MRR Alc.

Hispanic Society of America. Printed books, 1468-1700, in the Hispanic Society of America: New York, 1965. xlii, 614 p. 018.1 65-22528
Z1012 .H58 MRR Alc.

Hispanic society of America. Library. List of books printed 1601-1700, in the library of the Hispanic society of America, New York, Printed by order of the trustees, 1938. xxvi, 972 p. 015.46 38-15765
Z2682 .H671 MRR Alc.

Hispanic Society of America. Library. List of books printed before 1601 in the Library of the Hispanic Society of America. Offset reissue, with additions. New York, Printed by order of the trustees, the Hispanic Society of America, 1955. xiv, 305 p. 015.46 56-583
Z2682 .H67 1955 MRR Alc.

Scotland. National Library, Edinburgh. A short-title catalogue of foreign books printed up to 1600; Edinburgh, H.M. Stationery Off., 1970. viii, 545 p. [£17/-/-] 018/.1 77-579020
Z1014 .S35 MRR Alc.

Thacher, John Boyd, Catalogue of the John Boyd Thacher collection of incunabula. Washington, Govt. print. off., 1915. 329 p. incl. illus., facsim. in colors. 14-30012
Z663.4 .C2 MRR Alc.

United States. Library of Congress. Early printed books of the Low Countries Washington, 1858. vi, 37 p. 016.09 58-60011
Z663.4 .E2 MRR Alc.

United States. National Library of Medicine. Index-catalogue of the Library of the Surgeon-General's Office, United States Army: authors and subjects. Washington, Govt. Print. Off., 1880-1961. 61 v. 016.61 01-2344
Z6676 .U6 MRR Alc (DK 33).

INCUNABULA--BIBLIOGRAPHY--UNION LISTS.
Pellechet, Marie Leontine Catherine, Catalogue general des incunables des bibliotheques publiques de France. Paris, A. Picard et fils, 1897-1909. 3 v. 06-2931
Z240 .P38 MRR Alc.

Pollard, Alfred William, A short-title catalogue of books printed in England, Scotland, & Ireland and of English books printed abroad, 1475-1640, London, Bibliographical Society, 1946. xviii, 609 p. 015.42 47-20884
Z2002 .P77 1946 MRR Alc.

INCUNABULA--FACSIMILES.
Bible. Latin. ca. 1454-55. Mainz. Gutenberg (42 lines). 1962. Exact facsimile of the first page of Genesis from the Library of Congress copy of the Gutenberg Bible. Washington, Library of Congress. 1962. [1] l., col. facsim. 093 72-612485
Z663.B5 MRR Alc.

Bible. Latin. ca. 1454-55. Mainz. Gutenberg (42 lines). 1972. The Gutenberg Bible: [Washington] Library of Congress [1972] 1 p. in portfolio. 093 72-7352
Z663 .B5 1972 MRR Alc.

INDEX LIBRORUM PROHIBITORUM.
Burke, Redmond Ambrose, What is the Index? Milwaukee, Bruce [1952] x, 129 p. 098.11 52-9314
Z1019 .B95 MRR Alc.

INDEX MAPS.
International maps and atlases in
print. London, New York, Bowker
Publishing Co. [1974] 864 p.
[£15.00] 016.912 73-13336
Z6021 .I596 MRR Alc.

INDEX NUMBERS (ECONOMICS)
Crowe, Walter Ramsey. Index numbers;
London, Macdonald & Evans, 1965.
xiv, 368 p. 65-87793
HB225 .C7 MRR Alc.

INDEX OF AMERICAN DESIGN.
Christensen, Erwin Ottomar, The
Index of American Design. New York,
Macmillan, 1950. xviii, 229 p. 745
50-10215
NK1403 .C5 MRR Alc.

INDEX TRANSLATIONUM--INDEXES.
Cumulative index to English
translations, 1948-1968. Boston, G.
K. Hall, 1973. 2 v. 016.011 74-
167325
Z6514.T7 C8 MRR Alc.

INDEXES.
American library association. The
"A.L.A." index. 2d ed., greatly enl.
and brought down to January 1, 1900.
Boston, American library association,
1905. iv, 679 p. 15-5096
AI3 .A3 1905 MRR Alc.

Baer, Eleanora A. Titles in series;
2. ed. New York, Scarecrow Press,
1964. 2 v. (1530 p.) 011 64-11789
AI3 .B3 1964 MRR Alc.

Foulché-Delbosc, Raymond, Manuel de
l'hispanisant. New York, G. P.
Putnam's sons, 1920- v. 20-
16867
Z2681.A1 F7 MRR Alc.

Index of archaeological papers
published 1891-1910, [1st]-20th
issue; 1892-1914. [London] 08-10988
Z2027.A8 I7 MRR Alc Full set

Index to the contemporary scene. v.
1- 1973- Detroit, Gale Research
Co. [$14.00] 016.3 73-645955
Z7161 .I52 MRR Alc Full set

Wall, C. Edward. A.L.A. index to
general literature; cumulative author
index. Ann Arbor, Mich., Pierian
Press, 1972. vii, 192 p. 011 79-
143240
AI3 .W28 MRR Alc.

INDEXES--BIBLIOGRAPHY.
American Library Association. Junior
Members Round Table. Local indexes
in American libraries; Boston, F. W.
Faxon Co., 1947. xxxiv, 221 p.
016.01 47-30800
Z6293 .A5 MRR Alc.

United States. Library of Congress.
Processing Dept. Unpublished
bibliographical tools in certain
archives and libraries of Europe;
Washington, 1952. iv, 25 p. 016.01
52-60036
Z663.7 .U62 MRR Alc.

INDEXES, CARD
see Catalogs, Card

see Files and filing (Documents)

INDEXING.
see also Files and filing (Documents)

Bourne, Charles P. Methods of
information handling. New York, J.
Wiley [1963] xiv, 241 p. 010.78
63-20628
Z699 .B65 MRR Alc.

Collison, Robert Lewis. Indexes and
indexing; 3rd revised ed. London,
Benn; New York, De Graff, 1969. 223
p. [35/-] 029.5 75-400100
Z695.9 .C63 1969 MRR Alc.

Foskett, Antony Charles. The subject
approach to information 2d ed., rev.
and enl. [Hamden, Conn.] Linnet
Books [1972, c1971] 429 p. 025.33
71-31243
Z695 .F66 1972 MRR Alc.

Kahn, Gilbert, Progressive filing
8th ed. New York, Gregg Division
[1969] ix, 118 p. 651/.5 68-15469
HF5736 .K28 1969 MRR Alc.

INDIA.
American University, Washington, D.C.
Foreign Areas Studies Division. Area
handbook for India. Washington, For
sale by the Supt. of Docs., U.S.
Govt. Print. Off., 1964. xiv, 802 p.
67-115029
DS407 .A67 MRR Alc.

India (Republic). Ministry of
Information and Broadcasting. Facts
about India. [Delhi] sa 65-3133
Began publication in 1951.
DS401 .A3626 MRR Alc Latest
edition

India, 1953- [Delhi] Ministry of
Information and Broadcasting. 915.4
54-2074
DS405 .I64 MRR Alc Latest edition

India at a glance; [New Delhi,
Commercial Publications Bureau, 1967]
1 v. (various pagings) [21.50]
915.4/03/4 sa 68-14406
DS407 .I513 MRR Alc.

Spate, Oskar Hermann Khristian.
India and Pakistan: 3rd ed. revised
and completely reset. London,
Methuen, 1967. xxxiii, 877 p.
[£6/6/-] 915.4 68-86324
DS407 .S67 1967 MRR Alc.

INDIA--BIBLIOGRAPHY.
Fürer-Haimendorf, Elizabeth von. An
anthropological bibliography of South
Asia, Paris, Mouton, 1958-70. 3 v.
[fl. 130.00 (v. 3)] a 59-1034
Z5115 .F83 MRR Alc.

Indian national bibliography. v. 1-
Jan./Mar. 1958- [Calcutta] Central
Reference Library. 015.54 sa 68-6846
Z3201.A2 I5 MRR Alc Latest edition

Mahar, J. Michael. India; a critical
bibliography, Tucson, University of
Arizona Press [1964] 119 p.
016.9154 62-17992
Z3201 .M3 MRR Alc.

INDIA--BIOGRAPHY.
The Asylum Press almanack and
commercial directory. Madras, Sayee
Press [etc.] sa 63-1638
Began publication in 1801.
DS405 .A85 MRR Alc Latest edition

Buckland, Charles Edward, Dictionary
of Indian biography. Detroit, Gale
Research Co., 1968. xii, 494 p.
920.054 68-23140
DS434 .B8 1968 MRR Biog.

Directory of booksellers, publishers,
libraries & librarians in India. 1st-
ed.; 1968/69- New Delhi, Premier
Publishers. 655.4/025/54 73-900620
Z455 .D49 MRR Alc Latest edition

India: who's who. New Delhi, INFA
Publications. 73-906738
CT1506 .I53 MRR Biog Latest
edition

INDIA--BIOGRAPHY--DICTIONARIES.
Bhattacharya, Sachchidananda. A
dictionary of Indian history. [1st
American ed.] New York, G. Braziller
[c1967] xii, 888 p. 954/.003 68-
19984
DS433 .B49 1967b MRR Alc.

India (Republic). Parliament. Council
of States. Who's who. New Delhi,
Rajya Sabha Secretariat. sa 62-815
Began publication with vol. for
1952.
JQ261 .A55 MRR Biog Latest edition

Sahitya Akademi. Who's who of Indian
writers. Honolulu, East-West Center
Press [1964, c1961] 410 p. 928.914
64-7590
PK2903 .S3 1964 MRR Biog.

Sen, Siba Pada. Dictionary of
national biography. Calcutta,
Institute of Historical Studies, 1972-
v. [Rs100.00 ($20.00 U.S.) per
vol.] 920/.054 72-906859
CT1502 .S46 MRR Biog.

Sharma, Jagdish Saran, Encyclopaedia
of India's struggle for freedom,
[1st ed.] New Delhi, S. Chand [1971]
xii, 258 p. [Rs40.00] 73-923680
DS405 .S53 MRR Alc.

Sharma, Jagdish Saran, The national
biographical dictionary of India.
[1st ed.] New Delhi, Sterling
Publishers [1972] 302 p. [Rs40.00]
920/.054 72-901576
CT1503 .S48 MRR Biog.

INDIA--CIVILIZATION.
Basham, Arthur Llewellyn. The wonder
that was India: 3rd revised ed.
London, Sidgwick & Jackson, 1967.
xxv, 572 p. [63/-] 954 68-86859
DS425 .B33 1967 MRR Alc.

The History and culture of the Indian
people. [2d ed.] Bombay, Bharatiya
Vidya Bhavan [1964- v. 1, 1965] v.
sa 65-3169
DS436.A1 H52 MRR Alc.

INDIA--COMMERCE--DIRECTORIES.
India (Republic). Dept. of Commercial
Intelligence and Statistics.
Directory of exporters of Indian
produce and manufactures. Delhi,
Manager of Publications. 382 43-
21688
First ed. published in 1919.
HF3783 .A3 MRR Alc Latest edition

The Indian export directory, 1st
ed.; 1951- Baroda. 53-29078
HC432 I6 MRR Alc Latest edition

Trade Indian directory. New Delhi,
Trade Builders. 59-21191
HC432 .T7 MRR Alc Latest edition

INDIA--DESCRIPTION AND TRAVEL--TO 1000.
Arrianus, Flavius. Arrian, London,
W. Heinemann, ltd.; New York, G. P.
Putnam's sons, 1929-33. 2 v. 888.9
30-5835
PA3612 .A83 1929 MRR Alc.

INDIA--DESCRIPTION AND TRAVEL--1947- --GUIDE-BOOKS.
Fodor's India. New York, D. McKay.
915.4/04/4 74-22559
DS406 .F62 MRR Alc Latest edition

INDIA--DESCRIPTION AND TRAVEL--GUIDE-BOOKS.
Fodor's India. New York, D. McKay.
915.4/04/4 74-22559
DS406 .F62 MRR Alc Latest edition

A Handbook for travellers in India,
Pakistan, Burma and Ceylon. New York
[etc.] Barnes & Noble [etc.] 63-875
Began publication in 1892.
DS406 .H3 MRR Alc Latest edition

Kaul, S. N. Tourist India; [2d rev.
enl. ed. Bombay, S. N. Kaul for
Tourist India International, 1968]
viii, 387 p. [15.00 ($3.00)]
915.4/04/4 72-902594
DS406 .K3 1968 MRR Alc.

INDIA--DICTIONARIES AND ENCYCLOPEDIAS.
Sharma, Jagdish Saran, Encyclopaedia
of India's struggle for freedom,
[1st ed.] New Delhi, S. Chand [1971]
xii, 258 p. [Rs40.00] 73-923680
DS405 .S53 MRR Alc.

Walker, George Benjamin, The Hindu
world; New York, Praeger [1968] 2
v. [$35.00] 294.5/03 68-26182
BL1105 .W34 1968 MRR Alc.

INDIA--DIRECTORIES.
The Asylum Press almanack and
commercial directory. Madras, Sayee
Press [etc.] sa 63-1638
Began publication in 1801.
DS405 .A85 MRR Alc Latest edition

INDIA--ECONOMIC CONDITIONS.
Singh, V. B., ed. Economic history
of India, 1857-1956. Bombay, New
York, Allied Publishers [1965]
xxxiv, 795 p. 330.954 sa 65-10475
HC435 .S5524 MRR Alc.

INDIA--FOREIGN RELATIONS--CHINA.
Rowland, John, A history of Sino-
Indian relations; Princeton, N.J.,
Van Nostrand [1967] xv, 248 p.
327.51/054 66-29857
DS450.C5 R6 MRR Alc.

INDIA--GAZETTEERS.
United States. Office of Geography.
India; Washington, 1952. 2 v. 70-
10027
DS405 .U55 MRR Alc.

INDIA--GOVERNMENT PUBLICATIONS.
Singh, Mohinder, M.A. Government
publications of India; [1st ed.]
Delhi, Metropolitan Book Co. [1967]
iv, ii, ii, 270 p. [Rs22.50 $4]
015/.54 sa 68-3724
Z3205 .S63 MRR Alc.

INDIA--HISTORY.
The Cambridge history of India.
Cambridge [Eng.] University Press,
1922- v. 954 22-11272
DS436 .C22 MRR Alc.

The History and culture of the Indian
people. [2d ed.] Bombay, Bharatiya
Vidya Bhavan [1964- v. 1, 1965] v.
sa 65-3169
DS436.A1 H52 MRR Alc.

Smith, Vincent Arthur, The Oxford
history of India. 3d ed., Oxford,
Clarendon Press, 1958. xiii, 898 p.
954 58-4883
DS436 .S55 1958 MRR Alc.

Spear, Thomas George Percival.
India: New ed., rev. and enl. Ann
Arbor, University of Michigan Press
[1972] x, 511, xix p. [$10.00]
954 72-81334
DS436 .S68 1972 MRR Alc.

INDIA--HISTORY--TO 324 B.C.
Basham, Arthur Llewellyn. The wonder
that was India: 3rd revised ed.
London, Sidgwick & Jackson, 1967.
xxv, 572 p. [63/-] 954 68-86859
DS425 .B33 1967 MRR Alc.

INDIA--HISTORY--324 B.C.-1000 A.D.
Basham, Arthur Llewellyn. The wonder
that was India: 3rd revised ed.
London, Sidgwick & Jackson, 1967.
xxv, 572 p. [63/-] 954 68-86859
DS425 .B33 1967 MRR Alc.

INDIA--HISTORY--20TH CENTURY.
Singh, V. B., ed. Economic history
of India, 1857-1956. Bombay, New
York, Allied Publishers [1965]
xxxiv, 795 p. 330.954 sa 65-10475
HC435 .S5524 MRR Alc.

INDIA--HISTORY--1947- --SOURCES.
India (Dominion) India, 1947-50.
[London] Oxford University Press,
1959. 2 v. 954.04 60-1910
DS480.84 .A5 1959 MRR Alc.

INDIA--HISTORY--BIBLIOGRAPHY.
Case, Margaret H. South Asian
history, 1750-1950: Princeton, N.J.,
Princeton University Press, 1968.
xiii, 561 p. 016.954 67-21019
Z3185 .C3 MRR Alc.

INDIA--HISTORY--CHRONOLOGY.
Bhattacharya, Sachchidananda. A
dictionary of Indian history. [1st
American ed.] New York, G. Braziller
[c1967] xii, 888 p. 954/.003 68-
19984
DS433 .B49 1967b MRR Alc.

Rickmers, Christian Mabel (Duff) The
chronology of Indian history, from
the earliest times to the beginning
of the sixteenth century. Delhi,
Cosmo Publications, 1972. xi, 409 p.
[Rs65.00] 954.02 72-907831
DS433 .R5 1972 MRR Alc.

Sharma, Jagdish Saran. India since
the advent of the British: [1st ed.]
Delhi, S. Chand, 1970. xxx, 817 p.
[60.00] 954/.02/02 78-121820
DS433 .S47 MRR Alc.

INDIA--HISTORY--DICTIONARIES.
Bhattacharya, Sachchidananda. A
dictionary of Indian history. [1st
American ed.] New York, G. Braziller
[c1967] xii, 888 p. 954/.003 68-
19984
DS433 .B49 1967b MRR Alc.

INDIA--HISTORY--SOURCES--BIBLIOGRAPHY.
Wainwright, Mary Doreen. A guide to
Western manuscripts and documents in
the British Isles relating to South
and South East Asia. London, New
York, Oxford University Press, 1965.
xix, 532 p. 016.915 65-3147
CD1048.A8 W3 MRR Alc.

INDIA--IMPRINTS.
Diehl, Katharine Smith. Early Indian
imprints New York, Scarecrow Press,
1964. 533 p. 015.54 64-11786
Z3202. .D5 MRR Alc.

Impex reference catalogue of Indian
books. 1st- ed.; Mar. 1960- New
Delhi, Indian Book Export and Import
Co. 62-4286
Z3201 .I57 MRR Alc Full set

Indian national bibliography. v. 1-
Jan./Mar. 1958- [Calcutta] Central
Reference Library. 015.54 sa 68-6846
Z3201.A2 I5 MRR Alc Latest edition

The National bibliography of Indian
literature, 1901-1953. [1st ed.]
New Delhi, Sahitya Akademi [1962- v.
sa 63-1991
Z3201 .N3 MRR Alc.

Sher Singh. Indian books in print,
1955-67; Delhi, Indian Bureau of
Bibliographies [1969] 1116 p.
[100.00] 015/.54 78-104779
Z3201 .S47 MRR Alc.

United States. Library of Congress.
American Libraries Book Procurement
Center, Delhi. Accessions list,
India. v. 1- July 1962- New
Delhi. 63-24164
Z663.767.I5 A25 MRR Alc MRR Alc
Full set

United States. Library of Congress.
American Libraries Book Procurement
Center, Delhi. Accessions list,
India. Annual supplement: cumulative
list of serials. 1969- New Delhi.
74-643583
Z663.767.I5 A25 MRR Alc MRR Alc
Full set

INDIA--INDUSTRIES--DIRECTORIES.
The Indian export directory. 1st-
ed.; 1951- Baroda. 53-29078
HC432 I6 MRR Alc Latest edition

Trade Indian directory. New Delhi,
Trade Builders. 58-21191
HC432 .T7 MRR Alc Latest edition

INDIA--INDUSTRIES--YEARBOOKS.
Kothari's economic and industrial
guide of India. 29th- ed.; 1971/72-
Madras, Kothari. [$25.00]
338/.0954 72-904460
HG5731 .I57 MRR Alc Latest edition

INDIA--KINGS AND RULERS.
Rickmers, Christian Mabel (Duff) The
chronology of Indian history, from
the earliest times to the beginning
of the sixteenth century. Delhi,
Cosmo Publications, 1972. xi 409 p.
[Rs65.00] 954.02 72-907831
DS433 .R5 1972 MRR Alc.

INDIA--LEARNED INSTITUTIONS AND
SOCIETIES.
Universities handbook; India &
Ceylon. (1st]- ed.; 1927- New
Delhi [etc.], Inter-university Board
of India & Ceylon [etc.] e 35-209
L961.I4 U55 MRR Alc Latest edition

INDIA--MANUFACTURES--DIRECTORIES.
The Asylum Press almanack and
commercial directory. Madras, Sayee
Press [etc.] sa 63-1638
Began publication in 1801.
DS405 .A85 MRR Alc Latest edition

India (Republic). Dept. of Commercial
Intelligence and Statistics.
Directory of exporters of Indian
produce and manufactures. Delhi,
Manager of Publications. 382 43-
21688
First ed. published in 1919.
HF3783 .A3 MRR Alc Latest edition

INDIA--POLITICS AND GOVERNMENT--1947-
Kochanek, Stanley A. The Congress
party of India; Princeton, N.J.,
Princeton University Press, 1968.
xxv, 516 p. 329.9/54 68-10393
JQ298.I5 K6 MRR Alc.

INDIA--POLITICS AND GOVERNMENT--
DICTIONARIES.
Sharma, Jagdish Saran. Encyclopaedia
of India's struggle for freedom.
[1st ed.] New Delhi, S. Chand [1971]
xii, 258 p. [Rs40.00] 73-923680
DS405 .S53 MRR Alc.

INDIA--REGISTERS.
India: who's who. New Delhi, INFA
Publications. 73-906738
CT1506 .I53 MRR Biog Latest
edition

INDIA--STATISTICS.
India (Republic). Central Statistical
Organization. Statistical abstract,
India. New ser., v. 1- 1949-
Delhi, Manager of Publications.
315.4 52-40419
HA1713 .A732 MRR Alc Latest
edition

INDIA--STATISTICS--PERIODICALS.
India; a statistical outline.
Calcutta, Oxford & IBH Publishing Co.
[etc.] 70-912219
HA1724 .I49 MRR Alc Latest edition

INDIA (REPUBLIC). PARLIAMENT. COUNCIL
OF STATES--BIOGRAPHIES.
India (Republic). Parliament. Council
of States. Who's who. New Delhi,
Rajya Sabha Secretariat. sa 62-815
Began publication with vol. for
1952.
JQ261 .A55 MRR Biog Latest edition

INDIAN LITERATURE--UNITED STATES--
BIBLIOGRAPHY.
Hirschfelder, Arlene B. American
Indian authors; New York,
Association on American Indian
Affairs [1970] 45 p. 016.81 78-
121863
Z7118 .H55 MRR Alc.

INDIAN NATIONAL CONGRESS.
Kochanek, Stanley A. The Congress
party of India; Princeton, N.J.,
Princeton University Press, 1968.
xxv, 516 p. 329.9/54 68-10393
JQ298.I5 K6 MRR Alc.

INDIANA.
Indiana almanac and fact book. 1st-
ed.; 1967- Indianapolis, E. Leary &
Associates. 917.72/03 67-21436
F526 .I3955 MRR Alc Latest edition

Writers' program. Indiana. Indiana,
a guide to the Hoosier state; New
York, Oxford university press [1945]
xxvi, 548 (i.e. 564) p. 917.72 46-
5683
F526 .W93 1945 MRR Ref Desk.

INDIANA--BIBLIOGRAPHY.
Byrd, Cecil K. A bibliography of
Indiana imprints, 1804-1853,
Indianapolis, 1955. xxi, 479 p. 015.772
55-4194
Z1281 .B8 MRR Alc.

INDIANA--BIBLIOGRAPHY--CATALOGS.
United States. Library of Congress.
Indiana, the sesquicentennial of the
establishment of the Territorial
Government; Washington, U.S. Govt.
Print. Off., 1950. iv, 58 p.
016.9772 50-62974
Z663.15.A6I6 1950 MRR Alc.

INDIANA--BIOGRAPHY--DICTIONARIES.
Hepburn, William Murray, ed. Who's
who in Indiana: Hopkinsville, Ky.,
Historical Record Association [1957]
248 p. 920.0772 59-51286
F525 .H4 MRR Biog.

INDIANA--CENTENNIAL CELEBRATIONS, ETC.
United States. Library of Congress.
Indiana, the sesquicentennial of the
establishment of the Territorial
Government; Washington, U.S. Govt.
Print. Off., 1950. iv, 58 p.
016.9772 50-62974
Z663.15.A6I6 1950 MRR Alc.

INDIANA--COMMERCE--DIRECTORIES.
The Indiana industrial directory.
Indianapolis, Ind., Indiana State
Chamber of Commerce. 670.9772 42-
6661
T12 .I63 Sci RR Latest edition /
MRR Alc Latest edition

INDIANA--DESCRIPTION AND TRAVEL--GUIDE-
BOOKS.
Hoosier guide, 1968-1969, Indiana;
[Ray, Ind., Hoosier Guide Pub. Co.,
1968] 224 p. 917.72/04/4 68-3107

F524.3 .H6 MRR Alc.

Writers' program. Indiana. Indiana,
a guide to the Hoosier state, New
York, Oxford university press [1945]
xxvi, 548 (i.e. 564) p. 917.72 46-
5683
F526 .W93 1945 MRR Ref Desk.

INDIANA--EXECUTIVES.
Pitchell, Robert J., ed. Indiana
votes; Bloomington, Bureau of
Government Research, Indiana
University [1960] 103 p.
324.209772 62-62552
JK5693 1960 .P5 MRR Alc.

INDIANA--GAZETTEERS.
The Indiana industrial directory.
Indianapolis, Ind., Indiana State
Chamber of Commerce. 670.9772 42-
6661
T12 .I63 Sci RR Latest edition /
MRR Alc Latest edition

INDIANA--IMPRINTS.
Byrd, Cecil K. A bibliography of
Indiana imprints, 1804-1853,
Indianapolis, Indiana Historical
Bureau, 1955. xxi, 479 p. 015.772
55-4194
Z1281 .B8 MRR Alc.

INDIANA--MANUFACTURES--DIRECTORIES.
The Indiana industrial directory.
Indianapolis, Ind., Indiana State
Chamber of Commerce. 670.9772 42-
6661
T12 .I63 Sci RR Latest edition /
MRR Alc Latest edition

Midwest manufacturers and industrial
directory buyers guide. [Detroit,
Industrial Directory Publishers]
338.4/0977 72-626483
HC107.A15 M5 MRR Alc Latest
edition

INDIANA--POLITICS AND GOVERNMENT--
YEARBOOKS.
Indiana almanac and government guide.
1st- ed.; 1961- [Indianapolis,
Republican Citizens' Finance
Committee of Indiana] 64-32364
JK5630 .I5 MRR Alc Latest edition

INDIANA--REGISTERS.
Indiana. State Board of Accounts.
Roster of State and local officials
of the State of Indiana.
[Indianapolis?] 35-27733
JK5630 .A3 MRR Alc Latest edition

Indiana almanac and government guide.
1st- ed.; 1961- [Indianapolis,
Republican Citizens' Finance
Committee of Indiana] 64-32364
JK5630 .I5 MRR Alc Latest edition

INDIANA--STATISTICS.
Indiana almanac and government guide.
1st- ed.; 1961- [Indianapolis,
Republican Citizens' Finance
Committee of Indiana] 64-32364
JK5630 .I5 MRR Alc Latest edition

INDIANS.
Encyclopedia of Indians of the
Americas. St. Clair Shores, Mich.,
Scholarly Press [1974- v.
[$700.00 (set)] 970.1/03 74-5088
E54.5 .E52 MRR Alc.

INDIANS. (Cont.)
National Geographic Society,
Washington, D.C. National Geographic
on Indians of the Americas;
Washington, c1961. 431 p.   970.1
61-15830
    E58 .N3 1961 MRR Alc.

INDIANS--ANTIQUITIES.
Kelemen. Pal. Medieval American
art; New York, Macmillan, 1956.
xxii, 414, 33 p.   970.6571 57-335
    E59.A7 K4 1956 MRR Alc.

Willey, Gordon Randolph, A history
of American archaeology San
Francisco, W. H. Freeman [1974] 252
p.   913/.031 73-17493
    E61 .W67 1974b MRR Alc.

Willey, Gordon Randolph, An
introduction to American archaeology
Englewood Cliffs, N.J., Prentice-Hall
[1966-71] 2 v. [$24.00 (v. 2)]
970.1 66-10096
    E61 .W68 MRR Alc.

INDIANS--ANTIQUITIES--ADDRESSES,
ESSAYS, LECTURES.
Deuel, Leo, comp. Conquistadors
without swords: New York, St.
Martin's Press, 1967. xix, 647 p.
970.1 67-22577
    E61 .D46 MRR Alc.

Leone, Mark P., comp. Contemporary
archaeology; a guide to theory and
contributions. Carbondale, Southern
Illinois University Press [1972] xv,
460 p. [$15.00]   913/.031 79-
156779
    GN739 .L46 MRR Alc.

William Marsh Rice University,
Houston, Tex. Prehistoric man in the
New World. Chicago] Published for
William Marsh Rice University by the
University of Chicago Press [1964]
x, 633 p.   913.7082 63-18852
    E61 .W717 MRR Alc.

INDIANS--ART.
Kelemen. Pal. Medieval American
art: New York, Macmillan, 1956.
xxii, 414, 33 p.   970.6571 57-335
    E59.A7 K4 1956 MRR Alc.

Kubler, George, The art and
architecture of ancient America;
Baltimore, Penguin Books [1962] xxv,
396 p.   970.67 62-5022
    E59.A7 K8 MRR Alc.

INDIANS--BIBLIOGRAPHY.
Index to literature on the American
Indian. 1970- [San Francisco]
Indian Historian Press. 016.9701 70-
141292
    Z1209 .I53 MRR Alc Full set

INDIANS--BIBLIOGRAPHY--CATALOGS.
Field, Thomas Warren, An essay
towards an Indian bibliography;
Detroit, Gale Research Co., 1967.
iv, 430 p.   016.9701 67-14026
    Z1209 .F45 1967 MRR Alc.

Newberry Library, Chicago. Edward E.
Ayer Collection. Dictionary catalog
of the Edward E. Ayer Collection of
Americana and American Indians in the
Newberry Library. Boston, G. K.
Hall, 1961. 16 v. (8062 p.)   76-
4986
    Z1201 .N45 MRR Alc (Dk 33)

INDIANS--FILM CATALOGS.
Brigham Young University, Provo,
Utah. Instructional Development
Program. Bibliography of nonprint
instructional materials on the
American Indian. Provo [1972] v,
221 p.   016.9701 72-197915
    Z1209 .B728 MRR Alc.

INDIANS--HISTORY.
Josephy, Alvin M., The Indian
heritage of America [1st ed.] New
York, Knopf, 1968. xiii, 384, xiv p.
[$10.00]   970.1 68-12661
    E58 .J6 MRR Alc.

INDIANS--HISTORY--CHRONOLOGY.
Encyclopedia of Indians of the
Americas. St. Clair Shores, Mich.,
Scholarly Press [1974- v.
[$700.00 (set)]   970.1/03 74-5088
    E54.5 .E52 MRR Alc.

INDIANS--INDEXES.
United States. Bureau of American
Ethnology. Bulletin. (Indexes) Index
to Bulletins 1-100 of the Bureau of
American Ethnology; Washington, U.S.
Govt. Print. Off., 1963. vi, 726 p.
64-60461
    Z1209 .U49 MRR Alc.

INDIANS--INDEXES--PERIODICALS.
Index to literature on the American
Indian. 1970- [San Francisco]
Indian Historian Press. 016.9701 70-
141292
    Z1209 .I53 MRR Alc Full set

INDIANS--PERIODICALS--INDEXES.
Index to literature on the American
Indian. 1970- [San Francisco]
Indian Historian Press. 016.9701 70-
141292
    Z1209 .I53 MRR Alc Full set

INDIANS--PICTURES, ILLUSTRATIONS, ETC.
National Geographic Society,
Washington, D.C. National Geographic
on Indians of the Americas;
Washington, c1961. 431 p.   970.1
61-15830
    E58 .N3 1961 MRR Alc.

INDIANS--STUDY AND TEACHING--AUDIO-
VISUAL AIDS--BIBLIOGRAPHY.
Brigham Young University, Provo,
Utah. Instructional Development
Program. Bibliography of nonprint
instructional materials on the
American Indian. Provo [1972] v,
221 p.   016.9701 72-197915
    Z1209 .B728 MRR Alc.

INDIANS OF CENTRAL AMERICA.
Driver, Harold Edson, Indians of
North America 2d ed., rev. Chicago,
University of Chicago Press [1969]
xvii, 632 p.   970.1 79-76207
    E58 .D68 1969 MRR Alc.

Handbook of Middle American Indians.
Austin, University of Texas Press
[1964- v. [$15.00 per vol.]
970.4/2 64-10316
    F1434 .H3 MRR Alc.

Steward, Julian Haynes, ed. Handbook
of South American Indians,
Washington, U.S. Govt. Print. Off.,
1946-59. 7 v.   980.1 46-26504
    E51 .U6 no. 143 MRR Alc.

INDIANS OF CENTRAL AMERICA--
BIBLIOGRAPHY.
Bernal, Ignacio. Bibliografía de
arqueología y etnografía: Mexico,
Instituto Nacional de Antropología e
Historia, 1962. xvi, 634 p.   63-
39894
    Z1209 .B45 MRR Alc.

INDIANS OF CENTRAL AMERICA--RELIGION
AND MYTHOLOGY.
Alexander, Hartley Burr, Latin-
American [mythology] Boston,
Marshall Jones company, 1920. xvi,
424 p. incl. 1 illus., table.   20-
16109
    BL25 .M8 vol. 11 MRR Alc.

INDIANS OF MEXICO.
Driver, Harold Edson, Indians of
North America 2d ed., rev. Chicago,
University of Chicago Press [1969]
xvii, 632 p.   970.1 79-76207
    E58 .D68 1969 MRR Alc.

Handbook of Middle American Indians.
Austin, University of Texas Press
[1964- v. [$15.00 per vol.]
970.4/2 64-10316
    F1434 .H3 MRR Alc.

INDIANS OF MEXICO--BIBLIOGRAPHY.
Bernal, Ignacio. Bibliografía de
arqueología y etnografía: Mexico,
Instituto Nacional de Antropología e
Historia, 1962. xvi, 634 p.   63-
39894
    Z1209 .B45 MRR Alc.

INDIANS OF MEXICO--RELIGION AND
MYTHOLOGY.
Alexander, Hartley Burr, Latin-
American [mythology] Boston,
Marshall Jones company, 1920. xvi,
424 p. incl. 1 illus., table.   20-
16109
    BL25 .M8 vol. 11 MRR Alc.

INDIANS OF NORTH AMERICA.
see also Eskimos

Driver, Harold Edson, Indians of
North America 2d ed., rev. Chicago,
University of Chicago Press [1969]
xvii, 632 p.   970.1 79-76207
    E58 .D68 1969 MRR Alc.

Encyclopedia of Indians of the
Americas. St. Clair Shores, Mich.,
Scholarly Press [1974- v.
[$700.00 (set)]   970.1/03 74-5088
    E54.5 .E52 MRR Alc.

Gabriel, Ralph Henry, The lure of
the frontier; New Haven, Yale
university press; [etc., etc.] 1929.
3 p. l., 327 p.   29-22308
    E178.5 .P2 vol. 2 MRR Alc.

Lowery, Woodbury, The Spanish
settlements within the present limits
of the United States, 1513-1561, New
York, London, G. P. Putnam's sons,
1901. xiii, 515 p.   973.16 01-
11942
    E123 .L91 MRR Alc.

Spanish explorers in the southern
United States, 1528-1543: New York,
C. Scribner's sons, 1907. xx, 411 p.
07-10607
    E187.07 S7 MRR Alc.

Swanton, John Reed, The Indian
tribes of North America. Washington,
U.S. Govt. Print. Off., 1952. vi,
726 p.   970.1 52-61970
    E77 .S94 MRR Alc.

Wissler, Clark, Adventures in the
wilderness. New Haven, Yale
university press; [etc., etc.] 1925.
3 p. l., 369 p.   26-1142
    E178.5 .P2 vol. 1 MRR Alc.

INDIANS OF NORTH AMERICA--ANTIQUITIES.
Brennan, Louis A. Beginner's guide
to archaeology; [Harrisburg, Pa.]
Stackpole Books [1973] 318 p.
[$9.95]   913/.031 73-4193
    E77.9 .B73 MRR Alc.

Griffin, James Bennett, ed.
Archeology of eastern United States.
[Chicago] University of Chicago Press
[1952] x, 392 p.   913.73 973.1* 52-
14698
    E53 .G7 MRR Alc.

Robbins, Maurice. The amateur
archaeologist's handbook 2d ed. New
York, Crowell [1973] xiv, 288 p.
[$7.95]   913/.031/028 73-245
    E77.9 .R6 1973 MRR Alc.

INDIANS OF NORTH AMERICA--BIBLIOGRAPHY.
American Indian index.   -147/48;
-Oct./Nov. 1968. River Grove, Ill.
[etc.] R. L. Knor [etc.]   72-8243
    Z1209 .A4 MRR Alc Full set

Murdock, George Peter, Ethnographic
bibliography of North America. 3d
ed. New Haven, Human Relations Area
Files, 1960. xxiii, 393 p.
016.9701 60-16689
    Z1209 .M8 1960 MRR Alc.

Rader, Jesse Lee, South of forty,
[1st ed.] Norman, Univ. of Oklahoma
Press, 1947. xi, 336 p.   016.976
47-5360
    Z1251.S83 R3 MRR Alc.

Reference encyclopedia of the
American Indian, B. Klein
[1967] 536 p.   970.1/03 67-17326
    E76.2 .R4 MRR Alc.

United States. Bureau of American
Ethnology. List of publications of
the Bureau of American Ethnology
1894- Washington, U.S. Govt. Print.
Off.   23-27414
    E51 .U65 MRR Ref Desk Latest
      edition

INDIANS OF NORTH AMERICA--BIBLIOGRAPHY--
CATALOGS.
Newberry Library, Chicago. Edward E.
Ayer Collection. Dictionary catalog
of the Edward E. Ayer Collection of
Americana and American Indians in the
Newberry Library. Boston, G. K.
Hall, 1961. 16 v. (8062 p.)   76-
4986
    Z1201 .N45 MRR Alc (Dk 33)

United States. Dept. of the Interior.
Library. Biographical and historical
index of American Indians and persons
involved in Indian affairs. Boston,
G. K. Hall, 1966. 8 v.   016.9701
77-5470
    Z1209 .U494 MRR Alc (Dk 33)

INDIANS OF NORTH AMERICA--BIOGRAPHY.
Gridley, Marion Eleanor,
Contemporary American Indian leaders
New York, Dodd, Mead [1972] xix, 201
p. [$4.95]   970.3 B 72-3148
    E89 .G74 MRR Biog.

Stensland, Anna Lee, Literature by
and about the American Indian;
[Urbana, Ill.] National Council of
Teachers of English [1973] x, 208 p.
[$3.95]   016.9701 73-83285
    Z1209 .S73 MRR Alc.

INDIANS OF NORTH AMERICA--BIOGRAPHY--
DICTIONARIES.
Reference encyclopedia of the
American Indian. New York, B. Klein
[1967] 536 p.   970.1/03 67-17326
    E76.2 .R4 MRR Alc.

INDIANS OF NORTH AMERICA--BIOGRAPHY--
INDEXES.
United States. Dept. of the Interior.
Library. Biographical and historical
index of American Indians and persons
involved in Indian affairs. Boston,
G. K. Hall, 1966. 8 v.   016.9701
77-5470
    Z1209 .U494 MRR Alc (Dk 33)

INDIANS OF NORTH AMERICA--BIOGRAPHY--
JUVENILE LITERATURE.
Gridley, Marion Eleanor,
Contemporary American Indian leaders
New York, Dodd, Mead [1972] xix, 201
p. [$4.95]   970.3 B 72-3148
    E89 .G74 MRR Biog.

INDIANS OF NORTH AMERICA--DICTIONARIES.
Hodge, Frederick Webb, ed. Handbook of American Indians north of Mexico. Grosse Pointe, Mich., Scholarly Press, 1868. 2 v. 970.1/03 72-3141
E77 .H693 MRR Ref Desk.

INDIANS OF NORTH AMERICA--DICTIONARIES AND ENCYCLOPEDIAS.
Hodge, Frederick Webb, ed. Handbook of American Indians north of Mexico. Washington, Govt. print. off., 1907-10. 2 v. 07-35198
E77 .H68 MRR Alc.

INDIANS OF NORTH AMERICA--DICTIONARIES AND ENCYCLOPEDIAS.
Hodge, Frederick Webb, ed. Handbook of American Indians north of Mexico. Grosse Pointe, Mich., Scholarly Press, 1868. 2 v. 970.1/03 72-3141
E77 .H693 MRR Ref Desk.

INDIANS OF NORTH AMERICA--DIRECTORIES.
Reference encyclopedia of the American Indian. New York, B. Klein [1967] 536 p. 970.1/03 67-17326
E76.2 .R4 MRR Alc.

INDIANS OF NORTH AMERICA--ECONOMIC CONDITIONS--BIBLIOGRAPHY.
Snodgrass, Marjorie P. Economic development of American Indians and Eskimos, 1930 through 1967; [Washington, U.S. Bureau of Indian Affairs; for sale by the Supt. of Docs., U.S. Govt. Print. Off.] 1968 [i.e. 1969] v, 263 p. [2.00] 330.9 78-601798
Z1209 .S56 MRR Alc.

INDIANS OF NORTH AMERICA--GOVERNMENT RELATIONS.
Royce, Charles C., comp. Indian land cessions in the United States, 13-23487
HD231 .R7 1899 MRR Alc.

Taylor, Theodore W. The States and their Indian citizens Washington, U.S. Bureau of Indian Affairs; [for sale by the Supt. of Docs., U.S. Govt. Print. Off.] 1972. xxi, 307 p. 970.5 73-600607
E93 .T27 MRR Alc.

Washburn, Wilcomb E., comp. The American Indian and the United States; [1st ed.] New York, Random House [1973] 4 v. (xiv, 3119 p.) 970.5 72-10259
E93 .W27 MRR Alc.

INDIANS OF NORTH AMERICA--GOVERNMENT RELATIONS--1789-1868.
Prucha, Francis Paul. American Indian policy in the formative years: Cambridge, Harvard University Press, 1962. viii, 303 p. 970.5 62-9428
E93 .P965 MRR Alc.

INDIANS OF NORTH AMERICA--HISTORY.
North American Indians in historical perspective. [1st ed.] New York, Random House [1971] xi, 498 p. 970.1 70-130187
E77 .N63 MRR Alc.

Terrell, John Upton. American Indian almanac. New York, World Pub. Co. [1971] xiv, 494 p. [$15.00] 970.4/3 70-142135
E77 .T34 1871 MRR Alc.

Washburn, Wilcomb E., comp. The American Indian and the United States; [1st ed.] New York, Random House [1973] 4 v. (xiv, 3119 p.) 970.5 72-10259
E93 .W27 MRR Alc.

Wissler, Clark, Indians of the United States. Rev. ed. Garden City, N.Y., Doubleday, 1966. 336 p. 970.43 66-12215
E77 .W799 1966 MRR Alc.

INDIANS OF NORTH AMERICA--HISTORY--SOURCES.
Washburn, Wilcomb E., comp. The American Indian and the United States; [1st ed.] New York, Random House [1973] 4 v. (xiv, 3119 p.) 970.5 72-10259
E93 .W27 MRR Alc.

INDIANS OF NORTH AMERICA--JUVENILE LITERATURE--BIBLIOGRAPHY.
Stensland, Anna Lee, Literature by and about the American Indian; [Urbana, Ill.] National Council of Teachers of English [1973] x, 208 p. [$3.95] 016.9701 73-83285
Z1209 .S73 MRR Alc.

INDIANS OF NORTH AMERICA--LAND TRANSFERS.
Royce, Charles C., comp. Indian land cessions in the United States, 13-23487
HD231 .R7 1899 MRR Alc.

INDIANS OF NORTH AMERICA--LANGUAGES--BIBLIOGRAPHY.
Pilling, James Constantine, Bibliographies of the languages of the North American Indians. New York, AMS Press [1973] 3 v. 016.497 76-174200
Z7118 .P6 MRR Alc.

INDIANS OF NORTH AMERICA--LEGAL STATUS, LAWS, ETC.
United States. Laws, statutes, etc. Indian affairs. Laws and treaties. Washington, Govt. print. off., 1903-41. 5 v. 342/.73/087 03-13067
KF8203 1903 MRR Alc.

INDIANS OF NORTH AMERICA--MUSEUMS.
Reference encyclopedia of the American Indian. New York, B. Klein [1967] 536 p. 970.1/03 67-17326
E76.2 .R4 MRR Alc.

INDIANS OF NORTH AMERICA--MUSIC.
Rhodes, Willard, Music of the American Indian:Kiowa. Washington, Library of Congress, Music Division, Recording Laboratory, Archives of American Folksong, in cooperation with the Bureau of Indian Affairs [195-] 32 p. 58-43368
Z663.378 .M79 MRR Alc.

Rhodes, Willard, Music of the American Indian, Northwest, Puget Sound. Washington, Library of Congress, Music Division, Recording Laboratory, Archives of American Folksong, in cooperation with the Bureau of Indian Affairs and the Indian Arts and Crafts Board [1954] 36 p. 781.71 55-60151
Z663.378 .M8 MRR Alc.

INDIANS OF NORTH AMERICA--MUSIC--BIBLIOGRAPHY.
Haywood, Charles, A bibliography of North American folklore and folksong. 2d rev. ed. New York, Dover Publications [1961] 2 v. (xxx, 1301 p.) 016.398 62-3483
Z5984.U5 H32 MRR Alc.

INDIANS OF NORTH AMERICA--NEWSPAPERS--BIBLIOGRAPHY.
Princeton University. Library. American Indian periodicals in the Princeton University Library; Princeton, N.J., 1970. 78 p. 016.9701 76-26143
Z1209 .P75 MRR Alc.

INDIANS OF NORTH AMERICA--PERIODICALS--BIBLIOGRAPHY.
Princeton University. Library. American Indian periodicals in the Princeton University Library; Princeton, N.J., 1970. 78 p. 016.9701 76-26143
Z1209 .P75 MRR Alc.

INDIANS OF NORTH AMERICA--RELIGION AND MYTHOLOGY.
Alexander, Hartley Burr, North American [mythology] Boston, Marshall Jones company, 1916. xxiv p., 1 l., 325 p. [$6.00] 16-13983
BL25 .M8 vol. 10 MRR Alc.

INDIANS OF NORTH AMERICA--SOCIAL CONDITIONS.
North American Indians in historical perspective. [1st ed.] New York, Random House [1971] xi, 498 p. 970.1 70-130187
E77 .N63 MRR Alc.

INDIANS OF NORTH AMERICA--SOCIAL LIFE AND CUSTOMS.
Wissler, Clark, Indians of the United States. Rev. ed. Garden City, N.Y., Doubleday, 1966. 336 p. 970.43 66-12215
E77 .W799 1966 MRR Alc.

INDIANS OF NORTH AMERICA--STATISTICS.
United States. Laws, statutes, etc. Indian affairs. Laws and treaties. Washington, Govt. print. off., 1903-41. 5 v. 342/.73/087 03-13067
KF8203 1903 MRR Alc.

INDIANS OF NORTH AMERICA--TREATIES.
Prucha, Francis Paul. American Indian policy in the formative years: Cambridge, Harvard University Press, 1962. viii, 303 p. 970.5 62-9428
E93 .P965 MRR Alc.

United States. Laws, statutes, etc. Indian affairs. Laws and treaties. Washington, Govt. print. off., 1903-41. 5 v. 342/.73/087 03-13067
KF8203 1903 MRR Alc.

Washburn, Wilcomb E., comp. The American Indian and the United States; [1st ed.] New York, Random House [1973] 4 v. (xiv, 3119 p.) 970.5 72-10259
E93 .W27 MRR Alc.

INDIANS OF NORTH AMERICA--WARS.
Peters, Joseph P., comp. Indian battles and skirmishes on the American frontier, 1790-1898. New York, Published for University Microfilms, Ann Arbor, by Argonaut Press, 1966. 26, 112, 65, 51 p. 970.5 66-29882
E81 .P4 MRR Alc.

Tebbel, John William, The compact history of the Indian Wars. [1st ed.] New York, Hawthorn Books [1966] 334 p. 970.5 66-543
E81 .T42 MRR Alc.

INDIANS OF NORTH AMERICA--CANADA.
Champlain, Samuel de, Voyages of Samuel de Champlain, 1604-1618; New York, C. Scribner's sons, 1907. viii, 377 p. 07-22899
E187.07 C5 MRR Alc.

INDIANS OF NORTH AMERICA--SOUTHERN STATES.
Swanton, John Reed, The Indians of the Southeastern United States. Grosse Pointe, Mich., Scholarly Press, 1969. xiii, 943 p. 970.4/5 72-6336
E78.S65 S9 1969 MRR Alc.

INDIANS OF NORTH AMERICA--WEST--WARS.
United States. National Park Service. Soldier and brave; [1st ed.] New York, Harper & Row, 1963. xviii, 279 p. 978 63-10600
F591 .U59 MRR Alc.

INDIANS OF SOUTH AMERICA.
Encyclopedia of Indians of the Americas. St. Clair Shores, Mich., Scholarly Press [1974- v. [$700.00 (set)] 970.1/03 74-5088
E54.5 .E52 MRR Alc.

Murdock, George Peter, Outline of South American cultures. New Haven, Human Relations Area Files, 1951. 148 p. 52-972
H62 .B36 vol. 2, 1951 MRR Alc.

Steward, Julian Haynes, ed. Handbook of South American Indians. Washington, U.S. Govt. Print. Off., 1946-59. 7 v. 980.1 46-26504
E51 .U6 no. 143 MRR Alc.

INDIANS OF SOUTH AMERICA--BIBLIOGRAPHY--CATALOGS.
Newberry Library, Chicago. Edward E. Ayer Collection. Dictionary catalog of the Edward E. Ayer Collection of Americana and American Indians in the Newberry Library. Boston, G. K. Hall, 1961. 16 v. (8062 p.) 76-4986
Z1201 .N45 MRR Alc (Dk 33)

INDIANS OF SOUTH AMERICA--RELIGION AND MYTHOLOGY.
Alexander, Hartley Burr, Latin-American [mythology] Boston, Marshall Jones company, 1920. xvi, 424 p. incl. 1 illus., table. 20-16109
BL25 .M8 vol. 11 MRR Alc.

INDIANS OF THE WEST INDIES.
Driver, Harold Edson, Indians of North America 2d ed., rev. Chicago, University of Chicago Press [1969] xvii, 632 p. 970.1 79-76207
E58 .D68 1969 MRR Alc.

INDIC DRAMA--HISTORY AND CRITICISM.
India (Republic). Ministry of Information and Broadcasting. Indian drama. [Delhi] Publications Division, Ministry of Information and Broadcasting, Govt. of India [1956] 120 p. 58-25931
PK5421 .A52 1956 MRR Alc.

INDIC LITERATURE--HISTORY AND CRITICISM.
Gowen, Herbert Henry, A history of Indian literature from Vedic times to the present day, New York, London, D. Appleton and company, 1931. xvi p., 1 l., 593 p. 891.109 31-29769
PK2903 .G6 MRR Alc.

INDIC NEWSPAPERS--BIBLIOGRAPHY.
I N F A press and advertisers year book. 1962- New Delhi, INFA Publications. sa 63-2244
PN4709 .I2 MRR Alc Latest edition

INDIC PERIODICALS--BIBLIOGRAPHY.
I N F A press and advertisers year book. 1962- New Delhi, INFA Publications. sa 63-2244
PN4709 .I2 MRR Alc Latest edition

United States. Library of Congress. American Libraries Book Procurement Center, Delhi. Accessions list, India. v. 1- July 1962- New Delhi. 63-24164
Z663.767.I5 A25 MRR Alc MRR Alc Full set

INDIC PERIODICALS--BIBLIOGRAPHY. (Cont.)
United States. Library of Congress.
American Libraries Book Procurement
Center, Delhi. Accessions list,
India. Annual supplement: cumulative
list of serials. 1969- New Delhi.
74-643583
Z663.767.I5 A25 MRR Alc   MRR Alc
Full set

INDIC PERIODICALS--DIRECTORIES.
Gandhi, H. N. D., Indian periodicals
in print, 1973 Delhi, Vidya Mandal
[1973] 2 v.   016.052   73-904001
Z6958.I4 G35 MRR Alc.

INDIC PERIODICALS--INDEXES.
Prasher, Ram Gopal, Indian library
literature; New Delhi, Today &
Tomorrow's Printers & Publishers
[1971]   xii, 504 p.   [Rs40.00]
016.020/054   74-926208
Z666 .P88 MRR Alc.

INDICATORS AND TEST-PAPERS.
see also Chemical tests and reagents

INDIVIDUALISM.
see also Communism

INDIVIDUALITY.
see also Personality

INDO-ARYAN LANGUAGES--DICTIONARIES--
ENGLISH.
Turner, Ralph Lilley, Sir, A
comparative dictionary of the Indo-
Aryan languages: London, New York,
Oxford U.P., 1971. 231 p. [£6.00]
491.1   79-587452
PK175 .T8 1971 MRR Alc.

Turner, Ralph Lilley, Sir, A
comparative dictionary of the Indo-
Aryan languages London, New York,
Oxford University Press, 1966. xx,
841 p.   491.1   67-5371
PK175 .T8 MRR Alc.

INDO-ARYAN LANGUAGES--ETYMOLOGY--
DICTIONARIES.
Turner, Ralph Lilley, Sir, A
comparative dictionary of the Indo-
Aryan languages London, New York,
Oxford University Press, 1966. xx,
841 p.   491.1   67-5371
PK175 .T8 MRR Alc.

INDO-ARYAN LANGUAGES--PHONOLOGY.
Turner, Ralph Lilley, Sir, A
comparative dictionary of the Indo-
Aryan languages: London, New York,
Oxford U.P., 1971. 231 p. [£6.00]
491.1   79-587452
PK175 .T8 1971 MRR Alc.

INDOCHINA
see Asia, Southeastern

INDOCHINA, FRENCH--BIBLIOGRAPHY.
United States. Library of Congress.
Reference Dept. Indochina; a
bibliography of the land and people,
Washington, 1950. xii, 367 p.
016.9159   51-60006
Z3221 .U53 1950 MRR Alc.

INDOCHINA, FRENCH--REGISTERS.
Buttinger, Joseph. Vietnam: a dragon
embattled. London, Pall Mall P.,
1967. 2 v. [£6/10/-]   959.7   68-
70118
DS557.A5 B83 1967b MRR Alc.

INDONESIA.
Grant, Bruce. Indonesia. [2nd ed.
Carlton, Melbourne] Melbourne
University; London, New York,
Cambridge University Press [1966]
ix, 204 p. [$3.50 Aust.]   919.1   66-
29036
DS615 .G67 1966 MRR Alc.

Henderson, John William, Area
handbook for Indonesia. Washington;
For sale by the Supt. of Docs., U.S.
Govt. Print. Off., 1970. xviii, 569
p. [4.00]   959.8/03   73-608279
DS615 .H44 MRR Alc.

INDONESIA--BIBLIOGRAPHY.
United States. Library of Congress.
Orientalia Division. Southeast Asia
subject catalog. Boston, G. K. Hall,
1972- v.   016.9159/03   72-5257
Z3221 .U525 MRR Alc (Dk 33)

INDONESIA--CIVILIZATION.
Neill, Wilfred T. Twentieth-century
Indonesia New York, Columbia
University Press, 1973. xiv, 413 p.
[$15.00]   915.98/03/3   72-11718
DS634 .N45 1873 MRR Alc.

INDONESIA--GAZETTEERS.
United States. Office of Geography.
Indonesia and Portuguese Timor;
official standard names approved by
the United States Board on Geographic
Names. 2d ed. Washington, 1968.
viii, 901 p.   919.1/003   68-61196
DS614 .U64 1968 MRR Alc.

INDONESIA--HISTORY.
Neill, Wilfred T. Twentieth-century
Indonesia New York, Columbia
University Press, 1973. xiv, 413 p.
[$15.00]   915.98/03/3   72-11718
DS634 .N45 1873 MRR Alc.

Robertson, J. B. A history of
Indonesia, Melbourne, London [etc.]
Macmillan; New York, St. Martin's
Press, 1967. 258 p. [$2.50 Aust.]
991   67-97087
DS634 .R6 1967 MRR Alc.

Zainu'ddin, Ailsa Gwennyth. A short
history of Indonesia New York,
Praeger Publishers [1970, c1968]
xii, 299 p. [8.50]   991   78-117479
DS634 .Z3 1970 MRR Alc.

INDONESIA--IMPRINTS.
United States. Library of Congress.
Library of Congress Office, Djakarta.
Accessions list, Indonesia,
Malaysia, Singapore, and Brunei. v.
1- July 1964- Djakarta. sa 66-444
Z663.767.I6 A25 MRR Alc   MRR Alc
Full set

United States. Library of Congress.
Library of Congress Office, Djakarta.
Accessions list, Indonesia,
Malaysia, Singapore, and Brunei.
Cumulative list of serials. Jan.
1964/Sept. 1966-1964/68. Djakarta.
74-643581
Z663.767.I6 A252 MRR Alc   MRR Alc
Full set

INDONESIA--STATISTICS.
Indonesia. Biro Pusat Statistik.
Statistical pocket book of Indonesia.
1957- Djakarta. 319.1   60-18985
HA1811 .A34   MRR Alc Latest edition

INDONESIAN LANGUAGE--DICTIONARIES--
ENGLISH.
Echols, John M. An Indonesian-
English dictionary, 2d ed. Ithaca,
N.Y., Cornell University Press [1963]
xviii, 431 p.   499.2   63-8235
PL5076 .E25 1963 MRR Alc.

Van Goor's kamus Inggeris ketjil.
Rutland, Vt., C. E. Tuttle Co. [1966]
359 p.   499.22132   66-23535
PL5125 .V29 1966 MRR Alc.

Wittermans-Pino, Elizabeth. Kamus
inggeris, 3rd ed. Groningen, J. B.
Wolters, 1963. 2 v.   499.22132   65-
6750
PL5076 .W5 1963 MRR Alc.

INDOOR GAMES.
Foster, Robert Frederick, Foster's
complete Hoyle; Rev. and enl.
Philadelphia, Lippincott [1963]
xxiv, 697 p.   795   75-19113
GV1243 .F77 1963 MRR Alc.

Frey, Richard L., ed. The new
complete Hoyle; [Rev. ed.] Garden
City, N.Y., Garden City Books [1956]
740 p.   795   55-11330
GV1243 .F85 1956 MRR Alc.

INDUSTRIAL ACCIDENTS.
International Labor Office.
Encyclopaedia of occupational health
and safety. New York, McGraw-Hill
[1971-72] 2 v. (xiii, 1621 p.)
613.6/2/03   74-39329
RC963 .I6 1971b MRR Alc.

INDUSTRIAL ARBITRATION
see Arbitration, Industrial

INDUSTRIAL ARCHAEOLOGY--EUROPE.
Hudson, Kenneth. A guide to the
industrial archaeology of Europe.
[1st American ed.] Madison [N.J.]
Fairleigh Dickinson University Press
[1971]   xi, 186 p. [$15.00]   609/.4
76-160459
T26.A1 H8 1971b MRR Alc.

INDUSTRIAL ARTS.
see also Agriculture

see also Engineering

see also Machinery

see also Manufactures

see also Mechanical engineering

see also Printing

see also Technology

Hiscox, Gardner Dexter, ed. Henley's
twentieth century book of formulas,
processes and trade secrets; New
rev. and enl. ed. New York, Books,
Inc., 1970. 867, [67] p.   602/.02
76-18904
T49 .H6 1970 MRR Alc.

INDUSTRIAL ARTS--BIBLIOGRAPHY.
How-to-do-it books; 3d ed. rev. New
York, R. R. Bowker Co., 1963. xxi,
265 p.   016   63-15626
Z7911 .H6 1963 MRR Alc.

INDUSTRIAL ARTS--FILM CATALOGS.
National Information Center for
Educational Media. Index to
vocational and technical education
(multimedia). 1st ed. Los Angeles,
1972. x, 298 p.   016.6   72-190628
T65.5.M6 N28 1972 MRR Alc.

INDUSTRIAL ARTS--PERIODICALS--INDEXES.
Applied science & technology index.
v. 1-   Feb. 1913-   [Bronx, N.Y.,
etc.] H. W. Wilson [etc.]   016.6   14-
5408
Z7913 .I7 MRR Circ Partial set /
Sci RR Partial set

INDUSTRIAL ARTS--STUDY AND TEACHING--
HISTORY.
Barlow, Melvin L. History of
industrial education in the United
States Peoria, Ill., C. A. Bennett
[1967]   512 p.   607   67-10595
T73 .B377 MRR Alc.

INDUSTRIAL CHEMISTRY
see Chemical engineering

INDUSTRIAL DESIGN
see Design, Industrial

INDUSTRIAL DISTRICTS--UNITED STATES--
PERIODICALS.
Guide to industrial parks and area
development. 1st- ed.; 1969-
[Princeton, N.J., Resource
Publications, inc.]   338/.0973   78-
78651
HC101. G87 MRR Alc Latest edition

INDUSTRIAL ENGINEERING--ABBREVIATIONS.
Dictionary of industrial engineering
abbreviations; New York, Odyssey
Press [1967]   xviii, 898 p.
658.5/001/48   65-19183
T58 .D5 MRR Alc.

INDUSTRIAL ENGINEERING--NOTATION.
Dictionary of industrial engineering
abbreviations; New York, Odyssey
Press [1967]   xviii, 898 p.
658.5/001/48   65-19183
T58 .D5 MRR Alc.

INDUSTRIAL EQUIPMENT--UNITED STATES--
DIRECTORIES.
Municipal index; [1st]- ed.; 1924-
[Pittsfield, Mass., etc.] Buttenheim
Pub. Corp. [etc.]   24-14253
TD1 .M927 MRR Alc Latest edition

INDUSTRIAL HYGIENE--BIBLIOGRAPHY.
United States. Library of Congress.
General Reference and Bibliography
Division. A bibliography of writings
by the speakers participating in the
conference on the relation of
environment to work, November 6-10,
1960. Washington, 1950. 29 p.
016.33I2   50-61524
Z663.28 .B524 1950 MRR Alc.

INDUSTRIAL MANAGEMENT.
see also Business

see also Communication in management

see also Executives

see also Marketing

Fenner, Terrence W. Inventor's
handbook New York, Chemical Pub.
Co., 1969. xi, 309 p. [7.50]
608.7   73-5567
T212 .F44 MRR Alc.

Horton, Forest W. Reference guide to
advanced management methods [New
York] American Management Association
[1972]   xii, 333 p. [$17.50]   658.4
70-162473
HD31 .H653 MRR Alc.

INDUSTRIAL MANAGEMENT--BIBLIOGRAPHY.
Bakewell, K. G. B. How to find out:
management and productivity; 2d ed.
Oxford, New York, Pergamon Press
[1970]   x, 389 p.   016.6585   78-
89775
Z7164.O7 B2 1970 MRR Alc.

Bibliography of publications of
university bureaus of business and
economic research. [Boulder, Colo.,
etc.] Business Research Division,
University of Colorado.
016.33/007/2073   77-635614
Z7165.U5 A8 MRR Alc Full set

Coman, Edwin Truman, Sources of
business information, Rev. ed.
Berkeley, University of California
Press, 1964. xii, 330 p.   016.65
64-18639
Z7164.C81 C75 1964 MRR Alc.

European directory of economic and
corporate planning, 1973-74; Epping,
Gower Press, 1973. xvii, 442 p.
[£8.50]   309.2/12/0254   74-162022
HD31 .E83 1973 MRR Alc.

INDUSTRIAL MANAGEMENT--BIBLIOGRAPHY--
CATALOGS.
Harvard University. Graduate School
of Business Administration. Baker
Library. Subject catalog of the
Baker Library, Graduate School of
Business Administration, Harvard
University. Boston, G. K. Hall,
1971. 10 v.   016.33 70-170935
Z7164.C81 H275 MRR Alc (Dk 33)

INDUSTRIAL MANAGEMENT--BIOGRAPHY.
Urwick, Lyndall Fownes. The golden
book of management; London, N. Neame
[1956] xix, 198 p.   926.58 a 56-
4045
HD31 .U75 1956 MRR Biog.

INDUSTRIAL MANAGEMENT--DICTIONARIES.
Benn, A. E. The management
dictionary; New York, Exposition
Press [1952] 381 p.   658.03 51-
11831
HD19 .B4 MRR Alc.

Heyel, Carl, ed. The encyclopedia of
management. 2d ed. New York, Van
Nostrand Reinhold Co. [1973] xxvii,
1161 p.   658/.003 72-11784
HD19 .H4 1973 MRR alc.

Johannsen, Hano. Management
glossary. New York, American
Elsevier Pub. Co., 1968. 146 p.
658/.003 68-57418
HD19 .J6 1968 MRR Alc.

Lindemann, A. J. Encyclopaedic
dictionary of management and
manufacturing terms 2d ed. Dubuque,
Iowa, Kendall/Hunt Pub. Co. [1974]
vii, 150 p.   658.4/003 74-167262
HD19 .L5 1974 MRR Alc.

Mueller, Robert Kirk. Buzzwords;
New York, Van Nostrand Reinhold Co.
[1974] viii, 172 p.   658.4/003 74-
1403
HD19 .M75 MRR Alc.

Newnes encyclopaedia of business
management; London, Newnes, 1967.
637 p.   [6/6/-] 650/.03 67-97096
HD19 .N48 MRR Alc.

Prentice-Hall, inc. Encyclopedic
dictionary of systems and procedures,
Englewood Cliffs, N.J. [1966] 673
p.   658.5003 66-27954
HD19 .P72 MRR Alc.

Sommer, Werner. Management
dictionary. 3., durchgesehene und
erw. Aufl. Berlin, De Gruyter, 1966-
68. 2 v.   [DM 18.00 per vol.]
658.003 67-73661
HF1002 .S622 MRR Alc.

INDUSTRIAL MANAGEMENT--DICTIONARIES--
GERMAN.
Sommer, Werner. Management
dictionary. 3., durchgesehene und
erw. Aufl. Berlin, De Gruyter, 1966-
68. 2 v.   [DM 18.00 per vol.]
658.003 67-73661
HF1002 .S622 MRR Alc.

INDUSTRIAL MANAGEMENT--DIRECTORIES.
European directory of economic and
corporate planning, 1973-74; Epping,
Gower Press, 1973. xvii, 442 p.
[£8.50] 309.2/12/0254 74-162022
HD31 .E83 1973 MRR Alc.

INDUSTRIAL MANAGEMENT--PERIODICALS--
BIBLIOGRAPHY--CATALOGS.
Harvard University. Graduate School
of Business Administration. Baker
Library. Current periodical
publications in Baker Library.
1971/72- [Boston] 016.33/005 72-
620452
Z7164.C81 H266 MRR Alc Latest
edition

INDUSTRIAL MANAGEMENT--GREAT BRITAIN.
Newnes encyclopaedia of business
management; London, Newnes, 1967.
637 p.   [6/6/-] 650/.03 67-97096
HD19 .N48 MRR Alc.

INDUSTRIAL MANAGEMENT--UNITED STATES.
American Institute of Management.
Manual of excellent managements. New
York. 658.02 56-14078
HD2791 .A6 MRR Alc Latest edition

Dun and Bradstreet, inc. Business
Education Division. A guide to
management services. New York [1968]
260 p.   [1.95] 658.4/6 73-92724
HD69.C6 D85 MRR Alc.

INDUSTRIAL MATERIALS
see Materials

INDUSTRIAL MUSEUMS.
Coleman, Laurence Vail. Company
museums. Washington, D.C., The
American association of museums,
1943. viii, 173 p.   069 43-51215
T179 .C6 MRR Alc.

INDUSTRIAL PRODUCTIVITY CENTERS--
DIRECTORIES.
McNulty, Nancy G. Training managers;
[1st ed.] New York, Harper & Row
[1969] x, 572 p.   [12.95]
658.4/0071/5 70-83612
HD20 .M253 MRR Alc.

INDUSTRIAL PROMOTION--CARIBBEAN AREA--
HANDBOOKS, MANUALS, ETC.
Jonnard, Claude M. Caribbean
investment handbook Park Ridge,
N.J., Noyes Data Corporation, 1974.
xii, 306 p.   [$24.00]
332.6/73/09729 74-75903
HG5242 .J66 MRR Alc.

INDUSTRIAL PROMOTION--DISTRICT OF
COLUMBIA--DIRECTORIES.
Howard University, Washington, D.C.
Minority Economic Resource Center.
The District of Columbia directory of
inner city organizations active in
the field of minority business-
economic development. 3d ed.
Washington, 1972. iv, 20 p.
338/.04/025753 73-170762
HD2346.U52 D54 1972 MRR Alc.

INDUSTRIAL PROMOTION--UNITED STATES--
DICTIONARIES.
Collison, Koder M. The developers'
dictionary and handbook Lexington,
Mass., Lexington Books [1974] xiii,
175 p.   338/.0025/73 73-21866
HD1393.5 .C64 MRR Alc.

INDUSTRIAL PROPERTY--HANDBOOKS,
MANUALS, ETC.
Katsarov, Konstantin. Manual and
directory on industrial property all
over the world. 7th- ed.; 1970-
[Geneva, Switzerland] 608/.7/0202
72-625377
T201 .K3 MRR Alc Latest edition

INDUSTRIAL PUBLICITY.
see also Advertising

see also Public relations

INDUSTRIAL RELATIONS.
see also Labor and laboring classes

see also Trade-unions

INDUSTRIAL RELATIONS--BIBLIOGRAPHY.
Industrial relations theses and
dissertations accepted at
universities. Berkeley, Institute of
Industrial Relations, University of
California. 016.331 52-62063
Z7914.A2 I53 MRR Alc Latest
edition

INDUSTRIAL RELATIONS--BIBLIOGRAPHY--
CATALOGS.
Cornell University. New York State
School of Industrial and Labor
Relations. Library. Library catalog.
Boston, G. K. Hall, 1967. 12 v.
016.331 72-185899
Z7164.L1 C84 MRR Alc (Dk 33)

INDUSTRIAL RELATIONS--DICTIONARIES.
Becker, Esther R. Dictionary of
personnel and industrial relations.
New York, Philosophical Library
[1958] 366 p.   658.303 58-59649
HF5549 .B3418 MRR Alc.

Roberts, Harold Selig. Roberts'
dictionary of industrial relations.
Rev. ed. Washington, Bureau of
National Affairs [c1971] xv, 599 p.
331/.03 78-175029
HD4839 .R612 1971 MRR Alc.

INDUSTRIAL RELATIONS--DICTIONARIES--
POLYGLOT.
Associazione industriale lombarda.
Glossario del lavoro: italiano,
francese, inglese, tedesco. Milano,
1964. 1335 p.   67-43249
HD4839 .A78 MRR Alc.

INDUSTRIAL RELATIONS--LATIN AMERICA--
BIBLIOGRAPHY.
Morris, James Oliver. Bibliography
of industrial relations in Latin
America, Ithaca, New York State
School of Industrial and Labor
Relations, Cornell University [1967]
xv, 290 p.   016.6580098 67-64729
Z7164.L1 M69 MRR Alc.

INDUSTRIAL RELATIONS--UNITED STATES.
Chamberlain, Neil W., ed. Sourcebook
on labor New York, McGraw-Hill Book
Co. [1964] x, 382 p.   331.1973 64-
21013
HD8072 .C38 1964 MRR Alc.

Morgan, Chester A. Labor economics
3d ed. Austin, Tex., Business
Publications [1970] xiii, 662 p.
331 71-105541
HD4901 .M86 1970 MRR Alc.

INDUSTRIAL RELATIONS--UNITED STATES--
BIOGRAPHY.
Industrial Relations Research
Association. Membership directory.
Oct. 1949- [Madison, Wis., etc]
331.06273 50-20362
HD4802 .I66 MRR Biog Latest
edition

INDUSTRIAL RELATIONS--UNITED STATES--
DIRECTORIES.
Roberts, Harold Selig. Who's who in
industrial relations, [Honolulu]
Industrial Relations Center, College
of Business Administration,
University of Hawaii, 1966-67. 2 v.
331.102573 67-63128
HD8061 .R6 MRR Biog.

INDUSTRIAL RELATIONS--UNITED STATES--
YEARBOOKS.
Labor relations yearbook. 1965-
Washington, Bureau of National
Affairs. 331.1973 66-18726
HD8059 .L33 MRR Alc Latest edition

INDUSTRIAL RESEARCH
see Research, Industrial

INDUSTRIAL SAFETY.
see also Hazardous substances

International Labor Office.
Encyclopaedia of occupational health
and safety. New York, McGraw-Hill
[1971-72] 2 v. (xiii, 1621 p.)
613.6/2/03 74-39329
RC963 .I6 1971b MRR Alc.

INDUSTRIAL SAFETY--UNITED STATES--
DIRECTORIES.
Best's safety directory; Morristown,
N.J., A.M. Best Co.
338.4/7/620860257 73-642584
T55.A1 B4 MRR Alc Latest edition

INDUSTRIAL SITES--UNITED STATES--
DICTIONARIES.
Collison, Koder M. The developers'
dictionary and handbook Lexington,
Mass., Lexington Books [1974] xiii,
175 p.   338/.0025/73 73-21866
HD1393.5 .C64 MRR Alc.

INDUSTRIAL STATISTICS.
Econtel Research. World industrial
production. London, Econtel
Research, 1969. 20 p.   [60/- ($8.00
U.S.)] 338/.09/045 79-557483
HA40.I6 E3 MRR Alc.

Gallatin Service. Gallatin
statistical indicators. [New York,
Copley International Corporation,
1967- v.   310 72-12086
HA42 .G32 MRR Alc.

Organization for Economic Cooperation
and Development. Industrial
production. [Paris,] Organisation
for Economic Co-operation and
Development, 1968. 308 p. [14.00]
338/.09 76-422848
HC240 .O693 MRR Alc.

Trade Relations Council of the United
States. General Counsel. Employment,
output, and foreign trade of U.S.
manufacturing industries.
Washington. 338/.0973 73-30363
HC101 .T68 MRR Alc Latest edition

Troy, Leo. Almanac of business and
industrial financial ratios. 1972
ed. Englewood Cliffs, N.J., Prentice-
Hall [1971] xxi, 169 p.   338.5/0973
72-181403
HF5681.R25 T68 1971 MRR Alc.

U. S. industrial outlook.
Washington, Bureau of Competitive
Assessment and Business Policy, for
sale by the Supt. of Docs., U.S.
Govt. Print. Off. 338/.0973 74-
644570
HC106.6 .A23 MRR Alc Latest
edition

United Nations. Statistical Office.
The growth of world industry. 1967
ed. New York, United Nations, 1968-
69 [v. 1, 1969] 2 v.   338 77-7739
HC59 .U458 MRR Alc.

United Nations. Statistical Office.
The growth of world industry, 1938-
1961. New York, United Nations,
1963. xvi, 849 p.   338.4083 63-
25411
HC59 .U46 MRR Alc.

United Nations. Statistical Office.
Patterns of industrial growth. New
York, United Nations, 1960. viii,
471 p.   338.019 60-50248
HC58 .U5112 MRR Alc.

United Nations. Statistical Office.
Statistical yearbook. 1st issue;
1948- New York [etc.] 50-2746
HA12.5 .U63 MRR Ref Desk Latest
edition

United States. Bureau of Domestic
Commerce. Industry profiles.
1958/68- [Washington, For sale by
the Supt. of Docs., U.S. Govt. Print.
Off.] 338/.0973 72-626646
HC106.5 .A168 MRR Alc Latest
edition

INDUSTRIAL STATISTICS. (Cont.)
United States. Bureau of Labor Statistics. BLS handbook of methods for surveys and studies. Washington, For sale by the Superintendent of Documents, U.S. Govt. Print Off., 1966. v, 238 p. 331/.0973 67-60373
    HD8064 .A52 1966 MRR Alc.

United States. Bureau of the Census. County business patterns; 1946-[Washington] 49-45747
    HC101 .A184 MRR Alc Latest edition

United States. Bureau of the Census. Manufacturers' shipments, inventories, and orders; 1961-1968. Washington] U.S. Dept. of Commerce; [for sale by the Supt. of Docs., U.S. Govt. Print. Off., 1968] iii, 92 p. [1.00] 338.4/7/6700973 70-607789
    HD9724 .A4 1961 MRR alc.

United States. Bureau of the Census. Economic Statistics and Surveys Division. Enterprise statistics: 1967. [Washington; For sale by the Supt. of Docs., U.S. Govt. Print. Off., Washington, 1971- [v. 1, 1972] v. [$7.75 (v. 1)] 338/.0973 79-186224
    HC106.6 .U55 1972 MRR Alc.

INDUSTRIAL SUPPLY HOUSES--DIRECTORIES.
Directory of industrial distributors. New York. 650.58 53-40422
    HF5035 .D485 MRR Alc Latest edition

INDUSTRIALIZATION.
see also Underdeveloped areas

INDUSTRIALIZATION--BIBLIOGRAPHY.
Brode, John. The process of modernization; Cambridge, Mass., Harvard University Press, 1969. x, 378 p. [6.50] 016.3092 69-13765
    Z7164.U5 B7 MRR Alc.

INDUSTRIES
see Aerospace industries

see Construction industry

INDUSTRIES, LOCATION OF--UNITED STATES.
Kuznets, Simon Smith, ed. Population redistribution and economic growth: Philadelphia, American Philosophical Society, 1957-64. 3 v. 312.8 301.32* 57-10071
    HB1965 .K8 MRR Alc.

INDUSTRIES, PRIMITIVE.
see also Man, Prehistoric

INDUSTRIES, SERVICE
see Service industries

INDUSTRIES, SIZE OF.
see also Big business

INDUSTRY.
United Nations. Statistical Office. The growth of world industry. 1967 ed. New York, United Nations, 1968-69 [v. 1, 1968] 2 v. 338 77-7739
    HC59 .U458 MRR Alc.

INDUSTRY--BIBLIOGRAPHY.
Fundaburk, Emma Lila, Reference materials and periodicals in economics; Metuchen, N.J., Scarecrow Press, 1971- v. 016.33 78-142232
    Z7164.E2 F83 MRR Alc.

INDUSTRY--CLASSIFICATION.
United States. Bureau of the Census. Numerical list of manufactured products. [Washington, 1968] 165, A141, B2 p. 338.4/0973 a 68-7403
    HD9724 .A4 1967 MRR Alc.

United States. Office of Management and Budget. Statistical Policy Division. Standard industrial classification manual. [Washington; For sale by the Supt. of Docs., U.S. Govt. Print. Off.] 1972. 649 p. [$6.75] 338./02/0973 72-601529
    HF1042 .A55 1972 MRR Alc.

INDUSTRY--DICTIONARIES.
United States. Bureau of Labor Statistics. Guide to employment statistics of BLS; [Washington] 1961. i, 134 p. l 62-75
    HD8064 .A52 1961 MRR Alc.

INDUSTRY--DIRECTORIES.
Marconi's international register. New York [etc.] 31-15824
Began publication in 1917.
    HE7710 .I6 MRR Alc Latest edition

INDUSTRY--HISTORY.
United Nations. Statistical Office. Patterns of industrial growth. New York, United Nations, 1960. viii, 471 p. 338.019 60-50248
    HC58 .U5112 MRR Alc.

INDUSTRY--INDEXES.
United States. Bureau of the Census. 1970 census of population. [Washington, U.S. Bureau of the Census, Population Division; for sale by the Supt. of Docs., U.S. Govt. Print. Off.] 1971. xiv, 165, 201 p. [$3.00] 331.1/1/0973 74-612012
    HA201 1970 .A565 MRR Alc.

INDUSTRY--PERIODICALS--INDEXES.
Business periodicals index. v. 1-Jan. 1958- New York, H. W. Wilson Co. 016.6505 58-12645
    Z7164.C81 B983 MRR Circ Full set

F & S index international: industries, countries, companies. 1st- ed.; 1968- Cleveland, Predicasts. 016.338 74-644265
    Z7164.C81 F13 MRR Alc Full set / Sci RR Partial set

Wall Street Journal. (Indexes) Index. [New York] Dow Jones & Co. 59-35162
    HG1 .W26 MRR Alc Full set

INDUSTRY--SOCIAL ASPECTS--UNITED STATES.
Human Resources Network. Profiles of involvement. [Philadelphia, 1972] 3 v. (843 p.) [$50.00] 658.4/08 72-87222
    HD60.5.U5 H85 MRR Alc.

INDUSTRY--SOCIAL ASPECTS--UNITED STATES--CASE STUDIES.
Council on Economic Priorities. Guide to corporations. [1st ed.] Chicago, Swallow Press [1974] iii, 393 p. [$4.95] 301.5/5 73-13212
    HD60.5.U5 C7 1974 MRR Alc.

INDUSTRY AND STATE.
see also Agriculture and state

see also Economic policy

INDUSTRY AND STATE--BIBLIOGRAPHY.
Universal Reference System. Economic regulation: business and government; Princeton, N.J., Princeton Research Pub. Corp [1969] xx, llll p. 016.33 68-57824
    Z7161 .U64 vol. 8 MRR Alc.

INDUSTRY AND STATE--CANADA.
Organization for Economic Cooperation and Development. The industrial policies of 14 member countries. [Paris, 1971] 385 p. [$5.75 (U.S.)] 338.94 74-882853
    HD3616.E83 O73 MRR Alc.

INDUSTRY AND STATE--EUROPE.
Organization for Economic Cooperation and Development. The industrial policies of 14 member countries. [Paris, 1971] 385 p. [$5.75 (U.S.)] 338.94 74-882853
    HD3616.E83 O73 MRR Alc.

INDUSTRY AND STATE--UNITED STATES.
Cossman, E. Joseph. How to get $50,000 worth of services free, each year, from the U.S. Government, New York; F. Fell [1965, c1964] 233 p. 658.02 64-8781
    HF5353 .C7 MRR Alc.

INFANT EDUCATION
see Education, Preschool

INFANTICIDE.
see also Abortion

INFANTS--CARE AND HYGIENE.
see also Prenatal care

Boston. Children's Hospital Medical Center. Pregnancy, birth & the newborn baby [New York] Delacorte Press [1972] 474 p. [$10.00] 613 71-175649
    RG525 .B645 MRR Alc.

Levine, Milton Isra, The parents' encyclopedia of infancy, childhood, and adolescence New York, Crowell [1973] 619 p. [$10.00] 649/.1/03 72-83769
    RJ61 .L552 MRR Alc.

INFECTIOUS DISEASES
see Communicable diseases

INFIRMARIES
see Hospitals

INFLAMMABLE MATERIALS.
Factory Mutual Engineering Corporation. Handbook of industrial loss prevention; 2d ed. New York, McGraw-Hill [1967] 1 v. (various paging) 628/.92 66-23623
    TH9445.M4 F3 1967 MRR Alc.

Meidl, James H. Hazardous materials handbook Beverly Hills, Calif., Glencoe Press [1972] xviii, 349 p. 604/.7/0202 72-177437
    TH9446.I47 M44 MRR Alc.

INFORMATION AND RETRIEVAL SYSTEMS.
see also Computers

INFORMATION, FREEDOM OF
see Freedom of information

INFORMATION SCIENCE.
see also Electronic data processing

INFORMATION SCIENCE--ABBREVIATIONS.
Pugh, Eric. A dictionary of acronyms & abbreviations; 2d, rev. and expanded ed. [Hamden, Conn.] Archon Books [1970] 389 p. 601/.48 72-16645
    T8 .P8 1970 MRR Alc.

Pugh, Eric. Second dictionary of acronyms & abbreviations; [Hamden, Conn.] Archon Books [1974] 410 p. 601/.48 74-4271
    T8 .P82 MRR Alc.

INFORMATION SCIENCE--ABSTRACTS--PERIODICALS.
Library & information science abstracts. 1- Jan./Feb. 1969-London, Library Association. 016.02 78-228730
    Z671 .L6 MRR Alc Full set*

INFORMATION SCIENCE--BIBLIOGRAPHY.
Schutze, Gertrude. Information and library science source book; Metuchen, N.J., Scarecrow Press, 1972. ix, 483 p. 016.02 72-1157
    Z666 .S373 MRR Alc.

INFORMATION SCIENCE--COLLECTIONS.
Annual review of information science and technology. v. 1- 1966-Chicago [etc.] Encyclopaedia Britannica, inc. [etc.] 029.708 66-25096
    Z699 .A1A65 Sci RR Full set / MRR Alc Latest edition

INFORMATION SCIENCE--DICTIONARIES.
Casey, Florence, Compilation of terms in information sciences technology. [Springfield, Va.] National Technical Information Service, 1970. 470 l. on [240] p. 001.5/03 77-612498
    Z1006 .C38 MRR Alc.

Encyclopedia of library and information science. New York, M. Dekker [1968- v. 020/.3 68-31232
    Z1006 .E57 MRR Alc.

INFORMATION SCIENCE--RESEARCH--PERIODICALS.
LIST; library and information science today. 1971- [New York] Science Associates/International. 71-143963
    Z669.7 .L18 Sci RR Latest edition / MRR Alc Latest edition

INFORMATION SERVICES.
see also Libraries

see also Research

Angel, Juvenal Londoño, The handbook of international business and investment facts and information sources, New York, World Trade Academy Press; distributed by Simon & Schuster [1967] 565 p. 382 66-28172
    HF1411 .A5 MRR Alc.

Encyclopedia of business information sources; Detroit, Gale Research Co., 1970. 2 v. (xxi, 689 p.) 016.33 79-127922
    HF5353 .E52 MRR Ref Desk.

Kaplan, Stuart R., ed. A guide to information sources in mining, minerals, and geosciences, New York, Interscience Publishers [1965] xiv, 599 p. 016.622 65-24304
    Z7401 .O83 vol. 2 MRR Alc.

INFORMATION SERVICES--DIRECTORIES.
United Nations Educational, Scientific and Cultural Organization. World guide to science information and documentation services. [Paris, 1965] 211 p. 507.2 65-9614
    Q223 .U45 MRR Alc.

United States. Library of Congress. International Organizations Section. International scientific organizations; Washington, General Reference and Bibliography Division, Reference Dept.,Library of Congress; [for sale by the Superintendent of Documents, U.S. Govt. Print. Off.] 1962 [i.e. 1963] xi, 794 p. 506 62-64648
    Z663.295 .I5 MRR Alc.

INFORMATION SERVICES--CALIFORNIA.
The California handbook. 1st- ed.; 1969- [Claremont] Center for California Public Affairs. 917.94 75-171691
    HC107.C2 C253 MRR Alc Latest edition

INFORMATION SERVICES--CANADA.
Directory of business and financial services. [1st]- ed.; 1924- New York [etc.] Special Libraries Association. 25-4599
HF5003 .H3   MRR Ref Desk Latest edition / MRR Ref Desk Latest edition

INFORMATION SERVICES--CANADA--DIRECTORIES.
Young, Margaret Labash. Directory of special libraries and information centers. 3d ed.   Detroit, Gale Research Co. [1974- v.   [$48.00] 026/.00025/7. 74-3240
Z731 .Y68 1974 MRR Ref Desk.

INFORMATION SERVICES--CHICAGO METROPOLITAN AREA--DIRECTORIES.
Hamilton, Beth A. Libraries and information centers in the Chicago metropolitan area. Hinsdale, Illinois Regional Library Council, 1973.   499 p.   021/.0025/77311 73-89540
Z732.I2 H35 MRR Alc.

INFORMATION SERVICES--EUROPE.
Williams, Colin H. Guide to European sources of technical information. 3d ed. [Guernsey] Francis Hodgson [1970] 309 p. [$20.00 (U.S.)]   607 77-105217
T10.65.E8 W5 1970 MRR Alc.

INFORMATION SERVICES--FRANCE--DIRECTORIES.
Paris. Bibliothèque nationale. Répertoire des bibliothèques et organismes de documentation. Paris, 1971.   733 p.   020/.25/44 76-501813

Z797 .A1P35 1971 MRR Alc.

INFORMATION SERVICES--GREAT BRITAIN.
Burkett, Jack, ed. Special library and information services in the United Kingdom, 2d, rev. ed. [London] Library Association [1965] 366 p.   66-53653
Z781 .B9 1965 MRR Alc.

Davinson, Donald Edward. Commercial information; [1st ed.] Oxford, New York, Pergamon Press [1965] viii, 164 p.   380.0942 65-22918
HF3507 .D3 1965 MRR Alc.

Directory of newspaper and magazine personnel and data. London, Haymarket Publishing Group, [etc.] 072.058 59-18302
Z6956.E5 D5 MRR Alc Latest edition

Snape, Wilfrid Handley. How to find out about local government, [1st ed.] Oxford, New York, Pergamon Press [1969] xv, 173 p. 352/.000942 69-20482
JS3113 .S58 1969 MRR Alc.

Wills, Gordon, comp. Sources of U.K. marketing information; London, Nelson, 1969. xiii, 304 p. [60/-] 658.83/9/42 70-412725
HF5415.12.G7 W5 MRR Alc.

INFORMATION SERVICES--GREAT BRITAIN--BIBLIOGRAPHY.
Aslib. Aslib publications in and out of print. London. 65-51810
Z673 .A62712 MRR Alc Latest edition

INFORMATION SERVICES--GREAT BRITAIN--DIRECTORIES.
Aslib. Aslib directory; London, 1957. 2 v.   026.006242 58-2664
Z791 .A788 MRR Alc.

Who's who in journalism. 1968- [London] 070/.025/42 71-11173
Z6956.G6 W5 MRR Alc Latest edition

INFORMATION SERVICES--INDIA--DIRECTORIES.
Indian Association of Special Libraries and Information Centres. Directory of special and research libraries in India. [1st ed.] Calcutta, sole selling agent: Oxford Book & stationery Co., 1962. iii, 282 p. sa 63-1553
Z955 .I45 MRR Alc.

INFORMATION SERVICES--ITALY--DIRECTORIES.
Associazione italiana per le biblioteche. Guida delle biblioteche scientifiche e tecniche e dei centri di documentazione italiani, Roma, Consiglio nazionale delle ricerche, 1965. viii, 610 p.   68-130514
Z809 .A1A78 MRR Alc.

INFORMATION SERVICES--SWITZERLAND.
Schweizerische Vereinigung für Dokumentation. Archive, Bibliotheken und Dokumentationsstellen der Schweiz. 3. Aufl. Bern, 1958. xvi, 144 p.   59-45785
Z837 .S44 1958 MRR Alc.

INFORMATION SERVICES--UNITED STATES.
Chamber of Commerce of the United States of America. Foreign Commerce Dept. Guide to foreign information sources. [Rev. Washington] Chamber of Commerce of the United States [1960] 26 p.   327.73 61-25832
E744 .C46 1960 MRR Alc.

Cossman, E. Joseph. How to get $50,000 worth of services free, each year, from the U.S. Government, New York, F. Fell [1965, c1964] 233 p. 658.02 64-8781
HF5353 .C7 MRR Alc.

Directory of business and financial services. [1st]- ed.; 1924- New York [etc.] Special Libraries Association. 25-4599
HF5003 .H3   MRR Ref Desk Latest edition / MRR Ref Desk Latest edition

Dun and Bradstreet, inc. Business Education Division. A guide to management services. New York [1968] 260 p. [1.95] 658.4/6 73-92724
HD69.C6 D85 MRR Alc.

Frank, Nathalie D., Market analysis: a handbook of current data sources, New York, Scarecrow Press, 1964. 268 p. 658.83 64-21969
HF5415 .F686 MRR Alc.

Herner, Saul. Selected Federal computer-based information systems, Washington, Information Resources Press, 1972. ix, 215 p.   027.5 72-85016
Z699 .H47 MRR Alc.

Investment information and advice: [1st]- ed.; 1962- Whittier, Calif. [etc.] FIR Pub. Co. 62-16904
HG4509 .I65 MRR Ref Desk Latest edition

Knight, Douglas M., comp. Libraries at large: New York, Bowker, 1969. xxiv, 664 p.   021/.00973 70-79429
Z731 .K56 MRR Alc.

National Council for Community Services to International Visitors. National directory of community organizations serving short-term international visitors. Washington. 64-55675
Began publication in 1960.
E744.5 .N35 MRR Alc Latest edition

Pinson, William M. Resource guide to current social issues, Waco, Tex., Word Books [1968] 272 p. 016.301 67-30735
Z7164.S66 P47 MRR Alc.

Sources of information and unusual services; New York, Informational Directory Co. 917.4741 53-4208
AG521 .S6   MRR Ref Desk Latest edition

United States. Library of Congress. National Referral Center. A directory of information resources in the United States: biological sciences. Washington, Library of Congress; [for sale by the Supt. of Docs., U.S. Govt. Print. Off.] 1972. iv, 577 p. [$5.00] 570/.7 72-2659

Z663.379 .D46 MRR Alc.

United States. Library of Congress. National Referral Center. A directory of information resources in the United States: social sciences. Rev. ed. Washington, Library of Congress; [for sale by the Supt. of Docs., U.S. Govt. Print. Off.] 1973. iv, 700 p. [$6.90] 300/.7 73-3297

Z663.379 .D53 1973 MRR Alc.

United States. Library of Congress. National Referral Center for Science and Technology. A directory of information resources in the United States: general toxicology. Washington, Library of Congress; for sale by the Supt. of Docs., U.S. Govt. Print. Off.] 1969. v, 293 p. [3.00] 615.8/007 73-602563
Z663.379 .D49 MRR Alc

United States. Library of Congress. National Referral Center for Science and Technology. A directory of information resources in the United States: water. [Washington, For sale by the Superintendent of Documents, U.S. Govt. Print. Off.] 1966. v, 248 p.   66-61638
Z663.379 .D55 MRR Alc.

White, Alex Sandri. Fact-finding made easy; New, updated ed. Allenhurst, N.J., Aurea Publications [1967] 129 l.   016.016 67-3292
Z1002 .W45 1967 MRR Alc.

Winser, Marian (Manley) Business information, [1st ed.] New York, Harper [1955] xvi, 265 p.   016.65 55-11399
HF5353 .W56 MRR Alc.

INFORMATION SERVICES--UNITED STATES--DIRECTORIES.
Battelle Memorial Institute, Columbus, Ohio. Dept. of Economics and Information Research. Specialized science information services in the United States; Washington, National Science Foundation, Office of Science Information Service, 1961. ix, 528 p.   505.873 61-64862
AG521 .B3 MRR Alc.

Clearinghouse and Laboratory for Census Data. Census processing center catalog. Rev. ed. Arlington, Va. [1974] 1 v. (unpaged) 026/.312/0973 74-180379
HA37.U55 C564 1974 MRR Alc.

Kruzas, Anthony Thomas. Encyclopedia of information systems and services. 2d international ed. Ann Arbor, Mich., A. T. Kruzas Associates, order fulfillment by Edwards Bros. [1974] xii, 1271 p. 029/.025/73 73-3732
Z674.3 .K78 1974 MRR Alc.

Miller, Roy. Lawyers' source book; New York, M. Bender, 1971- 2 v. (loose-leaf) 060 75-179681
AS22 .M54 MRR alc.

United States. Library of Congress. National Referral Center. A directory of information resources in the United States: Federal Government, Rev. ed. Washington, Library of Congress; [for sale by the Supt. of Docs., U.S. Govt. Print. Off.] 1974. iv, 416 p.   001.4/3 73-22041
Z663.379 .D48 1974 MRR Ref Desk.

Weiner, Richard. Professional's guide to public relations services. 2d ed. Englewood Cliffs, N.J., Prentice-Hall [1971] 239 p. 659.2/025/73 71-136585
HD59 .W38 1971 MRR Alc.

Wolff, Garwood R. Environmental information sources handbook. [New York] Simon and Schuster [1974] 568 p.   301.31/07 73-3951
GF503 .W64 MRR Alc.

Young, Margaret Labash. Directory of special libraries and information centers. 3d ed. Detroit, Gale Research Co. [1974- v.   [$48.00] 026/.00025/7 74-3240
Z731 .Y68 1974 MRR Ref Desk.

INFORMATION SERVICES--WASHINGTON, D.C.
International Visitors Service Council. Organizations serving international visitors in the National Capital area. [4th ed.] Washington [1973] vii p., 151 l., 155-191 p. 917.53/04/4025 72-96925

F191 .I57 1973 MRR Alc.

INFORMATION STORAGE AND RETRIEVAL SYSTEMS.
see also Electronic data processing

see also Punched card systems

Bourne, Charles P. Methods of information handling. New York, J. Wiley [1963] xiv, 241 p.   010.78 63-20628
Z699 .B65 MRR Alc.

Conference on Libraries and Automation, Airlie Foundation, 1963. Libraries and automation; Washington, Library of Congress, 1964. xii, 268 p.   64-62653
Z663 .L4 MRR Alc.

Herner, Saul. Selected Federal computer-based information systems, Washington, Information Resources Press, 1972. ix, 215 p.   027.5 72-85016
Z699 .H47 MRR Alc.

Lancaster, Frederick Wilfred, Information retrieval systems; New York, Wiley [1968] xiv, 222 p. 029.7 68-31645
Z699 .L35 MRR Alc.

Reichmann, Felix, Notched cards, New Brunswick, N.J., Graduate School of Library Service, Rutgers, the State University, 1961. 5 v. in 1. 010.78 60-16772
Z695.92 .R4 MRR Alc.

Schultheiss, Louis Avery, Advanced data processing in the university library, New York, Scarecrow Press, 1962. 388 p.   025.078 62-10128
Z699 .S35 MRR Alc.

INFORMATION STORAGE AND (Cont.)
Vickery, Brian Campbell. On
retrieval system theory. 2d ed.
London, Archon Books [1968, c1965]
xii, 191 p.   029.7 68-2703
Z699 .V5 1968 MRR Alc.

INFORMATION STORAGE AND RETRIEVAL
SYSTEMS--BIBLIOGRAPHY.
Balz, Charles F. Literature on
information retrieval and machine
translation, [White Plains, N.Y.]
International Business Machines
Corp., 1962. 117 p.   63-2625
Z699.2 .B3 MRR Alc.

Bourne, Charles P. Bibliography on
the mechanization of information
retrieval, Menlo Park, Calif.,
Stanford Research Institute, 1958-
[62] 5 v. in 1.   65-73592
Z699.2 .B6 MRR Alc.

Service Bureau Corporation.
Literature on information retrieval
and machine translation; 2d ed.
[New York] 1959. 38 p.   016.01078
60-3612
Z699.2 .S4 1959 MRR Alc.

Western Reserve University,
Cleveland. Center for Documentation
and Communication Research. A
selected bibliography of
documentation & information
retrieval. [Rev.] Cleveland, 1964.
10 l.   65-5680
Z699.2 .W4 1964 MRR Alc.

Zell, Hans M. An international
bibliography of non-periodical
literature on documentation &
information, Oxford, R. Maxwell
[1965] vi, 284 p.   016.0297 66-
2713
Z699.2 .Z4 MRR Alc.

INFORMATION STORAGE AND RETRIEVAL
SYSTEMS--CARTOGRAPHY.
United States. Library of Congress.
Information Systems Office. Maps, a
MARC format; Washington; [For sale
by the Supt. of Docs., U.S. Govt.
Print. Off.] 1970. 45 p. [0.50]
526.8/018 77-607327
Z663.172 .M27 MRR Alc.

INFORMATION STORAGE AND RETRIEVAL
SYSTEMS--COLLECTIONS.
Annual review of information science
and technology. v. 1- 1966-
Chicago [etc.] Encyclopaedia
Britannica, inc. [etc.] 029.708 66-
25096
Z699 .A1A65 Sci RR Full set / MRR
Alc Latest edition

INFORMATION STORAGE AND RETRIEVAL
SYSTEMS--DIRECTORIES.
Kruzas, Anthony Thomas. Encyclopedia
of information systems and services.
2d international ed. Ann Arbor,
Mich., A. T. Kruzas Associates; order
fulfillment by Edwards Bros. [1974]
xii, 1271 p.   029/.025/73 73-3732
Z674.3 .K78 1974 MRR Alc.

INFORMATION STORAGE AND RETRIEVAL
SYSTEMS--SCIENCE--PERIODICALS.
Current research and development in
scientific documentation. July 1957-
1969. Washington. 010.78 58-2427
Z699.5.S3 C8 Sci RR Latest edition
/ MRR Alc Partial set

INFORMATION STORAGE AND RETRIEVAL
SYSTEMS--SOCIAL SCIENCES--DIRECTORIES.
Sessions, Vivian S. Directory of
data bases in the social and
behavioral sciences. [New York]
Published in cooperation with the
City University of New York [by]
Science Associates/International
[1974] xv, 300 p. [$35.00]
029/.9/30025 72-86759
Z699.5.S65 S47 MRR Alc.

INFORMATION STORAGE AND RETRIEVAL
SYSTEMS--TERMINOLOGY.
Thompson, Dana L. Glossary of STINFO
terminology. [Washington, Office of
Aerospace Research, U.S. Air Force,
1963] vii, 154 p.   63-65366
Z699 .T5 MRR Alc.

INFORMATION THEORY.
see also Telecommunication

INFORMATION THEORY--DICTIONARIES.
Meetham, A. R. Encyclopaedia of
linguistics, information, and
control. [1st ed.] Oxford, New
York, Pergamon Press [1969] xiv, 718
p.   001.5/39/03 68-18528
Q360 .M35 1969 MRR Alc.

INFRA-RED RAYS--BIBLIOGRAPHY.
United States. Library of Congress.
Technical Information Division.
Infrared, a bibliography.
Washington, 1954-57. 2 v.   016.5356
55-60478
Z663.49 .I58 MRR Alc.

United States. Library of Congress.
Technical Information Division.
Infrared in relation to skin and
underlying tissue; Washington, 1952.
vii p., 20 l.   016.612014482 52-
60026
Z663.49 .I583 MRR Alc.

INITIALISMS
see Acronyms

INJUNCTIONS--BIBLIOGARPHY.
United States. Library of Congress.
Division of bibliography. ... Select
list of references on boycotts and
injunctions in labor disputes;
Washington, Govt. print. off., 1911.
iii, 3-69 p.   10-35010
Z663.28 .S357 MRR Alc.

INJURIOUS INSECTS
see Insects, Injurious and beneficial

INLAND NAVIGATION--ATLANTIC STATES.
Waterway guide. Middle Atlantic
edition. no. 1- 1963- Chesapeake,
Va. [etc.] Waterway Guide Inc. [etc.]
64-2891
GV835 .W35 MRR Alc Latest edition

INLAND NAVIGATION--UNITED STATES.
Waterway guide. Northern edition.
[Fort Lauderdale, Fla.] Inland
Waterway Guide, inc.] 623.89/29/73
73-641441
VK994 .I55 MRR Alc Latest edition

INLAND WATER TRANSPORTATION--UNITED
STATES.
Interstate port handbook. [Chicago]
368.2 44-33741
HE554.A5 I5 MRR Alc Latest edition

INNS
see Hotels, taverns, etc.

INQUISITION--HISTORY.
Lea, Henry Charles, The Inquisition
of the Middle Ages; London, Eyre &
Spottiswoode, 1963. 326 p. 272.2
65-1333
BX1711 .L415 1963 MRR Alc.

INSECTS.
see also Beetles

Klots, Alexander Barrett, 1001
questions answered about insects,
New York, Dodd, Mead, 1961. 260 p.
595.7076 61-15997
QL467 .K58 MRR Alc.

Linsenmaier, Walter. Insects of the
world; New York, McGraw-Hill [1972]
392 p. [$25.00] 595.7 78-178047
QL463 .L4615 MRR Alc.

INSECTS--TERMINOLOGY.
De la Torre-Bueno, José Rollin, A
glossary of entomology; Lancaster,
Penna., Printed by the Science press
printing co., 1937. ix, 336 p.
595.703 38-8454
QL462.3 .D4 MRR Alc.

INSECTS--NORTH AMERICA.
Swan, Lester A. The common insects
of North America, [1st ed.] New
York, Harper & Row [1972] xiii, 750
p. [$15.00] 595.7/09/7 75-138765

QL473 .S9 MRR Alc.

INSECTS--NORTH AMERICA--IDENTIFICATION.
Swan, Lester A. The common insects
of North America, [1st ed.] New
York, Harper & Row [1972] xiii, 750
p. [$15.00] 595.7/09/7 75-138765

QL473 .S9 MRR Alc.

INSECTS--UNITED STATES.
Borror, Donald Joyce, An
introduction to the study of insects
3d ed. New York, Holt, Rinehart and
Winston [1971] xiii, 812 p. 595.7
73-96139
QL463 .B69 1971 MRR Alc.

INSECTS, INJURIOUS AND BENEFICIAL.
Metcalf, Clell Lee, Destructive and
useful insects: 4th ed. New York,
McGraw-Hill, 1962. 1087 p. 632.7
61-14049
SB931 .M45 1962 MRR Alc.

INSECTS, INJURIOUS AND BENEFICIAL--
CONTROL.
Mallis, Arnold. Handbook of pest
control; 5th ed. New York, MacNair-
Dorland Co. [1969] 1158 p. 648/.7
79-10395
TX325 .M3 1969 MRR Alc.

INSECTS AS CARRIERS OF DISEASE.
James, Maurice Theodore, Herms's
medical entomology 6th ed. [New
York] Macmillan [1969] viii, 484 p.
614.4/32 69-12641
RA639.5 .J35 1969 MRR Alc.

INSECTS, INJURIOUS AND BENEFICIAL.
Little, Van Allen, General and
applied entomology 3d ed. New York,
Harper & Row [1972] xi, 527 p.
595.7 79-181540
QL463 .L5 1972 MRR Alc.

INSIGNIA.
see also Emblems, National

American Society of Military Insignia
Collectors. Catalog of distinctive
insignia of the U.S. Army. [1st ed.
Spokane, c1960- 1 v. (loose-leaf)
61-41520
UC533 .A48 MRR Alc.

Blakeslee, Fred Gilbert, Uniforms of
the world, New York, E. P. Dutton &
company, inc. [c1929] xxii, 449 p.
29-10410
UC480 .B65 MRR Alc.

Clapp, Jane. Professional ethics and
insignia. Metuchen, N.J., Scarecrow
Press, 1974. xii, 851 p.   061/.3
74-10501
HD6504 .A194 MRR Ref Desk.

Dyer, Frederick Charles, The petty
officer's guide. 6th ed.
[Harrisburg, Pa.] Stackpole Books
[1966] 392 p.   359.338 66-18190
V123 .D9 1966 MRR Alc.

Kerrigan, Evans E. American badges
and insignia, New York, Viking Press
[1967] xvii, 286 p.   355.1/34 67-
13505
UC533 .K45 MRR Alc.

Tily, James C., The uniforms of the
United States Navy. New York, T.
Yoseloff [1964] 338 p.   359.140973
63-18235
VC303 .T5 MRR Alc.

INSIGNIA--GREAT BRITAIN.
Milton, Roger. The English
ceremonial book; Newton Abbot [Eng.]
David & Charles [1972] 216 p.
[£3.50] 391/.022/0942 72-185055
CR492 .M5 MRR Alc.

INSTALMENT PLAN--UNITED STATES--
DIRECTORIES.
Instalment lending directory. New
York, Instalment Credit Committee,
American Bankers Association. 53-
29979
HF5568 .A6 MRR Alc Latest edition

INSTITUTIONAL CARE.
see also Hospitals

INSTITUTIONAL INVESTMENTS--DIRECTORIES.
Money market directory. 1971- New
York, Money Market Directories.
332.67/025 76-146228
HG4509 .M65 MRR Alc Latest edition

INSTITUTIONS, CHARITABLE AND
PHILANTHROPIC
see Charities

INSTITUTIONS, INTERNATIONAL
see International agencies

INSTITUTIONS, SOCIAL
see Social institutions

INSTITUTIONS, ASSOCIATIONS, ETC.
see Associations, institutions, etc.

INSTRUCTION
see Teaching

INSTRUCTIONAL MATERIALS CENTERS.
Wynar, Christine L. Guide to
reference books for school media
centers Littleton, Colo., Libraries
Unlimited, 1973. xviii, 473 p.
[$17.50] 011/.02 73-87523
Z1035.1 .W97 MRR Alc.

INSTRUCTIVE GAMES
see Educational games

INSTRUMENTAL MUSIC--DICTIONARIES.
Ewen, David, Encyclopedia of concert
music, New York, Hill and Wang
[1959] ix, 566 p.   785.03 59-12597

ML100 .E85 MRR Alc.

INSTRUMENTAL MUSIC--HISTORY AND
CRITICISM.
see also Musical instruments

INSTRUMENTAL MUSIC--THEMATIC CATALOGS.
Barlow, Harold. A dictionary of
musical themes, New York, Crown
Publishers [1948] 656 p.   781.97
48-6784
ML128.I65 B3 MRR Alc.

INSTRUMENTAL MUSIC--UNITED STATES--
DIRECTORIES.
The National directory for the
performing arts and civic centers.
Dallas, Handel & Co.   790.2/0973 73-
646635
PN2289 .N38 MRR Alc Latest edition

INSTRUMENTS, ELECTRIC
see Electric apparatus and appliances

INSTRUMENTS, MEDICAL
see Medical instruments and apparatus

INSTRUMENTS, MUSICAL
see Musical instruments

INSTRUMENTS, PHYSICAL
  see Physical instruments

INSURANCE.
  Mehr, Robert Irwin, Principles of
  insurance, 4th ed. Homewood, Ill.,
  R. D. Irwin, 1966. xviii, 994 p.
  368 66-14546
    HG8051 .M4 1966 MRR Alc.

  Riegel, Robert, Insurance principles
  and practices 5th ed. Englewood
  Cliffs, N.J., Prentice-Hall [1966]
  xvii, 867 p.   368 66-13943
    HG8051 .R5 1966 MRR Alc.

INSURANCE--ADJUSTMENT OF CLAIMS.
  Best's recommended independent
  insurance adjusters. 43d- ed.;
  1973- Morristown, N.J., A. M. Best
  Co. 368/.014 73-644344
    HG8525 .B35 MRR Alc Latest edition

  National Association of Independent
  Insurance Adjusters. Membership
  directory. [Chicago] 63-50175
    HG8525 .N3 MRR Alc Latest edition

INSURANCE--ADJUSTMENT OF CLAIMS--
DIRECTORIES.
  Blue book of adjusters. [Chicago]
  National Association of Independent
  Insurance Adjusters. 368/.014/02573
  72-626059
    HG8525 .B52 MRR Alc Latest edition

INSURANCE--BIBLIOGRAPHY.
  United States. Library of Congress.
  Division of bibliography. List of
  works relating to government
  regulation of insurance, United
  States and foreign countries.
  Washington, Govt. print. off., 1906.
  46 p.   06-35008
    Z663.28 .L588 1906 MRR Alc.

INSURANCE--BIOGRAPHY.
  Who's who in insurance. 1948- New
  York, Underwriter Print. and Pub. Co.
  368.058 48-3960
    HG8523 .W5 MRR Alc Latest edition

INSURANCE--DICTIONARIES.
  Chamber of Commerce of the United
  States of America. Insurance Dept.
  Dictionary of insurance terms.
  Washington [1949] 74 p. 368.03 49-
  15848
    HG8025 .C45 MRR Alc.

  Davids, Lewis E. Dictionary of
  insurance, [4th ed.] Totowa, N.J.,
  Littlefield, Adams, 1974. v, 276 p.
  [$2.95]   368/.003 74-176125
    HG8025 .D3 1974 MRR Alc.

  Mutual of Omaha Insurance Company.
  Glossary of insurance terms. Omaha,
  c1950. 130 p. 368.03 51-15992
    HG8025 .M8 MRR Alc.

  Osler, Robert Willard, Glossary of
  insurance terms. [Santa Monica,
  Calif., Insurors Press, c1972] ix,
  175 p.   368/.003 73-160759
    HG8025 .O84 MRR Alc.

INSURANCE--DICTIONARIES--POLYGLOT.
  International insurance dictionary:
  [n.p., European Conference of
  Insurance Supervisory Services, 1959]
  xxxi, 1083 p.   368.03 61-35675
    HG8025 .I5 MRR Alc.

INSURANCE--PERIODICALS--INDEXES.
  Insurance periodicals index. Boston,
  Special Libraries Association,
  Insurance Division. 65-4638
    Began publication with 1963 vol.
    HG8011 .I545 MRR Alc Full set

INSURANCE--SOCIETIES, ETC.
  The Insurance almanac: who, what,
  when and where in insurance; [1st]-
  1913- New York, Underwriter Print.
  and Pub. Co. 13-15895
    HG8019 .I5 MRR Alc Latest edition

INSURANCE--STATISTICS.
  Ferguson, Elizabeth, ed. Sources of
  insurance statistics. [New York]
  Special Libraries Association, 1965.
  v, 191 p.   368.00212 65-25313
    HG8045 .F45 MRR Alc.

INSURANCE--STATISTICS--BIBLIOGRAPHY.
  Ferguson, Elizabeth, ed. Sources of
  insurance statistics. [New York]
  Special Libraries Association, 1965.
  v, 191 p.   368.00212 65-25313
    HG8045 .F45 MRR Alc.

INSURANCE--YEARBOOKS.
  Anuario español de seguros.
  Barcelona [Graficas marina, s.a.]
  368.058 47-20472
    HG8677 .A55 MRR Alc Latest edition

  The Insurance almanac: who, what,
  when and where in insurance; [1st]-
  1913- New York, Underwriter Print.
  and Pub. Co. 13-15895
    HG8019 .I5 MRR Alc Latest edition

The Insurance directory & year book.
London [etc.] Buckley Press [etc.]
368.058 51-18382
  Began publication in 1840.
    HG8596 .I53 MRR Alc Latest edition

National Underwriter Company.
Agent's and buyer's guide. 1948-
ed. Cincinnati. 368.058 49-140
    HG8523 .N3 MRR Alc Latest edition

INSURANCE--CANADA--DIRECTORIES.
  Breitner, Ruby Church, ed. National
  insurance organizations in the United
  States and Canada. New York, Special
  Libraries Association [c1957] vi, 65
  p. 57-14850
    HG8525 .B7 MRR Alc.

  Stone & Cox general insurance year
  book, Canada. Toronto, Stone & Cox
  Ltd. 368/.971 72-626343
    HG9783 .S8 MRR Alc Latest edition

INSURANCE--CANADA--YEARBOOKS.
  Stone & Cox general insurance year
  book, Canada. Toronto, Stone & Cox
  Ltd. 368/.971 72-626343
    HG9783 .S8 MRR Alc Latest edition

INSURANCE--GREAT BRITAIN--DIRECTORIES.
  The Insurance directory & year book.
  London [etc.] Buckley Press [etc.]
  368.058 51-18382
    Began publication in 1840.
    HG8596 .I53 MRR Alc Latest edition

INSURANCE--SPAIN.
  Anuario español de seguros.
  Barcelona [Graficas marina, s.a.]
  368.058 47-20472
    HG8677 .A55 MRR Alc Latest edition

INSURANCE--UNITED STATES.
  National Underwriter Company.
  Agent's and buyer's guide. 1948-
  ed. Cincinnati. 368.058 49-140
    HG8523 .N3 MRR Alc Latest edition

INSURANCE--UNITED STATES--AGENTS.
  Eastman, Richard W. The professional
  independent insurance agents in the
  United States. Verona, Va., McClure
  Press [1970] 290 p. 368/.065 75-
  128795
    HG8525 .E18 MRR Alc.

INSURANCE--UNITED STATES--BIBLIOGRAPHY.
  Thomas, Roy Edwin, comp. Insurance
  information sources. Detroit, Mich.,
  Gale Research Co. [1971] 332 p.
  [$14.50] 016.368/9/73 75-137575
    Z7164.I7 T48 MRR Alc.

INSURANCE--UNITED STATES--BIOGRAPHY.
  Eastman, Richard W. The professional
  independent insurance agents in the
  United States. Verona, Va., McClure
  Press [1970] 290 p. 368/.065 75-
  128795
    HG8525 .E18 MRR Alc.

  Who's who in risk management.
  Englewood, N.J. [etc.] Underwriter
  Printing and Pub. Co. 368/.81/002573
  70-648918
    HG8059.B8 W5 MRR Biog Latest
    edition

INSURANCE--UNITED STATES--DIRECTORIES.
  Best's key rating guide; property-
  liability. 62d- ed.; 1868-
  Morristown, N.J., A. M. Best Co.
  368/.8/73 72-627014
    HG9765 .B4 MRR Alc Latest edition

  Best's recommended independent
  insurance adjusters. 43d- ed.;
  1973- Morristown, N.J., A. M. Best
  Co. 368/.014 73-644344
    HG8525 .B35 MRR Alc Latest edition

  Best's recommended insurance
  attorneys. 1st- ed.; 1929-
  Morristown, N.J. [etc.] A. M. Best
  Co. 29-5672
    HG8525 .B4 MRR Alc Latest edition

  Best's reproductions of convention
  statements; property-liability.
  Morristown, N.J., A. M. Best Co.
  368/.9/73 72-627024
    HG9965.U5 B4 MRR Alc Latest
    edition

  Blue book of adjusters. [Chicago]
  National Association of Independent
  Insurance Adjusters. 368/.014/02573
  72-626059
    HG8525 .B52 MRR Alc Latest edition

  Breitner, Ruby Church, ed. National
  insurance organizations in the United
  States and Canada. New York, Special
  Libraries Association [c1957] vi, 65
  p. 57-14850
    HG8525 .B7 MRR Alc.

  Eastman, Richard W. The professional
  independent insurance agents in the
  United States. Verona, Va., McClure
  Press [1970] 290 p. 368/.065 75-
  128795
    HG8525 .E18 MRR Alc.

Hine's insurance counsel. Glen
Ellyn, Ill, [etc.] Hine's Legal
Directory [etc.] 07-28505
  Began publication in 1907?
    KF195.I5 H55 MRR Alc Latest
    edition

The Insurance almanac: who, what,
when and where in insurance; [1st]-
1913- New York, Underwriter Print.
and Pub. Co. 13-15895
    HG8019 .I5 MRR Alc Latest edition

National Association of Independent
Insurance Adjusters. Membership
directory. [Chicago] 63-50175
    HG8525 .N3 MRR Alc Latest edition

INSURANCE, BUSINESS--UNITED STATES--
DIRECTORIES.
  Who's who in risk management.
  Englewood, N.J. [etc.] Underwriter
  Printing and Pub. Co. 368/.81/002573
  70-648918
    HG8059.B8 W5 MRR Biog Latest
    edition

INSURANCE, CASUALTY.
  Elliott, Curtis Miller, Property and
  casualty insurance. New York, McGraw-
  Hill, 1960. 200 p. 368 60-12768
    HG8051 .E48 MRR Alc.

  Gordis, Philip, Property and
  casualty insurance; 17th ed., [rev.
  Indianapolis] Rough Notes [1970] 669
  p. 368/.973 76-21025
    HG8051 .G62 1970 MRR Alc.

INSURANCE, CASUALTY--CANADA--YEARBOOKS.
  Best's insurance reports; property-
  liability. [1st]- ed.; 1899/1900-
  Morristown, N.J. [etc.] A. M. Best
  Co. 368.1/0065 00-3410
    HG9655 .B5 MRR Alc Latest edition

INSURANCE, CASUALTY--UNITED STATES.
  Conning and Company, Hartford. A
  record of earnings and other
  financial data on fire and casualty
  insurance companies. [Hartford]
  368.1 58-38085
    HG9755 .C63 MRR Alc Latest edition

INSURANCE, CASUALTY--UNITED STATES--
STATISTICS.
  Best's fire and casualty aggregates &
  averages. 1st- annual ed.; 1940-
  Morristown, N.J. [etc.] Alfred M.
  Best Company. 368.0973 41-7002
    HG9755 .B4 MRR Alc Latest edition

  Dunne's international insurance
  reports: Fire and casualty edition.
  Louisville, Ky., The Insurance Index.
  368/.973 72-622884
    HG9765 .D8 MRR Alc Latest edition

INSURANCE, CASUALTY--UNITED STATES--
YEARBOOKS.
  Best's insurance reports; property-
  liability. [1st]- ed.; 1899/1900-
  Morristown, N.J. [etc.] A. M. Best
  Co. 368.1/0065 00-3410
    HG9655 .B5 MRR Alc Latest edition

INSURANCE, FIRE.
  Lincoln, Walter Osborn, Insurance
  inspection and underwriting; 8th
  ed., rev., condensed, Philadelphia,
  The Spectator [c1965] xiv, 1290 p.
  65-24092
    HG9715 .L5 1965 MRR Alc.

INSURANCE, FIRE--HISTORY.
  Bulau, Alwin E. Footprints of
  assurance. New York, Macmillan,
  1953. xiii, 319 p. 368.109 53-
  1691
    HG9660 .B8 MRR Alc.

INSURANCE, FIRE--INSPECTORS.
  Lincoln, Walter Osborn, Insurance
  inspection and underwriting; 8th
  ed., rev., condensed, Philadelphia,
  The Spectator [c1965] xiv, 1290 p.
  65-24092
    HG9715 .L5 1965 MRR Alc.

INSURANCE, FIRE--CANADA--YEARBOOKS.
  Best's insurance reports; property-
  liability. [1st]- ed.; 1899/1900-
  Morristown, N.J. [etc.] A. M. Best
  Co. 368.1/0065 00-3410
    HG9655 .B5 MRR Alc Latest edition

INSURANCE, FIRE--UNITED STATES.
  Conning and Company, Hartford. A
  record of earnings and other
  financial data on fire and casualty
  insurance companies. [Hartford]
  368.1 58-38085
    HG9755 .C63 MRR Alc Latest edition

INSURANCE, FIRE--UNITED STATES--
STATISTICS.
  Best's fire and casualty aggregates &
  averages. 1st- annual ed.; 1940-
  Morristown, N.J. [etc.] Alfred M.
  Best Company. 368.0973 41-7002
    HG9755 .B4 MRR Alc Latest edition

  Dunne's international insurance
  reports: Fire and casualty edition.
  Louisville, Ky., The Insurance Index.
  368/.973 72-622884
    HG9765 .D8 MRR Alc Latest edition

INSURANCE, FIRE--UNITED STATES--YEARBOOKS.
Best's insurance reports, property-liability. [1st]- ed.: 1899/1900-
Morristown, N.J. [etc.] A. M. Best
Co. 368.1/0065 00-3410
HG9655 .B5 MRR Alc Latest edition

INSURANCE, FRATERNAL--UNITED STATES.
Fraternal monitor. Combined statistics and consolidated chart of fraternal societies. 1958-
Indianapolis. 58-45886
HG9226 .F72 MRR Alc Latest edition

INSURANCE, HEALTH.
see also Medical care

Huebner, Solomon Stephen, Life insurance 8th ed. [New York] Appleton-Century-Crofts [1972]
xxxviii, 827 p. 368.3/2 72-181734

HG8771 .H8 1972 MRR Alc.

INSURANCE, HEALTH--DICTIONARIES.
Levy, Michael H. A handbook of personal insurance terminology,
Lynbrook, N.Y., Farnsworth Pub. Co.,
1968. xi, 595 p. 368.3/2/0014 68-3253
HG8759 .L4 MRR Alc.

INSURANCE, HEALTH--POLICIES.
National Underwriter Company. Time saver for health insurance. 37th-
ed.; 1960- Cincinnati. 368.3/8 72-623809
HG9336 .N3 MRR Alc Latest edition

National Underwriter Company. Who writes what? [1st- ed.]; 1942-
Cincinnati, O., Boston [etc.]
National underwriter company,
Statistical division. 368.30973 42-15064
HG8861 .N3 MRR Alc Latest edition

INSURANCE, HEALTH--UNITED STATES,
Employee benefits fact book. [New York] 331.2/52 76-118375
HD7125 .E57 MRR Alc Latest edition

Schwartz, Jerome L. Medical plans and health care; Springfield, Ill.,
Thomas [1968] xxxiii, 349 p.
658/.91/368382 67-12707
HG9396 .S3 MRR Alc.

INSURANCE, HEALTH--UNITED STATES--DIRECTORIES.
Best's insurance reports, life-health. 1st- ed.; 1906/07-
Morristown, N.J. [etc.] A. M. Best
Co. [etc.] 368.3/2/0065 06-37901
HG8943 .B3 MRR Alc Latest edition

INSURANCE, LIABILITY.
Magee, John Henry, Property and liability insurance 4th ed.
Homewood, Ill., R. D. Irwin, 1967.
xix, 944 p. 368 67-15838
HG8051 .M2 1967 MRR Alc.

INSURANCE, LIABILITY--UNITED STATES.
Best's key rating guide; property-liability. 62d- ed.; 1968-
Morristown, N.J., A. M. Best Co.
368/.9/73 72-627014
HG9765 .B4 MRR Alc Latest edition

INSURANCE, LIABILITY--UNITED STATES--DIRECTORIES.
Best (A. M.) Company. Best's executive data service. B series-
custom summary. Morristown, N.J.
368.1/025/73 70-618338
HG8525. B32 MRR Alc Latest edition

INSURANCE, LIABILITY--UNITED STATES--STATISTICS.
Best (A.M.) Company. Best's executive data service. Report A6-
Comparative experience by State (State leaders) Morristown, N.J.
368.1/00973 74-645117
HG8535 .B45a MRR Alc Latest edition

Best's reproductions of convention statements; property-liability.
Morristown, N.J., A. M. Best Co.
368/.9/73 72-627024
HG9965.U5 B4 MRR Alc Latest edition

INSURANCE, LIABILITY--UNITED STATES--YEARBOOKS.
Best's insurance reports, property-liability. [1st]- ed.: 1899/1900-
Morristown, N.J. [etc.] A. M. Best
Co. 368.1/0065 00-3410
HG9655 .B5 MRR Alc Latest edition

INSURANCE, LIFE.
Huebner, Solomon Stephen, Life insurance 8th ed. [New York]
Appleton-Century-Crofts [1972]
xxxviii, 827 p. 368.3/2 72-181734

HG8771 .H8 1972 MRR Alc.

McGill, Dan Mays. Life insurance,
Rev. ed. Homewood, Ill., R. D.
Irwin, 1967 [c1966] xxi, 1023 p.
368.32 66-28630
HG8771 .M26 1967 MRR Alc.

INSURANCE, LIFE--DICTIONARIES.
Levy, Michael H. A handbook of personal insurance terminology,
Lynbrook, N.Y., Farnsworth Pub. Co.,
1968. xi, 595 p. 368.3/2/0014 68-3253
HG8759 .L4 MRR Alc.

INSURANCE, LIFE--DICTIONARIES--POLYGLOT.
Sachs, Wolfgang, ed.
Lebensversicherungstechnisches
Worterbuch. Wurzburg, K. Thiltsch,
1954. 308 p. 56-16246
HG8759 .S3 MRR Alc.

INSURANCE, LIFE--POLICIES.
National Underwriter Company. Who writes what? [1st- ed.]; 1942-
Cincinnati, O., Boston [etc.]
National underwriter company,
Statistical division. 368.30973 42-15064
HG8861 .N3 MRR Alc Latest edition

INSURANCE, LIFE--RATES AND TABLES.
Best (A. M.) Company. Best's settlement options manual. [1]-
ed.; 1940- Morristown, N.J. [etc.]
44-31968
HG8853 .F63 MRR Alc Latest edition

Life rates & data. 1971-
[Cincinnati, National Underwriter
Co.] 368.3/2/011 77-615134
HG8853 .L52 MRR Alc Latest edition

Life reports, financial and operating results of life insurers.
[Cincinnati, National Underwriter
Company] 368.3/2/006573 72-624711
Began with vol. for 1971.
HG8955 .U5 MRR Alc Latest edition

The Spectator handy guide to standard and special contracts, premium rates,
non-forfeiture values, annuities and war risk provisions. [1st]- ed.;
1891- Philadelphia, Pa., The
Spectator [etc.] 99-2345
HG8881 .S84 MRR Alc Latest edition

INSURANCE, LIFE--YEARBOOKS.
Life insurance fact book. 1946-
[New York] 368.3058 47-27134
HG8943 .L5 MRR Alc Latest edition

INSURANCE, LIFE--CANADA--FINANCE--PERIODICALS.
Best's agents guide to life insurance companies. 1st- ed.; 1974-
Morristown, N.J., Na.M. Best Co.
368/9/73 74-647421
HG8943 .B27 MRR Alc Latest edition

INSURANCE, LIFE--CANADA--STATISTICS.
Dunne's international insurance reports, Louisville, Ky. [etc.]
Dunne's International Insurance
Reports. [etc.] 368.30973 35-13753

HG8943 .D8 MRR Alc Latest edition

INSURANCE, LIFE--CANADA--YEARBOOKS.
Best's insurance reports, life-health. 1st- ed.; 1906/07-
Morristown, N.J. [etc.] A. M. Best
Co. [etc.] 368.3/2/0065 06-37901
HG8943 .B3 MRR Alc Latest edition

INSURANCE, LIFE--TEXAS.
The Texas life record; Dallas,
Record Pub. Co. 368.3 51-17253
HG8961.T4 T4 MRR Alc Latest edition

INSURANCE, LIFE--UNITED STATES.
Life insurance fact book. 1946-
[New York] 368.3058 47-27134
HG8943 .L5 MRR Alc Latest edition

Life reports, financial and operating results of life insurers.
[Cincinnati, National Underwriter
Company] 368.3/2/006573 72-624711
Began with vol. for 1971.
HG8955 .U5 MRR Alc Latest edition

National Underwriter Company. Who writes what? [1st- ed.]; 1942-
Cincinnati, O., Boston [etc.]
National underwriter company,
Statistical division. 368.30973 42-15064
HG8861 .N3 MRR Alc Latest edition

The Spectator handy guide to standard and special contracts, premium rates,
non-forfeiture values, annuities and war risk provisions. [1st]- ed.;
1891- Philadelphia, Pa., The
Spectator [etc.] 99-2345
HG8881 .S84 MRR Alc Latest edition

INSURANCE, LIFE--UNITED STATES--DIRECTORIES.
Best's flitcraft compend.
Morristown, N.J., A. M. Best Co.
368.3/2/002573 72-626406
HG8881 .F68 MRR Alc Latest edition

Best's insurance reports, life-health. 1st- ed.; 1906/07-
Morristown, N.J. [etc.] A. M. Best
Co. [etc.] 368.3/2/0065 06-37901
HG8943 .B3 MRR Alc Latest edition

INSURANCE, LIFE--UNITED STATES--FINANCE--PERIODICALS.
Best's agents guide to life insurance companies. 1st- ed.; 1974-
Morristown, N.J., Na.M. Best Co.
368/9/73 74-647421
HG8943 .B27 MRR Alc Latest edition

INSURANCE, LIFE--UNITED STATES--STATISTICS.
Dunne's international insurance reports, Louisville, Ky. [etc.]
Dunne's International Insurance
Reports. [etc.] 368.30973 35-13753

HG8943 .D8 MRR Alc Latest edition

Fraternal monitor. Combined statistics and consolidated chart of fraternal societies. 1958-
Indianapolis. 58-45886
HG9226 .F72 MRR Alc Latest edition

INSURANCE, LIFE--UNITED STATES--YEARBOOKS.
Best's insurance reports, life-health. 1st- ed.; 1906/07-
Morristown, N.J. [etc.] A. M. Best
Co. [etc.] 368.3/2/0065 06-37901
HG8943 .B3 MRR Alc Latest edition

Best's recommended life insurance companies. Morristown, N.J., A. M.
Best Co. 332.6/722 72-627064
HG8943 .B28 MRR Alc Latest edition

INSURANCE, MARINE--DICTIONARIES.
Brown, Robert Henry, Dictionary of marine insurance terms. [London]
Witherby [1962] vi, 313 p. 62-48927
HE567 .B7 MRR Alc

INSURANCE, MARINE--PERIODICALS.
Lloyd's register of shipping,
London, Wyman and sons [etc.] ca 08-1387
"Founded 1760. Re-constituted
1834."
HE565.A3 L7 MRR Alc Latest edition

INSURANCE, MARINE--UNITED STATES--STATISTICS.
Best's fire and casualty aggregates & averages. 1st- annual ed.; 1940-
Morristown, N.J. [etc.], Alfred M.
Best Company. 368.0973 41-7002
HG9755 .B4 MRR Alc Latest edition

INSURANCE, PROPERTY.
Elliott, Curtis Miller, Property and casualty insurance. New York, McGraw-Hill, 1960. 200 p. 368 60-12768
HG8051 .E48 MRR Alc.

Gordis, Philip, Property and casualty insurance; 17th ed. [rev.]
Indianapolis] Rough Notes [1970] 669 p. 368/.973 76-21025
HG8051 .G62 1970 MRR Alc.

Magee, John Henry, Property and liability insurance 4th ed.
Homewood, Ill., R. D. Irwin, 1967.
xix, 944 p. 368 67-15838
HG8051 .M2 1967 MRR Alc.

INSURANCE, PROPERTY--UNITED STATES.
Best's key rating guide; property-liability. 62d- ed.; 1968-
Morristown, N.J., A. M. Best Co.
368/.9/73 72-627014
HG9765 .B4 MRR Alc Latest edition

INSURANCE, PROPERTY--UNITED STATES--DIRECTORIES.
Best (A. M.) Company. Best's executive data service. B series-
custom summary. Morristown, N.J.
368.1/025/73 70-618338
HG8525. B32 MRR Alc Latest edition

INSURANCE, PROPERTY--UNITED STATES--STATISTICS.
Best (A.M.) Company. Best's executive data service. Report A6-
Comparative experience by State (State leaders) Morristown, N.J.
368.1/00973 74-645117
HG8535 .B45a MRR Alc Latest edition

Best's reproductions of convention statements; property-liability.
Morristown, N.J., A. M. Best Co.
368/.9/73 72-627024
HG9965.U5 B4 MRR Alc Latest edition

INSURANCE, PROPERTY--UNITED STATES--YEARBOOKS.
Best's insurance reports, property-liability. [1st]- ed.; 1899/1900-
Morristown, N.J. [etc.] A. M. Best
Co. 368.1/0065 00-3410
HG9655 .B5 MRR Alc Latest edition

INSURANCE, SOCIAL--STATISTICS.
Employee benefits fact book. [New York] 331.2/52 76-118375
HD7125 .E57 MRR Alc Latest edition

INSURANCE, SOCIAL--UNITED STATES.
Boggess, Louise. Your social
security benefits. New York, Funk &
Wagnalls [1968, c1968] xii, 116 p.
[5.95]   368.4/3/00973   68-31077
    HD7125 .B57 MRR Alc.

Employee benefits fact book. [New
York]   331.2/52   76-118375
    HD7125 .E57 MRR Alc Latest edition

Lasser (J. K.) Institute, New York.
J. K. Lasser's Your social security
and medicare guide. New York, Simon
and Schuster [1966] 136 p.   368.4
66-21820
    HD7125 .L35 MRR Alc.

[Newman, Joseph] Social security and
medicare simplified; [New York]
Collier Books [1970] 240 p. [2.95]
368.4/26/00873   73-129344
    HD7125 .N45 1970 MRR Alc.

Turnbull, John Gudert. Economic and
social security 4th ed. New York,
Ronald Press Co. [1973] v, 728 p.
368.4/00873   73-76680
    HD7125 .T84 1973 MRR Alc.

United States. Social Security
Administration. Office of Research
and Statistics. Social security
programs in the United States.
[Washington] U.S. Social Security
Administration; [for sale by the
Supt. of Docs., U.S. Govt. Print.
Off.] 1968. v, 120 p. [0.55]
368.4/00873   hew68-100
    HD7123 .A52 1968 MRR Alc.

INSURANCE COMPANIES--CANADA.
Stone & Cox general insurance year
book, Canada. Toronto, Stone & Cox
Ltd. 368/.871   72-626343
    HG9783 .S8 MRR Alc Latest edition

INSURANCE COMPANIES--EUROPE.
Esslen, Rainer. A guide to marketing
securities in Europe, 1971-1972. New
York, Wall Street Reports Pub. Corp.
[1971] viii, 215 p.   332.67/34/073
79-178914
    HG4538 .E76 MRR Alc.

INSURANCE COMPANIES--GREAT BRITAIN.
The Insurance directory & year book.
London [etc.] Buckley Press [etc.]
368.058   51-18382
Began publication in 1840.
    HG8596 .I53 MRR Alc Latest edition

INSURANCE COMPANIES--SPAIN.
Anuario espanol de seguros.
Barcelona [Graficas marina, s.a.]
368.058   47-20472
    HG8677 .A55 MRR Alc Latest edition

INSURANCE COMPANIES--TEXAS.
The Texas life record; Dallas,
Record Pub. Co. 368.3   51-17253
    HG8961.T4 T4 MRR Alc Latest
    edition

INSURANCE COMPANIES--UNITED STATES.
Best's agents guide to life insurance
companies. 1st- ed.; 1974-
Morristown, N.J., Na.M. Best Co.
368/8/73   74-647421
    HG8943 .B27 MRR Alc Latest edition

Best's flitcraft compend.
Morristown, N.J., A. M. Best Co.
368.3/2/002573   72-626406
    HG8881 .F68 MRR Alc Latest edition

Best's insurance reports, life-
health. 1st- ed.; 1806/07-
Morristown, N.J. [etc.] A. M. Best
Co. [etc.] 368.3/2/0065   06-37901
    HG8943 .B3 MRR Alc Latest edition

Best's insurance reports, property-
liability. [1st]- ed.; 1899/1900-
Morristown, N.J. [etc.] A. M. Best
Co. 368.1/0065   00-3410
    HG9655 .B5 MRR Alc Latest edition

Best's recommended independent
insurance adjusters. 43d- ed.;
1973- Morristown, N.J., A. M. Best
Co. 368/.014   73-644344
    HG8525 .B35 MRR Alc Latest edition

Best's recommended life insurance
companies. Morristown, N.J., A. M.
Best Co. 332.6/722   72-627064
    HG8943 .B28 MRR Alc Latest edition

Best's reproductions of convention
statements; property-liability.
Morristown, N.J., A. M. Best Co.
368/.9/73   72-627024
    HG9965.U5 B4 MRR Alc Latest
    edition

Conning and Company, Hartford. A
record of earnings and other
financial data on fire and casualty
insurance companies. [Hartford]
368.1   58-38085
    HG9755 .C63 MRR Alc Latest edition

Dunne's international insurance
reports; Louisville, Ky. [etc.]
Dunne's International Insurance
Reports. [etc.]   368.30973   35-13753

    HG8943 .D8 MRR Alc Latest edition

Dunne's international insurance
reports: Fire and casualty edition.
Louisville, Ky., The Insurance Index.
368/.973   72-622884
    HG9765 .D8 MRR Alc Latest edition

The Insurance almanac: who, what,
when and where in insurance; [1st]-
1913- New York, Underwriter Print.
and Pub. Co.   13-15895
    HG8019 .I5 MRR Alc Latest edition

Life reports, financial and operating
results of life insurers.
[Cincinnati, National Underwriter
Company] 368.3/2/006573   72-624711
Began with vol. for 1971.
    HG8955 .U5 MRR Alc Latest edition

National Association of Independent
Insurance Adjusters. Membership
directory. [Chicago]   63-50175
    HG8525 .N3 MRR Alc Latest edition

**INSURANCE COMPANIES--UNITED STATES--
FINANCE.**
Purchases & sales, corporate [and]
municipal, of insurance companies.
1st- ed.; 1949- New York, United
Statistical Associates.   50-1912
    HG8078 .P87 MRR Alc Latest edition

**INSURANCE COMPANIES--UNITED STATES--
INVESTMENTS.**
Corporate holdings of insurance
companies. 1st- ed.; 1948-
Morristown, N.J. [etc.] United
Statistical Associates.   332.63 49-
13782
    HG8078 .C6 MRR Alc Latest edition

**INSURANCE COMPANIES--UNITED STATES--
INVESTMENTS--YEARBOOKS.**
Best's market guide. 1st- ed.;
1970- Morristown, N.J., United
Statistical Associates.   332.67 79-
613273
    HG4926.A3 B4 MRR Alc Latest
    Edition

**INSURANCE COMPANIES--UNITED STATES--
YEARBOOKS.**
Moody's bank & finance manual;
American and foreign. New York,
Moody's Investors Service.   56-14722

    HG4961 .M65 MRR Alc Latest edition

INSURANCE ENGINEERING.
see also Fire extinction

INSURANCE LAW--BIBLIOGRAPHY.
United States. Library of Congress.
Division of bibliography. List of
works relating to government
regulation of insurance, United
States and foreign countries.
Washington, Govt. print. off., 1906.
46 p.   06-35008
    Z663.28 .L588 1906 MRR Alc.

INSURANCE LAW--UNITED STATES.
Best's recommended insurance
attorneys. 1st- ed.; 1929-
Morristown, N.J. [etc.] A. M. Best
Co. 29-5672
    HG8525 .B4 MRR Alc Latest edition

**INSURANCE LAW--UNITED STATES--
BIBLIOGRAPHY.**
Life, health and accident insurance
law; v. [1]- 1906/31- New York,
Association of Life Insurance
Counsel. 016.368   35-25985
    Z7164.I7 L5 MRR Alc Latest edition

INSURANCE POLICIES--UNITED STATES.
National Underwriter Company.
Agent's and buyer's guide. 1948-
ed. Cincinnati. 368.058   49-140
    HG8523 .N3 MRR Alc Latest edition

INSURANCE STOCKS--UNITED STATES.
Best (A. M.) Company. Best's
insurance securities research
service; 2d ed.] Morristown, N.J.,
1969- 1 v. (loose-leaf)   332.63/2
70-11694
    HG5123.I6 B392 MRR Alc.

Best (A. M.) Company. Best's
insurance securities research
service. 1972 ed. Morristown, N.J.
[1972- 1 v. (loose-leaf)   332.6/722
72-170016
    HG5123.I6 B3932 MRR Alc.

**INSURANCE STOCKS--UNITED STATES--
STATISTICS.**
Best (A. M.) Company. Best's
insurance securities research
service; 2d ed.] Morristown, N.J.,
1969- 1 v. (loose-leaf)   332.63/2
70-11694
    HG5123.I6 B392 MRR Alc.

INSURRECTIONS
see Revolutions

INTEGRATED DATA PROCESSING
see Electronic data processing

INTEGRATION, RACIAL
see Race problems

INTELLECT.
Robb, George Paul, Assessment of
individual mental ability Scranton,
Intext Educational Publishers [1972]
xiv, 354 p. [$8.00] 153.9/32 73-
177298
    BF431 .R52 MRR Alc.

Wechsler, David, Wechsler's
Measurement and appraisal of adult
intelligence 5th and enl. ed.
Baltimore, Williams & Wilkins [1972]
x, 572 p.   153.9/3   72-77316
    BF431 .W35 1972 MRR Alc.

INTELLECTUAL COOPERATION.
Institute of International Education.
Open doors; foreign students,
foreign doctors, foreign faculty
members in the United States, U.S.
students, U.S. faculty members
abroad. [New York?] 378.3 55-4594

    LB2283 .I615 MRR Alc Latest
    edition

**INTELLECTUAL COOPERATION--SOCIETIES,
ETC.--DIRECTORIES.**
Council on foreign relations.
American agencies interested in
international affairs. 1931- New
York, [etc.] Frederick A. Praeger,
[etc.] 341.06   31-26874
    JX27 .C62 MRR Ref Desk Latest
    edition

INTELLECTUAL FREEDOM
see Freedom of information

INTELLECTUAL LIFE.
Johnson, Edgar Nathaniel, An
introduction to the history of
Western tradition. Boston, Ginn
[1959] 2 v.   901.9   59-16066
    CB245 .J58 MRR Alc.

INTELLECTUAL LIFE--STATISTICS.
United Nations Educational,
Scientific and Cultural Organization.
Statistical yearbook. 1963-
[Paris]   65-3517
    AZ361 .U45 MRR Ref Desk Latest
    edition

INTELLECTUALS.
Huszar, George Bernard de, ed. The
intellectuals; Glencoe, Ill., Free
Press [1960] viii, 543 p.   301.445
60-8590
    HM213 .H8 MRR Alc.

INTELLECTUALS--UNITED STATES.
Jacobs, Paul, The new radicals; New
York, Random House [1966] 333 p.
320.973   66-18328
    E839.5 .J3 MRR Alc.

INTELLIGENCE LEVELS--TESTING
see Mental tests

INTELLIGENCE SERVICE--UNITED STATES.
United States. Commission on
Organization of the Executive Branch
of the Government (1953-1955)
Intelligence activities.
[Washington, U.S. Govt. Print. Off.]
1955. ix, 76 p.   55-61682
    JK468.I6 A52 MRR Alc.

INTER-LIBRARY LOANS.
Brummel, Leendert, Guide des
catalogues collectifs et du prêt
international La Haye, M. Nijhoff,
1961. 89 p.   64-43892
    Z695.83 .B68 MRR Ref Desk.

Nitecki, Joseph Z. Directory of
library reprographic services. 5th
ed. [Weston, Conn.] Published for
the Reproduction of Library Materials
Section, American Library Association
by Microform Review Inc. [1974,
c1973] 105 p.   025.1/29 73-2059
    Z265 .N58 1974 MRR Ref Desk.

**INTER-LIBRARY LOANS--HANDBOOKS,
MANUALS, ETC.**
Thomson, Sarah Katharine,
Interlibrary loan procedure manual.
Chicago, Interlibrary Loan Committee,
American Library Association, 1970.
xi, 116 p.   024/.6/0973 71-125942
    Z713 .T45 MRR Alc.

INTEREST AND USURY.
Homer, Sidney, A history of interest
rates. New Brunswick, N.J., Rutgers
University Press [1963] xvi, 617 p.
332.809   62-21247
    HG1621 .H6 MRR Alc.

Rosen, Lawrence R. Dow Jones-Irwin
guide to interest; Homewood, Ill.,
Dow Jones-Irwin, 1974. x, 183 p.
[$7.95]   332.8/2   73-89120
    HG1628 .R77 MRR Alc.

INTEREST AND USURY--TABLES, ETC.
Bledsoe, Charles Wade. Bankers'
interest-calculating system.
[Sherman, Tex., 1959] 240 p.
511.8083   58-31963
HG1628 .B6 1959 MRR Alc.

Coffin, John E. Interest tables:
Rev. ed. Philadelphia, John C.
Winston Co. [1959] 139 p.   511.8083
59-7286
HG1628 .C69 1959 MRR Alc.

[Delbridge, Charles Lomax] Delbridge
interest tables, St. Louis, Mo.,
Delbridge calculating systems, inc.
[1944] xvi, 296 p. 332.82083 44-
45368
HG1626 .D4 MRR Alc.

Econtel Research. World interest
rates. London, Econtel Research,
1971. 20 p. [£3.00] 332.8/2 72-
200943
HG1626 .E25 MRR Alc.

Financial Publishing Company.
Constant annual percent loan
amortization schedules 2d ed.
Boston [1954] vi, 817 p.   332.82083
55-17611
HG1634 .F448 1954 MRR Alc.

Financial Publishing Company. Direct
reduction loan amortization schedules
3d ed. Boston [1955, c1954] 1 v.
332.8083 55-22204
HG1634 .F45 1955 MRR Alc.

Financial Publishing Company.
Financial amortization schedules for
monthly payment mortgages; 1st ed.
Boston [1959] 857 p.   332.72083 60-
708
HG1634 .F459 MRR Alc.

Financial Publishing Company.
Financial compound interest and
annuity tables, 5th ed. Boston
[1970] xiii, 884 p.   511/.8/0212
77-13316
HG1634 .F46 1970 MRR Alc.

Financial Publishing Company.
Financial simple interest table,
Boston [c1959] 912 p.   511.8083 60-
2187
HG1628 .F443 MRR Alc.

Financial Publishing Company.
Monthly payment direct reduction loan
amortization schedules, showing equal
monthly payment necessary to amortize
a loan of $1,000; [1st]- ed.; 1938-
Boston. 332.80835 38-15325
HG1634 .F47 MRR Alc Latest edition

GLS Enterprises, inc., Browerville,
Minn. GLS interest tables.
Browerville, Minn. [1962] unpaged.
62-39830
HG1628 .G2 MRR Alc.

Hart, William Le Roy, Tables for
Mathematics of investment. 4th ed.
Boston, Heath [1958] 150 p.   510.83
58-3601
HG1632 .H3 1958 MRR Alc.

Rosen, Lawrence R. Dow Jones-Irwin
guide to interest; Homewood, Ill.,
Dow Jones-Irwin, 1974. x, 183 p.
[$7.95] 332.8/2 73-89120
HG1628 .R77 MRR Alc.

INTERIOR DECORATION.
see also Furniture

see also House furnishings

Derieux, Mary, The complete book of
interior decorating. New and rev.
ed. New York, Greystone Press [1964]
x, 466 p.   747 64-13281
NK2110 .D4 1964 MRR Alc.

Savage, George. A concise history of
interior decoration. London, Thames
& Hudson [1966] 285 p. [35/-]
747.2 66-67475
NK1710 .S3 MRR Alc.

Whiton, Augustus Sherrill, Interior
design and decoration. 4th ed.
Philadelphia, Lippincott [1974] vi,
699 p.   747 73-19987
NK2110 .W55 1974 MRR Alc.

INTERIOR DECORATION--AMATEURS' MANUALS.
Goodheart-Willcox's painting and
decorating encyclopedia; Homewood,
Ill., Goodheart-Willcox Co. [1964]
288 p.   698 64-22379
TT320 .G6 1964 MRR Alc.

INTERIOR DECORATION--DICTIONARIES.
Pegler, Martin M. The dictionary of
interior design. London, Barker,
1967. [8], 500 p. [55/-] 747/.03
67-110479
NK1165 .P4 1967 MRR Alc.

**INTERIOR DECORATION--UNITED STATES--
DIRECTORIES.**
The Interior decorators' handbook.
New York, Clifford & Lawton. 44-
15433
NK1127 .I5   MRR Alc Latest edition

**INTERIOR DECORATORS--UNITED STATES--
DIRECTORIES.**
American Institute of Interior
Designers. Membership directory.
New York. 747.06273 56-1632
NK1700 .A54 MRR Alc Latest edition

**INTERLINGUA (INTERNATIONAL AUXILIARY
LANGUAGE ASSOCIATION)--DICTIONARIES--
ENGLISH.**
International Auxiliary Language
Association. Interlingua-English;
New York, Storm Publishers [1951]
lxiv, 415 p.   408.9 51-2430
PM8037 .I5 MRR Alc.

INTERNAL COMBUSTION ENGINES
see Gas and oil engines

INTERNAL MEDICINE.
Harrison, Tinsley Randolph, ed.
Harrison's principles of internal
medicine. 7th ed. New York, McGraw-
Hill [1974] xxix, 2044, [87] p.
616/.026 73-18001
RC46 .H32 1974 MRR Alc.

Harrison, Tinsley Randolph, ed.
Harrison's principles of internal
medicine. 7th ed. New York, McGraw-
Hill [1974] xxix, 2044, [87] p.
616/.026 73-18001
RC46 .H32 1974 MRR Alc.

McCombs, Robert Pratt, Fundamentals
of internal medicine; 4th ed.
Chicago, Year Book Medical Publishers
[1971] xvi, 923 p.   616/.026 74-
115098
RC46 .M15 1971 MRR Alc.

INTERNAL MIGRATION
see Migration, Internal

INTERNAL PRACTICE.
Cecil, Russell La Fayette, Cecil-
Loeb textbook of medicine. 12th ed.
Philadelphia, Saunders, 1967. xxxix,
liv, 1738 p.   616 67-10429
RC46 .C4 1967 MRR Alc.

INTERNAL REVENUE.
see also Income tax

INTERNAL REVENUE--UNITED STATES.
Seybert, Adam, Statistical annals,
New York, B. Franklin [1969] xxvii,
803 p.   317.3 68-56774
HA215 .S5 1969 MRR Alc.

INTERNAL SECURITY--EUROPE.
United States. Library of Congress.
Law Library. Legislation for the
protection of the state in various
European countries; Washington,
Library of Congress, Law Library,
Foreign Law Section, 1956. v, 155 l.
016.35175 016.36413* 56-61203
Z663.5 .L4 MRR Alc.

**INTERNAL SECURITY--UNITED STATES--
BIBLIOGRAPHY.**
United States. Congress. Senate.
Committee on the Judiciary.
Cumulative index to published
hearings and reports Washington,
U.S. Govt. Print. Off., 1957. ii,
844 p.   327.1 57-60563
Z7165.U5 U484 MRR Ref Desk.

INTERNATIONAL AGENCIES.
Directory of Soviet international
front organisations. [n.p., 1970] 1
v. (various pagings)   335.43/062/1
78-27355
HX11 .D523 1970 MRR Alc.

The Europa year book. 1959- London,
Europa Publications. 341.184 59-
2942
JN1 .E85 Sci RR Latest edition /
MRR Ref Desk Latest edition

Everyman's United Nations. [1st]-
ed.; 1948- New York, United Nations
Dept. of Public Information [etc.]
341.13 48-10196
JX1977.A37 E9 MRR Ref Desk Latest
edition

International Chamber of Commerce.
United States Council. International
economic organizations & terms
glossary. [New York, 1964] 48 p.
64-54675
HB61 .I6 1964 MRR Alc.

International organisation and
integration. Deventer, Æ. E. Kluwer;
Leiden, A. W. Sijthoff, 1968 [1969]
xxvi, 1146 p. [67.30] 341.13 68-
25399
JX171 .I54 MRR Alc.

The International year book and
statesmen's who's who. 1953-
London, Burke's Peerage. 305.8 53-
1425
JA51 .I57 MRR Biog Latest edition

Lawson, Ruth Catherine,
International regional organizations:
New York, Praeger [1962] xviii, 387
p.   341.18 62-13746
JX1979 .L3 MRR Alc.

Meerhaeghe, Marcel Alfons Gilbert
van, International economic
institutions London, Longmans, 1966.
xx, 404 p. [50/-] 338.91 67-
77500
HF1411 .M433 MRR Alc.

The Middle East and North Africa.
[1st]- ed:, 1948- London, Europa
Publications. 48-3250
DS49 .M5 MRR Alc Latest edition

Peaslee, Amos Jenkins, ed.
International governmental
organizations: constitutional
documents. Rev. 2d ed. [The Hague,
M. Nijhoff, c1961] 2 v. (lviii, 1962
p.) 341.11 62-32304
JX1995 .P4 1961 MRR Ref Desk.

Political handbook and atlas of the
world. Jan. 1, 1927- New York,
Simon and Schuster [etc.] for Council
on Foreign Relations. 28-12165
JF37 .P6 MRR Ref Desk Latest
edition / MRR Alc Latest edition

Taschenbuch für den Gemeinsamen
Markt EWG, EURATOM, Montan-Union.
Recklinghausen, Kommunal-Verlag
[etc.] 60-26020
HC240 .T32 MRR Alc Latest edition

Treaties and alliances of the world;
[2d ed.] [Bristol] Keesing's
Publications; New York, Scribner
[1974] xv, 235 p.   341.3/7 73-
15927
JX4005 .T72 1974 MRR Alc.

White, Lyman Cromwell, International
non-governmental organizations; New
Brunswick, Rutgers University Press,
1951. xi, 325 p.   060 51-10977
JX1995 .W48 MRR Alc.

The World this year. 1971- New
York, Simon and Schuster. 320.9/046
76-649587
JF37 .W65 MRR Ref Desk Latest
edition

INTERNATIONAL AGENCIES--ABBREVIATIONS.
Ruppert, Fritz, writer on
international organizations.
Initials. München-Pullach, Verlag
Dokumentation; Essen, Vulkan Verlag,
1966. 220 p. [DM 14.60] 060.25
67-71860
JX1995 .R87 MRR Ref Desk.

INTERNATIONAL AGENCIES--BIBLIOGRAPHY.
Dimitrov, Theodore Delchev.
Documents of international
organisations: London, International
University Publications; Chicago,
American Library Association, 1973.
xv, 301 p.   016.05 73-175089
Z6481 .D56 MRR Alc.

Haas, Michael, International
organization; Stanford, Calif.,
Hoover Institution Press [c1971]
xxiv, 944 p.   016.3412 68-28099
Z6464.I6 H3 MRR Alc.

Woodrow Wilson International Center
for Scholars. The human environment.
Washington, 1972. 2 v. [$5.00 per
vol.] 016.30131 72-601602
Z5118.A5 W66 1972 MRR Alc.

Yearbook of international congress
proceedings. 1st- ed.; 1960/67-
Brussels, Union of International
Associations. 060 70-21167
Z5051 .Y4 MRR Alc Full set

**INTERNATIONAL AGENCIES--BIBLIOGRAPHY--
CATALOGS.**
Foreign Relations Library. Catalog
of the Foreign Relations Library.
Boston, G. K. Hall, 1969. 9 v.
016.327 75-6133
Z6209 .F656 MRR Alc (Dk 33)

INTERNATIONAL AGENCIES--DIRECTORIES.
American Council on Education.
Overseas Liaison Committee.
International directory for
educational liaison. Washington
[1972, c1973] xxii, 474 p.
378/.006/21 72-92152
L900 .A47 1973 MRR Alc.

Angel, Juvenal Londoño, Directory
of international agencies. 1st ed.
New York, Simon & Schuster [1970]
447 p. [$25.00] 341/.24/025 70-
121774
AS8 .A5 MRR Alc.

Bilan du monde. [2. éd.] [Tournai]
Casterman, 1964. 2 v.   65-87638
G122 .B442 MRR Alc.

The Diplomat's annual. London. 54-
43085
Began publication in 1950.
JX1783 .A153 MRR Alc Latest
edition

INTERNATIONAL AGENCIES-- (Cont.)
International Film and Television
Council. Le répertoire C.I.C.T. des
organisations internationales de
cinéma et de télévision et de
leurs branches nationales.   1964-
[London] Film Centre. 65-71067
    PN1998 .I5 MRR Alc Latest edition

Phelps-Fetherston, Iain. Soviet
international front organizations.
New York, Praeger [1965] 178 p.
335.44 65-20503
    HX11 .P5 MRR Alc.

Sable, Martin Howard. Master
directory for Latin America. Los
Angeles, Latin American Center,
University of California, 1965. xxi,
438 p.   818.03306 66-25
    F1406.5 .S3 MRR Alc.

Unesco handbook of international
exchanges. 1-   1965- [Paris]
Unesco. 65-5337
    AS8 .U35 MRR Alc Latest edition

Union of International Associations.
Directory of periodicals published by
international organizations. 3d ed.
Brussels [1969] xii, 240 p. 016.05
70-480186
    AS8 .U38 1969 MRR Alc.

United States. Library of Congress.
International Organizations Section.
International scientific
organizations; Washington, General
Reference and Bibliography Division,
Reference Dept.,Library of Congress;
[for sale by the Superintendent of
Documents, U.S. Govt. Print. Off.]
1962 [i.e. 1963] xi, 794 p.   506
62-64648
    Z663.285 .I5 MRR Alc.

Wilkes, Ian B. British initials and
abbreviations. 3d ed. London, Hill,
1971. 346 p. [£5.50 ($17.50 U.S.)]
060/.25/42 71-25205
    AS118 .W5 1971 MRR Alc.

INTERNATIONAL AGENCIES--YEARBOOKS.
United Nations. Yearbook. 1946/47-
New York [etc.]   47-7191
    JX1977.A37 Y4 MRR Ref Desk Latest
    edition

Yearbook of international
organizations. 1st- year; 1948-
Brussels [etc.] Union of
International Associations. 49-22132

    JX1904 .A42 Sci RR Latest edition
    / MRR Alc Latest edition

INTERNATIONAL AGENCIES--EUROPE.
Political and Economic Planning.
European unity; [Revised ed.]
London, Political and Economic
Planning; Allen & Unwin, 1968. 3-519
p.   [63/-]   068/.4 68-111444
    JN94 .P6 1968 MRR Alc.

INTERNATIONAL AGENCIES IN ASIA.
The Far East and Australasia. 1st
ed.; 1969- London, Europa
Publications. 915/.03/05 74-417170

    DS1 .F3 MRR Alc Latest edition

INTERNATIONAL AGENCIES IN EUROPE.
Robertson, Arthur Henry. European
institutions: co-operation,
integration, unification. [3d ed.]
London, Stevens & Sons; New York,
Matthew Bender, 1973. xix, 478 p.
341.24/2 72-94556
    JN15 .R58 1973 MRR Alc.

INTERNATIONAL AGENCIES IN EUROPE--
BIBLIOGRAPHY.
Roussier, Michel. Les publications
officielles des institutions
européennes. [Paris, Dotation
Carnegie pour la paix internationale,
Centre européen, 1954] 73 p.   54-
1117
    Z2000 .R6 MRR Alc.

INTERNATIONAL AGENCIES IN EUROPE--
YEARBOOKS.
Annuaire européen. v. 1-   1955-
La Haye, Nijhoff. 55-3837
    JN3 .A5 MRR Alc Latest edition

INTERNATIONAL BUSINESS ENTERPRISES.
see also Investments, Foreign

INTERNATIONAL BUSINESS ENTERPRISES--
DIRECTORIES.
Who owns whom. North American
edition. London, O. W. Roskill.
332.6/73/025 74-646353
    HG4538 .W423 MRR Alc Latest
    edition

INTERNATIONAL BUSINESS ENTERPRISES--
STATISTICS.
Vaupel, James W. The world's
multinational enterprises; Boston,
Division of Research, Graduate School
of Business Administration, Harvard
University, 1973. xxxiii, 505 p.
[$25.00]   338.8/8 73-76600
    HD69.I7 V36 MRR Alc.

INTERNATIONAL CATALOGUE OF SCIENTIFIC
LITERATURE.
Royal society of London. Catalogue
of scientific papers, 1800-1900.
Cambridge, University press, 1908-
v.   08-24586
    Z7403 .R8812 MRR Alc.

INTERNATIONAL COOPERATION.
see also Reconstruction (1939-1951)

INTERNATIONAL COOPERATION--SOCIETIES,
ETC.--DIRECTORIES.
Angel, Juvenal Londoño, Directory
of international agencies. 1st ed.
New York, Simon & Schuster [1970]
447 p. [$25.00] 341./24/025 70-
121774
    AS8 .A5 MRR Alc.

Council on foreign relations.
American agencies interested in
international affairs. 1931- New
York, [etc.] Frederick A. Praeger,
[etc.] 341.06 31-26874
    JX27 .C62 MRR Ref Desk Latest
    edition

Great Britain. Dept. of Education and
Science. Sources of information on
international and commonwealth
organisations. [London] Department
of Education and Science [1973] v,
45 p.   060/.25 74-164179
    AS8 .G74 1973 MRR Alc.

INTERNATIONAL ECONOMIC INTEGRATION.
Meerhaeghe, Marcel Alfons Gilbert
van, International economic
institutions London, Longmans, 1966.
xx, 404 p. [50/-] 338.91 67-
77500
    HF1411 .M433 MRR Alc.

INTERNATIONAL ECONOMIC RELATIONS.
see also Economic assistance

Lary, Hal Buckner, Imports of
manufactures from less developed
countries New York, National Bureau
of Economic Research; distributed by
Columbia University Press, 1968.
xvii, 286 p.   382/.09172/401722 67-
28434
    HF1411 .L36 MRR Alc.

Meerhaeghe, Marcel Alfons Gilbert
van, International economic
institutions London, Longmans, 1966.
xx, 404 p. [50/-] 338.91 67-
77500
    HF1411 .M433 MRR Alc.

INTERNATIONAL ECONOMIC RELATIONS--
DICTIONARIES.
International Chamber of Commerce.
United States Council. International
economic organizations & terms
glossary. [New York, 1964] 48 p.
64-54675
    HB61 .I6 1964 MRR Alc.

INTERNATIONAL ECONOMIC RELATIONS--
HANDBOOKS, MANUALS, ETC.
Angel, Juvenal Londoño, The
handbook of international business
and investment facts and information
sources, New York, World Trade
Academy Press; distributed by Simon &
Schuster [1967] 565 p.   382 66-
28172
    HF1411 .A5 MRR Alc.

INTERNATIONAL ECONOMIC RELATIONS--
STATISTICS.
International Monetary Fund. Balance
of payments yearbook. 1946/47-
Washington. 382 49-6612
    HF1014 .I5 MRR Alc Latest edition

INTERNATIONAL FINANCE.
Hirsch, Fred. Money international.
London, Penguin P., 1967. 443 p.
[70/-] 332.4/5 68-86128
    HG3881 .H5 MRR Alc.

INTERNATIONAL FINANCE--ADDRESSES,
ESSAYS, LECTURES.
Nehrt, Lee Charles, ed.
International finance for
multinational business. 2d ed.
Scranton, Intext Educational
Publishers [c1972] xviii, 804 p.
[$11.00] 332/.08 72-177307
    HG3881 .N37 1972 MRR Alc.

INTERNATIONAL GEOPHYSICAL YEAR, 1957-
1958--BIBLIOGRAPHY.
United States. Library of Congress.
Science and Technology Division. An
interim bibliography on the
International Geophysical Year.
Washington, National Academy of
Sciences, 1958. v, 56 p. 016.551
58-60070
    Z663.41 .I5 MRR Alc.

INTERNATIONAL LABOR OFFICE. LIBRARY.
INTERNATIONAL LABOUR DOCUMENTATION--
INDEXES.
International Labor Office. Library.
Subject index to International labour
documentation, 1957-1964. Boston, G.
K. Hall, 1968. 2 v.   mrr01-76
    Z7164.L1 I646 MRR Alc.

INTERNATIONAL LABOR OFFICE--
BIBLIOGRAPHY.
International Labor Office. Central
Library and Documentation Branch.
Subject guide to publications of the
International Labour Office, 1919-
1964. Geneva, 1967. ii, 478 p.
[unpriced] 016.331 71-446416
    Z7164.L1 I56 MRR Alc.

INTERNATIONAL LAW.
Hackworth, Green Haywood, Digest of
international law. Washington, U.S.
Govt. Print. Off., 1940-44. 8 v.
341.02 41-50552
    JX237 .H3 MRR Alc.

Moore, John Bassett, A digest of
international law Washington, Govt.
print. off., 1906. 8 v.   30-10322
    JX237 .M7 1906a MRR Alc.

Whiteman, Marjorie Millace. Digest
of international law. [Washington,
U.S. Dept. of State; for sale by the
Superintendent of Documents, U.S.
Govt. Print. Off., 1963- v.
[$6.25 (v. 14) varies] 341.02 63-
62002
    JX237 .W55 MRR Alc.

INTERNATIONAL LAW--BIBLIOGRAPHY.
Carnegie Endowment for International
Peace. Publications of the Carnegie
Endowment for International Peace,
1910-1967, including International
conciliation, 1924-1967. New York,
1971. 229 p.   016.327/172 70-
153501
    Z6461 .C27 MRR Alc.

Institut Juridique international,
Hague, Repertoire général des
traités et autres actes
diplomatiques conclus depuis 1895
jusqu'en 1920, Harlem (Pays-Bas) H.
D. Tjeenk Willink & fils; La Haye
(Pays-Bas) M. Nijhoff, 1926. xix,
516 p.   27-9742
    Z6464.T8 I6 MRR Alc.

United States. Library of Congress.
Law library. The bibliography of
international law and continental
law, Washington, Govt. print. off.,
1913. 93 p.   12-35015
    Z663.5 .B5 MRR Alc.

INTERNATIONAL LAW--DICTIONARIES--GERMAN.
Strupp, Karl, Wörterbuch des
Völkerrechts. In völlig neu bearb.
2. Aufl. Berlin, De Gruyter, 1960-
62. 4 v.   61-38291
    JX1226 .S72 MRR Alc.

INTERNATIONAL LAW--SOURCES.
International organisation and
integration. Deventer, Æ. E. Kluwer;
Leiden, A. W. Sijthoff, 1968 [1969]
xxvi, 1146 p. [67.30] 341.13 68-
25399
    JX171 .I54 MRR Alc.

INTERNATIONAL OFFENSES--BIBLIOGRAPHY.
Schutter, Bart de. Bibliography on
international Criminal law. Leiden,
Sijthoff, 1972. li, 423 p.
[f158.00] 016.34/77 72-80997
    Z6464.C8 S38 MRR Alc.

INTERNATIONAL ORGANIZATION.
Goodspeed, Stephen S. The nature and
function of international
organization. 2d ed. New York,
Oxford University Press, 1967. xii,
733 p.   341.1/1 67-10856
    JX1954 .G62 1967 MRR Alc.

Harley, John Eugene, Documentary
textbook on the United Nations; 2d
ed., rev. and enl. Los Angeles,
Auspices of the Center for
International Understanding [1950]
xxvii, 1470 p.   341.1 50-10302
    JX1977 .H3 1950 MRR Alc.

INTERNATIONAL ORGANIZATION--
BIBLIOGRAPHY.
Haas, Michael, International
organization; Stanford, Calif.,
Hoover Institution Press [c1971]
xxiv, 944 p.   016.3412 68-28099
    Z6464.I6 H3 MRR Alc.

Roussier, Michel. Les publications
officielles des institutions
européennes. [Paris, Dotation
Carnegie pour la paix internationale,
Centre européen, 1954] 73 p.   54-
1117
    Z2000 .R6 MRR Alc.

INTERNATIONAL ORGANIZATION--COLLECTIONS.
Watkins, James Thomas, ed. General
international organization,
Princeton, Van Nostrand [1956] xi,
248 p.   341.11* 56-9730
    JX1937 .W3 MRR Alc.

INTERNATIONAL PAYMENTS, BALANCE OF
see Balance of payments

INTERNATIONAL POLICE.
Wainhouse, David Walter,
International peace observation;
Baltimore, Johns Hopkins Press, 1966.
xvii, 663 p.   341.11   66-14376
JX1981.P7 W25 MRR Alc.

INTERNATIONAL RELATIONS.
see also Diplomacy

see also Nationalism

see also Peace

Prosser, Michael H., comp. Sow the
wind, reap the whirlwind; New York,
Morrow, 1970. 2 v. (xviii, 1467 p.)
[$100.00]   341.1/08   73-118271
JX1977 .P728 MRR Alc.

Vincent, Jack Ernest. A handbook of
international relations; Woodbury,
N.Y., Barron's Educational Series,
inc. [1969] vii, 456 p. [2.95 (3.50
Can.)]   327   68-8679
JX1395 .V53 MRR Alc.

Wainhouse, David Walter,
International peace observation;
Baltimore, Johns Hopkins Press, 1966.
xvii, 663 p.   341.11   66-14376
JX1981.P7 W25 MRR Alc.

INTERNATIONAL RELATIONS--BIBLIOGRAPHY.
Arms control & disarmament. v. 1-
winter 1964/65- [Washington, For
sale by the Superintendent of
Documents, U.S. Govt. Print. Off.]
64-62746
Z663.28 .A23 MRR Alc   MRR Alc Full
set

Carnegie Endowment for International
Peace. Publications of the Carnegie
Endowment for International Peace,
1910-1967, including International
conciliation, 1924-1967. New York,
1971. 229 p.   016.327/172   70-
153501
Z6461 .C27 MRR Alc.

Cook, Blanche Wiesen. Bibliography
on peace research in history. Santa
Barbara, Calif., ABC-Clio [c1969] v,
72 p. [6.50]   016.3411   72-93481
Z6464.Z9 C7 MRR Alc.

Dimitrov, Théodore Delchev.
Documents of international
organisations: London, International
University Publications; Chicago,
American Library Association, 1973.
xv, 301 p.   016.05   73-175089
Z6481 .D56 MRR Alc.

The Foreign affairs 50-year
bibliography; New York, Published
for the Council on Foreign Relations
by R. R. Bowker Co., 1972. xxviii,
936 p.   016.327/09/04   75-163904
Z6461 .F62 MRR Alc.

Foreign affairs bibliography;
1919/32-1852/62. New York, Published
for the Council on Foreign Relations
by R. R. Bowker [etc.]   016.327
[016.9]   33-7094
Z6463 .F73 MRR Alc Full set

Harmon, Robert Bartlett, The art and
practice of diplomacy: Metuchen,
N.J., Scarecrow Press, 1971. xii,
355 p.   327/.2   75-142234
JX1662 .H273 MRR Alc.

Mason, John Brown, Research
resources: Santa Barbara, Calif.,
ABC-Clio, 1968- v.   [3.00]
016.327/.08/04 68-9685
Z7161 .M36 MRR Ref Desk.

Royal Institute of International
Affairs. Library. Index to
periodical articles 1950-1964 in the
Library of the Royal Institute of
International Affairs. Boston, G. K.
Hall, 1964. 2 v.   65-9436
AI3 .R6 MRR Alc.

Royal Institute of International
Affairs. Library. Index to
periodical articles 1965-1972 in the
Library of the Royal Institute of
International Affairs. Boston, G. K.
Hall, 1973. xxix, 879 p.   016.05
73-166442
AI3 .R6 1973 MRR Alc.

United States. Library of Congress.
General Reference and Bibliography
Division. A guide to bibliographic
tools for research in foreign
affairs, 2d ed. with suppl.
Washington, 1958. 145, 15 p.
016.341 58-60091
Z663.28 .G78 1958 MRR Alc.

Universal Reference System.
International affairs; [2d ed.]
Princeton, N.J., Princeton Research
Pub. Co. [1969] xx, 1206 p.
016.327 68-57819
Z7161 .U64 vol. 1 MRR Alc.

Wynar, Lubomyr Roman, Guide to
reference materials in political
science: Denver, Colorado
Bibliographic Institute, 1966-68. 2
v.   016.32 66-1321
Z7161 .W9 MRR Alc.

Zawodny, Janusz Kazimierz. Guide to
the study of international relations
San Francisco, Chandler Pub. Co.
[1965, c1966] xii, 151 p.   016.327
65-16765
Z6461 .Z3 MRR Alc.

**INTERNATIONAL RELATIONS--BIBLIOGRAPHY--
CATALOGS.**
Foreign Relations Library. Catalog
of the Foreign Relations Library.
Boston, G. K. Hall, 1969. 9 v.
016.327 75-6133
Z6209 .F656 MRR Alc (Dk 33)

Great Britain. Foreign Office.
Library. Catalogue of the Foreign
Office Library, 1826-1968. Boston,
G. K. Hall, 1972. 8 v.   019/.1 73-
160726
Z921 .G682 1972 MRR Alc (Dk 33)

INTERNATIONAL RELATIONS--DICTIONARIES.
Elliott, Florence. A dictionary of
politics. 6th ed. Harmondsworth,
Penguin, 1971. 480 p. [10/-]
320/.03 72-186214
D419 .E4 1971 MRR Alc.

Gamboa, Melquiades Jereos, Elements
of diplomatic and consular practice;
Quezon City, Philippines, Central
Lawbook Pub. Co.; [distributed by
Central Book Supply, inc., Manila,
1966] xxxv, 488 p.   327.2/03 67-
3357
JX1226 .G3 MRR Alc.

Plano, Jack C. The international
relations dictionary New York, Holt,
Rinehart and Winston [1969] xiv, 337
p.   327/.03 69-17657
JX1226 .P55 MRR Alc.

Vincent, Jack Ernest. A handbook of
international relations; Woodbury,
N.Y., Barron's Educational Series,
inc. [1969] vii, 456 p. [2.95 (3.50
Can.)]   327 68-8679
JX1395 .V53 MRR Alc.

**INTERNATIONAL RELATIONS--DICTIONARIES--
FRENCH.**
Academie diplomatique
internationale. Dictionnaire
diplomatique, Paris [1933] 2 v.
341.03 33-36212
JX1226 .A312 vol. 3 MRR Biog.

**INTERNATIONAL RELATIONS--DICTIONARIES--
POLYGLOT.**
Haensch, Günther. Dictionary of
international relations and politics;
Amsterdam, New York, Elsevier Pub.
Co., 1965. xv, 638 p.   320.03 64-
8710
JX1226 .H26 MRR Alc.

**INTERNATIONAL RELATIONS--PERIODICALS--
INDEXES.**
International bibliography of
political science. v. 1- 1953-
London, Tavistock Publications;
Chicago, Aldine Pub. Co. 54-14355
Z7163 .I64 MRR Alc Full set

INTERNATIONAL RELATIONS--RESEARCH.
Council on foreign relations.
American agencies interested in
international affairs. 1931- New
York, [etc.] Frederick A. Praeger,
[etc.] 341.06 31-28874
JX27 .C62 MRR Ref Desk Latest
edition

**INTERNATIONAL RELATIONS--RESEARCH--
DIRECTORIES.**
United States. Dept. of State. Office
of External Research. Foreign
affairs research, a directory of
governmental resources. [Washington,
For sale by the Supt. of Docs., U.S.
Govt. Print. Off.] 1967. vii, 83 p.
327/.025 67-61715
JX1293.U6 A527 MRR Ref Desk.

INTERNATIONAL RELATIONS--SOURCES.
Documents on international affairs.
1928- London, New York [etc.] Oxford
University Press. 341.08 30-10814
D442 .S82 MRR Alc Full set

Hartmann, Frederick H., ed. Basic
documents of international relations.
1st ed. New York, McGraw-Hill,
1951. xv, 312 p.   341.082 51-9293

JX68 .H35 MRR Alc.

**INTERNATIONAL RELATIONS--STUDY AND
TEACHING--DIRECTORIES.**
United States. Dept. of State. Office
of External Research. University
centers of foreign affairs research:
a selective directory. [Washington,
Dept. of State; for sale by the Supt.
of Docs., U.S. Govt. Print. Off.]
1968. xvi, 139 p.   327/.025/73 68-
60080
JX1293.U6 A54 MRR Alc.

**INTERNATIONAL RELATIONS--VOCATIONAL
GUIDANCE.**
Sakell, Achilles Nicholas. Careers
in the Foreign Service. New York, H.
A. Walck, 1962. 118 p.   341.7 62-
21793
JX1417 .S2 MRR Alc.

INTERNATIONAL RELATIONS--YEARBOOKS.
The United States in world affairs.
1931- New York, Simon & Schuster
[etc.] 32-26065
E744 .U66 MRR Alc Full set

The Year book of world affairs. v. 1-
1947- London, Stevens. 341.058
47-29156
JX21 .Y4 MRR Alc Latest edition

INTERNATIONAL SYSTEM OF UNITS.
Le Maraic, A. L., The complete
metric system with the international
system of units (SI). [Rev. and
expanded ed.] Somers, N.Y., Abbey
Books [1973] xiii, 184 p.   389/.152
72-97799
QC91 .L44 1973 MRR Alc.

INTERNATIONAL TRAVEL REGULATIONS.
United States. Passport Office. Visa
requirements of foreign governments.
Washington; [for sale by the Supt. of
Docs., U.S. Govt. Print. Off.] 1973.
8 p. [$0.20]   323.6/7 73-602727
JX4251 .U57 1973 MRR Ref Desk.

INTERNATIONAL VISITORS
see Visitors, Foreign

INTERNATIONALISM.
see also Nationalism

INTERNS.
Lewchuk, Ross C., National register
of internships and experiential
education. Washington, Acropolis
Books [1973] 175 p. [$3.95]
378.1/03/02573 73-6911
L901 .L45 MRR Alc.

INTERPLANETARY VOYAGES.
see also Rockets (Aeronautics)

see also Space flight

INTERPRETATIVE SPEECH
see Oral interpretation

INTERURBAN RAILROADS
see Street-railroads

INTERVIEWING.
see also Counseling

INTOXICANTS
see Alcohol

see Liquors

INTOXICATION
see Alcoholism

see Liquor problem

see Narcotic habit

INTRODUCTION OF SPEAKERS
Lyle, Guy Redvers, comp. I am happy
to present; New York, Wilson, 1953.
265 p.   808.84 53-5513
PN6122 .L9 MRR Alc.

INVALIDS.
see also Handicapped

INVENTIONS.
Fenner, Terrence W. Inventor's
handbook New York, Chemical Pub.
Co., 1969. xi, 309 p. [7.50]
608.7 73-5567
T212 .F44 MRR Alc.

Garrison, Webb B. How it started
Nashville, Abingdon Press [1972] 237
p. [$4.95]   390/.09 72-173951
GT75 .G3 MRR Alc.

Kessler, Kenneth O. The successful
inventor's guide; Englewood Cliffs,
N.J., Prentice-Hall [1965] xv, 224
p.   608.773 64-24939
T339 .K46 MRR Alc.

INVENTIONS--DICTIONARIES.
Carter, Ernest Frank. Dictionary of
inventions and discoveries Revised
ed. London, Muller, 1969. [7], 204
p. [25/-]   608.7/03 78-415875
T9 .C335 1969 MRR Alc.

INVENTIONS--HISTORY.
Crowther, James Gerald, Discoveries
and inventions of the 20th century.
4th ed., entirely rev. and rewritten.
London, Routledge & Paul [1955] 432
p.   608 55-2421
T20 .C82 1955 MRR Alc.

Wilson, Mitchell A. American science
and invention, a pictorial history;
New York, Simon and Schuster [1954]
ix, 437 p.   509/.73 54-9812
Q125 .W7914 MRR Alc.

INVENTIONS--PICTORIAL WORKS.
Wilson, Mitchell A. American science
and invention, a pictorial history;
New York, Simon and Schuster [1954]
ix, 437 p. 509.73 54-9812
Q125 .W7914 MRR Alc.

INVENTORIES.
United States. Bureau of the Census.
Manufacturers' shipments,
inventories, and orders: 1961-1968.
Washington] U.S. Dept. of Commerce.
[for sale by the Supt. of Docs., U.S.
Govt. Print. Off., 1968] iii, 92 p.
[1.00] 338.4/7/6700973 70-607789
HD9724 .A4 1961 MRR alc.

INVENTORS.
see also Engineers

INVENTORS, AMERICAN.
Haber, Louis. The role of the
American Negro in the fields of
science. [New York?] 1966. 70 l.
509/.22 B 67-62053
Q141 .H212 MRR Biog.

INVERTEBRATES.
see also Insects

Meglitsch, Paul Allen, Invertebrate
zoology New York, Oxford University
Press, 1967. xx, 961 p. 592 67-
15633
QL362 .M4 MRR Alc.

INVESTIGATIONS.
see also Governmental investigations

INVESTMENT ADVISERS--UNITED STATES--
DIRECTORIES.
Investment information and advice:
[1st]- ed.; 1962- Whittier, Calif.
[etc.] FIR Pub. Co. 62-16904
HG4509 .I65 MRR Ref Desk Latest
edition

INVESTMENT AND SAVING
see Saving and investment

INVESTMENT BANKING--UNITED STATES.
Hillstrom, Roger. 1960-1969, a
decade of corporate and international
finance. New York, IDD [1972] 381
p. 332 72-175335
HG4907 .H54 MRR Alc.

INVESTMENT TRUSTS.
Casey, William J. Mutual funds desk
book, New rev. ed. New York,
Institute for Business Planning
[1968, c1969] xii, 243, G47 p.
332.63/27 74-3890
HG4530 .C32 1969 MRR Alc.

International fund year book.
London, Throgmorton Publications.
332.6/327/05 72-623092
HG4530 .I148 MRR Alc Latest edition

INVESTMENT TRUSTS--DIRECTORIES.
Money market directory. 1971- New
York, Money Market Directories.
332.67/025 76-146228
HG4509 .M65 MRR Alc Latest edition

INVESTMENT TRUSTS--YEARBOOKS.
Investment companies international
yearbook. New York, Scheinman
Ciaramella International. 332.6/327
72-92661
HG4530 .I1525 MRR Alc Latest
edition

INVESTMENT TRUSTS--CANADA.
Survey of investment funds. v. 1-
1962- Toronto, Maclean-Hunter Pub.
Co. 64-35314
HG4530 .S88 MRR Alc Latest edition

INVESTMENT TRUSTS--EUROPE--DIRECTORIES.
Esslen, Rainer. A guide to marketing
securities in Europe, 1871-1972. New
York, Wall Street Reports Pub. Corp.
[1971] viii, 215 p. 332.67/34/073
79-178914
HG4538 .E76 MRR Alc.

Noyes Data Corporation. European
mutual funds. Park Ridge, N.J.,
1973. vii, 448 p. [$36.00]
332.6/327/094 72-82810
HG5424.5 .N68 MRR Alc.

INVESTMENT TRUSTS--GREAT BRITAIN--
YEARBOOKS.
The Unit trust year book. London,
Index Ltd.[etc.] 332.63/27 77-
200493
HG5436.5 .U54 MRR Alc Latest
edition

INVESTMENT TRUSTS--UNITED STATES.
Hirsch, Yale. Mutual funds almanac.
3rd- ed.; 1971/72- Old Tappan,
N.J., The Hirsch Organization, Inc.
332.6/327 72-622174
HG4930 .H57 MRR Alc Latest edition

Investment Statistics Laboratory.
ISL daily stock price index: over-the-
counter. [New York] 332.63/22 76-
25091
HG4915 .I6 MRR Alc Full set

Johnson's investment company charts.
Buffalo, Johnson's Charts, inc.
[etc.] 332.14 332.66* 53-34817
HG4530 .J6 MRR Alc Latest edition

Mutual funds; [New York] A.
Wiesenberger. 61-1614
HG4530 .I52 MRR Alc Latest edition

Standard and Poor's Corporation.
Daily stock price record: over-the-
counter. [New York] 332.6/322/0973
72-627516
HG4915 .S665 MRR Alc Full set

The U.S. news & world report guide to
stocks, bonds & mutual funds.
Washington, Books by U.S. News &
World Report [1972] 191 p. [$2.95]
332.6/78/0973 79-188880
HG4921 .U65 MRR Alc.

INVESTMENT TRUSTS--UNITED STATES--
DIRECTORIES.
Kelley, Richard E. The SBIC national
directory, [2d ed.] Los Angeles,
Keyfax Publications [1963] vii, 281
p. 332.672 76-12935
HG3729.U5 K38 1963 MRR Alc.

INVESTMENT TRUSTS--UNITED STATES--
YEARBOOKS.
Investment companies. New York,
Wiesenberger Services, Inc. 43-14373

Began publication in 1941.
HG4530 .I5 MRR Alc Latest edition

Moody's bank & finance manual:
American and foreign. New York,
Moody's Investors Service. 56-14722

HG4961 .M65 MRR Alc Latest edition

INVESTMENTS.
see also Securities

see also Stock-exchange

see also Stocks

Christy, George A. Introduction to
investments 6th ed. New York,
McGraw-Hill [1973, c1974] viii, 688
p. 332.6 73-15710
HG4521 .C455 1974 MRR Alc.

D'Ambrosio, Charles A. A guide to
successful investing Englewood
Cliffs, N.J., Prentice-Hall [1970]
xiii, 332 p. 332.67/8 72-85280
HG4521 .D123 MRR Alc.

Dougall, Herbert Edward. Investments
8th ed. Englewood Cliffs, N.J.,
Prentice-Hall [1968] xiv, 586 p.
332.67/8 68-10274
HG4521 .D65 1968 MRR Alc.

The U.S. news & world report guide to
stocks, bonds & mutual funds.
Washington, Books by U.S. News &
World Report [1972] 191 p. [$2.95]
332.6/78/0973 79-188880
HG4921 .U65 MRR Alc.

INVESTMENTS--BIBLIOGRAPHY.
Burgess, Norman. How to find out
about banking and investment. [1st
ed.] Oxford, New York, Pergamon
Press [1969] xii, 300 p. 016.332
68-55021
Z7164.F5 B84 1969 MRR Alc.

Woy, James B. Investment
information: Detroit, Gale Research
Co. [1970] 231 p. [$11.50]
016.33267 79-118791
Z7164.F5 W93 MRR Ref Desk.

Woy, James B. Investment methods;
New York, R. R. Bowker, 1973. viii,
220 p. 016.3326 73-9607
Z7164.F5 W94 MRR Alc.

Zerden, Sheldon. Best books on the
stock market: New York, Bowker,
1972. xii, 168 p. 016.3326/42/0973
72-8275
Z7164.F5 Z46 MRR Alc.

INVESTMENTS--DICTIONARIES.
Low, Janet. The investor's
dictionary. New York, Simon and
Schuster, 1964. vi, 217 p. 332.603
64-11197
HG4513 .L6 MRR Alc.

Rudman, Jack. Handbook of the stock
market: Brooklyn, N.Y., National
Learning Corp. [1970] xxii, 134 p.
[$4.95] 332.6 76-120548
HG4513 .R8 MRR Alc.

Woy, James B. Investment methods;
New York, R. R. Bowker, 1973. viii,
220 p. 016.3326 73-9607
Z7164.F5 W94 MRR Alc.

Wyckoff, Peter. The language of Wall
Street. New York, Hopkinson and
Blake [1973] 247 p. [$5.95]
332.6/03 73-76037
HG4513 .W92 MRR Alc.

INVESTMENTS--DICTIONARIES--POLYGLOT.
Elsevier's lexicon of stock-market
terms: Amsterdam, New York, Elsevier
Pub. Co., 1965. 131 p. 332.603 65-
13892
HG4513 .E4 MRR Alc.

INVESTMENTS--TABLES, ETC.
Financial Publishing Company.
Financial bond yields based on
premium redemption. Boston [1968]
1305 p. 332.63/23/0212 68-7192
HG4537 .F5347 MRR Alc.

White, Wilson, White's tax exempt
bond market ratings. 1st- ed.;1954-
New York, Standard & Poor's
Corp.[etc.] 65-47879
HG4537 .W5 MRR Alc Latest edition

INVESTMENTS--YEARBOOKS.
The Stock exchange official yearbook. [List] 1934- Croydon, Eng.
[etc.] T. Skinner [etc.] 332.6305
34-16479
HG5431 .S82 MRR Alc Latest edition

INVESTMENTS--EUROPE--YEARBOOKS.
Jane's major companies of Europe.
1st- ed.;1965- London, S. Marston
& Co. [etc.] 65-2174
HG5421 .J35 MRR Alc Latest edition

INVESTMENTS--INDIA--YEARBOOKS.
Kothari's economic and industrial
guide of India. 29th- ed.; 1971/72-
Madras Kothari. [$25.00]
338//0954 72-904460
HG5731 .I57 MRR Alc Latest edition

INVESTMENTS--UNITED STATES.
The 1971 encyclopedia of stock market
techniques. Larchmont, N.Y.,
Investors Intelligence [1970] 733 p.
[$24.95] 332.67/8 79-133412
HG4521 .E55 1970 MRR Alc.

The Stock market handbook: Homewood,
Ill., Dow Jones-Irwin, 1970. xxxi,
1073 p. [$27.50] 332.6/0973 78-
83128
HG4921 .S794 MRR Alc.

Vaughn, Donald E. Survey of
investments New York, Holt, Rinehart
and Winston [1967] xx, 490 p.
332.6/0973 67-21578
HG4921 .V3 MRR Alc.

INVESTMENTS--UNITED STATES--
BIBLIOGRAPHY.
Investment information and advice:
[1st]- ed.; 1962- Whittier, Calif.
[etc.] FIR Pub. Co. 62-16904
HG4509 .I65 MRR Ref Desk Latest
edition

INVESTMENTS--UNITED STATES--DIRECTORIES.
Goodman, Steven E. Financial market
place; New York, Bowker, 1972. x,
363 p. 332/.025/73 72-1736
HG65 .G62 MRR Ref Desk.

INVESTMENTS, EUROPEAN--UNITED STATES.
Esslen, Rainer. A guide to marketing
securities in Europe, 1971-1972. New
York, Wall Street Reports Pub. Corp.
[1971] viii, 215 p. 332.67/34/073
79-178914
HG4538 .E76 MRR Alc.

INVESTMENTS, FOREIGN--STATISTICS.
Vaupel, James W. The world's
multinational enterprises; Boston,
Division of Research, Graduate School
of Business Administration, Harvard
University, 1973. xxxiii, 505 p.
[$25.00] 338.8/8 73-76600
HD69.I7 V36 MRR Alc.

INVESTMENTS, FOREIGN--CARIBBEAN AREA--
HANDBOOKS, MANUALS, ETC.
Jonnard, Claude M. Caribbean
investment handbook Park Ridge,
N.J., Noyes Data Corporation, 1974.
xii, 306 p. [$24.00]
332.6/73/09729 74-75903
HG5242 .J66 MRR Alc.

INVESTMENTS, FOREIGN--UNITED STATES--
DIRECTORIES.
Probe directory of foreign direct
investment in the United States.
[Washington] Probe International,
inc. 332.6/73/0973 74-645092
HG4907 .P74 MRR Alc Latest edition

United States. Office of
International Investment. List of
foreign firms with some
interest/control in American
manufacturing and petroleum companies
in the United States. [Washington]
1972. 61 p. 332.6/73/02573 72-
603415
HG4909 .A5 1972 MRR Ref Desk.

INVESTORS
see Capitalists and financiers

IOWA--BIBLIOGRAPHY.
Historical records survey. A check
list of Iowa imprints 1838-1860,
Chicago, The WPA Historical records
survey project, 1940. 84 (i.e. 85)
numb. l. 015.777 42-17567
Z1215 .H67 no. 15 MRR Alc.

IOWA--BIBLIOGRAPHY. (Cont.)
Petersen, William John, Iowa history
reference guide. Iowa City, State
Historical Society of Iowa, 1952.
192 p. 016.9777 52-62980
Z1283 .P46 1952 MRR Alc.

IOWA--BIBLIOGRAPHY--CATALOGS.
United States. Library of Congress.
Iowa centennial exhibition.
Washington, U.S. Govt. Print. Off.,
1947. 84 p. 016.9777 47-46708
Z663.15.A6I8 1947 MRR Alc.

IOWA--BIOGRAPHY.
Iowa. Secretary of State. Official
register. 1886- Des Moines [etc.]
10-11583
JK6331 MRR Alc Latest edition

IOWA--CENTENNIAL CELEBRATIONS, ETC.
United States. Library of Congress.
Iowa centennial exhibition.
Washington, U.S. Govt. Print. Off.,
1947. 84 p. 016.9777 47-46708
Z663.15.A6I8 1947 MRR Alc.

IOWA--HISTORY.
Cole, Cyrenus, Iowa through the
years, Iowa City, Ia., The State
historical society of Iowa, 1940.
547 p. 977.7 40-28128
F621 .C68 MRR Alc.

Sage, Leland Livingston, A history
of Iowa [1st ed.] Ames, The Iowa
State University Press, 1974. xii,
376 p. 977.7 73-14984
F621 .S15 MRR Alc.

IOWA--HISTORY--BIBLIOGRAPHY.
Petersen, William John, Iowa history
reference guide. Iowa City, State
Historical Society of Iowa, 1952.
192 p. 016.9777 52-62980
Z1283 .P46 1952 MRR Alc.

IOWA--IMPRINTS.
Historical records survey. A check
list of Iowa imprints 1838-1860,
Chicago, The WPA Historical records
survey project, 1940. 84 (i.e. 85)
numb. l. 015.777 42-17567
Z1215 .H67 no. 15 MRR Alc.

IOWA--POLITICS AND GOVERNMENT.
Iowa. Secretary of State. Official
register. 1886- Des Moines [etc.]
10-11583
JK6331 MRR Alc Latest edition

IOWA--REGISTERS.
Iowa. Secretary of State. Official
register. 1886- Des Moines [etc.]
10-11583
JK6331 MRR Alc Latest edition

IPSWICH, ENG.--DIRECTORIES.
Kelly's directory of Ipswich and
neighbourhood. Kingston upon Thames
[etc.] Kelly's directories Limited.
53-28500
DA690.I6 K45 MRR Alc Latest
edition

IRAN.
Iran almanac and book of facts. 1st
ed.; 1961- Tehran, Echo of Iran.
62-50366
AY1185 .I7 MRR Alc Latest edition

Smith, Harvey Henry, Area handbook
for Iran. Washington; For sale by
the Supt. of Docs., U.S. Govt. Print.
Off., 1971. xxii, 653 p. [$4.00]
915.5/03/5 72-608678
DS254.5 .S6 1971 MRR Alc.

IRAN--BIBLIOGRAPHY.
Handley-Taylor, Geoffrey, comp.
Bibliography of Iran; Coronation
edition, revised and enlarged.
London, Bibliography of Iran, 1967.
[2], xviii, 34 p. [25/-]
016.9155/03 67-112633
Z3366 .H3 1967 MRR Alc.

Saba, Mohsen. English
bibliography of Iran. [Teheran?
196-   xlix, 313 p. 016.9155 78-
221539
Z3366 .S23 MRR Alc.

United States. Library of Congress.
General Reference and Bibliography
Division. Iran; a selected and
annotated bibliography, Washington,
1951. ix, 100 p. 016.955 52-60003

Z663.28 .I7 1951 MRR Alc.

IRAN--COMMERCE--DIRECTORIES.
Regional trade directory: 1968-
382/.025/5 sa 68-5897
HF3883 .R4 MRR Alc Latest edition

IRAN--DESCRIPTION AND TRAVEL--GUIDE-
BOOKS.
Fodor's Islamic Asia: Iran,
Afghanistan, Pakistan. 1973- New
York, D. McKay. [$12.95] 915 74-
641031
DS254 .F642 MRR Alc Latest edition

IRAN--GAZETTEERS.
United States. Office of Geography.
Iran; Washington, U.S. Govt. Print.
Off., 1956. iv, 578 p. 915.5 56-
61987
DS253 .U5 MRR Alc.

IRAN--HISTORY--TO 640 A.D.
Arrianus, Flavius. Arrian, London,
W. Heinemann, ltd.; New York, G. P.
Putnam's sons, 1929-33. 2 v. 888.9
30-5835
PA3612 .A83 1929 MRR Alc.

Olmstead, Albert Ten Eyck, History
of the Persian Empire, Achaemenid
period. Chicago, University of
Chicago Press [1948] xix, 576 p.
935 48-7317
DS281 .O4 MRR Alc.

IRAQ.
Smith, Harvey Henry, Area handbook
for Iraq. Washington, For sale by
the Supt. of Docs., U.S. Govt. Print.
Off.; 1969. xvi, 411 p. [3.50]
915.67/03/4 72-602177
DS70.6 .S6 MRR Alc.

IRAQ--GAZETTEERS.
United States. Office of Geography.
Iraq; Washington, U.S. Govt. Print.
Off., 1957. iii, 175 p. 915.67 57-
60597
DS67.8 .U5 MRR Alc.

IRELAND.
Encyclopaedia of Ireland. Dublin, A.
Figgis; New York, McGraw-Hill, 1968.
463 p. 914.15 68-54316
DA979 .E5 MRR Alc.

IRELAND--ANTIQUITIES.
Evans, Emyr Estyn. Prehistoric and
early Christian Ireland: London,
Batsford, 1966. xiv, 241 p. [45/-]
913.36 66-75526
DA920 .E9 MRR Alc.

IRELAND--BIBLIOGRAPHY.
Eager, Alan R. A guide to Irish
bibliographical material, London,
Library Association, 1964. xiii, 392
p. 016.91415 65-2507
Z2031 .E16 MRR Alc.

IRELAND--BIOGRAPHY.
Crone, John Smyth, A concise
dictionary of Irish biography,
London [etc.] Longmans, Green and co.
ltd., 1928. viii, 270 p. 28-20678

DA916 .C7 MRR Biog.

Thom's commercial directory. 116th-
1961/62- Dublin. 338.4/025/415
72-627097
HF3533 .T46 MRR Alc Latest edition

IRELAND--BIOGRAPHY--DICTIONARIES.
Hayes, Richard. Biographical
dictionary of Irishmen in France.
Dublin, M. H. Gill, 1949. 332 p.
325.24150944 50-17250
DC34.5.I7 H3 MRR Biog.

Strickland, Walter G., A dictionary
of Irish artists. New York, Hacker
Art Books [1969, c1968] 2 v.
709/.22 78-94898
N6782 .S7 1969 MRR Biog.

IRELAND--CHURCH HISTORY--BIBLIOGRAPHY.
Kenney, James Francis, The sources
for the early history of Ireland;
New York, Columbia University Press,
1929. xvi, 807 p. 29-30667
Z2041 .K36 MRR Alc.

IRELAND--CIVILIZATION--PERIODICALS--
INDEXES.
Hayes, Richard J., Sources for the
history of Irish civilisation;
Boston, G. K. Hall, 1970. 9 v.
016.91415/03 74-22260
Z2034 .H35 MRR Alc (Dk 33)

IRELAND--COMMERCE--DIRECTORIES.
Macdonald's Irish directory and
gazetteer. Edinburgh [etc.] W.
Macdonald & Co., ltd. ca 08-3135
HF5163 .M2 MRR Alc Latest edition

Thom's commercial directory. 116th-
1961/62- Dublin. 338.4/025/415
72-627097
HF3533 .T46 MRR Alc Latest edition

IRELAND--DESCRIPTION AND TRAVEL--1901-
1950.
Freeman, Thomas Walter. Ireland: a
general and regional geography 4th
ed. London, Methuen, 1969. xix, 557
p. [5/-/-] 914.15 77-395403
DA977 .F72 1969 MRR Alc.

IRELAND--DESCRIPTION AND TRAVEL--1951-
Freeman, Thomas Walter. Ireland: a
general and regional geography 4th
ed. London, Methuen, 1969. xix, 557
p. [5/-/-] 914.15 77-395403
DA977 .F72 1969 MRR Alc.

Rees, Henry, The British Isles: a
regional geography. 2nd ed., revised
and metricated. London, Harrap,
1972. xii, 404 p. [£2.30] 914.2
73-150498
DA631 .R4 1972 MRR Alc.

IRELAND--DESCRIPTION AND TRAVEL--1951- -
-GUIDE-BOOKS.
Aer Lingus. The complete Ireland:
3rd ed: London, Sydney, Ward Lock,
1968. 320 p. [21/-] 914.15/04/9
70-400679
DA980 .A3 1968 MRR Alc.

Fodor's Ireland. 1969- New York, D.
McKay. 914.15/04/9 73-640610
DA978 .I7 MRR Alc Latest edition

Killanin, Michael Morris, Baron, The
Shell guide to Ireland, 2nd ed.
revised and reset. London, Ebury P.
in association with George Rainbird,
1967. 512 p. [50/-] 914.15/04/903
68-70832
DA980 .K5 1967 MRR Alc.

Piehler, Hermann Augustine, Ireland
for everyman, 4th ed. reprinted
(with corrections). London, Dent;
New York, W. W. Norton, 1966. xvi,
238 p. [15/-] 914.15049 66-67349
DA980 .P5 1966 MRR Alc.

IRELAND--DESCRIPTION AND TRAVEL--GUIDE-
BOOKS.
Automobile Association. AA guide to
hotels & restaurants in Great Britain
and Ireland. [Basingstoke, Eng.:
Distributed in the U.S.A. by Harper &
Row, New York, 1974] 671, 48 p.
[£1.95 ($7.95 U.S.)] 647/.9442 74-
167286
TX910.G7 A8 1974 MRR Alc.

Automobile Association. Illustrated
road book of Ireland, [2d
illustrated ed. (rev.)] Dublin; [New
York, American Heritage Press] 1970.
285, v, 32 p. [$9.95] 914.15/04/9
75-25939
GV1025.I6 A82 1970 MRR Alc.

Automobile Association. Treasures of
Britain and treasures of Ireland.
[2d American ed.] New York, Norton
[1972] 680 p. [$17.50] 914.2 72-
193038
DA650 .A92 1972 MRR Alc.

Evans, Emyr Estyn. Prehistoric and
early Christian Ireland: London,
Batsford, 1966. xiv, 241 p. [45/-]
913.36 66-75526
DA920 .E9 MRR Alc.

Fodor's Ireland. 1969- New York, D.
McKay. 914.15/04/9 73-640610
DA978 .I7 MRR Alc Latest edition

IRELAND--DIRECTORIES.
Thom's directory of Ireland:
Professional directory. 116th- ;
1960- Dublin. 72-627098
DA979.5 .T57 MRR Alc Latest
edition

IRELAND--GAZETTEERS.
Automobile Association. Illustrated
road book of Ireland, [2d
illustrated ed. (rev.)] Dublin; [New
York, American Heritage Press] 1970.
285, v, 32 p. [$9.95] 914.15/04/9
75-25939
GV1025.I6 A82 1970 MRR Alc.

Automobile Association. Treasures of
Britain and treasures of Ireland.
[2d American ed.] New York, Norton
[1972] 680 p. [$17.50] 914.2 72-
193038
DA650 .A92 1972 MRR Alc.

Bartholomew, John George, Gazetteer
of the British Isles. 9th ed.,
reprinted, Edinburgh, J.
Bartholomew, 1963. xxxii, 748 p.
65-53267
DA640 .B23 1963 MRR Alc.

Dublin and district trades'
directory. Edinburgh, Town and
County Directories. 650.584183 60-
30162
HC258.D8 D8 MRR Alc Latest edition

Macdonald's Irish directory and
gazetteer. Edinburgh [etc.] W.
Macdonald & Co., ltd. ca 08-3135
HF5163 .M2 MRR Alc Latest edition

United States. Office of Geography.
Ireland; Washington, 1950. 189 p.
914.15/003 79-10005
DA879 .U5 MRR Alc.

IRELAND--HISTORY.
Costigan, Giovanni. A history of
modern Ireland; New York, Pegasus
[1969] xiii, 380 p. [7.95] 941.5
69-15699
DA910 .C85 MRR Alc.

IRELAND--HISTORY. (Cont.)
Inglis, Brian, The story of Ireland.
2nd ed. London, Faber, 1966. 274
p. [25/-] 941.5 66-70166
DA910 .I54 1966 MRR Alc.

IRELAND--HISTORY--TO 1172--BIBLIOGRAPHY.
Kenney, James Francis, The sources
for the early history of Ireland;
New York, Columbia University Press,
1929. xvi, 807 p. 29-30667
Z2041 .K36 MRR Alc.

IRELAND--HISTORY--18TH CENTURY.
Gipson, Lawrence Henry, The British
Empire before the American
Revolution. [Completely rev.] New
York, Knopf, 1958- v. 942.072
58-9670
DA500 .G52 MRR Alc.

Gipson, Lawrence Henry, The British
Empire before the American
Revolution. Caldwell, Id., Caxton
Printers, 1936-70. 15 v. 942.07/2
36-20870
DA500 .G5 MRR Alc.

IRELAND--HISTORY--BIBLIOGRAPHY.
Bell, S. Peter. Dissertations on
British history, 1815-1914;
Metuchen, N.J., Scarecrow Press,
1974. xii, 232 p. 016.9142/03 74-
16104
Z2016 .B43 MRR Alc.

IRELAND--HISTORY--SOURCES.
Curtis, Edmund, ed. Irish historical
documents, 1172-1922, New York,
Barnes & Noble [1968] 331 p. [8.00]
941.5/08 68-6C07
DA905 .C8 1968b MRR Alc.

IRELAND--HISTORY--SOURCES--BIBLIOGRAPHY.
Kenney, James Francis, The sources
for the early history of Ireland;
New York, Columbia University Press,
1929. xvi, 807 p. 29-30667
Z2041 .K36 MRR Alc.

IRELAND--HISTORY, LOCAL--BIBLIOGRAPHY.
Martin, Geoffrey Haward. A
bibliography of British and Irish
municipal history Leicester,
Leicester University Press, 1972- v.
[£12.50 (v. 1)] 016.30136/0942
73-156398
Z2023 .M26 MRR Alc.

IRELAND--IMPRINTS.
Black, R. D. Collison. A catalogue
of pamphlets on economic subjects
published between 1750 and 1900 and
now housed in Irish libraries, New
York, A. M. Kelley, 1969. ix, 632 p.
016.33 79-81989
Z7164.E2 B6 MRR Alc.

IRELAND--INDUSTRIES--DIRECTORIES--
YEARBOOKS.
Irish industrial year book. Dublin,
McEvoy Press Ltd, [etc.]
380.1/025/415 74-642474
Began with vol. for 1934
HC257 .I6A23 MRR Alc Latest
edition

IRELAND--MANUFACTURES--DIRECTORIES.
Irish industrial year book. Dublin,
McEvoy Press Ltd, [etc.]
380.1/025/415 74-642474
Began with vol. for 1934
HC257 .I6A23 MRR Alc Latest
edition

Macdonald's Irish directory and
gazetteer. Edinburgh [etc.] W.
Macdonald & Co., ltd. ca 08-3135
HF5163 .M2 MRR Alc Latest edition

IRELAND--POLITICS AND GOVERNMENT--1922-
1949.
Chubb, Basil. The government &
politics of Ireland. Stanford,
Calif., Stanford University Press,
1970. xii, 364 p. [10.00]
320.9/415 77-93493
JN1415 .C48 MRR Alc.

IRELAND--POLITICS AND GOVERNMENT--1949-
Chubb, Basil. The government &
politics of Ireland. Stanford,
Calif., Stanford University Press,
1970. xii, 364 p. [10.00]
320.9/415 77-93493
JN1415 .C48 MRR Alc.

IRELAND--SOCIAL LIFE AND CUSTOMS--
BIBLIOGRAPHY.
Brown, Stephen James Meredith,
Ireland in fiction; New ed. Dublin,
London, Maunsel and company, limited,
1919. xx, 362 p. 20-4278
Z2039.F4 B8 1919 MRR Alc.

IRISH IN FRANCE.
Hayes, Richard. Biographical
dictionary of Irishmen in France.
Dublin, M. H. Gill, 1949. 332 p.
325.24150844 50-17250
DC34.5.I7 H3 MRR Biog.

IRISH IN THE UNITED STATES.
Wittke, Carl Frederick, The Irish in
America. Baton Rouge, Louisiana
State University Press [c1956] xi,
319 p. 325.24150973 56-6199
E184.I6 W5 MRR Alc.

IRISH LANGUAGE--DICTIONARIES--ENGLISH.
Dinneen, Patrick Stephen, [Focloir
Gaedhilge agus Bearla (romanized
form)] New ed., rev. and greatly
enl. Dublin [etc.] Pub. for the
Irish texts society by the
Educational company of Ireland, ltd.,
1927. 4 p. l., [vii]-xxx, 1340 p.
28-14495
PB1291 .D5 1927 MRR Alc.

Fournier d'Albe, Edmund Edward, An
English-Irish dictionary and phrase
book, Dublin, The Celtic
association 1903. viii p., 1 l.,
338 p. 28-12337
PB1291 .F65 MRR Alc.

Ó Siochfhradha, Micheál, Irish-
English, English-Irish dictionary.
[New ed. Dublin, Talbot Press, 1972]
131, x, 190 p. [£1.70]
491.6/2/321 73-171932
PB1291 .O83 MRR Alc.

O'Reilly, Edward, An Irish-English
dictionary, A new ed., carefully
rev. and cor. Dublin, J. Duffy and
co., limited [181-] 3 p. l., 5-724,
[2] p. 14-11541
PB1291 .O8 MRR Alc.

IRISH LITERATURE--HISTORY AND CRITICISM.
Hyde, Douglas, Pres. Irish Free
State, A literary history of Ireland
from earliest times to the present
day. New ed. London, Benn, 1967.
xliii, 654 p. [70/-] 67-86298
PB1306 .H8 1967 MRR Alc.

IRISH LITERATURE (ENGLISH)--HISTORY AND
CRITICISM.
Howarth, Herbert. The Irish writers,
1880-1940; London, Rockliff [1958]
x, 318 p. 820.903 a 59-4779
PR8753 .H6 MRR Alc.

Taylor, Estella Ruth. The modern
Irish writers; Lawrence, University
of Kansas Press, 1954. 176 p.
820.904 54-8406
PR8753 .T3 MRR Alc.

IRISH PERIODICALS--INDEXES.
Hayes, Richard J., Sources for the
history of Irish civilisation;
Boston, G. K. Hall, 1970. 9 v.
016.91415/03 74-22260
Z2034 .H35 MRR Alc (Dk 33)

IRISH POETRY (ENGLISH)
Taylor, Geoffrey, ed. Irish poets of
the nineteenth century. London,
Routledge and Paul [1951] viii, 406
p. 821.7082 51-2435
PR8857 .T3 1951 MRR Alc.

IRISH UNIVERSITY PRESS SERIES OF
BRITISH PARLIAMENTARY PAPERS--INDEXES.
Irish University Press. Checklist of
British parliamentary papers in the
Irish University Press 1000-volume
series, 1801-1899. Shannon, Ireland
[1972] xii, 218 p. 015.42 73-
150718
Z2019 .I73 MRR Ref Desk.

Irish University Press series of
British parliamentary papers.
Shannon, Irish University Press
[1968] 8 v. 016.32842/01 77-
456705
Z2019 .I74 MRR Alc.

IRON.
see also Steel

IRON--DICTIONARIES.
Kohler, Eduard Ludwig, English-
German and German-English dictionary
for the iron and steel industry,
Vienna, Springer, 1955. xii, 168,
162 p. 55-6643
TN609 .K6 MRR Alc.

Osborne, Alice Katherine. An
encyclopaedia of the iron & steel
industry, 2nd ed. London, Technical
P., 1967. lxiii, 558 p. [84/-]
669.1/03 67-89452
TN609 .O8 1967 MRR Alc.

IRON--DICTIONARIES--GERMAN.
Kohler, Eduard Ludwig, English-
German and German-English dictionary
for the iron and steel industry,
Vienna, Springer, 1955. xii, 168,
162 p. a 55-6643
TN609 .K6 MRR Alc.

IRON AGE.
see also Archaeology

IRON CURTAIN LANDS
see Communist countries

IRON INDUSTRY AND TRADE.
Pounds, Norman John Greville. The
geography of iron and steel 3rd
impression (revised ed.) London,
Hutchinson, 1966. 192 p. [25/- 10/6
(pbk.)] 338.476681 66-73525
HD9510.5 .P6 1966 MRR Alc.

IRON INDUSTRY AND TRADE--DIRECTORIES.
Directory [of] iron and steel plants.
Pittsburgh, Steel Publications
[etc.] 16-18550
TS301 .D35 Sci RR Latest edition /
MRR Alc Latest edition

IRON INDUSTRY AND TRADE--STATISTICS.
American Iron and Steel Institute,
New York. Annual Statistical report.
1912- Washington [etc.] 14-3046
HD9514 .A5 MRR Alc Latest edition

IRON INDUSTRY AND TRADE--UNITED STATES--
BIBLIOGRAPHY.
United States. Library of Congress.
Division of Bibliography. Select
list of books, with references to
periodicals, relating to iron and
steel in commerce. Washington, Govt.
Print. Off., 1907. 25 p. 07-35003
Z663.28 .S35 MRR Alc.

IRON INDUSTRY AND TRADE--UNITED STATES--
DIRECTORIES.
Directory [of] iron and steel plants.
Pittsburgh, Steel Publications
[etc.] 16-18550
TS301 .D35 Sci RR Latest edition /
MRR Alc Latest edition

IRON-WORKS--CANADA--DIRECTORIES.
Directory of iron and steel works of
the United States and Canada. [1st]-
ed.; 1873- Washington [etc.]
American Iron and Steel Institute
[etc.] 01-1428
TS301 .A6 Sci RR Latest edition /
MRR Alc Latest edition

IRON-WORKS--UNITED STATES--DIRECTORIES.
Directory of iron and steel works of
the United States and Canada. [1st]-
ed.; 1873- Washington [etc.]
American Iron and Steel Institute
[etc.] 01-1428
TS301 .A6 Sci RR Latest edition /
MRR Alc Latest edition

IRS
see United States. Internal Revenue
Service

ISLAM.
Williams, John Alden, ed. Islam.
New York, G. Braziller, 1961. 256 p.
297.082 61-15500
BP161.2 .W5 MRR Alc.

ISLAM--DICTIONARIES.
The Encyclopaedia of Islam; Leyden,
E. J. Brill ltd.; London, Luzac & co,
1913- v. 26-26918
DS37 .E5 MRR Alc.

Hughes, Thomas Patrick, A dictionary
of Islam; 2d ed. London, W. H.
Allen & co., limited, 1896. vii p.,
1 l., 750 p. 01-14622
BP40 .H8 1896 MRR Alc.

Shorter encyclopaedia of Islam.
Ithaca, N.Y., Cornell University
Press [c1953] viii, 671 p. 297.03
57-59109
DS37 .E52 1953a MRR Alc.

ISLAMIC COUNTRIES--DICTIONARIES AND
ENCYCLOPEDIAS.
The Encyclopaedia of Islam; Leyden,
E. J. Brill ltd.; London, Luzac & co,
1913- v. 26-26918
DS37 .E5 MRR Alc.

ISLAMIC COUNTRIES--HISTORY.
The Cambridge history of Islam;
Cambridge [Eng.] University Press,
1970. 2 v. [£13/-/- ($39.00 U.S.)]
910.03/176/7 73-77291
DS35.6 .C3 MRR Alc.

ISLAMIC COUNTRIES--PERIODICALS--INDEXES.
London. University. School of
Oriental and African Studies.
Library. Index Islamicus, 1906-1955;
Cambridge, Eng., W. Heffer [1958]
xxxvi, 897 p. 016.9156 59-23014
Z7835.M6 L6 MRR Alc.

ISLAMIC EMPIRE--BIBLIOGRAPHY.
Sauvaget, Jean, Introduction to the
history of the Muslim East:
Berkeley, University of California
Press, 1965. xxi, 252 p. 64-25271
Z3013 .S314 MRR Alc.

ISLAMIC EMPIRE--HISTORY.
Hitti, Philip Khuri, History of the
Arabs from the earliest times to the
present 10th ed. [London]
Macmillan; [New York] St. Martin's
Press [1970] xxiv, 822 p. [$12.50]
953 74-102765
DS37.7 .H58 1970 MRR Alc.

ISLANDS.
Huxley, Anthony Julian, ed. Standard
encyclopedia of the world's oceans
and islands. London, Weidenfeld &
Nicolson [1963, c1962] 383 p.   63-
24429
GB471 .H9 1963 MRR Alc.

ISLANDS OF THE PACIFIC.
The Pacific islands year book. [1st]-
ed.; 1932- Sydney, Australia
[etc.] Pacific Publications [etc.]
32-24429
DU1 .P15 MRR Alc Latest edition

ISLANDS OF THE PACIFIC--BIBLIOGRAPHY.
Dickson, Diane. World catalogue of
theses on the Pacific Islands,
Canberra, Australian National
University Press, 1970. xii, 123 p.
[$3.90]   016.919 70-128370
Z4501 .D52 MRR Alc.

Taylor, Clyde Romer Hughes, A
Pacific bibliography; 2nd ed.
Oxford, Clarendon Press, 1965. xxx,
692 p.   016.919 66-1568
Z4501 .T3 1965 MRR Alc.

**ISLANDS OF THE PACIFIC--COMMERCE--
DIRECTORIES.**
Pacific Islands business directory.
Auckland, Universal Business
Directories Ltd. 338/.0099 72-
622889
HF5319 .U54 MRR Alc Latest edition

**ISLANDS OF THE PACIFIC--DESCRIPTION AND
TRAVEL.**
Harris, Neil Vernon. The tropical
Pacific London, University of London
P. [1866] 176 p. [20/-] 919 66-
69488
DU23 .H3 MRR Alc.

**ISLANDS OF THE PACIFIC--DESCRIPTION AND
TRAVEL--GUIDE-BOOKS.**
Clark, Sydney Aylmer, All the best
in the South Pacific New York, Dodd,
Mead [1971] xii, 338 p. [$6.95]
919 76-151283
DU15 .C6 1971 MRR Alc.

Waldo, Myra. Travel guide to the
Orient and the Pacific, 1970-71,
[Rev. ed. New York] Macmillan [1970]
xxii, 712 p. 915/.04/42 70-93723
DS4 .W3 1970 MRR Alc.

ISLANDS OF THE PACIFIC--GAZETTEERS.
United States. Office of Geography.
South Pacific; Washington, U.S.
Govt. Print. Off., 1957. iii, 68 p.
919 57-60873
DU10 .U66 MRR Alc.

United States. Office of Geography.
Southwest Pacific; Washington, U.S.
Govt. Print. Off., 1956 [i.e. 1957]
v, 368 p.   919 57-61177
DU10 .U68 MRR Alc.

United States. Office of Geography.
West Pacific islands; Washington,
Central Intelligence Agency, 1957.
ii, 170 p.   919.6 72-8436
DU10 .U665 MRR Alc.

ISOBARS
see Atmospheric pressure

ISRAEL.
Prittie, Terence Cornelius Farmer,
Hon., Israel; miracle in the desert
New York, Praeger [1967] 246 p.
956.94/05 66-26554
DS126.5 .P7 MRR Alc.

Smith, Harvey Henry, Area handbook
for Israel. [Washington; For sale by
the Supt. of Docs., U.S. Govt. Print.
Off.] 1970. xvi, 456 p. [$3.50]
309.1/5694/05 78-607520
DS126.5 .S6 MRR Alc.

ISRAEL--BIOGRAPHY.
Who's who Israel. 1945/46- Tel Aviv
[etc.] Bronfman & Cohen [etc.]
920.0569 46-6380
DS125.3.A2 W53 MRR Biog Latest
edition

ISRAEL--COMMERCE--DIRECTORIES.
The Directory of Israeli merchants
and manufacturers Tel-Aviv, N.A.
Etrogy. he 66-1345
HF3861.P2 D5 MRR Alc Latest
edition

The Israel directory, Tel-Aviv,
Register of Commerce and Industry in
Israel [etc.] 46-28585
Began publication with issue for
1935.
HF5268.P3 I8 MRR Alc Latest
edition

Israel export directory. Tel-Aviv,
Israel Publications [etc.] he 67-1270
HF3861.P2 I72 MRR Alc Bind/Label

**ISRAEL--DESCRIPTION AND TRAVEL--GUIDE-
BOOKS.**
Comay, Joan. Introducing Israel;
2nd revised ed. London, Methuen,
1969. 303 p. [50/-] 915.694/04/5
78-453347
DS103 .C59 1969 MRR Alc.

Comay, Joan. Israel: an uncommon
guide. New York, Random House
[c1968] xvii, 333 p. [6.95]
915.694/03/5 69-16461
DS103 .C593 MRR Alc.

Fodor's Israel. 1969- New York, D.
McKay. 915.694/04/5 75-5266
DS103 .F62 MRR Alc Latest edition

Rand, Abby. The American traveler's
guide to Israel. New York, Scribner
[1972] vii, 296 p. [$8.95]
915.694/04/5 70-37228
DS103 .R35 MRR Alc.

Vilnay, Zev, The guide to Israel.
[1st]- ed.; 1955- Jerusalem [etc.]
915.694/04/5 56-25288
DS103 .V475 MRR Alc Latest edition

ISRAEL--DICTIONARIES AND ENCYCLOPEDIAS.
Encyclopedia of Zionism and Israel.
New York, Herzl Press, 1971- v.
956.94/001/03 68-55271
DS149 .E597 MRR Alc.

ISRAEL--EXECUTIVE DEPARTMENTS.
Israel. Government yearbook. 1950-
Jerusalem. 56-40420
J693.P22213 MRR Alc Latest edition

ISRAEL--HISTORICAL GEOGRAPHY--MAPS.
Vilnay, Zev, The new Israel atlas;
New York, McGraw-Hill Book Co., 1969
[c1968] 112 p. [7.95] 912.5694
79-653239
G2235 .V52 1969 MRR Alc Atlas.

ISRAEL--HISTORY--YEARBOOKS.
The Israel yearbook. 1950/51- [Tel
Aviv] 915.69 53-28951
DS101 .I68 MRR Alc Latest edition

ISRAEL--IMPRINTS.
United States. Library of Congress.
American Libraries Book Procurement
Center, Tel-Aviv. Accessions list,
Israel. v. 1- Apr. 1964- Tel-
Aviv. he 66-1615
Z663.767.I8 A25 MRR Alc   MRR Alc
Full set

ISRAEL--INDUSTRIES--DIRECTORIES.
Israel export directory. Tel-Aviv,
Israel Publications [etc.] he 67-1270
HF3861.P2 I72 MRR Alc Bind/Label

ISRAEL--MANUFACTURES--DIRECTORIES.
The Directory of Israeli merchants
and manufacturers Tel-Aviv, N.A.
Etrogy. he 66-1345
HF3861.P2 D5 MRR Alc Latest
edition

Who represents whom in Israel and
abroad. 1st- ed.; 1968/69- Tel-
Aviv, A. L. Tanne. 382/.025/5694 78-
950757
HF3861.P2 A37 MRR Alc Latest
edition

ISRAEL--MAPS.
Vilnay, Zev, The new Israel atlas;
New York, McGraw-Hill Book Co., 1969
[c1968] 112 p. [7.95] 912.5694
79-653239
G2235 .V52 1969 MRR Alc Atlas.

ISRAEL--POLITICS AND GOVERNMENT.
Freudenheim, Yehoshu a. Government
in Israel. Dobbs Ferry, N.Y., Oceana
Publications, 1967. x, 309 p.
320.9/5694 66-17246
JQ1825.P3 F713 MRR Alc.

**ISRAEL--POLITICS AND GOVERNMENT--
YEARBOOKS.**
Israel. Government yearbook. 1950-
Jerusalem. 56-40420
J693.P22213 MRR Alc Latest edition

ISRAEL--REGISTERS.
Israel. Government yearbook. 1950-
Jerusalem. 56-40420
J693.P22213 MRR Alc Latest edition

ISRAELI PERIODICALS--BIBLIOGRAPHY.
Tronik, Ruth. Israeli periodicals &
serials in English & other European
languages: Metuchen, N.J., Scarecrow
Press, 1974. xiii, 193 p. 016.05
73-14901
Z6958.I8 T76 MRR Alc.

United States. Library of Congress.
American Libraries Book Procurement
Center, Tel-Aviv. Accessions list,
Israel. v. 1- Apr. 1964- Tel-
Aviv. he 66-1615
Z663.767.I8 A25 MRR Alc   MRR Alc
Full set

United States. Library of Congress.
American Libraries Book Procurement
Center, Tel-Aviv. Serial titles
submitted; Dec. 31, 1965- Tel-Aviv.
016.059924 he 66-10
Z663.767.I8 A45 MRR Alc   MRR Alc
Full set

ISRAELITES
see Jews

ISTANBUL--DESCRIPTION--GUIDE-BOOKS.
Istanbul et ses environs Paris,
Hachette, 1967. 183 p. [14,59 F.]
914.96/1/043 67-79909
DR718 .I8 1967 MRR Alc.

**ITALIAN DRAMA--EARLY TO 1700--
BIBLIOGRAPHY.**
Herrick, Marvin Theodore, Italian
plays, 1500-1700, in the University
of Illinois Library, Urbana,
University of Illinois Press, 1966.
92 p. 016.852 66-17248
Z2354.D7 H4 MRR Alc.

ITALIAN DRAMA--HISTORY AND CRITICISM.
Kennard, Joseph Spencer, The Italian
theatre, New York, W. E. Rudge,
1932. 2 v. 852.09 792.0945 32-
13803
PQ4134 .K4 MRR Alc.

ITALIAN IMPRINTS--CATALOGS.
British Museum. Dept. of Printed
Books. Short-title catalogue of
books printed in Italy London,
Trustees of the British Museum, 1958.
viii, 992 p. 015.45 a 60-1778
Z2342 .B7 MRR Alc.

ITALIAN IMPRINTS--FRANCE.
Michel, Suzanne, P. Repertoire des
ouvrages imprimes en langue
italienne au XVIIe siecle Firenze,
L. S. Olschki, 1970- v. [L17500
(v. 1)] 70-558790
Z2342 .M52 MRR Alc.

Michel, Suzanne, P. Répertoire des
ouvrages imprimés en langue
italienne au XVIIe siècle conservés
dans les bibliothèques de France
Paris, Éditions du Centre national
de la recherche scientifique, 1967-
v. [38.00 (v. 1) varies]
015/.45 67-69528
Z2342 .M5 MRR Alc.

ITALIAN LANGUAGE--BIBLIOGRAPHY.
Hall, Robert Anderson, Bibliografia
della linguistica italiana. 2. ed
riv. e aggiornata. Firenze, Sansoni,
1958. 3 v. 58-42410
Z2355.A2 H315 MRR Alc.

**ITALIAN LANGUAGE--CONVERSATION AND
PHRASE BOOKS.**
Glendening, P. J. T. Beyond the
dictionary in Italian, New York,
Funk & Wagnalls [1964, c1963] 159 p.
458.3 64-15860
PC1680 .G5 1964 MRR Alc.

ITALIAN LANGUAGE--DICTIONARIES.
Albertoni, Alberto. Vocabolario
della lingua italiana. 10. ed.
Firenze, F. Le Monnier, 1968. vi,
1071 p. [2300] 77-447164
PC1625 .A55 1968 MRR Alc.

Battaglia, Salvatore. Grande
dizionario della lingua italiana.
Torino] Unione tipografico-editrice
torinese [1961- v.   61-35046
PC1625 .B3 MRR Alc.

Devoto, Giacomo. Vocabolario
illustrato della lingua italiana,
Milano, Selezione dal Reader's
Digest, 1967. 2 v. 453 68-86771
PC1625 .D4 MRR Alc.

Dizionario Garzanti della lingua
italiana. Milano, Garzanti, 1971.
994 p. [L2700] 72-326322
PC1625 .D5 1971 MRR Alc.

Enciclopedia Sansoni illustrata.
Firenze, Sansoni, 1968. 4 v.
[48000] 73-390457
AE35 .E53 MRR Alc.

Modernissimo dizionario illustrato
... Novara, Istituto geografico De
Agostini, 1968. 2 v. [9000] 77-
436091
PC1625 .M6 MRR Alc.

Palazzi, Fernando, Novissimo
dizionario della lingua italiana. 2.
edizione riveduta, aggiornata e
corretta. Milano, Ceschina, 1969.
xiv, 1404, 47 p., leaf inserted. 77-
542889
PC1625 .P17 1969 MRR Alc.

Tommaseo, Niccolò, Dizionario dei
sinonimi della lingua italiana.
Nuovissima ed., accuratamente corr.
Milano, Bietti [1935] lviii, [2],
1330 p. 454 37-16087
PC1591 .T65 1935 MRR Alc.

ITALIAN LANGUAGE--DICTIONARIES. (Cont.)

Tommaseo, Niccolò. Dizionario della
lingua italiana, Torino [etc.]
Unione tipografico-editrice [1861-79]
4 v. in 8.   01-19877
   PC1625 .T6 1861 MRR Alc.

Zingarelli, Nicola, Vocabolario
della lingua italiana. Novissima ed.
(8) aggiornata ed annotata Bologna,
Zanichelli [1959] 1786 p.   a   59-
7512
   PC1625 .Z5 1959 MRR Alc.

ITALIAN LANGUAGE--DICTIONARIES--ENGLISH.

Aghina, Luisa. Dizionario tecnico
italiano-inglese. [Firenze]
Vallecchi [1961] 431 p.   a   61-3420
   TP9 .A35 MRR Alc.

Artschwager, Ernst Friedrich,
Dictionary of botanical equivalents,
Baltimore, The Williams & Wilkins
company, 1925. 5 p. l., 9-124 p.
25-11598
   QK9 .A7 1925 MRR Alc.

Cassell's Italian dictionary: Italian-
English, English-Italian. New York,
Funk & Wagnalls [1959, c1958] xxi,
1079 p.   453.2   59-12386
   PC1640 .C33 1959 MRR Ref Desk.

Cassell's Italian-English, English-
Italian dictionary; 7th ed. London,
Cassell, 1967. xxi, 1096 p.   [42/-]
453/.2   70-382670
   PC1640 .C33 1967 MRR Ref Desk.

Cassell's Italian-English, English-
Italian dictionary. London, Cassell
[1958] xxi, 1079 p.   453.2   58-4262

   PC1640 .C33 MRR Ref Desk.

Dizionario Garzanti italiano-inglese,
inglese-italiano. Edizione minore.
Milano, Garzanti, 1968. 1067 p.   [L
1900]   68-133578
   PC1640 .D5 1968 MRR Alc.

Hazon, Mario, Grande dizionario
inglese-italiano, italiano-inglese.
Milano Garzanti, 1969. x, 2100 p.
[7800]   76-508865
   PC1640 .H35 1969 MRR Alc.

Hoare, Alfred, A short Italian
dictionary. [New York] Cambridge
University Press, 1957. xxxii, 443,
v, 421 p.   453.2   58-2938
   PC1640 .H63 1957 MRR Alc.

Lysle, Andrea de Roever, called A. de
R., Nuovo dizionario moderno delle
lingue italiana e inglese. Ed. riv.
e aggiornata con aggiunta di un
supplemento commerciale Torino, F.
Casanova, 1951. 2 v.   56-29687
   PC1640 .L8 1951 MRR Alc.

Marolli, Giorgio. Dizionario tecnico
inglese-italiano, italiano-inglese
... 9. edizione riveduta e ampliata.
Firenze, F. Le Monnier, 1968. xxii,
1841 p.   [16000]   603   70-378230
   T9 .M18 1968 MRR Alc.

Moth, Axel Fredrik Carl Mathias,
Glossary of library terms, English,
Danish, Dutch, French, German,
Italian, Spanish, Swedish, Boston,
The Boston book company, 1915. 58 p.
15-3471
   Z1006 .M72 MRR Alc.

Motta, Giuseppe, teacher of English.
Dizionario commerciale: inglese-
italiano, italiano-inglese. Milano,
C. Signorelli [1961] x, 1050 p.   61-
33500
   HF1002 .M6 MRR Alc.

Orlandi, Giuseppe, Dizionario
italiano-inglese, inglese-italiano;
3. ed. riv., corr. e interamente
ricomposta. Milano, C. Signorelli
[1957] xiv, 2130 p.   57-24559
   PC1640 .O7 1957 MRR Ref Desk.

Pekelis, Carla. A dictionary of
colorful Italian idioms; New York,
G. Braziller [1965] 226 p.   453.1
65-14601
   PC1460 .P4 MRR Alc.

Ragazzini, Giuseppe. Dizionario
inglese e italiano. Concise edition
Bologna, Zanichelli; [London]
Longman, [1972] xiii, 1200 p.
[L2700]   73-307395
   PC1640 .R26 1972 MRR Alc.

Reynolds, Barbara. The Cambridge
Italian dictionary. Cambridge,
University Press, 1962-   v.
453.2   62-2528
   PC1640 .R4 MRR Ref Desk.

Sansoni-Harrap standard Italian and
English dictionary; London, Harrap
1970-   v.   [17/-/- (pt. 1, v. 1)]
453/.2   70-534485
   PC1640 .S3 MRR Alc.

Spinelli, Nicola, Dizionario
italiano-inglese, inglese-italiano.
3. ed. interamente rifatta. Torino,
Società editrice internazionale
[1955] 2 v.   a   55-8274
   PC1640 .S7 1955 MRR Alc.

Walter, Frank Keller, Abbreviations
and technical terms used in book
catalogs and bibliographies, in eight
languages, 1917 handy edition.
Boston, The Boston book company
[1919?] 2 v. in 1.   27-13479
   Z1006 .W261 1919 MRR Alc.

ITALIAN LANGUAGE--DICTIONARIES--POLYGLOT.

Associazione industriale lombarda.
Glossario del lavoro: italiano,
francese, inglese, tedesco. Milano
1964.   1335 p.   67-43249
   HD4839 .A78 MRR Alc.

Band-Kuzmany, Karin R. M. Glossary
of the theatre. Amsterdam, New York,
Elsevier Pub. Co., 1969. 140 p.
[31.20]   792/.03   68-57152
   PN2035 .B3 MRR Alc.

Bari, G. Dizionario commerciale
italiano-inglese-francese-tedesco.
2. ed. Milano, L. di G. Pirolo,
1970. 865 p., leaf inserted.   [8500]
70-488606
   HF1002 .B28 1970 MRR Alc.

Britannica world language dictionary,
[Chicago, 1958] 1483-2015 p.   413
58-4491
   P361 .B7 1958 MRR Alc.

Capitol's concise dictionary.
Bologna, Capitol, 1972.   1051 (i.e.
1207) p.   413   72-172231
   P361 .C3 MRR Alc.

Clason, W. E., Elsevier's dictionary
of computers, automatic control and
data processing. 2d rev. ed. of The
dictionary of automation, computers,
control and measuring. Amsterdam,
New York, Elsevier Pub. Co., 1971.
484 p.   [fl78.00]   001.6/4/03   73-
151733
   TJ212.5 .C55 1971 MRR Alc.

Clason, W. E., Supplement to the
Elsevier dictionaries of electronics,
nucleonics and telecommunication.
Amsterdam, New York, Elsevier Pub.
Co., 1963. 633 p.   603   63-11369
   T10 .C55 MRR Alc.

Conference terminology, 2d ed., rev.
and augm. Amsterdam, New York,
Elsevier Pub. Co.; [sole distributors
for the U.S.: American Elsevier Pub.
Co., New York] 1962. 162 p.   413
63-8568
   PB324.C6 C6 1962 MRR Alc.

Dictionnaire à l'usage de la
librairie ancienne pour les langues:
française, anglaise, allemande,
suédoise, danoise, italienne,
espagnole, hollandaise. Paris, Ligue
internationale de la librairie
ancienne, 1956. 190 p.   655.403   57-
2275
   Z282 .D5 MRR Alc.

The Duden pictorial encyclopedia in
five languages: English, French,
German, Italian, Spanish. 2d, enl.
ed. New York, F. Ungar Pub. Co.
[1958] 2 v.   413   58-11093
   P361 .D8 1958 MRR Alc.

Elektrotechnik und Elektrochemie.
München, R. Oldenbourg, 1955. xxiv,
1304 p.   57-18208
   TK9 .E42 1955 MRR Alc.

Elsevier's automobile dictionary in
eight languages: Amsterdam, New
York, Elsevier Pub. Co.; [distributed
by Van Nostrand, Princeton, N.J.]
1960. 946 p.   629.203   59-8946
   TL9 .E43 MRR Alc.

Elsevier's banking dictionary in six
languages: Amsterdam, New York,
Elsevier Pub. Co., 1966. 302 p.
332.103   65-20139
   HG151 .E45 MRR Alc.

Elsevier's dictionary of aeronautics
in six languages: Amsterdam, New
York, Elsevier Pub. Co., 1964. 842
p.   629.1303   63-22063
   TL509 .E4 MRR Alc.

Elsevier's dictionary of chemical
engineering. Amsterdam, New York,
1968. 2 v.   [62.50 per vol.]
660/.2/03   68-54865
   TP9 .E38 MRR Alc.

Elsevier's dictionary of cinema,
sound, and music, in six languages:
Amsterdam, New York, Elsevier Pub.
Co., 1956. 948 p.   778.503   56-
13141
   TR847 .E4 MRR Alc.

Elsevier's dictionary of criminal
science, in eight languages:
Amsterdam, New York, Elsevier Pub.
Co.; [distributed by Van Nostrand,
Princeton, N.J.] 1960. xv, 1460 p.
364.03   59-1258
   HV6017 .E4 MRR Alc.

Elsevier's dictionary of electronics
and waveguides, 2d ed., rev. and
enl. Amsterdam, New York, Elsevier
Pub. Co., 1966 [i.e. 1965] 833 p.
621.38103   65-20142
   TK7804 .E4 1965 MRR Alc.

Elsevier's dictionary of general
physics in six languages: Amsterdam,
New York, Elsevier Pub. Co., 1962.
859 p.   530.3   62-13015
   QC5 .E46 MRR Alc.

Elsevier's dictionary of nuclear
science and technology. 2d rev. ed.
Amsterdam, New York, Elsevier Pub.
Co., 1970. 787 p.   [85.00]
539.7/03   72-103357
   QC772 .E4 1970 MRR Alc.

Elsevier's dictionary of television,
radar, and antennas, in six
languages: Amsterdam, New York,
Elsevier Pub. Co., 1955. 760 p.
621.38803   55-6216
   TK6634 .E4 MRR Alc.

Elsevier's lexicon of archive
terminology: Amsterdam, New York,
Elsevier Pub. Co., 1964. 83 p.
025.171014   64-56714
   CD945 .E4 MRR Alc.

Elsevier's medical dictionary in five
languages: Amsterdam, New York,
Elsevier Pub. Co., 1964. 1588 p.
610.3   62-13022
   R121 .E5 1964 MRR Alc.

Elsevier's wood dictionary in seven
languages: Amsterdam, New York,
Elsevier Pub. Co., 1964-   v.
634.903   64-14178
   SD431 .E4 MRR Alc.

Frey, Albert Romer, Dictionary of
numismatic names, [New York] Barnes
& Noble [1947] ix, 311, 94 p.
737.03   48-5357
   CJ67 .F7 1947 MRR Alc.

Great Britain. Naval intelligence
division. A dictionary of naval
equivalents covering English, French,
Italian, Spanish, Russian, Swedish,
Danish, Dutch, German. London, H.M.
Stationery off., 1924. 2 v.   24-
23792
   V24 .G7 MRR Alc.

Hétnyelvű sportszótár: Budapest,
Terra, 1960-   v.   61-21333
   GV567 .H45 MRR Alc.

International Chamber of Commerce.
Dictionary of advertising and
distribution, Basel, Verlag für
Recht und Gesellschaft, 1954. 1 v.
(unpaged)   659.103   54-24644
   HF5803 .I58 1954 MRR Alc.

International Commission on Large
Dams. Dictionnaire technique des
barrages. 2. ed. [Paris, 1960?]
380 p.   627.803   61-805
   TC540 .I45 1960 MRR Alc.

International insurance dictionary:
[n.p., European Conference of
Insurance Supervisory Services, 1959]
xxxi, 1083 p.   368.03   61-35675
   HG8025 .I5 MRR Alc.

International Railway Documentation
Bureau. Lexique général des termes
ferroviaires, [2. éd. entièrement
refondue et augm.] Amsterdam, J. H.
De Bussy, 1965. 1357 p.   625.1003
66-87434
   TF9 .I46 1965 MRR Alc.

Jacks, Graham Vernon. Multilingual
vocabulary of soil science. [2d ed.,
rev. Rome] Land & Water Division,
Food and Agriculture Organization of
the United Nations [1960] xxiii, 428
p.   631.403   60-50105
   S591 .J26 1960 MRR Alc.

Kleczek, Josip. Astronomical
dictionary. [Vyd. 1.] Praha, Nakl.
Československé akademie věd, 1961.
972 p.   62-25391
   QB14 .K55 MRR Alc.

Labarre, E. J. Dictionary and
encyclopædia of paper and paper-
making, 2d ed., rev. and enl.
London, Oxford University Press,
1952. xxi, 488 p.   676.03   53-29414

   TS1085 .L3 1952a MRR Alc.

Lana, Gabriella. Glossary of
geographical names in six languages:
Amsterdam, New York, Elsevier Pub.
Co., 1967. 184 p.   910/.003   66-
25762
   G104.5 .L3 MRR Ref Desk.

ITALIAN LANGUAGE--DICTIONARIES-- (Cont.)
Lexicon opthalmologicum; Basel, New York, S. Karger, 1959. 223 p.
617.703 59-4669
RE21 .L45 MRR Alc.

Pisant, Emmanuel. International dictionary. Paris, Editions Moderninter [1958] 373 p. 413 58-26075
P361 .P5 MRR Alc.

Rae, Kenneth, ed. Lexique international de termes techniques de theatre Bruxelles, Elsevier [1959] 139 p. 60-26926
PN2035 .R3 MRR Alc.

Sachs, Wolfgang, ed. Lgbensversicherungstechnisches Worterbuch. Wurzburg, K. Thiltsch, 1954. 308 p. 56-16246
HG8759 .S3 MRR Alc.

Six-language dictionary of automation, electronics and scientific instruments; London, Iliffe Books; Englewood Cliffs, N.J., Prentice-Hall [1962] 732 p.
621.3803 63-5414
TK7804 .S5 1962 MRR Alc.

Skandinaviska banken, a.-b. Banking terms: French, German, Italian, Spanish, Swedish. Stockholm [1964] 65 p. 65-87814
HG151 .S46 MRR Alc.

Smith, William James, A dictionary of musical terms in four languages. London, Hutchinson [1961] 195 p. 61-65056
ML108 .S64D5 MRR Alc.

Townsend, Derek. Advertising and public relations; London, A. Redman [1964] xvi, 152 p. 65-6026
HF5803 .T6 MRR Alc.

ITALIAN LANGUAGE--ETYMOLOGY--DICTIONARIES.
Devoto, Giacomo. Avviamento alla etimologia italiana. 2. edizione riveduta e ampliata. Firenze, F. Le Monnier, 1968. xii, 501 p. [4800] 452/.03 74-418072
PC1580 .D4 1968 MRR Alc.

Olivieri, Dante. Dizionario etimologico italiano, Milano, Ceschina [1953] 811 p. 452.03 54-15334
PC1580 .O4 MRR Alc.

Satta, Luciano. Come si dice. Firenze, Sansoni, 1968. xi, 420 p. [3800] 70-418060
PC1460 .S35 MRR Alc.

ITALIAN LANGUAGE--GLOSSARIES, VOCABULARIES, ETC.
Glendening, P. J. T. Beyond the dictionary in Italian, New York, Funk & Wagnalls [1964, c1963] 159 p. 458.3 64-15860
PC1680 .G5 1964 MRR Alc.

ITALIAN LANGUAGE--GLOSSARIES, VOCABULARIES, ETC.--POLYGLOT.
Lessere, Samuel E. Harian's foreign language speak-easy, [3d ed.] Greenlawn, N.Y., Harian Publications [1957] 106 p. 418.24 57-14033
PE1635 .L4 1957 MRR Alc.

ITALIAN LANGUAGE--IDIOMS, CORRECTIONS, ERRORS.
Pekelis, Carla. A dictionary of colorful Italian idioms; New York, G. Braziller [1965] 226 p. 453.1 65-14601
PC1460 .P4 MRR Alc.

Satta, Luciano. Come si dice. Firenze, Sansoni, 1968. xi, 420 p. [3800] 70-418060
PC1460 .S35 MRR Alc.

ITALIAN LANGUAGE--SPOKEN ITALIAN.
Glendening, P. J. T. Beyond the dictionary in Italian, New York, Funk & Wagnalls [1964, c1963] 159 p. 458.3 64-15860
PC1680 .G5 1964 MRR Alc.

ITALIAN LANGUAGE--SYNONYMS AND ANTONYMS.
Gabrielli, Aldo, Dizionario dei sinonimi e dei contrari, Milano, IEI, 1967. 866 p. [L10000] 453.1 68-115990
PC1591 .G3 MRR Alc.

Tommaseo, Niccolò, Dizionario dei sinonimi della lingua italiana. Nuovissima ed., accuratamente corr. Milano, Bietti [1935] lviii, [2], 1330 p. 454 37-16097
PC1591 .T65 1935 MRR Alc.

ITALIAN LITERATURE--19TH CENTURY--BIBLIOGRAPHY.
Pagliaini, Attilio, Catalogo generale della libreria italiana dall'anno 1847 a tutto il 1899, Milano, Associazione tipografico-libraria italiana, 1901-05. 3 v. it 01-21
Z2341 .A85 MRR Alc.

ITALIAN LITERATURE--20TH CENTURY--BIBLIOGRAPHY.
Pagliaini, Attilio, Catalogo generale della libreria italiana dall'anno 1847 a tutto il 1899, Milano, Associazione tipografico-libraria italiana, 1901-05. 3 v. it 01-21
Z2341 .A85 MRR Alc.

United States. Library of Congress. Acquisitions Dept. European imprints for the war years Washington, 1945-46. 3 v. 015.4 45-37835
Z663.76 .E8 MRR Alc.

ITALIAN LITERATURE--20TH CENTURY--BIO-BIBLIOGRAPHY.
Triggiani, Domenico, Dizionario degli scrittori. [1. ed.] Bari, Triggiani editore [1960] 221 p. 61-28580
PQ4057 .T7 MRR Biog.

ITALIAN LITERATURE--BIBLIOGRAPHY.
Frattarolo, Renzo. Introduzione bibliografica alla letteratura italiana. [Roma] Edizioni dell'Ateneo [1963] 194 p. 64-54820

Z2351 .F7 MRR Alc.

Golden, Herbert Hershel, Modern Italian language and literature; Cambridge, Harvard University Press, 1959. x, 207 p. 016.4504 59-14742

Z2355.A2 G6 MRR Alc.

Libri d'Italia; 1947-58. [Firenze] Sansoni. 52-23153
Z2341 .L53 MRR Alc Full set

Ottino, Giuseppe, Bibliotheca bibliographica Italica; Graz, Akademische Druck- u. Verlangsanstalt, 1957. 6 v. in 1. 58-42417
Z2341.A1 O8 1957 MRR Alc.

ITALIAN LITERATURE--BIBLIOGRAPHY--CATALOGS.
Associazione italiana editori. Catalogo collettivo della libreria italiana, 1959. Milano, Società anonima per pubblicazioni bibliografico-editoriali [1959?] 3 v. (11, dxxvii, 62, 3105 p.) 62-45507
Z2341 .A83 1959 MRR Alc.

ITALIAN LITERATURE--BIO-BIBLIOGRAPHY.
Dizionario degli scrittori italiani d'oggi. Cosenza, Pellegrini, 1969. 269 p. [10000] 74-449684
Z2350 .D58 MRR Biog.

Fusco, Enrico M. Scrittori e idee; Torino, Società editrice internazionale [1956] xii, 626 p. 56-41593
PQ4006 .F8 MRR Biog.

ITALIAN LITERATURE--BIO-BIBLIOGRAPHY--INDEXES.
Ferrari, Luigi, Onomasticon; Milano, U. Hoepli, 1947. xlvi, 708 p. 015.45 49-17429
Z2350 .F4 1947 MRR Alc.

ITALIAN LITERATURE--DICTIONARIES, INDEXES, ETC.
Fusco, Enrico M. Scrittori e idee; Torino, Società editrice internazionale [1956] xii, 626 p. 56-41593
PQ4006 .F8 MRR Biog.

ITALIAN LITERATURE--HISTORY AND CRITICISM.
De Sanctis, Francesco, History of Italian literature New York, Basic Books [1960, c1958] 2 v. (viii, 972 p.) 850.9 60-16100
PQ4037 .D413 1960 MRR Alc.

Wilkins, Ernest Hatch, A history of Italian literature. Cambridge, Harvard University Press, 1954. 523 p. 850.9 54-5185
PQ4038 .W5 MRR Alc.

ITALIAN LITERATURE--HISTORY AND CRITICISM--BIBLIOGRAPHY.
Prezzolini, Giuseppe, Repertorio bibliografico della storia e della critica della letteratura italiana ... Roma, Edizioni Roma [1937-48] 4 v. 016.8509 40-5586
Z2351 .P93 MRR Alc.

ITALIAN NEWSPAPERS--DIRECTORIES.
Repertorio analitico della stampa italiana, quotidiani e periodici. 1964- Milano, Messaggerie italiane. 65-34474
Z6956.I8 R4 MRR Alc Latest edition / MRR Alc Latest edition

ITALIAN PERIODICALS--DIRECTORIES.
Repertorio analitico della stampa italiana, quotidiani e periodici. 1964- Milano, Messaggerie italiane. 65-34474
Z6956.I8 R4 MRR Alc Latest edition / MRR Alc Latest edition

ITALIAN PHILOLOGY--BIBLIOGRAPHY.
Golden, Herbert Hershel, Modern Italian language and literature; Cambridge, Harvard University Press, 1959. x, 207 p. 016.4504 59-14742

Z2355.A2 G6 MRR Alc.

ITALIAN POETRY.
The Oxford book of Italian verse, 2d ed., rev. Oxford, Clarendon Press, 1952. xxxvi, 615 p. 851.082 52-14934
PQ4208 .O8 1952 MRR Alc.

ITALIAN POETRY--20TH CENTURY.
Golino, Carlo Luigi, ed. Contemporary Italian poetry; Berkeley, University of California Press, 1962. 223 p. 851.91082 62-7436
PQ4214 .G6 MRR Alc.

Spagnoletti, Giacinto, ed. Poesia italiana contemporanea, 1909-1959. [Parma] Guanda [1961] 1003 p. 62-43979
PQ4214 .S63 MRR Alc.

ITALIAN POETRY--TRANSLATIONS INTO ENGLISH.
Golino, Carlo Luigi, ed. Contemporary Italian poetry; Berkeley, University of California Press, 1962. 223 p. 851.91082 62-7436
PQ4214 .G6 MRR Alc.

ITALIANS IN THE UNITED STATES.
Italian-American who's who; New York, Vigo Press. 325.2450973 [920.073] 38-15649
E184.I8 I7 MRR Biog Latest edition

Musmanno, Michael Angelo. The story of the Italians in America [1st ed.] Garden City, N.Y., Doubleday, 1965. x, 300 p. 873.09745 65-17234
E184.I8 M8 MRR Alc.

ITALY.
Grindrod, Muriel. Italy. London, Benn, 1968. 260 p. [42/-] 914.5 68-112732
DG417 .G7 1968 MRR Alc.

ITALY--ADMINISTRATIVE AND POLITICAL DIVISIONS.
Nuovo dizionario dei comuni e frazioni di comune con le circoscrizioni amministrative. Roma, Dizionario Voghera dei comuni [etc.] 12-20395
DG415.N82 MRR Alc Latest edition

ITALY--BIBLIOGRAPHY.
Borroni, Fabia. "Il Cicognara," Firenze, Sansoni, 1954- v. 55-18980
Z2357 .B6 MRR Alc.

Cruger, Doris M. A list of American doctoral dissertations on Africa, Ann Arbor, Mich., Xerox, University Microfilms Library Services, 1967. 36 p. 016.378/24 67-5644
Z5055.U49 C75 MRR Alc.

Enciclopedia biografica e bibliografica "Italiana." Milano, E.B.B.I., Istituto editoriale italiano B. C. Tosi, s.a. [1936- v. 920.045 42-5536
CT1123 .E6 MRR Biog.

Ottino, Giuseppe, Bibliotheca bibliographica Italica; Graz, Akademische Druck- u. Verlangsanstalt, 1957. 6 v. in 1. 58-42417
Z2341.A1 O8 1957 MRR Alc.

Pagliaini, Attilio, Catalogo generale della libreria italiana dall'anno 1847 a tutto il 1899, Milano, Associazione tipografico-libraria italiana, 1901-05. 3 v. it 01-21
Z2341 .A85 MRR Alc.

ITALY--BIO-BIBLIOGRAPHY.
Gubernatis, Angelo de, conte, Dictionnaire international des ecrivains du monde latin, Rome, Chez l'auteur; [etc., etc.] 1905. xii, 1506 p. 06-46763
Z1010 .G93 MRR Biog.

ITALY--BIO-BIBLIOGRAPHY. (Cont.)
Gubernatis, Angelo de, conte,
Dizionario biografico degli scrittori
contemporanei. Firenze, Coi tipi dei
successori Le Monier, 1879. xxxii,
1276 p.   02-2811
Z1010 .G92 MRR Biog.

ITALY--BIOGRAPHY.
Il Chi è? nella finanza italiana.
1955- Milano, Casa Editrice Nuova
Mercurio, [etc.]   56-33152
HG186.I8 C47 MRR Alc Latest
edition

Confederazione fascista dei
professionisti e degli artisti.
Dizionario dei Siciliani illustri.
Palermo, F. Ciuni, libraio editore,
1939. 3 p. l., [9]-537 p., 3 l.   ac
40-2374
CT1135.S5 C6 MRR Biog.

Dizionario biografico degli Italiani.
Roma, Istituto della Enciclopedia
italiana [1960- v.   61-34965
CT1123 .D5 MRR Biog.

Garollo, Gottardo, Dizionario
biografico universale. Milano, U.
Hoepli, 1907. 2 v.   08-25727
CT163 .G3 MRR Biog.

Gastaldi, Mario. Dizionario delle
scrittrici italiane contemporanee
Milano, Gastaldi [1957] 247 p.   59-
30423
CT3450 .G3 1957 MRR Biog.

Vaccaro, Gennaro, ed. Panorama
biografico degli italiani d'oggi.
Roma, A. Curcio [1956] 2 v. (xv,
1648 p.) 57-25416
CT1133 .V3 MRR Biog.

Who's who in Italy. 1957/58-
Milano, Intercontinental Book & Pub.
920.045 60-3514
DG578 .W5 MRR Biog Latest edition

ITALY--BIOGRAPHY--DICTIONARIES.
Chi è? 1928- Roma, Filippo Scarano
Editore [etc.]   29-25790
DG463 .C62 MRR Biog Latest edition

Cosenza, Mario Emilio, Biographical
and bibliographical dictionary of the
Italian humanists [2d ed., rev. and
enl. Boston, G. K. Hall, 1962]-67.
6 v.   820.045 62-13227
Z7128.H9 C6 MRR Alc.

Dizionario degli scrittori italiani
d'oggi. Cosenza, Pellegrini, 1969.
269 p. [10000]   74-448684
Z2350 .D58 MRR Biog.

Enciclopedia biografica e
bibliografica "Italiana." Milano,
E.B.B.I., Istituto editoriale
italiano B. C. Tosi, s.a. [1936- v.
820.045 42-5536
CT1123 .E6 MRR Biog.

The New Century Italian Renaissance
encyclopedia. New York, Appleton-
Century-Crofts [1972] xiii, 978 p.
914.5/03/503 76-181735
DG537.8.A1 N48 MRR Biog.

ITALY--COMMERCE--DIRECTORIES.
Guida economica della Sicilia,
Sardegna e Mezzogiorno d'Italia.
[1.]- ed.; 1946- Roma [etc.]
G.I.P.I 49-17748
HC307.S5 G8 MRR Alc Latest edition

Guida Monaci. Roma. 54-54206
"Fondata nel 1871."
DG804 .G8 MRR Alc Latest edition

Kompass; repertorio generale
dell'economia italiana; register of
Italian industry and commerce.
Milano, ETAS-KOMPASS Edizioni per
l'informazione economica. 65-30593
Began publication with 1962/63
edition.
HF3583 .K6 MRR Alc Latest edition

ITALY--COMMERCE--UNITED STATES.
United States-Italy trade directory.
1st- 1955- [New York] 56-2988
HF3101 .A583 MRR Alc Latest
edition

ITALY--DESCRIPTION AND TRAVEL.
Walker, Donald Smith. A geography of
Italy. 2nd ed. London, Methuen,
1967. xi, 296 p. [70/-] 914.5 67-
99883
DG418 .W3 1967 MRR Alc.

**ITALY--DESCRIPTION AND TRAVEL--1945- --
GUIDE-BOOKS.**
Clark, Sydney Aylmer, All the best
in Italy New York, Dodd, Mead [1968]
x, 572 p. [7.95] 914.5/04/92 68-
24865
DG416 .C6 1968 MRR Alc.

Guida del turista; Milano, Editrice
Vogarte italiana [etc.] 57-28620
DG416 .G79 MRR Alc Latest edition

Michelin: Italie. 1967- Paris, Pneu
Michelin, Services de Tourisme.
914.5/04/92 72-627451
DG416 .I8148 MRR Alc Latest
edition

Touring club italiano. Vademecum del
turista. [Milano] 57-48011
DG413 .T6 MRR Alc Latest edition

**ITALY--DESCRIPTION AND TRAVEL--GUIDE-
BOOKS.**
Barbieri, Pietro, Guide de l'Italie
catholique, 2. ed. Ed. française
rev, Paris, Éditions du Témoignage
chrétien, 1950. xii, 1338 p.   282
51-28419
BX842 .B314 1950 MRR Alc.

Fodor's Italy. New York, D. McKay.
914.5/04/92 72-622644
DG416 .I817 MRR Alc Latest edition

Olson, Harvey Stuart, Olson's
complete motoring guide to France,
Switzerland & Italy, [1st ed.]
Philadelphia, Lippincott [1967] xiv,
964 p. 914.4/04/83 66-16661
GV1025.F7 O4 MRR Alc.

ITALY--DESCRIPTION AND TRAVEL--TOURS.
Gibbons annual index of daily sight-
seeing tours: Rome, Paris, Florence,
London. [Los Angeles] 914 72-80819

D909 .G5 MRR Alc Latest edition

ITALY--DIRECTORIES.
Guida Monaci. Roma. 54-54206
"Fondata nel 1871."
DG804 .G8 MRR Alc Latest edition

Touring club italiano. Vademecum del
turista. [Milano] 57-48011
DG413 .T6 MRR Alc Latest edition

ITALY--ECONOMIC CONDITIONS--1945-
Grindrod, Muriel. Italy. London,
Benn, 1968. 260 p. [42/-] 914.5
68-112732
DG417 .G7 1968 MRR Alc.

**ITALY--ECONOMIC CONDITIONS--1945- --
YEARBOOKS.**
Organization for Economic Cooperation
and Development. Economic surveys:
Italy. 1954- [Paris] 55-28
HC301 .O69 MRR Alc Latest edition

**ITALY--EXECUTIVE DEPARTMENTS--
DIRECTORIES.**
Italy. Parlamento. Annuario
parlamentare. 1948/49- Roma,
Segretariato generale della Camera
dei deputati.   50-30921
JN5445 .A33 MRR Alc Latest edition

ITALY--GAZETTEERS.
Nuovo dizionario dei comuni e
frazioni di comune con le
circoscrizioni amministrative. Roma,
Dizionario Voghera dei comuni [etc.]
12-20395
DG415.N82 MRR Alc Latest edition

United States. Office of Geography.
Italy and associated areas;
Washington, U.S. Govt. Print. Off.,
1956. vi, 369 p. 914.5 56-63926
DG415 .U5 MRR Alc.

ITALY--HISTORY.
Grindrod, Muriel. Italy. London,
Benn, 1968. 260 p. [42/-] 914.5
68-112732
DG417 .G7 1968 MRR Alc.

Mack Smith, Denis, Italy; a modern
history. New ed. rev. and enl. Ann
Arbor, University of Michigan Press
[1969] xi, 542, xxx p. [8.50] 945
69-15851
DG467 .M3 1969 MRR Alc.

Musmanno, Michael Angelo. The story
of the Italians in America [1st ed.]
Garden City, N.Y., Doubleday, 1965.
x, 300 p. 973.09745 65-17234
E184.I8 M8 MRR Alc.

Trevelyan, Janet Penrose (Ward) A
short history of the Italian people,
Rev. [i.e. 4th] ed. London, Allen &
Unwin [1956] 425 p. 945 56-3772
DG468 .T7 1956 MRR Alc.

ITALY--HISTORY--1870-1915.
Seton-Watson, Christopher. Italy
from liberalism to fascism, 1870-
1925. London, Methuen; New York,
Barnes & Noble, 1967. x, 772 p.
[£6/-/-] 945.09 67-114393
DG555 .S4 1967 MRR Alc.

ITALY--HISTORY--1914-1945.
Seton-Watson, Christopher. Italy
from liberalism to fascism, 1870-
1925. London, Methuen; New York,
Barnes & Noble, 1967. x, 772 p.
[£6/-/-] 945.09 67-114393
DG555 .S4 1967 MRR Alc.

ITALY--HISTORY--1945-
Kogan, Norman. A political history
of postwar Italy. London, Pall Mall
P.; 1966. x, 252 p. [42/-]
945.092 67-72567
DG577 .K6 1966a MRR Alc.

ITALY--HISTORY--BIBLIOGRAPHY.
Bertocci, Giuseppe. Repertorio
bibliografico delle opere stampate in
Italia nel secolo XIX, Roma,
Tipografia di M. Armanni, 1876-87. 3
v. in 2   03-25848
Z2356 .B45 MRR Alc.

Bibliografia storica nazionale. Bari
[etc.] Gius. Laterza & Figli. 52-
23151
Z6201 .B54 MRR Alc Full set
Began publication in 1939.

ITALY--HISTORY--DICTIONARIES.
Freri, Orlando, Dizionario storico
italiano. Milano, Ceschina [1940] 4
p. l., [11]-399, [1] p.   945.003 44-
45073
DG461 .F7 MRR Alc.

ITALY--IMPRINTS.
Associazione italiana editori.
Catalogo collettivo della libreria
italiana, 1959. Milano, Società
anonima per pubblicazioni
bibliografico-editoriali [1959?] 3
v. (11, dxxvii, 62, 3105 p.) 62-
45507
Z2341 .A83 1959 MRR Alc.

Associazione italiana editori.
Catalogo dei libri italiani in
commercio. Milano, Associazione
italiana editori, 1970- v.   71-
19147
Z2341 .A833 MRR Alc.

Florence. Biblioteca nazionale
centrale. Catalogo cumulativo 1886-
1957 del Bollettino delle
pubblicazioni italiane Nendeln,
Liechtenstein, Kraus Reprint, 1968-
69. 41 v.   015/.45 68-28680
Z2345 .F65 MRR Alc.

Michel, Suzanne,P. Répertoire des
ouvrages imprimés en langue
italienne au XVIIe siecle Firenze,
L. S. Olschki, 1970- v.   [L17500
(v. 1)]   70-558790
Z2342 .M52 MRR Alc.

Michel, Suzanne,P. Répertoire des
ouvrages imprimés en langue
italienne au XVIIe siecle conservés
dans les bibliotheques de France
Paris, Éditions du Centre national
de la recherche scientifique, 1967-
v.   [38.00 (v. 1) varies]
015/.45 67-69528
Z2342 .M5 MRR Alc.

The National union catalog, pre-1956
imprints; London, Mansell, 1968- v.
021.6/4 67-30001
Z663.7.L5115 MRR Alc (Dk 33)

Ottino, Giuseppe, Biblioteca
bibliographica Italica; Graz,
Akademische Druck- u.
Verlagsanstalt, 1957. 6 v. in 1.
58-42417
Z2341.A1 O8 1957 MRR Alc.

Rome (City) Centro nazionale per il
catalogo unico delle biblioteche
italiane e per le informazioni
bibliografiche. Primo catalogo
collettivo delle biblioteche
italiane. Roma, 1962- v.   63-
50852
Z933 .A1R6 MRR Alc (Dk 33).

United States. Library of Congress.
Acquisitions Dept. European imprints
for the war years Washington, 1945-
46. 3 v. 015.4 45-37835
Z663.76 .E8 MRR Alc.

ITALY--INDUSTRIES.
Confederazione generale
dell'industria italiana. Annuario.
Roma. 29-16715
HC305 .C65 MRR Alc Latest edition

ITALY--INDUSTRIES--DIRECTORIES.
Annuario politecnico italiano;
Milano. 605.8 46-43840
Publication began in 1916.
T12.5.I75 A5 MRR Alc Latest
edition

ITALY--INDUSTRY--DIRECTORIES.
Kompass; repertorio generale
dell'economia italiana; register of
Italian industry and commerce.
Milano, ETAS-KOMPASS Edizioni per
l'informazione economica. 65-30593
Began publication with 1962/63
edition.
HF3583 .K6 MRR Alc Latest edition

ITALY--INTELLECTUAL LIFE--DIRECTORIES.
Triggiani, Domenico, Dizionario
degli scrittori. [1. ed.] Bari,
Triggiani editore [1960] 221 p.   61-
28580
PQ4057 .T7 MRR Biog.

ITALY--MANUFACTURES--DIRECTORIES.
Annuario politecnico italiano;
Milano . 605.8 46-43840
Publication began in 1916.
T12.5.I75 A5 MRR Alc Latest
edition

ITALY--POLITICS AND GOVERNMENT--20TH
CENTURY.
Hughes, Serge. The fall and rise of
modern Italy. New York, Macmillan
[1967] xiv, 322 p. 320.9/45 67-
26058
DG555 .H8 MRR Alc.

ITALY--POLITICS AND GOVERNMENT--1945-
Grindrod, Muriel. Italy. London,
Benn, 1968. 260 p. [42/-] 914.5
68-112732
DG417 .G7 1968 MRR Alc.

ITALY--POLITICS AND GOVERNMENT--
HANDBOOKS, MANUALS, ETC.
Italy. Parlamento. Annuario
parlamentare. 1948/49- Roma,
Segretariato generale della Camera
dei deputati. 50-30921
JN5445 .A33 MRR Alc Latest edition

ITALY--REGISTERS.
Italy. Parlamento. Annuario
parlamentare. 1948/49- Roma,
Segretariato generale della Camera
dei deputati. 50-30921
JN5445 .A33 MRR Alc Latest edition

ITALY--STATISTICS.
Compendio statistico italiano.
[Roma] Istituto centrale di
statistica. 74-642448
HA1362 .A32 MRR Alc Latest edition

Organization for Economic Cooperation
and Development. Economic surveys:
Italy. 1954- [Paris] 55-28
HC301 .O69 MRR Alc Latest edition

ITALY--STATISTICS--YEARBOOKS.
Italy. Istituto centrale di
statistica. Annuario statistico
italiano. 3.- serie; 1927- Roma.
314.5 35-32461
HA1367 .A3 MRR Alc Latest edition

ITALY--IMPRINTS.
Libri d'Italia; 1947-58. [Firenze]
Sansoni. 52-23153
Z2341 .L53 MRR Alc Full set

ITALY, SOUTHERN--DESCRIPTION AND TRAVEL-
-GUIDE-BOOKS.
Gunn, Peter. The companion guide to
Southern Italy. London, Collins,
1969. 446 p. [45/-] 914.5/7/0492
74-438796
DG416 .G86 MRR Alc.

ITALY, SOUTHERN--ECONOMIC CONDITIONS--
YEARBOOKS.
Guida economica della Sicilia,
Sardegna e Mezzogiorno d'Italia.
[1.]- ed.; 1946- Roma [etc.]
G.I.P.I. 49-17748
HC307.S5 G8 MRR Alc Latest edition

IVORY COAST.
Roberts, Thomas Duval, Area handbook
for Ivory Coast. 2d ed.
[Washington; For sale by the Supt. of
Docs., U.S. Govt. Print. Off., 1973.
lxvi, 449 p. [$6.35] 916.66/8/035
73-600169
DT545 .R58 1973 MRR Alc.

IVORY COAST--GAZETTEERS.
United States. Office of Geography.
Ivory Coast; official standard names
approved by the United States Board
on Geographic Names. Washington,
1965. iv, 250 p. 65-61753
DT545.2 .U5 MRR Alc.

JACKSON, ANDREW, PRES. U.S., 1767-1845.
Bassett, John Spencer, The life of
Andrew Jackson. [Hamden, Conn.]
Archon Books, 1967. xix, 766 p.
973.5/6/0924 B 67-26659
E382 .B35 1967 MRR Alc.

James, Marquis, Andrew Jackson,
portrait of a president,
Indianapolis, New York, The Bobbs-
Merrill company [c1937] 627 p.
923.173 37-28638
E382 .J27 MRR Alc.

Van Deusen, Glyndon Garlock, The
Jacksonian era, 1828-1848. [1st ed.]
New York, Harper [1959] 291 p.
973.56 58-13810
E338 .V2 MRR Alc.

JAILS
see Prisons

JAMAICA--BIOGRAPHY.
Who's who in Canada; Toronto,
International Press Limited. 17-
16282
Began publication in 1910.
F1033 .W62 Sci RR Latest edition /
MRR Biog Latest edition

Who's who Jamaica, British West
Indies. Kingston, Jamaica, B. W. I.,
Who's who (Jamaica) ltd. [etc.]
920.07292 41-24194
Publication began with issue for
1934/35.
F1865 .W63 MRR Biog Latest edition

JAMAICA--HISTORY.
Black, Clinton Vane de Brosse, The
story of Jamaica from prehistory to
the present [Rev. ed.] London,
Collins, 1965. 255 p. 66-36376
F1881 .B79 1965 MRR Alc.

JAMAICA--POLITICS AND GOVERNMENT.
The Handbook of Jamaica, Jamaica,
Govt. Print. Off., New York [etc.]
Gillespie Co. [etc.] 13-9047
Began publication in 1881.
F1861 .H23 MRR Alc Latest edition

JAMAICA--REGISTERS.
The Handbook of Jamaica, Jamaica,
Govt. Print. Off., New York [etc.]
Gillespie Co. [etc.] 13-9047
Began publication in 1881.
F1861 .H23 MRR Alc Latest edition

JAMAICA--STATISTICS.
The Handbook of Jamaica, Jamaica,
Govt. Print. Off., New York [etc.]
Gillespie Co. [etc.] 13-9047
Began publication in 1881.
F1861 .H23 MRR Alc Latest edition

JAMAICA--STATISTICS--PERIODICALS.
Statistical yearbook of Jamaica.
1973- [Kingston] 317.292 74-646385
HA891 .C45a MRR Alc Latest edition

JAPAN.
Chaffee, Frederic H. Area handbook
for Japan. Revision] Washington,
For sale by the Supt. of Docs., U.S.
Govt. Print. Off., 1969. xvi, 628 p.
[4.25] 309.1/51 73-605269
DS806 .C48 MRR Alc.

Japan. Mombushō. Nihon Yunesuko
Kokunai Iinkai. Japan: its land,
people and culture, [Rev. ed.
Tokyo] Print. Bureau, Ministry of
Finance [1964] 885, 200 p. 65-
71358
DS806 .A54 1964 MRR Alc.

Nippon; 1936- Tokyo, Kokusei-sha.
330.952 37-6132
DS801 .N43 MRR Alc Latest edition

JAPAN--BIBLIOGRAPHY.
Borton, Hugh. A selected list of
books and articles on Japan in
English, French, and German, Rev.
and enl. Cambridge, Published by the
Harvard University Press for the
Harvard-Yenching Institute, 1954.
xiv, 272 p. 016.952 53-5055
Z3306 .B67 1954 MRR Alc.

Kerner, Robert Joseph, Northeastern
Asia, a selected bibliography;
Berkeley, Calif., University of
California press, 1939. 2 v.
016.95 39-33136
Z3001 .K38 MRR Alc.

Nihon no Sankō Tosho Henshū Iinkai.
Guide to Japanese reference books.
Chicago, American Library
Association, 1966. 303 p. 66-23396
Z3306 .N5 1966 MRR Alc.

Silberman, Bernard S., Japan and
Korea; a critical bibliography.
Tucson, University of Arizona Press,
1962. xiv, 120 p. 016.95 61-11821
Z3301 .S55 MRR Alc.

United States. Library of Congress.
Far Eastern languages catalog.
Boston, G. K. Hall, 1972. 22 v.
019.1/09753 72-5364
Z3009 .U56 MRR Alc (Dk 33)

United States. Library of Congress.
Division of bibliography.
Bibliography of China, Japan and the
Philippine Islands, [Concord, N.H.,
1925] i. 214-246. 27-14560
Z663.28 .B52 MRR Alc.

JAPAN--BIBLIOGRAPHY--CATALOGS.
Harvard University. Library. China,
Japan, and Korea; classification
schedule. Cambridge, Distributed by
Harvard University Press, 1968. 494
p. 017/.1 68-14151
Z3109 .H3 MRR Alc.

JAPAN--BIO-BIBLIOGRAPHY.
Teng, Ssu-yu, Japanese studies on
Japan & the Far East; [Hong Kong]
Hong Kong University Press, 1961. x,
485 p. 016.915 61-66803
Z3306 .T4 MRR Alc.

JAPAN--BIOGRAPHY.
Japan company directory. 1957-
[Tokyo] Oriental economist. 62-29293
HC161 .J35 MRR Alc Latest edition

JAPAN--BIOGRAPHY--DICTIONARIES.
Japan. Mombushō. Nihon Yunesuko
Kokunai Iinkai. Who's who among
Japanese writers. [Tokyo, 1957] 140
p. 63-48768
PL723 .J3 MRR Biog.

The Japan biographical encyclopedia &
who's who. 1st- ed.; 1958- Tokyo,
Japan Biographical Research Dept.,
Rengo Press. 920.052 58-1808
DS834 .J7 MRR Biog Latest edition

JAPAN--COMMERCE--DIRECTORIES.
Japan company directory. 1957-
[Tokyo] Oriental economist. 62-29293
HC161 .J35 MRR Alc Latest edition

The Japan times directory of foreign
residents, business firms &
organizations. Tokyo, Japan Times,
ltd. 915.2 72-627115
HE9463 .J3 MRR Alc Latest edition

O. K. business directory. Hongkong
[O.K. Print Press] 53-30505
HF3779.H65 O15 MRR Alc Latest
edition

The Oriental economist's Japan
economic yearbook. [Tokyo] Oriental
economist. 55-40192
HC461 .O65 MRR Alc Latest edition

Standard trade index of Japan.
Tokyo, Japan Chamber of Commerce and
Industry. 55-36368
HF3823 .S7 MRR Alc Latest edition

Tokyo news business directory. 1950-
Tokyo, Tokyo News Service.
338/.0025 51-14706
HF5257.T6 T57 MRR Alc Latest
edition

JAPAN--DESCRIPTION AND TRAVEL--1945-
Trewartha, Glenn Thomas, Japan, a
geography Madison, University of
Wisconsin Press, 1965. x, 652 p.
915.2 65-11200
DS811 .T72 MRR Alc.

JAPAN--DESCRIPTION AND TRAVEL--GUIDE-
BOOKS.
The New official guide: Japan. 1964-
Tokyo, Japan Travel Bureau. 66-
19335
DS805.2 .N47 MRR Alc Latest
edition

Roberts, Dorothy E. A scholar's
guide to Japan, Rev. ed. Boston,
Christopher Pub. House [1969] viii,
125 p. 915.2/04/4 68-58963
DS811 .R58 1969 MRR Alc.

JAPAN--DESCRIPTION AND TRAVEL--GUIDE-
BOOKS--PERIODICALS.
Fodor's Japan and East Asia. 1972-
New York, D. McKay. 915.2/04/4 72-
621341
DS805.2 F64 MRR Alc Latest edition

JAPAN--DICTIONARIES AND ENCYCLOPEDIAS.
Bush, Lewis William, Japanalia; a
concise cyclopaedia [6th, rev. and
enl. ed. Tokyo] Tokyo News Service
[1965] xi, 420 p. 915.2003 65-
29262
DS805 .B8 1965 MRR Alc.

Papinot, Edmond, Historical and
geographical dictionary of Japan.
Ann Arbor, Overbeck Co., 1948. xiv,
842 p. 952.003 49-3327
DS833 .P3 1948 MRR Alc.

JAPAN--ECONOMIC CONDITIONS--1918-
Japan trade guide, with a
comprehensive mercantile directory.
1935- [Tokyo] JiJi Press [etc.]
338.0952 35-20033
HF3823 .J35 MRR Alc Latest edition

JAPAN--ECONOMIC CONDITIONS--1945-
Japan: a businessman's guide. New
York, American Heritage Press [1970]
xviii, 269 p. [6.95] 330.952 71-
109173
HC462.9 .J3 1970 MRR Alc.

JAPAN--ECONOMIC CONDITIONS--1945- --
YEARBOOKS.
The President directory. [Tokyo,
Diamond-Time Co.] [$8.00]
338.7/4/02552 73-645008
Began in 1967.
HC461 .P83 MRR Alc Latest edition

JAPAN--ECONOMIC CONDITIONS--
BIBLIOGRAPHY.
United States. Library of Congress.
Division of bibliography. Japan--
economic development and foreign
policy, Washington, 1940. 36 p.
016.330952 41-14197
Z663.28 .J18 MRR Alc.

United States. Library of Congress.
Division of bibliography. ... The
Japanese empire: industries and
transportation, Washington, 1943. 1
p. l., 56 p. 016.330952 43-50835
Z663.28 .J2 MRR Alc.

JAPAN--ECONOMIC CONDITIONS--YEARBOOKS.
The Oriental economist's Japan
economic yearbook. [Tokyo] Oriental
economist. 55-40192
    HC461 .O65 MRR Alc Latest edition

JAPAN--FOREIGN RELATIONS--BIBLIOGRAPHY.
United States. Library of Congress.
Division of bibliography. Japan--
economic development and foreign
policy. Washington, 1940. 36 p.
016.330952 41-14187
    Z663.28 .J18 MRR Alc.

Uyehara, Cecil H., comp. Checklist
of archives in the Japanese Ministry
of Foreign Affairs, Tokyo, Japan,
1868-1945: Washington,
Photoduplication Service, Library of
Congress, 1954. xii, 262 p.
016.32752 53-60045
    Z663.96 .C5 MRR Alc.

JAPAN--FOREIGN RELATIONS--UNITED STATES.
Reischauer, Edwin Oldfather, The
United States and Japan. Rev. ed.
Cambridge, Harvard University Press,
1957. 394 p. 327.730952 57-9082
    E183.8.J3 R4 1957 MRR Alc.

JAPAN--GAZETTEERS.
United States. Office of Geography.
Japan; Washington, U.S. Govt. Print.
Off., 1955. 3,731 p. 915.2 55-
63681
    DS805 .U525 MRR Alc.

JAPAN--HISTORY.
Borton, Hugh. Japan's modern
century; 2d ed. New York, Ronald
Press [1970] x, 610 p. 952.03 70-
110544
    DS835 .B6 1970 MRR Alc.

Hane, Mikiso. Japan; a historical
survey. [New York] Scribner [1972]
xlv, 650 p. [$15.00] 915.2/03 79-
37178
    DS835 .H266 MRR Alc.

Sansom, George Bailey, Sir, A
history of Japan. Stanford, Calif.,
Stanford University press, 1958-63.
3 v. 952 58-11694
    DS835 .S27 MRR Alc.

Tomlin, Eric Walter Frederick, Japan
New York, Walker [1973] 176 p.
[$8.50] 915.2/03 72-87517
    DS835 .T57 1973b MRR Alc.

JAPAN--HISTORY--BIBLIOGRAPHY.
Hall, John Whitney, Japanese
history: Ann Arbor, University of
Michigan Press, 1954. xi, 165 p.
016.952 54-62413
    Z3301 .H3 MRR Alc.

JAPAN--HISTORY--SOURCES--BIBLIOGRAPHY.
Uyehara, Cecil H., comp. Checklist
of archives in the Japanese Ministry
of Foreign Affairs, Tokyo, Japan,
1868-1945: Washington,
Photoduplication Service, Library of
Congress, 1954. xii, 262 p.
016.32752 53-60045
    Z663.96 .C5 MRR Alc.

JAPAN--IMPRINTS.
Ceadel, Eric B. Classified catalogue
of modern Japanese books in Cambridge
University Library. Cambridge, W.
Heffer [c1961] xxvii, 552 p.
015.52 62-6217
    Z3309 .C4 MRR Alc.

United States. Library of Congress.
Far Eastern languages catalog.
Boston, G. K. Hall, 1972. 22 v.
019.1/09753 72-5364
    Z3009 .U56 MRR Alc (Dk 33)

JAPAN--INDUSTRIES.
Japan: a businessman's guide. New
York, American Heritage Press [1970]
xviii, 269 p. [6.95] 330.952 71-
109173
    HC462.9 .J3 1970 MRR Alc.

Japan trade guide, with a
comprehensive mercantile directory.
1935- [Tokyo] JiJi Press [etc.]
338.0952 35-20033
    HF3823 .J35 MRR Alc Latest edition

Organization for Economic Cooperation
and Development. Industrial
production. [Paris,] Organisation
for Economic Co-operation and
Development, 1968. 308 p. [14.00]
338/.09 76-422848
    HC240 .O693 MRR Alc.

JAPAN--INDUSTRIES--DIRECTORIES.
J I T: Tokyo, [Kojunsha
International Publishers]
382/.025/52 68-51013
    HF54.J3 J2 MRR Alc Latest edition

Japan company directory. 1857-
[Tokyo] Oriental economist. 62-29293
    HC161 .J35 MRR Alc Latest edition

Japan trade guide, with a
comprehensive mercantile directory.
1935- [Tokyo] JiJi Press [etc.]
338.0952 35-20033
    HF3823 .J35 MRR Alc Latest edition

JAPAN--INDUSTRIES--YEARBOOKS.
Nippon: 1936- Tokyo, Kokusei-sha.
330.952 37-6132
    DS801 .N43 MRR Alc Latest edition

JAPAN--LEARNED INSTITUTIONS AND
SOCIETIES.
Japan. Mombushō. Nihon Yunesuko
Kokunai Iinkai. Directory of
researchers and research institutes
on Oriental studies in Japan.
[Tokyo] Japanese National Commission
for UNESCO [1957] 50 p. 068.52 61-
32041
    AS548 .A543 MRR Alc.

Japan. Mombushō. Nihon Yunesuko
Kokunai Iinkai. Museums in Japan.
[Tokyo] Japanese National Commission
for Unesco, 1960. 123 p. 63-34675

    AM77 .A55 MRR Alc.

Roberts, Dorothy E. A scholar's
guide to Japan. Rev. ed. Boston,
Christopher Pub. House [1969] viii,
125 p. 915.2/04/4 68-58963
    DS811 .R58 1969 MRR Alc.

JAPAN--MANUFACTURES--DIRECTORIES.
J I T: Tokyo, [Kojunsha
International Publishers]
382/.025/52 68-51013
    HF54.J3 J2 MRR Alc Latest edition

Japan trade guide, with a
comprehensive mercantile directory.
1935- [Tokyo] JiJi Press [etc.]
338.0952 35-20033
    HF3823 .J35 MRR Alc Latest edition

Standard trade index of Japan.
Tokyo, Japan Chamber of Commerce and
Industry. 55-36368
    HF3823 .S7 MRR Alc Latest edition

JAPAN--POLITICS AND GOVERNMENT--1945-
Japan: a businessman's guide. New
York, American Heritage Press [1970]
xviii, 269 p. [6.95] 330.952 71-
109173
    HC462.9 .J3 1970 MRR Alc.

JAPAN--REGISTERS.
Bidwell, Robin Leonard. The major
powers and western Europe, 1900-1971:
[London] F. Cass, [1973] xi, 297 p.
354/.4/002 72-92958
    JN12 .B5 MRR Ref Desk.

The Japan biographical encyclopedia &
who's who. 1st- ed.; 1958- Tokyo,
Japan Biographical Research Dept.,
Rengo Press. 920.052 58-1808
    DS834 .J7 MRR Biog Latest edition

JAPAN--SOCIAL LIFE AND CUSTOMS.
Japan: a businessman's guide. New
York, American Heritage Press [1970]
xviii, 269 p. [6.95] 330.952 71-
109173
    HC462.9 .J3 1970 MRR Alc.

Jōya, Moku. Mock Joya's Things
Japanese. [2d rev. ed.] Tokyo,
Tokyo News Service [1960] 732 p.
915.2 60-32123
    DS821 .J645 1960 MRR Alc.

JAPAN--STATISTICS.
Nippon: 1936- Tokyo, Kokusei-sha.
330.952 37-6132
    DS801 .N43 MRR Alc Latest edition

Organization for Economic Cooperation
and Development. Basic statistics of
energy, 1950-1964. Paris, O.E.C.D.
[London, H.M.S.O.] 1966. 363 p.
[24/-] 333.8 66-66031
    HD9555.A4 O7 MRR Alc.

Organization for Economic Cooperation
and Development. National accounts
statistics 1950-1968. [Paris, 1970]
415 p. [$7.50 (U.S.)] 339.3 73-
535302
    HC79.I5 O674 MRR Alc.

Organization for Economic Cooperation
and Development. National accounts
statistics, 1960-1971. [Paris, 1973]
471 p. [$7.50 (U.S.)] 339.3 74-
158206
    HC79.I5 O7 1973 MRR Alc.

Organization for Economic Cooperation
and Development. Statistics of
energy, 1953-1967. Paris, 1969. 265
p. 333.8 71-459605
    HD9540.4 .O73 1969 MRR Alc.

The Oriental economist's Japan
economic yearbook. [Tokyo] Oriental
economist. 55-40192
    HC461 .O65 MRR Alc Latest edition

Statistical Office of the European
Communities. Basic statistics of the
community; 8th ed. [Brussels, 1967]
218 p. [unpriced] 314 75-386707

    HA1107 .S7 1967 MRR Alc.

JAPAN. KAIGUN.
Watts, Anthony John. Japanese
warships of World War II Garden
City, N.Y., Doubleday [1967] 400 p.
623.82/5/0952 67-23821
    VA653 .W33 1967 MRR Alc.

JAPANESE ART
see Art, Japanese

JAPANESE IMPRINTS--CATALOGS.
United States. Library of Congress.
Far Eastern languages catalog.
Boston, G. K. Hall, 1972. 22 v.
019.1/09753 72-5364
    Z3009 .U56 MRR Alc (Dk 33)

JAPANESE LANGUAGE--DICTIONARIES--
ENGLISH.
Kenkyusha's new Japanese-English
dictionary. An entirely new ed.
Tokyo, Kenkyusha, 1963 [c1954] xvi,
2136 p. J 63-892
    PL679 .K4 1963 MRR Alc.

Nelson, Andrew Nathaniel. The modern
reader's Japanese-English character
dictionary. 1st ed. Tokyo, Rutland,
Vt., C. E. Tuttle Co. [1962] 1048 p.
495.632 61-11973
    PL679 .N4 MRR Alc.

Rose-Innes, Arthur. Beginners'
directory of Chinese-Japanese
characters, American ed. Cambridge,
Mass., Harvard university press,
1942. 8 p. l., xix, [3], 507, A-1--A-
25 p. 495.632 A 42-3493
    PL679 .R6 1942 MRR Alc.

JAPANESE LANGUAGE--DICTIONARIES--
POLYGLOT.
Elsevier's automobile dictionary in
eight languages: Amsterdam, New
York, Elsevier Pub. Co.; [distributed
by Van Nostrand, Princeton, N.J.]
1960. 946 p. 629.203 59-8946
    TL9 .E43 MRR Alc.

United States. Air Force. 6004th Air
Intelligence Service Squadron.
Dictionary of common oriental terms:
[n. p.] 1956. 1v. (various pagings)
495 57-60108
    PL493 .U52 MRR Alc.

JAPANESE LITERATURE--BIBLIOGRAPHY--
CATALOGS.
Ceadel, Eric B. Classified catalogue
of modern Japanese books in Cambridge
University Library. Cambridge, W.
Heffer [c1961] xxvii, 552 p.
015.52 62-6217
    Z3309 .C4 MRR Alc.

JAPANESE LITERATURE--HISTORY AND
CRITICISM.
Keene, Donald. Japanese literature;
New York, Grove Press [c1955] 114 p.
895.609 55-6276
    PL855 .K4 1955 MRR Alc.

JAPANESE LITERATURE--TRANSLATIONS INTO
FOREIGN LANGUAGES--BIBLIOGRAPHY.
Nihon PEN Kurabu. Japanese
literature in European languages,
[Tokyo? 1957?] ix, 69 p. 016.8956
61-32222
    Z3308.T7 N5 MRR Alc.

JAPANESE PERIODICALS--BIBLIOGRAPHY.
Nihon kagaku gijutsu kankei chikuji
kankobutsu mokuroku. 1962- [Tokyo]
National Diet Library. J 68-5037
    Z7403 .N5 Sci RR Latest edition /
    MRR Alc Latest edition

United States. Library of Congress.
Japanese scientific and technical
serial publications in the
collections of the Library of
Congress. Washington, Science and
Technology Division, Reference Dept.,
Library of Congress, 1962. v, 247 p.
62-60085
    Z663.41 .J2 MRR Alc.

United States. Library of Congress.
Science and Technology Division.
Journals in science and technology
published in Japan and mainland
China: Washington, 1961. 47 p.
016.505 61-60647
    Z663.41 .J6 MRR Alc.

JAZZ MUSIC.
see also Blues (Songs, etc.)

JAZZ MUSIC--DICTIONARIES.
Gold, Robert S. A Jazz lexicon.
[1st ed.] New York, A. A. Knopf,
1964. xxvi, 363 p. 781.5703 63-
9129
    ML102.J3 G6 MRR Alc.

Panassié, Hugues. Guide to Jazz,
Boston, Houghton Mifflin, 1956. vii,
312 p. 781.5 785.42* 56-10291
    ML102.J3 P33 MRR Alc.

JAZZ MUSIC--DISCOGRAPHY.
Feather, Leonard G. The encyclopedia
of jazz in the sixties. New York,
Horizon Press [1966] 312 p.
785.420922   66-26705
ML105 .F35 MRR Alc.

Panassié, Hugues. Guide to jazz,
Boston, Houghton Mifflin, 1956. v. 1,
312 p.   781.5 785.42*   56-10291
ML102.J3 P33 MRR Alc.

JAZZ MUSIC--PICTORIAL WORKS.
Keepnews, Orrin. A pictorial history
of jazz; New ed. rev. New York,
Crown Publishers [1966] 297 p.
781.570873   66-4300
ML3561.J3 K4 1966 MRR Alc.

JAZZ MUSICIANS.
Alphabeat: who's who in pop. London,
Century 21 Publishing Ltd., 1969.
[126] p. (chiefly ports. (some col.)
[12/6]   780/.922   70-484370
ML105 .A44 MRR Biog.

Panassié, Hugues. Guide to jazz,
Boston, Houghton Mifflin, 1956. vii,
312 p.   781.5 785.42*   56-10291
ML102.J3 P33 MRR Alc.

JAZZ MUSICIANS--BIOGRAPHY.
Burton, Jack, The blue book of Tin
Pan Alley, [Expanded new ed.]
Watkins Glen, N.Y., Century House
[1962-65]   2 v.   784   62-16426
ML390 .B963 MRR Alc.

Feather, Leonard G. The encyclopedia
of jazz in the sixties. New York,
Horizon Press [1966] 312 p.
785.420922   66-26705
ML105 .F35 MRR Alc.

JEFFERSON, THOMAS, PRES. U.S., 1743-
1826.
Hawke, David Freeman. A transaction
of free men; New York, Scribner
[1964] 282 p.   973.313   64-13632
E221 .H26 MRR Alc.

Malone, Dumas, Jefferson and his
time. [1st ed.] Boston, Little,
Brown, 1948- v.   [$14.50 (v. 5)]
973.4/6/0924 B   48-5972
E332 .M25 MRR Alc.

Schachner, Nathan, Thomas Jefferson,
New York, T. Yoseloff [1957] xiv,
1070 p. .923.173   57-14046
E332 .S32 1957 MRR Alc.

Winter, Ezra Augustus, The Thomas
Jefferson murals in the Thomas
Jefferson Room, Library of Congress.
Washington [U.S. Govt. Print. Off.]
1946. folder ([4] p.)   751.73 51-
60090
Z663 .T47 MRR Alc.

JEFFERSON, THOMAS, PRES. U.S., 1743-
1826--ANNIVERSARIES, ETC.
United States. Library of Congress.
The Thomas Jefferson bicentennial,
1743-1943. Washington, U.S. Govt.
Print. Off., 1943. iii, 170 p.
823.173   44-40602
Z663 .T45 MRR Alc.

JEFFERSON, THOMAS, PRES. U.S., 1743-
1826--ARCHIVES.
Virginia. University. Library. The
Jefferson papers of the University of
Virginia. Charlottesville, Published
for the University of Virginia
Library [by] the University Press of
Virginia [1973] xvi, 496 p.
016.9734/6/0924   72-91896
Z6616.J4 V55 1973 MRR Alc.

JEFFERSON, THOMAS, PRES. U.S., 1743-
1826--LIBRARY.
United States. Library of Congress.
Jefferson Collection. Catalogue of
the library of Thomas Jefferson.
Washington, Library of Congress, 1952-
59. 5 v.   017.1 52-60000
Z663.4 .C4 MRR Alc.

JEHOVAH'S WITNESSES--YEARBOOKS.
Yearbook of Jehovah's Witnesses.
Brooklyn, Watch Tower Bible & Tract
Society [etc.] 289.9 27-671
BX8525 .Y4 MRR Alc Latest edition

JEST-BOOKS
see Wit and humor

JESUS CHRIST--ART.
Maus, Cynthia Pearl, Christ and the
fine arts; Rev. and enl. ed. New
York, Harper [1959] 813 p.   232.9
59-5221
BT199 .M3 1959 MRR Alc.

JESUS CHRIST--BIOGRAPHY.
Laymon, Charles M. The life and
teachings of Jesus. Rev. ed. New
York, Abingdon Press [1962] 336 p.
232.9 62-7439
BT301.2 .L28 1962 MRR Alc.

Maus, Cynthia Pearl, Christ and the
fine arts; Rev. and enl. ed. New
York, Harper [1959] 813 p.   232.9
59-5221
BT199 .M3 1959 MRR Alc.

JESUS CHRIST--NAME.
Sabourin, Leopold. The names and
titles of Jesus; New York, Macmillan
[1967] xviii, 334 p.   232 66-22534
BT590.N2 S2 MRR Alc.

JESUS CHRIST--NATIVITY.
see also Christmas

JESUS CHRIST--POETRY.
Maus, Cynthia Pearl, Christ and the
fine arts; Rev. and enl. ed. New
York, Harper [1959] 813 p.   232.9
59-5221
BT199 .M3 1959 MRR Alc.

JESUS CHRIST--TEACHINGS.
Laymon, Charles M. The life and
teachings of Jesus. Rev. ed. New
York, Abingdon Press [1962] 336 p.
232.9 62-7439
BT301.2 .L28 1962 MRR Alc.

JEWELERS.
Cutten, George Barton, The
silversmiths of Virginia, Richmond,
Dietz Press, 1952. xxiv, 259 p.
739.23 52-14077
NK7112 .C86 MRR Alc.

JEWELRY--DICTIONARIES.
The Jewelers' manual. 1st- ed.;
1964- [Los Angeles] Gemological
Institute of America. 65-33618
TS725 .J4 MRR Alc Latest edition

Mason, Anita. An illustrated
dictionary of jewellery. [1st U.S.
ed.] New York, Harper & Row [1974]
388, [1] p. [$8.95] 739.27/03 73-
11590
NK7304 .M37 1974 MRR Alc.

JEWELRY--HISTORY.
Hughes, Graham. Modern jewelry;
Rev. ed. London, Studio Vista, 1968.
256 p. [70/-]   739.27/09/04 68-
97220
NK7310 .H8 1968 MRR Alc.

JEWELRY MAKING--HANDBOOKS, MANUALS ETC.
The Jewelers' manual. 1st- ed.;
1964- [Los Angeles] Gemological
Institute of America. 65-33618
TS725 .J4 MRR Alc Latest edition

JEWELRY TRADE--AFRICA--DIRECTORIES.
Africa-bijoux. Paris. 60-45606
HD9747.A6 A4 MRR Alc Latest
edition

JEWELRY TRADE--FRANCE--DIRECTORIES.
Annuaire Azur; Paris, Azur-
Éditions [etc.] 53-28461
HD9474.F7 A6 MRR Alc Latest
edition

Annuaire Paris-bijoux, publiant;
Paris. 53-28486
HD9747.F7 A65 MRR Alc Latest
edition

JEWELRY TRADE--UNITED STATES--CREDIT
GUIDES.
Jewelers Board of Trade. Reference
book of the jewelry trade in the
United States. Mar. 1933-
Providence [etc.] 658.9173927 44-
14869
HF5585.J4 J37 MRR Alc Latest
edition

JEWELS
see Precious stones

JEWISH-ARAB RELATIONS--1917- --HISTORY--
SOURCES.
United States. Library of Congress.
Foreign Affairs Division. A select
chronology and background documents
relating to the Middle East. 1st
rev. ed. Washington, U.S. Govt.
Print. Off., 1969. vii, 287 p.
[1.25] 956/.002 76-602249
DS62.8 .U55 1969 MRR Alc.

JEWISH-ARAB RELATIONS--COLLECTIONS.
Laqueur, Walter Ze'ev, comp. The
Israel-Arab reader; New York,
Citadel Press [1969] xi, 371 p.
[7.95] 956 68-25146
DS119.7 .L3 MRR Alc.

JEWISH FAMILIES--ADDRESSES, ESSAYS,
LECTURES.
Schlesinger, Benjamin. The Jewish
family; [Toronto] University of
Toronto Press [1971] xii, 175 p.
[$7.50] 301.42 79-151389
HQ525.J4 S47 MRR Alc.

JEWISH FAMILIES--BIBLIOGRAPHY.
Schlesinger, Benjamin. The Jewish
family; [Toronto] University of
Toronto Press [1971] xii, 175 p.
[$7.50] 301.42 79-151389
HQ525.J4 S47 MRR Alc.

JEWISH LIBRARIES.
Fraenkel, Josef. Guide to the Jewish
libraries of the world. [1st ed.]
London, Cultural Dept. of the World
Jewish Congress [1959] 64 p. 63-
2058
Z675.J4 F7 MRR Alc.

JEWISH LITERATURE.
see also Bible

JEWISH LITERATURE--BIBLIOGRAPHY.
Shunami, Shlomo. Bibliography of
Jewish bibliographies. 2d ed. enl.
Jerusalem, Magnes Press, 1965. xxiv, 992, xxiii
p. he 65-1493
Z7070.A1 S5 1965 MRR Alc.

JEWISH LITERATURE--HISTORY AND
CRITICISM.
Waxman, Meyer, A history of Jewish
literature. New York, T. Yoseloff
[c1960] 5 v. in 6. 892.409 61-
1793
PJ5008 .W323 MRR Alc.

JEWISH NEWSPAPERS--DIRECTORIES.
Fraenkel, Josef. The Jewish press of
the world / 7th ed. London :
Cultural Dept. of the World Jewish
Congress, 1972. 128 p. : [£1.00]
070/.025 74-190296
Z6367 .F7 1972 TJ Rm.

JEWISH PERIODICALS--DIRECTORIES.
Fraenkel, Josef. The Jewish press of
the world / 7th ed. London :
Cultural Dept. of the World Jewish
Congress, 1972. 128 p. : [£1.00]
070/.025 74-190296
Z6367 .F7 1972 TJ Rm.

JEWISH PERIODICALS--INDEXES.
Index to Jewish periodicals. v. 1-
June/Aug. 1963- Cleveland Heights
[etc.] Ohio, College of Jewish
Studies Press [etc.] 68-41603
Z6367 .I5 MRR Alc Full set

JEWISH WIT AND HUMOR.
Rosten, Leo Calvin. The joys of
Yiddish; [1st ed.] New York, McGraw-
Hill [1968] xxxix, 533 p.
492.49/3/2 68-29915
PN6231.J5 R67 MRR Alc.

JEWS--BIBLIOGRAPHY.
Schwab, Moïse. Index of articles
relative to Jewish history and
literature published in periodicals,
from 1665 to 1900. Augmented ed.,
New York, Ktav Pub. House [1971, i.e.
1972] xvi, 539, 409-613 p.
016.91/0039/24 74-114721
Z6366 .S413 MRR Alc.

Shunami, Shlomo. Bibliography of
Jewish bibliographies. 2d ed. enl.
Jerusalem, Magnes Press, 1965. xxiv, 992, xxiii
p. he 65-1493
Z7070.A1 S5 1965 MRR Alc.

JEWS--BIOGRAPHY.
The Israel honorarium. [Jerusalem,
Israeli Pub. Institute; New York,
Educational Pub. Institute, 1968] 5
v. (895 p.) 920 68-24276
E184.J5 I85 1968 MRR Biog.

Rubin, Eli. 140 Jewish marshals,
generals & admirals. London, De Vero
Books [1952] 300 p. 923.5 52-
67186
DS115 .R78 MRR Biog.

Who's who in world Jewry. 1955- New
York. 922.96 54-12036
DS125.3.A2 W5 MRR Biog Latest
edition

JEWS--BIOGRAPHY--DICTIONARIES.
Comay, Joan. Who's who in Jewish
history; [1st American ed.] New
York, D. McKay Co. [1974] 448 p.
920/.0092/924 73-93915
DS115 .C6 1974 MRR Biog.

JEWS--DICTIONARIES AND ENCYCLOPEDIAS.
Ausubel, Nathan, The book of Jewish
knowledge; New York, Crown
Publishers [1964] vii, 560 p.
915.693 64-23807
BM50 .A8 MRR Alc.

Comay, Joan. Who's who in Jewish
history; [1st American ed.] New
York, D. McKay Co. [1974] 448 p.
920/.0092/924 73-93915
DS115 .C6 1974 MRR Biog.

Encyclopaedia Judaica. Jerusalem,
Encyclopaedia Judaica; [New York]
Macmillan [c1971-72, v. 1, c1972] 16
v. 296/.03 72-177492
DS102.8 .E496 MRR Alc.

The Jewish encyclopedia; New ed.
New York, London, Funk and Wagnalls
company [c1925] 12 v. 25-14669
DS102.8 .J65 1925 MRR Alc.

The New Jewish encyclopedia. New
York, Behrman House [1962] xvi, 541
p. 296.03 62-17079
DS102.8 .N4 MRR Alc.

The New standard Jewish encyclopedia.
New., rev. ed. Jerusalem, Massada
Pub. Co., 1970. 30, 2027 columns.
910.09/174/924 70-16986
DS102.8 .S73 1970 MRR Alc.

JEWS--DICTIONARIES AND (Cont.)
Runes, Dagobert David, ed. Concise
dictionary of Judaism. New York,
Philosophical Library [c1959] 237 p.
   296.03 58-59474
   BM50 .R8 MRR Alc.

The Universal Jewish encyclopedia ...
New York, The Universal Jewish
encyclopedia, inc. [c1939-43] 10 v.
   296.03 40-5070
   DS102.8 .U5 MRR Alc.

JEWS--HISTORY.
Dubnov, Semen Markovich, History of
the Jews. South Brunswick [N.J.] T.
Yoseloff [1967-73] 5 v. $12.00 (v.
5)] 910/.03/924 66-14785
   DS117 .D7213 MRR Alc.

Eban, Abba Solomon, My people: the
story of the Jews, [New York]
Behrman House [1968] v, 534 p.
[$17.50] 909/.09/74924 68-27328
   DS117 .E2 MRR Alc.

Grayzel, Solomon, A history of the
Jews, [2d ed.] Philadelphia, Jewish
Publication Society of America, 1968.
xxv, 881 p. 909/.09/74924 68-5480

   DS118 .G875 1968 MRR Alc.

Roth, Cecil, A short history of the
Jewish people. [New] ed. revised and
enlarged. London, East & West
Library, 1969. xx, 494 p., 103
plates. [75/-] 909/.09/74924 77-
487564
   DS118 .R6 1969 MRR Alc.

The World history of the Jewish
people. [Tel-Aviv?] Jewish History
Publications [1964- c1963- v.
[$20.00 per vol.] ne 64-3260
   DS117 .W6 MRR Alc.

Wurmbrand, Max. The Jewish people:
New York, Shengold Publishers [1967,
c1966] 462 p. 909/.09/74924 67-
16635
   DS118 .W8 1967 MRR Alc.

JEWS--HISTORY--TO 70 A.D.
Grollenberg, Lucas Hendricus, Atlas
of the Bible. [London] Nelson, 1956.
165 p. 220.93 56-14320
   BS621 .G712 1956 MRR Alc.

JEWS--HISTORY--1789-1945.
Sachar, Howard Morley, The course of
modern Jewish history. [1st ed.]
Cleveland, World Pub. Co. [1958] 617
p. 296.09 58-6757
   DS125 .S28 MRR Alc.

JEWS--HISTORY--1945-
Sachar, Howard Morley, The course of
modern Jewish history. [1st ed.]
Cleveland, World Pub. Co. [1958] 617
p. 296.09 58-6757
   DS125 .S28 MRR Alc.

JEWS--PERIODICALS--INDEXES.
Index to Jewish periodicals. v. 1-
June/Aug. 1863- Cleveland Heights
[etc.] Ohio, College of Jewish
Studies Press [etc.] 68-41603
   Z6367 .I5 MRR Alc Full set

Schwab, Moïse, Index of articles
relative to Jewish history and
literature published in periodicals,
from 1665 to 1900. Augmented ed.,
New York, Ktav Pub. House [1971, i.e.
1972] xvi, 539, 408-613 p.
016.91/0039/24 74-114721
   Z6366 .S413 MRR Alc.

JEWS--POLITICAL AND SOCIAL CONDITIONS--
1948-
Institute of Jewish Affairs. The
Jewish communities of the world:
demography, political and
organizational status, religious
institutions, education, press. 3rd
revised ed. London, Deutsch for the
Institute of Jewish Affairs in
association with the World Jewish
Congress, 1871. 127 p. [£1.50]
910/.039/24 72-179973
   DS143 .I55 MRR Alc.

JEWS--RECREATION.
The Jewish travel guide. London,
Jewish Chronicle Publications. 910.2
52-44383
   Began publication with 1951 issue.
   G153 .J4 MRR Alc Latest edition

JEWS--STATISTICS.
Institute of Jewish Affairs. The
Jewish communities of the world:
demography, political and
organizational status, religious
institutions, education, press. 3rd
revised ed. London, Deutsch for the
Institute of Jewish Affairs in
association with the World Jewish
Congress, 1871. 127 p. [£1.50]
910/.039/24 72-179973
   DS143 .I55 MRR Alc.

JEWS--YEARBOOKS.
The Jewish year book. 1896- London,
Jewish Chronical Publications [etc.]
14-2382
   DS135.E5A3 MRR Alc Latest edition

JEWS IN CANADA--SOCIETIES, ETC.--
DIRECTORIES.
American Jewish organizations
directory. [1st]- ed.; 1957- New
York, L. Frenkel. 296.6 57-34944
   E184.J5 A35 MRR Alc Latest edition

JEWS IN GERMANY--HISTORY--1933-1945--
BIBLIOGRAPHY.
Robinson, Jacob, Guide to Jewish
history under Nazi impact. New York
[Yivo Institute for Jewish Research]
1960. xxxi, 425 p. 016.940535693
61-65976
   Z6207.W8 R56 MRR Alc.

JEWS IN GREAT BRITAIN--YEARBOOKS.
The Jewish year book. 1896- London,
Jewish Chronical Publications [etc.]
14-2382
   DS135.E5A3 MRR Alc Latest edition

JEWS IN THE UNITED STATES--BIOGRAPHY.
Development Corporation for Israel.
Who's who, 1958 trustees of Israel;
New York, State of Israel Bond
Organization [1959] 215 p.
336.31095694 59-46141
   HG5811.P3 D4 MRR Biog.

The Israel honorarium. [Jerusalem,
Israeli Pub. Institute; New York,
Educational Pub. Institute, 1968] 5
v. (895 p.) 920 68-24276
   E184.J5 I85 1968 MRR Biog.

Rosenbloom, Joseph R. A biographical
dictionary of early American Jews,
[Lexington] University of Kentucky
Press [1960] xii, 175 p. 920.05693
60-8517
   E184.J5 R63 MRR Biog.

Simonhoff, Harry. Jewish notables in
America, 1776-1865; New York,
Greenberg [1956] 402 p. 296 55-
12359
   E184.J5 S53 MRR Biog.

Simonhoff, Harry. Saga of American
Jewry, 1865-1914; New York, Arco
Pub. Co. [1959] 403 p.
325.256930973 58-13918
   E184.J5 S54 MRR Biog.

JEWS IN THE UNITED STATES--EDUCATION--
DIRECTORIES.
Jewish education register and
directory. 1951- New York, American
Association for Jewish Education.
371.98 52-13492
   LC741 .J47 MRR Alc Latest edition

JEWS IN THE UNITED STATES--HISTORY.
Goldberg, Israel, The Jews in
America; New York, KTAV Pub. House,
1972. xiv, 422 p. 917.3/06/924 72-
181613
   E184.J5 G613 1972 MRR Alc.

Handlin, Oscar, Adventure in
freedom; New York, McGraw-Hill
[1954] 282 p. 296 54-10634
   E184.J5 H29 MRR Alc.

Levitan, Tina Nellie, The firsts of
American Jewish history. [2d ed.]
Brooklyn, Charuth Press [1957] 285
p. 286 57-9129
   E184.J5 L6644 1957 MRR Alc.

Segal, Charles M. Fascinating facts
about American Jewish history. New
York, Twayne Publishers [1955] 159
p. 296 55-872
   E184.J5 S4 MRR Alc.

JEWS IN THE UNITED STATES--HISTORY--
SOURCES.
Schappes, Morris Urman, ed. A
documentary history of the Jews in
the United States, 1654-1875. 3d
ed.; [1st Schocken ed.] New York,
Schocken Books [1971] xxiv, 766 p.
917.3/06/924 72-122332
   E184.J5 S35 1971 MRR Alc.

JEWS IN THE UNITED STATES--SOCIETIES,
ETC.--DIRECTORIES.
American Jewish organizations
directory. [1st]- ed.; 1957- New
York, L. Frenkel. 296.6 57-34944
   E184.J5 A35 MRR Alc Latest edition

JEWS IN THE UNITED STATES--YEARBOOKS.
American Jewish year book. v. [1]-
1899/1900- New York [etc.] American
Jewish Committee [etc.] 99-4040
   E184.J5 A6 MRR Ref Desk Latest
   edition

JOANNES XXI, POPE, D. 1277. PRACTICA
MEDICINAE.
Rosenwald, Lessing Julius, The 19th
book: Tesoro de poveri. [Washington]
Published for the Library of
Congress, 1961. 123 p. 62-60686
   Z663.4 .N5 MRR Alc.

JOB DESCRIPTIONS.
Ross, E. E. Encyclopedia of job
descriptions in manufacturing,
Milwaukee, Wis., Sextant Systems
[1969] 865 p. 658.3 79-6832
   HF5549.5.J6 R67 MRR Alc.

United States. Bureau of Employment
Security. Selected characteristics
of occupations (physical demands,
working conditions, training time);
Washington; For sale by the Supt. of
Docs., U.S. Govt. Print. Off., 1966.
xii, 280, 8 p. 331.1/14/0973 70-
601497
   HB2595 .A35 1966 MRR Ref Desk.

Whitfield, Edwin A. Guide to careers
through vocational training [1st
ed.] San Diego, Calif., R. R. Knapp
[1968] viii, 312 p. 331.702/0973
68-15874
   HF5382.5.U5 W5 MRR Alc.

JOB DISCRIMINATION
see Discrimination in employment

JOB VACANCIES--UNITED STATES.
Directory of United States employers,
New York, Simon and Schuster [c1970]
823 p. 338/.0025/73 78-24980
   HC102 .K7 MRR Alc.

JOHNSON, ANDREW, PRES. U.S., 1808-1875.
McKitrick, Eric L. Andrew Johnson
and reconstruction. [Chicago]
University of Chicago Press [1960]
ix, 533 p. 973.81 60-5467
   E668 .M156 MRR Alc.

Steele, Robert V. P. The first
President Johnson; New York, Morrow,
1968. x, 676 p. [12.50]
973.8/1/0924 B 68-25487
   E667 .S7 1968 MRR Alc.

Stryker, Lloyd Paul. Andrew Johnson;
a study in courage, New York, The
Macmillan company, 1929. xvi p., 1
l., 881 p. 30-6280
   E667 .S923 MRR Alc.

JOHNSON, CLAUDIA ALTA (TAYLOR) 1912-
Montgomery, Ruth (Shick) Mrs. L. B.
J. [1st ed.] New York, Holt,
Rinehart and Winston [1964] 212 p.
920.7 64-15307
   E848.J6 M6 MRR Alc.

Smith, Marie D. The President's
lady; New York, Random House [1964]
vi, 243 p. 920.7 64-17940
   E848.J6 S55 MRR Alc.

JOHNSON, LYNDON BAINES, PRES. U.S.,
1908-
Amrine, Michael. This awesome
challenge. New York, Putnam [1964]
283 p. 973.923 64-18001
   E846 .A6 MRR Alc.

Bell, Jack, The Johnson treatment;
[1st ed.] New York, Harper & Row
[1965] 305 p. 923.173 64-25107
   E846 .B4 MRR Alc.

Kluckhohn, Frank L. Lyndon's legacy;
New York, Devin-Adair Co., 1964.
xiv, 335 p. 320.973 64-23751
   E846 .K55 1964a MRR Alc.

Mooney, Booth, The Lyndon Johnson
story. New York, Farrar, Straus
[1964] xxii, 198 p. 923.173 64-
15356
   E847 .M6 1964 MRR Alc.

Newlon, Clarke. L. B. J., Rev. and
enl. ed. New York, Dodd, Mead [1966]
x, 244 p. 973.9230924 66-20511
   E847 .N4 1966 MRR Alc.

Provence, Harry. Lyndon B. Johnson,
New York, Fleet Pub. Corp. [1964]
192 p. 923.173 64-15704
   E847 .P7 MRR Alc.

Roberts, Charles Wesley, LBJ's inner
circle. New York, Delacorte Press
[1965] 223 p. 973.9230922 65-
21935
   E846 .R56 MRR Alc.

Singer, Kurt D., Lyndon Baines
Johnson, man of reason. Minneapolis,
T. S. Denison [1964] 384 p.
923.173 64-17743
   E847 .S5 MRR Alc.

Steinberg, Alfred, Sam Johnson's
boy; New York, Macmillan [1968] 871
p. 973.923/0924 B 68-21306
   E847 .S7 MRR Alc.

White, William Smith. The
professional: Lyndon B. Johnson.
Boston, Houghton Mifflin, 1964. 273
p. 923.173 64-21165
   E847 .W5 MRR Alc.

JOHNSON, SAMUEL, 1709-1784--
CONCORDANCES.
Naugle, Helen Harrold. A concordance
to the poems of Samuel Johnson.
Ithaca, [N.Y.] Cornell University
Press [1973] xxx, 578 p. [$13.50]
821/.6 72-13383
PR3532 .N3 1973 MRR Alc.

JOINERS.
see also Cabinet-workers

JOINERY.
see also Cabinet-work

see also Furniture making

JOINT OPERATIONS (MILITARY SCIENCE)
see Amphibious warfare

JOINTS (ENGINEERING)--DIRECTORIES--
PERIODICALS.
Assembly engineering master catalog.
[Wheaton, Ill., Hitchcock Pub. Co.]
338.4/7/62188025 72-622720
TJ1320 .H5 MRR Alc Latest edition
/ Sci RR Latest edition

JOINVILLE, JEAN, SIRE DE, 1224?-1317?
L'HISTOIRE ET CHRONIQUE DU ... ROY S.
LOYS.
Du Cange, Charles Du Fresne, sieur,
Glossarium mediæ et infimæ
latinitatis. Editio nova, aucta
pluribus verbis aliorum scriptorum
Paris, Librairie des sciences et des
arts, 1937-38. 10 v. in 11. 40-
3397
PA2889 .D8 1937 Mrr Alc.

JOKES
see Wit and humor

JONES, JOHN PAUL, 1747-1792--
BIBLIOGRAPHY.
United States. Library of Congress.
Manuscript Division. A calendar of
John Paul Jones manuscripts in the
Library of Congress. Washington,
Govt. Print. Off., 1903. 316 p.
012 03-19074
Z663.34.J6 MRR Alc.

JORDAN.
Systems Research Corporation. Area
handbook for the Hashemit Kingdom of
Jordan. Washington, For sale by the
Supt. of Docs., U.S. Govt. Print.
Off., 1969. xvi, 370 p. 309.1/5695
79-606088
DS153 .S95 MRR Alc.

JORDAN--GAZETTEERS.
United States. Geographic Names
Division. Jordan: official standard
names Washington, 1971. xvii, 419
p. 915.685/003 70-614714
DS153.2 .U48 MRR Alc.

JOURNALISM.
see also Newspapers

see also Periodicals

see also Press

see also Reporters and reporting

Byerly, Kenneth R. Community
Journalism. [1st ed.] Philadelphia,
Chilton Co., Book Division [1961]
435 p. 070.48 61-7188
PN4784.C73 B9 MRR Alc.

MacDougall, Curtis Daniel,
Interpretive reporting [by] 5th
ed. New York, Macmillan [c1968] ix,
515 p. 070.4/3 68-10070
PN4781 .M153 1968 MRR Alc.

JOURNALISM--ABSTRACTS--PERIODICALS.
Journalism abstracts. v. 1- 1963-
[Chapel Hill, N.C.] Association for
Education in Journalism. [$2.50]
070/.08 74-642577
PN4725 .J67 MRR Alc Full set

JOURNALISM--AUTHORSHIP.
Bernstein, Theodore Menline, Watch
your language; Great Neck, N.Y.,
Channel Press [1958] 276 p. 428.3
58-12309
PE1460 .B463 MRR Alc.

JOURNALISM--BIBLIOGRAPHY.
Price, Warren C. An annotated
journalism bibliography, 1958-1968
Minneapolis, University of Minnesota
Press [1970] x, 285 p. [$12.75]
016.07 70-120810
Z6940 .P69 MRR Alc.

Price, Warren C. The literature of
journalism. Minneapolis, University
of Minnesota Press [1959] xiii, 489
p. 016.07 59-13522
Z6940 .P7 MRR Alc.

JOURNALISM--DICTIONARIES.
Kent, Ruth Kimball. The language of
journalism; [1st ed.] Kent, Ohio]
Kent State University Press [1971,
c1970] xvi, 186 p. [$5.00]
070/.03 71-100624
PN4728 .K4 MRR Alc.

Pepper, William M. Dictionary of
newspaper and printing terms; New
York, Columbia University Press
[1959] 344 p. 070.03 59-16345
PN4728 .P4 MRR Alc.

JOURNALISM--DICTIONARIES--POLYGLOT.
Beeck, Peter. Fachausdrucke der
Presse. [3. Aufl.] Frankfurt am
Main, Polygraph Verlag, 1950. 174 p.
070.03 51-16343
PN4728 .B43 1950 MRR Alc.

JOURNALISM--DICTIONARIES--SPANISH.
Pepper, William M. Dictionary of
newspaper and printing terms; New
York, Columbia University Press
[1959] 344 p. 070.03 59-16345
PN4728 .P4 MRR Alc.

JOURNALISM--HANDBOOKS, MANUALS, ETC.
Ayer Press. Ayer public relations
and publicity style book.
Philadelphia, 1974. 1 v. (unpaged)
[$8.90] 808/.02 74-161785
PN4783 .A9 1974 MRR Alc.

New York times. Style book. New
York, McGraw-Hill Book Co. 655.25
38-30140
Z253 .N56 MRR Ref Desk Latest
edition

JOURNALISM--PERIODICALS.
Editor & publisher. 1920/21- [New
York] 74-643525
PN4700 .E4 MRR Ref Desk Latest
edition / Sci RR Latest edition

JOURNALISM--CANADA--BIBLIOGRAPHY.
Price, Warren C. The literature of
journalism. Minneapolis, University
of Minnesota Press [1959] xiii, 489
p. 016.07 59-13522
Z6940 .P7 MRR Alc.

JOURNALISM--GREAT BRITAIN.
Frank, Joseph. The beginnings of the
English newspaper; 1620-1660.
Cambridge, Harvard University Press,
1961. x, 384 p. 072 61-13735
PN5115 .F7 1961 MRR Alc.

JOURNALISM--GREAT BRITAIN--BIBLIOGRAPHY.
Price, Warren C. The literature of
journalism. Minneapolis, University
of Minnesota Press [1959] xiii, 489
p. 016.07 59-13522
Z6940 .P7 MRR Alc.

JOURNALISM--GREAT BRITAIN--DIRECTORIES.
Who's who in journalism. 1969-
[London] 070/.025/42 71-11173
Z6956.G6 W5 MRR Alc Latest edition

JOURNALISM--UNITED STATES.
Hohenberg, John, ed. The Pulitzer
prize story; New York, Columbia
University Press, 1959. 375 p.
070.431 59-7702
PS647.N4 H6 MRR Alc.

Kobre, Sidney, Development of
American journalism. Dubuque, Iowa,
W. C. Brown Co. [1969] xiv, 767 p.
071/.3 68-28705
PN4855 .K585 MRR Alc.

Mott, Frank Luther, American
journalism; 3d ed. New York,
Macmillan [1962] 901 p. 071.3 62-
7157
PN4855 .M63 1962 MRR Alc.

Tebbel, John William, The compact
history of the American newspaper
New and rev. ed. New York, Hawthorn
Books [1969] 286 p. [6.95] 071/.3
69-20347
PN4855 .T4 1969 MRR Alc.

JOURNALISM--UNITED STATES--BIBLIOGRAPHY.
Price, Warren C. The literature of
journalism. Minneapolis, University
of Minnesota Press [1959] xiii, 489
p. 016.07 59-13522
Z6940 .P7 MRR Alc.

JOURNALISTS--GREAT BRITAIN--DIRECTORIES.
Directory of newspaper and magazine
personnel and data. London,
Haymarket Publishing Group, [etc.]
072.058 59-18302
Z6956.E5 D5 MRR Alc Latest edition

JOURNALISTS--UNITED STATES--BIOGRAPHY.
Association of Radio News Analysts.
History, constitution, and
membership, 1942-1954. New York
[1954] 73 p. 070.46 070.41* 55-
27032
PN4841 .A89 MRR Biog.

JOURNALISTS--UNITED STATES--DIRECTORIES.
Columbia University. Graduate School
of Journalism. Journalism alumni
directory, 1913-1956; New York]
Columbia University [1956] 185 p.
070.711747 57-43669
PN4791 .C78 MRR Biog.

Overseas Press Club of America.
Directory of [the] Overseas Press
Club of America and American
correspondents overseas. 1966- [New
York] 070.4/3/02573 66-18719
PN4871 O882 MRR Alc Latest edition

The Working press of the nation.
[1945]- Burlington, Iowa [etc.]
National Research Bureau [etc.]
071.47 46-7041
Z6951 .W6 MRR Alc Latest edition

JUDAISM--DICTIONARIES.
Ausubel, Nathan, The book of Jewish
knowledge; New York, Crown
Publishers [1964] vii, 560 p.
915.693 64-23807
BM50 .A8 MRR Alc.

Runes, Dagobert David, ed. Concise
dictionary of Judaism. New York,
Philosophical Library [c1959] 237 p.
296.03 58-59474
BM50 .R8 MRR Alc.

Werblowsky, Raphael Jehudah Zwi, ed.
The encyclopedia of the Jewish
religion; London, Phoenix House,
1967. [7], 415 p. [70/-] 296/.03
68-102358
BM50 .W45 1967 MRR Alc.

JUDAISM--HANDBOOKS, MANUALS, ETC.
Pearl, Chaim, The guide to Jewish
knowledge, [1st American ed.]
Bridgeport, Conn., Hartmore House
[1972, c1958] 123 p. 296 75-
187866
BM570 .P4 1972 MRR Alc.

JUDAISM--HISTORY--TO 70 A.D.
Finegan, Jack, Light from the
ancient past; [2d ed. Princeton,
N.J.] Princeton University Press,
1959. xxxvii, 638 p. 220.93 59-
11072
BS635 .F5 1959 MRR Alc.

JUDAISM--STUDY AND TEACHING.
Pearl, Chaim, The guide to Jewish
knowledge, [1st American ed.]
Bridgeport, Conn., Hartmore House
[1972, c1958] 123 p. 296 75-
187866
BM570 .P4 1972 MRR Alc.

JUDGES.
see also Courts

JUDGES--UNITED STATES.
Ewing, Cortez Arthur Milton, The
judges of the Supreme court, 1789-
1937; Minneapolis, The University of
Minnesota press [c1938] 3 p. l., 3-
124 p. 38-28601
KF8744 .E9 MRR Alc.

JUDGES--UNITED STATES--DIRECTORIES.
Notable names in American history;
3d ed. of White's conspectus of
American biography. [Clifton, N.J.]
J. T. White, 1973. 725 p. 920/.073
73-6885
E176 .N89 1973 MRR Biog.

JUDGES--VIRGINIA.
Dodson, Edward Griffith, The General
Assembly of the Commonwealth of
Virginia, 1885-1918. Richmond, State
Publication, 1960. 517 p. 328.755
a 61-9339
JK3931 1960 .D6 MRR Alc.

Dodson, Edward Griffith, The General
Assembly of the Commonwealth of
Virginia, 1940-1960. Richmond, State
Publication, 1961. 1152 p. a 64-
7405
JK3931 1961 .D6 MRR Alc.

JUDICIAL INVESTIGATIONS
see Governmental investigations

JUDICIAL POWER.
see also Separation of powers

JUDICIAL REVIEW.
see also Legislative power

JUDICIAL STATISTICS--UNITED STATES.
United States. Bureau of the Census.
National survey of court
organization. [Washington] U.S.
National Criminal Justice Information
and Statistics Service; [for sale by
the Supt. of Docs., U.S. Govt. Print.
Off.] 1973. 257 p. [$2.40]
347/.73/1 73-600321
KF8719 .A32 MRR Alc.

JUDICIARY
see Courts

JUGENDSTIL
see Art nouveau

JUNIOR COLLEGE LIBRARIES.
Pirie, James W., Books for junior
college libraries; Chicago, American
Library Association, 1969. x, 452 p.
[35.00] 011 76-82133
Z1035 .P448 MRR Alc.

Bertalan, Frank J. The Junior
college library collection. 1970 ed.
Newark, N.J., Bro-Dart Foundation,
1970. xiv, 503, [129] p. 011 76-
122455
Z1035 .B443 1970 MRR Alc.

**JUNIOR COLLEGE STUDENTS--UNITED STATES--
DIRECTORIES.**
Who's who among students in American
junior colleges. 1966/67-   ed.
Tuscaloosa, Ala., Randall Pub. Co.
378.1/98/025   73-200965
    LA2311 .W42   MRR Biog Latest
        edition

JUNIOR COLLEGES--DIRECTORIES.
American junior colleges. 1st-
ed.; 1940-   [Washington] American
Council on Education. 378.73   40-
33685
    L901 .A53   MRR Ref Desk Latest
        edition

JUNIOR COLLEGES--CANADA.
Campbell, Gordon. Community colleges
in Canada. Toronto, New York,
Ryerson Press [1971]   xx, 346 p.
[$6.00]   378.71   79-26176
    LA417.5 .C35 MRR Alc.

JUNIOR COLLEGES--CANADA--DIRECTORIES.
Community and junior college
directory. Washington,
Communications Division, American
Association of Community and Junior
Colleges. [$5.00]   378.1/543/02573
73-643804
    LB2328.A1 J8   MRR Alc Latest
        edition

**JUNIOR COLLEGES--UNITED STATES--
CURRICULA.**
Graham, R. William, Barron's guide
to the two-year colleges, Completely
rev. and enl. Woodbury, N.Y.,
Barron's Educational Series, inc.
[1972]   2 v.   [$3.95 (v. 1) $2.50 (v.
2)]   378.1/543/02573   72-188709
    L901 .G73 1972 MRR Alc.

**JUNIOR COLLEGES--UNITED STATES--
DIRECTORIES.**
American junior colleges. 1st-
ed.: 1940-   [Washington] American
Council on Education. 378.73   40-
33685
    L901 .A53   MRR Ref Desk Latest
        edition

Cass, James. Comparative guide to
junior and two-year community
colleges. New York, Harper & Row
[c1972]   xix, 396 p.   [$10.00]
378.1/543   72-79651
    LB2328 .C355 1972 MRR Ref Desk.

Cass, James. Comparative guide to
two-year colleges & four-year
specialized schools and programs,
[1st ed.] New York, Harper & Row
[1969]   xxii, 275 p.   [$7.95]   378.73
69-15301
    LB2328 .C36 MRR Ref Desk.

Community and junior college
directory. Washington,
Communications Division, American
Association of Community and Junior
Colleges. [$5.00]   378.1/543/02573
73-643804
    LB2328.A1 J8   MRR Alc Latest
        edition

Graham, R. William, Barron's guide
to the two-year colleges, Completely
rev. and enl. Woodbury, N.Y.,
Barron's Educational Series, inc.
[1972]   2 v.   [$3.95 (v. 1) $2.50 (v.
2)]   378.1/543/02573   72-188709
    L901 .G73 1972 MRR Alc.

**JUNIOR COLLEGES--UNITED STATES--
STATISTICS.**
Community and junior college
directory. Washington,
Communications Division, American
Association of Community and Junior
Colleges. [$5.00]   378.1/543/02573
73-643804
    LB2328.A1 J8   MRR Alc Latest
        edition

JUNIOR HIGH SCHOOLS.
Wilson, H. W., firm, publishers.
Junior high school library catalog.
2d ed. New York, 1970.   xii, 808 p.
[30.00]   028.52   75-126356
    Z1037 .W765 1970 MRR Alc.

**JUNIOR HIGH SCHOOLS--UNITED STATES--
DIRECTORIES.**
Gertler, Diane (Bochner) Directory:
public elementary and secondary day
schools, 1968-69. [Washington] U.S.
National Center for Educational
Statistics; [for sale by the Supt. of
Docs., U.S. Govt. Print. Off., 1970-
v.   [2.00]   371/.01/02573   70-
607482
    L901 .G39 MRR Alc.

JURISPRUDENCE.
    see also Law

JURISPRUDENCE, MEDICAL
    see Medical jurisprudence

JURISTS
    see Lawyers

JUSTICE, ADMINISTRATION OF.
    see also Courts

    see also Governmental investigations

JUSTICE, ADMINISTRATION OF--CHINA.
Hsia, Tao-t'ai. Guide to selected
legal sources of Mainland China:
Washington, Library of Congress; [for
sale by the Supt. of Docs., U.S.
Govt. Print. Off.] 1967.   viii, 357
p.   340/.0951   67-60042
    Z663.5.G8C53 MRR Alc.

**JUSTINIANUS I, EMPEROR OF THE EAST,
483?-565.**
Procopius, of Caesarea. Procopius,
Cambridge, Mass., Harvard University
Press; London, W. Heinemann, 1953-62
[v. 1, 1961]   7 v.   949.61   64-3759

    PA3613 .P85 1953 MRR Alc.

JUVENALIS, DECIMUS JUNIUS--CONCORDANCES.
Kelling, Lucile, Index verborum
Iuvenalis. Chapel Hill, University
of North Carolina Press, 1951.   vii,
139 p.   877.7   51-8087
    PA6448.Z8 1951 MRR Alc.

JUVENILE DELINQUENCY.
    see also Child welfare

JUVENILE DELINQUENCY--BIBLIOGRAPHY.
Crime and delinquency abstracts.   v.
1-   Jan. 1963-   [Bethesda, Md.,
etc.] National Clearinghouse for
Mental Health Information [etc.]   66-
3911
    Z5118.C9 I55   MRR Alc Full set

**JUVENILE DELINQUENCY--UNITED STATES--
ADDRESSES, ESSAYS, LECTURES.**
Tyler, Gus, ed. Organized crime in
America, Ann Arbor, University of
Michigan Press [1962]   421 p.
364.10973   60-15778
    HV6777 .T9 MRR Alc.

JUVENILE LITERATURE
    see Children's literature

KANSAS.
Federal Writers' Project. Kansas.
Kansas; a guide to the Sunflower
State, New York, Hastings House
[1949]   xviii, 538 p.   917.81   49-
5821
    F686 .F45 1949 MRR Ref Desk.

Kansas directory. July 1, 1891-
[Topeka]   52-62636
    JK6830 .A25   MRR Alc Latest edition

KANSAS--BIBLIOGRAPHY.
Historical Records Survey. Check
list of Kansas imprints, 1854-1876.
Topeka, WPA Historical Records Survey
Project, 1939.   xxxvii, 773 l.   40-
3090
    Z1215 .H67 no. 10 MRR Alc.

United States. Library of Congress.
Kansas and Nebraska, centennial of
the Territories, 1894-1954;
Washington, 1954.   vi, 71 p.
016.9781   54-60003
    Z663.15.A6K3 MRR Alc.

KANSAS--CENTENNIAL CELEBRATIONS, ETC.
United States. Library of Congress.
Kansas and Nebraska, centennial of
the Territories, 1894-1954;
Washington, 1954.   vi, 71 p.
016.9781   54-60003
    Z663.15.A6K3 MRR Alc.

**KANSAS--DESCRIPTION AND TRAVEL--GUIDE-
BOOKS.**
Federal Writers' Project. Kansas.
Kansas; a guide to the Sunflower
State, New York, Hastings House
[1949]   xviii, 538 p.   917.81   49-
5821
    F686 .F45 1949 MRR Ref Desk.

KANSAS--EXECUTIVE DEPARTMENTS.
Kansas. Report covering all agencies
of the government of the State of
Kansas. 1958/60-   [Topeka] 353.9781
61-64392
    JK6835 .A3   MRR Alc Latest edition*

**KANSAS--GOVERNMENT PUBLICATIONS--
BIBLIOGRAPHY.**
Wilder, Bessie E. Bibliography of
the official publications of Kansas,
1854-1958, [Lawrence] Governmental
Research Center, University of
Kansas, 1965-   v.   015.781   65-
63730
    Z1285 .W5 MRR Alc.

KANSAS--GOVERNORS--ELECTION.
Hein, Clarence Jacob. Kansas votes;
[Lawrence] Governmental Research
Center, University of Kansas, 1958.
103 p. (chiefly tables)   324.781   59-
62811
    JK6853.E6 H4 MRR Alc.

KANSAS--HISTORY.
Zornow, William Frank. Kansas; [1st
ed.] Norman, University of Oklahoma
Press [1957]   417 p.   978.1   57-7334

    F681 .Z6 MRR Alc.

KANSAS--IMPRINTS.
Historical Records Survey. Check
list of Kansas imprints, 1854-1876.
Topeka, WPA Historical Records Survey
Project, 1939.   xxxvii, 773 l.   40-
3090
    Z1215 .H67 no. 10 MRR Alc.

KANSAS--MANUFACTURES--DIRECTORIES.
Kansas. Dept. of Economic
Development. Directory of Kansas
manufacturers and products. Topeka.
43-53152
    T12 .K2   Sci RR Latest edition* /
        MRR Alc Latest edition

KANSAS--POLITICS AND GOVERNMENT--1951-
Kansas. Report covering all agencies
of the government of the State of
Kansas. 1958/60-   [Topeka]   353.9781
61-64392
    JK6835 .A3   MRR Alc Latest edition*

KANSAS--REGISTERS.
Directory of Kansas public officials.
Topeka, Kan., League of Kansas
Municipalities.   353.9/781/002   72-
626508
    JK6830 .K2   MRR Alc Latest edition

Kansas directory. July 1, 1891-
[Topeka]   52-62636
    JK6830 .A25   MRR Alc Latest edition

KASSEL--DIRECTORIES.
Kasseler Adressbuch. Kassel-
Wilhelmshöhe, H. Schönhoven.   62-
59907
    DD901.K33 K3   MRR Alc Latest
        edition

KEATS, JOHN, 1795-1821--CONCORDANCES.
Baldwin, Dane Lewis. A concordance
to the poems of John Keats.
Gloucester, Mass., P. Smith, 1963.
xxi, 437 p.   821.7   63-6084
    PR4836.A3 1963 MRR Alc.

**KENNEDY, JOHN FITZGERALD, PRES. U.S.,
1917-1963.**
Burns, James MacGregor. John
Kennedy: a political profile. New
York, Harcourt, Brace & World [1961]
xxiii, 309 p.   923.173   61-65170
    E842 .B8 1961 MRR Alc.

Sidey, Hugh. John F. Kennedy,
President. New ed. New York,
Atheneum, 1964.   x, 434 p.   973.922
64-772
    E842 .S5 1964 MRR Alc.

Sorensen, Theodore C. Kennedy [1st
ed.] New York, Harper & Row [1965]
viii, 783 p.   973.922   65-14660
    E841 .S6 MRR Alc.

**KENNEDY, JOHN FITZGERALD, PRES. U.S.,
1917-1963--ASSASSINATION.**
Meagher, Sylvia. Subject index to
the Warren report and hearings &
exhibits. New York, Scarecrow Press,
1966.   150 p.   364.1524   66-13736
    E842.9 .M4 MRR Alc.

United States. Warren Commission.
Report of the President's Commission
on the Assassination of President
John F. Kennedy. Washington, U.S.
Govt. Print. Off. [1964]   xxiv, 888
p.   64-62670
    E842.9 .A55 MRR Alc.

**KENNEDY, JOHN FITZGERALD, PRES. U.S.,
1917-1963--BIBLIOGRAPHY.**
United States. Library of Congress.
Bibliography and Reference
Correspondence Section. John
Fitzgerald Kennedy, 1917-1963; a
chronological list of references.
Washington, General Reference and
Bibliography Division, Reference
Dept., Library of Congress; [for sale
by the Superintendent of Documents,
U.S. Govt. Print. Off.] 1964.   viii,
68 p.   64-60056
    Z663.28 .K4 MRR Alc.

KENNEDY FAMILY--BIBLIOGRAPHY.
Sable, Martin Howard. A bio-
bibliography of the Kennedy family,
Metuchen, N.J., Scarecrow Press,
1969.   330 p.   016.973922/0922   78-
7234
    Z5315.K4 S3 MRR Alc.

KENTUCKY.
Federal Writers' Project. Kentucky.
Kentucky, St. Clair Shores, Mich.,
Somerset Publishers, 1973 [c1939]
xxix, 489 p.   917.69/04/4   72-84474

    F456 .F44 1973 MRR Alc.

Federal Writers' Project. Kentucky.
Kentucky; a guide to the Bluegrass
State, [Rev. ed.] New York,
Hastings House [1954]   xxix, 492 p.
917.69   54-1591
    F456 .F44 1954 MRR Ref Desk.

KENTUCKY--BIBLIOGRAPHY.
Coleman, John Winston, A
bibliography of Kentucky history.
Lexington, University of Kentucky
Press, 1949. xvi, 516 p.   016.9769
49-11965
Z1287 .C6 MRR Alc.

Historical records survey. Kentucky.
Supplemental check list of Kentucky
imprints, 1788-1820; Louisville,
Ky., Historical records survey,
Service division, Work projects
administration, 1942. 2 p. l., xii
(i.e. xiii) p., 1 l., 241 p. incl.
tables.   015.769   43-2549
Z1215 .H67 no. 38 MRR Alc.

McMurtrie, Douglas Crawford, Check
list of Kentucky imprints, 1787-1810,
Louisville, The Historical records
survey, 1939. xxvii, 205 p.
015.769   39-4909
Z1215 .H67 no. 5 MRR Alc.

KENTUCKY--BIOGRAPHY.
Richey, Ish. Kentucky literature,
1784-1963. Tompkinsville, Ky.,
Printed by Monroe County Press, 1963.
236 p.   64-3008
PS266.K4 R5 MRR Biog.

KENTUCKY--DESCRIPTION AND TRAVEL--GUIDE-
BOOKS.
Federal Writers' Project. Kentucky.
Kentucky, St. Clair Shores, Mich.,
Somerset Publishers, 1973 [c1939]
xxix, 489 p.   917.69/04/4 72-84474

F456 .F44 1973 MRR Alc.

Federal Writers' Project. Kentucky.
Kentucky; a guide to the Bluegrass
State, [Rev. ed.] New York,
Hastings House [1954] xxix, 492 p.
917.69   54-1581
F456 .F44 1954 MRR Ref Desk.

KENTUCKY--DIRECTORIES.
State directory of Kentucky. Pewee
Valley, Ky. [etc.] Directories, inc.
[etc.]   64-51705
JK5330 .S8 MRR Alc Latest edition

KENTUCKY--HISTORY.
Clark, Thomas Dionysius, A history
of Kentucky. [Rev. ed.] Lexington,
Ky., John Bradford Press, 1960. xi,
516 p.   976.9   61-1846
F451 .C63 1960 MRR Alc.

Clark, Thomas Dionysius, Kentucky,
land of contrast, [1st ed.] New
York, Harper & Row [1968] xii, 304
p. 917.69/03 67-28804
F451 .C645 MRR Alc.

KENTUCKY--HISTORY--BIBLIOGRAPHY.
Coleman, John Winston, A
bibliography of Kentucky history.
Lexington, University of Kentucky
Press, 1949. xvi, 516 p.   016.9769
49-11965
Z1287 .C6 MRR Alc.

KENTUCKY--HISTORY--SOURCES--
BIBLIOGRAPHY.
Kentucky Historical Society. Guide
to the manuscripts of the Kentucky
Historical Society Frankfort, 1955.
iv, 185 p.   016.9769 55-62791
Z1287 .K37 MRR Alc.

KENTUCKY--IMPRINTS.
Historical records survey. Kentucky.
Supplemental check list of Kentucky
imprints, 1788-1820; Louisville,
Ky., Historical records survey,
Service division, Work projects
administration, 1942. 2 p. l., xii
(i.e. xiii) p., 1 l., 241 p. incl.
tables.   015.769   43-2549
Z1215 .H67 no. 38 MRR Alc.

McMurtrie, Douglas Crawford, Check
list of Kentucky imprints, 1787-1810,
Louisville, The Historical records
survey, 1939. xxvii, 205 p.
015.769   39-4909
Z1215 .H67 no. 5 MRR Alc.

KENTUCKY--MANUFACTURES--DIRECTORIES.
Kentucky directory of manufacturers.
1949- Frankfort. 602/.5/769 52-
62224
T12 .K56 Sci RR Latest edition* /
MRR Alc Latest edition

KENTUCKY--REGISTERS.
State directory of Kentucky. Pewee
Valley, Ky. [etc.] Directories, inc.
[etc.]   64-51705
JK5330 .S8 MRR Alc Latest edition

KENTUCKY. GENERAL ASSEMBLY.
Kentucky. Legislative Research
Commission. Legislative handbook for
the Kentucky General Assembly. 1951-
Frankfort. 328.7698 52-62784
JK5330 .A33   MRR Alc Latest edition

KENYA--DESCRIPTION AND TRAVEL--GUIDE-
BOOKS.
Horrobin, David F. A guide to Kenya
and northern Tanzania [Aylesbury,
Eng., Medical and Technical Pub.,
1971] 304 p. [£3.25 ($10.00 U.S.)]
916.76/2/044   70-29461
DT434.E22 H59 MRR Alc.

KENYA--GAZETTEERS.
United States. Office of Geography.
Kenya; official standard names
approved by the United States Board
on Geographic Names Washington [U.S.
Govt. Print. Off.] 1964. vi, 367 p.
64-62504
DT434.E22 U5 MRR Alc.

KENYA COLONY AND PROTECTORATE--
GOVERNMENT PUBLICATIONS.
United States. Library of Congress.
African Section. Official
publications of British East Africa,
Washington, General Reference and
Bibliography Division, Reference
Dept., Library of Congress, 1960-63.
4 v. 015.676 61-60009
Z663.285 .O3 MRR Alc.

KHRUSHCHEV, NIKITA SERGEEVICH, 1894-
Pistrak, Lazar. The grand tactician;
Khrushchev's rise to power. New
York, Praeger [1961] 296 p.
923.247 61-9229
DK275.K5 P5 MRR Alc.

KIEL--DIRECTORIES.
Kieler Adressbuch. Kiel, Schmidt &
Klausing [etc.]   54-17318
DD901.K48 K35 MRR Alc Latest
edition

KIMBERLY--DIRECTORIES.
Braby's Orange Free State and
Northern Cape directory. Durban. 53-
32833
DT891 .B73 MRR Alc Latest edition

KINDERGARTEN.
see also Child study

see also Education, Preschool

KINDERGARTENS--UNITED STATES--
DIRECTORIES.
LaCrosse, E. Robert. Early childhood
education directory; 1st ed. New
York, R. R. Bowker Co., 1971. xiv,
455 p. [$19.50] 372.21/025/73 77-
126012
L901 .L3 MRR Ref Desk.

KING, JUDSON--BIBLIOGRAPHY.
United States. Library of Congress.
Manuscript Division. Judson King: a
register of his papers in the Library
of Congress. Washington, 1960. 10
l.   60-60019
Z663.34 .K5 MRR Alc.

KING PHILIP'S WAR, 1675-1676.
Lincoln, Charles Henry, ed.
Narratives of the Indian wars, 1675-
1699; New York, C. Scribner's sons,
1913. xii p., 2 l., 3-316 p.
[$3.00] 13-24819
E187.O7 L5 MRR Alc.

KINGDOM OF GOD.
Augustinus, Aurelius, Saint, Bp. of
Hippo. The city of God against the
pagans. Cambridge, Harvard
University Press, 1957-72. 7 v.
239.3 239.1* a 57-8616
PA6156.A82 MRR Alc.

KINGS AND RULERS.
see also Presidents

Bickerman, Elias Joseph, Chronology
of the ancient world London, Thames
& Hudson, 1968. 253 p. [57/6]
529/.32 68-78121
D54.5 .B5 MRR Alc.

Hall, Daniel George Edward, A
history of South-east Asia, 3rd ed.
London, Melbourne [etc.] Macmillan;
New York, St. Martin's P., 1968.
xxiv, 1019 p. 959 68-15302
DS511 .H15 1968 MRR Alc.

Haydn, Joseph Timothy, The book of
dignities, containing lists of the
official personages of the British
empire ... from the earliest periods
to the present time; 3d ed. London,
W. H. Allen & co., limited, 1894. 2
p. l., [iii]-xxviii, 1170 p. 09-
6387
DA34 .H32 MRR Alc.

Saillot, Jacques. Chronologie
universelle des souverains et chefs
d'etat. [Angers, H. Siraudeau,
1961] 411 p.   63-37133
D11 .S13 MRR Alc.

Spuler, Bertold, Regenten und
Regierungen der Welt. Wurzburg, A.
G. Ploetz [196 v.   63-5493
D11 .S78 MRR Alc.

Webster's biographical dictionary.
Springfield, Mass., G. & C. Merriam
Co. [1974] xxxvi, 1697 p. [$12.95]
920/.02 73-14908
CT103 .W4 1974 MRR Ref Desk.

Wise, Leonard F. Kings, rulers, and
statesmen. New York, Sterling Pub.
Co. [1967] 446 p. 920.02 67-16020

D107 .W5 MRR Ref Desk.

Wise, Leonard F. World rulers: from
ancient times to the present,
London, Ward Lock, 1967. 224 p.
[12/6] 929.7 67-111874
D107 .W5 1967b MRR Alc.

KINGS AND RULERS--BIOGRAPHY.
Valko, William G. The illustrated
who's who in reigning royalty;
Philadelphia, Community Press, 1969.
263 p. [2.25] 929.7 71-82314
D412.7 .V28 MRR Biog.

KINGS AND RULERS--GENEALOGY.
The Cambridge modern history, New
York, The Macmillan company; London,
Macmillan & co., ltd., 1902-12. 13
v. and atlas.   04-21616
D208 .C17 MRR Alc.

Toynbee, Paget Jackson, A dictionary
of proper names and notable matters
in the works of Dante. [New ed.]
Oxford, Clarendon P., 1968. xxv, 722
p. [5/15/6] 851/.1 68-81646
PQ4333 .T7 1968 MRR Alc.

KINROSS-SHIRE, SCOT.--COMMERCE--
DIRECTORIES.
Fife and Kinross trades' directory,
including the counties of Stirling
and Clackmannan, Edinburgh, Town and
County Directories, Limited. 59-
31510
HF5161 .F5 MRR Alc Latest edition

KINSHIP.
see also Family

KIOWA INDIANS.
Rhodes, Willard, Music of the
American Indian:Kiowa. Washington,
Library of Congress, Music Division,
Recording Laboratory, Archives of
American Folksong, in cooperation
with the Bureau of Indian Affairs
[195-] 32 p. 58-43368
Z663.378 .M79 MRR Alc.

KIPLING, RUDYARD, 1865-1936--
BIBLIOGRAPHY.
Chandler, Lloyd Horwitz, A summary
of the work of Rudyard Kipling, New
York, The Grolier club, 1930. 4 p.
l., xi-xxvii, 465 p. 012 30-28215

PR4856 .A219 MRR Alc.

Young, William Arthur, A Kipling
dictionary Revised ed. London,
Melbourne [etc.] Macmillan; New York,
St. Martin's P., 1967. x, 230 p.
[50/-] 828/.8/09 67-11840
PR4856 .A28 1967 MRR Alc.

KIPLING, RUDYARD, 1865-1936--
DICTIONARIES.
Young, William Arthur, A Kipling
dictionary Revised ed. London,
Melbourne [etc.] Macmillan; New York,
St. Martin's P., 1967. x, 230 p.
[50/-] 828/.8/09 67-11840
PR4856 .A28 1967 MRR Alc.

KIPLING, RUDYARD, 1865-1936--
DICTIONARIES, INDEXES, ETC.
Chandler, Lloyd Horwitz, A summary
of the work of Rudyard Kipling, New
York, The Grolier club, 1930. 4 p.
l., xi-xxvii, 465 p. 012 30-28215

PR4856 .A219 MRR Alc.

KITCHEN UTENSILS.
Lantz, Louise K. Old American
kitchenware 1725-1925 Camden, T.
Nelson [1970] 289 p. 683/.82 75-
101527
NK806 .L29 MRR Alc.

KITCHEN UTENSILS--UNITED STATES--
HISTORY.
Phipps, Frances, Colonial kitchens,
their furnishings, and their gardens,
New York, Hawthorn Books [1972]
xxii, 346 p. [$12.95] 643/.3/0974
78-158021
TX653 .P48 1972 MRR Alc.

KITCHENS--UNITED STATES--HISTORY.
Phipps, Frances, Colonial kitchens,
their furnishings, and their gardens,
New York, Hawthorn Books [1972]
xxii, 346 p. [$12.95] 643/.3/0974
78-158021
TX653 .P48 1972 MRR Alc.

KNIGHTS AND KNIGHTHOOD.
see also Heraldry

KNIGHTS AND KNIGHTHOOD--BIOGRAPHY.
Uden, Grant. A dictionary of
chivalry. New York, Crowell [1969,
c1968] 352 p. 394/.7/03 70-10564

CR13 .U3 1969 MRR Alc.

Uden, Grant. A dictionary of
chivalry. New York, Crowell [1969,
c1968] 352 p. 394/.7/03 70-10564

CR13 .U3 1969 MRR Alc.

KNIGHTS AND KNIGHTHOOD--GREAT BRITAIN.
Debrett's peerage, baronetage,
knightage, and companionage ...
Kingston upon Thames, Surrey, Kelly's
Directories [etc.] 929.72 42-17925

CS420 .D32 MRR Biog Latest edition

KNIT GOODS INDUSTRY--DIRECTORIES.
Davison's knit goods trade, "The
Standard." [Office ed.] Ridgewood,
N.J. [etc.] Davison Pub. Co. 08-
32658
TT695 .D26 Sci RR Latest edition /
MRR Alc Latest edition

Skinner's hosiery and knit goods
directory. Croydon, Eng. [etc.] T.
Skinner. 338.4767766 51-18825
TT679 .S5 MRR Alc Latest edition

KNOTS AND SPLICES.
Ashley, Clifford Warren, The Ashley
book of knots, Garden City, New
York, Doubleday, Doran & company,
inc., 1944. x p., 1 l., 620 p.
677.7 44-6788
VM533 .A8 MRR Alc.

KNOWLEDGE, THEORY OF.
see also Concepts

see also Intellect

KNOX, DUDLEY WRIGHT, 1877-1960--
MANUSCRIPTS.
United States. Library of Congress.
Manuscript Division. Dudley Wright
Knox: a register of his papers in the
Library of Congress, Washington,
Library of Congress, 1971. 16 p.
016.359/007/22 70-173823
Z663.34 .K66 MRR Alc.

KOMMUNISTICHESKAĬA PARTIĬA
SOVETSKOGO SOĬUZA.
Armstrong, John Alexander, The
politics of totalitarianism; New
York, Random House [1961] xvi, 458
p. 947.0842 61-6242
JN6598.K7 A67 MRR Alc.

Meissner, Boris. The Communist Party
of the Soviet Union; New York,
Praeger [1956] 276 p. 329.947 55-
12173
JN6598.K7 M415 MRR Alc.

KOMMUNISTICHESKAĬA PARTIĬA
SOVETSKOGO SOĬUZA--HISTORY.
Schapiro, Leonard Bertram, The
Communist Party of the Soviet Union.
London, Eyre & Spottiswoode [1960]
631 p. 329.947 60-4742
JN6598.K7 S35 1960 MRR Alc.

KOMMUNISTICHESKAĬA PARTIĬA
SOVETSKOGO SOĬUZA--MEMBERSHIP--
DIRECTORIES.
Institut zur Erforschung der UdSSR.
Party and government officials of the
Soviet Union, 1917-1967. Metuchen,
N.J., Scarecrow Press [1969] 214 p.
354.47/002 71-5787
JN6598.K7 I54 MRR Alc.

United States. Central Intelligence
Agency. Directory of Soviet
officials. [Washington?] 1973- v.
354/.47/002 73-603419
JN6521 .U55 1973 MRR Alc.

KOMUNISTICKÁ STRANA ČESKOSLOVENSKA--
MEMBERSHIP--DIRECTORIES.
Directory of Czechoslovak officials.
[n.p.] 1970. xi, 280 p.
354.437/002 74-16206
JN2217 .D5 1970 MRR Alc.

KOREA.
Clare, Kenneth G., Area handbook for
the Republic of Korea. Washington;
For sale by the Supt. of Docs., U.S.
Govt. Print. Off., 1969. xiv, 492 p.
[3.75] 915.19/03/43 78-604178
DS902 .C58 1969 MRR Alc.

Korea annual. 1964- Seoul, Hapdong
News Agency. 64-6162
DS901 .K67 MRR Alc Latest edition

KOREA--BIBLIOGRAPHY.
Chung, Yong Sun. Publications on
Korea in the era of political
revolutions, 1959-1963; [Kalamazoo,
Mich.] Korea Research and
Publication, inc. [1965] x, 117 p.
68-2879
Z3316 .C55 1965b MRR Alc.

Koh, Hesung Chun. Korea; an
analytical guide to bibliographies.
New Haven, Human Relations Area Files
Press, 1971. xviii, 334 p.
016.01691519 70-125119
Z3316.A1 K64 MRR Alc.

Silberman, Bernard S., Japan and
Korea; a critical bibliography.
Tucson, University of Arizona Press,
1962. xiv, 120 p. 016.95 61-11821

Z3301 .S55 MRR Alc.

United States. Library of Congress.
Far Eastern languages catalog.
Boston, G. K. Hall, 1972. 22 v.
019.1/09753 72-5364
Z3009 .U56 MRR Alc (Dk 33)

United States. Library of Congress.
Reference Dept. Korea, a preliminary
bibliography, Washington, 1950. iv,
107 p. 016.91519 50-61050
Z663.28 .K6 MRR Alc.

United States. Library of Congress.
Reference Dept. Korea, an annotated
bibliography ... Washington, 1950.
3 v. 016.91519 50-62963
Z663.28 .K63 MRR Alc.

KOREA--BIBLIOGRAPHY--CATALOGS.
Harvard University. Library. China,
Japan, and Korea; classification
schedule, Cambridge, Distributed by
Harvard University Press, 1968. 494
p. 017/.1 68-14151
Z3109 .H3 MRR Alc.

KOREA--BIOGRAPHY.
Korea annual. 1964- Seoul, Hapdong
News Agency. 64-6162
DS901 .K67 MRR Alc Latest edition

KOREA--CIVILIZATION.
Henthorn, William E. A history of
Korea New York, Free Press [1971]
xiv, 256 p. 915.19/03 75-143511
DS907 .H45 1971 MRR Alc.

KOREA--COMMERCE--DIRECTORIES.
The Korea directory. 1968- Seoul,
Korea Directory Company. 915.19 68-
57222
DS901 .K68 MRR Alc Latest edition

Korean trade directory. 1st- ed.;
1959- Seoul, Korean Traders
Association. 60-45910
HF3865 .K6 MRR Alc Latest edition

KOREA--COMMERCE--HANDBOOKS, MANUALS,
ETC.
Korean trade directory. 1st- ed.;
1959- Seoul, Korean Traders
Association. 60-45910
HF3865 .K6 MRR Alc Latest edition

KOREA--DIRECTORIES.
The Korea directory. 1968- Seoul,
Korea Directory Company. 915.19 68-
57222
DS901 .K68 MRR Alc Latest edition

KOREA--ECONOMIC CONDITIONS--
BIBLIOGRAPHY.
United States. Library of Congress.
Division of bibliography. ... The
Japanese empire: industries and
transportation, Washington, 1943. 1
p. l., 56 p. 016.330952 43-50835
Z663.28 .J2 MRR Alc.

KOREA--GAZETTEERS.
United States. Office of Geography.
South Korea; official standard names
approved by the United States Board
on Geographic names. Washington,
[U.S. Govt. Print. Off.] 1965 [i.e.
1966] iv, 370 p. 66-60727
DS901.8 .U49 MRR Alc.

KOREA--HISTORY.
Gale, James Scarth, James Scarth
Gale and his History of the Korean
people. Seoul, Royal Asiatic
Society, Korea Branch, 1972. xi, 396
p. [$8.00] 915.19/03 72-85805
DS907 .G33 1972 MRR Alc.

Henthorn, William E. A history of
Korea New York, Free Press [1971]
xiv, 256 p. 915.19/03 75-143511
DS907 .H45 1971 MRR Alc.

KOREA--IMPRINTS.
United States. Library of Congress.
Far Eastern languages catalog.
Boston, G. K. Hall, 1972. 22 v.
019.1/09753 72-5364
Z3009 .U56 MRR Alc (Dk 33)

KOREA--STATISTICS.
Korea annual. 1964- Seoul, Hapdong
News Agency. 64-6162
DS901 .K67 MRR Alc Latest edition

KOREA (DEMOCRATIC PEOPLE'S REPUBLIC)
Shinn, Rinn-Sup. Area handbook for
North Korea. Washington; For sale by
the Supt. of Docs., U.S. Govt. Print.
Off., 1969. xvi, 481 p. [3.75]
915.19/03/43 75-605343
DS932 .S5 MRR Alc.

KOREA (DEMOCRATIC PEOPLE'S REPUBLIC)--
GAZETTEERS.
United States. Office of Geography.
North Korea; official standard names
approved by the United States Board
on Geographic Names. Washington,
1963. iv, 380 p. 63-65234
DS932 .U5 MRR Alc.

KOREAN IMPRINTS--CATALOGS.
United States. Library of Congress.
Far Eastern languages catalog.
Boston, G. K. Hall, 1972. 22 v.
019.1/09753 72-5364
Z3009 .U56 MRR Alc (Dk 33)

KOREAN LANGUAGE--DICTIONARIES--ENGLISH.
Martin, Samuel Elmo, A Korean-
English dictionary, New Haven, Yale
University Press, 1967. xviii, 1902
p. 495.7/32 67-24503
PL937.E5 M3 MRR Alc.

KOREAN LANGUAGE--DICTIONARIES--POLYGLOT.
United States. Air Force. 6004th Air
Intelligence Service Squadron.
Dictionary of common oriental terms;
[n. p.] 1956. 1v. (various pagings)
495 57-60108
PL493 .U52 MRR Alc.

KOREAN WAR, 1950-1953--AERIAL
OPERATIONS.
Futrell, Robert Frank. The United
States Air Force in Korea, 1950-1953,
[1st ed.] New York, Duell, Sloan
and Pearce [1961] xxi, 774 p.
951.9042 61-16831
DS920.2.U5 F8 MRR Alc.

KOREAN WAR, 1950-1953--REGIMENTAL
HISTORIES--UNITED STATES--BIBLIOGRAPHY.
Dornbusch, Charles Emil, Histories,
personal narratives: United States
Army; Cornwallville, N.Y., Hope Farm
Press, 1967. [15]-399 p. 016.355
67-5273
Z1249.M5 D6 1967 MRR Ref Desk.

KU-KLUX KLAN.
Randel, William Peirce, The Ku Klux
Klan; [1st ed.] Philadelphia,
Chilton Books [1965] xvii, 300 p.
363.973 65-13920
E668 .R18 MRR Alc.

KU KLUX KLAN (1915-)
Randel, William Peirce, The Ku Klux
Klan; [1st ed.] Philadelphia,
Chilton Books [1965] xvii, 300 p.
363.973 65-13920
E668 .R18 MRR Alc.

LA RIOJA, SPAIN (DISTRICT)--DIRECTORIES.
Guía-anuario de Aragón, Rioja,
Navarra, Alava, Guipuzcoa y Vizcaya.
Zaragoza, E. Gallegos. 51-22040
DP11 .G78 MRR Alc Latest edition

LABADISTS.
Danckaerts, Jasper, b. 1639. Journal
of Jasper Danckaerts, 1679-1680; New
York, C. Scribner's sons, 1913.
xxxi, 313 p. 13-13556
E187.O7 D3 MRR Alc.

LABOR--UNITED STATES--STATISTICS.
United States. Bureau of Labor
Statistics. Guide to area employment
statistics; [Washington] 1960. iii,
227 p. l 60-70
HD8064 .A52 1960b MRR Alc.

United States. Bureau of Labor
Statistics. Guide to employment
statistics of BLS; [Washington]
1961. i, 134 p. l 62-75
HD8064 .A52 1961 MRR Alc.

LABOR (OBSTETRICS)
see also Childbirth

LABOR ACTION (NEW YORK, 1940-58)--
INDEXES.
Indexes to independent Socialist
periodicals. Berkeley, Calif.,
Independent Socialist Press [1969]
221 p. [9.5] 016.3091 77-16046
HX15 .I43 no. 4 MRR Alc.

LABOR AND LABORING CLASSES.
see also Occupations

see also Poor

see also Trade-unions

see also Unemployed

see also Woman--Employment

LABOR AND LABORING CLASSES--
BIBLIOGRAPHY.
International Labor Office. Central
Library and Documentation Branch.
Subject guide to publications of the
International Labour Office, 1919-
1964. Geneva, 1967. ii, 478 p.
[unpriced] 016.331 71-446416
Z7164.L1 I56 MRR Alc.

McBrearty, James C. American labor
history and comparative labor
movements; Tucson, Ariz., University
of Arizona Press [1973] ix, 262 p.
016.331/0973 78-190624
Z7164.L1 M15 MRR Alc.

LABOR AND LABORING CLASSES-- (Cont.)
United States. Library of Congress.
Division of bibliography. Select
list of books (with references to
periodicals) on labor, Washington,
Govt. print. off., 1903. 65 p.   03-
16881
Z663.28 .S28 MRR Alc.

LABOR AND LABORING CLASSES--
BIBLIOGRAPHY--CATALOGS.
International Institute for Social
History. Alphabetical catalog of the
books and pamphlets of the
International Institute of Social
History, Amsterdam. Boston, G. K.
Hall, 1970. 12 v.   019/.1 74-
169213
Z7164.S66 I5 1970 MRR alc (Dk 33)

LABOR AND LABORING CLASSES--DWELLINGS.
see also Housing

LABOR AND LABORING CLASSES--MEDICAL
CARE.
International Labor Office.
Encyclopaedia of occupational health
and safety. New York, McGraw-Hill
[1971-72] 2 v. (xiii, 1621 p.)
613.6/2/03 74-39329
RC963 .I6 1971b MRR Alc.

LABOR AND LABORING CLASSES--PERIODICALS-
-INDEXES.
Cornell University. New York State
School of Industrial and Labor
Relations Library. Library catalog.
Boston, G. K. Hall, 1967. 12 v.
016.331 72-185999
Z7164.L1 C84 MRR Alc (Dk 33)

International Labor Office. Library.
International labour documentation:
cumulative edition. Boston, Mass.,
G. K. Hall. 72-625702
H91 .I56 MRR Alc Full set

International Labor Office. Library.
Subject index to International labour
documentation, 1957-1964. Boston, G.
K. Hall, 1868. 2 v.   arr01-76
Z7164.L1 I646 MRR Alc.

McBrearty, James C. American labor
history and comparative labor
movements; Tucson, Ariz., University
of Arizona Press [1973] ix, 262 p.
016.331/0973 78-190624
Z7164.L1 M15 MRR Alc.

Michigan index to labor union
periodicals. Jan. 1960- Ann Arbor,
Bureau of Industrial Relations,
Graduate School of Business
Administration, University of
Michigan. 62-63689
Z7164.T7 U6 MRR Alc Full set

LABOR AND LABORING CLASSES--STATISTICS.
Deldycke, Tilo. La population active
et sa structure. Bruxelles, Centre
d'économie politique (de l')
Université libre de Bruxelles,
(1968) viii, 236 p.   [360.00]
331.11/12/0212 70-395436
HD4826 .D34 MRR Alc.

International Labor Office.
Technical guide: Geneva, 1968- v.
[unpriced]   331/.021/6 77-391010

HD4826 .I62 MRR Alc.

International Labor Office. Year
book of labour statistics. [1st]-
1935/36- Geneva.   l 36-130
HD4826 .I63 MRR Alc Latest edition

LABOR AND LABORING CLASSES--WAGES
see Wages

LABOR AND LABORING CLASSES--EUROPE--
STATISTICS.
Organization for Economic Cooperation
and Development. Manpower
statistics. 1950/60-1954/64. Paris.
66-202
HD5764.A6 O59 MRR Alc Latest
edition

LABOR AND LABORING CLASSES--FRANCE--
BIOGRAPHY.
Maitron, Jean, ed. Dictionnaire
biographique du mouvement ouvrier
français. Paris, Editions
ouvrieres [1864- v.   65-30024
HD8433.A1 M3 MRR Biog.

LABOR AND LABORING CLASSES--GREAT
BRITAIN--BIOGRAPHY--COLLECTIONS.
Bellamy, Joyce M. Dictionary of
labour biography [Clifton] N.J., A.
M. Kelley, 1972- v.   331/.092/2
B 78-185417
HD8393.A1 B44 MRR Biog.

LABOR AND LABORING CLASSES--GREAT
BRITAIN--HISTORY.
Cole, George Douglas Howard, comp.
British working class movements;
London, Macmillan, 1951. xxii, 628
p.   331.8 52-2264
HD8388 .C62 MRR Alc.

LABOR AND LABORING CLASSES--GREAT
BRITAIN--HISTORY--STATISTICS.
Great Britain. Dept. of Employment
and Productivity. British labour
statistics: London, H.M. Stationery
Off., 1971. 436 p.   [£7.00]
331/.0942 75-860907
HD8388 .A5 MRR Alc.

LABOR AND LABORING CLASSES--LATIN
AMERICA--BIBLIOGRAPHY.
Morris, James Oliver. Bibliography
of industrial relations in Latin
America, Ithaca, New York State
School of Industrial and Labor
Relations, Cornell University [1967]
xv, 290 p.   016.6580098 67-64729
Z7164.L1 M68 MRR Alc.

LABOR AND LABORING CLASSES--UNITED
STATES.
Cohen, Sanford. Labor in the United
States. 3d ed. Columbus, Ohio, C.
E. Merrill Pub. Co [1970] xii, 660
p.   331/.0973 70-104060
HD8072 .C72 1970 MRR Alc.

Commons, John Rogers. History of
labour in the United States, New
York, A. M. Kelley, 1966. 4 v.
331.0973 66-18557
HD8066 .C7 1966 MRR Alc.

Keir, Robert Malcolm. The epic of
industry. New Haven, Yale university
press: [etc., etc.] 1926. 3 p. l.,
329 p.   26-10707
E178.5 .P2 vol. 5 MRR Alc.

LABOR AND LABORING CLASSES--UNITED
STATES--1914-
Twentieth Century Fund. Employment
and wages in the United States, New
York, 1953. xxxii, 777 p.   331 53-
7170
HD8072 .T8 MRR Alc.

LABOR AND LABORING CLASSES--UNITED
STATES--BIBLIOGRAPHY.
Cornell University. New York State
School of Industrial and Labor
Relations. Library. Library catalog.
Boston, G. K. Hall, 1967. 12 v.
016.331 72-185999
Z7164.L1 C84 MRR Alc (Dk 33)

Lovett, Robert Woodberry. American
economic and business history
information sources: Detroit, Gale
Research Co. [1971] 323 p. [$14.50]
016.330973 78-137573
Z7165.U5 L66 MRR Alc.

Neufeld, Maurice F. A representative
bibliography of American labor
history Ithaca [New York State
School of Industrial and Labor
Relations] Cornell University, 1964.
ix, 146 p.   64-63608
Z7164.L1 N55 MRR Alc.

P H R A: poverty and human resources
abstracts. v. 1- Jan./Feb. 1966-
Beverly Hills, Cal., [etc.] Sage Pub.
[etc.] 66-9955
Z7165.U5 P2 MRR Alc Full set

LABOR AND LABORING CLASSES--UNITED
STATES--BIOGRAPHY.
Fink, Gary M. Biographical
dictionary of American labor leaders.
Westport, Conn., Greenwood Press
[1974] xiv, 559 p.   331.88/092/2 B
74-9322
HD8073.A1 F56 MRR Biog.

Madison, Charles Allan. American
labor leaders: 2d, enl. ed. New
York, Ungar [1962] 506 p.
331.880973 62-14081
HD8073.A1 M3 1962 MRR Alc.

Paradis, Adrian A. The labor
reference book [1st ed.]
Philadelphia, Chilton Book Co. [1927]
234 p. [$5.95]   331.1/1/0973 72-
6984
HD8066 .P37 MRR Alc.

LABOR AND LABORING CLASSES--UNITED
STATES--DICTIONARIES.
Paradis, Adrian A. The labor
reference book [1st ed.]
Philadelphia, Chilton Book Co. [1927]
234 p. [$5.95]   331.1/1/0973 72-
6984
HD8066 .P37 MRR Alc.

Roberts, Harold Selig. Roberts'
dictionary of industrial relations.
Rev. ed. Washington, Bureau of
National Affairs [c1971] xv, 599 p.
331/.03 78-175029
HD4839 .R612 1971 MRR Alc.

LABOR AND LABORING CLASSES--UNITED
STATES--HISTORY.
Foner, Phillip Sheldon. History of
the labor movement in the United
States ... New York, International
publishers [1947- v.   331.880973
47-19381
HD6508 .F57 MRR Alc.

Rayback, Joseph G. A history of
American labor. New York, Macmillan,
1959. 459 p.   331.880973 59-5344
HD8066 .R3 MRR Alc.

LABOR AND LABORING CLASSES--UNITED
STATES--HISTORY--BIBLIOGRAPHY.
McBrearty, James C. American labor
history and comparative labor
movements; Tucson, Ariz., University
of Arizona Press [1973] ix, 262 p.
016.331/0973 78-190624
Z7164.L1 M15 MRR Alc.

LABOR AND LABORING CLASSES--UNITED
STATES--SOURCES.
Chamberlain, Neil W., ed. Sourcebook
on labor New York, McGraw-Hill Book
Co [1964] x, 382 p.   331.1973 64-
21013
HD8072 .C38 1964 MRR Alc.

LABOR AND LABORING CLASSES--UNITED
STATES--INDEXES.
United States. Bureau of Labor.
Index of all reports issued by
bureaus of labor statistics in the
United States prior to March 1, 1902.
New York, Johnson Reprint Corp.,
1970. viii, 287 p.   016.331/0973
70-125418
Z7164.L1 U6 1970 MRR Alc.

LABOR AND LABORING CLASSES--UNITED
STATES--PERIODICALS--HISTORY.
The American radical press, 1880-
1960. Westport, Conn., Greenwood
Press [1974] 2 v. (xiv, 720 p.)
335/.00973 72-9825
HX1 .A49 MRR Alc.

LABOR AND LABORING CLASSES--UNITED
STATES--STATISTICAL SERVICES.
United States. Bureau of Labor
Statistics. BLS handbook of methods
for surveys and studies. Washington,
For sale by the Superintendent of
Documents, U.S. Govt. Print Off.,
1966. v, 238 p.   331/.0973 67-
60373
HD8064 .A52 1966 MRR Alc.

LABOR AND LABORING CLASSES--UNITED
STATES--STATISTICS.
Employee benefits fact book. [New
York] 331.2/52 76-118375
HD7125 .E57 MRR Alc Latest edition

Labor relations yearbook. 1965-
Washington, Bureau of National
Affairs. 331.1973 66-19726
HD8059 .L33 MRR Alc Latest edition

United States. Bureau of Labor
Statistics. Characteristics of
agreements covering 1,000 workers or
more. Washington, For sale by the
Supt. of Docs., U.S. Govt. Print.
Off. 331/.0973 s 331.89/0973 74-
600823
HD8051 .A62 subser HD6501 MRR Alc
Latest edition

United States. Bureau of Labor
Statistics. Employment and earnings
statistics for the United States.
1909/60- Washington, For sale by the
Superintendent of Documents, U.S.
Govt. Print. Off. l 64-5
HD5723 .A27 MRR Alc MRR Alc Latest
edition

United States. Bureau of Labor
Statistics. Guide to area employment
statistics: [Washington] 1960. iii,
227 p. l 60-70
HD8064 .A52 1960b MRR Alc.

United States. Bureau of Labor
Statistics. Guide to employment
statistics of BLS; [Washington]
1961. i, 134 p. l 62-75
HD8064 .A52 1961 MRR Alc.

United States. Bureau of Labor
Statistics. Handbook of labor
statistics. 1924/26- Washington,
U.S. Govt. Print. Off. l 27-328
HD8064 .A3 MRR Ref Desk MRR Ref
Desk Latest edition

United States. Bureau of the Census.
County business patterns: 1946-
[Washington] 49-45747
HC101 .A184 MRR Alc Latest edition

United States. President. Manpower
report of the President, and a Report
on manpower requirements, resources,
utilization, and training; by the
U.S. Dept. of Labor. 1963-
[Washington, For sale by the
Superintendent of Documents, U.S.
Govt. Print. Off.] l 63-45
HD5723 .A43 MRR Alc Latest edition

LABOR CONTRACT--DICTIONARIES--POLYGLOT.
Associazione industriale lombarda.
Glossario del lavoro: italiano,
francese, inglese, tedesco. Milano,
1964. 1335 p.   67-43249
HD4839 .A78 MRR Alc.

LABOR ECONOMICS.
Morgan, Chester A. Labor economics
3d ed. Austin, Tex., Business
Publications [1970] xiii, 662 p.
331 71-105541
HD4901 .M86 1970 MRR Alc.

LABOR ECONOMICS--BIBLIOGRAPHY--CATALOGS.
Cornell University. New York State
School of Industrial and Labor
Relations. Library. Library catalog.
Boston, G. K. Hall, 1967. 12 v.
016.331 72-185999
Z7164.L1 C84 MRR Alc (Dk 33)

LABOR EXCHANGES
see Employment agencies

LABOR POLICY--BIBLIOGRAPHY.
International Labor Office. Central
Library and Documentation Branch.
Subject guide to publications of the
International Labour Office, 1919-
1964. Geneva, 1967. il, 478 p.
[unpriced] 016.331 71-446416
Z7164.L1 I56 MRR Alc.

LABOR PRODUCTIVITY--BIBLIOGRAPHY.
Bakewell, K. G. B. How to find out:
management and productivity; 2d ed.
Oxford, New York, Pergamon Press
[1970] x, 389 p. 016.6585 78-
89775
Z7164.O7 B2 1970 MRR Alc.

LABOR PRODUCTIVITY--UNITED STATES.
Fabricant, Solomon. Employment in
manufacturing, 1899-1939, New York,
National bureau of economic research,
inc., 1942. xix, 362 p. 338.4 43-
6978
HD9724 .F27 MRR Alc.

LABOR RELATIONS
see Industrial relations

LABOR SUPPLY.
see also Manpower

LABOR SUPPLY--STATISTICS.
Deldycke, Tilo. La population active
et sa structure. Bruxelles, Centre
d'economie politique (de l')
Universite libre de Bruxelles,
(1968) viii, 236 p. [360.00]
331.1/12/0212 70-395436
HD4826 .D34 MRR Alc.

Organization for European Economic
Cooperation. Manpower population.
Paris, 1959. vii, 20 p. 331.112
59-65495
HD5712 .O73 MRR Alc.

LABOR SUPPLY--EUROPE.
Organization for Economic Cooperation
and Development. Manpower
statistics. 1950/60-1954/64. Paris.
66-202
HD5764.A6 O59 MRR Alc Latest
edition

LABOR SUPPLY--UNITED STATES.
Kuznets, Simon Smith, ed. Population
redistribution and economic growth;
Philadelphia, American Philosophical
Society, 1957-64. 3 v. 312.8
301.32* 57-10071
HB1965 .K8 MRR Alc.

Twentieth Century Fund. Employment
and wages in the United States, New
York, 1953. xxxii, 777 p. 331 53-
7170
HD8072 .T8 MRR Alc.

Wolfbein, Seymour Louis, Employment
and unemployment in the United
States; Chicago, Science Research
Associates [1964] 339 p.
331.1120973 64-12588
HD5724 .W6 MRR Alc.

LABOR SUPPLY--UNITED STATES--[(1960-)]
United States. President. Manpower
report of the President, and a Report
on manpower requirements, resources,
utilization, and training, by the
U.S. Dept. of Labor. 1963-
[Washington, For sale by the
Superintendent of Documents, U.S.
Govt. Print. Off.] l 63-45
HD5723 .A43 MRR Alc Latest edition

LABOR SUPPLY--UNITED STATES--
DIRECTORIES.
Directory of United States employers,
New York, Simon and Schuster [c1970]
823 p. 338/.0025/73 78-24980
HC102 .K7 MRR Alc.

LABOR SUPPLY--UNITED STATES--STATISTICS.
Ashby, Lowell De Witt. Growth
patterns in employment by county,
1940-1950 and 1950-1960,
[Washington] U.S. Dept. of Commerce,
Office of Business Economics,
Regional Economics Division; [for
sale by the Superintendent of
Documents, U.S. Govt. Print. Off.,
1965-66] 8 v. 65-61774
HD5723 .A63 MRR Alc.

United States. Bureau of Labor
Statistics. Employment and earnings
statistics for the United States.
1909/60- Washington, For sale by the
Superintendent of Documents, U.S.
Govt. Print. Off. l 64-5
HD5723 .A27 MRR Alc MRR Alc Latest
edition

United States. Bureau of Labor
Statistics. Handbook of labor
statistics. 1924/26- Washington,
U.S. Govt. Print. Off. l 27-328
HD8064 .A3 MRR Ref Desk MRR Ref
Desk Latest edition

United States. Bureau of the Census.
County business patterns; 1946-
[Washington] 49-45747
HC101 .A184 MRR Alc Latest edition

LABORATORIES--RUSSIA--DIRECTORIES.
United States. Library of Congress.
Aerospace Technology Division.
Scientific institutes and
laboratories in Moscow. [Washington]
1963. ix, 133 p. 64-60333
Z663.23 .S35 MRR Alc.

LABORATORIES--UNITED STATES--
DIRECTORIES.
American Council of Independent
Laboratories. Directory.
[Washington] 607.273 58-4459
TA416 .A54 Sci RR Latest edition /
MRR Alc Latest edition

Industrial research laboratories of
the United States. [1st]- ed.;
1920- Tempe, Ariz. [etc.] Jaques
Cattell Press [etc.] 21-26022
T176 .I65 Sci RR Latest edition /
MRR Ref Desk Latest edition

LABOUR PARTY (GT. BRIT.)
Cole, George Douglas Howard, A
history of the Labour Party from
1914. New York, A. M. Kelley [1969]
x, 517 p. 329.9/42 73-90407
JN1129.L32 C6 1969b MRR Alc.

LABRADOR--COMMERCE--DIRECTORIES.
Newfoundland and Labrador business
directory and buyers guide. St.
John's [Maritimes Directories]
380.1/025/718 73-642979
HF3229.N5 A45 MRR Alc Latest
edition

LACE AND LACE MAKING.
Clifford, Chandler Robbins, The lace
dictionary / Pocket ed., New York,
Clifford & Lawton [c1913] 156 p.
incl. front., illus. [$2.00] 14-7

NK9404 .C5 MRR Alc.

Powys, Marian, Lace and lace-making.
Boston, C. T. Branford Co., 1953.
219 p. 746.2 52-14187
NK9404 .P75 MRR Alc.

LACQUER AND LACQUERING--DICTIONARIES.
Martin, John Henry, Guide to
pigments and to varnish and lacquer
constituents, London, L. Hill, 1954.
127 p. 667.603 54-42002
TP934.3 .M3 MRR Alc.

Merz, Otto, Deutsch-englisches und
englisch-deutsches Fachwörterbuch
für Fachausdrücke aus dem Lack- und
Farbengebiet. 2., neubearb. und
erweiterte Aufl. Stuttgart,
Wissenschaftliche Verlagsgesellschaft, 1954. 351 p. 55-
22330
TP935 .M45 1954 MRR Alc.

LACQUER AND LACQUERING--DICTIONARIES--
GERMAN.
Merz, Otto, Deutsch-englisches und
englisch-deutsches Fachwörterbuch
für Fachausdrücke aus dem Lack- und
Farbengebiet. 2., neubearb. und
erweiterte Aufl. Stuttgart,
Wissenschaftliche Verlagsgesellschaft, 1954. 351 p. 55-
22330
TP935 .M45 1954 MRR Alc.

LACQUER AND LACQUERING--ORIENTAL.
Herberts, Kurt. Das Buch der
ostasiatischen Lackkunst,
Düsseldorf, Econ-Verlag [c1959] 549
p. 745.59 60-22168
NK9900 .H4 MRR Alc.

LADINO LANGUAGE--BIBLIOGRAPHY.
Besso, Henry V. Ladino books in the
Library of Congress; Washington,
Hispanic Foundation, Reference Dept.,
Library of Congress; [for sale by the
Superintendent of Documents, U.S.
Govt. Print. Off.] 1963 [i.e. 1964]
vii, 44 p. 63-62107
Z663.32 .A5 no. 7 MRR Alc.

LADINO LITERATURE--BIBLIOGRAPHY.
Besso, Henry V. Ladino books in the
Library of Congress; Washington,
Hispanic Foundation, Reference Dept.,
Library of Congress; [for sale by the
Superintendent of Documents, U.S.
Govt. Print. Off.] 1963 [i.e. 1964]
vii, 44 p. 63-62107
Z663.32 .A5 no. 7 MRR Alc.

LAKES--DICTIONARIES.
Gresswell, R. Kay, ed. Standard
encyclopedia of the world's rivers
and lakes; 1st ed. London,
Weidenfeld & Nicolson, 1965 [i.e.
1966] 384 p. [50/-] 910.091683
66-70378
GB1203 .G73 1966a MRR Alc.

LAMP-CHIMNEYS, GLOBES, ETC.--CATALOGS.
Lamps & other lighting devices, 1850-
1906. [1st ed.] Princeton [N.J.]
Pyne Press; distributed by Scribner,
New York [1972] 156 p. [$4.95]
621.32/3 72-76874
TP746 .L35 MRR Alc.

LAMPS.
Thwing, Leroy Livingstone, A
dictionary of old lamps and other
lighting devices, [Cambridge? Mass.]
c1952. 15 p. 665.603 52-40082
TP746 .T48 MRR Alc.

LAMPS--CATALOGS.
Lamps & other lighting devices, 1850-
1906. [1st ed.] Princeton [N.J.]
Pyne Press; distributed by Scribner,
New York [1972] 156 p. [$4.95]
621.32/3 72-76874
TP746 .L35 MRR Alc.

LAMPS--HISTORY.
Thwing, Leroy Livingstone, A
dictionary of old lamps and other
lighting devices, [Cambridge? Mass.]
c1952. 15 p. 665.603 52-40082
TP746 .T48 MRR Alc.

LAND, EMORY SCOTT, 1879- --BIBLIOGRAPHY.
United States. Library of Congress.
Manuscript Division. Emory Scott
Land; a register of his papers in the
Library of Congress. Washington,
1958. 7 l. 012 58-60039
Z663.34 .L3 MRR Alc.

LAND.
see also Agriculture

see also Real estate business

LAND GRANTS--UNITED STATES--HISTORY--
SOURCES--INDEXES.
McMullin, Phillip W. Grassroots of
America; Salt Lake City, Gendex
Corp., 1972. xxvii, 489 p.
333.1/0973 71-186588
J33 .M3 MRR Alc.

LAND REFORM.
see also Agriculture and state

LAND SETTLEMENT.
see also Migration, Internal

LAND TENURE--UNITED STATES.
Chandler, Alfred Noblit, Land title
origins, New York, Robert
Schalkenbach foundation, 1945. xvi
p., 1 l., 550 p. 333.3 46-902
HD194 .C5 MRR Alc.

LAND TITLES--REGISTRATION AND TRANSFER--
IRELAND.
Thomson, William, bank inspector.
Thomson's Dictionary of banking.
11th ed. London, Pitman [1965] ix,
641 p. 332.103 66-3511
HG1601 .T4 1965 MRR Alc.

LAND TITLES--UNITED STATES.
Chandler, Alfred Noblit, Land title
origins, New York, Robert
Schalkenbach foundation, 1945. xvi
p., 1 l., 550 p. 333.3 46-902
HD194 .C5 MRR Alc.

LANDFORMS.
see also Mountains

LANDSCAPE ARCHITECTURE.
see also Plants, Ornamental

see also Shrubs

LANDSCAPE ARCHITECTURE--BIBLIOGRAPHY.
Harvard University. Graduate School
of Design. Library. Catalogue of the
Library of the Graduate School of
Design, Harvard University. Boston,
Mass., G. K. Hall, 1968. 44 v.
019/.1 73-169433
Z5945 .H28 1968 MRR Alc (Dk 33)

LANDSCAPE PAINTERS--GREAT BRITAIN--
BIOGRAPHY--DICTIONARIES.
Berea, T. B. Handbook of 17th, 18th,
and 19th century British landscape
painters & watercolorists
[Chattanooga? Tenn., 1970] 72 p.
758/.1/0942 78-13623
ND496 .B4 MRR Biog.

LANGMUIR, IRVING, 1881-1957--
BIBLIOGRAPHY.
United States. Library of Congress.
Manuscript Division. Irving
Langmuir; a register of his papers in
the Library of Congress. Washington,
1962. 9 l. 62-60070
Z663.34 .L33 MRR Alc.

LANGUAGE, UNIVERSAL.
Ogden, Charles Kay. The general
Basic English dictionary. New York,
W. W. Norton & company, inc. [1942]
x, 441 p.   428.25 423   42-36402
   PE1073.5 .O372 1942 MRR Alc.

LANGUAGE, UNIVERSAL--BIBLIOGRAPHY.
Alston, R. C. Logic, philosophy,
epistemology, universal language
Bradford, Printed for the author by
E. Cummins [1967] xvi, 111 p.   68-
105634
   Z2015.A1 A4 no. 7 MRR Alc.

LANGUAGE AND LANGUAGES.
see also Bilingualism

   see also Communication

   see also English language

   see also Writing

Bodmer, Frederick. The loom of the
language, New York, W. W. Norton &
company, inc. [1944] x, 692 p. incl.
front., illus., diagrs.   400   44-
40079
   P121 .B6 1944 MRR Alc.

Book, Julius Nicholas. Modern
American grammar and usage New York,
Ronald Press Co. [1956] 475 p.   425
56-6265
   PE1111 .H638 MRR Alc.

Meillet, Antoine, ed. Les langues du
monde. Nouvelle edition, augmentée
d'un index. Paris, Centre national
de la recherche scientifique; H.
Champion, depositaire, 1952. xlii,
1294 p. and atlas (26 maps (part
fold., part col.))   a   53-8197
   P201 .M4 1852 MRR Alc.

Muller, Siegfried Hermann. The
world's living languages; New York,
Ungar [1964] xii, 212 p.   410 64-
15694
   P201 .M84 MRR Alc.

Nida, Eugene Albert. The Book of a
thousand tongues. Rev. ed. [London]
United Bible Societies [1972] xviii,
536 p.   220.5 73-160367
   P352.A2 N6 1972 MRR Alc.

Pei, Mario Andrew. The story of
language. Rev. ed. Philadelphia,
Lippincott [1965] 491 p.   400 65-
12599
   P121 .P37 1965 MRR Alc.

Pei, Mario Andrew. The world's chief
languages; 3d ed. London, G. Allen
& Unwin [1949] 663 p.   410 49-
28175
   P121 .P36 1949 MRR Ref Desk.

Piette, J. R. F. A guide to foreign
languages for science librarians and
bibliographers, [New ed.] revised
and enlarged London, Published on
behalf of the Welsh Plant Breeding
Station, Aberystwyth, by Aslib, 1965.
[5] 53 p. [27/6 21/- (to members)]
66-68259
   P201 .P5 MRR Alc.

LANGUAGE AND LANGUAGES--ABSTRACTS--
PERIODICALS.
Abstracts in anthropology. v. 1-
Feb. 1970- Farmingdale, N.Y.,
Baywood Publishing Co. [etc.] 77-
20528
   GN1 .A15 MRR Alc Full set

LANGUAGE AND LANGUAGES--BIBLIOGRAPHY.
Blass, Birgit A. A provisional
survey of materials for the study of
neglected languages, Washington,
Center for Applied Linguistics
[c1969] vi, 414 p.   016.41 78-
113390
   Z7001 .B59 MRR Alc.

Permanent International Committee of
Linguists. Bibliographie
linguistique. 1939/47- Utrecht,
Spectrum. 016.4 a 50-3972
   Z7001 .P4 MRR Alc Full set

Rutherford, Phillip R. A
bibliography of American doctoral
dissertations in linguistics, 1900-
1964. Washington, Center for Applied
Linguistics, 1968. iv, 139 p.
016.41 68-27431
   Z7001 .R8 MRR Alc.

LANGUAGE AND LANGUAGES--DICTIONARIES.
Hartmann, R. R. K. Dictionary of
language and linguistics New York,
Wiley [1972] xviii, 302 p.   410/.3
72-6251
   P29 .H34 MRR Alc.

Pei, Mario Andrew. Glossary of
linguistic terminology Garden City,
N.Y., Anchor Books, 1966. xvi, 299
p.   410.3 66-21013
   P29 .P39 MRR Alc.

LANGUAGE AND LANGUAGES--GLOSSARIES,
VOCABULARIES, ETC.
Bodmer, Frederick. The loom of the
language, New York, W. W. Norton &
company, inc. [1944] x, 692 p. incl.
front., illus., diagrs.   400 44-
40079
   P121 .B6 1944 MRR Alc.

Pei, Mario Andrew. The world's chief
languages; 3d ed. London, G. Allen
& Unwin [1949] 663 p.   410 49-
28175
   P121 .P36 1949 MRR Ref Desk.

LANGUAGE AND LANGUAGES--GRAMMARS--
BIBLIOGRAPHY.
Walford, Albert John. A guide to
foreign language grammars and
dictionaries, 2nd ed., revised and
enlarged. London, Library
Association, 1967. 240 p. [60/-]
016.415 68-86136
   Z7004.G7 W3 1967 MRR Alc.

LANGUAGE AND LANGUAGES--HANDBOOKS,
MANUALS, ETC.
Von Ostermann, George Frederick,
Manual of foreign languages 4th ed.,
rev. and enl. New York, Central Book
Co., 1952. 414 p.   402/.02 52-2409
   Z253 .V94 1952 MRR Alc.

LANGUAGE AND LANGUAGES--STATISTICS.
Hartmann, R. R. K. Dictionary of
language and linguistics New York,
Wiley [1972] xviii, 302 p.   410/.3
72-6251
   P29 .H34 MRR Alc.

LANGUAGE AND LANGUAGES--STUDY AND
TEACHING.
Pei, Mario Andrew. How to learn
languages and what languages to
learn, Enl. ed. New York, Harper &
Row [1973] x, 299 p. [$6.95]   407
72-79685
   P53 .P38 1973 MRR Alc.

LANGUAGE AND LANGUAGES--STUDY AND
TEACHING--AUDIO-VISUAL AIDS--
BIBLIOGRAPHY.
Walford, Albert John. A guide to
foreign language grammars and
dictionaries, 2nd ed., revised and
enlarged. London, Library
Association, 1967. 240 p. [60/-]
016.415 68-86136
   Z7004.G7 W3 1967 MRR Alc.

LANGUAGE AND LANGUAGES--STUDY AND
TEACHING--UNITED STATES.
Grognet, Allene Guss. University
resources in the United States and
Canada for the study of linguistics;
1971-1972. [7th rev. ed. Arlington,
Va.] Center for Applied Linguistics
[1972] iv, 289 p.   410/.7/1173 72-
93471
   P57.U7 G7 1972 MRR Alc.

LANGUAGE ARTS.
see also Reading

LANGUAGE ARTS.
see Speech

LANGUAGE DATA PROCESSING.
see also Electronic data processing

LANGUAGE DATA PROCESSING--BIBLIOGRAPHY.
Bourne, Charles P. Bibliography on
the mechanization of information
retrieval, Menlo Park, Calif.,
Stanford Research Institute, 1958-
[62] 5 v. in 1.   65-73592
   Z699.2 .B6 MRR Alc.

LANGUAGES, MODERN.
Piette, J. R. F. A guide to foreign
languages for science librarians and
bibliographers, [New ed.] revised
and enlarged London, Published on
behalf of the Welsh Plant Breeding
Station, Aberystwyth, by Aslib, 1965.
[5] 53 p. [27/6 21/- (to members)]
66-68259
   P201 .P5 MRR Alc.

LANGUAGES, MODERN--BIBLIOGRAPHY.
The Year's work in modern language
studies. 1929/30- [Leeds, Eng.,
etc.] Modern Humanities Research
Association [etc.] 405.8 31-32540
   PB1 .Y45 MRR Alc Full set

LANGUAGES, MODERN--CONVERSATION AND
PHRASE BOOKS--POLYGLOT.
Lyall, Archibald. A guide to 25
languages of Europe. Rev. ed.
[Harrisburg, Pa.] Stackpole Co.
[1966] viii, 407 p.   413 66-20847
   PB73 .L85 1966 MRR Alc.

LANGUAGES, MODERN--GLOSSARIES,
VOCABULARIES, ETC.
Conference terminology, 2d ed., rev.
and augm. Amsterdam, New York,
Elsevier Pub. Co.: [sole distributors
for the U.S.: American Elsevier Pub.
Co., New York] 1962. 162 p.   413
63-8568
   PB324.C6 C6 1962 MRR Alc.

Lessere, Samuel E. Harlan's foreign
language speak-easy, [3d ed.]
Greenlawn, N.Y., Harlan Publications
[1957] 106 p.   418.24 57-14033
   PE1635 .L4 1957 MRR Alc.

Lyall, Archibald, A guide to 25
languages of Europe. Rev. ed.
[Harrisburg, Pa.] Stackpole Co.
[1966] viii, 407 p.   413 66-20847
   PB73 .L85 1966 MRR Alc.

LANGUAGES, MODERN--HANDBOOKS, MANUALS,
ETC.
Von Ostermann, George Frederick,
Manual of foreign languages 4th ed.,
rev. and enl. New York, Central Book
Co., 1952. 414 p.   402/.02 52-2409
   Z253 .V94 1952 MRR Alc.

LANGUAGES, MODERN--STUDY AND TEACHING--
BIBLIOGRAPHY.
Blass, Birgit A. A provisional
survey of materials for the study of
neglected languages, Washington,
Center for Applied Linguistics
[c1969] vi, 414 p.   016.41 78-
113390
   Z7001 .B59 MRR Alc.

Centre for Information on Language
Teaching. A language-teaching
bibliography, 2d ed. Cambridge
[Eng.] University Press, 1972. x,
242 p.   016.407 76-152633
   Z5814.L26 C45 1972 MRR Alc.

Walford, Albert John. A guide to
foreign language grammars and
dictionaries, 2nd ed., revised and
enlarged. London, Library
Association, 1967. 240 p. [60/-]
016.415 68-86136
   Z7004.G7 W3 1967 MRR Alc.

LANGUAGES, MODERN--STUDY AND TEACHING--
UNITED STATES.
Language and area studies, East
Central and Southeastern Europe;
Chicago, University of Chicago Press
[1969] xix, 483 p.   914.7 72-81222
   DR34.8 .L33 MRR Alc.

LANGUAGES, MODERN--YEARBOOKS.
The Year's work in modern language
studies, 1929/30- [Leeds, Eng.,
etc.] Modern Humanities Research
Association [etc.] 405.8 31-32540
   PB1 .Y45 MRR Alc Full set

LANTERN SLIDES--CATALOGS.
American Library Color Slide Company,
inc., New York. The American Library
compendium and index of world art;
New York, American Archives of World
Art [c1961] xv, 465 p.   016.704973
61-18783
   N4040 .A45 MRR Alc.

United States. Library of Congress.
Prints and photographs division. The
colonial art of Latin America.
Washington, D.C., The Library of
Congress, 1945. xii, 43 p.   709.8
46-25650
   Z663.39 .C6 MRR Alc.

LAO LANGUAGE--DICTIONARIES--ENGLISH.
Marcus, Russell. English-Lao, Lao-
English dictionary. Rutland, Vt., C.
E. Tuttle Co. [1970] 416 p. [5.00]
495/.919 77-116487
   PL4251.L34 M3 1970 MRR Alc.

LAOS.
Roberts, Thomas Duval. Area handbook
for Laos. Washington, For sale by
the Supt. of Docs., U.S. Govt. Print.
Off., 1967. ix, 349 p.   915.95 68-
60604
   DS557.L2 R6 MRR Alc.

Whitaker, Donald P. Area handbook
for Laos. Washington, For sale by
the Supt. of Docs., U.S. Govt. Print.
Off., 1972. xiv, 337 p. [$4.50]
915.94/03/4 72-600173
   DS557.L2 W5 MRR Alc.

LAOS--BIBLIOGRAPHY.
United States. Library of Congress.
Orientalia Division. Southeast Asia
subject catalog. Boston, G. K. Hall,
1972- v.   016.9159/03 72-5257
   Z3221 .U525 MRR Alc (Dk 33)

LAOS--GAZETTEERS.
United States. Office of Geography.
Laos; Washington, 1963. v, 214 p.
915.94/003 71-10003
   DS557.L22 U5 1963 MRR Alc.

LAST WORDS.
Conrad, Barnaby, comp. Famous last
words. [1st ed.] Garden City, N.Y.,
Doubleday, 1961. 208 p.   808.88 61-
12505
   PN6328.L3 C65 MRR Alc.

LAST WORDS. (Cont.)
Marvin, Frederic Rowland, The last words (real and traditional) of distinguished men and women, New York, Chicago [etc.] F. H. Revell co., 1901. 3 p. l., 336 p. 01-22886
 PN6328.L8 M8 1901 MRR Alc.

LATIN AMERICA.
James, Preston Everett, Latin America. 4th ed. New York, Odyssey Press [1969] xx, 947 p. 818 69-10222
 F1408 .J28 1969 MRR Alc.

The South American handbook. [1st]-annual ed.; 1924- London, Trade & Travel Pub. [etc.] 25-514
 F1401 .S71 MRR Alc Latest edition

United States. Library of Congress. Legislative reference service. Latin American abstracts ... [Washington] Library of Congress, Legislative reference service, 1943- v. 918 44-6896
 Z663.6 .L3 MRR Alc.

Véliz, Claudio. Latin America and the Caribbean; New York, Praeger [1968] xxiv, 840 p. 918/.03 68-14143
 F1408 .V43 MRR Alc.

LATIN AMERICA--ANTIQUITIES.
Kubler, George, The art and architecture of ancient America; Baltimore, Penguin Books [1962] xxv, 396 p. 970.67 62-5022
 E59.A7 K8 MRR Alc.

LATIN AMERICA--BIBLIOGRAPHY.
American Universities Field Staff. A select bibliography: Asia, Africa, Eastern Europe, Latin America. New York [1960] ix, 534 p. 016.9019 60-10482
 Z5579 .A5 MRR Alc.

Andrews, David H. Latin America; a bibliography of paperback books, Washington, Hispanic Foundation, Reference Dept., Library of Congress; [for sale by the Superintendent of Documents, U.S. Govt. Print. Off.] 1964. v, 38 p. 64-60047
 Z663.32 .A5 no. 9 MRR Alc.

Bayitch, S. A. Latin America and the Caribbean; Coral Gables, Fla., University of Miami Press, 1967. xxviii, 943 p. 016.918/03 67-28900
 Z1601 .B35 MRR Alc.

Birkos, Alexander S. Latin American studies. [Kent, Ohio] Kent State University Press [1971] 359 p. 808.02/5 70-160685
 Z1601 .B54 MRR Alc.

Brunn, Stanley D. Urbanization in developing countries; East Lansing, Latin American Studies Center, Michigan State University, 1971. xviii, 693 p. 016.30136/3/091724 79-172535
 Z7164.U7 B7 MRR Alc.

Chilcote, Ronald H. Revolution and structural change in Latin America; Stanford, Calif., Hoover Institution on War, Revolution and Peace, Stanford University, 1970. 2 v. 016.3091/8/03 68-28100
 Z1601 .C496 MRR Alc.

Dorn, Georgette M. Latin America; an annotated bibliography of paperback books, Washington, Library of Congress; [for sale by the Supt. of Docs., U.S. Govt. Print. Off.] 1967. 77 p. 016.918 67-60082
 Z663.32 .A5 no. 11 MRR Alc.

Dorn, Georgette M. Latin America, Spain, and Portugal; an annotated bibliography of paperback books. Washington, Library of Congress, 1971. 180 p. [$0.75] 016.918 71-37945
 Z663.32 .A5 no. 32 MRR Alc.

Griffin, Charles Carroll, Latin America: a guide to the historical literature. Austin, Published for the Conference on Latin American History by the University of Texas Press [c1971] xxx, 700 p. [$25.00] 016.98 71-165916
 Z1601 .G75 MRR Alc.

Gropp, Arthur Eric, A bibliography of Latin American bibliographies, Metuchen, N.J., Scarecrow Press, 1968. ix, 515 p. 016.01698 68-9330
 Z1601.A2 G76 1968 MRR Alc.

Hispanic Foundation bibliographical series: no. 1- 1942- Washington, Library of Congress, Reference Dept. 42-38547
 Z663.32 .A5 MRR Alc MRR Alc Full set

Mason, Lois E., comp. Bibliography of Latin America, 1955-1964; Columbus, Dept. of Geography, Ohio State University, 1965. vi, 232 l. 016.918 65-64902
 Z1601 .M33 MRR Alc.

Morris, James Oliver, Bibliography of industrial relations in Latin America, Ithaca, New York State School of Industrial and Labor Relations, Cornell University [1967] xv, 290 p. 016.6580098 67-64729
 Z7164.L1 M69 MRR Alc.

Okinshevich, Leo, Latin America in Soviet writings; Baltimore, Published for the Library of Congress by the Johns Hopkins Press [1966] 2 v. 016.91803 66-16039
 Z1601 .O55 MRR Alc.

Okinshevich, Leo, Latin America in Soviet writings, 1945-1958; Washington, Slavic and Central European Division and the Hispanic Foundation, Reference Dept., Library of Congress, 1959. xii, 257 p. 016.98 59-64248
 Z663.32 .A5 no. 5 MRR Alc.

Palau y Dulcet, Antonio, 1867-1954. Manual del librero hispano-americano; 2. ed. corr. y aumentada por el autor. Barcelona, A. Palau, 1948- v. 015.46 49-2664
 Z2681 .P16 MRR Alc.

Pan American Union. Columbus Memorial Library. Index to Latin American periodical literature, 1929-1960. Boston, G. K. Hall, 1962. 8 v. (xv, 6030 p.) 016.918 63-590
 Z1601 .P16 MRR Alc.

Sable, Martin Howard. Latin American urbanization: Metuchen, N.J., Scarecrow Press, 1971. 1077 p. 016.3013/6/098 74-145643
 Z7165.L3 S28 MRR Alc.

United States. Dept. of the Army. Latin America and the Caribbean; Washington; [For sale by the Supt. of Docs., U.S. Govt. Print. Off.] 1969. vii, 319 p. 016.918 76-603569
 Z1601 .U63 MRR Alc.

LATIN AMERICA--BIOGRAPHY.
Enciclopedia vniversal ilvstrada evropeo-americana; Barcelona, J. Espasa [1907?-30] 70 v. in 72. 036 32-11302
 AE61 .E6 MRR Alc.

Encyclopedia of Latin America. New York, McGraw-Hill [1974] ix, 651 p. 918/.03/03 74-1036
 F1406 .E52 MRR Alc.

Latin American government leaders. Tempe, Center for Latin American Studies of Arizona State University, 1970. 60 p. 73-631271
 F1407 .L37 MRR Biog.

Martin, Michael Rheta, Encyclopedia of Latin-American history Rev. ed. Indianapolis, Bobbs-Merrill [1968] vi, 348 p. 980/.003 66-28231
 F1408 .M36 1968 MRR Alc.

LATIN AMERICA--BIOGRAPHY--BIBLIOGRAPHY.
Peña Cámara, José María de la. A list of Spanish residencias in the Archives of the Indies, 1516-1775; Washington, Library of Congress, Reference Dept., 1955. x, 109 p. 016.98 55-60017
 Z663.32 .S7 MRR Alc.

Toro, Josefina del, A bibliography of the collective biography of Spanish America, Rio Piedras, P.R., The University [1938] viii, 140 p. 016.92808 39-28101
 Z1609.B6 T6 MRR Biog.

LATIN AMERICA--BIOGRAPHY--DICTIONARIES.
Dictionary of Latin American and Caribbean biography. 2d ed. London, Melrose Press, 1971. 458 p. [£8.50 ($20.00 U.S.)] 920.08 75-28705
 F1407 .D5 1971 MRR Biog.

Who's who in Latin America; 3d ed. Detroit, B. Ethridge, 1971 [c1945] 2 v. 920.08 76-165656
 CT506 .W48 1971 MRR Biog.

LATIN AMERICA--CENSUS--BIBLIOGRAPHY.
United States. Library of Congress. Census library project. General censuses and vital statistics in the Americas. Washington, U.S. Govt. print. off., 1943. ix, 151 p. 016.312 44-40643
 Z7553.C3 U45 MRR Alc.

LATIN AMERICA--CIVILIZATION.
Bailey, Helen Miller. Latin America; 2d ed. Englewood Cliffs, N.J., Prentice-Hall [1968] 822 p. 980 67-12678
 F1408 .B16 1968 MRR Alc.

Henríquez-Ureña, Pedro, Literary currents in Hispanic America. Cambridge, Mass., Harvard university press, 1945. vi , 2 l., [3]-345 p. 860.9 a 45-2956
 PQ7081 .H39 MRR Alc.

Hilton, Ronald, ed. Handbook of Hispanic source materials and research organizations in the United States. 2d ed. Stanford, Calif., Stanford University press, 1956. xiv, 448 p. 980 56-6178
 F1408.3 .H65 1956 MRR Alc.

LATIN AMERICA--CIVILIZATION--HISTORY.
Arciniegas, German, Latin America: a cultural history. [1st American ed.] New York, Knopf, 1967 [c1966] xxvii, 594 p. 918/.03 66-11342
 F1408.3 .A663 MRR Alc.

LATIN AMERICA--COMMERCE--DIRECTORIES.
Anuario comercial iberoamericano. [Madrid] OFICE. 380.1/025 74-644606
 HF3683 .A48 MRR Alc Latest edition

Chico, Vicente V. International importers & exporters; 1st ed. Manila, Nationwide Business Agency [1971] 1068 p. 382/.025 76-31299
 HF54.P6 C54 MRR Alc.

Dun and Bradstreet, inc. International market guide; v. 1- 1938- New York. 38-18610
 HF54.U5 D8 MRR Alc Latest edition

The International telex book. Americas edition. v. 1- 1974- Atlanta, International Telex Corp. 384.1/4 74-645911
 HE7621 .I59 MRR Alc Latest edition

LATIN AMERICA--DESCRIPTION AND TRAVEL--1951-
Robinson, Harry, Latin America; a geographical survey, [Rev. ed.] New York, Praeger [1967] xii, 499 p. 918 67-24686
 F1409.2 .R6 1967 MRR Alc.

LATIN AMERICA--DESCRIPTION AND TRAVEL--GUIDE-BOOKS.
Fodor's South America. 1970- New York, D. McKay. 918/.04/3 72-622642
 F2211 .F6 MRR Alc Latest edition

Kane, Robert S. South America, A to Z. Rev. ed. Garden City, N.Y., Doubleday [1971] xiii, 346 p. [$7.95] 918/.04/3 70-84391
 F2211 .K3 1971 MRR Alc.

The South American handbook. [1st]-annual ed.; 1924- London, Trade & Travel Pub. [etc.] 25-514
 F1401 .S71 MRR Alc Latest edition

LATIN AMERICA--DICTIONARIES AND ENCYCLOPEDIAS.
Encyclopedia of Latin America. New York, McGraw-Hill [1974] ix, 651 p. 918/.03/03 74-1036
 F1406 .E52 MRR Alc.

Martin, Michael Rheta, Encyclopedia of Latin-American history Rev. ed. Indianapolis, Bobbs-Merrill [1968] vi, 348 p. 980/.003 66-28231
 F1408 .M36 1968 MRR Alc.

LATIN AMERICA--DIRECTORIES.
The Europa year book. 1959- London, Europa Publications. 341.184 59-2942
 JN1 .E85 Sci RR Latest edition / MRR Ref Desk Latest edition

Latin America technical assistance programs of U.S. nonprofit organizations. New York, Technical Assistance Information Clearing House. 309.2/23 72-4820
 HC122 .L3 MRR Alc Latest edition

Sable, Martin Howard. Master directory for Latin America. Los Angeles, Latin American Center, University of California, 1965. xxi, 438 p. 918.03306 66-25
 F1406.5 .S3 MRR Alc.

LATIN AMERICA--DISCOVERY AND EXPLORATION
see America--Discovery and exploration

LATIN AMERICA--ECONOMIC CONDITIONS--1945-
Grunwald, Joseph, Natural resources in Latin American development, Baltimore, Published for Resources for the Future, Inc., by the Johns Hopkins Press [1970] xvii, 494 p. [20.00] 330.98 77-108381
 HC125 .G72 MRR Alc.

LATIN AMERICA--ECONOMIC CONDITIONS--BIBLIOGRAPHY.
Kiel. Universität. Institut für Weltwirtschaft. Bibliothek. Regionenkatalog. Boston, G. K. Hall, 1967. 52 v. 017/.5 67-9425
 Z929 .K52 1967 MRR Alc. (Dk 33).

LATIN AMERICA--ECONOMIC CONDITIONS--OUTLINES, SYLLABI, ETC.
Wilgus, Alva Curtis. Historical atlas of Latin America: [New and enl. ed.] New York, Cooper Square Pbulishers, 1967. xi, 365 p.
911/.8 66-30784
F1408 .W66 1967 MRR Alc.

LATIN AMERICA--ECONOMIC CONDITIONS--PERIODICALS--BIBLIOGRAPHY.
Committee on Latin America. Latin American economic & social serials: London, Published on behalf of COLA by Bingley, 1969. 189 p. [50/-]
016.3091/8 74-382598
Z7165.L3 C65 MRR Alc.

LATIN AMERICA--FOREIGN RELATIONS--TREATIES.
Manning, William Ray, ed. Arbitration treaties among the American nations, to the close of the year 1910. New York [etc.] Oxford university press, 1924. xl, 472 p.
24-6749
JX1985 .M3 MRR Alc.

LATIN AMERICA--FOREIGN RELATIONS--UNITED STATES.
Gantenbein, James Watson, ed. The evolution of our Latin-American policy. New York, Columbia University Press, 1950. xxvii, 979 p.
327.73098 49-50406
F1418 .G2 MRR Alc.

LATIN AMERICA--FOREIGN RELATIONS--UNITED STATES--BIBLIOGRAPHY.
Trask, David F. A bibliography of United States-Latin American relations since 1810: Lincoln, University of Nebraska Press [1968] xxxi, 441 p. [$14.95] 016.32773/08
67-14421
Z1609.R4 T7 MRR Alc.

LATIN AMERICA--GOVERNMENT PUBLICATIONS--BIBLIOGRAPHY.
United States. Library of Congress. A guide to the official publications of the other American republics.
Washington, [1945]- v. in 015.8
45-36618
Z1605 .U64 MRR Alc.

LATIN AMERICA--HANDBOOKS, MANUALS, ETC.
Worldmark encyclopedia of the nations. [4th ed.] New York, Worldmark Press, [1971] 5 v.
910/.3 76-152128
G103 .W65 1971 MRR Ref Desk.

A Year book of the Commonwealth.
1969- London, H.M. Stationery Off.
320.9/171/242 79-7332
JN248 .C5912 MRR Alc Latest edition

LATIN AMERICA--HISTORICAL GEOGRAPHY--MAPS.
Wilgus, Alva Curtis, Historical atlas of Latin America: [New and enl. ed.] New York, Cooper Square Pbulishers, 1967. xi, 365 p.
911/.8 66-30784
F1408 .W66 1967 MRR Alc.

LATIN AMERICA--HISTORY.
Bailey, Helen Miller. Latin America; 2d ed. Englewood Cliffs, N.J., Prentice-Hall [1968] 822 p. 980
67-12678
F1408 .E16 1968 MRR Alc.

Fagg, John Edwin. Latin America, a general history. 2d ed. [New York] Macmillan [1969] xiii, 814 p. 980
69-10455
F1410 .F25 1969 MRR Alc.

Rippy, James Fred. Latin America; a modern history. New ed., rev. and enl. Ann Arbor, University of Michigan Press [1968] xiv, 594, xxii p. [$10.00] 980 68-29268
F1410 .R454 1968 MRR Alc.

LATIN AMERICA--HISTORY--TO 1800--SOURCES--BIBLIOGRAPHY.
Peña Cámara, José María de la. A list of Spanish residencias in the Archives of the Indies, 1516-1775; Washington, Library of Congress, Reference Dept., 1955. x, 109 p.
016.98 55-60017
Z663.32.S7 MRR Alc.

LATIN AMERICA--HISTORY--TO 1830--BIBLIOGRAPHY--CATALOGS.
Hispanic Society of America. Library. Catalogue of the library. Boston, G. K. Hall, 1962. 10 v. (10048 p.)
62-52682
Z881 .N639 MRR Alc (Dk33)

LATIN AMERICA--HISTORY--1948-
Latin America. 1972- New York, Facts on File, inc. 918/.005 73-83047
F1401 .L325 MRR Alc Latest edition

LATIN AMERICA--HISTORY--BIBLIOGRAPHY.
Griffin, Charles Carroll, Latin America: a guide to the historical literature. Austin, Published for the Conference on Latin American History by the University of Texas Press [c1971] xxx, 700 p. [$25.00]
016.98 71-165916
Z1601 .G75 MRR Alc.

Indice histórico español. Bibliografía histórica de España e Hispanoamérica. v. 1- enero/marzo 1953- [Barcelona] Editorial Teide.
57-34741
Z2696 .I6 MRR Alc Full set

LATIN AMERICA--HISTORY--BIBLIOGRAPHY--CATALOGS.
New York. Public Library. Reference Dept. Dictionary catalog of the history of the Americas. Boston, G. K. Hall, 1961. 28 v. 016.97 61-4957
Z1201 .N4 MRR Alc (Dk 33).

LATIN AMERICA--HISTORY--BIO-BIBLIOGRAPHY.
Cline, Howard Francis, comp. Historians of Latin America in the United States, 1965; Durham, N.C., Published for the Conference on Latin American History [by] Duke University Press, 1966. xiv, 105 p.
980.0720922 66-22489
F1409.8.A2 C55 MRR Biog.

LATIN AMERICA--HISTORY--OUTLINES, SYLLABI, ETC.
Wilgus, Alva Curtis, Historical atlas of Latin America: [New and enl. ed.] New York, Cooper Square Pbulishers, 1967. xi, 365 p.
911/.8 66-30784
F1408 .W66 1967 MRR Alc.

LATIN AMERICA--HISTORY--SOURCES.
Thomas, Norman F., comp. Selected documents in the history of Latin America. [Tacoma? Wash.] c1961. 174 p. 62-1117
F1410 .T5 MRR Alc.

LATIN AMERICA--IMPRINTS.
Brown University. Library. List of Latin American imprints before 1800, Providence, 1952. iv, 140 p. 015.8 a 53-2246
Z1610 .B695 MRR Alc.

Libros en venta en Hispanoamérica y España; [1. ed.] New York, R. R. Bowker Co., 1964. 1891 p. 015.8 64-3492
Z1601 .L59 MRR Alc.

Palau y Dulcet, Antonio, 1867-1954. Manual del librero hispano-americano; 2. ed. corr. y aumentada por el autor. Barcelona, A. Palau, 1948-v. 015.46 49-2664
Z2681 .P16 MRR Alc.

LATIN AMERICA--OFFICIALS AND EMPLOYEES--BIBLIOGRAPHY.
Peña Cámara, José María de la. A list of Spanish residencias in the Archives of the Indies, 1516-1775; Washington, Library of Congress, Reference Dept., 1955. x, 109 p.
016.98 55-60017
Z663.32.S7 MRR Alc.

LATIN AMERICA--PERIODICALS.
Latin America. 1972- New York, Facts on File, inc. 918/.005 73-83047
F1401 .L325 MRR Alc Latest edition

LATIN AMERICA--PERIODICALS--BIBLIOGRAPHY.
Birkos, Alexander S. Latin American studies. [Kent, Ohio] Kent State University Press [1971] 359 p.
808.02/5 70-160685
Z1601 .B54 MRR Alc.

LATIN AMERICA--PERIODICALS--INDEXES.
Chilcote, Ronald H. Revolution and structural change in Latin America; Stanford, Calif., Hoover Institution on War, Revolution and Peace, Stanford University, 1970. 2 v.
016.3091/8/03 68-28100
Z1601 .C496 MRR Alc.

Griffin, Charles Carroll, Latin America: a guide to the historical literature. Austin, Published for the Conference on Latin American History by the University of Texas Press [c1971] xxx, 700 p. [$25.00]
016.98 71-165916
Z1601 .G75 MRR Alc.

Indice general de publicaciones periódicas latinoamericanas; v. 1- 1961- New York [etc.] Scarecrow Press [etc.] 056.1 65-13548
Z1605 .I55 MRR Alc Full set

Pan American Union. Columbus Memorial Library. Index to Latin American periodical literature, 1929-1960. Boston, G. K. Hall, 1962. 8 v. (xv, 6030 p.) 016.918 63-590
Z1601 .P16 MRR Alc.

LATIN AMERICA--POLITICS.
Kantor, Harry. Patterns of politics and political systems in Latin America. Chicago, Rand McNally [1969] xiii, 742 p. 320.3/098 68-16840
JF51 .K3 MRR Alc.

LATIN AMERICA--POLITICS--1948-
Latin America. 1972- New York, Facts on File, inc. 918/.005 73-83047
F1401 .L325 MRR Alc Latest edition

Latin American political guide. Manitou Springs, Col. [etc.] Juniper Editions [etc.] 31-34267
F1414 .L28 MRR Alc Latest edition

Needler, Martin C., ed. Political systems of Latin America. 2d ed. New York, Van Nostrand Reinhold Co. [1970] xviii, 621 p. 320.9/8 78-90774
F1414.2 .N4 1970 MRR Alc.

LATIN AMERICA--POLITICS--BIBLIOGRAPHY.
Chilcote, Ronald H. Revolution and structural change in Latin America; Stanford, Calif., Hoover Institution on War, Revolution and Peace, Stanford University, 1970. 2 v.
016.3091/8/03 68-28100
Z1601 .C496 MRR Alc.

Kantor, Harry. Latin American political parties; a bibliography, [Gainesville] Reference and Bibliography Dept., University of Florida Libraries, 1968. ix, 113 p.
016.3299/8 a 68-7771
Z7165.L3 K3 MRR Alc.

LATIN AMERICA--RELATIONS (GENERAL) WITH THE UNITED STATES.
Sable, Martin Howard. Master directory for Latin America, Los Angeles, Latin American Center, University of California 1965. xxi, 438 p. 918.03306 66-25
F1406.5 .S3 MRR Alc.

LATIN AMERICA--SOCIAL CONDITIONS--1945-
Needler, Martin C., ed. Political systems of Latin America. 2d ed. New York, Van Nostrand Reinhold Co. [1970] xviii, 621 p. 320.9/8 78-90774
F1414.2 .N4 1970 MRR Alc.

LATIN AMERICA--SOCIAL CONDITIONS--PERIODICALS--BIBLIOGRAPHY.
Committee on Latin America. Latin American economic & social serials: London, Published on behalf of COLA by Bingley, 1969. 189 p. [50/-]
016.3091/8 74-382598
Z7165.L3 C65 MRR Alc.

LATIN AMERICA--STATISTICS.
Deldycke, Tilo. La population active et sa structure. Bruxelles, Centre d'économie politique (de l') Université libre de Bruxelles, (1968) viii, 236 p. [360.00]
331.1/12/0212 70-395436
HD4826 .D34 MRR Alc.

Food and Agriculture Organization of the United Nations. Trade yearbook. v. 12- 1958- Rome. 338.14058 59-3598
HD9000.4 .F58 Sci RR Partial set / MRR Alc Latest edition

Grunwald, Joseph, Natural resources in Latin American development, Baltimore, Published for Resources for the Future, inc., by the Johns Hopkins Press [1970] xvii, 494 p. [20.00] 330.98 77-108381
HC125 .G72 MRR Alc.

International Labor Office. Year book of labour statistics. [1st]-1935/36- Geneva. l 36-130
HD4826 .I63 MRR Alc Latest edition

International Monetary Fund. Balance of payments yearbook. 1946/47-Washington. 382 49-6612
HF1014 .I5 MRR Alc Latest edition

Keyfitz, Nathan, Population: facts and methods of demography San Francisco, W. H. Freeman [1971] x, 613 p. [$13.50] 301.3/2/072 70-141154
HB885 .K43 MRR Alc.

Organization for Economic Cooperation and Development. Foreign trade. Commerce extérieur. Series C. Commodity trade. Commerce par produits. [Paris] 382/.021/2 72-626755
HF91 .O67 MRR Latest edition

Predicasts, inc. World food supply & demand / Cleveland : Predicasts, inc., 1974. v, 90 leaves ; 338.1/9 74-187853
HD9000.4 .P73 1974 MRR Alc.

LATIN AMERICA--STATISTICS. (Cont.)
Showers, Victor. The world in
figures. New York, Wiley [1973]
xii, 585 p.   910/.21/2   73-9
   G109 .S52 MRR Ref Desk.

Statistical activities of the
American nations, 1940; Washington,
D.C., Inter American statistical
institute, 1941. xxxi, 842 p.
311.397   41-14318
   HA175 .S75 MRR Alc.

United Nations. Conference on Trade
and Development. Secretariat. Trade
prospects and capital needs of
developing countries; New York,
United Nations, 1968. ix, 614 p.
[8.00]   382/.09172/3   75-5813
   HF1413 .U52 MRR Alc.

United Nations. Statistical Office.
The growth of world industry, 1938-
1961; New York, United Nations,
1963. xvi, 849 p.   338.4083 63-
25411
   HC59 .U46 MRR Alc.

United Nations. Statistical Office.
Yearbook of international trade
statistics. 1st- issue; 1950- New
York. 382.058   51-8987
   JX1977 .A2 MRR Ref Desk Latest
      edition

United States. Bureau of the Census.
U.S. foreign trade: general imports,
world area by commodity groupings.
1970- [Washington, For sale by the
Supt. of Docs., U.S. Govt. Print.
Off.]   382/.5/0973   78-649732
   HF105 .C137172 MRR Alc Latest
      edition

United States. Bureau of the Census.
U.S. foreign trade: exports, SIC-
based products. 1870- [Washington,
For sale by the Supt. of Docs., U.S.
Govt. Print. Off.] 382/.6/0873 71-
648606
   HF105 .C137166 MRR Alc Latest
      edition

United States. Bureau of the Census.
U.S. foreign trade: exports, world
area by commodity groupings. 1970-
[Washington, For sale by the Supt. of
Docs., U.S. Govt. Print. Off.]
382/.6/0973   79-648608
   HF105 .C137132 MRR Alc Latest
      edition

United States. Dept. of Agriculture.
Economic Research Service. European
Economic Community: agricultural
trade statistics, 1961-67.
[Washington, 1969] 1 v. (unpaged)
382/.41/094 78-601937
   HD9015.A3 U46 MRR Alc.

United States. Dept. of Agriculture.
Economic Research Service. Foreign
Regional Analysis Division. Indices
of agricultural production for the
Western Hemisphere excluding the
United States; Washington] 1969.
ii, 33 p.   338.1/0918/12 72-601512

   HD1415 .U49 MRR Alc.

Véliz, Claudio. Latin America and
the Caribbean; New York, Praeger
[1968] xxiv, 840 p.   918/.03 68-
14143
   F1408 .V43 MRR Alc.

LATIN AMERICA--STATISTICS--BIBLIOGRAPHY.
Harvey, Joan M. Statistics America:
sources for market research (North,
Central & South America), Beckenham,
CBD Research, 1973. xii, 225 p.
[£6.00 ($22.00 U.S.)] 016.317 73-
180742
   Z7554.A5 H37 MRR Alc.

Inter American Statistical Institute.
Bibliography of selected statistical
sources of the American nations. 1st
ed. Washington, 1847. xvi, 689 p.
016.31   48-6568
   Z7554.S75 I4 1947 MRR Alc.

Texas. University. Population
Research Center. International
population census bibliography.
Austin, Bureau of Business Research,
University of Texas, 1965-67. 6 v.
016.312   66-63578
   Z7164.D3 T45 MRR Alc.

LATIN AMERICA--STATISTICS--YEARBOOKS.
The South American handbook. [1st]-
annual ed.; 1924- London, Trade &
Travel Pub. [etc.]   25-514
   F1401 .S71 MRR Alc Latest edition

Statistical abstract of Latin
America. [1st]- 1955- Los
Angeles.   56-63659
   HA935 .S8 MRR Ref Desk Latest
      edition / MRR Alc Latest edition

LATIN AMERICA--STATISTICS, VITAL.
Preston, Samuel H. Causes of death:
life tables for national population
New York, Seminar Press, 1972. xi,
787 p.   312/.2 72-80305
   HB1321 .P73 MRR Alc.

LATIN AMERICA--STATISTICS, VITAL--
BIBLIOGRAPHY.
United States. Library of Congress.
Census library project. General
censuses and vital statistics in the
Americas. Washington, U.S. Govt.
print. off., 1943. ix, 151 p.
016.312   44-40643
   Z7553.C3 U45 MRR Alc.

LATIN AMERICAN ART
   see Art, Latin American

LATIN AMERICAN LITERATURE--20TH CENTURY-
-PHONOTAPE CATALOGS.
United States. Library of Congress.
Latin American, Portuguese, and
Spanish Division. The Archive of
Hispanic Literature on Tape;
Washington, Library of Congress; [for
sale by the Supt. of Docs., U.S.
Govt. Print. Off.] 1974. xii, 516 p.
016.86/008   73-19812
   Z663.32 .A7 MRR Alc.

LATIN AMERICAN LITERATURE--BIBLIOGRAPHY.
Chatham, James R., Dissertations in
Hispanic languages and literatures;
[Lexington] University Press of
Kentucky [1970]   xiv, 120 p. [12.50]
016.46   70-80093
   Z2695 .A2C46 MRR Alc.

Grismer, Raymond Leonard, A
reference index to twelve thousand
Spanish American authors; New York,
The H. W. Wilson company, 1939. xvi
p., 1 l., 150 p.   016.86   39-32334
   Z1601 .G86 MRR Alc.

Simón Díaz, José. Bibliografía
de literatura hispánica. 2. ed.
corr. y aumentada. Madrid, Consejo
Superior de Investigaciones
Científicas, Instituto "Miguel de
Cervantes" de Filología Hispánica,
1960- v.   64-5767
   Z2691 .S52 MRR Alc.

LATIN AMERICAN LITERATURE--BIBLIOGRAPHY-
-CATALOGS.
Brown University. Library.
Dictionary catalog of the Harris
collection of American poetry and
plays, Brown University Library,
Providence, Rhode Island. Boston, G.
K. Hall, 1972. 13 v.   016.81 75-
184497
   Z1231.P7 B72 MRR Alc (Dk 33)

LATIN AMERICAN LITERATURE--BIO-
BIBLIOGRAPHY.
The Penguin companion to American
literature. New York, McGraw-Hill
[1971] 384 p. [$9.95] 809 70-
158062
   PN843 .P4 MRR Alc.

LATIN AMERICAN LITERATURE--HISTORY AND
CRITICISM.
Anderson Imbert, Enrique, Spanish-
American literature; 2d ed., rev and
updated Detroit, Wayne State
University Press, 1969- v.   [5.95
(v. 1)]   860.9   70-75087
   PQ7081 .A56342 MRR Alc.

Cejador y Frauca, Julio, Historia de
la lengua y literatura castellana ...
Madrid, Imprenta Radio, 1916-30. 14
v. in 15.   mrr01-65
   PQ6032 .C3 1916 MRR Alc.

Henríquez-Ureña, Pedro, Literary
currents in Hispanic America,
Cambridge, Mass., Harvard university
press 1945. vi p., 2 l., [3]-345 p.
860.9   a 45-2956
   PQ7081 .H39 MRR Alc.

LATIN AMERICAN LITERATURE--TRANSLATIONS
INTO ENGLISH--BIBLIOGRAPHY.
Granier, James Albert, Latin
American belles-lettres in English
translation; [2d rev. ed.]
Washington, 1943. ii, 33 p. 016.86
44-40918
   Z663.32 .A5 no. 1 1943 MRR Alc.

Levine, Suzanne Jill. Latin America
fiction & poetry in translation. New
York, Center for Inter-American
Relations [1970] 71 p. [1.25]
016.8608   75-121376
   Z1609.T7 L45 MRR Alc.

LATIN AMERICAN NEWSPAPERS--BIBLIOGRAPHY-
-UNION LISTS.
Gropp, Arthur Eric, comp. Union list
of Latin American newspapers in
libraries in the United States.
Washington, Dept. of Cultural
Affairs, Pan American Union, 1953.
x, 235 p.   016.0798   53-61715
   Z6945 .P18 MRR Alc.

Latin American newspapers in United
States libraries; Austin, Published
for the Conference on Latin American
History by the University of Texas
Press [1969, c1968] xiv, 619 p.
[20.00]   016.07918   69-63004
   Z6947 .C5 MRR Alc.

LATIN AMERICAN NEWSPAPERS--DIRECTORIES.
Feuereisen, Fritz. Die Presse in
Lateinamerika; 1. Ausg. Munchen-
Pullach, Verlag Dokumentation, 1968.
272 p.   68-132933
   Z6954.A1 F4 MRR Alc.

LATIN AMERICAN PERIODICALS--
BIBLIOGRAPHY.
Committee on Latin America. Latin
American economic & social serials:
London, Published on behalf of COLA
by Bingley, 1969. 189 p. [50/-]
016.05917L   74-382598
   Z7165.L3 C65 MRR Alc.

Pan American Union. Dept. of
Scientific Affairs. Guide to Latin
American scientific and technical
periodicals; Washington, Pan
American Union, 1962. xii, 187 p.
016.505   62-62414
   Z7407.S6 P3 MRR Alc.

Zimmerman, Irene, A guide to current
Latin American periodicals: [1st
ed.] Gainesville, Fla., Kallman Pub.
Co., 1961. x, 357 p.   61-15751
   Z6954.S8 Z5 MRR Alc.

LATIN AMERICAN PERIODICALS--
BIBLIOGRAPHY--CATALOGS.
United States. Library of Congress.
Latin American periodicals currently
received in the Library of Congress
and in the library of the Department
of agriculture. Washington, The
Library of Congress, 1944. vii, 249
p.   016.056   45-35735
   Z663.32 .L3 MRR Alc.

LATIN AMERICAN PERIODICALS--INDEXES.
Indice general de publicaciones
periodicas latinoamericanas; v. 1-
1961- New York [etc.] Scarecrow
Press [etc.]   056.1   65-13548
   Z1605 .I55 MRR Alc Full set

LATIN AMERICANISTS.
Cutolo, Vicente Osvaldo.
Historiadores argentinos y
americanos, 1963-65. Buenos Aires,
Casa Pardo, 1966. xxiii, 447 p.   66-
83008
   F1409.8.A2 C8 MRR Biog.

United States. Library of Congress.
Hispanic Foundation. National
directory of Latin Americanists;
Washington, [For sale by the
Superintendent of Documents, U.S.
Govt. Print. Off.] 1966. iii, 351 p.
920/.08   65-61762
   Z663.32.A5 no. 10 MRR Biog.

LATIN AMERICANISTS--UNITED STATES.
United States. Library of Congress.
Hispanic Foundation. National
directory of Latin Americanists; 2d
ed. Washington, Library of Congress;
[for sale by the Supt. of Docs., U.S.
Govt. Print. Off. 1971 [i.e. 1972]
684 p. [$4.25] 918/.03/072022 75-
37737
   Z663.32 .A5 no. 12 MRR Alc.

LATIN DRAMA--HISTORY AND CRITICISM.
Bieber, Margarete, The history of
the Greek and Roman theater. [2d
ed., rev. and enl.] Princeton, N.J.,
Princeton University Press, 1961.
xiv, 343 p.   882.09   60-9367
   PA3201 .B52 1961 MRR Alc.

Harsh, Philip Whaley, A handbook of
classical drama. Stanford
University, Calif., Stanford
university press; London, H. Milford,
Oxford university press [1944] xii,
526 p.   882.082 a 44-4250
   PA3024 .H3 MRR Alc.

Hathorn, Richmond Yancey, Crowell's
handbook of classical drama. New
York, Crowell [1967] 350 p.
882.003   67-12403
   PA3024 .H35 TJ Rm.

LATIN DRAMA, MEDIEVAL AND MODERN--
BIBLIOGRAPHY.
Baker, David Erskine, Biographia
dramatica; London, Longman, Hurst,
Rees, Orme, and Brown [etc.] 1812. 3
v. in 4.   04-14124
   Z2014.D7 B2 1812 MRR Alc.

Halliwell-Phillips, James Orchard, A
dictionary of old English plays,
existing either in print or in
manuscript, from the earliest times
to the close of the seventeenth
century; Naarden, [Turfpoortstraat
11] Anton W. van Bekhoven, 1968.
viii, 296 p. [65.00]   74-375761
   Z2014.D7 H12 1968 MRR Alc.

LATIN LANGUAGE.
Varro, Marcus Terentius. On the
Latin language, Cambridge, Mass.,
Harvard university press; London, W.
Heinemann, ltd., 1938. 2 v.   878.9
38-21516
PA6156.V275 1938 MRR Alc.

LATIN LANGUAGE--PRECLASSICAL TO CA.
B.C. 100.
Warmington, Eric Herbert, ed. and tr.
Remains of old Latin, Cambridge,
Mass., Harvard university press;
London, W. Heinemann, ltd., 1935-40.
4 v.   870.82 35-16198
PA6156.A1 1935 MRR Alc.

LATIN LANGUAGE--CHURCH LATIN.
Russo-Alesi, Anthony Ignatius,
Martyrology pronouncing dictionary.
New York, The Edward O'Toole company,
inc., 1939. xiv, 177 p.   922.2 39-
21766
BX4661 .R8 MRR Alc.

LATIN LANGUAGE--DICTIONARIES.
Merguet, Hugo, Lexikon zu Vergilius
mit angabe samtlicher stellen,
Leipzig-R., Kommissionsverlag von R.
Schmidt, 1912. 2 p. l., 786 p.   15-
13878
PA6852 .M4 MRR Alc.

Thesaurus linguae Latinae. Lipsiae,
In aedibus B. G. Teubneri, 1900- v.
in   77-11275
PA2361 .T4 MRR Alc.

LATIN LANGUAGE--DICTIONARIES--ENGLISH.
Andrews, Ethan Allen, Harper's Latin
dictionary. Rev., enl., and in great
part rewritten New York, Cincinnati
[etc.] American book company [1907]
xiii, [1], 2019 p.   475.2 17-28264

PA2365.E5 A7 1907a MRR Ref Desk.

Andrews, Ethan Allen, A Latin
dictionary founded on Andrews'
edition of Freund's Latin dictionary.
Rev., enl., and in great part
rewritten Oxford, Clarendon Press
[1955] xiv, 2019 p.   473.2 56-
58003
PA2365.E5 A7 1955 MRR Ref Desk.

Cassell's Latin dictionary, Latin-
English and English-Latin. New York,
Funk & Wagnalls [1957] xiv, 927 p.
473.2 58-1875
PA2365.E5 C3 1957 MRR Ref Desk.

Cassell's new Latin dictionary. New
York, Funk & Wagnalls [1960, c1959]
xvii, 883 p.   473.2 60-7805
PA2365.L3 C3 1960 MRR Alc.

Cassell's new Latin-English, English-
Latin dictionary, London, Cassell
[1959] xvii, 883 p.   473.2 59-
65014
PA2365.L3 C3 MRR Ref Desk.

Levine, Edwin B. Follett world-wide
Latin dictionary; Chicago, Follett
Pub. Co., 1867. 767 p.   473/.2 67-
15559
PA2365.E5 L65 MRR Alc.

Oxford Latin dictionary. Oxford,
London, Clarendon Pr., 1968- v.
[75/- fasc. 1]   473.2 68-31959
PA2365.E5 O9 MRR Alc.

Walter, Frank Keller, Abbreviations
and technical terms used in book
catalogs and bibliographies, in eight
languages, 1917 handy edition.
Boston, The Boston book company
[1919?] 2 v. in 1.   27-13479
Z1006 .W261 1919 MRR Alc.

LATIN LANGUAGE--DICTIONARIES--FRENCH.
Ernout, Alfred, Dictionnaire
etymologique de la langue latine,
4. ed. rev., corr. et augm. d'un
index. Paris, C. Klincksieck, 1959
[i.e. 1960] xviii, 820 p.   62-
31847
PA2342 .E7 1960 MRR Alc.

LATIN LANGUAGE--DICTIONARIES--GERMAN.
Merguet, Hugo, Handlexikon zu
Cicero, Leipzig, Dieterich, 1905. 2
p. l., 816 p.   06-33549
PA6366 .M45 MRR Alc.

LATIN LANGUAGE--DICTIONARIES--POLYGLOT.
Chalkiopoulos, Georgios.
[Pentaglosson lexilogion technikon
horon (romanized form)] [1960]
1030 p.   61-31355
T10 .C46 1960 MRR Alc.

Lexicon opthalmologicum; Basel, New
York, S. Karger, 1959. 223 p.
617.703 58-4669
RE21 .L45 MRR Alc.

Nijdam, J. Tuinbouwkundig
woordenboek in acht talen. Herziene
en uitgebreide uitg. van de
Woordenlijst voor de tuinbouw in
zeven talen. ['s-Gravenhage,
Staatsdrukkerij- en
Uitgeverijbedrijf; voor alle anderen
landen: Interscience Publishers, New
York] 1961. 504 p.   62-52704
SB45 .N673 MRR Alc.

LATIN LANGUAGE--ETYMOLOGY--DICTIONARIES.
Ernout, Alfred, Dictionnaire
etymologique de la langue latine,
4. ed. rev., corr. et augm. d'un
index. Paris, C. Klincksieck, 1959
[i.e. 1960] xviii, 820 p.   62-
31847
PA2342 .E7 1960 MRR Alc.

Walde, Alois, Lateinisches
etymologisches Worterbuch. 4. Aufl.
Heidelberg, C. Winter, 1965. 3 v.
[DM150.--] 472/.03 68-83380
PA2342 .W23 MRR Alc.

LATIN LANGUAGE--GLOSSARIES,
VOCABULARIES, ETC.
Britt, Matthew, ed. A dictionary of
the Psalter. New York, Cincinnati
[etc.] Benziger brothers, 1928.
xxxvi, 299 p.   29-1306
BX2033 .B7 MRR Alc.

LATIN LANGUAGE, MEDIEVAL AND MODERN--
DICTIONARIES.
Deferrari, Roy Joseph, A Latin-
English dictionary of St. Thomas
Aquinas. [Boston] St. Paul Editions
[1960] 1115 p.   189.4 60-1846
B765.T54 D39 MRR Alc.

Deferrari, Roy Joseph, A lexicon of
St. Thomas Aquinas [Washington,
Catholic University of America Press,
1948-53, c1949] 5 v.   189.4 a 49-
1297
B765.T54 D38 MRR Alc.

Du Cange, Charles du Fresne, sieur,
Glossarium ad scriptores mediæ &
infimæ Græcitatis ... [Graz,
Akademische Druck- u. Verlagsanstalt,
1958] 2 v. in 1 (x, p. 1793, 214,
101, 316 columns)   60-21441
PA1125 .D8 1688a MRR Alc.

Du Cange, Charles Du Fresne, sieur,
Glossarium mediæ et infimæ
latinitatis. Editio nova, aucta
pluribus verbis aliorum scriptorum
Paris, Librairie des sciences et des
arts, 1937-38. 10 v. in 11.   40-
3397
PA2889 .D8 1937 Mrr Alc.

LATIN LANGUAGE, MEDIEVAL AND MODERN--
DICTIONARIES--ENGLISH.
Latham, Ronald Edward, ed. Revised
Medieval Latin word-list from British
and Irish sources. London, Published
for the British Academy by the Oxford
University Press, 1965. xxiii, 524
p.   473.2 65-28937
PA2891 .L3 MRR Alc.

Martin, Charles Trice, The record
interpreter: 2d ed. London, Stevens
and sons, limited, 1910. xv, 464 p.
10-16320
Z111 .M23 MRR Alc.

LATIN LITERATURE--BIBLIOGRAPHY.
Engelmann, Wilhelm, Bibliotheca
scriptorum classicorum, 8. aufl.
Leipzig [etc.] W. Engelmann, 1880-82.
2 v.   01-16689
Z7016 .E58 1880 MRR Alc.

Lambraz, Scarlat. Bibliographie de
l'antiquite classique, 1896-1914.
Paris, Societe d'edition "Les
Belles Lettres," 1951- v.   a 52-
1454
Z7016 .L3 MRR Alc.

Marouzeau, Jules, Dix annees de
bibliographie classique, Paris,
Societe d'edition "Les belles
lettres," 1927-28. 2 v.   28-27582
Z7016 .M35 MRR Alc.

Nairn, John Arbuthnot, Classical
hand-list: 3d ed., rev. and enl.
Oxford, 1953. viii, 164 p.   016.88
54-14555
Z7016 .N17 1953 MRR Alc.

LATIN LITERATURE--DICTIONARIES.
Mantinband, James H. Dictionary of
Latin literature. New York,
Philosophical Library [1956] vi, 303
p.   870.3 56-14004
PA31 .M3 MRR Alc.

LATIN LITERATURE--HISTORY AND CRITICISM.
Rose, Herbert Jennings, A handbook
of Latin literature: 3rd ed.
reprinted; London, Methuen; New
York, Dutton [1966] ix, 582 p. [42/-
]   870.9 67-76490
PA6003 .R6 1966 MRR Alc.

Wright, Frederick Adam, A history of
later Latin literature from the
middle of the fourth to the end of
the seventeenth century, New York,
The Macmillan company, 1931. vii,
417, [1] p.   879.09 36-16877
PA8015 .W7 1931a MRR Alc.

LATIN LITERATURE--HISTORY AND CRITICISM-
-BIBLIOGRAPHY.
L'Annee philologique; 1.- annee;
1924/26- Paris, Societe d'edition
"Les Belles lettres."   29-9941
Z7016 .M35A MRR Alc Full set

Fifty years (and twelve) of classical
scholarship; [2d ed.] New York,
Barnes & Noble, 1968. xiv, 523 p.
68-5952
PA3001 .F5 1968 MRR Alc.

Gwinup, Thomas. Greek and Roman
authors; Metuchen, N.J., Scarecrow
Press, 1973. x, 194 p.   016.88/009
72-10156
Z7016 .G9 MRR Alc.

Marouzeau, Jules, Dix annees de
bibliographie classique; New York,
B. Franklin [1969] 2 v. (xv, 1286
p.) 68-57915
Z7016 .M35 1969 MRR Alc.

LATIN LITERATURE, MEDIEVAL AND MODERN--
HISTORY AND CRITICISM.
Wright, Frederick Adam, A history of
later Latin literature from the
middle of the fourth to the end of
the seventeenth century, New York,
The Macmillan company, 1931. vii,
417, [1] p.   879.09 36-16877
PA8015 .W7 1931a MRR Alc.

LATIN POETRY.
Duff, John Wight, ed. and tr. Minor
Latin poets; Cambridge, Mass.,
Harvard university press; London, W.
Heinemann, ltd., 1934. xii, 838 p.,
1 l.   871.0822 35-178
PA6156.A2 1934 MRR Alc.

LATIN POETRY--DICTIONARIES.
Swanson, Donald Carl Eugene, The
names in Roman verse; Madison,
University of Wisconsin Press, 1967.
xix, 425 p.   871/.003 67-25942
PA2379 .S9 MRR Alc.

LATIN POETRY--TRANSLATIONS INTO ENGLISH.
Duff, John Wight, ed. and tr. Minor
Latin poets; Cambridge, Mass.,
Harvard university press; London, W.
Heinemann, ltd., 1934. xii, 838 p.,
1 l.   871.0822 35-178
PA6156.A2 1934 MRR Alc.

LATIN POETRY, MEDIEVAL AND MODERN.
The Oxford book of medieval Latin
verse. Oxford, Clarendon Press,
1959. 512 p.   879.1082 59-1256
PA8185 .O9 1959 MRR Alc.

LATVIA.
Rutkis, Janis, Latvia: country and
people. Stockholm, Latvian National
Foundation, [1967] xv, 681 p.
[85.00 skr] 914.7/43 68-73905
DK511.L16 R848 MRR Alc.

LATVIA--HISTORY.
Bilmanis, Alfreds, A history of
Latvia. Princeton, Princeton
University Press, 1951. x, 441 p.
947.4 51-14774
DK511.L17 B48 MRR Alc.

LATVIAN LANGUAGE--CONVERSATION AND
PHRASE BOOKS--POLYGLOT.
Lyall, Archibald, A guide to 25
languages of Europe. Rev. ed.
[Harrisburg, Pa.] Stackpole Co.
[1966] viii, 407 p.   413 66-20847
PB73 .L85 1966 MRR Alc.

LATVIAN LANGUAGE--DICTIONARIES--ENGLISH.
Turkina, Eizenija, Latviesu-anglu
vardnica, Parstradats un
papildinats 2. izdevums Riga,
Latvijas valsts izdevnieciba, 1962.
775 p.   63-36157
PG8979 .T83 1962 MRR Alc.

LAUSANNE--DIRECTORIES.
Annuaire; Livre d'adresses de
Lausanne et du canton de Vaud.
Lausanne, Societe de l'annuaire
vaudois.   53-28491
DQ724 .A6 MRR Alc Latest edition

LAW.
see also Courts

see also Legislation

LAW--BIBLIOGRAPHY--CATALOGS.
United States. Library of Congress.
Law library. The bibliography of
international law and continental
law, Washington, Govt. print. off.,
1913. 93 p.   12-35015
Z663.5 .B5 MRR Alc.

LAW--DICTIONARIES.
Herbst, Robert. Dictionary of
commercial, financial, and legal
terms 3rd ed. rev. Zug, Translegal
[1968-   v.   [unpriced] 330/.03
76-410368
HB61 .H463 MRR Alc.

Salottolo, A. Lawrence. Modern
police service encyclopedia; Rev.
ed. New York, Arco Pub. Co. [1970]
276 p.   363.2/03 70-125939
HV8133 .S2 1970 MRR Alc.

LAW--DICTIONARIES--POLYGLOT.
Herbst, Robert. Dictionary of
commercial, financial, and legal
terms; 2d ed. Zug, Translegal
[1966-   v.   330/.03 67-8369
HB61 .H462 MRR Alc.

LAW--DIGESTS.
Martindale-Hubbell law directory.
Summit, N.J. [etc.] 31-6356
KF190 .H813 MRR Biog Latest
    edition

LAW--PERIODICALS--INDEXES.
Crime and delinquency abstracts. v.
1-   Jan. 1863- [Bethesda, Md.,
etc.] National Clearinghouse for
Mental Health Information [etc.] 66-
3911
Z5118.C9 I55 MRR Alc Full set

Hsia, Tao-t'ai. Guide to selected
legal sources of Mainland China;
Washington, Library of Congress; [for
sale by the Supt. of Docs., U.S.
Govt. Print. Off.] 1967. viii, 357
p.   340/.0951 67-60042
Z663.5.G8C53 MRR Alc.

Schutter, Bart de. Bibliography on
international criminal law. Leiden,
Sijthoff, 1972. li, 423 p.
[fl58.00] 016.34/77 72-80997
KZ6464.C8 S38 MRR Alc.

LAW--QUOTATIONS.
Mead, Leon, comp. Manual of forensic
quotations, New York, J. F. Taylor &
company, 1903. xiv, 207 p.   03-
10774
LAW MRR Alc.

LAW--TERMS AND PHRASES.
Heimanson, Rudolph. Dictionary of
political science and law. Dobbs
Ferry, N.Y., Oceana Publications,
1967. 188 p.   320/.03 67-14401
JA61 .H4 MRR Ref Desk.

LAW--ARGENTINE REPUBLIC--BIBLIOGRAPHY.
United States. Library of Congress.
Law library. Guide to the law and
legal literature of Argentina, Brazil
and Chile, Washington, Govt. print.
off., 1917. 523 p.   16-26005
Z663.5.G8A5 MRR Alc.

LAW--ARGENTINE REPUBLIC--HISTORY AND
CRITICISM.
United States. Library of Congress.
Law library. Guide to the law and
legal literature of Argentina, Brazil
and Chile, Washington, Govt. print.
off., 1917. 523 p.   16-26005
Z663.5.G8A5 MRR Alc.

LAW--BRAZIL--BIBLIOGRAPHY.
United States. Library of Congress.
Law library. Guide to the law and
legal literature of Argentina, Brazil
and Chile, Washington, Govt. print.
off., 1917. 523 p.   16-26005
Z663.5.G8A5 MRR Alc.

LAW--BRAZIL--HISTORY AND CRITICISM.
United States. Library of Congress.
Law library. Guide to the law and
legal literature of Argentina, Brazil
and Chile, Washington, Govt. print.
off., 1917. 523 p.   16-26005
Z663.5.G8A5 MRR Alc.

LAW--CHILE--BIBLIOGRAPHY.
Clagett, Helen (Lord) A guide to the
law and legal literature of Chile,
1917-1946. Washington, The Library
of Congress, 1947. viii, 103 p.
016.34983 48-50091
Z663.5.G8 C5 MRR Alc.

United States. Library of Congress.
Law library. Guide to the law and
legal literature of Argentina, Brazil
and Chile, Washington, Govt. print.
off., 1917. 523 p.   16-26005
Z663.5.G8A5 MRR Alc.

LAW--CHILE--HISTORY AND CRITICISM.
Clagett, Helen (Lord) A guide to the
law and legal literature of Chile,
1917-1946. Washington, The Library
of Congress, 1947. viii, 103 p.
016.34983 48-50091
Z663.5.G8 C5 MRR Alc.

United States. Library of Congress.
Law library. Guide to the law and
legal literature of Argentina, Brazil
and Chile, Washington, Govt. print.
off., 1917. 523 p.   16-26005
Z663.5.G8A5 MRR Alc.

LAW--CHINA--BIBLIOGRAPHY.
Hsia, Tao-t'ai. Guide to selected
legal sources of Mainland China;
Washington, Library of Congress; [for
sale by the Supt. of Docs., U.S.
Govt. Print. Off.] 1967. viii, 357
p.   340/.0951 67-60042
Z663.5.G8C53 MRR Alc.

LAW--DISTRICT OF COLUMBIA.
District of Columbia. Laws, statutes,
etc. District of Columbia code,
annotated. 1973 ed., Washington,
U.S. Govt. Print. Off., 1973- v.
348/.753/023 73-174270
KFD1230 1973 .A2 MRR Alc.

LAW--EUROPE, EASTERN--PERIODICALS.
Highlights of current legislation and
activities in mid-Europe. v. 1-
June 1853- Washington. 58-14279
Z663.55 .H5 MRR Alc MRR Alc Full
set

LAW--FRANCE--BIBLIOGRAPHY.
Stumberg, George Wilfred. ... Guide
to the law and legal literature of
France, Washington, U.S. Govt.
print. off., 1931. v, 242 p.
016.3470944 30-26002
Z663.5.G8F7 MRR Alc.

LAW--FRANCE--HISTORY AND CRITICISM.
Stumberg, George Wilfred. ... Guide
to the law and legal literature of
France, Washington, U.S. Govt.
print. off., 1931. v, 242 p.
016.3470944 30-26002
Z663.5.G8F7 MRR Alc.

LAW--GERMANY--BIBLIOGRAPHY.
United States. Library of Congress.
Law library. ... Guide to the law
and legal literature of Germany,
Washington, Govt. print. off., 1912.
266 p.   12-35003
Z663.5.G8G4 MRR Alc.

LAW--GERMANY--HISTORY AND CRITICISM.
United States. Library of Congress.
Law library. ... Guide to the law
and legal literature of Germany,
Washington, Govt. print. off., 1912.
266 p.   12-35003
Z663.5.G8G4 MRR Alc.

LAW--GREAT BRITAIN--BIBLIOGRAPHY.
United States. Library of Congress.
Law library. Anglo-American legal
bibliographies, Washington, U.S.
Govt. print. off., 1944. xii, 166 p.
016.01634 44-41314
Z663.5 .A5 MRR Alc.

LAW--GREAT BRITAIN--CLASSIFICATION.
United States. Library of Congress.
Subject Cataloging Division.
Classification. Washington, Library
of Congress; [for sale by the Card
Division] 1973, ix p.; 114 l., 115-
163 p. [$5.75] 025.4/6/3400942 73-
8416
Z663.78.C5 K 1973 MRR Alc.

LAW--MEXICO--BIBLIOGRAPHY.
Clagett, Helen (Lord) A revised
guide to the law & legal literature
of Mexico, Washington, Library of
Congress; [for sale by the Supt. of
Docs., U.S. Govt. Print. Off.] 1973.
xii, 463 p. [$6.95] 016.34/00972
72-12763
Z663.5.G8 M4 1973 MRR Alc.

LAW--MEXICO--HISTORY AND CRITICISM.
Clagett, Helen (Lord) A revised
guide to the law & legal literature
of Mexico, Washington, Library of
Congress; [for sale by the Supt. of
Docs., U.S. Govt. Print. Off.] 1973.
xii, 463 p. [$6.95] 016.34/00972
72-12763
Z663.5.G8 M4 1973 MRR Alc.

LAW--SPAIN--BIBLIOGRAPHY.
Palmer, Thomas Waverly, Guide to the
law and legal literature of Spain,
Washington, Govt. print. off., 1915.
174 p.   15-26001
Z663.5.G8S7 MRR Alc.

LAW--SPAIN--HISTORY AND CRITICISM.
Palmer, Thomas Waverly, Guide to the
law and legal literature of Spain,
Washington, Govt. print. off., 1915.
174 p.   15-26001
Z663.5.G8S7 MRR Alc.

LAW--UNITED STATES.
United States. Laws, statutes, etc.
United States code. 1970 ed.,
containing the general and permanent
laws of the United States in force on
January 20, 1971. Washington, U.S.
Govt. Print. Off., 1971. 15 v.
(lxix, 17728 p.)   348/.73/23 73-
25452
KF62 1970 .A2 MRR Alc.

Warren, Charles, The Supreme court
in United States history, Rev. ed.
Boston, Little, Brown, and company,
1935. 2 v.   347.99 353.5 37-1848
JK1561 .W3 1935 MRR Alc.

LAW--UNITED STATES--BIBLIOGRAPHY.
Chicago. University. Library.
Official publications relating to
American state constitutional
conventions, New York, The H. W.
Wilson company, 1936. 3 p. l., 91 p.
016.342732 37-4455
Z4457.A1 C5 MRR Alc.

National association of state
libraries. Public document clearing
house committee. Check-list of
legislative journals of states of the
United States of America,
Providence, the Oxford press, 1938.
3 p. l., 274 p.   016.32873 38-38809

Z1223.5.A1 N27 1938 MRR Ref Desk.

Roorbach, Orville Augustus,
Bibliotheca americana. New York, P.
Smith, 1939. xi, 652 p.   015.73 39-
27504
Z1215 .A3 1939 MRR Ref Desk.

Roorbach, Orville Augustus,
Bibliotheca Americana: Metuchen,
N.J., Mini-Print Corp., 1967. 1 v.
(various pagings) 015.73 67-8332
Z1215 .A3 1967 MRR Alc.

United States. Library of Congress.
A guide to the microfilm collection
of early state records, [Washington]
Library of Congress, Photoduplication
Service, 1950. 1 v. (various
pagings) 016.01573 50-62956
Z663.96 .G8 MRR Alc.

United States. Library of Congress.
Law library. Anglo-American legal
bibliographies, Washington, U.S.
Govt. print. off., 1944. xii, 166 p.
016.01634 44-41314
Z663.5 .A5 MRR Alc.

LAW--UNITED STATES--COMPENDS.
United States. Laws, statutes, etc.
United States statutes at large,
containing the laws and concurrent
resolutions ... and reorganization
plan, amendment to the Constitution,
and proclamations. v. 1- 1789/1845-
Washington, U.S. Govt. Print. Off.
07-35353
LAW MRR Alc (Dk 33) Full set

LAW--UNITED STATES--DIGESTS.
Martindale-Hubbell law directory.
Summit, N.J. [etc.] 31-6356
KF190 .H813 MRR Biog Latest
    edition

LAW--UNITED STATES--INDEXES.
Congressional Information Service.
CIS annual. 1970- Washington.
348/.731 79-158879
KF49 .C62 MRR Ref Desk Full set

LAW--UNITED STATES--INTERPRETATION AND
CONSTRUCTION.
Folsom, Gwendolyn B. Legislative
history; Charlottesville, University
Press of Virginia [1972] viii, 136
p. 348/.73/1 72-80386
KF425 .F64 MRR Ref Desk.

LAW--UNITED STATES--POPULAR WORKS.
Kling, Samuel G., The complete guide
to everyday law, 3d ed. Chicago,
Follett Pub. Co. [1973] 709 p.
[$9.95] 340/.0973 72-93376
KF387 .K55 1973 MRR Alc.

LAW--UNITED STATES--STATES--INDEXES.
State law index. v. 1-12; 1925/26-
1947/48. Washington, U.S. Govt.
Print. Off. 30-2750
Z663.6 .A63 MRR Alc MRR Alc Full
set

LAW, CORPORATION
see Corporation law

LAW, CRIMINAL
see Criminal law

LAW ENFORCEMENT--STUDY AND TEACHING--
UNITED STATES.
Law enforcement education directory.
Washington, International Association
of Chiefs of Police, Professional
Standards Division. 363.2/071/173
78-649322
HV8143 .L36 MRR Alc Latest edition

LAW PARTNERSHIP--UNITED STATES--
DIRECTORIES.
Best's recommended insurance
attorneys. 1st- ed.; 1929-
Morristown, N.J. [etc.] A. M. Best
Co. 29-5672
HG8525 .B4 MRR Alc Latest edition

The Clearing house quarterly.
Minneapolis, Minn., Attorneys'
National Clearing House Co. 08-15550

KF195.C57 C4 MRR Alc Latest
    edition

Hine's insurance counsel. Glen
Ellyn, Ill. [etc.] Hine's Legal
Directory [etc.] 07-28505
Began publication in 1907?
KF195.I5 H55 MRR Alc Latest
    edition

LAWN TENNIS
see Tennis

LAWNS.
see also Ground cover plants

LAWRENCE, DAVID HERBERT, 1885-1930—CONCORDANCES.
Garcia, Reloy. A concordance to the poetry of D. H. Lawrence. Lincoln, University of Nebraska Press [c1970] xvi, 523 p. 821/.9/12 70-120277
PR6023.A93 Z49 MRR Alc.

LAWYERS—DIRECTORIES.
Martindale-Hubbell law directory. Summit, N.J. [etc.] 31-6356
KF190 .H813 MRR Biog Latest edition

LAWYERS—UNITED STATES—BIOGRAPHY.
Thomas, Dorothy, pseud., ed. Women lawyers in the United States. [1st ed.] New York, Scarecrow Press, 1957. xxx, 747 p. 347.058 57-6625
LAW MRR Biog.

LAWYERS—UNITED STATES—DIRECTORIES.
Best's recommended insurance attorneys. 1st- ed.; 1929- Morristown, N.J. [etc.] A. M. Best Co. 29-5672
HG8525 .B4 MRR Alc Latest edition

The Clearing house quarterly. Minneapolis, Minn., Attorneys National Clearing House Co. 08-15550
KF195.C57 C4 MRR Alc Latest edition

Hine's insurance counsel. Glen Ellyn, Ill. [etc.] Hine's Legal Directory [etc.] 07-28505
Began publication in 1907?
KF195.I5 H55 MRR Alc Latest edition

Martindale-Hubbell law directory. Summit, N.J. [etc.] 31-6356
KF190 .H813 MRR Biog Latest edition

Thomas, Dorothy, pseud., ed. Women lawyers in the United States. [1st ed.] New York, Scarecrow Press, 1957. xxx, 747 p. 347.058 57-6625
LAW MRR Biog.

LEADERSHIP.
see also Discussion

Pierson, George Wilson. The education of American leaders; New York, Praeger [1969] xxxii, 261 p. 331.7/6 68-17173
LA226 .P5 MRR Alc.

LEAF PRINTS.
Marx, David S. A modern American herbal: useful trees and shrubs. South Brunswick, A. S. Barnes [1973] 190 p. 582/.1609/73 71-86305
QK482 .M43 MRR Alc.

LEAGUE OF NATIONS—BIBLIOGRAPHY.
Aufricht, Hans. Guide to League of Nations publications; New York, Columbia University Press, 1951. xix, 682 p. 016.34112 51-14811
Z6473 .A85 MRR Alc.

Ghébali, Victor Yves. A repertoire of League of Nations serial documents, 1919-1947. Dobbs Ferry, N.Y., Oceana Publications, 1973 [c1972] 2 v. (xiv, 773 p.) [$60.00] 016.05 73-7839
Z6473 .G45 MRR Alc.

Reno, Edward A. League of Nations documents, 1919-1946; New Haven, Conn., Research Publications, 1973- v. 016.34112 73-3061
Z6473 .R45 MRR Alc.

LEAGUE OF NATIONS—HISTORY.
Walters, Francis Paul. A history of the League of Nations. London, New York, Oxford University Press, 1952. 2 v. (xv, 833 p.) 341.1209 52-7354
JX1975 .W28 MRR Alc.

LEARNED INSTITUTIONS AND SOCIETIES.
Handbook of learned societies and institutions: America. Washington, D.C., Carnegie institution of Washington, 1908. viii, 592 p. 08-21011
Z5055.U39 H2 MRR Alc.

The World of learning. [1st]- 1947- London, Europa Publications [etc.] 47-30172
AS2 .W6 Sci RR Latest edition / MRR Ref Desk Latest edition

LEARNED INSTITUTIONS AND SOCIETIES—BIBLIOGRAPHY.
Royal Society of London. Catalogue of scientific papers. London, C. J. Clay, 1867-1925. 19 v. 02-11462
Z7403 .R88 MRR Alc.

Royal society of London. Catalogue of scientific papers, 1800-1900. Cambridge, University press, 1908- v. 08-24586
Z7403 .R8812 MRR Alc.

LEARNED INSTITUTIONS AND SOCIETIES—BIBLIOGRAPHY—CATALOGS.
Royal society of London. Library. Catalogue of the periodical publications in the library of the Royal society of London. London, Printed for the Royal society at the Oxford university press, 1912. viii, 455, [1] p. 13-19466
Z7403 .R888 MRR Alc.

LEARNED INSTITUTIONS AND SOCIETIES—BIBLIOGRAPHY—UNION LISTS.
World list of scientific periodicals published in the years 1900-1960. 4th ed. Washington, Butterworths, 1963-65. 3 v. (xxv, 1824 p.) 016.505 64-9729
Z7403 .W923 MRR Alc.

LEARNED INSTITUTIONS AND SOCIETIES—DIRECTORIES.
Ljunggren, Florence, ed. An international directory of institutes and societies interested in the Middle East. Amsterdam, Djambatan [1962] 159 p. 060 63-36286
DS41 .L5 MRR Alc.

Minerva: internationales Verzeichnis wissenschaftlicher Institutionen. Forschungsinstitute. 33.- Ausg. (Jahrg.); 1972- Berlin, New York, W. de Gruyter. 72-76041
AS2 .M57 MRR Ref Desk Latest edition / MRR Alc Latest edition

Minerva: internationales Verzeichnis wissenschaftlicher Institutionen. Wissenschaftliche Gesellschaften. 33.- Ausg. (Jahrg.); 1972- Berlin, New York, de Gruyter. 060/.25 72-624841
AS2 .M58 MRR Ref Desk Latest edition / MRR Alc Latest edition

Organization for Economic Co-operation and Development. Development Centre. Catalogue of social and economic development training institutes and programmes. Paris, O.E.C.D.; London, H.M.S.O., 1968. [2], 344 p. [31/-] 309.2/23/0711 68-140061
HD82 .O66 MRR Alc.

Organization for Economic Cooperation and Development. Development Centre. Catalogue of social and economic development institutes and programmes: research. Paris, Development Centre of the Organization for Economic Co-operation and Development, 1968. 413 p. [$4.50] 338.9/0072 75-417969
HD82 .O656 MRR Alc.

Unesco handbook of international exchanges. 1- 1965- [Paris] Unesco. 65-5337
AS8 .U35 MRR Alc Latest edition

LEARNED INSTITUTIONS AND SOCIETIES—DIRECTORIES—BIBLIOGRAPHY.
Hellstrom, Kajsa. Bibliography of directories of sources of information The Hague, International Federation for Documentation, 1960. 22 p. 016.06058 62-1923
Z5051 .H45 MRR Alc.

LEARNED INSTITUTIONS AND SOCIETIES—YEARBOOKS.
Minerva; 1- Jahrg.; 1891/92- Berlin [etc.] W. de Gruyter [etc.] 06-13219
AS2 .M6 MRR Alc Latest edition / MRR Ref Desk Latest edition

LEARNED INSTITUTIONS AND SOCIETIES—EUROPE.
European research index; 3d ed. [St. Peter Port, Guernsey] Francis Hodgson [1973] 2 v. (2293 p.) 507/.204 70-190255
Q180.E9 E9 1973 MRR Alc.

LEARNING, PSYCHOLOGY OF.
see also Programmed instruction

LEARNING AND SCHOLARSHIP.
Jocher, Christian Gottlieb, Allgemeines gelehrten-lexicon; Leipzig, 1750-1897. 11 v. 06-3520
Z1010 .J63 MRR Biog.

LEARNING AND SCHOLARSHIP—BOOK REVIEWS—INDEXES.
Internationale Bibliographie der Rezensionen wissenschaftlicher Literatur. Jahrg. 1.- 1971- Osnabrück, F. Dietrich Verlag. 72-623124
Z5051 .I64 MRR Alc Full set

LEATHER INDUSTRY AND TRADE.
see also Boots and shoes

LEATHER INDUSTRY AND TRADE—YEARBOOKS.
Leather and leathergoods directory. London, Benn Brothers Ltd. 72-626494
TS945 .L385 MRR Alc Latest edition

LEATHER INDUSTRY AND TRADE—GREAT BRITAIN—DIRECTORIES.
The Shoe trades directory & diary. London, Shoe & leather news. 23 cm. 54-17271
TS945 .S45 MRR Alc Latest edition

LEAVES.
Marx, David S. A modern American herbal: useful trees and shrubs. South Brunswick, A. S. Barnes [1973] 190 p. 582/.1609/73 71-86305
QK482 .M43 MRR Alc.

LEBANON.
Smith, Harvey Henry. Area handbook for Lebanon. Washington, For sale by the Supt. of Docs., U.S. Govt. Print. Off., 1969. xviii, 352 p. [3.25] 915.692 72-603935
DS80 .S63 MRR Alc.

LEBANON—GAZETTEERS.
United States. Geographic Names Division. Lebanon: official standard names approved by the United States Board on Geographic Names. Washington [U.S. Govt. Print. Off.] 1970. xiii, 676 p. 915.692 77-610513
DS80.A5 U5 MRR Alc.

LEBANON—HISTORY.
Hitti, Philip Khuri. Lebanon in history: 3rd ed. London, Melbourne [etc.] Macmillan; New York, St. Martin's P., 1967. xx, 550 p. [84/-] 956.92 67-21542
DS80.9 .H5 1967 MRR Alc.

LEE, ROBERT EDWARD, 1807-1870.
Freeman, Douglas Southall. R. E. Lee, a biography. New York, London, C. Scribner's sons, 1934-35. 4 v. 923.573 34-33660
E467.1.L4 F83 MRR Alc.

LEE, SAMUEL PHILLIPS, 1812-1897—BIBLIOGRAPHY.
United States. Library of Congress. Manuscript Division. Samuel P. Lee: a register of his papers in the Library of Congress. Washington, Library of Congress, 1967. 15 l. 016.3593/3/20924 67-62763
Z663.34 .L4 MRR Alc.

LEGAL HOLIDAYS
see Holidays

LEGAL PROFESSION
see Lawyers

LEGAL TENDER.
see also Money

see also Paper money

LEGENDS.
see also Fairy tales

see also Folk-lore

see also Mythology

Waters, Clara (Erskine) Clement. A handbook of legendary and mythological art. [14th impression] Boston, New York, Houghton, Mifflin and company [189-?] xii, 575 p. 04-11646
N7760 .W33 MRR Alc.

LEGENDS—INDEXES.
Eastman, Mary Huse. Index to fairy tales, myths, and legends. 2d ed., rev. and enl. Boston, F. W. Faxon Co., 1926. ix, 610 p. 016.398 26-11491
Z5983.F17 E2 1926 MRR Alc.

LEGENDS—GREAT BRITAIN.
Folklore, myths and legends of Britain. [1st ed. London] Reader's Digest Association [1973] 552 p. 390/.0942 73-177007
GR141 .F65 MRR Alc.

LEGENDS AND STORIES OF ANIMALS
see Animals, Legends and stories of

LÉGER, ALEXIS SAINT-LÉGER, 1889-
Emmanuel, Pierre. Saint-John Perse: praise and presence. Washington, Published for the Library of Congress by the Gertrude Clarke Whittall Poetry and Literature Fund [for sale by the Supt. of Docs., U.S. Govt. Print. Off., 1971. iii, 82 p. [$0.45] 848/.9/1209 72-174226
Z663.293 .P38 MRR Alc.

LEGERDEMAIN
see Conjuring

see Magic

LEGISLATION.
see also Governmental investigations

see also Law

LEGISLATION--BIBLIOGRAPHY.
Public Affairs Information Service.
Bulletin ... annual cumulation. 1st-
1915- New York [etc.] 16-920
Z7163 .P9 MRR Circ Full set

LEGISLATION--CHINA--BIBLIOGRAPHY.
Hsia, Tao-t'ai. Guide to selected
legal sources of Mainland China;
Washington, Library of Congress; [for
sale by the Supt. of Docs., U.S.
Govt./Print. Off.] 1967. viii, 357
p. 340/.0951 67-60042
Z663.5.G8C53 MRR Alc

LEGISLATION--EUROPE, EASTERN--
PERIODICALS.
Highlights of current legislation and
activities in mid-Europe. v. 1-
June 1953- Washington. 58-14279
Z663.55 .B5 MRR Alc MRR Alc Full
set

LEGISLATION--GREAT BRITAIN--INDEXES.
Great Britain. Parliament. House of
Commons. Library. General index to
the Bills, Reports and papers printed
by order of the House of Commons
London, H.M. Stationery Off., 1960.
viii, 893 p. 328.4204 61-3087
LAW MRR Ref Desk.

LEGISLATION--NEW YORK (STATE).
New York state legislative annual.
1946- New York, New York Legislative
Service, inc. 328.747 47-20115
JK3401 .N48 MRR Alc Latest edition

LEGISLATION--UNITED STATES.
C Q weekly report. Washington,
Congressional Quarterly Inc. [etc.]
328.73 52-36903
JK1 .C15 MRR Ref Desk Partial set

Congressional Information Service.
CIS annual. 1970- Washington.
348/.731 79-158879
KF49 .C62 MRR Ref Desk Full set

Congressional quarterly almanac. v.
1- Jan./Mar. 1945- Washington.
328.73 47-41081
JK1 .C66 Sci RR Latest edition /
MRR Alc Full set

Congressional Quarterly Service,
Washington, D.C. Congress and the
Nation; [1st ed.] Washington [1965-
69] 2 v. 320.9/73 65-22351
KF49 .C653 MRR Ref Desk.

Congressional Quarterly Service,
Washington, D.C. Congressional roll
call; a chronology and analysis of
votes in the House and Senate, 91st
Congress, second session. Washington
[1971] 52, 71S, 91H, 4A p. [$8.00]
328.73/077 75-156289
JK1059 91st .C65 MRR Alc.

Smith, George Howard Edward,
Congress in action; Manassas, Va.,
National Capitol Publishers [1948]
87 p. 328.373 48-782
JK1096 .S55 MRR Alc.

United States. Library of Congress.
Congressional Research Service.
Digest of public general bills and
resolutions. 92d- Congress; 1971-
[Washington, Library of Congress; for
sale by the Supt. of Docs., U.S.
Govt. Print. Off.] 348/.73/1 79-
611725
KF18 .L5 Sci RR Full set / MRR Alc
Full set

LEGISLATION--UNITED STATES--PERIODICALS.
Congressional Quarterly, inc.
Congressional roll call. Washington.
328.73/07/75 72-77849
JK1 .C6635 MRR Alc Full set

National journal reports. v. 5, no.
30- July 28, 1973- [Washington,
Government Research Corporation]
320.9/73 73-645726
JK1 .N28 MRR Alc Full set

LEGISLATION, DRUG--UNITED STATES.
Brecher, Edward M. Licit and illicit
drugs; [1st ed.] Boston, Little,
Brown [1972] xv, 623 p. [$12.50]
362.2/9 75-186972
HV5825 .B72 MRR Alc.

LEGISLATIVE ADVOCATES
see Lobbyists

LEGISLATIVE BODIES.
Institute of Electoral Research.
Parliaments and electoral systems,
[London] 1962. 128 p. 64-53190
JF511 .I555 MRR Alc.

Inter-parliamentary Union.
Parliaments: a comparative study on
the structure and functioning of
representative institutions in fifty-
five countries. 2d ed. (rev. and
enl.)] London, published for the
Inter-parliamentary Union by Cassell,
1966. xii,346 p. [42/-] 328.3 66-
73619
JF511 .I57 1966 MRR Alc.

Political handbook and atlas of the
world. Jan. 1, 1927- New York,
Simon and Schuster [etc.] for Council
on Foreign Relations. 28-12165
JF37 .P6 MRR Ref Desk Latest
edition / MRR Alc Latest edition

LEGISLATIVE BODIES--RULES AND PRACTICE
see Parliamentary practice

LEGISLATIVE BODIES--UNITED STATES.
Blair, George S. American
legislatures; New York, Harper & Row
[1967] x, 449 p. 328.73/07 67-
13472
JK2488 .B55 MRR Alc.

LEGISLATIVE BODIES--UNITED STATES--
BIBLIOGRAPHY.
National association of state
libraries. Public document clearing
house committee. Check-list of
legislative journals of states of the
United States of America,
Providence, the Oxford press, 1938.
3 p. l., 274 p. 016.32873 38-38809

Z1223.5.A1 N27 1938 MRR Ref Desk.

United States. Library of Congress.
A guide to the microfilm collection
of early state records, [Washington]
Library of Congress, Photoduplication
Service, 1950. 1 v. (various
pagings) 016.01573 50-62956
Z663.96 .G8 MRR Alc.

LEGISLATIVE BODIES--UNITED STATES--
STATES.
The Legislative system; New York,
Wiley [1962] xii, 517 p. 328.73
62-15335
JK2488 .L4 MRR Alc.

LEGISLATIVE BODIES AS COURTS.
see also Impeachments

LEGISLATIVE, EXECUTIVE, AND JUDICIAL
APPROPRIATION BILLS
see United States--Appropriations and
expenditures

LEGISLATIVE HEARINGS--UNITED STATES.
United States. Congress Hearings.
78th- Cong. 1943- Washington. 49-
654
J74 .A23 MRR Alc (Dk 33) Full set

LEGISLATIVE HEARINGS--UNITED STATES--
BIBLIOGRAPHY.
South, Charles E. Hearings in the
records of the U.S. Senate and joint
committees of Congress, Washington,
National Archives, 1972. vii, 91 p.
016.348/73/1 72-600240
KF40 .S68 MRR Ref Desk.

Thomen, Harold Ordell, Checklist of
hearings before congressional
committees through the Sixty-seventh
Congress Washington, Reference
Dept., General Reference and
Bibliography Division, Library of
Congress, 1957-59 [pts. 1-3, 1959] 9
pts. in 1 v. 016.3283742 43-52170

Z1223.Z7 T5 MRR Ref Desk.

United States. Congress. House.
Library. Index to congressional
committee hearings in the Library of
the United States House of
Representatives. Jan. 5, 1937-
Washington, U.S. Govt. Print. Off.
016.32873 38-26099
Z1223.A1 A3 MRR Ref Desk Partial
set

LEGISLATIVE HEARINGS--UNITED STATES--
INDEXES.
Congressional Information Service.
CIS annual. 1970- Washington.
348/.731 79-158879
KF49 .C62 MRR Ref Desk Full set

United States. Congress. House.
Committee on Un-American Activities.
Cumulative index to publications of
the Committee on Un-American
Activities. 1939/41- Washington,
U.S. Govt. Print. Off. 42-13283
E743.5 .A28 MRR Ref Desk Latest
edition

United States. Congress. Senate.
Committee on the Judiciary.
Cumulative index to published
hearings and reports Washington,
U.S. Govt. Print. Off., 1957. ii,
844 p. 327.1 57-60563
Z7165.U5 U484 MRR Ref Desk.

United States. Congress. Senate
.Library. Cumulative index of
congressional committee hearings (not
confidential in character) from
Seventy-fourth Congress (January 3,
1935) through Eithty-fifth Congress
(January 3, 1959) in the United
States Senate Library. Washington,
U.S. Govt. Print. Off., 1959. v, 823
p. 59-61946
KF40 .H8 MRR Ref Desk.

United States. Congress. Senate.
Library. Index of congressional
committee hearings (not confidential
in character) prior to January 3,
1935 in the United States Senate
library. Washington, U.S. Govt.
print. off., 1935. ii, 1056 p.
015.73 35-26894
Z1223 .A 1935 MRR Ref Desk.

LEGISLATIVE HISTORIES--UNITED STATES.
Folsom, Gwendolyn B. Legislative
history; Charlottesville, University
Press of Virginia [1972] viii, 136
p. 348/.73/1 72-80386
KF425 .F64 MRR Ref Desk.

LEGISLATIVE HISTORIES--UNITED STATES--
BIBLIOGRAPHY.
Congressional Information Service.
CIS annual. 1970- Washington.
348/.731 79-158879
KF49 .C62 MRR Ref Desk Full set

LEGISLATIVE JOURNALS--UNITED STATES--
BIBLIOGRAPHY.
National association of state
libraries. Public document clearing
house committee. Check-list of
legislative journals of states of the
United States of America,
Providence, the Oxford press, 1938.
3 p. l., 274 p. 016.32873 38-38809

Z1223.5.A1 N27 1938 MRR Ref Desk.

LEGISLATIVE POWER.
see also Separation of powers

see also State governments

LEGISLATIVE POWER--UNITED STATES.
Congressional Quarterly, inc. Guide
to the Congress of the United States;
[1st ed.] Washington, Congressional
Quarterly Service [1971] xxxi, 639,
323a, 21b p. [$35.00] 328.73 78-
167743
JK1021 .C56 MRR Ref Desk.

Fisher, Louis. President and
Congress; New York, Free Press
[1972] xvi, 347 p. 353.03/72 78-
142362
JK305 .F55 MRR Alc.

Horn, John Stephen. The Cabinet and
Congress. New York, Columbia
University Press, 1960. 310 p.
353.02 60-13237
JK616 .H6 MRR Alc.

LEGISLATORS--UNITED STATES.
Barone, Michael. The almanac of
American politics: [2d ed.] Boston,
Gambit [c1973] xxiii, 1240 p.
[$15.00] 328.73 72-96875
JK271 .B343 1974 MRR Ref Desk.

Christopher, Maurine. America's
Black congressmen. New York, Crowell
[1971] xvi, 283 p. [$8.95]
328.73/0922 70-146280
E185.96 .C5 1971 MRR Biog.

LEGISLATORS--UNITED STATES--BIOGRAPHY.
Who's who in American politics. 1st-
ed.; 1967/68- New York, Bowker.
320/.0922 67-25024
E176 .W6424 MRR Biog Latest
edition

LEGISLATORS--UNITED STATES--DIRECTORIES.
Clements, John. Taylor's
encyclopedia of Government officials,
Federal and State. v. 1- 1967/68-
Dallas, Political Research, inc. 67-
22269
JK6 .T36 Sci RR Latest edition /
MRR Alc Latest edition

Rosenbloom, David L. The political
marketplace. [New York] Quadrangle
Books [1972] xix, 948 p. [$25.00]
328/.0025/73 72-77926
JK2283 .R64 MRR Ref Desk.

LEGISLATORS--YUGOSLAVIA.
Sedma sjla, Novinsko-izdavačko
preduzeće Belgrad. Savezna i
republičke skupstine. Beograd,
1964. 311 p. 65-83351
JN9673 .S45 MRR Alc.

LEICA CAMERA.
Leica manual. Hastings-on-Hudson,
N.Y., Morgan & Morgan. 771.3/1 74-
644639
TR146 .M77 MRR Alc Latest edition
/ Sci RR Latest edition

LEINSTER, IRE.--COMMERCE--DIRECTORIES.
Dublin, Leinster and Connaught
trades' directory, Edinburgh,
Trades' Directories. 57-36641
HF5164.D8 D8 MRR Alc Latest
edition

LEISLER, JACOB, D. 1691.
Andrews, Charles McLean, ed.
Narratives of the insurrections, 1675-
1690, New York, C. Scribner's sons,
1915. 1x p., 2 l., 3-414 p. 973.2
15-4852
E187.07 A6 MRR Alc.

LEISURE.
see also Recreation

LEITH, SCOTLAND--DIRECTORIES.
Edinburgh & Leith post office directory. Edinburgh, Meill [etc.] 34-38962
DA890.E3 E15 MRR Alc Latest edition

LEPIDOPTERA DIURNA
see Butterflies

LESOTHO--DIRECTORIES.
Braby's Orange Free State and Northern Cape directory. Durban. 53-32833
DT891 .B73 MRR Alc Latest edition

LESOTHO--GAZETTEERS.
United States. Office of Geography. South Africa; Washington, 1954. 2 v. (1081 p.) 916.8/003 73-10017
DT752 .U65 MRR Alc.

LESOTHO--GOVERNMENT PUBLICATIONS--BIBLIOGRAPHY--UNION LISTS.
Balima, Mildred Grimes. Botswana, Lesotho, and Swaziland; a guide to official publications, 1868-1968. Washington, General Reference and Bibliography Division, Library of Congress; [for sale by the Supt. of Docs., U.S. Govt. Print. Off.] 1971. xvi, 84 p. [$1.00] 016.9168 74-171029
Z663.285 .B6 MRR Alc.

LESS DEVELOPED COUNTRIES
see Underdeveloped areas

LETTER-WRITING.
Blumenthal, Lassor A. The complete book of personal letter-writing and modern correspondence [1st ed.] Garden City, N.Y., Doubleday, 1969. xv, 313 p. [5.95] 808.6 68-18080
PE1483 .B55 MRR Alc.

Sheff, Alexander L. How to write letters for all occasions. New ed., rev. Garden City, N.Y., Doubleday [1961] 239 p. 651.75 61-10015
HF5726 .S465 1961 MRR Ref Desk.

Watson, Lillian (Eichler) Standard book of letter writing and correct social forms. Rev. and enl. ed. Englewood Cliffs, N.J., Prentice-Hall [1958] 713 p. 395 58-10199
BJ2101 .W33 1958 MRR Alc.

LETTERS OF THE ALPHABET
see Alphabet

LEVANT--DESCRIPTION AND TRAVEL--GUIDE-BOOKS.
The Eastern Mediterranean. Paris, Hachette, 1967. 463 p. [27.23 F.]
910.09/1/6613 68-76526
DS43 .M3813 MRR Alc.

LEVANT--DIRECTORIES.
Le Guide arabe pour le commerce, l'industrie & les professions liberales dans les pays arabes. Beyrouth. 53-32838
Began publication with issue for 1945 in Arabic.
DS43 .G85 MRR Alc Latest edition

LIBERIA.
American University, Washington, D.C. Foreign Areas Studies Division. Area handbook for Liberia. Washington, For sale by the Supt. of Docs., U.S. Govt. Print. Off., 1964. xiii, 419 p. 67-115013
DT624 .A62 MRR Alc.

LIBERIA--GAZETTEERS.
United States. Geographic Names Division. Liberia; Washington, 1968. iii, 61 p. 916.6/6/003 68-62724
DT623 .U48 MRR Alc.

LIBERTY.
see also Civil rights

Madison, Charles Allan. Critics & crusaders; 2d ed. New York, Ungar [1959] 662 p. 920.073 58-14283
E176 .M22 1959 MRR Alc.

Rossiter, Clinton Lawrence. Seedtime of the Republic; [1st ed.] New York, Harcourt, Brace [1953] xiv, 558 p. 342.739 320.973* 53-5647
JK31 .R6 MRR Alc.

LIBERTY--YEARBOOKS.
Yearbook on human rights. 1946- New York [etc.] United Nations. 323.4058 48-4455
JC571 .U4 MRR Ref Desk Latest edition

LIBERTY OF SPEECH.
Downs, Robert Bingham, ed. The first freedom; Chicago, American Library Association, 1960. xiii, 469 p.
323.445 59-13653
Z657 .D76 MRR Alc.

LIBERTY OF SPEECH--BIBLIOGRAPHY.
Schroeder, Theodore Albert, Free speech bibliography. New York, The H. W. Wilson company; London, Grafton & co., 1922. 4 p. l., 247 p. 22-8066
Z657 .S383 MRR Alc.

LIBERTY OF THE PRESS.
see also Freedom of information

Downs, Robert Bingham, ed. The first freedom; Chicago, American Library Association, 1960. xiii, 469 p.
323.445 59-13653
Z657 .D76 MRR Alc.

LIBERTY OF THE PRESS--BIBLIOGRAPHY.
Schroeder, Theodore Albert, Free speech bibliography. New York, The H. W. Wilson company; London, Grafton & co., 1922. 4 p. l., 247 p. 22-8066
Z657 .S383 MRR Alc.

LIBRARIANS.
Encyclopedia of library and information science. New York, M. Dekker [1968- v. 020/.3 68-31232
Z1006 .E57 MRR Alc.

LIBRARIANS--DIRECTORIES.
School library supervisors directory. 1st- ed.; 1966- New York, R. R. Bowker Co. 027.8/025/73 66-27557
Z675.S3 S375 MRR Alc Latest edition

LIBRARIANS--AUSTRALIA.
Kose, Geza Attila. Who's who in Australian libraries. Sydney, Library Association of Australia, 1968. xiv, 181 p. [5.40]
021/.0025/94 75-398852
Z720.A46A85 MRR Biog.

LIBRARIANS--AUSTRIA--DIRECTORIES.
Jahrbuch der deutschen Bibliotheken. 1.- Jahrg.; 1902- Wiesbaden [etc.] O. Harrassowitz. 02-17084
Z801 .J2 MRR Alc Latest edition

LIBRARIANS--CANADA--DIRECTORIES.
A Biographical directory of librarians in the United States and Canada. 5th ed. Chicago, American Library Association, 1970. xviii, 1250 p. 020/.922 B 79-118854
Z720.A4 W47 1970 MRR Ref Desk.

LIBRARIANS--GERMANY--DIRECTORIES.
Jahrbuch der deutschen Bibliotheken. 1.- Jahrg.; 1902- Wiesbaden [etc.] O. Harrassowitz. 02-17084
Z801 .J2 MRR Alc Latest edition

LIBRARIANS--GREAT BRITAIN--BIOGRAPHY.
Landau, Thomas. Who's who in librarianship and information science; 2nd ed. London, New York, Abelard-Schuman, 1972. v, 311 p. [£5.50] 020/.92/2 70-184398
Z720.A46 G75 1972 MRR Biog.

LIBRARIANS--GREAT BRITAIN--DIRECTORIES.
Library Association. The Library Association year book. London. 01-15606
Z673 .L7Y MRR Alc Latest edition / MRR Alc Latest edition

LIBRARIANS--INDIA--DIRECTORIES.
Directory of booksellers, publishers, libraries & librarians in India. 1st- ed.; 1968/69- New Delhi, Premier Publishers. 655.4/025/54 73-900620
Z455 .D49 MRR Alc Latest edition

LIBRARIANS--SWEDEN--DIRECTORIES.
Svensk biblioteksmatrikel 1966. Lund, Bibliotekstjanst, 1967. 318 p. [55.-skr] 67-91543
Z827 .A1S8 MRR Alc.

LIBRARIANS--UNITED STATES.
A Biographical directory of librarians in the field of Slavic and East European studies. Chicago, American Library Association, 1967. xv, 80 p. 026/.000922 67-28101
Z675.A2 B5 MRR Biog.

LIBRARIANS--UNITED STATES--DIRECTORIES.
A.L.A. membership directory. 1949- Chicago, American Library Association. 020.622 50-3095
Z720 .A4U37 Sci RR Latest edition / MRR Ref Desk Latest edition

Academic Media, Orange, N.J. Worldwide directory of Federal libraries. 1st ed. Orange, N.J. [1973] xiv, 411 p. 027.5/025/73 72-75955
Z675.G7 A2 MRR Alc.

A Biographical directory of librarians in the United States and Canada. 5th ed. Chicago, American Library Association, 1970. xviii, 1250 p. 020/.922 B 79-118854
Z720.A4 W47 1970 MRR Ref Desk.

Young, Margaret Labash. Directory of special libraries and information centers. 3d ed. Detroit, Gale Research Co. [1974- v. [$48.00]
026/.00025/7 74-3240
Z731 .Y68 1974 MRR Ref Desk.

LIBRARIANS--WASHINGTON, D.C. METROPOLITAN AREA--DIRECTORIES.
Special Libraries Association. Washington, D.C., Chapter. Directory and handbook. 1966- [Washington]
026/.006/2753 72-620935
Z673 .S817 MRR Alc Latest edition / Sci RR Latest edition

LIBRARIANS, AMERICAN--DIRECTORIES.
Foreign service directory of American librarians. Pittsburgh, University of Pittsburgh Book Center.
020/.25/73 67-28996
Began in 1958.
Z720.A4 F6 MRR Alc Latest edition / MRR Ref Desk Latest edition

LIBRARIES, UNIVERSITY AND COLLEGE.
Carey, R. J. P. Library guiding; [Hamden, Conn.] Linnet Books [1974] 186 p. 028.7 73-18477
Z711.2 .C36 MRR Alc.

LIBRARIES.
see also Information services

see also School libraries

Gates, Jean Key. Introduction to librarianship. New York, McGraw-Hill [1968] xii, 415 p. 021 67-12623
Z721 .G33 MRR Alc.

LIBRARIES--ADDRESSES, ESSAYS, LECTURES.
MacLeish, Archibald. Libraries in the contemporary crisis; [Washington] U.S. Govt. print. off., 1939. 11, [1] p. 020.4 39-29265
Z663 .L43 1939 MRR Alc.

LIBRARIES--ARRANGEMENT OF BOOKS ON SHELVES
see Shelf-listing (Library science)

LIBRARIES--AUTOMATION.
Conference on Libraries and Automation, Airlie Foundation, 1963. Libraries and automation; Washington, Library of Congress, 1964. xii, 268 p. 64-62653
Z663 .L4 MRR Alc.

King, Gilbert William, Automation and the Library of Congress. Washington, Library of Congress; [for sale by the Superintendent of Documents, U.S. Govt. Print. Off.] 1963 [i.e. 1964] vii, 88 p. 64-60015
Z663 .A9 MRR Alc.

United States. Library of Congress. Information Systems Office. Terminals requirements for the Library of Congress' central bibliographic system. Washington, 1970. 110 p. 025/.02 71-610454
Z699.3 .U5 MRR Alc.

LIBRARIES--AUTOMATION--BIBLIOGRAPHY.
Cayless, Colin Frederick. Bibliography of library automation, 1964-1967; London, British National Bibliography, 1968 [i.e. 1969] 107 p. [28/-] 016.0297 78-399413
Z699.2 .C37 MRR Alc.

LIBRARIES--AUTOMATION--COLLECTIONS.
Annual review of information science and technology. v. 1- 1966- Chicago [etc.] Encyclopaedia Britannica, inc. [etc.] 029.708 66-25096
Z699 .A1A65 Sci RR Full set / MRR Alc Latest edition

LIBRARIES--BIBLIOGRAPHY.
Five years' work in librarianship. 1951/55- London, Library Association. 016.02 58-2169
Z666 .F5 MRR Alc Full set

United States. Library of Congress. General Reference and Bibliography Division. Safeguarding our cultural heritage; a bibliography Washington, 1952. x, 117 p. 016.355232* 52-60017
Z663.28 .S3 MRR Alc.

LIBRARIES--DIRECTORIES.
American library directory; New York, R. R. Bowker. 23-3581
Z731 .A53 Sci RR Latest edition / MRR Ref Desk Latest edition

Cockx, August. Telecode and telex address book; 2d ed. Sevenoaks (Kent), International Federation of Library Associations, 1966. 191 p. [42/-] 020.25 66-69653
Z731 .C6 MRR Alc.

Fraenkel, Josef. Guide to the Jewish libraries of the world. [1st ed.] London, Cultural Dept. of the World Jewish Congress [1959] 64 p. 63-2058
Z675.J4 F7 MRR Alc.

LIBRARIES--DIRECTORIES. (Cont.)
International Association of
Agricultural Librarians and
Documentalists. World directory of
agricultural libraries &
documentation centres; Harpenden,
Herts, 1960. 280 p. 026.63 60-
3301
    Z675.A8 I55 MRR Alc.

International Federation for
Documentation. Photocopies from
abroad; 3d and rev. ed. The Hague
[1963 or 4] 28 p. 64-4609
    Z265 .I55 1964 MRR Ref Desk.

International library directory. 1st
ed.; 1963- London, A. P. Wales
Organization, Pub. Division. 63-
23734
    Z721 .I6 MRR Ref Desk Latest
    edition

Internationales Bibligthek-Handbuch.
2.- Ausg.; 1968- Munchen-Pullach,
Verlag Dokumentation. 72-627058
    Z721 .I63 MRR Ref Desk Latest
    edition

United Nations Educational,
Scientific and Cultural Organization.
Guide to national bibliographical
information centres. 3d rev. ed.
[Paris, 1970] 195 p. [18F ($4.50
US)] 021.6/4 74-583949
    Z674.5.A2 U52 1970 MRR Ref Desk.

The World of learning. [1st]- 1947-
London, Europa Publications [etc.]
47-30172
    AS2 .W6 Sci RR Latest edition /
    MRR Ref Desk Latest edition

LIBRARIES--DIRECTORIES--BIBLIOGRAPHY.
Internationales Bibligthek-Handbuch.
2.- Ausg.; 1968- Munchen-Pullach,
Verlag Dokumentation. 72-627058
    Z721 .I63 MRR Ref Desk Latest
    edition

Lewanski, Richard Casimir, Library
directories. Santa Barbara, Calif.
[American Bibliographical Center]
1967. 49 p. 016.021/0025 67-20728
    Z719 .L4 1967 MRR Alc.

LIBRARIES--HANDBOOKS, MANUALS, ETC.
Aldrich, Ella Virginia, Using books
and libraries 5th ed. Englewood
Cliffs, N.J., Prentice-Hall [1967]
viii, 147 p. 028.7 67-12587
    Z710 .A36 1967 MRR Alc.

Gates, Jean Key. Guide to the use of
books and libraries. 3d ed. New
York, McGraw-Hill [1974] xii, 308 p.
028.7 73-9502
    Z710 .G27 1974 MRR Alc.

Todd, Alden. Finding facts fast;
New York, Morrow, 1972. xii, 108 p.
[$5.95] 028.7 71-188180
    Z710 .T6 MRR Alc.

LIBRARIES--HISTORY.
Encyclopedia of library and
information science. New York, M.
Dekker [1968- v. 020/.3 68-
31232
    Z1006 .E57 MRR Alc.

Hessel, Alfred, A history of
libraries; Washington, Scarecrow
Press [1950] v, 198 p. 020.9 50-
8938
    Z721 .H582 MRR Alc.

Hobson, Anthony Robert Alwyn. Great
libraries London, Weidenfeld &
Nicolson, 1970. 320 p. [£7/10/-]
027/.009 74-543163
    Z721 .H66 1970b MRR Alc.

Johnson, Elmer D. Communication; 3d
ed. New York, Scarecrow Press, 1966.
304 p. 027.009 66-13742
    Z721 .J6 1966 MRR Alc.

Smith, Josephine Metcalfe. A
chronology of librarianship.
Metuchen, N.J., Scarecrow Press,
1968. 263 p. 020/.9 67-12062
    Z665 .S58 MRR Alc.

LIBRARIES--PERIODICALS--BIBLIOGRAPHY.
Springman, Mary Adele. The directory
of library periodicals.
[Philadelphia] Drexel Press, 1967.
iv, 192 p. 016.020/5 67-24822
    Z674 .D7 no. 23 MRR Alc.

Temple, Phillis Lumsden. A
directory of library periodicals
published in the continental United
States. Pittsburg, Kan., State
College Library, 1957. 44 p.
016.0205 57-63232
    Z719 .T37 MRR Alc.

LIBRARIES--REFERENCE DEPT.
Wynar, Bohdan S. Introduction to
bibliography and reference work; 4th
rev.ed. Rochester, N.Y., Libraries
Unlimited, 1967. 310 p. 016.0287
67-20763
    Z1035 .W95 1967b MRR Alc.

LIBRARIES--SPECIAL COLLECTIONS.
Ash, Lee, comp. Subject collections;
3d ed., rev. and enl. New York,
Bowker, 1967. ix, 1221 p. 026 67-
27563
    Z688.A2 A8 1967 MRR Ref Desk.

Association for Recorded Sound
Collections. A preliminary directory
of sound recordings collections in
the United States and Canada. [New
York] New York Public Library, 1967.
157 p. 026/.7899/0257 67-31297
    ML19 .A85 MRR Alc.

Downs, Robert Bingham, American
library resources; Chicago, American
Library Association, 1951. 428 p.
016.016 51-11156
    Z1002 .D6 MRR Alc.

Downs, Robert Bingham, British
library resources; Chicago, American
Library Association, 1973 [i.e. 1974]
xvi, 332 p. 016.016 73-1598
    Z1002 .D63 MRR Alc.

Downs, Robert Bingham, ed. Resources
of southern libraries; Chicago,
American library association, 1938.
xii, 370 p. 027.075 38-27568
    Z731 .D75 MRR Alc.

George Washington University,
Washington, D.C. Biological Sciences
Communication Project. A study of
resources and major subject holdings
available in U.S. Federal libraries
Washington, U.S. Office of Education,
Bureau of Research, 1970. ix, 670 p.
011 79-609579
    Z881.A1 G4 1970b MRR Alc.

Lewanski, Richard Casimir, Subject
collections in European libraries;
[New York] R. R. Bowker Co., 1965.
xl, 789 p. 017.1094 64-22710
    Z789 .L4 MRR Alc.

Philip, Alexander John, An index to
the special collections in libraries,
museums and art galleries (public,
private and official) in Great
Britain and Ireland. London, Pub.
for the author by F. G. Brown [1949]
viii, 190 p. 016 49-48107
    AM213 .P5 MRR Alc.

Race Relations Information Center.
Directory of Afro-American resources.
New York, R. R. Bowker Co. [1970]
xv, 485 p. 917.3/06/96073 71-
126008
    Z1361.N39 R3 MRR Alc.

Special libraries association.
Special library resources ... New
York, Special libraries association
[1941]-47. 4 v. 026.0087 41-23807
    Z675.A2 S65 MRR Alc.

United States. Library of Congress.
Reference Dept. A guide to special
book collections in the Library of
Congress, Washington, 1949. 2, 66
p. 027.5753 50-60175
    Z663.2 .G78 MRR Alc.

Young, Margaret Labash. Directory of
special libraries and information
centers. 3d ed. Detroit, Gale
Research Co. [1974- v. [$48.00]
026/.00025/7 74-3240
    Z731 .Y68 1974 MRR Ref Desk.

LIBRARIES--SPECIAL COLLECTIONS--
CHILDREN'S LITERATURE.
Field, Carolyn W., Subject
collections in children's literature.
New York, Bowker, 1969. 142 p.
[6.50] 028.5 68-56955
    Z688.C47 F5 MRR Alc.

LIBRARIES--SPECIAL COLLECTIONS--
HISPANIC MATERIALS.
Hilton, Ronald, ed. Handbook of
Hispanic source materials and
research organizations in the United
States. 2d ed. Stanford, Calif.,
Stanford University press, 1956.
xiv, 448 p. 980 56-6178
    F1408.3 .H65 1956 MRR Alc.

LIBRARIES--SPECIAL COLLECTIONS--
PICTURES.
Special Libraries Association.
Picture Division. Picture sources.
2d ed. New York, Special Libraries
Association [1964] viii, 216 p. 64-
15089
    N4000 .S7 1964 MRR Ref Desk.

United States. Library of Congress.
Prints and Photographs Division.
Pictorial Americana; 2d ed.
Washington, Library of Congress,
1955. 68 p. 973.084 55-60012
    Z663.39 .P5 1955 MRR Alc.

United States. Library of Congress.
Reference Dept. Guide to the special
collections of prints & photographs
in the Library of Congress,
Washington, 1955. v, 200 p.
016.779 54-60020
    Z663.2 .G8 MRR Alc.

LIBRARIES--SPECIAL COLLECTIONS--THEATER.
Gilder, Rosamond. Theatre
collections in libraries and museums,
New York, Theatre arts inc. [c1936]
4 p. l., 182 p. 792.074 36-21492
    Z688.T6 G5 MRR Alc.

International Federation of Library
Associations. Section for Theatrical
Libraries and Museums.
Bibliotheques et musees des arts du
spectacle dans le monde ... 2e
edition revue et augmentee Paris,
Editions du Centre national de la
recherche scientifique, 1967. 803 p.
[90 F] 016.792 70-362547
    Z675.T36 I5 1967 MRR Alc.

Young, William C., American
theatrical arts; Chicago, American
Library Association, 1971. ix, 166
p. 016.7902 78-161234
    Z6935 .Y68 MRR Alc.

LIBRARIES--SPECIAL COLLECTIONS--AFRICA.
Standing Conference on Library
Materials on Africa. The Scolma
directory of libraries and special
collections on Africa. 2d ed.
Hamden, Conn., Archon Books, 1967.
92 p. 015.6 67-676
    Z3501 .S8 1967 MRR Alc.

LIBRARIES--STATISTICS.
United Nations Educational,
Scientific and Cultural Organization.
Statistics on libraries. [Paris,
c1959] 128 p. 027.0083 60-50226
    Z721 .U5 MRR Alc.

LIBRARIES--AFRICA--BIBLIOGRAPHY.
United States. Library of Congress.
African Section. African libraries,
book production, and archives;
Washington, General Reference and
Bibliography Division, Reference
Dept; Library of Congress, 1962.
vi, 64 p. 016.02096 62-64603
    Z663.285 .A73 MRR Alc.

LIBRARIES--AFRICA--DIRECTORIES.
Dadzie, E. W. Directory of archives,
libraries, and schools of
librarianship in Africa. [Paris]
UNESCO [1965] 112 p. 65-5420
    Z857.A1 D3 MRR Alc.

LIBRARIES--AFRICA, SOUTH--DIRECTORIES.
Directory of scientific research
organizations in South Africa. 1971-
Pretoria, South African Council for
Scientific and Industrial Research.
507/.2068 72-621812
    Q180.A55 D53 MRR Alc Latest
    edition

Pretoria. State Library. Handbook of
Southern African libraries.
Pretoria, State Library, 1970.
[cxiv] 939 p. [20.00] 75-14937
    Z674 .P72 no. 10 MRR Alc.

South African Library Association.
Orange Free State Branch. Adresboek
van Vrystaatse biblioteke.
Bloemfontein, Suid-Afrikaanse
Biblioteekvereniging (O.V.S. Tak)
1960. 39 l. 62-32128
    Z857.O7 S6 MRR Alc.

LIBRARIES--AFRICA, SOUTH--ORANGE FREE
STATE--DIRECTORIES.
South African Library Association.
Orange Free State Branch. Adresboek
van Vrystaatse biblioteke.
Bloemfontein, Suid-Afrikaanse
Biblioteekvereniging (O.V.S. Tak)
1960. 39 l. 62-32128
    Z857.O7 S6 MRR Alc.

LIBRARIES--AFRICA, SOUTHERN--
DIRECTORIES.
Pretoria. State Library. Handbook of
Southern African libraries.
Pretoria, State Library, 1970.
[cxiv] 939 p. [20.00] 75-14937
    Z674 .P72 no. 10 MRR Alc.

LIBRARIES--AUSTRALIA.
Tauber, Maurice Falcolm, Resources
of Australian libraries: Canberra,
Australian Advisory Council on
Bibliographical Services, 1963. 42
p. 64-2248
    Z870 .T4 MRR Alc.

LIBRARIES--AUSTRALIA--DIRECTORIES.
Kosa, Geza Attila, Who's who in
Australian libraries, Sydney,
Library Association of Australia,
1968. xiv, 181 p. [5.40]
021/.0025/94 75-398852
    Z720.A46A85 MRR Biog.

Library Association of Australia.
Committee on Library Statistics for
Unesco. Register of libraries in
Australia. Sydney, Library
Association of Australia, 1963. 2.
144 l. 66-49125
    Z870 .L48 MRR Alc.

LIBRARIES--AUSTRIA--DIRECTORIES.
Handbuch der österreichischen
Wissenschaft. 1.- Bd.; 1947/48-
Wien, Österreichischer Bundesverlag
für Unterricht, Wissenschaft und
Kunst. 50-18117
    AS132 .J3 MRR Alc Latest edition

Jahrbuch der deutschen Bibliotheken.
1.- Jahrg.; 1902- Wiesbaden [etc.]
O. Harrassowitz. 02-17084
    Z801 .J2 MRR Alc Latest edition

LIBRARIES--BELGIUM.
Polain, Louis. Catalogue des livres
imprimés au quinzième siècle des
bibliothèques de Belgique.
Bruxelles, Pour la Société des
bibliophiles & iconophiles de
Belgique, 1932. 4 v. 016.093 33-
18424
    Z240 .P76 MRR Alc.

LIBRARIES--CANADA.
Campbell, Henry Cummings. Canadian
libraries. 2nd ed. fully revised and
expanded. London, Bingley, 1971.
114 p. [£1.75] 021/.00971 76-
872034
    Z735.A1 C29 1971b MRR Alc.

Downs, Robert Bingham. Resources of
Canadian academic and research
libraries Ottawa, Association of
Universities and Colleges of Canada,
1967. xi, 301 p. [5.00]
026/.000971 70-359019
    Z735.A1 D6 MRR Alc.

International congresses and
conferences, 1840-1937; New York,
The H. W. Wilson company, 1938. 3 p.
l., 229 p. 016.06 38-1264
    Z5051 .I58 MRR Alc.

Ottawa. National Library.
Periodicals in the social sciences
and humanities currently received by
Canadian libraries. [Ottawa, Queen's
Printer] 1968. 2 v. [unpriced]
016.300/5 68-105183
    Z6945 .O895 MRR Alc.

Ricci, Seymour de, Census of
medieval and renaissance manuscripts
in the United States and Canada, New
York, H. W. Wilson, 1935-40. 3 v.
35-31886
    Z6620.U5 R5 MRR Alc.

Union list of serials in libraries of
the United States and Canada, 3d ed.
New York, H. W. Wilson Co., 1965. 5
v. (4649 p.) 016.05 65-10150
    Z6945 .U45 1965 MRR Circ.

Young, Margaret Labash. Directory of
special libraries and information
centers. 3d ed. Detroit, Gale
Research Co. [1974- v. [$48.00]
026/.00025/7 74-3240
    Z731 .Y68 1974 MRR Ref Desk.

LIBRARIES--CANADA--ABBREVIATIONS.
National union catalog. Register of
additional locations. June 1965-
Washington, Library of Congress.
018/.1 74-646916
    Z881.A1 U3722 MRR Alc (Dk 33)
    Partial set

Symbols of American libraries. [1st]-
ed.; 1932- Washington, Library of
Congress. 018/.1 33-13797
    Z663.79 .S9 MRR Alc MRR Alc
    Partial set

LIBRARIES--CANADA--DIRECTORIES.
Anderson, Beryl L. Special libraries
and information centres in Canada:
1970 revision. Ottawa, Canadian
Library Association, 1970. 168 p.
[$7.50] 026/.00025/71 72-197100
    Z735.A1 A55 MRR Alc.

LIBRARIES--EGYPT--DIRECTORIES.
Jam' Iyat al-Maktabat al-Miṣrīyah.
Directory of libraries in Cairo.
Cairo, 1950. 35 l. 027.062 51-
31798
    Z857 .J3 MRR Alc.

**LIBRARIES--ENGLAND--MONMOUTHSHIRE--
DIRECTORIES.**
Library Association. Reference,
Special and Information Section.
Western Group. Library resources in
Wales and Monmouthshire. London,
Library Association (Reference,
Special and Information Section,
Western Group), 1967. [2], v, 61 p.
[16/-] 021/.0025/429 78-354478
    Z791.W3 L5 MRR Alc.

LIBRARIES--EUROPE.
United States. Library of Congress.
Processing Dept. Unpublished
bibliographical tools in certain
archives and libraries of Europe;
Washington, 1952. iv, 25 p. 016.01
52-60036
    Z663.7 .U62 MRR Alc.

LIBRARIES--EUROPE--DIRECTORIES.
Lewanski, Richard Casimir, European
library directory. Firenze, L. S.
Olschki, 1968. xxvi, 774 p.
021/.0025/4 68-138998
    Z789 .L39 MRR Ref Desk.

Lewanski, Richard Casimir, Subject
collections in European libraries;
[New York] R. R. Bowker Co., 1965.
xl, 789 p. 017.1094 64-22710
    Z789 .L4 MRR Alc.

LIBRARIES--FRANCE.
Paris. Bibliothèque nationale.
Département des périodiques.
Catalogue collectif des périodiques
du début du XVIIe siècle à 1939,
Paris, Bibliothèque nationale, 1967-
v. [250.00 (v. 4)] 016.05 67-
104498
    Z6945 .P236 MRR Alc.

Pellechet, Marie Léontine Catherine,
Catalogue général des incunables
des bibliothèques publiques de
France. Paris, A. Picard et fils,
1887-1909. 3 v. 06-2931
    Z240 .P38 MRR Alc.

LIBRARIES--FRANCE--DIRECTORIES.
Paris. Bibliothèque nationale.
Répertoire des bibliothèques et
organismes de documentation. Paris,
1971. 733 p. 020/.25/44 76-501813

    Z797 .A1P35 1971 MRR Alc.

LIBRARIES--GERMANY.
Berlin. Institut für
zeitungswissenschaft.
Standortskatalog wichtiger
zeitungsbestände in deutschen
bibliotheken. Leipzig, K. W.
Hiersemann, 1933. xxxi, 254 p., 1 l.
016.073 33-24972
    Z6945 .B46 MRR Alc.

Deutscher gesamtkatalog, Berlin,
Preussische druckerei- und verlags-
aktiengesellschaft, 1931- v.
019.1 32-9323
    Z929 .A1D4 MRR Alc (Dk 33).

LIBRARIES--GERMANY--DIRECTORIES.
Berlin. Stadtbibliothek. Führer
durch die Bibliotheken und
Literaturstellen der Hauptstadt
Berlin. Leipzig, Verlag für Buch-
und Bibliothekswesen] 1963. 254 p.
63-41869
    Z802 .B44B4 MRR Alc.

Jahrbuch der deutschen Bibliotheken.
1.- Jahrg.; 1902- Wiesbaden [etc.]
O. Harrassowitz. 02-17084
    Z801 .J2 MRR Alc Latest edition

Lullies, Hildegard, Verzeichnis der
Bibliotheken in Berlin <West>
Berlin, Spitzing, 1966. 301 p. [DM
24.90] 027/.043/155 67-86023
    Z801.B4 L8 MRR Alc.

LIBRARIES--GERMANY--STATISTICS.
Jahrbuch der deutschen Bibliotheken.
1.- Jahrg.; 1902- Wiesbaden [etc.]
O. Harrassowitz. 02-17084
    Z801 .J2 MRR Alc Latest edition

**LIBRARIES--GERMANY (FEDERAL REPUBLIC,
1949-)**
Busse, Gisela von. West German
library developments since 1945,
Washington, Slavic and Central
European Division, Reference Dept.,
Library of Congress, 1962. vii, 82
p. 027 61-60081
    Z663.47 .W4 MRR Alc.

LIBRARIES--GREAT BRITAIN.
Ashworth, Wilfred. Handbook of
special librarianship and information
work. 3rd ed. London, Aslib, 1967.
[5] 624 p. [98/- 80/-(to members)]
026 67-89439
    Z665 .A73 1967 MRR Alc.

British librarianship and information
science, 1966-1970; London, Library
Association, 1972. xly, 712, [4] p.,
[5] leaves (4 fold.) [£8.50] 020
73-157654
    Z791.A1 B74 MRR Alc.

Downs, Robert Bingham, British
library resources; Chicago, American
Library Association, 1973 [i.e. 1974]
xvi, 332 p. 016.016 73-1598
    Z1002 .D63 MRR Alc.

Hewitt, Arthur R. Union list of
Commonwealth newspapers in London,
Oxford, and Cambridge. [London]
Published for the Institute of
Commonwealth Studies [by] the Athlone
Press, University of London, 1960.
ix, 101 p. 016.072 60-51452
    Z6945 .H55 1960 MRR Alc.

The Libraries, museums and art
galleries year book. 1897- London
[etc.] J. Clarke [etc.] 28-11281
    Z791 .L7 MRR Alc Latest edition

Library Association. The Library
Association year book. London. 01-
15606
    Z673 .L7Y MRR Alc Latest edition /
    MRR Alc Latest edition

McColvin, Kenneth Roy. The library
student's London, [London] Greater
London Division, Association of
Assistant Librarians, 1961. 132 p.
020.9421 62-53439
    Z791 .M22 MRR Alc.

Morgan, Paul. Oxford libraries
outside the Bodleian; Oxford [Eng.]
Oxford Bibliographical Society and
the Bodleian Library, 1973. xx, 250
p. 027.7425/72 74-164911
    Z791.098 M67 MRR Alc.

Philip, Alexander John, An index to
the special collections in libraries,
museums and art galleries (public,
private and official) in Great
Britain and Ireland. London, Pub.
for the author by F. G. Brown [1949]
viii, 190 p. 016 49-48107
    AM213 .P5 MRR Alc.

Standing Conference on Library
Materials on Africa. The Scolma
directory of libraries and special
collections on Africa. 2d ed.
Hamden, Conn., Archon Books, 1967.
92 p. 015.6 67-676
    Z3501 .S8 1967 MRR Alc.

United States. Library of Congress.
Manuscript division. A guide to
manuscripts relating to American
history in British depositories
reproduced for the Division of
manuscripts of the Library of
Congress. [Washington] The Library
of Congress, 1946. xvi, 313 p.
016.973 46-27863
    CD1048.U5 A35 1946 MRR Alc.

LIBRARIES--GREAT BRITAIN--DIRECTORIES.
Aslib. Aslib directory; London,
1957. 2 v. 026.006242 58-2664
    Z791 .A788 MRR Alc.

Industrial research in Britain. 7th
ed. [St. Peter Port, Guernsey] F.
Hodgson [1972] 889 p. 607/.2/42
73-190253
    T177.G7 I52 1972 MRR Alc.

Library Association. Complete
address list of public library
authorities in Great Britain and
Northern Ireland, London, Library
Association [1966] [2], 30 p. [5/-]
027.002542 66-76987
    Z791 .L713 MRR Alc.

Library Association. Medical Section.
Directory of medical libraries in
the British Isles. 2d ed. London,
Library Association, 1965. vii, 113
p. 66-39871
    Z675.M4 L5 1965 MRR Alc.

McColvin, Kenneth Roy. The library
student's London, [London] Greater
London Division, Association of
Assistant Librarians, 1961. 132 p.
020.9421 62-53439
    Z791 .M22 MRR Alc.

Nunn, George Walter Arthur, ed.
British sources of photographs and
pictures. London, Cassell [1952]
viii, 220 p. 770.58 53-25373
    TR12 .N8 MRR Alc.

LIBRARIES--GREAT BRITAIN--HISTORY.
Ogilvy, Jack David Angus. Books
known to the English, 597-1066
Cambridge, Mass., Mediaeval Academy
of America, 1967. xx, 300 p. 011
65-19630
    Z6602 .O35 MRR Alc.

LIBRARIES--HONGKONG.
Kan, Lai-bing, Libraries in Hong
Kong; [Hong Kong] Hong Kong Library
Association, 1963. 98 p. 64-55482

    Z845.H6 K3 MRR Alc.

**LIBRARIES--ILLINOIS--CHICAGO
METROPOLITAN AREA--DIRECTORIES.**
Hamilton, Beth A. Libraries and
information centers in the Chicago
metropolitan area. Hinsdale,
Illinois Regional Library Council,
1973. 499 p. 021/.0025/77311 73-
89540
    Z732.I2 H35 MRR Alc.

LIBRARIES--INDIA--BIBLIOGRAPHY.
Prasher, Ram Gopal, Indian library
literature; New Delhi, Today &
Tomorrow's Printers & Publishers
[1971] xiii, 504 p. [Rs40.00]
016.020/954 74-926208
    Z666 .P88 MRR Alc.

LIBRARIES--INDIA--DIRECTORIES.
Directory of booksellers, publishers,
libraries & librarians in India. 1st-
ed.; 1968/69- New Delhi, Premier
Publishers. 655.4/025/54 73-900620

    Z455 .D49 MRR Alc Latest edition

LIBRARIES--IRELAND.
Black, R. D. Collison. A catalogue
of pamphlets on economic subjects
published between 1750 and 1900 and
now housed in Irish libraries, New
York, A. M. Kelley, 1969. ix, 632 p.
016.33 78-81989
Z7164.E2 B6 MRR Alc.

Philip, Alexander John, An index to
the special collections in libraries,
museums and art galleries (public,
private and official) in Great
Britain and Ireland. London, Pub.
for the author by F. G. Brown [1949]
viii, 180 p. 016 49-48107
AM213 .P5 MRR Alc.

LIBRARIES--ITALY.
Italy. Direzione generale delle
accademie e biblioteche. Annuario
delle biblioteche italiane. [1.]-
ed.[1949]- Roma, Fratelli Palombi
Editori, 027.045 51-30361
Z809 .I763 MRR Alc Latest edition

Rome (City) Centro nazionale per il
catalogo unico delle biblioteche
italiane e per le informazioni
bibliografiche. Primo catalogo
collettivo delle biblioteche
italiane. Roma, 1962- v. 63-
50852
Z933 .A1R6 MRR Alc (Dk 33).

LIBRARIES--ITALY--DIRECTORIES.
Associazione italiana per le
biblioteche. Guida delle biblioteche
scientifiche e tecniche e dei centri
di documentazione italiani, Roma,
Consiglio nazionale delle ricerche,
1965. viii, 610 p. 68-130514
Z809 .A1A78 MRR Alc.

LIBRARIES--MEXICO--DIRECTORIES.
Mexico. Departamento de Bibliotecas.
Directorio de bibliotecas de la
Republica Mexicana; [Mexico] 1962.
iii, 154 l. 64-46987
Z739 .M6114 MRR Alc.

Parsons, Mary D., comp. Directorio
de bibliotecas de la Ciudad de
Mexico; Mexico, Mexico City
College Press, 1858. xix, 85 p. 59-
37909
Z740.M58 P3 MRR Alc.

LIBRARIES--NEAR EAST.
Daghir, Yusuf As'ad. Répertoire
des bibliothèques du Proche et du
Moyen-Orient, Paris, Organisation
des nations unies pour l'education,
la science et la culture, 1951. xi,
182 p. 027.05 51-36549
Z843 .D3 MRR Alc.

LIBRARIES--NETHERLANDS.
Nederlandse Vereniging van
Bibliothecarissen. Libraries and
documentation centres in the
Netherlands. The Hague, 1966. 61 p.
021/.009492 68-1366
Z815 .N395 1966 MRR Alc.

LIBRARIES--NETHERLANDS--DIRECTORIES.
Bibliotheek- en documentatiegids voor
Nederland, Suriname en de Nederlandse
Antillen. 2. druk. 's-Gravenhage,
Bezuidenhoutseweg 43, NIDER, 1966.
444 p. [fl 27.50] 027/.09492 67-
107049
Z815 .B52 1966 MRR Alc.

Bibliotheek- en documentatiegids voor
Nederland, Suriname en de Nederlandse
Antillen. 's-Gravenhage, NIDER. 67-
107049
Z815.A1 B5 MRR Alc Latest edition

LIBRARIES--NETHERLANDS ANTILLES--
DIRECTORIES.
Bibliotheek- en documentatiegids voor
Nederland, Suriname en de Nederlandse
Antillen. 's-Gravenhage, NIDER. 67-
107049
Z815.A1 B5 MRR Alc Latest edition

Bibliotheek- en documentatiegids voor
Nederland, Suriname en de Nederlandse
Antillen. 2. druk. 's-Gravenhage,
Bezuidenhoutseweg 43, NIDER, 1966.
444 p. [fl 27.50] 027/.09492 67-
107049
Z815 .B52 1966 MRR Alc.

LIBRARIES--NEW ENGLAND--HISTORY.
Shera, Jesse Hauk. Foundations of
the public library; [Hamden, Conn.]
Shoe String Press, 1965 [c1949] xv,
308 p. 027.474 65-17879
Z631 .S55 1965 MRR Alc.

LIBRARIES--NEW YORK (CITY)
Special libraries directory of
Greater New York. 12th- ed.; 1972-
New York, Special Libraries
Association, New York Chapter.
021/.0025/747 74-644548
Z732.N75 S6 MRR Alc Latest edition

LIBRARIES--NEW YORK (STATE)
Fessler, Aaron L. Current
newspapers; United States and
foreign; Provisional ed. New York,
New York Public Library, 1957. 66 p.
016.07 57-14848
Z6945 .F4 MRR Alc.

New York State union list of serials.
New York, CCM Information Corp.
[1970] 2 v. 016.05 76-135198
Z6945 .N685 MRR Alc.

Union list of serials [in] the
libraries of the State University of
New York. 1st- ed.; 1966-
[Syracuse] 011 67-65593
Z6945 .U454 MRR Alc Latest edition

LIBRARIES--NORTHERN IRELAND--
DIRECTORIES.
Library Association. Northern Ireland
Branch. Directory of Northern
Ireland libraries. Belfast, Library
Association (Northern Ireland
Branch), 1967. [4], 22 p. [10/-]
021/.0025/416 67-105639
Z791.N87 L5 MRR Alc.

LIBRARIES--NORTHWEST, PACIFIC.
Inland Empire Council of Teachers of
English. Northwest books, [2d ed.]
Portland, Or., Binfords & Mort [1942]
356 p. 016.81 42-21718
Z1251.N7 I6 MRR Alc.

LIBRARIES--PAKISTAN--DIRECTORIES.
Shamsuddoulah, A. B. M., Pakistan
library directory; 1st ed. Dacca,
Great Eastern Books, 1970. 156 p.
[8.00 ($3.00)] 71-931634
Z845.P28 S48 MRR Alc.

LIBRARIES--PENNSYLVANIA.
Special Libraries Council of
Philadelphia and Vicinity. Directory
of libraries and informational
sources. [1st, 3d]- ed.; 1920,
1923- Philadelphia [etc.] 026.0058
24-5378
Z732.P6 P5 MRR Alc Latest edition

LIBRARIES--RUSSIA.
Horecky, Paul Louis, Libraries and
bibliographic centers in the Soviet
Union. [Bloomington, Indiana
University, 1959] xviii, 287 p.
027.047 59-63389
Z819 .H6 MRR Alc.

Ruggles, Melville J., Soviet
libraries and librarianship;
Chicago, American Library
Association, 1962. x, 147 p.
020.947 62-21564
Z819 .R77 MRR Alc.

LIBRARIES--SOUTH CAROLINA.
Moore, John Hammond. Research
materials in South Carolina; [1st
ed.] Columbia, University of South
Carolina Press, 1967. xiv, 346 p.
016.05 67-25916
Z732.S72 M6 MRR Alc.

LIBRARIES--SOUTHERN STATES.
Downs, Robert Bingham, ed. Resources
of southern libraries; Chicago,
American Library association, 1938.
xli, 370 p. 027.075 38-27568
Z731 .D75 MRR Alc.

Southern Regional Education Board. A
Southeastern supplement to the Union
list of serials; Atlanta, 1959.
xviii, 447 p. 016.05 59-9979
Z6945 .S614 MRR Alc.

LIBRARIES--SPAIN--BIBLIOGRAPHY.
Foulché-Delbosc, Raymond, Manuel de
l'hispanisant. New York, G. P.
Putnam's sons, 1920- v. 20-
16867
Z2681.A1 F7 MRR Alc.

LIBRARIES--SURINAM--DIRECTORIES.
Bibliotheek- en documentatiegids voor
Nederland, Suriname en de Nederlandse
Antillen. 's-Gravenhage, NIDER. 67-
107049
Z815.A1 B5 MRR Alc Latest edition

Bibliotheek- en documentatiegids voor
Nederland, Suriname en de Nederlandse
Antillen. 2. druk. 's-Gravenhage,
Bezuidenhoutseweg 43, NIDER, 1966.
444 p. [fl 27.50] 027/.09492 67-
107049
Z815 .B52 1966 MRR Alc.

LIBRARIES--SWEDEN.
Ottervik, Gösta, Libraries and
archives in Sweden Stockholm,
Swedish Institute, 1954. 216 p.
027.0485 55-14224
Z827 .O8 MRR Alc.

LIBRARIES--SWEDEN--DIRECTORIES.
Svensk biblioteksmatrikel 1966.
Lund, Bibliotekstjanst, 1967. 318
p. [55-skr] 67-91543
Z827 .A1S8 MRR Alc.

LIBRARIES--SWITZERLAND.
Schweizerische Vereinigung für
Dokumentation. Archive, Bibliotheken
und Dokumentationsstellen der
Schweiz. 3. Aufl. Bern, 1958. xvi,
144 p. 59-45785
Z837 .S44 1958 MRR Alc.

LIBRARIES--TENNESSEE.
Historical records survey. Tennessee.
List of Tennessee imprints, 1793-
1840, in Tennessee libraries.
Nashville, Tenn., The Tennessee
Historical records survey, 1941.
viii, 97 numb. l. 015.768 41-52927
Z1215 .H67 no. 16 MRR Alc.

LIBRARIES--UGANDA.
Trowell, Kathleen Margaret, comp. A
handbook of the museums and libraries
of Uganda. Kampala, Uganda Museum,
1957. 16 p. 58-29016
Z858.U4 T7 MRR Alc.

LIBRARIES--UNITED STATES.
American Library Association. Junior
Members Round Table. Local indexes
in American libraries; Boston, F. W.
Faxon Co., 1947. xxxiv, 221 p.
016.01 47-30800
Z6293 .A5 MRR Alc.

Downs, Robert Bingham, American
library resources; Chicago, American
Library Association, 1951. 428 p.
016.016 51-11156
Z1002 .D6 MRR Alc.

Duignan, Peter. Handbook of American
resources for African studies.
[Stanford, Calif.] Hoover Institution
on War, Revolution, and Peace,
Stanford University, 1967. xvii, 218
p. 016.916 66-20901
Z3501 .D8 MRR Alc.

Gropp, Arthur Eric, comp. Union list
of Latin American newspapers in
libraries in the United States.
Washington, Dept. of Cultural
Affairs, Pan American Union, 1953.
x, 235 p. 016.0798 53-61715
Z6945 .P18 MRR Alc.

International congresses and
conferences, 1840-1937; New York,
The H. W. Wilson company, 1938. 3 p.
l., 229 p. 016.06 39-1264
Z5051 .I58 MRR Alc.

Knight, Douglas M., comp. Libraries
at large; New York, Bowker, 1969.
xxiv, 664 p. 027/.00973 70-79429
Z731 .K56 MRR Alc.

Latin American newspapers in United
States libraries; Austin, Published
for the Conference on Latin American
History by the University of Texas
Press [1969, c1968] xiv, 619 p.
[20.00] 016.07918 69-63004
Z6947 .C5 MRR Alc.

Library of Congress and National
union catalog author lists, 1942-
1962; Detroit, Gale Research Co.,
1969-71. 152 v. 018/.1/0973 73-
82135
Z881.A1 L63 MRR Alc (Dk 33)

Malia, Martin Edward. Report, to the
Joint Committee on Slavic Studies and
to the Library of Congress, on
methods for improving Soviet book
acquisitions by American research
libraries, February-March, 1956.
[Washington?] 1956. 2 l., 79 p. 63-
61735
Z663 .R394 MRR Alc.

Philadelphia Bibliographical Center
and Union Library Catalogue.
Committee on Microphotography. Union
list of microfilms; Ann Arbor,
Mich., J. W. Edwards, 1961. 2 v.
(xviii p., 2800 columns) 016.099
62-1343
Z1033.M5 P5 1961 MRR Alc.

Ricci, Seymour de, Census of
medieval and renaissance manuscripts
in the United States and Canada, New
York, H. W. Wilson, 1935-40. 3 v.
35-31986
Z6620.U5 R5 MRR Alc.

Smits, Rudolf, Half a century of
Soviet serials, 1917-1968;
Washington, Library of Congress: [for
sale by the Supt. of Docs., U.S.
Govt. Print. Off.] 1968. 2 v. (xv,
1661 p.) [16.00] 016.057 68-62169
Z663.23 .H3 MRR Alc.

Special Libraries Association.
Geography and Map Division. Directory
Revision Committee. Map collections
in the United States and Canada; 2d
ed. New York, Special Libraries
Association, 1970. xiii, 159 p.
026/.912/02573 72-101336
GA193.U5 S68 1970 MRR Alc.

LIBRARIES--UNITED STATES. (Cont.)
Union list of serials in libraries of
the United States and Canada. 3d ed.
New York, H. W. Wilson Co., 1965. 5
v. (4648 p.)   016.05 65-10150
Z6945 .U45 1965 MRR Circ.

United States. Library of Congress.
American Libraries Book Procurement
Center, Delhi. Accessions list,
Bangladesh. v. 1-   1972-   New
Delhi. 018/.1 73-902218
Z3186 .U55 MRR Alc Full set

United States. Library of Congress.
American Libraries Book Procurement
Center, Delhi. Accessions list, Sri
Lanka. v. 7-   Feb. 1973-   New
Delhi. 015/.549/3 73-929618
Z3211 .U5 MRR Alc Full set

United States. Library of Congress.
Cyrillic Bibliographic Project.
Serial publications of the Soviet
Union, 1939-1957; [New expanded ed.]
Washington, 1958. ix, 459 p.
016.057 58-60013
Z663.7 .S4 1958 MRR Alc.

LIBRARIES--UNITED STATES--ABBREVIATIONS.
National union catalog. Register of
additional locations. June 1965-
Washington, Library of Congress.
018/.1 74-646916
Z881.A1 U3722 MRR Alc (Dk 33)
     Partial set

Symbols of American libraries. [1st]-
ed.; 1932- Washington, Library of
Congress. 018/.1 33-13797
Z663.79 .S9 MRR Alc MRR Alc
     Partial set

LIBRARIES--UNITED STATES--DIRECTORIES.
Academic Media, Orange, N.J.
Worldwide directory of Federal
libraries. 1st ed. Orange, N.J.
[1973] xiv, 411 p.   027.5/025/73
72-75955
Z675.G7 A2 MRR Alc.

American library directory; New
York, R. R. Bowker. 23-3581
Z731 .A53 Sci RR Latest edition /
MRR Ref Desk Latest edition

American school library directory;
New York, R. R. Bowker Co., 1952-57.
4 v.   027.82058 52-6286
Z675.S3 A63 MRR Alc.

American school library directory;
Rev. ed. New York, R. R. Bowker Co.,
1959- v. in   65-1486
Z675.S3 A632 MRR Alc.

Ash, Lee, comp. Subject collections;
3d ed., rev. and enl. New York,
Bowker, 1967. ix, 1221 p.   026 67-
27563
Z688.A2 A8 1967 MRR Ref Desk.

The Bowker annual of library and book
trade information. 1955/56-   New
York, R. R. Bowker. 020.58 55-12434

     Z731 .A47 Sci RR Latest edition /
     MRR Alc Latest edition / MRR Ref
     Desk Latest edition

Haro, Robert P. Latin Americana
research in the United States and
Canada: Chicago, American Library
Association, 1971. x, 111 p.
918/.03/07 72-138653
Z1601 .H35 MRR Alc.

Medical Library Association.
Directory. 2d ed. Hamden, Conn.,
Shoe String Press, 1959. xxxi, 274
p.   026.61058 59-15362
Z675.M4 M43 1959 MRR Alc.

Shaw, Elizabeth Miller. Directory of
documents librarians in the United
States. Chicago, RSD/RTSD
Interdivisional Committee on Public
Documents, American Library
Association, 1967. 93 p.   020/.922
79-23647
Z675.D4 S55 MRR Biog.

System Development Corporation.
Directory of educational information
resources. [Rev. and updated ed.]
New York, CCM Information Corp.,
1971. ix, 181 p.   370/.7 70-136093

L901 .S95 1972 MRR Alc.

United States. Library of Congress.
National Referral Center. A
directory of information resources in
the United States: social sciences.
Rev. ed. Washington, Library of
Congress; [for sale by the Supt. of
Docs., U.S. Govt. Print. Off.] 1973.
iv, 700 p. [$6.90]   300/.7 73-3297

Z663.379 .D53 1973 MRR Alc.

Young, Margaret Labash. Directory of
special libraries and information
centers. 3d ed. Detroit, Gale
Research Co. [1974- v.   [$48.00]
026/.00025/7 74-3240
Z731 .Y68 1974 MRR Ref Desk.

LIBRARIES--UNITED STATES--HISTORY.
Daniel, Hawthorne, Public libraries
for everyone; [1st ed.] Garden
City, N.Y., Doubleday, 1961. 192 p.
027.473 61-8881
Z731 .D35 MRR Alc.

LIBRARIES--UNITED STATES--HISTORY--
BIBLIOGRAPHY.
Harris, Michael H. A guide to
research in American library history,
Metuchen, N.J., Scarecrow Press,
1968. 186 p.   016.021/009 67-12068

Z731 .H3 MRR Alc.

LIBRARIES--UNITED STATES--STATISTICS.
The Bowker annual of library and book
trade information. 1955/56-   New
York, R. R. Bowker. 020.58 55-12434

     Z731 .A47 Sci RR Latest edition /
     MRR Alc Latest edition / MRR Ref
     Desk Latest edition

LIBRARIES--WALES--DIRECTORIES.
Library Association. Reference,
Special and Information Section.
Western Group. Library resources in
Wales and Monmouthshire. London,
Library Association (Reference,
Special and Information Section,
Western Group), 1967. [2], v, 61 p.
[16/-]   021/.0025/429 78-354478
Z791.W3 L5 MRR Alc.

LIBRARIES--WISCONSIN--DIRECTORIES.
Long, Marie Ann. Directory of
library resources in Wisconsin.
[Madison] College & University
Section, Wisconsin Library
Association; [distributed by Madison
Public Library] 1964. 1 v. (unpaged)
64-64469
Z732.W8 L6 MRR Alc.

LIBRARIES, CHILDREN'S.
see also Books and reading for
children

     see also Children's literature

LIBRARIES, CHILDREN'S--BIBLIOGRAPHY.
Pellowski, Anne. The world of
children's literature. New York,
Bowker, 1968. x, 538 p. [$18.75
U.S. and Can. ($20.65 elsewhere)]
028.52 67-25022
Z1037 .P37 MRR Alc.

LIBRARIES, DEPOSITORY--UNITED STATES--
DIRECTORIES.
Burke, John Gordon, The monthly
catalog of United States Government
publications; [Hamden, Conn.] Linnet
Books, 1973. vi, 113 p.   015/.73
72-11690
Z1223 .A184 MRR Ref Desk.

Shaw, Elizabeth Miller. Directory of
documents librarians in the United
States. Chicago, RSD/RTSD
Interdivisional Committee on Public
Documents, American Library
Association, 1967. 93 p.   020/.922
79-23647
Z675.D4 S55 MRR Biog.

LIBRARIES, GOVERNMENTAL,
ADMINISTRATIVE, ETC.--AUSTRALIA.
Johnston, Barbara. Libraries of
Australian government departments and
agencies. Sydney, James Bennett
[1969] 52 p. [1.50]   027.5/0994
79-479929
Z870 .A1J6 MRR Alc.

LIBRARIES, GOVERNMENTAL,
ADMINISTRATIVE, ETC.--GREAT BRITAIN--
DIRECTORIES.
Great Britain. Treasury. Organization
and Methods Division. A guide to
Government libraries. [2d ed.]
London, H.M. Stationery Off., 1958.
viii, 139 p.   027.542 59-31093
Z675.G7 G7 1958 MRR Alc.

LIBRARIES, GOVERNMENTAL,
ADMINISTRATIVE, ETC.--UNITED STATES.
George Washington University,
Washington, D.C. Biological Sciences
Communication Project. A study of
resources and major subject holdings
available in U.S. Federal libraries
Washington, U.S. Office of Education,
Bureau of Research, 1970. ix, 670 p.
011 79-609579
Z881.A1 G4 1970b MRR Alc.

LIBRARIES, GOVERNMENTAL,
ADMINISTRATIVE, ETC.--UNITED STATES--
DIRECTORIES.
Academic Media, Orange, N.J.
Worldwide directory of Federal
libraries. 1st ed. Orange, N.J.
[1973] xiv, 411 p.   027.5/025/73
72-75955
Z675.G7 A2 MRR Alc.

LIBRARIES, GOVERNMENTAL,
ADMINISTRATIVE, ETC.-- WASHINGTON, D.C.--
-DIRECTORIES.
Library and reference facilities in
the area of the District of Columbia.
[1st]- ed.; 1943- Washington.
021/.0025/753 44-41159
Z732.D62 U63 Sci RR Latest edition
/ MRR Alc Latest edition

LIBRARIES, NATIONAL.
Esdaile, Arundell James Kennedy,
National libraries of the world; 2d
ed., completely rev. London, Library
Association, 1957. xv, 413 p.
027.5 58-1073
Z721 .E74 1957 MRR Alc.

United States. Library of Congress.
General Reference and Bibliography
Division. Functions of selected
national libraries. Washington,
1959. iii, ii, 103 p.   61-61111
Z675.N2 U5 MRR Alc.

LIBRARIES, PRIVATE--UNITED STATES.
McKay, George Leslie, American book
auction catalogues, 1713-1934; New
York, The New York public library,
1937. xxxii, 540 p.   016.0173 37-
33888
Z999 .A1M2 MRR Alc.

LIBRARIES, SPECIAL.
Ashworth, Wilfred. Handbook of
special librarianship and information
work. 3rd ed. London, Aslib, 1967.
[5], 624 p. [98/- 80/-(to members)]
026 67-89439
Z665 .A73 1967 MRR Alc.

Johns, Ada Winifred. Special
libraries: development of the
concept, their organizations, and
their services. Metuchen, N.J.,
Scarecrow Press, 1968. 245 p.   026
68-12628
Z675.A2 J57 MRR Alc.

Philip, Alexander John, An index to
the special collections in libraries,
museums and art galleries (public,
private and official) in Great
Britain and Ireland. London, Pub.
for the author by F. G. Brown [1949]
viii, 190 p.   016 49-48107
AM213 .P5 MRR Alc.

Special libraries association.
Special library resources ... New
York, Special libraries association
[1941]-47. 4 v.   026.0097 41-23807

Z675.A2 S65 MRR Alc.

Special Libraries Association.
Illinois Chapter. Special libraries:
a guide for management; New York,
Special Libraries Association, 1966.
viii, 63 p.   026 66-17107
Z675.A2 S75 MRR Alc.

LIBRARIES, SPECIAL--DIRECTORIES.
Ruoss, George Martin. A world
directory of theological libraries,
Metuchen, N.J., Scarecrow Press,
1968. 220 p.   027.6/7/025 68-12632

Z675.T4 R8 MRR Alc.

LIBRARIES, SPECIAL--AFRICA, SOUTH--
TRANSVAAL--DIRECTORIES.
Musiker, Reuben. Directory of
libraries in the southern Transvaal.
Potchefstroom, South African Library
Association, 1963. 2, 41 l. 64-
55507
Z857.T75 M8 MRR Alc.

LIBRARIES, SPECIAL--AUSTRALIA.
Johnston, Barbara. Libraries of
Australian government departments and
agencies. Sydney, James Bennett
[1969] 52 p. [1.50]   027.5/0994
79-479929
Z870 .A1J6 MRR Alc.

LIBRARIES, SPECIAL--BRAZIL--DIRECTORIES.
Rio de Janeiro. Instituto Brasileiro
de Bibliografia e Documentação.
Bibliotecas especializadas
brasileiras; Rio de Janeiro, 1962.
375 p.   64-28145
Z769 .R54 MRR Alc.

LIBRARIES, SPECIAL--CANADA--DIRECTORIES.
Anderson, Beryl L. Special libraries
and information centres in Canada:
1970 revision. Ottawa, Canadian
Library Association, 1970. 168 p.
[$7.50] 026/.00025/71 72-197100
Z735.A1 A55 MRR Alc.

Ash, Lee, comp. Subject collections;
3d ed.; rev. and enl. New York,
Bowker, 1967. ix, 1221 p.   026 67-
27563
Z688.A2 A8 1967 MRR Ref Desk.

Young, Margaret Labash. Directory of
special libraries and information
centers. 3d ed. Detroit, Gale
Research Co. [1974- v.   [$48.00]
026/.00025/7 74-3240
Z731 .Y68 1974 MRR Ref Desk.

LIBRARIES, SPECIAL--DELAWARE.
Special Libraries Council of
Philadelphia and Vicinity. Directory
of libraries and informational
sources. (1st, 3d)- ed.; 1920,
1923- Philadelphia [etc.] 026.0058
24-5378
    Z732.P6 P5 MRR Alc Latest edition

LIBRARIES, SPECIAL--GREAT BRITAIN.
Burkett, Jack, ed. Special library
and information services in the
United Kingdom. 2d. rev. ed.
[London] Library Association [1965]
366 p. 66-53653
    Z791 .B9 1965 MRR Alc.

Irwin, Raymond, ed. The libraries of
London. 2d. rev. ed. London,
Library Association, 1961. 332 p.
027.0421 62-1104
    Z791 .L852 1961 MRR Alc.

LIBRARIES, SPECIAL--INDIA--DIRECTORIES.
Indian Association of Special
Libraries and Information Centres.
Directory of special and research
libraries in India. [1st ed.]
Calcutta, sole selling agent: Oxford
Book & stationery Co., 1962. iii,
282 p. sa 63-1553
    Z955 .I45 MRR Alc.

**LIBRARIES, SPECIAL--NEW JERSEY--
DIRECTORIES.**
Special Libraries Council of
Philadelphia and Vicinity. Directory
of libraries and informational
sources. (1st, 3d)- ed.; 1920,
1923- Philadelphia [etc.] 026.0058
24-5378
    Z732.P6 P5 MRR Alc Latest edition

**LIBRARIES, SPECIAL--NEW YORK
METROPOLITAN AREA--DIRECTORIES.**
Special libraries directory of
Greater New York. 12th- ed.; 1972-
New York, Special Libraries
Association, New York Chapter.
021/.0025/747 74-644549
    Z732.N75 S6 MRR Alc Latest edition

**LIBRARIES, SPECIAL--PENNSYLVANIA--
DIRECTORIES.**
Special Libraries Council of
Philadelphia and Vicinity. Directory
of libraries and informational
sources. (1st, 3d)- ed.; 1920,
1923- Philadelphia [etc.] 026.0058
24-5378
    Z732.P6 P5 MRR Alc Latest edition

**LIBRARIES, SPECIAL--UNITED STATES--
DIRECTORIES.**
Ash, Lee, comp. Subject collections;
3d ed., rev. and enl. New York,
Bowker, 1967. ix, 1221 p. 026 67-
27563
    Z688.A2 A8 1967 MRR Ref Desk.

Young, Margaret Labash. Directory of
special libraries and information
centers. 3d ed. Detroit, Gale
Research Co. [1974- v.   [$48.00]
026/.00025/7 74-3240
    Z731 .Y68 1974 MRR Ref Desk.

**LIBRARIES, SPECIAL--WASHINGTON, D.C.
METROPOLITAN AREA--DIRECTORIES.**
Special Libraries Association.
Washington, D.C., Chapter. Directory
and handbook 1966- [Washington]
026/.006/2753 72-620935
    Z673 .S817 MRR Alc Latest edition
    / Sci RR Latest edition

LIBRARIES, THEATRICAL.
Gilder, Rosamond. Theatre
collections in libraries and museums,
New York, Theatre arts inc. [c1936]
4 p. l., 182 p. 792.074 36-21492
    Z688.T6 G5 MRR Alc.

International Federation of Library
Associations. Section for Theatrical
Libraries and Museums.
Bibliothèques et musées des arts du
spectacle dans le monde ... 2e
édition revue et augmentée Paris,
Éditions du Centre national de la
recherche scientifique, 1967. 803 p.
[90 F] 016.792 70-362547
    Z675.T36 I5 1967 MRR Alc.

Young, William C., American
theatrical arts; Chicago, American
Library Association, 1971. ix, 166
p. 016.7902 78-161234
    Z6935 .Y68 MRR Alc.

LIBRARIES, UNIVERSITY AND COLLEGE.
Books for college libraries;
Chicago, American Library
Association, 1967. ix, 1056 p.
016.028 66-30781
    Z1035 .B72 MRR Alc.

Farber, Evan Ira. Classified list of
periodicals for the college library,
5th ed., rev. and enl. Westwood,
Mass.; F. W. Faxon Co., 1972. xvii,
449 p. 016.05 72-76264
    Z6941 .F25 1972 MRR Alc.

Metcalf, Keyes DeWitt, Planning
academic and research library
buildings New York, McGraw-Hill
[1965] xv, 431 p. 022 64-7868
    Z679 .M38 MRR Alc.

Wheeler, Helen Rippier. A basic book
collection for the community college
library, [Hamden, Conn.] Shoe String
Press, 1968. x, 317 p. 011 67-
24193
    Z1035 .W47 MRR Alc.

Wilson, Louis Round, The university
library; 2d ed. New York, Columbia
University Press, 1956. xiii, 641 p.
027.7 55-11184
    Z675.U5 W745 1956 MRR Alc.

**LIBRARIES, UNIVERSITY AND COLLEGE--
ADMINISTRATION.**
Lyle, Guy Redvers, The
administration of the college
library, 3d ed. New York, Wilson,
1961. xiii, 419 p. 027.7 61-11121
    Z675.U5 L88 1961 MRR Alc.

**LIBRARIES, UNIVERSITY AND COLLEGE--
CANADA.**
Downs, Robert Bingham, Resources of
Canadian academic and research
libraries Ottawa, Association of
Universities and Colleges of Canada,
1967. xi, 301 p. [5.00]
026/.000971 70-359019
    Z735.A1 D6 MRR Alc.

Ottawa. National Library. Research
collections in Canadian libraries.
[Ottawa, Information Canada, 1972-
v. in [$1.00 (v. 1) varies]
027.7/0971 74-159990
    Z735.A1 O88 1972 MRR Alc.

**LIBRARIES, UNIVERSITY AND COLLEGE--
UNITED STATES.**
Delanoy, Diana D. Directory of
academic library consortia, Santa
Monica, Calif., System Development
Corp. [c1972] 304 p. 021.6/4/0873
73-164534
    Z675.U5 D39 MRR Alc.

Princeton University. Library. Julian
Street Library. The Julian Street
Library; a preliminary list of
titles, New York, Bowker, 1966. 789
p. 017.5 66-13551
    Z881.P942 J8 MRR Alc.

**LIBRARIES, UNIVERSITY AND COLLEGE--
UNITED STATES--STATISTICS.**
American Library Association. Library
Administration Division. Library
statistics of colleges and
universities, 1965-66; Chicago,
American Library Association, 1967.
viii, 234 p. 027.7/021/2 67-6695
    Z675.U5 A585 MRR Alc.

LIBRARIES AND MOVING-PICTURES.
United States. Library of Congress.
Stack and Reader Division. Libraries
and library services on film; 2d ed.
Washington, Reference Dept., Library
of Congress, 1957. 19 p. 020.84
57-60043
    Z663.48 .L5 1957 MRR Alc.

LIBRARIES AND READERS.
Hook, Lucyle. The research paper;
4th ed. Englewood Cliffs, N.J.,
Prentice-Hall [1969] viii, 120 p.
808+.023/3 69-20488
    PE1478 .H6 1969 MRR Alc.

LIBRARIES AND SCHOOLS.
see also Children's literature

LIBRARIES AND STATE--UNITED STATES.
Temple, Phillips Lumsden, Federal
services to libraries; Chicago,
American Library Association, 1954.
xxvii, 227 p. 021.8 54-8697
    Z731 .T56 MRR Alc.

**LIBRARIES AND THE PHYSICALLY
HANDICAPPED--UNITED STATES--DIRECTORIES.**
Directory of library resources for
the blind and physically handicapped.
Washington, Library of Congress,
Division for the Blind and Physically
Handicapped. 027.6/63/02573 70-
615605
    Z675.B6 D5 MRR Alc Latest edition

LIBRARY ADMINISTRATION.
Bowler, Roberta, ed. Local public
library administration. 1st ed.
Chicago International City Managers'
Association, 1964. xiii, 375 p.
027+.4 64-21804
    Z678 .B8 MRR Alc.

LIBRARY ADMINISTRATION--CONGRESSES.
Rutgers University, New Brunswick,
N.J. Graduate School of Library
Service. Studies in library
administrative problems; New
Brunswick, N.J., 1960. 210 p.
025.082 60-7275
    Z678 .R8 MRR Alc.

LIBRARY ARCHITECTURE.
Ellsworth, Ralph Eugene, Buildings,
New Brunswick, N.J., Graduate School
of Library Service, Rutgers, the
State University, 1960. 3 v. in 1.
022.082 60-7279
    Z679 .E4 MRR Alc.

Thompson, Anthony. Library buildings
of Britain and Europe; London,
Butterworths, 1963. xii, 326 p.
022.3 64-9681
    Z679 .T5 MRR Alc.

LIBRARY ASSOCIATION--BIBLIOGRAPHY.
Cole, George Watson, An index to
bibliographical papers published by
the Bibliographical society and the
Library association, London, 1877-
1932, Chicago, Ill., Pub. for the
Bibliographical society of America at
the University of Chicago press
[1933] ix, 262 p. 016.01 33-33065
    Z1008 .B585 MRR Alc.

LIBRARY ASSOCIATIONS.
Fang, Josephine R. Handbook of
national and international library
associations Prelim. ed. Chicago,
American Library Association, 1973.
xxvi, 326 p. [$8.50] 020/.6 73-
5619
    Z673.A1 F3 MRR Alc.

Library Association. The Library
Association year book. London. 01-
15606
    Z673 .L7Y MRR Alc Latest edition /
    MRR Alc Latest edition

LIBRARY ASSOCIATIONS--DIRECTORIES.
A.L.A. membership directory. 1949-
Chicago, American Library
Association. 020.622 50-3095
    Z720 .A4U37 Sci RR Latest edition
    / MRR Ref Desk Latest edition

Internationales Bibliothek-Handbuch.
2.- Ausg.; 1968- München-Pullach,
Verlag Dokumentation. 72-627058
    Z721 .I63 MRR Ref Desk Latest
    edition

LIBRARY CATALOGS.
see also Catalogs, Card

American Antiquarian Society,
Worcester, Mass. Library. A
dictionary catalog of American books
pertaining to the 17th through 19th
centuries. Westport, Conn.,
Greenwood Pub. Corp. [1971] 20 v.
015/.73 76-103920
    Z1215 .A264 MRR Alc (Dk 33)

California. University. Library.
Author-title catalog. Boston, G. K.
Hall, 1963. 115 v. 018/.1 73-
153193
    Z881 .C1532 1963 MRR Alc (Dk 33)

Chicago. Center for Research
Libraries. The Center for Research
Libraries catalogue; monographs.
Chicago, 1969-70. 5 v. 018/.1 76-
13486
    Z881 .C512 MRR Alc (DK 33)

Deutscher gesamtkatalog, Berlin,
Preussische druckerei- und verlags-
aktiengesellschaft, 1931- v.
018.1 32-9323
    Z929 .A1D4 MRR Alc (Dk 33).

Library Association. Library.
Catalogue. London, 1958. vii, 519
p. 017.1 58-40138
    Z921 .L323 MRR Alc.

London library. Catalogue of the
London library, London, 1913-14. 2
v. 14-5422
    Z921 .L6 1913 MRR Alc (DK33).

New York (City). Public Library.
Research Libraries. Dictionary
catalog of the Research Libraries.
Jan. 1972- [New York] 019/.1 72-
620418
    Z881.N588 D5 MRR Alc (Dk 33)
    Latest edition

New York Academy of Medicine.
Library. Catalog of biographies.
Boston, G. K. Hall, 1960. 165 p.
016.9261 60-50505
    R134 .N4 MRR Biog.

Princeton University. Library. Julian
Street Library. The Julian Street
Library; a preliminary list of
titles, New York, Bowker, 1966. 789
p. 017.5 66-13551
    Z881.P942 J8 MRR Alc.

Stanford University. Hoover
Institution on War, Revolution, and
Peace. The library catalogs of the
Hoover Institution on War,
Revolution, and Peace, Stanford
University: Boston, G. K. Hall, 1969-
v. 017./5 77-17709
    Z881.S785 1969e MRR Alc (Dk 33)

LIBRARY CATALOGS. (Cont.)
United States. Congress. Senate.
Library. Catalogue of the library of
the United States Senate. Washington
[Govt. print. off.] 1924. 1210 p.
24-1209
Z881 .U58 1924 MRR Alc.

LIBRARY CATALOGS--BIBLIOGRAPHY.
Downs, Robert Bingham. British
library resources; Chicago, American
Library Association, 1973 [i.e. 1974]
xvi, 332 p. 016.016 73-1598
Z1002 .D63 MRR Alc.

United States. Library of Congress.
Processing Dept. Unpublished
bibliographical tools in certain
archives and libraries of Europe;
Washington, 1952. iv, 25 p. 016.01
52-60036
Z663.7 .U62 MRR Alc.

LIBRARY COOPERATION--UNITED STATES--
DIRECTORIES.
Delanoy, Diana D. Directory of
academic library consortia, Santa
Monica, Calif., System Development
Corp. [c1972] 304 p. 021.6/4/0973
73-164534
Z675.U5 D39 MRR Alc.

LIBRARY EDUCATION--ENGLAND--LONDON.
McColvin, Kenneth Roy. The library
student's London, [London] Greater
London Division, Association of
Assistant Librarians, 1961. 132 p.
020.9421 62-53439
Z791 .M22 MRR Alc.

LIBRARY OF CONGRESS CLASSIFICATION
see Classification, Library of
Congress

LIBRARY ORIENTATION.
Carey, R. J. P. Library guiding;
[Hamden, Conn.] Linnet Books [1974]
186 p. 028.7 73-18477
Z711.2 .C36 MRR Alc.

LIBRARY PLANNING.
Metcalf, Keyes DeWitt. Planning
academic and research library
buildings New York, McGraw-Hill
[1965] xv, 431 p. 022 64-7868
Z679 .M38 MRR Alc.

LIBRARY RECORDS.
United States. Library of Congress.
Information Systems Office.
Terminals requirements for the
Library of Congress' central
bibliographic system. Washington,
1970. 110 p. 025/.02 71-610454
Z699.3 .U5 MRR Alc.

LIBRARY RESOURCES--CANADA--STATISTICS.
Ottawa. National Library. Research
collections in Canadian libraries.
[Ottawa, Information Canada, 1972-
v. in [$1.00 (v. 1) varies]
027.7/0971 74-159990
Z735.A1 O88 1972 MRR Alc.

LIBRARY RESOURCES--GREAT BRITAIN.
Downs, Robert Bingham. British
library resources; Chicago, American
Library Association, 1973 [i.e. 1974]
xvi, 332 p. 016.016 73-1598
Z1002 .D63 MRR Alc.

LIBRARY RESOURCES--OXFORD.
Morgan, Paul. Oxford libraries
outside the Bodleian; Oxford [Eng.]
Oxford Bibliographical Society and
the Bodleian Library, 1973. xx, 250
p. 027.7425/72 74-164911
Z791.O98 M67 MRR Alc.

LIBRARY RESOURCES ON AFRICA--EUROPE.
Witherell, Julian W. Africana
acquisitions; Washington, Library of
Congress, 1973. 122 p. 016.916/007
73-9620
Z663.285 .A74 MRR Alc.

LIBRARY RESOURCES ON AFRICA--FRANCE.
Carson, Patricia. Materials for West
African history in French archives.
London, Athlone P.; distributed by
Constable, 1968. viii, 170 p. [42/-
] 016.9166 68-99964
CD2491.W4 C3 1968 MRR Alc.

LIBRARY RESOURCES ON AFRICA--GREAT
BRITAIN.
Standing Conference on Library
Materials on Africa. The Scolma
directory of libraries and special
collections on Africa. 2d ed.
Hamden, Conn., Archon Books, 1967.
92 p. 015.6 67-676
Z3501 .S8 1967 MRR Alc.

LIBRARY RESOURCES ON AFRICA--UNITED
STATES.
Duignan, Peter. Handbook of American
resources for African studies.
[Stanford, Calif.] Hoover Institution
on War, Revolution, and Peace,
Stanford University, 1967. xvii, 218
p. 016.816 66-20901
Z3501 .D8 MRR Alc.

LIBRARY RESOURCES ON AFRO-AMERICAN
STUDIES.
Race Relations Information Center.
Directory of Afro-American resources.
New York, R. R. Bowker Co. [1970]
xv, 485 p. 917.3/06/96073 71-
126008
Z1361.N39 R3 MRR Alc.

LIBRARY RESOURCES ON AMERICA--PARIS.
Leland, Waldo Gifford. Guide to
materials for American history in the
libraries and archives of Paris,
Washington, D.C., Carnegie
Institution of Washington, 1932- v.
016.97 32-15616
CD1198.U6 L4 MRR Alc.

LIBRARY RESOURCES ON ASIA.
Pearson, James Douglas. Oriental and
Asian bibliography; Hamden, Conn.,
Archon Books, 1966. xvi, 261 p.
016.915 66-1006
Z7046 .P4 MRR Alc.

LIBRARY RESOURCES ON ASIA--GREAT
BRITAIN.
Wainwright, Mary Doreen. A guide to
Western manuscripts and documents in
the British Isles relating to South
and South East Asia. London, New
York, Oxford University Press, 1965.
xix, 532 p. 016.915 65-3147
CD1048.A8 W3 MRR Alc.

LIBRARY RESOURCES ON ASIA--NEW YORK
(CITY)
Asia Society. Libraries in New York
City, New York, 1962. 23 p. 67-
46335
Z3001 .A8 MRR Alc.

LIBRARY RESOURCES ON ASIA--UNITED
STATES.
Yang, Winston L. Y. Asian resources
in American libraries; New York
[Foreign Area Materials Center,
University of the State of New York]
1968. ix, 122 p. 016.915 68-16584

Z1009 .N54 no. 9 MRR Alc.

LIBRARY RESOURCES ON CHINA.
Nathan, Andrew James. Modern China,
1840-1972; Ann Arbor, Center for
Chinese Studies, University of
Michigan, 1973. vi, 95 p. [$2.00]
016.9151 74-167311
Z3106 .N32 MRR Alc.

LIBRARY RESOURCES ON CUBA--CONGRESSES.
International Conference on Cuban
Acquisitions and Bibliography.
Library of Congress, 1970. Cuban
acquisitions and bibliography;
Washington, Library of Congress,
1970. viii, 164 p. 016.917291/03
76-609231
Z663.32 .C85 1970 MRR Alc.

LIBRARY RESOURCES ON EASTERN EUROPE--
UNITED STATES.
Ruggles, Melville J., Russian and
East European publications in the
libraries of the United States New
York, Columbia University Press,
1960. xv, 396 p. 016.947 60-13887

Z2483 .R82 1960 MRR Alc.

LIBRARY RESOURCES ON LATIN AMERICA.
Haro, Robert P. Latin Americana
research in the United States and
Canada; Chicago, American Library
Association, 1971. x, 111 p.
918/.03/07 72-138653
Z1601 .H35 MRR Alc.

Hilton, Ronald, ed. Handbook of
Hispanic source materials and
research organizations in the United
States. 2d ed. Stanford, Calif.,
Stanford University press, 1956.
xiv, 448 p. 980 56-6178
F1408.3 .H65 1956 MRR Alc.

LIBRARY RESOURCES ON RUSSIA--UNITED
STATES.
Ruggles, Melville J., Russian and
East European publications in the
libraries of the United States New
York, Columbia University Press,
1960. xv, 396 p. 016.947 60-13887

Z2483 .R82 1960 MRR Alc.

LIBRARY RESOURCES ON THE PERFORMING
ARTS--CANADA.
Young, William C., American
theatrical arts; Chicago, American
Library Association, 1971. ix, 166
p. 016.7902 78-161234
Z6935 .Y68 MRR Alc.

LIBRARY RESOURCES ON THE PERFORMING
ARTS--UNITED STATES.
Young, William C., American
theatrical arts; Chicago, American
Library Association, 1971. ix, 166
p. 016.7902 78-161234
Z6935 .Y68 MRR Alc.

LIBRARY RULES AND REGULATIONS.
United States. Library of Congress.
Information for readers in the
Library of Congress. 1910-
[Washington, U.S. Govt. Print. Off.]
14-30003
Z663.48 I5 MRR Alc MRR Alc Latest
edition

United States. Library of Congress.
Special facilities for research.
1928- Washington. 027.5753 28-
16952
Z663.48 .S6 MRR Alc MRR Alc Latest
edition

LIBRARY SCHOOLS--DIRECTORIES.
American library directory; New
York, R. R. Bowker. 23-3581
Z731 .A53 Sci RR Latest edition /
MRR Ref Desk Latest edition

United Nations Educational,
Scientific and Cultural Organization.
World guide to library schools and
training courses in documentation.
Paris, Unesco; London, Clive Bingley
[1972] 245 p. [3 British pounds]
020/.7/11 73-155165
Z668 .U56 MRR Alc.

LIBRARY SCHOOLS--AFRICA--DIRECTORIES.
Dadzie, E. W. Directory of archives,
libraries, and schools of
librarianship in Africa. [Paris]
UNESCO [1965] 112 p. 65-5420
Z857.A1 D3 MRR Alc.

LIBRARY SCIENCE.
see also Shelf-listing (Library
science)

Asheim, Lester Eugene, The
humanities and the library; Chicago,
American Library Association, 1957.
xix, 278 p. 020 56-12395
Z665 .A727 MRR Alc.

Ashworth, Wilfred. Handbook of
special librarianship and information
work. 3rd ed. London, Aslib, 1967.
[5] 624 p. [98/- 80/-(to members)]
025 67-89439
Z665 .A73 1967 MRR Alc.

Esdaile, Arundell James Kennedy,
Esdaile's manual of bibliography.
4th revised ed., London, Allen &
Unwin, 1967 [i.e. 1968] 336 p. [50/-
] 010 68-114662
Z1001 .E75 1968 MRR Alc.

McColvin, Kenneth Roy. The library
student's London, [London] Greater
London Division, Association of
Assistant Librarians, 1961. 132 p.
020.9421 62-53439
Z791 .M22 MRR Alc.

Ruggles, Melville J., Soviet
libraries and librarianship;
Chicago, American Library
Association, 1962. x, 147 p.
020.947 62-21564
Z819 .R77 MRR Alc.

LIBRARY SCIENCE--ABSTRACTS.
Schlachter, Gail A. Library science
dissertations, 1925-1972; Littleton,
Colo., Libraries Unlimited, 1974.
293 p. 020.8 s 016.02 73-90497
Z674 .R4 no. 12 MRR Alc.

LIBRARY SCIENCE--ABSTRACTS--PERIODICALS.
Library & information science
abstracts. 1- Jan./Feb. 1969-
London, Library Association. 016.02
78-228730
Z671 .L6 MRR Alc Full set*

LIBRARY SCIENCE--ADDRESSES, ESSAYS,
LECTURES.
Bonn, George Schlegel. Training
laymen in use of the library, New
Brunswick, N.J., Graduate School of
Library Service, Rutgers, the State
University, 1960. 2 v. in 1.
020.82 60-7280
Z665 .B697 MRR Alc.

LIBRARY SCIENCE--BIBLIOGRAPHY.
American library association. Junior
members round table. Library
literature 1921-1932; Chicago,
American Library association, 1934.
x, [2] 430 p. 016.02 34-5185
Z666 .C21 1927 Suppl. MRR Alc.

Aslib. Aslib publications in and out
of print. London. 65-51810
Z673 .A62712 MRR Alc Latest
edition

Canadian Library Association.
Reference Section. Canadian library
literature index. Ottawa, Canadian
Library Association, 1956. iv, 79 p.
016.02 58-41202
Z666 .C18 MRR Alc.

Cannons, Harry George Turner.
Bibliography of library economy;
Chicago, American library
association, 1927. 4 p. l., 11-680
p. 26-26901
Z666 .C21 1927 MRR Alc.

LIBRARY SCIENCE--BIBLIOGRAPHY. (Cont.)
Cohen, Nathan Marshall, Library
science dissertations, 1925-60;
[Washington] U.S. Dept. of Health,
Education, and Welfare, Office of
Education; [for sale by the
Superintendent of Documents, U.S.
Govt. Print. Off., 1963] viii, 120
p.   hew63-119
    Z666 .C67 MRR Alc.

Cole, George Watson, An index to
bibliographical papers published by
the Bibliographical society and the
Library association, London, 1877-
1932. Chicago, Ill. Pub. for the
Bibliographical society of America at
the University of Chicago press
[1933] ix, 262 p.   016.01 33-33065

    Z1008 .B585 MRR Alc.

Columbia University. Libraries.
Library Service Library. Dictionary
catalog. Boston, G. K. Hall, 1962-
v.   016.02   63-2444
    Z881.N6295 1962 MRR Alc. (Deck 33)

Danton, J. Periam, Index to
Festschriften in librarianship New
York, R. R. Bowker Co., 1970. xi,
461 p.   016.02 75-88796
    Z666 .D35 MRR Alc.

Five years' work in librarianship.
1951/55- London, Library
Association. 016.02 58-2169
    Z666 .F5 MRR Alc Full set

Library & information science
abstracts. 1- Jan./Feb. 1969-
London, Library Association. 016.02
78-228730
    Z671 .L6 MRR Alc Full set*

Library literature; 1933/35- New
York, H. W. Wilson Co. 016.02   36-
27468
    Z666 .C211 MRR Alc Full set

Library science abstracts. v. 1-19;
Jan./Mar. 1950-Oct./Dec. 1968.
London, Library Association. 016.02
53-33079
    Z671 .L617 MRR Alc Full set*

Prasher, Ram Gopal, Indian library
literature; New Delhi, Today &
Tomorrow's Printers & Publishers
[1971] xiii, 504 p. [Rs40.00]
016.020/854 74-926208
    Z666 .P88 MRR Alc.

Schlachter, Gail A. Library science
dissertations, 1925-1972; Littleton,
Colo., Libraries Unlimited, 1974.
292 p.   020.8 s 016.02 73-90497
    Z674 .R4 no. 12 MRR Alc.

Schutze, Gertrude. Documentation
source book. New York, Scarecrow
Press, 1965. 554 p.   016.02 65-
13551
    Z666 .S37 MRR Alc.

Schutze, Gertrude. Information and
library science source book;
Metuchen, N.J., Scarecrow Press,
1972. ix, 483 p.   016.02 72-1157
    Z666 .S373 MRR Alc.

LIBRARY SCIENCE--DICTIONARIES.
American library association.
Editorial committee. Subcommittee on
library terminology. A.L.A. glossary
of library terms, Chicago, Ill.,
American library association, 1943.
viii, 159, [1] p.   020.3 43-51260
    Z1006 .A5 MRR Ref Desk.

The Bookman's concise dictionary.
New York, Philosophical Library
[1956] 318 p.   010.3 57-678
    Z1006 .B59 1956a MRR Ref Desk.

Carter, John, ABC for book-
collectors. [3d ed., rev.] London,
R. Hart-Davis [1961] 208 p.   62-
6733
    Z1006 .C37 1961a MRR Alc.

Encyclopedia of library and
information science. New York, M.
Dekker [1968- v.   020/.3 68-
31232
    Z1006 .E57 MRR Alc.

Harrod, Leonard Montague, The
librarians glossary. [2d rev. ed.]
London, Grafton, 1959. 332 p.
010.3 59-2822
    Z1006 .H32 1959 MRR Ref Desk.

LIBRARY SCIENCE--DICTIONARIES--
BIBLIOGRAPHY.
Lewanski, Richard Casimir, Library
directories. Santa Barbara, Calif.
(American Bibliographical Center)
1967. 49 p.   016.021/0025 67-20728

    Z719 .L4 1967 MRR Alc.

LIBRARY SCIENCE--DICTIONARIES--GERMAN.
Lexikon des Buchwesens, Stuttgart,
Hiersemann, 1952-56. 4 v.   010.3
53-17416
    Z118 .L65 MRR Alc.

Lexikon des gesamten Buchwesens.
Leipzig, K. W. Hiersemann, 1935 [i.e.
1934]-37. 3 v.   34-28790
    Z118 .L67 MRR Alc.

LIBRARY SCIENCE--DICTIONARIES--POLYGLOT.
The Bookman's glossary. 4th ed.,
rev. and enl. New York, R. R. Bowker
[1961] viii, 212 p.   010.3 61-
13239
    Z1006 .B6 1961 MRR Alc.

Cowles, Barbara (Pehotsky)
Bibliographers' glossary of foreign
words and phrases; New York, R. R.
Bowker company, 1935. 3 p. l., 82
numb. l.   010.3 41-5736
    Z1006 .C87 1935 MRR Alc.

Lexikon des Bibliothekswesens.
Leipzig, VEB Verlag für Buch- und
Bibliothekswesen, 1969. xiii, 769 p.
[42.00]   70-423794
    Z1006 .L46 MRR Alc.

Moth, Axel Fredrik Carl Mathias,
Glossary of library terms, English,
Danish, Dutch, French, German,
Italian, Spanish, Swedish, Boston,
The Boston book company, 1915. 58 p.
15-3471
    Z1006 .M72 MRR Alc.

Orne, Jerrold, The language of the
foreign book trade: 2d ed. Chicago,
American Library Association, 1962.
213 p.   010.3 61-12881
    Z1006 .O7 1962 MRR Alc.

Pipics, Zoltán. Dictionarium
bibliothecarii practicum: ad usum
internationalem in XXII linguis. 6.,
rev. and enlarged ed. Pullach
(München) Verlag Dokumentation,
1974. 385 p. [DM98.00] 74-322719

    Z1006 .P67 1974 MRR Ref Desk.

Thompson, Anthony. Vocabularium
bibliothecarii. 2d ed. [Paris]
UNESCO, 1962. 627 p.   63-5650
    Z1006 .T47 1962a MRR Alc.

Walter, Frank Keller, Abbreviations
and technical terms used in book
catalogs and bibliographies, in eight
languages, 1917 handy edition.
Boston, The Boston book company
[1919?] 2 v. in 1.   27-13479
    Z1006 .W261 1919 MRR Alc.

LIBRARY SCIENCE--HISTORY.
Smith, Josephine Metcalfe. A
chronology of librarianship.
Metuchen, N.J., Scarecrow Press,
1968. 263 p.   020/.9 67-12062
    Z665 .S58 MRR Alc.

LIBRARY SCIENCE--INDEXES.
Library work. 09-32253
    Z671 .L7182 MRR Alc.

LIBRARY SCIENCE--PERIODICALS.
Library science abstracts. v. 1-19;
Jan./Mar. 1950-Oct./Dec. 1968.
London, Library Association. 016.02
53-33079
    Z671 .L617 MRR Alc Full set*

LIBRARY SCIENCE--PERIODICALS--
BIBLIOGRAPHY.
International Federation for
Documentation. Library and
documentation journals. 2d rev. ed.
Hague, 1961. 30 p.   63-52506
    Z666 .I55 1961 MRR Alc.

Springman, Mary Adele. The directory
of library periodicals.
[Philadelphia] Drexel Press, 1967,
iv, 192 p.   016.020/5 67-24822
    Z674 .D7 no. 23 MRR Alc.

Winckler, Paul A. Library
periodicals directory; Brookville,
N.Y., Graduate Library School of Long
Island University, 1967. v. 76 l.
67-7215
    Z666 .W5 1967 MRR Alc.

LIBRARY SCIENCE--PERIODICALS--
DIRECTORIES.
Hernon, Peter. Library and library-
related publications; Littleton,
Colo., Libraries Unlimited, 1973.
216 p. [$10.00] 020/.5 73-84183
    Z666 .H4 MRR Alc.

LIBRARY SCIENCE--PERIODICALS--INDEXES.
American library association. Junior
members round table. Library
literature, 1921-1932; Chicago,
American library association, 1934.
x, [2], 430 p.   016.02 34-5185
    Z666 .C21 1927 Suppl. MRR Alc.

Cannons, Harry George Turner.
Bibliography of library economy;
Chicago, American library
association, 1927. 4 p. l., 11-680
p.   26-26901
    Z666 .C21 1927 MRR Alc.

Library & information science
abstracts. 1- Jan./Feb. 1969-
London, Library Association. 016.02
78-228730
    Z671 .L6 MRR Alc Full set*

Library literature; 1933/35- New
York, H. W. Wilson Co. 016.02   36-
27468
    Z666 .C211 MRR Alc Full set

Library science abstracts. v. 1-19;
Jan./Mar. 1950-Oct./Dec. 1968.
London, Library Association. 016.02
53-33079
    Z671 .L617 MRR Alc Full set*

Library work. 09-32253
    Z671 .L7182 MRR Alc.

Schutze, Gertrude. Information and
library science source book;
Metuchen, N.J., Scarecrow Press,
1972. ix, 483 p.   016.02 72-1157
    Z666 .S373 MRR Alc.

LIBRARY SCIENCE--RESEARCH--PERIODICALS.
LIST: library and information science
today. 1971- [New York] Science
Associates/International. 71-143963

    Z669.7 .L18 Sci RR Latest edition
    / MRR Alc Latest edition

LIBRARY SCIENCE--SCHOLARSHIPS,
FELLOWSHIPS, ETC.
American Association of School
Librarians. Awards and Scholarships
Committee. Scholarships,
fellowships, loans, grants-in-aid for
school librarianship. Chicago,
American Library Association, 1963.
40 p.   64-4534
    Z668 .A35 MRR Alc.

LIBRARY SCIENCE--YEARBOOKS.
Progress in library science. 1965-
London [etc.] Butterworths; [Hamden,
Conn.] Archon Books. 020.5 66-2926

    Z671 .P76 MRR Alc Full set

LIBRARY SCIENCE AS A PROFESSION.
Gates, Jean Key. Introduction to
librarianship. New York, McGraw-Hill
[1968] xii, 415 p.   021 67-12623
    Z721 .G33 MRR Alc.

LIBRARY STATISTICS.
American Library Association.
Statistics Coordinating Project.
Library statistics: Chicago,
American Library Association, 1966.
xv, 160 p.   021.00182 66-22724
    Z721 .A53 MRR Alc.

LIBRETTISTS, AMERICAN.
Green, Stanley. The world of musical
comedy; New York, Ziff-Davis Pub.
Co. [1960] xvi, 391 p.   782.810973
60-10522
    ML1711 .G74 MRR Alc.

LIBRETTOS--BIBLIOGRAPHY.
United States. Library of Congress.
Music division. Catalogue of opera
librettos printed before 1800,
Washington, Govt. print. off., 1914.
2 v.   13-35009
    Z663.37 .C34 MRR Alc.

LIBYA.
Blunsum, Terence. Libya: the country
and its people. London, Queen Anne
P., 1968. xii, 117 p. [12/6]
916.1/2 68-101155
    DT215 .B55 MRR Alc.

Nyrop, Richard F. Area handbook for
Libya. 2d ed. [Washington, For sale
by the Supt. of Docs., U.S. Govt.
Print. Off.] 1973. xv, 317 p.
[$3.60]   916.1/2/034 72-600386
    DT215 .N97 1973 MRR Alc.

LIBYA--BIBLIOGRAPHY.
Schlüter, Hans. Index Libycus:
Bibliography of Libya, 1957-1969,
Boston, G. K. Hall, 1972. viii, 305
p.   016.9161/2 72-2778
    Z3971 .S36 MRR Alc.

LIBYA--COMMERCE--DIRECTORIES.
Contact Mediterranean directory:
Malta, Libya, Sicily. 1966-
Valletta, Associated Publicity
Services.   380/.09/1822 67-115040
    HC244.5.A1 C6 MRR Alc Latest
    edition

LIBYA--GAZETTEERS.
United States. Office of Geography.
Libya; Washington, U.S. Govt. Print.
Off., 1958. v, 161 p.   916.1 58-
61875
    DT214 .U54 MRR Alc.

LIBYA--HISTORY.
Wright, John L. Libya, New York,
Praeger [1969] 304 p. [7.50]
961.2 79-79075
    DT224 .W7 1969b MRR Alc.

LICENSES--UNITED STATES--DIRECTORIES.
Angel, Juvenal Londono, Directory
of professional and occupational
licensing in the United States, New
York, World Trade Academy Press;
distributed by Simon & Schuster
[1970] 755 p. 75-93680
HD7824.U5 A75 MRR alc.

LIECHTENSTEIN.
The Principality of Liechtenstein;
Vaduz] Press and Information Office
of the Government of the Principality
of Liechtenstein, 1967. 142 p.
914.36/48 71-379561
DB540.5 .P7 MRR Alc.

LIECHTENSTEIN--BIOGRAPHY--DICTIONARIES.
Who's who in Switzerland, including
the Principality of Liechtenstein.
1950/51- Geneva [etc.] Nagel
Publishers [etc.] 920.0494 52-39693
DQ52 .W5 MRR Biog Latest edition

LIÈGE (PROVINCE)--DIRECTORIES.
Annuaire du commerce et de
l'industrie de la province de Liège
Lasalle. Liège, Édition Lasalle.
53-28345
DH801.L5 A65 MRR Alc Latest
edition

LIFE.
see also Conduct of life
see also Ethics

LIFE, SPIRITUAL
see Spiritual life

LIFE (BIOLOGY)
see also Biology
see also Genetics
see also Old age
see also Reproduction

LIFE INSURANCE
see Insurance, Life

LIFE-LONG EDUCATION
see Adult education

LIFE ON OTHER PLANETS--BIBLIOGRAPHY.
Sable, Martin Howard. UFO guide:
1947-1967; 1st ed. Beverly Hills,
Calif., Rainbow Press Co., 1967. 100
p. 016.001/9 67-30550
Z5064.F5 S3 MRR Alc.

LIFE SCIENCES.
see also Agriculture
see also Medicine

LIGHT.
see also Color

LIGHTHOUSES.
The Lights and tides of the world,
including a description of all the
fog-signals. London, Imray, Laurie,
Norie & Wilson, ltd. ca 08-3141
VK1150 .L7 MRR Alc Latest edition

LIGNITE.
see also Coal

LINCOLN, ABRAHAM, PRES. U.S., 1809-1865.
Angle, Paul McClelland, ed. The
Lincoln reader, New Brunswick,
Rutgers university press, 1947. xii,
564 p. 923.173 47-30067
E457 .A58 MRR Alc.

Mearns, David Chambers, The Lincoln
papers; [1st ed.] Garden City,
N.Y., Doubleday, 1948. 2 v. (xvii,
681 p.) 973.7 48-9019
E457.92 1948 MRR Alc.

Nevins, Allan, The emergence of
Lincoln. New York, Scribner, 1950.
2 v. 973.68 50-9920
E415.7 .N38 MRR Alc.

Pratt, Harry Edward, The personal
finances of Abraham Lincoln,
Springfield, Ill., The Abraham
Lincoln association 1943. xiii, 198
p. 923.173 43-4814
E457.2 .P9 1943a MRR Alc.

Randall, James Garfield, Lincoln,
the President. New York, Dodd, Mead,
1945-55. 4 v. 923.173 45-10041
E457 .R2 MRR Alc.

Sandburg, Carl, Abraham Lincoln; the
war years, New York, Harcourt, Brace
& company [c1939] 4 v. 923.173
mrr01-44
E457.4 .S364 MRR Alc.

Sandburg, Carl, Abraham Lincoln, the
prairie years, New York, Harcourt,
Brace & company [c1926] 2 v. 26-
3885
E457.3 .S22 MRR Alc.

Sandburg, Carl, Abraham Lincoln; the
prairie years and the war years.
[1st ed.] New York, Harcourt, Brace
[1954] xiv, 762 p. 923.173 54-
9720
E457 .S215 MRR Alc.

Thomas, Benjamin Platt, Abraham
Lincoln, a biography. [1st ed.] New
York, Knopf, 1952. xiv, 548, xii p.
923.173 52-6425
E457 .T427 1952a MRR Alc.

LINCOLN, ABRAHAM, PRES. U.S., 1809-1865-
-ANNIVERSARIES, ETC.
United States. Library of Congress.
Abraham Lincoln; an exhibition at the
Library of Congress in honor of the
150th anniversary of his birth.
Washington, 1959. 94 p. 923.173
59-60260
Z663.15 .L5 MRR Alc.

LINCOLN, ABRAHAM, PRES. U.S., 1809-1865-
-ASSASSINATION.
Kunhardt, Dorothy (Meserve) Twenty
days; [1st ed.] New York, Harper &
Row [1965] 312 p. 973.70924 62-
15660
E457.5 .K8 MRR Alc.

LINCOLN, ABRAHAM, PRES. U.S., 1809-1865-
-BIBLIOGRAPHY.
Monaghan, James, Lincoln
bibliography, 1839-1939.
Springfield, Ill., Illinois state
historical library, 1943-45. 2 v.
012 a 45-103
F536 .I25 vol. 31-32 MRR Alc.

United States. Library of Congress.
A catalog of the Alfred Whital Stern
collection of Lincolniana.
Washington, 1960. xi, 498 p. 012
60-60024
Z663 .C27 MRR Alc.

United States. Library of Congress.
A list of Lincolniana in the Library
of Congress, Rev. ed., with
supplement. Washington, Govt. print.
off., 1906. 86 p. 06-35010
Z663 .L49 1906 MRR Alc.

LINCOLN, ABRAHAM, PRES. U.S., 1809-1865-
-BIBLIOGRAPHY--CATALOGS.
California. University, Santa
Barbara. Library. The William Wyles
collection. Westport, Conn.,
Greenwood Pub. Corp., 1970] 5 v.
016.9173/03 70-19247
Z1236 .C23 MRR Alc (Dk 33)

United States. Library of Congress.
Abraham Lincoln; an exhibition at the
Library of Congress in honor of the
150th anniversary of his birth.
Washington, 1959. 94 p. 923.173
59-60260
Z663.15 .L5 MRR Alc.

LINCOLN, ABRAHAM, PRES. U.S., 1809-1865-
-CHRONOLOGY.
United States. Lincoln
Sesquicentennial Commission. Lincoln
day by day; Washington, 1960. 3 v.
923.173 60-60023
E457 .U66 MRR Alc.

LINCOLN, ABRAHAM, PRES. U.S., 1809-1865-
-DICTIONARIES, INDEXES, ETC.
Winn, Ralph Bubrich, A concise
Lincoln dictionary: thoughts and
statements. New York, Philosophical
Library [1959] 152 p. 923.173 59-
1859
E457.92 1959a MRR Ref Desk.

LINCOLN, ABRAHAM, PRES. U.S., 1809-1865-
-FUNERAL JOURNEY TO SPRINGFIELD.
Kunhardt, Dorothy (Meserve) Twenty
days; [1st ed.] New York, Harper &
Row [1965] 312 p. 973.70924 62-
15660
E457.5 .K8 MRR Alc.

LINCOLN, ABRAHAM, PRES. U.S., 1809-1865-
-MUSEUMS, RELICS, ETC.
United States. Library of Congress.
Abraham Lincoln; an exhibition at the
Library of Congress in honor of the
150th anniversary of his birth.
Washington, 1959. 94 p. 923.173
59-60260
Z663.15 .L5 MRR Alc.

LINCOLN, ABRAHAM, PRES. U.S., 1809-1865-
-PORTRAITS.
Meredith, Roy, Mr. Lincoln's
contemporaries; New York, Scribner,
1951. xii, 233 p. 973.7 51-12294
E415.8 .M4 MRR Alc.

LINCOLN, ROBERT TODD, 1843-1926.
Mearns, David Chambers, The Lincoln
papers; [1st ed.] Garden City,
N.Y., Doubleday, 1948. 2 v. (xvii,
681 p.) 973.7 48-9019
E457.92 1948 MRR Alc.

LINGELBACH, WILLIAM EZRA, 1871-
Thomas, Daniel H., ed. Guide to the
diplomatic archives of Western
Europe. Philadelphia, University of
Pennsylvania Press [1959] xii, 389
p. 940.2 57-9123
CD1001 .T4 MRR Alc.

LINGUISTIC GEOGRAPHY.
Spencer, Robert F. An ethno-atlas;
Dubuque, Iowa, W. C. Brown Co. [1958,
c1956] iii, 42 p. 572.084 56-
12496
GN11 .S75 MRR Alc.

LINGUISTICS--BIBLIOGRAPHY.
Alston, R. C. Punctuation,
concordances, works on language in
general, origin of language, theory
of grammar Menston [Eng.] Printed
for the author by Scolar Press [1971]
xii, 66 p. 016.42 s 016.41 72-
185541
Z2015.A1 A4 vol. 3, pt. 2 MRR Alc.

Modern Language Association of
America. MLA abstracts of articles
in scholarly journals. [New York]
408 72-624077
P1 .M64 MRR Alc Full set

Permanent International Committee of
Linguists. Bibliographie
linguistique. 1939/47- Utrecht,
Spectrum. 016.4 a 50-3972
Z7001 .P4 MRR Alc Full set

Rutherford, Phillip R. A
bibliography of American doctoral
dissertations in linguistics, 1900-
1964. Washington, Center for Applied
Linguistics, 1968. iv, 139 p.
016.41 68-27431
Z7001 .R8 MRR Alc.

Wawrzyszko, Aleksandra K.
Bibliography of general linguistics;
[Hamden, Conn.] Archon Books, 1971.
xii, 120 p. 016.41 75-150766
Z7001 .W35 MRR Alc.

LINGUISTICS--DICTIONARIES.
Gerson, Stanley. A glossary of
grammatical terms; [St. Lucia, Q.]
University of Queensland Press [1969]
73 p. 415/.03 78-497971
P29 .G4 MRR Alc.

Hartmann, R. R. K. Dictionary of
language and linguistics New York,
Wiley [1972] xviii, 302 p. 410/.3
72-6251
P29 .H34 MRR Alc.

Meetham, A. R. Encyclopaedia of
linguistics, information, and
control. [1st ed.] Oxford, New
York, Pergamon Press [1969] xiv, 718
p. 001.5/39/03 68-18528
Q360 .M35 1969 MRR Alc.

Pei, Mario Andrew, Glossary of
linguistic terminology. Garden City,
N.Y., Anchor Books, 1966. xvi, 299
p. 410.3 66-21013
P29 .P39 MRR Alc.

LINGUISTICS--DICTIONARIES--POLYGLOT.
Nash, Rose. Multilingual lexicon of
linguistics and philology: English,
Russian, German, French. Coral
Gables, Fla., University of Miami
Press [1968] xxvi, 390 p. 413 68-
31044
P29 .N34 MRR Alc.

LINGUISTICS--PERIODICALS--BIBLIOGRAPHY.
Maison des sciences de l'homme,
Paris. Service d'échange
d'informations scientifiques. Liste
mondiale des périodiques
spécialisés: linguistique. Paris,
Mouton [1971] 243 p. 72-323495
Z7003 .M34 MRR Alc.

LINGUISTICS--PERIODICALS--INDEXES.
Abstracts in anthropology. v. 1-
Feb. 1970- Farmingdale, N.Y.,
Baywood Publishing Co. [etc.] 77-
20528
GN1 .A15 MRR Alc Full set

LINGUISTICS--STUDY AND TEACHING
(HIGHER)--CANADA--DIRECTORIES.
Grognet, Allene Guss. University
resources in the United States and
Canada for the study of linguistics:
1971-1972, [7th rev. ed. Arlington,
Va.] Center for Applied Linguistics
[1972] iv, 289 p. 410/.7/1173 72-
93471
P57.U7 G7 1972 MRR Alc.

LINGUISTICS--STUDY AND TEACHING
(HIGHER)--UNITED STATES--DIRECTORIES.
Grognet, Allene Guss. University
resources in the United States and
Canada for the study of linguistics:
1971-1972, [7th rev. ed. Arlington,
Va.] Center for Applied Linguistics
[1972] iv, 289 p. 410/.7/1173 72-
93471
P57.U7 G7 1972 MRR Alc.

LINGUISTICS--TERMINOLOGY.
Hamp, Eric P. A glossary of American
technical linguistic usage, 1925-
1950, [3rd ed.] Utrecht, Antwerp,
Het Spectrum, 1966. 72 p. [f19.50]
410/.3 67-83571
P29 .H3 1866 MRR Alc.

LINGUISTS.
Sebeok, Thomas Albert, ed. Portraits
of linguists; Bloomington, Indiana
University Press [1966] 2 v.
410.822 64-64663
P83 .S4 MRR Biog.

LIQUEFIED PETROLEUM GAS INDUSTRY--
UNITED STATES--DIRECTORIES.
L P-gas motor fuel station directory.
Chicago, Liquefied Petroleum Gas
Association. 58-39759
HD9579.P43U6 MRR Alc Latest
edition

LIQUID FUELS.
see also Gasoline

LIQUOR LAWS--NEW YORK (STATE)
Beverage media. Blue book. New
York. 178.4 51-38397
HD9352 .B4 MRR Alc latest edition

LIQUOR LAWS--UNITED STATES.
Red book: encyclopaedic directory of
the wine and liquor industries. New
York, Schwartz Publications, inc.
[$19.50] 338.4/7/663102573 73-
646025
HD9373 .R43 MRR Alc Latest edition

LIQUOR PROBLEM.
see also Alcoholism

LIQUOR PROBLEM--ABSTRACTS.
The Alcoholism digest annual. v. 1-
1972/73- Rockville, Md.,
Information Planning Associates.
362.2/92 74-644283
HV5001 .A34 MRR Alc Full set

LIQUOR PROBLEM--BIBLIOGRAPHY.
International bibliography of studies
on alcohol. New Brunswick, N.J.,
Publications Division, Rutgers Center
of Alcohol Studies [1966- v.
016.61381 60-14437
Z7721 .I5 MRR Alc.

LIQUOR PROBLEM--UNITED STATES--
STATISTICS.
Efron, Vera, Selected statistics on
consumption of alcohol (1850-1968)
and on alcoholism (1930-1968) New
Brunswick, N.J., Publications
Division, Rutgers Center of Alcohol
Studies [1970] 18 p. [$2.00]
362.2/92/0973 70-277380
HV5292 .E36 MRR Alc.

LIQUOR TRAFFIC--DIRECTORIES.
Harpers directory and manual.
London, Harper Trade Journals.
663/.2/0025 78-3865
Began in 1914.
TP500.5 .H37 MRR Alc Latest
edition

LIQUOR TRAFFIC--YEARBOOKS.
Beverage media. Blue book. New
York. 178.4 51-38397
HD9352 .B4 MRR Alc latest edition

LIQUOR TRAFFIC--UNITED STATES.
Beverage media. Blue book. New
York. 178.4 51-38397
HD9352 .B4 MRR Alc latest edition

Brewers' almanac. [Washington, etc.]
United States Brewers' Association.
338.476633 45-51432
Publication began in 1940?
HD9397.U5 B7 MRR Alc Latest
edition

LIQUOR TRAFFIC--UNITED STATES--
STATISTICS.
Brewers' almanac. [Washington, etc.]
United States Brewers' Association.
338.476633 45-51432
Publication began in 1940?
HD9397.U5 B7 MRR Alc Latest
edition

Distilled Spirits Institute, inc.,
Washington, D.C. Public revenue from
alcoholic beverages. [Washington]
336.27 38-17702
HD9350.8.U5 A12 MRR Alc Latest
edition

Red book: encyclopaedic directory of
the wine and liquor industries. New
York, Schwartz Publications, inc.
[$19.50] 338.4/7/663102573 73-
646025
HD9373 .R43 MRR Alc Latest edition

LIQUOR TRAFFIC--UNITED STATES--
YEARBOOKS.
The Liquor handbook. New York [etc.]
Gavin-Jobson Associates, inc. [etc.]
338.476635 59-16930
HD9352 .L5 MRR Alc latest edition

LIQUORS.
Mario, Thomas. Playboy's host & bar
book. [1st ed. Chicago] Playboy
Press [c1971] vii, 339 p. - [$12.95]
641.8/74 75-167615
TX951 .M266 MRR Alc.

Old Mr. Boston deluxe official
bartender's guide / New world wide
ed. Boston : Mr. Boston Distiller
Corp., 1974. 216 p. : [$2.50]
641.8/74 74-80666
TX951 .O4 1974 MRR Alc.

LITERARY CHARACTERS
see Characters and characteristics in
literature

LITERARY CURIOSA.
Bombaugh, Charles Carroll, Gleanings
for the curious from the harvestfields of literature; Author's
unabridged ed. 1st ser. Detroit,
Gale Research Co., 1970. 864 p.
808.8 68-23465
PN43 .B62 1970 MRR Alc.

LITERARY FORGERIES AND MYSTIFICATIONS.
Thomas, Ralph, Handbook of
fictitious names; Detroit, Gale
Research Co., 1969. xiv, 235 p.
929.4 70-90248
Z1065 .T46 1969 MRR Alc.

LITERARY LANDMARKS--EUROPE.
Crosland, Margaret, A guide to
literary Europe, Philadelphia,
Chilton Books [1966] 3 v. in 1.
914/.04/55 66-22874
PN164 .C7 MRR Alc.

LITERARY LANDMARKS--GREAT BRITAIN.
Briscoe, John D'Auby, A mapbook of
English literature. New York, H.
Holt and company [1936] 47 p.
820.9 36-18473
PR109 .B7 MRR Alc.

Hardwick, John Michael Drinkrow, A
literary atlas & gazetteer of the
British Isles Newton Abbot, David &
Charles [1973] 216 p. [£4.95]
820/.3 73-181081
PR109 .H25 MRR Alc.

LITERARY LANDMARKS--GREAT BRITAIN--MAPS.
Hardwick, John Michael Drinkrow, A
literary atlas & gazetteer of the
British Isles Newton Abbot, David &
Charles [1973] 216 p. [£4.95]
820/.3 73-181081
PR109 .H25 MRR Alc.

LITERARY LANDMARKS--LONDON.
Williams, George Guion. Guide to
literary London London, Batsford,
1973. [7], 406 p. [£4.00]
914.21/04/85 74-159176
PR110.L6 W5 MRR Alc.

LITERARY PRIZES.
Bonin, Jane F. Prize-winning
American drama: Metuchen, N.J.,
Scarecrow Press, 1973. xii, 222 p.
812/.5/09 73-3111
PS351 .B6 MRR Alc.

Children's Book Council, New York.
Children's books: awards & prizes.
[New York, 1969] [32] p. [$4.95]
028.52 78-24483
Z1037.A2 C52 MRR Alc.

Clapp, Jane. International
dictionary of literary awards. New
York, Scarecrow Press, 1963. 545 p.
807.9 63-7468
PN171.P75 C5 MRR Ref Desk.

Guide des prix littéraires; [1.]-
ed.; 1952- Paris, Cercle de la
librairie. a 58-6283
PN171.P75 G8 MRR Alc Latest
edition

International literary market place.
1965- New York, R. R. Bowker Co. 65-
28326
Z291.5 I5 MRR Ref Desk Latest
edition

Kürschners deutscher Literatur-
kalender. 1.- Jahrg.; 1879-
Berlin, Leipzig [etc.] 06-44821
Z2230 .K92 MRR Biog Latest edition

Literary and library prizes. 1935-
New York, R. R. Bowker Co. 807.9 59-
11370
PN171.P75 L5 MRR Ref Desk Latest
edition

Literary market place; [1st]- ed.;
1940- New York, Bowker. 655.473 41-
51571
PN161 .L5 Sci RR Partial set / MRR
Ref Desk Latest edition

LITERARY PRIZES--DIRECTORIES--
PERIODICALS.
Grants and awards available to
foreign writers. 1973- [New York,
PEN American Center] [$2.00] 807/.9
74-641041
PN171.P75 G74 MRR Alc Latest
edition

LITERARY PRIZES--PERIODICALS.
Grants and awards available to
American writers. [New York, P.E.N.
American Center] [$2.00] 001.4/4
73-648098
PN171.P75 G73 MRR Alc Latest
edition

LITERARY RECREATIONS.
see also Riddles

LITERARY STYLE
see Style, Literary

LITERATURE.
see also Authorship

see also Characters and
characteristics in literature

see also Essays

see also Poetry

see also Wit and humor

LITERATURE--ADDRESSES, ESSAYS, LECTURES.
Literary lectures presented at the
Library of Congress. Washington,
Library of Congress: [for sale by the
Supt. of Docs., U.S. Govt. Print.
Off.] 1973. ix, 602 p. [$7.55]
809 72-14365
Z663 .L54 MRR Alc.

LITERATURE--ANECDOTES, FACETIAE,
SATIRE, ETC.
Disraeli, Isaac, Curiosities of
literature, New York, London, D.
Appleton and company, 1932. xx p., 1
l., 312 p. 828.7 32-28946
PN43 .D5 1932 MRR Alc.

LITERATURE--BIBLIOGRAPHY.
Rogers, A. Robert, The humanities;
Littleton, Colo., Libraries
Unlimited, 1974. 400 p. [$9.50]
016.0013 74-78393
Z5579 .R63 MRR Alc.

Watt, Robert, Bibliotheca
Britannica; New York, B. Franklin
[1965] 4 v. 011 77-6557
Z2001 .W34 1965 MRR Alc.

The Year's work in modern language
studies, 1929/30- [Leeds, Eng.,
etc.] Modern Humanities Research
Association [etc.] 405.8 31-32540
PB1 .Y45 MRR Alc Full set

LITERATURE--BIO-BIBLIOGRAPHY.
Cassell's encyclopaedia of world
literature. Rev. and enl. New York,
Morrow, [1973] 3 v. 803 73-10405

PN41 .C3 1972 MRR Biog.

Concise dictionary of literature New
York, Philosophical Library [1963]
526 p. 016.8 60-15958
PN41 .C63 MRR Biog.

Dictionnaire biographique des auteurs
[2. ed.] Paris, Société
d'édition de dictionnaires et
encyclopedies [1964, c1956] 2 v.
66-98043
PN41 .D48 1964 MRR Alc.

Dizionario letterario Bompiani degli
autori di tutti i tempi e di tutte le
letterature. Milano, V. Bompiani,
1956-57. 3 v. 58-16111
Z1010 .D5 MRR Biog.

Gidel, Charles Antoine, Dictionnaire-
manuel-illustré des écrivains et
des littératures. Paris, A. Colin &
cie 1898. 2 p. l., 908 p. f 01-
3144
Z1010 .G453 MRR Biog.

Kosch, Wilhelm, Deutsches Literatur-
Lexikon. Ausg. in einem Band Bern,
Francke [1963] 511 p. 63-48267
Z2231 .K66 1963 MRR Alc.

Kosch, Wilhelm, Deutsches Literatur-
Lexikon; 2., vollständig neubearb.
und stark erweiterte Aufl. Bern, A.
Francke, 1949 [i.e. 1947]-58. 4 v.
a 48-4168
Z2230 .K862 MRR Biog.

Lectuur-repertorium; [2. en
definitieve uitg. Antwerpen,
Vlaamsche Boekcentrale, 1952-54] 3
v. 011 53-15682
Z1010 .L43 MRR Biog.

Magill, Frank Northen, ed.
Cyclopedia of world authors. Rev.
ed. Englewood Cliffs, N.J., Salem
Press [1974] 3 v. (vii, 1973, xi p.)
803 74-174980
PN451 .M36 1974 MRR Biog.

Magnus, Laurie, A dictionary of
European literature, 2d impression,
rev., with addenda. London, G.
Routledge & sons, ltd.; New York, E.
P. Dutton & co., 1927. xii, 605 p.
803 30-22114
PN41 .M3 1927 MRR Alc.

LITERATURE--BIO-BIBLIOGRAPHY. (Cont.)
Meyers Handbuch über die Literatur.
2a, neu bearb. Aufl. Mannheim, Wien,
Zürich, Bibliographisches Inst.
(1970) 987 p. [36.00]   79-483796
   PN41 .M45 1870 MRR Biog.

The Penguin companion to European
literature. New York, McGraw-Hill
[1971, c1969] 907 p. [$11.95]
809.8/94 74-158063
   PN41 .P43 1971 MRR Alc.

Ruiz, Luis Alberto. Diccionario de
la literatura universal. Buenos
Aires, Editorial Raigal, 1955-56. 3
v.   57-41563
   PN41 .R8 MRR Alc.

Tod, Thomas Miller. A necrology of
literary celebrities, 1321-1943.
Perth [Scot.] Printed by Munro &
Scott [1948] 67, xiii p.   928 49-
1212
   PN452 .T6 MRR Biog.

Tod, Thomas Miller. A necrology of
literary celebrities, 1321-1943.
[Folcroft, Pa.] Folcroft Press [1969]
67, xiii p.   820/.9 B 72-195326
   PN41 .T6 1969 MRR Biog.

Die Weltliteratur; Wien, Brüder
Hollinek [1951-54] 3 v.   52-24550
   PN41 .W4 MRR Alc.

Wilpert, Gero von. Lexikon der
Weltliteratur. Stuttgart, A. Kröner
[1963-68] 2 v.   63-49901
   PN41 .W48 MRR Alc.

LITERATURE--BIOGRAPHY
see Authors

LITERATURE--COLLECTIONS.
Hammerton, John Alexander, Sir, ed.
Outline of great books, New York,
Wise & co., 1937. vii p., 1 l., 902
p.   808.8 37-8816
   PN44 .H3 MRR Alc.

Mack, Maynard, ed. World
masterpieces Rev. New York, Norton
[1965] 2 v.   808.8 64-10888
   PN6014 .M1382 v. 1 MRR Alc.

Singleton, Ralph H., ed. An
introduction to literature,
Cleveland, World Pub. Co. [1966]
xxxi, 1237 p.   808.8 66-18877
   PN6014 .S52 MRR Alc.

The Standard home library of the
world's greatest literature. New
York, Standard Reference Works Pub.
Co., 1958. 20 v.   808.83 58-46060

   PN44 .W62 MRR Alc.

LITERATURE--COMPETITIONS.
Clapp, Jane. International
dictionary of literary awards. New
York, Scarecrow Press, 1963. 545 p.
807.9 63-7468
   PN171.P75 C5 MRR Ref Desk.

Guide des prix littéraires; [1.]-
ed.; 1952- Paris, Cercle de la
librairie. a 58-6283
   PN171.P75 G8 MRR Alc Latest
   edition

LITERATURE--DICTIONARIES.
Beckson, Karl E., A reader's guide
to literary terms, New York, Noonday
Press [1861, c1960] 230 p.   803 60-
14127
   PN41 .B33 MRR Alc.

Benét, William Rose, ed. The
reader's encyclopedia, New York, T.
Y. Crowell Co. [1955] vii, 1270 p.
803 55-10502
   PN41 .B4 1955 MRR Alc.

Benét, William Rose, ed. The
reader's encyclopedia. 2d ed. New
York, Crowell [1965] viii, 1118 p.
803 65-12510
   PN41 .B4 1965 MRR Ref Desk.

Bombaugh, Charles Carroll, Facts and
fancies for the curious from the
harvestfields of literature;
Philadelphia, London, J. B.
Lippincott company [1905] 647 p.
05-34162
   PN43 .B6 MRR Alc.

Brewer, Ebenezer Cobham, Brewer's
dictionary of phrase and fable.
Centenary ed. (completely revised);
London, Cassell, 1870. xvi, 1175 p.,
plate. [60/-]   803 73-529591
   PN43 .B65 1870 MRR Ref Desk.

Brewer, Ebenezer Cobham, The
reader's handbook of famous names in
fiction, A new ed., rev. throughout
and greatly enl. Detroit,
Republished by Gale Research Co.,
1966. 2 v. (viii, 1243 p.) 803 71-
134907
   PN43 .B7 1965 MRR Alc.

Cassell's encyclopaedia of world
literature. Rev. and enl. New York,
Morrow, [1973] 3 v.   803 73-10405

   PN41 .C3 1972 MRR Biog.

Concise dictionary of literature New
York, Philosophical Library [1963]
526 p.   016.8 60-15958
   PN41 .C63 MRR Biog.

Dictionnaire biographique des auteurs
[2. ed.] Paris, Société
d'édition de dictionnaires et
encyclopédies [1964, c1956] 2 v.
66-98043
   PN41 .D48 1964 MRR Biog.

Dizionario letterario Bompiani delle
opere e dei personaggi di tutti i
tempi e di tutte le letterature ...
[Milano] V. Bompiani, 1947 [c1946]-
50. 9 v.   803 47-20998
   PN41 .D5 MRR Alc.

Fowler, Roger. A dictionary of
modern critical terms; London,
Boston, Routledge & Kegan Paul [1973]
ix, 208 p.   801/.95 73-89184
   PN41 .F6 MRR Alc.

Frey, Albert Romer, Sobriquets and
nicknames, Detroit, Republished by
Gale Research Co., 1966. iii, 482 p.
929.403 66-22671
   CT108 .F7 1966 MRR Alc.

Gerwig, Henrietta, ed. Crowell's
handbook for readers and writers;
New York, Thomas Y. Crowell company
[c1925] vi, 728 p.   25-20161
   PN41 .G4 MRR Alc.

Holman, Clarence Hugh, A handbook to
literature, 3d ed. Indianapolis,
Odyssey Press [1972] viii, 646 p.
803 73-175226
   PN41 .H6 1972 MRR Alc.

Keller, Helen Rex, ed. The reader's
digest of books, New and greatly
enl. ed. New York, The Macmillan
company, 1940. 3 p. l., 1447 p.
803 40-7463
   PN44 .K4 1940 MRR Alc.

Magill, Frank Northen, ed.
Masterplots cyclopedia of literary
characters. New York, Salem Press
[1963] 2 v.   803 64-120
   PN44 .M3 1963a MRR Alc.

Magnus, Laurie, A dictionary of
European literature, 2d impression,
rev. with addenda. London, G.
Routledge & sons, ltd.; New York, E.
P. Dutton & co., 1927. xii, 605 p.
803 30-22114
   PN41 .M3 1927 MRR Alc.

Payton, Geoffrey. Payton's proper
names. London, New York, F. Warne,
1969. vii, 502 p. [45/-]   032 69-
20109
   PE1660 .P3 MRR Alc.

Payton, Geoffrey. Webster's
dictionary of proper names.
Springfield, Mass., G. & C. Merriam
Co. [c1970] 752 p.   423.1 72-22048

   PE1660 .P34 MRR Ref Desk.

The Penguin companion to European
literature. New York, McGraw-Hill
[1971, c1969] 907 p. [$11.95]
809.8/94 74-158063
   PN41 .P43 1971 MRR Alc.

The Reader's companion to world
literature. 2d ed., rev. and updated
New York, New American Library
[1973] 577 p. [$1.95] 803 73-
173311
   PN41 .R4 1973 MRR Alc.

Shipley, Joseph Twadell, Dictionary
of world literary terms, forms,
technique, criticism. Completely
rev. and enl. ed. Boston, Writer
[1970] xiii, 466 p. [12.95]   803
75-91879
   PN41 .S5 1970 MRR Alc.

Shipley, Joseph Twadell, ed.
Encyclopedia of literature, New
York, Philosophy library [1946] 2 v.
809 47-3870
   PN41 .S52 MRR Alc.

Walsh, William Shepard, Handy-book
of literary curiosities, Detroit,
Gale Research Co., 1966. 1104 p.
803 66-24370
   PN43 .W3 1966 MRR Alc.

Walsh, William Shepard, Heroes and
heroines of fiction. Detroit,
Republished by Gale Research Co.,
1966. 2 v.   803 66-29782
   PN43 .W33 1966 MRR Alc.

Warner, Charles Dudley, ed.
Biographical dictionary and synopsis
of books, ancient and modern.
Detroit, Gale Research Co., 1965-
[i.e. 1966- v.   803 66-4326
   PN41 .W3 MRR Biog.

Wheeler, William Adolphus, An
explanatory and pronouncing
dictionary of the noted names of
fiction, Detroit, Gale Research Co.,
1966. xxxii, 440 p.   803 66-25811

   PN43 .W4 1966 MRR Alc.

Wolf, Martin L. Dictionary of the
arts; New York, Philosophical
Library [1951] xiii, 797 p.   703
51-13402
   N33 .W6 MRR Alc.

LITERATURE--DICTIONARIES--FRENCH.
Dictionnaire des œvres de tous les
temps et de tous les pays; [1. ed.]
Paris, S.E.D.E. [1952-68] 5 v.   55-
15784
   AE25 .D52 MRR Alc.

Dictionnaire des personnages
littéraires et dramatiques de tous
les temps et de tous les pays; 1.
ed.] Paris, Société d'édition de
dictionnaires et encyclopédies
[1960] 668 p.   62-27565
   PN41 .D485 MRR Alc.

Gidel, Charles Antoine, Dictionnaire-
manuel-illustré des écrivains et
des littératures. Paris, A. Colin &
cie 1898. 2 p. l., 908 p.   f 01-
3144
   Z1010 .G453 MRR Biog.

LITERATURE--DICTIONARIES--GERMAN.
Giebisch Hans, ed. Kleines
österreichisches Literaturlexikon,
Wien, Hollinek, 1948. viii, 550 p.
016.83 49-2882
   Z2110 .G5 MRR Biog.

Kindlers Literatur Lexikon. Zürich,
Kindler [1965- v.   66-45488
   PN41 .K43 MRR Alc.

Koch, Willi August, Musisches
Lexikon: Künstler, Kunstwerke und
Motive aus Dichtung, Musik und
bildender Kunst, 2., veränderte und
ergänzerte Aufl. Stuttgart, A.,
Kröner [c1964] 1250 columns, xxxx
p.   65-69991
   N31 .K57 1964 MRR Alc.

Meyers Handbuch über die Literatur.
2a, neu bearb. Aufl. Mannheim, Wien,
Zürich, Bibliographisches Inst.
(1970) 987 p. [36.00]   79-483796
   PN41 .M45 1970 MRR Biog.

Die Weltliteratur; Wien, Brüder
Hollinek [1951-54] 3 v.   52-24550
   PN41 .W4 MRR Alc.

Wilpert, Gero von. Lexikon der
Weltliteratur. Stuttgart, A. Kröner
[1963-68] 2 v.   63-49901
   PN41 .W48 MRR Alc.

LITERATURE--DICTIONARIES--ITALIAN.
Bazzarelli, Eridano, Dizionario
Motta della lettertura universale.
Milano, F. Motta, 1972- v.   74-
316700
   PN564 .B3 MRR Alc.

LITERATURE--DICTIONARIES--SPANISH.
Ruiz, Luis Alberto. Diccionario de
la literatura universal. Buenos
Aires, Editorial Raigal, 1955-56. 3
v.   57-41563
   PN41 .R8 MRR Alc.

**LITERATURE--EXAMINATIONS, QUESTIONS,
ETC.**
American notes & queries. v. 1-
Sept. 1962- [New Haven, Conn.]
[$6.50] 031/.02 74-642751
   Z1034 .A4 MRR Alc Full set

Notes and queries; v. 1- Nov. 3,
1849- London [etc.] Oxford Univ.
Press [etc.] 12-25307
   AG305 .N7 MRR Alc Full set

LITERATURE--HISTORY AND CRITICISM.
Bazzarelli, Eridano, Dizionario
Motta della lettertura universale.
Milano, F. Motta, 1972- v.   74-
316700
   PN564 .B3 MRR Alc.

Drinkwater, John, ed. The outline of
literature. [Rev. ed.] London,
Newnes [1957] xiv, 871 p.   809 58-
1973
   PN524 .D7 1957 MRR Alc.

Horton, Rod William, Backgrounds of
European literature; New York,
Appleton-Century-Crofts [1954] 462
p.   901 54-9623
   CB53 .H6 MRR Alc.

LITERATURE—HISTORY AND (Cont.)
Laird, Charlton Grant, ed. The world
through literature. Freeport, N.Y.,
Books for Libraries Press [1969,
c1951] xx, 506 p. 809 77-99639
   PN501 .L3 1969 MRR Alc.

Les écrivains célèbres ... 3e
édition.] Paris, L. Mazenod, 1966.
3 v. [130 F per vol.] 68-123034
   PN503 .E3 1966 MRR Biog.

Shipley, Joseph Twadell, ed.
Encyclopedia of literature. New
York, Philosophy library [1946] 2 v.
   809 47-3870
   PN41 .S52 MRR Alc.

Wimsatt, William Kurtz, Literary
criticism; [1st ed.] New York,
Knopf, 1957. 757 p. 801 57-5286
   PN86 .W5 MRR Alc.

**LITERATURE—HISTORY AND CRITICISM—
BIBLIOGRAPHY.**
Milic, Louis Tonko. Style and
stylistics; New York, Free Press
[1967] 199 p. 016.808 67-19233
   Z6514.S8 M49 MRR Alc.

Modern Language Association of
America. MLA abstracts of articles
in scholarly journals. [New York]
408 72-624077
   P1 .M64 MRR Alc Full set

Pownall, David E., Articles on
twentieth century literature: an
annotated bibliography, 1954 to 1970.
New York, Kraus-Thomson
Organization, 1973- v.
016.809/04 73-6588
   Z6519 .P66 MRR Alc.

Romanische Bibliographie. 1961/62-
Tübingen, M. Niemeyer Verlag. 72-
620927
   Z7032 .Z45 MRR Alc Full set

Die Weltliteratur; Wien, Brüder
Hollinek [1951-54] 3 v. 52-24550
   PN41 .W4 MRR Alc.

Zeitschrift für romanische
Philologie. Supplementheft.
Bibliographie. 1-72/76; 1875/76-
1956/60. Tübingen [etc.] M.
Niemeyer. 74-643524
   Z7032 .Z45 MRR Alc Full set

**LITERATURE—HISTORY AND CRITICISM—
INDEXES.**
Combs, Richard E. Authors: critical
and biographical references;
Metuchen, N.J., Scarecrow Press,
1971. 221 p. 016.809 73-167644
   PN524 .C58 MRR Alc.

LITERATURE—INDEXES.
American library association. The
"A.L.A." index. 2d ed., greatly enl.
and brought down to January 1, 1900.
Boston, American library association,
1905. iv, 679 p. 15-5096
   AI3 .A3 1905 MRR Alc.

Essay and general literature index;
v. 1- 1930/33- New York, H. W.
Wilson Co. 016 34-14581
   AI3 .E752 MRR Alc Full set

The Great ideas; Chicago,
Encyclopædia Britannica [1955, c1952]
2 v. 028.3 55-10313
   AC1 .G72 vol. 2-3 MRR Alc.

LITERATURE—MISCELLANEA.
Bombaugh, Charles Carroll, Facts and
fancies for the curious from the
harvestfields of literature;
Philadelphia, London, J. B.
Lippincott company [1905] 647 p.
05-34162
   PN43 .B6 MRR Alc.

LITERATURE—MISCELLANEA—PERIODICALS.
American notes & queries; v. 1-
Sept. 1962- [New Haven, Conn.]
[$6.50] 031/.02 74-642751
   Z1034 .A4 MRR Alc Full set

LITERATURE—OUTLINES, SYLLABI, ETC.
Dizionario letterario Bompiani delle
opere e dei personaggi di tutti i
tempi e di tutte le letterature ...
[Milano] V. Bompiani, 1947 [c1946]-
50. 9 v. 803 47-20998
   PN41 .D5 MRR Alc.

LITERATURE—STORIES, PLOTS, ETC.
Bazzarelli, Eridano, Dizionario
Motta della lettertura universale.
Milano, F. Motta, 1972- v. 74-
316700
   PN564 .B3 MRR Alc.

Cohen, Sam D., ed. The digest of the
world's great classics. [New York?]
Daily Compass, 1950. 833 p. 808.83
51-86653
   PN44 .C6 MRR Alc.

Dictionnaire des œuvres
contemporaines de tous les pays.
Paris, Société d'édition de
dictionnaires et encyclopédies,
1967. viii, 767 p. [155 F] 703
68-118409
   AG25 .D552 MRR Alc.

Hammerton, John Alexander, Sir, ed.
Outline of great books. New York,
Wise & co., 1937. vii p., 1 l., 902
p. 808.8 37-8816
   PN44 .H3 MRR Alc.

Hardwick, John Michael Drinkrow, The
Charles Dickens companion London, J.
Murray [1965] xiii, 250 p. 823.8
66-10009
   PR4581 .H34 MRR Alc.

Heiney, Donald W., Essentials of
contemporary literature. Great Neck,
N.Y., Barron's Educational Series,
inc. [1955, c1954] 555 p. 55-1318

   PN771 .H4 MRR Alc.

Johnson, Rossiter, ed. Authors
digest; Metuchen, N.J., Mini-Print
Corp. 1970 [c1909] 21 v. in 5.
808.83 70-12099
   PN44 .J7 1970 MRR Alc.

Keller, Helen Rex, ed. The reader's
digest of books. New and greatly
enl. ed. New York, The Macmillan
company, 1940. 3 p. l., 1447 p.
803 40-7463
   PN44 .K4 1940 MRR Alc.

Magill, Frank Northen, Masterpieces
of world literature in digest form.
New York, Harper [1952-59] 4 v.
808.8 51-12454
   PN44 .M3 1952 MRR Alc.

Magill, Frank Northen, Masterplots.
New York, Salem Press [1964] 6 v.
808.8 64-54679
   PN44 .M32 MRR Alc.

Magill, Frank Northen, ed.
Masterplots cyclopedia of literary
characters. New York, Salem Press
[1963] 2 v. 803 64-120
   PN44 .M3 1963a MRR Alc.

Magill, Frank Northen, comp. Survey
of contemporary literature; New
York, Salem Press [1971] 7 v. (xlv,
5194, xviii p.) 809/.04 75-25876
   PN44 .M34 MRR Alc.

Magill, Frank Northern, ed.
Masterplots; [Definitive ed.] New
York, Salem Press [1968] 8 v. (ix,
5795, xxii p.) 68-8171
   PN44 .M33 MRR Alc.

Masterplots annual. 1954- New York,
Salem Press. 55-41212
   Z1219 .M33 MRR Alc Latest edition

Masterplots annual. 1954- New York,
Salem Press. 55-41212
   Z1219 .M33 MRR Alc Latest edition

Richardson, Kenneth Ridley.
Twentieth century writing; London,
New York [etc.] Newnes, 1969. viii,
751 p. [63/-] 809/.04 70-431735
   PN771 .R5 MRR Biog.

Smith, Guy E. English literature;
Paterson, N.J., Littlefield, Adams,
1959. 2 v. 820.2 59-33833
   PR87 .S65 1959 MRR Alc.

The Standard home library of the
world's greatest literature; New
York, Standard Reference Works Pub.
Co., 1958. 20 v. 808.83 58-46060

   PN44 .W62 MRR Alc.

Stanford, Barbara Dodds. Negro
literature for high school students.
[Champaign, Ill.] National Council of
Teachers of English [1968] ix, 157
p. [$2.00] 016.810/9/9 68-7786
   Z1361.N39 S75 MRR Alc.

Ward, Alfred Charles, Longman
companion to twentieth century
literature; Harlow, Longman, 1970.
[5,] 593 p. [65/-] 820.9/008/1 76-
554609
   PN771 .W28 MRR Alc.

Wilson, Barbara Logan, Capsule
classics; [1st ed.] Cleveland,
World Pub. Co. [1952] 306 p. 808.8
52-5178
   PN44 .W5 MRR Alc.

**LITERATURE—STORIES, PLOTS, ETC.—
INDEXES.**
Koehmstedt, Carol L. Plot summary
index. Metuchen, N.J., Scarecrow
Press, 1973. 312 p. 809 72-13726

   Z6514.P66 K63 MRR Ref Desk.

LITERATURE—TERMINOLOGY.
Abrams, Meyer Howard. A glossary of
literary terms 3d ed. New York,
Holt, Rinehart and Winston [1971]
vi, 193 p. 803 70-124358
   PN44.5 .A2 1971 MRR Alc.

Barnet, Sylvan. A dictionary of
literary, dramatic, and cinematic
terms 2d ed. Boston, Little, Brown
[1971] 124 p. 801/.4 74-145572
   PN44.5 .B3 1971 MRR Alc.

Beckson, Karl E., A reader's guide
to literary terms. New York, Noonday
Press [1961, c1960] 230 p. 803 60-
14127
   PN41 .B33 MRR Alc.

Deutsch, Babette, Poetry handbook;
4th ed. New York, Funk & Wagnalls
[1974] xix, 203 p. 808.1/01/4 73-
13970
   PN44.5 .D4 1974b MRR Alc.

Fowler, Roger. A dictionary of
modern critical terms; London,
Boston, Routledge & Kegan Paul [1973]
ix, 208 p. 801/.95 73-89194
   PN41 .F6 MRR Alc.

Holman, Clarence Hugh. A handbook to
literature, 3d ed. Indianapolis,
Odyssey Press [1972] viii, 646 p.
803 73-175226
   PN41 .H6 1972 MRR Alc.

Jones, Rhodri. English language
reference book. London, Blackie,
1970. xi, 243 p. [13/9] 428/.003
70-566676
   PE1460 .J6 MRR Alc.

Lazarus, Arnold Leslie. Modern
English; New York, Grosset & Dunlap
[1971] 462 p. [$10.00] 423 78-
86706
   PE31 .L3 MRR Ref Desk.

Lemon, Lee T. A glossary for the
study of English New York, Oxford
University Press, 1971. xi, 138 p.
803 71-151186
   PN44.5 .L4 MRR Alc.

Liberman, Myron M. A modern lexicon
of literary terms [Glenview, Ill.]
Scott, Foresman [1968] 138 p.
801/.4 68-17741
   PN44.5 .L46 MRR Alc.

Malof, Joseph, A manual of English
meters. Bloomington, Indiana
University Press [1970] xvi, 236 p.
[8.50] 426 70-98979
   PE1505 .M3 1970 MRR Alc.

Meyers Handbuch über die Literatur.
2., neu bearb. Aufl. Mannheim, Wien,
Zürich, Bibliographisches Inst.
[1970] 987 p. [36.00] 79-483796
   PN41 .M45 1970 MRR Biog.

National Poetry Association.
Dictionary of poetry terms Los
Angeles [1959] 142 p. 808.1 59-
3155
   PN1021 .N3 MRR Alc.

Scott, Arthur Finley. Current
literary terms; London, Macmillan;
New York, St Martin's Press, 1965.
vii, 324 p. 803 65-24300
   PN44.5 .S3 1965 MRR Alc.

Shaw, Harry, Dictionary of literary
terms. New York, McGraw-Hill [1972]
402 p. [$12.50] 803 72-179884
   PN44.5 .S46 MRR Alc.

Shipley, Joseph Twadell, Dictionary
of world literary terms, forms,
technique, criticism. Completely
rev. and enl. ed. Boston, Writer
[1970] xiii, 466 p. [12.95] 803
75-91879
   PN41 .S5 1970 MRR Alc.

Taaffe, James G. A student's guide
to literary terms Cleveland, World
Pub. Co. [1967] v, 165 p. 802 67-
13631
   PN44.5 .T3 MRR Alc.

Yelland, Hedley Lowry. A handbook of
literary terms; Sydney, Angus and
Robertson [1950] 221, [3] p. 803
51-4351
   PN41 .Y4 MRR Alc.

LITERATURE—TRANSLATIONS INTO SPANISH.
Ruiz, Luis Alberto. Diccionario de
la literatura universal. Buenos
Aires, Editorial Raigal, 1955-56. 3
v. 57-41563
   PN41 .R8 MRR Alc.

LITERATURE—YEARBOOKS.
The Author's & writer's who's who.
[1934]- London, Burke's Peerage,
ltd. [etc.] 928.2 34-38025
   Z2011 .A91 MRR Biog Latest edition

Who's who in literature. 1924-34.
Liverpool, Literary Year Books Press.
26-26968
   Z2011 .L78 MRR Biog Latest edition

LITERATURE, COMPARATIVE.
Chyzhevs'kyi, Dmytro. Outline of
comparative Slavic literatures.
Boston, American Academy of Arts and
Sciences, 1952. 143 p.   a 53-1570
PG502 .C35 MRR Alc

LITERATURE, COMPARATIVE--BIBLIOGRAPHY.
Baldensperger, Fernand. Bibliography
of comparative literature. New York,
Russell & Russell, 1960 [c1950]
xxiv, 705 p.   016.809 60-5270
Z6514.C7 B3 1960 MRR Alc.

LITERATURE, COMPARATIVE--CLASSICAL AND
MODERN.
Highet, Gilbert. The classical
tradition. New York, Oxford
University Press, 1949. xxxviii, 763
p.   809 49-11655
PN883 .H5 MRR Alc.

LITERATURE, COMPARATIVE--ENGLISH AND
SPANISH.
Williams, Stanley Thomas. The
Spanish background of American
literature. [Hamden, Conn.] Archon
Books, 1968 [c1955] 2 v. 810.9 68-
16337
PS159.S7 W5 1968 MRR Alc.

LITERATURE, COMPARATIVE--MODERN AND
CLASSICAL.
Highet, Gilbert. The classical
tradition. New York, Oxford
University Press, 1949. xxxviii, 763
p.   809 49-11655
PN883 .H5 MRR Alc.

LITERATURE, COMPARATIVE--SPANISH AND
ENGLISH.
Williams, Stanley Thomas. The
Spanish background of American
literature. [Hamden, Conn.] Archon
Books, 1968 [c1955] 2 v. 810.9 68-
16337
PS159.S7 W5 1968 MRR Alc.

LITERATURE, MEDIEVAL--BIBLIOGRAPHY.
Fisher, John H., ed. The medieval
literature of western Europe; [New
York] Published for the Modern
Language Association of America by
the New York University Press, 1966.
xvi, 432 p.   808.02 66-22346
PN671 .F5 MRR Alc.

International guide to medieval
studies. v. 1- June 1961- Darien,
Conn., American Bibliographic
Service. 63-24615
Z6203 .I6 MRR Alc Full set

LITERATURE, MEDIEVAL--DICTIONARIES.
Spence, Lewis. A dictionary of
medieval romance and romance writers.
London; G. Routledge & sons,
limited; New York, E. P. Dutton & co.
[1913] vi, 395 p.   14-6809
PN669 .S6 MRR Alc.

Walsh, William Shepard. Heroes and
heroines of fiction. Detroit,
Republished by Gale Research Co.,
1966. 2 v.   803 66-28782
PN43 .W33 1966 MRR Alc.

LITERATURE, MEDIEVAL--HISTORY AND
CRITICISM.
Edwardes, Marian, comp. A summary of
the literatures of modern Europe
(England, France, Germany, Italy,
Spain) London; J. M. Dent & co.,
1907. xvi, 532 p.   07-20870
PN671 .E4 MRR Alc.

Fisher, John H., ed. The medieval
literature of western Europe; [New
York] Published for the Modern
Language Association of America by
the New York University Press, 1966.
xvi, 432 p.   808.02 66-22346
PN671 .F5 MRR Alc.

Jackson, William Thomas Hobdell. The
literature of the Middle Ages. New
York, Columbia University Press,
1960. 432 p.   809.02 60-13153
PN671 .J3 1960 MRR Alc.

LITERATURE, MEDIEVAL--TRANSLATIONS INTO
ENGLISH--BIBLIOGRAPHY.
Farrar, Clarissa Palmer.
Bibliography of English translations
from medieval sources. New York,
Columbia university press, 1946.
xiii, 534 p.   016.8 a 46-1541
Z6517 .F3 MRR Alc.

Ferguson, Mary Anne. Bibliography of
English translations from medieval
sources, 1943-1967. New York,
Columbia University Press, 1974. x,
274 p.   016.08 73-7751
Z6517 .F47 MRR Alc.

LITERATURE, MODERN--19TH CENTURY--
HISTORY AND CRITICISM.
Seymour-Smith, Martin. Funk &
Wagnalls Guide to modern world
literature. New York, Funk &
Wagnalls [1973] xxi, 1206 p.
[$13.95] 809.034 73-5931
PN761 .S43 1973 MRR Alc.

LITERATURE, MODERN--20TH CENTURY.
Wallis, Charles Langworthy, ed.
Speaker's resources from contemporary
literature. [1st ed.] New York,
Harper & Row [1965] xvi, 282 p.
808.882 65-20460
PN6081 .W28 MRR Ref Desk.

LITERATURE, MODERN--20TH CENTURY--
ADDRESSES, ESSAYS, LECTURES.
Frenz, Horst, comp. Literature 1901-
1967; Amsterdam, New York, published
for the Nobel Foundation by Elsevier
Pub. Co., 1969. xxi, 640 p. [40.00]
808.9 68-20649
PN771 .F74 MRR Alc.

United States. Library of Congress.
Gertrude Clarke Whittall Poetry and
Literature Fund. Perspectives:
recent literature of Russia, China,
Italy, and Spain; Washington,
Reference Dept., Library of Congress,
1961. v, 57 p.   809.04 61-60040
Z663.293 .P4 MRR Alc.

LITERATURE, MODERN--20TH CENTURY--
BIBLIOGRAPHY.
Krawitz, Henry. A post-symbolist
bibliography. Metuchen, N.J.,
Scarecrow Press, 1973. 284 p.
016.809/04 73-1181
Z6520.S9 K7 MRR Alc.

LITERATURE, MODERN--20TH CENTURY--BIO-
BIBLIOGRAPHY.
The Concise encyclopedia of modern
world literature. [2d ed.] New
York, Hawthorn Books [1971, c1963]
430 p. [$12.95] 809/.04 B 76-
28851
PN771 .C58 1971 MRR Alc.

Écrivains contemporains. Paris,
Éditions d'art L. Mazenod [1965]
763 p.   67-45173
PN773 .E3 MRR Biog.

Encyclopedia of world literature in
the 20th century. New York, F. Ungar
Pub. Co. [1967-71] 3 v.   803 67-
13615
PN774 .L433 MRR Alc.

Harte, Barbara, comp. 200
contemporary authors; Detroit,
Mich., Gale Research Co. [1969] 306
p.   809/.04 75-94113
PN771 .H28 MRR Biog.

Heiney, Donald W. Essentials of
contemporary literature. Great Neck,
N.Y., Barron's Educational Series,
inc. [1955, c1954] 555 p.   55-1318

PN771 .H4 MRR Alc.

Kunitz, Stanley Jasspon, ed.
Twentieth century authors. New York,
Wilson, 1942. vii, 1577 p.   928 ac
43-51003
PN771 .K86 MRR Alc.

Kunitz, Stanley Jasspon, ed.
Twentieth century authors. New York,
Wilson, 1942. vii, 1577 p.   928 920
43-51003
PN771 .K86 MRR Alc.

Richardson, Kenneth Ridley.
Twentieth century writing; London,
New York [etc.] Newnes, 1969. viii,
751 p. [63/-] 809/.04 70-431735
PN771 .R5 MRR Biog.

LITERATURE, MODERN--20TH CENTURY--
BIOGRAPHY.
Kunitz, Stanley Jasspon, ed.
Twentieth century authors. New York,
Wilson, 1942. vii, 1577 p.   928 ac
43-51003
PN771 .K86 MRR Alc.

Kunitz, Stanley Jasspon, ed.
Twentieth century authors. New York,
Wilson, 1942. vii, 1577 p.   928 920
43-51003
PN771 .K86 MRR Alc.

LITERATURE, MODERN--20TH CENTURY--
DICTIONARIES.
The Concise encyclopedia of modern
world literature. [2d ed.] New
York, Hawthorn Books [1971, c1963]
430 p. [$12.95] 809/.04 B 76-
28851
PN771 .C58 1971 MRR Alc.

Dictionnaire des œuvres
contemporaines de tous les pays.
Paris, Société d'édition de
dictionnaires et encyclopédies,
1967. viii, 767 p. [155 F] 703
68-119409
AG25 .D552 MRR Alc.

Encyclopedia of world literature in
the 20th century. New York, F. Ungar
Pub. Co. [1967-71] 3 v.   803 67-
13615
PN774 .L433 MRR Alc.

Ward, Alfred Charles. Longman
companion to twentieth century
literature. Harlow, Longman, 1970.
[6], 593 p. [65/-] 820.9/009/1 76-
554609
PN771 .W28 MRR Alc.

LITERATURE, MODERN--20TH CENTURY--
DICTIONARIES--GERMAN.
Encyclopedia of world literature in
the 20th century. New York, F. Ungar
Pub. Co. [1967-71] 3 v.   803 67-
13615
PN774 .L433 MRR Alc.

LITERATURE, MODERN--20TH CENTURY--
HISTORY AND CRITICISM.
Curley, Dorothy Nyren, comp. Modern
Romance literatures. New York, F.
Ungar Pub. Co. [1967] x, 510 p.
875.9/09 67-14053
PN813 .C8 MRR Alc.

Heiney, Donald W. Essentials of
contemporary literature. Great Neck,
N.Y., Barron's Educational Series,
inc. [1955, c1954] 555 p.   55-1318

PN771 .H4 MRR Alc.

Ivask, Ivar. World literature since
1945; New York, F. Ungar Pub. Co.
[1973] xii, 724 p.   809/.04 72-
79930
PN771 .I9 MRR Alc.

Seymour-Smith, Martin. Funk &
Wagnalls Guide to modern world
literature. New York, Funk &
Wagnalls [1973] xxi, 1206 p.
[$13.95] 809/.034 73-5931
PN761 .S43 1973 MRR Alc.

LITERATURE, MODERN--20TH CENTURY--
HISTORY AND CRITICISM--PERIODICALS.
Contemporary literary criticism. CLC
1- 1973- Detroit, Gale Research
Co. 809/.04 76-38938
PN771 .C59 MRR Alc Full set

LITERATURE, MODERN--20TH CENTURY--
HISTORY AND CRITICISM--PERIODICALS--
BIBLIOGRAPHY.
Pownall, David E., Articles on
twentieth century literature: an
annotated bibliography, 1954 to 1970,
New York, Kraus-Thomson
Organization, 1973- v.
016.809/04 73-6588
Z6519 .P66 MRR Alc.

LITERATURE, MODERN--BIBLIOGRAPHY--UNION
LISTS.
United States. Library of Congress.
Acquisitions Dept. European imprints
for the war years. Washington, 1945-
46. 3 v. 015.4 45-37835
Z663.76 .E8 MRR Alc.

LITERATURE, MODERN--BIO-BIBLIOGRAPHY.
Dizionario universale della
letteratura contemporanea. 1. ed.
Milano] A. Mondadori [1959-63] 5 v.
60-644
PN41 .D53 MRR Alc.

Hargreaves-Mawdsley, W. N.
Everyman's dictionary of European
writers. London, Dent; New York, E.
P. Dutton & Co., 1968. vi, 561 p.
[38/-] 803 68-59559
PN451 .H3 MRR Biog.

LITERATURE, MODERN--DICTIONARIES.
Dizionario universale della
letteratura contemporanea. 1. ed.
Milano] A. Mondadori [1959-63] 5 v.
60-644
PN41 .D53 MRR Alc.

LITERATURE, MODERN--DICTIONARIES,
INDEXES, ETC.
Walsh, William Shepard. Heroes and
heroines of fiction. Detroit,
Republished by Gale Research Co.,
1966. 2 v.   803 66-28782
PN43 .W33 1966 MRR Alc.

LITERATURE, MODERN--HISTORY AND
CRITICISM.
Kranz, Gisbert. Europas christliche
Literatur, 1500-1960. Aschaffenburg,
P. Pattloch [1961] 637 p.   65-33366

PN704 .K7 MRR Alc.

Wellek, René. A history of modern
criticism: 1750-1950. New Haven,
Yale University Press, 1955- v.
801 55-5989
PN86 .W4 MRR Alc.

LITERATURE, PRIMITIVE.
see also Folk-lore

LITERATURE AS A PROFESSION
see Authorship

see Journalism

LITHERLAND, ENG.--DIRECTORIES.
Kelly's (Gore's) directory of
Liverpool, including Bootle,
Birkenhead, Wallasey and environs.
Kingston upon Thames, Surrey [etc.]
Kelly's Directories Ltd. 35-15072
DA690.L8 K4 MRR Alc Latest edition

LITHOGRAPHERS, AMERICAN.
Warman, Edwin G., Print price guide;
Uniontown, Pa., Warman Pub. Co.
[1955] 136 p. 763.085 56-521
NE2415.C7 W36 MRR Alc.

LITHOGRAPHS--CATALOGS.
Conningham, Frederic Arthur, Currier
& Ives prints; [Rev. ed.] New York,
Crown Publishers [1970] xx, 300 p.
[12.50] 769/.02/8 77-105858
NE2415.C7 C62 1970 MRR Alc.

LITHOGRAPHS--PRICES.
Warman, Edwin G., Print price guide;
Uniontown, Pa., Warman Pub. Co.
[1955] 136 p. 763.085 56-521
NE2415.C7 W36 MRR Alc.

LITHOGRAPHY.
Shapiro, Charles, comp. The
lithographers manual. 4th ed.
Pittsburgh, Graphic Arts Technical
Foundation [1970, c1968] 1 v.
(various pagings) 686.2/315 68-
57213
TR940 .S47 1970 MRR Alc.

LITHOLOGY
see Petrology

LITHUANIA--BIOGRAPHY.
Encyclopedia Lituanica. Boston [J.
Kapocius, 1970- v.
914.7/5/0303 74-114275
DK511.L2 E5 MRR Alc.

**LITHUANIA--DICTIONARIES AND
ENCYCLOPEDIAS.**
Encyclopedia Lituanica. Boston [J.
Kapocius, 1970- v.
914.7/5/0303 74-114275
DK511.L2 E5 MRR Alc.

**LITHUANIA--HISTORY--ADDRESSES, ESSAYS,
LECTURES.**
Gerutis, Albertas, Lithuania 700
years. New York, Manyland Books
[1969] xii, 474 p. 947/.5 75-
80057
DK511.L2 G5 MRR Alc.

LITHUANIA--POLITICS AND GOVERNMENT.
Vardys, Vytas Stanley, ed. Lithuania
under the Soviets; New York, Praeger
[1965] ix, 299 p. 309.1475 65-
14060
DK511.L27 V35 MRR Alc.

**LITHUANIAN LANGUAGE--CONVERSATION AND
PHRASE BOOKS--POLYGLOT.**
Lyall, Archibald, A guide to 25
languages of Europe. Rev. ed.
[Harrisburg, Pa.] Stackpole Co.
[1966] viii, 407 p. 413 66-20847
PB73 .L85 1966 MRR Alc.

**LITHUANIAN LANGUAGE--DICTIONARIES--
ENGLISH.**
Lalis, Anthony, Lietuviškos ir
angliškos kalbu žodynas. 3.,
išnaujo taisytas ir gausiai
papildytas, spaudimas. Chicago,
Ill., Turtu ir spauda "Lietuvos,"
1915. 2 pt. in 1 v. 20-5148
PG8679 .L33 1915 MRR Alc.

LITTERATEURS.
see also Authors

see also Poets

Disraeli, Isaac, Curiosities of
literature, New York, London, D.
Appleton and company, 1932. xx p., 1
l., 312 p. 828.7 32-28946
PN43 .D5 1932 MRR Alc.

LITTLE MAGAZINES--BIBLIOGRAPHY.
Hoffman, Frederick John. The little
magazine; Princeton, N.J., Princeton
university press, 1946. ix p., 2 l.,
440 p. 052 a 46-17
PN4836 .H6 MRR Alc.

**LITTLE MAGAZINES--BIBLIOGRAPHY--UNION
LISTS.**
Indiana. University. Library. Union
list of little magazines, Chicago,
Midwest Inter-Library Center, 1956.
iii, 98 l. a 57-2877
Z6944.L5 I53 MRR Alc

LITTLE MAGAZINES--DIRECTORIES.
International directory of little
magazines & small presses. 9th-
ed.: 1973/74- [Paradise, Calif.,
Dustbooks] [$3.50] 051/.025 73-
645432
Z6944.L5 D5 MRR Alc Latest edition

LITTLE MAGAZINES--HISTORY.
Hoffman, Frederick John. The little
magazine; Princeton, N.J., Princeton
university press, 1946. ix p., 2 l.,
440 p. 052 a 46-17
PN4836 .H6 MRR Alc.

LITTLE PRESSES--DIRECTORIES.
International directory of little
magazines & small presses. 9th-
ed.: 1973/74- [Paradise, Calif.,
Dustbooks] [$3.50] 051/.025 73-
645432
Z6944.L5 D5 MRR Alc Latest edition

LITURGICAL OBJECTS--DICTIONARIES.
Lee, Frederick George, A glossary of
liturgical and ecclesiastical terms.
Detroit, Tower Books, 1971. xxxix,
452 p. 200/.3 76-174069
BR95 .L4 1971 MRR Alc.

LITURGICAL YEAR
see Church year

LITURGICS.
see also Church music

LITURGICS--DICTIONARIES.
Davies, John Gordon, A dictionary of
liturgy and worship. [1st American
ed.] New York, Macmillan [1972] ix,
385 p. [$10.00] 264/.003 72-90276

BV173 .D28 1972 MRR Alc.

LITURGIES--DICTIONARIES.
Podhradsky, Gerhard. New dictionary
of the liturgy. English ed. Staten
Island, N.Y., Alba House [1967,
c1966] 208 p. 264/.003 67-5547
BV173 .P613 1967 MRR Alc.

LIVERPOOL--DIRECTORIES.
Kelly's (Gore's) directory of
Liverpool, including Bootle,
Birkenhead, Wallasey and environs.
Kingston upon Thames, Surrey [etc.]
Kelly's Directories Ltd. 35-15072
DA690.L8 K4 MRR Alc Latest edition

LIVESTOCK
see Domestic animals

LIVESTOCK BREEDS
see also Cattle breeds

LIVESTOCK DISEASES
see Veterinary medicine

LIVING, STANDARD OF
see Cost and standard of living

LIVRES À CLEF--BIBLIOGRAPHY.
Walbridge, Earle Francis, Literary
characters drawn from life; New
York, H. W. Wilson Co., 1936. 192 p.
098.5 36-10273
Z1026 .W15 MRR Alc.

LOANS--FRANCE.
Annuaire Desfossés; Paris, Cote
Desfossés [etc.] 332.63 46-39086
HG5471 .A64 MRR Alc Latest edition

LOANS--UNITED STATES--DIRECTORIES.
Instalment lending directory. New
York, Instalment Credit Committee,
American Bankers Association. 53-
29979
HF5568 .A6 MRR Alc Latest edition

**LOANS, PERSONAL--UNITED STATES--
DIRECTORIES.**
Instalment lending directory. New
York, Instalment Credit Committee,
American Bankers Association. 53-
29979
HF5568 .A6 MRR Alc Latest edition

National directory of finance
companies. 1951- Montpelier, Ohio,
Inter-state Service Co. 332.31
332.35* 52-18620
HG2066 .N285 MRR Alc Latest
edition

LOBBYING.
Key, Valdimer Orlando, Politics,
parties, & pressure groups. 5th ed.
New York, Crowell [1964] xiii, 738
p. 329 64-11799
JF2051 .K4 1964 MRR Alc.

Truman, David Bicknell, The
governmental process; [1st ed.] New
York, Knopf, 1951. xvi, 544, xv p.
328.368 51-4187
JK1118 .T7 MRR Alc.

**LOBBYING--LAW AND LEGISLATION--UNITED
STATES.**
Congressional Quarterly, inc. The
Washington lobby Washington,
Congressional Quarterly [1971] 123
p. [$4.00] 328.73/07/8 78-168708

KF4948 .Z9C6 MRR Alc.

Directory of registered federal and
state lobbyists. 1st- ed.; 1973-
Orange, N.J. Academic Media.
328/.38/02573 72-75953
JK1118 .D56 MRR Ref Desk Latest
edition

LOBBYING--UNITED STATES.
Congressional Quarterly, inc. The
Washington lobby Washington,
Congressional Quarterly [1971] 123
p. [$4.00] 328.73/07/8 78-168708

KF4948 .Z9C6 MRR Alc.

LOBBYISTS--UNITED STATES--DIRECTORIES.
Directory of registered federal and
state lobbyists. 1st- ed.; 1973-
Orange, N.J. Academic Media.
328/.38/02573 72-75953
JK1118 .D56 MRR Ref Desk Latest
edition

LOCAL FINANCE--NEW ZEALAND--STATISTICS.
New Zealand. Dept. of Statistics.
Local authority statistics.
Wellington. 336.931 72-626670
JS10 .N8 MRR Alc Latest edition

**LOCAL FINANCE--UNITED STATES--
STATISTICS.**
United States. Bureau of the Census.
1972 census of governments.
[Washington, U.S. Govt. Print. Off.]
1973- v. [$1.25 (v. 2, pt. 1)
varies] 317.3 73-600080
JS3 .A244 MRR Alc.

LOCAL GOVERNMENT.
see also Cities and towns

see also Mayors

see also Municipal government

see also Public administration

LOCAL GOVERNMENT--BIBLIOGRAPHY.
Leif, Irving P., Community power and
decision-making: Metuchen, N.J.,
Scarecrow Press, 1974. vi, 170 p.
016.30115/5 74-4171
Z7164.C842 L43 MRR Alc.

LOCAL GOVERNMENT--YEARBOOKS.
The County & municipal year book for
Scotland. Coupar Angus. 352.041 49-
20531
Began publication with 1933 issue.
JS4101 .C6 MRR Alc Latest edition

LOCAL GOVERNMENT--ARIZONA--REGISTERS.
League of Arizona Cities and Towns.
Directory of Arizona city and town
officials. Phoenix. 64-37719
JS451.A63 L4 MRR Alc Latest
edition

LOCAL GOVERNMENT--GREAT BRITAIN.
Clarke, John Joseph, Outlines of
local government of the United
Kingdom, 20th ed. London, Pitman,
1969. x, 245 p. [40/-]
352/.000942 77-386962
JS3113 .C5 1969 MRR Alc.

**LOCAL GOVERNMENT--GREAT BRITAIN--
DIRECTORIES.**
The Oyez directory of local
authorities in England and Wales,
1968. 3rd ed. London, Oyez
Publications, 1968. 96 p. [25/-]
352/.00025/42 72-436378
JS3137 .O9 1968 MRR Alc.

**LOCAL GOVERNMENT--GREAT BRITAIN--
INFORMATION SERVICES.**
Snape, Wilfrid Handley. How to find
out about local government, [1st
ed.] Oxford, New York, Pergamon
Press [1969] xv, 175 p.
352/.000942 69-20482
JS3113 .S58 1969 MRR Alc.

**LOCAL GOVERNMENT--GREAT BRITAIN--
YEARBOOKS.**
The Local government manual and
directory. 1923- London, Shaw &
Sons Ltd. 352.042 72-622949
JS3003 .M8 MRR Alc Latest edition

The Municipal year book and public
utilities directory. London,
Municipal Journal [etc.] 352.042 07-
24315
Began publication in 1897.
JS3003 .M8 MRR Alc Latest edition

**LOCAL GOVERNMENT--NEW ZEALAND--
STATISTICS.**
New Zealand. Dept. of Statistics.
Local authority statistics.
Wellington. 336.931 72-626670
JS10 .N8 MRR Alc Latest edition

LOCAL GOVERNMENT--OHIO.
Rose, Albert Henry, Ohio government,
State and local 3d ed. [Dayton]
University of Dayton Press [1966]
xviii, 590 p. 320.9771 66-8580
JK5525 1966 .R6 MRR Alc.

LOCAL GOVERNMENT--SCOTLAND.
The County & municipal year book for
Scotland. Coupar Angus. 352.041 49-
20531
Began publication with 1933 issue.
JS4101 .C6 MRR Alc Latest edition

LOCAL GOVERNMENT--UNITED STATES.
Adrian, Charles R. Governing our
fifty States and their communities
[2d ed.] New York, McGraw-Hill
[1967] 133 p. 353.9 67-18389
JK2408 .A28 1967 MRR Alc.

Adrian, Charles R. State and local
governments 2d ed. New York, McGraw-
Hill [c1967] vii, 607 p. 353.9 66-
25472
JK2408 .A3 1967 MRR Alc.

Dye, Thomas R. Politics in States
and communities 2d ed. Englewood
Cliffs, N.J., Prentice-Hall [1973]
xii, 548 p. [$10.95] 320.4/73 72-
11912
JK2408 .D82 1973 MRR Alc.

LOCAL GOVERNMENT--UNITED STATES. (Cont.)
Ogg, Frederic Austin. Ogg and Ray's
Introduction to American Government.
13th ed. New York, Appleton-Century-
Crofts [1966] x, 979 p. 353 66-
16282
   JK421 .O5 1966 MRR Alc.

LOCAL GOVERNMENT--UNITED STATES--
ADDRESSES, ESSAYS, LECTURES.
Feeler, James William, ed. The 50
States and their local governments.
New York, Knopf [1967] xviii, 603 p.
353.9 66-12816
   JK2408 .F4 1967 MRR Alc.

LOCAL GOVERNMENT--UNITED STATES--
STATISTICS.
United States. Bureau of the Census.
1967 census of governments.
[Washington, For sale by the Supt. of
Docs., U.S. Govt. Print. Off., 1968-
v. in 353.000021/2 a 68-7201
   JS3.A257 MRR Alc.

United States. Bureau of the Census.
1972 census of governments.
[Washington, U.S. Govt. Print. Off.]
1973- v. [$1.25 (v. 2, pt. 1)
varies] 317.3 73-600080
   JS3 .A244 MRR Alc.

LOCAL GOVERNMENT--VERMONT.
Nuquist, Andrew Edgerton. Vermont
State Government and administration;
Burlington, Government Research
Center, University of Vermont, 1966.
xlv, 644 p. 353.9743 65-29199
   JK3025 1966 .N8 MRR Alc.

LOCAL GOVERNMENT--WASHINGTON (STATE)--
HANDBOOKS, MANUALS, ETC.
The Research Council's handbook. 1st
ed.; 1961/62- Seattle, Washington
State Research Council. 64-20640
   JK8230 .R46 MRR Alc Latest edition

LOCAL OFFICIALS AND EMPLOYEES--UNITED
STATES--STATISTICS.
United States. Bureau of the Census.
1967 census of governments.
[Washington, For sale by the Supt. of
Docs., U.S. Govt. Print. Off., 1968-
v. in 353.000021/2 a 68-7201
   JS3.A257 MRR Alc.

United States. Bureau of the Census.
1972 census of governments.
[Washington, U.S. Govt. Print. Off.]
1973- v. [$1.25 (v. 2, pt. 1)
varies] 317.3 73-600080
   JS3 .A244 MRR Alc.

LOCAL TRANSIT.
   see also Motor bus lines

   see also Street-railroads

LOCAL TRANSIT--STATISTICS.
International Union of Public
Transport. Statistiques des
transports publics urbains. (2e
ed.). Bruxelles, Union
internationale des transports
publics (1968). 211 p. 388/.021/2
76-393786
   HE4211 .I56 1968 MRR Alc.

LOCOMOTION.
   see also Automobiles

   see also Boats and boating

LOCOMOTIVE WORKS--DIRECTORIES.
Arnold, Ian. Locomotive, trolley,
and rail car builders, [Los Angeles,
Trans-Anglo Books, 1965] 64 p.
625.2025573 65-17586
   TF355 .A7 MRR Alc.

LOCOMOTIVES--HISTORY.
Lucas, Walter Arndt, ed. 100 years
of steam locomotives. New York,
Simmons-Boardman Pub. Corp. [1957]
278 p. 621.132973 625.26* 57-12355

   TJ603 .L77 MRR Alc.

LOCOMOTIVES--UNITED STATES.
Bruce, Alfred W. The steam
locomotive in America: [1st ed.]
New York, Norton [1952] 443 p.
621.132973 625.26* 52-14477
   TJ605 .B78 MRR Alc.

LODGING-HOUSES--EUROPE.
Women's Rest Tour Association,
Boston. Foreign lodging list.
Boston. 647.94094 ca 35-238
   D910 .W82 MRR Alc Latest edition

LOENING, GROVER CLEVELAND, 1888- --
BIBLIOGRAPHY.
United States. Library of Congress.
Manuscript Division. Grover C.
Loening; a register of his papers in
the Library of Congress. Washington,
1959. 9 l. 016.62913 58-60050
   Z663.34 .L6 MRR Alc.

LOGARITHMS.
Hart, William Le Roy. Tables for
Mathematics of investment. 4th ed.
Boston, Heath [1958] 150 p. 510.83
58-3601
   HG1632 .H3 1958 MRR Alc.

Smoley, Constantine Kenneth.
Segmental functions; Chautauqua,
N.Y., C. K. Smoley, 1962. 255, 179,
193 p. 510.83 62-53086
   QA342 .S65 1962 MRR Alc.

LOGGING
   see Lumbering

LOGIC.
Copi, Irving M. Introduction to
logic 4th ed. New York, Macmillan
[1972] xii, 540 p. [$8.95] 160
70-171565
   BC108 .C69 1972 MRR Alc.

LOGIC--EARLY WORKS TO 1800.
Aristoteles. The Organon.
Cambridge, Harvard University Press,
1938- v. 160 38-12666
   PA3612 .A807 1938 MRR Alc.

LOGIC--HISTORY.
Bochenski, Innocentius M., A
history of formal logic. [Notre
Dame, Ind.] University of Notre Dame
Press, 1961. xxii, 657 p. 160.9
58-14183
   BC15 .B643 MRR Alc.

LOGIC, SYMBOLIC AND MATHEMATICAL.
Copi, Irving M. Symbolic logic 3d
ed. New York, Macmillan [1968,
c1967] xvi, 400 p. 164 67-21418
   BC135 .C58 1968 MRR Alc.

LONDON--ANTIQUITIES.
Harben, Henry Andrade, A dictionary
of London; London, H. Jenkins
limited, 1918. 2 p. l., vii-xxiv p.,
2 l., 641 p. 18-7018
   DA679 .H3 MRR Alc.

LONDON--BIOGRAPHY.
City of London directory and diary
and livery companies guide. London,
City Press [etc.] 53-29778
   DA679 .A12 MRR Alc Biog Latest edition

LONDON--COMMERCE--DIRECTORIES.
Kelly's manufacturers and merchants
directory, 82d- ed.; 1968/69-
Kingston upon Thames, Kelly's
Directories. 380.1/025 72-622824
   HF54.G7 K4 MRR Alc Latest edition

Kelly's post office London directory.
London, Kelly's Directories.
914.21/0025 72-626566
   DA679 .A14 MRR Alc Latest edition

London and suburbs trades' directory.
Edinburgh, Town and County
Directories. 61-45501
   HF5159.L6 L6 MRR Alc Latest
   edition

South-eastern counties of England
trades' directory, including London,
London surburbs, Brighton and
Reading. Edinburgh, Trades'
Directories. 55-26292
   HF5159.L6 S6 MRR Alc Latest
   Edition

Trades register of London. London,
Trades Register of London, ltd. 57-
34104
   HC258.L6 T7 MRR Alc Latest edition

LONDON--DESCRIPTION.
Clunn, Harold Philip. The face of
London. A completely new ed. rev.
London, Spring Books [1962] 630 p.
942.1 62-51022
   DA683 .C6 1962 MRR Alc.

LONDON--DESCRIPTION--1951-
Kent, William, ed. An encyclopaedia
of London. Revised [ed.]; London,
Dent, 1970. [11], 618 p., 32 plates.
[50/-] 914.21/003 71-527323
   DA679 .A127 1970 MRR Alc.

LONDON--DESCRIPTION--1951- --GUIDE-
BOOKS.
The City of London official guide.
4th ed. Cheltenham, E. J. Burrow
[1962] 336 p. 63-5163
   DA679 .A1216 MRR Alc.

Piper, David. Fodor's London; [Rev.
ed.] New York, McKay [1971, c1964]
540 p. [$3.95] 914.21/04/85 72-
148997
   DA679 .P5 1971 MRR Alc.

Piper, David. London. [1st ed.]
New York, Holt, Rinehart and Winston
[1971] 288 p. [$9.95]
914.21/04/85 77-155540
   N6770 .P5 MRR Alc.

Rossiter, Stuart, ed. London. 9th
ed. London, E. Benn; [distributed in
the U.S.A. by Rand McNally] 1965.
xlii, 317 p. 67-1667
   DA679 .B7 1965 MRR Alc.

Simon, Kate. London places &
pleasures; New York, Putnam [1968]
348 p. 914.21/04/85 68-15522
   DA679 .S58 1968 MRR Alc.

Ward, Lock and Company, ltd. London.
64th ed. London, Ward, Lock [1967]
287 p. [12/6] 914.21/04/85 67-
108475
   DA679 .W3 1967 MRR Alc.

LONDON--DESCRIPTION--GUIDE-BOOKS.
The City of London: the official
guide. 6th ed. Cheltenham, London,
Burrow [1968] 204 p.
914.21/2/0485 68-118308
   DA679 .C5 1968 MRR Alc.

Coe's guide to London bookshops.
Market Harborough (Leics.), Gerald
Coe Ltd., 1967. [86] p. [7/6]
658.8/09/655570254212 68-112509
   Z327 .C6 MRR Alc.

LONDON--DESCRIPTION--TOURS.
Gibbons annual index of daily sight-
seeing tours: Rome, Paris, Florence,
London. [Los Angeles] 914 72-80819

   D909 .G5 MRR Alc Latest edition

Williams, George Guion. Guide to
literary London. London, Batsford,
1973. [7], 406 p. [£4.00]
914.21/04/85 74-159176
   PR110.L6 W5 MRR Alc.

LONDON--DICTIONARIES AND ENCYCLOPEDIAS.
Kent, William, ed. An encyclopaedia
of London. Revised [ed.]; London,
Dent, 1970. [11], 618 p., 32 plates.
[50/-] 914.21/003 71-527323
   DA679 .A127 1970 MRR Alc.

LONDON--DIRECTORIES.
City of London directory and diary
and livery companies guide. London,
City Press [etc.] 53-29778
   DA679 .A12 MRR Alc Biog Latest edition

The City of London official guide.
4th ed. Cheltenham, E. J. Burrow
[1962] 336 p. 63-5163
   DA679 .A1216 MRR Alc.

Kelly's post office London directory.
London, Kelly's Directories.
914.21/0025 72-626566
   DA679 .A14 MRR Alc Latest edition

The London directory & international
register of commerce. 1973- London.
338/.0025/421 73-642810
   DA679 .A1315 MRR Alc Latest edition

LONDON--GAZETTEERS.
Harben, Henry Andrade, A dictionary
of London; London, H. Jenkins
limited, 1918. 2 p. l., vii-xxiv p.,
2 l., 641 p. 18-7018
   DA679 .H3 MRR Alc.

LONDON--HISTORIC HOUSES, ETC.
Williams, George Guion. Guide to
literary London. London, Batsford,
1973. [7], 406 p. [£4.00]
914.21/04/85 74-159176
   PR110.L6 W5 MRR Alc.

LONDON--HISTORY.
Clunn, Harold Philip. The face of
London. A completely new ed. rev.
London, Spring Books [1962] 630 p.
942.1 62-51022
   DA683 .C6 1962 MRR Alc.

Harben, Henry Andrade, A dictionary
of London; London, H. Jenkins
limited, 1918. 2 p. l., vii-xxiv p.,
2 l., 641 p. 18-7018
   DA679 .H3 MRR Alc.

LONDON--HOTELS, TAVERNS, ETC.
Hotels and restaurants in London.
1954- ed. London, British Travel &
Holidays Association. 647.94058 55-
22331
   TX910.G7 H6 MRR Alc Latest edition

LONDON--INDUSTRIES--DIRECTORIES.
South-eastern counties of England
trades' directory, including London,
London surburbs, Brighton and
Reading. Edinburgh, Trades'
Directories. 55-26292
   HF5159.L6 S6 MRR Alc Latest
   Edition

Trades register of London. London,
Trades Register of London, ltd. 57-
34104
   HC258.L6 T7 MRR Alc Latest edition

LONDON--LIBRARIES.
Irwin, Raymond, ed. The libraries of
London, 2d, rev. ed. London,
Library Association, 1961. 332 p.
027.0421 62-1104
   Z791 .L852 1961 MRR Alc.

McColvin, Kenneth Roy. The library
student's London, [London] Greater
London Division, Association of
Assistant Librarians, 1961. 132 p.
020.9421 62-53439
   Z791 .M22 MRR Alc.

LONDON--MANUFACTURES--DIRECTORIES.
The London directory & international
register of commerce. 1973- London.
338/.0025/421 73-642810
   D679 .A1315 MRR Alc Latest edition

LONDON--MAPS.
Bartholomew (John) and Son, ltd.
Reference atlas of Greater London.
7th- ed.; 1940- Edinburgh. map62-
261
   G1819.L7 B3 MRR Atlas Case Latest
     edition

Sugden, Edward Holdsworth, A
topographical dictionary to the works
of Shakespeare and his fellow
dramatists, Manchester, The
University press; London, New York,
etc., Longmans, Green & co., 1925.
xix, 580 p.   25-9716
   PR2892 .S8 MRR Alc.

LONDON--POLITICS AND GOVERNMENT.
The City of London: the official
guide. 6th ed. Cheltenham, London,
Burrow, [1968] 204 p.
914.21/2/0485   68-118308
   DA679 .C5 1968 MRR Alc.

LONDON--REGISTERS.
Kelly's post office London directory.
London, Kelly's Directories.
814.21/0025   72-626566
   DA679 .A14 MRR Alc Latest edition

LONDON--RESTAURANTS, LUNCH ROOMS, ETC.
Hotels and restaurants in London.
1954- ed. London, British Travel &
Holidays Association. 647.94058 55-
22331
   TX910.G7 H6 MRR Alc Latest edition

Where to eat in London, 1968;
London, Regency P., 1968. [i] 241
p. [3/6] 647.95421 76-369012
   TX910.G7 W45 1968 MRR Alc.

LONDON--STREETS.
Bebbington, Gillian. London street
names. London, Batsford, 1972.
viii, 367, 8, 8 p. [£4.50]
914.21/003 73-150423
   DA685.A1 B4 1972 MRR Alc.

Clunn, Harold Philip. The face of
London. A completely new ed. rev.
London, Spring Books [1962] 630 p.
942.1 62-51022
   DA683 .C6 1962 MRR Alc.

Ekwall, Eilert, Street-names of the
city of London. Oxford, Clarendon
Press, 1954. xvi, 209 p. a 55-3054
   DA685.A1 E39 MRR Alc.

London. County Council. Names of
streets and places in the
administrative county of London, 4th
ed.; London, 1955. 870 p.   56-
39305
   DA679 .A18 1955 MRR Alc.

Smith, Al. Dictionary of City of
London street names. Newton Abbot,
David & Charles, 1970. 219 p., 2
fold. plates. [50/-] 914.21/2 74-
503725
   DA685.A1 S62 1970b MRR Alc.

LONDON--THEATERS.
Mander, Raymond. The theatres of
London [2d ed., rev.] London, Hart-
Davis, 1963. 292 p.   64-6934
   PN2596.L6 M35 1963 MRR Alc.

Who's who in the theatre; [1st]-
ed.; 1912- London, I. Pitman.
927.92 12-22402
   PN2012 .W5 MRR Biog Latest edition

**LONDON. CORPORATION OF LONDON RECORDS
OFFICE.**
Jones, Philip E. A guide to the
records in the Corporation of London
Records Office and the Guildhall
Library Muniment Room, London,
English Universities Press [1951]
203 p. 016.352042 51-8290
   CD1067.L65 J6 MRR Alc.

LONDON. GUILDHALL LIBRARY.
Jones, Philip E. A guide to the
records in the Corporation of London
Records Office and the Guildhall
Library Muniment Room, London,
English Universities Press [1951]
203 p. 016.352042 51-8290
   CD1067.L65 J6 MRR Alc.

**LONG-RANGE WEATHER FORECASTS--
PERIODICALS.**
Weather outlook. spring/summer 1969-
New York, Grosset & Dunlap.
551.6/365/0973 71-89524
   QC997 .W4 MRR Alc Latest edition

LONGEVITY.
see also Aging

LOS ANGELES--DESCRIPTION--GUIDE-BOOKS.
Writers' Program. California. Los
Angeles; St. Clair Shores, Mich.,
Somerset Publishers, 1972. liii, 419
p. 917.84/94/045 72-84475
   F869.L83 W74 1972 MRR Alc.

Writers' Program. California. Los
Angeles; a guide to the city and its
environs, 2d ed. New York, Hastings
House [1951] liv, 441 p. 917.9494
51-11827
   F869.L8 W85 1951 MRR Ref Desk.

LOS ANGELES--DIRECTORIES.
Gast, Monte. Getting the best of
L.A. [Los Angeles, Calif.] J. P.
Tarcher [1972] 208 p.
917.94/94/0025 73-189108
   F869.L83 G3 MRR Alc.

LOS ANGELES--POLITICS AND GOVERNMENT.
Rosien, Barbara. Greater Los Angeles
public service guide. 1972-73 ed.
Los Angeles, Public Service
Publications [1972] xvi, 688 p.
[$10.95] 352.0794/93 72-184514
   JS1002.A2 R66 MRR Alc.

**LOS ANGELES CO., CALIF.--POLITICS AND
GOVERNMENT.**
Rosien, Barbara. Greater Los Angeles
public service guide. 1972-73 ed.
Los Angeles, Public Service
Publications [1972] xvi, 688 p.
[$10.95] 352.0794/93 72-184514
   JS1002.A2 R66 MRR Alc.

LOUISIANA.
Louisiana almanac and fact book.
1949- New Orleans. a 50-7997
   F375 .L9435 MRR Alc Latest edition

LOUISIANA--COMMERCE--DIRECTORIES.
Louisiana. State University in New
Orleans. International Marketing
Institute. Louisiana international
trade directory. [1st ed.] New
Orleans [1973] 159 p. 382/.025/763
73-179263
   HF5065.L8 L66 1973 MRR Alc.

**LOUISIANA--DESCRIPTION AND TRAVEL--
GUIDE-BOOKS.**
Writers' program. Louisiana.
Louisiana; a guide to the state, New
York, Hastings house, 1941. xxx, 746
p. incl. illus., maps. 917.63 41-
52389
   F375 .W8 MRR Ref Desk.

**LOUISIANA--GOVERNMENT PUBLICATIONS--
BIBLIOGRAPHY.**
Foote, Lucy Brown, comp.
Bibliography of the official
publications of Louisiana, 1803-1934.
Baton Rouge, La., Hill memorial
library, Louisiana state university,
1942. 4 p. l., [vii]-xiv, 579, [3]
p. 015.763 42-19598
   Z1215 .H67 no. 19 MRR Alc.

LOUISIANA--HISTORY.
Davis, Edwin Adams, Louisiana, a
narrative history. 3d ed. Baton
Rouge, Claitor's Pub. Division, 1971.
xi, 413 p. [$12.50] 917.63/03 73-
159524
   F369 .D24 1971 MRR Alc.

LOUISIANA--HISTORY--CHRONOLOGY.
Louisiana almanac and fact book.
1949- New Orleans. a 50-7997
   F375 .L9435 MRR Alc Latest edition

LOUISIANA--IMPRINTS.
Foote, Lucy Brown, comp.
Bibliography of the official
publications of Louisiana, 1803-1934.
Baton Rouge, La., Hill memorial
library, Louisiana state university,
1942. 4 p. l., [vii]-xiv, 579, [3]
p. 015.763 42-19598
   Z1215 .H67 no. 19 MRR Alc.

LOUISIANA--INDUSTRIES--CLASSIFICATION.
Louisiana. State University in New
Orleans. International Marketing
Institute. Louisiana international
trade directory. [1st ed.] New
Orleans [1973] 159 p. 382/.025/763
73-179263
   HF5065.L8 L66 1973 MRR Alc.

LOUISIANA--REGISTERS.
Louisiana. Dept. of State. Roster of
officials. [New Orleans] 353.9763
37-27684
   JK4730 .A32 MRR Alc Latest edition

Louisiana almanac and fact book.
1949- New Orleans. a 50-7997
   F375 .L9435 MRR Alc Latest edition

LOUISIANA--STATISTICS.
Louisiana. State University in New
Orleans. Division of Business and
Economic Research. Statistical
abstract of Louisiana. 1st- 1965-
New Orleans. 65-65408
   HA405.L6 L6 MRR Alc Latest edition

Louisiana almanac and fact book.
1949- New Orleans. a 50-7997
   F375 .L9435 MRR Alc Latest edition

LOUISIANA PURCHASE--BIBLIOGRAPHY.
Rader, Jesse Lee, South of forty,
[1st ed.] Norman, Univ. of Oklahoma
Press, 1947. xi, 336 p. 016.976
47-5360
   Z1251.S83 R3 MRR Alc.

**LOUISIANA PURCHASE--BIBLIOGRAPHY--
CATALOGS.**
United States. Library of Congress.
Louisiana Purchase sesquicentennial,
1803-1953, Washington, 1953. v, 47
p. 016.97346 53-60041
   Z663.15 .L6 MRR Alc.

**LOUISIANA PURCHASE--CENTENNIAL
CELEBRATIONS, ETC.**
United States. Library of Congress.
Louisiana Purchase sesquicentennial,
1803-1953, Washington, 1953. v, 47
p. 016.97346 53-60041
   Z663.15 .L6 MRR Alc.

LOW INCOME HOUSING
see Housing

LOW TEMPERATURE ENGINEERING.
see also Refrigeration and
refrigerating machinery

**LOWER HUTT, N.Z.--INDUSTRIES--
DIRECTORIES.**
Universal business directory for
Wellington, Hutt [and] Petone.
Auckland, Universal Business
Directories. 53-30822
   HC623.W45 U5 MRR Alc Latest
     edition

LÜBECK--DIRECTORIES.
Lübecker Adressbuch. Lübeck,
M.Schmidt-Römhild. 56-38099
Began publication in 1798.
   DD901.L84 L8 MRR Alc Latest
     edition

**LUBETZKY, SEYMOUR. CODE OF CATALOGING
RULES.**
United States. Library of Congress.
Descriptive Cataloging Division.
Synoptic table of rules:
[Washington] 1958. iii, 46 p.
025.32 59-64161
   Z695 .U4737 MRR Alc.

LUCANUS, MARCUS ANNAEUS--CONCORDANCES.
Deferrari, Roy Joseph, A concordance
of Lucan, Washington, The Catholic
university of America press, 1940.
vii, 602 p. 873.2 40-31224
   PA6480 .D4 MRR Alc.

**LUCE, STEPHEN BLEECKER, 1827-1917--
MANUSCRIPTS.**
United States. Library of Congress.
Manuscript Division. David Foote
Sellers, Stephen B. Luce; a register
of their papers in the Library of
Congress. Washington, Library of
Congress, 1969. 7, 8 l.
016.3593/31/0924   79-601361
   Z663.34 .S43 MRR Alc.

LUCERNE--DIRECTORIES.
Luzerner Adressbuch für Stadt und
Kanton Luzern. Luzern, Buchdr.
Keller. 42-31507
   DQ509.2 .L8 MRR Alc Latest edition

LUCERNE (CANTON)--DIRECTORIES.
Luzerner Adressbuch für Stadt und
Kanton Luzern. Luzern, Buchdr.
Keller. 42-31507
   DQ509.2 .L8 MRR Alc Latest edition

LUDICROUS, THE
see Wit and humor

LUGGAGE--DIRECTORIES.
Sources of supply directory [for
manufacturers of luggage & leather
goods] New York, Haire Pub. Co.
685.5058 48-31663
   TS945 .L8 MRR Alc Latest edition

**LUGGAGE INDUSTRY--UNITED STATES--
DIRECTORIES.**
Sources of supply directory [for
manufacturers of luggage & leather
goods] New York, Haire Pub. Co.
685.5058 48-31663
   TS945 .L8 MRR Alc Latest edition

LUMBER.
see also Sawmills

see also Timber

see also Woodwork

LUMBER--DICTIONARIES--POLYGLOT.
Elsevier's wood dictionary in seven
languages: Amsterdam, New York,
Elsevier Pub. Co., 1964- v.
634.903 64-14178
   SD431 .E4 MRR Alc.

LUMBER TRADE.
see also Woodwork

Organization for Economic Cooperation
and Development. Bois tropicaux.
[Paris, 1969] 179 p. [$3.20] 74-
458866
   HD9750.5 .O68 1969 MRR Alc.

LUMBER TRADE--DICTIONARIES--POLYGLOT.
Elsevier's wood dictionary in seven
languages: Amsterdam, New York,
Elsevier Pub. Co., 1964- v.
634.903 64-14178
   SD431 .E4 MRR Alc.

LUMBER TRADE--DIRECTORIES.
Timber trades directory, London, The
Timber trades journal office. 338.1
40-20668
   HD9761.3 .T5 MRR Alc Latest
     edition

LUMBER TRADE--STATISTICS.
Organization for Economic Cooperation
and Development. Bois tropicaux.
[Paris, 1969] 179 p. [$3.20] 74-
458866
HD9750.5 .O68 1969 MRR Alc.

Yearbook of forest products
statistics. 1947- Rome, [etc.] Food
and Agriculture Organization of the
United Nations. 338.17498 48-28149
HD9750.4 .Y4 MRR Alc Latest
edition

LUMBER TRADE--CANADA--YEARBOOKS.
Lumber requirements of factory
consumers in the United States &
Canada. 10th- ed.; 1959- Memphis,
Lumber Requirements Co.
338.1/7/490873 72-622539
HD9752.L8 MRR Alc Latest edition

LUMBER TRADE--FRANCE--DIRECTORIES.
France-bois. [Paris, Editions A. R.
de Chapassol] 674.058 46-39212
Fondé en 1922.
HD9762.3 .F7 MRR Alc Latest
edition

LUMBER TRADE--GREAT BRITAIN--
DIRECTORIES.
Timber trades directory. London, The
Timber trades journal office. 338.1
40-20668
HD9761.3 .T5 MRR Alc Latest
edition

LUMBER TRADE--UNITED STATES--CREDIT
GUIDES.
The Lumbermen's national red book
service reference book. Chicago,
Lumbermen's Credit Association.
338.47674 02-19114
"Established 1876."
HF5585.L8 L7 MRR Alc Latest
edition

LUMBER TRADE--UNITED STATES--
DIRECTORIES.
Directory: home centers & hardware
chains, auto supply chains. 1974-
[New York, Business Guides, inc.]
[$59.00] 381/.45/629202573 74-
647308
HD9745.U4 D485 MRR Alc Latest
edition

Directory of the forest products
industry. San Francisco [etc.] M.
Freeman Publications [etc.] 21-10771
TS803 .D5 Sci RR Latest edition /
MRR Alc Latest edition

Dun and Bradstreet, inc. Reference
book: lumber and wood products
industries. [spring] 1968- New
York. 338.7/67/4002573 72-489
HD9753 .D85 MRR Alc Latest edition

Lumber requirements of factory
consumers in the United States &
Canada. 10th- ed.; 1959- Memphis,
Lumber Requirements Co.
338.1/7/490873 72-622539
HD9752.L8 MRR Alc Latest edition

LUMBER TRADE--UNITED STATES--YEARBOOKS.
Lumber requirements of factory
consumers in the United States &
Canada. 10th- ed.; 1959- Memphis,
Lumber Requirements Co.
338.1/7/490873 72-622539
HD9752.L8 MRR Alc Latest edition

LUMBERING--TERMINOLOGY.
McCulloch, Walter Fraser. Woods
words; [Portland] Oregon Historical
Society, 1958. vi, 219 p. 427.9
58-63667
PE3727.L8 M3 MRR Alc.

LUMBERING--UNITED STATES--DIRECTORIES.
Directory of the forest products
industry. San Francisco [etc.] M.
Freeman Publications [etc.] 21-10771
TS803 .D5 Sci RR Latest edition /
MRR Alc Latest edition

LUMBERMEN--LANGUAGE (NEW WORDS, SLANG,
ETC.)
McCulloch, Walter Fraser. Woods
words; [Portland] Oregon Historical
Society, 1958. vi, 219 p. 427.9
58-63667
PE3727.L8 M3 MRR Alc.

LUNAR ORBIT RENDEZVOUS
see Project Apollo

LUTHER, MARTIN, 1483-1546--BIBLIOGRAPHY.
Benzing, Josef. Lutherbibliographie.
Baden-Baden, Heitz, 1966. xl, 512
p. [DM 170.00 (unb. DM 100.00)]
016.284/1/0924 68-73875
Z8528 .B45 MRR Alc.

LUTHER, MARTIN, 1483-1546--
DICTIONARIES, INDEXES, ETC.
Luther, Martin. What Luther says.
Saint Louis, Concordia Pub. House
[c1959] 3 v. (xxvi, 1667 p.)
230.41 57-8854
BR324 .P6 MRR Alc.

LUTHERAN CHURCH--DICTIONARIES.
Bodensieck, Julius, ed. The
encyclopedia of the Lutheran Church.
Minneapolis, Augsburg Pub. House
[1965] 3 v. (xxii, 2575 p.)
284.103 64-21500
BX8007 .B6 MRR Alc.

The Concordia cyclopedia; St. Louis,
Concordia Pub. House, 1927. iv, 848
p. 27-13940
BX8007 .C6 MRR Alc.

LUTHERAN CHURCH--DOCTRINAL AND
CONTROVERSIAL WORKS.
Mayer, Frederick Emanuel. The
religious bodies of America. 4th
ed.; rev. Saint Louis, Concordia
Pub. House, 1961. xiii, 598 p. 280
61-15535
BR516.5 .M3 1961 MRR Alc.

LUTHERAN CHURCH--HISTORY.
Lutheran churches of the world.
Minneapolis, Augsburg Pub. House
[1957] x, 333 p. 284.1 57-9727
BX8018 .L78 MRR Alc.

LUTHERAN CHURCH--YEARBOOKS.
American Lutheran Church (1961-
Yearbook. 1961- Minneapolis,
Augsburg Pub. House. 65-5070
BX8008 .A542 MRR Alc Latest
edition

LUTHERAN CHURCH IN AMERICA--STATISTICS.
Lutheran Church in America.
Yearbook. 1963- Philadelphia, Board
of Publication of the Lutheran Church
in America. 63-25562
BX8048.2 .A35 MRR Alc Latest
edition

LUTHERAN CHURCH IN AMERICA--YEARBOOKS.
Lutheran Church in America.
Yearbook. 1963- Philadelphia, Board
of Publication of the Lutheran Church
in America. 63-25562
BX8048.2 .A35 MRR Alc Latest
edition

LUTHERAN CHURCH IN THE UNITED STATES--
HISTORY.
Wentz, Abdel Ross. A basic history
of Lutheranism in America. Rev. ed.
Philadelphia, Fortress Press [1964]
viii, 439 p. 284.173 64-12996
BX8041 .W38 1964 MRR Alc.

LUXEMBURG--BIOGRAPHY.
Who's who in Belgium and Grand Duchy
of Luxembourg. [1st]- ed.; 1957/58-
Brussels, Intercontinental Book &
Pub. Co. 920.0493 59-3017
DH513 .W45 MRR Biog Latest edition

LUXEMBURG--DESCRIPTION AND TRAVEL--
GUIDE-BOOKS.
Belgique, Luxembourg. [8. éd.]
Paris, Hachette, 1971. 730 p.
[46.00F] 74-24119
DH416 .B4 1971 MRR Alc.

Benelux. Paris [etc.] Pneu Michelin,
Services de tourisme [etc.] 56-50955
GV1025.B43 B4 MRR Alc Latest
edition

Fodor's Belgium and Luxembourg. 1969-
New York, D. McKay Co. 914.93/04/4
72-622746
DH416 .B43 MRR Alc Latest edition

LUXEMBURG--GAZETTEERS.
United States. Office of Geography.
Luxembourg; Washington, 1951. 35 p.
76-10007
DH903 .U5 MRR Alc.

LUXEMBURG--STATISTICS.
Luxemburg. Service central de la
statistique et des etudes
economiques. Annuaire statistique
du Luxembourg. 1964- [Luxembourg]
72-627048
HA1411 .A4 MRR Alc Latest edition

LYNCHING--BIBLIOGRAPHY.
Williams, Daniel T. Eight Negro
bibliographies. New York, Kraus
Reprint Co., 1970. 1 v. (various
pagings) 016.301451/96/073 71-
107893
Z1361.N39 W54 MRR Alc.

LYNCHING--STATISTICS.
Williams, Daniel T. Eight Negro
bibliographies. New York, Kraus
Reprint Co., 1970. 1 v. (various
pagings) 016.301451/96/073 71-
107893
Z1361.N39 W54 MRR Alc.

LYRIC DRAMA
see Opera

LYRIC POETRY.
Edmonds, John Maxwell, ed. and tr.
Elegy and iambus. London, W.
Heinemann, ltd.; New York, G. P.
Putnam's sons, 1931. 2 v. 881.08
mrr01-26
PA3611.A14 1931d MRR Alc.

Edmonds, John Maxwell, ed. and tr.
Lyra graeca; London, W. Heinemann;
Cambridge, Mass., Harvard University
Press, 1927-1934 [v. 1, 1934] 3 v.
mrr01-23
PA3611.A15 1927d MRR Alc.

MACDOWELL, EDWARD ALEXANDER, 1861-1908--
BIBLIOGRAPHY.
United States. Library of Congress.
Music division. Catalogue of first
editions of Edward MacDowell (1861-
1908) Washington, Govt. print. off.,
1917. 89 p. 17-26002
Z663.37.M2 MRR Alc.

MACHINE-READABLE BIBLIOGRAPHIC DATA--
CATALOGS.
Schneider, John Hoke. Survey of
commercially available computer-
readable bibliographic data bases.
[Washington] American Society for
Information Science [1973] 181 p.
029.7/53/02573 72-97793
Z699.22 .S35 MRR Alc.

MACHINE-READABLE BIBLIOGRAPHIC DATA--
STANDARDS.
United States. Library of Congress.
Marc Development Office. Books: a
MARC format; 5th ed. Washington
[for sale by the Supt. of Docs., U.S.
Govt. Print. Off.] 1972. 106 p.
[$1.00] 025.3/0285 73-39649
Z663.757 .B66 1972a MRR Alc.

United States. Library of Congress.
Marc Development Office.
Manuscripts: a MARC format;
Washington, Library of Congress; for
sale by the Supt. of Docs., U.S.
Govt. Print. Off., 1973. v, 47 p.
[$0.80] 025.3/4/102854 72-13497
Z663.757 .M36 MRR Alc.

MACHINE-SHOP PRACTICE--DICTIONARIES.
Colvin, Fred Herbert. The machinist
dictionary; New York, Simmons-
Boardman Pub. Corp. [c1956] vi, 496
p. 621.03 55-10428
TJ9 .C56 MRR Alc.

Freeman, Henry George. Wörterbuch
Werkzeuge; 2. Aufl. Essen, W.
Girardet [1960] 658 p. 621.7503
61-1734
TJ9 .F72 1960 MRR Alc.

MACHINE-SHOP PRACTICE--DICTIONARIES--
GERMAN.
Freeman, Henry George. Wörterbuch
Werkzeuge; 2. Aufl. Essen, W.
Girardet [1960] 658 p. 621.7503
61-1734
TJ9 .F72 1960 MRR Alc.

MACHINE THEORY.
see also Electronic data processing

MACHINE-TOOLS--DIRECTORIES.
Hitchcock's machine and tool
directory and specifications catalog.
v. 18- 1968- [Wheaton, Ill.,
Hitchcock Pub. Co.] 621.9/02/02573
74-618600
TJ1180 .A1M26 MRR Alc Latest
edition / Sci RR Latest edition

MACHINE TRANSLATING--BIBLIOGRAPHY.
Balz, Charles F. Literature on
information retrieval and machine
translation. [White Plains, N.Y.]
International Business Machines
Corp., 1962. 117 p. 63-2625
Z699.2 .B3 MRR Alc.

Service Bureau Corporation.
Literature on information retrieval
and machine translation; 2d ed.
[New York] 1959. 38 p. 016.01078
60-3612
Z699.2 .S4 1959 MRR Alc.

MACHINE TRANSLATING--PERIODICALS.
Current research and development in
scientific documentation. July 1957-
1969. Washington. 010.78 58-2427
Z699.5.S3 C8 Sci RR Latest edition
/ MRR Alc Partial set

MACHINERY.
Bibliographisches Institut A.G.,
Mannheim. The way things work; New
York, Simon and Schuster [1967] 590
p. 600 67-27972
T47 .B552 MRR Alc.

MACHINERY--CATALOGS.
Mechanical engineers' catalog and
product directory. 1962- New York,
American Society of Mechanical
Engineers, United Engineering Center.
338.4/7/62102573 72-621604
TJ168 .A2 MRR Alc Latest edition /
Sci RR Latest edition

MACHINERY--DICTIONARIES.
Colvin, Fred Herbert. The machinist
dictionary; New York, Simmons-
Boardman Pub. Corp. [c1956] vi, 496
p. 621.03 55-10428
TJ9 .C56 MRR Alc.

MACHINERY--DICTIONARIES. (Cont.)
Palestrant, Simon S., Practical
pictorial guide to mechanisms and
machines. New York, University Books
[1956] 256 p.   621.03 56-13016
   TJ9 .P3 1856 MRR Alc.

MACHINERY--TRADE AND MANUFACTURE--
DIRECTORIES.
Directory of manufacturers agents
serving the field of energy systems
engineering. New York, Power.
381/.45/62102573 66-1052
   HD9705.U6 P6 MRR Alc Latest
   edition

Mechanical engineers' catalog and
product directory. 1962- New York,
American Society of Mechanical
Engineers. United Engineering Center.
338.4/7/62102573   72-621604
   TJ168 .A2 MRR Alc Latest edition /
   Sci RR Latest edition

Wer baut Maschinen. Darmstadt,
Hoppenstedt. 53-30932
   TJ1170 .W4 MRR Alc Latest edition

MACHINERY--TRADE AND MANUFACTURE--
GERMANY--DIRECTORIES.
Wer baut Maschinen. Darmstadt,
Hoppenstedt. 53-30932
   TJ1170 .W4 MRR Alc Latest edition

MACHINERY--TRADE AND MANUFACTURE--GREAT
BRITAIN--DIRECTORIES.
Machinery's annual buyers' guide.
[London, Machinery Pub. Co.]
338.4/7/621802542 72-626508
   TJ13.G7 M3 MRR Alc Latest edition

MACHINERY--TRADE AND MANUFACTURE--
UNITED STATES.
A E D handbook. Oak Brook, Ill.
[etc.] Associated Equipment
Distributors. 62-45431
   HD9705.U6 A6 MRR Alc Latest
   edition

MADAGASCAR.
Nelson, Harold D. Area handbook for
the Malagasy Republic. 1st ed.
[Washington, For sale by the Supt. of
Docs., U.S. Govt. Print. Off.] 1973.
xiv, 327 p. [$3.85] 916.9/1/035
73-600012
   DT469.M26 N4 MRR Alc.

MADAGASCAR--BIBLIOGRAPHY.
International African Institute.
South-east Central Africa and
Madagascar: general,
ethnography/sociology, linguistics,
London, 1961. v, 53 l.   016.91676
61-65578
   Z3516 .I53 MRR Alc.

MADAGASCAR--COMMERCE--DIRECTORIES.
Malagasy Republic. Annuaire
national. [Strasbourg, Impr.
strasbourgeoise] 67-58848
   DT469.M21 M3 MRR Alc Latest
   edition

MADAGASCAR--DESCRIPTION AND TRAVEL--
GAZETTEERS.
United States, Office of Geography.
Madagascar, Reunion, and the Comoro
Islands; official standard names
approved by the United States Board
on Geographic Names. Washington,
1955. 498 p.   55-61720
   DT469.M24 U5 MRR Alc.

MADAGASCAR--DIRECTORIES.
Malagasy Republic. Annuaire
national. [Strasbourg, Impr.
strasbourgeoise] 67-59848
   DT469.M21 M3 MRR Alc Latest
   edition

MADAGASCAR--GOVERNMENT PUBLICATIONS--
BIBLIOGRAPHY.
United States. Library of Congress.
African Section. Madagascar and
adjacent islands; Washington,
General Reference and Bibliography
Division, Reference Department,
Library of Congress;[for sale by the
Superintendent of Documents, U.S.
Govt. Print. Off.] 1965. xiii, 58 p.
65-61703
   Z663.285 .M3 MRR Alc.

MADISON, JAMES, PRES. U.S., 1751-1836.
Brant, Irving, James Madison.
Indianapolis, Bobbs-Merrill [1941-61]
6 v.   920.173 41-19278
   E342 .B7 MRR Alc.

MADRAS--DIRECTORIES.
The Asylum Press almanack and
commercial directory. Madras, Sayee
Press [etc.] sa 63-1638
Began publication in 1801.
   DS405 .A85 MRR Alc Latest edition

MAGAZINES
see Periodicals

MAGIC.
see also Conjuring

see also Occult sciences

Frazer, James George, Sir,
Aftermath; London, Macmillan and
co., limited, 1936. xx, 494 p.   291
37-2300
   BL310 .F715 1936 MRR Alc.

[Frazer, James George Sir,] The
golden bough; 3d ed. [New York, The 291
Macmillan company, 1935] 12 v.
35-35398
   BL310 .F7 1935 MRR Alc.

MAGIC--HISTORY.
Christopher, Milbourne. The
illustrated history of magic. New
York, Crowell [1973] 452 p.
[$14.95]   793.8 73-10390
   GV1543 .C45 MRR Alc.

MAGISTRATES
see Judges

MAIL-ORDER BUSINESS.
see also Sales letters

Hart, Harold H., Catalog of the
unusual New York, Hart Pub. Co.
[1973] 351 p. [$6.95] 380.1/025
73-80023
   HF1041 .H297 MRR Alc.

MAIL-ORDER BUSINESS--DIRECTORIES.
De La Iglesia, Maria Elena. The
catalogue of catalogues; [1st ed.]
New York, Random House [1973] 191 p.
[$10.00]   380.1/025   72-1817
   HF5466 .D45 MRR Alc.

Mail order business directory. New
York, B. Klein. 55-43557
   HF5466 .M28 MRR Alc Latest edition

MAIL-ORDER BUSINESS--UNITED STATES--
DIRECTORIES.
O'Callaghan, Dorothy. Mail order
USA; [2d ed. Washington, 1973] 141
p. [$3.00] 381   73-181593
   HF5466 .O25 1973 MRR Alc.

MAIL-ORDER BUSINSS--DIRECTORIES.
Lyons, Delphine C. The whole world
catalog [New York] Quadrangle [1973]
167 p. [$5.00]   380.1/025 73-
79934
   HF5466 .L9 1973 MRR Alc.

MAIL SERVICE
see Postal service

MAILING LISTS--UNITED STATES--
DIRECTORIES.
Directory of mailing lists. 1967-
[New York] M. W. Lads Pub. Co.
659.13/3 67-5375
   HF5863 .D5 MRR Alc Latest edition

MAINE.
Maine League of Historical Societies
and Museums. Maine, a guide "down
east." 2d ed. Rockland, Me.,
Courier-Gazette, 1970. xxiv, 510 p.
[$6.50] 917.41/03 70-24552
   F17.3 .M3 1970 MRR Ref Desk.

MAINE--BIBLIOGRAPHY--CATALOGS.
United States. Library of Congress.
Maine: the sesquicentennial of
statehood; Washington; [For sale by
the Supt. of Docs., U.S. Govt. Print.
Off.] 1970 [i.e. 1971] 86 p.
[$1.00] 016.91741/03 72-608482
   Z663.15.A6M2 MRR Alc.

MAINE--CENTENNIAL CELEBRATIONS, ETC.
United States. Library of Congress.
Maine: the sesquicentennial of
statehood; Washington; [For sale by
the Supt. of Docs., U.S. Govt. Print.
Off.] 1970 [i.e. 1971] 86 p.
[$1.00] 016.91741/03 72-608482
   Z663.15.A6M2 MRR Alc.

MAINE--COMMERCE--DIRECTORIES.
Maine. Maine register, state year-
book and legislative manual. 1870-
Portland. 99-4262
   JK2831 date MRR Alc Latest
   edition

MAINE--DESCRIPTION AND TRAVEL--GUIDE-
BOOKS.
Maine League of Historical Societies
and Museums. Maine, a guide "down
east." 2d ed. Rockland, Me.,
Courier-Gazette, 1970. xxiv, 510 p.
[$6.50] 917.41/03 70-24552
   F17.3 .M3 1970 MRR Ref Desk.

MAINE--DIRECTORIES.
Maine. Maine register, state year-
book and legislative manual. 1870-
Portland. 99-4262
   JK2831 date MRR Alc Latest
   edition

MAINE--ECONOMIC CONDITIONS.
Maine pocket data book. 1969-
[Augusta, Maine Dept. of Economic
Development. Planning, Research and
Program Assistance Division] 317.41
72-629891
   HA414 .A3 MRR Alc Latest edition

MAINE--MANUFACTURES--DIRECTORIES.
Directory of New England
manufacturers. Boston, Mass., G. D.
Hall, inc. 338.40974 36-5085
   HD9723 .D45 Sci RR Latest edition
   / MRR Alc Latest edition

MAINE--REGISTERS.
Maine. Maine register, state year-
book and legislative manual. 1870-
Portland. 99-4262
   JK2831 date MRR Alc Latest
   edition

MAINE--STATISTICS.
The Maine handbook, a statistical
abstract. 1968- Augusta, Maine
Dept. of Economic Development.
317.41 75-625377
   HA411 .A3 MRR Alc Latest edition

Maine pocket data book. 1969-
[Augusta, Maine Dept. of Economic
Development. Planning, Research and
Program Assistance Division] 317.41
72-629891
   HA414 .A3 MRR Alc Latest edition

MAINTENANCE.
see also Automobiles--Maintenance and
repair

MAJOR ORDERS
see Clergy

MAJORITIES
see also Minorities

MAKE-UP, THEATRICAL.
Liszt, Rudolph G. The last word in
make-up. [Rev.] New York,
Dramatists Play Service [1959] 118
p. 792.027 59-1768
   PN2068 .L5 1959 MRR Alc.

MAKE-UP (COSMETICS)
see Cosmetics

MALAWI.
Pike, John G. Malawi; a political
and economic history New York, F. A.
Praeger [1968] viii, 248 p.
916.89/7 68-21904
   DT858 .P53 MRR Alc.

MALAWI--DIRECTORIES.
The Rhodesia-Zambia-Malawi directory
(including Botswana and Mocambique).
Bulawayo, Publications (Central
Africa) [etc.] 916.89/0025 38-1460

"First published in 1910."
   DT947 .R5 MRR Alc Latest edition

MALAWI--GAZETTEERS.
United States. Geographic Names
Division. Malawi; offical standard
names approved by the U.S. Board on
Geographic Names. Washington, 1970.
iii, 161 p. 916.89/7/003 70-607550

   DT857.5 .U55 MRR Alc.

MALAWI--GOVERNMENT PUBLICATIONS--
BIBLIOGRAPHY.
United States. Library of Congress.
African Section. The Rhodesias and
Nyasaland; Washington, General
Reference and Bibliography Division,
Reference Dept., Library of Congress:
[for sale by the Superintendent of
Documents, U.S. Govt. Print. Off.]
1965. xv, 285 p.   65-60089
   Z663.285 .R5 MRR Alc.

MALAWI--MANUFACTURES--DIRECTORIES.
The A R N I register of
manufacturers. 1959- Salisbury,
Association of Rhodesian Industries.
[etc.] 66-47368
   HD9737.R5 A2 MRR Alc Latest
   edition

MALAY LANGUAGE--DICTIONARIES--ENGLISH.
Winstedt, Richard Olof, Sir, A
practical modern Malay-English
dictionary. 2d ed.; rev. and enl.
Singapore, Marican [1957] 203 p.
499.22132 59-37520
   PL5125 .W69 1957 MRR Alc.

MALAY PENINSULA--COMMERCE--DIRECTORIES.
The Straits times directory of
Malaysia. [Singapore] 53-30515
   HF5239.M36 S8 MRR Alc Latest
   edition

MALAY PENINSULA--HISTORY.
Moorhead, Francis Joseph. A history
of Malaya and her neighbours [Kuala
Lumpur] Longmans of Malaysia [1965]
2 v.   68-34730
   DS596 .M62 MRR Alc.

MALAYA--BIBLIOGRAPHY.
Cheeseman, Harold Ambrose Robinson.
Bibliography of Malaya, London, New
York, Published for the British
Association of Malaya by Longmans,
Green [1959] xi, 234 p. 016.9191
60-27688
   Z3246 .C5 MRR Alc.

MALAYA--HISTORY.
Kennedy, Joseph, A history of
Malaya, A.D. 1400-1959. London,
Macmillan; New York. St Martin's
Press, 1962. 311 p.   959.5 62-4230

     DS596 .K4 1962 MRR Alc.

MALAYALAM LANGUAGE--DICTIONARIES--
ENGLISH.
Gundert, Hermann, A Malayalam and
English dictionary, Mangalore, C.
Stolz; London, Trübner & co.; [etc.,
etc.] 1872. xviii, 1116 p.   03-
18077
     PL4716 .G8 MRR Alc.

MALAYSIA.
Maday, Bela C. Area handbook for
Malaysia and Singapore. Washington,
For sale by the Supt. of Docs., U.S.
Govt. Print. Off., 1965 [i.e. 1966]
xii, 745 p. [2.75]   915.95035 66-
61930
     DS592 .M16 MRR Alc.

MALAYSIA--BIBLIOGRAPHY.
Pelzer, Karl Josef, West Malaysia
and Singapore: a selected
bibliography. New Haven, Human
Relations Area Files Press, 1971.
vi, 394 p.   016.91595/1/03 72-87853

     Z3246 .P4 MRR Alc.

United States. Library of Congress.
Orientalia Division. Southeast Asia
subject catalog. Boston, G. K. Hall,
1972- v.   016.9159/03 72-5257
     Z3221 .U525 MRR Alc (Dk 33)

MALAYSIA--BIOGRAPHY.
The Who's who, Malaysia and
Singapore. Kuala Lumpur, J. V.
Morais.   820/.0595 72-627182
     DS595.5 .L4 MRR Biog Latest
     edition

MALAYSIA--COMMERCE--DIRECTORIES.
The Straits times directory of
Malaysia. [Singapore] 53-30515
     HF5239.M36 S8 MRR Alc Latest
     edition

MALAYSIA--HISTORY.
Gullick, J. M. Malaysia, London,
Benn, 1969. 304 p. [45/-]   959.5
79-387734
     DS596 .G83 MRR Alc.

MALAYSIA--IMPRINTS.
United States. Library of Congress.
Library of Congress Office, Djakarta.
Accessions list, Indonesia,
Malaysia, Singapore, and Brunei. v.
1-   July 1964- Djakarta. sa 66-444
     Z663.767.I6 A25 MRR Alc   MRR Alc
     Full set

United States. Library of Congress.
Library of Congress Office, Djakarta.
Accessions list, Indonesia,
Malaysia, Singapore, and Brunei.
Cumulative list of serials. Jan.
1964/Sept. 1966-1964/68. Djakarta.
74-643581
     Z663.767.I6 A252 MRR Alc   MRR Alc
     Full set

MALAYSIA--PERIODICALS--INDEXES.
Pelzer, Karl Josef, West Malaysia
and Singapore: a selected
bibliography. New Haven, Human
Relations Area Files Press, 1971.
vi, 394 p.   016.91595/1/03 72-87853

     Z3246 .P4 MRR Alc.

MALAYSIA--POLITICS AND GOVERNMENT.
Gullick, J. M. Malaysia, London,
Benn, 1969. 304 p. [45/-]   959.5
79-387734
     DS596 .G83 MRR Alc.

MALAYSIA--REGISTERS.
The Straits times directory of
Malaysia. [Singapore] 53-30515
     HF5239.M36 S8 MRR Alc Latest
     edition

MALAYSIA--YEARBOOKS.
Malaysia. Official year book. v. 1-
1961- Kuala Lumpur, Printed at the
Govt. Press.   915.95/005 62-41053
     DS591.A27 MRR Alc Latest edition

MALI--GAZETTEERS.
United States. Office of Geography.
Mali; official standard names
approved by the United States Board
on Geographic Names. Washington
[U.S. Govt. Print. Off.] 1965. v,
263 p.   916.62 66-60437
     DT551.2 .U5 MRR Alc.

MALTA.
The Malta year book. 1953- St.
Julian's, St. Michael's College
Publications [etc.] 314.585 59-
47535
     DG987 .M33 MRR Alc Latest edition

MALTA--BIOGRAPHY.
Malta who's who. 1st-   1964-
Valetta, Progress Press Co. 65-1547

     DG988 .M3 MRR Biog Latest edition

MALTA--COMMERCE--DIRECTORIES.
Contact Mediterranean directory:
Malta, Libya, Sicily. 1966-
Valletta, Associated Publicity
Services.   380/.09/1822 67-115040
     HC244.5.A1 C6 MRR Alc Latest
     edition

MALTA--DESCRIPTION AND TRAVEL--GUIDE-
BOOKS.
Balls, Bryan. Traveller's guide to
Malta; Valleta, T. Cox, 1969] 112
p.   914.58/5/04 78-5406
     DG989 .B23 MRR Alc.

MALTA--ECONOMIC CONDITIONS--PERIODICALS.
Contact Mediterranean directory:
Malta, Libya, Sicily. 1966-
Valletta, Associated Publicity
Services.   380/.09/1822 67-115040
     HC244.5.A1 C6 MRR Alc Latest
     edition

MAMMALS.
Grzimek, Bernhard. Grzimek's animal
life encyclopedia. New York, Van
Nostrand Reinhold Co. [1972- v. 13,
1972] v.   [$29.95 per vol.] 591
79-183178
     QL3 .G7813 MRR Alc.

Morris, Desmond. The mammals; [1st
ed.] New York, Harper & Row [1965]
448 p.   599 65-20508
     QL703 .M68 1965 MRR Alc.

Walker, Ernest Pillsbury, Mammals of
the world. Revision for 2d ed. by
John L. Paradiso. Baltimore, Johns
Hopkins Press, 1968- v.   599 67-
26860
     QL703 .W222 MRR Alc.

MAMMALS--BIBLIOGRAPHY.
Walker, Ernest Pillsbury, Mammals of
the world. Revision for 2d ed. by
John L. Paradiso. Baltimore, Johns
Hopkins Press, 1968- v.   599 67-
26860
     QL703 .W222 MRR Alc.

MAMMALS--DICTIONARIES.
Wender, Leo. Animal encyclopaedia;
[1st American ed.] New York, Oxford
University Press, 1949 [c1947] 266
p.   599.03 49-6161
     QL703 .W45 1949 MRR Alc.

MAMMALS--ANTILLES.
Hall, Eugene Raymond, The mammals of
North America New York, Ronald Press
Co. [1959] 2 v.   599.097 58-5832
     QL715 .H15 MRR Alc.

MAMMALS--NORTH AMERICA.
Hall, Eugene Raymond, The mammals of
North America New York, Ronald Press
Co. [1959] 2 v.   599.097 58-5832
     QL715 .H15 MRR Alc.

Rue, Leonard Lee. Sportsman's guide
to game animals; New York, Outdoor
Life Books [1968] 655 p. 599/.097
68-12140
     QL715 .R83 MRR Alc.

MAN, ISLE OF--POLITICS AND GOVERNMENT--
YEARBOOKS.
N.M.P. Manx year book. Douglas, I.
o. M., Norris Modern Press. 354.4289
52-16110
     JN1573.M3 N2 MRR Alc Latest
     edition

MAN.
     see also Anthropology

     see also Ethnology

MAN--INFLUENCE OF ENVIRONMENT.
     see also Anthropo-geography

Rand McNally and Company. The earth
and man; New York [1972]   439 p.
[$35.00]   912 70-654432
     G1019 .R26 1972 MRR Alc Atlas.

MAN--INFLUENCE ON NATURE.
     see also Environmental policy

     see also Pollution

Nobile, Philip, comp. The complete
ecology fact book. [1st ed.] Garden
City, N.Y., Doubleday 1972. xx, 472
p. [$10.00]   301.31 73-175364
     TD174 .N6 MRR Alc.

MAN--INFLUENCE ON NATURE--BIBLIOGRAPHY.
Morrison, Denton E. Environment:
Washington, Office of Research and
Monitoring, U.S. Environmental
Protection Agency; for sale by the
Supt. of Docs., U.S. Govt. Print.
Off., 1974, c1973. vii, 860 p.
[$7.45]   016.3 74-601576
     Z7161 .M56 1974 MRR Alc.

Woodrow Wilson International Center
for Scholars. The human environment.
Washington, 1972- 2 v.   [$5.00 per
vol.]   016.30131 72-601602
     Z5118.A5 W66 1972 MRR Alc.

MAN--MIGRATIONS.
     see also Migration, Internal

MAN, PREHISTORIC.
Brace, C. Loring. The stages of
human evolution; Englewood Cliffs,
N.J., Prentice-Hall [1967] xi, 116
p.   573/.8 67-22426
     GN741 .B68 MRR Alc.

Childe, Vere Gordon, The dawn of
European civilization. [6th ed.
rev.] London, Routledge & Paul
[1957] xiii, 368 p.   901 58-872
     D65 .C5 1957 MRR Alc.

Day, Michael H. Guide to fossil man;
2nd ed. London, Cassell, 1967 [i.
e. 1968] xvi, 289 p. [42/-]
569/.9 71-375416
     GN75.A2 D3 1968 MRR Alc.

Hole, Frank. An introduction to
prehistoric archeology New York,
Holt, Rinehart and Winston [1965] x,
306 p.   571 65-11842
     CC165 .H64 MRR Alc.

Howells, William White, Back of
history; Rev. ed. Garden City,
N.Y., Doubleday [1963] 384 p.   571
63-11257
     GN743 .H78 1963 MRR Alc.

Koenigswald, Gustav Heinrich Ralph
von, Meeting prehistoric man. New
York, Harper [c1956] 216 p.   573.7
56-8769
     GN75.A2 K63 1956a MRR Alc.

Mellersh, H. E. L. The story of
early man; New York, Viking Press,
1960 [c1959] 256 p.   573.3 60-5837

     GN743 .M4 1960 MRR Alc.

Morgan, Jacques Jean Marie de,
Prehistoric man; London, K. Paul,
Trench, Trubner & co., ltd.; New
York; A. A. Knopf, 1924. xxiii, 304
p.   25-2564
     GN738 .M785 MRR Alc.

Murray, Raymond William, Man's
unknown ancestors; Milwaukee, The
Bruce publishing company [1943] xiv,
384 p. incl. plates, diagrs.   571
43-11405
     GN738 .M97 MRR Alc.

MAN, PREHISTORIC--AMERICA.
     see also Indians

MAN, PREHISTORIC--EUROPE.
Coon, Carleton Stevens, The races of
Europe New York, The Macmillan
company, 1939. xvi, 399 p., [28],
400-739 p. incl. illus. (incl. maps)
tables, diagrs.   572.94 39-10651
     GN575 .C6 MRR Alc.

MAN, PREHISTORIC--NORTH AMERICA.
     see also Indians of North America

MAN, PREHISTORIC--SOUTH AMERICA.
     see also Indians of South America

MAN, PRIMITIVE.
Murdock, George Peter, Our primitive
contemporaries, New York, The
Macmillan company, 1934. xxii p., 1
l., 614 p.   572.7 34-2549
     GN400 .M8 MRR Alc.

MANAGEMENT.
     see also Business

     see also Executives

     see also Industrial management

Horton, Forest W. Reference guide to
advanced management methods [New
York] American Management Association
[1972] xii, 333 p. [$17.50] 658.4
70-162473
     HD31 .H653 MRR Alc.

Whiteside, Conon Doyle. Accountant's
guide to profitable management
advisory services Englewood Cliffs,
N.J., Prentice-Hall [1969] ix, 430
p. [29.95]   658.4/6 69-14584
     HF5657 .W48 MRR Alc.

MANAGEMENT--ABBREVIATIONS.
Pugh, Eric. A dictionary of acronyms
& abbreviations; 2d, rev. and
expanded ed. [Hamden, Conn.] Archon
Books [1970] 389 p.   601/.48 72-
16645
     T8 .P8 1970 MRR Alc.

Pugh, Eric. Second dictionary of
acronyms & abbreviations; [Hamden,
Conn.] Archon Books [1974] 410 p.
601/.48 74-4271
     T8 .P82 MRR Alc.

MANAGEMENT--ANECDOTES, FACETIAE,
SATIRE, ETC.
Martin, Thomas Lyle. Malice in
Blunderland, New York, McGraw-Hill
[1973] vii, 143 p. [$5.95]
658.4/002/07 73-4376
     PN6231.M2 M3 MRR Ref Desk.

MANAGEMENT--BIBLIOGRAPHY.
Bakewell, K. G. B. How to find out:
management and productivity; 2d ed.
Oxford, New York, Pergamon Press
[1970] x, 389 p. 016.6585 78-
89775
Z7164.O7 E2 1970 MRR Alc.

Morrill, Chester. Systems &
procedures including office
management: information sources;
Detroit, Gale Research Co. [1967]
375 p. 016.658 67-31261
Z7914.A2 M65 MRR Alc.

MANAGEMENT--BIBLIOGRAPHY--CATALOGS.
Harvard University. Graduate School
of Business Administration. Baker
Library. Business reference sources;
[Boston] 1871. 108 p. [$3.00]
016.65/008 s 016.65/008 75-30038
Z7164.C81 H273 no. 27 MRR Alc.

Harvard University. Graduate School
of Business Administration. Baker
Library. Subject catalog of the
Baker Library, Graduate School of
Business Administration, Harvard
University. Boston, G. K. Hall,
1971. 10 v. 016.33 70-170935
Z7164.C81 H275 MRR Alc (Dk 33)

MANAGEMENT--BIOGRAPHY.
Urwick, Lyndall Fownes, The golden
book of management; London, N. Neame
[1956] xix, 198 p. 926.58 s 56-
4045
HD31 .U75 1956 MRR Biog.

MANAGEMENT--DICTIONARIES.
Heyel, Carl, ed. The encyclopedia of
management. 2d ed. New York, Van
Nostrand Reinhold Co. [1973] xxvii,
1161 p. 658/.003 72-11784
HD19 .H4 1973 MRR alc.

Johannsen, Hano. Management
glossary. New York, American
Elsevier Pub. Co., 1968. 146 p.
658/.003 68-57418
HD19 .J6 1968 MRR Alc.

Lindemann, A. J. Encyclopaedic
dictionary of management and
manufacturing terms 2d ed. Dubuque,
Iowa, Kendall/Hunt Pub. Co. [1974]
vii, 150 p. 658.4/003 74-167262
HD19 .L5 1974 MRR Alc.

Mueller, Robert Kirk. Buzzwords;
New York, Van Nostrand Reinhold Co.
[1974] viii, 172 p. 658.4/003 74-
1403
HD19 .M75 MRR Alc.

MANAGEMENT--DIRECTORIES.
Anderson, Ian Gibson. Marketing &
management: Beckenham (Kent), C.B.D.
Research, 1969. iii-xii, 228 p.
[60/-] 658/.006 78-465981
HF5415 .A616 MRR Alc.

MANAGEMENT--HANDBOOKS, MANUALS, ETC.
Vancil, Richard F. Financial
executive's handbook. Homewood,
Ill., Dow Jones-Irwin, 1970. xxxv,
1314 p. [27.50] 658.1/5/0202 69-
15541
HD31 .V34 MRR Alc.

**MANAGEMENT--STUDY AND TEACHING--
DIRECTORIES.**
McNulty, Nancy G. Training managers:
[1st ed.] New York, Harper & Row
[1969] 71, 572 p. [12.95]
658.4/0071/5 70-83612
HD20 .M253 MRR Alc.

**MANAGEMENT--STUDY AND TEACHING--UNITED
STATES--DIRECTORIES.**
Bricker, George W. Bricker's
directory of university-sponsored
executive development programs. 1970-
Wilton, Conn. 658.4/0071/173 73-
110249
HD20.15.U5 B7 MRR Alc Latest
edition

MANAGEMENT, INDUSTRIAL
see Industrial management

MANAGEMENT, SALES
see Sales management

MANAGEMENT ENGINEERING
see Industrial engineering

MANAGEMENT GAMES--BIBLIOGRAPHY.
Belch, Jean. Contemporary games;
Detroit, Gale Research Co. [1973- v.
371.3/078 72-6353
LB1029.G3 B44 MRR Alc.

MANAGEMENT GAMES--DIRECTORIES.
Belch, Jean. Contemporary games;
Detroit, Gale Research Co. [1973- v.
371.3/078 72-6353
LB1029.G3 B44 MRR Alc.

MANCHESTER, ENG.--DIRECTORIES.
Kelly's (Slater's) directory of
Manchester, Salford and suburbs.
Kingston upon Thames, Surrey [etc.]
Kelly's Directories Limited. 34-
33227
DA690.M4 K4 MRR Alc Latest edition

The Manchester, Salford, and district
red book. Manchester, Littlebury
Bros. 19 cm. 61-27275
DA690.M4 M23 MRR Alc Latest
edition

MANCHURIA--BIBLIOGRAPHY.
United States. Library of Congress.
Reference Dept. Manchuria; an
annotated bibliography. Washington,
1951. xii, 187 p. 016.9518 51-
60031
Z663.2 .M27 MRR Alc.

**MANCHURIA--ECONOMIC CONDITIONS--
BIBLIOGRAPHY.**
United States. Library of Congress.
Division of bibliography. ... The
Japanese empire: industries and
transportation, Washington, 1943. 1
p. l., 56 p. 016.330952 43-50835
Z663.28 .J2 MRR Alc.

MANIC-DEPRESSIVE PSYCHOSES.
see also Psychology, Pathological

MANNED SPACE FLIGHT.
see also Astronauts

see also Project Apollo

MANNERS AND CUSTOMS.
see also Clothing and dress

see also Costume

see also Etiquette

see also Festivals.

see also Funeral rites and ceremonies

see also Holidays

see also Rites and ceremonies

see also Students

Brasch, Rudolph, How did it begin?
[Croydon, Australia] Longmans [1965]
352 p. 390 66-3994
GT75 .B7 MRR Alc.

Harper, Howard V. Days and customs
of all faiths. New York, Fleet Pub.
Corp. [1957] 399 p. 264 57-14777

GR930 .H3 MRR Alc.

Origin of things familiar;
Cincinnati, O., United book
corporation [c1934] 4 p. l., 280 p.
031 35-2154
AG5 .O7 MRR Alc.

Textor, Robert B., comp. A cross-
cultural summary. New Haven, HRAF
Press [1967] 1 v. (various pagings)
390 67-18560
GN307 .T4 MRR Alc.

Walsh, William Shepard, Curiosities
of popular customs Detroit, Gale
Research Co., 1966. 1018 p. 390
66-23951
GT31 .W2 1898b MRR Alc.

Watson, Lillian (Eichler) The
customs of mankind. De luxe ed.
Garden City, N.Y., Garden City
publishing company, inc. [1937]
xvii, [2], 753 p. 390 37-15874
GT75 .W35 1937 MRR Alc.

MANNERS AND CUSTOMS--HISTORY.
Garrison, Webb B. How it started
Nashville, Abingdon Press [1972] 237
p. [$4.95] 390/.09 72-173951
GT75 .G3 MRR Alc.

MANNHEIM--DIRECTORIES.
Mannheimer Adressbuch, Mannheim, Dr.
Haas [etc.] 53-30182
DD901.M27 M3 MRR Alc Latest
edition

MANPOWER.
see also Labor supply

see also Military service, Compulsory

MANPOWER--EUROPE--STATISTICS.
Organization for Economic Cooperation
and Development. Manpower
statistics. 1950/60-1854/64. Paris.
66-202
HD5764.A6 O59 MRR Alc Latest
edition

MANPOWER--UNITED STATES--STATISTICS.
United States. President. Manpower
report of the President, and a Report
on manpower requirements, resources,
utilization, and training by the
U.S. Dept. of Labor. 1963-
[Washington, For sale by the
Superintendent of Documents, U.S.
Govt. Print. Off.] l 63-45
HD5723 .A43 MRR Alc Latest edition

**MANPOWER POLICY--UNITED STATES--
DIRECTORIES--PERIODICALS.**
Directory of special programs for
minority group members: Career
information services, employment
skills banks, financial aid. 1974-
[Garrett Park, Md., Garrett Park
Press] [$6.95] 331.7/02/02573 73-
93533
HD5724 .D56 MRR Alc Latest edition

MANUFACTURERS--LONDON--DIRECTORIES.
The London directory & international
register of commerce. 1973- London.
338/.0025/421 73-642810
D679 .A1315 MRR Alc Latest edition

MANUFACTURERS' AGENTS--DIRECTORIES.
Directory of manufacturers agents
serving the field of energy systems
engineering. New York, Power.
381/.45/62102573 66-1052
HD9705.U6 P6 MRR Alc Latest
edition

Manufacturers' Agent Publishing
Company, New York. Verified
directory of manufacturers'
representatives (agents) 1957- New
York. 57-17305
HD9723 .M33 MRR Alc Latest edition

MANUFACTURES.
see also Commerce

see also Prices

Lary, Hal Buckner, Imports of
manufactures from less developed
countries New York, National Bureau
of Economic Research; distributed by
Columbia University Press, 1968.
xvii, 286 p. 382/.09172/401722 67-
28434
HF1411 .L36 MRR Alc.

MANUFACTURES--BIBLIOGRAPHY.
United States. Library of Congress.
Reference Dept. Manufacturing and
mechanical engineering in the Soviet
Union; Washington, 1953. xii, 234
p. 016.621 53-60040
Z663.2 .M3 MRR Alc.

MANUFACTURES--CATALOGS.
Sweet's product design file. [New
York, Sweet's Industrial Division,
Catalog Systems, McGraw-Hill
Information Systems Company] 670 72-
626782
TS199 .S93 MRR Alc Latest edition

MANUFACTURES--CATALOGS--BIBLIOGRAPHY.
Romaine, Lawrence B. A guide to
American trade catalogs, 1744-1900.
New York, R. R. Bowker, 1960. xxiii,
422 p. 016.65085 60-16893
Z7164.C8 R6 MRR Alc.

MANUFACTURES--CLASSIFICATION.
United States. Bureau of the Census.
Alphabetic index of manufactured
products: [Washington, For sale by
the Supt. of Docs., U.S. Govt. Print.
Off., 1968] 192 p. [50]
338.4/7/67025573 70-601986
HD9724 .A4 1967c MRR Alc.

United States. Bureau of the Census.
Numerical list of manufactured
products. [Washington, 1968] 165,
A141, B2 p. 338.4/0973 s 68-7403
HD9724 .A4 1967 MRR Alc.

United States. Office of Management
and Budget. Statistical Policy
Division. Standard industrial
classification manual. [Washington;
For sale by the Supt. of Docs., U.S.
Govt. Print. Off., 1972. 649 p.
[$6.75] 338/.02/0973 72-601529
HF1042 .A55 1972 MRR Alc.

MANUFACTURES--DIRECTORIES.
Bottin. Bottin international. 1947-
Paris, Société Didot-Bottin [etc.]
48-24844
HF54.F8 B6 Sci RR Latest edition /
MRR Alc Latest edition

Cenypres trading register of the
United Nations countries. London,
Cenypres. 380.025 66-85954
HF54.G7 C4 MRR Alc Latest edition

International yellow pages. New York
[etc.] R. H. Donnelly Telephone
Directory Co. [etc.] 64-8064
Began publication with 1963/64 vol.
HE8721 .I67 MRR Alc Latest edition

Marconi's international register.
New York [etc.] 31-15824
Began publication in 1917.
HE7710 .I6 MRR Alc Latest edition

Product design & development. PD&D
product encyclopedia; [Philadelphia,
1961] 253, 10, 10 p. 61-59873
T12 .P8 MRR Alc.

Westminster directory of the world.
London, Tamar Publishing Co. Ltd.,
1968. 564 p. [unpriced] 380.1/025
73-403663
HF54.G7 W46 MRR Alc.

MANUFACTURING PROCESSES.
   see also Machine-tools

MANUSCRIPTS.
   Diringer, David, The illuminated
   book: Rev. ed. New York, Praeger
   [1967] 514 p.   745.6/7/09 66-12525

      ND2920 .D55 1967 MRR Alc.

MANUSCRIPTS--BIBLIOGRAPHY.
   Oesterley, Hermann, Wegweiser durch
   die literatur der urkundensammlungen,
   Berlin, G. Reimer, 1885-86. 2 v.
   03-7358
      CD995 .O3 MRR Alc.

MANUSCRIPTS--CATALOGS.
   Clark, Kenneth Willis, ed. Checklist
   of manuscripts in the libraries of
   the Greek and Armenian Patriarchates
   in Jerusalem, Washington,
   Photoduplication Service, Library of
   Congress, 1953. xi, 44 p.   016.091
   52-60045
      Z663.96 .C54 MRR Alc.

   Morgan, William Thomas, A
   bibliography of British history (1700-
   1715) Bloomington, Ind., 1934-42. 5
   v.   016.942069 35-27707
      Z2019 .M85 1934 MRR Alc.

MANUSCRIPTS--CATALOGS--BIBLIOGRAPHY.
   Kristeller, Paul Oskar, Latin
   manuscript books before 1600; 3d ed.
   New York, Fordham University Press
   [1965] xxvi, 284 p. 016.091 66-
   3585
      Z6601.A1 K7 1965 MRR Alc.

MANUSCRIPTS--COLLECTORS AND COLLECTING.
   Hamilton, Charles, Collecting
   autographs and manuscripts. [1st
   ed.] Norman, University of Oklahoma
   Press [1961] xviii, 269 p. 091.5
   61-9007
      Z41 .H34 MRR Alc.

   Manuscript Society. M S directory.
   New York. 091.058 53-3518
      Z41 .M25 MRR Alc Latest edition

MANUSCRIPTS--PRICES.
   American book prices current. v. 1-
   1894/85- New York, Bancroft-Parkman
   [etc.] 018/.3 03-14557
      Z1000 .A51 MRR Alc Partial set

MANUSCRIPTS--CANADA--BIBLIOGRAPHY.
   Ricci, Seymour de, Census of
   medieval and renaissance manuscripts
   in the United States and Canada, New
   York, H. W. Wilson, 1935-40. 3 v.
   35-31986
      Z6620.U5 R5 MRR Alc.

MANUSCRIPTS--CANADA--CATALOGS.
   Union list of manuscripts in Canadian
   repositories. Ottawa [Queen's
   Printer] 1968. x, 734 p. [10.00]
   091/.0971 74-410102
      CD3622 .U5 MRR Alc.

MANUSCRIPTS--EUROPE--CATALOGS--
   BIBLIOGRAPHY.
   United States. Library of Congress.
   Processing Dept. Unpublished
   bibliographical tools in certain
   archives and libraries of Europe;
   Washington, 1952. iv, 25 p.   016.01
   52-60036
      Z663.7 .U62 MRR Alc.

MANUSCRIPTS--FRANCE--CATALOGS.
   Carson, Patricia. Materials for West
   African history in French archives.
   London, Athlone P.; distributed by
   Constable, 1968. viii, 170 p. [42/-
   ] 016.9166 68-89964
      CD2491.W4 C3 1968 MRR Alc.

MANUSCRIPTS--GREAT BRITAIN.
   Gilson, Julius Parnell, A student's
   guide to the manuscripts of the
   British museum, London, Society for
   promoting Christian knowledge; New
   York, The Macmillan company, 1920.
   v, 7-48 p.   21-5619
      Z6621.B88 G MRR Alc.

   Morgan, Paul, Oxford libraries
   outside the Bodleian; Oxford [Eng.]
   Oxford Bibliographical Society and
   the Bodleian Library, 1973. xx, 250
   p.   027.7425/72 74-164911
      Z791.O98 M67 MRR Alc.

   Ogilvy, Jack David Angus. Books
   known to the English, 597-1066
   Cambridge, Mass., Mediaeval Academy
   of America, 1967. xx, 300 p.   011
   65-19630
      Z6602 .O35 MRR Alc.

MANUSCRIPTS--GREAT BRITAIN--
   BIBLIOGRAPHY.
   Downs, Robert Bingham, British
   library resources; Chicago, American
   Library Association, 1973 [i.e. 1974]
   xvi, 332 p. 016.016 73-1598
      Z1002 .D63 MRR Alc.

United States. Library of Congress.
   Manuscript division. A guide to
   manuscripts relating to American
   history in British depositories
   reproduced for the Division of
   manuscripts of the Library of
   Congress. [Washington] The Library
   of Congress, 1946. xvi, 313 p.
   016.973 46-27863
      CD1048.U5 A35 1946 MRR Alc.

MANUSCRIPTS--GREAT BRITAIN--CATALOGS.
   Andrews, Charles McLean, comp. Guide
   to the manuscript materials for the
   history of the United States to 1783,
   Washington, D.C., The Carnegie
   institution of Washington, 1908.
   xiv, 499 p.   09-6049
      CD1048.U5 A55 MRR Alc.

   Great Britain. Historical Manuscripts
   Commission. Guide to the reports of
   the Royal Commission on Historical
   Manuscripts, 1911-1957. London,
   H.M.S.O., 1966-   v.   [£10/10/-
   (pt. 2)] 942.082/08 67-31924
      DA25 .M252 MRR Alc.

   Great Britain. Historical Manuscripts
   Commission. A guide to the reports
   on collections of manuscripts of
   private families, corporations and
   institutions in Great Britain and
   Ireland London, H.M. Stationery
   Off., 1914-38. 2 pts. in 3.   15-
   7434
      DA25 .M25 MRR Alc.

   Pugh, Ralph Bernard, The records of
   the Colonial and Dominions Offices
   London, H.M. Stationery Off., 1964.
   v, 118 p.   325.342 64-4582
      JV1011 .P8 MRR Alc.

   United States. Library of Congress.
   Processing Dept. British manuscripts
   project; New York, Greenwood Press
   [1968] xvii, 179 p.   016.02517/1
   68-55138
      Z6620.G7 U5 1968 MRR Alc.

   United States. Library of Congress.
   Processing Dept. British manuscripts
   project; Washington, Library of
   Congress, 1955. xvii, 179 p.
   016.025179 55-60041
      Z663.7 .B7 MRR Alc.

   Wainwright, Mary Doreen. A guide to
   Western manuscripts and documents in
   the British Isles relating to South
   and South East Asia. London, New
   York, Oxford University Press, 1965.
   xix, 532 p.   016.915 65-3147
      CD1048.A8 W3 MRR Alc.

MANUSCRIPTS--GREAT BRITAIN--CATALOGS--
   BIBLIOGRAPHY.
   British Museum. Dept. of Manuscripts.
   The catalogues of the manuscript
   collections London] The Trustees of
   the British Museum, 1951. 43 p.
   016.016091 52-23464
      Z6621 .B844 MRR Alc.

MANUSCRIPTS--GREAT BRITAIN--YORKSHIRE.
   Society of Archivists. A brief guide
   to Yorkshire Record Offices; York,
   University of York (Borthwick
   Institute of Historical Research),
   1968. [i], iv, 41 l. [5/-]
   016.91427/4/03 70-455717
      CD1065.Y6 S6 MRR Alc.

MANUSCRIPTS--ILLINOIS--BIBLIOGRAPHY.
   Burton, William Lester, Descriptive
   bibliography of Civil War manuscripts
   in Illinois. [Evanston, Ill.]
   Published for the Civil War
   Centennial Commission of Illinois
   [Springfield] by Northwestern
   University Press [1966] xv, 393 p.
   016.9737 65-24627
      Z1242 .B95 MRR Alc.

MANUSCRIPTS--ISRAEL--CATALOGS.
   Clark, Kenneth Willis, ed. Checklist
   of manuscripts in the libraries of
   the Greek and Armenian Patriarchates
   in Jerusalem, Washington,
   Photoduplication Service, Library of
   Congress, 1953. xi, 44 p. 016.091
   52-60045
      Z663.96 .C54 MRR Alc.

MANUSCRIPTS--KENTUCKY--CATALOGS.
   Kentucky Historical Society. Guide
   to the manuscripts of the Kentucky
   Historical Society Frankfort, 1955.
   iv, 185 p.   016.9769 55-62791
      Z1287 .K37 MRR Alc.

MANUSCRIPTS--PALESTINE--CATALOGS.
   Clark, Kenneth Willis, ed. Checklist
   of manuscripts in the libraries of
   the Greek and Armenian Patriarchates
   in Jerusalem, Washington,
   Photoduplication Service, Library of
   Congress, 1953. xi, 44 p. 016.091
   52-60045
      Z663.96 .C54 MRR Alc.

MANUSCRIPTS--PENNSYLVANIA--CATALOGS.
   Historical Records Survey.
   Pennsylvania. Guide to the
   manuscript collections of the
   Historical Society of Pennsylvania.
   2d ed. Philadelphia, Historical
   Society of Pennsylvania, 1949. 1 v.
   (unpaged) 016.9748 49-49681
      Z1329 .H68 1949 MRR Alc.

MANUSCRIPTS--RUSSIA.
   Grimsted, Patricia Kennedy. Archives
   and manuscript repositories in the
   USSR, Moscow and Leningrad.
   Princeton, Princeton University Press
   [1972] xxx, 436 p. [$22.50]
   947/.007 73-166375
      CD1711 .G7 MRR Alc.

MANUSCRIPTS--SINAITIC PENINSULA--
   CATALOGS.
   Clark, Kenneth Willis, ed. Checklist
   of manuscripts in St. Catherine's
   monastery, Mount Sinai, Washington,
   Library of Congress Photoduplication
   Service, Library of Congress, 1952.
   ix, 53 p.   016.091 52-60038
      Z663.96 .C53 MRR Alc.

MANUSCRIPTS--SPAIN.
   Robertson, James Alexander, List of
   documents in Spanish archives
   relating to the history of the United
   States, Washington, D.C., Carnegie
   institution of Washington, 1910. xv,
   368 p.   10-16322
      CD1858.U6 R6 MRR Alc.

MANUSCRIPTS--UNITED STATES.
   United States. Library of Congress.
   Manuscript division. The Declaration
   of independence, the Constitution of
   the United States, and other historic
   material in the Division of
   manuscripts of the Library of
   Congress. [Washington] The Library
   of Congress, Division of manuscripts
   [1941] 14, 2 p.   027.5753 091 41-
   50007
      Z663.34 .D4 MRR Alc.

   [United States. Library of Congress.
   Manuscript Division] The manuscript
   collections in the Library of
   Congress. Washington, Govt. Print.
   Off., 1916. 9 p.   16-26002
      Z663.34 .M27 MRR Alc.

   United States. National Historical
   Publications Commission. A guide to
   archives and manuscripts in the
   United States. New Haven, Yale
   University Press, 1961. xxiii, 775
   p.   025.171 61-6878
      CD3022 .A45 MRR Ref Desk.

MANUSCRIPTS--UNITED STATES--
   BIBLIOGRAPHY.
   Billington, Ray Allen, Guides to
   American history manuscript
   collections in libraries of the
   United States. New York, P. Smith,
   1952. 467-496 p.   016.973 52-2323

      Z1236 .B5 MRR Alc.

   Greene, Evarts Boutell, A guide to
   the principal sources for early
   American history (1600-1800) in the
   city of New York, New York, Columbia
   university press, 1929. xxv, 357,
   [1] p.   29-17492
      Z1236 .G82 MRR Alc.

   Hale, Richard Walden, ed. Guide to
   photocopied historical materials in
   the United States and Canada.
   Ithaca, N.Y., published for the
   American Historical Association [by]
   Cornell University Press [1961]
   xxxiv, 241 p.   016.9 61-17269
      Z6209 .H3 MRR Alc.

   Krichmar, Albert. The women's rights
   movement in the United States, 1848-
   1970; Metuchen, N.J., Scarecrow
   Press, 1972. ix, 436 p.
   016.3014L/2/0973 72-4702
      Z7964.U49 K75 MRR Alc.

   Matthews, William, American diaries
   in manuscript, 1580-1954; Athens,
   University of Georgia Press [1974]
   xvi, 176 p.   016.92/0073 73-76782
      Z5305.U5 M32 MRR Alc.

   Ricci, Seymour de, Census of
   medieval and renaissance manuscripts
   in the United States and Canada, New
   York, H. W. Wilson, 1935-40. 3 v.
   35-31986
      Z6620.U5 R5 MRR Alc.

   United States. Library of Congress.
   Manuscript division. List of
   manuscript collections in the Library
   of Congress to July, 1931,
   Washington, U.S. Govt. print. off.,
   1932. 1 p. l., 123-249 p. 016.091
   32-7818
      Z6621 .U56 MRR Alc.

MANUSCRIPTS--UNITED STATES-- (Cont.)
United States. Library of Congress.
Manuscript division. List of
manuscript collections received in
the Library of Congress, July 1931 to
July 1938. Washington, U.S. Govt.
print. off., 1939. v, 33 p.
016.091 016.973 39-26002
Z663.34 .L482 MRR Alc.

United States. Library of Congress.
Manuscript division. Manuscripts in
public and private collections in the
United States. Washington, Govt.
print. off., 1924. ix, 98 p. 24-
26001
Z663.34 .M3 MRR Alc.

Young, William C., American
theatrical arts; Chicago, American
Library Association. 1971. ix, 166
p. 01.7002 78-161234
Z6935 .Y68 MRR Alc.

MANUSCRIPTS--UNITED STATES--CATALOGS.
Historical Records Survey.
Pennsylvania. Guide to the
manuscript collections of the
Historical Society of Pennsylvania.
2d ed. Philadelphia, Historical
Society of Pennsylvania, 1949. 1 v.
(unpaged) 016.9748 49-49681
Z1329 .H68 1949 MRR Alc.

McCoy, Garnett. Archives of American
art; New York, Bowker, 1972. ix,
163 p. 016.7/0973 72-5125
Z6611.A7 M3 MRR Alc.

Michigan. University. William L.
Clements Library. Author/title
catalog of Americana, 1493-1860, in
the William L. Clements Library,
Boston, G. K. Hall, 1970. 7 v.
016.9173/03 73-156668
Z1236 .M53 MRR Alc (Dk 33)

Modern Language Association of
America. American Literature Group.
Committee on Manuscript Holdings.
American literary manuscripts;
Austin, University of Texas Press
[1961, c1960] xxviii, 421 p.
016.81 60-10356
Z6620.U5 M6 MRR Alc.

The National union catalog of
manuscript collections. 1959/61-
Washington [etc.] The Library of
Congress [etc.] 62-17486
Z6620.U5 N3 MRR Alc Full set / MRR
Alc Full set

Race Relations Information Center.
Directory of Afro-American resources.
New York, R. R. Bowker Co. [1970]
xv, 485 p. 917.3/06/96073 71-
126008
Z1361.N39 R3 MRR Alc.

United States. Library of Congress.
Manuscript Division. Accessions of
manuscripts, broadsides and British
transcripts. July 1920/21-1925.
Washington, Govt. Print. Off.,
Library Branch. 22-26001
Z663.34 .A25 MRR Alc   MRR Alc Full
set

United States. Library of Congress.
Manuscript division. Calendar of the
correspondence of George Washington,
commander in chief of the Continental
army, with the officers. Washington,
Govt. print. off., 1915. 4 v. 10-
35016
Z663.34 .C28 MRR Alc.

United States. Library of Congress.
Manuscript Division. Calendar of the
papers of John Jordan Crittenden.
Washington, Govt. print. off., 1913.
355 p. 12-35010
Z663.34 .C7 MRR Alc.

United States. Library of Congress.
Manuscript division. Calendar of the
papers of Martin Van Buren,
Washington, Govt. print. off., 1910.
757 p. 012 10-35009
Z663.34 .V2 MRR Alc.

United States. Library of Congress.
Manuscript division. Handbook of
manuscripts in the Library of
Congress. Washington, Govt. print.
off., 1918. xvi, 750 p. 17-26010
Z6621 .U55 MRR Alc.

United States. Library of Congress.
Manuscript division. The Harkness
collection in the Library of
Congress. Washington, U.S. Govt.
print. off., 1932. x, 336 p.
016.985 32-26175
Z663.34 .H28 MRR Alc.

United States. Library of Congress.
Manuscript division. List of the
Benjamin Franklin papers in the
Library of Congress. Washington,
Govt. print. off., 1905. 322 p. 05-
20007
Z663.34 .L5 MRR Alc.

United States. Library of Congress.
Manuscript division. List of the
Vernon-Wager manuscripts in the
Library of Congress. Washington,
Govt. print. off., 1904. 148 p. 05-
3073
Z663.34 .V4 MRR Alc.

United States. Library of Congress.
Manuscript division. List of the
Washington manuscripts from the year
1592 to 1775. Washington, Govt.
print. off., 1919. iii, 137 p. 19-
26005
Z663.34 .W35 MRR Alc.

United States. Library of Congress.
Manuscript Divison. Calendar of the
papers of Franklin Pierce,
Washington, Govt. print. off., 1917.
102 p. 17-26003
Z663.34 .P5 MRR Alc.

Yale University. Library. A
catalogue of manuscripts in the
collection of western Americana New
Haven, Yale University Press, 1952.
x, 398 p. 016.978 52-5370
Z1251.W5 Y3 MRR Alc.

MANUSCRIPTS, GREEK--CATALOGS.
Clark, Kenneth Willis, ed. Checklist
of manuscripts in the libraries of
the Greek and Armenian Patriarchates
in Jerusalem, Washington,
Photoduplication Service, Library of
Congress, 1953. xi, 44 p. 016.091
52-60045
Z663.96 .C54 MRR Alc.

United States. Library of Congress.
A descriptive checklist of selected
manuscripts in the monasteries of
Mount Athos Washington, Library of
Congress, Photoduplication Service,
1957. xii, 36 p. 016.091 57-
60041
Z663.96 .D4 MRR Alc.

MANUSCRIPTS, GREEK (PAPYRI)
Hunt, Arthur Surridge, ed. and tr.
Select papyri, London, W. Heinemann;
New York, G. P. Putnam's sons;
Cambridge, Mass. Harvard University
Press, 1932- v. mrr01-21
PA3611.A9 1932d MRR Alc.

Page, Denys Lionel, comp. Greek
literary papyri in two volumes. I.
Cambridge, Harvard University Press,
1942. xix, 617 p. a 42-4500
PA3611.A22 1942 MRR Alc.

MANUSCRIPTS, IRISH.
Kenney, James Francis, The sources
for the early history of Ireland;
New York, Columbia University Press,
1929. xvi, 807 p. 29-30667
Z2041 .K36 MRR Alc.

**MANUSCRIPTS, LATIN--CATALOGS--
BIBLIOGRAPHY.**
Kristeller, Paul Oskar, Latin
manuscript books before 1600; 3d ed.
New York, Fordham University Press
[1965] xxvi, 284 p. 016.091 66-
3585
Z6601.A1 K7 1965 MRR Alc.

MANUSCRIPTS, MEXICAN--CATALOGS.
United States. Library of Congress.
Manuscript Division. The Harkness
Collection in the Library of
Congress; Washington, Library of
Congress; [for sale by the Supt. of
Docs., U.S. Govt. Print. Off.] 1974.
xi, 315 p. 016.972/02 73-6747
Z663.34 .H293 MRR Alc.

MANUSCRIPTS, PERSIAN--FACSIMILES.
Browne, Edward Granville, A literary
history of Persia ... Cambridge
[Eng.] The University press, 1928-
1930. 4 v. mrr01-34
PK6097 .B73 MRR Alc.

MANUSCRIPTS, SPANISH--CATALOGS.
United States. Library of Congress.
Manuscript Division. The Harkness
Collection in the Library of
Congress; Washington, Library of
Congress; [for sale by the Supt. of
Docs., U.S. Govt. Print. Off.] 1974.
xi, 315 p. 016.972/02 73-6747
Z663.34 .H293 MRR Alc.

United States. Library of Congress.
Manuscript division. The Harkness
collection in the Library of
Congress. Washington, U.S. Govt.
print. off., 1932. x, 336 p.
016.985 32-26175
Z663.34 .H28 MRR Alc.

MANUSCRIPTS ON MICROFILM--CATALOGS.
United States. Library of Congress.
Processing Dept. British manuscripts
project; Washington, Library of
Congress, 1955. xvii, 179 p.
016.025179 55-60041
Z663.7 .B7 MRR Alc.

United States. Library of Congress.
Processing Dept. British manuscripts
project; New York, Greenwood Press
[1968] xvii, 179 p. 016.02517/1
68-55138
Z6620.G7 U5 1968 MRR Alc.

MAO, TSE-TUNG, 1893-
Payne, Pierre Stephen Robert, Mao
Tse-tung New York, Weybright and
Talley [1969] vii, 343 p. [10.00]
951.05/0924 B 68-17753
DS778.M3 P32 1969 MRR Alc.

Schram, Stuart R. Mao Tse-tung
London, Allen Lane the Penguin P.,
1967. 3-351 p. [50/-] 951.05/0924
67-105785
DS778.M3 S3 1967b MRR Alc.

MAORI LANGUAGE--DICTIONARIES--ENGLISH.
Williams, Herbert William, Bp., A
dictionary of the Maori language,
7th ed., Wellington, A. R. Shearer,
Govt. printer, 1971. xi, 499 p.
[$4.50] 499/.4 76-882911
PL6465.Z5 W58 1971 MRR Alc.

Williams, Herbert William, Bp., A
dictionary of the Maori language.
6th ed., rev. and augm. Wellington,
N.Z., R. E. Owen, Govt. printer,
1957. 499 p. 57-58498
PL6465 .W48 1957 MRR Alc.

Williams, Herbert William, Bp., A
dictionary of the Maori language.
6th ed., rev. and augm. Wellington,
N.Z., R. E. Owen, Govt. printer,
1957. 499 p. 57-58498
PL6465 .W48 1957 MRR Alc.

MAP COLLECTIONS.
Special Libraries Association.
Geography and Map Division. Directory
Revision Committee. Map collections
in the United States and Canada; 2d
ed. New York, Special Libraries
Association 1970. xiii 159 p.
026/.912/02573 72-101336
GA193.U5 S68 1970 MRR Alc.

MAPS.
see also Cartography

Bagrow, Leo. History of cartography.
London, C. A. Watts, 1964. 312 p.
526.809 64-56112
GA201 .B313 1964a MRR Alc.

Greenhood, David. Mapping. Chicago,
University of Chicago Press [1964]
xiii, 289 p. 526.8 63-20905
GA151 .G7 1964 MRR Alc.

MAPS--BIBLIOGRAPHY.
International maps and atlases in
print. London, New York, Bowker
Publishing Co. [1974] 864 p.
[£15.00] 016.912 73-13336
Z6021 .I596 MRR Alc.

United States. Library of Congress.
Library of Congress catalog; Maps and
atlases. 1953-55. Washington.
016.912 53-60010
Z663.35 .L45 MRR Alc   MRR Alc Full
set

United States. Library of Congress.
Map Division. The Hotchkiss map
collection; Washington, 1951. 67 p.
016.91273 51-60026
Z663.35 .H6 MRR Alc.

United States. Library of Congress.
Map division. A list of atlases and
maps applicable to the world war;
Washington, Govt. print. off., 1918.
202 p. 18-26005
Z663.35 .L54 MRR Alc.

United States. Library of Congress.
Map Division. A list of geographical
atlases in the Library of Congress,
Washington, Govt. Print. Off., 1909-
v. 016.912 09-35009
Z663.35 .L5 MRR Alc.

United States. Library of Congress.
Map Division. A list of maps of
America in the Library of Congress.
New York, B. Franklin [1967?] 2 v.
in 1 (1137 p.) 016.91273 67-7211
Z663.35 .L55 1967 MRR Alc.

United States Library of Congress.
Map Division. Noteworthy maps; no.
[1]-3: 1925/26-1927/28. Washington,
U.S. Govt. Print. Off. 27-26417
Z663.35 .N6 MRR Alc   MRR Alc
Partial set

Wheat, James Clements. Maps and
charts published in America before
1800; New Haven, Yale University
Press, 1969. xxii, 215 p. [30.00]
016.5268 69-15464
Z6027.A5 W68 MRR Alc.

MAPS--BIBLIOGRAPHY--CATALOGS.
Ristow, Walter William, Facsimiles
of rare historical maps; 3d ed.,
rev. and enl. Washington [Library of
Congress] 1968. 20 p. 016.911 70-
602104
Z663.35 .F3 1968 MRR Alc.

MAPS--BIBLIOGRAPHY--CATALOGS. (Cont.)
United States. National Archives.
Guide to cartographic records in the
National Archives Washington,
National Archives, National Archives
and Records Service; for sale by the
Supt. of Docs., U.S. Govt. Print.
Off. 1971. xi, 444 p. [$3.25]
016.91273 76-611061
Z6028 .U575 MRR Alc.

MAPS--CONSERVATION AND RESTORATION.
United States. Library of Congress.
Map Division. Maps; their care,
repair, and preservation in
libraries. Rev. ed. Washington,
1956. ix, 75 p. 025.176 56-60030

Z663.35 .M28 1956 MRR Alc.

MAPS--TERMINOLOGY.
United States. Defense Intelligence
Agency. A DOD glossary of mapping,
charting and geodetic terms. 1st ed.
[Washington] 1967. v, 243 p.
526/.01/4 68-60382
G108.A2 U5 MRR Alc.

MAPS, EARLY--ADDRESSES, ESSAYS,
LECTURES.
Ristow, Walter William, comp. A la
carte; Washington, Library of
Congress [for sale by the Supt. of
Docs., U.S. Govt. Print. Off.] 1972.
x, 232 p. [$4.00] 912.73 75-
173026
Z663.35 .S42 MRR Alc.

MARC SYSTEM.
RECON Pilot Project. RECON Pilot
Project; Washington, Library of
Congress [for sale by the Supt. of
Docs., U.S. Govt. Print. Off.] 1972.
vii, 49 p. [$1.50] 029.7 72-7314

Z663.172 .R4 MRR Alc.

RECON Working Task Force. Conversion
of retrospective catalog records to
machine-readable form; Washington,
Library of Congress; [for sale by the
Supt. of Docs., U.S. Govt. Print.
Off.] 1969. x, 230 p. [2.25]
029.7 70-601790
Z663.172 .R2 MRR Alc.

RECON Working Task Force. National
aspects of creating and using
MARC/RECON records; Washington,
Library of Congress; [for sale by the
Supt. of Docs., U.S. Govt. Print.
Off.] 1973. v, 48 p. [$2.75]
029.7 73-3381
Z663.172 .R45 MRR Alc.

United States. Library of Congress.
Information Systems Office. Maps, a
MARC format; Washington; [For sale
by the Supt. of Docs., U.S. Govt.
Print. Off.] 1970. 45 p. [0.50]
526.8/018 77-607327
Z663.172 .M27 MRR Alc.

United States. Library of Congress.
Information Systems Office. The MARC
pilot experience; Washington,
Library of Congress, 1968. 15 p.
029.7 68-61783
Z663.172 .M28 MRR Alc.

United States. Library of Congress.
Information Systems Office. The MARC
pilot project; Washington, Library
of Congress; [for sale by the Supt.
of Docs., U.S. Govt. Print. Off.]
1968 [i.e. 1869] 183 p. [3.50]
029.7 68-67367
Z663.172 .M29 MRR Alc.

United States. Library of Congress.
Marc Development Office. Serials: a
MARC format; 2d ed. Washington,
Library of Congress; [for sale by the
Supt. of Docs., U.S. Govt. Print.
Off.] 1974. 104 p. 025.3/4/3 74-
7176
Z663.757 .S47 1974 MRR Alc.

MARC SYSTEM--BIBLIOGRAPHY.
United States. Library of Congress.
Marc Development Office. Information
on the MARC system, 4th ed.
Washington, Library of Congress,
1974. iv, 48 p. 025.3/028/54 74-
10624
Z663.757 .I5 1974 MRR Alc.

MARC SYSTEM--UNITED STATES.
United States. Library of Congress.
Information Systems Office. A
preliminary report on the MARC
(Machine-Readable Catalog) pilot
project; Washington, 1966. iv, 101
p. 029.7 68-60289
Z663.14 .P7 MRR Alc.

United States. Library of Congress.
Information Systems Office. Project
MARC; Washington, Library of
Congress, 1967. 16, [1] p. 029.7
67-62769
Z663.14 .P73 MRR Alc.

United States. Library of Congress.
Marc Development Office. Information
on the MARC system, 4th ed.
Washington, Library of Congress,
1974. iv, 48 p. 025.3/028/54 74-
10624
Z663.757 .I5 1974 MRR Alc.

United States. Library of Congress.
Marc Development Office. Information
on the MARC system, 3d ed.
Washington, Library of Congress,
1973. 44 p. 025.3/028/54 73-5544

Z663.757 .I5 1973 MRR Alc.

United States. Library of Congress.
Marc Development Office. MARC user
survey, 1972. Washington, Library of
Congress, 1972. 58 p. 025.3/028/54
72-13832
Z663.757 .M17 MRR Alc.

MARC SYSTEM--UNITED STATES--CONGRESSES.
Conference on Machine-Readable
Catalog Copy. Proceedings of the
Conference on Machine-Readable
Catalog Copy. Washington, Library of
Congress, 1965-66. 2 v. 029.7 68-
3828
Z663.172 .C6 MRR Alc.

MARC SYSTEM--UNITED STATES--FORMAT.
United States. Library of Congress.
Information Systems Office. The MARC
II format; Washington, Library of
Congress, 1968. 167 p. 029.7 68-
61408
Z663.172 .M3 MRR Alc.

United States. Library of Congress.
Information Systems Office. Serials:
a MARC format. Preliminary ed.
Washington, Library of Congress; [for
sale by the Supt. of Docs., U.S.
Govt. Print. Off.] 1970. 72 p.
[$0.70] 025.3/4/3 73-606842
Z663.172 .S4 MRR Alc.

United States. Library of Congress.
Marc Development Office. Books: a
MARC format; 5th ed. Washington
[for sale by the Supt. of Docs., U.S.
Govt. Print. Off.] 1972. 106 p.
[$1.00] 025.3/0285 73-38649
Z663.757 .B66 1972a MRR Alc.

United States. Library of Congress.
Marc Development Office. Films: a
MARC format; Washington; [For sale
by the Supt. of Docs., U.S. Govt.
Print. Off.] 1970 [i.e. 1971] 65 p.
[$0.65] 025.3/4/7 77-611336
Z663.757 .F5 MRR Alc.

United States. Library of Congress.
Marc Development Office.
Manuscripts: a MARC format;
Washington, Library of Congress; for
sale by the Supt. of Docs., U.S.
Govt. Print. Off., 1973. v, 47 p.
[$0.80] 025.3/4/102854 72-13497
Z663.757 .M36 MRR Alc.

MARC SYSTEM--UNITED STATES--HANDBOOKS,
MANUALS, ETC.
Carrington, David K. Data
preparation manual for the conversion
of map cataloging records to machine-
readable form. Washington, Library
of Congress; [for sale by the Supt.
of Docs., U.S. Govt. Print. Off.]
1971. v, 317 p. [$2.75] 025.3/46
79-169093
Z663.35 .D3 MRR Alc.

MARCO, OF MONTEGALLO, 1425-1496. LIBRO
DEI COMANDAMENTI DI DIO.
Rosenwald, Lessing Julius, The 19th
book: Tesoro de poveri. [Washington]
Published for the Library of
Congress, 1961. 123 p. 62-60686
Z663.4 .N5 MRR Alc.

MARCO, OF MONTEGALLO, 1425-1496. TABULA
DELLA SALUTE.
Rosenwald, Lessing Julius, The 19th
book: Tesoro de poveri. [Washington]
Published for the Library of
Congress, 1961. 123 p. 62-60686
Z663.4 .N5 MRR Alc.

MARINE ARCHITECTURE
see Ship-building

MARINE BIOLOGY.
see also Seashore biology

Hardy, Alister Clavering, Sir. The
open sea; London, Fontana, 1970-71.
2 v. [15/- (v. 1)] 574.92 75-
857351
QH91 .H293 MRR Alc.

MARINE BIOLOGY--BIBLIOGRAPHY.
Selected references to literature on
marine expeditions, 1700-1960.
Boston, G. K. Hall, 1972. iv, 517 p.
016.5514/6 72-6452
Z5971 .S4 MRR Alc.

MARINE BORERS--BIBLIOGRAPHY.
United States. Library of Congress.
Science and Technology Division.
Marine borers; Washington [U.S.
Govt. Print Off.] 1963. xii, 1136 p.
63-60040
Z663.41 .M28 MRR Alc.

United States. Library of Congress.
Technical Information Division.
Marine borers, a preliminary
bibliography, Washington, 1956- v.
016.632732 56-60020
Z663.43 .M3 MRR Alc.

MARINE ENGINEERING--CATALOGS.
Marine catalog and buyers' directory.
1st- ed.; 1943- New York, N.Y.
[etc.] Simmons-Boardman publishing
corporation. 623.8085 43-19016
VM12 .M33 MRR Alc Latest edition

MARINE ENGINEERING--DIRECTORIES.
Marine catalog and buyers' directory.
1st- ed.; 1943- New York, N.Y.
[etc.] Simmons-Boardman publishing
corporation. 623.8085 43-19016
VM12 .M33 MRR Alc Latest edition

MARINE ENGINEERS.
Bennett, Frank Marion, The steam
navy of the United States. 2d ed.
Pittsburgh, Pa., Warren & company,
1897. 2 v. 08-29480
VA55 .B49 1897 MRR Alc.

MARINE ENGINES.
The Motor ship reference book.
London, Temple press ltd. 25-22579
VM315 .A2 MRR Alc Latest edition

MARINE FAUNA.
see also Fishes

Miner, Roy Waldo, Field book of
seashore life. New York, Putnam
[1950] xv, 888 p. 591.92 50-10405

QH91 .M5 1950 MRR Alc.

MARINE RADIO STATIONS--DIRECTORIES.
International Telecommunication
Union. General Secretariat.
Nomenclature des stations côtières
et de navire. 1st- ed.; Sept.
1933- Genève, Union internationale
des télécommunications. 36-15706
VK397 .I55 MRR Alc Latest edition

MARINE RESOURCES.
see also Fisheries

MARINE RESOURCES--DICTIONARIES.
Firth, Frank E. The encyclopedia of
marine resources. New York, Van
Nostrand Reinhold Co. [1969] xi, 740
p. 551.4/6/003 70-78014
SH201 .F56 1969 MRR Alc.

MARINE TRANSPORTATION
see Shipping

MARIONETTES
see Puppets and puppet-plays

MARKET SURVEYS.
Angel, Juvenal Londoño,
International marketing guide for
technical, management and other
consultants. 1st ed. New York,
World Trade Academy Press;
distributed by Simon & Schuster
[1971] 600 p. [$25.00] 658.4/03
77-111350
HD69.C6 A676 MRR Alc.

Angel, Juvenal Londoño, Looking for
employment in foreign countries
reference handbook. 6th ed., rev.
and enl. New York, World Trade
Academy Press; distributed by Simon &
Schuster [1972] 727 p. [$25.00]
331.7/02 70-111351
HF5381 .A7847 1972 MRR Alc.

Bradford's directory of marketing
research agencies in the United
States and the world. [1st- ed.;
1944- Fairfax, Va. [etc.] 658.83058
44-5426
HF5415.A2 B7 MRR Ref Desk Latest
edition

International reference handbook of
services, organizations, diplomatic
representation, marketing, and
advertising channels. 1954- New
York, World Trade Academy Press. a
55-1568
HF54.U5 I52 MRR Alc Latest edition

MARKET SURVEYS--BIBLIOGRAPHY.
International Trade Centre. Market
surveys by products and countries;
Geneva, 1969. ix, 203 p. [$5.00]
(U.S.) 016.6588/3 72-186218
Z7164.M18 I5 1969 MRR Alc.

MARKET SURVEYS--SOCIETIES, ETC.--
DIRECTORIES.
American University, Washington, D.C.
Bureau of Social Science Research.
Directory of organizations in
opinion, and related research outside
the United States. Washington,
c1956. 1 v. (various pagings) 57-
17609
   HM263 .A77 MRR Alc.

MARKET SURVEYS--CANADA.
Dhalla, Nariman K. These Canadians;
Toronto, New York, McGraw-Hill Co. of
Canada [1966] 749 p.   308.171 66-
14580
   HC115 .D54 MRR Alc.

Survey of markets and business year
book. Toronto, Maclean-Hunter Ltd.
330.9/71/0644 72-626543
   HC111 .B8 MRR Alc Latest edition

MARKET SURVEYS--EUROPE.
Agence Havas. Keys to European
markets. [Paris, Havas Conseil, 1969]
327 p. [206.25F] 330.9/4 72-
183572
   HC240 .A584 MRR Alc.

MARKET SURVEYS--UNITED STATES.
Bradford's directory of marketing
research agencies in the United
States and the world. [1st-   ed.;
1944- Fairfax, Va. [etc.] 658.83058
44-5426
   HF5415.A2 B7 MRR Ref Desk Latest
   edition

Dun & Bradstreet International. Dun
& Bradstreet exporters'
encyclopaedia: United States
marketing guide. 1973- New York.
382/.6/0973 73-642857
   HF3031 .D86a MRR Alc Latest
   edition

Editor & publisher. Market guide.
v. [1]-   1924- New York. 658.8 45-
44873
   HF5905 .E38 MRR Ref Desk Latest
   edition

Goldenthal, Allan B. The handbook of
U.S. markets and industrial growth
areas [New York] Regents Pub. Co.
[1969] v.   330.973 71-85525
   HC106.6 .G64 MRR Alc.

Military market facts. [Washington]
Army Times Pub. Co. 65-5288
   UC263 .M46 MRR Alc Latest edition

National Industrial Conference Board.
Graphic guide to consumer markets.
1960- New York. 658.83973 61-4523

   HC101 .N3183 MRR Alc Latest
   edition

Standard Rate and Data Service, inc.
S R D S newspaper circulation
analysis. Skokie, Ill. 67-6743
   HF5415.3 .S7 MRR Ref Desk Latest
   edition

MARKET SURVEYS--UNITED STATES--MAPS--
BIBLIOGRAPHY.
United States. Library of Congress.
Map Division. Marketing maps of the
United States; [1st]- 1851-
Washington. 016.6588 52-60015
   Z663.35 .M3 MRR Alc   MRR Alc Full
   set

MARKET SURVEYS--UNITED STATES--
YEARBOOKS.
American Newspaper Markets, inc.,
Northfield, Ill. Circulation.
Northfield. 65-36529
   Began publication with 1962 volume.
   HF5905 .A57 MRR Alc Latest edition

MARKETING.
see also Consumers

see also Export marketing

see also Retail trade

see also Sales promotion

MARKETING--ADDRESSES, ESSAYS, LECTURES.
Handbook of modern marketing. New
York, McGraw-Hill [1970] v.
(various pagings) [$27.50]
658.8/008 78-96238
   HF5415 .H1867 MRR Alc.

MARKETING--BIBLIOGRAPHY.
Frank, Nathalie D., Data sources for
business and market analysis, 2d ed.
Metuchen, N.J., Scarecrow Press,
1969. 361 p.   016.65883/9/73 73-
5855
   HF5415.1 .F7 1969 MRR Alc.

Frank, Nathalie D., Market analysis:
a handbook of current data sources,
New York, Scarecrow Press, 1964. 268
p.   658.83 64-21969
   HF5415 .F686 MRR Alc.

Pennington, Allan L. Reference guide
to marketing literature Braintree,
Mass., D. H. Mark Pub. Co. [1970] v,
13, [109] p.   016.6588 77-100576
   Z7164.M18 P44 MRR Alc.

Sandeau, Georges. International
bibliography of marketing and
distribution. [Bruxelles, Presses
universitaires de Bruxelles]
Distributed exclusively in North
America and South America [by] R. R.
Bowker Co., New York, 1971. 1 v.
(various pagings) 016.6588 73-
159927
   Z7164.M18 S2 1971b MRR Alc.

Wills, Gordon, comp. Sources of U.K.
marketing information; London,
Nelson, 1969. xiii, 304 p. [60/-]
658.83/9/42 72-626543
   HF5415.12.G7 W5 MRR Alc.

MARKETING--BIOGRAPHY.
American Marketing Association.
Membership roster. Chicago.
338.4/06/273 72-626734
   HF5415.A2 A57 MRR Alc Latest
   edition

MARKETING--CASE STUDIES--BIBLIOGRAPHY.
Berman, Linda. Case studies in
marketing; Metuchen, N.J., Scarecrow
Press, 1971. 211 p.   016.6588 79-
155282
   Z7164.M18 B46 MRR Alc.

MARKETING--CASE STUDIES--INDEXES.
Berman, Linda. Case studies in
marketing; Metuchen, N.J., Scarecrow
Press, 1971. 211 p.   016.6588 79-
155282
   Z7164.M18 B46 MRR Alc.

MARKETING--DICTIONARIES.
Shapiro, Irving J. Marketing terms:
definitions, explanations, and/or
aspects 3d ed. [West Long Branch,
N.J., S-M-C Pub. Co., 1973] 185 p.
658.8/003 73-75371
   HF5415 .S397 1973 MRR Alc.

Strand, Stanley. Marketing
dictionary. New York, Philosophical
Library [1962] 810 p.   658.803 61-
15251
   HF5415 .S868 MRR Alc.

Vigrolio, Tom. Marketing and
communications media dictionary,
[Norfolk, Mass., NBS Co., 1969]
xvii, 415 p. 658.8/003 76-80076
   HF5415 .V52 MRR Alc.

MARKETING--DIRECTORIES.
American Marketing Association.
Membership roster. Chicago.
338.4/06/273 72-626734
   HF5415.A2 A57 MRR Alc Latest
   edition

Anderson, Ian Gibson. Marketing &
management: Beckenham (Kent), C.B.D.
Research, 1969. iii-xii, 228 p.
[60/-] 658/.006 78-465981
   HF5415 .A616 MRR Alc.

MARKETING--INFORMATION SERVICES.
Frank, Nathalie D., Market analysis:
a handbook of current data sources,
New York, Scarecrow Press, 1964. 268
p.   658.83 64-21969
   HF5415 .F686 MRR Alc.

International reference handbook of
services, organizations, diplomatic
representation, marketing, and
advertising channels. 1954- New
York, World Trade Academy Press. a
55-1568
   HF54.U5 I52 MRR Alc Latest edition

MARKETING--INFORMATION SERVICES--UNITED
STATES.
Frank, Nathalie D., Data sources for
business and market analysis, 2d ed.
Metuchen, N.J., Scarecrow Press,
1969. 361 p.   016.65883/9/73 73-
5855
   HF5415.1 .F7 1969 MRR Alc.

MARKETING--PERIODICALS--INDEXES.
Pennington, Allan L. Reference guide
to marketing literature Braintree,
Mass., D. H. Mark Pub. Co. [1970] v,
13, [109] p.   016.6588 77-100576
   Z7164.M18 P44 MRR Alc.

Sandeau, Georges. International
bibliography of marketing and
distribution. [Bruxelles, Presses
universitaires de Bruxelles]
Distributed exclusively in North
America and South America [by] R. R.
Bowker Co., New York, 1971. 1 v.
(various pagings) 016.6588 73-
159927
   Z7164.M18 S2 1971b MRR Alc.

MARKETING--GREAT BRITAIN--INFORMATION
SERVICES.
Wills, Gordon, comp. Sources of U.K.
marketing information; London,
Nelson, 1969. xiii, 304 p. [60/-]
658.83/9/42 70-412725
   HF5415.12.G7 W5 MRR Alc.

MARKETING--NEW ENGLAND--DIRECTORIES.
The Book of names. Wellesley, Mass.,
New England Marketing Publications.
[$7.50]   380.1/025/74 74-644293
   HF5806.A11 B65 MRR Alc Latest
   edition

MARKETING--UNITED STATES.
Dun & Bradstreet International. Dun
& Bradstreet exporters'
encyclopaedia: United States
marketing guide. 1973- New York.
382/.6/0973 73-642857
   HF3031 .D86a MRR Alc Latest
   edition

MARKETING (HOME ECONOMICS)
see also Consumer education

see also Shopping

MARKETING (HOME ECONOMICS)--UNITED
STATES--DIRECTORIES.
The Organic directory, [Completely
rev. ed.] Emmaus, Pa., Rodale Press
[1974] 229 p. [$2.95] 641.3/1 74-
166399
   TX356 .O69 1974 MRR Alc.

MARKETING RESEARCH--BIBLIOGRAPHY.
A Basic bibliography on marketing
research / [3d ed.], 1974 revision.
[Chicago] : American Marketing
Association, 1974. x, 299 p. ;
016.6588/3 74-187908
   Z7164.M18 B35 1974 MRR Alc.

MARKETING RESEARCH--DIRECTORIES.
Annuaire du marketing europeen.
[Amsterdam] ESOMAR 72-624633
   HF5415.2 .A49 MRR Alc Latest
   edition

Bradford's directory of marketing
research agencies in the United
States and the world. [1st-   ed.;
1944- Fairfax, Va. [etc.] 658.83058
44-5426
   HF5415.A2 B7 MRR Ref Desk Latest
   edition

International reference handbook of
services, organizations, diplomatic
representation, marketing, and
advertising channels. 1954- New
York, World Trade Academy Press. a
55-1568
   HF54.U5 I52 MRR Alc Latest edition

MARKETS--EUROPE--DIRECTORIES.
Byrns, John H. Europe's hidden flea
markets and budget antique shops,
[1st ed. New York, R. P. Long; trade
distributor: Hastings House, 1968]
112 p.   914/.04/55 68-2401
   HF5152 .B9 MRR Alc.

MARKS OF ORIGIN.
Macdonald-Taylor, Margaret Stephens,
ed. A dictionary of marks:
metalwork, furniture, ceramics.
London, Connoisseur [c1962] 318 p.
63-1876
   NK7210 .M25 1962a MRR Alc.

MARLBOROUGH, N.Z. (PROVINCE)--COMMERCE--
DIRECTORIES.
Universal business directory for
Nelson-Marlborough-west coast.
Auckland, Universal Business
Directories. 52-38722
   HF5298 .U55 MRR Alc Latest edition

MARLBOROUGH, N.Z. (PROVINCIAL DISTRICT)--
COMMERCE--DIRECTORIES.
Universal business directory for
Nelson-Marlborough-west coast.
Auckland, Universal Business
Directories. 52-38722
   HF5298 .U55 MRR Alc Latest edition

MARRIAGE.
see also Family

see also Sex

Bowman, Henry Adelbert, Marriage for
moderns 6th ed. New York, McGraw-
Hill [1970] xii, 628 p.   301.42/6
70-95795
   HQ734 .B76 1970 MRR Alc.

Kirkpatrick, Clifford, The family as
process and institution, 2d ed. New
York, Ronald Press Co. [1963] 705 p.
301.42 63-10429
   HQ728 .K48 1963 MRR Alc.

Murdock, George Peter, Social
structure. New York, Macmillan Co.,
1949. xvii, 387 p.   392 49-9317
   GN27 .M95 MRR Alc.

MARRIAGE--BIBLIOGRAPHY.
Aldous, Joan. International
bibliography of research in marriage
and the family, 1900-1964
[Minneapolis] Distributed by the
University of Minnesota Press for the
Minnesota Family Study Center and the
Institute of Life Insurance [1967]
508 p.   016.30142 67-63014
   Z7164.M2 A48 MRR Alc.

MARRIAGE--BIBLIOGRAPHY. (Cont.)
Israel, Stanley. A bibliography on
divorce. New York, Bloch Pub. Co.
[1974] xiv, 300 p. [$10.95]
016.30142/84   73-77287
Z7164.M2 I76 MRR Alc.

Mogey, John M. Sociology of marriage
and family behaviour 1957-1968; The
Hague, Mouton [1971] 364 p.
016.30142   78-28387
Z7164.M2 M64 MRR Alc.

MARRIAGE--UNITED STATES.
Jacobson, Paul Harold, American
marriage and divorce. New York,
Rinehart [1959] xviii, 188 p.
301.42   59-9748
HQ535 .J3 MRR Alc.

United States. Division of Vital
Statistics. Vital statistics of the
United States. 1937- [Washington,
U.S. Govt. Print. Off.]   40-26272
HA203 .A22 MRR Alc Latest edition

MARRIAGE--UNITED STATES--STATISTICS.
Jacobson, Paul Harold, American
marriage and divorce. New York,
Rinehart [1959] xviii, 188 p.
301.42   59-9748
HQ535 .J3 MRR Alc.

Women's rights almanac. 1974-
Bethesda, Md., Elizabeth Cady Stanton
Pub. Co. [$4.95]   301.41/2/0973 74-
75527
HQ1406 .W65 MRR Ref Desk Latest
edition

MARRIAGE, PROMISE OF
see Betrothal

MARRIAGE LAW.
see also Divorce

MARRIAGE LICENSES--UNITED STATES.
United States. Health Services and
Mental Health Administration. Where
to write for marriage records; United
States and outlying areas.
[Washington, For sale by the Supt. of
Docs., U.S. Govt. Print. Off.]
312/.5/0973   73-615003
HA38 .A25 MRR Ref Desk Latest
edition

MARSHALL PLAN
see Economic assistance, American

MARTYRS--DICTIONARIES.
Russo-Alesi, Anthony Ignatius,
Martyrology pronouncing dictionary.
New York, The Edward O'Toole company,
inc., 1939. xiv, 177 p.   922.2 39-
21766
BX4661 .R8 MRR Alc.

MARVELL, ANDREW, 1621-1678--
CONCORDANCES.
Guffey, George Robert. A concordance
to the English poems of Andrew
Marvell. Chapel Hill, University of
North Carolina Press [1974] xiv, 623
p.   821/.4   73-21550
PR3546 .G77 MRR Alc.

MARX, KARL, 1818-1883--DICTIONARIES,
INDEXES, ETC.
Marx, Karl. Karl Marx dictionary,
New York, Philosophical Library
[1965] vii,273 p.   335.403 65-
10660
HX39.5 .A38 1965 MRR Alc.

MARXISM
see Communism

MARY, VIRGIN--DICTIONARIES.
Attwater, Donald, A dictionary of
Mary. New York, Kenedy [1956] viii,
312 p.   232.931 56-10460
BT599 .A9 MRR Alc.

MARYLAND.
Writers' program. Maryland.
Maryland, a guide to the old line
state, New York, Oxford university
press [c1940] xxviii, 561 p.
917.52   40-13919
F181 .W75 MRR Ref Desk.

MARYLAND--BIBLIOGRAPHY.
Bristol, Roger Pattrell. Maryland
imprints, 1801-1810.
Charlottesville, Published by the
University of Virginia Press for the
Bibliographical Society of the
University of Virginia, 1953.
xxviii, 310 p.   015.752 53-7130
Z1293 .B75 MRR Alc.

MARYLAND--DESCRIPTION AND TRAVEL.
Sprouse, Edith Moore. Potomac
sampler; [Alexandria, Va.] c1961.
29 l.   62-27127
F227 .S74 MRR Alc.

MARYLAND--DESCRIPTION AND TRAVEL--GUIDE-
BOOKS.
Living in Washington; 1st ed.]
Richmond, Westover Pub. Co. [1972]
vii, 259 p. [$3.50]   917.53 72-
188108
F192.3 .L58 MRR Ref Desk.

Writers' program. Maryland.
Maryland, a guide to the old line
state, New York, Oxford university
press [c1940] xxviii, 561 p.
917.52   40-13919
F181 .W75 MRR Ref Desk.

MARYLAND--EXECUTIVE DEPARTMENTS--
DIRECTORIES.
Maryland manual. [Baltimore, etc.]
10-6200
JK3831 MRR Alc Latest edition

MARYLAND--GOVERNMENT PUBLICATIONS--
BIBLIOGRAPHY.
Maryland manual. [Baltimore, etc.]
10-6200
JK3831 MRR Alc Latest edition

MARYLAND--HISTORIC HOUSES, ETC.
Sprouse, Edith Moore. Potomac
sampler; [Alexandria, Va.] c1961.
29 l.   62-27127
F227 .S74 MRR Alc.

MARYLAND--HISTORY--COLONIAL PERIOD, CA.
1600-1775--BIBLIOGRAPHY.
Baer, Elizabeth. Seventeenth century
Maryland; Baltimore, John Work
Garrett Library, 1949. xxix, 219 p.
016.9752   49-6516
Z1293 .B3 MRR Alc.

MARYLAND--HISTORY--COLONIAL PERIOD, CA.
1600-1775--SOURCES.
Hall, Clayton Colman, ed. Narratives
of early Maryland, 1633-1684, New
York, Charles Scribner's sons, 1910.
ix p., 2 l., 3-460 p.   10-23763
E187.Q7 H3 MRR Alc.

MARYLAND--IMPRINTS.
Bristol, Roger Pattrell. Maryland
imprints, 1801-1810.
Charlottesville, Published by the
University of Virginia Press for the
Bibliographical Society of the
University of Virginia, 1953.
xxviii, 310 p.   015.752 53-7130
Z1293 .B75 MRR Alc.

MARYLAND--MANUFACTURES--DIRECTORIES.
Directory of Central Atlantic States
manufacturers; 1.- ed.; 1950-
Baltimore, T. K. Sanderson
Organization.   670.58 50-2706
T12 .D485 Sci RR Latest edition /
MRR Alc Latest edition

MARYLAND--POLITICS AND GOVERNMENT.
League of Women Voters of
Metropolitan Washington.
Metropolitan Washington: District of
Columbia, Maryland, Virginia.
Washington, League of Women Voters
Education Fund [1970] 52 p. [$0.25]
320.4/753   77-27912
JK2725 1970 .L4 MRR Ref Desk.

Maryland manual. [Baltimore, etc.]
10-6200
JK3831 MRR Alc Latest edition

MARYLAND--REGISTERS.
Maryland manual. [Baltimore, etc.]
10-6200
JK3831 MRR Alc Latest edition

MASARYK, TOMÁŠ GARRIGUE, PRES.
CZECHOSLOVAK REPUBLIC, 1850-1937.
Jesina, Cestmir, comp. The birth of
Czechoslovakia. [Washington]
Czechoslovak National Council of
America, Washington, D.C. Chapter,
1968. ix, 110 p. [5.00]   74-18574

DB215.2 .J48 MRR Alc.

MASONRY.
see also Bricklaying

see also Concrete

Dezettel, Louis M. Masons and
builders library, Indianapolis, T.
Audel [1972] 2 v.   693 78-186134
TH5311 .D48 MRR Alc.

MASS COMMUNICATION
see Communication

see Telecommunication

MASS FEEDING
see Food service

MASS MEDIA.
see also Moving-pictures

see also Newspapers

see also Television broadcasting

Handbook of communication. Chicago,
Rand McNally College Pub. Co. [c1973]
ix, 1011 p.   001.5/02/02 72-7851
P90 .H293 MRR Alc.

MASS MEDIA--BIBLIOGRAPHY.
Brockett, Oscar Gross, A
bibliographical guide to research in
speech and dramatic art Chicago,
Scott, Foresman [1963] 118 p.   016
63-14554
Z1002 .B87 MRR Alc.

Journalism abstracts. v. 1- 1963-
[Chapel Hill, N.C.] Association for
Education in Journalism. [$2.50]
070/.08   74-642577
PN4725 .J67 MRR Alc Full set

MASS MEDIA--DICTIONARIES.
Biddlecombe, Peter. International
public relations encyclopedia.
London, Grant Helm, 1968. 220 p.
[37/6]   659.2/03 77-364516
HD59 .B5 MRR Alc.

Curtis, Ron. Media dictionary; Red
Oak, Southwest Iowa Learning
Resources Center [1973] 290 p.
301.16/1/03   73-158317
P87.5 .C8 MRR Alc.

Jacobson, Howard Boone, ed. A mass
communications dictionary; New York,
Greenwood Press [1969, c1961] xxvi,
377 p.   301.16 70-90536
P87.5 .J3 1969 MRR Alc.

MASS MEDIA--DIRECTORIES.
Black list; New York, Panther House
[1970] 289 p. [$12.50 (pbk)]
001.5/025/6   73-112479
P88.8 .B6 MRR Alc.

MASS MEDIA--METHODOLOGY.
Nafziger, Ralph O., ed. Introduction
to mass communications research.
[Rev. ed.] Baton Rouge, Louisiana
State University Press [1963] 281 p.
070/72   63-8223
PN4853 .J6 no. 6 1963 MRR Alc.

MASS MEDIA--CALIFORNIA--DIRECTORIES.
California publicity outlets. 1972-
Los Angeles, Unicorn Systems Co.,
Information Services Division.
659.2/025/794   76-186163
HM263 .C2 MRR Alc Latest edition

West coast theatrical directory.
1970- Los Angeles, Tarcher/Gousha
Guides. 917.94/0025   70-109344
PN1582.U6 W4 MRR Alc Latest
edition

MASS MEDIA--UNITED STATES--BIOGRAPHY.
Foremost women in communications;
New York, Foremost Americans Pub.
Corp. [1970] xvii, 788 p.
001.5/0922   79-125936
P92.5.A1 F6 MRR Biog.

MASS MEDIA--UNITED STATES--DIRECTORIES.
Rosenbloom, David L. The political
marketplace. [New York] Quadrangle
Books [1972] xix, 948 p. [$25.00]
329/.0025/73   72-77926
JK2283 .R64 MRR Ref Desk.

United States. Office of Minority
Business Enterprise. Directory of
minority media. [Washington]; for
sale by the Supt. of Docs., U.S.
Govt. Print. Off., 1973. ix, 89 p.
[$1.25]   301.16/1/02573   73-602686
P88.8 .U55 MRR Alc.

Weiner, Richard, Professional's
guide to public relations services.
2d ed. Englewood Cliffs, N.J.,
Prentice-Hall [1971] 239 p.
659.2/025/73   71-136585
HD59 .W38 1971 MRR Alc.

MASS PSYCHOLOGY
see Social psychology

MASSACHUSETTS.
Massachusetts: a guide to the Pilgram
State. 2d ed., rev. and enl.
Boston, Houghton Mifflin, 1971. xiv,
525 p. [$10.00]   917.44/04/4 68-
16270
F70 .M425 1971 MRR Ref Desk.

MASSACHUSETTS--BIBLIOGRAPHY.
American imprints inventory project.
Massachusetts. A check list of
Massachusetts imprints, 1801.
Boston, Mass., 1942. xxxiii, 157
numb. l., 5 l.   015.744 44-5151
Z1215 .H67 no. 40 MRR Alc.

American imprints inventory project.
Massachusetts. A check list of
Massachusetts imprints, 1802.
Boston, Mass., 1942. xxxiii, 158
numb. l., 5 l.   015.744 43-444
Z1215 .H67 no. 45 MRR Alc.

MASSACHUSETTS--DESCRIPTION AND TRAVEL--
1951- --GUIDE-BOOKS.
Rubin, Jerome. A guide to
Massachusetts museums, historic
houses, points of interest, [Newton,
Mass., Emporium Publications, 1972]
126 p. [$1.95]   917.44/044 72-
81231
F61.5 .R8 MRR Alc.

MASSACHUSETTS--DESCRIPTION AND TRAVEL--
GUIDE-BOOKS.
Massachusetts: a guide to the Pilgram
State. 2d ed., rev. and enl.
Boston, Houghton Mifflin, 1971. xiv,
525 p. [$10.00]   917.44/04/4 68-
16270
F70 .M425 1971 MRR Ref Desk.

MASSACHUSETTS--HISTORIC HOUSES, ETC.--
DIRECTORIES.
Rubin, Jerome. A guide to
Massachusetts museums, historic
houses, points of interest, [Newton,
Mass., Emporium Publications, 1972]
126 p. [$1.95] 917.44/044 72-
81231
  F61.5 .R8 MRR Alc.

MASSACHUSETTS--HISTORY.
Howe, Henry Forbush, Massachusetts:
there she is--behold her. [1st ed.]
New York, Harper [1960] 290 p.
974.4 60-13447
  F64 .H75 MRR Alc.

MASSACHUSETTS--HISTORY--COLONIAL
PERIOD, CA. 1600-1775.
Johnson, Edward, Johnson's Wonder-
working providence, 1628-1651; New
York, C. Scribner's sons, 1910. viii
p., 2 l., 3-285 p. [$3.00] 10-9809

  E187.07 J6 MRR Alc.

Winthrop, John, Winthrop's journal,
"History of New England," 1630-1649;
New York, C. Scribner's sons, 1908.
2 v. 08-17771
  E187.07 W5 MRR Alc.

MASSACHUSETTS--HISTORY--NEW PLYMOUTH,
1620-1691.
Bradford, William, Bradford's
history of Plymouth plantation, 1606-
1646; New York, C. Scribner's sons,
1908. xv p., 2 l., 3-437 p. 08-
7375
  E187.07 B7 MRR Alc.

Willison, George Findlay, Saints and
strangers: [Revised ed.] London,
Heinemann, 1866. xii, 307 p. [36/-]
974.402 66-77420
  F68 .W75 1866 MRR Alc.

MASSACHUSETTS--IMPRINTS.
American imprints inventory project.
Massachusetts. A check list of
Massachusetts imprints, 1801.
Boston, Mass., 1942. xxxiii, 157
numb. l., 5 l.   015.744 44-5151
  Z1215 .H67 no. 40 MRR Alc.

American imprints inventory project.
Massachusetts. A check list of
Massachusetts imprints, 1802.
Boston, Mass., 1942. xxxiii, 158
numb. l., 5 l.   015.744 43-444
  Z1215 .H67 no. 45 MRR Alc.

MASSACHUSETTS--MANUFACTURES--
DIRECTORIES.
Directory of New England
manufacturers. Boston, Mass., G. D.
Hall, inc. 338.40974 36-5085
  HD8723 .D45 Sci RR Latest edition
  / MRR Alc Latest edition

Massachusetts industrial directory.
[Boston, Massachusetts Dept. of
Commerce and Development]
380.1/025/744 72-626567
  HD8727.M4 A25 Sci RR Latest
  edition / MRR Alc Latest edition

MASSACHUSETTS--POLITICS AND GOVERNMENT.
Massachusetts. General Court. Manual
for the use of the general court.
Boston. 08-8771
  JK3131 MRR Alc Latest edition

MASSACHUSETTS--REGISTERS.
Massachusetts. General Court. Manual
for the use of the general court.
Boston. 08-8771
  JK3131 MRR Alc Latest edition

MĂT TRĂN DĂN TŎC GI'AI PH'ONG
MIĚN NAM VIĚT NAM.
Pike, Douglas Eugene, Viet Cong;
Cambridge, Mass., M.I.T. Press [1966]
xx, 490 p. 959.704 66-28896
  DS557.A6 P54 MRR Alc.

MATERIA MEDICA.
see also Drugs

see also Pharmacology.

see also Poisons

see also Therapeutics

The Merck index; 8th ed. Rahway,
N.J., Merck, 1968. xii, 1713 p.
615/.1/03 68-12252
  RS356 .M524 1968 MRR Alc.

Modern drug encyclopedia and
therapeutic index. 1st- ed.; 1934-
New York, R. H. Donnelley [etc.] 34-
12823
  RS153 .M57 Sci RR Latest edition /
  MRR Alc Latest edition

Physicians' desk reference to
pharmaceutical specialties and
biologicals. 1st- ed.; 1847-
Oradell [etc.] N.J., Medical
economics. 60-784
  RS75 .P5 Sci RR latest edition /
  MRR Ref Desk Latest edition

MATERIA MEDICA--DICTIONARIES.
Hocking, George Macdonald. A
dictionary of terms in pharmacognosy
and other divisions of economic
botany; Springfield, Ill., C. C.
Thomas [1955] xxv, 284 p. 581.603
55-7453
  QK99 .H69 1955 MRR Alc.

MATERIA MEDICA, VEGETABLE.
see also Botany, Medical

Grieve, Maud. A modern herbal; New
York, Hafner Pub. Co., 1959. 2 v.
(xvi, 888 p.) 581.6303 59-15624
  QK9 .G7 1959 MRR Alc.

Loewenfeld, Claire. The complete
book of herbs and spices / New York
: Putnam, [1974] 313 p., [4] leaves
of plates : [$14.95] 581.6/3 74-
78005
  SB351.H5 L67 MRR Alc.

MATERIALS.
United States. Library of Congress.
Science and Technology Division.
Materials research chronology, 1917-
1957. Dayton, Directorate of
Materials and Processes, Aeronautical
Systems Division, Wright Patterson
Air Force Base, 1962. viii, 59 p.
620.1 63-60204
  Z663.41 .M33 MRR Alc.

MATERIALS--ABSTRACTS.
United States. Library of Congress.
Science and Technology Division.
Materials research abstracts,
[Washington] Published for
Directorate of Materials and
Processes, Aeronautical Systems
Division, Wright-Patterson Air Force
Base, Ohio, 1962. vii, 534 p.
620.1 63-60205
  Z663.41 .M3 MRR Alc.

MATERIALS--DICTIONARIES.
Brady, George Stuart, Materials
handbook; 1st- ed.; 1929- New
York, McGraw-Hill. 29-1603
  TA403 .B75 Sci RR Latest edition /
  MRR Alc Latest edition

MATERIALS--STANDARDS.
American Society for Testing and
Materials. Book of A.S.T.M.
standards, with related material.
1939- Philadelphia. 40-10712
  TA401 .A653 Sci RR Latest edition
  / MRR Alc Latest edition

MATERIALS--TESTING.
American Society for Testing and
Materials. Book of A.S.T.M.
standards, with related material.
1939- Philadelphia. 40-10712
  TA401 .A653 Sci RR Latest edition
  / MRR Alc Latest edition

United States. Library of Congress.
Science and Technology Division.
Materials research abstracts,
[Washington] Published for
Directorate of Materials and
Processes, Aeronautical Systems
Division, Wright-Patterson Air Force
Base, Ohio, 1962. vii, 534 p.
620.1 63-60205
  Z663.41 .M3 MRR Alc.

MATERIALS--TESTING--COLLECTED WORKS.
United States. Library of Congress.
Science and Technology Division.
Charles J. Cleary awards for papers
on material sciences. [Washington]
Published for Directorate of
Materials and Processes, Aeronautical
Systems Division, Wright-Patterson
Air Force Base, Ohio, 1962. vii, 219
p. 620.1 63-60206
  Z663.41 .C43 MRR Alc.

MATERIALS HANDLING--DIRECTORIES.
Material handling engineering
directory & handbook. 1st- ed.;
1948- Cleveland, Industrial
Publishing [etc.] 621.86058 50-
11696
  TS149 .M28 MRR Alc Latest edition

MATERNITY HOMES--UNITED STATES--
DIRECTORIES.
National Council on Illegitimacy.
Maternity homes and residential
facilities for unmarried mothers:
directory; New York, 1966. 206 p.
362.8302573 66-8903
  HV700.5 .N34 MRR Alc.

MATHEMATICAL PHYSICS.
see also Sound

MATHEMATICAL RECREATIONS.
see also Chess

MATHEMATICAL SYMBOLS
see Abbreviations

MATHEMATICIANS--BIOGRAPHY.
Fang, Joong. Mathematicans from
antiquity to today A prelim. ed.
[Hauppauge, N.Y.] Paideia [1972- v.
  [$12.80 (v. 1)] 510/.92/2 B 70-
131575
  QA28 .F3 MRR Biog.

MATHEMATICIANS, AMERICAN.
American Mathematical Society.
Combined membership list.
[Providence?] 56-23632
  QA1 .A523 Sci RR Latest edition /
  MRR Alc Latest edition

MATHEMATICS.
see also Equations

see also Metric system

see also Trigonometry

Miller, Leslie Haynes. Understanding
basic mathematics. New York, Holt,
Rinehart and Winston [1961] 499 p.
510 61-6363
  QA39 .M522 MRR Alc.

MATHEMATICS--DICTIONARIES.
Ballentyne, Denis William George. A
dictionary of named effects and laws
in chemistry, physics and mathematics
3rd ed. London, Chapman & Hall,
1970. iii-viii, 355 p. [£3.00]
500.2/03 71-552485
  Q123 .B3 1970 MRR Alc.

Herland, Leo Joseph. Dictionary of
mathematical sciences 2d ed.; rev.
and enl. New York, F. Ungar Pub. Co.
[1965- v.   510.3 65-16622
  QA5 .H42 MRR Alc.

Herland, Leo Joseph. Dictionary of
mathematical sciences. New York, F.
Ungar Pub. Co. [1951-54] 2 v.
510.3 51-13545
  QA5 .H4 MRR Alc.

James, Glenn, ed. Mathematics
dictionary, Multilingual ed.
Princeton, N.J., Van Nostrand [1959]
546 p.   510.3 59-8656
  QA5 .J32 1959 MRR Alc.

Millington, T. Alaric. Dictionary of
mathematics, London, Cassell, 1966.
x, 259 p. [21/-] 510.03 66-2548
  QA5 .M495 MRR Alc.

The Universal encyclopedia of
mathematics. New York, Simon and
Schuster, 1964. 715 p. 510.3 63-
21086
  QA5 .U5413 MRR Alc.

MATHEMATICS--DICTIONARIES--GERMAN.
Herland, Leo Joseph. Dictionary of
mathematical sciences. New York, F.
Ungar Pub. Co. [1951-54] 2 v.
510.3 51-13545
  QA5 .H4 MRR Alc.

Herland, Leo Joseph. Dictionary of
mathematical sciences 2d ed.; rev.
and enl. New York, F. Ungar Pub. Co.
[1965- v.   510.3 65-16622
  QA5 .H42 MRR Alc.

MATHEMATICS--DICTIONARIES--POLYGLOT.
The International dictionary of
applied mathematics, Princeton,
N.J., Van Nostrand [1960] 1173 p.
510.3 60-16931
  QA5 .I5 MRR Alc.

James, Glenn, ed. Mathematics
dictionary, Multilingual ed.
Princeton, N.J., Van Nostrand [1959]
546 p.   510.3 59-8656
  QA5 .J32 1959 MRR Alc.

MATHEMATICS--FORMULAE.
Burington, Richard Stevens, Handbook
of mathematical tables and formulas.
5th ed. New York, McGraw-Hill
[c1973] x, 500 p. [$5.50]
510/.21/2 78-39634
  QA47 .B8 1972 MRR Alc.

The Universal encyclopedia of
mathematics. New York, Simon and
Schuster, 1964. 715 p. 510.3 63-
21086
  QA5 .U5413 MRR Alc.

MATHEMATICS--HANDBOOKS, MANUALS, ETC.
Korn, Granino Arthur, Mathematical
handbook for scientists and
engineers; 2d, enl. and rev. ed.
New York, McGraw-Hill [c1968] xvii,
1130 p. 510/.02/02 67-16304
  QA40 .K598 1968 MRR Alc.

Levine, Sol, Mathematics handbook.
[1st ed.] New York, R. Rosen Press
[1972] 224 p.   510/.2/02 76-116618

  QA40 .L48 MRR Alc.

MATHEMATICS--HISTORY.
Eves, Howard Whitley, An
introduction to the history of
mathematics 3d ed. New York, Holt,
Rinehart and Winston [1969] xv, 464
p. 510/.09 69-14523
  QA21 .E8 1969 MRR Alc.

Hogben, Lancelot Thomas, Mathematics
for the million 4th ed. extensively
revised London, Allen & Unwin, 1967.
649 p. [40/-] 510 68-88418
  QA36 .H6 1967 MRR Alc.

MATHEMATICS--HISTORY. (Cont.)
Kline, Morris. Mathematical thought from ancient to modern times. New York, Oxford University Press, 1972. xvii, 1238 p. [$35.00] 510/.9 77-170263
QA21 .K516 MRR Alc.

MATHEMATICS--POPULAR WORKS.
Hogben, Lancelot Thomas. Mathematics for the million 4th ed. extensively revised London, Allen & Unwin, 1967. 649 p. [40/-] 510 68-88418
QA36 .H6 1967 MRR Alc.

MATHEMATICS--PROBLEMS, EXERCISES, ETC.
Eves, Howard Whitley. An introduction to the history of mathematics 3d ed. New York, Holt, Rinehart and Winston [1969] xv, 464 p. 510/.09 69-14523
QA21 .E8 1969 MRR Alc.

MATHEMATICS--TABLES, ETC.
Burington, Richard Stevens. Handbook of mathematical tables and formulas. 5th ed. New York, McGraw-Hill [c1973] x, 500 p. [$5.50] 510/.21/2 78-39634
QA47 .B8 1972 MRR Alc.

C.R.C. standard mathematical tables. [1st]- ed.: 1931- Cleveland, Chemical Rubber Co. [etc.] 510.83 30-4052
QA47 .M315 MRR Alc Latest edition / Sci RR Latest edition

Carlsten, Kirk Finley. Book computer, Denver, Metron Instrument Co. [1960] 999 p. 510.83 60-12305
QA49 .C2 MRR Alc.

Cox, Edwin Burk. Basic tables in business and economics, New York, McGraw-Hill [1967] xiv, 399 p. 511/.8 66-18284
HF5699 .C892 MRR Alc.

Damm, John A., ed. The practical and technical encyclopedia, New York, W. H. Wise, 1848. vi, 632 p. 603 48-3757
T9 .D3 MRR Alc.

[Delbridge, Charles Lomax] Delbridge interest tables, St. Louis, Mo., Delbridge calculating systems, inc. [1944] xvi, 296 p. 332.82083 44-45368
HG1626 .D4 MRR Alc.

Hof, Hans, Powers, roots, reciprocals, from 1-15000: 1st ed. [Jenkintown, Pa.; Professional Supply Co., 1956] unpaged. 510.83 56-45578
QA49 .H68 MRR Alc.

Smoley, Constantine Kenneth, Smoley's four combined tables for engineers, architects, and students, Chautauqua, N.Y., C. K. Smoley & Sons, 1956. 1 v. (various pagings) 510.835 56-14448
TA332 .S56 1956 MRR Alc.

The Universal encyclopedia of mathematics. New York, Simon and Schuster, 1964. 715 p. 510.3 63-21086
QA5 .U5413 MRR Alc.

MATHEMATICS--TABLES, ETC.--COLLECTED WORKS.
Handbook of tables for mathematics. 3d- ed.: 1967- Cleveland, Chemical Rubber Co. 510/.21/2 72-620937
QA47 .H32 Sci RR Latest edition / MRR Alc Latest edition

MATHEMATICS--TABLES, ETC.--INDEXES.
Fletcher, Alan, An index of mathematical tables. 2d ed. Reading, Mass., For Scientific Computing Service [by] Addison-Wesley Pub. Co., 1862. 2 v. (xi, 994 p.) 510.83 62-13521
QA47 .F55 1962 MRR Alc.

MATHEMATICS, GREEK.
Bulmer-Thomas, Ivor, ed. and tr. Selections illustrating the history of Greek mathematics Cambridge, Mass., Harvard university press; London, W. Heinemann, ltd., 1939-41. 2 v. 510.938 39-23451
PA3611 .A95 1939 MRR Alc.

MATRIARCHY.
see also Family

MAUPASSANT, GUY DE, 1850-1893--DICTIONARIES, INDEXES, ETC.
Los Angeles. Public Library. Fiction Dept. Index to the stories of Guy de Maupassant. Boston, G. K. Hall, 1960. 105 p. 843.8 60-51767
PQ2356 .L6 MRR Alc.

MAURITANIA.
Curran, Brian Dean. Area handbook for Mauritania. [Washington; For sale by the Supt. of Docs., U.S. Govt. Print. Off.] 1972. xiv, 185 p. [$2.25] 916.61/03/5 72-600188
DT553.M2 C87 MRR Alc.

Gerteiny, Alfred G. Mauritania New York, Praeger [1967] x, 243 p. 916.6/1 67-23574
DT553.M2 G4 MRR Alc.

MAURITANIA--GAZETTEERS.
United States. Office of Geography. Mauritania; official standard names approved by the United States Board on Geographic Names. Washington, 1966. vii, 149 p. 916.6/1/003 66-62751
DT553.M22 U5 MRR Alc.

MAURITIUS--GOVERNMENT PUBLICATIONS--BIBLIOGRAPHY.
United States. Library of Congress. African Section. Madagascar and adjacent islands; Washington General Reference and Bibliography Division, Reference Department, Library of Congress;[for sale by the Superintendent of Documents, U.S. Govt. Print. Off.] 1965. xiii, 58 p. 65-61703
Z663.285 .M3 MRR Alc.

MAXIMS.
Lawson, James Gilchrist, comp. The world's best proverbs and maxims, New York, George H. Doran company [c1926] xvi p., 1 l., 19-364 p. 26-12534
PN6405 .L3 MRR Alc.

Plotkin, David George, Dictionary of American maxims, New York, Philosophical Library [1955] 597 p. 398.9 55-13882
PN6271 .P6 MRR Ref Desk.

Stevenson, Burton Egbert, ed. The home book of proverbs, maxims and familiar phrases. New York, Macmillan Co., 1948. viii, 2957 p. 398.9 48-8717
PN6405 .S8 MRR Alc.

Stevenson, Burton Egbert, ed. The Macmillan book of proverbs, maxims, and famous phrases. New York, Macmillan [1965, c1948] viii, 2957 p. 808.88 65-3787
PN6405 .S8 1965 MRR Ref Desk.

MAXIMS, GERMAN--DICTIONARIES.
Röhrich, Lutz. Lexikon der sprichwörtlichen Redensarten. Freiburg, Herder [1973] 2 v. (1255 p.) 73-364707
PF689 .R6 MRR Alc.

MAXIMS, SANSKRIT.
Apte, Vaman Shivaram, The practical Sanskrit-English dictionary. Rev. and enl. ed. Poona, Prasad Prakashan, 1957-59. 3 v. 491.232 58-20492
PK933 .A65 MRR Alc.

MAYORS--UNITED STATES.
Who's who in American politics. 1st-ed.: 1967/68- New York, Bowker. 320/.0922 67-25024
E176 .W6424 MRR Biog Latest edition

MAYORS--UNITED STATES--DIRECTORIES.
Notable names in American history; 3d ed of White's conspectus of American biography. [Clifton, N.J.] J. T. White, 1973. 725 p. 920/.073 73-6885
E176 .N89 1973 MRR Biog.

Rosenbloom, David L. The political marketplace. [New York] Quadrangle Books [1972] xix, 948 p. [$25.00] 329/.0025/73 72-77926
JK2283 .R64 MRR Ref Desk.

MCADOO, WILLIAM GIBBS, 1863-1941--MANUSCRIPTS.
United States. Library of Congress. Manuscript Division. William Gibbs McAdoo: a register of his papers in the Library of Congress. Washington, 1959. 35 p. 012 59-60038
Z663.34 .M2 MRR Alc.

MCGILL UNIVERSITY, MONTREAL. LIBRARY.
McGill University, Montreal. Library. The Lawrence Lande collection of Canadiana in the Redpath Library of McGill University; Montreal, Lawrence Lande Foundation for Canadian Historical Research, 1965. xxxv, 301 p. 65-18258
Z1365 .M14 MRR Alc.

MCGOVERN, GEORGE STANLEY, 1922-
Anson, Robert Sam, McGovern: [1st ed.] New York, Holt, Rinehart and Winston [1972] xiii, 303 p. [$7.95] 328.73/092/4 B 72-183538
E840.8.M34 A8 1972 MRR Alc.

MCGOWAN, SAMUEL, 1870-1934--MANUSCRIPTS.
United States. Library of Congress. Manuscript Division. Colby Mitchell Chester, William Freeland Fullam, Samuel McGowan, Henry Croskey Mustin: a register of their papers in the Library of Congress. Washington, Library of Congress, 1973. iii, 4, 6, 7, 5 p. 016.359 73-2939
Z663.34 .C48 MRR Alc.

MCKINLEY, WILLIAM, PRES. U.S., 1843-1901.
Leech, Margaret. In the days of McKinley. [1st ed.] New York, Harper [1959] viii, 686 p. 923.173 59-6310
E711.6 .L4 MRR Alc.

Morgan, Howard Wayne. William McKinley and his America. [Syracuse, N.Y.] Syracuse University Press, 1963. xi, 595 p. 923.173 63-19723
E711.6 .M7 MRR Alc.

Olcott, Charles Sumner, The life of William McKinley, Boston, New York, Houghton Mifflin company, 1916. 2 v. 16-10505
E711.6 .O43 MRR Alc.

MEASUREMENT, MENTAL
see Psychometrics

MEASUREMENTS, PHYSICAL
see Physical measurements

MECHANICAL DRAWING.
see also Design, Industrial

see also Graphic methods

MECHANICAL ENGINEERING.
see also Chemical engineering

see also Machinery

MECHANICAL ENGINEERING--ABBREVIATIONS.
Dictionary of mechanical engineering abbreviations: New York, Odyssey Press [1967] xviii, 725 p. 621/.01/48 65-18844
TJ9 .D5 MRR Alc.

MECHANICAL ENGINEERING--BIBLIOGRAPHY.
United States. Library of Congress. Reference Dept. Manufacturing and mechanical engineering in the Soviet Union; Washington, 1953. xii, 234 p. 016.621 53-60040
Z663.2 .M3 MRR Alc.

MECHANICAL ENGINEERING--DICTIONARIES.
Del Vecchio, Alfred. Dictionary of mechanical engineering, New York, Philosophical Library [1961] 346 p. 621.03 60-13664
TJ9 .D38 MRR Alc.

Nayler, Joseph Lawrence, Dictionary of mechanical engineering, London, Newnes, 1967. [5], 406 p. [45/-] 621/.03 67-86836
TJ9 .N3 MRR Alc.

MECHANICAL ENGINEERING--DICTIONARIES--POLYGLOT.
Cooper, S. A. Concise international dictionary of mechanics & geology: New York, Philosophical Library [1958] viii, 400 p. 621.03 58-3594
TJ9 .C6 1958 MRR Alc.

MECHANICAL ENGINEERING--HANDBOOKS, MANUALS, ETC.
Machinery's handbook. 16th- ed.: 1959- New York, Industrial Press. 621.8/02 72-622276
TJ151 .M3 MRR Alc Latest edition / Sci RR Latest edition

Standard handbook for mechanical engineers. 1st- ed.: 1916- New York, McGraw-Hill. 502/.4/621 16-12915
TJ151 .S82 Sci RR Latest edition / MRR Alc Latest edition

MECHANICAL ENGINEERING--INDEXES.
American Society of Mechanical Engineers. Seventy-seven year index: technical papers, 1880-1956. New York [1957] 382 p. 621.06273 57-59509
TJ1 .A774 MRR Alc.

MECHANICAL ENGINEERING--JUVENILE LITERATURE.
Boumphrey, Geoffrey Maxwell, Engines and how they work. New York, F. Watts [1967] 256 p. 67-5972
TJ147 .B68 1967 MRR Alc.

MECHANICAL ENGINEERS--UNITED STATES--DIRECTORIES.
American Society of Mechanical Engineers. Committee on Professional Practice of Consulting Engineering. Directory of consulting engineers. New York, American Society of Mechanical Engineers [1957] 42 p. 57-2083
TJ11 .A7 MRR Biog.

MECHANICAL MOVEMENTS.
Graf, Rudolf F. How it works,
illustrated: everyday devices and
mechanisms. New York, Popular
science [1974] viii, 184 p.
[$10.95] 620 73-80716
TX298 .G68 MRR Alc.

MECHANIZATION.
see also Automation

MEDAL OF HONOR.
Blakeney, Jane. Heroes, U.S. Marine
Corps, 1861-1955; [1st ed.]
Washington, 1957] xviii, 621 p.
359.96 57-13185
VE23 .B56 MRR Biog.

Kerrigan, Evans E. The Medal of
Honor in Vietnam, [1st ed.] Noroton
Heights, Conn., Medallic Pub. Co.
[1971- v. 958.7/0434/0922 B 77-
173048
DS557.A6315 K45 MRR Biog.

Lee, Irvin H. Negro Medal of Honor
men, 3d ed., new and enl. New York,
Dodd, Mead [1969] xii, 156 p.
[4.50] 355.1/34 68-58447
UB433 .L4 1969 MRR Alc.

Schott, Joseph L. Above and beyond:
the story of the Congressional Medal
of Honor. New York, Putnam [1963]
314 p. 355.134 62-18293
E181 .S35 MRR Alc.

United States. Bureau of Naval
Personnel. Medal of honor, 1861-
1949, the Navy. [Washington, 1950?]
ix, 327 p. 359.134 50-61099
VB333 .A532 MRR Biog.

United States. Congress. Senate.
Committee on Veterans' Affairs.
Medal of Honor recipients, 1863-1973:
Washington, U.S. Govt. Print. Off.,
1973. xix, 1231 p. [$8.50]
355.1/34 73-603149
UB433 .U55 1973b MRR Biog.

United States. Dept. of the Army.
Public Information Division. The
Medal of Honor of the United States
Army. [Washington, U.S. Govt. Print.
Off., 1948] vii, 468 p. 355.134
48-45817
UB433 .A52 1948 MRR Biog.

MEDALS.
Werlich, Robert. Orders and
decorations of all nations: ancient
and modern, civil and military. 2d
ed. [Washington, Quaker Press, 1974]
476 p. 929.8 74-177291
CR4509 .W4 1974 MRR Ref Desk.

MEDALS--DENMARK.
Forlaget Liber, Copenhagen. De
kongelige danske ridderordener og
medailler. København, Forlaget
liber, 1865. 611 p. 73-332590
CR5750 .F62 MRR Alc.

Forlaget Liber, Copenhagen. De
kongelige danske ridderordener og
medailler. [1964-1968]. København,
Liber, 1970. 591 p. [kr722.20] 72-
300129
CR5750 .F6 1970 MRR Alc.

MEDALS--GERMANY.
Doehle, Heinrich, Die Orden und
Ehrenzeichen des Grossdeutschen
Reichs. Berlin, Berliner Buch- und
Zeitschriften-Verlag, 1941. 128 p.
737.2 52-55855
CR5109 .D57 1941 MRR Alc.

MEDALS--GREAT BRITAIN.
Abbott, Peter Edward. British
gallantry awards Enfield, Guiness
Superlatives; London, Seaby, 1971.
359 p.; [£6.00] 355.1/34 72-
872853
CR4801 .A63 MRR Alc.

British orders and awards: 2nd
entirely revised ed. London, Kaye &
Ward, 1968. [5], 183 p. [30/-]
737/.2/0942 72-352008
CR4801 .B7 1968 MRR Alc.

Jocelyn, Arthur. Awards of honour;
London, A. and C. Black, 1956. xix,
276 p. 928.72 57-268
CR4529.G7 J6 MRR Alc.

Joslin, Edward C. The standard
catalogue of British orders,
decorations and medals 1969, London,
Spink, 1969. xiv, 114 p. chiefly
illus. [unpriced] 737.2 74-448443

CR4801 .J6 MRR Alc.

MEDALS--UNITED STATES.
Dusterberg, Richard B. The official
inaugural medals of the presidents of
the United States; [1st ed.]
Cincinnati, Ohio, Medallion Press
[1971] viii, 107 p. 737/.2 72-
24531
CJ5813 .D87 MRR Alc.

Failor, Kenneth M. Medals of the
United States Mint, [Washington; For
sale by the Supt. of Docs., U.S.
Govt. Print. Off., 1969] v, 274 p.
[3.50] 928.8 74-602460
CJ5805 .F3 MRR Alc

Hibler, Harold E. So-called dollars:
[1st ed.] New York, Coin and
Currency Institute [c1963] xi, 156
p. 737.2085 63-11546
CJ5806 .H5 MRR Alc.

Kerrigan, Evans E. American war
medals and decorations, Newly rev.
and expanded. New York, Viking Press
[1971] xiv, 173 p. [$8.50]
355.1/34 77-124322
CJ5805 .K4 1971 MRR Ref Desk.

MEDALS, MILITARY AND NAVAL.
Abbott, Peter Edward. British
gallantry awards Enfield, Guiness
Superlatives; London, Seaby, 1971.
359 p.; [£6.00] 355.1/34 72-
872853
CR4801 .A63 MRR Alc.

Blakeney, Jane. Heroes, U.S. Marine
Corps, 1861-1955; [1st ed.
Washington, 1957] xviii, 621 p.
359.96 57-13185
VE23 .B56 MRR Biog.

Dorling, Henry Taprell, Ribbons and
medals; This ed. rev. under the
editorship of Francis K. Mason.
Garden City, N.Y., Doubleday, 1974.
359 p. [$14.95] 355.1/34/09 73-
20952
UC530 .D63 1974 MRR Ref Desk.

Gordon, Lawrence L. British battles
and medals, 4th ed., rev. London,
Spink, 1971. xiv, 440 p. 355.1/34
72-180227
UB435.G8 G6 1971 MRR Alc.

Joslin, Edward C. The standard
catalogue of British orders,
decorations and medals 1969, London,
Spink, 1969. xiv, 114 p. chiefly
illus. [unpriced] 737.2 74-448443

CR4801 .J6 MRR Alc.

Kerrigan, Evans E. American war
medals and decorations, Newly rev.
and expanded. New York, Viking Press
[1971] xiv, 173 p. [$8.50]
355.1/34 77-124322
CJ5805 .K4 1971 MRR Ref Desk.

Werlich, Robert. Orders and
decorations of all nations: ancient
and modern, civil and military. 2d
ed. [Washington, Quaker Press, 1974]
476 p. 929.8 74-177291
CR4509 .W4 1974 MRR Ref Desk.

MEDICAL ASSISTANCE PROGRAMS
see Insurance, Social

MEDICAL CARE--UNITED STATES--
DIRECTORIES.
Gaver, Jessyca Russell. The complete
directory of medical and health
services. New York [Award Books,
1970] 281 p. [0.95 (pbk)] 362 79-
15698
RA445 .G38 MRR Alc.

The Medical and healthcare stock
market guide. 1972/73- ed.
Arcadia, Calif., International Biomedical Information Service.
332.6/7/22 72-84884
HG5123.M4 M44 MRR Alc Latest
edition

MEDICAL CARE--UNITED STATES--STATISTICS.
Employee benefits fact book. [New
York] 331.2/52 76-118375
HD7125 .E57 MRR Alc Latest edition

MEDICAL CARE, COST OF--UNITED STATES--
STATISTICS.
Employee benefits fact book. [New
York] 331.2/52 76-118375
HD7125 .E57 MRR Alc Latest edition

MEDICAL CENTERS--UNITED STATES--
DIRECTORIES.
American Association of Medical
Clinics. Directory. Alexandria, Va.
[etc.] 61-30176
Began publication with 1952 issue.
RA981.A2 A62 MRR Alc Latest
edition

MEDICAL COLLEGES--DIRECTORIES.
World directory of medical schools.
Geneve, World Health Organization.
610.71 54-441
R711 .W6 MRR Alc Latest edition

MEDICAL COLLEGES--CANADA--ENTRANCE
REQUIREMENTS.
Medical school admission
requirements, U.S.A. and Canada.
[1st]- ed.; 1951- Washington
[etc.] Association of American
Medical Colleges. 51-7778
R745 .A8 Sci RR Latest Edition /
MRR Ref Desk Latest edition

MEDICAL COLLEGES--UNITED STATES--
DIRECTORIES.
Association of American Medical
Colleges. Directory. Washington,
D.C., etc.] 55-25506
R712.A1 A8 MRR Alc Latest edition

White, Alex Sandri. The new
directory of medical schools, New
1974 ed. Allenhurst, N.J., Aurea
Publications [1973] 143 p. [$5.95]
610/.7/1173 73-175214
R712.A1 W5 1974 MRR Ref Desk.

MEDICAL COLLEGES--UNITED STATES--
ENTRANCE REQUIREMENTS.
Medical school admission
requirements, U.S.A. and Canada.
[1st]- ed.; 1951- Washington
[etc.] Association of American
Medical Colleges. 51-7778
R745 .A8 Sci RR Latest Edition /
MRR Ref Desk Latest edition

MEDICAL EMERGENCIES.
see also First aid in illness and
injury

Gardiner-Hill, Harold, Compendium of
emergencies. 3d ed. New York,
Appleton-Century-Crofts [1971] xii,
427 p. 616/.025 77-22601
RC87 .G32 1971 MRR Alc.

MEDICAL ETHICS--BIBLIOGRAPHY--
PERIODICALS.
Bibliography of society, ethics and
the life sciences. Hastings-on-the
Hudson, N.Y., Institute of Society,
Ethics and the Life Sciences.
016.174/2 73-160650
Z5322.B5 B52 MRR Alc Full set /
Sci RR Full set

MEDICAL INSTRUMENTS AND APPARATUS--
DIRECTORIES--YEARBOOKS.
The Hospitals yearbook and directory
of hospital suppliers. 1968-
London. 362.1/1/02542 72-622672
RA986.A1 H6 MRR Alc Latest edition

MEDICAL INSTRUMENTS AND APPARATUS
INDUSTRY--UNITED STATES--DIRECTORIES.
The Medical and healthcare stock
market guide. 1972/73- ed.
Arcadia, Calif., International Biomedical Information Service.
332.6/7/22 72-84884
HG5123.M4 M44 MRR Alc Latest
edition

MEDICAL JURISPRUDENCE--INDEXES.
Nick, William V., Index of legal
medicine, 1940-1970; Columbus, Ohio,
Legal Medicine Press [c1970] iv, 694
p. 016.61 71-148391
Z6672.J9 N53 MRR Alc.

MEDICAL LAWS AND LEGISLATION--UNITED
STATES.
American Medical Association.
Committee on Human Sexuality. Human
sexuality. [Chicago, Ill., 1972]
xv, 246 p. 301.41/7 72-90176
HQ31 .A496 MRR Alc.

MEDICAL LIBRARIES.
Medical Library Association.
Handbook of medical library practice,
2d ed., rev. and enl. Chicago,
American Library Association, 1956.
xv, 601 p. 026.61 55-6491
Z675.M4 M45 1956 MRR Alc.

MEDICAL LIBRARIES--DIRECTORIES.
Library Association. Medical Section.
Directory of medical libraries in
the British Isles. 2d ed. London,
Library Association, 1965. vii, 113
p. 66-39871
Z675.M4 L5 1965 MRR Alc.

Medical Library Association.
Directory. 2d ed. Hamden, Conn.,
Shoe String Press, 1959. xxxi, 274
p. 026.61058 59-15362
Z675.M4 M43 1959 MRR Alc.

MEDICAL MICROBIOLOGY.
Microbiology; including immunology
and molecular genetics 2d ed.
Hagerstown, Md., Medical Dept.,
Harper & Row [1973] xv, 1562 p.
576 73-6349
QR41.2 .M49 1973 MRR Alc.

MEDICAL MYCOLOGY.
Dubos, Rene Jules, ed. Bacterial
and mycotic infections of man. 4th
ed. Philadelphia, Lippincott [1965]
xiii, 1025 p. 616.01 64-23602
RC115 .D75 1965 MRR Alc.

MEDICAL PARASITOLOGY.
Craig, Charles Franklin, Craig and
Faust's Clinical parasitology 8th
ed., thoroughly rev. Philadelphia,
Lea & Febiger, 1970. viii, 890 p.
616.9/6 76-85841
RC119 .C68 1970 MRR Alc.

MEDICAL PERSONNEL.
see also Dentists

see also Physicians

see also Public health personnel

MEDICAL RESEARCH--MORAL AND RELIGIOUS
ASPECTS--BIBLIOGRAPHY--PERIODICALS.
Bibliography of society, ethics and
the life sciences. Hastings-on-the
Hudson, N.Y., Institute of Society,
Ethics and the Life Sciences.
016.174/2 73-160650
     Z5322.B5 B52 MRR Alc Full set /
     Sci RR Full set

MEDICAL SOCIETIES--DIRECTORIES.
Health organizations of the United
States, Canada and internationally.
[1st]-   1961- Ithaca, N.Y.,
Graduate School of Business and
Public Administration, Cornell
University. 610.62 61-3260
     R711 .H4 Sci RR Latest edition /
     MRR Alc Latest edition

MEDICAL SOCIETIES--UNITED STATES--
DIRECTORIES.
American Medical Association.
Directory. Chicago. 610.6806273 63-
6472
     R15 .A4385 MRR Alc Latest edition

MEDICAL SOCIETIES--UNITES STATES--
DIRECTORIES.
Gale Research Company. Encyclopedia
of associations. 8th ed. Detroit,
Mich. [1973-   v.   [$45.00 (v. 1)
$28.50 (v. 2)] 061/.3 73-7400
     HS17 .G334 1973 MRR Ref Desk.

MEDICAL STATISTICS--YEARBOOKS.
World health statistics annual. 1962-
Geneva, World Health Organization.
312/.2/05 72-624373
     RA651.A485 MRR Alc Latest edition
     / Sci RR Latest edition

MEDICARE.
Lasser (J. K.) Institute, New York.
J. K. Lasser's Your social security
and medicare guide. New York, Simon
and Schuster [1966] 136 p. 368.4
66-21820
     HD7125 .L35 MRR Alc.

MEDICINE.
   see also Dentistry

   see also Hospitals

   see also Hygiene

   see also Nurses and nursing

   see also Physiology

MEDICINE--15TH-18TH CENTURIES--
BIBLIOGRAPHY.
Guerra, Francisco. American medical
bibliography 1639-1783. New York, L.
C. Harper, 1862. 885 p. 016.61 61-
17786
     Z6659 .G8 MRR Alc.

United States. National Library of
Medicine. Index-catalogue of the
Library of the Surgeon-General's
Office, United States Army: authors
and subjects. Washington, Govt.
Print. Off., 1880-1961. 61 v.
016.61 01-2344
     Z6676 .U6 MRR Alc (DK 33).

MEDICINE--ABBREVIATIONS.
Medical abbreviations; 2d ed. [Ann
Arbor, Michigan Occupational Therapy
Association] 1967. vii, 165 p.
610/.1/48 67-66290
     R121 .M49 1967 MRR Alc.

MEDICINE--BIBLIOGRAPHY.
Bowker's medical books in print.
1972- New York, R.R. Bowker Co.
016.61 78-37613
     Z6658 .B65 MRR Alc Latest edition
     / Sci RR Latest edition

Cumulated Index medicus. v. 1-
1960-   62-4404
     Z660 .I422 Sci RR Full set / MRR
     Alc Full set

Ebert, Myrl, An introduction to the
literature of the medical sciences.
2d ed. Chapel Hill [University of
North Carolina Book Exchange] 1967.
119 p. 016.61 67-64481
     Z6658 .E22 1967 MRR Alc.

Garrison, Fielding Hudson, A medical
bibliography 3d ed. [London] A.
Deutsch [1970] 872 p. [£12.60]
016.61 75-864894
     Z6658 .G243 1970b MRR Alc.

Medical Library Association.
Handbook of medical library practice,
2d ed., rev. and enl. Chicago,
American Library Association, 1956.
xv, 601 p. 026.61 55-6491
     Z675.M4 M45 1956 MRR Alc.

United States. National Library of
Medicine. Bibliography of medical
reviews. v. [1]-12, 1955-1967.
Washington. 016.61 56-61913
     Z6658 .U52 Sci RR Full set / MRR
     Alc Full set

United States. National Library of
Medicine. Early American medical
imprints; Washington, U.S. Dept. of
Health, Education, and Welfare,
Public Health Service, 1961. x, 240
p. 016.610973 62-60123
     Z6661.U5 A44 MRR Alc.

World Health Organization.
Publications; 1947/57- Geneva. 58-
4871
     Z6660 .W57 MRR Alc Full set

MEDICINE--BIBLIOGRAPHY--CATALOGS.
Physician's book compendium. 1969/70-
New York. 016.61 72-9669
     Z6676.Z9 P5 Sci RR Full set / MRR
     Alc Latest edition

United States. National Library of
Medicine. Catalog. Apr./Dec. 1948-
1965. Washington, Library of
Congress 016.61 51-60145
     Z663.7 .C33 MRR Alc MRR Alc Full
     set / Sci RR Full set / MRR Alc
     (Deck 33) Full set

United States. National Library of
Medicine. Current catalog. 1966-
Bethesda, Md. [For sale by the Supt.
of Docs., U.S. Govt. Print. Off.,
Washington] 67-62762
     Z675.M4 U552 Sci RR Full set / MRR
     Alc Full set

United States. National Library of
Medicine. Current catalog: 1968/70-
Bethesda, Md. 016.61 77-618570
     Z675.M4 U553 Sci RR Full set / MRR
     Alc (Dk 33) Full set

United States. National Library of
Medicine. Index-catalogue of the
Library of the Surgeon-General's
Office, United States Army: authors
and subjects. Washington, Govt.
Print. Off., 1880-1961. 61 v.
016.61 01-2344
     Z6676 .U6 MRR Alc (DK 33).

MEDICINE--BIBLIOGRAPHY--PERIODICALS.
Current list of medical literature.
v. 1-36; Jan. 1, 1941-Dec. 1959.
Washington. 44-11211
     Z6660 .C8 Sci RR Partial set / MRR
     Alc Partial set

Index medicus. new ser., v. 1-
Jan. 1960- Washington, National
Library of Medicine. 016.61 61-
60337
     Z6660 .I42 Sci RR Current issues /
     MRR Ref Desk Current issues

Quarterly cumulative index to current
medical literature. v. 1-12;
Jan./Mar. 1916-July/Dec. 1926.
Chicago, American Medical
Association. sg 16-72
     Z6660 .A5 MRR Alc Full set

MEDICINE--BIO-BIBLIOGRAPHY.
Biographisches Lexikon der
hervorragenden arzte aller zeiten
und völker. 2. aufl. durchgesehen
und ergänzt Berlin, Wien, Urban &
Schwarzenberg, 1929-34. 5 v.
016.61 32-1892
     Z6658 .B61 1929 MRR Biog.

Fischer, Isidor, ed. Biographisches
Lexikon der hervorragenden arzte der
letzten fünfzig Jahre, Berlin,
Wien, Urban & Schwarzenberg, 1932-33.
2 v. 016.61 32-20791
     Z6658 .B62 MRR Biog.

Kelly, Emerson Crosby, Encyclopedia
of medical sources. Baltimore,
Williams & Wilkins Co., 1948. v, 476
p. 016.61 48-2235
     Z6658 .K4 MRR Alc.

MEDICINE--BIOGRAPHY.
Garrison, Fielding Hudson, An
introduction to the history of
medicine, 4th ed., rev. and enl.
Philadelphia, London, W. B. Saunders
company, 1929. 996 p. 29-3665
     R131 .G3 1929 MRR Alc.

Stevenson, Lloyd G. Nobel prize
winners in medicine and physiology,
1901-1950. New York, H. Schuman
[1953] 291 p. 926.1 378.32 53-
10370
     R134 .S77 MRR Alc.

Talbott, John Harold, A biographical
history of medicine: New York, Grune
& Stratton [1970] 1211 p. 610/.922
B 78-109574
     R134 .T35 MRR Biog.

United States. National Library of
Medicine. Index-catalogue of the
Library of the Surgeon-General's
Office, United States Army: authors
and subjects. Washington, Govt.
Print. Off., 1880-1961. 61 v.
016.61 01-2344
     Z6676 .U6 MRR Alc (DK 33).

MEDICINE--COLLECTED WORKS.
Hippocrates. Hippocrates, London,
Heinemann; New York, Putnam, 1923-31.
4 v. 23-12030
     PA3612 .H65 1923 MRR Alc.

MEDICINE--DICTIONARIES.
Black's medical dictionary. London,
A. & C. Black. 610.3 59-167
Began publication in 1906.
     R121 .B598 Sci RR Latest edition /
     MRR Ref Desk Latest edition

Blakiston's Gould medical dictionary;
3d ed. New York, McGraw-Hill [1972]
xxi, 1828 p. 610/.3 78-37376
     R121 .B62 1972 MRR Ref Desk.

Dorland's illustrated medical
dictionary. [1st]- ed.; 1900-
Philadelphia, Saunders. 610.3 00-
6382
     R121 .D73 Sci RR Latest edition /
     MRR Ref Desk Latest edition

Fishbein, Morris, The handy home
medical adviser, and concise medical
encyclopedia: New rev. ed. Garden
City, N.Y., Doubleday [1973] xix,
410 p. [$5.95] 616 72-92209
     RC81 .F527 1973 MRR Alc.

Fishbein, Morris, The popular
medical encyclopedia. 1946- Garden
City, N.Y., Doubleday. 616.02 61-
17378
     RC87 .F538 MRR Alc Latest edition

Jablonski, Stanley. Illustrated
dictionary of eponymic syndromes, and
diseases, and their synonyms,
Philadelphia, Saunders [1969] viii,
335 p. 610/.3 69-12884
     R121 .J24 MRR Alc.

LeJeune, Fritz, Deutsch-Englisches,
Englisch-Deutsches Wörterbuch für
Arzte. 2. völlig neubearb. Aufl.
Stuttgart, Thieme, 1968-   v.   [DM
64.00] 610/.3 68-69803
     R121 .L372 MRR Alc.

Lépine, Pierre. Dictionnaire
français-anglais, anglais-français,
des termes medicaux et biologiques;
Paris, Flammarion [1952] 829 p. 52-
3756
     R121 .L39 MRR Alc.

Medical abbreviations; 2d ed. [Ann
Arbor, Michigan Occupational Therapy
Association] 1967. vii, 165 p.
610/.1/48 67-66290
     R121 .M49 1967 MRR Alc.

Miller, Benjamin Frank, Encyclopedia
and dictionary of medicine and
nursing, Philadelphia, Saunders,
1972. x, 1089 p. 610/.3 73-103569
     R121 .M65 MRR Alc.

Reader's digest family health guide.
[1st ed.] London, Reader's Digest
Association [1972] 599 p. 610 73-
152900
     R121 .R38 MRR Alc.

Schmidt, Jacob Edward, Medical
discoveries: Springfield, Ill.,
Thomas [1959] ix, 555 p. 610.9 58-
14086
     R131 .S35 1959 MRR Alc.

Schmidt, Jacob Edward, Reversicon: a
medical word finder. Springfield,
Ill., Thomas [1958] 440 p. 610.3
58-8433
     R121 .S34 1958 MRR Alc.

Stedman, Thomas Lathrop, Stedman's
medical dictionary; 22d ed.,
completely rev. Baltimore, Williams
& Wilkins [1972] lii, 1533 p.
610/.3 78-176294
     R121 .S8 1972 MRR Ref Desk.

Taber's cyclopedic medical
dictionary. [1st]- ed.; 1940-
Philadelphia, Davis. 62-8364
     R121 .T18 Sci RR Latest edition /
     MRR Alc Latest edition

Wain, Harry, The story behind the
word; Springfield, Ill., Thomas
[1958] viii, 342 p. 610.14 57-
12557
     R123 .W2 1958 MRR Alc.

MEDICINE--DICTIONARIES--FRENCH.
Lépine, Pierre. Dictionnaire
français-anglais, anglais-français,
des termes medicaux et biologiques;
Paris, Flammarion [1952] 829 p. 52-
3756
     R121 .L39 MRR Alc.

MEDICINE--DICTIONARIES--GERMAN.
Goulden, William Owen. German-
English medical dictionary. London,
J. & A. Churchill, 1955. vi, 513 p.
610.3 56-2079
     R121 .G73 1955 MRR Alc.

MEDICINE--DICTIONARIES--GERMAN. (Cont.)
Lejeune, Fritz, Deutsch-Englisches,
Englisch-Deutsches Worterbuch fur
Arzte. 2. vollig neubearb. Aufl.
Stuttgart, Thieme, 1968- v.   [DM
64.00]   610/.3   68-69803
    R121 .L372 MRR Alc

MEDICINE--DICTIONARIES--POLYGLOT.
Elsevier's medical dictionary in five
languages: Amsterdam, New York,
Elsevier Pub. Co., 1964.   1588 p.
610.3   62-13022
    R121 .E5 1964 MRR Alc.

Nobel, Albert, Dictionnaire
medical. 5. ed. rev. et augm.
Paris, Masson, 1970 [c1969]   xxii,
1329 p.   [200.00]   77-93556
    R121 .N6 1970 MRR Alc.

MEDICINE--DICTIONARIES--RUSSIAN.
Carpovich, Eugene A., Russian-
English biological & medical
dictionary. 1st ed. New York,
Technical Dictionaries Co., 1958.
400 p.   574.03   58-7915
    QH13 .C37 1958 MRR Alc.

Jablonski, Stanley. Russian-English
medical dictionary. New York,
Academic Press, 1958.   xi, 423 p.
610.3   58-10411
    R121 .J25 MRR Alc.

MEDICINE--FORMULAE, RECEIPTS,
PRESCRIPTIONS.
Meyer, Clarence, comp.   American folk
medicine. New York, Crowell [1973]
296 p.   [$8.95]   615/.882/0973   73-
4300
    R152 .M49 MRR Alc.

National formulary, 1st-   ed.; 1888-
Washington [etc.] American
Pharmaceutical Association [etc.]
615.1373   55-4116
    RS141.2 N3   MRR Alc Latest edition

Pharmaceutical Society of Great
Britain, London.   British
pharmaceutical codex, 1973.   London,
Pharmaceutical Press [1973]   xxxix,
983 p.   [£10.50]   615/.12/42   73-
171134
    RS151.3 .P54 1973 MRR Alc.

MEDICINE--HANDBOOKS, MANUALS, ETC.
Physician's handbook. 1st-   1941-
Los Altos, Calif. [etc.] Lange
Medical Publications [etc.]   616.075
41-9970
    RC55 .P4 MRR Alc Latest edition

MEDICINE--HISTORY.
Castiglioni, Arturo, A history of
medicine. New York, A. A. Knopf,
1941.   3 p. l., v-xxviii, 1013, xl
p., 1 l.   610.9   41-2602
    R131 .C272 MRR Alc.

Garrison, Fielding Hudson, An
introduction to the history of
medicine, 4th ed., rev. and enl.
Philadelphia, London, W. B. Saunders
company, 1929.   996 p.   29-3665
    R131 .G3 1929 MRR Alc.

Schmidt, Jacob Edward, Medical
discoveries: Springfield, Ill.,
Thomas [1959]   ix, 555 p.   610.9   58-
14086
    R131 .S35 1959 MRR Alc.

Singer, Charles Joseph, A short
history of medicine, 2d ed.   Oxford,
Clarendon Press, 1962.   854 p.
610.9   63-313
    R131 .S55 1962a MRR Alc.

MEDICINE--HISTORY--BIBLIOGRAPHY.
Ash, Lee, Serial publications
containing medical classics; New
Haven, Antiquarium, 1961.   xxiv, 147
p.   016.61   61-8290
    Z6658 .G26 MRR Alc.

Garrison, Fielding Hudson, A medical
bibliography 3d ed. [London] A.
Deutsch [1970]   872 p.   [£12.60]
016.61   75-864894
    Z6658 .G243 1970b MRR Alc.

Gilbert, Judson Bennett, Disease and
destiny; London, Dawsons of Pall
Mall, 1962.   535 p.   016.92   62-4082

    Z6664.A1 G5 MRR Alc.

MEDICINE--PERIODICALS--BIBLIOGRAPHY.
World medical periodicals. 3d ed.
[New York] World Medical Association,
1961.   xli, 407 p.   016.6105 a   63-
269
    Z6660 .W6 1961 MRR Alc.

MEDICINE--PERIODICALS--BIBLIOGRAPHY--
PERIODICALS.
Bibliography of medical reviews.
1966/70- Bethesda, Md., National
Library of Medicine; for sale by the
Supt. of Docs., U.S. Govt. Print.
Off. 016.61   72-627542
    Z6660 .B5817 Sci RR Full set / MRR
    Alc Full set

MEDICINE--PERIODICALS--INDEXES.
American Hospital Association.
Library, Asa S. Bacon Memorial.
Cumulative index of hospital
literature. Chicago.   016.3621   50-
11277
    Z6675.H7 A5 MRR Alc Partial set /
    Sci RR Full set

Ash, Lee, Serial publications
containing medical classics; New
Haven, Antiquarium, 1961.   xxiv, 147
p.   016.61   61-8290
    Z6658 .G26 MRR Alc.

Bibliography of medical reviews.
1966/70- Bethesda, Md., National
Library of Medicine; for sale by the
Supt. of Docs., U.S. Govt. Print.
Off. 016.61   72-627542
    Z6660 .B5817 Sci RR Full set / MRR
    Alc Full set

Bibliography of society, ethics and
the life sciences. Hastings-on-the
Hudson, N.Y., Institute of Society,
Ethics and the Life Sciences.
016.174/2   73-160650
    Z5322.B5 B52 MRR Alc Full set /
    Sci RR Full set

Cumulative index to nursing
literature. v. 1/5-   1956/60-
[Glendale, Calif.] Seventh-Day
Adventist Hospital Association.   62-
147
    Z6675 .N7C8 Sci RR Full set / MRR
    Alc Full set

Current list of medical literature.
v. 1-36; Jan. 1, 1941-Dec. 1959.
Washington.   44-11211
    Z6660 .C8 Sci RR Partial set / MRR
    Alc Partial set

Garrison, Fielding Hudson, A medical
bibliography 3d ed. [London] A.
Deutsch [1970]   872 p.   [£12.60]
016.61   75-864894
    Z6658 .G243 1970b MRR Alc.

Goode, Stephen H., Venereal disease
bibliography. 1966/70- Troy, N.Y.,
Whitston Pub. Co. [$10.00]
016.6169/51   71-189843
    Z6664 .V45 G66 MRR Alc Full set

Index medicus. new ser., v. 1-
Jan. 1960- Washington, National
Library of Medicine. 016.61   61-
60337
    Z6660 .I42 Sci RR Current issues /
    MRR Ref Desk Current issues

Kelly, Emerson Crosby, Encyclopedia
of medical sources. Baltimore,
Williams & Wilkins Co., 1948.   v, 476
p.   016.61   48-2235
    Z6658 .K4 MRR Alc.

Mental retardation abstracts. v. 1-
Jan./Mar. 1964- [Bethesda, Md.] for
sale by Superintendent of Documents,
U.S. Govt. Print. Off., Washington]
66-60248
    RC570 .M4 MRR Alc Full set / Sci
    RR Full set

Nick, William V., Index of legal
medicine, 1940-1970; Columbus, Ohio,
Legal Medicine Press [c1970]   iv, 694
p.   016.61   71-148391
    Z6672.J9 N53 MRR Alc.

Quarterly cumulative index medicus.
v. 1-60; Jan. 1927-1956. Chicago,
American Medical Association. 016.61
27-18521
    Z6660 .A51 MRR Alc Full set

Quarterly cumulative index to current
medical literature. v. 1-12;
Jan./Mar. 1916-July/Dec. 1926.
Chicago, American Medical
Association. sg 16-72
    Z6660 .A5 MRR Alc Full set

United States. National Institutes of
Health. Division of Research Grants.
Research grants index. 1961-
Bethesda, Md. [etc., For sale by the
Supt. of Docs., U.S. Govt. Print.
Off., Washington] 614   61-64708
    RA440.6 .U47 Sci RR Latest edition
    / MRR Alc Latest edition

United States. National Library of
Medicine. Index-catalogue of the
Library of the Surgeon-General's
Office, United States Army; authors
and subjects. Washington, Govt.
Print. Off., 1880-1961. 61 v.
016.61   01-2344
    Z6676 .U6 MRR Alc (DK 33).

MEDICINE--POPULAR WORKS.
Frank, Arthur. The people's handbook
of medical care [1st ed.] New York,
Random House [1972]   xiv, 494 p.
[$8.95]   616   72-4593
    RC81 .F82 1972 MRR Alc.

The Medicine show Rev. ed. New
York, Pantheon Books, 1974.   384 p.
610   74-10418
    RC81 .M496 1974 MRR Alc.

MEDICINE--PRACTICE.
    see also Diagnosis

MEDICINE--QUOTATIONS, MAXIMS, ETC.
Strauss, Maurice Benjamin, comp.
Familiar medical quotations, [1st
ed.] Boston, Little, Brown [1968]
xix, 968 p.   610/.2   68-21620
    R707 .S75 MRR Ref Desk.

MEDICINE--RESEARCH GRANTS.
United States. National Institutes of
Health. Division of Research Grants.
Research grants index. 1961-
Bethesda, Md. [etc., For sale by the
Supt. of Docs., U.S. Govt. Print.
Off., Washington] 614   61-64708
    RA440.6 .U47 Sci RR Latest edition
    / MRR Alc Latest edition

MEDICINE--SPECIALITIES AND SPECIALISTS--
UNITED STATES--DIRECTORIES.
Directory of medical specialists
holding certification by American
specialty boards. v. 1- 1939-
Chicago [etc.] Marquis-Who's Who
[etc.]   610/.922   40-9671
    R712.A1 D5 Sci RR Latest edition /
    MRR Biog Latest edition

MEDICINE--STUDY AND TEACHING.
World directory of medical schools.
Geneva, World Health Organization.
610.71   54-441
    R711 .W6 MRR Alc Latest edition

MEDICINE--STUDY AND TEACHING--UNITED
STATES--DIRECTORIES.
White, Alex Sandri. The new
directory of medical schools, New
1974 ed. Allenhurst, N.J., Aurea
Publications [1973]   143 p.   [$5.95]
610/.7/1173   73-175214
    R712.A1 W5 1974 MRR Ref Desk.

MEDICINE--TERMINOLOGY.
Dellinger, Edith V. Manual of
medical terminology. Columbia, S.C.
[1968]   xi, 209 p.   610/.1/4   68-
57284
    R123 .D45 MRR Alc.

Lamela, Alberto. Handbook of medical
and anatomical terminology, [New
York? c1967]   240 p.   610/.1/4   68-
1195
    R123 .L35 MRR Alc.

Skinner, Henry Alan. The origin of
medical terms. 2d ed. Baltimore,
Williams & Wilkins, 1961. x, 438 p.
610.14   61-10562
    R123 .S54 1961 MRR Alc.

Wain, Harry, The story behind the
word; Springfield, Ill. Thomas
[1958]   viii, 342 p.   610.14   57-
12557
    R123 .W2 1958 MRR Alc.

MEDICINE--AMERICA--BIOGRAPHY.
American men of medicine. 1st-
ed.; 1945- Farmingdale, N.Y. [etc.]
Institute for Research in Biography.
45-41506
    R150 .W5 Sci RR Latest edition /
    MRR Biog Latest edition

MEDICINE--CANADA--DIRECTORIES.
Canadian medical directory. 1st-
ed.; 1955- Toronto, Seccombe House
[etc.]   55-3605
    R713.01 .C3 MRR Alc Latest edition

U. S. medical directory. Miami,
Fla., U.S. Directory Service.
610/.25/73   77-23057
    R712.A1 U5 MRR Alc Latest edition
    / Sci RR Latest edition

MEDICINE--FRANCE--DIRECTORIES.
Guide médical et pharmaceutique
Rosenwald. Paris, L'Expansion
scientifique française [etc.]
610.58   46-33186
    Publication began with the guide
    for 1887.
    R713.43 .A6G8 MRR Alc Latest
    edition

MEDICINE--GREAT BRITAIN--DIRECTORIES.
The Medical directory. London, J. &
A. Churchill ltd.   35-7636
    R713.29 .M4 MRR Biog Latest
    edition

MEDICINE--UNITED STATES.
Thacher, James, American medical
biography; New York, Milford House,
1967.   2 v. in 1.   610/.922   67-
30787
    R153 .T3 1967 MRR Biog.

Williams, Stephen West, American
medical biography; New York, Milford
House, 1967.   xv, 664 p.   610/.922
67-30786
    R153 .W5 1967 MRR Biog.

MEDICINE--UNITED STATES--BIBLIOGRAPHY.
Guerra, Francisco. American medical
bibliography 1639-1783. New York, L.
C. Harper, 1962.   885 p.   016.61   61-
17786
    Z6659 .G8 MRR Alc.

MEDICINE--UNITED STATES-- (Cont.)
United States. National Library of
Medicine. Early American medical
imprints; Washington, U.S. Dept. of
Health, Education, and Welfare,
Public Health Service, 1961. x, 240
p.   016.610973   62-60123
Z6661.U5 A44 MRR Alc.

MEDICINE--UNITED STATES--DIRECTORIES.
U. S. medical directory. Miami,
Fla., U.S. Directory Service.
610/.25/73   77-23057
R712.A1 U5   MRR Alc Latest edition
/ Sci RR Latest edition

MEDICINE, CLINICAL.
see also Pathology

MEDICINE, GREEK AND ROMAN.
Celsus, Aulus Cornelius. De
medicina, Cambridge, Mass., Harvard
university press; London, W.
Heinemann, ltd., 1935-38. 3 v.
878.9   36-4458
PA6156.C4 1935a MRR Alc.

Galenus. Galen On the natural
faculties, London, W. Heinemann; New
York, G. P. Putnam's sons, 1916. iv,
339, [1] p.   17-16
PA3612 .G2 1916 MRR Alc.

Hippocrates. Hippocrates, London,
Heinemann; New York, Putnam, 1923-31.
4 v.   23-12030
PA3612 .H65 1923 MRR Alc.

MEDICINE, INDUSTRIAL.
International Labor Office.
Encyclopaedia of occupational health
and safety. New York, McGraw-Hill
[1971-72] 2 v. (xiii, 1621 p.)
613.6/2/03   74-38329
RC963 .I6 1971b MRR Alc.

MEDICINE, MILITARY.
Beebe, Gilbert Wheeler, Battle
casualties; Springfield, Ill.,
Thomas [1952] xxiii, 277 p.
940.5475   52-11968
D805.U5 B4 MRR Alc.

MEDICINE, POPULAR.
Dublin, Louis Israel, Factbook on
man, 2d ed. New York, Macmillan
[1965] xiv, 465 p.   312 65-16561
HB3505 .D78 1965 MRR Alc.

Fishbein, Morris, The handy home
medical adviser, and concise medical
encyclopedia; New rev. ed. Garden
City, N.Y., Doubleday [1973] xix,
410 p. [$5.95] 616 72-92209
RC81 .F527 1973 MRR Alc.

Fishbein, Morris, ed. Modern home
medical adviser; New, rev. ed.
Garden City, N.Y., Doubleday, 1969.
xxxi, 997 p. [8.95] 610 69-10978

RC81 .F53 1969 MRR Alc.

Fishbein, Morris, The popular
medical encyclopedia. 1946- Garden
City, N.Y., Doubleday. 616.02 61-
17378
RC87 .F538 MRR Alc Latest edition

Frank, Arthur. The people's handbook
of medical care [1st ed.] New York,
Random House [1972] xiv, 494 p.
[$8.95] 616 72-4593
RC81 .F82 1972 MRR Alc.

Gaver, Jessyca Russell. The complete
directory of medical and health
services. New York [Award Books,
1970] 281 p. [0.95 (pbk)] 362 79-
15698
RA445 .G38 MRR Alc.

Gomez, Joan. Dictionary of symptoms;
Arundel (Sx.), Centaur P.; 1967.
xxiv, 383 p. [45/-] 616.07/2/03
67-106674
RC82 .G6 MRR Alc.

Hudson, Ian Donald. What to do until
the doctor comes Princeton, N.J.
[Auerbach, 1970, c1969] xvi, 269 p.
[$7.95] 614.8/8 79-124624
RC81 .H9214 1970 MRR Alc.

The Medicine show Rev. ed. New
York, Pantheon Books, 1974. 384 p.
610 74-10418
RC81 .M496 1974 MRR Alc.

Miller, Benjamin Frank, The complete
medical guide Rev. New York, Simon
and Schuster [1967] 633 p. 610/.24
67-13210
RC81 .M66 1967 MRR Alc.

Miller, Benjamin Frank, The family
book of preventive medicine; New
York, Simon and Schuster [1971] 704
p. [$12.95] 613 70-139644
RC81 .M664 MRR Alc.

The New concise family health &
medical guide. Chicago, J. G.
Ferguson Pub. Co. [1972] xi, 404 p.
[$9.95] 616 73-155618
RC81 .N52 1972 MRR Alc.

Reader's digest family health guide.
[1st ed.] London, Reader's Digest
Association [1972] 599 p.   610 73-
152900
R121 .R38 MRR Alc.

Rothenberg, Robert E. The new
illustrated medical encyclopedia for
home use : Enl. and rev. ed. New
York : Abradale Press, [1974] 4 v.
(1634 p., [14] leaves of plates) :
616/.024 74-188880
RC81.A2 R67 1974 MRR Alc.

MEDICINE, POPULAR--DICTIONARIES.
Family health encyclopedia.
Philadelphia, Lippincott [1970] 2
v., (526 p.) 610/.3 70-123630
RC81.A2 F35 MRR Alc.

MEDICINE, VETERINARY
see Veterinary medicine

MEDIEVAL ARCHITECTURE
see Architecture, Medieval

MEDIEVAL CIVILIZATION
see Civilization, Medieval

MEDIEVAL ILLUMINATION OF BOOKS AND
MANUSCRIPTS
see Illumination of books and
manuscripts, Medieval

MEDITERRANEAN REGION--DESCRIPTION AND
TRAVEL.
Pounds, Norman John Greville. Europe
and the Soviet Union 2d ed. New
York, McGraw-Hill [1966] 528 p.
914 65-24529
D921 .P6835 1966 MRR Alc.

MEDITERRANEAN REGION--DESCRIPTION AND
TRAVEL--GUIDEBOOKS.
Clark, Sydney Aylmer, All the best
in the Mediterranean New York, Dodd,
Mead [1966] xii, 500 p. 66-31637
D972 .C58 1966 MRR Alc.

MEDITERRANEAN REGION--ECONOMIC
CONDITIONS--PERIODICALS.
Contact Mediterranean directory:
Malta, Libya, Sicily. 1966-
Valletta, Associated Publicity
Services. 380/.09/1822 67-115040
HC244.5.A1 C6 MRR Alc Latest
edition

MEDIUMS--UNITED STATES.
Holzer, Hans W., The directory of
the occult Chicago, H. Regnery Co.
[1974] x, 201 p.   133/.025/73 74-
6895
BF1409 .H6 MRR Alc.

MEDWAY VALLEY--DIRECTORIES.
Kelly's directory of Medway towns.
Kingston upon Thames. [-/27/6]
914.22/3/0025 73-642686
DA670.M4 K45 MRR Alc Latest
edition

MEETINGS.
see also Discussion

see also Leadership

Association executives buyers' guide
and meeting planner. v. 1- 1973-
[Washington, Columbia Books] [$7.50]
658.4 72-92834
HD2743 .A75 MRR Alc Latest edition

MEMOIRS
see Biography

MEMORIALS.
see also Holidays

MENNONITES--BIOGRAPHY.
Kauffman, Daniel, bp., ed. Mennonite
cyclopedic dictionary; Scottdale,
Pa., Mennonite publishing house,
1937. 3 p. l., ix-xi, [1], 433, [8]
p. 289.703 37-17937
BX8106 .K3 MRR Alc.

MENNONITES--DICTIONARIES.
Kauffman, Daniel, bp., ed. Mennonite
cyclopedic dictionary; Scottdale,
Pa., Mennonite publishing house,
1937. 3 p. l., ix-xi, [1], 433, [8]
p. 289.703 37-17937
BX8106 .K3 MRR Alc.

The Mennonite encyclopedia;
Hillsboro, Kan., Mennonite Brethren
Pub. House, 1955-59. 4 v. 289.703
55-4563
BX8106 .M37 MRR Alc.

MENNONITES--HISTORY.
Smith, Charles Henry, The story of
the Mennonites. 3d ed., rev. and
enl. Newton, Kan., Mennonite
Publication Office, 1950. x, 856 p.
289.709 51-3348
BX8115 .S65 1950 MRR Alc.

MENNONITES--YEARBOOKS.
Mennonite year-book and directory.
Scottdale, Pa., Mennonite Pub. House.
ca 19-23
BX8107 .M4 MRR Alc Latest edition

MEN'S CLOTHING.
Salesman's Guide, inc., New York.
Nationwide directory, exclusive of
New York metropolitan area, [of]
men's and boys' wear buyers. New
York. 687.1105873 65-684
HD9940.U4 S23 MRR Alc Latest
edition

Schoeffler, O. E., Esquire's
encyclopedia of 20th century men's
fashions New York, McGraw-Hill
[1973] x, 709 p. [$35.00]
391/.07/10904 72-9811
TT617 .S36 MRR Alc.

MEN'S CLOTHING--DIRECTORIES.
G Q guide to fashion sources. New
York, Gentlemen's quarterly.
687/.11/02573 67-116689
TT495 .G2 MRR Alc Latest edition

MENTAL DEFICIENCY--ABSTRACTS--
PERIODICALS.
Mental retardation abstracts. v. 1-
Jan./Mar. 1964- [Bethesda, Md.] for
sale by Superintendent of Documents,
U.S. Govt. Print. Off., Washington]
66-60248
RC570 .M4 MRR Alc Full set / Sci
RR Full set

MENTAL DEFICIENCY--BIBLIOGRAPHY.
Bibliography of world literature on
mental retardation. Washington,
Published for the President's Panel
on Mental Retardation by the U.S.
Dept. of Health, Education, and
Welfare, Public Health Service; for
sale by the Superintendent of
Documents, U.S. Govt. Print. Off.,
1963] vii, 564 p.   64-60331
Z6677 .B5 MRR Alc.

MENTAL DISEASES
see Psychology, Pathological

MENTAL DISORDERS.
Novello, Joseph R. A practical
handbook of psychiatry. Springfield,
Ill., C. C. Thomas [1974] xxiv, 621
p. 616.8/9/00202 73-7518
RC454 .N676 MRR Alc.

MENTAL HEALING.
see also Psychotherapy

MENTAL HYGIENE.
see also Community mental health
services

MENTAL HYGIENE--BOOK REVIEWS--INDEXES--
PERIODICALS.
Mental health book review index. v.
[1]- (no. 1-) Jan./Feb. 1956-
[New York] 66-9162
Z6664.N5 M49 MRR Circ Full set

MENTAL HYGIENE--UNITED STATES--FINANCE--
DIRECTORIES.
Wilson, Paul T., Money and
information for mental health;
Washington, American Psychiatric
Association [1971] xvi, 150 p.
362.2/072/073 72-152415
RA790.6 .W5 MRR Alc.

MENTAL PHILOSOPHY
see Psychology

MENTAL TESTS.
see also Educational tests and
measurements

Buros, Oscar Krisen, Personality
tests and reviews; Highland Park,
N.J., Gryphon Press [1970] xxxi,
1659 p. 155.28 74-13192
BF698.5 .B87 MRR Alc.

Freeman, Frank Samuel, Theory and
practice of psychological testing.
3d ed. New York, Holt, Rinehart and
Winston [1962] 697 p. 151.2 62-
10000
BF431 .F655 1962 MRR Alc.

Goldman, Bert A. Directory of
unpublished experimental mental
measures. v. 1- 1974- New York,
Behavioral Publications. 152.8 73-
17342
BF431 .G625 MRR Alc Latest edition

Johnson, Orval G., Tests and
measurements in child development;
[1st ed.] San Francisco, Jossey-
Bass, 1971. xiii, 518 p. 155.41
78-110636
BF722 .J64 MRR Alc.

Robb, George Paul, Assessment of
individual mental ability Scranton,
Intext Educational Publishers [1972]
xiv, 354 p. [$8.00] 153.9/32 73-
177298
BF431 .R52 MRR Alc.

Wechsler, David, Wechsler's
Measurement and appraisal of adult
intelligence 5th and enl. ed.
Baltimore, Williams & Wilkins [1972]
x, 572 p. 153.9/3 72-77316
BF431 .W35 1972 MRR Alc.

MENTAL TESTS--BIBLIOGRAPHY.
Buros, Oscar Krisen, ed. The mental
measurements yearbook. [1st]- 1938-
Highland Park, N.J. [etc.] Gryphon
Press [etc.] 016.1512 016.159928 39-
3422
Z5814.P8 B932 MRR Alc Partial set

Goldman, Bert A. Directory of
unpublished experimental mental
measures. v. 1- 1974- New York,
Behavioral Publications. 152.8 73-
17342
BF431 .G625 MRR Alc Latest edition

MENTALLY HANDICAPPED--ABSTRACTS--
PERIODICALS.
Mental retardation abstracts. v. 1-
Jan./Mar. 1964- [Bethesda, Md.] for
sale by Superintendent of Documents,
U.S. Govt. Print. Off., Washington]
66-60248
RC570 .M4 MRR Alc Full set / Sci
RR Full set

MENTALLY HANDICAPPED--BIBLIOGRAPHY.
Bibliography of world literature on
mental retardation. Washington,
Published for the President's Panel
on Mental Retardation by the U.S.
Dept. of Health, Education, and
Welfare, Public Health Service; for
sale by the Superintendent of
Documents, U.S. Govt. Print. Off.,
1963] vii, 564 p.   64-60331
Z6677 .B5 MRR Alc.

MENTALLY HANDICAPPED--PERIODICALS--
INDEXES.
Mental retardation abstracts. v. 1-
Jan./Mar. 1964- [Bethesda, Md.] for
sale by Superintendent of Documents,
U.S. Govt. Print. Off., Washington]
66-60248
RC570 .M4 MRR Alc Full set / Sci
RR Full set

MENUS.
Dale, Martin. How to read a French
menu. [1st ed.] New York, Appleton-
Century [1966] 95 p. 641.5944 65-
26808
TX652.7 .D3 MRR Alc.

MERCHANDISE
see Commercial products

MERCHANT MARINE.
see also Harbors

see also Shipping

MERCHANT MARINE--BIBLIOGRAPHY.
Albion, Robert Greenhalgh, Naval &
maritime history; 4th ed., rev. and
expanded. Mystic, Conn., Munson
Institute of American Maritime
History, 1972. ix, 370 p. [$15.00]
016.387/09 73-186863
Z6834.H5 A4 1972 MRR Alc.

MERCHANT MARINE--YEARBOOKS.
Merchant ships: v. [1]- 1952-
London, A. Coles in association with
Hart-Davis; Tuckahoe, N.Y., De Graff
[etc.] 623.824058 54-3765
VM1 .M54 Sci RR Latest edition /
MRR Alc Latest edition

Navis; annuaire de la marine
marchande, de la construction navale
et des ports maritimes. Paris, R.
Moreux. 56-27553
HE730 .N35 MRR Alc Latest edition

MERCHANT MARINE--NETHERLANDS--YEARBOOKS.
Moormans jaarboek voor scheepvaart en
scheepsbouw. Den Haag, Verenigde
Periodieke Pers N.V. 51-20638
Began publication in 1923.
HE730 .M6 MRR Alc Latest edition

MERCHANT MARINE--UNITED STATES.
Cutler, Carl C., Five hundred
sailing records of American built
ships. Mystic, Conn., Marine
Historical Association, 1952. 114 p.
623.822 52-30285
VK23 .C79 MRR Alc.

Heyl, Erik. Early American steamers.
Buffalo, 1953- v.   387.24 53-
3672
VM23 .H4 MRR Alc.

Matthews, Frederick C. American
merchant ships, 1850-1900. Salem,
Mass., Marine research society, 1930-
31. 2 v. 387.50973 623.82209 31-
87
VM23 .M3 MRR Alc.

United States. Maritime
Administration. Essential United
States foreign trade routes. [1946]-
Washington, For sale by the
Superintendent of Documents, U.S.
Govt. Print. Off. [etc.] 60-62459
HE745 .A184 MRR Alc Latest edition

MERCHANT MARINE--UNITED STATES--HISTORY.
Cutler, Carl C. Queens of the
western ocean; Annapolis, U.S. Naval
Institute [1961] xxi, 672 p.
387.50973 61-11247
HE745 .C8 MRR Alc.

MERCHANT SHIPS.
La Dage, John Hoffman, Merchant
ships, 2d ed. Cambridge, Md.,
Cornell Maritime Press, 1968. xxv,
481 p. 623.82/4 68-8314
VM378 .L3 1968 MRR Alc.

MERCHANT SHIPS--YEARBOOKS.
Merchant ships: v. [1]- 1952-
London, A. Coles in association with
Hart-Davis; Tuckahoe, N.Y., De Graff
[etc.] 623.824058 54-3765
VM1 .M54 Sci RR Latest edition /
MRR Alc Latest edition

MERCHANT SHIPS--UNITED STATES.
Merchant vessels of the United States
(including yachts) Washington, For
sale by the Supt. of Docs., U.S.
Govt. Print. Off. 387.2/4/02573 76-
606560
HE565.U5 A27 MRR Alc Latest
edition

MERCHANT SHIPS, AMERICAN.
Lytle, William M., Merchant steam
vessels of the United States, 1807-
1868. Mystic, Conn., Steamship
Historical Society of America, 1952
[i.e. 1953] 294 p. 387.24 53-1846

VM7 .S74 no. 6 MRR Alc.

United States. National Archives.
List of American-flag merchant
vessels that received certificates of
enrollment or registry at the Port of
New York, 1789-1867 Washington,
1968. 2 v. (vii, 804 p.)
387.2/097471 a 68-7106
HE565.U5A43 MRR Alc.

MERCHANTS, AMERICAN.
Mahoney, Tom. The great merchants;
New and enl. ed. New York, Harper &
Row [1966] ix, 374 p. 658.8700973
67-11328
HF5429 .M288 1966 MRR Alc.

METABOLISM.
see also Nutrition

METABOLISM, DISORDERS OF.
Duncan, Garfield George, Duncan's
Diseases of metabolism. 7th ed.
Philadelphia, Saunders, 1974. 2 v.
616.3/9 72-80787
RB147 .D8 1974 MRR Alc.

METAL INDUSTRIES
see Mineral industries

METAL TRADE--DICTIONARIES.
Crispin, Frederic Swing, Dictionary
of technical terms. 11th ed., rev.
New York, Bruce Pub. Co. [1970] vi,
455 p. 603 73-104870
T9 .C885 1970 MRR Alc.

METAL TRADE--STATISTICS.
American bureau of Metal Statistics.
Year book. 1st- 1920- New York.
21-15719
HD9506.U6 A37 MRR Alc Latest
edition

Metallgesellschaft A.G., Frankfurt am
Main. Metal statistics. 54th
ed.; 1957/66- Frankfurt am Main. 72-
622829
HD9539.A1 M4 MRR Alc Latest
edition / Sci RR Latest edition

METAL TRADE--STATISTICS--BIBLIOGRAPHY.
International Trade Centre.
Compendium of sources: Geneva, 1967.
232 p. [unpriced] 016.3824 74-
431255
Z7164.C81 I58 MRR Alc.

METAL TRADE--EUROPE--DIRECTORIES.
European metals directory. [1st ed.]
London, Quin Press [1964] 375 p.
66-46321
TS370 .E8 MRR Alc.

METAL TRADE--GREAT BRITAIN--DIRECTORIES.
Ryland's coal, iron, steel, tinplate,
metal, engineering, foundry, hardware
and allied trades directory, with
brands and trade marks. London,
Industrial Newspapers. 605.8 51-
22142
Began publication with 1881 ed.
TN12 .R9 MRR Alc Latest edition

METAL TRADE--UNITED STATES.
American bureau of Metal Statistics.
Year book. 1st- 1920- New York.
21-15719
HD9506.U6 A37 MRR Alc Latest
edition

METAL TRADE--UNITED STATES--DIRECTORIES.
Dun and Bradstreet, inc.
Metalworking directory. New York.
62-533
Began publication with vol. for
1960.
TS203 .D8 MRR Alc Latest edition /
Sci RR Latest edition

METAL TRADE--UNITED STATES--STATISTICS.
Commodity year book. 1st- ed.;
1939- New York, Commodity Research
Bureau, inc. 338.0973 39-11418
HF1041 .C56 MRR Alc Latest edition

Dun and Bradstreet, inc.
Metalworking directory. New York.
62-533
Began publication with vol. for
1960.
TS203 .D8 MRR Alc Latest edition /
Sci RR Latest edition

METAL-WORK.
see also Electroplating

METAL-WORK--DICTIONARIES--RUSSIAN.
Massachusetts Institute of
Technology. Center for International
Studies. Russian-English glossary of
metallurgical and metalworking terms.
Cambridge, 1955. iii, 175 p.   55-
4386
TN609 .M39 MRR Alc.

METAL-WORK--HISTORY.
Aitchison, Leslie. A history of
metals. New York, Interscience
Publishers, 1960. 2 v. (xxi, 647 p.)
669.09 60-3041
TN615 .A5 MRR Alc.

METAL-WORK--UNITED STATES--DIRECTORIES.
Dun and Bradstreet, inc.
Metalworking directory. New York.
62-533
Began publication with vol. for
1960.
TS203 .D8 MRR Alc Latest edition /
Sci RR Latest edition

METAL-WORK, ART
see Art metal-work

METAL-WORKING MACHINERY.
see also Machine-tools

METALLURGICAL PLANTS--EUROPE--
DIRECTORIES.
European metals directory. [1st ed.]
London, Quin Press [1964] 375 p.
66-46321
TS370 .E8 MRR Alc.

METALLURGY--DICTIONARIES.
Henderson, J. G., Metallurgical
dictionary. New York, Reinhold Pub.
Corp., 1953. xi, 396 p. 669.03 53-
12371
TN609 .H4 MRR Alc.

Merriman, Arthur Douglas. A
dictionary of metallurgy. London,
MacDonald & Evans, 1958. xv, 401 p.
669.03 59-480
TN609 .M475 MRR Alc.

METALLURGY--DICTIONARIES--RUSSIAN.
Massachusetts Institute of
Technology. Center for International
Studies. Russian-English glossary of
metallurgical and metalworking terms.
Cambridge, 1955. iii, 175 p.   55-
4386
TN609 .M39 MRR Alc.

METALLURGY--HISTORY.
Aitchison, Leslie. A history of
metals. New York, Interscience
Publishers, 1960. 2 v. (xxi, 647 p.)
669.09 60-3041
TN615 .A5 MRR Alc.

METALLURGY--TABLES, CALCULATIONS, ETC.
Smithells, Colin James, ed. Metals
reference book 4th ed. New York,
Plenum Press, 1967. 3 v. (xvi, 1147
p.) 669/.0021/2 67-23290
TN671 .S55 1967 MRR Alc.

METALS.
American Society for Metals. Metals
handbook. [1st]- ed.; [1927]-
Metals Park, Ohio [etc.] 27-12046
TA459 .A5 Sci RR Latest edition /
MRR Alc Latest edition

Hampel, Clifford A., ed. Rare metals
handbook. 2d ed. [New York]
Reinhold Pub. Corp. [1961] xvi, 15
p. 669.7 61-10449
TA459 .H28 1961 MRR Alc.

METAPHOR.
Dickey, James. Metaphor as pure
adventure; Washington, Library of
Congress; [for sale by the Supt. of
Docs., U.S. Govt. Print. Off.] 1968.
20 p. [$0.25] 808.1 68-61809
Z663.293 .M4 MRR Alc.

Rodale, Jerome Irving. The phrase
finder; Emmaus, Pa., Rodale Press
[c1953] 1325 p. 423 54-2348
PE1689 .R63 MRR Alc.

METAPHYSICS--EARLY WORKS TO 1800.
Aristoteles. The Metaphysics ...
London, W. Heinemann, ltd.; New York,
G. P. Putnam's sons, 1933-35. 2 v.
33-17911
PA3612 .A8A13 1933 MRR Alc.

METAPSYCHOLOGY
see Psychical research

METEORITES.
Middlehurst, Barbara M., ed. The moon, meteorites, and comets, Chicago, University of Chicago Press [1963] xxii, 810 p.   523 62-18117
QB501 .S6 vol. 4 MRR Alc.

METEOROLOGY.
see also Air

see also Atmospheric pressure

see also Climatology

see also Tornadoes

see also Weather

see also Weather control

METEOROLOGY--DICTIONARIES.
Fairbridge, Rhodes Whitmore, The encyclopedia of atmospheric sciences and astrogeology, New York, Reinhold Pub. Corp. [1967] xv, 1200 p. 551.5/03 68-1126
QC854 .F34 MRR Alc.

METEOROLOGY--EARLY WORKS TO 1800.
Aristoteles. Meteorologica. Cambridge, Harvard University Press, 1952. xxx, 432 p.   888.5 52-14795
PA3612.A8 M47 MRR Alc.

METEOROLOGY--OBSERVATIONS.
Great Britain. Meteorological Office. Tables of temperature, relative humidity and precipitation for the world. 2nd ed. London, H.M.S.O., 1966-   v.   [1/5/- (pt. 3) 1/15- (pt. 4) 15/6 (pt. 5)] 551.5/021/2 76-385248
QC982.5 .G732 MRR Alc.

World weather records. 1921/30- Washington. 551.59083 59-65360
QC982 .W6 MRR Alc Latest edition / Sci RR Full set

METER
see Versification

METHODISM--HISTORY.
Cameron, Richard Morgan, comp. The rise of Methodism. New York, Philosophical Library [1954] xv, 397 p.   287.09 54-8668
BX8231 .C3 MRR Alc.

The History of American Methodism. New York, Abingdon Press [1964] 3 v. 64-10013
BX8235 .H5 MRR Alc.

Sweet, William Warren, Methodism in American history. Revision of 1953. Nashville, Abingdon Press [1954] 472 p.   287 54-5943
BX8235 .S9 1953 MRR Alc.

METHODIST CHURCH (UNITED STATES)-- DISCIPLINE.
Methodist Church (United States). Doctrines and discipline. 1939- Nashville [etc.] Methodist Pub. House. 287.673 39-32498
BX8388 .A5 MRR Alc Latest edition

METHODIST CHURCH (UNITED STATES)-- DOCTRINAL AND CONTROVERSIAL WORKS.
Methodist Church (United States). Doctrines and discipline. 1939- Nashville [etc.] Methodist Pub. House. 287.673 39-32498
BX8388 .A5 MRR Alc Latest edition

METHODIST CHURCH (UNITED STATES)-- HISTORY.
The History of American Methodism. New York, Abingdon Press [1964] 3 v. 64-10013
BX8235 .H5 MRR Alc.

METHODIST CHURCH--BIOGRAPHY-- DICTIONARIES.
Who's who in the Methodist Church. Nashville, Abingdon Press [1966] vii, 1489 p. 287.0922 66-26876
BX8213 .W52 1966 MRR Biog.

METHODIST CHURCH--PERIODICALS--INDEXES.
The Methodist periodical index. v. 1- 8 Jan./Mar. 1961-June/Aug. 1968. Nashville, Methodist Pub. House. 287/.05 76-2484
Z7845.M5 M516 MRR Alc Full set

The United Methodist periodical index. v. 9- Sept./Nov. 1968- Nashville, Methodist Pub. House. 287/.6/05 72-626947
Z7845.M5 M516 MRR Alc Full set

METHODIST CHURCH IN THE UNITED STATES-- HISTORY.
The History of American Methodism. New York, Abingdon Press [1964] 3 v. 64-10013
BX8235 .H5 MRR Alc.

METHODISTS IN THE UNITED STATES.
Sweet, William Warren, Methodism in American history. Revision of 1953. Nashville, Abingdon Press [1954] 472 p.   287 54-5943
BX8235 .S9 1953 MRR Alc.

METHODOLOGY.
see also Research

METRIC SYSTEM.
see also International system of units

Le Maraic, A. L., The complete metric system with the international system of units (SI). [Rev. and expanded ed.] Somers, N.Y., Abbey Books [1973] xiii, 184 p.   389/.152 72-97799
QC91 .L44 1973 MRR Alc.

METRIC SYSTEM--CONVERSION TABLES.
Le Maraic, A. L., The complete metric system with the international system of units (SI). [Rev. and expanded ed.] Somers, N.Y., Abbey Books [1973] xiii, 184 p.   389/.152 72-97799
QC91 .L44 1973 MRR Alc.

Malgorn, Guy Marie, Lexique technique anglais-français: 4. éd. rev. et corr. Paris, Gauthier- Villars, 1956. xxxiv, 483 p.   57- 155
T9 .M16 1956 MRR Alc.

Malgorn, Guy Marie, Lexique technique français-anglais: Paris, Gauthier-Villars, 1956. xxviii, 475 p.   57-156
T9 .M163 MRR Alc.

METRIC SYSTEM--PERIODICALS.
Specification. Metric edition. 71st- 1970- (London, Architectural Press) 692/.3/05 72-622381
TH425 .S65 MRR Alc Latest edition / Sci RR Latest edition*

METRO-GOLDWYN-MAYER, INC.
Parish, James Robert. The MGM stock company; New Rochelle, N.Y., Arlington House [1973] 862 p. [$14.95] 791.43/028/0922 B 72- 91640
PN1998.A2 P394 MRR Alc.

METROLOGY
see Weights and measures

METROPOLITAN AREAS.
see also Urban renewal

METROPOLITAN AREAS--STATISTICS.
Annuaire de statistique internationale des grandes villes. v. 1- 1961- La Haye. 66-88394
HA42 .A55 MRR Alc Latest edition

Davis, Kingsley, World urbanization, 1950-1970. Berkeley, Institute of International Studies, University of California [1969-72] 2 v. [$6.00] 301.36 71-627843
HB2161 .D37 MRR Alc.

METROPOLITAN AREAS--ATLANTIC STATES.
Gottmann, Jean. Megalopolis; the urbanized northeastern seaboard of the United States. New York, Twentieth Century Fund, 1961. xi, 810 p.   301.36 61-17298
HT123.5.A12 G6 MRR Alc.

METROPOLITAN AREAS--UNITED STATES.
Government Affairs Foundation. Metropolitan surveys: Chicago, Public Administration Service, c1958. xvi, 256 p.   352.073 58-14374
HN29 .G65 MRR Alc.

United States. Bureau of the Census. Directory of Federal statistics for local areas. [Washington, For sale by the Supt. of Docs., U.S. Govt. Print. Off.] 1966. vi, 156 p. a 66-7475
HB2175 .A5 1966 TJ Rm.

METROPOLITAN AREAS--UNITED STATES-- BIBLIOGRAPHY.
Government Affairs Foundation. Metropolitan communities: Chicago, Public Administration Service [1957, c1956] xviii, 392 p.   016.352073 56-13382
Z7164.L8 G66 MRR Alc.

METROPOLITAN AREAS--UNITED STATES-- STATISTICS.
The Municipal year book; 1934- Washington, D.C. [etc.] International city manager's association. 34-27121

JS344.C5 A24 MRR Ref Desk Latest edition / MRR Alc Latest edition

United States. Bureau of the Budget. Office of Statistical Standards. Standard metropolitan statistical areas. [Washington, U.S. Govt. Print. Off.] 61-60569
HB2175 .A3 MRR Alc Latest edition

United States. Bureau of the Census. 1960 census of housing. [Washington, 1961-63] 6 v. in 66 pts. and 1 v. in 420 pts. a 61-9347
HD7293 .A4884 MRR Alc.

United States. Bureau of the Census. 1967 census of business. [Washington; For sale by the Supt. of Docs., U.S. Govt. Print. Off., 1970- 71] 5 v. in 9 [$9.50 (v. 1) varies] 338/.0973 72-608032
HF3007 .U55 1970 MRR Alc.

United States. Bureau of the Census. 1967 census of governments. [Washington, For sale by the Supt. of Docs., U.S. Govt. Print. Off., 1968- v. in 353.000021/2 a 68-7201
JS3.A257 MRR Alc.

United States. Bureau of the Census. 1970 census of housing. [Washington; For sale by the Supt. of Docs., U.S. Govt. Print Off., 1972- v. 301.5/4/09791 72-600057
HD7293 .A512 1972 MRR Alc.

United States. Bureau of the Census. 1970 census of population. Washington; For sale by the Supt. of Docs., U.S. Govt. Print. Off., 1972- 2 v. in 312/.0973 72-600036
HA201 1970 .A568 MRR Alc.

United States. Bureau of the Census. 1970 census of population and housing. [Washington; For sale by the Supt. of Docs., U.S. Govt. Print. Off.] 1971-   v. [$1.00 (v. 5) varies] 312/.9/0973 73-186611
HA201 1970 .A542 MRR Alc.

United States. Bureau of the Census. 1972 census of governments. [Washington, U.S. Govt. Print. Off.] 1973-   v. [$1.25 (v. 2, pt. 1) varies] 317.3 73-600080
JS3 .A244 MRR Alc.

United States. Bureau of the Census. County and city data book. 1949- [Washington, U.S. Govt. Print. Off.] 317.3 52-4576
HA202 .A36 MRR Desk Latest edition / MRR Desk Latest edition / MRR Alc Latest edition

United States. Bureau of the Census. County business patterns; 1946- [Washington] 49-45747
HC101 .A184 MRR Alc Latest edition

METROPOLITAN GOVERNMENT.
see also Municipal government

METROPOLITAN TRANSPORTATION
see Urban transportation

MEXICAN AMERICANS.
Grebler, Leo. The Mexican-American people, New York, Free Press [1970] xvii, 777 p., illus., forms, maps. 301.453/72/073 73-81931
E184.M5 G68 MRR Alc.

Newman, Patty. Do it up brown! San Diego, Calif., Viewpoint Books [1971] 392 p. [$3.95] 301.451/6872/073 72-164889
E184.M5 N4 MRR Alc.

MEXICAN AMERICANS--BIBLIOGRAPHY.
Grebler, Leo. The Mexican-American people, New York, Free Press [1970] xvii, 777 p., illus., forms, maps. 301.453/72/073 73-81931
E184.M5 G68 MRR Alc.

Jordan, Lois B. Mexican Americans; resources to build cultural understanding, Littleton, Colo., Libraries Unlimited, 1973. 265 p. 016.9172/03 72-94302
Z1361.M4 J67 MRR Alc.

Stanford University. Center for Latin American Studies. The Mexican American: a selected and annotated bibliography. 2d ed. [rev. and enl.] Stanford, Stanford University; available through Stanford Bookstore, 1971 [c1969] xii, 162 p. [$2.00] 016.30145/16/872073 72-177730
Z1361.M4 S77 1971 MRR Alc.

United States. Cabinet Committee on Opportunity for the Spanish Speaking. The Spanish speaking in the United States: a guide to materials. Washington, 1971. iv, 175 p. 016.9173/06/68 75-614612
Z1361.S7 U54 MRR Alc.

MEXICAN AMERICANS--BIBLIOGRAPHY-- CATALOGS.
California. State College, Long Beach. Library. Chicano bibliography; Long Beach, 1970. 45 p.   016.9173/09/746 70-633370
Z1361.M4 C3 MRR Alc.

Utah. University. Library. Chicano bibliography. [Salt Lake City, 1973] 295 p.   016.9172/06/68 73-623051
Z1361.M4 U78 1973 MRR Alc.

MEXICAN AMERICANS--BIOGRAPHY.
Jordan, Lois B. Mexican Americans;
resources to build cultural
understanding. Littleton, Colo.,
Libraries Unlimited, 1973. 265 p.
016.9172/03 72-94302
Z1361.M4 J67 MRR Alc.

MEXICAN AMERICANS--HISTORY.
Moquin, Wayne, comp. A documentary
history of the Mexican Americans.
New York, Praeger [1971] xiv, 399 p.
[$13.50] 973.04/687/2 78-101671
E184.M5 M63 1971 MRR Alc.

MEXICAN AMERICANS--SOCIETIES, ETC.--
DIRECTORIES.
Jordan, Lois B. Mexican Americans;
resources to build cultural
understanding. Littleton, Colo.,
Libraries Unlimited, 1973. 265 p.
016.9172/03 72-94302
Z1361.M4 J67 MRR Alc.

Newman, Patty. Do it up brown! San
Diego, Calif., Viewpoint Books [1971]
392 p. [$3.95] 301.451/6872/073
72-164989
E184.M5 N4 MRR Alc.

United States. Cabinet Committee on
Opportunity for the Spanish Speaking.
Directory of Spanish speaking
organizations in the United States.
Washington, 1970. x, 224 p. 061
77-608446
E184.S75 A44 MRR Alc.

MEXICAN LITERATURE--BIBLIOGRAPHY.
Berroa, Josefina. Mexico
bibliografico, 1957-1960; Mexico,
1961. xxi, 189 p. 61-65546
Z1411 .B4 MRR Alc.

MEXICAN LITERATURE--PERIODICALS--
INDEXES.
Forster, Merlin H. An index to
Mexican literary periodicals, New
York, Scarecrow Press, 1966. 276 p.
860 65-22755
Z1421 .F6 MRR Alc.

MEXICAN NEWSPAPERS--MEXICO (CITY).
Audit Bureau of Circulations. A.B.C.
blue book, [Chicago?] 071 45-53615
Z6951 .A67 MRR Alc Latest edition

MEXICANS IN THE UNITED STATES.
Grebler, Leo. The Mexican-American
people, New York, Free Press [1970]
xvii, 777 p., illus., forms, maps.
301.453/72/073 73-81931
E184.M5 G68 MRR Alc.

MEXICO.
Ewing, Russell C., ed. Six faces of
Mexico; Tucson] University of
Arizona Press [1966] 320 p.
917.20382 66-18533
F1208 .E9 MRR Alc.

MEXICO--ANTIQUITIES--BIBLIOGRAPHY.
Bernal, Ignacio. Bibliografia de
arqueologia y etnografia: Mexico,
Instituto Nacional de Antropologia e
Historia, 1962. xvi, 634 p. 63-
39894
Z1209 .B45 MRR Alc.

MEXICO--BIBLIOGRAPHY.
Biblioteca Nacional de Antropologia
e Historia. Catalogos de la
Biblioteca Nacional de Antropologia
e Historia, Mexico. Boston, G. K.
Hall, 1972. 10 v. 74-225152
Z885.A1 B5 1972 MRR Alc (Dk 33)

González y González, Luis. Fuentes
de la historia contemporanea de
Mexico; [1. ed. Mexico] El
Colegio de Mexico [1961-62] 3 v.
61-29162
Z1426.5 .G6 MRR Alc.

MEXICO--BIO-BIBLIOGRAPHY.
Beristain de Souza, José Mariano,
Biblioteca hispano americana
septentrional; [3. ed.] Mexico,
Editorial Fuente Cultural [1947] 5
v. in 2. 015.72 48-8774
Z1412 .B53 MRR Alc.

MEXICO--BIOGRAPHY.
Alisky, Marvin. Who's who in Mexican
government. Tempe, Center for Latin
American Studies of Arizona State
University, 1969. 64 p.
354.72/060922 77-625171
F1235.5.A2 A4 MRR Biog.

Morales Díaz, Carlos. Quién es
quién en la nomenclatura de la
ciudad de México; [México] 1962.
ix, 582 p. 63-28910
F1386 .M74 MRR Biog.

MEXICO--BIOGRAPHY--BIBLIOGRAPHY.
Iguiniz, Juan Bautista,
Bibliografia biografica mexicana
[1. ed.] Mexico, Universidad
Nacional Autonoma de Mexico,
Instituto de Investigaciones
Historicas, 1969. 431 p. 71-
482904
Z5305.M6 I22 MRR Biog.

MEXICO--BIOGRAPHY--DICTIONARIES.
Diccionario biografico de Mexico.
v. [1]- [1968]- Monterrey,
Editorial Revesa 77-426594
CT550 .D5 MRR Biog Latest edition

Diccionario Porrúa de historia,
biografia y geografia de Mexico.
3. ed. corr. y aumentada. Mexico,
Editorial Porrúa [1971, c1970] 2 v.
(xxxi, 2465 p., p. 2455-2465
advertisements) 70-599848
F1204 .D56 1971 MRR Alc.

MEXICO--COMMERCE--DIRECTORIES.
Anglo-American directory of Mexico.
Mexico, D.F., Talleres tipograficos
de "Excélsior." 917.2 42-34594
F1204.5 .A4 MRR Alc Latest edition

Dun and Bradstreet, inc.
International market guide: Mexico.
New York. 380.1/025/72 72-621019
HC132 .D84 MRR Alc Latest edition

MEXICO--DESCRIPTION AND TRAVEL--1951- --
GUIDE-BOOKS.
Boulanger, Robert, Mexico. Paris,
Hachette, 1968. 927 p. 917.2/04/82
76-373963
F1386.A4 B6 MRR Alc.

Carlson, Loraine. Mexico: an
extraordinary guide. Chicago, Rand
McNally [1971] 416 p. [$9.95]
917.2/04/82 75-160263
F1209 .C25 MRR Alc.

Clark, Sydney Aylmer, All the best
in Mexico, New York, Dodd, Mead
[1974] viii, 320 p. [$7.95]
917.2/04/82 74-2600
F1209 .C6 1974 MRR Alc.

Ford, Norman D Fabulous Mexico,
where everything costs less. 1960-
Greenlawn, N.Y., Harian Publications;
trade distributor: Grosset & Dunlap,
New York. 61-16021
F1209 .F6 MRR Alc Latest edition

Sannebeck, Norvelle. Everything you
ever wanted to know about living in
Mexico. [1st ed.] Anderson, S.C.,
Droke House, distributed by Grosset &
Dunlap, New York [1970] 250
[4.95] 917.2/04/82 73-118204
F1209 .S24 MRR Alc.

Wilhelm, John. Guide to all Mexico.
4th ed., rev, and enl. New York,
McGraw-Hill [1973] x, 425 p.
[$8.95] 917.2/04/82 72-11528
F1209 .W74 1973 MRR Alc.

MEXICO--DESCRIPTION AND TRAVEL--GUIDE-
BOOKS.
Clark, Sydney Aylmer, All the best
in Mexico, New York, Dodd, Mead
[1974] viii, 320 p. [$7.95]
917.2/04/82 74-2600
F1209 .C6 1974 MRR Alc.

Fodor's Mexico. 1972- New York, D.
McKay. 917.2/04/82 72-623954
F1216 .F58 MRR Alc Latest edition

Ford, Norman D. Mexico and Guatemala
by car; Greenlawn, N.Y., Harian
Publications; trade distributors:
Crown Publishers, 1963. 159 p.
917.2 63-5328
GV1025.M4 F6 1963 MRR Alc.

Mexico and Central America:
Washington, American Automobile
Association. 917.2 35-8488
GV1025.M4 A6 MRR Alc Latest
edition

Rand McNally vacation guide:
Chicago. 917.3 60-2943
E158 .R3 MRR Alc Latest edition

Toor, Frances, New guide to Mexico,
including Lower California. 8th ed.,
augm. and completely rev. New York,
Crown Publishers [1967] ix, 342 p.
917.2/04/82 67-6217
F1209 .T65 1967 MRR Alc.

MEXICO--DICTIONARIES AND ENCYCLOPEDIAS.
Diccionario Porrúa de historia,
biografia y geografia de Mexico.
3. ed. corr. y. aumentada. Mexico,
Editorial Porrúa [1971, c1970] 2 v.
(xxxi, 2465 p., p. 2455-2465
advertisements) 70-599848
F1204 .D56 1971 MRR Alc.

MEXICO--DIRECTORIES.
Anglo-American directory of Mexico.
Mexico, D.F., Talleres tipograficos
de "Excélsior." 917.2 42-34594
F1204.5 .A4 MRR Alc Latest edition

MEXICO--FOREIGN RELATIONS--UNITED
STATES.
Cline, Howard Francis. The United
States and Mexico. Rev. ed., enl.
New York, Atheneum, 1963. 484 p.
63-24587
F1226 .C6 1963 MRR Alc.

MEXICO--GAZETTEERS,
Diccionario Porrúa de historia,
biografia y geografia de Mexico.
3. ed. corr. y.aumentada. Mexico,
Editorial Porrúa [1971, c1970] 2 v.
(xxxi, 2465 p., p. 2455-2465
advertisements) 70-599848
F1204 .D56 1971 MRR Alc.

United States. Office of Geography.
Mexico; Washington, U.S. Govt.
Print. Off., 1956. iii, 750 p.
917.2 56-61174
F1204 .U5 MRR Alc.

MEXICO--GOVERNMENT PUBLICATIONS--
BIBLIOGRAPHY.
Ker, Annita Melville, Mexican
government publications. Washington,
U.S. Govt. print. off., 1940. xxi,
333 p. 015.72 40-26001
Z663 .M4 MRR Alc.

MEXICO--HISTORY.
Alba, Victor. The Mexicans, New
York, Praeger [1967] vii, 268 p.
917.2/03 67-20469
F1226 .A4 MRR Alc.

Cline, Howard Francis. The United
States and Mexico. Rev. ed., enl.
New York, Atheneum, 1963. 484 p.
63-24587
F1226 .C6 1963 MRR Alc.

Fehrenbach, T. R. Fire and blood;
New York, Macmillan [1973] x, 675 p.
917.2/03 72-91265
F1226 .F43 MRR Alc.

MEXICO--HISTORY--SPANISH COLONY, 1540-
1810.
Lowery, Woodbury, The Spanish
settlements within the present limits
of the United States, 1513-1561, New
York, London, G. P. Putnam's sons,
1901. xiii, 515 p. 973.16 01-
11942
E123 .L91 MRR Alc.

MEXICO--HISTORY--SPANISH COLONY, 1540-
1810--SOURCES.
United States. Library of Congress.
Manuscript Division. The Harkness
Collection in the Library of
Congress; Washington, Library of
Congress; [for sale by the Supt. of
Docs., U.S. Govt. Print. Off.] 1974.
xi, 315 p. 016.972/02 73-6747
Z663.34 .H293 MRR Alc.

MEXICO--HISTORY--BIBLIOGRAPHY.
California. University. Bancroft
Library. Catalog of printed books.
Boston, G. K. Hall, 1964. 22 v.
016.9178 67-52922
Z881 .C1523 MRR Alc (DK33)

Jordan, Lois B. Mexican Americans;
resources to build cultural
understanding, Littleton, Colo.,
Libraries Unlimited, 1973. 265 p.
016.9172/03 72-94302
Z1361.M4 J67 MRR Alc.

MEXICO--IMPRINTS.
Berroa, Josefina. Mexico
bibliografico, 1957-1960; Mexico,
1961. xxi, 189 p. 61-65546
Z1411 .B4 MRR Alc.

Streeter, Thomas Winthrop,
Bibliography of Texas, 1795-1845.
Cambridge, Harvard University Press,
1955-60. 3 pts. in 5 v. 016.9764
56-13552
Z1339 .S8 MRR Alc.

MEXICO--INDUSTRIES--DIRECTORIES.
Dun and Bradstreet, inc.
International market guide: Mexico.
New York. 380.1/025/72 72-621019
HC132 .D84 MRR Alc Latest edition

MEXICO--LEARNED INSTITUTIONS AND
SOCIETIES.
Salas Ortega, Guadalupe, ed.
Directorio de asociaciones e
institutos cientificos y culturales
de la Republica Mexicana. [1. ed.]
Mexico, Dirección General de
Publicaciones, 1959. 242 p. 60-
30892
AS63.A7 S3 MRR Alc.

MEXICO--MAPS.
Rand, McNally and Company. Road
atlas of the United States, Canada
and Mexico. 1926- Chicago. 629.281
map26-19
G1201.P2 R35 MRR Ref Desk Latest
edition / Sci RR Latest edition

MEXICO--POLITICS AND GOVERNMENT.
Ker, Annita Melville, Mexican
government publications. Washington,
U.S. Govt. print. off., 1940. xxi,
333 p. 015.72 40-26001
Z663 .M4 MRR Alc.

MEXICO--POLITICS AND GOVERNMENT--1910-
1946.
Dulles, John W. F. Yesterday in
Mexico; Austin, University of Texas
Press [1961] 805 p. 972.082 60-
14309
F1234 .D9 MRR Alc.

MEXICO--POLITICS AND GOVERNMENT--1946-
Alisky, Marvin. Who's who in Mexican
government. Tempe, Center for Latin
American Studies of Arizona State
University, 1969. 64 p.
354.72/000822 77-625171
    F1235.5.A2 A4 MRR Biog.

MEXICO--REGISTERS.
Directorio del poder ejecutivo
federal. Mexico, Secretaría del
Patrimonio Nacional. 48-44044
    JL1221 .A24 MRR Alc Latest edition

**MEXICO--RELATIONS (GENERAL) WITH THE
UNITED STATES.**
Cline, Howard Francis. The United
States and Mexico. Rev. ed., enl.
New York, Atheneum, 1963. 484 p.
63-24587
    F1226 .C6 1963 MRR Alc.

MEXICO--STATISTICS--BIBLIOGRAPHY.
Harvey, Joan M. Statistics America:
sources for market research (North,
Central & South America), Beckenham,
CBD Research, 1973. xii, 225 p.
[£6.00 ($22.00 U.S.)] 016.317 73-
180742
    Z7554.A5 H37 MRR Alc.

MEXICO (CITY)--LIBRARIES.
Parsons, Mary D., comp. Directorio
de bibliotecas de la Ciudad de
México; México, Mexico City
College Press, 1958. xix, 85 p. 59-
37909
    Z740.M58 P3 MRR Alc.

MEXICO (CITY)--STREETS.
Morales Díaz, Carlos. Quién es
quién en la nomenclatura de la
ciudad de México; [Mexico] 1962.
ix, 582 p. 63-28910
    F1386 .M74 MRR Biog.

MICHIGAN.
Writers' Program. Michigan.
Michigan, a guide to the Wolverine
State. St. Clair Shores, Mich.,
Somerset Publishers, 1973 [c1941]
xxxvi, 682 p. 917.74/04/4 72-84482

    F566 .W9 1973 MRR Ref Desk.

MICHIGAN--BIBLIOGRAPHY.
Historical records survey. Michigan.
Preliminary check list of Michigan
imprints, 1796-1850. Detroit, Mich.,
The Michigan Historical records
survey project, 1942. vii, 224 p., 4
numb. l. 015.774 44-41415
    Z1215 .H67 no. 52 MRR Alc.

MICHIGAN--BIBLIOGRAPHY--CATALOGS.
United States. Library of Congress.
Michigan [from wilderness to center
of industry], Washington, 1955.
vii, 70 p. 016.9774 55-60061
    Z663.15.A6M5 MRR Alc.

MICHIGAN--BIOGRAPHY.
Michigan manual. 1959/60-
[Lansing?] 353.9/774/0202 72-623543
    JK5830 .A32 MRR Alc Latest edition

MICHIGAN--CENTENNIAL CELEBRATIONS, ETC.
United States. Library of Congress.
Michigan [from wilderness to center
of industry], Washington, 1955.
vii, 70 p. 016.9774 55-60061
    Z663.15.A6M5 MRR Alc.

**MICHIGAN--DESCRIPTION AND TRAVEL--GUIDE-
BOOKS.**
Writers' Program. Michigan.
Michigan, a guide to the Wolverine
State. St. Clair Shores, Mich.,
Somerset Publishers, 1973 [c1941]
xxxvi, 682 p. 817.74/04/4 72-84482

    F566 .W9 1973 MRR Ref Desk.

MICHIGAN--HISTORY.
Dunbar, Willis Frederick, Michigan:
a history of the Wolverine State.
Grand Rapids, W. B. Eerdmans Pub. Co.
[1965] 800 p. 977.4 64-8579
    F566 .D84 MRR Alc.

MICHIGAN--HISTORY--BIBLIOGRAPHY.
Greenly, Albert Harry, A selective
bibliography of important books,
pamphlets, and broadsides relating to
Michigan history. Lunenburg, Vt.,
Stinehour Press, 1958. xvii, 165 p.
016.9774 58-33867
    Z1297 .G7 MRR Alc.

MICHIGAN--IMPRINTS.
Historical records survey. Michigan.
Preliminary check list of Michigan
imprints, 1796-1850. Detroit, Mich.,
The Michigan Historical records
survey project, 1942. vii, 224 p., 4
numb. l. 015.774 44-41415
    Z1215 .H67 no. 52 MRR Alc.

MICHIGAN--MANUFACTURES--DIRECTORIES.
The Directory of Michigan
manufacturers. Detroit, Mich.,
Manufacturer Pub. Co. 338.409774 41-
12488
    HD9723 .D43 Sci RR Latest edition
    / MRR Alc Latest edition

Midwest manufacturers and industrial
directory buyers guide. [Detroit,
Industrial Directory Publishers]
338.4/0977 72-626483
    HC107.A15 M5 MRR Alc Latest
    edition

MICHIGAN--OFFICIALS AND EMPLOYEES.
Michigan Municipal League. Annual
directory of Michigan municipal
officials. Ann Arbor. 352.0774 43-
35863
    JS303.M5 M52 no. 1 MRR Alc Latest
    edition

**MICHIGAN--OFFICIALS AND EMPLOYEES--
REGISTERS.**
Michigan. Dept. of State. List of
elective and appointive state
officers, boards and commissions,
state, federal and municipal courts,
state institutions, legislative and
county officers. Lansing, Mich.
353.9774 26-10622
    JK5830 .A3 MRR Alc Latest edition

**MICHIGAN--POLITICS AND GOVERNMENT--1951-
--HANDBOOKS, MANUALS, ETC.**
Michigan manual. 1959/60-
[Lansing?] 353.9/774/0202 72-623543

    JK5830 .A32 MRR Alc Latest edition

MICHIGAN--REGISTERS.
Michigan. Dept. of State. List of
elective and appointive state
officers, boards and commissions,
state, federal and municipal courts,
state institutions, legislative and
county officers. Lansing, Mich.
353.9774 26-10622
    JK5830 .A3 MRR Alc Latest edition

Michigan Municipal League. Annual
directory of Michigan municipal
officials. Ann Arbor. 352.0774 43-
35863
    JS303.M5 M52 no. 1 MRR Alc Latest
    edition

MICHIGAN--STATISTICS.
Michigan. State University, East
Lansing. Graduate School of Business
Administration. Division of Research.
Michigan statistical abstract. 8th
ed.; 1970- [East Lansing] [$5.25]
317.74 74-644904
    HA441 .M53 MRR Alc Latest edition

MICRO-ORGANISMS.
see also Bacteria

MICRO-ORGANISMS, PATHOGENIC.
see also Bacteria, Pathogenic

MICROBES
see Bacteria

see Bacteriology

MICROBIOLOGY.
Microbiology; including immunology
and molecular genetics 2d ed.
Hagerstown, Md., Medical Dept.,
Harper & Row [1973] xv, 1562 p.
576 73-6349
    QR41.2 .M49 1973 MRR Alc.

Stanier, Roger Y. The microbial
world 3d ed. Englewood Cliffs,
N.J., Prentice-Hall [1970] vii, 873
p. [15.95] 576 70-110090
    QR41.2 .S775 1970 MRR Alc.

MICROBIOLOGY--DICTIONARIES.
Jacobs, Morris Boris, Dictionary of
microbiology Princeton, N.J., Van
Nostrand [1957] 276 p. 589.9503
576.03* 56-12482
    QR9 .J18 MRR Alc.

MICROCARDS--BIBLIOGRAPHY.
United States. Library of Congress.
General Reference and Bibliography
Division. Microfilms and microcards,
their use in research; Washington,
1950. v, 81 p. 016.025179 50-
62951
    Z663.28 .M5 MRR Alc.

MICROCARDS--CATALOGS.
Guide to microforms in print. 1961-
Washington, Microcard Editions.
016.099 61-7082
    Z1033.M5 G8 Sci RR Latest edition
    / MRR Alc Latest edition

MICROCARDS--UNION LISTS.
Tilton, Eva Maude, comp. A union
list of publications in opaque
microforms. 2d ed. New York,
Scarecrow Press, 1964. ix, 744 p.
016.099 64-11788
    Z1033.M5 T5 1964 MRR Alc.

MICROCLIMATOLOGY.
United States. Library of Congress.
Science and Technology Division.
Cold weather agriculture.
Washington, U.S. Govt. Print. Off.,
1960. v, 48 p. 631.0911 60-61031

    Z663.41 .C6 MRR Alc.

MICROFILM PROJECTORS.
Stewart, Jean Falconer. Reading
devices for micro-images, New
Brunswick, N.J., Graduate School of
Library Service, Rutgers, the State
University; distributed by Rutgers
University Press, 1960. viii, 205 p.
025.179 60-7276
    Z265 .S78 MRR Alc.

MICROFILM SERVICES--DIRECTORIES.
International Federation for
Documentation. Photocopies from
abroad; 3d and rev. ed. The Hague
[1963 or 4] 28 p. 64-4609
    Z265 .I55 1964 MRR Ref Desk.

Microfilm source book. [New York,
Microfilm Pub. Co.] 338.4/7/68643
72-624065
    Z265 .M563 MRR Alc Latest edition
    / Sci RR Latest edition

Nitecki, Joseph Z. Directory of
library reprographic services. 5th
ed. [Weston, Conn.] Published for
the Reproduction of Library Materials
Section, American Library Association
by Microform Review Inc. [1974,
c1973] 105 p. 025.1/29 73-2059
    Z265 .N58 1974 MRR Ref Desk.

MICROFILMS--BIBLIOGRAPHY.
Canadiana. Jan. 15, 1951- [Ottawa]
015.71 53-35723
    Z1365 .C23 MRR Alc Full set

National register of microform
masters. Sept. 1965- Washington,
Library of Congress. 65-29419
    Z663 .A43 MRR Alc MRR Alc Full set

United States. Library of Congress.
A guide to the microfilm collection
of early state records. [Washington]
Library of Congress, Photoduplication
Service 1950. 1 v. (various
pagings) 016.01573 50-62956
    Z663.96 .G8 MRR Alc.

MICROFILMS--CATALOGS.
American Studies Association.
Committee on Microfilm Bibliography.
Bibliography of American culture,
1493-1875. Ann Arbor, Mich.,
University Microfilms, 1957. xvi,
228 p. 016.9173 57-4827
    Z1215 .A585 MRR Alc.

Reno, Edward A. League of Nations
documents, 1919-1946; New Haven,
Conn., Research Publications, 1973-
v. 016.34122 73-3061
    Z6473 .R45 MRR Alc.

United States. Library of Congress.
A descriptive checklist of selected
manuscripts in the monasteries of
Mount Athos Washington, Library of
Congress, Photoduplication Service,
1957. xiii, 36 p. 016.091 57-
60041
    Z663.96 .D4 MRR Alc.

United States. National Archives.
List of National Archives microfilm
publications. 1947- Washington.
016.026973 a 61-9222
    CD3027 .M514 MRR Alc Latest
    edition

MICROFILMS--DIRECTORIES.
Microfilm source book. [New York,
Microfilm Pub. Co.] 338.4/7/68643
72-624065
    Z265 .M563 MRR Alc Latest edition
    / Sci RR Latest edition

MICROFORMS--BIBLIOGRAPHY.
Reichmann, Felix, Bibliographic
control of microforms, Westport,
Conn., Greenwood Press, Pub. Division
[1972] 256 p. 016.02517/9 72-2463

    Z1033.M5 R43 MRR Alc.

Subject guide to microforms in print.
1962/63- Washington, Microcard
Editions. 016.099 62-21624
    Z1033.M5 S8 Sci RR Latest edition
    / MRR Alc Latest edition

MICROFORMS--CATALOGS.
Guide to microforms in print. 1961-
Washington, Microcard Editions.
016.099 61-7082
    Z1033.M5 G8 Sci RR Latest edition
    / MRR Alc Latest edition

United States. Library of Congress.
General Reference and Bibliography
Division. Microfilms and microcards,
their use in research; Washington,
1950. v, 81 p. 016.025179 50-
62951
    Z663.28 .M5 MRR Alc.

MICROPHOTOGRAPHY.
see also Filmstrips

Salmon, Stephen R. Specifications
for Library of Congress microfilming.
Washington Library of Congress;
[for sale by the Superintendent of
Documents, U.S. Govt. Print. Off.]
1964. v, 21 p. 64-60058
    Z663.96 .S6 MRR Alc.

MICROPHOTOGRAPHY. (Cont.)
United States. Library of Congress.
Photoduplication Service.
Specifications for the microfilming
of books and pamphlets in the Library
of Congress. Washington, Library of
Congress; [for sale by the Supt. of
Docs., U.S. Govt. Print. Off.] 1973.
iii, 16 p. [$0.40]   686.43 73-9756

    Z663.86 .S68 MRR Alc.

MICROPHOTOGRAPHY--DIRECTORIES.
Microfilm source book. [New York,
Microfilm Pub. Co.] 338.4/7/68643
72-624065
    Z265 .M563 MRR Alc Latest edition
    / Sci RR Latest edition

MICROSCOPE AND MICROSCOPY--DICTIONARIES.
Clark, George Lindenberg, ed. The
encyclopedia of microscopy. New
York, Reinhold Pub. Corp. [1961] 693
p. 578.03 61-9698
    QH211 .C54 MRR Alc.

MICROSCOPIC ANATOMY
see Histology

MICROTONIC MUSIC.
see also Music, Oriental

MIDDLE AGE.
see also Aging

MIDDLE AGES.
see also Civilization, Medieval

    see also Renaissance

MIDDLE AGES--BIBLIOGRAPHY.
Chevalier, Cyr Ulysse Joseph,
Répertoire des sources historiques
du moyen age, Paris, 1877-1903. 2
pt. in 3 v. 02-2025
    Z6203 .C52 MRR Alc.

International Medieval Bibliography.
International medieval bibliography
1967- Leeds, 1968. 160 p.
[unpriced] 016.914/03/1 s 70-
462591
    Z6203 .I63 MRR Alc.

Paetow, Louis John, A guide to the
study of medieval history, Rev. ed.,
New York, F. S. Crofts & co., 1931.
xvii p., 2 l., 3-643 p. 016.9401
31-14070
    Z6203 .P19 1931 MRR Alc.

Potthast, August, Bibliotheca
historica medii nevi. 2. verb. und
verm. aufl. Berlin, W. Weber, 1896.
2 v. 02-5027
    Z6203 .P87 MRR Alc.

Williams, Harry Franklin, An index
of mediaeval studies published in
Festschriften, 1865-1946, Berkeley,
University of California Press, 1951.
x, 165 p. 016.9401 51-62136
    Z6203 .W5 MRR Alc.

MIDDLE AGES--BIBLIOGRAPHY--PERIODICALS.
International guide to medieval
studies. v. 1- June 1961- Darien,
Conn., American Bibliographic
Service. 63-24615
    Z6203 .I6 MRR Alc Full set

Rouse, Richard H. Serial
bibliographies for medieval studies
Berkeley, University of California
Press 1969. xiii, 150 p.
016.016814/03/1 68-31637
    Z6203 .R66 MRR Alc.

MIDDLE AGES--BIOGRAPHY.
Jocher, Christian Gottlieb,
Allgemeines gelehrten-lexicon ...
Leipzig, 1750-1897. 11 v. 06-3520

    Z1010 .J63 MRR Biog.

MIDDLE AGES--HISTORY.
see also Feudalism

The Cambridge medieval history, New
York, The Macmillan company, 1911-36.
8 v. 11-29851
    D117 .C3 MRR Alc.

Cantor, Norman F. Medieval history;
2d ed. [New York] Macmillan [1969]
xxiii, 584 p. 914/.03/1 68-10930
    D118 .C3 1969 MRR Alc.

Larousse encyclopedia of ancient and
medieval history. London, P. Hamlyn
[1963] 413 p. 64-363
    D59 .H553 1963a MRR Alc.

Previté-Orton, Charles William, The
shorter Cambridge medieval history.
Cambridge [Eng.] University Press,
1952. 2 v. (xxi, 1202 p.) 940.1
52-12272
    D117 .P75 MRR Alc.

Thompson, James Westfall, Economic
and social history of the Middle
Ages, 300-1300. New York, Ungar
[1959] 2 v. (ix, 900 p.) 940.1 59-
10886
    D117 .T5 1959 MRR Alc.

MIDDLE AGES--HISTORY--CHRONOLOGY.
Storey, R. L. Chronology of the
medieval world: 800 to 1491 [1st
American ed.] New York, D. McKay Co.
[1973] xii, 705 p. 909.07 72-
90909
    D118 .S855 1973b MRR Ref Desk.

MIDDLE AGES--HISTORY--DICTIONARIES.
Fines, John. Who's who in the Middle
Ages. London, Blond, 1970. xii, 218
p. 940.1/0922 B 70-540350
    D115 .F5 1970 MRR Biog.

Wedeck, Harry Ezekiel, Concise
dictionary of medieval history [1st
British Commonwealth ed.] London, P.
Owen [1964, c1963] 377 p. 67-40280

    D114 .W4 1964 MRR Alc.

MIDDLE AGES--HISTORY--OUTLINES,
SYLLABI, ETC.
Paetow, Louis John, A guide to the
study of medieval history, Rev. ed.,
New York, F. S. Crofts & co., 1931.
xvii p., 2 l., 3-643 p. 016.9401
31-14070
    Z6203 .P19 1931 MRR Alc.

MIDDLE AGES--HISTORY--SOURCES.
Downs, Norton, ed. Basic documents
in medieval history, Princeton,
N.J., Van Nostrand [1959] 189 p.
940.1082 59-9758
    D113.5 .D6 MRR Alc.

Ogg, Frederic Austin, ed. A source
book of medieval history; New York,
Cincinnati [etc.] American book
company [1908?] 504 p. 08-12576
    D113 .O3 MRR Alc.

Pullan, Brian S., ed. Sources for
the history of medieval Europe from
the mid-eighth to the mid-thirteenth
century Oxford, Blackwell [1966] x,
277 p. [35/-] 940.14 66-75453
    D113.5 .P8 MRR Alc.

White, Donald A., ed. Medieval
history; Homewood, Ill., Dorsey
Press, 1965. ix, 575 p. 901.921
65-6954
    D113.5 .W5 MRR Alc.

MIDDLE ATLANTIC STATES--BIOGRAPHY--
DICTIONARIES.
Who's who in the East and Eastern
Canada. 1st- ed.; 1942/43-
Chicago [etc.] Marquis-Who's Who
[etc.] 920.07 43-18522
    E176 .W643 MRR Biog Latest edition

MIDDLE ATLANTIC STATES--DESCRIPTION AND
TRAVEL--GUIDE-BOOKS.
American Automobile Association.
Mideastern tour book. Washington.
917.4 59-43016
    F106 .A5 MRR Alc Latest edition

Shosteck, Robert, Weekender's guide;
places of historic, scenic, and
recreational interest within 200
miles of the Washington-Baltimore
area. Washington, Potomac Books
[c1973] xiii, 400 p. [$2.90]
917.5 74-159051
    F106 .S53 1973 MRR Alc.

MIDDLE ATLANTIC STATES--MANUFACTURES--
DIRECTORIES.
Directory of Central Atlantic States
manufacturers; 1- ed.; 1950-
Baltimore, T. K. Sanderson
Organization. 670.58 50-2706
    T12 .D485 Sci RR Latest edition /
    MRR Alc Latest edition

MIDDLE WEST.
Peirce, Neal R. The Great Plains
States of America: people, politics,
and power in the nine Great Plains
States [1st ed.] New York, Norton
[1973] 402 p. 917.8 72-13928
    F595.2 .P44 MRR Alc.

MIDDLE WEST--BIOGRAPHY--DICTIONARIES.
Personalities of the West and
Midwest. Raleigh, N.C., News Pub.
Co. 920.078 68-56857
    CT213 .P4 MRR Biog Latest edition

Who's who in the Midwest and Central
Canada. 1st- ed.; 1947- Chicago,
Marquis-Who's Who [etc.] 920.07 50-
289
    E176 .W644 MRR Biog Latest edition

MIDDLE WEST--DESCRIPTION AND TRAVEL--
GUIDE-BOOKS.
American Automobile Association.
Mideastern tour book. Washington.
917.4 59-43016
    F106 .A5 MRR Alc Latest edition

American Automobile Association.
South central tour book. Washington.
917.6 59-43018
    F396 .A6 MRR Alc Latest edition

North Central States. 1969/70-
[Washington] AAA. 917.7/04 72-
622646
    GV1024 .N82 MRR Alc Latest edition

MIDDLE WEST--INDUSTRIES--DIRECTORIES.
Midwest manufacturers and industrial
directory buyers guide. [Detroit,
Industrial Directory Publishers]
338.4/0977 72-626483
    HC107.A15 M5 MRR Alc Latest
    edition

MIDDLE WEST--MANUFACTURES--DIRECTORIES.
Midwest manufacturers and industrial
directory buyers guide. [Detroit,
Industrial Directory Publishers]
338.4/0977 72-626483
    HC107.A15 M5 MRR Alc Latest
    edition

MIDLANDS--COMMERCE--DIRECTORIES.
Chambers trades register of the
Midlands. London, Chambers Trades
Registers & Directories Ltd. 61-
30725
    HC257.M5 C5 MRR Alc Latest edition

MIDLANDS--INDUSTRIES--DIRECTORIES.
Chambers trades register of the
Midlands. London, Chambers Trades
Registers & Directories Ltd. 61-
30725
    HC257.M5 C5 MRR Alc Latest edition

MIGRANT LABOR.
see also Migration, Internal

MIGRATION, INTERNAL.
see also Cities and towns--Growth

MIGRATION, INTERNAL--BIBLIOGRAPHY.
Mangalam, J. J. Human migration;
Lexington, University of Kentucky
Press, 1968. 194 p. [15.00]
016.3013/2 67-23777
    Z7164.D3 M36 MRR Alc.

MIGRATION, INTERNAL--UNITED STATES.
Kuznets, Simon Smith, ed. Population
redistribution and economic growth:
Philadelphia, American Philosophical
Society, 1957-64. 3 v. 312.8
301.32* 57-10071
    HB1965 .K8 MRR Alc.

MILAN--DESCRIPTION--GUIDE-BOOKS.
Guida di Milano e provincia. Milano,
S. di Fontana. 49-35529
    Began publication in 1879.
    DG652 .G8 MRR Alc Latest edition

MILAN--DESCRIPTION--GUIDE-BOOKS.
Guida di Milano e provincia. Milano,
S. di Fontana. 49-35529
    Began publication in 1879.
    DG652 .G8 MRR Alc Latest edition

MILAN (PROVINCE)--INDUSTRIES--
DIRECTORIES.
Annuario industriale della provincia
di Milano. [Milano, Associazione
industriale lombarda] a 52-7615
    HC307.M5 A5 MRR Alc Latest edition

MILITARISM--YEARBOOKS.
International Institute for Peace and
Conflict Research. S I P R I
yearbook of world armaments and
disarmaments. 1968/69- New York,
Humanities Press. 341.6/7/05 76-
12210
    UA10 .I55 MRR Alc Latest edition

MILITARY--BIBLIOGRAPHY.
Stuttgart. Bibliothek für
Zeitgeschichte. Bibliothek für
Zeitgeschichte--Weltkriegsbücherei,
Stuttgart; systematischer Katalog.
Boston, G. K. Hall, 1968. 20 v. 74-
225445
    Z6204 .S8 1968 MRR Alc (Dk 33)

MILITARY AERONAUTICS
see Aeronautics, Military

MILITARY AEROPLANES
see Aeroplanes, Military

MILITARY AIR BASES
see Air bases

MILITARY ART AND SCIENCE.
see also Armaments

    see also Arms and armor

    see also Battles

    see also Fortification

    see also War

Dupuy, Richard Ernest, Military
heritage of America New York, McGraw-
Hill, 1956. xv, 794 p. 973 55-
11169
    E181 .D8 MRR Alc.

Inter-University Seminar on Armed
Forces and Society. Handbook of
military institutions. Beverly
Hills, Calif., Sage Publications
[1971] 607 p. 301.5/98 78-127989
    U102 .I65 MRR Alc.

MILITARY ART AND SCIENCE--DICTIONARIES.
Farrow, Edward Samuel, Farrow's
military encyclopedia; New York, The
author, 1885. 3 v. 01-9732
    U24 .F24 MRR Alc.

MILITARY ART AND SCIENCE-- (Cont.)
France. Armée. Direction technique des armes et de l'instruction. Lexique militaire moderne français-anglais. Paris, Charles-Lavauzelle et Cie, 1968. 544 p. [25 F] 355/.0003 68-118881
U25 .F66 MRR Alc.

Garber, Max Bruce, A modern military dictionary, Washington, D.C., P. S. Bond publishing co., 1942. 2 p. l., 272 p. 355.03 42-21115
U24 .G3 1942 MRR Alc.

Gaynor, Frank, The new military and naval dictionary. New York, Philosophical Library [1951] viii, 295 p. 355.03 51-13233
U24 .G34 MRR Alc.

Luttwak, Edward. A dictionary of modern war. [1st U.S. ed.] New York, Harper & Row [1971] 224 p. [$7.95] 355/.003 77-159574
U24 .L93 1971 MRR Alc.

Partridge, Eric, A dictionary of Forces' slang, 1939-1945. Freeport, N.Y., Books for Libraries Press [1970] xi, 212 p. 427.09 75-117899
PE3727.S7 P25 1970 MRR Alc.

Quick, John, Dictionary of weapons and military terms. New York, McGraw-Hill [1973] xii, 515 p. 623/.03 73-8757
U24 .Q5 MRR Alc.

Scott, Henry Lee, Military dictionary. New York, Greenwood Press [1968] 674 p. 355/.003 68-54782
U24 .S42 1968 MRR Alc.

MILITARY ART AND SCIENCE--DICTIONARIES--FRENCH.
France. Armée. Direction technique des armes et de l'instruction. Lexique militaire moderne français-anglais. Paris, Charles-Lavauzelle et Cie, 1968. 544 p. [25 F] 355/.0003 68-118881
U25 .F66 MRR Alc.

MILITARY ART AND SCIENCE--EARLY WORKS TO 1800.
Aeneas Tacticus. Aeneas Tacticus, Asclepiodotus, Onasander, London, W. Heinemann; New York, G. P. Putnam's sons, 1923. x, 531, [1] p. 24-2508

PA3612 .A2 1923 MRR Alc.

Frontinus, Sextus Julius. The Stratagems. London, W. Heinemann; New York, G. P. Putnam's sons, 1925. xl, 483, [1] p. 25-15482
PA6156.F6 1925 MRR Alc.

MILITARY ART AND SCIENCE--PERIODICALS--BIBLIOGRAPHY.
United States. Air University. Library. Union list of military periodicals. Maxwell Air Force Base, Ala., Air University Library, 1960. viii, 121 p. 016.35505 60-62431
Z6723 .U32 MRR Alc.

MILITARY ART AND SCIENCE--QUOTATIONS, MAXIMS, ETC.
Heinl, Robert Debs, comp. Dictionary of military and naval quotations. Annapolis, United States Naval Institute [c1966] xl, 367 p. 355.0008 66-22342
U19 .H4 MRR Ref Desk.

Taylor, Anna Marjorie, The language of World War II; Rev. and enl. ed. New York, H. W. Wilson Co., 1948. 265 p. 940.53014 48-8265
PE3727.S7 T3 1948 MRR Alc.

MILITARY ART AND SCIENCE--TERMINOLOGY.
Fraser, Edward, comp. Soldier and sailor words and phrases; London, G. Routledge and sons, ltd., 1925. vii, 372 p. 25-8719
PE3727.S7 F7 MRR Alc.

Taylor, Anna Marjorie, The language of World War II; Rev. and enl. ed. New York, H. W. Wilson Co., 1948. 265 p. 940.53014 48-8265
PE3727.S7 T3 1948 MRR Alc.

MILITARY ART AND SCIENCE--YEARBOOKS.
Brassey's annual. 1st- year; 1886- New York [etc.] Praeger [etc.] 359.058 12-30905
V10 .N3 MRR Alc Latest edition

MILITARY BALLOONS
see Balloons

MILITARY BASES--UNITED STATES--DIRECTORIES.
Taussig, Joseph K., Rand McNally travel guide for servicemen. [Chicago, Rand McNally, 1972] 64, 96 p. [$2.95] 917.3/04/924 72-189287
E169.02 .T4 1972 MRR Alc.

MILITARY BIOGRAPHY.
Blakeney, Jane, Heroes, U.S. Marine Corps, 1861-1955; [1st ed. Washington, 1957] xviii, 621 p. 359.96 57-13185
VE23 .B56 MRR Biog.

Greene, Robert Ewell, Black defenders of America, 1775-1973. Chicago, Johnson Pub. Co., 1974. 416 p. 355.1 73-15607
E185.63 .G73 MRR Alc.

Martell, Paul. World military leaders / New York : Bowker, [1974] 268 p. ; 355/.0092/2 B 74-78392
U51 .M35 MRR Biog.

Rubin, Eli. 140 Jewish marshals, generals & admirals. London, De Vero Books [1952] 300 p. 923.5 52-67186
DS115 .R78 MRR Biog.

United States. Congress. Senate. Committee on Veterans' Affairs. Medal of Honor recipients, 1863-1973: Washington, U.S. Govt. Print. Off., 1973. xix, 1231 p. [$8.50] 355.1/34 73-603149
UB433 .U55 1973b MRR Biog.

MILITARY CEREMONIES, HONORS, AND SALUTES--UNITED STATES.
Boatner, Mark Mayo, Military customs and traditions. New York, D. McKay Co. [1956] 176 p. 355.1 56-14010

U353 .B6 MRR Alc.

Bunkley, Joel William, Military and naval recognition book; 2d ed. New York, D. Van Nostrand company, inc., 1942. xiv, 309 p. incl. col. front., illus. (part col.) 355.14 42-24955

UC530 .B8 1942a MRR Alc.

Moss, James Alfred, Origin and significance of military customs, including military miscellany of interest to soldiers and civilians, Menasha, Wis., George Banta publishing company [c1917] 78 p. 18-5608
U766 .M6 MRR Alc.

MILITARY CHAPLAINS
see Chaplains, Military

MILITARY FUNERALS--UNITED STATES.
Mossman, B. C. The last salute: civil and military funerals, 1921-1969, Washington, Dept. of the Army; [for sale by the Supt. of Docs. U.S. Govt. Print. Off.] 1971 [i.e. 1972] xxii, 428 p. [$5.75] 393/.0973 77-606843
GT3203 .M67 MRR Alc.

United States. Army. Military District of Washington. State, official, special military funeral policies and implementation plans. [Washington] 1958. 1 v. 355.17 58-62023
U353 .A53 MRR Alc.

MILITARY HISTORY.
Coggins, Jack. The fighting man; [1st ed.] Garden City, N.Y., Doubleday [1966] xii, 372 p. 355.0009 66-20936
U750 .C6 MRR Alc.

Dupuy, Richard Ernest, The encyclopedia of military history; [1st ed.] New York, Harper & Row [1970] xiii, 1406 p. [20.00] 355/.0009 74-81871
D25.A2 D8 MRR Ref Desk.

Fuller, John Frederick Charles, A military history of the Western World. New York, Funk & Wagnalls, 1954-56. 3 v. 909 54-9733
D25 .F935 MRR Alc.

MILITARY HISTORY--BIBLIOGRAPHY.
Higham, Robin D. S. Official histories; essays and bibliographies from around the world. Manhattan, Kansas State University Library, 1970. xi, 644 p. 016.355/009 74-634493
Z6724.H6 H5 MRR Alc.

MILITARY HISTORY--DICTIONARIES.
Ruffner, Frederick G., ed. Code names dictionary; Detroit, Gale Research Co. [1963] 555 p. 423 63-21847
PE1693 .R9 MRR Alc.

MILITARY HISTORY--HISTORIOGRAPHY.
Higham, Robin D. S. Official histories; essays and bibliographies from around the world. Manhattan, Kansas State University Library, 1970. xi, 644 p. 016.355/009 74-634493
Z6724.H6 H5 MRR Alc.

MILITARY HISTORY, MODERN.
Bodart, Gaston, Losses of life in modern wars, Austria-Hungary; France, Oxford, The Clarendon press; London, New York [etc.] H. Milford, 1916. x, 207, 6 p. incl. tables. 16-20885
D25.5 .B6 MRR Alc.

MILITARY INTELLIGENCE.
see also Photographic interpretation (Military science)

MILITARY LIFE
see Soldiers

MILITARY MUSEUMS.
Association of Museums of Arms and Military History. Repertory of museums of arms and military history. Copenhagen, 1960. 158 p. 355.074 61-24144
U13.A1 A7 MRR Alc.

MILITARY POSTS.
Army times, Washington, D.C. Guide to Army posts. [2d ed. Harrisburg, Pa.] Stackpole Books [1966] 383 p. 355.7 65-13382
UA26.A6 A7 1966 MRR Alc.

MILITARY POSTS--UNITED STATES.
Air Force bases; [3d ed.] Harrisburg, Pa., Stackpole Co. [1965] 224 p. 358.417058 65-13381
UG634.5.A1 A7 1965 MRR Alc.

Allen, Mary Moore. Origin of names of Army and Air Corps posts; camps, and stations in World War II in United States. Goldsboro, N.C. [1958?] 352 p. 59-1054
UA26.A6 A4 MRR Alc.

Army times, Washington, D.C. Guide to Army posts. [2d ed. Harrisburg, Pa.] Stackpole Books [1966] 383 p. 355.7 65-13382
UA26.A6 A7 1966 MRR Alc.

Prucha, Francis Paul. A guide to the military posts of the United States, 1789-1895. Madison, State Historical Society of Wisconsin, 1964. xiii, 178 p. 355.70973 64-63571
UA26.A6 P7 MRR Alc.

MILITARY POSTS--WEST.
United States. National Park Service. Soldier and brave; [1st ed.] New York, Harper & Row, 1963. xviii, 279 p. 978 63-10600
F591 .U59 MRR Alc.

MILITARY RESEARCH--ABBREVIATIONS.
Jacobs, Horace. Missile and space projects guide New York, Plenum Press, 1962. x, 235 p. 629.403 62-13473
TL788 .J3 MRR Alc.

MILITARY RESEARCH--UNITED STATES.
United States. Library of Congress. Science and Technology Division. Materials research abstracts, [Washington] Published for Directorate of Materials and Processes, Aeronautical Systems Division, Wright-Patterson Air Force Base, Ohio, 1962. vii, 534 p. 620.1 63-60205
Z663.41 .M3 MRR Alc.

MILITARY RESEARCH--UNITED STATES--BIBLIOGRAPHY.
United States. Library of Congress. Science and Technology Division. Air Force scientific research bibliography, Washington, U.S. Govt. Print. Off., 1961- v. 016.5 61-60038
Z663.41 .A36 MRR Alc.

MILITARY RESERVATIONS.
see also National parks and reserves

MILITARY SERVICE, COMPULSORY--UNITED STATES.
Tatum, Arlo. Guide to the draft, Boston, Beacon Press [1969] xx, 281 p. [$.95] 355.2/23/0973 69-17998

UB343 .T37 MRR Alc.

MILITARY STATISTICS.
Dupuy, Trevor Nevitt, The almanac of world military power 2d ed. New York, R. R. Bowker Co., 1972. xii, 373 p. 355.03/32/09047 72-2636
UA15 .D9 1972 MRR Ref Desk.

The Military balance. London, International Institute for Strategic Studies. 355.03/32/05 79-617319
UA15 .L652 MRR Ref Desk Latest edition

Military market facts. [Washington] Army Times Pub. Co. 65-5288
UC263 .M46 MRR Alc Latest edition

The Reference handbook of the armed forces of the world. 1966- New York [etc.] Praeger, [etc.] 66-17547
UA15 .R43 MRR Alc Latest edition

MILITARY STATISTICS. (Cont.)
Singer, Joel David, The wages of war, 1816-1965: New York, Wiley [1972] xii, 419 p. 301.6/334 75-39120
U21.2 .S57 MRR Alc.

United States. Arms Control and Disarmament Agency. Bureau of Economic Affairs. World military expenditures. 1970- [Washington, For sale by the Supt. of Docs., U.S. Govt. Print. Off.] 338.4/7/355005 70-649143
UA17 .U42 MRR Ref Desk Latest edition

MILITARY VEHICLES
see Vehicles, Military

MILK.
see also Cheese

MILLINERY.
see also Hats

MILLS AND MILL-WORK.
see also Machinery

MILTON, GEORGE FORT, 1894-1955--BIBLIOGRAPHY.
United States. Library of Congress. Manuscript Division. George Fort Milton: a register of his papers in the Library of Congress. Washington, 1958. 7 p. 012 58-60067
Z663.34 .M5 MRR Alc.

MILTON, JOHN, 1608-1674--CONCORDANCES.
Bradshaw, John, A concordance to the poetical works of John Milton. [1st ed. new impression] London, Allen & Unwin, 1965. [4], 412 p. [42/-] 67-78888
PR3595 .B7 1965a MRR Alc.

MILTON, JOHN, 1608-1674--DICTIONARIES, INDEXES, ETC.
Lockwood, Laura Emma, Lexicon to the English poetical works of John Milton. New York, B. Franklin [1968] xii, 671 p. 821/.4 68-56596
PR3580 .L7 1968 MRR Alc.

MIND
see Intellect

MIND AND BODY.
see also Dreams

see also Psychoanalysis

MINERAL INDUSTRIES.
see also Ceramic industries

MINERAL INDUSTRIES--DICTIONARIES.
Thrush, Paul W. A dictionary of mining, mineral, and related terms. [Washington, U.S. Bureau of Mines; for sale by the Supt. of Docs., U.S. Govt. Print. Off.] 1968. vii, 1269 p. [$8.50] 622/.03 68-67091
TN9 .T5 MRR Alc.

MINERAL INDUSTRIES--DIRECTORIES.
Walter R. Skinner's mining international year book. 86th-1972/73- London [Ft Business Publications Ltd.] 338.2/025 72-627354
TN13 .M7 MRR Alc Latest edition / Sci RR Latest edition

MINERAL INDUSTRIES--SOCIETIES, ETC.--DIRECTORIES.
Kaplan, Stuart R., ed. A guide to information sources in mining, minerals, and geosciences. New York, Interscience Publishers [1965] xiv, 599 p. 016.622 65-24304
Z7401 .G83 vol. 2 MRR Alc.

MINERAL INDUSTRIES--STATISTICS.
Great Britain. Institute of Geological Sciences. Mineral Resources Division. Statistical summary of the mineral industry. 1961/66- London, H. M. Stationery Off. 338.2/021/2 70-613320
HD9506 .A1G742 MRR Alc Latest edition

Metal bulletin handbook. 1st- ed.; 1968- London, Metal Bulletin Ltd. 338.4/5669 70-2106
HD9506.4 .M4 Sci RR Latest edition / MRR Alc Latest edition*

Minerais et métaux, s.a., Paris. Statistiques. Paris. 49-41772
HD9539 .A1M5 MRR Alc Latest edition

Minerals yearbook. 1932/33- [Washington, U.S. Govt. Print. Off.] 33-26551
TN23 .U612 MRR Alc Latest edition / Sci RR Partial set

MINERAL INDUSTRIES--STUDY AND TEACHING--DIRECTORIES.
Worldwide directory of mineral industries education and research. Houston, Gulf Pub. Co., 1968. x, 451 p. 668/.007 68-9304
TN165 .W66 MRR Alc.

MINERAL INDUSTRIES--YEARBOOKS.
Mining year book. London, W. E. Skinner [etc.] 338.2058 50-18583 "Established 1887."
TN13 .M7 MRR Alc Latest edition / Sci RR Latest edition

Mining year book. 1933- Denver, Colorado Mining Association. 622.058 46-33675
TN24.C6 M5 MRR Alc Latest edition

South African mining and engineering year book and directory. Johannesburg. 622 gs 29-261
TN119.S7 A7 MRR Alc Latest edition

MINERAL INDUSTRIES--CANADA--YEARBOOKS.
Canadian mining journal reference manual & buyers' guide. 83d- ed.; 1973- Quebec, National Business Publications Ltd. [$20.00] 338.2/025/71 74-641184
TN26 .C29 MRR Alc Latest edition

MINERAL INDUSTRIES--GERMANY--YEARBOOKS.
Jahrbuch für Bergbau, Energie, Mineralöl und Chemie. Essen, Glückauf [etc.] 338.2/025 53-31420

Began in 1893.
TN73 .J34 MRR Alc Latest edition

MINERAL INDUSTRIES--GREAT BRITAIN--DIRECTORIES.
Ryland's coal, iron, steel, tinplate, metal, engineering, foundry, hardware and allied trades directory, with brands and trade marks. London, Industrial Newspapers. 605.8 51-22142

Began publication with 1881 ed.
TN12 .R9 MRR Alc Latest edition

MINERAL INDUSTRIES--UNITED STATES.
Minerals yearbook. 1932/33- [Washington, U.S. Govt. Print. Off.] 33-26551
TN23 .U612 MRR Alc Latest edition / Sci RR Partial set

United States. Bureau of the Census. List of materials: consumption items; [Washington, For sale by the Supt. of Docs., U.S. Govt. Print. Off., 1969] 304 p. 339.4 77-601181
HD9724 .A4 1967b MRR Alc.

MINERAL INDUSTRIES--UNITED STATES--DIRECTORIES.
Pit and quarry. Directory of the nonmetallic minerals industries. Chicago. 58-20992
TN12 .P5 Sci RR Latest edition / MRR Alc Latest edition

MINERAL INDUSTRIES--UNITED STATES--STATISTICS.
United States. Bureau of the Census. 1963 census of mineral industries. [Washington, For sale by the Supt. of Docs., U.S. Govt. Print. Off., 1967] 2 v. 338.2/0873 a 66-7829
HD9506.U62 A36 1963 MRR Alc.

MINERAL OILS.
see also Petroleum

MINERALOGISTS--DIRECTORIES.
International Mineralogical Association. World directory of mineralogists. Barcelona, Published for the I.M.A. by Editorial Jover, 1970. xl, 170 p. 549/.025 73-31273
QE361.A1 I5 1970 MRR Biog.

MINERALOGY.
see also Precious stones

Dana, James Dwight, Manual of mineralogy. 17th ed., rev. New York, Wiley [1959] 609 p. 549 59-11820
QE372 .D2 1959 MRR Alc.

Pearl, Richard Maxwell, 1001 questions answered about the mineral kingdom. New York, Dodd, Mead, 1959. 326 p. 549.076 59-12156
QE365 .P33 MRR Alc.

Pearl, Richard Maxwell, Gems, minerals, crystals, and ores; New York, Golden Press [1967] 320 p. 549 64-14672
QE392 .P357 1967 MRR Alc.

MINERALOGY--COLLECTING OF SPECIMENS.
Nicolay, H. H. Rocks and minerals; South Brunswick [N.J.] A. S. Barnes [1967] 255 p. 549/.075 67-10619
QE364 .N49 1967 MRR Alc.

MINERALOGY--COLLECTORS AND COLLECTING.
Fay, Gordon S. The rockhound's manual [1st ed.] New York, Harper & Row [1972] x, 290 p. [$7.95] 549/.075 77-157080
QE365 .F22 MRR Alc.

MINERALOGY--COLLECTORS AND COLLECTING--UNITED STATES.
Carlisle, Norman V., The complete guide to treasure hunting Chicago, H. Regnery Co. [1973] 280 p. 917.3/04 73-6452
E159.5 .C37 MRR Alc.

MINERALOGY--DICTIONARIES.
Pearl, Richard Maxwell, Gems, minerals, crystals, and ores; New York, Golden Press [1967] 320 p. 549 64-14672
QE392 .P357 1967 MRR Alc.

Roberts, Willard Lincoln. Encyclopedia of minerals. New York, Van Nostrand Reinhold Co. [1974] xxv, 693, 128 p. 549/.03 74-1155
QE355 .R6 MRR Alc.

MINERALOGY--NORTH AMERICA--BIBLIOGRAPHY.
United States. Geological Survey. Bibliography of North American geology. 1785/1918-1950/59. Washington, U.S. Govt. Print. Off. 016.557 gs 24-38
Z6034.U49 U45 Sci RR Sci RR Partial set / MRR Alc Partial set

United States. Geological Survey. Bibliography of North American geology. 1906- Washington, U.S. Govt. Print. Off. 016.557 gs 09-427
QE75 .B9 MRR Alc Partial set / Sci RR Partial set

MINERALOGY--UNITED STATES.
Nicolay, H. H. Rocks and minerals; South Brunswick [N.J.] A. S. Barnes [1967] 255 p. 549/.075 67-10619
QE364 .N49 1967 MRR Alc.

MINERALOGY, DETERMINATIVE.
Liddicoat, Richard Thomas, Handbook of gem identification, [8th ed.] Los Angeles. Gemological Institute of America [1969] xv, 430 p. 549.1 73-13583
QE392 .L5 1969 MRR Alc.

MINES AND MINERAL RESOURCES.
see also Prospecting

Bertin, Léon, Larousse encyclopedia of the earth. London, P. Hamlyn [1961] 419 p. 550.3 61-66629
QE501 .B563 1961a MRR Alc.

MINES AND MINERAL RESOURCES--INFORMATION SERVICES.
Kaplan, Stuart R., ed. A guide to information sources in mining, minerals, and geosciences. New York, Interscience Publishers [1965] xiv, 599 p. 016.622 65-24304
Z7401 .G83 vol. 2 MRR Alc.

MINES AND MINERAL RESOURCES--MAPS.
Van Royen, William, Atlas of the world's resources. New York, Published by Prentice-Hall for the University of Maryland, 1952- v. 338 52-9034
G1046.G3 V3 1952 MRR Alc Atlas.

MINES AND MINERAL RESOURCES--STATISTICS.
Great Britain. Institute of Geological Sciences. Mineral Resources Division. Statistical summary of the mineral industry. 1961/66- London, H. M. Stationery Off. 338.2/021/2 70-613320
HD9506 .A1G742 MRR Alc Latest edition

Minerais et métaux, s.a., Paris. Statistiques. Paris. 49-41772
HD9539 .A1M5 MRR Alc Latest edition

MINES AND MINERAL RESOURCES--CANADA.
Canadian mining journal reference manual & buyers' guide. 83d- ed.; 1973- Quebec, National Business Publications Ltd. [$20.00] 338.2/025/71 74-641184
TN26 .C29 MRR Alc Latest edition

MINES AND MINERAL RESOURCES--COLORADO.
Mining year book. 1933- Denver, Colorado Mining Association. 622.058 46-33675
TN24.C6 M5 MRR Alc Latest edition

MINES AND MINERAL RESOURCES--NORTH AMERICA.
Mines register. [1900]- Somerset, N.J. [etc.] American Metal Market Co. [etc.] 01-30837
TN13 .M65 MRR Alc Latest edition / Sci RR Latest edition

MINES AND MINERAL RESOURCES--SOUTH AFRICA.
South African mining and engineering year book and directory. Johannesburg. 622 gs 29-261
TN119.S7 A7 MRR Alc Latest edition

MINES AND MINERAL RESOURCES--UNITED STATES.
Brobst, Donald Albert, United States mineral resources. Washington, U.S. Govt. Print. Off., 1973. viii, 722 p. [$8.50] 333.8/0973 73-600060
TN23 .B76 MRR Alc.

MINES AND MINERAL RESOURCES-- (Cont.)
Minerals yearbook. 1932/33-
[Washington, U.S. Govt. Print. Off.]
33-26551
TN23 .U612 MRR Alc Latest edition
/ Sci RR Partial set

**MINES AND MINERAL RESOURCES--UNITED
STATES--STATISTICS.**
United States. Bureau of the Census.
1963 census of mineral industries.
[Washington, For sale by the Supt. of
Docs., U.S. Govt. Print. Off., 1967]
2 v. 338.2/0973 a 66-7829
HD9506.U62 A36 1963 MRR Alc.

MINIATURE PAINTERS--DICTIONARIES.
Foster, Joshua James, A dictionary
of painters of miniatures (1525-1850)
London, P. Allan & co., ltd., 1926.
xv, 330 p. 26-14138
N7616 .F72 MRR Alc.

**MINIATURE PAINTERS, BRITISH--BIOGRAPHY--
DICTIONARIES.**
Foskett, Daphne. A dictionary of
British miniature painters. New
York, Praeger Publishers [1972] 2 v.
[$135.00] 759.2 72-112634
ND1337.G7 F463 1972 MRR Alc.

MINIATURE PAINTING.
Foster, Joshua James, A dictionary
of painters of miniatures (1525-1850)
London, P. Allan & co., ltd., 1926.
xv, 330 p. 26-14138
N7616 .F72 MRR Alc.

MINIATURE PAINTING, AMERICAN.
Wehle, Harry Brandeis, American
miniatures, 1730-1850; Garden City,
N.Y., Garden City publishing company,
inc. [1937] xxv p., 1 l., 127 p.
757.0973 37-6103
ND1337.U5 W4 1937 MRR Alc.

MINIATURE PAINTING, BRITISH.
Foskett, Daphne. A dictionary of
British miniature painters. New
York, Praeger Publishers [1972] 2 v.
[$135.00] 759.2 72-112634
ND1337.G7 F463 1972 MRR Alc.

MINING CORPORATIONS--DIRECTORIES.
Jane's world mining: 1970- London,
S. Low, Marston; New York, McGraw-
Hill. 338.2 74-146474
HG4811.A3 J35 Sci RR Latest
edition / MRR Alc Latest edition

Mines register. [1900]- Somerset,
N.J. [etc.] American Metal Market Co.
[etc.] 01-30837
TN13 .M65 MRR Alc Latest edition /
Sci RR Latest edition

**MINING CORPORATIONS--CANADA--
DIRECTORIES.**
Northern Miner Press Limited,
Toronto. Canadian mines register of
dormant and defunct companies.
Toronto [1960] 419 p. 622.065 60-
23311
HD9506.C22 N6 1960 MRR Alc.

MINING ENGINEERING--DICTIONARIES.
Nelson, Archibald. Dictionary of
applied geology: mining and civil
engineering. London, Newnes, 1967.
vii, 421 p. [45/-] 550/.3 68-
86619
QE5 .N44 1967 MRR Alc.

Nelson, Archibald. Dictionary of
mining. New York, Philosophical
Library [1965] 523 p. 622.03 65-
4207
TN9 .N44 1965 MRR Alc.

Thrush, Paul W. A dictionary of
mining, mineral, and related terms.
[Washington, U.S. Bureau of Mines;
for sale by the Supt. of Docs., U.S.
Govt. Print. Off.] 1968. vii, 1269
p. [$8.50] 622/.03 68-67091
TN9 .T5 MRR Alc.

MINING INDUSTRY AND FINANCE.
Mines register. [1900]- Somerset,
N.J. [etc.] American Metal Market Co.
[etc.] 01-30837
TN13 .M65 MRR Alc Latest edition /
Sci RR Latest edition

**MINING INDUSTRY AND FINANCE--
DIRECTORIES.**
Jane's world mining: 1970- London,
S. Low, Marston; New York, McGraw-
Hill. 338.2 74-146474
HG4811.A3 J35 Sci RR Latest
edition / MRR Alc Latest edition

Mining year book. London, W. E.
Skinner [etc.] 338.2058 50-18583
"Established 1887."
TN13 .M7 MRR Alc Latest edition /
Sci RR Latest edition

MINING INDUSTRY AND FINANCE--YEARBOOKS.
Walter R. Skinner's mining
international year book. 86th-
1972/73- London [Ft Business
Publications Ltd.] 338.2/025 72-
627354
TN13 .M7 MRR Alc Latest edition /
Sci RR Latest edition

**MINING INDUSTRY AND FINANCE--AFRICA,
SOUTH--YEARBOOKS.**
Beerman's all mining year book.
Johannesburg [etc.] Combined
Publishers [etc.] 55-32931
HD9506.A5 R5 Sci RR Latest edition
/ MRR Alc Latest edition

**MINING INDUSTRY AND FINANCE--AUSTRALIA--
YEARBOOKS.**
Jobson's mining year book. Sydney,
Jobson's Financial Services. 66-2200
HG5899.M4 J6 MRR Alc Latest
edition

**MINING INDUSTRY AND FINANCE--CANADA--
DIRECTORIES.**
Canadian mines handbook. 1935-
Toronto. 338.2065 35-19088
HG5159.M4C3 MRR Alc Latest edition

Northern Miner Press Limited,
Toronto. Canadian mines register of
dormant and defunct companies.
Toronto [1960] 419 p. 622.065 60-
23311
HD9506.C22 N6 1960 MRR Alc.

**MINING INDUSTRY AND FINANCE--MISSOURI--
DIRECTORIES.**
Missouri directory of manufacturers
and mining operations. Jefferson
City, Missouri Division of Commerce
and Industrial Development. [$15.00]
338.4/025/778 74-644525
T12 .M56 MRR Alc Latest edition

**MINING INDUSTRY AND FINANCE--NEW
ZEALAND--YEARBOOKS.**
Jobson's mining year book. Sydney,
Jobson's Financial Services. 66-2200
HG5899.M4 J6 MRR Alc Latest
edition

MINISTERS OF STATE
see Cabinet officers

MINISTRY
see Clergy

MINNEAPOLIS--DESCRIPTION--GUIDE-BOOKS.
Ervin, Jean. The Twin Cities
explored; Minneapolis, Adams Press
[1972] 200 p. [$8.95]
917.76/579/045 73-150443
F614.M6 E78 MRR Alc.

MINNESOTA--BIBLIOGRAPHY--CATALOGS.
United States. Library of Congress.
Centennial of the Territory of
Minnesota exhibition, March 5, 1949-
June 15, 1949. Washington, U.S.
Govt. Print. Off., 1949. iii, 74 p.
016.9776 49-45821
Z663.15.A6M6 1949 MRR Alc.

MINNESOTA--BIOGRAPHY.
The Minnesota legislative manual.
1967/68- [St. Paul] 328/.776/05 72-
623459
JK6130.A36 MRR Alc Latest edition

MINNESOTA--CENTENNIAL CELEBRATIONS, ETC.
United States. Library of Congress.
Centennial of the Territory of
Minnesota exhibition, March 5, 1949-
June 15, 1949. Washington, U.S.
Govt. Print. Off., 1949. iii, 74 p.
016.9776 49-45821
Z663.15.A6M6 1949 MRR Alc.

**MINNESOTA--DESCRIPTION AND TRAVEL--
GUIDE-BOOKS.**
Federal Writers' Project. Minnesota.
Minnesota, a State guide. [Rev. ed.]
New York, Hastings House [1954]
xxx, 545 p. 917.76 54-589
F606 .F44 1954 MRR Ref Desk.

MINNESOTA--HISTORY.
Blegen, Theodore Christian,
Minnesota; a history of the State.
[Minneapolis] University of Minnesota
Press [1963] 688 p. 977.6 63-
13124
F606 .B668 MRR Alc.

Folwell, William Watts, A history of
Minnesota. [Rev. ed.] St. Paul,
Minnesota Historical Society, 1956-
69. 4 v. 977.6 56-57334
F606 .F679 MRR Alc.

MINNESOTA--IMPRINTS.
Martin, Mamie Ruth. ... Check list
of Minnesota imprints, 1849-1865,
Chicago, The Historical records
survey, 1938. ix, 219 p. 015.776
38-22260
Z1215 .H67 no. 2 MRR Alc.

MINNESOTA--MANUFACTURES--DIRECTORIES.
Midwest manufacturers and industrial
directory buyers guide. [Detroit,
Industrial Directory Publishers]
338.4/0977 72-626483
HC107.A15 M5 MRR Alc Latest
edition

**MINNESOTA--POLITICS AND GOVERNMENT--
1951- --HANDBOOKS, MANUALS, ETC.**
The Minnesota legislative manual.
1967/68- [St. Paul] 328/.776/05 72-
623459
JK6130.A36 MRR Alc Latest edition

MINNESOTA--STATISTICS.
Minnesota pocket data book. 1973-
[St. Paul] Minnesota State Planning
Agency, Development Planning
Division. 317.76 74-645305
HA454 .M55 MRR Alc Latest edition

MINORITIES.
see also Nationalism

Simpson, George Eaton, Racial and
cultural minorities; 4th ed. New
York, Harper & Row [1972] viii, 775
p. 301.45/1/042 72-76373
HT1521 .S53 1972 MRR Alc.

**MINORITIES--EDUCATION--UNITED STATES--
DIRECTORIES.**
Directory of special programs for
minority group members; Career
information services, employment
skills banks, financial aid. 1974-
[Garrett Park, Md., Garrett Park
Press] [$6.95] 331.7/02/02573 73-
93533
HD5724 .D56 MRR Alc Latest edition

**MINORITIES--EDUCATION (HIGHER)--UNITED
STATES.**
Graduate & professional school
opportunities for minority students.
Princeton, N.J., Educational Testing
Service. 378.1/553/02573 73-642558
L901 .G717 MRR Ref Desk Latest
edition

MINORITIES--EMPLOYMENT--UNITED STATES.
Council on Economic Priorities.
Guide to corporations; [1st ed.]
Chicago, Swallow Press [1974] iii,
393 p. [$4.95] 301.5/5 73-13212
HD60.5.U5 C7 1974 MRR Alc.

United States. Civil Service
Commission. Minority group
employment in the Federal Government.
May 1970- Washington, For sale by
the Supt. of Docs., U.S. Govt. Print.
Off. 331.1/33/0973 72-622550
JK639 .A42 subser MRR Alc Latest
edition

United States. Office of Minority
Business Enterprise. Special catalog
of Federal programs assisting
minority enterprise. Washington; For
sale by the Supt. of Docs., U.S.
Govt. Print. Off., 1971. xiii, 89 p.
[$1.00] 338.973 77-614023
HC110.P63 A57 MRR Alc.

**MINORITIES--EMPLOYMENT--UNITED STATES--
DIRECTORIES.**
United States. Bureau of
Apprenticeship and Training.
Directory for reaching minority
groups. [Washington; For sale by the
Supt. of Docs., U.S. Govt. Print.
Off.] 1973. 214 p. [$2.85] 331.6
73-602280
HD6305.M5 U53 1973 MRR alc.

**MINORITIES--EMPLOYMENT--UNITED STATES--
DIRECTORIES--PERIODICALS.**
Directory of special programs for
minority group members; Career
information services, employment
skills banks, financial aid. 1974-
[Garrett Park, Md., Garrett Park
Press] [$6.95] 331.7/02/02573 73-
93533
HD5724 .D56 MRR Alc Latest edition

**MINORITIES--SCHOLARSHIPS, FELLOWSHIPS,
ETC.--UNITED STATES--DIRECTORIES.**
United States. Office of Minority
Business Enterprise. Higher
education aid for minority business;
Washington; [For sale by the Supt. of
Docs., U.S. Govt. Print. Off.] 1970.
viii, 103 p. [1.00] 650/.071/1 78-
607539
HF1131 .A55 MRR Alc.

**MINORITIES--SCHOLARSHIPS, FELLOWSHIPS,
ETC.--UNITED STATES--DIRECTORIES--
PERIODICALS.**
Directory of special programs for
minority group members; Career
information services, employment
skills banks, financial aid. 1974-
[Garrett Park, Md., Garrett Park
Press] [$6.95] 331.7/02/02573 73-
93533
HD5724 .D56 MRR Alc Latest edition

MINORITIES--CANADA--BIBLIOGRAPHY.
Takle, John A. Ethnic and racial
minorities in North America;
[Monticello, Ill., Council of
Planning Librarians] 1973. 71 p.
[$7.00] 016.3092/08 s
016.30145/1/0420973 74-160797
Z5942 .C68 no. 459-460 MRR Alc.

MINORITIES--UNITED STATES.
Gossett, Thomas F. Race; the history
of an idea in America. Dallas,
Southern Methodist University Press,
1963. ix, 512 p. 63-21187
E184.A1 G6 MRR Alc.

MINORITIES--UNITED STATES--BIBLIOGRAPHY.
Kinton, Jack F. American ethnic groups and the revival of cultural pluralism: 4th ed. [Aurora, Ill., Social Science & Sociological Resources] 1974. 206 p.
016.9173/06   74-171031
Z1361.E4 K55 1974 MRR Alc.

Los Angeles. University of Southern California. Library. An introduction to materials for ethnic studies in the University of Southern California Library. Los Angeles, 1970. ii, 196 p.   016.30145/0873   76-278151
Z7164.R12 L66 MRR Alc.

Takle, John A. Ethnic and racial minorities in North America: [Monticello, Ill., Council of Planning Librarians] 1973. 71 p. [$7.00]   016.3092/08 s
016.30145/1/0420973   74-160797
Z5942 .C68 no. 459-460 MRR Alc.

MINORITIES--UNITED STATES--COLLECTIONS.
Brown, Francis James, ed. One America: 3d ed. New York, Prentice-Hall, 1952. xvi, 764 p.   325.73 52-1682
E184.A1 B87 1952 MRR Alc.

MINORITIES--UNITED STATES--INFORMATION SERVICES--DIRECTORIES.
United States. Bureau of Apprenticeship and Training. Directory for reaching minority groups. [Washington] For sale by the Supt. of Docs., U.S. Govt. Print. Off.] 1973. 214 p. [$2.85]   331.6 73-602280
HD6305.M5 U53 1973 MRR alc.

MINORITIES--UNITED STATES--JUVENILE LITERATURE--BIBLIOGRAPHY.
Keating, Charlotte Matthews. Building bridges of understanding. Tucson, Ariz., Palo Verde Pub. Co., 1967. xvii, 134 p.   016.813/008/03 67-27778
Z1037.A1 K4 MRR Alc.

MINORITY BUSINESS ENTERPRISES.
United States. Office of Minority Business Enterprise. Directory of minority media. [Washington]; for sale by the Supt. of Docs., U.S. Govt. Print. Off., 1973. ix, 89 p. [$1.25]   301.16/1/02573 73-602686
P88.8 .U55 MRR Alc.

MINORITY BUSINESS ENTERPRISES--DISTRICT OF COLUMBIA.
Howard University, Washington, D.C. Minority Economic Resource Center. The District of Columbia directory of inner city organizations active in the field of minority business-economic development. 3d ed. Washington, 1972. iv, 20 p.   338/.04/025753 73-170762
HD2346.U52 D54 1872 MRR Alc.

MINORITY BUSINESS ENTERPRISES--UNITED STATES--DIRECTORIES.
National minority business directory. 1972- [Minneapolis, National Minority Business Campaign] 338/.0025/73 76-182148
HD2346.U5 N34 MRR Alc Latest edition

United States. Office of Minority Business Enterprise. National roster: minority professional consulting firms Washington, 1973. ix, 121 p.   658.4/03 73-601615
HD69.C6 U56 1973 MRR Alc.

MINORITY BUSINESS ENTERPRISES--UNITED STATES--DIRECTORIES--PERIODICALS.
National directory of minority manufacturers. [Washington] Office of Minority Business Enterprise.
338/.0025/73 74-645920
HD2346.U5 N33 MRR Alc Latest edition

MINORITY BUSINESS ENTERPRISES--UNITED STATES--FINANCE--DIRECTORIES.
United States. Office of Minority Business Enterprise. Directory of private programs assisting minority business. Washington; For sale by the Supt. of Docs., U.S. Govt. Print. Off., 1970. iv, 364 p. [$2.50]
658.4/6/02573 72-602355
HD69.C6 U545 MRR Alc.

MINORITY BUSINESS ENTERPRISES--WASHINGTON METROPOLITAN AREA--DIRECTORIES--PERIODICALS.
Impact directory. [Washington, Impact Press] 338.7/6/025753 74-645912
HD2346.U52 W355 MRR Alc Latest edition

MINSTREL SHOWS
see Musical revues, comedies, etc.

MINTS.
see also Coinage

MINTS--UNITED STATES.
United States. Bureau of the Mint. Domestic and foreign coins manufactured by mints of the United States, 1793-1970. [Washington, U.S. Govt. Print. Off., 1972] vi, 138 p. [$0.75]   338.47/7374973 72-603132
HG459 .U56 1972 MRR Alc.

MINTS--UNITED STATES--DIRECTORIES.
Davis, Norman M., The complete book of United States coin collecting New York, Macmillan [1971] xii, 336 p. [$7.95]   737.49/73 70-117863
CJ1830 .D36 MRR Alc.

MISCONDUCT IN OFFICE.
see also Corruption (in politics)

MISDEMEANORS (LAW)
see Criminal law

MISSIONARIES.
Neill, Stephen Charles, Bp. Concise dictionary of the Christian world mission. Nashville, Abingdon Press [1971] xxi, 682 p. [$10.50]
266/.003 76-21888
BV2040 .N44 MRR Alc.

MISSIONS.
see also Salvation Army

New York. Missionary Research Library. Protestant churches of Asia, the Middle East, Africa, Latin America, and the Pacific area. New York, 1959. 75 p.   284 59-44072
BX4805.2 .N45 1959 MRR Alc.

MISSIONS--DICTIONARIES.
The Encyclopedia of modern Christian missions; Camden, N.J., T. Nelson [1967] xix, 743 p.   266/.003 67-29099
BV2040 .E53 MRR Alc.

Neill, Stephen Charles, Bp. Concise dictionary of the Christian world mission. Nashville, Abingdon Press [1971] xxi, 682 p. [$10.50]
266/.003 76-21888
BV2040 .N44 MRR Alc.

MISSIONS--STATISTICS.
World Christian handbook. 1949-London, World Dominion Press. 270.8 49-6861
BR481 .W6 MRR Alc Latest edition

MISSIONS--AFRICA.
Duignan, Peter. Handbook of American resources for African studies. [Stanford, Calif.] Hoover Institution on War, Revolution, and Peace, Stanford University, 1967. xvii, 218 p.   016.916 66-20901
Z3501 .D8 MRR Alc.

MISSIONS--AFRICA--BIBLIOGRAPHY--UNION LISTS.
Williams, Ethel L. Afro-American religious studies: Metuchen, N.J., Scarecrow Press, 1972. 454 p.
016.301451/96073 78-166072
Z1361.N39 W55 MRR Alc.

MISSIONS--ASIA--DIRECTORIES.
Technical Assistance Information Clearing House. Far East technical assistance programs of U.S. nonprofit organizations, New York, 1966. viii, 274 p.   309.2/23 67-60359
HC411 .T4 MRR Alc.

MISSIONS--CHINA--HISTORY--SOURCES.
Marchant, Leslie Ronald. A guide to the archives and records of Protestant Christian missions [Nedlands, W.A.] University of Western Australia Press [1966] xi, 134 p. [3.50]   016.2664 66-18025
Z7817 .M3 MRR Alc.

MISSIONS, BRITISH--HISTORY--SOURCES.
Marchant, Leslie Ronald. A guide to the archives and records of Protestant Christian missions [Nedlands, W.A.] University of Western Australia Press [1966] xi, 134 p. [3.50]   016.2664 66-18025
Z7817 .M3 MRR Alc.

MISSISSIPPI.
Federal writers' project. Mississippi. Mississippi; a guide to the Magnolia state, New York, The Viking press, 1938. 4 p. l., [vii]-xxiv, 545 p.   917.62 38-12400
F341 .F45 MRR Ref Desk.

MISSISSIPPI--BIBLIOGRAPHY--CATALOGS.
United States. Library of Congress. Mississippi; the sesquicentennial of statehood. Washington; [For sale by the Supt. of Docs., U.S. Govt. Print. Off.] 1967. viii, 61 p. [0.45]
976.2/0074/0153 67-62576
Z663.15.A6M655 MRR Alc.

MISSISSIPPI--CENTENNIAL CELEBRATIONS, ETC.
United States. Library of Congress. Mississippi; the sesquicentennial of statehood. Washington; [For sale by the Supt. of Docs., U.S. Govt. Print. Off.] 1967. viii, 61 p. [0.45]
976.2/0074/0153 67-62576
Z663.15.A6M655 MRR Alc.

MISSISSIPPI--DESCRIPTION AND TRAVEL--GUIDE-BOOKS.
Federal writers' project. Mississippi. Mississippi; a guide to the Magnolia state, New York, The Viking press, 1938. 4 p. l., [vii]-xxiv, 545 p.   917.62 38-12400
F341 .F45 MRR Ref Desk.

MISSISSIPPI--HISTORY.
Bettersworth, John Knox, Mississippi: a history. Austin, Tex., Steck Co. [1959] 595, 32 p. 976.2 59-502
F341 .B58 MRR Alc.

MISSISSIPPI--MANUFACTURES--DIRECTORIES.
Mississippi industrial directory. Jackson, Miss. 670.58 54-62882 First ed. published 1942.
T12 .M54 MRR Alc Latest edition

MISSISSIPPI--POLITICS AND GOVERNMENT.
Highsaw, Robert Baker, The government and administration of Mississippi New York, Crowell [1954] 414 p.   342.762 320.9762* 54-11152
JK4625 1954 .H5 MRR Alc.

MISSISSIPPI--POLITICS AND GOVERNMENT--YEARBOOKS.
Mississippi official and statistical register. [Jackson] 10-33135
J87 .M74a MRR Alc Latest edition

MISSISSIPPI--REGISTERS.
Mississippi. University. Bureau of Governmental Research. A directory of Mississippi municipalities. 1949-University. 352.0762 50-63282
JS451.M79 A2 MRR Alc Latest edition

Mississippi official and statistical register. [Jackson] 10-33135
J87 .M74a MRR Alc Latest edition

MISSISSIPPI--STATISTICS.
Abney, F. Glenn. Mississippi election statistics, 1900-1967, University, Miss. [Bureau of Governmental Research, 1968] vi, 480 p.   324/.2021/762 68-66456
JK4693 1968.A62 MRR Alc.

MISSISSIPPI--STATISTICS--PERIODICALS.
Mississippi statistical abstract. Mississippi State, Miss. 317.62 75-629881
HA465 .A25 MRR Alc Latest edition

MISSISSIPPI RIVER.
Botkin, Benjamin Albert, ed. A treasury of Mississippi River folklore; New York, Crown Publishers [1955] xx, 620 p.   398 55-10172
GR109 .B58 MRR Alc.

MISSISSIPPI RIVER--NAVIGATION.
Inland river record: 1945- (Sewickley, Pa.] 386.224 45-7239
VM23 .I5 MRR Alc Latest edition

MISSISSIPPI VALLEY--HISTORY--1803-1865.
Billington, Ray Allen, Westward expansion; 3d ed. New York, Macmillan [c1967] xvii, 933 p.   973 67-12337
E179.5 .B63 1967 MRR Alc.

MISSOURI--BIBLIOGRAPHY.
Historical records survey. ... A preliminary check list of Missouri imprints 1808-1850. Washington, D.C., The historical records survey, 1937. ix, 225 p.   015.778 39-4905
Z1215 .H67 no. 1 MRR Alc.

MISSOURI--BIOGRAPHY.
Missouri. State Dept. Official manual. 1878- [Jefferson City, etc.] 353.9778 54-47364
JK5431 date MRR Alc Latest edition

MISSOURI--CENTENNIAL CELEBRATIONS, ETC.--EXHIBITIONS.
United States. Library of Congress. Missouri: the sesquicentennial of statehood; Washington; [For sale by the Supt. of Docs., U.S. Govt. Print. Off.] 1971. viii, 93 p. [$1.00]
917.78/03 72-37388
Z663.15.A6M85 MRR Alc.

MISSOURI--EXECUTIVE DEPARTMENTS.
Missouri. State Dept. Official manual. 1878- [Jefferson City, etc.] 353.9778 54-47364
JK5431 date MRR Alc Latest edition

MISSOURI--HISTORY.
Meyer, Duane Gilbert, The heritage
of Missouri. Saint Louis, State Pub.
Co., 1963. 843 p.   977.8 63-1213
F466 .M578 MRR Alc

MISSOURI--HISTORY--EXHIBITIONS.
United States. Library of Congress.
Missouri: the sesquicentennial of
statehood; Washington; [For sale by
the Supt. of Docs., U.S. Govt. Print.
Off.] 1971. viii, 93 p. [$1.00]
917.78/03 72-37388
Z663.15.A6M85 MRR Alc.

MISSOURI--MANUFACTURES--DIRECTORIES.
Midwest manufacturers and industrial
directory buyers guide. [Detroit,
Industrial Directory Publishers]
338.4/0977 72-626483
HC107.A15 M5 MRR Alc Latest
edition

Missouri directory of manufacturers
and mining operations. Jefferson
City, Missouri Division of Commerce
and Industrial Development. [$15.00]
338.4/025/778 74-645525
T12 .M56 MRR Alc Latest edition

MISSOURI--POLITICS AND GOVERNMENT.
Missouri. State Dept. Official
manual. 1878- [Jefferson City,
etc.] 353.9778 54-47364
JK5431 date MRR Alc Latest
edition

MISSOURI--POLITICS AND GOVERNMENT--1951-
Karsch, Robert Frederick, The
Government of Missouri. 12th ed.
Columbia, Mo., Lucas Bros.
Publishers, 1974. iii, 263 p.
320.4/778 74-166453
JK5425 1974 .K3 MRR Alc.

MISSOURI--REGISTERS.
Missouri. State Dept. Official
manual. 1878- [Jefferson City,
etc.] 353.9778 54-47364
JK5431 date MRR Alc Latest
edition

Missouri. State Dept. Roster of
State, district and county officers
of the State of Missouri. [Jefferson
City] 43-30785
Began publication in 1893.
JK5430.A33 MRR Alc Latest edition

MISTAKES
see Errors, Popular

MITCHELL, WILLIAM, 1879-1936--
BIBLIOGRAPHY.
United States. Library of Congress.
Division of bibliography. ... A list
of references on Brigadier General
William Mitchell, 1879-1936.
[Washington] 1942. 1 p. l., 33 p.
012 42-38080
Z663.28 .L575 MRR Alc.

MOBILE HOME INDUSTRY--DIRECTORIES.
The Mobile home dealers of the United
States and Canada. Detroit.
338.4769226 56-21768
HD9715.7.U6 M6 MRR Alc Latest
edition

MOBILE HOME PARKS--CANADA--DIRECTORIES.
Woodall's directory of mobile home
communities. 24th- ed.; 1971-
Highland Park, Ill., Woodall Pub. Co.
[$5.95] 647/.9473 74-645024
TX907 .W66 MRR Alc Latest edition

MOBILE HOME PARKS--MEXICO--DIRECTORIES.
Woodall's directory of mobile home
communities. 24th- ed.; 1971-
Highland Park, Ill., Woodall Pub. Co.
[$5.95] 647/.9473 74-645024
TX907 .W66 MRR Alc Latest edition

MOBILE HOME PARKS--UNITED STATES--
DIRECTORIES.
Woodall's directory of mobile home
communities. 24th- ed.; 1971-
Highland Park, Ill., Woodall Pub. Co.
[$5.95] 647/.9473 74-645024
TX907 .W66 MRR Alc Latest edition

MOBILE HOMES--HANDBOOKS, MANUALS, ETC.
Nulsen, Robert Hovey. The mobile
home manual. [Beverly Hills, Calif.,
Trail-R-Club of America, 1972] 2 v.
[$4.50 per vol.] 643 72-187894
TL197 .N8163 MRR Alc.

MOBILE HOMES--UNITED STATES.
Drury, Margaret J. Mobile homes;
Rev. ed. New York, Praeger, 1972.
xv, 234 p. 301.5/4 72-153392
HD7395.M6 D7 1972 MRR Alc.

MOBILITY
see Migration, Internal.

MOBS.
see also Riots

MODEL CITIES
see Cities and towns--Planning

MODELS, FASHION--YEARBOOKS.
International model. 1958- London
Haymarket Press Ltd. [etc.] 58-46808
HD6073.M7 I5 MRR Alc Latest
edition

MODELS AND MODELMAKING--INDEXES.
Lovell, Eleanor Cook, comp. Index to
handicrafts, modelmaking, and
workshop projects, Boston, Faxon,
1936. 476 p. 016.6 36-27324
Z7911 .L89 MRR Alc.

MODERN ARCHITECTURE
see Architecture, Modern

MODERN ART
see Art, Modern

MODERN CIVILIZATION
see Civilization, Modern

MODERN DANCE--DICTIONARIES.
Love, Paul Van Derveer, Modern dance
terminology, [New York] Kamin Dance
Publishers [1953] 96 p. 793.303
53-11674
GV1585 .L65 MRR Alc.

MODERN HISTORY
see History, Modern

MODERN LANGUAGES
see Languages, Modern

MODERN PAINTING
see Painting, Modern

MODERN POETRY
see Poetry, Modern

MODERN SCULPTURE
see Sculpture, Modern

MODERNISM (ART)
see also Architecture, Modern--20th
century

see also Art, Abstract

see also Art, Modern

see also Expressionism (Art)

MODULAR COORDINATION (ARCHITECTURE)
De Chiara, Joseph, Time-saver
standards for building types. New
York, McGraw-Hill [1973] xiii, 1065
p. [$27.50] 729/.2 73-6663
NA2760 .D42 MRR Alc.

MOHAMMEDAN COUNTRIES.
see also Arab countries

MOHAMMEDANISM
see Islam

MOLDING (CHEMICAL TECHNOLOGY)--
BIBLIOGRAPHY.
United States. Library of Congress.
Technical Information Division.
Casting techniques for explosives and
other nonmetallic materials.
Washington, 1956. vii, 50 p.
016.660284 56-60021
Z663.49 C3 MRR Alc.

MOLLUSKS.
see also Shells

Grzimek, Bernhard. Grzimek's animal
life encyclopedia. New York, Van
Nostrand Reinhold Co. [1972- v. 13,
1972] v. [$29.95 per vol.] 591
79-183178
QL3 .G7813 MRR Alc.

MOLLUSKS--CARIBBEAN SEA.
Warmke, Germaine Le Clerc. Caribbean
seashells; Narberth, Pa., Livingston
Pub. Co. [1961] x, 346 p.
594.09729 61-13006
QL423.C3 W3 MRR Alc.

MOLLUSKS--NORTH AMERICA.
Abbott, Robert Tucker, American
seashells. New York, Van Nostrand
[1954] xiv, 541 p. 594 54-5780
QL414 .A2 MRR Alc.

MOLLUSKS--NORTH AMERICA--PICTORIAL
WORKS.
Abbott, Robert Tucker, Seashells of
North America; New York, Golden
Press [c1968] 280 p. [3.95]
594/.09/7 68-10083
QL404 .A2 MRR Alc.

MOLLUSKS--PUERTO RICO.
Warmke, Germaine Le Clerc. Caribbean
seashells; Narberth, Pa., Livingston
Pub. Co. [1961] x, 346 p.
594.09729 61-13006
QL423.C3 W3 MRR Alc.

MOLLUSKS--UNITED STATES.
Abbott, Robert Tucker, American
seashells. New York, Van Nostrand
[1954] xiv, 541 p. 594 54-5780
QL414 .A2 MRR Alc.

MONACO--BIOGRAPHY--DICTIONARIES.
Who's who in France. 1.- ed.;
1953/54- Paris, J. Lafitte. 920.044
54-17054
DC705.A1 W46 MRR Biog Latest
edition

MONASTIC AND RELIGIOUS LIFE.
Dirks, Walter, The monk and the
world; New York, D. McKay Co.
[1954] 234 p. 271 53-11381
BX2431 .D513 MRR Alc.

MONASTICISM AND RELIGIOUS ORDERS.
King, Archdale Arthur, Liturgies of
the religious orders. London, New
York, Longmans, Green [1955] xii,
431 p. 264.02 55-4576
BX2049.A1 K5 1955 MRR Alc.

MONASTICISM AND RELIGIOUS ORDERS--
DICTIONARIES.
Kapsner, Oliver Leonard, Catholic
religious orders; 2d ed., enl.
Collegeville, Minn., St. John's Abbey
Press, 1957. xxxviii, 594 p.
271.03 57-1997
BX2420 .K3 1957 MRR Alc.

MONASTICISM AND RELIGIOUS ORDERS--GREAT
BRITAIN--DIRECTORIES.
Directory of religious orders,
congregations and societies of Great
Britain and Ireland. [1st]- [1955]-
Glasgow, J. S. Burns 271 56-23821
BX2592 .D5 MRR Alc Latest edition

MONASTICISM AND RELIGIOUS ORDERS--
IRELAND--DIRECTORIES.
Directory of religious orders,
congregations and societies of Great
Britain and Ireland. [1st]- [1955]-
Glasgow, J. S. Burns 271 56-23821
BX2592 .D5 MRR Alc Latest edition

MONASTICISM AND RELIGIOUS ORDERS--
UNITED STATES.
McCarthy, Thomas Patrick, Guide to
the Catholic sisterhoods in the
United States. [5th ed.] rev. and
enl. Washington, Catholic University
of America Press, 1964. xii, 404 p.
271.905873 64-15336
BX4220.U6 M3 1964 MRR Alc.

MONASTICISM AND RELIGIOUS ORDERS,
ANGLICAN.
Anson, Peter Frederick, The call of
the cloister; London, S.P.C.K.,
1955. xvi, 641 p. 271.83 56-287
BX5183 .A55 MRR Alc.

MONASTICISM AND RELIGIOUS ORDERS FOR
WOMEN--UNITED STATES.
McCarthy, Thomas Patrick, Guide to
the Catholic sisterhoods in the
United States. [5th ed.] rev. and
enl. Washington, Catholic University
of America Press, 1964. xii, 404 p.
271.905873 64-15336
BX4220.U6 M3 1964 MRR Alc.

MONEY.
see also Banks and banking

see also Credit

see also Finance

see also Prices

see also Tokens

Kent, Raymond P., Money and banking
6th ed. New York, Holt, Rinehart and
Winston [1972] xvi, 624 p. 332.1
73-183628
HG221 .K385 1972 MRR Alc.

Prather, Charles Lee, Money and
banking 9th ed. Homewood, Ill., R.
D. Irwin, 1969. xviii, 738 p. 332
69-15547
HG221 .P93 1969 MRR Alc.

MONEY--BIBLIOGRAPHY.
Burgess, Norman. How to find out
about banking and investment. [1st
ed.] Oxford, New York, Pergamon
Press [1969] xii, 300 p. 016.332
68-55021
Z7164.F5 B84 1969 MRR Alc.

MONEY--DICTIONARIES.
Pick, Franz. All the monies of the
world; [2d ed.] New York, Pick Pub.
Corp. [1971] xviii, 613 p.
332.4/03 72-154984
HG216 .P614 1971 MRR Alc.

MONEY--HISTORY.
Burns, Arthur Robert, Money and
monetary policy in early times,
London, K. Paul, Trench, Trubner &
co., ltd.; New York, A. A. Knopf,
1927. xiii, 517 p. 27-21334
HG237 .B86 MRR Alc.

MONEY--TABLES, ETC.
American International Investment
Corporation, San Francisco. World
currency charts. [5th ed.] San
Francisco [1970] 77 fold. l.
332.4/5 74-285254
HG3863 .A652 1970 MRR Alc.

MONEY--TABLES, ETC. (Cont.)
Bidwell, Robin Leonard. Currency
conversion tables: London, Rex
Collings Ltd., 1970. v, 66 p. [20/-
]   389/.15   78-489912
HG219 .B5 MRR Ref Desk.

Felber, John Edward. The American's
tourist manual for the U.S.S.R.,
[10th ed.] Newark, N.J.,
International Intertrade Index [1972,
c1973] 192 p.   914.7/04/85 72-
78512
DK16 .F4 1973 MRR Alc.

International Finance Institute.
Handbook of world currency, banking
and foreign exchange. Washington
[1970] vii, 212 p.   332.1/02/02 70-
113538
HG219 .I53 MRR Ref Desk.

Money converter and tipping guide for
European travel. [1st]- ed.; 1953-
[New York] Dover Publications.
332.4083 58-4482
HG219 .M58 MRR Alc Latest edition

Naft, Stephen, International
conversion tables; New York, Duell,
Sloan and Pearce [1961] xii, 372 p.
389   61-10391
HF5714 .N3 1961 MRR Alc.

Perera's official illustrated foreign
money guide, New York, Random House
[1970] 1 v. (unpaged) [1.95]
332.4/021/2 75-102307
HG219 .P46 MRR Ref Desk.

Richard Joseph's world wide money
converter and tipping guide. 1953-
Garden City, N.Y., Doubleday. 332.45
52-13383
HG219 .R5 MRR Ref Desk Latest
edition

Robertson, James, of London.
Dictionary for international
commercial quotations, London, New
York [etc.] H. Milford, Oxford
university press, 1918-19. 2 v.   19-
4807
HF5715.G7 R6 MRR Alc.

Swiss Bank Corporation. Values and
measures of the world; [London]
1959. 25 p.   332.4083 60-30644
HF5712 .S8 1959 MRR Alc.

The Economist (London) Guide to
weights and measures, [2d. ed.]
London [1962] 95 p.   65-87714
HF5712 .E25 1962 MRR Alc.

MONEY--YEARBOOKS.
Pick's currency yearbook. 1955- New
York, Pick Pub. Corp. [etc.]
332.4058 55-11013
HG219 .P5 MRR Ref Desk Latest
edition

MONEY--CONFEDERATE STATES OF AMERICA.
Reinfeld, Fred, The story of Civil
War money. New York, Sterling Pub.
Co. [1959] 93 p.   332.4973 59-
13003
HG219 .R36 MRR Alc.

MONEY--UNITED STATES.
Friedman, Milton, Monetary
statistics of the United States:
estimates, sources, methods New
York, National Bureau of Economic
Research, 1970. xx, 629 p. [15.00]
332.4/9/73 78-85410
HG538 .F863 MRR Alc.

Reinfeld, Fred, The story of Civil
War money, New York, Sterling Pub.
Co. [1959] 93 p.   332.4973 59-
13003
HG525 .R36 MRR Alc.

Shafer, Neil. A guide book of modern
United States currency. 5th ed.
Racine, Wis., Western Pub. Co. [1971]
160 p.   769/.559/73 70-28630
HG591 .S5 1971 MRR Ref Desk.

MONEY--UNITED STATES--HISTORY.
Krooss, Herman Edward, comp.
Documentary history of banking and
currency in the United States. New
York, Chelsea House Publishers [1969]
4 v. (xlii, 3232 p.)   332/.0973 69-
16011
HG2461 .K76 MRR Alc.

Nussbaum, Arthur, A history of the
dollar. New York, Columbia
University Press, 1957. 308 p.
332.4973 57-11693
HG501 .N8 MRR Alc.

MONEY--UNITED STATES--STATISTICS.
Friedman, Milton, Monetary
statistics of the United States:
estimates, sources, methods New
York, National Bureau of Economic
Research, 1970. xx, 629 p. [15.00]
332.4/8/73 78-85410
HG538 .F863 MRR Alc.

MONEY RAISING
see Fund raising

MONGOLIA (MONGOLIAN PEOPLE'S REPUBLIC)
Historical Evaluation and Research
Organization, Washington, D.C. Area
handbook for Mongolia. Washington,
For sale by the Supt. of Docs., U.S.
Govt. Print. Off., 1970. xiv, 500 p.
[3.75]   309.1/517/3 74-607921
DS798 .H57 MRR Alc.

**MONGOLIA (MONGOLIAN PEOPLE'S REPUBLIC)--
GAZETTEERS.**
United States. Geographic Names
Division. Mongolia; Washington,
1970. v, 256 p.   915.17/3/003 72-
611367
DS798 .U48 MRR Alc.

**MONGOLIA (MONGOLIAN PEOPLE'S REPUBLIC)--
HISTORY.**
Bawden, Charles R. The modern
history of Mongolia London,
Weidenfeld & Nicolson, 1968. xvii,
460 p. [63/-]   951.7/3 75-354157
DS798 .B53 MRR Alc.

**MONGOLIAN LANGUAGE--DICTIONARIES--
ENGLISH.**
Boberg, Folke. Mongolian-English
dictionary. Stockholm, Förlaget
Filadelfia [1954-55] 3 v.   494.2
55-36672
PL406 .B6 MRR Alc.

MONOGRAMS.
Bénézit, Emmanuel, Dictionnaire
critique et documentaire des
peintres, sculpteurs, dessinateurs et
graveurs de tous les temps et de tous
les pays, Nouv. éd. entièrement
refondue, rev. et corr. [Paris]
Gründ, 1948-55. 8 v.   927 49-
18054
N40 .B47 MRR Alc.

Goldstein, Franz. Monogramm-Lexikon;
Berlin, De Gruyter, 1964. 931 p.
65-47949
N45 .G6 MRR Alc.

MONOLOGUES--INDEXES.
Ireland, Norma (Olin) An index to
monologs and dialogs. Rev. and enl.
ed. Boston, F. W. Faxon Co., 1949.
xxv, 171 p.   016.815 49-8379
PN4305.M6 I64 1949 MRR Alc.

MONROE, JAMES, PRES. U.S., 1758-1831.
Cresson, William Penn, James Monroe,
Chapel Hill, The University of North
Carolina Press [1946] xiv, 577 p.
923.173 47-652
E372 .C7 MRR Alc.

**MONROE, JAMES, PRES. U.S., 1758-1831--
BIBLIOGRAPHY.**
United States. Library of Congress.
Manuscript Division. Papers of James
Monroe. Washington, Govt. print.
off., 1904. 114 p.   05-1169
Z663.34 .M6 MRR Alc.

MONTANA.
Federal writers' project. Montana.
Montana, a state guide book, New
York, The Viking press, 1939. 2 p.
l., vii-xxiii, [1], 430, [12] p.
917.86 39-27792
F731 .F44 MRR Ref Desk.

The Montana almanac. 1957-
Missoula, Montana State University.
917.86 57-63761
F726 .M75 MRR Alc Latest edition

The Montana almanac. Statistical
supplement. Missoula, Bureau of
Business and Economic Research,
School of Business Administration,
Montana State University. 917.86 74-
643556
F726 .M752 MRR Alc Latest edition

**MONTANA--DESCRIPTION AND TRAVEL--GUIDE-
BOOKS.**
Federal writers' project. Montana.
Montana, a state guide book, New
York, The Viking press, 1939. 2 p.
l., vii-xxiii, [1], 430, [12] p.
917.86 39-27792
F731 .F44 MRR Ref Desk.

MONTANA--EXECUTIVE DEPARTMENTS.
Montana directory of public affairs.
1864/1955- [Hamilton? Mont.] 56-
62504
JK7330 .M65 MRR Alc Latest edition

MONTANA--HISTORY.
Toole, Kenneth Ross, Montana: an
uncommon land. [1st ed.] Norman,
University of Oklahoma Press [1959]
278 p.   978.6 59-7489
F731 .T65 MRR Alc.

MONTANA--POLITICS AND GOVERNMENT.
Montana directory of public affairs.
1864/1955- [Hamilton? Mont.] 56-
62504
JK7330 .M65   MRR Alc Latest edition

Waldron, Ellis L., comp. Montana
politics since 1864; [Missoula]
Montana State University Press [1958]
x, 428 p.   324.786 58-45388
JK7392 .W3 MRR Alc.

MONTANA--REGISTERS.
Montana directory of public affairs.
1864/1955- [Hamilton? Mont.] 56-
62504
JK7330 .M65 MRR Alc Latest edition

MONTANA--STATISTICS.
The Montana almanac. 1957-
Missoula, Montana State University.
917.86 57-63761
F726 .M75 MRR Alc Latest edition

The Montana almanac. Statistical
supplement. Missoula, Bureau of
Business and Economic Research,
School of Business Administration,
Montana State University. 917.86 74-
643556
F726 .M752 MRR Alc Latest edition

MONTHS.
Krythe, Maymie Richardson. All about
the months [1st ed.] New York,
Harper & Row [1966] 222 p.   529.2
66-18584
GR930 .K7 MRR Alc.

MONUMENTS--WEST.
United States. National Park Service.
Soldier and brave; [1st ed.] New
York, Harper & Row, 1963. xviii, 279
p.   978 63-10600
F591 .U59 MRR Alc.

MOON.
Middlehurst, Barbara M., ed. The
moon, meteorites, and comets,
Chicago, University of Chicago Press
[1963] xvii, 810 p.   523 62-18117
QB501 .S6 vol. 4 MRR Alc.

MOON--PHOTOGRAPHS.
Alter, Dinsmore, Pictorial guide to
the moon. Updated and expanded [i.
e. 2d] ed. New York, Crowell [1967]
199 p.   523.39 67-13996
QB595 .A56 1967 MRR Alc.

MOON--TABLES.
Ward, Craig, The 200 year ephemeris,
New York, Macoy Pub. Co., 1949. vi,
420 p.   133.5083 49-8975
BF1715 .W3 MRR Alc.

**MOORE, MARIANNE, 1887-1972--
CONCORDANCES.**
Lane, Gary, A concordance to the
poems of Marianne Moore. New York,
Haskell House, 1972. 526 p.
811/.5/2 72-6438
PS3525.O5616 Z49 1972 MRR Alc.

MOORE, MERRILL, 1903-1957--MANUSCRIPTS.
United States. Library of Congress.
Manuscript Division. Merrill Moore:
a register of his papers in the
Library of Congress. Washington,
Library of Congress, 1972. iii, 99
p.   016.6168/9/00924 B 72-10870
Z663.34 .M65 MRR Alc.

MORAL CONDITIONS.
Brinton, Clarence Crane, A history
of Western morals. [1st ed.] New
York, Harcourt, Brace [1959] 502 p.
170.9 59-6421
BJ71 .B68 MRR Alc.

MORAL EDUCATION--BIBLIOGRAPHY.
Kircher, Clara J. Behavior patterns
in children's books; Washington,
Catholic University of America Press
[1966] v, 132 p.   016.6497 66-
18693
Z1037 .K55 MRR Alc.

MORAL PHILOSOPHY
see Ethics

**MORALITIES, ENGLISH--HISTORY AND
CRITICISM.**
Houle, Peter J. The English morality
and related drama; [Hamden, Conn.]
Archon Books, 1972. xviii, 195 p.
822/.051 70-38714
PR643.M7 H6 MRR Alc.

MORALS
see Conduct of life

MORAVIANS--CHURCH HISTORY.
Hamilton, John Taylor, History of
the Moravian Church; [Bethlehem,
Pa., Interprovincial Board of
Christian Education, Moravian Church
in America, 1967] 723 p.   284/.609
67-24086
BX8565 .H3 1967 MRR Alc.

MORMONS AND MORMONISM--DICTIONARIES.
Brooks, Melvin R. L.D.S. reference
encyclopedia. Salt Lake City,
Bookcraft, 1960-65. 2 v.   289.303
60-44463
BX8605.5 .B7 MRR Alc.

Jenson, Andrew, Encyclopedic history
of the Church of Jesus Christ of
latterday saints, Salt Lake City,
Utah, Printed by Deseret news
publishing company, 1941. iv p., 1
l., 976 p.   289.309 41-8948
BX8605.5 .J4 MRR Alc.

MORMONS AND MORMONISM-- (Cont.)
McConkie, Bruce R. Mormon doctrine, 2d ed. Salt Lake City, Bookcraft, 1966. 856 p. 230.9/3 67-2237
 BX8605.5 .M3 1966 MRR Alc.

MORMONS AND MORMONISM--DOCTRINAL AND CONTROVERSIAL WORKS.
McConkie, Bruce R. Mormon doctrine, 2d ed. Salt Lake City, Bookcraft, 1966. 856 p. 230.9/3 67-2237
 BX8605.5 .M3 1966 MRR Alc.

MORMONS AND MORMONISM--HISTORY.
Berrett, William Edwin, ed. Readings in L.D.S. Church history from original manuscripts. 1st ed. Salt Lake City, Deseret Book Co., 1953-58. 3 v. 289.309 53-23418
 BX8611 .B346 MRR Alc.

Davis, Inez (Smith) The story of the church; 6th ed. Independence, Mo., Herald Pub. House, 1959. 656 p. 289.3 59-4430
 BX8611 .D3 1959 MRR Alc.

MOROCCO.
Nyrop, Richard F. Area handbook for Morocco. Washington, For sale by the Supt. of Docs., U.S. Govt. Print. Off.] 1972. xiv, 403 p. [$3.25] 309.1/64/05 72-600025
 DT305 .A74 1972 MRR Alc.

MOROCCO--COMMERCE--DIRECTORIES.
Bottin du Maroc. Paris, Didot-Bottin. 58-44761
 HF5289.M6 B6 MRR Alc Latest edition

MOROCCO--DESCRIPTION AND TRAVEL--GUIDE-BOOKS.
Fodor's Morocco. New York, D. McKay. 916.4/04/5 70-648469
 DT304 .M652 MRR Alc Latest edition

MOROCCO--GAZETTEERS.
United States. Geographic Names Division. Morocco; Washington, 1970. ix, 923 p. 916.4 72-608974

 DT304 .U46 MRR Alc.

MORONS
see Mentally handicapped

MORTALITY.
Preston, Samuel H. Causes of death: life tables for national population New York, Seminar Press, 1972. xi, 787 p. 312/.2 72-80305
 HB1321 .P73 MRR Alc.

MORTUARY CUSTOMS
see Funeral rites and ceremonies

MOSCOW--DIRECTORIES.
Moskva; Moskva, Moskovskiĭ Rabochiĭ [etc.] 55-35470
 DK595 .M6 MRR Alc Latest edition

MOTEL MANAGEMENT--UNITED STATES--BIOGRAPHY.
Who's who among innkeepers 1st ed., 1974-1975. [New York, Rating Publications, 1974] 210 p. 647/.94/0922 73-89548
 TX910.3 .W48 MRR Biog.

MOTELS--DIRECTORIES.
Directory of hotel & motel systems. New York, American Hotel Association Directory Corp. 44-29752
 TX907 .D5 MRR Alc Latest edition

MOTELS--EUROPE--DIRECTORIES.
Motel guide officiel: Europe. Paris, Editions Ediservice. 647/.94 78-216033
 Began with 1962/63 issue as Motel-guide Europe.
 TX910.A1 M66 MRR Alc Latest edition

MOTELS--NETHERLANDS--DIRECTORIES.
Lasschuit's officieel adresboek: Bilthoven, J. G. Lasschuit. 67-37932
 Began publication with vol. for 1908.
 TX910.N4 L3 MRR Alc Latest edition

MOTELS--UNITED STATES.
Harris, Kerr, Forster and Company. Trends in the hotel-motel business. Atlanta [etc.] a 40-3316
 Began publication with 1936 issue?
 TX909.A1 H3 MRR Alc Latest edition

MOTELS--UNITED STATES--DIRECTORIES.
Auger, Bert Y. How to find better business meeting places; St. Paul, Business Services Press [1966] xvii, 637 p. 647.9473 66-24060
 TX907 .A8 MRR Alc.

Hotel & motel red book. 1886- New York, American Hotel Association Directory Corp. 98-295
 TX907 .O45 Sci RR Latest edition / MRR Ref Desk Latest edition

MOTHS--PICTORIAL WORKS.
Werner, Alfred. Butterflies and moths [3rd] further revised & enlarged ed. London, Deutsch, 1970. 138 p. [5/5/-] 595.78/022/2 77-523008
 QK543 .W47 1970 MRR Alc.

MOTION PICTURES
see Moving-pictures

MOTOR-BOAT RACING--YEARBOOKS.
American Power Boat Association. Rule book. 1962- Detroit. 797.1/25 72-622852
 VM320 .A54 MRR Alc Latest edition

MOTOR-BOATS.
Chapman, Charles Frederic, Piloting, seamanship and small boat handling; 1- ed.; 1922- New York, Motor boating. 797.125 42-49646
 VM341 .M9 vol. 5 MRR Alc Latest edition

The Mercantile Navy list. London, H.M. Stationery Off. [etc.] 387.23 50-33347
 Began publication with 1850 issue.
 HE565.G7 M5 MRR Alc Latest edition

MOTOR-BOATS--YEARBOOKS.
American Power Boat Association. Rule book. 1962- Detroit. 797.1/25 72-622852
 VM320 .A54 MRR Alc Latest edition

National power boat guide. 1st ed.: 1968- (Boston, Associated International Publishers Corporation] 623.82/31/05 68-43966
 VM320 .N3 MRR Alc Latest edition

MOTOR BUS LINES--GREAT BRITAIN--DIRECTORIES.
Passenger transport (London) Year book. London. 388.4058 61-20834
 Began publication in 1899.
 TP701 .P3 MRR Alc Latest edition

MOTOR BUS LINES--UNITED STATES--DIRECTORIES.
Standard Rate and Data Service, inc. Transit advertising rates and data. [Skokie, Ill.] 380.1/45/6591344 72-626448
 HF5905 .S75 MRR Ref Desk Latest edition

MOTOR-CARS
see Automobiles

MOTOR-SHIPS.
Baker, William A. The engine powered vessel; New York, Grosset & Dunlap [1965] 267 p. 387.24 65-21508
 VM315 .B3 MRR Alc.

Hardy, Alfred Cecil, History of motorshipping; London, Whitehall Technical Press [1955] 389 p. 623.823 56-29184
 VM315 .H23 MRR Alc.

Inland river record; 1945- [Sewickley, Pa.] 386.224 45-7239
 VM23 .I5 MRR Alc Latest edition

The Motor ship reference book. London, Temple press ltd. 25-22579
 VM315 .A2 MRR Alc Latest edition

MOTOR-TRUCKS.
see also Campers and coaches, Truck

MOTOR-TRUCKS--DICTIONARIES.
Tak, Montie. Truck talk; [1st ed.] Philadelphia, Chilton Book Co. [1971] xiv, 191 p. [$5.95] 388.3/24/014 72-169583
 PE3727.H5 T3 MRR Alc.

MOTOR-TRUCKS--MAINTENANCE AND REPAIR--PERIODICALS.
Motor's truck & diesel repair manual. 24th- ed.: 1971- [New York, Motor] 629.28/7/4 73-618596
 TL230.A1 M64 Sci RR Latest edition / MRR Alc Latest edition

MOTOR-TRUCKS--STATISTICS.
United States. Bureau of the Census. 1967 census of transportation. [Washington; For sale by the Supt. of Docs., U.S. Govt. Print. Off., 1970] 3 v. in 5 [$3.00 (v. 1) varies] 380.5/0973 76-607509
 HE18 1967 .A55 MRR Alc.

MOTOR VEHICLES.
see also Automobiles

MOTOR VEHICLES--MAINTENANCE AND REPAIR--PERIODICALS.
Motor handbook. [New York, Motor] 629.28/7/05 74-644571
 TL152 .M73 MRR Alc Latest edition

MOTOR VEHICLES--POLLUTION CONTROL DEVICES--MAINTENANCE AND REPAIR.
Chilton Book Company. Automotive Editorial Dept. Chilton's motor/age professional emission diagnostic and safety manual / Radnor, Pa. : Chilton Book Co., [1974] 1152 p. : 629.2/52 74-182330
 TL214.P6 C47 1974a MRR Alc.

MOTORCYCLE RACING.
Engel, Lyle Kenyon. The complete motorcycle book. New York, Four Winds Press [1974] 195 p. [$6.95] 629.22/75 73-88085
 TL440 .E5 MRR Alc.

MOTORCYCLES.
Engel, Lyle Kenyon. The complete motorcycle book. New York, Four Winds Press [1974] 195 p. [$6.95] 629.22/75 73-88085
 TL440 .E5 MRR Alc.

MOTORCYCLING.
Engel, Lyle Kenyon. The complete motorcycle book. New York, Four Winds Press [1974] 195 p. [$6.95] 629.22/75 73-88085
 TL440 .E5 MRR Alc.

MOTORS.
see also Automobiles--Motors
 see also Gas and oil engines
 see also Machinery

MOTTOES.
Shankle, George Earlie. American mottoes and slogans, New York, The H. W. Wilson company, 1941. 183 p. 973 41-26048
 E179 .S544 MRR Alc.

Shankle, George Earlie. State names, flags, seals, songs, birds, flowers, and other symbols; Rev. ed. New York, H. W. Wilson Co., 1941 [i.e. 1951, c1938] 524 p. 929.4 917.3* 52-52807
 E155 .S43 1951 MRR Alc.

MOUNTAIN WHITES (SOUTHERN STATES)--BIBLIOGRAPHY.
Munn, Robert F. The Southern Appalachians; Morgantown, West Virginia University Library, 1961. iii, 106 p. 016.9755 a 62-9041
 Z1251.A7 M8 MRR Alc.

MOUNTAINEERING.
see also Trails

Huxley, Anthony Julian, ed. Standard encyclopedia of the world's mountains. [1st ed.] New York, Putnam [1962] 383 p. 551.4303 62-7984
 GB501 .H8 MRR Alc.

MOUNTAINEERING--DICTIONARIES.
Collomb, Robin G. A dictionary of mountaineering; New York, Philosophical Library, 1958. 175 p. 796.5203 58-14718
 G508 .C6 1958 MRR Alc.

MOUNTAINS.
see also Volcanoes

Huxley, Anthony Julian, ed. Standard encyclopedia of the world's mountains. [1st ed.] New York, Putnam [1962] 383 p. 551.4303 62-7984
 GB501 .H8 MRR Alc.

MOURNING CUSTOMS.
see also Funeral rites and ceremonies

MOUTH--SURGERY--DIRECTORIES.
Oral surgery directory of the world. 1st- 1957- Pittsburgh. 617.53 617.6* 57-10598
 RD523 .O7 MRR Biog Latest edition / Sci RR Latest edition

MOVEMENTS OF ANIMALS
see Animal locomotion

MOVING-PICTURE ACTORS AND ACTRESSES.
Cawkwell, Tim. The world encyclopedia of the film / New York : Galahad Books, [1974] c1972. ix, 444 p. : [$25.00] 791.43/092/2 73-90832
 PN1998.A2 C38 1974 MRR Biog.

Chaneles, Sol. The movie makers Secaucus, N.J., Derbibooks [1974] 544 p. [$19.95] 791.43/028/0922 B 74-6443
 PN1998.A2 C46 MRR Biog.

Graham, Peter John, A dictionary of the cinema, [Rev. and reset] New York, A. S. Barnes [1968] 175 p. 68-15194
 PN1998.A2 G7 1968 MRR Alc.

Griffith, Richard, The movie stars. [1st ed.] Garden City, N.Y., Doubleday, 1970. xiii, 498 p. [19.95] 791.43/028/0922 72-126382
 PN1998.A2 G75 MRR Alc.

Halliwell, Leslie. The filmgoer's companion / 4th ed., entirely rev., reset and much enl. New York : Hill and Wang, [1974] xi, 873 p. : [$25.00] 791.43/03 74-185464
 PN1993.45 .H3 1974 MRR Biog.

MOVING-PICTURE ACTORS AND (Cont.)
The International encyclopedia of
film. 1st American ed.] New York,
Crown Publishers [1972] 574 p.
[$17.95] 791.43/03 70-187555
PN1993.45 .I5 1972 MRR Alc.

International motion picture almanac.
1929- New York [etc.] Quigley
Publications [etc.] 29-8663
PN1993.3 .I55 MRR Biog Latest
edition

Osborne, Robert A. Academy awards
Oscar annual. La Habre, Calif., ESE
California. 791.43/079 74-640065
Began with vol. for 1871.
PN1993 .O8 MRR Alc Latest edition

Twomey, Alfred E. The versatiles;
South Brunswick [N.J.] A. S. Barnes
[1969] 304 p. [10.00]
791.43/028/0922 68-27218
PN1998.A2 T9 MRR Biog.

Weaver, John T. Twenty years of
silents, 1908-1928. Metuchen, N.J.,
Scarecrow Press, 1971. 514 p.
016.79143/5 73-157729
PN1998.A2 W38 MRR alc.

**MOVING-PICTURE ACTORS AND ACTRESSES--
BIOGRAPHY.**
Truitt, Evelyn Mack. Who was who on
screen. New York, R. R. Bowker Co.,
1974. vii, 363 p. 791.43/028/0922
B 74-4325
PN1998.A2 T73 MRR Biog.

**MOVING-PICTURE ACTORS AND ACTRESSES--
BIOGRAPHY--BIBLIOGRAPHY.**
Schuster, Mel. Motion picture
performers; Metuchen, N.J., The
Scarecrow Press, 1971. 702 p.
016.79143/028/0922 70-154300
Z5784.M9 S35 MRR Biog.

**MOVING-PICTURE ACTORS AND ACTRESSES--
BIOGRAPHY--DICTIONARIES.**
Bousquinot, Roger. L'Encyclopédie du
cinema. Paris, Bordas, 1967- v.
[130 F (v. 1)] 791.43/03 68-89498

PN1993.45 .B6 MRR Alc.

Shipman, David. The great movie
stars -- the international years.
London, Angus and Robertson, 1972.
viii, 568 p. [£3.75]
791.43/028/0922 73-153923
PN1998.A2 S55 MRR Biog.

**MOVING-PICTURE ACTORS AND ACTRESSES--
DIRECTORIES.**
Academy of Motion Picture Arts and
Sciences. Academy players directory.
no. 1- Jan. 1937- Hollywood,
Calif. 791.4058 37-1400
PN1898.A1 A3 MRR Alc Latest
edition

Players' guide ... 1st- ed.; Aug.
1944- [New York] 792.058 47-34214

PN2289 .P55 MRR Alc Latest edition

**MOVING-PICTURE ACTORS AND ACTRESSES--
PORTRAITS, CARICATURES, ETC.**
The New York times film reviews, 1913-
1968. New York, The New York Times,
1970 [v. 6, 1970, c1971] 6 v. (4961
p.) 791.43/5 70-112777
PN1995 .N4 MRR Alc.

**MOVING-PICTURE ACTORS AND ACTRESSES--
UNITED STATES--BIOGRAPHY.**
Parish, James Robert. The MGM stock
company; New Rochelle, N.Y.,
Arlington House [1973] 862 p.
[$14.95] 791.43/028/0922 B 72-
91640
PN1998.A2 P394 MRR Alc.

**MOVING-PICTURE ACTORS AND ACTRESSES,
AMERICAN.**
Lamparski, Richard. Whatever became
of ...? Fourth series. New York,
Crown Publishers [1973] 206 p.
[$5.95] 790.2/092/2 B 72-96665
CT220 .L284 1973 MRR Biog.

Michael, Paul. The American movies
reference book; Englewood Cliffs,
N.J., Prentice-Hall [1969] 629 p.
[29.95] 791.43/0873 68-13401
PN1993.5.U6 M53 MRR Alc.

**MOVING-PICTURE ACTORS AND ACTRESSES,
ENGLISH.**
British film and television year
book. [1st]- ed; 1946- [London,
British and American Film Press,
etc.] 791.4058 792.93058* 46-4765
PN1993.3 .B7 MRR Biog Latest
edition

MOVING-PICTURE FESTIVALS.
Gottesman, Ronald. Guidebook to
film. New York, Holt, Rinehart and
Winston [1972] viii, 230 p.
016.79143 78-160462
Z5784.M9 G66 MRR Alc.

Neubaum, Frank Selwyn.
International calendar of film
festivals, contests, and awards.
[University Park, Pa.] University
Film Producers Association [1957] 20
p. 791.40791 792.93079* 57-39678
PN1993.4 .N4 MRR Alc.

MOVING-PICTURE INDUSTRY--DIRECTORIES.
Kemp's film and television year book
(International). London, Kemp's
Printing & Publishing Co.
338.4/7/7914305 72-624899
PN1998.A1 K39 MRR Alc Latest
edition

**MOVING-PICTURE INDUSTRY--AUSTRALIA--
DIRECTORIES.**
Film weekly (Sydney) Motion picture
directory; [Sydney] 56-56235
PN1998.A1 F49 MRR Alc Latest
edition

**MOVING-PICTURE INDUSTRY--CANADA--
YEARBOOKS.**
Year book [of the] Canadian
entertainment industry. Toronto,
Film Publications of Canada.
791.43/0971 53-30400
PN1993.3 .Y3 MRR Alc Latest
edition

**MOVING-PICTURE INDUSTRY--GREAT BRITAIN--
DIRECTORIES.**
British film and television year
book. [1st]- ed; 1946- [London,
British and American Film Press,
etc.] 791.4058 792.93058* 46-4765
PN1993.3 .B7 MRR Biog Latest
edition

Kinematograph and television year
book. London, Go Magazine ltd.
338.4/7/791430942 72-626476
PN1993.3 .K5 MRR Alc Latest
edition

**MOVING-PICTURE INDUSTRY--ITALY--
YEARBOOKS.**
Annuario del cinema italiano.
1950/51- [Roma, Cinedizione] 61-
44026
PN1993.5.I88 A7 MRR Alc Latest
edition

**MOVING-PICTURE INDUSTRY--SPAIN--
YEARBOOKS.**
Anuario español de cinematografía.
Madrid, Sindicato Nacional del
Espectaculo. 57-24397
PN1993.5.S7 A8 MRR Alc Latest
edition

**MOVING-PICTURE INDUSTRY--UNITED STATES--
DIRECTORIES.**
Gottesman, Ronald. Guidebook to
film. New York, Holt, Rinehart and
Winston [1972] viii, 230 p.
016.79143 78-160462
Z5784.M9 G66 MRR Alc.

International motion picture almanac.
1929- New York [etc.] Quigley
Publications [etc.] 29-8663
PN1993.3 .I55 MRR Biog Latest
edition

National Information Center for
Educational Media. Index to 16mm
educational films. 2d ed. New York,
R. R. Bowker Co., 1969. xi, 1111 p.
016.37133/523 71-91713
Z5814.M8 N35 1969 MRR Alc.

MOVING-PICTURE MUSIC--BIBLIOGRAPHY.
Limbacher, James L. Film music: from
violins to video. Metuchen, N.J.,
Scarecrow Press, 1974. 835 p.
782.8/5 73-16153
ML2075 .L54 MRR Alc.

**MOVING-PICTURE MUSIC--HISTORY AND
CRITICISM.**
Limbacher, James L. Film music: from
violins to video. Metuchen, N.J.,
Scarecrow Press, 1974. 835 p.
782.8/5 73-16153
ML2075 .L54 MRR Alc.

MOVING-PICTURE PLAYS--BIBLIOGRAPHY.
Dimmitt, Richard Bertrand. A title
guide to the talkies; New York,
Scarecrow Press, 1965. 2 v. (2133
p.) 791.438 65-13556
PN1998 .D55 MRR Alc.

McCarty, Clifford. Published
screenplays; [1st ed. Kent, Ohio]
Kent State University Press [1971]
xiii, 127 p. (p. 126-127
advertisements) [$6.50]
016.80882/3 73-138656
Z5784.M9 M3 MRR Alc.

Rehrauer, George. Cinema booklist.
Metuchen, N.J., Scarecrow Press,
1972. 473 p. 016.79143 70-188378

Z5784.M9 R43 MRR Alc.

Samples, Gordon. The drama scholars'
index to plays and filmscripts;
Metuchen, N.J., Scarecrow Press
[1974] xii, 448 p. 016.80882 73-
22165
Z5781 .S17 MRR Alc.

MOVING-PICTURE PLAYS--INDEXES.
Academy of Motion Picture Arts and
Sciences. Who wrote the movie and
what else did he write? Los Angeles,
1970. xix, 491 p. 016.812/5/209
78-27347
PN1998 .A53 MRR Alc.

MOVING-PICTURE PRODUCERS AND DIRECTORS.
Bousquinot, Roger. L'Encyclopédie du
cinema. Paris, Bordas, 1967- v.
[130 F (v. 1)] 791.43/03 68-89498

PN1993.45 .B6 MRR Alc.

Cawkwell, Tim. The world
encyclopedia of the film / New York
: Galahad Books, [1974] c1972. ix,
444 p. : [$25.00] 791.43/092/2
73-90832
PN1998.A2 C38 1974 MRR Biog.

Chaneles, Sol. The movie makers
Secaucus, N.J., Derbibooks [1974]
544 p. [$19.95] 791.43/028/0922 B
74-6443
PN1998.A2 C46 MRR Biog.

Graham, Peter John, A dictionary of
the cinema, [Rev. and reset] New
York, A. S. Barnes [1968] 175 p.
68-15194
PN1998.A2 G7 1968 MRR Alc.

Halliwell, Leslie. The filmgoer's
companion / 4th ed., entirely rev.,
reset and much enl. New York : Hill
and Wang, [1974] xi, 873 p. :
[$25.00] 791.43/03 74-185464
PN1993.45 .H3 1974 MRR Biog.

The International encyclopedia of
film. 1st American ed.] New York,
Crown Publishers [1972] 574 p.
[$17.95] 791.43/03 70-187555
PN1993.45 .I5 1972 MRR Alc.

Michael, Paul. The American movies
reference book; Englewood Cliffs,
N.J., Prentice-Hall [1969] 629 p.
[29.95] 791.43/0873 68-13401
PN1993.5.U6 M53 MRR Alc.

Sadoul, Georges, Dictionary of film
makers. Berkeley, University of
California Press [1972] viii, 288 p.
[$4.95 (pbk)] 791.43/03 78-136028

PN1993.45 .S313 MRR Biog.

**MOVING-PICTURE PRODUCERS AND DIRECTORS--
BIOGRAPHY--BIBLIOGRAPHY.**
Schuster, Mel. Motion picture
directors: Metuchen, N.J., Scarecrow
Press, 1973. 418 p.
016.79143/0233/0922 73-780
Z5784.M9 S34 MRR Biog.

**MOVING-PICTURE PRODUCERS AND DIRECTORS--
UNITED STATES.**
Hochman, Stanley, comp. American
film directors. New York, Ungar
[1974] xiv, 590 p. [$18.50]
791.43/0233/0922 73-82923
PN1995.9.P7 H57 MRR Alc.

MOVING-PICTURES.
Kracauer, Siegfried, Theory of film;
New York, Oxford University Press,
1960. 364 p. 791.43 60-13209
PN1994 .K7 MRR Alc.

MOVING-PICTURES--AWARDS.
Academy of Motion Picture Arts and
Sciences. Who wrote the movie and
what else did he write? Los Angeles,
1970. xix, 491 p. 016.812/5/209
78-27347
PN1998 .A53 MRR Alc.

Academy of Motion Picture Arts and
Sciences. Who wrote the movie and
what else did he write? Los Angeles,
1970. xix, 491 p. 016.812/5/209
78-27347
PN1998 .A53 MRR Alc.

Michael, Paul. The American movies
reference book; Englewood Cliffs,
N.J., Prentice-Hall [1969] 629 p.
[29.95] 791.43/0873 68-13401
PN1993.5.U6 M53 MRR Alc.

Neubaum, Frank Selwyn.
International calendar of film
festivals, contests, and awards.
[University Park, Pa.] University
Film Producers Association [1957] 20
p. 791.40791 792.93079* 57-39678
PN1993.4 .N4 MRR Alc.

The New York times film reviews, 1913-
1968. New York, The New York Times,
1970 [v. 6, 1970, c1971] 6 v. (4961
p.) 791.43/5 70-112777
PN1995 .N4 MRR Alc.

MOVING-PICTURES--BIBLIOGRAPHY.
Bukalski, Peter J. Film research;
Boston, G. K. Hall, 1972. 215 p.
016.79143 72-3784
Z5784.M9 B897 MRR Alc.

MOVING-PICTURES--BIBLIOGRAPHY. (Cont.)
Chicorel, Marietta. Chicorel
bibliography to the performing arts.
1st ed. New York, Chicorel Library
Pub. Corp. [1972] 498 p.   016.7902
73-155102
     Z6935 .C45 MRR Alc.

Gerlach, John C. The critical index;
New York, Teachers College Press
[1974] xlvi, 726 p. [$6.50 (pbk.)]
016.79143 74-1958
     Z5784.M8 G47 MRR Alc.

Gottesman, Ronald. Guidebook to
film; New York, Holt, Rinehart and
Winston [1972] viii, 230 p.
016.79143 78-160462
     Z5784.M9 G66 MRR Alc.

Limbacher, James L. A reference
guide to audiovisual information,
New York, Bowker. 1972. ix, 197 p.
016.00155/3 72-1737
     Z5814.V8 L55 MRR Alc.

Manchel, Frank. Film study:
Rutherford [N.J.] Fairleigh Dickinson
University Press [1973] 422 p.
791.43/07 72-3262
     Z5784.M9 M34 MRR Alc.

Rehrauer, George. Cinema booklist.
Metuchen, N.J., Scarecrow Press,
1972. 473 p.   016.79143 70-188378

     Z5784.M9 R43 MRR Alc.

Schoolcraft, Ralph Newman.
Performing arts/books in print: an
annotated bibliography. [1st ed.]
New York, Drama Book Specialists
[1973] xiii, 761 p.   016.7902 72-
78909
     Z6935 .S34 MRR Alc.

Writers' program. New York. The film
index, New York. The Museum of
modern art film library and the H. W.
Wilson company, 1941- v.
016.7914 41-8716
     Z5784.M9 W75 MRR Alc.

MOVING-PICTURES--BIOGRAPHY.
Chaneles, Sol. The movie makers
Secaucus, N.J., Derbibooks [1974]
544 p. [$18.95]   791.43/028/0922 B
74-6443
     PN1998.A2 C46 MRR Biog.

Filmlexicon degli autori e delle
opere. [1. ed.] Roma, Bianco e nero
[1958- v.   791.43/082/2 B a 59-
8549
     PN1998.A2 F53 MRR Alc.

Graham, Peter John. A dictionary of
the cinema, [Rev. and reset] New
York, A. S. Barnes [1968] 175 p.
68-15194
     PN1998.A2 G7 1968 MRR Alc.

The International encyclopedia of
film. 1st American ed.] New York,
Crown Publishers [1972] 574 p.
[$17.95]   791.43/03   70-187555
     PN1993.45 .I5 1972 MRR Alc.

International motion picture almanac.
1929- New York [etc.] Quigley
Publications [etc.] 29-8663
     PN1993.3 .I55   MRR Biog Latest
     edition

Kinematograph and television year
book. London, Go Magazine ltd.
338.4/7/791430942 72-626476
     PN1993.3 .K5 MRR Alc Latest
     edition

Osborne, Robert A. When who did
what, [Los Angeles, Stationers
corporation, 1944] 207 p.   44-53427

     E174.5 .O8 MRR Alc.

Pickard, Roy. A companion to the
movies, from 1903 to the present day
: New York : Hippocrene Books, 1974,
c1972. 287 p., [8] leaves of plates
: [$8.95] 791.43/092/2 74-76616

     PN1993.45 .P48 1974 MRR Alc.

MOVING-PICTURES--BIOGRAPHY--
DICTIONARIES.
Cawkwell, Tim. The world
encyclopedia of the film / New York
: Galahad Books, [1974] c1972. ix,
444 p. : [$25.00]   791.43/092/2
73-90832
     PN1998.A2 C38 1974 MRR Alc.

Halliwell, Leslie. The filmgoer's
companion / 4th ed., entirely rev.,
reset and much enl. New York : Hill
and Wang. [1974] xi, 873 p. :
[$25.00]   791.43/03 74-185464
     PN1993.45 .H3 1974 MRR Biog.

Sadoul, Georges. Dictionary of film
makers. Berkeley, University of
California Press [1972] viii, 288 p.
[$4.95 (pbk)] 791.43/03 78-136028

     PN1993.45 .S313 MRR Biog.

Twomey, Alfred E. The versatiles;
South Brunswick [N.J.] A. S. Barnes
[1969] 304 p. [10.00]
791.43/028/0922 68-27218
     PN1998.A2 T9 MRR Biog.

MOVING-PICTURES--BIOGRAPHY--INDEXES.
International index to film
periodicals. 1972- New York, R. R.
Bowker Co. 016.79143 72-1964
     Z5784.M9 I49 MRR Alc Full set

MOVING-PICTURES--BIOGRAPHY--PERIODICALS.
The New York times directory of the
film. 1971- [New York] Arno Press.
791.43 72-622071
     PN1995 .N39 MRR Alc Full set

MOVING-PICTURES--CATALGOS.
United States. Library of Congress.
Library of Congress catalog; Books:
authors. Jan. 1947-1955.
Washington.   47-32682
     Z663.7 .L5 MRR Alc MRR Alc (DK 33)
     Full set

MOVING-PICTURES--CATALOGS.
American Library Association. Audio-
Visual Committee. Films for
libraries, Chicago, American Library
Association, 1962. 81 p.   791.43
62-20326
     PN1998 .A653 MRR Alc.

Association-Sterling Films. Free
loan films. [New York] 011 74-
640978
     PN1998 .A7 MRR Alc Latest edition

AVRG; audio-visual resource guide for
use in religious education. [1st]-
ed.; 1948- [New York, etc.]
016.268635 58-13297
     BV1535 .A22 MRR Alc Latest edition

Baer, D. Richard. The film buff's
bible of motion pictures (1915-1972)
[1st ed.] Hollywood, Calif.,
Hollywood Film Archive [1972] x, 171
p. [$24.00] 791.43/0291/6 73-
153235
     PN1998 .B25 MRR Alc.

Barrot, Jean Pierre. Liste des films
recommandés pour les enfants et les
adolescents jusqu'à seize ans
d'après des sélections faltes dans
vingtdeux pays. [Paris] UNESCO
[1956] 118 p.   57-1061
     PN1998 .B3 1956 MRR Alc.

Dimmitt, Richard Bertrand. An actor
guide to the talkies; Metuchen,
N.J., Scarecrow Press, 1967-68. 2 v.
(1555 p.)   791.43/8 67-12057
     PN1998 .D53 MRR Alc.

Educators' guide to free films.
Randolph, Wis., Educators' Progress
Service. 371.335230838 45-412
Began with 1941 vol.
     LB1044 .E3 MRR Alc Latest edition

Feature films on 8 and 16; a
directory of feature films available
for rental, lease and sale in the
United States. [New York, R. R.
Bowker Co.] 68-58279
     MRR Alc Latest edition

Gifford, Denis. The British film
catalogue, 1895-1970; New York,
McGraw-Hill [1973] 1 v. (largely
unpaged) 791.43/0942 72-7861
     PN1993.5.G7 G5 MRR Alc.

International television almanac.
1956- New York, Quigley Pub. Co. 56-
2008
     HE8698 .I55 MRR Biog Latest
     edition

Kone, Grace Ann. 8mm film directory,
1969-70. [New York] Educational Film
Library Association; produced and
distributed by Comprehensive Service
Corp. [1969] xiv, 532 p.   791.43/8
68-58280
     PN1998 .K7 MRR Alc.

London. National Film Archive.
Catalogue. London, British Film
Institute, 1951- v.   792.93
791.4085 52-4264
     PN1998 .L58 MRR Alc.

National Information Center for
Educational Media. Index to 8mm
motion cartridges. New York, R. R.
Bowker Co., 1969. xv, 402 p.
371.33/523/0216 72-91716
     LB1044.Z9 N34 MRR Alc.

National Information Center for
Educational Media. Index to 16mm
educational films. 2d ed. New York,
R. R. Bowker Co., 1969. xi, 1111 p.
016.37133/523 71-91713
     Z5814.M8 N35 1969 MRR Alc.

Niver, Kemp R. Motion pictures from
the Library of Congress paper print
collection, 1894-1912, Berkeley,
University of California Press, 1967.
xxii, 402 p.   016.79143 66-28789
     Z5784.M9 N58 MRR Alc.

Pinson, William M. Resource guide to
current social issues, Waco, Tex.
Word Books [1968] 272 p.   016.301
67-30735
     Z7164.S66 P47 MRR Alc.

Sprecher, Daniel. Guide to films
(16mm) about famous people. [1st
ed.] Alexandria, Va., Serina Press
[1969] x, 206 p.   791.43/8 76-
110326
     PN1998 .S694 MRR Alc.

United States. Copyright Office.
Motion pictures. 1912/39-
[Washington] 53-60032
     PN1998 .U615 MRR Alc MRR Alc Full
     set / MRR Alc Partial set

United States. Library of Congress.
Library of Congress catalog: Motion
pictures and filmstrips; 1953-
Washington.   53-60011
     Z663.7 .L54 MRR Alc MRR Alc Full
     set

United States. Library of Congress.
Stack and Reader Division. The Civil
War in motion pictures; Washington,
1961. vi, 109 p.   973.79 61-60074

     Z663.48 .C5 MRR Alc.

United States. Library of Congress.
Stack and Reader Division. Libraries
and library services on film; 2d ed.
Washington, Reference Dept., Library
of Congress, 1957. 19 p.   020.84
57-60045
     Z663.48 .L5 1957 MRR Alc.

Walls, Howard Lamarr. Motion
pictures, 1894-1912, [Washington]
Copyright Office, Library of
Congress, 1953. xi, 92 p.
791.40838 792.9308* 53-60033
     Z663.8 .M6 MRR Alc.

MOVING-PICTURES--COSTUME
see Costume

MOVING-PICTURES--DICTIONARIES.
Curtis, Ron. Media dictionary; Red
Oak, Southwest Iowa Learning
Resources Center [1973] 290 p.
301.16/1/03 73-158317
     P87.5 .C8 MRR Alc.

Dimmitt, Richard Bertrand. An actor
guide to the talkies; Metuchen,
N.J., Scarecrow Press, 1967-68. 2 v.
(1555 p.)   791.43/8 67-12057
     PN1998 .D53 MRR Alc.

Dimmitt, Richard Bertrand. A title
guide to the talkies; New York,
Scarecrow Press, 1965. 2 v. (2133
p.)   791.438 65-13556
     PN1998 .D55 MRR Alc.

Enciclopedia dello spettacolo. Roma,
Casa editrice Le Maschere [1954-62]
9 v. a 55-2513
     PN1625 .E7 MRR Alc.

Filmlexicon degli autori e delle
opere. [1. ed.] Roma, Bianco e nero
[1958- v.   791.43/082/2 B a 59-
8549
     PN1998.A2 F53 MRR Alc.

The Focal encyclopedia of film &
television techniques. [1st American
ed.] New York, Hastings House [1969]
xxiv, 1100 p. [37.50]   778.5/03
73-7135
     TR847 .F62 1969 MRR Alc.

Graham, Peter John, A dictionary of
the cinema, [Rev. and reset] New
York, A. S. Barnes [1968] 175 p.
68-15194
     PN1998.A2 G7 1968 MRR Alc.

Halliwell, Leslie. The filmgoer's
companion / 4th ed., entirely rev.,
reset and much enl. New York : Hill
and Wang. [1974] xi, 873 p. :
[$25.00]   791.43/03 74-185464
     PN1993.45 .H3 1974 MRR Biog.

The International encyclopedia of
film. 1st American ed.] New York,
Crown Publishers [1972] 574 p.
[$17.95]   791.43/03   70-187555
     PN1993.45 .I5 1972 MRR Alc.

Pickard, Roy. A companion to the
movies, from 1903 to the present day
: New York : Hippocrene Books, 1974,
c1972. 287 p., [8] leaves of plates
: [$8.95]   791.43/092/2 74-76616

     PN1993.45 .P48 1974 MRR Alc.

Sadoul, Georges, Dictionary of
films. Berkeley, University of
California Press [1972] x, 432 p.
[$16.50] 791.43/03 74-136027
     PN1993.45 .S3213 MRR Alc.

MOVING-PICTURES--DICTIONARIES--FRENCH.
Bessy, Maurice, Dictionnaire du
cinéma et de la télévision
[Paris] J. J. Pauvert [1965-71] 4 v.
66-39201
     PN1993.45 .B4 MRR Alc.

MOVING-PICTURES--DICTIONARIES--(Cont.)
Bougsinot, Roger. L'Encyclopédie du
cinema, Paris, Bordas. 1967- v.
[130 F (v. 1)] 781.43/03 68-89498

    PN1993.45 .B6 MRR Alc

MOVING-PICTURES--DICTIONARIES--POLYGLOT.
Elsevier's dictionary of cinema,
sound, and music, in six languages:
Amsterdam, New York, Elsevier Pub.
Co., 1956. 948 p. 778.503 56-
13141
    TR847 .E4 MRR Alc.

MOVING-PICTURES--DIRECTORIES.
Gottesman, Ronald. Guidebook to
film. New York, Holt, Rinehart and
Winston [1972] viii, 230 p.
016.79143 78-160462
    Z5784.M9 G66 MRR Alc.

Kemp's film and television year book
(International). London, Kemp's
Printing & Publishing Co.
338.4/7/7914305 72-624899
    PN1998.A1 K39 MRR Alc Latest
    edition

MOVING-PICTURES--EDITING.
Reisz, Karel. The technique of film
editing; 2nd enlarged ed. London,
Focal P., 1868. 410 p. [63/-]
778.5/35 68-120302
    PN1996 .R43 1968b MRR Alc.

MOVING-PICTURES--EVALUATION.
Educational Film Library Association.
Film evaluation guide, 1946-1964.
[New York, 1965] xv, 528 p.
016.37133523 65-27898
    PN1995.9.E9 E3 MRR Alc.

MOVING-PICTURES--FANTASTIC FILMS
see Fantastic films

MOVING-PICTURES--HISTORY.
Blum, Daniel C. A pictorial history
of the silent screen. New York,
Putnam [1953] 334 p. (chiefly
illus.) 781.4084 792.93084* 53-
8156
    PN1993.5.U6 B6 MRR Alc.

Fulton, Albert Rondthaler, Motion
pictures; [1st ed.] Norman,
University of Oklahoma Press [1960]
320 p. 791.4309 60-13471
    PN1993.5.A1 F8 MRR Alc.

Knight, Arthur. The liveliest art;
New York, Macmillan, 1957. 383 p.
791.4309 57-12222
    PN1993.5.A1 K6 MRR Alc.

Rotha, Paul. The film till now: New
ed. London, Spring Books [1967] 831
p. [42/-] 791.43/09 68-85807
    PN1993.5.A1 R69 1967 MRR Alc.

MOVING-PICTURES--PERIODICALS.
Film review. London, W. H. Allen
[etc.] 791.4058 47-20688
    Publication began in 1944?
    PN1993 .F624 MRR Alc Latest
    edition

MOVING-PICTURES--PERIODICALS--
BIBLIOGRAPHY.
Reilly, Adam. Current film
periodicals in English. Rev. ed.
New York, Educational Film Library
Association [1972] 25 p.
016.79143/8 72-188994
    Z5784.M9 R43 1972 MRR Alc.

MOVING-PICTURES--PERIODICALS--INDEXES.
Gerlach, John C. The critical index;
New York, Teachers College Press
[1974] xlvi, 726 p. [$6.50 (pbk.)]
016.79143 74-1959
    Z5784.M9 G47 MRR Alc.

International index to film
periodicals. 1972- New York, R. R.
Bowker Co. 016.79143 72-1964
    Z5784.M9 I49 MRR Alc Full set

Writers' program. New York. The film
index, New York, The Museum of
modern art film library and the H. W.
Wilson company, 1941- v.
016.7914 41-8716
    Z5784.M9 W75 MRR Alc.

MOVING-PICTURES--PICTORIAL WORKS.
Blum, Daniel C. A new pictorial
history of the talkies. New York,
Putnam [1968] 339 p. [$10.00] 68-
21918
    PN1995.7 .B56 1968 MRR Alc.

Blum, Daniel C. A pictorial history
of the silent screen. New York,
Putnam [1953] 334 p. (chiefly
illus.) 781.4084 792.93084* 53-
8156
    PN1993.5.U6 B6 MRR Alc.

Michael, Paul, comp. The Academy
awards: a pictorial history.
Indianapolis, Bobbs-Merrill [1964]
341 p. 791.43079 64-8653
    PN1993.5.U6 M5 MRR Alc.

MOVING-PICTURES--PLOTS, THEMES, ETC.
American Film Institute. The
American Film Institute catalog of
motion pictures produced in the
United States. New York, R. R.
Bowker, 1971- v. in
016.7/9143/0973 79-128587
    PN1998 .A57 MRR Alc.

Annuario del cinema italiano.
1950/51- [Roma, Cinedizione] 61-
44026
    PN1993.5.I88 A7 MRR Alc Latest
    edition

Gifford, Denis. The British film
catalogue, 1895-1970: New York,
McGraw-Hill [1973] 1 v. (largely
unpaged) 791.43/0942 72-7861
    PN1993.5.G7 G5 MRR Alc.

Niver, Kemp R. Motion pictures from
the Library of Congress paper print
collection, 1894-1912, Berkeley,
University of California Press, 1967.
xxii, 402 p. 016.79143 66-28789
    Z5784.M9 N58 MRR Alc.

Parish, James Robert. The great spy
pictures, Metuchen, N.J., Scarecrow
Press, 1974. 585 p. 016.79143 73-
19509
    PN1998 .P26 MRR Alc.

Pickard, R. A. E. Dictionary of
1,000 best films New York,
Association Press [1971] 496 p.
[$12.00] 791.43/03 70-129433
    PN1997.8 .P5 MRR Alc.

Pickard, Roy. A companion to the
movies, from 1903 to the present day
: New York : Hippocrene Books, 1974,
c1972. 287 p. : [8] leaves of plates
: [$8.95] 791.43/092/2 74-76616

    PN1993.45 .P48 1974 MRR Alc.

Sadoul, Georges, Dictionary of
films. Berkeley, University of
California Press [1972] x, 432 p.
[$16.50] 781.43/03 74-136027
    PN1993.45 .S3213 MRR Alc.

MOVING-PICTURES--PLOTS, THEMES, ETC.--
HORROR.
Lee, Walt. Reference guide to
fantastic films: Los Angeles,
Chelsea-Lee Books, 1972- v.
016.79143 72-88775
    PN1995.9.F36 L4 MRR Alc.

MOVING-PICTURES--PLOTS, THEMES, ETC.--
SCIENCE FICTION.
Lee, Walt. Reference guide to
fantastic films: Los Angeles,
Chelsea-Lee Books, 1972- v.
016.79143 72-88775
    PN1995.9.F36 L4 MRR Alc.

MOVING-PICTURES--PRODUCTION AND
DIRECTION.
Hochman, Stanley, comp. American
film directors. New York, Ungar
[1974] xiv, 590 p. [$18.50]
791.43/0233/0922 73-92923
    PN1995.9.P7 H57 MRR Alc.

Manoogian, Haig P. The film-maker's
art New York, Basic Books [1966] x,
340 p. 791.43023 66-16372
    PN1995.9.P7 M3 MRR Alc.

Quick, John, Handbook of film
production New York, Macmillan
[1972] xii, 304 p. [$12.95]
791.43/0232 72-151694
    PN1995.9.P7 Q5 MRR Alc.

Sarris, Andrew. The American cinema;
[1st ed.] New York, Dutton, 1968.
383 p. [$7.95] 791.43/0233 69-
12603
    PN1993.5.U6 S3 MRR Alc.

MOVING-PICTURES--PRODUCTION AND
DIRECTION--DICTIONARIES.
Levitan, Eli L. An alphabetical
guide to motion picture, television,
and videotape production New York,
McGraw-Hill [1970] xvii, 797 p.
778.5/3/03 69-13610
    TR847 .L47 MRR Alc.

MOVING-PICTURES--REVIEWS.
The Catholic periodical and
literature index. July/Aug. 1968-
Haverford, Pa., Catholic Library
Association. 011 70-649588
    AI3 .C32 MRR Alc Full set

The Catholic periodical index,
1930/33-May/June 1968. Haverford,
Pa. [etc.] Catholic Library
Association [etc.] 40-15160
    AI3 .C32 MRR Alc Full set

Hochman, Stanley, comp. American
film directors. New York, Ungar
[1974] xiv, 590 p. [$18.50]
791.43/0233/0922 73-92923
    PN1995.9.P7 H57 MRR Alc.

The New York times directory of the
film. 1971- [New York] Arno Press.
791.43 72-622071
    PN1995 .N39 MRR Alc Full set

The New York times film reviews, 1913-
1968. New York, The New York Times,
1970 [v. 6, 1970, c1971] 6 v. (4961
p.) 791.43/5 70-112777
    PN1995 .N4 MRR Alc

MOVING-PICTURES--REVIEWS--INDEXES.
Johnson, Robert Owen. An index to
literature in the New Yorker, volumes
I-XV, 1925-1940. Metuchen, N.J.,
Scarecrow Press, 1969-71. 3 v. 051
71-7740
    AP2 .N6764 MRR Alc.

The New York times directory of the
film. 1971- [New York] Arno Press.
791.43 72-622071
    PN1995 .N39 MRR Alc Full set

Salem, James M. A guide to critical
reviews, 2d ed. Metuchen, N.J.,
Scarecrow Press, 1973- v.
016.809/2 73-3120
    Z5782 .S342 MRR Ref Desk.

Salem, James M. A guide to critical
reviews, New York, Scarecrow Press,
1966- v. [$4.50 (v. 1) varies]
016.8092 66-13733
    Z5782 .S34 MRR Ref Desk.

MOVING-PICTURES--REVIEWS--YEARBOOKS.
Film. 1967/68- New York, Simon and
Schuster. 791.43/05 68-19946
    PN1993.3 .F38 MRR Alc Full set

MOVING-PICTURES--SOCIETIES, ETC.--
DIRECTORIES.
International Film and Television
Council. Le repertoire C.I.C.T. des
organisations internationales de
cinema et de television et de
leurs branches nationales. 1964-
[London] Film Centre. 65-71067
    PN1998 .I5 MRR Alc Latest edition

MOVING-PICTURES--STUDY AND TEACHING.
Manchel, Frank. Film study:
Rutherford [N.J.] Fairleigh Dickinson
University Press [1973] 422 p.
791.43/07 73-3262
    Z5784.M9 M34 MRR Alc.

MOVING-PICTURES--STUDY AND TEACHING--
DIRECTORIES.
American Film Institute. The
American Film Institute guide to
college courses in film and
television. Washington, Acropolis
Books [1973] xv, 309 p. [$5.95]
791.4/07/1173 72-12391
    LB1043.Z9 A8 MRR Alc.

MOVING-PICTURES--TERMINOLOGY.
Barnet, Sylvan. A dictionary of
literary, dramatic and cinematic
terms 2d ed. Boston, Little, Brown
[1971] 124 p. 801/.4 74-145572
    PN44.5 .B3 1971 MRR Alc.

MOVING-PICTURES--TITLING.
Halliwell, Leslie. The filmgoer's
companion / 4th ed., entirely rev.;
reset and much enl. New York : Hill
and Wang, [1974] xi, 873 p. :
[$25.00] 791.43/03 74-185464
    PN1993.45 .H3 1974 MRR Biog.

MOVING-PICTURES--YEARBOOKS.
Fame: New York, Quigley Pub. Co. 53-
31048
    Began publication in 1933?
    PN1993.3 .B6 MRR Alc Latest
    edition

Film. 1967/68- New York, Simon and
Schuster. 791.43/05 68-19946
    PN1993.3 .F38 MRR Alc Full set

Film review. London, W. H. Allen
[etc.] 791.4058 47-20688
    Publication began in 1944?
    PN1993 .F624 MRR Alc Latest
    edition

International motion picture almanac.
1929- New York [etc.] Quigley
Publications [etc.] 29-8663
    PN1993.3 .I55 MRR Biog Latest
    edition

Jahrbuch der Schweizer Filmindustrie.
Geneve, Société anonyme de "La
Tribune de Geneve". 791.4058 47-
18842
    Publication began with issue for
    1938.
    PN1993.3 .J28 MRR Alc Latest
    edition

Kinematograph and television year
book. London, Go Magazine ltd.
338.4/7/791430942 72-626476
    PN1993.3 .K5 MRR Alc Latest
    edition

Screen world. v. 1- 1949- New
York [etc.] Crown Publishers [etc.]
791.43/05 50-3023
    PN1993.3 .D3 MRR Alc Full set

MOVING-PICTURES--CANADA--CATALOGS.
Canadian periodical index. v. 1-
Jan. 1948- Ottawa. 49-2133
    AI3 .C242 MRR Alc Full set

MOVING-PICTURES--FRANCE.
Annyaire du spectacle; [1]-
annee; 1942/43- Paris, Éditions
Raoult [etc.] 45-27035
PN2620 .A67 MRR Alc Latest edition

MOVING-PICTURES--GREAT BRITAIN.
Gifford, Denis. The British film
catalogue, 1895-1970; New York,
McGraw-Hill [1973] 1 v. (largely
unpaged) 791.43/0842 72-7861
PN1993.5.G7 G5 MRR Alc.

**MOVING-PICTURES--GREAT BRITAIN--
BIOGRAPHY.**
British film and television year
book. [1st]- ed; 1946- [London,
British and American Film Press,
etc.] 791.4058 792.93058* 46-4765
PN1993.3 .B7 MRR Biog Latest
edition

**MOVING-PICTURES--GREAT BRITAIN--
DIRECTORIES.**
British film and television year
book. [1st]- ed; 1946- [London,
British and American Film Press,
etc.] 791.4058 792.93058* 46-4765
PN1993.3 .B7 MRR Biog Latest
edition

MOVING-PICTURES--ITALY--YEARBOOKS.
Annuario del cinema italiano,
1950/51- [Roma, Cinedizione] 61-
44026
PN1993.5.I88 A7 MRR Alc Latest
edition

MOVING-PICTURES--SPAIN--YEARBOOKS.
Anuario español de cinematografia.
Madrid, Sindicato Nacional del
Espectaculo. 57-24397
PN1993.5.S7 A8 MRR Alc Latest
edition

MOVING-PICTURES--SWITZERLAND.
Jahrbuch der Schweizer Filmindustrie.
Geneve, Société anonyme de "La
Tribune de Genève". 791.4058 47-
18842
Publication began with issue for
1938.
PN1993.3 .J28 MRR Alc Latest
edition

MOVING-PICTURES--UNITED STATES.
Michael, Paul. The American movies
reference book; Englewood Cliffs,
N.J., Prentice-Hall [1969] 629 p.
[29.95] 791.43/0973 68-13401
PN1993.5.U6 M53 MRR Alc.

Sarris, Andrew. The American cinema;
[1st ed,] New York, Dutton, 1968.
383 p. [$7.95] 791.43/0233 69-
12602
PN1993.5.U6 S3 MRR Alc.

**MOVING-PICTURES--UNITED STATES--
BIOGRAPHY.**
Sarris, Andrew. The American cinema;
[1st ed,] New York, Dutton, 1968.
383 p. [$7.95] 791.43/0233 69-
12602
PN1993.5.U6 S3 MRR Alc.

**MOVING-PICTURES--UNITED STATES--
CATALOGS.**
American Film Institute. The
American Film Institute catalog of
motion pictures produced in the
United States. New York, R. R.
Bowker, 1971- v. in
016.7/9143/0873 79-128587
PN1998 .A57 MRR Alc.

Dimmitt, Richard Bertrand. A title
guide to the talkies; New York,
Scarecrow Press, 1965. 2 v. (2133
p.) 791.438 65-13556
PN1998 .D55 MRR Alc.

MOVING-PICTURES--UNITED STATES--HISTORY.
Bogle, Donald. Toms, coons,
mulattoes, mammies, and bucks; New
York, Viking Press [1973] xviii, 260
p. [$12.50] 791.43/0873 72-76776

PN1995.9.N4 B6 MRR Alc.

Griffith, Richard, The movies; New
York, Simon and Schuster, 1957.
[13], 442 p. 791.409 792.9309* 57-
10977
PN1993.5.U6 G78 MRR Alc.

Quigley, Martin, Films in America,
1929-1968 New York, Golden Press
[1970] 379 p. [$12.95] 791.43/09
78-125278
PN1993.5.U6 Q5 MRR Alc.

MOVING-PICTURES, DOCUMENTARY--CATALOGS.
London. National Film Archive.
Catalogue. London, British Film
Institute, 1951- v. 782.93
791.4085 52-4264
PN1998 .L58 MRR Alc.

**MOVING-PICTURES, DOCUMENTARY--
DIRECTORIES.**
United Nations Educational,
Scientific and Cultural Organization.
Mass Communication Techniques
Division. World film directory;
[Paris] UNESCO [1962] 66 p. 62-
4747
PN1995.9.D6 U47 MRR Alc.

**MOVING-PICTURES, DOCUMENTARY--
HANDBOOKS, MANUALS, ETC.**
Film Council of America. A guide to
film services of national
associations. Evanston, Ill. [1954]
xlix, 146 p. 791.4058 792.93058*
54-3752
PN1995.9.D6 F5 MRR Alc.

**MOVING-PICTURES, DOCUMENTARY--UNITED
STATES--CATALOGS.**
Guide to Government-loan film. 1st-
ed; 1969/70- [Alexandria, Va.,
Serina Press] 791.43/8 71-76544
PN1998 .G83 MRR Alc Latest edition

MOVING-PICTURES, SILENT--HISTORY.
Blum, Daniel C. A pictorial history
of the silent screen. New York,
Putnam [1953] 334 p. (chiefly
illus.) 791.4084 792.93084* 53-
8156
PN1993.5.U6 B6 MRR Alc.

MOVING-PICTURES, SILENT--UNITED STATES.
Weaver, John T. Twenty years of
silents, 1908-1928. Metuchen, N.J.,
Scarecrow Press, 1971. 514 p.
016.79143/5 73-157729
PN1998.A2 W38 MRR alc.

MOVING-PICTURES, TALKING--HISTORY.
Blum, Daniel C. A new pictorial
history of the talkies. New York,
Putnam [1968] 339 p. [$10.00] 68-
21918
PN1995.7 .B56 1968 MRR Alc.

MOVING-PICTURES IN EDUCATION.
American Library Association. Audio-
Visual Committee. Films for
libraries, Chicago, American Library
Association, 1962. 81 p. 791.43
62-20326
PN1998 .A653 MRR Alc.

Educators' guide to free films.
Randolph, Wis., Educators' Progress
Service. 371.335230838 45-412
Began with 1941 vol.
LB1044 .E3 MRR Alc Latest edition

Educators' guide to free filmstrips.
1st- 1949- Randolph, Wis.,
Educators' Progress Service.
371.3352 50-11650
LB1043.8 .E4 MRR Alc Latest
edition

**MOVING-PICTURES IN EDUCATION--
BIBLIOGRAPHY.**
Educational Media Council.
Educational media index. New York,
McGraw-Hill [1964] 14 v. 016.37133
64-17810
Z5814.V8 E3 MRR Alc.

MOVING-PICTURES IN EDUCATION--CATALOGS.
Educational Film Library Association.
Film evaluation guide, 1946-1964.
[New York, 1965] xv, 528 p.
016.37133523 65-27898
PN1995.9.E9 E3 MRR Alc.

National Information Center for
Educational Media. Index to 8mm
motion cartridges. New York, R. R.
Bowker Co., 1969. xv, 402 p.
371.33/523/0216 72-91716
LB1044.Z9 N34 MRR Alc.

National Information Center for
Educational Media. Index to
psychology; multimedia. 1st ed.
[Los Angeles, University of Southern
California] 1972. x, 461 p. 016.15
76-190637
BF77 .N37 1972 MRR Alc.

**MOVING-PICTURES IN EDUCATION--
HANDBOOKS, MANUALS, ETC.**
Film Council of America. A guide to
film services of national
associations. Evanston, Ill. [1954]
xlix, 146 p. 791.4058 792.93058*
54-3752
PN1995.9.D6 F5 MRR Alc.

MOZAMBIQUE.
Herrick, Allison Butler. Area
handbook for Mozambique. Washington,
For sale by the Supt. of Docs., U.S.
Govt. Print. Off., 1969. xiv, 351 p.
[3.25] 916.7/9 72-601780
DT453 .H4 MRR Alc.

MOZAMBIQUE--COMMERCE--DIRECTORIES.
Indicador economico de Moçambique.
no. 1- 1967- Lourenço Marques.
79-18488
HC578.M6 I5 MRR Alc Latest edition

MOZAMBIQUE--DIRECTORIES.
Anuario do Estado de Moçambique.
Lourenço Marques, A. W. Bayly. 74-
642869
DT451 .A55 MRR Alc Latest edition

The Rhodesia-Zambia-Malawi directory
(including Botswana and Mocambique).
Bulawayo, Publications (Central
Africa) [etc.] 916.89/0025 38-1460

"First published in 1910."
DT947 .R5 MRR Alc Latest edition

**MOZAMBIQUE--ECONOMIC CONDITIONS--
YEARBOOKS.**
Indicador económico de Moçambique.
no. 1- 1967- Lourenço Marques.
79-19488
HC578.M6 I5 MRR Alc Latest edition

MOZAMBIQUE--GAZETTEERS.
United States. Geographic Names
Division. Mozambique; Washington,
1969. iv, 505 p. 916.7/9/003 75-
603590
DT452 .U5 MRR Alc.

MOZAMBIQUE--INDUSTRIES--DIRECTORIES.
Indicador economico de Moçambique.
no. 1- 1967- Lourenço Marques.
79-19488
HC578.M6 I5 MRR Alc Latest edition

**MOZART, JOHANN CHRYSOSTOM WOLFGANG
AMADEUS, 1756-1791. OPERAS.**
Grout, Donald Jay. Mozart in the
history of opera; Washington,
Published for the Library of Congress
by the Louis Charles Elson Memorial
Fund, 1972 [c1971] iii, 20 p.
782.1/0924 75-38821
Z663.37 .A5 1970 MRR Alc.

MULTILINGUALISM.
see also Bilingualism

MULTINATIONAL CORPORATION
see International business enterprises

MULTIPLICATION.
Sprinkle, Leland W. Sprinkle's
conversion formulas, Philadelphia,
P. Blakiston's son & co., inc.
[c1938] xii, 122 p. 510.835 38-
8711
HF5699 .S75 MRR Ref Desk.

MULTIPLICATION--TABLES.
Carlsten, Kirk Finley. Book
computer, Denver, Metron Instrument
Co. [1960] 999 p. 510.83 60-12305

QA49 .C2 MRR Alc.

MUNICH--DESCRIPTION--GUIDE-BOOKS.
Clark, Sydney Aylmer, All the best
in Austria, 1973-1974 rev. ed. New
York, Dodd, Mead [1973] viii, 344 p.
[$9.95] 814.36/04/5 74-815
DB16 .C55 1973 MRR Alc.

MUNICH--DIRECTORIES.
Münchner Stadtadressbuch. München,
Adressbuchverlag der Industrie- und
Handelskammer München. ca 33-785
DD901.M74 M8 MRR Alc Latest
edition*

MUNICIPAL BONDS--UNITED STATES.
Directory: municipal bond dealers of
the United States. New York, The
Bond buyer. 332.6/2/02573 74-642470

HG4907 .D5 MRR Alc Latest edition

**MUNICIPAL BONDS--UNITED STATES--
YEARBOOKS.**
Moody's municipal & government
manual: American and foreign. 1955-
New York, Moody's Investors Service.
57-29
HG4931 .M58 MRR Alc Latest edition

MUNICIPAL ENGINEERING.
see also Housing

MUNICIPAL ENGINEERING--YEARBOOKS.
Municipal index; [1st]- ed.; 1924-
[Pittsfield, Mass., etc.] Buttenheim
Pub. Corp. [etc.] 24-14253
TD1 .M927 MRR Alc Latest edition

MUNICIPAL GOVERNMENT.
Robson, William Alexander, ed. Great
cities of the world; Beverly Hills,
Calif., Sage Publications [1972] 2
v. (1114 p.) 352/.008 75-167875
HT151 .R585 1972b MRR Alc.

MUNICIPAL GOVERNMENT--YEARBOOKS.
The Municipal year book; 1934-
Washington, D.C. [etc.] International
city manager's association. 34-27121

JS344.C5 A24 MRR Ref Desk Latest
edition / MRR Alc Latest edition

The Scottish municipal annual.
Edinburgh [etc.] 352.041 49-25439
JS4101 .S35 MRR Alc Latest edition

MUNICIPAL GOVERNMENT--AFRICA, SOUTH.
Official South African municipal year
book. Pretoria, [etc.] Sa.
Association of Municipal Employees
(non political) [etc.] 14-9587
JS7531 .A5 MRR Alc Latest edition

MUNICIPAL GOVERNMENT--CALIFORNIA.
California. Secretary of State.
Roster: Federal, state, county,
city, and township officials. 1858-
[Sacramento] 353.9/794/002 72-
622827
JK8730.A27 MRR Alc Latest edition

MUNICIPAL GOVERNMENT--DENMARK--
YEARBOOKS.
Kommunal aarbog. København. 52-
42501
Began publication with 1930 issue.
JS6151 .K65 MRR Alc Latest edition

MUNICIPAL GOVERNMENT--GREAT BRITAIN--
BIBLIOGRAPHY.
Martin, Geoffrey Haward. A
bibliography of British and Irish
municipal history Leicester,
Leicester University Press, 1972- v.
[£12.50 (v. 1)] 016.30136/0942
73-156398
Z2023 .M26 MRR Alc.

MUNICIPAL GOVERNMENT--GREAT BRITAIN--
YEARBOOKS.
The Municipal year book and public
utilities directory. London,
Municipal Journal [etc.] 352.042 07-
24315
Began publication in 1897.
JS3003 .M8 MRR Alc Latest edition

MUNICIPAL GOVERNMENT--IRELAND--
BIBLIOGRAPHY.
Martin, Geoffrey Haward. A
bibliography of British and Irish
municipal history Leicester,
Leicester University Press, 1972- v.
[£12.50 (v. 1)] 016.30136/0942
73-156398
Z2023 .M26 MRR Alc.

MUNICIPAL GOVERNMENT--MICHIGAN.
Michigan Municipal League. Annual
directory of Michigan municipal
officials. Ann Arbor. 352.0774 43-
35863
JS303.M5 M52 no. 1 MRR Alc Latest
edition

MUNICIPAL GOVERNMENT--MISSISSIPPI--
REGISTERS.
Mississippi. University. Bureau of
Governmental Research. A directory
of Mississippi municipalities. 1949-
University. 352.0762 50-63282
JS451.M78 A2 MRR Alc Latest
edition

MUNICIPAL GOVERNMENT--OHIO--REGISTERS.
Ohio. Secretary of State. Official
roster; [Columbus, etc.] 09-3257
JS451.O37 A28 MRR Alc Latest
edition

MUNICIPAL GOVERNMENT--SCOTLAND.
The Scottish municipal annual.
Edinburgh [etc.] 352.041 49-25439
JS4101 .S35 MRR Alc Latest edition

MUNICIPAL GOVERNMENT--SCOTLAND--
YEARBOOKS.
The County 8 municipal year book for
Scotland. Coupar Angus. 352.041 49-
20531
Began publication with 1933 issue.
JS4101 .C6 MRR Alc Latest edition

MUNICIPAL GOVERNMENT--UNITED STATES.
The Municipal year book; 1934-
Washington, D.C. [etc.] International
city manager's association. 34-27121
JS344.C5 A24 MRR Ref Desk Latest
edition / MRR Alc Latest edition

MUNICIPAL GOVERNMENT--UNITED STATES--
ADDRESSES, ESSAYS, LECTURES.
Banfield, Edward C., ed. Urban
government; Rev. ed. New York, Free
Press [1968, c1969] xvii, 718 p.
352/.008/0973 69-11169
JS308 .B2 1969 MRR Alc.

MUNICIPAL GOVERNMENT--UNITED STATES--
BIBLIOGRAPHY.
Government Affairs Foundation.
Metropolitan communities: Chicago,
Public Administration Service [1957,
c1956] xviii, 392 p. 016.352073
56-13382
Z7164.L8 G66 MRR Alc.

MUNICIPAL GOVERNMENT--UNITED STATES--
STATISTICS.
United States. Bureau of the Census.
1972 census of governments.
[Washington, U.S. Govt. Print. Off.]
1973- v. [$1.25 (v. 2, pt. 1)
varies] 317.3 73-600080
JS3 .A244 MFR Alc.

MUNICIPAL GOVERNMENT BY CITY MANAGER.
The Municipal year book; 1934-
Washington, D.C. [etc.] International
city manager's association. 34-27121
JS344.C5 A24 MRR Ref Desk Latest
edition / MRR Alc Latest edition

MUNICIPAL GOVERNMENT BY CITY MANAGER--
DIRECTORIES.
The Municipal management directory.
[Washington] International City
Management Association.
352/.0084/0973 79-612895
JS344.C5 A252 MRR Alc Latest
edition

MUNICIPAL GOVERNMENT BY CITY MANAGER--
PENNSYLVANIA--DIRECTORIES.
Directory of Pennsylvania council-
manager municipalities and municipal
managers. Pittsburgh. 59-26688
JS451.P3 D5 MRR Alc Latest edition

MUNICIPAL JUNIOR COLLEGES.
Cass, James. Comparative guide to
junior and two-year community
colleges New York, Harper & Row
[c1972] xii, 396 p. [$10.00]
378.1/543 72-79651
LB2328 .C355 1972 MRR Ref Desk.

MUNICIPAL JUNIOR COLLEGES--UNITED
STATES--DIRECTORIES.
Community and junior college
directory. Washington,
Communications Division, American
Association of Community and Junior
Colleges. [$5.00] 378.1/543/02573
73-643804
LB2328.A1 J8 MRR Alc Latest
edition

MUNICIPAL OFFICIALS AND EMPLOYEES--
UNITED STATES--DIRECTORIES.
Municipal index; [1st]- ed.; 1924-
[Pittsfield, Mass., etc.] Buttenheim
Pub. Corp. [etc.] 24-14253
TD1 .M827 MRR Alc Latest edition

MUNICIPAL OFFICIALS AND EMPLOYEES--UTAH-
-REGISTERS.
Directory of Utah municipal
officials. Salt Lake City, Utah
League of Cities and Towns.
352/.005/209792 72-623017
JS451.U87 D53 MRR Alc Latest
edition

MUNICIPAL OWNERSHIP--BIBLIOGRAPHY.
United States. Library of Congress.
Division of bibliography. ... Select
list of books on municipal affairs,
Washington, Govt. print. off., 1906.
34 p. 06-35001
Z663.28 .S32 MRR Alc.

MUNICIPAL RESEARCH.
Governmental Research Association.
Directory of organizations and
individuals professionally engaged in
governmental research and related
activities. 1935- New York [etc.]
350.6273 35-16469
JX3 .G627 MRR Alc Latest edition

MUNICIPAL RESEARCH--BIBLIOGRAPHY.
Index to current urban documents. v.
1- July/Oct. 1972- Westport,
Conn., Greenwood Press. [$75.00]
016.30136/0973 73-641453
Z7165.U5 I654 MRR Alc Full set

MUNICIPAL RESEARCH--DIRECTORIES.
Urban Institute. A directory of
university urban research centers.
Washington [1969] 141 p. [3.50]
301.3/64/072073 72-112409
HT110 .U7 MRR Alc.

MUNICIPAL SERVICES.
see also Fire-departments

see also Police

MUNICIPAL TRANSPORTATION
see Urban transportation

MUNICIPAL UNIVERSITIES AND COLLEGES.
Wheeler, Helen Rippier. A basic book
collection for the community college
library, [Hamden, Conn.] Shoe String
Press, 1968. x, 317 p. 011 67-
24183
Z1035 .W47 MRR Alc.

MUNICIPAL UNIVERSITIES AND COLLEGES--
CANADA--DIRECTORIES.
Campbell, Gordon, Community colleges
in Canada. Toronto, New York,
Ryerson Press [1971] xx, 346 p.
[$6.00] 378.71 79-26176
LA417.5 .C35 MRR Alc.

MUNICIPAL UNIVERSITIES AND COLLEGES--
UNITED STATES--DIRECTORIES.
Cass, James. Comparative guide to
two-year colleges & four-year
specialized schools and programs,
[1st ed.] New York, Harper & Row
[1969] xxii, 275 p. [7.95] 378.73
69-15301
LB2328 .C36 MRR Ref Desk.

MUNICIPAL UTILITIES
see Public utilities

MUNICIPALITIES
see Cities and towns

MUNITIONS.
Kirk, John, Great weapons of World
War II. New York, Walker [1961] 347
p. 623.4 61-16984
UF520 .K5 MRR Alc.

MUNITIONS--DICTIONARIES.
Quick, John, Dictionary of weapons
and military terms. New York, McGraw-
Hill [1973] xii, 515 p. 623/.03
73-8757
U24 .Q5 MRR Alc.

MÜNSTER--DIRECTORIES.
Adressbuch der Stadt Münster.
Münster. 914.3/56 70-649651
DD901.M696 E4 MRR Alc Latest
edition

MUNSTER, IRE.--COMMERCE--DIRECTORIES.
Cork and Munster trades' directory.
Edinburgh, Trades' Directories. 62-
38597
HF5163.M8 C6 MRR Alc Latest
edition

MURAL PAINTING AND DECORATION--
WASHINGTON, D.C.
Drake, Alice Hutchins. Mural
decorations in the Library of
Congress, [Washington, D.C., Printed
by J. C. Wood, c1932] 26 p.
027.573 32-17646
Z733.U58 D85 MRR Ref Desk.

United States. Library of Congress.
Hispanic foundation. Murals by
Cándido Portinari in the Hispanic
foundation of the Library of
Congress. Washington [U.S. Govt.
print. off.] 1943. 31, [1] p.
751.73 43-52050
Z663.32 .M8 MRR Alc.

Winter, Ezra Augustus, 1886- The
Canterbury pilgrims, Washington
[U.S. Govt. print. off.] 1946.
folder ([6] p.) 751.73 46-27985
Z663 .C2 MRR Alc.

Winter, Ezra Augustus. The Thomas
Jefferson murals in the Thomas
Jefferson Room. Library of Congress.
Washington [U.S. Govt. Print. Off.]
1946. folder ([4] p.) 751.73 51-
60090
Z663 .T47 MRR Alc.

MURDER.
Nash, Jay Robert. Bloodletters and
badmen; New York, M. Evans;
distributed in association with
Lippincott, Philadelphia [1973] 640
p. [$16.95] 364/.092/2 B 72-95977

HV6785 .N37 MRR Biog.

Wilson, Colin, Encyclopedia of
murder [1st American ed.] New York,
Putnam [1962, c1961] 576 p.
364.152 61-12748
HV6245 .W77 1962 MRR Alc.

MURDER--GREAT BRITAIN.
Shew, Edward Spencer, A companion to
murder; [1st American ed.] New
York, Knopf, 1961. 303 p. 364.152
61-14626
HV6945 .S48 1961 MRR Alc.

MUSEUMS.
see also Art--Galleries and museums

MUSEUMS--BIBLIOGRAPHY.
American association of museums. A
bibliography of museums and museum
work, Washington, D.C., The American
association of museums, 1928. 2 p.
l., vi, 302 p. 28-17186
Z5052 .A51 MRR Alc.

United States. Library of Congress.
General Reference and Bibliography
Division. Safeguarding our cultural
heritage; a bibliography Washington,
1952. x, 117 p. 016.355232* 52-
60017
Z663.28 .S3 MRR Alc.

MUSEUMS--DIRECTORIES.
The Archaeologists' year book. 1973-
[Park Ridge, N.J.] Noyes Press.
[$12.50] 913/.031/025 73-78778
CC120 .A67 MRR Alc Latest edition

Association of Museums of Arms and
Military History. Repertory of
museums of arms and military history.
Copenhagen, 1960. 158 p. 355.074
61-24144
U13.A1 A7 MRR Alc.

Cooper, Barbara, The world museums
guide, London, Threshold Books Ltd;
Sotheby Parke Bernet Publications
Ltd., 1973. 288 p. [£3.75] 708
74-174259
N405 .C66 MRR Alc.

Huenefeld, Irene Pennington.
International directory of historical
clothing. Metuchen, N.J., Scarecrow
Press, 1967. 175 p. 391/.0025 67-
10186
NK4700 .H8 MRR Alc.

Museums of the world; Pullach bei
München, Verlag Dokumentation; New
York, R. R. Bowker, 1973. 762 p.
069/.025 73-155445
AM1 .M76 MRR Ref Desk.

MUSEUMS--DIRECTORIES. (Cont.)
The World of learning. [1st]- 1947-
London, Europa Publications [etc.]
47-30172
AS2 .W6 Sci RR Latest edition /
MRR Ref Desk Latest edition

MUSEUMS--YEARBOOKS.
Museums Association. Museums
calendar. London. 64-36342
AM1 .M6734 MRR Alc Latest edition

MUSEUMS--AFRICA--DIRECTORIES.
Museums in Africa; [Bonn, German
Africa Society] 1970. ix, 594 p.
[40.00] 068/.025/6 76-478923
AM80.A2 M8 MRR Alc.

MUSEUMS--CANADA.
Canadian museums and related
institutions, 1968. [Ottawa,
Canadian Museums Association, c1968]
xii, 138 p. [unpriced] 069/.025/71
77-430168
AM21.A2 C3 MRR Alc.

MUSEUMS--CANADA--BIBLIOGRAPHY.
Clapp, Jane. Museum publications.
New York, Scarecrow Press, 1962. 2
v. 016.0687 62-10120
Z5051 .C5 MRR Alc.

Wasserman, Paul. Museum media; 1st
ed. Detroit, Gale Research Co.,
1973. vii, 455 p. 011 73-16335
Z5052 .W35 MRR alc.

MUSEUMS--CANADA--DIRECTORIES.
Coleman, Laurence Vail. Company
museums, Washington, D.C., The
American association of museums,
1943. viii, 173 p. 069 43-51215
T179 .C6 MRR Alc.

The Official museum directory. 1971-
[New York] American Association of
Museums and Crowell-Collier
Educational Corp. 069/.025/7 79-
144808
AM10.A2 O4 Sci RR Latest edition /
MRR Ref Desk Latest edition

MUSEUMS--CENTRAL EUROPE.
Birgit-Klogter, Gudrun. Handbuch der
Museen. München-Pullach, Berlin,
Verl. Dokumentation, 1971. 2 v.
(viii, 1300 p.) [DM60.00 (v. 1)]
069/.0943 72-204766
AM40 .B57 MRR Alc.

MUSEUMS--EUROPE.
Hudson, Kenneth. A guide to the
industrial archaeology of Europe.
[1st American ed.] Madison [N.J.]
Fairleigh Dickinson University Press
[1971] xi, 186 p. [$15.00] 609/.4
76-160459
T26.A1 H8 1971b MRR Alc.

MUSEUMS--FRANCE--DIRECTORIES.
Barnaud, Germaine, comp. Répertoire
des musées de France et de la
communauté. Paris, Institut
pédagogique national, 1959. x, 416
p. 60-24344
AM46 .B3 MRR Alc.

MUSEUMS--GREAT BRITAIN.
Directory of museums and art
galleries in the British Isles,
South Kensington, Museums Association
[1948] viii, 392 p. 069.0942 50-
395
AM41 .D52 1948 MRR Alc.

The Libraries, museums and art
galleries year book. 1897- London
[etc.] J. Clarke [etc.] 28-11281
Z791 .L7 MRR Alc Latest edition

Philip, Alexander John, An index to
the special collections in libraries,
museums and art galleries (public,
private and official) in Great
Britain and Ireland. London, Pub.
for the author by F. G. Brown [1949]
viii, 190 p. 016 49-48107
AM213 .P5 MRR Alc.

MUSEUMS--GREAT BRITAIN--DIRECTORIES.
Museums and galleries in Great
Britain and Ireland. London, Index
Publishers. 58-46843
Began publication with 1955 vol.
N1020 .M82 MRR Alc Latest edition

Museums Association. Museums
calendar. London. 64-36342
AM1 .M6734 MRR Alc Latest edition

Nunn, George Walter Arthur, ed.
British sources of photographs and
pictures. London, Cassell [1952]
viii, 220 p. 770.58 53-25373
TR12 .N8 MRR Alc.

MUSEUMS--INDIA--DIRECTORIES.
Sivaramamurti, C. Directory of
museums in India. New Delhi,
Ministry of Scientific Research &
Cultural Affairs, 1959. xi, 141 p.
sa 62-766
AM73.A2 S5 MRR Alc.

MUSEUMS--IRELAND.
Philip, Alexander John, An index to
the special collections in libraries,
museums and art galleries (public,
private and official) in Great
Britain and Ireland. London, Pub.
for the author by F. G. Brown [1949]
viii, 190 p. 016 49-48107
AM213 .P5 MRR Alc.

MUSEUMS--JAPAN.
Japan. Mombushō. Nihon Yunesuko
Kokunai Iinkai. Museums in Japan.
[Tokyo] Japanese National Commission
for Unesco, 1960. 123 p. 63-34675
AM77 .A55 MRR.Alc.

MUSEUMS--MASSACHUSETTS--DIRECTORIES.
Rubin, Jerome. A guide to
Massachusetts museums, historic
houses, points of interest, [Newton,
Mass., Emporium Publications, 1972]
126 p. [$1.95] 917.44/044 72-
81231
F61.5 .R8 MRR Alc.

MUSEUMS--NORTH AMERICA--BIBLIOGRAPHY.
Clapp, Jane. Museum publications.
New York, Scarecrow Press, 1962. 2
v. 016.0697 62-10120
Z5051 .C5 MRR Alc.

MUSEUMS--NORTH AMERICA--DIRECTORIES.
The Official museum directory. 1971-
[New York] American Association of
Museums and Crowell-Collier
Educational Corp. 069/.025/7 79-
144808
AM10.A2 O4 Sci RR Latest edition /
MRR Ref Desk Latest edition

MUSEUMS--UGANDA.
Trowell, Kathleen Margaret, comp. A
handbook of the museums and libraries
of Uganda. Kampala, Uganda Museum,
1957. 16 p. 58-29016
Z858.U4 T7 MRR Alc.

MUSEUMS--UNITED STATES.
Hilton, Ronald, ed. Handbook of
Hispanic source materials and
research organizations in the United
States. 2d ed. Stanford, Calif.,
Stanford University press, 1956.
xiv, 448 p. 980 56-6178
F1408.3 .H65 1956 MRR Alc.

Illustrated guide to the treasures of
America. Pleasantville, N.Y.,
Reader's Digest Association [1974]
624 p. [$11.97] 917.3/03 73-83812

E159 .I44 MRR Alc.

Katz, Herbert. Museums, U.S.A.;
[1st ed.] Garden City, N.Y.,
Doubleday, 1965. x, 395 p.
069.0973 65-12364
AM11 .K3 MRR Alc.

MUSEUMS--UNITED STATES--BIBLIOGRAPHY.
Clapp, Jane. Museum publications.
New York, Scarecrow Press, 1962. 2
v. 016.0697 62-10120
Z5051 .C5 MRR Alc.

Wasserman, Paul. Museum media; 1st
ed. Detroit, Gale Research Co.,
1973. vii, 455 p. 011 73-16335
Z5052 .W35 MRR alc.

MUSEUMS--UNITED STATES--DIRECTORIES.
Coleman, Laurence Vail, Company
museums, Washington, D.C., The
American association of museums,
1943. viii, 173 p. 069 43-51215
T179 .C6 MRR Alc.

Lewis, Guy. Sporting heritage;
South Brunswick, A. S. Barnes [1974]
181 p. 796/.074/013 72-6391
GV583 .L48 1974 MRR Alc.

The Official museum directory. 1971-
[New York] American Association of
Museums and Crowell-Collier
Educational Corp. 069/.025/7 79-
144808
AM10.A2 O4 Sci RR Latest edition /
MRR Ref Desk Latest edition

MUSHROOMS--UNITED STATES.
Thomas, William Sturgis, Field book
of common mushrooms; New and enl.
ed., New York London, G. P. Putnam's
sons, 1936. xx, 369 p. 589.222 36-
19008
QK617 .T5 1936 MRR Alc.

MUSHROOMS, EDIBLE--UNITED STATES.
Smith, Alexander Hanchett, The
mushroom hunter's field guide. Ann
Arbor, University of Michigan Press
[1958] 197 p. 589.222 57-7748
QK617 .S56 MRR Alc.

MUSHROOMS, POISONOUS--UNITED STATES.
Smith, Alexander Hanchett, The
mushroom hunter's field guide. Ann
Arbor, University of Michigan Press
[1958] 197 p. 589.222 57-7748
QK617 .S56 MRR Alc.

MUSIC--ADDRESSES, ESSAYS, LECTURES.
Barzun, Jacques. Music into words;
Washington, 1953. ill, 27 p. 780.1
53-60002
Z663.37 .A5 1951 MRR Alc.

Davison, Archibald Thompson, Words
and music, Washington [U.S. Govt.
Print. Off.] 1954. 24 p. 784 54-
60019
Z663.37 .A5 1954 MRR Alc.

Pincherle, Marc, Musical creation;
Washington, Library of Congress,
1961. ill, 23 p. 780 61-60093
Z663.37 .A5 1960 MRR Alc.

Pratt, Carroll Cornelius, Music as
the language of emotion; Washington
[U.S. Govt. Print. Off.] 1952. 26 p.
780.1 52-60021
Z663.37 .A5 1950 MRR Alc.

Stevenson, Robert Murrell.
Philosophies of American music
history, Washington, Published for
the Library of Congress by the Louis
Charles Elson Memorial Fund, 1970.
ill, 18 p. 780/.973 70-609941
Z663.37.A5 1969 MRR Alc.

Wellesz, Egon, The origins of
Schönberg's twelve-tone system;
Washington [U.S. Govt. Print. Off.]
1958. ill, 14 p. 781.22 58-60018
Z663.37 .A5 1957 MRR Alc.

Westrup, Jack Allan, Sir, Music, its
past and its present; Washington,
1964. ill, 24 p. 64-60042
Z663.37 .A5 1963 MRR Alc.

MUSIC--ALMANACS, YEARBOOKS, ETC.
Annuaire du spectacle; [1]-
année; 1942/43- Paris, Editions
Raoult [etc.] 45-27035
PN2620 .A67 MRR Alc Latest edition

MUSIC--ANALYSIS, APPRECIATION.
Ewen, David, The complete book of
classical music. Englewood Cliffs,
N.J., Prentice-Hall [1965] xx, 946
p. 780.9033 65-11033
MT6 .E89 MRR Alc.

Ewen, David, Musical masterworks;
[2d ed., rev. and reset] New York,
Arco Pub. Co. [1954] vi, 740 p.
780.3 54-12618
ML105 .E96 1954 MRR Alc.

MUSIC--BIBLIOGRAPHY.
Belknap, Sara (Yancey) Guide to the
musical arts; New York, Scarecrow
Press, 1957. 1 v. (unpaged) 016.78
57-6631
ML113 .B37 MRR Alc.

Berkowitz, Freda Pastor. Popular
titles and subtitles of musical
compositions. New York, Scarecrow
Press, 1962. 182 p. 016.78 62-
10121
ML113 .B39 MRR Alc.

Blum, Fred, Music monographs in
series; New York, Scarecrow Press,
1964. xiii, 197 p. 016.78 64-
11794
ML113 .B63 MRR Alc.

The British union-catalogue of early
music printed before the year 1801;
London, Butterworths Scientific
Publications, 1957. 2 v. (xx, 1178
p.) 781.97 58-526
ML116 .B7 MRR Alc.

Davies, J. H. Musicalia: 2d ed.,
rev. and enl. Oxford, New York,
Pergamon Press [1969] xii, 184 p.
016.78 76-77013
ML113.D383 M9 1969 MRR Alc.

Duckles, Vincent Harris, Music
reference and research materials; 2d
ed. New York, Free Press [1967]
xiii, 385 p. 016.78 67-17657
ML113 .D83 1967 MRR Alc.

Fuld, James J., The book of world-
famous music; New York, Crown
Publishers [1966] xi, 564 p.
016.78 65-24332
ML113 .F8 MRR Alc.

International inventory of musical
sources. [München, G. Henle, 1960-
[v. 1, 1971] v. 63-49368
ML113 .I6 MRR Alc.

Joint Committee of the Music Teachers
National Association and the American
Musicological Society. Doctoral
dissertations in musicology. 4th ed.
Philadelphia, American Musicological
Society, 1965. 152 p. 016.78001
66-1684
ML128.M8 J6 1965 MRR Alc.

Limbacher, James L. A reference
guide to audiovisual information,
New York, Bowker, 1972. ix, 197 p.
016.00155/3 72-1737
Z5814.V8 L55 MRR Alc.

MUSIC--BIBLIOGRAPHY--CATALOGS.
Barsortiments-Lagerkatalog.
Stuttgart [etc.] Koehler & Volckmar
[etc.] 015.43   46-38153
Z2221 .B3 MRR Alc Latest edition

United States. Library of Congress.
Catalogue of early books on music
(before 1800) Washington, Govt.
print. off., 1913. 312 p.   12-35008

Z663.37 .C28 MRR Alc.

United States. Library of Congress.
Library of Congress catalog; Books:
authors. Jan. 1947-1955.
Washington. 47-32682
Z663.7 .L5 MRR Alc   MRR Alc (DK 33)
Full set

United States. Library of Congress.
Library of Congress catalog: Music
and phonorecords; 1953- Washington.
53-60012
Z663.37 .A3 MRR Alc   MRR Alc Full
set

MUSIC--BIBLIOGRAPHY--MANUSCRIPTS.
International inventory of musical
sources. [München, G. Henle, 1960-
[v. 1, 1971] v.   63-49368
ML113 .I6 MRR Alc.

United States. Library of Congress.
Gertrude Clarke Whittall Foundation
Collection. Autograph musical scores
and autograph letters in the Whittall
Foundation Collection, Rev.
Washington, 1953. 18 p. 54-60005
Z663.375 .A8 1953 MRR Alc.

MUSIC--BIBLIOGRAPHY--UNION LISTS.
The British union-catalogue of early
music printed before the year 1801;
London, Butterworths Scientific
Publications, 1957. 2 v. (xx, 1178
p.)   781.97 58-526
ML116 .B7 MRR Alc.

MUSIC--BIO-BIBLIOGRAPHY.
Baker, Theodore, Biographical
dictionary of musicians. 5th ed.,
completely rev. New York, G.
Schirmer [1958] xv, 1855 p.
780.922 58-4953
ML105 .B16 1958 MRR Biog.

Cobbett, Walter Willson, ed.
Cobbett's cyclopedic survey of
chamber music, London, Oxford
university press, H. Milford, 1929-
30. 2 v.   29-14486
ML1100 .C7 MRR Alc.

Dizionario letterario Bompiani degli
autori di tutti i tempi e di tutte le
letterature. Milano, V. Bompiani,
1956-57. 3 v.   58-16111
Z1010 .D5 MRR Biog.

Ewen, David, Great composers, 1300-
1900; New York, H. W. Wilson Co.,
1966. 429 p.   780.922 65-24585
ML105 .E944 MRR Biog.

Ewen, David, Musical masterworks;
[2d ed., rev. and reset] New York,
Arco Pub. Co. [1954] vi, 740 p.
780.3 54-12618
ML105 .E96 1954 MRR Alc.

Feather, Leonard G. The encyclopedia
of jazz in the sixties, New York,
Horizon Press [1966] 312 p.
785.420922 66-26705
ML105 .F35 MRR Alc.

Grove, George, Sir, ed. Dictionary
of music and musicians. 5th ed.,
London, Macmillan; New York, St.
Martin's Press, 1954. 9 v.   780.3
54-11819
ML100 .G885 1954 MRR Alc.

Historical Records Survey. District
of Columbia. Bio-bibliographical
index of musicians in the United
States of America since colonial
times. 2d ed. Washington, Music
Section, Pan American Union, 1956.
xxiii, 439 p.   016.78071 pa 57-4
ML106.U3 H6 1956 MRR Biog.

Panassié, Hugues. Guide to jazz,
Boston, Houghton Mifflin, 1956. vii,
312 p.   781.5 785.42* 56-10291
ML102.J3 P33 MRR Alc.

Roxon, Lillian. Rock encyclopedia.
New York, Grosset & Dunlap [1971]
611 p. [$3.85]   784 76-26545
ML102.P66 R7 1971 MRR Alc.

Sainsbury, John S. A dictionary of
musicians from the earliest times,
New York, Da Capo Press, 1966. 2 v.
780.922 65-23396
ML105 .S2 1825a MRR Biog.

Sandved, Kjell Bloch, ed. The world
of music; [1st American ed.] New
York, Abradale Press [1963] 4 v.
(1516 p.)   780.3 63-14095
ML100 .S25 1963 MRR Alc.

Scholes, Percy Alfred, The concise
Oxford dictionary of music, 2d ed.,
London, New York, Oxford University
Press, 1964. xxx, 636 p.   780.3 64-
5946
ML100 .S367 1964 MRR Alc.

Scholes, Percy Alfred, The Oxford
companion to music, 9th ed.,
completely rev. and reset London,
New York, Oxford University Press,
1955. lx, 1195 p.   780.3 55-14499

ML100 .S37 1955 MRR Alc.

Stambler, Irwin. Encyclopedia of
popular music. New York, St.
Martin's Press [1965] xiii, 350 p.
780.3 65-20817
ML102.J3 S8 MRR Alc.

Thompson, Oscar, The international
cyclopedia of music and musicians.
New York, Dodd, Mead, 1964. 2476 p.
64-23285
ML100 .T47 1964 MRR Alc.

Westrup, Jack Allan, Sir, The new
college encyclopedia of music New
York, Norton [1960] xvii, 739 p.
780.3 60-10570
ML100 .W48 1960 MRR Alc.

MUSIC--BIO-BIBLIOGRAPHY--INDEXES.
Bull, Storm. Index to biographies of
contemporary composers. New York,
Scarecrow Press, 1964. 405 p.
016.9278 64-11781
ML105 .B9 MRR Biog.

MUSIC--BIOGRAPHY
see Composers

see Singers

MUSIC--CHRONOLOGY.
Slonimsky, Nicolas, Music since
1900. 4th ed. New York, C.
Scribner's Sons [1971] xvii, 1595 p.
[$49.50]   780/.904 70-114929
ML197 .S634 1971 MRR Alc.

MUSIC--DICTIONARIES.
Apel, Willi, Harvard dictionary of
music. 2d ed., rev. and enl.
Cambridge, Mass., Belknap Press of
Harvard University Press, 1969. xv,
935 p. [17.50]   780/.3 68-21970
ML100 .A64 1969 MRR Alc.

Benét, William Rose, ed. The
reader's encyclopedia. 2d ed. New
York, Crowell [1965] viii, 1118 p.
803 65-12510
PN41 .B4 1965 MRR Ref Desk.

Benét, William Rose, ed. The
reader's encyclopedia, New York, T.
Y. Crowell Co. [1955] vii, 1270 p.
803 55-10502
PN41 .B4 1955 MRR Alc.

Berkowitz, Freda Pastor. Popular
titles and subtitles of musical
compositions. New York, Scarecrow
Press, 1962. 182 p.   016.78 62-
10121
ML113 .B39 MRR Alc.

Blom, Eric, Everyman's dictionary of
music. [Rev. ed.] London, Dent; New
York, Dutton [1954] xiii, 687 p.
780.3 55-14271
ML100 .B47 1954 MRR Alc.

Cooper, Martin, ed. The concise
encyclopedia of music and musicians.
[1st ed.] New York, Hawthorn Books
[1958] 516 p.   780.3 58-5630
ML100 .C78 MRR Alc.

A dictionary of modern music and
musicians. London, Toronto, J. M.
Dent & sons, ltd.; New York, E. P.
Dutton & co., 1924. xvi, 543, [1] p.
25-2077
ML100 .D5 MRR Alc.

Ewen, David, Encyclopedia of concert
music, New York, Hill and Wang
[1959] ix, 566 p.   785.03 59-12597

ML100 .E85 MRR Alc.

Grove, George, Sir, ed. Dictionary
of music and musicians. 5th ed.,
London, Macmillan; New York, St.
Martin's Press, 1954. 9 v.   780.3
54-11819
ML100 .G885 1954 MRR Alc.

Sacher, Jack, ed. Music A to Z. New
York, Grosset & Dunlap [c1963] viii,
432 p.   64-1733
ML100 .S82 1963 MRR Alc.

Sandved, Kjell Bloch, ed. The world
of music; [1st American ed.] New
York, Abradale Press [1963] 4 v.
(1516 p.)   780.3 63-14095
ML100 .S25 1963 MRR Alc.

Scholes, Percy Alfred, The concise
Oxford dictionary of music, 2d ed.,
London, New York, Oxford University
Press, 1964. xxx, 636 p.   780.3 64-
5946
ML100 .S367 1964 MRR Alc.

Scholes, Percy Alfred, The Oxford
companion to music, 9th ed.,
completely rev. and reset London,
New York, Oxford University Press,
1955. lx, 1195 p.   780.3 55-14499

ML100· .S37 1955 MRR Alc.

Slonimsky, Nicolas, Music since
1900. 4th ed. New York, C.
Scribner's Sons [1971] xvii, 1595 p.
[$49.50]   780/.904 70-114929
ML197 .S634 1971 MRR Alc.

Thompson, Oscar, The international
cyclopedia of music and musicians.
New York, Dodd, Mead, 1964. 2476 p.
64-23285
ML100 .T47 1964 MRR Alc.

Westrup, Jack Allan, Sir, The new
college encyclopedia of music New
York, Norton [1960] xvii, 739 p.
780.3 60-10570
ML100 .W48 1960 MRR Alc.

Wolf, Martin L. Dictionary of the
arts; New York, Philosophical
Library [1951] xiii, 797 p.   703
51-13402
N33 .W6 MRR Alc.

MUSIC--DICTIONARIES--GERMAN.
Koch, Willi August, Musisches
Lexikon: Künstler, Kunstwerke und
Motive aus Dichtung, Musik und
bildender Kunst, 2., veränderte und
ergeiterte Aufl. Stuttgart, A.,
Kröner [c1964] 1250 columns, xxxx
p.   65-69991
N31 .K57 1964 MRR Alc.

MUSIC--DICTIONARIES--POLYGLOT.
Elsevier's dictionary of cinema,
sound, and music, in six languages:
Amsterdam, New York, Elsevier Pub.
Co., 1956. 948 p.   778.503 56-
13141
TR847 .E4 MRR Alc.

MUSIC--DISCOGRAPHY.
Ewen, David, Musical masterworks;
[2d ed., rev. and reset] New York,
Arco Pub. Co. [1954] vi, 740 p.
780.3 54-12618
ML105 .E96 1954 MRR Alc.

High fidelity. Records in review.
1955- Great Barrington, Mass. [etc.]
Wyeth Press [etc.] 789.913* 55-
10600
ML156.9 .H5 MRR Alc Partial set

MUSIC--HISTORIOGRAPHY.
Stevenson, Robert Murrell.
Philosophies of American music
history, Washington, Published for
the Library of Congress by the Louis
Charles Elson Memorial Fund, 1970.
iii, 18 p.   780/.973 70-608941
Z663.37.A5 1969 MRR Alc.

MUSIC--HISTORY AND CRITICISM.
Lang, Paul Henry, Music in western
civilization, New York, W. W. Norton
& company, inc. [c1941] xvi, 1107 p.
780.9 41-9128
ML160.L25 M8 MRR Alc.

New Oxford history of music.
[London, New York, Oxford University
Press, 1954- [v. 1, 1957] v.
780.9 54-12578
ML160 .N44 MRR Alc.

Sainsbury, John S. A dictionary of
musicians from the earliest times,
New York, Da Capo Press, 1966. 2 v.
780.922 65-23396
ML105 .S2 1825a MRR Biog.

MUSIC--HISTORY AND CRITICISM--TO 400.
Wellesz, Egon, ed. Ancient and
oriental music. London, New York,
Oxford University Press, 1957.
xxiii, 530 p.   781.8 780.93* 57-
4332
ML160 .N44 vol.1 MRR Alc.

**MUSIC--HISTORY AND CRITICISM--MEDIEVAL,
400-1500.**
Hughes, Anselm, ed. Ars nova and the
Renaissance, 1300-1540. London, New
York, Oxford University Press, 1960,
xiv, 565 p.   63-603
ML160.N44 vol. 3 MRR Alc.

Hughes, Anselm, ed. Early medieval
music, up to 1300. London, New York,
Oxford University Press, 1954.
xviii, 434 p.   54-14955
ML160 .N44 vol. 2 MRR Alc.

**MUSIC--HISTORY AND CRITICISM--20TH
CENTURY.**
see also Jazz music

MUSIC--HISTORY AND CRITICISM-- (Cont.)
Austin, William W. Music in the 20th
century. [1st ed.] New York, W. W.
Norton [1966] xx, 708 p. 780.904
65-18776
ML197 .A9 MRR Alc.

Ewen, David, The new book of modern
composers. 3d ed., rev. and enl.
New York, Knopf, 1961. 491 p.
927.8 61-15040
ML390 .E83 1961 MRR Biog.

Howard, John Tasker, Our
contemporary composers; New York,
Thomas Y. Crowell company, 1941. xv,
447 p. 780.973 41-6762
ML390 .H8 MRR Biog.

Slonimsky, Nicolas, Music since
1900. 4th ed. New York, C.
Scribner's Sons [1971] xvii, 1595 p.
[$49.50] 780/.904 70-114929
ML197 .S634 1971 MRR Alc.

MUSIC--HISTORY AND CRITICISM--SOURCES.
Slonimsky, Nicolas, Music since
1900. 4th ed. New York, C.
Scribner's Sons [1971] xvii, 1595 p.
[$49.50] 780/.904 70-114929
ML197 .S634 1971 MRR Alc.

MUSIC--INSTRUCTION AND STUDY--UNITED
STATES--DIRECTORIES.
The Musician's guide. 1st- ed.;
1954- New York, Music Information
Service. 54-14954
ML13 .M505 MRR Alc Latest edition

MUSIC--JEWS.
Wellesz, Egon, ed. Ancient and
oriental music. London, New York,
Oxford University Press, 1957.
xxiii, 530 p. 781.8 780.93* 57-
4332
ML160 .N44 vol.1 MRR Alc.

MUSIC--MANUSCRIPTS--UNITED STATES.
United States. Library of Congress.
Gertrude Clarke Whittall Foundation
Collection. Autograph musical scores
and autograph letters in the Whittall
Foundation Collection. Rev.
Washington, 1953. 18 p. 54-60005
Z663.375 .A8 1953 MRR Alc.

MUSIC--PERIODICALS--INDEXES.
Belknap, Sara (Yancey) Guide to the
musical arts. New York, Scarecrow
Press, 1957. 1 v. (unpaged) 016.78
57-6631
ML113 .B37 MRR Alc.

Guide to the performing arts. 1957-
Metuchen, N.J. [etc.] Scarecrow
Press. 016.78 60-7266
ML118 .G8 MRR Alc Full set

The Music index. v. 1- 1949-
Detroit, Information Coordinators,
inc.[etc.] 50-13627
ML118 .M84 MRR Alc Full set

MUSIC--SCHOLARSHIPS, FELLOWSHIPS, ETC.
The Musician's guide. 1st- ed.;
1954- New York, Music Information
Service. 54-14954
ML13 .M505 MRR Alc Latest edition

MUSIC--TERMINOLOGY.
Barach, Stephanie. An introduction
to the language of music.
Washington, E. B. Luce [1962] 120 p.
781.23 62-10216
ML108 .B25 MRR Alc.

Grant, Parks. Handbook of music
terms. Metuchen, N.J., Scarecrow
Press, 1967. 476 p. 781.2/3 67-
10187
ML108.G844 H3 MRR Alc.

Kaufmann, Helen (Loeb). The
listener's dictionary of musical
terms. New York, Grossett & Dunlap
[1960] 277 p. 780.3 60-51521
ML108 .K35 1960 MRR Alc.

Sacher, Jack, ed. Music A to Z. New
York, Grosset & Dunlap [c1863] viii,
432 p. 64-1733
ML100 .S82 1963 MRR Alc.

Smith, William James, A dictionary
of musical terms in four languages.
London, Hutchinson [1961] 195 p.
61-65086
ML108 .S64D5 MRR Alc.

MUSIC--THEMATIC CATALOGS.
Fuld, James J., The book of world-
famous music. New York, Crown
Publishers [1966] xi, 564 p.
016.78 65-24332
ML113 .F8 MRR Alc.

MUSIC--AFRICA, SUB-SAHARAN--
BIBLIOGRAPHY.
International African Institute. A
select bibliography of music in
Africa. London, 1965. 83 p. 66-
36908
ML120.A35 I6 MRR Alc.

MUSIC--FRANCE--BIO-BIBLIOGRAPHY.
Dictionnaire des musiciens français.
[Paris, Seghers, 1961] 379 p. 62-
44375
ML106.F8 D5 MRR Alc.

MUSIC--SWEDEN--BIBLIOGRAPHY.
Svensk bokkatalog. 1866/75-
Stockholm, Tidningsaktiebolaget
Svensk Bokhandel [etc.] 015.485 01-
10261
Z2621 .S95 MRR Alc Partial set

MUSIC--UNITED STATES--BIBLIOGRAPHY.
Sonneck, Oscar George Theodore, A
bibliography of early secular
American music 18th century. New
York, Da Capo Press, 1964. x, xvi,
616 p. 781.97 64-18992
ML120.U5 S6 1964 MRR Alc.

Wolfe, Richard J. Secular music in
America, 1801-1825; [1st ed.] New
York, The New York Public Library,
1964. 3 v. 781.97 64-25006
ML120.U5 W57 MRR Alc.

MUSIC--UNITED STATES--BIO-BIBLIOGRAPHY.
American Society of Composers,
Authors and Publishers. The ASCAP
biographical dictionary of composers,
authors and publishers. [3d ed.]
New York, 1966. 845 p. 780.922 66-
20214
ML106.U3 A5 1966 MRR Biog.

Historical Records Survey. District
of Columbia. Bio-bibliographical
index of musicians in the United
States of America since colonial
times. 2d ed. Washington, Music
Section, Pan American Union, 1956.
xxiii, 439 p. 016.78071 pa 57-4
ML106.U3 H6 1956 MRR Biog.

MUSIC--UNITED STATES--DIRECTORIES.
The Musician's guide. 1st- ed.;
1954- New York, Music Information
Service. 54-14954
ML13 .M505 MRR Alc Latest edition

MUSIC--UNITED STATES--HISTORY AND
CRITICISM.
Chase, Gilbert, America's music,
New York, McGraw-Hill [1955] xxiii,
733 p. 780.973 54-9707
ML200 .C5 MRR Alc.

Mattfeld, Julius, Variety music
cavalcade 1620-1961. Rev. ed.
Englewood Cliffs, N.J., Prentice-Hall
[1962] xxiii, 713 p. 781.97 62-
16317
ML128.V7 M4 1962 MRR Alc.

MUSIC, AFRICAN--BIBLIOGRAPHY.
United States. Library of Congress.
Music Division. African music.
Washington, 1964. xxvi, 55 p. 64-
60046
Z663.37 .A75 MRR Alc.

MUSIC, AMERICAN
Mather, Frank Jewett, The American
spirit in art, New Haven, Yale
university press; [etc., etc.] 1927.
3 p. l., 354 p. 27-5701
E178.5 .P2 vol. 12 MRR Alc.

MUSIC, AMERICAN--HISTORY AND CRITICISM.
Howard, John Tasker, Our
contemporary composers; New York,
Thomas Y. Crowell company, 1941. xv,
447 p. 780.973 41-6762
ML390 .H8 MRR Biog.

MUSIC, CHINESE--BIBLIOGRAPHY.
United States. Library of Congress.
Orientalia Division. Books on East
Asiatic music in the Library of
Congress printed before 1800.
[Washington, U.S. Govt. Print. Off.,
1945] 121-133 p. 016.78175 49-
53367
Z663.37 .B6 MRR Alc.

MUSIC, ELECTRONIC
see Electronic music

MUSIC, ENGLISH.
Chappell, William, Old English
popular music. A new ed., New York,
J. Brussel [c1961] 2 v. in 1.
784.3 62-3231
M1740 .C52 1961 MRR Alc.

MUSIC, GERMAN.
Bithell, Jethro, ed. Germany, a
companion to German studies. [5th
ed., rev., enl.] London, Methuen
[1955] xii, 578 p. 914.3 55-3335

DD61 .B56 1955 MRR Alc.

MUSIC, GREEK AND ROMAN.
Wellesz, Egon, ed. Ancient and
oriental music. London, New York,
Oxford University Press, 1957.
xxiii, 530 p. 781.8 780.93* 57-
4332
ML160 .N44 vol.1 MRR Alc.

MUSIC, ISLAMIC.
Wellesz, Egon, ed. Ancient and
oriental music. London, New York,
Oxford University Press, 1957.
xxiii, 530 p. 781.8 780.93* 57-
4332
ML160 .N44 vol.1 MRR Alc.

MUSIC, JAPANESE--BIBLIOGRAPHY.
United States. Library of Congress.
Orientalia Division. Books on East
Asiatic music in the Library of
Congress printed before 1800.
[Washington, U.S. Govt. Print. Off.,
1945] 121-133 p. 016.78175 49-
53367
Z663.37 .B6 MRR Alc.

MUSIC, NEGRO
see Negro music

MUSIC, ORIENTAL.
Wellesz, Egon, ed. Ancient and
oriental music. London, New York,
Oxford University Press, 1957.
xxiii, 530 p. 781.8 780.93* 57-
4332
ML160 .N44 vol.1 MRR Alc.

MUSIC, POPULAR (SONGS, ETC.)
see also Rock music

Alphabeat: who's who in pop. London,
Century 21 Publishing Ltd., 1969.
[126] p. (chiefly ports. (some col.)
[12/6] 780/.922 70-484370
ML105 .A44 MRR Biog.

MUSIC, POPULAR (SONGS, ETC.)--
BIBLIOGRAPHY.
Fuld, James J., The book of world-
famous music. New York, Crown
Publishers [1966] xi, 564 p.
016.78 65-24332
ML113 .F8 MRR Alc.

MUSIC, POPULAR (SONGS, ETC.)--
DICTIONARIES.
Roxon, Lillian. Rock encyclopedia.
New York, Grosset & Dunlap [1971]
611 p. [$3.95] 784 76-26545
ML102.P66 R7 1971 MRR Alc.

Stambler, Irwin. Encyclopedia of
popular music. New York, St.
Martin's Press [1965] xiii, 350 p.
780.3 65-20817
ML102.J3 S8 MRR Alc.

MUSIC, POPULAR (SONGS, ETC.)--
DISCOGRAPHY.
Burton, Jack, The blue book of Tin
Pan Alley. [Expanded new ed.]
Watkins Glen, N.Y., Century House
[1962-65] 2 v. 784 62-16426
ML390 .B963 MRR Alc.

Propes, Steve. Those oldies but
goodies; New York, Macmillan Co.
[1973] viii, 192 p. [$5.95]
789.9/12 72-93630
ML156.4.P6 P76 MRR Alc.

Rust, Brian A. L., The complete
entertainment discography, from the
mid-1890s to 1942 New Rochelle,
N.Y., Arlington House [1973] 677 p.
[$12.95] 016.7899/12 73-13239
ML156.4.P6 R88 MRR Alc.

Stambler, Irwin. Encyclopedia of
popular music. New York, St.
Martin's Press [1965] xiii, 350 p.
780.3 65-20817
ML102.J3 S8 MRR Alc.

Whitburn, Joel. Joel Whitburn's top
LP's, 1945-1972. Menomonee Falls,
Wis. Record Research, c1973. 224
p. 789.9/131 74-75179
ML156.4.P6 W494 MRR Alc.

Whitburn, Joel. Top rhythm & blues
records, 1949-1971. Menomonee Falls,
Wis., Record Research, c1973. 184 p.
016.7899/12 73-78333
ML156.4.P6 W53 MRR Alc.

MUSIC, POPULAR (SONGS, ETC.)--WRITING
AND PUBLISHING.
Holotcener, Lawrence. A practical
dictionary of rhymes. New York,
Crown Publishers [1960] 211 p.
426/03 59-14023
PE1519 .H6 MRR Alc.

MUSIC, POPULAR (SONGS, ETC.)--UNITED
STATES.
see also Blues (Songs, etc.)

MUSIC, POPULAR (SONGS, ETC.)--UNITED
STATES--BIBLIOGRAPHY.
Burton, Jack, The blue book of Tin
Pan Alley. [Expanded new ed.]
Watkins Glen, N.Y., Century House
[1962-65] 2 v. 784 62-16426
ML390 .B963 MRR Alc.

Chipman, John H., comp. Index to top-
hit tunes, 1900-1950. Boston, B.
Humphries [1962] 249 p. 016.784
61-11711
ML128.V7 C54 MRR Alc.

MUSIC, POPULAR (SONGS, ETC.)-- (Cont.)
Ewen, David, ed. American popular
songs from the Revolutionary War to
the present. New York, Random House
[1966] xiii, 507 p. 016.784 66-
12843
    ML128.N3 E8 MRR Alc.

Shapiro, Nat, ed. Popular music;
[1st ed. New York] Adrian Press
[1964]- v.   64-23761
    ML120.U5 S5 MRR Alc.

Stecheson, Anthony, comp. The
Stecheson classified song directory,
Hollywood, Calif., Music Industry
Press [1961] ix, 503 p.   016.784
62-753
    ML128.V7 S83 MRR Alc.

MUSIC, POPULAR (SONGS, ETC.)--UNITED
STATES--DIRECTORIES.
Official talent & booking directory.
1st- ed. 1970- Culver City, Cal.,
Specialty Publications, Inc.
780/.25/73 78-116585
    ML18 .O3 MRR Alc Latest edition

MUSIC, POPULAR (SONGS, ETC.)--UNITED
STATES--HISTORY AND CRITICISM.
Burton, Jack. The blue book of Tin
Pan Alley. [Expanded new ed.]
Watkins Glen, N.Y., Century House
[1962-65] 2 v.   784 62-16426
    ML390 .B963 MRR Alc.

Ewen, David, Great men of American
popular song; Englewood Cliffs,
N.J., Prentice-Hall [1970] x, 387 p.
[12.95]   784/.0922 79-110079
    ML3551 .E83 MRR Alc.

Mattfeld, Julius, Variety music
cavalcade 1620-1961. Rev. ed.
Englewood Cliffs, N.J., Prentice-Hall
[1962] xxiii, 713 p.   781.97 62-
16317
    ML128.V7 M4 1962 MRR Alc.

MUSIC, PRIMITIVE.
see also Ethnomusicology

Kunst, Jaap, Some sociological
aspects of music, Washington, 1958.
iii, 25 p.   780.07 58-60094
    Z663.37 .A5 1956a MRR Alc.

Wellesz, Egon, ed. Ancient and
oriental music. London, New York,
Oxford University Press, 1957.
xxiii, 530 p.   781.8 780.93* 57-
4332
    ML160 .N44 vol.1 MRR Alc.

MUSIC, RELIGIOUS
see Church music

MUSIC, SPANISH.
Peers, Edgar Allison, ed. Spain;
5th ed., rev. and enl. London,
Methuen [1956] xii, 319 p.   914.6
56-58806
    DP66 .P4 1956 MRR Alc.

MUSIC, THEATRICAL
see Opera

MUSIC AND LITERATURE.
Davison, Archibald Thompson, Words
and music. Washington [U.S. Govt.
Print. Off.] 1954. 24 p.   784 54-
60019
    Z663.37 .A5 1954 MRR Alc.

Hunger, Herbert, Lexikon der
griechischen und römischen
Mythologie. 6., erw. erg. Aufl.
Wien, Hollinek (1969). xii p., 64 p.
of illus. 444 p. [260.00] 76-
495586
    BL303 .H8 1869 MRR Alc.

MUSIC AND SOCIETY.
Kunst, Jaap, Some sociological
aspects of music, Washington, 1958.
iii, 25 p.   780.07 58-60094
    Z663.37 .A5 1956a MRR Alc.

MUSIC FESTIVALS.
The Musician's guide. 1st- ed.;
1954- New York, Music Information
Service. 54-14954
    ML13 .M505 MRR Alc Latest edition

MUSIC-HALLS--DIRECTORIES.
Stubs. Metropolitan New York
edition. [New York, M. Schattner,
etc.] 782./0295/7472 46-22521
Began publication in 1942.
    PN2277.N5 S8 MRR Alc Latest
    edition

MUSIC TRADE--UNITED STATES--DIRECTORIES.
The Musician's guide. 1st- ed.;
1954- New York, Music Information
Service. 54-14954
    ML13 .M505 MRR Alc Latest edition

Official talent & booking directory.
1st- ed. 1970- Culver City, Cal.,
Specialty Publications, Inc.
780/.25/73 78-116585
    ML18 .O3 MRR Alc Latest edition

The Purchaser's guide to the music
industries. 1897- New York, Music
Trades Corp. [etc.] 99-2406
    ML18 .P9 MRR Alc Latest edition

MUSICAL INSTRUMENTS.
Palestrant, Simon S., Practical
pictorial guide to mechanisms and
machines. New York, University Books
[1956] 256 p.   621.03 56-13016
    TJ9 .P3 1956 MRR Alc.

MUSICAL INSTRUMENTS--DICTIONARIES.
Marcuse, Sibyl. Musical instruments;
[1st ed.] Garden City, N.Y.,
Doubleday, 1964. xiv, 608 p.
781.9103 64-19290
    ML102.I5 M37 MRR Alc.

MUSICAL INSTRUMENTS--MAKERS.
The Purchaser's guide to the music
industries. 1897- New York, Music
Trades Corp. [etc.] 99-2406
    ML18 .P9 MRR Alc Latest edition

MUSICAL INSTRUMENTS, AFRICAN--
BIBLIOGRAPHY.
International African Institute. A
select bibliography of music in
Africa, London, 1965. 83 p. 66-
36908
    ML120.A35 I6 MRR Alc.

MUSICAL INSTRUMENTS, PRIMITIVE.
Kunst, Jaap, Some sociological
aspects of music, Washington, 1958.
iii, 25 p.   780.07 58-60094
    Z663.37 .A5 1956a MRR Alc.

MUSICAL NOTATION.
Scholes, Percy Alfred, The concise
Oxford dictionary of music, 2d ed.,
London, New York, Oxford University
Press, 1964. xxx, 636 p.   780.3 64-
5946
    ML100 .S367 1964 MRR Alc.

Scholes, Percy Alfred, The Oxford
companion to music, 9th ed.,
completely rev. and reset London,
New York, Oxford University Press,
1955. lx, 1195 p.   780.3 55-14499

    ML100 .S37 1955 MRR Alc.

MUSICAL REVUE, COMEDY, ETC.--
DICTIONARIES.
Sharp, Harold S., comp. Index to
characters in the performing arts,
New York, Scarecrow Press, 1966-73.
4 v. in 6.   808.8292703 66-13744
    PN1579 .S45 MRR Alc.

MUSICAL REVUE, COMEDY, ETC.--UNITED
STATES.
Ewen, David, New complete book of
the American musical theater. [1st
ed.] New York, Holt, Rinehart, and
Winston [1970] xxv, 800 p. [$15.00]
782.8/1/0973 70-117257
    ML1711 .E9 1970 MRR Alc.

Green, Stanley. The world of musical
comedy; New York, Ziff-Davis Pub.
Co. [1960] xvi, 391 p.   782.810973
60-10522
    ML1711 .G74 MRR Alc.

MUSICAL REVUE, COMEDY, ETC.--UNITED
STATES--HISTORY AND CRITICISM--
BIBLIOGRAPHY.
Salem, James M. A guide to critical
reviews. New York, Scarecrow Press,
1966- v.   [$4.50 (v. 1) varies]
016.8092 66-13733
    Z5782 .S34 MRR Ref Desk.

MUSICAL REVUES, COMEDIES, ETC.--
STORIES, PLOTS, ETC.
Ewen, David, New complete book of
the American musical theater. [1st
ed.] New York, Holt, Rinehart, and
Winston [1970] xxv, 800 p. [$15.00]
782.8/1/0973 70-117257
    ML1711 .E9 1970 MRR Alc.

Stambler, Irwin. Encyclopedia of
popular music. New York, St.
Martin's Press [1965] xiii, 350 p.
780.3 65-20817
    ML102.J3 S8 MRR Alc.

MUSICAL REVUES, COMEDIES, ETC--UNITED
STATES--BIBLIOGRAPHY.
Mattfeld, Julius, Variety music
cavalcade 1620-1961. Rev. ed.
Englewood Cliffs, N.J., Prentice-Hall
[1962] xxiii, 713 p.   781.97 62-
16317
    ML128.V7 M4 1962 MRR Alc.

MUSICAL SOCIETIES--UNITED STATES--
DIRECTORIES.
The National directory for the
performing arts and civic centers.
Dallas, Handel & Co. 790.2/0973 73-
646635
    PN2289 .N38 MRR Alc Latest edition

MUSICIANS.
see also Jazz musicians

MUSICIANS--BIO-BIBLIOGRAPHY.
Alphabeat: who's who in pop. London,
Century 21 Publishing Ltd., 1969.
[126] p. (chiefly ports. (some col.)
[12/6]   780/.922 70-484370
    ML105 .A44 MRR Biog.

MUSICIANS--BIOGRAPHY.
Cooper, Martin, ed. The concise
encyclopedia of music and musicians.
1st ed.] New York, Hawthorn Books
[1958] 516 p.   780.3 58-5630
    ML100 .C78 MRR Alc.

Grove, George, Sir, ed. Dictionary
of music and musicians. 5th ed.,
London, Macmillan; New York, St.
Martin's Press, 1954. 9 v.   780.3
54-11819
    ML100 .G885 1954 MRR Alc.

MUSICIANS--CORRESPONDENCE,
REMINISCENCES, ETC.
Spivacke, Harold, Paganiniana.
Washington [U.S. Govt. Print. Off.]
1945. 19 p.   927.8 45-36264
    Z663.375 .P3 MRR Alc.

MUSICIANS--DICTIONARIES.
Atlantic brief lives: a biographical
companion to the arts. [1st ed.]
Boston, Little, Brown [1971] xxii,
900 p. [$15.00]   700/.922 B 73-
154960
    NX90 .A73 1971 MRR Alc.

Baker, Theodore, Biographical
dictionary of musicians. 5th ed.,
completely rev. New York, G.
Schirmer [1958] xv, 1855 p.
780.922 58-4953
    ML105 .B16 1958 MRR Biog.

Cobbett, Walter Willson, ed.
Cobbett's cyclopedic survey of
chamber music, London, Oxford
university press, H. Milford, 1929-
30. 2 v.   29-14486
    ML1100 .C7 MRR Alc.

A dictionary of modern music and
musicians. London, Toronto, J. M.
Dent & sons, ltd.; New York, E. P.
Dutton & co., 1924. xvi, 543, [1] p.
25-2077
    ML100 .D5 MRR Alc.

Ewen, David, Great composers, 1300-
1900; New York, H. W. Wilson Co.,
1966. 429 p.   780.922 65-24585
    ML105 .E944 MRR Biog.

Koch, Willi August, Musisches
Lexikon: Künstler, Kunstwerke und
Motive aus Dichtung, Musik und
bildender Kunst, 2., veränderte und
ergeiterte Aufl. Stuttgart, A.,
Kröner [c1964] 1250 columns, xxxx
p. 65-68991
    N31 .K57 1964 MRR Alc.

Sainsbury, John S. A dictionary of
musicians from the earliest times,
New York, Da Capo Press, 1966. 2 v.
780.922 65-23396
    ML105 .S2 1825a MRR Biog.

Sandved, Kjell Bloch, ed. The world
of music; [1st American ed.] New
York, Abradale Press [1963] 4 v.
(1516 p.)   780.3 63-14095
    ML100 .S25 1963 MRR Alc.

MUSICIANS--PORTRAITS.
Cooper, Martin, ed. The concise
encyclopedia of music and musicians.
1st ed.] New York, Hawthorn Books
[1958] 516 p.   780.3 58-5630
    ML100 .C78 MRR Alc.

Keepnews, Orrin. A pictorial history
of jazz; New ed. rev. New York,
Crown Publishers [1966] 297 p.
781.570973 66-4300
    ML3561.J3 K4 1966 MRR Alc.

National Portrait Gallery,
Washington, D.C. Portraits of the
American stage, 1771-1971;
Washington, Smithsonian Institution
Press; [for sale by the Supt. of
Docs., U.S. Govt. Print. Off.] 1971.
203 p. [$4.50]   782/.0973 75-
170284
    PN1583.A2 N3 MRR Biog.

Scholes, Percy Alfred, The Oxford
companion to music, 9th ed.,
completely rev. and reset London,
New York, Oxford University Press,
1955. lx, 1195 p.   780.3 55-14499

    ML100 .S37 1955 MRR Alc.

Stambler, Irwin. Encyclopedia of
popular music. New York, St.
Martin's Press [1965] xiii, 350 p.
780.3 65-20817
    ML102.J3 S8 MR2 Alc.

MUSICIANS--UNITED STATES--DIRECTORIES.
Official talent & booking directory.
1st- ed. 1970- Culver City, Cal.,
Specialty Publications, Inc.
780/.25/73 78-116585
    ML18 .O3 MRR Alc Latest edition

MUSICIANS, AMERICAN.
American Society of Composers,
Authors and Publishers. The ASCAP
biographical dictionary of composers,
authors and publishers. [3d ed.]
New York, 1966. 845 p. 780.922 66-
20214
ML106.U3 A5 1966 MRR Biog.

Feather, Leonard G. The encyclopedia
of jazz in the sixties. New York,
Horizon Press [1966] 312 p.
785.420922 66-26705
ML105 .F35 MRR Alc.

Gentry, Linnell. A history and
encyclopedia of country, western, and
gospel music. 2d ed., completely
rev. [Nashville, Tenn., Clairmont
Corp., 1969] xiv, 598 p.
784.4/9/73 70-7208
ML200 .G4 1969 MRR Biog.

Historical Records Survey. District
of Columbia. Bio-bibliographical
index of musicians in the United
States of America since colonial
times. 2d ed. Washington, Music
Section, Pan American Union, 1956.
xxiii, 439 p. 016.78071 pa 57-4
ML106.U3 H6 1956 MRR Biog.

MUSICIANS, AMERICAN--BIOGRAPHY.
Ewen, David, New complete book of
the American musical theater. [1st
ed.] New York, Holt, Rinehart, and
Winston [1970] xxv, 800 p. [$15.00]
782.8/1/0973 70-117257
ML1711 .E9 1970 MRR Alc.

Metcalf, Frank Johnson, American
writers and compilers of sacred
music. New York, Cincinnati, The
Abingdon press [c1925] 373 p. 25-
18159
ML106.U3 M3 MRR Biog.

MUSICIANS, FRENCH--BIOGRAPHY.
Dictionnaire des musiciens français.
[Paris, Seghers, 1961] 379 p. 62-
44375
ML106.F8 D5 MRR Alc.

MUSICOLOGY.
see also Ethnomusicology

MUSICOLOGY--BIBLIOGRAPHY.
Joint Committee of the Music Teachers
National Association and the American
Musicological Society. Doctoral
dissertations in musicology. 4th ed.
Philadelphia, American Musicological
Society, 1965. 152 p. 016.78001
66-1684
ML128.M8 J6 1965 MRR Alc.

MUSLIM EMPIRE
see Islamic Empire

**MUSTIN, HENRY CROSKEY, 1874-1923--
MANUSCRIPTS.**
United States. Library of Congress.
Manuscript Division. Colby Mitchell
Chester, William Freeland Fullam,
Samuel McGowan, Henry Croskey Mustin:
a register of their papers in the
Library of Congress. Washington,
Library of Congress, 1973. iii, 4,
6, 7, 5 p. 016.359 73-2939
Z663.34 .C48 MRR Alc.

MUTUAL INSURANCE
see Insurance

MUTUAL SECURITY PROGRAM, 1951-
United States. Congress. House.
Committee on Foreign Affairs.
Collective defense treaties, with
maps, texts of treaties, a
chronology, status of forces
agreements, and comparative chart.
Rev.] Washington, U.S. Govt. Print.
Off., 1969. ix, 514 p. [2.50]
341.2 79-602271
JX171 .U39 1969 MRR Alc.

MYCENAEAN CIVILIZATION
see Civilization, Mycenaean

MYCOLOGY.
see also Medical mycology

MYCOLOGY--DICTIONARIES.
Snell, Walter Henry, A glossary of
mycology Cambridge, Harvard
University Press, 1957. xxxi, 171 p.
589.203 55-5063
QK603 .S53 MRR Alc.

MYSTICISM--BIBLIOGRAPHY.
Sharma, Umesh D. Mysticism: a select
bibliography, Waterloo, Ont.,
Waterloo Lutheran University, 1973.
109 p. 016.248/22 73-174548
Z7819 .S5 MRR Alc.

MYSTICISM--DICTIONARIES.
Gaynor, Frank, ed. Dictionary of
mysticism. New York, Philosophical
Library [1953] 208 p. 290.3 53-
13354
BL31 .G32 MRR Alc.

MYSTICISM--DICTIONARIES--FRENCH.
Dictionnaire de spiritualité
ascétique et mystique, Paris, G.
Beauchesne et ses fils, 1932- v.
282.03 38-24895
BX841 .D67 MRR Alc.

MYTHOLOGY.
see also Folk-lore

see also Heroes

see also Religion, Primitive

see also Symbolism in art

Bulfinch, Thomas, Mythology: The age
of fable; Garden City, N.Y.,
Doubleday, 1948. ix, 402 p. 290
48-2683
BL310 .B82 1948 MRR Alc.

Campbell, Joseph, The masks of God.
New York, Viking Press, 1959-[68] 4
v. 291/.13 59-8354
BL311 .C27 MRR Alc.

Frazer, James George, Sir,
Aftermath; London, Macmillan and
co., limited, 1936. xx, 494 p. 291
37-2300
BL310 .F715 1936 MRR Alc.

[Frazer, James George Sir,] The
golden bough; 3d ed. [New York, The
Macmillan company, 1935] 12 v. 291
35-35398
BL310 .F7 1935 MRR Alc.

Grimal, Pierre, ed. Larousse world
mythology. London, P. Hamlyn [1965]
560 p. 66-36182
BL311 .G683 1965a MRR Alc.

Jobes, Gertrude. Outer space: New
York, Scarecrow Press, 1964. 479 p.
291.212 64-11783
BL438 .J6 MRR Alc.

Larousse encyclopedia of mythology.
London, Batchworth Press [1959]
viii, 500 p. 59-4844
BL310 .L453 1959 MRR Alc.

The Mythology of all races, Boston,
Marshall Jones company, 1916-32. 13
v. 17-26477
BL25 .M8 MRR Alc.

New Larousse encyclopedia of
mythology. New ed. New York] Putnam
[1968, c1959] xi, 500 p. [17.95]
200.4/03 68-57758
BL311 .N43 1968 MRR Alc.

Waters, Clara (Erskine) Clement, A
handbook of legendary and
mythological art. [14th impression]
Boston, New York, Houghton, Mifflin
and company [189-?] xii, 575 p. 04-
11646
N7760 .W33 MRR Alc.

MYTHOLOGY--BIBLIOGRAPHY.
Diehl, Katharine Smith. Religions,
mythologies, folklores: an annotated
bibliography. 2d ed. New York,
Scarecrow Press, 1962. 573 p.
016.2 62-16003
Z7751 .D54 1962 MRR Alc.

MYTHOLOGY--DICTIONARIES.
Aken, Andreas Rudolphus Antonius van.
The encyclopedia of classical
mythology Englewood Cliffs, N.J.,
Prentice Hall [1965] 155 p. 292.03
64-23566
BL715 .A413 MRR Alc.

Bonnerjea, Biren. A dictionary of
superstitions and mythology. London,
Folk Press, Detroit, Singing Tree
Press, 1969. 314 p. 291/.13/03 69-
17755
BL303 .B6 1969 MRR Alc.

Bray, Frank Chapin, The world of
myths; New York, Thomas Y. Crowell
company [c1935] x, 323 p. 290.3
35-24306
BL303 .B67 MRR Alc.

Edwardes, Marian. A dictionary of
non-classical mythology, London, J.
M. Dent & sons, ltd.; New York, E. P.
Dutton & co. [1912] xii, 214 p., 1
l. incl. front., plates. 290.3 13-
8773
BL303 .E25 MRR Alc.

Evans, Bergen, Dictionary of
mythology, mainly classical. Lincoln
[Neb.] Centennial Press [1970]
xviii, 293 p. [$6.95] 398 70-
120115
BL303 .E9 MRR Alc.

Funk & Wagnalls standard dictionary
of folklore, mythology and legend.
New York, Funk & Wagnalls Co., 1949-
[50] 2 v. 398.03 49-48675
GR35 .F8 MRR Alc.

Jobes, Gertrude. Dictionary of
mythology, folklore and symbols. New
York, Scarecrow Press, 1961. 2 v.
(1759 p.] 398.03 61-860
GR35 .J6 MRR Alc.

Parrinder, Edward Geoffrey. A
dictionary of non-Christian
religions, Philadelphia, Westminster
Press [1973, c1971] 320 p. 290/.3
73-4781
BL31 .P36 1973 MRR Alc.

Sykes, Egerton. Everyman's
dictionary of non-classical
mythology. London, Dent; New York,
Dutton [1952] xviii, 262 p. 290.3
52-3946
BL303 .S9 MRR Alc.

Thomas, Joseph, Universal
pronouncing dictionary of biography
and mythology. 5th ed.
Philadelphia, London, J. B.
Lippincott company [c1930] 2 p. l.,
iii-xi, [1] p., 1 l., 5-2550 p.
920.01 30-22946
CT103 .L7 1930 MRR Biog.

Tripp, Edward. Crowell's handbook of
classical mythology. New York,
Crowell [1970] ix, 631 p. [$10.00]
398 74-127614
BL303 .T75 1970 MRR Alc.

Zimmerman, John Edward, Dictionary
of classical mythology. [1st ed.]
New York, Harper & Row [1964] xx,
300 p. 292.03 63-20319
BL715 .Z5 MRR Alc.

MYTHOLOGY--DICTIONARIES--ENGLISH.
Whittlesey, Eunice S. Symbols and
legends in Western art; New York,
Scribner [1972] ix, 367 p. [$7.95]
704.94 71-162764
N7740 .W53 MRR Alc.

MYTHOLOGY--DICTIONARIES--FRENCH.
Grimal, Pierre, Dictionnaire de la
mythologie grecque et romaine. 4e
édition revue. Paris, Presses
universitaires de France, 1969.
xxxii, 580 p. [50.00] 77-489526
BL715 .G7 1969 MRR Alc.

MYTHOLOGY--DICTIONARIES--GERMAN.
Hunger, Herbert, Lexikon der
griechischen und römischen
Mythologie. 6. erw. erg. Aufl.
Wien, Hollinek (1969). xii p., 64 p.
of illus., 444 p. [260.00] 76-
495596
BL303 .H8 1969 MRR Alc.

MYTHOLOGY--INDEXES.
Eastman, Mary Huse, Index to fairy
tales, myths, and legends. 2d ed.,
rev. and enl. Boston, F. W. Faxon
Co., 1926. ix, 610 p. 016.398 26-
11491
Z5983.F17 E2 1926 MRR Alc.

Ireland, Norma (Olin) Index to fairy
tales, 1949-1972; Westwood, Mass.,
F. W. Faxon Co., 1973. xxxviii, 741
p. 398.2/01/6 73-173454
Z5983.F17 I73 MRR Alc.

MYTHOLOGY, AFRICAN.
Ananikian, Mardiros Harootioon,
Armenian [mythology] Boston,
Archaeological institute of America,
Marshall Jones company, 1925. viii,
448 p. 299.154 25-19195
BL25 .M8 vol. 7 MRR Alc.

MYTHOLOGY, ARMENIAN.
Ananikian, Mardiros Harootioon,
Armenian [mythology] Boston,
Archaeological institute of America,
Marshall Jones company, 1925. viii,
448 p. 299.154 25-19195
BL25 .M8 vol. 7 MRR Alc.

MYTHOLOGY, ARYAN.
Keith, Arthur Berriedale, Indian
[mythology] Boston, Marshall Jones
company, 1917. ix, 404 p. 17-6787

BL25 .M8 vol. 6 MRR Alc.

MYTHOLOGY, BALTIC.
Macculloch, John Arnott, Celtic
[mythology] Boston, Marshall Jones
company 1918. x, 398 p. 299.16
18-14207
BL25 .M8 vol. 3 MRR Alc.

MYTHOLOGY, CELTIC.
Macculloch, John Arnott, Celtic
[mythology] Boston, Marshall Jones
company, 1918. x, 398 p. 299.16
18-14207
BL25 .M8 vol. 3 MRR Alc.

MYTHOLOGY, CHINESE.
Ferguson, John Calvin, Chinese
[mythology] Boston, Archaeological
institute of America, Marshall Jones
company 1938. xii, 416 p. 299.51
28-14539
BL25 .M8 vol. 8 MRR Alc.

MYTHOLOGY, CHINESE--DICTIONARIES.
Werner, Edward Theodore Chalmers, A
dictionary of Chinese mythology. New
York, Julian Press, 1961. xxiii, 627
p.   398.3 61-17239
   BL1801 .W35 1961 MRR Alc.

MYTHOLOGY, CLASSICAL.
Fox, William Sherwood, Greek and
Roman [mythology] Boston, Marshall
Jones company, 1916. lxii, 354 p.
16-15868
   BL25 .M8 vol. 1 MRR Alc.

MYTHOLOGY, CLASSICAL--DICTIONARIES.
Grant, Michael, Who's who in
classical mythology London,
Weidenfeld & Nicolson [1973]   447 p.
[£5.00]   292/.2/1103 73-177715
   BL715 .G68 MRR Alc.

The New Century classical handbook.
New York, Appleton-Century-Crofts
[1962] xiii, 1162 p.   913.3/8/003
62-10069
   DE5 .N4 MRR Alc.

Radice, Betty. Who's who in the
ancient world: Revised [ed.]
Harmondsworth, Penguin, 1973. 336,
[32] p. [£0.60] 920/.038 74-
161490
   DE7 .R33 1973 MRR Alc.

MYTHOLOGY, CLASSICAL, IN ART.
Mayerson, Philip. Classical
mythology in literature, art, and
music. Waltham, Mass., Xerox College
Pub. [1971] xv, 509 p.   700 77-
138393
   NX650.M9 M38 MRR Alc.

MYTHOLOGY, EGYPTIAN.
Müller, Wilhelm Max, Egyptian
[mythology] Boston, Marshall Jones
company, 1918. xiv p., 2 l., [3]-450
p. 18-8775
   BL25 .M8 vol. 12 MRR Alc.

MYTHOLOGY, FINNO-UGRIAN.
Harva, Uno, Finno-Ugric, Siberian
[mythology] Boston, Archaeological
institute of America, Marshall Jones
company, 1927. xxv, [3] 387 p.
291.1435 27-26450
   BL25 .M8 vol. 4 MRR Alc.

MYTHOLOGY, GREEK.
Apollodorus, of Athens. Apollodorus,
The library, London, W. Heinemann;
New York, G. P. Putnam's sons, 1921.
2 v. 21-15885
   PA3612 .A5 1921 MRR Alc.

Fontenrose, Joseph Eddy, Python; a
study of Delphic myth and its
origins. Berkeley, University of
California Press, 1959. xviii, 616
p. 398.4 59-5144
   GR830.D7 F6 MRR Alc.

Grant, Michael, Who's who in
classical mythology London,
Weidenfeld & Nicolson [1973]   447 p.
[£5.00]   292/.2/1103 73-177715
   BL715 .G68 MRR Alc.

Pfister, Friedrich, Greek gods and
heroes. London, Macgibbon & Kee,
1961. 272 p.   292 61-65881
   BL782 .P453 MRR Alc.

Rose, Herbert Jennings, A handbook
of Greek mythology, [6th ed.]
London, Methuen [1958] ix, 363 p.
292 58-1932
   BL781 .R65 1958 MRR Alc.

MYTHOLOGY, HINDU.
Keith, Arthur Berriedale, Indian
[mythology] Boston, Marshall Jones
company, 1917. ix, 404 p.   17-6787
   BL25 .M8 vol. 6 MRR Alc.

MYTHOLOGY, INDO-CHINESE.
Müller, Wilhelm Max, Egyptian
[mythology] Boston, Marshall Jones
company, 1918. xiv p., 2 l., [3]-450
p. 18-8775
   BL25 .M8 vol. 12 MRR Alc.

MYTHOLOGY, JAPANESE.
Ferguson, John Calvin, Chinese
[mythology] Boston, Archaeological
institute of America, Marshall Jones
company, 1938. xii, 416 p.   299.51
28-14539
   BL25 .M8 vol. 8 MRR Alc.

MYTHOLOGY, NORSE.
Macculloch, John Arnott, Eddic
[mythology] Boston, Archaeological
institute of America, Marshall Jones
company 1930. x p., 2 l., [3]-400
p. 293 30-9990
   BL25 .M8 vol. 2 MRR Alc.

MYTHOLOGY, OCEANIAN.
Dixon, Roland Burrage, Oceanic
[mythology] Boston, Marshall Jones
company, 1916. xv, 364 p.   16-22069

   BL25 .M8 vol. 9 MRR Alc.

MYTHOLOGY, ROMAN.
Grant, Michael, Who's who in
classical mythology London,
Weidenfeld & Nicolson [1973] 447 p.
[£5.00]   292/.2/1103 73-177715
   BL715 .G68 MRR Alc.

Rose, Herbert Jennings, A handbook
of Greek mythology, [6th ed.]
London, Methuen [1958] ix, 363 p.
292 58-1932
   BL781 .R65 1958 MRR Alc.

MYTHOLOGY, SEMITIC.
Langdon, Stephen Herbert, Semitic
[Mythology] Boston, Archaeological
institute of America, Marshall Jones
company, 1931. xx p., 1 l., 454 p.
299.2 31-25060
   BL25 .M8 vol. 5 MRR Alc.

MYTHOLOGY, SIBERIAN.
Harva, Uno, Finno-Ugric, Siberian
[mythology] Boston, Archaeological
institute of America, Marshall Jones
company 1927. xxv, [3] 387 p.
291.1435 27-26450
   BL25 .M8 vol. 4 MRR Alc.

MYTHOLOGY, SLAVIC.
Macculloch, John Arnott, Celtic
[mythology] Boston, Marshall Jones
company, 1918. x, 398 p.   299.16
18-14207
   BL25 .M8 vol. 3 MRR Alc.

MYTHOLOGY IN LITERATURE.
Hunger, Herbert, Lexikon der
griechischen und römischen
Mythologie. 6. erw. erg. Aufl.
Wien, Hollinek [1969]. xii p., 64 p.
of illus., 444 p. [260.00]   76-
485596
   BL303 .H8 1969 MRR Alc.

Mayerson, Philip. Classical
mythology in literature, art, and
music, Waltham, Mass., Xerox College
Pub. [1971] xv, 509 p.   700 77-
138393
   NX650.M9 M38 MRR Alc.

NAMES.
Blumberg, Dorothy Rose. Whose what?
[1st ed.] New York, Holt, Rinehart
and Winston [1969] 184 p. [3.95]
031/.02 68-12199
   AG105 .B72 MRR Alc.

The Century dictionary and
cyclopedia, [Rev. and enl. ed.] New
York, The Century co. [c1911] 12 v.
[$75.00]   11-31934
   PE1625 .C4 1911 MRR Alc.

Latham, Edward. A dictionary of
names, nicknames, and surnames of
persons, places and things. Detroit,
Republished by Gale Research Co.,
1966. vii, 334 p.   031.02 66-22674

   AG5 .L35 1966 MRR Alc.

NAMES--DICTIONARIES.
Brewer, Ebenezer Cobham, Brewer's
dictionary of phrase and fable.
Centenary ed. (completely revised);
London, Cassell, 1970. xvi, 1175 p.,
plate. [60/-]   803 73-529591
   PN43 .B65 1970 MRR Ref Desk.

Brewer, Ebenezer Cobham, The
reader's handbook of famous names in
fiction, A new ed., rev. throughout
and greatly enl. Detroit,
Republished by Gale Research Co.,
1966.   2 v. (viii, 1243 p.)   803 71-
134907
   PN43 .B7 1965 MRR Alc.

Funk, Charles Earle, What's the
name, please? New York, London, Funk
& Wagnalls company, 1936. x, 11-176
p.   421.5 929.4 36-27288
   PE1660 .F8 MRR Alc.

Jobes, Gertrude. Dictionary of
mythology, folklore and symbols. New
York, Scarecrow Press, 1961. 2 v.
(1759 p.)   398.03 61-860
   GR35 .J6 MRR Alc.

Johnson, Charles Benjamin, The
Harrap book of boys' and girls'
names, London, Harrap, 1973. xiii,
273 p. [£2.40] 929.4 74-159444
   CS2375.G7 J63 1973 MRR Ref Desk.

Mackey, Mary Stuart. The
pronunciation of 10,000 proper names,
New ed., New York, Dodd, Mead and
company, 1922. xiii, 329 p.   22-
22423
   PE1137 .M5 1922 MRR Alc.

Mawson, Christopher Orlando
Sylvester, International book of
names; New York, Thomas Y. Crowell
company [1942] xliv, 337 p.   423
929.4 42-18501
   PE1660 .M3 1942 MRR Alc.

The New Century cyclopedia of names,
New York, Appleton-Century-Crofts
[1954] 3 v. (xxviii, 4342 p.)
929.4 52-13879
   PE1625 .C43 1954 MRR Ref Desk.

Payton, Geoffrey. Payton's proper
names. London, New York, F. Warne,
1969. vii, 502 p. [45/-]   032 69-
20109
   PE1660 .P3 MRR Alc.

Payton, Geoffrey. Webster's
dictionary of proper names.
Springfield, Mass., G. & C. Merriam
Co. [c1970] 752 p.   423.1 72-22048
   PE1660 .P34 MRR Ref Desk.

Rodale, Jerome Irving, The phrase
finder; Emmaus, Pa., Rodale Press
[c1953] 1325 p.   423 54-2348
   PE1689 .R63 MRR Alc.

Toynbee, Paget Jackson, A dictionary
of proper names and notable matters
in the works of Dante. [New ed.]
Oxford, Clarendon P., 1968 xxv, 722
p. [5/15/6] 851/.1 68-81646
   PQ4333 .T7 1968 MRR Alc.

Wheeler, William Adolphus, An
explanatory and pronouncing
dictionary of the noted names of
fiction, Detroit, Gale Research Co.,
1966. xxxii, 440 p.   803 66-25811

   PN43 .W4 1966 MRR Alc.

NAMES--ETYMOLOGY.
Arthur, William, An etymological
dictionary of family and Christian
names; Detroit, Gale Research Co.,
1969. iv, 300 p.   929.4 68-17911
   CS2309 .A7 1969 MRR Alc.

Notes and queries; v. 1- Nov. 3,
1849- London [etc.] Oxford Univ.
Press [etc.] 12-25307
   AG305 .N7 MRR Alc Full set

NAMES--PRONUNCIATION.
British Broadcasting Corporation.
BBC pronouncing dictionary of British
names: London, Oxford University
Press, 1971. xxii, 171 p. [£2.00]
421/.55 74-575346
   PE1660 .B7 MRR Alc.

Greet, William Cabell, World words;
2d ed., rev. and enl. New York,
Columbia Univ. Press, 1948. liii,
608 p.   411.5 48-6140
   PE1660 .G7 1948 MRR Alc.

Mawson, Christopher Orlando
Sylvester, International book of
names; New York, Thomas Y. Crowell
company [1942] xliv, 337 p.   423
929.4 42-18501
   PE1660 .M3 1942 MRR Alc.

[Press association, inc.] PA
pronouncer. [New York, Press
association, inc., c1941] 2 p. l.,
58 p.   421.5 41-27547
   PE1660 .P7 MRR Alc.

NAMES--GREAT BRITAIN--DICTIONARIES.
British Broadcasting Corporation.
BBC pronouncing dictionary of British
names: London, Oxford University
Press, 1971. xxii, 171 p. [£2.00]
421/.55 74-575346
   PE1660 .B7 MRR Alc.

NAMES--UNITED STATES.
Emrich, Duncan, Folklore on the
American land. [1st ed.] Boston,
Little, Brown [1972] xxviii, 707 p.
[$15.00]   398/.0973 72-161865
   GR105 .E47 MRR Alc.

Mencken, Henry Louis, The American
language; [1st abridged ed.] New
York, Knopf, 1963. xxv, 777, cxxiv
p. 427.973 63-13628
   PE2808 .M43 MRR Alc.

Mencken, Henry Louis, The American
language; New York, A, A. Knopf,
1936. xi, 769, xxix, [1] p.   427.9
36-27236
   PE2808 .M4 1936 MRR Alc.

NAMES, ENGLISH.
Partridge, Eric, Name into word;
[2d ed., rev. and enl.] New York,
Macmillan, 1950. xv, 648 p.   422
53-31511
   PE1583 .P35 1950a MRR Alc.

Severn, William, People words, New
York, Washburn [1966] 184 p.
422.09 66-8757
   PE1574 .S4 MRR Alc.

NAMES, ENGLISH--DICTIONARIES.
British Broadcasting Corporation.
BBC pronouncing dictionary of British
names: London, Oxford University
Press, 1971. xxii, 171 p. [£2.00]
421/.55 74-575346
   PE1660 .B7 MRR Alc.

NAMES, GAELIC.

Dwelly, Edward, comp. The illustrated Gaelic-English dictionary; containing every Gaelic word and meaning given in all previously published dictionaries and a great number never in print before, to which is prefixed a concise Gaelic grammar; 7th ed. Glasgow, Gairm Publications, 1971. [2], xiv, 1034 p. [£5.50] 491.6/3/321 72-191085

PB1591 .D8 1971 MRR Alc.

Macbain, Alexander, An etymological dictionary of the Gaelic language, Stirling, E. Mackay, 1911. xvi, xxxvii. A-D p., 1 l., 412 p. 12-642

PB1583 .M33 MRR Alc.

NAMES, GEOGRAPHICAL.

Benagh, Christine L. 100 keys: names across the land Nashville, Abingdon Press [1973] 288 p. [$5.95] 917.3/003 70-186613

E180 .B45 MRR Alc.

Gleichen, Edward, Lord, Alphabets of foreign languages, 2d ed. 1933 reprinted with incorporation of supplement of 1938 London, The Royal geographical society [etc.] 1944. xvi, 82 p., 1 l. gs 46-161

P213 .G55 1944 MRR Alc.

Knox, Alexander, Glossary of geographical and topographical terms London, E. Stanford, 1904. xl, 432 p. 05-4475

G103 .K72 MMR Alc.

Peddie, Robert Alexander, Place names in imprints; London, Grafton & co., 1932. vii, [1] p., 1 l., 61 numb. l., 1 l. 929.4 32-11548

Z125 .P37 MRR Ref Desk.

Room, Adrian. Place names of the world. Newton Abbot, David & Charles [1974] 216 p. [£3.50] 910/.3 74-155897

G103 .R7 MRR Alc.

Severn, William. Place words New York, Washburn [1969] 148 p. [3.95] 422.4 75-82646

PE1574 .S42 MRR Alc.

Sugden, Edward Holdsworth, A topographical dictionary to the works of Shakespeare and his fellow dramatists, Manchester, The University press; London, New York, etc., Longmans, Green & co., 1925. xix, 580 p. 25-9716

PR2892 .S8 MRR Alc.

United States. Geographic Names Division. Undersea features. 2d ed. Washington, 1971 [i.e. 1972] vi, 182 p. 910/.02/162 72-601422

GC83 .U5 1972 MRR Alc.

NAMES, GEOGRAPHICAL--ENGLISH.

Irvine, Theodora Ursula. A pronouncing dictionary of Shakespearean proper names, New York, Barnes & Noble, inc., 1945. lviii, 387 p. incl. front. (facsim.) 822.33 46-104

PR3081 .I65 1945a MRR Alc.

NAMES, GEOGRAPHICAL--INDEXES.

Sealock, Richard Burl, Bibliography of place-name literature; 2d ed. Chicago, American Library Association, 1967. x, 352 p. 016.917 67-23000

Z6824 .S4 1967 MRR Alc.

NAMES, GEOGRAPHICAL--LATIN.

Grasse, Johann Georg Theodor, Orbis latinus; 2. aufl., Berlin, R. C. Schmidt & co.; New York, E. Steiger & co.: [etc., etc.] 1909. 4 p. l., 348 p. 10-4247

G107 .G8 MRR Ref Desk.

Grässe, Johann Georg Theodor, Orbis latinus; Grossausgabe, Braunschweig, Klinkhardt & Biermann [c1972] 3 v. 72-345986

G107 .G8 1972 MRR Alc.

Martin, Charles Trice, The record interpreter: 2d ed. London, Stevens and sons, limited, 1910. xv, 464 p. 10-16320

Z111 .M23 MRR Alc.

Peddie, Robert Alexander, Place names in imprints; London, Grafton & co., 1932. vii, [1] p., 1 l., 61 numb. l., 1 l. 929.4 32-11548

Z125 .P37 MRR Ref Desk.

Peddie, Robert Alexander, Fifteenth-century books; New York, B. Franklin [1969] 89 p. 016.016/.083 73-101890

Z240.A1 P4 1969 MRR Alc.

NAMES, GEOGRAPHICAL--RUSSIAN.

Telberg, Ina. Russian-English geographical-encyclopedia. New York, Telberg Book Co., c1960. x, 142 l. 914.7 60-9280

DK14 .T4 MRR Alc.

NAMES, GEOGRAPHICAL--ARIZONA.

Barnes, William Croft. Arizona place names. Tucson, University of Arizona Press, 1960. xix, 519 p. 917.91 59-63657

F809 .B27 1960 MRR Alc.

NAMES, GEOGRAPHICAL--CANADA.

Armstrong, George Henry, The origin and meaning of place names in Canada, Toronto, The Macmillan company of Canada limited, 1930. vii p., 1 l., 312 p. 929.4 32-7322

F1004 .A25 MRR Alc.

NAMES, GEOGRAPHICAL--CANADA--BIBLIOGRAPHY.

Sealock, Richard Burl, Bibliography of place-name literature; 2d ed. Chicago, American Library Association, 1967. x, 352 p. 016.917 67-23000

Z6824 .S4 1967 MRR Alc.

NAMES, GEOGRAPHICAL--ENGLAND.

Cameron, Kenneth, English place-names. London, Batsford [1861] 256 p. 914.2 61-18937

DA645 .C3 MRR Alc.

Ekwall, Eilert, The concise Oxford dictionary of English place-names. 4th ed. Oxford, Clarendon Press, 1960. L, 546 p. 914.2 60-2031

DA645 .E38 1860 MRR Alc.

NAMES, GEOGRAPHICAL--FRANCE.

Dauzat, Albert, Dictionnaire etymologique des noms de lieux en France, Paris, Librairie Larousse [1963] xii, 738 p. 65-33799

DC14 .D28 MRR Alc.

NAMES, GEOGRAPHICAL--JAPAN.

Papinot, Edmond, Historical and geographical dictionary of Japan. Ann Arbor, Overbeck Co., 1948. xiv, 842 p. 952.003 49-3327

DS833 .P3 1948 MRR Alc.

NAMES, GEOGRAPHICAL--MAURITANIA.

United States. Office of Geography. Mauritania; official standard names approved by the United States Board on Geographic Names. Washington, 1866. vii, 149 p. 916.6/1/003 66-62751

DT553.M22 U5 MRR Alc.

NAMES, GEOGRAPHICAL--NETHERLANDS.

Nederlandsch aardrijkskundig genootschap, Amsterdam. Lijst der aardrijkskundige namen van Nederland, Leiden, E. J. Brill, 1936. 3 p. l., [ix]-xiv, [2], 494 p. 929.4 38-9122

DJ15 .N35 MRR Alc.

NAMES, GEOGRAPHICAL--NEW MEXICO.

Pearce, Thomas Matthews ed. New Mexico place names; [1st ed. Albuquerque] University of New Mexico Press [c1965] xv, 187 p. 917.89003 64-17808

F794 .P4 MRR Alc.

NAMES, GEOGRAPHICAL--NORTH AMERICA--BIBLIOGRAPHY.

Sealock, Richard Burl, Bibliography of place-name literature; 2d ed. Chicago, American Library Association, 1967. x, 352 p. 016.917 67-23000

Z6824 .S4 1967 MRR Alc.

NAMES, GEOGRAPHICAL--NORTH CAROLINA.

Powell, William Stevens, The North Carolina gazetteer, Chapel Hill, University of North Carolina Press [1968] xviii, 561 p. [$12.50] 917.56/003 68-25916

F252 .P6 MRR Alc.

NAMES, GEOGRAPHICAL--SCOTLAND.

Johnston, James Brown, Place-names of Scotland, London, J. Murray, 1934. xvi, 335 p. 929.4 35-4015

DA869 .J72 1934 MRR Alc.

Johnston (W. and A. K.) and G. W. Bacon, ltd. Johnston's gazetteer of Scotland, [2d ed.] Edinburgh [1958] viii, 248 p. 914.1 58-45407

DA869 .J74 1958 MRR Alc.

NAMES, GEOGRAPHICAL--UNITED STATES.

Air Force bases: [3d ed.] Harrisburg, Pa.: Stackpole Co. [1965] 224 p. 358.417058 65-13381

UG634.5.A1 A7 1965 MRR Alc.

Alexander, Gerald L. Nicknames of American cities, New York, Special Libraries Association [1951] 74 p. 929.4 51-8763

E155 .A5 MRR Alc.

Allen, Mary Moore. Origin of names of Army and Air Corps posts, camps, and stations in World War II in United States. Goldsboro, N.C. [1958?] 352 p. 59-1054

UA26.A6 A4 MRR Alc.

Army times, Washington, D.C. Guide to Army posts. [2d ed. Harrisburg, Pa.] Stackpole Books [1966] 383 p. 355.7 65-13382

UA26.A6 A7 1966 MRR Alc.

Gannett, Henry, American names, [Washington] Public Affairs Press [1947] 334 p. 929.4 47-12236

E155 .G19 1947 MRR Alc.

Goff, John. A book of nicknames. Louisville, Ky., Courier-Journal Job printing co., 1892. 75 p. 08-30496

E179 .G61 MRR Ref Desk.

Holt, Alfred Hubbard, American place names, Detroit, Gale Research Co., 1969. 222 p. 917.3 68-26574

E155 .H65 1969 MRR Alc.

Kane, Joseph Nathan, The American counties; 3d ed. Metuchen, N.J., Scarecrow Press, 1972. 608 p. 917.3/03 70-186010

E180 .K3 1972 MRR Ref Desk.

Kane, Joseph Nathan, Nicknames and sobriquets of U.S. cities and States, 2d ed. Metuchen, N.J., Scarecrow Press, 1970. 456 p. 917.3/003 77-10357

E155 .K24 1970 MRR Alc.

Prucha, Francis Paul. A guide to the military posts of the United States, 1789-1895. Madison, State Historical Society of Wisconsin, 1964. xiii, 178 p. 355.70973 64-63571

UA26.A6 P7 MRR Alc.

Quimby, Myron J. Scratch Ankle, U.S.A.; South Brunswick [N.J.] A. S. Barnes [1969] 390 p. 917.3/03 68-23069

E155 .Q5 MRR Alc.

Shankle, George Earlie. American nicknames; New York, The H. W. Wilson company, 1937. v, [1],599 p. 929.4 37-36382

E179 .S545 MRR Alc.

Shankle, George Earlie. State names, flags, seals, songs, birds, flowers, and other symbols; Rev. ed. New York, H. W. Wilson Co., 1941 [i.e. 1951, c1938] 524 p. 929.4 917.3* 52-52807

E155 .S43 1951 MRR Alc.

Stewart, George Rippey, American place-names; New York, Oxford University Press, 1970. xl, 550 p. [12.50] 917.3/003 72-83018

E155 .S79 MRR Ref Desk.

Stewart, George Rippey, Names on the land; 3d ed. Boston, Houghton Mifflin, 1967. xiii, 511 p. 917.3 67-9180

E155 .S8 1967 MRR Alc.

NAMES, GEOGRAPHICAL--UNITED STATES--BIBLIOGRAPHY.

Sealock, Richard Burl, Bibliography of place-name literature; 2d ed. Chicago, American Library Association, 1967. x, 352 p. 016.917 67-23000

Z6824 .S4 1967 MRR Alc.

NAMES, GEOGRAPHICAL--UNITED STATES--JUVENILE LITERATURE.

Benagh, Christine L. 100 keys: names across the land Nashville, Abingdon Press [1973] 288 p. [$5.95] 917.3/003 70-186613

E180 .B45 MRR Alc.

NAMES, GEOGRAPHICAL--VIRGINIA.

Hanson, Raus McDill. Virginia place names; Verona, Va., McClure Press [1969] ix, 253 p. [5.95] 917.55 69-20401

F224 .H3 MRR Alc.

NAMES, GEOGRAPHICAL--WALES.

Wales. University. Board of Celtic Studies. Language and Literature Committee. Rhestr o enwau lleoedd. 3. arg. Caerdydd, Gwasg Prifysgol Cymru, 1967. xxxvii, 119 p. [15/-] 914.29/003 68-71418

DA734 .W3 1967 MRR Alc.

NAMES, LATIN--DICTIONARIES.

Swanson, Donald Carl Eugene, The names in Roman verse: Madison, University of Wisconsin Press, 1967. xix, 425 p. 871/.003 67-25942

PA2379 .S9 MRR Alc.

NAMES, LATIN--PRONUNCIATION.
Russo-Alesi, Anthony Ignatius,
Martyrology pronouncing dictionary.
New York, The Edward O'Toole company,
inc., 1939. xiv, 177 p.   922.2 39-
21766
    BX4661 .R8 MRR Alc.

NAMES, PERSONAL.
Arthur, William, An etymological
dictionary of family and Christian
names; Detroit, Gale Research Co.,
1969. iv, 300 p.   929.4 68-17911
    CS2309 .A7 1969 MRR Alc.

Burton, Dorothy. A new treasury of
names for the baby. Englewood
Cliffs, N.J., Prentice-Hall [1961]
187 p.   929.4 61-14577
    CS2377 .B8 MRR Alc.

Loughead, Flora (Haines) Apponyi,
Dictionary of given names, 2d ed.,
rev. and corr. Glendale, Calif., A.
H. Clark Co., 1958 [c1933] 248 p.
929.403 a 58-5638
    CS2367 .L6 1958 MRR Alc.

Schmidt, Jacob Edward, Baby name
finder. Springfield, Ill., Thomas
[1960] 390 p.   929.4 58-14934
    CS2377 .S28 1960 MRR Alc.

Shankle, George Earlie. American
nicknames; New York, The H. W.
Wilson company, 1937. v, [1],599 p.
929.4 37-36382
    E179 .S545 MRR Alc.

Stokes, Francis Griffin. A
dictionary of the characters & proper
names in the works of Shakespeare,
Boston, New York, Houghton Mifflin
company [pref. 1924] xv, 359, [1] p.
incl. geneal. tables.   822.33 31-
25861
    PR2892 .S67 1924a MRR Alc.

Wells, Evelyn. What to name the
baby. Garden City, N.Y., Garden City
Books [1953, c1946] 326 p.   929.4
53-1872
    CS2367 .W43 1953 MRR Alc.

Yonge, Charlotte Mary, History of
Christian names. London, Macmillan
and co., 1878. 2 v.   15-14136
    CS2367 .Y6 1878 MRR Alc.

NAMES, PERSONAL--BIBLIOGRAPHY.
Smith, Elsdon Coles, Personal names;
Detroit, Gale Research Co., 1965.
226 p.   016.9294 66-31855
    Z6824 .S55 1965 MRR Alc.

NAMES, PERSONAL--DICTIONARIES.
Ballentyne, Denis William George. A
dictionary of named effects and laws
in chemistry, physics and mathematics
3rd ed. London, Chapman & Hall,
1970. iii-viii, 355 p. [£3.00]
500.2/03 71-552485
    Q123 .B3 1870 MRR Alc.

Jablonski, Stanley. Illustrated
dictionary of eponymic syndromes, and
diseases, and their synonyms.
Philadelphia, Saunders [1969] viii,
335 p.   610/.3 69-12884
    R121 .J24 MRR Alc.

NAMES, PERSONAL--DICTIONARIES--POLYGLOT.
United States. Immigration and
Naturalization Service. Foreign
versions, variations, and diminutives
of English names. Rev. [Washington;
For sale by the Supt. of Docs., U.S.
Govt. Print. Off.] 1969 [i.e. 1970]
53 p. [1.00] 929.4 73-605932
    CS2309 .U55 1970 MRR Alc.

NAMES, PERSONAL--ENGLISH.
Bardsley, Charles Wareing Endell, A
dictionary of English and Welsh
surnames. Baltimore, Genealogical
Pub. Co., 1967. xvi, 837 p.
929.4/0942 67-25404
    CS2505 .B3 1967 MRR Alc.

Irvine, Theodora Ursula. A
pronouncing dictionary of
Shakespearean proper names, New
York, Barnes & Noble, inc., 1945.
lviii, 387 p. incl. front. (facsim.)
822.33 46-104
    PR3081 .I65 1945a MRR Alc.

Reaney, Percy Hide. A dictionary of
British surnames. London, Routledge
and Paul [1958] lix, 366 p.   929.4
58-3233
    CS2385 .R4 MRR Alc.

Withycombe, Elizabeth Gidley, The
Oxford dictionary of English
Christian names, New York, London,
Oxford university press, 1947.
xxxviii, 142 p.   929.4 47-2106
    CS2375.G7 W5 1947 MRR Alc.

NAMES, PERSONAL--GERMAN.
Gottschald, Max. Deutsche
Namenkunde, 3., verm. Aufl.,
Berlin, W. de Gruyter, 1954. 630 p.
54-4252
    CS2545 .G6 1954 MRR Alc.

NAMES, PERSONAL--GERMANIC--DICTIONARIES.
Gillespie, George T. A catalogue of
persons named in German heroic
literature (700-1600), including
named animals and objects and ethnic
names, Oxford, [Eng.] Clarendon
Press, 1973. xxxvii, 166 p. [£10.50
($33.75 U.S.)] 831/.009 73-173463
    PT204 .G5 1973 MRR Alc.

NAMES, PERSONAL--ITALIAN.
Fucilla, Joseph Guerin, Our Italian
surnames. Evanston, Ill., Chandler's
inc., 1949. xi, 299 p.   929.4 49-
6230
    CS2715 .F8 MRR Alc.

NAMES, PERSONAL--PRONUNCIATION.
Funk, Charles Earle, What's the
name, please? New York, London, Funk
& Wagnalls company, 1936. x, 11-176
p.   421.5 929.4 36-27288
    PE1660 .F8 MRR Alc.

NAMES, PERSONAL--ROMAN.
Jones, Arnold Hugh Martin, The
prosopography of the later Roman
Empire, Cambridge [Eng.] University
Press, 1971- v.   920.037 77-
118859
    DG203.5 .J6 MRR Alc.

NAMES, PERSONAL--SCOTTISH.
Black, George Fraser, The surnames
of Scotland; New York, The New York
public library, 1946. lxxi, [1], 838
p.   929.4 a 47-1716
    CS2435 .B55 MRR Alc.

NAMES, PERSONAL--WELSH.
Bardsley, Charles Wareing Endell, A
dictionary of English and Welsh
surnames, Baltimore, Genealogical
Pub. Co., 1967. xvi, 837 p.
928.4/0942 67-25404
    CS2505 .B3 1967 MRR Alc.

NAMES, PERSONAL--FRANCE.
Dauzat, Albert, Dictionnaire
étymologique des noms de famille et
prénoms de France. Paris, Larousse
[1951] xxii, [4], 604 p.   51-30087

    CS2691 .D3 MRR Alc.

NAMES, PERSONAL--GREAT BRITAIN.
Johnson, Charles Benjamin, The
Harrap book of boys' and girls'
names, London, Harrap, 1973. xiii,
273 p. [£2.40]   929.4 74-158444
    CS2375.G7 J63 1973 MRR Ref Desk.

NAMES, PERSONAL--UNITED STATES.
Goff, John. A book of nicknames.
Louisville, Ky., Courier-journal job
printing co., 1892. 75 p.   08-30496

    E179 .G61 MRR Ref Desk.

Keiser, Albert, College names, their
origin and significance. New York,
Bookman Associates [1952] 184 p.
378 52-11160
    LA225 .K37 MRR Alc.

Smith, Elsdon Coles, American
surnames [1st ed.] Philadelphia,
Chilton Book Co. [1969] xx, 370 p.
929.4 71-85245
    CS2485 .S63 MRR Alc.

Smith, Elsdon Coles, New dictionary
of American family names [1st ed.]
New York, Harper & Row [1972, c1973]
xxix, 570 p. [$12.95] 929/.4/0973
72-79693
    CS2481 .S55 1973 MRR Ref Desk.

NAPLES--DIRECTORIES.
Napoli e i napoletani. Napoli,
Marino Turchi; [etc.] 914.57 44-
45835
    DG842 .N3 MRR Alc Latest edition

NARCOTIC ADDICTS--LANGUAGE (NEW WORDS,
SLANG, ETC.)
Young, Kenn W. Naz's underground
dictionary; Vancouver, Wash. [Naz
Enterprises, 1973] vi, 67 p.
[$2.00] 427/.9/73 74-156957
    PE3727.N3 Y6 MRR Alc.

NARCOTIC ADDICTS--REHABILITATION--
UNITED STATES.
Andrews, Matthew, The parents' guide
to drugs. [1st ed.] Garden City,
N.Y., Doubleday, 1972. 186 p.
[$6.95] 362.2/93/0973 78-144245
    HV5825 .A7 MRR Alc.

NARCOTIC ADDICTS--REHABILITATION--
UNITED STATES--DIRECTORIES.
Keville, Kathleen. Where to get help
for a drug problem. New York, Award
Books [1971] 237 p. [$1.25]
362.2/93/02573 71-31889
    HV5815 .K44 MRR Alc.

NARCOTIC CLINICS--UNITED STATES--
DIRECTORIES.
Andrews, Matthew, The parents' guide
to drugs. [1st ed.] Garden City,
N.Y., Doubleday, 1972. 186 p.
[$6.95] 362.2/93/0973 78-144245
    HV5825 .A7 MRR Alc.

NARCOTIC HABIT.
Maurer, David W. Narcotics and
narcotic addiction, 4th ed.
Springfield, Ill. Thomas [1973] xv,
473 p.   616.86/3 73-7879
    RC566 .M3 1973 MRR Alc.

NARCOTIC HABIT--BIBLIOGRAPHY.
Menditto, Joseph. Drugs of addiction
and non-addiction, their use and
abuse; Troy, N.Y., Whitston Pub.
Co., 1970. 315 p.   016.6138/3 79-
116588
    Z7164.N17 M45 MRR Alc.

United States. National Clearinghouse
for Mental Health Information.
Bibliography on drug dependence and
abuse, 1928-1966. [Chevy Chase, Md.,
1969] 258 p.   016.6138/3 70-600726

    Z7164.N17 U56 MRR Alc.

NARCOTIC HABIT--DICTIONARIES.
Landy, Eugene E. The underground
dictionary, New York, Simon and
Schuster [1971] 206 p. [$5.95]
427.09 73-139637
    PE3721 .L3 MRR Alc.

Lingeman, Richard R. Drugs from A to
Z: Rev. & updated, 2d ed. New York,
McGraw-Hill [1974] xxii, 310 p.
613.8/3/03 74-13363
    HV5804 .L54 1974 MRR Alc.

Maurer, David W. Narcotics and
narcotic addiction, 4th ed.
Springfield, Ill., Thomas [1973] xv,
473 p.   616.86/3 73-7879
    RC566 .M3 1973 MRR Alc.

NARCOTICS.
Brecher, Edward M. Licit and illicit
drugs; [1st ed.] Boston, Little,
Brown [1972] xv, 623 p. [$12.50]
362.2/9 75-186972
    HV5825 .B72 MRR Alc.

Maurer, David W. Narcotics and
narcotic addiction, 4th ed.
Springfield, Ill., Thomas [1973] xv,
473 p.   616.86/3 73-7879
    RC566 .M3 1973 MRR Alc.

Maurer, David W. Narcotics and
narcotic addiction, 4th ed.
Springfield, Ill., Thomas [1973] xv,
473 p.   616.86/3 73-7879
    RC566 .M3 1973 MRR Alc.

NARCOTICS--BIBLIOGRAPHY.
Menditto, Joseph. Drugs of addiction
and non-addiction, their use and
abuse; Troy, N.Y., Whitston Pub.
Co., 1970. 315 p.   016.6138/3 79-
116588
    Z7164.N17 M45 MRR Alc.

NARCOTICS--DICTIONARIES.
Lingeman, Richard R. Drugs from A to
Z: Rev. & updated, 2d ed. New York,
McGraw-Hill [1974] xxii, 310 p.
613.8/3/03 74-13363
    HV5804 .L54 1974 MRR Alc.

NATIONAL ANTHEMS
see National songs

NATIONAL ASSOCIATION FOR THE
ADVANCEMENT OF COLORED PEOPLE.
Hughes, Langston, Fight for freedom;
New York, Norton [1962] 224 p.
325.2670973 62-14352
    E185.5.N276 H8 MRR Alc.

NATIONAL ASSOCIATION FOR THE
ADVANCEMENT OF COLORED PEOPLE--ARCHIVES.
United States. Library of Congress.
Manuscript Division. The National
Association for the Advancement of
Colored People: a register of its
records in the Library of Congress.
Washington, Library of Congress, 1972-
v.   016.30145/19/6073 72-13291

    Z663.34 .N28 MRR Alc.

NATIONAL ASSOCIATION OF SECURITIES
DEALERS.
Loll, Leo M. The over-the-counter
securities markets; 2d ed.
Englewood Cliffs, N.J., Prentice-Hall
[1967] vi, 426 p.   332.6/43 67-
22419
    HG4910 .L6 1967 MRR Alc.

NATIONAL BANK NOTES.
Friedberg, Robert, Paper money of
the United States. 7th ed., New
York, Coin and Currency Institute
[1972] 327 p.   769/.55973 72-80202

    HG591 .F7 1972 MRR Ref Desk.

NATIONAL BANKS (U.S.)
Friedberg, Robert, Paper money of
the United States. 7th ed., New
York, Coin and Currency Institute
[1972] 327 p.   769/.55973 72-80202

    HG591 .F7 1972 MRR Ref Desk.

NATIONAL CHARACTERISTICS.
Herman, Lewis Helmar, Foreign
dialects; New York, Theatre Arts
Books [1958? c1943] 415 p. 792.028
58-10332
PN2071.F6 H4 1958 MRR Alc.

International Research Associates.
The new Far East; [Hong Kong]
Reader's Digest [Far East ltd.];
distributors: C.E. Tuttle Co.,
Rutland, Vt. [c1966] 159 p.
339.42/085 67-7110
HD7049 .I53 MRR Alc.

NATIONAL CHARACTERISTICS, AMERICAN.
Billington, Ray Allen, America's
frontier heritage. [1st ed.] New
York, Holt, Rinehart and Winston
[1966] xiv, 302 p. 917.303 66-
13289
E179.5 .B62 MRR Alc.

Boorstin, Daniel Joseph, The
Americans; the colonial experience.
New York, Random House [1958] 434 p.
917.3 58-9884
E188 .B72 MRR Alc.

Boorstin, Daniel Joseph, The
Americans: the national experience,
New York, Random House [1965] 517 p.
917.303 65-17440
E301 .B6 MRR Alc.

Commager, Henry Steele, The American
mind; New Haven, Yale University
Press, 1950. ix, 476 p. 917.3 50-
6338
E169.1 .C673 MRR Alc.

NATIONAL CHARACTERISTICS, GERMAN.
Bithell, Jethro, ed. Germany, a
companion to German studies. [5th
ed., rev., enl.] London, Methuen
[1955] xii, 578 p. 914.3 55-3335
DD61 .B56 1955 MRR Alc.

NATIONAL COLLEGIATE ATHLETIC
ASSOCIATION.
National Collegiate Athletic
Association. The Official National
Collegiate Athletic Association
football rules interpretations which
supplements the NCAA official
football rules. Shawnee Mission,
Kan., NCAA Publishing Service.
796.33/202022 74-645430
GV956.8 .N36a MRR Alc Latest
edition

NATIONAL CONFERENCE ON SOCIAL WELFARE.
Bruno, Frank John, Trends in social
work, 1874-1956: [2d ed.] New York,
Columbia University Press, 1957.
xviii, 462 p. 360.973 57-9699
HV91 .B75 1957 MRR Alc.

NATIONAL EMBLEMS
see Emblems, National

NATIONAL FOOTBALL LEAGUE.
Treat, Roger L. The encyclopedia of
football / 12th rev. ed. / South
Brunswick [N.J.] : A. S. Barnes,
[1974] 723 p. : [$13.95]
796.33/264/0973 73-22593
GV954 .T7 1974 MRR Alc.

NATIONAL FOOTBALL LEAGUE--YEARBOOKS.
Smith, Don, N F L official
illustrated digest, New York, Poretz
& Ross Associates. 796.332/64 74-
7801
GV955.5.N35 S6 MRR Alc Latest
edition

NATIONAL FORESTS
see Forest reserves

NATIONAL HOCKEY LEAGUE.
Hollander, Zander. The complete
encyclopedia of ice hockey : Rev.
ed. Englewood Cliffs, N.J. :
Prentice-Hall, [1974] xi, 702 p. :
[$14.95] 796.9/62/03 73-15019
GV847.8.N3 H6 1974 MRR Alc.

NATIONAL HOLIDAYS
see Holidays

NATIONAL INCOME
see Income

NATIONAL INCOME--GREAT BRITAIN--
ACCOUNTING.
Great Britain. Central Statistical
Office. National accounts
statistics: London, H.M.S.O., 1968.
vii, 502 p. [45/-] 339.2/0942 79-
356609
HC260.I5 A45 MRR Alc.

NATIONAL INCOME--ORGANIZATION FOR
ECONOMIC COOPERATION AND DEVELOPMENT
COUNTRIES--ACCOUNTING.
Organization for Economic Cooperation
and Development. National accounts
statistics, 1960-1971. [Paris, 1973]
471 p. [$7.50 (U.S.)] 339.3 74-
158206
HC79.I5 O7 1973 MRR Alc.

NATIONAL MERIT SCHOLARSHIP QUALIFYING
TEST.
Tarr, Harry A. National merit
scholarship tests; 3d ed.] New
York, Arco [1968] 416 p. [$4.00]
371.26/42 68-7928
LB2353 .T3 1968 MRR Alc.

NATIONAL MONUMENTS--UNITED STATES.
Butcher, Devereux. Exploring our
national parks and monuments. 5th
ed. Boston, Houghton Mifflin, 1956.
288 p. 917.3 57-724
E160. B8 1956 MRR Alc.

NATIONAL MUSIC.
see also Folk dancing

NATIONAL PARKS AND RESERVES.
see also Wilderness areas

International Union for the
Conservation of Nature and Natural
Resources. Liste des Nations unies
des parcs nationaux et réserves
analogues. ([Bruxelles], Hayez,
1967). 550 p. [675.00] 79-393664
SB481 .I57 MRR Alc.

The World wildlife guide. London
(200 Buckingham Palace Rd, S.W.1),
Threshold Books Ltd, 1971. 416 p.
[£3.50] 639/.95 72-185519
SB481 .W63 1971 MRR Alc.

NATIONAL PARKS AND RESERVES--AFRICA,
EAST.
Williams, John George, A field guide
to the national parks of East Africa
London, Collins, 1967. 352 p. [45/-
] 591.967 68-76542
SB484.E3 W54 MRR Alc.

NATIONAL PARKS AND RESERVES--UNITED
STATES.
Butcher, Devereux. Exploring our
national parks and monuments. 5th
ed. Boston, Houghton Mifflin, 1956.
288 p. 917.3 57-724
E160. B8 1956 MRR Alc.

Frome, Michael. Rand McNally
national park guide. 1967- Chicago,
Rand McNally. 68-3748
E160 .F73 MRR Alc Latest edition

Ise, John, Our national park policy;
Baltimore, Published for Resources
for the Future by Johns Hopkins Press
[1961] xiii, 701 p. 333.78 60-
15704
SB482.A1 I75 MRR Alc.

National Geographic Society,
Washington, D.C. Book Service.
America's wonderlands; New enl. ed.
Washington, National Geographic
Society [1966] 552 p. 917.3 66-
17745
E160 .N24 1966 MRR Alc.

National parks & monuments; New 1973
revision, Menlo Park, Calif., 1973]
140 p. [$1.95] 917.3/04/92 73-
163780
E160 .N26 MRR Alc.

Udall, Stewart L. The national parks
of America [1st ed.] New York,
Putnam [1966] 225 p. 917.3 66-
27672
E160 .U3 MRR Alc.

NATIONAL PARKS AND RESERVES--UNITED
STATES--DIRECTORIES.
The National register of historic
places. 1969- Washington, National
Park Service. [For sale by the Supt.
of Docs., U.S. Govt. Print. Off.]
973/.025 78-603008
E159 .N34 MRR Alc Latest edition

NATIONAL PARKS AND RESERVES--UNITED
STATES--GUIDE-BOOKS.
Matthews, William Henry, A guide to
the national parks; Garden City,
N.Y., Doubleday, 1973. xx, 529 p.
[$5.95] 551.4/0973 72-89824
GB427.5 .M37 1973 MRR Alc.

NATIONAL PARKS AND RESERVES--WEST.
National parks of the West. [2d ed.]
Menlo Park, Calif., Lane Magazine &
Book Co., [1970] 286 p. [11.75]
719/.32/0978 76-108153
E160 .N36 1970 MRR Alc.

NATIONAL PLANNING
see Economic policy

NATIONAL RESOURCES.
see also Mines and mineral resources

NATIONAL RESTAURANT ASSOCIATION.
Who's who in food service in America.
Chicago, National Restaurant
Association. 72-626563
TX907 .N35 MRR Alc Latest edition

NATIONAL SOCIALISM.
Zentner, Kurt. Illustrierte
Geschichte des Dritten Reiches.
Wien, Buchgemeinschaft Donauland
[1966] 623 p. [S 125.00] 943.086
68-86744
DD256.5 .Z43 1966 MRR Alc.

NATIONAL SOCIALISM--HISTORY--SOURCES.
Remak, Joachim, comp. The Nazi
years; Englewood Cliffs, N.J.,
Prentice-Hall [1969] xi, 178 p.
[4.95] 943.086 69-11359
DD256.5 .R43 MRR Alc.

NATIONAL SONGS.
Shaw, Martin Fallas, ed. National
anthems of the world. London,
Blandford Press [1960] 330 p.
784.71 m 60-2155
M1627 .S55N33 MRR Alc.

NATIONAL SONGS--HISTORY AND CRITICISM.
Nettl, Paul, National anthems. 2d,
enl. ed. New York, Frederick Ungar
Pub. Co. [1967] xii, 261 p.
784.7/1 66-26509
ML3545 .N29 1967 MRR Alc.

NATIONAL SONGS, AMERICAN.
Preble, George Henry, Origin and
history of the American flag and of
the naval and yacht-club signals,
seals and arms, and principal
national songs of the United States,
New ed. in two volumes,
Philadelphia, N. L. Brown, 1917. 2
v. 17-21758
CR113 .P7 1917 MRR Alc.

NATIONAL UNION CATALOG, PRE-1956
IMPRINTS.
Prospectus for the National union
catalog, pre-1956 imprints. London,
Mansell, 1967. 96 p. 021.6/4 67-
30000
Z881.A1 U526 MRR Alc. (DK 33)

NATIONALISM.
see also Minorities

NATIONALISM--BIBLIOGRAPHY.
Deutsch, Karl Wolfgang, Nationalism
and national development; Cambridge,
Mass., MIT Press [1970] 519 p.
016.3201/58 79-90750
Z7164.N2 D43 MRR Alc.

NATIONALISM--AFRICA.
Wauthier, Claude, The literature and
thought of modern Africa; London,
Pall Mall P., 1966. 323 p. [45/-]
809.896 67-71993
DT21 .W313 1966 MRR Alc.

NATIONALISM--IRELAND.
Howarth, Herbert. The Irish writers,
1880-1940; London, Rockliff [1958]
x, 318 p. 820.903 a 59-4779
PR8753 .H6 MRR Alc.

NATIONALISM--UNITED STATES.
Dangerfield, George, The awakening
of American nationalism, 1815-1828.
[1st ed.] New York, Harper & Row
[c1965] xiii, 331 p. 973.5 64-
25112
E338 .D3 MRR Alc.

NATIONALISM AND EDUCATION.
see also Education and state

NATIONALITY (CITIZENSHIP)
see Citizenship

NATIVE RACES.
see also Ethnology

NATURAL AREAS.
see also Wildlife refuges

NATURAL GAS
see Gas, Natural

NATURAL HISTORY.
see also Biology

see also Botany

see also Geology

see also Marine biology

see also Paleontology

see also Zoology

The Book of popular sciences. New
York, Grolier [1969] 10 v. 500 69-
10053
Q162 .B68 1969 MRR Alc.

NATURAL HISTORY--BIBLIOGRAPHY--CATALOGS.
British museum (Natural History)
Library. Catalogue of the books,
manuscripts, maps and drawings in the
British museum (Natural history).
London, Printed by order of the
Trustees, 1903-15. 5 v. 04-18991
Z7409 .B85 MRR Alc.

NATURAL HISTORY--PICTORIAL WORKS--
INDEXES.
Ellis, Jessie (Croft) Nature and its
applications; Boston, F. W. Faxon
Co., 1949. xii, 861 p. 016.745 49-
9331
Z5956.D3 E53 MRR Alc.

NATURAL HISTORY--PRE-LINNEAN WORKS.
Plinius Secundus, C. Natural
history, Cambridge, Mass., Harvard
University Press; London, W.
Heinemann, 1938-63 [v. 10, 1962] 10
v.   38-5370
    PA6156.P65   1938 MRR Alc

NATURAL HISTORY--INDONESIA.
Neill, Wilfred T. Twentieth-century
Indonesia New York, Columbia
University Press, 1973. xiv, 413 p.
[$15.00]   915.98/03/3 72-11718
    DS634 .N45 1973 MRR Alc.

NATURAL HISTORY--KENYA.
Horrobin, David F. A guide to Kenya
and northern Tanzania [Aylesbury,
Eng. Medical and Technical Pub.,
1971] 304 p. [£3.25 ($10.00 U.S.)]
916.76/2/044 70-29461
    DT434.E22 H59 MRR Alc.

NATURAL HISTORY--TANZANIA.
Horrobin, David F. A guide to Kenya
and northern Tanzania [Aylesbury,
Eng. Medical and Technical Pub.,
1971] 304 p. [£3.25 ($10.00 U.S.)]
916.76/2/044 70-29461
    DT434.E22 H59 MRR Alc.

NATURAL HISTORY--UNITED STATES--
BIBLIOGRAPHY.
Meisel, Max, A bibliography of
American natural history; Brooklyn,
N.Y., The Premier publishing co.,
1924-29. 3 v.   24-30970
    Z7408.U5 M5 MRR Alc.

NATURAL HISTORY SOCIETIES--UNITED
STATES.
Meisel, Max, A bibliography of
American natural history; Brooklyn,
N.Y., The Premier publishing co.,
1924-29. 3 v.   24-30970
    Z7408.U5 M5 MRR Alc.

NATURAL LAW.
    see also Ethics

NATURAL MONUMENTS.
    see also National parks and reserves

NATURAL MONUMENTS--UNITED STATES.
National Geographic Society,
Washington, D.C. Book Service.
America's wonderlands; New enl. ed.
Washington, National Geographic
Society [1966] 552 p. 917.3 66-
17745
    E160 .N24 1966 MRR Alc.

United States. National Park Service.
Explorers and settlers; historic
places commemorating the early
exploration and settlement of the
United States. Washington [For sale
by the Supt. of Docs., U.S. Govt.
Print. Off.] 1968. xvi, 506 p.
917.3/04 66-60013
    E159 .U545 MRR Alc.

NATURAL RESOURCES.
    see also Commercial products

    see also Conservation of natural
    resources

    see also Fisheries

    see also Forests and forestry

    see also Marine resources

    see also Power resources

    see also Water resources development

    see also Water-supply

Van Royen, William, Atlas of the
world's resources. New York,
Published by Prentice-Hall for the
University of Maryland, 1952- v.
338 52-9034
    G1046.G3 V3 1952 MRR Alc Atlas.

NATURAL RESOURCES--DICTIONARIES.
Jackson, Nora. A dictionary of
natural resources and their principal
uses, [2d ed.] Oxford, New York,
Pergamon Press [1969] vii, 151 p.
333/.003 73-91463
    HF1051 .J3 1969 MRR Alc.

NATURAL RESOURCES--UTILIZATION.
United States. Dept. of Agriculture.
Outdoors USA. [Washington, U.S.
Govt. Print. Off., 1967] xxxix, 408
p. 333.7/2/0973 agr67-359
    S21.A35 1967 MRR Alc.

NATURAL RESOURCES--LATIN AMERICA.
Grunwald, Joseph, Natural resources
in Latin American development,
Baltimore, Published for Resources
for the Future, inc., by the Johns
Hopkins Press [1970] xvii, 494 p.
[20.00] 330.98 77-108381
    HC125 .G72 MRR Alc.

NATURAL SCIENCE
    see Physics

    see Science

NATURALISTS.
    see also Scientists

The Naturalists' directory. [1st]-
ed.; 1877- Phillipsburg, N.J. [etc.]
PCL Publications. [etc.] 505.8 05-
5997
    Q145 .S4   MRR Alc Latest edition

NATURALISTS, AMERICAN.
Meisel, Max, A bibliography of
American natural history; Brooklyn,
N.Y., The Premier publishing co.,
1924-29. 3 v.   24-30970
    Z7408.U5 M5 MRR Alc.

NATURALIZATION.
    see also Citizenship

NATURALIZATION--UNITED STATES.
How to become a citizen of the United
States. New York, American Council
for Nationalities Service. 26-11021
    JK1829 .C73   MRR Alc Latest edition

NATURALIZATION--UNITED STATES--
HANDBOOKS, MANUALS, ETC.
United States. Immigration and
Naturalization Service.
Naturalization requirements and
general information. [Rev. 5-1-67.
Washington, For sale by the Supt. of
Docs., U.S. Govt. Print. Off., 1967]
iv, 38 p.   70-600962
    JK1829 .A52 1967 MRR Alc.

NATURE.
    see also Man--Influence on nature

NATURE, EFFECT OF MAN ON
    see Man--Influence on nature

NATURE (AESTHETICS)--INDEXES.
Ellis, Jessie (Croft) Nature and its
applications; Boston, F. W. Faxon
Co., 1949. xii, 861 p. 016.745 49-
9331
    Z5956.D3 E53 MRR Alc.

Ellis, Jessie (Croft) comp. Nature
index; Boston, The F. W. Faxon
company, 1930. 4 p. l., 319 p.
016.745 30-20661
    Z5956.D3 E5 MRR Alc.

NATURE CONSERVATION--UNITED STATES--
YEARBOOKS.
Ecology USA 1971; New York, Special
Reports inc. [1972] xi, 610 p.
[$125.00] 333.7/2/0973 71-188164
    QH541.145 .E26 MRR Alc.

NATURE SOUNDS.
    see also Animal sounds

NATURE STUDY.
    see also Animals, Habits and behavior
    of

    see also Animals, Legends and stories
    of

NAUTICAL ALMANACS.
The Air almanac. Jan./Apr. 1953-
Washington, U.S. Govt. Print. Off.
52-61239
    TL587 .A36   MRR Alc Latest edition

Brown's nautical almanac Daily tide
tables. Glasgow, Brown, son &
Ferguson, ltd. 528.2 ca 32-280
    VK8 .B8   MRR Alc Latest edition

The Nautical almanac. Washington,
U.S. Govt. Print. Off. [etc.] 07-
35404
    Began publication with vol. for
1855.
    QB8 .U3   MRR Alc Partial set / Sci
    RR Partial set

United States. Nautical Almanac
Office. The American ephemeris and
nautical almanac. 1855- Washington.
07-35435
    QB8 .U1   Sci RR Partial set / MRR
    Alc Latest edition

NAUTICAL ASTRONOMY.
    see also Navigation

Norie, John William, Norie's
nautical tables with explanations of
their use. Revised ed.; Saint Ives,
Laurie, Norie and Wilson, 1973. lii,
608 p. 623.89/021/2 73-178120
    VK563 .N86 1973 MRR Alc.

NAUTICAL CHARTS--BIBLIOGRAPHY.
United States Library of Congress.
Map Division. Noteworthy maps; no.
[1]-3; 1925/26-1927/28. Washington,
U.S. Govt. Print. Off. 27-26417
    Z663.35 .N6 MRR Alc MRR Alc
    Partial set

NAUTICAL CHARTS--VIRGINIA.
Salt water sport fishing and boating
in Virginia. Alexandria, Va., 1971.
78 p. [$5.00] 623.89 73-654615
    G1291-L1 S2 1971 MRR Alc.

NAVAL AERONAUTICS
    see Aeronautics, Military

NAVAL ARCHITECTURE.
    see also Boat-building

NAVAL ARCHITECTURE--HISTORY.
Landstrom, Bjorn. The ship;
London] Allen & Unwin [1961] 309,
[10] p. 623.8109 61-66428
    VM15 .L213 1961a MRR Alc.

NAVAL ART AND SCIENCE.
    see also Navigation

Dorling, Henry Taprell, Salt water
quiz London] Hodder and Stoughton
[1952] 157 p. 387.076 53-6532
    V21 .D65 MRR Alc.

NAVAL ART AND SCIENCE--ABBREVIATIONS.
Wedertz, Bill. Dictionary of naval
abbreviations. 1970 ed. [Annapolis]
U.S. Naval Institute [1970] 249 p.
[3.50] 359/.001/48 72-96483
    V23 .W43 MRR Alc.

NAVAL ART AND SCIENCE--DICTIONARIES.
American association of port
authorities. Committee on
standardization and special research.
A port dictionary of technical
terms, New Orleans, La., The
American association of port
authorities, 1940. 2 p. l., 7-208 p.
656 40-33335
    V23 .A48 MRR Alc.

Bradford, Gershom, A glossary of sea
terms. London, Cassell [1954] 215
p. 359.03 54-4204
    V23 .B75 1954 MRR Alc.

Dyer, Frederick Charles, The petty
officer's guide. 6th ed.
[Harrisburg, Pa.] Stackpole Books
[1966] 392 p. 359.338 66-18190
    V123 .D9 1966 MRR Alc.

Gaynor, Frank, The new military and
naval dictionary. New York,
Philosophical Library [1951] viii,
295 p. 355.03 51-13233
    U24 .G34 MRR Alc.

Kerchove, René de, baron,
International maritime dictionary;
2d ed. Princeton, N.J., Van Nostrand
[1961] v, 1018 p. 623.803 61-
16272
    V23 .K4 1961 MRR Alc.

Layton, Cyril Walter Thomas.
Dictionary of nautical words and
terms. [1st ed.] Glasgow, Brown,
Son & Ferguson [1955] 413 p. 55-
4773
    V23 .L4 MRR Alc.

McEwen, William Alvin, Encyclopedia
of nautical knowledge, Cambridge,
Md., Cornell Maritime Press [1953]
618 p. 359.03 53-9685
    V23 .M25 MRR Alc.

Noel, John Vavasour, Naval terms
dictionary. 2d ed., rev. Annapolis,
U.S. Naval Institute [1966] 377 p.
359.003 66-27031
    V23 .N6 1966 MRR Alc.

Shay, Frank, A sailor's treasury;
[1st ed.] New York, Norton [1951]
196 p. 910.4 51-7454
    GR910 .S36 MRR Alc.

United States. Hydrographic Office.
Navigation dictionary. Washington,
1956 [i.e., 1955] iii, 253 p.
359.03 56-60471
    V23 .U54 MRR Alc.

United States. Naval Oceanographic
Office. Navigation dictionary. 2d
ed. Washington, U.S. Govt. Print.
Off., 1969. iv, 292 p. 623.89/03
71-603652
    V23 .U557 1969 MRR Alc.

NAVAL ART AND SCIENCE--DICTIONARIES--
POLYGLOT.
Great Britain. Naval intelligence
division. A dictionary of naval
equivalents covering English, French,
Italian, Spanish, Russian, Swedish,
Danish, Dutch, German. London, H.M.
Stationery off., 1924. 2 v. 24-
23792
    V24 .G7 MRR Alc.

Intergovernmental Maritime
Consultative Organization. Glossary
of maritime technical terms. London
[c1963] 118 p. 64-56993
    V24 .I5 MRR Alc.

NAVAL ART AND SCIENCE--QUOTATIONS,
MAXIMS, ETC.
Heinl, Robert Debs, comp. Dictionary
of military and naval quotations.
Annapolis, United States Naval
Institute [c1966] xl, 367 p.
355.0008 66-22342
    U19 .H4 MRR Ref Desk.

NAVAL ART AND SCIENCE--TERMINOLOGY.
Colcord, Joanna Carver. Sea language
comes ashore. New York, Cornell
maritime press [1945] ix, 213 p.
427.9   45-966
   PE1689 .C65 MRR Alc.

Lovette, Leland Pearson. Naval
customs, traditions & usage. [4th
ed.] Annapolis, Md., United States
Naval Institute [1959] xiv, 358 p.
359.0973   59-11628
   V310 .L6 1959 MRR Alc.

NAVAL ART AND SCIENCE--YEARBOOKS.
Brassey's annual. 1st- year; 1886-
New York [etc.] Praeger [etc.]
359.058   12-30905
   V10 .N3 MRR Alc Latest edition

NAVAL BIOGRAPHY.
Riverain, Jean. Dictionnaire des
marins célèbres. Paris, Larousse,
1967. 157 p. [N.T.]   68-137808
   V61 .R58 MRR Biog.

**NAVAL CEREMONIES, HONORS, AND SALUTES--
UNITED STATES.**
Lovette, Leland Pearson. Naval
customs, traditions & usage. [4th
ed.] Annapolis, Md., United States
Naval Institute [1959] xiv, 358 p.
359.0973   59-11628
   V310 .L6 1959 MRR Alc.

NAVAL CHAPLAINS
see Chaplains, Military

NAVAL CONSTRUCTION
see Ship-building

NAVAL DISTRICTS--UNITED STATES.
Carrison, Daniel J. The United
States Navy. New York, Praeger [1968]
x, 262 p.   359/.00973 68-16081
   VA55 .C3 MRR Alc.

NAVAL HISTORY.
Potter, Elmer Belmont, ed. Sea
power. Englewood Cliffs, N.J.,
Prentice-Hall, 1960. xii, 932 p.
359.09   60-15619
   D27 .P65 MRR Alc.

NAVAL HISTORY--BIBLIOGRAPHY.
Albion, Robert Greenhalgh. Naval &
maritime history; 4th ed., rev. and
expanded. Mystic, Conn., Munson
Institute of American Maritime
History, 1972. ix, 370 p. [$15.00]
016.387/09   73-186863
   Z6834.H5 A4 1972 MRR Alc.

NAVAL HISTORY--PICTORIAL WORKS.
Lloyd, Christopher. Ships & seamen.
London, Weidenfeld & Nicolson, c1961.
223 p.   64-39484
   D27 .L55 MRR Alc.

**NAVAL HISTORY--SOURCES--BIBLIOGRAPHY--
CATALOGS.**
United States. Library of Congress.
Manuscript Division. Dudley Wright
Knox: a register of his papers in the
Library of Congress. Washington,
Library of Congress, 1971. 16 p.
016.359/007/22   70-173823
   Z6834.34 .K66 MRR Alc.

NAVAL HISTORY, MODERN.
Potter, Elmer Belmont, ed. The
United States and world sea power.
Englewood Cliffs [N.J.] Prentice-
Hall, 1955. ix, 963 p.   973 55-
9323
   E182 .P8 MRR Alc.

NAVAL MUSEUMS.
Aymar, Brandt. A pictorial treasury
of the marine museums of the world;
New York, Crown Publishers [1967]
viii, 244 p.   623.8/074 67-27032
   VM307 .A94 MRR Alc.

NAVARRE (PROVINCE)--DIRECTORIES.
Guía-anuario de Aragón, Rioja,
Navarra, Alava, Guipúzcoa y Vizcaya.
Zaragoza, E. Gallegos.   51-22040
   DP11 .G78 MRR Alc Latest edition

NAVIES.
Blackman, Raymond V. B. The world's
warships 4th and completely rev. ed.
Garden City, N.Y., Doubleday [1970,
c1969] 159 p.   [5.95] 623.82/5 70-
7563
   VA40 .B55 1970 MRR Alc.

Breyer, Siegfried. Battleships and
battle cruisers, 1905-1970; Garden
City, N.Y., Doubleday [1973] 480 p.
[$25.00] 359.3/2/520904 72-84895
   V765 .B6813 MRR Alc.

Les Flottes de combat. Paris,
Éditions Maritimes et D'outre-Mer
[etc.] 623.825 11-13474
   VA40 .F64 MRR Alc Latest edition

Jane's fighting ships. [1st]- 1898-
London, S. Low, Marston and
Co. [etc.]   07-25192
   VA40 .F5 Sci RR Latest edition /
   MRR Alc Latest edition

Kafka, Roger, ed. Warships of the
world. Victory ed. New York,
Cornell maritime press [1946] x p.,
1 l., 1167 p.   623.825 47-119
   VA40 .K3 1946 MRR Alc.

NAVIES--STATISTICS.
The Military balance. London,
International Institute for Strategic
Studies.   355.03/32/05 79-617319
   UA15 .L652 MRR Ref Desk Latest
   edition

NAVIES--YEARBOOKS.
Weyer's warships of the world. 1968-
Annapolis, United States Naval
Institute.   623.82/5/05 67-14517
   V10 .W47 Sci RR Latest edition /
   MRR Alc Latest edition

NAVIES, COST OF--PERIODICALS.
United States. Arms Control and
Disarmament Agency. Bureau of
Economic Affairs. World military
expenditures. 1970- [Washington,
for sale by the Supt. of Docs., U.S.
Govt. Print. Off.] 338.4/7/355005
70-649143
   UA17 .U42 MRR Ref Desk Latest
   edition

NAVIGATION.
see also Harbors

see also Lighthouses

NAVIGATION--TABLES.
Norie, John William. Norie's
nautical tables with explanations of
their use. Revised ed.: Saint Ives,
Laurie, Norie and Wilson, 1973. lii,
608 p.   623.89/021/2 73-178120
   VK563 .N86 1973 MRR Alc.

NAVIGATION (AERONAUTICS)
see also Aeroplanes--Piloting

NAVIGATION (AERONAUTICS)--TABLES.
The Air almanac. Jan./Apr. 1953-
Washington, U.S. Govt. Print. Off.
52-61239
   TL587 .A36 MRR Alc Latest edition

NAVIGATION (ASTRONAUTICS)
see also Space flight

see also Space vehicles

NAVIGATION ACTS, 1649-1696.
Dickerson, Oliver Morton. The
navigation acts and the American
Revolution. Philadelphia, University
of Pennsylvania Press, 1951. xv, 344
p.   973.3112 51-13206
   E215.1 .D53 MRR Alc.

NEAR EAST.
see also Arab countries

see also Asia, Western

Adams, Michael. The Middle East;
New York, Praeger [1971] xiii, 633
p.   [$25.00] 915.6/03 77-134528
   DS44 .A3 1971b MRR Alc.

The Middle East and North Africa.
[1st]- ed.; 1948- London, Europa
Publications. 48-3250
   DS49 .M5 MRR Alc Latest edition

NEAR EAST--ANTIQUITIES--DICTIONARIES.
Pfeiffer, Charles F., ed. The
Biblical world; Grand Rapids, Baker
Book House [1966] 612 p. 220.9303
66-19312
   BS62 .P4 MRR Alc.

NEAR EAST--BIBLIOGRAPHY.
American University of Beirut.
Economic Research Institute. A
selected and annotated bibliography
of economic literature on the Arab
countries of the Middle East, 1953-
1965. Beirut, 1967. xvii, 458 p.
016.3309174/927 ne 68-4814
   Z7165.A67 A56 MRR Alc.

Sharabi, Hisham Bashir. A handbook
on the contemporary Middle East;
Washington, Georgetown University,
1956. vii, 113 p.   016.956 57-2001

   Z3013 .S47 MRR Alc.

United States. Library of Congress.
Introduction to the Near East
collections in the Library of
Congress. Washington, 1953. 5 p.
016.956 53-63370
   Z663.387 .I5 MRR Alc.

NEAR EAST--BIOGRAPHY.
Heravi, Mehdi. Concise encyclopedia
of the Middle East. Washington,
Public Affairs Press [1973] 336 p.
[$12.00] 915.6/03/03 73-82012
   DS43 .H47 MRR Alc.

The Middle East and North Africa.
[1st]- ed:, 1948- London, Europa
Publications. 48-3250
   DS49 .M5 MRR Alc Latest edition

Who's who in U.A.R. and the Near
East. Cairo. 354.62 45-33763
   DT44 .W47 MRR Biog Latest edition

NEAR EAST--BIOGRAPHY--DICTIONARIES.
Shimoni, Yaacov. Political
dictionary of the Middle East in the
twentieth century; London,
Weidenfeld and Nicolson, 1972. 434
p. [£5.00] 320.9/56 72-188540
   DS61 .S52 MRR Alc.

NEAR EAST--COMMERCE--DIRECTORIES.
The Eastern trade directory. [Cairo]
   ne 62-1365
   HF3760.8 .E25 MRR Alc Latest
   edition

Guide du commerce mondial pour les
professions liberales. Beyrouth,
Mansour. ne 66-1383
   HF3866 .G55 MRR Alc Latest edition

The Middle East trade directory.
1961/62- Beirut, Y. S. Karam. ne 63-
729
   HF3760.8 .M5 MRR Alc Latest
   edition

NEAR EAST--COMMERCE--YEARBOOKS.
Owen's commerce and travel and
international register. London,
Owen's Commerce & Travel Ltd.
380.1/025 72-626541
   HF3872 .P3 MRR Alc Latest edition

NEAR EAST--DESCRIPTION AND TRAVEL.
Fisher, William Bayne. The Middle
East: 5th ed. London, Methuen; New
York, Dutton, 1966. xiii, 568 p.
[63/-]   915.6 67-107597
   DS49 .F56 1966 MRR Alc.

**NEAR EAST--DESCRIPTION AND TRAVEL--
GUIDE-BOOKS.**
The Middle East, Lebanon, Syria,
Jordan, Iraq, Iran. Paris, Hachette
(impr. Brodard et Taupin), 1966.
1060 p. [37.95 F.] 915.6/04/3 68-
71419
   DS43 .M6813 1966 MRR Alc.

Showker, Kay. Complete reference
guide to the Arab Middle East: [1st
ed. New York] Pan American Airways;
[trade distribution in the U.S. and
Canada by Simon and Schuster, 1967]
191 p. 915.6/04 67-19408
   DS43 .S5 MRR Alc.

**NEAR EAST--DICTIONARIES AND
ENCYCLOPEDIAS.**
The Encyclopaedia of Islam; Leyden,
E. J. Brill ltd.; London, Luzac & co,
1913- v.   26-26918
   DS37 .E5 MRR Alc.

Heravi, Mehdi. Concise encyclopedia
of the Middle East. Washington,
Public Affairs Press [1973] 336 p.
[$12.00] 915.6/03/03 73-82012
   DS43 .H47 MRR Alc.

Shimoni, Yaacov. Political
dictionary of the Middle East in the
twentieth century; London,
Weidenfeld and Nicolson, 1972. 434
p. [£5.00] 320.9/56 72-188540
   DS61 .S52 MRR Alc.

NEAR EAST--ECONOMIC CONDITIONS.
Middle East and North Africa markets
review. [Epping, Eng.] Gower
Economic Publications. [£30.00]
330.9/56/04 74-640571
   HC410.7.A1 M48 MRR Alc Latest
   edition

The Middle East trade directory.
1961/62- Beirut, Y. S. Karam. ne 63-
729
   HF3760.8 .M5 MRR Alc Latest
   edition

NEAR EAST--FOREIGN RELATIONS.
Middle East record. v. 1- 1960-
Jerusalem [etc.]. 63-48859
   DS63 .M58 MRR Alc Full set

NEAR EAST--HISTORY.
Fisher, Sydney Nettleton. The Middle
East; a history. 2d ed. [rev. and
enl.] New York, Knopf [1968, c1969]
xiv, 749, xxx p. [$13.95] 956 68-
24673
   DS62 .F5 1969 MRR Alc.

Yale, William. The Near East; a
modern history. New ed., rev. and
enl. Ann Arbor, University of
Michigan Press [1968] x, 495, xxii
p. [$8.50] 956 68-29269
   DS62.4 .Y3 1968 MRR Alc.

NEAR EAST--HISTORY--622-1517
see Islamic Empire

NEAR EAST--HISTORY--1517- --SOURCES.
Hurewitz, Jacob Coleman, ed.
Diplomacy in the Near and Middle
East; New York, Octagon Books, 1972
[c1956] 2 v. 956 72-2494
   DS42 .H782 MRR Alc.

NEAR EAST--HISTORY--1517- -- (Cont.)
United States. Library of Congress.
Foreign Affairs Division. A select
chronology and background documents
relating to the Middle East. 1st
rev. ed. Washington, U.S. Govt.
Print. Off., 1969. vii, 287 p.
[1.25]   956/.002   76-602249
DS62.8 .U55 1969 MRR Alc.

NEAR EAST--HISTORY--CHRONOLOGY.
Mansoor, Menahem. Political and
diplomatic history of the Arab world,
1900-1967; [Washington] NCR
Microcard Editions, 1972. 7 v.
320.9/17/4927 72-184866
DS62.8 .M35 MRR Alc.

NEAR EAST--HISTORY--SOURCES.
Fisher, Carol Ann. Middle East in
crisis; [Syracuse] Syracuse
University Press [1959] 213 p.   956
59-9859
DS63 .F5 MRR Alc.

Higgins, Rosalyn. United Nations
peacekeeping, 1946-1967: London, New
York [etc.] issued under the auspices
of the Royal Institute of
International Affairs by Oxford U.P.,
1969-   v.   [5/10- (v. 1)]   341.6
76-396893
JX1981.P7 B5 MRR Alc.

NEAR EAST--IMPRINTS.
United States Library of Congress.
American Libraries Book Procurement
Center, Cairo. Accessions list,
Middle East. v. 1-   Jan. 1963-
Cairo.   63-24163
Z663.767.A1 A25 MRR Alc   MRR Alc
Full set

NEAR EAST--PERIODICALS--BIBLIOGRAPHY.
Ljunggren, Florence. Annotated guide
to journals dealing with the Middle
East and North Africa, Cairo,
American University in Cairo Press,
1964. viii, 105 p.   ne 65-2428
Z3013 .L655 MRR Alc.

NEAR EAST--PERIODICALS--INDEXES.
London. University. School of
Oriental and African Studies.
Library. Index Islamicus, 1906-1955;
Cambridge, Eng., W. Heffer [1958]
xxxvi, 897 p.   016.9156   59-23014
Z7835.M6 L6 MRR Alc.

NEAR EAST--POLITICS.
Abboushi, W. F., Political systems
of the Middle East in the 20th
century New York, Dodd, Mead, 1970.
xiii, 345 p.   320.9/56 71-108046
DS62.8 .A2 MRR Alc.

Fisher, Carol Ann. Middle East in
crisis; [Syracuse] Syracuse
University Press [1959] 213 p.   956
59-9859
DS63 .F5 MRR Alc.

NEAR EAST--POLITICS--COLLECTIONS.
Magnus, Ralph H., comp. Documents on
the Middle East, Washington,
American Enterprise Institute for
Public Policy Research, 1969. viii,
232 p. [3.00]   327.56/073 75-93191

DS42 .M3 MRR Alc.

NEAR EAST--POLITICS--DICTIONARIES.
Shimoni, Yaacov, Political
dictionary of the Middle East in the
twentieth century; London,
Weidenfeld and Nicolson, 1972.   434
p. [£5.00]   320.9/56   72-188540
DS61 .S52 MRR Alc.

NEAR EAST--POLITICS--SOURCES.
United States. Library of Congress.
Foreign Affairs Division. A select
chronology and background documents
relating to the Middle East. 1st
rev. ed. Washington, U.S. Govt.
Print. Off., 1969. vii, 287 p.
[1.25]   956/.002   76-602249
DS62.8 .U55 1969 MRR Alc.

NEAR EAST--POLITICS--YEARBOOKS.
Middle East record. v. 1-   1960-
Jerusalem [etc.] 63-48859
DS63 .M58 MRR Alc Full set

NEAR EAST--RELIGION.
James, Edwin Oliver, The ancient
gods; London, Weidenfeld and
Nicolson [1960] 359 p.   290 60-
4641
BL96 .J32 1960a MRR Alc.

NEAR EAST--SOCIETIES, ETC.--DIRECTORIES.
Ljunggren, Florence, ed. An
international directory of institutes
and societies interested in the
Middle East. Amsterdam, Djambatan
[1962] 159 p.   060 63-36286
DS41 .L5 MRR Alc.

NEAR EAST--STATISTICS.
Middle East and North Africa markets
review. [Epping, Eng.] Gower
Economic Publications. [£30.00]
330.9/56/04 74-640571
HC410.7.A1 M48   MRR Alc Latest
edition

NEBRASKA--BIBLIOGRAPHY.
Historical records survey. Nebraska.
A check list of Nebraska imprints,
1847-1876. Lincoln, Neb., 1942. 2
v.   015.782 42-16593
Z1215 .H67 no. 26-27 MRR Alc.

United States. Library of Congress.
Kansas and Nebraska, centennial of
the Territories, 1894-1954;
Washington, 1954. vi, 71 p.
016.9781 54-60003
Z663.15.A6K3 MRR Alc.

NEBRASKA--BIOGRAPHY.
Nebraska blue book. Lincoln, Neb.
353.9782 99-1456
JK6630 .N4 MRR Alc Latest edition

NEBRASKA--CENTENNIAL CELEBRATIONS, ETC.
United States. Library of Congress.
Kansas and Nebraska, centennial of
the Territories, 1894-1954;
Washington, 1954. vi, 71 p.
016.9781 54-60003
Z663.15.A6K3 MRR Alc.

NEBRASKA--DESCRIPTION AND TRAVEL--GUIDE-
BOOKS.
Federal writers' project. Nebraska.
Nebraska; a guide to the cornhusker
state; New York, The Viking press,
1939. xxiii, 424 p.   917.82 39-
27582
F666 .F46 MRR Ref Desk.

NEBRASKA--EXECUTIVE DEPARTMENTS.
Nebraska blue book. Lincoln, Neb.
353.9782 99-1456
JK6630 .N4 MRR Alc Latest edition

NEBRASKA--GOVERNMENT PUBLICATIONS--
BIBLIOGRAPHY.
Historical records survey. Nebraska.
A check list of Nebraska imprints,
1847-1876. Lincoln, Neb., 1942. 2
v.   015.782 42-16593
Z1215 .H67 no. 26-27 MRR Alc.

NEBRASKA--HISTORY.
Olson, James C. History of Nebraska,
[2d ed.] Lincoln, University of
Nebraska Press, 1966. xii, 387 p.
978.2 67-8965
F666 .048 1966 MRR Alc.

NEBRASKA--IMPRINTS.
Historical records survey. Nebraska.
A check list of Nebraska imprints,
1847-1876. Lincoln, Neb., 1942. 2
v.   015.782 42-16593
Z1215 .H67 no. 26-27 MRR Alc.

NEBRASKA--MANUFACTURES--DIRECTORIES.
A Directory of Nebraska manufacturers
and their products. Lincoln. 72-
625673
T12 .D62   MRR Alc Latest edition

NEBRASKA--POLITICS AND GOVERNMENT.
Nebraska blue book. Lincoln, Neb.
353.9782 99-1456
JK6630 .N4   MRR Alc Latest edition

NEBRASKA--REGISTERS.
Nebraska blue book. Lincoln, Neb.
353.9782 99-1456
JK6630 .N4 MRR Alc Latest edition

NECROMANCY
see Magic

NEEDLEPOINT.
Lent, D. Geneva, Needle point as a
hobby, New York, London, Harper &
brothers, 1942. xiii p., 1 l., 180
p.   746 42-13832
TT770 .L4 MRR Alc.

NEEDLEWORK.
see also Dressmaking

see also Sewing

Guild, Vera P. Good housekeeping's
complete book of needlecraft. New
York, Good Housekeeping, Book Dept.
[1959] 498 p.   746.4 59-6356
TT750 .G86 MRR Alc.

NEEDLEWORK, AMERICAN.
Harbeson, Georgiana (Brown) Mrs.,
American needlework; New York,
Coward-McCann, inc., 1938. xxxviii,
232 p.   746 38-29098
NK9212 .H3 MRR Alc.

NEGROES--BIOGRAPHY.
Burke, Joan Martin. Civil rights;
2d ed. New York, Bowker, 1974. xi,
266 p.   323.4/025/73 74-4053
JC599.U5 B85 1974 MRR Alc.

NEGRO ACTORS.
Bogle, Donald. Toms, coons,
mulattoes, mammies, and bucks; New
York, Viking Press [1973] xviii, 260
p. [$12.50]   791.43/0973 72-76776

PN1995.9.N4 B6 MRR Alc.

Hughes, Langston, Black magic;
Englewood Cliffs, N.J., Prentice-Hall
[1967] 375 p.   780.2/09174/86 67-
22993
PN2286 .H75 MRR Alc.

Patterson, Lindsay, comp. Anthology
of the American Negro in the theatre;
[2d ed.] New York, Publishers Co.
[1968] xiv, 306 p.   792.09174/96
68-2730
PN2226 .P3 1968 MRR Alc.

NEGRO AFRICA
see Africa, Sub-Saharan

NEGRO ART.
United States. Library of Congress.
75 years of freedom; [Washington,
U.S. Govt. print. off.; 1943] cover-
title, vi, 108 p.   325.260973 43-
52457
Z663 .S43 MRR Alc.

NEGRO ART--UNITED STATES.
Porter, James Amos, Modern Negro art
New York, Arno Press, 1969. viii,
272 p. [10.00]   709.73 69-18593
N6538.N5 P6 1969 MRR Alc.

NEGRO ARTISTS--BIBLIOGRAPHY.
Williams, Ora, American Black women
in the arts and social sciences: a
bibliographic survey. Metuchen,
N.J., Scarecrow Press, 1973. xix,
141 p.   016.3014/12/0922 73-4560
Z1361.N39 W56 1973 MRR Biog.

NEGRO ARTISTS--BIO-BIBLIOGRAPHY--
DIRECTORIES.
Cederholm, Theresa Dickason. Afro-
American artists; a bio-
bibliographical directory. [Boston]
Trustees of the Boston Public
Library, 1973. 348 p.   709/.73 73-
84951
N6538.N5 C42 MRR Biog.

NEGRO ARTISTS--UNITED STATES.
Patterson, Lindsay, comp. The Negro
in music and art. [1st ed.] New
York, Publishers Co. [1967] xvi, 304
p.   781.7/2/86 67-6841
ML3556 .P38 MRR Alc.

Porter, James Amos, Modern Negro art
New York, Arno Press, 1969. viii,
272 p. [10.00]   709.73 69-18593
N6538.N5 P6 1969 MRR Alc.

NEGRO ATHLETES.
Ploski, Harry A. Reference library
of Black America. [New York]
Bellwether Pub. Co.; for exclusive
distribution by Afro-American Press
[c1971] 5 v. 917.3/06/96073 74-
151239
E185 .P56 MRR Alc.

NEGRO AUTHORS.
Bailey, Leaonead Pack. Broadside
authors and artists; [1st ed.]
Detroit, Mich., Broadside Press
[1974] 125 p. [$9.95]   811/.5/409
B 70-108887
Z1229.N39 B34 MRR Biog.

Hatch, James V., comp. Black
theater, U.S.A.; forty-five plays by
black Americans, 1847-1974. New
York, Free Press [1974] x, 886 p.
[$19.95]   812/.008/0352 75-169234
PS628.N4 H3 MRR Alc.

Loggins, Vernon, The Negro author,
his development in America to 1900.
Port Washington, N.Y., Kennikat Press
[1964, c1959] ix, 480 p.   810.9 64-
15540
PS153.N5 L65 1964 MRR Alc.

Lomax, Alan, comp. 3000 years of
black poetry; New York, Dodd, Mead
[1970] xxvi, 261 p. [6.95]   808.81
76-95909
PN6109.7 .L6 MRR Alc.

Ploski, Harry A. Reference library
of Black America. [New York]
Bellwether Pub. Co.; for exclusive
distribution by Afro-American Press
[c1971] 5 v.   917.3/06/96073 74-
151239
E185 .P56 MRR Alc.

Shockley, Ann Allen. Living Black
American authors: New York, R. R.
Bowker Co., 1973. xv, 220 p.
810/.9/896073 73-17005
PS153.N5 S5 MRR Biog.

Turner, Darwin T., Afro-American
writers. New York, Appleton-Century-
Crofts, Educational Division [1970]
xviii, 117 p.   016.8108/091/7496 72-
78171
Z1361.N39 T78 MRR Alc.

NEGRO AUTHORS--BIBLIOGRAPHY.
Brignano, Russell Carl. Black
Americans in autobiography; Durham,
N.C., Duke University Press, 1974.
ix, 118 p. [$5.75]
016.9173/06/96073022 B 73-92535
Z1361.N39 B67 MRR Alc.

Howard University, Washington, D.C.
Library. Dictionary catalog of the
Arthur B. Spingarn Collection of
Negro Authors. Boston, G. K. Hall,
1970. 2 v.   016.909/.04/96 72-
187159
Z1361.N39 H78 MRR Alc (Dk 33)

NEGRO AUTHORS--BIBLIOGRAPHY. (Cont.)
Whitlow, Roger. Black American
literature; Chicago, Nelson Hall
[1973] xv, 287 p. [$8.95]
810/.9/896073 73-75525
PS153.N5 W45 MRR Alc.

Williams, Ora, American Black women
in the arts and social sciences: a
bibliographic survey. Metuchen,
N.J., Scarecrow Press, 1973. xix,
141 p. 016.3014/12/0922 73-4560
Z1361.N39 W56 1973 MRR Biog.

NEGRO AUTHORS--JUVENILE LITERATURE.
Rollins, Charlemae Hill. Famous
American Negro poets. New York,
Dodd, Mead [1965] 95 p. 928.1 65-
11811
PS153.N5 R6 MRR Biog.

NEGRO BUSINESSMEN--UNITED STATES--
DIRECTORIES.
National directory of minority
manufacturers. [Washington] Office
of Minority Business Enterprise.
338/.0025/73 74-645920
HD2346.U5 N33 MRR Alc Latest
edition

NEGRO BUSINESSMEN--WASHINGTON
METROPOLITAN AREA--DIRECTORIES--
PERIODICALS.
Impact directory. [Washington,
Impact Press] 338.7/6/025753 74-
645912
HD2346.U52 W355 MRR Alc Latest
edition

NEGRO CLERGY--UNITED STATES--BIOGRAPHY--
DICTIONARIES.
Williams, Ethel L. Biographical
directory of Negro ministers, 2d ed.
Metuchen, N.J., Scarecrow Press,
1970. 605 p. 262/.14/0922 B 78-
18496
BR563.N4 W5 1970 MRR Biog.

NEGRO DRAMA.
Patterson, Lindsay, comp. Anthology
of the American Negro in the theatre;
[2d ed.] New York, Publishers Co.
[1968] xiv, 306 p. 792.09174/96
68-2730
PN2226 .P3 1968 MRR Alc.

NEGRO DRAMA--BIBLIOGRAPHY.
Hatch, James Vernon. Black image on
the American stage; New York, DBS
Publications [1970] xiii, 162 p.
016.812/008 72-115695
Z5784.N4 H35 MRR Alc.

NEGRO INVENTORS.
Haber, Louis. The role of the
American Negro in the fields of
science. [New York?] 1966. 70 l.
509/.22 B 67-62053
Q141 .H212 MRR Biog.

Ploski, Harry A. Reference library
of Black America. [New York]
Bellwether Pub. Co.; for exclusive
distribution by Afro-American Press
[c1971] 5 v. 917.3/06/86073 74-
151239
E185 .P56 MRR Alc.

Salk, Erwin A. A layman's guide to
Negro history. New, enl. ed. New
York, McGraw-Hill [1967] xviii, 196
p. 016.91003/174/96 67-22967
Z1361.N39 S23 1967 MRR Alc.

NEGRO LITERATURE--BIBLIOGRAPHY.
Fontvieille, Jean Roger. Guide
bibliographique du Monde noir.
Yaoundé, Direction des affaires
culturelles, 1970 [cover 1971- v.
72-205179
Z5118.N4 F64 MRR Alc.

Jahn, Janheinz. A bibliography of
neo-African literature from Africa,
America, and the Caribbean. New
York, F. A. Praeger [1965] xxxv, 359
p. 016.80889917496 65-23927
Z3508.L5 J3 MRR Alc.

NEGRO LITERATURE--BIBLIOGRAPHY--
CATALOGS.
Howard University, Washington, D.C.
Library. Dictionary catalog of the
Arthur B. Spingarn Collection of
Negro Authors. Boston, G. K. Hall,
1970. 2 v. 016.909/.04/96 72-
187159
Z1361.N39 H78 MRR Alc (Dk 33)

NEGRO LITERATURE--HISTORY AND CRITICISM.
Jahn, Janheinz. Neo-African
literature; New York, Grove Press
[1969, c1968] 301 p. [7.50]
809.8/91/7496 68-58154
PL8010 .J313 1969 MRR Alc.

NEGRO LITERATURE--AFRICA, SUB-SAHARAN--
BIBLIOGRAPHY.
Abrash, Barbara. Black African
literature in English since 1952;
New York, Johnson Reprint Corp.,
1967. xiv, 92 p. 016.82 67-29100

Z3508.L5 A25 MRR Alc.

NEGRO MUSIC--BIBLIOGRAPHY--CATALOGS.
Howard University, Washington, D.C.
Library. Dictionary catalog of the
Arthur B. Spingarn Collection of
Negro Authors. Boston, G. K. Hall,
1970. 2 v. 016.909/.04/96 72-
187159
Z1361.N39 H78 MRR Alc (Dk 33)

NEGRO MUSIC--HISTORY AND CRITICISM.
Patterson, Lindsay, comp. The Negro
in music and art. [1st ed.] New
York, Publishers Co. [1967] xvi, 304
p. 781.7/2/96 67-6941
ML3556 .P38 MRR Alc.

NEGRO MUSICIANS.
Patterson, Lindsay, comp. The Negro
in music and art. [1st ed.] New
York, Publishers Co. [1967] xvi, 304
p. 781.7/2/96 67-6941
ML3556 .P38 MRR Alc.

NEGRO NEWSPAPERS (AMERICAN)--
BIBLIOGRAPHY.
[Pride, Armistead Scott] Negro
newspapers on microfilm; Washington,
Library of Congress, Photoduplication
Service, 1953. 8 p. 016.071 53-
60015
Z663.96 .N4 MRR Alc.

NEGRO NEWSPAPERS (AMERICAN)--
DIRECTORIES.
La Brie, Henry G. The Black
newspaper in America; 3d ed.
[Kennebunkport, Me.; Mercer House
Press] 1973. 84 p. [$5.00]
070/.02573 73-166319
Z6944.N39 L3 1973 MRR Alc.

NEGRO PERIODICALS (AMERICAN)--
BIBLIOGRAPHY.
Howard University, Washington, D.C.
Library. Moorland Foundation.
Dictionary catalog of the Jesse E.
Moorland Collection of Negro Life and
History, Howard University,
Washington, D.C. Boston, G. K. Hall,
1970. 9 v. 016.910/0396 72-195773

Z1361.N39 H82 MRR Alc (Dk 33)

NEGRO PERIODICALS (AMERICAN)--INDEXES.
A Guide to Negro periodical
literature. v. 1-4, no. 3; Feb. 1941-
Sept. 1946. Winston-Salem, N.C.
[etc.] 016.32526 45-41371
Z1361.N39 G8 MRR Alc Full set

Index to periodical articles by and
about Negroes. v. 17- 1966-
Boston, G. K. Hall. 051 72-627261
AI3 .O4 MRR Alc Full set

Ohio. Central State College,
Wilberforce. Library. Index to
selected periodicals. Mar. 1950-
Wilberforce. 50-62898
MRR Alc Full set

NEGRO POETRY.
Lomax, Alan, comp. 3000 years of
black poetry; New York, Dodd, Mead
[1970] xxvi, 261 p. [6.95] 808.81
76-95909
PN6109.7 .L6 MRR Alc.

NEGRO PRESS--DIRECTORIES.
Black list; New York, Panther House
[1970] 289 p. [$12.50 (pbk)]
001.5/025/6 73-112479
P88.8 .B6 MRR Alc.

NEGRO PRESS--UNITED STATES.
Dann, Martin E., comp. The Black
press, 1827-1890; New York, Putnam
[1971] 384 p. [$7.95]
301.451/96/073 72-127714
E185.5 .D35 1971 MRR Alc.

Detweiler, Frederick German. The
Negro press in the United States.
College Park, Md., McGrath Pub. Co.,
1968 [c1922] x, 274 p. 071/.3 68-
7818
PN4888.N4 D4 1968 MRR Alc.

Ploski, Harry A. Afro USA; [New
York] Bellwether Pub. Co.;
distributed by Afro-American Press
[1971] 1110 p. 301.45/19/60730022
70-151238
E185 .P55 1971 MRR Ref Desk.

Ploski, Harry A. The Negro almanac,
[1st ed.] New York, Bellwether Pub.
Co. [1967] xi, 1012 p. 973 66-
29721
E185 .P55 MRR Ref Desk.

Wolseley, Roland Edgar. The Black
press, U.S.A. [1st ed.] Ames, Iowa
State University Press [1971] xiii,
362 p. [$10.50] 070.4/84 74-
126160
PN4888.N4 W6 MRR Alc.

NEGRO PRESS--UNITED STATES--
BIBLIOGRAPHY.
Ayer directory of publications.
Philadelphia, Ayer Press. 071.3/025
73-640052
Z6951 .A97 Sci RR Latest edition /
MRR Ref Desk Latest edition / MRR
Alc Latest edition

NEGRO RACE--BIBLIOGRAPHY.
Encyclopedia of the Negro, Rev. and
enl. ed. New York, The Phelps-Stokes
fund, inc., 1946. 215, [1] p.
572.96 47-1133
HT1581 .E5 1946 MRR Alc.

Fontvieille, Jean Roger. Guide
bibliographique du Monde noir.
Yaoundé, Direction des affaires
culturelles, 1970 [cover 1971- v.
72-205179
Z5118.N4 F64 MRR Alc.

Thompson, Edgar Tristram. Race and
region. Chapel Hill, Univ. of North
Carolina Press, 1949. xii, 194 p.
016.32526097473 49-1367
Z1361.N39 T5 MRR Alc.

Work, Monroe Nathan. A bibliography
of the Negro in Africa and America.
New York, Octagon Books, 1965 [c1928]
xxi, 698 p. 016.9100917496 65-
28242
Z1361.N39 W8 1965 MRR Alc.

NEGRO RACE--BIOGRAPHY.
Rogers, Joel Augustus. World's great
men of color. New York, Macmillan
[1972, c1946-47] 2 v. 920/.0092/96
73-186437
DT18 .R592 MRR Biog.

NEGRO RACE--DICTIONARIES AND
ENCYCLOPEDIAS.
Encyclopedia of the Negro, Rev. and
enl. ed. New York, The Phelps-Stokes
fund, inc., 1946. 215, [1] p.
572.96 47-1133
HT1581 .E5 1946 MRR Alc.

NEGRO RACE--HISTORY--BIBLIOGRAPHY.
Fontvieille, Jean Roger. Guide
bibliographique du Monde noir.
Yaoundé, Direction des affaires
culturelles, 1970 [cover 1971- v.
72-205179
Z5118.N4 F64 MRR Alc.

NEGRO SCIENTISTS.
Haber, Louis. The role of the
American Negro in the fields of
science. [New York?] 1966. 70 l.
509/.22 B 67-62053
Q141 .H212 MRR Biog.

NEGRO SONGS.
see also Blues (Songs, etc.)

Lomax, John Avery, comp. American
ballads and folk songs. New York,
The Macmillan company, 1935. xxxix,
625 p. 784.4973 38-9495
M1629 .L85A52 MRR Alc.

United States. Library of Congress.
75 years of freedom; [Washington,
U.S. Govt. print. off., 1943] cover-
title, vi, 108 p. 325.260973 43-
52457
Z663 .S43 MRR Alc.

NEGRO SONGS--BIBLIOGRAPHY.
Haywood, Charles, A bibliography of
North American folklore and folksong.
2d rev. ed. New York, Dover
Publications [1961] 2 v. (xxx, 1301
p.) 016.398 62-3483
Z5984.U5 H32 MRR Alc.

NEGRO UNIVERSITIES AND COLLEGES--
DIRECTORIES.
Black list; New York, Panther House
[1970] 289 p. [$12.50 (pbk)]
001.5/025/6 73-112479
P88.8 .B6 MRR Alc.

NEGRO UNIVERSITIES AND COLLEGES--UNITED
STATES--DIRECTORIES.
Plans for Progress. Directory of
Negro colleges and universities,
March, 1967. Washington [1967] ii,
103 p. 378.73 67-61097
LC2801 .P55 1967 MRR Ref Desk.

United States. Bureau of
Apprenticeship and Training.
Directory for reaching minority
groups. [Washington; For sale by the
Supt. of Docs., U.S. Govt. Print.
Off.] 1973. 214 p. [$2.85] 331.6
73-602280
HD6305.M5 U53 1973 MRR alc.

NEGRO VOTING RIGHTS (UNITED STATES)
see Negroes--Politics and suffrage

NEGROES.
see also United States--Race question

Garrett, Romeo B. Famous first facts
about Negroes. New York, Arno Press,
1972. viii, 212 p. 301.45/19/6073
75-172613
E185 .G22 MRR Ref Desk.

Myrdal, Gunnar, An American dilemma;
20th anniversary ed. New York,
Harper & Row [1962] 1483 p.
301.451 62-18706
E185.6 .M95 1962 MRR Alc.

NEGROES. (Cont.)
Ploski, Harry A. Afro USA; [New York] Bellwether Pub. Co.; distributed by Afro-American Press [1971] 1110 p. 301.45/19/60730022 70-151238
     E185 .P55 1971 MRR Ref Desk.

Ploski, Harry A. The Negro almanac, [1st ed.] New York, Bellwether Pub. Co. [1967] xi, 1012 p. 873 66-29721
     E185 .P55 MRR Ref Desk.

Ploski, Harry A. Reference library of Black America. [New York] Bellwether Pub. Co.; for exclusive distribution by Afro-American Press [c1971] 5 v. 917.3/06/86073 74-151239
     E185 .P56 MRR Alc.

United States. Library of Congress. 75 years of freedom; [Washington, U.S. Govt. print. off., 1943] cover-title, vi, 108 p. 325.260873 43-52457
     Z663 .S43 MRR Alc.

NEGROES--ADDRESSES, ESSAYS, LECTURES.
Glenn, Norval D., comp. Blacks in the United States, San Francisco, Chandler Pub. Co.; distributed by Science Research Associates, Chicago [1969] xiii, 621 p. 301.451/96/073 69-15429
     E185.615 .G55 MRR Alc.

NEGROES--BIBLIOGRAPHY.
Baskin, Wade. Dictionary of Black culture, New York, Philosophical Library [1973] 493 p. [$15.00] 917.3/06/86003 72-78162
     E185.96 .B33 MRR Ref Desk.

Blacks in America; 1st ed.] Garden City, N.Y., Doubleday, 1971. xxii, 430 p. [$8.85] 016.9173/06/96073 70-164723
     Z1361.N39 B56 MRR Alc.

Enoch Pratt Free Library, Baltimore. The blacklist. Baltimore, 1969] [16] p. 016.301451/96 70-8465
     Z1361.N39 E5 MRR Alc.

Fontvieille, Jean Roger. Guide bibliographique du Monde noir. Yaounde, Direction des affaires culturelles, 1970 [cover 1971- v. 72-205179
     Z5118.N4 F64 MRR Alc.

Howard University, Washington, D.C. Library. Dictionary catalog of the Arthur B. Spingarn Collection of Negro Authors. Boston, G. K. Hall, 1970. 2 v. 016.909/.04/96 72-187159
     Z1361.N39 H78 MRR Alc (Dk 33)

Irwin, Leonard Bertram, Black studies: a bibliography. Brooklawn, N.J., McKinley Pub. Co., 1973. viii, 122 p. 016.9173/06/96073 73-160604
     Z1361.N39 I78 MRR Alc.

Kinton, Jack F. American ethnic groups and the revival of cultural pluralism; 4th ed. [Aurora, Ill., Social Science & Sociological Resources] 1974. 206 p. 016.9173/06 74-171031
     Z1361.E4 K55 1974 MRR Alc.

Los Angeles. University of Southern California. Library. An introduction to materials for ethnic studies in the University of Southern California Library. Los Angeles, 1970. ii, 196 p. 016.30145/0873 76-278151
     Z7164.R12 L66 MRR Alc.

Miller, Elizabeth W. The Negro in America; 2d ed., rev. and enl., Cambridge, Harvard University Press, 1970. xx, 351 p. [10.00] 016.301451/86/073 71-120319
     Z1361.N39 M5 1970 MRR Alc.

Miller, Kent S. Comparative studies of Blacks and whites in the United States. New York, Seminar Press, 1973. xiii, 572 p. 301.45/1/0420873 72-82126
     E185.86 .M53 MRR Alc.

Porter, Dorothy (Burnett), The Negro in the United States; Washington, Library of Congress; [for sale by the Supt. of Docs., U.S. Govt. Print. Off.] 1970. x, 313 p. [3.25] 016.9173/08/7496 78-606085
     Z1361.N38 P59 MRR Alc.

Porter, Dorothy (Burnett) A working bibliography on the Negro in the United States, [Ann Arbor, Mich.?] Xerox, University Microfilms, 1969. 202 p. 016.301451/96/073 68-55572

     Z1361.N39 P62 MRR Alc.

Race Relations Information Center. Directory of Afro-American resources. New York, R. R. Bowker Co. [1970] xv, 485 p. 917.3/06/96073 71-126008
     Z1361.N39 R3 MRR Alc.

Salk, Erwin A. A layman's guide to Negro history, New, enl. ed. New York, McGraw-Hill [1967] xviii, 196 p. 016.91003/174/96 67-22967
     Z1361.N39 S23 1967 MRR Alc.

Smith, Dwight La Vern, Afro-American history; Santa Barbara, Calif., ABC-Clio [1974] xvi, 856 p. 016.9173/06/96073 73-87155
     Z1361.N39 S56 MRR Alc.

Spangler, Earl. Bibliography of Negro history: Minneapolis, Ross and Haines, 1963. vii, 101 p. 016.967 63-2056
     Z1361.N39 S65 MRR Alc.

United States. Library of Congress. Division of bibliography. ... Select list of references on the Negro question. 2d issue, with additions. Washington, Govt. print. off., 1906. 61 p. 06-35017
     Z663.28 .S438 MRR Alc.

United States. National Clearinghouse for Mental Health Information. Bibliography on the urban crisis; Chevy Chase, Md., National Institute of Mental Health [1968] iv, 158 p. 016.3091/73 77-600665
     Z7164.S66 U57 MRR Alc.

Walton, Hanes, The study and analysis of Black politics: Metuchen, N.J., Scarecrow Press, 1973. xviii, 161 p. 016.32 73-12985
     Z1361.N39 W29 MRR Alc.

Welsch, Erwin K. The Negro in the United States; Bloomington, Indiana University Press, 1965. xiii, 142 p. 016.30145196073 65-23085
     Z1361.N39 W4 1965 MRR Alc.

West, Earle H. A bibliography of doctoral research on the Negro, 1933-1966. [Washington] Xerox, 1969. vii, 134 p. 016.301451/96/073 73-76349
     Z1361.N39 W44 MRR Alc.

Whitlow, Roger. Black American literature; Chicago, Nelson Hall [1973] xv, 287 p. [$8.95] 810/.9/896073 73-75525
     PS153.N5 W45 MRR Alc.

Williams, Daniel T. Eight Negro bibliographies. New York, Kraus Reprint Co., 1970. 1 v. (various pagings) 016.301451/96/073 71-107893
     Z1361.N39 W54 MRR Alc.

Williams, Ora, American Black women in the arts and social sciences: a bibliographic survey. Metuchen, N.J., Scarecrow Press, 1973. xix, 141 p. 016.3014/12/0922 73-4560
     Z1361.N39 W56 1973 MRR Biog.

NEGROES--BIBLIOGRAPHY--CATALOGS.
Howard University, Washington, D.C. Library. Moorland Foundation. Dictionary catalog of the Jesse E. Moorland Collection of Negro Life and History, Howard University, Washington, D.C. Boston, G. K. Hall, 1970. 9 v. 016.910/0396 72-195773

     Z1361.N39 H82 MRR Alc (Dk 33)

NEGROES--BIBLIOGRAPHY--PERIODICALS.
A Guide to Negro periodical literature. v. 1-4, no. 3; Feb. 1941-Sept. 1946. Winston-Salem, N.C. [etc.] 016.32526 45-41371
     Z1361.N39 G8 MRR Alc Full set

Index to periodical articles by and about Negroes. v. 17- 1966- Boston, G. K. Hall. 051 72-627261 AI3 .04 MRR Alc Full set

Ohio. Central State College, Wilberforce. Library. Index to selected periodicals. Mar. 1950- Wilberforce. 50-62898
     MRR Alc Full set

NEGROES--BIOGRAPHY.
1,000 successful Blacks. Chicago, Johnson Pub. Co., 1973. 341 p. 920/.073 73-5828
     E185.96 .O93 MRR Biog.

Adams, Russell L. Great Negroes, past and present, 3d ed. Chicago, Afro-Am Pub. Co., 1969. ix, 212 p. 920 72-87924
     E186.96 .A4 1969 MRR Biog.

Afro-American encyclopedia / 1st ed. North Miami, Fla. : Educational Book Publishers, [1974] 10 v. : 917.3/06/96073 70-94684
     E185 .A28 MRR Alc.

Baskin, Wade. Dictionary of Black culture, New York, Philosophical Library [1973] 493 p. [$15.00] 917.3/06/96003 72-78162
     E185.96 .B33 MRR Ref Desk.

Christmas, Walter, ed. Negroes in public affairs and government. [1st ed.] Yonkers [N.Y.] Educational Heritage [1966- v. 920.073 67-31903
     E185.96 .C47 MRR Biog.

Christopher, Maurine. America's Black congressmen. New York, Crowell [1971] xvi, 283 p. [$8.95] 328.73/0922 70-146280
     E185.96 .C5 1971 MRR Biog.

Dannett, Sylvia G. L., Profiles of Negro womanhood, [1st ed.] Yonkers, N.Y., Educational Heritage [1964-66] 2 v. 920.7 64-25013
     E185.96 .D25 MRR Alc.

Drotning, Phillip T. A guide to Negro history in America, [1st ed.] Garden City, N.Y., Doubleday, 1968. xiv, 247 p. [4.95] 917.3/04/923 68-14168
     E185 .D72 MRR Alc.

The Ebony handbook. Chicago, Johnson Pub. Co., 1974. 553 p. [$20.00] 917.3/06/96073 73-16179
     E185 .E22 MRR Ref Desk.

Fax, Elton C. Contemporary Black leaders New York, Dodd, Mead [1970] x, 243 p. [$4.95] 301.451/96/073 79-134322
     E185.96 .F38 MRR Biog.

Flynn, James J. Negroes of achievement in modern America, New York, Dodd, Mead [1970] 272 p. [4.50] 920.009174/96 70-111911
     E185.96 .F55 MRR Biog.

Garrett, Romeo B. Famous first facts about Negroes New York, Arno Press, 1972. viii, 212 p. 301.45/19/6073 75-172613
     E185 .G22 MRR Ref Desk.

Greene, Robert Ewell, Black defenders of America, 1775-1973. Chicago, Johnson Pub. Co., 1974. 416 p. 355.1 73-15607
     E185.63 .G73 MRR Alc.

Haber, Louis. The role of the American Negro in the fields of science. [New York?] 1966. 70 l. 509/.22 B 67-62053
     Q141 .H212 MRR Biog.

The National register; 1st- ed., 1952- Louisville, Ky., Register Publications. 325.260973 53-32943
     E185.96 .N37 MRR Biog Latest edition

Ploski, Harry A. Afro USA; [New York] Bellwether Pub. Co.; distributed by Afro-American Press [1971] 1110 p. 301.45/19/60730022 70-151238
     E185 .P55 1971 MRR Ref Desk.

Ploski, Harry A. The Negro almanac, [1st ed.] New York, Bellwether Pub. Co. [1967] xi, 1012 p. 873 66-29721
     E185 .P55 MRR Ref Desk.

Rogers, Joel Augustus, World's great men of color. New York, Macmillan [1972, c1946-47] 2 v. 920/.0092/96 73-156437
     DT18 .R592 MRR Biog.

Simmons, William J., Men of mark: New York, Arno Press, 1968. 1141 p. 920/.073 68-29017
     E185.96 .S45 1968 MRR Biog.

Stanford, Barbara Dodds. Negro literature for high school students. [Champaign, Ill.] National Council of Teachers of English [1968] ix, 157 p. [$2.00] 016.810/9/9 68-7786
     Z1361.N39 S75 MRR Alc.

Toppin, Edgar Allan, A biographical history of Blacks in America since 1528. New York, McKay [1971] x, 499 p. [$7.95] 917.3/06/96073 70-107402
     E185.96 .T66 MRR Alc.

Who's who in colored America; v. 1- 1927- Yonkers-on-Hudson, N.Y. Christian E. Burckel 27-8470
     E185.96 .W54 MRR Biog Latest edition

NEGROES--BIOGRAPHY--BIBLIOGRAPHY.
Bell, Barbara L. Black biographical sources: New Haven, Yale University Library, 1970. 20 p. [$2.00] 016.92/0073 70-130440
     Z1361.N39 B46 MRR Biog.

NEGROES--BIOGRAPHY-- (Cont.)
Brignano, Russell Carl. Black
Americans in autobiography: Durham,
N.C., Duke University Press, 1974.
ix, 118 p. [$5.75]
016.9173/06/86073022 B 73-92535
Z1361.N39 B67 MRR Alc.

NEGROES--BIOGRAPHY--DICTIONARIES.
Alford, Sterling G., Famous first
Blacks / 1st ed. New York : Vantage
Press [1974] 105 p. : [$3.95]
920/.073 74-186460
E185.96 .A514 MRR Ref Desk.

NEGROES--BIOGRAPHY--INDEXES.
Howard University, Washington, D.C.
Library. Moorland Foundation.
Dictionary catalog of the Jesse E.
Moorland Collection of Negro Life and
History, Howard University,
Washington, D.C. Boston, G. K. Hall,
1970. 9 v. 016.910/0396 72-195773

Z1361.N39 H82 MRR Alc (Dk 33)

Spradling, Mary Mace, In black and
white: Afro-Americans in print;
Kalamazoo, Mich., Kalamazoo Library
System, 1971. ix, 127 p. [$3.00]
016.920073 77-31475
Z1361.N39 S653 MRR Biog.

NEGROES--BIOGRAPHY--JUVENILE LITERATURE.
Adams, Russell L. Great Negroes,
past and present, 3d ed. Chicago,
Afro-Am Pub. Co., 1969. ix, 212 p.
920 72-87824
E186.96 .A4 1969 MRR Biog.

NEGROES--CIVIL RIGHTS.
Burke, Joan Martin. Civil rights;
2d ed. New York, Bowker, 1974. xi,
266 p. 323.4/025/73 74-4053
JC599.U5 B85 1974 MRR Alc.

Cain, Alfred E., ed. The winding
road to freedom; [1st ed.] Yonkers
[N.Y.] Educational Heritage [1965]
384 p. 973.097496 65-5735
E185 .C14 MRR Alc.

Friedman, Leon, comp. The civil
rights reader; New York, Walker
[1967] xxi, 348 p. 323.4/0973 67-
13235
E185.61 .F857 MRR Alc.

Hughes, Langston, Fight for freedom;
New York, Norton [1962] 224 p.
325.2670873 62-14352
E185.5.N276 H8 MRR Alc.

Ianniello, Lynne, ed. Milestones
along the march; New York, F. A.
Praeger [1965] xviii, 124 p.
323.408 65-24709
E185.61 .I2 MRR Alc.

Lewis, Anthony, Portrait of a
decade; New York, Random House
[1964] 322 p. 323.40973 64-14832

E185.61 .L52 1964 MRR Alc.

Vander, Harry Joseph. The political
and economic progress of the American
Negro, 1940-1963 Dubuque, Iowa, W.
C. Brown Book Co. [1968] ix, 111 p.
309.1/73 68-4951
JK2275.N4 V3 MRR Alc.

Wesley, Charles Harris, Negro
Americans in the Civil War; from
slavery to citizenship, [2d ed.
rev.] New York, Publishers Co.
[1969] xi, 291 p. 973.71/5 75-
6204
E540.N3 W4 1969 MRR Alc.

NEGROES--CIVIL RIGHTS--BIBLIOGRAPHY.
Williams, Daniel T. Eight Negro
bibliographies. New York, Kraus
Reprint Co., 1970. 1 v. (various
pagings) 016.301451/96/073 71-
107893
Z1361.N39 W54 MRR Alc.

NEGROES--CIVIL RIGHTS--HISTORY.
Chambers, Bradford, comp. Chronicles
of Negro protest; New York, Parents'
Magazine Press [1968] 319 p.
[$4.50] 322/.4 68-16998
E185.61 .C5 MRR Alc.

NEGROES--COLONIZATION--AFRICA.
Brotz, Howard, ed. Negro social and
political thought, 1850-1920; New
York, Basic Books [1966] ix, 593 p.
301.45196073 66-22070
E185 .B876 MRR Alc.

NEGROES--DICTIONARIES.
Baskin, Wade. Dictionary of Black
culture. New York, Philosophical
Library [1973] 493 p. [$15.00]
917.3/06/86003 72-78162
E185.96 .B33 MRR Ref Desk.

NEGROES--DICTIONARIES AND ENCYCLOPEDIAS.
Afro-American encyclopedia / 1st ed.
North Miami, Fla. : Educational Book
Publishers, [1974] 10 v. :
917.3/06/96073 70-94684
E185 .A28 MRR Alc.

NEGROES--DIRECTORIES.
Black list; New York, Panther House
[1970] 289 p. [$12.50 (pbk)]
001.5/025/6 73-112479
P88.8 .B6 MRR Alc.

The National register; 1st- ed.,
1952- Louisville, Ky., Register
Publications. 325.260973 53-32943
E185.96 .N37 MRR Biog Latest
edition

Rather, Ernest R., Chicago Negro
almanac and reference book,
[Chicago, Chicago Negro Almanac Pub.
Co., c1972] viii, 256 p.
917.73/11/0696073025 72-81384
F548.9.N3 R37 MRR Alc.

NEGROES--ECONOMIC CONDITIONS.
Cross, Theodore L., Black
capitalism; [1st ed.] New York,
Atheneum, 1969. xii, 274 p. [8.95]
658.42 72-80268
E185.8 .C9 MRR Alc.

Swinton, David H. Aggregate personal
income of the Black population in the
U.S.A., 1947-1980, [New York, Black
Economic Research Center, c1973]
viii, 75 p. [$3.00] 339.4/1/0973
74-157912
E185.8 .S98 MRR Alc.

NEGROES--ECONOMIC CONDITIONS--
ADDRESSES, ESSAYS, LECTURES.
Miller, Kent S. Comparative studies
of Blacks and whites in the United
States. New York, Seminar Press,
1973. xiii, 572 p.
301.45/1/0420973 72-82126
E185.86 .M53 MRR Alc.

NEGROES--ECONOMIC CONDITIONS--
STATISTICS.
United States. Bureau of the Census.
The social and economic status of the
Black population in the United
States, 1971. Washington; For sale
by the Supt. of Docs. U.S. Govt.
Print. Off., 1972] iv, 164 p.
[$1.25] 312/.0973 s 301.45/19/6073
72-602571
HA203 .A218 no. 42 MRR Alc.

NEGROES--EDUCATION.
see also Segregation in education

Johnson, Harry Alleyn. Multimedia
materials for Afro-American studies;
New York, R. R. Bowker Co., 1971.
353 p. 016.9173/06/96073 75-126009

LC2801 .J63 MRR Alc.

The National register; 1st- ed.,
1952- Louisville, Ky., Register
Publications. 325.260973 53-32943
E185.96 .N37 MRR Biog Latest
edition

Ploski, Harry A. Reference library
of Black America. [New York]
Bellwether Pub. Co.; for exclusive
distribution by Afro-American Press
[c1971] 5 v. 917.3/06/96073 74-
151239
E185 .P56 MRR Alc.

NEGROES--EDUCATION--ADDRESSES, ESSAYS,
LECTURES.
Miller, Kent S. Comparative studies
of Blacks and whites in the United
States. New York, Seminar Press,
1973. xiii, 572 p.
301.45/1/0420973 72-82126
E185.86 .M53 MRR Alc.

NEGROES--EDUCATION (HIGHER)--UNITED
STATES--DIRECTORIES.
Paynter, Julie. Graduate
opportunities for Black students,
1969-1970. Chicago [1970] xvi, 88
l. [3.00] 378.73 77-11563
LC2801 .P38 MRR Ref Desk.

NEGROES--EMPLOYMENT.
Ross, Arthur Max, ed. Employment,
race, and poverty. [1st ed. New
York, Harcourt, Brace & World, 1967]
ix, 598 p. 331.1130973 65-23537
E185.8 .R6 MRR Alc.

United States. Bureau of
Apprenticeship and Training.
Directory for reaching minority
groups. [Washington; For sale by the
Supt. of Docs., U.S. Govt. Print.
Off.] 1973. 214 p. [$2.85] 331.6
73-602280
HD6305.M5 U53 1973 MRR alc.

NEGROES--EMPLOYMENT--UNITED STATES.
Directory of special programs for
minority group members: Career
information services; employment
skills banks, financial aid. 1974-
[Garrett Park, Md., Garrett Park
Press] [$6.95] 331.7/02/02573 73-
93533
HD5724 .D56 MRR Alc Latest edition

NEGROES--ENCYCLOPEDIAS AND DICTIONARIES.
Afro-American encyclopedia / 1st ed.
North Miami, Fla. : Educational Book
Publishers, [1974] 10 v. :
917.3/06/96073 70-94684
E185 .A28 MRR Alc.

NEGROES--FILM CATALOGS.
Johnson, Harry Alleyn. Multimedia
materials for Afro-American studies;
New York, R. R. Bowker Co., 1971.
353 p. 016.9173/06/96073 75-126009

LC2801 .J63 MRR Alc.

NEGROES--HANDBOOKS, MANUALS, ETC.
Alford, Sterling G., Famous first
Blacks / 1st ed. New York : Vantage
Press [1974] 105 p. : [$3.95]
920/.073 74-186460
E185.96 .A514 MRR Ref Desk.

Davis, John Preston, ed. The
American Negro reference book,
Englewood Cliffs, N.J., Prentice-Hall
[1966] xxii, 969 p. 301.45196073
65-12819
E185 .D25 MRR Ref. Desk.

The Ebony handbook. Chicago, Johnson
Pub. Co., 1974. 553 p. [$20.00]
917.3/06/96073 73-16179
E185 .E22 MRR Ref Desk.

Miller, Kent S. Comparative studies
of Blacks and whites in the United
States. New York, Seminar Press,
1973. xiii, 572 p.
301.45/1/0420973 72-82126
E185.86 .M53 MRR Alc.

The National register; 1st- ed.,
1952- Louisville, Ky., Register
Publications. 325.260973 53-32943
E185.96 .N37 MRR Biog Latest
edition

Ploski, Harry A. Afro USA; [New
York] Bellwether Pub. Co.;
distributed by Afro-American Press
[1971] 1110 p. 301.45/19/60730022
70-151238
E185 .P55 1971 MRR Ref Desk.

Ploski, Harry A. The Negro almanac;
[1st ed.] New York, Bellwether Pub.
Co. [1967] xi, 1012 p. 973 66-
29721
E185 .P55 MRR Ref Desk.

Rather, Ernest R., Chicago Negro
almanac and reference book,
[Chicago, Chicago Negro Almanac Pub.
Co., c1972] viii, 256 p.
917.73/11/0696073025 72-81384
F548.9.N3 R37 MRR Alc.

Sloan, Irving J. Blacks in America,
1492-1970, [3d ed., rev. updated and
expanded] Dobbs Ferry, N.Y., Oceana
Publications, 1971. x, 149 p.
973/.04/96073 76-170877
E185 .S57 1971 MRR Alc.

NEGROES--HISTORY.
Chambers, Bradford, comp. Chronicles
of Negro protest; New York, Parents'
Magazine Press [1968] 319 p.
[$4.50] 322/.4 68-16998
E185.61 .C5 MRR Alc.

Cincinnati. Public Schools. The
Negro in American life New York,
Harcourt, Brace & World [1967] xii,
273 p. 301.451/96/073 67-18544
E185 .C56 1967 MRR Alc.

Drotning, Phillip T. A guide to
Negro history in America, [1st ed.]
Garden City, N.Y., Doubleday, 1968.
xiv, 247 p. [4.95] 917.3/04/923
68-14168
E185 .D72 MRR Alc.

Garrett, Romeo B. Famous first facts
about Negroes New York, Arno Press,
1972. viii, 212 p. 301.45/19/6073
75-172613
E185 .G22 MRR Ref Desk.

Hughes, Langston, A pictorial
history of Blackamericans 4th rev.
ed. of a pictorial history of the
Negro in America. New York, Crown
Publishers [1973] 377 p. [$7.95]
917.3/06/96073 73-82942
E185 .H83 1973 MRR Alc.

Lincoln, Charles Eric. The Negro
pilgrimage in America. New York,
Bantam Books [1967] 184 p.
973/.0974/96 67-28881
E185 .L47 MRR Alc.

Meier, August, From plantation to
ghetto. Rev. ed. New York, Hill and
Wang [1970] x, 340 p. [6.50]
973/.04/96073 71-106967
E185 .M4 1970 MRR Alc.

Ploski, Harry A. Afro USA; [New
York] Bellwether Pub. Co.;
distributed by Afro-American Press
[1971] 1110 p. 301.45/19/60730022
70-151238
E185 .P55 1971 MRR Ref Desk.

NEGROES--HISTORY. (Cont.)
Toppin, Edgar Allan, A biographical
history of Blacks in America since
1528, New York, McKay [1971] x, 499
p. [$7.95] 917.3/06/86073 70-
107402
   E185.96 .T66 MRR Alc.

Wesley, Charles Harris, Negro
Americans in the Civil War; from
slavery to citizenship, [2d ed.
rev.] New York, Publishers Co.
[1969] xi, 291 p. 973.71/5 75-
6204
   E540.N3 W4 1969 MRR Alc.

Woodson, Carter Godwin, The Negro in
our history, 10th ed., further rev.
and enl. Washington, Associated
Publishers [1962] 833 p. 326.973
62-3879
   E185 .W89 1962 MRR Alc.

NEGROES--HISTORY--TO 1863.
Litwack, Leon F. North of slavery;
[Chicago] University of Chicago Press
[1961] 318 p. 326.973 61-10869
   E185.9 .L5 MRR Alc.

Wesley, Charles Harris, In freedom's
footsteps, from the African
background to the Civil War, [1st
ed.] New York, Publishers Co. [1968]
xiii, 307 p. 973 68-56834
   E185 .W45 MRR Alc.

NEGROES--HISTORY--1877-1964.
Waskow, Arthur I. From race riot to
sit-in, 1919 and the 1960s; [1st
ed.] Garden City, N.Y., Doubleday,
1966. xviii, 380 p. 66-11737
   E185.61 .W24 MRR Alc.

Wesley, Charles Harris, The quest
for equality; [1st ed.] New York,
Publishers Co. [1968] xii, 307 p.
973 68-56835
   E185.6 .W4 MRR Alc.

NEGROES--HISTORY--1964-
Wesley, Charles Harris, The quest
for equality; [1st ed.] New York,
Publishers Co. [1968] xii, 307 p.
973 68-56835
   E185.6 .W4 MRR Alc.

NEGROES--HISTORY--ADDRESSES, ESSAYS,
LECTURES.
Brotz, Howard, ed. Negro social and
political thought, 1850-1920; New
York, Basic Books [1966] ix, 593 p.
301.45196073 66-22070
   E185 .B876 MRR Alc.

Davis, John Preston, ed. The
American Negro reference book,
Englewood Cliffs, N.J., Prentice-Hall
[1966] xxii, 969 p. 301.45196073
65-12919
   E185 .D25 MRR Ref. Desk.

Foner, Eric, comp. America's black
past; [1st ed.] New York, Harper &
Row [1970] xiv, 684 p. [12.50]
973/.09/7496 70-96804
   E185 .F59 1970 MRR Alc.

NEGROES--HISTORY--BIBLIOGRAPHY.
Blacks in America: 1st ed.] Garden
City, N.Y., Doubleday, 1971. xii,
430 p. [$8.95] 016.9173/06/96073
70-164723
   Z1361.N39 B56 MRR Alc.

Katz, William Loren. Teachers' guide
to American Negro history. [2d] rev.
ed. Chicago, Quadrangle Books [1971]
192 p. [$2.65] 973/.04/96 71-
32338
   E185 .K285 1971b MRR Alc.

Salk, Erwin A. A layman's guide to
Negro history, New, enl. ed. New
York, McGraw-Hill [1967] xviii, 196
p. 016.91003/174/96 67-22967
   Z1361.N39 S23 1967 MRR Alc.

Smith, Dwight La Vern, Afro-American
history; Santa Barbara, Calif., ABC-
Clio [1974] xvi, 856 p.
016.9173/06/96073 73-87155
   Z1361.N39 S56 MRR Alc.

Turner, Darwin T., Afro-American
writers, New York, Appleton-Century-
Crofts, Educational Division [1970]
xvii, 117 p. 016.8108/091/7496 72-
79171
   Z1361.N39 T78 MRR Alc.

Williams, Daniel T. Eight Negro
bibliographies. New York, Kraus
Reprint Co., 1970. 1 v. (various
pagings) 016.301451/96/073 71-
107893
   Z1361.N39 W54 MRR Alc.

NEGROES--HISTORY--CHRONOLOGY.
Afro-American encyclopedia / 1st ed.
North Miami, Fla. : Educational Book
Publishers, [1974] 10 v. :
917.3/06/86073 70-94684
   E185 .A28 MRR Alc.

Bergman, Peter M. The chronological
history of the Negro in America,
[1st ed.] New York, Harper & Row
[1969] 698 p. [12.00]
973/.09/7496 68-27434
   E185 .B46 MRR Ref Desk.

The Ebony handbook, Chicago, Johnson
Pub. Co.; 1974. 553 p. [$20.00]
917.3/06/86073 73-16179
   E185 .E22 MRR Ref Desk.

Hopkins, Lee Bennett. Important
dates in Afro-American history. New
York, F. Watts [1969] 188 p.
973/.09/7496 73-83648
   E185 .H6 MRR Alc.

Hornsby, Alton. The Black almanac.
Rev. and enl. Woodbury, N.Y.,
Barron's Educational Series, Inc.
[1973] xxiv, 247 p. [$2.95]
917.3/06/86073 74-154291
   E185 .H63 1973 MRR Alc.

Lincoln, Charles Eric. The Negro
pilgrimage in America, New York,
Bantam Books [1967] 184 p.
973/.0974/96 67-28881
   E185 .L47 MRR Alc.

Ploski, Harry A. Reference library
of Black America. [New York]
Bellwether Pub. Co.; for exclusive
distribution by Afro-American Press
[c1971] 5 v. 917.3/06/86073 74-
151239
   E185 .P56 MRR Alc.

Salk, Erwin A. A layman's guide to
Negro history, New, enl. ed. New
York, McGraw-Hill [1967] xviii, 196
p. 016.91003/174/96 67-22967
   Z1361.N39 S23 1967 MRR Alc.

Sloan, Irving J. Blacks in America,
1492-1970; [3d ed., rev. updated and
expanded] Dobbs Ferry, N.Y., Oceana
Publications 1971. x, 149 p.
973/.04/86073 76-170977
   E185 .S57 1971 MRR Alc.

NEGROES--HISTORY--CHRONOLOGY--JUVENILE
LITERATURE.
Hopkins, Lee Bennett. Important
dates in Afro-American history. New
York, F. Watts [1969] 188 p.
973/.09/7496 73-83648
   E185 .H6 MRR Alc.

NEGROES--HISTORY--PICTORIAL WORKS.
Hughes, Langston, A pictorial
history of Blackamericans 4th rev.
ed. of a pictorial history of the
Negro in America. New York, Crown
Publishers [1973] 377 p. [$7.95]
917.3/06/86073 73-82942
   E185 .H83 1973 MRR Alc.

NEGROES--HISTORY--SOURCES.
Cain, Alfred E., ed. The winding
road to freedom; [1st ed.] Yonkers
[N.Y.] Educational Heritage [1965]
384 p. 973.097496 65-5735
   E185 .C14 MRR Alc.

Katz, William Loren, comp.
Eyewitness; New York, Pitman Pub.
Corp. [1967] xix, 554 p.
301.451/96/073 67-10838
   E185 .K28 MRR Alc.

The Negro in American History.
[Chicago] Encyclopaedia Britannica
Educational Corp. [1969] 3 v.
973/.0974/96 68-56369
   E185 .N4 MRR Alc.

Ploski, Harry A. The Negro almanac,
[1st ed.] New York, Bellwether Pub.
Co. [1967] xi, 1012 p. 973 66-
29721
   E185 .P55 MRR Ref. Desk.

Romero, Patricia W., comp. I too am
America; [1st ed.] New York,
Publishers Co. [1968] xv, 304 p.
973 68-56836
   E185 .R76 MRR Alc.

NEGROES--HISTORY--STUDY AND TEACHING.
Katz, William Loren. Teachers' guide
to American Negro history. [2d] rev.
ed. Chicago, Quadrangle Books [1971]
192 p. [$2.65] 973/.04/96 71-
32338
   E185 .K285 1971b MRR Alc.

NEGROES--INTELLECTUAL LIFE.
Thorpe, Earl E. The mind of the
Negro; Baton Rouge, La., Printed by
Ortlieb Press [1961] 562 p.
325.2670973 61-16125
   E185.82 .T5 MRR Alc.

NEGROES--LANGUAGE (NEW WORDS, SLANG,
ETC.)
Major, Clarence. Dictionary of Afro-
American slang. [1st ed.] New York,
International Publishers [1970] 127
p. [$3.95] 427.09 79-130863
   PE3727.N4 M3 MRR Alc.

NEGROES--LEGAL STATUS, LAWS, ETC.
Ploski, Harry A. Reference library
of Black America. [New York]
Bellwether Pub. Co.; for exclusive
distribution by Afro-American Press
[c1971] 5 v. 917.3/06/86073 74-
151239
   E185 .P56 MRR Alc.

NEGROES--MORAL AND SOCIAL CONDITIONS.
Myrdal, Gunnar, An American dilemma;
20th anniversary ed. New York,
Harper & Row [1962] 1483 p.
301.451 62-19706
   E185.6 .M95 1962 MRR Alc.

NEGROES--PERIODICALS--ABSTRACTS.
Smith, Dwight La Vern, Afro-American
history; Santa Barbara, Calif., ABC-
Clio [1974] xvi, 856 p.
016.9173/06/96073 73-87155
   Z1361.N39 S56 MRR Alc.

NEGROES--POLITICS AND SUFFRAGE.
Stone, Chuck. Black political power
in America. Indianapolis, Bobbs-
Merrill [1968] 261 p. [8.50]
320.9/174/96 68-29291
   E185 .S84 MRR Alc.

Vander, Harry Joseph. The political
and economic progress of the American
Negro, 1940-1963 Dubuque, Iowa, W.
C. Brown Book Co. [1968] ix, 111 p.
308.1/73 68-4951
   JK2275.N4 V3 MRR Alc.

Walton, Hanes, Black political
parties; New York, Free Press [1972]
xi, 276 p. 329/.894 76-143514
   JK2261 .W33 MRR Alc.

NEGROES--POLITICS AND SUFFRAGE--
BIBLIOGRAPHY.
United States. Library of Congress.
Division of bibliography. ... List
of discussions of the fourteenth and
fifteenth amendments with special
reference to Negro suffrage.
Washington, Govt. print. off., 1906.
18 p. 06-35012
   Z663.28 .L568 MRR Alc.

Walton, Hanes, The study and
analysis of Black politics:
Metuchen, N.J., Scarecrow Press,
1973. xviii, 161 p. 016.32 73-
12985
   Z1361.N39 W29 MRR Alc.

NEGROES--POLITICS AND SUFFRAGE--
DIRECTORIES.
Rather, Ernest R., Chicago Negro
almanac and reference book,
[Chicago, Chicago Negro Almanac Pub.
Co., c1972] viii, 256 p.
917.73/11/0696073025 72-81384
   F548.9.N3 R37 MRR Alc.

NEGROES--POLITICS AND SUFFRAGE--
DIRECTORIES--PERIODICALS.
National roster of Black elected
officials. Washington, Joint Center
for Political Studies. [$6.00 (per
copy)] 353.002 73-83185
   JK1924 .N38 MRR Ref Desk Latest
edition

NEGROES--PSYCHOLOGY.
Thorpe, Earl E. The mind of the
Negro; Baton Rouge, La., Printed by
Ortlieb Press [1961] 562 p.
325.2670973 61-16125
   E185.82 .T5 MRR Alc.

NEGROES--PSYCHOLOGY--ADDRESSES, ESSAYS,
LECTURES.
Miller, Kent S. Comparative studies
of Blacks and whites in the United
States. New York, Seminar Press,
1973. xiii, 572 p.
301.45/1/0420973 72-82126
   E185.86 .M53 MRR Alc.

NEGROES--RACE IDENTITY.
Dann, Martin E., comp. The Black
press 1827-1890; New York, Putnam
[1971] 384 p. [$7.95]
301.451/96/073 72-127714
   E185.5 .D35 1971 MRR Alc.

NEGROES--RELIGION--BIBLIOGRAPHY--UNION
LISTS.
Williams, Ethel L. Afro-American
religious studies: Metuchen, N.J.,
Scarecrow Press, 1972. 454 p.
016.301451/86073 78-166072
   Z1361.N39 W55 MRR Alc.

NEGROES--SEGREGATION.
Hughes, Langston, Fight for freedom;
New York, Norton [1962] 224 p.
325.2670973 62-14352
   E185.5 .N276 H8 MRR Alc.

Lewis, Anthony, Portrait of a
decade; New York, Random House
[1964] 322 p. 323.40973 64-14832

   E185.61 .L52 1964 MRR Alc.

Litwack, Leon F. North of slavery;
[Chicago] University of Chicago Press
[1961] 318 p. 326.973 61-10869
   E185.9 .L5 MRR Alc.

NEGROES--SEGREGATION. (Cont.)
Woodward, Comer Vann, The strange
career of Jim Crow 3d rev. ed. New
York, Oxford University Press, 1974.
xvii, 233 p.   [$8.95]
301.45/18/6073 73-90370
    E185.61 .W86 1974 MRR Alc.

NEGROES--SOCIAL CONDITIONS--TO 1964.
Brotz, Howard, ed. Negro social and
political thought, 1850-1920; New
York, Basic Books [1966] ix, 593 p.
301.45196073 66-22070
    E185 .B876 MRR Alc.

NEGROES--SOCIAL CONDITIONS--1964-
Patterson, Lindsay, comp. Anthology
of the American Negro in the theatre;
[3d ed.] New York, Publishers Co.
[1968] xiv, 306 p. 782.09174/96
68-2730
    PN2226 .P3 1968 MRR Alc.

NEGROES--SOCIAL CONDITIONS--1964- --
ADDRESSES, ESSAYS, LECTURES.
Miller, Kent S. Comparative studies
of Blacks and whites in the United
States. New York, Seminar Press,
1973. xiii, 572 p.
301.45/1/0420973 72-82126
    E185.86 .M53 MRR Alc.

NEGROES--SOCIAL CONDITIONS--STATISTICS.
United States. Bureau of the Census.
The social and economic status of the
Black population in the United
States, 1871. Washington, For sale
by the Supt. of Docs. U.S. Govt.
Print. Off., 1972] iv, 164 p.
[$1.25] 312/.0973 s 301.45/19/6073
72-602571
    HA203 .A218 no. 42 MRR Alc.

NEGROES--SOCIETIES, ETC.
Ploski, Harry A. Afro USA; [New
York] Bellwether Pub. Co.;
distributed by Afro-American Press
[1971] 1110 p. 301.45/19/60730022
70-151238
    E185 .P55 1971 MRR Ref Desk

NEGROES--SOCIETIES, ETC.--DIRECTORIES.
Directory: National Black
organizations. 1972- Harlem, N. Y.,
Afram Associates. 301.45/19/607306
72-624646
    E185.5 .D5 MRR Ref Desk Latest
    edition

NEGROES--STATISTICS.
Davis, John Preston, ed. The
American Negro reference book.
Englewood Cliffs, N.J., Prentice-Hall
[1966] xxii, 969 p. 301.45196073
65-12918
    E185 .D25 MRR Ref. Desk.

The Ebony handbook. Chicago, Johnson
Pub. Co., 1974. 553 p. [$20.00]
917.3/06/96073 73-16179
    E185 .E22 MRR Ref Desk.

Events of 1969. [1st ed.] New York,
Publishers Co. [1970] xv, 455 p.
917.3/06/96073 77-25453
    E185.5.A86 E9 MRR Alc.

Glenn, Norval D., comp. Blacks in
the United States. San Francisco,
Chandler Pub. Co.; distributed by
Science Research Associates, Chicago
[1969] xiii, 621 p. 301.451/96/073
69-15428
    E185.615 .G55 MRR Alc.

Miller, Kent S. Comparative studies
of Blacks and whites in the United
States. New York, Seminar Press,
1973. xiii, 572 p.
301.45/1/0420973 72-82126
    E185.86 .M53 MRR Alc.

Ploski, Harry A. Afro USA; [New
York] Bellwether Pub. Co.;
distributed by Afro-American Press
[1971] 1110 p. 301.45/19/60730022
70-151238
    E185 .P55 1971 MRR Ref Desk.

Ploski, Harry A. The Negro almanac.
[1st ed.] New York, Bellwether Pub.
Co. [1967] xi, 1012 p. 973 66-
29721
    E185 .P55 MRR Ref Desk.

Swinton, David H. Aggregate personal
income of the Black population in the
U.S.A., 1947-1980. [New York, Black
Economic Research Center, c1973]
viii, 75 p. [$3.00] 339.4/1/0973
74-167812
    E185.8 .S98 MRR Alc.

United States. Bureau of Labor
Statistics. Black Americans; a
chartbook. Washington; For sale by
the Supt. of Docs., U.S. Govt. Print.
Off., 1971. x, 141 p. [$1.25]
301.451/36/073 71-613945
    E185.8 .U528 MRR Ref Desk.

United States. Bureau of the Census.
1970 census of population and
housing. [Washington; For sale by
the Supt. of Docs., U.S. Govt. Print.
Off.] 1971--   v. [$1.00 (v. 5)
varies] 312/.0973 73-186611
    HA201 1970 .A542 MRR Alc.

United States. Bureau of the Census.
Negro population 1790-1915.
Washington, Govt. print. off., 1918.
844 p. incl. maps, tables, diagrs.
18-26864
    E185 .U56 MRR Alc.

United States. Bureau of the Census.
Negro population in the United
States, 1790-1915. New York, Arno
Press, 1968. 844 p. 312/.9 68-
28892
    HA205 .A33 1968 MRR Alc.

United States. Bureau of the census.
Negroes in the United States, 1920-
32. Washington, U.S. Govt. print.
off., 1935. xvi, 845 p. 325.260973
35-26735
    HA205 .A33 1920-32 MRR Alc.

United States. Bureau of the Census.
The social and economic status of the
Black population in the United
States, 1871. Washington; For sale
by the Supt. of Docs. U.S. Govt.
Print. Off., 1972] iv, 164 p.
[$1.25] 312/.0973 s 301.45/19/6073
72-602571
    HA203 .A218 no. 42 MRR Alc.

NEGROES--STATISTICS, VITAL.
United States. Bureau of Labor
Statistics. Black Americans; a
chartbook. Washington; For sale by
the Supt. of Docs., U.S. Govt. Print.
Off., 1971. x, 141 p. [$1.25]
301.451/96/073 71-613945
    E185.8 .U528 MRR Ref Desk.

NEGROES--YEARBOOKS.
Events of 1969. [1st ed.] New York,
Publishers Co. [1970] xv, 455 p.
917.3/06/96073 77-25453
    E185.5.A86 E9 MRR Alc.

In Black America, 1968: [1st ed.]
New York, Publishers Co. [1969]
xvii, 445 p. 917.3/09/7496 69-
17399
    E185.5 .I52 MRR Alc.

NEGROES--CHICAGO--DIRECTORIES.
Rather, Ernest R., Chicago Negro
almanac and reference book,
[Chicago, Chicago Negro Almanac Pub.
Co., c1972] viii, 256 p.
917.73/11/0696073025 72-81384
    F548.9.N3 R37 MRR Alc.

NEGROES--MINNESOTA--BIBLIOGRAPHY.
Spangler, Earl. Bibliography of
Negro history: Minneapolis, Ross and
Haines, 1963. vii, 101 p. 016.967
63-2056
    Z1361.N39 S65 MRR Alc.

NEGROES AS BUSINESSMEN.
Cross, Theodore L., Black
capitalism; [1st ed.] New York,
Atheneum, 1969. xii, 274 p. [8.95]
658.42 72-80268
    E185.8 .C9 MRR Alc.

NEGROES AS BUSINESSMEN--DIRECTORIES.
National minority business directory.
1972- [Minneapolis, National
Minority Business Campaign]
338/.0025/73 76-182148
    HD2346.U5 N34 MRR Alc Latest
    edition

NEGROES AS SOLDIERS.
Greene, Robert Ewell, Black
defenders of America, 1775-1973.
Chicago, Johnson Pub. Co., 1974. 416
p. 355.1 73-15607
    E185.63 .G73 MRR Alc.

Lee, Irvin H. Negro Medal of Honor
men, 3d ed; new and enl. New York,
Dodd, Mead [1969] xii, 156 p.
[4.50] 355.1/34 68-58447
    UB433 .L4 1969 MRR Alc.

Lee, Ulysses Grant. The employment
of Negro troops, Washington, Office
of the Chief of Military History,
United States Army; [for sale by the
Superintendent of Documents, U.S.
Govt. Print. Off.] 1966. xix, 740 p.
940.5403 66-60003
    D810.N4 L4 MRR Alc.

Ploski, Harry A. Afro USA; [New
York] Bellwether Pub. Co.;
distributed by Afro-American Press
[1971] 1110 p. 301.45/19/60730022
70-151238
    E185 .P55 1971 MRR Ref Desk.

Quarles, Benjamin. The Negro in the
Civil War. [1st ed.] Boston,
Little, Brown [1953] xvi, 379 p.
973.715 53-7309
    E540.N3 Q3 MRR Alc.

Salk, Erwin A. A layman's guide to
Negro history. New, enl. ed. New
York, McGraw-Hill [1967] xviii, 196
p. 016.91003/174/96 67-22967
    Z1361.N39 S23 1967 MRR Alc.

Scott, Emmett Jay, Scott's official
history of the American Negro in the
World War. New York, Arno Press,
1969. 511 p. 940.4/03 69-18556
    D639.N4 S3 1969 MRR Alc.

NEGROES IN AFRICA.
see also Africa, Sub-Saharan

NEGROES IN AFRICA--BIOGRAPHY]
Adams, Russell L. Great Negroes,
past and present, 3d ed. Chicago,
Afro-Am Pub. Co., 1969. ix, 212 p.
920 72-87924
    E186.96 .A4 1969 MRR Biog.

NEGROES IN AFRICA--BIOGRAPHY--JUVENILE
LITERATURE.
Adams, Russell L. Great Negroes,
past and present, 3d ed. Chicago,
Afro-Am Pub. Co., 1969. ix, 212 p.
920 72-87924
    E186.96 .A4 1969 MRR Biog.

NEGROES IN LITERATURE--BIBLIOGRAPHY.
Hatch, James Vernon, Black image on
the American stage; New York, DBS
Publications [1970] xiii, 162 p.
016.812/008 72-115695
    Z5784.N4 H35 MRR Alc.

NEGROES IN MEDICINE.
Morais, Herbert Montfort, The
history of the Negro in medicine,
[3d ed.] New York, Publishers Co.
[1969] xiv, 322 p. 610/.973 76-
7527
    R695 .M6 1969 MRR Alc.

NEGROES IN MOVING-PICTURES.
Bogle, Donald. Toms, coons,
mulattoes, mammies, and bucks; New
York, Viking Press [1973] xviii, 260
p. [$12.50] 791.43/0973 72-76776
    PN1995.9.N4 B6 MRR Alc.

NEGROES IN POLITICS (UNITED STATES)
see Negroes--Politics and suffrage

NELSON, N.Z. (PROVINCIAL DISTRICT)--
COMMERCE--DIRECTORIES.
Universal business directory for
Nelson-Marlborough-west coast.
Auckland, Universal Business
Directories. 52-38722
    HF5298 .U55 MRR Alc Latest edition

NEO-IMPRESSIONISM (ART)
see Impressionism (Art)

NEOCLASSICISM (ART)--EUROPE.
Novotny, Fritz, Painting and
sculpture in Europe, 1780 to 1880.
2nd ed. Harmondsworth, Penguin,
1970. xxii, 290, 192 p., leaf.
[£5.75] 759.94 74-149800
    N6757 .N6813 1970 MRR Alc.

NEOLOGISMS
see Words, New

NEPAL.
American University, Washington, D.C.
Foreign Areas Studies Divison. Area
handbook for Nepal (with Sikkim and
Bhutan). Washington, For sale by the
Supt. of Docs., U.S. Govt. Print.
Off., 1964. xv, 448 p. 67-115014
    DS485.N4 A8 MRR Alc.

Harris, George Lawrence, Area
handbook for Nepal, Bhutan, and
Sikkim. 2d ed. [Washington; for
sale by the Supt. of Docs., U.S.
Govt. Print. Off.] 1973. lxxx, 431
p. [$6.85] 915.48/6/035 73-600139
    DS493.4 .H37 1973 MRR Alc.

NEPAL--BIBLIOGRAPHY.
Wood, Hugh Bernard, Nepal,
bibliography. Eugene, Or., American-
Nepal Education Foundation, 1959.
108 p. 016.915426 59-16488
    Z3207.N4 W6 MRR Alc.

NEPAL--BIOGRAPHY.
Hedrick, Basil Calvin, Historical
and cultural dictionary of Nepal,
Metuchen, N.J., Scarecrow Press,
1972. vii, 198 p. 954.9/6/003 72-
8499
    DS485.N44 H4 1973 MRR Alc.

NEPAL--DICTIONARIES AND ENCYCLOPEDIAS.
Hedrick, Basil Calvin, Historical
and cultural dictionary of Nepal,
Metuchen, N.J., Scarecrow Press,
1972. vii, 198 p. 954.9/6/003 72-
8499
    DS485.N44 H4 MRR Alc.

NEPAL--GAZETTEERS.
United States. Office of Geography.
India; Washington, 1952. 2 v. 70-
10027
    DS405 .U55 MRR Alc.

NEPAL--IMPRINTS.
United States. Library of Congress.
American Libraries Book Procurement
Center, Delhi. Accessions list,
Nepal. v. 1- Apr. 1966- New
Delhi. sa 66-4579
Z663.767.N4 A25 MRR Alc   MRR Alc
Full set

NEPALI LANGUAGE--DICTIONARIES--ENGLISH.
Turner, Ralph Lilley, Sir, A
comparative and etymological
dictionary of the Nepali language.
London, Routledge & K. Paul [1965]
xxiii, 932 p.   66-2990
PK2596 .T8 1965 MRR Alc.

NERVOUS SYSTEM--DISEASES.
Alpers, Bernard Jacob, Clinical
neurology 6th ed. Philadelphia, F.
A. Davis Co. [1971] xx, 1072 p.
616.8 73-103534
RC346 .A4 1971 MRR Alc.

NETHERLANDS--BIBLIOGRAPHY.
United States. Library of Congress.
Netherlands Studies Unit. A guide to
Dutch bibliographies. Washington,
1951. iii, 193 p.   015.492 51-
60014
Z2416 .U6 1951c MRR Alc.

NETHERLANDS--BIBLIOGRAPHY--CATALOGS.
United States. Library of Congress.
Early printed books of the Low
Countries Washington, 1958. vi, 37
p.   016.09 58-60011
Z663.4 .E2 MRR Alc.

NETHERLANDS--BIOGRAPHY.
Kobus, Jan Christiaan, Biographisch
woordenboek van Nederland Nieuwe
uitg. ... Arnhem-Nijmegen, Gebr. E.
& M. Cohen, 1886. 3 v.   02-23511
CT1143 .K6 MRR Biog.

Parlement en kiezer: Jaarboek. 's-
Gravenhage, Nijhoff. 74-642439
Began with vol. for 1911/12.
JN5873 .A3 MRR Alc Latest edition

Wie is dat? 1931- 's-Gravenhage, M.
Nijhoff. 920.0492 33-7538
DJ103 .W62 MRR Biog Latest edition

NETHERLANDS--BIOGRAPHY--DICTIONARIES.
Persoonlijkheden in het koninkrijk
der Nederlanden in woord en beeld.
Amsterdam, van Holkema & Warendorf
n.v., 1938. 1748 p., 1 l.   ac 39-
3032
CT1143 .P4 MRR Biog.

NETHERLANDS--COLONIES--BIBLIOGRAPHY.
United States. Library of Congress.
Netherlands Studies Unit. A guide to
Dutch bibliographies. Washington,
1951. iii, 193 p.   015.492 51-
60014
Z2416 .U6 1951c MRR Alc.

NETHERLANDS--COLONIES--STATISTICS.
Jaarcijfers voor Nederlanden. 's
Gravenhage. 08-6303
HA1381 .D-D5 MRR Alc Latest
edition

NETHERLANDS--COMMERCE--DIRECTORIES.
British & international buyers &
sellers guide. Manchester, Eng.
[etc.] C. G. Birn. 55-36686
HF54.G7 B7 MRR Alc Latest edition

Kompass; informatiewerk over het
Nederlandse bedrijfsleven. Den Haag,
Kompass Nederland N.V. 72-620607
Began with vol. for 1965/66.
HF3613 .K58 MRR Alc Latest edition

Nederlands abc voor handel en
industrie. Haarlem, ABC voor Handel
en Industrie. 63-36606
HF3613 .N4 MRR Alc Latest edition

Telexgids Nederland. ['s-Gravenhage]
Staatsbedrijf der Posterijen,
Telegrafie en Telefonie. 68-5730
HE7742 .T42 MRR Alc Latest edition

NETHERLANDS--COMMERCE--HANDBOOKS,
MANUALS, ETC.
Netherlands-British trade directory.
London, Netherlands Chamber of
Commerce in the United Kingdom.
382/.0942 73-645767
HF302 .N37 MRR Alc Latest edition

NETHERLANDS--DESCRIPTION AND TRAVEL--
GUIDE-BOOKS.
Benelux. Paris [etc.] Pneu Michelin,
Services de tourisme [etc.] 56-50955

GV1025.B43 B4 MRR Alc Latest
edition

Fodor's Holland. 1969- New York, D.
McKay. 849/.2/047 72-612644
DJ16 .H562 MRR Alc Latest edition

Holland. [4th ed.] Geneva, Paris
[etc.] Nagel Publishers [1968] vii,
679 p. [$6.95] 914.92/04/7 71-
431955
DJ16 .H57 1968 MRR Alc.

Muirhead, Litellus Russell, ed.
Holland. [2d ed.] London, Benn,
1961. lxiv, 219 p.   62-34821
DJ16 .M83 MRR Alc.

Netherlands (Kingdom, 1815-)
Departement van Onderwijs, Kunsten en
Wetenschappen. Guide to Dutch art.
2d rev. ed. Hague, Govt. Print. and
Pub. Off., 1953. 152 p.   709.492
58-42372
N6941 .A48 1953 MRR Alc.

NETHERLANDS--ECONOMIC CONDITIONS--
YEARBOOKS.
Economisch- en sociaal-historisch
jaarboek. deel 33- 1971- 's-
Gravenhage, M. Nijhoff. 72-622501
HC321 .E3 MRR Alc Latest edition

NETHERLANDS--EXECUTIVE DEPARTMENTS.
Netherlands (Kingdom, 1815-).
Staatsalmanak voor het koninkrijk der
Nederlanden. 1860- 's Gravenhage.
07-16339
JN5704 MRR Alc Latest edition

NETHERLANDS--GAZETTEERS.
United States. Office of Geography.
Netherlands; Washington, 1950. 145
p.   914.92/003 75-10039
DJ14 .U5 MRR Alc.

NETHERLANDS--IMPRINTS.
Brinkman's cumulatieve catalogus van
boeken, en verder in den boekhandel
voorkomende artikelen, die ... in
Nederland zijn uitgegeven of herdrukt
... voorts een alfabetische lijst van
nederlandsche boeken in België
uitgegeven ... Leiden, [etc.] A. W.
Sijthoff [etc.] 015.492 33-17363
Z2431 .A46 MRR Alc Partial set

British Museum. Dept. of Printed
Books. Short-title catalogue of
books printed in the Netherlands and
Belgium London, Trustees of the
British Museum, 1965. viii, 274 p.
66-44548
Z2402 .B7 MRR Alc.

Landwehr, John. Dutch emblem books;
a bibliography. Utrecht, Haentjens
Dekker & Gumbert [1962] xii, 98 p.
66-83333
Z2401 .L3 MR Alc.

NETHERLANDS--INDUSTRIES--DIRECTORIES.
Nederlands abc voor handel en
industrie. Haarlem, ABC voor Handel
en Industrie. 63-36606
HF3613 .N4 MRR Alc Latest edition

NETHERLANDS--MANUFACTURES--DIRECTORIES.
Kompass; informatiewerk over het
Nederlandse bedrijfsleven. Den Haag,
Kompass Nederland N.V. 72-620607
Began with vol. for 1965/66.
HF3613 .K58 MRR Alc Latest edition

NETHERLANDS--POLITICS AND GOVERNMENT--
YEARBOOKS.
Pyttersen's nederlandse almanak.
Zaltbommel, van de Garde. 46-18200
Began in 1900.
JN5703 .N4 MRR Alc Latest edition*

NETHERLANDS--REGISTERS.
Netherlands (Kingdom, 1815-).
Staatsalmanak voor het koninkrijk der
Nederlanden. 1860- 's Gravenhage.
07-16339
JN5704 MRR Alc Latest edition

Parlement en kiezer: Jaarboek. 's-
Gravenhage, Nijhoff. 74-642439
Began with vol. for 1911/12.
JN5873 .A3 MRR Alc Latest edition

Pyttersen's nederlandse almanak.
Zaltbommel, van de Garde. 46-18200
Began in 1900.
JN5703 .N4 MRR Alc Latest edition*

NETHERLANDS--SOCIAL CONDITIONS--
YEARBOOKS.
Economisch- en sociaal-historisch
Jaarboek. deel 33- 1971- 's-
Gravenhage, M. Nijhoff. 72-622501
HC321 .E3 MRR Alc Latest edition

NETHERLANDS--STATISTICS.
Jaarcijfers voor Nederlanden. 's
Gravenhage. 08-6303
HA1381 .D-D5 MRR Alc Latest
edition

NETHERLANDS (KINGDOM, 1815-). STATEN-
GENERAAL--REGISTERS--YEARBOOKS.
Parlement en kiezer: Jaarboek. 's-
Gravenhage, Nijhoff. 74-642439
Began with vol. for 1911/12.
JN5873 .A3 MRR Alc Latest edition

NETHERLANDS--BIOGRAPHY--DICTIONARIES.
Who's who in the Netherlands. 1st
ed.; 1962/63- [Montreal]
Intercontinental Book and Pub. Co.
64-6538
DJ289.A1 W5 MRR Biog Latest
edition

NETHERLANDS CHAMBER OF COMMERCE IN THE
UNITED KINGDOM.
Netherlands-British trade directory.
London, Netherlands Chamber of
Commerce in the United Kingdom.
382/.0942 73-645767
HF302 .N37 MRR Alc Latest edition

NEUMÜNSTER, GER.--DIRECTORIES.
Adreßbuch Neumünster und Umgebung.
Neumünster, K. Wachholtz. 57-40801

DD901.N575 A7 MRR Alc Latest
edition

NEUROLOGY.
Alpers, Bernard Jacob, Clinical
neurology 6th ed. Philadelphia, F.
A. Davis Co. [1971] xx, 1072 p.
616.8 73-103534
RC346 .A4 1971 MRR Alc.

Merritt, Hiram Houston, A textbook
of neurology 5th ed. Philadelphia,
Lea & Febiger, 1973. xxi, 841 p.
616.8 72-79352
RC346 .M4 1973 MRR Alc.

NEUROSES.
see also Phobias

NEVADA.
Writers' Program. Nevada. Nevada;
St. Clair Shores, Mich., Somerset
Publishers, 1973 [c1940] xviii, 315
p. 917.93/04/3 72-84489
F841 .W77 1973 MRR Ref Desk.

NEVADA--BIBLIOGRAPHY.
Historical records survey. A check
list of Nevada imprints, 1859-1890.
Chicago, The Historical records
survey, 1939. xv, 127 numb. l.
015.793 39-29057
Z1215 .H67 no. 7 MRR Alc.

NEVADA--BIBLIOGRAPHY--CATALOGS.
United States. Library of Congress.
Nevada: the centennial of statehood;
Washington: [For sale by the
Superintendent of Documents] 1965.
x, 66 p. 979-300740153 65-60081
Z663.15.A6N3 MRR Alc.

NEVADA--BIOGRAPHY.
Handbook of the Nevada Legislature.
Carson City, Nevada Legislative
Counsel Bureau. 328.793/05 72-
626560
JK8571 .A32 MRR Alc Latest edition

NEVADA--CENTENNIAL CELEBRATIONS, ETC.
United States. Library of Congress.
Nevada: the centennial of statehood;
Washington: [For sale by the
Superintendent of Documents] 1965.
x, 66 p. 979.300740153 65-60081
Z663.15.A6N3 MRR Alc.

NEVADA--DESCRIPTION AND TRAVEL--1951- --
GUIDE-BOOKS.
Mobil travel guide: California and
the west. 1969- [Bloomfield, N.J.]
Simon and Schuster. 917.94/04/5 72-
623503
F859.3 .M6 MRR Alc Latest edition

NEVADA--DESCRIPTION AND TRAVEL--GUIDE-
BOOKS.
American Automobile Association.
California-Nevada tour book,
Washington. 61-45102
GV1024 .A2314 MRR Alc Latest
edition

Writers' Program. Nevada. Nevada;
St. Clair Shores, Mich., Somerset
Publishers, 1973 [c1940] xviii, 315
p. 917.93/04/3 72-84489
F841 .W77 1973 MRR Ref Desk.

NEVADA--HISTORY.
Elliott, Russell R. History of
Nevada, Lincoln, Univeristy of
Nebraska Press, 1973. xii, 447 p.
[$9.50] 917.93 72-187809
F841 .E43 MRR Alc.

Ostrander, Gilman Marston, Nevada,
the great rotten borough, 1859-1964
[1st ed.] New York, Knopf, 1966.
xii, 247, [1], viii p. 879.3 66-
10747
F841 .O8 MRR Alc.

NEVADA--HISTORY--BIBLIOGRAPHY.
Elliott, Russell R. History of
Nevada, Lincoln, Univeristy of
Nebraska Press, 1973. xii, 447 p.
[$9.50] 917.93 72-187809
F841 .E43 MRR Alc.

NEVADA--IMPRINTS.
Historical records survey. A check
list of Nevada imprints, 1859-1890.
Chicago, The Historical records
survey, 1939. xv, 127 numb. l.
015.793 39-29057
Z1215 .H67 no. 7 MRR Alc.

NEVADA--OFFICIALS AND EMPLOYEES--
DIRECTORIES.
Nevada. Secretary of State.
Political history of Nevada. 5th ed.
Carson City, S[tate] P[rint.] O[ff.]
1965. 213 p. 67-64717
JK8516 .A5 1965 MRR Alc.

NEVADA--POLITICS AND GOVERNMENT.
Nevada. Secretary of State.
Political history of Nevada. 5th ed.
Carson City, S[tate] P[rint.] O[ff.]
1965. 213 p. 67-64717
JK8516 .A5 1965 MRR Alc.

Ostrander, Gilman Marston, Nevada,
the great rotten borough, 1859-1964
[1st ed.] New York, Knopf, 1966.
xii, 247, [1], viii p. 979.3 66-
10747
F841 .O8 MRR Alc.

NEVADA. LEGISLATURE--REGISTERS.
Handbook of the Nevada Legislature.
Carson City, Nevada Legislative
Counsel Bureau. 328.793/05 72-
626560
JK8571 .A32 MRR Alc Latest edition

NEVADA. LEGISLATURE--RULES AND PRACTICE.
Handbook of the Nevada Legislature.
Carson City, Nevada Legislative
Counsel Bureau. 328.793/05 72-
626560
JK8571 .A32 MRR Alc Latest edition

NEW CALEDONIA--BIBLIOGRAPHY.
O'Reilly, Patrick. Bibliographie
méthodique, analytique et critique
de la Nouvelle-Calédonie. Paris,
Musée de l'homme, 1955. ix, 361 p.
57-1374
Z4805 .O7 MRR Alc.

NEW CASTLE, DEL.--BIBLIOGRAPHY.
United States. Library of Congress.
Old New Castle and modern Delaware.
Washington, U.S. Govt. Print. Off.,
1951. iv, 58 p. 016.9751 51-60024
Z663.15.A6D3 1951 MRR Alc.

NEW CASTLE, DEL.--CENTENNIAL CELEBRATIONS, ETC.
United States. Library of Congress.
Old New Castle and modern Delaware.
Washington, U.S. Govt. Print. Off.,
1951. iv, 58 p. 016.9751 51-60024
Z663.15.A6D3 1951 MRR Alc.

NEW ENGLAND--BIOGRAPHY--DICTIONARIES.
Who's who in the East and Eastern
Canada. 1st- ed.; 1942/43-
Chicago [etc.] Marquis-Who's Who
[etc.] 920.07 43-18522
E176 .W643 MRR Biog Latest edition

NEW ENGLAND--COMMERCE--DIRECTORIES.
The Book of names. Wellesley, Mass.,
New England Marketing Publications.
[$7.50] 380.1/025/74 74-644283
HF5806.A11 B65 MRR Alc Latest edition

NEW ENGLAND--DESCRIPTION AND TRAVEL--GUIDE-BOOKS.
Faison, Samson Lane, A guide to the
art museums of New England. [1st
ed.] New York, Harcourt, Brace
[1958] xvii, 270 p. 708.14 58-8579
N510.5.N4 F2 MRR Alc.

Fodor, Eugene. New England; 2d,
rev. ed. Litchfield, Conn.] Fodor's
Modern Guides; distributors: D. McKay
Co., New York [1967] 411 p.
917.4/04/4 67-20077
F2.3 .F6 1967 MRR Alc.

Mobil travel guide: Northeastern
States. 1960- New York, Simon and
Schuster. 917.4 60-51602
F2.3 M6 MRR Alc Latest edition

Northeastern States. 1969/70-
[Washington, American Automobile
Association] 917.4/04/4 76-615943
GV1024 .N84 MRR Alc Latest edition

Northeastern tour book. [Washington,
American Automobile Association]
917.4/04/4 74-644520
GV1024 .N84 MRR Alc Latest edition

NEW ENGLAND--HISTORIC HOUSES, ETC.
Faison, Samson Lane, A guide to the
art museums of New England. [1st
ed.] New York, Harcourt, Brace
[1958] xvii, 270 p. 708.14 58-8579
N510.5.N4 F2 MRR Alc.

Webster, Isabel Stevens. Antique
collectors' guide to New England;
New York, Grosset & Dunlap [1961]
165 p. 708.051 61-3263
NK1127 .W4 MRR Alc.

NEW ENGLAND--HISTORY--COLONIAL PERIOD, CA. 1600-1775.
Winthrop, John, Winthrop's journal,
"History of New England," 1630-1649;
New York, C. Scribner's sons, 1908.
2 v. 08-17771
E187.O7 W5 MRR Alc.

NEW ENGLAND--HISTORY--COLONIAL PERIOD, CA. 1600-1775--HISTORIOGRAPHY.
Gay, Peter, A loss of mastery;
Berkeley, University of California
Press [1966] viii, 164 p.
974.02072 67-10969
E175.45 .G3 MRR Alc.

NEW ENGLAND--HISTORY--COLONIAL PERIOD, CA. 1600-1775--SOURCES.
Lincoln, Charles Henry, ed.
Narratives of the Indian wars, 1675-
1699; New York, C. Scribner's sons,
1913. xii p., 2 l., 3-316 p.
[$3.00] 13-24819
E187.O7 L5 MRR Alc.

NEW ENGLAND--INDUSTRIES--DIRECTORIES.
Eastern manufacturers' & industrial
directory New York, Bell Directory
Publishers. 54-35021
Began publication in 1936.
HC107.A11 E2 MRR Alc Latest edition

NEW ENGLAND--MANUFACTURES--DIRECTORIES.
Directory of New England
manufacturers. Boston, Mass., G. D.
Hall, inc. 338.40974 36-5085
HD9723 .D45 Sci RR Latest edition
/ MRR Alc Latest edition

NEW ENGLAND--SOCIAL LIFE AND CUSTOMS.
Botkin, Benjamin Albert, ed. A
treasury of New England folklore;
Rev. ed. New York, Crown Publishers
[1965] xxii, 618 p. 398 64-17848
GR106 .B6 1965 MRR Alc.

NEW FRANCE--DISCOVERY AND EXPLORATION.
Champlain, Samuel de, Voyages of
Samuel de Champlain, 1604-1618; New
York, C. Scribner's sons, 1907.
viii, 377 p. 07-22899
E187.O7 C5 MRR Alc.

NEW HAMPSHIRE.
Federal writers' project. New
Hampshire. New Hampshire, a guide to
the Granite state, Boston, Houghton
Mifflin company, 1938. xxix, 559 p.
917.42 38-6192
F39 .F43 MRR Ref Desk.

NEW HAMPSHIRE--COMMERCE--DIRECTORIES.
New Hampshire register, state year-
book and legislative manual. 1869-
Portland, Me. [etc.] F. L. Tower
Companies [etc.] 11-25112
JK2930 .N4 Sci RR Latest edition*
/ MRR Alc Latest edition

NEW HAMPSHIRE--DESCRIPTION AND TRAVEL--GUIDE-BOOKS.
Federal writers' project. New
Hampshire. New Hampshire, a guide to
the Granite state, Boston, Houghton
Mifflin company, 1938. xxix, 559 p.
917.42 38-6192
F39 .F43 MRR Ref Desk.

NEW HAMPSHIRE--INDUSTRIES--DIRECTORIES.
New Hampshire register, state year-
book and legislative manual. 1869-
Portland, Me. [etc.] F. L. Tower
Companies [etc.] 11-25112
JK2930 .N4 Sci RR Latest edition*
/ MRR Alc Latest edition

NEW HAMPSHIRE--MANUFACTURES--DIRECTORIES.
Directory of New England
manufacturers. Boston, Mass., G. D.
Hall, inc. 338.40974 36-5085
HD9723 .D45 Sci RR Latest edition
/ MRR Alc Latest edition

New Hampshire. Office of Industrial
Development. Made in New Hampshire;
[1st] ed.; 1940- Concord. 54-
33797
T12 .N4 MRR Alc Latest edition

NEW HAMPSHIRE--POLITICS AND GOVERNMENT.
New Hampshire. Secretary of State.
Manual for the General court. nq.
[1]- 1889- Concord N.H. [etc.] 13-
33250
JK2931 date e MRR Alc Latest edition

NEW HAMPSHIRE--REGISTERS.
New Hampshire. Secretary of State.
Manual for the General court. nq.
[1]- 1889- Concord N.H. [etc.] 13-
33250
JK2931 date e MRR Alc Latest edition

New Hampshire register, state year-
book and legislative manual. 1869-
Portland, Me. [etc.] F. L. Tower
Companies [etc.] 11-25112
JK2930 .N4 Sci RR Latest edition*
/ MRR Alc Latest edition

NEW HAMPSHIRE. GENERAL COURT.
New Hampshire. Secretary of State.
Manual for the General court. nq.
[1]- 1889- Concord N.H. [etc.] 13-
33250
JK2931 date e MRR Alc Latest edition

NEW HEBRIDES--BIBLIOGRAPHY.
O'Reilly, Patrick. Bibliographie
méthodique, analytique et critique
des Nouvelles-Hébrides. Paris,
Musée de l'homme, 1958. xi, 304 p.
58-41208
Z4820 .O7 MRR Alc.

NEW HEBRIDES--BIOGRAPHY--DICTIONARIES.
O'Reilly, Patrick. Hébridais;
répertoire bio-bibliographique des
Nouvelles-Hébrides. Paris, Musée
de l'homme, 1957. vii, 289 p. 57-
48614
DU50 .O7 MRR Biog.

NEW INTERNATIONAL--INDEXES.
Indexes to independent Socialist
periodicals. Berkeley, Calif.,
Independent Socialist Press [1969]
221 p. [9.75] 016.3091 77-16046
HX15 .I43 no. 4 MRR Alc.

NEW JERSEY--BIBLIOGRAPHY.
Burr, Nelson Rollin, A narrative and
descriptive bibliography of New
Jersey Princeton, N.J., Van
Nostrand, 1964. xxii, 266 p.
016.91749 65-862
Z1313 .B8 MRR Alc.

NEW JERSEY--BIOGRAPHY.
Manual of the Legislature of New
Jersey. Trenton, N.J. [etc.] 05-
11203
JK3531 MRR Alc Latest edition

NEW JERSEY--DESCRIPTION AND TRAVEL--GUIDE-BOOKS.
Federal writers' project. New Jersey.
New Jersey, a guide to its present
and past; New York, The Viking
Press, 1939. xxxii, 735 p. 917.49
39-20654
F139 .F45 MRR Ref Desk.

NEW JERSEY--DIRECTORIES.
Printing trades blue book.
Metropolitan ed., Greater New York
and New Jersey. [no. 1]- 1916-
New York, A. F. Lewis. 16-1684
Z475 .P8N MRR Alc Latest edition

NEW JERSEY--EXECUTIVE DEPARTMENTS.
Manual of the Legislature of New
Jersey. Trenton, N.J. [etc.] 05-
11203
JK3531 MRR Alc Latest edition

NEW JERSEY--HISTORY--COLONIAL PERIOD, CA. 1600-1775--SOURCES.
Myers, Albert Cook, ed. Narratives
of early Pennsylvania, West New
Jersey and Delaware, 1630-1707, New
York, C. Scribner's sons, 1912. xiv
p., 2 l., 3-476 p. 12-4611
E187.O7 M9 MRR Alc.

NEW JERSEY--INDUSTRIES--DIRECTORIES.
New Jersey State industrial
directory, New York [etc.] 13-33036
Began publication with 1901 issue.
HC107.N5 N45 Sci RR Latest edition
/ MRR Alc Latest edition

NEW JERSEY--POLITICS AND GOVERNMENT--1865-1950.
Manual of the Legislature of New
Jersey. Trenton, N.J. [etc.] 05-
11203
JK3531 MRR Alc Latest edition

NEW JERSEY--POLITICS AND GOVERNMENT--1951-
League of Women Voters of New Jersey.
New Jersey: spotlight on government.
[Rev. ed.] [New Brunswick, N.J.,
Rutgers University Press, 1972] 425
p. [$10.00] 320.4/749 71-188294
JK3525 1972 .L4 MRR Alc.

NEW JERSEY--REGISTERS.
Manual of the Legislature of New
Jersey. Trenton, N.J. [etc.] 05-
11203
JK3531 MRR Alc Latest edition

New Jersey. Dept. of state. State
officers, Judges, &c. [Trenton] ca
10-3334
JK3531 date c MRR Alc Latest edition

NEW JERSEY. LEGISLATURE--RULES AND PRACTICE.
Manual of the Legislature of New
Jersey. Trenton, N.J. [etc.] 05-
11203
JK3531 MRR Alc Latest edition

NEW LEFT
see Radicalism

NEW MEXICO--BIBLIOGRAPHY.
Historical records survey. Illinois.
Check list of New Mexico imprints and
publications, 1784-1876. [Detroit]
Michigan Historical records survey,
1942. 3 p. l., v-xiii, 115 p., 3 l.
015.798 43-5102
Z1215 .H67 no. 25 MRR Alc.

NEW MEXICO--DESCRIPTION AND TRAVEL--GUIDE-BOOKS.
Writers' Program. New Mexico. New
Mexico; a guide to the colorful
State. New and completely rev. ed.
New York, Hastings House, 1962.
xxxii, 472 p. 917.89 62-53065
F794.3 .W7 1962 MRR Ref Desk.

NEW MEXICO--GOVERNMENT PUBLICATIONS--
BIBLIOGRAPHY.
Shelton, Wilma Loy, Checklist of New
Mexico publications, 1850-1953.
[Albuquerque] University of New
Mexico Press, 1954. 240 p.   015.789
54-12989
Z1315 .S47 MRR Alc.

NEW MEXICO--HISTORY.
Beck, Warren A. New Mexico; a history
of four centuries. [1st ed.]
Norman, University of Oklahoma Press
[1962] 363 p.   978.9   62-16470
F786 .B4 MRR Alc.

NEW MEXICO--IMPRINTS.
Historical records survey. Illinois.
Check list of New Mexico imprints and
publications, 1784-1876. [Detroit]
Michigan Historical records survey,
1942. 3 p. l., v-xiii, 115 p., 3 l.
015.798   43-5102
Z1215 .H67 no. 25 MRR Alc.

NEW MEXICO--REGISTERS.
New Mexico blue book. [Santa Fe?]
Secretary of State.   72-626561
JK8030 .A22 MRR Alc Latest edition

NEW ORLEANS.
Federal Writers' Project. New
Orleans. New Orleans city guide.
Boston, Houghton Mifflin, 1952. lx,
416 p.   917.6335   52-14722
F379.N5 F34 1952 MRR Ref Desk.

NEW ORLEANS--DESCRIPTION--GUIDE-BOOKS.
Federal Writers' Project. New
Orleans. New Orleans city guide.
Boston, Houghton Mifflin, 1952. lx,
416 p.   917.6335   52-14722
F379.N5 F34 1952 MRR Ref Desk.

NEW PRODUCTS.
Growth & acquisition guide yearbook.
1968- Cleveland, Predicasts. 72-
14099
HG4028.M4 G74 MRR Alc Full set

NEW PRODUCTS--DIRECTORIES.
The New product directory of New York
Stock Exchange listed companies.
Concord, Mass., Marketing
Development. 338/.0025/73 74-647304
HD69.N4 N44 MRR Alc Latest edition

TTA Information Services Company.
Guide to locating new products. San
Mateo, Calif. [1971] 66 l.   338.4/7
71-153653
HD69.N4 T15 MRR Alc.

NEW SOUTH WALES.
Official year book of New South
Wales. [Sydney, Bureau of Census and
Statistics] 319.44 72-626839
DU150 .A3 MRR Alc Latest edition

NEW SOUTH WALES--COMMERCE--DIRECTORIES.
The Universal business directory for
central & southern New South Wales.
Sydney. 55-35122
HF5295 .U55 MRR Alc Latest edition

The Universal business directory of
New England, north & north-west
N.S.W. Sydney. 55-32913
HF5295 .U54 MRR Alc Latest edition

NEW SOUTH WALES--STATISTICS.
Official year book of New South
Wales. [Sydney, Bureau of Census and
Statistics] 319.44 72-626839
DU150 .A3 MRR Alc Latest edition

NEW SWEDEN--HISTORY--SOURCES.
Myers, Albert Cook, ed. Narratives
of early Pennsylvania, West New
Jersey and Delaware, 1630-1707. New
York, C. Scribner's sons, 1912. xlv
p., 2 l., 3-476 p.   12-4611
E187.O7 M9 MRR Alc.

NEW YEAR.
Gaster, Theodor Herzl, New Year: its
history, customs, and superstitions.
New York, Abelard-Schumann [1955]
138 p.   394.268 55-5069
GT4905 .G3 MRR Alc.

NEW YORK (CITY)--AMUSEMENTS--
DIRECTORIES.
Who's where. New York, L. Shull
Publications. 54-29736
Began publication in 1941.
PN2277.N5 A19 MRR Alc Latest
edition

NEW YORK (CITY)--BUILDINGS.
Goldstone, Harmon Hendricks, History
preserved; New York, Simon and
Schuster [1974] 576 p. [$12.95]
917.47/1/044 73-19096
F128.7 .G64 MRR Alc.

NEW YORK (CITY)--CHARITIES--DIRECTORIES.
Directory of social and health
agencies of New York City. [1st]-
ed.: 1883- [New York] 360.58 12-
37275
HV99.N59 N5 MRR Alc Latest edition

NEW YORK (CITY)--COMMERCE.
Custom house guide. New York. 99-
1545
HE953.N5 C8 MRR Alc Latest edition

NEW YORK (CITY)--COMMERCE--DIRECTORIES.
Brener, Carol. The underground
collector; New York, Simon and
Schuster [1970] 319 p. [2.95]
745.1/025/7471 72-107269
NK1127 .B64 MRR Alc.

Directory of New York importers.
1949- New York, Commerce and
Industry Association of New York.
382.058 50-4680
HF3163.N7 C617 MRR Alc Latest
edition

Scharlatt, Elizabeth Lohman, comp.
The passionate shopper; New York,
Dutton [1972] 257 p. [$2.95]
917.47/1/044 72-79127
HF5068.N5 S3 MRR Alc.

NEW YORK (CITY)--DESCRIPTION.
Ashton, Dore. New York. [1st ed.]
New York, Holt, Rinehart and Winston
[1972] 288 p. [$9.95]   709/.747/1
70-155541
N6535.N5 A9 MRR Alc.

NEW YORK (CITY)--DESCRIPTION--1951- --
GUIDE-BOOKS.
American Institute of Architects. New
York Chapter. AIA guide to New York
City. New York, Macmillan [1968]
xii, 464 p. [$6.95] 917.47/2 68-
58489
NA735.N5 A78 1968 MRR Alc.

Hepburn, Andrew. Complete guide to
New York City. New rev. ed. Garden
City, N.Y., Doubleday [1966] 192 p.
917.47104 65-26215
F128.18 .H4 1966 MRR Alc.

Hillman, Howard. The complete New
Yorker; New York, McKay Co. [1973,
c1972] ix, 273 p. [$5.95]
917.47/1/044 78-185129
F128.18 .H53 1973 MRR Alc.

Rinzler, Alan. The New York spy;
London, Blond, 1967. viii, 440 p.
[30/-]   917.471/04/4 67-106644
F128.18 .R5 1967b MRR Alc.

Tauber, Gilbert. The New York City
handbook; Rev. ed. Garden City,
N.Y., Doubleday, 1968. xxiii, 622 p.
917.471 67-23822
F128.18 .T3 1968 MRR Alc.

NEW YORK (CITY)--DESCRIPTION--GUIDE-
BOOKS.
Federal writers' project. New York
(City) New York city guide; New
York, Random house [1939] xx, 708 p.
917.471 39-27593
F128.5 .F376 MRR Ref Desk.

Gardner, Arron. Gardner's guide to
antiques and art buying in New York
City. Indianapolis, Bobbs-Merrill
[1969] xiii, 204 p. [5.95]
745.1/025/7471 69-13091
NK1127 .G3 MRR Alc.

Goldstone, Harmon Hendricks, History
preserved; New York, Simon and
Schuster [1974] 576 p. [$12.95]
917.47/1/044 73-19096
F128.7 .G64 MRR Alc.

McDarrah, Fred W., Museums in New
York; [1st ed.] New York, Dutton,
1967. 319 p.   917.471/04/4 66-
25127
F128.15 .M3 MRR Alc.

New York hackmen's and chauffeur's
guide. Scarsdale, N.Y. [etc.]
Thurston Pub. Co. [etc.] 917.471 60-
24961
F128.18 .N4 MRR Alc Latest edition

Osman, Randolph E., Art centers of
the world; New York Cleveland, World
Pub. Co. [1968] 192 p. [$7.95]
708.1471 68-26017
N600 .O8 MRR Alc.

Simon, Kate. New York places &
pleasures; 4th ed, rev. New York,
Harper & Row [1971] xxiii, 417 p.
[$7.95] 917.47/1/044 70-138761
F128.18 .S5 1971 MRR Alc.

NEW YORK (CITY)--DESCRIPTION--VIEWS.
Rizzuto, Angelo, Angelo Rizzuto's
New York; "In little old New York, by
Anthony Angel." Washington, Library
of Congress, 1972. 55 p. (chiefly
illus.) 917.47/1/0340222 72-3243
Z663.39 .N4 MRR Alc.

NEW YORK (CITY)--DIRECTORIES.
Directory of social and health
agencies of New York City. [1st]-
ed.: 1883- [New York] 360.58 12-
37275
HV99.N59 N5 MRR Alc Latest edition

New York hackmen's and chauffeur's
guide. Scarsdale, N.Y. [etc.]
Thurston Pub. Co. [etc.] 917.471 60-
24961
F128.18 .N4 MRR Alc Latest edition

Printing trades blue book.
Metropolitan ed., Greater New York
and New Jersey. [no. 1]- 1916-
New York, A. F. Lewis. 16-1684
Z475 .P8N MRR Alc Latest edition

NEW YORK (CITY)--DWELLINGS.
Goldstone, Harmon Hendricks, History
preserved; New York, Simon and
Schuster [1974] 576 p. [$12.95]
917.47/1/044 73-19096
F128.7 .G64 MRR Alc.

NEW YORK (CITY)--EXECUTIVE DEPARTMENTS.
New York (City). Official directory
of the City of New York. 1918- [New
York] 20-3855
JS1222 date c MRR Alc Latest
edition

NEW YORK (CITY)--GALLERIES AND MUSEUMS.
McDarrah, Fred W., Museums in New
York; [1st ed.] New York, Dutton,
1967. 319 p.   917.471/04/4 66-
25127
F128.15 .M3 MRR Alc.

Scott, Thomas J. Greater New York
art directory. [New York, Center for
Urban Education, 1968] 314 p.
[1.00]   700/.25/747 68-56339
N6535.N5 S27 MRR Alc.

NEW YORK (CITY)--HARBOR--YEARBOOKS.
New York port handbook. 1958- New
York, Port Resources Information
Committee. 387.12* 58-11356
HE554.N7 N55 MRR Alc Latest
edition

NEW YORK (CITY)--HISTORIC HOUSES, ETC.
Goldstone, Harmon Hendricks, History
preserved; New York, Simon and
Schuster [1974] 576 p. [$12.95]
917.47/1/044 73-19096
F128.7 .G64 MRR Alc.

McDarrah, Fred W., Museums in New
York; [1st ed.] New York, Dutton,
1967. 319 p.   917.471/04/4 66-
25127
F128.15 .M3 MRR Alc.

NEW YORK (CITY)--LIBRARIES.
Asia Society. Libraries in New York
City, New York, 1962. 23 p. 67-
46335
Z3001 .A8 MRR Alc.

Carman, Harry James, A guide to the
principal sources for American
civilization, 1800-1900, in the city
of New York; New York, Columbia
University Press, 1962. xlvi, 630 p.
016.973 62-10450
Z1236 .C25 1962 MRR Alc.

Columbia University. School of
Library Service. Libraries in New
York City. New York [1971] viii,
214 p. [$3.50] 0217.0097471 74-
21910
Z732.N75 N34 MRR Alc.

Greene, Evarts Boutell, A guide to
the principal sources for early
American history (1600-1800) in the
city of New York, New York, Columbia
university press, 1929. xxv, 357,
[1] p.   29-17492
Z1236 .G82 MRR Alc.

Special libraries directory of
Greater New York. 12th- ed.; 1972-
New York, Special Libraries
Association, New York Chapter.
021/.0025/747 74-644549
Z732.N75 S6 MRR Alc Latest edition

NEW YORK (CITY)--MAPS.
Hagstrom Company, inc., New York.
Hagstrom's Pocket atlas of the city
of New York; 3d ed. New York [1967]
143 p. (p. 3-96 col. maps) map67-
1081
G1254.N4 H25 1967 MRR Alc.

NEW YORK (CITY)--REGISTERS.
New York (City). Official directory
of the City of New York. 1918- [New
York] 20-3855
JS1222 date c MRR Alc Latest
edition

NEW YORK (CITY)--SOCIAL LIFE AND
CUSTOMS--PICTORIAL WORKS.
Rizzuto, Angelo, Angelo Rizzuto's
New York; "In little old New York, by
Anthony Angel." Washington, Library
of Congress, 1972. 55 p. (chiefly
illus.) 917.47/1/0340222 72-3243
Z663.39 .N4 MRR Alc.

NEW YORK (CITY)--THEATERS--DIRECTORIES.
Stubs. Metropolitan New York
edition. [New York, M. Schattner,
etc.] 792./0295/7472 46-22521
Began publication in 1942.
PN2277.N5 S8 MRR Alc Latest
edition

NEW YORK (CITY)--THEATERS-- (Cont.)
Who's where. New York, L. Shull
Publications. 54-29736
Began publication in 1941.
PN2277.N5 A19 MRR Alc Latest
edition

NEW YORK (CITY) AMERICAN STOCK EXCHANGE.
Standard and Poor's Corporation.
Daily stock price record: American
stock Exchange. [New York]
332.6/322/0873 72-627513
HG4915 .S66 MRR Alc Full set

NEW YORK (CITY). AMERICAN STOCK
EXCHANGE.
Standard and Poor's Corporation.
Standard & Poor's stock reports:
American Stock Exchange. Feb. 1973-
New York. 332.6/7 70-183942
HG4905 .S44 MRR Alc Latest edition

NEW YORK (CITY). PUBLIC LIBRARY.
New York (City). Public Library.
Research Libraries. Catalog of
Government publications in the
Research Libraries: Boston, G. K.
Hall, 1972. 40 v. 011 74-171015
Z7164.G7 N54 1972 MRR Alc (Dk 33)

NEW YORK (CITY). PUBLIC LIBRARY.
RESEARCH LIBRARIES.
New York (City). Public Library.
Research Libraries. Dictionary
catalog of the Research Libraries.
Jan. 1972- [New York] 019/.1 72-
620418
Z881.N588 D5 MRR Alc (Dk 33)
Latest edition

NEW YORK (CITY). STOCK EXCHANGE.
Standard and Poor's Corporation.
Daily stock price record: New York
Stock Exchange. [New York]
332.6/322/0873 72-627514
HG4915 .S664 MRR Alc Full set

NEW YORK (CITY) STOCK EXCHANGE.
Standard and Poor's Corporation.
Standard & Poor's stock reports: New
York Stock Exchange. Jan. 1973- New
York. 332.6/7 74-183943
HG4905 .S443 MRR Alc Latest
edition

NEW YORK (STATE)
Writers' program. New York. New
York, a guide to the Empire state,
New York, Oxford university press
[1940] xxxi, 782 p. 917.47 40-
28672
F124 .W89 MRR Ref Desk.

NEW YORK (STATE)--BIOGRAPHY.
The New York red book. Albany,
Williams Press, [etc.] 99-2308
JK3430 .N5 MRR Alc Latest edition

Who's who in New York (city and
state). 1st- ed.; 1904- New York
[etc.] Lewis Historical Pub. Co.
[etc.] 11-7854
F118 .W62 MRR Biog Latest edition

NEW YORK (STATE)--DESCRIPTION AND
TRAVEL.
Danckaerts, Jasper, b. 1638. Journal
of Jasper Danckaerts, 1679-1680; New
York, C. Scribner's sons, 1913.
xxxi, 313 p. 13-13556
E187.07 D3 MRR Alc.

NEW YORK (STATE)--DESCRIPTION AND
TRAVEL--GUIDE-BOOKS.
Mobil travel guide: Northeastern
States. 1960- New York, Simon and
Schuster. 917.4 60-51602
F2.3 M6 MRR Alc Latest edition

Writers' program. New York. New
York, a guide to the Empire state,
New York, Oxford university press
[1940] xxxi, 782 p. 917.47 40-
28672
F124 .W89 MRR Ref Desk.

NEW YORK (STATE)--DIRECTORIES.
Charitable organizations,
professional fund raisers, and
professional solicitors. [1st]-
ed.; 1955- Albany, N.Y.
361.7/3/025747 a 56-9301
HV89 .N44 MRR Alc Latest edition

NEW YORK (STATE)--EXECUTIVE DEPARTMENTS.
The New York red book. Albany,
Williams Press, [etc.] 99-2308
JK3430 .N5 MRR Alc Latest edition

NEW YORK (STATE)--GENEALOGY.
Belknap, Waldron Phoenix, American
colonial painting: Cambridge, Mass.,
Belknap Press of Harvard University
Press, 1959. xxi, 377 p. 759.13
59-10313
ND1311 .B39 MRR Alc.

NEW YORK (STATE)--GOVERNMENT
PUBLICATIONS--BIBLIOGRAPHY.
New York (State). State Library,
Albany. Official publications of the
State of New York. [Albany] 1969.
390 p. 015/.747 79-629176
Z1223.5.N57 N552 MRR Alc.

NEW YORK (STATE)--HISTORY.
Ellis, David Maldwyn. A history of
New York State Rev. ed.] Ithaca,
N.Y., Cornell University Press [1967]
xx, 732 p. 917.47/03 67-20587
F119 .E46 1967 MRR Alc.

NEW YORK (STATE)--HISTORY--COLONIAL
PERIOD, CA. 1600-1775.
Danckaerts, Jasper b. 1639. Journal
of Jasper Danckaerts, 1679-1680; New
York, C. Scribner's sons, 1913.
xxxi, 313 p. 13-13556
E187.07 D3 MRR Alc.

NEW YORK (STATE)--HISTORY--COLONIAL
PERIOD, CA. 1600-1775--SOURCES.
Jameson, John Franklin, ed.
Narratives of New Netherland, 1609-
1664; New York, C. Scribner's sons,
1909. xx p., 2 l., 3-478 p. 09-
24463
E187.07 J3 MRR Alc.

NEW YORK (STATE)--HISTORY--1865- --
SOURCES.
Roosevelt, Franklin Delano, Pres.
U.S., The public papers and
addresses of Franklin D. Roosevelt,
New York, Random House, 1938-[50] 13
v. 973.917 38-11227
E806 .R749 MRR Alc.

NEW YORK (STATE)--IMPRINTS.
Historical records survey. Illinois.
A check list of Utica imprints, 1799-
1830. Chicago, Ill., Illinois
Historical records survey, Illinois
public records project, 1942. viii,
179 p. 015.747 43-5103
Z1215 .H67 no. 36 MRR Alc.

NEW YORK (STATE)--INDUSTRIES--
DIRECTORIES.
New York State industrial directory.
New York. 64-39295
HC107.N7 N45 Sci RR Latest
edition* / MRR Alc Latest edition

NEW YORK (STATE)--MANUFACTURES--
DIRECTORIES.
New York State industrial directory.
New York. 64-39295
HC107.N7 N45 Sci RR Latest
edition* / MRR Alc Latest edition

NEW YORK (STATE)--POLITICS AND
GOVERNMENT.
The New York red book. Albany,
Williams Press, [etc.] 99-2308
JK3430 .N5 MRR Alc Latest edition

NEW YORK (STATE)--POLITICS AND
GOVERNMENT--YEARBOOKS.
New York state legislative annual.
1946- New York, New York Legislative
Service, inc. 328.747 47-20115
JK3401 .N48 MRR Alc Latest edition

NEW YORK (STATE)--REGISTERS.
New York (City). Official directory
of the City of New York. 1918- [New
York] 20-3855
JS1222 date c MRR Alc Latest
edition

The New York red book. Albany,
Williams Press, [etc.] 99-2308
JK3430 .N5 MRR Alc Latest edition

NEW YORK (STATE). STATE UNIVERSITY.
New York (State). State University.
Washington Office. Support for the
arts; Washington 1973. 164 p.
[$2.00] 338.4/7/7009747 73-176026

NX705.5.U62 N77 1973 MRR Alc.

NEW YORK HISTORICAL SOCIETY.
New York Historical Society.
Catalogue of American portraits in
the New York Historical Society. New
Haven : Published by the New York
Historical Society by Yale University
Press, 1974. 2 v. (ix, 964 p.) :
757/.9/0973 74-79974
N7593 .N5 1974 MRR Alc.

NEW YORK REVIEW OF BOOKS--INDEXES.
The New York review of books. Ten-
year cumulative index, February 1963-
January 1973. [New York] Arno Press,
1973. 90 p. mrr01-77
ZP2 .N6552 MRR Circ.

NEW YORKER--INDEXES.
Johnson, Robert Owen. An index to
literature in the New Yorker, volumes
I-XV, 1925-1940. Metuchen, N.J.,
Scarecrow Press, 1969-71. 3 v. 051
71-7740
AP2 .N6764 MRR Alc.

NEW YORKER (NEW YORK, 1925-)
Johnson, Robert Owen. An index to
profiles in the New Yorker.
Metuchen, N.J., Scarecrow Press,
1972. vi, 190 p. 016.920/073 71-
186947
Z5305.U5 J64 MRR Biog.

NEW ZEALAND.
The New Zealand official year-book.
[1st]- issue; 1892- Wellington.
07-21753
DU400 .A3 MRR Alc Latest edition

Osborne, Charles, Australia, New
Zealand, and the South Pacific; New
York, Praeger [1970] xi, 580 p.
[18.50] 919.4 69-12899
DU15 .08 1970b MRR Alc.

NEW ZEALAND--BIBLIOGRAPHY.
Index to New Zealand periodicals.
1966- Wellington, National Library
of New Zealand. 052 73-640533
Z6962.N5 I49 MRR Alc Full set

New Zealand national bibliography.
Wellington, Alexander Turnbull
Library. 015/.931 73-640530
Z4101 .N57 MRR Alc Full set

NEW ZEALAND--BIBLIOGRAPHY--BIBLIOGRAPHY.
New Zealand Library Association. A
bibliography of New Zealand
bibliographies. Prelim. ed.
Wellington, 1967. 58 p. [10/- 7/6
(to members N.Z.)] 016.016/91931
68-88968
Z4101.A1 N4 MRR Alc.

NEW ZEALAND--BIOGRAPHY.
Who's who in New Zealand. Wellington
[etc.] 920.0931 27-18903
"Established 1908."
DU402 .W5 MRR Biog Latest edition

NEW ZEALAND--BIOGRAPHY--DICTIONARIES.
Scholefield, Guy Hardy. A dictionary
of New Zealand biography,
Wellington, Dept. of internal
affairs: New Zealand, 1940. 2 v.
920.0931 41-1230
CT2886 .S35 MRR Biog.

NEW ZEALAND--COMMERCE--DIRECTORIES.
Lloyd's Australian and New Zealand
trade register. Sydney. 57-47262
HC602 .L55 MRR Alc Latest edition

The New Zealand index of trades,
industries, and professions.
Auckland, N.Z., Dodson and Cooper.
61-45521
HF3963 .N4 MRR Alc Latest edition

NEW ZEALAND--DESCRIPTION AND TRAVEL--
1951- --GUIDE-BOOKS.
Shadbolt, Maurice. The Shell guide
to New Zealand, London, Michael
Joseph Ltd., 1969. 336 p.; 17
plates. [50/-] 919.31/04/3 72-
487560
DU412 .S44 1969 MRR Alc.

NEW ZEALAND--DESCRIPTION AND TRAVEL--
GUIDE-BOOKS.
Brathwaite, Errol, The companion
guide to the North Island of New
Zealand. Auckland, Collins, 1970.
462 p. [$5.50] 70-598476
DU430.N6 B7 MRR Alc.

NEW ZEALAND--DICTIONARIES AND
ENCYCLOPEDIAS.
An Encyclopaedia of New Zealand.
Wellington, N.Z., R. E. Owen, Govt.
printer, 1966. 3 v. 919.31/003 67-
4443
DU405 .E5 MRR Alc.

The Modern encyclopædia of Australia
and New Zealand. Sydney, Horwitz-
Grahame [c1964] 1199 p. 65-2387
DU90 .M6 MRR Alc.

NEW ZEALAND--DIRECTORIES.
Wise's New Zealand post office
directory. Dunedin, H. Wise. 53-
28720
DU400 .W5 MRR Alc Latest edition

NEW ZEALAND--GAZETTEERS.
United States. Office of Geography.
New Zealand, official standard names
approved by the United States Board
on Geographic Names. Washington,
1954. 454 p. 919.31/003 75-10020

DU405 .U67 MRR Alc.

Wise's New Zealand guide. Dunedin,
H. Wise. 919.31/003 72-627324
DU405 .N55 MRR Alc Latest edition

NEW ZEALAND--HISTORY.
Oliver, William Hosking. The story
of New Zealand. New York, Roy
Publishers [1962, c1960] 301 p.
993.1 62-10707
DU420 .045 1962 MRR Alc.

NEW ZEALAND--IMPRINTS.
New Zealand books in print.
Wellington [etc.] Published for the
Associated Booksellers of New Zealand
by Price Milburn [etc.] 62-44889
Began publication in 1957.
Z4101 .N56 MRR Alc Latest edition

New Zealand national bibliography.
Wellington, Alexander Turnbull
Library. 015/.931 73-640530
Z4101 .N57 MRR Alc Full set

NEW ZEALAND--INDUSTRIES--DIRECTORIES.
Lloyd's Australian and New Zealand
trade register. Sydney. 57-47262
HC602 .L55 MRR Alc Latest edition

NEW ZEALAND--INDUSTRIES-- (Cont.)
The New Zealand business who's who.
Wellington, L. T. Watkins, ltd. 338
51-32889
Began in 1935.
HC621 .N4 MRR Alc Latest edition

The New Zealand index of trades,
industries, and professions.
Auckland, N.Z., Dodson and Cooper.
61-45521
HF3963 .N4 MRR Alc Latest edition

NEW ZEALAND--STATISTICS.
New Zealand. Dept. of Statistics.
Local authority statistics.
Wellington. 336.931 72-626670
JS10 .N8 MRR Alc Latest edition

The New Zealand official year-book.
[1st]-   issue: 1892- Wellington.
07-21753
DU400 .A3 MRR Alc Latest edition

NEW ZEALAND LITERATURE--HISTORY AND
CRITICISM.
McCormick, Eric Hall, New Zealand
literature, London, Oxford
University Press, 1959. 173 p.
820.9 59-2038
PR9606 .M3 MRR Alc.

NEW ZEALAND PERIODICALS--BIBLIOGRAPHY.
New Zealand national bibliography.
Wellington, Alexander Turnbull
Library. 015/.931 73-640530
Z4101 .N57 MRR Alc Full set

NEW ZEALAND PERIODICALS--INDEXES.
Index to New Zealand periodicals.
1966- Wellington, National Library
of New Zealand. 052 73-640533
Z6962.N5 I49 MRR Alc Full set

NEW ZEALAND POETRY.
Chapman, Robert McDonald, comp. An
anthology of New Zealand verse,
London, Oxford University Press,
1956. 341 p. 821.082 56-3148
PR9657 .C5 MRR Alc.

Murdoch, Walter, comp. A book of
Australian and New Zealand verse,
[4th ed.] London, Oxford University
Press [1950] 377 p. 821.082 53-
25334
PR9551 .M9 1950 MRR Alc.

NEW ZEALAND POETRY--BIBLIOGRAPHY.
Cuthbert, Eleonora Isabel. Index of
Australian and New Zealand poetry.
New York, Scarecrow Press, 1963. 453
p. 016.821 63-7469
Z4024.P7 C8 MRR Alc.

NEW ZEALAND POETRY--INDEXES.
Cuthbert, Eleonora Isabel. Index of
Australian and New Zealand poetry.
New York, Scarecrow Press, 1963. 453
p. 016.821 63-7469
Z4024.P7 C8 MRR Alc.

NEWBERY MEDAL BOOKS.
Kingman, Lee, ed. Newbery and
Caldecott medal books: 1956-1965,
Boston, Horn Book, 1965. xix, 300 p.
028.5 65-26759
Z1037.A2 K5 1965 MRR Alc.

Miller, Bertha E. (Mahony) ed.
Newbery medal books, 1922-1955,
Boston, Horn Book, inc., 1955. xvi,
458 p. 028.5 55-13968
Z1035.A2 M5 MRR Alc.

Smith, Irene, A history of the
Newbery and Caldecott medals. New
York, Viking Press [1957] 140 p.
028.5 57-4510
Z1037 .S648 MRR Alc.

NEWCASTLE-UPON-TYNE--DIRECTORIES.
Kelly's (incorporating "Ward's")
directory of the city of Newcastle
upon Tyne and Gosforth. Kingston
upon Thames, Surrey [etc.] Kelly's
Directories Ltd. 53-28852
DA690.N6 K4 MRR Alc Latest edition

NEWFOUNDLAND--BIOGRAPHY.
Who's who in Canada: Toronto,
International Press Limited. 17-
16282
Began publication in 1910.
F1033 .W62 Sci RR Latest edition /
MRR Blog Latest edition

NEWFOUNDLAND--COMMERCE--DIRECTORIES.
Newfoundland and Labrador business
directory and buyers guide. St.
John's [Maritimes Directories]
380.1/025/718 73-642979
HF3229.N5 A45 MRR Alc Latest
edition

NEWPORT NEWS, VA.--HARBOR.
Hampton Roads Maritime Association,
Norfolk, Va. The ports of Greater
Hampton Roads annual. 1925-
Norfolk, Va. 28-31191
HE554.H3 A25 MRR Alc Latest
edition

NEWS AGENCIES.
Merrill, John Calhoun, The foreign
press; Baton Rouge, Louisiana State
University Press [1970] 365 p.
070.9 76-96259
PN4736 .M39 1970 MRR Alc.

United Nations Educational,
Scientific and Cultural Organization.
News agencies, their structure and
operation. New York, Greenwood Press
[1969, c1953] 208 p. 070.04/3 76-
88957
PN4714.A1 U5 1969 MRR Alc.

NEWS AGENCIES--DIRECTORIES.
Directory of newspaper and magazine
personnel and data. London,
Haymarket Publishing Group, [etc.]
072.058 59-18302
Z6956.E5 D5 MRR Alc Latest edition

Esslen, Rainer. A guide to marketing
securities in Europe, 1971-1972. New
York, Wall Street Reports Pub. Corp.
[1971] viii, 215 p. 332.67/34/073
79-178914
HG4538 .E76 MRR Alc.

Hudson's Washington news media
contacts directory. 1968-
Washington. 071/.53 68-22594
Z6953.W2 H8 MRR Alc Latest edition

New York publicity outlets. New
York, Attention Inc. [etc.] 61-65657

Z6953.N6 N6 MRR Alc Latest edition

Union nationale des attachés de
presse. Annuaire. Paris. 64-1317
Began publication 1959?
PN5171 .U53 MRR Alc Latest edition

Weiner, Richard, News bureaus in the
U.S. [New York, 1974] vi, 143 p.
071/.3 74-170343
Z6951 .W4 1974 MRR Alc.

NEWS-LETTERS--BIBLIOGRAPHY.
National directory of newsletters and
reporting services. 1st- ed.; 1966-
Detroit, Gale Research Co. 66-
15458
Z6941 .N3 MRR Ref Desk Latest
edition

NEWS-LETTERS--DIRECTORIES.
Gebbie house magazine directory.
[Sioux City, Iowa, House Magazine
Pub. Co.] 016.0704/86 74-644438
Z7164.C81 N32 MRR Ref Desk Latest
edition

The Standard directory of
newsletters. 1st ed. New York,
Oxbridge Pub. Co. [1971, c1972] lvi,
210 p. [$20.00] 071/.025/73 71-
173896
Z6944.N44 S8 MRR Ref Desk.

NEWSPAPER ADVERTISING
see Advertising, Newspaper

NEWSPAPER AND PERIODICAL WHOLESALERS--
DIRECTORIES.
Bestsellers who's who in independent
distribution. 1969- [Philadelphia,
North American Pub. Co.]
658.8/08/655572 70-15822
PN4889 .B45 MRR Alc Latest edition

NEWSPAPER AND PERIODICAL WHOLESALERS--
UNITED STATES--DIRECTORIES.
Who's who in magazine distribution.
New York, Ziff-Davis Pub. Co. [1960]
304 p. 070.33 60-10057
PN4889 .W5 MRR Alc.

NEWSPAPER READING.
Stabler, Charles Norman, How to read
the financial news, 9th ed. New
York, Harper [1959] 210 p. 070.443
58-11049
PN4784.F5 S8 1959 MRR Alc.

NEWSPAPERS.
see also Periodicals

see also Press

see also Reporters and reporting

Merrill, John Calhoun, The foreign
press; Baton Rouge, Louisiana State
University Press [1970] 365 p.
070.9 76-96259
PN4736 .M39 1970 MRR Alc.

Merrill John Calhoun, A handbook of
the foreign press. [Baton Rouge]
Louisiana State University Press
[1959] viii, 394 p. 070.1 59-
14603
PN4736 .M4 1959 MRR Alc.

NEWSPAPERS--BIBLIOGRAPHY.
New York. Public library. Checklist
of newspapers and official gazettes
in the New York public library; [New
York] The New York public library,
1915. iv, 579 p. 16-1688
Z6945 .N6 MRR Alc.

Willing's press guide. London, J.
Willing, Ltd. [etc.] 53-36485
Began publication with issue for
1874.
Z6956.E5 W5 MRR Alc Latest edition

NEWSPAPERS--BIBLIOGRAPHY--CATALOGS.
Chicago. Center for Research
Libraries. The Center for Research
Libraries catalogue: newspapers.
Chicago, 1969. 176 p. 016.07 72-
13485
Z6945 .C533 MRR Alc (Dk 33)

Chicago. Center for Research
Libraries. The Center for Research
Libraries catalogue: serials.
Chicago, 1972. 2 v. 019 72-180872

Z6945 .C5335 MRR Alc (Dk 33).

Stanford University. Hoover
Institution on War, Revolution, and
Peace. The library catalogs of the
Hoover Institution on War,
Revolution, and Peace, Stanford
University: Boston, Mass., G. K.
Hall, 1969. 3 v. 016.05 79-17893

Z6945 .S7982 MRR Alc (Dk 33)

United States. Library of Congress.
Periodicals division. A check list
of foreign newspapers in the Library
of Congress, Washington, U.S. Govt.
print. off., 1929. vi, 209 p. 29-
14596
Z663.46 .C47 1929 MRR Alc.

United States. Library of Congress.
Serial Division. Newspapers
currently received & permanently
retained in the Library of Congress.
1968- Washington [For sale by the
Supt. of Docs., U.S. Govt. Print.
Off.] 016.07 68-61877
Z663.44 .A42 MRR Alc MRR Alc
Latest edition

NEWSPAPERS--BIBLIOGRAPHY--UNION LISTS.
American newspapers, 1821-1936: New
York, H. W. Wilson Co., 1937. xvi,
791 p. 37-12783
Z6945 .A53 MRR Alc.

Berlin. Institut für
zeitungswissenschaft.
Standortskatalog wichtiger
zeitungsbestände in deutschen
bibliotheken, Leipzig, K. W.
Hiersemann, 1933. xxxi, 254 p., 1 l.
016.073 33-24972
Z6945 .B46 MRR Alc.

Brigham, Clarence Saunders, History
and bibliography of American
newspapers, 1690-1820. Worcester,
Mass., American Antiquarian Society,
1947. 2 v. (xvii, 1508 p.) 016.071
47-4111
Z6951 .B86 MRR Alc.

Case, Margaret H. South Asian
history, 1750-1950; Princeton, N.J.,
Princeton University Press, 1968.
xiii, 561 p. 016.954 67-21019
Z3185 .C3 MRR Alc.

Fessler, Aaron L. Current
newspapers: United States and
foreign; Provisional ed. New York,
New York Public Library, 1957. 66 p.
016.07 57-14848
Z6945 .F4 MRR Alc.

Hewitt, Arthur R. Union list of
Commonwealth newspapers in London,
Oxford, and Cambridge. [London]
Published for the Institute of
Commonwealth Studies [by] the Athlone
Press, University of London, 1960.
ix, 101 p. 016.072 60-51452
Z6945 .H55 1960 MRR Alc.

[United States. Library of Congress.
Serial Division] Postwar foreign
newspapers; Washington, 1953. vi,
231 p. 53-60006
Z663.44 .P6 MRR Alc.

NEWSPAPERS--DICTIONARIES.
Pepper, William M. Dictionary of
newspaper and printing terms; New
York, Columbia University Press
[1959] 344 p. 070.03 59-16345
PN4728 .P4 MRR Alc.

NEWSPAPERS--DIRECTORIES.
Handbuch der Weltpresse. [5. Aufl.]
Köln, Westdeutscher Verlag, 1970. 2
v. 71-552170
Z6941 .H25 1970 MRR Alc.

Media Scandinavia. 16.- udg.; 1967-
København, Danske reklamebureauers
brancheforening. 72-623099
Z6941 .M4 MRR Alc Latest edition

The Newspaper press directory.
London, C. Mitchell [etc.] ca 07-6361
Z6956.E5 M6 MRR Alc Latest edition

Overseas newspapers and periodicals.
[London, Publishing & Distributing
Co.] 63-42121
Began publication with 1952 issue.
Z6941 .O9 MRR Alc Latest edition

NEWSPAPERS--DIRECTORIES. (Cont.)
Political handbook and atlas of the
world. Jan. 1, 1927- New York,
Simon and Schuster [etc.] for Council
on Foreign Relations. 28-12165
JF37 .P6 MRR Ref Desk Latest
edition / MRR Alc Latest edition

Wilcox, Dennis L. English language
newspapers abroad; Detroit, Gale
Research Co. [1967] 243 p.
017/.025 67-25558
Z6941 .W5 MRR Alc.

NEWSPAPERS--DIRECTORIES--BIBLIOGRAPHY.
Duprat, Gabrielle. Bibliographie des
répertoires nationaux de
périodiques en cours London, IFLA,
1969. 141 p. 73-858215
AS4.U8 A154 MRR Alc.

NEWSPAPERS--INDEXES.
New York times. (Indexes) The New
York times index for the published
news. v. 1- Jan./Mar. 1913- New
York. 13-13458
AI21 .N45 MRR Circ Full set / MRR
Circ Partial set

New York times. (Indexes) The New
York times index. New York,
Reprinted for the New York Times Co.
by R. R. Bowker Co. 66-41174
AI21 .N452 MRR Circ Partial set

New York tribune. New-York daily
tribune index. 1875-1906. New York,
Tribune Association. 12-37148
AI21 .N5 MRR Alc Full set

Paris. Université. Institut
français de presse. Section
d'histoire. Tables du journal Le
Temps. Paris, Éditions du Centre
national de la recherche
scientifique, 1966- v.   074.43/6
67-42357
AI21 .T375 MRR Alc.

Wall Street Journal. (Indexes)
Index. [New York] Dow Jones & Co.
59-35162
HG1 .W26 MRR Alc Full set

NEWSPAPERS--INDEXES--BIBLIOGRAPHY.
Brayer, Herbert Oliver. Preliminary
guide to indexed newspapers in the
United States, 1850-1900. [Cedar
Rapids? Ia., 1946?] 237-258 p.
016.071 48-12815
Z6293 .B7 MRR Alc.

NEWSPAPERS--SECTIONS, COLUMNS, ETC.--
FINANCE.
Stabler, Charles Norman, How to read
the financial news. 9th ed. New
York, Harper [1959] 210 p.   070.443
58-11049
PN4784.F5 S8 1959 MRR Alc.

NEWSPAPERS--EUROPE--BIBLIOGRAPHY.
United States. Library of Congress.
Slavic and Central European Division.
Newspapers of east central and
southeastern Europe in the Library of
Congress. Washington, 1965. vii,
204 p.   65-60088
Z663.47 .N37 MRR Alc.

NEWSPAPERS--EUROPE, EASTERN--
BIBLIOGRAPHY.
East European accessions index. v. 1-
Sept./Oct. 1951- Washington [U.S.
Govt. Print. Off.] 016.94 51-60032

Z663.7 .A3 MRR Alc MRR Alc Full
set

NEWSPAPERS--SCANDINAVIA--BIBLIOGRAPHY.
Media Scandinavia. 16.- udg.; 1967-
København, Danske reklamebureauers
brancheforening. 72-623099
Z6941 .M4 MRR Alc Latest edition

NEWSPAPERS IN MICROFORM--BIBLIOGRAPHY--
UNION LISTS.
United States. Library of Congress.
Catalog Publication Division.
Newspapers in microform: foreign
countries, 1948-1972. Washington,
Library of Congress, 1973. xix, 269
p. [$10.00] 016.05 73-13554
Z663.733 .N47 MRR Ref Desk.

United States. Library of Congress.
Catalog Publication Division.
Newspapers in microform: United
States, 1948-1972. Washington,
Library of Congress, 1973. xxiii,
1056 p. [$30.00] 016.071/3 73-
6936
Z663.733 .N48 MRR Ref Desk.

NEWSPAPERS ON MICROFILM.
Salmon, Stephen R. Specifications
for Library of Congress microfilming.
Washington, Library of Congress;
[for sale by the Superintendent of
Documents, U.S. Govt. Print. Off.]
1964. v, 21 p.   64-60058
Z663.96 .S6 MRR Alc.

NEWSPAPERS ON MICROFILM--BIBLIOGRAPHY.
Guide to microforms in print. 1961-
Washington, Microcard Editions.
016.099 61-7082
Z1033.M5 G8 Sci RR Latest edition
/ MRR Alc Latest edition

[Pride, Armistead Scott] Negro
newspapers on microfilm; Washington,
Library of Congress, Photoduplication
Service, 1953. 8 p.   016.071 53-
60015
Z663.96 .N4 MRR Alc.

Subject guide to microforms in print.
1962/63- Washington, Microcard
Editions. 016.099 62-21624
Z1033.M5 S8 Sci RR Latest edition
/ MRR Alc Latest edition

NEWSREELS--CATALOGS.
London. National Film Archive.
Catalogue. London, British Film
Institute, 1951- v.   792.93
791.4085 52-4264
PN1998 .L58 MRR Alc.

NICARAGUA--GAZETTEERS.
United States. Office of Geography.
Nicaragua; Washington, U.S. Govt.
Print. Off., 1956. ii, 49 p.
917.285 56-63928
F1522 .U5 MRR Alc.

NICKNAMES.
Abbatt, William, comp. The
colloquial who's who; Tarrytown,
N.Y., W. Abbatt, 1924-25. 2 v. 24-
23254
Z1045 .A12 MRR Alc.

Alexander, Gerald L. Nicknames of
American cities, New York, Special
Libraries Association [1951] 74 p.
929.4 51-8763
E155 .A5 MRR Alc.

Appleton's cyclopaedia of American
biography. Detroit, Gale Research
Co., 1868. 7 v. [168.00] 920.07
67-14061
E176 .A666 MRR Biog.

De Sola, Ralph, Abbreviations
dictionary; New international 4th
ed. New York, American Elsevier Pub.
Co. [1974] xiii, 428 p. 423/.1 73-
7687
PE1693 .D4 1974 MRR Ref Desk.

Franklyn, Julian. A dictionary of
nicknames. New York, British Book
Centre [1963] xx, 132 p. 427.09
63-10444
CT108 .F68 1963 MRR Alc.

Frey, Albert Romer, Sobriquets and
nicknames, Detroit, Republished by
Gale Research Co., 1966. iii, 482 p.
929.403 66-22671
CT108 .F7 1966 MRR Alc.

Goff, John. A book of nicknames.
Louisville, Ky., Courier-Journal Job
printing co., 1892. 75 p. 08-30496

E179 .G61 MRR Ref Desk.

Kane, Joseph Nathan, Nicknames and
sobriquets of U.S. cities and States,
2d ed. Methuchen, N.J., Scarecrow
Press, 1970. 456 p. 917.3/003 77-
10357
E155 .K24 1970 MRR Alc.

Latham, Edward. A dictionary of
names, nicknames, and surnames of
persons, places and things. Detroit,
Republished by Gale Research Co.,
1966. vii, 334 p. 031.02 66-22674

AG5 .L35 1966 MRR Alc.

Payton, Geoffrey. Webster's
dictionary of proper names.
Springfield, Mass., G. & C. Merriam
Co. [c1970] 752 p. 423.1 72-22048

PE1660 .P34 MRR Ref Desk.

Ruffner, Frederick G., ed. Code
names dictionary; Detroit, Gale
Research Co. [1963] 555 p. 423 63-
21847
PE1693 .R9 MRR Alc.

Shankle, George Earlie. American
nicknames; New York, The H. W.
Wilson company, 1937. v, [1],599 p.
929.4 37-36382
E179 .S545 MRR Alc.

Sharp, Harold S. Handbook of
pseudonyms and personal nicknames,
Metuchen, N.J., Scarecrow Press,
1972. 2 v. (1104 p.) 929.4 71-
189886
Z1041 .S43 MRR Ref Desk.

NIETZSCHE, FRIEDRICH WILHELM, 1844-1900.
United States. Library of Congress.
Gertrude Clarke Whittall Poetry and
Literature Fund. French and German
letters today; Washington, Reference
Dept., Library of Congress, 1960. v,
53 p.   840.9 60-60062
Z663.293 .F7 MRR Alc.

NIGER--GAZETTEERS.
United States. Office of Geography.
Niger; official standard names
approved by the United States Board
on Geographic Names. Washington,
1966. iv, 207 p. 916.6/26/003 66-
62657
DT547.2 .U2 MRR Alc.

NIGERIA.
The Diplomatic Press trade directory
of the Federal Republic of Nigeria
including classified trade index.
1960- London, Diplomatic Press and
Pub. Co. 60-51577
DT515 .A5613 MRR Alc Latest
edition

Nelson, Harold D. Area handbook for
Nigeria, Rev. 3d ed. Washington;
For sale by the Supt. of Docs., U.S.
Govt. Print. Off.] 1972. xvi, 485 p.
[$3.50] 309.1/669 77-183909
DT515 .N37 1972 MRR Alc.

Nigeria year book. Lagos, Times
Press ltd. (etc.] 55-23464
DT515 .N48 MRR Alc Latest edition

NIGERIA--BIBLIOGRAPHY.
Aguolu, Christian Chukwunedu,
Nigeria: a comprehensive bibliography
in the humanities and social
sciences, 1900-1971. Boston, G. K.
Hall, 1973. iv, 620 p.
016.91669/03 73-12843
Z3597 .A64 MRR Alc.

NIGERIA--BIOGRAPHY.
The Diplomatic Press trade directory
of the Federal Republic of Nigeria
including classified trade index.
1960- London, Diplomatic Press and
Pub. Co. 60-51577
DT515 .A5613 MRR Alc Latest
edition

NIGERIA--BIOGRAPHY--DICTIONARIES.
Who's who in Nigeria; [1st ed.]
Lagos, Nigerian Print. and Pub. Co.
[1956] 278 p. 62-5975
DT515.6.A1 W5 MRR Biog.

NIGERIA--DIRECTORIES.
Nigeria year book. Lagos, Times
Press ltd. (etc.] 55-23464
DT515 .N48 MRR Alc Latest edition

NIGERIA--FOREIGN RELATIONS--TREATIES.
Burns, Alan Cuthbert, Sir, History
of Nigeria 7th ed. London, Allen &
Unwin, 1969. 366 p. [45/-] 966/.9
79-410228
DT515 .B8 1969 MRR Alc.

NIGERIA--GAZETTEERS.
Nigeria. Survey Division. Gazetteer
[of the] Federal Republic of Nigeria.
Lagos, Director of Federal Surveys,
1965. 2 v. [5/- per vol.] 77-
268858
DT515.2 .A56 MRR Alc.

United States. Geographic Names
Division. Nigeria; official standard
names Washington [U.S. Board on
Geographic Names] 1971. iv, 641 p.
916.6/9/003 71-614382
DT515.2 .U55 MRR Alc.

NIGERIA--GOVERNMENT PUBLICATIONS--
BIBLIOGRAPHY.
United States. Library of Congress.
African Section. Nigeria: a guide to
official publications. Washington,
General Reference and Bibliography
Division. Reference Dept., Library of
Congress; [for sale by the
Superintendent of Documents, U.S.
Govt. Print. Off.] 1966. xii, 166 p.
016.354669 66-61703
Z663.285 .N5 MRR Alc.

United States. Library of Congress.
General Reference and Bibliography
Division. Nigerian official
publications, 1869-1959; Washington,
1959. xii, 153 p. 015.669 59-
60079
Z663.28 .N5 MRR Alc.

NIGERIA--HISTORY.
Burns, Alan Cuthbert, Sir, History
of Nigeria 7th ed. London, Allen &
Unwin, 1969. 366 p. [45/-] 966/.9
79-410228
DT515 .B8 1969 MRR Alc.

Crowder, Michael. The story of
Nigeria. 3rd. ed., revised, London,
Faber, 1973. 426, [8] p. [£5.00]
966.9 73-180515
DT515.5 .C7 1973 MRR Alc.

Crowder, Michael, The story of
Nigeria. London, Faber and Faber
[1962] 307 p. 966.9 62-4821
DT515.5 .C7 MRR Alc.

NIGERIA--INDUSTRIES--DIRECTORIES.
The Diplomatic Press trade directory
of the Federal Republic of Nigeria
including classified trade index.
1960- London, Diplomatic Press and
Pub. Co. 60-51577
DT515 .A5613 MRR Alc Latest
edition

NIGERIA--KINGS AND RULERS.
Burns, Alan Cuthbert, Sir, History
of Nigeria 7th ed. London, Allen &
Unwin, 1969. 366 p. [45/-] 966/.9
79-410228
DT515 .B8 1969 MRR Alc.

NIXON, RICHARD MILHOUS, 1913-
De Toledano, Ralph, One man alone:
Richard Nixon. New York, Funk &
Wagnalls [1969] 386 p. [6.95]
973.924/0924 B 71-87942
E856 .D4 MRR Alc.

Hughes, Arthur J. Richard M. Nixon,
New York, Dodd, Mead [1972] viii,
181 p. [$4.95] 973.924/0929/4 72-
3152
E856 .H83 MRR Alc.

Mazo, Earl, Nixon; a political
portrait [1st ed.] New York, Harper
& Row [1968] viii, 326 p.
973.92/0924 B 68-31363
E748.N5 M3 1968 MRR Ref Desk.

NOBEL PRIZES.
Farber, Eduard, Nobel prize winners
in chemistry, 1901-1961. Rev. ed.
London, New York, Abelard-Schuman
[1963] 341 p. 925.4 62-17263
QD21 .F37 1963 MRR Biog.

Frenz, Horst, comp. Literature 1901-
1967; Amsterdam, New York, published
for the Nobel Foundation by Elsevier
Pub. Co., 1969. xxi, 640 p. [40.00]
808.9 68-20649
PN771 .F74 MRR Alc.

Kaplan, Flora. Nobel prize winners:
Chicago, Ill., Nobelle publishing
company [c1941] xvi, 144 p. incl.
front. (port.), tables (1 fold.)
378.32 41-18559
AS911.N9 K3 1941 MRR Alc.

MacCallum, Thomas Watson, ed. The
Nobel prize-winners and the Nobel
foundation, 1901-1937, Zurich,
Central European Times Pub. Co.,
1938. xi, 589 p. 378.32 39-1224
AS911.N9 M3 MRR Alc.

Nobelstiftelsen, Stockholm. Nobel,
the man and his prizes. 3d ed. New
York, American Elsevier Pub. Co.
[1972] x, 659 p. 001.4/4 77-
169840
AS911 .N7553 1972 MRR Alc.

Peace. Amsterdam, New York, Elsevier
Publ. Co., 1972. 3 v. [fl83.20 per
vol.] 327/.172/08 68-20650
JX1937 .P38 MRR Alc.

Stevenson, Lloyd G. Nobel prize
winners in medicine and physiology,
1901-1950. New York, H. Schuman
[1953] 291 p. 926.1 378.32 53-
10370
R134 .S77 MRR Alc.

NOBELSTIFTELSEN, STOCKHOLM.
MacCallum, Thomas Watson, ed. The
Nobel prize-winners and the Nobel
foundation, 1901-1937, Zurich,
Central European Times Pub. Co.,
1938. xi, 589 p. 378.32 39-1224
AS911.N9 M3 MRR Alc.

NOBILITY.
The Royalty, peerage and aristocracy
of the world. London, Annuaire de
France. 929.7 74-644555
CS404 .R68 MRR Alc Latest edition

NOMINATIONS FOR OFFICE.
see also Political conventions

NOMINATIONS FOR OFFICE--UNITED STATES.
David, Paul Theodore, The politics
of national party conventions,
[Washington] Brookings Institution
[1960] xv, 592 p. 329 60-7422
JK2255 .D38 MRR Alc.

Judah, Charles Burnet, The unchosen
New York, Coward-McCann [1962] 377
p. 324.23 62-10947
JK2255 .J8 MRR Alc.

McKee, Thomas Hudson. The national
conventions and platforms of all
political parties, 1789 to 1905; New
York, B. Franklin [1971] 414, 33 p.
329/.02 75-132682
JK2255 .M2 1871 MRR Alc.

Pomper, Gerald M. Nominating the
President; [Evanston, Ill.]
Northwestern University Press, 1963.
xii, 292 p. 329/.022/0973 63-13558

JK521 .P6 MRR Alc.

United States. Congress. Senate.
Library. Nomination and election of
the President and Vice President of
the United States, including the
manner of selecting delegates to
national political conventions,
Washington, U.S. Govt. Print. Off.,
1972. v, 273 p. [$1.50]
329/.0221/0973 72-600557
JK2063 .A513 1872 MRR Ref Desk.

NON-OBJECTIVE PAINTINGS
see Art, Abstract

NON-WAGE PAYMENTS--UNITED STATES.
Employee benefits fact book. [New
York] 331.2/52 76-118375
HD7125 .E57 MRR Alc Latest edition

NONCONFORMISTS
see Dissenters

**NONFERROUS METAL INDUSTRIES--
DIRECTORIES.**
Non-ferrous metal works of the world.
1st- ed.; 1967- London, Metal
Bulletin Books. 68-39821
HD9539 .A1W62 MRR Alc Latest
edition

NONFERROUS METAL INDUSTRIES--STATISTICS.
Metallgesellschaft A.G., Frankfurt am
Main. Metal statistics. 54th-
ed.; 1957/66- Frankfurt am Main. 72-
622829
HD9539.A1 M4 MRR Alc Latest
edition / Sci RR Latest edition

**NONFERROUS METAL INDUSTRIES--EUROPE--
STATISTICS.**
Organization for Economic Cooperation
and Development. L'Industrie des
metaux non ferreux. Paris.
338.4/7/673 72-626357
HD9539.A1 O66a MRR Alc Latest
edition

**NONFERROUS METAL INDUSTRIES--JAPAN--
STATISTICS.**
Organization for Economic Cooperation
and Development. L'Industrie des
metaux non ferreux. Paris.
338.4/7/673 72-626357
HD9539.A1 O66a MRR Alc Latest
edition

**NONFERROUS METAL INDUSTRIES--NORTH
AMERICA--STATISTICS.**
Organization for Economic Cooperation
and Development. L'Industrie des
metaux non ferreux. Paris.
338.4/7/673 72-626357
HD9539.A1 O66a MRR Alc Latest
edition

NONFERROUS METALS--STATISTICS.
Minerais et metaux, s.a., Paris.
Statistiques. Paris. 49-41772
HD9539 .A1M5 MRR Alc Latest
edition

NONFERROUS METALS--YEARBOOKS.
Minerais et metaux, s.a., Paris.
Statistiques. Paris. 49-41772
HD9539 .A1M5 MRR Alc Latest
edition

NONFERROUS METALS--EUROPE--DIRECTORIES.
European metals directory, [1st ed.]
London, Quin Press [1964] 375 p.
66-46321
TS370 .E8 MRR Alc.

NONMETALLIC MINERALS--UNITED STATES.
Pit and quarry. Directory of the
nonmetallic minerals industries.
Chicago. 58-20992
TN12 .P5 Sci RR Latest edition /
MRR Alc Latest edition

NORFOLK, VA.--HARBOR.
Hampton Roads Maritime Association,
Norfolk, Va. The ports of Greater
Hampton Roads annual. 1925-
Norfolk, Va. 28-31191
HE554.H3 A25 MRR Alc Latest
edition

**NORMANDY--DESCRIPTION AND TRAVEL--GUIDE-
BOOKS.**
Normandie. Paris, Hachette, 1972.
768 p. [56.00F] 914.42/04/83 72-
350126
DC611.N848 N57 1972 MRR Alc.

NORTH AFRICA
see Africa, North

NORTH AMERICA--ANTIQUITIES.
Brennan, Louis A. Beginner's guide
to archaeology; [Harrisburg, Pa.]
Stackpole Books [1973] 318 p.
[$8.95] 913/.031 73-4193
E77.9 .B73 MRR Alc.

Robbins, Maurice. The amateur
archaeologist's handbook 2d ed. New
York, Crowell [1973] xiv, 288 p.
[$7.95] 913/.031/028 73-245
E77.9 .R6 1973 MRR Alc.

**NORTH AMERICA--DESCRIPTION AND TRAVEL--
1951-**
Watson, James Wreford. North
America, its countries and regions,
[London] Longmans [1963] xxi, 854 p.
64-57181
E41 .W25 MRR Alc.

NORTH AMERICA--DISCOVERY AND EXPLORATION
see America--Discovery and exploration

NORTH AMERICA--HISTORY--BIBLIOGRAPHY.
Church, Elihu Dwight, A catalogue of
books relating to the discovery and
early history of North and South
America, New York, P. Smith, 1951.
5 v. (vi, 2635 p.) 016.9731 51-
4055
Z1203 .C55 1951 MRR Ref Desk.

**NORTH AMERICA--HISTORY--FICTION--
BIBLIOGRAPHY.**
Hotchkiss, Jeanette. American
historical fiction and biography for
children and young people. Metuchen,
N.J., Scarecrow Press, 1973. 318 p.
016.9173/03 73-13715
Z1236 .H73 MRR Alc.

NORTH AMERICA--INDUSTRIES.
Organization for Economic Cooperation
and Development. Industrial
production. Paris, Organisation
for Economic Co-operation and
Development, 1968. 308 p. [14.00]
338/.09 76-422848
HC240 .O693 MRR Alc.

NORTH AMERICA--ROAD MAPS.
Leahy's hotel-motel guide & travel
atlas of the United States, Canada
and Mexico. Chicago, American Hotel
Register Co. 647.94 09-20539
TX907 .L5 MRR Alc Latest edition

NORTH AMERICA--STATISTICS.
Organization for Economic Cooperation
and Development. Statistics of
energy, 1953-1967. Paris, 1969. 265
p. 333.8 71-459605
HD9540.4 .O73 1969 MRR Alc.

NORTH AMERICAN INDIANS
see Indians of North America

NORTH ATLANTIC REGION--BIBLIOGRAPHY.
Conference on North Atlantic
Community, Bruges, 1957. The
Atlantic Community; Leiden, A. W.
Sythoff, 1961. 2 v. 62-39959
Z2000.6 .C6 1957i MRR Alc.

NORTH ATLANTIC TREATY ORGANIZATION.
North Atlantic Treaty Organization.
Information Service, NATO facts and
figures. Brussels [1969] 354 p.
[25.00 Dutch florins] 341.18/18/21
72-487997
UA646.3 .A559 MRR Alc.

Stanley, Timothy W. NATO in
transition: [1st ed.] New York,
Published for the Council on Foreign
Relations by F. A. Praeger [1965]
xii, 417 p. 341.184 65-15650
D845.2 .S8 MRR Alc.

NORTH CAROLINA.
Federal Writers' Project. North
Carolina. The North Carolina guide;
Chapel Hill, University of North
Carolina Press [1955] xxi, 649 p.
917.56 55-2216
F259 .F44 1955 MRR Ref Desk.

NORTH CAROLINA--BIBLIOGRAPHY.
Thornton, Mary Lindsay. A
bibliography of North Carolina, 1589-
1956. Chapel Hill, University of
North Carolina Press, 1958. viii,
597 p. 015.756 58-63590
Z1319 .T495 MRR Alc.

NORTH CAROLINA--BIOGRAPHY--DICTIONARIES.
Who's who in North Carolina. 1st-
ed.; 1973- Lexington, Ky., Names of
Distinction, inc. [$25.00]
920/.0756 73-86267
CT252 .W48 MRR Biog Latest edition

**NORTH CAROLINA--DESCRIPTION AND TRAVEL--
GUIDE-BOOKS.**
Federal Writers' Project. North
Carolina. The North Carolina guide;
Chapel Hill, University of North
Carolina Press [1955] xxi, 649 p.
917.56 55-2216
F259 .F44 1955 MRR Ref Desk.

NORTH CAROLINA--GAZETTEERS.
Powell, William Stevens, The North
Carolina gazetteer, Chapel Hill,
University of North Carolina Press
[1968] xviii, 561 p. [$12.50]
917.56/003 68-25916
F252 .P6 MRR Alc.

**NORTH CAROLINA--GOVERNMENT PUBLICATIONS-
-BIBLIOGRAPHY.**
Thornton, Mary Lindsay. Official
publications of the Colony and State
of North Carolina, 1749-1939; Chapel
Hill, University of North Carolina
Press, 1954. x, 347 p. 015.756 55-
14165
Z1319 .T5 MRR Alc.

NORTH CAROLINA--HISTORY.
Lefler, Hugh Talmage, North
Carolina, the history of a Southern
State, Rev. ed. Chapel Hill,
University of North Carolina Press
[1963] xii, 756 p. 975.6 63-3932

F254 .L39 1963 MRR Alc.

NORTH CAROLINA--HISTORY--COLONIAL
PERIOD, CA. 1600-1775--SOURCES.
Salley, Alexander Samuel, ed.
Narratives of early Carolina, 1650-
1708. New York, C. Scribner's sons,
1911. xi p., 2 l., 3-388 p.   11-
9548
    E187.07 S3 MRR Alc.

NORTH CAROLINA--HISTORY--BIBLIOGRAPHY.
Lefler, Hugh Talmage. A guide to the
study and reading of North Carolina
history. Rev. ed. Chapel Hill,
University of North Carolina Press
[1963] iv, 103 p. 016.9756 63-
24922
    Z1319 .L4 1963 MRR Alc.

NORTH CAROLINA--HISTORY--SOURCES.
Lefler, Hugh Talmage, ed. North
Carolina history told by
contemporaries. [4th ed., rev. and
enl.] Chapel Hill, University of
North Carolina Press [1965] xv, 580
p. 975.6 65-6351
    F254 .L37 1965 MRR Alc.

NORTH CAROLINA--IMPRINTS.
Thornton, Mary Lindsay. A
bibliography of North Carolina, 1589-
1956. Chapel Hill, University of
North Carolina Press, 1958. viii,
597 p. 015.756 58-63590
    Z1319 .T495 MRR Alc.

NORTH CAROLINA--MANUFACTURES--
DIRECTORIES.
Directory of Central Atlantic States
manufacturers; 1.- ed.; 1950-
Baltimore, T. K. Sanderson
Organization. 670.58 50-2706
    T12 .D485 Sci RR Latest edition /
    MRR Alc Latest edition

NORTH CAROLINA--POLITICS AND GOVERNMENT.
North Carolina. Secretary of State.
Directory of the state and county
officials of North Carolina.
Raleigh. 19-27251
    JK4130 .A25 MRR Alc Latest edition

North Carolina manual. 1874-
Raleigh. 14-31233
    JK4130 .N6 MRR Alc Latest edition

NORTH CAROLINA--REGISTERS.
North Carolina. Secretary of State.
Directory of the state and county
officials of North Carolina.
Raleigh. 19-27251
    JK4130 .A25 MRR Alc Latest edition

North Carolina manual. 1874-
Raleigh. 14-31233
    JK4130 .N6 MRR Alc Latest edition

NORTH CAROLINA--STATISTICS.
North Carolina. Office of State
Budget and Management. Statistical
Services Section. North Carolina
State government statistical
abstract. 2d ed. [Raleigh] 1973.
xvii, 367 p. 317.56 74-170351
    HA552 .C35 1973 MRR Alc.

NORTH CENTRAL STATES
see Middle West

NORTH DAKOTA.
Federal Writers' Project. North
Dakota. North Dakota, a guide to the
northern prairie state. [2d ed.]
New York, Oxford University Press,
1950. xix, 352 p. 917.84 50-9076
    F636 .F45 1950 MRR Ref Desk.

NORTH DAKOTA--BIOGRAPHY.
Who's who for North Dakota. 1955-
Bismarck, H. L. White. 920.0784 60-
51394
    F635 .W5 MRR Biog Latest edition

NORTH DAKOTA--DESCRIPTION AND TRAVEL--
GUIDE-BOOKS.
Federal Writers' Project. North
Dakota. North Dakota, a guide to the
northern prairie state. [2d ed.]
New York, Oxford University Press,
1950. xix, 352 p. 917.84 50-9076
    F636 .F45 1950 MRR Ref Desk.

NORTH DAKOTA--REGISTERS.
North Dakota. Dept. of State.
Directory of officials, boards and
institutions. Bismarck. 58-33224
    JK6430 .A25 MRR Alc Latest edition

NORTH ISLAND, N.Z.--DESCRIPTION AND
TRAVEL.
Brathwaite, Errol, The companion
guide to the North Island of New
Zealand. Auckland, Collins, 1970.
462 p. [$5.50] 70-598476
    DU430.N6 B7 MRR Alc.

NORTH POLE.
see also Arctic regions

NORTHEASTERN STATES.
see also Atlantic States

NORTHEASTERN STATES--DESCRIPTION AND
TRAVEL--GUIDE-BOOKS.
Northeastern States. 1969/70-
[Washington, American Automobile
Association] 917.4/04/4 76-615943
    GV1024 .N84 MRR Alc Latest edition

Northeastern tour book. [Washington,
American Automobile Association]
917.4/04/4 74-644520
    GV1024 .N84 MRR Alc Latest edition

NORTHERN IRELAND--COMMERCE--DIRECTORIES.
Northern Ireland Chamber of Commerce
and Industry. Yearbook. [Belfast]
380.1/025/415 74-615885
    HF302 .N68 MRR Alc Latest edition

NORTHERN IRELAND--DIRECTORIES.
Belfast and Northern Ireland
directory. Belfast, Century
Newspaper Ltd. [etc.] 53-32016
    "First published in May 1852."
    DA995.B5 B45 MRR Alc Latest
    edition

NORTHERN IRELAND--ECONOMIC CONDITIONS--
YEARBOOKS.
The Ulster year book; 1926-
Belfast, H.M. Stationery Off. 26-
19216
    HC257.I65 U4 MRR Alc Latest
    edition

NORTHERN IRELAND--INDUSTRIES--
DIRECTORIES.
Northern Ireland Chamber of Commerce
and Industry. Yearbook. [Belfast]
380.1/025/415 74-615885
    HF302 .N68 MRR Alc Latest edition

NORTHERN IRELAND--SOCIAL CONDITIONS--
YEARBOOKS.
The Ulster year book; 1926-
Belfast, H.M. Stationery Off. 26-
19216
    HC257.I65 U4 MRR Alc Latest
    edition

NORTHMEN.
see also Vikings

NORTHWEST, CANADIAN.
see also Prairie Provinces

NORTHWEST, CANADIAN--BIOGRAPHY.
Who's who in the West and Western
Canada. 1st- ed.; 1947- Chicago,
Marquis-Who's Who [etc.] 920.07 49-
48186
    E176 .W646 MRR Biog Latest edition

NORTHWEST, OLD.
see also Middle West

NORTHWEST, OLD--DISCOVERY AND
EXPLORATION.
Kellogg, Louise Phelps, ed. Early
narratives of the Northwest, 1634-
1699. New York, C. Scribner's sons,
1917. xiv, 382 p. [$3.00] 17-6235

    E187.07 K4 MRR Alc.

NORTHWEST, OLD--HISTORY.
Philbrick, Francis Samuel, The rise
of the West, 1754-1830, (1st ed.)
New York, Harper & Row [1965] xvii,
398 p. 973 65-21377
    E179.5 .P45 MRR Alc.

NORTHWEST, OLD--HISTORY--SOURCES.
Beers, Henry Putney, The French &
British in the Old Northwest;
Detroit, Wayne State University
Press, 1964. 297 p. 977 64-13305

    F478.2 .B4 MRR Alc.

NORTHWEST, PACIFIC--BIBLIOGRAPHY.
Inland Empire Council of Teachers of
English. Northwest books, [2d ed.]
Portland, Or., Binfords & Mort [1942]
356 p. 016.81 42-21718
    Z1251.N7 I6 MRR Alc.

NORTHWEST, PACIFIC--DESCRIPTION AND
TRAVEL--GUIDE-BOOKS.
Northwestern tour book. [Falls
Church, Va., American Automobile
Association] 917.8 74-644286
    GV1024 .N87 MRR Alc Latest edition

NORTHWEST, PACIFIC--DESCRIPTION AND
TRAVEL--GUIDEBOOKS.
Gartner, John F. Outdoor guide to
the Pacific Northwest Princeton,
N.J., Van Nostrand [1968] 300 p.
796.5/09795 68-19366
    GV54.N95 G3 MRR Alc.

NORTHWEST, PACIFIC--HISTORY.
Johansen, Dorothy O. Empire of the
Columbia; 2d ed. New York, Harper &
Row [1967] xiii, 654 p. 979.5 67-
12548
    F852 .J67 1967 MRR Alc.

NORTHWEST, PACIFIC--HISTORY--
BIBLIOGRAPHY.
Smith, Charles Wesley, Pacific
Northwest Americana; 3d ed., rev.
and extended Portland, Or., Binfords
& Mort, 1950. 381 p. 016.9795 51-
10154
    Z1251.N7 S62 1950 MRR Alc.

NORTHWESTERN STATES--DESCRIPTION AND
TRAVEL--GUIDE-BOOKS.
Mobil travel guide: Northwest and
Great Plains States; good food,
lodging and sightseeing. 1962/63-
New York, Simon and Schuster. 917.8
62-12969
    F597 .M7 MRR Alc Latest edition

NORTHWESTERN UNIVERSITY, EVANSTON, ILL.
LIBRARY.
Northwestern University, Evanston,
Ill. Library. Special Collections
Dept. Guide to underground
newspapers in the Special Collections
Department. Evanston, Northwestern
University Library, 1971. 60 p.
016.071/3 73-180306
    Z6951 .N9 1971 MRR Ref Desk.

NORWAY--BIOGRAPHY.
Norsk biografisk leksikon.
Kristiania, H. Aschehoug, 1923 [i.e.
1921]- v. 22-11836
    CT1293 .N6 MRR Biog.

NORWAY--BIOGRAPHY--BIBLIOGRAPHY.
Andresen, Harald, comp. Norsk
biografisk oppslagslitteratur.
[Oslo] Cammermeyer [1945] 218 p. a
48-3923
    Z5305.N6 A6 MRR Biog.

NORWAY--BIOGRAPHY--DICTIONARIES.
Dictionary of Scandinavian biography.
London, Melrose Press [1972] xxxv,
467 p. [£10.50] 920/.048 B 73-
189270
    CT1243 .D53 MRR Biog.

Hvem er hvem? [1912]- Oslo, H.
Aschehoug. 920.0481 12-9669
    DL444 .H8 MRR Biog Latest edition

Illustrert norsk kunstnerleksikon;
Oslo, Broen bokhandel, 1956. 261 p.
a 57-5084
    N7072 .I55 MRR Alc.

NORWAY--CIVILIZATION.
Popperwell, Ronald G. Norway, New
York, Praeger [1972] 335 p.
[$11.50] 914.81/03 72-154357
    DL431 .P66 MRR Alc.

NORWAY--COMMERCE--DIRECTORIES.
Nordisk handelskalender, København,
H. P. Bov. 49-23912
    Began with vol. for 1903.
    HF5193 .N6 MRR Alc Latest edition

Norges handels-kalender. Oslo
(Kristiania) S. M. Bryde. 66-4838
    Began publication in 1869.
    HF3663 .N7 MRR Alc Latest edition

NORWAY--DESCRIPTION AND TRAVEL--GUIDE-
BOOKS.
Hay, Doddy. Your guide to Norway.
New York, Funk & Wagnalls [1971,
c1968] 175 p. [$4.95] 914.81/04/4
68-27362
    DL407 .H35 1971 MRR Alc.

Welle-Strand, Erling. Motoring in
Norway. Oslo] Norway Travel
Association, 1967. 127 p. [7.50
nkr] 914.81/04/4 67-98157
    GV1025.N6 W383 MRR Alc.

NORWAY--GAZETTEERS.
United States. Office of Geography.
Norway; Svalbard, and Jan Mayen;
official standard names approved by
the United States Board on Geographic
Names. Washington [U.S. Govt. Print.
Off.] 1963. xiii, 1029 p. 64-62580
    DL405 .U5 MRR Alc.

NORWAY--GOVERNMENT PUBLICATIONS--
BIBLIOGRAPHY.
Oslo. Universitet. Bibliotek.
Bibliografi over Norges offentlige
publikasjoner. 1956- Oslo,
Universitetsforlaget. 57-46694
    Z2599 .O8 MRR Alc Full set

NORWAY--HISTORY.
Derry, Thomas Kingston, A short
history of Norway. London, G. Allen
& Unwin [1957] 281 p. 948.1 57-
3947
    DL448 .D4 MRR Alc.

Larsen, Karen, A history of Norway.
Princeton, Princeton University Press
for the American-Scandinavian
Foundation, 1948. x, 591 p. 948.1
48-9017
    DL448 .L3 MRR Alc.

NORWAY--LEARNED INSTITUTIONS AND
SOCIETIES--BIBLIOGRAPHY.
Oslo. Universitet. Bibliotek.
Bibliografi over Norges offentlige
publikasjoner. 1956- Oslo,
Universitetsforlaget. 57-46694
    Z2599 .O8 MRR Alc Full set

NORWAY--MANUFACTURES--DIRECTORIES.
Norges handels-kalender. Oslo
(Kristiania) S. M. Bryde. 66-4838
    Began publication in 1869.
    HF3663 .N7 MRR Alc Latest edition

NORWAY--REGISTERS.
Sweden. Sveriges statskalender.
Uppsala, Stockholm, Almquist &
Wiksell Informations-industri AB.   07-
16334
    JN7724   MRR Alc Latest edition

NORWAY--STATISTICS.
Norway. Statistisk sentralbyrå.
Statistisk arbok for Norge.   1.-
arg.;   1880-   Oslo.   06-20915
    HA1502 .A32   MRR Alc Latest edition

NORWEGIAN LANGUAGE--DICTIONARIES--
ENGLISH.
Ansteinson, John,   Norsk-engelsk
teknisk ordbok;   Trondheim, F. Brun,
1954.   327 p.   55-40305
    T9 .A625   MRR Alc.

Brynildsen, John,   Norsk-engelsk
ordbok.   3. omarb. utg.   Oslo, H.
Acheboug & co. (W. Nygaard) 1927.   4
p. l., 1228 p.   28-8395
    PD2691 .B8 1927 MRR Alc.

Follestad, Sverre.   Engelske idiomer;
[Oslo] Fabritius [1962]   512 p.   63-
28474
    PD2691 .F6 MRR Alc.

Gyldendal's English-Norwegian and
Norwegian-English dictionary.   New
York, McKay [1951]   2 v. in 1.
439.8232   a   51-7382
    PD2691 .G9 1951 MRR Alc.

Norwegian English dictionary;   2nd
American printing with addendum and
corrections.   Oslo,
Universitetsforlaget;   Madison,
University of Wisconsin Press [1967]
500 p.   [unpriced]   439.8/2/32   66-
13801
    PD2691 .N6 1967 MRR Alc.

NORWEGIAN LANGUAGE--DICTIONARIES--
POLYGLOT.
International insurance dictionary:
[n.p., European Conference of
Insurance Supervisory Services, 1959]
xxxi, 1083 p.   368.03   61-35675
    HG8025 .I5 MRR Alc.

NORWEGIAN LANGUAGE--ETYMOLOGY--
DICTIONARIES.
Falk, Hjalmar Sejersted,   Norwegisch-
dänisches etymologisches
Wörterbuch, 2. Aufl.   Oslo,
Universitetsforlaget, 1960.   2 v.
(1722 p.)   61-34051
    PD2683 .F33 1960 MRR Alc.

NORWEGIAN LITERATURE--HISTORY AND
CRITICISM.
Beyer, Harald,   A history of
Norwegian literature.   [New York] New
York University Press for the
American-Scandinavian Foundation,
1956 [i. e. 1957, c1956]   ix, 370 p.
839.8209   56-6801
    PT8360 .B42 MRR Alc.

NORWEGIAN LITERATURE--HISTORY AND
CRITICISM--BIBLIOGRAPHY.
Øksnevad, Reidar,   Norsk
litteraturhistorisk bibliografi.
Oslo, Gyldendal, 1951-58.   2 v.   a
52-5350
    Z2601 .O3 MRR Alc.

NORWEGIAN LITERATURE--TRANSLATIONS INTO
ENGLISH--BIBLIOGRAPHY.
Nordiska kulturkommissionen.
Oversettelse til engelsk av nordisk
skjønnlitteratur;   [Oslo, 1960]   143
p.   66-84821
    Z2604.T7 N58 MRR Alc.

NORWEGIANS IN THE UNITED STATES.
Qualey, Carlton Chester,   Norwegian
settlement in the United States,
Northfield, Minn., Norwegian-American
historical association, 1938.   xi p.,
2 l., 3-285 p. incl. illus., tables,
diagr.   325.24810973   38-6266
    E184.S2 Q8 MRR Alc.

NOTATION (FOR BOOKS IN LIBRARIES)
see Alphabeting

    see Shelf-listing (Library science)

NOTIONS (MERCHANDISE)--DIRECTORIES.
Chain drug stores buyers directory of
variety merchandise.   1961-   New
York, Directory Division,
Merchandiser Publications.   60-40115

    T12 .C43   MRR Alc Latest edition

Sheldon's jobbing and wholesale
trade.   87th-   ed.; 1960-   New York,
Phelon-Sheldon publications [etc.]
381   72-623015
    HF5421 .S5   MRR Alc Latest edition

NOVELISTS, AMERICAN.
Cournos, John,   Famous modern
American novelists.   New York, Dodd,
Mead, 1952.   181 p.   928.1   52-7209

    PS128 .C65 MRR Biog.

Johannsen, Albert,   The House of
Beadle and Adams and its dime and
nickel novels;   [1st ed.]   Norman,
University of Oklahoma Press [1950-
62]   3 v.   655.4747   50-8158
    Z1231.F4 J68 MRR Alc.

Vinson, James,   Contemporary
novelists.   New York, St. Martin's
Press [1972]   xvii, 1422 p.   [$30.00]
823./03   75-189694
    PR737 .V5 MRR Biog.

Warfel, Harry Redcay,   American
novelists of today.   New York,
American Book Co. [1951]   vii, 478 p.
813.509   51-10144
    PS379 .W3 MRR Biog.

NOVELISTS, CANADIAN.
Pierce, Lorne Albert,   An outline of
Canadian literature (French and
English)   Toronto, The Ryerson press,
1927.   6 p. l., 251 p.   28-2647
    PR9112 .P5 MRR Alc.

NOVELISTS, ENGLISH.
Vinson, James,   Contemporary
novelists.   New York, St. Martin's
Press [1972]   xvii, 1422 p.   [$30.00]
823./03   75-189694
    PR737 .V5 MRR Biog.

NOVELISTS, SPANISH.
Sainz de Robles, Federico Carlos,
La novela española en el siglo XX.
Madrid, Pegaso [c1957]   302 p.   a
58-2588
    PQ6144 .S3 MRR Alc.

NOVELS
see Fiction

NOVELTIES--CATALOGS.
American Booksellers Association.   A
B A sidelines directory.   1957-   New
York.   57-35344
    Z477 .A614   MRR Alc Latest edition

Christian Booksellers Association.   C
B A suppliers directory.   Colorado
Springs [etc.]   070.5/94   72-622387
    Z479 .C5   MRR Alc Latest edition

The Gift and decorative accessory
buyers directory.   [New York, Geyer-
McAllister Publications]
338.4/7/745502573   74-644351
    T12 .G46 MRR Alc Latest edition

NUCLEAR ENERGY
see Atomic energy

NUCLEAR ENGINEERING--DICTIONARIES.
Hughes, Leslie Ernest Charles.
Dictionary of electronics and
nucleonics   New York, Barnes & Noble
[1970, c1969]   viii, 443 p.
621.381/03   77-13060
    TK7804 .H84 1970 MRR Alc.

Sarbacher, Robert Irving.
Encyclopedic dictionary of
electronics and nuclear engineering.
Englewood Cliffs, N.J., Prentice-
Hall, 1959.   1417 p.   621.4803   59-
11990
    TK7804 .S3 MRR Alc.

NUCLEAR ENGINEERING--DICTIONARIES--
POLYGLOT.
Clason, W. E.,   Supplement to the
Elsevier dictionaries of electronics,
nucleonics and telecommunication.
Amsterdam, New York, Elsevier Pub.
Co., 1963.   633 p.   603   63-11369
    T10 .C55 MRR Alc.

Elsevier's dictionary of nuclear
science and technology.   2d rev. ed.
Amsterdam, New York, Elsevier Pub.
Co., 1970.   787 p.   [$85.00]
539.7/03   72-103357
    QC772 .E4 1970 MRR Alc.

Sube, Ralf.   Kernphysik und
Kerntechnik: Berlin, Verlag Technik
[1962]   1606 p.   62-2924
    QC772 .S9 MRR Alc.

NUCLEAR ENGINEERING--DICTIONARIES--
RUSSIAN.
Carpovich, Eugene A.,   Russian-
English atomic dictionary.   2d rev.
and enriched ed.   New York, Technical
Dictionaries Co., 1959.   317 p.
539.703   59-2755
    QC772 .C3 1959 MRR Alc.

NUCLEAR PHYSICS
see also Astronomy

NUCLEAR PHYSICS--BIOGRAPHY.
American Nuclear Society.   A N S
membership list.   Oak Ridge, Tenn.
539.706273   59-19570
    QC770 .A45   Sci RR Latest edition /
    MRR Alc Latest edition

Who's who in atoms.   1959-   London,
Harrap Research Publications [etc.]
925.3   59-2375
    QC774 .A1W5   Sci RR Latest edition
    / MRR Alc Latest edition

NUCLEAR PHYSICS--DICTIONARIES.
Del Vecchio, Alfred, ed.   Concise
dictionary of atomics.   New York,
Philosophical Library [1964]   ix, 262
p.   539.703   64-13328
    QC772 .D4 MRR Alc.

United States of America Standards
Institute.   USA standard glossary of
terms in nuclear science and
technology.   [New York, 1967]   111 p.
539./03   74-3790
    QC772 .U55 1967 MRR Alc.

NUCLEAR PHYSICS--DICTIONARIES--POLYGLOT.
Elsevier's dictionary of nuclear
science and technology.   2d rev. ed.
Amsterdam, New York, Elsevier Pub.
Co., 1970.   787 p.   [$85.00]
539.7/03   72-103357
    QC772 .E4 1970 MRR Alc.

Sube, Ralf.   Kernphysik und
Kerntechnik: Berlin, Verlag Technik
[1962]   1606 p.   62-2924
    QC772 .S9 MRR Alc.

NUCLEAR REACTOR SUPPLY INDUSTRY
see Atomic energy industries

NUDISM--DIRECTORIES.
American Sunbathing Association.
Nudist park guide;   Orlando, Fla.
[1974]   136 p.   917.3   74-166368
    GV450 .A493 1974 MRR Alc.

NULLIFICATION.
Freehling, William W.,   Prelude to
Civil War;   [1st ed.]   New York,
Harper & Row [1966]   xiii, 395 p.
973.561   66-10629
    E384.3 .F7 MRR Alc.

NUMERATION OF BOOKS IN LIBRARIES
see Alphabeting

NUMISMATICS.
Burns, Arthur Robert,   Money and
monetary policy in early times,
London, K. Paul, Trench, Trubner &
co., ltd.;   New York, A. A. Knopf,
1927.   xiii, 517 p.   27-21334
    HG237 .B86 MRR Alc.

Carson, Robert Andrew Glindinning.
Coins ancient, mediaeval & modern
2nd (revised) ed.   London,
Hutchinson, 1970.   xiii, 642 p., 64
plates.   [£6.00]   737.4/09   75-
862183
    CJ75 .C3 1970 MRR Alc.

NUMISMATICS--COLLECTORS AND COLLECTING.
Coffin, Joseph,   The complete book of
coin collecting.   2d rev. ed.   New
York, Coward-McCann [1967]   251 p.
737.4/075   67-21506
    CJ81 .C6 1967 MRR Alc.

Del Monte, Jacques,   Coins; a
complete guide to collecting.   [Los
Angeles, Trend Books, 1959]   128 p.
737.4075   59-36854
    CJ89 .D38 MRR Alc.

Reed, Fred Morton.   Coins: an
investor's & collector's guide
Chicago, Regnery [1973]   x, 403 p.
[$10.00]   737.4/973   72-11187
    CJ1830 .R417 MRR Alc.

NUMISMATICS--DICTIONARIES.
Chamberlain, Christopher Churchill.
Coin dictionary and guide   New York,
Barnes & Noble [1961]   256 p.
737.4075   61-18192
    CJ67 .C47 1961 MRR Alc.

Frey, Albert Romer,   Dictionary of
numismatic names,   [New York] Barnes
& Noble [1947]   ix, 311, 94 p.
737.03   48-5357
    CJ67 .F7 1947 MRR Alc.

Hobson, Burton.   Illustrated
encyclopedia of world coins   Garden
City, N.Y., Doubleday [1970]   512 p.
[$12.95]   737.4/03   78-81030
    CJ67 .H6 1970 MRR Alc.

Narbeth, Colin.   The coin collector's
encyclopaedia.   London, S. Paul,
1968.   [7] 232 p.   [35/-]   737.4/03
67-113305
    CJ89 .N15 MRR Alc.

Reed, Fred Morton.   Coins: an
investor's & collector's guide
Chicago, Regnery [1973]   x, 403 p.
[$10.00]   737.4/973   72-11187
    CJ1830 .R417 MRR Alc.

NUMISMATICS--AFRICA.
Davenport, John Stewart,   The dollars
of Africa, Asia, & Oceania
Galesburg, Ill., 1969.   208 p.
737.4   76-7369
    CJ1529 .D3 MRR Alc.

NUMISMATICS--ASIA.
Davenport, John Stewart,   The dollars
of Africa, Asia, & Oceania
Galesburg, Ill., 1969.   208 p.
737.4   76-7369
    CJ1529 .D3 MRR Alc.

NUMISMATICS--CENTRAL AMERICA.
Wallace, Holland. Central American
coinage since 1821. [Weslaco? Tex.]
1966 [c1965] 123, [2] p.   737.49728
66-4668
   CJ1816 .W3 1966 MRR Alc.

NUMISMATICS--GREAT BRITAIN--YEARBOOKS.
Coin yearbook. [Brentwood, Eng.,
Numismatic Pub. Co. [-/-/80]
737.4/8/42   74-644812
   CJ2471 .C6 MRR Alc Latest edition

NUMISMATICS--OCEANICA.
Davenport, John Stewart. The dollars
of Africa, Asia, & Oceania
Galesburg, Ill., 1969. 208 p.
737.4 76-7369
   CJ1529 .D3 MRR Alc.

NUMISMATICS--ROME--DICTIONARIES.
Stevenson, Seth William, A
dictionary of Roman coins, London,
G. Bell and sons, 1889. viii, 929 p.
01-25230
   CJ829 .S8 MRR Alc.

NUMISMATICS--UNITED STATES.
Bowers, Q. David. Coins and
collectors. [Johnson City, N.Y.,
Windsor Research Publications, 1964]
213 p.   737.4075 64-8501
   CJ1830 .B6 MRR Alc.

Coin collectors' handbook. Garden
City, N.Y. [etc.] Doubleday [etc.]
737.4075   60-11003
   CJ1830 .C65 MRR Ref Desk Latest
   edition

NUMISMATICS, GREEK.
Jenkins, G. Kenneth. Ancient Greek
coins, London, Barrie and Jenkins,
1972. 310 p. [£7.00]   737.4/9/38
73-160003
   CJ335 .J45 1972b MRR Alc.

NUMISMATICS, ROMAN.
Sear, David R. Roman coins and their
values, Revised ed. London, Seaby,
1970. 376 p., 13 plates. [48/-]
737.49/37   77-538139
   CJ833 .S4 1970 MRR Alc.

NUREMBERG--DIRECTORIES.
Einwohnerbuch der Stadt Nürnberg.
Nürnberg, W. Tummels Buchdr. und
Verlag. 61-30764
   DD901.N925 E4 MRR Alc Latest
   edition

NURSERY RHYMES.
Ireson, Barbara, ed. The Barnes book
of nursery verse. New York, Barnes
[1960] 286 p. 808.81 59-14348
   PN6110.C4 I7 MRR Alc.

Mother Goose. Mother Goose's nursery
rhymes, New York, Cupples & Leon
company [c1930] 384 p.   398.8 30-
17308
   PZ8.3 .M85Cs MRR Ref Desk.

Opie, Iona (Archibald) ed. The
Oxford dictionary of nursery rhymes,
Oxford, Clarendon Press, 1951.
xxvii, 467 p.   51-14126
   PZ8.3.C6 Ox MRR Ref Desk.

Opie, Iona (Archibald) comp. The
Oxford nursery rhyme book, New York,
Oxford University Press, 1955. xi,
223 p.   398.8 55-12050
   PN6110.C4 O53 MRR Alc.

NURSERY SCHOOLS.
see also Day nurseries

see also Education, Preschool

NURSERY SCHOOLS--DIRECTORIES.
LaCrosse, E. Robert. Early childhood
education directory; 1st ed. New
York, R. R. Bowker Co., 1971. xiv,
455 p. [$19.50] 372.21/025/73 77-
126012
   L901 .L3 MRR Ref Desk.

NURSES AND NURSING.
see also Diet in disease

see also Hospitals

American College of Hospital
Administrators. Directory. 1938-
Chicago. 362.06273 39-2135
   RA977 .A57 Sci RR Latest edition /
   MRR Biog Latest edition

NURSES AND NURSING--BIBLIOGRAPHY.
Bowker's medical books in print.
1972- New York, R.R. Bowker Co.
016.61 78-37613
   Z6658 .B65 MRR Alc Latest edition
   / Sci RR Latest edition

Nursing studies index; Philadelphia,
Lippincott [c1963-72. v. 1, 1872, v.
4, 1963] 4 v.   016.61073 62-22361

   Z6675.N7 N87 MRR Alc.

Thompson, Alice M. C. A bibliography
of nursing literature 1859-1960,
London, Library Association for the
Royal College of Nursing and National
Council of Nurses of the United
Kingdom in association with King
Edward's Hospital Fund for London,
1968. xx, 132 p. [80/- 65/- (to
members of the L.A. and the Royal
College of Nursing)]   016.61073 68-
141603
   Z6675.N7 T45 MRR Alc.

NURSES AND NURSING--HISTORY--COLLECTED
WORKS.
History of nursing. 12th- ed.;
1968- Philadelphia, W. B. Saunders,
610.73/09 72-627086
   RT31 .G578 MRR Alc Latest edition
   / Sci RR Latest edition

NURSES AND NURSING--INDEXES.
Nursing studies index; Philadelphia,
Lippincott [c1963-72. v. 1, 1872, v.
4, 1963] 4 v. 016.61073 62-22361
   Z6675.N7 N87 MRR Alc.

NURSES AND NURSING--PERIODICALS--
INDEXES.
Cumulative index to nursing
literature. v. 1/5- 1956/60-
[Glendale, Calif.] Seventh-Day
Adventist Hospital Association. 62-
147
   Z6675 .N7C8 Sci RR Full set / MRR
   Alc Full set

Nursing studies index; Philadelphia,
Lippincott [c1963-72. v. 1, 1872, v.
4, 1963] 4 v. 016.61073 62-22361

   Z6675.N7 N87 MRR Alc.

NURSES AND NURSING--STATISTICS--
PERIODICALS.
American Nurses' Association. Facts
about nursing. New York.
331.7/61/610730973 72-627049
   RT1 .A67 MRR Alc Latest edition

NURSES AND NURSING--UNITED STATES--
STATISTICS.
American Nurses' Association. Facts
about nursing. New York.
331.7/61/610730973 72-627049
   RT1 .A67 MRR Alc Latest edition

NURSING HOMES--CANADA--DIRECTORIES.
Modern nursing home directory of
nursing homes in the United States,
U.S. Possessions and Canada.
Chicago, McGraw-Hill. 362.1/6/02573
74-644553
   RA997.A2 D5 MRR Alc Latest edition

NURSING HOMES--UNITED STATES--
DIRECTORIES.
Greenberg, Dan. U.S. guide to
nursing homes. New York, Grosset &
Dunlap [1970] 3 v. [2.95 (each)]
362.1/6/02573 71-92386
   RA997.A2 G7 MRR Alc.

Modern nursing home directory of
nursing homes in the United States,
U.S. Possessions and Canada.
Chicago, McGraw-Hill. 362.1/6/02573
74-644553
   RA997.A2 D5 MRR Alc Latest edition

Musson, Noverre. The national
directory of retirement residences;
best places to live when you retire.
Rev. ed. New York, F. Fell [1973]
214 p. 362.6/15/02573 72-89943
   HV1465 .M87 1973 MRR Alc.

NURSING SCHOOLS--UNITED STATES--
DIRECTORIES.
White, Alex Sandri. The new
directory of medical schools, New
1974 ed. Allenhurst, N.J., Aurea
Publications [1973] 143 p. [$5.95]
610/.7/1173 73-175214
   R712.A1 W5 1974 MRR Ref Desk.

NUTRITION.
see also Diet

see also Food

Bogert, Lotta Jean, Nutrition and
physical fitness 9th ed.
Philadelphia, Saunders, 1973. xi,
598 p. 641.1 76-188385
   TX354 .B6 1973 MRR Alc.

Margolius, Sidney K. Health foods:
facts and fakes New York, Walker
[1973] 293 p. [$6.95] 641.3 75-
186187
   TX355 .M35 1973 MRR Alc.

National Research Council. Food and
Nutrition Board. Recommended dietary
allowances. 8th rev. ed.
Washington, National Academy of
Sciences, 1974. v, 128 p. 641.1
74-5170
   TX551 .N39 1974 MRR Alc.

Proudfit, Fairfax Throckmorton.
Proudfit-Robinson's Normal and
therapeutic nutrition. 13th ed. New
York, Macmillan [1967] xiv, 891 p.
641.1 67-16055
   RM216 .P83 1967 MRR Alc.

United States. Dept. of Agriculture.
Food for us all. [Washington; For
sale by the Supt. of Docs., U.S.
Govt. Print. Off., 1969] xxxix, 360
p. [3.50 641.3 76-604428
   S21 .A35 1969 MRR Alc.

Williams, Sue Rodwell. Nutrition and
diet therapy. 2d ed. Saint Louis,
Mosby, 1973. xviii, 693 p. 641.1
72-88510
   RM216 .M684 1973 MRR Alc.

Wohl, Michael Gershon, ed. Modern
nutrition in health and disease; 4th
ed. Philadelphia, Lea & Febiger,
1968. xv, 1240 p. 615/.854 68-
18869
   QP141 .W6 1968 MRR Alc.

NUTRITION--DICTIONARIES.
Bender, Arnold E. Dictionary of
nutrition and food technology 3rd
ed. London, Butterworths, 1968.
viii, 228 p. [50/-] 641/.03 79-
451065
   TX349 .B4 1968b MRR Alc.

NYANJA LANGUAGE--DICTIONARIES--ENGLISH.
Scott, David Clement Ruffelle,
Dictionary of the Nyanja language,
London, Toronto [etc.] The Religious
tract society [1929] vii, 612 p.
46-42629
   PL8593.Z5 S38 1929 MRR Alc.

OBITUARIES--INDEXES.
Columbia University. Libraries. Avery
Architectural Library. Avery
obituary index of architects and
artists. Boston, G. K. Hall, 1963.
338 p.   64-7017
   Z5841 .C64 MRR Biog.

Farrar, Robert Henry. An index to
the biographical and obituary notices
in the Gentleman's magazine, 1731-
1780. London, 1891 [i.e. 1886-91]
677 p.   10-20807
   AI3 .I4 vol. 15 MRR Alc.

The New York times obituaries index,
1858-1968. New York, New York times,
1970. 1136 p.   929.3 72-113422
   CT213 .N47 MRR Biog.

OBITUARIES--GERMANY.
Kürschners Deutscher Literatur-
Kalender; Berlin, New York, de
Gruyter, 1973. xiv, 871 p.
[DM220.00] 808 73-203144
   Z2233.3 .K83 MRR Biog.

OBSCENITY (LAW)--UNITED STATES--CASES.
De Grazia, Edward. Censorship
landmarks. New York, Bowker, 1969.
xxxii, 657 p.   340 71-79424
   KF9444.A7 D4 MRR Alc.

OBSEQUIES
see Funeral rites and ceremonies

OBSERVATORIES, ASTRONOMICAL
see Astronomical observatories

OBSTETRICIANS--UNITED STATES--
DIRECTORIES.
American directory of obstetricians
and gynecologists. 1st- ed.;
1954/55- Knoxville, Tenn., Joe T.
Smith. 614.24 55-27820
   RG32 .A5 Sci RR Latest edition /
   MRR Biog Latest edition

OBSTETRICS.
see also Abortion

see also Childbirth

see also Pregnancy

OCCIDENTAL CIVILIZATION
see Civilization, Occidental

OCCIDENTAL LANGUAGES
see Languages, Modern

OCCULT SCIENCES.
see also Demonology

see also Magic

see also Prophecies

see also Satanism

Cavendish, Richard. Encyclopedia of
the unexplained; London, Routledge &
K. Paul [1974] 304 p. [£7.95] 133
74-166662
   BF1411 .C32 1974b MRR Alc.

Mackay, Charles, Extraordinary
popular delusions and the madness of
crowds. London, G. G. Harrap [1956]
xxiv, 724 p. 301.15 133.7 57-1736
   AZ999 .M2 1956 MRR Alc.

OCCULT SCIENCES. (Cont.)
Villiers, Elizabeth. The book of
charms. [New York] Simon and
Schuster [1974, c1973] 144 p.
[$3.95] 133.4/4 74-171069
BF1561 .V5 1974 MRR Alc.

OCCULT SCIENCES--DICTIONARIES.
Abbot, A. E., pseud. Encyclopaedia
of the occult sciences. London,
Emerson press [c1960] 457 p.
133.03 61-4585
BF1025 .A2 MRR Alc.

Baskin, Wade. Dictionary of
Satanism. New York, Philosophical
Library [1971, c1972] 351 p.
[$12.50] 133.4/2/03 75-155971
BF1407 .B37 1972 MRR Alc.

Chambers, Howard V., An occult
dictionary for the millions. Los
Angeles, Sherbourne Press [1966] 160
p. 133 66-26077
BF1025 .C5 MRR Alc.

Gaynor, Frank, ed. Dictionary of
mysticism. New York, Philosophical
Library [1953] 208 p. 290.3 53-
13354
BL31 .G32 MRR Alc.

Wedeck, Harry Ezekiel, Dictionary of
spiritualism, New York,
Philosophical Library [1971] vi, 390
p. [$10.00] 133/.03 73-104365
BF1025 .W4 MRR Alc.

OCCULT SCIENCES--DIRECTORIES.
Cushing, A. I. The international
"mystery schools" directory. New
1970 ed. Boston, A.C. Publications
[1970] 1 v. (unpaged) 133/.062 70-
16742
BL35 .C86 MRR Alc.

Holzer, Hans W., The directory of
the occult Chicago, H. Regnery Co.
[1974] x, 201 p. 133/.025/73 74-
6895
BF1409 .H6 MRR Alc.

OCCUPATIONAL DISEASES.
International Labor Office.
Encyclopaedia of occupational health
and safety. New York, McGraw-Hill
[1971-72] 2 v. (xiii, 1621 p.)
613.6/2/03 74-39329
RC963 .I6 1971b MRR Alc.

OCCUPATIONS.
see also Civil service positions

see also Job descriptions

see also Professions

Angel, Juvenal Londoño, Students'
guide to occupational opportunities
and their lifetime earnings, New
York, World Trade Academy Press;
distributed by Simon & Schuster
[1967] 312 p. 331.702/0873 67-
25270
HF5382 .A57 MRR Alc.

The Encyclopedia of careers and
vocational guidance. Rev. ed.
Chicago, J. G. Ferguson Pub. Co.;
distributed to the book trade by
Doubleday [1972] 2 v. 331.7/02 72-
183086
HF5381 .E52 1972 MRR Alc.

How to travel and get paid for it.
1st- ed.; 1953- Greenlawn, N.Y.,
Harian Publications; distributed by
Grosset & Dunlap [etc., New York] 59-
11296
HF5382 .H69 MRR Alc Latest edition

Lederer, Muriel. The guide to career
education. [New York] Quadrangle/New
York Times Book Co. [1974] xiv, 401
p. [$9.95] 370.11/3 73-90169
LC1044 .L42 1974 MRR Alc.

Ross, E. E. Encyclopedia of job
descriptions in manufacturing.
Milwaukee, Wis., Sextant Systems
[1969] 865 p. 658.3 79-6832
HF5549.5.J6 R67 MRR Alc.

United States. Bureau of Employment
Security. Selected characteristics
of occupations (physical demands,
working conditions, training time);
Washington; For sale by the Supt. of
Docs., U.S. Govt. Print. Off., 1966.
xii, 280, 8 p. 331.1/14/0873 70-
601487
HB2595 .A35 1966 MRR Ref Desk.

Whitfield, Edwin A. Guide to careers
through vocational training [1st
ed.] San Diego, Calif., R. R. Knapp
[1968] viii, 312 p. 331.702/0873
68-15874
HF5382.5.U5 W5 MRR Alc.

OCCUPATIONS--BIBLIOGRAPHY.
Forrester, Gertrude, Occupational
literature; 1971 ed. New York, H.
W. Wilson Co., 1971. 619 p.
016.37142/5 79-149382
Z7164.V6 F67 1971 MRR Alc.

Mapp, Edward. Books for occupational
education programs; New York,
Bowker, 1971. xii, 308 p.
016.378/013 70-126013
Z5814.T4 M34 MRR Alc.

Modern vocational trends reference
handbook. New York, World Trade
Academy Press. 371.425058 55-3128
HF5381 .M565 MRR Ref Desk Latest
edition

Nicholsen, Margaret E. People in
books; New York, H. W. Wilson Co.,
1969. xviii, 498 p. 016.92 69-
15811
Z5301 .N53 MRR Biog.

United States. Civil Service
Commission. Guide to Federal career
literature. [Washington; for sale by
the Supt. of Docs., U.S. Govt. Print.
Off., 1972] 34 p. [$0.45]
016.3317/95/0873 72-603286
Z1223 .A199 1972 MRR Ref Desk.

OCCUPATIONS--CLASSIFICATION.
International Labor Office.
International standard classification
of occupations. Rev. ed. 1968.
Geneva, International Labour Office,
1969. vi, 355 p. [20.00]
331.7/001/2 71-476976
HB2581 .I63 1969 MRR Alc.

United States. Employment Service.
Dictionary of occupational titles.
3d ed. Washington, U.S. Dept. of
Labor, Manpower Administration,
Bureau of Employment Security; for
sale by the Superintendent of
Documents, U.S. Govt. Print. Off.,
1965. 2 v. 331.7003 l 66-20
HB2595 .A5 1965 MRR Ref Desk.

OCCUPATIONS--HISTORY.
Lockyer, Herbert. All the trades and
occupations of the Bible; Grand
Rapids, Zondervan Pub. House [c1969]
327 p. [4.95] 220.8/33/7 70-95038

BS680.03 L6 MRR Alc.

OCCUPATIONS--HYGIENIC ASPECTS
see Industrial hygiene

OCCUPATIONS--INDEXES.
United States. Bureau of the Census.
1970 census of population.
[Washington, U.S. Bureau of the
Census, Population Division; for sale
by the Supt. of Docs., U.S. Govt.
Print. Off.] 1971. xiv, 165, 201 p.
[$3.00] 331.1/1/0973 74-612012
HA201 1970 .A565 MRR Alc.

OCCUPATIONS--LICENSES--UNITED STATES--
DIRECTORIES.
Angel, Juvenal Londoño, Directory
of professional and occupational
licensing in the United States, New
York, World Trade Academy Press;
distributed by Simon & Schuster
[1970] 755 p. 75-93680
HD7824.U5 A75 MRR alc.

OCCUPATIONS--TERMINOLOGY.
United States. Employment Service.
Dictionary of occupational titles.
3d ed. Washington, U.S. Dept. of
Labor, Manpower Administration,
Bureau of Employment Security; for
sale by the Superintendent of
Documents, U.S. Govt. Print. Off.,
1965. 2 v. 331.7003 l 66-20
HB2595 .A5 1965 MRR Ref Desk.

OCEAN.
Huxley, Anthony Julian, ed. Standard
encyclopedia of the world's oceans
and islands. London, Weidenfeld &
Nicolson [1963, c1962] 383 p. 63-
276
GB471 .H9 1963 MRR Alc.

OCEAN BIRDS
see Sea birds

OCEAN BOTTOM.
United States. Geographic Names
Division. Undersea features. 2d ed.
Washington, 1971 [i.e. 1972] vi,
182 p. 910/.02/162 72-601422
GC83 .U5 1972 MRR Alc.

OCEAN ENGINEERING--DICTIONARIES.
Hunt, Lee M., ed. A glossary of
ocean science and undersea technology
terms; Arlington, Va., Compass
Publications, 1965. vii, 173 p.
551.46 65-25322
GC9 .H85 MRR Alc.

OCEAN LINERS.
Dunn, Laurence. Passenger liners.
[Rev. ed.] London, A. Coles [1965]
485 p. 65-9111
VM381 .D83 1965 MRR Alc.

Gibbs, Charles Robert Vernon.
Passenger liners of the Western
Ocean; 2d ed. [completely rev.]
London, Staples Press [1957] 434 p.
623.824 57-1880
VM18 .G5 1957 MRR Alc.

Worker, Colin F. The world's
passenger ships London, Allan,
[1967]. viii, 304 p. [63/-]
387.2/43 67-86845
VM381 .W6 MRR Alc.

OCEAN LINERS--REGISTERS.
Cairis, Nicholas T. North Atlantic
passenger liners since 1900 London,
Allan, 1972. 224 p. [£4.40]
387.2/43 72-193343
HE566.O25 C35 MRR Alc.

Emmons, Frederick. The Atlantic
liners, 1925-70. New York, Drake
Publishers [1972] 160 p. 387.2/43
72-182051
HE566.O25 E45 MRR Alc.

Moody, Bert. Ocean ships [New ed.].
London, Allan 1967. vii, 359 p.
[25/-] 387.2/4 72-472168
HE565 .A5M6 1967 MRR Alc.

Smith, Eugene Waldo, Passenger ships
of the world, [1st ed.] Boston, G.
H. Dean Co. [1963] ii, 1002 p.
387.243 63-3478
HE565.A3 S48 MRR Alc.

OCEAN TRANSPORTATION
see Shipping

OCEAN TRAVEL.
Freighter days. Greenlawn, N.Y.,
Hadrian Publications; trade
distributor; Grosset & Dunlap [etc.,
New York] 910.2
G550 .F73 MRR Alc Latest edition /
MRR Alc Latest edition

OCEANIAN NEWSPAPERS--DIRECTORIES.
Feuereisen, Fritz. Die Presse in
Asien und Ozeanien; 1. Ausg.
München-Pullach, Verlag
Dokumentation, 1968. 303 p. 79-
381760
Z6957 .F48 MRR Alc.

OCEANICA.
Osborne, Charles, Australia, New
Zealand, and the South Pacific; New
York, Praeger [1970] xi, 580 p.
[18.50] 919.4 69-12899
DU15 .O8 1970b MRR Alc.

The Pacific islands year book. [1st]-
ed.; 1932- Sydney, Australia
[etc.] Pacific Publications [etc.]
32-24429
DU1 .P15 MRR Alc Latest edition

OCEANICA--BIBLIOGRAPHY.
Cammack, Floyd M. Pacific island
bibliography. New York, Scarecrow
Press, 1962. 421 p. 016.99 62-
10126
Z4001 .C3 MRR Alc.

OCEANICA--COMMERCE--DIRECTORIES.
Pacific Islands business directory.
Auckland, Universal Business
Directories Ltd. 338/.0099 72-
622889
HF5319 .U54 MRR Alc Latest edition

OCEANICA--DESCRIPTION AND TRAVEL--1951-
--GUIDE-BOOKS.
Clark, Sydney Aylmer, All the best
in the South Pacific New York, Dodd,
Mead [1971] xii, 338 p. [$6.95]
919 76-151293
DU15 .C6 1971 MRR Alc.

OCEANICA--DESCRIPTION AND TRAVEL--GUIDE-
BOOKS.
Middle East, North Africa, Orient and
Pacific travel guide. [Washington,
D.C.] AAA World Wide Travel Dept.
910 72-622839
DS4 .M5 MRR Alc Latest edition

OCEANICA--DISCOVERY AND EXPLORATION.
Pacific voyages. Garden City, N.Y.,
Doubleday [1973, c1971] 488 p.
[$14.85] 910/.09/1823 72-93388
DU19 .P3 1973 MRR Alc.

OCEANICA--GAZETTEERS.
United States. Geographic Names
Division. Australia, New Zealand and
Oceania; Washington, 1972. iii, 48
p. 919/.03 72-602929
DU10 .U654 MRR Alc.

United States. Office of Geography.
South Pacific; Washington, U.S.
Govt. Print. Off., 1957. iii, 68 p.
919 57-60873
DU10 .U66 MRR Alc.

United States. Office of Geography.
Southwest Pacific; Washington, U.S.
Govt. Print. Off., 1956 [i.e. 1957]
v, 368 p. 919 57-61177
DU10 .U68 MRR Alc.

OCEANICA--INDUSTRIES--DIRECTORIES.
Pacific Islands business directory.
Auckland, Universal Business
Directories Ltd. 338/.0099 72-
622889
HF5319 .U54 MRR Alc Latest edition

OCEANICA--STATISTICS.
Deldycke, Tilo. La population active
et sa structure. Bruxelles, Centre
d'économie politique (de l')
Universite libre de Bruxelles,
(1968) viii, 236 p. [360.00]
331.1/12/0212 70-395436
HD4826 .D34 MRR Alc.

OCEANICA--YEARBOOKS.
The Far East and Australasia. 1st-
ed.; 1969- London, Europa
Publications. 915/.03/05 74-417170

DS1 .F3 MRR Alc Latest edition

OCEANOGRAPHIC RESEARCH--BIBLIOGRAPHY.
Selected references to literature on
marine expeditions, 1700-1960.
Boston, G. K. Hall, 1972. iv, 517 p.
016.5514/6 72-6452
Z5971 .S4 MRR Alc.

OCEANOGRAPHY.
see Marine biology

see also Marine resources

see also Navigation

see also Tides

OCEANOGRAPHY--DICTIONARIES.
Fairbridge, Rhodes Whitmore, The
encyclopedia of oceanography, New
York, Reinhold Pub. Co. [1966] xiii,
1021 p. 551.46003 66-26059
GC9 .F3 MRR Alc.

Hunt, Lee M., ed. A glossary of
ocean science and undersea technology
terms; Arlington, Va., Compass
Publications, 1965. vii, 173 p.
551.46 65-25322
GC9 .H85 MRR Alc.

United States. Naval Oceanographic
Office. Glossary of oceanographic
terms. 2d ed. Washington, U.S.
Naval Oceanographic Office, 1966.
vi, 204 p. 551.4/6/003 66-62513
GC9 .U5 1966 MRR Alc.

OCEANOGRAPHY--MISCELLANEA.
Taber, Robert W., 1001 questions
answered about the oceans and
oceanography, New York, Dodd, Mead
[1972] xiv, 269 p. [$7.50]
551.4/6 73-184136
GC21 .T3 MRR Alc.

ODENSE, DENMARK--DIRECTORIES.
Odense vejviser. Odense, Fyens
stiftsbogtrykkeri. 53-30584
DL291.O3 O35 MRR Alc Latest
edition

ODER-NEISSE AREA.
Gottinger Arbeitskreis. Eastern
Germany; a handbook. Wuerzburg,
Holzner-Verlag, 1960- [v. 1, 1961]
v. 943.1087 60-13392
DD801.O35 G59 MRR Alc.

OECOLOGY
see Ecology

OFFENSES AGAINST THE PERSON.
see also Abortion

OFFICE EQUIPMENT AND SUPPLIES--
DIRECTORIES.
Geyer's "who makes it" directory.
[New York, Geyer-McAllister
Publications] 338.4/7/651202573 74-
647065
TS1088 .W7 MRR Alc Latest edition

OFFICE FURNITURE--DIRECTORIES.
Geyer's "who makes it" directory.
[New York, Geyer-McAllister
Publications] 338.4/7/651202573 74-
647065
TS1088 .W7 MRR Alc Latest edition

OFFICE MANAGEMENT.
see also Secretaries

OFFICE PRACTICE.
see also Files and filing (Documents)

Hutchinson, Lois Irene. Standard
handbook for secretaries 8th ed.
[New York] McGraw-Hill, 1969. x, 638
p. 650 69-19201
HF5547 .H77 1969 MRR Ref Desk.

Taintor, Sarah Augusta. The
secretary's handbook; 9th ed. fully
rev. [New York] Macmillan [1969]
xi, 530 p. 651.7/402 69-10466
HF5547 .T25 1969 MRR Alc.

OHIO.
Ohio almanac. 1st-   ed.; 1968-
Lorain. 917.71/005 68-3162
AY271.L6 O5 MRR Alc Latest edition

Writers' program. Ohio. The Ohio
guide, New York, Oxford press [1946]
xxxi, 634 (i.e. 650) p. 917.71 46-
5681
F496 .W96 1946 MRR Ref Desk.

OHIO--BIBLIOGRAPHY.
Historical records survey. Ohio. A
check list of Ohio imprints, 1796-
1820. Columbus, O., Ohio Historical
records survey, 1941. 202 numb. l.
015.771 42-17565
Z1215 .H67 no. 17 MRR Alc.

OHIO--BIBLIOGRAPHY--CATALOGS.
United States. Library of Congress.
Ohio, the sesquicentennial of
statehood, 1803-1953; Washington,
U.S. Govt. Print. Off., 1953. iv, 76
p. 016.9771 52-60052
Z663.15.A603 MRR Alc.

OHIO--CENTENNIAL CELEBRATIONS, ETC.
United States. Library of Congress.
Ohio, the sesquicentennial of
statehood, 1803-1953; Washington,
U.S. Govt. Print. Off., 1953. iv, 76
p. 016.9771 52-60052
Z663.15.A603 MRR Alc.

OHIO--DESCRIPTION AND TRAVEL--GUIDE-
BOOKS.
Writers' program. Ohio. The Ohio
guide, New York, Oxford press [1946]
xxxi, 634 (i.e. 650) p. 917.71 46-
5681
F496 .W96 1946 MRR Ref Desk.

OHIO--EXECUTIVE DEPARTMENTS.
Ohio. Secretary of State. Official
roster; [Columbus, etc.] 09-3257
JS451.O37 A28 MRR Alc Latest
edition

Swanson, Patricia. Union
bibliography of Ohio printed State
documents, 1803-1970. Columbus, Ohio
Historical Society, 1973. xiii, 750
p. 015.771 73-93700
Z1323 .S9 MRR Alc.

OHIO--GOVERNMENT PUBLICATIONS--
BIBLIOGRAPHY.
Ohio. State Library, Columbus.
Checklist publications of the State
of Ohio, 1803-1952. Columbus, Ohio
Library Foundation, 1964. 131 p.
65-70943
Z1223.5.O4 A18 MRR Alc.

OHIO--GOVERNMENT PUBLICATIONS--
BIBLIOGRAPHY--UNION LISTS.
Swanson, Patricia. Union
bibliography of Ohio printed State
documents, 1803-1970. Columbus, Ohio
Historical Society, 1973. xiii, 750
p. 015.771 73-93700
Z1323 .S9 MRR Alc.

OHIO--IMPRINTS.
Historical records survey. Ohio. A
check list of Ohio imprints, 1796-
1820. Columbus, O., Ohio Historical
records survey, 1941. 202 numb. l.
015.771 42-17565
Z1215 .H67 no. 17 MRR Alc.

OHIO--MANUFACTURES--DIRECTORIES.
Directory of Ohio manufacturers. 22d-
ed.; 1964- [Columbus]
338.4/025/771 72-620308
T12 .O3 Sci RR Latest edition /
MRR Alc Latest edition

Midwest manufacturers and industrial
directory buyers guide. [Detroit,
Industrial Directory Publishers]
338.4/0977 72-626483
HC107.A15 M5 MRR Alc Latest
edition

OHIO--POLITICS AND GOVERNMENT--1865-
1950.
Rose, Albert Henry, Ohio government,
State and local 3d ed. [Dayton]
University of Dayton Press [1966]
xviii, 590 p. 320.9771 66-8580
JK5525 1966 .R6 MRR Alc.

OHIO--POLITICS AND GOVERNMENT--1951-
Rose, Albert Henry, Ohio government,
State and local 3d ed. [Dayton]
University of Dayton Press [1966]
xviii, 590 p. 320.9771 66-8580
JK5525 1966 .R6 MRR Alc.

OHIO--REGISTERS.
Ohio. Secretary of State. Official
roster; [Columbus, etc.] 09-3257
JS451.O37 A28 MRR Alc Latest
edition

OIL
see Petroleum

OIL ENGINES
see Gas and oil engines

OIL FIELDS--EQUIPMENT AND SUPPLIES--
CATALOGS.
Composite catalog of oil field
equipment & services. no. 1- 1929-
Houston, Tex. 31-702
TN871.5 .C6 Sci RR Latest edition
/ MRR Alc Latest edition

OIL INDUSTRIES.
see also Petroleum industry and trade

OIL INDUSTRIES--DIRECTORIES.
Chemical buyers directory. [1st]-
1913- New York, Schnell Pub. Co.
660/.025/73 13-5763
TP12 .O6 Sci RR Latest edition /
MRR Alc Latest edition

OIL-PAINTING
see Painting

OIL REFINERIES
see Petroleum refineries

OILS AND FATS.
see also Petroleum

Trademark directory. Washington
[etc.] 667.6058 14-18485
TP934.5 .T7 Sci RR Latest edition
/ MRR Alc Latest edition

Trademark directory. Supplement.
Washington [etc.] 667.6058 74-
643570
TP934.5 .T7 Sci RR Latest edition
/ MRR Alc Latest edition

OILS AND FATS, EDIBLE.
Directory of the edible oil industry
in the United States. Washington,
Institute of Shortening and Edible
Oils. 56-26580
TP670 .A1D5 MRR Alc Latest edition

OKLAHOMA.
Oklahoma almanac. 1908- Norman,
Okla. [etc.] 08-10798
F691 .O48 MRR Alc Latest edition

Ruth, Kent, ed. Oklahoma; a guide to
the Sooner State, [Rev. ed.]
Norman, University of Oklahoma Press
[1957] xxxv, 532 p. 917.66 57-
7333
F694 .R8 MRR Ref Desk.

OKLAHOMA--BIBLIOGRAPHY.
Hargrett, Lester, Oklahoma imprints,
1835-1890. New York, Published for
the Bibliographical Society of
America [by] Bowker, 1951. xvii, 267
p. 015.766 51-3747
Z1325 .H3 MRR Alc.

OKLAHOMA--BIBLIOGRAPHY--CATALOGS.
United States. Library of Congress.
Oklahoma, the semicentennial of
statehood, 1907-1957. Washington,
1957. vii, 70 p. 016.8766 57-
60056
Z663.15.A605 MRR Alc.

OKLAHOMA--CENTENNIAL CELEBRATIONS, ETC.
United States. Library of Congress.
Oklahoma, the semicentennial of
statehood, 1907-1957. Washington,
1957. vii, 70 p. 016.8766 57-
60056
Z663.15.A605 MRR Alc.

OKLAHOMA--DESCRIPTION AND TRAVEL--GUIDE-
BOOKS.
Ruth, Kent, ed. Oklahoma; a guide to
the Sooner State, [Rev. ed.]
Norman, University of Oklahoma Press
[1957] xxxv, 532 p. 917.66 57-
7333
F694 .R8 MRR Ref Desk.

OKLAHOMA--HISTORY.
McReynolds, Edwin C. Oklahoma; a
history of the Sooner State. [1st
ed.] Norman, University of Oklahoma
Press [1954] xii, 461 p. 976.6 54-
10052
F694 .M16 MRR Alc.

OKLAHOMA--IMPRINTS.
Hargrett, Lester, Oklahoma imprints,
1835-1890. New York, Published for
the Bibliographical Society of
America [by] Bowker, 1951. xvii, 267
p. 015.766 51-3747
Z1325 .H3 MRR Alc.

OKLAHOMA--MANUFACTURES--DIRECTORIES.
Oklahoma directory of manufacturers
and products. Oklahoma City,
Oklahoma Industrial Development and
Park Dept. 338.4/7/67025766 72-
620773
HD9727.O5 A28 MRR Alc Latest
edition

OKLAHOMA--REGISTERS.
Oklahoma. State Library, Oklahoma
City. Oklahoma State agencies,
boards, commissions, courts,
institutions, Legislature and
officers. St. Paul, West Pub. Co.
353.9766 53-29616
JK7130 .O4 MRR Alc Latest edition

OKLAHOMA--REGISTERS--PERIODICALS.
Directory of Oklahoma. 1973-
[Oklahoma City] State Election Board.
353.9 766/002 74-647993
JK7192 .A36 MRR Alc Latest edition

OLD AGE.
see also Aged

OLD AGE. (Cont.)
Cicero, Marcus Tullius. De
senectute, De amicitia, De
divinatione, Cambridge, Mass.,
Harvard University Press; London, W.
Heinemann, 1938. vii, 567 p.   mrr01-
1
    PA6156.C5 A2 1938d MRR Alc.

**OLD AGE HOMES--UNITED STATES--
DIRECTORIES.**
Active Retirement Executives
Association. Retirement facilities
register. Studio City, Calif., 1965]
331 p. 66-597
    HQ1062 .A35 MRR Alc.

Active Retirement Executives
Association. Retirement facilities
register. Los Angeles, 1964?] 224
p. 362.6105873 64-4960
    HD7287.9 .A26 MRR Alc.

Greenberg, Dan. U.S. guide to
nursing homes. New York, Grosset &
Dunlap [1970] 3 v. [2.95 (each)]
362.1/6/02573 71-92386
    RA997.A2 G7 MRR Alc.

Holter, Paul. Guide to retirement
living. Chicago, Rand McNally [1973]
xviii, 174 p. [$3.95]
362.6/15/02573 73-173331
    HQ1063 .H64 1973 MRR Alc.

Musson, Noverre. The national
directory of retirement residences:
best places to live when you retire.
Rev. ed. New York, F. Fell [1973]
214 p. 362.6/15/02573 72-89943
    HV1465 .M87 1973 MRR Alc.

OLD AGE PENSIONS--UNITED STATES.
U.S Labor-Management Services
Administration. Register of
retirement benefit plans,
Washington, For sale by the Supt. of
Docs., U.S. Govt. Print. Off. [1967]
ix, 550 p. 331.2/52/02573 68-60198

    HD7106.U5 A539 MRR Alc.

**OLD AGE SURVIVORS AND DISABILITY
INSURANCE**
see Insurance, Social

**OLMSTED, FREDERICK LAW, 1822-1903--
BIBLIOGRAPHY.**
United States. Library of Congress.
Manuscript Division. Frederick Law
Olmsted; a register of his papers in
the Library of Congress. Washington,
1963. 13 l. 63-65420
    Z663.34 .O4 MRR.Alc.

OLYMPIC GAMES.
Grombach, John V. The 1972 Olympic
guide New York, Paperback Library
[1972] 319 p. [$1.25] 796.4/8 77-
183373
    GV721.5 .G683 MRR Alc.

Kieran, John, The story of the
Olympic games, 776 B.C. to 1972,
[Rev. ed.] Philadelphia, Lippincott
[1973] 542 p. 796.4/8/09 73-1171

    GV23 .K5 1973 MRR Alc.

Guinness book of Olympic records;
New York, Sterling Pub. Co. [1964]
158 p. 796.48083 64-15104
    GV721.5 .G8 MRR Alc.

Schaap, Richard, An illustrated
history of the Olympics. 2d ed.,
rev. and enl. New York, Knopf [1967]
xlii, 338, v p. 796.4/8 67-18616

    GV721.5 .S35 1967 MRR Alc.

OLYMPIC GAMES--REVIVAL, 1896-
Chester, David. The Olympic games
handbook; New York, Scribner [1971]
227 p. 796.4/8 74-162947
    GV721.5 .C45 1971 MRR Alc.

Kamper, Erich. Encyclopedia of the
Olympic Games. [1st ed.] New York,
McGraw-Hill [1972] xix, 360 p.
[$25.00] 796.4/8/03 71-38508
    GV721.5 .K34 MRR Alc.

United States Olympic book. New York
[etc.] United States Olympic
Association [etc.] 796.48* 21-21618

    GV721.5 .U6 MRR Alc Latest edition

Weyand, Alexander M., The Olympic
pageant. New York, Macmillan, 1952.
347 p. 796.4 52-10353
    GV721.5 .W4 MRR Alc.

OLYMPIC GAMES--DICTIONARIES.
Watman, Melvyn Francis. The
encyclopaedia of athletics. [3d ed.]
London, Hale [1973] 244 p. [£2.50]
796.4/03 73-178722
    GV567 .W3 1973 MRR Alc.

OLYMPIC GAMES--DICTIONARIES--POLYGLOT.
Kamper, Erich. Encyclopedia of the
Olympic Games. [1st ed.] New York,
McGraw-Hill [1972] xix, 360 p.
[$25.00] 796.4/8/03 71-38508
    GV721.5 .K34 MRR Alc.

OLYMPIC GAMES--HISTORY.
Chester, David. The Olympic games
handbook; New York, Scribner [1971]
227 p. 796.4/8 74-162947
    GV721.5 .C45 1971 MRR Alc.

OMENS.
see also Dreams

OMNIBUS SERVICE
see Motor bus lines

ONE-ACT PLAYS, AMERICAN.
Cerf, Bennett Alfred, ed. 24
favorite one-act plays, [1st ed.]
Garden City, N.Y., Doubleday, 1958.
455 p. 808.82 58-13274
    PS634 .C43 MRR Alc.

ONE-ACT PLAYS, ENGLISH.
Cerf, Bennett Alfred, ed. 24
favorite one-act plays, [1st ed.]
Garden City, N.Y., Doubleday, 1958.
455 p. 808.82 58-13274
    PS634 .C43 MRR Alc.

**O'NEIL, CHARLES, 1842-1927--
BIBLIOGRAPHY.**
United States. Library of Congress.
Manuscript Division. Edmund Ross
Colhoun; Charles O'Neil: a register
of their papers in the Library of
Congress. Washington, Library of
Congress, 1967. 8, 9 l.
016.3593/3/20922 68-60020
    Z663.34 .C57 MRR Alc.

ONEIROMANCY
see Dreams

**ONTARIO--DESCRIPTION AND TRAVEL--GUIDE-
BOOKS.**
Hepburn, Andrew. The Toronto guide,
1966-67. Toronto, McClelland &
Stewart, c1966. 166 p. [$1.00 Can.]
917.13/541 67-79850
    F1059.5.T68 H4 MRR Alc.

ONTOLOGY.
see also Existentialism

OPERA.
Biancolli, Louis Leopold, ed. The
opera reader. New York, McGraw-Hill
Book Co. [1953] 678 p. 782.08 53-
9008
    ML1700 .B47 MRR Alc.

OPERA--ADDRESSES, ESSAYS, LECTURES.
Grout, Donald Jay. Mozart in the
history of opera; Washington,
Published for the Library of Congress
by the Louis Charles Elson Memorial
Fund, 1972 [c1971] iii, 20 p.
782.1/0924 75-38821
    Z663.37 .A5 1970 MRR Alc.

OPERA--BIBLIOGRAPHY.
United States. Library of Congress.
Music division. Catalogue of opera
librettos printed before 1800,
Washington, Govt. print. off., 1914.
2 v. 13-35009
    Z663.37 .C34 MRR Alc.

United States. Library of Congress.
Music Division. Dramatic music
(class M 1500, 1510, 1520)
Washington, Govt. Print. Off., 1908.
170 p. 08-35001
    Z663.37 .D7 MRR Alc.

OPERA--BIO-BIBLIOGRAPHY.
Kosch, Wilhelm, Deutsches Theater-
Lexikon; Klagenfurt, F. Kleinmayr,
1951- v.   a 52-1902
    PN2035 .K6 MRR Alc.

OPERA--DICTIONARIES.
Ewen, David, The new encyclopedia of
the opera. New York, Hill and Wang
[1971] viii, 759 p. [$15.00]
782.1/03 71-148237
    ML102.06 E9 1971 MRR Alc.

Moore, Frank Ledlie. Crowell's
handbook of world opera. New York,
Crowell [1961] 683 p. 782.03 61-
6139
    ML102.06 M6 MRR Alc.

Ross, Anne, ed. The opera directory.
New York, Sterling Pub. Co. [1961]
xii, 566 p. 782.058 61-12046
    ML102.06 R68 MRR Alc.

Sharp, Harold S., comp. Index to
characters in the performing arts.
New York, Scarecrow Press, 1966-73.
4 v. in 6. 808.8292703 66-13744
    PN1579 .S45 MRR Alc.

OPERA--DICTIONARIES--FRENCH.
Dictionnaire des personnages
litteraires et dramatiques de tous
les temps et de tous les pays; 1.
ed.] Paris, Societe d'edition de
dictionnaires et encyclopedies
[1960] 668 p. 62-27565
    PN41 .D485 MRR Alc.

OPERA--HISTORY AND CRITICISM.
Westerman, Gerhart von. Opera guide.
New York, E. P. Dutton [1965, c1964]
584 p. 782.1 65-1790
    ML1700 .W42 MRR Alc.

OPERA--RUSSIA--HISTORY AND CRITICISM.
Slonim, Marc, Russian theater, [1st
ed.] Cleveland, World Pub. Co.
[1961] 354 p. 792.0947 61-15304
    PN2721 .S55 MRR Alc.

OPERA--HOUSES
see Theaters

OPERAS--DICTIONARIES.
Loewenberg, Alfred. Annals of opera,
1597-1940, 2d ed., rev. and corr.
Geneve, Societas Bibliographica
[1955] 2 v.: xxv p., 1756 columns)
782.03 a 56-1141
    ML102.06 L6 1955 MRR Alc.

OPERAS--DISCOGRAPHY.
Moore, Frank Ledlie. Crowell's
handbook of world opera. New York,
Crowell [1961] 683 p. 782.03 61-
6139
    ML102.06 M6 MRR Alc.

**OPERAS--EXCERPTS--VOCAL SCORES WITH
PIANO.**
Sullivan, Arthur Seymour, Sir,
Martyn Green's treasury of Gilbert &
Sullivan. New York, Simon and
Schuster, 1961. 717 p. 782.12 m
61-1017
    M1507 .S95G7 MRR Alc.

OPERAS--LIBRETTOS.
Legerman, David G., ed. A treasury
of opera librettos. [1st ed.]
Garden City, N.Y., Doubleday [1962]
xvi, 1060 p. 782.12 61-13329
    ML48 .L37T7 1962 MRR Alc.

Sullivan, Arthur Seymour, Sir,
Martyn Green's treasury of Gilbert &
Sullivan. New York, Simon and
Schuster, 1961. 717 p. 782.12 m
61-1017
    M1507 .S95G7 MRR Alc.

OPERAS--LIBRETTOS--BIBLIOGRAPHY.
United States. Library of Congress.
Music division. Catalogue of opera
librettos printed before 1800,
Washington, Govt. print. off., 1914.
2 v. 13-35009
    Z663.37 .C34 MRR Alc.

OPERAS--STORIES, PLOTS, ETC.
Biancolli, Louis Leopold, ed. The
opera reader. New York, McGraw-Hill
Book Co. [1953] 678 p. 782.08 53-
9008
    ML1700 .B47 MRR Alc.

Cross, Milton John, The new Milton
Cross' complete stories of the great
operas. Rev. and enl. ed. Garden
City, N.Y., Doubleday [1955] xiii,
688 p. 782.08 55-10505
    MT95 .C76 1955 MRR Alc.

Moore, Frank Ledlie. Crowell's
handbook of world opera. New York,
Crowell [1961] 683 p. 782.03 61-
6139
    ML102.06 M6 MRR Alc.

Simon, Henry William, Festival of
opera. [1st ed.] Garden City, N.Y.,
Hanover House [1957] 704 p. 782.08
57-5524
    MT95 .S59 MRR Alc.

Westerman, Gerhart von. Opera guide.
New York, E. P. Dutton [1965, c1964]
584 p. 782.1 65-1790
    ML1700 .W42 MRR Alc.

OPERAS--THEMATIC CATALOGS.
Barlow, Harold. A dictionary of
opera and song themes. New York,
Crown Publishers [1966, c1950] 547
p. 781.97 66-18454
    ML128.V7 B3 1950a MRR Alc.

OPERAS--TO 1800--LIBRETTOS.
Legerman, David G., ed. A treasury
of opera librettos. [1st ed.]
Garden City, N.Y., Doubleday [1962]
xvi, 1060 p. 782.12 61-13329
    ML48 .L37T7 1962 MRR Alc.

OPERATIONS RESEARCH.
see also Simulation methods

OPERETTAS
see Musical revues, comedies, etc.

**OPHTHALMOLOGISTS--UNITED STATES--
DIRECTORIES.**
The red book of eye, ear, nose and
throat specialists. 1st- ed.; 1915-
Chicago, Professional Press, Inc.
[etc.] 15-6770
    RE22 .R3 MRR Alc Latest edition

OPHTHALMOLOGY--DICTIONARIES--POLYGLOT.
Lexicon opthalmologicum; Basel, New
York, S. Karger, 1959. 223 p.
617.703 59-4669
    RE21 .L45 MRR Alc.

OPIATES
see Narcotics

OPINION, PUBLIC
see Public opinion

OPPENHEIMER, J. ROBERT, 1904-1967--
BIBLIOGRAPHY.
United States. Library of Congress.
Manuscript Division. J. Robert
Oppenheimer; Washington, Library of
Congress, 1974. iii, 63 p.   016.53
74-8144
Z663.34 .O66 MRR Alc.

OPTICAL INSTRUMENTS.
see also Microscope and microscopy

OPTICAL TRADE--UNITED STATES--
DIRECTORIES.
The Optical industry and systems
directory. no. 1- 1954-
Pittsfield, Mass. [etc.] Optical Pub
Co.   a 54-6009
HD9998.O63U65   Sci RR Latest
edition / MRR Alc Latest edition

OPTICS.
see also Color

OPTICS--DICTIONARIES--POLYGLOT.
Schulz, Ernst, lexicographer.
Worterbuch der Optik und
Feinmechanik. Wiesbaden,
Brandstetter [1960-61] 3 v.   a 61-
3700
QC351.2 .S34 MRR Alc.

ORAL COMMUNICATION.
see also Speech

Bryant, Donald Cross, Oral
communication; 3d ed. New York,
Appleton-Century-Crofts [1962] 351
p.   808.5   62-7253
PN4121 .B776 1962 MRR Alc.

ORAL COMMUNICATION--DIRECTORIES.
Speech Communication Association.
Directory. 1971/72- New York.
808.5/06/13   73-640465
PN4073 .N253 MRR Alc Latest
edition

ORAL HISTORY--BIBLIOGRAPHY--CATALOGS.
Columbia University. Oral History
Research Office. The Oral History
Collection of Columbia University.
[3d ed.] New York; [Sold by
Microfilming Corp. of America, Glen
Rock, N.J.] 1973. xvii, 459 p.
016.9173/03 73-78480
Z6621 .C725 1973 MRR Alc.

ORAL HISTORY--DIRECTORIES.
Shumway, Gary L. Oral history in the
United States; New York, Oral
History Association, 1971. 120 p.
973/.025/73 71-162931
E175.4 .S58 MRR Alc.

ORAL INTERPRETATION.
Crocker, Lionel George, Oral
reading: discussion and principles,
2d ed. New York, Prentice-Hall,
1955. 492 p.   808.54* 55-7942
PN4145 .C75 1955 MRR Alc.

ORAL READING.
Crocker, Lionel George, Oral
reading: discussion and principles,
2d ed. New York, Prentice-Hall,
1955. 492 p.   808.54* 55-7942
PN4145 .C75 1955 MRR Alc.

ORANGE FREE STATE--DIRECTORIES.
Braby's Orange Free State and
Northern Cape directory. Durban. 53-
32833
DT891 .B73 MRR Alc Latest edition

ORATIONS.
Modern eloquence; Revised. New
York, P. F. Collier & son corporation
[c1941] 15 v.   808.85 41-9672
PN6121 .M63 1941 MRR Alc.

Peterson, Houston, ed. A treasury of
the world's great speeches. Rev. and
enl. ed. New York, Simon and
Schuster [1965] xxix, 866 p.
808.85   65-4344
PN6121 .P4 1965 MRR Alc.

ORATIONS--INDEXES.
Sutton, Roberta (Briggs) Speech
index; 4th ed., rev. and enl. New
York, Scarecrow Press, 1966. vii,
947 p.   016.80885   66-13749
AI3 .S85 1966 MRR Ref Desk.

ORATORIO--BIBLIOGRAPHY.
Baker, David Erskine, Biographia
dramatica: London, Longman, Hurst,
Rees, Orme, and Brown [etc.] 1812. 3
v. in 4.   04-14124
Z2014.D7 B2 1812 MRR Alc.

ORATORS, GREEK.
Minor Attic orators. Cambridge,
Harvard University Press, 1941-54. 2
v.   a 41-2546
PA3611.A93 1941 MRR Alc.

ORATORY.
see also Public speaking

Cicero, Marcus Tullius. Cicero. De
oratore. Cambridge, Mass., Harvard
university press; London, W.
Heinemann ltd., 1942. 2 v.   875.3
a 42-4498
PA6156.C6 D6 1942 MRR Alc.

ORBITAL RENDEZVOUS (SPACE FLIGHT)
see also Project Apollo

ORBITING VEHICLES
see Artificial satellites

ORBITS.
see also Planets

ORCHARDS
see Fruit-culture

ORCHESTRAL MUSIC--ANALYSIS,
APPRECIATION.
Biancolli, Louis Leopold, ed. The
analytical concert guide, [English
ed.] London, Cassell [1957] xxv,
769 p.   785.1 58-19721
MT125 .B46 1957 MRR Alc.

Frankenstein, Alfred Victor, A
modern guide to symphonic music,
[1st ed.] New York, Meredith Press
[c1966] xvii, 667 p.   785/.015 66-
13486
MT125 .F83M6 MRR Alc.

ORCHESTRAL MUSIC--BIBLIOGRAPHY--
CATALOGS.
United States. Library of Congress.
Music division. ... Orchestral music
(class M 1000-1268) catalogue.
Washington, Govt. print. off., 1912.
663 p.   11-35001
Z663.37 .O7 MRR Alc.

ORCHESTRAL MUSIC--THEMATIC CATALOGS.
Barlow, Harold. A dictionary of
musical themes. New York, Crown
Publishers [1948] 656 p.   781.97
48-6784
ML128.I65 B3 MRR Alc.

ORDERS, MAJOR
see Clergy

ORDERS, MONASTIC
see Monasticism and religious orders

ORDERS OF KNIGHTHOOD AND CHIVALRY.
Dycourtial, Claude. Ordres et
decorations ... 2e edition
augmentee et mise a jour. Paris,
Presses universitaires de France,
1968. 128 p. [3.30] 72-406717
CR4509 .D8 1968 MRR Alc.

ORDERS OF KNIGHTHOOD AND CHIVALRY--
DENMARK.
Forlaget Liber, Copenhagen. De
kongelige danske ridderordener og
medaljer. [1964-1968] København,
Liber, 1970. 591 p. [kr722.20] 72-
300129
CR5750 .F6 1970 MRR Alc.

Forlaget Liber, Copenhagen. De
kongelige danske ridderordener og
medaljer. København, Forlaget
liber, 1965. 611 p.   73-332590
CR5750 .F62 MRR Alc.

ORDERS OF KNIGHTHOOD AND CHIVALRY--
GREAT BRITAIN.
British orders and awards: 2nd
entirely revised ed. London, Kaye &
Ward, 1968. [5], 183 p. [30/-]
737/.2/0942 72-352008
CR4801 .B7 1968 MRR Alc.

ORDNANCE--DICTIONARIES.
Luttwak, Edward. A dictionary of
modern war. (1st U.S. ed.] New
York, Harper & Row [1971] 224 p.
[$7.95] 355/.003 77-159574
U24 .L93 1971 MRR Alc.

ORDNANCE--YEARBOOKS.
Jane's weapon systems. 1st- ed.;
1969/70- New York, McGraw-Hill.
623.4/05 79-12909
U104 .J35 Sci RR Latest edition /
MRR Alc Latest edition

OREGON--BIBLIOGRAPHY--CATALOGS.
United States. Library of Congress.
Centennial of the Oregon Territory
exhibition, September 11, 1948-
January 11, 1949. Washington, U.S.
Govt. Print. Off., 1948. 76 p.
016.9795 48-46991
Z663.15.A6O7 1948 MRR Alc.

OREGON--CENTENNIAL CELEBRATIONS, ETC.
United States. Library of Congress.
Centennial of the Oregon Territory
exhibition, September 11, 1948-
January 11, 1949. Washington, U.S.
Govt. Print. Off., 1948. 76 p.
016.9795 48-46991
Z663.15.A6O7 1948 MRR Alc.

OREGON--DESCRIPTION AND TRAVEL--GUIDE-
BOOKS.
Writers' Program. Oregon. Oregon;
end of the trail, St. Clair Shores,
Mich., Somerset Publishers, 1972
[c1940] xxxii, 549 p.   917.95/04/4
72-84501
F874.3 .W73 1972 MRR Alc.

Writers' Program. Oregon. Oregon,
end of the trail. Rev. ed,
Portland, Binfords & Mort [1951,
c1940] xxxii, 549 p.   917.95 52-
11474
F881 .W76 1951 MRR Ref Desk.

OREGON--ECONOMIC CONDITIONS.
Oregon. Secretary of State. The
Oregon blue book. 1911- Salem. 12-
33110
JK9031 MRR Alc Latest edition

OREGON--HISTORY--DICTIONARIES.
Corning, Howard McKinley, ed.
Dictionary of Oregon history.
Portland, Binfords & Mort [c1956]
281 p.   979.5O03 57-1975
F874 .C6 MRR Alc.

OREGON--MANUFACTURES--DIRECTORIES.
Directory of Oregon manufacturers.
Portland, Economic Development
Division. 338.4/7/6025795 72-627022

T12 .O7 MRR Alc Latest edition /
Sci RR Latest edition

OREGON--POLITICS AND GOVERNMENT.
Oregon. Secretary of State. The
Oregon blue book. 1911- Salem. 12-
33110
JK9031 MRR Alc Latest edition

OREGON--REGISTERS.
Oregon. Secretary of State. The
Oregon blue book. 1911- Salem. 12-
33110
JK9031 MRR Alc Latest edition

OREGON--STATISTICS.
Onstine, Burton W. Oregon votes:
1858-1972, election returns.
Portland, Oregon Historical Society,
1973. vii, 395 p.   324/.2021/795
73-88980
JK9092 .O55 MRR Alc.

ORES.
see also Metals

see also Mines and mineral resources

ORGANIC CHEMISTRY
see Chemistry, Organic

ORGANIC FARMING--UNITED STATES--
DIRECTORIES.
The Organic directory, [Completely
rev. ed.] Emmaus, Pa., Rodale Press
[1974] 229 p. [$2.95] 641.3/1 74-
166399
TX356 .O69 1974 MRR Alc.

ORGANIC GARDENING--UNITED STATES--
SOCIETIES, ETC.--DIRECTORIES.
The Organic directory, [Completely
rev. ed.] Emmaus, Pa., Rodale Press
[1974] 229 p. [$2.95] 641.3/1 74-
166399
TX356 .O69 1974 MRR Alc.

ORGANIZATION.
see also Industrial management

see also Management

ORGANIZATIONS
see Associations, institutions, etc.

ORGANIZED CAMPS
see Camps

ORGANIZED CRIME--UNITED STATES--
ADDRESSES, ESSAYS, LECTURES.
Tyler, Gus, ed. Organized crime in
America. Ann Arbor, University of
Michigan Press [1962] 421 p.
364.10973 60-15778
HV6777 .T9 MRR Alc.

ORGANOMETALLIC COMPOUNDS--HANDBOOKS,
MANUALS, ETC.
Kaufman, Herbert C. Handbook of
organometallic compounds. Princeton,
N.J., Van Nostrand [1961] iv, 1546
p.   547.45 61-3980
QD411 .K33 MRR Alc.

ORIENTAL CIVILIZATION
see Civilization, Oriental

ORIENTAL LANGUAGES--DICTIONARIES--
POLYGLOT.
Bergman, Peter M. The concise
dictionary of twenty-six languages in
simultaneous translations. New York,
Polyglot Library [1968] 406 p.   413
67-14284
P361 .B4 TJ Rm.

United States. Air Force. 6004th Air
Intelligence Service Squadron.
Dictionary of common oriental terms;
[n. p.] 1956. 1v. (various pagings)
495 57-60108
PL493 .U52 MRR Alc.

ORIENTAL LITERATURE--BIO-BIBLIOGRAPHY.
The Penguin companion to classical,
Oriental & African literature. New
York, McGraw-Hill [1971, c1969] 359
p.   [$9.95] 809 78-158064
PA31 .P4 1971 MRR Alc.

ORIENTAL LITERATURE--TRANSLATIONS INTO
ENGLISH.
Pritchard, James Bennett, ed.
Ancient Near Eastern texts relating
to the Old Testament. 2d ed., corr.
and enl. Princeton, Princeton
University Press, 1955. xxi, 544 p.
221.93 55-9033
BS1180 .P83 1955 MRR Alc.

ORIENTAL MUSIC
see Music, Oriental

ORIENTAL STUDIES.
see also Civilization, Oriental

ORIENTAL STUDIES--BIBLIOGRAPHY.
Pearson, James Douglas. Oriental and
Asian bibliography; Hamden, Conn.,
Archon Books, 1966. xvi, 261 p.
016.915 66-1006
Z7046 .P4 MRR Alc.

ORIENTAL STUDIES--SOCIETIES, ETC.
Japan. Mombusho. Nihon Yunesuko
Kokunai Iinkai. Directory of
researchers and research institutes
on Oriental studies in Japan.
[Tokyo] Japanese National Commission
for UNESCO [1957] 50 p. 068.52 61-
32041
AS548 .A543 MRR Alc.

ORIENTAL STUDIES--UNITED STATES.
Stucki, Curtis W. American doctoral
dissertations on Asia, 1933-1962,
Ithaca, N.Y., Southeast Asia Program,
Dept. of Asian Studies, Cornell
University, 1963. 204 p. 016.915
64-2901
Z3001 .S72 MRR Alc.

ORIENTAL STUDIES--UNITED STATES--
BIBLIOGRAPHY.
Stucki, Curtis W. American doctoral
dissertations on Asia, 1933-1962,
Ithaca, N.Y., Southeast Asia Program,
Dept. of Asian Studies, Cornell
University, 1963. 204 p. 016.915
64-2901
Z3001 .S72 MRR Alc.

ORIENTALISTS--DIRECTORIES.
Tilman, Robert O. International
biographical directory of Southeast
Asia specialists [Ann Arbor, Mich.]
Interuniversity Southeast Asia
Committee, Association for Asian
Studies. [Distributed by Southeast
Asia Studies Center for International
Studies, Ohio University, Athens,
Ohio] 1969. xxxv, 337 p.
815.9/0072/022 76-631592
DS510.7 .T5 MRR Biog.

ORIGIN OF MAN
see Man--Origin

ORLEANS (TER.)--GOVERNMENT PUBLICATIONS-
-BIBLIOGRAPHY.
Foote, Lucy Brown, comp.
Bibliography of the official
publications of Louisiana, 1803-1934.
Baton Rouge, La., Hill memorial
library, Louisiana state university,
1942. 4 p. l., [vii]-xiv, 579, [3]
p. 015.763 42-19598
Z1215 .H67 no. 19 MRR Alc.

ORNAMENT
see Decoration and ornament

ORNAMENTAL HORTICULTURE.
see also Landscape architecture

see also Plants, Ornamental

ORNAMENTAL TREE.
see also Flowering trees

ORNITHOLOGISTS.
Gruson, Edward S. Words for birds;
[New York] Quadrangle Books [1972]
xiv, 305 p. [$8.95] 598.2/97 72-
77537
QL677 .G78 1972 MRR Alc.

ORNITHOLOGY.
see also Birds

ORNITHOLOGY--EXAMINATIONS, QUESTIONS,
ETC.
Cruickshank, Allan D. 1001 questions
answered about birds, New York,
Dodd, Mead, 1958. 291 p. 598.2076
58-10784
QL673 .C7 MRR Alc.

OROLOGY
see Mountains

ORTHODOX EASTERN CHURCH--HISTORY.
Meyendorff, Jean, The Orthodox
Church, [New York] Pantheon Books
[1962] 244 p. 281.9 62-14260
BX290 .M413 MRR Alc.

ORTHODOX EASTERN CHURCH, RUSSIAN, IN
AMERICA--YEARBOOKS.
Russian Orthodox Greek Catholic
Church of America. Year book and
church directory. 1950- New York.
51-37234
BX496.A5 R8 MRR Alc Latest edition

OSLO--COMMERCE--DIRECTORIES.
S.M. Brydes fagfortegnelse over
næringsdrivende i Oslo. [Oslo] 53-
29067
HC368.08 A25 MRR Alc Latest
edition

OSLO--DIRECTORIES.
Oslo adressebok. 1934- [Oslo]
Nationaltrykkeriet. 35-25484
DL581 .A2065 MRR Alc Latest
edition

OSLO--INDUSTRIES--DIRECTORIES.
S.M. Brydes fagfortegnelse over
næringsdrivende i Oslo. [Oslo] 53-
29067
HC368.08 A25 MRR Alc Latest
edition

ØSTFOLD, NORWAY--DIRECTORIES.
Adressebok for Østfold fylke med
skatteligninger. Oslo, S. M. Bryde.
53-28838
DL576.04 A7 MRR Alc Latest edition

OSWALD, LEE HARVEY.
United States. Warren Commission.
Report of the President's Commission
on the Assassination of President
John F. Kennedy. Washington, U.S.
Govt. Print. Off. [1964] xxiv, 888
p. 64-62670
E842.9 .A55 MRR Alc.

OTAGO, N.Z.--COMMERCE--DIRECTORIES.
Universal business directory for
Otago-Southland. Auckland, Universal
Business Directories. 53-30674
HC623.08 U5 MRR Alc Latest edition

OTAGO, N.Z.--INDUSTRIES--DIRECTORIES.
Universal business directory for
Otago-Southland. Auckland, Universal
Business Directories. 53-30674
HC623.08 U5 MRR Alc Latest edition

OTOLARYNGOLOGISTS--UNITED STATES--
DIRECTORIES.
The red book of eye, ear, nose and
throat specialists. 1st- ed.; 1915-
Chicago, Professional Press, Inc.
[etc.] 15-6770
RE22 .R3 MRR Alc Latest edition

OUT-OF-PRINT BOOKS.
The A B bookman's yearbook. 1954-
Newark, N.J. 010.58 54-1676
Z990 .A18 MRR Alc Latest edition

Guide to reprints. 1967-
Washington, Microcard Editions. 011
66-29279
Z1000.5 .G8 MRR Ref Desk Latest
edition

Ostwald, Renate.
Nachdruckverzeichnis von
Einzelwerken, Serien und
Zeitschriften Wiesbaden, G. Nobis,
1965- v. 66-31825
Z1011 .078 MRR Alc.

OUTBOARD MOTOR-BOATS--PRICES--UNITED
STATES--YEARBOOKS.
Blue book official outboard boat
trade-in guide. Kansas City, Mo.,
Abos Marine Publications Div.,
Intertect Pub. Corp. [etc.] [$4.95]
338.4/3/62382130973 74-644650
VM348 .B52 MRR Alc Latest edition

OUTBOARD MOTORS.
Blue book, official outboard motor
trade-in guide. Kansas City, Mo.,
Abos Marine Publications Div.,
Intertect Pub. Corp. [etc.]
380.1/45/6238723 72-627123
HD9999.B5 085 MRR Alc Latest
edition

OUTDOOR EDUCATION.
see also Physical education and
training

OUTDOOR LIFE.
see also Hiking

see also Mountaineering

see also Wilderness survival

Herter, George Leonard. Professional
guide's manual, [1st ed. Waseca,
Minn.] Herter's [1960] 207 p. 799
60-21551
SK601 .H497 MRR Alc.

OUTDOOR RECREATION.
see also Camping

see also Parks

Sparano, Vin T. Complete outdoors
encyclopedia, New York, Outdoor
Life, Harper & Row [1972] 622 p.
[$13.95] 799/.03 72-90934
SK33 .S646 MRR Alc.

United States. Dept. of Agriculture.
Outdoors USA. [Washington, U.S.
Govt. Print. Off., 1967] xxxix, 408
p. 333.7/2/0973 agr67-359
S21.A35 1967 MRR Alc.

OUTDOOR RECREATION--DIRECTORIES--
BIBLIOGRAPHY.
United States. Bureau of Outdoor
Recreation. Guides to outdoor
recreation areas and facilities
Washington; [For sale by the Supt. of
Docs., U.S. Govt. Print. Off., 1973]
79 p. [$1.05] 301.5/7 73-603093
Z7514.08 U54 1973 MRR Alc.

OUTDOOR RECREATION--NORTHWEST, PACIFIC.
Gartner, John F. Outdoor guide to
the Pacific Northwest Princeton,
N.J., Van Nostrand [1968] 300 p.
796.5/09795 68-19366
GV54.N95 G3 MRR Alc.

OUTDOOR RECREATION--UNITED STATES.
United States. Bureau of Outdoor
Recreation. Federal outdoor
recreation programs and recreation-
related environmental programs. [1st
revision Washington; For sale by
the Supt. of Docs., U.S. Govt. Print.
Off.] 1970. 226 p. [2.75]
301.5/7/0973 70-607632
GV53 .A47 1970 MRR Alc.

OUTDOOR RECREATION--UNITED STATES--
DIRECTORIES.
Adventure trip guide. New York,
Adventure Guides, 1972 208 p.
[$2.95] 917.3/24/824 72-81137
E158 .A38 MRR Alc.

OUTDOOR RECREATION--UNITED STATES--
DIRECTORIES--BIBLIOGRAPHY.
United States. Bureau of Outdoor
Recreation. Guides to outdoor
recreation areas and facilities
Washington; [For sale by the Supt. of
Docs., U.S. Govt. Print. Off., 1973]
79 p. [$1.05] 301.5/7 73-603093
Z7514.08 U54 1973 MRR Alc.

OUTER SPACE.
Newlon, Clarke. 1001 questions
answered about space. Rev. ed. New
York, Dodd, Mead, 1964. x, 356 p.
64-1372
TL793 .N38 1964 MRR Alc.

OUTER SPACE--EXPLORATION.
Astronautics and aeronautics;
1915/60- Washington, Scientific and
Technical Information Division,
National Aeronautics and Space
Administration [etc.; for sale by the
Superintendent of Documents, U.S.
Govt. Print. Off.] 65-60308
TL521.3.A8 A3 MRR Alc Partial set

OUTER SPACE--EXPLORATION--DICTIONARIES.
The New space encyclopaedia; New,
rev. ed. New York, E. P. Dutton
[1973] 326 p. [$14.95] 520/.3 73-
12348
QB14 .S66 1973 MRR Alc.

OUTLAWS.
Hunter, John Marvin, The album of
gunfighters, [San Antonio? 1965]
xi, 236 p. 978.020922 66-3801
F591 .H935 1965 MRR Biog.

OUTLAWS--BIBLIOGRAPHY.
Adams, Ramon Frederick, Six-guns and
saddle leather: New ed., [Norman,
University of Oklahoma Press, 1969]
xxv, 808 p. [19.95] 016.3641 69-
16729
Z1251.W5 A3 1969 MRR Alc.

OUTLET STORES--CANADA--DIRECTORIES.
S.O.S. directory of factory outlet
stores in the entire United States
and Canada. [Dearborn, Mich., S.O.S.
Directory Inc.] [$4.95] 381 74-
75652
HF5421 .S2 MRR Alc Latest edition

OUTLET STORES--UNITED STATES--
DIRECTORIES.
S.O.S. directory of factory outlet
stores in the entire United States
and Canada. [Dearborn, Mich., S.O.S.
Directory Inc.] [$4.95] 381 74-
75652
HF5421 .S2 MRR Alc Latest edition

OUTSIDE BROKERS
see Brokers

OVER-THE-COUNTER MARKETS--DIRECTORIES.
Moody's OTC industrial manual. New
York, Moody's Investors Service.
332.67 77-649772
HG4961 .M7237 MRR Ref Desk Latest
edition

OVER-THE-COUNTER MARKETS--UNITED STATES.
Loll, Leo M. The over-the-counter
securities markets; 2d ed.
Englewood Cliffs, N.J., Prentice-Hall
[1967] vi, 426 p. 332.6/43 67-
22419
HG4910 .L6 1967 MRR Alc.

OVER-THE-COUNTER MARKETS--UNITED STATES--
PERIODICALS.
Investment Statistics Laboratory.
ISL daily stock price index: over-the-
counter. [New York] 332.63/22 76-
25091
HG4915 .I6 MRR Alc Full set

Standard and Poor's Corporation.
Daily stock price record: over-the-
counter. [New York] 332.6/322/0973
72-627516
HG4915 .S665 MRR Alc Full set

OVER-THE-COUNTER MARKETS-- (Cont.)
Standard and Poor's Corporation.
Standard & Poor's stock reports: over
the counter. Mar. 1973- New York.
332.6/7   78-183944
  HG4905 .S444 MRR Alc Latest
    edition

OXFORD--DIRECTORIES.
Kelly's directory of Oxford.
Kingston upon Thames [Eng., etc.] 53-
28823
  DA690.O88 K4 MRR Alc Latest
    edition

OXFORD--LIBRARIES.
Morgan, Paul, Oxford libraries
outside the Bodleian; Oxford [Eng.]
Oxford Bibliographical Society and
the Bodleian Library. 1973. xx, 250
p.   027.7425/72 74-164811
  Z791.O98 M67 MRR Alc.

OXFORD. UNIVERSITY.
Handbook to the University of Oxford.
1932- Oxford, Clarendon Press.
378.42   33-15048
  LF501 .C82 MRR Alc Latest edition

OXFORD. UNIVERSITY--LIBRARIES.
Morgan, Paul, Oxford libraries
outside the Bodleian; Oxford [Eng.]
Oxford Bibliographical Society and
the Bodleian Library. 1973. xx, 250
p.   027.7425/72 74-164811
  Z791.O98 M67 MRR Alc.

OXFORD. UNIVERSITY--REGISTERS.
Oxford. University. The historical
register of the University of Oxford,
Oxford, Clarendon Press, 1900. 914
p.   378.42   30-33089
  LF524.A2 1220-1900 MRR Alc.

OXFORD. UNIVERSITY. RHODES SCHOLARSHIPS.
Aydelotte, Frank, The American
Rhodes scholarships; Princeton,
N.J., Princeton university press,
1946. xvi, 208 p.   378.34 a 46-
4271
  LF503.F8 A9 MRR Alc.

PACIFIC COAST--DESCRIPTION AND TRAVEL--
GUIDE-BOOKS.
Clark, Sydney Aylmer, All the best
in South America, west coast; New
York, Dodd, Mead [1966] x, 271 p.
918.043 66-13264
  F2213 .C5 1966 MRR Alc.

National Automobile Club. Touring
guide of the Pacific coast. San
Francisco. 629.281 53-31891
  GV1024 .N325 MRR Alc Latest
    edition

PACIFIC ISLANDS (TER.)
Coulter, John Wesley, The Pacific
dependencies of the United States.
New York, Macmillan, 1957. 388 p.
996   57-9543
  F970 .C6 MRR Alc.

PACIFIC SETTLEMENT OF INTERNATIONAL
DISPUTES.
Wainhouse, David Walter,
International peace observation;
Baltimore, Johns Hopkins Press, 1966.
xvii, 663 p.   341.11 66-14376
  JX1981.P7 W25 MRR Alc.

PACIFIC STATES--DESCRIPTION AND TRAVEL--
GUIDE-BOOKS.
Fodor, Eugene. Pacific States: 2d,
rev. ed. Litchfield, Conn.] Fodor's
Modern Guides; distributor: D. McKay
Co., New York [1967] 480 p.
917.9/04/3 67-20084
  F851 .F6 1967 MRR Alc.

Sunset. Sunset beachcombers' guide
to the Pacific coast, Menlo Park,
Calif., Lane Books [1966] 112 p.
917.90946 66-15333
  F851 .S93 MRR Alc.

PACKAGED BUILDINGS
see Buildings, Prefabricated

PACKAGING--YEARBOOKS.
Modern packaging encyclopedia issue.
New York [etc.] McGraw-Hill [etc.]
35-547
  Began publication in 1929.
  TS1200 .A1M64 Sci RR Latest
    edition / MRR Alc Latest edition

PACKAGING MACHINERY--DIRECTORIES.
The Packaging machinery catalog.
(Chicago, A. J. Ray Pub. Co.] 65-
84682
  TJ1545 .P28 MRR Alc Latest edition

Packaging machinery directory.
Washington, Packaging Machinery
Manufacturers Institute.
338.4/7/621757025 72-624817
  TJ1545 .O35 MRR Alc Latest edition

PACKING (TRANSPORTATION)
see Backpacking

PAGANINI, NICOLÒ, 1782-1840.
Spivacke, Harold, Paganiniana.
Washington [U.S. Govt. Print. Off.]
1945. 19 p.   927.8 45-36264
  Z663.375 .P3 MRR Alc.

PAGANISM--DICTIONARIES.
Wedeck, Harry Ezekiel, Dictionary of
pagan religions, [1st ed.] New
York, Philosophical Library [1971]
363 p. ($10.00] 290/.3 79-86508
  BL31 .W4 MRR Alc.

PAGEANTS.
see also Festivals

PAGEANTS--BIBLIOGRAPHY.
Baker, Blanch (Merritt) Theatre and
allied arts; New York, Wilson, 1952.
xiii, 536 p.   016.792 52-6756
  Z5781 .B18 MRR Alc.

PAINT--DICTIONARIES.
Chatfield, Herbert Walter, Glossary
of terms used in the paint, varnish,
and allied trades. London, Scott,
Greenwood [1951] 200 p.   667.603
51-8149
  TP934.3 .C5 MRR Alc.

Merz, Otto, Deutsch-englisches und
englisch-deutsches Fachwörterbuch
für Fachausdrücke aus dem Lack- und
Farbengebiet. 2., neubearb. und
erweiterte Aufl. Stuttgart,
Wissenschaftliche Verlagsgesellschaft, 1954. 351 p.   55-
22330
  TP935 .M45 1954 MRR Alc.

Stewart, Jeffrey R., The national
paint dictionary; 3d ed.
Washington, Stewart Research
Laboratory, 1948. 704 p.   667.603
48-5243
  TP934.3 .S7 1948 MRR Alc.

PAINT--DICTIONARIES--GERMAN.
Merz, Otto, Deutsch-englisches und
englisch-deutsches Fachwörterbuch
für Fachausdrücke aus dem Lack- und
Farbengebiet. 2., neubearb. und
erweiterte Aufl. Stuttgart,
Wissenschaftliche Verlagsgesellschaft, 1954. 351 p.   55-
22330
  TP935 .M45 1954 MRR Alc.

PAINT--DICTIONARIES--POLYGLOT.
Raaff, J. J. Index vocabulorum
quadrilingius; verf en vernis, [Den
Haag] Vereniging van Vernis- en
Verffabrikanten in Nederland,
Exportgroep Verf, 1958. 898 p.
667.603 59-27978
  TP934.3 .R2 MRR Alc.

PAINT--DIRECTORIES.
Chemical buyers directory. [1st]-
1913- New York, Schnell Pub. Co.
660/.025/73 13-6763
  TP12 .O6 Sci RR Latest edition /
    MRR Alc Latest edition

PAINT--TRADE-MARKS.
Trademark directory. Washington
[etc.] 667.6058 14-18485
  TP934.5 .T7 Sci RR Latest edition
    / MRR Alc Latest edition

PAINT INDUSTRY AND TRADE--UNITED STATES.
Trademark directory. Washington
[etc.] 667.6058 14-18485
  TP934.5 .T7 Sci RR Latest edition
    / MRR Alc Latest edition

Trademark directory. Supplement.
Washington [etc.] 667.6058 74-
643570
  TP934.5 .T7 Sci RR Latest edition
    / MRR Alc Latest edition

PAINTERS.
see also Artists

Histoire de l'art contemporain;
Authorized reprint ed. in one volume.
New York, Arno Press [1968] 536 p.
68-9229
  ND195 .H5 1968 MRR Alc.

Les Peintres célèbres. [2, éd.
Paris] L. Mazenod [1953-64] 3 v.
54-25077
  ND50 .P4 MRR Alc.

PAINTERS--BIOGRAPHY.
Canaday, John Edwin, The lives of
the painters [1st ed.] New York,
Norton [1969] 4 v.   759 B 67-17666
  ND35 .C35 MRR Alc.

PAINTERS--DICTIONARIES.
Bryan, Michael, Dictionary of
painters and engravers. New ed.,
rev. and enl. Port Washington,
N.Y., Kennikat Press [1964] 5 v.
927.5   64-15534
  N40 .B945 MRR Alc.

Dictionary of modern painting. 3d
ed., rev. and enl.] New York, Tudor
Pub. Co. [1964] 416 p.   759.05 65-
1420
  ND30 .D515 1964 MRR Alc.

Encyclopedia of painting; New York,
Crown Publishers, 1955. 511 p.
750.3   55-12456
  ND30 .E5 MRR Alc.

Jakovsky, Anatole. Peintres naïfs;
New York, Universe Books [1967] 398
p.   759 67-15570
  ND35 .J28 MRR Alc.

New international illustrated
encyclopedia of art. New York,
Greystone Press [1967- v.   703
67-24201
  N31 .N4 MRR Alc.

Shorewood Publishers, inc., New York.
The Shorewood art reference guide.
Rev. and enl. 3d ed. New York,
Shorewood Reproductions [1970]
xviii, 600 p.   759 70-110685
  N5305 .S5 1970 MRR Alc.

PAINTERS--DICTIONARIES--FRENCH.
Berckelaers, Ferdinand Louis,
Dictionnaire de la peinture
abstraite. Paris, F. Hazan [1957]
305 p.   a 57-7206
  ND35 .B4 MRR Alc.

PAINTERS--DICTIONARIES--GERMAN.
Fernau, Joachim. The Praeger
encyclopedia of old masters. New
York, F. A. Praeger [1959] 334 p.
759.003 59-7456
  ND30 .F413 MRR Alc.

Kindlers Malerei Lexikon. Zürich,
Kindler Verlag [1964- v.   759.3
68-80855
  ND35 .K5 MRR Alc.

PAINTERS--DICTIONARIES--ITALIAN.
Enciclopedia della pittura italiana
[Milano] Garzanti [1950] 2 v.
759.5 51-17931
  ND622 .E5 MRR Alc.

PAINTERS--FRANCE--BIOGRAPHY--
DICTIONARIES.
Dictionnaire des peintres français.
[Paris, Seghers, 1961] 378 p.   62-
44444
  ND552 .D5 MRR Alc.

PAINTERS--UNITED STATES.
Lipman, Jean (Herzberg) comp.
Primitive painters in America, 1750-
1950: New York, Dodd, Mead [1950]
182 p.   759.13 50-58059
  ND236 .L7 MRR Alc.

PAINTERS, AMERICAN.
Belknap, Waldron Phoenix, American
colonial painting; Cambridge, Mass.,
Belknap Press of Harvard University
Press, 1959. xxi, 377 p.   759.13
59-10313
  ND1311 .B39 MRR Alc.

Fielding, Mantle, Dictionary of
American painters, sculptors and
engravers / Enl. ed. with over 2,500
new listings of seventeenth,
eighteenth, and nineteenth century
American artists / Greens Farms,
Conn. : Modern Books and Crafts,
[1974] vi, 455 p. : [$17.50]
709/.2/2 74-192539
  N6536 .F5 1974 MRR Biog.

Illinois. University at Urbana-
Champaign. College of Fine and
Applied Arts. Contemporary American
painting and sculpture. Urbana.
759.13 74-642877
  ND212.A1 I4 MRR Alc Latest edition

New York Historical Society.
Catalogue of American portraits in
the New York Historical Society. New
Haven : Published by the New York
Historical Society by Yale University
Press, 1974. 2 v. (ix, 964 p.) :
757/.9/0973 74-79974
  N7593 .N5 1974 MRR Alc.

Park, Esther Ailleen. Mural painters
in America. Pittsburg, Kansas State
Teachers College, 1949- pts.
016.75173 50-63160
  ND236 .P3 MRR Biog.

Watson, Ernest William, Color and
method in painting as seen in the
work of 12 American painters, New
York, Watson-Guptill publications,
inc., 1942. 6 p. l., 141 p. incl.
illus., col. plates, ports.   750 42-
25525
  ND1260 .W3 MRR Alc.

Wehle, Harry Brandeis, American
miniatures, 1730-1850; Garden City,
N.Y., Garden City publishing company,
inc. [1937] xxv p., 1 l., 127 p.
757.0873 37-6103
  ND1337.U5 W4 1937 MRR Alc.

PAINTERS, BRITISH.
Berea, T. B. Handbook of 17th, 18th,
and 19th century British landscape
painters & watercolorists
[Chattanooga? Tenn., 1970] 72 p.
758/.1/0942 78-13623
  ND496 .B4 MRR Biog.

PAINTERS, BRITISH. (Cont.)
Wood, Christopher. Dictionary of
Victorian painters; [Woodbridge]
Antique Collectors' Club, 1971. v-
xvi, 435 p. [£8.00] 759.2 72-
188506
ND35 .W6 MRR Biog.

PAINTERS, CHINESE.
Sirén, Osvald, Chinese painting:
New York, Ronald Press [1956- v.
759.951 s 57-1105
ND1040 .S49 MRR Alc.

PAINTERS, DUTCH.
Bernt, Walther. The Netherlandish
painters of the seventeenth century;
London, Phaidon, 1970- v. plates.
[15/-/- (v. 1)] 759.9482 76-105963

ND636 .B4315 MRR Alc.

Mander, Carel van, Dutch and Flemish
painters: New York, McFarlane,
Warde, McFarlane, 1936. lxix, 560 p.
759.9492 36-25229
ND625 .M24 MRR Alc.

PAINTERS, ENGLISH.
Fredeman, William Evan, Pre-
Raphaelitism; a bibliocritical study
Cambridge, Harvard University Press,
1965. xix, 327 p. 016.70942 64-
21242
Z5948.P9 F7 MRR Alc.

Rothenstein, John Knewstub Maurice,
Sir, Modern English painters.
London, Eyre & Spottiswoode, 1952-56.
2 v. 759.2 52-40976
ND496 .R65 MRR Alc.

PAINTERS, FLEMISH.
Bernt, Walther. The Netherlandish
painters of the seventeenth century;
London, Phaidon, 1970- v. plates.
[15/-/- (v. 1)] 759.9482 76-105963

ND636 .B4315 MRR Alc.

Mander, Carel van, Dutch and Flemish
painters: New York, McFarlane,
Warde, McFarlane, 1936. lxix, 560 p.
759.9492 36-25229
ND625 .M24 MRR Alc.

PAINTERS, FLEMISH--DICTIONARIES.
Wilenski, Reginald Howard, Flemish
painters, 1430-1830. London, Faber
and Faber [1960] 2 v. 759.9493 60-
51134
ND672 .W5 1960a MRR Alc.

PAINTERS, FRENCH.
Schurr, Gérald. 1820 [i.e. Dix-huit
cent vingt]-1920 [i.e. dix-neuf cent
vingt], les petits maîtres de la
peinture; [Paris, Editions de la
Gazette, c1969] 159 p. [120.00]
77-466202
ND547 .S473 MRR Alc.

PAINTERS, ITALIAN.
Enciclopedia della pittura italiana
[Milano] Garzanti [1950] 2 v.
759.5 51-17831
ND622 .E5 MRR Alc.

Schmeckebier, Laurence Eli, A
handbook of Italian renaissance
painting. New York, G. P. Putnam's
sons [c1938] xi, 362 p. 759.5 38-
27574
ND615 .S38 MRR Alc.

PAINTERS, SPANISH--BIOGRAPHY--
DICTIONARIES.
Pintores españoles contemporáneos;
Madrid, Estiarte [1972] 250 p.
759.6 73-314037
ND808 .P48 MRR Biog.

PAINTERS, VICTORIAN--BIOGRAPHY--
DICTIONARIES.
Wood, Christopher. Dictionary of
Victorian painters; [Woodbridge]
Antique Collectors' Club, 1971. v-
xvi, 435 p. [£8.00] 759.2 72-
188506
ND35 .W6 MRR Biog.

PAINTERS' MATERIALS
see Artists' materials

PAINTING.
see also Color

PAINTING--DICTIONARIES.
Barron, John N. The language of
painting; Cleveland, World Pub. Co.
[1967] 207 p. 750./3 67-21388
ND30 .B32 MRR Alc.

Encyclopedia of painting; New York,
Crown Publishers, 1955. 511 p.
750.3 55-12456
ND30 .E5 MRR Alc.

Wolf, Martin L. Dictionary of
painting. New York, Philosophical
Library [1958] viii, 335 p. 750.3
58-1338
ND30 .W6 MRR Alc.

PAINTING--DICTIONARIES--GERMAN.
Fernau, Joachim. The Praeger
encyclopedia of old masters. New
York, F. A. Praeger [1959] 334 p.
759.003 59-7456
ND30 .F413 MRR Alc.

Kindlers Malerei Lexikon. Zürich,
Kindler Verlag [1964- v. 759.3
68-80855
ND35 .K5 MRR Alc.

PAINTING--EARLY WORKS TO 1800.
Philostratus, Flavius. Philostratus,
Imagines: London, W. Heinemann,
ltd.; New York, G. P. Putnam's sons,
1931. xxxii, 429, [1] p. 888.9
183.1 32-3145
PA3612 .P38 1931 MRR Alc.

PAINTING--HISTORY.
Les Peintres célèbres. [2. éd.
Paris] L. Mazenod [1953-64] 3 v.
54-25077
ND50 .P4 MRR Alc.

Tudor history of painting in 1000
color reproductions. New York, Tudor
Pub. Co. [1961] 325, [8] p. 759
61-17425
ND1170 .H513 MRR Alc.

PAINTING--HISTORY--20TH CENTURY.
Berckelaers, Ferdinand Louis,
Dictionnaire de la peinture
abstraite, Paris, F. Hazan [1957]
305 p. a 57-7206
ND35 .B4 MRR Alc.

PAINTING--TECHNIQUE.
Mayer, Ralph, The artist's handbook
of materials and techniques. 3d ed.,
rev. and expanded. New York, Viking
Press [1970] xv, 750 p. [$12.50]
751.4 75-18183
ND1500 .M3 1970 MRR Alc.

Watson, Ernest William, Color and
method in painting as seen in the
work of 12 American painters, New
York, Watson-Guptill publications,
inc., 1942. 6 p. l., 141 p. incl.
illus., col. plates, ports. 750 42-
25525
ND1260 .W3 MRR Alc.

PAINTING--TECHNIQUE--DICTIONARIES.
Mayer, Ralph, A dictionary of art
terms and techniques. New York,
Crowell [1969] 447 p. [8.95] 703
69-15414
N33 .M36 MRR Alc.

Taubes, Frederic, The painter's
dictionary of materials and methods.
New York, Watson-Guptill Publications
[1971] 253 p. [$6.95] 703 71-
155142
ND1505 .T38 MRR Alc.

PAINTING--CHINA--HISTORY.
Sirén, Osvald, Chinese painting:
New York, Ronald Press [1956- v.
759.951 a 57-1105
ND1040 .S49 MRR Alc.

PAINTING--EUROPE--HISTORY.
Novotny, Fritz, Painting and
sculpture in Europe, 1780 to 1880.
2nd ed. Harmondsworth, Penguin,
1970. xxii, 290, 192 p., leaf.
[£5.75] 759.94 74-149800
N6757 .N6813 1970 MRR Alc.

Smith, Solomon Charles Kaines. An
outline history of painting in Europe
to the end of the XIX century,
London, Boston, The Medici society
[1928] xvi, 274 p., 1 l. 29-4896
ND50 .S6 MRR Alc.

PAINTING--FRANCE--HISTORY.
Wilenski, Reginald Howard, Modern
French painters. [3d ed.] [London]
Faber & Faber [1954] xxxv, 424 p.
759.4 54-38502
ND547 .W5 1954 MRR Alc.

PAINTING--GREAT BRITAIN.
Bubbard, Eric Hesketh, A hundred
years of British painting, 1851-1951.
London, New York, Longmans, Green
[1951] xii, 325 p. 750.942 51-
14717
ND467 .H85 MRR Alc.

PAINTING--ITALY--HISTORY.
Schmeckebier, Laurence Eli, A
handbook of Italian renaissance
painting, New York, G. P. Putnam's
sons [c1938] xi, 362 p. 759.5 38-
27574
ND615 .S38 MRR Alc.

PAINTING, AMERICAN.
Hunter, Sam, American art of the
20th century: New York, H. N. Abrams
[1973] 583 p. 709./73 73-10211
N6512 .H78 1973 MRR Alc.

Watson, Ernest William, Color and
method in painting as seen in the
work of 12 American painters, New
York, Watson-Guptill publications,
inc., 1942. 6 p. l., 141 p. incl.
illus., col. plates, ports. 750 42-
25525
ND1260 .W3 MRR Alc.

PAINTING, DECORATIVE
see Decoration and ornament

PAINTING, DUTCH--HISTORY.
Osten, Gert von der. Painting and
sculpture in Germany and the
Netherlands, 1500 to 1600
Harmondsworth, Penguin, 1969. xxii,
403 p., 193 plates. [7/7/-] 759.3
79-514834
N6925 .O813 1969 MRR Alc.

PAINTING, ENGLISH--HISTORY--
BIBLIOGRAPHY.
Fredeman, William Evan, Pre-
Raphaelitism; a bibliocritical study
Cambridge, Harvard University Press,
1965. xix, 327 p. 016.70942 64-
21242
Z5948.P9 F7 MRR Alc.

PAINTING, EUROPEAN--HISTORY.
Hamilton, George Heard. Painting and
sculpture in Europe, 1880-1940.
Baltimore, Penguin Books [1967]
xxiv, 443 p. 709.4 67-31947
ND457 .H3 MRR Alc.

PAINTING, FLEMISH--HISTORY.
Wilenski, Reginald Howard, Flemish
painters, 1430-1830. London, Faber
and Faber [1960] 2 v. 759.9493 60-
51134
ND672 .W5 1960a MRR Alc.

PAINTING, FRENCH--HISTORY.
Schurr, Gérald. 1820 [i.e. Dix-huit
cent vingt]-1920 [i.e. dix-neuf cent
vingt], les petits maîtres de la
peinture; [Paris, Editions de la
Gazette, c1969] 159 p. [120.00]
77-466202
ND547 .S473 MRR Alc.

PAINTING, GERMAN--HISTORY.
Osten, Gert von der. Painting and
sculpture in Germany and the
Netherlands, 1500 to 1600
Harmondsworth, Penguin, 1969. xxii,
403 p., 193 plates. [7/7/-] 759.3
79-514834
N6925 .O813 1969 MRR Alc.

PAINTING, INDUSTRIAL.
see also House painting

PAINTING, MODERN--17TH-18TH CENTURIES--
NETHERLANDS.
Bernt, Walther. The Netherlandish
painters of the seventeenth century;
London, Phaidon, 1970- v. plates.
[15/-/- (v. 1)] 759.9492 76-105963

ND636 .B4315 MRR Alc.

PAINTING, MODERN--19TH CENTURY.
Gowans, Alan. The restless art;
[1st ed.] Philadelphia, Lippincott
[1966] 414 p. 759.05 66-10346
ND190 .G6 MRR Alc.

PAINTING, MODERN--19TH CENTURY--FRANCE.
Schurr, Gérald. 1820 [i.e. Dix-huit
cent vingt]-1920 [i.e. dix-neuf cent
vingt], les petits maîtres de la
peinture; [Paris, Editions de la
Gazette, c1969] 159 p. [120.00]
77-466202
ND547 .S473 MRR Alc.

PAINTING, MODERN--20TH CENTURY.
Gowans, Alan. The restless art;
[1st ed.] Philadelphia, Lippincott
[1966] 414 p. 759.05 66-10346
ND190 .G6 MRR Alc.

Histoire de l'art contemporain;
Authorized reprint ed. in one volume.
New York, Arno Press [1968] 536 p.
68-9229
ND195 .H5 1968 MRR Alc.

PAINTING, MODERN--20TH CENTURY--
DICTIONARIES.
Dictionary of modern painting. 3d
ed., rev. and enl.] New York, Tudor
Pub. Co. [1964] 416 p. 759.05 65-
1420
HD30 .D515 1964 MRR Alc.

PAINTING, MODERN--20TH CENTURY--FRANCE.
Schurr, Gérald. 1820 [i.e. Dix-huit
cent vingt]-1920 [i.e. dix-neuf cent
vingt], les petits maîtres de la
peinture; [Paris, Editions de la
Gazette, c1969] 159 p. [120.00]
77-466202
ND547 .S473 MRR Alc.

PAINTING, MODERN--20TH CENTURY--SPAIN.
Pintores españoles contemporáneos;
Madrid, Estiarte [1972] 250 p.
759.6 73-314037
ND808 .P48 MRR Biog.

PAINTING, MODERN--20TH CENTURY--UNITED STATES.
Illinois. University at Urbana-Champaign. College of Fine and Applied Arts. Contemporary American painting and sculpture. Urbana. 759.13 74-642877
ND212.A1 I4 MRR Alc Latest edition

Watson, Ernest William. Color and method in painting as seen in the work of 12 American painters, New York, Watson-Guptill publications, inc., 1942. 6 p. l., 141 p. incl. illus., col. plates, ports. 750 42-25525
ND1260 .W3 MRR Alc.

PAINTING, RENAISSANCE.
Schmeckebier, Laurence Eli, A handbook of Italian renaissance painting, New York, G. P. Putnam's sons [c1938] xi, 362 p. 759.5 38-27574
ND615 .S38 MRR Alc.

PAINTINGS.
[Bilzer, Bert] ed. Paintings of the world's great galleries; London, Thames and Hudson [1961, c1960] 584 p. 759.074 62-6722
ND1170 .B513 1961a MRR Alc.

Kindlers Malerei Lexikon. Zürich, Kindler Verlag [1964- v. 759.3 68-80855
ND35 .K5 MRR Alc.

Shorewood Publishers, inc., New York. The Shorewood art reference guide. Rev. and enl. 3d ed. New York, Shorewood Reproductions [1970] xviii, 600 p. 759 70-110685
N5305 .S5 1970 MRR Alc.

Tudor history of painting in 1000 color reproductions. New York, Tudor Pub. Co. [1961] 325, [8] p. 759 61-17425
ND1170 .H513 MRR Alc.

PAINTINGS--COLOR REPRODUCTIONS
see Color prints

PAINTINGS--INDEXES.
Bartran, Margaret. A guide to color reproductions. 2d ed. Metuchen, N.J., Scarecrow Press, 1971. 625 p. 338.4/7/76902573 74-142231
NE1850 .B3 1971 MRR Ref Desk.

Braider, Donald, Putnam's guide to the art centers of Europe. New York, Putnam [1965] ix, 542 p. 708 64-18003
N6750 .B66 MRR Alc.

Clapp, Jane. Art reproductions. New York, Scarecrow Press, 1961. 350 p. 708.1 61-8714
N4000 .C5 MRR Ref Desk.

Hewlett-Woodmere Public Library. Index to art reproductions in books. Metuchen, N.J., Scarecrow Press, 1974. xii, 178 p. 709 74-1286
N7525 .H48 1974 MRR Alc.

Monro, Isabel Stevenson. Index to reproductions of American paintings; New York, H. W. Wilson Co., 1948. 731 p. 759.13 48-9663
ND205 .M57 MRR Ref Desk.

Monro, Isabel Stevenson. Index to reproductions of European paintings; New York, Wilson, 1956. 668 p. 016.759 55-6803
ND45 .M6 M44 Ref Desk.

PAINTINGS--PRICES.
Art prices current. v. [1]-8, 1907/08-1915/16; new ser., v. 1-1921/22- 704.938 09-23300
N8670 .A7 MRR Alc Partial set

International auction records. v. [1]- 1867- [London, etc. Editions E. M.-Publisol] 700/.29 78-2167
N8640 .I5 MRR Alc Full set

Reitlinger, Gerald, The economics of taste. London, Barrie and Rockliff [1961-70] 3 v. [50/- (v. 1) varies] 069/.51 62-4300
N8675 .R44 MRR Alc.

Schurr, Gérald. 1820 [i.e. Dix-huit cent vingt]-1920 [i.e. dix-neuf cent vingt], les petits maîtres de la peinture; [Paris, Editions de la Gazette, c1969] 159 p. [120.00] 77-466202
ND547 .S473 MRR Alc.

World collectors annuary. v. 1-1946/49- Delft, Brouwer. 759.085 52-494
ND47 .W6 MRR Alc Full set

PAINTINGS--NEW YORK (CITY)
Osman, Randolph E., Art centers of the world; New York Cleveland, World Pub. Co. [1868] 192 p. [$7.95] 708.1471 68-26017
N600 .08 MRR Alc.

PAINTINGS, ABSTRACT
see Art, Abstract

PAINTINGS, AMERICAN.
Monro, Isabel Stevenson. Index to reproductions of American paintings; New York, H. W. Wilson Co., 1948. 731 p. 759.13 48-9663
ND205 .M57 MRR Ref Desk.

Taft, Robert, Artists and illustrators of the Old West, 1850-1900. New York, Scribner, 1953. xvii, 400 p. 709.78 53-7577
N6510 .T27 MRR Alc.

PAINTINGS, AMERICAN--EXHIBITIONS.
Illinois. University at Urbana-Champaign. College of Fine and Applied Arts. Contemporary American painting and sculpture. Urbana. 759.13 74-642877
ND212.A1 I4 MRR Alc Latest edition

PAINTINGS, CHINESE.
Siren, Osvald, Chinese painting: New York, Ronald Press [1956- v. 759.951 a 57-1105
ND1040 .S49 MRR Alc.

PAINTINGS, DUTCH--CATALOGS.
Bernt, Walther. The Netherlandish painters of the seventeenth century; London, Phaidon, 1970- v. plates. [15/-/- (v. 1)] 759.9492 76-105963
ND636 .B4315 MRR Alc.

PAINTINGS, EUROPEAN.
Monro, Isabel Stevenson. Index to reproductions of European paintings; New York, Wilson, 1956. 668 p. 016.759 55-6803
ND45 .M6 M44 Ref Desk.

PAINTINGS, FLEMISH.
Wilenski, Reginald Howard, Flemish painters, 1430-1830. London, Faber and Faber [1960] 2 v. 759.9493 60-51134
ND672 .W5 1960a MRR Alc.

PAINTINGS, FLEMISH--CATALOGS.
Bernt, Walther. The Netherlandish painters of the seventeenth century; London, Phaidon, 1970- v. plates. [15/-/- (v. 1)] 759.9492 76-105963
ND636 .B4315 MRR Alc.

PAINTINGS, GRECO-ROMAN.
Philostratus, Flavius. Philostratus, Imagines; London, W. Heinemann, ltd.; New York, G. P. Putnam's sons, 1931. xxxii, 429, [1] p. 888.9 1B3.1 32-3145
PA3612 .P38 1931 MRR Alc.

PAKISTAN.
Nyrop, Richard F. Area handbook for Pakistan. Washington; For sale by the Supt. of Docs., U.S. Govt. Print. Off.] 1971. xvi, 691 p. [$4.25] 309.1/549 79-608677
DS377 .N97 MRR Alc.

Spate, Oskar Hermann Khristian. India and Pakistan: 3rd ed. revised and completely reset. London, Methuen, 1967. xxxiii, 877 p. [£6/6/-] 915.4 68-86324
DS407 .S67 1967 MRR Alc.

PAKISTAN--BIBLIOGRAPHY.
Moid, A. A guide to periodical publications and newspapers of Pakistan, Karachi, Pakistan Bibliographical Working Group [1953] iv, 60 p. 015.547* 54-19364
Z3193 .M6 MRR Alc.

PAKISTAN--BIOGRAPHY.
Biographical encyclopedia of Pakistan. 1955- [Lahore, Published by Biographical Research Institute, Pakistan for International Publishers (Pakistan)] sa 63-1749
DS381 .B5 MRR Biog Latest edition

Pakistan trade directory and who's who. 1949/50- Karachi, Barque. 650.58 49-54943
HF5239.P28 P3 MRR Alc Latest edition

The West Pakistan civil list. Karachi, West Pakistan Govt. Press. sa 62-1249
JQ559.W4 W37 MRR Alc Latest edition

PAKISTAN--COMMERCE--DIRECTORIES.
Ansari's trade & industrial directory of Pakistan. 1st- 1950/51- Karachi, Ansari Pub. House. sa 64-9
HC440.5 .A8 MRR Alc Latest edition

Pakistan trade directory and who's who. 1949/50- Karachi, Barque. 650.58 49-54943
HF5239.P28 P3 MRR Alc Latest edition

Regional trade directory: 1968-382/.025/5 sa 68-5997
HF3883 .R4 MRR Alc Latest edition

PAKISTAN--DESCRIPTION AND TRAVEL--GUIDE-BOOKS.
Fodor's Islamic Asia: Iran, Afghanistan, Pakistan. 1973- New York, D. McKay. [$12.95] 915 74-641031
DS254 .F642 MRR Alc Latest edition

PAKISTAN--GAZETTEERS.
United States. Office of Geography. Pakistan: official standard names approved by the United States Board on Geographic names. Washington, 1962. v, 883 p. 62-64576
DS376.8 .U6 MRR Alc.

PAKISTAN--HISTORY--BIBLIOGRAPHY.
Case, Margaret H. South Asian history, 1750-1950; Princeton, N.J., Princeton University Press, 1968. xiii, 561 p. 016.954 67-21019
Z3185 .C3 MRR Alc.

PAKISTAN--IMPRINTS.
Siddiqui, Akhtar H. A guide to reference books published in Pakistan Karachi, Pakistan Reference Publications, 1966. 41 p. 015.549 sa 66-7465
Z1035.9 .S5 MRR Alc.

United States. Library of Congress. American Libraries Book Procurement Center, Karachi. Accessions list; Pakistan. v. 1- July/Dec. 1962-Karachi, Dacca, American Libraries Book Procurement Centers. 015/.549 63-24162
Z663.767.P2 A25 MRR Alc MRR Alc Full set

United States. Library of Congress. American Libraries Book Procurement Center, Karachi. Accessions list, Pakistan. Annual supplement: cumulative list of serials. 1970-Karachi, Dacca, American Libraries Book Procurement Centers. 015/.549 74-643590
Z3191 .U53 suppl MRR Alc Full set

PAKISTAN--INDUSTRIES--DIRECTORIES.
Ansari's trade & industrial directory of Pakistan. 1st- 1950/51- Karachi, Ansari Pub. House. sa 64-9
HC440.5 .A8 MRR Alc Latest edition

PAKISTAN--OFFICIALS AND EMPLOYEES.
The West Pakistan civil list. Karachi, West Pakistan Govt. Press. sa 62-1249
JQ559.W4 W37 MRR Alc Latest edition

PAKISTAN--POLITICS AND GOVERNMENT.
Singhal, Damodar P. Pakistan Englewood Cliffs, N.J., Prentice-Hall [1972] ix, 214 p. [$6.95] 954.9/04 72-4625
DS384 .S49 MRR Alc.

PAKISTAN--REGISTERS.
The West Pakistan civil list. Karachi, West Pakistan Govt. Press. sa 62-1249
JQ559.W4 W37 MRR Alc Latest edition

PAKISTAN--STATISTICS.
Pakistan. Central Statistical Office. 20 years of Pakistan in statistics, 1947-1967. Karachi, Manager of Publications [1968] xiv, 333 p. [8.50] 315.49 sa 68-11815
HA1730.5 .A52 MRR Alc.

PAKISTAN NEWSPAPERS--BIBLIOGRAPHY.
Moid, A. A guide to periodical publications and newspapers of Pakistan, Karachi, Pakistan Bibliographical Working Group [1953] iv, 60 p. 015.547* 54-19364
Z3193 .M6 MRR Alc.

PAKISTAN PERIODICALS--BIBLIOGRAPHY.
Moid, A. A guide to periodical publications and newspapers of Pakistan, Karachi, Pakistan Bibliographical Working Group [1953] iv, 60 p. 015.547* 54-19364
Z3193 .M6 MRR Alc.

PALEOANTHROPOLOGY
see Man, Prehistoric

PALEOETHNOGRAPHY
see Archaeology

PALEOGRAPHY.
see also Alphabet

PALEOGRAPHY, ENGLISH.
Hall, Hubert, Studies in English official historical documents, Cambridge, University press, 1908. xv, [1] p., 1 l., 404 p. 09-4071
CD65 .H4 MRR Alc.

PALEOGRAPHY, ITALIAN.
Cappelli, Adriano. Lexicon abbreviaturarum. 6. ed. Milano, Hoepli, 1967. lxxiii, 531 p. 67-122585
Z111 .C24 1967 MRR Alc.

PALEOGRAPHY, LATIN.
Cappelli, Adriano. Lexicon
abbreviaturarum. 6. ed. Milano,
Hoepli, 1967. lxxiii, 531 p.   67-
122585
Z111 .C24 1967 MRR Alc.

PALEONTOLOGY.
Kummel, Bernhard, History of the
earth. San Francisco, W. H. Freeman
[1961] 610 p.   551.7 61-6783
QE501 .K79 MRR Alc.

PALEONTOLOGY--NORTH AMERICA--
BIBLIOGRAPHY.
United States. Geological Survey.
Bibliography of North American
geology. 1785/1918-1950/59.
Washington, U.S. Govt. Print. Off.
016.557   gs 24-38
Z6034.U49 U45 Sci RR Sci RR
Partial set / MRR Alc Partial set

United States. Geological Survey.
Bibliography of North American
geology. 1806- Washington, U.S.
Govt. Print. Off. 016.557 gs 08-427
QE75 .B9 MRR Alc Partial set / Sci
RR Partial set

PALESTINE--ANTIQUITIES.
Young, Robert, Analytical
concordance to the Bible 22d
American ed., rev. New York, Funk &
Wagnalls [1955] ix, 1090, 93, 23, 51
p.   220.2 55-5338
BS425 .Y7 1955 MRR Alc.

PALESTINE--ANTIQUITIES--DICTIONARIES.
Negev, Avraham. Archaeological
encyclopedia of the Holy Land. New
York, Putnam [1972] 354 p. [$15.95]
913.33/03/03 71-190101
DS111.A2 N38 MRR Alc.

PALESTINE--COMMERCE--DIRECTORIES.
The Israel directory, Tel-Aviv,
Register of Commerce and Industry in
Israel [etc.] 46-28585
Began publication with issue for
1935.
HF5268.P3 I8 MRR Alc Latest
edition

PALESTINE--DESCRIPTION AND TRAVEL--
GUIDE-BOOKS.
Comay, Joan. Israel: an uncommon
guide. New York, Random House
[c1969] xvii, 333 p. [6.95]
915.694/03/5 69-16461
DS103 .C593 MRR Alc.

PALESTINE--INDUSTRIES--DIRECTORIES.
The Israel directory, Tel-Aviv,
Register of Commerce and Industry in
Israel [etc.] 46-28585
Began publication with issue for
1935.
HF5268.P3 I8 MRR Alc Latest
edition

PALMER, THEODORE SHERMAN, 1868-1955--
BIBLIOGRAPHY.
United States. Library of Congress.
Manuscript Division. Theodore
Sherman Palmer; a register of his
papers in the Library of Congress.
Washington, 1958. 8 l.   012 58-
60080
Z663.34 .P3 MRR Alc.

PAMPHLETS--BIBLIOGRAPHY.
Black, R. D. Collison. A catalogue
of pamphlets on economic subjects
published between 1750 and 1900 and
now housed in Irish libraries. New
York, A. M. Kelley, 1969. ix, 632 p.
016.33 79-81989
Z7164.E2 B6 MRR Alc.

Canadiana. Jan. 15, 1951- [Ottawa]
015.71 53-35723
Z1365 .C23 MRR Alc Full set

Lindsay, Robert O. French political
pamphlets, 1547-1648; Madison,
University of Wisconsin Press, 1969.
xii, 510 p.   016.944/.03 78-84953
Z2177.5 .L54 MRR Alc.

United States. Library of Congress.
A descriptive list of the principal
pamphlet collections in the Library
of Congress in 1934. Washington,
D.C. 1934. 1 p. l., 6, 4 numb. l., 1
l.   mrr01-66
Z733.U63 P2 MRR Ref Desk.

Vertical file index. v. [1]-
1932/34- New York, H. W. Wilson.
016   45-40505
Z1231.P2 V48 MRR Alc Full set

PAN-AFRICANISM.
Legum, Colin. Pan-Africanism; New
York, Praeger [1962] 296 p.   960
62-13489
DT30 .L39 1962a MRR Alc.

PAN AMERICAN SOCIETIES--DIRECTORIES.
Pan American associations in the
United States; [1st]- ed.; 1955-
Washington, pa 56-7165
F1401 .F263 MRR Alc Latest edition

PANAMA--BIOGRAPHY.
Quién es quién en Venezuela,
Panamá, Ecuador, Columbia. Jun. 30,
1952- [Bogotá] O. Perry. 920.086
54-19781
F2205 .Q54 MRR Biog Latest edition

PANAMA--BIOGRAPHY--DICTIONARIES.
Hedrick, Basil Calvin, Historical
dictionary of Panama, Metuchen,
N.J., Scarecrow Press, 1970. 105 p.
918.62/03/03 70-19393
F1562 .H43 MRR Alc.

Mejía Robledo, Alfonso, Quién es
quién en Panamá, 1. ed.
Medellín, Colombia, Editorial
Bedout, 1949. 320 p.   920.086 51-
16665
F1562.7 .M4 MRR Biog.

PANAMA--DICTIONARIES AND ENCYCLOPEDIAS.
Hedrick, Basil Calvin, Historical
dictionary of Panama, Metuchen,
N.J., Scarecrow Press, 1970. 105 p.
918.62/03/03 70-19393
F1562 .H43 MRR Alc.

PANAMA--GAZETTEERS.
United States. Geographic Names
Division. Panama and the Canal Zone;
Washington, 1969. v, 323 p.
918.62/003 75-603156
F1562 .U5 MRR Alc.

PANAMA--HISTORY.
Howarth, David Armine, Panama; [1st
ed.] New York, McGraw-Hill [1966]
297 p.   986.2 65-28592
F1566 .H6 1966 MRR Alc.

PANAMA CANAL--GAZETTEERS.
United States. Geographic Names
Division. Panama and the Canal Zone;
Washington, 1969. v, 323 p.
918.62/003 75-603156
F1562 .U5 MRR Alc.

PANTOMIMES WITH MUSIC.
see also Ballets

PAPACY.
see also Catholic Church

PAPACY--HISTORY.
Burn-Murdoch, Hector, The
development of the papacy. London,
Faber and Faber [1954] 432 p.   282
54-1738
BX955 .B88 1954 MRR Alc.

Kühner, Hans. Encyclopedia of the
Papacy. New York, Philosophical
Library [1958] 248 p.   262.13 58-
4521
BX955 .K853 MRR Alc.

PAPAL DOCUMENTS--BIBLIOGRAPHY.
Carlen, Mary Claudia, Dictionary of
papal pronouncements, New York, P.
J. Kenedy [1958] 216 p.   262.82 58-
12095
BX873.7 .C3 MRR Alc.

PAPAL DOCUMENTS--INDEXES.
Carlen, Mary Claudia, Dictionary of
papal pronouncements, New York, P.
J. Kenedy [1958] 216 p.   262.82 58-
12095
BX873.7 .C3 MRR Alc.

PAPER.
Horne (Robert) and Company, ltd.,
London. Paper for books; [Rev. and
enl. ed.] London, 1961. 648 p.
655.53 61-59595
Z247 .H6 1961 MRR Alc.

PAPER--DICTIONARIES.
American Paper and Pulp Association.
The dictionary of paper, 3d ed. New
York, 1965. xii, 500 p.   676.03 65-
2940
TS1085 .A6 1965 MRR Alc.

PAPER--YEARBOOKS.
The Paper year book. [1st]- ed.;
1943- New York [etc.] Harcourt Brace
Janovich [etc.] 43-8343
TS1080 .P285 Sci RR Latest edition
/ MRR Alc Latest edition

PAPER MAKING AND TRADE--DICTIONARIES.
American Paper and Pulp Association.
The dictionary of paper, 3d ed. New
York, 1965. xii, 500 p.   676.03 65-
2940
TS1085 .A6 1965 MRR Alc.

PAPER MAKING AND TRADE--DICTIONARIES--
POLYGLOT.
Labarre, E. J. Dictionary and
encyclopædia of paper and paper-
making, 2d ed., rev. and enl.
London, Oxford University Press,
1952. xxi, 488 p.   676.03 53-29414

TS1085 .L3 1952a MRR Alc.

PAPER MAKING AND TRADE--DIRECTORIES.
Lockwood's directory of the paper and
allied trades. [1st]- ed.; 1873/74-
New York, Lockwood Pub. Co. [etc.]
676.058 01-12840
TS1088 .L82 Sci RR Latest edition
/ MRR Alc Latest edition

The Paper makers' & merchants'
directory of all nations. London,
Admark Directories Limited London
[etc.] 57-24181
TS1088 .P5 Sci RR Latest edition /
MRR Alc Latest edition

Phillips, S. C. & Co., London.
Phillips' paper trade directory of
the world. London. 338.4/7/6762025
74-642473
TS1088 .P8 MRR Alc Latest edition
/ Sci RR Latest edition

Phillips paper trade directory. 1974-
London, Benn Bros. Ltd. [10.50]
338.4/7/6762025 74-647730
HD9820.3 .P47 MRR Alc Latest
edition / Sci RR Latest edition

Post's pulp & paper directory. San
Francisco [etc.] M. Freeman
Publications [etc.] 03-6150
TS1088 .P85 Sci RR Latest edition
/ MRR Alc Latest edition

PAPER MAKING AND TRADE--HISTORY.
Hunter, Dard, Papermaking; 2d ed.,
rev. and enl. New York, A. A. Knopf,
1947. xxiv, 611, xxxvii p.   676 47-
6507
TS1090 .H816 1947 MRR Alc.

United States. Library of Congress.
Papermaking: art and craft;
Washington, 1968. 96 p.   676/.2/09
68-60043
Z663.15 .P3 MRR Alc.

PAPER MAKING AND TRADE--EUROPE--
DIRECTORIES.
"Birkner." Adressbuch der Papier-
industrie Europeas. Directory of the
paper industry of Europe. Annuaire de
l'industrie du papier en Europe.
Hamburg [etc.] 676.058 46-40558
Publication began in 1905?
TS1088 .B5 MRR Alc Latest edition

PAPER MAKING AND TRADE--FRANCE--
DIRECTORIES.
Annuaire Desechaliers ... Paris. 42-
34851
"Fondé en 1895.
Z308 .A75 MRR Alc Latest edition

PAPER MAKING AND TRADE--GERMANY--
DIRECTORIES.
"Birkner." Adressbuch der Papier-
industrie Europeas. Directory of the
paper industry of Europe. Annuaire de
l'industrie du papier en Europe.
Hamburg [etc.] 676.058 46-40558
Publication began in 1905?
TS1088 .B5 MRR Alc Latest edition

PAPER MAKING AND TRADE--UNITED STATES.
American Paper and Pulp Association.
The statistics of paper. [1st]-
1947- New York. 338.47676 48-11302

HD9824 .A7 MRR Alc Latest edition

PAPER MAKING AND TRADE--UNITED STATES--
CREDIT GUIDES.
Paper & Allied Trades Mercantile
Agency, inc., New York. P. A. T.
credit reference. New York. 27-9871

HF5585.P2 P3 MRR Alc Latest
edition

PAPER MAKING AND TRADE--UNITED STATES--
DIRECTORIES.
Lockwood's directory of the paper and
allied trades. [1st]- ed.; 1873/74-
New York, Lockwood Pub. Co. [etc.]
676.058 01-12840
TS1088 .L82 Sci RR Latest edition
/ MRR Alc Latest edition

Post's pulp & paper directory. San
Francisco [etc.] M. Freeman
Publications [etc.] 03-6150
TS1088 .P85 Sci RR Latest edition
/ MRR Alc Latest edition

PAPER MAKING AND TRADE--UNITED STATES--
STATISTICS.
American Paper and Pulp Association.
The statistics of paper. [1st]-
1947- New York. 338.47676 48-11302

HD9824 .A7 MRR Alc Latest edition

PAPER MONEY.
Keller, Arnold. Paper money of the
world; New York, Royal Coin Co.,
c1956-   332.53 57-20712
HG353 .K413 MRR Alc.

Sten, George J. Banknotes of the
world, 1368-1966; Menlo Park,
Calif., Shirjieh Publishers [1967-
v.   769/.55 67-7759
HG353 .S68 MRR Alc.

PAPER MONEY--CATALOGS.
Hessler, Gene, The comprehensive
catalog of U.S. paper money.
Chicago, H. Regnery Co. [1974] xiv,
456 p. [$20.00] 769/.55973 73-
6461
HG591 .H47 MRR Ref Desk.

PAPER MONEY--CATALOGS. (Cont.)
Loeb, Walter M. Catalog of paper
money around the world. Port
Washington, N.Y., Universal Pub. Co.
of Port Washington, c1961. 75 p.
62-2723
HG353 .L6 MRR Alc.

Pick, Albert. Catalogue of European
paper money since 1900. 2d ed. New
York, Sterling Pub. Co. [1974] 336
p. 769/.5594 74-178196
HG353 .P5213 1974 MRR Alc.

Sten, George J. Encyclopedia of
world paper money; Port Washington,
N.Y., Universal Pub. Co., 1965. 152
p. 768.550216 65-6034
HG353 .S7 MRR Alc.

PAPER MONEY--AMERICA--CATALOGS.
Pick, Albert. Papermoney; catalogue
of the Americas. Munich, E.
Battenberg [1973] 335 p. 769/.5597
74-167938
HG353 .P54 MRR Alc.

PAPER MONEY--CANADA.
Standard catalogue of Canadian coins,
tokens, and paper money. Racine,
Wis. [etc.] Whitman Hobby Division
[etc.] 737.4971 60-473
CJ1861 .S8 MRR Alc Latest edition

PAPER MONEY--CONFEDERATE STATES OF
AMERICA.
Criswell, Grover C. Confederate and
Southern State currency; 1st rev.
ed. [Iola, Wis., Krause
Publications,] 1964. 291 p.
332.530875 64-7583
HG526 .C73 MRR Alc.

Criswell, Grover C. The official
guide to Confederate money & Civil
War tokens, tradesmen & patriotic,
[1st ed.] [New York] HC Publishers
[1971] 144 p. [$1.00] 737.3/0975
79-181839
HG526 .C74 MRR Alc.

Fuller, Claud E., Confederate
currency and stamps, 1861-1865;
[Nashville, Published by the
Parthenon Press under the auspices of
the Tennessee Division, United
Daughters of the Confederacy, c1949]
236 p. 332.53 50-449
HG526 .F8 MRR Alc.

Slabaugh, Arlie R. Confederate
States paper money; Centennial ed.
Racine, Wis., Whitman Pub. Co. [1961]
64 p. 332.530875 61-3618
HG526 .S55 MRR Alc.

PAPER MONEY--EUROPE.
Pick, Albert. Catalogue of European
paper money since 1900. 2d ed. New
York, Sterling Pub. Co. [1974] 336
p. 769/.5594 74-178196
HG353 .P5213 1974 MRR Alc.

PAPER MONEY--LATIN AMERICA.
Pick, Albert. Papermoney; catalogue
of the Americas. Munich, E.
Battenberg [1973] 335 p. 769/.5597
74-167938
HG353 .P54 MRR Alc.

PAPER MONEY--NORTH AMERICA.
Criswell, Grover C. North American
currency; Iola, Wis., Krause
Publications [1965] 910 p. 769.55
64-66240
HG591 .C7 MRR Alc.

Pick, Albert. Papermoney; catalogue
of the Americas. Munich, E.
Battenberg [1973] 335 p. 769/.5597
74-167938
HG353 .P54 MRR Alc.

PAPER MONEY--UNITED STATES.
Criswell, Grover C. North American
currency; Iola, Wis., Krause
Publications [1965] 910 p. 769.55
64-66240
HG591 .C7 MRR Alc.

Friedberg, Robert, Paper money of
the United States; 7th ed., New
York, Coin and Currency Institute
[1972] 327 p. 769/.55973 72-80202

HG591 .F7 1972 MRR Ref Desk.

Hessler, Gene, The comprehensive
catalog of U.S. paper money.
Chicago, H. Regnery Co. [1974] xiv,
456 p. [$20.00] 769/.55973 73-
6461
HG591 .H47 MRR Ref Desk.

Shafer, Neil. A guide book of modern
United States currency. 5th ed,
Racine, Wis., Western Pub. Co. [1971]
160 p. 769/.559/73 70-28630
HG591 .S5 1971 MRR Ref Desk.

United States. Laws, statutes, etc.
Laws of the United States concerning
money, banking, and loans, 1778-1909;
Washington, Govt. print. off., 1910.
v. 267 p., 1 l., 269-812, xxii p.
10-36032
HG481 .A2 1910 MRR Alc.

PAPER MONEY--UNITED STATES--HISTORY.
Newman, Eric P. The early paper
money of America, [Racine, Wis.,
Whitman Pub. Co., 1967] 360 p.
332.5/3/0973 67-16064
HG591 .N45 MRR Alc.

Rothert, Matt. A guide book of
United States fractional currency;
Racine, Wis., Whitman Pub. Co. [1963]
81 p. 769.5 63-23600
HG613 .R6 MRR Alc.

PAPER PRODUCTS.
Lockwood's directory of the paper and
allied trades. [1st]- ed.; 1873/74-
New York, Lockwood Pub. Co. [etc.]
676.058 01-12840
TS1088 .L82 Sci RR Latest edition
/ MRR Alc Latest edition

The Paper year book. [1st]- ed.;
1943- New York [etc.] Harcourt Brace
Janovich [etc.] 43-8343
TS1080 .P285 Sci RR Latest edition
/ MRR Alc Latest edition

PAPERBACK WHOLESALERS--NORTH AMERICA--
DIRECTORIES.
Bestsellers who's who in independent
distribution. 1969- [Philadelphia,
North American Pub. Co.]
658.8/09/655572 70-15922
PN4889 .B45 MRR Alc Latest edition

PAPERBACK WHOLESALERS--UNITED STATES--
DIRECTORIES.
Gillespie, John Thomas, Paperback
books for young people; Chicago,
American Library Association, 1972.
viii, 177 p. 070.5/73 72-2390
Z479 .G55 MRR Alc.

PAPERBOARD INDUSTRY--UNITED STATES--
STATISTICS.
Paperboard industry statistics.
1932/41- Chicago. 338.47676 42-
14250
HD9839 .P33U55 MRR Alc Latest
edition

PAPERWEIGHTS, AMERICAN.
Melvin, Jean Sutherland. American
glass paperweights and their makers;
[New York] T. Nelson [1967] 192 p.
748/.8 67-22425
NK5440.P3 M4 MRR Alc.

PAPUA NEW GUINEA--DICTIONARIES AND
ENCYCLOPEDIAS.
Encyclopaedia of Papua and New
Guinea. [Melbourne] Melbourne
University Press in association with
the University of Papua and New
Guinea [1972] 3 v. 919.5/003 72-
188173
DU740 .E5 MRR Alc.

PAPUA-NEW GUINEA (TER.)--GAZETTEERS.
United States. Office of Geography.
Southwest Pacific; Washington, U.S.
Govt. Print. off., 1956 [i.e. 1957]
v, 368 p. 919 57-61177
DU10 .U68 MRR Alc.

PARAGUAY.
Pendle, George. Paraguay: a
riverside nation. 3rd ed. London,
New York [etc.] issued under the
auspices of the Royal Institute of
International Affairs [by] Oxford
U.P., 1967. ix, 96 p. [21/-]
918.92/03 67-76622
F2668 .P4 1967 MRR Alc.

Raine, Philip. Paraguay. New
Brunswick, N.J., Scarecrow Press,
1956. 443 p. 989.2 56-8692
F2668 .R3 MRR Alc.

PARAGUAY--BIOGRAPHY--DICTIONARIES.
Kolinski, Charles J. Historical
dictionary of Paraguay, Metuchen,
N.J., Scarecrow Press, 1973. vi, 282
p. 989.2/003 72-13238
F2664 .K64 MRR Alc.

Quién es quién en el Paraguay?
[1.]- tomo; 1941- [Buenos Aires]
F. Monte Domecq. 920.089 48-34888
F2665 .Q5 MRR Biog Latest edition

PARAGUAY--COMMERCE--DIRECTORIES.
Quién es quién en el Paraguay?
[1.]- tomo; 1941- [Buenos Aires]
F. Monte Domecq. 920.089 48-34888
F2665 .Q5 MRR Biog Latest edition

PARAGUAY--DICTIONARIES AND
ENCYCLOPEDIAS.
Kolinski, Charles J. Historical
dictionary of Paraguay, Metuchen,
N.J., Scarecrow Press, 1973. vi, 282
p. 989.2/003 72-13238
F2664 .K64 MRR Alc.

PARAGUAY--GAZETTEERS.
United States. Office of Geography.
Paraguay; Washington, 1957. ii, 32
p. 75-10012
F2664 .U5 1957b MRR Alc.

PARAGUAY--REGISTERS.
Quién es quién en el Paraguay?
[1.]- tomo; 1941- [Buenos Aires]
F. Monte Domecq. 920.089 48-34888
F2665 .Q5 MRR Biog Latest edition

PARAPSYCHOLOGY
see Psychical research

PARAPSYCHOLOGY--ABSTRACTS.
White, Rhea A. Parapsychology:
sources of information. Metuchen,
N.J., Scarecrow Press, 1973. 302 p.
016.1338 73-4853
Z6878.P8 W47 MRR Alc.

PARASITES.
see also Bacteriology

see also Insects, Injurious and
beneficial

Noble, Elmer Ray, Parasitology; 3d
ed. Philadelphia, Lea & Febiger,
1971. vii, 617 p. 591.5/24 75-
123417
QL757 .N6 1971 MRR Alc.

PARASITISM.
Noble, Elmer Ray, Parasitology; 3d
ed. Philadelphia, Lea & Febiger,
1971. vii, 617 p. 591.5/24 75-
123417
QL757 .N6 1971 MRR Alc.

PARASITOLOGY.
see also Medical parasitology

see also Veterinary medicine

PARCELS-POST--BIBLIOGRAPHY.
United States. Library of Congress.
Division of bibliography. Select
list of references on parcels post.
Washington, Govt. print. off., 1911.
1 p. l., 39 p. 11-35007
Z663.28 .S4 MRR Alc.

PARENT AND CHILD.
see also Adolescence

see also Children--Management

PARENT-CHILD RELATIONS--ENCYCLOPEDIA--
POPULAR WORKS.
Levine, Milton Isra, The parents'
encyclopedia of infancy, childhood,
and adolescence New York, Crowell
[1973] 619 p. [$10.00] 649/.1/03
72-83769
RJ61 .L552 MRR Alc.

PARIS--BIOGRAPHY.
Who's who in France. 1.- éd.;
1953/54- Paris, J. Lafitte. 920.044
54-17054
DC705.A1 W46 MRR Biog Latest
edition

PARIS--COMMERCE--DIRECTORIES.
Annuaire officiel français des
adresses télégraphiques [Paris]
Ministère des postes et
télécommunications. 72-622826
HF3553 .A77 MRR Alc Latest edition

Bottin. Paris, Société Didot-
Bottin [etc.] 50-49011
HF53 .B6 MRR Alc Latest edition

PARIS--DESCRIPTION--GUIDE-BOOKS.
Clebert, Jean Paul. Les rues de
Paris; [Paris] Club des libraires de
France [1958] 2 v. 59-33340
DC761 .C63 MRR Alc.

Cronin, Vincent. The companion guide
to Paris 3rd revised ed. London,
Collins, 1973. 256, [16] p. [£2.50]
914.4/36/0483 74-154567
DC708 .C77 1973 MRR Alc.

Gault, Henri, Julliard guide to
Paris [London] Studio Vista [1965]
623 p. 68-129245
DC708 .G313 1965b MRR Alc.

Huisman, Georges Maurice, Les
monuments de Paris [Paris] Hachette
[1966] 423 p. 66-80289
NA1050 .H8 1966 MRR Alc.

Monmarché, Georges, Paris, Hauts-de-
Seine, Seine-St. Denis, Val-de-Marne.
Paris, Hachette, 1972. 1002 p.
[58.00F] 72-358167
DC708 .M83 1972 MRR Alc.

Nagel Publishers. Paris and its
environs. [3rd ed.] Geneva, Paris
[etc., 1968] xvi, 366 p. [$6.95]
914.43/6/0483 70-438871
DC708 .N82 1968 MRR Alc.

Paris et sa proche banlieue. [8.
ed.] Paris, Hachette, 1963. cxlvi,
700 p. 63-46823
DC708 .P27 1963 MRR Alc.

Paris in a week, [English ed.
Paris, Hachette, 1964. 120 p. 64-
47374
DC708 .P2813 1964 MRR Alc.

Rossiter, Stuart. Paris, 3d ed.
revised. London, E. Benn; Chicago,
Rand McNally, 1968. lii, 236 p.
[32/6] 914.43/6/0483 78-353324
DC708 .R7 1968 MRR Alc.

PARIS--DESCRIPTION--TOURS.
Gibbons annual index of daily sight-
seeing tours: Rome, Paris, Florence,
London. [Los Angeles] 914 72-80819

    D909 .G5 MRR Alc Latest edition

PARIS--DICTIONARIES AND ENCYCLOPEDIAS.
Dictionnaire de Paris. Paris,
Larousse [1964] 591 p. 65-86700
DC704 .D5 MRR Alc.

PARIS--DIRECTORIES.
Bottin. Bottin mondain; Paris,
Annuaire du commerce Didot-Bottin
[etc.] 50-30663
    DC704 .A5 MRR Alc Latest edition

PARIS--HISTORIC HOUSES, ETC.
Dictionnaire de Paris. Paris,
Larousse [1964] 591 p. 65-86700
DC704 .D5 MRR Alc.

PARIS--HISTORY--COMMUNE, 1871--
DICTIONARIES.
Noel, Bernard, Dictionnaire de la
Commune. Paris, F. Hazan [1971]
365, [2] p. [78.00F] 71-595371
DC317 .N6 MRR Alc.

PARIS--LIBRARIES--DIRECTORIES.
Paris. Bibliothèque nationale.
Répertoire des bibliothèques et
organismes de documentation. Paris,
1971. 733 p. 020/.25/44 76-501813

    Z797 .A1P35 1971 MRR Alc.

PARIS--MAPS.
Hachette, firm, publishers, Paris.
Plan de Paris et de sa proche
banlieue, [2. ed., rev. et augm.
Paris, 1954] 95 p. map55-143
G1844.P3 H2 1954 MRR Alc Atlas.

PARIS--SOCIAL REGISTERS.
Bottin. Bottin mondain; Paris,
Annuaire du commerce Didot-Bottin
[etc.] 50-30663
    DC704 .A5 MRR Alc Latest edition

PARIS--STREETS.
Clébert, Jean Paul. Les rues de
Paris; [Paris] Club des libraires de
France [1958] 2 v. 59-33340
DC761 .C63 MRR Alc.

PARIS--SUBURBS AND ENVIRONS.
Ile de France, environs de Paris.
Paris, Hachette, 1858. lxxii, 758 p.
58-48587
DC768 .E52 MRR Alc.

PARIS, TREATY OF, 1783.
Morris, Richard Brandon, The
peacemakers; [1st ed.] New York,
Harper & Row [1965] xviii, 572 p.
973.317 65-20435
E249 .M68 MRR Alc.

PARKS.
see also National parks and reserves

The World wildlife guide. London
[200 Buckingham Palace Rd, S.W.1],
Threshold Books Ltd, 1971. 416 p.
[£3.50] 639/.95 72-185519
SB481 .W63 1971 MRR Alc.

PARKS--UNITED STATES.
Tilden, Freeman, The State parks,
[1st ed.] New York, Knopf, 1962.
496, xi p. 817.3 62-17547
E160 .T53 MRR Alc.

PARKS--UNITED STATES--DIRECTORIES.
Sloane, Howard N. The Goodyear guide
to State parks, New York, Crown
Publishers [1967- v.
352/.7/0974 66-26199
SK601 .S6 MRR Alc.

PARLIAMENTARY PRACTICE.
Demeter, George, Demeter's manual of
parliamentary law and procedure;
Blue book ed. rev., expanded and
updated. Boston, Little, Brown
[1969] viii, 374 p. [3.95] 328.1
69-15061
JF515 .D4 1969 MRR Alc.

Keesey, Ray E. Modern parliamentary
procedure Boston, Houghton Mifflin,
1974. xv, 176 p. 060.4/2 74-6250

    JF515 .K385 1974b MRR Alc.

McMonagle, James A. The membership
manual. [1st ed.] New York, Vantage
Press [1970] 289 p. [$4.50] 328.1
76-19420
JF515 .M22 MRR Alc.

Robert, Sarah Corbin. Robert's rules
of order, newly revised; a new and
enl. ed. [Glenview, Ill.] Scott,
Foresman [1970] xlii, 594 p. [5.95]
328.1 71-106451
JF515 .R692 MRR Ref Desk.

Whitney, Byrl Albert, Parliamentary
procedure; Washington, R. B. Luce
[1962] 269 p. 328.1 62-18963
JF515 .W53 MRR Alc.

PARLIAMENTARY PRACTICE--DICTIONARIES.
Abraham, Louis Arnold. A
parliamentary dictionary, 2d ed.
London, Butterworths, 1964. viii,
241 p. 65-1879
JN594 .A7 1964 MRR Alc.

PARLIAMENTARY PRACTICE--UNITED STATES.
Cannon, Clarence, Cannon's
Precedents of the House of
representatives of the United States
Washington, Govt. print. off., 1935-
41. 6 v. 328.735 41-13680
JK1438 .H62 vol. 6-11 MRR Alc.

Sturgis, Alice Fleenor. Sturgis
standard code of parliamentary
procedure, 2d ed. New York, McGraw-
Hill [1966] xxix, 283 p. 328.1 65-
24530
JF515 .S88 1966 MRR Alc.

PARLIAMENTS
see Legislative bodies

PARNELL, CHARLES STEWART, 1846-1891.
Howarth, Herbert. The Irish writers,
1880-1940; London, Rockliff [1958]
x, 318 p. 820.903 a 59-4779
PR8753 .H6 MRR Alc.

PARODIES.
Macdonald, Dwight, ed. Parodies:
New York, Random House [1960] 574 p.
827.082 60-12147
PN6231.P3 M3 MRR Alc.

PAROLE OFFICERS--CANADA--DIRECTORIES.
National Council on Crime and
Delinquency. Probation and parole
directory, United States and Canada.
1910- New York. 364.62 12-8793
HV9303 .N255 MRR Alc Latest
edition

PAROLE OFFICERS--UNITED STATES--
DIRECTORIES.
National Council on Crime and
Delinquency. Probation and parole
directory, United States and Canada.
1910- New York. 364.62 12-8793
HV9303 .N255 MRR Alc Latest
edition

PAROTID GLANDS.
see also Saliva

PARTIA E PUNËS SË SHQIPËRISË--
DIRECTORIES.
Directory of Albanian officials.
[n.p.] 1970. vii, 121 p.
354.496/5/002 79-13669
JN9684 .D55 MRR Alc.

PARTIALLY SEEING
see Visually handicapped

PARTIES
see Entertaining

PARTIES, POLITICAL
see Political parties

PARTURITION.
see also Childbirth

PARTY COMMITTEES--UNITED STATES.
Bone, Hugh Alvin, Party committees
and national politics. Seattle,
University of Washington Press, 1958.
xv, 256 p. 329 58-10481
JK2276 .B6 MRR Alc.

PASSIVE RESISTANCE TO GOVERNMENT.
Waskow, Arthur I. From race riot to
sit-in, 1919 and the 1960s; [1st
ed.] Garden City, N.Y., Doubleday,
1966. xviii, 380 p. 66-11737
E185.61 .W24 MRR Alc.

PASSPORTS.
United States. Passport Office. Visa
requirements of foreign governments.
Washington; [for sale by the Supt. of
Docs., U.S. Govt. Print. Off.] 1973.
8 p. [$0.20] 323.6/7 73-602727
JX4251 .U57 1973 MRR Ref Desk.

PASTIMES
see Games

PASTORAL POETRY, GREEK.
Theocritus. The Greek bucolic poets,
London, W. Heinemann, New York, G.
P. Putnam's sons, 1916. xxviii, 527,
[1] p. 19-6715
PA3611 .A3 1916 MRR Alc.

PASTORS
see Clergy

PASTURES.
United States. Dept. of Agriculture.
Grass. Washington, U.S. Govt. Print.
Off., 1948. xiv, 892 p. 633.2
agr55-8
S21 .A35 1948 MRR Alc.

PATENT LAWS AND LEGISLATION.
Katsarov, Konstantin. Manual and
directory on industrial property all
over the world. 7th- ed.; 1970-
[Geneva, Switzerland] 608/.7/0202
72-625377
    T201 .K3 MRR Alc Latest edition

PATENT LAWYERS--DIRECTORIES.
Martindale-Hubbell law directory.
Summit, N.J. [etc.] 31-6356
KF190 .H813 MRR Biog Latest
edition

PATENT LAWYERS--UNITED STATES--
DIRECTORIES.
Martindale-Hubbell law directory.
Summit, N.J. [etc.] 31-6356
KF190 .H813 MRR Biog Latest
edition

PATENTS.
Fenner, Terrence W. Inventor's
handbook New York, Chemical Pub.
Co., 1969. xi, 309 p. [7.50]
608.7 73-5567
T212 .F44 MRR Alc.

PATENTS--BIBLIOGRAPHY.
National Translations Center.
Consolidated index of translations
into English. New York, Special
Libraries Association, 1969. vi, 948
p. 016.5/05 76-101337
Z7403 .N273 MRR Alc.

PATENTS--HANDBOOKS, MANUALS, ETC.
Jones, Stacy V. The inventor's
patent handbook Rev. ed. New York,
Dial Press, 1969. ix, 229 p. [5.95]
608.7/73 72-8219
T339 .J74 1969 MRR Alc.

PATENTS--UNITED STATES.
Kessler, Kenneth O. The successful
inventor's guide; Englewood Cliffs,
N.J., Prentice-Hall [1965] xv, 224
p. 608.773 64-24939
T339 .K46 MRR Alc.

United States. Patent Office. Index
of patents issued from the United
States Patent office. 1920-
Washington, U. S. Govt. Print. Off.
608 30-26211
    T223 .D3 Sci RR Latest edition /
MRR Alc Latest edition

PATHOGENIC BACTERIA
see Bacteria, Pathogenic

PATHOLOGY.
see also Diagnosis

see also Diseases--Causes and
theories of causation

see also Histology

see also Medicine

Robbins, Stanley L. Pathology 3d
ed. Philadelpia, Saunders, 1867. x,
1434, xxvi, p. 616.07 67-10141
RB37 .R57 1967 MRR Alc.

PATHS
see Trails

PATIENCE (MIDDLE ENGLISH POEM)--
CONCORDANCES.
Kottler, Barnet. A concordance to
five Middle English poems:
[Pittsburgh] University of Pittsburgh
Press [1966] xxxiii, 761 p.
821.1016 66-13311
PR265 .K6 MRR Alc.

PATRIARCHY
see Family

PATRIOTIC SOCIETIES--BIOGRAPHY.
The Hereditary register of the United
States of America. 1972-
Washington, United States Hereditary
Register. 369/.1 76-184658
E172.7 .H47 MRR Alc Latest edition

PATRIOTIC SOCIETIES--DIRECTORIES.
The Hereditary register of the United
States of America. 1972-
Washington, United States Hereditary
Register. 369/.1 76-184658
E172.7 .H47 MRR Alc Latest edition

PATRIOTIC SONGS
see National songs

PATRIOTISM.
see also Nationalism

PATRONAGE, POLITICAL.
see also Corruption (in politics)

PATTERN GLASS.
Doubles, Malcolm Ray, Pattern glass
checklist. Richmond, 1959. 100 p.
748.2973 59-3293
NK5112 .D64 MRR Alc.

Kamm, Minnie Elizabeth (Watson) The
Kamm-Wood encyclopedia of antique
pattern glass. Watkins Glen, N.Y.,
Century House, c1961. 2 v.
748.2913 61-5439
NK5112 .K284 MRR Alc.

PATTERSON, DANIEL TODD, 1786-1839--
MANUSCRIPTS.
United States. Library of Congress.
Manuscript Division. Bladen Dulany,
Gustavus R. B. Horner, Daniel Todd
Patterson: a register of their papers
in the Library of Congress.
Washington, Library of Congress,
1970. 4, 8, 4 l.   016.3593/32/0922
78-606846
Z663.34 .D9 MRR Alc.

PAUPERISM
see Poor

PEACE--ADDRESSES, ESSAYS, LECTURES.
Peace. Amsterdam, New York, Elsevier
Publ. Co., 1972. 3 v. [f183.20 per
vol.]   327.172/08   68-20650
JX1937 .P38 MRR Alc.

PEACE--BIBLIOGRAPHY.
Arms control & disarmament. v. 1-
winter 1964/65- [Washington, For
sale by the Superintendent of
Documents, U.S. Govt. Print. Off.]
64-62746
Z663.28 .A23 MRR Alc MRR Alc Full
set

Carnegie Endowment for International
Peace. Publications of the Carnegie
Endowment for International Peace,
1910-1967, including International
conciliation, 1924-1967. New York,
1971. 229 p.   016.327/172 70-
153501
Z6461 .C27 MRR Alc.

Cook, Blanche Wiesen. Bibliography
on peace research in history. Santa
Barbara, Calif., ABC-Clio [c1969] v,
72 p. [6.50]   016.3411 72-93481
Z6464.Z9 C7 MRR Alc.

PEACE CORPS
see United States. Peace Corps

PEARL (MIDDLE ENGLISH POEM)--
CONCORDANCES.
Kottler, Barnet. A concordance to
five Middle English poems:
[Pittsburgh] University of Pittsburgh
Press [1966] xxxiii, 761 p.
821.1016 66-13311
PR265 .K6 MRR Alc.

PEDAGOGICAL LIBRARIES--DIRECTORIES.
System Development Corporation.
Directory of educational information
resources. [Rev. and updated ed.]
New York, CCM Information Corp.,
1971. ix, 181 p.   370/.7 70-136093

L901 .S95 1972 MRR Alc.

PEDAGOGY
see Teaching

PEDIATRICIANS--UNITED STATES--
DIRECTORIES.
American pediatric directory. 1st
ed.: 1935- Knoxville, Tenn., Joe T.
Smith [etc.]   614.24097 35-9541
R712.A1 A65 Sci RR Latest edition
/ MRR Biog Latest edition

PEDIATRICS.
see also Children--Care and hygiene

Barnett, Henry L. Pediatrics. 15th
ed. New York, Appleton-Century-
Crofts [1972] xxxi, 2070 p.
618.9/2 70-133170
RJ45 .B35 1972 MRR Alc.

PEDIATRICS--ENCYCLOPEDIA--POPULAR WORKS.
Levine, Milton Isra. The parents'
encyclopedia of infancy, childhood,
and adolescence New York, Crowell
[1973] 618 p. [$10.00] 649/.1/03
72-83768
RJ61 .L552 MRR Alc.

PEDIGREES
see Heraldry

PEDOLOGY (CHILD STUDY)
see Child study

see Children

PEERAGE.
The Royalty, peerage and aristocracy
of the world. London, Annuaire de
France. 929.7 74-644555
CS404 .R68 MRR Alc Latest edition

PEKING--DESCRIPTION--GUIDE-BOOKS.
Cail, Odile. Peking. [Rev. ed.]
New York, D. McKay Co. [1973] x, 210
p. [$6.85] 915.11/56/045 72-96171

DS795.A4 C34 1973 MRR Alc.

PENAL INSTITUTIONS
see Prisons

PENNELL, JOSEPH, 1857-1926.
United States. Library of Congress.
Joseph Pennell memorial exhibition.
Washington [Govt. print. off.] 1927.
vii, 46 p. 27-26356
Z663.39 .P4 MRR Alc.

PENNELL, JOSEPH, 1857-1926--
BIBLIOGRAPHY.
United States. Library of Congress.
Joseph Pennell memorial exhibition.
Washington [Govt. print. off.] 1927.
vii, 46 p. 27-26356
Z663.39 .P4 MRR Alc.

PENNSYLVANIA.
Writer's program. Pennsylvania.
Pennsylvania: a guide to the Keystone
state, New York, Oxford university
press [1940] xxxii, 660 p. 917.48
40-28760
F154 .W94 MRR Ref Desk.

PENNSYLVANIA--BIOGRAPHY.
The Pennsylvania manual. 1923/24-
Harrisburg. 25-4346
JK3630 .P4 MRR Alc Latest edition

PENNSYLVANIA--DESCRIPTION AND TRAVEL--
GUIDE-BOOKS.
Writer's program. Pennsylvania.
Pennsylvania: a guide to the Keystone
state, New York, Oxford university
press [1940] xxxii, 660 p. 917.48
40-28760
F154 .W94 MRR Ref Desk.

PENNSYLVANIA--HISTORY.
Klein, Philip Shriver, A history of
Pennsylvania New York, McGraw-Hill
[1973] xiv, 559 p. 917.48/03 72-
3991
F149 .K55 MRR Alc.

Stevens, Sylvester Kirby,
Pennsylvania, birthplace of a nation,
New York, Random House [1964] xiii,
399 p. 974.8 64-18930
F149 .S77 MRR Alc.

PENNSYLVANIA--HISTORY--COLONIAL PERIOD,
CA. 1600-1775--SOURCES.
Myers, Albert Cook, ed. Narratives
of early Pennsylvania, West New
Jersey and Delaware, 1630-1707, New
York, C. Scribner's sons, 1912. xiv
p., 2 l., 3-476 p. 12-4611
E187.07 M9 MRR Alc.

PENNSYLVANIA--HISTORY--SOURCES--
BIBLIOGRAPHY.
Historical Records Survey.
Pennsylvania. Guide to the
manuscript collections of the
Historical Society of Pennsylvania.
2d ed. Philadelphia, Historical
Society of Pennsylvania 1949. 1 v.
(unpaged) 016.9748 49-49681
Z1329 .H68 1949 MRR Alc.

PENNSYLVANIA--INDUSTRIES--DIRECTORIES.
Industrial directory of the
Commonwealth of Pennsylvania. 1st-
1913- Harrisburg. 14-31832
HC107.P4 A28 Sci RR Latest edition
/ MRR Alc Latest edition

PENNSYLVANIA--MANUFACTURES--DIRECTORIES.
Industrial directory of the
Commonwealth of Pennsylvania. 1st-
1913- Harrisburg. 14-31832
HC107.P4 A28 Sci RR Latest edition
/ MRR Alc Latest edition

PENNSYLVANIA--POLITICS AND GOVERNMENT.
Directory of Pennsylvania council-
manager municipalities and municipal
managers. Pittsburgh. 59-26688
JS451.P3 D5 MRR Alc Latest edition

The Pennsylvania manual. 1923/24-
Harrisburg. 25-4346
JK3630 .P4 MRR Alc Latest edition

PENNSYLVANIA--REGISTERS.
The Pennsylvania manual. 1923/24-
Harrisburg. 25-4346
JK3630 .P4 MRR Alc Latest edition

PENNSYLVANIA--STATISTICS.
Pennsylvania statistical abstract.
1958- [Harrisburg] 317.48 a 59-
9073
HA607 .P4 MRR Alc Latest edition

PENNSYLVANIA GERMANS--BIBLIOGRAPHY.
Meynen, Emil, Bibliographie des
deutschtums der kolonialzeitlichen
einwanderung in Nordamerika,
Leipzig, O. Harrassowitz, 1937.
xxxvi, 636 p. 016.3252430973 38-
7457
Z1361.G37 M6 MRR Alc.

PENSION TRUSTS--UNITED STATES--
DIRECTORIES.
Money market directory. 1971- New
York, Money Market Directories.
332.67/025 76-146228
HG4509 .M65 MRR Alc Latest edition

PENSION TRUSTS--UNITED STATES--
INVESTMENTS.
Investors Publishing Company, New
York. Pension funds, 1969. New
York, D. A. Campbell [c1969] xxxi,
930 p. 331.2/52 75-10552
HD7106.U5 I67 1969 MRR Alc.

PENSIONS.
see also Insurance, Social

PENSIONS--UNITED STATES.
Employee benefits fact book. [New
York] 331.2/52 76-118375
HD7125 .E57 MRR Alc Latest edition

PEOPLE'S DEMOCRACIES
see also Communist countries

PERCEPTION
see also Concepts

PERENNIALS.
Potter, Charles H. Perennials in the
garden for lasting beauty. New York,
Criterion Books [1959] 271 p.
635.932 59-6124
SB434 .P6 MRR Alc.

PERFORMING ARTS
see also Theater

PERFORMING ARTS--BIBLIOGRAPHY.
Chicorel, Marietta. Chicorel
bibliography to the performing arts.
1st ed. New York, Chicorel Library
Pub. Corp. [1972] 498 p. 016.7902
73-155102
Z6935 .C45 MRR Alc.

Rogers, A. Robert, The humanities;
Littleton, Colo., Libraries
Unlimited, 1974. 400 p. [$9.50]
016.0013 74-78393
Z5579 .R63 MRR Alc.

Schoolcraft, Ralph Newman.
Performing arts/books in print: an
annotated bibliography. [1st ed.]
New York, Drama Book Specialists
[1973] xiii, 761 p. 016.7902 72-
78909
Z6935 .S34 MRR Alc.

PERFORMING ARTS--BIBLIOGRAPHY--CATALOGS.
New York (City). Public Library.
Research Libraries. Catalog of the
theatre and drama collections.
Boston, G. K. Hall, 1967. 21 v.
016.700 68-5330
Z5785 .N56 MRR Alc. (DK 33).

PERFORMING ARTS--DICTIONARIES.
Enciclopedia dello spettacolo. Roma,
Casa editrice Le Maschere [1954-62]
9 v. a 55-2513
PN1625 .E7 MRR Alc.

The Language of show biz; Chicago,
Dramatic Pub. Co. [1973] xliii, 251
p. 790/.03 73-173320
PN1579 .L3 MRR Alc.

The Lincoln library of the arts.
[1st ed.] Columbus, Ohio, Frontier
Press Co. [1973] 2 v. (846 p.)
700/.3 73-78393
NX70 .L54 MRR Alc.

Sharp, Harold S., comp. Index to
characters in the performing arts,
New York, Scarecrow Press, 1966-73.
4 v. in 6. 808.8292703 66-13744
PN1579 .S45 MRR Alc.

PERFORMING ARTS--DICTIONARIES--POLYGLOT.
Giteau, Cécile. Dictionnaire des
arts du spectacle, français--anglais-
-allemand; Paris, Dunod, 1970. xxv,
429 p. [88.00] 78-499699
PN1579 .G5 MRR Alc.

PERFORMING ARTS--DIRECTORIES.
International Federation of Library
Associations. Section for Theatrical
Libraries and Museums.
Bibliothèques et musées des arts du
spectacle dans le monde ,.. 2e
edition revue et augmentée Paris,
Éditions du Centre national de la
recherche scientifique, 1967. 803 p.
[90 F] 016.792 70-362547
Z675.T36 I5 1967 MRR Alc.

Pride, Leo Bryan, International
theatre directory; New York, Simon
and Schuster [1973] xviii, 577 p.
[$35.00] 792/.025 70-157681
PN2052 .P7 MRR Alc.

Young, William C., American
theatrical arts; Chicago, American
Library Association, 1971. ix, 166
p. 016.7902 78-161234
Z6935 .Y68 MRR Alc.

PERFORMING ARTS--PERIODICALS--
BIBLIOGRAPHY.
Stratman, Carl Joseph, American
theatrical periodicals, 1798-1967;
Durham, N.C., Duke University Press,
1970. xxii, 133 p. 016.7902 72-
110577
Z6935 .S75 MRR Alc.

PERFORMING ARTS--PERIODICALS--INDEXES.
Belknap, Sara (Yancey) Guide to the
musical arts; New York, Scarecrow
Press, 1957. 1 v. (unpaged) 016.78
57-6631
ML113 .B37 MRR Alc.

Guide to the performing arts. 1957-
Metuchen, N.J. [etc.] Scarecrow
Press. 016.78 60-7266
ML118 .G8 MRR Alc Full set

PERFORMING ARTS--REVIEWS.
The New York times theater reviews, 1920-1970. New York, New York times, 1971- v. 792/.09747/1 72-166218
PN1581 .N4 MRR Alc.

PERFORMING ARTS--CALIFORNIA--DIRECTORIES.
West coast theatrical directory. 1970- Los Angeles, Tarcher/Gousha Guides. 917.94/0025 70-109344
PN1582.U6 W4 MRR Alc Latest edition

PERFORMING ARTS--CANADA--BIOGRAPHY.
Creative Canada; [Toronto] Published in association with McPherson Library, University of Victoria, by University of Toronto Press [1971- v. [$15.00 (v. 1)] 790/.871 71-151387
NX513.A1 C7 MRR Biog.

PERFORMING ARTS--FRANCE--DIRECTORIES.
Annuaire du spectacle; [1]- annee; 1942/43- Paris, Editions Raoult [etc.] 45-27035
PN2620 .A67 MRR Alc Latest edition

PERFORMING ARTS--GREAT BRITAIN--PERIODICALS--BIBLIOGRAPHY.
Stratman, Carl Joseph, Britain's theatrical periodicals, 1720-1967, New York, New York Public Library, 1972. xxiv, 160 p. 016.792/0942 72-134260
Z6935 .S76 1972 MRR Alc.

PERFORMING ARTS--UNITED STATES--BIOGRAPHY.
Lamparski, Richard. Whatever became of ...? Fourth series. New York, Crown Publishers [1973] 206 p. [$5.95] 790.2/092/2 B 72-96665
CT220 .L284 1973 MRR Biog.

PERFORMING ARTS--UNITED STATES--DIRECTORIES.
Who's who in show business: 1967/68- New York. 790.2/0922 72-220578
PN1583.A2 W5 MRR Alc Latest edition

PERFORMING ARTS--UNITED STATES--EXHIBITIONS.
United States. Library of Congress. Exhibits Office. The performing arts in 18th-century America; Washington, Library of Congress 1972. [28] p. 790.2/0973 72-10085
Z663.15 .P47 MRR Alc.

PERFORMING ARTS--UNITED STATES--SOCIETIES, ETC.--DIRECTORIES.
The National directory for the performing arts and civic centers. Dallas, Handel & Co. 790.2/0973 73-646635
PN2289 .N38 MRR Alc Latest edition

PERFUMES.
Gattefossé, René Maurice. Formulary of perfumery and of cosmetology. London, L. Hill, 1952. 252 p. 668.5 54-15112
TP983 .G29 MRR Alc.

PERIODICALS.
see also Newspapers

Davis, Sheldon Emmor, Educational periodicals during the nineteenth century. Metuchen, N.J., Scarecrow Reprint Corp., 1970. 125 p. 370/.5 79-18630
Z5811 .D36 1970 MRR Alc.

Ford, James L. Magazines for millions; Carbondale, Southern Illinois University Press [c1969] xvii, 320 p. [11.75] 051 79-76187
PN4877 .F6 MRR Alc.

Merrill, John Calhoun, The foreign press; Baton Rouge, Louisiana State University Press [1970] 365 p. 070.9 76-96259
PN4736 .M39 1970 MRR Alc.

Osborn, Andrew Delbridge, Serial publications; their place and treatment in libraries 2d ed., rev. Chicago, American Library Association, 1973. xx, 434 p. 025.17/3 72-4519
Z692.S5 O8 1973 MRR Alc.

PERIODICALS--ABBREVIATIONS OF TITLES.
Akademiia nauk SSSR. Institut nauchnoi informatsii. Index of abbreviated and full titles of scientific and technical periodical literature Wright-Patterson Air Force Base, Ohio, [1960?] 247 l. 60-60261
Z6945.A2 A43 MRR Alc.

Fondation nationale des sciences politiques. Bibliographie courante d'articles de periodiques posterieurs a 1944 sur les problemes politiques, economiques, et sociaux. Boston, G. K. Hall, 1968. 17 v. 70-409780
AI7 .F6 MRR Alc. (Dk 33).

Global Engineering Documentation Services. Directory of engineering document sources. Newport Beach, Calif., Global Engineering Documentation Services [1972] 1 v. (unpaged) [$29.95] 029.9/62 72-176333
Z5852 .G5 MRR Alc.

International African Institute. A select bibliography of music in Africa, London, 1965. 83 p. 66-36908
ML120.A35 I6 MRR Alc.

International catalogue of scientific literature. List of journals, London, Harrison and sons; [etc., etc.] 1903. 2 p. l., v-xv, 312 p. 03-19593
Z7403 .I61 MRR Alc.

Leistner, Otto. Internationale Titelabkurzungen von Zeitschriften, Zeitungen wichtigen Handbuchern, Worterbuchern, Gesetzen usw. Osnabruck, Biblio-Verlag, 1967- v. [28.00 (pt. 1)] 68-96819
Z6945.A2 L4 MRR Alc.

Royal Society of London. Catalogue of scientific papers. London, C. J. Clay, 1867-1925. 19 v. 02-11462
Z7403 .R88 MRR Alc.

Royal society of London. Catalogue of scientific papers, 1800-1900. Cambridge, University press, 1908- v. 08-24586
Z7403 .R8812 MRR Alc.

Ulving, Tor. Periodica philologica abbreviata; Stockholm, Almqvist & Wiksell [1963] 137 p. 64-1932
Z6945.A2 U5513 MRR Alc.

United States. Library of Congress. Technical Information Division. List of abbreviations and symbols, Washington, 1952. i, 14 l. 016.05 52-60047
Z663.49 .L48 MRR Alc.

Wall, C. Edward. Periodical title abbreviations. Detroit, Gale Research Co., 1969. 210 p. 050 78-86599
Z6945.A2 W34 MRR Ref Desk.

Whitlock, Carolyn, Abbreviations used in the Department of agriculture for titles of publications, Washington, D.C. [U.S. Govt. print. off., 1939] 278 p. 016.05 agr39-503
Z6945.A2 W5 MRR Alc.

World list of scientific periodicals published in the years 1900-1960. 4th ed. Washington, Butterworths, 1963-65. 3 v. (xxv, 1824 p.) 016.505 64-9729
Z7403 .W923 MRR Alc.

PERIODICALS--ABSTRACTS--INDEXES.
Chicorel, Marietta. Chicorel index to abstracting and indexing services: 1st ed. New York, Chicorel Library Pub.Corp. [1974] 2 v. (920 p.) 016.05 74-170434
Z6293 .C54 MRR Ref Desk.

PERIODICALS--BIBLIOGRAPHY.
American Library Association. Periodicals List Subcommittee. Periodicals for school libraries; Chicago, American Library Association, 1969. xvii, 217 p. 016.051 70-80870
Z6944.S8 A4 MRR Alc.

Andriot, John L. Guide to U.S. Government serials & periodicals, 1967 ed. McLean, Va., Documents Index [c1967] 2 v. (1631 p.) 015/.73 68-3862
Z1223.Z7 A573 MRR Ref Desk.

Arndt, Karl John Richard. German-American newspapers and periodicals, 1732-1955; Heidelberg, Quelle & Meyer, 1961. 794 p. 62-107
Z6953.5.G3 A7 MRR Alc.

Ayer directory of publications. Philadelphia, Ayer Press. 071.3/025 73-640052
Z6951 .A97 Sci RR Latest edition / MRR Ref Desk Latest edition / MRR Alc Latest edition

Bacon's publicity checker. 1933- Chicago, R. H. Bacon. 659.111 34-14702
HD59 .B3 MRR Alc Latest edition

Birkos, Alexander S. East European and Slavic studies. [Kent? Ohio] Kent State University Press [1973] 572 p. [$7.50] 016.9147/03/05 73-158303
Z2483 .B56 MRR Alc.

Birkos, Alexander S. Latin American studies. [Kent, Ohio] Kent State University Press [1971] 359 p. 808.02/5 70-160685
Z1601 .B54 MRR Alc.

Boehm, Eric H., Historical periodicals; Santa Barbara, Calif., Clio Press, 1961. xviii, 618 p. 016.905 59-8783
Z6205 .B6 MRR Alc.

Camp, William L. Guide to periodicals in education, Metuchen, N.J., Scarecrow Press, 1968. 419 p. 016.370/5 68-12625
Z5813 .C28 MRR Alc.

Caron, Pierre, ed. World list of historical periodicals and bibliographies. Oxford [Eng.] International committee of historical sciences, 1939 [i.e. 1940] xiv, [2], 391, [1] p. 016.905 41-4203
Z6201.A1 C3 MRR Alc.

The Catholic press directory. 1923- New York [etc.] Catholic Press Ass. [etc.] 23-11774
Z6951 .C36 MRR Alc Latest edition

Chicago. Center for Research Libraries. Rarely held scientific serials in the Midwest Inter-library Center. Chicago, 1963. vi, 197 p. 63-5712
Z7403 .C49 MRR Alc.

Committee on Latin America. Latin American economic & social serials: London, Published on behalf of COLA by Bingley, 1969. 189 p. [50/-] 016.3081/8 74-382598
Z7165.L3 C65 MRR Alc.

Crane, Ronald Salmon, A census of British newspapers and periodicals, 1620-1800, London, Holland P., 1966. 205 p. 016.072 67-112604
Z6956.E5 C8 1966 MRR Alc.

Deutschsprachige Zeitschriften. Marbach am Neckar, Verlag der Schillerbuchhandlung Hans Banger. 053.1/025 70-612760
Z6956.G3 A55 MRR Alc Latest edition

Directory of business and financial services. [1st]- ed.; 1924- New York [etc.] Special Libraries Association. 25-4599
HF5003 .H3 MRR Ref Desk Latest edition / MRR Ref Desk Latest edition

Directory of Canadian scientific and technical periodicals. 1961- Ottawa, National Research Council. 016.505 61-2342
Z7403 .D5 MRR Alc Latest edition

Dobler, Lavinia G. The Dobler world directory of youth periodicals, New York, Schulte Pub. Co., 1966. xi, 37 p. 65-28886
Z6944.C5 D6 1966 MRR Alc.

Educational Press Association of America. America's education press; [1st]- yearbook; 1925- Washington. 016.3705 41-9994
Z5813 .E24 MRR Alc Latest edition

Farber, Evan Ira. Classified list of periodicals for the college library, 5th ed., rev. and enl. Westwood, Mass., F. W. Faxon Co., 1972. xvii, 449 p. 016.05 72-76264
Z6841 .F25 1972 MRR Alc.

Fowler, Maureen J. Guides to scientific periodicals: London, Library Association [1966] xvi, 318 p. [84/- 63/- (to L.A. members)] 016.505 67-71339
Z7403 .F6 MRR Alc.

Gandhi, H. N. D., Indian periodicals in print, 1973 Delhi, Vidya Mandal [1973] 2 v. 016.052 73-904001
Z6958.I4 G35 MRR Alc.

Gilmer, Gertrude Cordelia, Checklist of southern periodicals to 1861, Boston, The F. W. Faxon company, 1934. 128 p. 016.051 34-23493
Z6951 .G48 MRR Alc.

Goggio, Emilio, A bibliography of Canadian cultural periodicals [Toronto] Dept. of Italian, Spanish and Portuguese, University of Toronto, 1955. 45 p. 016.051 55-2883
Z1369 .G6 MRR Alc.

Goldwater, Walter. Radical periodicals in America, 1890-1950; New Haven, Yale University Library, 1964. xv, 51 p. 64-6244
Z7164.S67 .G57 MRR Alc.

PERIODICALS--BIBLIOGRAPHY. (Cont.)
Gray, Richard A. Serial
bibliographies in the humanities and
social sciences. Ann Arbor, Mich.,
Pierian Press, 1969. xxiv, 345 p.
016.01605 68-58895
Z1002 .G814 MRR Ref Desk.

Handboek van de Nederlandse pers.
Feb. 1964- Barendrecht, Publiciteit.
66-93771
Z6956.N45 H35 MRR Alc Latest
edition

Harris, Chauncy Dennison,
International list of geographical
serials. 2d ed., rev., expanded, and
updated. [Chicago] University of
Chicago, Dept. of Geography, 1971.
xxvi, 267 p. [$4.50] 016.91/05 79-
163720
H31 .C514 no. 138 MRR Alc.

Harvard University. Graduate School
of Business Administration. Baker
Library. Current periodical
publications in Baker Library.
1971/72- [Boston] 016.33/005 72-
620452
Z7164.C81 H266 MRR Alc Latest
edition

Harvard University. Library.
Bibliography and bibliography
periodicals. Cambridge, Distributed
by the Harvard University Press,
1966. 1066 p. 017.1097444 66-
31367
Z1002 .H26 MRR Alc.

Harvard University. Library.
Education and education periodicals.
Cambridge; Distributed by Harvard
University Press, 1968. 2 v.
016.370/5 68-15925
Z5817 .H33 MRR Alc.

Hernon, Peter. Library and library-
related publications; Littleton,
Colo., Libraries Unlimited, 1973.
216 p. [$10.00] 020/.5 73-84183
Z666 .H4 MRR Alc.

Hiler, Hilaire, Bibliography of
costume; New York, B. Blom [1967]
xi, 911 p. 016.391 66-12285
Z5691 .H64 1967 MRR Alc.

Hollyfield, Jeanne. Poet's handbook;
[1st ed. Appalachia, Va., Young
Publications, 1969] 140 p. [3.00]
655.5/2 75-4171
PN161 .H6 MRR Alc.

Index bibliographiens. [1st]- ed.;
1925- Le Haye Federation
Internationale de Documentation.
016.01 25-8351
Z1002 .I38 MRR Alc Latest edition

International catalogue of scientific
literature. List of journals,
London, Harrison and sons; [etc.,
etc.] 1903. 2 p. l., v-xv, 312 p.
03-19593
Z7403 .I61 MRR Alc.

International Federation for
Documentation. Library and
documentation journals. 2d rev. ed.
Hague, 1961. 30 p. 63-52506
Z666 .I55 1961 MRR Alc.

Internationale Bibliographie der
Fachzeitschriften für Technik und
Wirtschaft. München-Pullach, Verlag
Dokumentation [etc.] 67-118312
Z7913 .I757 MRR Alc Latest edition

Katz, William Armstrong, Magazines
for libraries; 2d ed. New York, R.
R. Bowker, 1972. xviii, 822 p.
016.05 72-6607
Z6941 .K2 1972 MRR Alc.

Kirby, John Lavan. A guide to
historical periodicals in the English
language, [London] Historical
Association, 1970. 48 p. [6/-]
016.91003 70-22365
Z6205 .K55 MRR Alc.

Der Leitfaden für Presse und
Werbung. Essen, W. Stamm. 073 51-
17269
Z6956.G3 L4 MRR Alc Latest edition

Library-Anthropology Resource Group.
Serial publications in anthropology.
Chicago, University of Chicago Press
[1973] xi, 91 p. 016.3012/05 72-
91422
Z5112 .L53 1973 MRR Alc.

Literary market place; [1st]- ed.;
1940- New York, Bowker. 655.473 41-
51571
PN161 .L5 Sci RR Partial set / MRR
.Ref Desk Latest edition

Literature Service Associates, Bound
Brook, N.J. English language
equivalent editions of foreign
language serials, Bound Brook, N.J.
[1959] 81 p. 016.05 59-46914
Z1007 .L77355 MRR Alc.

Ljunggren, Florence. Annotated guide
to journals dealing with the Middle
East and North Africa, Cairo,
American University in Cairo Press,
1964. viii, 105 p. ne 65-2428
Z3013 .L655 MRR Alc.

London. University. Institute of
Germanic Studies. Union list of
periodicals dealing with Germanic
languages and literatures London,
1956. 58 p; (p. 56-58 blank for
"Additions") 57-39974
Z7036 .I6 MRR Alc.

Lowndes, William Thomas, The
bibliographer's manual of English
literature New ed., rev., cor. and
enl., London, H. G. Bohn, 1857-61;
Bell & Daldy, 1864-65. 10 v.
015.42 35-36009
Z2001 .L92 1857-65 MRR Alc.

Maison des sciences de l'homme,
Paris. Service d'échange
d'informations scientifiques.
Etudes africaines. Liste mondiale
des périodiques spécialises. La
Haye, Mouton, 1970. 214 p. [25.50]
73-498025
Z3503 .M32 MRR Alc.

Maison des sciences de l'homme,
Paris. Service d'échange
d'informations scientifiques. Liste
mondiale des périodiques
spécialises: linguistique. Paris,
Mouton [1971] 243 p. 72-323495
Z7003 .M34 MRR Alc.

Maréchal, Yvon, Répertoire
pratique des périodiques belges
edités en langue française.
Louvain-Bruxelles, Vander, (1970).
[v], 128 p. [200F] 74-564809
Z6956.B4 M27 MRR Alc.

Mason, John Brown, Research
resources; Santa Barbara, Calif.,
ABC-Clio, 1968- v. [3.00]
016.327/.09/04 68-9685
Z7161 .M36 MRR Ref Desk.

Michigan. State University, East
Lansing. Library. Research sources
for African studies; [East Lansing]
African Studies Center, Michigan
State University, 1969. vii, 384 p.
[3.00] 016.916/005 67-65352
Z3503 .M52 MRR Alc.

Naas, Bernard G. American labor
union periodicals, Ithaca, Cornell
University [1956] xv, 175 p.
016.3318805 56-63004
Z7164.L1 N14 MRR Alc.

National Translations Center.
Consolidated index of translations
into English. New York, Special
Libraries Association, 1969. vi, 948
p. 016.5/05 76-101337
Z7403 .N273 MRR Alc.

Nihon kagaku gijutsu kankei chikuji
kankobutsu mokuroku. 1862- [Tokyo]
National Diet Library. j 68-5037
Z7403 .N5 Sci RR Latest edition /
MRR Alc Latest edition

Österreichs Presse, Werbung,
Graphik; Handbuch. 15.- Jahrg.;
1967- Wien, Verband
österreichischer
Zeitungsherausgeber. 72-626652
Z6956.A9 H3 MRR Alc Latest edition

Ottawa. National Library.
Periodicals in the social sciences
and humanities currently received by
Canadian libraries. [Ottawa, Queen's
Printer] 1968. 2 v. [unpriced]
016.300/5 68-105183
Z6945 .O895 MRR Alc.

Pan American Union. Dept. of
Scientific Affairs. Guide to Latin
American scientific and technical
periodicals; Washington, Pan
American Union, 1962. xii, 187 p.
016.505 62-62414
Z7407.S6 P3 MRR Alc.

Paoletti, Odette. Périodiques et
publications en série concernant les
sciences sociales et humaines,
Paris, Maison des sciences de
l'homme, Service bibliothèque-
documentation, 1966. 2 v. (xxiv, 684
p.) [80.00F] 016.07 67-100583
Z6941 .P3 MRR Alc.

Philosophie. 's-Gravenhage, Mouton &
Co., 1967. 124 p. [fl 15.-]
016.1/05 68-77967
Z7127 .P52 MRR Alc.

Pinson, William M. Resource guide to
current social issues, Waco, Tex.,
Word Books [1968] 272 p. 016.301
67-30735
Z7164.S66 P47 MRR Alc.

Poole's index: date and volume key
Chicago, Association of College and
Reference Libraries, 1957. 61 p.
016.05 57-7157
Z674 .A75 no. 19 MRR Ref Desk.

Princeton University. Library.
American Indian periodicals in the
Princeton University Library;
Princeton, N.J., 1970. 78 p.
016.9701 76-26143
Z1209 .P75 MRR Alc.

Reilly, Adam. Current film
periodicals in English. Rev. ed.
New York, Educational Film Library
Association [1972] 25 p.
016.79143/8 72-188994
Z5784.M9 R43 1972 MRR Alc.

Répertoire de la presse et des
publications périodiques
françaises. [1.]- ed.; 1957-
Paris, La Documentation française.
a 58-3274
Z6956.F8 R39 MRR Alc Latest
edition

Repertorio analitico della stampa
italiana, quotidiani e periodici.
1964- Milano, Messaggerie italiane.
65-34474
Z6956.I8 R4 MRR Alc Latest edition
/ MRR Alc Latest edition

Schatoff, Michael. Half a century of
Russian serials, 1917-1968: [2d ed.,
rev.]. New York, Russian Book
Chamber Abroad, 1972- v.
016.057/1 72-195896
Z6956.R9 S352 MRR Alc.

Schatoff, Michael. Half a century of
Russian serials, 1917-1968; New
York, Russian Book Chamber Abroad,
1970-72. 4 v. (xiv, 687 p.)
016.057/1 68-59340
Z6956.R9 S35 MRR Alc.

Schmid, Hans, writer on sociology.
Verzeichnis von Fachzeitschriften aus
dem Gebiet der Psychologie und ihrer
Nachbarwissenschaften. Bern,
Schweizerischer Berufsverband für
angewandte Psychologie, 1967. 70 l.
[18.00] 016.300/5 79-371198
Z7203 .S25 MRR Alc.

Schweizer Zeitschriftenverzeichnis.
1951/55- Zürich, Schweizerischer
Buchhandler- und Verlegerverein. 58-
31348
Z6956.S92 S33 MRR Alc Latest
edition

Scudder, Samuel Hubbard, Catalogue
of scientific serials of all
countries, Cambridge, Library of
Harvard university, 1879. xii, 358
p. 02-7012
Z7403 .S43 MRR Alc.

Smits, Rudolf. Half a century of
Soviet serials, 1917-1968:
Washington, Library of Congress; [for
sale by the Supt. of Docs., U.S.
Govt. Print. Off.] 1968. 2 v. (xv,
1661 p.) [16.00] 016.057 68-62169

Z663.23 .H3 MRR Alc.

Special Libraries Association. New
York Chapter. Advertising and
Marketing Group. Guide to special
issues and indexes of periodicals;
New York, Special Libraries
Association, 1962. vi, 125 p. 050
62-12644
Z6951 .S755 MRR Alc.

Springman, Mary Adele. The directory
of library periodicals.
[Philadelphia] Drexel Press, 1967,
iv, 192 p. 016.020/5 67-24822
Z674 .D7 no. 23 MRR Alc.

The Standard directory of
newsletters. 1st ed. New York,
Oxbridge Pub. Co [1971, c1972] lvi,
210 p. [$20.00] 071/.025/73 71-
173886
Z6944.N44 S8 MRR Ref Desk.

Stanford University. Libraries.
German periodical publications;
Stanford, Calif., Hoover Institution
on War, Revolution, and Peace,
Stanford University, 1967. viii, 175
p. 016.053/1 66-28530
Z6956.G3 S78 MRR Alc.

Stratman, Carl Joseph, American
theatrical periodicals, 1798-1967;
Durham, N.C., Duke University Press,
1970. xxii, 133 p. 016.7902 72-
110577
Z6935 .S75 MRR Alc.

Temple, Phillips Lumsden, A
directory of library periodicals
published in the continental United
States, Pittsburg, Kan., State
College Library, 1957. 44 p.
016.0205 57-63232
Z719 .T37 MRR Alc.

PERIODICALS--BIBLIOGRAPHY. (Cont.)
The Times, London. Tercentenary
handlist of English & Welsh
newspapers, magazines & reviews ...
London, The Times, 1920. 212 p.; 1
l., L p., 1 l., [215]-324, xxxv p.
21-6520
Z6956.E5 T5 MRR Alc.

Tompkins, Margaret. A checklist of
serials in psychology and allied
fields. Troy, N.Y., Whitston Pub.
Co. 1969. viii, 261 p. [10.50]
016.1505 70-87477
Z7203 .T65 MRR Alc.

Tronik, Ruth. Israeli periodicals &
serials in English & other European
languages: Metuchen, N.J., Scarecrow
Press, 1974. xiii, 193 p. 016.05
73-14901
Z6858.I8 T76 MRR Alc.

Ulving, Tor. Periodica philologica
abbreviata; Stockholm, Almqvist &
Wiksell [1963] 137 p. 64-1932
Z6945.A2 U5513 MRR Alc.

Union of International Associations.
Directory of periodicals published by
international organizations. 3d ed.
Brussels [1969] xii, 240 p. 016.05
70-480186
AS8 .U38 1969 MRR Alc.

United Nations Educational,
Scientific and Cultural Organization.
Educational periodicals. [Paris?]
64-6395
   Began publication with 1957 issue.
Z5813 .U52 MRR Alc Latest edition

United Nations Educational,
Scientific and Cultural Organization.
Liste mondiale des périodiques
spécialisés dans les sciences
sociales. 3. ed., rev. et augm.
[Paris] Unesco [1966, c1952] 448 p.
67-51954
Z7163 .U52 1966 MRR Alc.

United States. Air University.
Library. Union list of military
periodicals. Maxwell Air Force Base,
Ala., Air University Library, 1960.
viii, 121 p. 016.35505 60-62431
Z6723 .U32 MRR Alc.

United States. Library of Congress.
Japanese scientific and technical
serial publications in the
collections of the Library of
Congress. Washington, Science and
Technology Division, Reference Dept.,
Library of Congress, 1962. v, 247 p.
62-60085
Z663.41 .J2 MRR Alc.

United States. Library of Congress.
Latin American periodicals currently
received in the Library of Congress
and in the library of the Department
of agriculture. Washington: The
Library of Congress, 1944. vii, 249
p. 016.056 45-35735
Z663.32 .L3 MRR Alc.

United States. Library of Congress.
African Section. Serials for African
studies. Washington, General
Reference and Bibliography Division,
Reference Dept., Library of Congress,
1961. viii, 163 p. 016.916 61-
60072
Z663.285 .S4 MRR Alc.

United States. Library of Congress.
African Section. Sub-Saharan Africa:
a guide to serials. Washington,
Library of Congress; [for sale by the
Supt. of Docs., U.S. Govt. Print.
Off.] 1970. xx, 409 p. [$5.25]
016.9167/03 70-607392
Z663.285 .S9 MRR Alc.

United States. Library of Congress.
Cyrillic Bibliographic Project.
Serial publications of the Soviet
Union, 1939-1957; [New expanded ed.]
Washington, 1958. ix, 459 p.
016.057 58-60013
Z663.7 .S4 1958 MRR Alc.

United States. Library of Congress.
Division for the Blind and Physically
Handicapped. Magazines: braille and
recorded. Washington, 1968. 12 l.
016.05 68-60035
Z663.25 .M28 MRR Alc.

United States. Library of Congress.
Division of Aeronautics. A checklist
of aeronautical periodicals and
serials in the Library of Congress,
Washington, 1948. 129 p.
016.6291305 48-46803
Z663.22 .C45 MRR Alc.

United States. Library of Congress.
European Affairs Division.
Continuing sources for research on
Africa, [Washington] 1952. 21 p.
016.916 52-60041
Z663.26 .C6 MRR Alc.

United States. Library of Congress.
European Affairs Division. The
European press today. Washington,
1949. 152 p. 016.07 49-46986
Z663.26 .E84 MRR Alc.

United States. Library of Congress.
European Affairs Division. Reference
notes on the press in European
countries participating in the
European recovery program;
[Washington] 1948. 39 p. 338.942
49-45627
Z663.26 .R4 MRR Alc.

[United States. Library of Congress.
General Reference and Bibliography
Division] Philosophical periodicals;
Washington, 1952. vi, 89 p.
016.105 52-60055
Z663.28 .P47 MRR Alc.

United States. Library of Congress.
Processing Dept. Russian periodicals
in the Helsinki University Library,
Washington, 1959. 120 p. 016.057
59-60791
Z663.7 .R8 MRR Alc.

United States. Library of Congress.
Reference Dept. Research and
information on Africa: Washington,
1954. vi, 70 p. 016.916 54-60024

Z663.26 .C62 MRR Alc.

United States. Library of Congress.
Science and Technology Division.
Aeronautical and space serial
publications; Washington, 1962. ix,
255 p. 61-60083
Z663.41 .A73 MRR Alc.

United States. Library of Congress.
Science and Technology Division.
Biological sciences serial
publications, Philadelphia,
Biological Abstracts, 1955. 269 p.
016.57405 55-60051
Z663.41 .B5 MRR Alc.

United States. Library of Congress.
Science and Technology Division.
Chinese scientific and technical
serial publications in the
collections of the Library of
Congress. Rev. ed. Washington,
1961. v, 107 p. 016.505 62-60011

Z663.41 .C45 1961 MRR Alc.

United States. Library of Congress.
Science and Technology Division. A
list of scientific and technical
serials currently received by the
Library of Congress. Washington,
1960. v, 186 p. 016.505 60-60055

Z663.41 .L5 MRR Alc.

United States. Library of Congress.
Science and Technology Division.
Scientific and technical serial
publications, Washington, 1954.
viii, 238 p. 016.505 54-60022
Z663.41 .S33 MRR Alc.

United States. Library of Congress.
Science and Technology Division.
Scientific and technical serial
publications, Washington, 1954.
viii, 118 p. 016.505 54-60015
Z663.41 .S3 MRR Alc.

United States. Library of Congress.
Science and Technology Division.
Scientific and technical serial
publications of the Soviet Union,
1945-1960. Washington [For sale by
the Superintendent of Documents, U.S.
Govt. Print. Off.] 1963. iv, 347 p.
63-61782
Z663.41 .S29 MRR Alc.

United States. Library of Congress.
Slavic and Central European Division.
East and East Central Europe:
periodicals Washington, 1958. v,
126p. 016.943 58-60065
Z663.47 .E2 MRR Alc.

United States. Library of Congress.
Slavic and Central European Division.
The USSR and Eastern Europe; 3d ed.
rev. and enl. Washington, Library of
Congress; [for sale by the Supt. of
Docs., U.S. Govt. Print. Off.] 1967.
89 p. 016.05 68-60045
Z663.47 .U22 1967 MRR Alc.

United States Historical Documents
Institute. U.S. Government serial
titles, 1789-1970; Washington [1972]
xii, 527 p. 015.73 s 74-190737
Z1223.Z7 L45 vol. 4 MRR Ref Desk.

Verzeichnis deutscher
wissenschaftlicher Zeitschriften.
[1.] Aufl.; 1939/52- Wiesbaden
[etc.] F. Steiner [etc.] 54-30714
   Z6956.G3 V45 MRR Alc Latest
   edition

Vesenyi, Paul E., European
periodical literature in the social
sciences and the humanities,
Metuchen, N.J., Scarecrow Press,
1969. 226 p. 016.052 79-7052
Z6955 .Z9V45 MRR Alc.

Ward, William Smith, Index and
finding list of serials published in
the British Isles, 1789-1832.
Lexington, University of Kentucky
Press [1953] xv, 180 p. 016.052
53-5521
Z6956.E5 W27 MRR Alc.

Willing's press guide. London, J.
Willing, Ltd. [etc.] 53-36485
   Began publication with issue for
1874.
Z6956.E5 W5 MRR Alc Latest edition

Winckler, Paul A. Library
periodicals directory; Brookville,
N.Y., Graduate Library School of Long
Island University, 1967. v. 76 l.
67-7215
Z666 .W5 1967 MRR Alc.

A World list of computer periodicals.
Manchester, National Computing
Centre, 1970. [1], 102 p. [£3.00]
016.0016/4/05 78-586322
Z6654.C17 W65 MRR Alc.

World medical periodicals. 3d ed.
[New York] World Medical Association,
1961. xli, 407 p. 016.6105 a 63-
269
Z6660 .W6 1961 MRR Alc.

The Writer's market. Cincinnati, O.,
Writer's digest. 051 [029.6] 31-
20772
   PN161 .W83 MRR Ref Desk Latest
   edition

Zeitungskatalog der Schweiz. 1943-
Zürich, [etc.] Verband
Schweizerischer Annoncen-
Expeditionen. 58-19529
   Z6956.S92 Z4 MRR Alc Latest
   edition

Zimmerman, Irene, A guide to current
Latin American periodicals: [1st
ed.] Gainesville, Fla., Kallman Pub.
Co., 1961. x, 357 p. 61-15751
Z6954.S8 Z5 MRR Alc.

PERIODICALS--BIBLIOGRAPHY--CATALOGS.
Archives de la ville de Bruxelles.
Catalogue des journaux et
periodiques conserves aux Archives
de la Ville de Bruxelles. Bruxelles,
[Ville de Bruxelles], 1965. 3 v.
74-366082
Z6945 .A76 MRR Alc.

Cambridge. University. Library.
Current serials available in the
University Library and in other
libraries connected with the
university. Cambridge. 016.05 74-
645183
   Began in 1970.
Z6945 .C175 MRR Alc Latest edition

Chicago. Center for Research
Libraries. The Center for Research
Libraries catalogue: serials.
Chicago, 1972. 2 v. 019 72-180872

Z6945 .C5335 MRR Alc (Dk 33).

Harvard University. Library.
Periodical classes; Cambridge;
Distributed by the Harvard University
Press, 1968. 758 p. 017 68-14152

Z6945 .H34 MRR Alc.

New serial titles, classed subject
arrangement. Jan./May 1955-
[Washington, Library of Congress]
016.05 55-60037
   Z663.7 .A48 MRR Alc MRR Alc Full
set

Royal society of London. Library.
Catalogue of the periodical
publications in the library of the
Royal society of London. London,
Printed for the Royal society at the
Oxford university press, 1912. viii,
455, [1] p. 13-19466
Z7403 .R888 MRR Alc.

Stanford University. Hoover
Institution on War, Revolution, and
Peace. The library catalogs of the
Hoover Institution on War,
Revolution, and Peace, Stanford
University: Boston, Mass., G. K.
Hall, 1969. 3 v. 016.05 79-17893

Z6945 .S7982 MRR Alc (Dk 33)

United States. Library of Congress.
Periodicals division. A check list
of foreign newspapers in the Library
of Congress, Washington, U.S. Govt.
print. off., 1929. vi, 209 p. 29-
14596
Z663.46 .C47 1929 MRR Alc.

PERIODICALS--BIBLIOGRAPHY--UNION LISTS.
British union-catalogue of
periodicals; London, Butterworths
Scientific Publications, 1955-58. 4
v. 016.05 56-1295
    Z6945 .B87 MRR Alc.

British union-catalogue of
periodicals; Mar. 1964- London,
Butterworths. 66-1557
    Z6945 .B874 Sci RR Full set / MRR
    Alc Partial set

California. University. Library.
University of California, Berkeley,
serials key word index. 1st- ed.;
1973- Berkeley. 016.05 73-645730
    Z6945 .C16a MRR Alc Latest edition

Consortium of Universities of the
Washington Metropolitan Area. Union
list of serials. 3d ed. Washington,
1974. 350 p. [$27.50] 016.05 74-
78294
    Z6945 .C763 1974 MRR Ref Desk.

List of the serial publications of
foreign governments, 1815-1931,
Millwood, N.Y., Kraus Reprint Co.,
1973. 720 p. 016.05 73-9866
    Z7164.G7 L7 1973 MRR Alc.

Moore, John Hammond. Research
materials in South Carolina; [1st
ed.] Columbia, University of South
Carolina Press 1967. xiv, 346 p.
016.05 67-25916
    Z732.S72 M6 MRR Alc.

New York State union list of serials.
New York, CCM Information Corp.
[1970] 2 v. 016.05 76-135188
    Z6945 .N685 MRR Alc.

Paris. Bibliothèque nationale.
Département des périodiques.
Catalogue collectif des périodiques
du début du XVIIe siècle à 1939,
Paris, Bibliothèque nationale, 1967-
v.   [250.00 (v. 4)] 016.05 67-
104498
    Z6945 .P236 MRR Alc.

Southan, Joyce E., comp. A survey of
classical periodicals; [London]
University of London, Institute of
Classical Studies, 1962. xii, 181 p.
65-9438
    Z2260 .S67 MRR Alc.

Southern Regional Education Board. A
Southeastern supplement to the Union
list of serials; Atlanta, 1959.
xviii, 447 p. 016.05 59-8979
    Z6945 .S614 MRR Alc.

Stratman, Carl Joseph, Britain's
theatrical periodicals, 1720-1967,
New York, New York Public Library,
1972. xxiv, 160 p. 016.792/0942
72-134260
    Z6935 .S76 1972 MRR Alc.

Union list of serials in libraries of
the United States and Canada, 3d ed.
New York, H. W. Wilson Co., 1965. 5
v. (4649 p.) 016.05 65-10150
    Z6945 .U45 1965 MRR Circ.

Union list of serials [in] the
libraries of the State University of
New York. 1st- ed.; 1866-
[Syracuse] 011 67-65593
    Z6945 .U454 MRR Alc Latest edition

United States. Library of Congress.
Division of bibliography. ... A
union list of periodicals,
transactions and allied publications
currently received in the principal
libraries of the District of
Columbia. Washington, Govt. print.
off., 1901. v; 315 p. 01-16622
    Z6663.28 .U5 MRR Alc.

United States. Library of Congress.
Reference Dept. Periodicals on
Africa currently received in selected
American libraries. Washington,
1956. iv, 34 p. 56-60035
    Z6663.2 .P4 MRR Alc.

World list of scientific periodicals;
1960/68- London, Butterworths.
016.505 70-20683
    Z7403 .W9 Sci RR Latest edition /
    MRR Alc Latest edition

World list of scientific periodicals
published in the years 1900-1960.
4th ed. Washington, Butterworths,
1963-65. 3 v. (xxv, 1824 p.)
016.505 64-9729
    Z7403 .W923 MRR Alc.

PERIODICALS--DIRECTORIES.
An Advertiser's guide to scholarly
periodicals. New York, American
University Press Services. 659.132
65-9732
    Began publication in 1958.
    Z6944.S3 A25 MRR Alc Latest
    edition

The Advertising & press annual of
Africa. Cape Town, National Pub. Co.
(Pty) Ltd. [etc.] 52-41681
    Z6959 .A65 MRR Alc Latest edition

Anuario de la prensa española.
[Madrid, Ministerio de Información y
Turismo, Secretaría General Técnica,
Sección de Planificación y
Documentación] 076/.1/025 74-
644556
    Z6956.S7 S65 MRR Alc Latest
    edition

Association des universités
entièrement ou partiellement de
langue française. Catalogue des
publications périodiques
universitaires de langue française.
[2. éd. Montréal, 1969] viii, 150
p.   77-478508
    Z6944.S3 A7 1969 MRR Alc.

Bowker serials bibliography
supplement. 1972- New York, R. R.
Bowker Co. 011 72-2677
    Z6941 .U522 MRR Alc Latest edition
    / MRR Ref Desk Latest edition /
    Sci RR Latest edition

Canadian serials directory.
[Toronto, Buffalo] University of
Toronto Press. 016.051 73-643405
    Z6954.C2 C23 MRR Alc Latest
    edition

Commonwealth Secretariat.
Commonwealth directory of
periodicals: London, Commonwealth
Secretariat, Publications Section,
1973. ix, 157 p. [£2.50] 016.05
74-168502
    Z6941 .C65 1973 MRR Alc.

Consumer magazine and farm
publication rates and data. v. 38,
no. 10- Oct. 1956- [Skokie, Ill.]
Standard Rate & Data Service, Inc.
659.1/025/73 72-622888
    HF5905 .S725 MRR Ref Desk Latest
    edition

Fraenkel, Josef. The Jewish press of
the world / 7th ed. London :
Cultural Dept. of the World Jewish
Congress, 1972. 128 p. : [£1.00]
070/.025 74-190296
    Z6367 .F7 1972 TJ Rm.

Gebbie house magazine directory.
[Sioux City, Iowa, House Magazine
Pub. Co.] 016.0704/86 74-644438
    Z7164.C81 N32 MRR Ref Desk Latest
    edition

Irregular serials & annuals; 1st-
ed.; 1967- New York, Bowker. 016.05
67-25026
    Z6941 .I78 Sci RR Latest edition /
    MRR Ref Desk Latest edition

Media Scandinavia. 16.- udg.; 1967-
København, Danske reklamebureauers
brancheforening. 72-623099
    Z6941 .M4 MRR Alc Latest edition

Muller, Robert H. From radical left
to extreme right; 2d ed. rev. and
enl. Ann Arbor, Campus Publishers
[c1970- v.   79-126558
    Z7165.U5 M82 MRR Ref Desk.

National directory of newsletters and
reporting services. 1st- ed.; 1966-
Detroit, Gale Research Co. 66-
15458
    Z6941 .N3 MRR Ref Desk Latest
    edition

New York publicity outlets. New
York, Attention Inc. [etc.] 61-65657
    Z6953.N6 N6 MRR Alc Latest edition

The Newspaper press directory.
London, C. Mitchell [etc.] ca 07-6361
    Z6956.E5 M6 MRR Alc Latest edition

Overseas newspapers and periodicals.
[London, Publishing & Distributing
Co.] 63-42121
    Began publication with 1952 issue.
    Z6941 .O9 MRR Alc Latest edition

La Presse française; 1965- [Paris,
Hachette] 65-80951
    Z6956.F8 P7 MRR Alc Latest edition

Ross, Mary Bucher, Directory of
publishing opportunities; 2d ed.
Orange, N.J., Academic Media [1973]
x, 722 p.   808/.025 73-13565
    Z479 .R67 1973 MRR Ref Desk.

The Standard periodical directory. 1-
ed.; 1964/65- New York, Oxbridge
Pub. Co. 016.051 64-7598
    Z6951 .S78 Sci RR Latest edition /
    MRR Ref desk Latest edition

Standard Rate and Data Service, inc.
Business publication rates and data.
v.33- Jan. 1951- Skokie, Ill.
[etc.] 659.132058 53-36930
    HF5905 .S723 MRR Ref Desk Latest
    edition

Ulrich's international periodicals
directory. [1st]- ed.; [1932]-
New York, Bowker. 011 32-16320
    Z6941 .U5 Sci RR Latest edition /
    MRR Ref Desk Latest edition / MRR
    Ref Desk Latest edition

Woodworth, David. Guide to current
British journals: 2nd ed. London,
Library Association, 1973. 2 v.
[£8.50 (v. 1) £4.50 (v. 2)] 016.052
74-159014
    Z6956.G6 W66 1973 MRR Alc.

The Writers and artists' year book;
[1st]- year; 1906- Boston [etc.]
The Writer, inc. [etc.] 08-22320
    PN12 .W8 MRR Ref Desk Latest
    edition

PERIODICALS--DIRECTORIES--BIBLIOGRAPHY.
Duprat, Gabrielle. Bibliographie des
répertoires nationaux de
périodiques en cours London, IFLA,
1969. 141 p. 73-858215
    AS4.U8 A154 MRR Alc.

Katz, William Armstrong, Magazines
for libraries; 2d ed. New York, R.
R. Bowker, 1972. xviii, 822 p.
016.05 72-6607
    Z6941 .K2 1972 MRR Alc.

PERIODICALS--INDEXES.
Abstracts for social workers. v. 1-
spring 1965- [New York] National
Association of Social Workers.
[$20.00] 361/.008 74-642752
    HV1 .A2 MRR Alc Full set

Abstracts in anthropology. v. 1-
Feb. 1970- Farmingdale, N.Y.,
Baywood Publishing Co. [etc.] 77-
20528
    GN1 .A15 MRR Alc Full set

Abstracts on criminology and
penology. Deventer. 364/.08 72-
626328
    Began in 1969.
    HV6001 .E9 MRR Alc Full set

Adelman, Irving. The contemporary
novel; Metuchen, N.J., Scarecrow
Press, 1972. 614 p. 016.823/03 72-
4451
    Z1231.F4 A34 MRR Ref Desk.

Adelman, Irving, comp. Modern drama;
Metuchen, N.J., Scarecrow Press,
1967. xvii, 370 p. 016.809/2/04
67-10189
    Z5781 .A35 MRR Ref Desk.

Aerospace medicine and biology; v.
[1]-11; 1952-1962/63. Washington.
016.61698021 56-60078
    Z6663.49 .A37 MRR Alc MRR Alc
    Partial set / Sci RR Full set

African abstracts. v. 1- Jan. 1950-
[London] 960 55-18105
    DT1 .I553 MRR Alc Full set

The African experience. Evanston,
Northwestern University Press, 1970-
v.   916/.03/3 70-98466
    DT14 .A37 MRR Alc.

Aguolu, Christian Chukwunedu, Ghana
in the humanities and social
sciences, 1900-1971: a bibliography.
Metuchen, N.J., Scarecrow Press,
1973. xi, 469 p. 016.91667 73-
9519
    Z3785 .A65 MRR Alc.

Aguolu, Christian Chukwunedu,
Nigeria: a comprehensive bibliography
in the humanities and social
sciences, 1900-1971. Boston, G. K.
Hall, 1973. iv, 620 p.
016.91669/03 73-12843
    Z3597 .A64 MRR Alc.

The Air pollution bibliography. v. 1-
1957- Washington. 016.62853 57-
60050
    Z6663.49 .A4 MRR Alc MRR Alc Full
    set

Ajami, Alfred M. Drugs: an annotated
bibliography and guide to the
literature, Boston, G. K. Hall,
1973. xxiv, 205 p. 615/.78 72-
13943
    RM300 .A47 MRR Alc.

Albrecht, Günter. Internationale
Bibliographie zur Geschichte der
deutschen Literatur von den Anfängen
bis zur Gegenwart, [1. Aufl.]
Berlin, Volk und Wissen, 1969- v.
76-430568
    Z2231 .A44 MRR Alc.

The Alcoholism digest annual. v. 1-
1972/73- Rockville, Md.,
Information Planning Associates.
362.2/92 74-644283
    HV5001 .A34 MRR Alc Full set

PERIODICALS--INDEXES. (Cont.)
Aldous, Joan.   International
bibliography of research in marriage
and the family, 1900-1964
[Minneapolis] Distributed by the
University of Minnesota Press for the
Minnesota Family Study Center and the
Institute of Life Insurance [1967]
508 p.   016.30142   67-63014
     Z7164.M2 A48 MRR Alc.

Allen, Victor Leonard.   International
bibliography of trade unionism.
London, Merlin, 1968.   vii, 180 p.
[73/6]   016.33188   71-403739
     Z7164.17 A38 MRR Alc.

Altbach, Philip G.   American
students. Lexington, Mass.,
Lexington Books [1973]   xiv, 537 p.
016.3781/98/1   73-7992
     Z5814.S86 A55 1973 MRR Alc.

America, history and life.   v. 1-
July 1964-   [Santa Barbara, Calif.]
016.917   64-25630
     Z1236 .A48   MRR Alc Full set

American Ceramic Society.   Indexes to
publications of the American Ceramic
Society: Columbus, Ohio, 1957.   131
p.   666.05   a   58-237
     TP785 .A643 MRR Alc.

American Educational Theatre
Association. Theatre arts
publications available in the United
States, 1953-1957; Evanston? Ill.,
c1964]   xiii, 188 p.   65-3361
     Z5781 .A52 MRR Alc.

American Geographical Society of New
York.   Current geographical
publications; v. 1-   Jan. 1938-
New York.   016.91   41-27154
     Z6009 .A47 MRR Alc Partial set*

The American historical review. v. 1-
Oct. 1895-   Washington [etc.]
973.05   05-18244
     E171 .A57 MRR Ref Desk Indexes
     only

American Hospital Association.
Library, Asa S. Bacon Memorial.
Cumulative index of hospital
literature. Chicago. 016.3621   50-
11277
     Z6675.H7 A5 MRR Alc Partial set /
     Sci RR Full set

American Indian index.   -147/48;
-Oct./Nov. 1968. River Grove, Ill.
[etc.] R. L. Knor [etc.] 72-8243
     Z1209 .A4 MRR Alc Full set

American Institute of Certified
Public Accountants.   Accountants'
index; [New York] American Institute
of Accountants, 1921.   1578 p.   21-
10690
     Z7164.C81 A5 MRR Alc.

American library association. Junior
members round table. Library
literature, 1921-1932: Chicago,
American library association, 1934.
x, [2], 430 p.   016.02   34-5185
     Z666 .C21 1927 Suppl. MRR Alc.

American literature; v. 1-   Mar.
1929-   [Durham, N.C. Duke University
Press] 810.5   30-20216
     PS1 .A6 MRR Ref Desk Indexes only

American Society of Mechanical
Engineers.   Seventy-seven year index:
technical papers, 1880-1956. New
York [1957]   382 p.   621.06273 57-
59509
     TJ1 .A774 MRR Alc.

American Studies Association.
Metropolitan New York Chapter.
Committee on Bibliography.   Articles
in American studies, 1954-1968; Ann
Arbor, Mich., Pierian Press, 1972. 2
v. (x, 898 p.)   016.9173/03/45 71-
172759
     Z1361.C6 A44 MRR Alc.

American Theological Library
Association. Index to religious
periodical literature; 1949/52
[Chicago]   a   54-6085
     Z7753 .A5 MRR Alc Full set

American University of Beirut.
Economic Research Institute.   A
selected and annotated bibliography
of economic literature on the Arab
countries of the Middle East, 1953-
1965. Beirut, 1967.   xvii, 458 p.
016.3309174/927   ne 68-4814
     Z7165.A67 A56 MRR Alc.

L'Année philologique; 1.-   année;
1924/26- Paris, Société d'édition
"Les Belles lettres."   29-9941
     Z7016 .M35A MRR Alc Full set

Antarctic bibliography. v. 1-   1965-
Washington, Library of Congress;
[For sale by the Supt. of Docs., U.S.
Govt. Print. Off.]   65-61825
     Z663.41 .A24 MRR Alc. Sci RR Full
     set / MRR Alc Full set

Applied science & technology index.
v. 1-   Feb. 1913-   [Bronx, N.Y.,
etc.] H. W. Wilson [etc.] 016.6 14-
5408
     Z7913 .I7 MRR Circ Partial set /
     Sci RR Partial set

The Architectural index.   [Berkeley,
Calif., etc.]   016.7205 51-33537
     Z5941 .A66 MRR Alc Full set

Arctic bibliography.   v.1-   1953-
Montreal [etc.] McGill-Queen's
University Press [etc.]   53-61783
     Z6005.P7 A72   Sci RR Full set / MRR
     Alc Full set

Arms control & disarmament.   v. 1-
winter 1964/65-   [Washington, For
sale by the Superintendent of
Documents, U.S. Govt. Print. Off.]
64-62746
     Z663.28 .A23 MRR Alc   MRR Alc Full
     set

Art index.   v. 1-   Jan. 1929/Sept.
1932-   New York, H. W. Wilson.   016.7
31-7513
     Z5937 .A78 MRR Circ Full set

Artbibliographies modern.   Santa
Barbara, Calif., American
Bibliographical Center.   016.709/04
74-647780
     Z5935 .L64 MRR Alc Full set

Ash, Lee,   Serial publications
containing medical classics; New
Haven, Antiquarium, 1961.   xxiv, 147
p.   016.61   61-8290
     Z6658 .G26 MRR Alc.

Astin, Helen S.,   Women; Washington,
Human Service Press [1971] v, 243 p.
[$5.95]   016.3314   76-30266
     Z7963.E7 A86 MRR Alc.

The Athenæum subject index to
periodicals ...   London, The
Athenæum, 1916.   2 p. l., [vii]-xv,
150 p.   16-24573
     AI3 .A7 MRR Alc.

Australian public affairs information
service; no. 1-   July 1945-
Canberra.   015.94   50-28427
     Z7165.A8 A8 MRR ALc Partial set

Barr, Ernest Scott,   An index to
biographical fragments in
unspecialized scientific journals,
University, Ala., University of
Alabama Press [c1973] vii, 294 p.
016.5/092/2 B   73-13434
     Q141 .B29 MRR Biog.

A Basic bibliography on marketing
research [3d ed.], 1974 revision.
[Chicago] : American Marketing
Association, 1974. x, 299 p. ;
016.6588/3   74-187908
     Z7164.M18 B35 1974 MRR Alc.

Bateson, Frederick Wilse,   The
Cambridge bibliography of English
literature, Cambridge [Eng.] The
University press, 1940-57. 5 v.
016.82   41-2592
     Z2011 .B28 vol. 5 MRR Alc.

Bateson, Frederick Wilse,   The
Cambridge bibliography of English
literature, New York, The Macmillan
company; Cambridge, Eng., The
University press, 1941.   4 v.
015.42   41-4948
     Z2011 .B3 1941 MRR Alc.

Bayitch, S. A.   Latin America and the
Caribbean; Coral Gables, Fla.,
University of Miami Press, 1967.
xxviii, 943 p.   016.918/03   67-28900
     Z1601 .B35 MRR Alc.

Belknap, Sara (Yancey) Guide to the
musical arts; New York, Scarecrow
Press, 1957. 1 v. (unpaged) 016.78
57-6631
     ML113 .B37 MRR Alc.

Bell, Inglis Freeman,   The English
novel, 1578-1956; Denver, A. Swallow
[1959] xii, 169 p.   016.82309 59-
8212
     Z2014.F4 B4 MRR Alc.

Belson, William A.   Bibliography on
methods of social and business
research London, London School of
Economics and Political Science;
Lockwood, 1973. viii, 300 p.
[£4.95]   016.3/001/8   73-155242
     Z7161 .B44 MRR Alc.

Berkowitz, Morris I.   Social
scientific studies of religion:
[Pittsburgh] University of Pittsburgh
Press [1967] xvii, 258 p.   016.2
67-18692
     Z7751 .B47 MRR Alc.

Bibliografia storica nazionale. Bari
[etc.] Gius. Laterza & Figli. 52-
23151
     Began publication in 1939.
     Z6201 .B54 MRR Alc Full set

Bibliographie de la littérature
française moderne (16.-20.
siècles). Paris, Librairie A.
Colin.   67-40990
     Began publication in 1962.
     Z2171 .B55 MRR Alc Full set

Bibliographie der deutschen
Bibliographien. Jahrg. 1-   1954-
Leipzig, Verlag für Buch- und
Bibliothekswesen.   59-43508
     Z1002 .B598 MRR Alc Full set

Bibliographie der deutschen
Literaturwissenschaft. Bd. [1]-8;
1945/53-1967/68. Frankfurt am Main,
V. Klostermann.   a   57-5262
     Z2231 .B5 MRR Alc Full set

Bibliographie der deutschen Sprach-
und Literaturwissenschaft. Bd. 9-
1969-   Frankfurt am Main, V.
Klostermann.   72-612758
     Z2231 .B5 MRR Alc Full set

Bibliographie der französischen
Literaturwissenschaft. Bd. 1-
1956/58- Frankfurt am Main, V.
Klostermann.   60-43852
     Z2171 .B56 MRR Alc Full set

Bibliographie der Rezensionen, nach
Titeln (alphabet der Verfasser)
geordnetes Verzeichnis von
Besprechungen deutscher und
ausländischer Bücher und Karten,
die ... in zumeist wissenschaftlichen
und kritischen Zeitschriften,
Zeitungen und Sammelwerken deutscher
Zunge erschienen sind ... 1.-
Supplementband; 1900-   Leipzig [etc.]
F. Dietrich.   01-15596
     AI9 .B6 MRR Alc Full set

Bibliographie géographique
internationale. [1.]-   1891-
Paris, Centre national de la
recherche scientifique [etc.] 25-
1167
     Z6001 .B57 MRR Alc Partial set

Bibliographie internationale de
l'Humanism et de la Renaissance. 1-
1965-   Genève, Librairie Droz. 68-
2326
     Z6207.R4 B5 MRR Alc Full set

Bibliography of medical reviews.
1966/70- Bethesda, Md., National
Library of Medicine; for sale by the
Supt. of Docs., U.S. Govt. Print.
Off. 016.61   72-627542
     Z6660 .B5817 Sci RR Full set / MRR
     Alc Full set

Bibliography of Old Norse-Icelandic
studies. Copenhagen, Munksgaard.
016.91003/175/396   68-45376
     Began in 1963.
     Z2556 .B5 MRR Alc Full set

Bibliography of publications of
university bureaus of business and
economic research. [Boulder, Colo.,
etc.] Business Research Division,
University of Colorado.
016.33/007/2073   77-635614
     Z7165.U5 A8 MRR Alc Full set

Bibliography of society, ethics and
the life sciences. Hastings-on-the
Hudson, N.Y., Institute of Society,
Ethics and the Life Sciences.
016.174/2   73-160650
     Z5322.B5 B52 MRR Alc Full set /
     Sci RR Full set

Bibliography of world literature on
mental retardation, Washington,
Published for the President's Panel
on Mental Retardation by the U.S.
Dept. of Health, Education, and
Welfare : Public Health Service; for
sale by the Superintendent of
Documents, U.S. Govt. Print. Off.,
1963] vii, 564 p.   64-60331
     Z6677 .B5 MRR Alc.

Bibliotheca celtica, 1909-1927/28;
new ser., v. 1-   1929/33-
Aberystwyth [National library of
Wales]   11-5717
     Z2071 .B56 MRR Alc Partial set

Biography index; v. 1-   Jan.
1946/July 1949- New York, H. W.
Wilson Co. 016.82   47-6532
     Z5301 .B5 MRR Biog Full set

Biological & agricultural index.
Jan. 1916-   [Bronx, N.Y., etc.] H. W.
Wilson Co.   17-8906
     Z5073 .A46 Sci RR Full set / MRR
     Alc Full set

Bodurgil, Abraham. Atatürk and
Turkey: Washington, Library of
Congress; [for sale by the Supt. of
Docs., U.S. Govt. Print. Off.] 1974.
74 p.   016.9561   73-18313
     Z663.387 .A8 MRR Alc.

Bonheim, Helmut W., The English
novel before Richardson; Metuchen,
N.J., Scarecrow Press, 1971. vi, 145
p.   016.823/03   75-19590
     Z2014.F4 B65 MRR Alc.

PERIODICALS--INDEXES. (Cont.)

Bonser, Wilfrid, An Anglo-Saxon and Celtic bibliography, 450-1087. Oxford, Blackwell, 1957. 2 v. 016.94201 a 58-1987
Z2017 .B6 MRR Alc.

Book review digest. Annual cumulation. v. 1- 1905- New York [etc.] H. W. Wilson Co. 06-9994
Z1219 .C96 MRR Circ Full set

Bossuat, Robert, Manuel bibliographique de la littérature française du Moyen Age. Melun, Librairie d'Argences, 1951. xxxiv, 638 p. 016.84 51-5797
Z2172 .B7 MRR Alc.

Branch, Melville Campbell, Comprehensive urban planning; a selective annotated bibliography Beverly Hills, Calif., Sage Publications [1970] 477 p. 016.711/4 73-92349
Z5942 .B7 MRR Alc.

Breed, Paul Francis, Dramatic criticism index; Detroit, Gale Research Co. [1972] 1022 p. 016.8092/04 79-127598
Z5781 .B8 MRR Ref Desk.

Bremner, Robert Hamlett, American social history since 1860. New York, Appleton-Century-Crofts [1971] xiv, 126 p. 016.917/03 70-146848
Z1361.C6 B7 MRR Alc.

British archaeological association. The journal of the British archaeological association. General index to volumes I to XXX. London, Printed for the Association, 1875. 225 p. 01-6360
DA20 .B83 Index MRR Alc.

British education index. v. 1- Aug. 1954/Nov. 1958- London, Library Association. 61-45718
Z5813 .B7 MRR Alc Full set

British humanities index. 1962- London, Library Association. 63-24940
AI3 .B7 MRR Alc Full set

British technology index. 1962- London, Library Association. 63-23735
Z7913 .B7 Sci RR Full set / MRR Alc Full set

Brode, John. The process of modernization; Cambridge, Mass., Harvard University Press, 1969. x, 378 p. [6.50] 016.3092 69-13765
Z7164.U5 E7 MRR Alc.

Brunn, Stanley D. Urbanization in developing countries; East Lansing, Latin American Studies Center, Michigan State University, 1971. xviii, 693 p. 016.30136/3/091724 79-172535
Z7164.U7 B7 MRR Alc.

Bulletin signalétique 519: Philosophie, sciences religieuses. v. 15-23; 1961-69. Paris, Centre de documentation du C.N.R.S. 75-10205
Z7127 .F712 MRR Alc Full set

Bulletin signalétique: Philosophie, sciences humaines. v. 1-14; 1947-60. Paris, Centre de documentation du C. N. R. S. 51-30077
Z7127 .F7 MRR Alc Full set

Buros, Oscar Krisen, Personality tests and reviews; Highland Park, N.J., Gryphon Press [1970] xxxi, 1659 p. 155.28 74-13192
BF698.5 .B87 MRR Alc.

Burr, Nelson Rollin, Religion in American life, New York, Appleton-Century-Crofts [1971] xix, 171 p. 016.2009/73 70-136219
Z7757.U5 B8 MRR Alc.

Business periodicals index. v. 1- Jan. 1958- New York, H. W. Wilson Co. 016.6505 58-12645
Z7164.C81 B983 MRR Circ Full set

California. University. Institute of Governmental Studies. Library. Subject catalog of the Institute of Governmental Studies Library, University of California, Berkeley. Boston, G. K. Hall, 1970 [pref. 1971] 26 v. 016.353 73-152341
Z7164.A2 C34 MRR Alc (Dk 33)

Canadian Library Association. Reference Section. Canadian library literature index; Ottawa, Canadian Library Association, 1956. iv, 79 p. 016.02 58-41202
Z666 .C18 MRR Alc.

Canadian periodical index. 1938-May 1947. Toronto, Public Libraries Branch, Ontario Department of Education. 40-17273
AI3 .C262 MRR Alc Full set

Canadian periodical index. v. 1- Jan. 1948- Ottawa. 49-2133
AI3 .C242 MRR Alc Full set

Cannons, Harry George Turner. Bibliography of library economy; Chicago, American library association, 1927. 4 p. l., 11-680 p. 26-26901
Z666 .C21 1927 MRR Alc.

Carter, Robert M. Communication in organizations; Detroit, Gale Research Co. [1972] ix, 272 p. [$14.50] 016.6584/5 73-161194
Z7164.C81 C27 MRR Alc.

Case, Margaret H. South Asian history, 1750-1950; Princeton, N.J., Princeton University Press, 1968. xiii, 561 p. 016.954 67-21019
Z3185 .C3 MRR Alc.

The Catholic periodical and literature index. July/Aug. 1968- Haverford, Pa., Catholic Library Association. 011 70-649588
AI3 .C32 MRR Alc Full set

The Catholic periodical index, 1930/33-May/June 1968. Haverford, Pa. [etc.] Catholic Library Association [etc.] 40-15160
AI3 .C32 MRR Alc Full set

Cayless, Colin Frederick. Bibliography of library automation, 1964-1967; London, British National Bibliography, 1968 [i.e. 1969] 107 p. [28/-] 016.0297 78-399413
Z699.2 .C37 MRR Alc.

Chicago. Art Institute. Ryerson Library. Index to art periodicals. Boston, G. K. Hall, 1962. 11 v. (xi, 9635 p.) 016.7 62-6346
Z5937 .C55 MRR Alc (Dk 33)

Chicorel, Marietta. Chicorel theater index to plays for young people in periodicals, anthologies, and collections; 1st ed. New York, Chicorel Library Pub. Corp., 1974. 489 p. 808/.82/016 74-173632
Z5784.C5 C55 MRR Alc.

Chicorel, Marietta. Chicorel theater index to plays in periodicals. 1st ed. New York, Chicorel Library Pub. Corp., 1973. 500 p. 808/.82/016 73-174118
Z5781 .C487 MRR Alc.

Chilcote, Ronald H. Revolution and structural change in Latin America; Stanford, Calif., Hoover Institution on War, Revolution and Peace, Stanford University, 1970. 2 v. 016.3091/8/03 68-28100
Z1601 .C496 MRR Alc.

Child development abstracts and bibliography. v. 1- June/Sept./Dec. 1927- Chicago, Ill. [etc.] Univ. of Chicago Press [etc.] 016.6491 46-31872
HQ750 .A1C47 MRR Alc Full set

Christian, Portia, Ethics in business conduct: Detroit, Gale Research Co. [c1970] 156 p. [$14.50] 016.174/4 77-127411
Z7164.C81 C524 MRR Alc.

Christian periodical index. 1958- [Buffalo, N.Y.] Christian Librarians' Fellowship. 203 60-36226
Z7753 .C5 MRR Alc Full set

Cioranescu, Alexandre. Bibliographie de la littérature française du dix-huitième siècle ... Paris, Editions du Centre national de la recherche scientifique, 1969- v. [120.00 (v. 1)] 70-453192
Z2172 .C48 MRR Alc.

Cline, Gloria Stark. An index to criticisms of British and American poetry. Metuchen, N.J., Scarecrow Press, 1973. x, 307 p. 821/.009 73-15542
PR89 .C5 MRR Ref Desk.

Coleman, Arthur, Drama criticism Denver, A. Swallow [1966-71] 2 v. [$7.50 (v. 1) $12.50 (v. 2)] 016.809/2 66-30426
Z5781 .C65 MRR Ref Desk.

Columbia University. Libraries. Avery Architectural Library. Avery index to architectural periodicals. 2d ed., rev. and enl. Boston, G. K. Hall, 1973- v. 016.72 74-152756
Z5945 .C653 1973 MRR Alc (Dk 33)

Columbia University. Libraries. Avery Architectural Library. Avery obituary index of architects and artists. Boston, G. K. Hall, 1963. 338 p. 64-7017
Z5941 .C64 MRR Biog.

Comitas, Lambros. Caribbeana 1900-1965, a topical bibliography. Seattle, Published for Research Institute for the Study of Man [by] University of Washington Press [1968] L, 909 p. 016.91729/03/5 68-14239
Z1501 .C6 MRR Alc.

Commerce Clearing House. Accounting articles, 1867-1970; New York [1971] 1 v. (various pagings) 016.657 78-26871
Z7164.C81 C782 MRR Alc.

Computer yearbook and directory. 1st ed.; 1966- [Detroit, American Data Processing] 651.8 66-25748
QA76 .C576 Sci RR Partial set / MRR Alc Latest edition

Cook, Frederick S., Fred Cook's index to the Wonder group, [Grand Haven, Mich., 1966] 239 p. 70-14090
Z5917.S36 C64 MRR Alc.

Cornell University. New York State School of Industrial and Labor Relations. Library. Library catalog. Boston, G. K. Hall, 1967. 12 v. 016.331 72-185999
Z7164.L1 C84 MRR Alc (Dk 33)

Crime and delinquency abstracts. v. 1- Jan. 1963- [Bethesda, Md., etc.] National Clearinghouse for Mental Health Information [etc.] 66-3911
Z5118.C9 I55 MRR Alc Full set

Cross, Lowell M., comp. A bibliography of electronic music. [Toronto] University of Toronto Press [1967] ix, 126 p. 016.7899 67-2573
ML128.E4 C76 MRR Alc.

Crowther, Peter A. A bibliography of works in English on early Russian history to 1800, Oxford, Basil Blackwell, 1969. xviii, 236 p. [60/-] 016.947 76-95558
Z2506 .C75 MRR Alc.

Cumulated Dramatic index, 1909-1949; Boston, G. K. Hall, 1965. 2 v. 68-4712
Z5781 .C8 MRR Alc.

Cumulated magazine subject index, 1907-1949; Boston, G. K. Hall, 1964. 2 v. 65-98
AI3 .C76 MRR Alc.

Cumulative bibliography of Asian studies, 1941-1965: Boston, Mass., G. K. Hall, 1969 [i.e. 1970] 4 v. 016.915 79-12105
Z3001 .C93 MRR Alc.

Cumulative index to a selected list of periodicals. v. -8; -June 1903. Cleveland, O., The Public Library [etc.], ca 17-9
AI3 .C8 MRR Alc Full set

Cumulative index to nursing literature. v. 1/5- 1956/60- [Glendale, Calif.] Seventh-Day Adventist Hospital Association. 62-147
Z6675 .N7C8 Sci RR Full set / MRR Alc Full set

Current index to journals in education. v. 1- 1968- New York, CCM Information Corp. 016.370/5 75-7532
Z5813 .C8 MRR Circ Full set

Current list of medical literature. v. 1-36; Jan. 1, 1941-Dec. 1959. Washington. 44-11211
Z6660 .C8 Sci RR Partial set / MRR Alc Partial set

Dahlmann, Friedrich Christoph, Dahlmann-Waitz. Quellenkunde der deutschen geschichte. 9. aufl. Leipzig, K. F. Koehler, 1931. xl, 992 p. 016.943 32-9099
Z2236 .D14 1931 MRR Alc.

Dania polyglotta; 1.-24. année; 1945-1968. Copenhague, Bibliothèque royale. 015.489 48-2634
Z2574.F6 D32 MRR Alc Partial set

Dania polyglotta. new ser.; 1- 1969- Copenhagen [Royal Library] 72-622671
Z2561 .D162 MRR Alc Full set

Dansk tidsskrift-index. København, Udgivet af Bibliotekscentralen [etc.] ca 18-1493
AI13. D3 MRR Alc Partial set

Day, Donald Byrne, Index to the science-fiction magazines, 1926-1950. Portland, Or., Perri Press [1952] xv, 184 p. 016.5 52-41880
Z5917.S36 D3 MRR Alc.

PERIODICALS--INDEXES. (Cont.)
Deardorff, John. United Nations
Economic and Social Council index;
Columbus] United Nations Collection,
O.S.U. Libraries, 1969. vii, 170 l.
330/.061/1 79-628081
HC59 .D425 MRR Alc.

Debate index. New ed. rev. New
York, Wilson, 1939. 130 p.   016.3
39-27689
Z7161.5 .D28 1939 MRR Alc.

Deutsch, Karl Wolfgang. Nationalism
and national development; Cambridge,
Mass., MIT Press [1970] 519 p.
016.3201/58 79-90750
Z7164.N2 D43 MRR Alc.

Deutsches Archäologisches Institut.
Römische Abteilung. Bibliothek.
Kataloge der Bibliothek des Deutschen
Archaeologischen Instituts, Rom:
Zeitschriften--Autorenkatalog.
Boston, G. K. Hall, 1969. 3 v.
016.91337 73-202659
Z5134 .R7642 MRR Alc (Dk 33)

Dreher, S. Bibliographie de la
litterature française, 1930-1939,
Lille, Giard, 1948- v.   a 49-
1233
Z2171 .D7 MRR Alc.

Driver, Edwin D. World population
policy; an annotated bibliography
Lexington, Mass., Lexington Books
[c1971] xxi, 1280 p.   016.30132 73-
184302
Z7164.D3 D75 MRR Alc.

Education index. Jan. 1929- New
York, H. W. Wilson Co. 016.3705 30-
23807
Z5813 .E23 MRR Circ Full set

Eichelberger, Clayton L., A guide to
critical reviews of United States
fiction, 1870-1910, Metuchen, N.J.,
Scarecrow Press, 1971. 415 p.
016.813/4/09 77-149998
Z1225 .E35 MRR Ref Desk.

Eichelberger, Clayton L., A guide to
critical reviews of United States
fiction, 1870-1910, Metuchen, N.J.,
Scarecrow Press, 1971. 415 p.
016.813/4/09 77-149998
Z1225 .E35 MRR Ref Desk.

Eicher, Joanne Bubolz. African
dress; [East Lansing] African
Studies Center, Michigan State
University, 1969. xi, 134 p.
[$4.00]   016.391/00967 73-631220
Z5694.A4 E53 MRR Alc.

Ellis, Jessie Croft, comp. General
index to illustrations; Boston, The
F. W. Faxon company, 1931. 4 p. l.,
467 p.   016.74 31-28562
NC996 .E6 MRR Ref Desk.

Ellis, Jessie (Croft) Index to
illustrations. Boston, F. W. Faxon
Co., 1966 [c1967] xi, 682 p.
741.6/01/6 66-11619
NC996 .E62 MRR Ref Desk.

Ellis, Jessie (Croft) Nature and its
applications; Boston, F. W. Faxon
Co., 1949. xii, 861 p.   016.745 49-
9331
Z5956.D3 E53 MRR Alc.

The Energy index. [New York,
Environment Information Center,
Energy Reference Dept.] [$50.00]
333.7 73-88098
HD9502.U5 E525 MRR Alc Full set /
Sci RR Full set

Engineering index. 1906- New York
[etc.] 07-38575
Z5851 .E62 Sci RR Full set / MRR
Alc (Dk 33) Partial set

English literature, 1660-1800;
Princeton, Princeton University
Press, 1950- v.   016.82 a 51-
6808
Z2011 .E6 MRR Alc.

Evanston, Ill. Transportation Center
at Northwestern University. Library.
Catalog. Boston, G. K. Hall, 1972.
12 v.   016.3805 74-171017
Z7164.T8 E83 1972 MRR Alc (Dk 33)

Excerpta criminologica. v. 1-8; 1961-
68. Amsterdam. 63-59273
HV6001 .E9 MRR Alc Full set

F & S index international:
industries, countries, companies.
1st   ed.; 1968- Cleveland,
Predicasts.   016.338 74-644265
Z7164.C81 F13 MRR Alc Full set /
Sci RR Partial set

Farrar, Robert Henry. An index to
the biographical and obituary notices
in the Gentleman's magazine, 1731-
1780. London, 1891 [i.e. 1886-91]
677 p.   10-20807
AI3 .I4 vol. 15 MRR Alc.

Ferguson, Elizabeth, ed. Sources of
insurance statistics. [New York]
Special Libraries Association, 1965.
v, 191 p.   368.00212 65-25313
HG8045 .F45 MRR Alc.

Fondation nationale des sciences
politiques. Bibliographie courante
d'articles de périodiques
postérieurs a 1944 sur les
problèmes politiques, économiques,
et sociaux. Boston, G. K. Hall,
1968. 17 v.   70-409780
AI7 .F6 MRR Alc. (Dk 33).

Forsman, John. Recipe index, 1970;
Detroit, Gale Research Co. [1972] x,
772 p.   641.5/01/6 72-884
TX651 .F63 MRR Alc.

Forsman, John. Recipe index, 1971;
Detroit, Gale Research Co. [c1973]
viii, 764 p.   641.5/01/6 74-164317
TX651 .F633 MRR Alc.

Forster, Merlin H. An index to
Mexican literary periodicals, New
York, Scarecrow Press, 1966. 276 p.
860 65-22755
Z1421 .F6 MRR Alc.

Freitag, Ruth S. Presidential
inaugurations; 3d ed., rev. and enl.
Washington, Library of Congress;
[for sale by the Supt. of Docs., U.S.
Govt. Print. Off.] 1969. vii, 230 p.
[2.00]   016.394/4 76-602825
Z663.28 .P68 1969 MRR Alc.

Fürer-Haimendorf, Elizabeth von. An
anthropological bibliography of South
Asia, Paris, Mouton, 1958-70. 3 v.
[fl. 130.00 (v. 3)]   a 58-1034
Z5115 .F83 MRR Alc.

Garrison, Fielding Hudson, A medical
bibliography 3d ed. [London] A.
Deutsch [1970] 872 p. [£12.60]
016.61 75-864894
Z6658 .G243 1970b MRR Alc.

Gephart, Ronald M. Periodical
literature on the American
Revolution: historical research and
changing interpretations, 1895-1970;
Washington, Library of Congress; [for
sale by the Supt. of Docs., U.S.
Govt. Print. Off.] 1971. iv, 93 p.
[$1.00]   016.9733 74-609228
Z663.28 .P4 MRR Alc.

Gerlach, John C. The critical index;
New York, Teachers College Press
[1974] xlvi, 726 p. [$6.50 (pbk.)]
016.79143 74-1959
Z5784.M9 G47 MRR Alc.

Gerstenberger, Donna Lorine. The
American novel, 1789-1959; Denver,
A. Swallow [1961-70] 2 v.
016.813/03 61-9356
Z1231.F4 G4 TJ Rm.

Gettens, Rutherford John, comp.
Abstracts of technical studies in art
and archaeology, 1943-1952,
Washington, 1955. viii, 408 p.
016.7 55-61312
N7428 .G44 MRR Alc.

Glenn, Norval D. Social
stratification: Berkeley, Calif.,
The Glendessary Press [1970] xi, 466
p.   016.30144 74-104325
Z7164.S64 G55 MRR Alc.

Gomme, George Laurence, Sir, Index
of archaeological papers, 1665-1890.
London, A. Constable & company, ltd.,
1907. xi, 910 p.   08-9803
Z2027.A8 I6 MRR Alc.

Goode, Stephen H., Venereal disease
bibliography. 1966/70- Troy, N.Y.,
Whitston Pub. Co. [$10.00]
016.6169/51 71-189843
Z6664.V45 G66 MRR Alc Full set

Greenwood, John, American defense
policy since 1945; Lawrence,
Published for the National Security
Education Program, by the University
Press of Kansas [1973] xv, 317 p.
016.3554 72-97468
Z1361.D4 G73 MRR Alc.

Griffin, Appleton Prentiss Clark,
Bibliography of American historical
societies 2d ed., rev. and enl.
[Washington, Govt. print. off., 1907]
1374 p.   08-7356
Z1236 .G86 MRR Alc.

Griffin, Charles Carroll, Latin
America: a guide to the historical
literature. Austin, Published for
the Conference on Latin American
History by the University of Texas
Press [c1971] xxx, 700 p. [$25.00]
016.98 71-165916
Z1601 .G75 MRR Alc.

Grinstein, Alexander. The index of
psychoanalytic writings. New York,
International Universities Press
[1956- v.   [$150.00 (v. 1-5) (v.
6-9) (v. 10-14)]   016.13134 56-8932

Z7204.P8 G7 MRR Alc.

A Guide to Negro periodical
literature. v. 1-4, no. 3; Feb. 1941-
Sept. 1946. Winston-Salem, N.C.
[etc.]   016.32526 45-41371
Z1361.N39 G8 MRR Alc Full set

Guide to religious and semi-religious
periodicals. Flint, Mich., National
Library of Religious Periodicals.
016.200/5 72-624925
Z7753 .G83 MRR Alc Full set

Guide to religious periodicals. v. 1-
Sept. 1964/Feb. 1965- Flint,
Mich. [etc.] National Library of
Religious Periodicals [etc.] 76-2563

Z7753 .G84 MRR Alc Full set

Guide to social science and religion
in periodical literature. Flint,
Mich., National Periodical Library.
016.2/005 73-641014
Z7753 .G83 MRR Alc Full set

Guide to the performing arts. 1957-
Metuchen, N.J. [etc.] Scarecrow
Press.   016.78 60-7266
ML118 .G8 MRR Alc Full set

Gwinup, Thomas. Greek and Roman
authors; Metuchen, N.J., Scarecrow
Press, 1973. x, 194 p.   016.88/009
72-10156
Z7016 .G9 MRR Alc.

Haas, Michael, International
organization; Stanford, Calif.,
Hoover Institution Press [c1971]
xxiv, 944 p.   016.3412 68-28099
Z6464.I6 H3 MRR Alc.

Hager, Anna Marie. The Historical
Society of Southern California
bibliography of all published works,
1884-1957, Los Angeles, Historical
Society of Southern California, 1958.
xix, 183 p.   016.9794 58-59890
Z1261 .H22 MRR Alc.

Halstead, John P. Modern European
imperialism: Boston, G. K. Hall,
1974. 2 v.   016.90908 73-19511
Z6204 .H35 MRR Alc.

Harvard University. Graduate School
of Design. Library. Catalogue of the
Library of the Graduate School of
Design, Harvard University. Boston,
Mass., G. K. Hall, 1968. 44 v.
019/.1 73-169433
Z5945 .H28 1968 MRR Alc (Dk 33)

Harvard University. Peabody Museum of
Archaeology and Ethnology. Library.
Catalogue: authors. Boston, G. K.
Hall, 1963. 26 v.   64-2646
Z5119 .H35 MRR Alc (DK 33).

Harvard University. Peabody Museum of
Archaeology and Ethnology. Library.
Catalogue: subjects. Boston, G. K.
Hall, 1963. 27 v.   018/1 64-2645
Z5119 .H36 MRR Alc (Dk 33)

Havlice, Patricia Pate. Art in Time.
Metuchen, N.J., Scarecrow Press,
1970. 350 p.   016.7 76-14885
N7225 .H38 MRR Alc.

Hay, Stephen N. Southeast Asian
history; New York, Praeger [1962]
vii, 138 p.   016.959 62-20439
Z3221 .H36 MRR Alc.

Hayes, Richard J., Sources for the
history of Irish civilisation;
Boston, G. K. Hall, 1970. 9 v.
016.91415/03 74-22260
Z2034 .H35 MRR Alc (Dk 33)

Heere, Wybo P. International
bibliography of air law 1900-1971.
Leiden, Sijthoff; Dobbs Ferry, N.Y.,
Oceana, 1972. xxvi, 569 p.
[fl78.00]   016.34146 72-86857
Z6464.A4 H43 MRR Alc.

Historical abstracts. v. 1- Mar.
1955- [Santa Barbara, Calif., etc.]
909.8082 56-56304
D299 .H5 MRR Alc Full set

Housing and planning references. new
ser. no. 1- July/Aug. 1965-
[Washington, U.S. Govt. Print. Off.]
016.3015/4 72-621364
Z7165.U5 A3 MRR Alc Full set

Howard University, Washington, D.C.
Library. Moorland Foundation.
Dictionary catalog of the Jesse E.
Moorland Collection of Negro Life and
History, Howard University,
Washington, D.C. Boston, G. K. Hall,
1970. 9 v.   016.910/0396 72-195773

Z1361.N39 H82 MRR Alc (Dk 33)

PERIODICALS--INDEXES. (Cont.)
Hsia, Tao-t'ai. Guide to selected
legal sources of Mainland China;
Washington, Library of Congress; [for
sale by the Supt. of Docs., U.S.
Govt. Print. Off.] 1967. viii, 357
p.   340/.0951   67-60042
Z663.5.G8C53 MRR Alc.

Index of American periodical verse.
1971- Metuchen, N.J., Scarecrow
Press. 016.811/5/4 73-3060
Z1231.P7 I47 MRR Alc Full set

Index of archæological papers
published 1891-1910. [1st]-20th
issue; 1892-1914. [London] 08-10988

Z2027.A8 I7 MRR Alc Full set

Index of economic articles. v. 7-A;
1964/65. Homewood, Ill., R. D.
Irwin. 73-14217
Z7164.E2 I45 MRR Alc Full set

Index of economic articles in
journals and collective volumes. v.
8- 1966- Homewood, Ill., R. D.
Irwin. 016.33 72-622847
Z7164.E2 I4812 MRR Alc Latest
edition

Index of economic journals. v. 1-7;
1886/1924-1864/65. Homewood, Ill.,
R. D. Irwin. 61-8020
Z7164.E2 I48 MRR Alc Full set

Index to American little magazines.
Troy, N.Y. [etc.] Whitston Pub. Co.
[etc.] 77-97476
AI3 .I54 MRR Alc Full set

Index to Commonwealth little
magazines. 1964/65- Troy, N.Y.
[etc.] Whitston Pub. Co. [etc.] 66-
28796
AI3 .I48 MRR Alc Latest edition

Index to dental literature. 1962-
Chicago, American Dental Association.
617.6/001/6 72-622063
Z6668 .I45 Sci RR Partial set /
MRR Alc Partial set

Index to Jewish periodicals. v. 1-
June/Aug. 1963- Cleveland Heights
[etc.] Ohio, College of Jewish
Studies Press [etc.] 68-41603
Z6367 .I5 MRR Alc Full set

Index to literature on the American
Indian. 1970- [San Francisco]
Indian Historian Press. 016.9701 70-
141292
Z1209 .I53 MRR Alc Full set

Index to New Zealand periodicals.
1966- Wellington, National Library
of New Zealand. 052 73-640533
Z6962.N5 I49 MRR Alc Full set

Index to periodical articles by and
about Negroes. v. 17- 1966-
Boston, G. K. Hall. 051 72-627261
AI3 .C4 MRR Alc Full set

Index to South African periodicals.
v. 1- 1940- Johannesburg [etc.]
052 41-26582
AI3 .I65 MRR Alc Partial set

Indexes to independent Socialist
periodicals. Berkeley, Calif.,
Independent Socialist Press [1969]
221 p. [8.75] 016.3091 77-16046
HX15 .I43 no. 4 MRR Alc

Indice general de publicaciones
periódicas latinoamericanas; v. 1-
1961- New York [etc.] Scarecrow
Press [etc.] 056.1 65-13548
Z1605 .I55 MRR Alc Full set

Indice histórico español.
Bibliografía histórica de España e
Hispanoamérica. v. 1- enero/marzo
1953- [Barcelona] Editorial Teide.
57-34741
Z2696 .I6 MRR Alc Full set

Inland Empire Council of Teachers of
English. Northwest books, [2d ed.]
Portland, Or., Binfords & Mort [1942]
356 p. 016.81 42-21718
Z1251.N7 I6 MRR Alc.

Insurance periodicals index. Boston,
Special Libraries Association,
Insurance Division. 65-4638
Began publication with 1863 vol.
HG8011 .I545 MRR Alc Full set

International African Institute.
East Africa: general, ethnography,
sociology, linguistics, London,
1960. iii, 61 l. 60-44644
Z3516 .I47 MRR Alc.

International African Institute.
North-east Africa: general,
ethnography, sociology, linguistics,
London, 1959. iii, 51 l. 016.91676
60-34932
Z3516 .I5 MRR Alc.

International African Institute.
South-east Central Africa and
Madagascar: general,
ethnography/sociology, linguistics,
London, 1961. v, 53 l. 016.91676
61-65578
Z3516 .I53 MRR Alc.

International African Institute.
West Africa: general, ethnography,
sociology, linguistics, London,
1958. v, 116 l. 016.9166 a 59-
4683
Z3516.5 .I5 MRR Alc.

International bibliography of
economics. v. 1- 1952- London,
Tavistock Publications; Chicago,
Aldine Pub. Co. 55-2317
Z7164.E2 I58 MRR Alc Full set

International bibliography of
historical sciences. 1st- year;
1926- Paris, A. Colin [etc.] 016.9
31-15829
Z6205 .I61 MRR Alc Full set

International bibliography of
political science. v. 1- 1953-
London, Tavistock Publications;
Chicago, Aldine Pub. Co. 54-14355
Z7163 .I64 MRR Alc Full set

International bibliography of social
and cultural anthropology. v. 1-
1955- London, Tavistock Pub.;
Chicago, Aldine Pub. Co. [etc.]
016.572 58-4366
Z7161 .I593 MRR Alc Full set

International bibliography of
sociology. London, Tavistock Pub.,
Chicago, Aldine Pub. Co. [etc.]
016.301 57-2949
Z7161 .I594 MRR Alc Full set

International bibliography of studies
on alcohol. New Brunswick, N.J.,
Publications Division, Rutgers Center
of Alcohol Studies [1966- v.
016.61381 60-14437
Z7721 .I5 MRR Alc.

International bibliography of the
history of religions. 1952- Leiden,
E. J. Brill. 016.29 56-19258
Z7833 .I53 MRR Alc Full set

International guide to classical
studies. v. 1- June 1961- Darien,
Conn., American Bibliographic
Service. 016.91338/03 64-6277
Z7016 .I5 MRR Alc Full set

International guide to medieval
studies. v. 1- June 1961- Darien,
Conn., American Bibliographic
Service. 63-24615
Z6203 .I6 MRR Alc Full set

International index to film
periodicals. 1972- New York, R. R.
Bowker Co. 016.79143 72-1964
Z5784.M9 I49 MRR Alc Full set

International Labor Office. Library.
International labour documentation:
cumulative edition. Boston, Mass.,
G. K. Hall. 72-625702
H91 .I56 MRR Alc Full set

International Labor Office. Library.
Subject index to International labour
documentation, 1957-1964. Boston, G.
K. Hall, 1968. 2 v. mrr01-76
Z7164.L1 I646 MRR Alc.

International Medieval Bibliography.
International medieval bibliography
1967. Leeds, 1968. 160 p.
[unpriced] 016.914/03/1 s 70-
462591
Z6203 .I63 MRR Alc.

International political science
abstracts. v. 1- 1951- Oxford
[etc.] Basil Blackwell [etc.] 320.82
54-3623
JA36 .I5 MRR Alc Full set

Internationale Bibliographie der
Rezensionen wissenschaftlicher
Literatur. Jahrg. 1- 1971-
Osnabrück, F. Dietrich Verlag. 72-
623124
Z5051 .I64 MRR Alc Full set

Internationale Bibliogrqaphie der
Zeitschriften-literatur aus allen
Gebieten des Wissens. Jahrg. 1-
1965- Osnabrück, F. Dietrich. 67-
1836
AI9 .I5 MRR Alc Full set

Internationale volkskundliche
Bibliographie. 1939/41- Bonn [etc.]
R. Habelt [etc.] 53-24243
Z5882 .I523 MRR Alc Full set

ISIS cumulative bibliography;
[London] Mansell, in conjunction with
the History of Science Society, 1971-
v. 016.509 72-186272
Z7405.H6 I2 MRR Biog.

Istituto nazionale di archeologia e
storia dell'arte, Rome. Biblioteca.
Annuario bibliografico di
archeologia. anno 1- 1952-
Modena. 55-22588
Z5132 .I782 MRR Alc Full set

Istituto nazionale di archeologia e
storia dell'arte, Rome. Biblioteca.
Annuario bibliografico di storia
dell'arte. anno 1- 1952- Modena.
55-58434
Z5931 .I73 MRR Alc Full set

Jaffe, Adrian H. Bibliography of
French literature in American
magazines in the 18th century. [East
Lansing] Michigan State College
Press, 1951. vii, 27 p. 016.84 51-
4374
Z2172 .J3 MRR Alc.

Johnson, Robert Owen. An index to
literature in the New Yorker, volumes
I-XV, 1925-1940. Metuchen, N.J.,
Scarecrow Press, 1969-71. 3 v. 051
71-7740
AP2 .N6764 MRR Alc.

Johnson, Robert Owen. An index to
profiles in the New Yorker.
Metuchen, N.J., Scarecrow Press,
1972. vi, 190 p. 016.920/073 71-
186947
Z5305.U5 J64 MRR Biog.

Journal of economic literature. v. 7-
Mar. 1969- Menasha, Wis. American
Economic Association] [$6.00] 330
73-646621
HB1 .J6 MRR Alc Full set

Kaid, Lynda Lee. Political campaign
communication: a bibliography and
guide to the literature. Metuchen,
N.J., Scarecrow Press, 1974. v, 206
p. 016.329/01/0973 73-22492
Z7165.U5 K34 MRR Alc.

Kantor, Harry. Latin American
political parties; a bibliography,
[Gainesville] Reference and
Bibliography Dept., University of
Florida Libraries, 1968. ix, 113 p.
016.3299/8 a 68-7771
Z7165.L3 K3 MRR Alc.

Keller, Dean H. Index to plays in
periodicals. Metuchen, N.J.,
Scarecrow Press, 1971. 558 p.
016.80882 72-142236
Z5781 .K43 MRR Alc.

Kelly, Emerson Crosby. Encyclopedia
of medical sources. Baltimore,
Williams & Wilkins Co., 1948. v, 476
p. 016.61 48-2235
Z6658 .K4 MRR Alc.

Kendall, Maurice George.
Bibliography of statistical
literature. Edinburgh, Oliver and
Boyd [1962- v. 63-853
Z7551 .K42 MRR Alc.

Kiel. Universität. Institut für
Weltwirtschaft. Bibliothek.
Personenkatalog. Boston, G. K. Hall,
1966. 30 v. 72-213362
Z7164.E2 K55 MRR Alc. (Dk 33)

Kiel. Universität. Institut für
Weltwirtschaft. Bibliothek.
Regionenkatalog. Boston, G. K. Hall,
1967. 52 v. 017/.5 67-9425
Z929 .K52 1967 MRR Alc. (Dk 33).

Krawitz, Henry. A post-symbolist
bibliography. Metuchen, N.J.,
Scarecrow Press, 1973. 284 p.
016.809/04 73-1181
Z6520.S9 K7 MRR Alc.

Krichmar, Albert. The women's rights
movement in the United States, 1848-
1970; Metuchen, N.J., Scarecrow
Press, 1972. ix, 436 p.
016.30141/2/0973 72-4702
Z7964.U49 K75 MRR Alc.

Kuntz, Joseph Marshall, Poetry
explication; Rev. ed. Denver, A.
Swallow, 1962. 331 p. 016.82109
62-12525
Z2014.P7 K8 MRR Alc.

Lanson, Gustave, Manuel
bibliographique de la littérature
française moderne, Nouv. éd. rev.
et cor. Paris, Hachette, 1931.
xxxii, 1820 p. 016.84 39-30135
Z2171 .L22 1931 MRR Alc.

Larson, Arthur D. National security
affairs: Detroit, Gale Research Co.,
[1973] 411 p. 016.35503/3/0973 70-
184013
Z1215 .L37 MRR Alc.

Leary, Lewis Gaston, Articles on
American literature, 1900-1950.
Durham, N.C., Duke University Press,
1954. 437 p. 016.81 54-5025
Z1225 .L49 MRR Ref Desk.

PERIODICALS--INDEXES. (Cont.)
Leary, Lewis Gaston. Articles on
American literature, 1950-1967.
Durham, N.C., Duke University Press,
1970. xxi, 751 p. 016.8109 70-
132027
Z1225 .L492 MRR Ref Desk.

Leif, Irving P., Community power and
decision-making; Metuchen, N.J.,
Scarecrow Press, 1974. vi, 170 p.
016.30115/5 74-4171
Z7164.C842 L43 MRR Alc.

Liboiron, Albert A. Federalism and
intergovernmental relations in
Australia, Canada, the United States
and other countries; Kingston, Ont.,
Institute of Intergovernmental
Relations, Queen's University, 1967.
vi, 231 l. [$3.00 Can.] 016.351
68-110060
Z7165.A8 L5 MRR Alc.

Library & information science
abstracts. 1- Jan./Feb. 1969-
London, Library Association. 016.02
78-228730
Z671 .L6 MRR Alc Full set*

Library literature; 1933/35- New
York, H. W. Wilson Co. 016.02 36-
27468
Z666 .C211 MRR Alc Full set

Library science abstracts. v. 1-19;
Jan./Mar. 1950-Oct./Dec. 1968.
London, Library Association. 016.02
53-33079
Z671 .L617 MRR Alc Full set*

Library work. 09-32253
Z671 .L7182 MRR Alc.

Life, health and accident insurance
law; v. [1]- 1906/31- New York,
Association of Life Insurance
Counsel. 016.368 35-25985
Z7164.I7 L5 MRR Alc Latest edition

Liniger-Goumaz, Max. Eurafrique:
bibliographie generale. Geneve,
Éditions du Temps, 1970. 160 p.
76-505812
Z3508.R4 L5 MRR Alc.

Literary history of the United
States. 4th ed., rev. New York,
Macmillan [1974] 2 v. 810/.9 73-
14014
PS88 .L522 1974 MRR Alc.

Liu, Chun-jo, Controversies in
modern Chinese intellectual history;
Cambridge, Published by the East
Asian Research Center, Harvard
University; distributed by Harvard
University Press, 1964. vii, 207 p.
64-56634
Z3108.A5 L5 MRR Alc.

London. University. School of
Oriental and African Studies.
Library. Index Islamicus, 1906-1955;
Cambridge, Eng., W. Heffer [1958]
xxxvi, 897 p. 016.9156 59-23014
Z7835.M6 L6 MRR Alc.

Los Angeles. Public Library.
Municipal Reference Library. Catalog
of the police library of the Los
Angeles Public Library; Boston, G.
K. Hall, 1972. 2 v. 016.3632 73-
158794
Z7164.P76 L58 MRR Alc (Dk 33)

Lust, John. Index Sinicus;
Cambridge, Eng., W. Heffer [1964]
xxx, 663 p. 64-7164
Z3101 .L8 MRR Alc.

Mackey, William Francis.
Bibliographie internationale sur le
bilinguisme; Quebec, Presses de
l'Universite Laval, 1972. xxviii,
337, 208, 203 p. 73-358929
Z7004.B5 M3 MRR Alc.

Marouzeau, Jules, Dix années de
bibliographie classique; New York,
B. Franklin [1969] 2 v. (xv, 1286
p.) 68-57915
Z7016 .M35 1969 MRR Alc.

Martin, Geoffrey Haward. A
bibliography of British and Irish
municipal history Leicester,
Leicester University Press, 1972- v.
[£12.50 (v. 1)] 016.30136/0942
73-156398
Z2023 .M26 MRR Alc.

Mason, Lois E., comp. Bibliography
of Latin America, 1955-1964;
Columbus, Dept. of Geography, Ohio
State University, 1965. vi, 232 l.
016.918 65-64902
Z1601 .M33 MRR Alc.

McBrearty, James C. American labor
history and comparative labor
movements; Tucson, Ariz., University
of Arizona Press [1973] ix, 262 p.
016.331/0973 78-190624
Z7164.L1 M15 MRR Alc.

Menditto, Joseph. Drugs of addiction
and non-addiction, their use and
abuse; Troy, N.Y., Whiteson Pub.
Co., 1970. 315 p. 016.6138/3 79-
116588
Z7164.N17 M45 MRR Alc.

Mental health book review index. v.
[1]- (no. 1-); Jan./Feb. 1956-
[New York] 66-9162
Z6664.N5 M49 MRR Circ Full set

Mental retardation abstracts. v. 1-
Jan./Mar. 1964- [Bethesda, Md.] for
sale by Superintendent of Documents,
U.S. Govt. Print. Off., Washington]
66-60248
RC570 .M4 MRR Alc Full set / Sci
RR Full set

The Methodist periodical index. v. 1-
8 Jan./Mar. 1961-June/Aug. 1968.
Nashville, Methodist Pub. House.
287/.05 76-2484
Z7845.M5 M516 MRR Alc Full set

Michigan index to labor union
periodicals. Jan. 1960- Ann Arbor,
Bureau of Industrial Relations,
Graduate School of Business
Administration, University of
Michigan. 62-63689
Z7164.T7 U6 MRR Alc Full set

Miller, Albert Jay. Confrontation,
conflict, and dissent: Metuchen,
N.J., Scarecrow Press, 1972. 567 p.
016.3091/73/092 78-189440
Z7165.U5 M53 MRR Alc.

Miller, Elizabeth W. The Negro in
America; 2d ed., rev. and enl.,
Cambridge, Harvard University Press,
1970. xx, 351 p. [10.00]
016.301451/96/073 71-120319
Z1361.N39 M5 1970 MRR Alc.

Milne, Alexander Taylor. A centenary
guide to the publications of the
Royal Historical Society, 1868-1968,
London, Royal Historical Society,
1968. xi, 249 p. [unpriced]
016.942 77-436189
Z5055.G6 R66 MRR Alc.

Modern Humanities Research
Association. Annual bibliography of
English Language and literature.
1920- [Leeds, Eng. etc.] 22-11861
Z2011 .M69 MRR Alc Full set

Modern Language Association of
America. MLA abstracts of articles
in scholarly journals. [New York]
408 72-624077
P1 .M64 MRR Alc Full set

Modern Language Association of
America. French III. Bibliography of
French seventeenth century studies.
no. 1- 1952/53- [n.p.] 54-35632
Z2172 .M6 MRR Alc Full set

Mogey, John M. Sociology of marriage
and family behaviour 1957-1968; The
Hague, Mouton [1971] 364 p.
016.30142 78-28387
Z7164.M2 M64 MRR Alc.

Morris, James Oliver, Bibliography
of industrial relations in Latin
America; Ithaca, New York State
School of Industrial and Labor
Relations, Cornell University [1967]
xv, 290 p. 016.6580098 67-64729
Z7164.L1 M69 MRR Alc.

Morrison, Denton E. Environment:
Washington, Office of Research and
Monitoring, U.S. Environmental
Protection Agency; for sale by the
Supt. of Docs., U.S. Govt. Print.
Off., 1974, c1973. vii, 860 p.
[$7.45] 016.3 74-601576
Z7161 .M56 1974 MRR Alc.

Morrow, William R., Behavior therapy
bibliography, 1950-1969; Columbia,
University of Missouri Press [1971]
165 p. [$10.00] 016.61689/1 73-
633730
Z6664.N5 M67 MRR Alc.

Munn, Robert F. Index to West
Virginiana. Charleston, W.Va.,
Education Foundation [1960] 154 p.
016.9754005 60-50809
Z1349 .M8 MRR Alc.

The Music index. v. 1- 1949-
Detroit, Information Coordinators,
inc.[etc.] 50-13627
ML118 .M84 MRR Alc Full set

National geographic magazine.
(Indexes) A guide to unit material
in the National geographic magazine.
Angwin, Calif. [etc.] Angwin Book
Bindery [etc.] 59-32783
G1 .N2712 MRR Alc Latest edition

The New Cambridge bibliography of
English literature. Cambridge [Eng.]
University Press, 1969- v. [10/-
/- $28.50 (U.S.) (v. 3)] 016.82 69-
10199
Z2011 .N45 MRR Alc.

New England Science Fiction
Association. Index to the science
fiction magazines, 1966-1970. [1st
ed. Cambridge, Mass.] 1971. ix, 82
p. [$5.00] 016.823/0876 74-30236

Z5917.S36 N42 1971 MRR Alc.

New York. Public Library. Reference
Dept. Dictionary catalog of the
history of the Americas. Boston, G.
K. Hall, 1961. 28 v. 016.97 61-
4957
Z1201 .N4 MRR Alc (Dk 33).

Nick, William V., Index of legal
medicine, 1940-1970; Columbus, Ohio,
Legal Medicine Press [c1970] lv, 694
p. 016.61 71-148391
Z6672.J9 N53 MRR Alc.

Nineteenth century readers' guide to
periodical literature, 1890-1899,
New York, The H. W. Wilson company,
1944. 2 v. 050 a 44-5439
AI3 .R496 MRR Alc.

Nursing studies index; Philadelphia,
Lippincott [c1963-72. v. 1, 1972, v.
4, 1963] 4 v. 016.61073 62-22361

Z6675.N7 N87 MRR Alc.

Ohio. Central State College,
Wilberforce. Library. Index to
selected periodicals. Mar. 1950-
Wilberforce. 50-62898
MRR Alc Full set

Osburn, Charles B. Research and
reference guide to French studies,
Metuchen, N. J., Scarecrow Press,
1968. 517 p. [$11.50] 016.44 68-
12638
Z2175.A2 O8 MRR Ref Desk.

P H R A; poverty and human resources
abstracts. v. 1- Jan./Feb. 1966-
Beverly Hills, Cal., [etc.] Sage Pub.
[etc.] 66-9955
Z7165.U5 P2 MRR Alc Full set

Palmer, Helen H. American drama
criticism; Hamden, Conn., Shoe
String Press, 1967. 239 p.
016.782/0873 67-16009
Z1231.D7 P3 MRR Ref Desk.

Palmer, Helen H. European drama
criticism, Hamden, Conn., Shoe
String Press, 1968. 460 p.
016.809/2 67-24188
Z5781 .P2 MRR Ref Desk.

Pan American Union. Columbus Memorial
Library. Index to Latin American
periodical literature, 1929-1960.
Boston, G. K. Hall, 1962. 8 v. (xv,
6030 p.) 016.918 63-590
Z1601 .P16 MRR Alc.

Park, Esther Ailleen. Mural painters
in America. Pittsburg, Kansas State
Teachers College, 1949- pts.
016.75173 50-63160
ND236 .P3 MRR Biog.

Parker, William. Homosexuality: a
selective bibliography of over 3,000
items. Metuchen, N.J., Scarecrow
Press, 1971. viii, 323 p.
016.30141/57 71-163430
Z7164.S42 P35 MRR Alc.

Patterson, Charlotte A. Plays in
periodicals; Boston, G. K. Hall,
1970. ix, 240 p. 016.22/9/108 76-
21033
Z5781 .P3 MRR Alc.

Paulus, Virginia. Housing: New
York, AMS Press [1974] xii, 339 p.
016.3015/4/0973 73-15863
Z7164.H8 P38 MRR Alc.

Peabody institute, Baltimore.
Library. Catalogue of the library of
the Peabody institute of the city of
Baltimore ... Baltimore [I.
Friedenwald] 1883-92. 5 v. 02-5028

Z881 .B2 MRR Alc (Dk33)

Peabody institute, Baltimore.
Library. Second catalogue of the
library of the Peabody institute of
the city of Baltimore, Baltimore,
1896-1905. 8 v. 02-5029
Z881 .B21 MRR Alc (Dk33)

Pelzer, Karl Josef, West Malaysia
and Singapore: a selected
bibliography, New Haven, Human
Relations Area Files Press, 1971.
vi, 394 p. 016.91595/1/03 72-87853

Z3246 .P4 MRR Alc.

Pennington, Allan L. Reference guide
to marketing literature Braintree,
Mass., D. H. Mark Pub. Co. [1970] v,
13, [109] p. 016.6588 77-100576
Z7164.M18 P44 MRR Alc.

PERIODICALS--INDEXES. (Cont.)
Permanent International Committee of
Linguists. Bibliographie
linguistique. 1939/47- Utrecht,
Spectrum. 016.4 a 50-3972
Z7001 .P4 MRR Alc Full set

Personnel management abstracts. v. 1-
Jan./Feb. 1955- Ann Arbor, Mich.
[etc.] 658.3082 57-36326
HF5549 .P452 MRR Alc Full set*

The Philosopher's index. Cumulative
ed. 1967/68- Bowling Green, Ohio,
Philosophy Documentation Center,
Bowling Green University [etc.]
016.105 74-250928
Z7127 .P47 MRR Alc Full set

Poole's index to periodical
literature; New York, P. Smith,
1938. xiii, 476 p. 38-32447
AI3 .P7 2d suppl. 1938 MRR Circ.

Poole's index to periodical
literature; New York, P. Smith,
1938. xiv, p., 1 l., 646 p. 38-
32449
AI3 .P7 4th Suppl. 1938 MRR Circ.

Poole's index to periodical
literature; New York, P. Smith,
1938. xix, 637 p. 38-32448
AI3 .P7 3d suppl. 1938 MRR Circ.

Poole's index to periodical
literature; New York, P. Smith,
1938. xv, 714 p. 38-32450
AI3 .P7 5th suppl. 1938 MRR Circ.

Poole's index to periodical
literature; New York, P. Smith,
1938. xiii, 483 p. 38-32446
AI3 .P7 1st suppl. 1938 MRR Circ.

Poole's index to periodical
literature. Rev. ed. New York, P.
Smith, 1938. 1 v. in 2. 38-32445
AI3 .P7 1938 MRR Circ.

Population index. v. 1- Jan. 20,
1935- [Princeton, N.J., etc.]
016.312 39-10247
Z7164.D3 P83 MRR Alc Partial set

Pownall, David E., Articles on
twentieth century literature: an
annotated bibliography, 1954 to 1970,
New York, Kraus-Thomson
Organization, 1973- v.
016.809/04 73-6588
Z6519 .P66 MRR Alc.

Princeton University. Office of
Population Research. Population
index bibliography, Boston, G. K.
Hall, 1971. 4 v. 016.312 75-26979

Z7164.D3 P85 MRR Alc (Dk 33)

Princeton University. Office of
Population Research. Population
index bibliography, Boston, G. K.
Hall, 1971. 5 v. 016.312 79-30213

Z7164.D3 P852 MRR Alc (Dk 33)

Psychological abstracts. v. 1-
Jan. 1927- Lancaster, Pa., American
Psychological Association. 29-23479

BF1 .P65 Sci RR Partial set / MRR
Alc Partial set

Psychological index. Columbus, O.,
Published by the American
psychological association, inc., Ohio
state university, 1841, '40. 2 v.
41-28061
Z7203 .P972 MRR Alc.

Public Affairs Information Service.
Bulletin ... annual cumulation. 1st-
1915- New York [etc.] 16-820
Z7163 .P9 MRR Circ Full set

Public Affairs Information Service.
Foreign language index. 1968/71-
New York. 016.3 72-626907
Z7164.E2 P8 MRR Circ Full set

Recent publications in the social and
behavioral sciences. 1966- [New
York] The American behavioral
scientist. 016.3 66-56737
Z7161 .A42 MRR Alc Full set

Reed, Henry Clay, A bibliography of
Delaware through 1960, Newark,
Published for the Institute of
Delaware History and Culture by the
University of Delaware Press, 1966.
vi, 196 p. 016.91751 66-18259
Z1267 .R4 MRR Alc.

Religious and theological abstracts.
v. 1- Mar. 1958- Youngstown, Ohio,
Theological Publications. 208.22 61-
35093
BR1 .R286 MRR Alc Partial set

Répertoire bibliographique de la
philosophie. t. 1- ,fev. 1949-
Louvain, Institut supérieur de
philosophie. 016.1 51-28726
Z7127 .R42 MRR Alc Full set

Revista de filología española.
(Indexes) Guía para la consulta de
la Revista de filología espanola,
1914-1960. [New York] New York
University Press, 1964. 835 p.
460.5 64-22265
PQ6001 .R452 MRR Alc.

Romanische Bibliographie. 1961/62-
Tübingen, M. Niemeyer Verlag. 72-
620927
Z7032 .Z45 MRR Alc Full set

The Romantic movement bibliography,
1936-1970; [Ann Arbor, Mich.]
Pierian Press, 1973. 7 v. (xiii,
3289 p.) 016.809/894 77-172773
Z6514.R6 R65 MRR Alc.

Royal Commonwealth Society. Library.
Biography catalogue of the Library of
the Royal Commonwealth Society,
London, Royal Commonwealth Society,
1961. xxiii, 511 p. 016.92002 61-
66062
Z5301 .R6 MRR Biog.

Royal Commonwealth Society. Library.
Subject catalogue of the Library of
the Royal Empire Society, [1st ed.
reprinted] London, Dawsons for the
Royal Commonwealth Society, 1967. 4
v. (60/-/- per set (16/-/- per
vol.)] 016.942 68-70847
Z7164.C7 R82 1967 MRR Alc.

Royal Commonwealth Society. Library.
Subject catalogue of the Royal
Commonwealth Society, London.
Boston, Mass., G. K. Hall, 1971. 7
v. 017.1 70-180198
Z7164.C7 R83 MRR Alc (Dk 33)

Royal Historical Society, London.
Writings on British history 1901-
1933: London, Cape, 1968- v.
[£5/5- (v. 1) 63/- (v.2) £5/5/- (v.
3)] 016.942 68-88411
Z2016 .R85 MRR Alc.

Royal Institute of International
Affairs. Library. Index to
periodical articles 1950-1964 in the
Library of the Royal Institute of
International Affairs. Boston, G. K.
Hall, 1964. 2 v. 65-9436
AI3 .R6 MRR Alc.

Royal Institute of International
Affairs. Library. Index to
periodical articles 1965-1972 in the
Library of the Royal Institute of
International Affairs. Boston, G. K.
Hall, 1973. xxix, 879 p. 016.05
73-166442
AI3 .R6 1973 MRR Alc.

Royal Society of London. Catalogue
of scientific papers. London, C. J.
Clay, 1867-1925. 19 v. 02-11462
Z7403 .R88 MRR Alc.

Royal society of London. Catalogue
of scientific papers, 1800-1900.
Cambridge, University press, 1908-
v. 08-24586
Z7403 .R8812 MRR Alc.

Ryan, Pat M. American drama
bibliography; Fort Wayne, Ind., Fort
Wayne Public Library, 1969. 240 p.
016.812 77-11267
Z1231.D7 R92 MRR Ref Desk.

Sable, Martin Howard. A bio-
bibliography of the Kennedy family,
Metuchen, N.J.; Scarecrow Press,
1969. 330 p. 016.973922/0922 78-
7234
Z5315.K4 S3 MRR Alc.

Sable, Martin Howard. Latin American
urbanization: Metuchen, N.J.,
Scarecrow Press, 1971. 1077 p.
016.3013/6/098 74-145643
Z7165.L3 S28 MRR Alc.

Sable, Martin Howard. UFO guide:
1947-1967; 1st ed. Beverly Hills,
Calif., Rainbow Press Co., 1967. 100
p. 016.001/9 67-30550
Z5064.F5 S3 MRR Alc.

Salem, James M. A guide to critical
reviews, 2d ed. Metuchen, N.J.,
Scarecrow Press, 1973- v.
016.809/2 73-3120
Z5782 .S342 MRR Ref Desk.

Salem, James M. A guide to critical
reviews, New York, Scarecrow Press,
1966- v. [$4.50 (v. 1) varies]
016.8092 66-13733
Z5782 .S34 MRR Ref Desk.

Samples, Gordon. The drama scholars'
index to plays and filmscripts:
Metuchen, N.J., Scarecrow Press
[1974] xii, 448 p. 016.80882 73-
22165
Z5781 .S17 MRR Alc.

Sandeau, Georges. International
bibliography of marketing and
distribution. [Bruxelles, Presses
universitaires de Bruxelles]
Distributed exclusively in North
America and South America [by] R. R.
Bowker Co., New York, 1971. 1 v.
(various pagings) 016.6588 73-
159927
Z7164.M18 S2 1971b MRR Alc.

Schlüter, Hans. Index Libycus:
Bibliography of Libya, 1957-1969,
Boston, G. K. Hall, 1972. viii, 305
p. 016.9161/2 72-2779
Z3971 .S36 MRR Alc.

Schuster, Mel. Motion picture
directors: Metuchen, N.J., Scarecrow
Press, 1973. 418 p.
016.79143/0233/0922 73-780
Z5784.M9 S34 MRR Biog.

Schuster, Mel. Motion picture
performers: Metuchen, N.J., The
Scarecrow Press, 1971. 702 p.
016.79143/028/0922 70-154300
Z5784.M9 S35 MRR Biog.

Schutter, Bart de. Bibliography on
international Criminal law. Leiden,
Sijthoff, 1972. li, 423 p.
[fl58.00] 016.34/77 72-80997
Z6464.C8 S38 MRR Alc.

Schutze, Gertrude. Information and
library science source book;
Metuchen, N.J., Scarecrow Press,
1972. ix, 483 p. 016.02 72-1157
Z666 .S373 MRR Alc.

Schwab, Moïse. Index of articles
relative to Jewish history and
literature published in periodicals,
from 1665 to 1900. Augmented ed.,
New York, Ktav Pub. House [1971, i.e.
1972] xvi, 539, 409-613 p.
016.91/0039/24 74-114721
Z6366 .S413 MRR Alc.

Scientific American. v.1-14, Aug.
28, 1845-June 25, 1859; new ser., v.1-
July 2, 1859- [New York] 505
04-17574
T1 .S5 MRR Alc Indexes only / Sci
RR Indexes only

Scott, Franklin Daniel, Guide to the
American historical review, 1895-
1945: 46-25831
E172 .A60 1944, vol. 1 MRR Ref
Desk.

Selected references to literature on
marine expeditions, 1700-1860.
Boston, G. K. Hall, 1972. iv, 517 p.
016.5514/6 72-6452
Z5971 .S4 MRR Alc.

Serís, Homero, Manual de
bibliografía de la literatura
española. Syracuse, N.Y., Centro de
Estudios Hispanicos, 1948- [c1949-
v. in 016.86 50-4332
Z2691 .S47 MRR Alc.

Sharma, Umesh D. Mysticism: a select
bibliography, Waterloo, Ont.,
Waterloo Lutheran University, 1973.
109 p. 016.248/22 73-174548
Z7819 .S5 MRR Alc.

Shaw, Thomas Shuler, Index to
profile sketches in New Yorker
magazine, Boston, The F. W. Faxon
company, 1946. 5 p. l., 100 p.
016.920073 47-450
Z5305.U5 S5 1946 MRR Biog.

Shepard, Frederick Job, comp. Index
to illustrations, Preliminary ed.
Chicago, American library
association, 1924. 89 p. 24-26753

NC996 .S5 MRR Ref Desk.

Smith, Dwight La Vern, Afro-American
history; Santa Barbara, Calif., ABC-
Clio [1974] xvi, 856 p.
016.9173/06/96073 73-87155
Z1361.N39 S56 MRR Alc.

Smith, Dwight La Vern, The American
political process; selected abstracts
of periodical literature, 1954-1971.
Santa Barbara, Calif., ABC-CLIO
[1972] xvi, 630 p. 016.329/00973
72-77549
JK2261 .S73 MRR Alc.

Smith, Myron J. The American Navy,
1865-1918: Metuchen, N.J., Scarecrow
Press, 1974. xiii, 372 p.
016.359/00973 74-4230
Z6835.U5 S62 MRR Alc.

Social Science Research Council.
Committee on Survey of Research on
Crime and Criminal Justice. A guide
to material on crime and criminal
justice. Montclair, N.J., Patterson
Smith, 1969 [c1929] 665 p.
016.364/9/73 69-16240
Z5118.8.C9 S6 1969 MRR Alc.

PERIODICALS--INDEXES. (Cont.)
Social sciences & humanities index.
v. 1-   1907/15-   New York [etc.] H.
W. Wilson Co.   17-4969
   AI3 .R49   MRR Circ Partial set /
   MRR Circ Partial set

Social sciences citation index.
Philadelphia, Institute for
Scientific Information.   016.3   73-
85287
   Z7161 .S65   MRR Alc Full set

Sociological abstracts.   v. 1-
Jan./Oct. 1953-   [New York]   301   58-
46404
   HM1 .S67   MRR Alc Full set

Special Libraries Association. New
York Chapter. Advertising and
Marketing Group.   Guide to special
issues and indexes of periodicals;
New York, Special Libraries
Association, 1962.   vi, 125 p.   050
62-12644
   Z6951 .S755   MRR Alc.

Spitz, Allan A.   Developmental
change; an annotated bibliography,
Lexington, University Press of
Kentucky [1969]   xi, 316 p.   [12.50]
   016.308   69-19766
   Z7164.E15 S615   MRR Alc.

Stratman, Carl Joseph,   Bibliography
of the American theatre,   [Chicago]
Loyola University Press [1965]   xv,
397 p.   016.7920973   65-3359
   Z1231.D7 S8   MRR Alc.

Stratman, Carl Joseph,   Restoration
and eighteenth century theatre
research: Carbondale, Southern
Illinois University Press [1971]   ix,
811 p.   [$25.00]   016.822/5/09   71-
112394
   Z2014.D7 S854   MRR Alc.

Stratman, Carl Joseph,   Bibliography
of medieval drama.   2d ed., rev. and
enl.   New York, F. Unger [1972]   2 v.
(xv, 1035 p.)   [$35.00]
016.80882/02   78-163141
   Z5782.A2 S8 1972   MRR Alc.

Strauss, Erwin S.   The MIT Science
Fiction Society's index to the s-f
magazines, 1951-1965.   [Cambridge,
Mass., MIT Science Fiction Society]
c1966.   iii, 207 p.   016.823/0876
73-174981
   Z5917.S36 S84   MRR Alc.

Subject index to children's
magazines.   v. 2, no. 8-   Mar./Aug.
1950-   Madison, Wis.   051   72-627331
   Z6944.C5 W5   MRR Alc Full set

The Subject index to periodicals.
1915/16-1961.   London, Library
Association.   29-19815
   AI3.A72   MRR Alc Full set

Svenska tidskriftsartiklar.   årg. 10-
1961-   [Lund] Bibliotekstjänst.
72-626677
   AI13 .S8   MRR Alc Partial set

Swem, Earl Gregg, comp.   Virginia
historical index ...   Roanoke, Va.,
Designed, printed, and bound by the
Stone printing and manufacturing
company, 1934-36.   2 v.   34-38514
   F221 .S93   MRR Ref Desk.

Szekely, Kalman S.   Electoral
college; Littleton, Colo., Libraries
Unlimited, 1970.   125 p.   016.324/21
79-136256
   Z7165.U5 S95   MRR Alc.

Takle, John A.   Ethnic and racial
minorities in North America:
[Monticello, Ill., Council of
Planning Librarians] 1973.   71 p.
[$7.00]   016.3092/08 s
016.30145/1/0420973   74-160787
   Z5942 .C68 no. 459-460   MRR Alc.

Talvart, Hector.   Bibliographie des
auteurs modernes de langue
française, Paris, Éditions de la
Chronique des lettres françaises,
1928-   v.   29-24892
   Z2173 .T3   MRR Alc.

Taylor, George Rogers,   American
economic history before 1860.   New
York, Appleton-Century-Crofts [1969]
xiv, 108 p.   016.330973   70-79173
   Z7165.U5 T37   MRR Alc.

The American behavioral scientist.
The ABS guide to recent publications
in the social and behavioral
sciences.   New York, 1965.   xxi, 781
p.   65-17168
   Z7161 .A4   MRR Alc.

Theodoratus, Robert J.,   Europe: a
selected ethnographic bibliography,
New Haven, Conn., Human Relations
Area Files, 1969.   xi, 544 p.
016.30129/4   75-87851
   Z5117 .T5   MRR Alc.

Thibault, Claude.   Bibliographia
Canadiana.   Don Mills, Ont., Longman
Canada, 1973.   lxiv, 795 p.   [$25.00]
   917.1/03   74-163122
   Z1382 .T47   MRR Alc.

Thieme, Hugo Paul,   Bibliographie de
la littérature française de 1800 à
1930,   Paris, E. Droz, 1933.   3 v.
015.44   33-11487
   Z2171 .T43 1933   MRR Alc.

Thurston, Jarvis A.   Short fiction
criticism;   Denver, A. Swallow [1960]
265 p.   016.80931   60-8070
   Z5917.S5 T5   MRR Alc.

Tompkins, Dorothy Louise (Campbell)
Culver.   Poverty in the United States
during the sixties;   [Berkeley]
Institute of Governmental Studies,
University of California, 1970.   ix,
542 p.   [$10.00]   016.3625/0973   74-
632910
   Z7165.U5 T62   MRR Alc.

Trask, David F.   A bibliography of
United States-Latin American
relations since 1810;   Lincoln,
University of Nebraska Press [1968]
xxxi, 441 p.   [$14.95]   016.32773/08
67-14421
   Z1609.R4 T7   MRR Alc.

Tregonning, K. G.   Southeast Asia;
Tucson, University of Arizona Press
[1969]   103 p.   016.9159   68-9845
   Z3221 .T7   MRR Alc.

Turner, Darwin T.,   Afro-American
writers,   New York, Appleton-Century-
Crofts, Educational Division [1970]
xvii, 117 p.   016.8108/081/7496   72-
79171
   Z1361.N39 T78   MRR Alc.

The United Methodist periodical
index.   v. 9-   Sept./Nov. 1968-
Nashville, Methodist Pub. House.
287/.6/05   72-626947
   Z7845.M5 M516   MRR Alc Full set

United States. Cabinet Committee on
Opportunity for the Spanish Speaking.
The Spanish speaking in the United
States: a guide to materials.
Washington, 1971.   v, 175 p.
016.9173/06/68   75-614612
   Z1361.S7 U54   MRR Alc.

United States. Dept. of Commerce.
Library.   Price sources;   New York,
B. Franklin [1968]   iv, 320 p.
016.33852   70-6381
   Z7164.P94 U56 1968   MRR Alc.

United States. Dept. of Housing and
Urban Development.   New communities;
Washington; For sale by the Supt. of
Docs., U.S. Govt. Print. Off. [1970]
iv, 84 p.   [0.75]   016.3092/6   75-
606174
   Z5942 .U584   MRR Alc.

United States. Dept. of the Army.
Communist China: a bibliographic
survey.   Washington; [For sale by the
Supt. of Docs., U.S. Govt. Print.
Off.] 1971.   x, 253 p.
016.9151/03/5   72-613755
   Z3108.A5 U48   MRR Alc.

United States. Dept. of the Army.
Communist Eastern Europe: analytical
survey of literature.   Washington;
[For sale by the Supt. of Docs., U.S.
Govt. Print. Off.] 1971.   xi, 367 p.
016.9147   78-611513
   Z2483 .U48   MRR Alc.

United States. Library of Congress.
Antarctic bibliography, 1951-1961.
Washington; [For sale by the Supt. of
Docs., U.S. Govt. Print. Off.] 1970.
vii, 349 p.   [4.75]   016.509/99   74-
606139
   Z663.41 .A76   MRR Alc.

United States. Library of Congress.
African Section.   Africa south of the
Sahara; index to periodical
literature, 1900-1970.   Boston, G. K.
Hall, 1971.   4 v.   016/.9167/03   74-
170939
   Z3503 .U47   MRR Alc (Dk 33).

United States. Library of Congress.
Geography and Map Division.   The
bibliography of cartography.   Boston,
G. K. Hall, 1973.   5 v.   016.526   73-
12977
   Z6028 .U49 1973   MRR Alc (Dk 33)

United States. Library of Congress.
Legislative reference service.
Abstracts of postwar literature.
[Washington] Library of Congress,
Legislative reference service, 1943-
v.   910.53144   44-6264
   Z663.6 .A73   MRR Alc.

United States. Library of Congress.
Legislative reference service.   Latin
American abstracts ...   [Washington]
Library of Congress, Legislative
reference service, 1943-   v.   918
44-6896
   Z663.6 .L3   MRR Alc.

United States. Library of Congress.
Legislative reference service.
Postwar abstracts, July 1942 to June,
1943.   [Washington] Legislative
reference service, Library of
Congress, 1943.   3 v.   940.53114   43-
16029
   Z663.6 .P6   MRR Alc.

United States. Library of Congress.
Orientalia Division.   Southeast Asia
subject catalog.   Boston, G. K. Hall,
1972-   v.   016.9159/03   72-5257
   Z3221 .U525   MRR Alc (Dk 33)

United States. Library of Congress.
Orientalia Division.   Southern Asia
accessions list.   v. 1-   Jan. 1952-
Washington.   016.95   52-60012
   Z663.38 .S8   MRR Alc   MRR Alc Full
set

United States. Library of Congress.
Processing Dept.   Monthly index of
Russian accessions.   v. 1-   Apr.
1948-   Washington [U.S. Govt. Print.
Off.]   015.47   48-46562
   Z663.7 .A45   MRR Alc   MRR Alc Full
set

United States. National Agricultural
Library.   Bibliography of
agriculture.   v. 1-   July 1942-   New
York [etc.] CCM Information Corp.
[etc.]   63-24851
   Z5073 .U572   Sci RR Partial set /
   MRR Alc (Dk 33) Full set

United States. National Clearinghouse
for Mental Health Information.
Bibliography on drug dependence and
abuse, 1928-1966.   [Chevy Chase, Md.,
1969]   258 p.   016.6138/3   70-600726

   Z7164.N17 U56   MRR Alc.

United States. National Clearinghouse
for Mental Health Information.
Bibliography on the urban crisis;
Chevy Chase, Md., National Institute
of Mental Health [1968]   iv, 158 p.
016.3091/73   77-600665
   Z7164.S66 U57   MRR Alc.

United States. National Institutes of
Health. Division of Research Grants.
Research grants index.   1961-
Bethesda, Md. [etc., For sale by the
Supt. of Docs., U.S. Govt. Print.
Off., Washington]   614   61-64708
   RA440.6 .U47   Sci RR Latest edition
   / MRR Alc Latest edition

United States. National Library of
Medicine.   Index-catalogue of the
Library of the Surgeon-General's
Office, United States Army: authors
and subjects.   Washington, Govt.
Print. Off., 1880-1961.   61 v.
016.61   01-2344
   Z6676 .U6   MRR Alc (DK 33).

United States and Canadian
publications on Africa.   1960-
[Stanford, Calif., etc.]   016.9167
62-60021
   Z3501 .U59   MRR Alc Full set

Universal Reference System.
Administrative management: public and
private bureaucracy;   Princeton,
N.J., Princeton Research Pub. Co.
[1969]   xx, 888 p.   011   68-57820
   Z7161 .U64 vol. 4   MRR Alc.

Universal Reference System.
Comparative government and cultures;
Princeton, N.J., Princeton Research
Pub. Co. [1969]   xxi, 1255 p.   016.3
68-57826
   Z7161 .U64 vol. 10   MRR Alc.

Universal Reference System.   Current
events and problems of modern
society;   Princeton, N.J., Princeton
Research Pub. Co. [1969]   xx, 935 p.
016.90982   68-57821
   Z7161 .U64 vol. 5   MRR Alc.

Universal Reference System.   Economic
regulation: business and government;
Princeton, N.J., Princeton Research
Pub. Co. [1969]   xx, 1111 p.   016.33
68-57824
   Z7161 .U64 vol. 8   MRR Alc.

Universal Reference System.
International affairs;   [2d ed.]
Princeton, N.J., Princeton Research
Pub. Co. [1969]   xx, 1206 p.
016.327   68-57819
   Z7161 .U64 vol. 1   MRR Alc.

PERIODICALS--INDEXES. (Cont.)
Universal Reference System.
Legislative process, representation,
and decision-making; Princeton,
N.J., Princeton Research Pub. Co.
[c1967] xv, 749 p. 016.32 67-29646
Z6461 .U64 vol. 2 MRR Alc.

Universal Reference System. Public
opinion, mass behavior, and political
psychology; Princeton, N.J.,
Princeton Research Pub. Co. [1969]
xxi, 1225 p. 016.30115/4 68-57822
Z7161 .U64 vol. 6 MRR Alc.

Universal Reference System. Public
policy and the management of science;
Princeton, N.J., Princeton Research
Pub. Co. [1969] xix, 594 p.
016.353008/5 68-57825
Z7161 .U64 vol. 9 MRR Alc.

Utah. University. Library. Chicano
bibliography. [Salt Lake City, 1973]
295 p. 016.9172/06/68 73-623051
Z1361.M4 U78 1973 MRR Alc.

Utz, Arthur Fridolin, Bibliographie
der Sozialethik. 1- 1956/59
Freiburg, New York, Herder. a 61-2645
Z7161 .U83 MRR Alc Full set

Vance, Lucile E. Illustration index,
2d ed. New York, Scarecrow Press,
1966. 527 p. 011 65-13558
N7525 .V3 1966 MRR Ref Desk.

Walker, Warren S. Twentieth-century
short story explication; 2d ed.
[Hamden, Conn.] Shoe String Press,
1967. v1, 687 p. 016.8093/1 67-24192
Z5917.S5 W33 MRR Ref Desk.

Wall, C. Edward. Cumulative author
index for Poole's index to periodical
literature, 1802-1906. Ann Arbor,
Mich., Pierian Press, 1971. ix, 488
p. 050 77-143237
AI3 .W3 MRR Circ.

Wall, C. Edward. Words and phrases
index; Ann Arbor, Mich., Pierian
Press, 1969- v. [17.95 (v. 1)]
016.423 68-58894
PE1689 .W3 MRR Alc.

Washington, D.C. Joint Library of the
International Monetary Fund and the
International Bank for Reconstruction
and Development. Economics and
finance; index to periodical
articles, 1947-1971. Boston, G. K.
Hall, 1972. 4 v. 016.33 73-156075
Z7164.E2 W34 MRR Alc (dk 33)

The Wellesley index to Victorian
periodicals, 1824-1900. [Toronto]
University of Toronto Press; [London]
Routledge & K. Paul [c1966- v.
[$75.00 Can. (v. 1)] 052 67-79381
AI3 .W45 MRR Alc.

Williams, Daniel T. Eight Negro
bibliographies. New York, Kraus
Reprint Co., 1970. 1 v. (various
pagings) 016.301451/96/073 71-107893
Z1361.N39 W54 MRR Alc.

Winther, Oscar Osburn, A classified
bibliography of the periodical
literature of the trans-Mississippi
West, 1811-1957. Bloomington,
Indiana University Press, 1961.
xxvi, 626 p. 016.9178 61-63869
Z1251.W5 W53 MRR Alc.

Work, Monroe Nathan, A bibliography
of the Negro in Africa and America,
New York, Octagon Books, 1965 [c1928]
xxi, 698 p. 016.9100817496 65-28242
Z1361.N39 W8 1965 MRR Alc.

World Health Organization.
Publications; 1947/57- Geneva. 58-4871
Z6660 .W57 MRR Alc Full set

Woy, James B. Investment
information: Detroit, Gale Research
Co. [1970] 231 p. [$11.50]
016.33267 79-118791
Z7164.F5 W93 MRR Ref Desk.

Woy, James B. Investment methods;
New York, R. R. Bowker, 1973. viii,
220 p. 016.3326 73-9607
Z7164.F5 W94 MRR Alc.

Wright, George Nelson.
Rehabilitation counselor functions:
annotated references Madison,
University of Wisconsin, Regional
Rehabilitation Research Institute,
1968. viii, 451 p. 016.3628/5 68-63360
HF7256.U6 W56 ser. 1, vol. 1 MRR
Alc.

Writers' program. New York. The film
index, New York, The Museum of
modern art film library and the H. W.
Wilson company, 1941- v.
016.7914 41-8716
Z5784.M9 W75 MRR Alc.

Writings on British history. 1901/33-
New York, Barnes & Noble. 61-2932
Z2016 .R88 MRR Alc Full set

The Year's work in modern language
studies, 1929/30- [Leeds, Eng.,
etc.] Modern Humanities Research
Association [etc.] 405.8 31-32540
PB1 .Y45 MRR Alc Full set

Zeitschrift für romanische
Philologie. Supplementheft.
Bibliographie. 1-72/76; 1875/76-
1956/60. Tübingen [etc.] M.
Niemeyer. 74-643524
Z7032 .Z45 MRR Alc Full set

PERIODICALS--INDEXES--BIBLIOGRAPHY.
Chicorel, Marietta. Chicorel index
to abstracting and indexing services:
1st ed. New York, Chicorel Library
Pub.Corp. [1974] 2 v. (920 p.)
016.05 74-170434
Z6293 .C54 MRR Ref Desk.

Kujoth, Jean Spealman. Subject guide
to periodical indexes and review
indexes. Metuchen, N.J., Scarecrow
Press, 1969. 129 p. 016.05 79-1268
Z6293 .K84 MRR Ref Desk.

New York. Public library. A check
list of cumulative indexes to
individual periodicals in the New
York public library; New York, The
New York public library, 1942. 3 p.
l., 370 p. 016.05 a 43-563
Z6293 .N45 MRR Alc.

Rouse, Richard H. Serial
bibliographies for medieval studies
Berkeley, University of California
Press 1969. xiii, 150 p.
016.016914/03/1 68-31637
Z6203 .R66 MRR Alc.

United States. Library of Congress.
Science and Technology Division. A
guide to the world's abstracting and
indexing services in science and
technology. Washington, 1963. viii,
183 p. 016.505 63-61148
Z663.41 .G78 MRR Alc.

Vesenyi, Paul E., European
periodical literature in the social
sciences and the humanities,
Metuchen, N.J., Scarecrow Press,
1969. 226 p. 016.052 79-7052
Z6955 .Z9V45 MRR Alc.

PERIODICALS--PRICES--PERIODICALS.
Bookman's price index. v. 1- 1964-
Detroit, Gale Research Co. 018 64-8723
Z1000 .B74 MRR Alc Full set

PERIODICALS--TRANSLATIONS--BIBLIOGRAPHY.
Groot-de Rook, A. S. de.
Translations journals; [Delft]
European Translations Centre, Centre
europeen des traductions, 1970. 44,
3, 3 p. 016.05 75-583148
Z6941 .G85 MRR Alc.

PERIODICALS--CEYLON--BIBLIOGRAPHY.
United States. Library of Congress.
American Libraries Book Procurement
Center, Delhi. Accessions list,
Ceylon. v. 1- Mar. 1967- New
Delhi. 015/.5493 sa 67-7489
Z663.767.C45 A25 MRR Alc MRR Alc
Full set

PERIODICALS--FRANCE--DIRECTORIES.
Paris. Bibliothèque nationale.
Département des périodiques.
Répertoire national des annuaires
français, 1958-1968. Paris,
Bibliothèque nationale, Editions
Mercure, 1970. 811 p. 76-501237
Z2174.Y4 P29 MRR Alc.

PERIODICALS--ISRAEL--BIBLIOGRAPHY.
United States. Library of Congress.
American Libraries Book Procurement
Center, Tel-Aviv. Serial titles
submitted; Dec. 31, 1965- Tel-Aviv.
016.059924 he 66-10
Z663.767.I8 A45 MRR Alc MRR Alc
Full set

PERIODICALS--NEPAL--BIBLIOGRAPHY.
United States. Library of Congress.
American Libraries Book Procurement
Center, Delhi. Accessions list,
Nepal. v. 1- Apr. 1966- New
Delhi. sa 66-4579
Z663.767.N4 A25 MRR Alc MRR Alc
Full set

PERIODICALS--PAKISTAN--BIBLIOGRAPHY.
United States. Library of Congress.
American Libraries Book Procurement
Center, Karachi. Accessions list,
Pakistan. v. 1- July/Dec. 1962-
Karachi, Dacca, American Libraries
Book Procurement Centers. 015/.549
63-24162
Z663.767.P2 A25 MRR Alc MRR Alc
Full set

United States. Library of Congress.
American Libraries Book Procurement
Center, Karachi. Accessions list,
Pakistan. Annual supplement:
cumulative list of serials. 1970-
Karachi, Dacca, American Libraries
Book Procurement Centers. 015/.549
74-643590
Z3191 .U53 suppl MRR Alc Full set

United States. Library of Congress.
American Libraries Book Procurement
Center, Karachi. Annual list of
serials. 1966- Karachi, Dacca,
American Libraries Book Procurement
Centers. 016.05 sa 66-6576
Z663.767.P2 A28 MRR Alc MRR Alc
Full set

PERIODICALS ON MICROFILM--BIBLIOGRAPHY.
Guide to microforms in print. 1961-
Washington, Microcard Editions.
016.099 61-7082
Z1033.M5 G8 Sci RR Latest edition
/ MRR Alc Latest edition

National register of microform
masters. Sept. 1965- Washington,
Library of Congress. 65-29419
Z663 .A43 MRR Alc MRR Alc Full set

Paoletti, Odette. Périodiques et
publications en série concernant les
sciences sociales et humaines,
Paris, Maison des sciences de
l'homme. Service bibliothèque-
documentation, 1966. 2 v. (xxiv, 684
p.) [80.00F] 016.07 67-100583
Z6941 .P3 MRR Alc.

Subject guide to microforms in print.
1962/63- Washington, Microcard
Editions. 016.099 62-21624
Z1033.M5 S8 Sci RR Latest edition
/ MRR Alc Latest edition

PERIODICALS ON MICROFILM--INDEXES.
United States Historical Documents
Institute. U.S. Government serial
titles, 1789-1970; Washington [1972]
xii, 527 p. 015.73 s 74-190737
Z1223.Z7 L45 vol. 4 MRR Ref Desk.

PERSIA
see Iran

PERSIAN LANGUAGE--DICTIONARIES--ENGLISH.
Steingass, Francis Joseph, A
comprehensive Persian-English
dictionary, Beirut, Librarie du
Liban [1970] viii, 1539 p. 77-273978
PK6379 .S7 1970 MRR Alc.

PERSIAN LITERATURE--HISTORY AND
CRITICISM.
Browne, Edward Granville, A literary
history of Persia ... Cambridge
[Eng.] The University press, 1928-
1930. 4 v. mrr01-34
PK6097 .B73 MRR Alc.

PERSIAN LITERATURE--TRANSLATIONS INTO
ENGLISH.
Browne, Edward Granville, A literary
history of Persia ... Cambridge
[Eng.] The University press, 1928-
1930. 4 v. mrr01-34
PK6097 .B73 MRR Alc.

PERSONAL FINANCE
see Finance, Personal

PERSONAL HYGIENE
see Hygiene

PERSONAL INCOME TAX
see Income tax

PERSONAL LIBERTY
see Liberty

PERSONALITY.
Eysenck, Hans Jurgen, The structure
of human personality. London,
Methuen; New York, Wiley [1953] xix,
348 p. 155.2/64 53-12674
BF698 .E97 MRR Alc.

PERSONALITY--ADDRESSES, ESSAYS,
LECTURES.
Borgatta, Edgar F., Handbook of
personality theory and research,
Chicago, Rand McNally [1968] xiv,
1232 p. 155.2 67-14685
BF698 .B623 MRR Alc.

PERSONALITY--BIBLIOGRAPHY.
Little, Lawrence Calvin, Researches
in personality, character and
religious education; [Pittsburgh]
University of Pittsburgh Press, 1962.
iv, 215 p. 013.3784886 62-12625
Z7849 .L54 MRR Alc.

PERSONALITY--DICTIONARIES.
Heidenreich, Charles A. A dictionary
of personality: behavior and
adjustment terms Dubuque, Iowa, W.
C. Brown Book Co. [1968] vii, 213 p.
150/.3 68-6353
BF31 .H43 MRR Alc.

PERSONALITY (LAW)
see also Civil rights

PERSONALITY ASSESSMENT.
Lanyon, Richard I. Personality
assessment New York, Wiley [1971]
xii, 267 p. 155.28 75-140552
BF698.4 .L34 MRR Alc.

PERSONALITY TESTS.
Buros, Oscar Krisen, Personality
tests and reviews; Highland Park,
N.J., Gryphon Press [1970] xxxi,
1659 p. 155.28 74-13192
BF698.5 .B87 MRR Alc.

Goldman, Bert A. Directory of
unpublished experimental mental
measures. v. 1- 1974- New York,
Behavioral Publications. 152.8 73-
17342
BF431 .G625 MRR Alc Latest edition

Johnson, Orval G. Tests and
measurements in child development:
[1st ed.] San Francisco, Jossey-
Bass, 1971. xiii, 518 p. 155.41
78-110636
BF722 .J64 MRR Alc.

Lake, Dale G. Measuring human
behavior; New York, Teachers College
Press [1973] xviii, 422 p. 155.2/8
72-82083
BF698.5 .L34 MRR Alc.

PERSONALITY TESTS--BIBLIOGRAPHY.
Buros, Oscar Krisen, ed. The mental
measurements yearbook. [1st]- 1938-
Highland Park, N.J. [etc.] Gryphon
Press [etc.] 016.1512 016.159928 39-
3422
Z5814.F8 B932 MRR Alc Partial set

Buros, Oscar Krisen, Personality
tests and reviews; Highland Park,
N.J., Gryphon Press [1970] xxxi,
1659 p. 155.28 74-13192
BF698.5 .B87 MRR Alc.

Goldman, Bert A. Directory of
unpublished experimental mental
measures. v. 1- 1974- New York,
Behavioral Publications. 152.8 73-
17342
BF431 .G625 MRR Alc Latest edition

PERSONNEL MANAGEMENT.
see also Applications for positions

see also Communication in management

see also Employment agencies

see also Executives

PERSONNEL MANAGEMENT--ABSTRACTS.
Personnel management abstracts. v. 1-
Jan./Feb. 1955- Ann Arbor, Mich.
[etc.] 658.3082 57-36326
HF5549 .P452 MRR Alc Full set*

PERSONNEL MANAGEMENT--DICTIONARIES.
Becker, Esther R. Dictionary of
personnel and industrial relations.
New York, Philosophical Library
[1958] 366 p. 658.303 58-59649
HF5549 .B3418 MRR Alc.

Benn, A. E. The management
dictionary; New York, Exposition
Press [1952] 381 p. 658.03 51-
11831
HD19 .B4 MRR Alc.

PERSONNEL MANAGEMENT--DIRECTORIES.
Public Personnel Association.
Membership directory. 1959-
Chicago. 59-41844
JK674.A7 A3 MRR Biog Latest
edition

PERSONNEL MANAGEMENT--HANDBOOKS,
MANUALS, ETC.
The Dartnell personnel director's
handbook [1st ed.] Chicago,
Dartnell Corp. [1969] 960 p. 658.3
76-77249
HF5549 .D3392 MRR Alc.

PERSONNEL RECORDS.
Marting, Elizabeth, ed. AMA book of
employment forms. New York] American
Management Association [1967] 702 p.
658.3 66-23998
HF5549.5.P4 M3 MRR Alc.

PERSONNEL SERVICE IN EDUCATION.
see also Counseling

see also Vocational guidance

Educators guide to free guidance
materials. 1st- ed.; 1962-
Randolph, Wis., Educators Progress
Service. 016.37142 62-18761
HF5381.A1 E3 MRR Alc Latest
edition

Traxler, Arthur Edwin, Techniques of
guidance 3d ed. New York, Harper &
Row [1966] xii, 377 p. 371.4 66-
12563
LB1027.5 .T7 1966 MRR Alc.

PERSONNEL SERVICE IN EDUCATION--
DICTIONARIES.
Hopke, William E. Dictionary of
personnel and guidance terms, [1st
ed.] Chicago, J. G. Ferguson Pub.
Co. [1968] xix, 464 p. 371.4/03
68-57491
LB15 .H66 MRR Alc.

PERSONNEL SERVICE IN HIGHER EDUCATION.
Zimmerman, Oswald Theodore, College
placement directory, 4th ed. Dover,
N.H., Industrial Research Service,
1965. vii, 643 p. 331.11502573 66-
919
LB2343.5 .Z5 1965 MRR Alc.

PERSUASION (PSYCHOLOGY)
see also Propaganda

PERU.
American University, Washington, D.C.
Foreign Areas Studies Division. Area
handbook for Peru. Washington, For
sale by the Supt. of Docs., U.S.
Govt. Print. Off.] 1972. xii, 429 p.
[$3.50] 916.5/03/63 72-600150
F3408 .A75 1972 MRR Alc.

PERU--BIOGRAPHY--DICTIONARIES.
González y Arjola, Víctor Jorge.
¿Quién es quién en el Perú? Lima,
Sociedad Hispano Americana de
Difusión Cultural y de R. L. [1960?-
v. 65-31427
F3405 .G68 MRR Biog.

PERU--COMMERCE--DIRECTORIES.
Dun and Bradstreet, inc.
International market guide; Peru.
New York. 380.1/025/85 72-621020
HC226 .D85 MRR Alc Latest edition

Field directorio gremial del Perú.
Lima, Field Ediciones. 61-21907
HF3463 .F5 MRR Alc Latest edition

Guía Lascano del Perú. Lima. 74-
642467
HF3463 .G8 MRR Alc Latest edition

PERU--DIRECTORIES.
Guía Lascano del Perú. Lima. 74-
642467
HF3463 .G8 MRR Alc Latest edition

PERU--GAZETTEERS.
United States. Office of Geography.
Peru; official standard names
approved by the United States Board
on Geographic Names. Washington,
Central Intelligence Agency, 1955.
609 p. 918.5/003 70-8182
F3404 .U5 MRR Alc.

PERU--HISTORY.
Marett, Robert Hugh Kirk, Sir, Peru,
New York, Praeger Publishers [1969]
288 p. [7.50] 985 71-85541
F3431 .M35 1969 MRR Alc.

Pike, Fredrick B. The modern history
of Peru London, Weidenfeld &
Nicolson [1967]. xix, 386 p. [55/-]
985 67-101020
F3431 .P52 1967b MRR Alc.

PERU--HISTORY--CONQUEST, 1522-1548--
SOURCES.
United States. Library of Congress.
Manuscript division. The Harkness
collection in the Library of
Congress. Washington, U.S. Govt.
print. off., 1936. xi, 253 p. 985
36-26004
Z663.34 .H29 MRR Alc.

PERU--HISTORY--1548-1820--SOURCES.
United States. Library of Congress.
Manuscript division. The Harkness
collection in the Library of
Congress. Washington, U.S. Govt.
print. off., 1936. xi, 253 p. 985
36-26004
Z663.34 .H29 MRR Alc.

PERU--HISTORY--SOURCES--BIBLIOGRAPHY.
United States. Library of Congress.
Manuscript division. The Harkness
collection in the Library of
Congress. Washington, U.S. Govt.
print. off., 1932. x, 336 p.
016.985 32-26175
Z663.34 .H28 MRR Alc.

PERU--INDUSTRIES--DIRECTORIES.
Dun and Bradstreet, inc.
International market guide; Peru.
New York. 380.1/025/85 72-621020
HC226 .D85 MRR Alc Latest edition

Field directorio gremial del Perú.
Lima, Field Ediciones. 61-21907
HF3463 .F5 MRR Alc Latest edition

Guía Lascano del Perú. Lima. 74-
642467
HF3463 .G8 MRR Alc Latest edition

PERU--REGISTERS.
Guía Lascano del Perú. Lima. 74-
642467
HF3463 .G8 MRR Alc Latest edition

PESTICIDES.
Nobile, Philip, comp, The complete
ecology fact book. [1st ed.] Garden
City, N.Y., Doubleday, 1972. xx, 472
p. [$10.00] 301.31 73-175364
TD174 .N6 MRR Alc.

PESTS.
see also Insects, Injurious and
beneficial

see also Parasites

PETONE, N.Z.--INDUSTRIES--DIRECTORIES.
Universal business directory for
Wellington, Hutt [and] Petone.
Auckland, Universal Business
Directories. 53-30822
HC623.W45 U5 MRR Alc Latest
edition

PETRARCA, FRANCESCO, 1304-1374--MUSICAL
SETTINGS--BIBLIOGRAPHY.
Newsom, Jon. Francesco Petrarca:
musical settings of his works from
Jacopa da Bologna to the present;
Washington, Library of Congress,
1974. iii, 29 p. 016.784/3 74-
6359
Z663.37 .P433 MRR Alc.

PETROLEUM.
see also Oil fields

PETROLEUM--DICTIONARIES.
Rueil-Malmaison, France. Institut
français du pétrole. Dictionnaire
technique des termes utilisés dans
l'industrie du pétrole, anglais-
français, français-anglais. Paris,
Editions Technip, 1963. xvi, 385 p.
64-56944
TN865 .R82 MRR Alc.

PETROLEUM--DICTIONARIES--FRENCH.
Rueil-Malmaison, France. Institut
français du pétrole. Dictionnaire
technique des termes utilisés dans
l'industrie du pétrole, anglais-
français, français-anglais. Paris,
Editions Technip, 1963. xvi, 385 p.
64-56944
TN865 .R82 MRR Alc.

PETROLEUM--PIPE LINES.
Directory of pipe line companies and
pipe line contractors. Tulsa, Okla.,
Midwest oil register [etc.] 58-35170
TN867 .D525 MRR Alc Latest edition

PETROLEUM--STATISTICS.
Darmstadter, Joel, Energy in the
world economy; Baltimore, Published
for Resources for the Future by the
Johns Hopkins Press [1971] x, 876 p.
[$22.50] 333.9 70-155848
HD9540.4 D37 MRR Alc.

PETROLEUM--STATISTICS--YEARBOOKS.
World petroleum report. v. 1-
1953/54- Dallas, M. Palmer.
338.2728 54-14745
HD9560.4 .W6 MRR Alc Latest
edition

PETROLEUM--YEARBOOKS.
International oil and gas
development. Austin, Tex. [etc.]
338.2728 32-22187
Began publication in 1930.
TN862 .N3 Sci RR Partial set / MRR
Alc Latest copy

PETROLEUM AS FUEL.
American Petroleum Institute.
Petroleum facts and figures. [1st]-
ed.; [1928]- New York. 338.2 41-
10749
HD9561 .A7 MRR Alc Latest edition

PETROLEUM ENGINES
see Gas and oil engines

PETROLEUM INDUSTRY AND TRADE.
see also Automobiles--Service stations

Barrows, Gordon Hensley.
International petroleum industry.
1st ed. New York, International
Petroleum Institute, 1965-67. 2 v.
65-28367
HD9560.5 .B27 MRR Alc.

International petroleum encyclopedia.
Tulsa, Okla., Petroleum Pub. Co.
[1972] 448 p. [$32.50]
338.2/7/282025 72-76602
HD9560.5 .I59 1972 MRR Alc.

International petroleum encyclopedia.
Tulsa, OK., Petroleum Pub. Co.
[1974] 468 p. [$32.50]
338.2/7/282025 74-77981
HD560.5 .I59 1974 MRR Alc.

PETROLEUM INDUSTRY AND TRADE--
ABBREVIATIONS.
  Atlantic Refining Company.
  Dictionary of abbreviations peculiar
  to the oil industry. [Dallas, 1963]
  62 p.   63-5675
    TN865 .A75 1963 MRR Alc.

PETROLEUM INDUSTRY AND TRADE--
BIBLIOGRAPHY.
  Special Libraries Association.
  Petroleum Section. Committee on U.S.
  Sources of Petroleum and Natural Gas
  Statistics. U.S. sources of
  petroleum and natural gas statistics,
  New York, Special Libraries
  Association, 1961. vii, 94 p.
  016.6655   61-15740
    Z6972 .S65 MRR Alc.

PETROLEUM INDUSTRY AND TRADE--
DIRECTORIES.
  The Geophysical directory. [Houston]
  622.1058   50-28141
    TN867 .G46 MRR Alc Latest edition

  International petroleum encyclopedia.
  Tulsa, Okla., Petroleum Pub. Co.
  [1972] 448 p.   [$32.50]
  338.2/7/282025 72-76602
    HD9560.5 .I59 1972 MRR Alc.

  International petroleum encyclopedia.
  Tulsa, OK., Petroleum Pub. Co.
  [1974] 468 p.   [$32.50]
  338.2/7/282025 74-77981
    HD560.5 .I59 1974 MRR Alc.

  International petroleum register.
  [1st]- ed.; 1917/18- New
  York[etc.] Palmer Publications [etc.]
  18-6917
    TN867 .P4 Sci RR Latest edition /
    MRR Alc Latest edition

  Oil directory of foreign companies
  outside the U. S. A. and Canada.
  Tulsa, Okla., Midwest oil register
  [etc.] 57-47989
    HD9560.3 .O36 MRR Alc Latest
    edition

  World-wide personnel directory,
  refining and gas processing. Tulsa,
  Okla. 51-28381
    TN867 .O487 Sci RR Latest edition
    / MRR Alc Latest edition

PETROLEUM INDUSTRY AND TRADE--
DIRECTORIES--PERIODICALS.
  The Oil & gas directory: worldwide
  exploration, drilling, producing
  coverage. [Houston, Tex.]
  338.2/7/28025 72-623151
    TN867 .C4853 MRR Alc Latest
    edition

PETROLEUM INDUSTRY AND TRADE--
STATISTICS.
  International petroleum encyclopedia.
  Tulsa, Okla., Petroleum Pub. Co.
  [1972] 448 p.   [$32.50]
  338.2/7/282025 72-76602
    HD9560.5 .I59 1972 MRR Alc.

PETROLEUM INDUSTRY AND TRADE--
STATISTICS--YEARBOOKS.
  World petroleum report. v. 1-
  1953/54- Dallas, M. Palmer.
  338.2728 54-14745
    HD9560.4 .W6 MRR Alc Latest
    edition

PETROLEUM INDUSTRY AND TRADE--YEARBOOKS.
  The Oil and petroleum year book.
  London ca 12-1196
    HG4821 .O4 MRR Alc Latest edition

PETROLEUM INDUSTRY AND TRADE--ALASKA--
DIRECTORIES.
  Oil directory of Alaska. Tulsa,
  Okla., Midwest oil register [etc.]
  338.27282 60-24552
    TN867 .O514 MRR Alc latest edition

PETROLEUM INDUSTRY AND TRADE--
CALIFORNIA--DIRECTORIES.
  California petroleum register. Los
  Angeles, Petroleum World. 49-54566
    TN867 .C28 MRR Alc Latest edition

  Personnel directory of California oil
  and gas producers. Los Angeles,
  Conservation Committee of California
  Oil Producers. 338.2/7/282025794 72-
  622324
    HD9567.C2 C6 MRR Alc Latest
    edition

PETROLEUM INDUSTRY AND TRADE--CANADA.
  The Financial post survey of oils.
  Montreal, New York, Maclean-Hunter
  Pub. Co. 338.2728 52-31385
    HD9574.C2 F5 MRR Alc Latest
    edition

PETROLEUM INDUSTRY AND TRADE--CANADA--
DIRECTORIES.
  Oil directory of Canada. Tulsa,
  Okla., C. L. Cooper. 57-49796
    TN867 .O52 Sci RR Latest edition /
    MRR Alc Latest edition

PETROLEUM INDUSTRY AND TRADE--KANSAS--
DIRECTORIES.
  Directory of producers and drilling
  contractors: Kansas. Tulsa, Okla.,
  Midwest oil register [etc.] 58-17958

    TN867 .D55 MRR Alc Latest edition

  Morrison petroleum directory of
  Kansas. Wichita, Kan. 44-35055
    TN872.K2 M6 MRR Alc Latest edition

PETROLEUM INDUSTRY AND TRADE--LATIN
AMERICA--DIRECTORIES.
  Latin America petroleum directory.
  1st ed.; 1971- Tulsa, Okla.,
  Petroleum Pub. Co. 338.2/7/2820258
  72-613215
    HD9574.L28 L33 MRR Alc Latest
    edition

PETROLEUM INDUSTRY AND TRADE--MIDDLE
STATES--DIRECTORIES.
  Directory of oil marketing and
  wholesale distributors. Tulsa,
  Okla., Midwest Oil Register. 63-
  36095
    HD9567.A3 D5 MRR Alc Latest
    edition

PETROLEUM INDUSTRY AND TRADE--MIDDLE
WEST--DIRECTORIES.
  Directory of producers and drilling
  contractors: Michigan, Indiana,
  Illinois, Kentucky. Tulsa, Okla.,
  Midwest oil register [etc.] 58-17949

    TN867 .D555 MRR Alc Latest edition

PETROLEUM INDUSTRY AND TRADE--OKLAHOMA--
DIRECTORIES.
  Directory of producers and drilling
  contractors: Oklahoma. Tulsa, Okla.,
  Midwest oil register. 58-17951
    TN867 .D557 MRR Alc Latest edition

  Oklahoma petroleum directory. 1946-
  Oklahoma City [Okla., etc.] Petroleum
  Records Co. 622.338 47-34260
    TN867 .O54 MRR Alc Latest edition

PETROLEUM INDUSTRY AND TRADE--SOUTHERN
STATES--DIRECTORIES.
  Directory of producers and drilling
  contractors: Louisiana, Mississippi,
  Arkansas, Florida, Georgia. Tulsa,
  Okla. Midwest oil register [etc.] 58-
  17957
    TN867 .D553 MRR Alc Latest edition

PETROLEUM INDUSTRY AND TRADE--TEXAS--
DIRECTORIES.
  Directory of producers and drilling
  contractors: Texas. Tulsa, Okla.,
  Midwest oil register [etc.] 622.3382
  59-23098
    Began publication in 1945.
    TN867 .D563 MRR Alc Latest edition

PETROLEUM INDUSTRY AND TRADE--THE WEST--
DIRECTORIES.
  Directory of producers and drilling
  contractors: Rocky Mountain Region,
  Williston Basin, New Mexico. Tulsa,
  Okla. Midwest oil register [etc.] 58-
  17950
    TN867 .D559 MRR Alc Latest edition

PETROLEUM INDUSTRY AND TRADE--UNITED
STATES.
  Williamson, Harold Francis, The
  American petroleum industry.
  Evanston [Ill.] Northwestern
  University Press [1959-63] 2 v.
  338.476655 59-12043
    HD9565 .W5 MRR Alc.

PETROLEUM INDUSTRY AND TRADE--UNITED
STATES--BIBLIOGRAPHY.
  Special Libraries Association.
  Petroleum Section. Committee on U.S.
  Sources of Petroleum and Natural Gas
  Statistics. U.S. sources of
  petroleum and natural gas statistics,
  New York, Special Libraries
  Association, 1961. vii, 94 p.
  016.6655 61-15740
    Z6972 .S65 MRR Alc.

PETROLEUM INDUSTRY AND TRADE--UNITED
STATES--DIRECTORIES.
  Directory of oil marketing and
  wholesale distributors. Tulsa,
  Okla., Midwest Oil Register. 63-
  36095
    HD9567.A3 D5 MRR Alc Latest
    edition

  Directory of oil refineries,
  construction, petrochemical and
  natural gas processing plants.
  Tulsa, Okla., Midwest oil register
  [etc.] 665.53058 58-33960
    TN867 .D48 MRR Alc Latest edition

  Directory of pipe line companies and
  pipe line contractors, Tulsa, Okla.,
  Midwest oil register [etc.] 58-35170

    TN867 .D525 MRR Alc Latest edition

  The Oil & gas directory: worldwide
  exploration, drilling, producing
  coverage. [Houston, Tex.]
  338.2/7/28025 72-623151
    TN867 .O4953 MRR Alc Latest
    edition

U.S.A. oil industry directory.
  Tulsa, Petroleum Pub. Co.
  338.2/7/2802573 72-621148
    HD9563 .U54 Sci RR Latest edition
    / MRR Alc Latest edition

  United States. Office of
  International Investment. List of
  foreign firms with some
  interest/control in American
  manufacturing and petroleum companies
  in the United States. [Washington]
  1972. 61 p. 332.6/73/02573 72-
  603415
    HG4909 .A5 1972 MRR Ref Desk.

PETROLEUM INDUSTRY AND TRADE--UNITED
STATES--STATISTICS.
  American Petroleum Institute.
  Petroleum facts and figures. [1st]-
  ed.; [1928]- New York. 338.2 41-
  10749
    HD9561 .A7 MRR Alc Latest edition

PETROLEUM REFINERIES--UNITED STATES.
  Directory of oil refineries,
  construction, petrochemical and
  natural gas processing plants.
  Tulsa, Okla., Midwest oil register
  [etc.] 665.53058 58-33960
    TN867 .D48 MRR Alc Latest edition

PETROLOGY.
  see also Geology

  see also Rocks

PETROLOGY--NORTH AMERICA--BIBLIOGRAPHY.
  United States. Geological Survey.
  Bibliography of North American
  geology. 1785/1918-1950/59.
  Washington, U.S. Govt. Print. Off.
  016.557 gs 24-38
    Z6034.U49 U45 Sci RR Sci RR
    Partial set / MRR Alc Partial set

  United States. Geological Survey.
  Bibliography of North American
  geology. 1906- Washington, U.S.
  Govt. Print. Off. 016.557 gs 09-427
    QE75 .B9 MRR Alc Partial set / Sci
    RR Partial set

PETS.
  see also Cats

  see also Dogs

  see also Domestic animals

  Guthrie, Esther L. Home book of
  animal care, [1st ed.] New York,
  Harper & Row [1966] xiv, 302 p.
  636.0887 66-11474
    SF413 .G85 MRR Alc.

PEWTER, AMERICAN.
  Jacobs, Carl. Guide to American
  pewter. New York, McBride, 1957.
  216 p. 739.53388 56-12017
    NK8412 .J3 MRR Alc.

  Laughlin, Ledlie Irwin. Pewter in
  America, Boston, Houghton Mifflin
  company, 1940. 2 v. 739 41-1939
    NK8412 .L3 MRR Alc.

  Laughlin, Ledlie Irwin. Pewter in
  America: its makers and their marks.
  Barre, Mass., Barre Publishers, 1969-
  71. 3 v. [27.50 per vol.]
  739/.533/0973 77-86912
    NK8412 .L33 MRR Alc.

  Thorn, C. Jordan. Handbook of
  American silver and pewter marks;
  New York, Tudor Pub. Co. [1949] xii,
  289 p. 739.23 50-5385
    NK7210 .T5 MRR Alc.

PEWTER, AMERICAN--DIRECTORIES.
  Kovel, Ralph M. A directory of
  American silver, pewter, and silver
  plate. New York, Crown Publishers
  [1961] 352 p. 739.205873 60-8620

    NK7112 .K66 MRR Alc.

PFORZHEIM, GER.--DIRECTORIES.
  Adressbuch von Pforzheim und
  Umgebung. Pforzheim, Pforzheimer
  Adressbuch Neumayer [etc.] 53-28335

    DD901.P5 A7 MRR Alc Latest edition

PHARMACISTS--FRANCE--DIRECTORIES.
  Guide medical et pharmaceutique
  Rosenwald. Paris, L'Expansion
  scientifique française [etc.]
  610.58 46-33196
    Publication began with the guide
    for 1887.
    R713.43 .A6G8 MRR Alc Latest
    edition

PHARMACOGNOSY--DICTIONARIES.
  Hocking, George Macdonald. A
  dictionary of terms in pharmacognosy
  and other divisions of economic
  botany; Springfield, Ill., C. C.
  Thomas [1955] xxv, 284 p. 581.603
  55-7453
    QK99 .H69 1955 MRR Alc.

PHARMACOLOGY.
  see also Drugs

PHARMACOLOGY. (Cont.)
see also Psychopharmacology

American Medical Association. Council
on Drugs. A M A drug evaluations.
1st- ed.; 1971- Chicago, American
Medical Association. 615/.1 75-
147249
RM300 .A553 MRR Alc Latest edition

Drugs of choice. St. Louis C. V.
Mosby Co. 615.1 58-6889
RM101 .D75 Sci RR Latest edition /
MRR Alc Latest edition

Goth, Andres. Medical pharmacology;
principles and concepts. 7th ed.
Saint Louis, Mosby, 1974. x, 753 p.
615/.7 73-20083
RM300 .G65 1974 MRR Alc.

Goth, Andres. Medical pharmacology;
principles and concepts. 7th ed.
Saint Louis, Mosby, 1974. x, 753 p.
615/.7 73-20083
RM300 .G65 1974 MRR Alc.

Musser, Ruth D. Pharmacology and
therapeutics 3d ed. New York,
Macmillan [1965] xvi, 878 p. 615
65-16932
RM101 .M87 1965 MRR Alc.

PHARMACOLOGY--PERIODICALS.
Drugs in current use and new drugs.
New York, Springer Pub. Co.
615/.1/05 72-622911
RS79 .D7 Sci RR Latest edition /
MRR Alc Latest edition

PHARMACOLOGY--YEARBOOKS.
Current drug handbook. 1958-
Philadelphia [etc.] W. B. Saunders
Co. 615.1 58-6390
RM300 .C8 Sci RR Latest edition /
MRR Alc Latest edition

PHARMACOPOEIAS--GREAT BRITAIN.
British pharmacopeia. London,
Published for the General Medical
Council by the Pharmaceutical Press
[etc.] 615.11 agr15-305
RS141.3 .B75 Sci RR Latest edition
/ MRR Alc Latest edition

Martindale, William, The extra
pharmacopoeia: incorporating Squire's
"Companion". 26th ed.; London,
Pharmaceutical Press, 1972. xxvi,
2320 p. [£14.00] 615/.11/42 72-
78897
RS141.3 .M4 1972 MRR Alc.

**PHARMACOPOEIAS--UNITED STATES--
COLLECTED WORKS.**
The United States dispensatory and
physicians' pharmacology. 26th
ed.; 1967- Philadelphia, J. B.
Lippincott Co. 615/.12/73 67-17443

RS151.2 .D5 MRR Alc Latest edition

PHARSALUS, BATTLE OF, 48 B.C.
Lucanus, Marcus Annaeus. Lucan,
London, W. Heinemann; New York, G. P.
Putnam's sons, 1928. 637 p. mrr01-
10
PA6156.L7 1928d MRR Alc.

PHENOMENOLOGY.
see also Existentialism

PHILADALPHIA--DESCRIPTION--GUIDE-BOOKS.
Hadley Group. Inside Philadelphia;
Philadelphia [1973] 323 p. [$2.95]
917.48/11/044 73-82969
F158.18 .H32 1973a MRR Alc.

PHILADELPHIA--BUILDINGS.
Marion, John Francis. Bicentennial
city : Princeton [N.J.] : Pyne Press
; [New York : distributed by
Scribner, 1874] xiii, 210 p. :
[$14.95. $4.95] 917.48/11/044 73-
91977
F158.18 .M37 MRR Alc.

**PHILADELPHIA--DESCRIPTION--1951- --
GUIDE-BOOKS.**
Hadley Group. Inside Philadelphia;
Philadelphia [1973] 323 p. [$2.95]
917.48/11/044 73-82969
F158.18 .H32 1973a MRR Alc.

Wilson, Robert H. Philadelphia;
official handbook for visitors, [New
rev. ed. Maplewood, N.J.] Hammond
[1972] 128 p. [$1.50]
917.48/11/044 72-186096
F158.18 .W5 1972 MRR Alc.

Wurman, Richard Saul, Man-made
Philadelphia; [Cambridge, Mass., MIT
Press, 1972] 104 p. [$3.95]
917.48/11/044 72-4534
F158.18 .W87 MRR Alc.

**PHILADELPHIA--DESCRIPTION--1951- --
TOURS.**
Marion, John Francis. Bicentennial
city : Princeton [N.J.] : Pyne Press
; [New York : distributed by
Scribner, 1874] xiii, 210 p. :
[$14.95. $4.95] 917.48/11/044 73-
91977
F158.18 .M37 MRR Alc.

PHILADELPHIA--DESCRIPTION--GUIDE-BOOKS.
Marion, John Francis. Bicentennial
city : Princeton [N.J.] : Pyne Press
; [New York : distributed by
Scribner, 1874] xiii, 210 p. :
[$14.95. $4.95] 917.48/11/044 73-
91977
F158.18 .M37 MRR Alc.

PHILADELPHIA--HOTELS, TAVERNS, ETC.
Hadley Group. Inside Philadelphia;
Philadelphia [1973] 323 p. [$2.95]
917.48/11/044 73-82969
F158.18 .H32 1973a MRR Alc.

PHILADELPHIA--LIBRARIES--DIRECTORIES.
Special Libraries Council of
Philadelphia and Vicinity. Directory
of libraries and informational
sources. [1st, 3d]- ed.; 1920,
1923- Philadelphia [etc.] 026.0058
24-5378
Z732.P6 P5 MRR Alc Latest edition

PHILADELPHIA--MAPS.
Wurman, Richard Saul, Man-made
Philadelphia; [Cambridge, Mass., MIT
Press, 1972] 104 p. [$3.95]
917.48/11/044 72-4534
F158.18 .W87 MRR Alc.

PHILADELPHIA--POLITICS AND GOVERNMENT.
The Bulletin ... almanac & year book.
1924- Philadelphia, The Evening and
Sunday bulletin. 352.0748 24-7750
AY286.P5 B9 MRR Alc Latest edition

PHILANTHROPY
see Charities

see Social service

PHILATELIC AGENCIES--DIRECTORIES.
Bedard Publications, Detroit.
Directory of worldwide philatelic
agencies. Detroit [1960] 16 l.
383.22058 60-3275
HE6209 .B4 MRR Alc.

PHILIPPINE ISLANDS.
Chaffee, Frederic H. Area handbook
for the Philippines, Washington, For
sale by the Supt. of Docs., U.S.
Govt. Print. Off., 1969. xiv, 413 p.
[3.50] 919.14/03 78-601326
DS655 .C4 MRR Alc.

PHILIPPINE ISLANDS--BIBLIOGRAPHY.
Bernardo, Gabriel Adriano,
Bibliography of Philippine
bibliographies, 1593-1961. Quezon
City, Ateneo University Press, 1968.
xiv, 182 p. 016.01691914/03 68-
17160
Z3291.A1 B45 MRR Alc.

Chicago. University. Philippine
Studies Program. Selected
bibliography of the Philippines,
Preliminary ed. New Haven, Human
Relations Area Files, 1956. vi, 138
p. 016.9914 57-4424
Z3291 .C45 MRR Alc.

Pardo de Tavera, Trinidad
Hermenegildo, Biblioteca filipina,
Washington, Govt. print. off., 1903.
439 p. 04-8772
Z3291 .P23 MRR Alc.

United States. Library of Congress.
Division of bibliography.
Bibliography of China, Japan and the
Philippine Islands, [Concord, N.H.,
1925] l. 214-246. 27-14560
Z663.28 .B52 MRR Alc.

United States. Library of Congress.
Orientalia Division. Southeast Asia
subject catalog. Boston, G. K. Hall,
1972- v. 016.9159/03 72-5257
Z3221 .U525 MRR Alc (Dk 33)

**PHILIPPINE ISLANDS--BIBLIOGRAPHY--
CATALOGS.**
Manila. Far Eastern University.
Library. Classified list of
Filipiniana books and pamphlets in
the Filipiniana Section, Far Eastern
University, as of December, 1960.
Manila, Far Eastern University, 1960.
v, 254 l. 017.1 62-4081
Z3299 .M3 MRR Alc.

Newberry Library, Chicago. A
catalogue of printed materials
relating to the Philippine Islands,
1519-1900, Chicago, 1959. viii, 179
p. 016.9914 58-11546
Z3299 .N4 MRR Alc.

**PHILIPPINE ISLANDS--BIBLIOGRAPHY--UNION
LISTS.**
Quezon, Philippines. University of
the Philippines. Interdepartmental
Reference Service. Union catalog of
Philippine materials of sixty-four
government agency libraries of the
Philippines. Manila, 1962. xvi, 718
p. 016.9914 64-3534
Z3299 .Q38 MRR Alc.

PHILIPPINE ISLANDS--BIOGRAPHY.
Eminent Filipinos, Manila [National
Historical Commission] 1965. xxvi,
294 p. 920/.0599 70-220561
CT1793 .E43 MRR Biog.

Manuel, E. Arsenio, Dictionary of
Philippine biography. Quezon City,
Filipiniana Publications, 1955- v.
920.0914 56-38083
DS653.7 .M3 MRR Biog.

Maring, Ester G. Historical and
cultural dictionary of the
Philippines, Metuchen, N.J.,
Scarecrow Press, 1973. vii, 240 p.
915.99/03/03 72-10544
DS654 .M27 MRR Alc.

Nicanor, Precioso M. Profiles of
notable Filipinos in the U.S.A. ...
[1st ed.] New York, Pre-Mer Pub. Co.
[c1963- v. 920.0914 63-22694
E184.F4 N5 MRR Biog.

Retizos, Isidro L. Philippines who's
who, [Manila] Capitol Pub. House
[1957?] xxxix, 327 p. 920.0914 58-
40279
DS686.6.A2 R4 MRR Biog.

Tableau; v. 1- 1957- Manila,
Philippines, National Souvenir
Publications. 60-41123
DS686.6 .A2T2 MRR Alc Latest
edition

Who's who in the Philippines; v. 1-
1936/37- Manila, Ramon Races, Inc.
[etc.] CT1790 .W5 39-14256
MRR Biog Latest edition

**PHILIPPINE ISLANDS--COMMERCE--
DIRECTORIES.**
A B commercial directory of the
Philippines. Manila, A. G. Briones.
338 51-15009
"Since 1946."
HF5253 .A2 MRR Alc Latest edition

**PHILIPPINE ISLANDS--DESCRIPTION AND
TRAVEL.**
Dobby, Ernest Henry George.
Southeast Asia 9th ed. London,
University of London P., [1966]. 415
p. [21/-] 915.9 67-85516
DS508 .D58 1966 MRR Alc.

Wernstedt, Frederick L. The
Philippine Island world: Berkeley,
University of California Press, 1967.
ix, 742 p. 919.14 67-14001
DS660 .W47 MRR Alc.

**PHILIPPINE ISLANDS--DICTIONARIES AND
ENCYCLOPEDIAS.**
Maring, Ester G. Historical and
cultural dictionary of the
Philippines, Metuchen, N.J.,
Scarecrow Press, 1973. vii, 240 p.
915.99/03/03 72-10544
DS654 .M27 MRR Alc.

PHILIPPINE ISLANDS--GAZETTEERS.
United States. Office of Geography.
Philippine Islands: Washington,
1953. 2 v. (1303 p.) 919.14/003
70-10051
DS654 .U59 MRR Alc.

**PHILIPPINE ISLANDS--GOVERNMENT
PUBLICATIONS--BIBLIOGRAPHY.**
Bibliographical Society of the
Philippines. Checklist of Philippine
Government documents, 1917-1949.
Quezon City, University of the
Philippines Library 1960. xv, 817
p. 016.9914 61-54831
Z3295 .B52 MRR Alc.

Philippine bibliography. 1963/64-
Dilman [Quezon] Library, University
of the Philippines. sa 67-3532
Z3291 .P48 MRR Alc Full set

PHILIPPINE ISLANDS--HISTORY.
Agoncillo, Teodoro A. History of the
Filipino people, [Rev. ed.] Quezon
City, Malaya Books, [1969, c1967]
xviii, 725 p. 991.4 76-10930
DS668 .A32 1969 MRR Alc.

**PHILIPPINE ISLANDS--HISTORY--1898- --
BIBLIOGRAPHY.**
United States. Library of Congress.
Division of bibliography. List of
works relating to the American
occupation of the Philippine islands,
1898-1903. Washington, Govt. print.
off., 1905. 100 p. 05-20003
Z663.28 .L5884 MRR Alc.

PHILIPPINE ISLANDS--IMPRINTS.
Manila. Far Eastern University.
Library. Classified list of
Filipiniana books and pamphlets in
the Filipiniana Section, Far Eastern
University, as of December, 1960.
Manila, Far Eastern University, 1960.
v, 254 l. 017.1 62-4081
Z3299 .M3 MRR Alc.

Philippine bibliography. 1963/64-
Dilman [Quezon] Library, University
of the Philippines. sa 67-3532
Z3291 .P48 MRR Alc Full set

PHILIPPINE ISLANDS--IMPRINTS. (Cont.)
Quezon, Philippines. University of
the Philippines. Interdepartmental
Reference Service. Union catalog of
Philippine materials of sixty-four
government agency libraries of the
Philippines. Manila, 1962. xvi, 718
p. 016.9914 64-3534
Z3289 .038 MRR Alc.

PHILIPPINE ISLANDS--INDUSTRIES--
DIRECTORIES.
Directory-catalog of Philippine
manufacturers and producers. 1st-
ed.; 1964- Manila, Philippine
Industry & Business Journals. sa 64-
4132
T12.5.P5 D5 MRR Alc Latest edition

PHILIPPINE ISLANDS--MANUFACTURES--
DIRECTORIES.
Directory-catalog of Philippine
manufacturers and producers. 1st-
ed.; 1964- Manila, Philippine
Industry & Business Journals. sa 64-
4132
T12.5.P5 D5 MRR Alc Latest edition

PHILIPPINE ISLANDS--POLITICS AND
GOVERNMENT.
Liang, Ta-p'êng, Philippine parties
and politics; New ed., completely
rev. and enl. San Francisco,
Gladstone Co. [1971, c1970] xiii,
486 p. 329.9/599 75-139510
JQ1398.A1 L52 1971 MRR Alc.

PHILIPPINE LANGUAGES--BIBLIOGRAPHY.
Pardo de Tavera, Trinidad
Hermenegildo, Biblioteca filipina,
Washington, Govt. print. off., 1903.
439 p. 04-8772
Z3291 .P23 MRR Alc.

PHILIPPINE LITERATURE (SPANISH)--
BIBLIOGRAPHY.
Pardo de Tavera, Trinidad
Hermenegildo, Biblioteca filipina,
Washington, Govt. print. off., 1903.
439 p. 04-8772
Z3291 .P23 MRR Alc.

PHILOLOGY.
see also Archaeology

PHILOLOGY--ABSTRACTS--PERIODICALS.
Modern Language Association of
America. MLA abstracts of articles
in scholarly journals. [New York]
408 72-624077
P1 .M64 MRR Alc Full set

PHILOLOGY--DICTIONARIES--POLYGLOT.
Nash, Rose. Multilingual lexicon of
linguistics and philology: English,
Russian, German, French. Coral
Gables, Fla., University of Miami
Press [1968] xxvi, 390 p. 413 68-
31044
P29 .N34 MRR Alc.

PHILOLOGY--PERIODICALS--BIBLIOGRAPHY.
Ulving, Tor. Periodica philologica
abbreviata; Stockholm, Almqvist &
Wiksell [1963] 137 p. 64-1932
Z6945.A2 U5513 MRR Alc.

PHILOLOGY, COMPARATIVE.
see also Semantics

PHILOLOGY, MODERN.
see also Languages, Modern

PHILOLOGY, MODERN--BIBLIOGRAPHY.
The Year's work in modern language
studies, 1929/30- [Leeds, Eng.,
etc.] Modern Humanities Research
Association [etc.] 405.8 31-32540
PB1 .Y45 MRR Alc Full set

Zeitschrift für romanische
Philologie. Supplementheft.
Bibliographie. 1-72/76; 1875/76-
1956/60. Tubingen [etc.] M.
Niemeyer. 74-643524
Z7032 .Z45 MRR Alc Full set

PHILOLOGY, MODERN--BIBLIOGRAPHY--
PERIODICALS.
Romanische Bibliographie. 1961/62-
Tubingen, M. Niemeyer Verlag. 72-
620927
Z7032 .Z45 MRR Alc Full set

PHILOLOGY, MODERN--PERIODICALS.
Zeitschrift für romanische
Philologie. Supplementheft.
Bibliographie. 1-72/76; 1875/76-
1956/60. Tubingen [etc.] M.
Niemeyer. 74-643524
Z7032 .Z45 MRR Alc Full set

PHILOSOPHERS.
Jaspers, Karl, The great
philosophers. [1st American ed.]
New York, Harcourt, Brace & World
[1962- v. 109 62-9436
B82 .J313 MRR Alc.

Who's who in philosophy. [New York,
Philosophical library, 1942- v.
921 42-17400
B790 .W5 MRR Biog.

PHILOSOPHERS--BIO-BIBLIOGRAPHY.
Totok, Wilhelm. Handbuch der
Geschichte der Philosophie.
Frankfurt am Main, V. Klostermann
[1964- v. 64-52305
B82 .T6 MRR Alc.

PHILOSOPHERS--DICTIONARIES.
Elseviers filosofische en
psychologische encyclopedie.
Amsterdam, Elsevier, 1970. 271 p.
[fl4.50] 75-543438
BF31 .E45 MRR Alc.

Grooten, Johan, ed. New encyclopedia
of philosophy New York,
Philosophical Library [1972] 468 p.
[$20.00] 103 72-192726
B48.D8 G713 MRR Alc.

Kiernan, Thomas. Who's who in the
history of philosophy. [1st ed.]
New York, Philosophical Library
[1965] vii, 185 p. 109.22 B 65-
20325
B41 .K5 MRR Biog.

Thomas, Henry, Biographical
encyclopedia of philosophy. [1st
ed.] Garden City, N.Y., Doubleday,
1965. xii, 273 p. 921 64-22313
B41 .T5 MRR Biog.

PHILOSOPHERS--DICTIONARIES--GERMAN.
Philosophen-Lexikon; Berlin, W. de
Gruyter, 1949-50. 2 v. a 52-2075
B43 .P5 1949 MRR Alc.

Schmidt, Heinrich, Philosophisches
Wörterbuch. 18. Aufl., neu bearb.
Stuttgart, A. Kröner [1969] vii,
690 p. 79-400014
B43 .S3 1969 MRR Alc.

PHILOSOPHERS--DICTIONARIES--ITALIAN.
Enciclopedia filosofica. 2. edizione
interamente rielaborata ... Firenze,
G. C. Sansoni, 1968- v. [28000
(v. 1) varies] 70-387428
B44 .E52 MRR Alc.

PHILOSOPHERS--UNITED STATES.
Stroh, Guy W. American philosophy
from Edwards to Dewey, Princeton,
N.J., Van Nostrand [1968] x, 288 p.
191 68-21148
B851 .S8 MRR Alc.

PHILOSOPHERS--UNITED STATES--
DIRECTORIES.
Directory of American philosophers.
1- 1962/63- Albuquerque. 62-4947

B935 .D5 MRR Alc Latest edition

PHILOSOPHERS, AMERICAN.
American Catholic Philosophical
Association. Directory of members.
1- 1968- Washington. 106/.2/73
78-5394
B35 .A45 MRR Biog Latest edition

PHILOSOPHERS, AMERICAN--BIOGRAPHY--
DICTIONARIES.
Nauman, St. Elmo. Dictionary of
American philosophy, New York,
Philosophical Library [1972, c1973]
viii, 273 p. [$10.00] 191 B 72-
78169
B851 .N3 MRR Alc.

PHILOSOPHERS, ANCIENT.
Diogenes Laertius. Lives of eminent
philosphers, London, W. Heinemann;
Cambridge, Mass., Harvard University
Press, 1938-1931. 2 v. mrr01-38
PA3612 .D5 1931d MRR Alc.

PHILOSOPHICAL GRAMMAR
see Grammar, Comparative and general

PHILOSOPHY.
see also Aesthetics

see also Ethics

Conde Obregón, Ramón. Enciclopedia
de la filosofia. [1. ed.]
Barcelona, De Gassó Hnos. [1961]
363 p. 65-73857
B51 .C6 MRR Alc.

PHILOSOPHY--ABSTRACTS--PERIODICALS.
Bulletin signalétique 519:
Philosophie. v. 24- 1970- Paris
72-624427
Z7127 .F7118 MRR Alc Full set

Bulletin signalétique 519:
Philosophie, sciences religieuses.
v. 15-23; 1961-69. Paris, Centre de
documentation du C.N.R.S. 75-10205
Z7127 .F712 MRR Alc Full set

PHILOSOPHY--BIBLIOGRAPHY.
Alston, R. C. Logic, philosophy,
epistomology, universal language
Bradford, Printed for the author by
E. Cummins [1967] xvi, 111 p. 68-
105634
Z2015.A1 A4 no. 7 MRR Alc.

Baldwin, James Mark, ed. Dictionary
of philosophy and psychology; New
York, The Macmillan company; London,
Macmillan & co., ltd., 1901-05. 3 v.
in 4. 06-8753
Z7125 .R2 volume 3 MRR Alc.

Borchardt, Dietrich Hans, How to
find out in philosophy and
psychology, [1st ed.] Oxford, New
York, Pergamon Press [1968] vii, 97
p. 016.1 67-28659
Z7125 .B65 1968 MRR Alc.

Brie, G. A. de. Bibliographia
philosophica, 1934-1945. Bruxellis,
Editiones Spectrum, 1950-54. 2 v.
016.1 51-5842
Z7125 .B7 MRR Alc.

Koren, Henry J. Research in
philosophy; Pittsburgh, Duquesne
University Press [1966] 203 p.
016.1 66-28340
Z7125 .K65 MRR Alc.

Rogers, A. Robert, The humanities;
Littleton, Colo., Libraries
Unlimited, 1974. 400 p. [$9.50]
016.0013 74-78393
Z5579 .R63 MRR Alc.

Totok, Wilhelm. Handbuch der
Geschichte der Philosophie.
Frankfurt am Main, V. Klostermann
[1964- v. 64-52305
B82 .T6 MRR Alc.

Varet, Gilbert, Manuel de
bibliographie philosophique. [1.
ed.] Paris, Presses universitaires
de France, 1956. 2 v. (xx, 1058 p.)
a 57-1089
Z7125 .V3 MRR Alc.

PHILOSOPHY--BIBLIOGRAPHY--PERIODICALS.
Bibliographie de la philosophie.
[année] 1- jan./mar. 1954- Paris,
Librairie Philosophique J. Vrin. 58-
31345
Z7127 .B5 MRR Alc Full set

Bulletin signalétique 519:
Philosophie. v. 24- 1970- Paris
72-624427
Z7127 .F7118 MRR Alc Full set

Bulletin signalétique 519:
Philosophie, sciences religieuses.
v. 15-23; 1961-69. Paris, Centre de
documentation du C.N.R.S. 75-10205
Z7127 .F712 MRR Alc Full set

Bulletin signalétique: Philosophie,
sciences humaines. v. 1-14; 1947-60.
Paris, Centre de documentation du C.
N. R. S. 51-30077
Z7127 .F7 MRR Alc Full set

Répertoire bibliographique de la
philosophie. t. 1- ,fev. 1949-
Louvain, Institut supérieur de
philosophie. 016.1 51-28726
Z7127 .R42 MRR Alc Full set

PHILOSOPHY--BIO-BIBLIOGRAPHY.
Philosophen-Lexikon; Berlin, W. de
Gruyter, 1949-50. 2 v. a 52-2075
B43 .P5 1949 MRR Alc.

PHILOSOPHY--COLLECTIONS.
Kurtz, Paul W., ed. American thought
before 1900; [1st ed.] New York,
Macmillan [1966] 448 p. 191 65-
24106
B850 .K8 MRR Alc.

Magill, Frank Northen, ed.
Masterpieces of world philosophy in
summary form, [1st ed.] New York,
Salem Press [1961] 2 v. 108.2 61-
65279
B21 .M3 1961 MRR Alc.

PHILOSOPHY--DICTIONARIES.
Baldwin, James Mark, ed. Dictionary
of philosophy and psychology; New
York, The Macmillan company; London,
Macmillan & co., ltd., 1901-05. 3 v.
in 4. 06-8753
Z7125 .R2 volume 3 MRR Alc.

Briggs, Michael H. Handbook of
philosophy. New York, Philosophical
Library [1959] 214 p. 103 59-2040

B41 .B66 MRR Alc.

Brugger, Walter, ed. Philosophical
dictionary. Spokane, Wash., Gonzaga
University Press [1972] xxiii, 460
p. 103 72-82135
B43 .B713 MRR Alc.

Dictionary of the history of ideas;
New York, Scribner [1973] 4 v.
[$35.00 (per vol.)] 901.9 72-7943

CB5 .D52 MRR Alc.

The Encyclopedia of philosophy. New
York, Macmillan [1967] 8 v. 103
67-10059
B41 .E5 MRR Alc.

PHILOSOPHY--DICTIONARIES. (Cont.)
Runes, Dagobert David, ed.
Dictionary of philosophy. 15th ed.,
rev. New York, Philosophical Library
[1960] 342 p.   103 60-16583
   B41 .R8 1960 MRR Alc.

Spinoza, Benedictus de, Spinoza:
dictionary. New York, Philosophical
Library [1951] xiv, 309 p.   199.492
51-14421
   B3951 .S5 MRR Alc.

Urmson, J. O., ed. The concise
encyclopedia of Western philosophy
and philosophers. 1st ed.] New
York, Hawthorn Books [1960] 431 p.
190.3 60-6258
   B41 .U7 MRR Alc.

Wuellner, Bernard. A dictionary of
scholastic philosophy. 2d ed.
Milwaukee, Bruce Pub. Co. [1966]
xviii, 339 p. 188.403 66-24259
   B50.S35 W8 1966 MRR Alc.

PHILOSOPHY--DICTIONARIES--DUTCH.
Elseviers filosofische en
psychologische encyclopedie.
Amsterdam, Elsevier, 1970. 271 p.
[fl4.50]   75-543438
   BF31 .E45 MRR Alc.

PHILOSOPHY--DICTIONARIES--ENGLISH.
Grooten, Johan, ed. New encyclopedia
of philosophy New York,
Philosophical Library [1972] 468 p.
[$20.00]   103 72-192726
   B48.D8 G713 MRR Alc.

PHILOSOPHY--DICTIONARIES--FRENCH.
Foulquie, Paul, Dictionnaire de la
langue philosophique 2e edition
revue et augmentee. Paris, Presses
universitaires de France, 1969. xvi,
779 p. [53.00]   103 73-409415
   B42 .F6 1969 MRR Alc.

Lalande, André, Vocabulaire
technique et critique de la
philosophie, 10e edition revue et
augmentee. Paris, Presses
universitaires de France, 1967.
xxviii, 1324 p. [80 F] 103 68-
104260
   B42 .L3 1967 MRR Alc.

PHILOSOPHY--DICTIONARIES--GERMAN.
Eisler, Rudolf, Worterbuch der
philosophischen begriffe, historisch-
quellenmassig 4. vollig neubearb.
aufl. Berlin, E. S. Mittler & sohn,
1927-30. 3 v. 103 27-25034
   B43 .E4 1927 MRR Alc.

Schmidt, Heinrich, Philosophisches
Worterbuch. 18. Aufl., neu bearb.
Stuttgart, A. Kröner [1969] vii,
690 p. 79-400014
   B43 .S3 1969 MRR Alc.

PHILOSOPHY--DICTIONARIES--ITALIAN.
Abbagnano, Nicola, Dizionario di
filosofia. [Torino] Unione
tipografico-editrice torinese [1961]
xii, 905 p.   61-31385
   B44 .A2 MRR Alc.

Enciclopedia filosofica. 2. edizione
interamente rielaborata ... Firenze,
G. C. Sansoni, 1968- v.   [28000
(v. 1) varies] 70-387428
   B44 .E52 MRR Alc.

Enciclopedia filosofica. Venezia,
Istituto per la collaborazione
culturale [1957-58] 4 v. a 58-4987
   B44 .E5 MRR Alc.

Ranzoli, Cesare, Dizionario di
scienze filosofiche 6. ed. aumentata
e riv. Milano, Hoepli, 1963. xii,
1345 p.   67-121899
   B44 .R2 1963 MRR Alc.

PHILOSOPHY--DICTIONARIES--LATIN.
Deferrari, Roy Joseph, A Latin-
English dictionary of St. Thomas
Aquinas. [Boston] St. Paul Editions
[1960] 1115 p. 189.4 60-1846
   B765.T54 D39 MRR Alc.

Deferrari, Roy Joseph, A lexicon of
St. Thomas Aquinas [Washington,
Catholic University of America Press,
1948-53, c1949] 5 v. 189.4 a 49-
1297
   B765.T54 D38 MRR Alc.

PHILOSOPHY--DIRECTORIES.
American Catholic Philosophical
Association. Directory of members.
1- 1968- Washington. 106/.2/73
78-5394
   B35 .A45 MRR Biog Latest edition

International directory of philosophy
and philosophers. [1st]- ed.] 1966-
Bowling Green, Ohio [etc.] 102.5
66-18830
   B35 .I55 MRR Alc Latest edition

PHILOSOPHY--HISTORY.
Brehier, Émile, The history of
philosophy. Chicago, University of
Chicago Press [1963- v.   109 63-
20912
   B77 .B723 MRR Alc.

Copleston, Frederick Charles. A
history of philosophy. Westminster,
Md., Newman Bookshop, 1946- v.
109 47-875
   B72 .C62 MRR Alc.

Jaspers, Karl, The great
philosophers. [1st American ed.]
New York, Harcourt, Brace & World
[1962- v.   109 62-9436
   B82 .J313 MRR Alc.

O'Connor, Daniel John, ed. A
critical history of Western
philosophy. [New York] Free Press of
Glencoe [1964] vi, 604 p. 190 64-
13242
   B72 .O2 MRR Alc.

Passmore, John Arthur. A hundred
years of philosophy. 2nd ed.
London, Duckworth, 1966. 574 p.
[50/-]   109 66-67868
   B1615 .P3 1966 MRR Alc.

Totok, Wilhelm. Handbuch der
Geschichte der Philosophie.
Frankfurt am Main, V. Klostermann
[1964- v.   64-52305
   B82 .T6 MRR Alc.

PHILOSOPHY--HISTORY--CHINA--SOURCES.
Chan, Wing-tsit, comp. and tr. A
source book in Chinese philosophy.
Princeton, N.J., Princeton University
Press, 1963. xxv, 856 p.   181.11082
62-7398
   B125 .C45 MRR Alc.

PHILOSOPHY--HISTORY--UNITED STATES.
Schneider, Herbert Wallace, A
history of American philosophy. 2d
ed. New York, Columbia University
Press, 1963. 590 p. 191 63-14114

   B851 .S4 1963 MRR Alc.

PHILOSOPHY--INTRODUCTIONS.
Flew, Antony Gerrard Newton, An
introduction to Western philosophy.
[1st American ed.] Indianapolis,
Bobbs-Merrill [1971] 511 p. [$4.95]
190 74-142179
   BD21 .F59 1971b MRR Alc.

PHILOSOPHY--PERIODICALS--BIBLIOGRAPHY.
Philosophie. 's-Gravenhage, Mouton &
Co. 1867- 124 p. [fl 15.-]
016.1/05 68-77967
   Z7127 .P52 MRR Alc.

[United States. Library of Congress.
General Reference and Bibliography
Division] Philosophical periodicals;
Washington, 1952. vi, 89 p.
016.105 52-60055
   Z663.28 .P47 MRR Alc.

PHILOSOPHY--PERIODICALS--INDEXES.
Bulletin signalétique: Philosophie,
sciences humaines. v. 1-14; 1947-60.
Paris, Centre de documentation du C.
N. R. S.   51-30077
   Z7127 .F7 MRR Alc Full set

The Philosopher's index. Cumulative
ed. 1967/68- Bowling Green, Ohio,
Philosophy Documentation Center,
Bowling Green University [etc.]
016.105 74-250928
   Z7127 .P47 MRR Alc Full set

Répertoire bibliographique de la
philosophie. t. 1- fev. 1949-
Louvain, Institut supérieur de
philosophie. 016.1 51-28726
   Z7127 .R42 MRR Alc Full set

PHILOSOPHY--QUOTATIONS, MAXIMS, ETC.
Spinoza, Benedictus de, Spinoza:
dictionary. New York, Philosophical
Library [1951] xiv, 309 p.   199.492
51-14421
   B3951 .S5 MRR Alc.

PHILOSOPHY--STUDY AND TEACHING--UNITED
STATES.
Directory of American philosophers.
1- 1962/63- Albuquerque. 62-4947

   B935 .D5 MRR Alc Latest edition

PHILOSOPHY--TERMINOLOGY.
Peters, Francis E. Greek
philosophical terms; New York, New
York University Press, 1967. xii,
234 p.   103 67-25043
   B49 .P4 MRR Alc.

PHILOSOPHY, AMERICAN.
Kurtz, Paul W., ed. American thought
before 1900; [1st ed.] New York,
Macmillan [1966] 448 p. 191 65-
24106
   B850 .K8 MRR Alc.

Parrington, Vernon Louis, Main
currents in American thought; [New
York, Harcourt, Brace and company,
1927-30] 3 v.   27-8440
   PS88 .P3 MRR Alc.

Schneider, Herbert Wallace, A
history of American philosophy. 2d
ed. New York, Columbia University
Press, 1963. 590 p. 191 63-14114

   B851 .S4 1963 MRR Alc.

Stroh, Guy W. American philosophy
from Edwards to Dewey, Princeton,
N.J., Van Nostrand [1968] x, 288 p.
191 68-21148
   B851 .S8 MRR Alc.

PHILOSOPHY, ANCIENT.
Diogenes Laertius. Lives of eminent
philosophers, London, W. Heinemann;
Cambridge, Mass., Harvard University
Press, 1938-1931. 2 v. arr01-38
   PA3612 .D5 1931d MRR Alc.

Guthrie, William Keith Chambers, A
history of Greek philosophy.
Cambridge, University Press, 1962-
v.   182 62-52735
   B171 .G83 MRR Alc.

Peters, Francis E. Greek
philosophical terms; New York, New
York University Press, 1967. xii,
234 p.   103 67-25043
   B49 .P4 MRR Alc.

PHILOSOPHY, ANCIENT--ADDRESSES, ESSAYS,
LECTURES.
Armstrong, Arthur Hilary. The
Cambridge history of later Greek and
early medieval philosophy; London,
Cambridge U.P., 1967. xiv, 711 p.
[95/-]   182 66-12305
   B171 .A79 MRR Alc.

PHILOSOPHY, ANCIENT--BIBLIOGRAPHY.
London. University. Warburg
Institute. Library. Catalogue. [2d
ed.] Boston, G. K. Hall, 1967. 12
v.   019/.2 68-4522
   Z921 .L66 1967 MRR Alc (Dk 33)

PHILOSOPHY, CHINESE--ADDRESSES, ESSAYS,
LECTURES.
East-West Philosophers' Conference.
The Chinese mind; Honolulu, East-
West Center Press [1967] ix, 402 p.
181/.11 66-24011
   B125 .E25 MRR Alc.

PHILOSOPHY, CHINESE--COLLECTIONS.
Chan, Wing-tsit, comp. and tr. A
source book in Chinese philosophy.
Princeton, N.J., Princeton University
Press, 1963. xxv, 856 p.   181.11082
62-7398
   B125 .C45 MRR Alc.

PHILOSOPHY, ENGLISH--20TH CENTURY.
Passmore, John Arthur. A hundred
years of philosophy. 2nd ed.
London, Duckworth, 1966. 574 p.
[50/-]   109 66-67868
   B1615 .P3 1966 MRR Alc.

PHILOSOPHY, HINDU.
Zimmer, Heinrich Robert,
Philosophies of India; [New York]
Pantheon Books [1951] xvii, 687 p.
181.4 51-13167
   B131 .Z52 MRR Alc.

PHILOSOPHY, HINDU--COLLECTIONS.
Radhakrishnan, Sarvepalli, Pres.
India, ed. A source book in Indian
philosophy, Princeton, N.J.,
Princeton University Press, 1957.
xxix, 683 p.   181.4 55-6698
   B130 .R3 MRR Alc.

PHILOSOPHY, INDIC.
Radhakrishnan, Sarvepalli, Pres.
India, ed. A source book in Indian
philosophy, Princeton, N.J.,
Princeton University Press, 1957.
xxix, 683 p.   181.4 55-6698
   B130 .R3 MRR Alc.

Sharma, Chandradhar. Indian
philosophy; [New York] Barnes &
Noble [1962] 405 p. 181.4 62-
18222
   B131 .S48 1962 MRR Alc.

PHILOSOPHY, ISLAMIC--HISTORY.
Fakhry, Majid. A history of Islamic
philosophy. New York, Columbia
University Press, 1970. xv, 427 p.
[$15.00]   181/.07 71-110144
   B741 .F23 1970 MRR Alc.

PHILOSOPHY, MEDIEVAL.
Copleston, Frederick Charles. A
history of medieval philosophy
London, Methuen [1972] 399 p.
[£4.00]   189/.09 72-181267
   B721 .C57 1972 MRR Alc.

PHILOSOPHY, MEDIEVAL--ADDRESSES, ESSAYS, LECTURES.
Armstrong, Arthur Hilary. The Cambridge history of later Greek and early medieval philosophy; London, Cambridge U.P., 1967. xiv, 711 p. [95/-] 182 66-12305
B171 .A79 MRR Alc.

PHILOSOPHY, MODERN--20TH CENTURY.
Moyrre, Michel, ed. Dictionnaire des idees contemporaines Nouvelle edition mise a jour. Paris, Editions universitaires 1966. 720 p. [35 F.] 103 67-87698
B804 .M65 1966 MRR Alc.

PHILOSOPHY, MODERN--20TH CENTURY--BIBLIOGRAPHY.
McLean, George F., comp. An annotated bibliography of philosophy in Catholic thought, 1900-1964, New York, F. Ungar Pub. Co. [1967] xiv, 371 p. 016.201 67-24185
Z7821 .M25 MRR Alc.

PHILOSOPHY, MODERN--20TH CENTURY--COLLECTIONS.
Runes, Dagobert David, ed. Twentieth century philosophy; New York, Philosophical library [1943] 571 p. 190.82 43-15977
B790 .R8 MRR Alc.

PHILOSOPHY, MODERN--DICTIONARIES--FRENCH.
Moyrre, Michel, ed. Dictionnaire des idees contemporaines Nouvelle edition mise a jour. Paris, Editions universitaires 1966. 720 p. [35 F.] 103 67-87698
B804 .M65 1966 MRR Alc.

PHILOSOPHY, MODERN--HISTORY.
Randall, John Herman, The career of philosophy. New York, Columbia University Press, 1962- v.
190.9 62-10454
B791 .R25 MRR Alc.

PHILOSOPHY, MORAL
see Ethics

PHILOSOPHY, ORIENTAL.
Koller, John M. Oriental philosophies, New York, Scribner [1970] xiii, 303 p. [8.95] 181 70-99010
B121 .K56 1970 MRR Alc.

PHOBIAS.
Blakiston's Gould medical dictionary; 3d ed. New York, McGraw-Hill [1972] xxi, 1828 p. 610/.3 78-37376
R121 .B62 1972 MRR Ref Desk.

Sheffield, Eng. Free Public Libraries and Museum. 'Isms: a dictionary of words ending in -ism, -ology, and -phobia, 2nd ed. Sheffield, Corporation of Sheffield; Wakefield, EP Publishing Ltd, 1972. 100 p. [£1.50] 423/.1 73-159939
PE1680 .S37 1972b MRR Ref Desk.

PHONOGRAPH IN EDUCATION.
National Information Center for Educational Media. Index to educational records. 2d ed. Los Angeles, 1972. viii, 536 p. 371.33/32/0216 78-190632
LB1044.3.Z9 N33 1972 MRR Alc.

PHONORECORDS--BIBLIOGRAPHY.
High fidelity. Records in review. 1955- Great Barrington, Mass. [etc.] Wyeth Press [etc.] 789.913* 55-10600
ML156.9 .H5 MRR Alc Partial set

Whitburn, Joel. Top rhythm & blues records, 1949-1971. Menomonee Falls, Wis., Record Research, c1973. 184 p. 016.7899/12 73-78333
ML156.4.P6 W53 MRR Alc.

PHONORECORDS--CATALOGS.
Educators guide to free tapes, scripts and transcriptions. 1st-ed.; Jan. 1955- Randolph, Wis., Educators' Progress Service. 789.913* 55-2784
LB1044.2 .E3 MRR Alc Latest edition

National Information Center for Educational Media. Index to educational records. 2d ed. Los Angeles, 1972. viii, 536 p. 371.33/32/0216 78-190632
LB1044.3.Z9 N33 1972 MRR Alc.

PHONORECORDS--CATALOGS--DIRECTORIES.
Association for Recorded Sound Collections. A preliminary directory of sound recordings collections in the United States and Canada [New York] New York Public Library, 1967. 157 p. 026/.7899/0257 67-31297
ML19 .A85 MRR Alc.

PHONORECORDS--CATALOGS AND COLLECTIONS.
United States. Library of Congress. Library of Congress catalog: Music and phonorecords; 1953- Washington. 53-60012
Z663.37 .A3 MRR Alc MRR Alc Full set

PHONORECORDS--PRESERVATION AND STORAGE.
Pickett, Andrew G. Preservation and storage of sound recordings; Washington, Library of Congress, 1959. vii, 74 p. 025.178 59-62190
Z663.378 .P7 MRR Alc.

PHONORECORDS--PRICES.
Propes, Steve. Those oldies but goodies; New York, Macmillan Co. [1973] viii, 192 p. [$5.95] 789.9/12 72-93630
ML156.4.P6 P76 MRR Alc.

PHONORECORDS--REVIEWS.
High fidelity. Records in review. 1955- Great Barrington, Mass. [etc.] Wyeth Press [etc.] 789.913* 55-10600
ML156.9 .H5 MRR Alc Partial set

PHONOTAPES--CATALOGS.
Educators guide to free tapes, scripts and transcriptions. 1st-ed.; Jan. 1955- Randolph, Wis., Educators' Progress Service. 789.913* 55-2784
LB1044.2 .E3 MRR Alc Latest edition

United States. Library of Congress. Division for the Blind. Books on magnetic tape; [Washington] 1962. x, 127 p. 789.913 62-60084
Z663.25 .B65 MRR Alc.

United States. Library of Congress. Division for the Blind. Books on magnetic tape; Washington, 1961. 24 p. 61-60071
Z663.25 .B66 MRR Alc.

United States. Library of Congress. Hispanic Foundation. Voces de poetas y prosistas ibericos y latinoamericanos en el archivo de literatura hispanica en cinta magnetica de la Fundacion Hispanica. Washington, 1960. viii, 33 p. 60-60075
Z663.32 .V6 MRR Alc.

PHOTOCOPYING SERVICES--DIRECTORIES.
International Federation for Documentation. Photocopies from abroad; 3d and rev. ed. The Hague [1963 or 4] 28 p. 64-46050
Z265 .I55 1964 MRR Ref Desk.

Nitecki, Joseph Z. Directory of library reprographic services. 5th ed. [Weston, Conn.] Published for the Reproduction of Library Materials Section, American Library Association by Microform Review Inc. [1974, c1973] 105 p. 025.1/29 73-2059
Z265 .N58 1974 MRR Ref Desk.

PHOTOGRAPH COLLECTIONS.
United Nations Educational, Scientific and Cultural Organization. Repertoire international des archives photographiques d'oeuvres d'art. Paris, Dunod, 1950. xx, 667 p. 704.94 50-12760
N4000 .U5 MRR Alc.

PHOTOGRAPHERS--DIRECTORIES.
Art directors handbook: Europe. v. 1- 1965- New York, P. Glenn Publications. 659.112 65-1527
HF5804 .A7 MRR Alc Latest edition

Director's Art Institute, New York. Who's who in commercial art and photography: [2d ed.] New York, 1964. 192 p. 66-235
NC997 .D5 1964 MRR Biog.

Society of Photographic Scientists and Engineers. A directory for members. 1st- 1959- Washington. 770.6273 59-42214
TR1 .S76A3 MRR Alc Latest edition

PHOTOGRAPHIC INTERPRETATION--BIBLIOGRAPHY.
United States. Library of Congress. Technical Information Division. Photo interpretation techniques, Washington, 1956. x, 162 p. 56-60077
Z663.49 .P4 MRR Alc.

PHOTOGRAPHS.
Nunn, George Walter Arthur, ed. British sources of photographs and pictures. London, Cassell [1952] viii, 220 p. 770.58 53-25373
TR12 .N8 MRR Alc.

United Nations Educational, Scientific and Cultural Organization. Repertoire international des archives photographiques d'oeuvres d'art. Paris, Dunod, 1950. xx, 667 p. 704.94 50-12760
N4000 .U5 MRR Alc.

PHOTOGRAPHS--CATALOGS.
Clapp, Jane. Art reproductions. New York, Scarecrow Press, 1961. 350 p. 708.1 61-8714
N4000 .C5 MRR Ref Desk.

United States. Library of Congress. Image of America: Washington, 1957. viii, 88 p. 917.3 57-60038
Z663.15 .I5 MRR Alc.

United States. Library of Congress. Prints and Photographs Division. Civil War photographs, 1861-1865; Washington, Reference Dept., Library of Congress, 1961. x, 74 p. 973.79085 61-60002
Z663.39 .C5 MRR Alc.

United States. Library of Congress. Prints and Photographs Division. Pictorial Americana: 2d ed. Washington, Library of Congress, 1955. 68 p. 973.084 55-60012
Z663.39 .P5 1955 MRR Alc.

United States. Library of Congress. Prints and Photographs Division. Pictorial Americana; Washington, 1945. 38 l. 973.084 46-12463
Z663.39 .P5 1945 MRR Alc.

United States. Library of Congress. Prints and Photographs Division. Selective checklist of prints and photographs recently cataloged and made available for reference. lots 2280- 1949- [Washington] 016.779 49-47008
Z663.39 .S4 MRR Alc MRR Alc Full set

United States. Library of Congress. Reference Dept. Guide to the special collections of prints & photographs in the Library of Congress, Washington, 1955. v, 200 p. 016.779 54-60020
Z663.2 .G8 MRR Alc.

PHOTOGRAPHS--COLLECTORS AND COLLECTING--DIRECTORIES.
Special Libraries Association. Picture Division. Picture sources. 2d ed. New York, Special Libraries Association [1964] viii, 216 p. 64-15089
N4000 .S7 1964 MRR Ref Desk.

PHOTOGRAPHY--ANIMATED PICTURES
see Moving-pictures

PHOTOGRAPHY--APPARATUS AND SUPPLIES--DIRECTORIES.
Photography directory & buying guide. 1954- New York, etc., Ziff-Davis Pub. Co.] 55-333
TR12 .P53 Sci RR Latest edition / MRR Alc Latest edition

Society of Photographic Scientists and Engineers. A directory for members. 1st- 1959- Washington. 770.6273 59-42214
TR1 .S76A3 MRR Alc Latest edition

PHOTOGRAPHY--BIBLIOGRAPHY.
Boni, Albert, Photographic literature; 1st ed. New York, Morgan & Morgan [1962] xvi, 335 p. 016.77 62-21351
Z7134 .B6 MRR Alc.

PHOTOGRAPHY--DICTIONARIES.
The Focal encyclopedia of photography. Revised desk ed. London, New York, Focal P., 1969. xi, 1699 p. [70/-] 770/.3 77-381067
TR9 .F6 1969 MRR Alc.

Sowerby, Arthur Lindsay McRae. Dictionary of photography: [19th ed.] London, Iliffe [1961] vi, 715 p. 62-68245
TR9 .S74 1961 MRR Alc.

Stroebel, Leslie. Dictionary of contemporary photography / Dobbs Ferry, N.Y.: Morgan & Morgan, [1974] 217 p. : [$20.00] 770/.3 73-93536
TR9 .S88 MRR Alc.

PHOTOGRAPHY--DICTIONARIES--POLYGLOT.
Dictionary of photography and cinematography: London, New York, Focal Press [1961] 1 v. (various pagings) 770.3 63-24356
TR9 .D5 MRR Alc.

Elsevier's dictionary of photography in three languages: Amsterdam, New York, Elsevier Pub. Co.: distributed by American Elsevier Pub. Co., New York, 1965. 660 p. 770.3 63-16076
TR9 .E46 MRR Alc.

PHOTOGRAPHY--DIRECTORIES.
Levitan, Eli L. An alphabetical guide to motion picture, television, and videotape production New York, McGraw-Hill [1970] xvii, 797 p. 778.5/3/03 69-13610
TR847 .L47 MRR Alc.

PHOTOGRAPHY--DIRECTORIES. (Cont.)
Nunn, George Walter Arthur, ed.
British sources of photographs and
pictures. London, Cassell [1952]
viii, 220 p.   770.58 53-25373
   TR12 .N8 MRR Alc.

PHOTOGRAPHY--EXHIBITIONS.
United States. Library of Congress.
Image of America; Washington, 1957.
viii, 88 p.   917.3 57-60038
   Z663.15 .I5 MRR Alc.

PHOTOGRAPHY--FILMS.
see also Microfilms

PHOTOGRAPHY--HANDBOOKS, MANUALS, ETC.
Leica manual. Hastings-on-Hudson,
N.Y., Morgan & Morgan. 771.3/1 74-
644639
   TR146 .M77 MRR Alc Latest edition
   / Sci RR Latest edition

PHOTOGRAPHY--HISTORY.
Gassan, Arnold. A chronology of
photography; a critical survey of the
history of photography as a medium of
art. Athens, Ohio, Handbook Co.;
[distributed by Light Impressions,
Rochester, N.Y., 1972] 373 p.
770/.9 72-83426
   TR15 .G33 MRR Alc.

Gernsheim, Helmut, The history of
photography from the camera obscura
to the beginning of the modern era,
Revised and enlarged ed. London,
Thames & Hudson, 1969. 599 p. [6/6/-
] 770/.9 71-452052
   TR15 .G37 1969b MRR Alc.

PHOTOGRAPHY--MOVING PICTURES
see Cinematography

PHOTOGRAPHY--PORTRAITS.
Berühmte Köpfe; 3200 Männer und
Frauen im Bild. [1. Aufl.
Gütersloh] C. Bertelsmann [1959]
413 p. 920 60-26257
   N7575 .B47 MRR Alc.

PHOTOGRAPHY--SOCIETIES, ETC.
Society of Photographic Scientists
and Engineers. A directory for
members. 1st- 1959- Washington.
770.6273 59-42214
   TR1 .S76A3 MRR Alc Latest edition

PHOTOGRAPHY, ARTISTIC--EXHIBITIONS.
United States. Library of Congress.
Contemporary photographs from Sweden;
Washington, 1971. [18] p.
779/.09485/0740153 70-37008
   Z663.38 .C62 MRR Alc.

PHOTOGRAPHY, JOURNALISTIC.
Ahlers, Arvel W., Where and how to
sell your pictures. 4th ed. rev.
New York, American Photographic Book
Pub. Co.; book trade: Garden City
Books, Garden City, N.Y. [1959] 142
p. 770.68 59-4237
   TR820 .A35 1959 MRR Alc.

PHOTOLITHOGRAPHY.
Shapiro, Charles, comp. The
lithographers manual. 4th ed.
Pittsburgh, Graphic Arts Technical
Foundation [1970, c1968] 1 v.
(various pagings) 686.2/315 68-
57213
   TR940 .S47 1970 MRR Alc.

PHOTOMETRY.
see also Color

PHOTOMICROGRAPHY.
see also Microscope and microscopy

PHOTOTYPESETTING.
Visual Graphics Corporation. The
world-famous photo typositor alphabet
library. New ed. [North Miami,
Fla.] c1973. xi, 270 p. 686.2/24
74-75683
   Z250 .V67 1973 MRR Alc.

PHYLOGENY.
see also Paleontology

PHYSICAL ANTHROPOLOGY.
Garn, Stanley M. Human races, 2d
ed. Springfield, Ill., Thomas [1965]
xiv, 155 p. 573 65-18056
   GN315 .G3 1965 MRR Alc.

Montagu, Ashley, An introduction to
physical anthropology. 3d ed.
Springfield, Ill., Thomas [1960] 771
p. 573 59-14204
   GN60 .M6 1960 MRR Alc.

PHYSICAL DISTRIBUTION OF GOODS.
see also Packaging

PHYSICAL EDUCATION AND TRAINING.
see also Games

see also Health education

PHYSICAL EDUCATION AND TRAINING--
BIBLIOGRAPHY.
Educators guide to free health,
physical education and recreation
materials. 1st- ed.; 1968-
Randolph, Wis., Educators Progress
Service. 011 68-57948
   Z6121 .E38 MRR Alc Latest edition

Zeigler, Earle F. Research in the
history, philosophy, and
international aspects of physical
education and sport; bibliographies
and techniques. Champaign, Ill.,
Stipes Pub. Co. [1971] vi, 350 p.
016.6137 76-26892
   Z6121 .Z45 MRR Alc.

PHYSICAL EDUCATION AND TRAINING--
HISTORY--BIBLIOGRAPHY.
Zeigler, Earle F. Research in the
history, philosophy, and
international aspects of physical
education and sport; bibliographies
and techniques. Champaign, Ill.,
Stipes Pub. Co. [1971] vi, 350 p.
016.6137 76-26892
   Z6121 .Z45 MRR Alc.

PHYSICAL GEOGRAPHY.
see also Climatology

see also Earth

see also Earthquakes

see also Geomorphology

see also Man--Influence on nature

see also Meteorology

see also Mountains

see also Ocean

see also Oceanography

see also Rivers

see also Volcanoes

Monkhouse, Francis John. Principles
of physical geography 7th ed.
London, University of London Press,
1970. ix, 570 p., 57 plates.
[£2.10] 551 73-567039
   GB53 .M6 1970 MRR Alc.

PHYSICAL GEOGRAPHY--DICTIONARIES.
Moore, Wilfred George, A dictionary
of geography; [New ed.] revised and
enlarged, London, Black, 1967. [8],
246 p. [30/-] 910.02/03 67-95321

   G103 .M65 1967b MRR Alc.

PHYSICAL GEOGRAPHY--TEXT-BOOKS--1945-
James, Preston Everett, A geography
of man 3d ed. Waltham, Mass.,
Blaisdell Pub. Co. [1966] xvii, 581
p. 910 65-14575
   GB55 .J3 1966 MRR Alc.

Strahler, Arthur Newell, Physical
geography 3d ed. New York, Wiley
[1969, c1969] ix, 733 p. 551 68-
28507
   GB56 .S75 1969 MRR Alc.

PHYSICAL GEOGRAPHY--CENTRAL EUROPE.
Mutton, Alice Florence Adelaide.
Central Europe; a regional and human
geography, 2nd ed. London,
Longmans, 1968. xxiv, 488 p. [65/-]
914 68-85425
   D922 .M87 1968 MRR Alc.

PHYSICAL GEOGRAPHY--UNITED STATES.
Douglas, Edward Morehouse.
Boundaries, areas, geographic centers
and altitudes of the United States
and several states, 2d ed.
Washington, U.S. Govt. print. off.,
1930. vii, 265 p. incl. illus.,
maps, tables. gs 30-275
   E179.5 .D73 1930 MRR Ref Desk.

PHYSICAL INSTRUMENTS.
see also Electronic apparatus and
appliances

Indicateur suisse de l'horlogerie.
Bienne, L.C. Calame. 51-36795
   TS543.S9 I5 MRR Alc Latest edition

Palestrant, Simon S., Practical
pictorial guide to mechanisms and
machines. New York, University Books
[1956] 256 p. 621.03 56-13016
   TJ9 .P3 1956 MRR Alc.

PHYSICAL INSTRUMENTS--BIBLIOGRAPHY.
United States. Library of Congress.
Technical Information Division.
Instrumentation literature and its
use; Washington, 1952. 129 p. 53-
63562
   Z663.49 .I6 MRR Alc.

PHYSICAL MEASUREMENTS--DICTIONARIES--
POLYGLOT.
Elsevier's lexicon of international
and national units; Amsterdam, New
York, Elsevier Pub. Co., 1964. 75 p.
389.103 63-11366
   QC82 .E37 MRR Alc.

PHYSICAL OCEANOGRAPHY
see Oceanography

PHYSICAL THERAPISTS--DIRECTORIES.
Licht, Sidney Herman, ed. World
directory of physical medicine
specialists. New Haven, E. Licht,
1960. xxii, 241 p. 615.8058 60-
8329
   RM697.A2 L5 MRR Biog.

PHYSICALLY HANDICAPPED.
see also Blind

PHYSICALLY HANDICAPPED--EMPLOYMENT--
BIBLIOGRAPHY.
United States. President's Committee
on Employment of the Physically
Handicapped. Employment of the
physically handicapped; [Washington,
U.S. Govt. Print. Off., 1957] vii,
93 p. 331.86 371.91* 57-62036
   Z663.28 .E5 MRR Alc.

PHYSICIANS.
Schmidt, Jacob Edward, Medical
discoveries; Springfield, Ill.,
Thomas [1959] ix, 555 p. 610.9 58-
14086
   R131 .S35 1959 MRR Alc.

Stevenson, Lloyd G. Nobel prize
winners in medicine and physiology,
1901-1950. New York, H. Schuman
[1953] 291 p. 926.1 378.32 53-
10370
   R134 .S77 MRR Alc.

PHYSICIANS--BIOGRAPHY--CATALOGS.
New York Academy of Medicine.
Library. Catalog of biographies.
Boston, G. K. Hall, 1960. 165 p.
016.9261 60-50505
   R134 .N4 MRR Biog.

PHYSICIANS--BIOGRAPHY--DICTIONARIES.
Fischer, Isidor, ed. Biographisches
Lexikon der hervorragenden Ärzte der
letzten fünfzig Jahre, Berlin,
Wien, Urban & Schwarzenberg, 1932-33.
2 v. 016.61 32-20791
   Z6658 .B62 MRR Biog.

PHYSICIANS--AMERICA.
American men of medicine. 1st-
ed.; 1945- Farmingdale, N.Y. [etc.]
Institute for Research in Biography.
45-4406
   R150 .W5 Sci RR Latest edition /
   MRR Biog Latest edition

PHYSICIANS--CANADA.
Kelly, Howard Atwood, Dictionary of
American medical biography; Boston,
Milford House [1971] xxx, 1364 p.
610/.922 B 74-78618
   R153 .K3 1971 MRR Biog.

PHYSICIANS--CANADA--DIRECTORIES.
American pediatric directory. 1st-
ed.; 1935- Knoxville, Tenn., Joe T.
Smith [etc.] 614.24097 35-9541
   R712.A1 A65 Sci RR Latest edition
   / MRR Biog Latest edition

Canadian medical directory. 1st-
ed.; 1955- Toronto, Seccombe House
[etc.] 55-3605
   R713.01 .C3 MRR Alc Latest edition

PHYSICIANS--FRANCE--DIRECTORIES.
Guide medical et pharmaceutique
Rosenwald. Paris, L'Expansion
scientifique française [etc.]
610.58 46-33196
   Publication began with the guide
   for 1887.
   R713.43 .A6G8 MRR Alc Latest
   edition

PHYSICIANS--GREAT BRITAIN--DIRECTORIES.
Great Britain General Council of
Medical Education and Registration.
The medical register: London Mackie
and co., ltd. ca 08-3152
   R713.29 .G7 MRR Alc Latest edition

The Medical directory. London, J. &
A. Churchill ltd. 35-7636
   R713.29 .M4 MRR Biog Latest
   edition

PHYSICIANS--UNITED STATES.
American College of Hospital
Administrators. Directory. 1938-
Chicago. 362.06273 39-2135
   RA977 .A57 Sci RR Latest edition /
   MRR Biog Latest edition

Kelly, Howard Atwood, Dictionary of
American medical biography; Boston,
Milford House [1971] xxx, 1364 p.
610/.922 B 74-78618
   R153 .K3 1971 MRR Biog.

Thacher, James, American medical
biography; New York, Milford House,
1967. 2 v. in 1. 610/.922 67-
30787
   R153 .T3 1967 MRR Biog.

Williams, Stephen West, American
medical biography; New York, Milford
House, 1967. xv, 664 p. 610/.922
67-30786
   R153 .W5 1967 MRR Biog.

PHYSICIANS--UNITED STATES--BIO-
BIBLIOGRAPHY.
Stone, Richard French, Biography of
eminent American physicians and
surgeons, Indianapolis, Carlon &
Hollenbeck, 1894. xxii, 729 p. 38-
1873
R153 .S8 MRR Biog.

PHYSICIANS--UNITED STATES--BIOGRAPHY.
American directory of obstetricians
and gynecologists. 1st- ed.;
1954/55- Knoxville, Tenn., Joe T.
Smith. 614.24 55-27820
RG32 .A5 Sci RR Latest edition /
MRR Biog Latest edition

American men of medicine. 1st-
ed.; 1945- Farmingdale, N.Y. [etc.]
Institute for Research in Biography.
45-4406
R150 .W5 Sci RR Latest edition /
MRR Biog Latest edition

PHYSICIANS--UNITED STATES--DIRECTORIES.
American medical directory. 1st-
ed.; 1906- Chicago, American Medical
Association [etc.] 07-10295
R712.A1 A6 Sci RR Latest edition /
MRR Biog Latest edition

American pediatric directory. 1st-
ed.; 1935- Knoxville, Tenn., Joe T.
Smith [etc.] 614.24097 35-9541
R712.A1 A65 Sci RR Latest edition
/ MRR Biog Latest edition

Directory of medical specialists
holding certification by American
specialty boards. v. 1- 1939-
Chicago [etc.] Marquis-Who's Who
[etc.] 610/.822 40-9671
R712.A1 D5 Sci RR Latest edition /
MRR Biog Latest edition

Oral surgery directory of the world.
1st- 1957- Pittsburgh. 617.53
617.6* 57-10598
RD523 .O7 MRR Biog Latest edition
/ Sci RR Latest edition

The red book of eye, ear, nose and
throat specialists. 1st- ed.; 1915-
Chicago, Professional Press, Inc.
[etc.] 15-6770
RE22 .R3 MRR Alc Latest edition

U. S. medical directory. Miami,
Fla., U.S. Directory Service.
610/.25/73 77-23057
R712.A1 U5 MRR Alc Latest edition
/ Sci RR Latest edition

PHYSICS.
see also Electricity

Condon, Edward Uhler, Handbook of
physics, 2d ed. New York, McGraw-
Hill [1967] 1 v. (various pagings)
530 66-20002
QC21 .C7 1967 MRR Alc.

PHYSICS--ABSTRACTS.
United States. Library of Congress.
European Affairs Division. Physics
and chemical sciences in Western
Germany; Washington, 1954. 123 p.
507.2 54-60012
Z663.26 .N3 1954 MRR Alc.

PHYSICS--BIBLIOGRAPHY.
Marckworth, M. Lois. Dissertations
in physics; Stanford, Calif.,
Stanford University Press, 1961.
xii, 803 p. 016.53 61-6530
Z7141 .M3 MRR Alc.

Whitford, Robert H. Physics
literature; 2d ed. Metuchen, N.J.,
Scarecrow Press, 1968. 272 p.
016.53 68-12636
Z7141 .W47 1968 MRR Alc.

Yates, Bryan, How to find out about
physics; [1st ed.] Oxford, New
York, Pergamon Press [1965] x, 175
p. 016.53 65-25338
Z7141 .Y3 1965 MRR Alc.

PHYSICS--DICTIONARIES.
[Anglo-russkiĭ fizicheskiĭ slovar'
(romanized form)] 1968. 848 p.
[3.13] 70-382641
QC5 .A55 MRR Alc.

Ballentyne, Denis William George. A
dictionary of named effects and laws
in chemistry, physics and mathematics
3rd ed. London, Chapman & Hall,
1970. iii-viii, 355 p. [£3.00]
500.2/03 71-552485
Q123 .B3 1970 MRR Alc.

Dictionary of physics and allied
sciences. London, P. Owen [1958-62]
2 v. 530.3 58-35180
QC5 .D52 MRR Alc.

Gray, Harold James, Dictionary of
physics, London, New York, Longmans,
Green [1958] x, 544 p. 530.3 58-
3300
QC5 .G7 MRR Alc.

The International dictionary of
physics and electronics. 2d ed.
Princeton, N.J., Van Nostrand [1961]
1355 p. 530.3 61-2485
QC5 .I5 1961 MRR Alc.

PHYSICS--DICTIONARIES--GERMAN.
Dictionary of physics and allied
sciences. London, P. Owen [1958-62]
2 v. 530.3 58-35180
QC5 .D52 MRR Alc.

PHYSICS--DICTIONARIES--POLYGLOT.
Elsevier's dictionary of general
physics in six languages: Amsterdam,
New York, Elsevier Pub. Co., 1962.
859 p. 530.3 62-13015
QC5 .E46 MRR Alc.

Sube, Ralf. Wörterbuch Physik;
Zürich, H. Deutsch, 1973. 3 v. 74-
320539
QC5 .S9 MRR Alc.

PHYSICS--EARLY WORKS TO 1800.
Aristoteles. Aristotle, the Physics,
London, W. Heinemann, ltd; New York,
G. P. Putnam's sons, 1929-34. 2 v.
888.5 30-5834
PA3612 .A8P3 1929 MRR Alc.

PHYSICS--HANDBOOKS, MANUALS, ETC.
American Institute of Physics.
American Institute of Physics
handbook. 3d ed. New York, McGraw-
Hill [1972] 1 v. (various pagings)
[$49.50] 016.5301/5 72-3248
QC61 .A5 1972 MRR Alc.

PHYSICS--STUDY AND TEACHING.
Whitford, Robert H. Physics
literature; 2d ed. Metuchen, N.J.,
Scarecrow Press, 1968. 272 p.
016.53 68-12636
Z7141 .W47 1968 MRR Alc.

PHYSICS--TABLES, ETC.
Handbook of chemistry and physics;
[1st]- ed.; 1913- Cleveland,
Chemical Rubber Co. [etc.] 541.9 13-
11056
QD65 .H3 Sci RR Latest edition /
MRR Alc Latest edition

Zimmerman, Oswald Theodore,
Industrial Research Service's
conversion factors and tables, 3d
ed. Dover, N.H., Industrial Research
Service, 1961. 680 p. 530.83 61-
2586
QC61 .Z5 1961 MRR Ref Desk.

PHYSICS, NUCLEAR
see Nuclear physics

PHYSIOGRAPHY
see Geology

PHYSIOLOGICAL CHEMISTRY.
see also Biological chemistry

see also Chemistry, Organic

PHYSIOLOGISTS.
Stevenson, Lloyd G. Nobel prize
winners in medicine and physiology,
1901-1950. New York, H. Schuman
[1953] 291 p. 926.1 378.32 53-
10370
R134 .S77 MRR Alc.

PHYSIOLOGY.
see also Heart

see also Human physiology

see also Nervous system

see also Nutrition

see also Reproduction

De Coursey, Russell Myles, The human
organism. 4th ed. New York, McGraw-
Hill [1974] xi, 644 p. 612 73-
23016
QP34.5 .D38 1974 MRR Alc.

Greisheimer, Esther Maud, Physiology
& anatomy 9th ed. Philadelphia,
Lippincott [1972] xv, 678 p.
[$13.50] 612 73-101355
QP34 .G63 1972 MRR Alc.

Smith, Anthony, The body. New York,
Walker [1968] xiii, 524 p. 612 68-
13972
QP38 .S67 1968b MRR Alc.

PHYTOGRAPHY
see Botany

PHYTOLOGY
see Botany

PIANISTS.
Bie, Oskar, A history of the
pianoforte and pianoforte players.
New York, Da Capo Press, 1966. xi,
336 p. 786.2109 66-28445
ML700 .B586 1899a MRR Alc.

PIANO.
Pierce piano atlas. [1st]- ed.;
1947- Long Beach, Calif., B. Pierce.
65-25465
ML652 .P53 MRR Alc Latest edition

PIANO--HISTORY.
Bie, Oskar, A history of the
pianoforte and pianoforte players.
New York, Da Capo Press, 1966. xi,
336 p. 786.2109 66-28445
ML700 .B586 1899a MRR Alc.

PIANO MAKERS.
Pierce piano atlas. [1st]- ed.;
1947- Long Beach, Calif., B. Pierce.
65-25465
ML652 .P53 MRR Alc Latest edition

PICKERING--BIBLIOGRAPHY.
United States. Library of Congress.
Division of bibliography. ... Select
list of references on boycotts and
injunctions in labor disputes;
Washington, Govt. print. off., 1911.
iii, 3-69 p. 10-35010
Z663.28 .S357 MRR Alc.

PICKLING
see Canning and preserving

PICKUP CAMPERS
see Campers and coaches, Truck

PICTURE-BOOKS FOR CHILDREN.
see also Nursery rhymes

PICTURE DICTIONARIES, ENGLISH.
De Vries, Harold, ed. Picture
library (encyclopedia pictoria) New
York, Research Book Co., c1955.
unpaged (chiefly illus.) 793.73 55-
37210
PE1629 .D4 MRR Alc.

Engelska Duden. Örebro, I.P.C.
[1966] 672, 128, 85 (2) p. [29.75
skr] 67-84395
PE1629 .E519 MRR Alc.

Mann's pictorial dictionary and
cyclopedia. Brooklyn, National
Library Publications, c1960. 2 v.
66-50384
AG250 .M26 MRR Alc.

Picture book supplement. [Cleveland]
Specialty Publications, c1951. 36 p.
of illus. 793.73 52-17464
PE1629 .C62 MRR Alc.

The Picture dictionary; Brooklyn,
National Library Publications, c1952.
2 v. (3008 p.) 423 56-43702
AG250 .P48 MRR Alc.

PICTURE DICTIONARIES, POLYGLOT.
The Duden pictorial encyclopedia in
five languages: English, French,
German, Italian, Spanish. 2d, enl.
ed. New York, F. Ungar Pub. Co.
[1958] 2 v. 413 58-11093
P361 .D8 1958 MRR Alc.

PICTURE FRAMES AND FRAMING.
Kass, Benjamin. The complete guide
to free prints. New York, Citadel
Press [1958] 112 p. 769.5 58-
10598
NE1860.A2 K3 MRR Alc.

PICTURE-GALLERIES
see Art--Galleries and museums

PICTURES--CATALOGS.
Special Libraries Association.
Picture Division. Picture sources.
2d ed. New York, Special Libraries
Association [1964] viii, 216 p. 64-
15089
N4000 .S7 1964 MRR Ref Desk.

PICTURES--INDEXES.
Belknap, Sara (Yancey) Guide to the
musical arts; New York, Scarecrow
Press, 1957. 1 v. (unpaged) 016.78
57-6631
ML113 .B37 MRR Alc.

Clapp, Jane. Sculpture index.
Metuchen, N.J., Scarecrow Press, 1970
[c1970-71] 2 v. in 3. 730/.16 79-
9538
NB36 .C55 MRR Alc.

Ellis, Jessie Croft, comp. General
index to illustrations; Boston, The
F. W. Faxon company, 1931. 4 p. l.,
467 p. 016.74 31-28562
NC996 .E6 MRR Ref Desk.

Ellis, Jessie (Croft) Index to
illustrations. Boston, F. W. Faxon
Co., 1966 [c1967] xi, 682 p.
741.6/01/6 66-11619
NC996 .E62 MRR Ref Desk.

Ellis, Jessie (Croft) Nature and its
applications; Boston, F. W. Faxon
Co., 1949. xii, 861 p. 016.745 49-
9331
Z5956.D3 E53 MRR Alc.

Greer, Roger C., Illustration index,
3d ed. Metuchen, N.J., Scarecrow
Press, 1973. 164 p. 011 72-10918

N7525 .G72 1973 MRR Ref Desk.

Havlice, Patricia Pate. Art in Time.
Metuchen, N.J., Scarecrow Press,
1970. 350 p. 016.7 76-14885
N7225 .H38 MRR Alc.

PICTURES--INDEXES. (Cont.)
Hewlett-Woodmere Public Library.
Index to art reproductions in books.
Metuchen, N.J., Scarecrow Press,
1974. xii, 178 p.   709 74-1286
N7525 .H48 1974 MRR Alc.

Monro, Isabel Stevenson, ed. Costume
index; New York, H. W. Wilson Co.,
1937. x, 338 p.   016.391 37-7142
Z5691 .M75 MRR Alc.

Shepard, Frederick Job, comp. Index
to illustrations. Preliminary ed.
Chicago, American library
association, 1924. 89 p.   24-26753

NC996 .S5 MRR Ref Desk.

Vance, Lucile E. Illustration index,
2d ed. New York, Scarecrow Press,
1966. 527 p.   011 65-13558
N7525 .V3 1966 MRR Ref Desk.

PIERCE, FRANKLIN, PRES. U.S., 1804-1869.
Nichols, Roy Franklin. Franklin
Pierce, [2d ed., completely rev.]
Philadelphia, University of
Pennsylvania Press [1958] xvii, 625
p.   923.173 58-7750
E432 .N63 1958 MRR Alc.

PIERCE, FRANKLIN, PRES. U.S., 1804-1869-
-BIBLIOGRAPHY.
United States. Library of Congress.
Manuscript Divison. Calendar of the
papers of Franklin Pierce,
Washington, Govt. print. off., 1917.
102 p.   17-26003
Z663.34 .P5 MRR Alc.

PIGMENTS--DICTIONARIES.
Martin, John Henry. Guide to
pigments and to varnish and lacquer
constituents, London, L. Hill, 1954.
127 p.   667.603 54-42002
TP934.3 .M3 MRR Alc.

PILGRIM FATHERS.
Willison, George Findlay. Saints and
strangers: [Revised ed.] London,
Heinemann, 1966. xii, 307 p. [36/-]
974.402 66-77420
F68 .W75 1966 MRR Alc.

PILGRIMS AND PILGRIMAGES--FRANCE.
Guide religieux de la France,
[Paris,] Hachette, 1967. xvi, 1240
p. [48.63 F.] 274.4 67-113748
BR843 .G8 MRR Alc.

PILOT GUIDES.
see also Air-pilot guides

PILOT GUIDES--ATLANTIC STATES.
Waterway guide. Middle Atlantic
edition. no. 1- 1963- Chesapeake,
Va. [etc.] Waterway Guide Inc. [etc.]
64-2891
GV835 .W35 MRR Alc Latest edition

PILOT GUIDES--UNITED STATES.
Waterway guide. Northern edition.
[Fort Lauderdale, Fla., Inland
Waterway Guide, inc.] 623.89/29/73
73-641441
VK984 .I55 MRR Alc Latest edition

The Yachtsman's guide. New York
[etc.] Motor boating [etc.]
797.1/25/05 01-8330
Began publication in 1877.
GV825 .Y12 MRR Alc Latest edition

PILOTS AND PILOTAGE.
see also Navigation

PIONEERS.
see also Frontier and pioneer life

PIONEERS--CALIFORNIA.
Bancroft, Hubert Howe. Register of
pioneer inhabitants of California,
1542 to 1848. Los Angeles, Dawson's
Book Shop, 1964. 683-795, 733-792,
688-786, 687-784 p.   920.0794 64-
3538
F861 .B21 1964 MRR Biog.

PIPE LINES--DIRECTORIES.
Directory of pipe line companies and
pipe line contractors. Tulsa, Okla.,
Midwest oil register [etc.] 58-35170

TN867 .D525   MRR Alc Latest edition

PIPE LINES--DIRECTORIES--YEARBOOKS.
Annual directory of pipelines.
[Bayonne, N.J., Oildom Pub. Co.] 72-
626549
TJ930 .P53 Sci RR Latest edition /
MRR Alc Latest edition

PIPE LINES--EQUIPMENT AND SUPPLIES--
CATALOGS.
Pipe line catalog. 1st- revision;
1957/58- Houston, Tex., Pipe line
industry. 621.8672 58-26871
TJ933 .P5 MRR Alc Latest edition

PIPE LINES--EQUIPMENT AND SUPPLIES--
DIRECTORIES.
Directory of gas utility companies
and pipe line contractors. Tulsa,
Okla., Midwest oil register [etc.]
61-46648
TP714 .D55 MRR Alc Latest edition

PISCES
see Fishes

PISTOLS.
Blair, Claude. Pistols of the world.
London, Batsford, 1968. x, 206 p.
[8/8/-]   623.4/43 71-357174
TS537 .B53 MRR Alc.

Smith, Walter Harold Black. Book of
pistols and revolvers. [7th ed.]
Harrisburg, Pa., Stackpole Books
[1968] xvi, 816 p.   623.4/43 68-
18959
TS537 .S54 1968 MRR Alc.

PISTOLS, AMERICAN.
Gluckman, Arcadi. United States
martial pistols and revolvers.
Harrisburg, Pa., Stackpole Co., 1956.
249, xxxvii, [1] p.   623.443 56-
3215
UD413 .G5 1956 MRR Alc.

PITTSBURGH--COMMERCE--DIRECTORIES.
Official directors register of
Pittsburgh. 1st- annual ed.; 1935-
Pittsburgh, Pa., Directory Pub. Co.
[etc.]   332.0974886 36-387
HG4058 .P64 MRR Alc Latest edition

PITTSBURGH--DIRECTORIES.
Official directors register of
Pittsburgh. 1st- annual ed.; 1935-
Pittsburgh, Pa., Directory Pub. Co.
[etc.]   332.0974886 36-387
HG4058 .P64 MRR Alc Latest edition

PITTSBURGH. CARNEGIE INSTITUTE.
MacLeish, Archibald. Libraries in
the contemporary crisis;
[Washington] U.S. Govt. print. off.,
1939. 11, [1] p.   020.4 39-29265
Z663 .L43 1939 MRR Alc.

PIZARRO FAMILY.
United States. Library of Congress.
Manuscript division. The Harkness
collection in the Library of
Congress. Washington, U.S. Govt.
print. off., 1936. xi, 253 p.   985
36-26004
Z663.34 .H29 MRR Alc.

PLACES OF RETIREMENT
see Retirement, Places of

PLAINS.
see also Deserts

PLANETS.
see also Life on other planets

Kuiper, Gerard Peter, ed. Planets
and satellites. Chicago, University
of Chicago Press [1961] xx, 601 p.
523.4 61-56677
QB501 .S6 vol. 3 MRR Alc.

PLANETS--EPHEMERIDES.
Simmons, A. LeRoi. Ephemerides, 1890-
1950. Dallas, Galaxis Pub. Co.
[c1970] viii, 407 p.   133.5/5 71-
172375
QB603 .S55 MRR Alc.

Stahlman, William D. Solar and
planetary longitudes for years--2500
to +2000 by 10-day intervals.
Madison, University of Wisconsin
Press, 1963. 566 p.   528.1 63-
10534
QB7 .S73 MRR Alc.

PLANKTON.
Hardy, Alister Clavering, Sir. The
open sea: London, Fontana, 1870-71.
2 v. [15/- (v. 1)] 574.92 75-
857351
QH91 .H293 MRR Alc.

PLANNED PARENTHOOD
see Birth control

PLANNING--BIBLIOGRAPHY.
European directory of economic and
corporate planning, 1973-74; Epping,
Gower Press, 1973. xvii, 442 p.
[£8.50] 309.2/12/0254 74-162022
HD31 .E83 1973 MRR Alc.

PLANNING--DIRECTORIES.
European directory of economic and
corporate planning, 1973-74; Epping,
Gower Press, 1973. xvii, 442 p.
[£8.50] 309.2/12/0254 74-162022
HD31 .E83 1973 MRR Alc.

PLANNING--STUDY AND TEACHING--
DIRECTORIES.
European directory of economic and
corporate planning, 1973-74; Epping,
Gower Press, 1973. xvii, 442 p.
[£8.50] 309.2/12/0254 74-162022
HD31 .E83 1973 MRR Alc.

PLANNING, ECONOMIC
see Economic policy

PLANNING, REGIONAL
see Regional planning

PLANS
see Maps

PLANT DISEASES--RESEARCH--UNITED STATES.
United States. Dept. of Agriculture.
Plant diseases. Washington [U.S.
Govt. Print. Off., 1953] xviii, 940
p.   632 agr55-3
S21 .A35 1953 MRR Alc.

PLANT DISEASES--UNITED STATES.
United States. Dept. of Agriculture.
Plant diseases. Washington [U.S.
Govt. Print. Off., 1953] xviii, 940
p.   632 agr55-3
S21 .A35 1953 MRR Alc.

PLANT ENGINEERING--DIRECTORIES.
Sweet's industrial construction &
renovation file with plant
engineering extension market list.
1974- [New York, Sweet's Division,
McGraw-Hill Information Systems Co.]
338.4/7/69002573 74-645493
TH12 .S93 MRR Alc Latest edition /
Sci RR Latest edition

PLANT LORE.
Coats, Alice M. Flowers and their
histories, [New ed.] London, Black,
1968. xiii, 346 p. [42/-]
635.9/09 68-119595
SB404.5 .C6 1968 MRR Alc.

Lehner, Ernst. Folklore and
symbolism of flowers, plants and
trees. New York, Tudor Pub. Co.
[1960] 128 p.   581.508 60-15038
QK83 .L4 MRR Alc.

Limburg, Peter R. What's in the
names of flowers. New York, Coward,
McCann & Geoghegan [1974] 189 p.
[$4.64 (lib. bdg.)] 582/.13 73-
88535
QK13 .L5 1974

Peattie, Donald Culross. A natural
history of trees of eastern and
central North America; Boston,
Houghton Mifflin, 1950. xv, 606 p.
582.16 50-10354
QK481 .P4 MRR Alc.

PLANT LORE--JUVENILE LITERATURE.
Limburg, Peter R. What's in the
names of flowers. New York, Coward,
McCann & Geoghegan [1974] 189 p.
[$4.64 (lib. bdg.)] 582/.13 73-
88535
QK13 .L5 1974

PLANT NAMES, POPULAR.
Healey, B. J. A gardener's guide to
plant names New York, Scribner
[1972] 284 p. [$7.95] 581/.01/4
72-1202
QK11 .H4 MRR Alc.

Plowden, C. Chicheley. A manual of
plant names. London, Allen & Unwin,
1968. 260 p. [55/-] 581/.01/4 77-
384870
QK96 .P57 MRR Alc.

PLANT NAMES, POPULAR--JUVENILE
LITERATURE.
Limburg, Peter R. What's in the
names of flowers. New York, Coward,
McCann & Geoghegan [1974] 189 p.
[$4.64 (lib. bdg.)] 582/.13 73-
88535
QK13 .L5 1974

PLANT PROPAGATION.
see also Seeds

PLANTATION LIFE--SOUTHERN STATES.
Phillips, Ulrich Bonnell. American
Negro slavery; New York, London, D.
Appleton and company, 1918. xi, 529
p.   18-11187
E441 .P549 MRR Alc.

PLANTING
see Agriculture

see Gardening

PLANTS.
see also Botany

see also Flowers

see also House plants

Manning, Stanley A. Systematic guide
to flowering plants of the world,
[1st American ed.] New York,
Taplinger Pub. Co. [1965, c1964] 302
p.   582.13 65-17028
QK97 .M3 1965 MRR Alc.

PLANTS, CULTIVATED.
see also Annuals (Plants)

PLANTS, EDIBLE--CANADA.
Fernald, Merritt Lyndon. Edible wild
plants of Eastern North America. New
York, Harper [1958] xii, 452 p.
581.632 58-7977
QK98.5 .F4 1968 MRR Alc.

PLANTS, EDIBLE--UNITED STATES.
Fernald, Merritt Lyndon. Edible wild
plants of Eastern North America. New
York, Harper [1958] xii, 452 p.
581.632 58-7977
QK98.5 .F4 1968 MRR Alc.

PLANTS, MEDICINAL
see Botany, Medical

PLANTS, ORNAMENTAL.
see also Ground cover plants

Edwards, Alexander, Rock gardens;
New York, Abelard-Schuman [1958] 255
p.   635.9672 58-3848
SB421 .E3 1958 MRR Alc.

Preston, F. G., ed. The greenhouse;
New York, Abelard-Schuman [1958] 640
p.   635.982 58-3807
SB415 .P7 MRR Alc.

PLANTS, ORNAMENTAL--DICTIONARIES.
Hay, Roy. The dictionary of garden
plants in colour, with house and
greenhouse plants London, Ebury P.;
Joseph, 1969. xvi, 373 p. [60/-]
635.83 75-413044
SB407 .H292 MRR Alc.

PLANTS, ORNAMENTAL--PICTORIAL WORKS.
Graf, Alfred Byrd. Exotica, series
3; 6th ed. E. Rutherford, N.J.,
Roehrs Co. [1973] 1834 p.   635.9/65
72-90669
SB407 .G7 1973 MRR Alc.

Hay, Roy. The dictionary of garden
plants in colour, with house and
greenhouse plants London, Ebury P.;
Joseph, 1968. xvi, 373 p. [60/-]
635.83 75-413044
SB407 .H292 MRR Alc.

The New illustrated encyclopedia of
gardening (unabridged). [New and
rev. ed.] New York, Greystone Press
[1972-73] 26 v. (4206 p.)   635/.03
72-182032
SB45 .N424 MRR Alc.

Skinner, Henry Thomas, ed. Garden
plants in color. 1st ed. Portland,
Or., Sweeney, Krist, and Dimm, 1958-
v.   635.9084 58-59510
SB407 .S55 MRR Alc.

PLANTS, ORNAMENTAL--UNITED STATES.
Skinner, Henry Thomas, ed. Garden
plants in color. 1st ed. Portland,
Or., Sweeney, Krist, and Dimm, 1958-
v.   635.9084 58-59510
SB407 .S55 MRR Alc.

PLANTS, PROTECTION OF--LAW AND
LEGISLATION.
see also National parks and reserves

PLANTS, PROTECTION OF--UNITED STATES.
United States. Dept. of Agriculture.
Protecting our food. [Washington]
U.S. Govt. Print. Off. [1966] xiii,
386 p.   641.3 agr66-345
S21 .A35 1966 MRR Alc.

PLANTS, PROTECTION OF--UNITED STATES--
STATES.
Burns, Ethel Magwood. National plant
conservation guide. [1st ed.]
Philadelphia, National Council Books,
1961. unpaged.   580 61-8123
QK86 .B8 MRR Alc.

PLANTS, USEFUL
see Botany, Economic

PLANTS IN THE BIBLE
see Bible--Natural history

PLASTIC FOAMS--DIRECTORIES.
International foamed plastic markets
& directory. 1963- Stamford, Conn.,
Technomic Pub. Co.   63-59134
TP1183.F6 I55 MRR Alc Latest
edition

PLASTICS.
Simonds, Herbert Rumsey, A concise
guide to plastics 2d ed. New York,
Reinhold Pub. Corp. [1963] 392 p.
668.4 63-13447
TP986.A2 S47 1963 MRR Alc.

PLASTICS--DICTIONARIES.
Whittington, Lloyd R. Whittington's
dictionary of plastics. [1st ed.]
Stamford, Conn., Technomic Pub. Co.
[1968] 261 p.   668/.4/03 67-31745

TP1110 .W46 MRR Alc.

PLASTICS--DICTIONARIES--POLYGLOT.
Wittfoht, Annemarie,
Kunststofftechnisches Wörterbuch.
München, C. Hanser, 1956- v.   a
56-5235
TP986 .A15W48 MRR Alc.

PLASTICS INDUSTRY AND TRADE--
DIRECTORIES.
International plastics directory.
[1st]- ed.; 1958- Zürich, Verlag
für Internationale
Wirtschaftsliteratur.   61-28711
TP1112 .I57 Sci RR Latest edition
/ MRR Alc Latest edition

PLASTICS INDUSTRY AND TRADE--CANADA--
DIRECTORIES.
Society of the Plastics Industry.
Directory. 1943/44- New York.
338.4/7/668402573 43-18308
TP986.A1 S6 MRR Alc Latest edition

PLASTICS INDUSTRY AND TRADE--UNITED
STATES--DIRECTORIES.
Society of the Plastics Industry.
Directory. 1943/44- New York.
338.4/7/668402573 43-18308
TP986.A1 S6 MRR Alc Latest edition

PLATE.
Wyler, Seymour B. The book of old
silver, English, American, foreign,
New York, Crown publishers [c1937] x
p., 1 l., 447 p. incl. illus.,
plates.   739 37-24775
NK7230 .W9 MRR Alc.

PLATE--GREAT BRITAIN.
Bradbury, Frederick, British and
Irish silver assay office marks, 1544-
1968. 12th ed. Sheffield, Northend,
1968. 93 p. [24/-] 739.2/3/0278
78-391328
NK7210 .B74 1968 MRR Alc.

PLATE--GREAT BRITAIN--HISTORY.
Jackson, Charles James, Sir, English
goldsmiths and their marks; 2d ed.,
rev. and enl. New York, Dover
Publications [1964, c1921] xvi, 747
p.   739.22742 64-18852
NK7143 .J15 1964 MRR Alc.

PLATE, FRENCH.
New York. Metropolitan Museum of Art.
Three centuries of French domestic
silver; New York, 1960. 2 v.
739.23744 60-9288
NK7149 .N42 MRR Alc.

PLATE NUMBERS (POSTAGE-STAMPS)
Durland standard plate number
catalog; Boston [etc.] Sterling
Stamp Co. [etc.] 55-22466
HE6230 .D8 MRR Alc Latest editions

PLATING.
see also Electroplating

PLATO--DICTIONARIES, INDEXES, ETC.
Stockhammer, Morris, ed. Plato
dictionary. New York, Philosophical
Library [1963] xv, 287 p.   888 63-
11488
B351 .S7 MRR Alc.

PLAY.
see also Games

see also Recreation

PLAY BILLS--LONDON.
Who's who in the theatre; [1st]-
ed.; 1912- London, I. Pitman.
927.92 12-22402
PN2012 .W5 MRR Biog Latest edition

PLAYING-CARDS
see Cards

PLAYS
see Drama

PLAYS FOR CHILDREN
see Children's plays

PLAYWRITING.
Busfield, Roger M. The playwright's
art; New York, Harper [1958] 260 p.
808.2 58-6918
PN1661 .B8 MRR Alc.

Niggli, Josephina. New pointers on
playwriting. Boston, The Writer,
inc. [1967] 166 p.   808.2 67-24454

PN1661 .N5 MRR Alc.

PLEBISCITE.
see also Elections

PLOTS (DRAMA, NOVEL, ETC.)
see also Characters and
characteristics in literature

PLUMBING--CATALOGS.
D E catalog directory. 1923-
[Chicago, Medalist Publications,
etc.]   22-21100
TH6112 .D6 Sci RR Latest edition /
MRR Alc Latest edition

PLUMBING--EQUIPMENT AND SUPPLIES--
CATALOGS.
M P C; Manhasset, N.Y., Hutton Pub.
Co. 696/.00028 68-7522
Began with 1964 vol.
TH6010 .M2 MRR Alc Latest edition

PLUMBING--LAWS AND REGULATIONS--UNITED
STATES.
National plumbing code illustrated.
1952- St. Petersburg, Fla. [etc.]
Manas Publications. 696.973 58-
20251
TH6164 .N3 MRR Alc Latest edition

PLYMOUTH, MASS.--HISTORY.
Bradford, William, Bradford's
history of Plymouth plantation, 1606-
1646; New York, C. Scribner's sons,
1908. xv p., 2 l., 3-437 p.   08-
7375
F187.O7 B7 MRR Alc.

PLYMOUTH AUTOMOBILE.
Fix your Plymouth. Homewood, Ill.
[etc.] Goodheart-Wilcox Co. 629.287
62-12428
TL215.P65 F5 MRR Alc Latest
edition

POE, EDGAR ALLAN, 1809-1849.
United States. Library of Congress.
Gertrude Clarke Whittall Poetry and
Literature Fund. Anniversary
lectures, 1959. Washington,
Reference Dept., Library of Congress,
1959. iii, 56 p.   821.082 59-60090

Z663.293 .A55 MRR Alc.

POE, EDGAR ALLAN, 1809-1949--
CONCORDANCES.
Booth, Bradford Allen, A concordance
of the poetical works of Edgar Allan
Poe, Baltimore, The Johns Hopkins
press, 1941. xiv, 211 p.   811.32
41-11711
PS2645 .B6 MRR Alc.

POETICS.
Deutsch, Babette, Poetry handbook;
4th ed. New York, Funk & Wagnalls
[1974] xix, 203 p.   808.1/01/4 73-
13970
PN44.5 .D4 1974b MRR Alc.

Johnson Burges, New rhyming
dictionary and poets' handbook. Rev.
ed. New York, Harper [1957] x, 464
p.   426.603 808.1* 57-9585
PE1519 .J6 1957 MRR Alc.

Shapiro, Karl Jay, A prosody
handbook New York, Harper & Row
[1965] x, 214 p.   416 64-24535
PN1042 .S57 MRR Alc.

POETICS--DICTIONARIES.
Encyclopedia of poetry and poetics.
Princeton, N.J., Princeton University
Press, 1965. xxiv, 906 p.   809.103
63-7076
PN1021 .E5 MRR Alc.

POETRY.
see also Children's poetry

see also English poetry

Untermeyer, Louis, The pursuit of
poetry; New York, Simon and Schuster
[1969] 318 p. [6.95] 808.1 78-
79640
PN1031 .U54 MRR Alc.

Whittemore, Reed, Ways of
misunderstanding poetry. Washington,
Reference Dept., Library of Congress;
[for sale by the Superintendent of
Documents, U.S. Govt. Print. Off.]
1965. 13 p.   65-60044
Z663.293 .W35 MRR Alc.

POETRY--ADDRESSES, ESSAYS, LECTURES.
Spender, Stephen, The imagination in
the modern world; Washington,
Reference Dept., Library of Congress;
[for sale by the Superintendent of
Documents, U.S. Govt. Print. Off.]
1962. iii, 40 p.   62-64964
Z663.293 .I5 MRR Alc.

United States. Library of Congress.
Gertrude Clarke Whittall Poetry and
Literature Fund. American poetry at
mid-century, Washington, Reference
Dept., Library of Congress, 1958. 49
p.   811.504 58-60074
Z663.293 .A5 MRR Alc.

POETRY--BIBLIOGRAPHY--PERIODICALS.
Index of American periodical verse.
1971- Metuchen, N.J., Scarecrow
Press. 016.811/5/4 73-3060
Z1231.P7 147 MRR Alc Full set

POETRY--COLLECTIONS.
Bryant, Al, comp. Sourcebook of
poetry, Grand Rapids, Zondervan Pub.
House [c1968] 767 p. [9.95]
808.81/5 68-27462
PN6101 .B78 MRR Alc.

POETRY--DICTIONARIES.
Coles Publishing Company. Dictionary
of poetical terms. Toronto, c1967.
99 p. [$1.25 Can.] 808.1/03 68-
80900
PN1021 .C6 MRR Alc.

Deutsch, Babette, Poetry handbook;
4th ed. New York, Funk & Wagnalls
[1974] xix, 203 p. 808.1/01/4 73-
13970
PN44.5 .D4 1974b MRR Alc.

Encyclopedia of poetry and poetics.
Princeton, N.J., Princeton University
Press, 1965. xxiv, 906 p.   809.103
63-7076
PN1021 .E5 MRR Alc.

National Poetry Association.
Dictionary of poetry terms Los
Angeles [1959] 142 p.   808.1 59-
3155
PN1021 .N3 MRR Alc.

POETRY—DICTIONARIES. (Cont.)
Untermeyer, Louis, The pursuit of
poetry; New York, Simon and Schuster
[1969] 318 p. [6.95] 808.1 78-
79640
PN1031 .U54 MRR Alc.

POETRY—DISCOGRAPHY.
The International who's who in
poetry. v. 1– 1958– London. 928
59-16302
PS324 .I5 MRR Biog Latest edition

POETRY—DISCOGRAPHY—INDEXES.
Chicorel, Marietta. Chicorel index
to poetry in collections in print, on
discs and tapes: 1st ed. New York,
Chicorel Library Pub. Corp., 1972.
443 p. 016.80882 73-160763
PR1175.8 .C4 MRR Alc.

POETRY—EARLY WORKS TO 1800.
Aristoteles. Aristotle: The poetics.
London, W. Heinemann, New York, G.
P. Putnam's sons, 1932. xx, 500 p.
808.1 mrr01-41
PA3612 .A8P5 1932d MRR Alc.

POETRY—HISTORY AND CRITICISM.
Encyclopedia of poetry and poetics.
Princeton, N.J., Princeton University
Press, 1965. xxiv, 906 p. 809.103
63-7097
PN1021 .E5 MRR Alc.

POETRY—HISTORY AND CRITICISM—
DICTIONARIES.
The Explicator. The Explicator
cyclopedia. Chicago, Quadrangle
Books, 1966– v. 820.9 66-11875
PR401 .E9 MRR Alc.

POETRY—INDEXES.
Abbott, Edwin, A concordance to the
works of Alexander Pope, London,
Chapman & Hall, 1875. xviii, 365,
[1] p. 01-22779
PR3632 .A73 MRR Alc.

American Library Association.
Subject index to poetry for children
and young people, Chicago, 1957.
582 p. 016.80881 57-8798
PN1023 .A5 MRR Alc.

Baker, Arthur Ernest, A concordance
to the poetical and dramatic works of
Alfred, Lord Tennyson, New York,
Barnes & Noble [1966] xvi, 1212 p.
821.8 66-2700
PR5580 .B3 1966 MRR Alc.

Baldwin, Dane Lewis. A concordance
to the poems of John Keats.
Gloucester, Mass., P. Smith, 1963.
xxi, 437 p. 821.7 63-6084
PR4836.A3 1963 MRR Alc.

Bartlett, John, A complete
concordance or verbal index to words,
phrases, and passages in the dramatic
works of Shakespeare, New York, St.
Martin's Press, 1953. 1910 p.
822.33 53-2095
PR2892 .B34 1953 MRR Alc.

Bartlett, John, A new and complete
concordance or verbal index to words,
phrases, & passages in the dramatic
works of Shakespeare. London,
Macmillan and co., limited 1937. 4
p. l., 1910 p. 822.33 38-5787
PR2892 .B34 1937 MRR Ref Desk.

Booth, Bradford Allen, comp. A
concordance of the poetical works of
William Collins; Berkeley, Calif.,
University of California press, 1939.
vi p., 1 l., 126 p. 821.57 40-344
PR3353.A3 B6 MRR Alc.

Booth, Bradford Allen, A concordance
of the poetical works of Edgar Allan
Poe. Baltimore, The Johns Hopkins
press, 1941. xiv, 211 p. 811.32
41-11711
PS2645 .B6 MRR Alc.

Bradshaw, John, A concordance to the
poetical works of John Milton. [1st
ed. new impression] London, Allen &
Unwin, 1965. [4], 412 p. [42/-]
67-79888
PR3595 .B7 1965a MRR Alc.

Brewton, John Edmund, Index to
children's poetry; New York, Wilson,
1942. xxxii, 965 p. 821.0016 42-
20148
PN1023 .B7 MRR Alc.

Brewton, John Edmund, Index to
poetry for children and young people,
1964-1969; New York, Wilson, 1972.
xxx, 575 p. 821/.001/6 71-161574
PN1023 .B72 MRR Alc.

Brown, Carleton Fairchild, The index
of Middle English verse. New York,
Printed for the Index Society by
Columbia University Press, 1943.
xix, 785 p. 016.821/1 43-16653
Z2012 .B86 MRR Alc.

Bruncken, Herbert, Subject index to
poetry; Chicago, American library
association, 1940. xix, [1], 201,
[1] p. 808.81 40-27835
PN1021 .B7 MRR Ref Desk.

Chicorel, Marietta. Chicorel index
to poetry in collections in print, on
discs and tapes: 1st ed. New York,
Chicorel Library Pub. Corp., 1972.
443 p. 016.80882 73-160763
PR1175.8 .C4 MRR Alc.

Combs, Homer Carroll. A concordance
to the English poems of John Donne,
New York, Haskell House, 1969. ix,
418 p. 821/.3 74-92960
PR2248 .A3 1969 MRR Alc.

Cook, Albert Stanburrough, A
concordance to the English poems of
Thomas Gray. Gloucester, Mass., P.
Smith, 1967 [c1908] x, 160 p.
821/.6 67-8967
PR3504 .C6 1967 MRR Alc.

Cooper, Lane, ed. A concordance of
the works of Horace, Washington, The
Carnegie institution of Washington,
1916. ix, [1], 593 p. 16-20920
PA6444 .C6 MRR Alc.

Cooper, Lane, ed. A concordance to
the poems of William Wordsworth,
London, Smith, Elder & co., 1911.
xiii, 1136 p. 11-28703
PR5880 .C6 MRR Alc.

Cuthbert, Eleonora Isabel. Index of
Australian and New Zealand poetry.
New York, Scarecrow Press, 1963. 453
p. 016.821 63-7469
Z4024.P7 C8 MRR Alc.

Deferrari, Roy Joseph, A concordance
of Lucan, Washington, The Catholic
university of America press, 1940.
vii, 602 p. 873.2 40-31224
PA6480 .D4 MRR Alc.

Dilligan, Robert J. A concordance to
the English poetry of Gerard Manley
Hopkins, Madison, University of
Wisconsin Press, 1970. xx, 321 p.
[10.00] 821/.8 70-101504
PR4803.H44 Z49 1970 MRR Alc.

Dunbar, Henry, comp. A complete
concordance to the Odyssey and Hymns
of Homer. Oxford, Clarendon press,
1880. iv, 419 p. 01-3069
PA4209 .D7 MRR Alc.

Durfee, Charles Augustus, A concise
poetical concordance to the principal
poets of the world, New York, J. B.
Alden, 1885. 639 p. 17-13881
PN1021 .D8 1885 MRR Alc.

Eby, Edwin Harold. A concordance of
Walt Whitman's Leaves of grass and
selected prose writings. New York,
Greenwood Press [1969] xiii, 964 p.
811/.3 76-90500
PS3245 .E2 1969 MRR Alc.

Ellis, Frederick Startridge, A
lexical concordance to the poetical
works of Percy Bysshe Shelley,
London, B. Quaritch, 1892. xi, 818
p. 13-24598
PR5430 .E5 MRR Alc.

Ellison, John William, Nelson's
complete concordance of the Revised
standard version of the Bible. New
York, Nelson [c1957] 2157 p. 220.2
57-7122
BS425 .E4 1957 MRR Ref Desk.

Erdman, David V. A concordance to
the writings of William Blake,
Ithaca, N.Y., Cornell University
Press [1967] 2 v. (xxxvi, 2317 p.)
828/.7/09 66-18608
PR4146 .A25 MRR Alc.

First-line index of English poetry,
1500-1800, in manuscripts of the
Bodleian Library, Oxford; Oxford,
Clarendon P., 1969. 2 v. (xi, 1257
p.) [11/5/-] 821/.0016 72-397656
Z2014.P7 F5 MRR Alc.

Furness, Helen Kate (Rogers) A
concordance to Shakespeare's poems:
<3d ed.> Philadelphia [etc.] J. B.
Lippincott company [1902] iv, 422 p.
02-10022
PR2892 .F8 1902 MRR Alc.

Garcia, Reloy. A concordance to the
poetry of D. H. Lawrence, Lincoln,
University of Nebraska Press [c1970]
xvi, 523 p. 821/.9/12 70-120277
PR6023.A93 Z49 1970 MRR Alc.

Granger, Edith. Granger's index to
poetry. 6th ed., completely rev. and
enl., indexing anthologies published
through December 31, 1970. New York,
Columbia University Press, 1973.
xxxvii, 2223 p. [$80.00]
808.81/0016 73-4186
PN1022 .G7 1973 MRR Ref Desk.

Granger, Edith. Granger's index to
poetry. 5th ed., completely rev. and
enl., New York, Columbia University
Press, 1962. xxxix, 2123 p. 808.81
62-3885
PN1021 .G7 1962 MRR Ref Desk.

Granger, Edith. Granger's Index to
poetry and recitations; 3d ed.,
completely rev. and enl., Chicago,
A. C. McClurg & co. [c1940] 2 p. l.,
vii-xxiv p., 1 l., 1525 p. 808.8
40-5254
PN4321 .G8 1940 MRR Ref Desk.

Granger, Edith. Index to poetry.
4th ed., completely rev. & enl., New
York, Columbia University Press,
1953. xxxvii, 1832 p. 808.81 53-
987
PN4321 .G8 1953 MRR Ref Desk.

Granger, Edith. An index to poetry
and recitations, Rev. and enl. ed.
Chicago, A. C. McClurg & co., 1927.
3 p. l., [v]-xv, 1059 p. 28-3385
PN4321 .G8 1927 MRR Ref Desk.

Granger, Edith. An index to poetry
and recitations, Rev. and enl. ed.
Chicago, A. C. McClurg & company,
1918. xiv p., 1 l., 1059 p.
[$10.00] 18-23538
PN4321 .G8 1918 MRR Ref Desk.

Granger, Edith. An index to poetry
and recitations; Chicago, A. C.
McClurg & company, 1904. 970 p. 04-
24547
PN4321 .G8 MRR Ref Desk.

Guffey, George Robert. A concordance
to the English poems of Andrew
Marvell. Chapel Hill, University of
North Carolina Press [1974] xiv, 623
p. 821/.4 73-21550
PR3546 .G77 MRR Alc.

Hubbell, George Shelton. A
concordance to the poems of Ralph
Waldo Emerson. New York, Russell &
Russell [1967] x, 478 p. 811/.3
67-18293
PS1645 .H8 1967 MRR Alc.

Hyder, Clyde Kenneth, ed. A
concordance to the poems of A. E.
Housman. Gloucester, Mass., P.
Smith 1966 [c1940] vii, 133 p.
821.912 66-9388
PR4809.H15 H9 1966 MRR Alc.

Index of American periodical verse.
1971– Metuchen, N.J., Scarecrow
Press. 016.811/5/4 73-3060
Z1231.P7 I47 MRR Alc Full set

Johnson, Robert Owen. An index to
literature in the New Yorker, volumes
1-XV, 1925-1940. Metuchen, N.J.,
Scarecrow Press, 1969-71. 3 v. 051
71-7740
AP2 .N6764 MRR Alc.

Kottler, Barnet. A concordance to
five Middle English poems:
[Pittsburgh] University of Pittsburgh
Press [1966] xxxiii, 761 p.
821.1016 66-13311
PR265 .K6 MRR Alc.

Landry, Hilton. A concordance to the
poems of Hart Crane. Metuchen, N.J.,
Scarecrow Press, 1973. viii, 379 p.
811/.5/2 72-10663
PS3505.R272 Z49 1973 MRR Alc.

Lane, Gary, A concordance to the
poems of Marianne Moore. New York,
Haskell House, 1972. 526 p.
811/.5/2 72-6438
PS3525.O5616 Z49 1972 MRR Alc.

Lane, Gary, A concordance to the
poems of Theodore Roethke. Metuchen,
N.J., Scarecrow Press, 1972. v, 484
p. 811/.5/4 77-188503
PS3535.O39 Z49 1972 MRR Alc.

Lathem, Edward Connery. A
concordance to The poetry of Robert
Frost. New York, Holt Information
Systems [1971] x, 640 p. [$30.00]
811/.5/2 75-177494
PS3511.R94 Z49 1971 MRR Alc.

Lockwood, Laura Emma, Lexicon to the
English poetical works of John
Milton. New York, B. Franklin [1968]
xii, 671 p. 821/.4 68-56596
PR3580 .L7 1968 MRR Alc.

Logan, Eugenia, sister. A
concordance to the poetry of Samuel
Taylor Coleridge, Saint Mary-of-the-
Woods, Ind. [Priv. print.] 1940.
xvi, 901 p. 821.72 40-5258
PR4482 .L6 MRR Alc.

MacLeod, Malcolm Lorimer, A
concordance to the poems of Robert
Herrick, New York, Oxford university
press, 1936. xviii p., 1 l., 299 p.
821.43 36-24656
PR3513.A3 M2 1936 MRR Alc.

POETRY--INDEXES. (Cont.)
Macpherson, Maud Russell. Children's
poetry index, Boston, The F. W.
Faxon company, 1938. xiii, 453 p.
808.81 38-9870
PN1023 .M25 MRR Alc.

Merguet, Hugg, Lexikon zu Vergilius
mit angebe samtlicher stellen,
Leipzig-R., Kommissionsverlag von R.
Schmidt, 1912. 2 p. l., 786 p. 15-
13878
PA6952 .M4 MRR Alc.

Molineux, Marie Ada. A phrase book
from the poetic and dramatic works of
Robert Browning, Ann Arbor, Mich.,
Gryphon Books, 1971. xiii, 520 p.
821/.8 71-145523
PR4230 .M6 1896ab MRR Alc.

Montgomery, Guy, comp. Concordance
to the poetical works of John Dryden,
New York, Russell & Russell [1967,
c1957] 722 p. 821/.4 66-27126
PR3422 .M6 1967 MRR Alc.

Morris, Helen (Soutar) Where's that
poem? Oxford, Blackwell, 1967.
xxxv, 300 p. [25/-] 016.821 67-
78385
PN1023 .M6 MRR Alc.

Naugle, Helen Harrold. A concordance
to the poems of Samuel Johnson.
Ithaca, [N.Y.] Cornell University
Press [1973] xxx, 578 p. [$13.50]
821/.6 72-13383
PR3532 .N3 1973 MRR Alc.

Neve, John. A concordance to the
poetical works of William Cowper.
New York, B. Franklin [1969] viii,
504 p. 821/.6 68-58237
PR3383.A2 N4 1969 MRR Alc.

Paden, William Doremus, ed. A
concordance to the poems of Oliver
Goldsmith, Gloucester, Mass., P.
Smith 1966 [c1940] xii, 180 p.
821.6 66-9077
PR3492 .P3 1966 MRR Alc.

Parrish, Stephen Maxfield. A
concordance to the poems of Matthew
Arnold. Ithaca, N.Y., Cornell
University Press [1959] xxi, 965 p.
821.8 59-4899
PR4023.A3 P3 MRR Alc.

Parrish, Stephen Maxfield. A
concordance to the poems of W. B.
Yeats. Ithaca, N.Y., Cornell
University Press [1963] xxxvii, 967
p. 821.912 63-11493
PR5907 .P35 MRR Alc.

Prendergast, Guy Lushington. A
complete concordance to the Iliad of
Homer. London, Longmans, Green, and
co., 1875. 3 p. l., 416 p. 03-
15393
PA4209 .P7 MRR Alc.

Reid, J. B. A complete word and
phrase concordance to the poems and
songs of Robert Burns, New York, B.
Franklin [1968] 568 p. 821/.6 68-
58477
PR4345 .R4 1968 MRR Alc.

Rosenbaum, Stanford Patrick. A
concordance to the poems of Emily
Dickinson, Ithaca, N.Y., Cornell
University Press [1964] xxii, 899 p.
811.4 64-25335
PS1541.Z49 R6 MRR Alc.

Spevack, Marvin. A complete and
systematic concordance to the works
of Shakespeare. Hildesheim, Georg
Olms, 1968- v. 822.3/3 68-
108766
PR2892 .S6 MRR Alc.

Spevack, Marvin. The Harvard
concordance to Shakespeare.
Cambridge, Mass., Belknap Press of
Harvard University Press, 1973. ix,
1600 p. [$45.00] 822.3/3 73-76385

PR2892 .S62 MRR Alc.

Tatlock, John Strong Perry, A
concordance to the complete works of
Geoffrey Chaucer Washington,
Carnegie institution of Washington,
1927. xiii, 1110 p., 1 l. 27-6088

PR1941 .T3 MRR Alc.

Walsh, Thomas F. Concordance to the
poetry of Wallace Stevens.
University Park, Pa., Pennsylvania
State University Press, 1963. xx,
341 p. 811.52 63-18744
PS3537.T4753 Z9 MRR Alc.

Wetmore, Monroe Nichols, Index
verborum Vergilianus, New Haven,
Yale university press; [etc., etc.]
1911. x, 554 p., 1 l. [$4.00] 11-
2238
PA6952 .W4 MRR Alc.

Whitman, Charles Huntington, A
subject-index to the poems of Edmund
Spenser. New York, Russell &
Russell, 1966. xi, 261 p. 821.3
66-13245
PR2362 .W5 1966 MRR Alc.

Wilkins, Ernest Hatch, A concordance
to the Divine comedy of Dante
Alighieri. Cambridge, Belknap Press
of Harvard University Press, 1965.
ix, 636 p. 851.1 65-11195
PQ4464 .W5 MRR Alc.

Williams, Robert Coleman. A
concordance to the Collected poems of
Dylan Thomas, Lincoln, University of
Nebraska Press [1967] xiii, 579 p.
821/.9/12 66-19268
PR6039.H52 Z49 MRR Alc.

Young, Ione (Dodson) A concordance
to the poetry of Byron. Austin,
Tex., Pemberton Press, 1965. 4 v.
(xv, 1698 p.) 821.7 66-674
PR4395 .Y6 MRR Alc.

POETRY--MARKETING.
Hollyfield, Jeanne. Poet's handbook;
[1st ed. Appalachia, Va., Young
Publications, 1969] 140 p. [3.00]
655.5/2 75-4171
PN161 .H6 MRR Alc.

POETRY--PERIODICALS--BIBLIOGRAPHY.
Hollyfield, Jeanne. Poet's handbook;
[1st ed. Appalachia, Va., Young
Publications, 1969] 140 p. [3.00]
655.5/2 75-4171
PN161 .H6 MRR Alc.

The International who's who in
poetry. v. 1- 1958- London. 928
59-16302
PS324 .I5 MRR Biog Latest edition

POETRY--SOCIETIES, ETC.
The International who's who in
poetry. v. 1- 1958- London. 928
59-16302
PS324 .I5 MRR Biog Latest edition

POETRY--TRANSLATING.
Tate, Allen, The translation of
poetry. Washington, Published for
the Library of Congress by the
Gertrude Clarke Whittall Poetry and
Literature Fund; [for sale by the
Supt. of Docs., U.S. Govt. Print.
Off.] 1972. v, 40 p. [$0.30]
418/.02 72-38779
Z663.293 .T7 MRR Alc.

POETRY, MODERN--HISTORY AND CRITICISM.
Spender, Stephen, The imagination in
the modern world; Washington,
Reference Dept., Library of Congress;
[for sale by the Superintendent of
Documents, U.S. Govt. Print. Off.]
1962. iii, 40 p. 62-64964
Z663.293 .I5 MRR Alc.

POETRY FOR CHILDREN
see Children's poetry

see Nursery rhymes

POETS.
The International who's who in
poetry. v. 1- 1958- London. 928
59-16302
PS324 .I5 MRR Biog Latest edition

Opie, Iona (Archibald), comp. The
Oxford book of children's verse;
Oxford, Clarendon Press, 1973.
xxxii, 407 p. [£2.25] 821/.008 73-
172900
PN6110.C4 O529 1973b MRR Alc.

POETS, AMERICAN.
The biographical dictionary of
contemporary poets; New York, Avon
house, 1938. 4 p. l., 536 p. 928.1
38-23392
PS324 .B5 MRR Biog.

Brinnin, John Malcolm, comp.
Twentieth century poetry: American
and British (1900-1970); New York,
McGraw-Hill [1970] xx, 515 p.
[$8.95] 821/.9/108 73-124305
PS613 .B7 1970b MRR Alc.

Contemporary poets of the English
language. Chicago, St. James Press
[1970] xvii, 1243 p. [$25.00]
821/.9/109 79-23734
Z2014.P7 C63 MRR Biog.

Malkoff, Karl. Crowell's handbook of
contemporary American poetry. New
York, Crowell [1973] ix, 338 p.
[$10.00] 811/.5/409 73-14787
PS323.5 .M3 MRR Biog.

Spender, Stephen, ed. The concise
encyclopedia of English and American
poets and poetry, [1st ed.] New
York, Hawthorn Books [1963] 415 p.
821.003 63-8015
PR19 .S6 MRR Alc.

Untermeyer, Louis, Lives of the
poets; New York, Simon and Schuster,
1959. 757 p. 821.09 59-11205
PR502 .U5 MRR Biog.

Untermeyer, Louis, ed. Modern
American poetry. New and enl. ed.
New York, Harcourt, Brace & World
[c1969] xxvi, 710 p. 811/.008 69-
13702
PS611 .U6 1969 MRR Alc.

POETS, AMERICAN--DIRECTORIES.
Poets and Writers, inc. A directory
of American poets, New York, 1973.
xi, 119 p. [$4.00] 811/.5/409 B
72-96830
PS323.5 .P6 1973 MRR Biog.

POETS, CANADIAN.
Garvin, John William, ed. Canadian
poets, Toronto, McClelland &
Stewart, limited [c1926] xi, 536 p.,
1 l. 27-26597
PR9258 .G3 1926 MRR Alc.

Pierce, Lorne Albert, An outline of
Canadian literature (French and
English) Toronto, The Ryerson press,
1927. 6 p. l., 251 p. 28-2647
PR9112 .P5 MRR Alc.

Smith, Arthur James Marshall, ed.
The book of Canadian poetry, 3d ed.,
rev. and enl. Toronto, W. J. Gage
[c1957] xxv, 532 p. 811.082 59-
20696
PR9250 .S58 1957 MRR Alc.

POETS, ENGLISH.
Brinnin, John Malcolm, comp.
Twentieth century poetry: American
and British (1900-1970); New York,
McGraw-Hill [1970] xx, 515 p.
[$8.95] 821/.9/108 73-124305
PS613 .B7 1970b MRR Alc.

Contemporary poets of the English
language. Chicago, St. James Press
[1970] xvii, 1243 p. [$25.00]
821/.9/109 79-23734
Z2014.P7 C63 MRR Biog.

Spender, Stephen, ed. The concise
encyclopedia of English and American
poets and poetry, [1st ed.] New
York, Hawthorn Books [1963] 415 p.
821.003 63-8015
PR19 .S6 MRR Alc.

Untermeyer, Louis, Lives of the
poets; New York, Simon and Schuster,
1959. 757 p. 821.09 59-11205
PR502 .U5 MRR Biog.

Untermeyer, Louis, ed. Modern
British poetry. New and enl. ed.
New York, Harcourt, Brace & World
[c1969] xxiii, 548 p. 821/.9/109
69-13703
PR1224 .U6 1969 MRR Alc.

Who's who in English speaking poets.
Los Angeles, National Poetry
Association [1958] 140 p. 016.821
58-38323
Z2014.P7 W5 MRR Biog.

POETS, FRENCH.
Brereton, Geoffrey. An introduction
to the French poets: Villon to the
present day. 2nd ed. London,
Methuen, 1973. xii, 320 p. [£3.80]
841/.009 73-162190
PQ401 .B7 1973 MRR Alc.

Rousselot, Jean, Dictionnaire de la
poésie française contemporaine.
Paris, Larousse, 1968. 256 p.
[9.90F] 841/.9/103 68-106149
PQ41 .R6 MRR Biog.

POETS, IRISH.
Taylor, Geoffrey, ed. Irish poets of
the nineteenth century. London,
Routledge and Paul [1951] viii, 406
p. 821.7082 51-2435
PR8857 .T3 1951 MRR Alc.

POETS, IRISH--BIO-BIBLIOGRAPHY.
O'Donoghue, David James, The poets
of Ireland; Dublin, Hodges, Figgis &
co., ltd.; [etc., etc.] 1912. 3 p.
l., iv, 504 p. 12-24411
PR8706 .O3 MRR Alc.

POETS, LATIN AMERICAN.
United States. Library of Congress.
Hispanic Foundation. Voces de poetas
y prosistas ibericos y
latinoamericanos en el archivo de
literatura hispanica en cinta
magnetica de la Fundación
Hispanica. Washington, 1960. viii,
33 p. 60-60075
Z663.32 .V6 MRR Alc.

United States. Library of Congress.
Latin American, Portuguese, and
Spanish Division. The Archive of
Hispanic Literature on Tape;
Washington, Library of Congress; [for
sale by the Supt. of Docs., U.S.
Govt. Print. Off.] 1974. xii, 516 p.
016.86/008 73-19812
Z663.32 .A7 MRR Alc.

POETS, RUSSIAN.
Poggioli, Renato. The poets of
Russia, 1890-1930. Cambridge, Mass.,
Harvard University Press, 1960. xix,
383 p.   891.71309 60-8000
    PG3056 .P6 MRR Alc

POETS, SPANISH.
United States. Library of Congress.
Hispanic Foundation. Voces de poetas
y prosistas ibericos y
latinoamericanos en el archivo de
literatura hispanica en cinta
magnetica de la Fundación
Hispanica. Washington, 1960. viii,
33 p. 60-60075
    Z663.32 .V6 MRR Alc.

United States. Library of Congress.
Latin American, Portuguese, and
Spanish Division. The Archive of
Hispanic Literature on Tape;
Washington, Library of Congress; [for
sale by the Supt. of Docs., U.S.
Govt. Print. Off.] 1974. xii, 516 p.
016.86/008 73-19812
    Z663.32 .A7 MRR Alc.

POISON CONTROL CENTERS--UNITED STATES--
DIRECTORIES.
Arena, Jay M. Poisoning: toxicology--
symptoms--treatments, 3d ed.
Springfield, Ill., Thomas [1974]
xxv, 804 p.   615.9 73-4213
    RA1216 .A69 1974 MRR Alc.

Levine, Milton Isra. The parents'
encyclopedia of infancy, childhood,
and adolescence New York, Crowell
[1973] 619 p. [$10.00] 649/.1/03
72-83769
    RJ61 .L552 MRR Alc.

U. S. medical directory. Miami,
Fla., U.S. Directory Service.
610/.25/73 77-23057
    R712.A1 U5 MRR Alc Latest edition
    / Sci RR Latest edition

POISONING.
Arena, Jay M. Poisoning: toxicology--
symptoms--treatments, 3d ed.
Springfield, Ill., Thomas [1974]
xxv, 804 p.   615.9 73-4213
    RA1216 .A69 1974 MRR Alc.

POISONS.
Arena, Jay M. Poisoning: toxicology--
symptoms--treatments, 3d ed.
Springfield, Ill., Thomas [1974]
xxv, 804 p.   615.9 73-4213
    RA1216 .A69 1974 MRR Alc.

Dreisbach, Robert Hastings. Handbook
of poisoning: diagnosis & treatment.
4th ed. Los Altos, Calif., Lange
Medical Publications, 1963. 467 p.
615.9 63-18896
    RA1211 .D7 1963 MRR Alc.

POISONS, ECONOMIC
see Pesticides

POLAND.
Keefe, Eugene K. Area handbook for
Poland. 1st ed. [Washington, For
sale by the Supt. of Docs., U.S.
Govt. Print. Off.] 1973. xiv, 335 p.
[$3.85] 914.38/03/5 72-600380
    DK443 .K38 MRR Alc.

Świdzińska, Natalia. Poland: facts
and figures. Warsaw, Interpress
Publishers, 1971. 63 p.
914.38/03/5 73-151713
    DK404 .S8813 MRR Alc.

POLAND--BIBLIOGRAPHY.
Estreicher, Karol Józef Teofil,
Bibliografia polska ,.. Kraków, W
Druk. Uniw. Jagiellońskiego, 1870-
v.   05-5187
    Z2521 .E82 MRR Alc.

Estreicher, Karol Józef Teofil,
Bibliografia polska,XIX stulecia.
Wyd. 2. Kraków [Państwowe Wydawn.
Naukowe, Oddział w Krakowie] 1959-
v.   60-40706
    Z2521 .E85 MRR Alc.

Hahn, Wiktor, Bibliografia
bibliografij polskich. Wyd. 2.,
znacznie rozsz. Wrocław, Zakład im.
Ossolinskich, 1956. xxii, 645 p.
56-33462
    Z2521.A1 H3 1956 MRR Alc.

Horecky, Paul Louis. East Central
Europe; a guide to basic
publications. Chicago, University of
Chicago Press [1969] xxv, 856 p.
016.9143 70-79472
    Z2483 .H56 MRR Alc.

Polish University College, London.
Library. Bibliography of books in
Polish or relating to Poland,
London, 1953- v.   016.91438 54-
1761
    Z2528.A5 P6 MRR Alc.

POLAND--BIBLIOGRAPHY--CATALOGS.
United States. Library of Congress.
Poland in the collections of the
Library of Congress; Washington,
[For sale by the Supt. of Docs., U.S.
Govt. Print. Off. 1968 (i.e.1969]
iii, 26 p. [0.40] 016.91438/63 69-
60009
    Z663 .P6 MRR Alc.

POLAND--BIOGRAPHY.
Wielka encyklopedia powszechna PWN.
Wyd. 1.] Warszawa, Państwowe
Wydawn. Naukowe [1962]-[70] 13 v.
039/.918/5 63-37817
    AE53 .W44 MRR Alc.

POLAND--BIOGRAPHY--DICTIONARIES.
Polska Akademia Umiejętności,
Kraków. Polski słownik biograficzny.
Kraków, Skład główny w księg.
Gebethnera i Wolffa, 1935- v.
50-39826
    CT1230 .P65 MRR Bilg.

POLAND--DESCRIPTION AND TRAVEL--GUIDE-
BOOKS.
Bajcar, Adam. Poland; Warsaw,
Interpress Publishers, 1972. 226 p.
[zł42.00] 914.38/04/5 72-170457
    DK403 .B3413 1972 MRR Alc.

Poland. New York, McGraw-Hill [1964]
383 p.   914.38 65-286
    DK403 .P6 MRR Alc.

Poland; travel guide. Warszawa,
Sport i Turystyka, 1970. x, 439 p.
[zł110.00] 78-27966
    DK403 .P57 MRR Alc.

POLAND--DICTIONARIES AND ENCYCLOPEDIAS.
Polska Ludowa; Wyd. 1. Warszawa]
Wiedza Powszechna, 1965. xi, 482 p.
65-80770
    DK403 .P63 MRR Alc.

POLAND--EXECUTIVE DEPARTMENTS--
DIRECTORIES.
Directory of Polish officials.
[n.p.] 1970. viii, 346 p.
354.438/002 74-11435
    JN6757 1970 .D56 MRR Alc.

POLAND--FOREIGN RELATIONS--TREATIES.
Horak, Stephan M., Poland's
international affairs, 1919-1960;
Bloomington, Indiana University,
1964. xviii, 248 p.   341.2438 64-
63009
    JX760.P7 H6 MRR Alc.

POLAND--HISTORY.
History of Poland, Warszawa, PWN,
Polish Scientific Publishers, 1968.
783 p.   943.8 68-6941
    DK414 .H618 MRR Alc.

POLAND--HISTORY--20TH CENTURY.
Roos, Hans. A history of modern
Poland, from the foundation of the
State in the First World War to the
present day. [1st American ed.] New
York, Knopf, 1966. xii, 303 p.
943.804 65-11131
    DK440 .R6173 1966a MRR Alc.

POLAND--HISTORY--BIBLIOGRAPHY.
Polska Akademia Nauk. Instytut
Historii. Bibliografia historii
Polski. Wyd. 1.] Warszawa,
Państwowe Wydawn. Naukowe, 1965- v.
65-57158
    Z2526 .P64 MRR Alc.

POLAND--IMPRINTS.
Estreicher, Karol Józef Teofil,
Bibliografia polska ,.. Kraków, W
Druk. Uniw. Jagiellońskiego, 1870-
v.   05-5187
    Z2521 .E82 MRR Alc.

Estreicher, Karol Józef Teofil,
Bibliografia polska,XIX stulecia.
Wyd. 2. Kraków [Państwowe Wydawn.
Naukowe, Oddział w Krakowie] 1959-
v.   60-40706
    Z2521 .E85 MRR Alc.

POLAND--LEARNED INSTITUTIONS AND
SOCIETIES.
Polish research guide. 1964-
Warszawa, Państwowe Wydawn. Naukowe.
64-2698
    AS258 .P6 MRR Alc Latest edition

Wepsiec, Jan. Polish institutions of
higher learning. New York, Polish
Institute of Arts and Sciences in
America, 1959. 110 p.   063.8 59-
37794
    AS258 .W4 MRR Alc.

POLAND--OFFICIALS AND EMPLOYEES--
DIRECTORIES.
Directory of Polish officials.
[n.p.] 1970. viii, 346 p.
354.438/002 74-11435
    JN6757 1970 .D56 MRR Alc.

POLAND--POLITICS AND GOVERNMENT--
YEARBOOKS.
Rocznik polityczny i gospodarczy.
1932- [Warszawa] Państwowe Wydawn.
Ekonomiczne [etc.] 44-30771
    JN6751 .A17 MRR Alc Latest edition

POLAND--REGISTERS.
Directory of Polish officials.
[n.p.] 1970. viii, 346 p.
354.438/002 74-11435
    JN6757 1970 .D56 MRR Alc.

Rocznik polityczny i gospodarczy.
1932- [Warszawa] Państwowe Wydawn.
Ekonomiczne [etc.] 44-30771
    JN6751 .A17 MRR Alc Latest edition

POLAND--STATISTICS.
Concise statistical year book of the
Polish People's Republic. 1930-Sept.
1939/June 1941; 1947- Warsaw.
314.38 49-25078
    HA1451 .S8 MRR Alc Latest edition

POLAR EXPEDITIONS
see Antarctic regions

    see Arctic regions

    see Scientific expeditions

POLAR REGIONS.
see also Arctic regions

POLES--BIOGRAPHY.
McLean, William Moore. Notable
personages of Polish ancestry
Detroit, The Unique press, inc.,
1938. 2 p. l., vii-xvi p., 1 l., 186
p.   920.0438 38-13303
    CT1230 .M25 MRR Biog.

POLICE--BIBLIOGRAPHY.
Wright, Martin. Use of criminology
literature. London, Butterworths
[1974] 242 p. [£5.50] 016.364 74-
174958
    Z5118.C9 W74 1974b MRR Alc.

POLICE--BIBLIOGRAPHY--CATALOGS.
Evanston, Ill. Transportation Center
at Northwestern University. Library.
Catalog. Boston, G. K. Hall, 1972.
12 v. 016.3805 74-171017
    Z7164.T8 E83 1972 MRR Alc (Dk 33)

Los Angeles. Public Library.
Municipal Reference Library. Catalog
of the police library of the Los
Angeles Public Library; Boston, G.
K. Hall, 1972. 2 v. 016.3632 73-
158794
    Z7164.P76 L58 MRR Alc (Dk 33)

POLICE--DICTIONARIES.
Salottolo, A. Lawrence. Modern
police service encyclopedia; Rev.
ed. New York, Arco Pub. Co. [1970]
276 p.   363.2/03 70-125939
    HV8133 .S2 1970 MRR Alc.

POLICE--DIRECTORIES.
Directory of identification bureaus
of the world. Chicago. 573.6 47-
26908
    HV8073 .D5 MRR Alc Latest edition

International security directory.
London, Security Gazette, ltd.
363.2/025 75-20715
    HV7900 .I63 MRR Alc Bind/Label

POLICE--EQUIPMENT AND SUPPLIES.
International Association of Chiefs
of Police. Police Weapons Center.
The Police Weapons Center data
service. Gaithersburg, Md.,
International Association of Chiefs
of Police, Research Services Section
[1972] 1 v. (loose leaf) [$30.00
per year.] 363.2/028 72-86295
    HV7936.E7 I58 MRR Alc.

POLICE--EQUIPMENT AND SUPPLIES--
DIRECTORIES.
International Association of Chiefs
of Police. Police Weapons Center.
The Police Weapons Center data
service. Gaithersburg, Md.,
International Association of Chiefs
of Police, Research Services Section
[1972] 1 v. (loose leaf) [$30.00
per year.] 363.2/028 72-86295
    HV7936.E7 I58 MRR Alc.

POLICE--STUDY AND TEACHING--UNITED
STATES--DIRECTORIES.
Law enforcement education directory.
Washington, International Association
of Chiefs of Police, Professional
Standards Division. 363.2/071/173
78-649322
    HV8143 .L36 MRR Alc Latest edition

POLICE--UNITED STATES--BIBLIOGRAPHY.
Hewitt, William H. A bibliography of
police administration, public safety,
and criminology to July 1, 1965,
Springfield, Ill., Thomas [1967]
xiv, 242 p. 016.350/74 66-24629
    Z7164.P76 H4 MRR Alc.

POLICE, PRIVATE--DIRECTORIES.
International security directory.
London, Security Gazette, ltd.
363.2/025 75-20715
    HV7900 .I63 MRR Alc Bind/Label

POLICE ADMINISTRATION.
Wilson, Orlando Winfield, Police
administration. 2d ed. New York,
McGraw-Hill [1963] 528 p. 351.74
63-9827
HV7935 .W48 1963 MRR Alc.

POLICE ADMINISTRATION--BIBLIOGRAPHY.
Hewitt, William H. A bibliography of
police administration, public safety,
and criminology to July 1, 1965,
Springfield, Ill., Thomas [1967]
xiv, 242 p. 016.350/74 66-24629
Z7164.P76 H4 MRR Alc.

POLICY SCIENCES.
see also Decision-making

POLISH LANGUAGE--DICTIONARIES--ENGLISH.
The Kosciuszko Foundation
dictionary: New York, 1960-62. 2 v.
491.8532 60-1190
PG6640 .K652 MRR Alc.

Stanisławski, Jan. Wielki słownik
polsko-angielski. [Wyd. 1]
Warszawa Wiedza Powszechna, 1969.
xvi, 1583 p. [240.00] 481.8/5/32
76-420311
PG6640 .S84 MRR Alc.

POLISH LANGUAGE--DICTIONARIES--POLYGLOT.
Dictionary of chemistry and chemical
technology, in six languages: [Rev.
ed.] Oxford, New York, Pergamon
Press [1966] 1325 p. 540.3 65-
29008
QD5 .D5 1966 MRR Alc.

Fabierkiewicz, Wacław. Podręczny
słownik włókienniczy w 5 językach:
[Wyd. 1] [Warszawa] Państwowe
Wydawn. Techniczne [1955] xlvii, 305
p. 55-38912
TS1309 .F3 MRR Alc.

Orne, Jerrold, The language of the
foreign book trade: 2d ed. Chicago,
American Library Association, 1962.
213 p. 010.3 61-12881
Z1006 .O7 1962 MRR Alc.

Stowarzyszenie Geodetów Polskich.
Słownik geodezyjny w 5 [i.e. pięciu]
językach: polskim, rosyjskim,
niemieckim, angielskim, francuskim.
Warszawa, Państwowe
Przedsiębiorstwo Wydawn.
Kartograficznych, 1954. xv, 525 p.
55-34784
QB279 .S8 MRR Alc.

Zboiński, A., ed. Dictionary of
architecture and building trades in
four languages: English, German,
Polish, Russian. Oxford, New York,
Pergamon Press; [distributed in the
Western Hemisphere by Macmillan, New
York, 1963] 491 p. 63-22975
NA31 .Z34 MRR Alc.

Żytka, Romuald. Geological
dictionary Warszawa, Wydawnictwa
Geologiczne, 1970. 1439 p.
[zł1250.00] 550/.3 72-31794
QE5 .Z9 MRR Alc.

POLISH LITERATURE--BIBLIOGRAPHY.
Estreicher, Karol Józef Teofil,
Bibliografia polska,XIX stulecia.
Wyd. 2. Kraków [Państwowe Wydawn.
Naukowe, Oddział w Krakowie] 1959-
v. 60-40706
Z2521 .E85 MRR Alc.

POLISH LITERATURE--BIO-BIBLIOGRAPHY.
Estreicher, Karol Józef Teofil,
Bibliografia polska,... Kraków, W
Druk. Uniw. Jagiellońskiego, 1870-
v. 05-5187
Z2521 .E82 MRR Alc.

Korzeniewska, Ewa, ed. Słownik
współczesnych pisarzy polskich.
Warszawa, Państwowe Wydawn. Naukowe,
1963-1966. 4 v. 64-31836
Z2528.L5 K6 MRR Alc.

POLISH LITERATURE--HISTORY AND
CRITICISM.
Kridl, Manfred, A survey of Polish
literature and culture. New York,
Columbia University Press, 1956.
viii, 525 p. 891.8509 55-11748
PG7012 .K713 MRR Alc.

POLISH LITERATURE IN FOREIGN COUNTRIES--
BIBLIOGRAPHY.
Polish University College, London.
Library. Bibliography of books in
Polish or relating to Poland,
London, 1953- v. 016.91438 54-
1761
Z2528.A5 P6 MRR Alc.

POLITICAL CONVENTIONS.
Bain, Richard C. Convention
decisions and voting records 2d ed.
Washington, Brookings Institution
[1973] x, 350, [120] p. [$14.95]
329/.0221 73-1082
JK2255 .B3 1973 MRR Alc.

David, Paul Theodore, The politics
of national party conventions,
[Washington] Brookings Institution
[1960] xv, 592 p. 329 60-7422
JK2255 .D39 MRR Alc.

Judah, Charles Burnet, The unchosen
New York, Coward-McCann [1962] 377
p. 324.23 62-10947
JK2255 .J8 MRR Alc.

Martin, Ralph G., Ballots &
bandwagons. Chicago, Rand McNally
[1964] 480 p. 973.9 64-10021
E743 .M275 MRR Alc.

McKee, Thomas Hudson. The national
conventions and platforms of all
political parties, 1789 to 1905; New
York, B. Franklin [1971] 414, 33 p.
329/.02 75-132682
JK2255 .M2 1971 MRR Alc.

Pomper, Gerald M. Nominating the
President; [Evanston, Ill.]
Northwestern University Press, 1963.
xii, 292 p. 329/.022/0973 63-13558

JK521 .P6 MRR Alc.

Runyon, John H. Source book of
American presidential campaign and
election statistics, 1948-1968. New
York, F. Ungar [1971] xiv, 380 p.
329/.023/0212 73-155093
JK524 .R83 MRR Alc.

United States. Congress. Senate.
Library. Nomination and election of
the President and Vice President of
the United States, including the
manner of selecting delegates to
national political conventions,
Washington, U.S. Govt. Print. Off.,
1972. v, 273 p. [$1.50]
329/.0221/0973 72-600557
JK2063 .A513 1972 MRR Ref Desk.

POLITICAL CRIMES AND OFFENSES.
see also Corruption (in politics)

see also Impeachments

POLITICAL CRIMES AND OFFENSES--EUROPE.
United States. Library of Congress.
Law Library. Legislation for the
protection of the state in various
European countries; Washington,
Library of Congress, Law Library,
Foreign Law Section, 1956. v, 155 l.
016.35175 016.36413* 56-61203
Z2663.5 .L4 MRR Alc.

POLITICAL ETHICS.
Weinberg, Albert Katz. Manifest
destiny: Baltimore, The Johns
Hopkins press, 1935. xiii, 559 p.
973 35-9403
E179.5 .W45 MRR Alc.

POLITICAL PARTICIPATION--UNITED STATES--
DIRECTORIES.
Youth info digest. 1972-
[Washington] Washington Workshops
Press. 309/.025/73 74-185964
HN55 .Y68 MRR Alc Latest edition

POLITICAL PARTIES.
Political handbook and atlas of the
world. Jan. 1, 1927- New York,
Simon and Schuster [etc.] for Council
on Foreign Relations. 28-12165
JF37 .P6 MRR Ref Desk Latest
edition / MRR Alc Latest edition

United States. Dept. of State. Bureau
of Intelligence and Research. World
strength of the Communist Party
organizations; annual report.
[Washington] 329/.07 56-60986
HX40 .U626 MRR Alc Latest edition

POLITICAL PARTIES--AFRICA.
Segal, Ronald, Political Africa;
London, Stevens, 1961. ix, 475 p.
920.06 62-1394
DT18 .S4 1961a MRR Biog.

POLITICAL PARTIES--AFRICA, SUB-SAHARAN.
Coleman, James Smoot, ed. Political
parties and national integration in
tropical Africa. Berkeley,
University of California Press, 1964.
xiii, 730 p. 329.96 64-19636
DT352 .C56 MRR Alc.

POLITICAL PARTIES--CALIFORNIA.
Owens, John Robert, California
politics and parties [New York]
Macmillan [1970] xiii, 338 p.
329/.009794 77-97764
JK8725 1970 .O93 MRR Alc.

POLITICAL PARTIES--CANADA--HISTORY.
Carrigan, D. Owen, comp. Canadian
party platforms 1867-1968, [Toronto]
Copp Clark [1968] xi, 363 p.
329.9/71 68-55645
JL195 .C3 1968b MRR Alc.

POLITICAL PARTIES--EUROPE.
European political parties; New
York, Praeger [1970, c1969] 565 p.
[13.50] 329.9/4 76-97185
JN94.A979 E85 1970 MRR Alc.

Rogger, Hans, ed. The European
right; Berkeley, University of
California Press, 1965. vi, 589 p.
320.52094 65-18562
JN12 .R6 MRR Alc.

POLITICAL PARTIES--FRANCE.
Coston, Henry. Dictionnaire de la
politique française, Paris,
Publications H. Coston (Diffusion: la
Librairie française) 1967- v.
[90.00F (v. 1) varies] 320.9/44 67-
99935
DC55 .C72 MRR Alc.

POLITICAL PARTIES--GERMANY.
Treue, Wolfgang, ed. Deutsche
Parteiprogramme seit 1861 [i. e.
achtzehnhunderteinundsechzig. 4.,
erw. Aufl.] Göttingen,
Musterschmidt-Verlag [1968, c1954]
506 p. 329.9/43 77-369618
JN3931 .T7 1968 MRR Alc.

POLITICAL PARTIES--GREAT BRITAIN.
Butler, David E. British political
facts, 1900-1968. 3rd ed. London,
Macmillan; New York, St Martin's P.,
1969. xlix, 314 p. [70/-] 320.9/42
74-82434
JN231 .B8 1969 MRR Alc.

POLITICAL PARTIES--GREAT BRITAIN--
HISTORY.
Craig, Fred W. S., comp. British
general election manifestos 1918-
1966, Chichester [Eng.] Political
Reference Publications, 1970. xii,
303 p. [75/- ($12.00 U.S.)]
329.9/42 70-77467
JN1121 .C73 MRR Alc.

POLITICAL PARTIES--LATIN AMERICA--
BIBLIOGRAPHY.
Kantor, Harry. Latin American
political parties; a bibliography,
[Gainesville] Reference and
Bibliography Dept., University of
Florida Libraries, 1968. ix, 113 p.
016.3299/8 a 68-7771
Z7165.L3 K3 MRR Alc.

POLITICAL PARTIES--NETHERLANDS.
Parlement en kiezer: Jaarboek. 's-
Gravenhage, Nijhoff. 74-642439
Began with vol. for 1911/12.
JN5873 .A3 MRR Alc Latest edition

POLITICAL PARTIES--PHILIPPINE ISLANDS.
Liang, Ta-p'eng, Philippine parties
and politics; New ed., completely
rev. and enl. San Francisco,
Gladstone Co. [1971, c1970] xiii,
486 p. 329.9/599 75-139510
JQ1398.A1 L52 1971 MRR Alc.

POLITICAL PARTIES--UNITED STATES.
Bain, Richard C. Convention
decisions and voting records 2d ed.
Washington, Brookings Institution
[1973] x, 350, [120] p. [$14.95]
329/.0221 73-1082
JK2255 .B3 1973 MRR Alc.

Binkley, Wilfred Ellsworth, American
political parties, 4th ed., enl.
New York, Knopf, 1962. 486 p. 329
62-52807
JK2261 .B5 1962 MRR Alc.

Bone, Hugh Alvin, American politics
and the party system 3d ed. New
York, McGraw-Hill [1965] x, 684 p.
329 64-7727
JK2265 .B6 1965 MRR Alc.

Goodman, William, The two-party
system in the United States. 3d ed.
Princeton, N.J., Van Nostrand [1964]
xvi, 672 p. 329 64-17062
JK2265 .G6 1964 MRR Alc.

Key, Valdimer Orlando, Politics,
parties, & pressure groups. 5th ed.
New York, Crowell [1964] xiii, 738
p. 329 64-11799
JF2051 .K4 1964 MRR Alc.

McKee, Thomas Hudson. The national
conventions and platforms of all
political parties, 1789 to 1905; New
York, B. Franklin [1971] 414, 33 p.
329/.02 75-132682
JK2255 .M2 1971 MRR Alc.

Robinson, Edgar Eugene, The
evolution of American political
parties; New York, Harcourt, Brace
and company [c1924] viii p., 2 l., 3-
382 p. 24-25538
JK2261 .R6 MRR Alc.

Sorauf, Francis Joseph, Party
politics in America Boston, Little,
Brown [1968] ix, 438 p.
329/.02/0973 68-14138
JK2265 .S65 MRR Alc.

Thayer, George, The farther shores
of politics; New York, Simon and
Schuster [1967] 610 p. 320.9/73
67-16728
JK2261 .T47 1967 MRR Alc.

POLITICAL PARTIES--UNITED (Cont.)
Theis, Paul A., All about politics;
New York, Bowker, 1972. xii, 228 p.
320   72-8470
JK1726 .T48 MRR Alc.

POLITICAL PARTIES--UNITED STATES--
ABSTRACTS.
Smith, Dwight La Vern, The American
political process: selected abstracts
of periodical literature, 1954-1971.
Santa Barbara, Calif., ABC-CLIO
[1972]   xvi, 630 p.   016.329/00973
72-77548
JK2261 .S73 MRR Alc.

POLITICAL PARTIES--UNITED STATES--
BIBLIOGRAPHY.
Wynar, Lubomyr Roman, American
political parties; Littleton, Colo.,
Libraries Unlimited, 1969.   427 p.
016.329/02/0973   75-96954
Z7166.U5 W88 MRR Alc.

POLITICAL PARTIES--UNITED STATES--
DIRECTORIES.
Rosenbloom, David L. The political
marketplace. [New York] Quadrangle
Books [1972]   xix, 948 p.   [$25.00]
329/.0025/73   72-77926
JK2283 .R64 MRR Ref Desk.

POLITICAL PARTIES--UNITED STATES--
HISTORY.
Cunningham, Noble E., The
Jeffersonian Republicans; Chapel
Hill. Published for the Institute of
Early American History and Culture at
Williamsburg by the University of
North Carolina Press [c1957] x, 279
p.   329.3 58-1263
JK2316 .C8 MRR Alc.

Johnson, Donald Bruce, comp.
National party platforms, 1840-1972.
[5th. ed.] Urbana, University of
Illinois Press [c1973]   xii, 889 p.
329/.0213/0973   73-81566
JK2255 .J64 1973 MRR Alc.

McCormick, Richard Patrick, The
second American party system; Chapel
Hill, University of North Carolina
Press [1966] x, 389 p.   329/.02 66-
10962
JK2261 .M165 MRR Alc.

Schlesinger, Arthur Meier, History
of U.S. political parties. New York,
Chelsea House Publishers, 1973. 4 v.
(liv, 3544 p.)   329/.02 72-8682
JK2261 .S35 MRR Alc.

Walton, Hanes, Black political
parties; New York, Free Press [1972]
xi, 276 p.   329/.894 76-143514
JK2261 .W33 MRR Alc.

POLITICAL PARTIES--UNITED STATES--
HISTORY--ADDRESSES, ESSAYS, LECTURES.
Bernhard, Winfred E. A., comp.
Political parties in American
history. New York, Putnam [1974,
c1973-74] 3 v. (xliv, 1324 p.)
[$8.95 per vol.]   329/.02 73-76139

JK2261 .B47 MRR Alc.

POLITICAL PARTIES--UNITED STATES--
HISTORY--SOURCES.
Schlesinger, Arthur Meier, History
of U.S. political parties. New York,
Chelsea House Publishers, 1973. 4 v.
(liv, 3544 p.)   329/.02 72-8682
JK2261 .S35 MRR Alc.

POLITICAL PARTIES--VIETNAM--DIRECTORIES.
Buttinger, Joseph. Vietnam: a dragon
embattled. London, Pall Mall P.,
1967. 2 v. [£6/10/-]   959.7 68-
70118
DS557.A5 B83 1967b MRR Alc.

POLITICAL PSYCHOLOGY--BIBLIOGRAPHY.
Universal Reference System. Public
opinion, mass behavior, and political
psychology; Princeton, N.J.,
Princeton Research Pub. Co. [1969]
xxi, 1225 p.   016.30115/4 68-57822

Z7161 .U64 vol. 6 MRR Alc.

POLITICAL SCIENCE.
    see also Bureaucracy

    see also Citizenship

    see also Civil rights

    see also Communism

    see also Legislation

    see also Nationalism

    see also Public administration

    see also Radicalism

    see also Separation of powers

    see also State governments

    see also World politics

Aristoteles. The Politics, London,
W. Heinemann, ltd.; New York, G. P.
Putnam's sons, 1932. xxiii, 683, [1]
p.   888.5 mrr01-62
PA3612.A8 P8 1932d MRR Alc.

Lipson, Leslie, The great issues of
politics: 4th ed. Englewood Cliffs,
N.J., Prentice-Hall [1970] xx, 458
p.   [7.95]   320/.01 79-110123
JA66 .L55 1970 MRR Alc.

McDonald, Lee Cameron. Western
political theory: from its origins to
the present. New York, Harcourt,
Brace & World [1968] xiv, 653 p.
320/.01 68-19235
JA71 .M15 1968 MRR Alc.

Plato. The Republic, Cambridge,
Mass., Harvard University Press;
London, W. Heinemann, 1935-37. 2 v.
321.07   mrr01-59
PA3612 .P67 1935d MRR Alc.

POLITICAL SCIENCE--ABSTRACTS.
International political science
abstracts. v. 1-   1951- Oxford
[etc.] Basil Blackwell [etc.] 320.82
54-3623
JA36 .I5 MRR Alc Full set

POLITICAL SCIENCE--ADDRESSES, ESSAYS,
LECTURES.
Ebenstein, William, ed. Modern
political thought, 2d ed. New York,
Holt, Rinehart and Winston [1960]
875 p.   320.4 60-15510
JA37 .E2 1960 MRR Alc.

POLITICAL SCIENCE--BIBLIOGRAPHY.
Brock, Clifton. The literature of
political science; New York, Bowker,
1969. xii, 232 p.   016.32 79-79426

Z7161 .B83 MRR Alc.

Harmon, Robert Bartlett, Political
science; New York, Scarecrow Press,
1965. 388 p.   016.32 65-13557
Z7161 .H27 MRR Alc.

Harmon, Robert Bartlett, Political
science bibliographies, Metuchen,
N.J., Scarecrow Press, 1973- v.
016.01632 72-8849
Z7161.A1 H35 MRR Alc.

International bibliography of
political science. v. 1-   1953-
London, Tavistock Publications;
Chicago, Aldine Pub. Co.   54-14355
Z7163 .I64 MRR Alc Full set

Public Affairs Information Service.
Bulletin ... annual cumulation. 1st-
1915- New York [etc.] 16-920
Z7163 .P9 MRR Circ Full set

Public Affairs Information Service.
Foreign language index. 1968/71-
New York.   016.3 72-626907
Z7164.E2 P8 MRR Circ Full set

Universal Reference System.
Bibliography of bibliographies in
political science, government, and
public policy; Princeton, N.J.,
Princeton Research Pub. Co. [1968]
xix, 927 p.   016.3 67-29647
Z7161 .U64 vol. 3 MRR Alc.

Universal Reference System.
Legislative process, representation,
and decision-making; Princeton,
N.J., Princeton Research Pub. Co.
[c1967] xv, 749 p.   016.32 67-
29646
Z6461 .U64 vol. 2 MRR Alc.

Utz, Arthur Fridolin, Bibliographie
der Sozialethik. 1-   1956/59
Freiburg, New York, Herder. a 61-
2645
Z7161 .U83 MRR Alc Full set

Wynar, Lubomyr Roman, Guide to
reference materials in political
science; Denver, Colorado
Bibliographic Institute, 1966-68. 2
v.   016.32 66-1321
Z7161 .W9 MRR Alc.

POLITICAL SCIENCE--DICTIONARIES.
Dunner, Joseph, ed. Dictionary of
political science. New York,
Philosophical Library [1964] xxii,
585 p.   320.03 63-15600
JA61 .D8 MRR Alc.

Elliott, Florence. A dictionary of
politics. 6th ed. Harmondsworth,
Penguin 1971. 480 p.   [10/-]
320/.03 72-186214
D419 .E4 1971 MRR Alc.

Heimanson, Rudolph. Dictionary of
political science and law. Dobbs
Ferry, N.Y., Oceana Publications,
1967. 188 p.   320/.03 67-14401
JA61 .H4 MRR Ref Desk.

Holt, Solomon. Dictionary of
American government Rev. ed. [New
York, Macfadden-Bartell Corp.] 1970.
304 p. [0.95]   353/.003 72-17208
JK9 .H6 1970 MRR Ref Desk.

Jefferson, Thomas, pres. U.S., The
Jeffersonian cyclopedia. New York,
London, Funk & Wagnalls company
[1900?] 4 p. l., [xiii]-xxii, [2],
1009 p.   mrr01-50
JK113 .J4 1900b MRR Alc.

Marxism, Communism, and Western
society; [New York] Herder and
Herder [1972-73] 8 v.   300/.3 79-
176368
AE5 .M27 MRR Alc.

McCarthy, Eugene J., The crescent
dictionary of American politics. New
York, Macmillan, 1962. x, 182 p.
320.3 62-10644
JK9 .M2 MRR Alc.

Montgomery, Hugh. A dictionary of
political phrases and allusions with
a short bibliography, London, S.
Sonnenschein & co. ltd., 1906. 3 p.
l., 406 p. w 07-84
JN114 .M7 MRR Alc.

Norton, Charles Ledyard, Political
Americanisms; New York, London,
Longmans, Green & co., 1890. viii,
135 p.   10-31868
PE2835 .N8 MRR Alc.

Raghu Vira. A comprehensive English-
Hindi dictionary of governmental &
educational words & phrases ...
[Nagpur, Lokesh Chandra,
International Academy of Indian
Culture, 1955] 189, 1579 p.
491.4332 56-19893
PK1937 .R3 MRR Alc.

Roberts, Geoffrey K. A dictionary of
political analysis New York, St.
Martin's Press [1971] xxii, 229 p.
320/.03 70-151309
JA61 .R62 1971b MRR Alc.

Spaull, Hebe, The new ABC of civics;
New and enl. ed. London, Barrie and
Rockliff [1963] 136 p.   64-32552
JA61 .S63 1963 MRR Alc.

White, Wilbur Wallace, White's
Political dictionary, Cleveland,
World Pub. Co. [1947] 378 p.   320.3
47-30518
D419 .W5 MRR Alc.

POLITICAL SCIENCE--DICTIONARIES--ARABIC.
Lewis, Bernard. A handbook of
diplomatic and political Arabic.
[London] Luzac, 1947. 72, [1] p.
492.732 49-6894
PJ6680 .L4 MRR Alc.

POLITICAL SCIENCE--DICTIONARIES--GERMAN.
Handwörterbuch der
Sozialwissenschaften. Stuttgart, G.
Fisher, 1952- v.   a 53-7990
H45 .H18 MRR Alc.

Staatslexikon, 5., von grund aus
neubearb. aufl. ... Freiburg im
Breisgau, Herder & co., g.m.b.h.,
1926- v.   28-29832
JA63 .S8 1926 MRR Alc.

POLITICAL SCIENCE--DICTIONARIES--
POLYGLOT.
Haensch, Günther. Dictionary of
international relations and politics;
Amsterdam, New York, Elsevier Pub.
Co., 1965. xv, 638 p.   320.03 64-
8710
JX1226 .H26 MRR Alc.

Polec. 2., verb. und erw. Aufl.
Berlin, de Gruyter, 1967. xvi, 1037
p. with map. [DM 48.-] 330/.03 68-
70864
H40 .P6 1967 MRR Alc.

POLITICAL SCIENCE--DICTIONARIES--
SPANISH.
Sell, Lewis L., Español-inglés
diccionario para especialistas en
seguros, finanzas, derecho, trabajo,
política, comercio; New York, D.
McKay Co. [1957] 650 p.   330.3 57-
3078
HB61 .S4 MRR Alc.

POLITICAL SCIENCE--HANDBOOKS, MANUALS,
ETC.
Political handbook and atlas of the
world. Jan. 1, 1927- New York,
Simon and Schuster [etc.] for Council
on Foreign Relations. 28-12165
JF37 .P6 MRR Ref Desk Latest
    edition / MRR Alc Latest edition

POLITICAL SCIENCE--HISTORY.
Burns, Edward McNall, Ideas in
conflict; [1st ed.] New York,
Norton [1960] 587 p.   320.1 60-
7571
JA83 .B85 MRR Alc.

McDonald, Lee Cameron. Western
political theory: from its origins to
the present. New York, Harcourt,
Brace & World [1968] xiv, 653 p.
320/.01 68-19235
JA71 .M15 1968 MRR Alc.

POLITICAL SCIENCE--HISTORY. (Cont.)
Schmandt, Henry J. A history of
political philosophy. Milwaukee,
Bruce Pub. Co. [1960] 499 p. 320.9
60-10556
JA81 .S338 MRR Alc.

POLITICAL SCIENCE--HISTORY--GERMANY
(FEDERAL REPUBLIC, 1949-)
Gurland, Arcadius Rudolph Lang.
Political science in Western Germany;
Washington, Library of Congress,
Reference Dept., European Affairs
Division, 1952. 118 p. 320.943 52-
60058
Z663.26 .P6 MRR Alc.

POLITICAL SCIENCE--HISTORY--RUSSIA.
Anderson, Thornton. Russian
political thought. Ithaca, N.Y.,
Cornell University Press [1967]
xiii, 444 p. 320.9/47 67-12902
JA84.R9 A7 MRR Alc.

POLITICAL SCIENCE--HISTORY--UNITED
STATES.
Grimes, Alan Pendleton. American
political thought. Rev. ed. New
York, Holt, Rinehart and Winston
[1960] 556 p. 320.973 60-7493
JA84.U5 G7 1960 MRR Alc.

Rossiter, Clinton Lawrence. Seedtime
of the Republic; [1st ed.] New
York, Harcourt, Brace [1953] xiv,
558 p. 342.739 320.973* 53-5647
JK31 .R6 MRR Alc.

Weinberg, Albert Katz. Manifest
destiny; Baltimore, The Johns
Hopkins press, 1935. xiii, 559 p.
973 35-8403
E179.5 .W45 MRR Alc.

Wood, Gordon S. The creation of the
American Republic, 1776-1787. Chapel
Hill, Published for the Institute of
Early American History and Culture at
Williamsburg, Va., by the University
of North Carolina Press [1969] xiv,
653 p. [15.00] 320/.0973 71-78861
JA84.U5 W6 MRR Alc.

POLITICAL SCIENCE--HISTORY--UNITED
STATES--CONGRESSES.
Library of Congress Symposia on the
American Revolution, 2d, 1973.
Fundamental testaments of the
American Revolution; Washington,
Library of Congress, 1973. 119 p.
[$3.50] 973.3/11 73-18173
Z663.115 .F85 1973 MRR Alc.

POLITICAL SCIENCE--PERIODICALS--INDEXES.
Deutsch, Karl Wolfgang. Nationalism
and national development; Cambridge,
Mass., MIT Press [1970] 519 p.
016.3201/58 79-90750
Z7164.N2 D43 MRR Alc.

Fondation nationale des sciences
politiques. Bibliographie courante
d'articles de périodiques
postérieurs à 1944 sur les
problèmes politiques, économiques,
et sociaux. Boston, G. K. Hall,
1968. 17 v. 70-409780
AI7 .F6 MRR Alc. (Dk 33).

International bibliography of
political science. v. 1- 1953-
London, Tavistock Publications;
Chicago, Aldine Pub. Co. 54-14355
Z7163 .I64 MRR Alc Full set

Liboiron, Albert A. Federalism and
intergovernmental relations in
Australia, Canada, the United States
and other countries; Kingston, Ont.,
Institute of Intergovernmental
Relations, Queen's University, 1967.
vi, 231 l. [$3.00 Can.] 016.351
68-10060
Z7165.A8 L5 MRR Alc.

Public Affairs Information Service.
Bulletin ... annual cumulation. 1st-
1915- New York [etc.] 16-920
Z7163 .P9 MRR Circ Full set

Public Affairs Information Service.
Foreign language index. 1968/71-
New York. 016.3 72-626907
Z7164.E2 P8 MRR Circ Full set

POLITICAL SCIENCE--QUOTATIONS, MAXIMS,
ETC.
Bingham, Colin, comp. Men and
affairs; Sydney, Currawong Pub. Co.
[1967] xv, 464 p. [$6.95 Aust.]
808.88/2 68-81441
PN6081 .B5 MRR Ref Desk.

Jefferson, Thomas, pres. U.S., The
Jeffersonian cyclopedia. New York,
London, Funk & Wagnalls company
[1900?] 4 p. l., [xiii]--xxii, [2],
1009 p. mrr01-50
JK113 .J4 1900b MRR Alc.

POLITICAL SCIENCE--SOCIETIES, ETC.
American Political Science
Association. Biographical directory.
[1st]- ed.: 1945- Washington
[etc.] 46-38
JA28 .A56 MRR Biog Latest edition

Governmental Research Association.
Directory of organizations and
individuals professionally engaged in
governmental research and related
activities. 1935- New York [etc.]
350.6273 35-16469
JK3 .G627 MRR Alc Latest edition

POLITICAL SCIENCE--STUDY AND TEACHING--
UNITED STATES.
National Association of Schools of
Public Affairs and Administration.
Graduate school programs in public
affairs and public administration.
Washington. [$5.00] 350/.0007/1173
74-80861
JF1338.A2 N28a MRR Alc Latest
edition

POLITICAL SCIENCE--TERMINOLOGY.
Cranston, Maurice William, ed. A
glossary of political ideas. New
York, Basic Books [1969] xii, 180 p.
[5.95] 320/.03 76-78455
JA61 .C7 1969 MRR Alc.

POLITICAL SCIENCE--YEARBOOKS.
The International year book and
statesmen's who's who. 1953-
London, Burke's Peerage. 305.8 53-
1425
JA51 .I57 MRR Biog Latest edition

The Statesman's year-book; [1st]-
1864- London, Macmillan; New York,
St. Martin's Press [etc.] 04-3776
JA51 .S7 MRR Ref Desk Latest
edition / MRR Ref Desk Latest
edition

POLITICAL SCIENCE RESEARCH--DIRECTORIES.
Governmental Research Association.
Directory of organizations and
individuals professionally engaged in
governmental research and related
activities. 1935- New York [etc.]
350.6273 35-16469
JK3 .G627 MRR Alc Latest edition

POLITICAL SCIENCE RESEARCH--WASHINGTON
METROPOLITAN AREA--DIRECTORIES.
Maryland. University. Dept. of
Government and Politics. University
of Maryland guide to political
science research. [College Park,
Md., 1969] 47 l. 320/.072/0753 73-
626301
JA88.U6 M35 MRR Alc.

POLITICAL SCIENTISTS--UNITED STATES--
DIRECTORIES.
American Political Science
Association. APSA directory of
members. Washington. 320/.06/273
74-646061
JA28 .A562 MRR Biog Latest edition

American Political Science
Association. Biographical directory.
[1st]- ed.; 1945- Washington
[etc.] 46-38
JA28 .A56 MRR Biog Latest edition

Governmental Research Association.
Directory of organizations and
individuals professionally engaged in
governmental research and related
activities. 1935- New York [etc.]
350.6273 35-16469
JK3 .G627 MRR Alc Latest edition

POLITICIANS
see Statesmen

POLITICS, PRACTICAL.
see also Campaign management

see also Electioneering

see also Voting

Key, Valdimer Orlando. Politics,
parties, & pressure groups. 5th ed.
New York, Crowell [1964] xiii, 738
p. 329 64-11799
JF2051 .K4 1964 MRR Alc.

Theis, Paul A., All about politics;
New York, Bowker, 1972. xii, 228 p.
320 72-8470
JK1726 .T48 MRR Alc.

POLK, JAMES KNOX, PRES. U.S., 1795-1849.
McCormac, Eugene Irving. James K.
Polk, a political biography.
Berkeley, Calif., University of
California press, 1922. x, 746 p.
a 22-821
E417 .M12 MRR Alc.

McCoy, Charles Allan, Polk and the
Presidency. Austin, University of
Texas Press [c1960] 238 p. 973.61
60-9515
E417 .M15 MRR Alc.

Sellers, Charles Grier. James K.
Polk, Jacksonian, 1795-1843.
Princeton, N.J., Princeton University
Press, 1957- v. 973.610924 B
57-5457
E417 .S4 MRR Alc.

POLK, JAMES KNOX, PRES. U.S., 1795-1849-
-MANUSCRIPTS--INDEXES.
United States. Library of Congress.
Manuscript Division. Index to the
James K. Polk papers. Washington
[For sale by the Supt. of Docs., U.S.
Govt. Print. Off.] 1969. xvi, 91 p.
[$1.25] 016.9736/1/0924 67-60016
Z663.34 .P6 MRR Alc.

POLLARD, ALFRED WILLIAM, 1859-1944
COMP. A SHORT-TITLE CATALOGUE OF BOOKS
PRINTED IN ENGLAND, SCOTLAND & IRELAND
AND OF ENGLISH BOOKS PRINTED ABROAD,
1475-1640--INDEXES.
Early English books 1475-1640,
selected from Pollard and Redgrave's
short-title catalogue; cross index to
reels. 1- 1972- Ann Arbor,
University Microfilms. 015/.42 72-
627329
Z2002 .U574 MRR Alc Latest edition

POLLS
see Voting

POLLUTION.
see also Environmental engineering

Nobile, Philip, comp. The complete
ecology fact book. [1st ed.] Garden
City, N.Y., Doubleday, 1972. xx, 472
p. [$10.00] 301.31 73-175364
TD174 .N6 MRR Alc.

POLLUTION--BIBLIOGRAPHY.
The Energy index. [New York,
Environment Information Center,
Energy Reference Dept.] [$50.00]
333.7 73-89088
HD9502.U5 E525 MRR Alc Full set /
Sci RR Full set

POLLUTION--DICTIONARIES.
Sarnoff, Paul. The New York times
encyclopedic dictionary of the
environment. New York, Quadrangle
Books [c1971] 352 p. [$10.00]
628.5/03 74-178736
TD173 .S27 1971 MRR Alc.

POLLUTION--RESEARCH--DIRECTORIES.
CCM Information Corporation.
Environmental pollution; New York,
1971. vii, 851 p. 628.5/07/2 71-
180288
TD178.5 .C2 MRR Alc.

POLLUTION--UNITED STATES.
Directory of Government agencies
safeguarding consumer and
environment. 1st- ed.; 1968-
Alexandria, Va., Serina Press.
339.4/7/02573 68-20372
HC110.C6 D5 MRR Alc Latest edition

POLLUTION--UNITED STATES--CASES.
Council on Economic Priorities.
Guide to corporations; [1st ed.]
Chicago, Swallow Press [1974] iii,
393 p. [$4.95] 301.575 73-13212
HD60.5.U5 C7 1974 MRR Alc.

POLLUTION--UNITED STATES--DIRECTORIES.
1971 directory of national
organizations concerned with land
pollution control. New York, Freed
Pub. Co. [1971] 36 p. [$7.00]
614/.776/02573 76-28602
TD173.5 .N55 MRR Alc.

1971 directory of State agencies
concerned with land pollution
control. New York, Freed Pub. Co.
[1971] 19 p. 614/.776/02573 70-
28603
TD173.5 .N57 MRR Alc.

POLLUTION--UNITED STATES--PERIODICALS.
Your government and the environment.
v. 1- 1971- Arlington, Va., Output
Systems Corp. 301.3/1 77-166183
HC110.E5 Y6 Sci RR Latest edition
/ MRR Alc Latest edition

POLLUTION CONTROL EQUIPMENT.
see also Motor vehicles--Pollution
control devices

POLYGLOT GLOSSARIES, PHRASE BOOKS, ETC.
The Bookman's glossary. 4th ed.,
rev. and enl. New York, R. R. Bowker
[1961] viii, 212 p. 010.3 61-
13239
Z1006 .B6 1961 MRR Alc.

Cowles, Barbara (Pehotsky)
Bibliographers' glossary of foreign
words and phrases; New York, R. R.
Bowker company, 1935. 3 p. l., 82
numb. l. 010.3 41-5736
Z1006 .C87 1935 MRR Alc.

Dony, Yvonne P. de. Léxico del
lenguaje figurado, comparado, Buenos
Aires, Ediciones Desclée, De Brouwer
[1951] 804 p. 52-21901
PB331 .D6 MRR Alc.

POLYGLOT TEXTS, SELECTIONS, QUOTATIONS,
ETC.
Nida, Eugene Albert. The Book of a
thousand tongues Rev. ed. [London]
United Bible Societies [1972] xviii,
536 p. 220.5 73-160367
P352.A2 N6 1972 MRR Alc.

POLYMERS AND POLYMERIZATION.
see also Plastics

POLYNESIA--BIBLIOGRAPHY.
O'Reilly, Patrick. Bibliographie de Tahiti et de la Polynesie française Paris, Musee de l'Homme, 1867. 1048 p. [400 F]   016.996 68-91315

Z4501 .072 MRR Alc.

POMFRET, JOHN EDWIN, 1898-
Billington, Ray Allen, ed. The reinterpretation of early American history; San Marino, Calif. Huntington Library, 1966. viii, 264 p.   973.20722 66-31501
E175 .B5 MRR Alc.

POMOLOGY
see Fruit-culture

POOLE, ENG. (DORSETSHIRE)--DIRECTORIES.
Kelly's directory of Bournemouth and Poole. Kingston upon Thames [Eng., etc.]   55-28315
DA690.B685 K4 MRR Alc Latest edition

POOLE'S INDEX TO PERIODICAL LITERATURE.
Poole's index: date and volume key Chicago, Association of College and Reference Libraries, 1957. 61 p.   016.05 57-7157
Z674 .A75 no. 19 MRR Ref Desk.

POOR.
see also Labor and laboring classes

see also Unemployed

POOR--UNITED STATES.
United States. Congress. Senate. Select Committee on Nutrition and Human Needs. Poverty, malnutrition, and Federal food assistance programs: Washington, U.S. Govt. Print. Off., 1969. v, 56 p.   338.1/9/73 78-603619
HD9006 .A5256 1969 MRR Alc.

POOR--UNITED STATES--BIBLIOGRAPHY.
Tompkins, Dorothy Louise (Campbell) Culver. Poverty in the United States during the sixties: [Berkeley] Institute of Governmental Studies, University of California, 1970. ix, 542 p. [$10.00] 016.3625/0973 74-632910
Z7165.U5 T62 MRR Alc.

POOR--UNITED STATES--BIBLIOGRAPHY--PERIODICALS.
P H R A; poverty and human resources abstracts. v. 1- Jan./Feb. 1966- Beverly Hills, Cal., [etc.] Sage Pub. [etc.] 66-9955
Z7165.U5 P2 MRR Alc Full set

POOR RELIEF
see Charities

POPE, ALEXANDER--CONCORDANCES.
Abbott, Edwin. A concordance to the works of Alexander Pope, London, Chapman & Hall, 1875. xviii, 365, [1] p.   01-22779
PR3632 .A73 MRR Alc.

POPES.
John, Eric, ed. The Popes, a concise biographical history. 1st ed.] New York, Hawthorn Books [1964] 496 p. 262.1309 64-12422
BX955.2 .J58 MRR Biog.

POPULAR CULTURE--BIBLIOGRAPHY--INDEXES.
Index to the contemporary scene. v. 1- 1973- Detroit, Gale Research Co. [$14.00] 016.3 73-645955
Z7161 .I52 MRR Alc Full set

POPULAR ERRORS
see Errors, Popular

POPULAR MUSIC
see Music, Popular (Songs, etc.)

POPULATION.
see also Birth control

see also Migration, Internal

Carr-Saunders, Alexander Morris, World population; Oxford, The Clarendon press, 1936. xv, 336 p. 312 37-8100
HB881 .C3 MRR Alc.

Chandler, Tertius. 3000 years of urban growth New York, Academic Press [1974] ix, 431 p. 301.36/1 72-84378
HB2161 .C45 1974 MRR alc.

Clark, Colin, Population growth and land use. London, Melbourne [etc.] Macmillan; New York, St. Martin's P., 1967. 406 p. [70/-] 301.3/2 67-15941
HB871 .C58 1967 MRR Alc.

Clarke, John Innes. Population geography, [2d ed.] Oxford, New York, Pergamon Press [1972] xi, 176 p.   301.32 70-183339
HB1951 .C5 1972 MRR Alc.

Davis, Kingsley, World urbanization, 1950-1970. Berkeley, Institute of International Studies, University of California [1969-72] 2 v. [$6.00] 301.36 71-627843
HB2161 .D37 MRR Alc.

Hauser, Philip Morris, ed. The study of population: [Chicago] University of Chicago Press [1959] 864 p. 312 58-11949
HB871 .H37 MRR Alc.

Petersen, William. Population. 2d ed. [New York] Macmillan [1969] xv, 735 p.   301.3/2 69-10542
HB851 .P46 1969 MRR Alc.

Trewartha, Glenn Thomas, A geography of population: world patterns New York, Wiley [1969] 186 p. 301.3/2 75-88319
HB851 .T7 MRR Alc.

POPULATION--ADDRESSES, ESSAYS, LECTURES.
Berelson, Bernard, Population policy in developed countries. New York, McGraw-Hill [1974] xiii, 783 p. 301.32 73-18368
HB851 .B45 MRR Alc.

POPULATION--BIBLIOGRAPHY.
Fogle, Catherine. International directory of population information and library resources, 1st ed. [Chapel Hill] Carolina Population Center, 1972. xiii, 324 p. 301.32/025 79-190722
HB850 .F6 MRR Alc.

Population index. v. 1- Jan. 20, 1935- [Princeton, N.J., etc.] 016.312 39-10247
Z7164.D3 P83 MRR Alc Partial set

Princeton University. Office of Population Research. Population index bibliography, Boston, G. K. Hall, 1971. 4 v. 016.312 75-26979

Z7164.D3 P85 MRR Alc (Dk 33)

Princeton University. Office of Population Research. Population index bibliography, Boston, G. K. Hall, 1971. 5 v. 016.312 79-30213

Z7164.D3 P852 MRR Alc (Dk 33)

Texas. University. Population Research Center. International population census bibliography. Austin, Bureau of Business Research, University of Texas, 1965-67. 6 v. 016.312 66-63578
Z7164.D3 T45 MRR Alc.

POPULATION--HISTORY.
Reinhard, Marcel R., Histoire generale de la population mondiale (3e edition] Paris, Montchrestien, 1968. x, 709 p. [90 F] 301.3/29 68-119418
HB881 .R43 1968 MRR Alc.

POPULATION--PERIODICALS--BIBLIOGRAPHY.
Fogle, Catherine. International directory of population information and library resources, 1st ed. [Chapel Hill] Carolina Population Center, 1972. xiii, 324 p. 301.32/025 79-190722
HB850 .F6 MRR Alc.

POPULATION--SOCIETIES, ETC.--DIRECTORIES.
Fogle, Catherine. International directory of population information and library resources, 1st ed. [Chapel Hill] Carolina Population Center, 1972. xiii, 324 p. 301.32/025 79-190722
HB850 .F6 MRR Alc.

POPULATION--STATISTICS.
Chandler, Tertius. 3000 years of urban growth New York, Academic Press [1974] ix, 431 p. 301.36/1 72-84378
HB2161 .C45 1974 MRR alc.

Davis, Kingsley, World urbanization, 1950-1970. Berkeley, Institute of International Studies, University of California [1969-72] 2 v. [$6.00] 301.36 71-627843
HB2161 .D37 MRR Alc.

Keyfitz, Nathan, Population: facts and methods of demography San Francisco, W. H. Freeman [1971] x, 613 p. [$13.50] 301.3/2/072 70-141154
HB885 .K43 MRR Alc.

Keyfitz, Nathan, World population; Chicago, University of Chicago Press [1968] xi, 672 p. 312 68-14010
HB881 .K48 TJ Rm.

Nobile, Philip, comp, The complete ecology fact book. [1st ed.] Garden City, N.Y., Doubleday, 1972. xx, 472 p. [$10.00] 301.31 73-175364
TD174 .N6 MRR Alc.

Organization for European Economic Cooperation. Manpower population. Paris, 1959. vii, 20 p.   331.112 59-65495
HD5712 .073 MRR Alc.

Taylor, Charles Lewis. World handbook of political and social indicators; 2d ed. New Haven, Yale University Press, 1972. xiv, 443 p. [$15.00] 301/.01/8 70-179479
HN15 .T37 1972 MRR Alc.

Wolfenden, Hugh Herbert. Population statistics and their compilation. Rev. ed.; [Chicago] Published for the Society of Actuaries by the University of Chicago Press, 1954. 258 p.   312 54-10735
HB881 .W64 1954 MRR Alc.

POPULATION--YEARBOOKS.
Demographic yearbook. 1948- Lake Success. 312.058 50-641
HA17 .D45 MRR Ref Desk Latest edition

POPULATION, FOREIGN
see Emigration and immigration

POPULATION POLICY--BIBLIOGRAPHY.
Driver, Edwin D. World population policy; an annotated bibliography Lexington, Mass.; Lexington Books [c1971] xxi, 1280 p. 016.30132 73-184302
Z7164.D3 D75 MRR Alc.

POPULATION RESEARCH--DIRECTORIES.
Fogle, Catherine. International directory of population information and library resources, 1st ed. [Chapel Hill] Carolina Population Center, 1972. xiii, 324 p. 301.32/025 79-190722
HB850 .F6 MRR Alc.

PORCELAIN--COLLECTORS AND COLLECTING.
Boger, Louise Ade. House & garden's antiques: questions & answers. New York, Simon and Schuster [1973] viii, 429 p. [$8.95] 745.1 73-180214
NK1125 .B56 MRR Alc.

Penkala, Maria. European porcelain; [2d ed.] Rutland, Vt., C. E. Tuttle Co. [1968] 256 p. [12.50] 738.2/094 69-19604
NK4230 .P4 1968 MRR Alc.

PORCELAIN--COLLECTORS AND COLLECTING--UNITED STATES.
Ray, Marcia. Collectible ceramics; New York, Crown Publishers [1974] 256 p. [$9.95] 738/.03 73-92104
NK3770 .R38 MRR Alc.

PORCELAIN--DICTIONARIES.
Boger, Louise Ade. The dictionary of world pottery and porcelain. New York, Scribner [1971] 533 p. [$22.50] 738/.03 72-123829
NK3770 .B64 MRR Alc.

Ray, Marcia. Collectible ceramics; New York, Crown Publishers [1974] 256 p. [$9.95] 738/.03 73-92104
NK3770 .R38 MRR Alc.

Savage, George, An illustrated dictionary of ceramics; New York, Van Nostrand Reinhold Co. [1974] 319 p. [$18.95] 738/.03 73-17999
NK3770 .S38 1974b MRR Alc.

PORCELAIN--HISTORY.
Chaffers, William, Marks & monograms on European and oriental pottery and porcelain. 15th rev. ed. London, W. Reeves [1965] 2 v. 738.0278 66-38182
NK4215 .C46 1965 MRR Alc.

PORCELAIN--MARKS.
[Burton, William] Collector's handbook to marks on porcelain and pottery. Greens Farms, Conn., Modern Books and Crafts [1974] [10], 213 p. [$10.00] 738.2/02/78 74-180368
NK4215 .B8 1974 MRR Alc.

Chaffers, William, Marks & monograms on European and oriental pottery and porcelain. 15th rev. ed. London, W. Reeves [1965] 2 v. 738.0278 66-38182
NK4215 .C46 1965 MRR Alc.

Cushion, John Patrick. Handbook of pottery and porcelain marks, [3d rev. ed.] London, Faber and Faber [1965] 477 p. 66-1611
NK4215 .C8 1965 MRR Alc.

Godden, Geoffrey A. The handbook of British pottery and porcelain marks London, Jenkins, 1968. 197 p. [25/-] 738.0278 68-112982
NK4085 .G635 MRR Alc.

Kovel, Ralph M. Dictionary of marks: pottery and porcelain, New York, Crown Publishers [1953] x, 278 p. 738.88 53-5247
NK4215 .K68 MRR Alc.

PORCELAIN--MARKS. (Cont.)
Penkala, Maria. European porcelain;
[2d ed.] Rutland, Vt., C. E. Tuttle
Co. [1968] 256 p. [12.50]
738.2/094 68-19604
NK4230 .P4 1968 MRR Alc.

Savage, George, The antique
collector's handbook; New revised
ed. Feltham, Spring Books, 1968.
304 p. [25/-] 745.1 70-510278
NK1125 .S3 1968 MRR Alc.

PORCELAIN--EUROPE.
Penkala, Maria. European porcelain;
[2d ed.] Rutland, Vt., C. E. Tuttle
Co. [1968] 256 p. [12.50]
738.2/094 68-19604
NK4230 .P4 1968 MRR Alc.

PORCELAIN, BRITISH.
Godden, Geoffrey A. An illustrated
encyclopedia of British pottery and
porcelain New York, Crown [1966]
xxvi, 390 p. 738.2 66-23065
NK4085 .G64 1966a MRR Alc.

PORCELAIN, BRITISH--HANDBOOKS, MANUALS,
ETC.
Godden, Geoffrey A. The handbook of
British pottery and porcelain marks
London, Jenkins, 1968. 197 p. [25/-
] 738.0278 68-112982
NK4085 .G635 MRR Alc.

PORCELAIN, ENGLISH--DICTIONARIES.
Mankowitz, Wolf. The concise
encyclopedia of English pottery and
porcelain, New York, Hawthorn Books
[1957] xv, 312 p. 738 57-6366
NK4085 .M34 MRR Alc.

PORCELAIN, EUROPEAN--DICTIONARIES.
Haggar, Reginald George, The concise
encyclopedia of continental pottery
and porcelain. [1st ed.] New York,
Hawthorn Books [1960] 533 p.
738.37 60-10340
NK4083 .H3 1960 MRR Alc.

PORCELAIN, ORIENTAL.
Chaffers, William, Marks & monograms
on European and oriental pottery and
porcelain. 15th rev. ed. London, W.
Reeves [1965] 2 v. 738.0278 66-
38182
NK4215 .C46 1965 MRR Alc.

PORT ELIZABETH, SOUTH AFRICA --
DIRECTORIES.
Donaldson's Port Elizabeth directory.
Durban, Natal [etc.] A.C. Braby
(Pty.) Ltd. [etc.] 57-24327
DT848.P7 D6 MRR Alc Latest edition

PORTFOLIO
see Investments

PORTINARI, CANDIDO, 1903-
United States. Library of Congress.
Hispanic foundation. Murals by
Candido Portinari in the Hispanic
foundation of the Library of
Congress. Washington [U.S. Govt.
print. off.] 1943. 31, [1] p.
751.73 43-52050
Z663.32 .M8 MRR Alc.

PORTRAIT-PAINTERS, AMERICAN.
Belknap, Waldron Phoenix, American
colonial painting: Cambridge, Mass.,
Belknap Press of Harvard University
Press, 1959. xxi, 377 p. 759.13
59-10313
ND1311 .B39 MRR Alc.

New York Historical Society.
Catalogue of American portraits in
the New York Historical Society. New
Haven : Published by the New York
Historical Society by Yale University
Press, 1974. 2 v. (ix, 964 p.) :
757/.9/0973 74-79974
N7593 .N5 1974 MRR Alc.

Wehle, Harry Brandeis, American
miniatures, 1730-1850; Garden City,
N.Y., Garden City publishing company,
inc. [1937] xxv p., 1 l., 127 p.
757.0873 37-6103
ND1337.US W4 1937 MRR Alc.

PORTRAIT PAINTING, AMERICAN--HISTORY.
Belknap, Waldron Phoenix, American
colonial painting: Cambridge, Mass.,
Belknap Press of Harvard University
Press, 1959. xxi, 377 p. 759.13
59-10313
ND1311 .B39 MRR Alc.

PORTRAITS.
Berühmte Köpfe; 3200 Männer und
Frauen im Bild. [1. Aufl.
Gütersloh] C. Bertelsmann [1959]
413 p. 920 60-26257
N7575 .B47 MRR Alc.

The McGraw-Hill encyclopedia of world
biography; New York, McGraw-Hill
[1973] 12 v. 920/.02 70-37402
CT103 .M27 MRR Biog.

Nisenson, Samuel. The dictionary of
1001 famous people; [New York] Lion
Press [1966] 267 p. 920.02/03 920
71-4426
CT107 .N58 1966 MRR Biog.

PORTRAITS--CATALOGS.
A.L.A. portrait index; Washington,
Govt. print. off., 1906. lxxiv p., 1
l., 1600 p., 1 l. 06-35019
N7620 .A2 MRR Alc.

Harvard university. Library. Theatre
collection. Catalogue of dramatic
portraits in the Theatre collection
of the Harvard college library,
Cambridge, Mass., Harvard university
press, 1930- v. 927.92 30-
13380
PN2205 .H35 MRR Alc.

National Portrait Gallery,
Washington, D.C. Portraits of the
American stage, 1771-1971;
Washington, Smithsonian Institution
Press; [for sale by the Supt. of
Docs., U.S. Govt. Print. Off.] 1971.
203 p. [$4.50] 792/.0973 75-
170284
PN1583.A2 N3 MRR Biog.

Singer, Hans Wolfgang, Neuer
bildniskatalog. Leipzig, K. W.
Hiersemann, 1937-38. 5 v. 757.0838
ac 37-1659
N7575 .S56 MRR Alc.

United States. Library of Congress.
Prints and photographs division.
Catalog of the Gardiner Greene
Hubbard collection of engravings,
presented to the Library of Congress
by Mrs. Gardiner Greene Hubbard.
Washington, Govt. print. off., 1905.
xxiii, 517 p. 05-20002
Z663.39 .C28 MRR Alc.

PORTRAITS--INDEXES.
A.L.A. portrait index; Washington,
Govt. print. off., 1906. lxxiv p., 1
l., 1600 p., 1 l. 06-35019
N7620 .A2 MRR Alc.

Belknap, Sara (Yancey) Guide to the
musical arts; New York, Scarecrow
Press, 1957. 1 v. (unpaged) 016.78
57-6631
ML113 .B37 MRR Alc.

PORTRAITS--NEW YORK (CITY)--CATALOGS.
New York Historical Society.
Catalogue of American portraits in
the New York Historical Society. New
Haven : Published by the New York
Historical Society by Yale University
Press, 1974. 2 v. (ix, 964 p.) :
757/.9/0973 74-79974
N7593 .N5 1974 MRR Alc.

PORTRAITS--UNITED STATES--INDEXES.
Lee, Cuthbert. Portrait register.
[Asheville, N.C.] Biltmore Press
[1968- v. 757/.016 73-3014
N7620 .L4 MRR Alc.

PORTRAITS, AMERICAN.
Cirker, Hayward. Dictionary of
American portraits. New York, Dover
Publications [1967] xlv, 756 p.
(chiefly ports.) 704.9/42/0973 66-
30514
N7593 .C53 MRR Alc.

PORTRAITS, AMERICAN--CATALOGS.
New York Historical Society.
Catalogue of American portraits in
the New York Historical Society. New
Haven : Published by the New York
Historical Society by Yale University
Press, 1974. 2 v. (ix, 964 p.) :
757/.9/0973 74-79974
N7593 .N5 1974 MRR Alc.

PORTS
see Harbors

PORTSMOUTH, ENG.--DIRECTORIES.
Kelly's directory of Portsmouth and
Southsea. Kingston upon Thames,
Surrey [etc.] Kelly's Directories
Limited [etc.] 53-28830
DA690.P8 K4 MRR Alc Latest edition

PORTSMOUTH, VA.--HARBOR.
Hampton Roads Maritime Association,
Norfolk, Va. The ports of Greater
Hampton Roads annual. 1925-
Norfolk, Va. 28-31191
HE554.H3 A25 MRR Alc Latest
edition

PORTUGAL--BIBLIOGRAPHY.
Dorn, Georgette M. Latin America,
Spain, and Portugal; an annotated
bibliography of paperback books.
Washington, Library of Congress,
1971. 180 p. [$0.75] 016.918 71-
37945
Z663.32 .A5 no. 32 MRR Alc.

Hispanic Foundation bibliographical
series. no. 1- 1942- Washington,
Library of Congress, Reference Dept.
42-38547
Z663.32 .A5 MRR Alc   MRR Alc Full
set

PORTUGAL--BIOGRAPHY.
Verbo; enciclopedia luso-brasileira
de cultura. Lisboa, Editorial Verbo
[1963- v. 65-47647
AE37 .V4 MRR Alc.

PORTUGAL--CIVILIZATION--BIBLIOGRAPHY--
CATALOGS.
Hispanic Society of America. Library.
Catalogue of the library. Boston,
G. K. Hall, 1962. 10 v. (10048 p.)
62-52682
Z881 .N639 MRR Alc (Dk33)

PORTUGAL--COLONIES--COMMERCE--
DIRECTORIES.
Anuario comercial de Portugal.
Lisboa. 380.1/025/469 07-21409
DP513 .A5 MRR Alc Latest edition

PORTUGAL--COLONIES--DIRECTORIES.
Anuario do ultramar portugues.
[Lisboa] Empresa Nacional de
Publicidade [etc.] 42-29
Began publication 1935?
JV4201 .A6 MRR Alc Latest edition

PORTUGAL--COMMERCE--DIRECTORIES.
Anuario comercial de Portugal.
Lisboa. 380.1/025/469 07-21409
DP513 .A5 MRR Alc Latest edition

Anuario comercial iberoamericano.
[Madrid] OFICE. 380.1/025 74-644606

HF3683 .A48 MRR Alc Latest edition

Dun and Bradstreet, inc.
International market guide; Portugal.
New York. 380.1/025/469 72-621021

HC391 .D84 MRR Alc Latest edition

Export directory of Portugal. 1960-
Lisbon. 67-4908
HF3693 .E9 MRR Alc Latest edition

Guia dos correios, telégrafos e
telefones Lisboa, Grafica Santelmo.
383.058 44-33738
HE7123 .G8 MRR Alc Latest edition

Spanish Lusitanian American trade
directory. 1st- ed.; 1961/62-
Madrid. 63-34152
HF54.S7 S6 MRR Alc Latest edition

PORTUGAL--DESCRIPTION AND TRAVEL--1951-
Pillement, Georges, Unknown
Portugal; London, Johnson, 1967.
248 p. [35/-] 914.69/04/4 67-
81550
DP526 .P5313 MRR Alc.

PORTUGAL--DESCRIPTION AND TRAVEL--1951-
--GUIDE-BOOKS.
Fodor's Portugal. 1969- New York,
D. McKay. 914.69/04/4 72-626459
DP516 .P57 MRR Alc Latest edition

PORTUGAL--DESCRIPTION AND TRAVEL--GUIDE-
BOOKS.
Warne, Osmund Hornby, Portugal. 2d
ed.] Geneva, Paris [etc.] Nagel
Publishers [1968] viii, 229 p.
[6.95] 914.69/04/4 77-432687
DP516 .W3 1968 MRR Alc.

PORTUGAL--DIRECTORIES.
Guia dos correios, telégrafos e
telefones Lisboa, Grafica Santelmo.
383.058 44-33738
HE7123 .G8 MRR Alc Latest edition

PORTUGAL--GAZETTEERS.
United States. Office of Geography.
Portugal and the Cape Verde Islands;
official standard names approved by
the United States Board on Geographic
Names. Washington, U.S. Govt. Print.
Off., 1961. v, 321 p. 914.69 61-
61738
DP514 .U6 MRR Alc.

PORTUGAL--HISTORY.
Marques, Antonio Henrique R. de
Oliveira. History of Portugal New
York, Columbia University Press,
1972. 2 v. [$12.50 (v. 1) $15.00
(v. 2)] 946.9 77-184748
DP538 .M37 MRR Alc.

PORTUGAL--INDUSTRIES--DIRECTORIES.
Dun and Bradstreet, inc.
International market guide; Portugal.
New York. 380.1/025/469 72-621021

HC391 .D84 MRR Alc Latest edition

PORTUGAL--MANUFACTURES--DIRECTORIES.
Export directory of Portugal. 1960-
Lisbon. 67-4908
HF3693 .E9 MRR Alc Latest edition

PORTUGAL--STATISTICS.
Portugal. Instituto Nacional de
Estatistica. Anuario estatistico.
1875- Lisboa. 13-12678
HA1571 .A285 MRR Alc Latest
edition

PORTUGUESE LANGUAGE--DICTIONARIES.
Figueiredo, Candido de, Novo
dicionario da lingua portuguesa,
6. ed., actualizada na grafia e
copiosamente ampliada ... Lisboa,
Livraria Bertrand [194-] 2 v.
469.3 47-36338
PC5327 .F514 MRR Alc.

PORTUGUESE LANGUAGE-- (Cont.)
Lima, Hildebrando de, Pequeno
dicionario brasileiro da lingua
portuguesa. 11. ed. 2. impr.
supervisionada e consideravelmente
aum. Rio de Janeiro, Ed.
Civilizacao Brasileira, 1967. 3
v. (xxxvi, 1301 p.) 469.3 68-93713
    PC5327 .L5 1967b MRR Alc.

Machado, Aires da Mata, Dicionario
didatico e popular da lingua
portuguesa 2. ed. Sao Paulo, Ed.
Brasiliense, 1968. xliii, 1123 p.
[16.00] 71-384622
    PC5327 .M3 1968 MRR Alc.

Moraes e Silva, Antonio de, Grande
dicionario da lingua portuguesa.
10. ed. rev., corrigida, muito
aumentada e actualizada [Lisboa]
Editorial Confluencia [1949-59] 12
v. 469.3 50-26313
    PC5327 .M733 MRR Alc.

**PORTUGUESE LANGUAGE--DICTIONARIES--
ENGLISH.**
Grande dictionario portugues_
ingles, ingles-portugues. Sao
Paulo, Li-Bra [1968] 4 v. 79-
357089
    PC5333 .G7 MRR Alc.

Houaiss, Antonio, ed. The new
Appleton dictionary of the English
and Portuguese languages. New York,
Appleton-Century-Crofts, 1964. xx,
636, 665 p. 469.32 64-25814
    PC5333 .H6 MRR Ref Desk.

The New Barsa dictionary of the
English and Portuguese languages.
New York, Appleton-Century-Crofts,
1967. 2 v. 469.3/2 67-8024
    PC5333 .N4 1967 MRR Alc.

Novo Michaelis, dicionario
ilustrado. Sao Paulo, Edicoes
Melhoramentos [c1958- 2 v. 59-
39106
    PC5333 .N6 1958 MRR Alc.

**PORTUGUESE LANGUAGE--DICTIONARIES--
POLYGLOT.**
Byecken, Francisco J. Vocabulario
tecnico portugues-ingles-frances-
alemao. 4. ed. rev. [Sao Paulo]
Edicoes Melhoramentos [1961] 600
p. 603 62-3680
    T10 .B82 1961 MRR Alc.

Elsevier's automobile dictionary in
eight languages: Amsterdam, New
York, Elsevier Pub. Co.; [distributed
by Van Nostrand, Princeton, N.J.]
1960. 946 p. 628.203 59-8946
    TL9 .E43 MRR Alc.

Elsevier's dictionary of aeronautics
in six languages: Amsterdam, New
York, Elsevier Pub. Co., 1964. 842
p. 628.1303 63-22063
    TL509 .E4 MRR Alc.

Elsevier's dictionary of criminal
science, in eight languages:
Amsterdam, New York, Elsevier Pub.
Co.; [distributed by Van Nostrand,
Princeton, N.J.] 1960. xv, 1460 p.
364.03 59-12582
    HV6017 .E4 MRR Alc.

Inter-American Statistical Institute.
Statistical vocabulary. 2d ed.
Washington, Pan American Union, 1960.
xi, 83 p. 310.3 pa 60-56
    HA17 .I6 1960 MRR Alc.

International Chamber of Commerce.
Dictionary of advertising and
distribution, Basel, Verlag fur
Recht und Gesellschaft, 1954. 1 v.
(unpaged) 659.103 54-24644
    HF5803 .I58 1954 MRR Alc.

International Commission on Large
Dams. Dictionnaire technique des
barrages. 2. ed. [Paris, 1960?]
380 p. 627.803 61-805
    TC540 .I45 1960 MRR Alc.

International insurance dictionary:
[n.p., European Conference of
Insurance Supervisory Services, 1959]
xxxi, 1083 p. 368.03 61-35675
    HG8025 .I5 MRR Alc.

Jacks, Graham Vernon. Multilingual
vocabulary of soil science. [2d ed.,
rev. Rome] Land & Water Division,
Food and Agriculture Organization of
the United Nations [1960] xxiii, 428
p. 631.403 60-50105
    S591 .J26 1960 MRR Alc.

PORTUGUESE LANGUAGE--HISTORY.
Entwistle, William James, The
Spanish language, [2d ed.] London,
Faber & Faber [1962] vi, 367 p.
460 63-6431
    PC4075 .E5 1962 MRR Alc.

**PORTUGUESE LANGUAGE--SYNONYMS AND
ANTONYMS.**
Fernandes, Francisco. Dicionario de
sinonimos, e antonimos da lingua
portuguesa. 2. ed. 8. imp. Porto
Alegre, Ed. Globo [1967] 823 p.
[NCr$23.00] 469.31 68-117580
    PC5315 .F47 1967 MRR Alc.

**PORTUGUESE LITERATURE--20TH CENTURY--
PHONOTAPE CATALOGS.**
United States. Library of Congress.
Latin American, Portuguese, and
Spanish Division. The Archive of
Hispanic Literature on Tape;
Washington, Library of Congress; [for
sale by the Supt. of Docs., U.S.
Govt. Print. Off.] 1974. xii, 516 p.
016.86/008 73-19812
    Z663.32 .A7 MRR Alc.

**PORTUGUESE LITERATURE--HISTORY AND
CRITICISM.**
Bell, Aubrey Fitz Gerald, Portuguese
literature, Oxford, The Clarendon
press, 1922. 375, [1] p. 22-12776
    PQ9011 .B4 MRR Alc.

**PORTUGUESE LITERATURE--TRANSLATIONS
FROM ENGLISH--BIBLIOGRAPHY.**
United States. Library of Congress.
Hispanic Foundation. A provisional
bibliography of United States books
translated into Portuguese.
Washington, Library of Congress,
Reference Dept., 1957. vii, 182 p.
015.73 57-60009
    Z663.32 .A5 no. 2 MRR Alc.

United States. Library of Congress.
Hispanic Foundation. Spanish and
Portuguese translations of United
States books, 1955-1962; Washington,
Library of Congress, 1963. xv, 506
p. 63-60091
    Z663.32 .A5 no. 8 MRR Alc.

PORTUGUESE PHILOLOGY--BIBLIOGRAPHY.
Chatham, James R., Dissertations in
Hispanic languages and literatures;
[Lexington] University Press of
Kentucky [1970] xiv, 120 p. [12.50]
016.46 70-80093
    Z2695 .A2C46 MRR Alc.

POST EXCHANGES--STATISTICS.
Military market facts. [Washington]
Army Times Pub. Co. 65-5288
    UC263 .M46 MRR Alc Latest edition

POST-IMPRESSIONISM (ART)
see also Expressionism (Art)

Bowness, Alan, ed. Impressionists
and post-impressionists. New York,
F. Watts [1965] 286 p. 709.034 65-
10269
    ND1265 .B67 MRR Alc.

POSTAGE-STAMPS.
Hertsch, Max. Famous stamps of the
world. Berne, Hallwag [1968] 8 p.
769/.56 68-116672
    HE6182 .H413 MRR Alc.

Thorsen, Harry D., All nations stamp
finder and dictionary. Chicago, H.
Cohn, c1952] 32 p. 383.22 53-
17589
    HE6215 .T53 MRR Alc.

POSTAGE-STAMPS--BIOGRAPHY.
Stiles, Kent B. Postal saints and
sinners; Brooklyn, T. Gaus' Sons,
1964. ix, 295 p. 383.22 64-7712
    HE6215 .S7 MRR Alc.

POSTAGE-STAMPS--CATALOGS.
A F A Europa frimærkekatalog.
Aarhus, Aarhus frimærkehandel. 51-
19739
    HE6224 .A13 MRR Alc Latest edition

Minkus new world-wide postage stamp
catalog. New York, Minkus
Publications. 338.4/3769/56 72-
626485
    HE6224 .N4 MRR Alc Latest edition

Scott Publishing Co. Scott's
standard postage stamp catalogue.
New York. 380.1/45/76956 72-623819
    HE6226 .S48 MRR Alc Latest edition

Stanley Gibbons priced postage stamp
catalogue. London [etc.] S. Gibbons
[etc.] 08-21091
    HE6226 .G5 MRR Alc Latest edition

Stanley Gibbons stamps of the world.
London, Stanley Gibbons Ltd. 769/.56
72-627259
    HE6224 .G5 MRR Alc Latest edition

Yvert et compagnie, publishers,
Amiens. Catalogue de timbres-poste.
Amiens, Yvert et Tellier [etc.]
383.22085 18-17889
    Publication began with issue for
1877?
    HE6226 .Y8 MRR Alc Latest edition

**POSTAGE-STAMPS--COLLECTORS AND
COLLECTING.**
Cabeen, Richard McP. Standard
handbook of stamp collecting. Rev.
New York, T. Y. Crowell Co. [1965]
xii, 628 p. 769.56075 65-26492
    HE6215 .C2 1965 MRR Alc.

Grossman, Samuel. The stamp
collector's handbook; New York,
Longacre Pub. Co. [1967] 192 p.
383.22 57-9037
    HE6215 .G84 MRR Alc.

Scott's new handbook for
philatelists. New York, Simon and
Schuster [1967] 192 p. 769/.56 67-
19818
    HE6215 .S33 MRR Alc.

Stiles, Kent B. Postal saints and
sinners; Brooklyn, T. Gaus' Sons,
1964. ix, 295 p. 383.22 64-7712
    HE6215 .S7 MRR Alc.

Thorp, Prescott Holden. The complete
guide to stamp collecting. New York,
Minkus Publications [1965] xiii, 198
p. 769.56 66-7043
    HE6213 .T48 1965 MRR Alc.

**POSTAGE-STAMPS--COLLECTORS AND
COLLECTING--EUROPE--HANDBOOKS, MANUALS,
ETC.**
Allen, Jon L. Stamp collector's
guide to Europe New York, Arco
[1974] ix, 309 p. 769/.56/075 73-
78494
    HE6215 .A45 MRR Alc.

POSTAGE-STAMPS--DEALERS--DIRECTORIES.
International Federation of Stamp
Dealers' Associations. Handbook.
1956- Paris. 59-25520
    HE6194 .I5 MRR Alc Latest edition

International stamp dealers'
directory. 1st- ed.; 1948-
London, Harris Publications.
383.22058 51-17246
    HE6209 .I575 MRR Alc Latest
edition

POSTAGE-STAMPS--DEALERS--SOCIETIES, ETC.
International Federation of Stamp
Dealers' Associations. Handbook.
1956- Paris. 59-25520
    HE6194 .I5 MRR Alc Latest edition

POSTAGE-STAMPS--DICTIONARIES.
Sutton, Richard John. The stamp
collector's encyclopaedia; 6th ed.
London, S. Paul, 1966. 372 p. [42/-
] 769.5603 66-74938
    HE6196 .S85 1966a MRR Alc.

Thorsen, Harry D., All nations stamp
finder and dictionary. Chicago, H.
Cohn, c1952] 32 p. 383.22 53-
17589
    HE6215 .T53 MRR Alc.

Tuya, Oscar C. de, ed. Tuya
international philatelic dictionary.
Habana, Cuba [1957?] xiv, 155 p.
383.2203 58-35196
    HE6196 .T8 MRR Alc.

POSTAGE-STAMPS--HISTORY.
Schenk, Gustav, The romance of the
postage stamp. Garden City, N.Y.,
Doubleday [1962] 231 p. 383.209
62-11466
    HE6182 .S313 MRR Alc.

POSTAGE-STAMPS--TOPICS--PORTRAITS.
Stiles, Kent B. Postal saints and
sinners; Brooklyn, T. Gaus' Sons,
1964. ix, 295 p. 383.22 64-7712
    HE6215 .S7 MRR Alc.

POSTAGE-STAMPS--TOPICS--SPORTS.
Bateman, Robert. The encyclopedia of
sports stamps, London, Paul, 1969.
[8], 173 p. [35/-] 769/.564 70-
402231
    HE6183 .B32 MRR Alc.

POSTAGE-STAMPS--CANADA--CATALOGS.
Holmes, Laurence Sealewyn, ed.
Specialized philatelic catalogue of
Canada and British North America,
9th ed. Toronto, Ryerson Press,
1960. 410 p. 383.22971 60-4895
    HE6185.C2 H58 MRR Alc.

**POSTAGE-STAMPS--COMMONWEALTH OF NATIONS--
CATALOGS.**
Stanley Gibbons priced postage stamp
catalogue. London [etc.] S. Gibbons
[etc.] 08-21091
    HE6226 .G5 MRR Alc Latest edition

**POSTAGE-STAMPS--CONFEDERATE STATES OF
AMERICA.**
Dietz Confederate States catalog and
handbook of the postage stamps and
envelopes of the Confederate States
of America. 1931- Richmond, Dietz
Press [etc.] 31-20545
    HE6185.U6 D5 MRR Alc Latest
edition

POSTAGE-STAMPS--CONFEDERATE (Cont.)
Fuller, Claud E., Confederate
currency and stamps, 1861-1865;
[Nashville, Published by the
Parthenon Press under the auspices of
the Tennessee Division, United
Daughters of the Confederacy, c1949]
236 p.   332.53   50-449
HG526 .F8 MRR Alc.

POSTAGE-STAMPS--EUROPE.
A F A Europa frimerkekatalog.
Aarhus, Aarhus frimærkehandel. 51-
1973§
HE6224 .A13 MRR Alc Latest edition

POSTAGE-STAMPS--EUROPE--CATALOGS.
Michel Europa-Katalog. München,
Schwaneberger Verlag GMBH 74-642464

HE6226 .M6 MRR Alc Latest edition

Stanley Gibbons priced postage stamp
catalogue. London [etc.] S. Gibbons
[etc.]   08-21091
HE6226 .G5 MRR Alc Latest edition

POSTAGE-STAMPS--EUROPE--HANDBOOKS,
MANUALS, ETC.
Allen, Jon L. Stamp collector's
guide to Europe New York, Arco
[1974]   ix, 309 p.   769/.56/075 73-
78494
HE6215 .A45 MRR Alc.

POSTAGE-STAMPS--UNITED STATES.
Thorp, Prescott Holden. Catalogue of
the 20th century stamped envelopes
and wrappers of the United States,
1st ed. Netcong, N.J. [1968] 205 p.
769/.569/73 68-2697
HE6185.U6 T46 MRR Alc.

POSTAGE-STAMPS--UNITED STATES--CATALOGS.
Bartels, John Murray, Thorp-Bartels
Catalogue of the stamped envelopes
and wrappers of the United States;
6th (Century) ed. Netcong, N.J.; H.
Thorp [1954] 597 p.   383.22 54-
37552
HE6185.U6 B32 1954 MRR Alc.

Durland standard plate number
catalog; Boston [etc.] Sterling
Stamp Co. [etc.]   55-212466
HE6230 .D8 MRR Alc Latest editions

Minkus new American stamp catalog.
New York, Minkus Publications.
338.4/3769/56873 72-626482
HE6185.U5 N4 MRR Alc Latest
edition

Scott's specialized catalogue of
United States stamps. 1st- ed.;
1923- New York, Scott Publications.
35-6933
HE6185.U5 S3 MRR Ref Desk latest
edition

United States Postal Service.
Postage stamps of the United States.
1970- Washington, U.S. Govt. Print.
Off.   383/.08 s [769/.569/73] 78-
617343
HE6311.A312 HE6185.U5 MRR Ref Desk
Latest edition

POSTAGE-STAMPS--UNITED STATES--HISTORY.
Rothert, Matt. A guide book of
United States fractional currency;
Racine, Wis., Whitman Pub. Co. [1963]
81 p.   769.5 63-23600
HG613 .R6 MRR Alc.

POSTAL CARDS.
Burdick, Jefferson R., ed. Pioneer
post cards; Franklin Square, N.Y.,
Nostalgia Press [1964] 200 p.
741.68 64-55184
NC1872 .B83 1964 MRR Alc.

POSTAL SERVICE--DIRECTORIES.
Union postale universelle.
Nomenclature internationale des
bureaux de poste. Edition 1968.
Berne, 1968. 3 v. (2101 p.)
383/.025 68-115303
HE6031 .U59 MRR Alc.

POSTAL SERVICE--RATES.
Dun & Bradstreet exporters'
encyclopaedia. New York, Dun and
Bradstreet International. 382/.6 72-
622175
HF3011 .E9 MRR Alc Latest edition

The Exporters year book - export
data. 55th- 1971- London, Benn
Bros. 382/.6/05 72-622714
HF53 .S9 MRR Alc Latest edition

Leonard's guide, parcel post,
express, freight rates and routing.
1st- ed.; 1923- Northbrook, Ill.
[etc.] G. R. Leonard. 383.1 23-6413

HE9.U5 L46 MRR Alc Latest edition

POSTAL SERVICE--EUROPE--HANDBOOKS,
MANUALS, ETC.
Allen, Jon L. Stamp collector's
guide to Europe New York, Arco
[1974] ix, 309 p.   769/.56/075 73-
78494
HE6215 .A45 MRR Alc.

POSTAL SERVICE--PORTUGAL.
Guia dos correios, telegrafos e
telefones Lisboa, Gráfica Santelmo.
383.058 44-33738
HE7123 .G8 MRR Alc Latest edition

POSTAL SERVICE--SWEDEN--GUIDES.
Posthandboken. Malmö. 52-43821
Began publication with 1913/14
issue.
HE7253 .P6 MRR Alc Latest edition

POSTAL SERVICE--UNITED STATES--
DIRECTORIES.
Bullinger's postal and shippers guide
for the United States and Canada and
Newfoundland. Westwood, N.J. [etc.]
Bullinger's Guides, inc. [etc.] 02-
3726
HE9.U5 B83 MRR Alc Latest edition

Directory of post offices (with Zip
codes) 1970- Washington, United
States Postal Service [For sale by
the Supt. of Docs., U.S. Govt. Print.
Off.] 383/.08 s 383/.025/73 73-
644964
HE6311 .A312 subser HD6951 MRR Ref
Desk Latest edition / MRR Ref
Desk Latest edition

Leonard's guide, parcel post,
express, freight rates and routing.
1st- ed.; 1923- Northbrook, Ill.
[etc.] G. R. Leonard. 383.1 23-6413

HE9.U5 L46 MRR Alc Latest edition

POSTAL SERVICE--UNITED STATES--HISTORY.
Fuller, Wayne Edison, The American
mail; Chicago, University of Chicago
Press [1972] xi, 378 p.   383/.49/73
72-78254
HE6371 .F84 MRR alc.

POSTERS--HISTORY.
Barnicoat, John, A concise history
of posters; 1870-1970. New York, H.
N. Abrams [1972] 288 p.   741.67 75-
173889
NC1810 .B3 1972b MRR Alc.

POSTMARKS--UNITED STATES.
Simpson, Tracy Whittelsey. U.S.
postal markings 1851-61 and related
mail services, Berkeley, Calif.
[1959] 177 p.   383.22973 59-42054

HE6185.U5 S5 MRR Alc.

POTOMAC RIVER.
Gutheim, Frederick Albert, The
Potomac; New York, Rinehart [1949]
436 p.   975.49 49-11856
F187.P8 G8 MRR Alc.

POTTERS.
Boger, Louise Ade. The dictionary of
world pottery and porcelain. New
York, Scribner [1971] 533 p.
[$22.50] 738/.03 72-123829
NK3770 .B64 MRR Alc.

Ray, Marcia. Collectible ceramics;
New York, Crown Publishers [1974]
256 p.   [$9.95] 738/.03 73-92104
NK3770 .R38 MRR Alc.

POTTERS--ENGLAND.
Bunt, Cyril George Edward, British
potters & pottery today. Leigh-on-
Sea, Eng., F. Lewis [1956] 78 p.
738 56-3257
NK4085 .B858 MRR Alc.

POTTERS--EUROPE.
Honey, William Bowyer, European
ceramic art, London, Faber and Faber
[1949-52] 2 v.   738 49-6149
NK4083 .H6 MRR Alc.

POTTERS--UNITED STATES.
Barber, Edwin Atlee, Marks of
American potters. Southampton, N.Y.,
Cracker Barrel Press [1971?] 174 p.
[$3.00] 738/.027/8 70-21077
NK4215 .B3 1971 MRR Alc.

Ramsay, John, American potters and
pottery, [Boston] Hale, Cushman &
Flint [c1939] xx, 304 p.   738 39-
18186
NK4005 .R3 MRR Alc.

POTTERY--COLLECTORS AND COLLECTING--
UNITED STATES.
Ray, Marcia. Collectible ceramics;
New York, Crown Publishers [1974]
256 p.   [$9.95] 738/.03 73-92104
NK3770 .R38 MRR Alc.

POTTERY--DICTIONARIES.
Barber, Edwin Atlee, The ceramic
collector's glossary. New York, Da
Capo Press, 1967. 119 p.   738/.03
67-27448
NK3770 .B3 1967 MRR Alc.

Boger, Louise Ade. The dictionary of
world pottery and porcelain. New
York, Scribner [1971] 533 p.
[$22.50] 738/.03 72-123829
NK3770 .B64 MRR Alc.

Honey, William Bowyer, European
ceramic art, London, Faber and Faber
[1949-52] 2 v.   738 49-6149
NK4083 .H6 MRR Alc.

Ray, Marcia. Collectible ceramics;
New York, Crown Publishers [1974]
256 p.   [$9.95] 738/.03 73-92104
NK3770 .R38 MRR Alc.

Savage, George, An illustrated
dictionary of ceramics; New York,
Van Nostrand Reinhold Co. [1974] 319
p.   [$18.95] 738/.03 73-17999
NK3770 .S38 1974b MRR Alc.

Searle, Alfred Broadhead, An
encyclopaedia of the ceramic
industries, London, E. Benn,
limited, 1929-30. 3 v.   666.03 30-
8476
TP788 .S4 MRR Alc.

POTTERY--HISTORY.
Chaffers, William, Marks & monograms
on European and oriental pottery and
porcelain. 15th rev. ed. London, W.
Reeves [1965] 2 v.   738.0278 66-
38182
NK4215 .C46 1965 MRR Alc.

POTTERY--MARKS.
Barber, Edwin Atlee, Marks of
American potters. Southampton, N.Y.,
Cracker Barrel Press [1971?] 174 p.
[$3.00] 738/.027/8 70-21077
NK4215 .B3 1971 MRR Alc.

[Burton, William] Collector's
handbook to marks on porcelain and
pottery. Greens Farms, Conn., Modern
Books and Crafts [1974] [10], 213 p.
[$10.00] 738.2/02/78 74-180368
NK4215 .B8 1974 MRR Alc.

Chaffers, William, Marks & monograms
on European and oriental pottery and
porcelain. 15th rev. ed. London, W.
Reeves [1965] 2 v.   738.0278 66-
38182
NK4215 .C46 1965 MRR Alc.

Cushion, John Patrick. Handbook of
pottery and porcelain marks, [3d
rev. ed.] London, Faber and Faber
[1965] 477 p.   66-1611
NK4215 .C8 1965 MRR Alc.

Cushion, John Patrick. Pocket book
of English ceramic marks London,
Faber and Faber [1959] 154 p.
738.880942 59-3962
NK4085 .C8 MRR Alc.

Godden, Geoffrey A. The handbook of
British pottery and porcelain marks
London, Jenkins, 1968. 197 p.   [25/-
] 738.0278 68-112982
NK4085 .G635 MRR Alc.

Hughes, George Bernard, The
collector's encyclopaedia of English
ceramics London, Lutterworth Press
[1956] 172 p.   738 57-743
NK4085 .H83 MRR Alc.

Kovel, Ralph M. Dictionary of marks:
pottery and porcelain, New York,
Crown Publishers [1953] x, 278 p.
738.88 53-5247
NK4215 .K68 MRR Alc.

Macdonald-Taylor, Margaret Stephens,
ed. A dictionary of marks:
metalwork, furniture, ceramics.
London, Connoisseur [c1962] 318 p.
63-1876
NK7210 .M25 1962a MRR Alc.

Penkala, Maria. European pottery;
[2d ed.] Rutland, Vt., C. E. Tuttle
Co. [1969, c1968] 472 p.   [15.00]
738/.027/8 69-19602
NK4215 .P4 MRR Alc.

POTTERY--ENGLAND.
Bunt, Cyril George Edward, British
potters & pottery today. Leigh-on-
Sea, Eng., F. Lewis [1956] 78 p.
738 56-3257
NK4085 .B858 MRR Alc.

POTTERY--ENGLAND--CATALOGS.
Laidacker, Samuel H., The standard
catalogue of Anglo-American china.
1938 ed. Scranton, Pa. [1938]-51. 2
v.   738.3 38-5740
NK4087.S6 L25 MRR Alc.

POTTERY--EUROPE.
Honey, William Bowyer, European
ceramic art, London, Faber and Faber
[1949-52] 2 v.   738 49-6149
NK4083 .H6 MRR Alc.

POTTERY--EUROPE--HISTORY.
Penkala, Maria. European pottery;
[2d ed.] Rutland, Vt., C. E. Tuttle
Co. [1969, c1968] 472 p.   [15.00]
738/.027/8 69-19602
NK4215 .P4 MRR Alc.

POTTERY--GREAT BRITAIN--DIRECTORIES.
Pottery gazette and glass trade
review reference book and directory.
London, S. Greenwood. 666.6058
666.3058*   47-41231
     TP785 .P83 MRR Alc Latest edition

POTTERY--UNITED STATES.
Ramsay, John. American potters and
pottery. [Boston] Hale, Cushman &
Flint [c1939] xx, 304 p.   738 39-
18186
     NK4005 .R3 MRR Alc.

POTTERY--UNITED STATES--CATALOGS.
Laidacker, Samuel H. The standard
catalogue of Anglo-American china.
1938 ed. Scranton, Pa. [1938]--51. 2
v.   738.3 38-5740
     NK4087.S6 L25 MRR Alc.

POTTERY, AMERICAN.
Guilland, Harold F. Early American
folk pottery [1st ed.]
Philadelphia, Chilton Book Co. [1971]
xii, 321 p.   738.3/0973 70-159513

     NK4006 .G8 1971 MRR Alc.

POTTERY, BRITISH.
Cushion, John Patrick. Pocket book
of English ceramic marks London,
Faber and Faber [1959] 154 p.
738.880942 59-3962
     NK4085 .C8 MRR Alc.

Godden, Geoffrey A. An illustrated
encyclopedia of British pottery and
porcelain New York, Crown [1966]
xxvi, 390 p.   738.2 66-23065
     NK4085 .G64 1966a MRR Alc.

POTTERY, BRITISH--HANDBOOKS, MANUALS,
ETC.
Godden, Geoffrey A. The handbook of
British pottery and porcelain marks
London, Jenkins, 1968. 197 p. [25/-
] 738.0278 68-112982
     NK4085 .G635 MRR Alc.

POTTERY, ENGLISH.
Larsen, Ellouise Baker. American
historical views on Staffordshire
china. New rev. and enl. ed. Garden
City, N.Y., Doubleday, 1950. xxx,
317 p.   738.27 50-11741
     NK4087.S6 L3 1950 MRR Alc.

POTTERY, ENGLISH--DICTIONARIES.
Hughes, George Bernard. The
collector's encyclopaedia of English
ceramics London, Lutterworth Press
[1956] 172 p.   738 57-743
     NK4085 .H83 MRR Alc.

Mankowitz, Wolf. The concise
encyclopedia of English pottery and
porcelain, New York, Hawthorn Books
[1957] xv, 312 p.   738 57-6366
     NK4085 .M34 MRR Alc.

POTTERY, EUROPEAN--DICTIONARIES.
Haggar, Reginald George, The concise
encyclopedia of continental pottery
and porcelain. [1st ed.] New York,
Hawthorn Books [1960] 533 p.
738.37 60-10340
     NK4083 .H3 1960 MRR Alc.

POTTERY, ORIENTAL.
Chaffers, William, Marks & monograms
on European and oriental pottery and
porcelain. 15th rev. ed. London, W.
Reeves [1965] 2 v.   738.0278 66-
38182
     NK4215 .C46 1965 MRR Alc.

POULTRY INDUSTRY--UNITED STATES.
Who's who in the egg and poultry
industries. Mt. Morris, Ill. [etc.]
Watt Pub. Co. [etc.]   29-14796
     HD9284.U4 W5 MRR Alc Latest
     edition

POVERTY.
see also Poor

Ross, Arthur Max, ed. Employment,
race, and poverty. [1st ed. New
York, Harcourt, Brace & World, 1967]
ix, 598 p.   331.1130973 65-23537
     E185.8 .R6 MRR Alc.

POVERTY--BIBLIOGRAPHY.
Tompkins, Dorothy Louise (Campbell)
Culver. Poverty in the United States
during the sixties: [Berkeley]
Institute of Governmental Studies,
University of California, 1970. ix,
542 p. [$10.00] 016.3625/0973 74-
632910
     Z7165.U5 T62 MRR Alc.

POWEL, MARY EDITH, 1846-1931--
MANUSCRIPTS.
United States. Library of Congress.
Manuscript Division. Dudley Wright
Knox: a register of his papers in the
Library of Congress, Washington,
Library of Congress, 1971. 16 p.
016.359/007/22 70-173823
     Z663.34 .K66 MRR Alc.

POWER, EXECUTIVE
see Executive power

POWER, LEGISLATIVE
see Legislative power

POWER (MECHANICS)
see also Electric power

see also Machinery

POWER (SOCIAL SCIENCES)--BIBLIOGRAPHY.
Leif, Irving P., Community power and
decision-making: Metuchen, N.J.,
Scarecrow Press, 1974. vi, 170 p.
016.30115/5 74-4171
     Z7164.C842 L43 MRR Alc.

POWER RESOURCES.
see also Fuel

POWER RESOURCES--ABSTRACTS--PERIODICALS.
The Energy index. [New York,
Environment Information Center,
Energy Reference Dept.] [$50.00]
333.7 73-89098
     HD9502.U5 E525 MRR Alc Full set /
     Sci RR Full set

POWER RESOURCES--BIBLIOGRAPHY--
PERIODICALS.
The Energy index. [New York,
Environment Information Center,
Energy Reference Dept.] [$50.00]
333.7 73-89098
     HD9502.U5 E525 MRR Alc Full set /
     Sci RR Full set

POWER RESOURCES--INDEXES--PERIODICALS.
The Energy index. [New York,
Environment Information Center,
Energy Reference Dept.] [$50.00]
333.7 73-89098
     HD9502.U5 E525 MRR Alc Full set /
     Sci RR Full set

POWER RESOURCES--STATISTICS.
Darmstadter, Joel, Energy in the
world economy: Baltimore, Published
for Resources for the Future by the
Johns Hopkins Press [1971] x, 876 p.
[$22.50] 333.9 70-155848
     HD9540.4 D37 MRR Alc.

POWER RESOURCES--EUROPE--STATISTICS.
Organization for Economic Cooperation
and Development. Basic statistics of
energy, 1950-1964. Paris, O.E.C.D.
[London, H.M.S.O.] 1966. 363 p.
[24/-] 333.8 66-66031
     HD9555.A4 O7 MRR Alc.

Organization for Economic Cooperation
and Development. Statistics of
energy, 1953-1967. Paris, 1969. 265
p.   333.8 71-459605
     HD9540.4 .O73 1969 MRR Alc.

POWER RESOURCES--JAPAN--STATISTICS.
Organization for Economic Cooperation
and Development. Basic statistics of
energy, 1950-1964. Paris, O.E.C.D.
[London, H.M.S.O.] 1966. 363 p.
[24/-] 333.8 66-66031
     HD9555.A4 O7 MRR Alc.

Organization for Economic Cooperation
and Development. Statistics of
energy, 1953-1967. Paris, 1969. 265
p.   333.8 71-459605
     HD9540.4 .O73 1969 MRR Alc.

POWER RESOURCES--NORTH AMERICA--
STATISTICS.
Organization for Economic Cooperation
and Development. Basic statistics of
energy, 1950-1964. Paris, O.E.C.D.
[London, H.M.S.O.] 1966. 363 p.
[24/-] 333.8 66-66031
     HD9555.A4 O7 MRR Alc.

Organization for Economic Cooperation
and Development. Statistics of
energy, 1953-1967. Paris, 1969. 265
p.   333.8 71-459605
     HD9540.4 .O73 1969 MRR Alc.

POWER RESOURCES--UNITED STATES.
National Petroleum Council. Committee
on U.S. Energy Outlook. U.S. energy
outlook; [Washington] 1972. 381 p.
333.8/2/0923 73-162777
     HD9545 .N33 MRR Alc.

Resources for the Future. Energy in
the American economy, 1850-1975;
Baltimore, Johns Hopkins Press [1960]
xxii, 774 p.   338.272 60-14304
     HD9545 .R45 MRR Alc.

POWER RESOURCES--UNITED STATES--
STATISTICS--PERIODICALS.
The Energy index. [New York,
Environment Information Center,
Energy Reference Dept.] [$50.00]
333.7 73-89098
     HD9502.U5 E525 MRR Alc Full set /
     Sci RR Full set

POWERS, SEPARATION OF
see Separation of powers

PRACTICAL POLITICS
see Politics, Practical

PRAGUE--DESCRIPTION--GUIDE-BOOKS.
Praha; guidebook 2d rev. ed.]
Praha, Sportovni a turisticke
nakladatelstvi, 1960 [c1958] 188 p.
914.371 60-4226
     DB879.P8 P688 1960 MRR Alc.

Svoboda, Alois. Prague: Prague,
Olympia, 1968. 302 p. [28.50] 70-
488831
     DB879.P8 S8913 1968 MRR Alc.

PRAIRIE PROVINCES--BIBLIOGRAPHY.
Peel, Bruce Braden, A bibliography
of the Prairie Provinces to 1953.
[Toronto] University of Toronto Press
[1956] xix, 680 p.   016.9712 56-
2717
     Z1365 .P4 MRR Alc.

PRAYERS.
Aldrich, Donald Bradshaw, ed. The
golden book of prayer; New York,
Dodd, Mead & company, 1941. xvi p.,
2 l., 3-275 p.   264.1 41-26726
     BV245 .A4 MRR Alc.

Bishop, James Alonzo, ed. Go with
God. [1st ed.] New York, McGraw-
Hill [1958] 410 p.   291.3 58-13856

     BL560 .B5 MRR Alc.

PRECANCELS--CANADA--CATALOGS.
Official catalog of Canada
precancels. Winter Park, Fla., G. W.
Noble. 383.22871 60-19904
     HE6185.C2 O35 MRR Alc Latest
     edition

PRECANCELS--UNITED STATES.
The Noble official catalog of bureau
precancels. Findlay, Ohio [etc.] G.
W. Noble [etc.] 383.22 56-31207
     HE6185.U6 M5 MRR Alc Latest
     edition

PRECIEUSES.
Schmidt, Jacob Edward, 1000 elegant
phrases, Springfield, Ill., C. C.
Thomas [1965] x, 223 p.   423.1 65-
12384
     PE1670 .S3 MRR Alc.

PRECIOUS STONES.
Liddicoat, Richard Thomas, Handbook
of gem identification, [8th ed.]
Los Angeles. Gemological Institute of
America [1969] xv, 430 p.   549.1
73-13583
     QE392 .L5 1969 MRR Alc.

Pearl, Richard Maxwell, Gems,
minerals, crystals, and ores; New
York, Golden Press [1967] 320 p.
549 64-14672
     QE392 .P357 1967 MRR Alc.

Smith, George Frederick Herbert,
Gemstones, 14th ed., London,
Chapman and Hall, 1972. xii, 580
[31] p. [£7.50] 549 73-155658
     QE392 .S7 1972 MRR Alc.

PRECIOUS STONES--CATALOGS.
Sinkankas, John. Van Nostrand's
standard catalog of gems, Princeton,
N.J., Van Nostrand [1968] xiii, 286
p.   553/.8 68-19369
     TS752 .S53 1968 MRR Alc.

PRECIOUS STONES--COLLECTORS AND
COLLECTING.
Fay, Gordon S. The rockhound's
manual [1st ed.] New York, Harper &
Row [1972] x, 290 p. [$7.95]
549/.075 77-157080
     QE365 .F22 MRR Alc.

PRECIOUS STONES--COLLECTORS AND
COLLECTING--UNITED STATES.
MacFall, Russell P. Gem hunter's
guide; 4th rev. ed. New York,
Crowell [1969] 279 p. [5.95]
549.9/73 78-81943
     QE392.5.U5 M3 1969 MRR Alc.

PRECIPITATION (METEOROLOGY)--STATISTICS.
Conway, Hobart McKinley, ed. The
weather handbook : Rev. ed. Atlanta
; Conway Research, 1974. 255 p.
[$25.00] 551.6/9/1732 74-187773
     QC982.5 .C6 1974 MRR Alc.

United States. National Oceanic and
Atmospheric Administration. Climates
of the States; [Port Washington,
N.Y., Water Information Center, 1974]
2 v. (975 p.) 551.6/9/73 73-93482

     QC983 .U58 1974 MRR Alc.

World weather records. 1921/30-
Washington. 551.59083 59-65360
     QC982 .W6 MRR Alc Latest edition /
     Sci RR Full set

PRECOCITY
see Gifted children

PREDICTIONS
see Prophecies

PREFABRICATED BUILDINGS
see Buildings, Prefabricated

PREGNANCY.
Boston. Children's Hospital Medical
Center. Pregnancy, birth & the
newborn baby [New York] Delacorte
Press [1972] 474 p. [$10.00] 613
71-175649
RG525 .B645 MRR Alc.

Guttmacher, Alan Frank, Pregnancy,
birth, and family planning; New
York, Viking Press [1973] xv, 365 p.
[$10.00] 612.6/3 72-79006
RG525 .G82 1973 MRR Alc.

Newton, Niles, The family book of
child care. [1st ed.] New York,
Harper [1957] 477 p. 649.1 55-
8058
RG525 .N43 MRR Alc.

PREHISTORIC ANTIQUITIES
see Archaeology

see Man, Prehistoric

PREHISTORIC FAUNA
see Paleontology

PREMIUMS (RETAIL TRADE)--UNITED STATES--
DIRECTORIES.
Directory of premium and incentive
buyers. 1970/71- New York,
Salesman's Guide. [$100.00] 658.8/2
73-645791
HF6146.P7 D57 MRR Alc Latest
edition

PRENATAL CARE.
Guttmacher, Alan Frank, Pregnancy,
birth, and family planning; New
York, Viking Press [1973] xv, 365 p.
[$10.00] 612.6/3 72-79006
RG525 .G82 1973 MRR Alc.

PRERAPHAELITISM--BIBLIOGRAPHY.
Fredeman, William Evan, Pre-
Raphaelitism; a bibliocritical study
Cambridge, Harvard University Press,
1965. xix, 327 p. 016.70942 64-
21242
Z5948.P8 F7 MRR Alc.

PRESBYTERIAN CHURCH--BIOGRAPHY.
Presbyterian Church in the U.S.
Ministerial directory of the
Presbyterian Church, U.S., 1861-1967.
Doraville, Ga., Foote & Davies,
1967. vii, 648 p. 285/.133/02573
68-3645
BX8220 .P7 1967 MRR Biog.

PRESBYTERIAN CHURCH IN THE U.S.--
BIOGRAPHY.
Presbyterian Church in the U.S.
Ministerial directory of the
Presbyterian Church, U.S., 1861-1967.
Doraville, Ga., Foote & Davies,
1967. vii, 648 p. 285/.133/02573
68-3645
BX8220 .P7 1967 MRR Biog.

PRESBYTERIAN CHURCH IN THE U.S.A.--
DICTIONARIES.
Nevin, Alfred, ed. Encyclopaedia of
the Presbyterian church in the United
States of America: including the
northern and southern assemblies.
Philadelphia, Presbyterian
encyclopaedia publishing co., 1884.
viii, 9-1248 p. 10-31801
BX8909 .N4 MRR Alc.

PRESBYTERIAN CHURCH IN THE U.S.A.--
DISCIPLINE.
Presbyterian Church in the U.S.A.
General Assembly. A digest of the
acts and proceedings of the General
Assembly of the Presbyterian Church
in the United States, 1861-1965.
Atlanta, 1966. ix, 489 p. 262.9851
66-5073
BX8956 .A5 1966a MRR Alc.

PRESBYTERIAN CHURCH IN THE UNITED
STATES--YEARBOOKS.
Presbyterian Church in the U.S.
General Assembly. Minutes. 1st-
meeting; 1861- Richmond, Va.,
Presbyterian Committee of
Publication. 09-17948
BX8861.A3 MRR Alc Latest edition

PRESBYTERIAN CHURCH IN THE UNITED
STATES (GENERAL)--HISTORY.
Slosser, Gaius Jackson, ed. They
seek a country; New York, Macmillan,
1955. xvi, 330 p. 285 55-14554
BX8935 .S55 MRR Alc.

PRESCHOOL EDUCATION
see Education, Preschool

PRESCRIPTION PRICING.
Burack, Richard. The new handbook of
prescription drugs: official names,
prices, and sources for patient and
doctor. [Rev. ed.] New York,
Pantheon Books [1970] xiv, 362 p.
[7.95] 615/.1 76-15606
RS91 .B916 1970 MRR Alc.

PRESERVING
see Canning and preserving

PRESIDENTS--INAUGURATION.
Durbin, Louise. Inaugural cavalcade.
New York, Dodd, Mead [1971] xii,
210 p. [$5.50] 394/.4 76-162611
F196 .D87 MRR Alc.

PRESIDENTS--PRESS CONFERENCES.
Stein, Meyer L. When Presidents meet
the press. New York, Messner [1969]
190 p. [3.95] 070.11 70-79701
JK518 .S72 MRR Alc.

PRESIDENTS--UNITED STATES.
Bailey, Thomas Andrew, Presidential
greatness; [1st ed.] New York,
Appleton-Century [1966] xi, 368 p.
973 66-19996
E176.1 .B17 MRR Alc.

Collins, Herbert Ridgeway,
Presidents on wheels. Washington,
Acropolis Books [1971] 224 p.
[$15.00] 629.2/0973 75-146442
TL23 .C597 MRR Alc.

Corwin, Edward Samuel, The
President, office and powers, 1787-
1948; [3d ed., rev.] New York, New
York Univ. Press [1948] xvii, 552 p.
353.03 48-7474
JK516 .C63 1948 MRR Alc.

Curley, Harold Thomas, Presidential
quiz. Washington, History Quiz,
c1951. 102 p. 353.03 51-2967
JK515 .C8 MRR Alc.

Filler, Louis, ed. The President
speaks: New York, Putnam [1964] 416
p. 973.082 64-13025
E173 .F5 MRR Alc.

Hurd, Charles, The White House
story. [1st ed.] New York, Hawthorn
Books [1966] 240 p. 975.3 66-
15233
F204.W5 H82 MRR Alc.

Johnson, Walter, 1600 Pennsylvania
Avenue; [1st ed.] Boston, Little,
Brown [1960] 390 p. 973.91 60-
6525
E743 .J6 MRR Alc.

Kallenbach, Joseph Ernest, The
American Chief Executive; New York,
Harper & Row [1966] xii, 622 p.
353.032 66-10838
JK516 .K3 MRR Alc.

Kane, Joseph, Nathan, Facts about
the Presidents; New York, H. W.
Wilson Co., 1959. x, 348 p.
923.173 59-12483
E176.1 .K3 MRR Alc.

Kane, Joseph Nathan, Facts about the
Presidents; 3d ed. New York, H. W.
Wilson Co., 1974. viii, 407 p.
973/.0992 74-5287
E176.1 .K3 1974 MRR Ref Desk.

Longaker, Richard P. The Presidency
and individual liberties. Ithaca,
N.Y., Cornell University Press [1961]
239 p. 353.03 61-8206
JK518 .L6 MRR Alc.

Morris, Richard Brandon, Great
Presidential decisions; New and enl.
ed. New York, Harper & Row [1973]
508 p. [$1.50] 973 73-176031
E173 .M93 1973 MRR Alc.

Plischke, Elmer, Summit diplomacy;
College Park, Bureau of Governmental
Research, College of Business and
Public Administration, University of
Maryland, 1958. viii, 125 p.
327.73 58-63026
JK570 .P58 MRR Alc.

Pollard, James Edward, The
presidents and the press. New York,
The Macmillan company, 1947. xiii,
866 p. 071 47-1213
PN4888.P7 P6 MRR Alc.

Singleton, Esther, The story of the
White House. New York, The McClure
company, 1907. 2 v. 07-37719
F204.W5 S6 MRR Ref Desk.

Smith, John Malcolm. Powers of the
President during crises. Washington,
Public Affairs Press [1960] viii,
184 p. 353.032 59-14964
JK516 .S66 MRR Alc.

Townsend, Malcolm, comp. Handbook of
the United States political history
for readers and students; Boston,
Lothrop, Lee & Shepard co. [c1905]
11, 441 p. 05-33512
JK9 .T7 MRR Alc.

Tugwell, Rexford Guy, The
enlargement of the Presidency. [1st
ed.] Garden City, N.Y., Doubleday,
1960. 508 p. 353.03 60-11391
JK516 .T8 MRR Alc.

United States. Congress. Senate.
Library. Presidential vetoes;
Washington, U.S. Govt. Print. Off.,
1969. viii, 252 p. [1.00]
353/.032 70-602991
KF42.2 1969 MRR Ref Desk.

United States. President. Public
papers of the Presidents of the
United States, containing the public
messages, speeches, and statements of
the President. Washington, U.S.
Govt. Print. Off. 353.03 58-61050
J80 .A283 MRR Alc Full set

United States. President, 1929-1933
(Hoover) Herbert Hoover :
Washington : U.S. Govt. Print. Off.,
1974. 2 v. (iii, 1566 p.) : [$24.55
] 353.03/5 74-602466
J82 .D5 1974 MRR Alc.

Walker, Kenneth Roland. The days the
Presidents died; [Little Rock? Ark.]
1966. xi, 175 p. 973 65-29072
E176.1 .W27 MRR Alc.

Warren, Sidney, The President as
world leader. [1st ed.]
Philadelphia, Lippincott [1964] xii,
480 p. 327.73 64-22183
E744 .W295 MRR Alc.

Weekly compilation of Presidential
documents. v. 1- Aug. 2, 1965-
[Washington, Office of the Federal
Register; distributed by Supt. of
Docs., Govt. Print. Off.] 65-9929
J80 .A284 MRR Alc Partial set

PRESIDENTS--UNITED STATES--ADDRESSES,
ESSAYS, LECTURES.
Haight, David E., ed. The President,
roles and powers. Chicago, Rand
McNally [1965] x, 400 p. 353.03
65-14098
JK511 .H25 MRR Alc.

PRESIDENTS--UNITED STATES--ARCHIVES.
United States. Library of Congress.
Manuscript Division. The
Presidential papers program of the
Library of Congress. [Washington,
1960] [4] p. 61-61189
Z663.34 .P7 MRR Alc.

PRESIDENTS--UNITED STATES--
ASSASSINATION.
Donovan, Robert J. The assassins
[New York, Popular Library, 1964]
254 p. 364.152 64-6177
HV6278 .D6 1964 MRR Alc.

PRESIDENTS--UNITED STATES--BIBLIOGRAPHY.
Historical records survey. New
Jersey. List and index of
presidential executive orders,
Newark, N.J., Historical records
survey, Work projects administration
[1943] 1 p. l., xiv p., 1 l., 388,
[2] p. 016.353 43-13029
Z6455.A4 H5 MRR Alc.

United States. Library of Congress.
General Reference and Bibliography
Division. The Presidents of the
United States, 1789-1962; Washington
[For sale by the Superintendent of
Documents, U.S. Govt. Print. Off.]
1963. xviii, 159 p. 63-61781
Z663.28 .P73 MRR Alc.

PRESIDENTS--UNITED STATES--BIOGRAPHY.
America's historic houses; New York,
Putnam [1967] 194 p. 973 67-26315

E159 .A4 MRR Alc.

Armbruster, Maxim Ethan, The
Presidents of the United States, and
their administrations from Washington
to Nixon. 5th ed., rev. New York,
Horizon Press [1973] 378 p. [$7.95]
973/.0992 B 73-82069
E176.1 .A75 1973 MRR Alc.

Bassett, Margaret Byrd, Profiles &
portraits of American Presidents &
their wives. Freeport, Me., B.
Wheelwright Co.; distributed by
Grosset & Dunlap, New York [1969] x,
449 p. [10.00] 973 B 68-11104
E176.1 .B24 MRR Alc.

Bergere, Thea. Homes of the
Presidents. New York, Dodd, Mead
[1962] 94 p. 917.3 62-16684
E159 .B43 MRR Alc.

Durant, John, Pictorial history of
American Presidents. 5th rev. ed.
South Brunswick [N.J.] A. S. Barnes
[1969] 370 p. [12.50] 973 69-
19632
E176.1 .D9 1969 MRR Alc.

Freidel, Frank Burt. The Presidents
of the United States of America. [2d
ed.] Washington, White House
Historical Association [1969] 82 p.
973 79-2265
E176.1 .F8 1969 MRR Alc.

Golson, K. K. Presidents are people
New York, Carlton Press [1964] 270
p. 923.173 64-56026
E176.1 .G637 MRR Alc.

PRESIDENTS--UNITED STATES-- (Cont.)
Haskin Service, Washington, D.C. The
Presidents and their wives;
[Washington, 1961] 66 p.   923.173
61-9629
  E176.1 .H343 1961 MRR Alc.

Jensen, Amy (La Follette) The White
House and its thirty-four families.
New enl. ed. New York, McGraw-Hill
[1965] 301, [8] p. 975.3 65-22957

  F204.W5 J4 1965 MRR Alc.

Jones, Cranston. Homes of the
American Presidents. New York,
McGraw-Hill [1962] 232 p.   923.173
62-18158
  E159 .J6 MRR Alc.

Kittler, Glenn D. Hail to the Chief!
[1st ed.] Philadelphia, Chilton
Books [1965] 242 p.   353.03 65-
15941
  E176.1 .K55 MRR Alc.

Miller, Hope Ridings. Scandals in
the highest office; [1st ed.] New
York, Random House [1973] 280 p.
[$6.95] 973/.0992 B 73-5022
  E176.1 .M647 MRR Alc.

Morgan, James. Our Presidents; 2d
enl. ed. New York, Macmillan, 1958.
470 p.   923.173 58-13113
  E176.1 .M84 1958 MRR Alc.

Smith, Don. Peculiarities of the
presidents; [4th ed.] Van Wert,
Ohio, 1947, c1946] 185 p.   923.173
47-28190
  E176.1 .S647 1947 MRR Alc.

Taylor, Tim. The book of presidents.
[1st ed.] New York, Arno Press,
1972. viii, 703 p.   [$12.95]
973/.099 B 74-164708
  E176.1 .T226 MRR Ref Desk.

Whitney, David C. The graphic story
of the American Presidents. Chicago,
J. G. Ferguson Pub. Co.; distributed
to the book trade by Doubleday [1973]
vii, 543 p.   [$19.95] 973/.0992
74-155403
  E176.1 .W6 1973 MRR Alc.

Wold, Karl Christian, Mr. President,
how is your health? St. Paul, Bruce
Pub. Co., 1948. x, 214 p.   923.173
48-3848
  E176.1 .W84 MRR Alc.

PRESIDENTS--UNITED STATES--CHILDREN.
Sadler, Christine. Children in the
White House. New York, Putnam [1967]
316 p.   973 67-15118
  E176.1 .S12 MRR Alc.

PRESIDENTS--UNITED STATES--ELECTION.
Bain, Richard C. Convention
decisions and voting records 2d ed.
Washington, Brookings Institution
[1973] x, 350, [120] p.   [$14.95]
329/.0221 73-1082
  JK2255 .B3 1973 MRR Alc.

Bean, Louis Hyman, How America votes
in presidential elections, Metuchen,
N.J., Scarecrow Press, 1968. 152 p.
324/.2/0873 68-12641
  JK1967 .B42 MRR Alc.

Burnham, Walter Dean. Presidential
ballots, 1836-1892. Baltimore, Johns
Hopkins Press [1955] xix, 956 p.
324.73 55-8428
  JK524 .B8 MRR Alc.

Governmental Affairs Institute,
Washington, D.C. Elections Research
Center. America at the polls;
Pittsburgh, University of Pittsburgh
Press, 1965. 521 p.   324.202173 65-
27801
  JK524 .G6 MRR Alc.

Hatch, Louis Clinton, A history of
the vice-presidency of the United
States, New York, The American
historical society, inc., 1934. viii
p., 2 l., [3]-437 p.   353.03 34-
8999
  E176 .H35 MRR Alc.

Judah, Charles Burnet, The unchosen
New York, Coward-McCann [1962] 377
p.   324.23 62-10947
  JK2255 .J8 MRR Alc.

McKee, Thomas Hudson. The national
conventions and platforms of all
political parties, 1789 to 1905; New
York, B. Franklin [1971] 414, 33 p.
329/.02 75-132682
  JK2255 .M2 1971 MRR Alc.

Mosher, Robert Brent, comp.
Executive register of the United
States, 1789-1902; Baltimore, Md.,
The Friedenwald company [1903] 1 p.
l., x, 351 p.   03-10230
  JK661 1902 MRR Alc.

Petersen, Svend, A statistical
history of the American presidential
elections. New York, Ungar [1963]
xxiii, 247 p.   324.73 62-21786
  JK1967 .P4 1963 MRR Alc.

Pomper, Gerald M. Nominating the
President; [Evanston, Ill.]
Northwestern University Press, 1963.
xii, 282 p.   329/.022/0973 63-13558

  JK521 .P6 MRR Alc.

Robinson, Edgar Eugene, The
presidential vote, 1896-1932,
Stanford University, Calif., Stanford
university press; London, H. Milford,
Oxford university press [c1934] ix,
403 p.   324.73 34-35830
  JK524 .R6 MRR Alc.

Roseboom, Eugene Holloway, A history
of presidential elections, from
George Washington to Richard M. Nixon
[3d ed. New York] Macmillan [1970]
viii, 639 p.   329/.023 78-101726
  E183 .R69 1970 MRR Alc.

Sayre, Wallace Stanley, Voting for
President; Washington, Brookings
Institution [1970] 169 p.   [$5.95]
324/.21/0973 78-139815
  JK528 .S28 MRR Alc.

Stanwood, Edward, A history of the
presidency, New ed.; rev. Boston,
New York, Houghton Mifflin company,
1928. 2 v.   28-26954
  JK511 .S7 1928 MRR Alc.

Stone, Irving, They also ran:
Garden City, N.Y., Doubleday [1966]
xi, 434 p.   973 66-21914
  E176 .S87 1966 MRR Alc.

Taylor, Tim, The book of presidents.
[1st ed.] New York, Arno Press,
1972. viii, 703 p.   [$12.95]
973/.099 B 74-164708
  E176.1 .T226 MRR Ref Desk.

United States. Congress. House.
Statistics of the presidential and
congressional election of November 2,
1920- Showing the highest vote for
presidential electors, and the vote
cast for each nominee for United
states senator, representative,
delegate, and resident commissioner
to the Sixty-seventh- Congress,
together with a recapitulation
thereof, including the electoral
vote. 1921- Washington, U.S. Govt.
Print Off.   324.73 21-26389
  JK1967 .A3 MRR Alc Partial set

United States. Congress. Senate.
Library. Nomination and election of
the President and Vice President of
the United States, including the
manner of selecting delegates to
national political conventions,
Washington, U.S. Govt. Print. Off.,
1972. v, 273 p.   [$1.50]
329/.0221/0973 72-600557
  JK2063 .A513 1972 MRR Ref Desk.

Weisbord, Marvin Ross. Campaigning
for president; [Rev. and expanded
ed.] New York, Washington Square
Press [1966] xv, 447 p.   329.023
67-519
  E183 .W4 1966 MRR Alc.

PRESIDENTS--UNITED STATES--ELECTION--
1964.
White, Theodore Harold, The making
of the President, 1964 [1st ed.]
New York, Atheneum Publishers, 1965.
xi, 431 p.   973.923 65-18328
  E850 .W5 MRR Alc.

PRESIDENTS--UNITED STATES--ELECTION--
1968.
Alexander, Herbert E. Financing the
1968 election Lexington, Mass.,
Heath Lexington Books [1971] xv, 355
p.   329/.025/0973 76-151790
  JK1991 .A683 1971 MRR Alc.

Congressional Quarterly Service,
Washington, D.C. Candidates 1968;
Rev. Washington, 1968. 136 p.
329/.00922 68-5150
  E840.6 .C6 1968 MRR Biog.

PRESIDENTS--UNITED STATES--ELECTION--
1972.
see also Watergate Affair, 1972-

[Newman, Joseph.] Guide to the '72
elections. Washington, Books by U.S.
News & World Report [1972] 255 p.
[$2.95] 329 79-186772
  E859 .N4 MRR Ref Desk.

Sobel, Lester A., comp. Money &
politics : New York : Facts on File,
[1974] 204 p. ;   [$7.95.]
329/.025/0973 74-81147
  JK1994 .S64 MRR Alc.

United States. Office of Federal
Elections. Federal election campaign
act of 1971 (Public law 92-225):
alphabetical listing of 1972
presidential campaign receipts.
[Washington; For sale by the Supt. of
Docs., U.S. Govt. Print. Off., 1974]
2 v.   [$17.40 per set]
329/.025/0973 74-601308
  JK1991 .U54 1974 MRR Alc.

White, Theodore Harold, The making
of the President, 1972 [1st ed.]
New York, Atheneum Publishers, 1973.
xix, 391 p.   [$10.00]
329/.023/730924 72-94252
  E859 .W47 1973 MRR Alc.

PRESIDENTS--UNITED STATES--ELECTION--
BIBLIOGRAPHY.
Kaid, Lynda Lee. Political campaign
communication: a bibliography and
guide to the literature. Metuchen,
N.J.; Scarecrow Press, 1974. v, 206
p.   016.329/01/0973 73-22492
  Z7165.U5 K34 MRR Alc.

Szekely, Kalman S. Electoral
college; Littleton, Colo., Libraries
Unlimited, 1970. 125 p.   016.324/21
79-136256
  Z7165.U5 S95 MRR Alc.

PRESIDENTS--UNITED STATES--ELECTION--
HISTORY.
Schlesinger, Arthur Meier, The
coming to power; [1st ed.] New
York, Chelsea House Publishers [1972]
xxi, 550 p.   329/.023/73 70-39588

  E183 .S28114 MRR Alc.

Schlesinger, Arthur Meier, History
of American presidential elections,
1789-1968. New York, Chelsea House
[1971] 4 v. (xxxvii, 3959 p.)
329/.023/73 70-139269
  E183 .S28 MRR Alc.

PRESIDENTS--UNITED STATES--ELECTION--
PICTORIAL WORKS.
Lorant, Stefan, The glorious burden:
the American Presidency. New York,
Harper & Row [1968] 959 p.   [25.00]
320.9/73 68-15963
  E183 .L64 MRR Alc.

Lorant, Stefan, The Presidency; New
York, Macmillan, 1951. 775 p.   973
51-12817
  E183 .L65 MRR Alc.

PRESIDENTS--UNITED STATES--ELECTION--
STATISTICS.
Runyon, John H. Source book of
American presidential campaign and
election statistics, 1948-1968. New
York, F. Ungar [1971] xiv, 380 p.
329/.023/0212 73-155093
  JK524 .R83 MRR Alc.

PRESIDENTS--UNITED STATES--GENEALOGY.
Zorn, Walter Lewis. The descendants
of the Presidents of the United
States of America. Monroe, Mich.,
1954. 149 p.   929.2 55-355
  CS59 .Z6 MRR Alc.

PRESIDENTS--UNITED STATES--HEALTH.
Marx, Rudolph, The health of the
Presidents. New York, Putnam [1961,
c1960] 376 p.   923.173 60-8476
  E176.1 .M38 MRR Alc.

Wold, Karl Christian, Mr. President,
how is your health? St. Paul, Bruce
Pub. Co., 1948. x, 214 p.   923.173
48-3848
  E176.1 .W84 MRR Alc.

PRESIDENTS--UNITED STATES--HISTORY--
SOURCES.
Tourtellot, Arthur Bernon. The
Presidents on the Presidency. [1st
ed.] Garden City, N.Y., Doubleday,
1964. xiv, 505 p.   353.032082 64-
11392
  JK511 .T6 MRR Ref Desk.

PRESIDENTS--UNITED STATES--ICONOGRAPHY.
Durant, John, Pictorial history of
American Presidents, 5th rev. ed.
South Brunswick [N.J.] A. S. Barnes
[1969] 370 p.   [12.50] 973 69-
19632
  E176.1 .D9 1969 MRR Alc.

PRESIDENTS--UNITED STATES--INAUGURAL
ADDRESSES.
United States. President. The Chief
Executive; New York, Crown
Publishers [1965] viii, 312 p.
353.035 65-24323
  J81 .C65 MRR Alc.

United States. President. The
Presidents speak: the inaugural
addresses of the American Presidents,
from Washington to Nixon. [3d ed.]
New York, Holt, Rinehart and Winston
[1969] xi, 308 p.   [10.00] 973 71-
80334
  J81 .C62 1969 MRR Alc.

PRESIDENTS--UNITED STATES--INAUGURATION.
Durbin, Louise. Inaugural cavalcade.
New York, Dodd, Mead [1971] xii,
210 p. [$5.50] 394/.4 76-162611
F186 .D87 MRR Alc.

Dusterberg, Richard B. The official
inaugural medals of the presidents of
the United States; [1st ed.]
Cincinnati, Ohio, Medallion Press
[1971] viii, 107 p. 737/.2 72-
24531
CJ5813 .D87 MRR Alc.

Kittler, Glenn D. Hail to the Chief!
[1st ed.] Philadelphia, Chilton
Books [1965] 242 p. 353.03 65-
15941
E176.1 .K55 MRR Alc.

PRESIDENTS--UNITED STATES--INAUGURATION-
-BIBLIOGRAPHY.
Freitag, Ruth S. Presidential
inaugurations; 3d ed., rev. and enl.
Washington, Library of Congress;
[for sale by the Supt. of Docs., U.S.
Govt. Print. Off.] 1969. vii, 230 p.
[2.00] 016.394/4 76-602825
Z663.28 .F68 1969 MRR Alc.

Holland, Carolyn M. Presidential
inaugurations; [Washington] 1964.
12 p. 65-60985
Z663.28 .F69 1964 MRR Alc.

United States. Library of Congress.
General Reference and Bibliography
Division. Presidential
inaugurations; Rev. ed. Washington,
1960. v, 72 p. 016.3944 60-60085
Z663.28 .F69 1960 MRR Alc.

PRESIDENTS--UNITED STATES--MEDALS.
Dusterberg, Richard B. The official
inaugural medals of the presidents of
the United States; [1st ed.]
Cincinnati, Ohio, Medallion Press
[1971] viii, 107 p. 737/.2 72-
24531
CJ5813 .D87 MRR Alc.

PRESIDENTS--UNITED STATES--MESSAGES.
United States. President. The State
of the Union messages of the
Presidents, 1790-1966. New York,
Chelsea House, 1966. 3 v. (xii, 3264
p.) 353.035 66-20309
J81 .C66 MRR Alc.

PRESIDENTS--UNITED STATES--PORTRAITS.
Armbruster, Maxim Ethan. The
Presidents of the United States, and
their administrations from Washington
to Nixon. 5th ed., rev. New York,
Horizon Press [1973] 378 p. [$7.95]
973/.0992 B 73-82069
E176.1 .A75 1973 MRR Alc.

Berger, Oscar, comp. The Presidents,
from George Washington to the
present. New York, Crown Publishers
[1968] 96 p. [$3.95] 741.4973 68-
9068
E176.1 .B46 MRR Alc.

PRESIDENTS--UNITED STATES--PRESS
CONFERENCES.
Kennedy, John Fitzgerald, Pres. U.S.,
Kennedy and the press; New York,
Crowell [1965] 555 p. 973.922 65-
12271
E841 .K37 MRR Alc.

Pollard, James Edward, The
Presidents and the press,
Washington, Public Affairs Press
[1964] 125 p. 353.03 64-8753
JK518 .P6 MRR Alc.

Stein, Meyer L. When Presidents meet
the press, New York, Messner [1969]
190 p. [3.95] 070.11 70-79701
JK518 .S72 MRR Alc.

PRESIDENTS--UNITED STATES--QUOTATIONS.
Fell, Frederick Victor, comp. The
wit and wisdom of the Presidents,
New York, F. Fell [1966] 206 p.
973.00207 66-11923
E176.1 .F4 MRR Alc.

Harnsberger, Caroline (Thomas) ed.
Treasury of presidential quotations.
Chicago, Follett Pub. Co., 1964.
xix, 384 p. 308.22 64-23607
E176.1 .H3 MRR Ref Desk.

PRESIDENTS--UNITED STATES--RACIAL
ATTITUDES.
Sinkler, George, The racial
attitudes of American Presidents,
[1st ed.] Garden City, N.Y.,
Doubleday, 1971. xiii, 413 p.
[8.95] 301.15/43/301451 74-139061
E176.1 .S57 MRR Alc.

PRESIDENTS--UNITED STATES--RELIGION.
Fuller, Edmund, God in the White
House; New York, Crown [1968] 246
p. [5.95] 973 B 68-9088
E176.1 .F93 MRR Alc.

Jones, Olga Anna. Churches of the
Presidents in Washington; [2d enl.
ed.] New York, Exposition Press
[1961] 128 p. 277.53 61-66359
F203.2.A1 J63 1961 MRR Alc.

PRESIDENTS--UNITED STATES--STAFF.
Fenno, Richard F., The President's
Cabinet; Cambridge, Mass., Harvard
University Press, 1959. 327 p.
353.05 59-9272
JK611 .F4 MRR Alc.

Kluckhohn, Frank L. Lyndon's legacy;
New York, Devin-Adair Co., 1964.
xiv, 335 p. 320.973 64-23751
E846 .K55 1964a MRR Alc.

PRESIDENTS--UNITED STATES--STAFF--
ADDRESSES, ESSAYS, LECTURES.
Cronin, Thomas E. comp. The
Presidential advisory system. New
York, Harper & Row [1969] xx, 375 p.
[6.95] 353/.03 69-18487
JK518 .C7 MRR Alc.

PRESIDENTS--UNITED STATES--SUCCESSION.
Feerick, John D. From failing hands;
New York, Fordham University Press
[1965] xiv, 368 p. 353.03 65-
14917
JK609 .F4 MRR Alc.

Harwood, Michael. In the shadow of
Presidents; [1st ed.] Philadelphia,
Lippincott [1966] x, 239 p. 353.03
ac 66-10025
JK609.5 .H3 MRR Alc.

PRESIDENTS--UNITED STATES--TRANSITION
PERIODS.
Henry, Laurin L. Presidential
transitions. Washington, Brookings
Institution [1960] xviii, 755 p.
353.032 60-53252
E743 .H4 MRR Alc.

PRESIDENTS--UNITED STATES--WIVES.
Barzman, Sol. The First Ladies.
[1st ed.] New York, Cowles Book Co.
[1970] xiii, 370 p. [8.95] 973 B
73-102817
E176.2 .B3 1970 MRR Alc.

Bassett, Margaret Byrd, Profiles &
portraits of American Presidents &
their wives, Freeport, Me., B.
Wheelwright Co.; distributed by
Grosset & Dunlap, New York [1969] x,
449 p. [10.00] 973 B 68-11104
E176.1 .B24 MRR Alc.

Haskin Service, Washington, D.C. The
Presidents and their wives,
[Washington, 1961] 66 p. 923.173
61-9629
E176.1 .H343 1961 MRR Alc.

Klapthor, Margaret (Brown) The
dresses of the First Ladies of the
White House, Washington, Smithsonian
Institution 1952. ix, 149 p.
391.2 52-61540
GT605 .K55 MRR Alc.

Means, Marianne. The woman in the
White House; New York, Random House
[1963] 299 p. 920.7 63-14143
E176.2 .M4 MRR Alc.

Ross, Ishbel. Sons of Adam,
daughters of Eve. [1st ed.] New
York, Harper & Row [1969] viii, 340
p. [7.95] 301.41/2/0922 67-13691
HQ1412 .R6 MRR Alc.

Taylor, Tim, The book of presidents.
[1st ed.] New York, Arno Press,
1972. viii, 703 p. [$12.95]
973/.099 B 74-164708
E176.1 .T226 MRR Ref Desk.

PRESIDENTS--UNITED STATES--WIVES--
JUVENILE LITERATURE.
McConnell, Jane (Tompkins) Our First
Ladies, from Martha Washington to
Lady Bird Johnson New York, Crowell
[1964] 373 p. 920.7 64-20800
E176.2 .M3 1964 MRR Alc.

PRESS.
see also Newspapers

see also Periodicals

Handbuch der Weltpresse. [5. Aufl.]
Köln, Westdeutscher Verlag, 1970. 2
v. 71-552170
Z6941 .H25 1970 MRR Alc.

Merrill, John Calhoun, The foreign
press; Baton Rouge, Louisiana State
University Press [1970] 365 p.
070.9 76-96259
PN4736 .M39 1970 MRR Alc.

Merrill John Calhoun, A handbook of
the foreign press. [Baton Rouge]
Louisiana State University Press
[1959] viii, 394 p. 070.1 59-
14603
PN4736 .M4 1959 MRR Alc.

PRESS--DIRECTORIES.
Union nationale des attachés de
presse. Annuaire. Paris. 64-1317
Began publication 1959?
PN5171 .U53 MRR Alc Latest edition

United Nations Educational,
Scientific and Cultural Organization.
News agencies, their structure and
operation. New York, Greenwood Press
[1969, c1953] 208 p. 070.04/3 76-
88957
PN4714.A1 U5 1969 MRR Alc.

PRESS--DIRECTORIES--BIBLIOGRAPHY
Duprat, Gabrielle. Bibliographie des
répertoires nationaux de
périodiques en cours London, IFLA,
1969. 141 p. 73-858215
AS4.U8 A154 MRR Alc.

PRESS--AFRICA.
United States. Joint Publications
Research Service. Abbreviations in
the African press. New York, CCM
Information Corp., 1972. ix, 108 p.
079.6/01/48 72-93345
P365 .U5 MRR Alc.

PRESS--EUROPE--DIRECTORIES.
Esslen, Rainer. A guide to marketing
securities in Europe, 1971-1972. New
York, Wall Street Reports Pub. Corp.
[1971] viii, 215 p. 332.67/34/073
79-178914
HG4538 .E76 MRR Alc.

PRESS--FRANCE--DIRECTORIES.
Union nationale des attachés de
presse. Annuaire. Paris. 64-1317
Began publication 1959?
PN5171 .U53 MRR Alc Latest edition

PRESS--FRANCE--YEARBOOKS.
Annuaire de la presse française et
étrangère. 1.- ed.; 1880-
Paris. 06-44929
Z6956.F8 A6 MRR Alc Latest edition

PRESS--GERMANY--DIRECTORIES.
Der Leitfaden für Presse und
Werbung. Essen, W. Stamm. 073 51-
17269
Z6956.G3 L4 MRR Alc Latest edition

PRESS--GREAT BRITAIN--DIRECTORIES.
Directory of newspaper and magazine
personnel and data. London,
Haymarket Publishing Group, [etc.]
072 c058 59-18302
Z6956.E5 D5 MRR Alc Latest edition

The Newspaper press directory.
London, C. Mitchell [etc.] ca 07-6361
Z6956.E5 M6 MRR Alc Latest edition

PRESS--INDIA--YEARBOOKS.
I N F A press and advertisers year
book. 1862- New Delhi, INFA
Publications. sa 63-2244
PN4709 .I2 MRR Alc Latest edition

PRESS--SPAIN--DIRECTORIES.
Anuario de la prensa española.
[Madrid, Ministerio de Información y
Turismo, Secretaría General Técnica,
Sección de Planificación y
Documentación] 076/.1/025 74-
644556
Z6956.S7 S65 MRR Alc Latest
edition

PRESS--SPANISH AMERICA.
United States. Joint Publications
Research Service. Abbreviations in
the Latin American press. New York,
CCM Information Corp., 1972. ix, 172
p. 463/.1 72-93344
P365 .U53 MRR Alc.

PRESS--UNITED STATES.
Emery, Edwin. The press and America,
3d ed. Englewood Cliffs, N.J.,
Prentice-Hall [1972] xi, 788 p.
071.3 77-38634
PN4855 .E6 1972 MRR Alc.

Mott, Frank Luther, American
journalism; 3d ed. New York,
Macmillan [1962] 901 p. 071.3 62-
7157
PN4855 .M63 1962 MRR Alc.

North, Simon Newton Dexter, History
and present condition of the
newspaper and periodical press of the
United States, [Elmsford, N.Y.,
Maxwell Reprint Co., 1971] vi, 446
p. 338/.0973 s 070.5/0973 73-
164452
HC105 .A66 vol. 9 MRR Alc.

PRESS--UNITED STATES--DIRECTORIES.
Ayer directory of publications.
Philadelphia, Ayer Press. 071.3/025
73-640052
Z6951 .A97 Sci RR Latest edition /
MRR Ref Desk Latest edition / MRR
Alc Latest edition

Weiner, Richard, News bureaus in the
U.S. [New York, 1974] vi, 143 p.
071/.3 74-170343
Z6951 .W4 1974 MRR Alc.

PRESS--UNITED STATES-- (Cont.)
The Working press of the nation.
[1945]- Burlington, Iowa [etc.]
National Research Bureau [etc.]
071.47   46-7041
Z6951 .W6 MRR Alc Latest edition

PRESS--WASHINGTON, D.C.--DIRECTORIES.
Hudson's Washington news media
contacts directory. 1968-
Washington. 071/.53 68-22594
Z6953.W2 H8 MRR Alc Latest edition

PRESS, LABOR--DIRECTORIES.
I L P A directory of member
publications. [1st]- 1957-
[Washington] International Labor
Press Association, AFL-CIO. 58-2503
PN4888.L3 L33 MRR Alc Latest
edition

PRESS AGENTS--FRANCE--SOCIETIES, ETC.
Union nationale des attachés de
presse. Annuaire. Paris. 64-1317
Began publication 1959?
PN5171 .U53 MRR Alc Latest edition

PRESS CENSORSHIP
see Liberty of the press

PRESS RELEASES.
Ayer Press. Ayer public relations
and publicity style book.
Philadelphia, 1974. 1 v. (unpaged)
[$8.90] 808/.02 74-161785
PN4783 .A9 1974 MRR Alc.

PRESSED GLASS.
Lee, Ruth Webb, Early American
pressed glass. Enl. and rev.
Northboro, Mass. The author [1946]
xxix, 666 p. 748.2 46-2536
NK5112 .L4 1946 MRR Alc.

PRESSURE.
see also Atmospheric pressure

PRESSURE GROUPS.
see also Lobbying

PRESTIDIGITATION
see Conjuring

see Magic

PRICE REGULATION.
see also Agricultural price supports

PRICE REGULATION--UNITED STATES.
[United States. Library of Congress.
Legislative Reference Service]
Materials relating to the debate
topic: "Resolved, that the Federal
government should adopt a permanent
program of price and wage control."
[Washington, 1951] 40 p. 338.526
52-60020
Z663.6 .M3 MRR Alc.

PRICES.
Commodity year book. 1st- ed.;
1939- New York, Commodity Research
Bureau, inc. 338.0973 39-11418
HF1041 .C56 MRR Alc Latest edition

PRICES--BIBLIOGRAPHY.
United States. Dept. of Commerce.
Library. Price sources; New York,
B. Franklin [1968] iv, 320 p.
016.33852 70-6381
Z7164.P94 U56 1968 MRR Alc.

United States. Library of Congress.
Division of bibliography. Select
list of references on the cost of
living and prices; Washington, Govt.
print. off., 1910. v, 107 p. 10-
35008
Z663.28 .S435 1910 MRR Alc.

Wasserman, Paul. Commodity prices:
Detroit, Gale Research Co. [1974]
xii, 200 p. [$15.00] 338.5/2/0973
73-19898
Z7164.P94 W33 MRR Alc.

PRICES--HISTORY.
Smith, Walter Buckingham.
Fluctuations in American business,
1790-1860. Cambridge, Harvard
university press, 1935. xxix, 195 p.
330.973 35-33983
HC105 .S65 MRR Alc.

PRICES--STATISTICS.
International Labor Office.
Technical guide; Geneva, 1968- v.
[unpriced] 331/.021/6 77-391010
HD4826 .I62 MRR Alc.

PRICES--GREAT BRITAIN--HISTORY.
Beveridge, William Henry Beveridge,
baron. Prices and wages in England
from the twelfth to the nineteenth
century London; New York [etc.]
Longmans, Green and co. [1939- v.
338.50942 39-16200
HB235.G7 B4 MRR Alc.

PRICES--UNITED STATES.
Smith, Walter Buckingham.
Fluctuations in American business,
1790-1860. Cambridge, Harvard
university press, 1935. xxix, 195 p.
330.973 35-33983
HC105 .S65 MRR Alc.

PRICES--UNITED STATES--SOURCES.
Special Libraries Association.
Business and Finance Division.
Committee on Sources of Commodity
Prices. Sources of commodity prices.
New York, Special Libraries
Association, 1959 [c1960] 170 p.
338.505873 60-8102
Z7164.P94 S6 MRR Alc.

Wasserman, Paul. Commodity prices:
Detroit, Gale Research Co. [1974]
xii, 200 p. [$15.00] 338.5/2/0973
73-19898
Z7164.P94 W33 MRR Alc.

PRICES--UNITED STATES--STATISTICS.
United States. Bureau of Labor
Statistics. Handbook of labor
statistics. 1924/26- Washington,
U.S. Govt. Print. Off. l 27-328
HD8064 .A3 MRR Ref Desk MRR Ref
Desk Latest edition

PRICES--UNITED STATES--YEARBOOKS.
Price buying directory. [Chicago]
Consumers Digest. 77-789
TX335.A1 P74 MRR Ref Desk Latest
edition

PRIMARIES.
United States. Congress. Senate.
Library. Nomination and election of
the President and Vice President of
the United States, including the
manner of selecting delegates to
national political conventions,
Washington, U.S. Govt. Print. Off.,
1972. v, 273 p. [$1.50]
329/.0221/0973 72-600557
JK2063 .A513 1972 MRR Ref Desk.

PRIMARIES--BIBLIOGRAPHY.
United States. Library of Congress.
Division of bibliography. ... List
of references on primary elections.
Washington, Govt. print. off., 1905.
25 p. 05-5186
Z663.28 .L577 MRR Alc.

PRIMARIES--UNITED STATES.
Runyon, John H. Source book of
American presidential campaign and
election statistics, 1948-1968. New
York, F. Unger [1971] xiv, 380 p.
329/.023/0212 73-155093
JK524 .R83 MRR Alc.

PRIME MINISTERS--CANADA--BIOGRAPHY.
Ondaatje, Christopher. The Prime
Ministers of Canada, 1867-1968
Toronto, Pagurian Press, 1968. 191
p. [unpriced] 971 79-396883
F1033 .O56 1968 MRR Biog.

PRIME MINISTERS--GREAT BRITAIN--
BIOGRAPHY.
Pike, Edgar Royston, Britain's Prime
Ministers from Walpole to Wilson
Feltham, Odhams, 1968. 487 p. [30/-
] 942.07/0922 B 79-435231
DA28.4 .P48 MRR Alc.

PRIMITIVE BAPTISTS--DIRECTORIES.
The Primitive Baptist church meeting
directory. 2d ed., rev. Elon
College, N.C., Primitive Baptist Pub.
House, 1959. 86 p. 286.405873 59-
39193
BX6380 .P67 1959 MRR Alc.

PRIMITIVE RELIGION
see Religion, Primitive

PRIMITIVE SCULPTURE
see Sculpture, Primitive

PRIMITIVE SOCIETY
see Society, Primitive

PRIMITIVISM IN ART.
Jakovsky, Anatole. Peintres naïfs;
New York, Universe Books [1967] 398
p. 759 67-15570
ND35 .J28 MRR Alc.

PRIMITIVISM IN ART--UNITED STATES.
Lipman, Jean (Herzberg) comp.
Primitive painters in America, 1750-
1950; New York, Dodd, Mead [1950]
182 p. 759.13 50-58059
ND236 .L7 MRR Alc.

PRINCETON UNIVERSITY--ALUMNI--
DIRECTORIES.
Princeton University. Alumni
directory. Princeton, N.J. 378.749
02-28149
First published in 1888.
LD4601 .A3 MRR Alc Latest edition

PRINTERS.
Benzing, Josef, Buchdruckerlexikon
des 16. Jahrhunderts Frankfurt am
Main, V. Klostermann [1952] 215 p.
52-41679
Z147 .B48 MRR Alc.

Clair, Colin. A chronology of
printing. London, Cassell, 1969.
228 p. [70/-] 655.1 78-425147
Z124 .C6 MRR Alc.

Jennett, Seán. Pioneers in
printing; London, Routledge & Paul
[1958] 196 p. 655.1 59-396
Z231 .J4 MRR Alc.

PRINTERS--ARKANSAS.
Historical records survey. Arkansas.
A check list of Arkansas imprints,
1821-1876. Little Rock, Ark., The
Arkansas Historical records survey,
1942. 6 p. l., 139 numb. l., 2 l.
015.767 42-17366
Z1215 .H67 no. 39 MRR Alc.

PRINTERS--GERMANY.
Benzing, Josef, Buchdruckerlexikon
des 16. Jahrhunderts Frankfurt am
Main, V. Klostermann [1952] 215 p.
52-41679
Z147 .B48 MRR Alc.

PRINTERS--GREAT BRITAIN.
Ames, Joseph, Typographical
antiquities; London, W. Miller, 1810-
19. 4 v. 02-2021
Z151 .A512 MRR Alc.

A dictionary of the printers and
booksellers who were at work in
England, Scotland and Ireland from
1726 to 1775; [Oxford] Printed for
the Bibliographical society at the
Oxford university press, 1932 [for
1930] xxi, 432 p. 655.142 32-
23320
Z151 .D54 MRR Alc.

Duff, Edward Gordon, A century of
the English book trade; [Folcroft,
Pa.] Folcroft Library Editions, 1972.
xxxv, 200 p. 686.2/092/2 72-
188912
Z151.2 .D83 1972 MRR Alc.

Duff, Edward Gordon, A century of
the English book trade. London,
Printed for the Bibliographical
society, by Blades, East & Blades,
1905. xxxv, [1], 200 p. 06-595
Z151 .D86 MRR Alc.

McKerrow, Ronald Brunlees, ed. A
dictionary of printers and
booksellers in England, Scotland and
Ireland, and of foreign printers of
English books 1557-1640. London,
Printed for the Bibliographical
society, by Blades, East & Blades,
1910. 2 p. l., [vii]-xxiii, 346 p.
11-5402
Z151 .D51 MRR Alc.

Plomer, Henry Robert, A dictionary
of the printers and booksellers who
were at work in England, Scotland and
Ireland from 1668 to 1725, [Oxford]
Printed for the Bibliographical
society, at the Oxford university
press, 1922. 2 p. l., [vii]-xii, 342
p. 23-5
Z151 .D53 MRR Alc.

Plomer, Henry Robert, A dictionary
of the booksellers and printers who
were at work in England, Scotland and
Ireland from 1641 to 1667. London,
Printed for the Bibliographical
society, by Blades, East & Blades,
1907. 2 p. l., [vii]-xxiii, [1], 199
p. 08-18568
Z151 .D52 MRR Alc.

Pollard, Alfred William, A short-
title catalogue of books printed in
England, Scotland, & Ireland and of
English books printed abroad, 1475-
1640. London, Bibliographical
Society, 1946. xviii, 609 p.
015.42 47-20884
Z2002 .P77 1946 MRR Alc.

Wing, Donald Goddard, Short-title
catalogue of books printed in
England, Scotland, Ireland, Wales,
and British America, and of English
books printed in other countries,
1641-1700. New York, Index Society,
1945-51. 3 v. 015.42 45-8773
Z2002 .W5 MRR Alc.

PRINTERS--GREAT BRITAIN--DIRECTORIES.
The Master printers annual. 44th-
year; 1963- London, British
Federation of Master Printers.
686.2/0942 72-623098
Z119.5 .M42 MRR Alc Latest edition

Printing and allied trades directory.
London, Benn Bros. 655/.025/42 68-
50160
Began in 1960.
Z327 .P7 MRR Alc Latest edition

PRINTERS--IOWA.
Historical records survey. A check
list of Iowa imprints 1838-1860,
Chicago, The WPA Historical records
survey project, 1940. 84 (i.e. 85)
numb. l. 015.777 42-17567
Z1215 .H67 no. 15 MRR Alc.

PRINTERS--MEXICO.
United States. Library of Congress.
Colonial printing in Mexico;
Washington, U.S. Govt. print. off.,
1939. 60 p. 655.172 39-29286
Z663.15 .C6 MRR Alc.

PRINTERS--OHIO.
Historical records survey. Ohio. A
check list of Ohio imprints, 1796-
1820. Columbus, O., Ohio Historical
records survey, 1941. 202 numb. l.
015.771 42-17565
Z1215 .H67 no. 17 MRR Alc.

PRINTERS--OKLAHOMA.
Hargrett, Lester. Oklahoma imprints,
1835-1890. New York, Published for
the Bibliographical Society of
America [by] Bowker, 1951. xvii, 267
p. 015.766 51-3747
Z1325 .H3 MRR Alc.

PRINTERS--PARIS.
Renouard, Philippe. Imprimeurs &
libraires parisiens du XVIe siècle;
Paris, 1964- v. 65-70946
Z305 .R4 MRR Alc.

PRINTERS--TENNESSEE.
Historical records survey. Tennessee.
Check list of Tennessee imprints,
1841-1850. Nashville, Tenn., The
Tennessee Historical records survey,
1941. 1 p. l., iii-xiii, 138 numb.
l. 015.768 42-17566
Z1215 .H67 no. 20 MRR Alc.

PRINTERS--UNITED STATES.
Brigham, Clarence Saunders. History
and bibliography of American
newspapers, 1690-1820. Worcester,
Mass., American Antiquarian Society,
1947. 2 v. (xvii, 1508 p.) 016.071
47-4111
Z6951 .B86 MRR Alc.

Bristol, Roger Pattrell. Supplement
to Charles Evans' American
bibliography. Charlottesville,
Published for the Bibliographical
Society of America and the
Bibliographical Society of the
University of Virginia [by]
University Press of Virginia [1970]
xix, 636 p. [35.00] 015.73 73-
94761
Z1215 .E92334 MRR Ref Desk (Alc. 6)

Evans, Charles. American
bibliography; Chicago, Priv. print.
for the author by the Blakely Press,
1903-59. 14 v. 03-32909
Z1215 .E92 MRR Ref Desk.

Evans, Charles. American
bibliography. Metuchen, N.J., Mini-
Print Corp., 1967. 13 v. in 1.
015.73 67-4309
Z1215 .E9232 1967 MRR Alc.

Oswald, John Clyde. Printing in the
Americas. New York, Hacker Art
Books, 1968. 565, xli p. 655.1/7
68-9008
Z205 .O86 1968 MRR Alc.

Thomas, Isaiah. The history of
printing in America. Barre, Mass.,
Imprint Society, 1970. xxi, 650 p.
686.2/0973 75-100491
Z205 .T56 1970 MRR Alc.

PRINTERS--UNITED STATES--BIBLIOGRAPHY.
Tanselle, George Thomas. Guide to
the study of United States imprints
Cambridge, Mass., Belknap Press of
Harvard University Press, 1971. 2 v.
(lxiv, 1050 p.) 016.015/73 79-
143232
Z1215.A2 T35 MRR Alc.

PRINTERS, ITALIAN.
Cosenza, Mario Emilio. Biographical
and bibliographical dictionary of the
Italian printers. Boston, G. K.
Hall, 1968 [c1967] vii, 679 p.
016.6551/45 67-17808
Z155 .C6 MRR Alc.

Norton, Frederick John. Italian
printers, 1501-1520. London, Bowes
and Bowes, 1958. xxxiv, 177 p.
655.145 58-1608
Z155 .N6 MRR Alc.

PRINTERS' MARKS.
Mumey, Nolie. A study of rare books,
Denver, The Clason publishing
company, 1930. xvii p., 2 l., 3-572
p. 090 30-25438
Z1012 .M95 MRR Alc.

PRINTING
see also Books

Jennett, Seán. The making of books.
[New ed. London] Faber & Faber
[1956] 474 p. 655 57-28023
Z116.A2 J47 1956 MRR Alc.

PRINTING--BIBLIOGRAPHY.
Bigmore, Edward Clements. A
bibliography of printing. London, B.
Quaritch, 1880-86. 3 v. 05-6634
Z117 .B59 MRR Alc.

PRINTING--DICTIONARIES.
Aldag, Keith A. Modern graphics
terminology [Hurstbridge, Vic.,
Hyphen Publishing, 1969] 350 p.
[8.40] 760.3 76-459625
Z118 .A53 MRR Alc.

Archambeaud, Pierre. Dictionnaire
anglais-français, français-anglais
des industries graphiques Paris,
Compagnie française d'editions,
[1968?] 200 p. [15.00] 77-550452

Z118 .A7 MRR Alc.

The Bookman's glossary. 4th ed.,
rev. and enl. New York, R. R. Bowker
[1961] viii, 212 p. 010.3 61-
13239
Z1006 .B6 1961 MRR Alc.

Carter, John. ABC for book-
collectors. [3d ed., rev.] London,
R. Hart-Davis [1961] 208 p. 62-
6733
Z1006 .C37 1961a MRR Alc.

Glaister, Geoffrey Ashall. Glossary
of the book; London, G. Allen and
Unwin [1960] 484 p. 655.03 61-
2811
Z118 .G55 1960a MRR Alc.

Graham, Irvin. Encyclopedia of
advertising; 2d ed. New York,
Fairchild Publications [1969] xiii,
494 p. [20.00] 659.1/03 68-14544

HF5803 .G68 1969 MRR Alc.

Harrod, Leonard Montague. The
librarians glossary. [2d rev. ed.]
London, Grafton, 1959. 332 p.
010.3 59-2822
Z1006 .H32 1959 MRR Ref Desk.

Hiller, Helmut. Wörterbuch des
Buches. 3., durchgesehene und erw.
Aufl. Frankfurt a. M., Klostermann
[1967.] 341 p. [DM 18.50 (unb. DM
16.50)] 68-96779
Z118 .H55 1967 MRR Alc.

Jacobi, Charles Thomas. The
printers' vocabulary; Detroit, Gale
Research Co., 1969. vi, 158 p.
655/.03 68-30613
Z118 .J18 1969 MRR Alc.

Kent, Ruth Kimball. The language of
journalism; [1st ed. Kent, Ohio]
Kent State University Press [1971,
c1970] xvi, 186 p. [$5.00]
070/.03 71-100624
PN4728 .K4 MRR Alc.

Melcher, Daniel. Printing and
promotion handbook; 2d ed. New
York, McGraw-Hill, 1956. xi, 438 p.
655.03 56-6966
Z118 .M4 1956 MRR Alc.

Pepper, William M. Dictionary of
newspaper and printing terms; New
York, Columbia University Press
[1959] 344 p. 070.03 59-16345
PN4728 .P4 MRR Alc.

Polygraph dictionary der graphischen
Techniken und der verwandten Gebiete.
2., durch die Polygraph-Redaktion
überarb., erg. und erw. Aufl.
Frankfurt am Main, Polygraph Verlag
[1967] 330 p. 68-123918
Z118 .P63 1967 MRR Alc.

Stevenson, George A. Graphic arts
encyclopedia New York, McGraw-Hill
[1968] xv, 492 p. 655/.003 67-
24445
Z118 .S82 MRR Alc.

Walter, Frank Keller. Abbreviations
and technical terms used in book
catalogs and bibliographies, in eight
languages, 1917 handy edition.
Boston, The Boston book company
[1919?] 2 v. in 1. 27-13479
Z1006 .W261 1919 MRR Alc.

PRINTING--DICTIONARIES--FRENCH.
Archambeaud, Pierre. Dictionnaire
anglais-français, français-anglais
des industries graphiques Paris,
Compagnie française d'editions,
[1968?] 200 p. [15.00] 77-550452

Z118 .A7 MRR Alc.

PRINTING--DICTIONARIES--GERMAN.
Polygraph dictionary der graphischen
Techniken und der verwandten Gebiete.
2., durch die Polygraph-Redaktion
überarb., erg. und erw. Aufl.
Frankfurt am Main, Polygraph Verlag
[1967] 330 p. 68-123918
Z118 .P63 1967 MRR Alc.

PRINTING--DICTIONARIES--POLYGLOT.
Orne, Jerrold. The language of the
foreign book trade: 2d ed. Chicago,
American Library Association, 1962.
213 p. 010.3 61-12881
Z1006 .O7 1962 MRR Alc.

PRINTING--DICTIONARIES--SPANISH.
Pepper, William M. Dictionary of
newspaper and printing terms; New
York, Columbia University Press
[1959] 344 p. 070.03 59-16345
PN4728 .P4 MRR Alc.

Rodríguez, César. Bilingual
dictionary of the graphic arts; New
and complete ed., rev. and enl.
Farmingdale, N.Y., G. A. Humphrey
[1966] 448 p. 655.03 66-27570
Z118 .R6 1966 MRR Alc.

PRINTING--HISTORY.
Bigmore, Edward Clements. A
bibliography of printing. London, B.
Quaritch, 1880-86. 3 v. 05-6634
Z117 .B59 MRR Alc.

Binns, Norman E. An introduction to
historical bibliography. 2d ed.,
rev. and enl. London, Association of
Assistant Librarians, 1962. 387 p.
63-25449
Z4 .B55 1962 MRR Alc.

Day, Kenneth, ed. Book typography,
1815-1965. London, Benn, 1966.
xxiii, 401 p. [5/5/-] 66-75818
Z116.A2 D313 1966 MRR Alc.

Esdaile, Arundell James Kennedy.
Esdaile's manual of bibliography.
4th revised ed. London, Allen &
Unwin, 1967 [i.e. 1968] 336 p. [50/-]
010 68-114662
Z1001 .E75 1968 MRR Alc.

Gaskell, Philip. A new introduction
to bibliography. New York, Oxford
University Press, 1972. 438 p.
686.2/09 73-153680
Z116.A2 G27 1972b MRR Alc.

Johnson, Elmer D. Communication; 3d
ed. New York, Scarecrow Press, 1966.
304 p. 027.009 66-13742
Z721 .J6 1966 MRR Alc.

McMurtrie, Douglas Crawford. The
book; New York, London [etc.] Oxford
university press [1943] xxx p., 1
l., 676 p. 1 l. 002 43-4110
Z4 .M15 1943 MRR Alc.

Updike, Daniel Berkeley. Printing
types, [3d ed.] Cambridge, Mass.,
Belknap Press, 1962. 2 v. 655.24
62-5866
Z250.A2 U6 1962 MRR Alc.

PRINTING--HISTORY--BIBLIOGRAPHY.
Besterman, Theodore. Early printed
books to the end of the sixteenth
century; 2d ed., rev. and much enl.
Genève, Societas Bibliographica,
1961. 344 p. 016.016093 62-2500
Z1002 .B562 1961 MRR Alc.

McMurtrie, Douglas Crawford, ed. The
invention of printing; New York, B.
Franklin [1962] xxiv, 413 p.
016.6551 63-12653
Z117 .M18 1962 MRR Alc.

Peddie, Robert Alexander. Fifteenth-
century books; New York, B. Franklin
[1969] 89 p. 016.016/.093 73-
101990
Z240.A1 P4 1969 MRR Alc.

Ulrich, Carolyn Farquhar. Books and
printing. Woodstock, Vt., W. E.
Rudge; New York, The New York Public
library, 1943. xi, [1], 244 p.
016.655 43-16214
Z1002 .U4 MRR Alc.

PRINTING--HISTORY--CHRONOLOGY.
Berry, William Turner. Annals of
printing; London, Blandford P.,
1966. xlix, 315 p. [84/-] 655.1
66-77876
Z124 .B45 MRR Alc.

Clair, Colin. A chronology of
printing. London, Cassell, 1969.
228 p. [70/-] 655.1 78-425147
Z124 .C4 MRR Alc.

PRINTING--HISTORY--GAZETTEERS.
Grasse, Johann Georg Theodor. Orbis
Latinus; Grossausgabe,
Braunschweig, Klinkhardt & Biermann
[c1972] 3 v. 72-345986
G107 .G8 1972 MRR Alc.

Parenti, Marino. Dizionario dei
luoghi di stampa falsi, inventati o
supposti in opere di autori e
traduttori italiani. Firenze,
Sansoni, 1951. 311 p. a 52-649
Z125 .P3 MRR Alc.

Peddie, Robert Alexander. Place
names in imprints; London, Grafton &
co., 1932. vii, [1] p., 1 l., 61
numb. l., 1 l. 929.4 32-11548
Z125 .P37 MRR Ref Desk.

PRINTING--HISTORY--ORIGIN AND ANTECEDENTS.
Carter, Thomas Francis, The invention of printing in China and its spread westward. 2d ed. New York, Ronald Press Co. [1955] xxiv, 293 p.   655.151 55-5418
     Z186.C5 C3 1955 MRR Alc.

PRINTING--HISTORY--AMERICA.
Oswald, John Clyde, Printing in the Americas. New York, Hacker Art Books, 1968. 565, xli p.   655.1/7 68-9008
     Z205 .O86 1968 MRR Alc.

Thomas, Isaiah, The history of printing in America. Barre, Mass., Imprint Society, 1970. xxi, 650 p. 686.2/0973 75-100491
     Z205 .T56 1970 MRR Alc.

PRINTING--HISTORY--CHINA.
Carter, Thomas Francis, The invention of printing in China and its spread westward. 2d ed. New York, Ronald Press Co. [1955] xxiv, 293 p.   655.151 55-5418
     Z186.C5 C3 1955 MRR Alc.

PRINTING--HISTORY--GREAT BRITAIN.
Ames, Joseph, Typographical antiquities; London, W. Miller, 1810-19. 4 v.   02-2021
     Z151 .A512 MRR Alc.

London. Stationers' Company. A transcript of the registers of the Company of Stationers of London, 1554-1640 A.D. [New York P. Smith, 1950] 5 v.   655.442 49-50201
     Z2002 .L64 MRR Alc.

London. Stationer's Company. A transcript of the registers of the worshipful Company of Stationers, from 1640-1708 A.D. [New York, P. Smith, 1950] 3 v.   655.442 50-37726
     Z2002 .L653 MRR Alc.

The Term catalogues, 1668-1709 A.D.; London, 1903-06. 3 v.   05-8720
     Z2002 .A31 MRR Alc.

PRINTING--HISTORY--HUNGARY.
Szabó, Károly, Régi magyar könyvtár . Budapest, A. M. Tud. Akademia Könyvkiado Hivatala, 1879-98. 3 v. in 4.   04-32267
     Z2142 .S98 MRR Alc.

PRINTING--HISTORY--ITALY.
Norton, Frederick John. Italian printers, 1501-1520; London, Bowes and Bowes, 1958. xxxiv, 177 p. 655.145 58-1608
     Z155 .N6 MRR Alc.

Parenti, Marino, Dizionario dei luoghi di stampa falsi, inventati o supposti in opere di autori e traduttori italiani, Firenze, Sansoni, 1951. 311 p.   a 52-649
     Z125 .P3 MRR Alc.

PRINTING--HISTORY--MEXICO.
United States. Library of Congress. Colonial printing in Mexico; Washington, U.S. Govt. print. off., 1939. 60 p.   655.172 39-29286
     Z663.15 .C6 MRR Alc.

PRINTING--HISTORY--NEW MEXICO.
Historical records survey. Illinois. Check list of New Mexico imprints and publications, 1784-1876. [Detroit] Michigan Historical records survey, 1942. 3 p. l., v-xiii, 115 p., 3 l. 015.798 43-5102
     Z1215 .H67 no. 25 MRR Alc.

PRINTING--HISTORY--POLAND.
Estreicher, Karol Jozef Teofil, Bibliografia polska ; Krakow, W Druk. Uniw. Jagiellonskiego, 1870-v.   05-5187
     Z2521 .E82 MRR Alc.

PRINTING--HISTORY--SPAIN--BIBLIOGRAPHY.
Foulché-Delbosc, Raymond, Manuel de l'hispanisant. New York, G. P. Putnam's sons, 1920- v.   20-16867
     Z2681.A1 F7 MRR Alc.

PRINTING--HISTORY--UNITED STATES.
Bristol, Roger Pattrell. Supplement to Charles Evans' American bibliography. Charlottesville, Published for the Bibliographical Society of America and the Bibliographical Society of the University of Virginia [by] University Press of Virginia [1970] xlx, 636 p. [35.00] 015.73 73-84761
     Z1215 .E92334 MRR Ref Desk (Alc. 6)

Evans, Charles, American bibliography. Metuchen, N.J., Mini-Print Corp., 1967. 13 v. in 1. 015.73 67-4308
     Z1215 .E9232 1967 MRR Alc.

Evans, Charles, American bibliography; Chicago, Priv. print. for the author by the Blakely Press, 1903-59. 14 v.   03-32909
     Z1215 .E92 MRR Ref Desk.

Lehmann-Haupt, Hellmut, The book in America; 2d [rev. and enl. American] ed. New York, Bowker, 1951. xlv, 493 p.   655.473 51-11308
     Z473 .L522 1951 MRR Alc.

Oswald, John Clyde, Printing in the Americas. New York, Hacker Art Books, 1968. 565, xli p.   655.1/7 68-9008
     Z205 .O86 1968 MRR Alc.

Thomas, Isaiah, The history of printing in America. Barre, Mass., Imprint Society, 1970. xxi, 650 p. 686.2/0973 75-100491
     Z205 .T56 1970 MRR Alc.

Trienens, Roger J. Pioneer imprints from fifty States, Washington, Library of Congress; [for sale by the Supt. of Docs., U.S. Govt. Print. Off.] 1973. 87 p. [$4.25] 686.2/0973 72-10069
     Z663 .P5 MRR Alc.

PRINTING--PRIVATE PRESSES.
Ransom, Will, Selective check list of press books; New York, P. C. Duschnes, 1945- pts.   015 46-583
     Z1028 .R3 MRR Alc.

PRINTING--SPECIMENS.
Jaspert, W. Pincus. The encyclopaedia of type faces [4th ed.], entirely restyled and greatly enl.] New York, Barnes & Noble [1970] xiii, 420 p. 686/.224 70-22018
     Z250 .J36 1970 MRR Alc.

Mumey, Nolie, A study of rare books, Denver, The Clason publishing company, 1930. xvii p., 2 l., 3-572 p. 090 30-25438
     Z1012 .M95 MRR Alc.

Nida, Eugene Albert, The Book of a thousand tongues Rev. ed. [London] United Bible Societies [1972] xviii, 536 p.   220.5 73-160367
     P352.A2 N6 1972 MRR Alc.

Robinson, Leslie John. A dictionary of graphical symbols London, Avis, 1972. 360 p. [£3.75] 001.56 73-165683
     Z250 .R683 MRR Ref Desk.

Updike, Daniel Berkeley, Printing types. [3d ed.] Cambridge, Mass., Belknap Press, 1962. 2 v.   655.24 62-5866
     Z250.A2 U6 1962 MRR Alc.

Visual Graphics Corporation. The world-famous photo typositor alphabet library. New ed. [North Miami, Fla.] c1973. xi, 270 p.   686.2/24 74-75693
     Z250 .V67 1973 MRR Alc.

PRINTING--YEARBOOKS.
The Master printers annual. 44th-year: 1963- London, British Federation of Master Printers. 686.2/0942 72-623098
     Z119.5 .M42 MRR Alc Latest edition

PRINTING--ITALY--BIO-BIBLIOGRAPHY.
Cosenza, Mario Emilio, Biographical and bibliographical dictionary of the Italian printers, Boston, G. K. Hall, 1968 [c1967] vii, 679 p. 016.6551/45 67-17808
     Z155 .C6 MRR Alc.

PRINTING, PRACTICAL.
Strauss, Victor. The printing industry; Washington, Printing Industries of America [1967] xiv, 814 p.   655 67-26209
     Z244 .S873 MRR Alc.

PRINTING, PRACTICAL--MAKE-UP.
Lee, Marshall, Bookmaking; New York, Bowker [1965] 399 p.   655 65-22380
     Z253.5 .L4 MRR Alc.

PRINTING, PRACTICAL--STYLE MANUALS.
Chicago. University. Press. A manual of style, [1st] ed.; 1906-Chicago. 655.25 06-40582
     Z253 .C57 MRR Ref Desk Latest edition

New York times. Style book. New York, McGraw-Hill Book Co. 655.25 38-30140
     Z253 .N56 MRR Ref Desk Latest edition

Oxford University Press. Rules for compositors & readers at the University Press, Oxford. London [etc.] 655.25 04-16812
     Z253 .O87 MRR Alc Latest edition

Skillin, Marjorie E. Words into type. 3d ed., completely rev. Englewood Cliffs, N.J., Prentice-Hall [1974] xx, 585 p.   808/.02 73-21726
     PN160 .S52 1974 MRR Ref Desk.

United States. Government Printing Office. Style manual. Rev. ed. Washington, 1973. viii, 548 p. [$4.25]   686.2/252 72-600382
     Z253 .U58 1973 MRR Ref Desk.

Von Ostermann, George Frederick, Manual of foreign languages 4th ed., rev. and enl. New York, Central Book Co., 1952. 414 p.   402/.02 52-2409
     Z253 .V94 1952 MRR Alc.

PRINTING, PUBLIC--UNITED STATES.
United States. Government Printing Office. 100 GPO years, 1861-1961; [Washington, 1961] xi, 164 p. 655.1753 61-19531
     Z232.U6 A5 1961 MRR Alc.

PRINTING INDUSTRY--DICTIONARIES.
Crispin, Frederic Swing, Dictionary of technical terms. 11th ed., rev. New York, Bruce Pub. Co. [1970] vi, 455 p.   603 73-104870
     T9 .C885 1970 MRR Alc.

PRINTING INDUSTRY--EUROPE--DIRECTORIES.
Polygraph Adressbuch der graphischen Industrie. 35.- Ausg.; 1969/70-[Frankfurt am Main] 72-623129
     Z291 .P6 MRR Alc Latest edition

PRINTING INDUSTRY--FRANCE--DIRECTORIES.
Annuaire Desechaliers ... Paris. 42-34851
"Fondé en 1895.
     Z308 .A75 MRR Alc Latest edition

PRINTING INDUSTRY--GREAT BRITAIN--DIRECTORIES.
Printing and allied trades directory. London, Benn Bros. 655/.025/42 68-50160
Began in 1960.
     Z327 .P7 MRR Alc Latest edition

PRINTING INDUSTRY--SPAIN--DIRECTORIES.
Catalogo del papel, prensa y artes graficas. 1957- [Barcelona, Abarca] 58-26342
     Z414 .C3 MRR Alc Latest edition

PRINTING INDUSTRY--UNITED STATES--CREDIT GUIDES.
Paper & Allied Trades Mercantile Agency, inc., New York. P. A. T. credit reference. New York. 27-9871
     HF5585.P2 P3 MRR Alc Latest edition

PRINTING INDUSTRY--UNITED STATES--DIRECTORIES.
Printing trades blue book. Southeastern edition. 1961/62- New York, A. F. Lewis. 62-52219
     Z475 .P79 MRR Alc Latest edition

Printing trades blue book. Northeastern edition. 1962/63- New York, A. F. Lewis. 62-52220
     Z475 .P78 MRR Alc Latest edition

Printing trades blue book. Metropolitan ed., Greater New York and New Jersey. [no. 1]- 1916-New York, A. F. Lewis. 16-1684
     Z475 .P8N MRR Alc Latest edition

PRINTING-INK.
Printing ink manual; 2nd ed. Cambridge, Heffer, 1969. ix, 848 p. [8/8/-]   667/.5 79-434695
     TP949 .B75 1969 MRR Alc.

PRINTING MACHINERY AND SUPPLIES--DIRECTORIES.
Weitpert, Hans, Lexograph, Internationales Handbuch für die graphische und papierverarbeitende Industrie. 2. Ausg. Stuttgart, Belser (1968). 602 p. with illus. [48.00]   76-422060
     Z249 .W4 1968 MRR Alc.

PRINTING PLANTS--DIRECTORIES.
Österreichs Presse, Werbung, Graphik; Handbuch. 15.- Jahrg.; 1967- Wien, Verband Österreichischer Zeitungsherausgeber. 72-626652
     Z6956.A9 H3 MRR Alc Latest edition

PRINTS--CATALOGS.
United States. Library of Congress. Prints and Photographs Division. Selective checklist of prints and photographs recently cataloged and made available for reference. lots 2280- 1949- [Washington] 016.779 49-47008
     Z663.39 .S4 MRR Alc   MRR Alc Full set

PRINTS--COLLECTORS AND COLLECTING.
Zigrosser, Carl, A guide to the
collecting and care of original
prints, New York, Crown Publishers
[1967, c1965] vi, 120 p. 769/.1
68-115
NE885 .Z5 1967 MRR Alc

PRINTS--TECHNIQUE.
Heller, Jules. Printmaking today,
2d ed. New York, Holt, Rinehart and
Winston [1972] viii, 344 p.
760/.28 73-171523
NE850 .H45 1972 MRR Alc.

Peterdi, Gabor. Printmaking: methods
old and new. Rev. ed. New York,
Macmillan [1971] xxxix, 342 p.
[$15.00] 760/.28 79-130950
NE850 .P4 1971 MRR Alc.

PRINTS--WASHINGTON, D.C.--CATALOGS.
United States. Library of Congress.
Prints and Photographs Division.
American prints in the Library of
Congress; Baltimore, Published for
the Library of Congress by the Johns
Hopkins Press [1970] xxi, 568 p.
769/.973 73-106134
NE505 .A47 MRR Alc.

United States. Library of Congress.
Prints and Photographs Division.
Selective checklist of prints and
photographs recently cataloged and
made available for reference. lots
2280- 1949- [Washington] 016.779
49-47008
Z663.39 .S4 MRR Alc MRR Alc Full
set

United States. Library of Congress.
Reference Dept. Guide to the special
collections of prints & photographs
in the Library of Congress,
Washington, 1955. v, 200 p.
016.779 54-60020
Z663.2 .08 MRR Alc.

PRINTS, AMERICAN--CATALOGS.
United States. Library of Congress.
Prints and Photographs Division.
American prints in the Library of
Congress; Baltimore, Published for
the Library of Congress by the Johns
Hopkins Press [1970] xxi, 568 p.
769/.973 73-106134
NE505 .A47 MRR Alc.

PRINTS, AMERICAN--EXHIBITIONS.
United States. Library of Congress.
Prints and Photographs Division.
Catalog of the national exhibition of
prints made during the current year,
1st- May 1/July 1, 1943-
Washington, 769.0838 43-16468
Z663.39 .C3 MRR Alc MRR Alc Full
set

PRISON INDUSTRIES
see Convict labor

PRISONERS--BIBLIOGRAPHY.
Abstracts on criminology and
penology. Deventer. 364/.08 72-
626328
Began in 1969.
HV6001 .E9 MRR Alc Full set

Crime and delinquency abstracts. v.
1- etc.] Jan. 1963- [Bethesda, Md.,
etc.] National Clearinghouse for
Mental Health Information [etc.] 66-
3911
Z5118.C9 I55 MRR Alc Full set

Excerpta criminologica. v. 1-8; 1961-
68. Amsterdam. 63-59273
HV6001 .E9 MRR Alc Full set

PRISONS--ENGLAND.
Tempest, Paul. Lag's lexicon;
London, Routledge & K. Paul [1950]
viii, 233 p. 427.09 51-5071
PE3726 .T4 MRR Alc.

PRIVATE FLYING.
America's flying book, New York,
Scribner [1972] xxvii, 365 p.
[$12.95] 629.132/5217 72-1213
TL721.4 .A4 MRR Alc.

Pryor, Louis R. Fly in Europe: your
guide to personal flying,
[Cleveland, Leisure Flying
Consultants] 1972. 235 p. [$5.95]
629.132/54/4 72-81620
TL726.15 .P78 MRR Alc.

PRIVATE PRESSES.
Ransom, Will, Private presses and
their books, New York, R. R. Bowker
company, 1929. 493, [1] p. 29-
24889
Z151 .R21 MRR Alc.

PRIVATE PRESSES--DIRECTORIES.
Private press books. 1959- [Pinner,
Eng. etc.] Private Libraries
Association. 015 60-31492
Z1028 .P7 MRR Alc Partial set

PRIVATE PRESSES--GREAT BRITAIN.
Ridler, William. British modern
press books: London, Covent Garden
Press, 1971. iii-xvi, 310 p.
[£5.25] 015/.42 72-179701
Z231.5.P7 R54 MRR Alc.

PRIVATE SCHOOLS--CANADA.
The Handbook of private schools. 1st-
1915- Boston, P. Sargent. 15-
12869
L901 .H3 MRR Ref Desk Latest
edition

PRIVATE SCHOOLS--FRANCE--DIRECTORIES.
Guide national de l'enseignement
privé. Académie de Paris. Paris,
Éditions Bereny. 62-50570
L927 .G85 MRR Alc Latest edition

PRIVATE SCHOOLS--GREAT BRITAIN--
DIRECTORIES.
The Girl's school year book (public
schools) London, Adam & Charles
Black, [etc.] ca 08-3162
LC2055 .A3 MRR Alc Latest edition

Paton's list of schools and tutors.
London, J. & J. Paton. ca 14-333
L915 .P3 MRR Alc Latest edition

The Public and preparatory schools
year book. 1935- London, Adam &
Charles Black [etc.] 373.2/22/02542
72-626709
L915 .P9 MRR Alc Latest edition

Schools; London, Truman & Knightley,
ltd. 370.942 [370.58] 34-29857
L915 .S43 MRR Alc Latest edition

The Schools of England, Wales,
Scotland and northern Ireland with
particulars of recommended schools on
the continent of Europe and tutors'
announcements; Cheltenham, Glos.
[etc.] Burrow's Scholastic Bureau. e
11-1602
L915 .S44 MRR Alc latest edition

PRIVATE SCHOOLS--GREAT BRITAIN--
YEARBOOKS.
Independent Schools Association.
Year book. London, A. & C. Black.
370.58 59-18884
Began publication with 1957 issue.
L915 .I5 MRR Alc Latest edition

PRIVATE SCHOOLS--NEW YORK (CITY)--
DIRECTORIES.
Hechinger, Grace. The New York times
guide to New York City private
schools, 1968- New York, Simon and
Schuster. 371/.02/0257471 68-14839

L903.N75 H4 MRR Alc Latest edition

PRIVATE SCHOOLS--UNITED STATES.
The Handbook of private schools. 1st-
1915- Boston, P. Sargent. 15-
12869
L901 .H3 MRR Ref Desk Latest
edition

PRIVATE SCHOOLS--UNITED STATES--
DIRECTORIES.
The Boarding school directory of the
United States and Canada. v. 3-
1969/72- Chicago, Educational
Bureau. 371/.02/0257 72-627132
L901 .B65 MRR Ref Desk Latest
edition

Bunting and Lyon. Bunting and Lyon's
guide to private independent schools.
1st- ed.: 1973- Wallingford,
Conn. [$4.95] 371/.02/02573 73-
77690
L901 .B86a MRR Ref Desk Latest
edition

Gertler, Diane (Bochner) Directory:
public elementary and secondary day
schools, 1968-69, [Washington] U.S.
National Center for Educational
Statistics; [for sale by the Supt. of
Docs., U.S. Govt. Print. Off., 1970-
v. [2.00] 371/.01/02573 70-
607482
L901 .G39 MRR Alc.

Leib, Robert J. U.S. private schools
classified, Los Angeles, Sherbourne
Press [1968] 192 p. 371/.02/02573
68-14283
L901 .L4 MRR Alc.

Lovejoy's prep school guide. 1958-
New York, Harper. 373.73 58-11044
L901 .L65 MRR Alc Latest edition

Private independent schools; A
directory and guide for parents and
teachers. 1943- Wallingford, Conn.
[etc.] J. E. Bunting & Lyon [etc.]
370.58 43-11107
L901 .P68 MRR Ref Desk Latest
edition

Summer studies in private independent
schools. 1st- ed.; 1964-
Wallingford, Conn., Bunting and Lyon.
373.2205873 64-20357
LC5751 .S8 MRR Alc Latest edition

PRIVATE SCHOOLS--WASHINGTON, D.C.--
DIRECTORIES.
Independent School Guides (Firm)
Washington area private schools;
Chevy Chase, Md., 1971. 99 p.
[$3.50] 371/.02/025753 73-26642
LC50.D6 I5 MRR Alc.

PRIVATE SCHOOLS--WASHINGTON
METROPOLITAN AREA--DIRECTORIES.
Independent School Guides (Firm)
Washington area private schools;
Chevy Chase, Md., 1971. 99 p.
[$3.50] 371/.02/025753 73-26642
LC50.D6 I5 MRR Alc.

PRIVATEERING.
Emmons, George Foster, The Navy of
the United States, from the
commencement, 1775 to 1853;
Washington, Printed by Gideon & co.,
1853. 4 p. l., 208 p. 02-7188
E182 .E54 MRR Alc.

PRIVATELY PRINTED BOOKS.
Lowndes, William Thomas, The
bibliographer's manual of English
literature New ed., rev., cor. and
enl., London, H. G. Bohn, 1857-61;
Bell & Daldy, 1864-65. 10 v.
015.42 35-36009
Z2001 .L92 1857-65 MRR Alc.

PRIVATELY PRINTED BOOKS--BIBLIOGRAPHY.
Private press books. 1959- [Pinner,
Eng. etc.] Private Libraries
Association. 015 60-31492
Z1028 .P7 MRR Alc Partial set

Ransom, Will, Selective check list
of press books; New York, P. C.
Duschnes, 1945- pts. 015 46-
583
Z1028 .R3 MRR Alc.

Ransom, Will, Private presses and
their books, New York, R. R. Bowker
company, 1929. 493, [1] p. 29-
24889
Z151 .R21 MRR Alc.

Ridler, William. British modern
press books: London, Covent Garden
Press, 1971. iii-xvi, 310 p.
[£5.25] 015/.42 72-179701
Z231.5.P7 R54 MRR Alc.

PRIZE-FIGHTING
see Boxing

PROBATION OFFICERS--CANADA--DIRECTORIES.
National Council on Crime and
Delinquency. Probation and parole
directory, United States and Canada.
1910- New York. 364.62 12-8793
HV9303 .N255 MRR Alc Latest
edition

PROBATION OFFICERS--UNITED STATES--
DIRECTORIES.
National Council on Crime and
Delinquency. Probation and parole
directory, United States and Canada.
1910- New York. 364.62 12-8793
HV9303 .N255 MRR Alc Latest
edition

PROBLEM CHILDREN.
see also Juvenile delinquency

PROCESSING (LIBRARIES)
Ruggles, Melville J., Russian and
East European publications in the
libraries of the United States New
York, Columbia University Press,
1960. xv, 396 p. 016.947 60-13887

Z2483 .R82 1960 MRR Alc.

Tauber, Maurice Falcolm, ed.
Technical services in libraries: New
York, Columbia University Press, 1954
[c1953] xvi, 487 p. 025 54-10328

Z665 .T28 1954 MRR Alc.

PROCESSIONS.
see also Festivals

PRODUCE
see Farm produce

PRODUCE EXCHANGES
see Commodity exchanges

PRODUCE TRADE.
see also Agricultural price supports

see also Farm produce

see also Food industry and trade

see also Food supply

PRODUCE TRADE--DICTIONARIES.
Henderson, Harry William, Dictionary
of international agricultural trade.
Washington, U.S. Foreign Agricultural
Service; [for sale by the Supt. of
Docs., U.S. Govt. Print. Off.] 1971.
170 p. 382/.41/014 76-612219
HF1002 .H38 1971 MRR Alc.

PRODUCE TRADE--STATISTICS.
Food and Agriculture Organization of
the United Nations. Trade yearbook.
v. 12- 1958- Rome. 338.14058 59-
3598
    HD9000.4 .F58 Sci RR Partial set /
    MRR Alc Latest edition

PRODUCE TRADE--STATISTICS--BIBLIOGRAPHY.
International Trade Centre.
Compendium of sources; Geneva, 1967.
232 p. [unpriced] 016.3824 74-
431255
    Z7164.C81 I58 MRR Alc.

Wasserman, Paul. Commodity prices:
Detroit, Gale Research Co. [1974]
xii, 200 p. [$15.00] 338.5/2/0973
73-19898
    Z7164.P94 W33 MRR Alc.

PRODUCE TRADE--EUROPEAN ECONOMIC
COMMUNITY COUNTRIES--STATISTICS.
United States. Dept. of Agriculture.
Economic Research Service. European
Economic Community; agricultural
trade statistics 1961-67.
[Washington, 1969] 1 v. (unpaged)
382/.41/094 78-601937
    HD9015.A3 U46 MRR Alc.

PRODUCE TRADE--FRANCE--DIRECTORIES.
Annuaire international fructidor.
Avignon. 72-627013
    HD9012.3 A6 MRR Alc Latest edition

PRODUCE TRADE--UNITED STATES.
United States. Dept. of Agriculture.
Marketing. [Washington, U.S. Govt.
Print. Off., 1954] xiv, 506 p.
631.18   agr55-4
    S21.A35 1954 MRR Alc.

PRODUCE TRADE--UNITED STATES--CREDIT
GUIDES.
Produce Reporter Company's semi-
annual blue book. 1905- Wheaton,
Ill. [etc.] 338.7/63 53-55972
    HF55.85.P7 P7 MRR Alc Latest
    edition

Produce Reporter Company's semi-
annual blue book. Supplement.
Wheaton, Ill. [etc.] 338.7/63 74-
643555
    HF5585.P7 P7 Suppl. MRR Alc
    Partial set

PRODUCE TRADE--UNITED STATES--
PERIODICALS.
Produce Reporter Company's semi-
annual blue book. 1905- Wheaton,
Ill. [etc.] 338.7/63 53-55972
    HF55.85.P7 P7 MRR Alc Latest
    edition

Produce Reporter Company's semi-
annual blue book. Supplement.
Wheaton, Ill. [etc.] 338.7/63 74-
643555
    HF5585.P7 P7 Suppl. MRR Alc
    Partial set

PRODUCERS, MOVING-PICTURE
see Moving-picture producers and
directors

PRODUCT MANAGEMENT.
see also New products

PRODUCTION CONTROL--DICTIONARIES.
Encyclopedic dictionary of production
and production control, Englewood
Cliffs, N.J., Prentice-Hall [1964]
vi, 569 p. 658.03 64-7566
    TS9 .E5 MRR Alc.

PRODUCTION MANAGEMENT--DICTIONARIES.
Encyclopedic dictionary of production
and production control, Englewood
Cliffs, N.J., Prentice-Hall [1964]
vi, 569 p. 658.03 64-7566
    TS9 .E5 MRR Alc.

PRODUCTS, COMMERCIAL
see Commercial products

PRODUCTS, MANUFACTURED
see Manufactures

PRODUCTS, NEW
see New products

PRODUCTS, WASTE
see Waste products

PROFESSIONAL EDUCATION--ARAB COUNTRIES.
Qubain, Fahim Issa, Education and
science in the Arab world Baltimore,
Johns Hopkins Press [1966] xxii, 539
p. 378.00917165 65-26182
    LA1101 .Q3 MRR Alc.

PROFESSIONAL EDUCATION--EUROPE--
DIRECTORIES.
Organization for Economic Cooperation
and Development. Inventory of
training possibilities in Europe.
[Paris, 1965] 896 p. 65-9050
    LC1071.E8 O7 MRR Alc.

PROFESSIONAL EDUCATION--UNITED STATES.
Colleges and specialized schools.
1st- 1952- Boston, P. Sargent. 52-
3398
    L901 .J8 MRR Ref Desk Latest
    edition / MRR Alc Latest edition

PROFESSIONAL EDUCATION--UNITED STATES--
DIRECTORIES.
Edfac Publishing Co. Edfac career
school directory. Colorado Springs
[1973, c1972] xlii, 305 p. [$12.95]
331.7/02 73-169423
    L901 .E33 1972 MRR Ref Desk.

Graduate & professional school
opportunities for minority students.
Princeton, N.J., Educational Testing
Service. 378.1/553/02573 73-642558
    L901 .G717 MRR Ref Desk Latest
    edition

Livesey, Herbert B. Guide to
American graduate schools, 2d ed.,
completely rev. and updated. New
York, Viking Press [1970] xxxviii,
410 p. [$5.95] 378.1/553/02573 70-
120742
    L901 .L5 1970 MRR Ref Desk.

Miller, Adeline Elizabeth. National
directory of schools and vocations,
2d ed. North Springfield, Pa., State
School Publications, 1963 viii, 703
p. 371.425058 63-19356
    L901 .M48 1963 MRR Ref Desk.

Searles, Aysel. Guide to financial
aids for students in arts & sciences
for graduate and professional study
Rev. ed. New York, Arco [1974] xii,
107 p. [$3.95] 378.3/025/73 74-
80776
    LB2338 .S4 1974 MRR Ref Desk.

PROFESSIONAL ETHICS.
see also Business ethics

PROFESSIONAL ETHICS--UNITED STATES.
Clapp, Jane. Professional ethics and
insignia. Metuchen, N.J., Scarecrow
Press, 1974. xii, 851 p. 061/.3
74-10501
    HD6504 .A194 MRR Ref Desk.

PROFESSIONALS.
see also Occupations

PROFESSIONS.
see also Vocational guidance

PROFESSIONS--LICENSES--UNITED STATES--
DIRECTORIES.
Angel, Juvenal Londoño, Directory
of professional and occupational
licensing in the United States, New
York, World Trade Academy Press;
distributed by Simon & Schuster
[1970] 755 p. 75-93680
    HD7824.U5 A75 MRR alc.

PROFESSIONS--NEW ZEALAND--DIRECTORIES.
The New Zealand index of trades,
industries, and professions.
Auckland, N.Z., Dodson and Cooper.
61-45521
    HF3963 .N4 MRR Alc Latest edition

PROFIT AND LOSS STATEMENTS
see Financial statements

PROGNOSIS.
see also Diagnosis

PROGRAM BUDGETING--UNITED STATES.
Novick, David, ed. Program
budgeting; [2d ed.] Cambridge,
Harvard University Press [c1967]
xxiv, 382 p. 353.007222 68-1604
    HJ2052 .N6 1967 MRR Alc.

PROGRAMMED INSTRUCTION--BIBLIOGRAPHY.
Gee, Ralph D. Teaching machines and
programmed learning; 2d ed.
Hatfield [Eng.] Hertfordshire County
Council, Technical Library &
Information Service. Hatfield College
of Technology, 1965. 128 p. 67-
103710
    Z5814.A85 G4 1965 MRR Alc.

Hendershot, Carl H. Programmed
learning and individually paced
instruction; 5th ed. [Bay City,
Mich., 1973- v.   [$30.00]
016.37139/442 73-77783
    LB1028.7 .H422 MRR Alc.

PROGRAMMED INSTRUCTION--CATALOGS.
Yearbook of educational and
instructional technology. [London]
Cornmarket Press. 370/.777 79-
224079
    LB1028.7 .Y4 MRR Alc Latest
    edition

PROGRAMS, RADIO
see Radio programs

PROGRAMS, TELEVISION
see Television programs

PROGRESSIVISM (U.S. POLITICS)
Shannon, David A., ed. Progressivism
and postwar disillusionment, 1898-
1928, New York, McGraw-Hill [1966]
383 p. 973.9108 65-26768
    E173 .D58 vol. 6 MRR Alc.

PROHIBITED BOOKS.
Burke, Redmond Ambrose, What is the
Index? Milwaukee, Bruce [1952] x,
129 p. 098.11 52-9314
    Z1019 .B95 MRR Alc.

PROHIBITED BOOKS--BIBLIOGRAPHY.
Burke, Redmond Ambrose, What is the
Index? Milwaukee, Bruce [1952] x,
129 p. 098.11 52-9314
    Z1019 .B95 MRR Alc.

Haight, Anne (Lyon) Banned books:
2d ed. rev. and enl. New York, R. R.
Bowker, 1955. xvii, 172 p. 098.1
54-11650
    Z1019 .H15 1955 MRR Alc.

Index librorum prohibitorum. Index
librorum prohibitorum, [In Civitate
Vaticana] Typis Polyglottis
Vaticanis, 1948. xxiv, 508 p.
098.11 a 52-648
    Z1020 .I948 MRR Alc.

PROJECT APOLLO.
Astronautics and aeronautics;
1915/60- Washington, Scientific and
Technical Information Division,
National Aeronautics and Space
Administration [etc.; for sale by the
Superintendent of Documents, U.S.
Govt. Print. Off.] 65-60308
    TL521.3.A8 A3 MRR Alc Partial set

PROJECTILES.
see also Rockets (Aeronautics)

PROLETARIAT.
see also Labor and laboring classes

PROMOTION OF SPECIAL EVENTS.
Leibert, Edwin Reisinger, Handbook
of special events for nonprofit
organizations; New York, Association
Press [1972] 224 p. [$12.95]
361.7/3 75-129437
    HV41 .L415 MRR Alc.

PROOF-READING.
Collins, Frederick Howard, Authors'
and printers' dictionary: 10th ed.,
rev. London, New York, Oxford
University Press, 1956. xlv, 442 p.
655.25 56-58185
    Z254 .C76 1956 MRR Alc.

PROPAGANDA.
see also Advertising

see also Public relations

PROPAGANDA, AMERICAN--CASE STUDIES.
Kominsky, Morris. The hoaxers: plain
liars, fancy liars, and damned liars.
Boston, Branden Press [1970] 735 p.
[$12.50] 909 76-109134
    E839.8 .K6 MRR Alc.

PROPERTY INSURANCE
see Insurance, Property

PROPORTIONAL REPRESENTATION.
see also Minorities

Lakeman, Enid. How democracies vote:
3rd ed. London, Faber, 1970. 3-
318 p. [45/-] 324/.21 73-481393
    JF1001 .L27 1970 MRR Alc.

PROSE LITERATURE--TECHNIQUE.
see also Fiction--Technique

PROSODY
see Versification

PROSPECTING.
see also Mineralogy, Determinative

Carlisle, Norman V., The complete
guide to treasure hunting Chicago,
H. Regnery Co. [1973] 280 p.
917.3/04 73-6452
    E159.5 .C37 MRR Alc.

Pearl, Richard Maxwell, Handbook for
prospectors 5th ed. New York,
McGraw-Hill [1973] viii, 472 p.
622/.1 72-11749
    TN270 .P4 1973 MRR Alc.

PROSPECTING--GEOPHYSICAL METHODS.
The Geophysical directory. [Houston]
622.1058 50-28141
    TN867 .G46 MRR Alc Latest edition

PROTECTION OF ENVIRONMENT
see Environmental protection

PROTECTION OF NATURE
see Nature conservation

PROTEST MOVEMENTS (VIETNAMESE CONFLICT,
1961-)
see Vietnamese Conflict, 1961- --
Protest movements

PROTESTANT CHURCHES.
New York. Missionary Research
Library. Protestant churches of
Asia, the Middle East, Africa, Latin
America, and the Pacific area. New
York, 1959. 75 p. 284 59-44072
    BX4805.2 .N45 1959 MRR Alc.

PROTESTANT CHURCHES--FRANCE--DIRECTORIES.
Annuaire protestant. Paris, Centrale du livre protestant [etc.]
280/.4/0944 74-642446
BX4843.A2 A55 MRR Alc Latest edition

PROTESTANT CHURCHES--UNITED STATES.
Hardon, John A. The Protestant churches of America Rev. ed. Garden City, N.Y., Image Books [1969] 439 p. [1.45] 280/.4/0973 69-12858
BR516.5 .H3 1969 MRR Alc.

PROTESTANT EPISCOPAL CHURCH IN THE U.S.A.--BIOGRAPHY.
Barnes, Calvin Rankin, The General Convention: offices and officers, 1785-1950. Philadelphia, Church Historical Society [1951] vi, 148 p.
283.73 51-10469
BX5820 .A4B3 MRR Biog.

PROTESTANT EPISCOPAL CHURCH IN THE U.S.A.--BIOGRAPHY--DICTIONARIES.
The Episcopal clergy directory. 1971/72- [New York] Church Hymnal Corp. 283/.092/2 72-621280
BX5990 .E5 MRR Biog Latest edition

PROTESTANT EPISCOPAL CHURCH IN THE U.S.A.--DICTIONARIES.
A Dictionary of the Episcopal Church. Philadelphia [etc.] Trefoil Publishing Society. 283.03 55-15394

BX5007 .D5 MRR Alc Latest edition

PROTESTANT EPISCOPAL CHURCH IN THE U.S.A.--EDUCATION --DIRECTORIES.
Directory of Episcopal church schools. [New York] National Association of Episcopal Schools.
377/.8/302573 78-10392
LC583 .D56 MRR Alc Latest Edition

PROTESTANT EPISCOPAL CHURCH IN THE U.S.A.--HISTORY.
Albright, Raymond Wolf, A history of the Protestant Episcopal Church New York, Macmillan [c1964] x, 406 p.
283.73 64-21168
BX5880 .A4 MRR Alc.

PROTESTANT EPISCOPAL CHURCH IN THE U.S.A.--HYMNS.
Protestant Episcopal Church in the U.S.A. Hymnal. The hymnal of the Protestant Episcopal Church in the United States of America. Greenwich, Conn., Seabury Press [1953, c1943] 673 p. 65-6189
BX5943.A1 1953 MRR Alc.

PROTESTANT EPISCOPAL CHURCH IN THE U.S.A.--YEARBOOKS.
The Episcopal Church annual. 1882- New York, Morehouse Barlow Co. [etc.] 283.058 46-33254
BX5830 .L5 MRR Alc Latest edition

Episcopal year. 1969- New York, Jarrow Press. 283/.73 72-122639
BX5830 .E64 MRR Alc Latest edition

PROTESTANT EPISCOPAL CHURCH IN THE U.S.A. BOOK OF COMMON PRAYER.
Protestant Episcopal Church in the U.S.A. Book of common prayer. The Oxford American prayer book commentary. New York, Oxford University Press, 1950. 1 v. (various pagings) 264.03 50-10192

BX5945 .S5 MRR Alc.

Suter, John Wallace, The American Book of common prayer; New York, Oxford Univ. Press, 1949. vii, 85 p. 264.039 49-3873
BX5145 .S8 MRR Alc.

PROTESTANT EPISCOPAL CHURCH IN THE U.S.A. GENERAL CONVENTION.
Barnes, Calvin Rankin, The General Convention: offices and officers, 1785-1950. Philadelphia, Church Historical Society [1951] vi, 148 p.
283.73 51-10469
BX5820 .A4B3 MRR Biog.

PROTESTANT REFORMATION
see Reformation

PROTESTANTISM.
Dunstan, John Leslie, ed. Protestantism. New York, G. Braziller, 1961. 255 p. 284 61-15497
BX4811 .D8 MRR Alc.

Ferm, Vergilius Ture Anselm, ed. Classics of Protestantism. New York, Philosophical Library [1959] ix, 587 p. 230.4 59-16427
BX4801 .F45 MRR Alc.

PROTESTANTISM--COLLECTIONS.
Magill, Frank Northen, ed. Masterpieces of Christian literature in summary form. [1st ed.] New York, Salem Press [1963] 2 v. (xxvi, 1193, v p.) 64-104
BR50 .M22 1963 MRR Alc.

PROTESTANTISM--DICTIONARIES.
Corpus dictionary of Western churches. Washington, Corpus Publications [1970] xviii, 820 p. [$25.00] 203 78-99501
BR95 .C67 MRR Alc.

Ferm, Vergilius Ture Anselm, Concise dictionary of religion; New York, Philosophical Library [1964? c1951] ix, 283 p. 203 64-4055
BR95 .F37 1964 MRR Alc.

The Westminster dictionary of church history. Philadelphia, Westminster Press [1971] xii, 887 p. [$17.50] 270/.03 69-11071
BR95 .W496 MRR Alc.

Wright, Charles Henry Hamilton, ed. The Protestant dictionary, New ed., London, The Harrison trust [1933] xix, 805, [1] p. 280.3 33-10289
BR95 .W7 1933 MRR Alc.

PROTESTANTISM--HISTORY.
Ferm, Vergilius Ture Anselm, Pictorial history of Protestantism; New York, Philosophical Library [1957] xi, 368 p. 284.09 57-14163
BX4805 .F4 MRR Alc.

Léonard, Émile G., A history of Protestantism London, Nelson, 1965 [i.e. 1966]- v. [90/- (v. 1)] 280.409 66-71795
BX4805.2 .L413 MRR Alc.

PROTESTANTISM--HISTORY--PICTURES, ILLUSTRATIONS, ETC.
Ferm, Vergilius Ture Anselm, Pictorial history of Protestantism; New York, Philosophical Library [1957] xi, 368 p. 284.09 57-14163
BX4805 .F4 MRR Alc.

PROTESTANTS IN THE UNITED STATES.
Gasper, Louis. The fundamentalist movement. The Hague, Mouton [1963] vii, 181 p. 230 63-24282
BT82.2 .G3 MRR Alc.

Who's who in the Protestant clergy. Encino, Calif., Nygaard Associates [1957] 264 p. 922 57-59372
BR569 .W5 MRR Biog.

PROVENÇAL LANGUAGE, MODERN--DICTIONARIES--FRENCH.
Mistral, Frédéric, Lou tresor dóu Felibrige Reimpression de l'edition 1879-1886. Osnabrück, Biblio-Verlag, 1966. 2 v. [DM 360.00] 67-84128
PC3376 .M72 MRR Alc.

PROVERBS.
Benham, William Gurney, Sir, Book of quotations, proverbs and household words. New and rev. ed. New York, Putnam [1949?] viii, 1384 p. 808.8 50-5072
PN6080 .B35 1949 MRR Ref Desk.

Bohn, Henry George, comp. A polyglot of foreign proverbs; Detroit, Gale Research Co., 1968. iv, 579 p.
398.9 67-23915
PN6404 .B7 1968b MRR Alc.

Champion, Selwyn Gurney, comp. Racial proverbs; [2d ed.] New York, Barnes & Noble [1964] cxxix, 767 p. 398.9 64-2057
PN6405 .C37 1964 MRR Alc.

Davidoff, Henry, comp. A world treasury of proverbs from twenty-five languages. London, Cassell [1953] 492 p. 398.9 54-24781
PN6405 .D3 1953 MRR Alc.

Lawson, James Gilchrist, comp. The world's best proverbs and maxims, New York, George H. Doran company [c1926] xvi p., 1 l., 19-364 p. 26-12534
PN6405 .L3 MRR Alc.

Lean, Vincent Stuckey, Lean's collectanea. Bristol, J. W. Arrowsmith; [etc., etc.] 1902-04. 4 v. in 5. 04-31340
PN6421 .L3 MRR Alc.

Pullar-Strecker, H. Proverbs for pleasure; London, C. Johnson [1954] 202 p. 398.9 55-19338
PN6405 .P8 MRR Alc.

Roback, Abraham Aaron, A dictionary of international slurs (ethnophaulisms Cambridge, Mass., Sci-art publishers [1944] 394 p. 323.1 44-8328
HT1523 .R6 MRR Alc.

Stevenson, Burton Egbert, ed. The home book of proverbs, maxims and familiar phrases. New York, Macmillan Co. 1948. viii, 2957 p.
398.9 48-8717
PN6405 .S8 MRR Alc.

Stevenson, Burton Egbert, ed. The Macmillan book of proverbs, maxims, and famous phrases. New York, Macmillan [1965, c1948] viii, 2957 p. 808.88 65-3787
PN6405 .S8 1965 MRR Ref Desk.

PROVERBS--BIBLIOGRAPHY--CATALOGS.
Cleveland. Public Library. John G. White Dept. Catalog of folklore and folk songs. Boston, G. K. Hall, 1964. 2 v. 65-4290
Z5985 .C5 MRR Alc (Dk 33).

PROVERBS--DICTIONARIES.
Browning, David Clayton, Everyman's dictionary of quotations and proverbs. London, Dent; New York, Dutton [1951] x, 766 p. 808.8 51-12780
PN6081 .B75 MRR Alc.

Tilley, Morris Palmer, A dictionary of the proverbs in England in the sixteenth and seventeenth centuries; Ann Arbor, University of Michigan Press, 1950. xiii, 854 p. 398.9 50-62722
PN6420 .T5 MRR Alc.

PROVERBS, AMERICAN.
Taylor, Archer, comp. A dictionary of American proverbs and proverbial phrases, 1820-1880, Cambridge, Belknap Press of Harvard University Press, 1958. xxii, 418 p. 398.903 58-10406
PN6426 .T28 MRR Alc.

PROVERBS, CHINESE.
Lai, T'ien-ch'ang, ed. and tr. [Ch'eng yu hsuan i (romanized form)] [Hong Kong] University Book Store, University of Hongkong, 1960. 191 p. 495.183 c 60-2495
PL1497 .L3 MRR Alc.

PROVERBS, ENGLISH.
The Dictionary of best known quotations & proverbs; New York, Garden City publishing co., inc. [c1939] vii, 380, 444 p. 808.8 39-33412
PN6081 .D5 MRR Alc.

Hazlitt, William Carew, English proverbs and proverbial phrases Detroit, Gale Research Co., 1969. xxx, 580 p. 398.9/2 73-78169
PN6421 .H3 1969 MRR Alc.

The Oxford dictionary of English proverbs. 3rd ed.; Oxford, Clarendon P., 1970. xix, 930 p. [£5/-/-] 398.9/2/03 75-18203
PN6421 .O9 1970 MRR Alc.

Ridout, Ronald. English proverbs explained. London, Heinemann, 1967. [5], 206 p. [25/-] 398.9/2/03 67-114581
PN6421 .R5 MRR Alc.

Taylor, Archer, comp. A dictionary of American proverbs and proverbial phrases, 1820-1880, Cambridge, Belknap Press of Harvard University Press, 1958. xxii, 418 p. 398.903 58-10406
PN6426 .T28 MRR Alc.

Whiting, Bartlett Jere, Proverbs, sentences, and proverbial phrases; Cambridge, Mass., Belknap Press of Harvard University Press, 1968. li, 733 p. [$25.00] 808.88/2 67-22874

PN6083 .W45 MRR Alc.

PROVERBS, GERMAN.
Kremer, Edmund Philipp, comp. German proverbs and proverbial phrases with their English counterparts. Stanford, Calif., Stanford University Press, 1955. 116 p. 398.9 55-6685

PN6461 .K75 MRR Alc.

Röhrich, Lutz. Lexikon der sprichwörtlichen Redensarten. Freiburg, Herder [1973] 2 v. (1255 p.) 73-364707
PF689 .R6 MRR Alc.

PROVERBS, JAPANESE.
Buchanan, Daniel Crump, ed. and tr. Japanese proverbs and sayings. [1st ed.] Norman, University of Oklahoma Press [1965] xvii, 280 p. 398.9956 65-24192
PN6519.J3 B8 MRR Alc.

Okada, Rokuo. Japanese proverbs and proverbial phrases. 1st- 1955- Tokyo, Japan Travel Bureau. 398.9 63-13226
PN6519.J3 O4 MRR Alc Latest edition

PROVERBS, MALAY.
Brown, Charles Cuthbert, Malay sayings. London, Routledge and K. Paul [1951] 274 p. 398.9 51-6834

PN6519.M26 B7 MRR Alc.

PROVERBS, PERSIAN.
Elwell-Sutton, Laurence Paul.
Persian proverbs. [1st ed.] London,
Murray [1954] 103 p.   398.9 55-338

    PN6519.P5 E4 MRR Alc.

PROVERBS, RUSSIAN.
Langnas, Izaak Abram, tr.   1200
Russian proverbs, New York,
Philosophical Library [1960] 91 p.
398.90947 60-2755
    PN6505.S5 L3 MRR Alc.

PROVERBS, SCOTTISH.
Carmichael, James, comp. The James
Carmichaell collection of proverbs in
Scots; Edinburgh, University Press,
1957. vii, 149 p.   398.9 a 58-2150
    PN6425.S4 C3 MRR Alc.

PSYCHIATRIC CLINICS--UNITED STATES--
DIRECTORIES.
Levine, Milton Isra, The parents'
encyclopedia of infancy, childhood,
and adolescence New York, Crowell
[1973] 619 p. [$10.00] 649/.1/03
72-83769
    RJ61 .L552 MRR Alc.

PSYCHIATRIC RESEARCH--RESEARCH GRANTS--
UNITED STATES--DIRECTORIES.
Wilson, Paul T., Money and
information for mental health;
Washington, American Psychiatric
Association [1971] xvi, 150 p.
362.2/072/073 72-152415
    RA790.6 .W5 MRR Alc.

PSYCHIATRIC SOCIAL WORK--WASHINGTON,
D.C.--DIRECTORIES.
Directory of psychiatrists and
clinical psychiatric facilities in
the Washington area. [Washington]
54-21311
    RC335 .D5 Sci RR Latest edition /
    MRR Ref Desk Latest edition

PSYCHIATRISTS--WASHINGTON, D.C.--
DIRECTORIES.
Directory of psychiatrists and
clinical psychiatric facilities in
the Washington area. [Washington]
54-21311
    RC335 .D5 Sci RR Latest edition /
    MRR Ref Desk Latest edition

PSYCHIATRISTS, AMERICAN--BIO-
BIBLIOGRAPHY.
American Psychiatric Association.
Biographical directory of fellows &
members. New York, R. R. Bowker Co.
616.806273 63-12595
    RC326 .A56 Sci RR Latest edition /
    MRR Biog Latest edition

PSYCHIATRY.
see also Mental hygiene
Freedman, Alfred M. Comprehensive
textbook of psychiatry. Baltimore,
Williams & Wilkins Co., 1967. xxv,
1666 p. 616.89 66-28162
    RC454 .F74 MRR Alc.

Freedman, Alfred M. Modern synopsis
of Comprehensive textbook of
psychiatry Baltimore, Williams &
Wilkins [1972] xvi, 853 p. [$15.95
(pbk)] 616.8/9 72-80881
    RC454 .F742 MRR Alc.

Noyes, Arthur Percy, Modern clinical
psychiatry 5th ed. Philadelphia,
Saunders, 1963. 586 p. 616.89 63-
9492
    RC454 .N68 1963 MRR Alc.

Redlich, Fredrick Carl, The theory
and practice of psychiatry New York,
Basic Books [1966] xii, 880 p.
616.89 66-13833
    RC454 .R4 MRR Alc.

Sim, Myre. Guide to psychiatry / 3d
ed. Edinburgh : Churchill
Livingstone ; New York : distributed
by Longman, 1974. xi, 1223 p. ;
[£6.00 ($21.00 U.S.)] 616.8/9 73-
94257
    RC454 .S47 1974 MRR Alc.

PSYCHIATRY--ADDRESSES, ESSAYS, LECTURES.
Millon, Theodore, ed. Theories of
psychopathology; Philadelphia,
Saunders, 1967. xv, 444 p.
616.89/008 67-11770
    RC459 .M515 MRR Alc.

PSYCHIATRY--BIBLIOGRAPHY.
Bowker's medical books in print.
1972- New York, R.R. Bowker Co.
016.61 78-37613
    Z6658 .B65 MRR Alc Latest edition
    / Sci RR Latest edition

Ennis, Bernice, Guide to the
literature in psychiatry. Los
Angeles, Partridge Press, 1971. xi,
127 p. 016.61689 76-150718
    Z6664.N5 E6 MRR Alc.

Menninger, Karl, A guide to
psychiatric books in English 3d ed.
New York, Grune & Stratton [1972]
xviii, 238 p. 016.6168/9 78-168846

    Z6664.N5 M48 1972 MRR Alc.

Solomon, Philip, Handbook of
psychiatry. 2d ed. Los Altos,
Calif., Lange Medical Publications,
1971. 648 p. 616.89 73-152398
    RC457 .S58 1971 MRR Alc.

PSYCHIATRY--COLLECTED WORKS.
American handbook of psychiatry. 2d
ed. [rev. and expanded] New York,
Basic Books [1974- v.
616.8/9/008 73-78893
    RC435 .A562 MRR Alc.

American handbook of psychiatry. New
York, Basic Books, 1958-66. 3 v.
616.89008 59-9444
    RC435 .A56 MRR Alc.

PSYCHIATRY--DICTIONARIES.
American Psychiatric Association.
Committee on Public Information. A
psychiatric glossary; 3d ed.
Washington, American Psychiatric
Association, 1969. 102 p. [1.00]
616.89/003 73-82048
    RC437 .A5 1969 MRR Alc.

Brussel, James Arnold, The layman's
dictionary of psychiatry New York,
Barnes and Noble [1967] xlv, 269 p.
616.89/003 67-19539
    RC437 .B7 1967 MRR Alc.

Goldenson, Robert M. The
encyclopedia of human behavior; [1st
ed.] Garden City, N.Y., Doubleday,
1970. 2 v. (xxviii, 1472 p.)
150/.3 68-18077
    BF31 .G6 MRR Alc.

Hinsie, Leland Earl, Psychiatric
dictionary 4th ed. New York, Oxford
University Press, 1970. ix, 816 p.
616.89/03 78-83030
    RC437 .H5 1970 MRR Alc.

Rycroft, Charles. A critical
dictionary of psychoanalysis. New
York, Basic Books, inc. [1968] xxvi,
189 p. [$4.95] 616.89/17/03 68-
54155
    RC437 .R9 MRR Alc.

Wolman, Benjamin B. Dictionary of
behavioral science, New York, Van
Nostrand Reinhold Co. [1973] ix, 478
p. 150/.3 73-748
    BF31 .W64 MRR Alc.

PSYCHIATRY--DICTIONARIES--GERMAN.
Beigel, Hugo G. Dictionary of
psychology and related fields German-
English. New York, F. Unger Pub. Co.
[1971] 256 p. [$9.00] 150/.3 74-
115063
    BF31 .B27 MRR Alc.

Müller, Christian, Lexikon der
Psychiatrie: Berlin, Heidelberg, New
York: Springer, 1973. 592 p.
[DM98.00] 616.8/9/003 73-78065
    RC437 .M8 1973 MRR Alc.

PSYCHIATRY--HANDBOOKS, MANUALS, ETC.
Novello, Joseph R. A practical
handbook of psychiatry. Springfield,
Ill., C. C. Thomas [1974] xxiv, 621
p. 616.8/9/00202 73-7518
    RC454 .N676 MRR Alc.

Solomon, Philip, Handbook of
psychiatry. 2d ed. Los Altos,
Calif., Lange Medical Publications,
1971. 648 p. 616.89 73-152398
    RC457 .S58 1971 MRR Alc.

PSYCHIATRY--HISTORY.
Psychiatry and its history;
Springfield, Ill., C. C. Thomas
[1970] xviii, 283 p. 618.89/009
75-95512
    RC438 .P78 MRR Alc.

PSYCHIATRY--STUDY AND TEACHING.
Novello, Joseph R. A practical
handbook of psychiatry. Springfield,
Ill., C. C. Thomas [1974] xxiv, 621
p. 616.8/9/00202 73-7518
    RC454 .N676 MRR Alc.

PSYCHIATRY--UNITED STATES--DIRECTORIES.
Novello, Joseph R. A practical
handbook of psychiatry. Springfield,
Ill., C. C. Thomas [1974] xxiv, 621
p. 616.8/9/00202 73-7518
    RC454 .N676 MRR Alc.

PSYCHICAL RESEARCH.
see also Dreams

Ashby, Robert H. The guidebook for
the study of psychical research New
York, S. Weiser, 1972. 190 p.
[$2.95] 016.1339/072 72-78575
    BF1031 .A8 1972b MRR Alc.

Cavendish, Richard. Encyclopedia of
the unexplained; London, Routledge &
K. Paul [1974] 304 p. [£7.95] 133
74-166662
    BF1411 .C32 1974b MRR Alc.

PSYCHICAL RESEARCH--BIBLIOGRAPHY.
Ashby, Robert H. The guidebook for
the study of psychical research New
York, S. Weiser, 1972. 190 p.
[$2.95] 016.1339/072 72-78575
    BF1031 .A8 1972b MRR Alc.

White, Rhea A. Parapsychology:
sources of information. Metuchen,
N.J., Scarecrow Press, 1973. 302 p.
016.1338 73-4853
    Z6878.P8 W47 MRR Alc.

PSYCHICAL RESEARCH--BIOGRAPHY.
Ashby, Robert H. The guidebook for
the study of psychical research New
York, S. Weiser, 1972. 190 p.
[$2.95] 016.1339/072 72-78575
    BF1031 .A8 1972b MRR Alc.

Biographical dictionary of
parapsychology. 1964/66- New York,
Helix Press. 921 64-4288
    BF1026 .B5 MRR Biog Latest edition

PSYCHICAL RESEARCH--DICTIONARIES.
Fodor, Nandor. Encyclopaedia of
psychic science. [New Hyde Park,
N.Y.] University Books [1966] xxxix,
415 p. 133.903 66-16316
    BF1025 .F6 1966 MRR Alc.

PSYCHOANALYSIS.
see also Dreams

Freud, Sigmund, Abstracts of The
standard edition of the complete
psychological works of Sigmund Freud.
New York, J. Aronson [c1973] 315 p.
[$15.00] 150/.19/52 mrr01-78
    BF173 .F6253 Suppl. 3 MRR Alc.

Hendrick, Ives, Facts and theories
of psychoanalysis. 3d ed.; rev.,
expanded, and rewritten. New York,
Knopf, 1958. 385 p. 131.3462 57-
10307
    BF173 .H435 1958 MRR Alc.

PSYCHOANALYSIS--BIBLIOGRAPHY.
Grinstein, Alexander. The index of
psychoanalytic writings. New York,
International Universities Press
[1956- v. [$150.00 (v. 1-5) (v.
6-9) (v. 10-14)] 016.13134 56-8932

    Z7204.P8 G7 MRR Alc.

Hart, Henry Harper. Conceptual index
to psychoanalytic technique and
training, [Croton-on-Hudson, N.Y.]
North River Press, 1972. 5 v. (xxxi,
1584 p.) 016.6168/917 72-77268
    Z7204.P8 H37 MRR Alc.

Rickman, John, Index
psychoanalyticus 1893-1926, London,
Pub. by L. & V. Woolf at the Hogarth
press and the Institute of psychoanalysis, 1928. 276 p. 29-11023
    Z7204.P8 R5 MRR Alc.

PSYCHOANALYSIS--DICTIONARIES.
Eidelberg, Ludwig, Encyclopedia of
psychoanalysis. New York, Free Press
[1968] xxxvii, 571 p. 150.19/52
67-28874
    BF173 .E5 MRR Alc.

English, Horace Bidwell, A
comprehensive dictionary of
psychological and psychoanalytical
terms, New York, McKay [1964, c1958]
xiv, 594 p. 64-2463
    BF31 .E58 1964 MRR Alc.

Laplanche, Jean. The language of
psycho-analysis. New York, Norton
[1974, c1973] xv, 510 p. [$14.95]
616.8/917/03 73-18418
    RC437 .L313 1974 MRR Alc.

Laplanche, Jean. The language of
psycho-analysis, New York, Norton
[1974, c1973] xv, 510 p. [$14.95]
616.8/917/03 73-18418
    RC437 .L313 1974 MRR Alc.

Rycroft, Charles. A critical
dictionary of psychoanalysis. New
York, Basic Books, inc. [1968] xxvi,
189 p. [$4.95] 616.89/17/03 68-
54155
    RC437 .R9 MRR Alc.

PSYCHOANALYSIS--HISTORY.
Alexander, Franz Gabriel, ed.
Psychoanalytic pioneers, New York,
Basic Books [1966] 616 p.
150.1950922 66-11692
    BF175 .A65 MRR Alc.

PSYCHOANALYSIS--INDEXES.
Hart, Henry Harper. Conceptual index
to psychoanalytic technique and
training [Croton-on-Hudson, N.Y.]
North River Press, 1972. 5 v. (xxxi,
1584 p.) 016.6168/917 72-77268
    Z7204.P8 H37 MRR Alc.

PSYCHOANALYSIS--PERIODICALS--INDEXES.
Grinstein, Alexander. The index of psychoanalytic writings. New York, International Universities Press [1956-   v.   [$150.00 (v. 1-5) (v. 6-9) (v. 10-14)]   016.13134 56-8932

Z7204.P8 G7 MRR Alc.

PSYCHOANALYSIS--STUDY AND TEACHING--INDEXES.
Hart, Henry Harper. Conceptual index to psychoanalytic technique and training. [Croton-on-Hudson, N.Y.] North River Press, 1972. 5 v. (xxxi, 1584 p.) 016.6168/917 72-77268
Z7204.P8 H37 MRR Alc.

PSYCHOANALYSIS--YEARBOOKS.
The Annual survey of psychoanalysis. v. 1- 1950- New York, International Universities Press. 131.34058 52-12082
RC500 .A6 MRR Alc Full set

PSYCHOLOGICAL MEASUREMENT
see Psychometrics

PSYCHOLOGICAL RESEARCH.
American Psychological Association. International opportunities for advanced training and research in psychology. Washington [1966] ix, 395 p. 150/.72 66-28054
BF76.5 .A6 MRR Alc.

PSYCHOLOGICAL RESEARCH--BIBLIOGRAPHY.
Research annual on intergroup relations. Chicago [etc.] Quadrangle Books [etc.] 66-14164
HM131 .R45 MRR Alc Full set

PSYCHOLOGISTS--BIOGRAPHY--COLLECTED WORKS.
A History of psychology in autobiography. New York, Russell & Russell, 1961- [c1930]- v. 150/.922 B 61-12125
BF105 .H52 MRR Biog.

PSYCHOLOGISTS--DIRECTORIES.
International Union of Psychological Science. Committee on Publication and Communication. International directory of psychologists. 2nd ed. Assen, Van Gorcum & Comp, 1966. xxiv, 580 p. [fl 15.75] 150/.25 67-114170
BF30 .I54 1966 MRR Biog.

PSYCHOLOGISTS--CANADA--DIRECTORIES.
American Psychological Association. The consolidated roster for psychology in the United States and Canada; Washington [c1973] xxxii, 1077 p. [$15.00] 150/.25/73 74-168224
BF30 .A493 1973 MRR Biog.

PSYCHOLOGISTS--UNITED STATES--DIRECTORIES.
American Psychological Association. The consolidated roster for psychology in the United States and Canada; Washington [c1973] xxxii, 1077 p. [$15.00] 150/.25/73 74-168224
BF30 .A493 1973 MRR Biog.

American Psychological Association. Membership register. [Washington] 150/.6/273 72-623170
BF30 .A49 MRR Biog Latest edition

PSYCHOLOGISTS--UNITED STATES--DIRECTORIES--PERIODICALS.
American Psychological Association. Biographical directory. 1870- [Washington] [$30.00] 150/.6/273 73-642059
BF11 .A67 MRR Biog Latest edition / Sci RR Latest edition

PSYCHOLOGY.
see also Child study

see also Concepts

see also Personality

see also Psychical research

see also Social psychology

see also Violence

Berelson, Bernard, Human behavior; New York, Harcourt, Brace and World [c1964] xxiii, 712 p.   301 64-11621
HM51 .B42 MRR Alc.

Guilford, Joy Paul, Fundamental statistics in psychology and education 5th ed. New York, McGraw-Hill [1973] xii, 546 p.   519.5 72-6960
HA29 .G9 1973 MRR Alc.

Helson, Harry, ed. Contemporary approaches to psychology. Princeton, N.J., Van Nostrand [1967] xii, 596 p. 150 67-6959
BF121 .H42 MRR Alc.

Koch, Sigmund, ed. Psychology: a study of a science. New York, McGraw-Hill, 1959- v. 150.82 57-14691

BF38 .K6 MRR Alc.

Ruch, Floyd Leon, Psychology and life 7th ed. [Glenview, Ill.] Scott, Foresman [1967] 758 p.   150 67-15475
BF131 .R84 1967 MRR Alc.

Wolman, Benjamin B. Contemporary theories and systems in psychology. New York, Harper [1960] 613 p. 150.1 60-7017
BF38 .W78 MRR Alc.

Wolman, Benjamin B. Handbook of general psychology. Englewood Cliffs, N.J., Prentice-Hall [1973] xv, 1006 p. 150 74-166142
BF121 .W63 MRR Alc.

PSYCHOLOGY--ABSTRACTS.
Psychological abstracts. v. 1- Jan. 1927- Lancaster, Pa., American Psychological Association. 29-23479

BF1 .P65 Sci RR Partial set / MRR Alc Partial set

PSYCHOLOGY--ABSTRACTS--BIBLIOGRAPHY.
Psychological index. Columbus, O., Published by the American psychological association, inc., Ohio state university, 1941, '40. 2 v. 41-28061
Z7203 .P972 MRR Alc.

PSYCHOLOGY--BIBLIOGRAPHY.
Baldwin, James Mark, ed. Dictionary of philosophy and psychology; New York, The Macmillan company; London, Macmillan & co., ltd., 1901-05. 3 v. in 4. 06-8753
Z7125 .R2 volume 3 MRR Alc.

Bonjean, Charles M. Sociological measurement; San Francisco, Chandler Pub. Co. [1967] xiv, 580 p. 016.301 67-24968
Z7164.S68 B6 MRR Alc.

Borchardt, Dietrich Hans, How to find out in philosophy and psychology, [1st ed.] Oxford, New York, Pergamon Press [1968] vii, 97 p. 016.1 67-28659
Z7125 .B65 1968 MRR Alc.

Communications/Research/Machines, inc. PsychoSources; Toronto, New York, Bantam Books [1973] 215 p. [$5.00] 150/.8 72-88415
BF131 .C628 1973 MRR Alc.

Hart, Henry Harper. Conceptual index to psychoanalytic technique and training, [Croton-on-Hudson, N.Y.] North River Press, 1972. 5 v. (xxxi, 1584 p.) 016.6168/917 72-77268
Z7204.P8 H37 MRR Alc.

Harvard University. The Harvard list of books in psychology, 4th ed. Cambridge, Mass., Harvard University Press [1971] viii, 108 p. [$2.75] 016.15 71-152700
Z7201 .H28 1971 MRR Alc.

Menninger, Karl, A guide to psychiatric books in English 3d ed. New York, Grune & Stratton [1972] xviii, 238 p. 016.6168/9 78-168846

Z6664.N5 M48 1972 MRR Alc.

Morrow, William R., Behavior therapy bibliography; 1950-1969; Columbia, University of Missouri Press [1971] 165 p. [$10.00] 016.61689/1 73-633730
Z6664.N5 M67 MRR Alc.

Recent publications in the social and behavioral sciences. 1966- [New York] The American behavioral scientist. 016.3 66-56737
Z7161 .A42 MRR Alc Full set

The American behavioral scientist. The ABS guide to recent publications in the social and behavioral sciences. New York, 1965. xxi, 781 p. 65-17168
Z7161 .A4 MRR Alc.

PSYCHOLOGY--BOOK REVIEWS--INDEXES.
Mental health book review index. v. [1]- (no. 1-); Jan./Feb. 1956- [New York] 66-9162
Z6664.N5 M49 MRR Circ Full set

PSYCHOLOGY--DICTIONARIES.
Baldwin, James Mark, ed. Dictionary of philosophy and psychology; New York, The Macmillan company; London, Macmillan & co., ltd., 1901-05. 3 v. in 4. 06-8753
Z7125 .R2 volume 3 MRR Alc.

Encyclopedia of psychology, New York, Philosophical library [1946] 2 p. l., vii, 897 p. incl. illus., tables, diagrs. 150.3 46-11920
BF31 .E55 MRR Alc.

Encyclopedia of psychology. London, Search Press [1972] 3 v. [£8.00 per vol.] 150/.3 72-181419
BF31 .E52 MRR Alc.

English, Horace Bidwell, A comprehensive dictionary of psychological and psychoanalytical terms, New York, McKay [1964, c1958] xiv, 594 p. 64-2463
BF31 .E58 1964 MRR Alc.

Goldenson, Robert M. The encyclopedia of human behavior; [1st ed.] Garden City, N.Y., Doubleday, 1970. 2 v. (xxviii, 1472 p.) 150/.3 68-18077
BF31 .G6 MRR Alc.

Harriman, Philip Lawrence, Handbook of psychological terms, Totowa, N.J., Littlefield, Adams, 1965. 222 p. 150.3 65-24821
BF31 .H33 1965 MRR Alc.

Harriman, Philip Lawrence, Dictionary of psychology; 3rd ed. London, Owen, 1972. [3], 364 p. [£3.00] 150/.3 73-152139
BF31 .H34 1972 MRR Alc.

Heidenreich, Charles A. A dictionary of general psychology: basic terminology and key concepts Dubuque, Iowa, Kendall/Hunt Pub. Co. [1970] vii, 309 p. 150/.3 77-113765
BF31 .H427 MRR Alc.

Heidenreich, Charles A. A dictionary of personality: behavior and adjustment terms Dubuque, Iowa, W. C. Brown Book Co. [1968] vii, 213 p. 150/.3 68-6353
BF31 .H43 MRR Alc.

Hinsie, Leland Earl, Psychiatric dictionary 4th ed. New York, Oxford University Press, 1970. ix, 816 p. 616.89/03 78-83030
RC437 .H5 1970 MRR Alc.

Topetzes, Nick J. Definitions of professional terms in educational psychology, Dubuque, Iowa, Wm. C. Brown Co. [c1958] 116 p. 370.15014 59-1307
LB1055 .T6 MRR Alc.

Warren, Howard Crosby, ed. Dictionary of psychology. Boston, New York [etc.] Houghton Mifflin company [c1934] x, 371, [1] p. 150.3 159.903 34-42807
BF31 .W3 MRR Alc.

Wilkening, Howard. The psychology almanac; Monterey, Calif. Brooks/Cole Pub. Co. [1973] vii, 241 p. 150/.3 72-86775
BF31 .W49 MRR Alc.

Wolman, Benjamin B. Dictionary of behavioral science. New York, Van Nostrand Reinhold Co. [1973] ix, 478 p. 150/.3 73-748
BF31 .W64 MRR Alc.

Wulfeck, Joseph W. The language of dynamic psychology, 1st ed. New York, McGraw-Hill, 1954. 111 p. 150.3 54-8811
BF31 .W8 MRR Alc.

PSYCHOLOGY--DICTIONARIES--DUTCH.
Elseviers filosofische en psychologische encyclopedie. Amsterdam, Elsevier, 1970. 271 p. [fl4.50] 75-543438
BF31 .E45 MRR Alc.

PSYCHOLOGY--DICTIONARIES--ENGLISH.
Castonguay, Jacques. Dictionary of psychology and related sciences: English-French. St.-Hyacinthe; Quebec, Edisem; Paris, Maloine, 1973 (i.e. 1972). 153, 162 p. [$14.50] 150/.3 74-179864
BF31 .C34 MRR Alc.

PSYCHOLOGY--DICTIONARIES--FRENCH.
Castonguay, Jacques. Dictionary of psychology and related sciences: English-French. St.-Hyacinthe; Quebec, Edisem; Paris, Maloine, 1973 (i.e. 1972). 153, 162 p. [$14.50] 150/.3 74-179864
BF31 .C34 MRR Alc.

Piéron, Henri, Vocabulaire de la psychologie, 3d ed. entièrement rev. et augm. Paris, Presses universitaires de France, 1963 [c1951] xiii, 524 p. 65-55671
BF31 .P5 1963 MRR Alc.

La Psychologie moderne de A à Z Paris, Centre d'étude et de promotion de la lecture, 1971] 544 p. [45.25F] 74-501160
BF31 .P75 1971 MRR Alc.

PSYCHOLOGY--DICTIONARIES--GERMAN.
Beigel, Hugo G. Dictionary of
psychology and related fields: German-
English. New York, F. Ungar Pub. Co.
[1971] 256 p. [$9.00] 150/.3 74-
115063
BF31 .E27 MRR Alc.

Sury, Kurt F. von. Wörterbuch der
Psychologie und ihrer Grenzgebiete
3., volständig neu bearb. und stark
erw. Aufl. Basel, Stuttgart, Schwabe
(1967) 324 p. [sfr 28.50] 150/.3
67-82190
BF31 .S8 1967 MRR Alc.

PSYCHOLOGY--DICTIONARY.
Wolman, Benjamin B. Dictionary of
behavioral science. New York, Van
Nostrand Reinhold Co. [1973] ix, 478
p. 150/.3 73-748
BF31 .W64 MRR Alc.

PSYCHOLOGY--EARLY WORKS TO 1850.
Aristoteles. On the soul. [Rev.]
Cambridge, Harvard University Press,
1957. xiii, 527 p. 58-17
PA3612.A8 A13 1957 MRR Alc.

PSYCHOLOGY--HISTORY.
Klein, David Ballin, A history of
scientific psychology. New York,
Basic Books [1970] xii, 907 p.
[20.00] 150/.9 72-94296
BF81 .K5 MRR Alc.

Misiak, Henryk, History of
psychology; New York, Grune &
Stratton [1966] x, 499 p. 150.9
66-20174
BF81 .M5 MRR Alc.

PSYCHOLOGY--HISTORY--COLLECTED WORKS.
A History of psychology in
autobiography. New York, Russell &
Russell, 1961- [c1930]- v.
150/.922 B 61-12125
BF105 .H52 MRR Biog.

PSYCHOLOGY--HISTORY--UNITED STATES.
Roback, Abraham Aaron, History of
American psychology New, rev. ed.
New York, Collier Books [1964] 575
p. 150.973 64-16138
BF108.U5 R6 1964 MRR Alc.

PSYCHOLOGY--PERIODICALS--BIBLIOGRAPHY.
Schmid, Hans, writer on sociology.
Verzeichnis von Fachzeitschriften aus
dem Gebiet der Psychologie und ihrer
Nachbarwissenschaften. Bern,
Schweizerischer Berufsverband für
angewandte Psychologie, 1967. 70 l.
[18.00] 016.300/5 79-371198
Z7203 .S25 MRR Alc.

Tompkins, Margaret. A checklist of
serials in psychology and allied
fields. Troy, N.Y., Whitston Pub.
Co., 1969. viii, 261 p. [10.50]
016.1505 70-87477
Z7203 .T65 MRR Alc.

PSYCHOLOGY--PERIODICALS--INDEXES.
Abstracts for social workers. v. 1-
spring 1965- [New York] National
Association of Social Workers.
[$20.00] 361/.008 74-642752
HV1 .A2 MRR Alc Full set

Bulletin signalétique: Philosophie,
sciences humaines. v. 1-14; 1947-60.
Paris, Centre de documentation du C.
N. R. S. 51-30077
Z7127 .F7 MRR Alc Full set

Grinstein, Alexander. The index of
psychoanalytic writings. New York,
International Universities Press
[1956- v. [$150.00] (v. 1-5) (v.
6-9) (v. 10-14) 016.13134 56-8932

Z7204.P8 G7 MRR Alc.

Mental retardation abstracts. v. 1-
Jan./Mar. 1964- [Bethesda, Md.] for
sale by Superintendent of Documents,
U.S. Govt. Print. Off., Washington]
66-60248
RC570 .M4 MRR Alc Full set / Sci
RR Full set

Psychological abstracts. v. 1-
Jan. 1927- Lancaster, Pa., American
Psychological Association. 29-23479

BF1 .P65 Sci RR Partial set / MRR
Alc Partial set

Psychological index. Columbus, O.,
Published by the American
psychological association, inc., Ohio
state university, 1941, '40. 2 v.
41-28061
Z7203 .P972 MRR Alc.

PSYCHOLOGY--STUDY AND TEACHING.
American Psychological Association.
International opportunities for
advanced training and research in
psychology. Washington [1966] ix,
395 p. 150/.72 66-28054
BF76.5 .A6 MRR Alc.

PSYCHOLOGY--STUDY AND TEACHING--AUDIO-
VISUAL AIDS--INDEXES.
National Information Center for
Educational Media. Index to
psychology: multimedia. 1st ed.
[Los Angeles, University of Southern
California] 1972. x, 461 p. 016.15
76-190637
BF77 .N37 1972 MRR Alc.

PSYCHOLOGY--STUDY AND TEACHING--
PERIODICALS.
Graduate study in psychology.
Washington, D.C., Educational Affairs
Office, American Psychological
Association. 150/.7/1173 72-626834

Began with v. for 1968/69.
BF77 .G73 MRR Alc Latest edition

PSYCHOLOGY, APPLIED.
see also Counseling

PSYCHOLOGY, CHILD
see Child study

PSYCHOLOGY, EDUCATIONAL
see Educational psychology

PSYCHOLOGY, EXPERIMENTAL--HISTORY.
Boring, Edwin Garrigues, A history
of experimental psychology, New
York, London, The Century co. [c1929]
xvi, 699 p. 29-24651
BF95 .B6 MRR Alc.

PSYCHOLOGY, MILITARY.
see also Leadership

PSYCHOLOGY, PATHOLOGICAL.
Arieti, Silvano. Adult clinical
psychiatry / 2d ed., rev. and
expanded. New York : Basic Books,
[1974] xi, 896 p. : 616.8/9/008 s
616.8/9 74-189491
RC435 .A562 vol. 3 MRR Alc.

Eysenck, Hans Jurgen, ed. Handbook
of abnormal psychology, 2nd ed.
London, Pitman, 1973. xvi, 906 p.
[£20.00] 616.8/9 73-594933
RC454 .E97 1973 MRR Alc.

Garrison, Karl Claudius, The
psychology of exceptional children
4th ed. New York, Ronald Press Co.
[1965] vi, 571 p. 371.9 65-21809

LC3965 .G3 1965 MRR Alc.

Thorpe, Louis Peter, The psychology
of abnormal behavior; 2d ed. New
York, Ronald Press Co. [1961] 677 p.
132 61-9428
BF173 .T55 1961 MRR Alc.

PSYCHOLOGY, PATHOLOGICAL--BIBLIOGRAPHY.
Eysenck, Hans Jurgen, ed. Handbook
of abnormal psychology, 2nd ed.
London, Pitman, 1973. xvi, 906 p.
[£20.00] 616.8/9 73-594933
RC454 .E97 1973 MRR Alc.

PSYCHOLOGY, PHYSIOLOGICAL.
Hurlock, Elizabeth Bergner, Child
development 5th ed. New York,
McGraw-Hill [1972] 494 p. 155.4
79-38613
BF721 .H8 1972 MRR Alc.

PSYCHOLOGY, POLITICAL
see Political psychology

PSYCHOLOGY, SEXUAL
see Sex (Psychology)

PSYCHOMETRICS.
see also Educational tests and
measurements

Guilford, Joy Paul, Fundamental
statistics in psychology and
education 5th ed. New York, McGraw-
Hill [1973] xii, 546 p. 519.5 72-
6960
HA29 .G9 1973 MRR Alc.

Nunnally, Jum C. Introduction to
psychological measurement New York,
McGraw-Hill [1970] xv, 572 p.
152.8 77-100805
BF39 .N78 1970 MRR Alc.

PSYCHOPATHOLOGY.
Eysenck, Hans Jurgen, ed. Handbook
of abnormal psychology, 2nd ed.
London, Pitman, 1973. xvi, 906 p.
[£20.00] 616.8/9 73-594933
RC454 .E97 1973 MRR Alc.

PSYCHOPHARMACOLOGY.
Wilder-Smith, A. E. The drug users;
[1st ed.] Wheaton, Ill., H. Shaw
[1969] 294, [10] p. [5.95]
615/.78 73-86528
RM315 .W55 MRR Alc.

PSYCHOTHERAPY.
Thorpe, Louis Peter, The psychology
of abnormal behavior; 2d ed. New
York, Ronald Press Co. [1961] 677 p.
132 61-9428
BF173 .T55 1961 MRR Alc.

PTERIDOPHYTA.
see also Ferns

PUBERTY.
see also Adolescence

PUBLIC ADMINISTRATION.
see also Bureaucracy

see also Governmental investigations

see also Local government

PUBLIC ADMINISTRATION--BIBLIOGRAPHY.
Spitz, Allan A. Developmental
change; an annotated bibliography,
Lexington, University Press of
Kentucky [1969] xi, 316 p. [12.50]
016.309 69-19766
Z7164.E15 S615 MRR Alc.

Universal Reference System.
Administrative management: public and
private bureaucracy; Princeton,
N.J., Princeton Research Pub. Co.
[1969] xx, 888 p. 011 68-57820
Z7161 .U64 vol. 4 MRR Alc.

PUBLIC ADMINISTRATION--BIBLIOGRAPHY--
CATALOGS.
California. University. Institute of
Governmental Studies. Library.
Subject catalog of the Institute of
Governmental Studies Library,
University of California, Berkeley.
Boston, G. K. Hall, 1970 [pref. 1971]
26 v. 016.353 73-152341
Z7164.A2 C34 MRR Alc (Dk 33)

PUBLIC ADMINISTRATION--BIOGRAPHY.
International who's who in community
service. 1973/74- ed. London,
Eddison Press. [12.50] 361/.0025
78-189467
HV27 .I57 MRR Biog Latest edition

PUBLIC ADMINISTRATION--STUDY AND
TEACHING--UNITED STATES.
National Association of Schools of
Public Affairs and Administration.
Graduate school programs in public
affairs and public administration.
Washington. [$5.00] 350/.0007/1173
74-80861
JF1338.A2 N28a MRR Alc Latest
edition

PUBLIC AQUARIUMS
see Aquariums, Public

PUBLIC ASSISTANCE
see Public welfare

PUBLIC BUILDINGS--DIRECTORIES.
A A S G; [Cincinnati, Billboard Pub.
Co] 725/.8/02573 72-626501
GV182 .A74 MRR Alc Latest edition

PUBLIC CONTRACTS--UNITED STATES.
Riemer, W. H. Handbook of Government
contract administration Englewood
Cliffs, N.J., Prentice-Hall [1968]
viii, 1087 p. 353.007/11 68-12882

HD3858 .R5 MRR Alc.

PUBLIC CONTRACTS--UNITED STATES--
DIRECTORIES.
Government Data Publications,
Washington, D.C. Government
production prime contractors
directory. Washington, c1969. 75,
72 p. 338/.0025/73 77-16744
HD3858 .G625 1969 MRR Alc.

PUBLIC FINANCE
see Finance, Public

PUBLIC HEALTH PERSONNEL--UNITED STATES--
DIRECTORIES.
American Public Health Association.
Membership directory. New York
[etc.] 614.06273 52-42786
RA421 .A557 MRR Alc Latest edition

PUBLIC HOUSES
see Hotels, taverns, etc.

PUBLIC HYGIENE
see Hygiene, Public

PUBLIC INSTITUTIONS.
see also Hospitals

see also Prisons

see also Schools

PUBLIC LAND RECORDS--INDEXES.
McMullin, Phillip W. Grassroots of
America; Salt Lake City, Gendex
Corp., 1972. xxvii, 489 p.
333.1/0973 71-186588
J33 .M3 MRR Alc.

PUBLIC LANDS.
see also National parks and reserves

PUBLIC LIBRARIES.
American Library Association. Ad Hoc
Reference Books Review Committee.
Reference books for small and medium-
sized libraries. 2d ed., rev.
Chicago, American Library
Association, 1973. xii, 146 p.
011/.02 73-8906
Z1035.1 .A47 1973 MRR Alc.

PUBLIC LIBRARIES. (Cont.)
Public library catalog. 6th ed.,
1973. New York, H. W. Wilson Co.,
1974. x, 1543 p. 011 74-656
Z1035 .S83 1974 MRR Alc.

Ranganathan, Shiyali Ramamrita, Rao
Sahib, comp. Free book service for
all; [1st ed.] Bombay, New York,
Published for the Mysore Library
Association by Asia Pub. House [1968]
464 p. 027.4 sa 68-8813
Z721 .R28 1968 MRR Alc.

**PUBLIC LIBRARIES--AUSTRALIA--
DIRECTORIES.**
Ling, Kenneth J. Directory of public
reference & lending libraries in
Australia. Sydney, Library
Association of Australia [1961] [71]
p. 65-82476
Z870 .L55 MRR Alc.

PUBLIC LIBRARIES--UNITED STATES.
Nelson Associates, inc. Public
library systems in the United States;
Chicago, American Library
Association, 1969. xvi, 368 p.
027.4/73 68-54708
Z731 .N4 MRR Alc.

PUBLIC OPINION.
MacDougall, Curtis Daniel,
Understanding public opinion;
Dubuque, Iowa, W. C. Brown Co. [1966]
xiv, 582 p. 301.154 66-27678
HM263 .M23 1966 MRR Alc.

PUBLIC OPINION--BIBLIOGRAPHY.
Universal Reference System. Public
opinion, mass behavior, and political
psychology: Princeton, N.J.,
Princeton Research Pub. Co. [1969]
xxi, 1225 p. 016.30115/4 68-57822

Z7161 .U64 vol. 6 MRR Alc.

PUBLIC OPINION--YEARBOOKS.
What they said. 1969- [Beverly
Hills, Calif.] Monitor Book Co.
901.9/4 74-111080
D410 .W46 MRR Ref Desk Full set

PUBLIC OPINION--UNITED STATES.
Chandler, Robert, Public opinion;
changing attitudes on contemporary
political and social issues. New
York, R. R. Bowker Co., 1972. xi
195 p. 301.15/43/309173092 72-1739
HN90.P8 C54 MRR Alc.

Gallup, George Horace, The Gallup
Poll; public opinion, 1935-1971 [1st
ed.] New York, Random House [1972]
3 v. (xliv, 2388 p.)
301.15/43/32900973 77-39867
HN90.P8 G3 MRR Alc.

The Harris survey yearbook of public
opinion. 1870- New York, Louis
Harris and Associates.
301.15/43/309173092 73-184049
HN90.P8 H35 MRR Alc Full set

Truman, David Bicknell, The
governmental process; [1st ed.] New
York, Knopf, 1951. xvi, 544, xv p.
328.368 51-4187
JK1118 .T7 MRR Alc.

Weinberg, Albert Katz. Manifest
destiny; Baltimore, The Johns
Hopkins press, 1935. xiii, 559 p.
973 35-8403
E179.5 .W45 MRR Alc.

PUBLIC OPINION POLLS.
see also Market surveys

Chandler, Robert, Public opinion;
changing attitudes on contemporary
political and social issues. New
York, R. R. Bowker Co., 1972. xi
195 p. 301.15/43/309173092 72-1739

HN90.P8 C54 MRR Alc.

Gallup, George Horace, The Gallup
Poll; public opinion, 1935-1971 [1st
ed.] New York, Random House [1972]
3 v. (xliv, 2388 p.)
301.15/43/32900973 77-39867
HN90.P8 G3 MRR Alc.

Gallup opinion index; no. 1- June
1965- Princeton, N.J. 301.15/4 68-
5902
HM261.A1 G34 MRR Alc Partial set

The Harris survey yearbook of public
opinion. 1870- New York, Louis
Harris and Associates.
301.15/43/309173092 73-184049
HN90.P8 H35 MRR Alc Full set

Parten, Mildred Bernice, Surveys,
polls, and samples: practical
procedures. New York, Cooper Square
Publishers, 1966 [c1950] xii, 624 p.
311/.28 66-27603
HN29 .P3 1966 MRR Alc.

Runyon, John H. Source book of
American presidential campaign and
election statistics, 1948-1968. New
York, F. Ungar [1971] xiv, 380 p.
329/.023/0212 73-155093
JK524 .R83 MRR Alc.

**PUBLIC OPINION POLLS--SOCIETIES, ETC.--
DIRECTORIES.**
American University, Washington, D.C.
Bureau of Social Science Research.
Directory of organizations in
opinion, and related research outside
the United States. Washington,
c1956. 1 v. (various pagings) 57-
17609
HM263 .A77 MRR Alc.

PUBLIC POLICY
see Economic policy

see Environmental policy

PUBLIC RECORDS--GREAT BRITAIN.
Great Britain. Public Record Office.
Guide to the contents of the Public
Record Office. London, H.M.
Stationery Off., 1963. 3 v. [27/6
($4.95 U.S.) (v. 3)] 64-435
CD1043 .A553 MRR Alc.

PUBLIC RELATIONS.
Cutlip, Scott M. Effective public
relations 3d ed. Englewood Cliffs,
N.J., Prentice-Hall [1964] xvi, 512
p. 659.111 64-24066
HM263 .C78 1964 MRR Alc.

Hill and Knowlton, inc. Hill and
Knowlton International. Handbook on
international public relations. New
York, Praeger [1967-c1968] 2 v.
659.2 67-29430
HD59 .H53 MRR Alc.

Leibert, Edwin Reisinger, Handbook
of special events for nonprofit
organizations; New York, Association
Press [1972] 224 p. [$12.95]
361.7/3 75-129437
HV41 .L415 MRR Alc.

Lesly, Philip. Lesly's public
relations handbook. Englewood
Cliffs, N.J., Prentice-Hall [1971]
xvi, 557 p. 659.2 75-140169
HM263 .L46 1971 MRR Alc.

Stephenson, Howard, ed. Handbook of
public relations; 2d ed. New York,
McGraw-Hill [1971] xx, 836 p.
659.2 79-134602
HM263 .S85 1971 MRR Alc.

PUBLIC RELATIONS--BIBLIOGRAPHY.
Cutlip, Scott M. A public relations
bibliography, 2d ed. Madison,
University of Wisconsin Press, 1965.
xiv, 305 p. 016.3011523 65-16360
Z7164.P957 C8 1965 MRR Alc.

PUBLIC RELATIONS--BIOGRAPHY.
Who's who in public relations,
international. 1st- ed.; 1959/60-
Meriden, N.H., PR Pub. Co. 926.591
62-4348
HM263 .W45 MRR Biog Latest edition

**PUBLIC RELATIONS--CORPORATIONS--
DIRECTORIES.**
Analyst contact directory. 1968-
[New York, Kennington Pub. Corp.]
658.2 73-246112
HD59 .A53 MRR Alc Latest edition

PUBLIC RELATIONS--DICTIONARIES.
Biddlecombe, Peter. International
public relations encyclopedia.
London, Grant Helm, 1968. 220 p.
[37/6] 659.2/03 77-364516
HD59 .B5 MRR Alc.

Vigrolio, Tom. Marketing and
communications media dictionary,
[Norfolk, Mass., NBS Co., 1969]
xvii, 425 p. 658.8/003 76-80076
HF5414 .V52 MRR Alc.

**PUBLIC RELATIONS--HANDBOOKS, MANUALS,
ETC.**
Ayer Press. Ayer public relations
and publicity style book.
Philadelphia, 1974. 1 v. (unpaged)
[$8.90] 808/.02 74-161785
PN4783 .A9 1974 MRR Alc.

PUBLIC RELATIONS--SCHOOLS.
American College Public Relations
Association. Membership directory.
[Washington] 378/.006/273 59-48426

LB2301 .A34 MRR Alc Latest edition

**PUBLIC RELATIONS--UNITED STATES--
DIRECTORIES.**
Weiner, Richard, Professional's
guide to public relations services.
2d ed. Englewood Cliffs, N.J.,
Prentice-Hall [1971] 239 p.
659.2/025/73 71-136585
HD59 .W38 1971 MRR Alc.

**PUBLIC RELATIONS CONSULTANTS--
DIRECTORIES.**
P R blue book and supplement to the
international Who's who in public
relations. 1st- ed.; 1960-
Meriden, N.H.; PR Pub. Co. 659.111
60-10969
HM263 .P2 MRR Ref Desk Latest
edition

Public Relations Society of America.
Public relations register. New York.
301.154 301.152* 50-1638
HM263.A1 P853 MRR Ref Desk Latest
edition

PUBLIC RELATIONS CONSULTANTS--YEARBOOKS.
P R blue book and supplement to the
international Who's who in public
relations. 1st- ed.; 1960-
Meriden, N.H., PR Pub. Co. 659.111
60-10969
HM263 .P2 MRR Ref Desk Latest
edition

**PUBLIC SCHOOLS--UNITED STATES--
DIRECTORIES.**
Gertler, Diane (Bochner) Directory:
public elementary and secondary day
schools, 1968-69, [Washington] U.S.
National Center for Educational
Statistics; [for sale by the Supt. of
Docs., U.S. Govt. Print. Off., 1970-
v. [2.00] 371/.01/02573 70-
607482
L901 .G39 MRR Alc.

Gertler, Diane (Bochner) Directory:
public elementary and secondary
schools in large school districts
with enrollment and instructional
staff, by race: fall 1967,
[Washington] U.S. National Center for
Educational Statistics; [for sale by
the Supt. of Docs., U.S. Govt. Print.
Off., 1969] v, 840 p. [7.25]
371/.01/02573 72-604076
L901 .G38 MRR Alc.

**PUBLIC SCHOOLS--UNITED STATES--
STATISTICS.**
Gertler, Diane (Bochner) Directory:
public elementary and secondary
schools in large school districts
with enrollment and instructional
staff, by race: fall 1967,
[Washington] U.S. National Center for
Educational Statistics; [for sale by
the Supt. of Docs., U.S. Govt. Print.
Off., 1969] v, 840 p. [7.25]
371/.01/02573 72-604076
L901 .G38 MRR Alc.

PUBLIC SECURITIES
see Securities

PUBLIC SERVICES (LIBRARIES)
see Libraries and readers

PUBLIC SPEAKING.
see also Debates and debating

Bryant, Donald Cross, Oral
communication; 3d ed. New York,
Appleton-Century-Crofts [1962] 351
p. 808.5 62-7253
PN4121 .B776 1962 MRR Alc.

Reid, Loren Dudley, First principles
of public speaking. 2d ed.
Columbia, Mo., Artcraft Press [1962]
406 p. 808.5 62-15056
PN4121 .R428 1962 MRR Alc.

Sandford, William Phillips,
Effective business speech. 4th ed.
of Practical business speaking New
York, McGraw-Hill, 1960. 445 p.
808.5 60-8039
PN4193 .B8 S3 1960 MRR Alc.

**PUBLIC SPEAKING--HANDBOOKS, MANUALS,
ETC.**
Braude, Jacob Morton, ed. The
complete speaker's index to selected
stories for every occasion Englewood
Cliffs, N.J., Prentice-Hall [1967,
c1966] x, 353 p. 808.5/1/0202 66-
18166
PN4193.I5 B66 MRR Alc.

PUBLIC TELEVISION
see Television in education

PUBLIC UTILITIES.
see also Electric utilities

see also Gas companies

see also Railroads

see also Water-supply

**PUBLIC UTILITIES--UNITED STATES--
YEARBOOKS.**
Moody's public utility manual. 1954-
New York, Moody's Investors Service.
56-3927
HG4961 .M7245 MRR Alc Latest
edition

PUBLIC WELFARE.
see also Child welfare

see also Day nurseries

see also Poor

PUBLIC WELFARE. (Cont.)
   see also Social service

   see also Social workers

   see also Unemployed

PUBLIC WELFARE--GREAT BRITAIN--
YEARBOOKS.
   Family Welfare Association, London.
   Guide to the social services.
   London, MacDonald & Evans, Ltd.
   [etc.] 362.8 55-33805
     HV245.A2 F33 MRR Alc Latest
     edition

PUBLIC WELFARE--NEW YORK (CITY)--
DIRECTORIES.
   Directory of social and health
   agencies of New York City. [1st]-
   ed.; 1883- [New York] 360.58 12-
   37275
     HV99.N59 N5 MRR Alc Latest edition

PUBLIC WELFARE--UNITED STATES.
   Bruno, Frank John, Trends in social
   work, 1874-1956; [2d ed.] New York,
   Columbia University Press, 1957.
   xviii, 462 p. 360.973 57-9699
     HV91 .B75 1957 MRR Alc.

   Sampson, Timothy J., Welfare: a
   handbook for friend and foe.
   Philadelphia, United Church Press
   [1972] 203 p. 361.6/0973 72-8551

     HV91 .S24 MRR Alc.

PUBLIC WELFARE--UNITED STATES--
DIRECTORIES.
   American Public Welfare Association.
   The public welfare directory; 1940-
   Chicago. 360.58 41-4981
     HV89 .A55 MRR Alc Latest edition

PUBLIC WORKS--SOCIETIES, ETC.
   American Public Works Association.
   Yearbook. 1935- Chicago. 620.6273
   35-15769
     TD1 .A28 MRR Alc Latest edition

PUBLIC WORKS--YEARBOOKS.
   American Public Works Association.
   Yearbook. 1935- Chicago. 620.6273
   35-15769
     TD1 .A28 MRR Alc Latest edition

PUBLICITY.
   see also Advertising

   see also Journalism

   California publicity outlets. 1972-
   Los Angeles, Unicorn Systems Co.,
   Information Services Division.
   659.2/025/794 76-186163
     HM263 .C2 MRR Alc Latest edition

PUBLICITY--HANDBOOKS, MANUALS, ETC.
   Ayer Press. Ayer public relations
   and publicity style book.
   Philadelphia, 1974. 1 v. (unpaged)
   [$8.90] 808/.02 74-161785
     PN4783 .A9 1974 MRR Alc.

   Bacon's publicity checker. 1933-
   Chicago, R. H. Bacon. 659.111 34-
   14702
     HD59 .B3 MRR Alc Latest edition

   Weiner, Richard, Professional's
   guide to public relations services.
   2d ed. Englewood Cliffs, N.J.,
   Prentice-Hall [1971] 239 p.
   659.2/025/73 71-136585
     HD59 .W38 1971 MRR Alc.

PUBLISHERS AND PUBLISHING.
   see also Books

   see also Printing

   United States. Library of Congress.
   Technical Information Division.
   Final report on study of publications
   stemming from defense-related
   technical reports. [Washington]
   1956. 10 p. 620.09 57-60508
     Z663.49 .F5 MRR Alc.

   The Writer's handbook. [1936]-
   Boston, Mass., The Writer, inc.
   029.6 36-28596
     PN137 .W73 MRR Ref Desk Latest
     edition

PUBLISHERS AND PUBLISHING--DIRECTORIES.
   Cumulative book index. 1898/99- New
   York [etc.] H. W. Wilson Co. 05-
   33604
     Z1219 .W78 MRR Circ Partial set

   International bibliography of
   dictionaries. 5th, rev. ed. New
   York, R. R. Bowker Co., 1972. xxvi,
   511 p. 016.03 72-214468
     Z7004.D5 I55 1972 MRR Alc.

   International literary market place.
   1965- New York, R. R. Bowker Co. 65-
   28326
     Z291.5 I5 MRR Ref Desk Latest
     edition

   Internationale Bibliographie der
   Fachzeitschriften für Technik und
   Wirtschaft. München-Pullach, Verlag
   Dokumentation [etc.] 67-119312
     Z7913 .I757 MRR Alc Latest edition

   Internationales Verlagsadressbuch.
   München-Pullach, Verlag
   Dokumentationen der Technik. 67-
   47570
     Began with 1964 edition.
     Z282 .I65 MRR Ref Desk Latest
     edition

   Publishers international directory.
   New York, R. R. Bowker. 070.5/025
   79-649088
     Z282 .P78 MRR Ref Desk Latest
     edition

   Publishers' international year book.
   1st- ed.; 1960/6- London, A.P.
   Wales. 655.5058 61-542
     Z282 .P8 MRR Ref Desk Latest
     edition

   Répertoire international des
   éditeurs de langue française.
   Paris, Cercle de la librairie, 1971.
   xliv, 315 p. [51.66F] 070.5/025
   72-857877
     Z282 .R44 MRR Alc.

   Who is who in publishing. 1st ed.
   London, A. P. Wales, 1965. ix, 277
   p. 67-723
     Z282 .W48 MRR Biog.

   The Writers and artists' year book;
   [1st]- year; 1906- Boston [etc.]
   The Writer, inc. [etc.] 08-22320
     PN12 .W8 MRR Ref Desk Latest
     edition

   The Writers directory. 1971/73- New
   York, St. Martin's Press. London, St.
   James Press. 808 77-166289
     PS1 .W73 MRR Biog Latest edition

PUBLISHERS AND PUBLISHING--AFRICA--
DIRECTORIES.
   African book trade directory 1971.
   München-Pullach, Verlag
   Dokumentation; New York, Bowker,
   1971. 319 p. 338.7/61/0705730256
   73-142168
     Z465.5 .A45 MRR Alc.

PUBLISHERS AND PUBLISHING--ASIA--
DIRECTORIES.
   Asian book trade directory. [Bombay]
   Nirmala Sadanand Publishers.
   655.5/73/0255 sa 68-13864
     Began with 1964 vol.
     Z448.5 A75 MRR Alc Latest edition

   New India directory of publishers &
   booksellers. New Delhi, New Book
   Society of India [1952?] 224 p.
   655.454 52-40994
     Z455 .N4 1952 MRR Alc.

PUBLISHERS AND PUBLISHING--AUSTRIA--
DIRECTORIES.
   Vinz, Curt. Dokumentation
   deutschsprachiger Verlage. Ausg. 3.
   München, Wien, Olzog (1968). 588 p.
   [45.00] 72-569850
     Z317 .V5 1968 MRR Alc.

PUBLISHERS AND PUBLISHING--CANADA--
DIRECTORIES.
   Canadian serials directory.
   [Toronto, Buffalo] University of
   Toronto Press. 016.051 73-643405
     Z6954.C2 C23 MRR Alc Latest
     edition

PUBLISHERS AND PUBLISHING--COMMONWEALTH
OF NATIONS--DIRECTORIES.
   Cassell's directory of publishing in
   Great Britain, the Commwealth, and
   Ireland. 1st- ed.; 1960/61-
   London, Cassell. 655.442 60-52232
     Z326 .C3 MRR Ref Desk Latest
     edition

PUBLISHERS AND PUBLISHING--EUROPE--
DIRECTORIES.
   Adressbuch des deutschsprachigen
   Buchhandels. 1954- Frankfurt am
   Main, Buchhändler-Vereinigung. 54-
   38005
     Z282 .A28 MRR Alc Latest edition

   Cercle de la librairie, Paris. Le
   Livre de langue française, Paris,
   Cercle de la librairie, 1967. 213 p.
   655.4/025 68-116457
     Z282 .C42 MRR Alc.

   International literary market place.
   1965- New York, R. R. Bowker Co. 65-
   28326
     Z291.5 I5 MRR Ref Desk Latest
     edition

PUBLISHERS AND PUBLISHING--FRANCE--
DIRECTORIES.
   Annuaire Desechaliers ... Paris. 42-
   34851
     "Fondé en 1895.
     Z308 .A75 MRR Alc Latest edition

   Le Catalogue de l'édition
   française. 1.- ed.; 1970-
   [Paris] VPC livres, S.A.; [Port
   Washington, N.Y.] Paris Publications,
   Inc. 71-612834
     Z2165 .C3 MRR Alc Latest edition

   Cercle de la librairie, Paris.
   Repertoire des éditeurs et liste
   des collections. [Nouv. ed.] Paris
   [1963] 294 p. 64-48009
     Z307 .C4 1963 MRR Alc.

   La Librairie française; les livres
   de l'année. 1933/45- Paris, Cercle
   de la librairie. 48-11426
     Z2161 .L695 MRR Alc Full set

   Répertoire international des
   éditeurs de langue française.
   Paris, Cercle de la librairie, 1971.
   xliv, 315 p. [51.66F] 070.5/025
   72-857877
     Z282 .R44 MRR Alc.

PUBLISHERS AND PUBLISHING--GERMANY--
DIRECTORIES.
   Kürschners deutscher Gelehrten-
   Kalender. 1925- 1.- eng.
   Berlin, W. de Gruyter & Co. 25-15070

     Z2230 .K93 MRR Biog Latest edition

   Kürschners deutscher Literatur-
   kalender. 1.- Jahrg.; 1879-
   Berlin, Leipzig [etc.] 06-44921
     Z2230 .K92 MRR Biog Latest edition

PUBLISHERS AND PUBLISHING--GERMANY
(FEDERAL REPUBLIC, 1949-)--DIRECTORIES.
   Vinz, Curt. Dokumentation
   deutschsprachiger Verlage. Ausg. 3.
   München, Wien, Olzog (1968). 588 p.
   [45.00] 72-569850
     Z317 .V5 1968 MRR Alc.

PUBLISHERS AND PUBLISHING--GREAT
BRITAIN.
   Boutell, Henry Sherman, First
   editions of today and how to tell
   them; 4th ed., rev. and enl.
   Berkeley, Calif., Peacock Press, 1965
   [c1964] 227 p. 094.4 64-10193
     Z992 .B77 1965 MRR Alc.

   Growoll, Adolf, Three centuries of
   English booktrade bibliography: New
   York, Pub. for the Dibdin club, by M.
   L. Greenhalgh, 1903. xv p., 1 l.,
   195 p., 1 l. incl 6 facsim. 03-
   1395E
     Z2001.A1 G8 MRR Alc.

   London. Stationers' Company. A
   transcript of the registers of the
   Company of Stationers of London, 1554-
   1640 A.D. [New York P. Smith, 1950]
   5 v. 655.442 49-50201
     Z2002 .L64 MRR Alc.

   London. Stationer's Company. A
   transcript of the registers of the
   worshipful Company of Stationers;
   from 1640-1708 A.D. [New York, P.
   Smith, 1950] 3 v. 655.442 50-
   37726
     Z2002 .L653 MRR Alc.

   Pollard, Alfred William, A short-
   title catalogue of books printed in
   England, Scotland, & Ireland and of
   English books printed abroad, 1475-
   1640. London, Bibliographical
   Society, 1946. xviii, 609 p.
   015.42 47-20884
     Z2002 .P77 1946 MRR Alc.

   Wing, Donald Goddard, Short-title
   catalogue of books printed in
   England, Scotland, Ireland, Wales,
   and British America, and of English
   books printed in other countries,
   1641-1700. New York, Index Society,
   1945-51. 3 v. 015.42 45-8773
     Z2002 .W5 MRR Alc.

   The Writer's market. Cincinnati, O.,
   Writer's digest. 051 [029.6] 31-
   20772
     PN161 .W83 MRR Ref Desk Latest
     edition

PUBLISHERS AND PUBLISHING--GREAT
BRITAIN--DIRECTORIES.
   British books in print. 1874-
   London, Whitaker; New York, Bowker
   [etc.] 02-7496
     Z2001 .R33 MRR Ref Desk Partial
     set

   Cassell's directory of publishing in
   Great Britain, the Commwealth, and
   Ireland. 1st- ed.; 1960/61-
   London, Cassell. 655.442 60-52232
     Z326 .C3 MRR Ref Desk Latest
     edition

   Publishers in the United Kingdom and
   their addresses. 1965- London, J.
   Whitaker. 655.4/025/42 68-129544
     Z327 .P82 MRR Ref Desk Latest
     edition

PUBLISHERS AND PUBLISHING--GREAT (Cont.)
Woodworth, David. Guide to current
British journals; 2nd ed. London,
Library Association, 1973. 2 v.
[£8.50 (v. 1) £4.50 (v. 2)] 016.052
74-159014
Z6956.G6 W66 1973 MRR Alc.

**PUBLISHERS AND PUBLISHING--INDIA--
DIRECTORIES.**
Directory of booksellers, publishers,
libraries & librarians in India. 1st-
ed.: 1968/69- New Delhi, Premier
Publishers. 655.4/025/54 73-900620

Z455 .D49 MRR Alc Latest edition

Directory of Indian publishers. [1st
ed.] New Delhi, Federation of
Publishers & Booksellers Associations
in India: distributors: New Order
Book Co., Ahmedabad [1973] xv, 591
p. [Rs50.00] 070.5/025/54 74-
901329
Z455 .D494 MRR Alc.

Sher Singh, Indian books in print,
1955-67; Delhi, Indian Bureau of
Bibliographies [1969] 1116 p.
[100.00] 015/.54 78-104779
Z3201 .S47 MRR Alc.

**PUBLISHERS AND PUBLISHING--NEW ZEALAND--
DIRECTORIES.**
New Zealand books in print.
Wellington [etc.] Published for the
Associated Booksellers of New Zealand
by Price Milburn [etc.] 62-44889
Began publication in 1957.
Z4101 .N56 MRR Alc Latest edition

**PUBLISHERS AND PUBLISHING--PAKISTAN--
DIRECTORIES.**
Shamsuddoulah, A. B. M., Pakistan
library directory; 1st ed. Dacca,
Great Eastern Books, 1970. 156 p.
[8.00 ($3.00)] 71-931634
Z845.P28 S48 MRR Alc.

**PUBLISHERS AND PUBLISHING--SPAIN--
DIRECTORIES.**
Instituto Nacional del Libro
Español. Guía de editores y
libreros. [1.]- ed.: 1950-
Madrid. 50-21236
Z413 .I533 MRR Alc Latest edition

**PUBLISHERS AND PUBLISHING--SWITZERLAND--
DIRECTORIES.**
Vinz, Curt. Dokumentation
deutschsprachiger Verlage. Ausg. 3.
München, Wien Olzog (1968). 588 p.
[45.00] 72-569850
Z317 .V5 1968 MRR Alc.

**PUBLISHERS AND PUBLISHING--UNITED
STATES.**
Boutell, Henry Sherman, First
editions of today and how to tell
them; 4th ed., rev. and enl.
Berkeley, Calif., Peacock Press, 1965
[c1964] 227 p. 094.4 64-10193
Z992 .B77 1965 MRR Alc.

Burke, William Jeremiah, American
authors and books, 1640 to the
present day 3d rev. ed. New York,
Crown Publishers [c1972] 719 p.
[$12.50] 015/.73 75-168332
Z1224 .B87 1972 MRR Biog.

Grannis, Chandler B., ed. What
happens in book publishing. New
York, Columbia University Press,
1957. x, 414 p. 655.473 56-12739

Z471 .G7 MRR Alc.

Lehmann-Haupt, Hellmut, The book in
America; 2d [rev. and enl. American]
ed. New York, Bowker, 1951. xiv,
493 p. 655.473 51-11308
Z473 .L522 1951 MRR Alc.

Schick, Frank Leopold, The
paperbound book in America; New
York, R. R. Bowker Co., 1958. xviii,
262 p. 655.473 58-10097
Z1033.P3 S35 MRR Alc.

The Writer's market. Cincinnati, O.,
Writer's digest. 051 [029.6] 31-
20772
PN161 .W83 MRR Ref Desk Latest
edition

**PUBLISHERS AND PUBLISHING--UNITED
STATES--BIBLIOGRAPHY.**
Tanselle, George Thomas, Guide to
the study of United States imprints
Cambridge, Mass., Belknap Press of
Harvard University Press, 1971. 2 v.
(lxiv, 1050 p.) 016.015/73 79-
143232
Z1215.A2 T35 MRR Alc.

**PUBLISHERS AND PUBLISHING--UNITED
STATES--DIRECTORIES.**
American book trade directory. [1st]-
ed.: 1915- New York, R. R.
Bowker. 15-23627
Z475 .A5 Sci RR Latest edition /
MRR Ref Desk Latest edition

The American catalogue ... New York,
1941. 8 v. in 13. 015.73 a 42-
2938
Z1215 .A52 MRR Ref Desk.

Association of American University
Presses. Directory. [Baltimore] 54-
43046
Z475 .A88 MRR Alc Latest edition

Baer, Eleanora A. Titles in series;
2. ed. New York, Scarecrow Press,
1964. 2 v. (1530 p.) 011 64-11789

AI3 .B3 1964 MRR Alc.

Book buyer's handbook. 1947/48- New
York, American Booksellers' Assn.
655.473 48-512
Z475 .B6 MRR Alc Latest edition

Books in print; 1948- New York, R.
R. Bowker Co. 015.73 74-643574
Z1215 .P972 Sci RR Latest edition
/ MRR Alc Latest edition / MRR
Ref Desk Latest edition

Christian Booksellers Association. C
B A suppliers directory. Colorado
Springs [etc.] 070.5/94 72-622387
Z479 .C5 MRR Alc Latest edition

Cumulative book index. 1898/99- New
York [etc.] H. W. Wilson Co. 05-
33604
Z1219 .M78 MRR Circ Partial set

El-Hi textbooks in print. [56th]-
[1927- New York, Bowker [etc.]
016.378/156 57-4667
Z5813 .A51 MRR Alc Latest edition

Gillespie, John Thomas, Paperback
books for young people; Chicago,
American Library Association, 1972.
viii, 177 p. 070.5/73 72-2390
Z479 .G55 MRR Alc.

International directory of little
magazines & small presses. 9th
ed.: 1973/74- [Paradise, Calif.,
Dustbooks] [$3.50] 051/.025 73-
645432
Z6944.L5 D5 MRR Alc Latest edition

Literary market place; [1st]- ed.:
1940- New York, Bowker. 655.473 41-
51571
PN161 .L5 Sci RR Partial set / MRR
Ref Desk Latest edition

Names & numbers; 1952/53- New York,
Bowker. 655.473 61-1000
PN161 .L52 MRR Ref Desk Latest
edition / MRR Alc Latest edition

Nemeyer, Carol A., Scholarly reprint
publishing in the United States New
York, R. R. Bowker Co., 1972. ix,
262 p. 070.5/73 74-163901
Z479 .N44 MRR Alc.

Oleksy, Walter G., 1,000 tested
money-making markets for writers
West Nyack, N.Y., Parker Pub. Co.
[1973] 225 p. 808/.025/0973 72-
13005
PN161 .O5 MRR Alc.

Roorbach, Orville Augustus,
Bibliotheca americana. New York, P.
Smith, 1939. xi, 652 p. 015.73 39-
27504
Z1215 .A3 1939 MRR Ref Desk.

Shapiro, Nat, ed. Popular music;
[1st ed. New York] Adrian Press
[1964]- v. 64-23761
ML120.U5 S5 MRR Alc.

Stecheson, Anthony, comp. The
Stecheson classified song directory,
Hollywood, Calif., Music Industry
Press [1961] ix, 503 p. 016.784
62-753
ML128.V7 S83 MRR Alc.

The United States catalog; 4th ed.
New York, H. W. Wilson Co., 1928.
3164 p. 28-26655
Z1215 .U6 1928 MRR Circ.

The United States catalog; 3d ed.
Minneapolis, New York, The H. W.
Wilson company, 1912. 3 p. l., 2837
p. 12-35572
Z1215 .U6 1912a MRR Ref Desk (Alc.
6)

The United States catalog; books in
print 1902. 2d ed. Minneapolis, The
H. W. Wilson co., 1903. 2 p. l.,
2150 p. 03-28279
Z1215 .U6 1903 MRR Ref Desk.

**PUBLISHERS AND PUBLISHING--UNITED
STATES--HISTORY.**
Tebbel, John William, A history of
book publishing in the United States,
New York, R. R. Bowker Co. [1972-
v. 070.5/0973 71-163903
Z473 .T42 MRR Alc.

PUERTO RICAN LITERATURE--BIBLIOGRAPHY.
Pedreira, Antonio Salvador,
Bibliografía puertorriqueña (1493-
1830) New York, B. Franklin Reprints
[1974] xxxii, 707 p. 016.917295/03
72-82366
Z1551 .P37 1974 MRR Alc.

**PUERTO RICAN LITERATURE--BIO-
BIBLIOGRAPHY.**
Rivera de Alvarez, Josefina.
Diccionario de literatura
puertorriqueña. [1. ed. Rio
Pedras] Universidad de Puerto Rico
[1955] xviii, 499 p. 56-40818
PQ7424 .R5 MRR Alc.

**PUERTO RICAN LITERATURE--HISTORY AND
CRITICISM.**
Rivera de Alvarez, Josefina.
Diccionario de literatura
puertorriqueña. [1. ed. Rio
Pedras] Universidad de Puerto Rico
[1955] xviii, 499 p. 56-40818
PQ7424 .R5 MRR Alc.

PUERTO RICO.
Crampsey, Robert A. Puerto Rico.
Newton Abbot, David & Charles [1973]
206 p. [£3.75 ($8.95 U.S.)]
917.295/03/5 73-168726
F1958 .C72 MRR Alc.

United States. Puerto Rico
reconstruction administration.
Puerto Rico; a guide to the island of
Boriquén, New York, The University
society, inc., 1940. xli, 409 p.
917.295 40-35620
F1958 .U55 MRR Alc.

PUERTO RICO--BIBLIOGRAPHY.
Pedreira, Antonio Salvador,
Bibliografía puertorriqueña (1493-
1830) New York, B. Franklin Reprints
[1974] xxxii, 707 p. 016.917295/03
72-82366
Z1551 .P37 1974 MRR Alc.

PUERTO RICO--BIOGRAPHY.
Farr, Kenneth R. Historical
dictionary of Puerto Rico and the
U.S. Virgin Islands. Metuchen, N.J.,
Scarecrow Press, 1973. vii, 148 p.
917.28/003 73-7603
F1954 .F37 MRR Alc.

PUERTO RICO--COMMERCE--DIRECTORIES.
Puerto Rico official industrial
directory. San Juan, The Witcom
Group, inc. [$35.00] 380.1/025/7295
73-641037
HC157.P8 P596 MRR Alc Latest
edition

**PUERTO RICO--DESCRIPTION AND TRAVEL--
1951- --GUIDE-BOOKS.**
Rand, Abby. Abby Rand's guide to
Puerto Rico and the U.S. Virgin
Islands. New York, Scribner [1973]
ix, 276 p. [$8.95] 917.295/04/53
73-1357
F1959 .R36 1973 MRR Alc.

**PUERTO RICO--DESCRIPTION AND TRAVEL--
GUIDE-BOOKS.**
Chiesa de Pérez, Carmen. Enjoy
Puerto Rico; [1st ed.] New York,
Vantage Press [1961] 316 p.
917.295 61-12424
F1959 .C5 MRR Alc.

Marvel, Evalyn. Guide to Puerto Rico
and the Virgin Islands. Rev. ed.
New York, Crown Publishers [1963]
254 p. 917.295 63-24745
F1959 .M3 1963 MRR Alc.

Rand, Abby. Abby Rand's guide to
Puerto Rico and the U.S. Virgin
Islands. New York, Scribner [1973]
ix, 276 p. [$8.95] 917.295/04/53
73-1357
F1959 .R36 1973 MRR Alc.

United States. Puerto Rico
reconstruction administration.
Puerto Rico; a guide to the island of
Boriquén, New York, The University
society, inc., 1940. xli, 409 p.
917.295 40-35620
F1958 .U55 MRR Alc.

**PUERTO RICO--DICTIONARIES AND
ENCYCLOPEDIAS.**
Farr, Kenneth R. Historical
dictionary of Puerto Rico and the
U.S. Virgin Islands. Metuchen, N.J.,
Scarecrow Press, 1973. vii, 148 p.
917.28/003 73-7603
F1954 .F37 MRR Alc.

PUERTO RICO--HISTORY--CHRONOLOGY.
Ribes Tovar, Federico. A
chronological history of Puerto Rico.
[New York] Plus Ultra Educational
Publishers, c1973] 589 p. [$3.95]
972.95 74-156905
F1970 .R5213 MRR Alc.

PUERTO RICO--INDUSTRIES--DIRECTORIES.
Puerto Rico official industrial
directory. San Juan, The Witcom
Group, inc. [$35.00] 380.1/025/7295
73-641037
HC157.P8 P596 MRR Alc Latest
edition

PUGILISM
see Boxing

PUNCHED CARD SYSTEMS.
Reichmann, Felix, Notched cards,
New Brunswick, N.J., Graduate School
of Library Service, Rutgers, the
State University, 1961. 5 v. in 1.
010.78   60-16772
    Z695.92 .R4 MRR Alc.

PUNIC WAR, 2D, 218-201 B.C.--POETRY.
Silius Italicus, Tiberius Catius.
Punica, London, W. Heinemann, ltd.;
Cambridge, Mass. Harvard university
press, 1934. 2 v.   873.4 34-17332
    PA6156.S6 1934 MRR Alc.

PUNISHMENT.
see also Capital punishment

see also Prisons

PUPPETS AND PUPPET-PLAYS--BIBLIOGRAPHY.
Crothers, J. Francis. The
puppeteer's library guide; Metuchen,
N.J., Scarecrow Press, 1971-   v.
016.7915/3   71-149991
    Z5784.P9 C7 MRR Alc.

PUPPETS AND PUPPET-PLAYS--DICTIONARIES.
Philpott, Alexis Robert. Dictionary
of puppetry [1st American ed.]
Boston, Plays, inc. [1969] 286 p.
[8.95]   791.5/3/03 69-18110
    PN1972 .P47 1969b MRR Alc.

PUPPETS AND PUPPET-PLAYS--DIRECTORIES.
Puppeteers of America. Membership
directory. Ojai, Cal. 58-32541
    PN1979.D5 P8   MRR Alc Latest
    edition

PUPPETS AND PUPPET-PLAYS--UNITED STATES--
HISTORY.
McPharlin, Paul, The puppet theatre
in America: Boston, Plays, inc.
[1969] xi, 734 p. [12.95]
791.5/3/0973   79-97944
    PN1978.U6 M22 1969 MRR Alc.

PURCHASING.
see also Consumer education

see also Consumers

see also Shopping

Combs, Paul H. Handbook of
international purchasing, Boston,
Cahners Books [1971] viii, 168 p.
658.7/2   70-132670
    HF5437 .C585 MRR Alc.

PURCHASING AGENTS--UNITED STATES--
DIRECTORIES.
Phelon's resident buyers and
merchandise brokers of department
store merchandise, ready to wear,
millinery. New York, Phelon, Sheldon
& Marsar, inc. 380.1/45/68702573 72-
626495
    HD9940.U5 N736   MRR Alc Latest
    edition

Sheldon's retail directory of the
United States and Canada and Phelon's
resident buyers and merchandise
brokers. New York, Phelon; Sheldon &
Marsar. [$50.00]   381 74-644143
    HF5429.3 .S52 MRR Alc Latest
    edition

PUTNAM, HERBERT, 1861-1955.
Herbert Putnam, librarian of
Congress. [Washington, W. F. Roberts
company, 1939] 66, [1] p.   920.2
40-32838
    Z663 .P82 MRR Alc.

Herbert Putnam, Librarian of
Congress. [Washington, 1939] [12]
p.   920.2   39-20770
    Z663 .P8 MRR Alc.

United States. Library of Congress.
Herbert Putnam, 1861-1955;
Washington, 1956. vii, 94 p.   920.2
56-60027
    Z663 .H4 MRR Alc.

PUZZLES.
see also Educational games

QUACKS AND QUACKERY.
The Medicine show Rev. ed. New
York, Pantheon Books, 1974. 384 p.
610   74-10418
    RC81 .M496 1974 MRR Alc.

QUARRIES AND QUARRYING--DIRECTORIES.
Pit and quarry. Directory of the
nonmetallic minerals industries.
Chicago. 58-20992
    TN12 .P5 Sci RR Latest edition /
    MRR Alc Latest edition

QUEBEC (PROVINCE)--ECONOMIC CONDITIONS.
Quebec (Province). Bureau of
Statistics. Annuaire du Québec. 1.-
année; 1914- Quebec. 16-22513
    HA747 .Q3   MRR Alc Latest edition

QUEBEC (PROVINCE)--STATISTICS.
Quebec (Province). Bureau of
Statistics. Annuaire du Québec. 1.-
année; 1914- Quebec. 16-22513
    HA747 .Q3   MRR Alc Latest edition

QUEENSLAND--COMMERCE--DIRECTORIES.
Universal business directory for
North Central Queensland. Brisbane,
Universal Business Directories. 57-
36953
    HF5304 .U5   MRR Alc Latest edition

QUESTIONS AND ANSWERS.
Ackermann, Alfred Seabold Eli,
Popular fallacies; 4th ed. London,
Old Westminster Press; sole
distributors, S. Marshall, 1950. xv,
843 p.   133.7   50-32195
    AZ999 .A3 1950 MRR Alc.

Garrison, Webb B. The ignorance
book, New York, Morrow, 1971. 250
p. [$6.95]   031/.02   70-135148
    AG106 .G3 MRR Alc.

Schnapper, Morris Bartel, ed. The
facts of American life. Washington,
Public Affairs Press, [1960] vi, 420
p.   917.3   60-11398
    E169.1 .S345 MRR Alc.

Stimpson, George William, Nuggets of
knowledge, New York, G. Sully and
company [c1928] viii p., 1 l., 427
p.   28-24287
    AG105 .S85 MRR Ref Desk.

Stimpson, George William, Popular
questions answered, Detroit, Gale
Research Co., 1970. viii, 426 p.
031   74-109601
    AG195 .S74 1970 MRR Ref Desk.

QUESTIONS AND ANSWERS--ASTRONOMY.
Pickering, James Sayre. 1001
questions answered about astronomy,
Rev. ed. New York, Dodd, Mead, 1966.
xi, 420 p.   520.76   66-14989
    QB44 .P63 1966 MRR Alc.

QUESTIONS AND ANSWERS--METEOROLOGY.
Forrester, Frank H. 1001 questions
answered about the weather. New
York, Dodd, Mead, 1957.   419 p.
551.5076   57-11396
    QC863 .F72 MRR Alc.

QUESTIONS AND ANSWERS--PERIODICALS.
American notes & queries. v. 1-
Sept. 1962- [New Haven, Conn.]
[$6.50]   031/.02   74-642751
    Z1034 .A4   MRR Alc Full set

American notes & queries; v. 1-8;
Apr.-1941-Mar. 1950. [New York] 051
43-6120
    AG305 .A48   MRR Alc Full set

Notes and queries; v. 1- Nov. 3,
1849- London [etc.] Oxford Univ.
Press [etc.]   12-25307
    AG305 .N7   MRR Alc Full set

QUESTIONS AND ANSWERS--POLITICAL
SCIENCE.
Theis, Paul A., All about politics;
New York, Bowker, 1972. xii, 228 p.
320   72-8470
    JK1726 .T48 MRR Alc.

QUESTIONS AND ANSWERS--PRESIDENTS (U.S.)
Curley, Harold Thomas, Presidential
quiz. Washington, History Quiz,
c1951.   102 p.   353.03   51-2967
    JK515 .C8 MRR Alc.

QUOTATION.
Boller, Paul F. Quotemanship;
[Dallas] Southern Methodist
University Press [1967] xiii, 454 p.
66-29656
    PN171.Q6 B6 MRR Ref Desk.

QUOTATIONS.
Andriot, John L. Guide to the
building inscriptions of the Nation's
Capital. Arlington, Va., Jay-Way
Press, 1955.   57 p.   729   55-4877
    NA4050.I5 A55 MRR Ref Desk.

Auden, Wystan Hugh, ed. The Viking
book of aphorisms; New York, Viking
Press [1966] x, 431 p.   808.882 66-
3191
    PN6271 .A85 1966 MRR Alc.

Bartlett, John, comp. Familiar
quotations; 14th ed., rev. and enl.
Boston, Little, Brown [1968] xxviii,
1750 p.   808.88/2 68-15664
    PN6081 .B27 1968 MRR Ref Desk.

Belton, John Devoe, A literary
manual of foreign quotations, ancient
and modern, New York [etc.] G. P.
Putnam's sons, 1891. v1, 249 p.   11-
30769
    PN6080 .B3 MRR Alc.

Benham, William Gurney, Sir, Book of
quotations, proverbs and household
words. New and rev. ed. New York,
Putnam [1949?] viii, 1384 p.   808.8
50-5072
    PN6080 .B35 1949 MRR Ref Desk.

Benham, William Gurney, Sir,
Cassell's classified quotations from
authors of all nations and periods,
London, New York [etc.] Cassell and
company, limited, 1921. vi p., 1 l.,
653, [1] p.   21-10014
    PN6081 .C3 1921 MRR Alc.

Bent, Samuel Arthur, comp. Familiar
short sayings of great men, with
historical and explanatory notes,
Rev. and enl. ed. Boston, New York,
Houghton Mifflin company [191-] xix,
665 p.   21-8813
    PN6321 .B4 1910a MRR Alc.

Berrey, Lester V., ed. A treasury of
Biblical quotations; 1st ed.]
Garden City, N.Y., Doubleday, 1948.
viii, 240 p.   220.2   48-9181
    BS432 .B4 MRR Alc.

Bliss, Alan Joseph. A dictionary of
foreign words and phrases in current
English London, Routledge & K. Paul,
1966.   ix, 389 p.   [40/-]   422.4 66-
75485
    PE1670 .B55 MRR Ref Desk.

Braude, Jacob Morton, ed. Lifetime
speaker's encyclopedia. Englewood
Cliffs, N.J., Prentice-Hall [1962] 2
v. (xix, 1224 p.)   808.88 62-18248
    PN6081 .B667 MRR Alc.

Braude, Jacob Morton, New treasury
of stories for every speaking and
writing occasion. Englewood Cliffs,
N.J., Prentice-Hall [1959] 494 p.
808.88   59-13391
    PN6261 .B73 MRR Alc.

Braude, Jacob Morton, ed. Second
encyclopedia of stories, quotations,
and anecdotes. Englewood Cliffs,
N.J., Prentice-Hall, 1957.   468 p.
808.88*   57-5563
    PN6081 .B67 MRR Alc.

Büchmann, Georg, comp. Geflügelte
Worte; 32. Aufl., vollständig
neubearb. xvi, 1039 p.   72-337788
    PN6090 .B8 1972 MRR Alc.

Chapin, John, ed. The book of
Catholic quotations; New York,
Farrar, Straus and Cudahy [1956] x,
1073 p.   808.8   56-11061
    PN6084.C2 C5 MRR Alc.

Cohen, John Michael, comp. The
Penguin dictionary of quotations New
York, Atheneum, 1962 [c1960] v, 663
p.   808.88   62-8334
    PN6081 .C55 1962 MRR Ref Desk.

Conrad, Barnaby, comp. Famous last
words. [1st ed.] Garden City, N.Y.,
Doubleday, 1961.   208 p.   808.88 61-
12505
    PN6328.L3 C65 MRR Alc.

[Copeland, Lewis] ed. 5000
quotations for all occasions,
Philadelphia, Blakiston Co. [1945]
v, 346 p.   808.8   45-3728
    PN6081 .C68 MRR Alc.

Droke, Maxwell, ed. The Christian
leader's golden treasury,
Indianapolis, Droke House [1955] 620
p.   808.88*   55-11712
    PN6083 .D7 MRR Alc.

Edwards, Tryon, comp. The new
dictionary of thoughts; [New York]
Standard Book Co., 1957. xxxviii,
794 p.   808.88*   57-1131
    PN6331 .E2 1957 MRR Ref Desk.

Edwards, Tryon, comp. The new
dictionary of thoughts; [Collectors
ed. New York] Standard Book Co.,
1960. xxxviii, 794 p.   808.88 60-
2864
    PN6331 .E2 1960 MRR Alc.

Esar, Evan, ed. The dictionary of
humorous quotations. New York,
Horizon Press, 1853 [c1949] 270 p.
808.87   53-7005
    PN6084.H8 E8 1953 MRR Alc.

Flesch, Rudolf Franz, ed. The new
book of unusual quotations. [1st
ed.] New York, Harper & Row [1966]
x, 448 p.   808.882   66-20763
    PN6083 .F55 1966 MRR Ref Desk.

Fogg, Walter. One thousand sayings
of history presented as pictures in
prose, Boston, Mass., The Beacon
press, inc., 1929. vi, 819 p.   29-
1093
    PN6328.H5 F6 MRR Alc.

Fuller, Edmund, ed. Thesaurus of
epigrams. Garden City, N.Y., Garden
City Pub. Co. [1948] 382 p.   808.8
48-5656
    PN6281 .F8 1948 MRR Alc.

QUOTATIONS. (Cont.)

Gilbert, Mark, ed. Wisdom of the ages; London, Heinemann [1965] 431 p. 808.8 57-39679
PN6331 .G53 1956 MRR Alc.

The Great ideas; Chicago, Encyclopedia Britannica [1955, c1952] 2 v. 028.3 55-10313
AC1 .G72 vol. 2-3 MRR Alc.

Harbottle, Thomas Benfield, comp. Dictionary of quotations (classical) London, S. Sonnenschein & co., limited; New York, The Macmillan co., limited, 1897. 3 p. l., 648 p. 880.822 04-13800
PN6080 .H2 1897 MRR Alc.

Heinl, Robert Debs, comp. Dictionary of military and naval quotations. Annapolis, United States Naval Institute [c1966] xl, 367 p. 355.0008 66-22342
U19 .H4 MRR Ref Desk.

Hitchcock, Roswell Dwight, Hitchcock's Topical Bible and Cruden's Concordance. Grand Rapids, Baker Book House, 1959 [c1952] xxxvii, 685, 342 p. 220.2 56-12726

BS432 .H5 1959 MRR Alc.

Hovey, E. Paul, comp. The treasury for special days and occasions; [Westwood, N.J.] Revell [1961] 317 p. 808.88 61-9238
PN6083 .H73 MRR Alc.

Hovey, E. Paul, comp. The treasury of inspirational anecdotes, quotations, and illustrations, [Westwood, N.J.] Revell [1959] 316 p. 808.88 59-8725
PN6083 .H75 MRR Alc.

Hoyt, Jehiel Keeler, Hoyt's New cyclopedia of practical quotations New York, London, Funk & Wagnalls company [c1940] xxxi, 1343 p. 808.8 40-13383
PN6081 .H7 1940 MRR Ref Desk.

Hyman, Robin. A dictionary of famous quotations. London, Evans [1974] 515 p. [£2.80] 808.88/2 74-161201

PN6080 .H8 1974 MRR Ref Desk.

Hyman, Robin. A dictionary of famous quotations. London, Pan, 1967. 693 p. [7/6] 808.88/2 67-83680
PN6081 .H88 1967 MRR Alc.

Jones, Hugh Percy, ed. Dictionary of foreign phrases and classical quotations. New and rev. ed. Edinburgh, J. Grant, 1929. xx, 532 p. 808.8 30-31844
PN6080 .J6 1929 MRR Alc.

Joy, Charles Rhind, Harper's topical concordance. Rev. and enl. ed. New York, Harper [1962] ix, 628 p. 220.2 62-11129
BS432 .J63 1962 MRR Alc.

The Kenkyusha dictionary of English quotations. Tokyo, Kenkyusha, 1953 [i.e. 1957] xlix, 968 p. 808.88* 58-30594
PN6081 .K43 MRR Alc.

Kennedy, Gerald Hamilton, Bp., comp. A reader's notebook. [1st ed.] New York, Harper [1953] 340 p. 808.8 53-8373
PN6081 .K45 MRR Alc.

Kennedy, Gerald Hamilton, Bp., comp. A second reader's notebook. New York, Harper [1959] 362 p. 808.88 59-8254
PN6081 .K47 MRR Alc.

King, William Francis Henry, ed. and tr. Classical and foreign quotations; New York, Ungar [1958?] lxviii, 412 p. 808.88* 58-8962
PN6080 .K5 1958 MRR Ref Desk.

Kominsky, Morris. The hoaxers: plain liars, fancy liars, and damned liars. Boston, Branden Press [1970] 735 p. [$12.50] 909 76-109134
E839.8 .K6 MRR Alc.

Lawson, James Gilchrist, comp. The world's best proverbs and maxims, New York, George H. Doran company [c1926] xvi p., 1 l., 19-364 p. 26-12534
PN6405 .L3 MRR Alc.

Le Comte, Edward Semple, Dictionary of last words. New York, Philosophical Library [c1955] 267 p. 808.8 54-13452
PN6328.L3 L4 MRR Ref Desk.

Lean, Vincent Stuckey, Lean's collectanea. Bristol, J. W. Arrowsmith; [etc., etc.] 1902-04. 4 v. in 5. 04-31340
PN6421 .L3 MRR Alc.

Marvin, Frederic Rowland, The last words (real and traditional) of distinguished men and women, New York, Chicago [etc.] F. H. Revell co., 1901. 3 p. l., 336 p. 01-22886
PN6328.L8 M8 1901 MRR Alc.

McDormand, Thomas Bruce. Judson concordance to hymns Valley Forge, Judson Press [1965] 375 p. 245.203 65-15009
BV305 .M3 MRR Alc.

Mead, Frank Spencer, ed. The encyclopedia of religious quotations. Westwood, N.J., Revell [1965] 534 p. 808.882 65-23623
PN6084.R3 M4 MRR Ref Desk.

The Oxford dictionary of quotations. 2d ed. (rev.) London, New York, Oxford University Press [1959] xx, 1003 p. 808.88 62-2256
PN6081 .O9 1959 MRR Alc.

Partridge, Eric, ed. A book of essential quotations. [Rev. ed.] New York, Dutton, 1964. xii, 196 p. 65-4644
PN6081 .P19 1964 MRR Ref Desk.

Prochnow, Herbert Victor, comp. A dictionary of wit, wisdom & satire, [1st ed.] New York, Harper [1962] vi, 243 p. 808.88 62-9914
PN6081 .P7 MRR Ref Desk.

Prochnow, Herbert Victor, comp. Speaker's handbook of epigrams and witticisms. [1st ed.] New York, Harper [c1955] 332 p. 808.88* 54-12157
PN6271 .P7 MRR Alc.

Reynolds, George, A complete concordance of the Book of Mormon. Salt Lake City, Distributed by Deseret Book Co. [1957] iv, 852 p. 289.3 57-59334
BX8627.A1 R4 1957 MRR Alc.

Sattler, Wilhelm Ferdinand. Deutsch-englisches sachwörterbuch. Leipzig, Renger, 1904. xx, 1035 p. 05-16230

PF3640 .S3 MRR Alc.

Seitz, Rober, comp. Zitate von A bis Z. München, Sudwest-Verlag [1964] 512 p. 67-78325
PN6090 .S45 MRR Alc.

Simpson, James Beasley, comp. Contemporary quotations, New York, Crowell [1964] xi, 500 p. 808.88 64-16534
PN6081 .S47 MRR Alc.

Sites, Maud Kay. Quotations and inscriptions in the federal and public buildings on Capitol hill, Baltimore, Md., N.T.A. Munder [1934] 22, [2] p. 917.53 35-2954
F204 .A1S5 MRR Ref Desk.

Stevenson, Burton Egbert, comp. The home book of Bible quotations, New York, Harper [1949] xxiv, 645 p. 220.2 49-11832
BS432 .S667 MRR Alc.

Stevenson, Burton Egbert, ed. The home book of proverbs, maxims and familiar phrases. New York, Macmillan Co., 1948. viii, 2957 p. 398.9 48-8717
PN6405 .S8 MRR Alc.

Stevenson, Burton Egbert, comp. The home book of quotations, 10th ed. New York, Dodd, Mead, 1967. xlii, 2816 p. 808.88/2 67-13583
PN6081 .S73 1967 MRR Ref Desk.

Stevenson, Burton Egbert, ed. The Macmillan book of proverbs, maxims, and famous phrases. New York, Macmillan [1965, c1948] viii, 2957 p. 808.88 65-3787
PN6405 .S8 1965 MRR Ref Desk.

Strauss, Maurice Benjamin, comp. Familiar medical quotations, [1st ed.] Boston, Little, Brown [1968] xix, 968 p. 610/.2 68-21620
R707 .S75 MRR Ref Desk.

Wallis, Charles Langworthy, ed. Speaker's resources from contemporary literature. [1st ed.] New York, Harper & Row [1965] xvi, 282 p. 808.882 65-20460
PN6081 .W28 MRR Ref Desk.

Walter, Emily Loiseau, comp. A complete collection of the quotations and inscriptions in the Library of Congress, 10th rev. ed. Baltimore, S. J. Gaeng, 1925. 3 p. l., 11-47 p. 25-4054
Z733.U59 W2 1925 MRR Alc.

Walter, Emily Loiseau, comp. A complete collection of the quotations and inscriptions in the Library of Congress, 8th rev. ed. ... Baltimore, Williams & Wilkins company, 1907. 3 p. l., 11-45 p. 07-30624
Z733.U59 W2 1907 MRR Ref Desk.

Wood, James, Rev. Dictionary of quotations from ancient and modern English and foreign sources; London, New York, F. Warne and co., 1902. vii, [1], 658, [1] p. 05-35418
PN6080 .W6 MRR Alc.

QUOTATIONS--BIBLIOGRAPHY.
Guerlac, Othon Ggepp, Les citations françaises; 3. ed. Paris, A. Colin 1952 [c1931] 458 p. 848.08 52-43159
PN6086 .G8 1952 MRR Alc.

QUOTATIONS--PERIODICALS.
American notes & queries. v. 1- Sept. 1962- [New Haven, Conn.] [$6.50] 031/.02 74-642751
Z1034 .A4 MRR Alc Full set

Notes and queries; v. 1- Nov. 3, 1849- London [etc.] Oxford Univ. Press [etc.] 12-25307
AG305 .N7 MRR Alc Full set

QUOTATIONS, AMERICAN.
Bartlett, John Russell, Dictionary of Americanisms; 4th ed., greatly improved and enl. Boston, Little, Brown, and company, 1877. xlvi p., 1 l., 813 p. 11-7835
PE2835 .B3 1877 MRR Alc.

Berger, Oscar, comp. The Presidents, from George Washington to the present. New York, Crown Publishers [1968] 96 p. [$3.95] 741.4973 68-9068
E176.1 .B46 MRR Alc.

Bohle, Bruce, comp. The home book of American quotations, New York, Dodd, Mead, 1967. xv, 512 p. 818/.02 67-14310
PN6081 .B62 MRR Ref Desk.

[Clemens, Samuel Langhorne] Mark Twain at your fingertips, New York, Beechhurst Press [1948] xiv, 559 p. 817.44 48-5681
PS1303 .H3 MRR Alc.

Eisenhower, Dwight David, Pres. U.S., The quotable Dwight D. Eisenhower. [1st ed.] Anderson, S.C., Droke House; distributed by Grosset and Dunlap, New York [1967] vii, 242 p. 973.921/0924 67-13265
E836 .A25 G6 MRR Alc.

Fadiman, Clifton, ed. The American treasury, 1455-1955, [1st ed.] New York, Harper [1955] 1108 p. 810.82 55-8019
PS509.H5 F3 MRR Ref Desk.

Fell, Frederick Victor, comp. The wit and wisdom of the Presidents, New York, F. Fell [1966] 206 p. 973.00207 66-11923
E176.1 .F4 MRR Alc.

Harnsberger, Caroline (Thomas) ed. Treasury of presidential quotations. Chicago, Follett Pub. Co., 1964. xix, 394 p. 308.22 64-23607
E176.1 .H3 MRR Ref Desk.

Harris, Leon A. The fine art of political wit; [1st ed.] New York, Dutton, 1964. 288 p. 827.093 64-19532
PN6231.P6 H36 MRR Alc.

Hurd, Charles, A treasury of great American quotations; [1st ed.] New York, Hawthorn Books [1964] 318 p. 818.082 64-12420
PN6081 .H54 MRR Alc.

Jefferson, Thomas, pres. U.S., The Jeffersonian cyclopedia, New York, London, Funk & Wagnalls company [1900?] 4 p. l., [xiii]-xxii, [2], 1009 p. mrr01-50
JK113 .J4 1900b MRR Alc.

Jefferson, Thomas, Pres. U.S., The Jeffersonian cyclopedia; New York, Russell & Russell [1967] 2 v. (1009 p.) 973.46/0924 66-27664
E332.82 1967 MRR Ref Desk.

Johnson, Lyndon Baines, Pres. U.S., The Johnson wit. [1st ed.] New York, Citadel Press [1965] 94 p. 817.54 65-27093
E847 .A25 1965a MRR Alc.

Johnson, Lyndon Baines, Pres. U.S., The quotable Lyndon B. Johnson. [1st ed.] Anderson, S.C., Droke House; distributed by Grosset & Dunlap, New York [1968] vi, 311 p. 300/.8 67-13268
E847.J6 A25 MRR Alc.

QUOTATIONS, AMERICAN. (Cont.)
Kennedy, John Fitzgerald, Pres. U.S.,
Kennedy and the press; New York,
Crowell [1965] 555 p.   973.922 65-
12271
E837 .K37 MRR Alc.

Kennedy, John Fitzgerald, Pres. U.S.,
Memorable quotations of John F.
Kennedy. New York, Crowell [1965]
xii, 314 p.   300.8 65-21411
E842 .A25 1965b MRR Alc.

Kennedy, John Fitzgerald, Pres.,
U.S., More Kennedy wit, [1st ed.]
New York, Citadel Press [1965] 94 p.
923.173 65-20540
E842.A25 1965a MRR Alc.

Kennedy, John Fitzgerald, Pres. U.S.,
The quotable Kennedy, [1st ed.]
New York, Citadel Press [1965] 162
p.   818.5402 65-27090
E842.A25 G6 MRR Alc.

Lincoln, Abraham, Pres. U.S., The
Lincoln encyclopedia; New York,
Macmillan, 1950. xii, 395 p.   308.1
50-5351
E457.92 1950 MRR Alc.

Lincoln, Abraham, Pres. U.S., The
Lincoln treasury, [1st ed.]
Chicago, Wilcox & Follett [1950] ix,
372 p.   a 823.173 50-11878
E457.99 .H2 MRR Alc.

Lincoln, Abraham, Pres. U.S., A
treasury of Lincoln quotations. [1st
ed.] Garden City, N.Y., Doubleday
[1965] ix, 320 p.   813.3 65-13990
E457.92 1965a MRR Alc.

Madison, James, Pres. U.S., The
complete Madison; [1st ed.] New
York, Harper [1953] xi, 361 p.
308.1 53-5445
E302 .M17 MRR Alc.

Martin, Thomas Lyle. Malice in
Blunderland. New York, McGraw-Hill
[1973] vii, 143 p. [$5.95]
658.4/002/07 73-4376
PN6231.M2 M3 MRR Ref Desk.

Mitchell, Edwin Valentine, comp. An
encyclopedia of American politics.
New York, Greenwood Press, 1968
[c1946] 338 p.   320/.0973 69-10135

JK9 .M55 1968 MRR Alc.

Nixon, Richard Milhous, The quotable
Richard M. Nixon. [1st ed.]
Anderson, S.C., Droke House;
distributed by Grosset and Dunlap,
New York [1967] 199 p.   081 67-
13271
E748.N5 A29 MRR Alc.

Nixon, Richard Milhous, Quotations
from the would-be chairman: Richard
Milhous Nixon. Washington, Public
Affairs Press [1968] 168 p. [$1.00]
973.92/0924 68-55033
E748.N5 A293 MRR Alc.

Noble, Valerie, The effective echo;
New York, Special Libraries
Association, 1970. ix, 165 p.
659.1 71-110487
HF5828 .N62 MRR Alc.

Plotkin, David George, Dictionary of
American maxims. New York,
Philosophical Library [1955] 597 p.
398.9 55-13882
PN6271 .P6 MRR Ref Desk.

Representative American speeches.
1937/38- New York, H. W. Wilson Co.
815.5082 38-27962
PS668 .B3 MRR Alc Full set

Revolutionary quotations from the
thoughts of Uncle Sam. Cicero, Ill.,
Johnny Appleseed Patriotic
Publications [1969] xi, 113 p.
321/.09 74-5070
JC491 .R49 MRR Ref Desk.

Roosevelt, Franklin Delano, Pres.
U.S., Memorable quotations of
Franklin D. Roosevelt. New York,
Crowell [1965] 1 v. (various
pagings) 308.1 65-15221
E742.5 .R63 MRR Alc.

Roosevelt, Franklin Delano, pres.
U.S., "Quotations" from Franklin
Delano Roosevelt. Washington, D.C.,
Republican national committee [c1940]
128 p.   973.917 40-22770
E806 .R745 1940 MRR Alc.

Roosevelt, Franklin Delano, Pres.
U.S., The wit and wisdom of Franklin
D. Roosevelt. Boston, Beacon Press,
1950. 154 p.   308.1 50-10076
E806 .R79 MRR Alc.

Roosevelt, Theodore, pres. U.S.,
Theodore Roosevelt cyclopedia, New
York city, Roosevelt memorial
association [c1941] xiii p., 1 l.,
674 p.   308.1 41-4125
E757 .R82 MRR Alc.

Safire, William L. The new language
of politics; New York, Random House
[1968] xvi, 528 p.   320/.03 68-
14508
JK9 .S2 MRR Ref Desk.

Shankle, George Earlie. American
mottoes and slogans, New York, The
H. W. Wilson company, 1941. 183 p.
973 41-26048
E179 .S544 MRR Alc.

Shoemaker, Ralph Joseph, The
Presidents words, an index.
Louisville, Ky., E. De G. Shoemaker
and R. J. Shoemaker [1954- v.
973.92* 54-44837
E835 .S5 MRR Alc.

Sunners, William, American slogans;
New York, Paebar Co., 1949. 345 p.
659.103 49-3280
HF5823 .S9 MRR Alc.

Taylor, Archer, comp. A dictionary
of American proverbs and proverbial
phrases, 1820-1880. Cambridge,
Belknap Press of Harvard University
Press, 1958. xxii, 418 p.   398.903
58-10406
PN6426 .T28 MRR Alc.

Tourtellot, Arthur Bernon. The
Presidents on the Presidency. [1st
ed.] Garden City, N.Y., Doubleday,
1964. xiv, 505 p.   353.032082 64-
11392
JK511 .T6 MRR Ref Desk.

Truman, Harry S., Pres. U.S., The
quotable Harry S. Truman. [1st ed.]
Anderson, S.C., Droke House;
distributed by Grosset & Dunlap
[1967] vii, 190 p.   081 67-13275
E814.A25 S4 MRR Alc.

Washington, George, pres. U.S.,
Maxims of Washington, Mount Vernon,
Va., The Mount Vernon ladies'
association [1942] xxvii, 348 p.
incl. front. (port.) 308.1 42-
12912
E312.79 .W3127 1942 MRR Alc.

Washington, George, Pres. U.S., The
Washington papers; [1st ed.] New
York, Harper [1955] 430 p.   308.1
54-12149
E312.72 1955 MRR Alc.

What they said. 1969- [Beverly
Hills, Calif.] Monitor Book Co.
901.9/4 74-111080
D410 .W46 MRR Ref Desk Full set

Winn, Ralph Bubrich, A concise
Lincoln dictionary: thoughts and
statements. New York, Philosophical
Library [1959] 152 p.   823.173 59-
1859
E457.92 1959a MRR Ref Desk.

Woods, Henry Fitzwilliam, American
sayings; Rev. and enl. ed. New
York, Duell, Sloan and Pearce [1949]
vi, 312 p.   818.082 49-4322
PN6084.A5 W6 1949 MRR Ref Desk.

QUOTATIONS, ANGLO-SAXON.
Bosworth, Joseph, An Anglo-Saxon
dictionary; London, Oxford
University Press, 1972. [2], xiv,
1302 p.   [£11.00] 73-152962
PE279 .B52 1972 MRR Alc.

QUOTATIONS, ARABIC.
Field, Claud Herbert Alwyn, A
dictionary of Oriental quotations
(Arabic and Persian), London, S.
Sonnenschein & co., lim.; New York,
The Macmillan co., 1911. 3 p. l.,
351 p.   a 11-1070
PN6095.O7 F6 MRR Alc.

QUOTATIONS, CANADIAN.
Hamilton, Robert M., comp. Canadian
quotations and phrases, Toronto,
McClelland and Stewart [1965] xi,
272 p. [95c.] 818/.02 67-106497
PN6081 .H24 1965 MRR Alc.

QUOTATIONS, CHINESE.
Lai, T'ien-ch'ang, ed. and tr.
[Ch'eng yü hsüan i (romanized
form)] [Hong Kong] University Book
Store; University of Hongkong, 1960.
191 p.   495.183 c 60-2495
PL1487 .L3 MRR Alc.

Mao, Tse-tung, Quotations from
Chairman Mao Tse-tung. [1st U.S.
ed.] New York, Bantam Books [1967]
vi, 179 p.   951.05/0924 67-3426
DS778.M3 A31353 MRR Alc.

QUOTATIONS, DUTCH.
Spinoza, Benedictus de, Spinoza:
dictionary, New York, Philosophical
Library [1951] xiv, 309 p.   199.492
51-14421
B3951 .S5 MRR Alc.

QUOTATIONS, ENGLISH.
Abbatt, William, comp. The
colloquial who's who; Tarrytown,
N.Y., W. Abbatt, 1924-25. 2 v.   24-
23254
Z1045 .A12 MRR Alc.

Adams, A. K., comp. The home book of
humorous quotations, New York, Dodd,
Mead [1969] xii, 436 p. [10.00]
808.87 78-95912
PN6081 .A14 MRR Ref Desk.

Adams, Franklin Pierce, ed. FPA book
of quotations; New York, Funk &
Wagnalls [1952] xxx, 914 p.   808.88
52-10236
PN6081 .A15 MRR Ref Desk.

Allibone, Samuel Austin, Prose
quotations from Socrates to Macaulay;
Philadelphia, J. B. Lippincott
company, 1903. 2 p. l., ix-xi, 13-
764 p.   03-19988
PN6083 .A25 1903 MRR Alc.

The Barnhart dictionary of new
English since 1963. [1st ed.]
Bronxville, N.Y., Barnhart/Harper &
Row [1973] 512 p.   423 73-712
PE1630 .B3 MRR Ref Desk.

Baughman, Millard Dale, comp.
Educator's handbook of stories,
quotes and humor. Englewood Cliffs,
N.J., Prentice-Hall [c1963] xii, 340
p.   63-17504
LB1785 .B28 MRR Alc.

Bennett, Barbara, comp. Who said
what (and when, and where, and how)
in 1971. [New York] Quadrangle Books
[1972- v. [$12.50] 081 72-
78498
PN6083 .B4 MRR Ref Desk.

Bingham, Colin, comp. The affairs of
women; Sydney, Currawong Publishing
Co. [1969] xi, 400 p. [8.95]
808.88/2 77-453352
PN6084.W6 B5 MRR Alc.

Bingham, Colin, comp. Men and
affairs; Sydney, Currawong Pub. Co.
[1967] xv, 464 p. [$6.95 Aust.]
808.88/2 68-81441
PN6081 .B5 MRR Ref Desk.

Braude, Jacob Morton, comp. Braude's
source book for speakers and writers
Englewood Cliffs, N.J., Prentice-Hall
[1968] ix, 351 p. [$7.95]
808.88/2 68-19973
PN4193.I5 B64 MRR Alc.

Braude, Jacob Morton, ed. The
complete speaker's index to selected
stories for every occasion Englewood
Cliffs, N.J., Prentice-Hall [1967,
c1966] x, 353 p.   808.5/1/0202 66-
18166
PN4193.I5 B66 MRR Alc.

Browning, David Clayton, Everyman's
dictionary of quotations and
proverbs. London, Dent; New York,
Dutton [1951] x, 766 p.   808.8 51-
12780
PN6081 .B75 MRR Alc.

Brussell, Eugene E., comp.
Dictionary of quotable definitions.
Englewood Cliffs, N.J., Prentice-Hall
[1970] xl, 627 p.   808.88/2 76-
106471
PN6081 .B77 MRR Alc.

Churchill, Winston Leonard Spencer,
Sir, A Churchill reader; Boston,
Houghton Mifflin, 1954. 414 p.
923.242 54-11006
DA566.9.C5 A36 MRR Alc.

Churchill, Winston Leonard Spencer,
Sir, The Churchill wit, New York,
Coward-McCann [1965] 85 p.   827.912
65-18290
DA566.9.C5 A363 MRR Alc.

Churchill, Winston Leonard Spencer,
Sir, Irrepressible Churchill: [1st
ed.] Cleveland, World Pub. Co.
[1966] 372 p.   942.0820924 B 66-
18460
DA566.9.C5 A372 MRR Alc.

Churchill, Winston Leonard Spencer,
Sir, The wisdom of Winston
Churchill; London, Allen & Unwin
[1956] 427 p.   923.242 56-59232
DA566.9.C5 A29 MRR Alc.

The Compact edition of the Oxford
English dictionary: complete text
reproduced micrographically. Oxford,
Clarendon Press, 1971. 2 v. (xii,
4116 p.) [£28.00] 423 72-177361
PE1625 .N53 1971 MRR Ref Desk.

QUOTATIONS, ENGLISH. (Cont.)
D. U. W. ... Dictionary of unusual
words. Leigh-on-sea, Essex, The
Thames bank publishing company
limited, 1946-   v.   423 47-8357

PE1628 .D85 MRR Alc.

Dalbiac, Philip Hugh. Dictionary of
quotations (English) London, S.
Sonnenschein & co., lim.; New York,
The Macmillan co., 1899. 2 p. l.,
510 p.   04-178
PN6081 .D2 MRR Alc.

Davidoff, Henry, comp. A world
treasury of proverbs from twenty-five
languages. London, Cassell [1953]
492 p.   398.9   54-24781
PN6405 .D3 1953 MRR Alc.

Day, Edward Parsons, Day's collacon:
an encyclopaedia of prose quotations,
New York, International printing and
publishing office; [etc., etc.] 1884.
xv, [1], 1216 p.   10-4173
PN6083 .D2 1884 MRR Alc.

The Dictionary of best known
quotations & proverbs; New York,
Garden City publishing co., inc.
[c1939] vii, 380, 444 p.   808.8 39-
33412
PN6081 .D5 MRR Alc.

Ely, Virginia, comp. I quote, New
York, G. W. Stewart [c1947] xii, 404
p.   808.8 48-5073
PN6081 .E54 MRR Alc.

Esar, Evan, 20,000 quips and quotes.
[1st ed.] Garden City, N.Y.,
Doubleday, 1968. lxxvi, 908 p.
[7.95]   808.88/2 68-18096
PN6081 .E8 MRR Alc.

Evans, Bergen, Dictionary of
quotations, New York, Delacorte
Press [1968] lxxxix, 2029 p.
808.88/2 68-14825
PN6081 .E9 MRR Ref Desk.

Farmer, John Stephen, Dictionary of
slang & its analogues, past &
present: Rev. ed. New Hyde Park,
N.Y., University Books [1966- v.
427.09 65-24476
PE3721 .F32 MRR Alc.

Farmer, John Stephen, Slang and its
analogues [New York] Arno Press
[1970] 7 v. in 1. [8.95] 427.09
77-109023
PE3721 .F4 1970 MRR Alc.

Forman, Max Leon, comp, The world's
greatest quotations. [1st ed.] New
York, Exposition Press [1970] 720 p.
[12.50]   808.88/2 68-8003
PN6083 .F6 MRR Alc.

Funk & Wagnalls Standard encyclopedic
dictionary. Chicago, J. G. Ferguson
Pub. Co. [1970] xii, 1138 p.   423
72-10720
PE1625 .F8 1970 MRR Ref Desk.

Grizer, Leon, Wit and wisdom in
business; [1st ed.] New York,
Exposition Press [c1972] 509 p.
818/.02 75-146907
HF5391 .G74 MRR Ref Desk.

Hardwick, John Michael Drinkrow, The
Charles Dickens companion London, J.
Murray [1965] xiii, 250 p. 823.8
66-11009
PR4581 .H34 MRR Alc.

Harris, Leon A. The fine art of
political wit; [1st ed.] New York,
Dutton, 1964. 288 p.   827.093 64-
19532
PN6231.P6 H36 MRR Alc.

Hazlitt, William Carew, English
proverbs and proverbial phrases
Detroit, Gale Research Co., 1969.
xxx, 580 p.   398.9/2 73-78169
PN6421 .H3 1969 MRR Alc.

Hoyt, Jehiel Keeler, Hoyt's New
cyclopedia of practical quotations
New York, London, Funk & Wagnalls
company [c1940] xxxi, 1343 p.
808.8 40-13383
PN6081 .H7 1940 MRR Ref Desk.

Hyman, Robin. The quotation
dictionary. [1st American ed.] New
York, Macmillan [1965, c1962] 515 p.
828.02 65-23549
PN6081 .H9 1965 MRR Alc.

Kerber, August, comp. Quotable
quotes on education. Detroit, Wayne
State University Press, 1968. ix,
382 p.   370 67-26384
LB41 .K42 1968 MRR Alc.

Levinson, Leonard Louis, comp.
Bartlett's unfamiliar quotations.
[Chicago] Cowles Book Co. [1971] ix,
341 p. [$10.00] 808.88/2 70-
144314
PN6081 .L4 MRR Ref Desk.

Little, William, The shorter Oxford
English dictionary on historical
principles; 3rd. ed.; Oxford,
Clarendon Press, 1973. xxix, 2672 p.
[£10.00]   423 74-174806
PE1625 .L53 1973 MRR Alc.

Magill, Frank Northen, ed. Magill's
quotations in context, [1st ed.]
New York, Harper & Row [1969] lxvi,
1350 p. [11.95]   808.88/2 71-8539
PN6081 .M282 1969b MRR Ref Desk.

Magill, Frank Northen, ed. Magill's
quotations in context. [1st ed.]
New York, Salem Press [1965] 2 v.
(lxxxvi, 1230, xxvi p.) 828.02 66-
5744
PN6081 .M29 1965a MRR Ref Desk.

Mead, Leon, comp. Manual of forensic
quotations, New York, J. F. Taylor &
company, 1903. xiv, 207 p.   03-
10774
LAW MRR Alc.

Mencken, Henry Louis, ed. A new
dictionary of quotations on
historical principles from ancient
and modern sources, New York, A. A.
Knopf, 1942. xiii, 1347 p., 1 l.
808.8 42-8343
PN6081 .M49 MRR Alc.

Middle English dictionary. Ann
Arbor, University of Michigan Press
[1952- pts.   427.02* 53-62158
PE679 .M54 MRR Alc.

Montapert, Alfred Armand, ed.
Distilled wisdom. Englewood Cliffs,
N.J., Prentice-Hall [1964] ix, 355
p.   808.88 64-8181
BJ1548 .M6 MRR Alc.

The Oxford dictionary of English
proverbs. 3rd ed.; Oxford,
Clarendon P., 1970. xix, 930 p.
[£5/-/-]   398.9/2/03 75-18203
PN6421 .O9 1970 MRR Alc.

The Oxford dictionary of quotations.
2d ed. [rev.] London, New York,
Oxford University Press [1959] xx,
1003 p.   808.88 62-2256
PN6081 .O9 1959 MRR Alc.

The Oxford English dictionary;
Oxford, At the Clarendon press, 1933.
13 v.   423 a 33-3399
PE1625 .N53 1933 MRR Alc.

Perry, Whitall N., comp. A treasury
of traditional wisdom. New York,
Simon and Schuster [c1971] 1144 p.
[$15.00]   200/.8 70-93905
BL25 .P52 1971 MRR Alc.

Prochnow, Herbert Victor, comp. A
treasury of humorous quotations [1st
ed.] New York, Harper & Row [1968,
c1969] viii, 398 p. [6.95]
808.88/2 68-11822
PN6083 .P7 MRR Ref Desk.

Samuel, Herbert Louis Samuel,
viscount, Book of quotations. 2d
ed. London, J. Barrie, 1954. xvi,
284 p.   808.88 55-22316
PN6081 .S3 1954 MRR Alc.

Seldes, George, comp. The great
quotations. New York, L. Stuart
[1960] xi, 893 p.   808.88 58-10231

PN6081 .S4 MRR Ref Desk.

Shakespeare, William, Everyman's
dictionary of Shakespeare quotations,
London, Dent; New York, Dutton
[1953] xii, 560 p.   822.33 54-671

PR2768 .B73 MRR Alc.

Shakespeare, William, The home book
of Shakespeare quotations, New York,
C. Scribner's sons; London, C.
Scribner's sons, ltd. 1937. xl,
2055 p.   822.33 37-32691
PR2892 .S63 MRR Alc.

Simpson, James Beasley, comp.
Contemporary quotations / New York :
Galahad Books [1974] c1964. xi, 500
p. ; [$7.95]   808.88/2 74-77048
PN6083 .S5 1974 MRR Ref Desk.

The Speaker's desk book. New York,
Grosset & Dunlap [1967] 613 p.
808.8 66-20654
PN4193.I5 S6 1967 MRR Alc.

Stockhammer, Morris, ed. Thomas
Aquinas dictionary. New York,
Philosophical Library [1965] xiii,
219 p.   230.203 64-21468
BX1749.T324 S7 MRR Alc.

Stokes' cyclopædia of familiar
quotations, London, W. & R.
Chambers, limited; New York,
Frederick A. Stokes company, 1907.
x, 763, [1] p.   08-8544
PN6081 .S75 1907 MRR Alc.

Taylor, Anna Marjorie, The language
of World War II; Rev. and enl. ed.
New York, H. W. Wilson Co., 1948.
265 p.   940.53014 48-8265
PE3727.S7 T3 1948 MRR Alc.

Tripp, Rhoda Thomas. The
international thesaurus of
quotations, New York, Crowell [1970]
1088 p. [8.95] 808.88/2 73-
106587
PN6081 .T77 MRR Ref Desk.

Van Buren, Maud, Quotations for
special occasions, New York, The H.
W. Wilson company, 1938. 201 p.
808.8 38-27833
PN6084.O3 V3 MRR Alc.

Voss, Carl Hermann, comp. Quotations
of courage and vision; New York,
Association Press [1972] 270 p.
[$9.95]   808.88/2 72-7319
PN6081 .V6 MRR Alc.

Vale, William, ed. What great men
have said about great men; Detroit,
Gale Research Co., 1968. viii, 482
p.   808.88/2 68-17944
PN6084.G7 W2 1968 MRR Alc.

Walsh, William Shepard, comp.
International encyclopedia of prose
and poetical quotations, New York,
Greenwood Press [1968, c1951] xii,
1062 p.   808.88/2 68-14136
PN6081 .W3 1968 MRR Alc.

Webster's new dictionary of synonyms;
Springfield, Mass., Merriam [1973]
31a, 909 p. [$7.95]   423/.1 73-
180866
PE1591 .W4 1973 MRR Ref Desk.

Webster's new international
dictionary of the English language.
2d ed., unabridged ... Springfield,
Mass., G. & C. Merriam Co., 1953.
cxxxii, 3194 p.   423 53-369
PE1625 .W3 1953 MRR Ref Desk.

West, Emerson Roy, comp. Vital
quotations. Salt Lake City,
Bookcraft, 1968. xvii, 446 p.
[4.95]   808.88/2 68-59022
PN6083 .W4 MRR Alc.

What they said. 1969- [Beverly
Hills, Calif.] Monitor Book Co.
901.9/4 74-111080
D410 .W46 MRR Ref Desk Full set

Whiting, Bartlett Jere, Proverbs,
sentences, and proverbial phrases;
Cambridge, Mass., Belknap Press of
Harvard University Press, 1968. li,
733 p. [$25.00]   808.88/2 67-22874

PN6083 .W45 MRR Alc.

Wilstach, Frank Jenners, A
dictionary of similes. New ed. rev.
and enl. Boston, Little, Brown and
company, 1924. liv p., 1 l., 578 p.
[$4.00]   24-28476
PN6084.S5 W5 1924 MRR Alc.

Woods, Ralph Louis, ed. The world
treasury of religious quotations;
[1st ed.] New York, Hawthorn Books
[1966] xiv, 1106 p.   208 66-15355

BL29 .W6 MRR Ref Desk.

QUOTATIONS, FRENCH.
Dubois, Jean, grammarian.
Dictionnaire du français classique,
Paris, Larousse [1971] xxxi, 564 p.
[39.00F]   71-884265
PC2650 .D83 MRR Alc.

Dupré, P. Encyclopédie du bon
français dans l'usage contemporain;
Paris, Editions de Trévise [1972]
3 v. (2716 p.) [140F (v. 3)]   72-
339663
PC2460 .D88 MRR Alc.

Encyclopédie des citations Paris,
Editions de Trévise [1959] xlv,
[2], 701 p.   a   59-7389
PN6086 .E5 MRR Alc.

Godefroy, Frédéric Eugène,
Dictionnaire de l'ancienne langue
française, Paris, F. Vieweg, 1881-
1902. 10 v.   03-21764
PC2889 .G6 MRR Alc.

Grand Larousse de la langue
française en six volumes. Paris,
Larousse [1971- v.   [99.50F per
vol.]   71-854777
PC2625 .G7 MRR Alc.

Guerlac, Othon Goepp, Les citations
françaises; 3. éd. Paris, A.
Colin, 1952 [c1931] 458 p.   848.08
52-43159
PN6086 .G8 1952 MRR Alc.

Guterman, Norbert, comp. A book of
French quotations, [1st ed.] Garden
City, N.Y., Doubleday, 1963. vi, 442
p.   848 63-18210
PN6086 .G85 MRR Ref Desk.

QUOTATIONS, FRENCH. (Cont.)
Huguet, Edmond Eugène August,
Dictionnaire de la langue française
du seizième siècle ... Paris, E.
Champion, 1925-35. 2 v. and 2 pt.
26-5837
    PC2650 .H7 MRR Alc.

Imbs, Paul. Trésor de la langue
française; Paris, Éditions du
Centre national de la recherche
scientifique, 1971- v.   [200F (v.
1)] 72-327996
    PC2625 .I4 MRR Alc.

Nouveau dictionnaire de citations
françaises, Paris] Hachette-Tchou
[1970] 1606 p.   70-548715
    PN6086 .N6 MRR Alc.

Ramage, Craufurd Tait, comp.
Familiar quotations from French and
Italian authors, Detroit, Gale
Research, 1968. 619 p.   808.88/2
68-22042
    PN6080 .R3 1968 MRR Alc.

Robert, Paul, Dictionnaire
alphabétique et analogique de la
langue française; Paris, Société
du Nouveau Littré, 1970. 6 v.   70-
559630
    PC2625 .R552 1970 MRR Alc.

QUOTATIONS, GERMAN.
Büchmann, Georg, comp. Geflügelte
Worte; 32. Aufl., vollständig
neubearb. xvi, 1039 p.   72-337788

    PN6090 .B8 1972 MRR Alc.

Luther, Martin, What Luther says,
Saint Louis, Concordia Pub. House
[c1959] 3 v. (xxvi, 1667 p.)
230.41 57-8854
    BR324 .F6 MRR Alc.

Peltzer, Karl. Das treffende Zitat;
Thun, Ott [1957] 740 p.   58-26032
    PN6092 .P4 MRR Alc.

Ramage, Craufurd Tait, comp.
Beautiful thoughts from German and
Spanish authors, New rev. ed.
London, New York, G. Routledge and
sons, 1884. 3 p. l., [ix]-xvi, 559
p.   15-9871
    PN6080 .R32 1884 MRR Alc.

Remak, Joachim, comp. The Nazi
years; Englewood Cliffs, N.J.,
Prentice-Hall [1969] xi, 178 p.
[4.95] 943.086 69-11359
    DD256.5 .R43 MRR Alc.

QUOTATIONS, GREEK.
Aristoteles. Aristotle dictionary.
New York, Philosophical Library
[1962] 524 p. 185 61-10609
    PA3926.Z8 K53 1962 MRR Alc.

Harbottle, Thomas Benfield, comp.
Dictionary of quotations (classical)
London, S. Sonnenschein & co.,
limited; New York, The Macmillan co.,
limited, 1897. 3 p. l., 648 p.
880.822 04-13800
    PN6080 .H2 1897 MRR Alc.

Ramage, Craufurd Tait, comp.
Familiar quotations from Greek
authors, Detroit, Gale Research Co.,
1968. 588 p.   888/.002 68-22044
    PN6080 .R33 1968 MRR Alc.

Stockhammer, Morris, ed. Plato
dictionary. New York, Philosophical
Library [1963] xv, 287 p.   888 63-
11488
    B351 .S7 MRR Alc.

QUOTATIONS, ITALIAN.
Battaglia, Salvatore. Grande
dizionario della lingua italiana.
Torino] Unione tipografico-editrice
torinese [1861- v.   61-35046
    PC1625 .B3 MRR Alc.

Fumagalli, Giuseppe, ed. Chi l'ha
detto? 9. ed. Milano, U. Hoepli,
1946. xxvi, 841 p.   808.8 48-17531

    PN6080 .F8 1946 MRR Alc.

Ramage, Craufurd Tait, comp.
Familiar quotations from French and
Italian authors, Detroit, Gale
Research, 1968. 619 p.   808.88/2
68-22042
    PN6080 .R3 1968 MRR Alc.

Tommaseo, Niccolò, Dizionario della
lingua italiana, Torino [etc.]
Unione tipografico-editrice [1861-79]
4 v. in 8.   01-19877
    PC1625 .T6 1861 MRR Alc.

QUOTATIONS, JEWISH.
Baron, Joseph Louis, ed. A treasury
of Jewish quotations. New York,
Crown Publishers [1956] 623 p.
808.8 56-7194
    PN6095.J4 B3 MRR Alc.

Rosten, Leo Calvin, Leo Rosten's
treasury of Jewish quotations. New
York, McGraw-Hill [1972] xi, 716 p.
[$10.95] 808.88/2 72-298
    PN6095.J4 R6 MRR Ref Desk.

QUOTATIONS, LATIN.
Harbottle, Thomas Benfield, comp.
Dictionary of quotations (classical)
London, S. Sonnenschein & co.
limited; New York, The Macmillan co.,
limited, 1897. 3 p. l., [48 p.
880.822 04-13800
    PN6080 .H2 1897 MRR Alc.

Oxford Latin dictionary. Oxford,
London, Clarendon P., 1968- v.
[75/- fasc. 1]   473.2 68-31959
    PA2365.E5 O9 MRR Alc.

Thesaurus linguae Latinae. Lipsiae,
In aedibus B. G. Teubneri, 1900- v.
in   77-11275
    PA2361 .T4 MRR Alc.

QUOTATIONS, PERSIAN.
Field, Claud Herbert Alwyn, A
dictionary of Oriental quotations
(Arabic and Persian), London, S.
Sonnenschein & co., lim.; New York,
The Macmillan co., 1911. 3 p. l.,
351 p. a 11-1070
    PN6095.O7 F6 MRR Alc.

QUOTATIONS, PROVENÇAL.
Mistral, Frédéric. Lou tresor dóu
Felibrige Reimpression de
l'edition 1879-1886. Osnabrück,
Biblio-Verlag, 1966. 2 v. [DM
360.00] 67-84128
    PC3376 .M72 MRR Alc.

QUOTATIONS, SCOTTISH.
The Scottish national dictionary,
Edinburgh, The Scottish national
dictionary association limited [1931-
v.   427.9 36-20042
    PE2106 .S4 MRR Alc.

QUOTATIONS, SPANISH.
Goicoechea Romano, Cesáreo.
Diccionario de citas; Barcelona,
Editorial Labor, 1952. xvi, 716 p.
a 52-7471
    PN6095.S5 G6 MRR Alc.

Ramage, Craufurd Tait, comp.
Beautiful thoughts from German and
Spanish authors, New rev. ed.
London, New York, G. Routledge and
sons, 1884. 3 p. l., [ix]-xvi, 559
p.   15-9871
    PN6080 .R32 1884 MRR Alc.

RACE.
Garn, Stanley M. Human races, 2d
ed. Springfield, Ill., Thomas [1965]
xiv, 155 p.   573 65-18056
    GN315 .G3 1965 MRR Alc.

Gossett, Thomas F. Race; the history
of an idea in America. Dallas,
Southern Methodist University Press,
1963. ix, 512 p.   63-21187
    E184.A1 G6 MRR Alc.

Montagu, Ashley, Man's most
dangerous myth: 5th ed., rev. and
enl. New York, Oxford University
Press, 1974. xvi, 542 p. [$15.00]
572 73-92869
    GN280 .M59 1974 MRR Alc.

Montagu, Ashley, Man's most
dangerous myth: the fallacy of race.
4th ed., rev. and enl. Cleveland,
World Pub. Co. [1964] 499 p.   572
64-12067
    GN315 .M55 1964 MRR Alc.

RACE--BIBLIOGRAPHY.
Montagu, Ashley, Man's most
dangerous myth: 5th ed., rev. and
enl. New York, Oxford University
Press, 1974. xvi, 542 p. [$15.00]
572 73-92869
    GN280 .M59 1974 MRR Alc.

RACE--DICTIONARIES.
United States. Immigration
Commission, 1907-1910. Dictionary of
races or peoples. Detroit, Gale
Research Co., 1969. vii, 150 p.
572/.03 68-30665
    GN11 .U6 1969 MRR Alc.

RACE AWARENESS.
see also Negroes--Race identity

RACE HORSES.
see also Thoroughbred horse

The American racing annual. 1906-
Chicago, Daily Racing Form. 06-3772

    SF325 .A5 Sci RR Latest edition /
    MRR Alc Latest edition

Stoneridge, M. A. Great horses of
our time [1st ed.] Garden City,
N.Y., Doubleday, 1972. xiv, 543 p.
[$14.95] 798.4 73-175400
    SF338 .S76 MRR Alc.

RACE HORSES--DICTIONARIES.
Mortimer, Roger, comp. The
encyclopaedia of flat racing.
London, Hale, 1971. [8], 444 p., 16
plates. [£3.50]   798/.43/03 71-
568712
    SF321.5 .M67 1971 MRR Alc.

RACE PROBLEMS.
see also Emigration and immigration

see also Minorities

Montagu, Ashley, Man's most
dangerous myth: 5th ed., rev. and
enl. New York, Oxford University
Press, 1974. xvi, 542 p. [$15.00]
572 73-92869
    GN280 .M59 1974 MRR Alc.

Montagu, Ashley, Man's most
dangerous myth: the fallacy of race.
4th ed., rev. and enl. Cleveland,
World Pub. Co. [1964] 499 p.   572
64-12067
    GN315 .M55 1964 MRR Alc.

Roback, Abraham Aaron, A dictionary
of international slurs
(ethnophaulisms Cambridge, Mass.,
Sci-art publishers [1944] 394 p.
323.1 44-8328
    HT1523 .R6 MRR Alc.

Simpson, George Eaton, Racial and
cultural minorities: 4th ed. New
York, Harper & Row [1972] viii, 775
p.   301.45/1/042 72-76373
    HT1521 .S53 1972 MRR Alc.

RACE PROBLEMS--BIBLIOGRAPHY.
Thompson, Edgar Tristram, Race and
region, Chapel Hill, Univ. of North
Carolina Press, 1949. xii, 194 p.
016.325260973 49-1367
    Z1361.N39 T5 MRR Alc.

RACE PROBLEMS IN SCHOOL MANAGEMENT.
see also Segregation in education

RACES OF MAN
see Ethnology

RACIAL IDENTITY OF NEGROES
see Negroes--Race identity

RACING.
see also Automobile racing

RADAR--DICTIONARIES--POLYGLOT.
Elsevier's dictionary of television,
radar, and antennas, in six
languages: Amsterdam, New York,
Elsevier Pub. Co., 1955. 760 p.
621.38803 55-6216
    TK6634 .E4 MRR Alc.

RADAR--YEARBOOKS.
Jane's weapon systems. 1st- ed.;
1969/70- New York, McGraw-Hill.
623.4/405 78-12809
    U104 .J35 Sci RR Latest edition /
    MRR Alc Latest edition

RADICALISM--PERIODICALS--HISTORY.
The American radical press, 1880-
1960. Westport, Conn., Greenwood
Press [1974] 2 v. (xiv, 720 p.)
335/.00973 72-9825
    HX1 .A49 MRR Alc.

RADICALISM--UNITED STATES.
Jacobs, Paul. The new radicals; New
York, Random House [1966] 333 p.
320.973 66-18328
    E839.5 .J3 MRR Alc.

RADICALISM--UNITED STATES--ADDRESSES,
ESSAYS, LECTURES.
Teodori, Massimo, comp. The new
left: Indianapolis, Bobbs-Merrill
[1969] xiv, 501 p. [9.95]
301.15/3/0973 70-81291
    HN59 .T46 MRR Alc.

RADICALISM--UNITED STATES--PERIODICALS--
BIBLIOGRAPHY.
Muller, Robert H. From radical left
to extreme right; 2d ed. rev. and
enl. Ann Arbor, Campus Publishers
[c1970- v.   79-126558
    Z7165.U5 M82 MRR Ref Desk.

RADIO.
Anderson, Edwin P., Radiomans guide,
[3d ed.] Indianapolis, T. Audel
[1969] 502 p. [5.95] 621.384 72-
77587
    TK6550 .A65 1969 MRR Alc.

RADIO--AMATEURS' MANUALS.
American Radio Relay League. How to
become a radio amateur. 1st- 1930-
Newington, Conn. [etc.] 621.3841662
621.3845* 56-4149
    TK9956 .A6 MRR Alc Latest edition

RADIO--APPARATUS AND SUPPLIES--CATALOGS.
The Radio-electronic master. New
York, United Technical Publications
[etc.] 621.384085 39-15586
    TK6560.Z5 R35 Sci RR Latest
    edition / MRR Alc Latest edition

RADIO--BIBLIOGRAPHY.
United States. Library of Congress.
Division of bibliography. ... Radio
and radio broadcasting: a selected
list of references. [Washington]
1941. 1 p. l., 109 p.   016.621384
41-51408
Z663.28 .R2 1941 MRR Alc.

RADIO--DIAGRAMS.
Most-often-needed radio diagrams and
servicing information. v. [1]-
1926/38 [Highland Park, Ill., etc.]
Supreme Publications.   41-18326
TK6553.A1 B4 MRR Alc Latest
edition

RADIO--DIAGRAMS--PERIODICALS.
Most-often-needed radio diagrams and
servicing information. v. [1]-
1926/38 [Highland Park, Ill., etc.]
Supreme Publications.   41-18326
TK6553.A1 B4 MRR Alc Latest
edition

RADIO--DICTIONARIES.
Curtis, Ron. Media dictionary: Red
Oak, Southwest Iowa Learning
Resources Center [1973] 290 p.
301.16/1/03 73-158317
P87.5 .C8 MRR Alc.

Manly, Harold Phillips, Drake's
radio-television electronic
dictionary. Chicago, F. J. Drake Co.
[1960] 1 v. (unpaged) 621.3803 60-
4753
TK6544 .M33 1960 MRR Alc.

National Radio Institute, Washington,
D.C. Radio-television-electronics
dictionary. New York, J. F. Rider
[1962] 180 p. 621.38403 62-21929

TK6544 .N3 1962 MRR Alc.

Pannett, W. E. Dictionary of radio
and television, Amsterdam, Elsevier
Publishing Cy. [1967] 380 p.
[fl27.50] 621.38/03 67-95326
TK6544 .P28 1967b MRR Alc.

RADIO--DIRECTORIES.
The Working press of the nation.
[1945]- Burlington, Iowa [etc.]
National Research Bureau [etc.]
071.47 46-7041
Z6951 .W6 MRR Alc Latest edition

RADIO--EXAMINATIONS, QUESTIONS, ETC.
Swearer, Harvey F. Commercial FCC
license handbook, [2d ed.] Blue
Ridge Summit, Pa., G/L Tab Books
[1974] 444 p. 621.3845/076 73-
93692
TK6554.5 .S9 1974 MRR Alc.

RADIO--HANDBOOKS, MANUALS, ETC.
The Radio handbook. [1st]- ed.;
1935- New Augusta, Ind. [etc.]
Editors and Engineers, Ltd. [etc.]
621.38402 40-33904
TK6550 .R14 Sci RR Latest edition
/ MRR Alc Latest edition

Reference data for radio engineers.
1st- ed.; 1943- Indianapolis
[etc.] H. W. Sams. 621.384083 43-
14665
TK6552 .F4 Sci RR Latest edition /
MRR Alc Latest edition

RADIO--PERIODICALS.
British Broadcasting Corporation. B
B C handbook. 1955- [London]
384.54/0942 72-624368
TK6540 .B82 MRR Alc Latest edition

RADIO--REPAIRING--PERIODICALS.
Most-often-needed radio diagrams and
servicing information. v. [1]-
1926/38 [Highland Park, Ill., etc.]
Supreme Publications.   41-18326
TK6553.A1 B4 MRR Alc Latest
edition

RADIO--TABLES, CALCULATIONS, ETC.
Reference data for radio engineers.
1st- ed.; 1943- Indianapolis
[etc.] H. W. Sams. 621.384083 43-
14665
TK6552 .F4 Sci RR Latest edition /
MRR Alc Latest edition

RADIO--UNITED STATES--LAWS AND
REGULATIONS.
Kahn, Frank J., comp. Documents of
American broadcasting. 2d ed. New
York, Appleton-Century-Crofts [1973]
xv, 684 p.   343/.73/0994 72-12050
KF2804 .K3 1973 MRR Alc.

RADIO, SHORT WAVE--AMATEURS' MANUALS.
Bennett, Hank. The complete short
wave listener's handbook. [1st ed.]
Blue Ridge Summit, Pa., G/L Tab Books
[1974] 288 p. [$9.95] 384.5 74-
77023
TK9956 .B428 MRR Alc.

RADIO, SHORT WAVE--HANDBOOKS, MANUALS,
ETC.
The Radio amateur's handbook. 1st-
ed.; 1926- Newington, Conn. [etc.]
American Radio Relay League.
621.3841 41-3345
TK6550 .R18 Sci RR Latest edition
/ MRR Alc Latest edition

RADIO ADVERTISING--UNITED STATES--
DIRECTORIES.
National radio publicity directory.
1972- [New York?, Peter Glenn
Publications] 659.14/2/02573 72-
622772
HF6146.R3 N347 MRR Alc Latest
edition

RADIO ADVERTISING--UNITED STATES--
YEARBOOKS.
Broadcasting yearbook. [Washington,
Broadcasting Publications]
384.54/0973 71-649524
HF6146.R3 B73 MRR Ref Desk Latest
edition

RADIO AS A PROFESSION.
Lawton, Sherman Paxton. The modern
broadcaster: New York, Harper [1961]
351 p.   384.54 61-5463
PN1991.5 .L35 MRR Alc.

RADIO BROADCASTING.
see also Television broadcasting

Lawton, Sherman Paxton. The modern
broadcaster: New York, Harper [1961]
351 p.   384.54 61-5463
PN1991.5 .L35 MRR Alc.

Merrill, John Calhoun, The foreign
press; Baton Rouge, Louisiana State
University Press [1970] 365 p.
070.9 76-96259
PN4736 .M39 1970 MRR Alc.

World radio-television handbook, 1st-
ed.; winter 1947- Hellerup,
Denmark [etc.] World Radio-Television
Handbook Co., ltd. [etc.] 384.5 48-
20385
TK6540 .W67 Sci RR Latest edition*
/ MRR Alc Latest edition

RADIO BROADCASTING--BIBLIOGRAPHY.
United States. Library of Congress.
Division of bibliography. ... Radio
and radio broadcasting: a selected
list of references. [Washington]
1941. 1 p. l., 109 p.   016.621384
41-51408
Z663.28 .R2 1941 MRR Alc.

RADIO BROADCASTING--DIRECTORIES.
Internationales Handbuch für
Rundfunk und Fernsehen. 1957-
Hamburg, Hans Bredow-Institut. 60-
25306
HE8690 .I57 MRR Alc Latest edition

RADIO BROADCASTING--YEARBOOKS.
Fame; New York, Quigley Pub. Co. 53-
31048
Began publication in 1933?
PN1993.3 .B6 MRR Alc Latest
edition

Internationales Handbuch für
Rundfunk und Fernsehen. 1957-
Hamburg, Hans Bredow-Institut. 60-
25306
HE8690 .I57 MRR Alc Latest edition

RADIO BROADCASTING--FRANCE.
Annuaire du spectacle; [1]-
année; 1942/43- Paris, Éditions
Raoult [etc.]   45-27035
PN2620 .A67 MRR Alc Latest edition

RADIO BROADCASTING--UNITED STATES.
Kahn, Frank J., comp. Documents of
American broadcasting. 2d ed. New
York, Appleton-Century-Crofts [1973]
xv, 684 p.   343/.73/0994 72-12050
KF2804 .K3 1973 MRR Alc.

Standard Rate and Data Service, inc.
Network rates and data. v. 1- Feb.
1951- Skokie, Ill. [etc.] 54-32319

HE8698 .S75 MRR Ref Desk Latest
edition

RADIO BROADCASTING--UNITED STATES.--
DIRECTORIES.
The Working press of the nation.
[1945]- Burlington, Iowa [etc.]
National Research Bureau [etc.]
071.47 46-7041
Z6951 .W6 MRR Alc Latest edition

RADIO BROADCASTING--UNITED STATES--
HISTORY.
Settel, Irving. A pictorial history
of radio. New York, Grosset & Dunlap
[1967] 192 p.   791.44/0973 67-
23789
PN1991.3.U6 S4 1967 MRR Alc.

RADIO BROADCASTING--UNITED STATES--
YEARBOOKS.
Broadcasting yearbook. [Washington,
Broadcasting Publications]
384.54/0973 71-649524
HF6146.R3 B73 MRR Ref Desk Latest
edition

RADIO IN EDUCATION--UNITED STATES--
DIRECTORIES.
National Association of Educational
Broadcasters. N A E B directory of
members. Urbana, Ill. 61-22844
LB1044.5.A1 N316 MRR Alc Latest
edition

RADIO IN RELIGION--DIRECTORIES.
International Christian Broadcasters.
World directory of religious radio
and television broadcasting. South
Pasadena, Calif., William Carey
Library [1973] 808 p.   791.45/5 73-
8853
BV656 .I53 MRR Alc.

RADIO JOURNALISM--SOCIETIES, ETC.
Association of Radio News Analysts.
History, constitution, and
membership, 1942-1954. New York
[1954] 73 p.   070.46 070.41* 55-
27032
PN4841 .A89 MRR Biog.

RADIO METEOROLOGY--BIBLIOGRAPHY.
United States. Library of Congress.
Science and Technology Division.
Selected foreign references on
scatter propagation of ultrashort
waves, 1956-1960. Washington, 1961.
87 p.   016.62138411 61-60058
Z663.41 .S4 MRR Alc.

RADIO OPERATORS--UNITED STATES.
Swearer, Harvey F. Commercial FCC
license handbook, [2d ed.] Blue
Ridge Summit, Pa., G/L Tab Books
[1974] 444 p. 621.3845/076 73-
93692
TK6554.5 .S9 1974 MRR Alc.

RADIO PROGRAMS--DICTIONARIES.
Sharp, Harold S., comp. Index to
characters in the performing arts,
New York, Scarecrow Press, 1966-73.
4 v. in 6.   808.8292703 66-13744
PN1579 .S45 MRR Alc.

RADIO PROGRAMS--UNITED STATES.
Buxton, Frank. The big broadcast,
1920-1950. A new, rev., and greatly
expanded ed. of Radio's golden age,
the complete reference work. New
York, Viking Press [1972] xv, 301 p.
[$12.95] 791.44/0973 73-148272
PN1991.3.U6 B78 MRR Alc.

RADIO PROGRAMS--UNITED STATES--
DIRECTORIES.
National radio publicity directory.
1972- [New York?, Peter Glenn
Publications] 659.14/2/02573 72-
622772
HF6146.R3 N347 MRR Alc Latest
edition

RADIO SCRIPTS--BIBLIOGRAPHY.
Samples, Gordon. The drama scholars'
index to plays and filmscripts:
Metuchen, N.J., Scarecrow Press
[1974] xii, 448 p.   016.80882 73-
22165
Z5781 .S17 MRR Alc.

RADIO STATIONS--DIRECTORIES.
International Christian Broadcasters.
World directory of religious radio
and television broadcasting. South
Pasadena, Calif., William Carey
Library [1973] 808 p.   791.45/5 73-
8853
BV656 .I53 MRR Alc.

Wireless world. Guide to
broadcasting stations. London,
Iliffe. 384.5 54-19451
TK6555 .W67 MRR Alc Latest edition

World radio-television handbook, 1st-
ed.; winter 1947- Hellerup,
Denmark [etc.] World Radio-Television
Handbook Co., ltd. [etc.] 384.5 48-
20385
TK6540 .W67 Sci RR Latest edition*
/ MRR Alc Latest edition

RADIO STATIONS--CALIFORNIA--DIRECTORIES.
California publicity outlets. 1972-
Los Angeles, Unicorn Systems Co.,
Information Services Division.
659.2/025/794 76-186163
HM263 .C2 MRR Alc Latest edition

RADIO STATIONS--NORTH AMERICA--
DIRECTORIES.
A M - F M radio station directory.
Radnor, Pa. [etc.] Television digest.
621.38416 59-716
TK6555 .A22 MRR Alc Latest edition

Jones, Vane A. North American radio-
TV station guide. 1st- ed.; 1963-
Indianapolis, H. W. Sams. 621.38416
63-23371
TK6555 .J6 MRR Alc Latest edition

RADIO STATIONS--UNITED STATES--
DIRECTORIES.
A M - F M radio station directory.
Radnor, Pa. [etc.] Television digest.
621.38416 59-716
TK6555 .A22 MRR Alc Latest edition

RADIO STATIONS--UNITED STATES-- (Cont.)
Broadcasting yearbook. [Washington,
Broadcasting Publications]
384.54/0973 71-648524
HF6146.R3 B73 MRR Ref Desk Latest
edition

Jones, Vane A. North American radio-
TV station guide. 1st- ed.; 1963-
Indianapolis, H. W. Sams. 621.38416
63-23371
TK6555 .J6 MRR Alc Latest edition

National radio publicity directory.
1972- [New York?, Peter Glenn
Publications] 658.14/2/02573 72-
622772
HF6146.R3 N347 MRR Alc Latest
edition

United States. Office of Minority
Business Enterprise. Directory of
minority media. [Washington]; for
sale by the Supt. of Docs., U.S.
Govt. Print. Off., 1973. ix, 89 p.
[$1.25] 301.16/1/02573 73-602686
P88.8 .U55 MRR Alc.

RADIO STATIONS, SHORT WAVE--DIRECTORIES.
Woodruff, H. Charles. Shortwave
listener's guide, [5th ed.]
Indianapolis, H. W. Sams [1973] 128
p. [$2.85 ($3.75 Can)] 621.3841/8
72-88695
TK6555 .W68 1973 MRR Alc.

RADIO WAVES--SCATTERING--BIBLIOGRAPHY.
United States. Library of Congress.
Science and Technology Division.
Selected foreign references on
scatter propagation of ultrashort
waves, 1956-1960. Washington, 1961.
87 p. 016.62138411 61-60058
Z663.41 .S4 MRR Alc.

RADIOACTIVITY.
see also Nuclear physics.

RAGTIME MUSIC
see Jazz music

RAILROAD COMPANIES--UNITED STATES--
DIRECTORIES.
The Pocket list of railroad
officials. no. 1- 1885- New York,
The Railway Equipment and Publication
Co. 07-41367
HE2723 .P7 MRR Alc Latest edition

RAILROAD COMPANIES--UNITED STATES--
YEARBOOKS.
Moody's transportation manual:
American and foreign. 1954- New
York, Moody's Investors Service. 57-
15176
HG4871 .M74 MRR Alc Latest edition

RAILROADS--CARS.
Lucas, Walter Arndt, ed. 100 years
of railroad cars. New York, Simmons-
Boardman Pub. Corp. [1958] 196 p.
625.2209 58-14002
TF375 .L8 MRR Alc.

The Official railway equipment
register. New York, The Railway
Equipment and Publication Co. a 19-
162
TF340 .O5 MRR Alc Latest edition

RAILROADS--DICTIONARIES--POLYGLOT.
International Railway Documentation
Bureau. Lexique general des termes
ferroviaires, [2. ed. entierement
refondue et augm.] Amsterdam, J. H.
De Bussy, 1965. 1357 p. 625.1003
66-87434
TF9 .I46 1965 MRR Alc.

RAILROADS--DIRECTORIES.
Jane's world railways. 1st- ed.;
1950/51- London, B. P. C. Publishing
Ltd. [etc.] 385.05 51-29160
TF1 .J3 Sci RR Latest edition /
MRR Alc Latest edition

The Pocket list of railroad
officials. no. 1- 1885- New York,
The Railway Equipment and Publication
Co. 07-41367
HE2723 .P7 MRR Alc Latest edition

Railway directory & year book.
London, IPC Transport Press Ltd.
[etc.] 385/.025 72-622709
HE1009 .U6 MRR Alc Latest edition

RAILROADS--EQUIPMENT AND SUPPLIES.
The Official railway equipment
register. New York, The Railway
Equipment and Publication Co. a 19-
162
TF340 .O5 MRR Alc Latest edition

RAILROADS--FREIGHT.
see also Freight and freightage

RAILROADS--PERIODICALS.
The Official railway equipment
register. New York, The Railway
Equipment and Publication Co. a 19-
162
TF340 .O5 MRR Alc Latest edition

RAILROADS--PICTORIAL WORKS.
Ellis, Cuthbert Hamilton, The
pictorial encyclopedia of railways.
London, Hamlyn, 1968. 591 p.
(chiefly illus. (some col.)) [30/-]
625.1/022/2 68-101998
TF149 .E39 1968b MRR Alc.

Lucas, Walter Arndt, ed. Locomotives
and cars since 1900. New York,
Simmons-Boardman Pub. Corp. [1959]
[8], 119 p. (chiefly illus., diagrs.)
625.2084 59-9485
TF149 .L87 MRR Alc.

RAILROADS--RATES--BIBLIOGRAPHY.
United States. Library of Congress.
Division of Bibliography. Select
list of books on railroads in foreign
countries. Washington, Govt. Print.
Off., 1905. 72 p. 05-20008
Z663.28 .S33 MRR Alc.

RAILROADS--ROLLING-STOCK.
Lucas, Walter Arndt, ed. Locomotives
and cars since 1900. New York,
Simmons-Boardman Pub. Corp. [1959]
[8], 119 p. (chiefly illus., diagrs.)
625.2084 59-9485
TF149 .L87 MRR Alc.

RAILROADS--ROLLING-STOCK--DIRECTORIES.
Arnold, Ian. Locomotive, trolley,
and rail car builders, [Los Angeles,
Trans-Anglo Books, 1965] 64 p.
625.202573 65-17586
TF355 .A7 MRR Alc.

RAILROADS--STATISTICS.
Jane's world railways. 1st- ed.;
1950/51- London, B. P. C. Publishing
Ltd. [etc.] 385.05 51-29160
TF1 .J3 Sci RR Latest edition /
MRR Alc Latest edition

RAILROADS--TIME-TABLES.
Compagnie internationale des wagons-
lits et du tourisme. Guide. [Paris]
72-627197
HD9712.B34 C6 MRR Ref Desk Latest
edition

Cooks continental timetable. London,
Thos. Cook & Son. [$36.00]
385/.2042 73-645991
Began with Mar. 1873 issue.
HE3004 .C66 MRR Ref Desk Latest
edition

RAILROADS--YEARBOOKS.
Jane's world railways. 1st- ed.;
1950/51- London, B. P. C. Publishing
Ltd. [etc.] 385.05 51-29160
TF1 .J3 Sci RR Latest edition /
MRR Alc Latest edition

Yearbook of railroad facts. 1965-
Washington. a 66-7305
HE2713 .Y4 MRR Alc Latest edition

RAILROADS--AUSTRIA--DIRECTORIES.
GOF-Verlag, Vienna. GOF-
Ortsverzeichnis von Österreich für
wirtschaft und Verkehr. 5.,
neubearb. erweiterte und verb. Aufl.
Wien, GOF-Verlag (1966) 296 p. [S
175.00 DM 28.50] 914.36/003 67-
82158
DB14 .G2 1966 MRR Alc.

RAILROADS--CANADA--PASSENGER-CARS--
REGISTERS--PERIODICALS.
Railway passenger car annual. v. 1-
1973/74- Park Forest, Ill.
385/.33/0973 74-644911
TF455 .R3 MRR Alc Latest edition

RAILROADS--CANADA--TIME-TABLES.
The Official railway guide. North
American passenger travel edition.
v. 1- July/Aug. 1974- New York,
National Railway Publication Co.
[$28.00] 385/.2/042 74-645758
HE2727 .O32 MRR Ref Desk Latest
edition

RAILROADS--CONFEDERATE STATES OF
AMERICA.
Black, Robert C., The railroads of
the Confederacy. Chapel Hill,
University of North Carolina Press
[1952] xiv, 360 p. 973.7 52-3559
E545 .B55 MRR Alc.

RAILROADS--EUROPE.
Dunn, William J. Enjoy Europe by
train New York, Scribner [1974]
viii, 255 p. 914/.04/55 73-19289
TF55 .D8 1974 MRR Alc.

Farquhar, William Gordon. Enjoy
Europe by rail; London, I. Allan
[1965] 222 p. 914.04 66-7033
TF55 .F3 MRR Alc.

RAILROADS--EUROPE--TIME-TABLES.
Compagnie internationale des wagons-
lits et du tourisme. Guide. [Paris]
72-627197
HD9712.B34 C6 MRR Ref Desk Latest
edition

Cooks continental timetable. London,
Thos. Cook & Son. [$36.00]
385/.2042 73-645991
Began with Mar. 1873 issue.
HE3004 .C66 MRR Ref Desk Latest
edition

RAILROADS--GREAT BRITAIN--PASSENGER
TRAFFIC--HANDBOOKS, MANUALS, ETC.
Baxter, Robert G. Baxter's Britrail
pass travel guide, [1972-73 ed.]
Alexandria, Va., Rail-Europe, 1972]
162 p. [$2.95] 914.2/04/4 72-
83184
HE3014 .B38 1972 MRR Alc.

RAILROADS--GREAT BRITAIN--STATIONS--
DIRECTORIES.
The Railway & commercial gazetteer of
England, Scotland & Wales. 21st ed.
London, McCorquodale [1965] vi, 716
p. 385/.31 70-219483
HE3014 .R14 1965 MRR Alc.

RAILROADS--GREAT BRITAIN--YEARBOOKS.
Great Britain. British Railways
Board. Facts and figures about
British rail. [London] 57-43600
HE3011.A32 MRR Alc Latest edition

RAILROADS--MEXICO--TIME-TABLES.
The Official railway guide. North
American passenger travel edition.
v. 1- July/Aug. 1974- New York,
National Railway Publication Co.
[$28.00] 385/.2/042 74-645758
HE2727 .O32 MRR Ref Desk Latest
edition

RAILROADS--NORTH AMERICA--MAPS.
Leahy's hotel-motel guide & travel
atlas of the United States, Canada
and Mexico. Chicago, American Hotel
Register Co. 647.94 09-20538
TX907 .L5 MRR Alc Latest edition

RAILROADS--NORTH AMERICA--PASSENGER
TRAFFIC.
The Official railway guide. North
American passenger travel edition.
v. 1- July/Aug. 1974- New York,
National Railway Publication Co
[$28.00] 385/.2/042 74-645758
HE2727 .O32 MRR Ref Desk Latest
edition

RAILROADS--UNITED STATES.
Lewis, Robert Grier, The handbook of
American railroads. [2d. ed.] New
York, Simmons-Boardman Pub. Corp.
[1956] xii, 251 p. 385.1* 56-
12658
HE2751 .L45 1956 MRR Alc.

Lucas, Walter Arndt, ed. 100 years
of steam locomotives. New York,
Simmons-Boardman Pub. Corp. [1957]
278 p. 621.132973 625.26* 57-12355
TJ603 .L77 MRR Alc.

RAILROADS--UNITED STATES--BIOGRAPHY.
Who's who in railroading in North
America. [1st]- ed.; 1885- New
York [etc.] Simmons-Boardman Pub.
Corp. [etc.] 03-28609
HE2723 .W5 MRR Biog Latest edition

RAILROADS--UNITED STATES--EQUIPMENT AND
SUPPLIES.
The Pocket list of railroad
officials. no. 1- 1895- New York,
The Railway Equipment and Publication
Co. 07-41367
HE2723 .P7 MRR Alc Latest edition

RAILROADS--UNITED STATES--HANDBOOKS,
MANUALS, ETC.
Baxter, Robert G. Baxter's USA train
travel guide, [Alexandria, Va., Rail-
Europe, 1973] 255 p. [$3.95]
917.3/04/924 73-84776
HE2725 .B35 MRR alc.

RAILROADS--UNITED STATES--HISTORY.
Beebe, Lucius Morris, Hear the train
blow; New York, Grossett & Dunlap
[1958, c1952] 407 p. 385.1* 58-
4335
HE2751 .B4 1958 MRR Alc.

Stover, John F. American railroads.
[Chicago] University of Chicago Press
[1961] 302 p. 385.0973 61-8081
HE2751 .S7 MRR Alc.

RAILROADS--UNITED STATES--PASSENGER-
CARS.
Official register of passenger train
equipment. no. 1- Mar. 1943- New
York, Railway Equipment and
Publication Co. 385.22 54-26511
HE2583 .O33 MRR Alc Latest edition

RAILROADS--UNITED STATES--PASSENGER-
CARS--REGISTERS--PERIODICALS.
Railway passenger car annual. v. 1-
1973/74- Park Forest, Ill.
385/.33/0873 74-644911
TF455 .R3 MRR Alc Latest edition

RAILROADS--UNITED STATES--RATES.
Directory of class rail freight rates
by the publisher of Leonard's guide.
Chicago [etc.] G. R. Leonard.
385.1324 52-64052
TF664 .D5 MRR Alc Latest edition

RAILROADS--UNITED STATES--STATIONS.
Bullinger's postal and shippers guide
for the United States and Canada and
Newfoundland. Westwood, N.J. [etc.]
Bullinger's Guides, inc. [etc.] 02-
3726
HE9.U5 B83 MRR Alc Latest edition

RAILROADS--UNITED STATES--STATISTICS.
United States. Interstate Commerce
Commission. Bureau of Accounts.
Transport statistics in the United
States. Washington. 380.5/0973 72-
627360
HE2708 .I73 MRR Alc Latest edition

Yearbook of railroad facts. 1965-
Washington. a 66-7305
HE2713 .Y4 MRR Alc Latest edition

RAILROADS--UNITED STATES--TIME-TABLES.
The Official railway guide. North
American passenger travel edition.
1- July/Aug. 1974- New York,
National Railway Publication Co.
[$28.00] 385/.2/042 74-645758
HE2727 .O32 MRR Ref Desk Latest
edition

RAILROADS--UNITED STATES--VALUATION--
BIBLIOGRAPHY.
United States. Library of Congress.
Division of bibliography. ... Select
list of references on the valuation
and capitalization of railroads;
Washington. Govt. print. off., 1909.
28 p. 09-35001
Z663.28 .S446 MRR Alc.

RAILROADS, STREET
see Street-railroads

RAILROADS AND STATE--BIBLIOGRAPHY.
United States. Library of Congress.
Division of Bibliography. Select
list of books on railroads in foreign
countries. Washington, Govt. Print.
Off., 1905. 72 p. 05-20008
Z663.28 .S33 MRR Alc.

RAND CORPORATION--BIBLIOGRAPHY.
Rand Corporation. Index of selected
publications. v. 1, 1946/62. [Santa
Monica, Calif.?] 015.79493 63-1486

AS36 .R332 MRR Alc Full set

Rand Corporation. Selected Rand
abstracts. v. 1- 1963- Santa
Monica, Calif. 65-2088
AS36 .R284 MRR Alc Full set

RARE ANIMALS.
Nobile, Philip, comp. The complete
ecology fact book. [1st ed.] Garden
City, N.Y., Doubleday, 1972. xx, 472
p. [$10.00] 301.31 73-175364
TD174 .N6 MRR Alc.

RATIO ANALYSIS.
Troy, Leo. Almanac of business and
industrial financial ratios. 1972
ed. Englewood Cliffs, N.J., Prentice-
Hall [1971] xxi, 169 p. 338.5/0973
72-181403
HF5681.R25 T68 1971 MRR Alc.

Troy, Leo. Manual of performance
ratios for business analysis and
profit evaluation. Englewood Cliffs,
N.J., Prentice-Hall [1966] xvi, 736
p. 658.1513 66-26237
HF5681.R25 T7 MRR Alc.

RAW MATERIALS.
see also Farm produce

RAW MATERIALS--DICTIONARIES.
Jackson, Nora. A dictionary of
natural resources and their principal
uses. [2d ed.] Oxford, New York,
Pergamon Press [1969] vii, 151 p.
333/.003 73-91463
HF1051 .J3 1969 MRR Alc.

RAW MATERIALS--UNITED STATES--
STATISTICS.
Spencer, Vivian Eberle. Raw
materials in the United States
economy: 1900-1966. [Washington]
U.S. Bureau of the Census [1970] vi,
142 p. [1.50] 338 70-606828
HF1052 .S6 1970 MRR Alc.

Spencer, Vivian Eberle. Raw
materials in the United States
economy: 1900-1969. [Washington]
U.S. Bureau of the Census [1972] iv,
66 p. [$1.00] 338 72-602741
HF1052 .S62 MRR Alc.

RAW MATERIALS--UNITED STATES--
STATISTICS--BIBLIOGRAPHY.
Wasserman, Paul. Commodity prices:
Detroit, Gale Research Co. [1974]
xiii, 200 p. [$15.00] 338.5/2/0973
73-19898
Z7164.P94 W33 MRR Alc.

RAYON INDUSTRY AND TRADE--UNITED STATES-
-DIRECTORIES.
Davison's synthetic and silk red
book. 67th- ed.; 1962- Ridgewood,
N.J., Davison Pub. Co. 72-626449
TS1643 .D3 MRR Alc Latest edition

REACTIONS, CHEMICAL
see Chemical reactions

READERS--INDEXES.
Eakin, Mary K. Subject index to
books for intermediate grades. 3d
ed. Chicago, American Library
Association, 1963. vi, 308 p.
028.52 63-12951
Z1037 .E16 1963 MRR Alc.

Eakin, Mary K. Subject index to
books for primary grades. 3d ed.
Chicago, American Library
Association, 1967. viii, 113 p.
028.52 66-30062
Z1037 .E17 1967 MRR Alc.

READERS AND LIBRARIES
see Libraries and readers

READERS AND SPEAKERS--INDEXES.
Granger, Edith. An index to poetry
and recitations; Chicago, A. C.
McClurg & company, 1904. 970 p. 04-
24547
PN4321 .G8 MRR Ref Desk.

Granger, Edith. An index to poetry
and recitations, Rev. and enl. ed.
Chicago, A. C. McClurg & company,
1918. xiv p., 1 l., 1059 p.
[$10.00] 18-23538
PN4321 .G8 1918 MRR Ref Desk.

READING, ENG.--DIRECTORIES.
Kelly's directory of Reading,
Caversham and neighbourhood.
Kingston upon Thames, Surrey [etc.]
Kelly's Directories Limited [etc.]
53-30079
DA690.R28 K4 MRR Alc Latest
edition

READING--BIBLIOGRAPHY.
Davis, Bonnie M. A guide to
information sources for reading.
Newark, Del., International Reading
Association, 1972. 158 p.
016.4284/.025 72-176095
Z5814.R25 D37 MRR Alc.

Fay, Leo Charles. Doctoral studies
in reading, 1919 through 1960,
[Bloomington] Bureau of Educational
Studies and Testing, School of
Education, Indiana University, 1964.
vi, 80 p. 016.37241 64-64749
Z5814.R25 F35 MRR Alc.

READING--DICTIONARIES.
Schubert, Delwyn G. A dictionary of
terms and concepts in reading, 2d
ed. Springfield, Ill., Thomas [1969]
xv, 376 p. 428.4/03 68-55942
LB1050 .S3 1969 MRR Alc.

READING--DIRECTORIES.
Davis, Bonnie M. A guide to
information sources for reading.
Newark, Del., International Reading
Association, 1972. 158 p.
016.4284/.025 72-176095
Z5814.R25 D37 MRR Alc.

READING INTERESTS OF CHILDREN
see Books and reading for children

READY-RECKONERS.
see also Multiplication

Cox, Edwin Burk. Basic tables in
business and economics, New York,
McGraw-Hill [1967] xiv, 399 p.
511/.8 66-19284
HF5699 .C892 MRR Alc.

Robertson, James, of London.
Dictionary for international
commercial quotations, London, New
York [etc.] H. Milford, Oxford
university press, 1918-19. 2 v. 19-
4807
HF5715.G7 R6 MRR Alc.

Sprinkle, Leland W. Sprinkle's
conversion formulas, Philadelphia,
P. Blakiston's son & co., inc.
[c1938] xii, 122 p. 510.835 38-
8711
HF5699 .S75 MRR Ref Desk.

REAGENTS, CHEMICAL
see Chemical tests and reagents

REAL ESTATE AGENTS--UNITED STATES--
DIRECTORIES.
National roster of realtors. [Cedar
Rapids, Iowa, Stamats Pub. Co.]
[$25.00] 333.3/3 73-640148
HD253 .N34 MRR Alc Latest edition

Society of industrial Realtors.
Directory. Washington. 58-42493
HD251 .S6 MRR Alc Latest edition

REAL ESTATE BUSINESS.
see also House buying

Unger, Maurice Albert. Real estate
principles and practices. 4th ed.
Cincinnati, South-western Pub. Co.
[1969] xiii, 754 p. 333.3/3 69-
15469
HD1375 .U6 1969 MRR Alc.

REAL ESTATE BUSINESS--BIBLIOGRAPHY.
Babb, Janice B. Real estate
information sources. Detroit, Gale
Research Co. [1963] 317 p.
016.33333 63-16246
Z7164.L3 B2 MRR Alc.

REAL ESTATE BUSINESS--DICTIONARIES.
Gross, Jerome S. Illustrated
encyclopedic dictionary of real
estate terms. Englewood Cliffs, N.J.,
Prentice-Hall [1969] xi, 468 p.
333.3/3/03 69-16348
HD1375 .G73 MRR Alc.

Prentice-Hall, inc. Encyclopedic
dictionary of real estate practice,
Rev. and enl. Englewood Cliffs, N.J.
[1962] vi, 533 p. 333.3303 62-
17782
HD1375 .P67 1962 MRR Alc.

REAL ESTATE BUSINESS--FINANCE.
National Association of Real Estate
Investment Trusts. REIT handbook of
member trusts. Washington.
332.6/324 73-647773
HG5095 .N24 MRR Alc Latest edition

REAL ESTATE COUNSELORS--UNITED STATES--
DIRECTORIES.
American Society of Real Estate
Counselors. Geographical and
alphabetical directory. Chicago. 60-
20581
HD251 .A53 MRR Alc Latest edition

REAL ESTATE INVESTMENT.
Beaton, William R. Real estate
investment. Englewood Cliffs, N.J.,
Prentice-Hall [1971] xv, 296 p.
332.63/24 71-151510
HD1375 .B34 MRR Alc.

Harian's how to retire on real estate
profits. [1st] ed.; 1958-
Greenlawn, N.Y., Harian Publications;
trade distributor: Crown Publishers
[New York] 333.33 59-16156
HD1379 .H3 MRR Alc Latest edition

REAL ESTATE INVESTMENT--UNITED STATES--
YEARBOOKS.
Moody's bank & finance manual:
American and foreign. New York,
Moody's Investors Service. 56-14722
HG4961 .M65 MRR Alc Latest edition

REAL ESTATE INVESTMENT TRUSTS--UNITED
STATES.
National Association of Real Estate
Investment Trusts. REIT handbook of
member trusts. Washington.
332.6/324 73-647773
HG5095 .N24 MRR Alc Latest edition

REAL PROPERTY--ARLINGTON CO., VA.--
DIRECTORIES.
Lusk's northern Virginia real estate
directory service. Washington, R. S.
Lusk. 55-41843
HD266.V82A75 MRR Ref Desk Latest
edition

REAL PROPERTY--TERMINOLOGY.
American Institute of Real Estate
Appraisers. Appraisal terminology
and handbook. 5th ed. Chicago
[1967] 268 p. 333.3/32 67-7147
HD1387 .A58 1967 MRR Alc.

REAL PROPERTY--VALUATION.
American Institute of Real Estate
Appraisers. The appraisal of real
estate. 5th ed. Chicago [1967]
viii, 474 p. 333.3/32 67-7288
HD1387 .A56 1967 MRR Alc.

American Institute of Real Estate
Appraisers. Appraisal terminology
and handbook. 5th ed. Chicago
[1967] 268 p. 333.3/32 67-7147
HD1387 .A58 1967 MRR Alc.

REAL PROPERTY--VALUATION--COLLECTIONS.
Friedman, Edith Judith, ed.
Encyclopedia of real estate
appraising. Rev. and enl. Englewood
Cliffs, N.J., Prentice-Hall [1968]
xviii, 1160 p. 333.3/32/03 67-
24487
HD1387 .F69 1968 MRR Alc.

REAL PROPERTY--VALUATION--DICTIONARIES.
Cherney, Richard A. Appraisal and
assessment dictionary. Englewood
Cliffs, N.J., Prentice-Hall [1960]
vii, 337 p. 333.332 60-11976
HD1387 .C45 MRR Alc.

REAL PROPERTY--ALEXANDRIA, VA.--
DIRECTORIES.
Lusk's northern Virginia real estate
directory service. Washington, R. S.
Lusk. 55-41843
HD266.V82A75 MRR Ref Desk Latest
edition

REAL PROPERTY--FAIRFAX CO., VA.
Lusk's Fairfax County, Virginia real
estate directory service.
Washington, R. S. Lusk.
333.305875529 60-17443
HD266.V82F25 MRR Alc Partial set

REAL PROPERTY—MONTGOMERY CO., MD.—DIRECTORY.
Lusk's Montgomery County, Maryland real estate directory service. Washington, R. S. Lusk.   59-31046
HD266.M32 M6 MRR Ref Desk Partial set

REAL PROPERTY—PRINCE GEORGE'S CO., MD.—DIRECTORIES.
Lusk's Prince George's County real estate directory service. Washington, R. S. Lusk.   61-47964
HD266.M32P7 MRR Alc Latest edition

REAL PROPERTY—UNITED STATES—MAPS—BIBLIOGRAPHY.
United States. Library of Congress. Geography and Map Division. Land ownership maps, a checklist Washington [For sale by the Supt. of Docs., U.S. Govt. Print. Off.] 1967. xxv, 86 p.   016.91273 67-60091
Z663.35 .L37 MRR Alc.

REAL PROPERTY—WASHINGTON, D.C.
Lusk's D. C. assessment directory. Baltimore, Rufus S. Lusk & Son, inc. 352/.134 70-200538
HD268.W3 L86 MRR Ref Desk Latest edition

Lusk's District of Columbia real estate directory service. 1948- Washington, R. S. Lusk. 333.3/37/025753 73-200539
HD268.W3 L84 MRR Ref Desk Partial set

REAL PROPERTY TAX—DICTIONARIES.
Cherney, Richard A. Appraisal and assessment dictionary. Englewood Cliffs, N.J., Prentice-Hall [1960] vii, 337 p.   333.332 60-11976
HD1387 .C45 MRR Alc.

REAL PROPERTY TAX—AUST-AGDER, NORWAY.
Aust-Agder fylkes adressebok med skattelikninger. Trondheim, H. G. Moe.   54-16870
DL576.A8 A8   MRR Alc Latest edition

REBATES—UNITED STATES—DIRECTORIES.
Directory of premium and incentive buyers. 1970/71- New York, Salesman's Guide. [$100.00] 658.8/2 73-645791
HF6146.P7 D57 MRR Alc Latest edition

REBELS (SOCIAL PSYCHOLOGY)
see Dissenters

REBUSES.
Darly, Matthew, Two rebuses from the American Revolution in facsimile. Washington, Library of Congress, 1973. 1 portfolio (2 sheets) 973.3/02/07 73-603400
Z663 .T85 1973 MRR Alc.

RECEIPTS.
Belanger, Emil J. Modern manufacturing formulary, New York, Chemical Pub. Co., 1958. 399 p. 602 58-2072
T49 .E45 MRR Alc.

Bennett, Harry, The cosmetic formulary; New York, Chemical publishing co. of N.Y., inc., 1937- v.   668 37-2793
TP983 .B55 MRR Alc.

Freeman, Mitchell. New practical formulary. New York, Chemical Pub. Co., 1955. 376 p.   602 55-531
T49 .F74 MRR Alc.

Hiscox, Gardner Dexter, ed. Henley's twentieth century book of formulas, processes and trade secrets. New rev. and enl. ed. New York, Books, Inc., 1970. 867, [67] p.   602/.02 76-18904
T49 .H6 1970 MRR Alc.

Hopkins, Albert Allis, ed. The standard American encyclopedia of formulas. New York, Grosset & Dunlap [1953] 1077 p.   602 53-12855
T49 .H8 1953 MRR Alc.

Minrath, William R., ed. Van Nostrand's practical formulary, Princeton, N.J., Van Nostrand [1957] 336 p.   602 57-12492
T49 .M56 MRR Alc.

RECIPROCITY—BIBLIOGRAPHY.
United States. Library of Congress. Division of bibliography. ... List of references on reciprocity: Washington, Govt. print. off., 1902. 38 p.   02-18910
Z663.28 .L582 MRR Alc.

United States. Library of Congress. Division of bibliography. ... Select list of books, with references to periodicals, on reciprocity with Canada. Washington, Govt. print. off., 1907. 14 p.   07-35004
Z663.28 .S344 MRR Alc.

RECITATIONS.
Crocker, Lionel George, Oral reading: discussion and principles, 2d ed. New York, Prentice-Hall, 1955. 492 p.   808.54* 55-7942
PN4145 .C75 1955 MRR Alc.

RECITATIONS—INDEXES.
Granger, Edith. Granger's Index to poetry and recitations; 3d ed., completely rev. and enl., Chicago, A. C. McClurg & co. [c1940] 2 p. l., vii-xxiv p., 1 l., 1525 p.   808.8 40-5254
PN4321 .G8 1940 MRR Ref Desk.

Granger, Edith. An index to poetry and recitations; Chicago, A. C. McClurg & company, 1904. 970 p.   04-24547
PN4321 .G8 MRR Ref Desk.

Granger, Edith. An index to poetry and recitations, Rev. and enl. ed. Chicago, A. C. McClurg & co., 1927. 3 p. l., [v]-xv, 1059 p.   28-3385
PN4321 .G8 1927 MRR Ref Desk.

Granger, Edith. An index to poetry and recitations, Rev. and enl. ed. Chicago, A. C. McClurg & company, 1918. xiv p., 1 l., 1059 p. [$10.00]   18-23538
PN4321 .G8 1918 MRR Ref Desk.

RECONSTRUCTION.
see also Ku Klux Klan

see also Negroes

Coulter, Ellis Merton, The South during reconstruction, 1865-1877. [Baton Rouge] Louisiana State University Press, 1947. xii, 426 p. 975 48-5161
F216 .C6 MRR Alc.

Fleming, Walter Lynwood, ed. Documentary history of Reconstruction: Gloucester, Mass., P. Smith, 1960 [c1935] 2 v. in 1. 973.81082 60-52262
E668 .F58 1960 MRR Alc.

Franklin, John Hope, Reconstruction: after the Civil War. [Chicago] University of Chicago Press [1961] 258 p.   973.8 61-15931
E668 .F7 MRR Alc.

McKitrick, Eric L. Andrew Johnson and reconstruction. [Chicago] University of Chicago Press [1960] ix, 533 p.   973.81 60-5467
E668 .M156 MRR Alc.

McPherson, Edward, The political history of the United States of America during the period of reconstruction, (from April 15, 1865, to July 15, 1870,) 2d ed. Washington, Solomons & Chapman, 1875. v, 6-8, 648 p.   04-7498
E668 .M17 MRR Alc.

Welles, Gideon, Diary. New York, W. W. Norton [1960] 3 v.   923.273 60-6275
E468 .W444 MRR Alc.

RECONSTRUCTION (1939-1951)
United States. Library of Congress. Legislative reference service. Abstracts of postwar literature. [Washington] Library of Congress, Legislative reference service, 1943- v.   910.53144 44-6264
Z663.6 .A73 MRR Alc.

United States. Library of Congress. Legislative reference service. Postwar abstracts, July 1942 to June, 1943. [Washington] Legislative reference service, Library of Congress, 1943. 3 v.   940.53114 43-16029
Z663.6 .P6 MRR Alc.

RECONSTRUCTION (1939-1951)—AUSTRIA.
Heissenberger, Franz. The economic reconstruction of Austria, 1945-1952; Washington, Library of Congress, Reference Dept., European Affairs Division, 1953. xii, 153 p. 330.9436 53-60025
Z663.26 .E35 MRR Alc.

Hiscocks, Richard. The rebirth of Austria. London, New York, Oxford University Press, 1953. 263 p. 943.6 53-4436
DB99.1 .H5 MRR Alc.

RECONSTRUCTION (1939-1951)—EUROPE.
United States. Library of Congress. European Affairs Division. Reference notes on the press in European countries participating in the European recovery program; [Washington] 1948. 39 p.   338.942 49-45627
Z663.26 .R4 MRR Alc.

RECORDS, PHONOGRAPH
see Phonorecords

RECREATION.
see also Educational games

RECREATION—APPARATUS AND EQUIPMENT.
Explorers Ltd. The Explorers Ltd. source book. 1st ed. New York, Harper & Row [c1973] 384 p. [$4.95] 790/.028 72-9115
GV187 .E95 1973 MRR Alc.

RECREATION—BIBLIOGRAPHY.
Educators guide to free health, physical education and recreation materials. 1st- ed.; 1968- Randolph, Wis., Educators Progress Service. 011 68-57948
Z6121 .E38 MRR Alc Latest edition

A Guide to books on recreation. 10th- ed.; 1965/66- Washington, National Recreation and Park Association. 016.79 72-623100
Z7511 .N33 MRR Alc Latest edition

Nueckel, Susan. Selected guide to sports and recreation books. New York, Fleet Press Corp. [1974] 168 p.   016.7901 73-3735
Z7511 .N83 MRR Alc.

RECREATION—DICTIONARIES.
Duran, Dorothy B. The new encyclopedia of successful program ideas. New York, Association Press [1967] 511 p.   790/.03 67-21141
GV11 .D8 1967 MRR Alc.

RECREATION—YEARBOOKS.
Recreation and park yearbook. 1908- Washington [etc.] 790.58 52-20639
GV185 .R4 MRR Alc Latest edition

RECREATION—UNITED STATES—DIRECTORIES.
Recreation and park yearbook. 1908- Washington [etc.] 790.58 52-20639
GV185 .R4 MRR Alc Latest edition

RECREATION AGENCIES—UNITED STATES.
Recreation and park yearbook. 1908- Washington [etc.] 790.58 52-20639
GV185 .R4 MRR Alc Latest edition

RECREATION AREAS.
see also National parks and reserves

see also Outdoor recreation

see also Parks

RECREATIONAL FISHING
see Fishing

RECREATIONS
see Games

RECREATIONS, GEOGRAPHICAL
see Geographical recreations

RECRUITING AND ENLISTMENT.
see also Military service, Compulsory

RECRUITING OF EMPLOYEES.
see also Employment agencies

RECTORS
see Clergy

REDEVELOPMENT, URBAN
see Cities and towns—Planning

REFERENCE BOOKS.
see also Encyclopedias and dictionaries

Aldrich, Ella Virginia, Using books and libraries 5th ed. Englewood Cliffs, N.J., Prentice-Hall [1967] viii, 147 p.   028.7 67-12587
Z710 .A36 1967 MRR Alc.

Bagley, William Alfred, Facts and how to find them; 7th ed. London, Pitman [1964] xii, 148 p.   65-68024
Z1035.1 .B3 1964 MRR Alc.

Burke, Arvid James, Documentation in education New York, Teachers College Press, Teachers College, Columbia University [1967] xiv, 413 p. 028.7 67-17818
Z711 .B93 1967 MRR Alc.

Cook, Margaret Gerry, The new library key. 2d ed. New York, H. W. Wilson, 1963. vi, 184 p.   028.7 62-15045
Z711.2 .C75 1963 MRR Alc.

Encyclopedia of library and information science. New York, M. Dekker [1968-   v.   020/.3 68-31232
Z1006 .E57 MRR Alc.

Galin, Saul. Reference books: New York, Random House [1969] xxi, 312 p. [7.95] 011/.02 69-16443
Z1035.1 .G3 MRR Alc.

Gates, Jean Key. Guide to the use of books and libraries. 3d ed. New York, McGraw-Hill [1974] xii, 308 p. 028.7 73-9502
Z710 .G27 1974 MRR Alc.

REFERENCE BOOKS. (Cont.)
Hutchinson, Helene D. The Hutchinson
guide to writing research papers New
York, Glencoe Press [1973] xii, 233
p. 808/.02 72-86030
LB2369 .H85 MRR Alc.

Katz, William Armstrong,
Introduction to reference work New
York, McGraw-Hill [1969] 2 v.
011/.02 69-13223
Z711 .K32 MRR Alc.

Lock, Clara Beatrice Muriel,
Reference material for young people.
[Hamden, Conn.] Archon Books [1967]
189 p. 028.7 67-41
Z1037.1 .L8 MRR Alc.

McCormick, Mona. Who-what-when-where-
how-why made easy: Chicago,
Quadrangle Books [1971] 192 p.
[$5.95] 011/.02 70-138903
Z1035.1 .M17 MRR Alc.

Todd, Alden. Finding facts fast:
New York, Morrow, 1972. xii, 108 p.
[$5.95] 028.7 71-188180
Z710 .T6 MRR Alc.

REFERENCE BOOKS--AMERICAN LITERATURE.
Spargo, John Webster, A
bibliographical manual for students
of the language and literature of
England and the United States: 3d
ed. New York, Hendricks House, 1956.
x, 285 p. 016.82 56-14402
Z2011 .S73 1956 MRR Alc.

REFERENCE BOOKS--BIBLIOGRAPHY.
American Library Association. Ad Hoc
Reference Books Review Committee.
Reference books for small and medium-
sized libraries. 2d ed., rev.
Chicago, American Library
Association, 1973. xii, 146 p.
011/.02 73-8906
Z1035.1 .A47 1973 MRR Alc.

Boehm, Inge P. Reference works:
history and related fields, Santa
Barbara, Calif., ABC-Clio Press,
1967. vi, 58 p. 016.0287 67-20730
Z1035 .B655 MRR Alc.

Chandler, George. How to find out:
4th ed. Oxford, New York, Pergamon
Press [1974] xiv, 194 p. 011/.02
73-19918
Z1035.1 .C47 1974 MRR Alc.

Chandler, George. How to find out:
2nd ed. Oxford, New York [etc.]
Pergamon, 1966. xiv, 198 p. [17/6]
016.0287 66-76421
Z1035.1 .C44 1966 MRR Alc.

Cheney, Frances (Neel) Fundamental
reference sources. Chicago, American
Library Association, 1971. x, 318 p.
011/.02 73-151051
Z1035.1 .C5 MRR Alc.

Columbia University. Libraries.
Library Service Library. Dictionary
catalog. Boston, G. K. Hall, 1962-
v. 016.02 63-2444
Z881.N6295 1962 MRR Alc. (Deck 33)

Encyclopedia of business information
sources: Detroit, Gale Research Co.,
1970. 2 v. (xxi, 689 p.) 016.33
79-127922
HF5353 .E52 MRR Ref Desk.

Enoch Pratt Free Library, Baltimore.
Reference books: [1st] ed.: 1947-
Baltimore. 016 54-4633
Z1035.1 .E5 MRR Ref Desk Latest
edition / MRR Alc Latest edition

Garde, P. K. Directory of reference
works published in Asia. [Paris]
UNESCO [1956] xxvii, 139 p. 016 a
57-2357
Z1035 .G27 MRR Alc.

Jenkins, Frances Briggs, Science
reference sources. 4th ed.
Champaign, Ill., Distributed by
Illini Union Bookstore [c1965] xvi,
143 p. 016.5 66-966
Z7401 .J4 1965 MRR Alc.

Jenkins, Frances Briggs, Science
reference sources. 5th ed.
Cambridge, Mass., M.I.T. Press [1969]
xvi, 231 p. 016.5 73-95001
Z7401 .J4 1969 MRR Alc.

Library Association. Reference,
Special and Information Section.
Basic stock for the reference
library. 3d ed. London, Library
Association (Reference, Special and
Information Section), 1967 [i.e.
1968]. 24 p. [1/6] 011/.02 68-
105269
Z1035.1 .L6 1968 MRR Alc.

Malclès, Louise Noëlle. Cours de
bibliographie à l'intention des
étudiants de l'université et des
candidats aux examens de
bibliothécaire. Genève, E. Droz,
1954. xii, 350 p. a 55-2888
Z1035 .M117 MRR Alc.

Malclès, Louise Noëlle. Les
sources du travail bibliographique.
Genève, E. Droz, 1950-58. 3 v. in
4. 016.01 51-17035
Z1002 .M4 MRR Ref Desk.

Melnyk, Peter. Economics:
bibliographic guide to reference
books and information resources.
Littleton, Colo., Libraries
Unlimited, 1971. 263 p. 016.33 71-
144203
Z7164.E2 M45 MRR Alc.

National Book League, London.
Commonwealth reference books and
bibliographical guide. London, 1965.
54 p. 011.02 66-85951
Z1035 .N29 MRR Alc.

Neiswender, Rosemary. Guide to
Russian reference and language aids.
New York, Special Libraries
Association, 1962. iv, 92 p.
016.4917 62-21081
Z2505 .N4 1962 MRR Alc.

New reference tools for librarians.
1962/63- Oxford, New York, R.
Maxwell. 016.0287 64-55672
Z1035.1 .N48 MRR Alc Full set

Nihon no Sankō Tosho Henshū Iinkai.
Guide to Japanese reference books.
Chicago, American Library
Association, 1966. 303 p. 66-23396
Z3306 .N5 1966 MRR Alc.

Perkins, Ralph. The new concept
guide to reference books: [n.p.,
1965] 68 l. 011.02 65-6500
Z1035 .P4 MRR Alc.

Peterson, Carolyn Sue, Reference
books for elementary and junior high
school libraries. Metuchen, N.J.,
Scarecrow Press, 1970. 191 p.
028.52 72-8294
Z1037.1 .P4 MRR Alc.

Poulton, Helen J. The historian's
handbook: [1st ed.] Norman,
University of Oklahoma Press [1972]
xi, 304 p. 016.9 71-165774
Z6201 .P65 MRR Alc.

Rogers, A. Robert, The humanities:
Littleton, Colo., Libraries
Unlimited, 1974. 400 p. [$9.50]
016.0013 74-78393
Z5579 .R63 MRR Alc.

Schneider, Georg. Handbuch der
bibliographie, 4., ganzlich
veranderte und stark verm. aufl.
Leipzig, K. W. Hiersemann, 1930. ix,
674 p. : 1 l. 010.2 31-10631
Z1001 .S35 1930 MRR Alc.

Shores, Louis, Basic reference
sources: Chicago, American Library
Association, 1954. ix, 378 p.
028.7 53-7487
Z1035 .S49 1954 MRR Alc.

Siddiqui, Akhtar H. A guide to
reference books published in Pakistan
Karachi, Pakistan Reference
Publications, 1966. 41 p. 015.549
sa 66-7465
Z1035.9 .S5 MRR Alc.

Stevens, Rolland Elwell, Reference
books in the social sciences and
humanities 3d ed. Champaign, Ill.,
Distributed by Illini Union Bookstore
[1971] v, 188 p. 016.3 74-151299
Z1035.1 .S85 1971 MRR Ref Desk.

Szentmihályi, János. Útmutató a
tudományos munka magyar es
nemezetközi irodalmahoz Budapest,
Gondolat, 1963. 730 p. 65-84718
Z1035.1 .S97 MRR Alc.

Totok, Wilhelm. Handbuch der
bibliographischen Nachschlagewerke.
4., erw., völlig neu bearb. Aufl.
Frankfurt am Main, V. Klostermann
[c1972] xxxiv, 367 p. 72-371275
Z1002 .T68 1972 MRR Alc.

United States. Library of Congress.
General Reference and Bibliography
Division. Biographical sources for
the United States. Washington, 1961.
v, 58 p. 016.920073 61-60065
Z663.28 .B53 MRR Alc.

Walford, Albert John, ed. Guide to
reference material. 3d ed. [London]
Library Association, 1973- v.
011/.02 73-174024
Z1035.1 .W33 MRR Ref Desk.

Walford, Albert John, ed. Guide to
reference material. 2nd ed. London,
Library Association, 1966-1970. 3 v.
[£15/-/-] 011/.02 66-71608
Z1035 .W252 MRR Alc.

Walsh, James Patrick. Home reference
books in print: New York, R. R.
Bowker Co., 1969. x, 284 p. [9.75]
011/.02 68-56427
Z1035.1 .W35 MRR Alc.

White, Alex Sandri. Fact-finding
made easy; New, updated ed.
Allenhurst, N.J., Aurea Publications
[1967] 129 l. 016.016 67-3292
Z1002 .W45 1967 MRR Alc.

Williams, Cecil Brown, A research
manual for college studies and
papers. 3d ed. New York, Harper &
Row [1963] 212 p. 808.06 63-14052
LB2369 .W5 1963 MRR Alc.

Winchell, Constance Mabel, Guide to
reference books 8th ed. Chicago,
American Library Association, 1967.
xx, 741 p. 011/.02 66-29240
Z1035 .W79 1967 MRR Alc.

Wisconsin. University. Library
School. Reference syllabus for use
in advanced reference classes. 2d
ed. Madison, College Print. and
Typing Co. [1965] 273 p. 028.7 65-
6718
Z1035 .W864 1965 MRR Alc.

Wynar, Bohdan S. Introduction to
bibliography and reference work; 4th
rev. ed. Rochester, N.Y., Libraries
Unlimited, 1967. 310 p. 016.0287
67-20763
Z1035 .W95 1967b MRR Alc.

Wynar, Bohdan S. Reference books in
paperback: an annotated guide.
Littleton, Colo., Libraries
Unlimited, 1972. 199 p. [$4.75]
011.02 74-189257
Z1035.1 .W95 1972 MRR Alc.

Wynar, Christine L. Guide to
reference books for school media
centers Littleton, Colo., Libraries
Unlimited, 1973. xviii, 473 p.
[$17.50] 011/.02 73-87523
Z1035.1 .W97 MRR Alc.

Wynar, Lubomyr Roman, Guide to
reference materials in political
science: Denver, Colorado
Bibliographic Institute, 1966-68. 2
v. 016.32 66-1321
Z7161 .W9 MRR Alc.

Ziskind, Sylvia, Reference
readiness: [Hamden, Conn.] Linnet
Books, 1971. xiii, 310 p. [$10.00]
011/.02 72-134871
Z1035.1 .Z56 MRR Alc.

REFERENCE BOOKS--BIBLIOGRAPHY--CATALOGS.
Cambridge University. Library.
Subject guide to class 'Ref' (current
reference books) in the University
Library Cambridge. Cambridge,
Cambridge University Library, 1968.
[6], 106 leaves. [5/-] 011/.02 72-
354270
Z1035.1 .C35 MRR Alc.

Colchester, Eng. University of Essex.
Library. Comparative and social
studies: Colchester, University of
Essex (Library), 1969- [4], xiv, 407
p. 017/.1 70-506935
Z1035.1 .C63 1969 MRR Alc.

Harvard University. Library.
Reference collections shelved in the
Reading Room and Acquisitions
Department. Cambridge, Distributed
by the Harvard University Press,
1966. 187 p. 011.02 66-31368
Z1035.1 .H27 MRR Ref Desk.

REFERENCE BOOKS--BIBLIOGRAPHY--
PERIODICALS.
American reference books annual.
1970- Littleton, Colo., Libraries
Unlimited. 011/.02 75-120328
Z1035.1 .A55 MRR Alc Full set

REFERENCE BOOKS--CATHOLIC LITERATURE.
McCabe, James Patrick. Critical
guide to Catholic reference books.
Littleton, Colo., Libraries
Unlimited, 1971. 287 p. 011/.02
78-144202
Z674 .R4 no. 2 MRR Alc.

REFERENCE BOOKS--CHEMISTRY.
American Chemical Society. Division
of Chemical Literature. Searching
the chemical literature. Rev. and
enl. ed. Washington, American
Chemical Society, 1961. vi, 326 p.
016.54 61-11330
QD1 .A355 no. 30 MRR Alc.

REFERENCE BOOKS--CHILDREN'S LITERATURE.
Haviland, Virginia, Children's
literature; a guide to reference
sources. Washington, Library of
Congress; [for sale by the
Superintendent of Documents, U.S.
Govt. Print. Off.] 1966. x, 341 p.
016.8098/828/2 66-62734
Z663.292 .H35 MRR Alc.

REFERENCE BOOKS--ECONOMICS.
Coman, Edwin Truman, Sources of
business information. Rev. ed.
Berkeley, University of California
Press, 1964. xii, 330 p. 016.65
64-18639
Z7164.C81 C75 1964 MRR Alc.

REFERENCE BOOKS--ENGLISH LITERATURE.
Spargo, John Webster, A
bibliographical manual for students
of the language and literature of
England and the United States; 3d
ed. New York, Kendricks House, 1956.
x, 285 p. 016.82 56-14402
Z2011 .S73 1956 MRR Alc.

REFERENCE BOOKS--GOVERNMENT
PUBLICATIONS.
Wynkoop, Sally. Subject guide to
government reference books.
Littleton, Colo., Libraries
Unlimited, 1972. 276 p. 015.73 72-
83382
Z1223.Z7 W95 MRR Alc.

REFERENCE BOOKS--REVIEWS.
Reference and subscription books
reviews. 1668/70- Chicago, American
Library Association. 028.1 73-
159565
Z1035.1 .S822 MRR Ref Desk Latest
edition

Subscription books bulletin reviews.
1956/60-1968. Chicago, American
Library Association. 028.7082 61-
2636
Z1035.1 .S92 MRR Ref Desk Full set

REFERENCE BOOKS--CANADA.
Ryder, Dorothy E. Canadian reference
sources; Ottawa, Canadian Library
Association, 1973. x, 185 p.
011/.02/0971 73-169642
Z1365 .R8 MRR Alc.

REFERENCE BOOKS--CHINA.
Nathan, Andrew James. Modern China,
1840-1972; Ann Arbor, Center for
Chinese Studies, University of
Michigan, 1973. vi, 95 p. [$2.00]
016.9151 74-167311
Z3106 .N32 MRR Alc.

REFERENCE BOOKS, RUSSIAN--BIBLIOGRAPHY.
Maichel, Karol. Guide to Russian
reference books. [Stanford, Calif.]
Hoover Institution on War,
Revolution, and Peace, Stanford
University, 1962- v. 016.9147
62-14067
Z2491 .M25 MRR Alc.

REFERENCE SERVICES (LIBRARIES)
Hutchins, Margaret, Introduction to
reference work, Chicago, American
library association, 1944. xii, 214
p., 1 l. 025.5 44-5262
Z711 .H985 MRR Alc.

Katz, William Armstrong,
Introduction to reference work New
York, McGraw-Hill [1969] 2 v.
011/.02 69-13223
Z711 .K32 MRR Alc.

Shores, Louis, Basic reference
sources; Chicago, American Library
Association, 1954. ix, 378 p.
028.7 53-7487
Z1035 .S49 1954 MRR Alc.

REFERENCE SERVICES (LIBRARIES)--CASE
STUDIES.
Grogan, Denis Joseph. Case studies
in reference work Melbourne,
Cheshire [1967] 166 p. [4.00]
025.5/2/0186 75-356998
Z711 .G8 1967b MRR Alc.

REFERENDUM--RHODESIA, SOUTHERN.
Passmore, Gloria C. Source book of
parliamentary elections and referenda
in Southern Rhodesia, 1898-1962.
[Salisbury] Dept. of Government,
University College of Rhodesia and
Nyasaland, 1963. ii, 255 p. 64-
53188
JQ2921 .A23 no. 1 MRR Alc.

REFORESTATION.
see also Forests and forestry

REFORM, SOCIAL
see Social problems

REFORMATION--GERMANY.
Ranke, Leopold von, History of the
reformation in Germany, London, G.
Routledge and sons. limited; New
York, E. P. Dutton & co., 1905.
xxiv, 792 p. 06-15
BR305 .R4 1905 MRR Alc.

REFORMATORIES.
see also Juvenile delinquency

REFORMED CHURCH--DOCTRINAL AND
CONTROVERSIAL WORKS.
Calvin, Jean, A compend of the
Institutes of the Christian religion.
Philadelphia, Westminster Press
[1964] viii, 228 p. 230.42 65-
3389
BX9420 .I652 1964 MRR Alc.

REFORMED CHURCH IN AMERICA--DIRECTORIES.
Reformed Church in America.
Commission on History. Historical
directory of the Reformed Church in
America, 1628-1965. New Brunswick,
N.J. [1966] xix, 348 p. 285.732025
66-21948
BX9507 .A55 MRR Alc.

REFORMERS.
Jacobs, Paul, The new radicals; New
York, Random House [1966] 333 p.
320.973 66-18328
E839.5 .J3 MRR Alc.

REFRACTORIES INDUSTRY--UNITED STATES--
DIRECTORIES.
Product directory of the refractories
industry in the United States.
Pittsburgh, Refractories Institute.
62-38586
TP789 .P7 MRR Alc Latest edition

REFRACTORY MATERIALS--DIRECTORIES.
Product directory of the refractories
industry in the United States.
Pittsburgh, Refractories Institute.
62-38586
TP789 .P7 MRR Alc Latest edition

REFRIGERATION AND REFRIGERATING
MACHINERY.
see also Air conditioning

REFRIGERATION AND REFRIGERATING
MACHINERY--HANDBOOKS, MANUALS, ETC.
American Society of Heating,
Refrigerating and Air-Conditioning
Engineers. ASHRAE handbook & product
directory. 1973- New York; 697 73-
644272
TH7011 .A4 MRR Alc Latest edition
/ Sci RR Latest edition

REFUGES, WILDLIFE
see Wildlife refuges

REFUSE AND REFUSE DISPOSAL.
see also Pollution

REGALIA (INSIGNIA)--GREAT BRITAIN.
Milton, Roger. The English
ceremonial book; Newton Abbot [Eng.]
David & Charles [1972] 216 p.
[£3.50] 391/.022/0842 72-185055
CR492 .M5 MRR Alc.

REGIONAL PLANNING.
see also Cities and towns--Planning

REGIONAL PLANNING--UNITED STATES--
BIBLIOGRAPHY--CATALOGS.
United States. Dept. of Housing and
Urban Development. Library and
Information Division. The dictionary
catalog of the United States
Department of Housing and Urban
Development, Library and Information
Division, Boston, G. K. Hall, 1972.
19 v. 016.30154 73-152937
Z7164.H8 U4494 MRR Alc (Dk 33)

REGIONALISM (INTERNATIONAL ORGANIZATION)
Lawson, Ruth Catherine,
International regional organizations;
New York, Praeger [1962] xviii, 387
p. 341.18 62-13746
JX1979 .L3 MRR Alc.

REGISTERS OF BIRTH, ETC.--UNITED STATES.
United States. Public Health Service.
Where to write for birth and death
records: United States and outlying
areas. [Washington, For sale by the
Supt. of Docs., U.S. Govt. Print.
Off.] 312/.1/072073 77-649981
HA38 .A232 MRR Ref Desk Latest
edition

REGISTERS OF BIRTHS, ETC.--UNITED
STATES--DIRECTORIES.
United States. Health Services and
Mental Health Administration. Where
to write for marriage records; United
States and outlying areas.
[Washington, For sale by the Supt. of
Docs., U.S. Govt. Print. Off.]
312/.5/0973 73-615003
HA38 .A25 MRR Ref Desk Latest
edition

REHABILITATION, RURAL.
see also Community development

REHABILITATION, RURAL--UNITED STATES.
Baker, John Austin, Guide to Federal
programs for rural development;
Washington, U.S. Govt. Print. Off.,
1971 [i.e. 1972] ii, 576 p. [$2.50
(paper cover)] 309.2/63/0973 72-
601448
HN90.C6 B352 MRR Alc.

REHABILITATION CENTERS--UNITED STATES--
DIRECTORIES.
The Easter seal directory of resident
camps for persons with special health
needs. Chicago, National Easter Seal
Society for Crippled Children and
Adults. 796.54/22/02573 72-627459
GV197.H3 D5 MRR Alc Latest edition

REHABILITATION COUNSELING--BIBLIOGRAPHY.
Wright, George Nelson.
Rehabilitation counselor functions:
annotated references Madison,
University of Wisconsin, Regional
Rehabilitation Research Institute,
1968. viii, 451 p. 016.3628/5 68-
63360
HF7256.U6 W56 ser. 1, vol. 1 MRR
Alc.

REID, WHITELAW, 1837-1912--BIBLIOGRAPHY.
United States. Library of Congress.
Manuscript Division. Whitelaw Reid;
a register of his papers in the
Library of Congress. Washington,
1958. 62 p. 012 58-60047
Z663.34 .R4 MRR Alc.

RELATIONISM.
see also Existentialism

RELIEF (AID)
see Charities

RELIEF MODELS.
United States. Library of Congress.
Map Division. Three-dimensional
maps; 2d ed., rev. and enl.
Washington [For sale by the
Superintendent of Documents, U.S.
Govt. Print. Off.] 1964 [i.e. 1965]
x, 38 p. 64-65535
Z663.35 .T5 1965 MRR Alc.

RELIGION.
see also Spiritual life

see also Theology

RELIGION--BIBLIOGRAPHY.
Berkowitz, Morris I. Social
scientific studies of religion:
[Pittsburgh] University of Pittsburgh
Press [1967] xvii, 258 p. 016.2
67-18692
Z7751 .B47 MRR Alc.

Council on Graduate Studies in
Religion. Doctoral dissertations in
the field of religion, 1940-1952:
[New York] Columbia University Press
for the Council on Graduate Studies
in Religion in cooperation with the
National Council on Religion in
Higher Education [1954] iv, 194 p.
016.2 55-542
Z7751 .C7 MRR Alc.

Diehl, Katharine Smith. Religions,
mythologies, folklores: an annotated
bibliography. 2d ed. New York,
Scarecrow Press, 1962. 573 p.
016.2 62-16003
Z7751 .D54 1962 MRR Alc.

Little, Lawrence Calvin, Researches
in personality, character and
religious education; [Pittsburgh]
University of Pittsburgh Press, 1962.
iv, 215 p. 013.3784886 62-12625
Z7849 .L54 MRR Alc.

London. University. Warburg
Institute. Library. Catalogue. [2d
ed.] Boston, G. K. Hall, 1967. 12
v. 019/.2 68-4522
Z921 .L66 1967 MRR Alc (Dk 33)

Rogers, A. Robert, The humanities;
Littleton, Colo., Libraries
Unlimited, 1974. 400 p. [$9.50]
016.0013 74-78393
Z5579 .R63 MRR Alc.

Sharma, Umesh D. Mysticism: a select
bibliography. Waterloo, Ont.,
Waterloo Lutheran University, 1973.
109 p. 016.248/22 73-174548
Z7819 .S5 MRR Alc.

RELIGION--COLLECTIONS.
Perry, Whitall N., comp. A treasury
of traditional wisdom. New York,
Simon and Schuster [c1971] 1144 p.
[$15.00] 200/.8 70-93905
BL25 .P52 1971 MRR Alc.

RELIGION--DICTIONARIES.
Bumpus, John Skelton, A dictionary
of ecclesiastical terms; London, T.
W. Laurie [1910] 2 p. l., 323 [1] p.
11-2155
BR95 .B8 MRR Alc.

A Dictionary of the Episcopal Church.
Philadelphia [etc.] Trefoil
Publishing Society. 283.03 55-15394

BX5007 .D5 MRR Alc Latest edition

Encyclopaedie of religion and ethics,
Edinburgh, T. & T. Clark; New York,
C. Scribner's sons, 1908-26. 13 v.
08-35833
BL31 .E4 MRR Alc.

RELIGION--DICTIONARIES. (Cont.)
Ferm, Vergillius Ture Anselm, ed. An
encyclopedia of religion. New York,
The Philosophical library [c1945]
xix, 844 p. 203 46-3249
BL31 .F4 MRR Alc.

Gaynor, Frank, ed. Dictionary of
mysticism. New York, Philosophical
Library [1953] 208 p. 290.3 53-
13354
BL31 .G32 MRR Alc.

Kauffman, Donald T. The dictionary
of religious terms London,
Edinburgh, Marshall, Morgan & Scott,
1967. 445 p. [60/-] 200/.3 68-
85136
BL31 .K34 1967b MRR Alc.

Mathews, Shailer, ed. A dictionary
of religion and ethics. New York,
The Macmillan company, 1923. 2 p.
l., iii-vii, 513 p. 203 31-24963
BL31 .M3 1923 MRR Alc.

Pike, Edgar Royston, Encyclopaedia
of religion and religions. New York,
Meridian Books [1958] 406 p. 203
58-8530
BL31 .P5 1958 MRR Alc.

RELIGION--DICTIONARIES--GERMAN.
Die Religion in Geschichte und
Gegenwart; 3., völlig neu
bearbeitete Aufl., Tubingen, Mohr,
1957-65. 7 v. a 59-1577
BL31 .R42 MRR Alc.

RELIGION--PERIODICALS--INDEXES.
American Theological Library
Association. Index to religious
periodical literature; 1949/52
[Chicago] a 54-6085
Z7753 .A5 MRR Alc Full set

Burr, Nelson Rollin, Religion in
American life. New York, Appleton-
Century-Crofts [1971] xix, 171 p.
016.2008/73 70-136219
Z7757.U5 B8 MRR Alc.

Christian periodical index. 1958-
[Buffalo, N.Y.] Christian Librarians'
Fellowship. 203 60-36226
Z7753 .C5 MRR Alc Full set

Guide to religious and semi-religious
periodicals. Flint, Mich., National
Library of Religious Periodicals.
016.200/5 72-624925
Z7753 .G83 MRR Alc Full set

Guide to religious periodicals. v. 1-
Sept. 1964/Feb. 1965- Flint,
Mich. [etc.] National Library of
Religious Periodicals [etc.] 76-2563

Z7753 .G84 MRR Alc Full set

Guide to social science and religion
in periodical literature. Flint,
Mich., National Periodical Library.
016.2/005 73-641014
Z7753 .G83 MRR Alc Full set

Religious and theological abstracts.
v. 1- Mar. 1958- Youngstown, Ohio,
Theological Publications. 208.22 61-
35093
BR1 .R286 MRR Alc Partial set

Williams, Ethel L. Afro-American
religious studies: Metuchen, N.J.,
Scarecrow Press, 1972. 454 p.
016.301451/86073 78-166072
Z1361.N39 W55 MRR Alc.

RELIGION--PHILOSOPHY.
MacGregor, Geddes. Introduction to
religious philosophy. Boston,
Houghton Mifflin [1959] 366 p. 201
59-9231
BL51 .M214 MRR Alc.

RELIGION--QUOTATIONS, MAXIMS, ETC.
Berrey, Lester V., ed. A treasury of
Biblical quotations. [1st ed.]
Garden City, N.Y., Doubleday, 1948.
viii, 240 p. 220.2 48-9181
BS432 .B4 MRR Alc.

Gaer, Joseph, The wisdom of the
living religions. New York, Dodd,
Mead, 1956. 338 p. 290.82 56-8362

BL29 .G27 MRR Alc.

Luther, Martin, What Luther says,
Saint Louis, Concordia Pub. House
[c1959] 3 v. (xxvi, 1667 p.)
230.41 57-8854
BR324 .P6 MRR Alc.

Mead, Frank Spencer, ed. The
encyclopedia of religious quotations.
Westwood, N.J., Revell [1965] 534
p. 808.882 65-23623
PN6084.R3 M4 MRR Ref Desk.

Perry, Whitall N., comp. A treasury
of traditional wisdom. New York,
Simon and Schuster [c1971] 1144 p.
[$15.00] 200/.8 70-93905
BL25 .P52 1971 MRR Alc.

Stockhammer, Morris, ed. Thomas
Aquinas dictionary. New York,
Philosophical Library [1965] xiii,
219 p. 230.203 64-21468
BX1749.T324 S7 MRR Alc.

Woods, Ralph Louis, ed. The world
treasury of religious quotations;
[1st ed.] New York, Hawthorn Books
[1966] xiv, 1106 p. 208 66-15355
BL29 .W6 MRR Ref Desk.

RELIGION--STUDY AND TEACHING--UNITED
STATES.
Holbrook, Clyde A. Religion, a
humanistic field. Englewood Cliffs,
N.J., Prentice-Hall [1963] xvi, 299
p. 207 63-12269
BL41 .H6 MRR Alc.

Ramsey, Paul, ed. Religion.
Englewood Cliffs, N.J., Prentice-Hall
[1965] x, 468 p. 207.2 64-23553
BL41 .R3 MRR Alc.

RELIGION, PRIMITIVE.
see also Superstition

Frazer, James George, Sir,
Aftermath; London, Macmillan and
co., limited, 1936. xx, 494 p. 291
37-2300
BL310 .F715 1936 MRR Alc.

[Frazer, James George Sir,] The
golden bough; 3d ed. [New York, The
Macmillan company, 1935] 12 v. 291
35-35398
BL310 .F7 1935 MRR Alc.

Howells, William White, The
heathens, [1st ed.] Garden City,
N.Y., Doubleday, 1948. 306 p. 290
48-5578
GN470 .H6 MRR Alc.

RELIGION AND PSYCHOLOGY
see Psychology, Religious

RELIGION AND SCIENCE.
see also Man--Origin

RELIGION AND SOCIAL PROBLEMS
see Church and social problems

RELIGION AND SOCIOLOGY.
Knudten, Richard D., comp. The
sociology of religion. New York,
Appleton-Century-Crofts [1967] xiii,
560 p. 261 67-14572
BL60 .K55 MRR Alc.

RELIGION AND STATE--BIBLIOGRAPHY.
LaNoue, George R. A bibliography of
doctoral dissertations undertaken in
American and Canadian universities,
1940-1962, [New York, Published for
the Dept. of Religious Liberty by the
Office of Publication and
Distribution, National Council of the
Churches of Christ in the U.S.A.,
1963] v, 49 p. 016.322 63-21606
Z7776.72 .L36 MRR Alc.

RELIGION IN THE PUBLIC SCHOOLS--UNITED
STATES--BIBLIOGRAPHY.
Little, Lawrence Calvin, Religion
and public education; 3d ed., rev.
and enl. Pittsburgh, University of
Pittsburgh Book Center, 1968. v, 214
p. 016.377/0873 68-1933
Z5814.C57 L5 1968 MRR Alc.

RELIGIONS.
see also Buddha and Buddhism

see also Christianity

see also Hinduism

see also Judaism

see also Mythology

Bach, Marcus, Strange sects and
curious cults. New York, Dodd, Mead,
1961. 277 p. 209 61-7167
BL85 .B3 MRR Alc.

Hutchison, John Alexander, Ways of
faith; 2d ed. New York, Ronald
Press Co. [1960] 597 p. 290 60-
7770
BL80.2 .H8 1960 MRR Alc.

Lyon, Quinter Marcellus. The great
religions. [1st ed.] New York,
Odyssey Press [1957] 732 p. 290
57-1753
BL80 .L9 MRR Alc.

McCasland, Selby Vernon, Religions
of the world New York, Random House
[1969] xviii, 760 p. [8.50]
200/.9 69-10524
BL80.2 .M27 MRR Alc.

Watts, Harold Holliday, The modern
reader's guide to religions. New
York, Barnes & Noble [1964] xi, 620
p. 290 64-17645
BL80.2 .W3 MRR Alc.

Zaehner, Robert Charles, ed. The
concise encyclopedia of living
faiths; 2nd ed. (revised in new
format). London, Hutchinson, 1971.
xxi, 436 p. [£3.00] 200 70-878039

BL80.2 .Z3 1971 MRR Alc.

RELIGIONS--BIBLIOGRAPHY.
Adams, Charles J., ed. A reader's
guide to the great religions. New
York, Free Press [1965] xv, 364 p.
016.2 65-15440
Z7833 .A35 MRR Alc.

International bibliography of the
history of religions. 1952- Leiden,
E. J. Brill. 016.29 56-19258
Z7833 .I53 MRR Alc Full set

RELIGIONS--DICTIONARIES.
A dictionary of comparative religion.
London, Weidenfeld & Nicolson [1970]
704 p. [5/10/-] 291/.03 75-
499655
BL31 .D54 MRR Alc.

Parrinder, Edward Geoffrey. A
dictionary of non-Christian
religions; Philadelphia, Westminster
Press [1973, c1971] 320 p. 290/.3
73-4781
BL31 .P36 1973 MRR Alc.

Pike, Edgar Royston, Encyclopaedia
of religion and religions. New York,
Meridian Books [1958] 406 p. 203
58-8530
BL31 .P5 1958 MRR Alc.

Wedeck, Harry Ezekiel, Dictionary of
pagan religions. [1st ed.] New
York, Philosophical Library [1971]
363 p. [$10.00] 290/.3 78-86508
BL31 .W4 MRR Alc.

Winternitz, Moriz, comp. A concise
dictionary of Eastern religion,
Oxford, The Clarendon press, 1910
[1925] xiv, [2], 683, [1] p. 290.8
ca 32-293
BL1010 .S32 MRR Alc.

RELIGIONS--DIRECTORIES.
Cushing, A. I. The international
"mystery schools" directory. New
1970 ed. Boston, A.C. Publications
[1970] 1 v. (unpaged) 133/.062 70-
16742
BL35 .C86 MRR Alc.

Friedlander, Ira. Year one catalog;
[1st ed.] New York, Harper & Row
[1972] 152 p. [$1.95] 200/.25/73
73-150151
BP602 .F74 1972 MRR Alc.

World Christian handbook. 1949-
London, World Dominion Press. 270.8
49-6861
BR481 .W6 MRR Alc Latest edition

RELIGIONS--HISTORY.
Finegan, Jack, The archeology of
world religions; Princeton,
Princeton University Press, 1952.
xl, 599 p. 290.9 52-5839
BL80 .F5 MRR Alc.

James, Edwin Oliver, The ancient
gods; London, Weidenfeld and
Nicolson [1960] 359 p. 290 60-
4641
BL96 .J32 1960a MRR Alc.

RELIGIONS--HISTORY--BIBLIOGRAPHY.
International bibliography of the
history of religions. 1952- Leiden,
E. J. Brill. 016.29 56-19258
Z7833 .I53 MRR Alc Full set

RELIGIONS--PERIODICALS--INDEXES.
Bulletin signalétique 527: Sciences
religieuses. v. 24- 1970- Paris,
Centre de documentation du C.N.R.S.
70-258523
Z7751 .B85 MRR Alc Full set

Guide to religious and semi-religious
periodicals. Flint, Mich., National
Library of Religious Periodicals.
016.200/5 72-624925
Z7753 .G83 MRR Alc Full set

Guide to social science and religion
in periodical literature. Flint,
Mich., National Periodical Library.
016.2/005 73-641014
Z7753 .G83 MRR Alc Full set

RELIGIOUS ART
see Church architecture

RELIGIOUS CAMPS, JEWISH--DIRECTORIES.
National directory of Jewish camps.
[Norfolk, Va., Camp Advisory Bureau]
796.5405873 60-28907
SK601.A1 N38 MRR Alc Latest
edition

RELIGIOUS EDUCATION--AUDIO-VISUAL AIDS.
AVRG; audio-visual resource guide for
use in religious education. [1st]-
ed.; 1949- [New York, etc.]
016.268635 58-13297
BV1535 .A22 MRR Alc Latest edition

RELIGIOUS EDUCATION--BIBLIOGRAPHY.
Little, Lawrence Calvin, Researches
in personality, character and
religious education; [Pittsburgh]
University of Pittsburgh Press, 1962.
iv, 215 p.   013.3784886 62-12625
Z7849 .L54 MRR Alc.

RELIGIOUS HISTORY
see Church history

RELIGIOUS LIBERTY--UNITED STATES.
Blakely, William Addison, ed.
American state papers and related
documents on freedom in religion.
4th rev. ed. Washington, Published
for the Religious Liberty Association
by the Review and Herald, 1949. 915
p.   263.8 50-206
BV133 .B6 1949 MRR Alc.

RELIGIOUS LIFE
see Monastic and religious life

RELIGIOUS LITERATURE.
Gaer, Joseph, The wisdom of the
living religions. New York, Dodd,
Mead, 1956. 338 p.   290.82 56-8362

BL29 .G27 MRR Alc.

Mead, Frank Spencer, ed. The
encyclopedia of religious quotations.
Westwood, N.J., Revell [1965] 534
p.   808.882 65-23623
PN6084.R3 M4 MRR Ref Desk.

RELIGIOUS LITERATURE--BIBLIOGRAPHY.
Guide to religious and semi-religious
periodicals. Flint, Mich., National
Library of Religious Periodicals.
016.200/5 72-624925
Z7753 .G83 MRR Alc Full set

Guide to social science and religion
in periodical literature. Flint,
Mich., National Periodical Library.
016.2/005 73-641014
Z7753 .G83 MRR Alc Full set

**RELIGIOUS LITERATURE, ENGLISH--HISTORY
AND CRITICISM--BIBLIOGRAPHY.**
A Manual of the writings in Middle
English, 1050-1500. New Haven,
Connecticut Academy of Arts and
Sciences [order from: Archon Books,
Hamden, Conn.] 1967- v.
016.820/9/001 67-7687
PR255 .M3 MRR Alc.

**RELIGIOUS LITERATURE, IRISH--
BIBLIOGRAPHY.**
Kenney, James Francis, The sources
for the early history of Ireland;
New York, Columbia University Press,
1929. xvi, 807 p.   29-30667
Z2041 .K36 MRR Alc.

RELIGIOUS MUSIC
see Church music

**RELIGIOUS NEWSPAPERS AND PERIODICALS--
DIRECTORIES.**
Associated Church Press. Directory.
Chicago [etc.] 56-40660
Z7753 .A7 MRR Alc Latest edition

RELIGIOUS ORDERS
see Monasticism and religious orders

RELIGIOUS POETRY.
Morrison, James Dalton, ed.
Masterpieces of religious verse.
[1st ed.] New York, Harper [1948]
xiv, 706 p.   808.81 48-8937
PN6110.R4 M6 MRR Alc.

RELIGIOUS POETRY, ENGLISH.
Hill, Caroline (Miles) ed. The
world's great religious poetry. New
York, The Macmillan company, 1938.
xxxix p., 1 l., 836 p.   808.81 40-
31228
PN6110.R4 H5 1938a MRR Alc.

**RELIGIOUS POETRY, ENGLISH--MIDDLE
ENGLISH, 1100-1500--BIBLIOGRAPHY.**
Brown, Carleton Fairchild, The index
of Middle English verse New York,
Printed for the Index Society by
Columbia University Press, 1943.
xix, 785 p.   016.821/1 43-16653
Z2012 .B86 MRR Alc.

RENAISSANCE.
see also Civilization, Medieval

see also Civilization, Modern

see also Painting, Renaissance

RENAISSANCE--BIBLIOGRAPHY--YEARBOOKS.
Bibliographie internationale de
l'Humanism et de la Renaissance. 1-
1965- Geneve, Librairie Droz. 68-
2326
Z6207.R4 B5 MRR Alc Full set

RENAISSANCE--BIOGRAPHY.
The New Century Italian Renaissance
encyclopedia. New York, Appleton-
Century-Crofts [1972] xiii, 978 p.
914.5/03/503 76-181735
DG537.8.A1 N48 MRR Biog.

Schweitzer, Frederick M., comp.
Dictionary of the Renaissance. New
York, Philosophical Library [1967]
xxii, 646 p.   914/.03/2103 64-20429

CB361 .S45 MRR Biog.

RENAISSANCE--DICTIONARIES.
Schweitzer, Frederick M., comp.
Dictionary of the Renaissance. New
York, Philosophical Library [1967]
xxii, 646 p.   914/.03/2103 64-20429

CB361 .S45 MRR Biog.

RENAISSANCE--ITALY.
Horizon (New York, 1958-) The
Horizon book of the Renaissance, New
York, American Heritage Pub. Co.;
book trade distribution by Doubleday
[1961] 431 p.   945.05 61-11489
DG533 .H6 MRR Alc.

RENAISSANCE--ITALY--DICTIONARIES.
The New Century Italian Renaissance
encyclopedia. New York, Appleton-
Century-Crofts [1972] xiii, 978 p.
914.5/03/503 76-181735
DG537.8.A1 N48 MRR Biog.

RENAISSANCE ART
see Art, Renaissance

**REORGANIZED CHURCH OF JESUS CHRIST OF
LATTER-DAY SAINTS--HISTORY.**
Davis, Inez (Smith) The story of the
church; 6th ed. Independence, Mo.,
Herald Pub. House, 1959. 656 p.
289.3 59-4430
BX8611 .D3 1959 MRR Alc.

REPAIRING.
see also Automobiles--Maintenance and
repair

REPAIRING--AMATEURS' MANUALS.
Popular mechanics do-it-yourself
encyclopedia. New York, Book
Division, Hearst Magazines [1968- v.
680/.2/02 68-3759
TT155 .P75 MRR Alc.

The Family handyman. America's
handyman book, New York, Scribner
[1961] 513 p.   643.7 61-7215
TT151 .F3 MRR Alc.

The Family handyman. America's
handyman book, Rev. ed. New York,
Scribner [1970] xiii, 529 p.
[$10.00] 643/.7 70-85277
TH4817 .F28 1970 MRR Alc.

Waugh, Andrew. Handyman's
encyclopaedia. Sydney, New York,
Paul Hamlyn [1971] 512 p. [$7.95]
643/.7 72-178656
TT151 .W38 MRR Alc.

**REPAIRING--AMATEURS' MANUALS--
BIBLIOGRAPHY.**
Nueckel, Susan. Selected guide to
make-it, fix-it, do-it-yourself
books. New York, Fleet Press Corp.
[1973] 213 p.   016.643/7 72-82609

Z6151 .N83 MRR Alc.

REPORT WRITING.
Allen, George Richard, The graduate
students' guide to theses and
dissertations; [1st ed.] San
Francisco, Jossey-Bass, 1973. xi,
108 p.   808/.02 73-3774
LB2369 .A595 MRR Alc.

Chicago. University. Press. A manual
of style, [1st]- ed.; 1906-
Chicago. 655.25 06-40582
Z253 .C57 MRR Ref Desk Latest
edition

Gatner, Elliott S. M. Research and
report writing New York, Barnes &
Noble [1963] vii, 142 p.   378.242
63-20520
LB2369 .G3 1963 MRR Alc.

Graves, Harold Frank, Report writing
4th ed. Englewood Cliffs, N.J.,
Prentice-Hall [1965] viii, 286 p.
808.066 65-11494
PE1478 .G7 MRR Alc.

Hendrickson, John Raymond. The
research paper. New York, Holt
[1957] 76 p.   029.6 808.06* 57-
5707
LB2369 .H4 MRR Alc.

Hook, Lucyle. The research paper;
4th ed. Englewood Cliffs, N.J.,
Prentice-Hall [1969] viii, 120 p.
808.02/3 69-20488
PE1478 .H6 1969 MRR Alc.

Hurt, Peyton, Bibliography and
footnotes; 3d ed., rev. and enl.
Berkeley, University of California
Press, 1968. xii, 163 p.   010 67-
26633
Z1001 .H95 1968 MRR Alc.

Hutchinson, Helene D. The Hutchinson
guide to writing research papers New
York, Glencoe Press [1973] xii, 233
p.   808/.02 72-86030
LB2369 .H85 MRR Alc.

Seeber, Edward Derbyshire, A style
manual for students, 2d ed., rev.
Bloomington, Indiana University Press
[1968, c1967] 94 p.   [1.00] 808.02
67-11623
LB2369 .S4 1968 MRR Ref Desk.

Thurston, Marjorie H. The
preparation of term papers and
reports, 6th ed. Minneapolis,
Burgess Pub. Co. [1970] vi, 63 p.
808.02 74-104333
LB2369 .T5 1970 MRR Ref Desk.

Turabian, Kate L. Student's guide
for writing college papers. Chicago,
University of Chicago Press [1963]
vii, 172 p.   029.6 63-19753
LB2369 .T82 1963 MRR Ref Desk.

Williams, Cecil Brown, A research
manual for college studies and
papers. 3d ed. New York, Harper &
Row [1963] 212 p.   808.06 63-14052

LB2369 .W5 1963 MRR Alc.

REPORTERS AND REPORTING.
MacDougall, Curtis Daniel,
Interpretative reporting [by] 5th
ed. New York, Macmillan [c1968] ix,
515 p.   070.4/3 68-10070
PN4781 .M153 1968 MRR Alc.

Warren, Carl Nelson. Modern news
reporting. 3d ed. New York, Harper
[1959] 480 p.   070.42 58-59883
PN4781 .W32 1959 MRR Alc.

**REPRESENTATIVE GOVERNMENT AND
REPRESENTATION.**
see also Elections

see also Legislative bodies

REPRINTS (PUBLICATIONS)
The A B bookman's yearbook. 1954-
Newark, N.J. 010.58 54-1676
Z990 .A18 MRR Alc Latest edition

Catalog of reprints in series. [1st]-
ed.; 1940- Metuchen, N.J. [etc.]
Scarecrow Press [etc.] 011 61-8715

Z1033.S5 C3 MRR Alc Latest edition

Guide to reprints. 1967-
Washington, Microcard Editions. 011
66-29279
Z1000.5 .G8 MRR Ref Desk Latest
edition

Nemeyer, Carol A., Scholarly reprint
publishing in the United States New
York, R. R. Bowker Co., 1972. ix,
262 p.   070.5/73 74-163901
Z479 .N44 MRR Alc.

REPRINTS (PUBLICATIONS)--BIBLIOGRAPHY.
Catalog of reprints in series. [1st]-
ed.; 1940- Metuchen, N.J. [etc.]
Scarecrow Press [etc.] 011 61-8715

Z1033.S5 C3 MRR Alc Latest edition

Ostwald, Renate.
Nachdruckverzeichnis von
Einzelwerken, Serien und
Zeitschriften Wiesbaden, G. Nobis,
1965- v.   66-31825
Z1011 .O78 MRR Alc.

REPRODUCTION
see also Genetics

see also Pregnancy

see also Sex

Aristoteles. Generation of animals,
Cambridge, Mass., Harvard University
Press; London, W. Heinemann ltd.,
1943. lxxviii, 607, [1] p.   591.16
888.5 a 44-1496
PA3612 .A8D28 1943 MRR Alc.

REPTILES.
see also Snakes

Grzimek, Bernhard. Grzimek's animal
life encyclopedia. New York, Van
Nostrand Reinhold Co. [1972- v. 13,
1972] v.   [$29.95 per vol.] 591
79-183178
QL3 .G7813 MRR Alc.

REPTILES--IDENTIFICATION.
Conant, Roger, A field guide to
reptiles and amphibians of the United
States and Canada east of the 100th
meridian. Boston, Houghton Mifflin,
1958. xv, 366 p.   597.6 58-6416
QL651 .C65 MRR Alc.

REPTILES--NORTH AMERICA.
Conant, Roger, A field guide to
reptiles and amphibians of the United
States and Canada east of the 100th
meridian. Boston, Houghton Mifflin,
1958. xv, 366 p.   597.6 58-6416
QL651 .C65 MRR Alc.

REPUBLICAN PARTY--HISTORY.
Mayer, George H. The Republican Party, 1854-1966 2d ed. New York, Oxford University Press, 1967. xi, 604 p. 329.6/009 67-25300
JK2356 .M3 1967 MRR Alc.

Moos, Malcolm Charles, The Republicans; New York, Random House [1956] 564 p. 329.6 56-5195
JK2356 .M6 MRR Alc.

RESCUE WORK.
see also First aid in illness and injury

RESEARCH.
see also Agricultural research

see also Information services

see also Psychical research

Allen, George Richard, The graduate students' guide to theses and dissertations; [1st ed.] San Francisco, Jossey-Bass, 1973. xi, 108 p. 808/.02 73-3774
LB2369 .A595 MRR Alc.

Bagley, William Alfred, Facts and how to find them; 7th ed. London, Pitman [1964] xii, 148 p. 65-68024

Z1035.1 .B3 1964 MRR Alc.

Brimmer, Brenda. A guide to the use of United Nations documents Dobbs Ferry, N.Y., Oceana Publications, 1962. xv, 272 p. 025.173 63-3667

Z674 .B7 1962a MRR Alc.

Cook, Margaret Gerry, The new library key. 2d ed. New York, H. W. Wilson, 1963. vi, 184 p. 028.7 62-15045
Z711.2 .C75 1963 MRR Alc.

Gatner, Elliott S. M. Research and report writing New York, Barnes & Noble [1963] vii, 142 p. 378.242 63-20520
LB2369 .G3 1963 MRR Alc.

Good, Carter Victor, Methods of research: educational, psychological, sociological, New York, Appleton-Century-Crofts [1954] 920 p. 007 001* 54-6255
AZ105 .G6 MRR Alc.

Hook, Lucyle. The research paper; 4th ed. Englewood Cliffs, N.J., Prentice-Hall [1969] viii, 120 p. 808.02/3 69-20488
PE1478 .H6 1969 MRR Alc.

Hutchinson, Helene D. The Hutchinson guide to writing research papers New York, Glencoe Press [1973] xii, 233 p. 808/.02 72-86030
LB2369 .H85 MRR Alc.

Todd, Alden. Finding facts fast; New York, Morrow, 1972. xii, 108 p. [$5.95] 028.7 71-188180
Z710 .T6 MRR Alc.

United States. Work projects administration. Index of research projects ... [Washington, U.S. Govt. print. off., 1938-39. 3 v. 351.80873 38-26877
HD3881 .A56 1938 MRR Alc.

Williams, Cecil Brown, A research manual for college studies and papers. 3d ed. New York, Harper & Row [1963] 212 p. 808.06 63-14052

LB2369 .W5 1963 MRR Alc.

RESEARCH--DIRECTORIES.
Minerva: internationales Verzeichnis wissenschaftlicher Institutionen. Forschungsinstitute. 33.- Ausg. (Jahrg.): 1872- Berlin, New York, W. de Gruyter. 72-76041
AS2 .M57 MRR Ref Desk Latest edition / MRR Alc Latest edition

Organization for Economic Co-operation and Development. Development Centre. Catalogue of social and economic development training institutes and programmes. Paris, O.E.C.D.; London, H.M.S.O., 1968. [2], 344 p. [31/-] 309.2/23/0711 68-140061
HD82 .O66 MRR Alc.

Organization for Economic Cooperation and Development. Development Centre. Catalogue of social and economic development institutes and programmes: research. Paris, Development Centre of the Organization for Economic Co-operation and Development, 1968. 413 p. [$4.50] 338.9/0072 75-417969
HD82 .O656 MRR Alc.

Wilson, William K. World directory of environmental research centers, 2d ed. New York, Oryx Press; distributed by R. R. Bowker Co., 1974. xi, 330 p. 301.31/025 72-87536
HC79.E5 W54 1974 MRR Alc.

Worldwide directory of mineral industries education and research. Houston, Gulf Pub. Co., 1968. x, 451 p. 668/.007 68-9304
TN165 .W66 MRR Alc.

RESEARCH--LAW AND LEGISLATION--YUGOSLAVIA.
Yugoslav scientific research guide 1970 Belgrade, Nolit Pub. House, 1972. xii, 634 p. 507/.2/0497 73-158775
Q180.Y8 Y83 MRR Alc.

RESEARCH--SOCIETIES, ETC.--DIRECTORIES.
American University, Washington, D.C. Bureau of Social Science Research. Directory of organizations in opinion, and related research outside the United States. Washington, c1956. 1 v. (various pagings) 57-17609
HM263 .A77 MRR Alc.

RESEARCH--AFRICA, SOUTH--DIRECTORIES.
Directory of scientific research organizations in South Africa. 1971- Pretoria, South African Council for Scientific and Industrial Research. 507/.2068 72-621812
Q180.A55 D53 MRR Alc Latest edition

RESEARCH--CHINA.
Surveys and Research Corporation, Washington, D.C. Directory of selected scientific institutions in mainland China. Stanford, Calif., Published for the National Science Foundation by the Hoover Institution Press [c1970] xxii, 469 p. [$19.50] 502/.4/51 76-138410
Q72 .S9 MRR Alc.

RESEARCH--CHINA--DIRECTORIES.
United States. Library of Congress. Science and Technology Division. Mainland China organizations of higher learning in science and technology and their publications. Washington, 1961. vi, 104 p. 61-60070
Z663.41 .M2 MRR Alc.

RESEARCH--EUROPE--DIRECTORIES.
European research index; 3d ed. [St. Peter Port, Guernsey] Francis Hodgson [1973] 2 v. (2293 p.) 507/.204 70-190255
Q180.E9 E9 1973 MRR Alc.

RESEARCH--EUROPE, EASTERN.
National Academy of Sciences, Washington, D.C. Office of the Foreign Secretary. The Eastern European academies of sciences; Washington, National Academy of Sciences-National Research Council, 1963. 148 p. 067.058 63-60058
AS98 .N3 MRR Alc.

RESEARCH--EUROPE, EASTERN--DIRECTORIES.
Little (Arthur D.) inc. Directory of selected research institutes in Eastern Europe; New York, Columbia University Press, 1967. x, 445 p. 507.204 66-20496
Q180.E9 L5 MRR Alc.

RESEARCH--GERMANY.
Ueberreiter, Kurt, A statistical postwar survey on the natural sciences and German universities. [Washington] Library of Congress, European Affairs Division [1950] 31 p. 507.2 50-61523
Z663.26 .S7 MRR Alc.

United States. Library of Congress. European Affairs Division. The natural sciences in Western Germany; [Washington, 1951] 127 p. 507.2 51-60019
Z663.26 .N3 1951 MRR Alc.

United States. Library of Congress. European Affairs Division. Physics and chemical sciences in Western Germany; Washington, 1954. 123 p. 507.2 54-60012
Z663.26 .N3 1954 MRR Alc.

Vademecum deutscher Lehr- und Forschungsstätten. [1.]- Ausg.; 1853- Essen [etc.] Stifterverband für die Deutsche Wissenschaft [etc.] 58-26815
AS178 .V35 Sci RR Latest edition / MRR Alc Latest edition

RESEARCH--GREAT BRITAIN--DIRECTORIES.
Industrial research in Britain. 7th ed. [St. Peter Port, Guernsey] F. Hodgson [1972] 889 p. 607/.2/42 73-190253
T177.G7 I52 1972 MRR Alc.

RESEARCH--JAPAN--DIRECTORIES.
Japan. Mombushō. Nihon Yunesuko Kokunai Iinkai. Directory of researchers and research institutes on Oriental studies in Japan. [Tokyo] Japanese National Commission for UNESCO [1957] 50 p. 068.52 61-32041
AS548 .A543 MRR Alc.

RESEARCH--MARYLAND--DIRECTORIES.
Directory [of] scientific resources in the Washington, D.C. area. 1961/62- Washington. 61-19684
Q180.U5 D5 MRR Alc Latest edition / Sci RR Latest edition

RESEARCH--POLAND.
Polish research guide. 1964- Warszawa, Panstwowe Wydawn. Naukowe. 64-2698
AS258 .P6 MRR Alc Latest edition

RESEARCH--POLAND--DIRECTORIES.
Wepsiec, Jan, Polish institutions of higher learning. New York, Polish Institute of Arts and Sciences in America, 1959. 110 p. 063.8 59-37794
AS258 .W4 MRR Alc.

RESEARCH--RUSSIA--DIRECTORIES.
United States. Library of Congress. Aerospace Technology Division. Scientific institutes and laboratories in Moscow. [Washington] 1963. ix, 133 p. 64-60333
Z663.23 .S35 MRR Alc.

United States. Library of Congress. Aerospace Technology Division. Scientific research institutes of the USSR. [Washington] 63-61636 Began publication in Feb. 1960.
Z663.23 .A27 MRR Alc MRR Alc Latest edition

RESEARCH--SCANDINAVIA--DIRECTORIES.
Scandinavian Council for Applied Research. Scandinavian research guide. 2d rev. ed. Copenhagen, Nordforsk [1965] 12, 438 p. [77.00dkr] 507.2048 66-68485
Q180.S3 S3 1965 MRR Alc.

RESEARCH--UNITED STATES.
CCM Information Corporation. Environmental pollution; New York, 1971. vii, 851 p. 628.5/07/2 71-180288
TD178.5 .C2 MRR Alc.

Governmental Research Association. Directory of organizations and individuals professionally engaged in governmental research and related activities. 1935- New York [etc.] 350.6273 35-16469
JK3 .G627 MRR Alc Latest edition

RESEARCH--UNITED STATES--DIRECTORIES.
Battelle Memorial Institute, Columbus, Ohio. Dept. of Economics and Information Research. Specialized science information services in the United States; Washington, National Science Foundation, Office of Science Information Service, 1961. ix, 528 p. 505.873 61-64862
AG521 .B3 MRR Alc.

New research centers. May 1965- Detroit, Gale Research Co. 74-643580

AS25 .D52 Sci RR Full set / MRR Ref Desk Full set

Research centers directory. 1st ed.; 1960- Detroit, Gale Research Co. 60-14807
AS25 .D5 Sci RR Latest edition / MRR Ref Desk Latest edition

United States. Dept. of State. Office of External Research. University centers of foreign affairs research: a selective directory. [Washington, Dept. of State; for sale by the Supt. of Docs., U.S. Govt. Print. Off.] 1968. xvi, 139 p. 327/.025/73 68-60080
JX1293.U6 A54 MRR Alc.

United States. Library of Congress. National Referral Center. A directory of information resources in the United States: biological sciences. Washington, Library of Congress; [for sale by the Supt. of Docs., U.S. Govt. Print. Off.] 1972. iv, 577 p. [$5.00] 570/.7 72-2659

Z663.379 .D46 MRR Alc.

United States. Library of Congress. National Referral Center. A directory of information resources in the United States: physical sciences, engineering. Washington, Library of Congress; [for sale by the Supt. of Docs., U.S. Govt. Print. Off.] 1971. iv, 803 p. [$6.50] 500.2/07 78-611209
Z663.379 .D5 1971 MRR Alc.

RESEARCH--UNITED STATES-- (Cont.)
United States. Library of Congress.
National Referral Center for Science
and Technology. A directory of
information resources in the United
States: general toxicology.
Washington, Library of Congress; for
sale by the Supt. of Docs., U.S.
Govt. Print. Off.] 1969. v, 293 p.
[3.00]   615.9/007   73-602563
Z663.379 .D49 MRR Alc

United States. Library of Congress.
National Referral Center for Science
and Technology. A directory of
information resources in the United
States: water. [Washington, For sale
by the Superintendent of Documents,
U.S. Govt. Print. Off.] 1966. v, 248
p.   66-61638
Z663.379 .D55 MRR Alc

RESEARCH--VIRGINIA--DIRECTORIES.
Directory [of] scientific resources
in the Washington, D.C. area.
1961/62- Washington.   61-19684
Q180.U5 D5 MRR Ref Desk Latest
edition / Sci RR Latest edition

RESEARCH--WASHINGTON, D.C.--DIRECTORIES.
Directory [of] scientific resources
in the Washington, D.C. area.
1961/62- Washington.   61-19684
Q180.U5 D5 MRR Ref Desk Latest
edition / Sci RR Latest edition

RESEARCH--YUGOSLAVIA--DIRECTORIES.
Yugoslav scientific research
directory. 1964- Belgrad [Published
for the National Library of Medicine,
Washington, by the NOLIT Pub. House;
available from the National Technical
Information Service, etc.,
Springfield, Va.]   64-6496
Q180.Y8 Y8 Sci RR Latest edition /
MRR Alc Latest edition

Yugoslav scientific research guide
1970 Belgrade, Nolit Pub. House,
1972. xii, 634 p.   507/.2/0497 73-
159775
Q180.Y8 Y83 MRR Alc.

RESEARCH, AERONAUTICAL
see Aeronautical research

RESEARCH, INDUSTRIAL.
see also Inventions

see also Marketing research

RESEARCH, INDUSTRIAL--MANAGEMENT--
BIBLIOGRAPHY.
United States. Library of Congress.
Science and Technology Division.
Scientific personnel, a bibliography.
Washington, 1950. vii, 164 p.
016.5069   50-61484
Z663.49 .S35 MRR Alc.

RESEARCH, INDUSTRIAL--EUROPE--
DIRECTORIES.
Williams, Colin H. Guide to European
sources of technical information. 3d
ed. [Guernsey] Francis Hodgson
[1970] 309 p. [$20.00 (U.S.)]   607
77-105217
T10.65.E8 W5 1970 MRR Alc.

RESEARCH, INDUSTRIAL--GREAT BRITAIN--
DIRECTORIES.
Industrial research in Britain. 7th
ed. [St. Peter Port, Guernsey] F.
Hodgson [1972] 889 p. 607/.2/42
73-190253
T177.G7 I52 1972 MRR Alc.

RESEARCH, INDUSTRIAL--SCANDINAVIA--
DIRECTORIES.
Scandinavian Council for Applied
Research. Scandinavian research
guide. 2d rev. ed. Copenhagen,
Nordforsk [1965] 12, 438 p.
[77.00dkr]   507.2048 66-68485
Q180.S3 S3 1965 MRR Alc.

RESEARCH, INDUSTRIAL--UNITED STATES.
United States. Dept. of Agriculture.
Crops in peace and war. Washington,
U.S. Govt. Print. Off. [1951] 942 p.
630.72   agr55-9
S21 .A35 1950-1951 MRR Alc.

RESEARCH, INDUSTRIAL--UNITED STATES--
LABORATORIES.
Industrial research laboratories of
the United States. [1st]- ed.;
1920- Tempe, Ariz. [etc.] Jaques
Cattell Press [etc.]   21-26022
T176 .I65 Sci RR Latest edition /
MRR Ref Desk Latest edition

RESEARCH, MEDICAL
see Medical research

RESEARCH, MILITARY
see Military research

RESEARCH BUILDINGS
see Laboratories

RESEARCH GRANTS.
Grantsmanship: money and how to get
it. Orange, N.J., Academic Media
[1973] 27 p. [$5.00]   001.4/4 72-
13214
HG174 .G72 MRR Alc.

RESEARCH GRANTS--UNITED STATES.
Renetzky, Alvin. NASA factbook;
Orange, N.J., Academic Media [1971]
456 p.   629.4/072/073 70-165274
TL521.312 .R45 MRR Alc.

Renetzky, Alvin. NSF factbook;
Orange, N.J., Academic Media [1971]
425 p.   507/.2/073 77-165273
Q11.U84 R45 MRR Alc.

Toy, Henry, Federal dollars for
scholars [1st ed.] Washington, Nu-
Toy [1970] vii, 54 p., 292 columns.
378.3/0973 77-112985
LB2338 .T6 MRR Alc.

United States. National Institutes of
Health. Division of Research Grants.
Research grants index. 1961-
Bethesda, Md. [etc. For sale by the
Supt. of Docs., U.S. Govt. Print.
Off., Washington] 614 61-64708
RA440.6 .U47 Sci RR Latest edition
/ MRR Alc Latest edition

RESEARCH GRANTS--UNITED STATES--
DIRECTORIES.
Annual register of grant support.
1969- Orange, N.J. [etc.] Academic
Media. 001.4/4 69-18307
AS911 .A267 Sci RR Latest edition
/ MRR Ref Desk Latest edition

Foundation Research Service.
Foundation research service.
[Washington, Lawson & Williams
Associates, 1972- 4 v. (loose-leaf)
507/.2073 72-184024
Q180.U5 F68 MRR Alc.

Wilson, Paul T., Money and
information for mental health;
Washington, American Psychiatric
Association [1971] xvi, 150 p.
362.2/072/073 72-152415
RA790.6 .W5 MRR Alc.

RESEARCH LIBRARIES--CANADA.
Downs, Robert Bingham, Resources of
Canadian academic and research
libraries Ottawa, Association of
Universities and Colleges of Canada,
1967. xi, 301 p. [5.00]
026/.000971 70-359019
Z735.A1 D6 MRR Alc.

RESOURCE MANAGEMENT
see Conservation of natural resources

RESOURCES, MARINE
see Marine resources

RESOURCES, NATURAL
see Natural resources

REST HOMES.
see also Nursing homes

RESTAURANTS, LUNCH ROOMS, ETC.
see also Hotels, taverns, etc.

RESTAURANTS, LUNCH ROOMS, ETC.--FRANCE--
DIRECTORIES.
Auto-Journal. Guide gastronomique;
[Paris] 64-36835
TX907 .A89 MRR Alc Latest edition

Guide bleu France. [Paris] Hachette.
914.4/04/8305 73-643708
DC16 .F69 MRR Alc Latest edition

Guide Kléber: France. 1969-
[Neuilly-sur-Seine] 647/.9444 72-
622708
TX910.F8 G822 MRR Alc Latest
edition

RESTAURANTS, LUNCH ROOMS, ETC.--GERMANY
(FEDERAL REPUBLIC, 1949-)--DIRECTORIES.
Varta-Führer. Stuttgart, Mairs
Geographischer Verlag. 647/.944 74-
644633
TX910.G4 V3 MRR Alc Latest edition

RESTAURANTS, LUNCH ROOMS, ETC.--GREAT
BRITAIN.
Hotels and restaurants in the British
Isles. 1951- London, British Travel
and Holidays Association. 647.9442
52-21171
TX910.G7 H64 MRR Alc Latest
edition

RESTAURANTS, LUNCH ROOMS, ETC.--GREAT
BRITAIN--DIRECTORIES.
Automobile Association. AA guide to
hotels & restaurants in Great Britain
and Ireland. [Basingstoke, Eng.;
Distributed in the U.S.A. by Harper &
Row, New York, 1974] 671, 48 p.
[£1.95 ($7.95 U.S.)]   647/.9442 74-
167286
TX910.G7 A8 1974 MRR Alc.

The Good food guide. London,
Cassell. 59-30230
Began publication with 1951/52
issue.
TX910.G7 G6 MRR Alc Latest edition

RESTAURANTS, LUNCH ROOMS, ETC.--
HOUSTON, TEX.
Coates, Felicia. Texas monthly's
Guide to Houston Austin, Texas
monthly 1973] 382 p. [$2.95]
917.64/1411/046 73-179186
F394.H8 C63 MRR Alc.

RESTAURANTS, LUNCH ROOMS, ETC.--IRELAND--
DIRECTORIES.
Automobile Association. AA guide to
hotels & restaurants in Great Britain
and Ireland. [Basingstoke, Eng.:
Distributed in the U.S.A. by Harper &
Row, New York, 1974] 671, 48 p.
[£1.95 ($7.95 U.S.)]   647/.9442 74-
167286
TX910.G7 A8 1974 MRR Alc.

RESTAURANTS, LUNCH ROOMS, ETC.--ITALY--
DIRECTORIES.
Touring club italiano. Vademecum del
turista. [Milano] 57-48011
DG413 .T6 MRR Alc Latest edition

RESTAURANTS, LUNCH ROOMS, ETC.--
NETHERLANDS--DIRECTORIES.
Lasschuit's officieel adresboek:
Bilthoven, J. G. Lasschuit. 67-37932

Began publication with vol. for
1908.
TX910.N4 L3 MRR Alc Latest edition

RESTAURANTS, LUNCH ROOMS, ETC.--NEW
YORK (CITY)
Simon, Kate. New York places &
pleasures; 4th ed. rev. New York,
Harper & Row [1971] xxiii, 417 p.
[$7.95]   917.47/1/044 70-138761
F128.18 .S5 1971 MRR Alc.

RESTAURANTS, LUNCH ROOMS, ETC.--
PHILADELPHIA.
Hadley Group. Inside Philadelphia;
Philadelphia [1973] 323 p. [$2.95]
917.48/11/044 73-82969
F158.18 .H32 1973a MRR Alc.

RESTAURANTS, LUNCH ROOMS, ETC.--UNITED
STATES--DIRECTORIES.
Chain store guide; [New York,
Business Guides] 647.9505873 62-
4170
TX907 .C54 MRR Alc Latest edition

Who's who in food service in America.
Chicago, National Restaurant
Association. 72-626563
TX907 .N35 MRR Alc Latest edition

RESTAURANTS, LUNCH ROOMS, ETC.--WEST--
DIRECTORIES.
TravelVision. Humble vacation guide
U.S.A.; favorite West Central
recreation regions. Houston, Tex.,
Humble Travel Club [1970] 224 p.
647/.9478 77-17741
TX907 .T8526 1970 MRR Alc.

RÉSUMÉS (EMPLOYMENT)
Angel, Juvenal Londoño, Looking for
employment in foreign countries
reference handbook, 6th ed., rev.
and enl. New York, World Trade
Academy Press; distributed by Simon &
Schuster [1972] 727 p. [$25.00]
331.7/02 70-111351
HF5381 .A7847 1972 MRR Alc.

Angel, Juvenal Londoño, Specialized
resumes for executives and
professionals, [New York] Regents
Pub. Co. [1967] 160 p. 331.1/15
66-25832
HF5383 .A57 MRR Alc.

Angel, Juvenal Londoño, Why and how
to prepare an effective job resume;
5th ed., rev. and enl. New York,
World Trade Academy Press,
distributed by Simon & Schuster
[1972] 506 p. 331.1/28 70-179618

HF5383 .A6 1972 MRR Ref Desk.

Bjegojeisen, Jacob Israel, Job
resumes; New York, Grosset &
Dunlap [1969] 96 p. [1.95]
331.1/15 70-75335
HF5383 .B46 MRR Alc.

Brennan, Lawrence David, Résumés
for better jobs New York, Simon and
Schuster [1973] 187 p. [$2.95]
331.1/28 73-174889
HF5383 .B68 MRR Alc.

Jameson, Robert, The professional
job changing system; [3d ed.
Verona, N.J., Performance Dynamics,
1974] 280 p. 650/.14 73-92380
HF5383 .J28 1974 MRR Alc.

RETAIL ADVERTISING
see Advertising

RETAIL TRADE.
see also Shopping

RETAIL TRADE--ACCOUNTING.
Portfolio of accounting systems for
small and medium-sized businesses.
Englewood Cliffs, N.J., Prentice-Hall
[1968] 2 v. (1392 p.) [$35.00]
657.8/3 68-18738
HF5635 .P86 MRR Alc.

RETAIL TRADE--DIRECTORIES.
Stores of the world. London, Newman
Books. 380.1025 66-9836
Began publication in 1961.
HF54.G7 S8 MRR Alc Latest edition

RETAIL TRADE--CANADA--DIRECTORIES.
Sheldon's retail directory of the
United States and Canada and Phelon's
resident buyers and merchandise
brokers. New York, Phelon, Sheldon &
Marsar. [$50.00] 381 74-644143
HF5429.3 .S52 MRR Alc Latest
edition

RETAIL TRADE--EUROPE.
Temple Fielding's selective shopping
guide to Europe. 1957/58- ed. New
York, Fielding Publications [etc.]
658.87058 57-9112
HF5341 .T4 MRR Alc Latest edition

RETAIL TRADE--GREAT BRITAIN--
DIRECTORIES.
Stores, shops, supermarkets retail
directory. 21st- ed.; 1967-
London, Newman Books Ltd. 381 72-
623101
HF5155 .S8 MRR Alc Latest edition

RETAIL TRADE--NEW YORK (CITY)--
DIRECTORIES.
Brener, Carol. The underground
collector; New York, Simon and
Schuster [1970] 319 p. [2.95]
745.1/025/7471 72-107269
NK1127 .B64 MRR Alc.

RETAIL TRADE--UNITED STATES.
Fairchild's financial manual of
retail stores. New York, Fairchild
Publications. 658.8705873 59-4791
HG4961 .F3 MRR Alc Latest edition

Mahoney, Tom. The great merchants;
New and enl. ed. New York, Harper &
Row [1966] ix, 374 p. 658.8700973
67-11328
HF5429 .M288 1966 MRR Alc.

United States. Bureau of the Census.
1963 census of business.
[Washington, For sale by the
Superintendent of Documents, U.S.
Govt. Print. Off., 1966] 7 v. in 17.
381.0973 a 66-7302
HF3007 .A5 1963 MRR Alc.

RETAIL TRADE--UNITED STATES--
DIRECTORIES.
Consumers digest guide to discount
buying, [Chicago, Consumers Digest,
inc.] [$4.95] 640.73 74-647121
HF5429.3 .C66 MRR Ref Desk Latest
edition

S.O.S. directory of factory outlet
stores in the entire United States
and Canada. [Dearborn, Mich., S.O.S.
Directory Inc.] [$4.95] 381 74-
75652
HF5421 .S2 MRR Alc Latest edition

The Salesman's guide nationwide
directory of major mass market
merchandisers (exclusive of New York
metropolitan area) New York,
Salesman's Guide, inc. 380.1/025/73
73-640394
HF5468 .S27 MRR Alc Latest edition

Sheldon's retail directory of the
United States and Canada and Phelon's
resident buyers and merchandise
brokers. New York, Phelon, Sheldon &
Marsar. [$50.00] 381 74-644143
HF5429.3 .S52 MRR Alc Latest
edition

RETAIL TRADE--UNITED STATES--STATISTICS.
Robert Morris Associates. Annual
statement studies. [Philadelphia]
338/.0973 72-626355
HF5681.B2 R6 MRR Alc Latest
edition

United States. Bureau of the Census.
1967 census of business.
[Washington; For sale by the Supt. of
Docs., U.S. Govt. Print. Off., 1970-
71] 5 v. in 9 [$8.50 (v. 1) varies]
338/.0973 72-608032
HF3007 .U55 1970 MRR Alc.

RETAIL TRADING AREAS
see Market surveys

RETIREMENT.
Active Retirement Executives
Association. Retirement facilities
register, Studio City, Calif., 1965]
331 p. 66-587
HQ1062 .A35 MRR Alc.

Buckley, Joseph C. The retirement
handbook; 5th ed. New York, Barnes
& Noble Books [1974, c1973] xv, 363
p. [$2.50 ($2.75 Can)] 301.43/5
73-10767
HQ1064.U5 B8 1974 MRR Alc.

RETIREMENT, PLACES OF--UNITED STATES.
Where to retire on a small income.
[1st]- ed.; 1950- Greenlawn, N.Y.,
Harian Publications; distributed by
Grosset & Dunlap [etc., New York]
917.3 60-146
E169 .W53 MRR Alc Latest edition

RETIREMENT, PLACES OF--UNITED STATES--
DIRECTORIES.
Active Retirement Executives
Association. Retirement facilities
register, Studio City, Calif., 1965]
331 p. 66-597
HQ1062 .A35 MRR Alc.

Active Retirement Executives
Association. Retirement facilities
register. Los Angeles, 1964?] 224
p. 362.6105873 64-4960
HD7287.9 .A26 MRR Alc.

Holter, Paul. Guide to retirement
living. Chicago, Rand McNally [1973]
xviii, 174 p. [$3.95]
362.6/15/02573 73-173331
HQ1063 .H64 1973 MRR Alc.

Musson, Noverre. The national
directory of retirement residences:
best places to live when you retire.
Rev. ed. New York, F. Fell [1973]
214 p. 362.6/15/02573 72-89943
HV1465 .M87 1973 MRR Alc.

RETRAINING, OCCUPATIONAL--UNITED STATES.
United States. President. Manpower
report of the President, and a Report
on manpower requirements, resources,
utilization, and training, by the
U.S. Dept. of Labor. 1963-
[Washington, For sale by the
Superintendent of Documents, U.S.
Govt. Print. Off.] l 63-61591
HD5723 .A43 MRR Alc Latest edition

RETREATS--DIRECTORIES.
Deemer, Philip. Ecumenical directory
of retreat and conference centers.
Boston, Jarrow Press [1974- v.
269/.6/02573 74-76974
BV1652 .D43 MRR Alc.

RÉUNION--DESCRIPTION AND TRAVEL--
GAZETTEERS.
United States. Office of Geography.
Madagascar, Réunion, and the Comoro
Islands; official standard names
approved by the United States Board
on Geographic Names. Washington,
1955. 498 p. 55-61720
DT469.M24 U5 MRR Alc.

RÉUNION--GOVERNMENT PUBLICATIONS--
BIBLIOGRAPHY.
United States. Library of Congress.
African Section. Madagascar and
adjacent islands; Washington,
General Reference and Bibliography
Division, Reference Department,
Library of Congress;[for sale by the
Superintendent of Documents, U.S.
Govt. Print. Off.] 1965. xiii, 58 p.
65-61703
Z663.285 .M3 MRR Alc.

REVENUE.
see also Taxation

REVENUE--UNITED STATES.
Firestone, John Mitchell. Federal
receipts and expenditures during
business cycles, 1879-1958.
Princeton [N.J.] Princeton University
Press, 1960. xvi, 176 p. 336.73
60-8391
HJ2051 .F48 MRR Alc.

REVERE, PAUL, 1735-1818. BOSTON
MASSACRE.
Revere, Paul, The Boston Massacre,
1770, [Washington] Library of
Congress [1970] col. plate (in
portfolio) 769/.924 78-606227
Z663.34 .R45 MRR Alc.

REVIVAL OF LETTERS
see Renaissance

REVIVALS--UNITED STATES.
McLoughlin, William Gerald. Modern
revivalism; New York, Ronald Press
Co. [1959] 551 p. 269.20973 58-
12959
BV3773 .M3 MRR Alc.

REVOLUTIONISTS.
Hyams, Edward S. A dictionary of
modern revolution New York,
Taplinger Pub. Co. [1973] 322 p.
[$8.95] 335.43/03 73-6175
HX17 .H9 1973 MRR Alc.

REVOLUTIONS--ADDRESSES, ESSAYS,
LECTURES.
Revolutionary quotations from the
thoughts of Uncle Sam. Cicero, Ill.,
Johnny Appleseed Patriotic
Publications [1969] xi, 113 p.
321/.09 74-5070
JC491 .R49 MRR Ref Desk.

REVOLUTIONS--DICTIONARIES.
Hyams, Edward S. A dictionary of
modern revolution, New York,
Taplinger Pub. Co. [1973] 322 p.
[$9.95] 335.43/03 73-6175
HX17 .H9 1973 MRR Alc.

REVOLUTIONS--EUROPE--HISTORY--SOURCES.
Postgate, Raymond William, ed.
Revolution from 1789 to 1906:
Gloucester, Mass., P. Smith, 1969.
xvi, 398 p. 940.2/7 70-10678
D351 .P86 1969 MRR Alc.

REVOLUTIONS--UNITED STATES--ADDRESSES,
ESSAYS, LECTURES.
Revolutionary quotations from the
thoughts of Uncle Sam. Cicero, Ill.,
Johnny Appleseed Patriotic
Publications [1969] xi, 113 p.
321/.09 74-5070
JC491 .R49 MRR Ref Desk.

REVOLVERS.
Smith, Walter Harold Black. Book of
pistols and revolvers. [7th ed.]
Harrisburg, Pa.; Stackpole Books
[1968] xvi, 816 p. 623.4/43 68-
18959
TS537 .S54 1968 MRR Alc.

REVOLVERS, AMERICAN.
Gluckman, Arcadi. United States
martial pistols and revolvers.
Harrisburg, Pa.; Stackpole Co., 1956.
249, xxxvii, [1] p. 623.443 56-
3215
UD413 .G5 1956 MRR Alc.

REWARDS (PRIZES, ETC.)
Guide des prix littéraires: [1.]-
ed.; 1952- Paris, Cercle de la
librairie. a 58-6283
PN171.P75 G8 MRR Alc Latest
edition

REWARDS (PRIZES, ETC.)--CANADA.
Special libraries Association.
Science-Technology Division.
Handbook of scientific and technical
awards in the United States and
Canada, 1900-1952. New York, Special
Libraries Association [1956] xxiv,
491 p. 507.9 56-7004
Q141 .S63 MRR Alc.

Wasserman, Paul. Awards, honors, and
prizes: 2d ed. Detroit, Gale
Research Co. 1972. vii, 579 p.
001.4/4 72-283
AS8 .W38 1972 MRR Ref Desk.

REWARDS (PRIZES, ETC.)--GREAT BRITAIN.
Millard, Patricia. Awards and
prizes. Havant, K. Mason, 1970. 249
p. [5/-/-] 001.4/4 70-498024
AS118 .M54 MRR Alc.

REWARDS (PRIZES, ETC.)--UNITED STATES.
Literary and library prizes. 1935-
New York, R. R. Bowker Co. 807.9 59-
11370
PN171.P75 L5 MRR Ref Desk Latest
edition

Notable names in American history;
3d ed. of White's conspectus of
American biography. [Clifton, N.J.]
J. T. White, 1973. 725 p. 920/.073
73-6885
E176 .N89 1973 MRR Biog.

Special libraries Association.
Science-Technology Division.
Handbook of scientific and technical
awards in the United States and
Canada, 1900-1952. New York, Special
Libraries Association [1956] xxiv,
491 p. 507.9 56-7004
Q141 .S63 MRR Alc.

Wasserman, Paul. Awards, honors, and
prizes: 2d ed. Detroit, Gale
Research Co. 1972. vii, 579 p.
001.4/4 72-283
AS8 .W38 1972 MRR Ref Desk.

REWARDS (PRIZES, ETC.)--UNITED STATES--
PERIODICALS.
Grants and awards available to
American writers. [New York, P.E.N.
American Center] [$2.00] 001.4/4
73-648098
PN171.P75 G73 MRR Alc Latest
edition

RHETORIC.
see also Figures of speech

RHETORIC, ANCIENT.
Aristoteles. Aristotle, London, W.
Heinemann; New York, G. P. Putnam's
sons, 1926. xlvii, 491, [1] p. 27-
2022
PA3612 .A8R4 1926 MRR Alc.

Cicero, Marcus Tullius. Cicero, De
oratore. Cambridge, Mass., Harvard
university press; London, W.
Heinemann ltd., 1942. 2 v. 875.3
a 42-4498
PA6156.C6 D6 1942 MRR Alc.

RHINELAND-PALATINATE--COMMERCE--
DIRECTORIES.
Firmenhandbuch Rheinland-Pfalz und
Saarland. Hannover, Industrie- und
Handelsverlag. 74-615207
HF3569.R55 A45 MRR Alc Latest
edition

RHODE ISLAND.
Federal writers' project. Rhode
Island. Rhode Island, a guide to the
smallest state. Boston, Houghton
Mifflin company, 1937. xxvi, 500 p.
917.45 37-28463
F79 .F38 MRR Ref Desk.

RHODE ISLAND--BIOGRAPHY.
Mohr, Ralph S. Governors for three
hundred years, 1638-1959; Rev. ed.
[Providence] Oxford Press, c1959.
339 p. 923.273 60-1466
JK3251 .M6 1959 MRR Alc.

Rhode Island. Dept. of State.
Manual, with rules and orders, for
the use of the General Assembly of
the state of Rhode Island. 1867/68-
Providence. 328.7455 09-34249
JK3230 .A25 MRR Alc Latest edition

RHODE ISLAND--DESCRIPTION AND TRAVEL--
GUIDE-BOOKS.
Federal writers' project. Rhode
Island. Rhode Island, a guide to the
smallest state. Boston, Houghton
Mifflin company, 1937. xxvi, 500 p.
917.45 37-28463
F79 .F38 MRR Ref Desk.

RHODE ISLAND--GOVERNORS.
Mohr, Ralph S. Governors for three
hundred years, 1638-1959; Rev. ed.
[Providence] Oxford Press, c1959.
339 p. 923.273 60-1466
JK3251 .M6 1959 MRR Alc.

RHODE ISLAND--HISTORY.
Mohr, Ralph S. Governors for three
hundred years, 1638-1959; Rev. ed.
[Providence] Oxford Press, c1959.
339 p. 923.273 60-1466
JK3251 .M6 1959 MRR Alc.

RHODE ISLAND--HISTORY--CHRONOLOGY.
Rhode Island. Dept. of State.
Manual, with rules and orders, for
the use of the General Assembly of
the state of Rhode Island. 1867/68-
Providence. 328.7455 09-34249
JK3230 .A25 MRR Alc Latest edition

RHODE ISLAND--INDUSTRIES--DIRECTORIES.
Rhode Island directory of
manufacturers and list of commercial
establishments. Providence.
670.58745 59-62618
HC107 .R4A158 Sci RR Latest
edition / MRR Alc Latest edition

RHODE ISLAND--MANUFACTURES--DIRECTORIES.
Directory of New England
manufacturers. Boston, Mass., G. D.
Hall, inc. 338.40874 36-5085
HD9723 .D45 Sci RR Latest edition
/ MRR Alc Latest edition

Rhode Island directory of
manufacturers and list of commercial
establishments. Providence.
670.58745 59-62618
HC107 .R4A158 Sci RR Latest
edition / MRR Alc Latest edition

RHODE ISLAND--POLITICS AND GOVERNMENT.
Rhode Island. Dept. of State.
Manual, with rules and orders, for
the use of the General Assembly of
the state of Rhode Island. 1867/68-
Providence. 328.7455 09-34249
JK3230 .A25 MRR Alc Latest edition

RHODE ISLAND--REGISTERS.
Rhode Island. Dept. of State.
Manual, with rules and orders, for
the use of the General Assembly of
the state of Rhode Island. 1867/68-
Providence. 328.7455 09-34249
JK3230 .A25 MRR Alc Latest edition

RHODE ISLAND. GENERAL ASSEMBLY--RULES
AND PRACTICE.
Rhode Island. Dept. of State.
Manual, with rules and orders, for
the use of the General Assembly of
the state of Rhode Island. 1867/68-
Providence. 328.7455 09-34249
JK3230 .A25 MRR Alc Latest edition

RHODESIA--DIRECTORIES.
The Rhodesia-Zambia-Malawi directory
(including Botswana and Mocambique).
Bulawayo, Publications (Central
Africa) [etc.] 916.89/0025 38-1460
"First published in 1910."
DT947 .R5 MRR Alc Latest edition

RHODESIA, SOUTHERN--GOVERNMENT
PUBLICATIONS--BIBLIOGRAPHY.
United States. Library of Congress.
African Section. The Rhodesias and
Nyasaland; Washington, General
Reference and Bibliography Division,
Reference Dept., Library of Congress;
[for sale by the Superintendent of
Documents, U.S. Govt. Print. Off.]
1965. xv, 285 p. 65-60089
Z663.285 .R5 MRR Alc.

Willson, Francis Michael Glenn.
Catalogue of the parliamentary papers
of Southern Rhodesia, 1899-1953,
Salisbury, Dept. of Govt., University
College of Rhodesia and Nyasaland,
1965. xxx, 484 p. 66-51416
JQ2921 .A23 no. 2 MRR Alc.

RHODESIA, SOUTHERN--INDUSTRIES--
DIRECTORIES.
The Business blue-book's national
trade index of South Africa &
Rhodesia. [Cape Town], National Pub.
Co.] 380.1/45/0002568 72-627238
HC517.S7 N22 MRR Alc Latest
edition

RHODESIA, SOUTHERN--MANUFACTURES--
DIRECTORIES.
The A R N I register of
manufacturers. 1959- Salisbury,
Association of Rhodesian Industries.
[etc.] 66-47368
HD9737.R5 A2 MRR Alc Latest
edition

RHODESIA AND NYASALAND--GOVERNMENT
PUBLICATIONS--BIBLIOGRAPHY.
United States. Library of Congress.
African Section. The Rhodesias and
Nyasaland; Washington, General
Reference and Bibliography Division,
Reference Dept., Library of Congress;
[for sale by the Superintendent of
Documents, U.S. Govt. Print. Off.]
1965. xv, 285 p. 65-60089
Z663.285 .R5 MRR Alc.

RHODESIA AND NYASALAND--MANUFACTURES--
DIRECTORIES.
The A R N I register of
manufacturers. 1959- Salisbury,
Association of Rhodesian Industries.
[etc.] 66-47368
HD9737.R5 A2 MRR Alc Latest
edition

RICHES
see Wealth

RICHMOND, ENG. (SURREY)--DIRECTORIES.
Kelly's directory of Richmond, Kew,
Petersham and Ham. Kingston upon
Thames. [-/15/-] 914.22/1 73-
642687
DA690.R5 K44 MRR Alc Latest
edition

RICKETTSIAE.
see also Bacteria

RIDDLES.
Taylor, Archer, English riddles from
oral tradition. Berkeley, University
of California Press, 1951. xxxi, 959
p. 398.6 51-2752
PN6371 .T3 MRR Alc.

Withers, Carl, comp. Riddles of many
lands. New York, Abelard-Schuman
[1956] 160 p. 398.6 56-5101
PN6371 .W59 MRR Alc.

RIDGELY, CHARLES GOODWIN, 1784-1848--
MANUSCRIPTS.
United States. Library of Congress.
Manuscript Division. Charles Goodwin
Ridgely, Francis Asbury Roe, John
Grimes Walker: a register of their
papers in the Library of Congress.
Washington, Library of Congress,
1970. 4, 5, 5 l. 359.2/0922 76-
607856
Z663.34 .R5 MRR Alc.

RIDICULOUS, THE
see Wit and humor

RIDING
see Horsemanship

RIFLES.
Gluckman, Arcadi, Identifying old
U.S. muskets, rifles & carbines.
Harrisburg, Pa., Stackpole Books
[1965] 487 p. 623.4425 65-20534
UD383 .G5 1965 MRR Alc.

Smith, Walter Harold Black, The book
of rifles [4th ed.] Harrisburg,
Pa., Stackpole [1972] xi, 689 p.
[$12.50] 683/.42 72-172068
TS535 .S548 1972 MRR Alc.

RIGHT AND LEFT (POLITICAL SCIENCE)
Chilcote, Ronald H. Revolution and
structural change in Latin America;
Stanford, Calif., Hoover Institution
on War, Revolution and Peace,
Stanford University, 1970. 2 v.
016.3091/8/03 68-28100
Z1601 .C496 MRR Alc.

First national directory of
"rightist" groups, publications, and
some individuals in the United States
and some foreign countries. 4th ed.
Sausalito, Calif., Distributed by the
Noontide Press, 1962. 36 p. 62-
2510
E743.5 .F48 1962 MRR Ref Desk.

Forster, Arnold. Danger on the
Right, New York, Random House [1964]
xviii, 294 p. 320 64-7549
E743 .F68 MRR Alc.

Jacobs, Paul, The new radicals; New
York, Random House [1966] 333 p.
320.973 66-18328
E839.5 .J3 MRR Alc.

Rogger, Hans, ed. The European
right; Berkeley, University of
California Press, 1965. vi, 589 p.
320.52094 65-18562
JN12 .R6 MRR Alc.

Solara, Ferdinand V. Key influences
in the American right, Denver,
Polifax Press [1972] xv, 68 p.
[$4.95] 320.5/12/0973 72-189989
E839.5 .S64 1972 MRR Ref Desk.

Teodori, Massimo, comp. The new
left; Indianapolis, Bobbs-Merrill
[1969] xiv, 501 p. [9.95]
301.15/3/0973 70-81291
HN59 .T46 MRR Alc.

Thayer, George, The farther shores
of politics; New York, Simon and
Schuster [1967] 610 p. 320.9/73
67-16728
JK2261 .T47 1967 MRR Alc.

RIGHT AND LEFT (POLITICAL SCIENCE)--
PERIODICALS--BIBLIOGRAPHY.
Muller, Robert H. From radical left
to extreme right; 2d ed. rev. and
enl. Ann Arbor, Campus Publishers
[c1970- v. 79-126558
Z7165.U5 M82 MRR Ref Desk.

RIGHTS, CIVIL
see Civil rights

RIGHTS OF WOMEN
see Woman--Rights of women

RIO DE JANEIRO METROPOLITAN AREA,
BRAZIL--COMMERCE--DIRECTORIES--
PERIODICALS.
AIC; anuario da indústria e
comércio: Centro. [Rio de Janeiro,
S. S. Moreira] 338.4/025/815 74-
645596
HC189.R4 A18 MRR Alc Latest
edition

RIO DE JANEIRO METROPOLITAN AREA,
BRAZIL--INDUSTRIES--DIRECTORIES--
PERIODICALS.
AIC; anuario da indústria e
comércio: Centro. [Rio de Janeiro,
S. S. Moreira] 338.4/025/815 74-
645596
HC189.R4 A18 MRR Alc Latest
edition

RIOTS--HISTORY.
Heaps, Willard Allison, Riots,
U.S.A., 1765-1970, Rev. ed. New
York, Seabury Press [1970] vi, 214
p. [4.95] 973 69-13444
HV6477 .H53 1970 MRR Alc.

RIOTS--UNITED STATES.
Waskow, Arthur I. From race riot to
sit-in, 1919 and the 1960s; [1st
ed.] Garden City, N.Y., Doubleday,
1966. xviii, 380 p. 66-11737
E185.61 .W24 MRR Alc.

RIOTS--UNITED STATES--BIBLIOGRAPHY.
United States. National Clearinghouse
for Mental Health Information.
Bibliography on the urban crisis;
Chevy Chase, Md., National Institute
of Mental Health [1968] iv, 158 p.
016.3091/73 77-600665
Z7164.S66 U57 MRR Alc.

RIOTS--UNITED STATES--HISTORY.
Platt, Anthony M., comp. The
politics of riot commissions, 1917-
1970: New York, Macmillan [1971] x,
534 p. 364.14/3 79-150069
HV6477 .P5 MRR Alc.

RIOTS--UNITED STATES--HISTORY--JUVENILE
LITERATURE.
Heaps, Willard Allison, Riots,
U.S.A., 1765-1970, Rev. ed. New
York, Seabury Press [1970] vi, 214
p. [4.95] 973 69-13444
HV6477 .H53 1970 MRR Alc.

RISK (INSURANCE)--UNITED STATES--
DIRECTORIES.
Who's who in risk management.
Englewood, N.J. [etc.] Underwriter
Printing and Pub. Co. 368/.81/002573
70-648918
HG8059.B8 W5 MRR Biog Latest
edition

RITES AND CEREMONIES.
see also Funeral rites and ceremonies

RITES AND CEREMONIES--GREAT BRITAIN.
Milton, Roger. The English
ceremonial book; Newton Abbot [Eng.]
David & Charles [1972] 216 p.
[£3.50] 391/.022/0942 72-185055
CR492 .M5 MRR Alc.

RITUAL.
see also Liturgics

RIVER BOATS--UNITED STATES.
Donovan, Frank Robert. River boats
of America. New York, Crowell [1966]
298 p. 386.22 66-25432
VM461 .D6 MRR Alc.

RIVER STEAMERS--MISSISSIPPI RIVER.
Inland river record; 1945-
[Sewickley, Pa.] 386.224 45-7239
VM23 .I5 MRR Alc Latest edition

RIVERS--DICTIONARIES.
Gresswell, R. Kay, ed. Standard
encyclopedia of the world's rivers
and lakes; 1st ed. London,
Weidenfeld & Nicolson, 1965 [i.e.
1966] 384 p. [50/-] 910.091693
66-70378
GB1203 .G73 1966a MRR Alc.

ROAD TRAFFIC
see Traffic engineering

ROAD TRANSPORTATION
see Transportation, Automotive

ROADS--UNITED STATES.
American Association of State Highway
Officials. United States numbered
highways. Washington [1955- 1 v.
(loose-leaf) 388.1 55-3274
HE355 .A616 MRR Alc.

ROADS--UNITED STATES--MAPS--
BIBLIOGRAPHY.
United States. Library of Congress.
Map Division. Maps showing
explorers' routes, trails & early
roads in the United States;
Washington, For sale by the
Superintendent of Documents, U.S.
Govt. Print. Off., 1962. vi, 137 p.
62-60066
Z663.35 .M26 MRR Alc.

ROBINSON, EDWIN ARLINGTON, 1869-1935.
United States. Library of Congress.
Edwin Arlington Robinson: a
reappraisal, Washington [For sale by
the Superintendent of Documents, U.S.
Govt. Print. Off.] 1963. 39 p. 63-
60045
Z663 .R6 MRR Alc.

ROBOTS
see Automation

ROCHESTER, ENG.--DIRECTORIES.
Kelly's directory of Medway towns.
Kingston upon Thames. [-/27/6]
914.22/3/0025 73-642686
DA670.M4 K45 MRR Alc Latest
edition

ROCK CLIMBING.
see also Mountaineering

ROCK GARDENS.
Edwards, Alexander. Rock gardens;
New York, Abelard-Schuman [1958] 255
p. 635.9672 58-3848
SB421 .E3 1958 MRR Alc.

ROCK MUSIC--DICTIONARIES.
Roxon, Lillian. Rock encyclopedia.
New York, Grosset & Dunlap [1971]
611 p. [$3.95] 784 76-26545
ML102.P66 R7 1971 MRR Alc.

ROCK MUSIC--ENGLAND--HISTORY AND
CRITICISM.
Jahn, Mike. Rock; [New York]
Quadrangle [c1973] x, 326 p.
[$9.95] 784 72-90449
ML3561.R62 J25 MRR Alc.

ROCK MUSIC--UNITED STATES--HISTORY AND
CRITICISM.
Jahn, Mike. Rock; [New York]
Quadrangle [c1973] x, 326 p.
[$9.95] 784 72-90449
ML3561.R62 J25 MRR Alc.

ROCKET FLIGHT
see Space flight

ROCKETRY.
see also Space vehicles

Ley, Willy. Rockets, missiles, and
men in space. [Newly rev. and
expanded ed.] New York, Viking Press
[1968] xvii, 557 p. 629.4 67-
20676
TL782 .L43 1968 MRR Alc.

Ordway, Frederick Ira. International
missile and spacecraft guide New
York, McGraw-Hill, 1960. 1 v.
(various pagings) 623.4513 59-
14463
UG630 .C67 MRR Alc.

ROCKETRY--DICTIONARIES--RUSSIAN.
Konarski, Michael M. Russian-English
dictionary of modern terms in
aeronautics and rocketry. Oxford,
New York, Pergamon Press, 1962. xi,
515 p. 629.1303 62-16918
TL509 .K62 1962a MRR Alc.

United States. Library of Congress.
Reference Dept. Russian-English
glossary of guided missile, rocket,
and satellite terms, Washington,
1958. vi, 352 p. 629.1333803
629.1435303* 58-60055
Z663.2 .R83 MRR Alc.

ROCKETRY--HISTORY.
Von Braun, Wernher. History of
rocketry & space travel Rev. ed.
New York, Crowell [1969] xi, 276 p.
[17.50] 629.4/09 76-94786
TK781 .V6 1969 MRR Alc.

ROCKETS (AERONAUTICS)
Bergaust, Erik, ed. The new
illustrated space encyclopedia.
[Rev. ed.] New York, Putnam [1970]
190 p. 629.4/03 68-26072
TL788 .B39 1970 MRR Alc.

Bowman, Norman John. The handbook of
rockets and guided missiles. 2d ed.
Newtown Square, Pa., Perastadion
Press, 1963. 1008 p. 629.13338 63-
3212
TL782 .B6 1963 MRR Alc.

ROCKETS (AERONAUTICS)--DICTIONARIES.
Herrick, John W., ed. Rocket
encyclopedia, Los Angeles, Aero
Publishers [1959] 607 p.
629.134354 59-8488
TL780.5 .H4 MRR Alc.

ROCKETS (AERONAUTICS)--YEARBOOKS.
Jane's all the world's aircraft.
[1st]- issue; 1909- London [etc.]
S. Low, Marston & Co. 629.133058 10-
8268
TL501 .J3 MRR Alc Latest edition /
Sci RR Latest edition

ROCKETS (ORDNANCE)--YEARBOOKS.
Jane's weapon systems. 1st- ed.;
1969/70- New York, McGraw-Hill.
623.4/05 79-12909
U104 .J35 Sci RR Latest edition /
MRR Alc Latest edition

ROCKS.
see also Geology

ROCKS--AGE
see Geology, Stratigraphic

ROCKY MOUNTAIN REGION--DESCRIPTION AND
TRAVEL--GUIDE-BOOKS.
Fodor, Eugene. Rockies and plains:
2d, rev. ed. Litchfield, Conn.]
Fodor's Modern Guides; distributor:
D. McKay Co., New York [1967] 432 p.
917.8/04/3 67-20083
F721 .F6 1967 MRR Alc.

ROE, FRANCIS ASBURY, 1823-1901--
MANUSCRIPTS.
United States. Library of Congress.
Manuscript Division. Charles Goodwin
Ridgely, Francis Asbury Roe, John
Grimes Walker: a register of their
papers in the Library of Congress.
Washington, Library of Congress,
1970. 4, 5, 1. 359.2/0922 76-
607856
Z663.34 .R5 MRR Alc.

ROETHKE, THEODORE, 1908-1963--
CONCORDANCES.
Lane, Gary. A concordance to the
poems of Theodore Roethke. Metuchen,
N.J., Scarecrow Press, 1972. v, 484
p. 811/.5/4 77-188503
PS3535.O39 Z49 1972 MRR Alc.

ROGALAND, NORWAY--DIRECTORIES.
Adressebok for Rogaland fylke med
skatteligninger. Oslo, S. M. Bryde.
53-30845
DL576.R65 A7 MRR Alc Latest
edition

ROLLING-STOCK
see Locomotives

ROMAN ALPHABET
see Alphabet

ROMAN ART
see Art, Roman

ROMAN CATHOLIC CHURCH
see Catholic Church

ROMAN DE LA ROSE--CONCORDANCES.
Tatlock, John Strong Perry. A
concordance to the complete works of
Geoffrey Chaucer Washington,
Carnegie Institution of Washington,
1927. xiii, 1110 p., 1 l. 27-6088
PR1941 .T3 MRR Alc.

ROMAN EMPERORS.
Scriptores historiae augustae. The
Scriptores historiae augustae,
London, W. Heinemann; New York, G. P.
Putnam's sons, 1922-32. 3 v. 878
22-11196
PA6156.A4 1922 MRR Alc.

Suetonius Tranquillus, C. Suetonius,
Cambridge, Mass., Harvard University
Press; London, W. Heinemann, 1930-
1935. 2 v. mrr01-3
PA6156.S9 1930d MRR Alc.

ROMAN LAW--BIBLIOGRAPHY.
Rounds, Dorothy. Articles on
antiquity in Festschriften, an index;
Cambridge, Harvard University Press,
1962. 560 p. 62-7193
Z6202 .R6 MRR Alc.

ROMANCE LANGUAGES--BIBLIOGRAPHY.
Romanische Bibliographie. 1961/62-
Tubingen, M. Niemeyer Verlag. 72-
620927
Z7032 .Z45 MRR Alc Full set

Zeitschrift für romanische
Philologie. Supplementheft.
Bibliographie. 1-72/76; 1875/76-
1956/60. Tubingen [etc.] M.
Niemeyer. 74-643524
Z7032 .Z45 MRR Alc Full set

ROMANCE LANGUAGES--CONVERSATION AND
PHRASE BOOKS--POLYGLOT.
Lyall, Archibald. A guide to 25
languages of Europe. Rev. ed.
[Harrisburg, Pa.] Stackpole Co.
[1966] viii, 407 p. 413 66-20847
PB73 .L85 1966 MRR Alc.

ROMANCE LANGUAGES--DICTIONARIES--
POLYGLOT.
Bergman, Peter M. The concise
dictionary of twenty-six languages in
simultaneous translations. New York,
Polyglot Library [1968] 406 p. 413
67-14284
P361 .B4 TJ Rm.

Orne, Jerrold. The language of the
foreign book trade: 2d ed. Chicago,
American Library Association, 1962.
213 p. 010.3 61-12881
Z1006 .O7 1962 MRR Alc.

Ouseg, H. L. 21-language dictionary.
London, P. Owen [1962] xxxi, 333 p.
63-1285
P361 .O85 1962 MRR Alc.

ROMANCE LANGUAGES--STUDY AND TEACHING--
BIBLIOGRAPHY.
Centre for Information on Language
Teaching. A language-teaching
bibliography, 2d ed. Cambridge
[Eng.] University Press, 1972. x,
242 p. 016.407 76-152633
Z5814.L26 C45 1972 MRR Alc.

ROMANCE LITERATURE--BIBLIOGRAPHY.
The Year's work in modern language
studies, 1929/30- [Leeds, Eng.,
etc.] Modern Humanities Research
Association [etc.] 405.8 31-32540
PB1 .Y45 MRR Alc Full set

Zeitschrift für romanische
Philologie. Supplementheft.
Bibliographie. 1-72/76; 1875/76-
1956/60. Tubingen [etc.] M.
Niemeyer. 74-643524
Z7032 .Z45 MRR Alc Full set

ROMANCE LITERATURE--BOOK REVIEWS.
Curley, Dorothy Nyren, comp. Modern
Romance literatures, New York, F.
Ungar Pub. Co. [1967] x, 510 p.
879.9/09 67-14053
PN813 .C8 MRR Alc.

ROMANCE LITERATURE--HISTORY AND
CRITICISM--BIBLIOGRAPHY.
Romanische Bibliographie. 1961/62-
Tubingen, M. Niemeyer Verlag. 72-
620927
Z7032 .Z45 MRR Alc Full set

Zeitschrift für romanische
Philologie. Supplementheft.
Bibliographie. 1-72/76; 1875/76-
1956/60. Tubingen [etc.] M.
Niemeyer. 74-643524
Z7032 .Z45 MRR Alc Full set

ROMANCE LITERATURE--TRANSLATIONS INTO
ENGLISH--BIBLIOGRAPHY.
Parks, George Bruner. The Romance
literatures. New York, F. Ungar Pub.
Co. [1970] 2 v. [$45.00]
016.84009 70-98341
Z7033.T7E65 MRR Alc.

ROMANCE PHILOLOGY--BIBLIOGRAPHY.
Golden, Herbert Hershel. Modern
Iberian language and literature;
Cambridge, Harvard University Press,
1958. x, 184 p. 016.46 58-12978
Z7031 .G6 MRR Alc.

ROMANCE PHILOLOGY--BIBLIOGRAPHY. (Cont.)
Zeitschrift für romanische
Philologie. Supplementheft.
Bibliographie. 1-72/76; 1875/76-
1956/60. Tübingen [etc.] M.
Niemeyer. 74-645524
Z7032 .Z45 MRR Alc Full set

ROMANCE PHILOLOGY--BIBLIOGRAPHY--
PERIODICALS.
Romanische Bibliographie. 1961/62-
Tübingen, M. Niemeyer Verlag. 72-
620927
Z7032 .Z45 MRR Alc Full set

ROMANCE PHILOLOGY--PERIODICALS.
Zeitschrift für romanische
Philologie. Supplementheft.
Bibliographie. 1-72/76; 1875/76-
1956/60. Tübingen [etc.] M.
Niemeyer. 74-645524
Z7032 .Z45 MRR Alc Full set

ROMANCES--BIBLIOGRAPHY--CATALOGS.
Cleveland. Public Library. John G.
White Dept. Catalog of folklore and
folk songs. Boston, G. K. Hall,
1964. 2 v. 65-4290
Z5985 .C5 MRR Alc (Dk 33).

ROMANCES--DICTIONARIES.
Spence, Lewis, A dictionary of
medieval romance and romance writers,
London, G. Routledge & sons,
limited; New York, E. P. Dutton & co.
[1913] vi, 395 p. 14-6809
PN669 .S6 MRR Alc.

ROMANCES, ENGLISH--HISTORY AND
CRITICISM--BIBLIOGRAPHY.
A Manual of the writings in Middle
English, 1050-1500. New Haven,
Connecticut Academy of Arts and
Sciences [order from: Archon Books,
Hamden, Conn.] 1967- v.
016.820/9/001 67-7687
PR255 .M3 MRR Alc.

ROMANIA.
Keefe, Eugene K. Area handbook for
Romania. Washington, For sale by the
Supt. of Docs., U.S. Govt. Print.
Off. 1972. xiv, 319 p. [$2.75]
914.98 72-600095
DR205 .K43 MRR Alc.

ROMANIA--BIBLIOGRAPHY.
United States. Library of Congress.
Slavic and Central European Division.
Rumania; a bibliographic guide.
Washington [For sale by the
Superintendent of Documents, U.S.
Govt. Print. Off.] 1963. vii, 75 p.
63-60076
Z663.47 .R83 MRR Alc.

ROMANIA--DESCRIPTION AND TRAVEL--GUIDE-
BOOKS.
Nagel Publishers. Rumania. 2d ed.
Geneva, Nagel [c1968] 368 p.
[$12.95] 914.98/04/3 72-442251
DR204.5 .N3 1968 MRR Alc.

ROMANIA--DICTIONARIES AND ENCYCLOPEDIAS.
Enciclopedia Romanigi. [Bucuresti,
Imprimeria Nationala, 1936- v.
949.8 48-38672
DR205 .E5 MRR Alc.

ROMANIA--STATISTICS--YEARBOOKS.
Romania. Directia Centrala de
Statistica. Anuarul statistic al
Republicii Socialiste Romania.
[Bucuresti] 72-627423
HA1641 .A2 MRR Alc Latest edition

ROMANIAN LANGUAGE--DICTIONARIES--
ENGLISH.
Levitchi, Leon. Dictionar român-
englez. Ediția a 3-a revizuita
București, Editura științifica,
1973. 1088 p. [lei 58.00] 74-
323938
PC779 .L4 1973 MRR Alc.

Levitchi, Leon. Dictionar român-
englez. Ed. a 2-a revazuta și
adaugita București, Editura
Științifica, 1965. xii, [1], 600
p. 66-93943
PC779 .L4 1965 MRR Alc.

ROMANTICISM--BIBLIOGRAPHY.
The Romantic movement bibliography,
1936-1970; [Ann Arbor, Mich.]
Pierian Press, 1973. 7 v. (xiii,
3289 p.) 016.809/894 77-172773
Z6514.R6 R65 MRR Alc.

ROMANTICISM--ENGLAND.
Bernbaum, Ernest, Guide through the
romantic movement. 2d ed., rev. and
enl. New York, Ronald Press [1949]
xi, 351 p. 820.903 49-8022
PR447 .B55 1949 MRR Alc.

Houtchens, Carolyn Washburn, ed. The
English Romantic poets & essayists;
Rev. ed. [New York] Published for
the Modern Language Association of
America by New York University Press,
1966. xviii, 395 p. 820.9007 66-
12599
PR590 .H6 1966 MRR Alc.

Raysor, Thomas Middleton, ed. The
English romantic poets; Rev. [i.e.
2d] ed. New York, Modern Language
Association of America, 1956. 307 p.
016.8217 57-4146
PR590 .R3 1956 MRR Alc.

ROMANTICISM--ENGLAND--BIBLIOGRAPHY.
Fogle, Richard Harter. Romantic
poets and prose writers. New York,
Appleton-Century-Crofts [1967] viii,
87 p. 016.8208008 66-29743
Z2013. F6 MRR Alc.

ROME--ANTIQUITIES.
Baumeister, August, ed. Denkmäler
des klassischen altertums zur
erläuterung des lebens der Griechen
und Römer in religion, kunst und
sitte. München, Leipzig, R.
Oldenbourg, 1885-1888. 3 v. 04-
35149
DE5 .B34 MRR Alc.

Daremberg, Charles Victor,
Dictionnaire des antiquités grecques
et romaines Graz, Akademische Druck-
u. Verlagsanstalt, 1962-63. 6 v. in
10. 64-44287
DE5 .D22 MRR Alc.

Dionysius, of Halicarnassus. The
Roman antiquities of Dionysius of
Halicarnassus, Cambridge, Mass.,
Harvard university press; London, W.
Heinemann, ltd., 1937-50. 7 v.
888.9 38-42
PA3612 .D53 1937 MRR Alc.

ROME--BIBLIOGRAPHY.
Rounds, Dorothy. Articles on
antiquity in Festschriften, an index;
Cambridge, Harvard University Press,
1962. 560 p. 62-7193
Z6202 .R6 MRR Alc.

ROME--BIOGRAPHY.
Jones, Arnold Hugh Martin, The
prosopography of the later Roman
Empire, Cambridge [Eng.] University
Press, 1971- v. 920.037 77-
118859
DG203.5 .J6 MRR Alc.

Plutarchus. Plutarch's Lives,
London, Heinemann; New York, Putnam,
1915-1928. 11 v. mrr01-69
PA3612 .P7 1915d MRR Alc.

ROME--BIOGRAPHY--DICTIONARIES.
Radice, Betty. Who's who in the
ancient world; Revised [ed.]
Harmondsworth, Penguin, 1973. 336,
[32] p. [£0.60] 920/.038 74-
161490
DE7 .R33 1973 MRR Alc.

ROME--CIVILIZATION.
Grant, Michael, The world of Rome.
London, Weidenfeld and Nicolson
[1960] xxi, 321 p. 937.06 60-
51841
DG77 .G62 1960 MRR Alc.

Grimal, Pierre, The civilization of
Rome. New York, Simon and Schuster,
1963. 531 p. 913.37 63-11905
DG77 .G733 MRR Alc.

ROME--DESCRIPTION--GUIDE-BOOKS.
Thynne, Roger. The churches of Rome,
London, K. Paul, Trench, Trubner &
co., ltd.; New York, E. P. Dutton &
co., 1924. xxxii, 460 p. 25-3760
BX4634.R6 T5 MRR Alc.

ROME--DESCRIPTION--TOURS.
Gibbons annual index of daily sight-
seeing tours: Rome, Paris, Florence.
London. [Los Angeles] 914 72-80819

D909 .G5 MRR Alc Latest edition

ROME--ECONOMIC CONDITIONS.
Frank, Tenney, ed. An economic
survey of ancient Rome, Baltimore,
The Johns Hopkins press [1933-40. 6
v. 937 330.937 33-17382
DG107 .F7 MRR Alc.

Rostovtsev, Mikhail Ivanovich, The
social and economic history of the
Roman Empire. 2d ed. rev. Oxford,
Clarendon Press, 1957. 2 v. (xxxi,
847 p.) 937.06 58-362
DG271 .R6 1957 MRR Alc.

ROME--HISTORY.
Appianus, of Alexandria. Appian's
Roman history; London, W. Heinemann;
New York, The Macmillan co., 1912-13.
4 v. 13-5584
PA3612 .A64 1912 MRR Alc.

Cassius Dio Cocceianus. Dio's Roman
history, London, W. Heinemann; New
York, The Macmillan co., 1914-27. 9
v. 14-4947
PA3612 .C3 1914 MRR Alc.

Dionysius, of Halicarnassus. The
Roman antiquities of Dionysius of
Halicarnassus, Cambridge, Mass.,
Harvard university press; London, W.
Heinemann, ltd., 1937-50. 7 v.
888.9 38-42
PA3612 .D53 1937 MRR Alc.

Livius, Titus. Livy, London,
Heinemann; New York, Putnam, 1919-59.
14 v. 937 20-2836
PA6156.L5 1919 MRR Alc.

Velleius Paterculus, C. Compendium
of Roman history; London, W.
Heinemann; New York, G. P. Putnam's
sons, 1924. xx, 431, [1] p. 937
878.9 24-16052
PA6156.V3 1924 MRR Alc.

ROME--HISTORY--REPUBLIC, B.C. 510-30.
Florus, Lucius Annaeus. Lucius
Annaeus Florus, Epitome of Roman
history. London, W. Heinemann, ltd.;
New York, G. P. Putnam's sons, 1929.
xv, 743, [1] p. 30-5836
PA6156.F5 1929 MRR Alc.

Polybius. The histories, London, W.
Heinemann; New York, G. P. Putnam's
sons, 1922-27. 6 v. 23-2839
PA3612 .P8 1922 MRR Alc.

ROME--HISTORY--REPUBLIC, 265-30 B.C.
Marsh, Frank Burr, A history of the
Roman world from 146 to 30 B. C. [3d
ed.] London, Methuen; New York,
Barnes & Noble [1963] 472 p.
937.05 63-3016
DG254 .M34 1963 MRR Alc.

ROME--HISTORY--CIVIL WAR, 49-48 B.C.
Caesar, C. Julius. Caesar. The civil
wars, London, W. Heinemann; New
York, G. P. Putnam's sons, 1928. 369
p. mrr01-13
PA6156.C18 1928d MRR Alc.

Lucanus, Marcus Annaeus. Lucan,
London, W. Heinemann; New York, G. P.
Putnam's sons, 1928. 637 p. mrr01-
10
PA6156.L7 1928d MRR Alc.

ROME--HISTORY--AUGUSTUS, 30 B.C.-14 A.D.
Velleius Paterculus, C. Compendium
of Roman history; London, W.
Heinemann; New York, G. P. Putnam's
sons, 1924. xx, 431, [1] p. 937
878.9 24-16052
PA6156.V3 1924 MRR Alc.

ROME--HISTORY--EMPIRE, 30 B.C.-284 A.D.
Herodianus. Herodian. Cambridge,
Mass. Harvard University Press, 1969-
70. 2 v. ($4.00 (v. 1); $5.00 (v.
2)) 937/.06 74-7907
PA3612 .H49 1969 MRR Alc.

Salmon, Edward Togo. A history of
the Roman world from 30 B.C. to A.D.
138, 6th ed. London, Methuen, 1968.
xv, 367 p. [50/- 21/- pbk.)]
937/.07 73-355498
DG276 .S26 1968 MRR Alc.

Scriptores historiae augustae. The
Scriptores' historiae augustae,
London, W. Heinemann; New York, G. P.
Putnam's sons, 1922-32. 3 v. 878
22-11196
PA6156.A4 1922 MRR Alc.

ROME--HISTORY--EMPIRE, 30 B.C.-476 A.D.
Gibbon, Edward, The decline and fall
of the Roman Empire. New York,
Modern Library [1932?] 3 v. 937 a
50-7554
DG311 .G5 1932a MRR Alc.

Parker, Henry Michael Denne. A
history of the Roman world from A.D.
138 to 337. London, Methuen [1958]
xii, 424 p. 937.06 a 59-8368
DG276 .P3 1958 MRR Alc.

Rostovtsev, Mikhail Ivanovich, The
social and economic history of the
Roman Empire. 2d ed. rev. Oxford,
Clarendon Press, 1957. 2 v. (xxxi,
847 p.) 937.06 58-362
DG271 .R6 1957 MRR Alc.

ROME--HISTORY--FLAVIANS, 69-96.
Tacitus, Cornelius. The Histories,
London, W. Heinemann; New York, G. P.
Putnam's sons, 1925-37. 4 v. 878.6
937.07 26-7877
PA6156.T25 1925 MRR Alc.

ROME--HISTORY--EMPIRE, 284-476.
Ammianus Marcellinus. Ammianus
Marcellinus; Cambridge, Mass.,
Harvard university press; London, W.
Heinemann ltd., 1935-39. 3 v.
878.9 36-2106
PA6156.A6 1935 MRR Alc.

Bury, John Bagnell, History of the
later Roman Empire from the death of
Theodosius I. to the death of
Justinian. New York, Dover
Publications [1958] 2 v. 937.08
58-11273
DG311 .B98 1958 MRR Alc.

ROME--HISTORY--CHRONOLOGY.
Grimal, Pierre, The civilization of
Rome. New York, Simon and Schuster,
1963. 531 p. 813.37 63-11905
DG77 .G733 MRR Alc.

ROME--HISTORY--DICTIONARIES.
The Oxford classical dictionary. 2d
ed. Oxford [Eng.] Clarendon Press,
1970. xxii, 1176 p. 913.38003 73-
18819
DE5 .O9 1970 MRR Ref Desk.

ROME--HISTORY--SOURCES.
Frank, Tenney, ed. An economic
survey of ancient Rome. Baltimore,
The Johns Hopkins press, 1933-40. 6
v. 937 330.937 33-17382
DG107 .F7 MRR Alc.

ROME--POLITICS AND GOVERNMENT.
Dionysius, of Halicarnassus. The
Roman antiquities of Dionysius of
Halicarnassus. Cambridge, Mass.,
Harvard university press; London, W.
Heinemann, ltd., 1937-50. 7 v.
888.9 38-42
PA3612 .D53 1937 MRR Alc.

ROME--SOCIAL CONDITIONS.
Rostovtsev, Mikhail Ivanovich. The
social and economic history of the
Roman Empire. 2d ed. rev. Oxford,
Clarendon Press, 1957. 2 v. (xxxi,
847 p.) 937.06 58-362
DG271 .R6 1957 MRR Alc.

ROME--SOCIAL LIFE AND CUSTOMS.
Cowell, Frank Richard. Everyday life
in ancient Rome. London, Batsford
[1961] 207 p. 913.37 61-4496
DG78 .C6 1961a MRR Alc.

ROME (CITY)--ANTIQUITIES.
Platner, Samuel Ball. A
topographical dictionary of ancient
Rome. London, Oxford university
press, H. Milford, 1929. xxiii, 609
p. 913.376 30-10804
DG16 .P685 MRR Alc.

ROME (CITY)--CHURCHES.
Thynne, Roger. The churches of Rome.
London, K. Paul, Trench, Trubner &
co., ltd.; New York, E. P. Dutton &
co., 1924. xxxii, 460 p. 25-3760
BX4634.R6 T5 MRR Alc.

ROME (CITY)--DESCRIPTION.
Platner, Samuel Ball. A
topographical dictionary of ancient
Rome. London, Oxford university
press, H. Milford, 1929. xxiii, 609
p. 913.376 30-10804
DG16 .P685 MRR Alc.

ROME (CITY)--DESCRIPTION--GUIDE-BOOKS.
Gessi, Leone. The Vatican City. 4th
ed. Rome] Istituto Poligrafico dello
Stato [c1954] 136 p. 914.56 55-
3455
DG800 .G36 1954 MRR Alc.

Masson, Georgina. Fodor's Rome;
[Rev. ed.] New York, Mckay [1971,
c1965] 592 p. [$3.95]
914.56/32/0482 76-148998
DG804 .M34 1971 MRR Alc.

Rome and its environs. 4th ed.]
Geneva, Paris [etc.] Nagel Publishers
[1968] 736 p. [$8.95]
914.56/32/0482 76-432684
DG804 .R68 1968 MRR Alc.

Simon, Kate. Rome: places and
pleasures. [1st ed.] New York,
Knopf, 1972. xv, 442, xvii p.
[$8.95] 914.5/632/0492 70-38320
DG804 .S47 MRR Alc.

ROME (CITY)--DIRECTORIES.
Guida Monaci. Roma. 54-54206
"Fondata nel 1871."
DG804 .G8 MRR Alc Latest edition

ROME (CITY)--WATER-SUPPLY.
Frontinus, Sextus Julius. The
Stratagems. London, W. Heinemann;
New York, G. P. Putnam's sons, 1925.
xl, 483, [1] p. 25-15482
PA6156.F6 1925 MRR Alc.

ROOFING--DIRECTORIES.
National Roofing Contractors
Association. N R C A directory. Oak
Park, Ill. [etc.] 60-21391
TH2430.N3 A3 MRR Alc Latest
edition

ROOMING HOUSES
see Hotels, taverns, etc.

**ROOSEVELT, FRANKLIN DELANO, PRES. U.S.,
1882-1945.**
Burns, James MacGregor. Roosevelt:
the lion and the fox. [1st ed.] New
York, Harcourt, Brace [1956] 553 p.
923.173 56-7920
E807 .B835 MRR Alc.

Freidel, Frank Burt. Franklin D.
Roosevelt. [1st ed.] Boston,
Little, Brown [1952- v. 923.173
52-5521
E807 .F74 MRR Alc.

Schlesinger, Arthur Meier. The age
of Roosevelt. Boston, Houghton,
Mifflin, 1957- v. 973.917 56-
10293
E806 .S34 MRR Alc.

**ROOSEVELT, THEODORE, PRES. U.S., 1858-
1919.**
Beale, Howard Kennedy. Theodore
Roosevelt and the rise of America to
world power. Baltimore, Johns
Hopkins Press, 1956. 600 p.
973.911 56-10255
E757 .B4 MRR Alc.

Mowry, George Edwin. The era of
Theodore Roosevelt, 1900-1912. [1st
ed.] New York, Harper [1958] 330 p.
973.911 58-8835
E756 .M85 MRR Alc.

United States. President, 1901-1909
(Roosevelt) Theodore Roosevelt, 1858-
1919; Dobbs Ferry, N.Y., Oceana
Publications, 1969. 120 p. [4.00]
971.91/1/0924 69-15392
E756 .U68 MRR Alc.

**ROOSEVELT, THEODORE, PRES. U.S., 1858-
1919--MANUSCRIPTS--INDEXES.**
United States. Library of Congress.
Manuscript Division. Index to the
Theodore Roosevelt papers.
Washington; [for sale by the Supt. of
Docs., U.S. Govt. Print. Off.] 1969
[i.e. 1970] 3 v. (xxvi, 1322 p.)
[12.75] 016.97391/1/0924 68-60026
Z663.34 .R6 MRR Alc.

ROSES--VARIETIES.
McFarland (J. Horace) Company.
Harrisburg, Pa. Modern roses 6;
Harrisburg, 1965. xvii, 497 p.
635.9333 65-3670
SB411 .M25 1965 MRR Alc.

ROSKILDE, DENMARK--DIRECTORIES.
Roskilde vejviser. 1.- aarg.; 1946-
[Roskilde] 53-30342
DL291.R6 R6 MRR Alc Latest edition

ROTARY INTERNATIONAL--DIRECTORIES.
Rotary International. The official
directory for 19< > Chicago [etc.]
650.621 30-25473
HF5001 .R762 MRR Biog Latest
edition

ROTHERHAM, ENG.--DIRECTORIES.
Kelly's directory of Sheffield and
Rotherham and the surrounding
parishes, townships, villages and
hamlets, Kingston upon Thames,
Surrey [etc.] Kelly's Directories
[etc.] 34-41846
DA690.S54 A15 MRR Alc Latest
edition

**ROYAL HISTORICAL SOCIETY, LONDON--
BIBLIOGRAPHY.**
Milne, Alexander Taylor. A centenary
guide to the publications of the
Royal Historical Society, 1868-1968,
London, Royal Historical Society,
1968. xi, 249 p. [unpriced]
016.942 77-436189
Z5055.G6 R66 MRR Alc.

ROYAL HOUSES.
Curley, Walter J. P. Monarchs-in-
waiting New York, Dodd, Mead [1973]
xv, 238 p. [$7.95] 929.7/094 73-
11549
D412.7 .C87 MRR Alc.

**ROYAL INSTITUTE OF INTERNATIONAL
AFFAIRS.**
Carr-Saunders, Alexander Morris,
World population; Oxford, The
Clarendon press, 1936. xv, 336 p.
312 37-8100
HB881 .C3 MRR Alc.

**ROYAL INSTITUTE OF INTERNATIONAL
AFFAIRS. LIBRARY.**
Royal Institute of International
Affairs. Library. Index to
periodical articles 1965-1972 in the
Library of the Royal Institute of
International Affairs. Boston, G. K.
Hall, 1973. xxix, 879 p. 016.05
73-166442
AI3 .R6 1973 MRR Alc.

RUBBER--BIBLIOGRAPHY.
Rubber red book; [1st]- ed.; 1937-
New York, Palmerton Pub. Co.
678.058 43-12783
TS1877 .R85 Sci RR Latest edition
/ MRR Alc Latest edition

RUBBER INDUSTRY AND TRADE--BIBLIOGRAPHY.
Rubber red book; [1st]- ed.; 1937-
New York, Palmerton Pub. Co.
678.058 43-12783
TS1877 .R85 Sci RR Latest edition
/ MRR Alc Latest edition

RUBBER INDUSTRY AND TRADE--DIRECTORIES.
Rubber red book; [1st]- ed.; 1937-
New York, Palmerton Pub. Co.
678.058 43-12783
TS1877 .R85 Sci RR Latest edition
/ MRR Alc Latest edition

**RUBBER INDUSTRY AND TRADE--GREAT
BRITAIN--DIRECTORIES.**
Rubber directory of Great Britain.
1966- Croyden [Eng.] Maclaren.
338.4/7/67802573 70-617227
TS1877 .R8752 MRR Alc Latest
edition

RUG AND CARPET INDUSTRY--DIRECTORIES.
Carpet annual. 1935- London,
Haymarket Pub. Ltd. [etc.] 677.64
35-15655
TS1772 .C33 MRR Alc Latest edition

RUGBY FOOTBALL.
see also Football

RUGS.
see also Carpets

Carpet annual. 1935- London,
Haymarket Pub. Ltd. [etc.] 677.64
35-15655
TS1772 .C33 MRR Alc Latest edition

RUGS, AMERICAN.
Weeks, Jeanne G. Rugs and carpets of
Europe and the Western World [1st
ed.] Philadelphia, Chilton Book Co.
[1969] ix, 251 p. [17.50]
746.7/9/1821 70-99605
NK2842 .W4 MRR Alc.

RUGS, EUROPEAN.
Weeks, Jeanne G. Rugs and carpets of
Europe and the Western World [1st
ed.] Philadelphia, Chilton Book Co.
[1969] ix, 251 p. [17.50]
746.7/9/1821 70-99605
NK2842 .W4 MRR Alc.

RUGS, ORIENTAL.
Jacobsen, Charles W. Oriental rugs;
[1st ed.] Tokyo, Rutland, Vt., C. E.
Tuttle Co. [1962] 479 p. 746.75
62-14117
NK2808 .J3113 MRR Alc.

RUGS, ORIENTAL--DICTIONARIES.
Jacoby, Heinrich. How to know
Oriental carpets and rugs. English
ed. London, Allen & Unwin [1952]
148 p. 745.52643 54-476
NK2808 .J3133 MRR Alc.

RUGS, ORIENTAL--HISTORY.
Hubel, Reinhard G. The book of
carpets. London, Barrie & Jenkins,
1971. 348 p. [£5.00] 746.7/5 73-
163462
NK2800 .H813 1971 MRR Alc.

RUINS
see Archaeology

RUMANIA--BIBLIOGRAPHY.
Horecky, Paul Louis. Southeastern
Europe; Chicago, University of
Chicago Press [1969] xxii, 755 p.
016.91496 73-110336
Z2831 .H67 MRR Alc.

RUMANIA--GAZETTEERS.
United States. Office of Geography.
Rumania; official standard names
approved by the United States Board
on Geographic Names. Washington,
U.S. Govt. Print. Off., 1960. iii,
450 p. 914.98 60-62205
DR204 .U5 MRR Alc.

**RUMANIAN LANGUAGE--DICTIONARIES--
POLYGLOT.**
Dictionar tehnic poliglot: Ediiția
a 2-a. Bucuresti, Editura Tehnica,
1967. xv, 1233 p. 603 68-2971
T10 .D54 1967 MRR Alc.

RUNAWAY CHILDREN.
see also Juvenile delinquency

RURAL ECONOMIC DEVELOPMENT
see Community development

RURAL LIFE
see Outdoor life

RURAL-URBAN MIGRATION.
see also Urbanization

RUSSIA.
Keefe, Eugene K. Area handbook for
the Soviet Union. Washington; For
sale by the Supt. of Docs., U.S.
Govt. Print. Off.] 1971. xviii, 827
p. [$5.25] 914.7/03/85 71-609246
DK18 .K43 MRR Alc.

The Soviet Union and Eastern Europe;
New York, Praeger [1970] xii, 614 p.
[$25.00] 914.7 70-100941
DK17 .S64 1970b MRR Alc.

**RUSSIA--ADMINISTRATIVE AND POLITICAL
DIVISIONS.**
SSSR; administrativnoterritorial'noe
delenie soluznykh respublik.
Moskva, Izvestija Sovetov deputatov
trudiashchikhsia SSSR [etc.] 49-
33696
JS6052 .A13 MRR Alc Latest edition

RUSSIA--BIBLIOGRAPHY.
Dossick, Jesse John. Doctoral
research on Russia and the Soviet
Union. [New York] New York
University Press, 1960. 248 p.
016.9147 60-14319
Z2491. D6 MRR Alc.

RUSSIA--BIBLIOGRAPHY. (Cont.)
Horak, Stephan M., Junior Slavica;
Rochester, N.Y., Libraries Unlimited,
1968. 244 p. [$7.85] 016.9147 68-
26959
   Z2491 .B58 MRR Alc.

Horecky, Paul Louis. Basic Russian
publications; Chicago] University of
Chicago Press [1962] xxvi, 313 p.
016.9147 62-20022
   Z2491 .H6 MRR Alc.

Horecky, Paul Louis, ed. Russia and
the Soviet Union; a bibliographic
guide to Western-language
publications. Chicago, University of
Chicago Press [1965] xxiv, 473 p.
016.9147 65-12041
   Z2491 .H64 MRR Alc.

Kerner, Robert Joseph, Northeastern
Asia, a selected bibliography;
Berkeley, Calif., University of
California press, 1939. 2 v.
016.95 39-33136
   Z3001 .K38 MRR Alc.

Maichel, Karol. Guide to Russian
reference books. [Stanford, Calif.]
Hoover Institution on War,
Revolution, and Peace, Stanford
University, 1962- v. 016.9147
62-14067
   Z2491 .M25 MRR Alc.

Simmons, John Simon Gabriel. Russian
bibliography, libraries and archives:
Twickenham, Anthony C. Hall, 1973.
xviii, 76 p. [£1.00] 016.0169147
74-162047
   Z2491.A1 S54 MRR Alc.

Spector, Sherman David, Checklist of
paperbound books on Russia, Albany,
University of the State of New York,
State Education Dept., 1964. iii, 63
p. 65-63612
   Z2491 .S69 MRR Alc.

United States. Library of Congress.
Division of bibliography. ... Soviet
Russia: a selected list of recent
references. Washington, 1943. 3 p.
l., 85 p. 016.947084 43-50549
   Z663.28 .S59 MRR Alc.

United States. Library of Congress.
General Reference and Bibliography
Division. Guide to Soviet
bibliographies; Washington, 1950.
v. 158 p. 016.01547 50-62955
   Z663.28 .G8 MRR Alc.

RUSSIA--BIO-BIBLIOGRAPHY--BIBLIOGRAPHY.
Kaufman, Isaak Mikhailovich.
[Russkie biograficheskie i
biobibliograficheskie slovari
(romanized form)] 1955. 751 p. 56-
45002
   Z5305.R9 K32 MRR Biog.

RUSSIA--BIOGRAPHY.
Institut zur Erforschung der UdSSR.
Biographic directory of the USSR,
New York, Scarecrow Press, 1958. ix,
782 p. 920.047 58-7804
   DK268.A1 I5 MRR Biog.

Koch, Hans, ed. 5000 [i.e.
Fünftausend] Sowjetkopfe; Köln,
Deutsche Industrieverlags-GmbH [1959]
xiv, 862 p. a 59-7663
   DK275.A1 K6 MRR Biog.

Simmonds, George W. Soviet leaders,
New York, T. Y. Crowell Co. [1967]
x, 405 p. 920.047 67-12409
   DK275.A1 S5 MRR Biog.

RUSSIA--BIOGRAPHY--DICTIONARIES.
Dox, Georg. Die russische
Sowjetliteratur: Berlin, De Gruyter,
1961. 184 p. 61-49174
   PG3024 .D6 MRR Biog.

Institut zur Erforschung der UdSSR.
Who was who in the USSR; Metuchen,
N.J., Scarecrow Press, 1972. 677 p.
920.047 70-161563
   CT1212 .I57 MRR Biog.

McGraw-Hill encyclopedia of Russia
and the Soviet Union. [1st ed.] New
York, McGraw-Hill [1961] xiv, 624 p.
914.7 61-18169
   DK14 .M26 MRR Alc.

Prominent personalities in the U S S
R. 1868- Metuchen, N.J., Scarecrow
Press. 920.047 68-12639
   DK275.A1 W534 MRR Biog Latest
edition

Turkevich, John, Soviet men of
science; Princeton, N.J., Van
Nostrand [1963] 441 p. 925 63-
24873
   Q141 .T83 MRR Biog.

Who's who in Soviet science and
technology. [2d ed., rev. and enl.
New York, Telberg Book Co. [1964]
vi, 301 l. 925 64-13006
   Q127.R9 W5 1964 MRR Biog.

Who's who in Soviet social sciences,
humanities, art and government. [New
York, Telberg Book Co., 1961] v, 147
l. 920.047 61-16892
   DK275.A1 W5 MRR Biog.

RUSSIA--BIOGRAPHY--DICTIONARIES--
BIBLIOGRAPHY.
Kaufman, Isaak Mikhailovich.
[Russkie biograficheskie i
biobibliograficheskie slovari
(romanized form)] 1955. 751 p. 56-
45002
   Z5305.R9 K32 MRR Biog.

RUSSIA--COMMERCE.
Marer, Paul. Soviet and East
European foreign trade, 1946-1969;
Bloomington, Indiana University Press
[1973, c1972] xviii, 408 p.
[$15.00] 382/.0947 72-76845
   HF3626.5 .M37 MRR Alc.

RUSSIA--COMMERCE--DIRECTORIES.
United States. Central Intelligence
Agency. Directory of USSR foreign
trade organizations and officials.
[Washington] 1974. vi, 71 p.
354/.47/00827025 74-600845
   HF3623 .U53 1974 MRR Alc.

RUSSIA--COMMERCIAL TREATIES.
Mid-European Law Project. Economic
treaties and agreements of the Soviet
bloc in Eastern Europe, 1945-1951.
2d ed. New York, Mid-European
Studies Center, 1952. xliii, 138 p.
382 52-60057
   Z663.55 .E3 MRR Alc.

RUSSIA--DESCRIPTION AND TRAVEL--1945-
Petrov, Victor P. Geography of the
Soviet Union Washington, V. P.
Kamkin, sole distributors, 1959- [v.
1, 1964] v. 64-8664
   DK28 .P393 MRR Alc.

RUSSIA--DESCRIPTION AND TRAVEL--1970- --
GUIDE-BOOKS.
Felber, John Edward. The American's
tourist manual for the U.S.S.R.,
[10th ed.] Newark, N.J.,
International Intertrade Index [1972,
c1973] 192 p. 914.7/04/85 72-
78512
   DK16 .F4 1973 MRR Alc.

RUSSIA--DESCRIPTION AND TRAVEL--
BIBLIOGRAPHY.
United States. Library of Congress.
Reference Dept. Soviet geography;
Washington, 1951. 2 v. (xii, 668 p.)
016.9147 51-62891
   Z663.2 .S63 MRR Alc.

RUSSIA--DESCRIPTION AND TRAVEL--GUIDE-
BOOKS.
Felber, John Edward. The American's
tourist manual for the U.S.S.R.,
[10th ed.] Newark, N.J.,
International Intertrade Index [1972,
c1973] 192 p. 914.7/04/85 72-
78512
   DK16 .F4 1973 MRR Alc.

Kane, Robert S. Eastern Europe, A to
Z: [1st ed.] Garden City, N.Y.,
Doubleday [1968] x, 348 p. 914.7
67-19081
   DR7 .K3 MRR Alc.

Louis, Victor E. A motorist's guide
to the Soviet Union, [1st ed.]
Oxford, New York, Pergamon Press
[1967] x, 368 p. and portfolio (4
fold. maps (1 col.)) 914.7/04/85
65-16215
   GV1025.R8 L6 1967 MRR Alc.

U.S.S.R. New York, McGraw-Hill
[c1965] 831 p. 914.70485 66-499
   DK16 .U23 1965 MRR Alc.

Whelpton, Peter. Tourists' guide to
Russia; London, MacGibbon & Kee,
1967 [i.e. 1968]. 183 p. [36/-]
914.7/04/85 68-87334
   DK16 .W45 MRR Alc.

RUSSIA--DICTIONARIES AND ENCYCLOPEDIAS.
Maxwell, Robert, ed. Information
U.S.S.R.; Oxford, New York, Pergamon
Press, 1962. xii, 982 p. 947.003
62-9879
   DK14 .M38 1962 MRR Alc.

McGraw-Hill encyclopedia of Russia
and the Soviet Union. 1st ed.] New
York, McGraw-Hill [1961] xiv, 624 p.
914.7 61-18169
   DK14 .M26 MRR Alc.

Utechin, Sergej, Everyman's concise
encyclopaedia of Russia, London,
Dent; New York, Dutton [1961] xxvi,
623 p. 947.003 61-4391
   DK28 .U83 MRR Alc.

RUSSIA--ECONOMIC CONDITIONS.
Jorré, Georges, The Soviet Union:
the land and its people; 3rd ed.
revised London, Longmans, 1967.
xxvi, 379 p. [52/6] 914.7 67-
114496
   DK17 .J613 1967 MRR Alc.

RUSSIA--ECONOMIC CONDITIONS--1917-
Clarke, Roger A. Soviet economic
facts, 1917-1970 [London] Macmillan
[1972] xi, 151 p. [£3.95]
330.9/47/084 73-151597
   HC335 .C518 1972b MRR Alc.

RUSSIA--ECONOMIC CONDITIONS--
BIBLIOGRAPHY.
Kiel. Universität. Institut für
Weltwirtschaft. Bibliothek.
Regionenkatalog. Boston, G. K. Hall,
1967. 52 v. 017/.5 67-9425
   Z929 .K52 1967 MRR Alc. (Dk 33).

RUSSIA--ECONOMIC POLICY.
Bauer, Raymond Augustine, How the
Soviet system works; Cambridge,
Harvard University Press, 1956. xiv,
274 p. 947.085* 56-8549
   DK266 .B26 MRR Alc.

RUSSIA--ECONOMIC POLICY--1951-1955.
Current digest of the Soviet press.
Current Soviet policies: 19th-
1952- New York, F. A. Praeger.
947.085* 53-6440
   JN6598 .K5 1952f MRR Alc Full set

RUSSIA--ECONOMIC POLICY--1959-1965.
Kommunisticheskaia partiia
Sovetskogo Soiuza. 22. s ezd,
Moscow, 1961. Russia enters the
1960s; [1st ed.] Philadelphia,
Lippincott [1962] ix, 278 p. 62-
11329
   JN6598 .K5 1961c MRR Alc.

RUSSIA--EXECUTIVE DEPARTMENTS.
Institut zur Erforschung der UdSSR.
Party and government officials of the
Soviet Union, 1917-1967. Metuchen,
N.J., Scarecrow Press [1969] 214 p.
354/.47/002 71-5797
   JN6598 .K7 I54 MRR Alc.

Koch, Hans, ed. 5000 [i.e.
Fünftausend] Sowjetkopfe; Köln,
Deutsche Industrieverlags-GmbH [1959]
xiv, 862 p. a 59-7663
   DK275.A1 K6 MRR Biog.

United States. Central Intelligence
Agency. Directory of Soviet
officials. [Washington?] 1973- v.
354/.47/002 73-603419
   JN6521 .U55 1973 MRR Alc.

RUSSIA--FOREIGN ECONOMIC RELATIONS--
BIBLIOGRAPHY.
Hammond, Thomas Taylor. Soviet
foreign relations and world
communism; Princeton, N.J.,
Princeton University Press, 1965.
xxiv, 1240 p. 016.32747 63-7069
   Z2517.R4 H3 MRR Alc.

RUSSIA--FOREIGN RELATIONS--1917-1945.
Degras, Jane (Tabrisky) ed. Soviet
documents on foreign policy. London,
New York, Oxford University Press,
1951-53. 3 v. 327.47 51-3107
   JX1555.A2 D4 MRR Alc.

Kulski, Władysław Wszebór, Peaceful
co-existence; Chicago, H. Regnery
Co., 1959. xxi, 662 p. 59-13052
   DK266 .K8 MRR Alc.

Rubinstein, Alvin Z., ed. The
foreign policy of the Soviet Union,
2d ed. New York, Random House [1966]
xx, 458 p. 327.47 66-15810
   DK63.3 .R8 1966 MRR Alc.

RUSSIA--FOREIGN RELATIONS--1917-1945--
BIBLIOGRAPHY.
Clemens, Walter C. Soviet
disarmament policy, 1917-1963;
[Stanford, Calif.] Hoover Institution
on War, Revolution and Peace,
Stanford University, 1965. xxvii,
151 p. 016.32747 65-12623
   Z2517.R4 C4 MRR Alc.

Hammond, Thomas Taylor. Soviet
foreign relations and world
communism; Princeton, N.J.,
Princeton University Press, 1965.
xxiv, 1240 p. 016.32747 63-7069
   Z2517.R4 H3 MRR Alc.

RUSSIA--FOREIGN RELATIONS--1945-
Kulski, Władysław Wszebór, Peaceful
co-existence; Chicago, H. Regnery
Co., 1959. xxi, 662 p. 59-13052
   DK266 .K8 MRR Alc.

Rubinstein, Alvin Z., ed. The
foreign policy of the Soviet Union,
2d ed. New York, Random House [1966]
xx, 458 p. 327.47 66-15810
   DK63.3 .R8 1966 MRR Alc.

RUSSIA--FOREIGN RELATIONS--1945- --
BIBLIOGRAPHY.
Clemens, Walter C. Soviet
disarmament policy, 1917-1963;
[Stanford, Calif.] Hoover Institution
on War, Revolution and Peace,
Stanford University, 1965. xxvii,
151 p. 016.32747 65-12623
   Z2517.R4 C4 MRR Alc.

RUSSIA--FOREIGN RELATIONS--1945-- (Cont.)
Hammond, Thomas Taylor. Soviet foreign relations and world communism; Princeton, N.J., Princeton University Press, 1965. xxiv, 1240 p.   016.32747 63-7069
Z2517.R4 H3 MRR Alc.

RUSSIA--FOREIGN RELATIONS--TREATIES.
Mid-European Law Project. Economic treaties and agreements of the Soviet bloc in Eastern Europe, 1945-1951. 2d ed. New York, Mid-European Studies Center, 1952. xliii, 138 p.
382 52-60057
Z663.55 .E3 MRR Alc.

Russia (1917- R.S.F.S.R.) Treaties, etc. Soviet treaty series; Washington, Georgetown University Press, 1850- v.   341.247 50-2664
JX756 1850 MRR Alc.

Slusser, Robert M. A calendar of Soviet treaties, 1917-1957 Stanford, Calif., Stanford University Press, 1959. xii, 530 p.   341.247 59-10638
JX756 1917 MRR Alc.

RUSSIA--FOREIGN RELATIONS--CHINA.
Gittings, John. Survey of the Sino-Soviet dispute; London, New York [etc.] issued under the auspices of the Royal Institute of International Affairs [by] Oxford U.P., 1968. xix, 410 p. [84/-] 327.51/047 75-356659
DS740.5.R8 G5 MRR Alc.

RUSSIA--FOREIGN RELATIONS--UNITED STATES.
Jados, Stanley S., ed. Documents on Russian-American relations, Washington, Catholic University of America Press [1965] viii, 416 p.
327.47073 65-12569
E183.8.R9 J3 MRR Alc.

United States. Dept. of State. The Soviet Union, 1933-1939. Washington, U.S. Govt. Print. Off., 1952. cii, 1034 p.   327.730947 52-61069
JX233.A6R83 MRR Alc.

RUSSIA--GAZETTEERS.
Telberg, Ina. Russian-English geographical-encyclopedia. New York, Telberg Book Co., c1960. x, 142 l.
914.7 60-8280
DK14 .T4 MRR Alc.

United States. Geographic Names Division. Europe and U.S.S.R.; official standard names Washington, 1971. iii, 151 p.   914/.003 70-30251
D904 .U5 MRR Alc.

United States. Geographic Names Division. U.S.S.R.; 2d ed. Washington, 1970- v.   914.7 78-608761
DK14 .U562 MRR Alc.

RUSSIA--HISTORICAL GEOGRAPHY.
Jorré, Georges, The Soviet Union: the land and its people; 3rd ed. revised London, Longmans, 1967. xxvi, 379 p. [52/6] 914.7 67-114496
DK17 .J613 1967 MRR Alc.

RUSSIA--HISTORICAL GEOGRAPHY--MAPS.
Adams, Arthur E. An atlas of Russian and East European history New York, Praeger [1967, c1966] 204 p. map67-61
G2111.S1 A2 1967 MRR Alc.

RUSSIA--HISTORY.
Clarkson, Jesse Dunsmore, A history of Russia. 2d ed. New York, Random House [1969] xxii, 886 p. [14.00]
947 69-11101
DK41 .C55 1969 MRR Alc.

Florinsky, Michael T., Russia: a short history 2d ed. [New York] Macmillan [1969] xiii, 699 p.   947 69-18818
DK41 .F6 1969 MRR Alc.

Harcave, Sidney Samuel, Russia, a history, 6th ed. Philadelphia, Lippincott [1968] xv, 787 p.   947 68-27861
DK41 .H3 1968 MRR Alc.

Miliukov, Pavel Nikolaevich, History of Russia. New York, Funk & Wagnalls [1868-69] 3 v. [10.00 per vol.] 947 68-22178
DK40 .M4613 MRR Alc.

Riasanovsky, Nicholas Valentine, A history of Russia 2d ed. New York, Oxford University Press, 1969. xviii, 748 p. [13.50] 947 69-17179
DK40 .R5 1969 MRR Alc.

Vernadsky, George, A history of Russia, [New Haven, Yale university press; London, H. Milford, Oxford university press, 1943- v.   947 a 43-1903
DK40 .V44 MRR Alc.

Walsh, Warren Bartlett, Russia and the Soviet Union; New ed., rev. and enl. Ann Arbor, University of Michigan Press [1968] xvi, 682, xxiv p. [10.00] 947 68-29267
DK41 .W33 1968 MRR Alc.

RUSSIA--HISTORY--19TH CENTURY.
Seton-Watson, Hugh. The Russian empire, 1801-1917. Oxford, Clarendon P., 1967. xx, 813 p. [55/-]
947/.08 67-93682
DK189 .S44 MRR Alc.

RUSSIA--HISTORY--19TH CENTURY--BIBLIOGRAPHY.
Shapiro, David. A select bibliography of works in English on Russian history, 1801-1917. Oxford, Blackwell, 1962. xii, 166 p.   63-2265
Z2509 .S5 MRR Alc.

RUSSIA--HISTORY--NICHOLAS II, 1894-1917.
Seton-Watson, Hugh. The Russian empire, 1801-1917. Oxford, Clarendon P., 1967. xx, 813 p. [55/-]
947/.08 67-93682
DK189 .S44 MRR Alc.

RUSSIA--HISTORY--NICHOLAS II, 1894-1917---BIBLIOGRAPHY.
Shapiro, David. A select bibliography of works in English on Russian history, 1801-1917. Oxford, Blackwell, 1962. xii, 166 p.   63-2265
Z2509 .S5 MRR Alc.

RUSSIA--HISTORY--1917-1921--BIBLIOGRAPHY.
United States. Library of Congress. Division of bibliography. ... Soviet Russia: a selected list of recent references. Washington, 1943. 3 p. l., 85 p. 016.947084 43-50549
Z663.28 .S59 MRR Alc.

RUSSIA--HISTORY--REVOLUTION, 1917-1921--INFLUENCE.
The Impact of the Russian Revolution, 1917-1967. London, New York [etc.] Oxford U.P., 1967. vi, 357 p. [unpriced] 335.43 67-104862
DK265.9.I5 I5 MRR Alc.

RUSSIA--HISTORY--1917-
Dmytryshyn, Basil, USSR: a concise history. 2d ed. New York, Scribner [1971] xv, 584 p. [$12.50]
947.084 77-162787
DK266 .D465 1971 MRR Alc.

Grey, Ian, The first fifty years: Soviet Russia, 1917-67. London, Hodder & Stoughton [1967] xvii, 558 p. [55/-] 947.084 67-109121
DK266 .G717 MRR Alc.

RUSSIA--HISTORY--1917- --BIBLIOGRAPHY.
Harvard University. Library. Russian history since 1917; Cambridge, Distributed by the Harvard University Press, 1966. 698 p. 016.947084 67-2882
Z2510 .H35 MRR Alc.

RUSSIA--HISTORY--BIBLIOGRAPHY.
Crowther, Peter A. A bibliography of works in English on early Russian history to 1800, Oxford, Basil Blackwell, 1969. xviii, 236 p. [60/-] 016.947 76-95558
Z2506 .C75 MRR Alc.

Maichel, Karol. Guide to Russian reference books. [Stanford, Calif.] Hoover Institution on War, Revolution, and Peace, Stanford University, 1962- v.   016.9147 62-14067
Z2491 .M25 MRR Alc.

Morley, Charles, Guide to research in Russian history. [Syracuse] Syracuse University Press [1951] xiii, 227 p. 016.947 51-12526
Z2506 .M85 MRR Alc.

RUSSIA--HISTORY--DICTIONARIES.
Pushkarev, Sergei Germanovich, Dictionary of Russian historical terms from the eleventh century to 1917. New Haven, Yale University Press, 1970. xi, 199 p. [12.50] 947/.003 73-81426
DK36 .P78 1970 MRR Alc.

RUSSIA--HISTORY--SOURCES--BIBLIOGRAPHY.
Grimsted, Patricia Kennedy. Archives and manuscript repositories in the USSR, Moscow and Leningrad. Princeton, Princeton University Press [1972] xxx, 436 p. [$22.50]
947/.007 73-166375
CD1711 .G7 MRR Alc.

Grimsted, Patricia Kennedy. Archives and manuscript repositories in the USSR, Moscow and Leningrad. Princeton, Princeton University Press [1972] xxx, 436 p. [$22.50]
947/.007 73-166375
CD1711 .G7 MRR Alc.

RUSSIA--IMPRINTS.
Okinshevich, Leo, Latin America in Soviet writings; Baltimore, Published for the Library of Congress by the Johns Hopkins Press [1966] 2 v. 016.91803 66-16039
Z1601 .O55 MRR Alc.

Okinshevich, Leo, Latin America in Soviet writings, 1945-1958; Washington, Slavic and Central European Division and the Hispanic Foundation, Reference Dept., Library of Congress, 1959. xii, 257 p.
016.98 59-64248
Z663.32 .A5 no. 5 MRR Alc.

Paris. Bibliothèque nationale. Catalogue général des livres imprimés: Paris, 1965- v.
018/.1 67-52152
Z927 .P1957 MRR Alc (Dk33)

United States. Library of Congress. Eighteenth century Russian publications in the Library of Congress; Washington, Slavic and Central European Division, Reference Dept., Library of Congress, 1961. xvi, 157 p.   61-60095
Z663.47 .E35 MRR Alc.

United States. Library of Congress. Processing Dept. Monthly index of Russian accessions. v. 1- Apr. 1948- Washington [U.S. Govt. Print. Off.] 015.47 48-46562
Z663.7 .A45 MRR Alc MRR Alc Full set

United States. Library of Congress. Reference Dept. Manufacturing and mechanical engineering in the Soviet Union; Washington, 1953. xii, 234 p. 016.621 53-60040
Z663.2 .M3 MRR Alc.

Yüan, T'ung-li, Russian works on China, 1918-1960, New Haven, Far Eastern Publications, Yale University, 1961. xiv, 162 p.
016.9151 61-16699
Z3106 .Y83 MRR Alc.

RUSSIA--LEARNED INSTITUTIONS AND SOCIETIES.
Koch, Hans, ed. 5000 [i.e. Fünftausend] Sowjetköpfe; Köln, Deutsche Industrieverlags-GmbH [1959] xiv, 862 p. a 59-7663
DK275.A1 K6 MRR Biog.

RUSSIA--LEARNED INSTITUTIONS AND SOCIETIES--DIRECTORIES.
Battelle Memorial Institute, Columbus, Ohio. Directory of selected scientific institutions in the U.S.S.R. [Columbus, C. E. Merrill Books] 1963. 1 v. (various pagings) 506 63-24824
060 .B36 MRR Alc.

A Guide to the Soviet academies. Rev. [n.p.] 1961. 103 p.   63-61190
AS258 .G82 MRR Alc.

United States. Library of Congress. Aerospace Technology Division. Scientific institutes and laboratories in Moscow. [Washington] 1963. ix, 133 p.   64-60333
Z663.23 .S35 MRR Alc.

United States. Library of Congress. Aerospace Technology Division. Scientific research institutes of the USSR. [Washington] 63-61636
Began publication in Feb. 1960.
Z663.23 .A27 MRR Alc MRR Alc Latest edition

RUSSIA--MANUFACTURES--BIBLIOGRAPHY.
United States. Library of Congress. Reference Dept. Manufacturing and mechanical engineering in the Soviet Union; Washington, 1953. xii, 234 p. 016.621 53-60040
Z663.2 .M3 MRR Alc.

RUSSIA--MAPS.
Adams, Arthur E. An atlas of Russian and East European history New York, Praeger [1967, c1966] 204 p. map67-61
G2111.S1 A2 1967 MRR Alc.

RUSSIA--OFFICIALS AND EMPLOYEES--DIRECTORIES.
Institut zur Erforschung der UdSSR. Party and government officials of the Soviet Union, 1917-1967. Metuchen, N.J., Scarecrow Press [1969] 214 p.
354.47/002 71-5797
JN6598.K7 I54 MRR Alc.

RUSSIA--OFFICIALS AND EMPLOYEES- (Cont.)
United States. Central Intelligence
Agency. Directory of Soviet
officials. [Washington?] 1973- v.
354/.47/002 73-603419
JN6521 .U55 1973 MRR Alc.

RUSSIA--PERIODICALS--BIBLIOGRAPHY.
Birkos, Alexander S. East European
and Slavic studies. [Kent? Ohio]
Kent State University Press [1973]
572 p. [$7.50]   016.9147/03/05 73-
158303
Z2483 .B56 MRR Alc.

RUSSIA--POLITICS AND GOVERNMENT.
Beer, Samuel Hutchison, ed. Patterns
of government; 3d ed. New York,
Random House [1973] xv, 778 p.
320.3 72-681
JN12 .B4 1973 MRR Alc.

Carter, Gwendolen Margaret, Major
foreign powers 6th ed. New York,
Harcourt Brace Jovanovich [1972]
xvi, 743 p. 320.3 78-179411
JF51 .C3 1972 MRR Alc.

RUSSIA--POLITICS AND GOVERNMENT--1917-
Hulicka, Karel. Soviet institutions,
the individual and society. Boston,
Christopher Pub. House [1967] xviii,
680 p. 320.9/47 67-13544
JN6515 1967 .H8 MRR Alc.

RUSSIA--POLITICS AND GOVERNMENT--1936-
1953.
Armstrong, John Alexander, The
politics of totalitarianism; New
York, Random House [1961] xvi, 458
p. 947.0842 61-6242
JN6598.K7 A67 MRR Alc.

RUSSIA--POLITICS AND GOVERNMENT--1945-
Current digest of the Soviet press.
Current Soviet policies; 19th-
1952- New York, F. A. Praeger.
947.085* 53-6440
JN6598 .K5 1952f MRR Alc Full set

RUSSIA--POLITICS AND GOVERNMENT--1953-
Armstrong, John Alexander, The
politics of totalitarianism; New
York, Random House [1961] xvi, 458
p. 947.0842 61-6242
JN6598.K7 A67 MRR Alc.

Kommunisticheskaia partiia
Sovetskogo Soiuza. 22. s"ezd,
Moscow, 1961. Russia enters the
1960s; [1st ed.] Philadelphia,
Lippincott [1962] ix, 278 p. 62-
11329
JN6598 .K5 1961c MRR Alc.

RUSSIA--REGISTERS.
Institut zur Erforschung der UdSSR.
Party and government officials of the
Soviet Union, 1917-1967. Metuchen,
N.J., Scarecrow Press [1969] 214 p.
354.47/002 71-5787
JN6598.K7 I54 MRR Alc.

Prominent personalities in the U S S
R. 1968- Metuchen, N.J., Scarecrow
Press. 920.047 68-12639
DK275.A1 W534 MRR Biog Latest
edition

United States. Central Intelligence
Agency. Directory of Soviet
officials. [Washington?] 1973- v.
354/.47/002 73-603419
JN6521 .U55 1973 MRR Alc.

United States. Central Intelligence
Agency. Directory of USSR foreign
trade organizations and officials.
[Washington] 1974. vi, 71 p.
354/.47/00827025 74-600845
HF3623 .U53 1974 MRR Alc.

RUSSIA--STATISTICS.
Clarke, Roger A. Soviet economic
facts, 1917-1970 [London] Macmillan
[1972] xi, 151 p. [£3.95]
330.9/47/084 73-151597
HC335 .C518 1972b MRR Alc.

Clarke, Roger A. Soviet economic
facts, 1917-1970 [London] Macmillan
[1972] xi, 151 p. [£3.95]
330.9/47/084 73-151597
HC335 .C518 1972b MRR Alc.

Marer, Paul. Soviet and East
European foreign trade, 1946-1969;
Bloomington, Indiana University Press
[1973, c1972] xviii, 408 p.
[$15.00] 382/.0947 72-76945
HF3626.5 .M37 MRR Alc.

Russia (1923- U.S.S.R.)
TSentral'noe statisticheskoe
upravlenie. Soviet Union 50 years;
Moscow, Progress Publishers [1969]
342 p. [unpriced] 314.7 78-433758
HA1435 .A5313 MRR Alc.

Statistical Office of the European
Communities. Basic statistics of the
community; 8th ed. [Brussels, 1967]
218 p. [unpriced] 314 75-386707
HA1107 .S7 1967 MRR Alc.

United States. Dept. of Agriculture.
Economic Research Service.
Agricultural statistics of Eastern
Europe and the Soviet Union, 1950-66.
Washington, 1969] vi, 110 p.
338.1/094 70-601060
HD1916 .U65 MRR Alc.

RUSSIA (1917- R.S.F.S.R.)--REGISTERS.
United States. Central Intelligence
Agency. Directory of Soviet
officials. [Washington?] 1973- v.
354/.47/002 73-603419
JN6521 .U55 1973 MRR Alc.

RUSSIA (1923- U.S.S.R.). MINISTERSTVO
VNESHNEI TORGOVLI--REGISTERS.
United States. Central Intelligence
Agency. Directory of USSR foreign
trade organizations and officials.
[Washington] 1974. vi, 71 p.
354/.47/00827025 74-600845
HF3623 .U53 1974 MRR Alc.

RUSSIAN LANGUAGE--ACRONYMS.
United States. Library of Congress.
Aerospace Technology Division.
Glossary of Russian abbreviations and
acronyms. Washington, Library of
Congress: [for sale by the Supt. of
Docs., U.S. Govt. Print. Off.] 1967.
x, 806 p. 491.731 68-60006
PG2693 .U47 MRR Alc.

RUSSIAN LANGUAGE--BIBLIOGRAPHY.
Neiswender, Rosemary. Guide to
Russian reference and language aids.
New York, Special Libraries
Association, 1962. iv, 82 p.
016.4917 62-21081
Z2505 .N4 1962 MRR Alc.

Unbegaun, Boris Ottokar, A
bibliographical guide to the Russian
language. Oxford, Clarendon Press,
1953. xi, 174 p. 016.4917 53-2211
Z2505 .U5 MRR Alc.

RUSSIAN LANGUAGE--DICTIONARIES.
Dal', Vladimir Ivanovich, [Tolkovyi
slovar zhivogo velikorusskogo
iazyka (romanized form)] 1955. 4
v. 56-41067
PG2625 .D33 MRR Alc.

RUSSIAN LANGUAGE--DICTIONARIES--ENGLISH.
Aleksandrov, A., pseud. [Poenyi
russko angliiskii (romanized
form)] 6th ed., rev. and enl. New
York, N.Y., Max N. Maisel, 1927. 2
p. l., 765, [1] p. 491.732 31-
24829
PG2640 .A5 1927 MRR Alc.

Carpovich, Eugene A., Russian-
English atomic dictionary. 2d rev.
and enriched ed. New York, Technical
Dictionaries Co., 1959. 317 p.
539.703 59-2755
QC772 .C3 1959 MRR Alc.

Carpovich, Eugene A., Russian-
English biological & medical
dictionary. 1st ed. New York,
Technical Dictionaries Co., 1958.
400 p. 574.03 58-7915
QH13 .C37 1958 MRR Alc.

Carpovich, Eugene A., Russian-
English chemical dictionary: 2d
improved ed. New York, Technical
Dictionaries Co., 1963. 352 p.
660.2803 63-4199
TP9 .C33 1963 MRR Alc.

Hoseh, Mordecai. Russian-English
dictionary of chemistry and chemical
technology. New York, Reinhold Pub.
Corp. [1964] xiii, 522 p. 540.3
64-22149
QD5 .H6 MRR Alc.

International encyclopedia of
chemical science. Princeton, N.J.,
Van Nostrand [1964] 1331 p. 540.3
64-1619
QD5 .I5 1964 MRR Alc.

Jablonski, Stanley. Russian-English
medical dictionary. New York,
Academic Press, 1958. xi, 423 p.
610.3 58-10411
R121 .J25 MRR Alc.

Konarski, Michael M. Russian-English
dictionary of modern terms in
aeronautics and rocketry. Oxford,
New York, Pergamon Press, 1962. xi,
515 p. 629.1303 62-16918
TL509 .K62 1962a MRR Alc.

Kotz, Samuel. Russian-English
dictionary of statistical terms and
expressions, Chapel Hill, University
of North Carolina Press [1964]
xviii, 115 p. 311.03 64-16840
HA17 .K6 MRR Alc.

Langenscheidt's Russian-English,
English-Russian dictionary. [1st
ed.] Berlin, Langenscheidt [1964]
505 p. 491.732 64-56693
PG2640 .L3 1964 MRR Alc.

Massachusetts Institute of
Technology. Center for International
Studies. Russian-English glossary of
metallurgical and metalworking terms.
Cambridge, 1955. iii, 175 p. 55-
4386
TN609 .M39 MRR Alc.

Pushkarev, Sergei Germanovich,
Dictionary of Russian historical
terms from the eleventh century to
1917. New Haven, Yale University
Press, 1970. xi, 199 p. [12.50]
947/.003 73-81426
DK36 .P78 1970 MRR Alc.

Russian-English aerospace dictionary.
Berlin, W. de Gruyter, 1965. xvi,
407 p. 65-73606
TL509 .R83 MRR Alc.

Schacht, Sigrid. The dictionary of
exceptions to rules of Russian
grammar. New York, American Elsevier
Pub. Co. [1968] xxvi, 196 p.
491.7/31 68-55062
PG2640 .S27 MRR Alc.

Segal, Louis. New complete Russian-
English dictionary (new orthography)
[Pocket ed.] New York, Praeger
[1959] 2 v. in 1. 491.732 59-8959
PG2640 .S42 MRR Alc.

Smirnitskii, Aleksandr Ivanovich,
ed. [Russko-angliiskii slovar
(romanized form)] 1965. 766 p. 65-
78896
PG2640 .S5 1965 MRR Alc.

United States. Library of Congress.
Aerospace Technology Division.
Soviet Russian scientific and
technical terms; Sept. 1958-63.
Washington [For sale by the Supt. of
Docs., U.S. Govt. Print. Off., etc.]
60-60977
Q123 .U46 Sci RR Latest edition /
MRR Alc Latest edition

United States. Library of Congress.
Reference Dept. Russian-English
glossary and Soviet classification of
ice found at sea. Washington, 1959.
vi, 30 p. 551.3403 59-60067
Z663.2 .R825 MRR Alc.

United States. Library of Congress.
Reference Dept. Russian-English
glossary of guided missile, rocket,
and satellite terms, Washington,
1958. vi, 352 p. 629.1333803
629.1435303* 58-60055
Z663.2 .R83 MRR Alc.

Wheeler, Marcus. The Oxford Russian-
English dictionary, London,
Clarendon Press, 1972. xiii, 918 p.
[£5.00] 491.7/32/1 72-191016
PG2640 .W5 MRR Ref Desk

Wolkonsky, Catherine A., comp.
Handbook of Russian roots, New York,
Columbia University Press, 1961.
xxiii, [iii], 414 p. 491.72 61-
1403
PG2580 .W6 1961 MRR Alc.

RUSSIAN LANGUAGE--DICTIONARIES--FRENCH.
Shcherba, Lev Vladimirovich. [Russko-
frantsuzskii slovar (romanized
form)] 1955. 783 p. 56-32808
PG2645.F5 S5 1955 MRR Alc.

RUSSIAN LANGUAGE--DICTIONARIES--
POLYGLOT.
Burger, Erich. Technical dictionary
of data processing, computers, office
machines. [1st ed.] Oxford, New
York, Pergamon Press [1970] 1463 p.
651.8/03 75-81247
QA76.15 .B46 1970 MRR Alc.

Conference terminology, 2d ed., rev.
and augm. Amsterdam, New York,
Elsevier Pub. Co.; [sole distributors
for the U.S.: American Elsevier Pub.
Co., New York] 1962. 162 p. 413
63-8568
PB324.C6 C6 1962 MRR Alc.

Dictionar tehnic poliglot: Editia
a 2-a. Bucuresti, Editura Tehnica,
1967. xv, 1233 p. 603 68-2971
T10 .D54 1967 MRR Alc.

Dictionary of chemistry and chemical
technology, in six languages: [Rev.
ed.] Oxford, New York, Pergamon
Press [1966] 1325 p. 540.3 65-
29008
QD5 .D5 1866 MRR Alc.

Dictionary of photography and
cinematography: London, New York,
Focal Press [1961] 1 v. (various
pagings) 770.3 63-24356
TR9 .D5 MRR Alc.

Elektrotechnik und Elektrochemie.
München, R. Oldenbourg, 1955. xxiv,
1304 p. 57-18208
TK9 .E42 1955 MRR Alc.

RUSSIAN LANGUAGE--DICTIONARIES-- (Cont.)
Elsevier's automobile dictionary in eight languages: Amsterdam, New York, Elsevier Pub. Co.; [distributed by Van Nostrand, Princeton, N.J.] 1960. 946 p. 629.203 59-8046
TL9 .E43 MRR Alc.

Fabierkiewicz, Wacław. Podręczny słownik włókienniczy w 5 językach: [Wyd. 1] [Warszawa] Państwowe Wydawn. Techniczne [1955] xlvii, 305 p. 55-38912
TS1309 .F3 MRR Alc.

Great Britain. Naval intelligence division. A dictionary of naval equivalents covering English, French, Italian, Spanish, Russian, Swedish, Danish, Dutch, German. London, H.M. Stationery off., 1924. 2 v. 24-23792
V24 .G7 MRR Alc.

Hétnyelvű sportszótár: Budapest, Terra, 1960- v. 61-21333
GV567 .H45 MRR Alc.

Intergovernmental Maritime Consultative Organization. Glossary of maritime technical terms. London [c1963] 118 p. 64-56893
V24 .I5 MRR Alc.

James, Glenn, ed. Mathematics dictionary, Multilingual ed. Princeton, N.J., Van Nostrand [1959] 546 p. 510.3 59-8656
QA5 .J32 1959 MRR Alc.

Kleczek, Josip. Astronomical dictionary. [Vyd. 1.] Praha, Nakl. Československé akademie věd, 1961. 972 p. 62-25391
QB14 .K55 MRR Alc.

Lexikon des Bibliothekswesens. Leipzig, VEB Verlag für Buch- und Bibliothekswesen, 1969. xiii, 769 p. [42.00] 70-423784
Z1006 .L46 MRR Alc.

Nash, Rose. Multilingual lexicon of linguistics and philology: English, Russian, German, French. Coral Gables, Fla., University of Miami Press [1968] xxvi, 390 p. 413 68-31044
P29 .N34 MRR Alc.

Orne, Jerrold. The language of the foreign book trade: 2d ed. Chicago, American Library Association, 1962. 213 p. 010.3 61-12881
Z1006 .O7 1962 MRR Alc.

Six-language dictionary of automation, electronics and scientific instruments: London, Iliffe Books; Englewood Cliffs, N.J., Prentice-Hall [1962] 732 p. 621.3803 63-5414
TK7804 .S5 1962 MRR Alc.

Stowarzyszenie Geodetów Polskich. Słownik geodezyjny w 5 [i.e. pięciu] językach: polskim, rosyjskim, niemieckim, angielskim, francuskim. Warszawa, Państwowe Przedsiębiorstwo Wydawn. Kartograficznych, 1954. xv, 525 p. 55-34784
QB279 .S8 MRR Alc.

Sube, Ralf. Kernphysik und Kerntechnik: Berlin, Verlag Technik [1962] 1606 p. 62-2924
QC772 .S9 MRR Alc.

Sube, Ralf. Wörterbuch Physik; Zurich, H. Deutsch, 1973. 3 v. 74-320539
QC5 .S9 MRR Alc.

Thompson, Anthony. Vocabularium bibliothecarii. 2d ed. [Paris] UNESCO, 1962. 627 p. 63-5650
Z1006 .T47 1962a MRR Alc.

Zatucki, Henryk. Dictionary of russian technical and scientific abbreviations Amsterdam, New York [etc.] Elsevier Pub. Co., 1968. 400 p. 601/.48 67-12784
PG2693 .Z3 MRR Alc.

Zboiński, A., ed. Dictionary of architecture and building trades in four languages: English, German, Polish, Russian. Oxford, New York, Pergamon Press; [distributed in the Western Hemisphere by Macmillan, New York, 1963] 491 p. 63-22875
NA31 .Z34 MRR Alc.

Żytka, Romuald. Geological dictionary Warszawa, Wydawnictwa Geologiczne, 1970. 1438 p. [zł1250.00] 550/.3 72-31794
QE5 .Z9 MRR Alc.

RUSSIAN LANGUAGE--ETYMOLOGY--DICTIONARIES.
Preobrazhenskiĭ, Aleksandr Grigor'evich, Etymological dictionary of the Russian language. New York, Columbia University Press, 1951. 1 v. (various pagings) a 52-3699
PG2580 .P7 MRR Alc.

Wolkonsky, Catherine A., comp. Handbook of Russian roots, New York, Columbia University Press, 1961. xxiii, [iii], 414 p. 491.72 61-1403
PG2580 .W6 1961 MRR Alc.

RUSSIAN LANGUAGE--STUDY AND TEACHING--BIBLIOGRAPHY.
Centre for Information on Language Teaching. A language-teaching bibliography, 2d ed. Cambridge [Eng.] University Press, 1972. x, 242 p. 016.407 76-152633
Z5814.L26 C45 1972 MRR Alc.

RUSSIAN LANGUAGE--TRANSLITERATION INTO ENGLISH.
Shaw, Joseph Thomas, The transliteration of modern Russian for English-language publications Madison, University of Wisconsin Press, 1967 [i.e. 1966] 15 p. 491.71/1 66-22858
PG2154 .S5 MRR Alc.

RUSSIAN LANGUAGE--WORD FORMATION.
Schacht, Sigrid. The dictionary of exceptions to rules of Russian grammar. New York, American Elsevier Pub. Co. [1968] xxvi, 196 p. 491.7/31 68-55062
PG2640 .S27 MRR Alc.

Wolkonsky, Catherine A., comp. Handbook of Russian roots, New York, Columbia University Press, 1961. xxiii, [iii], 414 p. 491.72 61-1403
PG2580 .W6 1961 MRR Alc.

RUSSIAN LITERATURE--TO 1700--HISTORY AND CRITICISM.
Gudziĭ, Nikolaĭ Kallinikovich, History of early Russian literature, New York, Octagon Books, 1970 [c1949] xix, 545 p. 891.7/09001 70-120620
PG3001 .G762 1970 MRR Alc.

RUSSIAN LITERATURE--18TH CENTURY--BIBLIOGRAPHY--CATALOGS.
United States. Library of Congress. Eighteenth century Russian publications in the Library of Congress; Washington, Slavic and Central European Division, Reference Dept., Library of Congress, 1961. xvi, 157 p. 61-60095
Z2663.47 .E35 MRR Alc.

RUSSIAN LITERATURE--19TH CENTURY--HISTORY AND CRITICISM.
Slonim, Marc, Modern Russia literature, New York, Oxford University Press, 1953. ix, 467 p. 891.709 53-6433
PG3011 .S538 MRR Alc.

RUSSIAN LITERATURE--20TH CENTURY--BIBLIOGRAPHY--CATALOGS.
Harvard University. Library. Twentieth century Russian literature: Cambridge, Distributed by the Harvard University Press, 1965. 142, 139, 140 p. 016.891709004 66-6980
Z2503.3 .H3 MRR Alc.

RUSSIAN LITERATURE--20TH CENTURY--BIO-BIBLIOGRAPHY.
Dox, Georg. Die russische Sowjetliteratur: Berlin, De Gruyter, 1961. 184 p. 61-49174
PG3024 .D6 MRR Biog.

RUSSIAN LITERATURE--20TH CENTURY--HISTORY AND CRITICISM.
Modern Slavic literatures. New York, F. Ungar Pub. Co. [c1972- v. [$15.00] 891.7/09/004 72-170319
PG501 .M518 MRR Alc.

Slonim, Marc, Modern Russia literature, New York, Oxford University Press, 1953. ix, 467 p. 891.709 53-6433
PG3011 .S538 MRR Alc.

RUSSIAN LITERATURE--BIBLIOGRAPHY.
Bibliography of Russian literature in English translation to 1945. Totowa, N.J., Rowman and Littlefield [1972] 74, 96 p. 016.8917/08 72-180612
Z2504.T8 B53 MRR Alc.

Horecky, Paul Louis, Basic Russian publications; [Chicago] University of Chicago Press [1962] xxvi, 313 p. 016.9147 62-20022
Z2491 .H6 MRR Alc.

Horecky, Paul Louis, ed. Russia and the Soviet Union; a bibliographic guide to Western-language publications. Chicago, University of Chicago Press [1965] xxiv, 473 p. 016.9147 65-12041
Z2491 .H64 MRR Alc.

Magner, Thomas F. Soviet dissertations for advanced degrees in Russian literature and Slavic linguistics, 1934-1962, University Park, Dept. of Slavic Languages, Pennsylvania State University, 1966. iii, 100 p. 016.4918 68-66174
Z2505.A2 M3 MRR Alc.

United States. Library of Congress. General Reference and Bibliography Division. Guide to Soviet bibliographies; Washington, 1950. v, 158 p. 016.01547 50-62955
Z663.28 .G8 MRR Alc.

RUSSIAN LITERATURE--BIBLIOGRAPHY--CATALOGS.
Harvard University. Library. The Kilgour collection of Russian literature, 1750-1920; Cambridge, Mass., Harvard College Library; distributed by the Harvard University Press, 1959. 1 v. (unpaged) 016.8917 59-942
Z2491.5 .H3 MRR Alc.

RUSSIAN LITERATURE--BIBLIOGRAPHY--PERIODICALS.
United States. Library of Congress. Processing Dept. Monthly index of Russian accessions, v. 1- Apr. 1948- Washington [U.S. Govt. Print. Off.] 015.47 48-46562
Z663.7 .A45 MRR Alc MRR Alc Full set

RUSSIAN LITERATURE--HISTORY AND CRITICISM.
Slonim, Marc, The epic of Russian literature from its origins through Tolstoy. New York, Oxford University Press, 1964 [c1950] vi, 369 p. 891.7/09 74-8762
PG2951 .S5 1964 MRR Alc.

RUSSIAN LITERATURE--HISTORY AND CRITICISM--BIBLIOGRAPHY.
Gibian, George. Soviet Russian literature in English: Ithaca, N.Y. Center for International Studies, Cornell University, 1967. iv, 118 p. 016.8917 67-20209
Z2504.T8 G5 MRR Alc.

RUSSIAN LITERATURE--TRANSLATIONS INTO ENGLISH--BIBLIOGRAPHY.
Bibliography of Russian literature in English translation to 1945. Totowa, N.J., Rowman and Littlefield [1972] 74, 96 p. 016.8917/08 72-180612
Z2504.T8 B53 MRR Alc.

Gibian, George. Soviet Russian literature in English: Ithaca, N.Y. Center for International Studies, Cornell University, 1967. iv, 118 p. 016.8917 67-20209
Z2504.T8 G5 MRR Alc.

United States. Library of Congress. Scientific Translations Center. Bibliography of translations from Russian scientific and technical literature. list no. 1-39; Oct. 1953-Dec. 1956. Washington. 016.5 53-60044
Z663.41 .U5 MRR Alc MRR Alc Partial set

RUSSIAN NEWSPAPERS--BIBLIOGRAPHY.
United States. Library of Congress. Slavic and Central European Division. Preliminary checklist of Russian, Ukrainian, and Belorussian newspapers published since January 1, 1917, Washington, 1952. iv, 97 l. 016.077 52-60042
Z663.47 .P7 MRR Alc.

United States. Library of Congress. Slavic and Central European Division. Russian, Ukrainian, and Belorussian newspapers, 1917-1953; Washington, 1953. xi, 218 p. 016.077 54-60001
Z663.47 .R85 MRR Alc.

RUSSIAN NEWSPAPERS--BIBLIOGRAPHY--CATALOGS.
Stanford University. Hoover Institution on War, Revolution, and Peace. Soviet and Russian newspapers at the Hoover Institution, [Stanford, Calif.] 1966. x, 235 p. 016.077 66-26281
Z6945 .S7983 MRR Alc.

United States. Library of Congress. Newspapers of the Soviet Union in the Library of Congress Washington, Slavic and Central European Division, and Serial Division, Reference Dept., Library of Congress [For sale by the Superintendent of Documents, U.S. Govt. Print. Off.] 1962. iv, 73 p. 62-60087
Z663.47 .N4 MRR Alc.

RUSSIAN PERIODICALS--BIBLIOGRAPHY.
Akademija nauk SSSR. Institut
nauchnoi informatsii. Index of
abbreviated and full titles of
scientific and technical periodical
literature Wright-Patterson Air
Force Base, Ohio, 1960?] 247 l.   60-
60261
   Z6945.A2 A43 MRR Alc

United States. Library of Congress.
Science and Technology Division.
Scientific and technical serial
publications, Washington, 1954.
viii, 118 p.   016.505 54-60015
   Z663.41 .S3 MRR Alc.

United States. Library of Congress.
Science and Technology Division.
Scientific and technical serial
publications of the Soviet Union,
1945-1960. Washington [For sale by
the Superintendent of Documents, U.S.
Govt. Print. Off.] 1963. iv, 347 p.
63-61782
   Z663.41 .S29 MRR Alc.

**RUSSIAN PERIODICALS--BIBLIOGRAPHY--
CATALOGS.**
United States. Library of Congress.
Processing Dept. Russian periodicals
in the Helsinki University Library,
Washington, 1959. 120 p.   016.057
59-60791
   Z663.7 .R8 MRR Alc.

United States. Library of Congress.
Slavic and Central European Division.
The USSR and Eastern Europe; 3d ed.
rev. and enl. Washington, Library of
Congress; [for sale by the Supt. of
Docs., U.S. Govt. Print. Off.] 1967.
89 p.   016.05 68-60045
   Z663.47 .U22 1967 MRR Alc.

**RUSSIAN PERIODICALS--BIBLIOGRAPHY--
UNION LISTS.**
Smits, Rudolf, Half a century of
Soviet serials, 1917-1968;
Washington, Library of Congress; [for
sale by the Supt. of Docs., U.S.
Govt. Print. Off,] 1968. 2 v. (xv,
1661 p.) [16.00]   016.057 68-62169

   Z663.23 .H3 MRR Alc.

United States. Library of Congress.
Cyrillic Bibliographic Project.
Serial publications of the Soviet
Union, 1939-1957; [New expanded ed.]
Washington, 1958. ix, 459 p.
016.057 58-60013
   Z663.7 .S4 1958 MRR Alc.

RUSSIAN PERIODICALS--INDEXES.
United States. Library of Congress.
Processing Dept. Monthly index of
Russian accessions; v. 1- Apr.
1948- Washington [U.S. Govt. Print.
Off.] 015.47 48-46562
   Z663.7 .A45 MRR Alc MRR Alc Full
set

**RUSSIAN PERIODICALS--TRANSLATIONS INTO
ENGLISH--BIBLIOGRAPHY.**
United States. Library of Congress.
Science and Technology Division.
List of Russian serials being
translated into English, and other
Western languages. [2d] ed.; 1960-
Washington. 60-60095
   Z663.41 .L47 MRR Alc MRR Alc
Latest edition

**RUSSIAN PERIODICALS IN FOREIGN
COUNTRIES--BIBLIOGRAPHY.**
Schatoff, Michael. Half a century of
Russian serials, 1917-1968; [2d ed.,
rev.]. New York, Russian Book
Chamber Abroad, 1972- v.
016.057/1 72-195896
   Z6956.R8 S352 MRR Alc.

Schatoff, Michael. Half a century of
Russian serials, 1917-1968; New
York, Russian Book Chamber Abroad,
1970-72. 4 v. (xiv, 697 p.)
016.057/1 68-59340
   Z6956.R9 S35 MRR Alc.

RUSSIAN PHILOLOGY--BIBLIOGRAPHY.
Magner, Thomas F. Soviet
dissertations for advanced degrees in
Russian literature and Slavic
linguistics, 1934-1962. [University
Park, Dept. of Slavic Languages,
Pennsylvania State University, 1966.
iii, 100 p.   016.4918 68-66174
   Z2505.A2 M3 MRR Alc.

RUSSIAN POETRY--HISTORY AND CRITICISM.
Poggioli, Renato, The poets of
Russia, 1890-1930. Cambridge, Mass.,
Harvard University Press, 1960. xix,
383 p.   891.71309 60-8000
   PG3056 .P6 MRR Alc.

**RUSSIAN POETRY--TRANSLATIONS INTO
ENGLISH.**
Yarmolinsky, Avrahm, ed. Two
centuries of Russian verse; New
York, Random House [1966] lxxv, 322
p.   891.71008 66-10992
   PG3237.E5 Y3 1966 MRR Alc.

RUSSIAN SATELLITES
see Communist countries

**RUSSO-FINNISH WAR, 1939-1940--
BIBLIOGRAPHY.**
United States. Library of Congress.
European Affairs Division.
Political, economic and social
writings in postwar Finland;
[Washington, 1952] vi, 41 p.   016.3
52-60040
   Z663.26 .P58 MRR Alc.

RWANDA.
Nyrop, Richard F. Area handbook for
Rwanda. Washington, For sale by the
Supt. of Docs., U.S. Govt. Print.
Off., 1969. xv, 212 p.   916.7/571
72-606089
   DT449.R9 N9 MRR Alc.

RWANDA--GAZETTEERS.
United States. Office of Geography.
Rwanda; official standard names
approved by the United States Board
on Geographic Names. Washington
[U.S. Govt. Print. Off.] 1964. iii,
44 p.   65-60657
   DT449.R9 U5 MRR Alc.

**RWANDA--GOVERNMENT PUBLICATIONS--
BIBLIOGRAPHY--UNION LISTS.**
Witherell, Julian W. French-speaking
central Africa; Washington, General
Reference and Bibliography Division,
Library of Congress; [for sale by the
Supt. of Docs., U.S. Govt. Print.
Off.] 1973. xiv, 314 p. [$3.70]
015./67 72-5766
   Z663.285 .F7 MRR Alc.

SAARLAND--COMMERCE--DIRECTORIES.
Firmenhandbuch Rheinland-Pfalz und
Saarland. Hannover, Industrie- und
Handelsverlag.   74-615207
   HF3569.R55 A45 MRR Alc Latest
edition

SACRAMENTS.
see also Marriage

SACRED BOOKS OF THE EAST--INDEXES.
Winternitz, Moriz, comp. A concise
dictionary of Eastern religion,
Oxford, The Clarendon press, 1910
[1925] xiv, [2], 683, [1] p.   290.8
ca 32-293
   BL1010 .S32 MRR Alc.

SACRED VOCAL MUSIC.
see also Carols

SAFETY APPLIANCES--CATALOGS.
Best's safety directory; Morristown,
N.J., A.M. Best Co.
338.4/7/620860257 73-642584
   T55.A1 B4 MRR Alc Latest edition

SAFETY REGULATIONS--UNITED STATES.
Best's safety directory; Morristown,
N.J., A.M. Best Co.
338.4/7/620860257 73-642584
   T55.A1 B4 MRR Alc Latest edition

SAHARA--DESCRIPTION AND TRAVEL.
Briggs, Lloyd Cabot, Tribes of the
Sahara. Cambridge, Harvard
University Press, 1960. xx, 295 p.
572.96611 60-7988
   DT337 .B7 MRR Alc.

SAILING.
see also Boats and boating

see also Navigation

Encyclopedia of sailing, [1st ed.]
New York, Harper & Row [1971] viii,
468 p. [$13.95]   797.1/24/03 70-
156549
   GV811 .E52 1971 MRR Alc.

SAILING SHIPS.
Chapelle, Howard Irving. The history
of the American sailing Navy; [1st
ed.] New York, Norton [1949] xxiii,
558 p.   623.822 49-48709
   VA56 .C5 MRR Alc.

Cutler, Carl C., Five hundred
sailing records of American built
ships. Mystic, Conn., Marine
Historical Association, 1952. 114 p.
623.822 52-30285
   VK23 .C79 MRR Alc.

Schauffelen, Otmar. Great sailing
ships; New York, Praeger [1969] 279
p. [12.50]   387.2/03 75-79074
   VM145 .S2913 MRR Alc.

SAINTS.
Butler, Alban, Lives of the saints.
Complete ed. [New York, Kenedy,
1962] 4 v.   922.22 62-51171
   BX4654 .B8 1962 MRR Biog.

Ferguson, George Wells, Signs &
symbols in Christian art. New York,
Oxford University Press [1954] xiii,
346 p.   704.9482 54-13072
   N7830 .F37 MRR Alc.

Harton, Sibyl, Stars appearing;
London, Hodder and Stoughton [1954]
237 p.   922.22 54-37082
   BR1710 .H35 1954 MRR Biog.

Réay, Louis, Iconographie de l'art
chrétien. [1. éd.] Paris, Presses
universitaires de France, 1955-59. 3
v. in 6. a 56-1728
   N7830 .R37 MRR Alc.

The Saints; [1st ed.] New York,
Hawthorn Books [1958] 496 p.
922.22 58-5626
   BX4655 .S28 MRR Biog.

SAINTS--ART.
Réay, Louis, Iconographie de l'art
chrétien. [1. éd.] Paris, Presses
universitaires de France, 1955-59. 3
v. in 6. a 56-1728
   N7830 .R37 MRR Alc.

SAINTS--CALENDAR.
Englebert, Omer, The lives of the
saints. New York, D. McKay Co.
[1951] xi, 532 p.   922.22 51-11328
   BX4655 .E513 MRR Alc.

SAINTS--DICTIONARIES.
Attwater, Donald, A dictionary of
saints; New York, P. J. Kenedy
[1958] vii, 280 p.   922.22 58-
12556
   BX4654 .B8 1958 Index MRR Alc.

The Book of saints; 5th ed.,
entirely rev. and re-set. New York,
Crowell [1966] xii, 740 p.   235.203
66-22140
   BX4655 .B6 1966 MRR Alc.

SALES LETTERS.
Nauheim, Ferd. Salesman's complete
model letter handbook. West Nyack,
N.Y., Parker Pub. Co. [1967] xiii,
203 p.   651.7/5 67-23727
   HF5730 .N3 MRR Alc.

SALES MANAGEMENT.
Dartnell Corporation. The sales
manager's handbook. [1st-] ed.;
1934- Chicago. 658.81 56-59050
   HF5415 .D32 MRR Alc Latest edition

SALES MANAGEMENT--BIBLIOGRAPHY.
Sandeau, Georges. International
bibliography of marketing and
distribution. [Bruxelles, Presses
universitaires de Bruxelles]
Distributed exclusively in North
America and South America [by] R. R.
Bowker Co., New York, 1971. 1 v.
(various pagings) 016.6588 73-
159927
   Z7164.M18 S2 1871b MRR Alc.

SALES PROMOTION.
Dartnell Corporation. The Dartnell
sales promotion handbook. 5th ed.
Chicago, 1966. 1080 p.   658.8/2 67-
5059
   HF5415 .D325 1966 MRR Alc.

SALESMAN AND SALESMANSHIP--HISTORY.
Scull, Penrose. From peddlers to
merchant princes; Chicago, Follett
Pub. Co., 1967. x, 274 p.
658.85/09 67-20837
   HF5438 .S292 MRR Alc.

SALESMEN AND SALESMANSHIP.
see also Advertising

see also Marketing

SALFORD, ENG. (LANCASHIRE)--DIRECTORIES.
Kelly's (Slater's) directory of
Manchester, Salford and suburbs.
Kingston upon Thames, Surrey [etc.]
Kelly's Directories Limited. 34-
33227
   DA690.M4 K4 MRR Alc Latest edition

The Manchester, Salford, and district
red book. Manchester, Littlebury
Bros. 19 cm.   61-27275
   DA690.M4 M23 MRR Alc Latest
edition

SALISBURY, ENG.--DIRECTORIES.
Kelly's directory of Salisbury and
neighbourhood. Kingston upon Thames,
Surrey [etc.] Kelly's Directories
Limited [etc.]   53-28202
   DA690.S16 K4 MRR Alc Latest
edition

SALIVA--BIBLIOGRAPHY.
United States. Library of Congress.
Science and Technology Division.
Bibliography on saliva, Washington,
Office of Naval Research, Dept. of
the Navy, 1960. iii, 447 p.
016.612313 60-61532
   Z663.41 .B46 MRR Alc.

SALOONS
see Hotels, taverns, etc.

SALT-WATER FISHING--MAPS.
Salt water sport fishing and boating
in Virginia. Alexandria, Va., 1971.
78 p. [$5.00]   623.89 73-654615
   G1291.L1 S2 1971 MRR Alc.

SALVADOR.
Blutstein, Howard I. Area handbook
for El Salvador. Washington; For
sale by the Supt. of Docs., U.S.
Govt. Print. Off.] 1971. xii, 259 p.
[$2.50] 309.1/7284/05 78-609951
F1483 .B55 MRR Alc.

SALVADOR--BIOGRAPHY--DICTIONARIES.
Flemion, Philip F. Historical
dictionary of El Salvador. Metuchen,
N.J., Scarecrow Press, 1972. 157 p.
972.84/003 78-189546
F1482 .F55 MRR Alc.

**SALVADOR--DICTIONARIES AND
ENCYCLOPEDIAS.**
Flemion, Philip F. Historical
dictionary of El Salvador. Metuchen,
N.J., Scarecrow Press, 1972. 157 p.
972.84/003 78-189546
F1482 .F55 MRR Alc.

SALVADOR--GAZETTEERS.
Flemion, Philip F. Historical
dictionary of El Salvador. Metuchen,
N.J., Scarecrow Press, 1972. 157 p.
972.84/003 78-189546
F1482 .F55 MRR Alc.

United States. Office of Geography.
El Salvador; Washington, U.S. Govt.
Print. Off., 1956. ii, 65 p.
917.284 56-63929
F1482 .U5 MRR Alc.

SALVATION ARMY.
The Salvation army year book.
London. Simpkin, Marshall, Hamilton,
Kent [etc.] ca 08-2994
HV4330 .S3 MRR Alc Latest edition

SALZBURG--COMMERCE--DIRECTORIES.
Herold Adressbuch von Salzburg für
Industrie, Handel, Gewerbe. Wien,
Herold. 72-622320
HF3549.S3 A45 MRR Alc Latest
editon

**SALZBURG (PROVINCE)--COMMERCE--
DIRECTORIES.**
Salzburger Amts-Kalender. Salzburg,
Mayrische Buchhandlung. 53-30514
JN2041.S3 S33 MRR Alc Latest
edition

SALZBURG (PROVINCE)--REGISTERS.
Salzburger Amts-Kalender. Salzburg,
Mayrische Buchhandlung. 53-30514
JN2041.S3 S33 MRR Alc Latest
edition

SAMOYEDIC LANGUAGES.
Collinder, Björn, An introduction
to the Uralic languages. Berkeley,
University of California Press, 1965.
xii, 167 p. 494.4 65-21136
PH14. C58 MRR Alc.

SAN FRANCISCO--DESCRIPTION--GUIDE-BOOKS.
Benet, James Walker. A guide to San
Francisco and the Bay region, [Rev.
ed.] New York, Random House [1966]
xxxii, 498 p. 917.94/6/045 67-9585

F868.S156 B4 1966 MRR Alc.

Writers' Program. California. San
Francisco, the bay and its cities.
New rev. ed. New York, Hastings
House [1973] xiv, 496 p. [$12.50]
917.94/6 72-5854
F869.S3 W85 1973 MRR Ref Desk.

**SAN FRANCISCO BAY REGION--DESCRIPTION
AND TRAVEL--GUIDE-BOOKS.**
Benet, James Walker. A guide to San
Francisco and the Bay region, [Rev.
ed.] New York, Random House [1966]
xxxii, 498 p. 917.94/6/045 67-9585

F868.S156 B4 1966 MRR Alc.

Writers' Program. California. San
Francisco, the bay and its cities.
New rev. ed. New York, Hastings
House [1973] xiv, 496 p. [$12.50]
917.94/6 72-5854
F869.S3 W85 1973 MRR Ref Desk.

**SANCTUARIES, WILDLIFE
see Wildlife refuges**

SANDBURG, CARL, 1878-1967.
Van Doren, Mark, Carl Sandburg.
Washington, Published for the Library
of Congress by the Gertrude Clarke
Whittall Poetry and Literature Fund;
[for sale by the Supt. of Docs., U.S.
Govt. Print. Off.] 1969. vi, 83 p.
[0.50] 811./5/2 71-600851
Z663.375 .C3 MRR Alc.

SANDBURG, CARL, 1878-1967--BIBLIOGRAPHY.
Van Doren, Mark, Carl Sandburg.
Washington, Published for the Library
of Congress by the Gertrude Clarke
Whittall Poetry and Literature Fund;
[for sale by the Supt. of Docs., U.S.
Govt. Print. Off.] 1969. vi, 83 p.
[0.50] 811./5/2 71-600851
Z663.375 .C3 MRR Alc.

**SANITATION.
see also Hygiene

see also Pollution**

**SANSKRIT LANGUAGE--DICTIONARIES--
ENGLISH.**
Apte, Vaman Shivaram, The practical
Sanskrit-English dictionary. Rev.
and enl. ed. Poona, Prasad
Prakashan, 1957-59. 3 v. 491.232
58-20492
PK933 .A65 MRR Alc.

SANSKRIT LANGUAGE--GRAMMAR.
Burrow, Thomas. The Sanskrit
language, 2nd ed. London, Faber,
1965 [i.e. 1966] vii, 426 p. [70/-]
491.25 66-72363
PK663 .B8 1966 MRR Alc.

**SANSKRIT LITERATURE--HISTORY AND
CRITICISM.**
Gowen, Herbert Henry, A history of
Indian literature from Vedic times to
the present day, New York, London,
D. Appleton and company, 1931. xvi
p., 1 l., 593 p. 891.109 31-29769

PK2903 .G6 MRR Alc.

**SÃO THOMÉ E PRINCIPE (PROVINCE--
DESCRIPTION AND TRAVEL--GAZETTEERS.**
United States. Office of Geography,
Rio Muni, Fernando Po, and São Tomé
e Principe; official standard names
approved by the United States Board
on Geographic Names. Washington,
U.S. Govt. Print. Off., 1962. iv, 95
p. 62-62087
DT619 .U47 MRR Alc.

SARDINIA--COMMERCE--DIRECTORIES.
Guida economica della Sicilia,
Sardegna e Mezzogiorno d'Italia.
[1.]- ed.; 1946- Roma [etc.]
G.I.P.I. 49-17748
HC307.S5 G8 MRR Alc Latest edition

SATANISM--DICTIONARIES.
Baskin, Wade. Dictionary of
Satanism. New York, Philosophical
Library [1971, c1972] 351 p.
[$12.50] 133.4/2/03 75-155971
BF1407 .B37 1972 MRR Alc.

**SATELLITES.
see also Artificial satellites**

Kuiper, Gerard Peter, ed. Planets
and satellites, Chicago, University
of Chicago Press [1961] xx, 601 p.
520.4 61-66777
QB501 .S6 vol. 3 MRR Alc.

**SATELLITES, ARTIFICIAL
see Artificial satellites**

**SAVEZ KOMUNISTA JUGOSLAVIJE--
DIRECTORIES.**
Directory of Yugoslav officials.
[n.p.] 1970- v. 216 p.
354.497/002 73-13670
JN9667 .D55 MRR Alc.

**SAVING AND INVESTMENT.
see also Investments**

SAVING AND INVESTMENT--UNITED STATES.
Surveys of consumers. 1971/72- [Ann
Arbor, Mich., Institute for Social
Research, University of Michigan]
658.8/3973 72-619718
HC110.S3 A3 MRR Alc Latest edition

**SAVINGS-BANKS--UNITED STATES--
DIRECTORIES.**
Directory of the mutual savings banks
of the United States. New York,
National Association of Mutual
Savings Banks. [$17.00] 332.2/1 74-
640216
HG2441 .D5 MRR Alc Latest edition

SAWMILLS--UNITED STATES--DIRECTORIES.
Directory of the forest products
industry. San Francisco [etc.] M.
Freeman Publications [etc.] 21-10771

TS803 .D5 Sci RR Latest edition /
MRR Alc Latest edition

SAXONY, LOWER--COMMERCE--DIRECTORIES.
Firmenhandbuch Niedersachsen und Land
Bremen. Hannover, Industrie- und
Handelsverlag. 53-29246
HC287.S3 F5 MRR Alc Latest edition

SAXONY, LOWER--INDUSTRIES--DIRECTORIES.
Firmenhandbuch Niedersachsen und Land
Bremen. Hannover, Industrie- und
Handelsverlag. 53-29246
HC287.S3 F5 MRR Alc Latest edition

**SAYRE, FRANCIS BOWES, 1885- --
BIBLIOGRAPHY.**
United States. Library of Congress.
Manuscript Division. Francis Bowes
Sayre: a register of his papers in
the Library of Congress. Washington,
1965. 11 l. 012 65-62943
Z663.34 .S35 MRR Alc.

**SCALES (WEIGHING INSTRUMENTS)--
DICTIONARIES.**
Scale Manufacturers Association,
Washington D.C. Terminology
Committee. Terms and definitions for
the weighing industry. [Washington,
1964] 115 p. 681.12 65-56089
TS410 .S28 1964 MRR Alc.

SCANDINAVIA.
Sømme, Axel Christian Zetlitz, The
geography of Norden; London
Heinemann [1961] 363 p. 914.8 62-
5819
DL5 .S6 1961a MRR Alc.

SCANDINAVIA--BIOGRAPHY--DICTIONARIES.
Dictionary of Scandinavian biography.
London, Melrose Press [1972] xxxv,
467 p. [£10.50] 920/.048 B 73-
189270
CT1243 .D53 MRR Biog.

SCANDINAVIA--CIVILIZATION--DICTIONARIES.
Kulturhistorisk leksikon for nordisk
middelalder fra vikingetid til
reformationstid. København,
Rosenkilde og Bagger, 1956- v.
56-58225
DL30 .K8 MRR Alc.

SCANDINAVIA--COMMERCE--DIRECTORIES.
British & international buyers &
sellers guide. Manchester, Eng.
[etc.] C. G. Birn. 55-36686
HF54.G7 B7 MRR Alc Latest edition

Nordisk handelskalender, København,
H. P. Bov. 49-23912
Began with vol. for 1903.
HF5193 .N6 MRR Alc Latest edition

**SCANDINAVIA--COMMERCE--HANDBOOKS,
MANUALS, ETC.**
Trade handbook for East Europe and
Scandinavia. 1971- [Copenhagen]
Wilkenschildt Publishers. 72-626883

HF3497 .T73 MRR Alc Latest edition

**SCANDINAVIA--DESCRIPTION AND TRAVEL--
GUIDE-BOOKS.**
Clark, Sydney Aylmer, All the best
in Scandinavia New York, Dodd, Mead
[1968] xi, 678 p. 914.8/04/8 68-
24864
DL4 .C58 1968 MRR Alc.

Fodor's Scandinavia. 1969- New
York, D. McKay. 914.8/04/8 72-
622912
DL4 .S35 MRR Alc Latest edition

**SCANDINAVIA--LEARNED INSTITUTIONS AND
SOCIETIES--DIRECTORIES.**
Scandinavian Council for Applied
Research. Scandinavian research
guide. 2d rev. ed. Copenhagen,
Nordforsk [1965] 12, 438 p.
[77.00dkr] 507.2048 66-68485
Q180.S3 S3 1965 MRR Alc.

SCANDINAVIA--STATISTICS.
Trade handbook for East Europe and
Scandinavia. 1971- [Copenhagen]
Wilkenschildt Publishers. 72-626883

HF3497 .T73 MRR Alc Latest edition

**SCANDINAVIAN LANGUAGES--CONVERSATION
AND PHRASE BOOKS--POLYGLOT.**
Lyall, Archibald, A guide to 25
languages of Europe. Rev. ed.
[Harrisburg, Pa.] Stackpole Co.
[1966] viii, 407 p. 413 66-20847

PB73 .L85 1966 MRR Alc.

**SCANDINAVIAN LANGUAGES--DICTIONARIES--
ENGLISH.**
Walter, Frank Keller, Abbreviations
and technical terms used in book
catalogs and bibliographies, in eight
languages, 1917 handy edition.
Boston, The Boston book company
[1919?] 2 v. in 1. 27-13479
Z1006 .W261 1919 MRR Alc.

**SCANDINAVIAN LANGUAGES--DICTIONARIES--
POLYGLOT.**
Bergmann, Peter M. The concise
dictionary of twenty-six languages in
simultaneous translations, New York,
Polyglot Library [1968] 406 p. 413
67-14284
P361 .B4 TJ Rm.

Great Britain. Naval intelligence
division. A dictionary of naval
equivalents covering English, French,
Italian, Spanish, Russian, Swedish,
Danish, Dutch, German. London, H.M.
Stationery off., 1924. 2 v. 24-
23792
V24 .G7 MRR Alc.

Orne, Jerrold, The language of the
foreign book trade: 2d ed. Chicago,
American Library Association, 1962.
213 p. 010.3 61-12881
Z1006 .O7 1962 MRR Alc.

Ouseg, H. L. 21-language dictionary.
London, P. Owen [1962] xxxi, 333 p.
63-1285
P361 .O85 1962 MRR Alc.

**SCANDINAVIAN LITERATURE--HISTORY AND
CRITICISM.**
Bredsdorff, Elias. An introduction
to Scandinavian literature, from the
earliest time to our day, Westport,
Conn., Greenwood Press [1970] 245 p.
839./5/09 78-98748
PT7063 .B7 1970 MRR Alc.

SCANDINAVIAN LITERATURE-- (Cont.)
Litteraturen i Danmark og de øvrige
nordiske lande. 4. udg. København,
Politiken, 1967. 536 p. [21.45 dkr]
68-85482
PT7060 .L5 1967 MRR Alc.

SCANDINAVIAN PERIODICALS--BIBLIOGRAPHY.
Media Scandinavia. 16.- udg.; 1967-
København, Danske reklamebureauers
brancheforening. 72-623099
Z6941 .M4 MRR Alc Latest edition

SCHIZOMYCETES.
Bergey's manual of determinative
bacteriology. 8th ed. Baltimore,
Williams & Wilkins Co. [1974] xxvi,
1246 p. 589.9/001/2 73-20173
QR81 .A5 1974 MRR Alc.

SCHLESWIG-HOLSTEIN--BIBLIOGRAPHY.
Erichsen, Balder Vermund Aage. Dansk
historisk bibliografi, [Ny udg.]
København, I kommission hos G. E. C.
Gad, 1929. 3 v. 53-48097
Z2576 .E682 MRR Alc.

SCHOLARLY PERIODICALS--DIRECTORIES.
An Advertiser's guide to scholarly
periodicals. New York, American
University Press Services. 659.132
65-9732
Began publication in 1958.
Z6944.S3 A25 MRR Alc Latest
edition

Association des universités
entièrement ou partiellement de
langue française. Catalogue des
publications périodiques
universitaires de langue française.
[2. ed. Montréal, 1969] viii, 150
p. 77-478508
Z6944.S3 A7 1969 MRR Alc.

SCHOLARLY PUBLISHING--UNITED STATES.
Nemeyer, Carol A., Scholarly reprint
publishing in the United States New
York, R. R. Bowker Co., 1972. lx,
262 p. 070.5/73 74-163901
Z479 .N44 MRR Alc.

**SCHOLARLY PUBLISHING--UNITED STATES--
DIRECTORIES.**
Ross, Mary Bucher, Directory of
publishing opportunities; 2d ed.
Orange, N.J., Academic Media [1973]
x, 722 p. 808/.025 72-13565
Z479 .R67 1973 MRR Ref Desk.

SCHOLARS.
Dawson, Warren Royal, Who was who in
Egyptology. London, Egypt
Exploration Society, 1951. x, 172 p.
920.02 52-27063
DT58 .D3 MRR Biog.

United Nations Educational,
Scientific and Cultural Organization.
Secretariat. Social scientists
specializing in African studies;
[Paris, École pratique des hautes
études, 1963. 375 p. 64-4339
DT19.5 .U5 MRR Biog.

Zischka, Gert A. Allgemeines
Gelehrten-Lexikon; Stuttgart, A.
Kroner [1961] viii, 710 p. 62-
31158
CT3990.A2 Z5 MRR Biog.

SCHOLARS--UNITED STATES.
Foreign Area Fellowship Program.
Directory, foreign area fellows.
[1st]- ed.; 1952/59- New York.
378.35 63-12636
CT83 .F6 MRR Biog Latest edition

SCHOLARS--UNITED STATES--DIRECTORIES.
Directory of American scholars;
[1st]- ed.; 1942- New York [etc.]
Jaques Cattell Press [etc.] 57-9125

LA2311 .C32 Sci RR Latest edition
/ MRR Biog Latest edition

SCHOLARS, AMERICAN--DIRECTORIES.
United States. Library of Congress.
Hispanic Foundation. National
directory of Latin Americanists;
Washington, [For sale by the
Superintendent of Documents, U.S.
Govt. Print. Off.] 1966. iii, 351 p.
920/.08 65-61762
Z663.32.A5 no. 10 MRR Biog.

SCHOLARS, EAST EUROPEAN.
National Academy of Sciences,
Washington, D.C. Office of the
Foreign Secretary. The Eastern
European academies of sciences;
Washington, National Academy of
Sciences-National Research Council,
1963. 148 p. 067.058 63-60058
AS98 .N3 MRR Alc.

SCHOLARS, ITALIAN.
Cosenza, Mario Emilio, Biographical
and bibliographical dictionary of the
Italian humanists [2d ed.; rev. and
enl. Boston, G. K. Hall, 1962]-67.
6 v. 920.045 62-13227
Z7128.H9 C6 MRR Alc.

SCHOLARSHIPS.
American Association of School
Librarians. Awards and Scholarships
Committee. Scholarships,
fellowships, loans, grants-in-aid for
school librarianship. Chicago,
American Library Association, 1963.
40 p. 64-4534
Z668 .A35 MRR Alc.

The College blue book. [1st]- 1923-
New York [etc.] CCM Information
Corp. [etc.] 378.73 24-223
LA226 .C685 MRR Ref Desk Latest
edition

The Grants register. 1969/70-
Chicago, St. James Press. 378.34 77-
12055
LB2338 .G7 MRR Alc Latest edition

Handbook on international study.
1955- [New York] Institute of
International Education. 55-8482
LB2376 .H3 MRR Ref Desk Latest
edition

Institute of International Education.
Directory of international
scholarships in the arts. New York,
1958. 120 p. 707.9 59-38191
N347 .I5 MRR Alc.

Study abroad. v. 1- 1948- [Paris]
UNESCO. 378.3 49-2511
LB2338 .S86 MRR Ref Desk Latest
edition / MRR Alc Latest edition

Vacation study abroad. [Paris,
United Nations Educational,
Scientific and Cultural Organization]
370.18/62 72-627046
LB2338 .V3 MRR Ref Desk Latest
edition

World-wide graduate award directory.
v. 1- 1957- Brooklyn, Advancement
and Placement Institute. 58-2475
LB2338 .W6 MRR Alc Latest edition

SCHOLARSHIPS--GREAT BRITAIN.
Millard, Patricia. Awards and
prizes. Havant, K. Mason, 1970. 249
p. [5/-/-] 001.4/4 70-498024
AS118 .M54 MRR Alc.

United Kingdom postgraduate awards.
London, Association of Commonwealth
Universities. 378.3/3/0942 72-
623777
LB2339.G7 A75 MRR Alc Latest
edition

SCHOLARSHIPS--UNITED STATES.
Aid-to-education programs of some
leading business concerns. New York.
378.1 62-4102
LB2342 .C6744 MRR Alc Latest
edition

American Council on Education.
Fellowships in the arts and sciences.
1st-10th ed.; 1957-1967/68
Washington [etc.] 58-461
LB2338 .F43 MRR Ref Desk Latest
edition

Angel, Juvenal Londoño, How and
where to get scholarships & loans,
2d ed. [New York] Regents Pub. Co.
[1968] 221 p. 378.3 68-19307
LB2848 .A65 1968 MRR Alc.

Annual register of grant support.
1969- Orange, N.J. [etc.] Academic
Media. 001.4/4 69-18307
AS911 .A2A67 Sci RR Latest edition
/ MRR Ref Desk Latest edition

Current financial aids for
undergraduate students. 1969/70-
Moline, Ill., etc., M & L
Enterprises, etc. 378.3/025/73 73-
2076
LB2338 .C8 MRR Ref Desk Latest
edition

Directory of special programs for
minority group members: Career
information services, employment
skills banks, financial aid. 1974-
[Garrett Park, Md., Garrett Park
Press] [$6.95] 331.7/02/02573 73-
93533
HD5724 .D56 MRR Alc Latest edition

Feingold, S. Norman, Scholarships,
fellowships, and loans. 1st ed.
Boston, Bellman Pub. Co. [1949- v.
378.330973 49-49180
LB2338 .F4 MRR Alc.

Keeslar, Oreon Pierre, Financial
aids for higher education, 74-75
catalog [Dubuque, Iowa] W. C. Brown
Co. [1974] lxviii, 629 p. [$13.95]
378.3/0973 73-82709
LB2338 .K4 1974 MRR Ref Desk.

Literary market place; [1st]- ed.;
1940- New York, Bowker. 655.473 41-
51571
PN161 .L5 Sci RR Partial set / MRR
Ref Desk Latest edition

Lovejoy's scholarship guide. 1957-
New York, Simon and Schuster. 57-
10980
LB2338 .L6 MRR Alc Latest edition
/ MRR Ref Desk Latest edition

National register of scholarships and
fellowships. New York, World Trade
Academy Press. 378.33 58-900
LB2948 .N3 MRR Alc Latest edition

Proia, Nicholas C. Barron's handbook
of American college financial aid
Rev. Woodbury, N.Y., Barron's
Educational Series, inc. [1974] 508
p. [$6.95] 378.3/0973 74-165306
LB2338 .P72 1974 MRR Ref Desk.

Shapiro, Sandra. Directory of
financial aid in higher education;
Waltham, Mass., African Studies
Association, Research Liaison
Committee, Brandeis University [1973]
v, 166 p. 378.3/025/73 73-166271

LB2338 .S46 MRR Alc.

Toy, Henry, Federal dollars for
scholars [1st ed.] Washington, Nu-
Toy [1970] vii, 54 p., 292 columns.
378.3/0973 77-112985
LB2338 .T6 MRR Alc.

Turner, David Reuben, College
scholarships; [1st ed.] New York,
Arco [1966] 1 v. (various pagings)
378.340973 66-17179
LB2338 .T78 MRR Alc.

United States. Library of Congress.
Education and Public Welfare
Division. Student assistance
handbook; Rev. Washington, U.S.
Govt. Print. Off., 1965. vi, 241 p.
65-62199
L901.A4 1965 MRR Alc.

**SCHOLARSHIPS--UNITED STATES--
BIBLIOGRAPHY.**
Education Services Press, St. Paul.
Guide to support programs for
education. St. Paul [1966] 160 p.
371 66-18553
Z5814.F5 E18 MRR Alc.

Searles, Aysel. Guide to financial
aids for students in arts & sciences
for graduate and professional study
Rev. ed. New York, Arco [1974] xii,
107 p. [$3.95] 378.3/025/73 74-
80776
LB2338 .S4 1974 MRR Ref Desk.

**SCHOLARSHIPS--UNITED STATES--
DIRECTORIES.**
Grants and aid to individuals in the
arts. 1st- ed.; 1970- Washington.
378.3 70-112695
NX398 .G7 MRR Ref Desk Latest
edition

Institute of International Education.
International awards in the arts;
[New York, 1969] 105 p. 707/.9 68-
57352
NX398 .I5 MRR Ref Desk.

Searles, Aysel. Guide to financial
aids for students in arts & sciences
for graduate and professional study
Rev. ed. New York, Arco [1974] xii,
107 p. [$3.95] 378.3/025/73 74-
80776
LB2338 .S4 1974 MRR Ref Desk.

United States. Office of Minority
Business Enterprise. Higher
education aid for minority business;
Washington; [For sale by the Supt. of
Docs., U.S. Govt. Print. Off.] 1970.
viii, 103 p. [1.00] 650/.071/1 78-
607539
HF1131 .A55 MRR Alc.

SCHOLARSHIPS--UNITED STATES--YEARBOOKS.
Need a lift? Indianapolis. 67-6704
Began in 1951.
LB2338 .N37 MRR Alc Latest edition

SCHOLASTIC APTITUDE TEST.
Brownstein, Samuel C., How to
prepare for college entrance
examinations 4th ed., enl. and
completely rev. Woodbury, N.Y.,
Barron's Educational Series, inc.
[1969] 538 p. [3.95] 378.1/6/42
68-56405
LB2353 .B75 1969 MRR Alc.

Brownstein, Samuel C., How to
prepare for the graduate record
examination Woodbury, N.Y., Barron's
Educational Series, inc. [1967] 267
p. 378.1/05/7 66-20916
LB2367 .B75 MRR Alc.

College Entrance Examination Board.
A description of the College Board
achievement tests. 1956-
[Princeton, N.J.] 371.26 59-4353
LB2367 .C6 MRR Alc Latest edition

SCHOLASTIC APTITUDE TEST. (Cont.)
Turner, David Reuben, College
scholarships; [1st ed.] New York,
Arco [1966] 1 v. (various pagings)
378.340973 66-17179
LB2338 .T78 MRR Alc.

SCHOLASTICISM--DICTIONARIES.
Wuellner, Bernard. A dictionary of
scholastic philosophy. 2d ed.
Milwaukee, Bruce Pub. Co. [1966]
xviii, 339 p. 189.403 66-24259
B50.S35 W8 1966 MRR Alc.

SCHÖNBERG, ARNOLD, 1874-1951.
Wellesz, Egon, The origins of
Schönberg's twelve-tone system;
Washington [U.S. Govt. Print. Off.]
1958. iii, 14 p. 781.22 58-60018

Z663.37 .A5 1957 MRR Alc.

SCHOOL ADMINISTRATORS--UNITED STATES--
DIRECTORIES.
American Association of School
Administrators. Roster of members.
[Washington] 371.147206273 58-7789

L13 .A366 MRR Alc Latest edition

SCHOOL BUSINESS ADMINISTRATORS--
DIRECTORIES.
Association of School Business
Officials of the United States and
Canada. Official membership
directory. Chicago [etc.] 61-45663

LB2803.A3 A8 MRR Alc Latest
edition

SCHOOL CENSUS--UNITED STATES--
STATISTICS.
Gertler, Diane (Bochner) Directory:
public elementary and secondary
schools in large school districts
with enrollment and instructional
staff, by race; fall 1967.
[Washington] U.S. National Center for
Educational Statistics; [for sale by
the Supt. of Docs., U.S. Govt. Print.
Off., 1968] v, 840 p. [7.25]
371/.01/02573 72-604076
L901 .G38 MRR Alc.

SCHOOL CREDITS.
American Association of Collegiate
Registrars and Admissions Officers.
Report on the credit given by
educational institutions. [n.p.] 57-
46346
LB2360 .A48 MRR Alc Latest edition

SCHOOL DECORATION--UNITED STATES.
Fundaburk, Emma Lila, Art at
educational institutions in the
United States; Metuchen, N.J.,
Scarecrow Press, 1974. xv, 670 p.
709/.73 74-3187
N510 .F86 MRR Alc.

SCHOOL DISTRICTS--UNITED STATES--
FINANCE.
Rowland, Howard S. Federal aid for
schools, 1967-1968 guide; New York,
Macmillan [1967] xv, 396 p.
379/.121/0973 67-19680
LB2825 .R64 MRR Alc.

SCHOOL DISTRICTS--UNITED STATES--
STATISTICS.
United States. Bureau of the Census.
1972 census of governments.
[Washington, U.S. Govt. Print. Off.]
1973- v. [$1.25 (v. 2, pt. 1)
varies] 317.3 73-600080
JS3 .A244 MRR Alc.

SCHOOL EMPLOYEES.
see also Teachers

SCHOOL INTEGRATION.
see also Segregation in education

SCHOOL LANDS--UNITED STATES.
Eddy, Edward Danforth. Colleges for
our land and time; [1st ed.] New
York, Harper [1957] xiv, 328 p.
379.123 57-6739
LA226 .E38 MRR Alc.

SCHOOL LIBRARIES.
see also Libraries, Children's

American Library Association.
Periodicals List Subcommittee.
Periodicals for school libraries;
Chicago, American Library
Association, 1969. xvii, 217 p.
016.051 70-80870
Z6944.S8 A4 MRR Alc.

The Elementary school library
collection, phases 1-2-3; 8th ed.
New Brunswick, N.J., Bro-Dart
Foundation, 1973. xxviii, 780 p.
028.52 73-8819
Z1037 .E4 1973 MRR Alc.

Hodges, Elizabeth D., Books for
elementary school libraries:
Chicago, American Library
Association, 1969. xiii, 321 p.
[7.50 (pbk)] 028.52 76-77273
Z1037 .B65 MRR Alc.

Wynar, Christine L. Guide to
reference books for school media
centers Littleton, Colo., Libraries
Unlimited, 1973. xviii, 473 p.
[$17.50] 011/.02 73-87523
Z1035.1 .W97 MRR Alc.

SCHOOL LIBRARIES--UNITED STATES.
American Association of School
Librarians. Awards and Scholarships
Committee. Scholarships,
fellowships, loans, grants-in-aid for
school librarianship. Chicago,
American Library Association, 1963.
40 p. 64-4534
Z668 .A35 MRR Alc.

SCHOOL LIBRARIES--UNITED STATES--
DIRECTORIES.
American school library directory;
Rev. ed. New York, R. R. Bowker Co.,
1959- v. in 65-1486
Z675.S3 A632 MRR Alc.

American school library directory;
New York, R. R. Bowker Co., 1952-57.
4 v. 027.82058 52-6286
Z675.S3 A63 MRR Alc.

SCHOOL LIBRARIES--UNITED STATES--
STATISTICS.
School library supervisors directory.
1st- ed.; 1966- New York, R. R.
Bowker Co. 027.8/025/73 66-27557
Z675.S3 S375 MRR Alc Latest
edition

SCHOOL LIBRARIES (HIGH SCHOOL)
Independent Schools Education Board.
3000 books for secondary school
libraries; New York, R. R. Bowker
Co. [1961] 134 p. 028.52 61-66741

Z1037 .I33 MRR Alc.

National Association of Independent
Schools. Library Committee. Books
for secondary school libraries. 4th
ed. New York, R. R. Bowker Co.,
1971. viii, 308 p. 028.52 71-
27321
Z1035 .N2 1971 MRR Alc.

Senior high school library catalog.
10th ed. New York, H. W. Wilson Co.,
1972. xii, 1214 p. 028.52 72-3819

Z1035 .S42 1972 MRR Alc.

Wilson, H. W., firm, publishers.
Junior high school library catalog.
2d ed. New York, 1970. xii, 808 p.
[30.00] 028.52 75-126356
Z1037 .W765 1970 MRR Alc.

SCHOOL LIFE
see Students

SCHOOL MANAGEMENT AND ORGANIZATION.
see also Teaching

Miller, Van, The public
administration of American school
systems 2d ed. New York, Macmillan
[1972] x, 428 p. [$8.95] 371.2
70-156834
LB2805 .M47 1972 MRR Alc.

Sharp, Theodore. The country index;
North Hollywood, Calif.,
International Education Research
Foundation [1971] xii, 217 p.
378.1/50/7 68-28836
LB2805 .S576 MRR Alc.

SCHOOL PLAYS
see Children's plays

SCHOOL SPORTS.
see also Football

SCHOOL-TEACHING
see Teaching

SCHOOL YEARBOOKS--UNITED STATES--
DIRECTORIES.
Directory of the college student
press in America. 1967/68- New York
[etc.] Oxbridge Pub. Co. [etc.]
378.1/98/87705 76-10981
L901 .D52 MRR Ref Desk Latest
edition

SCHOOLCRAFT, HENRY ROWE, 1793-1864--
MANUSCRIPTS.
Schoolcraft, Henry Rowe, The papers
of Henry Rowe Schoolcraft.
[Washington, Photoduplication
Service, Library of Congress, 1973]
69 reels. 016.9705/092/4 73-20014

Z663.34 .S38 MRR Alc.

SCHOOLS.
see also Kindergartens

see also Public schools

SCHOOLS--FURNITURE, EQUIPMENT, ETC.--
DIRECTORIES.
Where to buy supplies for educational
institutions. Boston, P. Sargent.
379.153 54-38611
LB3280 .W5 MRR Alc Latest edition

SCHURZ, CARL, 1829-1906--MANUSCRIPTS.
United States. Library of Congress.
Manuscript Division. Carl Schurz; a
register of his papers in the Library
of Congress. Washington, 1966. 17
p. 012 66-62983
Z663.34 .S4 MRR Alc.

SCIENCE.
see also Biology

see also Chemistry

see also Ethnology

see also Geology

see also Mathematics

see also Paleontology

see also Physics

see also Physiology

see also Technology

Asimov, Isaac, The new intelligent
man's guide to science. New York, 500
Basic Books [1965] xvi, 864 p.
65-23045
Q162 .A8 1965 MRR Alc.

The Book of popular sciences. New
York, Grolier [1969] 10 v. 500 69-
10053
Q162 .B68 1969 MRR Alc.

Cowles encyclopedia of science,
industry, and technology. New enl.
ed. New York, Cowles Book Co. [1969]
639 p. [17.50] 500 69-17310
Q158 .C6 1969 MRR Alc.

Woodbury, David Oakes, 1001
questions answered about the new
science. New York, Docc, Mead, 1959.
358 p. 507.6 59-6182
Q162 .W75 MRR Alc.

SCIENCE--ABBREVIATIONS.
Zatucki, Henryk. Dictionary of
russian technical and scientific
abbreviations Amsterdam, New York
[etc.] Elsevier Pub. Co., 1968. 400
p. 601/.48 67-12784
PG2693 .Z3 MRR Alc.

SCIENCE--ABSTRACTING AND INDEXING.
International Federation for
Documentation. Abstracting services.
[2d ed.] The Hague, 1969. 2 v.
029/.9/5 73-168592
Z695.93 .I58 1969 MRR Ref Desk.

United States. Library of Congress.
Science and Technology Division. A
guide to the world's abstracting and
indexing services in science and
technology. Washington 1963. viii,
183 p. 016.505 63-61149
Z663.41 .G78 MRR Alc.

SCIENCE--ABSTRACTS.
United States. Library of Congress.
European Affairs Division. The
natural sciences in Western Germany;
[Washington, 1951] 127 p. 507.2
51-60019
Z663.26 .N3 1951 MRR Alc.

SCIENCE--BIBLIOGRAPHY.
Blanchard, Joy Richard, Literature
of agricultural research, Berkeley,
University of California Press, 1958.
x, 231 p. 016.63 57-12942
Z5071 .B5 MRR Alc.

Clapp, Jane. Museum publications.
New York, Scarecrow Press, 1962. 2
v. 016.0697 62-10120
Z5051 .C5 MRR Alc.

Jenkins, Frances Briggs, Science
reference sources. 4th ed.
Champaign, Ill., Distributed by
Illini Union Bookstore [c1965] xvi,
143 p. 016.5 66-966
Z7401 .J4 1965 MRR Alc.

Jenkins, Frances Briggs, Science
reference sources. 5th ed.
Cambridge, Mass., M.I.T. Press [1969]
xvi, 231 p. 016.5 73-95001
Z7401 .J4 1969 MRR Alc.

Kyed, James M., Scientific,
technical, and engineering societies
publications in print, New York, R.
R. Bowker Co., 1974. x, 223 p.
016.5 74-5094
Z7911 .K92 MRR Alc.

Royal Society of London. Catalogue
of scientific papers. London, C. J.
Clay, 1867-1925. 19 v. 02-11462
Z7403 .R88 MRR Alc.

Royal society of London. Catalogue
of scientific papers, 1800-1900.
Cambridge, University press, 1908-
v. 08-24586
Z7403 .R8812 MRR Alc.

SCIENCE--BIBLIOGRAPHY. (Cont.)
Scientific and technical books in print. 1972- New York, R. R. Bowker Co. 016.5 71-37614
  Z7401 .S573 MRR Alc Latest edition / Sci RR Latest edition

Thornton, John Leonard. Scientific books, libraries and collectors; 2d rev. ed. London, Library Association, 1962. xiii, 406 p. 63-23658
  Z7401 .T45 1962 MRR Alc.

United States. Library of Congress. Japanese scientific and technical serial publications in the collections of the Library of Congress. Washington, Science and Technology Division, Reference Dept., Library of Congress, 1962. v, 247 p. 62-60085
  Z663.41 .J2 MRR Alc.

United States. Library of Congress. Science in the Library of Congress. Washington, Science Division, Reference Dept., Library of Congress, 1954. iii, 15 p. 027.5753 54-60008
  Z663.41 .S28 MRR Alc.

United States. Library of Congress. Science and Technology Division. Air Force scientific research bibliography. Washington, U.S. Govt. Print. Off., 1961- v. 016.5 61-60038
  Z663.41 .A36 MRR Alc.

United States. Library of Congress. Science and Technology Division. Scientific and technical serial publications. Washington, 1954. viii, 118 p. 016.505 54-60015
  Z663.41 .S3 MRR Alc.

SCIENCE--BIBLIOGRAPHY--CATALOGS.
British museum (Natural History) Library. Catalogue of the books, manuscripts, maps and drawings in the British museum (Natural history). London, Printed by order of the Trustees, 1903-15. 5 v. 04-18991
  Z7409 .B85 MRR Alc.

SCIENCE--BIO-BIBLIOGRAPHY.
Directorio de cientificos e instituciones de Argentina. 1966, fasc. 2- Montevideo, Centro de Cooperación Científica de la Unesco para América Latina. 72-621605
  Q33 .D5 MRR Alc Latest edition / Sci RR Latest edition

SCIENCE--BIO-BIBLIOGRAPHY--INDEXES.
Ireland, Norma (Olin) Index to scientists of the world, from ancient to modern times: Boston, F. W. Faxon Co. [1962. xliii, 662 p. 016.925 62-13662
  Z7404 .I7 MRR Biog.

SCIENCE--BIOGRAPHY--BIBLIOGRAPHY.
Pittsburgh. Carnegie library. Men of science and industry. Pittsburgh, Carnegie library, 1915. 189, [3] p. 15-6134
  Z7404 .A1P6 MRR Biog.

SCIENCE--DICTIONARIES.
Cowles encyclopedia of science, industry, and technology. New enl. ed. New York, Cowles Book Co. [1969] 639 p. [17.50] 500 69-17310
  Q158 .C6 1969 MRR Alc.

Dictionary of science and technology; Edinburgh, W. and R. Chambers, 1971. xvi, 1328 p. [£6.50] 503 72-180510
  Q123 .D53 1971 MRR Ref Desk.

The Harper encyclopedia of science, Rev. ed. New York, Harper & Row, 1967. ix, 1379 p. 503 67-22504
  Q123 .H26 1967 MRR Alc.

McGraw-Hill encyclopedia of science and technology; [Rev. ed.] New York, McGraw-Hill [1966] 15 v. 503 65-26484
  Q121 .M3 1966 MRR Alc.

Pei, Mario Andrew, ed. Language of the specialists; [New York] Funk & Wagnalls [1966] xii, 388 p. 423.1 66-22943
  PE1680 .P4 MRR Alc.

Raghu Vira. A comprehensive English-Hindi dictionary of governmental & educational words & phrases ... [Nagpur, Lokesh Chandra, International Academy of Indian Culture, 1955] 189, 1579 p. 491.4332 56-19893
  PK1937 .R3 MRR Alc.

Speck, Gerald Eugene, ed. A dictionary of science terms, [1st ed.] New York, Hawthorn Books [1965] 272 p. 503 65-22787
  Q123 .S6 1865a MRR Alc.

Tver, David F. Dictionary of business & scientific terms, 2d ed. Houston, Tex., Gulf Pub. Co. [1968] xi, 528 p. 503 68-6988
  Q123 .T85 1968 MRR Alc.

Van Nostrand's scientific encyclopedia; 4th ed. Princeton, N.J., Van Nostrand [1968] ix, 2008 p. 503 68-20822
  Q121 .V3 1968 MRR Alc.

SCIENCE--DICTIONARIES--BIBLIOGRAPHY.
Turnbull, William R. Scientific and technical dictionaries; San Bernardino, Calif., Bibliothek Press, 1966- v. 016.503 67-25830
  Z7401 .T8 MRR Alc.

SCIENCE--DICTIONARIES--FRENCH.
De Vries, Louis, French-English science dictionary for students in agricultural, biological, and physical sciences, 3d ed. New York, McGraw-Hill [1962] 655 p. 503 61-17943
  Q123 .D37 1962 MRR Alc.

SCIENCE--DICTIONARIES--GERMAN.
De Vries, Louis, German-English science dictionary for students in chemistry, physics, biology, agriculture, and related sciences 3d ed. xliii, 592 p. 503 59-9412
  Q123 .D4 1959 MRR Alc.

SCIENCE--DICTIONARIES--POLYGLOT.
The International dictionary of applied mathematics, Princeton, N.J., Van Nostrand [1960] 1173 p. 510.3 60-16931
  QA5 .I5 MRR Alc.

SCIENCE--DICTIONARIES--POLYGLOT--BIBLIOGRAPHY.
Bibliography of interlingual scientific and technical dictionaries. [1st]- 1951- [Paris] UNESCO. 54-11648
  Z7405.D5 B5 Sci RR Latest edition / MRR Alc Latest edition

SCIENCE--DICTIONARIES--RUSSIAN.
Carpovich, Eugene A., Russian-English atomic dictionary. 2d rev. and enriched ed. New York, Technical Dictionaries Co., 1959. 317 p. 539.703 59-2755
  QC772 .C3 1959 MRR Alc.

Hoseh, Mordecai. Russian-English dictionary of chemistry and chemical technology New York, Reinhold Pub. Corp. [1964] xiii, 522 p. 540.3 64-22149
  QD5 .H6 MRR Alc.

United States. Library of Congress. Aerospace Technology Division. Soviet Russian scientific and technical terms; Sept. 1958-63. Washington [For sale by the Supt. of Docs., U.S. Govt. Print. Off., etc.] 60-60977
  Q123 .U46 Sci RR Latest edition / MRR Alc Latest edition

Zatucki, Henryk. Dictionary of russian technical and scientific abbreviations Amsterdam, New York [etc.] Elsevier Pub. Co., 1968. 400 p. 601/.48 67-12784
  PG2683 .Z3 MRR Alc.

SCIENCE--DICTIONARIES, JUVENILE.
Compton's illustrated science dictionary. Chicago, Encyclopaedia Britannica Educational Corp. [1969] viii, 632 p. 503 68-58351
  Q123 .C65 1969 MRR Alc.

SCIENCE--DIRECTORIES.
United Nations Educational, Scientific and Cultural Organization. World directory of national science policymaking bodies. Paris, Unesco; Guernsey, Hodgson, 1966- [i.e. 1967- v. [65/- (v. 1)] 506/.1 67-78504
  Q10 .U455 MRR Alc.

SCIENCE--DIRECTORIES--BIBLIOGRAPHY.
Harvey, Anthony P. Directory of scientific directories. St. Peter Port, Guernsey, C.I., Francis Hodgson, 1969. 272 p. [unpriced] 016.5/025 68-8600
  Z7405.D55 H37 MRR Ref Desk.

Klein, Bernard. Guide to American scientific and technical directories. 1st ed. Rye, N.Y., B. Klein Publications [1972] v, 324 p. 016.3384/7/6702573 72-91671
  Z7914.M3 K53 MRR Ref Desk.

United States. Library of Congress. Science and Technology Division. Directories in science and technology; Washington [For sale by the Superintendent of Documents, U.S. Govt. Print. Off.] 1963. vi, 65 p. 63-65164
  Z663.41 .D5 MRR Alc.

SCIENCE--HISTORY.
Sarton, George, A guide to the history of science; Waltham, Mass., Chronica Botanica Co. 1952. xvii, 316 p. 509 52-10902
  Q125 .S24 MRR Alc.

Sarton, George, Introduction to the history of science ... Baltimore, Pub. for the Carnegie institution of Washington, by the Williams & Wilkins company [c1927- v. 27-11418
  Q125 .S32 MRR Alc.

Schmidt, Jacob Edward, Medical discoveries; Springfield, Ill., Thomas [1959] ix, 555 p. 610.9 58-14086
  R131 .S35 1959 MRR Alc.

Wilson, Mitchell A. American science and invention, a pictorial history; New York, Simon and Schuster [1954] ix, 437 p. 509.73 54-9812
  Q125 .W7914 MRR Alc.

SCIENCE--HISTORY--BIBLIOGRAPHY.
Sarton, George, A guide to the history of science; Waltham, Mass., Chronica Botanica Co. 1952. xvii, 316 p. 509 52-10902
  Q125 .S24 MRR Alc.

SCIENCE--HISTORY--BIBLIOGRAPHY--COLLECTED WORKS.
ISIS cumulative bibliography; [London] Mansell, in conjunction with the History of Science Society, 1971- v. 016.509 72-186272
  Z7405.H6 I2 MRR Biog.

SCIENCE--HISTORY--UNITED STATES.
Jaffe, Bernard, Men of science in America; Rev. ed. New York, Simon and Schuster, 1958. 715 p. 509.73 58-59443
  Q127.U6 J27 1958 MRR Biog.

SCIENCE--INDEXES.
Scientific and technical books in print. 1972- New York, R. R. Bowker Co. 016.5 71-37614
  Z7401 .S573 MRR Alc Latest edition / Sci RR Latest edition

SCIENCE--INDEXES--PERIODICALS.
Government reports index, v. 71-1971- [Springfield, Va.] National Technical Information Service. 507/.2073 72-627325
  Z7405.R4 US13 Sci RR Latest edition / MRR Alc Full set

SCIENCE--INFORMATION SERVICES--DIRECTORIES.
Battelle Memorial Institute, Columbus, Ohio. Dept. of Economics and Information Research. Specialized science information services in the United States; Washington, National Science Foundation, Office of Science Information Service, 1961. ix, 528 p. 505.873 61-64862
  AG521 .B3 MRR Alc.

National Research Council, Canada. Technical Information Service. National technical information services worldwide directory. 3d ed. The Hague, Federation internationale de documentation, [1970] 61 p. [fl.25.00] 025.5/2 72-178268
  Q223 .N37 1970 MRR Alc.

United Nations Educational, Scientific and Cultural Organization. World guide to science information and documentation services. [Paris, 1965] 211 p. 507.2 65-9614
  Q223 .U45 MRR Alc.

United States. Library of Congress. International Organizations Section. International scientific organizations; Washington, General Reference and Bibliography Division, Reference Dept., Library of Congress; [for sale by the Superintendent of Documents, U.S. Govt. Print. Off.] 1962 [i.e. 1963] xi, 794 p. 506 62-64648
  Z663.295 .I5 MRR Alc.

SCIENCE--MISCELLANEA.
Woodbury, David Oakes, 1001 questions answered about the new science. New York, Docc, Mead, 1959. 358 p. 507.6 59-6182
  Q162 .W75 MRR Alc.

SCIENCE--PERIODICALS.
Foreign science bulletin. v. 1-Jan. 1965- [Washington] Aerospace Technology Division, Library of Congress. 65-9850
  Z663.23 .A23 MRR Alc MRR Alc Full set

Scientific American. v.1-14, Aug. 28, 1845-June 25, 1859; new ser., v.1-July 2, 1859- [New York] 505 04-17574
  T1 .S5 MRR Alc Indexes only / Sci RR Indexes only

SCIENCE--PERIODICALS--BIBLIOGRAPHY.
Akademija nauk SSSR. Institut nauchnoĭ informatsii. Index of abbreviated and full titles of scientific and technical periodical literature Wright-Patterson Air Force Base, Ohio, 1960?] 247 l. 60-60261
Z6945.A2 A43 MRR Alc.

Directory of Canadian scientific and technical periodicals. 1961- Ottawa, National Research Council. 016.505 61-2342
Z7403 .D5 MRR Alc Latest edition

Fowler, Maureen J. Guides to scientific periodicals London, Library Association [1966] xvi, 318 p. [84/- 63/- (to L.A. members)] 016.505 67-71339
Z7403 .F6 MRR Alc.

International catalogue of scientific literature. List of journals, London, Harrison and sons; [etc., etc.] 1903. 2 p. l., v-xv, 312 p. 03-19593
Z7403 .I61 MRR Alc.

Internationale Bibliographie der Fachzeitschriften für Technik und Wirtschaft. München-Pullach, Verlag Dokumentation [etc.] 67-118312
Z7913 .I757 MRR Alc Latest edition

Nihon kagaku gijutsu kankei chikuji kankōbutsu mokuroku. 1962- [Tokyo] National Diet Library. J 68-5037
Z7403 .N5 Sci RR Latest edition / MRR Alc Latest edition

Pan American Union. Dept. of Scientific Affairs. Guide to Latin American scientific and technical periodicals; Washington, Pan American Union, 1962. xii, 187 p. 016.505 62-62414
Z7407.S6 P3 MRR Alc.

Royal society of London. Catalogue of scientific papers, 1800-1900. Cambridge, University press, 1908- v. 08-24586
Z7403 .R8812 MRR Alc.

Royal society of London. Library. Catalogue of the periodical publications in the library of the Royal society of London. London, Printed for the Royal society at the Oxford university press, 1912. viii, 455, [1] p. 13-18466
Z7403 .R888 MRR Alc.

Scudder, Samuel Hubbard. Catalogue of scientific serials of all countries, Cambridge, Library of Harvard university, 1879. xii, 358 p. 02-7012
Z7403 .S43 MRR Alc.

Ueberreiter, Kurt. A statistical postwar survey on the natural sciences and German universities. [Washington] Library of Congress, European Affairs Division [1950] 31 p. 507.2 50-61523
Z663.26 .S7 MRR Alc.

United States. Library of Congress. Science and Technology Division. Chinese scientific and technical serial publications in the collections of the Library of Congress. Rev. ed. Washington, 1961. v, 107 p. 016.505 62-60011
Z663.41 .C45 1961 MRR Alc.

United States. Library of Congress. Science and Technology Division. Journals in science and technology published in Japan and mainland China; Washington, 1961. 47 p. 016.505 61-60647
Z663.41 .J6 MRR Alc.

United States. Library of Congress. Science and Technology Division. A list of scientific and technical serials currently received by the Library of Congress. Washington, 1960. v, 186 p. 016.505 60-60055
Z663.41 .L5 MRR Alc.

United States. Library of Congress. Science and Technology Division. Scientific and technical serial publications. Washington, 1954. viii, 238 p. 016.505 54-60022
Z663.41 .S33 MRR Alc.

United States. Library of Congress. Science and Technology Division. Scientific and technical serial publications, Washington, 1954. viii, 118 p. 016.505 54-60015
Z663.41 .S3 MRR Alc.

United States. Library of Congress. Science and Technology Division. Scientific and technical serial publications of the Soviet Union, 1945-1960. Washington [For sale by the Superintendent of Documents, U.S. Govt. Print. Off.] 1963. iv, 347 p. 63-61782
Z663.41 .S29 MRR Alc.

World list of scientific periodicals published in the years 1900-1960. 4th ed. Washington, Butterworths, 1963-65. 3 v. (xxv, 1824 p.) 016.505 64-8729
Z7403 .W923 MRR Alc.

SCIENCE--PERIODICALS--BIBLIOGRAPHY--CATALOGS.
Chicago. Center for Research Libraries. Rarely held scientific serials in the Midwest Inter-library Center. Chicago, 1963. vi, 187 p. 63-5712
Z7403 .C49 MRR Alc.

SCIENCE--PERIODICALS--BIBLIOGRAPHY--UNION LISTS.
World list of scientific periodicals; 1960/68- London, Butterworths. 016.505 70-20683
Z7403 .W9 Sci RR Latest edition / MRR Alc Latest edition

SCIENCE--PERIODICALS--INDEXES.
Royal Society of London. Catalogue of scientific papers. London, C. J. Clay, 1867-1925. 19 v. 02-11462
Z7403 .R88 MRR Alc.

Royal society of London. Catalogue of scientific papers, 1800-1900. Cambridge, University press, 1908- v. 08-24586
Z7403 .R8812 MRR Alc.

Scientific American. v.1-14, Aug. 28, 1845-June 25, 1859; new ser., v.1-July 2, 1859- [New York] 505 04-17574
T1 .S5 MRR Alc Indexes only / Sci RR Indexes only

SCIENCE--PERIODICALS--TRANSLATIONS INTO ENGLISH--BIBLIOGRAPHY.
National Translations Center. Consolidated index of translations into English. New York, Special Libraries Association, 1969. vi, 948 p. 016.5/05 76-101337
Z7403 .N273 MRR Alc.

SCIENCE--PICTORIAL WORKS.
Wilson, Mitchell A. American science and invention, a pictorial history; New York, Simon and Schuster [1954] ix, 437 p. 509.73 54-9812
Q125 .W7914 MRR Alc.

SCIENCE--RESEARCH GRANTS--UNITED STATES--INDEXES.
Foundation Research Service. Foundation research service. [Washington, Lawson & Williams Associates, 1972- 4 v. (loose-leaf) 507/.2073 72-184024
Q180.U5 F68 MRR Alc.

SCIENCE--SCHOLARSHIPS, FELLOWSHIPS, ETC.--UNITED STATES--DIRECTORIES.
American Council on Education. Fellowships in the arts and sciences. 1st-10th ed.; 1957-1967/68 Washington [etc.] 58-461
LB2338 .F43 MRR Ref Desk Latest edition

SCIENCE--STUDY AND TEACHING.
Educators guide to free science materials. 1st- ed.;1960- Randolph, Wis., Educators Progress Service. 507 61-919
Q181.A1 E3 MRR Alc Latest edition

SCIENCE--STUDY AND TEACHING--DIRECTORIES.
Worldwide directory of mineral industries education and research. Houston, Gulf Pub. Co., 1968. x, 451 p. 669/.007 68-9304
TN165 .W66 MRR Alc.

SCIENCE--STUDY AND TEACHING--UNITED STATES--DIRECTORIES.
The Annual guides to graduate study. 1966/67- Princeton, N.J., Peterson's Guides Inc. 378.73 68-1823
L901 .P46 MRR Alc Latest edition

SCIENCE--TERMINOLOGY.
Brown, Roland Wilbur. Composition of scientific words; [Rev. ed. Washington, 1956] 882 p. 422.03 56-56233
PE1580 .B7 1956 MRR Alc.

SCIENCE--TRANSLATIONS INTO ENGLISH--BIBLIOGRAPHY.
United States. Library of Congress. Scientific Translations Center. Bibliography of translations from Russian scientific and technical literature. list no. 1-39; Oct. 1953-Dec. 1956. Washington. 016.5 53-60044
Z663.41 .U5 MRR Alc MRR Alc Partial set

SCIENCE--YEARBOOKS.
McGraw-Hill yearbook of science and technology. 1962- New York, McGraw-Hill Book Co. 505.8 62-12028
Q121 .M312 Sci RR Partial set / MRR Alc Full set

SCIENCE--CANADA--PERIODICALS--BIBLIOGRAPHY.
Directory of Canadian scientific and technical periodicals. 1961- Ottawa, National Research Council. 016.505 61-2342
Z7403 .D5 MRR Alc Latest edition

SCIENCE--CHINA--BIBLIOGRAPHY.
Wang, Chi. Nuclear science in mainland China; Washington, Library of Congress; [for sale by the Supt. of Docs., U.S. Govt. Print. Off.] 1968. vi, 70 p. [$0.70] 621.48/0951 68-62146
Z663.41 .W3 MRR Alc.

SCIENCE--JAPAN--PERIODICALS--BIBLIOGRAPHY.
Nihon kagaku gijutsu kankei chikuji kankōbutsu mokuroku. 1962- [Tokyo] National Diet Library. J 68-5037
Z7403 .N5 Sci RR Latest edition / MRR Alc Latest edition

SCIENCE--RUSSIA--BIBLIOGRAPHY.
Maichel, Karol. Guide to Russian reference books. [Stanford, Calif.] Hoover Institution on War, Revolution, and Peace, Stanford University, 1962- v. 016.9147 62-14067
Z2491 .M25 MRR Alc.

United States. Library of Congress. Science and Technology Division. Soviet science and technology; Washington, 1962. 209 p. 016.5 62-60058
Z663.41 .S6 MRR Alc.

SCIENCE--UNITED STATES--HISTORY.
Wilson, Mitchell A. American science and invention, a pictorial history; New York, Simon and Schuster [1954] ix, 437 p. 509.73 54-9812
Q125 .W7914 MRR Alc.

SCIENCE--UNITED STATES--INFORMATION SERVICES.
United States. Library of Congress. National Referral Center. A directory of information resources in the United States: physical sciences, engineering; Washington, Library of Congress; [for sale by the Supt. of Docs., U.S. Govt. Print. Off.] 1971. iv, 803 p. [$6.50] 500.2/07 78-611209
Z663.379 .D5 1971 MRR Alc.

SCIENCE, COMMUNICATION IN
see Communication in science

SCIENCE, MORAL
see Ethics

SCIENCE, POLITICAL
see Political science

SCIENCE, SOCIAL
see Sociology

SCIENCE AND CIVILIZATION.
Bernal, John Desmond. Science in history [3d ed.] New York, Hawthorn Books [1965] xxviii, 1039 p. 901.9 65-22660
CB151 .B4 1965 MRR Alc.

SCIENCE AND STATE--UNITED STATES.
Schaffter, Dorothy. The National Science Foundation. New York, Praeger [1969] xii, 278 p. [7.95] 353.008/5 68-8137
Q11.U84 S3 MRR Alc.

SCIENCE AND STATE--UNITED STATES--BIBLIOGRAPHY.
Universal Reference System. Public policy and the management of science; Princeton, N.J., Princeton Research Pub. Co. [1969] xix, 584 p. 016.353008/5 68-57825
Z7161 .U64 vol. 9 MRR Alc.

SCIENCE FICTION.
McGhan, Barry. Science fiction and fantasy pseudonyms. [Flint? Mich.] c1971. iv, 34 p. [$1.00] 823/.009 72-176242
Z1041 .M28 MRR Alc.

SCIENCE FICTION--BIBLIOGRAPHY.
Bleiler, Everett Franklin, ed. The checklist of fantastic literature; [1st ed.] Chicago, Shasta Publishers, 1948. xix, 455 p. 016.8083 48-6709
Z5917.F3 B55 MRR Alc.

Cole, Walter R. A checklist of science-fiction anthologies, [Brooklyn? 1964] xvi, 374 p. 016.823082 65-1442
Z5917.S36 C6 MRR Alc.

SCIENCE FICTION--BIBLIOGRAPHY. (Cont.)
Day, Bradford M. The supplemental
checklist of fantastic literature.
Denver, N.Y., Science-Fiction &
Fantasy Publications [1963] 155 p.
64-46968
Z5917.F3 D35 MRR Alc.

Tuck, Donald Henry. The encyclopedia
of science fiction and fantasy
through 1968: [1st ed.] Chicago,
Advent: Publishers, 1974- v.
016.80883/876 73-91828
Z5917.S36 T83 MRR Alc.

SCIENCE FICTION--BIO-BIBLIOGRAPHY.
Tuck, Donald Henry. The encyclopedia
of science fiction and fantasy
through 1968: [1st ed.] Chicago,
Advent: Publishers, 1974- v.
016.80883/876 73-91828
Z5917.S36 T83 MRR Alc.

**SCIENCE FICTION--HISTORY AND CRITICISM--
BIBLIOGRAPHY.**
Clareson, Thomas D. Science fiction
criticism; an annotated checklist,
[1st ed.- Kent, Ohio] Kent State
University Press [1972] xiii, 225 p.
016.8093/876 71-181084
Z5917.S36 C55 MRR Alc.

SCIENCE FICTION--INDEXES.
Cook, Frederick S., Fred Cook's
index to the Wonder group. [Grand
Haven, Mich., 1966] 239 p. 70-
14090
Z5917.S36 C64 MRR Alc.

SCIENCE FICTION--PERIODICALS--INDEXES.
Day, Donald Byrne. Index to the
science-fiction magazines, 1926-1950.
Portland, Or., Perri Press [1952]
xv, 184 p. 016.5 52-41880
Z5917.S36 D3 MRR Alc.

New England Science Fiction
Association. Index to the science
fiction magazines, 1966-1970. [1st
ed.- Cambridge, Mass.] 1971. x, 82
p. [$5.00] 016.823/0876 74-30236

Z5917.S36 N42 1971 MRR Alc.

Strauss, Erwin S. The MIT Science
Fiction Society's index to the s-f
magazines, 1851-1965. [Cambridge,
Mass., MIT Science Fiction Society]
c1966. iii, 207 p. 016.823/0876
73-174981
Z5917.S36 S84 MRR Alc.

**SCIENCE FICTION, AMERICAN--HISTORY AND
CRITICISM.**
Ketterer, David. New worlds for old:
Bloomington, Indiana University
Press [1974] xii, 347 p. 813/.0876
73-16717
PS374.S35 K4 MRR Alc.

SCIENCE FICTION, AMERICAN--INDEXES.
Siemon, Frederick. Science fiction
story index, 1950-1968. Chicago,
American Library Association, 1971.
x, 274 p. 016.823/0876 70-162470
Z5917.S36 S5 MRR Alc.

SCIENCE FICTION, ENGLISH--INDEXES.
Siemon, Frederick. Science fiction
story index, 1950-1968. Chicago,
American Library Association, 1971.
x, 274 p. 016.823/0876 70-162470
Z5917.S36 S5 MRR Alc.

SCIENCE FICTION FILMS--CATALOGS.
Willis, Donald C. Horror and science
fiction films: Metuchen, N.J.,
Scarecrow Press, 1972. x, 612 p.
791.43/0909/16 72-3682
PN1995.9.H6 W5 MRR Alc.

SCIENCES, OCCULT
see Occult sciences

SCIENCES, SOCIAL
see Social sciences

SCIENTIFIC APPARATUS AND INSTRUMENTS.
see also Electric apparatus and
appliances

see also Electronic apparatus and
appliances

see also Medical instruments and
apparatus

**SCIENTIFIC APPARATUS AND INSTRUMENTS--
BIBLIOGRAPHY.**
United States. Library of Congress.
Technical Information Division.
Instrumentation literature and its
use; Washington, 1952. 129 p. 53-
63562
Z663.49 .I6 MRR Alc.

**SCIENTIFIC APPARATUS AND INSTRUMENTS--
DICTIONARIES--POLYGLOT.**
Schulz, Ernst, lexicographer.
Wörterbuch der Optik und
Feinmechanik. Wiesbaden,
Brandstetter [1960-61] 3 v. a 61-
3700
QC351.2 .S34 MRR Alc.

Six-language dictionary of
automation, electronics and
scientific instruments; London,
Iliffe Books; Englewood Cliffs, N.J.,
Prentice-Hall [1962] 732 p.
621.3803 63-5414
TK7804 .S5 1962 MRR Alc.

SCIENTIFIC EXPEDITIONS--BIBLIOGRAPHY.
Selected references to literature on
marine expeditions, 1700-1960.
Boston, G. K. Hall, 1972. iv, 517 p.
016.5514/6 72-6452
Z5971 .S4 MRR Alc.

SCIENTIFIC LIBRARIES.
Strauss, Lucille (Jackson)
Scientific and technical libraries:
New York, Interscience Publishers
[1964] xi, 398 p. 026.5 64-15421

Z675.T3 S8 MRR Alc.

Thornton, John Leonard. Scientific
books, libraries and collectors; 2d
rev. ed. London, Library
Association, 1962. xiii, 406 p. 63-
23658
Z7401 .T45 1962 MRR Alc.

United Nations Educational,
Scientific and Cultural Organization.
World guide to science information
and documentation services. [Paris,
1965] 211 p. 507.2 65-9614
Q223 .U45 MRR Alc.

SCIENTIFIC LIBRARIES--DIRECTORIES.
Associazione italiana per le
biblioteche. Guida delle biblioteche
scientifiche e tecniche e dei centri
di documentazione italiani, Roma,
Consiglio nazionale delle ricerche,
1965. viii, 610 p. 68-130514
Z809 .A1A78 MRR Alc.

United States. Library of Congress.
National Referral Center. A
directory of information resources in
the United States: biological
sciences. Washington, Library of
Congress; [for sale by the Supt. of
Docs., U.S. Govt. Print. Off.] 1972.
iv, 577 p. [$5.00] 570/.7 72-2659

Z663.379 .D46 MRR Alc.

United States. Library of Congress.
National Referral Center. A
directory of information resources in
the United States: physical sciences,
engineering. Washington, Library of
Congress; [for sale by the Supt. of
Docs. U.S. Govt. Print. Off.] 1971.
iv, 803 p. [$6.50] 500.2/07 78-
611209
Z663.379 .D5 1971 MRR Alc.

SCIENTIFIC MANAGEMENT
see Industrial management

SCIENTIFIC SOCIETIES--BIBLIOGRAPHY.
[ISIS cumulative bibliography]
[London] Mansell, in conjunction with
the History of Science Society, 1971-
v. 016.509 72-186272
Z7405.H6 I2 MRR Biog.

Scudder, Samuel Hubbard, Catalogue
of scientific serials of all
countries, Cambridge, Library of
Harvard university, 1879. xii, 358
p. 02-7012
Z7403 .S43 MRR Alc.

SCIENTIFIC SOCIETIES--DIRECTORIES.
Minerva: internationales Verzeichnis
wissenschaftlicher Institutionen.
Forschungsinstitute. 33.- Ausg.
(Jahrg.); 1972- Berlin, New York, W.
de Gruyter. 72-76041
AS2 .M57 MRR Ref Desk Latest
edition / MRR Alc Latest edition

Minerva: internationales Verzeichnis
wissenschaftlicher Institutionen.
Wissenschaftliche Gesellschaften.
33.- Ausg. (Jahrg.); 1972- Berlin,
New York, de Gruyter. 060/.25 72-
624841
AS2 .M58 MRR Ref Desk Latest
edition / MRR Alc Latest edition

National Research Council, Canada.
Technical Information Service.
National technical information
services worldwide directory. 3d ed.
The Hague, Federation
internationale de documentation.
[1970] 61 p. [fl.25.00] 025.5/2
72-179268
Q223 .N37 1970 MRR Alc.

United Nations Educational,
Scientific and Cultural Organization.
World directory of national science
policymaking bodies. Paris, Unesco;
Guernsey, Hodgson, 1966- (i.e. 1967-
v. [65/- (v. 1)] 506/.1 67-
78504
Q10 .U455 MRR Alc.

United States. Library of Congress.
International Organizations Section.
International scientific
organizations; Washington, General
Reference and Bibliography Division,
Reference Dept.,Library of Congress;
[for sale by the Superintendent of
Documents, U.S. Govt. Print. Off.]
1962 [i.e. 1963] xi, 794 p. 506
62-64648
Z663.295 .I5 MRR Alc.

Verbände und Gesellschaften der
Wissenschaft: ein internat. Verz. 1
Ausg. [Pullach (Isartal)] Verlag
Dokumentation, 1974. xii, 481 p.
[DM98.00] 74-338569
Q145 .V45 MRR Ref Desk.

Wilson, William K. World directory
of environmental research centers,
2d ed. New York, Oryx Press;
distributed by R. R. Bowker Co.,
1974. xi, 330 p. 301.31/025 72-
87536
HC79.E5 W54 1974 MRR Alc.

**SCIENTIFIC SOCIETIES--AFRICA, SOUTH--
DIRECTORIES.**
Directory of scientific research
organizations in South Africa. 1971-
Pretoria, South African Council for
Scientific and Industrial Research.
507/.2068 72-621812
Q180.A55 D53 MRR Alc Latest
edition

**SCIENTIFIC SOCIETIES--ARGENTINE
REPUBLIC--DIRECTORIES.**
Directorio de científicos e
instituciones de Argentina. 1966,
fasc. 2- Montevideo, Centro de
Cooperación Científica de la Unesco
para America Latina. 72-621605
Q33 .D5 MRR Alc Latest edition /
Sci RR Latest edition

**SCIENTIFIC SOCIETIES--CANADA--
DIRECTORIES.**
Scientific and technical societies of
Canada. 1968- Ottawa, National
Research Council of Canada.
506/.2/71 72-649212
AS40 .S34 Sci RR Latest edition /
MRR Alc Latest edition

**SCIENTIFIC SOCIETIES--CHINA--
BIBLIOGRAPHY.**
United States. Library of Congress.
Science and Technology Division.
Mainland China organizations of
higher learning in science and
technology and their publications,
Washington, 1961. vi, 104 p. 61-
60070
Z663.41 .M2 MRR Alc.

**SCIENTIFIC SOCIETIES--CHINA--
DIRECTORIES.**
Surveys and Research Corporation,
Washington, D.C. Directory of
selected scientific institutions in
mainland China. Stanford, Calif.,
Published for the National Science
Foundation by the Hoover Institution
Press [c1970] xxii, 469 p. [$19.50]
502/.4/51 76-138410
Q72 .S9 MRR Alc.

United States. Library of Congress.
Science and Technology Division.
Mainland China organizations of
higher learning in science and
technology and their publications,
Washington, 1961. vi, 104 p. 61-
60070
Z663.41 .M2 MRR Alc.

**SCIENTIFIC SOCIETIES--EUROPE--
DIRECTORIES.**
European research index; 3d ed.
[St. Peter Port, Guernsey] Francis
Hodgson [1973] 2 v. (2293 p.)
507/.204 70-190255
Q180.E9 E9 1973 MRR Alc.

Williams, Colin H. Guide to European
sources of scientific information. 3d
ed. [Guernsey] Francis Hodgson
[1970] 309 p. [$20.00 (U.S.)] 607
77-105217
T10.65.E8 W5 1970 MRR Alc.

SCIENTIFIC SOCIETIES--EUROPE, EASTERN.
National Academy of Sciences,
Washington, D.C. Office of the
Foreign Secretary. The Eastern
European academies of sciences;
Washington, National Academy of
Sciences-National Research Council,
1963. 148 p. 067.058 63-60050
AS98 .N3 MRR Alc.

**SCIENTIFIC SOCIETIES--EUROPE, EASTERN--
DIRECTORIES.**
Little (Arthur D.) inc. Directory of
selected research institutes in
Eastern Europe, New York, Columbia
University Press, 1967. x, 445 p.
507.204 66-20496
Q180.E9 L5 MRR Alc.

SCIENTIFIC SOCIETIES--GREAT BRITAIN--
DIRECTORIES.
Scientific and learned societies of
Great Britain; 1st-   ed.; 1884-
London, Allen & Unwin [etc.] 062 01-
15597
AS115 .S313 MRR Ref Desk Latest
edition

SCIENTIFIC SOCIETIES--RUSSIA--
DIRECTORIES.
Battelle Memorial Institute,
Columbus, Ohio. Directory of
selected scientific institutions in
the U.S.S.R. [Columbus, C. E.
Merrill Books] 1963. 1 v. (various
pagings) 506 63-24824
Q60 .E36 MRR Alc.

A Guide to the Soviet academies.
Rev. [n.p.] 1961. 103 p. 63-61190

AS258 .G82 MRR Alc.

United States. Library of Congress.
Aerospace Technology Division.
Scientific institutes and
laboratories in Moscow. [Washington]
1963. ix, 133 p. 64-60333
Z663.23 .S35 MRR Alc.

United States. Library of Congress.
Aerospace Technology Division.
Scientific research institutes of the
USSR. [Washington] 63-61636
Began publication in Feb. 1960.
Z663.23 .A27 MRR Alc MRR Alc
Latest edition

SCIENTIFIC SOCIETIES--SCANDINAVIA--
DIRECTORIES.
Scandinavian Council for Applied
Research. Scandinavian research
guide. 2d rev. ed. Copenhagen,
Nordforsk [1965] 12, 438 p.
[77.00dkr] 507.2048 66-68485
Q180.S3 S3 1965 MRR Alc.

SCIENTIFIC SOCIETIES--UNITED STATES.
Bates, Ralph Samuel. Scientific
societies in the United States 3d
ed. Cambridge, Mass., M.I.T. Press
[1965] 326 p. 506.273 65-8325
Q11.A1 B3 1965 MRR Alc.

Kyed, James M., Scientific,
technical, and engineering societies
publications in print, New York, R.
R. Bowker Co., 1974. x, 223 p.
016.5 74-5094
Z7911 .K92 MRR Alc.

SCIENTIFIC SOCIETIES--UNITED STATES--
DIRECTORIES.
Battelle Memorial Institute,
Columbus, Ohio. Dept. of Economics
and Information Research.
Specialized science information
services in the United States;
Washington, National Science
Foundation, Office of Science
Information Service, 1961. ix, 528
p. 505.873 61-64862
AG521 .B3 MRR Alc.

Gale Research Company. Encyclopedia
of associations. 8th ed. Detroit,
Mich. [1973-   v.   [$45.00 (v. 1)
$28.50 (v. 2)] 061/.3 73-7400
HS17 .G334 1973 MRR Ref Desk.

Scientific and technical societies of
the United States. 8th-   ed.; 1968-
Washington, National Academy of
Sciences. 506 72-620448
AS25 .S33 Sci RR Latest edition /
MRR Ref Desk Latest edition / MRR
Alc Latest edition

United States. Library of Congress.
National Referral Center. A
directory of information resources in
the United States: biological
sciences. Washington, Library of
Congress; [for sale by the Supt. of
Docs., U.S. Govt. Print. Off.] 1972.
iv, 577 p. [$5.00] 570/.7 72-2659

Z663.379 .D46 MRR Alc.

United States. Library of Congress.
National Referral Center. A
directory of information resources in
the United States: physical sciences,
engineering. Washington, Library of
Congress; [for sale by the Supt. of
Docs., U.S. Govt. Print. Off.] 1971.
iv, 803 p. [$6.50] 500.2/07 78-
611209
Z663.379 .D5 1971 MRR Alc.

United States. Library of Congress.
National Referral Center for Science
and Technology. A directory of
information resources in the United
States: water. [Washington, For sale
by the Superintendent of Documents,
U.S. Govt. Print. Off.] 1966. v, 248
p. 66-61638
Z663.379 .D55 MRR Alc.

Wolff, Garwood R. Environmental
information sources handbook. [New
York] Simon and Schuster [1974] 568
p. 301.31/07 73-3951
GF503 .W64 MRR Alc.

SCIENTIFIC SOCIETIES--YUGOSLAVIA.
Babic, Ivo. Scientific institutions
in Yugoslavia Beograd, Edition
Jugoslavija, 1958. 148 p. 58-43852

AS346 .B25 MRR Alc.

SCIENTIFIC WRITING
see Technical writing

SCIENTISTS.
Ireland, Norma (Olin) Index to
scientists of the world, from ancient
to modern times: Boston, F. W. Faxon
Co., 1962. xliii, 662 p. 016.925
62-13662
Z7404 .I7 MRR Biog.

McGraw-Hill modern men of science,
New York, McGraw-Hill [1966-68] 2 v.
509.22 66-14808
Q141 .M15 MRR Biog.

Sarton, George, Introduction to the
history of science ... Baltimore,
Pub. for the Carnegie institution of
Washington, by the Williams & Wilkins
company [c1927-   v.   27-11418
Q125 .S32 MRR Alc.

Schmidt, Jacob Edward, Medical
discoveries: Springfield, Ill.,
Thomas [1959] ix, 555 p. 610.9 58-
14086
R131 .S35 1959 MRR Alc.

Zischka, Gert A. Allgemeines
Gelehrten-Lexikon; Stuttgart, A.
Kröner [1961] viii, 710 p. 62-
31158
CT3990.A2 Z5 MRR Biog.

SCIENTISTS--BIBLIOGRAPHY.
ISIS cumulative bibliography;
[London] Mansell, in conjunction with
the History of Science Society, 1971-
v.   016.509 72-186272
Z7405.H6 I2 MRR Biog.

SCIENTISTS--BIOGRAPHY.
Asimov, Isaac, Asimov's biographical
encyclopedia of science and
technology; New rev. ed. Garden
City, N.Y., Doubleday, 1972. xxviii,
805 p. [$12.95] 509/.2/2 B 78-
139003
Q141 .A74 1972 MRR Biog.

Talbott, John Harold, A biographical
history of medicine; New York, Grune
& Stratton [1970] 1211 p. 610/.922
B 78-109574
R134 .T35 MRR Biog.

Who's who in atoms. 1959- London,
Harrap Research Publications [etc.]
925.3 59-2375
QC774 .A1W5 Sci RR Latest edition
/ MRR Alc Latest edition

SCIENTISTS--BIOGRAPHY--DICTIONARIES.
Dictionary of scientific biography.
New York, Scribner [1970-   v.
[35.00 per vol.] 509/.22 B 69-
18090
Q141 .D5 MRR Biog.

Williams, Trevor Illtyd. A
biographical dictionary of
scientists, [New York] Wiley-
Interscience [1969] xi, 592 p.
509/.22 B 69-19757
Q141 .W62 1969b MRR Biog.

SCIENTISTS--BIOGRAPHY--DIRECTORIES.
World who's who in science: 1st ed.
Chicago, Marquis-Who's Who, inc.
[1968] xvi, 1855 p. 509/.22 68-
56149
Q141 .W7 MRR Biog.

SCIENTISTS--BIOGRAPHY--INDEXES.
Barr, Ernest Scott, An index to
biographical fragments in
unspecialized scientific journals,
University, Ala., University of
Alabama Press [c1973] vii, 294 p.
016.5/092/2 B 73-13434
Q141 .B29 MRR Biog.

Pittsburgh. Carnegie library. Men of
science and industry; Pittsburgh,
Carnegie library, 1915. 189, [3] p.
15-6134
Z7404 .A1P6 MRR Biog.

SCIENTISTS--DIRECTORIES.
The Naturalists' directory. [1st]-
ed.; 1877- Phillipsburg, N.J. [etc.]
PCL Publications. [etc.] 505.8 05-
5987
Q145 .S4 MRR Alc Latest edition

SCIENTISTS--EUROPE--DIRECTORIES.
Who's who in science in Europe:
Guernsey, F. Hodgson, 1967. 3 v.
[£10/-/- (v. 1-2) unpriced (v. 3)]
502/.5/4 67-27363
Q145 .W5 MRR Biog.

SCIENTISTS--EUROPE, EASTERN.
National Academy of Sciences,
Washington, D.C. Office of the
Foreign Secretary. The Eastern
European academies of sciences;
Washington, National Academy of
Sciences-National Research Council,
1963. 148 p. 067.058 63-60058
AS98 .N3 MRR Alc.

SCIENTISTS--GREAT BRITAIN--DIRECTORIES--
PERIODICALS.
Who's who of British scientists.
1969/70- [London] Longman. 509/.22
71-10910
Q145 .D52 Sci RR Latest edition /
MRR Biog Latest edition

SCIENTISTS--RUSSIA.
Turkevich, John, Soviet men of
science; Princeton, N.J., Van
Nostrand [1963] 441 p. 925 63-
24873
Q141 .T83 MRR Biog.

SCIENTISTS--UNITED STATES.
Haber, Louis. The role of the
American Negro in the fields of
science. [New York?] 1966. 70 l.
509/.22 B 67-62053
Q141 .H212 MRR Biog.

SCIENTISTS, AMERICAN.
Jaffe, Bernard, Men of science in
America; Rev. ed. New York, Simon
and Schuster, 1958. 715 p. 509.73
58-59443
Q127.U6 J27 1958 MRR Biog.

Meisel, Max, A bibliography of
American natural history; Brooklyn,
N.Y., The Premier publishing co.,
1924-29. 3 v.   24-30970
Z7408.U5 M5 MRR Alc.

National Academy of Sciences,
Washington, D.C. Biographical
memoirs. v. 1-   1877- New York,
London, [etc.] Columbia University
Press. 05-26629
Q141 .N2 MRR Biog Partial set

Special libraries Association.
Science-Technology Division.
Handbook of scientific and technical
awards in the United States and
Canada, 1900-1952. New York, Special
Libraries Association [1956] xxiv,
491 p. 507.9 56-7004
Q141 .S63 MRR Alc.

SCIENTISTS, AMERICAN--DIRECTORIES.
American men and women of science.
12th-   ed.; 1971- New York, Bowker.
509/.2/2 [B] 72-622716
Q141 .A47 MRR Ref Desk Latest
edition / Sci RR Latest edition

Leaders in American Science. v. 1-
1953/54- Hattiesburg, Miss. [etc.]
Who's who in American Education, inc.
925 54-724
Q141 .L43 Sci RR Latest edition /
MRR Biog Latest edition

National Association of Science
Writers. Membership list. Sea
Cliff, N.Y. [etc.] 63-36780
T11 .N35 MRR Alc Latest edition

SCIENTISTS, ARGENTINE--DIRECTORIES.
Directorio de científicos e
instituciones de Argentina. 1966,
fasc. 2- Montevideo, Centro de
Cooperación Científica de la Unesco
para América Latina. 72-621605
Q33 .D5 MRR Alc Latest edition /
Sci RR Latest edition

SCIENTISTS, JEWISH.
Cohen, Harry, ed. Jews in the world
of science; New York, Monde
Publishers [1956] xxiv, 264 p. 503
56-9332
Q128 .C65 MRR Biog.

SCIENTISTS, RUSSIAN.
Who's who in Soviet science and
technology. [2d ed.; rev. and enl.
New York, Telberg Book Co. [1964]
vi, 301 l. 925 64-13006
Q127.R9 W5 1964 MRR Biog.

SCIENTISTS, SWEDISH.
Lindroth, Sten, ed. Swedish men of
science, 1650-1950. Stockholm,
Swedish Institute, 1952. 295 p.
925 53-16761
Q127.S85 L5 MRR Biog.

SCOTCH IN IRELAND.
Leyburn, James Graham. The Scotch-
Irish: a social history. Chapel
Hill, University of North Carolina
Press [1962] xix, 377 p. 301.45
62-16063
E184.S4 L5 MRR Alc.

SCOTCH-IRISH IN THE UNITED STATES.
Leyburn, James Graham. The Scotch-
Irish: a social history. Chapel
Hill, University of North Carolina
Press [1962] xix, 377 p. 301.45
62-16063
E184.S4 L5 MRR Alc.

SCOTLAND.
Kellas, James G. Modern Scotland;
New York, Praeger [1968] 284 p.
[6.50] 941/.08 68-9439
DA821 .K44 1968b MRR Alc.

SCOTLAND--ANTIQUITIES.
Childe, Vere Gordon, Scotland, 5th
ed. Edinburgh, London, H.M.S.O.,
1967. 139 p. [10/- 6/- (pbk)]
913/.3 67-98401
DA770 .C53 1967 MRR Alc.

SCOTLAND--BIBLIOGRAPHY.
Hancock, P. D. A bibliography of
works relating to Scotland, 1916-
1950. Edinburgh, University Press
[c1959-60] 2 v. 016.9141 a 60-
8611
Z2061 .H3 MRR Alc.

Matheson, Cyril, A catalogue of the
publications of Scottish historical
and kindred clubs and societies,
Aberdeen, Milne and Hutchinson, 1928.
viii, 232 p. 28-23797
Z2061 .T34 MRR Alc.

National Book League, London.
Reader's guide to Scotland: London,
National Book League, 1968. 127 p.
[21/-] 016.9141/03 72-374943
Z2051 .N37 MRR Alc.

Terry, Charles Sanford, A catalogue
of the publications of Scottish
historical and kindred clubs and
societies, Glasgow, J. MacLehose and
sons, 1909. xiii, 253 p. 10-1995
Z2061 .T32 MRR Alc.

SCOTLAND--BIOGRAPHY.
Anderson, William, The Scottish
nation; Edinburgh [etc.] A.
Fullarton & co. [1859]-63. 3 v. in
9. 27-11180
CT813 .A6 MRR Biog.

Donaldson, Gordon. Who's who in
Scottish history Oxford, Blackwell
[1973] xx, 254 p. [£4.25]
941/.00992 74-167088
DA758 .D66 MRR Biog.

SCOTLAND--CIVILIZATION.
Craig, David, Scottish literature
and the Scottish people, 1680-1830.
London, Chatto & Windus, 1961. 339
p. 820.9 62-6437
PR8511 .C7 MRR Alc.

SCOTLAND--COMMERCE--DIRECTORIES.
Glasgow and west of Scotland trades'
directory including the counties of
Argyll, Ayr, Bute, Dunbarton,
Dumfries, Kirkcudbright, Lanark,
Renfrew and Wigtown, accompanied with
a gazetteer of Scotland. Edinburgh,
Trades' Directories [etc.] 57-44904

    HF5162.G6 G6 MRR Alc Latest
    edition

Macdonald's Scottish directory and
gazetteer. Edinburgh, W. Macdonald.
ca 08-3136
HF5161 .M2 MRR Alc Latest edition

The Scottish national register of
classified trades. London, Sells
Publications [etc.] 26 cm. 338.058
51-15820
    Began publication in 1938.
HF3523 .S35 MRR Alc Latest edition

SCOTLAND--DESCRIPTION AND TRAVEL.
Groome, Francis Hindes, Ordnance
gazetteer of Scotland; New ed., with
census appendix 1901. Edinburgh, T.
C. and E. C. Jack, 1901. 2 p. l.,
1762 p., 1 l. 02-6700
DA865 .G87 MRR Alc.

**SCOTLAND--DESCRIPTION AND TRAVEL--1951-
--GUIDE-BOOKS.**
The Complete Scotland. 1st- ed.;
1933- London, Ward, Lock and Co. 58-
35111
DA870 .C7 MRR Alc Latest edition

McLaren, Moray. The Shell guide to
Scotland: 2nd (fully revised) ed,
London, Ebury Press, 1973. 496, [32]
p. [£3.50] 914.1/04/81 74-167397

    DA870 .M3 1973 MRR Alc.

Muirhead, Litellus Russell,
Scotland, 5th ed. London, Benn;
Chicago, Rand McNally, 1967. liv,
474; 32 p. [50/-] 914/.1/0481 67-
93013
DA870 .M92 1967 MRR Alc.

**SCOTLAND--DESCRIPTION AND TRAVEL--
BIBLIOGRAPHY.**
Hancock, P. D. A bibliography of
works relating to Scotland, 1916-
1950. Edinburgh, University Press
[c1959-60] 2 v. 016.9141 a 60-
8611
    Z2061 .H3 MRR Alc.

**SCOTLAND--DESCRIPTION AND TRAVEL--GUIDE-
BOOKS.**
Childe, Vere Gordon, Scotland, 5th
ed. Edinburgh, London, H.M.S.O.,
1967. 139 p. [10/- 6/- (pbk)]
913/.3 67-99401
DA770 .C53 1967 MRR Alc.

McLaren, Moray. The Shell guide to
Scotland; 2nd (fully revised) ed,
London, Ebury Press, 1973. 496, [32]
p. [£3.50] 914.1/04/81 74-167397

DA870 .M3 1973 MRR Alc.

Murray, William Hutchison. The
companion guide to the West Highlands
of Scotland; [5th ed.] London,
Collins [1973, c1968] 415 p.
[£2.75] 914.11/04/81 73-178899
DA880.H7 M95 MRR Alc.

Ward, Lock and Company, ltd. The
Highlands of Scotland, 13th ed.
London [1961] 191 p. 914.1 62-
41052
DA880.H7 W34 1961 MRR Alc.

SCOTLAND--GAZETTEERS.
Fife and Kinross trades' directory,
including the counties of Stirling
and Clackmannan, Edinburgh, Town and
County Directories, Limited. 59-
31510
HF5161 .F5 MRR Alc Latest edition

Groome, Francis Hindes, Ordnance
gazetteer of Scotland; New ed., with
census appendix 1901. Edinburgh, T.
C. and E. C. Jack, 1901. 2 p. l.,
1762 p., 1 l. 02-6700
DA865 .G87 MRR Alc.

Jack, May Violet, Chamber's guide to
Scotland, [1st American ed., rev.]
New York, Simmons-Boardman Pub. Corp.
[1963, c1957] 284 p. 914.1 63-
15445
DA869 .J3 1963 MRR Alc.

Johnston (W. and A. K.) and G. W.
Bacon, ltd. Johnston's gazetteer of
Scotland, [2d ed.] Edinburgh [1958]
viii, 248 p. 914.1 58-45407
DA869 .J74 1958 MRR Alc.

Macdonald's Scottish directory and
gazetteer. Edinburgh, W. Macdonald.
ca 08-3136
HF5161 .M2 MRR Alc Latest edition

McLaren, Moray. The Shell guide to
Scotland; 2nd (fully revised) ed,
London, Ebury Press, 1973. 496, [32]
p. [£3.50] 914.1/04/81 74-167397

DA870 .M3 1973 MRR Alc.

SCOTLAND--GENEALOGY.
Anderson, William, The Scottish
nation; Edinburgh [etc.] A.
Fullarton & co. [1859]-63. 3 v. in
9. 27-11180
CT813 .A6 MRR Biog.

Bain, Robert. The clans and tartans
of Scotland. London, Collins [1954]
320 p. 941 55-1011
DA880.H76 B3 1954 MRR Alc.

Innes, Thomas, Sir, The tartans of
the clans and families of Scotland.
5th ed. Edinburgh, W. & A. K.
Johnston, 1950. iv, 300 p. 929.2
51-3429
DA880.H76 I5 1950 MRR Alc.

SCOTLAND--HISTORIC HOUSES, ETC.
Childe, Vere Gordon, Scotland, 5th
ed. Edinburgh, London, H.M.S.O.,
1967. 139 p. [10/- 6/- (pbk)]
913/.3 67-99401
DA770 .C53 1967 MRR Alc.

SCOTLAND--HISTORY.
Donaldson, Gordon. Who's who in
Scottish history Oxford, Blackwell
[1973] xx, 254 p. [£4.25]
941/.00992 74-167088
DA758 .D66 MRR Biog.

Glover, Janet Reavley. The story of
Scotland. London, Faber and Faber
[1960] 399 p. 941 60-27718
DA760 .G6 MRR Alc.

SCOTLAND--HISTORY--BIBLIOGRAPHY.
Matheson, Cyril, A catalogue of the
publications of Scottish historical
and kindred clubs and societies,
Aberdeen, Milne and Hutchinson, 1928.
viii, 232 p. 28-23797
Z2061 .T34 MRR Alc.

Terry, Charles Sanford, A catalogue
of the publications of Scottish
historical and kindred clubs and
societies, Glasgow, J. MacLehose and
sons, 1909. xiii, 253 p. 10-1995
Z2061 .T32 MRR Alc.

SCOTLAND--HISTORY--SOURCES.
Dickinson, William Croft, ed. A
source book of Scottish history, [2d
ed. rev. and enl.] London, T. Nelson
[1958-61] 3 v. 62-6746
DA755 .D52 MRR Alc.

Scotland. General registry office of
births, deaths and marriages. A
guide to the public records of
Scotland deposited in H.M. General
register house, Edinburgh;
Edinburgh, H.M. General register
house; 1905. xxvii, 233 p. 05-
41700
CD1072 .A3 MRR Alc.

SCOTLAND--HISTORY, LOCAL--BIBLIOGRAPHY.
Hancock, P. D. A bibliography of
works relating to Scotland, 1916-
1950. Edinburgh, University Press
[c1959-60] 2 v. 016.9141 a 60-
8611
Z2061 .H3 MRR Alc.

SCOTLAND--IMPRINTS.
Aldis, Harry Gidney, A list of books
printed in Scotland before 1700,
[Edinburgh] Printed for the Edinburgh
bibliographical society, 1904. xvi,
153 p. 05-9350
Z2051 .A55 MRR Alc.

Matheson, Cyril, A catalogue of the
publications of Scottish historical
and kindred clubs and societies,
Aberdeen, Milne and Hutchinson, 1928.
viii, 232 p. 28-23797
Z2061 .T34 MRR Alc.

Terry, Charles Sanford, A catalogue
of the publications of Scottish
historical and kindred clubs and
societies, Glasgow, J. MacLehose and
sons, 1909. xiii, 253 p. 10-1995
Z2061 .T32 MRR Alc.

SCOTLAND--INDUSTRIES--DIRECTORIES.
The Scottish national register of
classified trades. London, Sells
Publications [etc.] 26 cm. 338.058
51-15820
    Began publication in 1938.
HF3523 .S35 MRR Alc Latest edition

**SCOTLAND--LEARNED INSTITUTIONS AND
SOCIETIES--BIBLIOGRAPHY.**
Matheson, Cyril, A catalogue of the
publications of Scottish historical
and kindred clubs and societies,
Aberdeen, Milne and Hutchinson, 1928.
viii, 232 p. 28-23797
Z2061 .T34 MRR Alc.

Terry, Charles Sanford, A catalogue
of the publications of Scottish
historical and kindred clubs and
societies, Glasgow, J. MacLehose and
sons, 1909. xiii, 253 p. 10-1995
Z2061 .T32 MRR Alc.

SCOTLAND--MANUFACTURERS--DIRECTORIES.
Macdonald's Scottish directory and
gazetteer. Edinburgh, W. Macdonald.
ca 08-3136
HF5161 .M2 MRR Alc Latest edition

**SCOTLAND--POLITICS AND GOVERNMENT--
YEARBOOKS.**
The Year book for Scotland and
Scottish parliamentary election
manual. Edinburgh. 58-24072
JN1371.U5 Y4 MRR Alc Latest
edition

SCOTLAND--REGISTERS.
The Scottish municipal annual.
Edinburgh [etc.] 352.041 49-25439
JS4101 .S35 MRR Alc Latest edition

SCOTLAND--SOCIAL CONDITIONS.
Leyburn, James Graham. The Scotch-
Irish: a social history. Chapel
Hill, University of North Carolina
Press [1962] xix, 377 p. 301.45
62-16063
E184.S4 L5 MRR Alc.

SCOTTISH BALLADS AND SONGS.
Bronson, Bertrand Harris, ed. The
traditional tunes of the Child
ballads; Princeton, N.J.; Princeton
University Press, 1959- v.
784.3 57-5468
ML3650 .B82 MRR Alc.

Leach, MacEdward, ed. The ballad
book. New York, Harper, 1955. 842
p. 821.04 55-6778
PR1181 .L4 MRR Alc.

**SCOTTISH LITERATURE--HISTORY AND
CRITICISM.**
Craig, David, Scottish literature
and the Scottish people, 1680-1830.
London, Chatto & Windus, 1961. 339
p. 820.9 62-6437
PR8511 .C7 MRR Alc.

Millar, John Hepburn, A literary
history of Scotland, London, T. F.
Unwin, 1903. xv, 703 p. 03-17604
PR8561 .M5 MRR Alc.

SCOTTISH POETRY.
Dixon, William Macneile, ed. The
Edinburgh book of Scottish verse,
1300-1900. London, Meiklejohn and
Holden, 1910. xx, 938 p. a 11-1394
PR8651 .D5 MRR Alc.

SCRAP METAL INDUSTRY--SOCIETIES, ETC.
Institute of Scrap Iron and Steel.
Yearbook. [1st]-   ed.: 1939-
Washington [etc.]   338.47672 40-4188

    TS200 .I64 Sci RR Latest edition /
    MRR Alc Latest edition

SCRAP METAL INDUSTRY--UNITED STATES--
DIRECTORIES.
Institute of Scrap Iron and Steel.
Directory [of members] [Washington]
56-25957
    HD9511 .I526 MRR Alc Latest
    edition

SCRAP METAL INDUSTRY--UNITED STATES--
STATISTICS.
Institute of Scrap Iron and Steel.
Yearbook. [1st]-   ed.: 1939-
Washington [etc.]   338.47672 40-4188

    TS200 .I64 Sci RR Latest edition /
    MRR Alc Latest edition

SCREEN WRITERS.
Academy of Motion Picture Arts and
Sciences. Who wrote the movie and
what else did he write? Los Angeles,
1970. xix, 491 p.   016.812/5/209
78-27347
    PN1998 .A53 MRR Alc.

SCRIPTURES, HOLY
see Bible

SCULPTORS.
Albright-Knox Art Gallery.
Contemporary art, 1942-72; New York,
Praeger [1973, c1972] 479 p.
[$25.00] 709/.04/074014797 70-
189286
    N6487.B83 A42 MRR Alc.

SCULPTORS--BIOGRAPHY.
Pyke, E. J. A biographical
dictionary of wax modellers Oxford,
Clarendon Press, 1973. lxvi, 216,
[79] p.   [£20.00] 736/.93/0922 73-
174552
    NK9580 .P94 MRR Biog.

SCULPTORS--DICTIONARIES.
New dictionary of modern sculpture.
New York, Tudor Pub. Co. [1971] 328
p.   730/.922 70-153118
    NB50 .N6813 MRR Biog.

SCULPTORS, AMERICAN.
Fielding, Mantle, Dictionary of
American painters, sculptors and
engravers / Enl. ed. with over 2,500
new listings of seventeenth,
eighteenth, and nineteenth century
American artists / Greens Farms,
Conn : Modern Books and Crafts,
[1974] vi, 455 p. ; [$17.50]
709/.2/2 74-182539
    N6536 .F5 1974 MRR Biog.

Goode, James M. The outdoor
sculpture of Washington, D.C. [1st
ed.] Washington, Smithsonian
Institution Press [distributed by G.
Braziller] 1974. 615 p.   917.53 74-
5111
    NB235.W3 G66 MRR Ref Desk.

Illinois. University at Urbana-
Champaign. College of Fine and
Applied Arts. Contemporary American
painting and sculpture. Urbana.
759.13 74-642877
    ND212.A1 I4 MRR Alc Latest edition

SCULPTORS, AMERICAN--DICTIONARIES.
Young, William, A dictionary of
American artists, sculptors and
engravers: Cambridge, Mass., W.
Young [1968] 515 p.   709/.73 68-
3733
    N6536 .Y7 MRR Biog.

SCULPTORS, BRITISH.
Grant, Maurice Harold, A dictionary
of British sculptors London,
Rockliff [1953] 317 p.   927.3 53-
30728
    NB496 .G7 1953 MRR Alc.

SCULPTORS, BRITISH--DICTIONARIES.
Gunnis, Rupert. Dictionary of
British sculptors, 1660-1851. New
revised ed. London, [Murrays Book
Sales], 1968. 515 p. [30/-]
730/.922 78-381295
    NB496 .G55 1968 MRR Biog.

SCULPTORS, GREEK.
Richter, Gisela Marie Augusta, The
sculpture and sculptors of the
Greeks. New rev. ed. New Haven,
Yale University Press, 1950. xxxvi,
625 p.   733.3 50-10289
    NB90 .R54 1950 MRR Alc.

SCULPTURE--CATALOGS.
International auction records. v.
[1]-   1867- [London, etc.,
Editions E. M.-Publisol] 700/.29
78-2167
    N8640 .I5 MRR Alc Full set

SCULPTURE--HISTORY.
Cheney, Sheldon, Sculpture of the
world: London, Thames & Hudson,
1968. xi, 538 p. [5/5/-]   730/.9
73-401267
    NB60 .C55 1968b MRR Alc.

SCULPTURE--INDEXES.
Clapp, Jane. Sculpture index.
Metuchen, N.J., Scarecrow Press, 1970
[c1970-71] 2 v. in 3.   730/.16 79-
9538
    NB36 .C55 MRR Alc.

SCULPTURE--FRANCE.
Müller, Theodor, Sculpture in the
Netherlands, Germany, France, and
Spain: 1400 to 1500; Harmondsworth,
Penguin, 1966. xxiv, 262 p. [£5/5/-
]   735.21 66-68067
    NB180 .M82 MRR Alc.

SCULPTURE--GERMANY.
Müller, Theodor, Sculpture in the
Netherlands, Germany, France, and
Spain 1400 to 1500; Harmondsworth,
Penguin, 1966. xxiv, 262 p. [£5/5/-
]   735.21 66-68067
    NB180 .M82 MRR Alc.

SCULPTURE--GREAT BRITAIN.
Stone, Lawrence. Sculpture in
Britain: the Middle Ages.
[Baltimore] Penguin Books [1955]
xxi, 297 p.   730/.942 55-3485
    NB463 .S8 MRR Alc.

SCULPTURE--NETHERLANDS.
Müller, Theodor, Sculpture in the
Netherlands, Germany, France, and
Spain: 1400 to 1500; Harmondsworth,
Penguin, 1966. xxiv, 262 p. [£5/5/-
]   735.21 66-68067
    NB180 .M82 MRR Alc.

SCULPTURE--SPAIN.
Müller, Theodor, Sculpture in the
Netherlands, Germany, France, and
Spain: 1400 to 1500; Harmondsworth,
Penguin, 1966. xxiv, 262 p. [£5/5/-
]   735.21 66-68067
    NB180 .M82 MRR Alc.

SCULPTURE--UNITED STATES--HISTORY.
Taft, Lorado, The history of
American sculpture, New ed., New
York, The Macmillan company, 1930.
xiii, 622 p. incl. illus., plates.
735.0973 30-32611
    NB205 .T3 1930 MRR Alc.

SCULPTURE--WASHINGTON, D.C.
Goode, James M. The outdoor
sculpture of Washington, D.C. [1st
ed.] Washington, Smithsonian
Institution Press [distributed by G.
Braziller] 1974. 615 p.   917.53 74-
5111
    NB235.W3 G66 MRR Ref Desk.

Murdock, Myrtle M. (Cheney) National
Statuary Hall in the Nation's
Capitol. Washington, Monumental
Press, 1955. 128 p.   917.53 55-
1697
    NB235.W3 M8 MRR Ref Desk.

SCULPTURE, AFRICAN.
Segy, Ladislas. African sculpture
speaks. 3d ed., enl. and fully rev.
New York, Hill and Wang [1969] 315
p. [14.95] 732/.2 68-14790
    NB1080 .S4 1969 MRR Alc.

SCULPTURE, AMERICAN.
Hunter, Sam, American art of the
20th century: New York, H. N. Abrams
[1973] 583 p.   709/.73 73-10211
    N6512 .H78 1973 MRR Alc.

Taft, Lorado, The history of
American sculpture, New ed., New
York, The Macmillan company, 1930.
xiii, 622 p. incl. illus., plates.
735.0973 30-32611
    NB205 .T3 1930 MRR Alc.

SCULPTURE, AMERICAN--EXHIBITIONS.
Illinois. University at Urbana-
Champaign. College of Fine and
Applied Arts. Contemporary American
painting and sculpture. Urbana.
759.13 74-642877
    ND212.A1 I4 MRR Alc Latest edition

SCULPTURE, DUTCH--HISTORY.
Osten, Gert von der. Painting and
sculpture in Germany and the
Netherlands, 1500 to 1600
Harmondsworth, Penguin, 1969. xxii,
403 p., 193 plates. [7/7/-] 759.3
79-514834
    N6925 .O813 1969 MRR Alc.

SCULPTURE, EUROPEAN--HISTORY.
Hamilton, George Heard. Painting and
sculpture in Europe, 1880-1940,
Baltimore, Penguin Books [1967]
xxiv, 443 p.   709.4 67-31947
    ND457 .H3 MRR Alc.

Novotny, Fritz, Painting and
sculpture in Europe, 1780 to 1880.
2nd ed. Harmondsworth, Penguin,
1970. xxii, 290, 192 p., leaf.
[£5.75]   759.94 74-149800
    N6757 .N6813 1970 MRR Alc.

SCULPTURE, GERMAN--HISTORY.
Osten, Gert von der. Painting and
sculpture in Germany and the
Netherlands, 1500 to 1600
Harmondsworth, Penguin, 1969. xxii,
403 p., 193 plates. [7/7/-] 759.3
79-514834
    N6925 .O813 1969 MRR Alc.

SCULPTURE, GOTHIC.
Müller, Theodor, Sculpture in the
Netherlands, Germany, France, and
Spain: 1400 to 1500; Harmondsworth,
Penguin, 1966. xxiv, 262 p. [£5/5/-
]   735.21 66-68067
    NB180 .M82 MRR Alc.

SCULPTURE, GREEK.
Richter, Gisela Marie Augusta, The
sculpture and sculptors of the
Greeks. New rev. ed. New Haven,
Yale University Press, 1950. xxxvi,
625 p.   733.3 50-10289
    NB90 .R54 1950 MRR Alc.

SCULPTURE, MEDIEVAL--GREAT BRITAIN.
Stone, Lawrence. Sculpture in
Britain: the Middle Ages.
[Baltimore] Penguin Books [1955]
xxi, 297 p.   730/.942 55-3485
    NB463 .S8 MRR Alc.

SCULPTURE, MODERN--20TH CENTURY.
New dictionary of modern sculpture.
New York, Tudor Pub. Co. [1971] 328
p.   730/.922 70-153118
    NB50 .N6813 MRR Biog.

SCULPTURE, MODERN--20TH CENTURY--UNITED
STATES.
Illinois. University at Urbana-
Champaign. College of Fine and
Applied Arts. Contemporary American
painting and sculpture. Urbana.
759.13 74-642877
    ND212.A1 I4 MRR Alc Latest edition

SCULPTURE, PRIMITIVE--AFRICA.
Segy, Ladislas. African sculpture
speaks. 3d ed., enl. and fully rev.
New York, Hill and Wang [1969] 315
p. [14.95] 732/.2 68-14790
    NB1080 .S4 1969 MRR Alc.

SCULPTURE, RENAISSANCE.
Müller, Theodor, Sculpture in the
Netherlands, Germany, France, and
Spain: 1400 to 1500; Harmondsworth,
Penguin, 1966. xxiv, 262 p. [£5/5/-
]   735.21 66-68067
    NB180 .M82 MRR Alc.

SEA
see Ocean

SEA-FISHERIES
see Fisheries

SEA ICE--DICTIONARIES--RUSSIAN.
United States. Library of Congress.
Reference Dept. Russian-English
glossary and Soviet classification of
ice found at sea, Washington, 1959.
vi, 30 p.   551.3403 59-60067
    Z663.2 .R825 MRR Alc.

SEA RESOURCES
see Marine resources

SEA TRAVEL
see Ocean travel

SEAFARING LIFE.
Shay, Frank, A sailor's treasury;
[1st ed.] New York, Norton [1951]
196 p.   910.4 51-7454
    GR910 .S36 MRR Alc.

SEAFARING LIFE--DICTIONARIES.
Colcord, Joanna Carver, Sea language
comes ashore New York, Cornell
maritime press [1945] ix, 213 p.
427.9 45-966
    PE1689 .C65 MRR Alc.

SEALING (TECHNOLOGY)--DIRECTORIES--
PERIODICALS.
Assembly engineering master catalog.
[Wheaton, Ill., Hitchcock Pub. Co.]
338.4/7/62188025 72-622720
    TJ1320 .H5 MRR Alc Latest edition
    / Sci RR Latest edition

SEALS (NUMISMATICS)
see also Emblems, National

Hope, A. Guy. Symbols of the
nations, Washington, Public Affairs
Press [1973] 348 p. [$10.00]
929.8 73-82015
    JC345 .H66 MRR Alc.

SEALS (NUMISMATICS)--UNITED STATES.
Preble, George Henry, Origin and
history of the American flag and of
the naval and yacht-club signals,
seals and arms, and principal
national songs of the United States,
New ed. in two volumes.
Philadelphia, N. L. Brown, 1917. 2
v.   17-21758
    CR113 .P7 1917 MRR Alc.

SEALS (NUMISMATICS)--UNITED (Cont.)
Shankle, George Earlie. State names,
flags, seals, songs, birds, flowers,
and other symbols; Rev. ed. New
York, H. W. Wilson Co., 1941 [i.e.
1951, c1938] 524 p. 929.4 917.3*
52-52807
E155 .S43 1951 MRR Alc

Smith, Whitney. The flag book of the
United States. New York, Morrow
[1970] xiii, 306 p. [12.95]
929.9/0973 78-86879
JC346.Z3 S63 MRR Alc

SEAMANSHIP.
see also Navigation

Chapman, Charles Frederic. Piloting,
seamanship and small boat handling;
1- ed.; 1922- New York, Motor
boating. 787.125 42-48646
VM341 .M9 vol. 5 MRR Alc Latest
edition

Knight, Austin Melvin, Modern
seamanship. 15th ed. New York, Van
Nostrand Reinhold [1972] xi, 684 p.
623.88 75-189513
VK541 .K73 1972 MRR Alc

United States. Coast Guard. Official
U.S. Coast Guard recreational boating
guide. New York, Grosset & Dunlap
[1967] 124 p. 623.88 67-3310
GV775 .U59 1967 MRR Alc

SEASHELL COLLECTING
see Shells

SEASHORE.
see also Beaches

SEASHORE BIOLOGY.
Berrill, Norman John, 1001 questions
answered about the seashore, New
York, Dodd, Mead, 1957. 305 p.
574.92 57-7448
QH91.5 .B4 MRR Alc

Miner, Roy Waldo, Field book of
seashore life. New York, Putnam
[1950] xv, 888 p. 591.92 50-10405
QH91 .M5 1950 MRR Alc

SEASHORE BIOLOGY--PACIFIC COAST.
Sunset. Sunset beachcombers' guide
to the Pacific coast, Menlo Park,
Calif., Lane Books [1966] 112 p.
917.90946 66-15333
F851 .S93 MRR Alc

SEASONS--POETRY.
Cole, William, ed. Poems for seasons
and celebrations. [1st ed.]
Cleveland, World Pub. Co. [1961] 191
p. 808.81 (J) 61-12012
PS595.H6 C6 MRR Alc

SECOND SIGHT.
see also Prophecies

SECONDARY EDUCATION
see Education, Secondary

SECONDARY SCHOOLS
see High schools

SECONDHAND TRADE--UNITED STATES--
DIRECTORIES.
Mack, Jerry. What's it worth? [San
Angelo? Tex.] Educator Books, c1970.
94 p. [$3.95] 380.1/025/73 74-
138825
HF5482 .M3 MRR Alc

SECRET SERVICE--GREAT BRITAIN.
Van Doren, Carl Clinton, Secret
history of the American revolution,
New York, The Viking press, 1941. 3
p. l., [3]-xiv p., 2 l., [3]-534 p.
41-24478
E277 .V23 1941 MRR Alc

SECRET SOCIETIES.
Graebner, Theodore Conrad, A
handbook of organizations; Saint
Louis, Concordia Pub. House, 1948.
xl, 368 p. 366 49-14011
HS191 .G7 1948 MRR Alc

Heckethorn, Charles William. The
secret societies of all ages and
countries, New Hyde Park, N.Y.,
University Books, [1965] 2 v.
366.9 65-22572
HS125 .H45 1965 MRR Alc

MacKenzie, Norman Ian. Secret
societies, [1st ed.] New York,
Holt, Rinehart and Winston [1968,
c1967] 350 p. 336 68-10787
HS126 .M3 MRR Alc

Preuss, Arthur, comp. A dictionary
of secret and other societies, St.
Louis, Mo., London, B. Herder book
co., 1924. xi, 543 p. 24-9579
HS12 .P6 MRR Alc

SECRET SOCIETIES--UNITED STATES.
Stevens, Albert Clark, ed. The
cyclopædia of fraternities; 2d ed.,
rev. to date. Detroit; Republished
by the Gale Research Co., 1966.
xxiii, 444 p. 366.973 66-20332
HS122 .S7 MRR Alc

Whalen, William Joseph. Handbook of
secret organizations. Milwaukee,
Bruce Pub. Co. [1966] viii, 169 p.
366.0973 66-26658
HS204 .W45 MRR Alc

SECRETARIAL PRACTICE
see Office practice

SECRETARIES--HANDBOOKS, MANUALS, ETC.
Cook, Fred Solomon, The Dartnell
professional secretary's handbook
Chicago, Dartnell Corp. [1971] 224
p. [$8.50] 651/.3741 76-140224
HF5547.5 .C65 MRR Alc

Hutchinson, Lois Irene. Standard
handbook for secretaries 8th ed.
[New York] McGraw-Hill, 1969. x, 638
p. 650 69-19201
HF5547 .H77 1969 MRR Ref Desk

Taintor, Sarah Augusta. The
secretary's handbook; 9th ed. fully
rev. [New York] Macmillan [1969]
xi, 530 p. 651.7/402 69-10466
HF5547 .T25 1969 MRR Alc

SECRETARIES OF STATE
see Cabinet officers

SECRETARIES OF STATE (STATE
GOVERNMENTS)--SOCIETIES, ETC.
National Association of Secretaries
of State. Handbook. [n.p.] 59-
63517
Began publication with 1958 issue.
JK2403 .N353 MRR Alc Latest
edition

SECTIONALISM (U.S.)
Craven, Avery Odelle, The growth of
Southern nationalism, 1848-1862.
[Baton Rouge] Louisiana State
University Press [and] the
Littlefield Fund for Southern History
of the University of Texas [Austin]
1953. xi, 433 p. 975 53-11470
F213 .C75 MRR Alc

Sydnor, Charles Sackett, The
development of Southern sectionalism,
1819-1848. [Baton Rouge] Louisiana
State University Press, 1948. xii,
400 p. 975 48-7627
F213 .S92 MRR Alc

SECTS.
Anson, Peter Frederick, Bishops at
large; London, Faber and Faber
[1964] 593 p. 65-5071
BR157 .A56 1964 MRR Alc

Bach, Marcus, Strange sects and
curious cults. New York, Dodd, Mead,
1961. 277 p. 209 61-7167
BL85 .B3 MRR Alc

Gerstner, John H. The theology of
the major sects. Grand Rapids, Baker
Book House, 1960. 206 p. 230 59-
15527
BR157 .G45 MRR Alc

Lehrburger, Egon, Strange sects and
cults: New York, Hart Pub. Co.
[1972, c1971] 245 p. [$5.95] 280
79-189636
BR157 .L44 1972 MRR Alc

Molland, Einar, Christendom; New
York, Philosophical Library [1959]
418 p. 280 59-65285
BR157 .M613 MRR Alc

SECTS--DIRECTORIES.
Friedlander, Ira. Year one catalog;
[1st ed.] New York, Harper & Row
[1972] 152 p. [$1.95] 200/.25/73
73-150151
BP602 .F74 1972 MRR Alc

SECTS--CANADA--DIRECTORIES.
Yearbook of American and Canadian
churches. 41st- 1973- Nashville,
Abingdon Press. [$8.95] 277/.05 75-
640866
BR513 .Y4 MRR Ref Cat Latest
edition

SECTS--TRANSVAAL.
Skota, Mweli T. D. The African who's
who; [Johannesburg] Distributed by
Central News Agency [196-] 373 p.
67-58880
DT913 .S55 1960z MRR Biog.

SECTS--UNITED STATES.
Braden, Charles Samuel, These also
believe; New York, Macmillan Co.,
1949. xv, 491 p. 280.973 49-8917
BR516 .B697 MRR Alc

Clark, Elmer Talmage, The small
sects in America. Rev. ed. New
York, Abingdon-Cokesbury Press [1949]
256 p. 280.973 49-10200
BR516 .C57 1949 MRR Alc

Hardon, John A. The Protestant
churches of America Rev. ed. Garden
City, N.Y., Image Books [1969] 439
p. [1.45] 280/.4/0973 69-12858
BR516.5 .H3 1969 MRR Alc

Judah, J. Stillson. The history and
philosophy of the metaphysical
movements in America, Philadelphia,
Westminster Press [1967] 317 p.
280/.0973 67-11672
BR516.5 .J8 MRR Alc

Landis, Benson Young, Religion in
the United States New York, Barnes &
Noble [1965] viii, 120 p. 280.973
65-14270
BR516.5 .L3 MRR Alc

Look. Religions in America; New
York, Simon and Schuster, 1963. 415
p. 280.973 63-10852
BR516 .L77 1963 MRR Alc

Mathison, Richard R. Faiths, cults,
and sects of America: [1st ed.]
Indianapolis, Bobbs-Merrill [1960]
384 p. 209.73 60-13589
BR516.5 .M29 MRR Alc

Mayer, Frederick Emanuel, The
religious bodies of America. 4th
ed., rev. Saint Louis, Concordia
Pub. House, 1961. xiii, 598 p. 280
61-15535
BR516.5 .M3 1961 MRR Alc

Mead, Frank Spencer, Handbook of
denominations in the United States
New 5th ed. Nashville, Abingdon
Press [1970] 265 p. [3.95]
200/.973 70-109675
BR516.5 .M38 1970 MRR Ref Desk.

SECTS--UNITED STATES--DIRECTORIES.
Cushing, A. I. The international
"mystery schools" directory. New
1970 ed. Boston, A.C. Publications
[1970] 1 v. (unpaged) 133/.062 70-
16742
BL35 .C86 MRR Alc

White, Alex Sandri. The seeker's
guide to groups and societies.
Central Valley, N.Y., Aurea
Publications. 060.58 62-3443
HS17 .W47 MRR Alc Latest edition

Yearbook of American and Canadian
churches. 41st- 1973- Nashville,
Abingdon Press. [$8.95] 277/.05 75-
640866
BR513 .Y4 MRR Ref Cat Latest
edition

SECTS--UNITED STATES--STATISTICS.
Johnson, Douglas W., Churches &
church membership in the United
States: Washington, Glenmary
Research Center [1974] xiv, 237 p.
[$15.00] 280/.0973 73-94224
BR526 .J64 MRR Alc

National Council of the Churches of
Christ in the United States of
America. Bureau of Research and
Survey. Churches and church
membership in the United States; New
York, 1956-58. 80 no. 56-12497
BR526 .N3 MRR Alc

SECURITIES.
see also Bonds

Christy, George A. Introduction to
investments 6th ed. New York,
McGraw-Hill [1973, c1974] viii, 688
p. 332.6 73-15710
HG4521 .C455 1974 MRR Alc

Financial stock guide serivce.
Jersey City, N.J., Financial
Information, inc. 332.6/7/0973 74-
644692
HG4512 .R4 MRR Alc Latest edition

SECURITIES--BIBLIOGRAPHY.
Woy, James B. Investment
information: Detroit, Gale Research
Co. [1970] 231 p. [$11.50]
016.33267 79-118791
Z7164.F5 W93 MRR Ref Desk.

Woy, James B. Investment methods;
New York, R. R. Bowker, 1973. viii,
220 p. 016.3326 73-9607
Z7164.F5 W94 MRR Alc

SECURITIES--PERIODICALS--BIBLIOGRAPHY.
Directory of business and financial
services. [1st]- ed.; 1924- New
York [etc.] Special Libraries
Association. 25-4599
HF5003 .H3 MRR Ref Desk Latest
edition / MRR Ref Desk Latest
edition

SECURITIES--YEARBOOKS.
Annuaire-Chaix. Paris, Imprimerie
Chaix. ca 18-193
HG5471 .A6 MRR Alc Latest edition

Handbook for investors. 61st-
issue; 1960- [London, Fredc. C.
Mathieson & Sons] 332.6/7 72-623829
HG5431 .M3 MRR Alc Latest edition

SECURITIES--YEARBOOKS. (Cont.)
Handbuch der deutschen Aktien-
Gesellschaften. Darmstadt [etc.]
Hoppenstedt [etc.] ca 15-275
HG5491 .H4 MRR Alc Latest edition

The Oil and petroleum year book.
London ca 12-1196
HG4821 .O4 MRR Alc Latest edition

Le Recueil financier; Bruxelles, É.
Bruylant. 332.63 49-52017
Began publication in 1893.
HG5551 .R42 MRR Alc Latest edition

Répertoire général alphabétique
des valeurs cotées en France et es
valeurs non cotées. Paris,
Éditions financières alphabetiques.
47-42094
HG5471 .R4 MRR Alc Latest edition

The Stock exchange official yearbook. [1st]- 1934- Croydon, Eng.
[etc.] T. Skinner [etc.] 332.6305
34-16479
HG5431 .S82 MRR Alc Latest edition

SECURITIES--AFRICA, SOUTH.
Johannesburg. Stock Exchange. The
Stock Exchange handbook. 1967-
Johannesburg, Flesch Financial
Publications. 332.63/0968 68-130426

HG5841 .J63 MRR Alc Latest edition

SECURITIES--AUSTRIA--YEARBOOKS.
Finanz-Compass: 79.- Jahrg.; 1950-
Wien, Compass-Verlag. 54-17734
HG5451 .F5 MRR Alc Latest edition

SECURITIES--FRANCE.
Annuaire Desfossés; Paris, Cote
Desfossés [etc.] 332.63 46-39086
HG5471 .A64 MRR Alc Latest edition

Répertoire général alphabétique
des valeurs cotées en France et es
valeurs non cotées. Paris,
Éditions financières alphabetiques.
47-42094
HG5471 .R4 MRR Alc Latest edition

SECURITIES--GREAT BRITAIN--YEARBOOKS.
Moodies investment digest. 1966-
[London] Moodies Services. 332.67
68-119818
HG5431 .M6 MRR Alc Latest edition
/ MRR Alc Latest edition

The Times issuing house year book.
12th- ed; 1948- London, Times
Newspapers Ltd. [etc.] 332.6/32/0942
72-626344
HG5431 .I7 MRR Alc Latest edition

SECURITIES--INDIA--YEARBOOKS.
Calcutta. Stock Exchange. Official
year book. Calcutta, Calcutta Stock
Exchange Assn. 332.6 49-39127
HG5740 .C3 MRR Alc Latest edition

SECURITIES--IRELAND--YEARBOOKS.
Handbook of Irish securities, etc.
London, Straker Bros. Ltd. 55-32941

HG5443.I7 H3 MRR Alc Latest
edition

SECURITIES--SPAIN.
Anuario financiero y de sociedades
anónimas de España. Madrid,
Editorial Sopec. 74-642352
Began with 1916.
HG5631 .A47 MRR Alc Latest edition

SECURITIES--SPAIN--YEARBOOKS.
Anuario financiero. Bilbao, Spain.
31-28812
"Founded in 1914."
HG61 .A6 MRR Alc Latest edition

SECURITIES--SWEDEN.
Some prominent Swedish companies.
Stockholm, P. A. Norstedt.
338.7/09485 78-276274
HC372 .S64 MRR Alc Latest edition

SECURITIES--THE WEST--YEARBOOKS.
Walker's manual of Western
corporations & securities. 65th-
ed.; 1973- San Francisco.
332.6/7/0878 74-640659
HG5128.C2 W2 MRR Alc Latest
edition

SECURITIES--UNITED STATES.
Badger, Ralph Eastman. The complete
guide to investment analysis New
York, McGraw-Hill [1967] viii, 504
p. 332.6 67-15850
HG4521 .B3432 MRR Alc.

Financial daily card service; Jersey
City, N.J. Financial Information. 74-
642472
HG4905 .F45 MRR Alc Latest edition

First Boston Corporation. Handbook
of securities of the United States
government and federal agencies, 22d-
edition; 1966- [New York] 332.6/323
72-622502
HG4836 .F5 MRR Alc Latest edition

Harris Trust and Savings Bank.
Investment Dept. Government Bond
Division. The U.S. Government
securities market. [Chicago, 1973]
106 p. 332.6/323 73-160711
HG4936 .H36 MRR Alc.

Hillstrom, Roger. 1960-1969, a
decade of corporate and international
finance. New York, IDD [1972] 381
p. 332 72-175335
HG4907 .H54 MRR Alc.

Klinger, Oliver C. Obsolete
securities, New York City, Oildom
publishing co., inc., c1923. 431 p.
24-31861
HG4927 .K4 MRR Alc.

Kraus, Albert L. The New York times
guide to business and finance; [1st
ed.] New York, Harper & Row [1972]
viii, 280 p. [$8.95] 330.9/73/092
70-138745
HG181 .K7 1972 MRR Alc.

The National monthly stock summary.
New York [etc.] The National
Quotation Bureau Inc. 332.63 42-241
HG4905 .N34 MRR Alc Latest edition

New York. Stock Exchange. Listing
statements of the New York Stock
Exchange. New York, F. E. Fitch,
inc., ca 24-283
HG4501 .N4 MRR Alc Partial set

Robbins, Sidney M. The securities
markets; New York, Free Press [1966]
xvi, 303 p. 332.64 66-15499
HG4910 .R617 MRR Alc.

Robert D. Fisher manual of valuable &
worthless securities. v. 1- 1926-
New York, R. D. Fisher [etc.] 26-
5238
HG4055 .R6 MRR Alc Full set

Smythe, Roland Mulville. Valuable
extinct securities; New York, 1929.
v p., 1 l., 398 p. 30-1926
HG4927 .S63 MRR Alc.

Standard and Poor's Corporation.
Standard & Poor's stock market
encyclopedia. 14th ed. New York
[1971] 1 v. (unpaged) [$25.00]
332.6/ 70-23142
HG4921 .S68 1971 MRR Ref Desk.

Standard and Poor's Corporation.
Standard & Poor's stock market
encyclopedia. New York 332.6/7 70-
23142
HG4921 .S68 MRR Ref Desk Latest
edition

Standard and Poor's Corporation.
Status of bonds under the federal
income and state taxes and coupon
directory. 1942- ed. New York.
332.630973 42-15584
HG4921 .S67 MRR Alc Latest edition

Vaughn, Donald E. Survey of
investments New York, Holt, Rinehart
and Winston [1967] xx, 490 p.
332.6/0973 67-21578
HG4921 .V3 MRR Alc.

Your investments. [1st]- ed.; 1954-
New York, American Research
Council, Publications Division.
332.670973 58-1074
HG4905 .Y6 MRR Alc Latest edition

SECURITIES--UNITED STATES--BIBLIOGRAPHY.
Wall Street Journal. (Indexes)
Index. [New York] Dow Jones & Co.
59-35162
HG1 .W26 MRR Alc Full set

SECURITIES--UNITED STATES--HANDBOOKS,
MANUALS, ETC.
The Stock market handbook; Homewood,
Ill., Dow Jones-Irwin, 1970. xxxi,
1073 p. [$27.50] 332.6/0973 78-
83128
HG4921 .S794 MRR Alc.

SECURITIES--UNITED STATES--PERIODICALS.
Directory of obsolete securities.
1970- [n.p.] Financial Information,
inc. 332.67 72-612940
HG4961 .D56 MRR Alc Latest edition

Media General Financial Services.
Industriscope. v. 1- May 1973-
[Richmond, Va.] 332.6/322/0973 74-
644661
HG4915 .M5a MRR Alc Latest edition

Moody's OTC industrial manual. New
York, Moody's Investors Service.
332.67 77-649772
HG4961 .M7237 MRR Ref Desk Latest
edition

SECURITIES--UNITED STATES--STATISTICS.
Dow, Jones & Co., New York. The Dow
Jones investor's handbook.
Princeton, N.J. [etc.] Dow Jones
Books [etc.] 332.67/8 66-17650
HG4921 .D66 MRR Alc Latest edition

SECURITIES--UNITED STATES--YEARBOOKS.
Moody's bank & finance manual;
American and foreign. New York,
Moody's Investors Service. 56-14722

HG4961 .M65 MRR Alc Latest edition

Moody's industrial manual: 1954-
New York, Moody's Investors Service.
56-14721
HG4961 .M67 MRR Alc Latest edition

Moody's public utility manual. 1954-
New York, Moody's Investors Service.
56-3927
HG4961 .M7245 MRR Alc Latest
edition

Moody's transportation manual:
American and foreign. 1954- New
York, Moody's Investors Service. 57-
15176
HG4971 .M74 MRR Alc Latest edition

SECURITIES, TAX-EXEMPT--UNITED STATES.
Standard and Poor's Corporation.
Status of bonds under the federal
income and state taxes and coupon
directory. 1942- ed. New York.
332.630973 42-15584
HG4821 .S67 MRR Alc Latest edition

White, Wilson. White's tax exempt
bond market ratings. 1st- ed.;1954-
New York, Standard & Poor's
Corp.[etc.] 65-47879
HG4537 .W5 MRR Alc Latest edition

SECURITY, INTERNATIONAL.
see also Peace

SEED INDUSTRY AND TRADE--LAW AND
LEGISLATION--UNITED STATES.
Seed trade buyers guide & directory.
La Grange, Ill. [etc.] Seed World
Publications. 38-33966
SB115 .S4 Sci RR Latest edition /
MRR Alc Latest edition

SEEDS.
United States. Dept. of Agriculture.
Seeds. Washington [U.S. Govt. Print.
Off., 1961] xiv, 591 p. 631.52
agr61-260
S21 .A35 1961 MRR Alc.

SEEDS--CATALOGS.
Seed trade buyers guide & directory.
La Grange, Ill. [etc.] Seed World
Publications. 38-33966
SB115 .S4 Sci RR Latest edition /
MRR Alc Latest edition

SEGREGATION.
see also Minorities

SEGREGATION IN EDUCATION--BIBLIOGRAPHY.
Weinberg, Meyer. School integration;
Chicago, Integrated Education
Associates, 1967. iv, 137 p.
016.37019/342 67-29000
Z5814.D5 W4 MRR Alc.

SEISMOLOGY.
see also Earthquakes

see also Volcanoes

SELECTIVE SERVICE
see Military service, Compulsory

SELENOLOGY
see Moon

SELF.
see also Personality

SELF-CULTURE--BIBLIOGRAPHY.
Smith, Frank Seymour. Know-how
books; London, Thames and Hudson
[1956] xi, 306 p. 028 57-17217
Z1035.9 .S6 1956 MRR Alc.

United States. Library of Congress.
Division for the Blind and Physically
Handicapped. Talking books to profit
by. Washington [1971] 11 p. 011
70-613706
Z663.25 .T34 MRR Alc.

SELF-DEFENSE.
see also Boxing

SELF-DETERMINATION, NATIONAL.
see also Minorities

SELF MEDICATION--POPULAR WORKS.
The Medicine show Rev. ed. New
York, Pantheon Books, 1974. 384 p.
610 74-10418
RC81 .M496 1974 MRR Alc.

SELF-SERVICE STORES--DIRECTORIES.
Directory of discount houses and self-
service department stores. 1st-
ed.; 1961- Chicago, Directory
Division, National Research Bureau.
62-2505
HF5035 .D47 MRR Alc Latest edition

SELFRIDGE, THOMAS OLIVER, 1804-1902--
MANUSCRIPTS.
United States. Library of Congress.
Manuscript Division. Thomas Oliver
Selfridge, Sr. [and] Thomas Oliver
Selfridge, Jr.; Washington, Library
of Congress, 1969. 8, 7 l.
016.3593/31/0924 70-603258
Z663.34 .S42 MRR Alc.

SELFRIDGE, THOMAS OLIVER, 1836-1924--
MANUSCRIPTS.
United States. Library of Congress.
Manuscript Division. Thomas Oliver
Selfridge, Sr. [and] Thomas Oliver
Selfridge, Jr.; Washington, Library
of Congress, 1969. 8, 7 l.
016.3593/31/0924 70-603258
Z663.34 .S42 MRR Alc.

SELLERS, DAVID FOOTE, 1874-1949--
MANUSCRIPTS.
United States. Library of Congress.
Manuscript Division. David Foote
Sellers, Stephen B. Luce: a register
of their papers in the Library of
Congress. Washington, Library of
Congress, 1868. 7, 8 l.
016.3593/31/0924 79-601361
Z663.34 .S43 MRR Alc.

SEMANTICS.
see also Words, New

SEMANTICS (PHILOSOPHY)
see also Communication

SEMI-PRECIOUS STONES
see Precious stones

SEMIOLOGY.
see also Diagnosis

Gomez, Joan. Dictionary of symptoms:
Arundel (Sx.), Centaur P., 1967.
xxiv, 383 p. [45/-] 616.07/2/03
67-106674
RC82 .G6 MRR Alc.

Yater, Wallace Mason. Symptom
diagnosis 5th ed. New York,
Appleton-Century-Crofts [1961] 1035
p. 616.075 60-11757
RC71 .Y3 1961 MRR Alc.

SEMITES.
see also Jews

SEMITES--RELIGION.
see also Judaism

SENEGAL.
American University, Washington, D.C.
Foreign Areas Studies Division. Area
handbook for Senegal. [Washington,
For sale by the Supt. of Docs., U.S.
Govt. Print. Off.] 1963. xiv, 489 p.
67-117133
DT549 .A58 MRR Alc.

SENEGAL--GAZETTEERS.
United States. Office of Geography.
Senegal; official standard names
approved by the United States Board
on Geographic Names. Washington
[U.S. Govt. Print. Off.] 1965. iv,
194 p. 65-61415
DT549.2 .U5 MRR Alc.

SENESCENCE
see Aging

see Old age

SENIOR CITIZENS
see Aged

SEOUL, KOREA--DIRECTORIES.
The Korea directory. 1968- Seoul,
Korea Directory Company. 915.19 68-
57222
DS901 .K68 MRR Alc Latest edition

SEPARATION (LAW)
see also Divorce

SEPARATION OF POWERS--UNITED STATES.
Fisher, Louis. President and
Congress; New York, Free Press
[1972] xvi, 347 p. 353.03/72 78-
142362
JK305 .F55 MRR Alc.

SEQUENTIAL MACHINE THEORY.
see also Electronic digital computers

SERBO-CROATIAN LANGUAGE--DICTIONARIES--
ENGLISH.
Benson, Morton. Srpskohrvatsko-
engleski recnik. Beograd, Prosveta,
1971. lvii, 807 p. 72-979501
PG1376 .B4 1971b MRR Alc.

Bogadek, Francis Aloysius. New
English-Croatian and Croatian-English
dictionary. 3d ed., enl. and corr.
New York, Hafner Pub. Co., 1949
[c1944] 2 v. in 1. 491.8332 50-
2223
PG1377 .B72 1949 MRR Alc.

Cahen, Louis. Džepni srpsko-
engleski i englesko-srpski rečnik,
[4th impression] London, K. Paul,
Trench, Trubner & co., ltd., 1920.
iv, 268 p. 22-13783
PG1376 .C3 1920 MRR Alc.

Drvodelić, Milan. Hrvatskogrpsko-
engleski rječnik. Zagreb, Skolska
knj., 1961. 912 p. 61-19047
PG1377 .D7915 MRR Alc.

Srpskohrvatsko-engleski recnik.
Beograd, Naucna knjiga, 1957. 369
p. 59-22656
PG1377 .S67 MRR Alc.

SERBO-CROATIAN LANGUAGE--GRAMMAR.
Benson, Morton. Srpskohrvatsko-
engleski recnik. Beograd, Prosveta,
1971. lvii, 807 p. 72-979501
PG1376 .B4 1971b MRR Alc.

SERIAL PUBLICATION OF BOOKS.
Foulche-Delbosc, Raymond, Manuel de
l'hispanisant. New York, G. P.
Putnam's sons, 1920- v. 20-
16867
Z2681.A1 F7 MRR Alc.

Lowndes, William Thomas. The
bibliographer's manual of English
literature New ed., rev., cor. and
enl., London, H. G. Bohn, 1857-61;
Bell & Daldy, 1864-65. 10 v.
015.42 35-36009
Z2001 .L92 1857-65 MRR Alc.

SERIALS
see Periodicals

SERUMTHERAPY.
see also Allergy

SERVICE, COMPULSORY
see Military service, Compulsory

SERVICE INDUSTRIES--UNITED STATES--
DIRECTORIES.
Rosenbloom, Joseph. Consumer
complaint guide. 1973. New York, CCM
Information Corp. [1972] iv, 476 p.
338.4/7/602573 73-154774
T12 .R66 1972 MRR Alc.

SERVICE INDUSTRIES--UNITED STATES--
STATISTICS.
Robert Morris Associates. Annual
statement studies. [Philadelphia]
338/.0973 72-626355
HF5681.B2 R6 MRR Alc Latest
edition

United States. Bureau of the Census.
1967 census of business.
[Washington; For sale by the Supt. of
Docs., U.S. Govt. Print. Off., 1970-
71] 5 v. in 9 [$9.50 (v. 1) varies]
338/.0973 72-608032
HF3007 .U55 1970 MRR Alc.

SERVICE INDUSTRIES--WASHINGTON, D.C.--
DIRECTORIES.
Mintz, Bettie. Top shops & secret
services, Washington, D.C. area.
[Washington, Manufactured by Plymouth
Print. Co., 1971] ix, 213 p.
[$3.75] 380.1/025/753 74-31990
HF5429.5.W3 M5 1971 MRR Alc.

SERVICE STATIONS, AUTOMOBILE
see Automobiles--Service stations

SERVICEMEN, MILITARY
see Soldiers

SEVENTEENTH CENTURY--BIBLIOGRAPHY.
Michel, Suzanne P. Repertoire des
ouvrages imprimes en langue
italienne au XVIIe siecle Firenze,
L. S. Olschki, 1970- v. [L17500
(v. 1)] 70-558790
Z2342 .M52 MRR Alc.

Michel, Suzanne P. Répertoire des
ouvrages imprimes en langue
italienne au XVIIe siecle conservés
dans les bibliothèques de France
Paris, Éditions du Centre national
de la recherche scientifique, 1967-
v. [38.00 (v. 1) varies]
015/.45 67-69528
Z2342 .M5 MRR Alc.

SEVENTH-DAY ADVENTISTS--DICTIONARIES.
Seventh-Day Adventist encyclopedia.
Washington, Review and Herald Pub.
Association, 1966. xviii, 1452 p.
286.73 66-17322
BX6154 .S39 MRR Alc.

SEVENTH-DAY ADVENTISTS--YEARBOOKS.
Seventh-Day Adventists. Year book of
the Seventh-Day Adventist
Denomination. Washington, Review and
Herald Pub. Association. 18-17399
Began publication in 1883.
BX6109 .S4 MRR Alc Latest edition

SEVENTH-DAY ADVENTISTS--HISTORY.
Spalding, Arthur Whitefield,
Captains of the host, Washington,
Review and Herald Pub. Association
[1949] 2 v. 286.709 49-2497
BX6153 .S615 MRR Alc.

SEWERAGE.
see also Plumbing

SEWING.
The Vogue sewing book. [1st ed.]
New York, Vogue Patterns;
distribution by Doubleday, Garden
City N.Y. [1970] 416 p. 646.4/04
70-124559
TT515 .V63 MRR Alc.

SEX.
see also Homosexuality

see also Reproduction

American Medical Association.
Committee on Human Sexuality. Human
sexuality. [Chicago, Ill., 1972]
xv, 246 p. 301.41/7 72-90176
HQ31 .A496 MRR Alc.

Katchadourian, Herant A.
Fundamentals of human sexuality New
York, Holt, Rinehart and Winston
[1972] viii, 514 p. 612.6 76-
163189
HQ31 .K36 MRR Alc.

McCary, James Leslie. Human
sexuality; physiological,
psychological, and sociological
factors. 2d ed. New York, Van
Nostrand [1973] xiii, 542 p. 612.6
72-7809
HQ21 .M115 1973 MRR Alc.

SEX--BIBLIOGRAPHY.
Seruya, Flora C. Sex and sex
education: a bibliography. New York,
R. R. Bowker Co., 1972. xiii, 336 p.
016.6126/007 72-8333
Z7164.S43 S38 MRR Alc.

SEX--DICTIONARIES.
A Dictionary of contemporary and
colloquial usage. [1st ed.]
Chicago, English-Language Institute
of America [1972] 32 p. 427.09 77-
38007
PE3721 .D5 MRR Alc.

Ellis, Albert, ed. The encyclopedia
of sexual behavior. [New 2d ed.]
New York, J. Aronson [1973] 1072 p.
[$25.00] 612.6/003 73-76666
HQ9 .E4 1973 MRR Alc.

Landy, Eugene E. The underground
dictionary. New York, Simon and
Schuster [1971] 206 p. [$5.95]
427.09 73-139637
PE3721 .L3 MRR Alc.

Schmidt, Jacob Edward. Cyclopedic
lexicon of sex; [2d ed.] New York,
Brussel & Brussel, 1967. viii, 389
p. [$10.00] 301.41/7/03 74-152205

HQ9 .S28 1967 MRR Alc.

Wilson, Robert Anton, Playboy's book
of forbidden words; [1st ed.
Chicago, Playboy Press; distributed
by Simon & Schuster; New York, c1972]
xi, 302 p. [$8.95] 72-81109
HQ9 .W54 MRR Alc.

SEX (BIOLOGY)
Masters, William H. Human sexual
response. [1st ed.] Boston, Little,
Brown [1966] xiii, 366 p. 612.6
66-18370
QP251 .M35 MRR Alc.

SEX (PSYCHOLOGY)
Masters, William H. Human sexual
response. [1st ed.] Boston, Little,
Brown [1966] xiii, 366 p. 612.6
66-18370
QP251 .M35 MRR Alc.

SEX AND LAW.
see also Abortion

SEX AND LAW--UNITED STATES.
American Medical Association.
Committee on Human Sexuality. Human
sexuality. [Chicago, Ill., 1972]
xv, 246 p. 301.41/7 72-90176
HQ31 .A496 MRR Alc.

SEXUAL ETHICS.
see also Birth control

SEXUAL HYGIENE
see Hygiene, Sexual

SEYCHELLES--GOVERNMENT PUBLICATIONS--
BIBLIOGRAPHY.
United States. Library of Congress.
African Section. Madagascar and
adjacent islands; Washington,
General Reference and Bibliography
Division, Reference Department,
Library of Congress;[for sale by the
Superintendent of Documents, U.S.
Govt. Print. Off.] 1965. xiii, 58 p.
65-61703
Z663.285 .M3 MRR Alc.

SHAFROTH, JOHN FRANKLIN, 1867-1967--
MANUSCRIPTS--CATALOGS.
United States. Library of Congress.
Manuscript Division. Claude Charles
Bloch, Julius Augustus Furer, John
Franklin Shafroth, William Harrison
Standley; a register of their papers
in the Library of Congress.
Washington, Library of Congress,
1973. iii, 6, 10, 4, 11, p.
016.359 73-4374
Z663.34 .B55 MRR Alc.

SHAKERS--DOCTRINAL AND CONTROVERSIAL
WORKS.
Whitson, Robley Edward. Shaker
theological sources; Bethlehem,
Conn., United Institute, 1969. ix,
52 l. 230.8/8 77-13052
BX9771 .W53 MRR Alc.

SHAKERS--HISTORY.
Andrews, Edward Deming. The people
called Shakers; New enl. ed. New
York, Dover Publications [1963] xvi,
351 p. 289.8 63-17896
BX8765 .A6 1963 MRR Alc.

SHAKESPEARE, WILLIAM, 1564-1616. POEMS--
CONCORDANCES.
Furness, Helen Kate (Rogers) A
concordance to Shakespeare's poems:
<3d ed.> Philadelphia [etc.] J. B.
Lippincott company [1902] iv, 422 p.
02-10022
PR2892 .F8 1902 MRR Alc.

SHAKESPEARE, WILLIAM, 1564-1616--
ALLUSIONS.
The Shakespere allusion-book;
London, H. Milford, Oxford university
press, 1932. 2 v. 822.33 32-31755
PR2959 .S5 1932 MRR Alc.

SHAKESPEARE, WILLIAM, 1564-1616--
BIBLIOGRAPHY.
Ebisch, Walther. A Shakespeare
bibliography, Oxford, The Clarendon
press, 1931. xviii, 294 p., 1 l.
012 822.33 31-26966
Z8811 .E18 MRR Alc.

Jaggard, William, Shakespeare
bibliography; New York, F. Ungar
Pub. Co. [1959] xxi, 729 p. 012
58-59877
Z8811 .J21 1959 MRR Alc.

The Shakespere allusion-book;
London, H. Milford, Oxford university
press, 1932. 2 v. 822.33 32-31755
PR2959 .S5 1932 MRR Alc.

Smith, Gordon Ross. A classified
Shakespeare bibliography, 1963-1958.
University Park, Pennsylvania State
University Press, 1963. lviii, 784
p. 016.82233 63-17265
Z8811 .S64 MRR Alc.

Wells, Stanley W., Shakespeare:
select bibliographical guides;
[London, New York] Oxford University
Press, 1973. 300 p. 016.8223/3 74-
159015
Z8811 .W44 MRR Alc.

SHAKESPEARE, WILLIAM, 1564-1616--
BIBLIOGRAPHY--CATALOGS.
Folger Shakespeare Library.
Washington, D.C. Catalog of the
Shakespeare collection. Boston, G.
K. Hall, 1972. 2 v. 016.8223/3 72-
6446
Z8811 .F65 MRR Alc.

SHAKESPEARE, WILLIAM, 1564-1616--
BIOGRAPHY.
Bentley, Gerald Eades, Shakespeare;
a biographical handbook. New Haven,
Yale University Press, 1961. 256 p.
928.2 61-14997
PR2894 .B4 MRR Alc.

SHAKESPEARE, WILLIAM, 1564-1616--
CHARACTERS.
Quennell, Peter, Who's who in
Shakespeare London, Weidenfeld and
Nicolson [1973] 287 p. [£3.95]
822.3/3 73-177798
PR2989 .Q4 MRR Alc.

Smith, Alfred Russell. A handbook
index to those characters who have
speaking parts assigned to them in
the first folio of Shakespeare's
plays 1623. London, A. R. Smith,
1904. 3 p. l., 133 p. 04-32201
PR2989 .S6 MRR Alc.

Stokes, Francis Griffin. A
dictionary of the characters & proper
names in the works of Shakespeare,
Boston, New York, Houghton Mifflin
company [pref. 1924] xv, 359, [1] p.
incl. geneal. tables. 822.33 31-
25861
PR2892 .S67 1924a MRR Alc.

SHAKESPEARE, WILLIAM, 1564-1616--
COMEDIES.
Spevack, Marvin. A complete and
systematic concordance to the works
of Shakespeare. Hildesheim, Georg
Olms, 1968- v. 822.3/3 68-
108766
PR2892 .S6 MRR Alc.

SHAKESPEARE, WILLIAM, 1564-1616--
CONCORDANCES.
Bartlett, John, A complete
concordance or verbal index to words,
phrases, and passages in the dramatic
works of Shakespeare, New York, St.
Martin's Press, 1953. 1910 p.
822.33 53-2095
PR2892 .B34 1953 MRR Alc.

Bartlett, John, A new and complete
concordance or verbal index to words,
phrases, & passages in the dramatic
works of Shakespeare, London,
Macmillan and co., limited, 1937. 4
p. l., 1910 p. 822.33 38-5787
PR2892 .B34 1937 MRR Ref Desk.

Cunliffe, Richard John. A new
Shakespearean dictionary, London,
Glasgow, Bombay, Blackie and son,
limited, 1910. xl, [1], 342 p. 10-
20199
PR2892 .C8 MRR Alc.

Furness, Helen Kate (Rogers) A
concordance to Shakespeare's poems:
<3d ed.> Philadelphia [etc.] J. B.
Lippincott company [1902] iv, 422 p.
02-10022
PR2892 .F8 1902 MRR Alc.

Shakespeare, William, The home book
of Shakespeare quotations, New York,
C. Scribner's sons; London, C.
Scribner's sons, ltd.; 1937. xl,
2055 p. 822.33 37-32691
PR2892 .S63 MRR Alc.

Spevack, Marvin. A complete and
systematic concordance to the works
of Shakespeare. Hildesheim, Georg
Olms, 1968- v. 822.3/3 68-
108766
PR2892 .S6 MRR Alc.

Spevack, Marvin. The Harvard
concordance to Shakespeare.
Cambridge, Mass., Belknap Press of
Harvard University Press, 1973. ix,
1600 p. [$45.00] 822.3/3 73-76385
PR2892 .S62 MRR Alc.

SHAKESPEARE, WILLIAM, 1564-1616--
CRITICISM AND INTERPRETATION.
Eastman, Arthur M., ed.
Shakespeare's critics; Ann Arbor,
University of Michigan Press [1964]
xviii, 346 p. 822.33 64-10651
PR2890 .E2 MRR Alc.

SHAKESPEARE, WILLIAM, 1564-1616--
CRITICISM AND INTERPRETATION--
BIBLIOGRAPHY.
Howard-Hill, Trevor Howard.
Shakespearian bibliography and
textual criticism: Oxford, Clarendon
Press, 1971. 322 p. [£4.25]
016.8223/3 79-858175
Z8811 .H67 MRR Alc.

Velz, John W. Shakespeare and the
classical tradition; Minneapolis,
University of Minnesota Press [1968]
xvii, 459 p. 016.8283/3/09 67-
14377
Z8811 .V4 1968 MRR Alc.

SHAKESPEARE, WILLIAM, 1564-1616--
DICTIONARIES, INDEXES, ETC.
Baker, Arthur Ernest, A Shakespeare
commentary ... New York, F. Ungar
Pub. Co. [1957] 2 v. (9, 964 p.)
822.33 57-9168
PR2892 .B2 1957 MRR Alc.

Campbell, Oscar James, ed. The
reader's encyclopedia of Shakespeare,
New York, Crowell [1966] xv, 1014
p. 822.33 66-11946
PR2892 .C3 MRR Alc.

Halliday, Frank Ernest. A
Shakespeare companion, 1564-1964
[Rev. ed.] New York, Schocken Books
[1964] 569 p. 822.33 64-14774
PR2892 .H3 1964a MRR Alc.

Irvine, Theodora Ursula. A
pronouncing dictionary of
Shakespearean proper names, New
York, Barnes & Noble, inc.; 1945.
lviii, 387 p. incl. front. (facsim.)
822.33 46-104
PR3081 .I65 1945a MRR Alc.

Nares, Robert, A glossary of words,
phrases, names, and allusions in the
works of English authors New ed.;
Detroit, Republished by Gale Research
Co.; 1966. ix, 981 p. 423.1 66-
25635
PE1667 .N32 MRR Alc.

Quennell, Peter, Who's who in
Shakespeare London, Weidenfeld and
Nicolson [1973] 287 p. [£3.95]
822.3/3 73-177798
PR2989 .Q4 MRR Alc.

Schmidt, Alexander, Shakespeare
lexicon; 3d ed. rev. and enl. New
York, B. Blom [1968] 2 v. (x, 1484
p.) 822.3/3 67-30463
PR2892 .S4 1968 MRR Alc.

Stokes, Francis Griffin. A
dictionary of the characters & proper
names in the works of Shakespeare,
Boston, New York, Houghton Mifflin
company [pref. 1924] xv, 359, [1] p.
incl. geneal. tables. 822.33 31-
25861
PR2892 .S67 1924a MRR Alc.

Sugden, Edward Holdsworth, A
topographical dictionary to the works
of Shakespeare and his fellow
dramatists, Manchester, The
University press; London, New York,
etc., Longmans, Green & co., 1925.
xix, 580 p. 25-9716
PR2892 .S8 MRR Alc.

SHAKESPEARE, WILLIAM, 1564-1616--
DRAMATURGY.
Shattuck, Charles Harlen, The
Shakespeare promptbooks; Urbana,
University of Illinois Press, 1965.
vii, 553 p. 016.792023 65-11737
PR3091 .S4 MRR Alc.

SHAKESPEARE, WILLIAM, 1564-1616--
LANGUAGE--GLOSSARIES, ETC.
Cunliffe, Richard John. A new
Shakespearean dictionary, London,
Glasgow, Bombay, Blackie and son,
limited, 1910. xl, [1], 342 p. 10-
20199
PR2892 .C8 MRR Alc.

Onions, Charles Talbut, A
Shakespeare glossary. Oxford, The
Clarendon press, 1911. xii, 259, [1]
p. w 12-65
PR2892 .O6 MRR Alc.

SHAKESPEARE, WILLIAM, 1564-1616--
LANGUAGE--PRONUNCIATION.
Irvine, Theodora Ursula. A
pronouncing dictionary of
Shakespearean proper names, New
York, Barnes & Noble, inc.; 1945.
lviii, 387 p. incl. front. (facsim.)
822.33 46-104
PR3081 .I65 1945a MRR Alc.

SHAKESPEARE, WILLIAM, 1564-1616--
QUOTATIONS.
Shakespeare, William, Everyman's
dictionary of Shakespeare quotations,
London, Dent; New York, Dutton
[1953] xii, 560 p. 822.33 54-671
PR2768 .B73 MRR Alc.

Shakespeare, William, The home book
of Shakespeare quotations, New York,
C. Scribner's sons; London, C.
Scribner's sons, ltd.; 1937. xl,
2055 p. 822.33 37-32691
PR2892 .S63 MRR Alc.

Spevack, Marvin. The Harvard
concordance to Shakespeare.
Cambridge, Mass., Belknap Press of
Harvard University Press, 1973. ix,
1600 p. [$45.00] 822.3/3 73-76385
PR2892 .S62 MRR Alc.

SHAKESPEARE, WILLIAM, 1564-1616--STAGE
HISTORY.
Shattuck, Charles Harlen, The
Shakespeare promptbooks; Urbana,
University of Illinois Press, 1965.
vii, 553 p. 016.792023 65-11737
PR3091 .S4 MRR Alc.

SHAW, GEORGE BERNARD, 1856-1950.
Henderson, Archibald, George Bernard
Shaw, man of the century.
Washington, Reference Dept., Library
of Congress, 1957. 15 p. 928.2 57-
60036
Z663.293 .S5 MRR Alc.

SHAW, GEORGE BERNARD, 1856-1950--
BIBLIOGRAPHY.
Broad, Lewis, Dictionary to the
plays and novels of Bernard Shaw,
New York, Haskell House, 1969. xi,
230 p. 822/.9/12 75-92947
PR5366 .A23 1969 MRR Alc.

SHAW, GEORGE BERNARD, 1856-1950--
CONCORDANCES.
Bevan, E. Dean. A concordance to the
plays and prefaces of Bernard Shaw.
Detroit, Gale Research Co. [c1971]
10 v. 822/.9/12 77-166191
PR5366 .A22 MRR Alc.

SHAW, GEORGE BERNARD, 1856-1950--
DICTIONARIES, INDEXES, ETC.
Broad, Lewis, Dictionary to the
plays and novels of Bernard Shaw,
New York, Haskell House, 1969. xi,
230 p. 822/.9/12 75-92947
PR5366 .A23 1969 MRR Alc.

SHAW, GEORGE BERNARD, 1856-1950--PLOTS.
Broad, Lewis, Dictionary to the
plays and novels of Bernard Shaw,
New York, Haskell House, 1969. xi,
230 p. 822/.9/12 75-92947
    PR5366 .A23 1969 MRR Alc.

SHEEP BREEDS.
Briggs, Hilton Marshall, Modern
breeds of livestock. Rev. ed. New
York, Macmillan [1958] 754 p.
636.08 58-5049
    SF105 .B7 1958 MRR Alc.

Mason, Ian Lauder. A world
dictionary of livestock breeds, types
and varieties, 2nd (revised) ed.
Farnham Royal, Commonwealth
Agricultural Bureaux, 1969. xviii,
268 p. [70/-] 636/.003 75-454433
    SF21 .M3 1969 MRR Alc.

SHEFFIELD, ENG.--DIRECTORIES.
Kelly's directory of Sheffield and
Rotherham and the surrounding
parishes, townships, villages and
hamlets. Kingston upon Thames,
Surrey [etc.] Kelly's Directories
[etc.] 34-41846
    DA690.S54 A15 MRR Alc Latest
    edition

SHEFFIELD PLATE.
Bradbury, Frederick, British and
Irish silver assay office marks, 1544-
1968. 12th ed. Sheffield, Northend,
1968. 93 p. [24/-] 739.2/3/0278
78-391328
    NK7210 .B74 1968 MRR Alc.

SHELF-LISTING (LIBRARY SCIENCE)
United States. Library of Congress.
Catalog Division. Shelf list rules.
[Washington] 1902. 2 l. 61-55644
    Z663.78 .S5 1902a MRR Alc.

SHELLEY, PERCY BYSSHE, 1792-1822--
CONCORDANCES.
Ellis, Frederick Startridge, A
lexical concordance to the poetical
works of Percy Bysshe Shelley;
London, B. Quaritch, 1892. xi, 818
p. 13-24598
    PR5430 .E5 MRR Alc.

SHELLS.
Abbott, Robert Tucker, American
seashells. New York, Van Nostrand
[1954] xiv, 541 p. 594 54-5780
    QL414 .A2 MRR Alc.

Warmke, Germaine Le Clerc. Caribbean
seashells; Narberth, Pa., Livingston
Pub. Co. [1961] x, 346 p.
594.09729 61-13006
    QL423.C3 W3 MRR Alc.

SHERIDAN, PHILIP HENRY, 1831-1888--
MANUSCRIPTS.
United States. Library of Congress.
Manuscript Division. Philip H.
Sheridan; a register of his papers in
the Library of Congress. Washington,
1962. 18 l. 62-60597
    Z6633.34 .S47 MRR Alc.

SHERMAN, WILLIAM TECUMSEH, 1820-1891--
BIBLIOGRAPHY.
United States. Library of Congress.
Manuscript Division. William T.
Sherman; a register of his papers in
the Library of Congress. Washington,
1965. 12 l. 65-60099
    Z6633.34 .S5 MRR Alc.

SHIP-BUILDING
see also Boat-building

SHIP-BUILDING--CONTRACTS AND
SPECIFICATIONS.
American Bureau of Shipping. Rules
for the classification and
construction of steel vessels. 1922-
New York. 22-21101
    VM287 .A43 Sci RR Latest edition /
    MRR Alc Latest edition

SHIP-BUILDING--DIRECTORIES.
American Bureau of Shipping. Record.
1969- New York. 99-230
    HE565.U5 A55 MRR Alc Latest
    edition / MRR Alc Latest edition

The Directory of shipowners,
shipbuilders, and marine engineers.
London, Engineering, Chemical &
Marine Press [etc.] 25-4199
    HE565.A3 D5 MRR Alc Latest edition

Lloyd's register of shipping.
London, Wyman and sons [etc.] ca 08-
1387
    "Founded 1760. Re-constituted
    1834."
    HE565.A3 L7 MRR Alc Latest edition

Marine Directory. [New York, Simmons-
Boardman Publ. Corp.]
338.4/7/6238025 72-623836
    HE565.U5 S5 MRR Alc Latest edition

SHIP-BUILDING--HISTORY.
Gibbs, Charles Robert Vernon.
Passenger liners of the Western
Ocean; 2d ed. [completely rev.]
London, Staples Press [1957] 434 p.
623.824 57-1880
    VM18 .G5 1957 MRR Alc.

SHIP-BUILDING--YEARBOOKS.
International shipping and
shipbuilding directory. London, Benn
Bros. [etc.] 48-41377
    HE951 .S55 Sci RR Latest edition /
    MRR Alc Latest edition

Lloyd's register of shipping. Rules
& regulations for the construction
and classification of steel vessels.
London. 07-17765
    HE565.A3 L75 MRR Alc Latest
    edition

Navis; annuaire de la marine
marchande, de la construction navale
et des ports maritimes. Paris, R.
Moreux. 56-27553
    HE730 .N35 MRR Alc Latest edition

SHIP-BUILDING--GREAT LAKES--DIRECTORIES.
The Great Lakes red book. 1902- St.
Clair Shores, Mich. [etc.] Fourth
Seacoast Pub. Co. [etc.] 02-13631
    HE565.U71 L7 MRR Alc Latest
    edition

SHIP-BUILDING--NETHERLANDS--YEARBOOKS.
Moormans Jaarboek voor scheepvaart en
scheepsbouw. Den Haag, Verenigde
Periodieke Pers N.V. 51-20638
    Began publication in 1923.
    HE730 .M6 MRR Alc Latest edition

SHIP-BUILDING--UNITED STATES--HISTORY.
Sawyer, Leonard Arthur. Victory
ships and tankers; Cambridge, Md.,
Cornell Maritime Press [1974] 230 p.
387.2/45/0973 73-22561
    VM391 .S39 1974 MRR Alc.

SHIP NAMES.
Manning, Thomas Davys, British
warship names London, Putnam;
[label: Cambridge, Md., Cornell
Maritime Press, 1959] 498 p.
359.32 59-13450
    VA456 .M27 MRR Alc.

SHIP REGISTERS.
The Bulk carrier register. London,
H. Clarkson & Co. 387.2/45 70-
618134
    HE566.F7 B79 MRR Alc Latest
    edition

Cairis, Nicholas T. North Atlantic
passenger liners since 1900 London,
Allan, 1972. 224 p. [£4.40]
387.2/43 72-193343
    HE566.O25 C35 MRR Alc.

Germanischer Lloyd. Register.
Hamburg [etc.] 52-30900
    Began in 1873.
    HE565.A3 G4 MRR Alc Latest edition

List of shipowners. London, Lloyd's
register of shipping. 386/.22 76-
618089
    HE565.A3 L56 MRR Alc Latest
    edition

Lloyd's confidential index of foreign
steam and motor vessels. London,
Lloyd's. 387.2 57-24350
    HE565.A3 L68 MRR Alc Latest
    edition

Lloyd's register of shipping.
London, Wyman and sons [etc.] ca 08-
1387
    "Founded 1760. Re-constituted
    1834."
    HE565.A3 L7 MRR Alc Latest edition

Merchant ships: v. [1]- 1952-
London, A. Coles in association with
Hart-Davis; Tuckahoe, N.Y., De Graff
[etc.] 623.824058 54-3765
    VM1 .M54 Sci RR Latest edition /
    MRR Alc Latest edition

Moody, Bert. Ocean ships [New ed.].
London, Allan 1967. vii, 359 p.
[25/-] 387.2/4 72-472168
    HE565 .A5M6 1967 MRR Alc.

Smith, Eugene Waldo, Passenger ships
of the world, [1st ed.] Boston, G.
H. Dean Co. [1963] ii, 1002 p.
387.243 63-3478
    HE565.A3 S48 MRR Alc.

The Tanker register; London, H.
Clarkson, 1969. xx, 389 p. [£10.00]
387.2/45 71-565903
    HE566.T3 T33 1969 MRR Alc.

SHIP REGISTERS--FINLAND.
Norske veritas, Oslo. Register over
norske, svenske, danske, finske og
islandske skip. Oslo. 656 50-23213
    Began publication in 1865.
    HE565.A3 N67 MRR Alc Latest
    edition

SHIP REGISTERS--GERMANY.
Die Deutsche Handelsflotte. 1952-
Hamburg, Seehafen-Verlag Erik
Blumenfeld, [etc.] 54-33604
    HE565.G3 D48 MRR Alc Latest
    edition

SHIP REGISTERS--GREAT BRITAIN.
Colledge, J. J. Ships of the Royal
Navy; New York, A. M. Kelley, 1969-
v. 359.32/0942 69-10859
    VA456 .C66 MRR Alc.

The Mercantile Navy list. London,
H.M. Stationery Off. [etc.] 387.23
50-33347
    Began publication with 1850 issue.
    HE565.G7 M5 MRR Alc Latest edition

SHIP REGISTERS--GREAT LAKES.
The Great Lakes red book. 1902- St.
Clair Shores, Mich. [etc.] Fourth
Seacoast Pub. Co. [etc.] 02-13631
    HE565.U71 L7 MRR Alc Latest
    edition

Green's Great Lakes and seaway
directory. [1st]- ed.; 1809-
[North Olmsted, Ohio, etc.] 656
387.52* 09-25161
    HE565.U71 G8 MRR Alc Latest
    edition

Greenwood, John Orville. Namesakes
II; Cleveland, Ohio, Freshwater
Press [1973] xiii, 667 p. [$19.75]
386/.22/40977 73-161361
    HE565.U71 G832 MRR Alc.

Greenwood, John Orville. Namesakes
of the Lakes; Cleveland, Ohio,
Freshwater Press [1970] xii, 433 p.
[14.75] 386/.22/40977 73-161369
    HE565.U71 G83 MRR Alc.

International Shipmasters'
Association of the Great Lakes.
Directory. [Detroit?] 386/.5/02577
72-626792
    HE565.U71 S5 MRR Alc Latest
    edition

SHIP REGISTERS--MISSISSIPPI RIVER.
Inland river record; 1945-
[Sewickley, Pa.] 386.224 45-7239
    VM23 .I5 MRR Alc Latest edition

SHIP REGISTERS--NETHERLANDS.
Moormans Jaarboek voor scheepvaart en
scheepsbouw. Den Haag, Verenigde
Periodieke Pers N.V. 51-20638
    Began publication in 1923.
    HE730 .M6 MRR Alc Latest edition

SHIP REGISTERS--NEW YORK (CITY)
United States. National Archives.
List of American-flag merchant
vessels that received certificates of
enrollment or registry at the Port of
New York, 1789-1867? Washington,
1968. 2 v. (vii, 804 p.)
387.2/097471 a 68-7106
    HE565.U5A43 MRR Alc.

SHIP REGISTERS--SCANDINAVIA.
Norske veritas, Oslo. Register over
norske, svenske, danske, finske og
islandske skip. Oslo. 656 50-23213
    Began publication in 1865.
    HE565.A3 N67 MRR Alc Latest
    edition

SHIP REGISTERS--SPAIN.
Spain. Subsecretaría de la Marina
Mercante. Lista oficial de buques.
[Madrid] 09-16189
    HE565.S7A2 MRR Alc Latest edition

SHIP REGISTERS--UNITED STATES.
American Bureau of Shipping. Record.
1969- New York. 99-230
    HE565.U5 A55 MRR Alc Latest
    edition / MRR Alc Latest edition

Emmons, George Foster, The Navy of
the United States, from the
commencement, 1775 to 1853;
Washington, Printed by Gideon & co.,
1853. 4 p. l., 208 p. 02-7188
    E182 .E54 MRR Alc.

Heyl, Erik. Early American steamers.
Buffalo, 1953- v. 387.24 53-
3672
    VM23 .H4 MRR Alc.

International Shipmasters'
Association of the Great Lakes.
Directory. [Detroit?] 386/.5/02577
72-626792
    HE565.U71 S5 MRR Alc Latest
    edition

Lloyd's register of American yachts;
New York, Lloyd's register of
shipping. 03-14412
    GV825 .L7 MRR Alc Latest edition

Lytle, William M., Merchant steam
vessels of the United States, 1807-
1868. Mystic, Conn., Steamship
Historical Society of America, 1952
[i.e. 1953] 294 p. 387.24 53-1846
    VM7 .S74 no. 6 MRR Alc.

SHIP REGISTERS--UNITED STATES. (Cont.)
Merchant vessels of the United States
(including yachts) Washington, For
sale by the Supt. of Docs., U.S.
Govt. Print. Off. 387.2/4/02573 76-
606560
HE565.U5 A27 MRR Alc Latest
edition

Sawyer, Leonard Arthur. Victory
ships and tankers; Cambridge, Md.,
Cornell Maritime Press [1974] 230 p.
387.2/45/0973 73-22561
VM391 .S39 1974 MRR Alc.

United States. Naval History
Division. Dictionary of American
naval fighting ships. Washington,
[For sale by the Supt. of Doc., U.S.
Govt. Print. Off.] 1959- v.
623.825 60-60198
VA61 .A53 MRR Alc.

SHIPMASTERS--GREAT LAKES--DIRECTORIES.
International Shipmasters'
Association of the Great Lakes.
Directory. [Detroit?] 386/.5/02577
72-626752
HE565.U71 S5 MRR Alc Latest
edition

SHIPMENT OF GOODS.
Murr, Alfred. Export/import traffic
management and forwarding. New rev.
ed. Cambridge, Md., Cornell Maritime
Press, 1967. ix, 595 p.
658/.91/387 67-18222
HE5999.A3 M8 1967 MRR Alc.

SHIPMENT OF GOODS--DIRECTORIES.
The Official directory of industrial
and commercial traffic executives.
Washington, Traffic Service
Corporation. 380.5/2 72-626342
HF5780.U6 C4 MRR Alc Latest
edition

SHIPMENT OF GOODS--SOCIETIES, ETC.
Shippers' Conference of Greater New
York. List of non-profit shipper
associations. New York [1870] 160
p. 380.5/025/73 70-21822
HF5780.U6 S45 MRR Alc.

SHIPMENT OF GOODS--STATISTICS.
United States. Bureau of the Census.
1967 census of transportation.
[Washington; For sale by the Supt. of
Docs., U.S. Govt. Print. Off., 1970]
3 v. in 5 [$3.00 (v. 1) varies]
380.5/0973 76-607509
HE18 1867 .A55 MRR Alc.

SHIPPERS' GUIDES--CANADA.
Bullinger's postal and shippers guide
for the United States and Canada and
Newfoundland. Westwood, N.J. [etc.]
Bullinger's Guides, inc. [etc.] 02-
3726
HE9.U5 B83 MRR Alc Latest edition

SHIPPERS' GUIDES--NEWFOUNDLAND.
Bullinger's postal and shippers guide
for the United States and Canada and
Newfoundland. Westwood, N.J. [etc.]
Bullinger's Guides, inc. [etc.] 02-
3726
HE9.U5 B83 MRR Alc Latest edition

SHIPPERS' GUIDES--UNITED STATES.
Bullinger's postal and shippers guide
for the United States and Canada and
Newfoundland. Westwood, N.J. [etc.]
Bullinger's Guides, inc. [etc.] 02-
3726
HE9.U5 B83 MRR Alc Latest edition

Leonard's guide, parcel post,
express, freight rates and routing.
1st- ed.; 1923- Northbrook, Ill.
[etc.] G. R. Leonard. 383.1 23-6413

HE9.U5 L46 MRR Alc Latest edition

Shippers' Conference of Greater New
York. List of non-profit shipper
associations. New York [1870] 160
p. 380.5/025/73 70-21822
HF5780.U6 S45 MRR Alc.

SHIPPING.
All about ships & shipping; 11th
ed., rev. and brought up to date.
London, Faber & Faber [1964] xii,
723 p. 387.5 64-56470
VK155 .A6 1964 MRR Alc.

SHIPPING--BIBLIOGRAPHY.
Albion, Robert Greenhalgh, Naval &
maritime history; 4th ed., rev. and
expanded. Mystic, Conn., Munson
Institute of American Maritime
History, 1972. ix, 370 p. [$15.00]
016.387/08 73-186863
Z6834.H5 A4 1972 MRR Alc.

SHIPPING--DICTIONARIES.
Brown, Robert Henry. Dictionary of
marine insurance terms. [London]
Witherby [1962] vi, 313 p. 62-
48927
HE567 .B7 MRR Alc.

Stevens, Edward Frank. Dictionary of
shipping terms and phrases. 2nd ed.
London, Pitman, 1971. 96 p. [£1.90]
387/.03 72-187552
HE567 .S8 1971 MRR Alc.

Woollam, W. G. Shipping terms and
abbreviations; Cambridge, Md.,
Cornell Maritime Press, 1963. x, 144
p. 387.5403 62-22181
HE567 .W6 MRR Alc.

SHIPPING--DICTIONARIES--GERMAN.
Bein, Gerhard. Wörterbuch des
internationalen Verkehrs. Leipzig,
Verlag Enzyklopädie VEB (1968). 232
p. [18.00] 380.5/03 71-410715
HE141 .B44 MRR Alc.

SHIPPING--DIRECTORIES.
The Directory of shipowners,
shipbuilders, and marine engineers.
London, Engineering, Chemical &
Marine Press [etc.] 25-4199
HE565.A3 D5 MRR Alc Latest edition

The Globe world directory for land,
sea and air traffic. 1st- ed.;
1948- Oslo, [etc.] Globe
Directories. 385.058 50-13703
HE9.A1 G5 MRR Alc Latest edition

List of shipowners. London, Lloyd's
register of shipping. 386/.22 76-
618089
HE565.A3 L56 MRR Alc Latest
edition

Lloyd's confidential index of foreign
steam and motor vessels. London,
Lloyd's. 387.2 57-24350
HE565.A3 L68 MRR Alc Latest
edition

Lloyd's register of shipping.
London, Wyman and sons [etc.] ca 08-
1387
"Founded 1760. Re-constituted
1834."
HE565.A3 L7 MRR Alc Latest edition

Marine Directory. [New York, Simmons-
Boardman Publ. Corp.]
338.4/7/6238025 72-623836
HE565.U5 S5 MRR Alc Latest edition

SHIPPING--MAPS.
Philip (George) and Son, ltd. The
mercantile marine atlas; 16th ed.
[rev.] London, 1959. xxvii, p., 41
plates (chiefly col. maps (part
fold.)), 23 p.   map59-990
G1060 .P5 1959 MRR Alc Atlas.

SHIPPING--PERIODICALS.
Lloyd's register of shipping.
London, Wyman and sons [etc.] ca 08-
1387
"Founded 1760. Re-constituted
1834."
HE565.A3 L7 MRR Alc Latest edition

SHIPPING--YEARBOOKS.
International shipping and
shipbuilding directory. London, Benn
Bros [etc.] 48-41377
Began with 1886 vol.
HE951 .S55 Sci RR Latest edition /
MRR Alc Latest edition

Lloyd's register of shipping. Rules
& regulations for the construction
and classification of steel vessels.
London. 07-17765
HE565.A3 L75 MRR Alc Latest
edition

SHIPPING--ATLANTIC OCEAN.
Bonsor, N. R. P. North Atlantic
seaway; Prescot, Lancashire, T.
Stephenson [1955] xxxii, 639 p.
387.74 56-3308
HE822 .B7 MRR Alc.

SHIPPING--CANADA--DIRECTORIES.
Canadian ports and seaway directory,
including United States ports on the
Great Lakes. [1st]- ed.: 1934-
Gardenvale, Quebec, National Business
Publications. 36-1220
HE553 .C32 MRR Alc Latest edition

SHIPPING--GREAT BRITAIN.
Lloyd's register of shipping.
London, Wyman and sons [etc.] ca 08-
1387
"Founded 1760. Re-constituted
1834."
HE565.A3 L7 MRR Alc Latest edition

SHIPPING--GREAT LAKES.
Green's Great Lakes and seaway
directory. [1st]- ed.; 1909-
[North Olmsted, Ohio, etc.] 656
387.52* 09-25161
HE565.U71 G8 MRR Alc Latest
edition

SHIPPING--GREAT LAKES--DIRECTORIES.
International Shipmasters'
Association of the Great Lakes.
Directory. [Detroit?] 386/.5/02577
72-626792
HE565.U71 S5 MRR Alc Latest
edition

SHIPPING--ILLINOIS RIVER.
Interstate port handbook. [Chicago]
368.2 44-33741
HE554.A5 I5 MRR Alc Latest edition

SHIPPING--MICHIGAN, LAKE.
Interstate port handbook. [Chicago]
368.2 44-33741
HE554.A5 I5 MRR Alc Latest edition

SHIPPING--NETHERLANDS--YEARBOOKS.
Moormans jaarboek voor scheepvaart en
scheepsbouw. Den Haag, Verenigde
Periodieke Pers N.V. 51-20638
Began publication in 1923.
HE730 .M6 MRR Alc Latest edition

SHIPPING--ST. LAWRENCE SEAWAY--
DIRECTORIES.
Seaway maritime directory. 1st
ed.: 1958- [St. Clair, Mich., etc.,
Fourth Seacoast Pub. Co., etc.]
386/.5/025714 58-21534
HE630.S17 S4 MRR Alc Latest
edition

SHIPPING--UNITED STATES.
Emmons, George Foster, The Navy of
the United States, from the
commencement, 1775 to 1853;
Washington, Printed by Gideon & co.,
1853. 4 p. l., 208 p. 02-7188
E182 .E54 MRR Alc.

United States. Bureau of the Census.
Foreign commerce and navigation of
the United States. 1865/66-
Washington, U.S. Govt. Print. Off.
07-19228
HF105 .A2 MRR Alc Latest edition

SHIPPING--UNITED STATES--DIRECTORIES.
Custom house guide. New York. 99-
1545
HE953.N5 C8 MRR Alc Latest edition

The Journal of commerce
transportation telephone tickler.
[New York] 53-34476
HE9.U5 N7 MRR Alc Latest edition

SHIPPING--UNITED STATES--STATISTICS.
United States. Interstate Commerce
Commission. Bureau of Accounts.
Transport statistics in the United
States. Washington. 380.5/0973 72-
627360
HE2708 .I73 MRR Alc Latest edition

SHIPS.
see also Boats and boating

see also Navigation

All about ships & shipping; 11th
ed., rev. and brought up to date.
London, Faber & Faber [1964] xii,
723 p. 387.5 64-56470
VK155 .A6 1964 MRR Alc.

Baker, William A. The engine powered
vessel; New York, Grosset & Dunlap
[1965] 267 p. 387.24 65-21508
VM315 .B3 MRR Alc.

Matthews, Frederick C. American
merchant ships, 1850-1900, Salem,
Mass., Marine research society, 1930-
31. 2 v. 387.50973 623.82209 31-
87
VM23 .M3 MRR Alc.

SHIPS--BIBLIOGRAPHY.
Lancour, Harold, A bibliography of
ship passenger lists, 1538-1825; 3d
ed., rev. and enl. New York, New
York Public Library, 1963. ix, 137
p. 016.32573 63-18141
Z7164.I3 L2 1963 MRR Alc.

Selected references to literature on
marine expeditions, 1700-1960.
Boston, G. K. Hall, 1972. iv, 517 p.
016.5514/6 72-6452
Z5971 .S4 MRR Alc.

SHIPS--EQUIPMENT AND SUPPLIES--CATALOGS.
Marine catalog and buyers' directory.
1st- ed.; 1943- New York, N.Y.
[etc.] Simmons-Boardman publishing
corporation. 623.8085 43-19016
VM12 .M33 MRR Alc Latest edition

SHIPS--HISTORY.
Landström, Björn. The ship;
London] Allen & Unwin [1961] 309,
[10] p. 623.8109 61-66428
VM15 .L213 1961a MRR Alc.

SHIPS--INSPECTION.
American Bureau of Shipping. Rules
for the classification and
construction of steel vessels. 1922-
New York. 22-21101
VM287 .A43 Sci RR Latest edition /
MRR Alc Latest edition

SHIPS--PICTORIAL WORKS.
Aymar, Brandt. A pictorial treasury
of the marine museums of the world;
New York, Crown Publishers [1967]
viii, 244 p. 623.8/074 67-27032
VM307 .A94 MRR Alc.

SHIPS--PICTORIAL WORKS. (Cont.)
Lloyd, Christopher, Ships & seamen,
London, Weidenfeld & Nicolson, c1961.
223 p.   64-39484
D27 .L55 MRR Alc.

SHIPS, IRON AND STEEL.
American Bureau of Shipping. Rules
for the classification and
construction of steel vessels. 1922-
New York. 22-21101
VM287 .A43 Sci RR Latest edition /
MRR Alc Latest edition

SHIPWRECKS.
Fleming, Robert M. A primer of
shipwreck research and records for
skin divers, Milwaukee, Wis., Global
MFG. Corp. [1971] 73 p. [$2.75]
910.4/53 75-25624
VK1250 .F55 MRR Alc.

Huntress, Keith Gibson, comp.
Narratives of shipwrecks and
disasters, 1586-1860. [1st ed.]
Ames, Iowa State University Press,
1974. xxxii, 249 p.   910/.453 73-
12084
G525 .H898 1974 MRR Alc.

Potter, John Stauffer, The treasure
diver's guide Rev. ed. Garden City,
N.Y., Doubleday, 1972. xxvi, 567 p.
[$15.00] 910/.453 72-97681
G525 .P58 1972 MRR Alc.

SHIPWRECKS--BIBLIOGRAPHY.
Cox, Edward Godfrey, A reference
guide to the literature of travel,
Seattle, The University of
Washington, 1935-49. 3 v.   016.91
36-27679
Z6011 .C87 MRR Alc.

Fleming, Robert M. A primer of
shipwreck research and records for
skin divers, Milwaukee, Wis., Global
MFG. Corp. [1971] 73 p. [$2.75]
910.4/53 75-25624
VK1250 .F55 MRR Alc.

SHIPWRECKS--GREAT LAKES.
Heden, Karl Erik. Directory of
shipwrecks of the Great Lakes,
Boston, Bruce Humphries Publishers
[1966] x, 116 p.   904 66-15922
VK1271 .H4 MRR Alc.

SHOES
see Boots and shoes

SHOOTING--YEARBOOKS.
Gun digest. (1st)- ed.: 1944-
Northfield, Ill. [etc.] 623.44 44-
32588
GV1174 .G8 MRR Alc Latest edition

SHOP MATHEMATICS.
Grazda, Edward E., ed. Handbook of
applied mathematics, 4th ed.
Princeton, N.J., Van Nostrand [1966]
vi, 1119 p.   510.0202 66-9325
TA330 .G7 1966 MRR Alc.

SHOPPERS' GUIDES
see Consumer education

SHOPPING.
see also Consumers

Temple Fieldings' selective shopping
guide to Europe. 1957/58- ed. New
York, Fielding Publications [etc.]
658.87058 57-9112
HF5341 .T4 MRR Alc Latest edition

SHOPPING--DIRECTORIES.
Stores of the world. London, Newman
Books. 380.1025 66-9836
Began publication in 1961.
HF54.G7 S8 MRR Alc Latest edition

SHOPPING--YEARBOOKS.
Price buying directory. [Chicago]
Consumers Digest. 77-789
TX335.A1 P74 MRR Ref Desk Latest
edition

SHOPPING--ASIA.
Asian buyers' guide to Republic of
China, Hong Kong, Japan, Republic of
Singapore, and Thailand. 1st- ed.;
1968- Hong Kong, International Pub.
Co. 670 .25/5 68-7584
HF3763 .A82 MRR Alc Latest edition

SHOPPING--BELGIUM--DIRECTORIES.
Annuaire general de la Belgique,
industrielle, commerciale, maritime.
Bruxelles. 53-34696
BC312. A55 MRR Alc Latest edition

SHOPPING--EUROPE.
American overseas guide. [New York]
American Overseas Tourist-Service of
New York. 910.2 56-43375
HF5341 .A65 MRR Alc Latest edition

SHOPPING--EUROPE--DIRECTORIES.
Byrns, John H. Europe's hidden flea
markets and budget antique shops.
[1st ed. New York, R. F. Long; trade
distributor: Hastings House, 1968]
112 p.   914/.04/55 68-2401
HF5152 .B9 MRR Alc.

SHOPPING--HOUSTON, TEX.
Coates, Felicia. Texas monthly's
Guide to Houston [Austin, Texas
monthly, 1973] 382 p.   [$2.95]
917.64/1411/046 73-179186
F394.H8 C63 MRR Alc.

SHOPPING--NEW YORK (CITY)
Gardner, Arron. Gardner's guide to
antiques and art buying in New York
City. Indianapolis, Bobbs-Merrill
[1969] xiii, 204 p.   [5.95]
745.1/025/7471 69-13091
NK1127 .G3 MRR Alc.

Simon, Kate. New York places &
pleasures; 4th ed. rev. New York,
Harper & Row [1971] xxiii, 417 p.
[$7.95] 917.47/1/044 70-138761
F128.18 .S5 1971 MRR Alc.

SHOPPING--NEW YORK (CITY)--DIRECTORIES.
Brener, Carol. The underground
collector: New York, Simon and
Schuster [1970] 319 p.   [2.95]
745.1/025/7471 72-107269
NK1127 .B64 MRR Alc.

Scharlatt, Elizabeth Lohman, comp.
The passionate shopper; New York,
Dutton [1972] 257 p.   [$2.95]
917.47/1/044 72-79127
HF5068.N5 S3 MRR Alc.

SHOPPING--PHILADELPHIA.
Hadley Group. Inside Philadelphia;
Philadelphia [1973] 323 p.   [$2.95]
917.48/11/044 73-82969
F158.18 .H32 1973a MRR Alc.

SHOPPING--UNITED STATES.
American Crafts Council. Research &
Education Dept. Craft shops,
galleries, USA; [4th ed. New York]
American Crafts Council [1973] 214
p.   745.5/025/73 73-175467
NK805 .A67 1973 MRR Alc.

SHOPPING--WASHINGTON, D.C.--DIRECTORIES.
Mintz, Bettie. Top shops & secret
services, Washington, D.C. area.
[Washington, Manufactured by Plymouth
Print. Co., 1971] ix, 213 p.
[$3.75] 380.1/025/753 74-31890
HF5429.5.W3 M5 1971 MRR Alc.

SHOPPING CENTERS--DIRECTORIES.
Directory of shopping centers in the
United States and Canada. v. 1-
1957/58- Chicago, Merchandising
Division, National Research Bureau.
58-2082
HF5035 .D53 MRR Alc Latest edition

SHORE PROTECTION.
see also Harbors

SHORT AIRPLANES.
Barnes, Christopher Henry. Shorts
aircraft since 1900 London, Putnam;
Fallbrook (Calif.), Aero Publishers,
1967. x, 532 p.   [84/-] 629.133/34
67-26135
TL686.S47 B3 1967 MRR Alc.

SHORT SELLING.
Gold, Gerald. Modern commodity
futures trading. [4th rev. ed.] New
York, Commodity Research Bureau
[1966, c1959] 255 p.   332.64 66-
7166
HG6046 .G59 1966 MRR Alc.

SHORT STORIES--BIBLIOGRAPHY.
American Library Association.
Subject and title index to short
stories for children. Chicago,
American Library Association, 1955.
vi, 333 p.   028.5 55-10208
Z1037 .A4924 MRR Alc.

Cole, Walter R. A checklist of
science-fiction anthologies,
[Brooklyn? 1964] xvi, 374 p.
016.823082 65-1442
Z5917.S36 C6 MRR Alc.

Cook, Dorothy Elizabeth, Short story
index; New York, H. W. Wilson, 1953.
1553 p.   016.80883 53-8981
Z5917.S5 C6 MRR Alc.

Cook, Frederick S., Fred Cook's
index to the Wonder group, [Grand
Haven, Mich., 1966] 239 p.   70-
14090
Z5917.S36 C64 MRR Alc.

Day, Donald Byrne, Index to the
science-fiction magazines, 1926-1950.
Portland, Or., Perri Press [1952]
xv, 184 p.   016.5 52-41880
Z5917.S36 D3 MRR Alc.

Firkins, Ina Ten Eyck, Index to
short stories. 2d and enl. ed., New
York, The H. W. Wilson company;
[etc., etc.] 1923. 2 p. l., [ix]-
xii, [2], 537 p.   23-27435
Z5917.S5 F5 1923 MRR Alc

Johnson, Robert Owen. An index to
literature in the New Yorker, volumes
I-XV, 1925-1940. Metuchen, N.J.,
Scarecrow Press, 1969-71. 3 v.   051
71-7740
AP2 .N6764 MRR Alc.

Mundell, E. H. A checklist of
detective short stories, Portage,
Ind. 1968. xii, 337 p.
016.80883/872 68-3329
Z5917.D5 M8 MRR Alc.

Mundell, E. H. The detective short
story : Manhattan : Kansas State
University Library, 1974. iv, 493 p.
; [$12.50] 016.823/.0872 74-
182860
Z5917.D5 M82 MRR Alc.

New England Science Fiction
Association. Index to the science
fiction magazines, 1966-1970. [1st
ed. Cambridge, Mass.] 1971. ix, 82
p. [$5.00] 016.823/0876 74-30236

Z5917.S36 N42 1971 MRR Alc.

Siemon, Fred. Ghost story index;
San Jose, Calif., Library Research
Associates, 1967. 141 p.
016.80883/872 67-30345
Z6514.G5 S5 MRR Alc.

Siemon, Frederick, Science fiction
story index, 1950-1968. Chicago,
American Library Association, 1971.
x, 274 p.   016.823/0876 70-162470
Z5917.S36 S5 MRR Alc.

Strauss, Erwin S. The MIT Science
Fiction Society's index to the s-f
magazines, 1951-1965. [Cambridge,
Mass., MIT Science Fiction Society]
c1966. iii, 207 p.   016.823/0876
73-174981
Z5917.S36 S84 MRR Alc.

Wren, Sheila. Short story index
compiled from the Canadian periodical
index, 1938-1947. Ottawa, Canadian
Library Association, 1967. 46 p.
813/.5/016 76-399974
Z1377.F4 W7 MRR Alc.

SHORT STORIES, AMERICAN--BIBLIOGRAPHY.
Hannigan, Francis James, comp. The
standard index of short stories, 1900-
1914, Boston, Small, Maynard &
company [c1918] 5 p. l., 334 p.
016.8083 18-10178
Z5917.S5 H2 MRR Alc.

SHORT STORIES, AMERICAN--HISTORY AND
CRITICISM.
O'Brien, Edward Joseph Harrington,
The advance of the American short
story. Rev. ed. New York, Dodd,
Mead and company, 1931. 7 p. l., 314
p.   31-28252
PS374.S5 O3 1931 MRR Alc.

Pattee, Fred Lewis, The development
of the American short story; New
York, Bilbo and Tannen, 1966. v, 388
p.   813/.01 66-13477
PS374.S5 P3 1966 MRR Alc.

West, Ray Benedict, The short story
in America, 1900-1950. Chicago, H.
Regnery Co., 1952. 147 p.   813.509
52-3551
PS374.S5 W4 MRR Alc.

SHORT STORIES, CANADIAN--INDEXES.
Wren, Sheila. Short story index
compiled from the Canadian periodical
index, 1938-1947. Ottawa, Canadian
Library Association, 1967. 46 p.
813/.5/016 76-399974
Z1377.F4 W7 MRR Alc.

SHORT STORY.
O'Brien, Edward Joseph Harrington,
The advance of the American short
story. Rev. ed. New York, Dodd,
Mead and company, 1931. 7 p. l., 314
p.   31-28252
PS374.S5 O3 1931 MRR Alc.

SHORT STORY--BIBLIOGRAPHY.
Thurston, Jarvis A. Short fiction
criticism; Denver, A. Swallow [1960]
265 p.   016.80931 60-8070
Z5917.S5 T5 MRR Alc.

Walker, Warren S. Twentieth-century
short story explication; 2d ed.
[Hamden, Conn.] Shoe String Press,
1967. vi, 697 p.   016.8093/1 67-
24192
Z5917.S5 W33 MRR Ref Desk.

SHORTENINGS
see Oils and fats, Edible

SHORTHAND--BIBLIOGRAPHY.
Alston, R. C. Treatises on shorthand Leeds, Printed for the author
by E. J. Arnold, c1966. xiii, 152 p.
016.653 67-109904
Z2015.A1 A4 vol. 8 MRR Alc.

SHORTHAND--PITMAN--DICTIONARIES.
Pitman, Isaac, Sir, Pitman's English
and shorthand dictionary. New era
ed., reprinted with enl. appendix of
additional words. London, Pitman
[1964] liii, 834 p.   65-6985
Z55.5 .P5 1964 MRR Alc.

SHOW JUMPERS (HORSES)
Stoneridge, M. A. Great horses of
our time [1st ed.] Garden City,
N.Y., Doubleday, 1972. xiv, 543 p.
[$14.95] 798.4 73-175400
SF338 .S76 MRR Alc.

SHRINES--CANADA.
Thornton, Francis Beauchesne,
Catholic shrines in the United States
and Canada. New York, W. Funk [1954]
xii, 340 p. 282.7 53-10386
BX2320 .T4 MRR Alc.

SHRINES--UNITED STATES.
Thornton, Francis Beauchesne,
Catholic shrines in the United States
and Canada. New York, W. Funk [1954]
xii, 340 p. 282.7 53-10386
BX2320 .T4 MRR Alc.

SHRUBS--IDENTIFICATION.
Symonds, George Wellington
Dillingham. The shrub identification
book: New York, M. Barrows [1963]
379 p. 582.17 63-7388
QK482 .S89 MRR Alc.

SHRUBS--CANADA.
Symonds, George Wellington
Dillingham. The shrub identification
book: New York, M. Barrows [1963]
379 p. 582.17 63-7388
QK482 .S89 MRR Alc.

SHRUBS--NORTH AMERICA.
Symonds, George Wellington
Dillingham. The shrub identification
book: New York, M. Barrows [1963]
379 p. 582.17 63-7388
QK482 .S89 MRR Alc.

SHRUBS--NORTH AMERICA--IDENTIFICATION.
Petrides, George A. A field guide to
trees and shrubs; 2d ed. Boston,
Houghton Mifflin, 1972. xxxii, 428
p. [$5.85] 582/.1609/7 76-157132

QK482 .P43 1972 MRR Alc.

SHRUBS--SOUTHERN STATES.
Dean, Blanche Evans. Trees and
shrubs in the heart of Dixie. Rev.
ed. Birmingham, Ala., Southern
University Press, 1968. xvi, 246 p.
[$7.50] 582/.15/0975 68-57837
QK484.S88 D4 1968 MRR Alc.

SHRUBS--UNITED STATES.
Grimm, William Carey. Home guide to
trees, shrubs, and wild flowers.
[Harrisburg, Pa.] Stackpole Books
[1970] 320 p. [9.95] 582/.09/73
76-100348
QK482 .G734 MRR Alc.

Marx, David S. A modern American
herbal: useful trees and shrubs.
South Brunswick, A. S. Barnes [1973]
190 p. 582/.1609/73 71-86305
QK482 .M43 MRR Alc.

Symonds, George Wellington
Dillingham. The shrub identification
book: New York, M. Barrows [1963]
379 p. 582.17 63-7388
QK482 .S89 MRR Alc.

SHRUBS--UNITED STATES--IDENTIFICATION.
Petrides, George A. A field guide to
trees and shrubs; 2d ed. Boston,
Houghton Mifflin, 1972. xxxii, 428
p. [$5.85] 582/.1609/7 76-157132

QK482 .P43 1972 MRR Alc.

**SHUFELDT, ROBERT WILSON, 1822-1895--
MANUSCRIPTS.**
United States. Library of Congress.
Manuscript Division. Robert Wilson
Shufeldt; a register of his papers in
the Library of Congress. Washington,
Library of Congress, 1969. 12 l.
016.3593/31/0924 72-601362
Z663.34 S55 MRR Alc.

SIBERIA--HISTORY.
Lessner, Erwin Christian, Cradle of
conquerors: Siberia. [1st ed.]
Garden City, N.Y., Doubleday, 1955.
774 p. 957 55-8407
DK761 .L4 MRR Alc.

SICILY--BIOGRAPHY.
Confederazione fascista dei
professionisti e degli artisti.
Dizionario dei Siciliani illustri.
Palermo, F. Ciuni, libraio editore,
1939. 3 p. l., [9]-537 p., 3 l. ac
40-2374
CT1135.S5 C6 MRR Biog.

SICILY--COMMERCE--DIRECTORIES.
Contact Mediterranean directory:
Malta, Libya, Sicily. 1966-
Valletta, Associated Publicity
Services. 380/.09/1822 67-115040
HC244.5.A1 C6 MRR Alc Latest
edition

**SICILY--DESCRIPTION AND TRAVEL--GUIDE-
BOOKS.**
Kininmouth, Christopher, Sicily;
travellers' guide. Revised ed.
London, Cape, 1972. 322 p.; [2]
fold. leaves. [£2.50] 914.58/04/92
74-158691
DG862 .K5 1972 MRR Alc.

SICILY--ECONOMIC CONDITIONS--YEARBOOKS.
Guida economica della Sicilia,
Sardegna e Mezzogiorno d'Italia.
[1.]- ed.; 1946- Roma [etc.]
G.I.P.I. 48-17748
HC307.S5 G8 MRR Alc Latest edition

SICK.
see also Hospitals

see also Nurses and nursing

SIEGES.
Connell, Charles, The world's
greatest sieges, London, Odhams,
1967. 271 p. [21/-] 904/.7 67-
87607
D25.5 .C58 MRR Alc.

SIERRA LEONE--BIBLIOGRAPHY.
Williams, Geoffrey J. A bibliography
of Sierra Leone, 1925-1967 New York,
Africana Pub. Corp. [1971] xxxii,
209 p. 016.9166/4/033 74-80858
Z3553.S5 W55 MRR Alc.

SIERRA LEONE--BIOGRAPHY.
Sierra Leone year book. [Freetown]
Daily mail. 62-41051
DT516 .A2S5 MRR Alc Latest edition

SIERRA LEONE--DIRECTORIES.
Sierra Leone year book. [Freetown]
Daily mail. 62-41051
DT516 .A2S5 MRR Alc Latest edition

SIERRA LEONE--GAZETTEERS.
United States. Office of Geography.
Sierra Leone: official standard names
approved by the United States Board
on Geographic Names. Washington,
1966. ii, 125 p. 916.6/4/003 66-
62649
DT516.2 .U5 MRR Alc.

**SIERRA LEONE--GOVERNMENT PUBLICATIONS--
BIBLIOGRAPHY.**
United States. Library of Congress.
African Section. Official
publications of Sierra Leone and
Gambia. Washington, General
Reference and Bibliography Division,
Reference Department, Library of
Congress [for sale by the
Superintendent of Documents, U.S.
Govt. Print. Off.] 1963. xii, 92 p.
63-60090
Z663.285 .O34 MRR Alc.

SIERRA LEONE--INDEXES.
Williams, Geoffrey J. A bibliography
of Sierra Leone, 1925-1967 New York,
Africana Pub. Corp. [1971] xxxii,
209 p. 016.9166/4/033 74-80858
Z3553.S5 W55 MRR Alc.

SIGHT-SAVING BOOKS--BIBLIOGRAPHY.
Landau, Robert A. Large type books
in print, New York, R. R. Bowker
Co., 1970. xxi, 193 p. 015/.73 74-
102773
Z5348 .L3 MRR Alc.

SIGNALS AND SIGNALING.
Preble, George Henry, Origin and
history of the American flag and of
the naval and yacht-club signals,
seals and arms, and principal
national songs of the United States,
New ed. in two volumes.
Philadelphia, N. L. Brown, 1917. 2
v. 17-21758
CR113 .P7 1917 MRR Alc.

SIGNS AND SIGN-BOARDS.
see also Posters

SIGNS AND SYMBOLS.
see also Symbolism in art

De Sola, Ralph, Abbreviations
dictionary: New international 4th
ed. New York, American Elsevier Pub.
Co. [1974] xiii, 428 p. 423/.1 73-
7687
PE1693 .D4 1974 MRR Ref Desk.

Dreyfuss, Henry, Symbol sourcebook;
New York, McGraw-Hill [1972] 292 p.
001.56 71-172261
AZ108 .D74 MRR Ref Desk.

Kamekura, Yūsaku, Trademarks and
symbols of the world. London, Studio
Vista, 1966. 291 p. [6/6/-]
741.68 66-71155
NE965 .K32 1966 MRR Alc.

Lehner, Ernst, comp. American
symbols; New York, W. Penn Pub. Co.
[1957] 95 p. 973.084 57-14579
E178.5 .L4 MRR Alc.

Lehner, Ernst, The picture book of
symbols. New York, Wm. Penn Pub.
Corp. [1956] 96 p. (chiefly illus.)
031 56-14454
AZ108 .L38 MRR Alc.

Lehner, Ernst, Symbols, signs and
signets. Cleveland, World Pub. Co.
[1950] xi, 220, [1] p. (chiefly
illus.) 704.946 50-9861
AZ108 .L4 MRR Alc.

Raphaelian, Harry M., Signs of life;
[1st ed.] New York, A. Sivas, 1957.
124 p. 704.946 57-6637
GR950.S5 R3 MRR Alc.

Shepherd, Walter. Shepherd's
glossary of graphic signs and
symbols. New York, Dover
Publications [1971] x, 597 p.
[$15.00] 001.5/6 74-153895
AZ108 .S53 1971b MRR Alc.

Whittick, Arnold, Symbols, signs,
and their meaning. London, L. Hill,
1960. xvi, 408 p. 704.946 60-
51135
N7740 .W52 MRR Alc.

SIGNS AND SYMBOLS--DICTIONARIES.
Chevalier, Jean, Dictionnaire des
symboles: [Paris] R. Laffont [1969]
xxxii, 844 p. [140.00] 79-463013
GR35 .C47 MRR Alc.

Hangen, Eva Catherine. Symbols: our
universal language. Wichita, Kan.
[McCormick-Armstrong] 1962. 308 p.
423 62-20744
CR29 .H3 MRR Alc.

Robinson, Leslie John. A dictionary
of graphical symbols London, Avis,
1972. 360 p. [£3.75] 001.56 73-
165683
Z250 .R683 MRR Ref Desk.

SIGNS AND SYMBOLS--UNITED STATES.
Carter, David E. The book of
American trade marks. Ashland, Ky.,
Century Communications Unlimited
[1972- v. (chiefly illus.)
602/.75 72-76493
T223.V13 C37 MRR Alc.

SIKKIM.
American University, Washington, D.C.
Foreign Areas Studies Division. Area
handbook for Nepal (with Sikkim and
Bhutan). Washington, For sale by the
Supt. of Docs., U.S. Govt. Print.
Off., 1964. xv, 448 p. 67-115014
DS485.N4 A8 MRR Alc.

Harris, George Lawrence, Area
handbook for Nepal, Bhutan, and
Sikkim. 2d ed. [Washington; for
sale by the Supt. of Docs., U.S.
Govt. Print. Off.] 1973. lxxx, 431
p. [$6.85] 915.49/6/035 73-600139

DS493.4 .H37 1973 MRR Alc.

**SILK MANUFACTURE AND TRADE--UNITED
STATES--DIRECTORIES.**
Davison's synthetic and silk red
book. 67th- ed.: 1962- Ridgewood,
N.J., Davison Pub. Co. 72-626449
TS1643 .D3 MRR Alc Latest edition

SILVER.
see also Money

Bratter, Herbert Max, Silver market
dictionary, New York, Commodity
exchange, inc., 1933. 4 p. l., 202
p. 332.41 34-1212
HG301 .B74 MRR Alc.

SILVER--STATISTICS.
Bratter, Herbert Max, Silver market
dictionary, New York, Commodity
exchange, inc., 1933. 4 p. l., 202
p. 332.41 34-1212
HG301 .B74 MRR Alc.

**SILVER ARTICLES--COLLECTORS AND
COLLECTING.**
Delieb, Eric. Investing in silver.
London, Barrie & Rockliff, 1967. 158
p. [50/-] 739.2/3/075 67-112022
NK7143 .D4 MRR Alc.

McClinton, Katharine (Morrison)
Collecting American 19th century
silver. New York, Scribner [1968]
viii, 280 p. [$12.50] 739.2/3/773
68-27787
NK7103 .M22 MRR Alc.

SILVER ARTICLES, AMERICAN.
Clayton, Michael. The collector's
dictionary of the silver and gold of
Great Britain and North America.
[1st Amer. ed.] New York, World Pub.
Co. [1971] 350 p. [$35.00]
739.2/0942 73-149055
NK7143 .C55 1971 MRR Alc.

Fales, Martha Gandy. Early American
silver. Rev. and enl. ed. New York,
Dutton, 1973 [c1970] x, 336 p.
[$7.95] 739.2/3/773 74-154280
NK7112 .F3 1973 MRR Alc.

Hood, Graham, American silver; New
York, Praeger [1971] 255 p.
[$15.00] 739.2/3/773 77-124854
NK7112 .H65 MRR Alc.

SILVER ARTICLES, AMERICAN. (Cont.)
McClinton, Katherine (Morrison)
Collecting American 19th century
silver. New York, Scribner [1968]
viii, 280 p. [$12.50] 739.2/3/773
68-27787
NK7103 .M22 MRR Alc.

SILVER ARTICLES, BRITISH.
Clayton, Michael. The collector's
dictionary of the silver and gold of
Great Britain and North America.
[1st Amer. ed.] New York, World Pub.
Co. [1971] 350 p. [$35.00]
738.2/0942 73-149055
NK7143 .C55 1971 MRR Alc.

Delieb, Eric. Investing in silver.
London, Barrie & Rockliff, 1967. 158
p. [50/-] 739.2/3/075 67-112022
NK7143 .D4 MRR Alc.

SILVER-PLATED WARE--UNITED STATES--
DIRECTORIES.
Kovel, Ralph M. A directory of
American silver, pewter, and silver
plate. New York, Crown Publishers
[1961] 352 p. 739.205873 60-8620

NK7112 .K66 MRR Alc.

SILVER-PLATING.
see also Electroplating

SILVERSMITHING.
see also Jewelry making

Wyler, Seymour B. The book of old
silver, English, American, foreign.
New York, Crown publishers [c1937] x
p., 1 l., 447 p. incl. illus.,
plates. 739 37-24775
NK7230 .W9 MRR Alc.

SILVERSMITHING--FRANCE--HISTORY.
New York. Metropolitan Museum of Art.
Three centuries of French domestic
silver. New York, 1960. 2 v.
739.23744 60-9288
NK7149 .N42 MRR Alc.

SILVERSMITHING--GREAT BRITAIN--
DICTIONARIES.
Clayton, Michael. The collector's
dictionary of the silver and gold of
Great Britain and North America.
[1st Amer. ed.] New York, World Pub.
Co. [1971] 350 p. [$35.00]
739.2/0942 73-149055
NK7143 .C55 1971 MRR Alc.

SILVERSMITHING--SCHLESWIG-HOLSTEIN.
Stierling, Hubert. Der Silberschmuck
der Nordseeküste hauptsächlich in
Schleswig-Holstein. Neumünster, K.
Wachholtz, 1935-55. v.   56-41823

NK7150 .S68 MRR Alc.

SILVERSMITHING--UNITED STATES.
Fales, Martha Gandy. Early American
silver. Rev. and enl. ed. New York,
Dutton, 1873 [c1970] xx, 336 p.
[$7.95] 739.2/3/773 74-154280
NK7112 .F3 1973 MRR Alc.

Thorn, C. Jordan. Handbook of
American silver and pewter marks.
New York, Tudor Pub. Co. [1949] xii,
289 p. 739.23 50-5385
NK7210 .T5 MRR Alc.

SILVERSMITHING--UNITED STATES--
DICTIONARIES.
Clayton, Michael. The collector's
dictionary of the silver and gold of
Great Britain and North America.
[1st Amer. ed.] New York, World Pub.
Co. [1971] 350 p. [$35.00]
739.2/0942 73-149055
NK7143 .C55 1971 MRR Alc.

SILVERSMITHING--UNITED STATES--HISTORY.
Hood, Graham. American silver; New
York, Praeger [1971] 255 p.
[$15.00] 739.2/3/773 77-124854
NK7112 .H65 MRR Alc.

SILVERSMITHS, AMERICAN.
Ensko, Stephen Guernsey Cook.
American silversmiths and their
marks. New York, Priv. print., 1927-
v. 739 27-13408
NK7112 .E65 MRR Alc.

SILVERSMITHS, AMERICAN--DIRECTORIES.
Kovel, Ralph M. A directory of
American silver, pewter, and silver
plate. New York, Crown Publishers
[1961] 352 p. 739.205873 60-8620

NK7112 .K66 MRR Alc.

SILVERSMITHS, AMERICAN--VIRGINIA.
Cutten, George Barton. The
silversmiths of Virginia. Richmond,
Dietz Press, 1952. xxiv, 259 p.
739.23 52-14077
NK7112 .C86 MRR Alc.

SILVERSMITHS, BRITISH.
Jackson, Charles James, Sir. English
goldsmiths and their marks; 2d ed.,
rev. and enl. New York, Dover
Publications [1964, c1921] xvi, 747
p. 738.22742 64-18852
NK7143 .J15 1864 MRR Alc.

SIMILE.
Wilstach, Frank Jenners. A
dictionary of similes. New ed. rev.
and enl. Boston, Little, Brown and
company, 1924. liv p., 1 l., 578 p.
[$4.00] 24-28476
PN6084.S5 W5 1924 MRR Alc.

SIMS, WILLIAM SOWDEN, 1858-1936--
MANUSCRIPTS.
United States. Library of Congress.
Manuscript Division. William Sowden
Sims: a register of his papers in the
Library of Congress. Washington,
Library of Congress, 1971. 28 p.
016.3593/3/10924 72-600006
Z663.34 .S57 MRR Alc.

SIMULATION METHODS.
Belch, Jean. Contemporary games;
Detroit, Gale Research Co. [1973- v.
371.3/078 72-6353
LB1029.G3 B44 MRR Alc.

SINGAPORE.
Maday, Bela C. Area handbook for
Malaysia and Singapore. Washington,
For sale by the Supt. of Docs., U.S.
Govt. Print. Off., 1965 [i.e. 1966]
xii, 745 p. [2.75] 915.95035 66-
61930
DS592 .M16 MRR Alc.

SINGAPORE--BIBLIOGRAPHY.
Cheeseman, Harold Ambrose Robinson.
Bibliography of Malaya. London, New
York, Published for the British
Association of Malaya by Longmans,
Green [1959] xi, 234 p. 016.9191
60-27688
Z3246 .C5 MRR Alc.

Pelzer, Karl Josef. West Malaysia
and Singapore: a selected
bibliography. New Haven, Human
Relations Area Files Press, 1971.
vi, 394 p. 016.91595/1/03 72-87853

Z3246 .P4 MRR Alc.

United States. Library of Congress.
Orientalia Division. Southeast Asia
subject catalog. Boston, G. K. Hall,
1972- v. 016.9159/03 72-5257
Z3221 .U525 MRR Alc (Dk 33)

SINGAPORE--BIOGRAPHY.
The Who's who, Malaysia and
Singapore. Kuala Lumpur, J. V.
Morais. 920/.0595 72-627192
DS595.5 .L4 MRR Biog Latest
edition

SINGAPORE--COMMERCE--DIRECTORIES.
The Straits times directory of
Malaysia. [Singapore] 53-30515
HF5239.M36 S8 MRR Alc Latest
edition

SINGAPORE--IMPRINTS.
United States. Library of Congress.
Library of Congress Office, Djakarta.
Accessions list, Indonesia,
Malaysia, Singapore, and Brunei. v.
1- July 1964- Djakarta. sa 66-444
Z663.767.I6 A25 MRR Alc MRR Alc
Full set

United States. Library of Congress.
Library of Congress Office, Djakarta.
Accessions list, Indonesia,
Malaysia, Singapore, and Brunei.
Cumulative list of serials. Jan.
1964/Sept. 1966-1964/68. Djakarta.
74-643581
Z663.767.I6 A252 MRR Alc MRR Alc
Full set

SINGAPORE--REGISTERS.
Singapore. Directory [of] Istana
Negara, Judicial cabinet, Legislative
Assembly, Public Service Commission,
audit, ministries, Industrial
Arbitration Court, statutory boards,
advisory committees, universities,
polytechnic, Commonwealth
representatives and foreign consuls.
Singapore. 56-29632
JQ745.S5 A35 MRR Alc Latest
edition

The Straits times directory of
Malaysia. [Singapore] 53-30515
HF5239.M36 S8 MRR Alc Latest
edition

SINGERS--BIOGRAPHY.
Davidson, Gladys. A treasury of
opera biography. New York, Citadel
Press [c1955] 352 p. 927.8 55-
11856
ML400 .D32 MRR Biog.

SINGERS--DICTIONARIES.
Ross, Anne, ed. The opera directory.
New York, Sterling Pub. Co. [1961]
xii, 566 p. 782.058 61-12046
ML102.06 R68 MRR Alc.

SINGERS, AMERICAN.
Propes, Steve. Those oldies but
goodies; New York, Macmillan Co.
[1973] viii, 192 p. [$5.95]
789.9/12 72-93630
ML156.4.P6 P76 MRR Alc.

Roxon, Lillian. Rock encyclopedia.
New York, Grosset & Dunlap [1971]
611 p. [$3.95] 784 76-26545
ML102.P66 R7 1971 MRR Alc.

Rust, Brian A. L. The complete
entertainment discography, from the
mid-1890s to 1942 New Rochelle,
N.Y., Arlington House [1973] 677 p.
[$12.95] 016.7899/12 73-13239
ML156.4.P6 R88 MRR Alc.

SINGERS, AMERICAN--BIOGRAPHY.
Lawless, Ray McKinley. Folksingers
and folksongs in America; New rev.
ed. New York, Duell, Sloan and
Pearce [1965] xviii, 750 p.
784.4973 65-21677
ML3550 .L4 1965 MRR Alc.

SINO-INDIAN BORDER DISPUTE,1957-
Rowland, John. A history of Sino-
Indian relations; Princeton, N.J.,
Van Nostrand [1967] xv, 248 p.
327.51/054 66-29857
DS450.C5 R6 MRR Alc.

SISTERHOODS.
see also Monasticism and religious
orders

SKELETAL REMAINS
see Man, Prehistoric

SKIN--BIBLIOGRAPHY.
United States. Library of Congress.
Technical Information Division.
Infrared in relation to skin and
underlying tissue; Washington, 1952.
viii p., 20 l. 016.612014482 52-
60026
Z663.49 .I583 MRR Alc.

SKIN--DISEASES.
Sauer, Gordon C. Manual of skin
diseases 3d ed. Philadelphia,
Lippincott [1973] xx, 357 p. 616.5
73-2568
RL71 .S2 1973 MRR Alc.

SKIN DISEASES.
Sauer, Gordon C. Manual of skin
diseases 3d ed. Philadelphia,
Lippincott [1973] xx, 357 p. 616.5
73-2568
RL71 .S2 1973 MRR Alc.

SKIS AND SKIING.
Ski. America's ski book. New York,
Scribner [1966] xi, 473 p. 796.93
66-22664
GV854.4 .S57 MRR Alc.

SKIS AND SKIING--DIRECTORIES.
Palmedo, Roland. Ski new horizons;
3d [rev.] ed. [New York, Pan
American Airways [c1968] 320 p.
796.9/3/025 73-7048
GV854.A2 P3 1968 MRR Alc.

SKIS AND SKIING--CANADA--DIRECTORIES.
Siggins, Maggie. Guide to eastern
ski resorts. New York, McGraw-Hill
[1969] viii, 231 p. [2.95]
796.9/3/0257 68-56179
GV854.5.N58 S5 MRR Alc.

SKIS AND SKIING--EUROPE.
Galin, Saul. Skiing in Europe; [1st
ed.] New York, Hawthorn Books [1967]
318 p. 796.9/3/094 67-27331
GV854.8.E9 G34 MRR Alc.

Rand, Abby. Ski guide to Europe.
New York, Award House; distributed by
Scribner [1970] 553 p. [$10.00]
914/.04/55 70-143191
GV854.8.E9 R3 1970 MRR Alc.

SKIS AND SKIING--NORTHEASTERN STATES--
DIRECTORIES.
Siggins, Maggie. Guide to eastern
ski resorts. New York, McGraw-Hill
[1969] viii, 231 p. [2.95]
796.9/3/0257 68-56179
GV854.5.N58 S5 MRR Alc.

SLANG.
Farmer, John Stephen. Slang and its
analogues [New York] Arno Press
[1970] 7 v. in 1. [8.95] 427.09
77-109023
PE3721 .F4 1970 MRR Alc.

SLAVE LABOR.
Phillips, Ulrich Bonnell. American
Negro slavery; New York, London, D.
Appleton and company, 1918. xi, 529
p. 18-11187
E441 .P549 MRR Alc.

SLAVE-TRADE--HISTORY--SOURCES.
Donnan, Elizabeth, ed. Documents
illustrative of the history of the
slave trade to America. New York,
Octagon Books, 1965. 4 v.
326.10973 65-15753
E441 .D69 MRR Alc.

SLAVE-TRADE--UNITED STATES.
Bancroft, Frederic. Slave trading in
the Old South. New York, Ungar
[1959] xiii, 415 p. 326.10975 59-
10883
E442 .B21 1959 MRR Alc.

SLAVE-TRADE--UNITED STATES--HISTORY--SOURCES.
Donnan, Elizabeth, ed. Documents illustrative of the history of the slave trade to America. New York, Octagon Books, 1965. 4 v.
326.10973 65-15753
E441 .D69 MRR Alc.

SLAVERY IN THE UNITED STATES.
see also Negroes

Craven, Avery Odelle, The coming of the Civil War. [2d ed. Chicago] University of Chicago Press [1957] 491 p. 973.711 57-8572
E338 .C92 1957 MRR Alc.

Nevins, Allan, The emergence of Lincoln. New York, Scribner, 1950. 2 v. 973.68 50-9920
E415.7 .N38 MRR Alc.

Nevins, Allan, Ordeal of the Union. New York, Scribner, 1947. 2 v. 973.6 47-11072
E415.7 .N4 MRR Alc.

Woodson, Carter Godwin, The Negro in our history. 10th ed., further rev. and enl. Washington, Associated Publishers [1962] 833 p. 326.973 62-3679
E185 .W89 1962 MRR Alc.

SLAVERY IN THE UNITED STATES--ANTI-SLAVERY MOVEMENTS.
Dumond, Dwight Lowell, Antislavery; Ann Arbor, University of Michigan Press [1961] x, 422 p. 326.973 61-5937
E441 .D84 MRR Alc.

Filler, Louis, The crusade against slavery, 1830-1860. [1st ed.] New York, Harper [1960] 318 p. 326.973 60-13441
E449 .F49 MRR Alc.

SLAVERY IN THE UNITED STATES--ANTI-SLAVERY MOVEMENTS--BIBLIOGRAPHY.
Dumond, Dwight Lowell, A bibliography of antislavery in America. Ann Arbor, University of Michigan Press [1961] 119 p.
016.326973 61-9306
Z1249.S6 D8 MRR Alc.

SLAVERY IN THE UNITED STATES--ECONOMIC ASPECTS.
Phillips, Ulrich Bonnell, American Negro slavery; New York, London, D. Appleton and company, 1918. xi, 529 p. 18-11187
E441 .P549 MRR Alc.

SLAVERY IN THE UNITED STATES--ECONOMIC ASPECTS--SOUTHERN STATES.
Stampp, Kenneth Milton. The peculiar institution; slavery in the antebellum South. [1st ed.] New York, Knopf, 1956. xi, 435, xiii p.
326.975 56-5800
E441 .S8 MRR Alc.

Woodman, Harold D., ed. Slavery and the Southern economy; New York, Harcourt, Brace & World [1966] x, 261 p. 326.0975 66-18864
E441 .W876 MRR Alc.

SLAVERY IN THE UNITED STATES--HISTORY--BIBLIOGRAPHY.
Blacks in America; 1st ed.] Garden City, N.Y., Doubleday, 1971. xxii, 430 p. [$8.95] 016.9173/06/96073 70-164723
Z1361.N39 B56 MRR Alc.

SLAVERY IN THE UNITED STATES--PERSONAL NARRATIVES--BIBLIOGRAPHY.
Brignano, Russell Carl. Black Americans in autobiography; Durham, N.C., Duke University Press, 1974. ix 118 p. [$6.75]
016.9173/06/96073022 B 73-92535
Z1361.N38 B67 MRR Alc.

SLAVERY IN THE UNITED STATES--SPEECHES IN CONGRESS.
Miller, Marion Mills, ed. Great debates in American history. [The national ed.] New York, Current literature publishing company [c1913] 14 v. 13-23912
E173 .M64 vol. 14 MRR Alc.

SLAVERY IN THE WEST INDIES.
Williams, Eric Eustace, From Columbus to Castro: [1st U.S. ed.] New York, Harper & Row [1971, c1970] 576 p. [$10.95] 972.9 75-138773
F1621 .W68 1970b MRR Alc.

SLAVIC LANGUAGES.
De Bray, Reginald George Arthur. Guide to the slavonic languages Revised ed. London, Dent; New York, Dutton, 1969. xxvi, 798 p. [8/-/-]
491.8 73-442806
PG53 .D4 1969 MRR Alc.

SLAVIC LANGUAGES--CONVERSATION AND PHRASE BOOKS--POLYGLOT.
Lyall, Archibald, A guide to 25 languages of Europe. Rev. ed. [Harrisburg, Pa.] Stackpole Co. [1966] viii, 407 p. 413 66-20847
PB73 .L85 1966 MRR Alc.

SLAVIC LANGUAGES--DICTIONARIES--POLYGLOT.
Bergman, Peter M. The concise dictionary of twenty-six languages in simultaneous translations, New York, Polyglot Library [1968] 406 p. 413 67-14284
P361 .B4 TJ Rm.

Ouseg, H. L. 21-language dictionary. London, P. Owen [1962] xxxi, 333 p. 63-1285
P361 .O85 1962 MRR Alc.

SLAVIC LITERATURE--20TH CENTURY--HISTORY AND CRITICISM.
Modern Slavic literatures. New York, F. Ungar Pub. Co. [c1972- v. [$15.00] 891.7/09/004 72-170319
PG501 .M518 MRR Alc.

SLAVIC LITERATURE--BIBLIOGRAPHY.
The Year's work in modern language studies, 1929/30- [Leeds, Eng., etc.] Modern Humanities Research Association [etc.] 405.8 31-32540
PB1 .Y45 MRR Alc Full set

SLAVIC LITERATURE--HISTORY AND CRITICISM.
Chyzhevs'kyĭ, Dmytro, Outline of comparative Slavic literatures. Boston, American Academy of Arts and Sciences, 1952. 143 p. a 53-1570
PG502 .C35 MRR Alc.

SLAVIC LITERATURE--TRANSLATIONS INTO ENGLISH--BIBLIOGRAPHY.
Lewanski, Richard Casimir, The Slavic literatures. New York, New York Public Library, and F. Ungar Pub. Co. [1967] xiii, 630 p.
016.8917 65-23122
Z7041 .L59 MRR Alc.

SLAVIC PHILOLOGY--BIBLIOGRAPHY.
Magner, Thomas F. Soviet dissertations for advanced degrees in Russian literature and Slavic linguistics, 1934-1962, University Park, Dept. of Slavic Languages, Pennsylvania State University, 1966. iii, 100 p. 016.4918 68-66174
Z2505.A2 M3 MRR Alc.

SLAVIC STUDIES--UNITED STATES.
A Biographical directory of librarians in the field of Slavic and East European studies. Chicago, American Library Association, 1967. xv, 80 p. 026/.000922 67-28101
Z675.A2 B5 MRR Biog.

SLAVS--BIOGRAPHY.
Kleine slavische Biographie. Wiesbaden, O. Harrassowitz, 1958. 832 p. 59-21195
CT205 .K53 MRR Biog.

SLAVS--DICTIONARIES AND ENCYCLOPEDIAS.
Slavonic encyclopaedia, New York, Philosophical Library [1949] xi, 1445 p. 936.7 48-6489
D377 .S58 MRR Alc.

SLEEP.
see also Dreams

SLEIGHT OF HAND
see Conjuring

see Magic

SLOGANS.
Noble, Valerie, The effective echo; New York, Special Libraries Association, 1970. ix, 165 p.
659.1 71-110487
HF5828 .N62 MRR Alc.

Safire, William L. The new language of politics; New York, Random House [1968] xvi, 528 p. 320/.03 68-14508
JK9 .S2 MRR Ref Desk.

Shankle, George Earlie. American mottoes and slogans, New York, The H. W. Wilson company, 1941. 183 p. 973 41-26048
E179 .S544 MRR Alc.

Sunners, William, American slogans; New York, Paebar Co., 1949. 345 p.
659.103 49-3280
HF5823 .S9 MRR Alc.

Woods, Henry Fitzwilliam, American sayings; Rev. and enl. ed. New York, Duell, Sloan and Pearce [1949] vi, 312 p. 818.082 49-4322
PN6084.A5 W6 1949 MRR Ref Desk.

SLOVAK LANGUAGE--DICTIONARIES--ENGLISH.
Konus, Joseph James, Slovak-English phraseological dictionary, [Passaic, N.J.] Slovak Catholic Sokol, 1969. 1664 p. 491.8/7/32 76-16260
PG5379 .K58 MRR Alc.

Slovensko-anglický slovník. 1. vyd.] Bratislava, Slovenské pedagogické nakl., 1959. 477 p. 60-680
PG5379 .S62 MRR Alc.

SLOVAKS.
Thomson, Samuel Harrison, Czechoslovakia in European history. [2d ed. enl.] Princeton, Princeton University Press, 1953. 485 p.
943.7 52-8780
DB205.1 .T48 1953 MRR Alc.

SLOVENIAN LANGUAGE--DICTIONARIES--ENGLISH.
Kotnik, Janko. Slovensko-angleški slovar. 6., [izpopol.] izd. Ljubljana, Državna založba Slovenije, 1967. [8], 831, [1] p. [YnD 52.-] 68-77725
PG1891 .K6 1967 MRR Alc.

SLOW LEARNING CHILDREN.
Ellingson, Careth. Directory of facilities for the learning-disabled and handicapped [1st ed.] New York, Harper & Row [1972] xii, 624 p. [$15.00] 371.9/045/0257 77-95952
L901 .E5 1972 MRR Alc.

SLOW LEARNING CHILDREN, BOOKS FOR--BIBLIOGRAPHY.
Strang, Ruth May, Gateways to readable books! [4th ed.] New York, H. W. Wilson Co., 1966. 245 p.
028.52 65-24136
Z1037 .S88 1966 MRR Alc.

SLUGS
see Tokens

SLUM CLEARANCE
see Housing

SMALL ARMS
see Firearms

SMALL BUSINESS--ACCOUNTING
see Accounting

SMALL BUSINESS--FINANCE--DIRECTORIES.
Levy, Robert S. Directory of State and Federal funds for business development, [New York] Pilot Books [1968] 64 p. 332.7/42 68-55429
HG3729.U5 L4 MRR Alc.

SMALL BUSINESS INVESTMENT COMPANIES--DIRECTORIES.
Kelley, Richard E. The SBIC national directory, [2d ed.] Los Angeles, Keyfax Publications [1963] vii, 281 p. 332.672 76-12935
HG3729.U5 K38 1963 MRR Alc.

Rubel, Stanley M. Guide to venture capital sources. 3d ed. [Chicago] Capital Pub. Corp. [1974] 334 p.
332.1/025/73 74-75808
HG65 .R8 1974 MRR Alc.

Venture capital. v. 1- 1970- [New York, Technimetrics, inc.]
332.1/025/73 74-20999
HG65 .V4 MRR Alc Latest edition

SMELTING.
see also Metallurgy

SMITH, GEORGE, 1824-1901.
The dictionary of national biography, London, Oxford university press [1921-27] 24 v. 920.042 30-29308
DA28 .D45 1921 MRR Biog.

SMITHSON, JAMES, 1765-1829.
Carmichael, Leonard, James Smithson and the Smithsonian story. New York, Putnam [1965] 316 p. 069.09753 65-20672
Q11.S8 C3 MRR Alc.

SMITHSONIAN INSTITUTION.
Carmichael, Leonard, James Smithson and the Smithsonian story, New York, Putnam [1965] 316 p. 069.09753 65-20672
Q11.S8 C3 MRR Alc.

Karp, Walter. The Smithsonian Institution; [Washington] Smithsonian Institution [1965] 125 p. 069.09753 65-61775
Q11.S8 K3 MRR Alc.

SMOG CONTROL DEVICES (MOTOR VEHICLES)
see Motor vehicles--Pollution control devices

SMOKING--BIBLIOGRAPHY.
Larson, Paul Stanley, Tobacco; experimental and clinical studies; Baltimore, Williams & Wilkins Co., 1961. xii, 932 p. 615.7 61-5057
QP981.T6 L3 MRR Alc.

SMOKING--PHYSIOLOGICAL EFFECT
see Tobacco--Physiological effect

SNAKES--CANADA.
Wright, Albert Hazen, Handbook of
snakes of the United States and
Canada, Ithaca, N.Y., Comstock Pub.
Associates, 1957- v.   598.12 57-
1635
    QL666.C6 W7 MRR Alc.

SNAKES--MEXICO.
Wright, Albert Hazen, Handbook of
snakes of the United States and
Canada, Ithaca, N.Y., Comstock Pub.
Associates, 1957- v.   598.12 57-
1635
    QL666.C6 W7 MRR Alc.

SNAKES--NORTH AMERICA.
Wright, Albert Hazen, Handbook of
snakes of the United States and
Canada, Ithaca, N.Y., Comstock Pub.
Associates, 1957- v.   598.12 57-
1635
    QL666.C6 W7 MRR Alc.

SNAKES--UNITED STATES.
Wright, Albert Hazen, Handbook of
snakes of the United States and
Canada, Ithaca, N.Y., Comstock Pub.
Associates, 1957- v.   598.12 57-
1635
    QL666.C6 W7 MRR Alc.

SNOWMOBILES.
Malo, John W. Snowmobiling; the
guide New York, Macmillan [1971]
185 p.   786.9 77-163228
    GV857.S6 M35 MRR Alc.

SOCCER--YEARBOOKS.
World football handbook. [London]
66-9366
    GV937 .W6 MRR Alc Latest edition

SOCIAL CASE WORK.
see also Counseling

SOCIAL CENTERS
see Community centers

SOCIAL CHANGE.
see also Community development

SOCIAL CHANGE--ADDRESSES, ESSAYS,
LECTURES.
Handbook on the study of social
problems. Chicago, Rand McNally
[1971] xvii, 734 p.   362/.042 72-
138487
    HM51 .H25 MRR Alc.

SOCIAL CHANGE--BIBLIOGRAPHY.
Brode, John. The process of
modernization; Cambridge, Mass.,
Harvard University Press, 1969. x,
378 p. [6.50] 016.3092 69-13765
    Z7164.U5 B7 MRR Alc.

Geiger, H. Kent. National
development, 1776-1966; Metuchen,
N.J., Scarecrow Press, 1969. 247 p.
016.309 77-5813
    Z7164.U5 G43 MRR Alc.

SOCIAL CLASSES--BIBLIOGRAPHY.
Glenn, Norval D. Social
stratification; Berkeley, Calif.,
The Glendessary Press [1970] xi, 466
p. 016.30144 74-104325
    Z7164.S64 G55 MRR Alc.

SOCIAL ECOLOGY
see Human ecology

SOCIAL ETHICS.
see also Political ethics

Messner, Johannes, Social ethics;
Rev. ed. St. Louis, B. Herder Book
Co. [1965] xvii, 1054 p.   170 65-
23383
    HM216 .M463 1965 MRR Alc.

SOCIAL GROUPS.
see also Leadership

Research annual on intergroup
relations. Chicago [etc.] Quadrangle
Books [etc.] 66-14164
    HM131 .R45 MRR Alc Full set

SOCIAL HISTORY.
see also Moral conditions

see also Poor

see also Urbanization

SOCIAL HISTORY--20TH CENTURY.
Taylor, Charles Lewis. World
handbook of political and social
indicators, 2d ed. New Haven, Yale
University Press, 1972. xiv, 443 p.
[$15.00] 301/.01/8 70-179479
    HN15 .T37 1972 MRR Alc.

SOCIAL HISTORY--20TH CENTURY--
BIBLIOGRAPHY.
Geiger, H. Kent. National
development, 1776-1966; Metuchen,
N.J., Scarecrow Press, 1969. 247 p.
016.309 77-5813
    Z7164.U5 G43 MRR Alc.

SOCIAL HISTORY--1945- --BIBLIOGRAPHY.
Universal Reference System. Current
events and problems of modern
society; Princeton, N.J., Princeton
Research Pub. Co. [1969] xx, 935 p.
016.90982 68-57821
    Z7161 .U64 vol. 5 MRR Alc.

SOCIAL HISTORY--1945- --STATISTICS.
Taylor, Charles Lewis. World
handbook of political and social
indicators, 2d ed. New Haven, Yale
University Press, 1972. xiv, 443 p.
[$15.00] 301/.01/8 70-179479
    HN15 .T37 1972 MRR Alc.

SOCIAL HISTORY--BIBLIOGRAPHY.
Schleiffer, Hedwig, Index to
economic history essays in
Festschriften, 1900-1950 Cambridge,
A. H. Cole; distributed by Harvard
University Press, 1953. 68 p.
016.3304 53-11201
    Z7164.E2 S36 MRR Alc.

United States. Library of Congress.
Reference Dept. International
economic and social development;
Washington, 1952. vi, 55 p.
016.3309 52-60016
    Z663.28 .I5 MRR Alc.

SOCIAL HISTORY--BIBLIOGRAPHY--CATALOGS.
International Institute for Social
History. Alphabetical catalog of the
books and pamphlets of the
International Institute of Social
History, Amsterdam. Boston, G. K.
Hall, 1970. 12 v.   019/.1 74-
169213
    Z7164.S66 I5 1970 MRR alc (Dk 33)

SOCIAL HYGIENE
see Hygiene

see Hygiene, Public

SOCIAL INSTITUTIONS--BRAZIL.
Smith, Thomas Lynn, Brazil; people
and institutions 4th ed. Baton
Rouge, Louisiana State University
Press, 1972. xx, 778 p. [$15.00]
309.1/81 73-168396
    HN283.5 .S58 1972 MRR Alc.

SOCIAL MOVEMENTS.
Acton, Jay. Mug shots; who's who in
the new earth, New York, World Pub.
[1972] 244 p. [$9.95] 920/.073
77-174672
    CT220 .A27 1972 MRR Biog.

SOCIAL PRESSURE.
see also Propaganda

SOCIAL PROBLEMS.
see also Crime and criminals

see also Emigration and immigration

see also Housing

see also Juvenile delinquency

see also Migration, Internal

see also Poor

see also Unemployed

SOCIAL PROBLEMS--ADDRESSES, ESSAYS,
LECTURES.
Handbook on the study of social
problems. Chicago, Rand McNally
[1971] xvii, 734 p.   362/.042 72-
138487
    HM51 .H25 MRR Alc.

SOCIAL PROBLEMS--BIBLIOGRAPHY.
Debate index, New ed. rev. New
York, Wilson, 1939. 130 p.   016.3
39-27689
    Z7161.5 .D28 1939 MRR Alc.

Pinson, William M. Resource guide to
current social issues, Waco, Tex.,
Word Books [1968] 272 p.   016.301
67-30735
    Z7164.S66 P47 MRR Alc.

SOCIAL PROBLEMS--DICTIONARIES.
Filler, Louis, A dictionary of
American social reform. New York,
Philosophical Library [1963] 854 p.
303 62-12824
    H41 .F5 MRR Alc.

SOCIAL PROBLEMS AND THE CHURCH
see Church and social problems

SOCIAL PSYCHIATRY.
Child and adolescent psychiatry,
sociocultural and community
psychiatry. 2d ed. [Rev. and
expanded] New York, Basic Books
[1974] xi, 858 p.   616.8/9/008 s
616.8/9 72-89188
    RC435 .A562 vol. 2 MRR Alc.

SOCIAL PSYCHOLOGY.
see also Public opinion

see also Violence

Lindzey, Gardner, ed. The handbook
of social psychology. 2d ed.
Reading, Mass., Addison-Wesley Pub.
Co. [1968-70, c1968-69] 5 v.   301.1
68-19347
    HM251 .L486 MRR Alc.

Mackay, Charles, Extraordinary
popular delusions and the madness of
crowds. London, G. G. Harrap [1956]
xxiv, 724 p.   301.15 133.7 57-1736
    AZ999 .M2 1956 MRR Alc.

SOCIAL PSYCHOLOGY--BIBLIOGRAPHY.
Universal Reference System. Public
opinion, mass behavior, and political
psychology; Princeton, N.J.,
Princeton Research Pub. Co. [1969]
xxi, 1225 p. 016.30115/4 68-57822
    Z7161 .U64 vol. 6 MRR Alc.

SOCIAL PSYCHOLOGY--HISTORY--GERMANY
(FEDERAL REPUBLIC, 1949-)
Bondy, Curt, Social psychology in
Western Germany Washington, Library
of Congress, Reference Dept., 1956.
vii, 84 p. 301.15 56-60076
    Z663.2 .S6 MRR Alc.

SOCIAL REGISTERS.
Royal blue book. Chicago [etc.] St.
James Press [etc.] 9207.0025 68-
6111
    CT103 .R64 MRR Biog Latest edition

SOCIAL SCIENCE--SCHOLARSHIPS,
FELLOWSHIPS, ETC.--UNITED STATES.
Social Science Research Council.
Fellows of the Social Science
Research Council, 1825-1951. New
York, 1951. x, 473 p.   307.2 52-
3372
    H57 .S6 1951 MRR Biog.

SOCIAL SCIENCE RESEARCH.
Main trends of research in the social
and human sciences. The Hague,
Mouton, 1970- v.   [fl 78.00 (pt.
1)] 300/.72 70-114641
    H62 .M243 MRR Alc.

SOCIAL SCIENCE RESEARCH--BIBLIOGRAPHY.
Belson, William A. Bibliography on
methods of social and business
research London, London School of
Economics and Political Science;
Lockwood, 1973. viii, 300 p.
[£4.95] 016.3/001/8 73-155242
    Z7161 .B44 MRR Alc.

Research annual on intergroup
relations. Chicago [etc.] Quadrangle
Books [etc.] 66-14164
    HM131 .R45 MRR Alc Full set

SOCIAL SCIENCE RESEARCH--DIRECTORIES.
Organization for Economic Cooperation and Development.
Development Centre. Catalogue of
social and economic development
training institutes and programmes.
Paris, O.E.C.D.; London, H.M.S.O.,
1968. [2], 344 p. [31/-]
309.2/23/0711 68-140061
    HD82 .O66 MRR Alc.

United Nations Educational,
Scientific and Cultural Organization.
World index of social science
institutions. Paris, Unesco, 1970-
1 v. (loose-leaf)   300/.6 75-882769
    H10 .U53 MRR Alc.

United States. Dept. of State. Office
of External Research. Foreign
affairs research, a directory of
governmental resources. [Washington,
For sale by the Supt. of Docs., U.S.
Govt. Print. Off., 1967. vii, 83 p.
327/.025 67-61715
    JX1293.U6 A527 MRR Ref Desk.

SOCIAL SCIENCE RESEARCH--CARIBBEAN AREA-
-DIRECTORIES.
Vigo-Cepeda, Luisa C. Directory of
institutes and centers devoted to the
social and economic research in the
Caribbean. Rio Piedras, Institute of
Caribbean Studies, University of
Puerto Rico, 1968. 1 v. (various
pagings) 300/.72/0729 74-627100
    H62 .V47 MRR Alc.

SOCIAL SCIENCES.
Hoselitz, Berthold Frank, ed. A
reader's guide to the social
sciences. Rev. ed. New York, Free
Press [1970] xiv, 425 p.   016.3 71-
15373
    H61 .H69 1970 MRR Alc.

SOCIAL SCIENCES--ABSTRACTING AND
INDEXING.
International Federation for
Documentation. Abstracting services.
[2d ed.] The Hague, 1969. 2 v.
029/.3/5 73-168852
    Z695.93 .I58 1969 MRR Ref Desk.

SOCIAL SCIENCES--ABSTRACTS.
International Labor Office. Library.
International labour documentation:
cumulative edition. Boston, Mass.,
G. K. Hall. 72-625702
H91 .I56 MRR Alc Full set

Utz, Arthur Fridolin, Bibliographie
der Sozialethik. 1- 1956/59
Freiburg, New York, Herder. a 61-
2645
Z7161 .U83 MRR Alc Full set

SOCIAL SCIENCES--BIBLIOGRAPHY.
Colchester, Eng. University of Essex.
Library. Comparative and social
studies: Colchester, University of
Essex (Library), 1969. [4], xiv, 407
p. 017/.1 70-506935
Z1035.1 .C63 1969 MRR Alc.

Communications/Research/Machines,
inc. PsychoSources; Toronto, New
York, Bantam Books [1973] 215 p.
[$5.00] 150/.8 72-88415
BF131 .C628 1973 MRR Alc.

Freides, Thelma. Literature and
bibliography of the social sciences.
Los Angeles, Melville Pub. Co. [1973]
xviii, 284 p. 300/.1/8 73-10111
H61 .F635 MRR Alc.

Frykholm, Lars. Översikt över
samhällsvetenskapliga bibliografiska
hjälpmedel. [Stockholm, I
distribution: C. E. Fritzes Kungl.
Hovbokhandel, 1960] 160 p. 65-
54808
Z7161 .F78 MRR Alc.

Gray, Richard A. Serial
bibliographies in the humanities and
social sciences. Ann Arbor, Mich.,
Pierian Press, 1969. xxiv, 345 p.
016.01605 68-58895
Z1002 .G814 MRR Ref Desk.

Hoselitz, Berthold Frank, ed. A
reader's guide to the social
sciences. Rev. ed. New York, Free
Press [1970] xiv, 425 p. 016.3 71-
15373
H61 .H69 1870 MRR Alc.

Lewis, Peter R. The literature of
the social sciences; London, Library
Association, 1960. 222 p. 016.3
60-3467
Z7161 .L45 MRR Alc.

London. University. Warburg
Institute. Library. Catalogue. [2d
ed.] Boston, G. K. Hall, 1967. 12
v. 019/.2 68-4522
Z921 .L66 1967 MRR Alc (Dk 33)

Mason, John Brown, Research
resources; Santa Barbara, Calif.,
ABC-Clio, 1968- v. [3.00]
016.327/.09/04 68-9685
Z7161 .M36 MRR Ref Desk.

Morrison, Denton E. Environment;
Washington, Office of Research and
Monitoring, U.S. Environmental
Protection Agency; for sale by the
Supt. of Docs., U.S. Govt. Print.
Off., 1974, c1973. vii, 860 p.
[$7.45] 016.3 74-601576
Z7161 .M56 1974 MRR Alc.

Princeton University. Office of
Population Research. Population
index bibliography. Boston, G. K.
Hall, 1971. 4 v. 016.312 75-26979

Z7164.D3 P85 MRR Alc (Dk 33)

Public Affairs Information Service.
Bulletin ... annual cumulation. 1st-
1915- New York [etc.] 16-820
Z7163 .P9 MRR Circ Full set

Public Affairs Information Service.
Foreign language index. 1968/71-
New York. 016.3 72-626907
Z7164.E2 P8 MRR Circ Full set

Recent publications in the social and
behavioral sciences. 1966- [New
York] The American behavioral
scientist. 016.3 66-56737
Z7161 .A42 MRR Alc Full set

Stevens, Rolland Elwell, Reference
books in the social sciences and
humanities 3d ed. Champaign, Ill.,
Distributed by Illini Union Bookstore
[1971] v, 188 p. 016.3 74-151299

Z1035.1 .S85 1971 MRR Ref Desk.

The American behavioral scientist.
The ABS guide to recent publications
in the social and behavioral
sciences. New York, 1965. xxi, 781
p. 65-17168
Z7161 .A4 MRR Alc.

United Nations Educational,
Scientific and Cultural Organization.
Theses de sciences sociales;
[Paris, 1952] 236 p. 016.3 52-
4847
Z7161 .U4 MRR Alc.

Utz, Arthur Fridolin, Bibliographie
der Sozialethik. 1- 1956/59
Freiburg, New York, Herder. a 61-
2645
Z7161 .U83 MRR Alc Full set

White, Carl Milton, Sources of
information in the social sciences, a
guide to the literature 2d ed.
Chicago, American Library
Association, 1973. xviii, 702 p.
016.3 73-9825
Z7161 .W49 1973 MRR Ref Desk.

Wynar, Lubomyr Roman, Guide to
reference materials in political
science: Denver, Colorado
Bibliographic Institute, 1966-68. 2
v. 016.32 66-1321
Z7161 .W9 MRR Alc.

SOCIAL SCIENCES--BIBLIOGRAPHY--CATALOGS.
California. University. Institute of
Governmental Studies. Library.
Subject catalog of the Institute of
Governmental Studies Library,
University of California, Berkeley.
Boston, G. K. Hall, 1970 [pref. 1971]
26 v. 016.353 73-152341
Z7164.A2 C34 MRR Alc (Dk 33)

Cornell University. New York State
School of Industrial and Labor
Relations. Library. Library catalog.
Boston, G. K. Hall, 1967. 12 v.
016.331 72-185999
Z7164.L1 C84 MRR Alc (Dk 33)

Stanford University. Hoover
Institution on War, Revolution, and
Peace. The library catalogs of the
Hoover Institution on War,
Revolution, and Peace; Stanford
University; Boston, G. K. Hall, 1969-
v. 017/.5 77-17709
Z881.S785 1969e MRR Alc (Dk 33)

SOCIAL SCIENCES--BIBLIOGRAPHY--INDEXES.
Index to the contemporary scene. v.
1- 1973- Detroit, Gale Research
Co. [$14.00] 016.3 73-645955
Z7161 .I52 MRR Alc Full set

SOCIAL SCIENCES--BIBLIOGRAPHY--
PERIODICALS.
Population index. v. 1- Jan. 20,
1935- [Princeton, N.J., etc.]
016.312 39-10247
Z7164.D3 P83 MRR Alc Partial set

SOCIAL SCIENCES--BIBLIOGRAPHY--UNION
LISTS.
A London bibliography of the social
sciences. v. 1- 1929- London,
Mansell Information/Publishing Ltd.
[etc.] 016.3 31-9970
Z7161 .L84 MRR Alc Full set

SOCIAL SCIENCES--COMPARATIVE STUDIES.
see also Comparative economics

SOCIAL SCIENCES--DICTIONARIES.
Dictionary of the history of ideas;
New York, Scribner [1973] 4 v.
[$35.00 (per vol.)] 901.9 72-7943

CB5 .D52 MRR Alc.

Encyclopedia of the social sciences,
New York, The Macmillan company,
1937. 15 v. in 8. 303 37-28589
H41 .E6 1937 MRR Alc.

Filler, Louis, A dictionary of
American social reform. New York,
Philosophical Library [1963] 854 p.
303 62-12824
H41 .F5 MRR Alc.

Gould, Julius, ed. A dictionary of
the social sciences. [New York] Free
Press of Glencoe [1964] xvi, 761 p.
303 64-20307
H41 .G6 MRR Ref Desk.

International encyclopedia of the
social sciences. [New York]
Macmillan [1968] 17 v. 300/.3 68-
10023
H40.A2 I5 MRR Alc.

Marxism, Communism, and Western
society; [New York] Herder and
Herder [1972-73] 8 v. 300/.3 79-
176368
AE5 .M27 MRR Alc.

Pei, Mario Andrew, ed. Language of
the specialists: [New York] Funk &
Wagnalls [1966] xii, 388 p. 423.1
66-22943
PE1680 .P4 MRR Alc.

Zadrozny, John Thomas, Dictionary of
social science. Washington, Public
Affairs Press [1959] viii, 367 p.
303 58-13401
H41 .Z3 MRR Alc.

SOCIAL SCIENCES--DICTIONARIES--GERMAN.
Handwörterbuch der
Sozialwissenschaften. Stuttgart, G.
Fisher, 1952- v. a 53-7990
H45 .H18 MRR Alc.

Staatslexikon. 5., von grund aus
neubearb. aufl. .. Freiburg im
Breisgau, Herder & co.; g.m.b.h.,
1926- v. 28-29832
JA63 .S8 1926 MRR Alc.

SOCIAL SCIENCES--DICTIONARIES--POLYGLOT.
Polec. 2., verb. und erw. Aufl.
Berlin, de Gruyter, 1967. xvi, 1037
p. with map. [DM 48.-] 330/.03 68-
70864
H40 .P6 1967 MRR Alc.

SOCIAL SCIENCES--DIRECTORIES.
International directory of behavior
and design research. 1974-
[Orangeburg, N.Y.] [$12.00] 300/.25
74-75207
H57 .I57 MRR Biog Latest edition /
Sci RR Latest edition

SOCIAL SCIENCES--FILM CATALOGS.
Pinson, William M. Resource guide to
current social issues, Waco, Tex.,
Word Books [1968] 272 p. 016.301
67-30735
Z7164.S66 P47 MRR Alc.

SOCIAL SCIENCES--HISTORY--AUSTRIA.
Westphalen zu Fürstenberg, Ferdinand
Aloys, Graf von, Sociology and
economics in Austria; Washington,
Library of Congress, Reference Dept.,
European Affairs Division, 1953. 50
p. 309.436 53-60004
Z663.26 .S6 MRR Alc.

SOCIAL SCIENCES--HISTORY--GERMANY.
Horkheimer, Max, Survey of the
social sciences in Western Germany;
Washington, Library of Congress,
Reference Dept., European Affairs
Division, 1952. ix, 225 p. 309.43
52-60025
Z663.26 .S8 MRR Alc.

SOCIAL SCIENCES--INDEXES.
Social sciences citation index.
Philadelphia, Institute for
Scientific Information. 016.3 73-
85287
Z7161 .S65 MRR Alc Full set

SOCIAL SCIENCES--INFORMATION SERVICES--
UNITED STATES--DIRECTORIES.
Sessions, Vivian S. Directory of
data bases in the social and
behavioral sciences. [New York]
Published in cooperation with the
City University of New York [by]
Science Associates/International
[1974] xv, 300 p. [$35.00]
029/.9/30025 72-86759
Z699.5.S65 S47 MRR Alc.

United States. Library of Congress.
National Referral Center. A
directory of information resources in
the United States: social sciences.
Rev. ed. Washington, Library of
Congress; [for sale by the Supt. of
Docs., U.S. Govt. Print. Off.] 1973.
iv, 700 p. [$6.90] 300/.7 73-3297

Z663.379 .D53 1973 MRR Alc.

SOCIAL SCIENCES--JUVENILE LITERATURE--
BIBLIOGRAPHY.
Huus, Helen, Children's books to
enrich the social studies; Rev. ed.
Washington, National Council for the
Social Studies [c1966] xiii, 201 p.
016.3728/3 67-8284
Z1037.9 .H8 1966 MRR Alc.

SOCIAL SCIENCES--METHODOLOGY--
BIBLIOGRAPHY.
Belson, William A. Bibliography on
methods of social and business
research London, London School of
Economics and Political Science;
Lockwood, 1973. viii, 300 p.
[£4.95] 016.3/001/8 73-155242
Z7161 .B44 MRR Alc.

SOCIAL SCIENCES--PERIODICALS--
BIBLIOGRAPHY.
Paoletti, Odette. Périodiques et
publications en série concernant les
sciences sociales et humaines,
Paris, Maison des sciences de
l'homme, Service bibliothèque-
documentation, 1966. 2 v. (xxiv, 684
p.) [80.00F] 016.07 67-100583
Z6941 .P3 MRR Alc.

Schmid, Hans, writer on sociology.
Verzeichnis von Fachzeitschriften aus
dem Gebiet der Psychologie und ihrer
Nachbarwissenschaften. Bern,
Schweizerischer Berufsverband für
angewandte Psychologie, 1967. 70 l.
[18.00] 016.300/5 79-371198
Z7203 .S25 MRR Alc.

United Nations Educational,
Scientific and Cultural Organization.
Liste mondiale des périodiques
spécialisés dans les sciences
sociales. 3. ed., rev. et augm.
[Paris] Unesco [1966, c1952] 448 p.
67-51954
Z7163 .U52 1966 MRR Alc.

SOCIAL SCIENCES--PERIODICALS-- (Cont.)
Zimmerman, Irene. A guide to current
Latin American periodicals. [1st
ed.] Gainesville, Fla., Kellman Pub.
Co., 1961. x, 357 p. 61-15751
Z6954.S8 Z5 MRR Alc.

SOCIAL SCIENCES--PERIODICALS--
BIBLIOGRAPHY--UNION LISTS.
Ottawa. National Library.
Periodicals in the social sciences
and humanities currently received by
Canadian libraries. [Ottawa, Queen's
Printer] 1968. 2 v. [unpriced]
016.300/5 68-105183
Z6945 .O895 MRR Alc.

SOCIAL SCIENCES--PERIODICALS--INDEXES.
Abstracts for social workers. v. 1-
spring 1965- [New York] National
Association of Social Workers.
[$20.00] 361/.008 74-642752
HV1 .A2 MRR Alc Full set

Bulletin signalétique 519:
Philosophie, sciences religieuses.
v. 15-23; 1861-69. Paris, Centre de
documentation du C.N.R.S. 75-10205
Z7127 .F712 MRR Alc Full set

Bulletin signalétique: Philosophie,
sciences humaines. v. 1-14; 1947-60.
Paris, Centre de documentation du C.
N. R. S. 51-30077
Z7127 .F7 MRR Alc Full set

Fondation nationale des sciences
politiques. Bibliographie courante
d'articles de periodiques
postérieurs a 1944 sur les
problemes politiques, economiques,
et sociaux. Boston, G. K. Hall,
1968. 17 v. 70-409780
AI7 .F6 MRR Alc. (Dk 33).

Guide to social science and religion
in periodical literature. Flint,
Mich., National Periodical Library.
016.2/005 73-641014
Z7753 .G83 MRR Alc Full set

International Labor Office. Library.
International labour documentation:
cumulative edition. Boston, Mass.,
G. K. Hall. 72-625702
H91 .I56 MRR Alc Full set

Public Affairs Information Service.
Bulletin ... annual cumulation. 1st-
1915- New York [etc.] 16-920
Z7163 .P8 MRR Circ Full set

Public Affairs Information Service.
Foreign language index. 1968/71-
New York. 016.3 72-626807
Z7164.E2 P8 MRR Circ Full set

Social sciences & humanities index.
v. 1- 1907/15- New York [etc.] H.
W. Wilson Co. 17-4869
AI3 .R49 MRR Circ Partial set /
MRR Circ Partial set

Social sciences citation index.
Philadelphia, Institute for
Scientific Information. 016.3 73-
85287
Z7161 .S65 MRR Alc Full set

SOCIAL SCIENCES--PERIODICALS--INDEXES--
BIBLIOGRAPHY.
Vesenyi, Paul E., European
periodical literature in the social
sciences and the humanities,
Metuchen, N.J., Scarecrow Press,
1969. 226 p. 016.052 79-7052
Z6955 .Z8V45 MRR Alc.

SOCIAL SCIENCES--SOCIETIES, ETC.--
DIRECTORIES.
United Nations Educational,
Scientific and Cultural Organization.
World index of social science
institutions. Paris, Unesco, 1970-
1 v. (loose-leaf) 300/.6 75-882769

H10 .U53 MRR Alc.

SOCIAL SCIENCES--STUDY AND TEACHING.
Educators guide to free social
studies materials. 1st- ed.; 1961-
Randolph, Wis., Educators Progress
Service. 307 61-65910
AG600 .E315 MRR Alc Latest edition

SOCIAL SCIENCES--STUDY AND TEACHING--
UNITED STATES--DIRECTORIES.
The Annual guides to graduate study.
1966/67- Princeton, N.J., Peterson's
Guides Inc. 378.73 68-1823
L901 .P46 MRR Alc Latest edition

SOCIAL SCIENCES--STUDY AND TEACHING
(ELEMENTARY)
Jarolimek, John. Social studies in
elementary education. 4th ed. New
York, Macmillan [1971] x, 534 p.
[$8.50] 372.8/3 70-126186
LB1584 .J3 1971 MRR Alc.

Jarolimek, John. Social studies in
elementary education. 3d ed. New
York, Macmillan [1967] xi, 464 p.
372.83 66-30144
LB1584 .J3 1967 MRR Alc.

SOCIAL SCIENCES--THEORY, METHODS, ETC.
Freides, Thelma. Literature and
bibliography of the social sciences.
Los Angeles, Melville Pub. Co. [1973]
xviii, 284 p. 300/.1/8 73-10111
H61 .F635 MRR Alc.

SOCIAL SCIENCES--TRANSLATIONS INTO
ENGLISH--BIBLIOGRAPHY.
Catalog cards in book form for United
States Joint Publications Research
Service translations. v. -8; -
Jan./June 1970. New York [etc.] CCM
Information Corp. [etc.] 75-104064
Began with vol. for 1957/61.
Z1223.Z8 K9 Sci RR Sci RR Partial
set / MRR Alc Full set

SOCIAL SCIENCES--UNITED STATES--
DIRECTORIES--BIBLIOGRAPHY.
Klein, Bernard. Guide to American
scientific and technical directories.
1st ed. Rye, N.Y., B. Klein
Publications [1972] v, 324 p.
016.3384/7/6702573 72-91671
Z7914.M3 K53 MRR Ref Desk.

SOCIAL SCIENTISTS--BIOGRAPHY.
International directory of behavior
and design research, 1974-
[Orangeburg, N.Y.] [$12.00] 300/.25
74-75207
H57 .I57 MRR Biog Latest edition /
Sci RR Latest edition

United Nations Educational,
Scientific and Cultural Organization.
Secretariat. Social scientists
specializing in African studies;
[Paris, École pratique des hautes
études, 1963. 375 p. 64-4339
DT19.5 .U5 MRR Biog.

SOCIAL SCIENTISTS--UNITED STATES.
Social Science Research Council.
Fellows of the Social Science
Research Council, 1925-1951. New
York, 1951. x, 473 p. 307.2 52-
3372
H57 .S6 1951 MRR Biog.

SOCIAL SECURITY
see Insurance, Social

SOCIAL SECURITY--UNITED STATES.
United States. Social Security
Administration. Office of Research
and Statistics. Social security
programs in the United States.
[Washington] U.S. Social Security
Administration; [for sale by the
Supt. of Docs., U.S. Govt. Print.
Off.] 1968. v, 120 p. [0.55]
368.4/00973 hew68-100
HD7123 .A52 1968 MRR Alc.

SOCIAL SERVICE--ABSTRACTS--PERIODICALS.
Abstracts for social workers. v. 1-
spring 1965- [New York] National
Association of Social Workers.
[$20.00] 361/.008 74-642752
HV1 .A2 MRR Alc Full set

SOCIAL SERVICE--DICTIONARIES.
Encyclopedia of social work. 1st-
issue; 1929- New York. 30-30948
HV35 .S6 MRR Alc Latest edition

SOCIAL SERVICE--DIRECTORIES.
National Association of Social
Workers. Directory of agencies: U.S.
voluntary, international voluntary,
intergovermental. Washington [1973]
96 p. 362/.025/73 73-83478
HV89 .N223 1973 MRR Alc.

SOCIAL SERVICE--PERIODICALS--INDEXES.
Abstracts for social workers. v. 1-
spring 1965- [New York] National
Association of Social Workers.
[$20.00] 361/.008 74-642752
HV1 .A2 MRR Alc Full set

SOCIAL SERVICE--SOCIETIES, ETC.--
DIRECTORIES.
Directory of social and health
agencies of New York City. [1st]-
ed.; 1883- [New York] 360.58 [2-
37275
HV99.N59 N5 MRR Alc Latest edition

Gale Research Company. Encyclopedia
of associations. 8th ed. Detroit,
Mich. [1973- v. [$45.00 (v. 1)
$28.50 (v. 2)] 061/.3 73-7400
HS17 .G334 1973 MRR Ref Desk.

SOCIAL SERVICE--YEARBOOKS.
Encyclopedia of social work. 1st-
issue; 1929- New York. 30-30948
HV35 .S6 MRR Alc Latest edition

SOCIAL SERVICE--CALIFORNIA--SOCIETIES,
ETC.--DIRECTORIES.
Yung, Judith. Directory of
California non-profit associations,
San Francisco, San Francisco Public
Library, 1970. iii, 217 p. 061.94
79-20791
HD2428.C3 Y84 MRR Alc.

SOCIAL SERVICE--CHICAGO METROPOLITAN
AREA--DIRECTORIES.
Social service directory metropolitan
Chicago. Chicago, Welfare Council of
Metropolitan Chicago. 72-626573
HV87.C5 S6 MRR Alc Latest edition

SOCIAL SERVICE--LOS ANGELES--
DIRECTORIES.
Gaat, Monte. Getting the best of
L.A. [Los Angeles, Calif.] J. P.
Tarcher [1972] 208 p.
917.94/94/0025 73-189108
F869.L83 G3 MRR Alc.

SOCIAL SERVICE--UNITED STATES--
DIRECTORIES.
National Association of Social
Workers. Directory of agencies: U.S.
voluntary, international voluntary,
intergovermental. Washington [1973]
96 p. 362/.025/73 73-83478
HV89 .N223 1973 MRR Alc.

SOCIAL SERVICE--UNITED STATES--
SOCIETIES, ETC.--DIRECTORIES.
National Social Welfare Assembly.
Service directory of national
organizations 1st- ed.; 1951- New
York. 360.58 52-3715
HV89 .N35 MRR Alc Latest edition

Public administration organizations,
a directory of unofficial
organizations in the field of public
administration in the United States
and Canada. [1st] ed.; 1932-
Chicago, Public Administration
Clearing House. 061 33-4186
AS18 .P8 MRR Alc Latest edition

SOCIAL SERVICES--BIOGRAPHY.
International who's who in community
service. 1973/74- ed. London,
Eddison Press. [12.50] 361/.0025
78-189467
HV27 .I57 MRR Biog Latest edition

SOCIAL SETTLEMENTS
see also Day nurseries

SOCIAL SETTLEMENTS--DIRECTORIES.
National Federation of Settlements
and Neighborhood Centers. Directory
of member houses. New York.
361/.0025/7 68-47249
HV4193 .N3 MRR Alc Latest edition

SOCIAL SURVEYS.
Government Affairs Foundation.
Metropolitan surveys: Chicago,
Public Administration Service, c1958.
xvi, 256 p. 352.073 58-14374
HN29 .G65 MRR Alc.

Parten, Mildred Bernice, Surveys,
polls, and samples: practical
procedures. New York, Cooper Square
Publishers, 1966 (c1950) xii, 624 p.
311/.28 66-27603
HN29 .P3 1966 MRR Alc.

SOCIAL SURVEYS--BIBLIOGRAPHY.
Belson, William A. Bibliography on
methods of social and business
research London, London School of
Economics and Political Science;
Lockwood, 1973. viii, 300 p.
[£4.95] 016.3/001/8 73-155242
Z7161 .B44 MRR Alc.

SOCIAL WELFARE
see Charities

SOCIAL WORK EDUCATION.
Stickney, Patricia J. World guide to
social work education. New York,
International Association of Schools
of Social Work [1974] xi, 297 p.
361/.007/1 74-158451
HV11 .S83 MRR Alc.

SOCIAL WORK EDUCATION--DIRECTORIES.
Stickney, Patricia J. World guide to
social work education. New York,
International Association of Schools
of Social Work [1974] xi, 297 p.
361/.007/1 74-158451
HV11 .S83 MRR Alc.

SOCIAL WORKERS--UNITED STATES--
DIRECTORIES.
N A S W directory of professional
social workers. 1960- New York,
National Association of Social
Workers. 360.69 60-3375
HV89 .N2 MRR Alc Latest edition

SOCIALISM.
see also Collective settlements

see also Communism

see also Labor and laboring classes

SOCIALISM--BIBLIOGRAPHY.
Egbert, Donald Drew, ed. Socialism
and American life. Princeton,
Princeton University Press, 1952. 2
v. 335 52-5828
HX83 .E45 MRR Alc.

Rappoport, Angelo Solomon,
Dictionary of socialism, London, T.
F. Unwin, ltd. [1924] xi, 271 p.
24-31970
HX17 .R3 MRR Alc.

SOCIALISM--DICTIONARIES.
Rappoport, Angelo Solomon,
Dictionary of socialism, London, T.
F. Unwin, ltd. [1924] xi, 271 p.
24-31970
HX17 .R3 MRR Alc.

SOCIALISM--HISTORY.
Cole, George Douglas Howard, A history of socialist thought. London, Macmillan; New York, St. Martin's Press, 1953- v. in 335   53-4167
    HX36 .C57 MRR Alc.

Egbert, Donald Drew, ed. Socialism and American life. Princeton, Princeton University Press, 1952. 2 v.   335 52-5828
    HX83 .E45 MRR Alc.

Laidler, Harry Wellington, History of socialism; [Updated and expanded ed.] New York, Crowell [1968] xx, 870 p. [12.50]   335/.009 67-29698
    HX21 .L37 1968 MRR Alc.

SOCIALISM--PERIODICALS--BIBLIOGRAPHY.
Goldwater, Walter. Radical periodicals in America, 1890-1950; New Haven, Yale University Library, 1964. xv, 51 p.   64-6244
    Z7164.S67 .G57 MRR Alc.

SOCIALISM--PERIODICALS--HISTORY.
The American radical press, 1880-1960. Westport, Conn., Greenwood Press [1974] 2 v. (xiv, 720 p.) 335/.00873 72-9825
    HX1 .A49 MRR Alc.

SOCIALISM--PERIODICALS--INDEXES.
Indexes to independent Socialist periodicals. Berkeley, Calif., Independent Socialist Press [1969] 221 p. [9.75]   016.3091 77-16046
    HX15 .I43 no. 4 MRR Alc.

SOCIALISM IN EUROPE--HISTORY.
Landauer, Carl, European socialism; Berkeley, University of California Press, 1959 [i.e. 1960] 2 v. (xviii, 1894 p.)   335.094 59-5744
    HX40 .L24 MRR Alc.

SOCIALISM IN THE UNITED STATES.
Quint, Howard H. The forging of American socialism; [2d ed.] Indianapolis, Bobbs-Merrill [1964, c1953] ix, 409 p.   335 64-16709
    HX83 .Q5 1964 MRR Alc.

SOCIALISM IN THE UNITED STATES--HISTORY.
Egbert, Donald Drew, ed. Socialism and American life. Princeton, Princeton University Press, 1952. 2 v.   335 52-5828
    HX83 .E45 MRR Alc.

SOCIALISTS.
Rappoport, Angelo Solomon, Dictionary of socialism, London, T. F. Unwin, ltd. [1924] xi, 271 p. 24-31970
    HX17 .R3 MRR Alc.

SOCIALISTS, FRENCH.
Maitron, Jean, ed. Dictionnaire biographique du mouvement ouvrier français. Paris, Editions ouvrières [1964- v.   65-30024
    HD8433.A1 M3 MRR Biog.

SOCIALLY HANDICAPPED CHILDREN--EDUCATION--BIBLIOGRAPHY.
Culturally disadvantaged; Detroit, Wayne State University Press, 1967. 803 p.   016.3719/6 66-27901
    Z5814.C52 C8 MRR Alc.

Prentice-Hall, inc. Educator's complete ERIC handbook, Englewood Cliffs, N.J. [1868, c1967] x, 862 p. 016.3719/6 67-30283
    Z5814.C52 P7 MRR Alc.

SOCIETIES--BIBLIOGRAPHY.
Handbook of learned societies and institutions: America. Washington, D.C., Carnegie Institution of Washington, 1908. viii, 592 p.   08-21011
    Z5055.U39 H2 MRR Alc.

Lowndes, William Thomas, The bibliographer's manual of English literature New ed., rev., cor. and enl. London, H. G. Bohn, 1857-61; Bell & Daldy, 1864-65. 10 v. 015.42 35-36009
    Z2001 .L92 1857-65 MRR Alc.

Royal Society of London. Catalogue of scientific papers. London, C. J. Clay, 1867-1925. 19 v.   02-11462
    Z7403 .R88 MRR Alc.

Royal society of London. Catalogue of scientific papers, 1800-1900. Cambridge, University press, 1908- v.   08-24586
    Z7403 .R8812 MRR Alc.

United States. Library of Congress. Division of bibliography. ... A union list of periodicals, transactions and allied publications currently received in the principal libraries of the District of Columbia. Washington, Govt. print. off., 1901. v, 315 p.   01-16622
    Z663.28 .U5 MRR Alc.

SOCIETIES--DIRECTORIES.
Verbände und Gesellschaften der Wissenschaft: ein internat. Verz. 1 Ausg. [Pullach (Isartal)] Verlag Dokumentation, 1974. xii, 481 p. [DM98.00]   74-338569
    Q145 .V45 MRR Ref Desk.

SOCIETIES--HISTORY, ORGANIZATION, ETC.
Graebner, Theodore Conrad, A handbook of organizations; Saint Louis, Concordia Pub. House, 1948. xi, 368 p.   366 49-14011
    HS191 .G7 1948 MRR Alc.

Preuss, Arthur, comp. A dictionary of secret and other societies, St. Louis, Mo., London, B. Herder book co., 1924. xi, 543 p.   24-9579
    HS12 .P6 MRR Alc.

SOCIETY, PRIMITIVE.
see also Man, Prehistoric

see also Religion, Primitive

Herskovits, Melville Jean, Cultural anthropology. New York, Knopf, 1955. 569 p.   572 55-5171
    GN400 .H588 MRR Alc.

Lips, Julius Ernst, The origin of things; London, Harrap [1949] 420 p.   572 50-17122
    GN400 .L75 1949 MRR Alc.

Murdock, George Peter, Our primitive contemporaries, New York, The Macmillan company, 1934. xxii p., 1 l., 614 p.   572.7 34-2549
    GN400 .M8 MRR Alc.

Sanders, Irwin Taylor, ed. Societies around the world. New York, Dryden Press [1953] 2 v.   572 53-8588
    GN400 .S273 MRR Alc.

SOCIETY EMBLEMS.
Clapp, Jane. Professional ethics and insignia. Metuchen, N.J., Scarecrow Press, 1974. xii, 851 p.   061/.3 74-10501
    HD6504 .A194 MRR Ref Desk.

SOCIOLOGICAL RESEARCH--BIBLIOGRAPHY.
BonJean, Charles M. Sociological measurement; San Francisco, Chandler Pub. Co. [1967] xiv, 580 p. 016.301 67-24968
    Z7164.S68 B6 MRR Alc.

SOCIOLOGISTS.
Internationales Soziologen Lexikon. Stuttgart, F. Enke, 1959. viii, 662 p.   a 60-980
    HM19 .I6 MRR Biog.

SOCIOLOGISTS--UNITED STATES--DIRECTORIES.
American Sociological Association. Directory. Dec. 1950- Washington, D. C.   301.06273   60-1821
    HM9 .A725 MRR Biog Latest edition

SOCIOLOGY--BIBLIOGRAPHY.
International bibliography of social and cultural anthropology. v. 1- 1955- London, Tavistock Pub.; Chicago, Aldine Pub. Co. [etc.] 016.572 58-4366
    Z7161 .I593 MRR Alc Full set

SOCIOLOGY.
see also Cities and towns

see also Communication

see also Educational sociology

see also Family

see also Poor

Berelson, Bernard, Human behavior; New York, Harcourt, Brace and World [c1964] xxiii, 712 p.   301 64-11621
    HM51 .B42 MRR Alc.

Lundberg, George Andrew, Sociology, 4th ed. New York, Harper & Row [1968] ix, 771 p.   301 68-11717
    HM51 .L83 1968 MRR Alc.

Ziegenfuss, Werner, ed. Handbuch der Soziologie; Stuttgart, F. Enke, 1956. xliv, 1243 p.   57-30231
    HM57 .Z54 MRR Alc.

SOCIOLOGY--ABSTRACTS.
Sociological abstracts. v. 1- Jan./Oct. 1953- [New York] 301 58-46404
    HM1 .S67 MRR Alc Full set

SOCIOLOGY--BIBLIOGRAPHY.
Abramson, Harold J. Index to sociology readers, 1960-1965, Metuchen, N.J., Scarecrow Press, 1973. 2 v. (1125 p.)   016.301 73-877
    Z7164.S68 A22 MRR Alc.

Berkowitz, Morris I. Social scientific studies of religion; [Pittsburgh] University of Pittsburgh Press [1967] xvii, 258 p.   016.2 67-18692
    Z7751 .B47 MRR Alc.

BonJean, Charles M. Sociological measurement; San Francisco, Chandler Pub. Co. [1967] xiv, 580 p. 016.301 67-24968
    Z7164.S68 B6 MRR Alc.

International bibliography of sociology. London, Tavistock Pub., Chicago, Aldine Pub. Co. [etc.] 016.301 57-2849
    Z7161 .I594 MRR Alc Full set

Little, Lawrence Calvin, Researches in personality, character and religious education; [Pittsburgh] University of Pittsburgh Press, 1962. iv, 215 p.   013.3784886 62-12625
    Z7849 .L54 MRR Alc.

Lunday, G. Albert. Sociology dissertations in American universities, 1893-1966 [Commerce, East Texas State University, 1969] x, 277 p.   016.301 74-630565
    Z7164.S68 L9 MRR Alc.

Odum, Howard Washington, American sociology; [1st ed.] New York, Longmans, Green, 1951. vi, 501 p. 301 51-12390
    HM22.U5 O4 1951 MRR Alc.

Recent publications in the social and behavioral sciences. 1966- [New York] The American behavioral scientist.   016.3 66-56737
    Z7161 .A42 MRR Alc Full set

Utz, Arthur Fridolin, Bibliographie der Sozialethik. 1- 1956/59 Freiburg, New York, Herder. a 61-2645
    Z7161 .U83 MRR Alc Full set

SOCIOLOGY--COLLECTIONS.
Parsons, Talcott, ed. Theories of society; New York, Free Press of Glencoe [1961] 2 v.   301.082 61-8171
    HM15 .P33 MRR Alc.

SOCIOLOGY--DICTIONARIES.
Encyclopedia of sociology. Guilford, Conn., Dushkin Pub. Group [1973, c1974] vi, 330 p.   301/.03 73-87072
    HM17 .E5 MRR Alc.

Fairchild, Henry Pratt, ed. Dictionary of sociology. New York city, Philosophical library [1944] 4 p., l., 342 p.   303 44-4755
    HM17 .F3 MRR Alc.

Hoult, Thomas Ford. Dictionary of modern sociology. Totowa, N.J., Littlefield, Adams, 1969. xviii, 408 p. [3.45] 301/.03 67-10018
    HM17 .H63 MRR Alc.

Mitchell, Geoffrey Duncan. A dictionary of sociology. Chicago, Aldine Pub. Co. [1968] viii, 224 p. 301/.03 67-30870
    HM17 .M56 1968b MRR Alc.

Theodorson, George A. A modern dictionary of sociology. New York, Crowell, [1969] viii, 469 p. [10.00]   301/.03 69-18672
    HM17 .T5 MRR Alc.

SOCIOLOGY--DICTIONARIES--GERMAN.
Bernsdorf, Wilhelm, Wörterbuch der Soziologie. 2., neubearb. und erw. Ausg. Stuttgart, F. Enke, 1969. xi, 1317 p.   78-386417
    HM17 .B44 1969 MRR Alc.

SOCIOLOGY--HISTORY.
Barnes, Harry Elmer, Social thought from lore to science, 3d ed. [expanded and rev.] New York, Dover Publications [1961] 3 v. (xxxiv, 1178 p.)   301 61-4323
    HM19 .B27 1961 MRR Alc.

Bogardus, Emory Stephen, The development of social thought. 4th ed. New York, Longmans, Green [1960] 689 p.   301.09 59-15214
    HM19 .B58 1960 MRR Alc.

SOCIOLOGY--HISTORY--UNITED STATES.
Odum, Howard Washington, American sociology; [1st ed.] New York, Longmans, Green, 1951. vi, 501 p. 301 51-12390
    HM22.U5 O4 1951 MRR Alc.

SOCIOLOGY--PERIODICALS--INDEXES.
Abstracts for social workers. v. 1- spring 1965- [New York] National Association of Social Workers. [20.00]   361/.008 74-642752
    HV1 .A2 MRR Alc Full set

SOCIOLOGY--PERIODICALS--INDEXES. (Cont.)
Fondation nationale des sciences
politiques. Bibliographie courante
d'articles de periodiques
postérieurs a 1944 sur les
problemes politiques, economiques,
et sociaux. Boston, G. K. Hall,
1968. 17 v.   70-409780
AI7 .F6 MRR Alc. (Dk 33).

Fürer-Haimendorf, Elizabeth von. An
anthropological bibliography of South
Asia. Paris, Mouton, 1958-70. 3 v.
[fl. 130.00 (v. 3)]   a 59-1034
Z5115 .F83 MRR Alc.

Glenn, Norval D. Social
stratification; Berkeley, Calif.,
The Glendessary Press [1970] xi, 466
p.   016.30144 74-104325
Z7164.S64 G55 MRR Alc.

International bibliography of social
and cultural anthropology. v. 1-
1955- London, Tavistock Pub.;
Chicago, Aldine Pub. Co. [etc.]
016.572 58-4366
Z7161 .I593 MRR Alc Full set

International bibliography of
sociology. London, Tavistock Pub.,
Chicago, Aldine Pub. Co. [etc.]
016.301 57-2949
Z7161 .I594 MRR Alc Full set

Mogey, John M. Sociology of marriage
and family behaviour 1957-1968; The
Hague, Mouton [1971] 364 p.
016.30142 78-28387
Z7164.M2 M64 MRR Alc.

Sociological abstracts. v. 1-
Jan./Oct. 1953- [New York] 301 58-
46404
HM1 .S67 MRR Alc Full set

SOCIOLOGY, CHRISTIAN--DICTIONARIES--
GERMAN.
Evangelisches Staatslexikon,
Stuttgart, Berlin, Kreuz-Verlag
(1966) lxiv, 2687 p. [DM 75.00]
203 66-67138
BR95 .E95 MRR Alc.

SOCIOLOGY, MILITARY.
Inter-University Seminar on Armed
Forces and Society. Handbook of
military institutions. Beverly
Hills, Calif., Sage Publications
[1971] 607 p.   301.5/98 78-127989
U102 .I65 MRR Alc.

SOCIOLOGY, RURAL.
see also Community development

SOCIOLOGY, RURAL--BIBLIOGRAPHY.
Brode, John. The process of
modernization; Cambridge, Mass.,
Harvard University Press, 1969. x,
378 p. [6.50] 016.3092 69-13765
Z7164.U5 B7 MRR Alc.

SOCIOLOGY, URBAN.
see also City and town life

see also Urban renewal

SOCIOLOGY, URBAN--BIBLIOGRAPHY.
Housing and planning references. new
ser. no. 1- July/Aug. 1965-
[Washington, U.S. Govt. Print. Off.]
016.3015/4 72-621364
Z7165.U5 A3 MRR Alc Full set

United States. National Clearinghouse
for Mental Health Information.
Bibliography on the urban crisis;
Chevy Chase, Md., National Institute
of Mental Health [1968] iv, 158 p.
016.3091/73 77-600665
Z7164.S66 U57 MRR Alc.

SOCIOLOGY, URBAN--DICTIONARIES.
Abrams, Charles, The language of
cities; a glossary of terms. New
York, Viking Press [1971] ix, 365 p.
[$10.00] 301.3/6/03 76-137500
HT108.5 .A24 MRR Alc.

SOFT DRINK INDUSTRY--UNITED STATES--
DIRECTORIES.
The United beverage bureau book.
Louisville, Ky. 663.065 28-11187
Began with 1922 vol.
HF5585.B65 U5 MRR Alc Latest
edition

SOGN OG FJORDANE, NORWAY--DIRECTORIES.
Adressebok for Sogn og Fjordane fylke
og Bergen med skattelikninger. Oslo,
S. M. Bryde. 53-30568
DL596.B4 A6 MRR Alc Latest edition

SOILS--DICTIONARIES--POLYGLOT.
Jacks, Graham Vernon. Multilingual
vocabulary of soil science. [2d ed.,
rev. Rome] Land & Water Division,
Food and Agriculture Organization of
the United Nations [1960] xxiii, 428
p. 631.403 60-50105
S591 .J26 1960 MRR Alc.

SOLAR PHYSICS
see Sun

SOLAR SYSTEM.
see also Planets

The Solar system. [Chicago,
University of Chicago Press, 1953-
v. 523.2 54-7183
QB501 .S6 MRR Alc.

SOLDIERS.
Coggins, Jack. The fighting man;
[1st ed.] Garden City, N.Y.,
Doubleday [1966] xii, 372 p.
355.0009 66-20936
U750 .C6 MRR Alc.

SOLDIERS--LANGUAGE (NEW WORDS, SLANG,
ETC.)
Partridge, Eric, A dictionary of
Forces' slang, 1939-1945, Freeport,
N.Y., Books for Libraries Press
[1970] xi, 212 p. 427.09 75-
117899
PE3727.S7 P25 1970 MRR Alc.

SOLDIERS--UNITED STATES.
Wiley, Bell Irvin, The common
soldier in the Civil War. New York,
Grosset & Dunlap [1958] 454, 444 p.
973.74 58-4364
E607 .W48 MRR Alc.

SOLDIERS--UNITED STATES--STATISTICS.
Military market facts. [Washington]
Army Times Pub. Co. 65-5288
UC263 .M46 MRR Alc Latest edition

SOLICITORS
see Lawyers

SOLVENTS.
Marsden, Cyril, ed. Solvents guide,
2d ed., rev. and extended. New York,
Interscience Publishers [1963] 633
p. 660.294 63-4133
TP247.5 .M3 1963 MRR Alc.

SOMALILAND--BIBLIOGRAPHY.
United States. Library of Congress.
General Reference and Bibliography
Division. North and Northeast
Africa; Washington, 1957. v, 182 p.
016.96 57-60062
Z663.28 .N6 MRR Alc.

SOMALILAND--GAZETTEERS.
United States. Office of Geography.
Ethiopia, Eritrea, and the
Somalilands; Washington, 1950. 498
p. 73-10041
DT378.2 .U5 MRR Alc.

SOMALILAND--GOVERNMENT PUBLICATIONS--
BIBLIOGRAPHY.
United States. Library of Congress.
General Reference and Bibliography
Division. Official publications of
Somaliland, 1941-1959; Washington,
1960. vii, 41 p. 015.677 60-60050
Z663.28 .035 MRR Alc.

SOMATOLOGY--BIBLIOGRAPHY--CATALOGS.
Harvard University. Peabody Museum of
Archaeology and Ethnology. Library.
Catalogue: authors. Boston, G. K.
Hall, 1963. 26 v.   64-2646
Z5119 .H35 MRR Alc (Dk 33).

Harvard University. Peabody Museum of
Archaeology and Ethnology. Library.
Catalogue: subjects. Boston, G. K.
Hall, 1963. 27 v.   018.1 64-2645
Z5119 .H36 MRR Alc (Dk 33)

SONGS.
see also Ballads

SONGS--INDEXES.
Leigh, Robert, writer on music, comp.
Index to song books; Stockton,
Calif., 1964. 237 p. 781.97 64-
3837
ML128.S3 L45 MRR Alc.

Sears, Minnie Earl, Song index;
[n.p.] Shoe String Press, 1966. 2 v.
in 1. 016.784 66-25185
ML128.S3 S31 1966 MRR Alc.

United States. Library of Congress.
Archive of American Folk Song. A
list of American folksongs currently
available on records, Washington,
Library of Congress, 1953. 176 p.
789.9/13 53-60041
Z663.373 .L5 MRR Alc.

SONGS--THEMATIC CATALOGS.
Barlow, Harold. A dictionary of
opera and song themes, New York,
Crown Publishers [1966, c1950] 547
p. 781.97 66-18454
ML128.V7 B3 1950a MRR Alc.

SONGS, AMERICAN.
see also Ballads, American

SONGS, AMERICAN--BIBLIOGRAPHY.
Chipman, John H., comp. Index to top-
hit tunes, 1900-1950. Boston, B.
Humphries [1962] 249 p. 016.784
61-11711
ML128.V7 C54 MRR Alc.

Ewen, David, ed. American popular
songs from the Revolutionary War to
the present. New York, Random House
[1966] xiii, 507 p. 016.784 66-
12843
ML128.N3 E9 MRR Alc.

Mattfeld, Julius, Variety music
cavalcade 1620-1961. Rev. ed.
Englewood Cliffs, N.J., Prentice-Hall
[1962] xxiii, 713 p. 781.97 62-
16317
ML128.V7 M4 1962 MRR Alc.

Shapiro, Nat, ed. Popular music;
[1st ed. New York] Adrian Press
[1964]- v.   64-23761
ML120.U5 S5 MRR Alc.

Whitburn, Joel. Top rhythm & blues
records, 1949-1971. Menomonee Falls,
Wis., Record Research, c1973. 184 p.
016.7899/12 73-78333
ML156.4.P6 W53 MRR Alc.

SONGS, ENGLISH.
see also Ballads, English

SONGS, ENGLISH--BIBLIOGRAPHY.
Stecheson, Anthony, comp. The
Stecheson classified song directory,
Hollywood, Calif., Music Industry
Press [1961] ix, 503 p. 016.784
62-753
ML128.V7 S83 MRR Alc.

SONGS, PATRIOTIC
see National songs

SONGS, POPULAR
see Music, Popular (Songs, etc.)

SONNETS, AMERICAN.
Bender, Robert M., ed. The sonnet;
New York, Washington Square Press,
1965 [i.e. 1966, c1965] xviii, 554
p. 821.008 65-22603
PR1195.S5 B4 MRR Alc.

SONNETS, ENGLISH.
Bender, Robert M., ed. The sonnet;
New York, Washington Square Press,
1965 [i.e. 1966, c1965] xviii, 554
p. 821.008 65-22603
PR1195.S5 B4 MRR Alc.

SOPHISTS (GREEK PHILOSOPHY).
Philostratus, Flavius. Philostratus
and Eunapius; London, W. Heinemann;
New York, G. P. Putnam's sons, 1922.
v p.; 2 l.; ix-xlii, 595, [1] p. 22-
12854
PA3612 .P42 1922 MRR Alc.

SØR-TRØNDELAG, NORWAY--DIRECTORIES.
Sør-Trøndelag fylkes adressebok med
skattelikninger. Trondheim, Moe. 51-
17989
DL576.S62 S6 MRR Alc Latest
edition

SORCERY
see Magic

SOTO, HERNANDO DE, 1500 (CA.)-1542.
Spanish explorers in the southern
United States, 1528-1543: New York,
C. Scribner's sons, 1907. xx, 411 p.
07-10607
E187.O7 S7 MRR Alc.

SOUL.
see also Spiritual life

SOUL MUSIC
see Blues (Songs, etc.)

SOUND--RECORDING AND REPRODUCTION--
DICTIONARIES.
Curtis, Ron. Media dictionary; Red
Oak, Southwest Iowa Learning
Resources Center [1973] 290 p.
301.16/1/03 73-158317
P87.5 .C8 MRR Alc.

SOUND MOTION PICTURES
see Moving pictures, Talking

SOUND PRODUCTION BY ANIMALS.
see also Animal sounds

SOUSA'S BAND.
Smart, James Robert, The Sousa Band,
Washington, Library of Congress [For
sale by the Supt. of Docs., U.S.
Govt. Print. Off.] 1970. v, 123 p.
[1.50] 789.9/136/50671 70-604228
Z663.37 .S6 MRR Alc.

SOUTH AFRICA
see Africa, South

SOUTH AFRICAN PERIODICALS--BIBLIOGRAPHY.
South African national bibliography.
1959- Pretoria, State Library. 72-
626530
Z3603 .P7 MRR Alc Full set

SOUTH AFRICAN PERIODICALS--INDEXES.
Index to South African periodicals.
v. 1- 1940- Johannesburg [etc.]
052 41-26592
AI3 .I65 MRR Alc Partial set

SOUTH AMERICA.
Gunther, John, Inside South America.
[1st ed.] New York, Harper & Row
[c1967] xvi, 610 p. 320.98 66-
10630
F2208 .G94 MRR Alc.

SOUTH AMERICA--DESCRIPTION AND TRAVEL--
1951-
Clark, Sydney Aylmer, All the best
in South America, east coast: New
York, Dodd, Mead [1966] x, 264 p.
918.043 66-13263
F2224 .C55 1966 MRR Alc.

SOUTH AMERICA--DESCRIPTION AND TRAVEL--
1951- --GUIDE-BOOKS.
Clark, Sydney Aylmer, All the best
in South America, west coast: New
York, Dodd, Mead [1966] x, 271 p.
918.043 66-13264
F2213 .C5 1966 MRR Alc.

, Kane, Robert S. South America, A to
Z Rev. ed., Garden City, N.Y.,
Doubleday [1971] xiii, 346 p.
[$7.95] 918/.04/3 70-84391
F2211 .K3 1971 MRR Alc.

Waldo, Myra. Travel guide to South
America. New York, Macmillan [1972]
456 p. [$7.95] 918/.04/3 70-
177439
F2211 .W3 1972 MRR Alc.

SOUTH AMERICA--DESCRIPTION AND TRAVEL--
GUIDE-BOOKS.
Fodor's South America. 1970- New
York, D. McKay. 918/.04/3 72-622642

F2211 .F6 MRR Alc Latest edition

SOUTH AMERICA--HISTORY--BIBLIOGRAPHY.
Church, Elihu Dwight, A catalogue of
books relating to the discovery and
early history of North and South
America. New York, P. Smith, 1951.
5 v. (vi, 2635 p.) 016.9731 51-
4055
Z1203 .C55 1951 MRR Ref Desk.

SOUTH AMERICA--LEARNED INSTITUTIONS AND
SOCIETIES.
Handbook of learned societies and
institutions: America. Washington,
D.C., Carnegie institution of
Washington, 1908. viii, 592 p. 08-
21011
Z5055.U39 H2 MRR Alc.

SOUTH ASIA--BIBLIOGRAPHY.
Fürer-Haimendorf, Elizabeth von. An
anthropological bibliography of South
Asia. Paris, Mouton, 1958-70. 3 v.
[fl. 130.00 (v. 3)] a 59-1034
Z5115 .F83 MRR Alc.

Harvard University. Library.
Southern Asia: Cambridge;
Distributed by Harvard University
Press, 1968. iv, 543 p. 016.954
68-15927
Z3185 .H3 MRR Alc.

SOUTH ASIA--BIBLIOGRAPHY--CATALOGS.
United States. Library of Congress.
Orientalia Division. Southern Asia
accessions list. v. 1- Jan. 1952-
Washington. 016.95 52-60012
Z663.38 .S8 MRR Alc MRR Alc Full
set

SOUTH ASIA--DESCRIPTION AND TRAVEL--
GUIDE-BOOKS.
A Handbook for travellers in India,
Pakistan, Burma and Ceylon. New York
[etc.] Barnes & Noble [etc.] 63-875

Began publication in 1892.
DS406 .H3 MRR Alc Latest edition

SOUTH ASIA--HISTORY--BIBLIOGRAPHY.
Case, Margaret H. South Asian
history, 1750-1950; Princeton, N.J.,
Princeton University Press, 1968.
xiii, 561 p. 016.954 67-21019
Z3185 .C3 MRR Alc.

SOUTH ATLANTIC REGION--GAZETTEERS.
United States. Office of Geography.
South Atlantic; Washington, U.S.
Govt. Print. Off., 1957. ii, 53 p.
919.7 57-61543
F3030 .U5 MRR Alc.

SOUTH AUSTRALIA--DIRECTORIES.
Sands & McDougall's directory of
South Australia. Adelaide. 53-28719

DU300 .S3 MRR Alc Latest edition

SOUTH AUSTRALIA--ECONOMIC CONDITIONS--
YEARBOOKS.
South Australian yearbook.
[Adelaide] Commonwealth Bureau of
Census and Statistics, South
Australian Office. 309.1/94/2 79-
709
Began in 1966.
HC636 .S6 MRR Alc Latest edition

SOUTH AUSTRALIA--STATISTICS--YEARBOOKS.
South Australian yearbook.
[Adelaide] Commonwealth Bureau of
Census and Statistics, South
Australian Office. 309.1/94/2 79-
709
Began in 1966.
HC636 .S6 MRR Alc Latest edition

SOUTH CAROLINA--BIBLIOGRAPHY.
Turnbull, Robert James, Bibliography
of South Carolina, 1563-1950.
Charlottesville, University of
Virginia Press [1956-60] 6 v.
016.9757 a 56-3897
Z1333 .T8 MRR Alc.

SOUTH CAROLINA--BIOGRAPHY.
Biographical directory of the South
Carolina House of Representatives.
[1st ed.] Columbia, University of
South Carolina Press [1974- v.
328.757/092/2 B 73-13630
JK4278 .B56 MRR Alc.

South Carolina. General assembly.
Legislative manual ... Columbia,
S.C. 16-27080
JK4271 .A4 MRR Alc Latest edition

SOUTH CAROLINA--BIOGRAPHY--DICTIONARIES.
Reynolds, Emily Bellinger.
Biographical directory of the Senate
of the State of South Carolina, 1776-
1964. Columbia, South Carolina
Archives Dept., 1964. ix, 358 p.
64-64629
JK4276 .R4 1964 MRR Biog.

SOUTH CAROLINA--DESCRIPTION AND TRAVEL--
GUIDE-BOOKS.
Writers' program. South Carolina.
South Carolina: a guide to the
Palmetto state, New York, Oxford
university press [1941] xxvii, 514
p. 917.57 41-52304
F269 .W7 MRR Ref Desk.

SOUTH CAROLINA--DIRECTORIES.
The South Carolina almanac. 1968-
Columbia, S.C., Pramac Associates.
917.57/003 70-15579
F269 .S75 MRR Alc Latest edition

SOUTH CAROLINA--EXECUTIVE DEPARTMENTS.
South Carolina. General assembly.
Legislative manual ... Columbia,
S.C. 16-27080
JK4271 .A4 MRR Alc Latest edition

The South Carolina almanac. 1968-
Columbia, S.C., Pramac Associates.
917.57/003 70-15579
F269 .S75 MRR Alc Latest edition

SOUTH CAROLINA--HISTORY.
Wallace, David Duncan, South
Carolina, a short history, 1520-1948.
Chapel Hill, University of North
Carolina Press, 1951. xi, 753 p.
975.7 51-13847
F269 .W26 MRR Alc.

SOUTH CAROLINA--HISTORY--COLONIAL
PERIOD, CA. 1600-1775--SOURCES.
Salley, Alexander Samuel, ed.
Narratives of early Carolina, 1650-
1708, New York, C. Scribner's sons,
1911. xi p., 2 l., 3-388 p. 11-
9548
E187.07 S3 MRR Alc.

SOUTH CAROLINA--HISTORY--BIBLIOGRAPHY.
Turnbull, Robert James, Bibliography
of South Carolina, 1563-1950.
Charlottesville, University of
Virginia Press [1956-60] 6 v.
016.9757 a 56-3897
Z1333 .T8 MRR Alc.

SOUTH CAROLINA--IMPRINTS.
Turnbull, Robert James, Bibliography
of South Carolina, 1563-1950.
Charlottesville, University of
Virginia Press [1956-60] 6 v.
016.9757 a 56-3897
Z1333 .T8 MRR Alc.

SOUTH CAROLINA--INDUSTRIES--DIRECTORIES.
Industrial directory of South
Carolina. Columbia, Research
Division, South Carolina State
Development Board. 338/.0025/757 75-
615660
HC107.S7A363 MRR Alc Latest
edition

SOUTH CAROLINA--MANUFACTURES--
DIRECTORIES.
Directory of Central Atlantic States
manufacturers; 1.- ed.; 1950-
Baltimore, T. K. Sanderson
Organization. 670.58 50-2706
T12 .D485 Sci RR Latest edition /
MRR Alc Latest edition

Industrial directory of South
Carolina. Columbia, Research
Division, South Carolina State
Development Board. 338/.0025/757 75-
615660
HC107.S7A363 MRR Alc Latest
edition

SOUTH CAROLINA--POLITICS AND GOVERNMENT.
The South Carolina almanac. 1968-
Columbia, S.C., Pramac Associates.
917.57/003 70-15579
F269 .S75 MRR Alc Latest edition

SOUTH CAROLINA--POLITICS AND GOVERNMENT-
-1775-1865.
Freehling, William W., Prelude to
Civil War: [1st ed.] New York,
Harper & Row [1966] xiii, 395 p.
973.561 66-10629
E384.3 .F7 MRR Alc.

SOUTH CAROLINA--REGISTERS.
Biographical directory of the South
Carolina House of Representatives.
[1st ed.] Columbia, University of
South Carolina Press [1974- v.
328.757/092/2 B 73-13630
JK4278 .B56 MRR Alc.

South Carolina. General assembly.
Legislative manual ... Columbia,
S.C. 16-27080
JK4271 .A4 MRR Alc Latest edition

The South Carolina almanac. 1968-
Columbia, S.C., Pramac Associates.
917.57/003 70-15579
F269 .S75 MRR Alc Latest edition

SOUTH CAROLINA--STATISTICS.
Conklin, J. Douglas. Selected South
Carolina economic data, [Columbia]
Bureau of Business and Economic
Research, University of South
Carolina, 1969. 114 p. [2.50]
330.9757 73-631385
HA626 .C63 MRR Alc.

The South Carolina almanac. 1968-
Columbia, S.C., Pramac Associates.
917.57/003 70-15579
F269 .S75 MRR Alc Latest edition

SOUTH CAROLINA. GENERAL ASSEMBLY--
REGISTERS.
South Carolina. General assembly.
Legislative manual ... Columbia,
S.C. 16-27080
JK4271 .A4 MRR Alc Latest edition

SOUTH CAROLINA. GENERAL ASSEMBLY--RULES
AND PRACTICE.
South Carolina. General assembly.
Legislative manual ... Columbia,
S.C. 16-27080
JK4271 .A4 MRR Alc Latest edition

SOUTH CAROLINA. GENERAL ASSEMBLY. HOUSE
OF REPRESENTATIVES--BIOGRAPHY--
COLLECTED WORKS.
Biographical directory of the South
Carolina House of Representatives.
[1st ed.] Columbia, University of
South Carolina Press [1974- v.
328.757/092/2 B 73-13630
JK4278 .B56 MRR Alc.

SOUTH CAROLINA. GENERAL ASSEMBLY. HOUSE
OF REPRESENTATIVES--HISTORY--COLLECTED
WORKS.
Biographical directory of the South
Carolina House of Representatives.
[1st ed.] Columbia, University of
South Carolina Press [1974- v.
328.757/092/2 B 73-13630
JK4278 .B56 MRR Alc.

SOUTH CAROLINA. GENERAL ASSEMBLY. HOUSE
OF REPRESENTATIVES--REGISTERS--
COLLECTED WORKS.
Biographical directory of the South
Carolina House of Representatives.
[1st ed.] Columbia, University of
South Carolina Press [1974- v.
328.757/092/2 B 73-13630
JK4278 .B56 MRR Alc.

SOUTH CAROLINA. GENERAL ASSEMBLY.
SENATE--HISTORY.
Reynolds, Emily Bellinger.
Biographical directory of the Senate
of the State of South Carolina, 1776-
1964. Columbia, South Carolina
Archives Dept., 1964. ix, 358 p.
64-64629
JK4276 .R4 1964 MRR Biog.

SOUTH DAKOTA.
Federal Writers' Project. South
Dakota. South Dakota, a guide to the
State. 2d ed. completely revised
New York, Hastings House [1952]
xxvii, 421 p. 917.83 52-7601
F656 .F45 1952 MRR Ref Desk.

SOUTH DAKOTA--DESCRIPTION AND TRAVEL--
GUIDE-BOOKS.
Federal Writers' Project. South
Dakota. South Dakota, a guide to the
State. 2d ed. completely revised
New York, Hastings House [1952]
xxvii, 421 p. 917.83 52-7601
F656 .F45 1952 MRR Ref Desk.

SOUTH DAKOTA--HISTORY.
Schell, Herbert Samuel, History of
South Dakota, [2d ed., rev.]
Lincoln, University of Nebraska
Press, 1968. xiii, 444 p. [6.95]
978.3 68-6401
F651 .S29 1968 MRR Alc.

SOUTH DAKOTA--POLITICS AND GOVERNMENT.
South Dakota. Legislature. South
Dakota legislative manual. [Pierre,
State Pub. Co.] ca 10-1009
   JK6531 MRR Alc Latest edition

SOUTH DAKOTA--REGISTERS.
South Dakota. Legislature. South
Dakota legislative manual. [Pierre,
State Pub. Co.] ca 10-1009
   JK6531 MRR Alc Latest edition

SOUTH-WEST AFRICA--GAZETTEERS.
United States. Office of Geography.
South Africa: Washington, 1954. 2
v. (1081 p.) 916.8/003 73-10017
   DT752 .U65 MRR Alc.

SOUTHAMPTON, ENG.--DIRECTORIES.
Kelly's directory of Southampton and
neighbourhood. Kingston upon Thames,
[Eng., etc.] 53-28204
   DA690.S69 K4 MRR Alc Latest
   edition

SOUTHEAST ASIAN STUDIES.
Tilman, Robert O. International
biographical directory of Southeast
Asia specialists [Ann Arbor, Mich.]
Interuniversity Southeast Asia
Committee, Association for Asian
Studies. [Distributed by Southeast
Asia Studies Center for International
Studies, Ohio University, Athens,
Ohio] 1968. xxxv, 337 p.
915.9/0072/022 76-631592
   DS510.7 .T5 MRR Biog.

SOUTHEASTERN ASIA
see Asia, Southeastern

SOUTHERN AFRICA
see Africa, Southern

SOUTHERN BAPTIST CONVENTION--
DICTIONARIES.
Encyclopedia of Southern Baptists.
Nashville, Broadman Press [1958-71]
3 v. (xxviii, 2064 p.) [$9.95 (v.
3)] 286.175 58-5417
   BX6211 .E5 MRR Alc.

SOUTHERN BAPTIST CONVENTION--HISTORY.
Barnes, William Wright. The Southern
Baptist Convention, 1845-1953.
Nashville, Broadman Press [1954] x,
330 p. 286.175 53-13534
   BX6207 .A4083 MRR Alc.

SOUTHERN STATES--BIBLIOGRAPHY.
Woodward, Comer Vann. Origins of the
new South, 1877-1913, [Baton Rouge]
Louisiana State University Press
[c1971] xi, 654 p. [$12.50]
917.5/03/4 77-168397
   F215 .W85 1971 MRR Alc.

SOUTHERN STATES--BIOGRAPHY--
DICTIONARIES.
Personalities of the South. Raleigh,
N.C. 920.075 73-4535
   CT213 .P38 MRR Biog Latest edition

Who's who in the South and Southwest.
1st ed.; 1947- Chicago, Marquis-
Who's Who [etc.] 920.073 50-58231
   E176 .W645 MRR Biog Latest edition

SOUTHERN STATES--CIVILIZATION.
Peirce, Neal R. The Deep South
States of America; [1st ed.] New
York, Norton [1974] 528 p.
917.6/03/4 73-18244
   F216.2 .P44 MRR Alc.

SOUTHERN STATES--DESCRIPTION AND TRAVEL-
-BIBLIOGRAPHY.
Clark, Thomas Dionysius, ed. Travels
in the new South, [1st ed.] Norman,
University of Oklahoma Press [1962]
2 v. 016.9175 62-10772
   Z1251.S7 C38 MRR Alc.

Clark, Thomas Dionysius, ed. Travels
in the Old South, [1st ed.] Norman,
University of Oklahoma Press [1956-
v. 016.9175 56-8016
   Z1251.S7 C4 MRR Alc.

Coulter, Ellis Merton. Travels in
the Confederate States, [1st ed.]
Norman, Univ. of Oklahoma Press,
1948. xiv, 289 p. 016.9175 48-
7183
   Z1251.S7 C68 MRR Alc.

SOUTHERN STATES--DESCRIPTION AND TRAVEL-
-GUIDE-BOOKS.
American Automobile Association.
Southeastern tour book including the
West Indies. Washington. 629.281
53-40435
   GV1024 .A215 MRR Alc Latest
   edition

Fodor, Eugene. Southeast: Florida,
South Carolina, Georgia, Alabama,
Mississippi 2d, rev. ed.
Litchfield, Conn.] Fodor's Modern
Guides; distributor: D. McKay Co.,
New York [1967] 399 p. 917.5/04/4
67-20080
   F207.3 .F6 1967 MRR Alc.

SOUTHERN STATES--ECONOMIC CONDITIONS.
Phillips, Ulrich Bonnell. American
Negro slavery; New York, London, D.
Appleton and company, 1918. xi, 529
p. 18-11187
   E441 .P549 MRR Alc.

Woodman, Harold D., ed. Slavery and
the Southern economy; New York,
Harcourt, Brace & World [1966] x,
261 p. 326.0975 66-18864
   E441 .W876 MRR Alc.

SOUTHERN STATES--HISTORY.
Simkins, Francis Butler, A history
of the South. 3d ed. New York,
Knopf, 1963. xiii, 675, xxiv p.
975 63-16714
   F209 .S5 1963 MRR Alc.

SOUTHERN STATES--HISTORY--COLONIAL
PERIOD, CA. 1600-1775.
Craven, Wesley Frank, The southern
colonies in the seventeenth century,
1607-1689. [Baton Rouge] Louisiana
State Univ. Press, 1949. xv, 451 p.
975 49-3595
   F212 .C7 MRR Alc.

SOUTHERN STATES--HISTORY--REVOLUTION,
1775-1783.
Alden, John Richard, The South in
the Revolution, 1763-1789. [Baton
Rouge] Louisiana State University
Press, 1957. xv, 442 p. 975 57-
12096
   F213 .A4 MRR Alc.

SOUTHERN STATES--HISTORY--1775-1865.
Abernethy, Thomas Perkins, The South
in the new nation, 1789-1819. [Baton
Rouge] Louisiana State University
Press, 1961. xvi, 529 p. 975 61-
15488
   F213 .A2 MRR Alc.

Sydnor, Charles Sackett, The
development of Southern sectionalism,
1819-1848. [Baton Rouge] Louisiana
State University Press, 1948. xii,
400 p. 975 48-7627
   F213 .S92 MRR Alc.

SOUTHERN STATES--HISTORY--1865-1877.
Coulter, Ellis Merton, The South
during reconstruction, 1865-1877.
[Baton Rouge] Louisiana State
University Press, 1947. xii, 426 p.
975 48-5161
   F216 .C6 MRR Alc.

SOUTHERN STATES--HISTORY--1865-
Clark, Thomas Dionysius, The South
since Appomattox; New York, Oxford
University Press, 1967. vii, 438 p.
975.04 66-22259
   F215 .C62 MRR Alc.

Woodward, Comer Vann, Origins of the
new South, 1877-1913, [Baton Rouge]
Louisiana State University Press
[c1971] xi, 654 p. [$12.50]
917.5/03/4 77-168397
   F215 .W85 1971 MRR Alc.

SOUTHERN STATES--INDUSTRIES.
Schwab, John Christopher, The
Confederate States of America, 1861-
1865; New York, B. Franklin [1968]
xi, 332 p. 330.975 68-56580
   HC105.65 .S38 1968 MRR Alc.

SOUTHERN STATES--POLITICS AND
GOVERNMENT--1775-1865.
Craven, Avery Odelle, The growth of
Southern nationalism, 1848-1862.
[Baton Rouge] Louisiana State
University Press [and] the
Littlefield Fund for Southern History
of the University of Texas [Austin]
1953. xi, 433 p. 975 53-11470
   F213 .C75 MRR Alc.

SOUTHERN STATES--POLITICS AND
GOVERNMENT--1951-
Peirce, Neal R. The Deep South
States of America; [1st ed.] New
York, Norton [1974] 528 p.
917.6/03/4 73-18244
   F216.2 .P44 MRR Alc.

SOUTHERN STATES--RACE QUESTION.
Peirce, Neal R. The Deep South
States of America; [1st ed.] New
York, Norton [1974] 528 p.
917.6/03/4 73-18244
   F216.2 .P44 MRR Alc.

SOUTHERN STATES--SOCIAL CONDITIONS.
Woodward, Comer Vann. Origins of the
new South, 1877-1913, [Baton Rouge]
Louisiana State University Press
[c1971] xi, 654 p. [$12.50]
917.5/03/4 77-168397
   F215 .W85 1971 MRR Alc.

SOUTHERN STATES--SOCIAL LIFE AND
CUSTOMS.
Botkin, Benjamin Albert, ed. A
treasury of southern folklore; New
York, Crown Publishers [1949] xxiv,
776 p. 398 49-11786
   GR108 .B6 MRR Alc.

SOUTHERN STATES--STATISTICS.
Dodd, Donald B. Historical
statistics of the South, 1790-1970;
University, University of Alabama
Press [1973] vi, 85 p. 317.5 73-
1575
   HA218 .D63 MRR Ref Desk.

SOUTHLAND, N.Z.--COMMERCE--DIRECTORIES.
Universal business directory for
Otago-Southland. Auckland, Universal
Business Directories. 53-30674
   HC623.08 U5 MRR Alc Latest edition

SOUTHLAND, N.Z.--INDUSTRIES--
DIRECTORIES.
Universal business directory for
Otago-Southland. Auckland, Universal
Business Directories. 53-30674
   HC623.08 U5 MRR Alc Latest edition

SOUTHWARK, ENG. GLOBE THEATRE.
Adams, John Cranford, The Globe
Playhouse: [2d ed.] New York,
Barnes & Noble, 1961. x, 435 p.
792.094216 61-14744
   PR2920 .A38 1961 MRR Alc.

SOUTHWEST, NEW--BIBLIOGRAPHY.
Edwards, Elza Ivan, The enduring
desert; [Los Angeles] W. Ritchie
Press, 1969. xiii, 306 p.
016.91794/09/154 68-8306
   Z1251.S8 E32 MRR Alc.

SOUTHWEST, NEW--BIOGRAPHY--DICTIONARIES.
Who's who in the South and Southwest.
1st ed.; 1947- Chicago, Marquis-
Who's Who [etc.] 920.073 50-58231
   E176 .W645 MRR Biog Latest edition

SOUTHWEST, NEW--DESCRIPTION AND TRAVEL--
GUIDE-BOOKS.
American Automobile Association.
Southwestern tour book. Washington.
917.9 59-48032
   F787 .A6 MRR Alc Latest edition

SOUTHWEST, NEW--DISCOVERY AND
EXPLORATION.
Bolton, Herbert Eugene, ed. Spanish
exploration in the Southwest, 1542-
1706, New York, C. Scribner's sons,
1916. xii p., 2 l., 3-487 p. 16-
6066
   E187.07 B6 MRR Alc.

SOUTHWEST, OLD--BIBLIOGRAPHY.
Rader, Jesse Lee, South of forty,
[1st ed.] Norman, Univ. of Oklahoma
Press, 1947. xi, 336 p. 016.976
47-5360
   Z1251.S83 R3 MRR Alc.

SOUTHWEST, OLD--DESCRIPTION AND TRAVEL--
GUIDE-BOOKS.
American Automobile Association.
South central tour book. Washington.
917.6 59-43018
   F396 .A6 MRR Alc Latest edition

SOUTHWEST, OLD--HISTORY.
Philbrick, Francis Samuel, The rise
of the West, 1754-1830, [1st ed.]
New York, Harper & Row [1965] xvii,
398 p. 973 65-21377
   E179.5 .P45 MRR Alc.

SOVIET BLOC
see Communist countries

SPACE BIOLOGY--BIBLIOGRAPHY.
Aerospace medicine and biology; v.
[1]-11; 1952-1962/63. Washington.
016.61698021 56-60078
   Z663.49 .A37 MRR Alc MRR Alc
   Partial set / Sci RR Full set

SPACE FLIGHT.
see also Astronautics

Astronautics and aeronautics;
1915/60- Washington, Scientific and
Technical Information Division,
National Aeronautics and Space
Administration [etc.; for sale by the
Superintendent of Documents, U.S.
Govt. Print. Off.] 65-60308
   TL521.3.A8 A3 MRR Alc Partial set

SPACE FLIGHT TO THE MOON.
see also Project Apollo

SPACE MEDICINE--BIBLIOGRAPHY.
Aerospace medicine and biology; v.
[1]-11; 1952-1962/63. Washington.
016.61698021 56-60078
   Z663.49 .A37 MRR Alc MRR Alc
   Partial set / Sci RR Full set

SPACE SCIENCES.
see also Astronomy

see also Outer space

SPACE SCIENCES--BIBLIOGRAPHY.
United States. Library of Congress.
Science and Technology Division.
Space science and technology books,
1957-1961; Washington [For sale by
the Superintendent of Documents, U.S.
Govt. Print. Off.] 1962 [i.e. 1963]
iii, 133 p. 016.6294 62-60086
   Z663.41 .S65 MRR Alc.

SPACE SHIPS--PILOTS
see Astronauts

SPACE VEHICLES.
see also Artificial satellites

Ordway, Frederick Ira. International
missile and spacecraft guide New
York, McGraw-Hill, 1960. 1 v.
(various pagings)   623.4513 59-
14463
UG630 .O67 MRR Alc.

SPACE VEHICLES--MATERIALS.
United States. Library of Congress.
Science and Technology Division.
Materials research chronology, 1917-
1957. Dayton, Directorate of
Materials and Processes, Aeronautical
Systems Division, Wright Patterson
Air Force Base, 1962. viii, 59 p.
620.1 63-60204
Z663.41 .M33 MRR Alc.

SPACE VEHICLES--PROPULSION SYSTEMS.
see also Rocketry

SPAIN--BIBLIOGRAPHY.
Dorn, Georgette M. Latin America,
Spain, and Portugal; an annotated
bibliography of paperback books.
Washington, Library of Congress,
1971. 180 p. [$0.75] 016.818 71-
37945
Z663.32 .A5 no. 32 MRR Alc.

Foulché-Delbosc, Raymond, Manuel de
l'hispanisant. New York, G. P.
Putnam's sons, 1920- v.   20-
16867
Z2681.A1 F7 MRR Alc.

Hispanic Foundation bibliographical
series. no. 1- 1942- Washington,
Library of Congress, Reference Dept.
42-38547
Z663.32 .A5 MRR Alc   MRR Alc Full
set

Palau y Dulcet, Antonio, 1867-1954.
Manual del librero hispano-americano;
2. ed. corr. y aumentada por el
autor. Barcelona, A. Palau, 1948-
v.   015.46 49-2664
Z2681 .P16 MRR Alc.

SPAIN--BIBLIOGRAPHY--CATALOGS.
Harvard University. Library. Spanish
history and literature; Cambridge;
distributed by the Harvard University
Press, 1972. 771 p.   016.9146/03
72-75827
Z2709 .H35 MRR Alc.

SPAIN--BIBLIOGRAPHY--PERIODICALS.
Bibliografía española. 1958-
Madrid, Direccion General de
Archivos y Bibliotecas. 60-44645
Z2685 .B583 MRR Alc Full set

SPAIN--BIO-BIBLIOGRAPHY.
San Vicente, Faustina. Diccionario
de literatura española. Madrid,
Ediciones Boris Bureba [1954] 212 p.
55-42212
Z2690 .S3 MRR Alc.

SPAIN--BIOGRAPHY.
Agramonte y Cortijo, Francisco,
Diccionario cronológico biográfico
universal; [2. ed. corr. y muy
aumentada] [Madrid, Aguilar [1952]
1266 p.   57-18055
CT183 .A4 1952 MRR Biog.

Diccionario de historia de España.
2. ed., corr. y aum. Madrid,
Ediciones de la Revista de Occidente
[1968?] 3 v.   73-367315
DP56 .D5 1968 MRR Alc.

Directorio de consejeros y
directores. ed. 1861/62- Madrid.
64-36554
HC382 .D5 MRR Alc Latest edition

Heráldica; Madrid. 53-25105
DP11 .H4 MRR Biog Latest edition

SPAIN--BIOGRAPHY--DICTIONARIES.
Esperabe Arteaga, Enrique,
Diccionario enciclopédico ilustrado
y crítico de los hombres de España.
[Nueva ed., reformada, ampliada y
completada] Madrid, Artes Gráficas
Ibarra [1957?] 530 p.   57-27844
DP58 .E82 MRR Biog.

Pintores españoles contemporáneos;
Madrid, Estiarte [1972] 250 p.
759.6 73-314037
ND808 .P48 MRR Biog.

Who's who in Spain. 1st- ed.; 1963-
[Montreal] Intercontinental Book
and Pub. Co.   64-841
DP271.A2 W5 MRR Biog Latest
edition

SPAIN--CIVILIZATION--HISTORY.
Peers, Edgar Allison, ed. Spain;
5th ed., rev. and enl. London,
Methuen [1956] xii, 319 p.   914.6
56-58806
DP66 .P4 1956 MRR Alc.

SPAIN--COLONIES--OFFICIALS AND
EMPLOYEES--BIBLIOGRAPHY.
Pena Camara, Jose Maria de la. A
list of Spanish residencias in the
Archives of the Indies, 1516-1775;
Washington, Library of Congress,
Reference Dept.; 1955. x, 109 p.
016.98 55-60017
Z663.32.S7 MRR Alc.

SPAIN--COLONIES--AFRICA--GOVERNMENT
PUBLICATIONS--BIBLIOGRAPHY.
Rishworth, Susan Knoke. Spanish-
speaking Africa; Washington, Library
of Congress; for sale by the Supt. of
Docs., U.S. Govt. Print. Off., 1973.
xiii, 66 p. [$1.00] 015/.6 73-
10274
Z663.285 .S6 MRR Alc.

SPAIN--COLONIES--NORTH AMERICA.
Lowery, Woodbury, The Spanish
settlements within the present limits
of the United States, 1513-1561, New
York, London, G. P. Putnam's sons,
1901. xiii, 515 p. 973.16 01-
11942
E123 .L91 MRR Alc.

SPAIN--COMMERCE--DIRECTORIES.
Anuario comercial iberoamericano.
[Madrid] OFICE. 380.1/025 74-644606
HF3683 .A48 MRR Alc Latest edition

Anuario general de España "Bailly-
Bailliere--Riera." 2. epoca, ano 1-
1912- [Barcelona, Ediciones Ge.
Mon, etc.] 12-25419
DP11 .A7 MRR Alc Latest edition*

Guía industrial y comercial de
España. Barcelona. 48-33959
HF5208 .G8 MRR Alc Latest edition

Kompass; manual de información de la
economía española. 1.- ed.; 1960-
Madrid, Kompass España, S.A. 62-
65190
HF3683 .K6 MRR Alc Latest edition

Prodei; 1952- [Madrid] 52-38723
HF3683 .C32 MRR Alc Latest edition

Spanish Lusitanian American trade
directory. 1st- ed.; 1961/62-
Madrid. 63-34152
HF54.S7 S6 MRR Alc Latest edition

SPAIN--DESCRIPTION AND TRAVEL--1951- --
GUIDE-BOOKS.
Espagne. Paris, Hachette [1973]
1060 p.   914.6/04/82 73-169064
DP14 .E8 1973 MRR Alc.

Fodor's Spain. New York, D. McKay.
914.6/04/82 72-626505
DP14 .S629 MRR Alc Latest edition

Haggart, Stanley Mills. Spain on $5
a day, [New York, A. Frommer;
distributed by Simon and Schuster,
1968] 288 p.   914.6/04/82 68-4429

DP14 .H24 1968 MRR Alc.

SPAIN--DESCRIPTION AND TRAVEL--1951- --
TOURS.
Levi, Avraham. Bazak guide to Spain.
Tel Aviv, Bazak Israel Guidebook
Publishers; distributed by Harper &
Row, New York. [$4.95] 914.6/04/82
74-644071
DP14 .L48 MRR Alc Latest edition

SPAIN--DESCRIPTION AND TRAVEL--GUIDE-
BOOKS.
Espagne. 1952/53- Paris, Pneu
Michelin, Services de tourisme [etc.]
629.281 53-38884
GV1025.S7 E77 MRR Alc Latest
edition

Espagne. Paris, Hachette [1973]
1060 p.   914.6/04/82 73-169064
DP14 .E8 1973 MRR Alc.

Levi, Avraham. Bazak guide to Spain.
Tel Aviv, Bazak Israel Guidebook
Publishers; distributed by Harper &
Row, New York. [$4.95] 914.6/04/82
74-644071
DP14 .L48 MRR Alc Latest edition

Lowe, Alfonso. The companion guide
to the South of Spain. London,
Collins, 1973. [2], 445, [20] p.
[£3.00] 914.6/8/0482 73-177932
DP295 .L68 MRR Alc.

SPAIN--DIRECTORIES.
Anuario general de España "Bailly-
Bailliere--Riera." 2. epoca, ano 1-
1912- [Barcelona, Ediciones Ge.
Mon, etc.] 12-25419
DP11 .A7 MRR Alc Latest edition*

SPAIN--ECONOMIC CONDITIONS.
Vicens Vives, Jaime. An economic
history of Spain Princeton, N.J.,
Princeton University Press, 1969.
viii, 825 p.   330.946 66-10930
HC383 .V513 MRR Alc.

SPAIN--EXECUTIVE DEPARTMENTS.
Spain. Presidencia del Gobierno.
Guía de la administración del
Estado. 1960- Madrid. 64-50374
JN8104 .A32 MRR Alc Latest edition

SPAIN--FOREIGN RELATIONS--UNITED STATES.
Chadwick, French Ensor, The
relations of the United States and
Spain: the Spanish-American war, New
York, C. Scribner's sons, 1911. 2 v.
11-23013
E715 .C43 MRR Alc.

SPAIN--GAZETTEERS.
Anuario general de España "Bailly-
Bailliere--Riera." 2. epoca, ano 1-
1912- [Barcelona, Ediciones Ge.
Mon, etc.] 12-25419
DP11 .A7 MRR Alc Latest edition*

Diccionario geográfico de España.
Madrid, Ediciones Prensa Gráfica,
1956-61. 17 v.   58-27593
DP12 .D5 MRR Alc.

United States. Office of Geography.
Spain and Andorra; official standard
names approved by the United States
Board on Geographic Names.
Washington, 1961. ix, 651 p.   914.6
61-61785
DP12 .U6 MRR Alc.

SPAIN--HISTORY.
Hills, George. Spain. New York,
Praeger [1970] 480 p. [9.50]
946/.009 70-100936
DP66 .H55 1970b MRR Alc.

Livermore, Harold Victor, A history
of Spain. London, Allen & Unwin
[1958] 478 p. 946 59-189
DP66 .L66 1958 MRR Alc.

SPAIN--HISTORY--CIVIL WAR, 1936-1939--
REFUGEES.
Amo, Julián, La obra impresa de los
intelectuales españoles en América,
1936-1945; Stanford, Stanford
University Press [1950] xiii, 145 p.
013.973046 50-9025
Z1609.R38 A7 MRR Alc.

SPAIN--HISTORY--BIBLIOGRAPHY.
Indice histórico español.
Bibliografía histórica de España e
Hispanoamérica. v. 1- enero/marzo
1953- [Barcelona] Editorial Teide.
57-34741
Z2696 .I6 MRR Alc Full set

SPAIN--HISTORY--BIBLIOGRAPHY--CATALOGS.
Hispanic Society of America. Library.
Catalogue of the library. Boston,
G. K. Hall, 1962. 10 v. (10048 p.)
62-52682
Z881 .N639 MRR Alc (Dk33)

SPAIN--HISTORY--CHRONOLOGY.
Diccionario de historia de España.
2. ed., corr. y aum. Madrid,
Ediciones de la Revista de Occidente
[1968?] 3 v.   73-367315
DP56 .D5 1968 MRR Alc.

SPAIN--HISTORY--DICTIONARIES.
Diccionario de historia de España.
2. ed., corr. y aum. Madrid,
Ediciones de la Revista de Occidente
[1968?] 3 v.   73-367315
DP56 .D5 1968 MRR Alc.

SPAIN--IMPRINTS.
Bibliografía española. 1958-
Madrid, Direccion General de
Archivos y Bibliotecas. 60-44645
Z2685 .B583 MRR Alc Full set

Catálogo general de la librería
española, 1931-1950. Madrid,
Instituto Nacional del Libro
Español, 1957-65. 4 v.   58-24533
Z2681 .C34 MRR Alc.

Foulché-Delbosc, Raymond, Manuel de
l'hispanisant. New York, G. P.
Putnam's sons, 1920- v.   20-
16867
Z2681.A1 F7 MRR Alc.

Hispanic Society of America. Printed
books, 1468-1700, in the Hispanic
Society of America; New York, 1965.
xlii, 614 p.   018.1 65-22528
Z1012 .H58 MRR Alc.

Hispanic society of America. Library.
List of books printed 1601-1700, in
the library of the Hispanic society
of America, New York, Printed by
order of the trustees, 1938. xxvi,
972 p.   015.46 38-15765
Z2682 .H671 MRR Alc.

Libros en venta en Hispanoamérica y
España; [1. ed.] New York, R. R.
Bowker Co., 1964. 1891 p.   015.8
64-3492
Z1601 .L59 MRR Alc.

Libros españoles: catálogo ISBN.
1973- Madrid, Agencia Española del
International Standard Book Number
(ISBN) 74-644456
Z2681 .L53 MRR Alc Latest edition

SPAIN--IMPRINTS. (Cont.)
The National union catalog, pre-1956
imprints; London, Mansell, 1968- v.
021.6/4 67-30001
Z663.7.L5115 MRR Alc (Dk 33)

Palau y Dulcet, Antonio, 1867-1954.
Manual del librero hispano-americano;
2. ed. corr. y aumentada por el
autor. Barcelona, A. Palau, 1948-
v.   015.46 49-2664
Z2681 .P16 MRR Alc.

Simón Díaz, José. Bibliografía
de literatura hispánica. 2. ed.
corr. y aumentada. Madrid, Consejo
Superior de Investigaciones
Científicas, Instituto "Miguel de
Cervantes" de Filología Hispánica,
1960- v.   64-5767
Z2691 .S52 MRR Alc.

SPAIN--INDUSTRIES--DIRECTORIES.
Anuario espanol de empresas.
Madrid, Editorial Financiera Alfa
Omega. 338/.0025/46 74-646231
HG4216.Z5 A65 MRR Alc Latest
edition

Directorio de consejeros y
directores. ed. 1961/62- Madrid.
64-36554
HC382 .D5 MRR Alc Latest edition

Guía industrial y comercial de
España. Barcelona. 48-33959
HF5208 .G8 MRR Alc Latest edition

Prodei: 1952- [Madrid] 52-38723
HF3683 .C32 MRR Alc Latest edition

SPAIN--INDUSTRY--DIRECTORIES.
Kompass; manual de información de la
economía española. 1.- ed.; 1960-
Madrid, Kompass España, S.A. 62-
65190
HF3683 .K6 MRR Alc Latest edition

SPAIN--LANGUAGES.
Entwistle, William James. The
Spanish language, [2d ed.] London,
Faber & Faber [1962] vi, 367 p.
460 63-6431
PC4075 .E5 1962 MRR Alc.

SPAIN--NOBILITY.
Instituto Internacional de
Genealogía y Heráldica. Indice
nobiliario español. Madrid,
Ediciones Hidalguía, 1955. 754 p.
55-58623
CS947 .I5 MRR Alc.

Salvador y de Solá, Felipe de.
Títulos nobiliarios. Barcelona,
1955-56 [i.e. 1956] 984 p.   57-
20014
CS947 .S33 MRR Alc.

**SPAIN--POLITICS AND GOVERNMENT--19TH
CENTURY.**
Carr, Raymond. Spain: 1808-1939.
Oxford, Clarendon P., 1966. xxix,
766 p. [63/-]   946 66-72222
DP203 .C3 MRR Alc.

**SPAIN--POLITICS AND GOVERNMENT--20TH
CENTURY.**
Carr, Raymond. Spain: 1808-1939.
Oxford, Clarendon P., 1966. xxix,
766 p. [63/-]   946 66-72222
DP203 .C3 MRR Alc.

**SPAIN--POLITICS AND GOVERNMENT--
HANDBOOKS, MANUALS, ETC.**
Spain. Presidencia del Gobierno.
Guía de la administración del
Estado. 1960- Madrid. 64-50374
JN8104 .A32 MRR Alc Latest edition

SPAIN--REGISTERS.
Heráldica; Madrid. 53-25105
DP11 .H4 MRR Blog Latest edition

SPAIN--SOCIAL CONDITIONS.
Carr, Raymond. Spain: 1808-1939.
Oxford, Clarendon P., 1866. xxix,
766 p. [63/-]   946 66-72222
DP203 .C3 MRR Alc.

SPAIN--SOCIAL REGISTERS.
Heráldica; Madrid. 53-25105
DP11 .H4 MRR Blog Latest edition

SPAIN--STATISTICS.
Spain. Instituto Nacional de
Estadística. Anuario estadístico
de España. Año 1- 1912- Madrid.
39-21738
HA1543 .A5 MRR Alc Latest edition

Spain. Instituto National de
Estadística. Anuario estadístico
de España. Ed. manual. 1941-
[Madrid] 314.6 43-33553
HA1543 .A52 MRR Alc Latest edition

SPAIN. ARMADA--LISTS OF VESSELS.
Spain. Subsecretaría de la Marina
Mercante. Lista oficial de buques.
[Madrid] 09-16189
HE565.S7A2 MRR Alc Latest edition

SPAIN. ARMADA--SIGNALING.
Spain. Subsecretaría de la Marina
Mercante. Lista oficial de buques.
[Madrid] 09-16189
HE565.S7A2 MRR Alc Latest edition

**SPAIN, SOUTHERN--DESCRIPTION AND TRAVEL-
-GUIDE-BOOKS.**
Lowe, Alfonso. The companion guide
to the South of Spain. London,
Collins, 1973. [7], 445, [20] p.
[£3.00]   914.6/8/0482 73-177932
DP295 .L68 MRR Alc.

SPANIARDS IN AMERICA--BIBLIOGRAPHY.
Amo, Julián, La obra impresa de los
intelectuales españoles en América,
1936-1945; Stanford, Stanford
University Press [1950] xiii, 145 p.
013.973046 50-9025
Z1609.R38 A7 MRR Alc.

**SPANISH AMERICAN DRAMA--MICROCARD
CATALOGS.**
Thompson, Lawrence Sidney, A
bibliography of Spanish plays on
microcards, Hamden, Conn., Shoe
String Press, 1968. 490 p.   016.862
68-20280
Z2694.D7 T48 MRR Alc.

**SPANISH AMERICAN LITERATURE--20TH
CENTURY.**
Flakoll, Darwin J., ed. and tr. New
voices of Hispanic America, Boston,
Beacon Press [1962] 226 p.   860.82
62-7248
PQ7087.E5 F55 MRR Alc.

**SPANISH AMERICAN LITERATURE--
BIBLIOGRAPHY.**
Beristain de Souza, José Mariano,
Biblioteca hispano americana
septentrional; [3. ed.] Mexico,
Editorial Fuente Cultural [1947] 5
v. in 2. 015.72 48-9774
Z1412 .B53 MRR Alc.

Brown University. Library. List of
Latin American imprints before 1800,
Providence, 1952. iv, 140 p.   015.8
a 53-2246
Z1610 .B695 MRR Alc.

Cejador y Frauca, Julio, Historia de
la lengua y literatura castellana ...
Madrid, Imprenta Radio, 1916-30. 14
v. in 15.   mrr01-65
PQ6032 .C3 1916 MRR Alc.

**SPANISH AMERICAN LITERATURE--BIO-
BIBLIOGRAPHY.**
Pan American Union. Division of
Philosophy and Letters. Diccionario
de la literatura latinoamericana.
[Ed. provisional] Washington, Unión
Panamericana [1958]-63. 6 v. in 8.
pa 58-19
PQ7081 .P27 MRR Alc.

**SPANISH AMERICAN LITERATURE--
DICTIONARIES.**
Pan American Union. Division of
Philosophy and Letters. Diccionario
de la literatura latinoamericana.
[Ed. provisional] Washington, Unión
Panamericana [1958]-63. 6 v. in 8.
pa 58-19
PQ7081 .P27 MRR Alc.

**SPANISH AMERICAN LITERATURE--HISTORY
AND CRITICISM.**
Anderson Imbert, Enrique, Spanish-
American literature: 2d ed., rev and
updated Detroit, Wayne State
University Press, 1969- v.   [5.95
(v. 1)]   860.9 70-75087
PQ7081 .A56342 MRR Alc.

Cejador y Frauca, Julio, Historia de
la lengua y literatura castellana ...
Madrid, Imprenta Radio, 1916-30. 14
v. in 15.   mrr01-65
PQ6032 .C3 1916 MRR Alc.

SPANISH AMERICAN LITERATURE--INDEXES.
Grismer, Raymond Leonard, A
reference index to twelve thousand
Spanish American authors; New York,
The H. W. Wilson company, 1939. xvi
p., 1 l., 150 p.   016.86 39-32334
Z1601 .G86 MRR Alc.

**SPANISH AMERICAN LITERATURE--OUTLINES,
SYLLABI, ETC.**
Instituto internacional de literatura
iberoamericana. An outline history
of Spanish American literature, New
York, F. S. Crofts & co., 1941. xx
p., 1 l., 170 p.   860.9 41-26596
PQ7081 .I5 MRR Alc.

**SPANISH AMERICAN LITERATURE--
TRANSLATIONS INTO ENGLISH--BIBLIOGRAPHY.**
Granier, James Albert, Latin
American belles-lettres in English
translation; [2d rev. ed.]
Washington, 1943. ii, 33 p.   016.86
44-40918
Z663.32 .A5 no. 1 1943 MRR Alc.

**SPANISH-AMERICAN NEWSPAPERS--
BIBLIOGRAPHY.**
Jordan, Lois B. Mexican Americans;
resources to build cultural
understanding. Littleton, Colo.,
Libraries Unlimited, 1973. 265 p.
016.9172/03 72-94302
Z1361.M4 J67 MRR Alc.

**SPANISH AMERICAN NEWSPAPERS--
BIBLIOGRAPHY--UNION LISTS.**
Latin American newspapers in United
States libraries; Austin, Published
for the Conference on Latin American
History by the University of Texas
Press [1969, c1968] xiv, 619 p.
[20.00]   016.07918 69-63004
Z6947 .C5 MRR Alc.

SPANISH AMERICAN POETRY.
Cohen, John Michael, ed. The Penguin
book of Spanish verse.
[Harmondsworth, Middlesex] Penguin
Books [1956] xxxvi, 441 p.   861.082
57-25550
PQ6176 .C57 MRR Alc.

**SPANISH AMERICAN POETRY--TRANSLATIONS
INTO ENGLISH.**
Flakoll, Darwin J., ed. and tr. New
voices of Hispanic America, Boston,
Beacon Press [1962] 226 p.   860.82
62-7248
PQ7087.E5 F55 MRR Alc.

**SPANISH AMERICANS IN THE UNITED STATES--
BIBLIOGRAPHY.**
United States. Cabinet Committee on
Opportunity for the Spanish Speaking.
The Spanish speaking in the United
States: a guide to materials.
Washington, 1971. iv, 175 p.
016.9173/06/68 75-614612
Z1361.S7 U54 MRR Alc.

**SPANISH AMERICANS IN THE UNITED STATES--
SOCIETIES, ETC.--DIRECTORIES.**
United States. Cabinet Committee on
Opportunity for the Spanish Speaking.
Directory of Spanish speaking
organizations in the United States.
Washington, 1970. x, 224 p.   061
77-608446
E184.S75 A44 MRR Alc.

**SPANISH AMERICANS IN THE UNITED STATES--
STATISTICS.**
United States. Bureau of the Census.
1970 census of population and
housing. [Washington; For sale by
the Supt. of Docs., U.S. Govt. Print.
Off.] 1971- v. [$1.00 (v. 5)
varies]   312/.9/0973 73-186611
HA201 1970 .A542 MRR Alc.

SPANISH DRAMA--BIBLIOGRAPHY.
Thompson, Lawrence Sidney, A
bibliography of Spanish plays on
microcards, Hamden, Conn., Shoe
String Press, 1968. 490 p.   016.862
68-20280
Z2694.D7 T48 MRR Alc.

SPANISH DRAMA--HISTORY AND CRITICISM.
Valbuena Prat, Angel, Historia del
teatro español. [1. ed.]
Barcelona, Noguer [1956] 708 p.   a
57-1257
PN2781 .V3 MRR Alc.

SPANISH DRAMA--MICROCARD CATALOGS.
Thompson, Lawrence Sidney, A
bibliography of Spanish plays on
microcards, Hamden, Conn., Shoe
String Press, 1968. 490 p.   016.862
68-20280
Z2694.D7 T48 MRR Alc.

**SPANISH FICTION--20TH CENTURY--BIO-
BIBLIOGRAPHY.**
Sainz de Robles, Federico Carlos,
La novela española en el siglo XX.
Madrid, Pegaso [c1957] 302 p.   a
58-2588
PQ6144 .S3 MRR Alc.

**SPANISH FICTION--20TH CENTURY--HISTORY
AND CRITICISM.**
Sainz de Robles, Federico Carlos,
La novela española en el siglo XX.
Madrid, Pegaso [c1957] 302 p.   a
58-2588
PQ6144 .S3 MRR Alc.

**SPANISH LANGUAGE--CONVERSATION AND
PHRASE BOOKS.**
Gerrard, Arthur Bryson. Beyond the
dictionary in Spanish: 4th ed.
London, Cassell, 1967. 160 p. [16/-
]   468.3/42 68-83829
PC4680 .G4 1967 MRR Alc.

**SPANISH LANGUAGE--CONVERSATION AND
PHRASE BOOKS--POLYGLOT.**
Dony, Yvonne P. de. Léxico del
lenguaje figurado comparado, Buenos
Aires, Ediciones Desclée, De Brouwer
[1951] 804 p.   52-21901
PB331 .D6 MRR Alc.

SPANISH LANGUAGE--DICTIONARIES.
Academia Española, Madrid.
Diccionario de la lengua española.
[18. ed.] Madrid, 1970. xxix, 1424
p.   75-498386
PC4625 .A3 1970 MRR Alc.

SPANISH LANGUAGE--DICTIONARIES. (Cont.)
Alonso Pedraz, Martín. Enciclopedia
del idioma; Madrid, Aguilar, 1958.
3 v.   58-2215
    PC4667 .A4 MRR Alc.

Casares y Sánchez, Julio,
Diccionario ideológico de la lengua
española; 2. ed., corr., aumentada
y puesta al día. Barcelona,
Editorial G. Gili, 1959. lxxv, 482,
887 p.   59-51822
    PC4625 .C3 1959 MRR Alc.

Diccionario enciclopédico de la
lengua castellana; 3. ed. Paris,
Garnier hermanos, 1900. 2 v.   02-
18897
    PC4625 .D5 1900 MRR Alc.

Diccionario enciclopédico Salvat
universal Barcelona, etc. [Salvat,
1970-   v.   72-883776
    AE61 .D64 MRR Alc.

Enciclopedia universal Sopena;
Barcelona, R. Sopena [1963-   v.
64-49331
    PC4625 .E62 MRR Alc.

Kalveram, Carlos. Diccionario de
ideas y expresiones afines. Madrid,
Aguilar, 1956. xiv, 707 p.   a 57-
6324
    PC4591 .K3 MRR Alc.

Martínez Amador, Emilio María,
Diccionario gramatical, Barcelona,
R. Sopena [1954, c1953] 1498 p.   56-
42415
    PC4101 .M3 MRR Alc.

Moliner, María. Diccionario de uso
del español. Madrid, Editorial
Gredos [1966-67] 2 v.   67-58643
    PC4625 .M6 MRR Alc.

Santamaría, Francisco Javier,
Diccionario general de americanismos
... 1. ed. ... Mejico, D.F.,
Editorial P. Robredo, 1942 [i.e.
1943] 3 v.   467.9   a 43-2977
    PC4822 .S3 MRR Alc.

Vox. 2. ed. corr. y notablemente
ampliada Barcelona, Spes, 1953.
xxxix, 1815 p.   a 53-6116
    PC4625 .V6 1953 MRR Alc.

SPANISH LANGUAGE--DICTIONARIES--ENGLISH.
Cassell's Spanish-English, English-
Spanish dictionary; 6th ed. London,
Cassell, 1968. xv, 1477 p. [42/-]
463/.2 71-396569
    PC4640 .C35 1968 MRR Ref Desk.

Castilla's Spanish and English
technical dictionary. London,
Routledge & Paul [1958] 2 v.   603
58-2320
    T9 .C34 MRR Alc.

Corona Bustamante, Francisco. A new
dictionary of the Spanish-English and
English-Spanish languages. New ed.,
Baltimore, Ottenheimer Publishers,
c1959. 664, 536 p.   463.2 60-20298

    PC4640 .C58 1959 MRR Alc.

Cuyás, Arturo, Appleton's new
Cuyás English-Spanish and Spanish-
English dictionary. 5th ed.; rev.
New York, Appleton-Century-Crofts,
1972. 2 v. in 1. [$7.95] 463/.21
75-182137
    PC4640 .C8 1972 MRR Alc.

Cuyás, Arturo, Appleton's new
Cuyás English-Spanish and Spanish-
English dictionary. 5th ed. New
York, Appleton-Century-Crofts, 1966.
2 v. in 1.   463/.21 66-22193
    PC4640 .C8 1966 MRR Alc.

Diccionario moderno Langenscheidt de
los idiomas ingles y espanol.
Berlin, Munich, Zurich,
Langenscheidt, (1966). 568, 503 p.
[17.00] 79-390437
    PC4640 .D564 MRR Alc.

International encyclopedia of
chemical science. Princeton, N.J.,
Van Nostrand [1964] 1331 p.   540.3
64-1619
    QD5 .I5 1964 MRR Alc.

Moth, Axel Fredrik Carl Mathias,
Glossary of library terms, English,
Danish, Dutch, French, German,
Italian, Spanish, Swedish, Boston,
The Boston book company, 1915. 58 p.
15-3471
    Z1006 .M72 MRR Alc.

The New World Spanish-English and
English-Spanish dictionary. New
York, World Pub. Co. [1969] xvi,
257, 311 p. [$5.95 $6.95 (thumb
indexed)] 463.2 68-17418
    PC4640 .N4 MRR Ref Desk.

Nuevo diccionario general inglés-
español. [español-inglés] Madrid,
E.D.A.F. Ediciones-Distribuciones
[1966] 2 v.   67-51963
    PC4640 .N82 MRR Alc.

Pepper, William M. Dictionary of
newspaper and printing terms; New
York, Columbia University Press
[1959] 344 p.   070.03 59-16345
    PN4728 .P4 MRR Alc.

Sell, Lewis L., Español-inglés
diccionario para especialistas en
seguros, finanzas, derecho, trabajo,
política, comercio; New York, D.
McKay Co. [1957] 650 p.   330.3 57-
3078
    HB61 .S4 MRR Alc.

Simon and Schuster's international
dictionary. New York, Simon and
Schuster [1973] xviii, 1605 p.
[$12.95 (thumb-indexed)] 463/.21
71-180718
    PC4640 .S48 MRR Ref Desk.

Velázquez de la Cadena, Mariano,
New revised Velázquez Spanish and
English dictionary, Chicago, Follett
Pub. Co. [1974] 698, 788 p.
463/.21 74-78935
    PC4640 .V5 1974 MRR Ref Desk.

Vox modern college Spanish and
English dictionary. 2d ed. New
York, Scribner [1972, c1970] xxxi,
1417 p. [$9.95] 463/.21 75-38123

    PC4640 .V6813 1972 MRR Alc.

Walter, Frank Keller, Abbreviations
and technical terms used in book
catalogs and bibliographies, in eight
languages, 1917 handy edition.
Boston, The Boston book company
[1919?] 2 v. in 1.   27-13479
    Z1006 .W261 1919 MRR Alc.

Williams, Edwin Bucher, The Williams
Spanish & English dictionary;
Expanded ed. New York, Scribner
[1973, c1963] xvi, 623, lxiv, 620 p.
[$9.95] 463/.21 72-11299
    PC4640 .W55 1973 MRR Ref Desk.

**SPANISH LANGUAGE--DICTIONARIES--
POLYGLOT.**
Britannica world language dictionary,
[Chicago, 1958] 1483-2015 p.   413
58-4491
    P361 .B7 1958 MRR Alc.

Capitol's concise dictionary.
Bologna, Capitol, 1972. 1051 (i.e.
1207) p.   413 72-172231
    P361 .C3 MRR Alc.

Clason, W. E., Elsevier's dictionary
of computers, automatic control and
data processing. 2d rev. ed. of The
dictionary of automation, computers,
control and measuring. Amsterdam,
New York, Elsevier Pub. Co., 1971.
484 p. [fl78.00] 001.6/4/03 73-
151733
    TJ212.5 .C55 1971 MRR Alc.

Clason, W. E., Supplement to the
Elsevier dictionaries of electronics,
nucleonics and telecommunication.
Amsterdam, New York, Elsevier Pub.
Co., 1963. 633 p.   603 63-11369
    T10 .C55 MRR Alc.

Conference terminology, 2d ed., rev.
and augm. Amsterdam, New York,
Elsevier Pub. Co.; [sole distributors
for the U.S.: American Elsevier Pub.
Co., New York] 1962. 162 p.   413
63-8568
    PB324.C6 C6 1962 MRR Alc.

Cooper, S. A. Concise international
dictionary of mechanics & geology;
New York, Philosophical Library
[1958] viii, 400 p.   621.03 58-
3594
    TJ9 .C6 1958 MRR Alc.

Diccionario enciclopédico abreviado,
7. ed. Madrid, Espasa-Calpe, 1957
[c1954-55] 7 v.   71-205627
    AE61 .D45 1957 MRR Alc.

Dictionar tehnic poliglot: Ediţia
a 2-a. Bucureşti, Editura Tehnica,
1967. xv, 1233 p.   603 68-2971
    T10 .D54 1967 MRR Alc.

Dictionary of chemistry and chemical
technology, in six languages: [Rev.
ed.] Oxford, New York, Pergamon
Press [1966] 1325 p.   540.3 65-
29008
    QD5 .D5 1966 MRR Alc.

Dictionnaire à l'usage de la
librairie ancienne pour les langues:
française, anglaise, allemande,
suédoise, danoise, italienne,
espagnole, hollandaise, Paris, Ligue
internationale de la librairie
ancienne, 1956. 190 p.   655.403 57-
2275
    Z282 .D5 MRR Alc.

The Duden pictorial encyclopedia in
five languages: English, French,
German, Italian, Spanish. 2d enl.
ed. New York, F. Ungar Pub. Co.
[1958] 2 v.   413 58-11093
    P361 .D8 1958 MRR Alc.

Elektrotechnik und Elektrochemie.
München, R. Oldenbourg, 1955. xxiv,
1304 p.   57-18208
    TK9 .E42 1955 MRR Alc.

Elsevier's automobile dictionary in
eight languages: Amsterdam, New
York, Elsevier Pub. Co.; [distributed
by Van Nostrand, Princeton, N.J.]
1960. 946 p.   629.203 59-8946
    TL9 .E43 MRR Alc.

Elsevier's banking dictionary in six
languages: Amsterdam, New York,
Elsevier Pub. Co., 1966. 302 p.
332.103 65-20139
    HG151 .E45 MRR Alc.

Elsevier's dictionary of aeronautics
in six languages: Amsterdam, New
York, Elsevier Pub. Co., 1964. 842
p.   629.1303 63-22063
    TL509 .E4 MRR Alc.

Elsevier's dictionary of chemical
engineering. Amsterdam, New York,
1968. 2 v. [62.50 per vol.]
660/.2/03 68-54865
    TP9 .E38 MRR Alc.

Elsevier's dictionary of cinema,
sound, and music, in six languages:
Amsterdam, New York, Elsevier Pub.
Co., 1956. 948 p.   778.503 56-
13141
    TR847 .E4 MRR Alc.

Elsevier's dictionary of criminal
science, in eight languages:
Amsterdam, New York, Elsevier Pub.
Co.; [distributed by Van Nostrand,
Princeton, N.J.] 1960. xv, 1460 p.
364.03 59-12582
    HV6017 .E4 MRR Alc.

Elsevier's dictionary of electronics
and waveguides, 2d ed., rev. and
enl. Amsterdam, New York, Elsevier
Pub. Co., 1966 [i.e. 1965] 833 p.
621.38103 65-20142
    TK7804 .E4 1965 MRR Alc.

Elsevier's dictionary of general
physics in six languages: Amsterdam,
New York, Elsevier Pub. Co., 1962.
859 p.   530.3 62-13015
    QC5 .E46 MRR Alc.

Elsevier's dictionary of nuclear
science and technology. 2d rev. ed.
Amsterdam, New York, Elsevier Pub.
Co., 1970. 787 p. [$85.00]
539.7/03 72-103357
    QC772 .E4 1970 MRR Alc.

Elsevier's dictionary of television,
radar, and antennas, in six
languages: Amsterdam, New York,
Elsevier Pub. Co., 1955. 760 p.
621.38803 55-6216
    TK6634 .E4 MRR Alc.

Elsevier's lexicon of archive
terminology: Amsterdam, New York,
Elsevier Pub. Co., 1964. 83 p.
025.171014 64-56714
    CD945 .E4 MRR Alc.

Elsevier's medical dictionary in five
languages: Amsterdam, New York,
Elsevier Pub. Co., 1964. 1588 p.
610.3 62-13022
    R121 .E5 1964 MRR Alc.

Elsevier's wood dictionary in seven
languages: Amsterdam, New York,
Elsevier Pub. Co., 1964- v.
634.903 64-14178
    SD431 .E4 MRR Alc.

Great Britain. Naval intelligence
division. A dictionary of naval
equivalents covering English, French,
Italian, Spanish, Russian, Swedish,
Danish, Dutch, German. London, H.M.
Stationery off., 1924. 2 v.   24-
23792
    V24 .G7 MRR Alc.

Haensch, Günther. Dictionary of
international relations and politics;
Amsterdam, New York, Elsevier Pub.
Co., 1965. xv, 638 p.   320.03 64-
8710
    JX1226 .H26 MRR Alc.

Haensch, Günther. Wörterbuch der
Landwirtschaft: 3., überarb. Aufl.
München, Bayerischer
Landwirtschaftverlag [1966] xxiv,
746 p.   630/.3 68-96081
    S411 .H26 1966 MRR Alc.

Hétnyelvü sportszótár: Budapest,
Terra, 1960- v.   61-21333
    GV567 .H45 MRR Alc.

SPANISH LANGUAGE--DICTIONARIES-- (Cont.)
Horn, Stefan F., Glossary of
financial terms. Amsterdam, New
York, Elsevier Pub. Co., 1865. 271
p.   332.03 64-23405
HG151 .H6 MRR Alc.

Borten,Hans Ernest. Export-import
correspondence in four languages
London, Gower Press Ltd., 1970. xi,
2-316 p. [80/-]   382/.03 76-495482

HF1002 .H685 MRR Alc.

Inter-American Statistical Institute.
Statistical vocabulary. 2d ed.
Washington, Pan American Union, 1960.
xi, 83 p.   310.3 pa 60-56
HA17 .I6 1960 MRR Alc.

Intergovernmental Maritime
Consultative Organization. Glossary
of maritime technical terms. London
[c1963] 118 p.   64-56993
V24 .I5 MRR Alc.

International Chamber of Commerce.
Dictionary of advertising and
distribution. Basel, Verlag für
Recht und Gesellschaft, 1954. 1 v.
(unpaged) 659.103 54-24644
HF5803 .I58 1954 MRR Alc.

International Commission on Large
Dams. Dictionnaire technique des
barrages. 2. ed. [Paris, 1960?]
380 p.   627.803 61-805
TC540 .I45 1960 MRR Alc.

International insurance dictionary:
[n.p.: European Conference of
Insurance Supervisory Services, 1959]
xxxi, 1083 p.   368.03 61-35675
HG8025 .I5 MRR Alc.

International Railway Documentation
Bureau. Lexique général des termes
ferroviaires, [2. ed. entierement
refondue et augm.] Amsterdam, J. H.
De Bussy, 1965. 1357 p.   625.1003
66-87434
TF9 .I46 1965 MRR Alc.

Jacks, Graham Vernon. Multilingual
vocabulary of soil science. [2d ed.,
rev. Rome] Land & Water Division,
Food and Agriculture Organization of
the United Nations [1960] xxiii, 428
p.   631.403 60-50105
S591 .J26 1960 MRR Alc.

James, Glenn, ed. Mathematics
dictionary, Multilingual ed.
Princeton, N.J., Van Nostrand [1959]
546 p.   510.3 59-8656
QA5 .J32 1959 MRR Alc.

Labarre, E. J. Dictionary and
encyclopædia of paper and paper-
making. 2d ed., rev. and enl.
London, Oxford University Press,
1952. xxi, 488 p.   676.03 53-29414

TS1085 .L3 1952a MRR Alc.

Lane, Gabriella. Glossary of
geographical names in six languages:
Amsterdam, New York, Elsevier Pub.
Co., 1967. 184 p.   910/.003 66-
25762
G104.5 .L3 MRR Ref Desk.

Lexicon opthalmologicum: Basel, New
York, S. Karger, 1959. 223 p.
617.703 59-44669
RE21 .L45 MRR Alc.

Nijdam, J. Tuinbouwkundig
woordenboek in acht talen. Herziene
en uitgebreide uitg. van de
Woordenlijst voor de tuinbouw in
zeven talen. ['s-Gravenhage,
Staatsdrukkerij- en
Uitgeverijbedrijf; voor alle anderen
landen: Interscience Publishers, New
York] 1961. 504 p.   62-52704
SB45 .N673 MRR Alc.

Pisant, Emmanuel. International
dictionary. Paris, Editions
Moderninter [1958] 373 p.   413 58-
26075
P361 .P5 MRR Alc.

Rae, Kenneth, ed. Lexique
international de termes techniques de
theatre Bruxelles, Elsevier [1959]
139 p.   60-26926
PN2035 .R3 MRR Alc.

Sachs, Wolfgang, ed.
Lebensversicherungstechnisches
Worterbuch. Wurzburg, K. Thiltsch,
1954. 308 p.   56-16246
HG8759 .S3 MRR Alc.

Six-language dictionary of
automation, electronics and
scientific instruments: London,
Iliffe Books: Englewood Cliffs, N.J.,
Prentice-Hall [1962] 732 p.
621.3803 63-5414
TK7804 .S5 1962 MRR Alc.

Skandinaviska banken, a.-b. Banking
terms: French, German, Italian,
Spanish, Swedish. Stockholm [1964]
65 p.   65-87814
HG151 .S46 MRR Alc.

Thompson, Anthony. Vocabularium
bibliothecarii. 2d ed. [Paris]
UNESCO, 1962. 627 p.   63-5650
Z1006 .T47 1962a MRR Alc.

Union européenne des experts
comptables économiques et
financiers. Lexique U.E.C. Lexicon.
Dusseldorf, Verlagsbuchhandlung des
Instituts der Wirtschaftsprufer,
1961. 1 v. (various pagings) 63-
31440
HF5621 .U5 MRR Alc.

**SPANISH LANGUAGE--ETYMOLOGY--
DICTIONARIES.**
Corominas, Juan. Diccionario
crítico etimológico de la lengua
castellana. Madrid, Gredos [1954-57]
4 v.   a 55-4539
PC4580 .C6 MRR Alc.

**SPANISH LANGUAGE--GLOSSARIES,
VOCABULARIES, ETC.**
Gerrard, Arthur Bryson. Beyond the
dictionary in Spanish: 4th ed.
London, Cassell, 1967. 160 p. [16/-
] 468.3/42 68-83829
PC4680 .G4 1967 MRR Alc.

SPANISH LANGUAGE--GRAMMAR, HISTORICAL.
Martinez Amador, Emilio María,
Diccionario gramatical. Barcelona,
R. Sopena [1954, c1953] 1498 p. 56-
42415
PC4101 .M3 MRR Alc.

SPANISH LANGUAGE--HISTORY.
Cejador y Frauca, Julio, Historia de
la lengua y literatura castellana ...
Madrid, Imprenta Radio, 1916-30. 14
v. in 15. mrr01-65
PQ6032 .C3 1916 MRR Alc.

Entwistle, William James, The
Spanish language, [2d ed.] London,
Faber & Faber [1962] vi, 367 p.
460 63-6431
PC4075 .E5 1962 MRR Alc.

**SPANISH LANGUAGE--PROVINCIALISMS--
SPANISH AMERICA.**
Santamaría, Francisco Javier,
Diccionario general de americanismos
... 1. ed. ... Mejico, D.F.,
Editorial P. Robredo, 1942 [i.e.
1943] 3 v.   467.9 a 43-2977
PC4822 .S3 MRR Alc.

SPANISH LANGUAGE--SPOKEN SPANISH.
Gerrard, Arthur Bryson. Beyond the
dictionary in Spanish: 4th ed.
London, Cassell, 1967. 160 p. [16/-
] 468.3/42 68-83829
PC4680 .G4 1967 MRR Alc.

SPANISH LANGUAGE--SYNONYMS AND ANTONYMS.
Kalveram, Carlos. Diccionario de
ideas y expresiones afines. Madrid,
Aguilar, 1956. xiv, 707 p.   a 57-
6324
PC4591 .K3 MRR Alc.

Vox. Diccionario de sinónimos,
Barcelona, Publicaciones y Ediciones
Spes, 1958. xvi, 344 p.   58-42463
PC4591 .V6 MRR Alc.

**SPANISH LITERATURE--TO 1500--HISTORY
AND CRITICISM.**
Gonzalez Lopez, Emilio, Historia
de la literatura española: Edad
Media y Siglo de Oro. New York, Las
Americas Pub. Co., 1972. 840 p.
860/.9 72-93894
PQ6057 .G6 1972 MRR Alc.

**SPANISH LITERATURE--CLASSICAL PERIOD,
1500-1700--HISTORY AND CRITICISM.**
Gonzalez Lopez, Emilio, Historia
de la literatura española: Edad
Media y Siglo de Oro. New York, Las
Americas Pub. Co., 1972. 840 p.
860/.9 72-93894
PQ6057 .G6 1972 MRR Alc.

**SPANISH LITERATURE--20TH CENTURY--
HISTORY AND CRITICISM.**
Torrente Ballester, Gonzalo.
Literatura española contemporánea,
1898-1936. Madrid, A. Aguado [cover
1949] 464 p.   860.904 51-4916
PQ6072 .T6 MRR Alc.

**SPANISH LITERATURE--20TH CENTURY--
PHONOTAPE CATALOGS.**
United States. Library of Congress.
Latin American, Portuguese, and
Spanish Division. The Archive of
Hispanic Literature on Tape;
Washington, Library of Congress; [for
sale by the Supt. of Docs., U.S.
Govt. Print. Off.] 1974. xii, 516 p.
016.86/008 73-19812
Z663.32 .A7 MRR Alc.

SPANISH LITERATURE--BIBLIOGRAPHY.
Catálogo general de la librería
española, 1931-1950. Madrid,
Instituto Nacional del Libro
Español, 1957-65. 4 v.   58-24533
Z2681 .C34 MRR Alc.

Chatham, James R., Dissertations in
Hispanic languages and literatures;
[Lexington] University Press of
Kentucky [1970] xiv, 120 p. [12.50]
016.46 70-80093
Z2695 .A2C46 MRR Alc.

Foulché-Delbosc, Raymond, Manuel de
l'hispanisant. New York, G. P.
Putnam's sons, 1920- v.   20-
16867
Z2681.A1 F7 MRR Alc.

Golden, Herbert Hershel, Modern
Iberian language and literature;
Cambridge, Harvard University Press,
1958. x, 184 p.   016.46 58-12978
Z7031 .G6 MRR Alc.

Palau y Dulcet, Antonio, 1867-1954.
Manual del librero hispano-americano;
2. ed. corr. y aumentada por el
autor. Barcelona, A. Palau, 1948-
v.   015.46 49-2664
Z2681 .P16 MRR Alc.

Serís, Homero, Manual de
bibliografía de la literatura
española. Syracuse, N.Y., Centro de
Estudios Hispánicos, 1948- [c1949-
v. in   016.86 54-4332
Z2691 .S47 MRR Alc.

Simón Díaz, José. Bibliografía
de literatura hispánica. 2. ed.
corr. y aumentada. Madrid, Consejo
Superior de Investigaciones
Científicas, Instituto "Miguel de
Cervantes" de Filología Hispánica,
1960- v.   64-5767
Z2691 .S52 MRR Alc.

Simón Díaz, José. Manual de
bibliografía de la literatura
española. Barcelona, G. Gili, 1963.
vii, 603 p.   016.86 64-6635
Z2691 .S54 MRR Alc.

**SPANISH LITERATURE--BIBLIOGRAPHY--
CATALOGS.**
Harvard University. Library. Spanish
history and literature; Cambridge;
distributed by the Harvard University
Press, 1972. 771 p.   016.9146/03
72-75827
Z2709 .H35 MRR Alc.

Hispanic society of America. Library.
List of books printed 1601-1700, in
the library of the Hispanic society
of America, New York, Printed by
order of the trustees, 1938. xxvi,
972 p.   015.46 38-15765
Z2682 .H671 MRR Alc.

Hispanic Society of America. Library.
List of books printed before 1601 in
the Library of the Hispanic Society
of America, Offset reissue, with
additions. New York, Printed by
order of the trustees, the Hispanic
Society of America, 1955, xiv, 305
p.   015.46 56-583
Z2682 .H67 1955 MRR Alc.

United States. Library of Congress.
Hispanic Foundation. Voces de poetas
y prosistas ibericos y
latinoamericanos en el archivo de
literatura hispánica en cinta
magnética de la Fundación
Hispánica. Washington, 1960. viii,
33 p.   60-60075
Z663.32 .V6 MRR Alc.

**SPANISH LITERATURE--BIBLIOGRAPHY--
PERIODICALS.**
Bibliografía española. 1958-
Madrid, Dirección General de
Archivos y Bibliotecas.   60-44645
Z2685 .B583 MRR Alc Full set

SPANISH LITERATURE--BIO-BIBLIOGRAPHY.
Amo, Julian, La obra impresa de los
intelectuales españoles en América,
1936-1945; Stanford, Stanford
University Press [1950] xiii, 145 p.
013.973046 50-9025
Z1609.R38 A7 MRR Alc.

Chandler, Richard Eugene, A new
history of Spanish literature Baton
Rouge, Louisiana State University
Press [1961] 696 p.   860.9 61-
15756
PQ6033 .C45 MRR Alc.

Hurtado y Jiménez de la Serna, Juan,
Historia de la literatura española,
6. ed., corr. y aumentada. Madrid,
S.A.E.T.A., 1949. xv, 1102 p.
860.9 50-30913
PQ6032 .H8 1949 MRR Alc.

San Vicente, Faustina. Diccionario
de literatura española. Madrid,
Ediciones Boris Bureba [1954] 212 p.
55-42212
Z2690 .S3 MRR Biog.

SPANISH LITERATURE--DICTIONARIES.
Diccionario de literatura española.
Madrid, Revista de Occidente [1949]
xiii, 641 p.   860.3   50-1014
PQ6006 .D5 MRR Alc.

Newmark, Maxim. Dictionary of
Spanish literature. New York,
Philosophical Library [1956] vii,
352 p.   860.3   56-13978
PQ6006 .N4 MRR Alc.

SPANISH LITERATURE--HISTORY AND
CRITICISM.
Brenan, Gerald. The literature of
the Spanish people. [2d ed.]
Cambridge [Eng.] University Press,
1953. xxii, 494 p.   860.9 a 54-
10035
PQ6033 .B7 1953 MRR Alc.

Cejador y Frauca, Julio, Historia de
la lengua y literatura castellana ...
Madrid, Imprenta Radio, 1916-30. 14
v. in 15.   mrr01-65
PQ6032 .C3 1916 MRR Alc.

Chandler, Richard Eugene, A new
history of Spanish literature Baton
Rouge, Louisiana State University
Press [1961] 696 p.   860.9 61-
15756
PQ6033 .C45 MRR Alc.

Hurtado y Jiménez de la Serna, Juan,
Historia de la literatura española,
6. ed., corr. y aumentada. Madrid,
S.A.E.T.A., 1949. xv, 1102 p.
860.9 50-30913
PQ6032 .H8 1949 MRR Alc.

Peers, Edgar Allison, ed. Spain;
5th ed., rev. and enl. London,
Methuen [1956] xii, 319 p.   914.6
56-58806
DP66 .P4 1956 MRR Alc.

SPANISH LITERATURE--HISTORY AND
CRITICISM--BIBLIOGRAPHY.
González López, Emilio, Historia
de la literatura española: Edad
Media y Siglo de Oro. New York, Las
Américas Pub. Co., 1972. 840 p.
860/.9 72-93894
PQ6057 .G6 1972 MRR Alc.

Revista de filología española.
(Indexes) Guía para la consulta de
la Revista de filología española,
1914-1960. [New York] New York
University Press, 1964. 835 p.
460.5 64-22265
PQ6001 .R452 MRR Alc.

Serís, Homero, Manual de
bibliografía de la literatura
española. Syracuse, N.Y., Centro de
Estudios Hispánicos, 1948-   [c1949-
v. in   016.86 50-4332
Z2691 .S47 MRR Alc.

Simón Díaz, José. Bibliografía
de literatura hispánica. 2. ed.
corr. y aumentada. Madrid, Consejo
Superior de Investigaciones
Científicas, Instituto "Miguel de
Cervantes" de Filología Hispánica,
1960-   v.   64-5767
Z2691 .S52 MRR Alc.

SPANISH LITERATURE--TRANSLATIONS FROM
ENGLISH--BIBLIOGRAPHY.
United States. Library of Congress.
Hispanic Foundation. A provisional
bibliography of United States books
translated into Spanish. Washington,
Library of Congress, Reference Dept.,
1957. ix, 471 p.   015.73 57-60028

Z663.32 .A5 no. 3 MRR Alc.

United States. Library of Congress.
Hispanic Foundation. Spanish and
Portuguese translations of United
States books, 1955-1962; Washington,
Library of Congress, 1963. xv, 506
p.   63-60091
Z663.32 .A5 no. 8 MRR Alc.

SPANISH LITERATURE--TRANSLATIONS INTO
ENGLISH.
Ramage, Craufurd Tait, comp.
Beautiful thoughts from German and
Spanish authors, New rev. ed.
London, New York, G. Routledge and
sons, 1884. 3 p. l., [ix]-xvi, 559
p.   15-9871
PN6080 .R32 1884 MRR Alc.

SPANISH LITERATURE--TRANSLATIONS INTO
ENGLISH--BIBLIOGRAPHY.
Pane, Remigio Ugo. English
translations from the Spanish, 1484-
1943, New Brunswick, Rutgers
university press, 1944. vi, 218 p.
016.86 44-12659
Z2694.T7 P2 MRR Alc.

SPANISH MAIN--DESCRIPTION AND TRAVEL--
GUIDE-BOOKS.
Aspinall, Algernon Edward, Sir, The
pocket guide to the West Indies and
British Guiana, British Honduras,
Bermuda, the Spanish Main, Surinam,
the Panama Canal. [10th ed.] rev.
London, Methuen [1960] xx, 474 p.
917.29 61-19408
F1609 .A84 1960 MRR Alc.

SPANISH NEWSPAPERS--DIRECTORIES.
Anuario de la prensa española.
[Madrid, Ministerio de Información y
Turismo, Secretaría General Técnica,
Sección de Planificación y
Documentación] 076/.1/025 74-
644556
Z6956.S7 S65 MRR Alc Latest
edition

SPANISH PERIODICALS--DIRECTORIES.
Anuario de la prensa española.
[Madrid, Ministerio de Información y
Turismo, Secretaría General Técnica,
Sección de Planificación y
Documentación] 076/.1/025 74-
644556
Z6956.S7 S65 MRR Alc Latest
edition

Anuario español de la publicidad.
1960-   Madrid. 64-36955
HF5808.S62 A7 MRR Alc Latest
edition

SPANISH PHILOLOGY--BIBLIOGRAPHY.
Chatham, James R., Dissertations in
Hispanic languages and literatures;
[Lexington] University Press of
Kentucky [1970] xiv, 120 p. [12.50]
016.46 70-80093
Z2695 .A2C46 MRR Alc.

Revista de filología española.
(Indexes) Guía para la consulta de
la Revista de filología española,
1914-1960. [New York] New York
University Press, 1964. 835 p.
460.5 64-22265
PQ6001 .R452 MRR Alc.

SPANISH POETRY.
Cohen, John Michael, ed. The Penguin
book of Spanish verse.
[Harmondsworth, Middlesex] Penguin
Books [1956] xxxvi, 441 p. 861.082
57-2550
PQ6176 .C57 MRR Alc.

The Oxford book of Spanish verse,
XIIIth century-XXth century, 2d ed.
Oxford, The Clarendon press, 1940.
xl, 522 p., 1 l. 861.0822 41-20460

PQ6176 .O8 1940 MRR Alc.

Turnbull, Eleanor Laurelle, ed. Ten
centuries of Spanish poetry;
Baltimore, Johns Hopkins Press [1955]
452 p. 861.082 55-8424
PQ6267.E2 1955 MRR Alc.

SPANISH POETRY--INDEXES.
Simón Díaz, José. Bibliografía
de literature hispánica. 2. ed.
corr. y aumentada. Madrid, Consejo
Superior de Investigaciones
Científicas, Instituto "Miguel de
Cervantes" de Filología Hispánica,
1960-   v.   64-5767
Z2691 .S52 MRR Alc.

SPANISH POETRY--TRANSLATIONS INTO
ENGLISH.
Turnbull, Eleanor Laurelle, ed. Ten
centuries of Spanish poetry;
Baltimore, Johns Hopkins Press [1955]
452 p. 861.082 55-8424
PQ6267.E2 1955 MRR Alc.

SPANISH SAHARA--GAZETTEERS.
United States. Geographic Names
Division. Spanish Sahara; official
standard names approved by the United
States Board on Geographic Names.
Washington, 1969. v, 52 p. 916.4/8
77-603458
DT346.S7 U54 1969 MRR Alc.

SPARRING
see Boxing

SPEAKING
see Debates and debating

SPECIAL EDUCATION
see Handicapped children--Education

SPECIAL LIBRARIANS--DIRECTORIES.
A Biographical directory of
librarians in the field of Slavic and
East European studies, Chicago,
American Library Association, 1967.
xv, 80 p. 026/.000922 67-28101
Z675.A2 B5 MRR Biog.

SPECIAL LIBRARIANS--UNITED STATES--
DIRECTORIES.
Special Libraries Association.
Directory of members. New York.
026.0058 48-3103
Z673.S81 D5 MRR Ref Desk Latest
edition / MRR Alc Latest edition

SPECIAL LIBRARIES ASSOCIATION--
DIRECTORIES.
Special Libraries Association.
Official directory of personnel.
[New York?] 026.058 62-52221
Z673 .S8272 MRR Alc Latest edition

SPECIE
see Money

SPECIFICATIONS--PERIODICALS.
Specification. Metric edition. 71st-
1970-   (London, Architectural
Press) 692/.3/05 72-622381
TH425 .S65 MRR Alc Latest edition
/ Sci RR Latest edition*

SPECTRUM, INFRA-RED--BIBLIOGRAPHY.
United States. Library of Congress.
Technical Information Division.
Infrared, a bibliography,
Washington, 1954-57. 2 v.   016.5356
55-60478
Z663.49 .I58 MRR Alc.

SPECULATION.
see also Securities

SPEECH.
see also Oral communication
Sandford, William Phillips,
Effective business speech. 4th ed.
of Practical business speaking New
York, McGraw-Hill, 1960. 445 p.
808.5 60-8039
PN4193.B8 S3 1960 MRR Alc.

West, Robert William, Phonetics;
Rev. ed. New York, Harper [1960]
433 p. 421.5 60-7010
PE1135 .W4 1960 MRR Alc.

SPEECH--BIBLIOGRAPHY.
Brockett, Oscar Gross, A
bibliographical guide to research in
speech and dramatic art Chicago,
Scott, Foresman [1963] 118 p.   016
63-14554
Z1002 .B87 MRR Alc.

SPEECH--DIRECTORIES.
Speech Communication Association.
Directory. 1971/72-   New York.
808.5/06/13 73-640465
PN4073 .N253 MRR Alc Latest
edition

SPEECH--RESEARCH.
Auer, John Jeffery, An introduction
to research in speech. New York,
Harper [1959] 244 p. 808.5 59-
7024
PN4121 .A78 MRR Alc.

SPEECH--STUDY AND TEACHING--DIRECTORIES.
Speech Communication Association.
Directory. 1971/72-   New York.
808.5/06/13 73-640465
PN4073 .N253 MRR Alc Latest
edition

SPEECH, FIGURES OF
see Figures of speech

SPEECH COMMUNICATION ASSOCIATION.
Speech Communication Association.
Directory. 1971/72-   New York.
808.5/06/13 73-640465
PN4073 .N253 MRR Alc Latest
edition

SPEECH THERAPY--BIOGRAPHY.
American Speech and Hearing
Association. Directory. 1960-
[Washington] 62-5167
RF28 .A7 MRR Alc Latest edition

SPEECHES, ADDRESSES, ETC.
Belson, David. The chairman and
speaker's role made easy. New York,
Citadel Press [1964] 190 p.   808.5
64-15958
PN4305.O4 B38 1964 MRR Alc.

Hurd, Charles, ed. A treasury of
great American speeches. New and
rev. ed. New York, Hawthorn Books
[1970] 411 p. [10.00] 815/.01 77-
107901
PS662 .H8 1970 MRR Alc.

Modern eloquence; Revised. New
York, P. F. Collier & son corporation
[c1941] 15 v. 808.85 41-9672
PN6121 .M63 1941 MRR Alc.

Parrish, Wayland Maxfield, ed.
American speeches [1st ed.] New
York, Longmans, Green, 1954. 518 p.
815.082 54-10208
PN6122 .P3 MRR Alc.

Peterson, Houston, ed. A treasury of
the world's great speeches. Rev. and
enl. ed. New York, Simon and
Schuster [1965] xxix, 866 p.
808.85 65-4344
PN6121 .P4 1965 MRR Alc.

Prosser, Michael H., comp. Sow the
wind, reap the whirlwind: New York,
Morrow, 1970. 2 v. (xviii, 1467 p.)
[$100.00] 341.1/08 73-118271
JX1977 .P728 MRR Alc.

SPEECHES, ADDRESSES, ETC. (Cont.)
Representative American speeches.
1937/38-   New York, H. W. Wilson Co.
815.5082   38-27962
   PS668 .B3 MRR Alc Full set

Wrage, Ernest J., ed. Contemporary
forum; New York, Harper [1862] 376
p.   815.5082 62-10074
   PS668 .W7 MRR Alc.

SPEECHES, ADDRESSES, ETC.--INDEXES.
Sutton, Roberta (Briggs) Speech
index; 4th ed., rev. and enl. New
York, Scarecrow Press, 1966. vii,
947 p.   016.80885 66-13749
   AI3 .S85 1966 MRR Ref Desk.

SPELEOLOGY.
   see also Caves

SPELLERS.
Christoffers, Adele. A word
directory: spelling--division. [1st
ed.] New York, Exposition Press
[1957] 192 p.   428.1 56-7464
   PE1146 .C65 MRR Alc.

Hawley, Gessner Goodrich, Technical
speller, New York, Reinhold Pub.
Corp., 1955. 146 p.   428.1 55-
11714
   PE1146 .H33 MRR Alc.

SPELLERS--BIBLIOGRAPHY.
Alston, R. C. Spelling books
Bradford, Printed for the author by
E. Cummins, [1967]. xvi, 277 p. 68-
70375
   Z2015.A1 A4 vol. 4 MRR Alc.

SPELLING REFORM.
Noory, Samuel. Dictionary of
pronunciation. 2d ed. South
Brunswick, A. S. Barnes [1971]
xiii, 525 p.   [$7.95] 428/.1 76-
151120
   PE1137 .N65 1971 MRR Alc.

**SPENSER, EDMUND, 1552?-1599--
DICTIONARIES, INDEXES, ETC.**
Whitman, Charles Huntington, A
subject-index to the poems of Edmund
Spenser. New York, Russell &
Russell, 1966. xi, 261 p.   821.3
66-13245
   PR2362 .W5 1966 MRR Alc.

SPHERE.
   see also Circle

SPICES.
Loewenfeld, Claire. The complete
book of herbs and spices / New York
: Putnam, [1974] 313 p., [4] leaves
of plates : [$14.95] 581.6/3 74-
78005
   SB351.H5 L67 MRR Alc.

Rosengarten, Frederic. The book of
spices. Wynnewood, Pa., Livingston
Pub. Co., 1969. xiii, 489 p.
[20.00] 641.6/3/83 69-18867
   TX406 .R66 MRR Alc.

SPIDERS--IDENTIFICATION.
Kaston, Benjamin Julian, How to know
the spiders 2d ed. Dubuque, Iowa,
W. C. Brown [1972] x, 289 p.
595/.44 77-167732
   QL457.1 .K29 1972 MRR Alc.

SPIDERS--UNITED STATES--IDENTIFICATION.
Kaston, Benjamin Julian, How to know
the spiders 2d ed. Dubuque, Iowa,
W. C. Brown [1972] x, 289 p.
595/.44 77-167732
   QL457.1 .K29 1972 MRR Alc.

SPIES.
Seth, Ronald. Encyclopedia of
espionage. Garden City, N.Y.,
Doubleday [1974, c1972] 718 p.
[$10.00] 327/.12/03 76-131105
   UB270 .S4385 1974 MRR Biog.

SPINGARN, ARTHUR BARNETT, 1878-
Howard University, Washington, D.C.
Library. Dictionary catalog of the
Arthur B. Spingarn Collection of
Negro Authors. Boston, G. K. Hall,
1970. 2 v.   016.909/.04/96 72-
187159
   Z1361.N39 H78 MRR Alc (Dk 33)

SPIRITS, ALCOHOLIC
   see Liquors

SPIRITUAL LIFE.
   see also Christian life

SPIRITUAL LIFE--COLLECTIONS.
Perry, Whitall N., comp. A treasury
of traditional wisdom. New York,
Simon and Schuster [c1971] 1144 p.
[$15.00] 200/.8 70-93905
   BL25 .P52 1971 MRR Alc.

SPIRITUALISM.
   see also Psychical research

SPIRITUALISM--DICTIONARIES.
Blunsdon, Norman. A popular
dictionary of spiritualism. [1st
American ed.] New York, Citadel
Press [1963] 255, [1] p.   133.903
63-16730
   BF1025 .B58 1963 MRR Alc.

Fodor, Nandor. Encyclopedia of
psychic science. [New Hyde Park,
N.Y.] University Books [1966] xxxix,
415 p.   133.903 66-16316
   BF1025 .F6 1966 MRR Alc.

Wedeck, Harry Ezekiel, Dictionary of
spiritualism, New York,
Philosophical Library [1971] vi, 390
p.   [$10.00] 133/.03 73-104365
   BF1025 .W4 MRR Alc.

SPOILS SYSTEM
   see Corruption (in politics)

SPORTING GOODS--DIRECTORIES.
Explorers Ltd. The Explorers Ltd.
source book. 1st ed. New York,
Harper & Row [c1973] 384 p. [$4.95]
780/.028 72-9115
   GV187 .E95 1973 MRR Alc.

The Sporting goods jobbers' register.
St. Louis, C. C. Spink.   54-15170
   HD9999.S923U5 MRR Alc Latest
edition

**SPORTING GOODS INDUSTRY--UNITED STATES--
DIRECTORIES.**
The Sporting goods directory. [St.
Louis, C. C. Spink]
338.4/7/6887602573 72-622895
   GV744 .S6 MRR Alc Latest edition

SPORTS.
   see also Baseball

   see also Fishing

   see also Football

   see also Games

   see also Physical education and
   training

   see also Soccer

Litsky, Frank. The New York times
official sports record book 1967,
Toronto, New York, Bantam Books
[1967] viii, 360 p.   796 67-16073

   GV741 .L5 MRR Alc.

McWhirter, Norris Dewar, comp.
Guinness sports record book, 1974-
1975; [Rev. ed.] New York, Sterling
Pub. Co. [1974] 191 p.   796/.021/2
74-174979
   GV571 .M27 1974 MRR Alc.

Menke, Frank Grant, The encyclopedia
of sports. 3d rev. ed. New York,
Barnes [1963] 1044 p.   796.03 63-
9364
   GV11 .M4 1963 MRR Alc.

Menke, Frank Grant, The encyclopedia
of sports. 4th rev. ed. South
Brunswick [N.J.] A. S. Barnes [1969]
1100 p.   [20.00] 796/.03 68-27826

   GV11 .M4 1969 MRR Alc.

SPORTS--BIBLIOGRAPHY.
Nueckel, Susan. Selected guide to
sports and recreation books. New
York, Fleet Press Corp. [1974] 168
p.   016.7901 73-3735
   Z7511 .N83 MRR Alc.

Zeigler, Earle F. Research in the
history, philosophy, and
international aspects of physical
education and sport: bibliographies
and techniques. Champaign, Ill.,
Stipes Pub. Co. [1971] vi, 350 p.
016.6137 76-26892
   Z6121 .Z45 MRR Alc.

SPORTS--BIO-BIBLIOGRAPHY.
Higginson, Alexander Henry, British
and American sporting authors,
London, New York, Hutchinson, 1951.
xvii, 443 p.   016.7992 53-18485
   Z7511 .H55 1951 MRR Biog.

SPORTS--DICTIONARIES.
Avis, Frederick Compton. The
sportsman's glossary. London,
Souvenir Press [stamped: distributed
by Sportshelf, New Rochelle, N.Y.,
1961, c1960] 301 p.   796.03 61-
19835
   GV567 .A8 1961 MRR Alc.

Bateman, Robert. The encyclopedia of
sports stamps. London, Paul, 1969.
[8], 173 p.   [35/-] 769/.564 70-
402231
   HE6183 .B32 MRR Alc.

Burton, Bill, comp. The sportsman's
encyclopedia. New York, Grosset &
Dunlap [1971] 638 p.   [$7.95]
796/.03 75-26735
   GV701 .B8 MRR Alc.

Cummings, Parke, ed. The dictionary
of sports. New York, A. S. Barnes
[1949] xxi, 572 p.   796.03 49-8923

   GV567 .C85 1949 MRR Ref Desk.

Dawson, Jack C. Encyclopedia of
sport thrills; New York, Hart Pub.
Co. [1951] 223 p.   796.03 51-13909

   GV567 .D3 MRR Alc.

Encyclopaedia of Sport and sportsmen,
London, Sampson, Low: Purnell [1966]
624 p.   [10/6] 66-76009
   GV567 .E52 MRR Alc.

Harvey, Charles, ed. Sport
international. New York, A. S.
Barnes [1961] c1960. 415 p.
796.403 61-9620
   GV567 .H3 MRR Alc.

Salak, John S. Dictionary of
American sports. New York,
Philosophical Library [1961] xiv,
491 p.   796.03 60-13658
   GV567 .S3 MRR Alc.

Watman, Melvyn Francis. The
encyclopaedia of athletics, [3d ed.]
London, Hale [1973] 244 p. [£2.50]
796.4/03 73-178722
   GV567 .W3 1973 MRR Alc.

SPORTS--DICTIONARIES--POLYGLOT.
Hetnyelvu sportszotar: Budapest,
Terra, 1960- v.   61-21333
   GV567 .H45 MRR Alc.

SPORTS--HANDBOOKS, MANUALS, ETC.
Burton, Bill, comp. The sportsman's
encyclopedia. New York, Grosset &
Dunlap [1971] 638 p.   [$7.95]
796/.03 75-26735
   GV701 .B8 MRR Alc.

SPORTS--HISTORY.
Mullin, Willard, The junior
illustrated encyclopedia of sports.
[4th ed., rev. and enl.]
Indianapolis, Bobbs-Merrill [1970]
xii, 591 p.   [6.95] 796/.03 79-
103861
   GV576 .M8 1970 MRR Alc.

Willoughby, David P. The super-
athletes. South Brunswick, A. S.
Barnes [1970] 665 p.   [$15.00] 796
72-88302
   GV741 .W54 MRR Alc.

SPORTS--HISTORY--BIBLIOGRAPHY.
Zeigler, Earle F. Research in the
history, philosophy, and
international aspects of physical
education and sport: bibliographies
and techniques. Champaign, Ill.,
Stipes Pub. Co. [1971] vi, 350 p.
016.6137 76-26892
   Z6121 .Z45 MRR Alc.

SPORTS--HISTORY--MISCELLANEA.
Fetros, John G. This day in sports;
Novato, Calif., N. K. Gregg [1974]
264 p.   [$5.95] 796/.09 74-75882
   GV576 .F48 MRR Alc.

SPORTS--RECORDS.
Bland, Ernest A., ed. Fifty-two
years of sport; [London, Daily Mail,
1949] xxxi, 640 p.   790.9 49-5457

   GV741 .B47 1949 MRR Alc.

The Guinness book of records. 1955-
[Enfield, Eng., etc., Guinness
Superlatives Ltd., etc.] [£1.20
(single issue)] 001.9/3 56-19118
   AG243 .G86 MRR Ref Desk Latest
edition

Mullin, Willard, The junior
illustrated encyclopedia of sports.
[4th ed., rev. and enl.]
Indianapolis, Bobbs-Merrill [1970]
xii, 591 p.   [6.95] 796/.03 79-
103861
   GV576 .M8 1970 MRR Alc.

Richards, Jack W., Complete handbook
of sports scoring and record keeping
West Nyack, N.Y., Parker Pub. Co.
[1974] 266 p.   796/.021/2 73-14815

   GV741 .R47 MRR Alc.

SPORTS--RULES.
Official rules of sports and games.
New Rochelle, N.Y. [etc.] Sport Shelf
[etc.] 796 51-24610
   Began publication in 1949.
   GV731 .O27 MRR Alc Latest edition

Sports rules encyclopedia; Palo
Alto, Calif., National Press [1961]
x, 563 p.   796 61-19409
   GV731 .S75 MRR Alc.

SPORTS--STATISTICS.
McWhirter, Norris Dewar, comp.
Guinness sports record book, 1974-
1975; [Rev. ed.] New York, Sterling
Pub. Co. [1974] 191 p.   796/.021/2
74-174979
   GV571 .M27 1974 MRR Alc.

SPORTS--STATISTICS. (Cont.)
Menke, Frank Grant, The encyclopedia
of sports. 4th rev. ed. South
Brunswick [N.J.] A. S. Barnes [1969]
1100 p. [20.00]   796/.03 68-27826

GV11 .M4 1969 MRR Alc

Richards, Jack W., Complete handbook
of sports scoring and record keeping
West Nyack, N.Y., Parker Pub. Co.
[1974] 266 p. 796/.021/2 73-14815

GV741 .R47 MRR Alc.

Willoughby, David P. The super-
athletes. South Brunswick, A. S.
Barnes [1970] 665 p. [$15.00]   796
72-88302
GV741 .W54 MRR Alc.

SPORTS--YEARBOOKS.
Associated Press. The Official
Associated Press sports almanac,
1974- [New York, Dell Pub. Co.]
796/.021/2 74-83486
GV741 .A82a MRR Alc Latest edition

World sports. International
athletics annual. London. 796.058
56-23036
Began publication in 1951.
GV561 .W6 MRR Alc Latest edition

SPORTS--BIOGRAPHY.
Mullin, Willard, The junior
illustrated encyclopedia of sports.
[4th ed., rev. and enl.]
Indianapolis, Bobbs-Merrill [1970]
xii, 591 p. [6.95]   796/.03 79-
103861
GV576 .M8 1970 MRR Alc.

SPORTS--GREECE.
Gardiner, Edward Norman, Athletics
of the ancient world. Oxford, The
Clarendon press, 1930. x, 246 p.
796.093 30-32919
GV21 .G25 MRR Alc.

SPORTS--ROME.
Gardiner, Edward Norman, Athletics
of the ancient world. Oxford, The
Clarendon press, 1930. x, 246 p.
796.093 30-32919
GV21 .G25 MRR Alc.

SPORTS--UNITED STATES.
Krout, John Allen, Annals of
American sport. New Haven, Yale
university press; [etc., etc.] 1929.
4 p. l., 360 p.   29-22307
E178.5 .P2 vol. 15 MRR Alc.

SPORTS CAR EVENTS.
see also Automobile racing

SPORTS CARS.
Twite, M. L. The world's racing cars
4th ed., completely rev. Garden
City, N.Y., Doubleday [1971] viii,
190 p. [$3.95] 629.22/8 75-154706

TL236 .T9 1971 MRR Alc.

SPORTS CARS--HISTORY.
Georgano, G. N. A history of sports
cars. New York, Dutton, 1970. 320 p.
[14.85] 629.22/22 76-108425
TL236 .G45 1970 MRR Alc.

SPORTS MUSEUMS--CANADA--DIRECTORIES.
Lewis, Guy. Sporting heritage;
South Brunswick, A. S. Barnes [1974]
181 p. 796/.074/013 72-6391
GV583 .L48 1974 MRR Alc.

SPORTS MUSEUMS--UNITED STATES--
DIRECTORIES.
Lewis, Guy. Sporting heritage;
South Brunswick, A. S. Barnes [1974]
181 p. 796/.074/013 72-6391
GV583 .L48 1974 MRR Alc.

SPORTS OFFICIATING.
Richards, Jack W., Complete handbook
of sports scoring and record keeping
West Nyack, N.Y., Parker Pub. Co.
[1974] 266 p. 796/.021/2 73-14815

GV741 .R47 MRR Alc.

SPY FILMS--CATALOGS.
Parish, James Robert. The great spy
pictures. Metuchen, N.J., Scarecrow
Press, 1974. 585 p. 016.79143 73-
19508
PN1998 .P26 MRR Alc.

ST. ALBANS, ENG.--DIRECTORIES.
Kelly's directory of St. Albans.
Kingston upon Thames, Surrey [etc.]
53-28203
DA690.S13 K4 MRR Alc Latest
edition

ST. LAWRENCE SEAWAY.
Seaway maritime directory. 1st-
ed.: 1958- [St. Clair, Mich., etc.,
Fourth Seacoast Pub. Co., etc.]
386/.5/025714 58-21534
HE630.S17 S4 MRR Alc Latest
edition

ST. PAUL--DESCRIPTION--GUIDE-BOOKS.
Ervin, Jean. The Twin Cities
explored; Minneapolis, Adams Press
[1972] 200 p. [$8.95]
917.76/579/045 73-150443
F614.M6 E78 MRR Alc.

STABLES--DIRECTORIES.
United States Trotting Association.
Racing farm and stable names.
[Columbus, Ohio] 59-42692
SF321 .U52 MRR Alc Latest edition

STADIA--DIRECTORIES.
A A S G; [Cincinnati, Billboard Pub.
Co] 725/.8/02573 72-626501
GV182 .A74 MRR Alc Latest edition

Stubs. Metropolitan New York
edition. [New York, M. Schattner,
etc.] 792./0295/7472 46-22521
Began publication in 1942.
PN2277.N5 S8 MRR Alc Latest
edition

STAFFORDSHIRE POTTERY.
Laidacker, Samuel H., The standard
catalogue of Anglo-American china.
1938 ed. Scranton, Pa. [1938]-51. 2
v. 738.3 38-5740
NK4087.S6 L25 MRR Alc.

Larsen, Ellouise Baker. American
historical views on Staffordshire
china. New rev. and enl. ed. Garden
City, N.Y., Doubleday, 1950. xxx,
317 p. 738.27 50-11741
NK4087.S6 L3 1950 MRR Alc.

STAGE
see Acting

see Theater

STAGE COSTUME
see Costume

STAGE LIGHTING.
Rubin, Joel E. Theatrical lighting
practice, [New York, Theatre Arts
Books, c1954] 142 p. 792.92 55-
384
PN2091.E4 R8 MRR Alc.

STAGE MACHINERY--DICTIONARIES.
Lounsbury, Warren C. Theatre
backstage from A to Z. Rev. ed.
Seattle, University of Washington
Press [c1972] xxviii, 191 p.
[$10.00] 792/.025/03 73-159613
PN2035 .L6 1972 MRR Alc.

STAINS AND STAINING.
see also Wood finishing

STALIN, IOSIF, 1879-1953.
Payne, Pierre Stephen Robert, The
rise and fall of Stalin. New York,
Simon and Schuster [1965] 767 p.
947.08420924 E 65-17111
DK268.S8 P37 MRR Alc.

STALIN, IOSIF, 1879-1953--DICTIONARIES,
INDEXES, ETC.
Matlock, Jack F. An index to the
collected works of J. V. Stalin,
[Washington] External Research Staff,
Office of Intelligence Research,
Dept. of State, 1955. vii, 192 p.
016.3081 55-60804
JX231 .A3 no. 118 MRR Alc.

STALLIONS.
California turf directory and
stallion register. 1959- San Mateo,
Calif., N. Rayden [etc.] 636.10822
59-42113
SF321 .C3 MRR Alc Latest edition

STAMBUL
see Istanbul

STAMPED ENVELOPES.
Bartels, John Murray, Thorp-Bartels
Catalogue of the stamped envelopes
and wrappers of the United States;
6th (Century) ed. Netcong, N.J., H.
Thorp [1954] 597 p. 383.22 54-
37552
HE6185.U6 B32 1954 MRR Alc.

Thorp, Prescott Holden. Catalogue of
the 20th century stamped envelopes
and wrappers of the United States,
1st ed. Netcong, N.J. [1968] 205 p.
769/.568/73 68-2697
HE6185.U6 T46 MRR Alc.

STANDARD OF LIVING
see Cost and standard of living

STANDARD OF VALUE
see Money

STANDARDIZATION--UNITED STATES.
American Society for Testing and
Materials. Book of A.S.T.M.
standards, with related material.
1939- Philadelphia. 40-10712
TA401 .A653 Sci RR Latest edition
/ MRR Alc Latest edition

STANDARDIZATION--UNITED STATES--
DIRECTORIES.
Hartman, Joan E. Directory of United
States standardization activities
Washington [U.S. Dept. of Commerce,
National Bureau of Standards]; for
sale by the Supt. of Docs., U.S.
Govt. Print. Off., 1967. v, 276 p.
389/.6/02573 67-60370
QC100 .H33 MRR Alc.

STANDARDS, MILITARY.
Great Britain. Admiralty. Flags of
all nations. [Rev. ed.] London,
H.M.Stationery Off., 1955- v.
829.9 56-41972
V300 .G72 MRR Alc.

STANDARDS OF MASS.
see also Weights and measures

STANDLEY, WILLIAM H., 1872-1963--
MANUSCRIPTS--CATALOGS.
United States. Library of Congress.
Manuscript Division. Claude Charles
Bloch, Julius Augustus Furer, John
Franklin Shafroth, William Harrison
Standley: a register of their papers
in the Library of Congress.
Washington, Library of Congress,
1973. iii, 6, 10, 4, 11, p.
016.359 73-4374
Z663.34 .B55 MRR Alc.

STARS
see also Constellations

STARS--ATLASES.
Callatay, Vincent de. Atlas of the
sky. [1st ed.] London, Macmillan;
New York, St Martin's Press, 1959
[c1958] 157 p. (chiefly illus.,
charts, diagrs.) 523.89 62-51141
QB65 .C313 1959 MRR Alc.

Ernst, Bruno. Atlas of the universe
[London] Nelson, 1961. 226, [1] p.
523.1084 61-4868
QB65 .E713 MRR Alc.

STARS--EPHEMERIDES.
Apparent places of fundamental stars.
[1st]- 1941- Heidelberg,
Astronomisches Rechen-Institut.
523.8 41-25670
QB9.15 MRR Alc Latest edition

STARS (IN RELIGION, FOLK-LORE, ETC.)
Jobes, Gertrude. Outer space: New
York, Scarecrow Press, 1964. 479 p.
291.212 64-11783
BL438 .J6 MRR Alc.

Lum, Peter, The stars in our heaven.
London, Thames and Hudson [1951]
245 p. 291.2127 52-17434
GR625 .L8 1951 MRR Alc.

STATE AND AGRICULTURE
see Agriculture and state

STATE AND EDUCATION
see Education and state

STATE AND ENVIRONMENT
see Environmental policy

STATE AND SCIENCE
see Science and state

STATE BIRDS.
Burns, Ethel Magwood. National plant
conservation guide. [1st ed.]
Philadelphia, National Council Books,
1961. unpaged. 580 61-8123
QK86 .B8 MRR Alc.

Earle, Olive Lydia. State birds and
flowers. New York, Morrow, 1961. 64
p. 598.2973 61-8023
QL699 .E3 1961 MRR Ref Desk.

Shankle, George Earlie. State names,
flags, seals, songs, birds, flowers,
and other symbols; Rev. ed. New
York, H. W. Wilson Co., 1941 [i.e.
1951, c1938] 524 p. 929.4 917.3*
52-52807
E155 .S43 1951 MRR Alc.

STATE BONDS--UNITED STATES--YEARBOOKS.
Moody's municipal & government
manual: American and foreign. 1955-
New York, Moody's Investors Service.
57-29
HG4931 .M58 MRR Alc Latest edition

STATE ENCOURAGEMENT OF SCIENCE,
LITERATURE, AND ART--UNITED STATES.
Washington and the arts; New York]
Associated Councils of the Arts
[1971] vi, 176 p. [$6.50]
353.008/54/025753 79-163014
NX735 .W3 MRR Ref Desk.

STATE FARMS.
see also Collective farms

STATE FLOWERS.
Burns, Ethel Magwood. National plant
conservation guide. [1st ed.]
Philadelphia, National Council Books,
1961. unpaged. 580 61-8123
QK86 .B8 MRR Alc.

STATE FLOWERS. (Cont.)
Earle, Olive Lydia. State birds and flowers. New York, Morrow, 1961. 64 p.   598.2873 61-8023
QL699 .E3 1961 MRR Ref Desk.

Shankle, George Earlie. State names, flags, seals, songs, birds, flowers, and other symbols; Rev. ed. New York, H. W. Wilson Co., 1941 [i.e. 1951, c1938] 524 p.   929.4 917.3* 52-52807
E155 .S43 1951 MRR Alc.

STATE GOVERNMENTS.
see also Legislative power

Adrian, Charles R. Governing our fifty States and their communities [2d ed.] New York, McGraw-Hill [1967] 133 p.   353.9 67-18389
JK2408 .A28 1967 MRR Alc.

Adrian, Charles R. State and local governments 2d ed. New York, McGraw-Hill [c1967] vii, 607 p.   353.9 66-25472
JK2408 .A3 1967 MRR Alc.

Dye, Thomas R. Politics in States and communities 2d ed. Englewood Cliffs, N.J., Prentice-Hall [1973] xii, 548 p. [$10.85] 320.4/73 72-11912
JK2408 .D82 1973 MRR Alc.

Ewing, Cortez Arthur Milton, comp. Documentary source book in American government and politics, Boston, New York [etc.] D.C. Heath and company [c1931] xx, 823 p. 342.738 31-24918
JK11 1931 MRR Alc.

Nevins, Allan, The American states during and after the revolution, 1775-1789, New York, The Macmillan company, 1924. xviii p., 1 l., 728 p.   24-23941
E303 .N52 MRR Alc.

Ogg, Frederic Austin, Ogg and Ray's Introduction to American Government. 13th ed. New York, Appleton-Century-Crofts [1966] x, 879 p.   353 66-16282
JK421 .O5 1966 MRR Alc.

Peirce, Neal R. The megastates of America; [1st ed.] New York, Norton [1972] 745 p. [$12.95]   917.3/03/82 70-163375
E839.5 .P35 MRR Alc.

STATE GOVERNMENTS--ADDRESSES, ESSAYS, LECTURES.
Fesler, James William, ed. The 50 States and their local governments New York, Knopf [1967] xviii, 603 p.   353.9 66-12816
JK2408 .F4 1967 MRR Alc.

STATE GOVERNMENTS--BIBLIOGRAPHY.
Press, Charles. State manuals, blue books, and election results, Berkeley, Institute of Governmental Studies, University of California, 1962. i, 101 p. 016.3539 63-63225
Z7165.U5 P7 MRR Ref Desk.

STATE GOVERNMENTS--OFFICIALS AND EMPLOYEES.
Clements, John. Taylor's encyclopedia of Government officials, Federal and State. v. 1- 1967/68- Dallas, Political Research, inc. 67-22269
JK6 .T36 Sci RR Latest edition / MRR Alc Latest edition

State administrative officials; Oct. 1957- Lexington, Ky. [etc.] Council of State governments [etc.] 353.9 57-63470
JK2403 .S68 MRR Alc Latest edition / MRR Ref Desk Latest edition

Who's who in American politics. 1st-ed.; 1967/68- New York, Bowker. 320/.0922 67-25024
E176 .W6424 MRR Biog Latest edition

STATE GOVERNMENTS--REGISTERS.
Lukowski, Susan. State information and Federal region book. Washington, Potomac Books [1973] 90 p. [$5.00] (pbk)]   353.9/02 73-80718
JK2679 .L84 MRR Ref Desk.

State administrative officials; Oct. 1957- Lexington, Ky. [etc.] Council of State governments [etc.] 353.9 57-63470
JK2403 .S68 MRR Alc Latest edition / MRR Ref Desk Latest edition

STATE GOVERNMENTS--YEARBOOKS.
The Book of the States. v. 1- 1935- Lexington, Ky. [etc.], Council of State Governments. 353.9 35-11433
JK2403 .B6 MRR Alc Latest edition / MRR Ref Desk Latest edition

STATE GOVERNMENTS--INDIA.
Weiner, Myron. State politics in India. Princeton, N.J., Princeton University Press, 1968. xii, 520 p.   352/.000954 67-16954
JQ288.8 .W4 MRR Alc.

STATE GOVERNMENTS--UNITED STATES--BIBLIOGRAPHY.
Parish, David W. State government reference publications : Littleton, Colo. : Libraries Unlimited, 1974. 237 p. ; [$11.50] 015/.73 74-81322
Z1223.5.A1 P37 MRR Alc.

STATE GOVERNMENTS--UNITED STATES--DIRECTORIES.
Directory of consumer protection and environmental agencies. 1st ed. Orange, N.J., Academic Media [1973] xiii, 627 p.   381 72-75952
HC110.C63 D55 MRR Ref Desk.

STATE GOVERNMENTS--UNITED STATES--STATISTICS.
United States. Bureau of the Census. 1972 census of governments. [Washington, U.S. Govt. Print. Off.] 1973- v. [$1.25 (v. 2, pt. 1) varies] 317.3 73-600080
JS3 .A244 MRR Alc.

STATE LIBRARIES--CONGRESSES.
Assembly of State Librarians, Washington, D.C. Proceedings. 1st-1958- Washington, Exchange and Gift Division, Processing Dept., Library of Congress. 027.573 59-60924
Z663.75 .P7 MRR Alc MRR Alc Full set

STATE PARKS
see Parks

STATE PLANNING
see Economic policy

STATE RIGHTS.
United States. Supreme court. Judicial settlement of controversies between states of the American union; New York, London [etc.] Oxford university press, 1918. 2 v. 19-8255
JK310 .A3 MRR Alc.

STATE SONGS.
Shankle, George Earlie. State names, flags, seals, songs, birds, flowers, and other symbols; Rev. ed. New York, H. W. Wilson Co., 1941 [i.e. 1951, c1938] 524 p. 929.4 917.3* 52-52807
E155 .S43 1951 MRR Alc.

STATE TREES.
Harlow, William Morehouse, Textbook of dendrology, covering the important forest trees of the United States and Canada 5th ed. New York, McGraw-Hill [1968] xv, 512 p. 582.16/0973 68-17188
QK481 .H32 1968 MRR Alc.

STATES, NEW.
Afrique centrale; les républiques d'expression française. Paris, Hachette, 1962. clxxxiii, 533 p. 62-47850
DT546 .A68 MRR Alc.

see also Underdeveloped areas

STATESMEN.
Académie diplomatique internationale. Dictionnaire diplomatique. Paris [1933] 2 v. 341.03 33-36212
JX1226 .A312 vol. 3 MRR Biog.

Elliott, Florence. A dictionary of politics. 6th ed. Harmondsworth, Penguin, 1971. 480 p. [10/-] 320/.03 72-186214
D419 .E4 1971 MRR Alc.

Grant, Neil. World leaders of today. London, New York, F. Watts, 1972. [8], 310 p. [£2.75] 909.82/092/2 B 73-152399
D412.6 .G68 MRR Biog.

The International year book and statesmen's who's who. 1953- London, Burke's Peerage. 305.8 53-1425
JA51 .I57 MRR Biog Latest edition

Laqueur, Walter Ze'ev, A dictionary of politics / Rev. ed. New York : Free Press, 1974, c1973. 565 p. ; [$14.85] 320.9/04 74-8232
D419 .L36 1974 MRR Alc.

Wise, Leonard F. Kings, rulers, and statesmen, New York, Sterling Pub. Co. [1967] 446 p. 920.02 67-16020
D107 .W5 MRR Ref Desk.

STATESMEN--CANADA.
Centennial Commission (Canada) The founders and the guardians: fathers of confederation, governors general, prime ministers; [Ottawa, Queen's Printer, 1968] ii, 147 p. 971.05/0922 B 71-381935
F1033 .C52 MRR Biog.

STATESMEN--GERMANY--BIOGRAPHY.
Saur, Karl Otto. Who's who in German politics; New York, R. R. Bowker Co., 1971. x, 342 p. 329/.00922 B 72-204749
DD259.63 .S28 MRR Biog.

STATESMEN--LATIN AMERICA.
Latin American government leaders. Tempe, Center for Latin American Studies of Arizona State University, 1970. 60 p. 73-631271
F1407 .L37 MRR Alc.

STATESMEN--MEXICO.
Alisky, Marvin. Who's who in Mexican government. Tempe, Center for Latin American Studies of Arizona State University, 1969. 64 p. 354.72/000922 77-625171
F1235.5.A2 A4 MRR Biog.

STATESMEN--UNITED STATES.
Bemis, Samuel Flagg, ed. The American Secretaries of State and their diplomacy, New York, Pageant Book Co., 1958 [c1928] 10 v. in 5. 923.273 58-7201
E183.7 .B46 1958 MRR Alc.

Hatch, Louis Clinton, A history of the vice-presidency of the United States, New York, The American historical society, inc., 1934. viii p., 2 l., [3]-437 p. 353.03 34-8999
E176 .H35 MRR Alc.

Patterson, Richard Sharpe, comp. The Secretaries of State; [Washington, U.S. Govt. Print. Off., 1956] 124 p. 923.273 sd 57-2
E183.7 P3 MRR Biog.

Smith, William Henry, Speakers of the House of representatives of the United States, Baltimore, Md., S. J. Gaeng, 1928. 4 p. l., [xiii]-xvi, 261 p. 28-9295
E176 .S68 MRR Biog.

Who's who in United States politics and American political almanac. Chicago, Captiol House. 823.273 50-12020
E747 .W65 MRR Biog Latest edition

STATESMEN--UNITED STATES--DICTIONARIES.
Biographical directory of the United States executive branch, 1774-1971. Westport, Conn., Greenwood Pub. Co. [1971] x, 491 p. 973/.099 78-133495
E176 .B575 MRR Biog.

STATESMEN, AMERICAN.
Congressional Quarterly Service, Washington, D.C. Candidates 1968; Rev. Washington, 1968. 136 p. 329/.00922 68-5150
E840.6 .C6 1968 MRR Biog.

Douth, George. Leaders in profile: the United States Senate. 1972- ed. New York, Sperr & Douth. [etc.] 328/.73/0922 [B] 77-188152
JK1154 .D68 MRR Biog Latest edition

Graebner, Norman A., ed. An uncertain tradition: American Secretaries of State in the twentieth century. New York, McGraw-Hill, 1961. 341 p. 353.1 61-8654
E744 .G7 MRR Alc.

Smith, William Henry, History of the cabinet of the United States of America, from President Washington to President Coolidge; Baltimore, Md., The Industrial printing company, 1925. 537 p. 25-9781
JK611 .S5 MRR Biog.

Who's who in American politics. 1st-ed.; 1967/68- New York, Bowker. 320/.0922 67-25024
E176 .W6424 MRR Biog Latest edition

STATESMEN, ARAB.
Shimoni, Yaacov, Political dictionary of the Middle East in the twentieth century; London, Weidenfeld and Nicolson, 1972. 434 p. [£5.00] 320.9/56 72-188540
DS61 .S52 MRR Alc.

STATIONERY.
see also Paper

STATIONERY TRADE.
see also Paper making and trade

STATIONERY TRADE--UNITED STATES--
DIRECTORIES.
Geyer's "who makes it" directory.
[New York, Geyer-McAllister
Publications] 338.4/7/651202573 74-
647065
   TS1088 .W7 MRR Alc Latest edition

STATISTICAL SERVICES.
Statistics sources; Rev. 3d ed.
Detroit, Gale Research Co., 1971.
647 p. [$27.50] 016.31 72-127923

   Z7551 .S84 1971 MRR Ref Desk.

STATISTICIANS--DIRECTORIES.
Statisticians and others in allied
professions. Washington, D.C.,
American Statistical Association.
310/.62 70-618020
   HA1 .D52 MRR Alc Latest edition

STATISTICIANS--UNITED STATES--
DIRECTORIES.
Statisticians and others in allied
professions. Washington, D.C.,
American Statistical Association.
310/.62 70-618020
   HA1 .D52 MRR Alc Latest edition

STATISTICS.
Chandler, Tertius. 3000 years of
urban growth New York, Academic
Press [1974] ix, 431 p. 301.36/1
72-84378
   HB2161 .C45 1974 MRR alc.

Davis, Kingsley, World urbanization,
1950-1970. Berkeley, Institute of
International Studies, University of
California [1969-72] 2 v. [$6.00]
301.36 71-627843
   HB2161 .D37 MRR Alc.

Dupuy, Trevor Nevitt, The almanac of
world military power 2d ed. New
York, R. R. Bowker Co., 1972. xii,
373 p. 355.03/32/09047 72-2636
   UA15 .D9 1972 MRR Ref Desk.

Ernst, Morris Leopold, The
comparative international almanac
New York, Macmillan [1967] xli, 239
p. 910.03 67-21419
   HA42 .E7 MRR Ref Desk.

Gallatin Service. Gallatin
statistical indicators. [New York,
Copley International Corporation,
1967- v. 310 72-12086
   HA42 .G32 MRR Alc.

Guilford, Joy Paul, Fundamental
statistics in psychology and
education 5th ed. New York, McGraw-
Hill [1973] xii, 546 p. 519.5 72-
6960
   HA29 .G9 1973 MRR Alc.

Guilford, Joy Paul, Fundamental
statistics in psychology and
education 5th ed. New York, McGraw-
Hill [1973] xii, 546 p. 519.5 72-
6960
   HA29 .G9 1973 MRR Alc.

Guinness book of world records. New
York, Sterling Pub. Co. [etc.] 032
64-4984
   AG243 .G87 MRR Ref Desk Latest
edition

Oxford University Press. Oxford
economic atlas of the world; 4th
ed.; London, Oxford University
Press, 1972. viii, 239 p. [£5.75]
912/.1/33 72-169337
   G1046.G1 O92 1972 MRR Alc Atlas

Showers, Victor, The world in
figures. New York, Wiley [1973]
xii, 585 p. 910/.21/2 73-9
   G109 .S52 MRR Ref Desk.

Smith, C. Frank, Basic statistics
for business and economics Rev. ed.
Homewood, Ill., R. D. Irwin, 1964.
xiv, 479 p. 311.2 64-21022
   HA29 .S578 1964 MRR Alc.

Taylor, Charles Lewis. World
handbook of political and social
indicators, 2d ed. New Haven, Yale
University Press, 1972. xiv, 443 p.
[$15.00] 301/.01/8 70-179479
   HN15 .T37 1972 MRR Alc.

Yamane, Taro. Statistics; an
introductory analysis. 2d ed. New
York, Harper & Row [1967] xx, 919 p.
311 67-15794
   HA29 .Y2 1967 MRR Alc.

STATISTICS--BIBLIOGRAPHY.
Ball, Joyce. Foreign statistical
documents; Stanford, Calif., Hoover
Institution in War, Revolution and
Peace, Stanford University, 1967.
viii, 173 p. 016.3309 67-14234
   Z7551 .B3 MRR Alc.

Buros, Oscar Krisen, ed. The mental
measurements yearbook. [1st]- 1938-
Highland Park, N.J. [etc.] Gryphon
Press [etc.] 016.1512 016.158928 39-
3422
   Z5814.P8 B932 MRR Alc Partial set

Cormier, Reine. Les Sources des
statistiques actuelles, Paris,
Gauthier-Villars, 1969. 287 p.
[48.00] 016.3144 75-423353
   Z7551 .C65 MRR Alc.

Ferguson, Elizabeth, ed. Sources of
insurance statistics. [New York]
Special Libraries Association, 1965.
v, 191 p. 368.00212 65-25313
   HG8045 .F45 MRR Alc.

Harvey, Joan M. Sources of
statistics [Hamden, Conn.] Archon
Books [1969] 100 p. [4.00] 016.31
74-4258
   Z7554.G7 H3 1969b MRR Alc.

Harvey, Joan M. Statistics Africa:
Beckenham (Kent), C.B.D. Research
Ltd, 1970. iii-xii, 175 p. [80/-]
016.316 72-479012
   Z7554.A34 H37 MRR Alc.

Harvey, Joan M. Statistics America:
sources for market research (North,
Central & South America), Beckenham,
CBD Research, 1973. xii, 225 p.
[£6.00 ($22.00 U.S.)] 016.317 73-
180742
   Z7554.A5 H37 MRR Alc.

Harvey, Joan M. Statistics Europe:
sources for market research, 2nd
ed.; revised and enlarged. Beckenham
(154 High St., Beckenham, Kent):
C.B.D. Research Ltd, 1972. 255 p.
[£5.00 ($18.00 U.S.)] 016.314 72-
195848
   Z7554.E8 H35 1972 MRR Ref Desk.

Inter American Statistical Institute.
Bibliography of selected statistical
sources of the American nations. 1st
ed. Washington, 1947. xvi, 689 p.
016.31 48-6568
   Z7554.S75 I4 1947 MRR Alc.

International guide to electoral
statistics; The Hague, Mouton [c1969-
v. [$16.50 (v. 1)] 324/.2/021
73-101067
   JF1001 .I55 MRR Alc.

International Labor Office.
Technical guide; Geneva, 1968- v.
[unpriced] 331/.021/6 77-391010

   HD4826 .I62 MRR Alc.

International Trade Centre.
Compendium of sources: Geneva, 1967.
232 p. [unpriced] 016.3824 74-
431255
   Z7164.C81 I58 MRR Alc.

International Trade Centre.
Compendium of sources: international
trade statistics; Geneva, GATT
International Trade Centre, 1967.
150 p. [21.00] 016.382/021/2 73-
354490
   Z7164.C8 I64 MRR Alc.

Kendall, Maurice George.
Bibliography of statistical
literature Edinburgh, Oliver and
Boyd [1962- v. 63-853
   Z7551 .K42 MRR Alc.

Mason, John Brown, Research
resources; Santa Barbara, Calif.,
ABC-Clio, 1968- v. [3.00]
016.327/.09/04 68-9685
   Z7161 .M36 MRR Ref Desk.

Population index. v. 1- Jan. 20,
1935- [Princeton, N.J., etc.]
016.312 39-10247
   Z7164.D3 P83 MRR Alc Partial set

Princeton University. Office of
Population Research. Population
index bibliography, Boston, G. K.
Hall, 1971. 5 v. 016.312 79-30213

   Z7164.D3 P852 MRR Alc (Dk 33)

Special Libraries Association.
Business and Finance Division.
Committee on Sources of Commodity
Prices. Sources of commodity prices.
New York, Special Libraries
Association, 1959 [c1960] 170 p.
338.505873 60-8102
   Z7164.P94 S6 MRR Alc.

Statistics sources; Rev. 3d ed.
Detroit, Gale Research Co., 1971.
647 p. [$27.50] 016.31 72-127923

   Z7551 .S84 1971 MRR Ref Desk.

Texas. University. Population
Research Center. International
population census bibliography.
Austin, Bureau of Business Research,
University of Texas, 1965-67. 6 v.
016.312 66-63578
   Z7164.D3 T45 MRR Alc.

United States. Bureau of the Census.
Directory of non-Federal statistics
for States and local areas;
[Washington: For sale by the Supt. of
Docs., U.S. Govt. Print. Off., 1970]
viii, 678 p. [6.25] 317.3 76-
605082
   HA37 .U52 1970 MRR Ref Desk.

United States. Dept. of Commerce.
Library. Price sources; New York,
B. Franklin [1968] iv, 320 p.
016.33852 70-6381
   Z7164.P94 U56 1968 MRR Alc.

United States. Library of Congress.
Census Library Project. National
censuses and vital statistics in
Europe, 1918-1939; New York, B.
Franklin [1969] vii, 215, v, 48 p.
016.314 68-58214
   Z7553.C3 U46 1969 MRR Alc.

Verwey, Gerlof, The economist's
handbook, Amsterdam, The economist's
handbook, 1934. viii, p., 1 l., 460
p. 016.31 35-4837
   Z7553.E2 V6 MRR Alc.

Woy, James B. Investment
information; Detroit, Gale Research
Co. [1970] 231 p. [$11.50]
016.33267 79-118791
   Z7164.F5 W93 MRR Ref Desk.

STATISTICS--CATALOGS.
Canada. Bureau of Statistics.
Library. Historical catalogue of
Dominion Bureau of Statistics
publications, 1918-1960. Ottawa, DBS
Library [and] Canada Year Book
Division, 1966 [i.e. 1967] xiv, 298
p. [$2.50 Can.] 317.1 68-136228
   Z7554.C2 A5 MRR Alc.

STATISTICS--DICTIONARIES.
Freund, John E. Dictionary/outline
of basic statistics New York, McGraw-
Hill [1966] vii, 195 p. 310.03 66-
27574
   HA17 .F7 MRR Alc.

Kurtz, Albert Kenneth, Statistical
dictionary of terms and symbols, New
York, Hafner Pub. Co., 1967 [c1939]
xiii, 191 p. 310/.3 67-27317
   HA17 .K83 1967 MRR Alc.

Mulhall, Michael George, The
dictionary of statistics. 4th ed.,
rev. to Nov., 1898. Detroit, Gale
Research Co., 1969. 853 p. 310/.3
68-18013
   HA17 .M8 1969 MRR Ref Desk.

Nixon, James William. Glossary of
terms in official statistics, English-
French, French-English. Edinburgh,
Published for the International
Statistical Institute by Oliver &
Boyd [1964] xiv, 106 p. 65-50152
   HA17 .N5 MRR Alc.

Webb, Augustus Duncan, The new
dictionary of statistics; London, G.
Routledge and sons, limited; New
York, E. P. Dutton and co., 1911.
xi, [1], 682 p. 11-10376
   HA46 .M952 MRR Ref Desk.

STATISTICS--DICTIONARIES--RUSSIAN.
Kotz, Samuel. Russian-English
dictionary of statistical terms and
expressions, Chapel Hill, University
of North Carolina Press [1964]
xviii, 115 p. 311.03 64-16840
   HA17 .K6 MRR Alc.

STATISTICS--GRAPHIC METHODS.
Lockwood, Arthur. Diagrams: London,
Studio Vista; New York, Watson-
Guptill, 1969. 144 p. [84/-]
311/.26 77-82136
   HA31 .L58 1969 MRR Alc.

STATISTICS--INDEXES.
Dolby, J. L. The statistics cumindex
Los Altos, Calif., R & D Press
[1973] xviii, 498 p. 016.0014/22
72-86074
   Z7551 .D64 MRR Alc.

STATISTICS--TERMINOLOGY.
Howell, James M. Dictionary of
economic and statistical terms
Washington] U.S. Dept. of Commerce;
[for sale by the Supt. of Docs., U.S.
Govt. Print. Off.] 1969. 73 p.
[1.25] 330/.01/4 70-605347
   HB61 .H68 MRR Alc.

Inter-American Statistical Institute.
Statistical vocabulary. 2d ed.
Washington, Pan American Union, 1960.
xi, 83 p. 310.3 pa 60-56
   HA17 .I6 1960 MRR Alc.

STATISTICS--YEARBOOKS.
Annuaire de statistique
internationale des grandes villes.
v. 1- 1961- La Haye. 66-88394
   HA42 .A55 MRR Alc Latest edition

STATISTICS--YEARBOOKS. (Cont.)
The Book of the world. 1971- New
York, Collier Books [etc.] 910/.5
77-617076
  G1 .B65 MRR Ref Desk Latest
    edition

Demographic yearbook. 1948- Lake
Success. 312.058 50-641
  HA17 .D45 MRR Ref Desk Latest
    edition

The Economic almanac; 1940- New
York [etc.], Macmillan Co. [etc.]
330.58 40-30704
  HC101 .E38 MRR Ref Desk Latest
    edition

France. Institut national de la
statistique et des etudes
economiques. Annuaire statistique
de la France. v. 1- 1878- Paris
[etc.] 07-39079
  HA1213 .A4 MRR Alc Latest edition

The Guinness book of records. 1955-
[Enfield, Eng., etc., Guinness
Superlatives Ltd., etc.] [£1.20
(single issue)] 001.9/3 56-19118
  AG243 .G86 MRR Ref Desk Latest
    edition

India; a statistical outline.
Calcutta, Oxford & IBH Publishing Co.
[etc.] 70-912219
  HA1724 .I49 MRR Alc Latest edition

International Labor Office. Year
book of labour statistics. [1st]-
1935/36- Geneva. l 36-130
  HD4826 .I63 MRR Alc Latest edition

International Monetary Fund. Balance
of payments yearbook. 1946/47-
Washington. 382 49-6612
  HF1014 .I5 MRR Alc Latest edition

The International year book and
statesmen's who's who. 1953-
London, Burke's Peerage. 305.8 53-
1425
  JA51 .I57 MRR Biog Latest edition

The Military balance. London,
International Institute for Strategic
Studies. 355.03/32/05 78-617319
  UA15 .L652 MRR Ref Desk Latest
    edition

Political handbook and atlas of the
world. Jan. 1, 1927- New York,
Simon and Schuster [etc.] for Council
on Foreign Relations. 28-12165
  JF37 .P6 MRR Ref Desk Latest
    edition / MRR Alc Latest edition

The Reference handbook of the armed
forces of the world. 1966- New York
[etc.] Praeger, [etc.] 66-17547
  UA15 .R43 MRR Alc Latest edition

The Statesman's year-book; [1st]-
1864- London, Macmillan; New York,
St. Martin's Press [etc.] 04-3776
  JA51 .S7 MRR Ref Desk Latest
    edition / MRR Ref Desk Latest
    edition

United Nations. Statistical Office.
Statistical yearbook. 1st- issue;
1948- New York [etc.] 50-2746
  HA12.5 .U63 MRR Ref Desk Latest
    edition

United Nations. Statistical Office.
Yearbook of international trade
statistics. 1st- issue; 1950- New
York. 382.058 51-8987
  JX1977 .A2 MRR Ref Desk Latest
    edition

United Nations. Statistical Office.
Yearbook of national accounts
statistics. 1957- New York. 58-
3719
  HC79.I5 U53 MRR Ref Desk Latest
    edition / MRR Alc Latest edition

United Nations Educational,
Scientific and Cultural Organization.
Statistical yearbook. 1963-
[Paris] 65-3517
  AZ361 .U45 MRR Ref Desk Latest
    edition

United States. Arms Control and
Disarmament Agency. Bureau of
Economic Affairs. World military
expenditures. 1970- [Washington,
For sale by the Supt. of Docs., U.S.
Govt. Print. Off.] 338.4/7/355005
70-649143
  UA17 .U42 MRR Ref Desk Latest
    edition

The World almanac and book of facts.
New York, Newspaper Enterprise
Association [etc.] 04-3781
  AY67.N5 W7 Sci RR Latest edition
    / MRR Ref Desk Latest edition /
    MRR Alc Latest edition / MRR Ref
    Desk Latest edition / MRR Ref
    Desk Latest edition

STATISTICS--YEARBOOKS--BIBLIOGRAPHY.
United States. Library of Congress.
Census Library Project. Statistical
bulletins; Washington, 1954. x, 93
p. 016.31 54-60010
  Z663.29 .S83 MRR Alc.

United States. Library of Congress.
Census Library Project. Statistical
yearbooks; Washington, 1953. viii,
123 p. 016.31 53-60036
  Z663.29 .S85 MRR Alc.

STATISTICS, MATHEMATICAL
see Mathematical statistics

STATUES.
see also Sculpture

STEAM-NAVIGATION.
see also Navigation

  Custom house guide. New York. 99-
1545
  HE953.N5 C8 MRR Alc Latest edition

STEAM-NAVIGATION--UNITED STATES--
HISTORY.
Morrison, John Harrison, History of
American steam navigation. New York,
Stephen Daye Press [1958] 630 p.
387.509 58-11628
  VM623 .M87 1958 MRR Alc.

STEAMBOAT LINES.
All about ships & shipping; 11th
ed., rev. and brought up to date.
London, Faber & Faber [1964] xii,
723 p. 387.5 64-56470
  VK155 .A6 1964 MRR Alc.

The Bulk carrier register, London,
H. Clarkson & Co. Ltd. 1969. xxii
290 p. [10/-/-] 387.2/45/0216 71-
462684
  HE566.F7 B8 MRR Alc.

The Directory of shipowners,
shipbuilders, and marine engineers.
London, Engineering, Chemical &
Marine Press [etc.] 25-4199
  HE565.A3 D5 MRR Alc Latest edition

Dunn, Laurence. Passenger liners.
[Rev. ed.] London, A. Coles [1965]
495 p. 65-9111
  VM381 .D83 1965 MRR Alc.

Morton Allan directory of European
passenger steamship arrivals New
York, Immigration information bureau,
inc [c1931] 268 p., 2 l. 656 32-
6783
  HE945.A2 D5 1931 MRR Alc.

STEAMBOAT LINES--DIRECTORIES.
Lloyd's confidential index of foreign
steam and motor vessels. London,
Lloyd's. 387.2 57-24350
  HE565.A3 L68 MRR Alc Latest
    edition

Moody, Bert. Ocean ships [New ed.].
London, Allan 1967. vii, 359 p.
[25/-] 387.2/4 72-472168
  HE565 .A5M6 1967 MRR Alc.

STEAMBOAT LINES--PASSENGER LISTS.
Lancour, Harold, A bibliography of
ship passenger lists, 1538-1825; 3d
ed., rev. and enl. New York, New
York Public Library, 1963. ix, 137
p. 016.32573 63-18141
  Z7164.I3 L2 1963 MRR Alc.

STEAMBOAT LINES--ATLANTIC OCEAN.
Bonsor, N. R. P. North Atlantic
seaway; Prescot, Lancashire, T.
Stephenson [1955] xxxii, 639 p.
387.74 56-33908
  HE822 .B7 MRR Alc.

STEAMBOATS.
Bennett, Frank Marion, The steam
navy of the United States. 2d ed.
Pittsburgh, Pa., Warren & company,
1897. 2 v. 08-29480
  VA55 .B49 1897 MRR Alc.

Donovan, Frank Robert, River boats
of America. New York, Crowell [1966]
298 p. 386.22 66-25432
  VM461 .D6 MRR Alc.

Gibbs, Charles Robert Vernon.
Passenger liners of the Western
Ocean; 2d ed. [completely rev.]
London, Staples Press [1957] 434 p.
623.824 57-1880
  VM18 .G5 1957 MRR Alc.

Heyl, Erik. Early American steamers.
Buffalo, 1953- v. 387.24 53-
3672
  VM23 .H4 MRR Alc.

Lytle, William M., Merchant steam
vessels of the United States, 1807-
1868. Mystic, Conn., Steamship
Historical Society of America, 1952
[i.e. 1953] 294 p. 387.24 53-1846
  VM7 .S74 no. 6 MRR Alc.

STEEL.
see also Iron

American Society for Metals. Metals
handbook. [1st]- ed.; [1927]-
Metals Park, Ohio [etc.] 27-12046
  TA459 .A5 Sci RR Latest edition /
    MRR Alc Latest edition

STEEL--DICTIONARIES.
Kohler, Eduard Ludwig, English-
German and German-English dictionary
for the iron and steel industry.
Vienna, Springer, 1955. xii, 168,
162 p. a 55-6643
  TN609 .K6 MRR Alc.

Osborne, Alice Katherine. An
encyclopedia of the iron & steel
industry, 2nd ed. London, Technical
P., 1967. lxiii, 558 p. [84/-]
669.1/03 67-89452
  TN609 .O8 1967 MRR Alc.

STEEL--DICTIONARIES--GERMAN.
Kohler, Eduard Ludwig, English-
German and German-English dictionary
for the iron and steel industry,
Vienna, Springer, 1955. xii, 168,
162 p. a 55-6643
  TN609 .K6 MRR Alc.

STEEL INDUSTRY AND TRADE.
see also Iron industry and trade

Pounds, Norman John Greville. The
geography of iron and steel 3rd
impression (revised ed.) London,
Hutchinson, 1966. 192 p. [25/- 10/6
(pbk.)] 338.476691 66-73525
  HD9510.5 .P6 1966 MRR Alc.

STEEL INDUSTRY AND TRADE--DIRECTORIES.
Directory [of] iron and steel plants.
Pittsburgh, Steel Publications
[etc.] 16-18550
  TS301 .D35 Sci RR Latest edition /
    MRR Alc Latest edition

STEEL INDUSTRY AND TRADE--STATISTICS.
American Iron and Steel Institute,
New York. Annual Statistical report.
1912- Washington [etc.] 14-3046
  HD9514 .A5 MRR Alc Latest edition

United Nations. Economic Commission
for Europe. Statistics of world
trade in steel. 1913/59- 61-4874
  HD9510.4 .U529 MRR Alc Full set

STEEL INDUSTRY AND TRADE--YEARBOOKS.
Watkins cyclopedia of the steel
industry. 1st- ed.; 1947-
Pittsburgh, Steel Publications. 672
48-33449
  TN13 .W3 Sci RR Latest edition /
    MRR Alc Latest edition

STEEL INDUSTRY AND TRADE--UNITED STATES-
-BIBLIOGRAPHY.
United States. Library of Congress.
Division of Bibliography. Select
list of books, with references to
periodicals, relating to iron and
steel in commerce. Washington, Govt.
Print. Off., 1907. 25 p. 07-35003

  Z663.28 .S35 MRR Alc.

STEEL INDUSTRY AND TRADE--UNITED STATES-
-DIRECTORIES.
Directory [of] iron and steel plants.
Pittsburgh, Steel Publications
[etc.] 16-18550
  TS301 .D35 Sci RR Latest edition /
    MRR Alc Latest edition

STEEL-WORKS--UNITED STATES--DIRECTORIES.
Directory of iron and steel works of
the United States and Canada. [1st]-
ed.; 1873- Washington [etc.]
American Iron and Steel Institute
[etc.] 01-1428
  TS301 .A6 Sci RR Latest edition /
    MRR Alc Latest edition

STEREOCHEMISTRY.
see also Chemistry, Organic

STEREOPHONIC SOUND SYSTEMS--PERIODICALS.
Stereo directory & buying guide.
[New York, Ziff-Davis Pub. Co.]
[$1.50] 338.4/7/621393302573 73-
641957
  TK7881.8 .S73 MRR Alc Latest
    edition

STERLINGSHIRE, SCOT.--COMMERCE--
DIRECTORIES.
Fife and Kinross trades' directory,
including the counties of Stirling
and Clackmannan, Edinburgh, Town and
County Directories, Limited. 59-
31510
  HF5161 .F5 MRR Alc Latest edition

STEVENS, WALLACE, 1879-1955--
CONCORDANCES.
Walsh, Thomas F. Concordance to the
poetry of Wallace Stevens.
University Park, Pa., Pennsylvania
State University Press, 1963. xx,
341 p. 811.52 63-18744
  PS3537.T4753 Z9 MRR Alc.

STEVENSON, ADLAI EWING, 1900-1965.
Whitman, Alden. Portrait--Adlai E.
Stevenson: [1st ed.] New York,
Harper & Row [1965] ix, 289 p.
973.92 E 65-27638
E748.S84 W47 MRR Alc.

STOCK AND STOCK-BREEDING.
see also Veterinary medicine

Briggs, Hilton Marshall. Modern
breeds of livestock. Rev. ed. New
York, Macmillan [1958] 754 p.
636.08 58-5049
SF105 .B7 1958 MRR Alc.

STOCK BROKERS
see Brokers

STOCK COMPANIES--SPAIN--FINANCE.
Anuario financiero y de sociedades
anónimas de España. Madrid,
Editorial Sopec. 74-642352
Began with 1916.
HG5631 .A47 MRR Alc Latest edition

STOCK-EXCHANGE.
Leffler, George Leland. The stock
market. 3d ed., rev. New York,
Ronald Press Co. [1963] 654 p.
332.61 63-10640
HG4551 .L35 1963 MRR Alc.

Spray, David Eugene, ed. The
principal stock exchanges of the
world; [1st ed.] Washington,
International Economic Publishers,
1964. ix, 428 p. 332.61 64-25407
HG4551 .S65 1964a MRR Alc.

STOCK-EXCHANGE--BIBLIOGRAPHY.
Zerden, Sheldon. Best books on the
stock market. New York, Bowker,
1972. xii, 168 p. 016.3326/42/0973
72-8275
Z7164.F5 Z46 MRR Alc.

STOCK-EXCHANGE--DICTIONARIES.
Blahut, Robert. The A to Z of
finance, [Hackensack? N.J.; 1962] 1
v. (unpaged) 332.03 62-36848
HG151 .B5 MRR Alc.

Hanken, Richard. Wall Street
special; New York, HC Publishers
[c1972] 128 p. [$1.95] 332.6/42
73-157044
HG4513 .H35 MRR Alc.

Rudman, Jack. Handbook of the stock
market; Brooklyn, N.Y., National
Learning Corp. [1970] xxii, 134 p.
[$4.95] 332.6 76-120548
HG4513 .R8 MRR Alc.

Woy, James B. Investment methods;
New York, R. R. Bowker, 1973. viii,
220 p. 016.3326 73-9607
Z7164.F5 W94 MRR Alc.

Wyckoff, Peter. Dictionary of stock
market terms. Englewood Cliffs,
N.J., Prentice-Hall [1964] x, 301 p.
332.603 64-16432
HG4513 .W9 MRR Alc.

Wyckoff, Peter. The language of Wall
Street. New York, Hopkinson and
Blake [1973] 247 p. [$5.95]
332.6/03 73-76037
HG4513 .W82 MRR Alc.

STOCK-EXCHANGE--DICTIONARIES--POLYGLOT.
Elsevier's lexicon of stock-market
terms: Amsterdam, New York, Elsevier
Pub. Co.; 1965. 131 p. 332.603 65-
13892
HG4513 .E4 MRR Alc.

STOCK-EXCHANGE--YEARBOOKS.
The Stock exchange year-book of
Egypt. Cairo, Egypt. 332.63 45-
33051
Publication began with issue for
1939?
HG5831 .S75 MRR Alc Latest edition

STOCK-EXCHANGE--EGYPT.
The Stock exchange year-book of
Egypt. Cairo, Egypt. 332.63 45-
33051
Publication began with issue for
1939?
HG5831 .S75 MRR Alc Latest edition

STOCK-EXCHANGE--EUROPE.
Kent, C. H. European stock exchange
handbook Park Ridge, N.J., Noyes
Data Corp., 1973. xvii, 567 p.
332.6/42/094 72-75237
HG4551 .K45 MRR Alc.

STOCK-EXCHANGE--EUROPEAN ECONOMIC
COMMUNITY COUNTRIES.
Kent, C. H. European stock exchange
handbook Park Ridge, N.J., Noyes
Data Corp., 1973. xvii, 567 p.
332.6/42/094 72-75237
HG4551 .K45 MRR Alc.

STOCK-EXCHANGE--GERMANY--YEARBOOKS.
Handbuch der deutschen Aktien-
Gesellschaften. Darmstadt [etc.]
Hoppenstedt [etc.] ca 15-275
HG5491 .H4 MRR Alc Latest edition

STOCK-EXCHANGE--UNITED STATES.
The 1971 encyclopedia of stock market
techniques. Larchmont, N.Y.,
Investors Intelligence [1970] 733 p.
[$24.95] 332.6/7/8 79-133412
HG4521 .E55 1970 MRR Alc.

Hanken, Richard. Wall Street
special; New York, HC Publishers
[c1972] 128 p. [$1.95] 332.6/42
73-157044
HG4513 .H35 MRR Alc.

Robbins, Sidney M. The securities
markets; New York, Free Press [1966]
xvi, 303 p. 332.64 66-15499
HG4910 .R617 MRR Alc.

Vaughn, Donald E. Survey of
investments New York, Holt, Rinehart
and Winston [1967] xx, 490 p.
332.6/0973 67-21578
HG4921 .V3 MRR Alc.

STOCK-EXCHANGE--UNITED STATES--HISTORY.
Wyckoff, Peter. Wall Street and the
stock markets: [1st ed.]
Philadelphia, Chilton Book Co. [1972]
xiv, 304 p. 332.6/42/0973 72-8277
HG4572 .W87 MRR Alc.

STOCK TRANSFER--CANADA.
Financial stock guide serivce.
Jersey City, N.J., Financial
Information, inc. 332.6/7/0973 74-
644692
HG4512 .R4 MRR Alc Latest edition

STOCK TRANSFER--UNITED STATES.
Financial stock guide serivce.
Jersey City, N.J., Financial
Information, inc. 332.6/7/0973 74-
644692
HG4512 .R4 MRR Alc Latest edition

STOCKHOLM--DIRECTORIES.
Stockholms adresskalender. årg. 107-
1962- Stockholm. 73-646001
DL976 .H8 MRR Alc Latest edition

Stockholms kommunalkalender. 33-
1939- Stockholm, Kungl.
bgktryckeriet, P. A. Norstedt &
Söner. 72-623545
JS6271.A5 MRR Alc Latest edition

STOCKHOLM--OFFICIALS AND EMPLOYEES--
REGISTERS.
Stockholms kommunalkalender. 33-
1939- Stockholm, Kungl.
bgktryckeriet, P. A. Norstedt &
Söner. 72-623545
JS6271.A5 MRR Alc Latest edition

STOCKHOLM--POLITICS AND GOVERNMENT--
HANDBOOKS, MANUALS, ETC.
Stockholms kommunalkalender. 33-
1939- Stockholm, Kungl.
bgktryckeriet, P. A. Norstedt &
Söner. 72-623545
JS6271.A5 MRR Alc Latest edition

STOCKHOLM--STATISTICS.
Stockholm. Statistiska kontoret.
Statistisk årsbok för Stockholms
stad. ny ser. 1- 1904- Stockholm.
314.87 06-41074
HA1539 .S8A3 MRR Alc Latest
edition

STOCKS.
see also Bonds

see also Securities

STOCKS--PERIODICALS--BIBLIOGRAPHY.
Directory of business and financial
services. [1st]- ed.; 1924- New
York [etc.] Special Libraries
Association. 25-4599
HF5003 .H3 MRR Ref Desk Latest
edition / MRR Ref Desk Latest
edition

STOCKS--PRICES.
Wyckoff, Peter. Wall Street and the
stock markets: [1st ed.]
Philadelphia, Chilton Book Co. [1972]
xiv, 304 p. 332.6/42/0973 72-8277

HG4572 .W87 MRR Alc.

STOCKS--PRICES--UNITED STATES.
I S L daily stock price index:
American Stock Exchange. Jan./Mar.
1962- [New York, etc.] Standard &
Poor's Corp. [etc.] 66-91845
HG4915 .I22 MRR Alc Partial set

I S L daily stock price index: New
York Stock Exchange. 1961- [New
York, etc.] Standard & Poor's Corp.
[etc.] 62-39827
HG4915 .I23 MRR Alc Partial set

STOCKS--PRICES--UNITED STATES--
PERIODICALS.
Investment Statistics Laboratory.
ISL daily stock price index: over-the-
counter. [New York] 332.63/22 76-
25091
HG4915 .I6 MRR Alc Full set

Standard and Poor's Corporation.
Daily stock price record: American
stock Exchange. [New York]
332.6/322/0973 72-627513
HG4915 .S66 MRR Alc Full set

Standard and Poor's Corporation.
Daily stock price record: New York
Stock Exchange. [New York]
332.6/322/0973 72-627514
HG4915 .S664 MRR Alc Full set

Standard and Poor's Corporation.
Daily stock price record: over-the-
counter. [New York] 332.6/322/0973
72-627516
HG4915 .S665 MRR Alc Full set

STOCKS--AFRICA, SOUTH.
Beerman's financial year book of
southern Africa: 1947/48-
Johannesburg [etc.] Combined
Publishers [etc.] 332.6/0968 48-
17050
HG5850.S6 S67 MRR Alc Latest
edition

Johannesburg. Stock Exchange. The
Stock Exchange handbook. 1967-
Johannesburg, Flesch Financial
Publications. 332.63/0968 68-130426

HG5841 .J63 MRR Alc Latest edition

STOCKS--AUSTRALIA.
The "Digest" year book of public
companies of Australia & New Zealand.
Sydney, N.S.W., Jobson's
publications pty. limited. 338.058
45-26276
Publication began in 1928.
HD2927 .D5 MRR Alc Latest edition

Potter (Ian) & Company. Selected
Australian ordinary shares.
Melbourne. 66-99703
HG5894 .P6 MRR Alc Latest edition

STOCKS--AUSTRIA.
Finanz-Compass: 79.- Jahrg.; 1950-
Wien, Compass-Verlag. 54-17734
HG5451 .F5 MRR Alc Latest edition

STOCKS--CANADA.
The Financial post survey of oils.
Montreal, New York, Maclean-Hunter
Pub. Co. 338.2728 52-31395
HD9574.C2 F5 MRR Alc Latest
edition

Financial times of Canada, Montreal.
A guide to 100 Canadian stocks, [2d
rev. ed.] [Montreal] 1968. 61 p.
332.63/223/0971 71-499820
HG5158 .F53 1968 MRR Alc.

Standard and Poor's Corporation.
Annual dividend record. New York.
332.63058 44-24425
HG4908 .S77 MRR Alc Latest edition

STOCKS--EGYPT.
The Stock exchange year-book of
Egypt. Cairo, Egypt. 332.63 45-
33051
Publication began with issue for
1939?
HG5831 .S75 MRR Alc Latest edition

STOCKS--EUROPE.
Jane's major companies of Europe.
1st- ed.;1965- London, S. Marston
& Co. [etc.] 65-2174
HG5421 .J35 MRR Alc Latest edition

STOCKS--FRANCE.
Annuaire Desfossés; Paris, Cote
Desfosses [etc.] 332.63 46-39086
HG5471 .A64 MRR Alc Latest edition

Répertoire général alphabétique
des valeurs cotées en France et es
valeurs non cotées. Paris,
Éditions financières alphabetiques.
47-42094
HG5471 .R4 MRR Alc Latest edition

STOCKS--GERMANY.
Handbuch der deutschen Aktien-
Gesellschaften. Darmstadt [etc.]
Hoppenstedt [etc.] ca 15-275
HG5491 .H4 MRR Alc Latest edition

Saling Aktienführer. Darmstadt,
Hoppenstedt. 57-40599
Began publication with vol. for
1935/36;
HG5501 .S3 MRR Alc Latest edition

STOCKS--GREAT BRITAIN.
Handbook for investors. 61st-
issue; 1960- [London, Fredc. C.
Mathieson & Sons] 332.6/7 72-623829

HG5431 .M3 MRR Alc Latest edition

The Stock exchange official yearbook. [1st]- 1934- Croydon, Eng.
[etc.] T. Skinner [etc.] 332.6305
34-16479
HG5431 .S82 MRR Alc Latest edition

STOCKS--GREECE, MODERN.
Oikonomikos hodegos tōn en Helladi
anonymōn hetaireiōn kai
hetaireiōn perioramenes
euthynes. 1864- Athens, ICAP
Hellas Ltd. 70-401893
HF5175 .O4 MRR Alc Latest edition

STOCKS--INDIA.
Calcutta. Stock Exchange. Official
year book. Calcutta, Calcutta Stock
Exchange Assn. 332.6 49-39127
HG5740 .C3 MRR Alc Latest edition

Kothari's economic and industrial
guide of India. 29th- ed.: 1971/72-
Madras, Kothari. [$25.00]
338/.0954 72-904460
HG5731 .I57 MRR Alc Latest edition

STOCKS--IRELAND.
Handbook of Irish securities, etc.
London, Straker Bros. ltd. 55-32941
HG5443.I7 H3 MRR Alc Latest
edition

STOCKS--JAPAN.
Japan company directory. 1957-
[Tokyo] Oriental economist. 62-29293
HC161 .J35 MRR Alc Latest edition

STOCKS--NEW ZEALAND.
The "Digest" year book of public
companies of Australia & New Zealand.
Sydney, N.S.W., Jobson's
publications pty. limited. 338.058
45-26276
Publication began in 1928.
HD2927 .D5 MRR Alc Latest edition

STOCKS--NORWAY.
Haandbok over norske obligationer og
aktier. Oslo. 24-10346
HG4207 .H3 MRR Alc Latest edition

STOCKS--TEXAS.
Davis, James Walker. A money tree
grows in Texas; New York, Echo House
[1969] 352 p. [1.95]
338.7/4/09764 75-9616
HG5128.T4 D37 MRR Alc.

STOCKS--UNITED STATES.
American Apparel Manufacturers
Association. Apparel, textile and
retail financial survey. 1st- ed.;
1971- Arlington, Va.
338.4/7/6870973 72-626946
HD9940.U3 A567 MRR Alc Latest
edition

Best (A. M.) Company. Best's
insurance securities research
service. 1972 ed. Morristown, N.J.
[1972- 1 v. (loose-leaf) 332.6/722
72-170016
HG5123.I6 B3932 MRR Alc.

Corporate holdings of insurance
companies. 1st- ed.; 1948-
Morristown, N.J. [etc.] United
Statistical Associates. 332.63 49-
13782
HG8078 .C6 MRR Alc Latest edition

Directory of obsolete securities.
1970- [n.p.] Financial Information,
inc. 332.67 72-612940
HG4961 .D56 MRR Alc Latest edition

Dow, Jones & Co., New York. The Dow
Jones averages, 1885-1970. [New
York, 1972] 1 v. (unpaged)
332.6/322/0973 78-183053
HG4519 .D59 MRR Alc.

Dow, Jones & Co., New York. The Dow
Jones investor's handbook.
Princeton, N.J. [etc.] Dow Jones
Books [etc.] 332.67/8 66-17650
HG4921 .D66 MRR Alc Latest edition

Electronic news financial fact book &
directory. 1st- ed.; 1962- New
York, Book Division, Fairchild
Publications. 31 cm. 62-19605
HD9696.A1 E5 MRR Alc Latest
edition

Esslen, Rainer. A guide to marketing
securities in Europe, 1971-1972. New
York, Wall Street Reports Pub. Corp.
[1971] viii, 215 p. 332.67/34/073
79-178914
HG4538 .E76 MRR Alc.

Financial daily card service; Jersey
City, N.J. Financial Information. 74-
642472
HG4905 .F45 MRR Alc Latest edition

Financial stock guide serivce.
Jersey City, N.J., Financial
Information, inc. 332.6/7/0973 74-
644622
HG4512 .R4 MRR Alc Latest edition

Financial world stock factographs.
38th- ed.; 1952- New York,
Guenther Publ. Corp. 332.6/78 72-
623291
HG4905 .S68 MRR Alc Latest edition

Forbes guide to common stock profits.
New York, Investors Advisory
Institute. 332.678 60-596
HG4905 .F793 MRR Alc Latest
edition

Hanken, Richard. Wall Street
special; New York, HC Publishers
[c1972] 128 p. [$1.95] 332.6/42
73-157044
HG4513 .H35 MRR Alc.

Hudson's corporate mergers. New
York. 338.8/3/0973 74-644554
HG4915 .C67 MRR Alc Latest edition

The Medical and healthcare stock
market guide. 1972/73- ed.
Arcadia, Calif., International Biomedical Information Service.
332.6/7/22 72-84884
HG5123.M4 M44 MRR Alc Latest
edition

Moody's handbook of common stocks.
1965, 3d quarterly- ed. New York,
Moody's Investors Service, inc.
332.6/7 72-623694
HG4501 .M59 MRR Alc Latest edition

Moody's industrial manual: 1954-
New York, Moody's Investors Service.
56-14721
HG4961 .M67 MRR Alc Latest edition

Moody's OTC industrial manual. New
York, Moody's Investors Service.
332.67 77-649772
HG4961 .M7237 MRR Ref Desk Latest
edition

New York. Stock Exchange. Listing
Exchange. New York, F. E. Fitch,
inc. ca 24-283
HG4501 .N4 MRR Alc Partial set

Rosenberg, Claude N. Stock market
primer. Englewood Cliffs, N.J.,
Prentice-Hall [1962] 276 p.
332.678 62-12830
HG4921 .R58 MRR Alc.

Standard and Poor's Corporation.
Analysts handbook: composite
corporate per share data, by
industries. New York.
332.63/22/0973 67-212
HG4519 .S772 MRR Alc Latest
edition

Standard and Poor's Corporation.
Annual dividend record. New York.
332.63692 44-24425
HG4908 .S77 MRR Alc Latest edition

Standard and Poor's Corporation.
Standard & Poor's stock market
encyclopedia. New York 332.6/7 70-
23142
HG4921 .S68 MRR Ref Desk Latest
edition

Standard and Poor's Corporation.
Standard & Poor's stock market
encyclopedia. 14th ed. New York
[1971] 1 v. (unpaged) [$25.00]
332.67 70-23142
HG4921 .S68 1971 MRR Ref Desk.

The U.S. news & world report guide to
stocks, bonds & mutual funds.
Washington, Books by U.S. News &
World Report [1972] 191 p. [$2.95]
332.6/78/0973 79-188880
HG4921 .U65 MRR Alc.

Ultronic Systems Corporation. Stock
symbol guide: company to symbol,
symbol to company. [New York] 1967.
80 p. 332.6/2/0148 75-31662
HE7677.B2 U57 MRR Alc.

Walker's manual of Western
corporations & securities. 65th-
ed.: 1973- San Francisco.
332.6/7/0878 74-640659
HG5128.C2 W2 MRR Alc Latest
edition

STOCKS--UNITED STATES--PERIODICALS.
Media General Financial Services.
Industriscope. v. 1- May 1973-
[Richmond, Va.] 332.6/322/0973 74-
644661
HG4915 .M5a MRR Alc Latest edition

Standard and Poor's Corporation.
Standard & Poor's stock reports:
American Stock Exchange. Feb. 1973-
New York. 332.6/7 70-183942
HG4905 .S44 MRR Alc Latest edition

Standard and Poor's Corporation.
Standard & Poor's stock reports: New
York Stock Exchange. Jan. 1973- New
York. 332.6/7 74-183943
HG4905 .S443 MRR Alc Latest
edition

Standard and Poor's Corporation.
Standard & Poor's stock reports: over
the counter. Mar. 1973- New York.
332.6/7 78-183944
HG4905 .S444 MRR Alc Latest
edition

STOCKS--UNITED STATES--TABLES, ETC.
I S L daily stock price index:
American Stock Exchange. Jan./Mar.
1962- [New York, etc.] Standard &
Poor's Corp. [etc.] 66-91845
HG4915 .I22 MRR Alc Partial set

I S L daily stock price index: New
York Stock Exchange. 1961- [New
York, etc.] Standard & Poor's Corp.
[etc.] 62-39827
HG4915 .I23 MRR Alc Partial set

The National monthly stock summary.
New York [etc.] The National
Quotation Bureau Inc. 332.63 42-241
HG4905 .N34 MRR Alc Latest edition

Wyckoff, Peter. Wall Street and the
stock markets. [1st ed.]
Philadelphia, Chilton Book Co. [1972]
xiv, 304 p. 332.6/42/0973 72-8277
HG4572 .W87 MRR Alc.

STOCKS--UNITED STATES--TABLES, ETC.--
PERIODICALS.
Investment Statistics Laboratory.
ISL daily stock price index: over-the-
counter. [New York] 332.63/22 76-
25091
HG4915 .I6 MRR Alc Full set

STOCKS--UNITES STATES--YEARBOOKS.
Best's market guide. 1st- ed.;
1970- Morristown, N.J., United
Statistical Associates. 332.67 79-
613273
HG4926.A3 B4 MRR Alc Latest
Edition

STOCKS--WISCONSIN.
Financial briefs of Wisconsin
corporations. [Milwaukee] R. W.
Baird. 332.63 51-6093
HG4070.W5 F5 MRR Alc Latest
edition

STONE.
see also Rocks

STONE AGE.
see also Archaeology

see also Man, Prehistoric

STONE AGE--AMERICA
see Indians

STONES, PRECIOUS
see Precious stones

STONEWARE
see Pottery

STONEWORK, DECORATIVE
see Sculpture

STORAGE AND MOVING TRADE.
see also Transportation

STORAGE AND MOVING TRADE--UNITED STATES-
-DIRECTORIES.
Directory of movers. [Washington?]
American Movers Conference.
338.4/7/38832406273 74-4136
HE5623.A45 D572 MRR Alc Latest
edition

STORES, RETAIL--DIRECTORIES.
Chain store guide; directory of
leading chain stores in the United
States. 1959- [New York, Chain
Store Business Guide] 658.873058 58-
3958
HF5468 .C415 MRR Alc Latest
edition

Directory: General mdse., variety
and jr. dept. store chains. 36th-
ed.; 1970- [New York, Business
Guides, Inc.] 381 72-623621
HF5468.A1 C418 MRR Alc Latest
edition

Directory of department stores. 1955-
[New York, Department Store Guide]
55-39068
HF5465.U4 D47 MRR Alc Latest
edition / MRR Alc Latest edition

Directory of discount centers. 1961-
[New York, Business Guides, inc.]
63-41082
HF5035 .D46 MRR Alc Latest edition

Fairchild's financial manual of
retail stores. New York, Fairchild
Publications. 658.8705873 59-4791
HG4961 .F3 MRR Alc Latest edition

National travel guide to antique
shops. [Casper, Wyo., Antique
Enterprises] 65-4691
NK1127 .N3 MRR Alc Latest edition

Phelon's retail trade. 1st- ed.;
1960- New York, Phelon-Sheldon
Publications [etc.] 60-2106
HF5465.U4 P5 MRR Alc Latest
edition

STORES, RETAIL--DIRECTORIES. (Cont.)
Phelon's women's specialty stores.
1st-- ed.; 1963- New York, Phelon-
Sheldon & Marsar [etc.] 63-40375
HD9940.U3 P5 MRR Alc Latest
edition

Stores of the world. London, Newman
Books. 380.1025 66-9836
Began publication in 1961.
HF54.G7 S8 MRR Alc Latest edition

Stores, shops, supermarkets retail
directory. 21st-- ed.; 1967-
London, Newman Books Ltd. 381 72-
623101
HF5155 .S8 MRR Alc Latest edition

Variety department store merchandiser
buyers directory. 1947- New York,
Directory Division, Merchandiser Pub.
Co., [etc.] 338.4/7/670257 48-4264

T12 .S9 MRR Alc Latest edition

STORIES
see Children's stories

see Fables

see Fiction

see Ghost stories

see Tales

STORMS.
Tufty, Barbara. 1001 questions
answered about storms, and other
natural air disasters. New York,
Dodd, Mead [1970] xv, 368 p. [7.50]
551.5/5 74-112901
QC941 .T84 MRR Alc.

STORY, SHORT
see Short story

STORY-TELLING.
see also Children's stories

STRATEGY.
see also Military art and science

STRATIGRAPHIC GEOLOGY
see Geology, Stratigraphic

STREET FIGHTING (MILITARY SCIENCE)
see also Riots

STREET NAMES.
Morales Díaz, Carlos. Quién es
quién en la nomenclatura de la
ciudad de México; [Mexico] 1962.
ix, 582 p. 63-28910
F1386 .M74 MRR Biog.

STREET RAILROADS--PERIODICALS.
Passenger transport (London) Year
book. London. 388.4058 61-20834
Began publication in 1899.
TF701 .P3 MRR Alc Latest edition

STREET-RAILROADS--UNITED STATES--
HISTORY.
Middleton, William D., The time of
the trolley. [Milwaukee, Kalmbach
Pub. Co. 1967] 436 p.
388.4/6/0973 67-20155
TF723 .M5 MRR Alc.

STREET TRAFFIC
see Traffic engineering

STRETFORD, ENG.--DIRECTORIES.
Kelly's (Slater's) directory of
Manchester, Salford and suburbs.
Kingston upon Thames, Surrey [etc.]
Kelly's Directories Limited. 34-
33227
DA690.M4 K4 MRR Alc Latest edition

STRIKES AND LOCKOUTS.
see also Trade-unions

STRIKES AND LOCKOUTS--BIBLIOGRAPHY.
United States. Library of Congress.
Division of bibliography. Select
list of books (with references to
periodicals) on labor. Washington,
Govt. print. off., 1903. 65 p. 03-
16881
Z663.28 .S28 MRR Alc.

STRINGED INSTRUMENTS, BOWED.
see also Violin

STRUCTURAL ENGINEERING.
see also Building

see also Buildings

Parker, Harry, Simplified
engineering for architects and
builders. 4th ed. New York, Wiley
[1967] xvi, 361 p. 624/.17 67-
12568
TA633 .P3 1967 MRR Alc.

STRUCTURAL ENGINEERING--HANDBOOKS,
MANUALS, ETC.
Gaylord, Edwin Henry. Structural
engineering handbook. New York,
McGraw-Hill [1968] 1 v. (various
pagings) 624/.1 67-15423
TA635 .G3 MRR Alc.

STRUCTURAL FRAMES.
Condit, Carl W. American building
art: the twentieth century. New
York, Oxford University Press, 1961.
427 p. 624.10973 61-8369
TA23 .C57 MRR Alc.

STRUCTURAL MATERIALS
see Building materials

STUDENT AID--DIRECTORIES.
United States. Library of Congress.
Education and Public Welfare
Division. Student assistance
handbook; Rev. Washington, U.S.
Govt. Print. Off., 1965. vi, 241 p.
65-62199
L901.A4 1965 MRR Alc.

STUDENT AID--UNITED STATES.
College Entrance Examination Board.
Admissions and financial aid
requirements and procedures at
College Board member colleges [New
York] 378.1/05/70973 71-617254
LB2351.A1 C572 MRR Alc Latest
edition

Cooperative Program for Educational
Opportunity. Financial aid for
higher education. [Washington] U.S.
Office of Education; [for sale by the
Supt. of Docs., U.S. Govt. Print.
Off., 1969] iv, 110 p. [1.00]
379/.12142/0973 76-601801
LB2338 .C66 MRR Ref Desk.

Directory of special programs for
minority group members: Career
information services, employment
skills banks, financial aid. 1974-
[Garrett Park, Md., Garrett Park
Press] [$6.95] 331.7/02/02573 73-
93533
HD5724 .D56 MRR Alc Latest edition

Proia, Nicholas C. Barron's handbook
of American college financial aid
Rev. Woodbury, N.Y., Barron's
Educational Series, inc. [1974] 508
p. [$6.95] 378.3/0973 74-165306
LB2338 .P72 1974 MRR Ref Desk.

Toy, Henry, Federal dollars for
scholars [1st ed.] Washington, Nu-
Toy [1970] vii, 54 p., 292 columns.
378.3/0973 77-112985
LB2338 .T6 MRR Alc.

STUDENT AID--UNITED STATES--DIRECTORIES.
Searles, Aysel. Guide to financial
aids for students in arts & sciences
for graduate and professional study
Rev. ed. New York, Arco [1974] xii,
107 p. [$3.95] 378.3/025/73 74-
80776
LB2338 .S4 1974 MRR Ref Desk.

STUDENT AID--UNITED STATES--YEARBOOKS.
Need a lift? Indianapolis. 67-6704

Began in 1951.
LB2338 .N37 MRR Alc Latest edition

STUDENT COUNSELORS--DIRECTORIES.
The N A F S A directory.
[Washington, etc.] 61-24710
LB3602.N2 A52 MRR Alc Latest
edition

STUDENT GUIDANCE
see Personnel service in education

see Vocational guidance

STUDENT LOAN FUNDS--UNITED STATES.
Current financial aids for
undergraduate students. 1969/70-
Moline, Ill., etc., M & L
Enterprises, etc. 378.3/025/73 73-
2076
LB2338 .C8 MRR Ref Desk Latest
edition

STUDENT MOVEMENTS--UNITED STATES--
BIBLIOGRAPHY.
Miller, Albert Jay. Confrontation,
conflict, and dissent: Metuchen,
N.J., Scarecrow Press, 1972. 567 p.
016.3091/73/092 78-180440
Z7165.U5 M53 MRR Alc.

STUDENT PARTISAN--INDEXES.
Indexes to independent Socialist
periodicals. Berkeley, Calif.,
Independent Socialist Press [1969]
221 p. [9.75] 016.3091 77-16046
HX15 .I43 no. 4 MRR Alc.

STUDENT TRAVEL--YEARBOOKS.
United States National Student
Association. The student traveler
abroad; work, study, travel. New
York, Grosset & Dunlap. 370.19/62
72-626265
LB2376 .U7 MRR Ref Desk Latest
edition

STUDENTS.
see also College students

see also High school students

STUDENTS--POLITICAL ACTIVITY--
BIBLIOGRAPHY.
Altbach, Philip G. American
students: Lexington, Mass.,
Lexington Books [1973] xiv, 537 p.
016.3781/98/1 73-7992
Z5814.S86 A55 1973 MRR Alc.

STUDENTS--UNITED STATES.
Who's who among students in American
universities and colleges. v. 1-
1935- Washington [etc.] Randall Pub.
Co. [etc.] 35-8707
LA2311 .W43 MRR Biog Latest
edition

STUDENTS--UNITED STATES--DIRECTORIES.
Outstanding college athletes of
America. 1969- Washington, D.C.
796 79-94524
GV697.A1 O86 MRR Biog Latest
edition

Who's who among students in American
junior colleges. 1966/67-- ed.
Tuscaloosa, Ala., Randall Pub. Co.
378.1/98/025 73-200965
LA2311 .W42 MRR Biog Latest
edition

STUDENTS, FOREIGN.
see also Foreign study

Study abroad. v. 1- 1948- [Paris]
UNESCO. 378.3 49-2511
LB2338 .S86 MRR Ref Desk Latest
edition / MRR Alc Latest edition

STUDENTS, FOREIGN--YEARBOOKS.
United States National Student
Association. The student traveler
abroad; work, study, travel. New
York, Grosset & Dunlap. 370.19/62
72-626265
LB2376 .U7 MRR Ref Desk Latest
edition

STUDENTS, FOREIGN--SWEDEN.
Sverige-Amerika stiftelsen. Travel,
study and research in Sweden. 6. ed.
Stockholm, Sverige-Amerika stift.
[Nord. bokh., distr.)] 1965 [i. e.
1966] xi, 277, [2] p. [15.00] 67-
79953
L947 .S858 1965 MRR Alc.

STUDENTS, FOREIGN--UNITED STATES.
Institute of International Education.
Open doors; foreign students,
foreign doctors, foreign faculty
members in the United States, U.S.
students, U.S. faculty members
abroad. [New York?] 378.3 55-4594

LB2283 .I615 MRR Alc Latest
edition

The N A F S A directory.
[Washington, etc.] 61-24710
LB3602.N2 A52 MRR Alc Latest
edition

United States. Bureau of Educational
and Cultural Affairs. International
exchange. [Washington, For sale by
the Supt. of Docs. U.S. Govt. Print.
Off.] 370.19/6/0973 72-626994
LB2283 .U438 MRR Alc Latest
edition

STUDENTS, INTERCHANGE OF.
Handbook on international study.
1955- [New York] Institute of
International Education. 55-8482
LB2376 .H3 MRR Ref Desk Latest
edition

Institute of International Education.
Open doors; foreign students,
foreign doctors, foreign faculty
members in the United States, U.S.
students, U.S. faculty members
abroad. [New York?] 378.3 55-4594

LB2283 .I615 MRR Alc Latest
edition

International Association for the
Exchange of Students for Technical
Experience. Report. [London] 378.3
52-65801
Began publication in 1948.
LB2376 .I57 MRR Alc Latest edition

STUDENTS, RATING OF.
see also Educational tests and
measurements

STUDENTS, TRANSFER OF.
see also Transfer students

Proia, Nicholas C. Barron's handbook
of college transfer information.
Rev. ed. Woodbury, N.Y., Barron's
Educational Series [1971] viii, 271
p. [$3.95] 378.169/14/02573 75-
29430
L901 .P73 1971 MRR Alc.

STUTTGART. BIBLIOTHEK FÜR ZEITGESCHICHTE.
Stuttgart. Bibliothek für Zeitgeschichte. Bibliothek für Zeitgeschichte--Weltkriegsbücherei, Stuttgart; systematischer Katalog. Boston, G. K. Hall, 1968. 20 v. 74-225445
  Z6204 .S8 1968 MRR Alc (Dk 33)

STUTTGART--DIRECTORIES.
Adressbuch der Stadt Stuttgart. Stuttgart, Union Verlag 12-20383
  DD901.S96 A63 MRR Alc Latest edition

STYLE, LITERARY.
see also Letter-writing

STYLE, LITERARY--BIBLIOGRAPHY.
Milic, Louis Tonko. Style and stylistics; New York, Free Press [1967] 199 p. 016.808 67-19233
  Z6514.S8 M49 MRR Alc.

STYLE IN DRESS
see Costume

see Fashion

STYRIA--COMMERCE--DIRECTORIES.
Herold Adressbuch von Steiermark für Industrie, Handel, Gewerbe. Wien, Herold. 72-622308
  HF3549.S8 A45 MRR Alc Latest edition

SUB-SAHARAN AFRICA
see Africa, Sub-Saharan

SUBCONSCIOUSNESS.
see also Dreams

see also Psychoanalysis

SUBJECT CATALOGING.
Foskett, Antony Charles. The subject approach to information 2d ed., rev. and enl. [Hamden, Conn.] Linnet Books [1972, c1971] 429 p. 025.33 71-31243
  Z695 .F66 1972 MRR Alc.

SUBJECT HEADINGS.
Atkins, Thomas V. Cross-reference index: a subject heading guide; New York, R. R. Bowker Co., 1974. viii, 255 p. 025.3/3 73-23066
  Z695 .A954 MRR Alc.

Ball, Miriam Ogden, comp. Subject headings for the information file. 8th ed. New York, H. W. Wilson Co., 1956. 179 p. 025.33 56-7643
  Z695 .B24 1956 MRR Alc.

British Museum. Dept. of Printed Books. Subject index of the modern works added to the British museum library. [1st]- 1901/05- London, Trustees of the British Museum. 019.1 07-10319
  Z1035 .B8613 MRR Alc (Dk33) Full set

Eaton, Thelma, Cataloging and classification, 3d ed. Champaign, Ill., Distributed by the Illini Union Bookstore [1963] 199 p. 025.3 63-5885
  Z695 .E171 1963 MRR Alc.

Haykin, David Judson, Subject headings; a practical guide. Washington, U.S. Govt. Print. Off., 1951. v, 140 p. 025.33 52-60002
  Z663.78 .S7 MRR Alc.

London Library. Subject-index of the London Library, London, 1909. v. 10-177
  Z921 .L613 MRR Alc (Dk 33).

Metcalfe, John Wallace, Subject classifying and indexing of libraries and literature. New York, Scarecrow Press, 1959. 347 p. 025.4 59-65011
  Z696 .M59 MRR Alc.

Peabody institute, Baltimore. Library. Catalogue of the library of the Peabody institute of the city of Baltimore ... Baltimore [I. Friedenwald] 1883-92. 5 v. 02-5028

  Z881 .B2 MRR Alc (Dk33)

Peabody institute, Baltimore. Library. Second catalogue of the library of the Peabody institute of the city of Baltimore, Baltimore, 1896-1905. 8 v. 02-5029
  Z881 .B21 MRR Alc (Dk33)

Peddie, Robert Alexander, Subject index of books published up to and including 1880; London, Grafton & co., 1935. xv, [1], 857, [1] p. 36-890
  Z1035 .P37 2d ser. MRR Alc.

Peddie, Robert Alexander, Subject index of books published up to and including 1880. London, Grafton, 1948. vii, 872 p. 016 a 48-8762
  Z1035 .P38 MRR Alc.

Peddie, Robert Alexander, Subject index of books published up to and including 1880, A-Z, London, H. Pordes, 1962. xv, 745 p. 64-46978

  Z1035 .P37 1962 MRR Alc.

Sears, Minnie Earl, Sears List of subject headings. 10th ed., New York, H. W. Wilson Co., 1972. xliii, 590 p. 025.33 79-38376
  Z695 .S43 1972 MRR Alc.

Tauber, Maurice Falcolm, Cataloging and classification, New Brunswick, N.J., Graduate School of Library Service, Rutgers, the State University, 1960. 271, 92 p. 025.3 60-7278
  Z695 .T25 MRR Alc.

Taylor, Archer, General subject-indexes since 1548. Philadelphia, University of Pennsylvania Press [c1966] 336 p. 017 66-10221
  Z695 .T28 MRR Alc.

United States. Library of Congress. Catalog Division. Subject subdivisions: 6th ed., reprinted 1928. Washington, U.S. Govt. Print. Off., 1924 [i.e. 1928] 89 p. 62-56743
  Z663.74 .P7 1928 MRR Alc.

United States. Library of Congress. Subject Cataloging Division. Library of Congress subject headings supplements, 1966-1971 cumulation. Berkeley, University of California; for sale by University-Wide Library Automation Programs, Institute of Library Research] 1972. 793 p. [$40.00] 025.3/3 73-162768
  Z695 .U4739 MRR Ref Desk.

United States. Library of Congress. Subject Cataloging Division. Subject headings used in the dictionary catalogs of the Library of Congress [from 1897 through June 1964] 7th ed., Washington [for sale by the Card Division, Library of Congress] 1966. viii, 1432 p. 65-60043
  Z663.78 .S82 MRR Alc.

Vertical file index. v. [1]- 1932/34- New York, H. W. Wilson. 016 45-40505
  Z1231.P2 V48 MRR Alc Full set

Williams, James G. Classified Library of Congress subject headings, New York, M. Dekker, 1972. 2 v. 025.4 72-91323
  Z695.U48 W55 MRR Alc.

SUBJECT HEADINGS--ANTHROPOLOGY.
Harvard University. Peabody Museum of Archaeology and Ethnology. Library. Catalogue: subjects. Boston, G. K. Hall, 1963. 27 v. 018.1 64-2645
  Z5119 .H36 MRR Alc (Dk 33)

SUBJECT HEADINGS--BIBLIOGRAPHY.
Case Western Reserve University. Bibliographic Systems Center. Selected materials in classification; New York, Special Libraries Association [c1968] 142 p. 016.0254 68-19707
  Z696 .C3 MRR Alc.

Special Libraries Association. Guide to the SLA loan collection of classification schemes and subject heading lists 5th ed. New York, 1961. 97 p. 016.02543 61-13157
  Z696 .S8 1961 MRR Alc.

SUBJECT HEADINGS--CHILDREN'S LITERATURE.
United States. Library of Congress. Subject Cataloging Division. Subject headings for children's literature; Washington, Library of Congress, 1969. 30 p. [0.75] 025.33/0285 76-602013
  Z663.78 .C4 MRR Alc.

SUBJECT HEADINGS--ECONOMIC DEVELOPMENT.
Organization for Economic Cooperation and Development. Macrothesaurus; 1st English ed. [Paris, 1972] 17, 225 p. [$8.00 (U.S.)] 025.3/333 73-157089
  Z695.1.E2 O76 MRR Alc.

SUBJECT HEADINGS--EDUCATION.
Barhydt, Gordon C. Information retrieval thesaurus of education terms Cleveland, Press of Case Western Reserve University, 1968. vi, 133 p. [$5.50] 029.7 67-27797

  Z695.1.E3 B3 MRR Alc.

SUBJECT HEADINGS--LANGUAGE.
United States. Library of Congress. Catalog division. Literature subject headings with list for Shakespeare collections and Language subject headings. 5th ed. Washington, Govt. print. off., 1926. iii, 147 p. 26-26002
  Z663.74 .P68 1926 MRR Alc.

SUBJECT HEADINGS--LAW.
United States. Library of Congress. Law library. Tentative headings and cross-references for a subject catalogue of American and English law; Washington, Govt. print. off., 1911. 5 p. l., 7-150 numb. l. 11-35006
  Z663.5 .T4 MRR Alc.

SUBJECT HEADINGS--LITERATURE.
United States. Library of Congress. Catalog division. Literature subject headings with list for Shakespeare collections and Language subject headings. 5th ed. Washington, Govt. print. off., 1926. iii, 147 p. 26-26002
  Z663.74 .P68 1926 MRR Alc.

SUBJECT HEADINGS--MEDICINE.
Cumulated Index medicus. v. 1- 1960- 62-4404
  Z660 .I422 Sci RR Full set / MRR Alc Full set

SUBJECT HEADINGS--MUSEUMS.
American association of museums. A bibliography of museums and museum work, Washington, D.C., The American association of museums, 1928. 2 p. l., vi, 302 p. 28-17186
  Z5052 .A51 MRR Alc.

SUBJECT HEADINGS--MUSIC.
The Music index. v. 1- 1949- Detroit, Information Coordinators, inc.(etc.) 50-13627
  ML118 .M84 MRR Alc Full set

United States. Library of Congress. Subject Cataloging Division. Music subject headings used on printed catalog cards of the Library of Congress. Washington, 1952. x, 133 p. 025.33 52-60004
  Z663.78.M8 MRR Alc.

SUBJECT HEADINGS--NAMES, GEOGRAPHICAL.
United States. Library of Congress. Subject Cataloging Division. Period subdivisions under names of places Washington, U.S. Govt. Print. Off., 1950. iv, 75 p. 025.33 50-62964
  Z663.78 .P4 MRR Alc.

SUBJECT HEADINGS--NURSES AND NURSING.
Cumulative index to nursing literature. Nursing subject headings. [Glendale, Calif.] Seventh-Day Adventist Hospital Association. 610.73014 66-96923
  Z695.1.N8 C8 MRR Alc Latest edition

SUBJECT HEADINGS--SCIENCE.
United States. Library of Congress. Science and Technology Division. List of subject headings. 2d ed. Washington, 1950. v, 209 p. 025.335 50-61483
  Z663.49 .L5 1950 MRR Alc.

SUBJECT HEADINGS--TECHNOLOGY.
United States. Library of Congress. Science and Technology Division. List of subject headings. 2d ed. Washington, 1950. v, 209 p. 025.335 50-61483
  Z663.49 .L5 1950 MRR Alc.

SUBJECT HEADINGS--AFRICA.
Boston University. Libraries. Catalog of African government documents and African area index. 2d ed., rev. and enl. Boston, G. K. Hall, 1964. 471 p. 65-98838
  Z3508.G6 B6 1964 MRR Alc.

SUBMARINE ARCHAEOLOGY
see Underwater archaeology

SUBMARINE TOPOGRAPHY.
United States. Geographic Names Division. Undersea features. 2d ed. Washington, 1971 [i.e. 1972] vi, 182 p. 910/.02/162 72-601422
  GC83 .U5 1972 MRR Alc.

SUBSIDIARY CORPORATIONS--DIRECTORIES.
United States. Office of International Investment. List of foreign firms with some interest/control in American manufacturing and petroleum companies in the United States. [Washington] 1972. 61 p. 332.6/73/02573 72-603415
  HG4909 .A5 1972 MRR Ref Desk.

Who owns whom. North American edition. London, O. W. Roskill. 332.6/73/025 74-646353
  HG4538 .W423 MRR Alc Latest edition

SUBSIDIARY CORPORATIONS--STATISTICS.
Vaupel, James W. The world's multinational enterprises; Boston, Division of Research, Graduate School of Business Administration, Harvard University, 1973. xxxiii, 505 p. [$25.00] 338.8/8 73-76600
  HD69.17 V36 MRR Alc.

SUBSIDIARY CORPORATIONS--ASIA--
DIRECTORIES.
. Who owns whom: Australasia and Far
East. 1972- London, O. W. Roskill.
382/.025 74-642726
HD2927 .W48 MRR Alc Latest edition

SUBSIDIARY CORPORATIONS--AUSTRALASIA--
DIRECTORIES.
Who owns whom: Australasia and Far
East. 1972- London, O. W. Roskill.
382/.025 74-642726
HD2927 .W48 MRR Alc Latest edition

SUBSIDIARY CORPORATIONS--UNITED STATES.
Probe directory of foreign direct
investment in the United States.
[Washington] Probe International,
inc. 332.6/73/0973 74-645092
HG4907 .P74 MRR Alc Latest edition

SUBSIDIES.
Grantsmanship: money and how to get
it. Orange, N.J., Academic Media
[1973] 27 p. [$5.00] 001.4/4 72-
13214
HG174 .G72 MRR Alc

SUBSIDIES--UNITED STATES.
Roth, William V., 1969 listing of
operating Federal assistance programs
compiled during the Roth study.
Washington, U.S. Govt. Print. Off.,
1969. x, 1132 p. [4.50] 338.973
73-605845
HJ275 .R6 1969 MRR Ref Desk.

SUBVERSIVE ACTIVITIES--EUROPE.
United States. Library of Congress.
Law Library. Legislation for the
protection of the state in various
European countries; Washington,
Library of Congress, Law Library,
Foreign Law Section, 1956. v, 155 l.
016.35175 016.36413* 56-61203
Z663.5 .L4 MRR Alc.

SUBVERSIVE ACTIVITIES--UNITED STATES--
INDEXES.
United States. Congress. Senate.
Committee on Government Operations.
Congressional investigations of
communism and subversive activities;
Washington, U.S. Govt. Print. Off.,
1956. xvi, 382 p. 56-62374
Z7164.S67 U5 MRR Alc.

SUCCESS.
see also Applications for positions

see also Business

Businessmen around the globe.
[Harrisburg, Pa.] Stackpole Books
[1967] xiv, 252 p. 650/.1/0922 67-
21669
HF5386 .B88 1967 MRR Biog.

SUCCULENT PLANTS.
Jacobsen, Hermann, A handbook of
succulent plants; English ed. after
the 1st German ed., Jena 1954, rev.
and enl. London, Blandford Press
[1960] 3 v. (xiii, 1441 p.) 582.14
61-403
SB438 .J285 MRR Alc.

SUDAN.
American University, Washington, D.C.
Foreign Areas Studies Division. Area
handbook for the Republic of the
Sudan. 2d ed. Washington [Dept. of
the Army] for sale by the
Superintendent of Documents, U.S.
Govt. Print. Office, 1964. xi, 473
p. 65-60681
DT108.7 .A7 1964 MRR Alc.

SUDAN--BIBLIOGRAPHY.
United States. Library of Congress.
European Affairs Division. Egypt and
the Anglo-Egyptian Sudan, a selective
guide to background reading.
Washington, University Press of
Washington [1952] 26 p. 016.9162
52-60008
Z663.26 .E4 MRR Alc.

United States. Library of Congress.
General Reference and Bibliography
Division. North and Northeast
Africa; Washington, 1957. v, 182 p.
016.96 57-60062
Z663.28 .N6 MRR Alc.

SUDAN--BIOGRAPHY.
Hill, Richard Leslie. A biographical
dictionary of the Sudan 2nd ed.
London, Cass, 1967. 409 p. [90/-]
920.0624 67-94080
DT108.05.A2 H5 1967 MRR Biog.

SUDAN--COMMERCE--DIRECTORIES.
The Diplomatic Press Sudan trade
directory including classified trade
index. 8th- ed.; 1966/67- London,
Diplomatic Press and Pub. Co. 72-
626730
HF46 .D5 MRR Alc Latest edition

SUDAN--COMMERCE--YEARBOOKS.
The Diplomatic Press Sudan trade
directory including classified trade
index. 8th- ed.; 1966/67- London,
Diplomatic Press and Pub. Co. 72-
626730
HF46 .D5 MRR Alc Latest edition

SUDAN--GAZETTEERS.
United States. Office of Geography.
Sudan; official standard names
approved by the United States Board
on Geographic Names. Washington, For
sale by the Superintendent of
Documents, U.S. Govt. Print. Off.,
1962. xi, 358 p. 916.24 62-64495

DT119 .U5 MRR Alc.

SUDAN--HISTORY--1820-
Holt, Peter Malcolm. A modern
history of the Sudan. New York,
Grove Press [1961] 241 p. 962.4
61-11858
DT108 .H72 MRR Alc.

SUETONIUS TRANQUILLUS, C.
Howard, Albert Andrew, ed. Index
verborvm C. Svetoni Tranqvilli
stiliqve eivs proprietatvm
nonnvllarvm, Cantabrigiae
Massachvsettensivm, E typographeo
academiae harvardianae; [etc., etc.]
1922. 4 p. l., 273, [1] p. 22-
25830
PA6702.Z8 1922 MRR Alc.

SUFFRAGE.
see also Negroes--Politics and
suffrage

see also Voting

see also Woman--Suffrage

SUGAR--MANUFACTURE AND REFINING--
YEARBOOKS.
Sugar y azúcar. v. 36- 1968-
[New York, M. Palmer] 78-618348
TP375.3 .S85 MRR Alc Latest
edition / Sci RR Latest edition

SUGAR TRADE--DIRECTORIES.
Licht, F. O., firm. F. O. Licht's
Internationales zuckerstatistisches
Jahr- und Adressbuch. Ratzeburg. 51-
36145
HD9100.4 .L5 MRR Alc Latest
edition

Zucker-Jahrbuch. Hamburg, A. Röper.
60-28782
Began publication in 1954
HD9100.2 .Z8 MRR Alc Latest
edition

SUGAR TRADE--STATISTICS.
Licht, F. O., firm. F. O. Licht's
Internationales zuckerstatistisches
Jahr- und Adressbuch. Ratzeburg. 51-
36145
HD9100.4 .L5 MRR Alc Latest
edition

Sugar year book. London,
International Sugar Organization
[etc.] 338.476641 49-27323
HD9100.2 .P6 MRR Alc Latest
edition

SUGAR TRADE--YEARBOOKS.
Sugar year book. London,
International Sugar Organization
[etc.] 338.476641 49-27323
HD9100.2 .P6 MRR Alc Latest
edition

Zucker-Jahrbuch. Hamburg, A. Röper.
60-28782
Began publication in 1954
HD9100.2 .Z8 MRR Alc Latest
edition

SUMMER CAMPS
see Camps

SUMMER EMPLOYMENT--UNITED STATES--
DIRECTORIES.
Summer employment directory of the
United States. Cincinnati, National
Directory Service. 54-33991
HF5382.5U5 S76 MRR Alc Latest
edition

SUMMER SCHOOLS.
Garraty, John Arthur, The new guide
to study abroad; 1974-1975 ed. New
York, Harper & Row [1974] xliii, 422
p. [$10.95] 370.19/6 72-9117
LB2376 .G33 1974 MRR Ref Desk.

Vacation study abroad. [Paris,
United Nations Educational,
Scientific and Cultural Organization]
370.19/62 72-627046
LB2338 .V3 MRR Ref Desk Latest
edition

SUMMER SCHOOLS--DIRECTORIES.
Summer study abroad. New York,
Institute of International Education.
370.19/6/025 73-78423
LB2375 .S8 MRR Alc Latest edition

SUMMER SCHOOLS--UNITED STATES--
DIRECTORIES.
Summer studies in private independent
schools. 1st- ed.; 1964-
Wallingford, Conn., Bunting and Lyon.
373.2205873 64-20357
LC5751 .S8 MRR Alc Latest edition

SUMMERALL, CHARLES PELOT, 1867-1955--
BIBLIOGRAPHY.
United States. Library of Congress.
Manuscript Division. Charles Pelot
Summerall: a register of his papers
in the Library of Congress.
Washington, 1958. 9 l. 012 58-
60068
Z663.34 .S8 MRR Alc.

SUN.
Kuiper, Gerard Peter, ed. The sun.
Chicago, University of Chicago Press
[1953] xix, 745 p. 523.7 61-45072
QB501 .S6 vol. 1 MRR Alc.

SUNDAY LEGISLATION--UNITED STATES.
Blakely, William Addison, ed.
American state papers and related
documents on freedom in religion.
4th rev. ed. Washington, Published
for the Religious Liberty Association
by the Review and Herald, 1949. 915
p. 263.8 50-206
BV133 .B6 1949 MRR Alc.

SUNKEN CITIES
see Cities and towns, Ruined,
extinct, etc.

SUPERIOR CHILDREN
see Gifted children

SUPERMARKETS--DIRECTORIES.
Directory: Supermarket, grocery and
convenience store chains. 1956-
[New York, Business Guides, inc.]
381/.41/02573 72-623763
HD9321.3 .C43 MRR Alc Latest
edition

SUPERMARKETS--UNITED STATES--
DIRECTORIES.
Directory: Supermarket, grocery and
convenience store chains. 1956-
[New York, Business Guides, inc.]
381/.41/02573 72-623763
HD9321.3 .C43 MRR Alc Latest
edition

SUPERNATURAL.
see also Occult sciences

see also Prophecies

see also Psychical research

SUPERNATURAL IN LITERATURE.
Walbridge, Earle Francis, Literary
characters drawn from life; New
York, H. W. Wilson Co., 1936. 192 p.
098.5 36-10273
Z1026 .W15 MRR Alc.

SUPERNATURAL IN MOVING-PICTURES.
see also Fantastic films

SUPERSTITION.
see also Dreams

see also Folk-lore

Brasch, Rudolph, How did it begin?
[Croydon, Australia] Longmans [1965]
352 p. 390 66-3994
GT75 .B7 MRR Alc.

Chaundler, Christine. Every man's
book of superstitions; Oxford, A. R.
Mowbray & Co., Ltd., 1970. 174 p.
[30/-] 398.3/7 76-533357
AZ999 .C47 MRR Alc.

Frazer, James George, Sir,
Aftermath; London, Macmillan and
co., limited, 1936. xx, 494 p. 291
37-2300
BL310 .F715 1936 MRR Alc.

[Frazer, James George Sir,] The
golden bough; 3d ed. [New York, The
Macmillan company, 1935] 12 v. 291
35-35398
BL310 .F7 1935 MRR Alc.

Lys, Claudia de. A treasury of
American superstitions, New York,
Philosophical Library [1948] xxii,
494 p. 398.3 48-6722
BF1775 .L9 MRR Alc.

Lys, Claudia de. A treasury of
superstitions. New York,
Philosophical Library [1957] 317 p.
398.3 58-609
BF1775 .L92 MRR Alc.

SUPERSTITION--DICTIONARIES.
Bonnerjea, Biren. A dictionary of
superstitions and mythology. London,
Folk Press, Detroit, Singing Tree
Press, 1969. 314 p. 291/.13/03 69-
17755
BL303 .B6 1969 MRR Alc.

Ferm, Vergilius Ture Anselm, A brief
dictionary of American superstitions.
New York, Philosophical Library
[1959] 259 p. 398.303 59-16473
AZ999 .F45 MRR Alc.

Radford, Edwin, Encyclopaedia of
superstitions Chester Springs [Pa.]
Dufour Editions [1969, c1961] 384 p.
[8.95] 398.3/7/03 69-20013
BF1775 .R3 1969 MRR Alc.

SUPPLY AND DEMAND.
see also Consumption (Economics)

see also Prices

SURGEONS.
see also Physicians

**SURGEONS--UNITED STATES--BIO-
BIBLIOGRAPHY.**
Stone, Richard French, Biography of
eminent American physicians and
surgeons, Indianapolis, Carlon &
Hollenbeck, 1894. xxii, 729 p. 38-
1873
R153 .S8 MRR Biog.

SURGERY.
Surgery: principles and practice.
4th ed. Philadelphia, Lippincott
[1970] xxvii, 1864 p. 617 72-
108953
RD31 .S92 1970 MRR Alc.

**SURGICAL INSTRUMENTS AND APPARATUS--
DIRECTORIES.**
A.S.T.A. manufacturers directory.
[Chicago] American Surgical Trade
Association. 617.078 60-25245
RD76 .A2 Sci RR Latest edition* /
MRR Alc Latest edition

SURINAM--GAZETTEERS.
United States. Office of Geography.
The Guianas; Washington, 1954. 234
p. 918.8 78-10045
F2364 .U5 MRR Alc.

SURVEYS, EDUCATIONAL
see Educational surveys

SURVIVAL (HUMAN ECOLOGY)
see Human ecology

SWAHILI LANGUAGE--DICTIONARIES--ENGLISH.
Rechenbach, Charles William. Swahili-
English dictionary Washington,
Catholic University of America Press,
1967. xi, 641 p. 496/.923/2 67-
31438
PL8703 .R4 MRR Alc.

**SWAHILI LANGUAGE--DICTIONARIES--
POLYGLOT.**
Bergman, Peter M. The concise
dictionary of twenty-six languages in
simultaneous translations, New York,
Polyglot Library [1968] 406 p. 413
67-14284
P361 .B4 TJ Rm.

SWAZILAND--GAZETTEERS.
United States. Office of Geography.
South Africa; Washington, 1954. 2
v. (1081 p.) 916.8/003 73-10017
DT752 .U65 MRR Alc.

**SWAZILAND--GOVERNMENT PUBLICATIONS--
BIBLIOGRAPHY--UNION LISTS.**
Ballma, Mildred Grimes. Botswana,
Lesotho, and Swaziland: a guide to
official publications, 1868-1968,
Washington, General Reference and
Bibliography Division, Library of
Congress; [for sale by the Supt. of
Docs., U.S. Govt. Print. Off.] 1971.
xvi, 84 p. [$1.00] 016.9168 74-
171029
Z663.285 .B6 MRR Alc.

SWEDEN.
Nar-var-hur. 1.- arg.; 1945-
[Stockholm] Forum [etc.] 45-17468
AY982 .N3 MRR Alc Latest edition

Scobbie, Irene. Sweden. London,
Ernest Benn, 1972. 254, [16] p.
[£3.00] 948.5 73-153639
DL609 .S37 1972b MRR Alc.

Tidens kalender. Stockholm, Tidens
forlag. 529.43 46-36630
Publication began in 1922?
AY984 .T5 MRR Alc Latest edition

SWEDEN--BIO-BIBLIOGRAPHY.
Svenskt biografiskt lexikon ...
Stockholm, A. Bonnier [1918- v.
27-15141
CT1313 .S8 MRR Biog.

Svenskt forfattarlexikon; 1900/40-
Stockholm, Raben & Sjogren. 53-
34385
Z2630 .S92 MRR Alc Full set

SWEDEN--BIOGRAPHY.
Lindroth, Sten, ed. Swedish men of
science, 1650-1950. Stockholm,
Swedish Institute, 1952. 295 p.
925 53-16761
Q127.S85 L5 MRR Biog.

Svenskt forfattarlexikon; 1900/40-
Stockholm, Raben & Sjogren. 53-
34385
Z2630 .S92 MRR Alc Full set

SWEDEN--BIOGRAPHY--DICTIONARIES.
Dictionary of Scandinavian biography.
London, Melrose Press [1972] xxxv,
467 p. [£10.50] 920/.048 B 73-
188270
CT1243 .D53 MRR Biog.

Svenska man och kvinnor; Stockholm,
Bonnier [1842-55] 8 v. 920.0485
49-15252
CT1313 .S58 MRR Biog.

Svenskt biografiskt lexikon ...
Stockholm, A. Bonnier [1918- v.
27-15141
CT1313 .S8 MRR Biog.

Vem ar det? 1912- Stockholm, P. A.
Norstedt. 14-2846
DL644 .V4 MRR Biog Latest edition

SWEDEN--COMMERCE--DIRECTORIES.
Nordisk handelskalender, København,
H. P. Bov. 49-23912
Began with vol. for 1903.
HF5193 .N6 MRR Alc Latest edition

Swedish export directory. 28th-
ed.; 1846- Stockholm, General Export
Association of Sweden. 72-623267
HF3673 .S6 MRR Alc Latest edition

**SWEDEN--COMMERCE--DIRECTORIES--
YEARBOOKS.**
Sveriges handelskalender. Stockholm,
A. Bonniers forlag. 74-642440
Began in 1859.
HF3673 .S8 MRR Alc Latest edition

**SWEDEN--DESCRIPTION AND TRAVEL--GUIDE-
BOOKS.**
Sweden 3d ed.] Geneva, Paris [etc.]
Nagel Publishers [1968]. 135 p.
[4.95] 914.85/04/5 71-438869
DL607 .S9 1968 MRR Alc.

SWEDEN--DIRECTORIES.
Svenska institutet for kulturellt
utbyte med utlandet, Stockholm.
Where to get your facts about Sweden.
Stockholm, The Swedish Institute,
1968. 31 p. [gratis] 914.85/0025
73-383592
DL605 .S84 MRR Alc.

**SWEDEN--EXECUTIVE DEPARTMENTS--
DIRECTORIES.**
Sweden. Sveriges statskalender.
Uppsala, Stockholm, Almquist &
Wiksell Informations-industri AB. 07-
16334
JN7724 MRR Alc Latest edition

SWEDEN--GAZETTEERS.
Generalstabens litografiska anstalt,
Stockholm. Svenska orter; Stockholm
[Generalstabens litografiska anstalt]
1932- v. in and atlas. 914.85
ac 34-2254
DL605 .G4 MRR Alc.

United States. Office of Geography.
Sweden; official standard names
approved by the United States Board
on Geographic Names. [Washington,
U.S. Govt. Print. Off., 1963] vii,
1033 p. 63-65295
DL605 .U5 MRR Alc.

**SWEDEN--GOVERNMENT PUBLICATIONS--
BIBLIOGRAPHY.**
Sweden. Riksdagen. Biblioteket.
Forteckning over statliga
utredningar 1904-1945. Norrkoping,
Ostergotlands dagblads tryckeri,
1953. vi, 1405 p. 54-20125
Z2629 .S943 MRR Alc.

SWEDEN--HISTORY.
Andersson, Ingvar, A history of
Sweden. London, Weidenfeld and
Nicolson [1956] 461 p. 948.5 56-
2336
DL648 .A612 1956a MRR Alc.

Scobbie, Irene. Sweden. London,
Ernest Benn, 1972. 254, [16] p.
[£3.00] 948.5 73-153639
DL609 .S37 1972b MRR Alc.

SWEDEN--IMPRINTS.
Svensk bokkatalog. 1866/75-
Stockholm, Tidningsaktiebolaget
Svensk Bokhandel [etc.] 015.485 01-
10261
Z2621 .S95 MRR Alc Partial set

SWEDEN--INDUSTRIES--DIRECTORIES.
Some prominent Swedish companies.
Stockholm, P. A. Norstedt.
338.7/09485 78-276274
HC372 .S64 MRR Alc Latest edition

**SWEDEN--INDUSTRIES--DIRECTORIES--
YEARBOOKS.**
Svensk industrikalender. Stockholm,
P. A. Norstedt [etc.] 74-642462
HF3673 .S63 MRR Alc Latest edition

Sveriges handelskalender. Stockholm,
A. Bonniers forlag. 74-642440
Began in 1859.
HF3673 .S8 MRR Alc Latest edition

**SWEDEN--LEARNED INSTITUTIONS AND
SOCIETIES--DIRECTORIES.**
Sweden. Sveriges statskalender.
Uppsala, Stockholm, Almquist &
Wiksell Informations-industri AB. 07-
16334
JN7724 MRR Alc Latest edition

**SWEDEN--MANUFACTURES--DIRECTORIES--
YEARBOOKS.**
Svensk industrikalender. Stockholm,
P. A. Norstedt [etc.] 74-642462
HF3673 .S63 MRR Alc Latest edition

SWEDEN--MAPS.
Generalstabens litografiska anstalt,
Stockholm. Svenska orter; Stockholm
[Generalstabens litografiska anstalt]
1932- v. in and atlas. 914.85
ac 34-2254
DL605 .G4 MRR Alc.

SWEDEN--REGISTERS.
Svenska kalendern; Uppsala,
Stockholm, Almqvist & Wiksells
boktryckeri. ca 13-812
AY983 .S7 MRR Alc Latest edition

Sweden. Sveriges statskalender.
Uppsala, Stockholm, Almquist &
Wiksell Informations-industri AB. 07-
16334
JN7724 MRR Alc Latest edition

SWEDEN--STATISTICS.
Sweden. Statistiska centralbyran.
Statistisk arsbok for Sverige. 1.-
arg.; 1914- Stockholm. 14-17397
HA1523 .A46 MRR Alc Latest edition

SWEDES IN THE UNITED STATES.
American-Swedish handbook. v. [1]-
1943- Rock Island, Ill.
325.24850973 43-9752
E184.S23 A68 MRR Alc Latest
edition

Benson, Adolph Burnett, Americans
from Sweden [1st ed.] Philadelphia,
Lippincott, 1950 [c1949] 448 p.
325.24850973 50-5150
E184.S23 B328 MRR Alc.

SWEDISH LANGUAGE--DICTIONARIES.
Illustrerad svensk ordbok. 3. revid.
uppl. Stockholm, Natur och kultur
[1964] 1917 p. 66-34955
PD5625 .I4 1964 MRR Alc.

SWEDISH LANGUAGE--DICTIONARIES--ENGLISH.
Moth, Axel Fredrik Carl Mathias,
Glossary of library terms, English,
Danish, Dutch, French, German,
Italian, Spanish, Swedish, Boston,
The Boston book company, 1915. 58 p.
15-3471
Z1006 .M72 MRR Alc.

Nojd, Ruben, McKay's modern English-
Swedish and Swedish-English
dictionary. New York, D. McKay Co.
[1954] x, 248, 220 p. 439.732 53-
11359
PD5640 .N613 MRR Alc.

Reuter, Ole, Swedish-English
dictionary, 2nd revised ed. London,
Allen & Unwin, 1966. [8], 405 p.
[35/-] 439.732 66-72017
PD5640 .R42 1966 MRR Alc.

SWEDISH LANGUAGE--DICTIONARIES--FINNISH.
Lampen, Lea. Kuolulaisen
perussanakirja. Helsinki, W.
Soderstrom, 1972. (6) 724 p.
[Fmk40.00] 73-333264
PH278 .L3 MRR Alc.

**SWEDISH LANGUAGE--DICTIONARIES--
POLYGLOT.**
Britannica world language dictionary,
[Chicago, 1958] 1483-2015 p. 413
58-4491
P361 .B7 1958 MRR Alc.

Capitol's concise dictionary.
Bologna, Capitol, 1972. 1051 (i.e.
1207) p. 413 72-172231
P361 .C3 MRR Alc.

Dictionnaire à l'usage de la
librairie ancienne pour les langues:
francaise, anglaise, allemande,
suedoise, danoise, italienne,
espagnole, hollandaise, Paris, Ligue
internationale de la librairie
ancienne, 1956. 190 p. 655.403 57-
2275
Z282 .D5 MRR Alc.

Elsevier's dictionary of criminal
science, in eight languages:
Amsterdam, New York, Elsevier Pub.
Co.; [distributed by Van Nostrand,
Princeton, N.J.] 1960. xv, 1460 p.
364.03 59-12582
HV6017 .E4 MRR Alc.

Elsevier's wood dictionary in seven
languages: Amsterdam, New York,
Elsevier Pub. Co., 1964- v.
634.903 64-14178
SD431 .E4 MRR Alc.

Frey, Albert Romer, Dictionary of
numismatic names, [New York] Barnes
& Noble [1947] ix, 311, 94 p.
737.03 48-5357
CJ67 .F7 1947 MRR Alc.

SWEDISH LANGUAGE--DICTIONARIES-- (Cont.)
International Chamber of Commerce.
Dictionary of advertising and
distribution, Basel, Verlag für
Recht und Gesellschaft, 1954. 1 v.
(unpaged)   659.103 54-24644
HF5803 .I58 1954 MRR Alc.

International insurance dictionary:
[n.p., European Conference of
Insurance Supervisory Services, 1959]
xxxi, 1083 p.   368.03 61-35675
HG8025 .I5 MRR Alc.

Jacks, Graham Vernon. Multilingual
vocabulary of soil science. [2d ed.,
rev. Rome] Land & Water Division,
Food and Agriculture Organization of
the United Nations [1960] xxiii, 428
p.   631.403 60-50105
S591 .J26 1960 MRR Alc.

Labarre, E. J. Dictionary and
encyclopædia of paper and paper-
making. 2d ed., rev. and enl.
London, Oxford University Press,
1952. xxi, 488 p.   676.03 53-29414

TS1085 .L3 1952a MRR Alc.

Nijdam, J. Tuinbouwkundig
woordenboek in acht talen. Herziene
en uitgebreide uitg. van de
Woordenlijst voor de tuinbouw in
zeven talen. ['s-Gravenhage,
Staatsdrukkerij- en
Uitgeverijbedrijf; voor alle anderen
landen: Interscience Publishers, New
York] 1961. 504 p.   62-52704
SB45 .N673 MRR Alc.

Rae, Kenneth, ed. Lexique
international de termes techniques de
théâtre Bruxelles, Elsevier [1959]
139 p.   60-26926
PN2035 .R3 MRR Alc.

Skandinaviska banken, a.--b. Banking
terms: French, German, Italian,
Spanish, Swedish. Stockholm [1964]
65 p.   65-87814
HG151 .S46 MRR Alc.

SWEDISH LANGUAGE--SYNONYMS AND ANTONYMS.
Ord för ord; Stockholm, Nordiska
uppslagsböcker [1960] xx, 815 p.
60-27616
PD5591 .O7 MRR Alc.

SWEDISH LITERATURE--BIBLIOGRAPHY.
Svensk bokkatalog. 1866/75-
Stockholm, Tidningsaktiebolaget
Svensk Bokhandel [etc.] 015.485 01-
10261
Z2621 .S95 MRR Alc Partial set

SWEDISH LITERATURE--BIO-BIBLIOGRAPHY.
Svenskt författarlexikon; 1900/40-
Stockholm, Rabén & Sjögren. 53-
34385
Z2630 .S92 MRR Alc Full set

SWEDISH LITERATURE--HISTORY AND
CRITICISM.
Gustafson, Alrik, A history of
Swedish literature. Minneapolis,
Published for the American-
Scandinavian Foundation by the
University of Minnesota Press [1961]
xv, 708 p.   839.709 61-7722
PT9263 .G8 1961 MRR Alc.

SWEDISH LITERATURE--HISTORY AND
CRITICISM--BIBLIOGRAPHY.
Lund. Universitet.
Litteraturhistoriska institutionen.
Svensk litteraturhistorisk
bibliografi 1951-1960. [Lund,
Lundensiska litteratursällskapet;
(Universitets-biblioteket (distr.)]
1965. [1], 243 l.   67-70493
Z2636 .L8 MRR Alc.

SWEDISH NEWSPAPERS--DIRECTORIES.
Sweden. Sveriges statskalender.
Uppsala, Stockholm, Almquist &
Wiksell Informations-industri AB. 07-
16334
JN7724 MRR Alc Latest edition

SWEDISH PERIODICALS--INDEXES.
Svenska tidskriftsartiklar. årg. 10-
1961- [Lund] Bibliotekstjänst.
72-626677
AI13 .S8 MRR Alc Partial set

SWIMMING.
see also Diving

SWIMMING--DICTIONARIES.
Besford, Pat. Encyclopaedia of
swimming. [New York] St. Martin's
Press [1971] 235 p.   ($7.95)
797.21/03 78-157521
GV837 .B44 MRR Alc.

SWIMMING--RULES.
Amateur Athletic Union of the United
States. Rules for competitive and
synchronized swimming, diving ...
water polo. Indianapolis, Ind.
[etc.] A. A. U. House [etc.] 797.2
46-31932
Publication began in 1932.
GV837.A1 A45 MRR Alc Latest
edition

SWIMMING--STATISTICS.
Amateur Athletic Union of the United
States. Rules for competitive and
synchronized swimming, diving ...
water polo. Indianapolis, Ind.
[etc.] A. A. U. House [etc.] 797.2
46-31932
Publication began in 1932.
GV837.A1 A45 MRR Alc Latest
edition

SWIMMING POOLS--YEARBOOKS.
Swimming pool weekly and swimming
pool age data & reference annual.
38th-   ed.; 1972- [Fort Lauderdale,
Fla., Hoffman Publications] 643/.55
72-625041
TH4763 .S8 MRR Alc Latest edition

SWINDLERS AND SWINDLING.
Mackay, Charles, Extraordinary
popular delusions and the madness of
crowds. London, G. G. Harrap [1956]
xxiv, 724 p.   301.15 133.7 57-1736

AZ999 .M2 1956 MRR Alc.

SWINE BREEDS.
Briggs, Hilton Marshall, Modern
breeds of livestock. Rev. ed. New
York, Macmillan [1958] 754 p.
636.08 58-5049
SF105 .B7 1958 MRR Alc.

Mason, Ian Lauder. A world
dictionary of livestock breeds, types
and varieties, 2nd (revised) ed.
Farnham Royal, Commonwealth
Agricultural Bureaux, 1969. xviii,
268 p. [70/-] 636/.003 75-454433
SF21 .M3 1969 MRR Alc.

SWING MUSIC
see Jazz music

SWISS IN THE UNITED STATES--
BIBLIOGRAPHY.
Bern. Schweizerische
Landesbibliothek. Die Schweiz und
die Vereinigten Staaten von Amerika;
Bern, 1964. 58 p.   64-6083
ZI361.R4 B45 MRR Alc.

SWISS LITERATURE--BIBLIOGRAPHY--
CATALOGS.
Schweizer Bücherverzeichnis.
1948/50- Zurich, Schweizerischer
Buchhandler- und Verlegerverein. a
51-8855
Z949 .B56 MRR Alc Full set

SWISS NEWSPAPERS--BIBLIOGRAPHY.
Zeitungskatalog der Schweiz. 1943-
Zurich, [etc.] Verband
Schweizerischer Annoncen-
Expeditionen. 58-19529
Z6956.S92 Z4 MRR Alc Latest
edition

SWISS PERIODICALS--BIBLIOGRAPHY.
Deutschsprachige Zeitschriften.
Marbach am Neckar, Verlag der
Schillerbuchhandlung Hans Banger.
053.1/025 70-612760
Z6956.G3 A55 MRR Alc Latest
edition

Schweizer Zeitschriftenverzeichnis.
1951/55- Zurich, Schweizerischer
Buchhandler- und Verlegerverein. 58-
31348
Z6956.S92 S33 MRR Alc Latest
edition

Zeitungskatalog der Schweiz. 1943-
Zurich, [etc.] Verband
Schweizerischer Annoncen-
Expeditionen. 58-19529
Z6956.S92 Z4 MRR Alc Latest
edition

SWITZERLAND--BIBLIOGRAPHY--CATALOGS.
Schweizer Bücherverzeichnis.
1948/50- Zurich, Schweizerischer
Buchhandler- und Verlegerverein. a
51-8855
Z949 .B56 MRR Alc Full set

SWITZERLAND--BIOGRAPHY.
Biographisches Lexikon verstorbener
Schweizer. Zurich, Schweizerische
Industrie-Bibliothek, Departement
Lexikon, 1947- v.   920.0494 48-
27632
CT1383 .B5 MRR Biog.

Kosch, Wilhelm, Biographisches
Staatshandbuch; Bern, Francke [1963]
2 v. (1208 p.)   67-3923
DD85 .K6 MRR Biog.

Kürschners biographisches Theater-
Handbuch: Berlin, W. de Gruyter,
1956. xii, 840 p.   a 57-2818
PN2657 .K8 MRR Alc.

SWITZERLAND--BIOGRAPHY--DICTIONARIES.
Dictionnaire historique &
biographique de la Suisse,
Neuchatel, Administration du
Dictionnaire historique et
biographique de la Suisse; 1921 [i.e.
1920]-33. 7 v.   21-5108
DQ51 .D5 MRR Biog.

Who's who in Switzerland, including
the Principality of Liechtenstein.
1950/51- Geneva [etc.] Nagel
Publishers [etc.] 920.0494 52-39693

DQ52 .W5 MRR Biog Latest edition

SWITZERLAND--CIVILIZATION--BIBLIOGRAPHY.
Berchtold, Alfred. La suisse romande
au cap du XXe siecle; Lausanne,
Payot, 1963. 131 p.   66-80566
Z2771 .B4 MRR Alc.

SWITZERLAND--COMMERCE--DIRECTORIES.
Adressbuch der Schweiz für
Industrie, Gewerbe, Handel und
Export. Zurich, Mosse-Annoncen.
338.058 46-31151
"Gegründet 1888."
HF5214 .A62 MRR Alc Latest edition

British & international buyers &
sellers guide. Manchester, Eng.
[etc.] C. G. Birn. 55-36686
HF54.G7 B7 MRR Alc Latest edition

Directory of Swiss manufacturers and
producers. 1917- Zurich [etc.]
670.58 53-19872
HF3703 .D5 MRR Alc Latest edition

Kompass: Zürich, Éditions Kompass
Suisse S.A. [etc.] 51-19743
Began publication in 1947.
HF3703 .I5 MRR Alc Latest edition

Schweizerisches ragionenbuch.
Zürich, O. Füssli. 381.058 43-
15446
HF3703 .S3 MRR Alc Latest edition

SWITZERLAND--DESCRIPTION AND TRAVEL--
GUIDE-BOOKS.
Baedekers Autoführer-Verlag,
Stuttgart. Switzerland: official
handbook of the Automobile Club of
Switzerland. 2nd ed. Freiburg,
Baedeker; New York, Macmillan [etc.]
1967. 355 p. [45/-] 914.94/04/7
67-101220
GV1025.S8 B32 1967 MRR Alc.

Ferguson, Gwen. Switzerland London,
Charles Letts & Co., 1968. 96 p.
[6/-] 914.94/04/7 68-111720
DQ16 .F4 1968 MRR Alc.

Fodor's Switzerland. New York, D.
McKay. 914.94/04/7 72-649054
DQ16 .S833 MRR Alc Latest edition

Olson, Harvey Stuart, Olson's
complete motoring guide to France,
Switzerland & Italy, [1st ed.]
Philadelphia, Lippincott [1967] xiv,
964 p.   914.4/04/83 66-16661
GV1025.F7 O4 MRR Alc.

Pan American World Airways, inc.
Complete reference guide to Austria
and Switzerland, incl. Liechtenstein.
[2d rev. ed. New York, Trade
distribution by Simon & Schuster,
c1966] 128 p.   914.36/04/5 67-5271

DB16 .P3 1967 MRR Alc.

Suisse. Paris, Hachette, 1967. 860
p.   [38,90 F.] 914.94/04/7 67-
79908
DQ16 .S82 1967 MRR Alc.

SWITZERLAND--DICTIONARIES AND
ENCYCLOPEDIAS.
Dictionnaire historique &
biographique de la Suisse,
Neuchatel, Administration du
Dictionnaire historique et
biographique de la Suisse, 1921 [i.e.
1920]-33. 7 v.   21-5108
DQ51 .D5 MRR Biog.

SWITZERLAND--EXECUTIVE DEPARTMENTS.
Switzerland. Staats-kalender der
Schweizerischen Eidgenossenschaft.
18<52?>- Bern. 07-16335
JN8704 MRR Alc Latest edition

SWITZERLAND--GAZETTEERS.
Dictionnaire géographique de la
Suisse; Neuchatel, Attinger
freres, 1902-10. 6 v.   06-36945
DQ14 .D7 MRR Alc.

Jacot, Arthur, Schweizerisches
Ortslexikon mit Angabe der
Postleitzahlen und Verkehrskarte.
20. bis 22., neubearb. Aufl. Luzern,
C. J. Bucher, 1969. 32, 306 p.
[42.50] 75-430853
DQ14 .J2 1969 MRR Alc.

United States. Office of Geography.
Switzerland; Washington, 1950. 83
p.   77-280319
DQ14 .U55 MRR Alc.

SWITZERLAND--HISTORY.
Bonjour, Edgar, A short history of
Switzerland, Oxford, Clarendon
Press, 1952. 388 p.   949.4 52-
12224
DQ54 .B65 MRR Alc.

SWITZERLAND--HISTORY. (Cont.)
Dürrenmatt, Peter. Schweizer
Geschichte. Zürich, Schweizer Druck-
und Verlagshaus [1963] 735 p. 64-
53581
   DQ54 .D8 1963 MRR Alc.

Rimli, Eugen Theodor. Histoire de la
Confédération par le texte et par
l'image. (Reed. revue et augm.)
Zürich, Lausanne, Stauffacher, 1967.
562 p. [sfr 66.00] 949.4 67-
84456
   DQ54 .R512 1967 MRR Alc.

SWITZERLAND--HISTORY--DICTIONARIES.
Dictionnaire historique &
biographique de la Suisse,
Neuchatel, Administration du
Dictionnaire historique et
biographique de la Suisse, 1921 [i.e.
1920]-33. 7 v. 21-5108
   DQ51 .D5 MRR Biog.

SWITZERLAND--IMPRINTS.
British Museum. Dept. of Printed
Books. Short-title catalogue of
books printed in the German-speaking
countries London, Trustees of the
British Museum, 1962. viii, 1224 p.
63-24516
   Z2222 .B73 MRR Alc.

Deutsche Bibliographie; Jan./Juni
1951- Frankfurt a. M., Buchhändler-
Vereinigung. 52-39843
   Z2221 .F73 MRR Alc Full set

Deutsche Bibliographie; Fünfjahres-
Verzeichnis. 1945/50- Frankfurt a.
M., Buchhandler-Vereinigung. 53-
39084
   Z2221 .D47 MRR Alc Full set

Deutsches bücherverzeichnis: 1916-
[Leipzig] Börsenverein der deutschen
buchhandler zu Leipzig. 20-14984
   Z2221 .K25 MRR Alc Full set

Jahresverzeichnis des deutschen
Schrifttums. 1945/46- Leipzig,
Verlag des Börsenvereins der
Deutschen Buchhandler. 015.43 50-
38395
   Z2221 .J26 MRR Alc Full set

Schweizer Bücherverzeichnis.
1948/50- Zürich, Schweizerischer
Buchhändler- und Verlegerverein. a
51-8855
   Z949 .B56 MRR Alc Full set

SWITZERLAND--INDUSTRIES--DIRECTORIES.
Adressbuch der Schweiz für
Industrie, Gewerbe, Handel und
Export. Zürich, Mosse-Annoncen.
338.058 46-31151
   "Gegründet 1888."
   HF5214 .A62 MRR Alc Latest edition

Kompass; Zürich, Éditions Kompass
Suisse S.A. [etc.] 51-18743
   Began publication in 1947.
   HF3703 .I5 MRR Alc Latest edition

Schweizerisches regionenbuch.
Zürich, O. Füssli. 381.058 43-
15446
   HF3703 .S3 MRR Alc Latest edition

SWITZERLAND--MANUFACTURES--DIRECTORIES.
Directory of Swiss manufacturers and
producers, 1917- Zurich [etc.]
670.58 53-18872
   HF3703 .D5 MRR Alc Latest edition

SWITZERLAND--POLITICS AND GOVERNMENT.
Switzerland. Staats-kalender der
Schweizerischen Eidgenossenschaft.
18<522>- Bern. 07-16335
   JN8704 MRR Alc Latest edition

SWITZERLAND--REGISTERS.
Switzerland. Staats-kalender der
Schweizerischen Eidgenossenschaft.
18<522>- Bern. 07-16335
   JN8704 MRR Alc Latest edition

**SWITZERLAND--RELATIONS (GENERAL) WITH
THE UNITED STATES--BIBLIOGRAPHY.**
Bern. Schweizerische
Landesbibliothek. Die Schweiz und
die Vereinigten Staaten von Amerika;
Bern, 1964. 58 p. 64-6083
   Z1361.R4 B45 MRR Alc.

SWITZERLAND--STATISTICS.
Statistisches Jahrbuch der Schweiz.
1.- Jahrg.; 1891- Basel [etc.]
Birkhäuser [etc.] 06-39570
   HA1593. A4 MRR Alc Latest edition

SWORDS, AMERICAN.
Albaugh, William A., Confederate
arms. Harrisburg, Pa. [1957] xviii,
278 p. 623.4 57-13480
   UD383.5 .A6 MRR Alc.

Neumann, George C. The history of
weapons of the American Revolution,
[1st ed.] New York, Harper & Row
[1967] viii, 373 p. 623.4/4 67-
20829
   U815 .N4 MRR Alc.

SWORDSMITHS.
Gardner, Robert Edward. Five
centuries of gunsmiths, swordsmiths
and armourers, 1400-1900. [Columbus,
Ohio; V. F. Heer] 1948. 244 p. 399
48-15654
   U800 .G3 MRR Alc.

SYDNEY--COMMERCE--DIRECTORIES.
The Universal business directory for
Sydney city & suburbs. Sydney. 55-
32629
   HF5296.S9 .U55 MRR Alc Latest
   edition

SYLVICULTURE
see Forests and forestry

SYMBOLISM.
Garai, Jana. The book of symbols.
[New York] Simon and Schuster [1974,
c1973] 143 p. [$3.95] 398/.3 74-
171892
   GR950.S5 G37 1974 MRR Alc.

Villiers, Elizabeth. The book of
charms. [New York] Simon and
Schuster [1974, c1973] 144 p.
[$3.95] 133.4/4 74-171069
   BF1561 .V5 1974 MRR Alc.

Whittick, Arnold, Symbols, signs,
and their meaning. London, L. Hill,
1960. xvi, 408 p. 704.946 60-
51135
   N7740 .W52 MRR Alc.

Williams, Charles Alfred Speed.
Encyclopedia of Chinese symbolism and
art motives; New York, Julian Press,
1960 [i.e. 1961] xxi, 468 p.
398.30951 60-15987
   GR335 .W53 1961 MRR Alc.

SYMBOLISM--BIBLIOGRAPHY.
Lurker, Manfred. Bibliographie zur
Symbolkunde. [1. Aufl] Baden-Baden,
Verlag Heitz, 1964-68. 3 v. 67-
100109
   Z7660 .L8 MRR Alc.

SYMBOLISM--DICTIONARIES.
Cirlot, Juan Eduardo. A dictionary
of symbols, 2d ed. London,
Routledge & K. Paul [1971] lv. 419
p. [£3.75] 001.5/6 72-189383
   BF1623.S9 C513 1971 MRR Alc.

SYMBOLISM--DICTIONARIES--ENGLISH.
Whittlesey, Eunice S. Symbols and
legends in Western art; New York,
Scribner [1972] ix, 367 p. [$7.95]
704.94 71-162764
   N7740 .W53 MRR Alc.

SYMBOLISM IN ART.
Lemke, Antje B. Museum companion;
[New York] Hippocrene [1974] vii,
211 p. [$6.95] 703 73-76577
   N33 .L38 1974 MRR Alc.

Whittick, Arnold, Symbols, signs,
and their meaning. London, L. Hill,
1960. xvi, 408 p. 704.946 60-
51135
   N7740 .W52 MRR Alc.

Whittlesey, Eunice S. Symbols and
legends in Western art; New York,
Scribner [1972] ix, 367 p. [$7.95]
704.94 71-162764
   N7740 .W53 MRR Alc.

SYMBOLISM IN LITERATURE--BIBLIOGRAPHY.
Krawitz, Henry. A post-symbolist
bibliography. Metuchen, N.J.,
Scarecrow Press, 1973. 284 p.
016.809/04 73-1181
   Z6520.S9 K7 MRR Alc.

SYMBOLISM IN MUSIC.
Geiringer, Karl, Symbolism in the
music of Bach; Washington, 1956.
iii, 16 p. 780.81 56-60068
   Z663.37 .A5 1956 MRR Alc.

SYMBOLISM IN THE BIBLE.
Wilson, Walter Lewis, Wilson's
dictionary of Bible types. Grand
Rapids, Eerdmans [c1957] 519 p.
220.6 57-14495
   BS477 .W53 MRR Alc.

**SYMPHONY ORCHESTRAS--UNITED STATES--
DIRECTORIES.**
The National directory for the
performing arts and civic centers.
Dallas, Handel & Co. 790.2/0973 73-
646635
   PN2289 .N38 MRR Alc Latest edition

SYMPTOMS
see Diagnosis

SYNDICATES (FINANCE)--UNITED STATES.
Hillstrom, Roger. 1960-1969, a
decade of corporate and international
finance. New York, IDD [1972] 381
p. 332 72-175335
   HG4907 .H54 MRR Alc.

SYNTHETIC FABRICS.
Davison's synthetic and silk red
book. 67th- ed.; 1962- Ridgewood,
N.J., Davison Pub. Co. 72-626449
   TS1643 .D3 MRR Alc Latest edition

SYNTHETIC PRODUCTS.
see also Plastics

SYRIA.
American University, Washington. D.C.
Foreign Areas Studies Division. Area
handbook for Syria. Washington, For
sale by the Superintendent of
Documents, U.S. Govt. Print. Off.,
1965. x, 394 p. 915.691034 66-
60732
   DS93 .A65 MRR Alc.

SYRIA--GAZETTEERS.
United States. Office of Geography.
Syria; official standard names
approved by the United States Board
on Geographic Names. Washington,
1967. xi, 460 p. 915.691/003 68-
60902
   DS94 .U5 MRR Alc.

SYRIA--STATISTICS.
Syria. Mudīrīyat al-Ihṣāʾ . al-
Majmūʿah al-iḥṣāʾiyah .
Mudīrīyat al-Ihṣāʾ . al-sanah 1.-
1948- Dimashq, Maṭbaʿat al-
Ḥukūmah. 915.691 51-8191
   HA1941 .A32 MRR Alc Latest edition

**SYRIAC LANGUAGE, MODERN--DICTIONARIES--
ENGLISH.**
Maclean, Arthur John, bp. of Moray,
Ross, and Caithness, A dictionary of
the dialects of vernacular Syriac as
spoken by the eastern Syrians of
Kurdistan, northwest Persia, and the
plain of Mogul. Oxford, Clarendon
press, 1901. xxii p., 1 l., 334 p.,
1 l. 01-26182
   PJ5805 .M3 MRR Alc.

SYSTEMS ENGINEERING.
see also Design, Industrial

TABLE.
see also Cookery

see also Food

TABLE SETTING AND DECORATION.
see also Glassware

Pellaprat, Henri Paul. Modern French
culinary art. Cleveland, World Pub.
Co. [1966] xvi, 1171 p. 641.5944
65-25779
   TX719 .P3813 1966 MRR Alc.

TABLES, MATHEMATICAL
see Logarithms

TACTICS.
Steele, Matthew Forney, American
campaigns, Washington, B. S. Adams,
1909. vii p., 1 l., 731 p. and
atlas of xii p., 311 maps. war22-80
   E181 .S85 MRR Alc.

TADPOLES
see Frogs

see Toads

**TAFT, WILLIAM HOWARD, PRES. U.S., 1857-
1930.**
Pringle, Henry Fowles, The life and
times of William Howard Taft; New
York, Toronto, Farrar & Rinehart,
inc. [c1939] 2 v. 923.173 39-
27878
   E762 .P75 MRR Alc.

**TAFT, WILLIAM HOWARD, PRES. U.S., 1857-
1930--MANUSCRIPTS--INDEXES.**
United States. Library of Congress.
Manuscript Division. Index to the
William Howard Taft papers.
Washington; [For sale by the Supt. of
Docs., U.S. Govt. Print. Off.] 1972.
6 v. (xxxiii, 35, 2483 p.)
[$24.00/set] 016.97391/2/0924 70-
608096
   Z6663.34 .T25 MRR Alc.

TAHITI--BIBLIOGRAPHY.
O'Reilly, Patrick. Bibliographie de
Tahiti et de la Polynésie française
Paris, Musée de l'Homme, 1967.
1048 p. [400 F] 016.996 68-91315
   Z4501 .O72 MRR Alc.

TAILORING (WOMEN'S)
see also Dressmaking

TAIWAN.
Chaffee, Frederic H. Area handbook
for the Republic of China.
Washington, For sale by the Supt. of
Docs., U.S. Govt. Print. Off., 1969.
xiv, 435 p. [$3.25] 309.1/51/24905
72-600181
   DS895.F7 C4 MRR Alc.

China yearbook. 1937/43- Taipeh,
Taiwan [etc.] China Pub. Co. 43-
14605
   DS777.53 .C459 MRR Alc Latest
   edition

TAIWAN--BIBLIOGRAPHY.
Berton, Peter Alexander Menquez,
Contemporary China; Stanford,
Calif., Hoover Institution on War,
Revolution, and Peace, 1967. xxix,
695 p. 016.9151/03/5 67-14235
Z3106 .B39 MRR Alc

TAIWAN--BIOGRAPHY.
China yearbook. 1937/43- Taipeh,
Taiwan [etc.] China Pub. Co. 43-
14605
DS777.53 .C459 MRR Alc Latest
edition

TAIWAN--COMMERCE--DIRECTORIES.
Business directory of Taiwan. 1961-
[Taipei, E. T. Tsu, etc.]
650.5851249 61-18919
HF3828.F6 B8 MRR Alc Latest
edition

Businessman's directory, the Republic
of China. [Taipei, Tong-Hsing
Culture Press. Tung Hsing wen hua
ch'u pan she] [$8.50]
380.1/025/51249 74-898235
HF5237.5 .E87 MRR Alc Latest
edition

TAIWAN--DIRECTORIES.
Directory of Taiwan. 1951- Taipei
China news [etc.] 915.1249 52-20334
DS895.F7 D57 MRR Alc Latest
edition

TAIWAN--ECONOMIC CONDITIONS--
BIBLIOGRAPHY.
United States. Library of Congress.
Division of bibliography. ... The
Japanese empire: industries and
transportation, Washington, 1943. 1
p. l., 56 p. 016.330952 43-50835
Z663.28 .J2 MRR Alc.

TAIWAN--MANUFACTURES--DIRECTORIES.
Business directory of Taiwan. 1961-
[Taipei, E. T. Tsu, etc.]
650.5851249 61-18919
HF3828.F6 B8 MRR Alc Latest
edition

Taiwan buyer's guide. Taipei. 64-
9006
T12.5.F6 T3 MRR Alc Latest edition

TAIWAN--STATISTICS.
China yearbook. 1937/43- Taipeh,
Taiwan [etc.] China Pub. Co. 43-
14605
DS777.53 .C459 MRR Alc Latest
edition

TALENTED CHILDREN
see Gifted children

TALES--HISTORY AND CRITICISM.
Thompson, Stith. The folktale, New
York, The Dryden press, 1946. x, 510
p. 398.21 47-30175
PN1001 .T5 MRR Alc.

TALES, AMERICAN.
Emrich, Duncan. Folklore on the
American land. [1st ed.] Boston,
Little, Brown [1972] xxviii, 707 p.
[$15.00] 398/.0973 72-161865
GR105 .E47 MRR Alc.

TALES, AMERICAN--DISCOGRAPHY.
United States. Library of Congress.
Archive of American Folk Song. Folk
music; 1943- [Washington, For sale
by the Superintendent of Documents,
U.S. Govt. Print. Off.] 789.913 58-
60095
Z663.378 .F6 MRR Alc MRR Alc
Latest edition

TALES, BRAZILIAN--DISCOGRAPHY.
United States. Library of Congress.
Archive of American Folk Song. Folk
music; 1943- [Washington, For sale
by the Superintendent of Documents,
U.S. Govt. Print. Off.] 789.913 58-
60095
Z663.378 .F6 MRR Alc MRR Alc
Latest edition

TALES, FRENCH--BIBLIOGRAPHY.
Delarue, Paul. Le conte populaire
français; Paris, Érasme, 1957- v.
a 57-5342
Z2174.T3 D4 MRR Alc.

TALES, SPANISH-AMERICAN--DISCOGRAPHY.
United States. Library of Congress.
Archive of American Folk Song. Folk
music; 1943- [Washington, For sale
by the Superintendent of Documents,
U.S. Govt. Print. Off.] 789.913 58-
60095
Z663.378 .F6 MRR Alc MRR Alc
Latest edition

TALKING BOOK MACHINES.
United States. Library of Congress.
Division for the Blind and Physically
Handicapped. Technical Section.
Talking book machines. [Washington,
Library of Congress, 1970] [19] p.
362.4/1/028 72-607804
Z663.25 .T28 MRR Alc.

TALKING BOOKS--BIBLIOGRAPHY.
Joyce, Donald F., comp. The Civil
War; a list of one hundred books in
braille and on talking book records.
Washington, 1961. 7 p. 61-60075
Z663.25 .C5 MRR Alc

United States. Library of Congress.
Division for the Blind. Catalog of
talking books for the blind, 1934-
1948. Washington, U.S. Govt. Print.
Off., 1949. x, 188 p. 016.65538
789.9 49-46269
Z663.25 .C32 MRR Alc.

United States. Library of Congress.
Division for the Blind. Catalog of
talking books for the blind, 1953-57.
[Washington, U.S. Govt. Print. Off.,
1958] xvi, 145 p. 016.65538 58-
60041
Z663.25 .C33 MRR Alc.

United States. Library of Congress.
Division for the Blind. Counseling
and rehabilitation; Washington,
1962. ill, 9 p. 62-60018
Z663.25 .C6 MRR Alc.

United States. Library of Congress.
Division for the Blind. Talking
books for the blind placed in the
distributing libraries, Washington
[U.S. Govt. Print. Off.] 1943. x, 91
p. 016.65538 789.9 49-36641
Z663.25 .T332 MRR Alc.

United States. Library of Congress.
Division for the Blind and Physically
Handicapped. Talking books to profit
by. Washington [1971] 11 p. 011
70-613706
Z663.25 .T34 MRR Alc.

TALKING BOOKS--BIBLIOGRAPHY--CATALOGS.
Talking books: Adult. [New York]
Published for the Library of Congress
by the American Foundation for the
Blind. 017 72-605329
Z5347 .T3 MRR Alc Partial set

United States. Library of Congress.
Division for the Blind. Books on
magnetic tape; Washington, 1961. 24
p. 61-60071
Z663.25 .B66 MRR Alc.

United States. Library of Congress.
Division for the Blind. Books on
magnetic tape; [Washington] 1962.
x, 127 p. 789.913 62-60084
Z663.25 .B65 MRR Alc.

United States. Library of Congress.
Division for the Blind and Physically
Handicapped. Cassette books
[catalog] Washington, 1971. vii, 75
p. 011 70-616124
Z663.25 .C28 MRR Alc.

TALKING BOOKS--CONGRESSES.
Conference on Volunteer Activities in
Recording and Transcribing Books for
the Blind, Washington, D.C., 1952.
Proceedings. Washington, Library of
Congress, 1954. viii, 61 p. 54-
60014
Z663.25 .P7 MRR Alc.

TALKING PICTURES
see Moving pictures, Talking

TAMIL LANGUAGE--DICTIONARIES--ENGLISH.
Visvanatha Pillai, V. A
dictionary, Tamil and English, 4th
ed.--3,000 copies. Madras, The
Madras school book and literature
society, 1921. 1 p. l., 653 p. 24-
1034
PL4756 .V6 1921 MRR Alc.

TANGANYIKA--GOVERNMENT PUBLICATIONS.
United States. Library of Congress.
African Section. Official
publications of British East Africa,
Washington, General Reference and
Bibliography Division, Reference
Dept., Library of Congress, 1960-63.
4 v. 015.676 61-60009
Z663.285 .O3 MRR Alc.

TANGIER--DESCRIPTION--GUIDE-BOOKS.
Faggart, Stanley Mills. Spain on $5
a day, [New York, A. Frommer;
distributed by Simon and Schuster,
1968] 288 p. 914.6/04/82 68-4429
DP14 .H24 1968 MRR Alc.

TANK TRUCKS--DIRECTORIES.
National tank truck carrier
directory. 1st- ed.,; 1955-
Washington, National Tank Truck
Carriers. 55-32635
HE5623.A45 N33 MRR Alc Latest
edition

TANK-VESSELS--HISTORY.
Sawyer, Leonard Arthur. Victory
ships and tankers; Cambridge, Md.,
Cornell Maritime Press [1974] 230 p.
387.2/45/0873 73-22561
VM391 .S39 1974 MRR Alc.

TANK-VESSELS--REGISTERS.
Moody, Bert. Ocean ships [New ed.].
London, Allan 1967. vii, 359 p.
[25/-] 387.2/4 72-472168
HE565 .A5M6 1967 MRR Alc.

The Tanker register; London, H.
Clarkson, 1969. xx, 389 p. [£10.00]
387.2/45 71-565903
HE566.T3 T33 1969 MRR Alc.

TANKS (MILITARY SCIENCE)
Bradford, George. Armored vehicles
from their conception to the present
times. Bracknell [Berks.], Bellona
Publications, 1967. [24] p. [7/6]
623.7/475 68-75394
UG446.5 .B67 MRR Alc.

Crow, Duncan. AFV's of World War
One, Windsor, Eng., Profile
Publications [1970] viii, 164 p.
358/.18/08 s 358/.18/08041 72-181764
UG446.5 .A694 vol. 1 MRR Alc.

Crow, Duncan. American AFVs of World
War II, Windsor (Corburg House,
Sheet St., Windsor, Berks.), Profile
Publications Ltd., 1972. viii, 240,
63 p. [£6.00] 623.74/75/0973 73-
167485
UG446.5 .A694 Vol. 4 MRR Alc.

Crow, Duncan. British A.F.Vs, 1919-
40, Windsor, Profile Publications,
1970. viii, 176 p. [£3.75]
358/.18/0942 70-859341
UG446.5 .A694 vol. 2 MRR Alc.

Foss, Christopher F. Armoured
fighting vehicles of the world New
York, Scribner [1971] 192 p.
[$5.95] 623.74/75 73-162727
UG446.5 .F64 MRR Alc.

TANZANIA.
Herrick, Allison Butler. Area
handbook for Tanzania. Washington,
For sale by the Supt. of Docs., U.S.
Govt. Print. Off., 1968. xvi, 522 p.
[3.75] 309.1/678 68-67374
DT438 .H4 MRR Alc.

TANZANIA--DESCRIPTION AND TRAVEL--GUIDE-
BOOKS.
Horrobin, David F. A guide to Kenya
and northern Tanzania [Aylesbury,
Eng., Medical and Technical Pub.,
1971] 304 p. [£3.25 ($10.00 U.S.)]
916.76/2/044 70-29461
DT434.E22 H59 MRR Alc.

TANZANIA--GAZETTEERS.
United States. Office of Geography.
Tanzania: official standard names
approved by the United States Board
on Geographic Names. Washington
[U.S. Govt. Print. Off.] 1965. vi,
236 p. 65-62630
DT448.2 .U5 MRR Alc

TANZANIA--HISTORY.
Hatch, John Charles. Tanzania, a
profile. New York, Praeger [1972]
xix, 214 p. [$8.50] 916.78/03/4
70-118053
DT444 .H37 MRR Alc.

TARANAKI, N.Z. (PROVINCIAL DISTRICT)--
COMMERCE--DIRECTORIES.
Universal business directory for
Taranaki Province. Auckland,
Universal Business Directories. 52-
38580
HF5299.T37 U55 MRR Alc Latest
edition

TARIFF.
Annuaire de l'horlogerie suisse.
Genève, Chapalay & Mottier s.a.
681 105 46-34872
TS540 .A65 MRR Alc Latest edition

TARIFF--BIBLIOGRAPHY.
United States. Library of Congress.
Division of bibliography. ... List
of works on the tariffs of foreign
countries. Washington, Govt. print.
off., 1906. 42 p. 06-35002
Z663.28 .L587 MRR Alc.

TARIFF--CANADA.
McGoldrick's handbook of the Canadian
customs tariff and excise duties.
Montreal, McMullin Publishers.
382.7/0971 72-626409
HJ6092.A6 H3 MRR Alc Latest
edition

TARIFF--UNITED STATES.
Custom house guide. New York. 99-
1545
HE953.N5 C8 MRR Alc Latest edition

United States. Bureau of the Census.
U.S. foreign trade: imports, TSUSA
commodity by country. 1970-
[Washington, For sale by the Supt. of
Docs., U.S. Govt. Print. Off.]
382/.5/0973 74-649695
HF105 .C137232 MRR Alc Latest
edition

TARIFF--UNITED STATES--HISTORY.
Ratner, Sidney, The tariff in
American history. New York, Van
Nostrand [c1972] viii, 214 p.
382.7/0973   72-7968
    HF1753 .R37 MRR Alc.

TARIFF--UNITED STATES--HISTORY--
ADDRESSES, ESSAYS, LECTURES.
Ratner, Sidney, The tariff in
American history. New York, Van
Nostrand [c1972] viii, 214 p.
382.7/0973   72-7968
    HF1753 .R37 MRR Alc.

TARTANS.
Bain, Robert. The clans and tartans
of Scotland. London, Collins [1954]
320 p.   941   55-1011
    DA880.H76 B3 1954 MRR Alc.

Innes, Thomas, Sir, The tartans of
the clans and families of Scotland.
5th ed. Edinburgh, W. & A. K.
Johnston, 1950. iv, 300 p.   929.2
51-3429
    DA880.H76 I5 1950 MRR Alc.

TASMANIA--COMMERCE--DIRECTORIES.
Universal business directory for
Tasmania. Melbourne, Universal
Business Directories.   62-34871
    HF5310 .U6 MRR Alc Latest edition

TASMANIA--DIRECTORIES.
Walch's Tasmanian almanac. Hobart
[Tasmania] J. Walch [etc.]   07-21418
    JQ5102 .A3 MRR Alc Latest edition

TASTE (AESTHETICS)
see Aesthetics

TAVERNS
see Hotels, taverns, etc.

TAX CONSULTANTS--UNITED STATES--
DIRECTORIES.
Tax Executives Institute. Membership
list. Washington,D.C. [etc.] 55-
22247
    HJ2360 .T248 MRR Alc Latest
    edition

TAXATION.
see also Income tax

TAXATION--INDIANA--RATES AND TABLES.
Indiana almanac and government guide.
1st- ed.; 1961- [Indianapolis,
Republican Citizens' Finance
Committee of Indiana] 64-32364
    JK5630 .I5 MRR Alc Latest edition

TAXATION--UNITED STATES.
Schultz, William John, American
public finance 8th ed. Englewood
Cliffs N.J., Prentice-Hall [1965]
x, 565 p.   336.73   65-13570
    HJ241 .S3 1965 MRR Alc.

TAXATION--UNITED STATES--HISTORY.
Paul, Randolph Evernghim. Taxation
in the United States. Boston,
Little, Brown, 1954. xii, 830 p.
336.2   54-6282
    HJ2362 .P35 MRR Alc.

TAXATION--UNITED STATES--LAW.
Prentice-Hall, inc. Federal tax
handbook. 1947- Englewood Cliffs,
N.J. [etc.] 336.2   47-5117
    KF6289.A1 P73 MRR Alc Latest
    edition

TAXATION, EXEMPTION FROM.
Grundy, Milton. Grundy's tax havens:
2nd ed. London, Sweet and Maxwell;
New York, M. Bender, 1972. 173 p,
[£6.00] 336.2 72-78531
    HJ2336 .G78 MRR Alc.

TAYLOR, ZACHARY, PRES. U.S., 1784-1850.
Hamilton, Holman. Zachary Taylor.
[1st ed.] Indianapolis, Bobbs-
Merrill [1941-51] 2 v.   923.173 41-
2781
    E422 .H3 MRR Alc.

TEACHERS.
Mayer, Frederick, The great
teachers. [1st ed.] New York,
Citadel Press [1967] 384 p.   920.02
67-18085
    LA2303 .M35 MRR Alc.

TEACHERS--CERTIFICATION--UNITED STATES.
Woellner, Elizabeth H. Requirements
for certification: teachers, [1st]
ed.; 1935- [Chicago] University of
Chicago Press. a 43-1905
    LB1771 .W6 MRR Ref Desk Latest
    edition

TEACHERS--EXAMINATIONS
see Examinations

TEACHERS--UNITED STATES--BIOGRAPHY.
Leaders in education; 1st- ed.;
1932- Lancaster, Pa [etc.] Science
Press. 923.773   32-10194
    LA2311 .L4 MRR Biog Latest edition

Who's who in American education. v.
1-24; 1928-1867/68. Hattiesburg,
Miss. [etc.] 28-2351
    LA2311 .W45 MRR Biog Latest
    edition

TEACHERS--UNITED STATES--STATISTICS.
Gertler, Diane (Bochner) Directory:
public elementary and secondary
schools in large school districts
with enrollment and instructional
staff, by race: fall 1967,
[Washington] U.S. National Center for
Educational Statistics; [for sale by
the Supt. of Docs., U.S. Govt. Print.
Off., 1969] v, 840 p. [7.25]
371/.01/02573 72-604076
    L901 .G38 MRR Alc.

TEACHERS, INTERCHANGE OF--DIRECTORIES.
Conference Board of the Associated
Research Councils. Committee on
International Exchange of Persons.
Foreign scholars available under the
Fulbright-Hays Act for remunerative
positions in U.S. colleges and
universities. Washington. 64-57156
    LB2283 .C615 MRR Alc Latest
    edition

TEACHERS COLLEGES--GREAT BRITAIN--
DIRECTORIES.
Handbook of colleges and departments
of education. 1968- London,
Published for the Association of
Teachers in Colleges and Dept. of
Education by Methuen & Co.
370/73/02542 70-208256
    LB2224 .H35 MRR Alc Latest edition

TEACHING.
see also Audio-visual education

see also Child study

see also Examinations

Baughman, Millard Dale, comp.
Educator's handbook of stories,
quotes and humor. Englewood Cliffs,
N.J., Prentice-Hall [c1963] xii, 340
p.   63-17504
    LB1785 .B28 MRR Alc.

TEACHING--AIDS AND DEVICES.
see also Programmed instruction

see also Transparencies in education

TEACHING--AIDS AND DEVICES--
BIBLIOGRAPHY.
Educational Media Council.
Educational media index. New York,
McGraw-Hill [1964] 14 v. 016.37133
64-17810
    Z5814.V8 E3 MRR Alc.

TEACHING--AIDS AND DEVICES--CATALOGS.
Aubrey, Ruth H., ed. Selected free
materials for classroom teachers 3d
ed. Palo Alto, Calif., Fearon
Publishers [1969] 124 p. [2.00]
016.3713/078 77-91551
    Z5817.2 .A85 1969 MRR Alc.

Dever, Esther. Sources of free and
inexpensive educational materials.
4th ed. Grafton, W. Va. [1970]
iii, 538 p. [$6.30] 016.3713/078
70-21751
    AG600 .D45 1970 MRR Alc.

Educators grade guide to free
teaching aids. 1955- Randolph,
Wis., Educators Progress Service.
016.3713 56-2444
    AG600 .E3 MRR Alc Latest edition

Educators' guide to free films.
Randolph, Wis., Educators' Progress
Service. 371.335230838 45-412
Began with 1941 vol.
    LB1044 .E3 MRR Alc Latest edition

Educators' guide to free filmstrips.
1st- 1949- Randolph, Wis.,
Educators' Progress Service.
371.3352 50-11650
    LB1043.8 .E4 MRR Alc Latest
    edition

Educators guide to free science
materials. 1st- ed.;1960-
Randolph, Wis., Educators Progress
Service. 507 61-919
    Q181.A1 E3 MRR Alc Latest edition

Educators guide to free social
studies materials. 1st- ed.; 1961-
Randolph, Wis., Educators Progress
Service. 307 61-65910
    AG600 .E315 MRR Alc Latest edition

Educators guide to free tapes,
scripts and transcriptions. 1st-
ed.; Jan. 1955- Randolph, Wis.,
Educators' Progress Service.
789.913* 55-2784
    LB1044.2 .E3 MRR Alc Latest
    edition

Elementary teachers' guide for free
curriculum materials. 1st- ed.;
Sept. 1944- Randolph, Wis.,
Educators' Progress Service. 016.372
44-52255
    Z5817.2 .E45 MRR Alc Latest
    edition

Field Enterprises Educational
Corporation. Sources of free and
inexpensive educational materials.
Chicago [1958] 192 p.   58-1432
    Z5817.2 .F42 1958 MRR Alc.

Pepe, Thomas J. Free and inexpensive
educational aids. 4th rev. ed. New
York, Dover Publications [1970] xi,
173 p. [$2.00] 016.3713/078 70-
18964
    AG600 .P45 1970 MRR Alc.

TEACHING MACHINES--BIBLIOGRAPHY.
Gee, Ralph D. Teaching machines and
programmed learning; 2d ed.
Hatfield [Eng.] Hertfordshire County
Council, Technical Library &
Information Service, Hatfield College
of Technology, 1965. 128 p.   67-
103710
    Z5814.A85 G4 1965 MRR Alc.

TECHNICAL ASSISTANCE.
see also Community development

see also Underdeveloped areas

TECHNICAL ASSISTANCE--BIBLIOGRAPHY.
United States. Library of Congress.
Reference Dept. International
economic and social development;
Washington, 1952. vi, 55 p.
016.3309 52-60016
    Z663.28 .I5 MRR Alc.

TECHNICAL ASSISTANCE, AMERICAN.
see also United States. Peace Corps

TECHNICAL ASSISTANCE, AMERICAN--ASIA--
DIRECTORIES.
Technical Assistance Information
Clearing House. Far East technical
assistance programs of U.S. nonprofit
organizations, New York, 1966.
viii, 274 p.   309.2/23 67-60359
    HC411 .T4 MRR Alc.

TECHNICAL ASSISTANCE, AMERICAN--LATIN
AMERICA--DIRECTORIES.
Latin America technical assistance
programs of U.S. nonprofit
organizations. New York, Technical
Assistance Information Clearing
House. 309.2/23 72-4820
    HC122 .L3 MRR Alc Latest edition

TECHNICAL ASSISTANCE, CANADIAN--
DIRECTORIES.
Canadian Council for International Cooperation. Directory of Canadian non-
governmental organizations engaged in
international development assistance.
1970. Ottawa, 1970. 285 p. [$5.00]
309.2/233/7101724 79-855733
    HC60 .C2877 1970a MRR Alc.

TECHNICAL EDUCATION--FILM CATALOGS.
National Information Center for
Educational Media. Index to
vocational and technical education
(multimedia). 1st ed. Los Angeles,
1972. x, 298 p. 016.6 72-190628
    T65.5.M6 N28 1972 MRR Alc.

TECHNICAL EDUCATION--YEARBOOKS.
The Year book of technical education
and careers in industry. 1st- 1957-
London, A. and C. Black. 607.42
57-2770
    T61 .Y4 Sci RR Latest edition /
    MRR Alc Latest edition

TECHNICAL EDUCATION--GREAT BRITAIN.
The Year book of technical education
and careers in industry. 1st- 1957-
London, A. and C. Black. 607.42
57-2770
    T61 .Y4 Sci RR Latest edition /
    MRR Alc Latest edition

TECHNICAL EDUCATION--UNITED STATES--
DIRECTORIES.
American trade schools directory.
1st- ed.; 1953- Queens Village,
New York, Croner Publications.
607.73 53-8387
    T73 .A78 MRR Alc Latest edition

Cass, James. Comparative guide to
two-year colleges & four-year
specialized schools and programs,
[1st ed.] New York, Harper & Row
[1969] xxii, 275 p. [7.95] 378.73
69-15301
    LB2328 .C36 MRR Ref Desk.

TECHNICAL EDUCATION--UNITED STATES--
HISTORY.
Barlow, Melvin L. History of
industrial education in the United
States Peoria, Ill., C. A. Bennett
[1967] 512 p.   607 67-10595
    T73 .B377 MRR Alc.

TECHNICAL EDUCATION--UNITED STATES--YEARBOOKS.
Technician education yearbook.
1963/64- Ann Arbor, Mich., Prakken
Publications. 63-22652
T73 .T4 MRR Alc Latest edition

TECHNICAL INFORMATION PILOT.
United States. Library of Congress.
Technical Information Division. A
filing manual for TIP cards.
Washington, Documentation Research
Section, Technical Information
Division, Library of Congress, 1952.
12 p. 025.37 53-60016
Z663.49 .F47 MRR Alc.

TECHNICAL LIBRARIES.
Strauss, Lucille (Jackson)
Scientific and technical libraries:
New York, Interscience Publishers
[1964] xi, 398 p. 026.5 64-15421

Z675.T3 S8 MRR Alc.

TECHNICAL LIBRARIES--DIRECTORIES.
Associazione italiana per le
biblioteche. Guida delle biblioteche
scientifiche e tecniche e dei centri
di documentazione italiani, Roma,
Consiglio nazionale delle ricerche,
1965. viii, 610 p. 68-130514
Z809 .A1A78 MRR Alc.

**TECHNICAL REPORTS--ABBREVIATIONS OF
TITLES.**
Dictionary of report series codes,
2d ed. New York, Special Libraries
Association, 1973. vi, 645 p.
029.9/6 72-87401
Z6945.A2 D5 1973 MRR Alc.

TECHNICAL REPORTS--BIBLIOGRAPHY.
Global Engineering Documentation
Services. Directory of engineering
document sources. Newport Beach,
Calif., Global Engineering
Documentation Services [1972] 1 v.
(unpaged) [$29.95] 029.9/62 72-
176333
Z5852 .G5 MRR Alc.

Government reports index. v. 71-
1971- [Springfield, Va.] National
Technical Information Service.
507/.2073 72-627325
Z7405.R4 U513 Sci RR Latest
edition / MRR Alc Full set

Kyed, James M., Scientific,
technical, and engineering societies
publications in print, New York, R.
R. Bowker Co., 1974. x, 223 p.
016.5 74-5094
Z7911 .K92 MRR Alc.

Special Libraries Council of
Philadelphia and Vicinity.
Correlation index: document series
and PB reports, New York, Special
Libraries Association, 1953. x, 271
p. 016.6 53-10018
Z7916 .S65 MRR Alc.

United States. Dept. of Housing and
Urban Development. Library and
Information Division. The dictionary
catalog of the United States
Department of Housing and Urban
Development, Library and Information
Division, Boston, G. K. Hall, 1972.
19 v. 016.30154 73-152937
Z7164.H8 U4494 MRR Alc (Dk 33)

United States. Library of Congress.
Science and Technology Division. Air
Force scientific research
bibliography, Washington, U.S. Govt.
Print. Off., 1961- v. 016.5 61-
60038
Z663.41 .A36 MRR Alc.

United States. National Library of
Medicine. Current catalog: 1968/70-
Bethesda, Md. 016.61 77-618570
Z675.M4 U553 Sci RR Full set / MRR
Alc (Dk 33) Full set

TECHNICAL SOCIETIES--DIRECTORIES.
Kaplan, Stuart R., ed. A guide to
information sources in mining,
minerals, and geosciences, New York,
Interscience Publishers [1965] xiv,
599 p. 016.622 65-24304
Z7401 .G83 vol. 2 MRR Alc.

National Research Council, Canada.
Technical Information Service.
National technical information
services worldwide directory. 3d ed.
The Hague, Federation
internationale de documentation,
[1970] 61 p. [fl.25.00] 025.5/2
72-179268
Q223 .N37 1970 MRR Alc.

TECHNICAL SOCIETIES--CANADA.
Scientific and technical societies of
Canada. 1968- Ottawa, National
Research Council of Canada.
506/.2/71 72-649212
AS40 .S34 Sci RR Latest edition /
MRR Alc Latest edition

**TECHNICAL SOCIETIES--CHINA--
BIBLIOGRAPHY.**
United States. Library of Congress.
Science and Technology Division.
Mainland China organizations of
higher learning in science and
technology and their publications,
Washington, 1961. vi, 104 p. 61-
60070
Z663.41 .M2 MRR Alc.

TECHNICAL SOCIETIES--CHINA--DIRECTORIES.
United States. Library of Congress.
Science and Technology Division.
Mainland China organizations of
higher learning in science and
technology and their publications,
Washington, 1961. vi, 104 p. 61-
60070
Z663.41 .M2 MRR Alc.

**TECHNICAL SOCIETIES--EUROPE--
DIRECTORIES.**
European research index; 3d ed.
[St. Peter Port, Guernsey] Francis
Hodgson [1973] 2 v. (2293 p.)
507/.204 70-190255
Q180.E9 E9 1973 MRR Alc.

Williams, Colin H. Guide to European
sources of technical information. 3d
ed. [Guernsey] Francis Hodgson
[1970] 309 p. [$20.00 (U.S.)] 607
77-105217
T10.65.E8 W5 1970 MRR Alc.

TECHNICAL SOCIETIES--UNITED STATES.
Kyed, James M., Scientific,
technical, and engineering societies
publications in print, New York, R.
R. Bowker Co., 1974. x, 223 p.
016.5 74-5094
Z7911 .K92 MRR Alc.

Scientific and technical societies of
the United States. 8th- ed.; 1968-
Washington, National Academy of
Sciences. 506 72-620448
AS25 .S33 Sci RR Latest edition /
MRR Ref Desk Latest edition / MRR
Alc Latest edition

TECHNICAL WRITING.
Barzun, Jacques, The modern
researcher Rev. ed. New York,
Harcourt, Brace & World [1970] xvii,
430 p. [8.50] 907.2 72-115861
D13 .B334 1970 MRR Alc.

Durrenberger, Robert W. Geographical
research and writing New York,
Crowell [1971] ix, 246 p.
808.06/6/91 77-136033
G73 .D97 MRR Alc.

United States. Library of Congress.
Technical Information Division.
Final report on study of publications
stemming from defense-related
technical reports, [Washington]
1956. 10 p. 620.09 57-60508
Z663.49 .F5 MRR Alc.

**TECHNICAL WRITING--HANDBOOKS, MANUALS,
ETC.**
Jordan, Stello, Handbook of
technical writing practices. New
York, Wiley-Interscience [1971] 2 v.
(ix, 1374 p.) 808/.066/6021 75-
129051
T11 .J65 MRR Alc.

**TECHNICIANS IN INDUSTRY--UNITED STATES--
YEARBOOKS.**
Technician education yearbook.
1963/64- Ann Arbor, Mich., Prakken
Publications. 63-22652
T73 .T4 MRR Alc Latest edition

TECHNOLOGISTS, AMERICAN.
Special libraries Association.
Science-Technology Division.
Handbook of scientific and technical
awards in the United States and
Canada, 1900-1952. New York, Special
Libraries Association [1956] xxiv,
491 p. 507.9 56-7004
Q141 .S63 MRR Alc.

TECHNOLOGISTS, RUSSIAN.
Who's who in Soviet science and
technology. [2d ed., rev. and enl.
New York, Telberg Book Co. [1964]
vi, 301 l. 925 64-13006
Q127.R9 W5 1964 MRR Biog.

TECHNOLOGY.
see also Industrial management

see also Industry

see also Machinery

see also Manufactures

see also Mineral industries

see also Printing

Bibliographisches Institut A.G.,
Mannheim. The way things work; New
York, Simon and Schuster [1967] 590
p. 600 67-27972
T47 .B552 MRR Alc.

The Book of popular sciences. New
York, Grolier [1969] 10 v. 500 69-
10053
Q162 .B68 1969 MRR Alc.

Cowles encyclopedia of science,
industry, and technology. New enl.
ed. New York, Cowles Book Co. [1969]
639 p. [17.50] 500 69-17310
Q158 .C6 1969 MRR Alc.

TECHNOLOGY--ABBREVIATIONS.
Pugh, Eric. A dictionary of acronyms
& abbreviations; 2d, rev. and
expanded ed. [Hamden, Conn.] Archon
Books [1970] 389 p. 601/.48 72-
16645
T8 .P8 1970 MRR Alc.

Pugh, Eric. Second dictionary of
acronyms & abbreviations; [Hamden,
Conn.] Archon Books [1974] 410 p.
601/.48 74-4271
T8 .P82 MRR Alc.

Zatucki, Henryk. Dictionary of
russian technical and scientific
abbreviations Amsterdam, New York
[etc.] Elsevier Pub. Co., 1968. 400
p. 601/.48 67-12784
PG2693 .Z3 MRR Alc.

TECHNOLOGY--ABSTRACTING AND INDEXING.
United States. Library of Congress.
Science and Technology Division. A
guide to the world's abstracting and
indexing services in science and
technology. Washington, 1963. viii,
183 p. 016.505 63-61149
Z663.41 .G78 MRR Alc.

TECHNOLOGY--ACRONYMS.
White, Donald R. J. A glossary of
acronyms, abbreviations, and symbols,
1st ed. Germantown, Md., Don White
Consultants [1971] ix, 235 p.
620/.001/48 72-138444
T8 .W55 MRR Alc.

TECHNOLOGY--AUTHORSHIP
see Technical writing

TECHNOLOGY--BIBLIOGRAPHY.
Kyed, James M., Scientific,
technical, and engineering societies
publications in print, New York, R.
R. Bowker Co., 1974. x, 223 p.
016.5 74-5094
Z7911 .K92 MRR Alc.

Reinhart, Bruce, The vocational-
technical library collection:
Williamsport, Pa., Bro-Dart Pub. Co.,
1970. xiv, 377 p. 016.6 70-122456

Z7911 .R45 MRR Alc.

Scientific and technical books in
print. 1972- New York, R. R. Bowker
Co. 016.5 71-37614
Z7401 .S573 MRR Alc Latest edition
/ Sci RR Latest edition

United States. Library of Congress.
Japanese scientific and technical
serial publications in the
collections of the Library of
Congress. Washington, Science and
Technology Division, Reference Dept.,
Library of Congress, 1962. v, 247 p.
62-60085
Z663.41 .J2 MRR Alc.

TECHNOLOGY--BIBLIOGRAPHY--CATALOGS.
Technical books in print; London,
Whitaker, 1966. viii, 313 p. 78-
982
Z7916 .T42 1966 MRR Alc.

TECHNOLOGY--DICTIONARIES.
Audels new mechanical dictionary for
technical trades, New York, T. Audel
[1960] 736 p. 620.3 60-1970
T9 .A8 MRR Alc.

Breuer, Karl. Technisch-
wissenschaftliches
Taschenwörterbuch. 6., völlig
überarb. u. erg. Aufl. Berlin,
Bielefeld, Siemens (1971). 405 p.
[DM38.00] 75-587125
T10 .B77 1971 MRR Alc.

Castilla's Spanish and English
technical dictionary. London,
Routledge & Paul [1958] 2 v. 603
58-2320
T9 .C34 MRR Alc.

Chambers's technical dictionary.
[3d] rev. ed. with suppl. Edinburgh,
W. & R. Chambers [1958] vi, 1028 p.
59-1085
T9 .C5 1958 MRR Alc.

Cowles encyclopedia of science,
industry, and technology. New enl.
ed. New York, Cowles Book Co. [1969]
639 p. [17.50] 500 69-17310
Q158 .C6 1969 MRR Alc.

Crispin, Frederic Swing, Dictionary
of technical terms. 11th ed., rev.
New York, Bruce Pub. Co. [1970] vi,
455 p. 603 73-104870
T9 .C885 1970 MRR Alc.

TECHNOLOGY--DICTIONARIES. (Cont.)
Damm, John A., ed. The practical and technical encyclopedia, New York, W. H. Wise, 1948. vi, 632 p.   603 48-3757
   T9 .D3 MRR Alc.

De Vries, Louis, English-German technical and engineering dictionary, 2d ed., completely rev. and enl. New York, McGraw-Hill [c1967] 1154 p.   603 68-2779
   T9 .D47 1967 MRR Alc.

Dictionary of science and technology; Edinburgh, W. and R. Chambers, 1971. xvi, 1328 p. [£6.50] 503 72-180510
   Q123 .D53 1971 MRR Ref Desk.

Grande dicionário português-ingles, ingles-portugues. Sao Paulo, Li-Bra [1968] 4 v.   79-357089
   PC5333 .G7 MRR Alc.

The Harper encyclopedia of science, Rev. ed. New York, Harper & Row, 1967. ix, 1379 p.   503 67-22504
   Q123 .H26 1967 MRR Alc.

Malgorn, Guy Marie, Lexique technique anglais-français: 4. ed. rev. et corr. Paris, Gauthier-Villars, 1956. xxxiv, 493 p.   57-155
   T9 .M16 1956 MRR Alc.

Marolli, Giorgio. Dizionario tecnico inglese-italiano, italiano-inglese .. 9. edizione riveduta e ampliata. Firenze, F. Le Monnier, 1968. xxii, 1841 p. [16000] 603 70-378230
   T9 .M18 1868 MRR Alc.

McGraw-Hill encyclopedia of science and technology; [Rev. ed.] New York, McGraw-Hill [1966] 15 v. 503 65-26484
   Q121 .M3 1966 MRR Alc.

Oppermann, Alfred. Wörterbuch der modernen Technik. 3. Aufl. München-Pullach, Verlag Dokumentation, 1972- v.   603 72-306183
   TL509 .O623 MRR Alc.

Schwartz, Robert J. The dictionary of business and industry. New York, B. C. Forbes and Sons Pub. Co. [1954] xlvi, 561 p.   603 54-3133
   T9 .S38 MRR Alc.

Tver, David F. Dictionary of business & scientific terms, 2d ed. Houston, Tex., Gulf Pub. Co. [1968] xl, 528 p.   503 68-6988
   Q123 .T85 1968 MRR Alc.

Walther, Rudolf, lexicographer. Polytechnical dictionary, Oxford, New York, Pergamon Press [1968, c1967] 2 v.   603 67-25817
   T10 .W3 1968 MRR Alc.

TECHNOLOGY--DICTIONARIES--BIBLIOGRAPHY.
Turnbull, William R. Scientific and technical dictionaries; San Bernardino, Calif., Bibliothek Press, 1966- v.   016.503 67-25830
   Z7401 .T8 MRR Alc.

TECHNOLOGY--DICTIONARIES--CHINESE.
Modern Chinese-English technical and general dictionary. New York, McGraw-Hill [1863] 3 v.   495.132 63-19880

   PL1455 .M59 MRR Alc.

TECHNOLOGY--DICTIONARIES--CZECH.
Česko-anglický technický slovník. 2., preprac. a dopln. vyd. Praha, SNTL, t. Tisk 2, Brno, 1972. 946, [1] p.   [Kcs85.00] 73-316042
   T10 .C44 1972 MRR Alc.

TECHNOLOGY--DICTIONARIES--DANISH.
Warrern, Allan. Dansk-engelsk teknisk ordbog. 2. stærkt øgede udg. København, J. F. Clausen, 1957. 333p.   58-22125
   T9 .W26 1957 MRR Alc.

Warrern, Allan. Dansk-engelsk teknisk ordbog. 4. udg. København, J. Fr. Clausen, 1970. 368 p. [kr88.50] 76-861852
   T10 .W33 1970 MRR Alc.

TECHNOLOGY--DICTIONARIES--FRENCH.
Malgorn, Guy Marie, Lexique technique français-anglais: Paris, Gauthier-Villars, 1956. xxviii, 475 p.   57-156
   T9 .M163 MRR Alc.

TECHNOLOGY--DICTIONARIES--GERMAN.
Breuer, Karl. Technisch-wissenschaftliches Taschenwörterbuch. 6., völlig überarb. u. erg. Aufl. Berlin, Bielefeld, Siemens (1971). 405 p. [DM38.00] 75-597125
   T10 .B77 1971 MRR Alc.

De Vries, Louis, German-English technical and engineering dictionary, 2d ed., completely rev. and enl. New York, McGraw-Hill [1965, c1966] 1178 p.   603 65-23218
   T9 .D48 1966 MRR Alc.

Oppermann, Alfred. Wörterbuch der modernen Technik. 3. Aufl. München-Pullach, Verlag Dokumentation, 1972- v.   603 72-306183
   TL509 .O623 MRR Alc.

Walther, Rudolf, lexicographer. Polytechnical dictionary, Oxford, New York, Pergamon Press [1968, c1967] 2 v.   603 67-25817
   T10 .W3 1968 MRR Alc.

TECHNOLOGY--DICTIONARIES--HUNGARIAN.
Magyar-angol müszaki szótar. Budapest, Akadémiai Kiadó, 1957. viii, 752 p.   57-49792
   T9 .M14 MRR Alc.

TECHNOLOGY--DICTIONARIES--ITALIAN.
Marolli, Giorgio. Dizionario tecnico inglese-italiano, italiano-inglese .. 9. edizione riveduta e ampliata. Firenze, F. Le Monnier, 1968. xxii, 1841 p. [16000] 603 70-378230
   T9 .M18 1968 MRR Alc.

TECHNOLOGY--DICTIONARIES--NORWEGIAN.
Ansteinsson, John, Norsk-engelsk teknisk ordbok; Trondheim, F. Brun, 1954. 327 p.   55-40305
   T9 .A625 MRR Alc.

TECHNOLOGY--DICTIONARIES--POLYGLOT.
Bosch, Abraham ten, Viertalig technisch woordenboek. Deventer, Æ. E. Kluwer [1948-55] 4 v.   603 50-18447
   T10 .B72 MRR Alc.

Byecken, Francisco J. Vocabulário tecnico portugues-ingles-frances-alemão. 4. ed. rev. [São Paulo] Edições Melhoramentos [1961] 600 p.   603 62-3680
   T10 .B82 1961 MRR Alc.

Chalkiopoulos, Georgios. [Pentaglosson lexilogion technikon horon (romanized form)] [1960] 1030 p.   61-31355
   T10 .C46 1960 MRR Alc.

Dictionar tehnic poliglot: Ediţia a 2-a. Bucureşti, Editura Tehnica, 1967. xv, 1233 p.   603 68-2971
   T10 .D54 1967 MRR Alc.

Ernst, Richard. Wörterbuch der industriellen Technik, Wiesbaden, Brandstetter, 195 [c1948- v. 603 60-3617
   T10 .E75 Bd. 1-2 MRR Alc.

Ernst, Richard. Wörterbuch der industriellen Technik, Wiesbaden, Brandstetter [197]-[c1951]- v. 73-586747
   T10 .E76 MRR Alc.

2. uppl. Stockholm, Hedengren [1951] xix p., 1518 columns. 603 52-21624
   T10 .T358 1951 MRR Alc.

TECHNOLOGY--DICTIONARIES--POLYGLOT--BIBLIOGRAPHY.
Bibliography of interlingual scientific and technical dictionaries. [1st]- 1951- [Paris] UNESCO. 54-11648
   Z7405.D5 B5 Sci RR Latest edition / MRR Alc Latest edition

TECHNOLOGY--DICTIONARIES--RUSSIAN.
Hoseh, Mordecai. Russian-English dictionary of chemistry and chemical technology New York, Reinhold Pub. Corp. [1964] xlii, 522 p.   540.3 64-22149
   QD5 .H6 MRR Alc.

United States. Library of Congress. Aerospace Technology Division. Soviet Russian scientific and technical terms; Sept. 1958-63. Washington [For sale by the Supt. of Docs., U.S. Govt. Print. Off., etc.] 60-60877
   Q123 .U46 Sci RR Latest edition / MRR Alc Latest edition

Zatucki, Henryk. Dictionary of russian technical and scientific abbreviations, New York [etc.] Elsevier Pub. Co., 1968. 400 p.   601/.48 67-12784
   PG2693 .Z3 MRR Alc.

TECHNOLOGY--DICTIONARIES--SPANISH.
Castilla's Spanish and English technical dictionary. London, Routledge & Paul [1958] 2 v.   603 58-2320
   T9 .C34 MRR Alc.

TECHNOLOGY--DIRECTORIES--BIBLIOGRAPHY.
Klein, Bernard. Guide to American scientific and technical directories. 1st ed. Rye, N.Y: B. Klein Publications [1972] v., 324 p. 016.3384/7/6702573 72-91671
   Z7914.M3 K53 MRR Ref Desk.

United States. Library of Congress. Science and Technology Division. Directories in science and technology; Washington [For sale by the Superintendent of Documents, U.S. Govt. Print. Off.] 1963. vi, 65 p. 63-65164
   Z663.41 .D5 MRR Alc.

TECHNOLOGY--HISTORY.
Daumas, Maurice, ed. A history of technology & invention; New York, Crown Publishers [1970, c1969- v. [20.00 (v. 1-2)] 609 71-93403
   T15 .D2613 MRR Alc.

Derry, Thomas Kingston, A short history of technology from the earliest times to A.D. 1900, Oxford, Clarendon Press, 1960. xviii, 782 p. 609 61-3478
   T15 .D4 1960 MRR Alc.

Singer, Charles Joseph, ed. A history of technology, Oxford, Clarendon Press, 1954-1958. 5 v.   a 55-8645
   T15 .S53 MRR Alc.

TECHNOLOGY--HISTORY--BIBLIOGRAPHY.
Ferguson, Eugene S. Bibliography of the history of technology Cambridge, Mass., Society for the History of Technology [1968] xx, 347 p. 016.609 68-21558
   Z7914.H5 F4 MRR Alc.

TECHNOLOGY--INDEXES.
Scientific and technical books in print. 1972- New York, R. R. Bowker Co.   016.5 71-37614
   Z7401 .S573 MRR Alc Latest edition / Sci RR Latest edition

TECHNOLOGY--INDEXES--PERIODICALS.
Government reports index, v. 71-1971- [Springfield, Va.] National Technical Information Service. 507/.2073 72-627325
   Z7405.R4 U513 Sci RR Latest edition / MRR Alc Full set

TECHNOLOGY--INFORMATION SERVICES--DIRECTORIES.
National Research Council, Canada. Technical Information Service. National technical information services worldwide directory. 3d ed. The Hague, Federation internationale de documentation, [1970] 61 p. [fl.25.00] Q25.5/2 72-178268
   Q223 .N37 1970 MRR Alc.

TECHNOLOGY--INFORMATION SERVICES--EUROPE--DIRECTORIES.
Williams, Colin H. Guide to European sources of technical information. 3d ed. [Guernsey] Francis Hodgson [1970] 309 p. [$20.00 (U.S.)] 607 77-105217
   T10.65.E8 W5 1970 MRR Alc.

TECHNOLOGY--PERIODICALS.
Foreign science bulletin. v. 1- Jan. 1965- [Washington] Aerospace Technology Division, Library of Congress.   65-9850
   Z663.23 .A23 MRR Alc   MRR Alc Full set

Scientific American. v.1-14, Aug. 28, 1845-June 25, 1859; new ser., v.1- July 2, 1859- [New York]   505 04-17574
   T1 .S5 MRR Alc Indexes only / Sci RR Indexes only

TECHNOLOGY--PERIODICALS--BIBLIOGRAPHY.
Akademiia nauk SSSR. Institut nauchnoi informatsii. Index of abbreviated and full titles of scientific and technical periodical literature Wright-Patterson Air Force Base, Ohio, 1960? 247 l.   60-60261
   Z6945.A2 A43 MRR Alc.

Directory of Canadian scientific and technical periodicals. 1961- Ottawa, National Research Council. 016.505 61-2342
   Z7403 .D5 MRR Alc Latest edition

Internationale Bibliographie der Fachzeitschriften für Technik und Wirtschaft. München-Pullach, Verlag Dokumentation [etc.] 67-119312
   Z7913 .I757 MRR Alc Latest edition

Pan American Union. Dept. of Scientific Affairs. Guide to Latin American scientific and technical periodicals; Washington, Pan American Union, 1962. xii, 187 p. 016.505 62-62414
   Z7407.S6 P3 MRR Alc.

TECHNOLOGY--PERIODICALS-- (Cont.)
United States. Library of Congress.
Science and Technology Division.
Chinese scientific and technical
serial publications in the
collections of the Library of
Congress. Rev. ed. Washington,
1961. v, 107 p.   016.505 62-60011

Z663.41 .C45 1961 MRR Alc.

United States. Library of Congress.
Science and Technology Division.
Journals in science and technology
published in Japan and mainland
China; Washington, 1961. 47 p.
016.505 61-60647
Z663.41 .J6 MRR Alc.

United States. Library of Congress.
Science and Technology Division. A
list of scientific and technical
serials currently received by the
Library of Congress. Washington,
1960. v, 186 p.   016.505 60-60055

Z663.41 .L5 MRR Alc.

United States. Library of Congress.
Science and Technology Division.
Scientific and technical serial
publications. Washington, 1954.
viii, 118 p.   016.505 54-60015
Z663.41 .S3 MRR Alc.

United States. Library of Congress.
Science and Technology Division.
Scientific and technical serial
publications. Washington, 1954.
viii, 238 p.   016.505 54-60022
Z663.41 .S33 MRR Alc.

United States. Library of Congress.
Science and Technology Division.
Scientific and technical serial
publications of the Soviet Union,
1945-1960. Washington [For sale by
the Superintendent of Documents, U.S.
Govt. Print. Off.] 1963. iv, 347 p.
63-61782
Z663.41 .S29 MRR Alc.

World list of scientific periodicals
published in the years 1900-1960.
4th ed. Washington, Butterworths,
1963-65. 3 v. (xxv, 1824 p.)
016.505 64-9729
Z7403 .W923 MRR Alc.

**TECHNOLOGY--PERIODICALS--BIBLIOGRAPHY--
CATALOGS.**
Chicago. Center for Research
Libraries. Rarely held scientific
serials in the Midwest Inter-library
Center. Chicago, 1963. vi, 197 p.
63-5712
Z7403 .C49 MRR Alc.

TECHNOLOGY--PERIODICALS--INDEXES.
American Society of Mechanical
Engineers. Seventy-seven year index:
technical papers, 1880-1956. New
York [1957] 382 p.   621.06273 57-
59509
TJ1 .A774 MRR Alc.

Applied science & technology index.
v. 1-   Feb. 1913- [Bronx, N.Y.,
etc.] H. W. Wilson [etc.] 016.6 14-
5408
Z7813 .I7 MRR Circ Partial set /
Sci RR Partial set

British technology index. 1962-
London, Library Association. 63-
23735
Z7813 .B7 Sci RR Full set / MRR
Alc Full set

**TECHNOLOGY--PERIODICALS--TRANSLATIONS
INTO ENGLISH--BIBLIOGRAPHY.**
National Translations Center.
Consolidated index of translations
into English. New York, Special
Libraries Association 1969. vi, 948
p. 016.5/05 76-101337
Z7403 .N273 MRR Alc.

TECHNOLOGY--POPULAR WORKS.
Graf, Rudolf F. How it works,
illustrated: everyday devices and
mechanisms. New York, Popular
Science [1974] viii, 184 p.
[$10.95] 620 73-80716
TX298 .G68 MRR Alc.

**TECHNOLOGY--TRANSLATIONS INTO ENGLISH--
BIBLIOGRAPHY.**
United States. Library of Congress.
Scientific Translations Center.
Bibliography of translations from
Russian scientific and technical
literature. list no. 1-39; Oct. 1953-
Dec. 1956. Washington. 016.5 53-
60044
Z663.41 .U5 MRR Alc MRR Alc
Partial set

TECHNOLOGY--YEARBOOKS.
McGraw-Hill yearbook of science and
technology. 1962- New York, McGraw-
Hill book Co. 505.8 62-12028
Q121 .M312 Sci RR Partial set /
MRR Alc Full set

**TECHNOLOGY--CANADA--PERIODICALS--
BIBLIOGRAPHY.**
Directory of Canadian scientific and
technical periodicals. 1961-
Ottawa, National Research Council.
016.505 61-2342
Z7403 .D5 MRR Alc Latest edition

TECHNOLOGY--RUSSIA--BIBLIOGRAPHY.
Tolpin, Jacob Gerschon. Searching
the Russian technical literature.
[n. p., 1960] 81 l. 016.60847 60-
23665
Z7915.R9 T73 MRR Alc.

United States. Library of Congress.
Science and Technology Division.
Soviet science and technology;
Washington, 1962. 209 p.   016.5 62-
60058
Z663.41 .S6 MRR Alc.

**TECHNOLOGY--UNITED STATES--INFORMATION
SERVICES.**
United States. Library of Congress.
National Referral Center. A
directory of information resources in
the United States: physical sciences,
engineering. Washington, Library of
Congress; [for sale by the Supt. of
Docs., U.S. Govt. Print. Off.] 1971.
iv, 803 p. [$6.50] 500.2/07 78-
611209
Z663.379 .D5 1971 MRR Alc.

TECHNOLOGY TRANSFER.
see also New products

TECHOLOGICAL INNOVATIONS.
see also Research, Industrial

TEEN-AGE
see Adolescence

TEEN-AGERS
see Youth

TEETH.
see also Dentistry

TELECOMMUNICATION--DICTIONARIES.
Smith, Emerson Curtis. Glossary of
communications, [1st ed.] Chicago,
Telephony Pub. Corp. [1971] xiv, 547
p.   621.38/03 70-169786
TK5102 .S6 MRR Alc.

**TELECOMMUNICATION--DICTIONARIES--
POLYGLOT.**
Clason, W. E., Supplement to the
Elsevier dictionaries of electronics,
nucleonics and telecommunication.
Amsterdam, New York, Elsevier Pub.
Co., 1963. 633 p.   603 63-11369
T10 .C55 MRR Alc.

TELECOMMUNICATION--HISTORY.
International Telecommunication
Union. From semaphore to satellite.
Geneva, 1965. 343 p.   384 65-4299

HE7631 .I5 MRR Alc.

TELECOMMUNICATION--LAW AND LEGISLATION.
see also Freedom of information

TELEGRAPH--DIRECTORIES.
International Telecommunication
Union. General Secretariat. Official
list of telegraph offices opened for
international traffic. Geneva.
384.1 13-16092
HE7621 .I55 MRR Alc Latest edition

TELEGRAPH--RATES.
International Telecommunication
Union. Tableau B: taxes
télégraphiques du régime
extraeuropéen. 3. éd. Genève,
Union internationale des
télécommunications, 1966- 1 v.
(loose-leaf)   67-52493
HE7681 .I49 1966 MRR Alc.

TELEGRAPH--AUSTRIA--DIRECTORIES.
Österreichisches Telegramm-,
Fernschreiber-, Telex-Adressbuch.
[Salzburg, etc.] 53-28310
HE8133 .O8 MRR Alc Latest edition

TELEGRAPH--PORTUGAL.
Guia dos correios, telégrafos e
telefones Lisboa, Gráfica Santelmo.
383.058 44-33738
HE7123 .G8 MRR Alc Latest edition

TELEGRAPH CODE ADDRESSES.
Marconi's international register.
New York [etc.] 31-15824
Began publication in 1917.
HE7710 .I6 MRR Alc Latest edition

Peterson cable address directory.
Bogotá, N.J. [etc.] J. J. Ernau
[etc.] 26-3970
HE7677.B2 P45 MRR Alc Latest
edition

**TELEPHONE--APPARATUS AND SUPPLIES--
CATALOGS.**
Telephone engineer & management
directory. Wheaton, Ill. [etc.]
Harbrace Publications [etc.] 50-
23181
Began publication in 1936?
TK6195 .T45 MRR Alc Latest edition

TELEPHONE--DIRECTORIES.
International yellow pages. New York
[etc.] R. H. Donnelly Telephone
Directory Co. [etc.] 64-8064
Began publication with 1963/64 vol.
HE8721 .I67 MRR Alc Latest edition

Telephone engineer & management
directory. Wheaton, Ill. [etc.]
Harbrace Publications [etc.] 50-
23181
Began publication in 1936?
TK6195 .T45 MRR Alc Latest edition

Telephony's directory of the
telephone industry. Chicago,
Telephony Pub. Corp. [etc.] 10-7536

TK6011 .T24 MRR Alc Latest edition

TELEPHONE--ATLANTIC STATES--DIRECTORIES.
Eastern manufacturers' & industrial
directory New York, Bell Directory
Publishers. 54-35021
Began publication in 1936.
HC107.A11 E2 MRR Alc Latest
edition

TELEPHONE--JAPAN--DIRECTORIES.
The Japan times directory of foreign
residents, business firms &
organizations. Tokyo, Japan Times,
ltd. 915.2 72-627115
HE9463 .J3 MRR Alc Latest edition

TELEPHONE--NEW ENGLAND--DIRECTORIES.
Eastern manufacturers' & industrial
directory New York, Bell Directory
Publishers. 54-35021
Began publication in 1936.
HC107.A11 E2 MRR Alc Latest
edition

TELEPHONE--PORTUGAL.
Guia dos correios, telégrafos e
telefones Lisboa, Gráfica Santelmo.
383.058 44-33738
HE7123 .G8 MRR Alc Latest edition

TELEPHONE--UNITED STATES--DIRECTORIES.
Telephony's directory of the
telephone industry. Chicago,
Telephony Pub. Corp. [etc.] 10-7536

TK6011 .T24 MRR Alc Latest edition

TELEPHONE--UNITED STATES--STATISTICS.
United States Independent Telephone
Association. Statistics of the
independent telephone industry.
Washington. 56-19815
HE8815 .U55 MRR Alc Latest edition

TELEPHONE--UNITED STATES--YEARBOOKS.
Moody's public utility manual. 1954-
New York, Moody's Investors Service.
56-3927
HG4961 .M7245 MRR Alc Latest
edition

TELETYPE--DIRECTORIES.
Jaeger + Waldmann world telex. 16th
ed.; 1968- Darmstadt, Telex-Verlag
Jaeger + Waldmann. 384.1/4 72-
623533
HE7742 .I5 MRR Alc Latest edition

TELETYPE--AMERICA--DIRECTORIES.
The International telex book.
Americas edition. v. 1- 1974-
Atlanta, International Telex Corp.
384.1/4 74-645911
HE7621 .I59 MRR Alc Latest edition

TELETYPE--GREAT BRITAIN--DIRECTORIES.
United Kingdom telex directory.
London, General Post Office. 56-
26931
HE7742.G7 U55 MRR Alc Latest
edition

TELETYPE--LATIN AMERICA--DIRECTORIES.
The International telex book.
Americas edition. v. 1- 1974-
Atlanta, International Telex Corp.
384.1/4 74-645911
HE7621 .I59 MRR Alc Latest edition

TELETYPE--NETHERLANDS--DIRECTORIES.
Telexgids Nederland. ['s-Gravenhage]
Staatsbedrijf der Posterijen,
Telegrafie en Telefonie. 68-5730
HE7742 .T42 MRR Alc Latest edition

TELETYPE--UNITED STATES--DIRECTORIES.
The International telex book.
Americas edition. v. 1- 1974-
Atlanta, International Telex Corp.
384.1/4 74-645911
HE7621 .I59 MRR Alc Latest edition

TELETYPE IN LIBRARIES--DIRECTORIES.
Cockx, August. Telecode and telex
address book; 2d ed.; Sevenoaks
(Kent), International Federation of
Library Associations, 1966. 191 p.
[42/-]   020.25 66-69653
Z731 .C6 MRR Alc.

TELEVISION--APPARATUS AND SUPPLIES.
Official N A R D A T V blue book.
1953- Madison, Wis., National
Appliance Pub. Co. 621.3883085 55-
32756
HD9999.T37 N3 MRR Alc Latest
edition

TELEVISION--DICTIONARIES.
Curtis, Ron. Media dictionary; Red
Oak, Southwest Iowa Learning
Resources Center [1973] 290 p.
301.16/1/03   73-158317
P87.5 .C8 MRR Alc.

The Focal encyclopedia of film &
television techniques. [1st American
ed.] New York, Hastings House [1969]
xxiv, 1100 p. [37.50]   778.5/03
73-7135
TR847 .F62 1969 MRR Alc.

Levitan, Eli L. An alphabetical
guide to motion picture, television,
and videotape production New York,
McGraw-Hill [1970] xvii, 797 p.
778.5/3/03   68-13610
TR847 .L47 MRR Alc.

National Radio Institute, Washington,
D.C. Radio-television-electronics
dictionary. New York, J. F. Rider
[1962] 180 p.   621.38403   62-21929
TK6544 .N3 1962 MRR Alc.

Pannett, W. E. Dictionary of radio
and television, Amsterdam, Elsevier
Publishing Cy. [1967] 380 p.
[£27.50]   621.38/03   67-95326
TK6544 .P28 1967b MRR Alc.

TELEVISION--DICTIONARIES--POLYGLOT.
Elsevier's dictionary of television,
radar, and antennas, in six
languages: Amsterdam, New York,
Elsevier Pub. Co., 1955. 760 p.
621.38803   55-6216
TK6634 .E4 MRR Alc.

**TELEVISION--LAW AND LEGISLATION--UNITED
STATES.**
Kahn, Frank J., comp. Documents of
American broadcasting. 2d ed. New
York, Appleton-Century-Crofts [1973]
xv, 684 p.   343/.73/0994 72-12050
KF2804 .K3 1973 MRR Alc.

TELEVISION--PERIODICALS.
Television factbook. Washington,
Television Digest.   67-118025
TK6540 .T453 MRR Alc Latest
edition

TELEVISION--PRODUCTION AND DIRECTION.
Zettl, Herbert. Television
production handbook. 2d ed.
Belmont, Calif. Wadsworth Pub. Co.
[1968] xi, 541 p.   791.45/0232 68-
19446
PN1992.75 .Z4 1968 MRR Alc.

TELEVISION--RECEIVERS AND RECEPTION.
Johnson, J. Richard, How to
troubleshoot a TV receiver Rev. 3d
ed. New York, Hayden Book Co. [1971]
154 p. [$4.50]   621.388/8/7   79-
27591
TK6653 .J58 1971 MRR Alc.

TELEVISION--REPAIRING.
Johnson, J. Richard, How to
troubleshoot a TV receiver Rev. 3d
ed. New York, Hayden Book Co. [1971]
154 p. [$4.50]   621.388/8/7   79-
27591
TK6653 .J58 1971 MRR Alc.

TELEVISION--STAGE LIGHTING
see Stage lighting

TELEVISION ADVERTISING--DICTIONARIES.
Batten, Barton, Durstine and Osborn,
inc. Media Dept. One hundred basic
media terms defined; [New York]
1966. 44 p.   659.103   67-858
HF5803 .B3 MRR Alc.

**TELEVISION ADVERTISING--UNITED STATES--
DIRECTORIES.**
Boe, John Oliver. Television
sponsors directory. Everglades,
Fla., Everglades Pub. Co.
659.14/3/02573 72-622327
HF6146.T42 B6 MRR Alc Latest
edition

TELEVISION AS A PROFESSION.
Lawton, Sherman Paxton. The modern
broadcaster: New York, Harper [1961]
351 p.   384.54   61-5463
PN1991.5 .L35 MRR Alc.

TELEVISION AUTHORSHIP.
Bettinger, Hoyland, Television
techniques, New York, Harper [1955]
236 p.   791.4 792.95*   55-6964
PN1992.5 .B4 1955 MRR Alc.

TELEVISION BROADCASTING.
Bettinger, Hoyland, Television
techniques, New York, Harper [1955]
236 p.   791.4 792.95*   55-6964
PN1992.5 .B4 1955 MRR Alc.

Lawton, Sherman Paxton. The modern
broadcaster: New York, Harper [1961]
351 p.   384.54   61-5463
PN1991.5 .L35 MRR Alc.

TELEVISION BROADCASTING--DICTIONARIES.
Diamant, Lincoln. The broadcast
communications dictionary, New York,
Hastings House [1974] 128 p.
384.54/01/4 73-19610
P87.5 .D48 1974 MRR Alc.

Television dictionary/handbook for
sponsors, New York, Sponsor
Services, c1955. 48 p.   621.38803
55-3774
PN1992.18 .T2 1955 MRR Alc.

**TELEVISION BROADCASTING--DICTIONARIES--
FRENCH.**
Bessy, Maurice, Dictionnaire du
cinema et de la television
[Paris] J. J. Pauvert [1965-71] 4 v.
66-36201
PN1993.45 .B4 MRR Alc.

TELEVISION BROADCASTING--DIRECTORIES.
Internationales Handbuch für
Rundfunk und Fernsehen. 1957-
Hamburg, Hans Bredow-Institut. 60-
25306
HE8690 .I57 MRR Alc Latest edition

Kemp's film and television year book
(International). London, Kemp's
Printing & Publishing Co.
338.4/7/7914305 72-624899
PN1998.A1 K39 MRR Alc Latest
edition

World radio-television handbook, 1st-
ed.; winter 1947- Hellerup,
Denmark [etc.] World Radio-Television
Handbook Co., ltd. [etc.] 384.5 48-
20385
TK6540 .W67 Sci RR Latest edition*
/ MRR Alc Latest edition

**TELEVISION BROADCASTING--PICTORIAL
WORKS.**
Settel, Irving. A pictorial history
of television, New York, Grosset &
Dunlap [1969] xii, 209 p. [7.95]
791.45/0973 73-86710
PM1992.3.US S4 MRR Alc.

**TELEVISION BROADCASTING--SOCIETIES,
ETC.--DIRECTORIES.**
International Film and Television
Council. Le repertoire C.I.C.T. des
organisations internationales de
cinema et de television et de
leurs branches nationales. 1964-
[London] Film Centre. 65-71067
PN1998 .I5 MRR Alc Latest edition

**TELEVISION BROADCASTING--STUDY AND
TEACHING--DIRECTORIES.**
American Film Institute. The
American Film Institute guide to
college courses in film and
television. Washington, Acropolis
Books [1973] xv, 309 p. [$5.95]
791.4/07/1173 72-12391
LB1043.Z9 A8 MRR Alc.

TELEVISION BROADCASTING--YEARBOOKS.
Fame; New York, Quigley Pub. Co. 53-
31048
Began publication in 1933?
PN1993.3 .B6 MRR Alc Latest
edition

International motion picture almanac.
1929- New York [etc.] Quigley
Publications [etc.] 28-8663
PN1993.3 .I55 MRR Biog Latest
edition

Internationales Handbuch für
Rundfunk und Fernsehen. 1957-
Hamburg, Hans Bredow-Institut. 60-
25306
HE8690 .I57 MRR Alc Latest edition

**TELEVISION BROADCASTING--CANADA--
YEARBOOKS.**
Year book [of the] Canadian
entertainment industry. Toronto,
Film Publications of Canada.
791.43/0971 53-30400
PN1993.3 .Y3 MRR Alc Latest
edition

TELEVISION BROADCASTING--GREAT BRITAIN.
British Broadcasting Corporation. B
B C handbook. 1955- [London]
384.54/0942 72-624368
TK6540 .B82 MRR Alc Latest edition

**TELEVISION BROADCASTING--GREAT BRITAIN--
BIOGRAPHY.**
British film and television year
book. [1st]- ed; 1946- [London,
British and American Film Press,
etc.] 791.4058 792.93058* 46-4765
PN1993.3 .B7 MRR Biog Latest
edition

**TELEVISION BROADCASTING--GREAT BRITAIN--
DIRECTORIES.**
British film and television year
book. [1st]- ed; 1946- [London,
British and American Film Press,
etc.] 791.4058 792.93058* 46-4765
PN1993.3 .B7 MRR Biog Latest
edition

Commercial television year book. 16-
ed.; 1971/72- London, Admark
Directories Ltd. 384.55/4/02542 79-
617039
HE8700.9.G7 C6 MRR Alc Latest
edition

Directory of newspaper and magazine
personnel and data. London,
Haymarket Publishing Group, [etc.]
072.058 59-18302
Z6956.E5 D5 MRR Alc Latest edition

TELEVISION BROADCASTING--UNITED STATES.
35-mile CATV zone maps and full text
of FCC CATV inquiry; Washington,
Television Digest, Inc. [1969] 79 p.
[9.50]   384.55/4 78-80859
HE8700.8.U5 T45 MRR Alc.

Kahn, Frank J., comp. Documents of
American broadcasting. 2d ed. New
York, Appleton-Century-Crofts [1973]
xv, 684 p. 343/.73/0994 72-12050
KF2804 .K3 1973 MRR Alc.

Settel, Irving. A pictorial history
of television, New York, Grosset &
Dunlap [1969] xii, 209 p. [7.95]
791.45/0973 73-86710
PM1992.3.US S4 MRR Alc.

Standard Rate and Data Service, inc.
Network rates and data. v. 1- Feb.
1951- Skokie, Ill. [etc.] 54-32319
HE8698 .S75 MRR Ref Desk Latest
edition

**TELEVISION BROADCASTING--UNITED STATES--
BIOGRAPHY.**
International television almanac.
1956- New York, Quigley Pub. Co. 56-
2008
HE8698 .I55 MRR Biog Latest
edition

**TELEVISION BROADCASTING--UNITED STATES--
DIRECTORIES.**
Broadcasting sourcebook C A T V.
[Washington, Broadcasting
Publications Inc.] 384.55/47 73-
615665
HE8700.7.C6 B75 MRR Ref Desk
Latest edition

International television almanac.
1956- New York, Quigley Pub. Co. 56-
2008
HE8698 .I55 MRR Biog Latest
edition

The Working press of the nation.
[1945]- Burlington, Iowa [etc.]
National Research Bureau [etc.]
071.47 46-7041
Z6951 .W6 MRR Alc Latest edition

**TELEVISION BROADCASTING--UNITED STATES--
YEARBOOKS.**
Broadcasting yearbook. [Washington,
Broadcasting Publications]
384.54/0973 71-649524
HF6146.R3 B73 MRR Ref Desk Latest
edition

International television almanac.
1956- New York, Quigley Pub. Co. 56-
2008
HE8698 .I55 MRR Biog Latest
edition

**TELEVISION IN ADVERTISING--UNITED
STATES--YEARBOOKS.**
Broadcasting yearbook. [Washington,
Broadcasting Publications]
384.54/0973 71-649524
HF6146.R3 B73 MRR Ref Desk Latest
edition

**TELEVISION IN EDUCATION--UNITED STATES--
DIRECTORIES.**
National Association of Educational
Broadcasters. N A E B directory of
members. Urbana, Ill. 61-22844
LB1044.5.A1 N316 MRR Alc Latest
edition

TELEVISION IN RELIGION--DIRECTORIES.
International Christian Broadcasters.
World directory of religious radio
and television broadcasting. South
Pasadena, Calif., William Carey
Library [1973] 808 p. 791.45/5 73-
8853
BV656 .I53 MRR Alc.

TELEVISION INDUSTRY--DIRECTORIES.
Kemp's film and television year book
(International). London, Kemp's
Printing & Publishing Co.
338.4/7/7914305 72-624899
PN1998.A1 K39 MRR Alc Latest
edition

**TELEVISION INDUSTRY--GREAT BRITAIN--
DIRECTORIES.**
Kinematograph and television year
book. London, Go Magazine ltd.
338.4/7/791430942 72-626476
PN1993.3 .K5 MRR Alc Latest
edition

TELEVISION PROGRAMS--DICTIONARIES.
Sharp, Harold S., comp. Index to characters in the performing arts, New York, Scarecrow Press, 1966-73. 4 v. in 6. 808.8292703 66-13744
PN1579 .S45 MRR Alc.

TELEVISION PROGRAMS--UNITED STATES.
Parish, James Robert. Actors' television credits, 1950-1972. Metuchen, N.J., Scarecrow Press, 1973. x, 868 p. 791.45/028/0922 73-9914
PN1992.4.A2 P3 MRR Alc.

TELEVISION SCRIPTS--BIBLIOGRAPHY.
Samples, Gordon. The drama scholars' index to plays and filmscripts. Metuchen, N.J., Scarecrow Press [1974] xii, 448 p. 016.80882 73-22165
Z5781 .S17 MRR Alc.

TELEVISION STATIONS--CALIFORNIA-- DIRECTORIES.
California publicity outlets. 1972- Los Angeles, Unicorn Systems Co., Information Services Division. 659.2/025/794 76-186163
HM263 .C2 MRR Alc Latest edition

TELEVISION STATIONS--NORTH AMERICA-- DIRECTORIES.
Jones, Vane A. North American radio- TV station guide. 1st- ed.; 1963- Indianapolis, H. W. Sams. 621.38416 63-23371
TK6555 .J6 MRR Alc Latest edition

TELEVISION STATIONS--UNITED STATES-- DIRECTORIES.
Broadcasting yearbook. [Washington, Broadcasting Publications] 384.54/0873 71-649524
HF6146.R3 B73 MRR Ref Desk Latest edition

Jones, Vane A. North American radio- TV station guide. 1st- ed.; 1963- Indianapolis, H. W. Sams. 621.38416 63-23371
TK6555 .J6 MRR Alc Latest edition

United States. Office of Minority Business Enterprise. Directory of minority media. [Washington]; for sale by the Supt. of Docs., U.S. Govt. Print. Off., 1973. ix, 89 p. [$1.25] 301.16/1/02573 73-602686
P88.8 .U55 MRR Alc.

TEMPERANCE.
see also Alcoholism

TEMPERANCE--DICTIONARIES.
Keller, Mark. A dictionary of words about alcohol. New Brunswick, N.J., Publications Division, Rutgers Center of Alcohol Studies [1968] xxviii, 236 p. [$7.50] 362.2/92/03 68-64841
HV5017 .K42 MRR Alc.

TEMPS.
Paris. Université. Institut français de presse. Section d'histoire. Tables du journal Le Temps. Paris, Éditions du Centre national de la recherche scientifique, 1966- v. 074.43/6 67-42357
AI21 .T375 MRR Alc.

TENNESSEE.
Federal writers' project. Tennessee. Tennessee; a guide to the state, New York, The Viking press, 1939. xxiv, 558 p. 917.68 39-28847
F436 .F45 MRR Ref Desk.

TENNESSEE--BIBLIOGRAPHY.
Historical records survey. Illinois. A check list of Tennessee imprints, 1793-1840. Chicago, Ill., The Illinois Historical records survey, 1942. xv, 285 p. 015.768 43-4097
Z1215 .H67 no. 32 MRR Alc.

Historical records survey. Tennessee. Check list of Tennessee imprints, 1841-1850. Nashville, Tenn., The Tennessee Historical records survey, 1941. 1 p. l., iii-xiii, 138 numb. l. 015.768 42-17566
Z1215 .H67 no. 20 MRR Alc.

Historical records survey. Tennessee. List of Tennessee imprints, 1793-1840, in Tennessee libraries. Nashville, Tenn., The Tennessee Historical records survey, 1941. viii, 97 numb. l. 015.768 41-52927
Z1215 .H67 no. 16 MRR Alc.

Mitchell, Eleanor Drake. A preliminary checklist of Tennessee imprints, 1861-1866. Charlottesville, Bibliographical Society of the University of Virginia, 1953. 98 l. 015.768 53-7131
Z1337 .M58 MRR Alc.

TENNESSEE--BIBLIOGRAPHY--CATALOGS.
United States. Library of Congress. Tennessee's sesquicentennial exhibition, Washington, U.S. Govt. Print. Off., 1946. 71 p. 016.9768 46-26891
Z663.15.A6T2 1946 MRR Alc.

TENNESSEE--BIOGRAPHY.
Tennessee blue book. Nashville. 353.9768 28-11250
JK5230 .T4 MRR Alc Latest edition

TENNESSEE--CENTENNIAL CELEBRATIONS, ETC.
United States. Library of Congress. Tennessee's sesquicentennial exhibition, Washington, U.S. Govt. Print. Off., 1946. 71 p. 016.9768 46-26891
Z663.15.A6T2 1946 MRR Alc.

TENNESSEE--DESCRIPTION AND TRAVEL-- GUIDE-BOOKS.
Federal writers' project. Tennessee. Tennessee; a guide to the state, New York, The Viking press, 1939. xxiv, 558 p. 917.68 39-28847
F436 .F45 MRR Ref Desk.

TENNESSEE--ECONOMIC CONDITIONS.
Tennessee pocket data book. 1973- Knoxville, Center for Business and Economic Research, University of Tennessee. [$4.00] 330.9/768/05 72-98104
HC107.T3 T432 MRR Alc Latest edition

TENNESSEE--EXECUTIVE DEPARTMENTS.
Tennessee blue book. Nashville. 353.9768 28-11250
JK5230 .T4 MRR Alc Latest edition

TENNESSEE--HISTORY.
Burt, Jesse Clifton. Your Tennessee [Teacher's ed.] Austin, Tex., Steck-Vaughn Co. [1974] vi, 42, vi, 394 p. 917.68/03 74-158990
F436.3 .B87 1974 MRR Alc.

Folmsbee, Stanley John, Tennessee; Knoxville, University of Tennessee Press [1969] xv, 640 p. [15.00] 976.8 69-20114
F436 .F64 1969 MRR Alc.

TENNESSEE--HISTORY--CHRONOLOGY.
Tennessee blue book. Nashville. 353.9768 28-11250
JK5230 .T4 MRR Alc Latest edition

TENNESSEE--IMPRINTS.
Historical records survey. Illinois. A check list of Tennessee imprints, 1793-1840. Chicago, Ill., The Illinois Historical records survey, 1942. xv, 285 p. 015.768 43-4097
Z1215 .H67 no. 32 MRR Alc.

Historical records survey. Tennessee. Check list of Tennessee imprints, 1841-1850. Nashville, Tenn., The Tennessee Historical records survey, 1941. 1 p. l., iii-xiii, 138 numb. l. 015.768 42-17566
Z1215 .H67 no. 20 MRR Alc.

Historical records survey. Tennessee. List of Tennessee imprints, 1793-1840, in Tennessee libraries. Nashville, Tenn., The Tennessee Historical records survey, 1941. viii, 97 numb. l. 015.768 41-52927
Z1215 .H67 no. 16 MRR Alc.

Mitchell, Eleanor Drake. A preliminary checklist of Tennessee imprints, 1861-1866. Charlottesville, Bibliographical Society of the University of Virginia, 1953. 98 l. 015.768 53-7131
Z1337 .M58 MRR Alc.

TENNESSEE--POLITICS AND GOVERNMENT.
Burt, Jesse Clifton. Your Tennessee [Teacher's ed.] Austin, Tex., Steck-Vaughn Co. [1974] vi, 42, vi, 394 p. 917.68/03 74-158990
F436.3 .B87 1974 MRR Alc.

TENNESSEE--POLITICS AND GOVERNMENT-- 1951-
Greene, Lee Seifert. Government in Tennessee 2d ed. Knoxville, University of Tennessee Press [1966] viii, 371 p. 320.9768 66-21194
JK5225 1966 .G7 MRR Alc.

TENNESSEE--REGISTERS.
Tennessee blue book. Nashville. 353.9768 28-11250
JK5230 .T4 MRR Alc Latest edition

TENNESSEE--SOCIAL CONDITIONS.
Tennessee pocket data book. 1973- Knoxville, Center for Business and Economic Research, University of Tennessee. [$4.00] 330.9/768/05 72-98104
HC107.T3 T432 MRR Alc Latest edition

TENNESSEE--STATISTICS.
Tennessee pocket data book. 1973- Knoxville, Center for Business and Economic Research, University of Tennessee. [$4.00] 330.9/768/05 72-98104
HC107.T3 T432 MRR Alc Latest edition

Tennessee statistical abstract. 1969- [Knoxville] Center for Business and Economic Research, University of Tennessee. 68-66489
HA641 .T43 MRR Alc Latest edition

TENNIS.
Brady, Maurice. Lawn tennis encyclopaedia. South Brunswick, [N.J.] A. S. Barnes [1969] 221 p. [6.95] 796.34/2 71-79755
GV995 .B689 MRR Alc.

Danzig, Allison, comp. The fireside book of tennis. New York, Simon and Schuster [1972] xxxii, 1043 p. [$14.95] 796.34/2 70-165538
GV990 .D3 MRR Alc.

TENNIS--BIOGRAPHY.
Brady, Maurice. Lawn tennis encyclopaedia. South Brunswick, [N.J.] A. S. Barnes [1969] 221 p. [6.95] 796.34/2 71-79755
GV995 .B689 MRR Alc.

TENNIS--DICTIONARIES AND ENCYCLOPEDIAS.
United States Lawn Tennis Association. Official encyclopedia of tennis. [1st ed.] New York, Harper & Row [1972] viii, 472 p. [$13.95] 796.34/2/03 71-181644
GV990 .U5 1972 MRR Alc.

TENNIS--HISTORY.
Grimsley, Will. Tennis: its history, people and events. Englewood Cliffs, N.J., Prentice-Hall [1971] 380 p. [$12.50] 796.34/2/0922 76-144006
GV993 .G75 MRR Alc.

TENNYSON, ALFRED TENNYSON, BARON, 1809-1892--CONCORDANCES.
Baker, Arthur Ernest, A concordance to the poetical and dramatic works of Alfred, Lord Tennyson, New York, Barnes & Noble [1966] xvi, 1212 p. 821.8 66-2700
PR5580 .B3 1966 MRR Alc.

TERMINALS (TRANSPORTATION)
see also Airports

see also Harbors

TERMS AND PHRASES.
Blumberg, Dorothy Rose. Whose what? [1st ed.] New York, Holt, Rinehart and Winston [1969] 184 p. [3.95] 031/.02 68-12199
AG105 .B72 MRR Alc.

Origin of things familiar; Cincinnati, O., United book corporation [c1934] 4 p. l., 280 p. 031 35-2154
AG5 .O7 MRR Alc.

Roback, Abraham Aaron, A dictionary of international slurs (ethnophaulisms Cambridge, Mass., Sci-art publishers [1944] 394 p. 323.1 44-8328
HT1523 .R6 MRR Alc.

Stimpson, George William, Information roundup. [1st ed.] New York, Harper [1948] x, 587 p. 031 48-6728
AG5 .S85 MRR Alc.

TESTING.
see also Environmental engineering

see also Standardization

TESTING LABORATORIES--UNITED STATES-- DIRECTORIES.
American Council of Independent Laboratories. Directory; [Washington] 607.273 58-4459
TA416 .A54 Sci RR Latest edition / MRR Alc Latest edition

TESTS
see Examinations

TESTS, MENTAL
see Mental tests

TESTS AND MEASUREMENTS IN EDUCATION
see Educational tests and measurements

TEXAS.
Texas almanac. 1857- [Dallas, etc.] A. H. Belo Corp. [etc.] 10-3390
AY311.D3 T5 MRR Alc Latest edition

Writers' Program. Texas. Texas; New rev. ed. New York, Hastings House [1969] xxxiv, 717 p. [8.95] 917.64/04/6 68-31690
F391 .W95 1969 MRR Ref Desk.

TEXAS--BIBLIOGRAPHY.
Streeter, Thomas Winthrop,
Bibliography of Texas, 1795-1845.
Cambridge, Harvard University Press,
1955-60. 3 pts. in 5 v.   016.9764
56-13552
Z1339 .S8 MRR Alc.

TEXAS--BIBLIOGRAPHY--CATALOGS.
United States. Library of Congress.
Texas centennial exhibition.
Washington, U.S. Govt. print. off.,
1946. iii, 54 p.   976.4   46-26860
Z663.15.A6 T4 MRR Alc.

TEXAS--BIOGRAPHY.
Who's who in Texas today. 1st
ed.; 1968- Austin, Pemberton Press.
920.0764 68-20724
F385 .W55 MRR Biog Latest edition

TEXAS--BIOGRAPHY--DICTIONARIES.
Who's who in Texas. 1st ed.;
1973/74- Atlanta, Ga., United States
Public Relations Service. 920/.0764
73-93588
CT262 .W45 MRR Biog Latest edition

TEXAS--CENTENNIAL CELEBRATIONS, ETC.
United States. Library of Congress.
Texas centennial exhibition.
Washington, U.S. Govt. print. off.,
1946. iii, 54 p.   976.4   46-26860
Z663.15.A6 T4 MRR Alc.

TEXAS--DESCRIPTION AND TRAVEL--1951- --
GUIDE-BOOKS.
Writers' Program. Texas. Texas; New
rev. ed. New York, Hastings House
[1969] xxxiv, 717 p.   [8.85]
917.64/04/6 68-31690
F391 .W95 1969 MRR Ref Desk.

TEXAS--DESCRIPTION AND TRAVEL--GUIDE-
BOOKS.
[Almon, Millard H.] ed. The five
states guide to Texas; [Rev. Popular
ed.] Dallas, Five States of Texas
[1963] 511 p.   917.64 63-2476
F384.3 .A4 1963 MRR Alc.

TEXAS--DICTIONARIES AND ENCYCLOPEDIAS.
The Handbook of Texas. Austin, Texas
State Historical Association, 1952.
2 v.   917.64   53-483
F384 .H3 MRR Alc.

TEXAS--DIRECTORIES.
Directory of Texas manufacturers,
classified by cities and by products.
1932- Austin, Tex., Bureau of
Business research, the University of
Texas. 670.9764 34-27861
HD9727.T4 D5 MRR Alc Latest
edition

TEXAS--HISTORY.
Fehrenbach, T. R. Lone star; New
York, Macmillan [1968] xii, 751 p.
976.4 68-25222
F386 .F4 MRR Alc.

TEXAS--IMPRINTS.
Streeter, Thomas Winthrop,
Bibliography of Texas, 1795-1845.
Cambridge, Harvard University Press,
1955-60. 3 pts. in 5 v.   016.8764
56-13552
Z1339 .S8 MRR Alc.

TEXAS--MANUFACTURES--DIRECTORIES.
Directory of Texas manufacturers,
classified by cities and by products.
1932- Austin, Tex., Bureau of
Business research, the University of
Texas. 670.9764 34-27861
HD9727.T4 D5 MRR Alc Latest
edition

TEXAS--POLITICS AND GOVERNMENT.
Benton, Wilbourn E. Texas: its
government and politics 3d ed.
Englewood Cliffs, N.J., Prentice-Hall
[1972] xiv, 368 p. [$7.95]
320.4/764 72-372
JK4825 1972 .B4 MRR Alc.

TEXAS--STATISTICS.
Texas almanac. 1857- [Dallas, etc.]
A. H. Belo Corp. [etc.] 10-3390
AY311.D3 T5 MRR Alc Latest edition

TEXT-BOOKS--BIBLIOGRAPHY.
Clapp, Jane. College textbooks; New
York, Scarecrow Press, 1960. 1096 p.
016   60-7267
Z5817 .C6 MRR Alc.

El-Hi textbooks in print. [56th]-
[1927]- New York, Bowker [etc.]
016.379/156 57-4667
Z5813 .A51 MRR Alc Latest edition

TEXT-BOOKS--CATALOGS.
Barnes & Noble, inc., New York.
Textbook buying guide. New York.
016.37132 68-5106
Z5817 .B3 MRR Alc Latest edition

TEXT-BOOKS--UNITED STATES--HISTORY.
Nietz, John Alfred, Old textbooks;
[Pittsburgh] University of Pittsburgh
Press [1961] vii, 364 p.
371.320873 60-13851
LT23 .N5 MRR Alc.

TEXTILE FACTORIES--UNITED STATES--
DIRECTORIES.
Davison's textile blue book. United
States and Canada. [Office ed.] 1st-
annual ed.; 1888- Ridgewood, N.J.
[etc.] Davison Pub. Co. [etc.] 99-
3738
TS1312 .B6 MRR Alc Latest edition

TEXTILE FIBERS.
Hall, Archibald John. The standard
handbook of textiles 7th ed.
London, Heywood Books, 1969. 7, 370
p. [50/-] 677/.028 78-479366
TS1445 .H27 1969 MRR Alc.

TEXTILE FIBERS, SYNTHETIC.
Moncrieff, R. W. Man-made fibres,
[4th ed.] New York, Wiley, 1963. x,
742 p. 677.46 63-22956
TS1548.5 .M6 1963 MRR Alc.

United Piece Dye Works. Guidebook to
man-made textile fibers and textured
yarns of the world. 3d ed. New York,
[1969] 345 p. 677/.4 68-28677
TS1548.5 .U5 1969 MRR Alc.

TEXTILE INDUSTRY AND FABRICS.
American fabrics. AF encyclopedia of
textiles, Englewood Cliffs, N.J.,
Prentice-Hall [1960] xvi, 702 p.
677.03 59-8054
TS1445 .A45 MRR Alc.

American Home Economics Association.
Textiles and Clothing Section.
Textile handbook. 4th ed.
Washington, American Home Economics
Association [1970] vii, 115 p.
677/.002/02 71-129523
TS1445 .A46 1970 MRR Alc.

Hall, Archibald John. The standard
handbook of textiles 7th ed.
London, Heywood Books, 1969. 7, 370
p. [50/-] 677/.028 78-479366
TS1445 .H27 1969 MRR Alc.

TEXTILE INDUSTRY AND FABRICS--
DICTIONARIES.
Fairchild's dictionary of textiles.
New York, Fairchild Publications
[1967] vii, 662 p. 677/.003 67-
14640
TS1309 .F34 1967 MRR Alc.

Klapper, Marvin. Fabric almanac. 2d
ed. New York, Fairchild Publications
[1971] 181 p. [$6.95] 677/.002/02
72-132144
TS1451 .K53 1971 MRR Alc.

Linton, George Edward. The modern
textile dictionary. [1st ed.] New
York, Duell, Sloan and Pearce [1954]
xxii, 772 p. 677.03 54-8300
TS1309 .L743 MRR Alc.

Picken, Mary (Brooks) The fashion
dictionary; New York, Funk &
Wagnalls [1957] 397 p. 646.03 57-
10114
TT503 .P49 MRR Alc.

TEXTILE INDUSTRY AND FABRICS--
DICTIONARIES--GERMAN.
De Vries, Louis, Wörterbuch der
Textilindustrie. Wiesbaden,
Brandstetter [1959-60] 2 v.   677.03
59-42656
TS1309 .D43 MRR Alc.

TEXTILE INDUSTRY AND FABRICS--
DICTIONARIES--POLYGLOT.
Fabierkiewicz, Wacław. Podręczny
słownik włókienniczy w 5 językach:
[Wyd. 1] [Warszawa] Państwowe
Wydawn. Techniczne [1955] xlvii, 305
p.   55-38912
TS1309 .F3 MRR Alc.

TEXTILE INDUSTRY AND FABRICS--
DIRECTORIES.
Davison's textile blue book. United
States and Canada. [Office ed.] 1st-
annual ed.; 1888- Ridgewood, N.J.
[etc.] Davison Pub. Co. [etc.] 99-
3738
TS1312 .B6 MRR Alc Latest edition

Davison's textile catalogues and
buyers guide; Ridgewood, N.J. [etc.]
J. Davison publishing co. 677.085
13-18033
TS1312 .D25 MRR Alc Latest edition

Skinner's cotton and man-made fibres
directory of the world. 1923-
Croydon, Eng. [etc.] T. Skinner
Directories [etc.] 26-3388
HD9870.3 .S5 MRR Alc Latest
edition

United Piece Dye Works. Guidebook to
man-made textile fibers and textured
yarns of the world. 3d ed. New York,
[1969] 345 p. 677/.4 68-28677
TS1548.5 .U5 1969 MRR Alc.

TEXTILE INDUSTRY AND FABRICS--
HANDBOOKS, MANUALS, ETC.
Klapper, Marvin. Fabric almanac. 2d
ed. New York, Fairchild Publications
[1971] 181 p. [$6.95] 677/.002/02
72-132144
TS1451 .K53 1971 MRR Alc.

TEXTILE INDUSTRY AND FABRICS--GERMANY
(FEDERAL REPUBLIC, 1949-)--DIRECTORIES.
Jahresschau der deutschen Industrie.
[Darmstadt, Industrieschau-
Verlagsgesellschaft] 60-38682
HD9863.3 .J3 MRR Alc Latest
edition

TEXTILE INDUSTRY AND FABRICS--GREAT
BRITAIN--DIRECTORIES.
The British textile industry. 80th-
ed.; 1970/71- Croydon, Eng.; T.
Skinner. 677/.0025/42 71-649662
TS1312 .B76 MRR Alc Latest edition

Fabric & clothing trades index.
London. 55-58374
TS1312 .F3 MRR Alc Latest edition

Skinner's British textile register.
1st- ed.; 1973- Croydon, Eng.;
Thomas Skinner Directories. [£10.50]
338.4/7/677002542 74-644855
TS1312 .S55 MRR Alc Latest edition

TEXTILE INDUSTRY AND FABRICS--
NETHERLANDS--DIRECTORIES.
Textiel adresboek van de Nederlandse
textiel-industrie en groothandel. 6.
geheel opnieuw bewerkte uitg.
Amsterdam, Diligentia [1967] 674 p.
[fl 35.-]   68-81684
HD9865.N65 T4 1967 MRR Alc.

TEXTILE INDUSTRY AND FABRICS--UNITED
STATES--DIRECTORIES.
The Agent; [Chicago, Halper Pub.
Co.] 677.058 50-56303
TS1312 .A35 MRR Alc Latest edition

Davison's knit goods trade, "The
Standard." [Office ed.] Ridgewood,
N.J. [etc.] Davison Pub. Co. 08-
32658
TT695 .D26 Sci RR Latest edition /
MRR Alc Latest edition

Davison's synthetic and silk red
book. 67th- ed.; 1962- Ridgewood,
N.J., Davison Pub. Co. 72-626449
TS1643 .D3 MRR Alc Latest edition

Davison's textile blue book. United
States and Canada. [Office ed.] 1st-
annual ed.; 1888- Ridgewood, N.J.
[etc.] Davison Pub. Co. [etc.] 99-
3738
TS1312 .B6 MRR Alc Latest edition

Davison's textile directory for
executives and salesmen. [1st]-
ed.; 1911/12- Ridgewood, N.J. [etc.]
Davison Pub. Co. 677.058 11-19402
TS1312 .D3 MRR Alc Latest edition

TEXTILE MACHINERY--CATALOGS.
Davison's textile catalogues and
buyers guide; Ridgewood, N.J. [etc.]
J. Davison publishing co. 677.085
13-18033
TS1312 .D25 MRR Alc Latest edition

THAI LANGUAGE--DICTIONARIES--ENGLISH.
Haas, Mary Rosamond, Thai-English
student's dictionary. Stanford,
Calif., Stanford University Press,
1964. xxix, 638 p. 495.9132 64-
13554
PL4156 .H3 MRR Alc.

McFarland, George Bradley, Thai-
English dictionary; Stanford
University, Calif., Stanford
university press; London, H. Milford,
Oxford university press [1944] 2 p.
l., xxi, 1019 p., 1 l., 39 p.
495.9132 a 44-4738
PL4187 .M18 1944 MRR Alc.

Plang Phloyphrom. Modern standard
Thai-English dictionary. Prae
Bhitthaya [1959] 2, 1563 p. 71-
257127
PL4187 .P48 MRR Alc.

THAILAND.
Smith, Harvey Henry, Area handbook
for Thailand. 2d rev. ed.]
Washington, For sale by the Supt. of
Docs., U.S. Govt. Print. Off., 1968.
xvi, 558 p. [4.00] 309.1/593 74-
600099
DS571 .S58 1968 MRR Alc.

Thailand year book. 1964/65-
Bangkok, Temple Publicity Services.
sa 65-4965
DS561 .T57 MRR Alc Latest edition

THAILAND--BIBLIOGRAPHY.
Mason, John Brown, Thailand
bibliography, Gainesville, Fla.,
Dept. of Reference and Bibliography,
University of Florida Libraries,
1958. vii, 247 p. 016.9593 a 58-
9842
Z3236 .M3 MRR Alc.

United States. Library of Congress.
Orientalia Division. Southeast Asia
subject catalog. Boston, G. K. Hall,
1972- v.   016.9159/03 72-5257
Z3221 .U525 MRR Alc (Dk 33)

THAILAND--COMMERCE--DIRECTORIES.
The Siam directory. 1947- Bangkok,
Consumer International Ltd. [etc.]
915.93 48-11053
    DS563 .S53 MRR Alc Latest edition

Thai Chamber of Commerce. Directory.
[Bangkok] 52-18813
    HF331 .T45 MRR Alc Latest edition

Thailand. Dept. of Commercial
Intelligence. Commercial directory
of Thailand. 1st- ed.; 1920-
[Bangkok] 24-12684
    HF3868 A3 MRR Alc Latest edition

Thailand year book. 1964/65-
Bangkok, Temple Publicity Services.
sa 65-4965
    DS561 .T57 MRR Alc Latest edition

**THAILAND--COMMERCE--HANDBOOKS, MANUALS,
ETC.**
Thailand. Dept. of Commercial
Intelligence. Commercial directory
of Thailand. 1st- ed.; 1920-
[Bangkok] 24-12684
    HF3868 A3 MRR Alc Latest edition

THAILAND--DESCRIPTION AND TRAVEL.
Thai Chamber of Commerce. Directory.
[Bangkok] 52-18813
    HF331 .T45 MRR Alc Latest edition

**THAILAND--DIPLOMATIC AND CONSULAR
SERVICE.**
Thai Chamber of Commerce. Directory.
[Bangkok] 52-18813
    HF331 .T45 MRR Alc Latest edition

THAILAND--DIRECTORIES.
The Siam directory. 1947- Bangkok,
Consumer International Ltd. [etc.]
915.93 48-11053
    DS563 .S53 MRR Alc Latest edition

Thailand year book. 1964/65-
Bangkok, Temple Publicity Services.
sa 65-4965
    DS561 .T57 MRR Alc Latest edition

**THAILAND--ECONOMIC CONDITIONS--
YEARBOOKS.**
Thai Chamber of Commerce. Directory.
[Bangkok] 52-18813
    HF331 .T45 MRR Alc Latest edition

THAILAND--GAZETTEERS.
United States. Office of Geography.
Thailand; official standard names
approved by the United States Board
on Geographic Names. Washington,
1966. vi, 675 p. 915.93003 66-
62306
    DS563 .U5 MRR Alc.

THAILAND--POLITICS AND GOVERNMENT.
Wilson, David A. Politics in
Thailand. Ithaca, N.Y., Cornell
University Press [1962] 307 p.
959.3 62-20734
    JQ1745 .W5 MRR Alc.

THAILAND--STATISTICS.
Thailand. Central Statistical Office.
Statistical year book. Thailand.
no. 1-21, 1916-1939/44; new ser., v.
1- 1952- [Bangkok] 17-14291
    HA1781 .A3 MRR Alc Latest edition

**THE ARTS--SCHOLARSHIPS, FELLOWSHIPS,
ETC.--UNITED STATES--DIRECTORIES.**
Grants and aid to individuals in the
arts. 1st- ed.; 1970- Washington.
378.3 70-112695
    NX398 .G7 MRR Ref Desk Latest
    edition

American Council on Education.
Fellowships in the arts and sciences.
1st-10th ed.; 1957-1967/68
Washington [etc.] 58-461
    LB2338 .F43 MRR Ref Desk Latest
    edition

THE ARTS--RUSSIA--BIBLIOGRAPHY.
Bibliography of Russian literature in
English translation to 1945. Totowa,
N.J., Rowman and Littlefield [1972]
74, 96 p. 016.8917/08 72-180612
    Z2504.T8 B53 MRR Alc.

THE CHRISTIAN SCIENCE MONITOR--INDEXES.
The Christian Science monitor. Index.
[Boston, Mass.] Christian Science
Pub. Society. 051 74-644930
    AI21.C462 C45 MRR Alc Partial set

THE WEST--BIOGRAPHY
Who's who in the West and Western
Canada. 1st- ed.; 1947- Chicago,
Marquis-Who's Who [etc.] 920.07 49-
48186
    E176 .W646 MRR Biog Latest edition

THE WEST IN ART.
Dawdy, Doris Ostrander. Artists of
the American West : 1st ed. Chicago
: Sage Books, [1974] viii, 275 p. ;
[$12.50] 709/.2/2 72-91919
    N6536 .D38 MRR Biog.

THEATER.
see also Acting

see also Children's plays

see also Drama

Encyclopédie du théâtre
contemporain. [Paris, Publications
de France, 1957-[59] 2 v. 58-25160

    PN2020 .E63 MRR Alc.

Tennyson, G. B. An introduction to
drama New York, Holt, Rinehart and
Winston [c1967] viii, 134 p.
808.82 67-10599
    PN1655 .T4 MRR Alc.

Whiting, Frank M. An introduction to
the theatre. Rev. ed. New York,
Harper [1961] 369 p. 792 61-5460

    PN2037 .W5 1961 MRR Alc.

THEATER--AWARDS.
The New York times theater reviews,
1920-1970. New York, New York times,
1971- v. 792/.09747/1 72-
166218
    PN1581 .N4 MRR Alc.

THEATER--BIBLIOGRAPHY.
American Educational Theatre
Association. Theatre arts
publications available in the United
States, 1953-1957; Evanston? Ill.,
c1964] xiii, 188 p. 65-3361
    Z5781 .A52 MRR Alc.

Baker, Blanch (Merritt) Dramatic
bibliography; New York, The H. W.
Wilson company, 1933. xvi, 320 p.
016.792 33-3167
    Z5781 .B16 MRR Alc.

Baker, Blanch (Merritt) Theatre and
allied arts; New York, Wilson, 1952.
xiii, 536 p. 016.792 52-6756
    Z5781 .B18 MRR Alc.

British Drama League. Library. The
player's library; 1925- [London]
Faber and Faber [etc.] 016.822 26-
12434
    Z2014.D7 B8 MRR Alc Full set

British Drama League. Library. The
player's library; Supplement. 1st-
1951- [London] Faber and Faber
[etc.] 016.822 74-643566
    Z2014.D7 B8 Suppl. MRR Alc Full
    set

Cheshire, David F. Theatre; history,
criticism and reference London,
Bingley, 1967. 131 p. [25/-]
016.792 67-82149
    Z5781 .C48 1967a MRR Alc.

Chicorel, Marietta. Chicorel
bibliography to the performing arts.
1st ed. New York, Chicorel Library
Pub. Corp. [1972] 498 p. 016.7902
73-155102
    Z6935 .C45 MRR Alc.

Cumulated Dramatic index, 1909-1949;
Boston, G. K. Hall, 1965. 2 v. 68-
4712
    Z5781 .C8 MRR Alc.

Kindermann, Heinz, Theatergeschichte
Europas. (2., verb. und erg. Aufl.)
Salzburg, O. Müller, 1966- v.
[335.- (v.1) 210.- (v.3)] 67-88479

    PN2570 .K552 MRR Alc.

Litto, Fredric M., American
dissertations on the drama and the
theatre; [1st ed. Kent, Ohio] Kent
State University Press [1969] ix,
519 p. 016.8092 71-76761
    Z5781 .L56 MRR Alc.

Melnitz, William W. Theatre arts
publications in the United States,
1947-1952; [Dubuque? Iowa, c1959]
xiii, 91 p. 016.792 60-882
    Z5781 .M5 MRR Alc.

Palmer, Helen H. European drama
criticism, Hamden, Conn., Shoe
String Press, 1968. 460 p.
016.809/2 67-24188
    Z5781 .P2 MRR Ref Desk.

Schoolcraft, Ralph Newman.
Performing arts/books in print: an
annotated bibliography, [1st ed.]
New York, Drama Book Specialists
[1973] xiii, 761 p. 016.7902 72-
78809
    Z6935 .S34 MRR Alc.

THEATER--BIBLIOGRAPHY--CATALOGS.
Dramatists Play Service, New York.
Complete catalogue of plays. New
York. 016.812 63-289
    Z5785.Z9 D73 MRR Alc Latest
    edition

New York (City). Public Library.
Research Libraries. Catalog of the
theatre and drama collections.
Boston, G. K. Hall, 1967. 21 v.
016.700 68-5330
    Z5785 .N56 MRR Alc. (DK 33).

THEATER--COSTUME
see Theater

THEATER--DICTIONARIES.
Bowman, Walter Parker, Theatre
language; New York, Theatre Arts
Books [1961] xii, 428 p. 792.03
60-10495
    PN2035 .B6 MRR Alc.

Downs, Harold, ed. Theatre and
stage; London, Pitman [1951] 2 v.
(x, 1181 p.) 792.03 a 53-2461
    PN2035 .D6 1951 MRR Alc.

Granville, Wilfred. A dictionary of
theatrical terms. [London] A.
Deutsch [1952] 206 p. 792.03 53-
312
    PN2035 .G7 1952a MRR Alc.

Hartnoll, Phyllis. The Oxford
companion to the theatre, 3rd ed.
London, New York, [etc.] Oxford U.P.,
1967. xv, 1088 p. 792/.03 67-
31943
    PN2035 .H3 1967 MRR Ref Desk.

The Language of show biz, Chicago,
Dramatic Pub. Co. [1973] xliii, 251
p. 790/.03 73-173320
    PN1579 .L3 MRR Alc.

Melchinger, Siegfried. The concise
encyclopedia of modern drama;
London, Vision P., 1966. 288 p.
[70/-] 792.03 66-73655
    PN1861 .M4 1966 MRR Alc.

Sobel, Bernard, ed. The new theatre
handbook and digest of plays. [8th
ed., completely rev.] New York,
Crown Publishers, 1959. 749 p.
792.03 58-12876
    PN1625 .S6 1959 MRR Alc.

Taylor, John Russell. The Penguin
dictionary of the theatre,
Baltimore, Penguin Books [1966] 293
p. 809/.2/03 68-2861
    PN2035 .T3 1966b MRR Alc.

Wolf, Martin L. Dictionary of the
arts; New York, Philosophical
Library [1951] xiii, 797 p. 703
51-13402
    N33 .W6 MRR Alc.

THEATER--DICTIONARIES--FLEMISH.
Collet, Paul, Theater A-Z
Antwerpen, Boekengilde Die Poorte
[1959] 2 v. 60-29346
    PN1625 .C6 MRR Alc.

THEATER--DICTIONARIES--POLYGLOT.
Band-Kuzmany, Karin R. M. Glossary
of the theatre. Amsterdam, New York,
Elsevier Pub. Co., 1969. 140 p.
[31.20] 792/.03 68-57152
    PN2035 .B3 MRR Alc.

Rae, Kenneth, ed. Lexique
international de termes techniques de
théâtre Bruxelles, Elsevier [1959]
139 p. 60-26926
    PN2035 .R3 MRR Alc.

THEATER--DIRECTORIES.
Pride, Leo Bryan, International
theatre directory; New York, Simon
and Schuster [1973] xviii, 577 p.
[$35.00] 792/.025 70-157681
    PN2052 .P7 MRR Alc.

THEATER--HISTORY.
Brockett, Oscar Gross, History of
the theatre [Boston, Allyn and
Bacon, 1968] viii, 741 p. 792/.09
68-18812
    PN2101 .B68 MRR Alc.

Cleaver, James. Theatre through the
ages. New York, Hart Pub. Co. [1967]
xxi, 474 p. 792.09 67-20968
    PN2101 .C55 1967 MRR Alc.

Freedley, George, A history of the
theatre 3d newly rev. ed., New
York, Crown Publishers [1968] xvi,
1008 p. 792/.09 68-20482
    PN2010 .F7 1968 MRR Alc.

Gascoigne, Bamber. World theatre;
Boston, Little, Brown [1968] 335 p.
[15.00] 792.09 68-22899
    PN2101 .G3 MRR Alc.

Geisinger, Marion. Plays, players, &
playwrights; New York, Hart Pub. Co.
[1971] 767 p. [$20.00] 792/.09
77-162054
    PN2101 .G4 MRR Alc.

Kernodle, George Riley, Invitation
to the theatre New York, Harcourt,
Brace & World [1967] viii, 677 p.
792/.09 67-12523
    PN1655 .K4 MRR Alc.

Macgowan, Kenneth, The living stage;
New York, Prentice-Hall, 1955. 543
p. 792.09 55-5768
    PN2101 .M3 MRR Alc.

Nagler, Alois Maria, ed. Sources of
theatrical history. New York,
Theatre Annual [1952] xxiii, 611 p.
792.09 52-12506
    PN2101 .N3 MRR Alc.

THEATER--HISTORY. (Cont.)
Shipley, Joseph Twadell. Guide to great plays. Washington, Public Affairs Press [1956] xi, 867 p. 808.2 56-6595
PN6112.5 .S45 MRR Alc.

Southern, Richard. The seven ages of the theatre. New York, Hill and Wang [1961] 312 p. 792.09 61-14478
PN2101 .S6 MRR Alc.

Stephenson, Jim Bob, Chronological chart of theatre history. Ann Arbor, Ann Arbor Photo Lithographers, 1951. ii, 57 p. 792.09 51-4984
PN2115 .S8 MRR Alc.

THEATER--HISTORY--CHRONOLOGY.
Kindermann, Heinz, Theatergeschichte Europas. (2., verb. und erg. Aufl.) Salzburg, O. Müller, 1966- v. [335.- (v.1) 210.- (v.3)] 67-88479
PN2570 .K552 MRR Alc.

THEATER--LITTLE THEATER MOVEMENT.
Young, John Wray. The community theatre and how it works. [1st ed.] New York, Harper [1957] 166 p. 792 57-10361
PN2267 .Y6 MRR Alc.

THEATER--LITTLE THEATER MOVEMENT-- DIRECTORIES.
Havens, John F. Description of community theatres in the United States [Washington] U.S. Dept. of Health, Education, and Welfare, Office of Education, Bureau of Research, 1868. v, 5e, 164 p. 792/.0223/02573 70-602084
PN2267 .H3 MRR Alc.

THEATER--MUSEUMS AND COLLECTIONS.
Gilder, Rosamond. Theatre collections in libraries and museums, New York, Theatre arts inc. [c1936] 4 p. l., 182 p. 792.074 36-21492
Z688.T6 G5 MRR Alc.

International Federation of Library Associations. Section for Theatrical Libraries and Museums. Bibliothèques et musées des arts du spectacle dans le monde ... 2e édition revue et augmentée. Paris, Éditions du Centre national de la recherche scientifique, 1967. 803 p. [90 F] 016.792 70-362547
Z675.T36 I5 1967 MRR Alc.

Young, William C., American theatrical arts; Chicago, American Library Association, 1971. ix, 166 p. 016.7902 78-161234
Z6935 .Y68 MRR Alc.

THEATER--PERIODICALS--INDEXES.
Belknap, Sara (Yancey) Guide to the musical arts; New York, Scarecrow Press, 1957. 1 v. (unpaged) 016.78 57-6631
ML113 .B37 MRR Alc.

Guide to the performing arts. 1957- Metuchen, N.J. [etc.] Scarecrow Press. 016.78 60-7266
ML118 .G8 MRR Alc Full set

THEATER--PICTORIAL WORKS.
Sobel, Bernard. A pictorial history of vaudeville. New York, Citadel Press [1961] 224 p. 792.2 61-18015
PN1967 .S63 MRR Alc.

THEATER--PRODUCTION AND DIRECTION.
Dietrich, John E. Play direction. New York, Prentice-Hall, 1953. xii, 484 p. 792.92* 52-14043
PN2053 .D5 MRR Alc.

Gassner, John, Producing the play, Rev. ed. New York, Dryden Press [1953] 915 p. 792.02* 52-14799
PN2037 .G3 1953 MRR Alc.

Rowe, Kenneth Thorpe, A theater in your head. New York, Funk & Wagnalls [1960] 438 p. 808.2 60-7804
PN1731 .R6 MRR Alc.

THEATER--PRODUCTION AND DIRECTION-- DICTIONARIES.
Lounsbury, Warren C. Theatre backstage from A to Z. Rev. ed. Seattle, University of Washington Press [c1972] xxviii, 191 p. [$10.00] 792/.025/03 73-159613
PN2035 .L6 1972 MRR Alc.

THEATER--REVIEWS.
The Catholic periodical and literature index. July/Aug. 1968- Haverford, Pa., Catholic Library Association. 011 70-649588
AI3 .C32 MRR Alc Full set

The Catholic periodical index, 1930/33-May/June 1968. Haverford, Pa. [etc.] Catholic Library Association [etc.] 40-15160
AI3 .C32 MRR Alc Full set

New York theatre critics' reviews. v. 1- May 27, 1940- New York, N.Y., Critics' theatre reviews. 792 a 42-1744
PN2000 .N76 MRR Alc Partial set

Toohey, John L. A history of the Pulitzer Prize plays, [1st ed.] New York, Citadel Press [1967] viii, 344 p. 792/.097/3 67-25654
PN2266 .T6 MRR Alc.

THEATER--REVIEWS--INDEXES.
Johnson, Robert Owen. An index to literature in the New Yorker, volumes I-XV, 1925-1940. Metuchen, N.J., Scarecrow Press, 1969-71. 3 v. 051 71-7740
AP2 .N6764 MRR Alc.

Salem, James M. A guide to critical reviews, 2d ed. Metuchen, N.J., Scarecrow Press, 1973- v. 016.809/2 73-3120
Z5782 .S342 MRR Ref Desk.

Salem, James M. A guide to critical reviews. New York, Scarecrow Press, 1966- v. [$4.50 (v. 1) varies] 016.8092 66-13733
Z5782 .S34 MRR Ref Desk.

THEATER--STAGE LIGHTING
see Stage lighting

THEATER--STUDY AND TEACHING.
Directory of American college theatre. 1st ed.; 1960- Dallas, Tex. [etc.] American Educational Theatre Association. 792.0711 60-4683
PN2078.U6 D5 MRR Alc Latest edition

THEATER--TERMINOLOGY.
Rae, Kenneth, ed. Lexique international de termes techniques de théâtre Bruxelles, Elsevier [1959] 139 p. 60-26926
PN2035 .R3 MRR Alc.

THEATER--ASIA.
Bowers, Faubion, Theatre in the East; New York, T. Nelson [1956] 374 p. 792.095 56-8995
GV1689 .B6 MRR Alc.

THEATER--AUSTRIA--BIOGRAPHY.
Kürschners biographisches Theater-Handbuch: Berlin, W. de Gruyter, 1956. xii, 840 p. a 57-2818
PN2657 .K8 MRR Biog.

THEATER--ENGLAND--BIBLIOGRAPHY.
Stratman, Carl Joseph, Restoration and eighteenth century theatre research; Carbondale, Southern Illinois University Press [1971] ix, 811 p. [$25.00] 016.822/5/09 71-112384
Z2014.D7 S854 MRR Alc.

THEATER--ENGLAND--HISTORY.
Wickham, Glynne William Gladstone. Early English stages, 1300 to 1660. London, Routledge and Paul; New York, Columbia University Press, 1959- v. in 792.0942 59-2245
PN2587 .W53 MRR Alc.

THEATER--EUROPE--HISTORY.
Kindermann, Heinz, Theatergeschichte Europas. Salzburg, O. Müller [1957- v. 59-37129
PN2570 .K55 MRR Alc.

Kindermann, Heinz, Theatergeschichte Europas. (2., verb. und erg. Aufl.) Salzburg, O. Müller, 1966- v. [335.- (v.1) 210.- (v.3)] 67-88479
PN2570 .K552 MRR Alc.

THEATER--FRANCE.
Encyclopedie du théâtre contemporain. [Paris, Publications de France, 1957-[59] 2 v. 58-25160
PN2020 .E63 MRR Alc.

Fowlie, Wallace, Dionysus in Paris; New York, Meridian Books [1960] 314 p. 842.91082 60-6740
PQ556 .F6 MRR Alc.

THEATER--FRANCE--DICTIONARIES.
Centre français du théâtre. Dictionnaire des hommes de théâtre français contemporains. Paris, Librairie théâtrale [1957- v. 59-35428
PN2635 .C4 MRR Biog.

THEATER--FRANCE--YEARBOOKS.
Annuaire du spectacle; [1]- année; 1942/43- Paris, Éditions Raoult [etc.] 45-27035
PN2620 .A67 MRR Alc Latest edition

THEATER--GERMANY--BIO-BIBLIOGRAPHY.
Kosch, Wilhelm, Deutsches Theater-Lexikon; Klagenfurt, F. Kleinmayr, 1951- v. a 52-1902
PN2035 .K6 MRR Alc.

THEATER--GERMANY--BIOGRAPHY.
Kosch, Wilhelm, Deutsches Theater-Lexikon; Klagenfurt, F. Kleinmayr, 1951- v. a 52-1902
PN2035 .K6 MRR Alc.

Kürschners biographisches Theater-Handbuch: Berlin, W. de Gruyter, 1956. xii, 840 p. a 57-2818
PN2657 .K8 MRR Biog.

THEATER--GERMANY--DICTIONARIES.
Kosch, Wilhelm, Deutsches Theater-Lexikon; Klagenfurt, F. Kleinmayr, 1951- v. a 52-1902
PN2035 .K6 MRR Alc.

THEATER--GREAT BRITAIN.
Who's who in the theatre; [1st]- ed.; 1912- London, I. Pitman. 927.92 12-22402
PN2012 .W5 MRR Biog Latest edition

THEATER--GREAT BRITAIN--BIBLIOGRAPHY.
Arnott, James Fullarton, English theatrical literature, 1559-1900: London, Society for Theatre Research, 1970. xxii, 486 p. [£10/10/-] 016.792/0942 76-552584
Z2014.D7 A74 1970 MRR Alc.

Baker, David Erskine, Biographia dramatica; London, Longman, Hurst, Rees, Orme, and Brown [etc.] 1812. 3 v. in 4. 04-14124
Z2014.D7 B2 1812 MRR Alc.

THEATER--GREAT BRITAIN--BIO-BIBLIOGRAPHY.
Arnott, James Fullarton, English theatrical literature, 1559-1900: London, Society for Theatre Research, 1970. xxii, 486 p. [£10/10/-] 016.792/0942 76-552584
Z2014.D7 A74 1970 MRR Alc.

Lowe, Robert William, A bibliographical account of English theatrical literature Detroit, Republished by the Gale Research Co., 1966. x, 384 p. 016.792/0942 66-27665
Z2014.D7 L9 1966 MRR Alc.

THEATER--GREAT BRITAIN--BIOGRAPHY.
May, Robin. A companion to the theatre; Guildford, Lutterworth Press, 1973. 304 p. [16] p. of plates. [£2.40] 792/.0942 74-164747
PN2597 .M35 MRR Alc.

THEATER--GREAT BRITAIN--DICTIONARIES.
Halliday, Frank Ernest. A Shakespeare companion, 1564-1964 [Rev. ed.] New York, Schocken Books [1964] 569 p. 822.33 64-14774
PR2892 .H3 1964a MRR Alc.

THEATER--GREAT BRITAIN--DIRECTORIES.
The Stage year book. [London, Carson & Comerford Ltd.] ca 09-1341
PN2012 .S7 MRR Alc Latest edition

THEATER--GREAT BRITAIN--HISTORY.
Clunes, Alec. The British theatre. London, Cassell [1964] 187 p. 65-56188
PN2581 .C5 1964 MRR Alc.

Nicoll, Allardyce, A history of English drama, 1660-1900. Cambridge [Eng.] University Press, 1952-59. 6 v. 822.09 52-14525
PR625 .N52 1952 MRR Alc.

THEATER--GREAT BRITAIN--PERIODICALS--BIBLIOGRAPHY.
Stratman, Carl Joseph, Britain's theatrical periodicals, 1720-1967, New York, New York Public Library, 1972. xxiv, 160 p. 016.792/0942 72-124260
Z6935 .S76 1972 MRR Alc.

THEATER--GREECE.
Bieber, Margarete, The history of the Greek and Roman theater. [2d ed., rev. and enl.] Princeton, N.J., Princeton University Press, 1961. xiv, 343 p. 882.09 60-9367
PA3201 .B52 1961 MRR Alc.

THEATER--ITALY--HISTORY.
Kennard, Joseph Spencer, The Italian theatre, New York, W. E. Rudge, 1932. 2 v. 852.09 792.0945 32-13803
PQ4134 .K4 MRR Alc.

THEATER--LONDON.
Mander, Raymond. The theatres of London [2d ed., rev.] London, Hart-Davis, 1963. 292 p. 64-6934
PN2596.L6 M35 1963 MRR Alc.

Who's who in the theatre; [1st]- ed.; 1912- London, I. Pitman. 927.92 12-22402
PN2012 .W5 MRR Biog Latest edition

THEATER--NEW YORK (CITY)
Rigdon, Walter, ed. The biographical
encyclopaedia & who's who of the
American theatre. [1st ed.] New
York, J. H. Heineman [1966, c1965]
xiv, 1101 p.   792.0922 B 65-19390
PN2285 .R5 MRR Biog.

Who's who in the theatre; [1st]-
ed.: 1912- London, I. Pitman.
927.92 12-22402
PN2012 .W5 MRR Biog Latest edition

THEATER--NEW YORK (CITY)--HISTORY.
Atkinson, Justin Brooks, The lively
years, 1920-1973 New York,
Association Press [1973] viii, 312
p. [$12.50] 792/.09747/1 73-14659
PN2277.N5 A85 MRR Alc.

Odell, George Clinton Densmore,
Annals of the New York stage. 27-
5965
PN2277.N5 O4 Index MRR Alc.

Odell, George Clinton Densmore,
Annals of the New York stage. New
York, AMS Press [1970, c1927-49] 15
v. 792/.087471 77-116018
PN2277.N5 O4 1970 MRR Alc.

THEATER--NEW YORK (CITY)--PERIODICALS.
New York theatre critics' reviews.
v. 1- May 27, 1940- New York,
N.Y., Critics' theatre reviews. 792
a 42-1744
PN2000 .N76 MRR Alc Partial set

THEATER--NEW YORK (CITY)--REVIEWS.
The New York times theater reviews,
1920-1970. New York, New York times,
1971- v. 792/.09747/1 72-
166218
PN1581 .N4 MRR Alc.

THEATER--NEW YORK (CITY)--YEARBOOKS.
Theatre world. 1944/45- New York,
Crown Publishers [etc.] 792 46-
13321
PN2277.N5 A17 MRR Alc Partial set

THEATER--ROME.
Bieber, Margarete, The history of
the Greek and Roman theater. [2d
ed., rev. and enl.] Princeton, N.J.,
Princeton University Press, 1961.
xiv, 343 p.   882.09 60-9367
PA3201 .B52 1961 MRR Alc.

THEATER--RUSSIA--HISTORY.
Slonim, Marc, Russian theater, [1st
ed.] Cleveland, World Pub. Co.
[1961] 354 p.   792.0947 61-15304
PN2721 .S55 MRR Alc.

THEATER--SPAIN.
Valbuena Prat, Angel, Historia del
teatro español. [1. ed.]
Barcelona, Noguer [1956] 708 p. a
57-1257
PN2781 .V3 MRR Alc.

THEATER--SWITZERLAND--BIOGRAPHY.
Kurschners biographisches Theater-
Handbuch: Berlin, W. de Gruyter,
1956. xii, 840 p. a 57-2818
PN2657 .K8 MRR Biog.

THEATER--UNITED STATES.
National Portrait Gallery,
Washington, D.C. Portraits of the
American stage, 1771-1971;
Washington, Smithsonian Institution
Press; [for sale by the Supt. of
Docs., U.S. Govt. Print. Off.] 1971.
203 p. [$4.50] 792/.0973 75-
170284
PN1583.A2 N3 MRR Biog.

Patterson, Lindsay, comp. Anthology
of the American Negro in the theatre;
[2d ed.] New York, Publishers Co.
[1968] xiv, 306 p.   792.09174/96
68-2730
PN2226 .P3 1968 MRR Alc.

Sherman, Robert Lowery, Drama
cyclopedia, Chicago, The author
[1944] 1 p. l., iii, 612 p.   792
44-40134
PN2226 .S45 MRR Alc.

Theatre Communications Group,
Theatre profiles; [New York] 1973-
v. [$4.00 (v. 1)] 792/.0973 73-
91160
PN2266 .T48 MRR alc.

THEATER--UNITED STATES--BIBLIOGRAPHY.
Gohdes, Clarence Louis Frank,
Literature and theater of the States
and regions of the U.S.A.; Durham,
N.C., Duke University Press, 1967.
ix, 276 p.   016.8109 66-30584
Z1225 .G63 MRR Alc.

Melnitz, William W. Theatre arts
publications in the United States,
1947-1952; [Dubuque? Iowa, c1959]
xiii, 91 p.   016.792 60-882
Z5781 .M5 MRR Alc.

Palmer, Helen H. American drama
criticism; Hamden, Conn., Shoe
String Press, 1967. 239 p.
016.792/0873 67-16009
Z1231.D7 P3 MRR Ref Desk.

Stratman, Carl Joseph, Bibliography
of the American theatre, [Chicago]
Loyola University Press [1965] xv,
397 p.   016.7920973 65-3359
Z1231.D7 S8 MRR Alc.

THEATER--UNITED STATES--BIOGRAPHY.
May, Robin. A companion to the
theatre; Guildford, Lutterworth
Press, 1973. 304 p., [16] p. of
plates. [£2.40] 792/.0942 74-
164747
PN2597 .M35 MRR Alc.

THEATER--UNITED STATES--DICTIONARIES.
Rigdon, Walter, ed. The biographical
encyclopaedia & who's who of the
American theatre. [1st ed.] New
York, J. H. Heineman [1966, c1965]
xiv, 1101 p.   792.0922 B 65-19390
PN2285 .R5 MRR Biog.

THEATER--UNITED STATES--DIRECTORIES.
Simon's directory of theatrical
materials, services & information.
1st ed.; 1955- New York, Package
Publicity Service [etc.] 792.058 55-
12448
PN2289 .S5 MRR Ref Desk Latest
edition

THEATER--UNITED STATES--HISTORY.
Coad, Oral Sumner, The American
stage; New Haven, Yale university
press; [etc., etc.] 1929. 3 p. l.,
362 p.   29-22306
E178.5 .P2 vol. 14 MRR Alc.

Hewitt, Bernard Wolcott, Theatre
U.S.A., 1668 to 1957. New York,
McGraw-Hill, 1959. 528 p.   792.0873
58-11982
PN2221 .H4 MRR Alc.

Hughes, Glenn, A history of the
American theatre, 1700-1950. New
York, S. French [1951] ix, 562 p.
792 51-7975
PN2221 .H8 MRR Alc.

Morris, Lloyd R., Curtain time; New
York, Random House [1953] 380 p.
792.0973 53-6814
PN2221 .M68 MRR Alc.

Seilhamer, George Overcash, History
of the American theatre ...
Philadelphia, Globe printing house,
1888-91. 3 v.   11-19429
PN2221 .S4 MRR Alc.

Sherman, Robert Lowery, Actors and
authors, Chicago [1951] 433 p.
927.92 51-4020
PN2285 .S48 MRR Biog.

Taubman, Hyman Howard, The making of
the American theatre, New York,
Coward McCann [1965] 385 p.
792.0873 65-20410
PN2221 .T35 MRR Alc.

Toohey, John L. A history of the
Pulitzer Prize plays, [1st ed.] New
York, Citadel Press [1967] viii, 344
p.   792/.087/3 67-25654
PN2266 .T6 MRR Alc.

Wilson, Garff B. Three hundred years
of American drama and theatre, from
Ye bare and ye cubb to Hair
Englewood Cliffs, N.J., Prentice-Hall
[1973] viii, 536 p.   792/.0973 72-
3808
PN2221 .W5 MRR Alc.

Young, William C., Famous American
playhouses, 1716-1899 Chicago,
American Library Association. 1973.
xxii, 327 p.   792/.0973 72-9837
NA6830 .Y67 MRR Alc.

Young, William C., Famous American
playhouses, 1900-1971 Chicago,
American Library Association. 1973.
xii, 297 p. [$25.00] 792/.0973 73-
657
NA6830 .Y68 MRR Alc.

**THEATER--UNITED STATES--HISTORY--
PICTORIAL WORKS.**
Blum, Daniel C. A pictorial history
of the American theatre, 1860-1970,
New 3d ed., enl. and rev. New York,
Crown Publishers [1969] 416 p.
[12.50] 792/.0973 72-93394
PN2266 .B585 1969 MRR Alc.

THEATER--UNITED STATES--INDEXES.
Guernsey, Otis L., Directory of the
American theater, 1894-1971; New
York, Dodd, Mead [1971] vi, 343 p.
[$25.00] 812/.5/08 71-180734
PN6112 .B4524 MRR Alc.

**THEATER--UNITED STATES--PERIODICALS--
BIBLIOGRAPHY.**
Stratman, Carl Joseph, American
theatrical periodicals, 1798-1967;
Durham, N.C., Duke University Press,
1970. xxii, 133 p.   016.7902 72-
110577
Z6935 .S75 MRR Alc.

THEATER--UNITED STATES--YEARBOOKS.
The Best plays. 1894/99- New York
[etc.] Dodd, Mead [etc.] 812.5082
20-21432
PN6112 .B45 MRR Alc Partial set

THEATERS--DIRECTORIES.
A A S G; (Cincinnati, Billboard Pub.
Co) 725/.8/02573 72-626501
GV182 .A74 MRR Alc Latest edition

Pride, Leo Bryan, International
theatre directory; New York, Simon
and Schuster [1973] xviii, 577 p.
[$35.00] 792/.025 70-157681
PN2052 .P7 MRR Alc.

THEATERS--HISTORY.
Nicoll, Allardyce, The development
of the theatre; 5th ed., rev. New
York, Harcourt, Brace and World
[1967, c1966] xix, 292 p. 792/.09
67-10645
PN2101 .N5 1967 MRR Alc.

THEATERS--STAGE-SETTING AND SCENERY.
Cornberg, Sol, A stage crew
handbook, Rev. ed. New York, Harper
[c1957] 291 p.   792.92* 56-11926
PN2091.S8 C63 1957 MRR Alc.

Gassner, John, Producing the play,
Rev. ed. New York, Dryden Press
[1953] 915 p.   792.02* 52-14799
PN2037 .G3 1953 MRR Alc.

Philippi, Herbert. Stagecraft and
scene design. [Boston] Houghton
Mifflin [1953] 448 p.   792 53-6010
PN2091.S8 P48 MRR Alc.

Wickham, Glynne William Gladstone.
Early English stages, 1300 to 1660.
London, Routledge and Paul; New York,
Columbia University Press, 1959- v.
in   792.0942 59-2245
PN2587 .W53 MRR Alc.

**THEATERS--STAGE-SETTING AND SCENERY--
BIBLIOGRAPHY.**
Baker, Blanch (Merritt) Theatre and
allied arts; New York, Wilson, 1952.
xiii, 536 p.   016.792 52-6756
Z5781 .B18 MRR Alc.

**THEATERS--STAGE-SETTING AND SCENERY--
HISTORY.**
Nicoll, Allardyce, The development
of the theatre; 5th ed., rev. New
York, Harcourt, Brace and World
[1967, c1966] xix, 292 p. 792/.09
67-10645
PN2101 .N5 1967 MRR Alc.

THEATERS--GREAT BRITAIN--DIRECTORIES.
Holden, Michael. The Stage guide:
technical information on British
theatres; [New ed.]. London, Carson
and Comerford Ltd. 1971. 408 p.
792/.0942 72-195182
PN2595 .H64 MRR Alc.

The Stage year book. [London, Carson
& Comerford Ltd.] ca 09-1341
PN2012 .S7 MRR Alc Latest edition

THEATERS--GREECE.
Bieber, Margarete, The history of
the Greek and Roman theater. [2d
ed., rev. and enl.] Princeton, N.J.,
Princeton University Press, 1961.
xiv, 343 p.   882.09 60-9367
PA3201 .B52 1961 MRR Alc.

THEATERS--ROME.
Bieber, Margarete, The history of
the Greek and Roman theater. [2d
ed., rev. and enl.] Princeton, N.J.,
Princeton University Press, 1961.
xiv, 343 p.   882.09 60-9367
PA3201 .B52 1961 MRR Alc.

THEATERS--UNITED STATES--DIRECTORIES.
Havens, John F. Description of
community theatres in the United
States [Washington] U.S. Dept. of
Health, Education, and Welfare,
Office of Education, Bureau of
Research, 1968. v, 5e, 164 p.
792/.0223/02573 70-602084
PN2267 .H3 MRR Alc.

The National directory for the
performing arts and civic centers.
Dallas, Handel & Co. 790.2/0973 73-
646635
PN2289 .N38 MRR Alc Latest edition

THEATERS--UNITED STATES--HISTORY.
Young, William C., Famous American
playhouses, 1716-1899 Chicago,
American Library Association. 1973.
xxii, 327 p.   792/.0973 72-9837
NA6830 .Y67 MRR Alc.

THEATERS--UNITED STATES-- (Cont.)
Young, William C. Famous American
playhouses, 1900-1971 Chicago,
American Library Association, 1973.
xii, 287 p. [$25.00] 792/.0873 73-
657
NA6830 .Y68 MRR Alc.

THEATRICAL MAKE-UP
see Make-up, Theatrical

THEATRICAL MUSIC
see Opera

THEOLOGIANS.
Richardson, Alan, A dictionary of
Christian theology, Philadelphia,
Westminster Press [1969] xii, 364 p.
[8.50] 230/.03 69-19153
BR95 .R47 MRR Alc.

THEOLOGICAL EDUCATION
see Religious education

THEOLOGICAL LIBRARIES--DIRECTORIES.
Ruoss, George Martin. A world
directory of theological libraries,
Metuchen, N.J., Scarecrow Press,
1968. 220 p. 027.6/7/025 68-12632

Z675.T4 R8 MRR Alc.

THEOLOGICAL SEMINARIES--UNITED STATES--
DIRECTORIES.
White, Alex Sandri. Guide to
religious education: 1965-1966 ed.
Allenhurst, N.J., Aurea Publications
[1965] 82 l. 207.73025 65-5823
BV4030 .W46 MRR Alc.

THEOLOGY.
see also Bible

see also Ethics

see also Religion

THEOLOGY--20TH CENTURY.
O'Brien, Elmer, ed. Theology in
transition; [New York] Herder and
Herder [1965] 282 p. 230.209045
65-13486
BT28 .O2 MRR Alc.

THEOLOGY--ABSTRACTS.
Magill, Frank Northen, ed.
Masterpieces of Christian literature
in summary form. [1st ed.] New
York, Salem Press [1963] 2 v. (xxvi,
1193, v p.) 64-104
BR50 .M22 1963 MRR Alc.

Religious and theological abstracts.
v. 1- Mar. 1958- Youngstown, Ohio,
Theological Publications. 208.22 61-
35093
BR1 .R286 MRR Alc Partial set

THEOLOGY--BIBLIOGRAPHY.
O'Brien, Elmer, ed. Theology in
transition; [New York] Herder and
Herder [1965] 282 p. 230.209045
65-13486
BT28 .O2 MRR Alc.

THEOLOGY--BIBLIOGRAPHY--CATALOGS.
New York. Union theological seminary.
Library. Catalogue of the McAlpin
collection of British history and
theology, New York, 1927-30. 5 v.
29-29688
Z7757.E5 N5 MRR Alc.

THEOLOGY--COLLECTIONS.
Ferm, Vergilius Ture Anselm, ed.
Classics of Protestantism. New York,
Philosophical Library [1959] ix, 587
p. 230.4 59-16427
BX4801 .F45 MRR Alc.

THEOLOGY--DICTIONARIES.
Baker's dictionary of theology.
Grand Rapids, Baker Book House, 1960.
566 p. 203 60-7333
BR95 .B25 MRR Alc.

Bodensieck, Julius, ed. The
encyclopedia of the Lutheran Church,
Minneapolis, Augsburg Pub. House
[1965] 3 v. (xvii, 2575 p.)
284.103 64-21500
BX8007 .B6 MRR Alc.

Bouyer, Louis, Dictionary of
theology. [New York, Desclee Co.,
c1965] xi, 470 p. 230.203 66-
13370
BR95 .B6413 MRR Alc.

A Catholic dictionary of theology;
London, New York, Nelson [1962- v.
230.203 62-52257
BR85 .C27 MRR Alc.

Christian word book Nashville,
Abingdon Press [1969, c1968] 320 p.
[3.95] 230/.03 69-19739
BR95 .C53 1969 MRR Alc.

The Concordia cyclopedia; St. Louis,
Concordia Pub. House, 1927. iv, 848
p. 27-13940
BX8007 .C6 MRR Alc.

Corpus dictionary of Western
churches. Washington, Corpus
Publications [1970] xviii, 820 p.
[$25.00] 203 78-99501
BR95 .C67 MRR Alc.

Encyclopedie of religion and ethics,
Edinburgh, T. & T. Clark; New York,
C. Scribner's sons, 1908-26. 13 v.
08-35833
BL31 .E4 MRR Alc.

Encyclopedia of Southern Baptists.
Nashville, Broadman Press [1958-71]
3 v. (xxviii, 2064 p.) [$9.95 (v.
3)] 286.175 58-5417
BX6211 .E5 MRR Alc.

Ferm, Vergilius Ture Anselm, Concise
dictionary of religion; New York,
Philosophical Library [1964? c1951]
ix, 283 p. 203 64-4055
BR95 .F37 1964 MRR Alc.

Harvey, Van Austin. A handbook of
theological terms New York,
Macmillan [1964] 253 p. 230.03 64-
25193
BR95 .H32 MRR Alc.

Lee, Frederick George, A glossary of
liturgical and ecclesiastical terms.
Detroit, Tower Books, 1971. xxxix,
452 p. 200/.3 76-174069
BR95 .L4 1971 MRR Alc.

Léon-Dufour, Xavier. Dictionary of
Biblical theology; London, Dublin
[etc.] G. Chapman, 1967. xxix, 618
p. [63/-] 220.3 68-83461
BS543.A1 L413 MRR Alc.

Malloch, James M., comp. A practical
church dictionary, New York,
Morehouse-Barlow [1964] xiv, 520 p.
203 64-23926
BR95 .M37 MRR Alc.

The Oxford dictionary of the
Christian Church, 2d ed., London,
New York, Oxford University Press,
1974. xxxi, 1518 p. [£13.50] 203
74-163871
BR95 .O8 1974 MRR Alc.

Parente, Pietro, Abp. Dictionary of
dogmatic theology 1st English ed.
Milwaukee, Bruce [1951] xxvi, 310 p.
203 51-7704
BR95 .P3 MRR Alc.

Richardson, Alan, A dictionary of
Christian theology, Philadelphia,
Westminster Press [1969] xii, 364 p.
[8.50] 230/.03 69-19153
BR95 .R47 MRR Alc.

Sacramentum mundi: London, Burns &
Oates, 1968-70. 6 v. [£7/10/- per
vol.] 203 72-379493
BR95 .S23 MRR Alc.

Sacramentum mundi: London, Burns &
Oates, 1968-70. 6 v. [£7/10/- per
vol.] 203 72-379493
BR95 .S23 MRR Alc.

Schaff-Herzog encyclopedia. The new
Schaff-Herzog encyclopedia of
religious knowledge, Grand Rapids,
Mich., Baker, 1949-50. 13 v. 203
51-9847
BR95 .S435s MRR Alc.

Schaff-Herzog encyclopedia. The new
Schaff-Herzog encyclopedia of
religious knowledge, New York,
London, Funk and Wagnalls company
[1908-c14] 13 v. 08-20152
BR95 .S43 MRR Alc.

Shannon, Ellen C. A layman's guide
to Christian terms, South Brunswick
[N.J.] A. S. Barnes [1969] 347 p.
[10.00] 203 69-15776
BR95 .S45 MRR Alc.

White, Richard Clark, The vocabulary
of the church: New York, Macmillan,
1960. xiv, 178 p. 203 60-11810
BR95 .W53 MRR Alc.

Wright, Charles Henry Hamilton, ed.
The Protestant dictionary, New ed.,
London, The Harrison trust [1933]
xix, 805, [1] p. 280.3 33-10289
BR95 .W7 1933 MRR Alc.

THEOLOGY--DICTIONARIES--FRENCH.
Cabrol, Fernand, Dictionnaire
d'archeologie chrétienne et de
liturgie, Paris, Letouzey et Ané,
1907- v. 03-15097
BR95 .C2 MRR Alc.

THEOLOGY--DICTIONARIES--GERMAN.
Evangelisches Staatslexikon,
Stuttgart, Berlin, Kreuz-Verlag
[1966] lxiv, 2687 p. [DM 75.00]
203 66-67139
BR95 .E95 MRR Alc.

Lexikon für Theologie und Kirche;
2., vollig neu bearb. Aufl.,
Freiburg, Herder, 1957-65. 10 v.
58-41506
BR95 .L48 MRR Alc.

THEOLOGY--DICTIONARIES--LATIN.
Deferrari, Roy Joseph, A Latin-
English dictionary of St. Thomas
Aquinas, [Boston] St. Paul Editions
[1960] 1115 p. 189.4 60-1846
B765.T54 D39 MRR Alc.

Deferrari, Roy Joseph, A lexicon of
St. Thomas Aquinas [Washington,
Catholic University of America Press,
1948-53, c1949] 5 v. 189.4 a 49-
1297
B765.T54 D38 MRR Alc.

THEOLOGY--PERIODICALS--INDEXES.
American Theological Library
Association. Index to religious
periodical literature: 1949/52
[Chicago] a 54-6085
Z7753 .A5 MRR Alc Full set

Bulletin signalétique 527: Sciences
religieuses. v. 24- 1970- Paris,
Centre de documentation du C.N.R.S.
70-258523
Z7751 .B85 MRR Alc Full set

Christian periodical index. 1958-
[Buffalo, N.Y.] Christian Librarians'
Fellowship. 203 60-36226
Z7753 .C5 MRR Alc Full set

Religious and theological abstracts.
v. 1- Mar. 1958- Youngstown, Ohio,
Theological Publications. 208.22 61-
35093
BR1 .R286 MRR Alc Partial set

THEOLOGY--STUDY AND TEACHING--UNITED
STATES.
Ramsey, Paul, ed. Religion.
Englewood Cliffs, N.J., Prentice-Hall
[1965] x, 468 p. 207.2 64-23553
BL41 .R3 MRR Alc.

THEOLOGY, CATHOLIC--COLLECTIONS--
INDEXES.
Sprug, Joseph W. Index [to the
Twentieth century encyclopedia of
Catholicism]. [1st ed.] New York,
Hawthorn Books [1971] 412 p.
230/.2 58-14327
BX1751.2.A1 S67 MRR Alc.

THEOLOGY, DOCTRINAL.
see also Good and evil

see also Mysticism

Calvin, Jean, A compend of the
Institutes of the Christian religion.
Philadelphia, Westminster Press
[1964] viii, 228 p. 230.42 65-
3389
BX9420 .I652 1964 MRR Alc.

THEOLOGY, DOCTRINAL--HISTORY--EARLY
CHURCH, CA. 30-600.
Kelly, John Norman Davidson. Early
Christian doctrines. New York,
Harper [1959, c1958] 500 p. 230.11
58-12933
BT25 .K4 1959 MRR Alc.

THEOLOGY, MYSTICAL
see Mysticism

THEOLOGY, PRACTICAL.
see also Christian life

see also Spiritual life

THEOSOPHY.
see also Buddha and Buddhism

THERAPEUTICS.
see also Narcotics

see also Nurses and nursing

see also Nutrition

Drugs of choice. St. Louis C. V.
Mosby Co. 615.1 58-6889
RM101 .D75 Sci RR Latest edition /
MRR Alc Latest edition

Modern drug encyclopedia and
therapeutic index. 1st- ed.; 1934-
New York, R. H. Donnelley [etc.] 34-
12823
RS153 .M57 Sci RR Latest edition /
MRR Alc Latest edition

Musser, Ruth D. Pharmacology and
therapeutics 3d ed. New York,
Macmillan [1965] xvi, 878 p. 615
65-16932
RM101 .M87 1965 MRR Alc.

THERAPEUTICS, DENTAL--PERIODICALS.
Accepted dental therapeutics.
[Chicago, Council on Dental
Therapeutics of the American Dental
Association] 617.6/06/05 74-642043

RK701 .A3 MRR Alc Latest edition

THERAPEUTICS, PHYSIOLOGICAL.
see also Diet in disease

THERAPEUTICS, SUGGESTIVE.
see also Psychotherapy

THEROPHYTES
see Annuals (Plants)

THIRD WORLD
see Underdeveloped areas

THOMAS, DYLAN, 1914-1953--CONCORDANCES.
Williams, Robert Coleman. A
concordance to the Collected poems of
Dylan Thomas. Lincoln, University of
Nebraska Press [1967] xiii, 579 p.
821/.9/12   66-19268
PR6039.H52 Z49 MRR Alc.

THOMAS AQUINAS, SAINT, 1225?-1274--
DICTIONARIES, INDEXES, ETC.
Deferrari, Roy Joseph. A Latin-
English dictionary of St. Thomas
Aquinas. [Boston] St. Paul Editions
[1960] 1115 p.   189.4   60-1846
B765.T54 D39 MRR Alc.

Deferrari, Roy Joseph. A lexicon of
St. Thomas Aquinas [Washington,
Catholic University of America Press,
1948-53, c1949] 5 v.   189.4 a 49-
1297
B765.T54 D38 MRR Alc.

Stockhammer, Morris, ed. Thomas
Aquinas dictionary. New York,
Philosophical Library [1965] xiii,
219 p.   230.203 64-21468
BX1749.T324 S7 MRR Alc.

THOROUGHBRED HORSE.
Who's who in horsedom. v. [1]-
1948- Louisville, Ky. [etc.]
798.058 56-47235
SF31 .W45 MRR Alc Latest edition

Who's who in thoroughbred racing.
1st- ed.; 1946- Washington, D.C.,
Who's who in thoroughbred racing,
inc. 798.4   agr46-284
SF321 .W45 MRR Alc Latest edition

THOROUGHFARES
see Roads

THUCYDIDES--DICTIONARIES, INDEXES, ETC.
Essen, Martin Heinrich Nikolaus von,
Index Thucydideus Bekkeri Berolini,
apud Weidmannos, 1887. iv, 457, [1]
p.   05-5765
PA4486.Z8 1887 MRR Alc.

TIBET--CIVILIZATION--HISTORY.
Snellgrove, David L. A cultural
history of Tibet London, Weidenfeld
& Nicolson, 1968. 291 p. [63/-]
915.15/03 68-122119
DS786 .S6 MRR Alc.

TIBETAN LANGUAGE--DICTIONARIES--ENGLISH.
Zla-ba-bsam-'grub, Rai, An
English-Tibetan dictionary.
Calcutta, The University, 1919. xiv,
989 p.   24-1029
PL3637 .Z6 MRR Alc.

TIDES--TABLES.
Brown's nautical almanac Daily tide
tables. Glasgow, Brown, son &
Ferguson, ltd. 528.2 ca 32-280
VK8 .B8 MRR Alc Latest edition

The Lights and tides of the world,
including a description of all the
fog-signals. London, Imray, Laurie,
Norie & Wilson, ltd. ca 08-3141
VK1150 .L7 MRR Alc Latest edition

TILE LAYING.
Dezettel, Louis M. Masons and
builders library. Indianapolis, T.
Audel [1972] 2 v.   693   78-186134
TH5311 .D48 MRR Alc.

TIMBER.
see also Forests and forestry

see also Wood

TIMBER--DICTIONARIES--POLYGLOT.
Elsevier's wood dictionary in seven
languages: Amsterdam, New York,
Elsevier Pub. Co., 1964- v.
634.903 64-14178
SD431 .E4 MRR Alc.

TIMES, LONDON. THE TIMES ATLAS OF THE
WORLD--INDEXES.
Times, London. Index-gazetteer of
the world. London, Times Publishing
Co., 1965. xxxi, 964 p. [£10]
910.003 66-70286
G103 .T5 MRR Alc Atlas.

TIMOR, PORTUGUESE--GAZETTEERS.
United States. Office of Geography.
Indonesia and Portuguese Timor;
official standard names approved by
the United States Board on Geographic
Names. 2d ed. Washington, 1968.
viii, 901 p.   919.1/003 68-61196
DS614 .U64 1968 MRR Alc.

TIN--STATISTICS.
International Tin Council.
Statistical year book. 1959-
[London]   338.476736   60-3312
HD9539.T5 I36 MRR Alc Latest
edition

TIPPING.
Lessere, Samuel E. Harian's foreign
language speak-easy. [3d ed.]
Greenlawn, N.Y., Harian Publications
[1957] 106 p.   418.24   57-14033
PE1635 .L4 1957 MRR Alc.

Money converter and tipping guide for
European travel. [1st]- ed.; 1953-
[New York] Dover Publications.
332.4083   58-4482
HG219 .M58 MRR Alc Latest edition

Richard Joseph's world wide money
converter and tipping guide. 1953-
Garden City, N.Y., Doubleday. 332.45
52-13383
HG219 .R5 MRR Ref Desk Latest
edition

TITLE-PAGE.
Mumey, Nolie. A study of rare books.
Denver, The Clason publishing
company, 1930. xvii p., 2 l., 3-572
p.   090   30-25438
Z1012 .M95 MRR Alc.

TITLES OF BOOKS.
Ahnert, Heinz Jörg. Deutsches
Titelbuch 2. Berlin, Haude &
Spenersche Verlagsbuchhandlung (1966)
xii, 636 p. [DM 85.00]
016.83/090091 67-75457
Z2231 .A55 MRR Alc.

California. University. Library.
Author-title catalog. Boston, G. K.
Hall, 1963. 115 v.   018/.1 73-
153193
Z881 .C1532 1963 MRR Alc (Dk 33)

Peet, Louis Harman, Who's the
author? New York, T. Y. Crowell &
co. [c1901] iv, 317 p.   01-23523
Z1225 .P37 MRR Alc.

United States. Library of Congress.
English language books by title:
Detroit, Gale Research Co., 1971. 20
v.   018/.1   75-165487
Z881 .A1 C34 MRR Alc (Dk 33)

TITLES OF HONOR AND NOBILITY.
United States. Immigration and
Naturalization Service. Foreign
versions, variations, and diminutives
of English names. Rev. [Washington;
For sale by the Supt. of Docs., U.S.
Govt. Print. Off.] 1969 [i.e. 1970]
53 p. [1.00]   929.4 73-605932
CS2309 .U55 1970 MRR Alc.

TITLES OF HONOR AND NOBILITY--GREAT
BRITAIN.
Heywood, Valentine, British titles;
2d ed. London, A. and C. Black
[1953] 188 p.   929.7 53-32018
CR3891 .H4 1953 MRR Alc.

Pine, Leslie Gilbert. Guide to
titles, Kingswood, Surrey, Elliot's
Right Way Books [c1959] 124 p.
929.72 60-27721
CR3891 .P5 MRR Alc.

Titles and forms of address: 14th
ed. London, Black, 1971. xi, 188 p.
[£1.25] 395/.4 72-170772
CR3891 .T58 1971 MRR Alc.

TITLES OF MUSICAL COMPOSITIONS.
Berkowitz, Freda Pastor. Popular
titles and subtitles of musical
compositions. New York, Scarecrow
Press, 1962. 182 p.   016.78 62-
10121
ML113 .B39 MRR Alc.

TOASTS.
Copeland, Lewis, ed. 10,000 jokes,
toasts & stories. Garden City, N.Y.,
Doubleday [c1965] xi, 1020 p. 66-
737
PN6261 .C54 1965 MRR Alc.

Fuller, Edmund, ed. Thesaurus of
epigrams. Garden City, N.Y., Garden
City Pub. Co. [1948] 382 p. 808.8
48-5656
PN6281 .F8 1948 MRR Alc.

Koken, John Marshall, comp. Here's
to it! New York, Barnes [1960] 146
p.   808.85 60-11302
PN6341 .K6 MRR Alc.

TOBACCO.
see also Smoking

TOBACCO--BIBLIOGRAPHY.
Larson, Paul Stanley, Tobacco:
experimental and clinical studies;
Baltimore, Williams & Wilkins Co.,
1961. xii, 932 p.   615.7 61-5057
QP981.T6 L3 MRR Alc.

TOBACCO--DICTIONARIES.
Jahn, Raymond. Tobacco dictionary.
New York, Philosophical Library
[1954] 199 p.   679.137103 679.203*
54-11964
TS2240 .J3 MRR Alc.

TOBACCO--PHYSIOLOGICAL EFFECT.
Larson, Paul Stanley, Tobacco:
experimental and clinical studies;
Baltimore, Williams & Wilkins Co.,
1961. xii, 932 p. 615.7 61-5057
QP981.T6 L3 MRR Alc.

TOBACCO MANUFACTURE AND TRADE--
DIRECTORIES.
World tobacco directory. London
[etc.] Trade Publications Ltd. [etc.]
53-29978
Began with 1926 vol.
HD9133 .C6 MRR Alc Latest edition

TOBACCO MANUFACTURE AND TRADE--UNITED
STATES.
Heimann, Robert K. Tobacco and
Americans. [1st ed.] New York,
McGraw-Hill [1960] 265, [13] p.
338.476797 60-8114
TS2235.U5 H4 MRR Alc.

TOGO--BIBLIOGRAPHY.
United States. Library of Congress.
African Section. Official
publications of French Equatorial
Africa, French Cameroons, and Togo,
Washington, General Reference and
Bibliography Divison, Reference
Dept., Library of Congress; [for sale
by the Superintendent of Documents,
U.S. Govt. Print. Off.] 1964. xi, 78
p.   64-60029
Z663.285 .O32 MRR Alc.

TOGO--GAZETTEERS.
United States. Office of Geography.
Togo; official standard names
approved by the United States Board
on Geographic Names. Washington,
1966. iii, 100 p.   916.6/81 66-
62004
DT582.2 .U5 MRR Alc.

TOILET.
see also Costume

TOKENS--UNITED STATES.
Criswell, Grover C. The official
guide to Confederate money & Civil
War tokens, tradesmen & patriotic,
[1st ed.] [New York] HC Publishers
[1971] [44 p. [$1.00]   737.3/0975
79-181839
HG526 .C74 MRR Alc.

Fuld, George. Patriotic Civil War
tokens; Racine, Wis., Whitman Pub.
Co. [1960] 77 p.   737.3 60-1370
CJ4907 .F8 MRR Alc.

Taxay, Don. The comprehensive
catalogue and encyclopedia of United
States coins. 1st ed, New York,
Scott Pub. Co., 1971 (c1970] xiv,
397 p. [$15.00] 737.4/9/73 73-
176464
CJ1826 .T38 MRR Alc.

TOKYO--COMMERCE--DIRECTORIES.
Tokyo news business directory. 1950-
Tokyo, Tokyo News Service.
338/.0025 51-14706
HF5257.T6 T57 MRR Alc Latest
edition

TOLERATION.
see also Minorities

TONGA LANGUAGE (TONGA ISLANDS)
Churchward, Clerk Maxwell. Tongan
dictionary: London, Oxford
University Press, 1959. xiv, 836 p.
499.4 58-3277
PL6531 .C48 MRR Alc.

TONGA LANGUAGE (TONGA ISLANDS)--
DICTIONARIES--ENGLISH.
Churchward, Clerk Maxwell. Tongan
dictionary: London, Oxford
University Press, 1959. xiv, 836 p.
499.4 58-3277
PL6531 .C48 MRR Alc.

TOOLS.
see also Agricultural machinery

see also Machine-tools

TOOLS--DIRECTORIES.
Hitchcock's machine and tool
directory and specifications catalog.
v. 18- 1969- [Wheaton, Ill.,
Hitchcock Pub. Co.] 621.9/02/02573
74-618600
TJ1180 .A1M26 MRR Alc Latest
edition / Sci RR Latest edition

TORNADOES.
see also Storms

Flora, Snowden Dwight, Tornadoes of
the United States. [Rev. ed.]
Norman, University of Oklahoma Press
[1954] xvi, 221 p.   551.55 54-8922

QC955 .F6 1954 MRR Alc.

TORONTO--DESCRIPTION--GUIDE-BOOKS.
Hepburn, Andrew. The Toronto guide,
1966-67. Toronto, McClelland &
Stewart, c1966. 166 p. [$1.00 Can.]
917.13/541 67-79850
F1059.5.T68 H4 MRR Alc.

TOTALITARIANISM.
see also Communism

TOURIST CAMPS, HOSTELS, ETC.--DIRECTORIES.
Hotel & motel red book. 1886- New York, American Hotel Association Directory Corp. 98-295
TX907 .045 Sci RR Latest edition / MRR Ref Desk Latest edition

TOURIST CAMPS, HOSTELS, ETC.--NORTH AMERICA.
Woodall's trailering parks and campgrounds. 1st- ed.; 1967- Highland Park, Ill., Woodall Pub. Co. 917.3/04/92 67-3869
GV1025.A2 W65 MRR Alc Latest edition

TOURIST TRADE.
see also Visitors, Foreign

World Association of Travel Agencies. National tourist information and general tariff. Geneva. 61-65430
Began in 1853.
G155.A1 G4 MRR Alc Latest edition

TOURIST TRADE--DIRECTORIES.
Travel industry personnel directory. [New York, Travel Agent Magazine] 338.4/7/91009025 72-622913
G155 .A1T655 MRR Alc Latest edition

TOURIST TRADE--CANADA--STATISTICS.
Goeldner, Charles R. Travel trends in the United States and Canada, Boulder, Business Research Division, University of Colorado [1973] vi, 175 l. 338.4/7/9170453 73-166149
G155.U6 G6 1973 MRR Alc.

TOURIST TRADE--UNITED STATES--STATISTICS.
Goeldner, Charles R. Travel trends in the United States and Canada, Boulder, Business Research Division, University of Colorado [1973] vi, 175 l. 338.4/7/9170453 73-166149
G155.U6 G6 1973 MRR Alc.

TOWN LIFE
see City and town life

TOWN MEETING
see Local government

TOWNS
see Cities and towns

TOWNSHIP FINANCE
see Local finance

TOXIC AND INFLAMMABLE GOODS
see Hazardous substances

TOXICOLOGY.
Arena, Jay M. Poisoning: toxicology--symptoms--treatments, 3d ed. Springfield, Ill., Thomas [1974] xxv, 804 p. 615.9 73-4213
RA1216 .A69 1974 MRR Alc.

TOXICOLOGY--HANDBOOKS, MANUALS, ETC.
Dreisbach, Robert Hastings. Handbook of poisoning: diagnosis & treatment. 4th ed. Los Altos, Calif., Lange Medical Publications, 1963. 467 p. 615.9 63-18886
RA1211 .D7 1963 MRR Alc.

TOXICOLOGY--INFORMATION SERVICES.
United States. Library of Congress. National Referral Center for Science and Technology. A directory of information resources in the United States: general toxicology. Washington, Library of Congress; for sale by the Supt. of Docs., U.S. Govt. Print Off.] 1969. v, 293 p. [3.00] 615.8/007 73-602563
Z663.379 .D49 MRR Alc

TOY INDUSTRY--UNITED STATES--DIRECTORIES.
McClintock, Inez (Bertail) Toys in America. Washington, Public Affairs Press [1961] 480 p. 790 59-13657
GV1200 .M3 MRR Alc.

The Playthings directory of the toy industry. New York, Geyer-McAllister Publications, Inc. 25-22913
TS2301.T7 P5 MRR Alc Latest edition

Toys and novelties directory. 1961- New York, Harbrace, etc. 338.4/7/6687202573 73-21279
TS2301.T7 T632 MRR Alc Latest edition

TOYS--DIRECTORIES.
The Playthings directory of the toy industry. New York, Geyer-McAllister Publications, Inc. 25-22913
TS2301.T7 P5 MRR Alc Latest edition

TOYS--HISTORY.
Fritzsch, Karl Ewald. An illustrated history of toys. London, Abbey Library [Murray's Book Sales] 1966. 87 p. [84/-] 688.720943 66-31982
GV1200 .F7413 MRR Alc.

McClintock, Inez (Bertail) Toys in America. Washington, Public Affairs Press [1961] 480 p. 790 59-13657
GV1200 .M3 MRR Alc.

TRACK-ATHLETICS.
see also Weight throwing

The Official track and field guide. 1922- Phoenix, Ariz. [etc.] College Athletics Pub. Service [etc.] 796.4 23-8882
GV731 .O3 MRR Alc Latest edition

TRACK-ATHLETICS--BIOGRAPHY.
Hanley, Reid M., Who's who in track and field New Rochelle, N.Y., Arlington House [1973] 160 p. [$6.95] 796.4/2/0922 B 73-11872
GV697.A1 H34 MRR Biog.

TRACK-ATHLETICS--RULES.
The Official track and field guide. 1922- Phoenix, Ariz. [etc.] College Athletics Pub. Service [etc.] 796.4 23-8882
GV731 .O3 MRR Alc Latest edition

TRACK-ATHLETICS--YEARBOOKS.
High school track & field annual. Los Altos, Calif., Tafnews Press. 66-34217
Began publication in 1956.
GV1060.5 .H45 MRR Alc Latest edition

TRACTOR INDUSTRY--UNITED STATES.
National farm tractor and implement blue book. Chicago, National Market Reports. 62-32340
Began publication in 1939.
HD9486.U3 N3 MRR Alc Latest edition

TRACTORS--CATALOGS.
Official tractor and farm equipment guide. St. Louis, NRFEA Publications, Inc. 52-44515
S677 .O35 MRR Alc Latest edition

TRACTORS--MAINTENANCE AND REPAIR--PERIODICALS.
Motor's truck & diesel repair manual. 24th- ed.; 1971- [New York, Motor] 629.28/7/4 73-618596
TL230.A1 M64 Sci RR Latest edition / MRR Alc Latest edition

TRADE
see Business

see Commerce

TRADE AND PROFESSIONAL ASSOCIATIONS.
see also Associations, institutions, etc.

TRADE AND PROFESSIONAL ASSOCIATIONS--DIRECTORIES.
Angel, Juvenal Londoño, International marketing guide for technical, management and other consultants. 1st ed. New York, World Trade Academy Press; distributed by Simon & Schuster [1971] 600 p. [$25.00] 658.4/03 77-111350
HD69.C6 A676 MRR Alc.

International reference handbook of services, organizations, diplomatic representation, marketing, and advertising channels. 1954- New York, World Trade Academy Press. a 55-1568
HF54.U5 I52 MRR Alc Latest edition

International Trade Centre. World directory of industry and trade associations. [2d ed.] Geneva, 1970 viii, 370 p. [$5.00 (U.S.)] 338/.0062 70-590660
HF294 .I87 1970 MRR Alc.

World guide to trade associations. 1st- ed.; 1973- New York, R. R. Bowker Co. 380.1/06/2 74-644730
HD2421 .W67 MRR Ref Desk Latest edition

TRADE AND PROFESSIONAL ASSOCIATIONS--CALIFORNIA--DIRECTORIES.
Yung, Judith. Directory of California non-profit associations, San Francisco, San Francisco Public Library, 1970. iii, 217 p. 061.94 79-20791
HD2428.C3 Y84 MRR Alc.

TRADE AND PROFESSIONAL ASSOCIATIONS--CANADA--DIRECTORIES.
Public administration organizations, a directory of unofficial organizations in the field of public administration in the United States and Canada. [1st]- ed.; 1932- Chicago, Public Administration Clearing House. 061 33-4186
AS18 .P8 MRR Alc Latest edition

TRADE AND PROFESSIONAL ASSOCIATIONS--COMMONWEALTH OF NATIONS--DIRECTORIES.
Professional organisations in the Commonwealth; London, Published for The Commonwealth Foundation by Hutchinson, 1970. 511 p. [90/-] 060 72-525242
HD2421 .P73 MRR Alc.

TRADE AND PROFESSIONAL ASSOCIATIONS--EUROPE--DIRECTORIES.
Directory of European associations. 1971- Beckenham, Eng., CBD Research Ltd.; Detroit, Gale Research Co. 74-175919
AS98 .D55 MRR Ref Desk Latest edition

TRADE AND PROFESSIONAL ASSOCIATIONS--EUROPE, EASTERN--DIRECTORIES.
International Trade Centre. Foreign trade enterprises in Eastern Europe. [Revised ed.] Geneva [1968] 98 p. 76-503842
HF3493 .I5 MRR Alc.

TRADE AND PROFESSIONAL ASSOCIATIONS--FRANCE--DIRECTORIES.
Conseil national du patronat français. Annuaire. Paris, Union française d'annuaire professionnels [etc.] 62-25706
Began publication in 1949.
HD6683 .C6 MRR Alc Latest edition

TRADE AND PROFESSIONAL ASSOCIATIONS--GERMANY (FEDERAL REPUBLIC, 1949- --DIRECTORIES.
Verbande, Behörden. 1950- Darmstadt [etc.] Hoppenstedt. 51-24746
HD2429.G3 W5 MRR Alc Latest edition

TRADE AND PROFESSIONAL ASSOCIATIONS--GREAT BRITAIN--DIRECTORIES.
Millard, Patricia, ed. Trade associations & professional bodies of the United Kingdom. 3d ed., rev. and enl. Oxford, New York, Pergamon Press [1966] xiv, 372 p. 062.025 66-25830
HD2429.G7 M5 1966 MRR Alc.

TRADE AND PROFESSIONAL ASSOCIATIONS--UNITED STATES--DIRECTORIES.
Clapp, Jane. Professional ethics and insignia. Metuchen, N.J., Scarecrow Press, 1974. xii, 851 p. 061/.3 74-10501
HD6504 .A194 MRR Ref Desk.

Encyclopedia of business information sources; Detroit, Gale Research Co., 1970. 2 v. (xxi, 689 p.) 016.33 78-127922
HF5353 .E52 MRR Ref Desk.

Gale Research Company. Encyclopedia of associations. 8th ed. Detroit, Mich. [1973- v. [$45.00 (v. 1) $28.50 (v. 2)] 061/.3 73-7400
HS17 .G334 1973 MRR Ref Desk.

National trade and professional associations of the United States and labor unions. v. 7- 1972- Washington, D.C., Columbia Books, inc. [$15.00] 381/.06/273 74-647774
HD2425 .D53 MRR Ref Desk Latest edition

Public administration organizations, a directory of unofficial organizations in the field of public administration in the United States and Canada. [1st]- ed.; 1932- Chicago Public Administration Clearing House. 061 33-4186
AS18 .P8 MRR Alc Latest edition

United States trade associations. Loveland, Colo., Johnson Pub. Co. [$10.00] 338/.0025/73 74-642943
HD2425 .H53 MRR Alc Latest edition

Who's who in association management; membership directory. Washington. 56-1097
HD2425 .A573 MRR Alc Latest edition

TRADE AND PROFESSIONAL ASSOCIATIONS--UNITED STATES--HANDBOOKS, MANUALS, ETC.
Clapp, Jane. Professional ethics and insignia. Metuchen, N.J., Scarecrow Press, 1974. xii, 851 p. 061/.3 74-10501
HD6504 .A194 MRR Ref Desk.

TRADE FAIRS
see Fairs

TRADE-MARKS.
Kamekura, Yūsaku, Trademarks and symbols of the world. London, Studio Vista, 1966. 291 p. [6/6/-] 741.69 66-71155
NE965 .K32 1966 MRR Alc.

Katsarov, Konstantin. Manual and directory on industrial property all over the world. 7th- ed.; 1970- [Geneva, Switzerland] 608/.7/0202 72-625377
T201 .K3 MRR Alc Latest edition

United Piece Dye Works. Guidebook to man-made textile fibers and textured yarns of the world 3d ed. New York, [1969] 345 p. 677/.4 68-28677
TS1548.5 .U5 1969 MRR Alc.

United States Trademark Association. Trademark management; a guide for businessmen. [3d ed.] New York, [1960] 130 p. 608.87 61-3608
T325 .U66 1960 MRR Alc.

Zimmerman, Oswald Theodore, Industrial Research Service's handbook of material trade names, 1953 ed. Dover, N.H., Industrial Research Service, 1953. xvi, 794 p. 660.2 53-1074
TP151 .Z5 1953 MRR Alc.

TRADE-MARKS--DIRECTORIES.
Trade marks directory. London, Trade Marks Directory Service. 63-28216
T325 .I67 MRR Alc Latest edition

TRADE-MARKS--AFRICA.
The Business blue-book's national trade index of South Africa & Rhodesia. [Cape Town, National Pub. Co.] 380.1/45/0002568 72-627239
HC517.S7 N22 MRR Alc Latest edition

TRADE-MARKS--AUSTRALIA.
The Australasian manufacturers' directory. Sydney [etc.] Manufacturer Pub. Co. 23-10385
HD9738 .A2A8 MRR Alc Latest edition

Riddell's Australian purchasing year book. 1st- ed.; 1967- [Sydney, R. G. Riddell Pty. Ltd.] 602/.5/994 75-612957
T12.5.A8 R5 MRR Alc Latest edition

TRADE-MARKS--CANADA.
The National list of advertisers. Toronto, Maclean-Hunter Pub. Co. 56-46268
HF5808.C2 N3 MRR Alc Latest edition

TRADE-MARKS--GERMANY.
Deutschland liefert. Darmstadt, Gemeinschaftsverlag Deutsches Exportadressbuch. 57-18209
T12.5.G3 D43 MRR Alc Latest edition

Seibt export directory of German industries. Muenchen, Business Dictionaries Ltd. 338.4/7/602543 72-622306
T12.5.G3 E98 MRR Alc Latest edition

TRADE-MARKS--GREAT BRITAIN--INDEXES.
UK trade names. 1st- ed.; 1966- Croydon, Eng., Kompass Publishers Limited [etc.] 66-31719
T257.V4A27 MRR Alc Latest edition

TRADE-MARKS--JAPAN.
J I T: Tokyo, [Kojunsha International Publishers] 382/.025/52 68-51013
HF54.J3 J2 MRR Alc Latest edition

TRADE-MARKS--SWEDEN.
Swedish export directory. 28th- ed.; 1946- Stockholm, General Export Association of Sweden. 72-623267
HF3673 .S6 MRR Alc Latest edition

TRADE-MARKS--SWITZERLAND.
Directory of Swiss manufacturers and producers. 1817- Zurich [etc.] 670.58 53-19872
HF3703 .D5 MRR Alc Latest edition

TRADE-MARKS--UNITED STATES.
The Advertising specialty register. 1950- ed. Trevose, Pa. [etc.] Advertising Specialty Institute [etc.] 659.114 50-54758
HF6146.N7 A4 MRR Alc Latest edition

Boe, John Oliver. Television sponsors directory. Everglades, Fla., Everglades Pub. Co. 659.14/3/02573 72-622327
HF6146.T42 B6 MRR Alc Latest edition

Carter, David E. The book of American trade marks. Ashland, Ky., Century Communications Unlimited [1972- v. (chiefly illus.) 602/.75 72-76493
T223.V13 C37 MRR Alc.

Conover-Mast U.S. industrial purchasing directory. 1971- [New York, Cahners Publishing Co., etc.] 338.4/7/6702573 72-623800
T12 .C769 MRR Alc Latest edition

Grocery bulletin buying guide and reference issue. [Los Angeles, Grocery bulletin, etc.] 44-34611
HD9007.C2 G7 MRR Alc Latest edition

Grocery supermarket non-food buyers directory. 1961- New York, Directory Division, Merchandiser Publications. 60-41591
T12 .G75 MRR Alc Latest edition

Standard directory of advertisers. Jan. 1916- Skokie, Ill. [etc.] National Register Pub. Co. 659.102573 15-21147
HF5805 .S7 MRR Alc Latest edition

Thomas grocery register. 68th- ed.; 1966- New York, Thomas Publ. Co. 381/.45/664097 72-623125
HD9321.3 T5 MRR Alc Latest edition

Trademark directory. Washington [etc.] 667.6058 14-18485
TP934.5 .T7 Sci RR Latest edition / MRR Alc Latest edition

The Trademark register of the United States. 1967- Washington, Patent Searching Service. 602/.7/5 73-86256
T223.V4 A27 Sci RR Latest edition / MRR Alc Latest edition

United States. Patent office. Index of trade-marks issued from the United States Patent office. 1928- Washington, U.S. Govt. Print. Off. 655.620973 [608] 30-26198
T223.V4 A2 MRR Alc Latest edition

Wasserman, Paul. Consumer sourcebook; Detroit, Gale Research Co. [1974] xi, 593 p. 381/.3 74-10494
HC110.C63 W37 MRR Ref Desk.

TRADE-MARKS--UNITED STATES--HISTORY.
Franklin, Elizabeth. Why did they name it ...? New York, Fleet Pub. Corp. [1964] xv, 207 p. 608.87 64-12968
T223.V2 F7 MRR Alc.

TRADE REGULATION.
see also Consumer protection

TRADE ROUTES.
United States. Maritime Administration. Essential United States foreign trade routes. [1946]- Washington, For sale by the Superintendent of Documents, U.S. Govt. Print. Off. [etc.] 60-62459
HE745 .A184 MRR Alc Latest edition

TRADE-UNIONS--BIBLIOGRAPHY.
Allen, Victor Leonard. International bibliography of trade unionism. London, Merlin, 1968. vii, 180 p. [73/6] 016.33188 71-403739
Z7164.T7 A38 MRR Alc.

McBrearty, James C. American labor history and comparative labor movements: Tucson, Ariz., University of Arizona Press [1973] ix, 262 p. 016.331/0973 78-190624
Z7164.L1 M15 MRR Alc.

TRADE-UNIONS--PERIODICALS--INDEXES.
Michigan index to labor union periodicals. Jan. 1960- Ann Arbor, Bureau of Industrial Relations, Graduate School of Business Administration, University of Michigan. 62-63689
Z7164.T7 U6 MRR Alc Full set

TRADE-UNIONS--AFRICA--DIRECTORIES.
United States. Bureau of International Labor Affairs. Directory of labor organizations: Africa. Rev. ed. Washington, For sale by the Superintendent of Documents, U.S. Govt. Print. Off., 1966- 2 v. (loose-leaf) 66-62771
HD6856 .U63 MRR Alc.

TRADE-UNIONS--EUROPE--DIRECTORIES.
United States. Bureau of International Labor Affairs. Directory of labor organizations; Europe. Rev. ed. Washington, For sale by the Superintendent of Documents, U.S. Govt. Print. Off., 1965- 2 v. (loose-leaf) 65-81
HD6656 .A5 1965 MRR Alc.

TRADE-UNIONS--GREAT BRITAIN--HISTORY.
Cole, George Douglas Howard, comp. British working class movements; London, Macmillan, 1951. xxii, 628 p. 331.8 52-2264
HD8388 .C62 MRR Alc.

TRADE-UNIONS--UNITED STATES.
Commons, John Rogers, History of labour in the United States, New York, A. M. Kelley, 1966. 4 v. 331.0973 66-18557
HD8066 .C7 1966 MRR Alc.

TRADE-UNIONS--UNITED STATES-- BIBLIOGRAPHY.
Cornell University. New York State School of Industrial and Labor Relations. Library. Library catalog. Boston, G. K. Hall, 1967. 12 v. 016.331 72-185999
Z7164.L1 C84 MRR Alc (Dk 33)

Neufeld, Maurice F. A representative bibliography of American labor history Ithaca [New York State School of Industrial and Labor Relations] Cornell University, 1964. ix, 146 p. 64-63608
Z7164.L1 N55 MRR Alc.

Reynolds, Lloyd George, Trade union publications: Baltimore, The Johns Hopkins press, 1944-45. 3 v. 016.33188091 44-51461
Z7164.T7 R4 MRR Alc.

TRADE-UNIONS--UNITED STATES-- DICTIONARIES.
Paradis, Adrian A. The labor reference book [1st ed.] Philadelphia, Chilton Book Co. [1927] 234 p. [$5.95] 331.1/1/0973 72-6994
HD8066 .P37 MRR Alc.

Roberts, Harold Selig, Roberts' dictionary of industrial relations. Rev. ed. Washington, Bureau of National Affairs [c1971] xv, 599 p. 331/.03 78-175029
HD4839 .R612 1971 MRR Alc.

TRADE-UNIONS--UNITED STATES-- DIRECTORIES.
Directory of national unions and employee associations. 1971- Washington, U.S. Bureau of Labor Statistics; For sale by the Supt. of Docs., U.S. Govt. Print. Off. [$2.00] 331.88/025/73 73-641250
HD6504 .A15 MRR Ref Desk Latest edition

National trade and professional associations of the United States and labor unions. v. 7- 1972- Washington, D.C., Columbia Books, inc. [$15.00] 381/.06/273 74-647774
HD2425 .D53 MRR Ref Desk Latest edition

Reynolds, Lloyd George, Trade union publications: Baltimore, The Johns Hopkins press, 1944-45. 3 v. 016.33188091 44-51461
Z7164.T7 R4 MRR Alc.

TRADE-UNIONS--UNITED STATES--HISTORY.
Foner, Philip Sheldon, History of the labor movement in the United States ... New York, International publishers [1947- v. 331.880973 47-19381
HD6508 .F57 MRR Alc.

Rayback, Joseph G. A history of American labor. New York, Macmillan, 1959. 459 p. 331.880973 59-5344
HD8066 .R3 MRR Alc.

Reynolds, Lloyd George, Trade union publications: Baltimore, The Johns Hopkins press, 1944-45. 3 v. 016.33188091 44-51461
Z7164.T7 R4 MRR Alc.

Taft, Philip, Organized labor in American history. [1st ed.] New York, Harper & Row [1964] xxi, 818 p. 331.880973 64-12712
HD6508 .T25 MRR Alc.

TRADE-UNIONS--UNITED STATES--HISTORY-- BIBLIOGRAPHY.
McBrearty, James C. American labor history and comparative labor movements: Tucson, Ariz., University of Arizona Press [1973] ix, 262 p. 016.331/0973 78-190624
Z7164.L1 M15 MRR Alc.

TRADE-UNIONS--UNITED STATES-- PERIODICALS--BIBLIOGRAPHY.
Naas, Bernard G. American labor union periodicals. Ithaca, Cornell University [1956] xv, 175 p. 016.3318805 56-63004
Z7164.L1 N14 MRR Alc.

TRADE-UNIONS--UNITED STATES--STATISTICS.
Directory of national unions and employee associations. 1971- Washington, U.S. Bureau of Labor Statistics; For sale by the Supt. of Docs., U.S. Govt. Print. Off. [$2.00] 331.88/025/73 73-641250
HD6504 .A15 MRR Ref Desk Latest edition

TRADES
see Occupations

TRADITIONS
see Folk-lore

see Legends

see Superstition

TRAFFIC
see Communication and traffic

TRAFFIC ENGINEERING--DICTIONARIES.
Dictionary of highway traffic.
Evanston, Ill., Traffic Institute,
Northwestern University [1960] xv,
304 p.   388.312 60-4093
HE333 .D5 MRR Alc.

TRAFFIC ENGINEERING--YEARBOOKS.
Institute of Traffic Engineers.
Yearbook. Washington. 65-6787
HE331 .I45 MRR Alc Latest edition

TRAFFIC SAFETY--RESEARCH--DIRECTORIES.
Organization for Economic Cooperation
and Development. International road
safety research directory. 2nd ed.
Paris, O.E.C.D. [London, H.M.S.O.]
1966. 358 p. [44/-] 614.8/62/072
67-78356
HE5614 .O73 1966 MRR Alc.

TRAILER CAMPS--DIRECTORIES.
American Automobile Association.
Eastern campground directory: areas
in the Eastern United States and
Canada. [Washington, D.C.] 64-5093

SK601.A1 A514 MRR Alc Latest
edition

Hayes, Richard LoveJoy. Trailering
America's highways and byways.
[Beverly Hills, Calif., Trail-R-Club
of America, 1965-70. 2 v.
796.7/9/0973 66-1843
GV1024 .H38 MRR Alc.

Let's go camping, let's go
trailering. [Beverly Hills, Calif.,
Trail-R-Club of America] 796.5405873
58-87
SK601.A1 L4 MRR Alc Latest edition

Lippman, Paul. Camping guide to
Europe; [1st ed.] New York, Holt,
Rinehart and Winston [1968] x, 181
p. 914/.04/55 68-12211
GV1025.E9 L5 MRR Alc.

Rand McNally and Company. Campground
and trailer park guide. 1871- New
York. 917.3/04/924 78-613368
SK601 .R285 MRR Alc Latest edition

Rand McNally western campground &
trailering guide. 1970- [New York,
Rand McNally] 917.9/04/3 79-23951
SK601 .R29 MRR Alc Latest edition

Western camping and trailering areas
in Western United States and Canada
including location maps. 1964-
[Washington] American Automobile
Association. 64-5094
SK601 .W43 MRR Alc Latest edition

TRAILER CAMPS--NEW ENGLAND--DIRECTORIES.
Parry, Don. Don Parry's guide to
Northeast camping areas. Rocky Hill,
Conn., Outdoor Publishers.
796.54/0874 72-623299
SK601.A1 T4 MRR Alc Latest edition

TRAILER CAMPS--NEW YORK (STATE)--DIRECTORIES.
Parry, Don. Don Parry's guide to
Northeast camping areas. Rocky Hill,
Conn., Outdoor Publishers.
796.54/0874 72-623299
SK601.A1 T4 MRR Alc Latest edition

TRAILER CAMPS--UNITED STATES--DIRECTORIES.
Woodall's trailering parks and
campgrounds directory. Eastern
edition. [Highland Park, Ill.,
Woodall Pub. Co.] 647/.9473 74-
644615
GV191.35 .W66 MRR Alc Latest
edition

TRAILS.
Potomac Appalachian Trail Club,
Washington, D.C. Guide to the
Appalachian Trail: 7th ed.
Washington, 1970. vii, 190 p.
917.5 75-14141
F217.B6 P83 1970 MRR Alc.

TRAILS--UNITED STATES.
Colwell, Robert. Introduction to
foot trails in America. [Harrisburg,
Pa.] Stackpole Books [1972] 221 p.
[$5.95] 917.3/04/924 74-179603
E158 .C76 MRR Alc.

TRAILS--UNITED STATES--MAPS--BIBLIOGRAPHY.
United States. Library of Congress.
Map Division. Maps showing
explorers' routes, trails & early
roads in the United States;
Washington, For sale by the
Superintendent of Documents, U.S.
Govt. Print. Off., 1962. vi, 137 p.
62-60066
Z663.35 .M26 MRR Alc.

TRAINED NURSES
see Nurses and nursing

TRAINING, PHYSICAL
see Physical education and training

TRAINING OF EXECUTIVES
see Executives, Training of

TRAMPING
see Hiking

TRAMWAYS
see Street-railroads

TRANSFER STUDENTS--UNITED STATES.
Proia, Nicholas C. Barron's handbook
of college transfer information.
Rev. ed. Woodbury, N.Y., Barron's
Educational Series [1971] viii, 271
p. [$3.95] 378.169/14/02573 75-
29430
L901 .P73 1971 MRR Alc.

TRANSLATING AND INTERPRETING--BIBLIOGRAPHY.
Hoof, Henri van. Internationale
Bibliographie der Übersetzung. 1.
Ausg. Pullach bei München, Verlag
Dokumentation, 1973. xvi, 591 p.
73-205044
Z7004.T72 H66 MRR Alc.

TRANSLATING AND INTERPRETING--DIRECTORIES.
American Translators Association. A
T A professional services directory.
1965- New York. 67-2749
PN241 .A1A5 Sci RR Latest edition
/ MRR Alc Latest edition

TRANSLATING SERVICES--DIRECTORIES.
Kaiser, Frances E., ed. Translators
and translations: New York [Special
Libraries Association] 1959. iv, 60
p. 410.28 59-7523
PN241 .K27 MRR Alc.

TRANSLATIONS--BIBLIOGRAPHY.
Cumulative index to English
translations, 1948-1968. Boston, G.
K. Hall, 1973. 2 v. 016.011 74-
167325
Z6514.T7 C8 MRR Alc.

English, 1948-1964. 2d rev. ed.
Gottingen, Vandenhoeck & Ruprecht,
1968. 509 p. 016.9143/03 72-
590351
Z2221 .T73 no. 1 MRR Alc.

Ferguson, Mary Anne. Bibliography of
English translations from medieval
sources, 1943-1967. New York,
Columbia University Press, 1974. x,
274 p. 016.08 73-7751
Z6517 .F47 MRR Alc.

Fromm, Hans. Bibliographie deutscher
Übersetzungen aus dem
Französischen, 1700-1948. Baden-
Baden, Verlag für Kunst und
Wissenschaft, 1950- v.   51-24434

Z2174.T7 F7 MRR Alc.

Groot-de Rook, A. S. de.
Translations Journals: [Delft]
European Translations Centre, Centre
europeen des traductions, 1970. 44,
3, 3 p. 016.05 75-583148
Z6941 .G85 MRR Alc.

Index translationum. Nº 1-31; Juil.
1932-Jan. 1940. Paris, Société des
nations, Institut international de
cooperation intellectuelle [etc.]
016   32-32203
Z6514.T7 I4 MRR Alc Full set

Index translationum. 1-   1948-
Paris, UNESCO. 016 50-12446
Z6515.T7 I42 MRR Alc Full set

Levine, Suzanne Jill. Latin America
fiction & poetry in translation. New
York, Center for Inter-American
Relations [1970] 71 p. [1.25]
016.8608 75-121376
Z1609.T7 L45 MRR Alc.

Literature Service Associates, Bound
Brook, N.J. English language
equivalent editions of foreign
language serials. Bound Brook, N.J.
[1959] 81 p. 016.05 59-46914
Z1007 .L77355 MRR Alc.

Parks, George Bruner. The Romance
literatures. New York, F. Ungar Pub.
Co. [1970] 2 v. [$45.00]
016.84009 70-98341
Z7033.T7E65 MRR Alc.

Smith, Murray F., A selected
bibliography of German literature in
English translation, 1956-1960.
Metuchen, N.J.: Scarecrow Press,
1972. v, 398 p. 016.83 76-157727

Z2234.T7 S6 MRR Alc.

Translations from the German;
Gottingen, Vandenhoeck & Ruprecht,
1968- v. 76-590301
Z2221 .T73 MRR Alc.

White, Thomas N. Guide to United
States-J.P.R.S. research
translations, 1957-1966: Washington,
Research & Microfilm Publications
[1966] 67 p. 017 66-29498
Z1223.Z7 W55 MRR Alc.

TRANSLATIONS--BIBLIOGRAPHY--YEARBOOKS.
Chartotheca translationum
alphabetica. Frankfurt am Main, H.
W. Bentz. 66-89994
Began publication with vol. for
1961.
Z6514.T7 C48 MRR Alc Full set

TRANSLATIONS--INDEXES.
Transdex: v. 9-   July 1970- New
York, CCM Information Corp. 015/.73
77-612605
AS36 .U574 Sci RR Full Set / MRR
Alc Full set

TRANSLATORS--BIOGRAPHY.
Flegon, Alec. Who's who in
translating and interpreting:
London, Flegon P. [1967] 190 p.
418/.02/0922 68-71375
PN241 .F55 MRR Biog.

TRANSLATORS--DIRECTORIES.
American Translators Association. A
T A professional services directory.
1965- New York. 67-2749
PN241 .A1A5 Sci RR Latest edition
/ MRR Alc Latest edition

International Association of
Conference Interpreters. Yearbook.
Paris. 63-33765
P306.A1 I5 MRR Alc Latest edition

International directory of
translators and interpreters. 1967-
London, Pond Press. 68-39831
PN241.A1 I5 Sci RR Latest edition
/ MRR Alc Latest edition

Literary market place: [1st] ed.;
1940- New York, Bowker. 655.473 41-
51571
PN161 .L5 Sci RR Partial set / MRR
Ref Desk Latest edition

TRANSLITERATION.
see also Alphabet

Gleichen, Edward, Lord, Alphabets of
foreign languages, 2d ed. 1933
reprinted with incorporation of
supplement of 1938 London, The Royal
geographical society [etc.] 1944.
xvi, 82 p., 1 l. gs 46-161
P213 .G55 1944 MRR Alc.

TRANSPARENCIES--CATALOGS.
National Information Center for
Educational Media. Index to
educational overhead transparencies.
3d ed. [Los Angeles, University of
Southern California] 1973 (c1972]
viii, 757 p. 371.33/52/0216 75-
190634
LB1043.7.Z9 N3 1973 MRR Alc.

TRANSPARENCIES IN EDUCATION.
National Information Center for
Educational Media. Index to
educational overhead transparencies.
3d ed. [Los Angeles, University of
Southern California] 1973 (c1972]
viii, 757 p. 371.33/52/0216 75-
190634
LB1043.7.Z9 N3 1973 MRR Alc.

TRANSPORT PLANES.
Brooks, Peter W. The world's
airliners. London, Putnam [1963,
c1962] 585 p. 629.13334 63-25447

TL685.4 .B72 1963 MRR Alc.

TRANSPORTATION.
see also Aeronautics, Commercial

see also Automobiles

see also Commerce

see also Communication and traffic

see also Freight and freightage

see also Harbors

see also Railroads

see also Shipping

see also Urban transportation

TRANSPORTATION--BIBLIOGRAPHY.
Ad Hoc Committee of Librarians for
"Sources of information in
Transportation." Sources of
information in transportation.
[Evanston, Ill.] Published for the
Transportation Center at Northwestern
University by the Northwestern
University Press [1964] x, 262 p.
016.385 64-3945
Z7164.T8 A3 MRR Alc.

TRANSPORTATION--BIBLIOGRAPHY--CATALOGS.
Evanston, Ill. Transportation Center
at Northwestern University. Library.
Catalog. Boston, G. K. Hall, 1972.
12 v. 016.3805 74-171017
Z7164.T8 E83 1972 MRR Alc (Dk 33)

TRANSPORTATION--DICTIONARIES.
Stufflebeam, George Teele, ed. The
traffic dictionary; 4th ed., enl.
and rev. New York, Simmons-Boardman
[1950] 292 p. 380.3 50-8273
HE141 .S8 1950 MRR Alc.

TRANSPORTATION--DICTIONARIES--GERMAN.
Bein, Gerhard. Wörterbuch des
internationalen Verkehrs. Leipzig,
Verlag Enzyklopädie VEB (1968). 232
p. [18.00] 380.5/03 71-410715
HE141 .B44 MRR Alc.

TRANSPORTATION--DIRECTORIES.
The Globe world directory for land,
sea and air traffic. 1st- ed.;
1948- Oslo, [etc.] Globe
Directories. 385.058 50-13703
HE9.A1 G5 MRR Alc Latest edition

Jane's freight containers. 1st-
ed.; 1868/69- New York, McGraw-Hill
Book Co. 380.5/3 74-2497
TA1215 .J34 Sci RR Latest edition
/ MRR Alc Latest edition

TRANSPORTATION--FREIGHT
see Freight and freightage

TRANSPORTATION--HISTORY.
Keir, Robert Malcolm, The march of
commerce, New Haven, Yale university
press; [etc., etc.] 1927. 3 p. l.,
361 p. 28-866
E178.5 .P2 vol. 4 MRR Alc.

TRANSPORTATION--PERIODICALS--INDEXES.
Evanston, Ill. Transportation Center
at Northwestern University. Library.
Catalog. Boston, G. K. Hall, 1972.
12 v. 016.3805 74-171017
Z7164.T8 E83 1972 MRR Alc (Dk 33)

TRANSPORTATION--CANADA--DIRECTORIES.
The Journal of commerce
transportation telephone tickler.
[New York] 53-34476
HE9.U5 N7 MRR Alc Latest edition

TRANSPORTATION--EUROPE--STATISTICS.
United Nations. Economic Commission
for Europe. Annual bulletin of
transport statistics. 1st- year;
1949- Genève. 385 51-1244
HE242 .U5 MRR Alc Latest edition

TRANSPORTATION--RUSSIA--BIBLIOGRAPHY.
United States. Library of Congress.
Reference Dept. Soviet
transportation and communications;
Washington, 1952. xv, 330 p.
016.385 52-60024
Z663.28 .S6 MRR Alc.

TRANSPORTATION--UNITED STATES--
BIBLIOGRAPHY.
Flood, Kenneth U. Research in
transportation: legal/legislative and
economic sources and procedure
Detroit, Gale Research Co. [c1970]
126 p. [$11.50] 016.3805 72-
118792
Z7164.T8 F55 MRR Alc.

TRANSPORTATION--UNITED STATES--
DIRECTORIES.
Dun & Bradstreet reference book of
transportation. Washington, Trinc
Transportation Consultants.
380.5/2/02573 74-644693
HE5623.A45 D82 MRR Alc Latest
edition

The Journal of commerce
transportation telephone tickler.
[New York] 53-34476
HE9.U5 N7 MRR Alc Latest edition

The Official directory of industrial
and commercial traffic executives.
Washington, Traffic Service
Corporation. 380.5/2 72-626342
HF5780.U6 O4 MRR Alc Latest
edition

TRANSPORTATION--UNITED STATES--HISTORY.
Beebe, Lucius Morris, Hear the train
blow; New York, Grossett & Dunlap
[1958, c1952] 407 p. 385.1* 58-
4335
HE2751 .B4 1958 MRR Alc.

Dunbar, Seymour. A history of travel
in America. New York, Tudor
publishing company, 1937. L p., 2
l., 1530, [1] p. 385.0973 38-7081

HE203 .D77 1937 MRR Alc.

Taylor, George Rogers, The
transportation revolution, 1815-1860.
New York, Rinehart [1951] xvii, 490
p. 385.09 51-14038
HC103 .E25 vol. 4 MRR Alc.

Throm, Edward Louis, ed. Popular
mechanics' picture history of
American transportation. New York,
Simon and Schuster, 1952. 312 p.
385 52-14703
HE203 .T45 MRR Alc.

TRANSPORTATION--UNITED STATES--
PICTORIAL WORKS.
Hornung, Clarence Pearson. Wheels
across America. New York, A. S.
Barnes [1959] 341 p. 385.0973 58-
12391
HE203 .H6 MRR Alc.

TRANSPORTATION--UNITED STATES--
STATISTICS.
United States. Bureau of the Census.
1967 census of transportation.
[Washington; For sale by the Supt. of
Docs., U.S. Govt. Print. Off., 1970]
3 v. in 5 [$3.00 (v. 1) varies]
380.5/0973 76-607509
HE18 1967 .A55 MRR Alc.

United States. Interstate Commerce
Commission. Bureau of Accounts.
Transport statistics in the United
States. Washington. 380.5/0973 72-
627360
HE2708 .I73 MRR Alc Latest edition

TRANSPORTATION--UNITED STATES--
YEARBOOKS.
Moody's transportation manual:
American and foreign. 1954- New
York, Moody's Investors Service. 57-
15176
HG4971 .M74 MRR Alc Latest edition

TRANSPORTATION--UNITED STATES--
BIOGRAPHY.
Leading men in American
transportation. New York, Transport
Publishers Corp. [c1967] 164 p.
380.5/0922 68-4217
HE151.5 .A2L4 MRR Biog.

TRANSPORTATION, AUTOMOTIVE.
see also Motor bus lines

see also Motor vehicles

see also Traffic safety

TRANSPORTATION, AUTOMOTIVE--FREIGHT.
National highway and airway carriers
and routes. v. 1- Mar. 1942-
Chicago, National Highway Carriers
Directory. 388.3058 42-14688
HE5623.A45 N3 MRR Alc Latest
edition

TRANSPORTATION, AUTOMOTIVE--GREAT
BRITAIN--DIRECTORIES.
Passenger transport (London) Year
book. London. 388.4058 61-20834
Began publication in 1899.
TF701 .P3 MRR Alc Latest edition

TRANSPORTATION, AUTOMOTIVE--UNITED
STATES--DIRECTORIES.
American Trucking Associations. Dept.
of Research. Financial & operating
statistics, class I & II motor
carriers of property. Washington.
388.3 44-52021
HE5623 .A1A64 MRR Alc Latest
edition

National highway and airway carriers
and routes. v. 1- Mar. 1942-
Chicago, National Highway Carriers
Directory. 388.3058 42-14688
HE5623.A45 N3 MRR Alc Latest
edition

TRANSPORTATION, AUTOMOTIVE--UNITED
STATES--FREIGHT--DIRECTORIES.
American M C D; National edition.
[Atlanta] 338.3/24/02573 72-616915

HE5623.A45 A64 MRR Alc Latest
edition

Dun & Bradstreet reference book of
transportation. Washington, Trinc
Transportation Consultants.
380.5/2/02573 74-644693
HE5623.A45 D82 MRR Alc Latest
edition

TRANSPORTATION, AUTOMOTIVE--UNITED
STATES--STATISTICS.
American Trucking Associations. Dept.
of Research. Financial & operating
statistics, class I & II motor
carriers of property. Washington.
388.3 44-52021
HE5623 .A1A64 MRR Alc Latest
edition

American Trucking Associations. Dept.
of Research. Financial & operating
statistics, class I & II motor
carriers of property. Executive and
ownership section. 1956-
Washington. 388.3 74-643564
HE5623 .A1A642 MRR Alc Latest
edition

Trinc's blue book of the trucking
industry. Washington, Trinc
Associates. 60-2693
Began publication with vol. for
1944.
HE5623.A1 T685 MRR Alc Latest
edition

Trinc's red book of the trucking
industry. Washington, Trinc
Associates. 64-28389
HE5623.A1 T69 MRR Alc Latest
edition

United States. Interstate Commerce
Commission. Bureau of Accounts.
Transport statistics in the United
States. Washington. 380.5/0973 72-
627360
HE2708 .I73 MRR Alc Latest edition

TRANSPORTATION, AUTOMOTIVE--UNITED
STATES--YEARBOOKS.
Trinc's blue book of the trucking
industry. Washington, Trinc
Associates. 60-2693
Began publication with vol. for
1944.
HE5623.A1 T685 MRR Alc Latest
edition

Trinc's red book of the trucking
industry. Washington, Trinc
Associates. 64-28389
HE5623.A1 T69 MRR Alc Latest
edition

TRANSPORTATION, MILITARY.
see also Vehicles, Military

TRANSVAAL--BIOGRAPHY.
Skota, Mweli T. D. The African who's
who; [Johannesburg] Distributed by
Central News Agency [196-] 373 p.
67-58880
DT913 .S55 1960z MRR Biog.

TRANSVAAL--DIRECTORIES.
Skota, Mweli T. D. The African who's
who; [Johannesburg] Distributed by
Central News Agency [196-] 373 p.
67-58880
DT913 .S55 1960z MRR Biog.

TRANSVAAL--RELIGION.
Skota, Mweli T. D. The African who's
who; [Johannesburg] Distributed by
Central News Agency [196-] 373 p.
67-58880
DT913 .S55 1960z MRR Biog.

TRAPPING.
see also Hunting

Herter, George Leonard, Professional
guide's manual, [1st ed. Waseca,
Minn.] Herter's [1960] 207 p. 799
60-21551
SK601 .H497 MRR Alc.

TRAVEL.
Donovan, John. The businessman's
international travel guide. New
York, Stein and Day [1971] ix, 253
p. [$7.95] 910/.202 76-163347
G153 .D6 1971 MRR Alc.

Encyclopedia of world travel. 2d
rev. ed. Garden City, N.Y.,
Doubleday [1973] 2 v. [$12.95 per
vol.] 910/.202 73-76221
G153 .E5 1973 MRR Alc.

Freed's world travel catalog. 1965-
New York, Freed Publications. 910/.2
66-11940
G153 .F7 MRR Alc Latest edition

How to travel and get paid for it.
1st- ed.; 1953- Greenlawn, N.Y.,
Harian Publications; distributed by
Grosset & Dunlap [etc., New York] 59-
11296
HF5382 .H69 MRR Alc Latest edition

Jurgen, Jens. Air travel and charter
flight handbook; Kings Park, N.Y.,
Travel Information Bureau [1973] 192
p. [$4.95] 387.7/42 73-168342
HE9787 .J87 MRR Alc.

OAG travel planner & hotel/motel
guide. [Oak Brook, Ill.] R.H.
Donnelley Corp.] [$20.00] 910/.202
73-640442
G153 .O18 MRR Ref Desk Latest
edition

Pan Am's world guide: [New York,
Random House, 1974] 1012 p.
910/.202 74-176208
G153 .P32 1974b MRR Alc.

Pan Am's world guide: [1st ed.] New
York, Random House [1974, c1973]
1012 p. [$4.95] 910/.202 73-5004

G153 .P32 MRR Alc.

Stein, Howard, The budget guide to
Europe. Princeton, N.J., Van
Nostrand [c1962] 980 p. 910.2 62-
905
D909 .S82 1962 MRR Alc.

TRAVEL. (Cont.)
Travel routes around the world.
Greenlawn, N.Y. [etc.] Harlan
Publications. 42-44894
G153 .T75 MRR Alc Latest edition

World Association of Travel Agencies.
National tourist information and
general tariff. Geneva. 61-65430
Began in 1953.
G155.A1 G4 MRR Alc Latest edition

TRAVEL--BIBLIOGRAPHY.
Neal, Jack A., comp. Reference guide
for travellers. New York, Bowker,
1969. xi, 674 p. [17.50] 016.910
69-16399
Z6011 .N4 MRR Alc.

TRAVEL--YEARBOOKS.
World travel & vacation almanac.
1970- New York, Harper & Row. 910.2
78-111641
G153 .W897 MRR Alc Latest edition

TRAVEL AGENTS--DIRECTORIES.
International directory of travel
agents. [Hollywood, Calif., Robinson-
Ingledue Travel Publications, etc.]
[$16.00] 380.1/45/91025 73-647029
G154 .I56 MRR Alc Latest edition

Jurgen, Jens. Air travel and charter
flight handbook: Kings Park, N.Y.,
Travel Information Bureau [1973] 192
p. [$4.95] 387.7/42 73-168342
HE9787 .J87 MRR Alc.

Travel industry personnel directory.
[New York, Travel Agent Magazine]
338.4/7/91008025 72-622913
G155 .A1T655 MRR Alc Latest
edition

TRAVEL AGENTS--CANADA--DIRECTORIES.
American Society of Travel Agents.
Membership roster. [New York] 72-
626516
G154 .A46 MRR Alc Latest edition

TRAVEL AGENTS--UNITED STATES--
DIRECTORIES.
American Society of Travel Agents.
Membership roster. [New York] 72-
626516
G154 .A46 MRR Alc Latest edition

TRAVEL COSTS.
Ford, Norman D., 1921- Harian's
Today's best buys in travel in
Mexico, the West Indies, South
America, Europe, the Orient, Africa,
and around the world [by] Norman D.
Ford and Fredric E. Tyarks. 1960-
Greenlawn, N.Y., Harian Publications;
trade distributor: Crown Publishers
[New York] 910.202 61-836
G153 .F5925 MRR Alc Latest edition

Freed's world travel catalog. 1965-
New York, Freed Publications. 910/.2
66-111840
G153 .F7 MRR Alc Latest edition

How to travel without being rich.
Greenlawn, N.Y., Harian Publications;
Trade Distributor: Grosset & Dunlap
[etc., New York] 910.2 60-1057
G153 .H65 MRR Alc Latest edition

TRAVEL PHOTOGRAPHY.
Townsend, Derek. The photographer's
holiday guide to Europe: London,
Collins, Glasgow, 1967. 176 p. [25/-
] 914/.04/55 67-85313
D922 .T67 MRR Alc.

TRAVELS
see Scientific expeditions

TREASON--UNITED STATES.
Van Doren, Carl Clinton, Secret
history of the American revolution,
New York, The Viking press, 1941. 3
p. l., [v]-xiv p., 2 l., [3]-534 p.
41-24478
E277 .V23 1941 MRR Alc.

TREASURE-TROVE.
Coffman, Ferris La Verne. 1001 lost,
buried or sunken treasures; New
York, Nelson [1957] 277 p. 910.45
57-8128
G525 .C63 MRR Alc.

Potter, John Stauffer, The treasure
diver's guide Rev. ed. Garden City,
N.Y., Doubleday, 1972. xxvi, 567 p.
[$15.00] 910/.453 72-87681
G525 .P58 1972 MRR Alc.

Rieseberg, Harry Earl. Fell's
complete guide to buried treasure,
land end sea, New York, F. Fell
[1970] 235 p. [5.95] 398.3/24 67-
20435
G525 .R544 1970 MRR Alc.

TREASURE TROVE--BIBLIOGRAPHY.
Underbrink, Robert L. Treasure trove
: Carlinville, Ill. : Lamplighter
Press, [1974] 96 p. : 016.91/0453
74-80123
Z6016.T74 U5 MRR Alc.

TREASURE-TROVE--MAPS--BIBLIOGRAPHY.
United States. Library of Congress.
Map Division. A descriptive list of
treasure maps and charts, [in the
Library of Congress] Washington,
[For sale by the Superintendent of
Documents, U.S. Govt. Print. Off.]
1964. vii, 29 p. 64-60033
Z663.35 .T7 1964 MRR Alc.

TREASURE-TROVE--UNITED STATES.
Carlisle, Norman V. The complete
guide to treasure hunting Chicago,
H. Regnery Co. [1973] 280 p.
917.3/04 73-6452
E159.5 .C37 MRR Alc.

TREATIES.
Academie diplomatique
internationale. Dictionnaire
diplomatique, Paris [1933] 2 v.
341.03 33-36212
JX1226 .A312 vol. 3 MRR Biog.

Hertslet, Edward, Sir, The map of
Africa by treaty, 3d ed.: London,
Printed for H.M. Stationery off., by
Harrison and sons, 1909. 3 v. and
portfolio of maps. 10-833
JX1026 1896a MRR Alc.

Israel, Fred L., comp. Major peace
treaties of modern history, 1648-
1967. New York, Chelsea House
Publishers, 1967. 4 v. (xxix, 2880
p.) 341.2 67-27855
JX121 .I8 MRR Alc.

Toscano, Mario. The history of
treaties and international politics.
Baltimore, John Hopkins Press, 1966-
v. 327.209 66-15525
D217 .T613 MRR Alc.

Treaties and alliances of the world;
[2d ed.] [Bristol] Keesing's
Publications; New York, Scribner
[1974] xv, 235 p. 341.3/7 73-
15927
JX4005 .T72 1974 MRR Alc.

TREATIES--BIBLIOGRAPHY.
Institut Juridique international,
Hague, Repertoire general des
traites et autres actes
diplomatiques conclus depuis 1895
jusqu'en 1920, Harlem (Pays-Bas) H.
D. Tjeenk Willink & fils; La Haye
(Pays-Bas) M. Nijhoff, 1926. xix,
516 p. 27-9742
Z6464.T8 I6 MRR Alc.

United States. Library of Congress.
Division of bibliography. List of
references on the treaty-making
power, Washington, Govt. print.
off., 1920. 219 p. 20-26005
Z663.28 .L5827 MRR Alc.

TREATIES--CATALOGS.
Harvard University. Law School.
Library. Index to multilateral
treaties; Cambridge, Mass.;
[distributed by Oceana Publications,
Dobbs Ferry, N.Y.] 1965. x, 301 p.
341.2016 65-29763
JX171 .H35 MRR Ref Desk.

Hertslet, Edward, Sir, comp. The map
of Europe by treaty; London,
Butterworths [etc.] 1875-91. 4 v.
10-15038
JX626 1875 MRR Alc.

United States. Dept. of state.
Catalogue of treaties. 1814-1918.
Washington, Govt. print. off., 1919.
xxv, 3-716 p. 20-13106
JX171 .U4 1918 MRR Ref Desk.

United States. Dept. of State. Office
of the Legal Adviser. Treaties in
force; [Washington, U.S. Govt.
Print. Off.] 341.273 56-61604
Began publication with 1929 issue.
JX236 1929c MRR Alc Latest
edition

TREATIES--COLLECTIONS.
Council of Europe. European
conventions and agreements.
Strasbourg, 1971- v. 341.24/2
72-185347
JX626 1971 .C68 MRR Alc.

Davenport, Frances Gardiner, ed.
European treaties bearing on the
history of the United States and its
dependencies, Washington, D.C.,
Carnegie institution of Washington,
1917-37. 4 v. 18-3383
E173 .D24 MRR Alc.

Friedman, Leon, comp. The law of
war; a documentary history. [1st
ed.] New York, Random House [1972]
2 v. (xxv, 1764 p.) 341.6/026 72-
765
JX4505 .F7 MRR Alc.

Grenville, John Ashley Soames. The
major international treaties, 1914-
1973; New York, Stein and Day [1974]
xxix, 575 p. [$25.00] 341/.026
75-163352
JX171 .G74 MRR Alc.

Hartmann, Frederick H., ed. Basic
documents of international relations.
1st ed. New York, McGraw-Hill,
1951. xv, 312 p. 341.082 51-9293
JX68 .H35 MRR Alc.

Hudson, Manley Ottmer, ed.
International legislation;
Washington, Carnegie endowment for
international peace, 1931- v.
341.2 32-2976
JX171 .H8 MRR Alc.

Hurst, Michael, comp. Key treaties
for the great powers, 1814-1914. New
York, St. Martin's Press [1972] 2 v.
(xviii, 948 p.) [$31.50] 341/.026
72-188873
JX151 .H87 1972b MRR Alc.

International organisation and
integration. Deventer, Æ. E. Kluwer;
Leiden, A. W. Sijthoff, 1968 [1969]
xxvi, 1146 p. [67.30] 341.13 68-
25399
JX171 .I54 MRR Alc.

Russia (1917- R.S.F.S.R.) Treaties,
etc. Soviet treaty series;
Washington, Georgetown University
Press, 1950- v. 341.247 50-
2664
JX756 1950 MRR Alc.

United States. Congress. House.
Committee on Foreign Affairs.
Collective defense treaties, with
maps, texts of treaties, a
chronology, status of forces
agreements, and comparative chart.
Rev.] Washington, U.S. Govt. Print.
Off.] 1969. ix, 514 p. [2.50]
341.2 79-602271
JX171 .U39 1969 MRR Alc.

United States. Laws, statutes, etc.
United States statutes at large,
containing the laws and concurrent
resolutions ... and reorganization
plan, amendment to the Constitution,
and proclamations. v. 1- 1789/1845-
Washington, U.S. Govt. Print. Off.
07-35353
LAW MRR Alc (Dk 33) Full set

United States. Treaties, etc.
Treaties and other international acts
of the United States of America,
Washington, U.S. Govt. Print. Off.,
1931- v. 341.273 31-28592
JX236 1931a MRR Alc.

United States. Treaties, etc.
Treaties and other international
agreements of the United States of
America, 1776-1949. [Washington,
Dept. of State; for sale by the Supt.
of Docs., U.S. Govt. Print. Off.,
1968- v. [8.50 (v. 1) varies]
341/.0264/73 70-600742
JX236 1968 .A5 MRR Alc.

United States. Treaties, etc. United
States treaties and other
international agreements. v. 1-
1950- [Washington] Dept. of State.
341.273 53-60242
JX231 .A34 MRR Alc Full set

TREATIES--COLLECTIONS--BIBLIOGRAPHY.
Myers, Denys Peter, ed. Manual of
collections of treaties and of
collections relating to treaties,
Cambridge, Harvard university press
[etc.] 1922. xlvii, 685, [1] p. 22-
7754
Z6464.T8 M9 MRR Alc.

TREATIES--INDEXES.
American Bar Association. Committee
on Commercial Treaties. Commercial
treaty index. [Chicago] Section of
International Law, American Bar
Association [1973- 1 v. (loose-leaf)
341.7/54/026473 73-163891
JX236 1973 .A65 MRR Alc.

Harvard University. Law School.
Library. Index to multilateral
treaties; Cambridge, Mass.;
[distributed by Oceana Publications,
Dobbs Ferry, N.Y.] 1965. x, 301 p.
341.2016 65-29763
JX171 .H35 MRR Ref Desk.

Hertslet's commercial treaties.
London, 1827-1925. 31 v. 01-4024
JX636 1827 Vol. 22 & 31 MRR Alc.

Parry, Clive. An index of British
treaties, 1101-1968, London,
H.M.S.O., 1970. 1 v. in 3
341/.0264/42 75-873903
JX636 1970 .P37 MRR Alc.

United States. Dept. of state.
Catalogue of treaties. 1814-1918.
Washington, Govt. print. off., 1919.
xxv, 3-716 p. 20-13106
JX171 .U4 1918 MRR Ref Desk.

TREES.
see also Forests and forestry

see also Lumbering

TREES. (Cont.)
see also Wood

Platt, Rutherford Hayes, 1001
questions answered about trees. New
York, Dodd, Mead, 1959. 318 p.
582.16076 59-6900
QK475 .P55 MRR Alc.

TREES--DISEASES AND PESTS.
see also Insects, Injurious and
beneficial

TREES--IDENTIFICATION.
Symonds, George Wellington
Dillingham. The tree identification
book; New York, M. Barrows [1958]
272 p. 582.16084 58-5359
QK482 .S9 1958 MRR Alc.

TREES--NAMES.
Little, Elbert Luther, Check list of
native and naturalized trees of the
United States (including Alaska)
Washington, Forest Service, 1953.
472 p. 582.16 581.973* agr53-309
QK481 .L5 MRR Alc.

TREES--NOMENCLATURE (POPULAR)
Little, Elbert Luther, Check list of
native and naturalized trees of the
United States (including Alaska)
Washington, Forest Service, 1953.
472 p. 582.16 581.973* agr53-309
QK481 .L5 MRR Alc.

TREES--PICTORIAL WORKS.
Symonds, George Wellington
Dillingham. The tree identification
book; New York, M. Barrows [1958]
272 p. 582.16084 58-5359
QK482 .S9 1958 MRR Alc.

TREES--CANADA.
Peattie, Donald Culross, A natural
history of trees of eastern and
central North America; Boston,
Houghton Mifflin, 1950. xv, 606 p.
582.16 50-10354
QK481 .P4 MRR Alc.

Peattie, Donald Culross, A natural
history of western trees; Boston,
Houghton Mifflin, 1953. xiv, 751 p.
582.16 581.978* 52-5263
QK481 .P42 MRR Alc.

TREES--NORTH AMERICA.
Harlow, William Morehouse, Textbook
of dendrology, covering the important
forest trees of the United States and
Canada 5th ed. New York, McGraw-
Hill [1968] xv, 512 p. 582.16/0973
68-17188
QK481 .H32 1968 MRR Alc.

Hough, Romeyn Beck, Hough's
encyclopaedia of American woods,
[1st ed.] New York, R. Speller, 1957-
v. 634.98 57-10592
SD536 .H832 MRR Alc.

Peattie, Donald Culross, A natural
history of trees of eastern and
central North America; Boston,
Houghton Mifflin, 1950. xv, 606 p.
582.16 50-10354
QK481 .P4 MRR Alc.

TREES--NORTH AMERICA--IDENTIFICATION.
Petrides, George A. A field guide to
trees and shrubs; 2d ed. Boston,
Houghton Mifflin, 1972. xxxii, 428
p. [$5.95] 582/.1609/7 76-157132

QK482 .P43 1972 MRR Alc.

TREES--SOUTHERN STATES.
Dean, Blanche Evans. Trees and
shrubs in the heart of Dixie. Rev.
ed. Birmingham, Ala., Southern
University Press, 1968. xvi, 246 p.
[$7.50] 582/.15/0975 68-57837
QK484.S88 D4 1968 MRR Alc.

TREES--UNITED STATES.
Collingwood, George Harris, Knowing
your trees, Washington, American
Forestry Association, 1974. 374 p.
[$7.90] 582/.1609/73 73-83868
QK482 .C27 1974 MRR Alc.

Grimm, William Carey, Home guide to
trees, shrubs, and wild flowers.
[Harrisburg, Pa.] Stackpole Books
[1970] 320 p. [9.95] 582/.09/73
76-100348
QK482 .G734 MRR Alc.

Harlow, William Morehouse, Textbook
of dendrology, covering the important
forest trees of the United States and
Canada 5th ed. New York, McGraw-
Hill [1968] xv, 512 p. 582.16/0973
68-17188
QK481 .H32 1968 MRR Alc.

Little, Elbert Luther, Check list of
native and naturalized trees of the
United States (including Alaska)
Washington, Forest Service, 1953.
472 p. 582.16 581.973* agr53-309
QK481 .L5 MRR Alc.

Marx, David S. A modern American
herbal: useful trees and shrubs.
South Brunswick, A. S. Barnes [1973]
190 p. 582/.1609/73 71-86305
QK482 .M43 MRR Alc.

Peattie, Donald Culross, A natural
history of trees of eastern and
central North America. Boston,
Houghton Mifflin, 1950. xv, 606 p.
582.16 50-10354
QK481 .P4 MRR Alc.

Peattie, Donald Culross, A natural
history of western trees; Boston,
Houghton Mifflin, 1953. xiv, 751 p.
582.16 581.978* 52-5263
QK481 .P42 MRR Alc.

Symonds, George Wellington
Dillingham. The tree identification
book; New York, M. Barrows [1958]
272 p. 582.16084 58-5359
QK482 .S9 1958 MRR Alc.

United States. Dept. of Agriculture.
Trees, Washington, U.S. Govt. Print.
Off. [1949] xiv, 944 p. 634.90973
agr55-2
S21 .A35 1949 MRR Alc.

TREES--UNITED STATES--IDENTIFICATION.
Petrides, George A. A field guide to
trees and shrubs; 2d ed. Boston,
Houghton Mifflin, 1972. xxxii, 428
p. [$5.95] 582/.1609/7 76-157132

QK482 .P43 1972 MRR Alc.

TREES--WEST.
Peattie, Donald Culross, A natural
history of western trees; Boston,
Houghton Mifflin, 1953. xiv, 751 p.
582.16 581.978* 52-5263
QK481 .P42 MRR Alc.

TREES, FLOWERING
see Flowering trees

TRIBES AND TRIBAL SYSTEM.
see also Society, Primitive

TRIESTE--DIRECTORIES.
Guida generale di Trieste e della
Venezia Giulia. Trieste, Stab. tip.
nazionale. 53-32897
"Fondata nel 1894."
DB321 .G85 MRR Alc Latest edition

TRIGONOMETRY--TABLES, ETC.
see also Logarithms

Hof, Hans, Ten place natural
trigonometric tables; 1st ed.
[Jenkintown, Pa., Professional Supply
Co., c1959] 1083 p. 514.083 60-
21564
QA55 .H68 MRR Alc.

TRINIDAD AND TOBAGO--BIOGRAPHY.
Who's who in Canada; Toronto,
International Press Limited. 17-
16282
Began publication in 1910.
F1033 .W62 Sci RR Latest edition /
MRR Biog Latest edition

TROMS, NORWAY--DIRECTORIES.
Adressebok for Troms fylke med
skattelignlnger. Oslo, S. M. Bryde.
53-29107
DL576.T8 A7 MRR Alc Latest edition

TRONDHEIM--DIRECTORIES.
Trondheim adressebok. Trondheim, H.
G. Moe. 53-29105
DL596.T8 T7 MRR Alc Latest edition

TROOPS, LANDING OF
see Amphibious warfare

TROPICAL FISH.
Axelrod, Herbert R. Exotic tropical
fishes Jersey City, T. F. H.
Publications, distributed by Sterling
Pub. Co. [c1962] 1 v. (unpaged)
639.34 63-4310
SH167.T8 A9 MRR Alc.

Axelrod, Herbert R. Handbook of
tropical aquarium fishes New York,
McGraw-Hill [1955] xii, 718 p.
590.74 54-8817
QL78 .A87 MRR Alc.

Innes, William Thornton, Exotic
aquarium fishes; 1st- ed.; 1935-
Norristown, Pa.[etc.] Aquarium Pub.
Co. [etc.] 35-8711
QL78 .I5 Sci RR Latest edition /
MRR Alc Latest edition

TROPICAL PLANTS--PICTORIAL WORKS.
Graf, Alfred Byrd. Exotica, series
3; 6th ed. E. Rutherford, N.J.,
Roehrs Co. [1973] 1834 p. 635.9/65
72-90669
SB407 .G7 1973 MRR Alc.

TRUCK CAMPERS AND COACHES
see Campers and coaches, Truck

TRUCK TRAILERS--DIRECTORIES.
Truck Trailer Manufacturers
Association. T T M A directory.
Washington. 65-87690
HE5616 .T72 MRR Alc Latest edition

TRUMAN, HARRY S., PRES. U.S., 1884-
Steinberg, Alfred, The man from
Missouri; New York, Putnam [1962]
447 p. 923.173 62-8004
E814 .S74 MRR Alc.

Truman, Margaret, Harry S. Truman.
New York, Morrow, 1973 [c1972] 602
p. [$10.95] 973.918/0924 B 73-
170238
E814 .T8 MRR Alc.

**TRUMAN, HARRY S., PRES. U.S., 1884-1972-
-BIBLIOGRAPHY.**
Stapleton, Margaret L. The Truman
and Eisenhower years: 1945-1960;
Metuchen, N.J., Scarecrow Press,
1973. vii, 221 p. 016.973918 73-
1791
Z1245 .S7 MRR Alc.

TRUST COMPANIES--CANADA--DIRECTORIES.
Directory of trust institutions.
[New York] Trusts & Estates.
332.1/78 74-644898
HG4347 .A1 MRR Alc Latest edition

**TRUST COMPANIES--UNITED STATES--
DIRECTORIES.**
Directory of trust institutions.
[New York] Trusts & Estates.
332.1/78 74-644898
HG4347 .A1 MRR Alc Latest edition

TRUSTS, INDUSTRIAL.
see also Corporations

TRUSTS, INDUSTRIAL--LAW.
see also Corporation law

TRUSTS, INDUSTRIAL--AUSTRALIA.
Wheelwright, Edward Lawrence.
Anatomy of Australian manufacturing
industry; Sydney, Law Book Co.,
1967. xvii, 433 p. [$13.99 Aust.]
338.7/4/0994 67-95586
HD2927 .W45 MRR Alc.

**TRUSTS, INDUSTRIAL--GERMANY (FEDERAL
REPUBLIC, 1949-)**
Die Grossen 500 [i.e. Fünfhundert]
1970- Dusseldorf, Droste Verlag.
70-612586
HD2859 .G7 MRR Alc Latest edition

TRUSTS, INDUSTRIAL--JAPAN--DIRECTORIES.
1972 handbook of Japanese
financial/industrial combines; San
Francisco, Pacific Basin Reports
[1972] 83 l. [$25.00]
338.8/5/02552 73-150829
HD2756.J3 N55 MRR Alc.

TRUSTS AND TRUSTEES--DICTIONARIES.
American Bankers Association. Trust
Division. Glossary of fiduciary
terms. [New York, 1959] 52 p.
332.1403 59-34349
HG4485 .A56 MRR Alc.

**TUNISIA--DESCRIPTION AND TRAVEL--GUIDE-
BOOKS.**
Fodor's Tunisia. 1973- New York, D.
McKay. [$8.75] 916.1/1/04505 73-
640761
DT244 .F63 MRR Alc Latest edition

Tunisie. Paris, Hachette, 1967. 328
p. [21.40 F.] 916.1/1/045 68-
74343
DT244 .T8 1967 MRR Alc.

TUNISIA--DIRECTORIES.
Bottin de la Tunisie. 1959- Paris,
Société Didot Bottin. 60-35863
HC547.T8 B6 MRR Alc Latest edition

TUNISIA--GAZETTEERS.
United States. Office of Geography.
Tunisia; official standard names
approved by the United States Board
on Geographic Names. Washington
[U.S. Govt Print. Off.] 1964. xiii,
399 p. 64-62668
DT244 .U5 MRR Alc.

TUNISIA--INDUSTRIES--DIRECTORIES.
Bottin de la Tunisie. 1959- Paris,
Société Didot Bottin. 60-35863
HC547.T8 B6 MRR Alc Latest edition

TURKEY--BIOGRAPHY.
Who's who in Turkey. [1st]- ed.;
1958- Ankara, Cyclopedic
Publications. 920-0561 59-37265
DR592.A1 W5 MRR Biog Latest
edition

TURKEY--COMMERCE--DIRECTORIES.
Regional trade directory: 1968-
382/.025/5 sa 68-5997
HF3883 .R4 MRR Alc Latest edition

TURKEY--DESCRIPTION AND TRAVEL.
Lewis, Geoffrey L. Turkey, 3rd ed.
2nd impression (corrected) London,
Benn, 1966. xix, 21-230 p. [18/-]
956.1 66-69406
DR441 .L45 1966 MRR Alc.

TURKEY--DESCRIPTION AND TRAVEL--1960-
Williams, Gwyn. Turkey: a
traveller's guide and history.
London, Faber, 1967. 318 p. [50/-]
915.61 67-101521
DR429 .W5 MRR Alc.

TURKEY--DESCRIPTION AND TRAVEL--GUIDE-
BOOKS.
Ekvall, David H. Complete guide to
Eastern Europe New York, Hart Pub.
Co. [1970] 562 p. [9.85] 914.3
69-18898
DR7 .E37 MRR Alc.

Fodor's Turkey. 1969- New York, D.
McKay. 915.61 76-3702
DR416 .F62 MRR Alc Latest edition

Pan American World Airways, inc.
Complete reference guide to Greece,
Turkey, and Yugoslavia. [1st ed.]
New York, Trade distribution in the
U.S. and Canada by Simon and
Schuster, 1967] 159 p. 914.9 67-
19409
DF716 .P3 MRR Alc.

Trans-Balkan Highway: Yugoslavia,
Bulgaria, Turkey. Beograd,
Turisticka Stampa; Sofia, Resorts
Magazine [1967] 175 p. [unpriced]
914.96/04 78-391387
GV1025.A2 T7 MRR Alc.

TURKEY--GAZETTEERS.
United States. Office of Geography.
Turkey; official standard names
approved by the United States Board
on Geographic Names. Washington,
1960. iv, 665 p. 915.61 60-61214

DR414 .U5 MRR Alc.

TURKEY--HISTORY.
Lewis, Geoffrey L. Turkey, 3rd ed.
2nd impression (corrected) London,
Benn, 1966. xix, 21-230 p. [18/-]
956.1 66-68406
DR441 .L45 1966 MRR Alc.

Miller, William, The Ottoman Empire
and its successors, 1801-1927: 3rd
ed., new impression. London, Cass,
1966. xv, 616 p. [90/-] 956.101
66-67163
DR557 .M6 1966 MRR Alc.

Williams, Gwyn. Turkey: a
traveller's guide and history.
London, Faber, 1967. 318 p. [50/-]
915.61 67-101521
DR429 .W5 MRR Alc.

TURKEY--HISTORY--1918-1960--
BIBLIOGRAPHY.
Bodurgil, Abraham. Atatürk and
Turkey: Washington, Library of
Congress; [for sale by the Supt. of
Docs., U.S. Govt. Print. Off.] 1974.
74 p. 016.9561 73-18313
Z663.387 .A8 MRR Alc.

TURKEY--HISTORY--1960- --BIBLIOGRAPHY.
Bodurgil, Abraham. Atatürk and
Turkey: Washington, Library of
Congress; [for sale by the Supt. of
Docs., U.S. Govt. Print. Off.] 1974.
74 p. 016.9561 73-18313
Z663.387 .A8 MRR Alc.

TURKEY--HISTORY--BIBLIOGRAPHY.
Koray, Enver. Türkiye tarih
yayınları bibliyggrafyası, 1729-1950.
Ankara, Milli Egitim Basımevi,
1952. 548 p. 52-30135
Z2846 .K6 MRR Alc.

TURKISH LANGUAGE--CONVERSATION AND
PHRASE BOOKS--POLYGLOT.
Lyall, Archibald, A guide to 25
languages of Europe. Rev. ed.
[Harrisburg, Pa.] Stackpole Co.
[1966] viii, 407 p. 413 66-20847

PB73 .L85 1966 MRR Alc.

TURKISH LANGUAGE--DICTIONARIES--ENGLISH.
Hony, H. C. A Turkish-English
dictionary, 2d ed. Oxford,
Clarendon Press, 1957. xi, 419 p.
494.3532 57-1814
PL191 .H6 1957 MRR Alc.

TURKISH LANGUAGE--DICTIONARIES--
POLYGLOT.
Bergman, Peter M. The concise
dictionary of twenty-six languages in
simultaneous translations. New York,
Polyglot Library [1968] 406 p. 413
67-14284
P361 .B4 TJ Rm.

Ouseg, P. L. 21--anguage dictionary.
London, P. Owen [1962] xxxi, 333 p.
63-1285
P361 .O85 1962 MRR Alc.

TURKISH LITERATURE--BIBLIOGRAPHY.
Koray, Enver. Türkiye tarih
yayınları bibliyggrafyası, 1729-1950.
Ankara, Milli Egitim Basımevi,
1952. 548 p. 52-30135
Z2846 .K6 MRR Alc.

TURKISH LITERATURE--BIBLIOGRAPHY--
CATALOGS.
Türkiye biblyografyası, Istanbul,
Devlet matbaası, 1933. 359, ii p.
58-50156
Z2835 .T94 MRR Alc.

TURKISH NEWSPAPERS.
United States. Library of Congress.
European Affairs Division. The
European press today. Washington,
1949. 152 p. 016.07 49-46986
Z663.26 .E84 MRR Alc.

TURKISH PERIODICALS.
United States. Library of Congress.
European Affairs Division. The
European press today. Washington,
1949. 152 p. 016.07 49-46986
Z663.26 .E84 MRR Alc.

TURNER, FREDERICK JACKSON, 1861-1932.
THE FRONTIER IN AMERICAN HISTORY.
Billington, Ray Allen, ed. The
frontier thesis: valid interpretation
of American history? New York, Holt,
Rinehart and Winston [1966] 122 p.
973.01 66-21640
E179.5 .B625 MRR Alc.

TURNING.
see also Woodwork

TURTLES--NORTH AMERICA.
Carr, Archie Fairly, Handbook of
turtles; Ithaca, N.Y., Comstock Pub.
Associates, 1952. xv, 542 p.
598.13 52-9126
QL666.C5 C34 MRR Alc.

TUSKEGEE INSTITUTE.
United States. Library of Congress.
Manuscript Division. Booker T.
Washington: a register of his papers
in the Library of Congress.
Washington, 1958. 105 p. 012 58-
60037
Z663.34 .W3 MRR Alc.

Washington, Booker Taliaferro, Up
from slavery; New York, Dodd, Mead
[1965] 212 p. 923.773 65-21868
E185.97 .W3164 MRR Alc.

TWELVE-TONE SYSTEM.
Wellesz, Egon, The origins of
Schönberg's twelve-tone system;
Washington [U.S. Govt. Print. Off.]
1958. iii, 14 p. 781.22 58-60018

Z663.37 .A5 1957 MRR Alc.

TWENTIETH CENTURY--BIOGRAPHY
see Biography--20th century

TYLER, JOHN, PRES. U.S., 1790-1862.
Seager, Robert, And Tyler too; [1st
ed.] New York, McGraw-Hill [1963]
xvii, 681 p. 923.173 63-14259
E397 .S4 MRR Alc.

Tyler, Lyon Gardiner, The letters
and times of the Tylers. New York,
Da Capo Press, 1970 [c1884-86] 3 v.
973.5/8 71-75267
E397 .T982 MRR Alc.

TYLER, JULIA (GARDINER)
Seager, Robert, And Tyler too; [1st
ed.] New York, McGraw-Hill [1963]
xvii, 681 p. 923.173 63-14259
E397 .S4 MRR Alc.

TYLER FAMILY.
Tyler, Lyon Gardiner, The letters
and times of the Tylers. New York,
Da Capo Press, 1970 [c1884-86] 3 v.
973.5/8 71-75267
E397 .T982 MRR Alc.

TYPE AND TYPE-FOUNDING.
Jaspert, W. Pincus. The
encyclopaedia of type faces [4th
ed., entirely restyled and greatly
enl.] New York, Barnes & Noble
[1970] xiii, 420 p. 686/.224 70-
22018
Z250 .J36 1970 MRR Alc.

Updike, Daniel Berkeley, Printing
types, [3d ed.] Cambridge, Mass.,
Belknap Press, 1962. 2 v. 655.24
62-5866
Z250.A2 U6 1962 MRR Alc.

TYPE AND TYPE-FOUNDING--DICTIONARIES.
Robinson, Leslie John. A dictionary
of graphical symbols London, Avis,
1972. 360 p. [£3.75] 001.56 73-
165683
Z250 .R683 MRR Ref Desk.

TYPE AND TYPE-FOUNDING--DISPLAY TYPE.
Visual Graphics Corporation. The
world-famous photo typositor alphabet
library. New ed. [North Miami,
Fla.] c1973. xi, 270 p. 686.2/24
74-75683
Z250 .V67 1973 MRR Alc.

TYPOGRAPHY
see Printing

TYPOLOGY (THEOLOGY)
Wilson, Walter Lewis, Wilson's
dictionary of Bible types. Grand
Rapids, Eerdmans [c1957] 519 p.
220.6 57-14495
BS477 .W53 MRR Alc.

TYROL--COMMERCE--DIRECTORIES.
Herold Adressbuch von Tirol für
Industrie, Handel, Gewerbe. Wien,
Herold. 72-622311
HF3549.T9 A45 MRR Alc Latest
edition

TYROL, EAST--DIRECTORIES.
Karntner Amts-und Adressbuch mit
Osttirol. Klagenfurt, F. Kleinmayr
[etc.] 914.36/6/0025 74-642466
DB284.7 K33 MRR Alc Latest edition

U.N.
see United Nations

UGANDA.
Herrick, Allison Butler. Area
handbook for Uganda. Washington, For
sale by the Supt. of Docs., U.S.
Govt. Print. Off., 1969. xvi, 456 p.
[3.50] 916.76/1/03 73-601330
DT434.Y2 H4 MRR Alc.

UGANDA--GAZETTEERS.
United States. Office of Geography.
Uganda; official standard names
approved by the United States Board
on Geographic Names. Washington
[1964] iii, 167 p. 64-65500
DT434.U22 U5 MRR Alc.

UGANDA--GOVERNMENT PUBLICATIONS.
United States. Library of Congress.
African Section. Official
publications of British East Africa,
Washington, General Reference and
Bibliography Division, Reference
Dept., Library of Congress, 1960-63.
4 v. 015.676 61-60009
Z663.285 .O3 MRR Alc.

UGANDA--POLITICS AND GOVERNMENT.
Apter, David Ernest, The political
kingdom in Uganda; [2d ed.]
Princeton, N.J., Princeton University
Press [1967] xxii, 498 p.
320.9/676/1 67-18831
DT434.U25 A6 1967 MRR Alc.

UKRAINE--BIBLIOGRAPHY.
United States. Library of Congress.
Selected list of books on the Ukraine
published in English, French, German,
and Italian. Washington, 1941. 1 p.
l., 13 numb. l. 016.91477 44-30793

Z663.99.C6 Y2 MRR Alc.

UKRAINE--DICTIONARIES AND ENCYCLOPEDIAS.
Ukraine; a concise encyclopaedia.
[Toronto] Published for the Ukrainian
National Association, University of
Toronto Press [1963- v. 914.771
63-23686
DK508 .U413 MRR Alc.

UKRAINIAN LANGUAGE--DICTIONARIES--
ENGLISH.
Andrusyshen, C. H. [Ukraïns'ko-
anhliĭs kyĭ slovnyk (romanized
form)] Saskatoon, University of
Saskatchewan, 1955. 1163 p. 55-
34166
PG3891 .A7 MRR Alc.

Podveź'ko, M. L. [Ukraïns'ko-
anhliĭs kyĭ slovnyk (romanized
form)] [n.p.] 1954. 1011 p. 55-
18563
PG3891 .P63 MRR Alc.

UKRAINIAN NEWSPAPERS--BIBLIOGRAPHY.
United States. Library of Congress.
Slavic and Central European Division.
Preliminary checklist of Russian,
Ukrainian, and Belorussian newspapers
published since January 1, 1917,
Washington, 1952. iv, 87 l.
016.077 52-60042
Z663.47 .P7 MRR Alc.

United States. Library of Congress.
Slavic and Central European Division.
Russian, Ukrainian, and Belorussian
newspapers, 1917-1953; Washington,
1953. xi, 218 p. 016.077 54-60001

Z663.47 .R85 MRR Alc.

ULSTER, IRE.--DIRECTORIES.
Belfast and Northern Ireland
directory. Belfast, Century
Newspaper Ltd. [etc.] 53-32016
"First published in May 1852."
DA995.B5 B45 MRR Alc Latest
edition

UNDERDEVELOPED AREAS.
see also Community development

Higgins, Benjamin Howard, Economic
development; Rev. ed. New York, W.
W. Norton [1968] xvi, 918 p. 338.9
67-11081
HD82 .H45 1968 MRR Alc.

UNDERDEVELOPED AREAS--BIBLIOGRAPHY.
International Labor Office. Library.
International labour documentation:
cumulative edition. Boston, Mass.,
G. K. Hall. 72-625702
H91 .I56 MRR Alc Full set

UNDERDEVELOPED AREAS-- (Cont.)
ReQua, Eloise G. The developing
nations; Detroit, Gale Research Co.
[1965] 339 p. 016.33891 65-17576

Z7164.U5 R4 MRR Alc.

UNDERDEVELOPED AREAS--COMMERCE.
Lary, Hal Buckner. Imports of
manufactures from less developed
countries New York, National Bureau
of Economic Research; distributed by
Columbia University Press, 1968.
xvii, 286 p. 382/.09172/401722 67-
28434
HF1411 .L36 MRR Alc.

United Nations. Conference on Trade
and Development. Secretariat. Trade
prospects and capital needs of
developing countries; New York,
United Nations, 1968. ix, 614 p.
[8.00] 382/.09172/3 75-5913
HF1413 .U52 MRR Alc.

**UNDERDEVELOPED AREAS--EDUCATION--
DIRECTORIES.**
American Council on Education.
Overseas Liaison Committee.
International directory for
educational liaison. Washington
[1972, c1973] xxii, 474 p.
378/.006/21 72-92152
L900 .A47 1973 MRR Alc.

UNDERDEVELOPED AREAS--FINANCE.
Nyhart, J. Daniel. A global
directory of development finance
institutions in developing countries
Paris, Development Centre of the
Organisation for Economic Cooperation and Development, 1967. x,
453 p. [30.00] 332.1/025/1724 76-
386819
HG4517 .N82 1967b MRR Alc.

Organization for Economic Cooperation
and Development. Geographical
distribution of financial flows to
less developed countries
(disbursement) 1960-1964. Paris,
O.E.C.D.; [London, H.M.S.O.] 1966.
xvi, 179 p. [24/-] 338.91 67-
78951
HC60 .O65 MRR Alc.

United Nations. Conference on Trade
and Development. Secretariat. Trade
prospects and capital needs of
developing countries; New York,
United Nations, 1968. ix, 614 p.
[8.00] 382/.09172/3 75-5913
HF1413 .U52 MRR Alc.

**UNDERDEVELOPED AREAS--POLITICS AND
GOVERNMENT--BIBLIOGRAPHY.**
Spitz, Allan A. Developmental
change; an annotated bibliography,
Lexington, University Press of
Kentucky [1969] xi, 316 p. [12.50]
016.309 69-19766
Z7164.E15 S615 MRR Alc.

**UNDERDEVELOPED AREAS--SOCIAL CONDITIONS-
-BIBLIOGRAPHY.**
Brode, John. The process of
modernization; Cambridge, Mass.,
Harvard University Press, 1969. x,
378 p. [6.50] 016.3092 69-13765
Z7164.U5 B7 MRR Alc.

UNDERDEVELOPED AREAS--SOCIETIES, ETC.
OECD-ICVA directory; Paris, OECD,
1967. 1378 p. [90.00] 309.2/062
68-82889
HC60 .O2 TJ Rm.

**UNDERDEVELOPED AREAS--URBANIZATION--
BIBLIOGRAPHY.**
Brunn, Stanley D. Urbanization in
developing countries; East Lansing,
Latin American Studies Center,
Michigan State University, 1971.
xviii, 693 p. 016.30136/3/091724
79-172535
Z7164.U7 B7 MRR Alc.

UNDERGROUND PRESS--UNITED STATES.
Glessing, Robert J. The underground
press in America, Bloomington,
Indiana, University Press [1970]
xvi, 207 p. [6.50] 071/.3 71-
126209
PN4888.U5 G5 MRR Alc.

Leamer, Laurence. The paper
revolutionaries; New York, Simon and
Schuster [1972] 220 p. [$8.95]
071/.3 73-188751
PN4888.U5 L4 MRR Alc.

Muller, Robert H. From radical left
to extreme right; 2d ed. rev. and
enl. Ann Arbor, Campus Publishers
[c1970- v. 79-126558
Z7165.U5 M82 MRR Ref Desk.

Northwestern University, Evanston,
Ill. Library. Special Collections
Dept. Guide to underground
newspapers in the Special Collections
Department. Evanston, Northwestern
University Library, 1971. 60 p.
016.071/3 73-180306
Z6951 .N9 1971 MRR Ref Desk.

**UNDERGROUND PRESS--UNITED STATES--
DIRECTORIES.**
Glessing, Robert J. The underground
press in America, Bloomington,
Indiana, University Press [1970]
xvi, 207 p. [6.50] 071/.3 71-
126209
PN4888.U5 G5 MRR Alc.

UNDERPRIVILEGED CHILDREN
see Socially handicapped children

**UNDERTAKERS AND UNDERTAKING--UNITED
STATES--DIRECTORIES.**
Habenstein, Robert Wesley. Funeral
customs the world over [1st ed.]
Milwaukee, Bulfin Printers, 1960.
973 p. 393 60-53002
GT3150 .H28 MRR Alc.

The National directory of morticians.
Youngstown, Ohio. 53-31440
RA622.A7 N37 MRR Alc Latest
edition

UNDERWATER ARCHAEOLOGY.
Fleming, Robert M. A primer of
shipwreck research and records for
skin divers, Milwaukee, Wis., Global
MFG. Corp. [1971] 73 p. [$2.75]
910.4/53 75-25624
VK1250 .F55 MRR Alc.

UNDERWATER EXPLORATION.
see also Marine biology

UNDERWRITING
see Insurance

see Securities

UNEMPLOYED--UNITED STATES.
United States. President. Manpower
report of the President, and a Report
on manpower requirements, resources,
utilization, and training, by the
U.S. Dept. of Labor. 1963-
[Washington, for sale by the
Superintendent of Documents, U.S.
Govt. Print. Off.] 1 63-45
HD5723 .A43 MRR Alc Latest edition

Wolfbein, Seymour Louis. Employment
and unemployment in the United
States; Chicago, Science Research
Associates [1964] 339 p.
331.1120973 64-12588
HD5724 .W6 MRR Alc.

UNFINISHED BOOKS--BIBLIOGRAPHY.
Corns, Albert Reginald. A
bibliography of unfinished books in
the English language, New York, B.
Franklin [1969] xvi, 255 p. 011
69-17931
Z1033.U6 C7 1969 MRR Alc.

Walbridge, Earle Francis. Literary
characters drawn from life; New
York, H. W. Wilson Co., 1936. 192 p.
098.5 36-10273
Z1026 .W15 MRR Alc.

UNICAMERAL LEGISLATURES
see Legislative bodies

UNIFORMS.
see also Costume

Blakeslee, Fred Gilbert. Uniforms of
the world, New York, E. P. Dutton &
company, inc. [c1929] xxii, 449 p.
29-10410
UC480 .B65 MRR Alc.

UNIFORMS, CIVIL.
Blakeslee, Fred Gilbert. Uniforms of
the world, New York, E. P. Dutton &
company, inc. [c1929] xxii, 449 p.
29-10410
UC480 .B65 MRR Alc.

UNIFORMS, MILITARY.
Blakeslee, Fred Gilbert. Uniforms of
the world, New York, E. P. Dutton &
company, inc. [c1929] xxii, 449 p.
29-10410
UC480 .B65 MRR Alc.

Carman, W. Y. British military
uniforms from contemporary pictures:
Henry VII to the present day [1st
ed. reprinted]. Feltham, Spring
Books, 1968. iii-xix, 168 p. [35/-]
355.1/4/0942 75-386810
UC485.G7 C3 1968 MRR Alc.

Confederate States of America. War
Dept. Uniform and dress of the Army
and Navy of the Confederate States of
America. [Rev. ed,] Philadelphia,
R. Riling, 1960. [2] p., [4] p.
973.784 60-16421
UC483.5 .A223 MRR Alc.

Kannik, Preben. Military uniforms in
colour; London, Blandford P., 1968.
278 p. [30/-] 355.1/4/09 68-
107829
UC480 .K313 1968b MRR Alc.

Kredel, Fritz, illus. Soldiers of
the American Army, 1775-1954. [Rev.
ed.] Chicago, H. Regnery Co. [1954]
1 v. (unpaged) 355.14 54-13348
UC483 .K7 1954 MRR Alc.

Melegari, Vezio. The world's great
regiments. 1st American ed. New
York] Putnam [1969, c1968] 256 p.
[25.00] 355.3/5/09 69-15079
UA15 .M4413 1969b MRR Alc.

Mollo, John. Military fashion; New
York, Putnam [1972] 240 p. [$25.00]
355.1/4/094 76-188665
UC480 .M65 1972b MRR Alc.

Tily, James C. The uniforms of the
United States Navy. New York, T.
Yoseloff [1964] 338 p. 359.140973
63-18235
VC303 .T5 MRR Alc.

UNION POSTALE UNIVERSELLE.
Codding, George Arthur. The
Universal Postal Union, [New York]
New York University Press, 1964. ix,
296 p. 383.4 64-11670
HE6261 .C6 MRR Alc.

UNIONS, TRADE
see Trade-unions

UNITARIAN CHURCHES--DIRECTORIES.
Unitarian Universalist Association.
Directory. 1961/62- Boston. 62-
5422
BX9811 .U45 MRR Alc Latest edition

UNITED CHURCH OF CANADA--YEARBOOKS.
United Church of Canada. Year book.
Toronto. 280 38-37878
BX9881 .A16 MRR Alc Latest edition

UNITED NATIONS--REGISTERS.
United Nations. Permanent missions
to the United Nations. New York.
341.13 51-35159
JX1877.A2 MRR Ref Desk Latest
edition

UNITED NATIONS.
Coyle, David Cushman. The United
Nations and how it works. Rev. ed.,
with a foreword New York, Columbia
University Press, 1969. 256 p.
[7.50] 341.13 77-6959
JX1977 .C65 1969b MRR Alc.

Everyman's United Nations. [1st]-
ed.; 1948- New York, United Nations
Dept. of Public Information [etc.]
341.13 48-10196
JX1977.A37 E9 MRR Ref Desk Latest
edition

Goodspeed, Stephen S. The nature and
function of international
organization 2d ed. New York,
Oxford University Press, 1967. xii,
733 p. 341.1/1 67-10856
JX1954 .G62 1967 MRR Alc.

Gross, Franz B., ed. The United
States and the United Nations,
Norman, University of Oklahoma Press
[1964] x, 356 p. 341.13973 64-
20766
JX1977.2.U5 G7 MRR Alc.

Harley, John Eugene. Documentary
textbook on the United Nations; 2d
ed., rev. and enl. Los Angeles,
Auspices of the Center for
International Understanding [1950]
xxvii, 1470 p. 341.1 50-10302
JX1977 .H3 1950 MRR Alc.

International organisation and
integration. Deventer, A. E. Kluwer;
Leiden, A. W. Sijthoff, 1968 [1969]
xxvi, 1146 p. [67.30] 341.13 68-
25399
JX171 .I54 MRR Alc.

Prosser, Michael H., comp. Sow the
wind, reap the whirlwind; New York,
Morrow, 1970. 2 v. (xviii, 1467 p.)
[$100.00] 341.1/08 73-118271
JX1977 .P728 MRR Alc.

United Nations. Office of Public
Information. Basic facts about the
United Nations. May 15, 1947- New
York [etc.] 341.3 48-13440
JX1977.A37 B3 MRR Ref Desk Latest
edition

Vincent, Jack Ernest. A handbook of
the United Nations, Woodbury, N.Y.,
Barron's Educational Series, Inc.
[1969] ix, 211 p. [1.95] 341.13
68-8680
JX1977 .V48 MRR Alc.

Worldmark encyclopedia of the
nations. [4th ed.] New York,
Worldmark Press, [1971] 5 v.
910/.3 76-152128
G103 .W65 1971 MRR Ref Desk.

UNITED NATIONS--ARMED FORCES.
Bowett, D. W. United Nations forces;
New York, Praeger [1964] xxiv, 579
p. 341.65 64-22489
JX1981.P7 B68 1964a MRR Alc.

UNITED NATIONS--ARMED FORCES. (Cont.)
Higgins, Rosalyn. United Nations
peacekeeping, 1946-1967: London, New
York [etc.] issued under the auspices
of the Royal Institute of
International Affairs by Oxford U.P.,
1969- v.   [5/10- (v. 1)]   341.6
76-386893
  JX1981.P7 H5 MRR Alc.

Wainhouse, David Walter,
International peace observation;
Baltimore, Johns Hopkins Press, 1966.
xvii, 663 p.   341.11   66-14376
  JX1981.P7 W25 MRR Alc.

UNITED NATIONS--ARMED FORCES--
BIBLIOGRAPHY.
Legault, Albert. Peace-keeping
operations. Paris, International
Information Center on Peace-Keeping
Operations, 1967. 204 p. [25 F]
016.3553/57 68-108496
  JX1981.P7 L43 MRR Alc.

UNITED NATIONS--BIBLIOGRAPHY.
Brimmer, Brenda. A guide to the use
of United Nations documents Dobbs
Ferry, N.Y., Oceana Publications,
1962. xv, 272 p.   025.173 63-3667

  Z674 .B7 1962a MRR Alc.

Dimitrov, Théodore Delchev.
Documents of international
organisations: London, International
University Publications; Chicago,
American Library Association, 1973.
xv, 301 p.   016.05 73-175089
  Z6481 .D56 MRR Alc.

United Nations. UNDEX: United
Nations documents index. Series C:
list of documents issued. v. 1-
Jan. 1974- New York. [$80.00]
016.34123 74-645418
  JX1977 .A2 subser MRR Alc Full set

UNITED NATIONS--BIBLIOGRAPHY--CATALOGS.
United Nations. Office of Conference
Services. United Nations official
records. 1948-1962; New York, United
Nations, 1963. 107 p.   64-6035
  Z6485 .U53 MRR Alc.

United Nations. Office of Conference
Services. United Nations
publications, 1945-1963, New York,
United Nations, 1964. v, 71 p.   64-
57021
  Z6485 .U46 MRR Alc.

UNITED NATIONS--COLLECTIONS.
Cordier, Andrew Wellington, comp.
Public papers of the Secretaries-
General of the United Nations. New
York, Columbia University Press, 1969-
v.   [12.50 (v. 1)]   341.13/08
68-8873
  JX1977 .C62 MRR Alc.

UNITED NATIONS--HISTORY.
Chamberlin, Waldo, A chronology and
fact book of the United Nations, 1941-
1969 Dobbs Ferry, N.Y., Oceana
Publications, 1970. 234 p.   341/.23
73-127323
  JX1977 .C4822 MRR alc.

Russell, Ruth B. A history of the
United Nations Charter; Washington,
Brookings Institution [1958] xviii,
1140 p.   341.132* 58-14016
  JX1976 .R8 MRR Alc.

UNITED NATIONS--YEARBOOKS.
Annual review of United Nations
affairs. 1949- Dobbs Ferry, N.Y.
[etc.] Oceana Publications [etc.]
341.13058 50-548
  JX1977.A1 A5 MRR Alc Partial set

United Nations. Yearbook. 1946/47-
New York [etc.]   47-7191
  JX1977.A37 Y4 MRR Ref Desk Latest
edition

UNITED NATIONS--UNITED STATES.
Gross, Franz B., ed. The United
States and the United Nations,
Norman, University of Oklahoma Press
[1964] x, 356 p. 341.13873 64-
20766
  JX1977.2.U5 G7 MRR Alc.

Russell, Ruth B. A history of the
United Nations Charter; Washington,
Brookings Institution [1958] xviii,
1140 p. 341.132* 58-14016
  JX1976 .R8 MRR Alc.

UNITED NATIONS. CHARTER.
Russell, Ruth P. A history of the
United Nations Charter; Washington,
Brookings Institution [1958] xviii,
1140 p. 341.132* 58-14016
  JX1976 .R8 MRR Alc.

UNITED NATIONS. DAG HAMMARSKJOLD
LIBRARY.
Dale, Doris Cruger. The United
Nations Library; Chicago, American
Library Association, 1970. xvi, 236
p. [$10.00] 027.6/8 74-132060
  Z733.U45 D3 MRR Alc.

UNITED NATIONS. ECONOMIC AND SOCIAL
COUNCIL. OFFICIAL RECORDS--INDEXES.
Deardorff, John, United Nations
Economic and Social Council index;
Columbus] United Nations Collection,
O.S.U. Libraries, 1969. vii, 170 l.
330/.061/1 79-628081
  HC59 .D425 MRR Alc.

UNITED NATIONS EDUCATIONAL, SCIENTIFIC
AND CULTURAL ORGANIZATION--BIBLIOGRAPHY.
United Nations Educational,
Scientific and Cultural
Organization. Catalogue général
des publications de l'Unesco et des
publications parues sous les auspices
de l'Unesco. 1946/59- [Paris] 62-
2114
  Z6483 .U5A4 MRR Alc Full set

United Nations Educational,
Scientific and Cultural Organization.
Catalogue général des publications
de l'Unesco et des publications
parues sous les auspices de l'Unesco.
Supplement. 1960/63- [Paris] 74-
643554
  Z6483 .U5A42 MRR Alc Full set

UNITED PRESBYTERIAN CHURCH IN THE
UNITED STATES--YEARBOOKS.
United Presbyterian Church in the
U.S.A. General Assembly. Minutes.
New ser. v. 1-23, 1870-1900; ser. [2]
v. 1-21, 1901-21; ser. 3, v. 1-17,
1922-38; ser. 4, v. 1-13, 1939-1951;
ser 5, v. 1-6, 1952-57; ser. 6, v. 1-
1958- Philadelphia [etc.] 285.1
59-48588
  BX8951.A4 MRR Alc Latest edition*

UNITED STATES.
Fadiman, Clifton, ed. The American
treasury, 1455-1955, [1st ed.] New
York, Harper [1955] 1108 p.   810.82
55-8019
  PS509.H5 F3 MRR Ref Desk.

UNITED STATES--ADMINISTRATIVE AND
POLITICAL DIVISIONS.
United States. Bureau of the Census.
1967 census of governments.
[Washington, For sale by the Supt. of
Docs., U.S. Govt. Print. Off., 1968-
v. in 353.000021/2 a 68-7201
  JS3.A257 MRR Alc.

United States. Bureau of the Census.
1972 census of governments.
[Washington, U.S. Govt. Print. Off.]
1973- v.   [$1.25 (v. 2, pt. 1)
varies] 317.3 73-600080
  JS3 .A244 MRR Alc.

UNITED STATES--ALTITUDES.
Douglas, Edward Morehouse,
Boundaries, areas, geographic centers
and altitudes of the United States
and several states, 2d ed.
Washington, U.S. Govt. print. off.,
1930. vii, 265 p. incl. illus.,
maps, tables.   gs 30-275
  E179.5 .D73 1930 MRR Ref Desk.

Gannett, Henry, A dictionary of
altitudes in the United States. (4th
ed.) Washington, Govt. print. off.,
1906. 1072, ii p.   gs 06-397
  GB494 .G3 1906 MRR Alc.

UNITED STATES--ANTIQUITIES.
Carlisle, Norman V., The complete
guide to treasure hunting Chicago,
H. Regnery Co. [1973] 280 p.
917.3/04 73-6452
  E159.5 .C37 MRR Alc.

Griffin, James Bennett, ed.
Archeology of eastern United States.
[Chicago] University of Chicago Press
[1952] x, 392 p. 913.73 973.1* 52-
14698
  E53 .G7 MRR Alc.

Willey, Gordon Randolph, A history
of American archaeology San
Francisco, W. H. Freeman [1974] 252
p. 913/.031 73-17493
  E61 .W67 1974b MRR Alc.

UNITED STATES--ANTIQUITIES--
BIBLIOGRAPHY.
Hammond, Philip C. Archaeological
techniques for amateurs. Princeton,
N.J., Van Nostrand [1963] 329 p.
913.018 63-4293
  CC75 .H3 MRR Alc.

UNITED STATES--ANTIQUITIES--DIRECTORIES.
Hammond, Philip C. Archaeological
techniques for amateurs. Princeton,
N.J., Van Nostrand [1963] 329 p.
913.018 63-4293
  CC75 .H3 MRR Alc.

UNITED STATES--APPROPRIATIONS AND
EXPENDITURES.
Brown, William James, The Federal
budgeting and appropriations process,
New York, Dept. of Economics and
Research, American Bankers
Association [1967] xi, 50 p.
353.007/22 67-8435
  HJ2050 .B7 MRR Alc.

United States. Congress.
Appropriations, budget estimates,
etc. Statements. Washington, U.S.
Govt. Print Off. 07-1777
  HJ10.B6 MRR Alc Latest edition

United States. Office of Management
and Budget. The budget of the United
States Government. 1971/72-
[Washington,For sale by the Supt. of
Docs., U.S. Govt. Print. Off.]
353.007/22 70-611049
  HJ2051 .A59 MRR Ref Desk Latest
edition

United States. Office of Management
and Budget. The Budget of the United
States Government. Appendix. 1971/72-
[Washington, For sale by the Supt.
of Docs., U.S. Govt. Print. Off.]
353.007/22 74-643523
  HJ2051 .A59 Suppl. MRR Ref Desk
Latest Edition

United States. Treasury Dept. Bureau
of Accounts. Combined statement of
receipts, expenditures and balances
of the United States government.
1871/72- Washington. 10-11510
  HJ10 .A6 MRR Alc Latest edition

Wallace, Robert Ash, Congressional
control of Federal spending.
Detroit, Wayne State University
Press, 1960. x, 188 p.   328.341 60-
16509
  HJ2052 .W3 MRR Alc.

UNITED STATES--ARMED FORCES--
ABBREVIATIONS.
White, Donald R. J. A glossary of
acronyms, abbreviations, and symbols,
1st ed. Germantown, Md., Don White
Consultants [1971] ix, 235 p.
620/.001/48 72-138444
  T8 .W55 MRR Alc.

UNITED STATES--ARMED FORCES--BIOGRAPHY.
Allen, Mary Moore. Origin of names
of Army and Air Corps posts, camps,
and stations in World War II in
United States. Goldsboro, N.C.
[19582] 352 p.   59-1054
  UA26.A6 A4 MRR Alc.

Generals of the Army and the Air
Force and admirals of the Navy. v. 1-
3; Feb. 1953-Jan. 1956. [Washington]
923.573 56-23963
  U52 .G4 MRR Alc Full set

UNITED STATES--ARMED FORCES--HANDBOOKS,
MANUALS, ETC.
Bunkley, Joel William, Military and
naval recognition book; 2d ed. New
York, D. Van Nostrand company, inc.,
1942. xiv, 309 p. incl. col. front.,
illus. (part col.) 355.14 42-24955

  UC530 .B8 1942a MRR Alc.

UNITED STATES--ARMED FORCES--MEDALS,
BADGES, DECORATIONS, ETC.
Blakeney, Jane, Heroes, U.S. Marine
Corps, 1861-1955; [1st ed.]
Washington, 1957] xviii, 621 p.
359.96 57-13185
  VE23 .B56 MRR Biog.

Kerrigan, Evans E. American badges
and insignia, New York, Viking Press
[1967] xvii, 286 p. 355.1/34 67-
13505
  UC533 .K45 MRR Alc.

UNITED STATES--ARMED FORCES--MEDICAL
EXAMINATIONS.
Forster, Frank. The new 1972-73
draft; New York, Lancer Books [1972]
205 p. [$1.25] 355.2/236 72-
188366
  UB333 .F67 1972 MRR Alc.

UNITED STATES--ARMED FORCES--MILITARY
LIFE.
McCandless, Bruce. Service
etiquette; 2d ed. Annapolis, Md.,
United States Naval Institute [1963]
447 p. 355.13 63-13586
  U766 .M2 1963 MRR Alc.

UNITED STATES--ARMED FORCES--NEGROES.
Greene, Robert Ewell, Black
defenders of America, 1775-1973.
Chicago, Johnson Pub. Co., 1974. 416
p. 355.1 73-15607
  E185.63 .G73 MRR Alc.

Johnson, Jesse J., Black armed
forces officers, 1736-1971 Hampton,
Va., Distributed by J. J. Johnson
[c1971] x, 168 p. 355.3/32/0922
75-178014
  E185.63 .J62 MRR Alc.

Lee, Irvin H. Negro Medal of Honor
men, 3d ed.; new and enl. New York,
Dodd, Mead [1969] xii, 156 p.
[4.50] 355.1/34 68-58447
  UB433 .L4 1969 MRR Alc.

UNITED STATES--ARMED FORCES-- (Cont.)
Lee, Ulysses Grant. The employment
of Negro troops. Washington, Office
of the Chief of Military History,
United States Army; [for sale by the
Superintendent of Documents, U.S.
Govt. Print. Off.] 1966. xix, 740 p.
940.5403 66-60003
D810.N4 L4 MRR Alc.

UNITED STATES--ARMED FORCES--
PROCUREMENT.
Military market facts. [Washington]
Army Times Pub. Co. 65-5288
UC263 .M46 MRR Alc Latest edition

UNITED STATES--ARMED FORCES--STATISTICS.
Inter-University Seminar on Armed
Forces and Society. Handbook of
military institutions. Beverly
Hills, Calif., Sage Publications
[1971] 607 p. 301.5/98 78-127989

U102 .I65 MRR Alc.

Military market facts. [Washington]
Army Times Pub. Co. 65-5288
UC263 .M46 MRR Alc Latest edition

UNITED STATES--ARMED FORCES--YEARBOOKS.
Uniformed services almanac.
Washington. 59-28845
U9 .U5 MRR Alc Latest edition

UNITED STATES--BIBLIOGRAPHY.
The American catalogue ... New York,
1941. 8 v. in 13. 015.73 a 42-
2938
Z1215 .A52 MRR Ref Desk.

American Studies Association.
Committee on Microfilm Bibliography.
Bibliography of American culture,
1493-1875. Ann Arbor, Mich.,
University Microfilms, 1957. xvi,
228 p. 016.9173 57-4827
Z1215 .A585 MRR Alc.

American Studies Association.
Metropolitan New York Chapter.
Committee on Bibliography. Articles
in American studies, 1954-1968; Ann
Arbor, Mich., Pierian Press, 1972. 2
v. (x, 898 p.) 016.9173/03/45 71-
172769
Z1361.C6 A44 MRR Alc.

Fingerhut, Eugene R. The Fingerhut
guide: sources in American history
Santa Barbara, Calif., American
Bibliographical Center - Clio Press
[1973] xii, 148 p. 016.0169173/03
72-95266
Z1215.A2 F55 MRR Alc.

Gohdes, Clarence Louis Frank,
Bibliographical guide to the study of
the literature of the U.S.A. 3d ed.,
rev. and enl. Durham, N.C., Duke
University Press, 1970. x, 134 p.
[5.00] 016.81 79-110576
Z1225 .G6 1970 MRR Alc.

Historical records survey. American
imprints inventory. Washington,
D.C., [etc.] The Historical records
survey, 1937- v. 015.73 38-
6329
Z1215 .H67 MRR Alc.

Howes, Wright. U.S.iana, 1650-1950;
Rev. and enl. [i.e. 2d] ed. New
York, Bowker for the Newberry
Library, 1962. 652 p. 016.873 62-
10988
Z1215 .H75 1962 MRR Alc.

Rader, Jesse Lee, South of forty,
[1st ed.] Norman, Univ. of Oklahoma
Press, 1947. xi, 336 p. 016.876
47-5360
Z1251.S83 E3 MRR Alc.

United States. Library of Congress.
European Affairs Division.
Political, economic and social
writings in postwar Finland;
[Washington, 1952] vi, 41 p. 016.3
52-60040
Z663.26 .P58 MRR Alc.

United States. Library of Congress.
General Reference and Bibliography
Division. American history and
civilization; a list of guides 2d
(rev.) ed. Washington, 1951. 18 p.
016.016873 51-60033
Z663.28 .A64 1951 MRR Alc.

United States. Library of Congress.
General Reference and Bibliography
Division. A guide to the study of
the United States of America;
Washington, 1960. xv, 1193 p.
016.9173 60-60009
Z1215 .U53 MRR Alc.

United States. Treaties, etc.
Treaties and other international acts
of the United States of America.
Volume 1 (short print) Washington,
U.S. Govt. print. off., 1931. x, 201
p. 016.341273 31-28544
JX236 1931 MRR Alc.

The United States catalog: 3d ed.
Minneapolis, New York, The H. W.
Wilson company, 1912. 3 p. l., 2837
p. 12-35572
Z1215 .U6 1912a MRR Ref Desk (Alc.
6)

The United States catalog:
Minneapolis, H. W. Wilson [1900] 2
pt. in 1 v. 01-29127
Z1215 .U58 MRR Ref Desk.

The United States catalog; books in
print 1902. 2d ed. Minneapolis, The
H. W. Wilson co., 1903. 2 p. l.,
2150 p. 03-28279
Z1215 .U6 1903 MRR Ref Desk.

Writers' program. Catalogue, WPA
Writers' program publications, the
American guide series, the American
life series. [Washington, U.S. Govt.
print. off., 1942] 1 p. l., 54 p.
016.9173 42-37616
Z1236 .W75 MRR Alc.

UNITED STATES--BIBLIOGRAPHY--CATALOGS.
California. University. Institute of
Governmental Studies. Library.
Subject catalog of the Institute of
Governmental Studies Library,
University of California, Berkeley.
Boston, G. K. Hall, 1970 [pref. 1971]
26 v. 016.353 73-152341
Z7164.A2 C34 MRR Alc (Dk 33)

UNITED STATES--BIBLIOGRAPHY--
PERIODICALS.
The United States quarterly book
review. v. 1-12, no. 2; Mar. 1945-
June 1956. [Denver etc.] Swallow
Press [etc.] 015.73 48-46511
Z663 .A6 MRR Alc MRR Alc Full set

UNITED STATES--BIO-BIBLIOGRAPHY.
Contemporary authors; 1st revision.
Detroit, Gale Research Co. [1967- v.
810.9/005/2 67-9634
Z1224 .C59 MRR Biog.

Contemporary authors; v. 1- 1962-
Detroit, Gale Research. 928.1 62-
52046
Z1224 .C6 MRR Biog Full set

Duyckinck, Evert Augustus,
Cyclopedia of American literature,
Detroit, Gale Research Co., Book
Tower, 1965. 2 v. 66-31801
PS85 .D7 1965 MRR Biog.

Kirk, John Foster, A supplement to
Allibone's critical dictionary of
English literature and British and
American authors. Detroit, Gale
Research Co., 1965. 2 v. (x, 1562
p.) 820.3 67-286
Z1224 .A44 1891a MRR Biog.

Who's who among North American
authors. [1921]- Los Angeles,
Golden Syndicate Pub. Co. 22-1965
Z1124 .W62 MRR Biog Latest edition

UNITED STATES--BIOGRAPHY.
Acton, Jay. Mug shots; who's who in
the new earth. New York, World Pub.
[1972] 244 p. [$9.95] 920./073
77-174672
CT220 .A27 1972 MRR Biog.

Adams, Russell L. Great Negroes,
past and present. 3d ed. Chicago,
Afro-Am Pub. Co., 1969. ix, 212 p.
920 72-87924
E186.96 .A4 1969 MRR Biog.

Addis, Raymond E. Re-introducing our
signers of the Declaration of
independence. Holly, Mich., The
Holly herald [c1940] 132 p.
978.313 40-36029
E221 .A45 MRR Alc.

American biographical encyclopedia:
Phoenix, Ariz., P. W. Pollock [1967-
v. 920.073 68-1722
CT220 .A53 MRR Biog.

American biographies; Washington
[1950- v. 920.073 51-372
CT220 .A55 MRR Biog.

The American Catholic who's who.
1911- Grosse Point, Mich. [etc.] W.
Romig [etc.] 11-10944
E184.C3 A6 MRR Biog Latest edition

American directory of obstetricians
and gynecologists. 1st- ed.;
1954/55- Knoxville, Tenn., Joe T.
Smith. 614.24 55-27820
RG32 .A5 Sci RR Latest edition /
MRR Biog Latest edition

American Marketing Association.
Membership roster. Chicago.
338.4/06/273 72-626734
HF5415.A2 A57 MRR Alc Latest
edition

Barnes, Calvin Rankin, The General
Convention: offices and officers,
1785-1950. Philadelphia, Church
Historical Society [1951] vi, 148 p.
283.73 51-10469
BX5820 .A4B3 MRR Biog.

Barzman, Sol. Madmen and geniuses :
Chicago : Follett, [1974] xi, 335 p.
: [$8.95] 973/.0992 B 74-78583
E176 .B28 MRR Alc.

Billias, George Athan, ed. George
Washington's generals. New York, W.
Morrow, 1964. xvii, 327 p. 973.33
64-12038
E206 .B5 MRR Biog.

Blakeney, Jane. Heroes, U.S. Marine
Corps, 1861-1955; [1st ed.]
Washington, 1957] xviii, 621 p.
359.96 57-13185
VE23 .B56 MRR Biog.

Burke, Joan Martin. Civil rights;
2d ed. New York, Bowker, 1974. xi,
266 p. 323.4/025/73 74-4053
JC599.U5 B85 1974 MRR Alc.

Callahan, Edward William, ed. List
of officers of the Navy of the United
States and of the Marine Corps from
1775 to 1900; New York, Haskell
House, 1969. 749 p. 359.3/3/20973
68-31274
V11.U7 C2 1969 MRR Biog.

Christmas, Walter, ed. Negroes in
public affairs and government. [1st
ed.] Yonkers [N.Y.] Educational
Heritage [1966- v. 920.073 67-
31903
E185.96 .C47 MRR Biog.

Congressional staff directory. [1st]-
ed.; 1959- Washington [etc.]
328.738 59-13987
JK1012 MRR Ref Desk Latest edition
/ Sci RR Latest edition

Cournos, John. Famous modern
American novelists. New York, Dodd,
Mead, 1952. 181 p. 928.1 52-7209

PS128 .C65 MRR Biog.

Douth, George. Leaders in profile:
the United States Senate. 1972-
ed. New York, Sperr & Douth. [etc.]
328/.73/0922 [B] 77-188152
JK1154 .D68 MRR Biog Latest
edition

Dun and Bradstreet, inc. Dun's
reference book of corporate
managements. 1st- ed.; 1967- New
York. 658.1/145/02573 68-44776
HD2745 .D85 MRR Ref Desk Latest
edition

Duyckinck, Evert Augustus,
Cyclopedia of American literature,
Detroit, Gale Research Co., Book
Tower, 1965. 2 v. 66-31801
PS85 .D7 1965 MRR Biog.

Eminent Americans. [1st]- ed.;
1936- Palo Alto, Calif. [etc.] C. W.
Taylor. 920.073 36-9539
E176 .E55 MRR Biog Latest edition

Engelbarts, Rudolf. Women in the
United States Congress, 1917-1972:
Littleton, Colo., Libraries
Unlimited, 1974. 184 p.
328.73/092/2 73-93278
JK1030.A2 E5 MRR Biog.

Ewen, David, Great men of American
popular song; Englewood Cliffs,
N.J., Prentice-Hall [1970] x, 387 p.
[12.95] 784/.0922 79-110079
ML3551 .E83 MRR Alc.

Failor, Kenneth M. Medals of the
United States Mint, [Washington; For
sale by the Supt. of Docs., U.S.
Govt. Print. Off., 1969] v, 274 p.
[3.50] 928.6 74-602460
CJ5805 .F3 MRR Alc

Flynn, James J. Negroes of
achievement in modern America, New
York, Dodd, Mead [1970] 272 p.
[4.50] 920.009174/96 70-111911
E185.96 .F55 MRR Biog.

Foreign Area Fellowship Program.
Directory, foreign area fellows.
[1st]- ed.; 1952/59- New York.
378.35 63-12636
CT83 .F6 MRR Biog Latest edition

Friedman, Leon, comp. The justices
of the United States Supreme Court,
1789-1969. New York, Chelsea House
in association with Bowker, 1969. 4
v. (xxiv, 3373 p.) 347.99/22 69-
13699
KF8744 .F75 MRR Alc.

Gentry, Linnell. A history and
encyclopedia of country, western, and
gospel music. 2d ed., completely
rev. [Nashville, Tenn., Clairmont
Corp., 1969] xiv, 598 p.
784.4/9/73 70-7208
ML200 .G4 1969 MRR Biog.

Hunter, John Marvin, The album of
gunfighters, [San Antonio? 1965]
xi, 236 p. 978.020922 66-3801
F591 .H935 1965 MRR Biog.

UNITED STATES--BIOGRAPHY. (Cont.)
International television almanac.
1956- New York, Quigley Pub. Co.   56-
2008
  HE8698 .I55 MRR Biog Latest
  edition

The Israel honorarium. [Jerusalem,
Israeli Pub. Institute; New York,
Educational Pub. Institute, 1968] 5
v. (885 p.)   920   68-24276
  E184.J5 I85 1968 MRR Biog.

Jaffe, Bernard, Men of science in
America; Rev. ed. New York, Simon
and Schuster, 1958. 715 p.   509.73
58-59443
  Q127.U6 J27 1958 MRR Biog.

Jameson, John Franklin, Dictionary
of United States history; Rev. ed.
Detroit, Gale Research Co., 1971.
xi, 874 p.   973/.03 68-30658
  E174 .J32 MRR Alc.

John Simon Guggenheim Memorial
Foundation. Reports of the president
and the treasurer. 1961/62- New
York.   061/.3 72-622712
  AS911 .J6 MRR Alc Latest edition

Johnson, Thomas Herbert. The Oxford
companion to American history New
York, Oxford University Press, 1966.
vi, 906 p.   973.03 66-22263
  E174 .J6 MRR Ref Desk.

Kane, Joseph Nathan, The American
counties; 3d ed. Metuchen, N.J.,
Scarecrow Press, 1972. 608 p.
917.3/03 70-186010
  E180 .K3 1972 MRR Ref Desk.

Lamparski, Richard. Whatever became
of ...? New York, Crown Publishers
[1968] 206 p. [4.95] 920.073 68-
9092
  CT220 .L28 1968 MRR Biog.

Lamparski, Richard. Whatever became
of ...? Fourth series. New York,
Crown Publishers [1973] 206 p.
[$5.95]   790.2/092/2 B 72-96665
  CT220 .L284 1973 MRR Biog.

Lanman, Charles, Biographical annals
of the civil government of the United
States. 2d ed. Rev., enl. and
completed to date, New York, J. M.
Morrison, 1887. iv, [2], 568, cviii
p.   05-249
  E176 .L292 MRR Biog.

Madison, Charles Allan. American
labor leaders; 2d, enl. ed. New
York, Ungar [1962] 506 p.
331.880273 62-14081
  HD8073.A1 M3 1962 MRR Alc.

Madison, Charles Allan. Critics &
crusaders; 2d ed. New York, Ungar
[1959] 662 p. 920.073 58-14283
  E176 .M22 1959 MRR Alc.

Motor Vehicle Manufacturers
Association of the United States.
Automobiles of America: milestones,
pioneers, roll call, highlights. 4th
ed., rev. Detroit, Wayne State
University Press, 1974. 301 p.
629.22/22/0973 73-19838
  TL23 .M63 1974 MRR Alc.

National Academy of Sciences,
Washington, D.C. Biographical
memoirs. v. 1-   1877-   New York,
London, [etc.] Columbia University
Press. 05-26629
  Q141 .N2 MRR Biog Partial set

National Association of Secretaries
of State. Handbook. [n.p.] 59-
63517
  Began publication with 1958 issue.
  JK2403 .N353 MRR Alc Latest
  edition

National Portrait Gallery,
Washington, D.C. Portraits of the
American stage, 1771-1971;
Washington, Smithsonian Institution
Press; [for sale by the Supt. of
Docs., U.S. Govt. Print. Off.] 1971.
203 p. [$4.50] 792/.0973 75-
170284
  PN1583.A2 N3 1971 MRR Biog.

New York University. Hall of Fame.
The Hall of Fame for Great Americans
at New York University; official
handbook. Rev. ed. [New York] New
York University Press, 1967. 210 p.
920.073 67-10691
  LD3885.B3 A5 1967 MRR Alc.

Notable names in American history;
3d ed. of White's conspectus of
American biography. [Clifton, N.J.]
J. T. White, 1973. 725 p. 920/.073
73-6885
  E176 .N89 1973 MRR Biog.

Paradis, Adrian A. The labor
reference book [1st ed.]
Philadelphia, Chilton Book Co. [1927]
234 p. [$5.95] 331.1/1/0973 72-
6994
  HD8066 .P37 MRR Alc.

Patterson, Richard Sharpe, comp. The
Secretaries of State; [Washington,
U.S. Govt. Print. Off., 1956] 124 p.
823.273   sd 57-2
  E183.7 P3 MRR Biog.

Peterson, Clarence Stewart, First
governors of the forty-eight States.
New York, Hobson Book Press, 1947.
xviii, 110 p. 923.273 48-5475
  E176 .P49 MRR Biog.

Simmons, William J., Men of mark;
New York, Arno Press, 1968. 1141 p.
920/.073 68-29017
  E185.96 .S45 1968 MRR Biog.

Simonhoff, Harry. Jewish notables in
America, 1776-1865; New York,
Greenberg [1956] 402 p.   296 55-
12359
  E184.J5 S53 MRR Biog.

Simonhoff, Harry. Saga of American
Jewry, 1865-1914; New York, Arco
Pub. Co. [1959] 403 p.
325.256930973 58-13918
  E184.J5 S54 MRR Biog.

Smith, William Henry, History of the
cabinet of the United States of
America, from President Washington to
President Coolidge; Baltimore, Md.,
The industrial printing company,
1925. 537 p.   25-9781
  JK611 .S5 MRR Biog.

Smith, William Henry, Speakers of
the House of representatives of the
United States, Baltimore, Md.: S. J.
Gaeng, 1928. 4 p. l., [xiii]-xvi,
261 p.   28-8295
  E176 .S69 MRR Biog.

Social Science Research Council.
Fellows of the Social Science
Research Council, 1925-1951. New
York, 1951. x, 473 p.   307.2 52-
3372
  H57 .S6 1951 MRR Biog.

Stone, Irving, They also ran:
Garden City, N.Y., Doubleday [1966]
xi, 434 p.   973 66-21914
  E176 .S87 1966 MRR Biog.

Thacher, James, American medical
biography; New York, Milford House,
1967. 2 v. in 1.   610/.922 67-
30787
  R153 .T3 1967 MRR Biog.

The Evening star, Washington, D.C.
The New Frontiersmen; Washington,
Public Affairs Press [1961] 254 p.
923.273 61-11685
  E841 .E8 MRR Biog.

Toppin, Edgar Allan, A biographical
history of Blacks in America since
1528. New York, McKay [1971] x, 499
p. [$7.95] 917.3/06/96073 70-
107402
  E185.96 .T66 MRR Alc.

United States. 1st Congress, 1789-
1791. Senate. Senate executive
journal and related documents.
Baltimore, Johns Hopkins University
Press [1974] xvii, 574 p.
328.73/01 73-13443
  JK1059 1st .D6 vol. 2 MRR Alc.

United States. Bureau of Naval
Personnel. Medal of honor, 1861-
1949, the Navy. [Washington, 1950?]
ix, 327 p.   359.134 50-61099
  VB333 .A532 MRR Biog.

United States. Congress. Official
congressional directory. Washington,
U.S. Govt. Print. Off. [etc.] 328.73
06-35330
  JK1011 MRR Ref Desk Latest edition
  / MRR Ref Desk Latest edition /
  MRR Ref Desk Latest edition / MRR
  Alc Partial set / Sci RR Latest
  edition

United States. Congress. Senate.
Committee on Veterans' Affairs.
Medal of Honor recipients, 1863-1973:
Washington, U.S. Govt. Print. Off.,
1973. xix, 1231 p. [$8.50]
355.1/34 73-603149
  UB433 .U55 1973b MRR Biog.

United States. Dept. of the Army.
Public Information Division. The
Medal of Honor of the United States
Army. [Washington, U.S. Govt. Print.
Off., 1948] vii, 468 p.   355.134
48-45817
  UB433 .A52 1948 MRR Biog.

United States. National Park Service.
Signers of the Declaration;
Washington; [For sale by the Supt. of
Docs., U.S. Govt. Print. Off.] 1973
[i.e. 1974] xii, 310 p. [$5.65]
973.3/13/0922 B 73-600028
  E221 .U78 1974 MRR Alc.

Webster's guide to American history;
Springfield, Mass., G. & C. Merriam
Co. [1971] 1428 p.   973 76-24114
  E174.5 .W4 MRR Ref Desk.

Who's who among Pacific Northwest
authors. 2d ed. [Missoula, Mont.?]
Pacific Northwest Library
Association, Reference Division, 1969
[c1970] 105 p.   810.9/979 74-16021
  Z1251.N7 W5 1970 MRR Biog.

Who's who in American politics. 1st-
ed.; 1967/68- New York, Bowker.
320/.0922 67-25024
  E176 .W6424 MRR Biog Latest
  edition

Who's who in government. 1st ed.-
1972/73- Chicago, Marquis Who's Who.
920/.073 72-623344
  E747 .W512 MRR Biog Latest edition
  / MRR Biog Latest edition

Who's who in insurance. 1948- New
York, Underwriter Print. and Pub. Co.
368.058 48-3960
  HG8523 .W5 MRR Alc Latest edition

Who's who in United States politics
and American political almanac.
Chicago, Capitol House. 923.273 50-
12020
  E747 .W65 MRR Biog Latest edition

Willard, Frances Elizabeth, ed. A
woman of the century, Detroit, Gale
Research Co., 1967. 812 p.   920.073
67-21361
  E176 .W691 1967 MRR Biog.

Williams, Stephen West, American
medical biography; New York, Milford
House, 1967. xv, 664 p.   610/.922
67-30786
  R153 .W5 1967 MRR Biog.

Yale University. Living graduates
and non-graduates of Yale University.
New Haven, 1968. xv, 1620 p.
378.746 77-3504
  LD6322 1968 MRR Alc.

UNITED STATES--BIOGRAPHY--BIBLIOGRAPHY.
Bell, Barbara L. Black biographical
sources: New Haven, Yale University
Library, 1970. 20 p. [$2.00]
016.92/0073 70-130440
  Z1361.N39 B46 MRR Biog.

Columbia University. Oral History
Research Office. The Oral History
Collection of Columbia University.
[3d ed.] New York; [Sold by
Microfilming Corp. of America, Glen
Rock, N.J.] 1973. xvii, 459 p.
016.9173/03 73-78480
  Z6621 .C725 1973 MRR Alc.

Dargan, Marion. Guide to American
biography; Albuquerque, University
of New Mexico Press, 1949- v.
016.920073 49-48559
  Z5305.U5 D32 MRR Biog.

Harvard University. Graduate School
of Business Administration. Baker
Library. Studies in enterprise;
Boston, 1957. xiv, 169 p.
016.33874 57-11481
  Z7164.C81 H26 1957 MRR Alc.

Hotchkiss, Jeanette. American
historical fiction and biography for
children and young people. Metuchen,
N.J., Scarecrow Press, 1973. 318 p.
016.9173/03 73-13715
  Z1236 .H73 MRR Alc.

Hotchkiss, Jeanette. American
historical fiction and biography for
children and young people. Metuchen,
N.J., Scarecrow Press, 1973. 318 p.
016.9173/03 73-13715
  Z1236 .H73 MRR Alc.

Johnson, Robert Owen. An index to
profiles in the New Yorker.
Metuchen, N.J., Scarecrow Press,
1972. vi, 190 p. 016.920/073 71-
186947
  Z5305.U5 J64 MRR Biog.

Kaplan, Louis, A bibliography of
American autobiographies, Madison,
University of Wisconsin Press, 1961.
xii, 372 p. 016.920073 61-5499
  Z1224 .K3 MRR Alc.

Lillard, Richard Gordon, American
life in autobiography, Stanford,
Calif., Stanford University Press
[1956] v, 140 p.   016.92 56-8689
  Z5301 .L66 MRR Biog.

UNITED STATES--BIOGRAPHY-- (Cont.)
Matthews, William, American diaries;
Boston, J. S. Canner, 1959. xiv,
383 p. 016.820073 59-13345
  Z5305.U5 M3 1959 MRR Biog.

Plischke, Elmer, American diplomacy;
College Park, Bureau of Governmental
Research, College of business and
Public Adminstration, University of
Maryland, 1957. iv, 27 p.
016.32773 57-63088
  Z6465.U5 P48 MRR Alc.

Shaw, Thomas Shuler, Index to
profile sketches in New Yorker
magazine, Boston, The F. W. Faxon
company, 1946. 5 p. l., 100 p.
016.920073 47-450
  Z5305.U5 S5 1946 MRR Biog.

United States. Library of Congress.
General Reference and Bibliography
Division. Biographical sources for
the United States. Washington, 1961.
v, 58 p. 016.920073 61-60065
  Z663.28 .B53 MRR Alc.

UNITED STATES--BIOGRAPHY--DICTIONARIES.
1,000 successful Blacks. Chicago,
Johnson Pub. Co., 1973. 341 p.
820/.073 73-5828
  E185.96 .O93 MRR Biog.

Adams, Oscar Fay, A dictionary of
American authors. 5th ed. rev. and
enl. Detroit, Gale Research Co.,
1969. viii, 587 p. 810.9 68-21751

  Z1224 .A22 1969 MRR Biog.

Afro-American encyclopedia / 1st ed.
North Miami, Fla. : Educational Book
Publishers, [1974] 10 v. :
917.3/06/96073 70-94684
  E185 .A28 MRR Alc.

Allen, Mary Moore. Origin of names
of Army and Air Corps posts, camps,
and stations in World War II in
United States. Goldsboro, N.C.
[1958?] 352 p. 59-1054
  UA26.A6 A4 MRR Alc.

Allibone, Samuel Austin, A critical
dictionary of English literature and
British and American authors,
Detroit, Gale Research Co., 1965. 3
v. (3140 p.) 820.3 67-285
  Z1224 .A4317 MRR Biog.

American architects directory. 1st
ed.; 1956- New York, Published
under the sponsorship of American
Institute of Architects by R. R.
Bowker. 720.69 55-12270
  NA53 .A37 MRR Biog Latest edition

American College of Hospital
Administrators. Directory. 1938-
Chicago. 362.06273 39-2135
  RA977 .A57 Sci RR Latest edition /
  MRR Biog Latest edition

American economic association. Hand
book of the American economic
association. 1890/91, 1894-99, 1906-
[New York, etc.] 330.6273 08-25517

  HB1 .A585 MRR Biog Latest edition

American men and women of science;
economics. 1st- 1974- New York,
R. R. Bowker. 330/.092/2[B] 74-
645741
  HB119.A3 A43 MRR Biog Latest
  edition

American men in government,
[Washington] Public Affairs Press
[1949] xxiii, 472 p. 353 49-11779

  E747 .A68 MRR Biog.

American men of medicine. 1st-
ed.; 1945- Farmingdale, N.Y. [etc.]
Institute for Research in Biography.
45-4406
  R150 .W5 Sci RR Latest edition /
  MRR Biog Latest edition

American Political Science
Association. Biographical directory.
[1st]- ed.; 1945- Washington
[etc.] 46-38
  JA28 .A56 MRR Biog Latest edition

American Psychiatric Association.
Biographical directory of fellows &
members. New York, R. R. Bowker Co.
616.806273 60-12585
  RC326 .A56 Sci RR Latest edition /
  MRR Biog Latest edition

American Psychological Association.
Biographical directory. 1970-
[Washington] [$30.00] 150/.6/273
73-642059
  BF11 .A67 MRR Biog Latest edition
  / Sci RR Latest edition

American Society of Civil Engineers.
Committee on History and Heritage of
American Civil Engineering. A
biographical dictionary of American
civil engineers. New York, 1972. x,
163 p. [$5.00] 624/.092/2 B 72-
194203
  TA139 .A53 MRR Biog.

American Society of Composers,
Authors and Publishers. The ASCAP
biographical dictionary of composers,
authors and publishers. [3d ed.]
New York, 1966. 845 p. 780.922 66-
20214
  ML106.U3 A5 1966 MRR Biog.

American Sociological Association.
Directory. Dec. 1950- Washington,
D. C. 301.06273 60-1821
  HM9 .A725 MRR Biog Latest edition

Appleton's cyclopaedia of American
biography. Detroit, Gale Research
Co., 1968. 7 v. [168.00] 920.07
67-14061
  E176 .A666 MRR Biog.

A Biographical directory of clergymen
of The American Lutheran Church.
Minneapolis, Augsburg Pub. House,
1972. ix, 1054 p. 284/.131/0922 B
72-80314
  BX8047.7 .B56 MRR Biog.

A Biographical directory of
librarians in the field of Slavic and
East European studies, Chicago,
American Library Association, 1967.
xv, 80 p. 026/.000922 67-28101
  Z675.A2 B5 MRR Biog.

A Biographical directory of
librarians in the United States and
Canada. 5th ed. Chicago, American
Library Association, 1970. xviii,
1250 p. 020/.922 B 79-118854
  Z720.A4 W47 1970 MRR Ref Desk.

Biographical directory of the United
States executive branch, 1774-1971.
Westport, Conn., Greenwood Pub. Co.
[1971] x, 491 p. 973/.099 78-
133495
  E176 .B575 MRR Biog.

The Biographical encyclopedia of the
United States. [1st ed. New York,
Allied Publishers, 1968] 5 v. (1030
p.) 920.073 68-24277
  CT220 .B5 MRR Biog.

Boatner, Mark Mayo, The Civil War
dictionary. New York, D. McKay Co.
[1959] xvi, 974 p. 973.703 59-
12267
  E468 .B7 MRR Ref Desk.

Boatner, Mark Mayo, Encyclopedia of
the American Revolution.
Bicentennial ed. [rev. and expanded]
New York, D. McKay Co. [1974] xviii,
1290 p. [$17.50] 973.3/03 73-
91868
  E208 .B68 1974 MRR Ref Desk.

Brown, Thomas Allston, History of
the American stage; New York, Blom
[1969] 6, 6-421 p. 792/.028/0922
72-81206
  PN2285 .B75 1969 MRR Biog.

Browning, David Clayton, ed.
Everyman's dictionary of literary
biography; English & American.
London, Dent; New York, Dutton [1958]
x, 752 p. 928.2 a 58-2815
  PR19 .B7 MRR Biog.

Burke, William Jeremiah, American
authors and books, 1640 to the
present day 3d rev. ed. New York,
Crown Publishers [c1972] 719 p.
[$12.50] 015/.73 75-168332
  Z1224 .B87 1972 MRR Biog.

Cederholm, Theresa Dickason. Afro-
American artists; a bio-
bibliographical directory. [Boston]
Trustees of the Boston Public
Library, 1973. 348 p. 709/.73 73-
84951
  N6538.N5 C42 MRR Biog.

Celebrity register. 1959- New York,
Harper & Row [etc.] 920.02 59-15865

  CT120 .I46 MRR Biog Latest edition

Clepper, Henry Edward, comp. Leaders
of American conservation. New York,
Ronald Press Co. [1971] vii, 353 p.
333.7/2/0922 B 75-155206
  S926.A2 C54 MRR Biog.

Cline, Howard Francis, comp.
Historians of Latin America in the
United States, 1965; Durham, N.C.,
Published for the Conference on Latin
American History [by] Duke University
Press, 1966. xiv, 105 p.
980.0720922 66-22489
  F1409.8.A2 C55 MRR Biog.

Collins, Jimmie Lee, Women artists
in America; [Chattanooga? Tenn.,
1973] v. (unpaged) [$15.00]
709/.2/2 B 73-163882
  N43 .C64 MRR Biog.

Concise Dictionary of American
biography. New York, Scribner [1964]
viii, 1273 p. 920.073 64-10623
  E176 .D564 1964 MRR Alc.

Contemporary authors; 1st revision.
Detroit, Gale Research Co. [1967- v.
810.9/005/2 67-9634
  Z1224 .C59 MRR Biog.

Cummings, Paul. A dictionary of
contemporary American artists. 2d
ed. New York, St. Martin's Press
[1971] xv, 368 p. [$25.00]
709/.22 76-31377
  N6536 .C8 1971 MRR Biog.

Current biography yearbook. 1940-
New York, H. W. Wilson. 40-27432
  CT100 .C8 MRR Biog Full set

The Cyclopedia of American biography.
New enl. ed. New York, The Press
association compilers, inc., 1915-
v. 15-15825
  E176 .A665 MRR Biog.

Dawdy, Doris Ostrander. Artists of
the American West; 1st ed. Chicago
: Sage Books, [1974] viii, 275 p. ;
[$12.50] 709/.2/2 72-91919
  N6536 .D38 MRR Biog.

Development Corporation for Israel.
Who's who, 1958 trustees of Israel;
New York, State of Israel Bond
Organization [1959] 215 p.
336.31095694 59-46141
  HG5811.P3 D4 MRR Biog.

Dictionary of American biography.
New York, Scribner [1946?-58] 11 v.
920.073 60-2195
  E176 .D563 MRR Biog.

Dictionary of international
biography. [1st]- ed.; 1963-
London. 920.02 64-1109
  CT101 .D5 MRR Biog Latest edition
  / MRR Ref Desk Latest edition /
  MRR Alc Latest edition

Directory of American scholars;
[1st]- ed.; 1942- New York [etc.]
Jaques Cattell Press [etc.] 57-9125

  LA2311 .C32 Sci RR Latest edition
  / MRR Biog Latest edition

DuPre, Flint O. U.S. Air Force
biographical dictionary. New York,
F. Watts [1965] x, 273 p. 923.573
65-11718
  UG633 .D8 MRR Biog.

Eastman, Richard W. The professional
independent insurance agents in the
United States. Verona, Va., McClure
Press [1970] 290 p. 368/.065 75-
128795
  HG8525 .E18 MRR Alc.

Encyclopedia of American biography.
New series. New York, American
Historical Society, 1934- v.
920.073 34-4843
  E176 .E62 Index volumes MRR Biog.

Encyclopedia of American history.
Guilford, Conn., Dushkin Pub. Group
[1973] 405 p. 973/.03 73-85201
  E174 .E52 MRR Ref Desk.

Engineers Joint Council. Engineers
of distinction. 1st ed. New York
[1970] xx, 457 p. 620/.00922 B 75-
21290
  TA139 .E37 MRR Biog.

The Episcopal clergy directory.
1971/72- [New York] Church Hymnal
Corp. 283/.092/2 72-621280
  BX5990 .E5 MRR Biog Latest edition

Feather, Leonard G. The encyclopedia
of jazz in the sixties, New York,
Horizon Press [1966] 312 p.
785.420922 66-26705
  ML105 .F35 MRR Alc.

Fielding, Mantle, Dictionary of
American painters, sculptors and
engravers / Enl. ed. with over 2,500
new listings of seventeenth,
eighteenth, and nineteenth century
American artists / Greens Farms,
Conn. : Modern Books and Crafts,
[1974] vi, 455 p. ; [$17.50]
709/.2/2 74-192539
  N6536 .F5 1974 MRR Biog.

Foremost women in communications;
New York, Foremost Americans Pub.
Corp. [1970] xvii, 788 p.
001.5/0922 79-125936
  P92.5.A1 F6 MRR Biog.

UNITED STATES--BIOGRAPHY-- (Cont.)
Gannon, Francis Xavier. Biographical
dictionary of the left. Boston,
Western Islands [1969- v.   [8.00
(v. 1)]   920.73 76-12821
  E747 .G32 MRR Biog.

Garraty, John Arthur. Encyclopedia
of American biography. [1st ed.]
New York, Harper & Row [1974] xiv,
1241 p. [$22.50] 920.073 74-1807

  CT213 .G37 1974 MRR Biog.

Heitman, Francis Bernard.
Historical register and dictionary of
the United States Army, from its
organization, September 29, 1789, to
March 2, 1903. Urbana, University of
Illinois Press, 1965. 2 v.
355.3/0922 65-15575
  U11.U5 H6 1965 MRR Biog.

The Hereditary register of the United
States of America. 1972-
Washington, United States Hereditary
Register. 369/.1 76-184658
  E172.7 .H47 MRR Alc Latest edition

Hickok, Ralph. Who was who in
American sports. New York, Hawthorn
Books [1971] xlii, 338 p. [$9.95]
796/.0922 72-158009
  GV697.A1 H5 MRR Biog.

Industrial Relations Research
Association. Membership directory.
Oct. 1949- [Madison, Wis., etc]
331.06273 50-20362
  HD4802 .I66 MRR Biog Latest
    edition

International businessmen's who's
who. 1st- ed.; 1967- London,
Burke's Peerage ltd. 650/.0922 68-
2468
  HF5500 .I614 MRR Biog Latest
    edition

The International who's who. [1st]-
ed.; [1935]- London, Europa
Publications ltd. 920.01 35-10257
  CT120 .I5 Sci RR Latest edition /
    MRR Biog Latest edition

International who's who in community
service. 1873/74- ed. London,
Eddison Press. [12.50] 361/.0025
78-189467
  HV27 .I57 MRR Biog Latest edition

Italian-American who's who; New
York, Vigo Press. 325.2450973
[920.073] 38-15649
  E184.I8 I7 MRR Biog Latest edition

Kelly, Howard Atwood. Dictionary of
American medical biography; Boston,
Milford House [1971] xxx, 1364 p.
610/.922 B 74-78618
  R153 .K3 1971 MRR Biog.

Kirk, John Foster. A supplement to
Allibone's critical dictionary of
English literature and British and
American authors. Detroit, Gale
Research Co., 1965. 2 v. (x, 1562
p.) 820.3 67-296
  Z1224 .A44 1891a MRR Biog.

Kunitz, Stanley Jasspon, ed.
American authors, 1600-1900; New
York, The H. W. Wilson company, 1938.
vi, 846 p. 928.1 38-27938
  PS21 .K8 MRR Biog.

Leaders in American Science. v. 1-
1953/54- Hattiesburg, Miss. [etc.]
Who's who in American Education, inc.
925 54-724
  Q141 .L43 Sci RR Latest edition /
    MRR Biog Latest edition

Leaders in education; 1st- ed.;
1932- Lancaster, Pa. [etc.] Science
Press. 923.773 32-10194
  LA2311 .L4 MRR Biog Latest edition

Leading men in American
transportation. New York, Transport
Publishers Corp. [c1967] 164 p.
380.5/0922 68-4217
  HE151.5 .A2L4 MRR Biog.

Leading men in the United States of
America. [Providence? R.I.]
Riverhouse Pub. Co. [1965] 380 p.
920.073 65-19575
  E747 .L34 MRR Biog.

Lo, Samuel E. Asian who? in America.
[Roseland, N.J.] East-West Who?
[1971] 329 p. 920.0873 70-155285

  E184.O6 L6 MRR Biog.

Mader, Julius. Who's who in CIA;
Berlin, Julius Mader, 1066 Berlin W
66, Mauerstrasse 69, 1968. 604, [1]
p. [unpriced] 327/.12/0973 70-
389997
  JK468.I6 M323 MRR Biog.

Markotic, Vladimir. Biographical
directory of Americans and Canadians
of Croatian descent; 4th enl. and
rev. ed. Calgary, Alta., Research
Centre for Canadian Ethnic Studies,
1973. xlii, 204 p. 920/.071 74-
176543
  E184.C93 M3713 1973 MRR Biog.

May, Robin. A companion to the
theatre; Guildford, Lutterworth
Press, 1973. 304 p., [16] p. of
plates. [£2.40] 792/.0942 74-
164747
  PN2597 .M35 MRR Alc.

Merit's who's who among American high
school students. v. 1- 1966/67-
[Chicago, Merit Pub. Co.]
373.1/8/02573 68-43796
  LA2311 .M4 MRR Biog Latest edition

Morris, Richard Brandon, ed.
Encyclopedia of American history.
Updated and rev. New York, Harper &
Row [1965] xiv, 843 p. 973.03 65-
22859
  E174.5 .M847 1965 MRR Alc.

Morris, Richard Brandon, ed.
Encyclopedia of American history.
Enl. and updated. New York, Harper &
Row [1970] xiv, 850 p. [$8.89]
973/.03 73-95647
  E174.5 .M847 1970 MRR Ref Desk.

National register of educational
researchers. 1966- Bloomington,
Ind., Phi Delta Kappa. 370.780922
65-29124
  LB1028 .N32 MRR Alc Latest edition

National register of prominent
Americans and international notables.
Venice, Fla., National Register of
Prominent Americans and International
Notables Research Center. 920.02 74-
27338
  CT103 .N3 MRR Biog Latest edition

The National student register. 1st
ed; 1969- Baton Rouge, La., Magna
Pub. Co. 378.1/98/02573 72-84671
  L901 .N35 MRR Biog Latest edition

Nauman, St. Elmo. Dictionary of
American philosophy. New York,
Philosophical Library [1972, c1973]
viii, 273 p. [$10.00] 191 B 72-
78169
  B851 .N3 MRR Alc.

New York Historical Society.
Catalogue of American portraits in
the New York Historical Society. New
Haven : Published by the New York
Historical Society by Yale University
Press, 1974. 2 v. (ix, 964 p.) :
757/.9/0973 74-79974
  N7593 .N5 1974 MRR Alc.

Nicanor, Precioso M. Profiles of
notable Filipinos in the U.S.A. ...
[1st ed.] New York, Pre-Mer Pub. Co.
[c1963- v. 920.0914 63-22684
  E184.F4 N5 MRR Biog.

Notable American women, 1607-1950;
Cambridge, Mass., Belknap Press of
Harvard University Press, 1971. 3 v.
920.72/0873 76-152274
  CT3260 .N57 MRR Biog.

Outstanding civic leaders of America.
1968- ed. [Chicago, Outstanding
Americans Foundation] 920.073 68-
17375
  E747 .O8 MRR Biog Latest edition

Outstanding college athletes of
America. 1969- Washington, D.C.
796 79-94524
  GV697.A1 O86 MRR Biog Latest
    edition

Outstanding young men in America.
1965- Chicago [etc.] 65-3612
  E840.6 .O8 MRR Biog Latest edition

Outstanding young women of America.
1965- Washington, D.C., Outstanding
young women of America. 66-3374
  CT3260 .O75 MRR Biog Latest
    edition

Overseas Press Club of America.
Directory [of the] Overseas Press
Club of America and American
correspondents overseas. 1966- [New
York] 070.4/3/02573 66-18719
  PN4871 O882 MRR Alc Latest edition

The Penguin companion to American
literature. New York, McGraw-Hill
[1971] 384 p. [$9.95] 809 70-
158062
  PN843 .P4 MRR Alc.

Personalities of the South. Raleigh,
N.C. 920.075 73-4535
  CT213 .P38 MRR Biog Latest edition

Personalities of the West and
Midwest. Raleigh, N.C., News Pub.
Co. 920.078 68-56857
  CT213 .P4 MRR Biog Latest edition

Presbyterian Church in the U.S.
Ministerial directory of the
Presbyterian Church, U.S., 1861-1967.
Doraville, Ga., Foote & Davies,
1967. vii, 648 p. 285/.133/02573
68-3645
  BX9220 .P7 1967 MRR Biog.

Rigdon, Walter, ed. The biographical
encyclopaedia & who's who of the
American theatre. [1st ed.] New
York, J. H. Heineman [1966, c1965]
xlv, 1101 p. 792.0922 B 65-19390
  PN2285 .R5 MRR Biog.

Roberts, Harold Selig. Who's who in
industrial relations. [Honolulu]
Industrial Relations Center, College
of Business Administration,
University of Hawaii, 1966-67. 2 v.
331.102573 67-63128
  HD8061 .R6 MRR Biog.

Rosenbloom, Joseph R. A biographical
dictionary of early American Jews.
[Lexington] University of Kentucky
Press [1960] xii, 175 p. 920.05693
60-8517
  E184.J5 R63 MRR Biog.

Royal blue book. Chicago [etc.] St.
James Press [etc.] 920/.0025 68-
6111
  CT103 .R64 MRR Biog Latest edition

Schuon, Karl. U.S. Marine Corps
biographical dictionary. New York,
Watts [1963] vii, 278 p. 923.573
63-16921
  E182 .S39 MRR Biog.

Schuon, Karl. U.S. Navy biographical
dictionary. New York, F. Watts
[1965, c1964] 277 p. 923.573 64-
17396
  E182 .S45 MRR Biog.

Sherman, Robert Lowery. Actors and
authors. Chicago [1951] 433 p.
927.92 51-4020
  PN2285 .S48 MRR Biog.

Shockley, Ann Allen. Living Black
American authors: New York, R. R.
Bowker Co., 1973. xv, 220 p.
810/.9/896073 73-17005
  PS153.N5 S5 MRR Biog.

Spender, Stephen, ed. The concise
encyclopedia of English and American
poets and poetry. [1st ed.] New
York, Hawthorn Books [1963] 415 p.
821.003 63-8015
  PR19 .S6 MRR Alc.

Szy, Tibor, ed. Hungarians in
America; New York, Kossuth
Foundation [c1966] viii, 488 p.
920.00917494511 66-29798
  E184.H95 S9 1966 MRR Biog.

Thomas, Dorothy, pseud., ed. Women
lawyers in the United States. [1st
ed.] New York, Scarecrow Press,
1957. xxx, 747 p. 347.058 57-6625

  LAW MRR Biog.

The Twentieth century biographical
dictionary of notable Americans.
Detroit, Gale Research Co., 1968. 10
v. 920.073 68-19657
  E176 .C993 MRR Biog.

Twomey, Alfred E. The versatiles;
South Brunswick [N.J.] A. S. Barnes
[1969] 304 p. [10.00]
791.43/028/0922 68-27218
  PN1998.A2 T9 MRR Biog.

United States. Bureau of Naval
Personnel. The history of the
Chaplain Corps, United States Navy
[Washington, U.S. Govt. Print. Off.,
1948- v. 3, 1948] v. 359.34 48-
46297
  VG23 .A45 MRR Biog.

United States. Congress.
Biographical directory of the
American Congress, 1774-1971.
[Washington] U.S. Govt. Print. Off.,
1971. 1972 p. [$15.75]
328.73/0922 B 79-616224
  JK1010 .A5 MRR Biog.

United States. Library of Congress.
Hispanic Foundation. National
directory of Latin Americanists;
Washington. [For sale by the
Superintendent of Documents, U.S.
Govt. Print. Off.] 1966. iii, 351 p.
920/.08 65-61762
  Z663.32.A5 no. 10 MRR Biog.

United States. Library of Congress.
Hispanic Foundation. National
directory of Latin Americanists; 2d
ed. Washington, Library of Congress;
[for sale by the Supt. of Docs., U.S.
Govt. Print. Off. 1971 [i.e. 1972]
684 p. [$4.25] 918/.03/072022 75-
37737
  Z663.32 .A5 no. 12 MRR Alc.

UNITED STATES--BIOGRAPHY-- (Cont.)
Van Doren, Charles Lincoln.
Webster's American biographies.
Springfield, Mass., G. & C. Merriam
Co. [1974] xii, 1233 p. 820/.073
74-6341
　　CT213 .V36 MRR Biog.

Vinson, James, Contemporary
dramatists; London, St. James Press;
New York, St. Martin's Press [1973]
xv, 926 p. [£9.00 ($30.00 U.S.)]
822/.9/1409 B 73-80310
　　PR106 .V5 MRR Biog.

Wallace, William Stewart, A
dictionary of North American authors
deceased before 1950. Toronto,
Ryerson Press [1951] viii, 525 p.
928.1 51-7279
　　PS128 .W3 MRR Biog.

Ward, Martha Eads. Authors of books
for young people. 2d ed. Metuchen,
N.J., Scarecrow Press, 1971. 579 p.
808.8/9282 B 70-157057
　　PN452 .W35 1971 MRR Biog.

Warfel, Harry Redcay, American
novelists of today. New York,
American Book Co. [1951] vii, 478 p.
813.509 51-10144
　　PS379 .W3 MRR Biog.

Warner, Ezra J. Generals in gray;
[1st ed. Baton Rouge] Louisiana
State University Press [1959] xxvii,
420 p. 973.742 58-7551
　　E467 .W3 MRR Biog.

Who was who in America; 1607/1896-
Chicago, Marquis-Who's Who [etc.]
920.073 43-3788
　　E176 .W64 MRR Biog Full set / MRR
　　Biog Full set

Who's who among innkeepers 1st ed.,
1974-1975. [New York, Rating
Publications, 1974] 210 p.
647/.94/0922 73-88548
　　TX910.3 .W48 MRR Biog.

Who's who among students in American
junior colleges. 1966/67- ed.
Tuscaloosa, Ala., Randall Pub. Co.
378.1/98/025 73-200965
　　LA2311 .W42 MRR Biog Latest
　　edition

Who's who among students in American
universities and colleges. v. 1-
1935- Washington [etc.] Randall Pub.
Co. [etc.] 35-8707
　　LA2311 .W43 MRR Biog Latest
　　edition

Who's who in advertising. 1st-
ed.; 1963- New York. 926.591 63-
18786
　　HF5810.A2 W46 MRR Biog Latest
　　edition

Who's who in American college and
university administration. 1970/71-
[New York?] Crowell-Collier
Educational Corp. 378.1/1/0922 79-
114035
　　LA2311 .P72 MRR Biog Latest
　　edition

Who's who in American dentistry. Los
Angeles, Dale Dental Pub. Co., 1963.
xi, 198 p. 927.6 62-13884
　　RK41 .W6 MRR Biog.

Who's who in American education. v.
1-24; 1928-1967/68. Hattiesburg,
Miss. [etc.] 29-2351
　　LA2311 .W45 MRR Biog Latest
　　edition

Who's who in aviation. 1973- New
York, Harwood & Charles Pub. Co.
629.13/0092/2 B 73-88547
　　TL539 .W54 MRR Biog Latest edition
　　/ Sci RR Latest edition

Who's who in banking. 1966- New
York, Business Press. 66-24372
　　HG2463.A1 W55 MRR Biog Latest
　　edition

Who's who in colored America; v. 1-
1927- Yonkers-on-Hudson, N.Y.
Christian E. Burckel 27-8470
　　E185.86 .W54 MRR Biog Latest
　　edition

Who's who in computers and data
processing. [Chicago] Quadrangle
Books. 001.6/4/0922 [B] 70-648600
　　QA76.2 .A1W452 MRR Biog Latest
　　edition / Sci RR Latest edition

Who's who in engineering; [1st]-
ed.; 1922/23- New York, Lewis
Historical Pub. Co. [etc.] 22-14132

　　TA139 .W4 Sci RR Latest edition /
　　MRR Biog Latest edition

Who's who in finance and industry.
17th- ed.; 1972/73- Chicago,
Marquis Who's Who. 338/.00922 [B]
70-616550
　　HF3023.A2 W5 MRR Biog Latest
　　edition

Who's who in philosophy. [New York,
Philosophical library, 1942- v.
921 42-17400
　　B790 .W5 MRR Biog.

Who's who in public relations,
international. 1st- ed.; 1959/60-
Meriden, N.H., PR Pub. Co. 926.591
62-4348
　　HM263 .W45 MRR Biog Latest edition

Who's who in railroading in North
America. [1st]- ed.; 1885- New
York [etc.] Simmons-Boardman Pub.
Corp. [etc.] 03-28609
　　HE2723 .W5 MRR Biog Latest edition

Who's who in risk management.
Englewood, N.J. [etc.] Underwriter
Printing and Pub. Co. 368/.81/002573
70-648818
　　HG8059.B8 W5 MRR Biog Latest
　　edition

Who's who in the East and Eastern
Canada. 1st- ed.; 1942/43-
Chicago [etc.] Marquis-Who's Who
[etc.] 920.07 43-18522
　　E176 .W643 MRR Biog Latest edition

Who's who in the Methodist Church.
Nashville, Abingdon Press [1966]
vii, 1489 p. 287.0922 66-26876
　　BX8213 .W52 1966 MRR Biog.

Who's who in the Midwest and Central
Canada. 1st- ed.; 1947- Chicago,
Marquis-Who's Who [etc.] 920.07 50-
289
　　E176 .W644 MRR Biog Latest edition

Who's who in the Protestant clergy.
Encino, Calif., Nygaard Associates
[1957] 264 p. 922 57-59372
　　BR569 .W5 MRR Biog.

Who's who in the South and Southwest.
1st- ed.; 1947- Chicago, Marquis-
Who's Who [etc.] 920.073 50-58231
　　E176 .W645 MRR Biog Latest edition

Who's who in the West and Western
Canada. 1st- ed.; 1947- Chicago,
Marquis-Who's Who [etc.] 920.07 49-
48186
　　E176 .W646 MRR Biog Latest edition

Who's who in world Jewry. 1955- New
York. 922.96 54-12036
　　DS125.3.A2 W5 MRR Biog Latest
　　edition

Who's who of American women. 6th-
ed.; 1970/71- Chicago, Marquis Who's
Who, Inc. 920.72/0973 72-623128
　　E176 .W647 MRR Biog Latest edition

Williams, Ethel L. Biographical
directory of Negro ministers, 2d ed.
Metuchen, N.J., Scarecrow Press,
1970. 605 p. 262/.14/0922 B 78-
18496
　　BR563.N4 W5 1970 MRR Biog.

Withey, Henry F. Biographical
dictionary of American architects
(deceased) Los Angeles, New Age Pub.
Co. [c1956] 678 p. 927.2 A 57-
1854
　　NA736 .W5 MRR Biog.

The World who's who of women. v. 1-
1973- Cambridge, Eng., Melrose
Press. [$20.00] 920.72 74-643503
　　HQ1123 .W65 MRR Biog Latest
　　edition

The Writers directory. 1971/73- New
York, St. Martin's Press. London, St.
James Press. 808 77-166289
　　PS1 .W73 MRR Biog Latest edition

Young, William, A dictionary of
American artists, sculptors and
engravers: Cambridge, Mass., W.
Young [1968] 515 p. 709/.73 68-
3733
　　N6534 .Y7 MRR Biog.

UNITED STATES--BIOGRAPHY--DIRECTORIES.
Columbia University. Graduate School
of Journalism. Journalism alumni
directory, 1913-1956; [New York]
Columbia University [1956] 185 p.
070.711747 57-43669
　　PN4791 .C78 MRR Biog.

Statisticians and others in allied
professions. Washington, D.C.,
American Statistical Association.
310/.62 70-618020
　　HA1 .D52 MRR Alc Latest edition

UNITED STATES--BIOGRAPHY--INDEXES.
American biography; a new cyclopedia.
(Indexes) Index--volumes I-L. New
York, Pub. under the direction of the
American historical society, inc.,
1932. 2 p. l., 3-343 p. 920.073
mrr01-73
　　E176 .A47 Index MRR Biog.

Biography index; v. 1- Jan. --
1946/July 1949- New York, H. W.
Wilson Co. 016.92 47-6532
　　Z5301 .B5 MRR Biog Full set

Dargan, Marion. Guide to American
biography; Albuquerque, University
of New Mexico Press, 1949- v.
016.920073 49-48559
　　Z5305.U5 D32 MRR Biog.

Historical Records Survey. District
of Columbia. Bio-bibliographical
index of musicians in the United
States of America since colonial
times. 2d ed. Washington, Music
Section, Pan American Union, 1956.
xxiii, 439 p. 016.78071 pa 57-4
　　ML106.U3 H6 1956 MRR Biog.

The New York times obituaries index,
1858-1968. New York, New York times,
1970. 1136 p. 929.3 72-113422
　　CT213 .N47 MRR Biog.

Nicholsen, Margaret E. People in
books; New York, H. W. Wilson Co.,
1969. xviii, 498 p. 016.92 69-
15811
　　Z5301 .N53 MRR Biog.

Schuster, Mel. Motion picture
performers; Metuchen, N.J., The
Scarecrow Press, 1971. 702 p.
016.79143/028/0922 70-154300
　　Z5784.M9 S35 MRR Biog.

Spradling, Mary Mace, In black and
white: Afro-Americans in print;
Kalamazoo, Mich., Kalamazoo Library
System, 1971. ix, 127 p. [$3.00]
016.920073 77-31475
　　Z1361.N39 S653 MRR Biog.

UNITED STATES--BIOGRAPHY--PORTRAITS.
Cirker, Hayward. Dictionary of
American portraits. New York, Dover
Publications [1967] xiv, 756 p.
(chiefly ports.) 704.9/42/0973 66-
30514
　　N7593 .C53 MRR Biog.

Meredith, Roy, Mr. Lincoln's
contemporaries; New York, Scribner,
1951. xii, 233 p. 973.7 51-12294

　　E415.8 .M4 MRR Alc.

New York Historical Society.
Catalogue of American portraits in
the New York Historical Society. New
Haven : Published by the New York
Historical Society by Yale University
Press, 1974. 2 v. (ix, 964 p.) :
757/.9/0973 74-79974
　　N7593 .N5 1974 MRR Alc.

UNITED STATES--BOUNDARIES.
Douglas, Edward Morehouse.
Boundaries, areas, geographic centers
and altitudes of the United States
and several states, 2d ed.
Washington, U.S. Govt. print. off.,
1930. vii, 265 p. incl. illus.,
maps, tables. gs 30-275
　　E179.5 .D73 1930 MRR Ref Desk.

UNITED STATES--CENSUS.
Clearinghouse and Laboratory for
Census Data. Census processing
center catalog. Rev. ed. Arlington,
Va. [1974] 1 v. (unpaged)
026/.312/0973 74-180379
　　HA37.U55 C564 1974 MRR Alc.

Kirkham, E. Kay. The counties of the
United States: their derivation and
census schedules; [Salt Lake City,
Kay Pub. Co., 1961] a-e, 77 p. 61-
66794
　　E180 .K5 MRR Ref Desk.

United States. Bureau of the Census.
Census Bureau programs and
publications; [Washington; For sale
by the Supt. of Docs., U.S. Govt.
Print. Off., 1968] vi, 146 p.
[1.50] 311/.39/73 79-603950
　　HA37 .U52 1968 MRR Ref Desk.

United States. Bureau of the Census.
Census tract manual. [Washington,
For sale by the Supt. of Doc., U.S.
Govt. Print. Off.] 1966. 83 p. a
66-7119
　　HA37 .U52 1966 MRR Alc.

United States. Bureau of the Census.
A century of population growth,
Baltimore, Genealogical Pub. Co.,
1967. x, 303 p. 312/.0873 67-
25405
　　HA195 .A5 1967 MRR Alc.

United States. Bureau of the Census.
Population and housing inquiries in
U.S. decennial censuses, 1790-1970.
[Washington] U.S. Dept. of Commerce,
Social and Economic Statistics
Administration, Bureau of the Census
[1973] 179 p. [$2.50] 353.008/1
73-600280
　　HA37 .U52 1973 MRR Alc.

Wattenberg, Ben J. This U.S.A.:
[1st ed.] Garden City, N.Y.,
Doubleday, 1965. viii, 520 p.
317.3 65-19858
　　HA215 .W3 MRR Alc.

UNITED STATES--CENSUS--BIBLIOGRAPHY.
United States. Bureau of the Census. Bureau of the Census catalog. [Washington, For sale by the Supt. of Docs., U.S. Govt. Print. Off.] 016.3173 74-644649
   Z7554.U5 U32   MRR Alc Full set

United States. Bureau of the Census. Census Bureau programs and publications; [Washington; For sale by the Supt. of Docs., U.S. Govt. Print. Off., 1968] vi, 146 p. [1.50] 311/.39/73 79-603950
   HA37 .U52 1968 MRR Ref Desk.

United States. Library of Congress. Census Library Project. Catalog of United States census publications, 1790-1945, Washington, U.S. Govt.Print. Off., 1950. x, 320 p. 016.312 50-60600
   Z7554.U5 U62 MRR Alc.

United States. Library of Congress. Census Library Project. Catalog of United States census publications, 1790-1945. New York, B. Franklin [1971] x, 320 p. 016.3173 72-153029
   Z7554.U5 U62 1971 MRR Ref Desk.

United States. Library of Congress. Census Library Project. State censuses; an annotated bibliography Washington, U.S. Govt. Print. Off., 1948. v, 73 p. 016.312 48-46440
   Z7554.U5 U63 1948 MRR Alc.

UNITED STATES--CENSUS--BIBLIOGRAPHY-- CATALOGS.
Brewer, Mary Marie. Index to census schedules in printed form; Huntsville, Ark., Century Enterprises, Genealogical Services, 1969. 63 p. 929.3 72-2676
   Z7553.C3 B7 MRR Alc.

UNITED STATES--CENSUS--FILM CATALOGS.
United States. National Archives. Federal population censuses 1790-1890: a price list of microfilm copies of the schedules. Washington, 1969. ix, 186 p. 317.3 70-605086

   HA37 .U547 1969 MRR Alc.

UNITED STATES--CENSUS--FORMS, BLANKS, ETC.
United States. Bureau of the Census. 1970 census of population and housing: data-collection forms and procedures. Washington; For sale by the Supt. of Docs., U.S. Govt. Print. Off.] 1971. 115 p. [$1.25] 001.4/33 73-612497
   HA205 .A5 1971 MRR Alc.

UNITED STATES--CENSUS, 16TH, 1940.
United States. Bureau of the Census. Vital statistics rates in the United States, 1900-1940, Washington, U.S. Govt. Print. Off., 1943. vii, 1051 p. 312 43-50838
   HA201 1940 .A57 MRR Alc.

UNITED STATES--CENSUS, 19TH, 1970.
Dutka, Solomon. A marketer's guide to effective use of 1970 census data, [New York, Audits & Surveys, 1971] 19 p. [$0.50] 658.8/008 s 70-155028
   HF5415 .M546 no. 8 MRR Alc.

United States. Bureau of the Census. 1970 census of housing. [Washington; For sale by the Supt. of Docs., U.S. Govt. Print Off., 1972- v. 301.5/4/09791 72-600057
   HD7293 .A512 1972 MRR Alc.

United States. Bureau of the Census. 1970 census of population. Washington; For sale by the Supt. of Docs., U.S. Govt. Print. Off., 1972- 2 v. in 312/.0973 72-600036
   HA201 1970 .A568 MRR Alc.

United States. Bureau of the Census. 1970 census of population and housing. [Washington; For sale by the Supt. of Docs., U.S. Govt. Print. Off.] 1971- v. [$1.00 (v. 5) varies] 312/.8/0973 73-186611
   HA201 1970 .A542 MRR Alc.

United States. Bureau of the Census. 1970 census of population and housing: data-collection forms and procedures. Washington; For sale by the Supt. of Docs., U.S. Govt. Print. Off.] 1971. 115 p. [$1.25] 001.4/33 73-612497
   HA205 .A5 1971 MRR Alc.

United States. Bureau of the Census. 1970 census users' guide. [Washington; For Sale by the Supt. of Docs., U.S. Govt. Print. Off.] 1970. 2 v. [$1.25 (v. 1) $2.75 (v. 2)] 001.4/22 71-610123
   HA37 .U52 1970c MRR Alc.

UNITED STATES--CHURCH HISTORY.
Broderick, Robert C., Historic churches of the United States. New York, W. Funk [1958] 262 p. 726.5 58-7142
   NA5205 .B7 MRR Alc.

Gaustad, Edwin Scott. Historical atlas of religion in America. [1st ed.] New York, Harper & Row, [1962] 179 p. 209.73084 map62-51
   G1201.E4 G3 1962 MRR Alc Atlas.

Gaustad, Edwin Scott. A religious history of America. [1st ed.] New York, Harper & Row [1966] xxiii, 421 p. 277.3 66-11488
   BR515 .G3 MRR Alc.

Olmstead, Clifton E. History of religion in the United States. Englewood Cliffs, N.J., Prentice-Hall, 1960. 628 p. 209.73 60-10355
   BR515 .O4 MRR Alc.

Rose, Harold Wickliffe. The colonial houses of worship in America; New York, Hastings House [1964, c1963] xiv, 574 p. 726.50973 63-19175
   NA5207 .R6 MRR Alc.

Smith, Hilrie Shelton, American Christianity; New York, Scribner [1960-63] 2 v. 277.3 60-8117
   BR514 .S55 MRR Alc.

Weigle, Luther Allan, American idealism. New Haven, Yale university press; [etc., etc.] 1928. 3 p. l., 356 p. 28-25825
   E178.5 .P2 vol. 10 MRR Alc.

UNITED STATES--CHURCH HISTORY-- BIBLIOGRAPHY.
Mode, Peter George. Source book and bibliographical guide for American church history, Menasha, Wis., George Banta publishing company [c1921] xxiv, 735 p. 22-3718
   BR514 .M6 MRR Alc.

UNITED STATES--CHURCH HISTORY--SOURCES.
Mode, Peter George. Source book and bibliographical guide for American church history, Menasha, Wis., George Banta publishing company [c1921] xxiv, 735 p. 22-3718
   BR514 .M6 MRR Alc.

Smith, Hilrie Shelton, American Christianity; New York, Scribner [1960-63] 2 v. 277.3 60-8117
   BR514 .S55 MRR Alc.

UNITED STATES--CIVIL DEFENSE-- BIBLIOGRAPHY.
United States. Library of Congress. Reference Dept. Civil defense, 1951; a reading list of current material. Washington [1951] [30] p. 016.35523 51-60028
   Z663.2 .C5 MRR Alc.

UNITED STATES--CIVILIZATION.
Beard, Charles Austin, The American spirit, New York, The Macmillan company, 1942. vii p., 2 l., 696 p. 917.3 42-50003
   E169.1 .B285 MRR Alc.

Beard, Charles Austin, New basic history of the United States Garden City, N.Y., Doubleday, 1968. 571 p. 973 68-14172
   E178 .B39 1968 MRR Alc.

Beard, Charles Austin, The rise of American civilization, New ed., two volumes in one, rev. and enl. New York, The Macmillan company, 1933. xviii, 824, 865 p. incl. front. 973 33-4705
   E169.1 .B33 1933 MRR Alc.

Berky, Andrew S., ed. The historians' history of the United States, New York, Putnam [1966] 2 v. (1384 p.) 973.08 66-20295
   E178 .B48 MRR Alc.

Carman, Harry James, A history of the American people, 3d ed. New York, Knopf [1967] 2 v. 973 67-20622
   E178 .C284 1967 MRR Alc.

Commager, Henry Steele, The American mind; New Haven, Yale University Press, 1950. ix, 476 p. 917.3 50-6338
   E169.1 .C673 MRR Alc.

Curti, Merle Eugene, The growth of American thought, 3d ed. New York, Harper & Row [1964] xx, 939 p. 917.3 64-12786
   E169.1 .C87 1964 MRR Alc.

Ketchum, Richard M., The American heritage book of great historic places, New York, American Heritage Pub. Co. [1957] 376 p. 917.3 57-11274
   E169.1 .K418 MRR Alc.

Morison, Samuel Eliot, The Oxford history of the American people. New York, Oxford University Press, 1965. xxvii, 1150 p. 973 65-12468
   E178 .M855 MRR Alc.

Nevins, Allan, A short history of the United States, 5th ed., rev. and enl. New York, A. A. Knopf, 1966. xiv, 669, xxvi p. 973 64-12329
   E178 .N44 1966 MRR Alc.

The Pageant of America, a pictorial history of the United States; Liberty bell ed. [New Haven, Yale University Press, 1925-29] 15 v. 48-38521
   E178.5 .P2 MRR Alc.

Parrington, Vernon Louis, Main currents in American thought; [New York, Harcourt, Brace and company, 1927-30] 3 v. 27-8440
   PS88 .P3 MRR Alc.

Schneider, Herbert Wallace, A history of American philosophy. 2d ed. New York, Columbia University Press, 1963. 590 p. 191 63-14114

   B851 .S4 1963 MRR Alc.

Smith, James Ward, ed. Religion in American life. Princeton, N.J., Princeton University Press, 1961- v. in 277.3 61-5383
   BR515 .S6 MRR Alc.

Sullivan, Mark, Our Times; the United States, 1900-1925 ... New York [etc.] C. Scribner's sons, 1927-35. 6 v. mrr01-51
   E741 .S92 MRR Alc.

UNITED STATES--CIVILIZATION--TO 1783.
Alden, John Richard, Pioneer America, [1st ed.] New York, Knopf, 1966. xxix, 309, x p. 917.303 66-12396
   E169.1 .A468 MRR Alc.

Savelle, Max, Seeds of liberty; Seattle, University of Washington Press, 1965 [c1948] xvii, 618 p. 917.3032 65-23913
   E169.1 .S27 1965 MRR Alc.

UNITED STATES--CIVILIZATION--1783-1865.
Alden, John Richard, Pioneer America, [1st ed.] New York, Knopf, 1966. xxix, 309, x p. 917.303 66-12396
   E169.1 .A468 MRR Alc.

Boorstin, Daniel Joseph, The Americans: the national experience, New York, Random House [1965] 517 p. 917.303 65-17440
   E301 .B6 MRR Alc.

UNITED STATES--CIVILIZATION--19TH CENTURY.
United States. Library of Congress. Image of America: Washington, 1957. viii, 88 p. 917.3 57-60038
   Z663.15 .I5 MRR Alc.

UNITED STATES--CIVILIZATION--1945-
Schnapper, Morris Bartel, ed. The facts of American life. Washington, Public Affairs Press, [1960] vi, 420 p. 917.3 60-11398
   E169.1 .S345 MRR Alc.

UNITED STATES--CIVILIZATION--ADDRESSES, ESSAYS, LECTURES.
Commager, Henry Steele, ed. Living ideas in America. New, enl. ed. New York, Harper & Row [1964] xx, 872 p. 917.3 64-23898
   E173 .C67 1964 MRR Alc.

Larrabee, Eric, ed. American panorama; [New York] New York University Press, 1957. 436 p. 016.9173 57-11743
   Z1361.C6 L3 MRR Alc.

Wrage, Ernest J., ed. Contemporary forum; New York, Harper [1862] 376 p. 815.5082 62-10074
   PS668 .W7 MRR Alc.

UNITED STATES--CIVILIZATION-- BIBLIOGRAPHY.
Bremner, Robert Hamlett, American social history since 1860. New York, Appleton-Century-Crofts [1971] xiv, 126 p. 016.917/03 70-146848
   Z1361.C6 B7 MRR Alc.

Coan, Otis Welton. America in fiction; 5th ed. Palo Alto, Calif., Pacific Books, 1967. viii, 232 p. 016.813/00803 66-28118
   Z1361.C6 C6 1966 MRR Alc.

Institute of Early American History and Culture, Williamsburg, Va. Books about early America; [4th ed.] Williamsburg, Va., 1970. vi, 71 p. 016.9173/03 73-159365
   Z1237 .I58 1970 MRR Alc.

UNITED STATES--CIVILIZATION-- (Cont.)
Jones, Howard Mumford, Guide to
American literature and its
backgrounds since 1890 4th ed., rev.
and enl. Cambridge, Mass., Harvard
University Press, 1972. xii, 264 p.
016.81   72-85143
  Z1225 .J65 1972 MRR Alc.

Larrabee, Eric, ed. American
panorama; [New York] New York
University Press, 1957. 436 p.
016.9173 57-11743
  Z1361.C6 L3 MRR Alc.

[Library of American civilization.
Chicago, Library Resources, inc.,
1971-72] 12,474 sheets.
016.9173/03 71-170857
  Z1236 .L45 Suppl. MRR Alc.

UNITED STATES--CIVILIZATION--
BIBLIOGRAPHY--CATALOGS.
Columbia University. Oral History
Research Office. The Oral History
Collection of Columbia University.
[3d ed.] New York; [Sold by
Microfilming Corp. of America, Glen
Rock, N.J.] 1973. xvii, 459 p.
016.9173/03   73-78480
  Z6621 .C725 1973 MRR Alc.

UNITED STATES--CIVILIZATION--
BIBLIOGRAPHY--INDEXES.
American Studies Association.
Metropolitan New York Chapter.
Committee on Bibliography. Articles
in American studies, 1954-1968; Ann
Arbor, Mich., Pierian Press, 1972. 2
v. (x, 898 p.)   016.9173/03/45 71-
172769
  Z1361.C6 A44 MRR Alc.

UNITED STATES--CIVILIZATION--GERMAN
INFLUENCES--BIBLIOGRAPHY.
Pochmann, Henry August, Bibliography
of German culture in America to 1940;
Madison, University of Wisconsin
Press, 1953. xxxii, 483 p.
016.3252430873 53-12569
  Z1361.G37 P6 MRR Alc.

UNITED STATES--CIVILIZATION--HISTORY.
Barck, Oscar Theodore, Colonial
America 2d ed. New York, Macmillan
[1968] xi, 753 p.   973.2 68-10104

  E188 .B26 1968 MRR Alc.

Boorstin, Daniel Joseph, The
Americans; the colonial experience.
New York, Random House [1958] 434 p.
917.3 58-9884
  E188 .B72 MRR Alc.

Curti, Merle Eugene, A history of
American civilization New York,
Harper [1953] xv, 836 p. 917.3 52-
12769
  E169.1 .C875 MRR Alc.

Ross, Ishbel, Taste in America; New
York, Crowell [1967] 343 p.
390/.0973 67-23677
  E169.1 .R7773 MRR Alc.

Wish, Harvey, Society and thought in
America. [1st ed.] New York,
Longmans, Green, 1950-52. 2 v.
917.3 50-9881
  E169.1 .W65 MRR Alc.

UNITED STATES--CIVILIZATION--NEGRO
INFLUENCES.
Drotning, Phillip T. A guide to
Negro history in America, [1st ed.]
Garden City, N.Y., Doubleday, 1968.
xiv, 247 p. [4.95]   917.3/04/923
68-14168
  E185 .D72 MRR Alc.

UNITED STATES--CIVILIZATION--PICTORIAL
WORKS.
Lehner, Ernst, comp. American
symbols; New York, W. Penn Pub. Co.
[1957] 95 p. 973.084 57-14579
  E178.5 .L4 MRR Alc.

UNITED STATES--CLAIMS.
Digested summary and alphabetical
list of private claims which have
been presented to the House of
Representatives from the First to the
Thirty-first Congress, Baltimore,
Genealogical Pub. Co., 1970. 3 v.
929.3 79-135476
  KF4932.A25 1970 MRR Alc.

UNITED STATES--CLIMATE.
Conway, Hobart McKinley, ed. The
weather handbook ! Rev. ed. Atlanta
[Conway Research, 1974. 255 p.]
[$25.00]   551.6/9/1732 74-187773
  QC982.5 .C6 1974 MRR Alc.

Powers, Edward. Traveling
weatherwise in the U.S.A. with 150
weather maps, charts and tables New
York, Dodd, Mead [1972] xix, 299 p.
[$7.95]   551.6/9/73 73-153892
  QC983 .P68 MRR Alc.

United States. National Oceanic and
Atmospheric Administration. Climates
of the States; [Port Washington,
N.Y., Water Information Center, 1974]
2 v. (975 p.) 551.6/9/73 73-93482

  QC983 .U58 1974 MRR Alc.

Weather outlook. spring/summer 1969-
New York, Grosset & Dunlap.
551.6/365/0973 71-89524
  QC997 .W4 MRR Alc Latest edition

UNITED STATES--COLONIAL QUESTION--
BIBLIOGRAPHY.
United States. Library of Congress.
Division of bibliography. List of
works relating to the American
occupation of the Philippine islands,
1898-1903. Washington, Govt. print.
off., 1905. 100 p.   05-20003
  Z663.28 .L5884 MRR Alc.

UNITED STATES--COMMERCE.
Chamber of Commerce of the United
States of America. Foreign Commerce
Dept. Guide to foreign information
sources. [Rev. Washington] Chamber
of Commerce of the United States
[1960] 26 p.   327.73 61-25832
  E744 .C4 1960 MRR Alc.

Custom house guide. New York. 99-
1545
  HE953.N5 C8 MRR Alc Latest edition

Dun & Bradstreet exporters'
encyclopaedia. New York, Dun and
Bradstreet International. 382/.6 72-
622175
  HF3011 .E9 MRR Alc Latest edition

Dun & Bradstreet International. Dun
& Bradstreet exporters'
encyclopaedia: United States
marketing guide. 1973- New York.
382/.6/0973 73-642857
  HF3031 .D86a MRR Alc Latest
   edition

Foreign commerce handbook. 1922/1923-
[Washington, D.C.] Foreign commerce
department, Chamber of Commerce of
the United States. 22-23199
  HF3011 .F6 MRR Ref Desk Latest
   edition / MRR Alc Latest edition

Kraus, Albert L. The New York times
guide to business and finance; [1st
ed.] New York, Harper & Row [1972]
viii, 280 p. [$8.95] 330.9/73/092
70-138745
  HG181 .K7 1972 MRR Alc.

Lechter, Max. U.S. exports and
imports classified by OBE end-use
commodity categories, 1923-1968;
[Washington] U.S. Office of Business
Economics, Balance of Payments
Division; [for sale by the Supt. of
Docs., U.S. Govt. Print. Off.] 1970
[i.e. 1971] xxiii, 411 p. [$4.00]
382.4/0973 75-611180
  HF3001 .L43 MRR Alc.

Seybert, Adam, Statistical annals,
New York, B. Franklin [1969] xxvii,
803 p.   317.3 68-56774
  HA215 .S5 1969 MRR Alc.

Survey of current business. Business
statistics; 1951- Washington, U.S.
Govt. Print. Off. 330.5 74-643587
  HC101.A13122 MRR Alc Latest
   edition

Trade Relations Council of the United
States. General Counsel. Employment,
output, and foreign trade of U.S.
manufacturing industries.
Washington. 338/.0973 73-30363
  HC101 .T68 MRR Alc Latest edition

United States. Bureau of the Census.
Foreign commerce and navigation of
the United States. 1865/66-
Washington, U.S. Govt. Print. Off.
07-19228
  HF105 .A2 MRR Alc Latest edition

United States. Bureau of the Census.
U.S. exports and imports, 1958-1968;
[Washington, For sale by the Supt. of
Docs., U.S. Govt. Print. Off., 1969]
175 p. 382/.0973 s 68-7967
  HF3002 1969 .A53 MRR Alc.

United States. Bureau of the Census.
U.S. foreign trade: general imports,
commodity by world area.
[Washington, For sale by the Supt. of
Docs., U.S. Govt. Print. Off.]
382/.5/0973 75-648607
  HF105 .C137182 MRR Alc Latest
   edition

United States. Maritime
Administration. Essential United
States foreign trade routes. [1946]-
Washington, For sale by the
Superintendent of Documents, U.S.
Govt. Print. Off. [etc.] 60-62459
  HE745 .A184 MRR Alc Latest edition

UNITED STATES--COMMERCE--BIBLIOGRAPHY.
Special Libraries Association.
Business and Finance Division.
Committee on Sources of Commodity
Prices. Sources of commodity prices.
New York, Special Libraries
Association, 1959 [c1960] 170 p.
338.505873   60-8102
  Z7164.P94 S6 MRR Alc.

UNITED STATES--COMMERCE--DIRECTORIES.
American import directory. New York,
Costa's Directories Co. 66-83670
  HF3012 .A65 MRR Alc Latest edition

The American register of exporters
and importers. 1945/46- New York,
American Register of Exporters and
Importers, inc. 382.058 46-15595
  HF3010 .A6 MRR Alc Latest edition

Angel, Juvenal Londoño, Directory
of foreign firms operating in the
United States. New York, Simon &
Schuster [1971] 385 p.
338.7/4/02573 72-150331
  HG4057 .A155 MRR Alc.

Anglo-American trade directory. 1913-
London. 62-51858
  HF54.G7 A7 MRR Alc Latest edition

Anuario comercial iberoamericano.
[Madrid] OFICE. 380.1/025 74-644606

  HF3683 .A48 MRR Alc Latest edition

Belgian American trade directory.
1946- New York, Chamber of Commerce
in the United States inc. [etc.]
382.058 46-17126
  HF3603 .B4 MRR Alc Latest edition

Buyer's guide to imported German
products. 1957- New York, Nordeman
Pub. Co. 57-33277
  HF3563 .B8 MRR Alc Latest edition

D-U-N-S code book: New York, Dun &
Bradstreet. 64-5833
  HC102 .D22 MRR Alc Latest edition

Directory of American importers and
exporters. Medina, Wash., World Wide
Trade Service. 63-47591
  HF3010 .D5 MRR Alc Latest edition

Directory of industrial distributors.
New York. 650.58 53-40422
  HF5035 .D485 MRR Alc Latest
   edition

Directory of United States employers.
New York, Simon and Schuster [c1970]
823 p.   338/.0025/73 78-24980
  HC102 .K7 MRR Alc.

Dun and Bradstreet, inc. Middle
market directory. 1964- New York.
64-275
  HF5035 .D8 MRR Alc Latest edition

The International telex book.
Americas edition. v. 1-   1974-
Atlanta, International Telex Corp.
384.1/4 74-645911
  HE7621 .I59 MRR Alc Latest edition

Resource Publications, inc.
Franchise guide; Princeton, N.J.
[1969] 457 p. 658.87/0025/73 75-
78653
  HF5429.3 .R46 MRR Alc.

Shippers' Conference of Greater New
York. List of non-profit shipper
associations. New York [1970] 160
p. 380.5/025/73 70-21822
  HF5780.U6 S45 MRR Alc.

Spanish Lusitanian American trade
directory. 1st-   ed.; 1961/62-
Madrid. 63-34152
  HF54.S7 S6 MRR Alc Latest edition

TTA Information Services Company.
Guide to locating new products. San
Mateo, Calif. [1971] 66 l. 338.4/7
71-153653
  HD69.N4 T15 MRR Alc.

United States-Italy trade directory.
1st- 1955- [New York] 56-2988
  HF3101 .A583 MRR Alc Latest
   edition

UNITED STATES--COMMERCE--DIRECTORIES--
BIBLIOGRAPHY.
DeBoer, Lloyd Martin, National
directories for use in marketing
Rev.] Washington, Small Business
Administration [1971] 18 p.
016.65802208 s 016.380/025 75-614411

  HG3729.U5 A34 no.13 1971 MRR Ref
   Desk.

Prince, Martin. Commercial
directories of the United States.
[Cedarhurst, N.Y., WMD Publications,
1972, c1971] [44] 184, 28 p.
016.3801/025/73 71-185008
  Z7165.U5 P73 MRR Alc.

UNITED STATES--COMMERCE--DIRECTORIES--PERIODICALS.
Directory of United States importers.
New York, The Journal of commerce.
382.5/025/73   74-618556
HF3012 .D53   MRR Alc Latest edition

UNITED STATES--COMMERCE--HANDBOOKS, MANUALS, ETC.
Angel, Juvenal Londoño, The handbook of international business and investment facts and information sources, New York, World Trade Academy Press; distributed by Simon & Schuster [1967] 565 p.   382 66-28172
HF1411 .A5 MRR Alc.

UNITED STATES--COMMERCE--HISTORY.
Douglass, Elisha P. The coming of age of American business; Chapel Hill, University of North Carolina Press [1971] xii, 606 p. [$15.00]
338/.0973 78-132254
HF3021 .D63 MRR Alc.

Gras, Norman Scott Brien, Business history of the United States about 1650 to 1850's, [Ann Arbor, Mich., Lithographed by Edwards Bros.; distributed by the Lincoln Educational Foundation, New York, 1967] xxiv, 470 p.   650/.0973 67-8825
HF5343 .G7 MRR Alc.

Keir, Robert Malcolm, The march of commerce. New Haven, Yale university press; [etc., etc.] 1927. 3 p. l., 361 p.   28-966
E178.5 .P2 vol. 4 MRR Alc.

UNITED STATES--COMMERCE--PERIODICALS.
United States. Bureau of the Census. U.S. foreign trade: exports, commodity groupings by world area. 1970- [Washington, For sale by the Supt. of Docs., U.S. Govt. Print. Off.] 382/.6/0973 70-616577
HF105 .C137152 MRR Alc Latest edition

United States. Bureau of the Census. U.S. foreign trade: general imports, world area by commodity groupings. 1970- [Washington, For sale by the Supt. of Docs., U.S. Govt. Print. Off.] 382/.5/0973 78-649732
HF105 .C137172 MRR Alc Latest edition

United States. Bureau of the Census. U.S. foreign trade: imports, TSUSA commodity by country. 1970- [Washington, For sale by the Supt. of Docs., U.S. Govt. Print. Off.] 382/.5/0973 74-649695
HF105 .C137232 MRR Alc Latest edition

United States. Bureau of the Census. U.S. foreign trade: exports, SIC-based products. 1970- [Washington, For sale by the Supt. of Docs., U.S. Govt. Print. Off.] 382/.6/0973 71-648606
HF105 .C137166 MRR Alc Latest edition

United States. Bureau of the Census. U.S. foreign trade: exports, world area by commodity groupings. 1970- [Washington, For sale by the Supt. of Docs., U.S. Govt. Print. Off.] 382/.6/0973 79-648608
HF105 .C137132 MRR Alc Latest edition

UNITED STATES--COMMERCE--YEARBOOKS.
United States. Bureau of the Census. U.S. foreign trade: imports SIC-based products. [Washington, For sale by Supt. of Docs., U.S. Govt. Print. Off.] 382/.5/0973 72-626391
HF105 .C1371663 MRR Alc Latest edition

World trade data yearbook. [New York] 57-33273
HF3010 .W6 MRR Alc Latest edition / MRR Alc Latest edition

UNITED STATES--COMMERCE--CANADA--BIBLIOGRAPHY.
United States. Library of Congress. Division of bibliography. ... Select list of books, with references to periodicals, on reciprocity with Canada. Washington, Govt. print. off., 1907. 14 p.   07-35004
Z663.28 .S344 MRR Alc.

UNITED STATES--COMMERCE--GERMANY (FEDERAL REPUBLIC, 1949-)
Baudler, Paul G. Directory of American business in Germany. 4th ed. Munich, Selbt-Verlag [1971] xviii, 533 p.   338/.0025/43 72-178863
HF3099 .B3 1971 MRR Alc.

UNITED STATES--COMMERCE--ITALY.
United States-Italy trade directory. 1st-   1955- [New York] 56-2988
HF3101 .A583 MRR Alc Latest edition

UNITED STATES--COMMERCIAL POLICY.
Dun & Bradstreet International. Dun & Bradstreet exporters' encyclopaedia: United States marketing guide. 1973- New York. 382/.6/0973 73-642857
HF3031 .D86a MRR Alc Latest edition

UNITED STATES--COMMERCIAL POLICY--BIBLIOGRAPHY.
United States. Library of Congress. Division of bibliography. ... List of references on reciprocity; Washington, Govt. print. off., 1902. 38 p.   02-19910
Z663.28 .L582 MRR Alc.

UNITED STATES--COMMERCIAL TREATIES--INDEXES.
American Bar Association. Committee on Commercial Treaties. Commercial treaty index. [Chicago] Section of International Law, American Bar Association [1973- 1 v. (loose-leaf)
341.7/54/026473 73-163891
JX236 1973 .A65 MRR Alc.

UNITED STATES--CONSTITUTIONAL HISTORY.
Bordon, Morton, ed. The antifederalist papers. [East Lansing, Mich.] Michigan State University Press, 1965. xiv, 258 p.
342.7308 65-17929
JK116 .B6 MRR Alc.

Dumbauld, Edward, The Constitution of the United States. Norman, University of Oklahoma Press [1964] xiii, 502 p.   342.733 64-11324
JK31 .D8 MRR Alc.

Kelly, Alfred Hinsey, The American Constitution; 4th ed. New York, Norton [1970] xviii, 1211 p. [$10.95] 342/.73/09 72-102944
JK31 .K4 1970 MRR Alc.

Main, Jackson Turner. The antifederalists; Chapel Hill, Published for the Institute of Early American History and Culture at Williamsburg, Va., by the University of North Carolina Press [1961] xv, 308 p.   973.4 61-17904
JK116 .M2 MRR Alc.

Mitchell, Broadus, A biography of the Constitution of the United States: New York, Oxford University Press, 1964. xvii, 384 p.   342.739 64-11234
JK31 .M55 1964 MRR Alc.

Rossiter, Clinton Lawrence, Seedtime of the Republic. [1st ed.] New York, Harcourt, Brace [1953] xiv, 558 p.   342.739 320.973* 53-5647
JK31 .R6 MRR Alc.

Smith, John Malcolm. Powers of the President during crises, Washington, Public Affairs Press [1960] viii, 184 p.   353.032 59-14964
JK516 .S66 MRR Alc.

United States. Constitution sesquicentennial commission. History of the formation of the union under the Constitution [Washington, U.S. Govt. print. off., 1941] x, 885 p. incl. front., illus. (1 col.; incl. maps) ports., facsims., tables, diagrs.   342.73 41-50348
JK166 1941 MRR Alc.

UNITED STATES--CONSTITUTIONAL HISTORY--BIBLIOGRAPHY.
Browne, Cynthia E. State constitutional conventions from independence to the completion of the present Union, 1776-1959; Westport, Conn., Greenwood Press [1973] xl, 250 p.   016.342/73/024 73-9327
KF4501 .B76 MRR Alc.

UNITED STATES--CONSTITUTIONAL HISTORY--SOURCES.
Elliot, Jonathan, ed. The debates in the several State conventions on the adoption of the Federal Constitution as recommended by the general convention at Philadelphia in 1787 ... 2d ed., with considerable additions. Philadelphia, Lippincott, 1937. 5 v.   342.73/02 mrr01-64
JK141 1937 MRR Alc.

Schwartz, Bernard, comp. The Bill of Rights: a documentary history. New York, Chelsea House Publishers, 1971. 2 v. (xvii, 1234 p.)   342/.73/029 71-150209
KF4744 1971 MRR Alc.

United States. Bureau of rolls and library. Documentary history of the Constitution of the United States of America, 1786-1870. Washington, Department of state, 1894 [i.e. 1901]-05. 5 v.   02-10164
JK111 .A52 MRR Alc.

UNITED STATES--CONTINENTAL CONGRESS.
Journals of the Continental Congress, 1774-1789. Washington, Govt. print. off., 1904-37. 34 v.   05-59
J10 .A5 MRR Alc (Dk 33)

United States. Continental congress. Secret journals of the acts and proceedings of Congress. Boston: Printed and published by Thomas B. Wait, 1820-21. 4 v.   11-28751
J10 .A35 MRR Alc (Dk 33)

United States. Library of Congress. Legislative reference service. Documents illustrative of the formation of the union of the American states. Washington, Govt. print. off., 1927. x, 1115 p.   27-26258
JK11 1927 MRR Alc.

UNITED STATES--CONSTITUTIONAL LAW.
Federalist. The Federalist. Cambridge, Mass., Belknap Press of Harvard University Press, 1961. viii, 572 p.   342.733 61-6355
JK154 1961a MRR Alc.

Federalist. The Federalist. [1st ed.] Middletown, Conn., Wesleyan University Press [1961] xxx, 672 p.   342.733 61-6971
JK154 1961b MRR Alc.

Lieberman, Jethro Koller. Understanding our Constitution. New York, Walker [1967] 282 p.   342/.73 67-13236
KF4550 .L5 1967 MRR Alc.

Thorpe, Francis Newton. comp. The Federal and State constitutions, colonial charters, and other organic laws of the state, territories, and colonies now or heretofore forming the United States of America. Washington, Govt. Print. Off., 1909. 7 v.   09-35371
KF4541 .T48 MRR Alc.

United States. Constitution. The Constitution of the United States of America: analysis and interpretation. [Rev. ed.] Washington, U.S. Govt. Print. Off., 1973. xliv, 1961 p. [$20.50] 342/.73/023 74-601236
KF4527 .J39 1973 MRR Ref Desk.

United States. Supreme court. Judicial settlement of controversies between states of the American union; New York, London [etc.] Oxford university press, 1918. 2 v.   19-9255
JK310 .A3 MRR Alc.

UNITED STATES--DEFENSES.
United States. Congress. House. Committee on Foreign Affairs. Collective defense treaties, with maps, texts of treaties, a chronology, status of forces agreements, and comparative chart. Rev.] Washington, U.S. Govt. Print. Off., 1969. ix, 514 p. [2.50] 341.2 79-602271
JX171 .U39 1969 MRR Alc.

UNITED STATES--DEFENSES--BIBLIOGRAPHY.
Greenwood, John, American defense policy since 1945; Lawrence, Published for the National Security Education Program, by the University Press of Kansas [1973] xv, 317 p. 016.3554 72-97468
Z1361.D4 G73 MRR Alc.

Larson, Arthur D. National security affairs: Detroit, Gale Research Co., [1973] 411 p. 016.35503/3/0973 70-184013
Z1215 .L37 MRR Alc.

UNITED STATES--DEFENSES--INDEXES.
United States. Army. Corps of engineers. Analytical and topical index to the reports of the chief of engineers and officers of the Corps of engineers, United States Army,1866-1900 ... Washington, Govt. print. off., 1903. 3 v.   63-27840
TC23 .A3 1866-1900 MRR Alc.

UNITED STATES--DESCRIPTION AND TRAVEL.
Daniel, Jean Houston. Executive mansions and capitols of America, Waukesha, Wis., Country Beautiful; distributed by Putnam, New York [1969] 290 p. [25.00] 725/.1 71-77604
E159 .D3 MRR Alc.

National Geographic Society, Washington, D.C. Book Service. America's historylands: Washington, National Geographic Society [1962] 576 p.   917.3 62-7748
E159 .N3 MRR Alc.

Osborne, Robert A. When who did what, [Los Angeles, Stationers corporation, 1944] 207 p.   44-53427
E174.5 .O8 MRR Alc.

UNITED STATES--DESCRIPTION AND (Cont.)
The Reader's digest. These United
States. Pleasantville, N.Y.,
Reader's Digest Association [1968]
236 p.   912.73 map68-2
   G1200 .R4 1968 MRR Alc Atlas.

Townsend, Malcolm, comp. U.S. An
index to the United States of
America. Boston, D. Lothrop company
[c1890] 6 p. l., 9-482 (i.e. 484) p.
incl. illus., maps (part fold.). 01-
21543
   E174 .T74 MRR Alc.

White, Charles Langdon. Regional
geography of Anglo-America 4th ed.
Englewood Cliffs, N.J., Prentice-Hall
[1974] xv, 617 p. [$11.95] 917
73-3225
   E169 .W54 1974 MRR Alc.

UNITED STATES--DESCRIPTION AND TRAVEL--
TO 1783-
Danckaerts, Jasper, b. 1639. Journal
of Jasper Danckaerts, 1679-1680; New
York, C. Scribner's sons, 1913.
xxxi, 313 p.   13-13556
   E187.C7 D3 MRR Alc.

UNITED STATES--DESCRIPTION AND TRAVEL--
1940-1960.
Butcher, Devereux. Exploring our
national parks and monuments. 5th
ed. Boston, Houghton Mifflin, 1956.
288 p.   917.3 57-724
   E160. B8 1956 MRR Alc.

Ketchum, Richard M., The American
heritage book of great historic
places. New York, American Heritage
Pub. Co. [1957] 376 p.   917.3 57-
11274
   E169.1 .K418 MRR Alc.

Paterson, John Harris. North
America: a geography of Canada and
the United States 4th ed. London,
Oxford U.P., 1970. [16], 319 p., 16
plates.   [50/-] 917 77-129101
   E41 .P3 1970 MRR Alc.

UNITED STATES--DESCRIPTION AND TRAVEL--
1960-
America's historic houses; New York,
Putnam [1967] 194 p.   973 67-26315

   E159 .A4 MRR Alc.

National Geographic Society,
Washington, D.C. Book Service.
America's wonderlands; New enl. ed.
Washington, National Geographic
Society [1966] 552 p.   917.3 66-
17745
   E160 .N24 1966 MRR Alc.

Pollock, Paul W. The capital cities
of the United States. Phoenix,
Ariz., c1960. 206 p.   917.3 61-
22915
   E159 .P6 MRR Alc.

Tilden, Freeman, The State parks,
[1st ed.] New York, Knopf, 1962.
496, xi p.   917.3 62-17547
   E160 .T53 MRR Alc.

Watson, James Wreford. North
America, its countries and regions,
[London] Longmans [1963] xxi, 854 p.
64-57181
   E41 .W25 MRR Alc.

Williams, Henry Lionel. Great houses
of America, [1st ed.] New York,
Putnam [1966] 295 p.   728.80973 66-
19625
   E159 .W5 MRR Alc.

UNITED STATES--DESCRIPTION AND TRAVEL--
1960- --GUIDE-BOOKS.
Adventure trip guide. New York,
Adventure Guides. 1972] 208 p.
[$2.95] 917.3/24/924 72-81137
   E158 .A38 MRR Alc.

Automobile Legal Association, ALA
sights to see book. 1973- [Boston]
917.3/04/9205 73-642597
   E158 .A9a MRR Alc Latest edition

Baxter, Robert G. Baxter's USA train
travel guide. [Alexandria, Va., Rail-
Europe, 1973] 255 p. [$3.95]
917.3/04/924 73-84776
   HE2725 .B35 MRR alc.

Cromie, Alice Hamilton. A tour guide
to the Civil War. Chicago,
Quadrangle Books, 1965 [c1964] xxv,
372 p.   917.3 64-10926
   E468.9 .C8 MRR Alc.

Hayes, Bob. The Black American
travel guide. [1st ed. San
Francisco] Straight Arrow Books
[1971] 302 p. [$6.95]
917.3/04/924 73-158517
   E158 .H35 MRR Alc.

The Hertz survival manual for
traveling businessmen. 1967- New
York, Renaissance Editions, inc.
917.3/04/823 67-14478
   E158 .H57 MRR Alc Latest edition

Powers, Edward. Traveling
weatherwise in the U.S.A. with 150
weather maps, charts and tables New
York, Dodd, Mead [1972] xix, 299 p.
[$7.95] 551.6/9/773 73-153892
   QC983 .P68 MRR Alc.

Schwartz, Alvin, America's exciting
cities; New York, Crowell [1966]
270 p.   917.304923 66-14944
   E158 .S38 MRR Alc.

Stember, Sol. The bicentennial guide
to the American Revolution. [1st
ed.] New York, Saturday Review
Press; [distributed by] Dutton, 1974.
3 v.   973.3/3 73-23108
   E230 .S74 1974 MRR Alc.

Taussig, Joseph K., Rand McNally
travel guide for servicemen,
[Chicago, Rand McNally, 1972]   64,
96 p. [$2.95] 917.3/04/924 72-
189287
   E169.02 .T4 1972 MRR Alc.

UNITED STATES--DESCRIPTION AND TRAVEL--
GUIDE-BOOKS.
America by car. Greenlawn, N.Y.,
Harian Publications; trade
distributor: Grosset & Dunlap [etc.,
New York] 917 59-16154
   GV1024 .A198 MRR Alc Latest
   edition

Automobile Legal Association, ALA
sights to see book. 1973- [Boston]
917.3/04/9205 73-642597
   E158 .A9a MRR Alc Latest edition

Baxter, Robert G. Baxter's USA train
travel guide. [Alexandria, Va., Rail-
Europe, 1973] 255 p. [$3.95]
917.3/04/924 73-84776
   HE2725 .B35 MRR alc.

Boatner, Mark Mayo, Landmarks of the
American Revolution; [Harrisburg,
Pa.] Stackpole Books [1973] 608 p.
[$10.00] 917.3/03/3 73-6964
   E159 .B67 MRR Alc.

Carpenter, Ralph E. The fifty best
historic American houses, Colonial
and Federal, New York, Dutton, 1955.
112 p.   973 55-10288
   E159 .C3 MRR Alc.

Colwell, Robert. Introduction to
foot trails in America. [Harrisburg,
Pa.] Stackpole Books [1972] 221 p.
[$5.95] 917.3/04/924 74-179603
   E158 .C76 MRR Alc.

Drotning, Phillip T. A guide to
Negro history in America, [1st ed.]
Garden City, N.Y., Doubleday, 1968.
xiv, 247 p. [4.95] 917.3/04/823
68-14168
   E185 .D72 MRR Alc.

Franzen, Marilyn D. Capitol
capsules; Pierpont, S.D., Rushmore,
inc., 1964. 208 p.   973 64-2446
   E159 .F7 MRR Alc.

Frome, Michael. Rand McNally
national park guide. 1967- Chicago,
Rand McNally. 68-3748
   E160 .F73 MRR Alc Latest edition

Haas, Irvin. America's historic
houses and restorations. [1st ed.]
New York, Hawthorn Books [1967,
c1966] 271 p.   973 66-22320
   E159 .H12 MRR Alc.

Hayes, Richard Lovejoy, Trailering
America's highways and byways,
[Beverly Hills, Calif., Trail-R-Club
of America, 1965-70. 2 v.
796.7/9/0973 66-1943
   GV1024 .H38 MRR Alc.

Historic houses of America, New
York, American Heritage Pub. Co.
[1971] 320 p. [$6.95]
917.3/03/924 79-149725
   E159 .H7 MRR Alc.

Illustrated guide to the treasures of
America. Pleasantville, N.Y.,
Reader's Digest Association [1974]
624 p. [$11.97] 917.3/03 73-83812

   E159 .I44 MRR Alc.

Logan, Harry Britton, A traveler's
guide to North American gardens. New
York, Scribner [1974] vii, 253 p.
917/.04/53 73-1103
   SB446.U6 L63 MRR Alc.

Matthews, William Henry, A guide to
the national parks; Garden City,
N.Y., Doubleday, 1973. xx, 529 p.
[$5.95] 551.4/0973 72-89824
   GB427.5 .M37 1973 MRR Alc.

National parks & monuments; New 1973
revision, Menlo Park, Calif., 1973]
140 p. [$1.95] 917.3/04/92 73-
163780
   E160 .N26 MRR Alc.

Off the beaten path. [1st]- ed.;
1957- 1957- Greenlawn, N.Y., Harian
Publications; trade distributor:
Crown Publishers [etc.] 917 59-
16155
   E158 .O3 MRR Alc Latest edition

Pan American World Airways, inc. New
horizons U.S.A.; [1st]- ed.; 1956-
[New York, Distributed by Simon &
Schuster, etc.]   60-29847
   E158 .P25 MRR Alc Latest edition

Rand McNally vacation guide:
Chicago. 917.3 60-2943
   E158 .R3 MRR Alc Latest edition

Rose, Harold Wickliffe. The colonial
houses of worship in America; New
York, Hastings House [1964, c1963]
xiv, 574 p. 726.50973 63-19175
   NA5207 .R6 MRR Alc.

Sloane, Howard N. The Goodyear guide
to State parks, New York, Crown
Publishers [1967- v.
352/.7/0974 66-26199
   SK601 .S6 MRR Alc.

Sloane, Howard N. Visiting American
caves. New York, Crown Publishers
[1966] x, 246 p.   917.309144 66-
18457
   GB604 .S6 MRR Alc.

Spaeth, Eloise. American art
museums; Rev. ed. New York, McGraw-
Hill [1969] xiii, 321 p.   708.13
68-55274
   N510 .S6 1969 MRR Alc.

Stember, Sol. The bicentennial guide
to the American Revolution. [1st
ed.] New York, Saturday Review
Press; [distributed by] Dutton, 1974.
3 v.   973.3/3 73-23108
   E230 .S74 1974 MRR Alc.

Taussig, Joseph K., Rand McNally
travel guide for servicemen,
[Chicago, Rand McNally, 1972]   64,
96 p. [$2.95] 917.3/04/924 72-
189287
   E169.02 .T4 1972 MRR Alc.

United States. National Park Service.
Explorers and settlers; historic
places commemorating the early
exploration and settlement of the
United States. Washington [For sale
by the Supt. of Docs., U.S. Govt.
Print. Off.] 1968. xvi, 506 p.
917.3/04 66-60013
   E159 .U545 MRR Alc.

United States. National Park Service.
Signers of the Declaration;
Washington; [For sale by the Supt. of
Docs., U.S. Govt. Print. Off.] 1973
[i.e. 1974] xii, 310 p. [$5.65]
973.3/13/0922 B 73-600028
   E221 .U78 1974 MRR Alc.

UNITED STATES--DESCRIPTION AND TRAVEL--
GUIDE-BOOKS--BIBLIOGRAPHY.
United States. Bureau of Outdoor
Recreation. Guides to outdoor
recreation areas and facilities
Washington; [For sale by the Supt. of
Docs., U.S. Govt. Print. Off., 1973]
79 p. [$1.05] 301.5/7 73-603093
   Z7514.O8 U54 1973 MRR Alc.

United States. Library of Congress.
General reference and bibliography
division. The American guide series:
Washington, 1944. 1 p. l., 5 p.
016.9173 45-37859
   Z1236 .U615 MRR Alc.

Writers' program. Catalogue, WPA
Writers' program publications, the
American guide series, the American
life series. [Washington, U.S. Govt.
print. off., 1942] 1 p. l., 54 p.
016.9173 42-37616
   Z1236 .W75 MRR Alc.

UNITED STATES--DESCRIPTION AND TRAVEL--
VIEWS.
Ketchum, Richard M., The American
heritage book of great historic
places, New York, American Heritage
Pub. Co. [1957] 376 p.   917.3 57-
11274
   E169.1 .K418 MRR Alc.

Runyon, A. Milton, ed. Around the
U.S.A. in 1,000 pictures; Garden
City, N.Y., Doubleday [1956] 416 p.
(chiefly illus.) 917.3 56-8486
   E169 .R946 1956 MRR Alc.

Udall, Stewart L. The national parks
of America. [1st ed.] New York,
Putnam [1966] 225 p.   917.3 66-
27672
   E160 .U3 MRR Alc.

UNITED STATES--DESCRIPTION AND TRAVEL--
VIEWS--CATALOGS.
United States. Library of Congress.
Image of America; Washington, 1957.
viii, 88 p.   917.3 57-60038
   Z663.15 .I5 MRR Alc.

UNITED STATES--DESCRIPTION AND (Cont.)
United States. Library of Congress.
Prints and Photographs Division.
Pictorial Americana; Washington,
1945. 38 l.   973.084   46-12463
    Z663.39 .P5 1945 MRR Alc.

United States. Library of Congress.
Prints and Photographs Division.
Pictorial Americana; 2d ed.
Washington, Library of Congress,
1955. 68 p.   973.084   55-60012
    Z663.39 .P5 1955 MRR Alc.

UNITED STATES--DIPLOMATIC AND CONSULAR
SERVICE.
Barnes, William, The Foreign Service
of the United States: [Washington]
Historical Office, Bureau of Public
Affairs, Dept. of State [1961] xiii,
430 p.   341.70973 sd 61-22
    JX1705 .B35 MRR Alc.

Boyce, Richard Fyfe. The diplomat's
wife. [1st ed.] New York, Harper
[1956] 230 p.   341.7   56-6909
    JX1706 .B74 MRR Alc.

Plischke, Elmer, Conduct of American
diplomacy. 3d ed. Princeton, N.J.,
Van Nostrand [1967] xvii, 677 p.
353.008/92 67-6536
    JX1407 .P58 1967 MRR Alc.

Sakell, Achilles Nicholas, Careers
in the Foreign Service. New York, H.
A. Walck, 1962. 118 p.   341.7   62-
21793
    JX1417 .S2 MRR Alc.

UNITED STATES--DIPLOMATIC AND CONSULAR
SERVICE--BIO-BIBLIOGRAPHY.
Boyce, Richard Fyfe. American
foreign service authors; Metuchen,
N.J., Scarecrow Press, 1973. x, 321
p.   016.081 73-9780
    Z1224 .B68 MRR Alc.

UNITED STATES--DIPLOMATIC AND CONSULAR
SERVICE--REGISTERS.
United States. Dept. of State.
Foreign service list. Washington,
U.S. Govt. Print. Off.   10-16369
    JX1705 .A2 MRR Ref Desk Latest
    edition

United States. Dept. of State.
Historical Office. United States
Chiefs of Mission, 1778-1973
(complete to 31 March 1973)
[Washington] Dept. of State; [for
sale by the Supt. of Docs., U.S.
Govt. Print. Off.] 1973. v, 229 p.
[$2.70] 327.2/0973 73-602788
    JX1706.A59 U54 1973 MRR Ref Desk.

UNITED STATES--DIRECTORIES.
Sable, Martin Howard. Master
directory for Latin America, Los
Angeles, Latin American Center,
University of California, 1965. xxi,
438 p.   918.03306 66-25
    F1406.5 .S3 MRR Alc.

Sources of information and unusual
services; New York, Informational
Directory Co. 917.4741 53-4208
    AG521 .S6 MRR Ref Desk Latest
    edition

UNITED STATES--DIRECTORIES--
BIBLIOGRAPHY.
Association of North American
directory publishers. Catalog and
price list of city, county and state
directories published in North
America. New York. 43-47275
    Z5771 .A7 MRR Alc Latest edition

DeBoer, Lloyd Martin, National
directories for use in marketing
Rev.] Washington, Small Business
Administration [1971] 18 p.
016.65802208 s 016.380/025 75-614411

    HG3729.U5 A34 no.13 1971 MRR Ref
    Desk.

Encyclopedia of business information
sources; Detroit, Gale Research Co.,
1970. 2 v. (xxi, 689 p.)   016.33
79-127922
    HF5353 .E52 MRR Ref Desk.

Guide to American educational
directories. 1st- ;1963- New
York, B. Klein. 016.3705873 63-
14270
    Z5813 .G8 MRR Ref Desk Latest
    edition

Klein, Bernard. Guide to American
scientific and technical directories.
1st ed. Rye, N.Y., B. Klein
Publications [1972] v, 324 p.
016.3384/7/6702573 72-91671
    Z7914.M3 K53 MRR Ref Desk.

Prince, Martin. Commercial
directories of the United States.
[Cedarhurst, N.Y., WMD Publications,
1972, c1971] (44) 184, 28 p.
016.3801/025/73 71-185008
    Z7165.U5 P73 MRR Alc.

Smith, George Mayo. World wide
business publications directory, New
York, Simon and Schuster [1971] xvi,
593 p.   016.380/025 73-157682
    Z7164.C8 S55 MRR Ref Desk.

Spear, Dorothea N. Bibliography of
American directories through 1860.
Worcester, Mass., American
Antiquarian Society, 1961. 389 p.
016.9173 61-1054
    Z5771 .S7 MRR Alc.

Wynkoop, Sally. Directories of
Government agencies, Rochester,
N.Y., Libraries Unlimited, 1969. 242
p.   016.353/04/025 70-84652
    Z7165.U5 W9 MRR Alc.

UNITED STATES--DISCOVERY AND EXPLORATION
see America--Discovery and exploration

UNITED STATES--DISTANCES, ETC.
Whitten, Charles A. Air-line
distances between cities in the
United States. Washington, U.S.
Govt. Print. Off., 1947. vi, 246 p.
387.7 47-46569
    TL726.2 .W45 MRR Alc.

UNITED STATES--ECONOMIC CONDITIONS.
American economic growth; New York,
Harper & Row [1972] xvi, 683 p.
330.973 75-154879
    HC105 .A63 MRR Alc.

Davis, Lance Edwin. American
economic history; 3d ed. Homewood,
Ill., R. D. Irwin, 1969. xiii, 450
p.   330.973 68-56872
    HC103 .D35 1969 MRR Alc.

Dillard, Dudley D. Economic
development of the North Atlantic
community; Englewood Cliffs, N.J.,
Prentice-Hall [1967] viii, 747 p.
330/.0918/21 67-15169
    HC21 .D5 MRR Alc.

Douglas, Paul Howard, Real wages in
the United States, 1890-1926,
Boston, New York, Houghton Mifflin
company, 1930. xxviii, 682 p.
331.2973 30-12884
    HD4975 .D6 MRR Alc.

The Economic history of the United
States. New York, Toronto, Farrar &
Rinehart, inc. [19   v.   330.973
45-7376
    HC103 .E25 MRR Alc.

Groner, Alex. The American heritage
history of American business &
industry, New York, American
Heritage Pub. Co. [1972] 384 p.
[$20.00] 330.9/73 72-80699
    HC103 .G787 MRR Alc.

Kirkland, Edward Chase, A history of
American economic life, 4th ed. New
York, Appleton-Century-Crofts [1969]
xii, 623 p.   330.973 69-13070
    HC103 .K5 1969 MRR Alc.

Kirkland, Edward Chase, Industry
comes of age; New York, Holt,
Rinehart and Winston [1961] xiv, 445
p.   330.973 61-9816
    HC103 .E25 vol. 6 MRR Alc.

Long, Clarence Dickinson, Wages and
earnings in the United States, 1860-
1890. Princeton, Princeton
University Press, 1960. xvii, 169 p.
331.2973 60-5756
    HD4975 .L57 MRR Alc.

Lord, Clifford Lee, Historical atlas
of the United States, Rev. ed. New
York, Holt [1953] xv, 238 p. 53-
10208
    G1201.S1 L6 1953 MRR Ref Desk.

Miller, Marion Mills, ed. Great
debates in American history, [The
national ed.] New York, Current
literature publishing company [c1913]
14 v.   13-23912
    E173 .M64 vol. 14 MRR Alc.

Peterson, John M., Economic
development of the United States
Homewood, Ill., R. D. Irwin, 1969.
xiv, 551 p.   330.973 69-17159
    HC103 .P46 MRR Alc.

Robertson, Ross M. History of the
American economy. 2d ed. New York,
Harcourt, Brace & World [1964] xiii,
630 p.   330.973 64-15591
    HC103 .R58 1964 MRR Alc.

Smith, Walter Buckingham.
Fluctuations in American business,
1790-1860, Cambridge, Harvard
university press, 1935. xxix, 195 p.
330.973 35-33983
    HC105 .S65 MRR Alc.

United States. Bureau of labor
statistics. History of wages in the
United States from colonial times to
1928. Washington, U.S. Govt. print.
off., 1934. ix, 574 p. incl. tables.
331.2973 l 34-109
    HD4975 .A15 1933 MRR Alc.

Woytinsky, Emma (Shadkhan) Profile
of the U.S. economy: New York,
Praeger [1967] xiii, 601 p.
330.973 66-13673
    HC103 .W76 MRR Alc.

UNITED STATES--ECONOMIC CONDITIONS--TO
1865.
Nettels, Curtis Putnam. The
emergence of a national economy, 1775-
1815. New York, Holt, Rinehart and
Winston [1962] xvi, 424 p. 330.973
62-9523
    HC103 .E25 vol. 2 MRR Alc.

Seybert, Adam, Statistical annals;
New York, B. Franklin [1969] xxvii,
803 p.   317.3 68-56774
    HA215 .S5 1969 MRR Alc.

Taylor, George Rogers, The
transportation revolution, 1815-1860.
New York, Rinehart [1951] xvii, 490
p.   385.09 51-14038
    HC103 .E25 vol. 4 MRR Alc.

UNITED STATES--ECONOMIC CONDITIONS--TO
1865--BIBLIOGRAPHY.
Taylor, George Rogers, American
economic history before 1860. New
York, Appleton-Century-Crofts [1969]
xiv, 108 p.   016.330973 70-79173
    Z7165.U5 T37 MRR Alc.

UNITED STATES--ECONOMIC CONDITIONS--
1865-1918.
Faulkner, Harold Underwood, The
decline of laissez faire, 1897-1917.
New York, Rinehart [1951] xiv, 433
p.   330.973 51-5244
    HC103 .E25 vol. 7 MRR Alc.

UNITED STATES--ECONOMIC CONDITIONS--
1865-
Dorfman, Joseph, The economic mind
in American civilization. New York,
Viking Press, 1946-59. 5 v.
330.973 45-11318
    HB119.A2 D6 MRR Alc.

UNITED STATES--ECONOMIC CONDITIONS--
1918-1945.
Leuchtenburg, William Edward,
Franklin D. Roosevelt and the New
Deal, 1932-1940. [1st ed.] New
York, Harper & Row [1963] 393 p.
973.917 63-12053
    E806 .L475 MRR Alc.

Mitchell, Broadus, Depression
decade; New York, Rinehart [1947]
xviii, 462 p.   330.973 47-12331
    HC103 .E25 vol. 9 MRR Alc.

Soule, George Henry, Prosperity
decade; New York, Rinehart [1947]
xiv, 365 p.   330.973 47-5631
    HC103 .E25 vol. 8 MRR Alc.

UNITED STATES--ECONOMIC CONDITIONS--
1918-1945--PERIODICALS.
Survey of current business. Business
statistics; 1951- Washington, U.S.
Govt. Print. Off. 330.5 74-643587
    HC101.A13122 MRR Alc Latest
    edition

UNITED STATES--ECONOMIC CONDITIONS--
1945-
Ebasco Services Incorporated.
Business and economic charts.
Chicago. 59-44534
    HD9685.U7 E3 MRR Alc Latest
    edition

Goldenthal, Allan B. The handbook of
U.S. markets and industrial growth
areas [New York] Regents Pub. Co.
[1969-   v.   330.973 71-85525
    HC106.6 .G64 MRR Alc.

Harriss, Clement Lowell, The
American economy; 6th ed. Homewood,
Ill., R. D. Irwin, 1968. xv, 998 p.
330.973 68-14871
    HC106.5 .H325 1968 MRR Alc.

Moore, Geoffrey Hoyt, ed. Business
cycle indicators. Princeton [N.J.]
Princeton University Press, 1961. 2.
v.   338.540973 60-14062
    HB3711 .M58 MRR Alc.

National Industrial Conference Board.
Chartbook of weekly business
indicators. New York. 330.973 58-
24653
    HC106.5 .A2845 MRR Alc Latest
    edition

UNITED STATES--ECONOMIC CONDITIONS--
1945- --BIBLIOGRAPHY.
Business periodicals index. v. 1-
Jan. 1958- New York, H. W. Wilson
Co. 016.6505 58-12645
    Z7164.C81 B983 MRR Circ Full set

P H R A; poverty and human resources
abstracts. v. 1- Jan./Feb. 1966-
Beverly Hills, Cal., [etc.] Sage Pub.
[etc.] 66-9955
    Z7165.U5 P2 MRR Alc Full set

UNITED STATES--ECONOMIC CONDITIONS-- 1945- --PERIODICALS.
Survey of current business. Business statistics; 1951- Washington, U.S. Govt. Print. Off. 330.5 74-643587
HC101.A13122 MRR Alc Latest edition

UNITED STATES--ECONOMIC CONDITIONS-- 1961-
Peirce, Neal R. The megastates of America; [1st ed.] New York, Norton [1972] 745 p. [$12.95] 917.3/03/92 70-163375
E839.5 .P35 MRR Alc.

United States. Bureau of Labor Standards. State economic and social indicators: wages, and family income, educational attainment, projected growth in labor force, 1970-80 Washington; For sale by the Supt. of Docs., U.S. Govt. Print. Off.] 1970. vii, 96 p. [$1.00] 330/.973 71-610107
HA211 .A48 MRR Alc.

UNITED STATES--ECONOMIC CONDITIONS-- 1961- --BIBLIOGRAPHY.
Tompkins, Dorothy Louise (Campbell) Culver. Poverty in the United States during the sixties; [Berkeley] Institute of Governmental Studies, University of California, 1970. ix, 542 p. [$10.00] 016.3625/0973 74-632910
Z7165.U5 T62 MRR Alc.

United States. Office of Regional Development Planning. Guide to economic projections and forecasts. [Washington] U.S. Dept. of Commerce, Economic Development Administration [1968] iii, 113 p. 016.330973 77-600326
Z7165.U5 A48 MRR Alc.

UNITED STATES--ECONOMIC CONDITIONS-- BIBLIOGRAPHY.
Bibliography of publications of university bureaus of business and economic research. [Boulder, Colo., etc.] Business Research Division, University of Colorado. 016.33/007/2073 77-635614
Z7165.U5 A8 MRR Alc Full set

Frank, Nathalie D., Data sources for business and market analysis, 2d ed. Metuchen, N.J., Scarecrow Press, 1969. 361 p. 016.65883/9/73 73-5855
HF5415.1 .F7 1969 MRR Alc.

Kiel. Universität. Institut für Weltwirtschaft. Bibliothek. Regionenkatalog. Boston, G. K. Hall, 1967. 52 v. 017/.5 67-9425
Z929 .K52 1967 MRR Alc. (Dk 33).

Lovett, Robert Woodberry. American economic and business history information sources. Detroit, Gale Research Co. [1971] 323 p. [$14.50] 016.330873 78-137572
Z7165.U5 L66 MRR Alc.

Public Affairs Information Service. Bulletin ... annual cumulation. 1st-1915- New York [etc.] 16-920
Z7163 .P9 MRR Circ Full set

UNITED STATES--ECONOMIC CONDITIONS-- COLLECTIONS.
Letwin, William, ed. A documentary history of American economic policy since 1789. Chicago, Aldine Pub. Co. [1964, c1961] 406 p. 338.973 62-14752
HC103 .L37 1964 MRR Alc.

UNITED STATES--ECONOMIC CONDITIONS-- MAPS.
Oxford University Press. United States & Canada. Oxford, Clarendon P., 1967. [12], [35] p. [75/- (35/-pbk.)] 912.1/3309/73 map68-202
G1201.G1 O9 1967 MRR Alc Atlas.

UNITED STATES--ECONOMIC CONDITIONS-- YEARBOOKS.
The Economic almanac; 1940- New York [etc.], Macmillan Co. [etc.] 330.58 40-30704
HC101 .E38 MRR Ref Desk Latest edition

UNITED STATES--ECONOMIC POLICY.
Harriss, Clement Lowell, The American economy; 6th ed. Homewood, Ill., R. D. Irwin, 1968. xv, 988 p. 330.973 68-14871
HC106.5 .H325 1968 MRR Alc.

The United States in world affairs. 1931- New York, Simon & Schuster [etc.] 32-26065
E744 .U66 MRR Alc Full set

UNITED STATES--ECONOMIC POLICY--1933- 1945.
Moley, Raymond, The first New Deal [1st ed.] New York, Harcourt, Brace & World [1966] xxiii, 577 p. 973.917 66-22282
E806 .M68 MRR Alc.

Schlesinger, Arthur Meier, The age of Roosevelt. Boston, Houghton, Mifflin, 1957- v. 973.917 56-10293
E806 .S34 MRR Alc.

UNITED STATES--ECONOMIC POLICY--1945-1960.
Congressional Quarterly Service, Washington, D.C. Federal economic policy. 4th ed. Washington, 1969. 140 p. [2.95] 338.973 76-79759
HC106.5 .C67345 1969 MRR Alc.

UNITED STATES--ECONOMIC POLICY--1961-
Congressional Quarterly Service, Washington, D.C. Federal economic policy. 4th ed. Washington, 1969. 140 p. [2.95] 338.973 76-79759
HC106.5 .C67345 1969 MRR Alc.

UNITED STATES--ECONOMIC POLICY-- COLLECTIONS.
Letwin, William, ed. A documentary history of American economic policy since 1789. Chicago, Aldine Pub. Co. [1964, c1961] 406 p. 338.973 62-14752
HC103 .L37 1964 MRR Alc.

UNITED STATES--EMIGRATION AND IMMIGRATION.
George Washington University, Washington, D.C. A report on world population migrations as related to the United States of America; Washington [1956] v. 449 p. 016.32573 56-3432
Z7164.I3 G4 MRR Alc.

Handlin, Oscar, ed. Immigration as a factor in American history. Englewood Cliffs, N.J., Prentice-Hall, 1959. 206 p. 325.73 59-9516
E184.A1 H23 MRR Alc.

Jones, Maldwyn Allen. American immigration. [Chicago] University of Chicago Press [1960] 359 p. 325.73 60-8301
JV6450 .J6 MRR Alc.

Morton Allan directory of European passenger steamship arrivals New York, Immigration information bureau, inc [c1931] 268 p., 2 l. 656 32-6783
HE945.A2 D5 1931 MRR Alc.

UNITED STATES--EMIGRATION & IMMIGRATION.
United States. Bureau of the Census. Foreign commerce and navigation of the United States. 1865/66-Washington, U.S. Govt. Print. Off. 07-19228
HF105 .A2 MRR Alc Latest edition

UNITED STATES--EMIGRATION AND IMMIGRATION.
United States. Immigration Commission, 1907-1910. Dictionary of races or peoples. Detroit, Gale Research Co., 1969. vii, 150 p. 572/.03 68-30665
GN11 .U6 1969 MRR Alc.

Wittke, Carl Frederick, We who built America; [Rev. ed. Cleveland] Press of Western Reserve University [1964] xviii, 550 p. 64-20939
JV6455 .W55 1964 MRR Alc.

UNITED STATES--EMIGRATION AND IMMIGRATION--BIBLIOGRAPHY.
George Washington University, Washington, D.C. A report on world population migrations as related to the United States of America; Washington [1956] v. 449 p. 016.32573 56-3432
Z7164.I3 G4 MRR Alc.

Lancour, Harold, A bibliography of ship passenger lists, 1538-1825; 3d ed., rev. and enl. New York, New York Public Library, 1963. ix, 137 p. 016.32573 63-18141
Z7164.I3 L2 1963 MRR Alc.

United States. Library of Congress. Division of bibliography. ... A list of books (with references to periodicals) on immigration. 3d issue, with additions. Washington, Gov't. print. off., 1907. 157 p. 07-35001
Z7663.28 .L56 1907 MRR Alc.

United States. Library of Congress. Division of bibliography. Select list of references on Chinese immigration. Washington, Govt. Print. Off., 1904. 31 p. 04-5901
Z7663.28 .S36 MRR Alc.

UNITED STATES--EMIGRATION AND IMMIGRATION--COLLECTIONS.
Brown, Francis James, ed. One America; 3d ed. New York, Prentice-Hall, 1952. xvi, 764 p. 325.73 52-1682
E184.A1 B87 1952 MRR Alc.

UNITED STATES--EXECUTIVE DEPARTMENTS.
The Encyclopedia of U.S. Government benefits; [Union City, N.J.] W. H. Wise, 1967. viii, 1011 p. 353.0003 67-6136
JK424 .E55 1967 MRR Alc.

Kerbec, Matthew J., comp. Legally available U.S. Government information as a result of the Public Information Act. [1st ed.] Arlington, Va., Output Systems Corp. [1970] 2 v. 353/.0007 70-108181
KF5753 .A33 1970 MRR Alc.

Michael, James R. Working on the system; New York, Basic Books [1974] xxvi, 950 p. [$14.95] 353.09 73-81135
KF5407 .M52 MRR Alc.

Smith, William Henry, History of the cabinet of the United States of America, from President Washington to President Coolidge; Baltimore, Md., The Industrial printing company, 1925. 537 p. 25-9781
JK611 .S5 MRR Biog.

United States. Federal register. v. 1- March 14, 1936- [Washington, U.S. Govt. Print. off.] 353.005 36-26246
J1 .A2 MRR Alc (Dk 33) Full set

United States. Civil Service Commission. Official register of the United States. 1907-59. Washington, U.S. Govt. Print. Off. 08-35096
JK5 MRR Ref Desk Latest edition

United States. Congress. Official congressional directory. Washington, U.S. Govt. Print. Off. [etc.] 328.73 06-35330
JK1011 MRR Ref Desk Latest edition / MRR Ref Desk Latest edition / MRR Ref Desk Latest edition / MRR Alc Partial set / Sci RR Latest edition

United States. Dept. of State. Office of External Research. Foreign affairs research, a directory of governmental resources. [Washington, For sale by the Supt. of Docs., U.S. Govt. Print. Off.] 1967. vii, 83 p. 327/.025 67-61715
JX1293.U6 A527 MRR Ref Desk.

United States. Library of Congress. Legislative Reference Service. Federal educational policies, programs and proposals; Washington, U.S. Govt. Print. Off., 1968. 3 v. [0.75 (v. 1) varies] 379/.0973 76-600437
LC71 .U5332 MRR Alc.

United States. National Archives. Federal records of World War II. Washington [U.S. Govt. Print. Off.] 1950 [i.e. 1951] 2 v. 940.5373 a 51-9196
D735.A1 U52 1950 MRR Alc.

United States. National archives. Handbook of federal world war agencies and their records, 1917-1921. Washington, U.S. Govt. print. off., 1943. xiii, 666 p. 353 43-50551
JK464.1963 .A52 MRR Alc.

United States. Office of Management and Budget. The budget of the United States Government. 1971/72- [Washington, For sale by the Supt. of Docs., U.S. Govt. Print. Off.] 353.007/22 70-611048
HJ2051 .A59 MRR Ref Desk Latest edition

United States. Office of Management and Budget. The Budget of the United States Government. Appendix. 1971/72- [Washington, For sale by the Supt. of Docs., U.S. Govt. Print. Off.] 353.007/22 74-643523
HJ2051 .A59 Suppl. MRR Ref Desk Latest Edition

United States. Office of Science and Technology. Housing research and building technology activities of the Federal Government. Washington; [For sale by the Supt. of Docs., U.S. Govt. Print. Off.] 1970. 117 p. [1.25] 690/.072/073 75-608274
TH23 .A6 1970 MRR Alc.

United States. Treasury Dept. Bureau of Accounts. Combined statement of receipts, expenditures and balances of the United States government. 1871/72- Washington. 10-11510
HJ10 .A6 MRR Alc Latest edition

UNITED STATES--EXECUTIVE DEPARTMENTS-- BIBLIOGRAPHY.
Andriot, John L. Checklist of major U.S. Government series, McLean, Va., Documents Index, 1972- v. 015/.73 73-163950
Z1223.Z7 A544 MRR Alc.

UNITED STATES--EXECUTIVE (Cont.)
Munden, Kenneth White. Guide to
Federal archives relating to the
Civil War. Washington, National
Archives, National Archives and
Records Service, General Services
Administration, 1962. x, 721 p.
62-9432
   CD3047 .M8 MRR Alc.

United States. National Archives.
Guide to cartographic records in the
National Archives Washington,
National Archives and Records
Service; for sale by the
Supt. of Docs., U.S. Govt. Print.
Off., 1971. xi, 444 p. [$3.25]
016.91273 76-611061
   Z6028 .U575 MRR Alc.

UNITED STATES--EXECUTIVE DEPARTMENTS--
DIRECTORIES.
Congressional staff directory. [1st]-
ed.; 1959- Washington [etc.]
328.738 59-13987
   JK1012 MRR Ref Desk Latest edition
   / Sci RR Latest edition

Directory of consumer protection and
environmental agencies. 1st ed.
Orange, N.J., Academic Media [1973]
xiii, 627 p. 381 72-75952
   HC110.C63 D55 MRR Ref Desk.

Federal telephone directory. fall
1973- Washington, Consolidated
Directories, inc. [$60.00]
353.002/025 73-88404
   JK6 .F43 MRR Ref Desk Latest
   edition / Sci RR Latest edition

Lester, Daniel W. Departmental
keyword indexes to U.S. Government
author-organizations. Washington,
United States Historical Documents
Institute, 1972. xxxiii, 959 p.
015.73 s 72-2109
   Z1223.Z7 L45 vol. 3 MRR Ref Desk.

Lester, Daniel W. Master keyword
index to the publication-issuing
offices of the U.S. Government, 1789-
1970. Washington, United States
Historical Documents Institute, 1972.
xxxiii, 855 p. 015.73 s 72-2110
   Z1223.Z7 L45 vol. 5 MRR Ref Desk.

Lukowski, Susan. State information
and Federal region book. Washington,
Potomac Books [1973] 90 p. [$5.00
(pbk)] 353.9/02 73-80718
   JK2679 .L84 MRR Ref Desk.

United States. Library of Congress.
National Referral Center. A
directory of information resources in
the United States: Federal
Government, Rev. ed. Washington,
Library of Congress; [for sale by the
Supt. of Docs., U.S. Govt. Print.
Off.] 1974. iv, 416 p. 001.4/3 73-
22041
   Z663.379 .D48 1974 MRR Ref Desk.

United States. President's Committee
on Consumer Interests. Guide to
Federal consumer services.
[Washington] 1967. vii, 140 p.
353/.04/025 67-61903
   JK464 1967 .A5 MRR Alc.

United States Historical Documents
Institute. U.S. Government author-
organization index, 1789-1970.
Washington [1972] 015.73 s 72-
2108
   Z1223.Z7 L45 vol. 2 MRR Ref Desk.

UNITED STATES--EXECUTIVE DEPARTMENTS--
DIRECTORIES--BIBLIOGRAPHY.
Wynkoop, Sally. Directories of
Government agencies. Rochester,
N.Y., Libraries Unlimited, 1969. 242
p. 016.353/04/025 70-84652
   Z7165.U5 W9 MRR Alc.

UNITED STATES--EXECUTIVE DEPARTMENTS--
FILM CATALOGS.
Guide to Government-loan film. 1st
ed; 1969/70- [Alexandria, Va.,
Serina Press] 791.43/8 71-76544
   PN1998 .G83 MRR Alc Latest edition

UNITED STATES--EXECUTIVE DEPARTMENTS--
HANDBOOKS, MANUALS, ETC.
United States Government manual.
1973/74- [Washington] Office of the
Federal Register; [For sale by the
Supt. of Docs., U.S. Govt. Print.
Off.] [$4.00] 353 73-646537
   JK421 .A3 MRR Ref Desk Latest
   edition / MRR Ref Desk Latest
   edition

UNITED STATES--EXECUTIVE DEPARTMENTS--
PERIODICALS.
National Journal reports. v. 5, no.
30- July 28, 1973- [Washington,
Government Research Corporation]
320.9/73 73-645726
   JK1 .N28 MRR Alc Full set

UNITED STATES--EXECUTIVE DEPARTMENTS--
RECORDS AND CORRESPONDENCE.
United States. National Archives.
Guide to the records in the National
Archives. Washington, U.S. Govt.
Print. Off., 1948. xvi, 684 p. 353
a 49-10088
   CD3023 .A46 1948 MRR Ref Desk.

UNITED STATES--EXECUTIVE DEPARTMENTS--
STATISTICS.
United States. Civil Service
Commission. Minority group
employment in the Federal Government.
May 1970- Washington, For sale by
the Supt. of Docs., U.S. Govt. Print.
Off. 331.1/33/0973 72-622550
   JK639 .A42 subser MRR Alc Latest
   edition

United States. Division of Government
Financial Operations. Federal aid to
States. [Washington?] 338.973 72-
618404
   HJ275 .A36 MRR Ref Desk Latest
   edition

UNITED STATES--EXPLORING EXPEDITIONS.
Wright, Louis Booker, ed. The
Elizabethans' America: Cambridge,
Harvard University Press, 1965. xii,
295 p. 817.041 65-8877
   E141 .W7 MRR Alc.

UNITED STATES--EXPLORING EXPEDITIONS--
BIBLIOGRAPHY.
Church, Elihu Dwight, A catalogue of
books relating to the discovery and
early history of North and South
America, New York, P. Smith, 1951.
5 v. (vi, 2635 p.) 016.9731 51-
4055
   Z1203 .C55 1951 MRR Ref Desk.

United States. Library of Congress.
Map Division. Maps showing
explorers' routes, trails & early
roads in the United States;
Washington, For sale by the
Superintendent of Documents, U.S.
Govt. Print. Off., 1962. vi, 137 p.
62-60066
   Z663.35 .M26 MRR Alc.

Wagner, Henry Raup, The Plains and
the Rockies; 3d ed. Columbus, Ohio,
Long's College Book Co., 1953. 601
p. 016.9178 53-2473
   Z1251.W5 W2 1953 MRR Alc.

UNITED STATES--FAIRS--DIRECTORIES--
PERIODICALS.
Cavalcade and directory of fairs.
[Cincinnati, Billboard Publications,
etc.] 791 72-624676
   SF114 .D5 MRR Alc Latest edition

UNITED STATES--FOREIGN ECONOMIC
RELATIONS--CUBA.
Smith, Robert Freeman, The United
States and Cuba: New York, Bookman
Associates [1961, c1960] 256 p.
327.7307291 60-53477
   E183.8.C9 S6 MRR Alc.

UNITED STATES--FOREIGN POPULATION.
Handlin, Oscar, ed. Immigration as a
factor in American history.
Englewood Cliffs, N.J., Prentice-
Hall, 1959. 206 p. 325.73 59-9516
   E184.A1 H23 MRR Alc.

Hutchinson, Edward Prince,
Immigrants and their children, 1850-
1950, New York, Wiley [1956] xiv,
391 p. 331.62 56-6502
   HB2595 .H8 MRR Alc.

Wittke, Carl Frederick, We who built
America; [Rev. ed. Cleveland] Press
of Western Reserve University [1964]
xviii, 550 p. 64-20939
   JV6455 .W55 1964 MRR Alc.

UNITED STATES--FOREIGN POPULATION--
BIBLIOGRAPHY.
George Washington University,
Washington, D.C. A report on world
population migrations as related to
the United States of America:
Washington [1956] v. 449 p.
016.32573 56-3432
   Z7164.I3 G4 MRR Alc.

UNITED STATES--FOREIGN POPULATION--
COLLECTIONS.
Brown, Francis James, ed. One
America: 3d ed. New York, Prentice-
Hall, 1952. xvi, 764 p. 325.73 52-
1682
   E184.A1 B87 1952 MRR Alc.

UNITED STATES--FOREIGN RELATIONS.
Bailey, Thomas Andrew, A diplomatic
history of the American people 8th
ed. New York, Appleton-Century-
Crofts [1969] xl, 1015 p. 327.73
79-77535
   E183.7 .B29 1969 MRR Alc.

Bemis, Samuel Flagg, ed. The
American Secretaries of State and
their diplomacy. New York, Pageant
Book Co., 1958 [c1928] 10 v. in 5.
923.273 58-7201
   E183.7 .B46 1958 MRR Alc.

Bemis, Samuel Flagg, A diplomatic
history of the United States. 5th
ed. New York, Holt, Rinehart and
Winston [1965] x, 1062 p. 327.73
65-11841
   E183.7 .B4682 1965 MRR Alc.

Carroll, Holbert N. The House of
Representatives and foreign affairs.
Pittsburgh, University of Pittsburgh
[1958] 365 p. 328.73 58-10705
   JK1319 .C3 MRR Alc.

Chamber of Commerce of the United
States of America. Foreign Commerce
Dept. Guide to foreign information
sources. [Rev. Washington] Chamber
of Commerce of the United States
[1960] 26 p. 327.73 61-25832
   E744 .C46 1960 MRR Alc.

Council on foreign relations.
American agencies interested in
international affairs. 1931- New
York, [etc.] Frederick A. Praeger,
[etc.] 341.06 31-26874
   JX27 .C62 MRR Ref Desk Latest
   edition

De Conde, Alexander. A history of
American foreign policy. New York,
Scribner [1963] xi, 914 p. 327.73
63-7615
   E183.7 .D4 MRR Alc.

Farnsworth, David Nelson, The Senate
Committee on Foreign Relations.
Urbana, University of Illinois Press,
1961. vi, 189 p. 327.73 61-62766
   JK1240.F6 F3 MRR Alc.

Ferrell, Robert H. American
diplomacy; Rev., and expanded ed.
New York, Norton [1969] xiv, 930 p.
[9.50] 327.73 69-13018
   E183.7 .F4 1969 MRR Alc.

Hackworth, Green Haywood, Digest of
international law. Washington, U.S.
Govt. Print. Off., 1940-44. 8 v.
341.02 41-50552
   JX237 .H3 MRR Alc.

Moore, John Bassett, A digest of
international law Washington, Govt.
print. off., 1906. 8 v. 30-10322
   JX237 .M7'1906a MRR Alc.

Plischke, Elmer, Summit diplomacy;
College Park, Bureau of Governmental
Research, College of Business and
Public Administration, University of
Maryland, 1958. viii, 125 p.
327.73 58-63026
   JK570 .P58 MRR Alc.

United States. Dept. of State.
Foreign relations of the United
States. [1861]- Washington, U.S.
Govt. Print. Off. 327.73 10-3793
   JX233 .A3 MRR Alc Full set

United States. Treaties, etc.
Treaties, conventions, international
acts, protocols and agreements
between the United States of America
and other powers ... Grosse Pointe,
Mich., [Scholarly Press [1970?] 4 v.
(xxvi, 5755 p.) 341.2/73 78-121307
   JX236 1910c MRR Alc.

The United States in world affairs.
1931- New York, Simon & Schuster
[etc.] 32-26065
   E744 .U66 MRR Alc Full set

Whiteman, Marjorie Millace. Digest
of international law. [Washington,
U.S. Dept. of State; for sale by the
Superintendent of Documents, U.S.
Govt. Print. Off., 1963- v.
[$6.25 (v. 14) varies] 341.02 63-
62002
   JX237 .W55 MRR Alc.

UNITED STATES--FOREIGN RELATIONS--
REVOLUTION, 1775-1783.
Franklin, Benjamin, The writings of
Benjamin Franklin; New York, The
Macmillan company; London, Macmillan
& co., ltd., 1905-07. 10 v. 05-
35396
   E302 .F82 1905 MRR Alc.

Morris, Richard Brandon, The
peacemakers; [1st ed.] New York,
Harper & Row [1965] xviii, 572 p.
973.317 65-20435
   E249 .M68 MRR Alc.

UNITED STATES--FOREIGN RELATIONS--1783-
1865.
Adams, John Quincy, Pres. U.S.,
Diary, 1794-1845; New York,
Scribner, 1951. xxxv, 586 p.
973.5/5/0924 51-10345
   E377 .A213 MRR Alc.

Adams, John Quincy, pres. U.S.,
Memoirs of John Quincy Adams,
Philadelphia, J. B. Lippincott & co.,
1874-77. 12 v. 04-20138
   E377 .A19 MRR Alc.

UNITED STATES--FOREIGN (Cont.)
Bemis, Samuel Flagg. John Quincy
Adams and the foundations of American
foreign policy. [1st ed.] New York,
A. A. Knopf, 1949. xix, 588, xv p.
923.173   49-10664
    E377 .B45 1949 MRR Alc.

UNITED STATES--FOREIGN RELATIONS--
CONSTITUTIONAL PERIOD, 1789-1809.
State papers and publick documents of
the United States, from the accession
of George Washington to the
presidency, exhibiting a complete
view of our foreign relations since
that time. 3d ed. Boston, Printed
and published by Thomas B. Wait,
1819. 12 v. 27-5174
    J33 .W4 MRR Alc.

UNITED STATES--FOREIGN RELATIONS--1809-
1817.
State papers and publick documents of
the United States, from the accession
of George Washington to the
presidency, exhibiting a complete
view of our foreign relations since
that time. 3d ed. Boston, Printed
and published by Thomas B. Wait,
1819. 12 v. 27-5174
    J33 .W4 MRR Alc.

UNITED STATES--FOREIGN RELATIONS--20TH
CENTURY.
Graebner, Norman A., ed. An
uncertain tradition; American
Secretaries of State in the twentieth
century. New York, McGraw-Hill,
1961. 341 p. 353.1 61-8654
    E744 .G7 MRR Alc.

Johnson, Walter, 1600 Pennsylvania
Avenue; [1st ed.] Boston, Little,
Brown [1960] 390 p. 973.91 60-
6525
    E743 .J6 MRR Alc.

Warren, Sidney, The President as
world leader. [1st ed.]
Philadelphia Lippincott [1964] xii,
480 p. 327.73 64-22183
    E744 .W295 MRR Alc.

Wish, Harvey, Contemporary America;
4th ed. New York, Harper & Row
[1966] xx, 813 p. 973.9 66-15677
    E741 .W78 1966 MRR Alc.

UNITED STATES--FOREIGN RELATIONS--1901-
1909.
Beale, Howard Kennedy, Theodore
Roosevelt and the rise of America to
world power. Baltimore, Johns
Hopkins Press, 1956. 600 p.
973.911 56-10255
    E757 .B4 MRR Alc.

UNITED STATES--FOREIGN RELATIONS--1933-
1945.
United States. Congress. Senate.
Committee on Foreign Relations. A
decade of American foreign policy;
Washington, U.S. Govt. Print. Off.,
1950. xiv, 1381 p. 327.73 50-
60544
    JX1416 .A47 MRR Alc.

UNITED STATES--FOREIGN RELATIONS--1933-
1945--SOURCES.
Documents on American foreign
relations. 1938/39- New York, Simon
and Schuster [etc.] 39-28987
    JX231 .D6 MRR Alc Full set

UNITED STATES--FOREIGN RELATIONS--1945-
1953.
United States. Congress. Senate.
Committee on Foreign Relations. A
decade of American foreign policy;
Washington, U.S. Govt. Print. Off.,
1950. xiv, 1381 p. 327.73 50-
60544
    JX1416 .A47 MRR Alc.

UNITED STATES--FOREIGN RELATIONS--1945-
Crabb, Cecil Van Meter, American
foreign policy in the nuclear age 3d
ed. New York, Harper & Row [1972]
x, 528 p. 327.73 71-168366
    E744 .C793 1972 MRR Alc.

Gilbert, Amy M. Executive agreements
and treaties, 1946-1973; [Endicott,
N.Y.] Thomas-Newell [1973] x, 213 p.
327.73 73-82739
    JX1417 .G54 MRR Alc.

Gross, Franz B., ed. The United
States and the United Nations,
Norman, University of Oklahoma Press
[1964] x, 356 p. 341.13973 64-
20766
    JX1977.2.U5 G7 MRR Alc.

May, Ernest R., ed. Anxiety and
affluence: 1945-1965, New York,
McGraw-Hill [1966] xii, 404 p.
973.908 66-14810
    E173 .D58 vol. 8 MRR Alc.

United States. Dept. of State.
Historical Office. American foreign
policy; 1956- [Washington] 327.73
59-64042
    JX1417 .A33 MRR Alc Full set

UNITED STATES--FOREIGN RELATIONS--1945-
--ADDRESSES, ESSAYS, LECTURES.
Kertesz, Stephen Denis, ed. American
diplomacy in a new era. Notre Dame,
Ind.] University of Notre Dame Press,
1961. xi, 601 p. 327.73 61-8466
    E744 .K4 MRR Alc.

UNITED STATES--FOREIGN RELATIONS--1945-
--SOURCES.
Schlesinger, Arthur Meier, comp. The
dynamics of world power; New York,
Chelsea House Publishers, 1973- v.
[$149.00] 327.73 78-150208
    E744 .S395 MRR Alc.

United States. Dept. of State.
Historical Office. American foreign
policy, 1950-1955; Washington, U.S.
Govt. Print. Off., 1957] 2 v. (lix,
3244, xxv p.] 327.73 sd 57-10
    JX1417 .A55 MRR Alc.

UNITED STATES--FOREIGN RELATIONS--1953-
1961.
Eisenhower, Dwight David, Pres. U.S.,
The White House years. [1st ed.]
Garden City, N.Y., Doubleday, 1963-
65. 2 v. 973.921 63-18447
    E835 .E47 MRR Alc.

UNITED STATES--FOREIGN RELATIONS--1969-
1974.
Nixon, Richard Milhous, Nixon; the
fourth year of his Presidency.
Washington, Congressional Quarterly
[c1973] 46, 146 p. [$4.00]
320.9/73/0924 72-94077
    E855 .N494 MRR Alc.

UNITED STATES--FOREIGN RELATIONS--
BIBLIOGRAPHY.
Bemis, Samuel Flagg, Guide to the
diplomatic history of the United
States, 1775-1921, Washington, U.S.
Govt. print. off., 1935. xvii, 979
p. 016.32773 35-26001
    Z6465.U5 B4 MRR Ref Desk.

Hasse, Adelaide Rosalia, Index to
United States documents relating to
foreign affairs, 1828-1861, New
York, Kraus Reprint Corp., 1965. 3
v. 016.32773 67-163
    Z1223.Z7 H22 MRR Alc.

Larson, Arthur D. National security
affairs: Detroit, Gale Research Co.,
[1973] 411 p. 016.35503/3/0973 70-
184013
    Z1215 .L37 MRR Alc.

Plischke, Elmer, American diplomacy;
College Park, Bureau of Governmental
Research, College of business and
Public Adminstration, University of
Maryland, 1957. iv, 27 p.
016.32773 57-63088
    Z6465.U5 P48 MRR Alc.

Plischke, Elmer, American foreign
relations, College Park, Bureau of
Governmental Research, College of
Business and Public Administration,
University of Maryland [1956, c1955]
viii, 71 p. 016.32773 56-62681
    Z6465.U5 P5 MRR Alc.

United States. Library of Congress.
Division of Bibliography. Foreign
relations of the United States;
[Washington] 1929. 25 p. 016.32773
51-60036
    Z663.28 .F6 MRR Alc.

United States. Library of Congress.
Division of bibliography. ... List
of recent books on foreign relations
of the United States [Washington]
1940. 2 p. l., 55 p. 016.32773 41-
14163
    Z663.28 .L57 MRR Alc.

UNITED STATES--FOREIGN RELATIONS--
EXECUTIVE AGREEMENTS.
Gilbert, Amy M. Executive agreements
and treaties, 1946-1973; [Endicott,
N.Y.] Thomas-Newell [1973] x, 213 p.
327.73 73-82739
    JX1417 .G54 MRR Alc.

United States. Dept. of state.
Subject index of the Treaty series
and the Executive agreement series.
Washington, U.S. Govt. print. off.,
1932. v, 214 p. 341.273 32-26434
    JX235.9 .A3 Index 1931 MRR Ref
Desk.

United States. Laws, statutes, etc.
United States statutes at large,
containing the laws and concurrent
resolutions ... and reorganization
plan, amendment to the Constitution,
and proclamations. v. 1- 1789/1845-
Washington, U.S. Govt. Print. Off.
07-35353
    LAW MRR Alc (Dk 33) Full set

UNITED STATES--FOREIGN RELATIONS--
SOURCES.
Bartlett, Ruhl Jacob, ed. The record
of American diplomacy; 4th ed. enl.
New York, Knopf, 1964. xxiv, 892,
xxii p. 327.73 64-23887
    E183.7 .B35 1964 MRR Alc.

Documents on American foreign
relations. 1938/39- New York, Simon
and Schuster [etc.] 39-28987
    JX231 .D6 MRR Alc Full set

UNITED STATES--FOREIGN RELATIONS--
SPEECHES IN CONGRESS.
Miller, Marion Mills, ed. Great
debates in American history, [The
national ed.] New York, Current
literature publishing company [c1913]
14 v. 13-23912
    E173 .M64 vol. 14 MRR Alc.

UNITED STATES--FOREIGN RELATIONS--
TREATIES.
Davenport, Frances Gardiner, ed.
European treaties bearing on the
history of the United States and its
dependencies, Washington, D.C.,
Carnegie institution of Washington,
1917-37. 4 v. 18-3383
    E173 .D24 MRR Alc.

Gilbert, Amy M. Executive agreements
and treaties, 1946-1973; [Endicott,
N.Y.] Thomas-Newell [1973] x, 213 p.
327.73 73-82739
    JX1417 .G54 MRR Alc.

Manning, William Ray, ed.
Arbitration treaties among the
American nations, to the close of the
year 1910, New York [etc.] Oxford
university press, 1924. xl, 472 p.
24-6749
    JX1985 .M3 MRR Alc.

United States. Congress. House.
Committee on Foreign Affairs.
Collective defense treaties, with
maps, texts of treaties, a
chronology, status of forces
agreements, and comparative chart.
Rev.] Washington, U.S. Govt. Print.
Off., 1969. ix, 514 p. [2.50]
341.2 79-602271
    JX171 .U39 1969 MRR Alc.

United States. Dept. of state.
Catalogue of treaties. 1814-1918.
Washington, Govt. print. off., 1919.
xxv, 3-716 p. 20-13106
    JX171 .U4 1918 MRR Ref Desk.

United States. Dept. of state. List
of treaties submitted to the Senate,
1789-1934. Washington, U.S. Govt.
print. off., 1935. iii, 138 p.
341.273 35-26688
    JX236 1934b MRR Alc.

United States. Dept. of state.
Subject index of the Treaty series
and the Executive agreement series.
Washington, U.S. Govt. print. off.,
1932. v, 214 p. 341.273 32-26434
    JX235.9 .A3 Index 1931 MRR Ref
Desk.

United States. Dept. of State. Office
of the Legal Adviser. Treaties in
force; [Washington, U.S. Govt.
Print. Off.] 341.273 56-61604
Began publication with 1929 issue.
    JX236 1929c MRR Alc Latest
edition

United States. Laws, statutes, etc.
United States statutes at large,
containing the laws and concurrent
resolutions ... and reorganization
plan, amendment to the Constitution,
and proclamations. v. 1- 1789/1845-
Washington, U.S. Govt. Print. Off.
07-35353
    LAW MRR Alc (Dk 33) Full set

United States. Treaties, etc.
Treaties and other international acts
of the United States of America.
Washington, U.S. Govt. Print. Off.,
1931- v. 341.273 31-28592
    JX236 1931a MRR Alc.

United States. Treaties, etc.
Treaties and other international
agreements of the United States of
America, 1776-1949. [Washington,
Dept. of State; for sale by the Supt.
of Docs., U.S. Govt. Print. Off.,
1968- v. [8.50 (v. 1) varies]
341/.0264/73 70-600742
    JX236 1968 .A5 MRR Alc.

United States. Treaties, etc.
Treaties, conventions, international
acts, protocols and agreements
between the United States of America
and other powers ... Grosse Pointe,
Mich., Scholarly Press [1970?] 4 v.
(xxvi, 5755 p.] 341.2/73 78-121307
    JX236 1910c MRR Alc.

United States. Treaties, etc. United
States treaties and other
international agreements. v. 1-
1950- [Washington] Dept. of State.
341.273 53-60242
    JX231 .A34 MRR Alc Full set

UNITED STATES--FOREIGN RELATIONS--
TREATIES--BIBLIOGRAPHY.
United States. Library of Congress.
Division of bibliography. List of
references on the treaty-making
power. Washington, Govt. print.
off., 1920. 219 p.   20-26005
Z663.28 .L5827 MRR Alc.

United States. Treaties, etc.
Treaties and other international acts
of the United States of America.
Volume 1 (short print) Washington,
U.S. Govt. print. off., 1931. x, 201
p.   016.341273   31-28544
JX236 1931 MRR Alc.

UNITED STATES--FOREIGN RELATIONS--
TREATIES--INDEXES.
American Bar Association. Committee
on Commercial Treaties. Commercial
treaty index. [Chicago] Section of
International Law American Bar
Association [1973-   1 v. (loose-leaf)
341.7/54/026473   73-163891
JX236 1973 .A65 MRR Alc.

UNITED STATES--FOREIGN RELATIONS--CHINA.
United States. Dept. of State. The
China white paper, August 1949.
Stanford, Calif., Stanford University
Press [1967] xli, 1079 p.
327.51/073 67-26650
E183.8.C5 U53 1967 MRR Alc.

United States. Dept. of State.
Historical Office. China, 1942-
Washington, U.S. Govt. Print. Off.,
1956-   v.   327.73051   57-61196
JX1428.C6 A54 MRR Alc.

UNITED STATES--FOREIGN RELATIONS--CUBA.
Smith, Robert Freeman. The United
States and Cuba: New York, Bookman
Associates [1861, c1960] 256 p.
327.7307291 60-53477
E183.8.C9 S6 MRR Alc.

UNITED STATES--FOREIGN RELATIONS--
FRANCE.
De Conde, Alexander. The quasi-war;
New York, Scribner [1966] xiv, 498
p.   973.45 66-24492
E323 .D4 MRR Alc.

France. Archives nationales. French
consuls in the United States:
Washington, Library of Congress; [for
sale by the Supt. of Docs., U.S.
Govt. Print. Off.] 1967. xi, 605 p.
327.73044 67-62310
E183.8.F8 A45 MRR Alc.

UNITED STATES--FOREIGN RELATIONS--GREAT
BRITAIN.
Allen, Harry Cranbrook. Great
Britain and the United States; New
York, St. Martin's Press, 1955. 1024
p.   327.730942 55-7753
E183.8.G7 A47 1955 MRR Alc.

UNITED STATES--FOREIGN RELATIONS--JAPAN.
Reischauer, Edwin Oldfather, The
United States and Japan. Rev. ed.
Cambridge, Harvard University Press,
1957. 394 p.   327.730952 57-9082
E183.8.J3 R4 1957 MRR Alc.

UNITED STATES--FOREIGN RELATIONS--LATIN
AMERICA.
Gantenbein, James Watson, ed. The
evolution of our Latin-American
policy. New York, Columbia
University Press 1950. xxvii, 979
p.   327.73098 49-50406
F1418 .G2 MRR Alc.

UNITED STATES--FOREIGN RELATIONS--LATIN
AMERICA--BIBLIOGRAPHY.
Trask, David F. A bibliography of
United States-Latin American
relations since 1810; Lincoln,
University of Nebraska Press [1968]
xxxi, 441 p. [$14.95] 016.32773/08
67-14421
Z1609.R4 T7 MRR Alc.

UNITED STATES--FOREIGN RELATIONS--
MEXICO.
Cline, Howard Francis. The United
States and Mexico. Rev. ed., enl.
New York, Atheneum, 1963. 484 p.
63-24587
F1226 .C6 1963 MRR Alc.

UNITED STATES--FOREIGN RELATIONS--
RUSSIA.
Jados, Stanley S., ed. Documents on
Russian-American relations,
Washington, Catholic University of
America Press [1965] viii, 416 p.
327.47073 65-12569
E183.8.R9 J3 MRR Alc.

United States. Dept. of State. The
Soviet Union, 1933-1939. Washington,
U.S. Govt. Print. Off., 1952. cii,
1034 p.   327.730947 52-61069
JX233.A6R93 MRR Alc.

UNITED STATES--FOREIGN RELATIONS--SPAIN.
Chadwick, French Ensor, The
relations of the United States and
Spain: the Spanish-American war, New
York, C. Scribner's sons, 1911. 2 v.
11-23013
E715 .C43 MRR Alc.

UNITED STATES--FOREIGN RELATIONS--
VIETNAM.
United States. Congress. Senate.
Committee on Foreign Relations.
Background information relating to
Southeast Asia and Vietnam. Jan. 14,
1965- Washington, For sale by the
Supt. of Docs., U.S. Govt. Print.
Off. 327.597/073 72-601275
E183.8.V5 A3 MRR Alc Latest
edition

UNITED STATES--FOREIGN RELATIONS
ADMINISTRATION.
Crabb, Cecil Van Meter, American
foreign policy in the nuclear age 3d
ed. New York, Harper & Row [1972]
x, 528 p.   327.73 71-168366
E744 .C793 1972 MRR Alc.

Plischke, Elmer, Conduct of American
diplomacy. 3d ed. Princeton, N.J.,
Van Nostrand [1967] xvii, 677 p.
353.008/92 67-6536
JX1407 .P58 1967 MRR Alc.

Sakell, Achilles Nicholas, Careers
in the Foreign Service. New York, H.
A. Walck, 1962. 118 p.   341.7 62-
21793
JX1417 .S2 MRR Alc.

UNITED STATES--FOREIGN RELATIONS
ADMINISTRATION--ADDRESSES, ESSAYS,
LECTURES.
Kertesz, Stephen Denis, ed. American
diplomacy in a new era. Notre Dame,
Ind.] University of Notre Dame Press,
1961. xi, 601 p.   327.73 61-8466
E744 .K4 MRR Alc.

UNITED STATES--FORESTRY
United States. Dept. of Agriculture.
Trees, Washington, U.S. Govt. Print.
Off. [1949] xiv, 944 p.   634.90973
agr55-2
S21 .A35 1949 MRR Alc.

UNITED STATES--GAZETTEERS.
Cromie, Alice Hamilton. A tour guide
to the Civil War. Chicago,
Quadrangle Books, 1965 [c1964] xxv,
372 p.   917.3 64-10926
E468.9 .C8 MRR Alc.

UNITED STATES--GENEALOGY.
Colket, Meredith Bright, Guide to
genealogical records in the National
Archives, Washington, National
Archives, National Archives and
Records Service, General Services
Administration; [for sale by the
Superintendent of Documents, U.S.
Govt. Print. Off.] 1964. x, 145 p.
a 64-7048
CS15 .C6 MRR Alc.

Zorn, Walter Lewis. The descendants
of the Presidents of the United
States of America. Monroe, Mich.,
1954. 149 p.   929.2 55-355
CS59 .Z6 MRR Alc.

UNITED STATES--GENEALOGY--BIBLIOGRAPHY.
Filby, P. William, American &
British genealogy & heraldry; a
selected list of books. Chicago,
American Library Association, 1970.
xix, 184 p. [10.00] 016.9291/097
75-106200
Z5311 .F55 MRR Alc.

Stevenson, Noel C. Search and
research, the researcher's handbook:
Rev. ed. Salt Lake City, Deseret
Book Co., 1959. 364 p.   929.1072
59-11137
Z5313.U5 S8 1959 MRR Ref Desk.

UNITED STATES--GENEALOGY--BIBLIOGRAPHY--
CATALOGS.
American Antiquarian Society,
Worcester, Mass. Library. A
dictionary catalog of American books
pertaining to the 17th through 19th
centuries. Westport, Conn.,
Greenwood Pub. Corp. [1971] 20 v.
015/.73 76-103820
Z1215 .A264 MRR Alc (Dk 33)

United States. Library of Congress.
American and English genealogies in
the Library of Congress, 2d ed.
Washington, Govt. print. off., 1919.
iv, 1332 p.   19-26004
Z663.74 .A5 1919 MRR Alc.

United States. Library of Congress.
Genealogies in the Library of
Congress; Baltimore, Md., Magna
Carta Book Co., 1972. 2 v.
016.929/1 74-187078
Z5319 .U53 MRR Alc.

UNITED STATES--GENEALOGY--SOURCES--
BIBLIOGRAPHY.
Brewer, Mary Marie. Index to census
schedules in printed form;
Huntsville, Ark., Century
Enterprises, Genealogical Services,
1969. 63 p.   929.3 72-2676
Z7553.C3 B7 MRR Alc.

Lancour, Harold, A bibliography of
ship passenger lists, 1538-1825: 3d
ed., rev. and enl. New York, New
York Public Library, 1963. ix, 137
p.   016.32573 63-18141
Z7164.13 L2 1963 MRR Alc.

UNITED STATES--GOVERNMENT PUBLICATIONS.
Boyd, Anne Morris, United States
Government publications. 3rd ed.
rev. New York, Wilson, 1949 [i.e.
1952] xx, 627 p.   015.73 55-694
Z1223.Z7 B7 1952 MRR Ref Desk.

Cossman, E. Joseph. How to get
$50,000 worth of services free, each
year, from the U.S. Government, New
York, F. Fell [1965, c1964] 233 p.
658.02 64-8781
HF5353 .C7 MRR Alc.

Folsom, Gwendolyn B. Legislative
history: Charlottesville, University
Press of Virginia [1972] viii, 136
p.   348/.73/1 72-80386
KF425 .F64 MRR Ref Desk.

Kerbec, Matthew J., comp. Legally
available U.S. Government information
as a result of the Public Information
Act. [lst ed.] Arlington, Va.,
Output Systems Corp. [1970] 2 v.
353/.0007 70-108181
KF5753 .A33 1970 MRR Alc.

Schmeckebier, Laurence Frederick,
Government publications and their
use, 2d, rev., ed. Washington,
D.C., The Brookings institution,
1939. xv, 479 p.   025.1734 015.73
39-22433
Z1223.Z7 S3 1939 MRR Ref Desk.

Schmeckebier, Laurence Frederick,
Government publications and their use
2d rev. ed. Washington, Brookings
Institution [1969] viii, 502 p.
[8.95] 025.17/3 69-19694
Z1223.Z7 S3 1969 MRR Ref Desk.

Schmeckebier, Laurence Frederick,
Government publications and their use
Rev. ed. Washington, D.C.,
Brookings Institution [1961] xi, 476
p.   025.173 61-7718
Z1223.Z7 S3 1961 MRR Ref Desk.

United States. Library of Congress.
Union Catalog Division. United
States author headings, [2d printed
ed.] Ann Arbor, Mich., Edwards
Bros., 1946. 211 p.   025.3 47-5580

Z663.79 .U5 1946 MRR Alc.

UNITED STATES--GOVERNMENT PUBLICATIONS--
BIBLIOGRAPHY.
The American catalogue ... New York,
1941. 8 v. in 13.   015.73 a 42-
2938
Z1215 .A52 MRR Ref Desk.

Andriot, John L. Checklist of major
U.S. Government series, McLean, Va.,
Documents Index, 1972- v.
015/.73 73-163950
Z1223.Z7 A544 MRR Alc.

Andriot, John L. Guide to popular
U.S. Government publications.
[Arlington, Va.] Documents Index,
1960. 125 p.   015.73 60-9768
Z1223.Z7 A545 MRR Alc.

Boyd, Anne Morris, United States
Government publications. 3rd ed.
rev. New York, Wilson, 1949 [i.e.
1952] xx, 627 p.   015.73 55-694
Z1223.Z7 B7 1952 MRR Ref Desk.

Catalog cards in book form for United
States Joint Publications Research
Service translations. v. -8; -
Jan./June 1970. New York [etc.] CCM
Information Corp. [etc.] 75-104064
Began with vol. for 1957/61.
Z1223.Z9 K9 Sci RR Sci RR Partial
set / MRR Alc Full set

Child, Sargent Burrage, Check list
of Historical Records Survey
publications; Baltimore,
Genealogical Pub. Co., 1969. vi, 110
p.   016.973/08 69-17126
Z1223.Z7 C52 MRR Alc.

Complete guide and index to ERIC
reports: Englewood Cliffs, N.J.,
Prentice-Hall [1970] 1338 p.
370/.78 79-123091
Z5814.R4 C6 MRR Ref Desk.

Frank, Nathalie D., Data sources for
business and market analysis, 2d ed.
Metuchen, N.J., Scarecrow Press,
1969. 361 p.   016.65883/9/73 73-
5855
HF5415.1 .F7 1969 MRR Alc.

Government publications guide.
Boston, G. K. Hall. 011 73-19397
Z7164.G7 G68 MRR Ref Desk Partial
set

UNITED STATES--GOVERNMENT (Cont.)
Greely, Adolphus Washington. Public
documents of the first fourteen
Congresses, 1789-1817. New York,
Johnson Reprint Corp. [1973] 903,
343-406 p. 016.32873 73-2634
Z1223 .A 1973 MRR Ref Desk

Greely, Adolphus Washington. Public
documents of the first fourteen
congresses, 1789-1817. Washington,
Govt. print. off., 1900. 903 p. 01-
20895
Z1223.A 1900 MRR Alc.

Das Grosse Duden-Lexikon in acht
Banden. Mannheim, Bibliographisches
Institut, 1946-69. 10 v. [33.00 (v.
3) varies] 033/.1 67-94115
AE27 .G693 vol. 9-10 MRR Alc.

Guide to U.S. Government statistics.
1956- [Arlington, Va.] Documents
Index. 016.3173 61-9066
Z7554.U5 G8 MRR Ref Desk Latest
edition

Hasse, Adelaide Rosalia. Index to
United States documents relating to
foreign affairs, 1828-1861, New
York, Kraus Reprint Corp., 1965. 3
v. 016.32773 67-163
Z1223.Z7 H22 MRR Alc.

Jackson, Ellen Pauline. Subject
guide to major United States
Government publications. Chicago,
American Library Association, 1968.
x, 175 p. 015/.73 68-25844
Z1223.Z7 J32 MRR Alc.

Mason, John Brown. Research
resources; Santa Barbara, Calif.,
ABC-Clio, 1968- v. [3.00]
016.327/.09/04 68-8685
Z7161 .M36 MRR Ref Desk.

New York (City). Public Library.
Research Libraries. Catalog of
Government publications in the
Research Libraries: Boston, G. K.
Hall, 1972. 40 v. 011 74-171015
Z7164.G7 N54 1972 MRR Alc (Dk 33)

O'Hara, Frederic J., Over 2000 free
publications, New York, New American
Library [1968] 352 p. [0.95]
015/.73 71-3122
Z1223.Z7 O5 MRR Alc.

Plischke, Elmer, American foreign
relations, College Park, Bureau of
Governmental Research, College of
Business and Public Administration,
University of Maryland [1956, c1955]
viii, 71 p. 016.32773 56-62681
Z6465.U5 P5 MRR Alc.

Poore, Benjamin Perley, A
descriptive catalogue of the
government publications of the United
States, September 5, 1774-March 4,
1881. Washington, Govt. print. off.,
1885. iv, 1392 p. 01-9291
Z1223.A 1885 MRR Ref Desk.

Poore, Benjamin Perley, A
descriptive catalogue of the
Government publications of the United
States, September 5, 1774-March 4,
1881, [Ann Arbor, J. W. Edwards,
1953] iv, 1392 p. 015.73 54-60536

Z1223 .A 1885c MRR Ref Desk.

Poore, Benjamin Perley, A
descriptive catalogue of the
Government publications of the United
States, September 5, 1774-March 4,
1881. New York, Johnson Reprint
Corp. [1970] 2 v. (iv, 1392 p.)
015/.73 74-29060
Z1223.A 1885d MRR Alc.

Schmeckebier, Laurence Frederick,
Government publications and their use
Rev. ed. Washington, D.C.,
Brookings Institution [1961] xi, 476
p. 025.173 61-7718
Z1223.Z7 S3 1961 MRR Ref Desk.

Schmeckebier, Laurence Frederick,
Government publications and their
use. 2d. rev., ed. Washington,
D.C., The Brookings institution,
1939. xv, 479 p. 025.1734 015.73
39-22433
Z1223.Z7 S3 1939 MRR Ref Desk.

Schmeckebier, Laurence Frederick,
Government publications and their use
2d rev. ed. Washington, Brookings
Institution [1969] viii, 502 p.
[8.95] 025.17/3 69-19694
Z1233.Z7 S3 1969 MRR Ref Desk.

Transdex; v. 8- July 1970- New
York, CCM Information Corp. 015/.73
77-612605
AS36 .U574 Sci RR Full Set / MRR
Alc Full set

United States. Bureau of American
Ethnology. List of publications of
the Bureau of American Ethnology
1894- Washington, U.S. Govt. Print.
Off. 23-27414
E51 .U65 MRR Ref Desk Latest
edition

United States. Bureau of the Budget.
Office of Statistical Standards.
Statistical services of the United
States Government. [Washington] 59-
61620
HA37 .U16 MRR Ref Desk Latest
edition

United States. Bureau of the Census.
Bureau of the Census catalog.
[Washington, For sale by the Supt. of
Docs., U.S. Govt. Print. Off.]
016.3173 74-644649
Z7554.U5 U32 MRR Alc Full set

United States. Bureau of the Census.
Census Bureau programs and
publications; [Washington; For sale
by the Supt. of Docs., U.S. Govt.
Print. Off., 1968] vi, 146 p.
[1.50] 311/.39/73 79-603950
HA37 .U52 1968 MRR Ref Desk.

United States. Bureau of the Census.
Directory of Federal statistics for
local areas, [Washington; For sale
by the Supt. of Docs., U.S. Govt.
Print. Off.] 1966. vi, 156 p. a
66-7475
HB2175 .A5 1966 TJ Rm.

United States. Bureau of the Census.
Directory of Federal statistics for
states; Washington, For sale by the
Supt. of Docs, U.S. Govt. Print.
Off., 1967] viii, 372 p. 317.3 a
67-7451
HA37 .U52 1967 MRR Ref Desk.

United States. Civil Service
Commission. Guide to Federal career
literature. [Washington; for sale by
the Supt. of Docs., U.S. Govt. Print.
Off., 1972] 34 p. [$0.45]
016.3317/95/0973 72-603286
Z1223 .A199 1972 MRR Ref Desk.

United States. Congress. House.
[Index to reports of committees of
the House of representatives,
Washington, Govt. print. off., 1887]
58 v. in 1.   05-41773
Z1223 .A4 1887 MRR Ref Desk.

United States. Congress. House.
Library. Index to congressional
committee hearings in the Library of
the United States House of
Representatives. Jan. 5, 1937-
Washington, U.S. Govt. Print. Off.
016.32873 38-26099
Z1223.A1 A3 MRR Ref Desk Partial
set

United States. Congress. Senate.
[Index to reports of committees of
the Senate, Washington, Govt. print.
off., 1887] 36 v. in 1. 05-41774
Z1223.A3 1887 MRR Ref Desk.

United States. Congress. Senate.
Library. Catalogue of the library of
the United States Senate. Washington
[Govt. print. off.] 1924. 1210 p.
24-1209
Z881 .U58 1924 MRR Alc.

United States. Congress. Senate.
Library. Index of congressional
committee hearings (not confidential
in character) prior to January 3,
1935 in the United States Senate
library. Washington, U.S. Govt.
print. off., 1935. ii, 1056 p.
015.73 35-26894
Z1223 .A 1935 MRR Ref Desk.

United States. Dept. of state.
Subject index of the Treaty series
and the Executive agreement series.
Washington, U.S. Govt. print. off.,
1932. v, 214 p. 341.273 32-26434

JX235.9 .A3 Index 1931 MRR Ref
Desk.

United States. Dept. of the Interior.
Division of Documents. Comprehensive
index to the publications of the
United States Government, 1881-1893,
Ann Arbor, J. W. Edwards, 1953. 2 v.
in 1 (v, 1590 p.) 015.73 54-61502

Z1223.A 1953 MRR Alc.

United States. Dept. of the Interior.
Division of Documents. Comprehensive
index to the publications of the
United States Government, 1881-1893,
New York, Johnson Reprint Corp.,
[1970] 2 v. (v, 159 p.) 015/.73
75-29071
Z1223.A 1970 MRR Ref Desk.

United States. Educational Research
Information Center. Office of
Education research reports, 1956-65,
ED 002 747-ED 003 960. [Washington,
U.S. Govt. Print. Off., 1967] 2 v.
016.370/78 hew67-155
Z5814.R4 U5 MRR Ref Desk.

United States. Library of Congress.
Census Library Project. Catalog of
United States census publications,
1790-1945, Washington, U.S.
Govt.Print. Off., 1950. x, 320 p.
016.312 50-60600
Z7554.U5 U62 MRR Alc.

United States. Library of Congress.
Census Library Project. Catalog of
United States census publications,
1790-1945. New York, B. Franklin
[1971] x, 320 p. 016.3173 72-
153029
Z7554.U5 U62 1971 MRR Ref Desk.

United States. Library of Congress.
General reference and bibliography
division. The American guide series:
Washington, 1944. 1 p. l., 5 p.
016.9173 45-37859
Z1236 .U615 MRR Alc.

United States. Library of Congress.
Science and Technology Division. A
catalog of OSRD reports. Washington,
1950- 1 v. (loose-leaf) 016.5072
50-60310
Z663.41 .C3 MRR Alc.

United States. Library of Congress.
Serial Division. Popular names of
U.S. Government reports; Rev. and
enl. Washington, Library of
Congress; [for sale by the Supt. of
Docs., U.S. Govt. Print. Off.] 1970.
v, 43 p. [$0.55] 015/.73 77-
608261
Z663.44 .P57 1970 MRR Alc.

United States. National Archives.
Federal population censuses 1790-
1890: a price list of microfilm
copies of the schedules. Washington,
1969. ix, 186 p. 317.3 70-605086

HA37 .U547 1969 MRR Alc.

United States. Office of Education.
Bibliography of publications of the
United States Office of Education,
1867-1959. Totowa, N.J., Rowman and
Littlefield, 1971. xiv, 57, x, 158,
v, 157 p. 016.37 73-28324
Z5815.U5 U5354 MRR Alc.

United States. Superintendent of
Documents. Catalog of the Public
documents of the Congress and of all
departments of the Government of the
United States; the Comprehensive
index provided for the Act of Jan.
12, 1895. no. [1]-25: Mar. 4,
1893/June 30, 1895-Jan. 1, 1939/Dec.
31, 1940. Washington, U.S. Govt.
Print. Off. 06-12151
Z1223 .A13 MRR Gallery Full set /
MRR Alc (Deck 33) Full set

United States. Superintendent of
documents. Checklist of United
States public documents 1789-1909,
3d ed., rev. and en.,- Washington,
Govt. print. off., 1911- v. 12-
35731
Z1223 .A113 MRR Ref Desk.

United States. Superintendent of
Documents. Index to the reports and
documents of the 54th Congress, 1st
session-72d Congress, 2d session,
Dec. 2, 1895-March 4, 1933 with
numerical lists and schedule of
volumes. Being no. [1]-43 of the
"Consolidated index" provided for by
the act of January 12, 1895. 1897-
1933. Washington [Govt. print. off.]
43 v. 06-20448
Z1223 .A14 Sci RR Full set / MRR
Alc (Deck 33) Full set

United States. Superintendent of
Documents. Monthly catalog of United
States Government publications. no.
[1]- Jan. 1895- Washington, U.S.
Govt. Print. Off. 04-18088
Z1223.A18 MRR Ref Desk Full set /
Sci RR Full set

United States. Superintendent of
Documents. Monthly catalog of United
States Government publications.
Supplement. 1941/42-1945/46.
Washington, U.S. Govt. Print. Off.
74-643567
Z1223.A18 Suppl. MRR Ref Desk Full
set / Sci RR Full set

United States. Superintendent of
Documents. Numerical lists and
schedule of volumes of the reports
and documents of the 73d- Congress
... 1933/34- Washington [U.S. Govt.
print. off.] 015.73 34-28260
Z1223 .A15 MRR Ref Desk

UNITED STATES--GOVERNMENT (Cont.)
United States. Superintendent of
documents. Tables of and annotated
index to the congressional series of
United States public documents.
Washington, Govt. print. off., 1902.
769 p.   02-13262
   Z1223.A 1902 MRR Ref Desk.

Vinge, Clarence L. U.S. Government
publications for research and
teaching in geography, Totowa, N.J.,
Littlefield, Adams, 1967. xiv, 360
p.   016.910/7 67-8345
   Z6001 .V5 1967 MRR Alc.

White, Thomas N. Guide to United
States-J.P.R.S. research
translations, 1957-1966: Washington,
Research & Microfilm Publications
[1966] 67 p.   017 66-29498
   Z1223.Z7 W55 MRR Alc.

Wood, Jennings. United States
Government publications; Chicago,
American Library Association, 1964.
86 p.   65-3360
   Z1223.Z7 W75 MRR Alc.

Writers' program. Catalogue, WPA
Writers' program publications, the
American guide series, the American
life series. [Washington, U.S. Govt.
print. off., 1942] 1 p. l., 54 p.
016.9173 42-37616
   Z1236 .W75 MRR Alc.

Wynkoop, Sally. Directories of
Government agencies, Rochester,
N.Y., Libraries Unlimited, 1969. 242
p.   016.353/04/025 70-84652
   Z7165.U5 W9 MRR Alc.

Wynkoop, Sally. Subject guide to
government reference books.
Littleton, Colo., Libraries
Unlimited, 1972. 276 p.   015.73 72-
83382
   Z1223.Z7 W95 MRR Alc.

UNITED STATES--GOVERNMENT PUBLICATIONS--
BIBLIOGRAPHY--CATALOGS.
United States. Library of Congress.
Exchange and Gift Division. Non-GPO
imprints received in the Library of
Congress; a selective checklist.
July 1967/69- Washington. [$1.25]
015/.73 73-600148
   Z1223.A1 U54a MRR Alc Full set

UNITED STATES--GOVERNMENT PUBLICATIONS--
INDEXES.
American statistics index. 1973-
Washington, Congressional Information
Service. 016.3173 73-82599
   Z7554.U5 A46 MRR Alc Full set /
      Sci RR Full set

Congressional Information Service.
CIS annual. 1970- Washington.
348/.731 79-158879
   KF49 .C62 MRR Ref Desk Full set

Government reports index. v. 71-
1971- [Springfield, Va.] National
Technical Information Service.
507/.2073 72-627325
   Z7405.R4 U513   Sci RR Latest
      edition / MRR Alc Full set

Lester, Daniel W. Departmental
keyword indexes to U.S. Government
author-organizations, Washington,
United States Historical Documents
Institute, 1972. xxxiii, 959 p.
015.73 s 72-2109
   Z1223.Z7 L45 vol. 3 MRR Ref Desk.

Lester, Daniel W. Master keyword
index to the publication-issuing
offices of the U.S. Government, 1789-
1970, Washington, United States
Historical Documents Institute, 1972.
xxxiii, 855 p.   015.73 s 72-2110
   Z1223.Z7 L45 vol. 5 MRR Ref Desk.

Lester, Daniel W. Superintendent of
Documents classification number index
of U.S. Government author-
organization. Washington, United
States Historical Documents
Institute, 1972. xxxiii, 312 p.
015.73 s 72-2107
   Z1223.Z7 L45 vol. 1 MRR Ref Desk.

United States. Army. Corps of
engineers. Analytical and topical
index to the reports of the chief of
engineers and officers of the Corps
of engineers, United States Army,1866-
1900 ... Washington, Govt. print.
off., 1903. 3 v.   03-27940
   TC23 .A3 1866-1900 MRR Alc.

United States. Bureau of Labor
Statistics. Guide to employment
statistics of BLS; [Washington]
1961. i, 134 p.   l 62-75
   HD8064 .A52 1961 MRR Alc.

United States. Congress. House.
Committee on Un-American Activities.
Cumulative index to publications of
the Committee on Un-American
Activities. 1939/41- Washington,
U.S. Govt. Print. Off.   42-13283
   E743.5 .A28 MRR Ref Desk Latest
      edition

United States. Congress. Senate.
Committee on the Judiciary.
Cumulative index to published
hearings and reports Washington,
U.S. Govt. Print. Off., 1957. ii,
844 p.   327.1 57-60563
   Z7165.U5 U484 MRR Ref Desk.

United States. Congress. Senate
.Library. Cumulative index of
congressional committee hearings (not
confidential in character) from
Seventy-fourth Congress (January 3,
1935) through Eithty-fifth Congress
(January 3, 1959) in the United
States Senate Library. Washington,
U.S. Govt. Print. Off., 1959. v, 823
p.   59-61946
   KF40 .H8 MRR Ref Desk.

United States. Dept. of the Interior.
Division of Documents. Comprehensive
index to the publications of the
United States Government, 1881-1893,
New York, Johnson Reprint Corp.,
[1970] 2 v. (v, 159 p.) 015/.73
75-29071
   Z1223.A 1970 MRR Ref Desk.

United States. Dept. of the Interior.
Division of Documents. Comprehensive
index to the publications of the
United States Government, 1881-1893,
Ann Arbor, J. W. Edwards, 1953. 2 v.
in 1 (v, 1590 p.) 015.73 54-61502

   Z1223.A 1953 MRR Alc.

United States. Library of Congress.
Legislative Reference Service. Index
to the Commission and Task Force
reports; Washington, U.S. Govt.
Print. Off.] 1955. iii, 85 p.   55-
63343
   JK643.C53 A55 1955h MRR Ref Desk.

United States. Work projects
administration. Index of research
projects ... [Washington, U.S.
Govt. print. off., 1938-39. 3 v.
351.80973 38-26877
   HD3881 .A56 1938 MRR Alc.

United States Historical Documents
Institute. U.S. Government author-
organization index, 1789-1970.
Washington [1972]   p. 015.73 s 72-
2108
   Z1223.Z7 L45 vol. 2 MRR Ref Desk.

UNITED STATES--GOVERNMENT PUBLICATIONS--
PERIODICALS--BIBLIOGRAPHY.
Andriot, John L. Guide to U.S.
Government serials & periodicals,
1967 ed. McLean, Va., Documents
Index [c1967] 2 v. (1631 p.)
015/.73 68-3862
   Z1223.Z7 A573 MRR Ref Desk.

United States Historical Documents
Institute. U.S. Government serial
titles, 1789-1970; Washington [1972]
xii, 527 p. 015.73 s 74-190737
   Z1223.Z7 L45 vol. 4 MRR Ref Desk.

UNITED STATES--GOVERNMENT PUBLICATIONS
(COUNTIES)--BIBLIOGRAPHY.
Hodgson, James Goodwin, comp. The
official publications of American
counties, Fort Collins, Col., 1937.
viii p., ix-xii numb. l., xiii-xxii,
594 p. 015.73 37-27440
   Z7164.L8 H72 MRR Alc.

Index to current urban documents. v.
1- July/Oct. 1972- Westport,
Conn., Greenwood Press. [$75.00]
016.30136/0973 73-641453
   Z7165.U5 I654 MRR Alc Full set

UNITED STATES--GOVERNMENT PUBLICATIONS
(MUNICIPAL GOVERNMENTS)--BIBLIOGRAPHY.
Index to current urban documents. v.
1- July/Oct. 1972- Westport,
Conn., Greenwood Press. [$75.00]
016.30136/0973 73-641453
   Z7165.U5 I654 MRR Alc Full set

UNITED STATES--GOVERNMENT PUBLICATIONS
(STATE GOVERNMENTS)--BIBLIOGRAPHY.
The American catalogue ... New York,
1941. 8 v. in 13. 015.73 a 42-
2938
   Z1215 .A52 MRR Ref Desk.

Bibliography of publications of
university bureaus of business and
economic research. [Boulder, Colo.,
etc.] Business Research Division,
University of Colorado.
016.33/007/2073 77-635614
   Z7165.U5 A8 MRR Alc Full set

Bowker, R[ichard] R[ogers] State
publications; New York, The
Publishers' weekly, 1908. 1 v. in 4.
00-98
   Z1223.5.A1 B7 MRR Alc.

Chicago. University. Library.
Official publications relating to
American state constitutional
conventions, New York, The H. W.
Wilson company, 1936. 3 p. l., 91 p.
016.342732 37-4455
   Z6457.A1 C5 MRR Alc.

Corbin, John Boyd, comp. An index of
state geological survey publications
issued in series. New York,
Scarecrow Press, 1965. xi, 667 p.
016.5573 65-13555
   Z6031 .C6 MRR Alc.

Government publications guide.
Boston, G. K. Hall. 011 73-19397
   Z7164.G7 G68 MRR Ref Desk Partial
      set

National Association of State
Libraries. Collected public
documents of the States; Boston,
1947. ix, 87 p. 015.73 48-3640
   Z1223.5.A1 N24 MRR Alc.

National association of state
libraries. Public document clearing
house committee. Check-list of
legislative journals of states of the
United States of America,
Providence, the Oxford press, 1938.
3 p. l., 274 p. 016.32873 38-38809

   Z1223.5.A1 N27 1938 MRR Ref Desk.

New York (City). Public Library.
Research Libraries. Catalog of
Government publications in the
Research Libraries: Boston, G. K.
Hall, 1972. 40 v. 011 74-171015
   Z7164.G7 N54 1972 MRR Alc (Dk 33)

Press, Charles. State manuals, blue
books, and election results,
Berkeley, Institute of Governmental
Studies, University of California,
1962. i, 101 p. 016.3539 63-63225

   Z7165.U5 P7 MRR Ref Desk.

United States. Bureau of the Census.
Directory of non-Federal statistics
for States and local areas;
[Washington; For sale by the Supt. of
Docs., U.S. Govt. Print. Off., 1970]
viii, 678 p. [6.25] 317.3 76-
605082
   HA37 .U52 1970 MRR Ref Desk.

United States. Library of Congress.
A guide to the microfilm collection
of early state records. [Washington]
Library of Congress, Photoduplication
Service, 1950. 1 v (various
pagings) 016.01573 50-62956
   Z663.96 .G8 MRR Alc.

United States. Library of Congress.
Exchange and Gift Division. Monthly
checklist of State publications. v.
1- Jan. 1910- Washington, U.S.
Govt. Print. Off. 015.73 10-8924
   Z1223.5.A1 U5 MRR Alc Full set

UNITED STATES--GOVERNMENT PUBLICATIONS
(STATE GOVERNMENTS)--INDEXES.
United States. Bureau of Labor.
Index of all reports issued by
bureaus of labor statistics in the
United States prior to March 1, 1902.
New York, Johnson Reprint Corp.,
1970. viii, 287 p. 016.331/0973
70-125418
   Z7164.L1 U6 1970 MRR Alc.

UNITED STATES--HISTORIC HOUSES, ETC.
America's historic houses; New York,
Putnam [1967] 194 p. 973 67-26315

   E159 .A4 MRR Alc.

Bergere, Thea. Homes of the
Presidents. New York, Dodd, Mead
[1962] 94 p. 917.3 62-16684
   E159 .B43 MRR Alc.

Boatner, Mark Mayo. Landmarks of the
American Revolution; [Harrisburg,
Pa.] Stackpole Books [1973] 608 p.
[$10.00] 917.3/03/3 73-6964
   E159 .B67 MRR Alc.

Carpenter, Ralph E. The fifty best
historic American houses, Colonial
and Federal, New York, Dutton, 1955.
112 p. 973 55-10288
   E159 .C3 MRR Alc.

Great Georgian houses of America.
New York, Printed by the Kalkhoff
Press, 1933-37. 2 v. (chiefly
illus., facsims., plans) 33-34801
   NA707 .G66 MRR Alc.

Haas, Irvin. America's historic
houses and restorations. [1st ed.]
New York, Hawthorn Books [1967,
c1966] 271 p. 973 66-22320
   E159 .H12 MRR Alc.

Hammond, John Martin. Quaint and
historic forts of North America,
Philadelphia, London, J. B.
Lippincott company, 1915. xiii, [1]
p., l l., 308, [1] p. 16-645
   E159 .H22 MRR Alc.

UNITED STATES--HISTORIC HOUSES, (Cont.)
Historic American Buildings Survey.
Documenting a legacy; [Washington,
Library of Congress, 1973] 269-294
p. 720/.973 73-17422
Z663 .D6 MRR Alc.

Historic American Buildings Survey.
Preservation through documentation.
Washington, Library of Congress; [for
sale by the Supt. of Docs., Govt.
Print. Off., 1968] [16] p. [0.25]
720/.973 68-62342
Z663 .P73 MRR Alc.

Illustrated guide to the treasures of
America. Pleasantville, N.Y.,
Reader's Digest Association [1974]
624 p. [$11.97] 917.3/03 73-83812

E159 .I44 MRR Alc.

Ketchum, Richard M., The American
heritage book of great historic
places. New York, American Heritage
Pub. Co. [1957] 376 p. 917.3 57-
11274
E169.1 .K418 MRR Alc.

Kimball, Sidney Fiske, Domestic
architecture of the American colonies
and of the early Republic. New York,
Dover Publications [1966, c1922] xx,
314 p. 728/.0973 66-29154
NA707 .K45 1966 MRR Alc.

National Geographic Society,
Washington, D.C. Book Service.
America's historylands; Washington,
National Geographic Society [1962]
576 p. 917.3 62-7748
E159 .N3 MRR Alc.

United States. National Park Service.
Explorers and settlers; historic
places commemorating the early
exploration and settlement of the
United States. Washington [For sale
by the Supt. of Docs., U.S. Govt.
Print. Off.] 1968. xvi, 506 p.
917.3/04 66-60013
E159 .U545 MRR Alc.

United States. National Park Service.
Signers of the Declaration;
Washington; [For sale by the Supt. of
Docs., U.S. Govt. Print. Off.] 1973
[i.e. 1974] xii, 310 p. [$5.65]
973.3/13/0922 B 73-600028
E221 .U78 1974 MRR Alc.

Williams, Henry Lionel. Great houses
of America, [1st ed.] New York,
Putnam [1966] 295 p. 728.80973 66-
19625
E159 .W5 MRR Alc.

UNITED STATES--HISTORIC HOUSES, ETC.--
DIRECTORIES.
The National register of historic
places. 1969- Washington, National
Park Service. [For sale by the Supt.
of Docs., U.S. Govt. Print. Off.]
973/.025 78-603008
E159 .N34 MRR Alc Latest edition

UNITED STATES--HISTORIC HOUSES, ETC.--
PICTORIAL WORKS.
Jones, Cranston. Homes of the
American Presidents. New York,
McGraw-Hill [1962] 232 p. 923.173
62-19158
E159 .J6 MRR Alc.

UNITED STATES--HISTORICAL GEOGRAPHY.
Klose, Nelson, A concise study guide
to the American frontier. Lincoln,
University of Nebraska Press, 1964.
xi, 269 p. 973 64-15180
E179.5 .K55 MRR Alc.

UNITED STATES--HISTORICAL GEOGRAPHY--
MAPS.
Adams, James Truslow, ed. Atlas of
American history. New York, C
Scribner's sons, 1943. xi, [1], 360
p. incl. maps. 911.73 map43-126
G1201.S1 A2 1943 MRR Ref Desk.

American heritage. The American
heritage pictorial atlas of United
States history, New York, American
Heritage Pub. Co.; book trade
distribution by McGraw-Hill Book Co.
[1966] 424 p. map66-29
G1201.S1 A4 1966 MRR Alc.

Catchpole, Brian. A map history of
the United States. London, Heinemann
Educational, 1972. vi, 130 p.
[£0.90] 917.3/03 73-330879
E178.2 .C34 MRR Alc.

Lord, Clifford Lee, Historical atlas
of the United States, Rev. ed. New
York, Holt [1953] xv, 238 p. 53-
10208
G1201.S1 L6 1953 MRR Ref Desk.

Paullin, Charles Oscar, Atlas of the
historical geography of the United
States, [Washington, D.C., New York]
Pub. Jointly by Carnegie institution
of Washington and the American
geographical society of New York,
1932. 2 p. l., iii-xv p., 1 l., 162
p., 1 l., 688 maps (part col.) on 166
plates (part double) 911.73 map32-
54
G1201.S1 P3 1932 MRR Alc Atlas.

Webster's guide to American history;
Springfield, Mass., G. & C. Merriam
Co. [1971] 1428 p. 973 76-24114
E174.5 .W4 MRR Ref Desk.

UNITED STATES--HISTORIOGRAPHY.
Eisenstadt, Abraham Seldin, ed. The
craft of American history; [1st ed.]
New York, Harper & Row [1966] 2 v.
973.072 66-6380
E175 .E4 MRR Alc.

Hockett, Homer Carey, The critical
method in historical research and
writing. New York, Macmillan [1955]
330 p. 973.072 55-13664
E175.7 .H6446 MRR Alc.

Skotheim, Robert Allen. American
intellectual histories and
historians. Princeton, N.J.,
Princeton University Press, 1966.
xi, 326 p. 973.072 66-11960
E175.45 .S5 MRR Alc.

Spielman, William Carl, Introduction
to sources of American history. New
York, Exposition Press [1951] 175 p.
973.07 51-11625
E175 .S6 MRR Alc.

Stevenson, Robert Murrell.
Philosophies of American music
history, Washington, Published for
the Library of Congress by the Louis
Charles Elson Memorial Fund, 1970.
iii, 18 p. 780/.973 70-609941
Z663.37.A5 1969 MRR Alc.

Wish, Harvey, The American
historian; New York, Oxford
University Press, 1960. 366 p.
973.072 60-13202
E175 .W5 MRR Alc.

UNITED STATES--HISTORIOGRAPHY--
ADDRESSES, ESSAYS, LECTURES.
Billington, Ray Allen, ed. The
reinterpretation of early American
history; San Marino, Calif.,
Huntington Library, 1966. viii, 264
p. 973.20722 66-31501
E175 .B5 MRR Alc.

UNITED STATES--HISTORY.
Album of American history. New York,
Scribner [1969- v. 973.022/2
74-91746
E178.5 .A482 MRR Alc.

Beard, Charles Austin, New basic
history of the United States Garden
City, N.Y., Doubleday, 1968. 571 p.
973 68-14172
E178 .B39 1968 MRR Alc.

Beard, Charles Austin, The rise of
American civilization, New ed., two
volumes in one, rev. and enl. New
York, The Macmillan company, 1933.
xviii, 824, 865 p. incl. front. 973
33-4705
E169.1 .B33 1933 MRR Alc.

Berky, Andrew S., ed. The
historians' history of the United
States, New York, Putnam [1966] 2
v. (1384 p.) 973.08 66-20295
E178 .B48 MRR Alc.

Billington, Ray Allen, Westward
expansion; 3d ed. New York,
Macmillan [c1967] xvii, 933 p. 973
67-12337
E179.5 .B63 1967 MRR Alc.

Butterfield, Roger Place, The
American past; [2d rev. and expanded
ed. New York] Simon and Schuster
[1966] 544 p. 973.0222 66-16146
E178 .B988 1966 MRR Alc.

Carman, Harry James, A history of
the American people, 3d ed. New
York, Knopf [1967] 2 v. 973 67-
20622
E178 .C284 1967 MRR Alc.

Channing, Edward, A history of the
United States, New York, The
Macmillan company, 1932-37. 6 v.
mrr01-48
E178 .C447 MRR Alc.

Ewing, Cortez Arthur Milton, The
judges of the Supreme court, 1789-
1937; Minneapolis, The University of
Minnesota press [c1938] 3 p. l., 3-
124 p. 38-28601
KF8744 .E9 MRR Alc.

Hofstadter, Richard, comp. American
violence; [1st ed.] New York,
Knopf, 1970. xiv, 478, xiii p.
[$10.00] 973 73-111238
E179 .H8 1970 MRR Alc.

Hofstadter, Richard, The United
States. 3d ed. Englewood Cliffs,
N.J., Prentice-Hall [1972] xvi, 879,
xvia-lxiii p. [$10.95] 973 79-
160528
E178.1 .H7 1972 MRR Alc.

Kraus, Michael, The United States to
1865. New ed. rev. and enl. Ann
Arbor, University of Michigan Press
[1969] xiii, 548, xi p. [8.50]
973 69-15849
E178 .K7 1969 MRR Alc.

Malone, Dumas, Empire for liberty;
New York, Appleton-Century-Crofts
[1960] 2 v. 973 60-5002
E178 .M26 MRR Alc.

Morison, Samuel Eliot, The growth of
the American Republic [6th ed.,
rev., and enl.] New York, Oxford
University Press, 1969. 2 v. 973
69-10494
E178 .M852 MRR Alc.

Morison, Samuel Eliot, The Oxford
history of the American people. New
York, Oxford University Press, 1965.
xxvii, 1150 p. 973 65-12468
E178 .M855 MRR Alc.

National Geographic Society,
Washington, D.C. Book Service.
America's historylands; Washington,
National Geographic Society [1962]
576 p. 917.3 62-7748
E159 .N3 MRR Alc.

Nevins, Allan, A short history of
the United States, 5th ed., rev. and
enl. New York, A. A. Knopf, 1966.
xiv, 669, xxvi p. 973 64-12329
E178 .N44 1966 MRR Alc.

Ogg, Frederic Austin, Builders of
the Republic, New Haven, Yale
university press; [etc., etc.] 1927.
3 p. l., 352 p. 27-9284
E178.5 .P2 vol. 8 MRR Alc.

Rhodes, James Ford, History of the
United States from the compromise of
1850 to the end of the Roosevelt
administration. new ed. in nine
volumes ... New York, The Macmillan
company; London, Macmillan & co.,
ltd., 1928, c1929. 9 v. mrr01-49
E178 .R4782 MRR Alc.

Townsend, Malcolm, comp. U.S. An
index to the United States of
America. Boston, D. Lothrop company
[c1890] 6 p. l., 9-482 (i.e. 484) p.
incl. illus., maps (part fold.). 01-
21543
E174 .T74 MRR Alc.

Turner, Frederick Jackson, The
frontier in American history, New
York, H. Holt and company, 1920. 4
p. l., 375 p. 20-18058
E179.5 .T95 MRR Alc.

Washington, George, pres. U.S., The
writings of George Washington from
the original manuscript sources, 1745-
1799; Washington, U.S. Govt. print.
off. [1931-44] 39 v. 308 32-11075

E312.7 1931 MRR Alc.

Williams, Thomas Harry, A history of
the United States 3d ed. New York,
Knopf [1969] 2 v. 973 69-11069
E178.1 .W7282 MRR Alc.

Winsor, Justin, ed. Narrative and
critical history of America,
Standard library ed. [Boston, New
York, Houghton, Mifflin and company,
1923, c1884-89] 8 v. 23-16194
E18 .W77 MRR Alc.

Wood, William Charles Henry, The
winning of freedom, New Haven, Yale
university press; [etc., etc.] 1927.
3 p. l., 366 p. 28-1990
E178.5 .P2 vol. 6 MRR Alc.

UNITED STATES--HISTORY--COLONIAL
PERIOD, CA. 1600-1775.
Andrews, Charles McLean, The
colonial background of the American
Revolution; New Haven, Yale
University Press [1961, c1958] 220
p. 973.311 61-19714
E210 .A55 1961 MRR Alc.

Andrews, Charles McLean, The
colonial period of American history,
New Haven, Yale University Press
[1964] 4 v. 973.2 64-54917
E188 .A5745 MRR Alc.

Barck, Oscar Theodore, Colonial
America 2d ed. New York, Macmillan
[1968] xi, 753 p. 973.2 68-10104

E188 .B26 1968 MRR Alc.

UNITED STATES--HISTORY--COLONIAL (Cont.)
Boorstin, Daniel Joseph, The
Americans; the colonial experience.
New York, Random House [1958] 434 p.
917.3 58-9884
E188 .B72 MRR Alc.

Gipson, Lawrence Henry, The British
Empire before the American
Revolution. [Completely rev.] New
York, Knopf, 1958- v.　942.072
58-9670
DA500 .G52 MRR Alc.

Gipson, Lawrence Henry, The British
Empire before the American
Revolution. Caldwell, Id., Caxton
Printers, 1936-70. 15 v.　942.07/2
36-20870
DA500 .G5 MRR Alc.

Greene, Evarts Boutell, American
population before the federal census
of 1790, New York, Columbia
university press, 1932.　xxii p., 2
l., [3]-228 p., 1 l.　312.0973　33-
718
HB3505 .G7 MRR Alc.

Jensen, Merrill. The founding of a
nation;　New York, Oxford University
Press, 1968.　xiii, 735 p.　[$13.50]
973.31/1　68-29720
E195 .J4 MRR Alc.

Osgood, Herbert Levi, The American
colonies in the eighteenth century,
New York, Columbia university press,
1924.　4 v.　973.2　24-3889
E195 .082 MRR Alc.

Osgood, Herbert Levi, The American
colonies in the seventeenth century;
London, Macmillan & co., ltd. 1904-
07.　3 v.　04-14597
E191 .082 MRR Alc.

Peterson, Harold Leslie, Arms and
armor in colonial America, 1526-1783.
Harrisburg, Pa., Stackpole Co.
[1956]　350 p.　399　56-11273
U818 .P4 MRR Alc.

Pomfret, John Edwin, Founding the
American colonies, 1583-1660, [1st
ed.] New York, Harper & Row [1970]
xvii, 380 p.　[$7.95]　973.2　68-
15968
E191 .P64 1970 MRR Alc.

Savelle, Max, A history of colonial
America, 3d ed. Hinsdale, Ill.,
Dryden Press [c1973]　xxx, 830 p.
973.2　73-5327
E188 .S29 1973 MRR alc.

Wissler, Clark, Adventures in the
wilderness, New Haven, Yale
university press; [etc., etc.] 1925.
3 p. l., 369 p.　26-1142
E178.5 .P2 vol. 1 MRR Alc.

Wright, Louis Booker, The American
heritage history of the Thirteen
Colonies, [New York] American
Heritage Pub. Co.; book trade
distribution by Simon and Schuster
[1967]　384 p.　917.3/03/2　67-23814

E188 .W79 MRR Alc.

UNITED STATES--HISTORY--COLONIAL
PERIOD, CA. 1600-1775--BIBLIOGRAPHY.
Institute of Early American History
and Culture, Williamsburg, Va.　Books
about early America; [4th ed.]
Williamsburg, Va., 1970.　vi, 71 p.
016.9173/03　73-158365
Z1237 .I58 1970 MRR Alc.

Meynen, Emil, Bibliographie des
deutschtums der kolonialzeitlichen
einwanderung in Nordamerika,
Leipzig, O. Harrassowitz, 1937.
xxxvi, 636 p.　016.3252430973　38-
7457
Z1361.G37 M6 MRR Alc.

UNITED STATES--HISTORY--COLONIAL
PERIOD, CA. 1600-1775--FICTION--
BIBLIOGRAPHY.
Van Derhoof, Jack Warner. A
bibliography of novels related to
American frontier and colonial
history, Troy, N.Y., Whitston Pub.
Co., 1971.　xii, 501 p.　016.813/03
70-150333
Z1231.F4 V3 MRR Alc.

UNITED STATES--HISTORY--COLONIAL
PERIOD, CA. 1600-1775--SOURCES.
Andrews, Charles McLean, comp.　Guide
to the manuscript materials for the
history of the United States to 1783,
Washington, D.C., The Carnegie
institution of Washington, 1908.
xiv, 499 p.　09-6049
CD1048.U5 A55 MRR Alc.

Andrews, Charles McLean, Guide to
the materials for American history,
to 1783, Washington, D.C., Carnegie
institution of Washington, 1912-14.
2 v.　13-35
CD1048.U5 A6 MRR Alc.

Andrews, Charles McLean, ed.
Narratives of the insurrections, 1675-
1690, New York, C. Scribner's sons
1915.　ix p., 2 l., 3-414 p.　973.2
15-4852
E187.O7 A6 MRR Alc.

Greene, Jack P., ed. Settlements to
society: 1584-1763, New York, McGraw-
Hill [1966] xiv, 386 p.　973.2　66-
22295
E173 .D58 vol. 1 MRR Alc.

Kavenagh, W. Keith.　Foundations of
colonial America: New York, Chelsea
House, 1973.　3 v.　[$95.00]
325/.342/0973　72-80866
JK49 .K38 MRR Alc.

Miller, John Chester, ed.　The
colonial image: New York, G.
Braziller, 1962.　500 p.　973.2　62-
9930
E187.O7 M5 MRR Alc.

UNITED STATES--HISTORY--KING WILLIAM'S
WAR, 1689-1697.
Lincoln, Charles Henry, ed.
Narratives of the Indian wars, 1675-
1699; New York, C. Scribner's sons,
1913.　xii p., 2 l., 3-316 p.
[$3.00]　13-24819
E187.O7 L5 MRR Alc.

UNITED STATES--HISTORY--REVOLUTION,
1775-1783.
Alden, John Richard, The American
Revolution, 1775-1783, [1st ed.]
New York, Harper [1954]　294 p.
973.3　53-11826
E208 .A35 MRR Alc.

Alden, John Richard, A history of
the American Revolution, [1st ed.]
New York, Knopf, 1969.　vii, 541, xvi
p.　[10.00]　973.3　69-10201
E208 .A38 MRR Alc.

Boatner, Mark Mayo, Landmarks of the
American Revolution; [Harrisburg,
Pa.] Stackpole Books [1973] 608 p.
[$10.00]　917.3/03/3　73-6964
E159 .B67 MRR Alc.

Higginbotham, Don. The war of
American independence; New York,
Macmillan [1971]　xvi, 509 p.
[$12.95]　973.3　74-132454
E210 .H63 MRR Alc.

Neumann, George C. The history of
weapons of the American Revolution,
[1st ed.] New York, Harper & Row
[1967]　viii, 373 p.　623.4/4　67-
20829
U815 .N4 MRR Alc.

Nevins, Allan, The American states
during and after the revolution, 1775-
1789, New York, The Macmillan
company, 1924.　xviii p., 1 l., 728
p.　24-23941
E303 .N52 MRR Alc.

Peterson, Harold Leslie, The book of
the Continental soldier; Harrisburg,
Pa., Stackpole Co. [1968]　287 p.
973.3/4　67-27697
UC263 .P47 MRR Alc.

Van Doren, Carl Clinton, Secret
history of the American revolution,
New York, The Viking press, 1941.　3
p. l., [v]-xiv p., 2 l., [3]-534 p.
41-24478
E277 .V23 1941 MRR Alc.

Washington, George, pres. U.S., The
writings of George Washington from
the original manuscript sources, 1745-
1799; Washington, U.S. Govt. print.
off. [1931-44]　39 v.　308　32-11075

E312.7 1931 MRR Alc.

UNITED STATES--HISTORY--REVOLUTION,
1775-1783--BIBLIOGRAPHY.
Institute of Early American History
and Culture, Williamsburg, Va.　Books
about early America; [4th ed.]
Williamsburg, Va., 1970.　vi, 71 p.
016.9173/03　73-158365
Z1237 .I58 1970 MRR Alc.

UNITED STATES--HISTORY--REVOLUTION,
1775-1783--BIOGRAPHY.
Billias, George Athan, ed.　George
Washington's generals. New York, W.
Morrow, 1964.　xvii, 327 p.　973.33
64-12038
E206 .B5 MRR Biog.

Boatner, Mark Mayo, Encyclopedia of
the American Revolution.
Bicentennial ed. [rev. and expanded]
New York, D. McKay Co. [1974] xviii,
1290 p.　[$17.50]　973.3/03　73-
91868
E208 .B68 1974 MRR Ref Desk.

UNITED STATES--HISTORY--REVOLUTION,
1775-1783--CAMPAIGNS AND BATTLES.
Furneaux, Rupert. The pictorial
history of the American Revolution as
told by eyewitnesses and
participants. Chicago, J. G.
Ferguson Pub. Co.; distributed by
Doubleday [Garden City, N.Y., 1973]
400 p.　[$19.95]　973.3/022/2　72-
89979
E230 .F87 MRR Alc.

Peckham, Howard Henry, The War for
Independence, [Chicago] University
of Chicago Press [1958]　226 p.
973.34　58-5685
E230 .P36 MRR Alc.

Stember, Sol. The bicentennial guide
to the American Revolution. [1st
ed.] New York, Saturday Review
Press; [distributed by] Dutton, 1974.
3 v.　973.3/3　73-23108
E230 .S74 1974 MRR Alc.

Ward, Christopher, The War of the
Revolution; New York, Macmillan,
1952.　2 v. (xiv, 989 p.)　973.33
52-14233
E230 .W34 MRR Alc.

UNITED STATES--HISTORY--REVOLUTION,
1775-1783--CAUSES.
Andrews, Charles McLean, The
colonial background of the American
Revolution; New Haven, Yale
University Press [1961, c1958]　220
p.　973.311　61-19714
E210 .A55 1961 MRR Alc.

Dickerson, Oliver Morton, The
navigation acts and the American
Revolution. Philadelphia, University
of Pennsylvania Press, 1951.　xv, 344
p.　973.3112　51-13206
E215.1 .D53 MRR Alc.

Gipson, Lawrence Henry, The coming
of the Revolution, 1763-1775. [1st
ed.] New York, Harper [1954] xiv,
287 p.　973.311　54-8952
E209 .G5 MRR Alc.

Jensen, Merrill. The founding of a
nation;　New York, Oxford University
Press, 1968.　xiii, 735 p.　[$13.50]
973.31/1　68-29720
E195 .J4 MRR Alc.

Knollenberg, Bernhard, Origin of the
American Revolution: 1759-1766.　New
York, Macmillan, 1960.　viii, 486 p.
973.311　59-10990
E210 .K65 MRR Alc.

Sosin, Jack M. Agents and merchants;
Lincoln, University of Nebraska
Press [1965.　xvi, 267 p.　973.3112
65-13913
E210 .S73 MRR Alc.

UNITED STATES--HISTORY--REVOLUTION,
1775-1783--CAUSES--BIBLIOGRAPHY.
Adams, Thomas Randolph, American
independence: the growth of an idea;
Providence, Brown University Press,
1965.　xxi, [2], 200 p.　916.973311
62-16995
Z1238 .A4 MRR Alc.

UNITED STATES--HISTORY--REVOLUTION,
1775-1783--CLAIMS.
Brown, Wallace, The king's friends;
Providence, Brown University Press,
1965.　x, 411 p.　973.314　66-10179

E277 .B82 MRR Alc.

UNITED STATES--HISTORY--REVOLUTION,
1775-1783--CONGRESSES.
Library of Congress Symposia on the
American Revolution, 1st, 1972.　The
development of a revolutionary
mentality; Washington, Library of
Congress, 1972.　157 p.　[$3.50]
973.3　72-11849
Z663.115 .D4 1972 MRR Alc.

Library of Congress Symposia on the
American Revolution, 2d, 1973.
Fundamental testaments of the
American Revolution; Washington,
Library of Congress, 1973.　119 p.
[$3.50]　973.3/11　73-18173
Z663.115 .F85 1973 MRR Alc.

UNITED STATES--HISTORY--REVOLUTION,
1775-1783--DICTIONARIES.
Boatner, Mark Mayo, Encyclopedia of
the American Revolution.
Bicentennial ed. [rev. and expanded]
New York, D. McKay Co. [1974] xviii,
1290 p.　[$17.50]　973.3/03　73-
91868
E208 .B68 1974 MRR Ref Desk.

UNITED STATES--HISTORY--REVOLUTION,
1775-1783--EXHIBITIONS.
United States. Library of Congress.
To set a country free: Washington,
1975 [i.e. 1974]　74 p.
973.3/074/0153　74-8556
Z663 .T6 MRR Alc.

UNITED STATES--HISTORY-- (Cont.)
United States. Library of Congress.
American Revolution Bicentennial
Office. Twelve flags of the American
Revolution. Washington, Library of
Congress, 1974. [16] p. 873.3/6
73-10402
Z663.115 .T93 MRR Alc.

UNITED STATES--HISTORY--REVOLUTION,
1775-1783--FOREIGN PUBLIC OPINION--
COLLECTIONS.
Smith, Paul Hubert, comp. English
defenders of American freedoms, 1774-
1778: Washington, Library of
Congress, 1972. 231 p. [$2.75]
301.15/43/8733 78-37002
Z663.115 .S5 MRR Alc.

UNITED STATES--HISTORY--REVOLUTION,
1775-1783--HUMOR, CARICATURES, ETC.
Darly, Matthew, Two rebuses from the
American Revolution in facsimile.
Washington, Library of Congress,
1973. 1 portfolio (2 sheets)
973.3/02/07 73-603400
Z663 .T85 1973 MRR Alc.

UNITED STATES--HISTORY--REVOLUTION,
1775-1783--INDEXES.
Gephart, Ronald M. Periodical
literature on the American
Revolution: historical research and
changing interpretations, 1895-1970;
Washington, Library of Congress; [for
sale by the Supt. of Docs., U.S.
Govt. Print. Off.] 1971. iv, 93 p.
[$1.00] 016.9733 74-609228
Z663.28 .P4 MRR Alc.

UNITED STATES--HISTORY--REVOLUTION,
1775-1783--JUVENILE LITERATURE--
BIBLIOGRAPHY.
Coughlan, Margaret N., Creating
independence, 1763-1789: background
reading for young people:
Washington, Library of Congress; [for
sale by the Supt. of Docs., U.S.
Govt. Print. Off.] 1972. 62 p.
[$0.75] 016.9733 72-3573
Z663.292 .C68 MRR Alc.

UNITED STATES--HISTORY--REVOLUTION,
1775-1783--MUSEUMS.
Stember, Sol. The bicentennial guide
to the American Revolution. [1st
ed.] New York, Saturday Review
Press; [distributed by] Dutton, 1974.
3 v. 973.3/3 73-23108
E230 .S74 1974 MRR Alc.

UNITED STATES--HISTORY--REVOLUTION,
1775-1783--NAVAL OPERATIONS.
United States. Naval History
Division. Naval documents of the
American Revolution. Washington [For
sale by the Supt. of Docs., U.S.
Govt. Print. Off.] 1964- v. 64-
60087
E271 .U583 MRR Alc.

UNITED STATES--HISTORY--REVOLUTION,
1775-1783--NAVAL OPERATIONS--SOURCES.
United States. Library of Congress.
Manuscript Division. Naval records
of the American revolution, 1775-
1788. Washington, Govt. print. off.,
1906. 549 p. 06-35020
Z1238 .U58 MRR Alc.

UNITED STATES--HISTORY--REVOLUTION,
1775-1783--PERSONAL NARRATIVES.
Commager, Henry Steele, ed. The
spirit of 'seventy-six: New York,
Harper & Row [1967] lii, 1348 p.
973.3/08 67-11325
E203 .C69 1967 MRR Alc.

UNITED STATES--HISTORY--REVOLUTION,
1775-1783--PICTORIAL WORKS.
Furneaux, Rupert. The pictorial
history of the American Revolution as
told by eyewitnesses and
participants. Chicago, J. G.
Ferguson Pub. Co.; distributed by
Doubleday [Garden City, N.Y., 1973]
400 p. [$19.95] 973.3/022/2 72-
89979
E230 .F87 MRR Alc.

UNITED STATES--HISTORY--REVOLUTION,
1775-1783--REGISTERS, LISTS, ETC.--
BIBLIOGRAPHY.
Doane, Gilbert Harry, Searching for
your ancestors: [3d ed.]
Minneapolis, University of Minnesota
Press [1960] 198 p. 929.1 60-
12200
CS16 .D6 1960 MRR Alc.

UNITED STATES--HISTORY--REVOLUTION,
1775-1783--SONGS AND MUSIC.
Moore, Frank, comp. The diary of the
American Revolution, 1775-1781. New
York, Washington Square Press, 1967.
xxxiv, 605 p. 973.3 66-22119
E203 .M68 1967 MRR Alc.

UNITED STATES--HISTORY--REVOLUTION,
1775-1783--SOURCES.
Adams, John, pres. U.S., The works
of John Adams, Boston, Little, Brown
and company [etc.] 1850-56 [v. 1,
'56] 10 v. 08-19755
E302 .A26 MRR Alc.

American archives: consisting of a
collection of authentick records,
state papers, debates, and letters
and other notices of publick affairs,
[New York, Johnson Reprint Corp.,
1972] 9 v. 973.2/7 74-181484
E203 .A5 1972 MRR Alc.

Andrews, Charles McLean, comp. Guide
to the manuscript materials for the
history of the United States to 1783,
Washington, D.C., The Carnegie
institution of Washington, 1908.
xiv, 499 p. 09-6049
CD1048.U5 A55 MRR Alc.

Andrews, Charles McLean, Guide to
the materials for American history,
to 1783. Washington, D.C., Carnegie
institution of Washington, 1912-14.
2 v. 13-35
CD1048.U5 A6 MRR Alc.

Burnett, Edmund Cody, ed. Letters of
members of the Continental Congress.
Gloucester, Mass., P. Smith, 1963. 8
v. 973.31 64-2503
JK1033 .B8 1963 MRR Alc.

Commager, Henry Steele, ed. The
spirit of 'seventy-six: New York,
Harper & Row [1967] lii, 1348 p.
973.3/08 67-11325
E203 .C69 1967 MRR Alc.

Franklin, Benjamin, The writings of
Benjamin Franklin; New York, The
Macmillan company; London, Macmillan
& co., ltd., 1905-07. 10 v. 05-
35396
E302 .F82 1905 MRR Alc.

Greene, Jack P., comp. Colonies to
nation, 1763-1789, New York, McGraw-
Hill [1967] xvii, 583 p. 973.3/08
67-24438
E173 .D58 vol. 2 MRR Alc.

Hamilton, Alexander, The works of
Alexander Hamilton, [Federal ed.]
New York, London, G. P. Putnam's
sons, 1904. 12 v. 04-19021
E302 .H24 MRR Alc.

Jefferson,Thomas, pres. U.S., The
writings of Thomas Jefferson.
Library ed., Washington, D.C.,
Issued under the auspices of the
Thomas Jefferson memorial association
of the United States, 1903-04. 20 v.
353.03 14-3171
E302 .J469 MRR Alc.

Moore, Frank, comp. The diary of the
American Revolution, 1775-1781. New
York, Washington Square Press, 1967.
xxxiv, 605 p. 973.3 66-22119
E203 .M68 1967 MRR Alc.

Morris, Richard Brandon, comp. The
American Revolution, 1763-1783; New
York, Harper & Row [1970] xix, 361
p. [$2.95] 973.3 70-20960
E203 .M87 MRR Alc.

United States. Continental congress.
Journals of the American congress:
from 1774 to 1788. Washington;
Printed and published by Way and
Gideon, 1823. 4 v. 17-23718
J10 .A3 MRR Alc.

United States. Continental congress.
Journals of the Continental Congress,
1774-1789. Washington, U.S. Govt.
print. off., 1904-37. 34 v. 05-59

J10 .A5 MRR Alc (Dk 33)

United States. Continental congress.
Secret journals of the acts and
proceedings of Congress, Boston;
Printed and published by Thomas B.
Wait, 1820-21. 4 v. 11-28751
J10 .A35 MRR Alc (Dk 33)

UNITED STATES--HISTORY--REVOLUTION,
1775-1783--SOURCES--BIBLIOGRAPHY.
United States. Library of Congress.
Manuscript division. Calendar of the
correspondence of George Washington,
Washington, Govt. print. off., 1906.
741 p. 06-35011
Z663.34 .C27 MRR Alc.

United States. Library of Congress.
Manuscript division. Calendar of the
correspondence of George Washington,
commander in chief of the Continental
army, with the officers. Washington,
Govt. print. off., 1915. 4 v. 10-
35016
Z663.34 .C28 MRR Alc.

UNITED STATES--HISTORY--CONFEDERATION,
1783-1789.
Bordon, Morton, ed. The
antifederalist papers. [East
Lansing, Mich.] Michigan State
University Press, 1965. xiv, 258 p.
342.7308 65-17929
JK116 .B6 MRR Alc.

Jensen, Merrill. The New Nation:
[1st ed.] New York, Knopf, 1950.
xvii, 433, xi p. 973.318 50-9344
E303 .J45 1950 MRR Alc.

Main, Jackson Turner. The
antifederalists; Chapel Hill,
Published for the Institute of Early
American History and Culture at
Williamsburg, Va., by the University
of North Carolina Press [1961] xv,
308 p. 973.4 61-17904
JK116 .M2 MRR Alc.

Nevins, Allan, The American states
during and after the revolution, 1775-
1789, New York, The Macmillan
company, 1924. xviii p., 1 l., 728
p. 24-23941
E303 .N52 MRR Alc.

UNITED STATES--HISTORY--CONFEDERATION,
1783-1789--SOURCES.
Franklin, Benjamin, The writings of
Benjamin Franklin; New York, The
Macmillan company; London, Macmillan
& co., ltd., 1905-07. 10 v. 05-
35396
E302 .F82 1905 MRR Alc.

Greene, Jack P., comp. Colonies to
nation, 1763-1789, New York, McGraw-
Hill [1967] xvii, 583 p. 973.3/08
67-24438
E173 .D58 vol. 2 MRR Alc.

UNITED STATES--HISTORY--1783-1815--
BIBLIOGRAPHY.
Institute of Early American History
and Culture, Williamsburg, Va. Books
about early America: [4th ed.]
Williamsburg, Va., 1970. vi, 71 p.
016.9173/03 73-159365
Z1237 .I58 1970 MRR Alc.

UNITED STATES--HISTORY--1783-1865.
Adams, John Quincy, Pres. U.S.,
Diary, 1794-1845: New York,
Scribner, 1951. xxxv, 586 p.
873.5/5/0924 51-10345
E377 .A213 MRR Alc.

Brant, Irving, James Madison.
Indianapolis, Bobbs-Merrill [1941-61]
6 v. 923.173 41-19279
E342 .B7 MRR Alc.

Cunliffe, Marcus. The Nation takes
shape, 1789-1837. [Chicago]
University of Chicago Press [1959]
222 p. 973.4 59-5770
E301 .C85 MRR Alc.

Seybert, Adam, Statistical annals,
New York, B. Franklin [1969] xxvii,
803 p. 317.3 68-56774
HA215 .S5 1969 MRR Alc.

Shepard, Edward Morse, Martin Van
Buren, [Rev. ed.] Boston, New York,
Houghton, Mifflin and company, 1900.
vii p., 1 l., 499, [1] p. 02-854
E387 .S55 MRR Alc.

UNITED STATES--HISTORY--1783-1865--
BIBLIOGRAPHY.
Carman, Harry James, A guide to the
principal sources for American
civilization, 1800-1900, in the city
of New York: New York, Columbia
University Press, 1962. xlvi, 630 p.
016.973 62-10450
Z1236 .C25 1962 MRR Alc.

UNITED STATES--HISTORY--1783-1865--
SOURCES.
Adams, John, pres. U.S., The works
of John Adams, Boston, Little, Brown
and company [etc.] 1850-56 [v. 1,
'56] 10 v. 08-19755
E302 .A26 MRR Alc.

Adams, John Quincy, pres. U.S.,
Memoirs of John Quincy Adams,
Philadelphia, J. B. Lippincott & co.,
1874-77. 12 v. 04-20138
E377 .A19 MRR Alc.

Jefferson,Thomas, pres. U.S., The
writings of Thomas Jefferson.
Library ed., Washington, D.C.,
Issued under the auspices of the
Thomas Jefferson memorial association
of the United States, 1903-04. 20 v.
353.03 14-3171
E302 .J469 MRR Alc.

Madison, James, pres. U.S., Letters
and other writings of James Madison.
Philadelphia, J. B. Lippincott & co.,
1865. 4 v. 06-24330
E302 .M18 MRR Alc.

Monroe, James, Pres. U.S., The
writings of James Monroe, including a
collection of his public and private
papers and correspondence, now for
the first time printed. New York,
AMS Press [1969] 7 v. 973.5/4 69-
18218
E302 .M74 1969 MRR Alc.

Paullin, Charles Oscar, Guide to the
materials in London archives for the
history of the United States since
1783. Washington, D.C., Carnegie
institution of Washington, 1914. xi,
642 p. 14-10535
CD1048.U5 P3 MRR Alc.

UNITED STATES--HISTORY--1783- (Cont.)
Washington, George, pres. U.S., The
writings of George Washington from
the original manuscript sources, 1745-
1799; Washington, U.S. Govt. print.
off. [1931-44] 39 v. 308 32-11075

   E312.7 1931 MRR Alc.

UNITED STATES--HISTORY--CONSTITUTIONAL
PERIOD, 1789-1809.
Brant, Irving, James Madison.
Indianapolis, Bobbs-Merrill [1941-61]
6 v. 923.173 41-19279
   E342 .B7 MRR Alc.

Miller, John Chester, The Federalist
era, 1789-1801. [1st ed.] New York,
Harper [1960] 304 p. 973.4 60-
15321
   E310 .M5 MRR Alc.

UNITED STATES--HISTORY--CONSTITUTIONAL
PERIOD, 1789-1809--BIBLIOGRAPHY.
Greely, Adolphus Washington, Public
documents of the first fourteen
Congresses, 1789-1817. New York,
Johnson Reprint Corp. [1973] 903,
343-406 p. 016.32873 73-2634
   Z1223 .A 1973 MRR Ref Desk.

Greely, Adolphus Washington, Public
documents of the first fourteen
congresses, 1789-1817. Washington,
Govt. print. off., 1900. 903 p. 01-
20895
   Z1223 .A 1900 MRR Alc.

UNITED STATES--HISTORY--CONSTITUTIONAL
PERIOD, 1789-1809--SOURCES.
France. Archives nationales. French
consuls in the United States:
Washington, Library of Congress: [for
sale by the Supt. of Docs., U.S.
Govt. Print. Off.] 1967. xi, 605 p.
327.73044 67-62310
   E183.8.F8 A45 MRR Alc.

Hamilton, Alexander, The works of
Alexander Hamilton. [Federal ed.]
New York, London, G. P. Putnam's
sons, 1904. 12 v. 04-19021
   E302 .H24 MRR Alc.

State papers and publick documents of
the United States, from the accession
of George Washington to the
presidency, exhibiting a complete
view of our foreign relations since
that time. 3d ed. Boston, Printed
and published by Thomas B. Wait,
1819. 12 v. 27-5174
   J33 .W4 MRR Alc.

UNITED STATES--HISTORY--WAR WITH
FRANCE, 1798-1800.
De Conde, Alexander, The quasi-war;
New York, Scribner [1966] xiv, 498
p. 973.45 66-24492
   E323 .D4 MRR Alc.

UNITED STATES--HISTORY--1801-1809.
Mayo, Bernard, Henry Clay, spokesman
of the new West. [Unaltered and
unabridged ed. Hamden, Conn.] Archon
Books, 1966 [c1937] 570 p.
973.40924 66-25184
   E340.C6 M2 1966 MRR Alc.

UNITED STATES--HISTORY--WAR OF 1812.
Beirne, Francis F., The War of 1812,
Hamden, Conn., Archon Books, 1965
[c1949] 410 p. 973.52 65-16896
   E354 .B44 1965 MRR Alc.

Coles, Harry Lewis, The War of 1812,
Chicago, University of Chicago Press
[1965] ix, 298 p. 973.52 65-17283

   E354 .C7 MRR Alc.

Tucker, Glenn. Poltroons and
patriots; [1st ed.] Indianapolis,
Bobbs-Merrill [1954] 2 v. (812 p.)
973.52 54-6059
   E354 .T8 MRR Alc.

UNITED STATES--HISTORY--WAR OF 1812--
CAUSES.
Mayo, Bernard, Henry Clay, spokesman
of the new West. [Unaltered and
unabridged ed. Hamden, Conn.] Archon
Books, 1966 [c1937] 570 p.
973.40924 66-25184
   E340.C6 M2 1966 MRR Alc.

UNITED STATES--HISTORY--WAR OF 1812--
SOURCES.
State papers and publick documents of
the United States, from the accession
of George Washington to the
presidency, exhibiting a complete
view of our foreign relations since
that time. 3d ed. Boston, Printed
and published by Thomas B. Wait,
1819. 12 v. 27-5174
   J33 .W4 MRR Alc.

UNITED STATES--HISTORY--1815-1861.
Craven, Avery Odelle, The coming of
the Civil War. [2d ed. Chicago,
University of Chicago Press [1957]
491 p. 973.711 57-8572
   E338 .C82 1957 MRR Alc.

Dangerfield, George, The awakening
of American nationalism, 1815-1828.
[1st ed.] New York, Harper & Row
[c1965] xiii, 331 p. 973.5 64-
25112
   E338 .D3 MRR Alc.

Fuess, Claude Moore, Daniel Webster.
Hamden, Conn., Archon Books, 1963
[c1958] 2 v. 923.273 63-17434
   E340.W4 F955 MRR Alc.

Klein, Philip Shriver, President
James Buchanan, University Park,
Pennsylvania State University Press
[1962] xviii, 506 p. 923.173 62-
12623
   E437 .K53 MRR Alc.

UNITED STATES--HISTORY--1815-1861--
SOURCES.
Buchanan, James, Pres. U.S., James
Buchanan, 1791-1868; Dobbs Ferry,
N.Y., Oceana Publications, 1968. v,
89 p. [$3.00] 973.6/8/08 68-21537

   E436 .B88 MRR Alc.

Grant, Ulysses Simpson, Pres. U.S.,
The papers of Ulysses S. Grant.
Carbondale, Southern Illinois
University Press [1967- v.
973.8/2/0924 67-10725
   E660 .G74 MRR Alc.

Van Buren, Martin, Pres. U.S.,
Martin Van Buren, 1782-1862; Dobbs
Ferry, N.Y., Oceana Publications,
1969. 116 p. [4.00] 973.5/7/0924
69-15391
   E386 .S55 MRR Alc.

UNITED STATES--HISTORY--1817-1825--
CHRONOLOGY.
Monroe, James, Pres. U.S., James
Monroe, 1758-1831; Dobbs Ferry,
N.Y., Oceana Publications, 1969. 86
p. [3.00] 973.5/4/0924 69-15393
   E371 .E4 MRR Alc.

UNITED STATES--HISTORY--1817-1825--
SOURCES.
Monroe, James, Pres. U.S., James
Monroe, 1758-1831; Dobbs Ferry,
N.Y., Oceana Publications, 1969. 86
p. [3.00] 973.5/4/0924 69-15393
   E371 .E4 MRR Alc.

UNITED STATES--HISTORY--WAR WITH
MEXICO, 1845-1848.
Brooks, Nathan Covington, A complete
history of the Mexican War, its
causes, conduct, and consequences.
Chicago, Rio Grande Press [1965]
xiv, 558 p. 973.62 65-20151
   E404 .B88 1965 MRR Alc.

Singletary, Otis A. The Mexican War.
[Chicago] University of Chicago
Press [1960] 181 p. 973.62 60-
7248
   E404 .S5 MRR Alc.

Smith, Justin Harvey, The war with
Mexico, New York, The Macmillan
company, 1919. 2 v. 973.62 19-
19605
   E404 .S66 MRR Alc.

UNITED STATES--HISTORY--1849-1877.
Garfield, James Abram, Pres. U.S.,
The diary of James A. Garfield.
[East Lansing] Michigan State
University, 1967- v. [$22.50 (v.
3)] 973.8/4/0924 B 67-12577
   E660 .G223 MRR Alc.

Nevins, Allan, The emergence of
Lincoln. New York, Scribner, 1950.
2 v. 973.68 50-9920
   E415.7 .N38 MRR Alc.

Nevins, Allan, Ordeal of the Union.
New York, Scribner, 1947. 2 v.
973.6 47-11072
   E415.7 .N4 MRR Alc.

Rhodes, James Ford, History of the
United States from the compromise of
1850 to the end of the Roosevelt
administration. New ed. in nine
volumes ... New York, The Macmillan
company; London, Macmillan & co.,
ltd., 1928, c1929. 9 v. mrr01-49
   E178 .R4782 MRR Alc.

UNITED STATES--HISTORY--1849-1877--
SOURCES.
Grant, Ulysses Simpson, Pres. U.S.,
Ulysses S. Grant, 1822-1885; Dobbs
Ferry, N.Y., Oceana Publications,
1968. 114 p. [$4.00] 973.8/2/08
68-23568
   E671 .M8 MRR Alc.

Johannsen, Robert Walter, comp.
Democracy on trial, 1845-1877, New
York, McGraw-Hill [1966] x, 405 p.
973.7 66-14534
   E173 .D58 vol. 4 MRR Alc.

Pierce, Franklin, Pres. U.S.,
Franklin Pierce, 1804-1869; Dobbs
Ferry, N.Y., Oceana Publications,
1968. v, 90 p. 973.6/6/08 68-
21539
   E415.6 .P6 1968 MRR Alc.

UNITED STATES--HISTORY--CIVIL WAR, 1861-
1865.
Basler, Roy Prentice, A short
history of the American Civil War
New York, Basic Books [1967] xix,
140 p. 973.7 67-12358
   E468 .B33 MRR Alc.

Catton, Bruce, The American heritage
picture history of the Civil War,
New York, American Heritage Pub. Co.;
book trade distribution by Doubleday
[1960] 630 p. 973.79 60-10751
   E468.7 .C3 1960 MRR Alc.

Catton, Bruce, The centennial
history of the Civil War. [1st ed.]
Garden City, N.Y., Doubleday, 1961-
65. 3 v. 973.7 61-12502
   E468 .C29 MRR Alc.

Coulter, Ellis Merton, The
Confederate States of America, 1861-
1865. [Baton Rouge] Louisiana State
University Press, 1950. x, 644 p.
973.713 50-6319
   E487 .C83 MRR Alc.

Eaton, Clement, A history of the
Southern Confederacy. New York,
Macmillan, 1954. 351 p. 973.713
54-8772
   E487 .E15 MRR Alc.

Foote, Shelby. The Civil War, New
York, Random House [1958- v.
973.7 58-9882
   E468 .F7 MRR Alc.

Hendrick, Burton Jesse, Statesmen of
the lost cause: Boston, Little,
Brown and company, 1939. xvii, 452
p. 923.273 39-28981
   E487 .H47 MRR Alc.

Livermore, Thomas Leonard, Numbers &
losses in the Civil War in America,
1861-65. Bloomington, Indiana
University Press, 1957. 150 p.
973.74 57-10726
   E491 .L77 1957 MRR Alc.

Lonn, Ella, Desertion during the
Civil War. Gloucester, Mass., P.
Smith, 1966 [c1928] vii, 251 p.
973.74 66-31671
   E468 .L86 1966 MRR Alc.

Lord, Francis Alfred, They fought
for the Union. [1st ed.]
Harrisburg, Pa., Stackpole Co. [1960]
375 p. 973.741 60-8813
   E491 .L89 MRR Alc.

Nevins, Allan, The War for the
Union. New York, Scribner [1959-71]
4 v. [$15.00 (v. 2)] 973.7 59-
3690
   E468 .N43 MRR Alc.

Randall, James Garfield, Lincoln,
the President. New York, Dodd, Mead,
1945-55. 4 v. 923.173 45-10041
   E457 .R2 MRR Alc.

The Rebellion record; New York, G.
P. Putnam, 1861-63; D. Van Nostrand,
1864-68. 11 v. 02-9069
   E468 .R29 MRR Alc.

Rhodes, James Ford, History of the
United States from the compromise of
1850 to the end of the Roosevelt
administration. New ed. in nine
volumes ... New York, The Macmillan
company; London, Macmillan & co.,
ltd., 1928, c1929. 9 v. mrr01-49
   E178 .R4782 MRR Alc.

Ripley, Warren, Artillery and
ammunition of the Civil War. New
York, Van Nostrand Reinhold Co.
[1970] 384 p. 623.4 75-90331
   UF23 .R56 1970 MRR Alc.

Sandburg, Carl, Abraham Lincoln; the
war years, New York, Harcourt, Brace
& company [c1939] 4 v. 923.173
mrr01-44
   E457.4 .S364 MRR Alc.

Wood, William Charles Henry, In
defense of liberty, New Haven, Yale
university press; [etc., etc.] 1928.
3 p. l. 370 p. 28-25826
   E178.5 .P2 vol. VII MRR Alc.

UNITED STATES--HISTORY--CIVIL WAR, 1861-
1865--ANECDOTES.
The Rebellion record; New York, G.
P. Putnam, 1861-63; D. Van Nostrand,
1864-68. 11 v. 02-9069
   E468 .R29 MRR Alc.

UNITED STATES--HISTORY--CIVIL WAR, 1861-
1865--BIBLIOGRAPHY.
Coulter, Ellis Merton, Travels in
the Confederate States, [1st ed.]
Norman, Univ. of Oklahoma Press,
1948. xiv, 289 p. 016.9175 48-
7183
   Z1251.S7 C68 MRR Alc.

UNITED STATES--HISTORY--CIVIL (Cont.)
Joyce, Donald F., comp. The Civil
War; a list of one hundred books in
braille and on talking book records.
Washington, 1961. 7 p.   61-60075
Z663.25 .C5 MRR Alc.

Kelly, James. The American catalogue
of books. New York, P. Smith, 1938.
2 v.   015.73 38-29060
Z1215 .A4 1938 MRR Ref Desk.

Mebane, John. Books relating to the
Civil War. New York, T. Yoseloff
[1963] 144 p. 016.9737 63-9375
Z1242 .M4 MRR Alc.

Nevins, Allan. Civil War books;
Baton Rouge, Published for the U.S.
Civil War Centennial Commission by
Louisiana State University Press
[1967-68] 2 v. 016.9737 67-10687

Z1242 .N35 MRR Alc.

United States. Library of Congress.
General Reference and Bibliography
Division. The American Civil War;
[Washington, 1960] 24 p. 016.9737
60-62340
Z663.28 .A6 MRR Alc.

United States. War dept. Library.
Bibliography of state participation
in the civil war 1861-1866. [3d ed.]
Washington, Govt. print. off., 1913.
x, 1140 p.   13-35640
Z1242 .U581 1913 MRR Alc.

UNITED STATES--HISTORY--CIVIL WAR,
1861-1865--BIBLIOGRAPHY--CATALOGS.
California. University, Santa
Barbara. Library. The William Wyles
collection. Westport, Conn.,
Greenwood Pub. Corp., 1970] 5 v.
016.9173/03 70-19247
Z1236 .C23 MRR Alc (Dk 33)

UNITED STATES--HISTORY--CIVIL WAR,
1861-1865--BIOGRAPHY.
Boatner, Mark Mayo. The Civil War
dictionary. New York, D. McKay Co.
[1959] xvi, 974 p. 973.703 59-
12267
E468 .B7 MRR Ref Desk.

Hamersly, Thomas Holdup Stevens,
comp. Complete regular army register
of the United States: for one hundred
years (1779 to 1879) Washington, T.
H. S. Hamersly, 1880. viii, 928,
381, xxxvi p.   07-12444
U11.U5 H3 MRR Biog.

Johnson, William T. Johnson's Civil
War book prices. Allegan, Mich.
[1962-65, pt. 3, 1965] 4 pts. 62-
1195
Z1242 .J6 MRR Alc.

Warner, Ezra J. Generals in blue;
lives of the Union commanders.
[Baton Rouge] Louisiana State
University Press [1964] xxiv, 679,
[1] p.   973.741 64-21593
E467 .W29 MRR Biog.

Warner, Ezra J. Generals in gray;
[1st ed. Baton Rouge] Louisiana
State University Press [1959] xxvii,
420 p. 973.742 58-7551
E467 .W3 MRR Biog.

UNITED STATES--HISTORY--CIVIL WAR, 1861-
1865--CAMPAIGNS AND BATTLES.
Battles and leaders of the Civil War.
New York, T. Yoseloff [1958-59,
c1956] 4 v. 973.7 57-59524
E470 .B347 MRR Alc.

Grant, Ulysses Simpson, Pres. U.S.,
Personal memoirs. [1st ed.]
Cleveland, World Pub. Co. [1952]
xxv, 608 p. 923.173 52-5191
E672 .G7617 MRR Alc.

Steele, Matthew Forney. American
campaigns. Washington, B. S. Adams,
1909. viii p., 1 l., 731 p. and
atlas of xii p., 311 maps. war22-80
E181 .S85 MRR Alc.

Strait, Newton Allen, comp.
Alphabetical list of battles, 1754-
1900; Washington, D.C., 1909. 1 p.
l., 252 p. 973.02 38-11790
E181 .S89 1909 MRR Ref Desk.

UNITED STATES--HISTORY--CIVIL WAR,
1861-1865--CAMPAIGNS AND BATTLES--LISTS.
Dyer, Frederick Henry, A compendium
of the War of the Rebellion. New
York, T. Yoseloff [1959] 3 v. (1796
p.) 973.7 59-12963
E491 .D99 1959 MRR Alc.

UNITED STATES--HISTORY--CIVIL WAR, 1861-
1865--CAMPAIGNS AND BATTLES--MAPS.
United States. Military Academy, West
Point. Dept. of Military Art and
Engineering. The West Point atlas of
the Civil War. New York, Praeger
[1962] 1 v. (various pagings)
973.78 map62-23
G1201.S5 U58 1962 MRR Alc.

UNITED STATES--HISTORY--CIVIL WAR, 1861-
1865--CASUALTIES (STATISTICS, ETC.)
Livermore, Thomas Leonard, Numbers &
losses in the Civil War in America,
1861-65. Bloomington, Indiana
University Press, 1957. 150 p.
973.74 57-10726
E491 .L77 1957 MRR Alc.

UNITED STATES--HISTORY--CIVIL WAR, 1861-
1865--CAUSES.
Craven, Avery Odelle, The coming of
the Civil War. [2d ed. Chicago]
University of Chicago Press [1957]
491 p. 973.711 57-8572
E338 .C92 1957 MRR Alc.

Nevins, Allan, Ordeal of the Union.
New York, Scribner, 1947. 2 v.
973.6 47-11072
E415.7 .N4 MRR Alc.

UNITED STATES--HISTORY--CIVIL WAR, 1861-
1865--CENTENNIAL CELEBRATIONS, ETC.
United States. Library of Congress.
The American Civil War; a centennial
exhibition. Washington, 1961. v, 88
p. 973.76 61-60091
Z663 .A83 MRR Alc.

UNITED STATES--HISTORY--CIVIL WAR, 1861-
1865--CHRONOLOGY.
Long, Everette B., The Civil War day
by day; [1st ed.] Garden City,
N.Y., Doubleday, 1971. xiii, 1135 p.
[$17.50] 973.7 73-163653
E468.3 .L6 MRR Alc.

UNITED STATES--HISTORY--CIVIL WAR, 1861-
1865--DICTIONARIES.
Boatner, Mark Mayo, The Civil War
dictionary. New York, D. McKay Co.
[1959] xvi, 974 p. 973.703 59-
12267
E468 .B7 MRR Ref Desk.

Cromie, Alice Hamilton. A tour guide
to the Civil War. Chicago,
Quadrangle Books, 1965 [c1964] xxv,
372 p. 917.3 64-10926
E468.9 .C8 MRR Alc.

UNITED STATES--HISTORY--CIVIL WAR, 1861-
1865--FILM CATALOGS.
United States. Library of Congress.
Stack and Reader Division. The Civil
War in motion pictures; Washington,
1961. vi, 109 p. 973.79 61-60074

Z663.48 .C5 MRR Alc.

UNITED STATES--HISTORY--CIVIL WAR, 1861-
1865--FINANCE, COMMERCE, CONFISCATIONS.
ETC.
Reinfeld, Fred, The story of Civil
War money. New York, Sterling Pub.
Co. [1959] 93 p. 332.4973 59-
13003
HG525 .R36 MRR Alc.

UNITED STATES--HISTORY--CIVIL WAR, 1861-
1865--HISTORIOGRAPHY.
Pressly, Thomas J. Americans
interpret their Civil War.
Princeton, Princeton University
Press, 1954. xvi, 347 p. 973.707
52-13166
E468.5 .P7 MRR Alc.

UNITED STATES--HISTORY--CIVIL WAR, 1861-
1865--MAPS.
Battles and leaders of the Civil War.
New York, T. Yoseloff [1958-59,
c1956] 4 v. 973.7 57-59524
E470 .B347 MRR Alc.

United States. War Dept. The
official atlas of the Civil War. New
York, T. Yoseloff [1958] [8] p.,
facsim.: 29 p., 175 plates (incl.
illus. (part col.) maps (part col.)
plans) map58-3
G1201.S5 U6 1958 MRR Alc.

United States. War dept. The war of
the rebellion: a compilation of the
official records of the Union and
Confederate armies. Washington,
Govt. print. off., 1880-1901. 70 v.
in 128.   03-3452
E464 .U6 Index MRR Ref Desk.

UNITED STATES--HISTORY--CIVIL WAR, 1861-
1865--MAPS--BIBLIOGRAPHY.
United States. Library of Congress.
Map Division. Civil War maps;
Washington, 1961. v, 138 p.
016.97379 61-60061
Z663.35 .C45 MRR Alc.

United States. Library of Congress.
Map Division. The Hotchkiss map
collection; Washington, 1951. 67 p.
016.91273 51-60026
Z663.35 .H6 MRR Alc.

UNITED STATES--HISTORY--CIVIL WAR, 1861-
1865--MISCELLANEA.
Fuld, George. Patriotic Civil War
tokens; Racine, Wis., Whitman Pub.
Co. [1960] 77 p. 737.3 60-1370
CJ4907 .F8 MRR Alc.

UNITED STATES--HISTORY--CIVIL WAR, 1861-
1865--NAVAL OPERATIONS.
Jones, Virgil Carrington, The Civil
War at sea. [1st ed.] New York,
Holt, Rinehart, Winston [1960-62] 3
v. 973.75 60-14457
E591 .J6 MRR Alc.

UNITED STATES--HISTORY--CIVIL WAR, 1861-
1865--NAVAL OPERATIONS--BIBLIOGRAPHY.
Smith, Myron J. American Civil War
navies: a bibliography. Metuchen,
N.J., Scarecrow Press, 1972. ix, 347
p. 016.9737/5 72-6063
Z1242 .S63 MRR Alc.

UNITED STATES--HISTORY--CIVIL WAR, 1861-
1865--NEGRO TROOPS.
Wesley, Charles Harris, Negro
Americans in the Civil War; from
slavery to citizenship, [2d ed.
rev.] New York, Publishers Co.
[1968] xi, 291 p. 973.71/5 75-
6204
E540.N3 W4 1969 MRR Alc.

UNITED STATES--HISTORY--CIVIL WAR, 1861-
1865--NEGROES.
Quarles, Benjamin. The Negro in the
Civil War. [1st ed.] Boston,
Little, Brown [1953] xvi, 379 p.
973.715 53-7309
E540.N3 Q3 MRR Alc.

Wesley, Charles Harris, Negro
Americans in the Civil War; from
slavery to citizenship, [2d ed.
rev.] New York, Publishers Co.
[1968] xi, 291 p. 973.71/5 75-
6204
E540.N3 W4 1969 MRR Alc.

UNITED STATES--HISTORY--CIVIL WAR, 1861-
1865--PERIODICALS.
The Rebellion record; New York, G.
P. Putnam, 1861-63; D. Van Nostrand,
1864-68. 11 v. 02-9069
E468 .R29 MRR Alc.

UNITED STATES--HISTORY--CIVIL WAR, 1861-
1865--PERSONAL NARRATIVES.
Battles and leaders of the Civil War.
New York, T. Yoseloff [1958-59,
c1956] 4 v. 973.7 57-59524
E470 .B347 MRR Alc.

Commager, Henry Steele, ed. The Blue
and the Gray; [1st ed.]
Indianapolis, Bobbs-Merrill [1950] 2
v. (1201 p.) 973.78 50-10710
E464 .C6 MRR Alc.

Eisenschiml, Otto, ed. Eyewitness:
the Civil War as we lived it. New
York, Grosset & Dunlap [c1956] 719
p. 973.7 60-29844
E468 .E4 1956 MRR Alc.

Wiley, Bell Irvin, The common
soldier in the Civil War. New York,
Grosset & Dunlap [1958] 454, 444 p.
973.74 58-4364
E607 .W48 MRR Alc.

UNITED STATES--HISTORY--CIVIL WAR, 1861-
1865--PERSONAL NARRATIVES--BIBLIOGRAPHY.
Dornbusch, Charles Emil, Regimental
publications & personal narratives of
the Civil War; New York, New York
Public Library, 1961-1962. 7 pts.
61-15574
Z1242 .D6 MRR Alc.

UNITED STATES--HISTORY--CIVIL WAR, 1861-
1865--PICTORIAL WORKS.
Catton, Bruce, The American heritage
picture history of the Civil War.
New York, American Heritage Pub. Co.;
book trade distribution by Doubleday
[1960] 630 p. 973.79 60-10751
E468.7 .C3 1960 MRR Alc.

Divided we fought; New York,
Macmillan [c1956] viii, 454 p.
973.7084 56-58591
E468.7 .D5 1956 MRR Alc.

UNITED STATES--HISTORY--CIVIL WAR, 1861-
1865--PICTORIAL WORKS--BIBLIOGRAPHY.
United States. Library of Congress.
General Reference and Bibliography
Division. The Civil War in pictures,
1861-1961; Washington, 1961. 30 p.
61-60076
Z663.28 .C53 MRR Alc.

UNITED STATES--HISTORY--CIVIL WAR, 1861-
1865--PICTORIAL WORKS--CATALOGS.
United States. Library of Congress.
Prints and Photographs Division.
Civil War photographs, 1861-1865;
Washington, Reference Dept., Library
of Congress, 1961. x, 74 p.
973.79085 61-60002
Z663.39 .C5 MRR Alc.

UNITED STATES--HISTORY--CIVIL WAR, 1861-
1865--POETRY.
The Rebellion record; New York, G.
P. Putnam, 1861-63; D. Van Nostrand,
1864-68. 11 v. 02-9069
E468 .R29 MRR Alc.

UNITED STATES--HISTORY--CIVIL WAR, 1861-1865--PORTRAITS.
Meredith, Roy, Mr. Lincoln's contemporaries; New York, Scribner, 1951. xii, 233 p. 973.7 51-12294

E415.8 .M4 MRR Alc.

UNITED STATES--HISTORY--CIVIL WAR, 1861-1865--REGIMENTAL HISTORIES.
Amann, William Frayne, ed. Personnel of the Civil War. New York, T. Yoseloff [1961] 2 v. 973.74 60-9890
E494 .A5 MRR Alc.

Dyer, Frederick Henry. A compendium of the war of the Rebellion. New York, T. Yoseloff [1959] 3 v. (1796 p.) 973.7 59-12963
E491 .D99 1959 MRR Alc.

Stubbs, Mary Lee. Armor-cavalry, Washington, Office of the Chief of Military History, U.S. Army; [for sale by the Supt. of Docs., U.S. Govt. Print. Off.] 1969- v. [6.75] 357./0973 69-60002
UA30 .S8 MRR Alc.

United States. Dept. of the Army. Office of Military History. The Army lineage book. Washington, U.S. Govt. Print. Off., 1953- v. 355.309 54-61235
UA25 .A516 MRR Alc.

UNITED STATES--HISTORY--CIVIL WAR, 1861-1865--REGIMENTAL HISTORIES--BIBLIOGRAPHY.
Dornbusch, Charles Emil, Regimental publications & personal narratives of the Civil War; New York, New York Public Library, 1961-1962. 7 pts. 61-15574
Z1242 .D6 MRR Alc.

Johnson, William T. Johnson's Civil War book prices, Allegan, Mich. [1962-65, pt. 3, 1965] 4 pts. 62-1195
Z1242 .J6 MRR Alc.

United States. War dept. Library. Bibliography of state participation in the civil war 1861-1866. [3d ed.] Washington, Govt. print. off., 1913. x, 1140 p. 13-35640
Z1242 .U581 1913 MRR Alc.

UNITED STATES--HISTORY--CIVIL WAR, 1861-1865--REGISTERS, LISTS, ETC.
Amann, William Frayne, ed. Personnel of the Civil War. New York, T. Yoseloff [1961] 2 v. 973.74 60-9890
E494 .A5 MRR Alc.

UNITED STATES--HISTORY--CIVIL WAR, 1861-1865--SOURCES.
Grant, Ulysses Simpson, Pres. U.S., The papers of Ulysses S. Grant. Carbondale, Southern Illinois University Press [1967- v. 973.8/2/0924 67-10725
E660 .G74 MRR Alc.

Mearns, David Chambers, The Lincoln papers. [1st ed.] Garden City, N.Y., Doubleday, 1948. 2 v. (xvii, 681 p.) 973.7 48-9019
E457.92 1948 MRR Alc.

United States. War dept. The war of the rebellion: a compilation of the official records of the Union and Confederate armies. Washington, Govt. print. off., 1880-1901. 70 v. in 128. 03-3452
E464 .U6 Index MRR Ref Desk.

Welles, Gideon, Diary. New York, W. W. Norton [1960] 3 v. 923.273 60-6275
E468 .W444 MRR Alc.

UNITED STATES--HISTORY--CIVIL WAR, 1861-1865--SOURCES--BIBLIOGRAPHY.
Beers, Henry Putney, Guide to the archives of the Government of the Confederate States of America. Washington, National Archives, General Services Administration; [for sale by the Supt. of Docs., U.S. Govt. Print. Off.] 1968. ix, 536 p. [3.75] 016.97371/3 a 68-7603
CD3047 .B4 MRR Alc.

Burton, William Lester, Descriptive bibliography of Civil War manuscripts in Illinois. [Evanston, Ill.] Published for the Civil War Centennial Commission of Illinois [Springfield] by Northwestern University Press [1966] xv, 393 p. 016.9737 65-24627
Z1242 .B95 MRR Alc.

Munden, Kenneth White. Guide to Federal archives relating to the Civil War. Washington, National Archives; National Archives and Records Service, General Services Administration, 1962. x, 721 p. a 62-9432
CD3047 .M8 MRR Alc.

UNITED STATES--HISTORY--CIVIL WAR, 1861-1865--STATISTICS.
Dyer, Frederick Henry, A compendium of the War of the Rebellion. New York, T. Yoseloff [1959] 3 v. (1796 p.) 973.7 59-12963
E491 .D99 1959 MRR Alc.

Livermore, Thomas Leonard, Numbers & losses in the Civil War in America, 1861-65. Bloomington, Indiana University Press, 1957. 150 p. 973.74 57-10726
E491 .L77 1957 MRR Alc.

UNITED STATES--HISTORY--CIVIL WAR, 1861-1865--SUPPLIES.
Lord, Francis Alfred, Civil War collector's encyclopedia; [1st ed.] Harrisburg, Pa., Stackpole Co. [1963] 360 p. 355.80973 63-14636
UC23 1861-65 .L6 MRR Alc.

UNITED STATES--HISTORY--CIVIL WAR, 1861-1865--TRANSPORTATION.
Black, Robert C., The railroads of the Confederacy. Chapel Hill, University of North Carolina Press [1952] xlv, 360 p. 973.7 52-3559

E545 .B55 MRR Alc.

UNITED STATES--HISTORY--1865-1898.
see also Reconstruction

Faulkner, Harold Underwood, Politics, reform, and expansion, 1890-1900. [1st ed.] New York, Harper [1959] 312 p. 973.8 56-6022
E661 .F3 MRR Alc.

Franklin, John Hope, Reconstruction: after the Civil War. [Chicago] University of Chicago Press [1961] 258 p. 973.8 61-15931
E668 .F7 MRR Alc.

McKitrick, Eric L. Andrew Johnson and reconstruction. [Chicago] University of Chicago Press [1960] ix, 533 p. 973.81 60-5467
E668 .M156 MRR Alc.

McPherson, Edward, The political history of the United States of America during the period of reconstruction, (from April 15, 1865, to July 15, 1870,) 2d ed. Washington, Solomons & Chapman, 1875. v, 6-9, 648 p. 04-7498
E668 .M17 MRR Alc.

Rhodes, James Ford, History of the United States from the compromise of 1850 to the end of the Roosevelt administration. New ed. in nine volumes ... New York, The Macmillan company; London, Macmillan & co., ltd., 1928, c1929. 9 v. mrr01-49
E178 .R4782 MRR Alc.

UNITED STATES--HISTORY--1865-1898--BIBLIOGRAPHY.
Carman, Harry James, A guide to the principal sources for American civilization, 1800-1900, in the city of New York; New York, Columbia University Press 1962. xlvi, 630 p. 016.973 62-10450
Z1236 .C25 1962 MRR Alc.

UNITED STATES--HISTORY--1865-1898--SOURCES.
Cleveland, Grover, Pres. U.S., Grover Cleveland, 1837-1908; Dobbs Ferry, N.Y., Oceana Publications, 1968. 118 p. 973.8/5/08 68-21538

E696 .C617 1968 MRR Alc.

Fleming, Walter Lynwood, ed. Documentary history of Reconstruction; Gloucester, Mass., P. Smith, 1960 [c1935] 2 v. in 1. 973.81082 60-52262
E668 .F58 1960 MRR Alc.

Furer, Howard B., comp. James A. Garfield, 1831-1881: Chester A. Arthur, 1830-1886; Dobbs Ferry, N.Y., Oceana Publications, 1970. v, 148 p. 973.8/4/0922 74-111214
E660.G25 F8 MRR Alc.

Hayes, Rutherford Birchard, Pres. U.S., Rutherford B. Hayes, 1822-1893; Dobb Ferry, N.Y., Oceana Publications, 1969. 90 p. [3.00] 973.8/3/0924 69-15394
E681 .B59 MRR Alc.

UNITED STATES--HISTORY--1865-
Bassett, John Spencer, Makers of a new nation, New Haven, Yale university press; [etc., etc.] 1928. 3 p. l., 344 p. 28-24814
E178.5 .P2 vol. 9 MRR Alc.

Dulles, Foster Rhea, The United States since 1865. New ed. rev. and enl. Ann Arbor, University of Michigan Press [1969] ix, 562, xx p. [8.50] 973 69-15850
E178 .D87 1969 MRR Alc.

Hicks, John Donald, The American Nation; 4th ed. Boston, Houghton Mifflin, 1965. xiii, 832, cix p., 973.8 66-3913
E661 .H55 1965 MRR Alc.

UNITED STATES--HISTORY--1865- --SOURCES.
Wilson, Woodrow, Pres. U.S., 1856-1924. The papers of Woodrow Wilson. Princeton, N.J., Princeton University Press, 1966- v. [$20.00 per vol.] 973.91/3/0924 66-10880
E660 .W717 MRR Alc.

UNITED STATES--HISTORY--WAR OF 1898.
Chadwick, French Ensor, The relations of the United States and Spain: the Spanish-American war, New York, C. Scribner's sons, 1911. 2 v. 11-23013
E715 .C43 MRR Alc.

Freidel, Frank Burt. The splendid little war. [1st ed.] Boston, Little, Brown [1958] 314 p. 973.89 58-10069
E715 .F7 MRR Alc.

Wood, William Charles Henry, In defense of liberty, New Haven, Yale university press; [etc., etc.] 1928. 3 p. l., 370 p. 28-25826
E178.5 .P2 vol. VII MRR Alc.

UNITED STATES--HISTORY--1898-
Lyons, Eugene, Herbert Hoover, a biography. [1st ed.] Garden City, N.Y. Doubleday, 1964. xii, 444 p. 923.173 64-15834
E802 .L82 MRR Alc.

UNITED STATES--HISTORY--20TH CENTURY.
Barck, Oscar Theodore, Since 1900; 4th ed. New York, Macmillan [1965] x, 963 p. 973.91 65-14074
E741 .B34 1965 MRR Alc.

Freidel, Frank Burt. America in the twentieth century, 2d ed. New York, Knopf, 1965. xxiv, 651, xxiv p. 973.9 65-11501
E741 .F7 1965 MRR Alc.

Freidel, Frank Burt. Franklin D. Roosevelt. [1st ed.] Boston, Little, Brown [1952- v. 923.173 52-5521
E807 .F74 MRR Alc.

Hohenberg, John, ed. The Pulitzer prize story; New York, Columbia University Press, 1959. 375 p. 070.431 59-7702
PS647.N4 H6 MRR Alc.

Link, Arthur Stanley. American epoch; 3d ed. New York, Knopf [1967] xxii, 926, xliv p. 973.91 67-12258
E741 .L55 1967 MRR Alc.

Link, Arthur Stanley. Wilson. Princeton, Princeton University Press, 1947- v. 923.173 47-3554
E767 .L65 MRR Alc.

Sinclair, Andrew. The available man; New York, Macmillan [1965] viii, 344 p. 923.173 65-14332
E786 .S5 MRR Alc.

Steinberg, Alfred, The man from Missouri; New York, Putnam [1962] 447 p. 923.173 62-8004
E814 .S74 MRR Alc.

Sullivan, Mark, Our Times; the United States, 1900-1925 ... New York [etc.] C. Scribner's sons, 1927-35. 6 v. mrr01-51
E741 .S92 MRR Alc.

Wish, Harvey, Contemporary America; 4th ed. New York, Harper & Row [1966] xx, 813 p. 973.9 66-15677

E741 .W78 1966 MRR Alc.

UNITED STATES--HISTORY--20TH CENTURY--SOURCES.
Roosevelt, Franklin Delano, Pres. U.S., F. D. R.: his personal letters. [1st ed.] New York, Duell, Sloan and Pearce [1947-50] 4 v. 923.173 47-11935
E807 .R649 MRR Alc.

Shannon, David A., ed. Progressivism and postwar disillusionment, 1898-1928, New York, McGraw-Hill [1966] 383 p. 973.9108 65-26768
E173 .D58 vol. 6 MRR Alc.

UNITED STATES--HISTORY--1901-1953--SOURCES.
United States. President, 1901-1909 (Roosevelt) Theodore Roosevelt, 1858-1919; Dobbs Ferry, N.Y., Oceana Publications, 1969. 120 p. [4.00] 971.91/1/0924 69-15392
E756 .U68 MRR Alc.

UNITED STATES--HISTORY--EUROPEAN WAR, 1914-1918
see European War, 1914-1918

UNITED STATES--HISTORY--1919-1933.
Emerson, Edwin, Hoover and his
times; Garden City, N.Y., Garden
City publishing company, inc., 1932.
xvi p., 1 l., 632 p.   923.173 32-
25411
   E801 .E75 MRR Alc.

Schlesinger, Arthur Meier, The age
of Roosevelt. Boston, Houghton,
Mifflin, 1957- v.   973.917 56-
10293
   E806 .S34 MRR Alc.

UNITED STATES--HISTORY--1919-1933--
SOURCES.
Rollins, Alfred Brooks, ed.
Depression, recovery, and war, 1929-
1945, New York, McGraw-Hill [1966]
xii, 404 p.   973.9108 66-14813
   E173 .D58 vol. 7 MRR Alc.

UNITED STATES--HISTORY--1933-1945.
Leuchtenburg, William Edward,
Franklin D. Roosevelt and the New
Deal, 1932-1940. [1st ed.] New
York, Harper & Row [1963] 393 p.
973.917 63-12053
   E806 .L475 MRR Alc.

Schlesinger, Arthur Meier, The age
of Roosevelt. Boston, Houghton,
Mifflin, 1957- v.   973.917 56-
10293
   E806 .S34 MRR Alc.

UNITED STATES--HISTORY--1933-1945--
SOURCES.
Rollins, Alfred Brooks, ed.
Depression, recovery, and war, 1929-
1945, New York, McGraw-Hill [1966]
xii, 404 p.   973.9108 66-14813
   E173 .D58 vol. 7 MRR Alc.

Roosevelt, Franklin Delano, Pres.
U.S., The public papers and
addresses of Franklin D. Roosevelt,
New York, Random House, 1938-[50] 13
v.   973.917 38-11227
   E806 .R749 MRR Alc.

UNITED STATES--HISTORY--1945-
O'Neill, William L. Coming apart;
Chicago, Quadrangle Books, 1971. ix,
442, xxvi p. [$12.50] 973.921 79-
152098
   E389 .O5 1971 MRR Alc.

Sorensen, Theodore C. Kennedy [1st
ed.] New York, Harper & Row [1965]
viii, 783 p.   973.922 65-14660
   E841 .S6 MRR Alc.

UNITED STATES--HISTORY--1945- --
BIBLIOGRAPHY.
Miller, Albert Jay. Confrontation,
conflict, and dissent: Metuchen,
N.J., Scarecrow Press, 1972. 567 p.
016.3091/73/092 78-189440
   Z7165.U5 M53 MRR Alc.

Stapleton, Margaret L. The Truman
and Eisenhower years: 1945-1960;
Metuchen, N.J., Scarecrow Press,
1973. vii, 221 p.   016.973918 73-
1791
   Z1245 .S7 MRR Alc.

UNITED STATES--HISTORY--1945- --SOURCES.
Historic documents. 1972-
[Washington] Congressional Quarterly,
inc. [$25.00]   917.3/03/9205 72-
97888
   E839.5 .H57 MRR Alc Full set

May, Ernest R., ed. Anxiety and
affluence: 1945-1965, New York,
McGraw-Hill [1966] xii, 404 p.
973.908 66-14810
   E173 .D58 vol. 8 MRR Alc.

Schlesinger, Arthur Meier, comp. The
dynamics of world power; New York,
Chelsea House Publishers, 1973- v.
[$149.00]   327.73 78-150208
   E744 .S395 MRR Alc.

United States. Dept. of State.
Historical Office. American foreign
policy; 1956- [Washington] 327.73
59-64042
   JX1417 .A33 MRR Alc Full set

UNITED STATES--HISTORY--ADDRESSES,
ESSAYS, LECTURES.
Hurd, Charles, ed. A treasury of
great American speeches. New and
rev. ed. New York, Hawthorn Books
[1970] 411 p. [10.00] 815/.01 77-
107901
   PS662 .H8 1970 MRR Alc.

UNITED STATES--HISTORY--BIBLIOGRAPHY.
Beers, Henry Putney, Bibliographies
in American history; [Rev. ed.
Paterson] N.J., Pageant Books, 1959
[c1938] xv, 487 p. 016.016973 59-
14179
   Z1236.A1 B4 1959 MRR Ref Desk.

California. University. Bancroft
Library. Catalog of printed books.
Boston, G. K. Hall, 1964. 22 v.
016.9178 67-52922
   Z881 .C1523 MRR Alc (DK33)

Church, Elihu Dwight, A catalogue of
books relating to the discovery and
early history of North and South
America. New York, P. Smith, 1951.
5 v. (vi, 2635 p.) 016.9731 51-
4055
   Z1203 .C55 1951 MRR Ref Desk.

Fingerhut, Eugene R. The Fingerhut
guide: sources in American history
Santa Barbara, Calif., American
Bibliographical Center - Clio Press
[1973] xii, 148 p. 016.0169173/03
72-95266
   Z1215.A2 F55 MRR Alc.

Freidel, Frank Burt. Harvard guide
to American history. Rev. ed.
Cambridge, Mass., Belknap Press of
Harvard University Press, 1974. 2 v.
(xxx, 1290 p.) 016.9173/03 72-
81272
   Z1236 .F77 1974 MRR Ref Desk.

Griffin, Appleton Prentiss Clark,
Bibliography of American historical
societies 2d ed., rev. and enl.
[Washington, Govt. print. off., 1907]
1374 p.   08-7356
   Z1236 .G86 MRR Alc.

Handlin, Oscar, Harvard guide to
American history Cambridge, Mass.,
Belknap Press, 1954. xxiv, 689 p.
016.973 53-5066
   Z1236 .H27 TJ Rm.

Hotchkiss, Jeanette. American
historical fiction and biography for
children and young people. Metuchen,
N.J., Scarecrow Press, 1973. 318 p.
016.9173/03 73-13715
   Z1236 .H73 MRR Alc.

Jones, Howard Mumford, Guide to
American literature and its
backgrounds since 1890 4th ed., rev.
and enl. Cambridge, Mass., Harvard
University Press, 1972. xii, 264 p.
016.81 72-85143
   Z1225 .J65 1972 MRR Alc.

Kuehl, Warren F., Dissertations in
history; [Lexington] University of
Kentucky Press, 1965-[72] 2 v.
016.9 65-11832
   Z6201 .K8 MRR Ref Desk.

Larned, Josephus Nelson, ed. The
literature of American history;
Columbus, Ohio, Long's College Book
Co., 1953 [c1902] ix, 588, 37 p.
016.973 55-45638
   Z1236 .L3 1953 MRR Alc.

List of doctoral dissertations in
history now in progress at
universities in the United States.
Washington [etc.] 016.9 10-12162
   Z5055.U49 L7 MRR Ref Desk Partial
set

Scott, Franklin Daniel, Guide to the
American historical review, 1895-
1945;   46-25831
   E172 .A60 1944, vol. 1 MRR Ref
Desk.

Taylor, George Rogers, American
economic history before 1860. New
York, Appleton-Century-Crofts [1969]
xiv, 108 p. 016.330973 70-79173
   Z7165.U5 T37 MRR Alc.

United States. Library of Congress.
General Reference and Bibliography
Division. American history and
civilization; a list of guides 2d
(rev.) ed. Washington, 1951. 18 p.
016.016973 51-60033
   Z663.28 .A64 1951 MRR Alc.

United States. Library of Congress.
General Reference and Bibliography
Division. A guide to the study of
the United States of America;
Washington, 1960. xv, 1193 p.
016.9173 60-60009
   Z1215 .U53 MRR Alc.

Vail, Robert William Glenroi, The
voice of the old frontier.
Philadelphia, University of
Pennsylvania Press, 1949. xii, 492
p. 016.9173 49-50000
   Z1249.F9 V3 MRR Alc.

Wiltz, John E. Books in American
history: Bloomington, Indiana
University Press [1964] ix, 150 p.
016.973 64-18817
   Z1236 .W53 MRR Alc.

Winsor, Justin, ed. Narrative and
critical history of America,
Standard library ed. [Boston, New
York, Houghton, Mifflin and company,
1923, c1884-89] 8 v.   23-16194
   E18 .W77 MRR Alc.

UNITED STATES--HISTORY--BIBLIOGRAPHY--
CATALOGS.
American Antiquarian Society,
Worcester, Mass. Library. A
dictionary catalog of American books
pertaining to the 17th through 19th
centuries. Westport, Conn.,
Greenwood Pub. Corp. [1971] 20 v.
015/.73 76-103820
   Z1215 .A264 MRR Alc (Dk 33)

California. University, Santa
Barbara. Library. The William Wyles
collection. Westport, Conn.,
Greenwood Pub. Corp., 1970] 5 v.
016.9173/03 70-19247
   Z1236 .C23 MRR Alc (Dk 33)

Harvard University. Library.
American history. Cambridge;
Distributed by the Harvard University
Press, 1967. 5 v. 016.973 67-
30955
   Z1236 .H28 MRR Alc.

[Library of American civilization.
Chicago, Library Resources, inc.,
1971-72] 12,474 sheets.
016.9173/03 71-170957
   Z1236 .L45 Suppl. MRR Alc.

Michigan. University. William L.
Clements Library. Author/title
catalog of Americana, 1493-1860, in
the William L. Clements Library,
Boston, G. K. Hall, 1970. 7 v.
016.9173/03 73-156668
   Z1236 .M53 MRR Alc (Dk 33)

New York. Public Library. Reference
Dept. Dictionary catalog of the
history of the Americas. Boston, G.
K. Hall, 1961. 28 v. 016.97 61-
4957
   Z1201 .N4 MRR Alc (Dk 33)

UNITED STATES--HISTORY--CHRONOLOGY.
Astronautics and aeronautics;
1915/60- Washington, Scientific and
Technical Information Division,
National Aeronautics and Space
Administration [etc.; for sale by the
Superintendent of Documents, U.S.
Govt. Print. Off.] 65-60308
   TL521.3.A8 A3 MRR Alc Partial set

Bergman, Peter M. The chronological
history of the Negro in America,
[1st ed.] New York, Harper & Row
[1969] 698 p. [12.00]
973/.09/7496 68-27434
   E185 .B46 MRR Ref Desk.

Burke, Joan Martin. Civil rights;
2d ed. New York, Bowker, 1974. xi,
266 p. 323.4/025/73 74-4053
   JC599.US B85 1974 MRR Alc.

Carruth, Gorton. The encyclopedia of
American facts and dates. 6th ed.,
New York, Crowell [1972] vi, 922 p.
[$8.95] 973/.02 72-78262
   E174.5 .C3 1972 MRR Ref Desk.

Curti, Merle Eugene, A history of
American civilization New York,
Harper [1953] xv, 836 p. 917.3 52-
12769
   E169.1 .C875 MRR Alc.

Damon, Charles Ripley, comp. The
American dictionary of dates, 458-
1920; Boston, R. G. Badger [c1921]
3 v.   21-21758
   E174.5 .D16 MRR Alc.

Dillon, Philip Robert, American
anniversaries; New York, The Philip
R. Dillon publishing company [c1918]
3 p. l., 349, xv p.   18-22970
   E174.5 .D57 MRR Alc.

Fetros, John G. This day in sports;
Novato, Calif., N. K. Gregg [1974]
264 p. [$5.95] 796/.09 74-75882
   GV576 .F48 MRR Alc.

Hart, James David, The Oxford
companion to American literature 4th
ed. [rev. and enl.] New York, Oxford
University Press, 1965. ix, 991 p.
810.3 65-22796
   PS21 .H3 1965 MRR Ref Desk.

Hopkins, Lee Bennett. Important
dates in Afro-American history. New
York, F. Watts [1969] 188 p.
973/.09/7496 73-83648
   E185 .H6 MRR Alc.

Hornsby, Alton. The Black almanac.
Rev. and enl. Woodbury, N.Y.,
Barron's Educational Series, inc.
[1973] xxiv, 247 p. [$2.95]
917.3/06/96073 74-154291
   E185 .H63 1973 MRR Alc.

Hunt, William Welch, comp. The book
of governors. (2d ed.) Los Angeles,
Calif., Printed by Washington
typographers [c1935] 84 p. 973.02
36-764
   E174.5 .H862 MRR Ref Desk.

UNITED STATES--HISTORY-- (Cont.)
Jameson, John Franklin, Dictionary of United States history; Rev. ed. Detroit, Gale Research Co., 1971. xi, 874 p.   973/.03   68-30658
E174 .J32 MRR Alc.

Kelley, Etna M. The business founding date directory. [1st ed.] Scarsdale, N.Y., Morgan & Morgan [1954]   x, 228 p.   650.58 54-6999
HD2785 .K4 MRR Ref Desk.

Kull, Irving Stoddard. A short chronology of American history, 1492-1950 New Brunswick, Rutgers University Press, 1952. 388 p. 973.02 52-9371
E174.5 .K8 MRR Ref Desk.

Little, Charles Eugene, Cyclopedia of classified dates with an exhaustive index. Detroit, Gale Research Co., 1967. vii, 1454 p. 902/.02   66-27839
D9 .L7 1967 MRR Alc.

Long, Everette B., The Civil War day by day; [1st ed.] Garden City, N.Y., Doubleday, 1971. xiii, 1135 p. [$17.50]   973.7 73-163653
E468.3 .L6 MRR Alc.

Morris, Richard Brandon, ed. Encyclopedia of American history. Enl. and updated. New York, Harper & Row [1970] xiv, 850 p. [$9.89] 973/.03   73-95647
E174.5 .M847 1970 MRR Ref Desk.

Morris, Richard Brandon, ed. Encyclopedia of American history, Updated and rev. New York, Harper & Row [1965] xiv, 843 p.   973.03 65-22859
E174.5 .M847 1965 MRR Alc.

Motor Vehicle Manufacturers Association of the United States. Automobiles of America: milestones, pioneers, roll call, highlights. 4th ed.; rev. Detroit, Wayne State University Press, 1974. 301 p. 629.22/22/0973 73-19838
TL23 .M63 1974 MRR Alc.

Osborne, Robert A. When who did what, [Los Angeles, Stationers corporation, 1944] 207 p.   44-53427

E174.5 .O8 MRR Alc.

Phelps, Robert, The literary life; New York, Farrar, Straus and Giroux, 1968.   244 p. [$15.00] 016.8209/009/1   68-27533
Z2013 .P48 MRR Alc.

Taylor, Tim, The book of presidents. [1st ed.] New York, Arno Press, 1972. viii, 703 p. [$12.95] 973/.099 B 74-164708
E176.1 .T226 MRR Ref Desk.

Thornton, Willis. Almanac for Americans New York, Greenberg [c1941] 5 p. l., 3-418 p. incl. front., illus.   973.02 41-23726
E174.5 .T5 MRR Alc.

Thornton, Willis. Almanac for Americans. [2d ed.] New York, Greenberg [1954] 440 p.   973.02 54-11015
E174.5 .T5 1954 MRR Alc.

The Times in review; New York, Arno Press, 1970-73 [v. 1, 1973; v. 5, 1970] 5 v.   909.82 74-139439
D427 .T5 MRR Alc.

United States. Bureau of Aeronautics (Navy Dept.) A calendar of significant events in the growth and development of United States naval aviation, 1898-1956. [Washington, 1956] 64 p.   623.74 628.13* 58-60324
VG93 .A62 1956 MRR Alc.

Webster's guide to American history; Springfield, Mass., G. & C. Merriam Co. [1971] 1428 p.   973 76-24114
E174.5 .W4 MRR Ref Desk.

Winsor, Justin, ed. Narrative and critical history of America, Standard library ed. [Boston, New York, Houghton, Mifflin and company, 1923, c1884-89] 8 v.   23-16194
E18 .W77 MRR Alc.

Wyckoff, Peter. Wall Street and the stock markets: [1st ed.] Philadelphia, Chilton Book Co. [1972] xiv, 304 p.   332.6/42/0973 72-8277

HG4572 .W87 MRR Alc.

UNITED STATES--HISTORY--DICTIONARIES.
Adams, James Truslow, ed. Concise dictionary of American history. New York, Scribner [1962] viii, 1156 p. 973.03 62-9635
E174 .A45 MRR Ref Desk.

Adams, James Truslow, ed. Dictionary of American history; 2nd ed. rev. New York, C. Scribner's sons, 1942-v.   973.03   44-1876
E174 .A43 1942 MRR Ref Desk.

Encyclopedia of American history. Guilford, Conn., Dushkin Pub. Group [1973] 405 p. 973/.03 73-85201
E174 .E52 MRR Ref Desk.

Hurwitz, Howard Lawrence, An encyclopedic dictionary of American history, New York, Washington Square Press [1968] xii, 882 p. [$10.00] 973/.03 68-18511
E174 .H8 MRR Alc.

Jameson, John Franklin, Dictionary of United States history; Rev. ed. Detroit, Gale Research Co., 1971. xi, 874 p.   973/.03   68-30658
E174 .J32 MRR Alc.

Johnson, Thomas Herbert. The Oxford companion to American history New York, Oxford University Press, 1966. vi, 906 p.   973.03 66-22263
E174 .J6 MRR Ref Desk.

Martin, Michael Rheta, The new dictionary of American history, New York, Philosophical Library [1965] vi, 714 p.   973.03 65-23770
E174 .M3 1965a MRR Alc.

Mitchell, Edwin Valentine, comp. An encyclopedia of American politics. New York, Greenwood Press, 1968 [c1946] 338 p.   320/.0973 69-10135

JK9 .M55 1968 MRR Alc.

Morris, Richard Brandon, ed. Encyclopedia of American history, Updated and rev. New York, Harper & Row [1965] xiv, 843 p.   973.03 65-22859
E174.5 .M847 1965 MRR Alc.

Morris, Richard Brandon, ed. Encyclopedia of American history. Enl. and updated. New York, Harper & Row [1970] xiv, 850 p. [$9.89] 973/.03   73-95647
E174.5 .M847 1970 MRR Ref Desk.

UNITED STATES--HISTORY--ERRORS, INVENTIONS, ETC.
Kominsky, Morris. The hoaxers: plain liars, fancy liars, and damned liars. Boston, Branden Press [1970] 735 p. [$12.50]   909 76-109134
E839.8 .K6 MRR Alc.

Lindquist, Orville Alvin. Common fallacies regarding United States history. Richmond, Dietz Press, 1948.   99 p.   973.0883 48-3411
E179 .L6 MRR Ref Desk.

UNITED STATES--HISTORY--EXAMINATIONS, QUESTIONS, ETC.
Schnapper, Morris Bartel, ed. The facts of American life. Washington, Public Affairs Press, [1960] vi, 420 p.   917.3   60-11398
E169.1 .S345 MRR Alc.

UNITED STATES--HISTORY--FICTION--BIBLIOGRAPHY.
Coan, Otis Welton. America in fiction; 5th ed. Palo Alto, Calif., Pacific Books, 1967. viii, 232 p. 016.813/00803   66-28118
Z1361.C6 C6 1966 MRR Alc.

Dickinson, A. T. American historical fiction, 3d ed. Metuchen, N.J., Scarecrow Press, 1971. 380 p. 016.813/03 78-146503
PS374.H5 D5 1971 MRR Alc.

Hotchkiss, Jeanette. American historical fiction and biography for children and young people. Metuchen, N.J., Scarecrow Press, 1973. 318 p. 016.9173/03 73-13715
Z1236 .H73 MRR Alc.

Hotchkiss, Jeanette. American historical fiction and biography for children and young people. Metuchen, N.J., Scarecrow Press, 1973. 318 p. 016.9173/03 73-13715
Z1236 .H73 MRR Alc.

UNITED STATES--HISTORY--JUVENILE LITERATURE--BIBLIOGRAPHY.
Metzner, Seymour. American history in juvenile books. New York, H. W. Wilson Co., 1966. 329 p.   016.973 66-12299
Z1037 .M32 MRR Alc.

UNITED STATES--HISTORY--MISCELLANEA.
Shankle, George Earlie. American mottoes and slogans, New York, The H. W. Wilson company, 1941. 183 p. 973 41-26048
E179 .S544 MRR Alc.

UNITED STATES--HISTORY--OUTLINES, SYLLABI, ETC.
Catchpole, Brian. A map history of the United States. London, Heinemann Educational, 1972. vi, 130 p. [£0.90]   917.3/03 73-330879
E178.2 .C34 MRR Alc.

Cole, Donald B. Handbook of American history New York, Harcourt, Brace & World [1968] xiii, 337 p. 973/.02/02 68-24778
E178.2 .C76 MRR Alc.

UNITED STATES--HISTORY--PERIODICALS.
The American historical review. v. 1-Oct. 1895- Washington [etc.] 973.05 05-18244
E171 .A57 MRR Ref Desk Indexes only

UNITED STATES--HISTORY--PERIODICALS--INDEXES.
America, history and life. v. 1-July 1964- [Santa Barbara, Calif.] 016.917 64-25630
Z1236 .A48 MRR Alc Full set

The American historical review. v. 1-Oct. 1895- Washington [etc.] 973.05 05-18244
E171 .A57 MRR Ref Desk Indexes only

Freidel, Frank Burt. Harvard guide to American history. Rev. ed. Cambridge, Mass., Belknap Press of Harvard University Press, 1974. 2 v. (xxx, 1290 p.) 016.9173/03 72-81272
Z1236 .F77 1974 MRR Ref Desk.

New York. Public Library. Reference Dept. Dictionary catalog of the history of the Americas. Boston, G. K. Hall, 1961. 28 v. 016.97 61-4957
Z1201 .N4 MRR Alc (Dk 33).

Smith, Dwight La Vern, Afro-American history; Santa Barbara, Calif., ABC-Clio [1974] xvi, 856 p. 016.9173/06/96073 73-87155
Z1361.N39 S56 MRR Alc.

Swem, Earl Gregg, comp. Virginia historical index ... Roanoke, Va., Designed, printed, and bound by the Stone printing and manufacturing company, 1934-36. 2 v. 34-38514
F221 .S93 MRR Ref Desk.

Winther, Oscar Osburn, A classified bibliography of the periodical literature of the trans-Mississippi West, 1811-1957. Bloomington, Indiana University Press, 1961. xxvi, 626 p.   016.9178 61-63869
Z1251.W5 W53 MRR Alc.

UNITED STATES--HISTORY--PHILOSOPHY.
Skotheim, Robert Allen. American intellectual histories and historians. Princeton, N.J., Princeton University Press, 1966. xi, 326 p.   973.072 66-11960
E175.45 .S5 MRR Alc.

UNITED STATES--HISTORY--PICTORIAL WORKS.
Album of American history New York, Scribner, 1944-60. 6 v.   973.084 44-706
E178.5 .A48 MRR Alc.

Album of American history. New York, Scribner [1969- v.   973.022/2 74-91746
E178.5 .A482 MRR Alc.

Butterfield, Roger Place, The American past; [2d rev. and expanded ed. New York] Simon and Schuster [1966] 544 p.   973.0222 66-16146
E178 .B988 1966 MRR Alc.

Faulkner, Harold Underwood, A visual history of the United States. 2d ed. New York, McGraw-Hill [1961] 188 p. 973.084   61-8652
E178.5 .F3 1961 MRR Alc.

Larsen, Ellouise Baker. American historical views on Staffordshire china. New rev. and enl. ed. Garden City, N.Y., Doubleday, 1950. xxx, 317 p.   738.27 50-11741
NK4087.S6 L3 1950 MRR Alc.

The Pageant of America, a pictorial history of the United States; Liberty bell ed. [New Haven, Yale University Press, 1925-29] 15 v. 48-38521
E178.5 .P2 MRR Alc.

UNITED STATES--HISTORY--PICTORIAL WORKS--CATALOGS.
United States. Library of Congress. Prints and Photographs Division. Pictorial Americana; Washington, 1945. 38 l.   973.084 46-12463
Z663.39 .P5 1945 MRR Alc.

UNITED STATES--HISTORY-- (Cont.)
United States. Library of Congress.
Prints and Photographs Division.
Pictorial Americana; 2d ed.
Washington, Library of Congress,
1955. 68 p.   973.084 55-60012
Z663.39 .P5 1955 MRR Alc.

UNITED STATES--HISTORY--SOCIETIES, ETC.
American Historical Association.
Annual report. 1889- Washington,
Smithsonian Institution Press [etc.]
04-18261
E172 .A60 MRR Ref Desk Partial set

Griffin, Appleton Prentiss Clark,
Bibliography of American historical
societies 2d ed., rev. and enl.
[Washington, Govt. print. off., 1907]
1374 p.   08-7356
Z1236 .G86 MRR Alc.

UNITED STATES--HISTORY--SOURCES.
Adams, John Quincy, Pres. U.S.,
Writings of John Quincy Adams. New
York, Greenwood Press [1968] 7 v.
973.4/0924 68-30993
E337.8 .A22 MRR Alc.

Angle, Paul McClelland, ed. By these
words; New York, Rand McNally [1954]
560 p.   973 54-10616
E173 .A79 MRR Alc.

Bartlett, Ruhl Jacob, ed. The record
of American diplomacy; 4th ed. enl.
New York, Knopf, 1964. xxiv, 892,
xxii p.   327.73 64-23857
E183.7 .B35 1964 MRR Alc.

Bell, Herbert Clifford Francis,
Guide to British West Indian archive
materials. Washington, D.C.,
Carnegie institution of Washington,
1926. ix, 435 p.   26-10272
CD1048.U5 B4 MRR Alc.

Boorstin, Daniel Joseph, ed. An
American primer. Chicago, University
of Chicago Press [1966] 2 v. (xvii,
994 p.)   917.303 66-20576
E173 .B7 MRR Alc.

Carter, Clarence Edwin, comp. The
territorial papers of the United
States. Washington, U.S. Govt.
Print. Off., 1934- v.   973.082
35-26191
E173 .C3 MRR Alc.

Commager, Henry Steele, ed.
Documents of American history. 9th
ed. New York, Appleton-Century-
Crofts [1973] xxiii, 815 p.
973/.08 73-11492
E173 .C66 1973 MRR Ref Desk.

Commager, Henry Steele, ed. Living
ideas in America. New, enl. ed. New
York, Harper & Row [1964] xx, 872 p.
917.3 64-23898
E173 .C67 1964 MRR Alc.

Davenport, Frances Gardiner, ed.
European treaties bearing on the
history of the United States and its
dependencies. Washington, D.C.,
Carnegie institution of Washington,
1917-37. 4 v.   18-3383
E173 .D24 MRR Alc.

A Documentary history of American
life. New York, McGraw-Hill [1966-
v.   973.08 66-1167
E173 .D58 MRR Alc.

Documents on American foreign
relations. 1938/39- New York, Simon
and Schuster [etc.]   39-28987
JX231 .D6 MRR Alc Full set

Filler, Louis, ed. The President
speaks; New York, Putnam [1964] 416
p.   973.082 64-13025
E173 .F5 MRR Alc.

Franklin, Benjamin, The papers of
Benjamin Franklin. New Haven, Yale
University Press, 1959- v.   081
59-12697
E302 .F82 1959 MRR Alc.

Griffin, Bulkley S., comp. Offbeat
history. Cleveland, World Pub. Co.
[1967] xiii, 360 p.   973 67-5205
E173 .G87 MRR Alc.

Handlin, Oscar, ed. Readings in
American history. 2d ed. New York,
Knopf [1970] 2 v.   973/.08 77-
107455
E173 .H23 1970 MRR Alc.

Hollingsworth, Joseph Rogers, ed.
American democracy. New York,
Crowell [1961-62] 2 v.   973.082 61-
16898
E173 .H77 MRR Alc.

Huszar, George Bernard de, ed. Basic
American documents. Ames, Iowa,
Littlefield, Adams [c1953] 365 p.
973 52-14779
E173 .H95 MRR Alc.

Jados, Stanley S., ed. Documents on
Russian-American relations,
Washington, Catholic University of
America Press [1965] viii, 416 p.
327.47073 65-12569
E183.8.R9 J3 MRR Alc.

Johnson, Andrew, Pres. U.S., The
papers of Andrew Johnson. Knoxville,
University of Tennessee Press, 1967-
v.   [$15.00] 973.8/1/0924 67-
25733
E415.6 .J65 1967 MRR Alc.

Leopold, Richard William, ed.
Problems in American history. 2d ed.
Englewood Cliffs, N.J., Prentice-
Hall, 1957. 706 p.   973 57-6544
E178 .L5 1957 MRR Alc.

Morris, Richard Brandon, Great
Presidential decisions; New and enl.
ed. New York, Harper & Row [1973]
508 p.   [$1.50] 973 73-176031
E173 .M93 1973 MRR Alc.

Robertson, James Alexander, List of
documents in Spanish archives
relating to the history of the United
States, Washington, D.C., Carnegie
institution of Washington, 1910. xv,
368 p.   10-16322
CD1858.U6 R6 MRR Alc.

Schlesinger, Arthur Meier, History
of U.S. political parties. New York,
Chelsea House Publishers, 1973. 4 v.
(liv, 3544 p.)   329/.02 72-8682
JK2261 .S35 MRR Alc.

Schwartz, Bernard, comp. The Bill of
Rights; a documentary history. New
York, Chelsea House Publishers, 1971.
2 v. (xvii, 1234 p.)   342/.73/029
71-150209
KF4744 1971 MRR Alc.

United States. Bureau of rolls and
library. Documentary history of the
Constitution of the United States of
America, 1786-1870. Washington,
Department of state, 1894 [i.e. 1901]-
05. 5 v.   02-10164
JK111 .A52 MRR Alc.

United States. Congress. American
state papers. Washington, Gales and
Seaton, 1832-61. 38 v.   09-33892
J33 MRR Alc.

United States. Dept. of State.
Foreign relations of the United
States. [1861]- Washington, U.S.
Govt. Print. Off. 327.73 10-3793
JX233 .A3 MRR Alc Full set

United States. Library of Congress.
Legislative reference service.
Documents illustrative of the
formation of the union of the
American states. Washington, Govt.
print. off., 1927. x, 1115 p.   27-
26258
JK11 1927 MRR Alc.

United States. Library of Congress.
Manuscript Division. A calendar of
John Paul Jones manuscripts in the
Library of Congress. Washington,
Govt. Print. Off., 1903. 316 p.
012 03-19074
Z663.34.J6 MRR Alc.

United States. Library of Congress.
Manuscript Division. Calendar of the
papers of John Jordan Crittenden.
Washington, Govt. print. off., 1913.
355 p.   12-35010
Z663.34 .C7 MRR Alc.

United States. Library of Congress.
Manuscript division. Calendar of the
papers of Martin Van Buren,
Washington, Govt. print. off., 1910.
757 p.   012 10-35009
Z663.34 .V2 MRR Alc.

United States. Library of Congress.
Manuscript division. The Declaration
of independence, the Constitution of
the United States, and other historic
material in the Division of
manuscripts of the Library of
Congress. [Washington] The Library
of Congress, Division of manuscripts
[1941] 14, 2 p.   027.5753 091 41-
50007
Z663.34 .D4 MRR Alc.

United States. Library of Congress.
Manuscript division. List of the
Benjamin Franklin papers in the
Library of Congress. Washington,
Govt. print. off., 1905. 322 p.   05-
20007
Z663.34 .L5 MRR Alc.

United States. Library of Congress.
Manuscript division. List of the
Washington manuscripts from the year
1592 to 1775. Washington, Govt.
print. off., 1919. iii, 137 p.   19-
26005
Z663.34 .W35 MRR Alc.

United States. Library of Congress.
Manuscript Division. Papers of James
Monroe. Washington, Govt. print.
off., 1904. 114 p.   05-1169
Z663.34 .M6 MRR Alc.

United States. Library of Congress.
Manuscript Divison. Calendar of the
papers of Franklin Pierce,
Washington, Govt. print. off., 1917.
102 p.   17-26003
Z663.34 .P5 MRR Alc.

United States. President. A
compilation of the messages and
papers of the presidents, New York,
Bureau of national literature, inc.
[191?7] 20 v.   353.03 17-7545
J81 .B97a MRR Alc.

United States. President. Public
papers of the Presidents of the
United States, containing the public
messages, speeches, and statements of
the President. Washington, U.S.
Govt. Print. Off. 353.03 58-61050
J80 .A283 MRR Alc Full set

United States. President. The State
of the Union messages of the
Presidents, 1790-1966. New York,
Chelsea House, 1966. 3 v. (xii, 3264
p.)   353.035 66-20309
J81 .C66 MRR Alc.

Washington, George, Pres. U.S.,
Diaries, 1748-1799. [Regents ed.]
Boston, Houghton Mifflin, 1925. 4 v.
25-21899
E312.8 1748-99 MRR Alc.

Washington, George, Pres. U.S., The
Washington papers; [1st ed.] New
York, Harper [1955] 430 p.   308.1
54-12149
E312.72 1955 MRR Alc.

Weekly compilation of Presidential
documents. v. 1- Aug. 2, 1965-
[Washington, Office of the Federal
Register; distributed by Supt. of
Docs., Govt. Print. Off.] 65-9929
J80 .A284 MRR Alc Partial set

UNITED STATES--HISTORY--SOURCES--
BIBLIOGRAPHY.
Billington, Ray Allen, Guides to
American history manuscript
collections in libraries of the
United States. New York, P. Smith,
1952. 467-496 p.   016.973 52-2323

Z1236 .B5 MRR Alc.

Crick, Bernard R., ed. A guide to
manuscripts relating to America in
Great Britain and Ireland. [London]
Published for the British Association
for American Studies by the Oxford
University Press, 1961. xxxvi, 667
p.   016.973 61-65029
CD1048.U5 C7 MRR Alc.

Greene, Evarts Boutell, A guide to
the principal sources for early
American history (1600-1800) in the
city of New York. New York, Columbia
university press, 1929. xxv, 357,
[1] p.   29-17492
Z1236 .G82 MRR Alc.

Hale, Richard Walden, ed. Guide to
photocopied historical materials in
the United States and Canada.
Ithaca, N.Y., published for the
American Historical Association [by]
Cornell University Press [1961]
xxxiv, 241 p.   016.9 61-17269
Z6209 .H3 MRR Alc.

Historical Records Survey.
Pennsylvania. Guide to the
manuscript collections of the
Historical Society of Pennsylvania.
2d ed. Philadelphia, Historical
Society of Pennsylvania, 1949. 1 v.
(unpaged) 016.9748 49-49681
Z1329 .H68 1949 MRR Alc.

Lancour, Harold, A bibliography of
ship passenger lists, 1538-1825; 3d
ed., rev. and enl. New York, New
York Public Library, 1963. ix, 137
p.   016.32573 63-18141
Z7164.I3 L2 1963 MRR Alc.

The National union catalog of
manuscript collections. 1959/61-
Washington [etc.] The Library of
Congress [etc.]   62-17486
Z6620.U5 N3 MRR Alc Full set / MRR
Alc Full set

Spielman, William Carl, Introduction
to sources of American history. New
York, Exposition Press [1951] 175 p.
973.07 51-11625
E175 .S6 MRR Alc.

Stevenson, Noel C. Search and
research, the researcher's handbook;
Rev. ed. Salt Lake City, Deseret
Book Co., 1959. 364 p.   929.1072
59-11137
Z5313.U5 S8 1959 MRR Ref Desk.

UNITED STATES--HISTORY--SOURCES- (Cont.)
United States. Library of Congress. A guide to the microfilm collection of early state records, [Washington] Library of Congress, Photoduplication Service, 1950. 1 v. (various pagings) 016.01573 50-62956
    Z663.96 .G8 MRR Alc.

United States. Library of Congress. Manuscript Division. Accessions of manuscripts, broadsides and British transcripts. July 1920/21-1925. Washington, Govt. Print. Off., Library Branch. 22-26001
    Z663.34 .A25 MRR Alc MRR Alc Full set

United States. Library of Congress. Manuscript Division. Carl William Ackerman: a register of his papers in the Library of Congress. Washington, Library of Congress, 1973. lii, 78 p. 016.070/92/4 73-4207
    Z663.34 .A27 MRR Alc.

United States. Library of Congress. Manuscript division. A guide to manuscripts relating to American history in British depositories reproduced for the Division of manuscripts of the Library of Congress. [Washington] The Library of Congress, 1946. xvi, 313 p. 016.973 46-27863
    CD1048.U5 A35 1946 MRR Alc.

United States. Library of Congress. Manuscript division. Handbook of manuscripts in the Library of Congress. Washington, Govt. print. off., 1918. xviii, 750 p. 17-26010
    Z6621 .U55 MRR Alc.

United States. Library of Congress. Manuscript division. List of manuscript collections in the Library of Congress to July, 1931. Washington, U.S. Govt. print. off., 1932. 1 p. l., 123-249 p. 016.091 32-7818
    Z6621 .U56 MRR Alc.

United States. Library of Congress. Manuscript division. List of manuscript collections received in the Library of Congress, July 1931 to July 1938, Washington, U.S. Govt. print. off., 1939. v, 33 p. 016.091 016.973 39-26002
    Z663.34 .L482 MRR Alc.

United States. Library of Congress. Manuscript division. Manuscripts in public and private collections in the United States. Washington, Govt. print. off., 1924. ix, 98 p. 24-26001
    Z663.34 .M3 MRR Alc.

United States. National Archives. Guide to the records in the National Archives. Washington, U.S. Govt. Print. Off., 1948. xvi, 684 p. 353 a 49-10088
    CD3023 .A46 1948 MRR Ref Desk.

United States. National Archives. Preliminary inventory of the records of the United States House of Representatives, 1789-1946 (Record group 233) Washington, 1959. 2 v. a 59-9361
    CD3026 .A32 no. 113 MRR Alc.

Van Tyne, Claude Halstead, Guide to the archives of the government of the United States in Washington, 2d ed. rev. and enl. [Washington] Carnegie institution of Washington, 1907. xiii, 327 p. 08-9062
    CD3024 .V3 1907 MRR Alc.

UNITED STATES--HISTORY--SOURCES--BIBLIOGRAPHY--CATALOGS.
Michigan. University. William L. Clements Library. Author/title catalog of Americana, 1493-1860, in the William L. Clements Library, Boston, G. K. Hall, 1970. 7 v. 016.9173/03 73-156668
    Z1236 .M53 MRR Alc (Dk 33)

United States. Library of Congress. Rare Book Division. Catalog of broadsides in the Rare Book Division. Boston, G. K. Hall 1972. 4 v. 011 72-6563
    Z1231.B7 A5 MRR Alc (Dk 33)

UNITED STATES--HISTORY--SOURCES--DIRECTORIES.
Shumway, Gary L. Oral history in the United States: New York, Oral History Association, 1971. 120 p. 973/.025/73 71-169931
    E175.4 .S58 MRR Alc.

UNITED STATES--HISTORY--STUDY AND TEACHING.
Handlin, Oscar, Harvard guide to American history Cambridge, Mass., Belknap Press, 1954. xxiv, 689 p. 016.973 53-5066
    Z2136 .H27 TJ Rm.

UNITED STATES--HISTORY, LOCAL.
Benagh, Christine L. 100 keys: names across the land Nashville, Abingdon Press [1973] 288 p. [$5.95] 917.3/003 70-186613
    E180 .B45 MRR Alc.

Franzen, Marilyn D. Capitol capsules; Pierpont, S.D., Rushmore, inc., 1964. 208 p. 973 64-2446
    E159 .F7 MRR Alc.

Kane, Joseph Nathan, The American counties; 3d ed. Metuchen, N.J., Scarecrow Press, 1972. 608 p. 917.3/03 70-186010
    E180 .K3 1972 MRR Ref Desk.

UNITED STATES--HISTORY, LOCAL--BIBLIOGRAPHY.
Bradford, Thomas Lindsley, The bibliographer's manual of American history, Philadelphia, S. V. Henkels & co., 1907-10. 5 v. 07-23470
    Z1250 .B85 MRR Alc.

Child, Sargent Burrage, Check list of Historical Records Survey publications; Baltimore, Genealogical Pub. Co., 1969. vi, 110 p. 016.973/08 69-17126
    Z1223.Z7 C52 MRR Alc.

Griffin, Appleton Prentiss Clark, Bibliography of American historical societies 2d ed., rev. and enl. [Washington, Govt. print. off., 1907] 1374 p. 08-7356
    Z1236 .G86 MRR Alc.

Historical records survey. American imprints inventory, Washington, D.C., [etc.] The Historical records survey, 1937- v. 015.73 38-6329
    Z1215 .H67 MRR Alc.

Hodgson, James Goodwin, comp. The official publications of American counties, Fort Collins, Col., 1937. viii p., ix-xii numb. l., xiii-xxii, 594 p. 015.73 37-27440
    Z7164.L8 H72 MRR Alc.

Peterson, Clarence Stewart, Consolidated bibliography of county histories in fifty States in 1961, consolidated 1935-1961. Baltimore, Genealogical Pub. Co., 1973 [c1961] 186 p. 016.929/3 73-8036
    Z1250 .P47 1973 MRR Alc.

Shankle, George Earlie. State names, flags, seals, songs, birds, flowers, and other symbols; Rev. ed. New York, H. W. Wilson Co., 1941 [i.e. 1951, c1938] 524 p. 929.4 917.3* 52-52807
    E155 .S43 1951 MRR Alc.

Writers' program. Catalogue, WPA Writers' program publications, the American guide series, the American life series. [Washington, U.S. Govt. print. off., 1942] 1 p. l., 54 p. 016.9173 42-37616
    Z1236 .W75 MRR Alc.

UNITED STATES--HISTORY, LOCAL--JUVENILE LITERATURE.
Benagh, Christine L. 100 keys: names across the land Nashville, Abingdon Press [1973] 288 p. [$5.95] 917.3/003 70-186613
    E180 .B45 MRR Alc.

UNITED STATES--HISTORY, LOCAL--SOURCES.
Kirkham, E. Kay. The counties of the United States: their derivation and census schedules; [Salt Lake City, Kay Pub. Co., 1961] a-e, 77 p. 61-66794
    E180 .K5 MRR Ref Desk.

UNITED STATES--HISTORY, LOCAL--SOURCES--BIBLIOGRAPHY.
Stevenson, Noel C. Search and research, the researcher's handbook; Rev. ed. Salt Lake City, Deseret Book Co., 1959. 364 p. 929.1072 59-11137
    Z5313.U5 S8 1959 MRR Ref Desk.

UNITED STATES--HISTORY, MILITARY.
Bernardo, C. Joseph, American military policy, its development since 1775 [2d ed.] Harrisburg, Pa., Military Service Division, Stackpole Co. [1961] 548 p. 355 61-15573
    UA23 .B43 1961 MRR Alc.

Dupuy, Richard Ernest, The compact history of the United States Army 2d rev. ed. New York, Hawthorn Books [1973] 346 p. [$9.95] 973 72-10984
    E181 .D78 1973 MRR Alc.

Dupuy, Richard Ernest, The little wars of the United States. [1st ed.] New York, Hawthorn Books [1968] 226 p. [6.95] 973 68-28130
    E181 .D79 MRR Alc.

Dupuy, Richard Ernest, Military heritage of America New York, McGraw-Hill, 1956. xv, 794 p. 973 55-11169
    E181 .D8 MRR Alc.

Ganoe, William Addleman, The history of the United States Army, Rev. ed. New York, London, D. Appleton-Century company, incorporated, 1942. xi, 640 p. 973 42-20792
    E181 .G17 1942 MRR Alc.

Hamersly, Thomas Holdup Stevens, comp. Complete regular army register of the United States: for one hundred years (1779 to 1879) Washington, T. H. S. Hamersly, 1880. viii, 928, 381, xxxvi p. 07-12444
    U11.U5 H3 MRR Biog.

Hinkel, John Vincent, Arlington: monument to heroes. New and enl. ed. Englewood Cliffs, N.J., Prentice-Hall [1970] x, 187 p. [5.95] 975.5/295 79-89542
    F234.A7 H6 1970 MRR Alc.

Leckie, Robert. The wars of America. [1st ed.] New York, Harper & Row [1967, c1968] xvii, 1052 p. 973 65-20433
    E181 .L45 MRR Alc.

Matloff, Maurice, American military history. Washington, Office of the Chief of Military History, U.S. Army; [for sale by the Supt. of Docs., U.S. Govt. Print. Off.] 1969. xvi, 701 p. [8.00] 355/.00973 76-600410
    E181 .M33 1969 MRR Alc.

Prucha, Francis Paul. A guide to the military posts of the United States, 1789-1895. Madison, State Historical Society of Wisconsin, 1964. xiii, 178 p. 355.70973 64-63571
    UA26.A6 P7 MRR Alc.

Steele, Matthew Forney, American campaigns, Washington, B. S. Adams, 1909. viii p., 1 l., 731 p. and atlas of xii p., 311 maps. war22-80
    E181 .S85 MRR Alc.

Stubbs, Mary Lee. Armor-cavalry, Washington, Office of the Chief of Military History, U.S. Army; [for sale by the Supt. of Docs., U.S. Govt. Print. Off.] 1969- v. [6.75] 357/.00973 69-60002
    UA30 .S8 MRR Alc.

United States. Dept. of the Army. Office of Military History. The Army lineage book. Washington, U.S. Govt. Print. Off., 1953- v. 355.309 54-61235
    UA25 .A516 MRR Alc.

United States. Library of Congress. An album of American battle art, 1755-1918. Washington, U.S. Govt. Print. Off., 1947. xvi, 319 p. 769.49973 48-45628
    Z663 .A8 MRR Alc.

Weigley, Russell Frank. History of the United States Army, New York, Macmillan [1967] xiv, 688 p. 355/.000973 67-16051
    UA25 .W35 MRR Alc.

Wood, William Charles Henry, In defense of liberty, New Haven, Yale university press; [etc., etc.] 1928. 3 p. l., 370 p. 28-25826
    E178.5 .P2 vol. VII MRR Alc.

UNITED STATES--HISTORY, MILITARY--TO 1900.
Peterson, Harold Leslie, Arms and armor in colonial America, 1526-1783. Harrisburg, Pa., Stackpole Co. [1956] 350 p. 399 56-11273
    U818 .P4 MRR Alc.

Strait, Newton Allen, comp. Alphabetical list of battles, 1754-1900; Washington, D.C., 1909. 1 p. l., 252 p. 973.02 38-11780
    E181 .S89 1909 MRR Ref Desk.

UNITED STATES--HISTORY, MILITARY--ANECDOTES.
Schott, Joseph L. Above and beyond: the story of the Congressional Medal of Honor. New York, Putnam [1963] 314 p. 355.134 62-18293
    E181 .S35 MRR Alc.

UNITED STATES--HISTORY, MILITARY--BIBLIOGRAPHY.
Dollen, Charles. Bibliography of the United States Marine Corps. New York, Scarecrow Press, 1963. 115 p. 016.35996 63-7464
    Z6725.U5 D6 MRR Alc.

Dornbusch, Charles Emil, Histories, personal narratives: United States Army; Cornwallville, N.Y., Hope Farm Press, 1967. [15]-399 p. 016.355 67-5273
    Z1249.M5 D6 1967 MRR Ref Desk.

UNITED STATES--HISTORY, MILITARY--DICTIONARIES.
Ruffner, Frederick G., ed. Code names dictionary; Detroit, Gale Research Co. [1963] 555 p.   423 63-21847
PE1693 .R9 MRR Alc.

UNITED STATES--HISTORY, MILITARY--MAPS.
United States. Military Academy, West Point. Dept. of Military Art and Engineering. The West Point atlas of American Wars. New York, Praeger [1959] 2 v.   912.73 59-7452
G1201.S1 U5 1959 MRR Alc.

UNITED STATES--HISTORY, NAVAL.
Pater, Alan Frederick. United States battleships; [1st ed.] Beverly Hills, Calif., Monitor Book Co. [1968] 279 p.   359.32/52/0973 68-17423
VA58 .P3 MRR Alc.

Potter, Elmer Belmont, The Naval Academy illustrated history of the United States Navy New York, Crowell [1971] 299 p. [$12.95] 359/.00973 72-146286
E182 .P78 MRR Alc.

Potter, Elmer Belmont, ed. The United States and world sea power. Englewood Cliffs [N.J.] Prentice-Hall, 1955. ix, 963 p.   973 55-9323
E182 .P8 MRR Alc.

Pratt, Fletcher, The compact history of the United States Navy. New and rev. ed. New York, Hawthorn Books [1962] 350 p.   973 62-9039
E182 .P84 1962 MRR Alc.

Pratt, Fletcher, The navy, a history; Garden City, N.Y., Garden City publishing co., inc. [1941] 4 p. l., xi-xvii, [2], 496 (i.e. 504) p.   359.0973 41-23977
VA55 .P7 1941 MRR Alc.

United States. Bureau of Naval Personnel. Medal of honor, 1861-1949, the Navy. [Washington, 1950?] ix, 327 p.   359.134 50-61099
VB333 .A532 MRR Biog.

United States. Naval History Division. Dictionary of American naval fighting ships. Washington, [For sale by the Supt. of Doc., U.S. Govt. Print. Off.] 1959- v.   623.825 60-60198
VA61 .A53 MRR Alc.

United States Naval Institute. Almanac of naval facts. Annapolis [1964] 305 p.   973 64-12269
E182 .U587 MRR Alc.

UNITED STATES--HISTORY, NAVAL--TO 1900.
Bennett, Frank Marion, The steam navy of the United States. 2d ed. Pittsburgh, Pa., Warren & company, 1897. 2 v.   08-29480
VA55 .B49 1897 MRR Alc.

UNITED STATES--HISTORY, NAVAL--ANECDOTES.
Schott, Joseph L. Above and beyond: the story of the Congressional Medal of Honor. New York, Putnam [1963] 314 p.   355.134 62-18293
E181 .S35 MRR Alc.

UNITED STATES--HISTORY, NAVAL--BIBLIOGRAPHY.
Albion, Robert Greenhalgh, Naval & maritime history; 4th ed., rev. and expanded. Mystic, Conn., Munson Institute of American Maritime History, 1972. ix, 370 p. [$15.00] 016.387/09 73-186863
Z6834.H5 A4 1972 MRR Alc.

Smith, Myron J. American Civil War navies: a bibliography, Metuchen, N.J., Scarecrow Press, 1972. ix, 347 p.   016.8737/5 72-6063
Z1242 .S63 MRR Alc.

Smith, Myron J. The American Navy, 1865-1918: Metuchen, N.J., Scarecrow Press, 1974. xiii, 372 p. 016.359/00973 74-4230
Z6835.U5 S62 MRR Alc.

UNITED STATES--HISTORY, NAVAL--CHRONOLOGY.
Cooney, David M. A chronology of the U.S. Navy, 1775-1965, New York, F. Watts [1965] 471 p.   359.00973 65-21636
E182 .C73 MRR Alc.

UNITED STATES--HISTORY, NAVAL--SOURCES.
United States. Naval History Division. Naval documents of the American Revolution. Washington [For sale by the Supt. of Docs., U.S. Govt. Print. Off.] 1964- v.   64-60087
E271 .U583 MRR Alc.

UNITED STATES--HISTORY, NAVAL--SOURCES--BIBLIOGRAPHY--CATALOGS.
United States. Library of Congress. Manuscript Division. Claude Charles Bloch, Julius Augustus Furer, John Franklin Shafroth, William Harrison Standley: a register of their papers in the Library of Congress. Washington, Library of Congress, 1971. iii, 6 l., 10, 4, 11, p.   016.359 73-4374
Z663.34 .B55 MRR Alc.

United States. Library of Congress. Manuscript Division. William Sowden Sims: a register of his papers in the Library of Congress. Washington, Library of Congress, 1971. 28 p.   016.3593/3/10924 72-600006
Z663.34 .S57 MRR Alc.

UNITED STATES--IMPRINTS.
Adams, Ramon Frederick, Six-guns and saddle leather; New ed., [Norman, University of Oklahoma Press, 1969] xxv, 808 p. [19.95] 016.3641 69-16729
Z1251.W5 A3 1969 MRR Alc.

Adams, Thomas Randolph, American independence: the growth of an idea; Providence, Brown University Press, 1965. xxi, [2], 200 p.   916.973311 62-16995
Z1238 .A4 MRR Alc.

American book publishing record. BPR annual cumulative. 1960/64- New York, Bowker. 015/.73 66-19741
Z1201 .A52 MRR Ref Desk Full set

The American catalogue ... New York, 1941. 8 v. in 13.   015.73 a 42-2938
Z1215 .A52 MRR Ref Desk.

Blanck, Jacob Nathaniel, Bibliography of American literature, New Haven, Yale University Press, 1955- v.   016.81 54-5283
Z1225 .B55 MRR Alc.

Bowker's medical books in print. 1972- New York, R.R. Bowker Co. 016.61 78-37613
Z6658 .B65 MRR Alc Latest edition / Sci RR Latest edition

Bristol, Roger Pattrell. Supplement to Charles Evans' American bibliography. Charlottesville, Published for the Bibliographical Society of America and the Bibliographical Society of the University of Virginia [by] University Press of Virginia [1970] xix, 636 p. [35.00] 015.73 73-94761
Z1215 .E92334 MRR Ref Desk (Alc. 6)

Brown, Eleanor Parker. Culinary Americana; New York, Roving Eye Press [c1961] xlv, 417 p.   64-54658

Z5776.G2 B7 MRR Alc.

Brown University. Library. Dictionary catalog of the Harris collection of American poetry and plays, Brown University Library, Providence, Rhode Island. Boston, G. K. Hall, 1972. 13 v.   016.81 75-184497
Z1231.P7 B72 MRR Alc (Dk 33)

A Catalog of books represented by Library of Congress printed cards issued to July 31, 1942. Ann Arbor, Mich., Edwards Bros., 1942-46. 167 v.   018.1 43-3338
Z881.A1 C3 MRR Alc. (DK 33)

Children's books in print. 1969- New York, R. R. Bowker Co. 028.52 70-101705
Z1037.A1 C482 MRR Alc Latest edition

Church, Elihu Dwight, A catalogue of books relating to the discovery and early history of North and South America, New York, P. Smith, 1951. 5 v. (vi, 2635 p.) 016.9731 51-4055
Z1203 .C55 1951 MRR Ref Desk.

Cooper, Gayle. A checklist of American imprints for 1830- Metuchen, N.J., Scarecrow Press, 1972- v.   015/.73 72-187094
Z1215 .C66 MRR Ref Desk (Alc 6)

Cumulative book index. 1898/99- New York [etc.] H. W. Wilson Co. 05-33604
Z1219 .M78 MRR Circ Partial set

Deodene, Frank. Black American fiction since 1952; Chatham, N.J., Chatham Bookseller, 1970. 25 p. 016.813/5/4 78-96384
Z1361.N39 D45 MRR Alc.

Deodene, Frank. Black American poetry since 1944; Chatham, N.J., Chatham Bookseller, 1971. 41 p. 016.811/5/408 76-175303
Z1229.N39 D46 MRR Alc.

Dickinson, A. T. American historical fiction, 3d ed. Metuchen, N.J., Scarecrow Press, 1971. 380 p. 016.813/03 78-146503
PS374.H5 D5 1971 MRR Alc.

Drake, Milton. Almanacs of the United States. New York, Scarecrow Press, 1962. 2 v. (L, 1397 p.) 016.051 62-10127
Z1231.A6 D7 MRR Alc.

Evans, Charles, American bibliography. Metuchen, N.J., Mini-Print Corp. 1967. 13 v. in 1. 015.73 67-4309
Z1215 .E9232 1967 MRR Alc.

Evans, Charles, American bibliography; Chicago, Priv. print. for the author by the Blakely Press, 1903-59. 14 v. 03-32909
Z1215 .E92 MRR Ref Desk.

Faxon, Frederick Winthrop, Literary annuals and gift books : [1st ed.] reprinted / Pinner (Ravelston, Southview Rd, Pinner, Middx) : Private Libraries Association, 1973. 352 p. in various pagings : [£6.00] 015/.42 74-186776
Z6520.G4 F3 1973 MRR Alc.

Foley, Patrick Kevin, American authors, 1795-1895; New York, Milford House, 1969. xvi, 350 p. 016.81 68-54462
Z1231.F5 F65 1969 MRR Alc.

Gaines, Pierce Welch. Political works of concealed authorship in the United States, 1789-1810, Rev. and enl. ed. Hamden, Conn., Shoe String Press, 1965. 190 p. 014.1 65-17720
Z1045 .G3 1965 MRR Alc.

Guerra, Francisco. American medical bibliography 1639-1783. New York, L. C. Harper, 1962. 885 p. 016.61 61-17786
Z6659 .G8 MRR Alc.

Guide to reprints. 1967- Washington, Microcard Editions. 011 66-29279
Z1000.5 .G8 MRR Ref Desk Latest edition

Harvard University. Library. English literature. Cambridge; Distributed by the Harvard University Press, 1971. 4 v. 016.82 74-128717
Z2011 .H36 MRR Alc.

Harwell, Richard Barksdale. More Confederate imprints. Richmond, Virginia State Library, 1957. 2 v. (xxxvi, 345 p.) 015.75 a 57-9084
Z1242.5 .H33 MRR Alc.

Heard, Joseph Norman, Bookman's guide to Americana [5th ed.] Metuchen, N.J., Scarecrow Press, 1969. ix, 472 p. 016.917 76-2468

Z998 .H42 1969 MRR Alc.

Hill, Frank Pierce, American plays printed 1714-1830; New York, B. Blom, 1968. xi, 152 p. 016.812 68-20229
Z1231.D7 H6 1968 MRR Alc.

Historical records survey. American imprints inventory, Washington, D.C., [etc.] The Historical records survey, 1937- v. 015.73 38-6329
Z1215 .H67 MRR Alc.

Hitchcock, Henry Russell, American architectural books; Minneapolis, University of Minnesota Press [1962] xii, 130 p. 016.72 62-11970
Z5941 .H67 1962 MRR Alc.

Inland Empire Council of Teachers of English. Northwest books, [2d ed.] Portland, Or., Binfords & Mort [1942] 356 p. 016.81 42-21718
Z1251.N7 I6 MRR Alc.

Johnson, James Gibson, Southern fiction prior to 1860: New York, Phaeton Press, 1968. vii, 126 p. 016.813/2 67-30904
Z1231.F4 J7 1968 MRR Alc.

Kelly, James, The American catalogue of books, New York, P. Smith, 1938. 2 v. 015.73 38-29060
Z1215 .A4 1938 MRR Ref Desk.

Kelly, James, The American catalogue of books, New York, P. Smith, 1938. 2 v. 015.73 38-29060
Z1215 .A4 1938 MRR Ref Desk.

UNITED STATES--IMPRINTS. (Cont.)
Library of Congress and National
union catalog author lists, 1942-
1962: Detroit, Gale Research Co.,
1969-71. 152 v.   018/.1/0873 73-
82135
   Z881.A1 L63 MRR Alc (Dk 33)

Lowenstein, Eleanor. Bibliography of
American cookery books, 1742-1860.
[3d ed.] Worcester [Mass.] American
Antiquarian Society, 1972. xii, 132
p.   016.6415 72-81730
   Z5776.G2 L68 1972 MRR Alc.

Michigan. University. William L.
Clements Library. Author/title
catalog of Americana, 1483-1860, in
the William L. Clements Library,
Boston, G. K. Hall, 1970. 7 v.
016.9173/03 73-156668
   Z1236 .M53 MRR Alc (Dk 33)

The National union catalog, Totowa,
N.J., Rowman and Littlefield [1970-
v.   018/.1/0973 76-141020
   Z881.A103742 MRR Alc (Dk 33)

The National union catalog, pre-1956
imprints: London, Mansell, 1968- v.
   021.6/4 67-30001
   Z663.7.L5115 MRR Alc (Dk 33)

Nevins, Allan, Civil War books;
Baton Rouge, Published for the U.S.
Civil War Centennial Commission by
Louisiana State University Press
[1967-69] 2 v.   016.9737 67-10687

   Z1242 .N35 MRR Alc.

New York (City). Public Library. Berg
Collection. Dictionary catalog of
the Henry W. and Albert A. Berg
Collection of English and American
literature. Boston, G. K. Hall,
1969. 5 v.   016.82 75-21408
   Z2011 .N55 MRR Alc (Dk 33)

Newberry Library, Chicago. A
catalogue of the Everett D. Graff
collection of Western Americana.
Chicago. Published for the Newberry
Library by the University of Chicago
Press, 1968. xxv, 854 p. 016.978
66-20577
   Z1251.W5 N43 MRR Alc.

Paperbound book guide for colleges.
New York, R. R. Bowker. 016 60-3050

   Z1033.P3 P3 MRR Alc Latest
      editions

Paperbound books in print. Mar. 1971-
[New York, Bowker] 011 71-649559

   Z1033.P3 P33 MRR Alc Latest
      edition / Sci RR Latest edition

Princeton University. Library. Early
American book illustrators and wood
engravers, 1670-1870; Princeton,
N.J., 1958. xlvii, 265 p. 761.2084
58-9784
   Z1023 .P9 1958 MRR Alc.

Ransom, Will, Selective check list
of press books: New York, P. C.
Duschnes, 1945- pts.   015 46-
583
   Z1028 .R3 MRR Alc.

Reginald, R. Cumulative paperback
index, 1939-1959; Detroit, Gale
Research Co. [1973] xxiv, 362 p.
018//4 73-6866
   Z1033.P3 R4 MRR Alc.

Roden, Robert F., Later American
plays, 1831-1900: New York, B.
Franklin [1969] 132 p. 016.812/3
71-6518
   Z1231.D7 W5 1969 MRR Alc.

Roorbach, Orville Augustus,
Bibliotheca americana. New York, P.
Smith, 1939. xi, 652 p.   015.73 39-
27504
   Z1215 .A3 1939 MRR Ref Desk.

Roorbach, Orville Augustus,
Bibliotheca Americana: Metuchen,
N.J., Mini-Print Corp., 1967. 1 v.
(various pagings) 015.73 67-8332
   Z1215 .A3 1967 MRR Alc.

Sabin, Joseph, A dictionary of books
relating to America, New York, 1868
[i.e. 1867]-1936. 29 v.   01-26958
   Z1201 .S2 MRR Ref Desk.

Shaw, Ralph Robert, American
bibliography, New York, Scarecrow
Press, 1958-66. 22 v.   015.73 58-
7809
   Z1215 .S48 MRR Ref Desk.

Shipton, Clifford Kenyon, National
index of American imprints through
1800; [Worcester, Mass.] American
Antiquarian Society, 1969. 2 v.
(xxv, 1028 p.) 015/.73 69-11248
   Z1215 .S485 MRR Ref Desk.

Shoemaker, Richard H. A checklist of
American imprints for 1820-1829. New
York, Scarecrow Press, 1964-71. 10
v.   015.73 64-11784
   Z1215 .S5 MRR Ref Desk (Alc. 6)

Sloane, William. Children's books in
England & America in the seventeenth
century: New York, King's Crown
Press, Columbia University, 1955.
ix, 251 p.   028.5 54-9938
   Z1037 .S62 MRR Alc.

Soliday, George W., A descriptive
check list, together with short title
index, describing almost 7500 items
of western Americana: [Reprinted
with corrections] New York,
Antiquarian Press, 1960. 1 v.
(various pagings) 016.97 61-45337

   Z1251.W5 S62 MRR Alc.

Streeter, Thomas Winthrop,
Bibliography of Texas, 1795-1845.
Cambridge, Harvard University Press,
1955-60. 3 pts. in 5 v.   016.9764
56-13552
   Z1339 .S8 MRR Alc.

Thompson, Lawrence Sidney, The new
Sabin; Troy, N.Y., Whitston Pub.
Co., 1974- v.   016.9173/03 73-
85960
   Z1201 .T45 MRR Ref Desk (Alc 6)

Thompson, Ralph, American literary
annuals & gift books, 1825-1865.
[Hamden, Conn.] Archon Books, 1967
[c1936] 190 p.   050 67-17791
   AY10 .T5 1967 MRR Alc.

United States. Library of Congress.
English language books by title:
Detroit, Gale Research Co., 1971. 20
v.   018/.1 75-165487
   Z881.A1 C34 MRR Alc (Dk 33)

United States. Library of Congress.
Exchange and Gift Division. Monthly
checklist of State publications. v.
1- Jan. 1910- Washington, U.S.
Govt. Print. Off. 015.73 10-8924
   Z1223.5.A1 U5 MRR Alc Full set

United States. Library of Congress.
Jefferson Collection. Catalogue of
the library of Thomas Jefferson.
Washington, Library of Congress, 1952-
59. 5 v.   017.1 52-60000
   Z663.4 .C4 MRR Alc.

United States. Library of Congress.
Map Division. United States atlases;
Washington, 1950- v.   016.91273
50-62950
   Z663.35 .U52 MRR Alc.

United States. National Agricultural
Library. Catalog. 1966/70- Totowa,
N.J., Rowman and Littlefield. 016.63
72-84831
   Z5076 .U632b MRR Alc (DK 33) Full
      set / Sci RR Full set

United States. National Agricultural
Library. Dictionary catalog of the
National Agricultural Library, 1862-
1965. New York, Rowman and
Littlefield, 1967-70. 73 v. 016.63
67-12454
   Z5076 .U63 MRR Alc (Dk 33)

United States. National Library of
Medicine. Early American medical
imprints: Washington, U.S. Dept. of
Health, Education, and Welfare,
Public Health Service, 1961. x, 240
p. 016.610973 62-60123
   Z6661.U5 A44 MRR Alc.

United States. National Library of
Medicine. Index-catalogue of the
Library of the Surgeon-General's
Office, United States Army: authors
and subjects. Washington, Govt.
Print. Off., 1880-1961. 61 v.
016.61 01-2344
   Z6676 .U6 MRR Alc (DK 33).

The United States catalog:
Minneapolis, H. W. Wilson [1900] 2
pt. in 1 v.   01-29127
   Z1215 .U58 MRR Ref Desk.

The United States catalog; 3d ed.
Minneapolis, New York, The H. W.
Wilson company, 1912. 3 p. l., 2837
p.   12-35572
   Z1215 .U6 1912a MRR Ref Desk (Alc.
      6)

The United States catalog; 4th ed.
New York, H. W. Wilson Co., 1928.
3164 p.   28-26655
   Z1215 .U6 1928 MRR Circ.

The United States catalog; books in
print 1902. 2d ed. Minneapolis, The
H. W. Wilson co., 1903. 2 p. l.,
2150 p.   03-28279
   Z1215 .U6 1903 MRR Ref Desk.

Vail, Robert William Glenroi, The
voice of the old frontier.
Philadelphia, University of
Pennsylvania Press, 1949. xii, 492
p.   016.9173 49-50000
   Z1249.F9 V3 MRR Alc.

Van Derhoof, Jack Warner. A
bibliography of novels related to
American frontier and colonial
history. Troy, N.Y., Whitston Pub.
Co., 1971. xii, 501 p. 016.813/03
70-150333
   Z1231.F4 V3 MRR Alc.

Vertical file index. v. [1]-
1932/34- New York, H. W. Wilson.
016 45-40505
   Z1231.P2 V48 MRR Alc Full set

Wasserman, Paul. Museum media; 1st
ed. Detroit, Gale Research Co.,
1973. vii, 455 p.   011 73-16335
   Z5052 .W35 MRR alc.

Wegelin, Oscar, Early American
plays, 1714-1830; New York, B.
Franklin [1970] xxvi, 113 p.
016.8121 70-130101
   Z1231.D7 W4 1970 MRR Alc.

Welch, D'Alté Aldridge, A
bibliography of American children's
books printed prior to 1821. [Barre?
Mass.] American Antiquarian Society
and Barre Publishers, 1972. lxvi,
516 p.   081 s 028.52 73-162761
   Z1232 .W44 1972b MRR Alc.

Wright, Lyle Henry, American
fiction, 1774-1850: 2d rev. ed. San
Marino, Calif., Huntington Library,
1969. xviii, 411 p. [10.00]
016.813/2 68-29777
   Z1231.F4 W9 1969 MRR Alc.

Wright, Lyle Henry, American
fiction, 1851-1875; San Marino,
Calif., Huntington Library, 1965.
xviii, 438 p. 016.8133/2 65-20870
   Z1231.F4 W92 1965 MRR Alc.

Wright, Lyle Henry, American
fiction, 1876-1900: San Marino,
Calif., Huntington Library, 1966.
xix, 683 p. 016.8134 66-24112
   Z1231.F4 W93 MRR Alc.

UNITED STATES--IMPRINTS--BIBLIOGRAPHY.
Tanselle, George Thomas, Guide to
the study of United States imprints
Cambridge, Mass., Belknap Press of
Harvard University Press, 1971. 2 v.
(lxiv, 1050 p.) 016.015/73 79-
143232
   Z1215.A2 T35 MRR Alc.

UNITED STATES--IMPRINTS--CATALOGS.
American Antiquarian Society,
Worcester, Mass. Library. A
dictionary catalog of American books
pertaining to the 17th through 19th
centuries. Westport, Conn.,
Greenwood Pub. Corp. [1871] 20 v.
015//73 76-103820
   Z1215 .A264 MRR Alc (Dk 33)

Books in print; 1948- New York, R.
R. Bowker Co. 015.73 74-643574
   Z1215 .P972 Sci RR Latest edition
      / MRR Alc Latest edition / MRR
      Ref Desk Latest edition

Books in print supplement: authors,
titles, subjects. 1972/73- New
York, R. R. Bowker Co. 015.73 74-
643521
   Z1215 .P974 MRR Alc Latest edition
      / MRR Ref Desk Latest edition

The Publishers' trade list annual.
[1st]- 1873- New York, R. R.
Bowker Co., Office of the Publisher's
Weekly [etc.] 015.73 04-12648
   Z1215 .P97 MRR Ref Desk Latest
      edition / Sci RR Latest edition

Subject guide to Books in print;
1957- New York, R. R. Bowker Co.
015.73 74-643573
   Z1215 .P973 MRR Alc Latest edition
      / MRR Ref Desk Latest edition /
      Sci RR Latest edition

UNITED STATES--INDUSTRIES.
Council on Economic Priorities.
Guide to corporations; [1st ed.]
Chicago, Swallow Press [1974] iii,
393 p. [$4.95] 301.5/5 73-13212
   HD60.5.U5 C7 1974 MRR Alc.

Goldenthal, Allan B. The handbook of
U.S. markets and industrial growth
areas [New York] Regents Pub. Co.
[1969- v.   330.973 71-85525
   HC106.6 .G64 MRR Alc.

Human Resources Network. Profiles of
involvement. [Philadelphia, 1972] 3
v. (843 p.) [$50.00] 658.4/08 72-
87222
   HD60.5.U5 H85 MRR Alc.

UNITED STATES--INDUSTRIES. (Cont.)
Keir, Robert Malcolm. The epic of
industry. New Haven, Yale university
press: [etc., etc.] 1926. 3 p. l.,
329 p.   26-10707
   E178.5 .P2 vol. 5 MRR Alc.

Shaw, William Howard, Value of
commodity output since 1869. [New
York] National Bureau of Economic
Research, 1947. x, 310 p.   48-566
   HD9724 .S45 MRR Alc.

Spencer, Vivian Eberle, Raw
materials in the United States
economy: 1900-1966. [Washington]
U.S. Bureau of the Census [1970] vi,
142 p. [1.50]   338 70-606828
   HF1052 .S6 1970 MRR Alc.

Spencer, Vivian Eberle, Raw
materials in the United States
economy: 1900-1969. [Washington]
U.S. Bureau of the Census [1972] iv,
66 p. [$1.00]   338 72-602741
   HF1052 .S62 MRR Alc.

Standard and Poor's Corporation.
Analysts handbook; composite
corporate per share data, by
industries. New York.
332.63/22/0973 67-212
   HG4519 .S772 MRR Alc Latest
   edition

Standard and Poor's Corporation.
Standard & Poor's industry surveys.
Jan. 1973- New York. 332.6/7 77-
183941
   HC106.6 .S74 MRR Alc Latest
   edition

Trade Relations Council of the United
States. General Counsel. Employment,
output, and foreign trade of U.S.
manufacturing industries.
Washington. 338/.0973 73-30363
   HC101 .T68 MRR Alc Latest edition

Troy, Leo. Almanac of business and
industrial financial ratios. 1972
ed. Englewood Cliffs, N.J., Prentice-
Hall [1971] xxi, 169 p.   338.5/0973
72-181403
   HF5681.R25 T68 1971 MRR Alc.

Troy, Leo. Manual of performance
ratios for business analysis and
profit evaluation. Englewood Cliffs,
N.J., Prentice-Hall [1966] xvi, 736
p. 658.1513 66-26237
   HF5681.R25 T7 1966 MRR Alc.

U. S. industrial outlook.
Washington, Bureau of Competitive
Assessment and Business Policy, for
sale by the Supt. of Docs., U.S.
Govt. Print. Off. 338/.0973 74-
644570
   HC106.6 .A23 MRR Alc Latest
   edition

United States. Bureau of Domestic
Commerce. Industry profiles.
1958/68- [Washington, For sale by
the Supt. of Docs., U.S. Govt. Print.
Off.] 338/.0973 72-626646
   HC106.5 .A168 MRR Alc Latest
   edition

United States. Bureau of Labor
Statistics. Employment and earnings
statistics for the United States.
1909/60- Washington, For sale by the
Superintendent of Documents, U.S.
Govt. Print. Off. l 64-5
   HD5723 .A27 MRR Alc MRR Alc Latest
   edition

United States. Bureau of Labor
Statistics. Guide to area employment
statistics; [Washington] 1960. iii,
227 p. l 60-70
   HD8064 .A52 1960b MRR Alc.

United States. Bureau of the Census.
1967 census of manufactures.
[Washington; For sale by the Supt. of
Docs., U.S. Govt. Print. Off.] 1971.
3 v. in 6 v. [$9.00 (varies)]
338.4/7/670973 74-609524
   HD9724 .A4445 MRR Alc.

United States. Bureau of the Census.
Annual survey of manufacturers.
1949/50- Washington, U.S. Govt.
Print. Off. 338.4 52-60884
   HD9724 .A211 MRR Alc Latest
   edition

United States. Bureau of the Census.
County business patterns; 1946-
[Washington] 49-45747
   HC101 .A184 MRR Alc Latest edition

United States. Bureau of the Census.
Enterprise statistics, 1963.
[Washington, For sale by the Supt. of
Docs., U.S. Govt. Print. Off., 1968-
70. 3 v. [2.75 (v. 1) varies]
338.4/0973 a 68-7228
   HC106.5 .A5393 MRR Alc.

United States. Bureau of the Census.
Manufacturers' shipments,
inventories, and orders: 1961-1968.
[Washington] U.S. Dept. of Commerce;
[for sale by the Supt. of Docs., U.S.
Govt. Print. Off., 1968] iii, 92 p.
[1.00]   338.4/7/6700973 70-607789
   HD9724 .A4 1961 MRR Alc.

United States. Bureau of the Census.
Economic Statistics and Surveys
Division. Enterprise statistics:
1967. [Washington; For sale by the
Supt. of Docs., U.S. Govt. Print.
Off., Washington, 1971-   [v. 1,
1972] v.   [$7.75 (v. 1)]
338/.0973 79-186224
   HC106.6 .U55 1972 MRR Alc.

UNITED STATES--INDUSTRIES--BIBLIOGRAPHY.
Encyclopedia of business information
sources; Detroit, Gale Research Co.,
1970. 2 v. (xxi, 689 p.) 016.33
79-127922
   HF5353 .E52 MRR Ref Desk.

Fundaburk, Emma Lila, Reference
materials and periodicals in
economics; Metuchen, N.J., Scarecrow
Press, 1971- v.   016.33 78-
142232
   Z7164.E2 F83 MRR Alc.

Lovett, Robert Woodberry. American
economic and business history
information sources; Detroit, Gale
Research Co. [1971] 323 p. [$14.50]
016.330973 78-137573
   Z7165.U5 L66 MRR Alc.

UNITED STATES--INDUSTRIES--
CLASSIFICATION.
United States. Bureau of Domestic
Commerce. Industry profiles.
1958/68- [Washington, For sale by
the Supt. of Docs., U.S. Govt. Print.
Off.] 338/.0973 72-626646
   HC106.5 .A168 MRR Alc Latest
   edition

United States. Bureau of the Census.
Alphabetic index of manufactured
products; [Washington, For sale by
the Supt. of Docs., U.S. Govt. Print.
Off., 1968] 192 p. [1.50]
338.4/7/6702573 70-601986
   HD9724 .A4 1967c MRR Alc.

United States. Bureau of the Census.
Numerical list of manufactured
products. [Washington, 1968] 165,
A141, B2 p. 338.4/0973 a 68-7403
   HD9724 .A4 1967 MRR Alc.

United States. Office of Management
and Budget. Statistical Policy
Division. Standard industrial
classification manual. [Washington;
For sale by the Supt. of Docs., U.S.
Govt. Print. Off.] 1972. 649 p.
[$6.75] 338/.02/0973 72-601529
   HF1042 .A55 1972 MRR Alc.

UNITED STATES--INDUSTRIES--DIRECTORIES.
Conover-Mast U.S. industrial
purchasing directory. 1971- [New
York, Cahners Publishing Co., etc.]
338.4/7/6702573 72-623800
   T12 .C769 MRR Alc Latest edition

D-U-N-S code book: New York, Dun &
Bradstreet. 64-5833
   HC102 .D22 MRR Alc Latest edition

Directory of United States employers.
New York, Simon and Schuster [c1970]
823 p. 338/.0025/73 78-24980
   HC102 .K7 MRR Alc.

Dun and Bradstreet, inc. Million
dollar directory. 1959- New York.
338.0973 59-3033
   HC102 .D8 MRR Ref Desk Latest
   edition

Government Data Publications,
Washington, D.C. Government
production prime contractors
directory. Washington, c1969. 75,
72 p. 338/.0025/73 77-16744
   HD3858 .G625 1969 MRR Alc.

Index of opportunity for engineers.
1968/69- New York, Macmillan.
620/.0025/73 76-1574
   TA157 .I43 MRR Alc Latest edition

MacRae's blue book. Western Springs,
Ill. [etc.] 56-36154
   T12 .M3 Sci RR Latest edition /
   MRR Alc Latest edition

Marketing economics key plants. 1973-
New York, Marketing Economics
Institute. 338.4/025/73 73-642154
   HC102 .M25 MRR Alc Latest edition

Moody's OTC industrial manual. New
York, Moody's Investors Service.
332.67 77-649772
   HG4961 .M7237 MRR Ref Desk Latest
   edition

Plant and product directory. 1961-
[New York?] Market Research Dept. of
Fortune. 338.05873 61-12113
   HC102 .P59 MRR Alc Latest edition

UNITED STATES--INDUSTRIES--DIRECTORIES--
BIBLIOGRAPHY.
Klein, Bernard. Guide to American
scientific and technical directories.
1st ed. Rye, N.Y., B. Klein
Publications [1972] v, 324 p.
016.3384/7/6702573 72-91671
   Z7914.M3 K53 MRR Ref Desk.

UNITED STATES--INDUSTRIES--HISTORY.
Clark, Victor Selden, History of
manufactures in the United States,
1929 ed. New York [etc.] Published
for the Carnegie institution of
Washington by the McGraw-Hill book
company, inc., 1929. 3 v.   29-10065

   HD9725 .C52 MRR Alc.

Douglass, Elisha P. The coming of
age of American business; Chapel
Hill, University of North Carolina
Press [1971] xii, 606 p. [$15.00]
338/.0973 78-132254
   HF3021 .D63 MRR Alc.

Groner, Alex. The American heritage
history of American business &
industry. New York, American
Heritage Pub. Co. [1972] 384 p.
[$20.00]   330.9/73 72-80699
   HC103 .G797 MRR Alc.

UNITED STATES--INDUSTRIES--HISTORY--
BIBLIOGRAPHY.
Larson, Henrietta Melia. Guide to
business history; Cambridge, Harvard
University Press, 1948. xxvi, 1181
p. 650.9 48-7565
   Z7164.C81 L25 MRR Alc.

UNITED STATES--INDUSTRIES--INDEXES.
United States. Bureau of the Census.
1970 census of population.
[Washington, U.S. Bureau of the
Census, Population Division; for sale
by the Supt. of Docs., U.S. Govt.
Print. Off., 1971. xiv, 165, 201 p.
[$3.00] 331.1/1/0973 74-612012
   HA201 1970 .A565 MRR Alc.

UNITED STATES--INDUSTRIES--PERIODICALS.
Moody's OTC industrial manual. New
York, Moody's Investors Service.
332.67 77-649772
   HG4961 .M7237 MRR Ref Desk Latest
   edition

UNITED STATES--INDUSTRIES--STATISTICS.
National Industrial Conference Board.
Chartbook of weekly business
indicators. New York. 330.973 58-
24653
   HC106.5 .A2845 MRR Alc Latest
   edition

UNITED STATES--INDUSTRIES--YEARBOOKS.
Moody's industrial manual: 1954-
New York, Moody's Investors Service.
56-14721
   HG4961 .M67 MRR Alc Latest edition

UNITED STATES--INSULAR POSSESSIONS.
Coulter, John Wesley, The Pacific
dependencies of the United States.
New York, Macmillan, 1957. 388 p.
996 57-9543
   F970 .C6 MRR Alc.

UNITED STATES--INTELLECTUAL LIFE.
Commager, Henry Steele, The American
mind; New Haven, Yale University
Press, 1950. ix, 476 p.   917.3 50-
6338
   E169.1 .C673 MRR Alc.

Curti, Merle Eugene, The growth of
American thought, 3d ed. New York,
Harper & Row [1964] xx, 939 p.
917.3 64-12796
   E169.1 .C87 1964 MRR Alc.

Savelle, Max, Seeds of liberty;
Seattle, University of Washington
Press, 1965 [c1948] xvii, 618 p.
917.3032 65-23913
   E169.1 .S27 1965 MRR Alc.

Wish, Harvey, Society and thought in
America. [1st ed.] New York,
Longmans, Green, 1950-52. 2 v.
917.3 50-9981
   E169.1 .W65 MRR Alc.

Wright, Louis Booker, The cultural
life of the American Colonies, 1607-
1763. [1st ed.] New York, Harper
[1957] xiv, 292 p. 973.2 57-250
   E162 .W89 MRR Alc.

UNITED STATES--LEARNED INSTITUTIONS AND
SOCIETIES.
Bates, Ralph Samuel. Scientific
societies in the United States 3d
ed. Cambridge, Mass., M.I.T. Press
[1965] 326 p. 506.273 65-8325
   Q11.A1 B3 1965 MRR Alc.

Burke, William Jeremiah, American
authors and books, 1640 to the
present day 3d rev. ed. New York,
Crown Publishers [c1972] 719 p.
[$12.50] 015/.73 75-168332
   Z1224 .B87 1972 MRR Biog.

UNITED STATES--LEARNED (Cont.)
Handbook of learned societies and
institutions: America. Washington,
D.C., Carnegie institution of
Washington, 1908. viii, 592 p.   08-
21011
    Z5055.U39 H2 MRR Alc.

Kiger, Joseph Charles. American
learned societies. Washington,
Public Affairs Press [1963] 291 p.
061.3   63-16497
    AS25 .K5 MRR Alc.

New research centers. May 1965-
Detroit, Gale Research Co.   74-643580

    AS25 .D52 Sci RR Full set / MRR
    Ref Desk Full set

Research centers directory. 1st-
ed.; 1960- Detroit, Gale Research
Co.   60-14807
    AS25 .D5 Sci RR Latest edition /
    MRR Ref Desk Latest edition

Scientific and technical societies of
the United States. 8th- ed.; 1968-
Washington, National Academy of
Sciences. 506 72-620448
    AS25 .S33 Sci RR Latest edition /
    MRR Ref Desk Latest edition / MRR
    Alc Latest edition

**UNITED STATES--LEARNED INSTITUTIONS AND
SOCIETIES--BIBLIOGRAPHY.**
The American catalogue ... New York,
1941. 8 v. in 13. 015.73 a 42-
2938
    Z1215 .A52 MRR Ref Desk.

Bowker, Richard Rogers, Publications
of societies; New York, Office of
the Publishers' weekly, 1899. v, 181
p.   00-465
    Z5055.U39 B7 MRR Alc.

Griffin, Appleton Prentiss Clark,
Bibliography of American historical
societies 2d ed.: rev. and enl.
[Washington, Govt. print. off., 1907]
1374 p.   08-7356
    Z1236 .G86 MRR Alc.

Kelly, James, The American catalogue
of books, New York, P. Smith, 1938.
2 v.   015.73 38-29060
    Z1215 .A4 1838 MRR Ref Desk.

**UNITED STATES--LEARNED INSTITUTIONS AND
SOCIETIES--DIRECTORIES.**
Asia Society. American institutions
and organizations interested in Asia,
2d ed. New York, Taplinger Pub.
Co., 1961. xii, 581 p.   950.06273
61-11435
    DS1 .C572 MRR Alc.

Battelle Memorial Institute,
Columbus, Ohio. Dept. of Economics
and Information Research.
Specialized science information
services in the United States:
Washington, National Science
Foundation, Office of Science
Information Service, 1961. ix, 528
p.   505.873 61-64862
    AG521 .B3 MRR Alc.

Council on foreign relations.
American agencies interested in
international affairs. 1931- New
York, [etc.] Frederick A. Praeger,
[etc.] 341.06 31-26874
    JX27 .C62 MRR Ref Desk Latest
    edition

United States. Dept. of State. Office
of External Research. University
centers of foreign affairs research:
a selective directory. [Washington,
Dept. of State; for sale by the Supt.
of Docs., U.S. Govt. Print. Off.]
1968. xvi, 139 p.   327/.025/73 68-
60080
    JX1293.U6 A54 MRR Alc.

United States. Library of Congress.
National Referral Center. A
directory of information resources in
the United States: social sciences.
Rev. ed. Washington, Library of
Congress; [for sale by the Supt. of
Docs., U.S. Govt. Print. Off.] 1973.
iv, 700 p. [$6.90]   300/.7 73-3297

    Z663.379 .D53 1973 MRR Alc.

United States. Library of Congress.
National Referral Center for Science
and Technology. A directory of
information resources in the United
States: general toxicology.
Washington, Library of Congress; for
sale by the Supt. of Docs., U.S.
Govt. Print. Off.] 1969. v, 293 p.
[3.00]   615.8/007 73-602563
    Z663.379 .D49 MRR Alc

UNITED STATES--LITERATURE.
    see also American literature

UNITED STATES--MANUFACTURERS--CATALOGS.
Sweet's product design file. [New
York, Sweet's Industrial Division,
Catalog Systems, McGraw-Hill
Information Systems Company] 670 72-
626782
    TS199 .S93 MRR Alc Latest edition

UNITED STATES--MANUFACTURES.
Fabricant, Solomon, Employment in
manufacturing, 1899-1939, New York,
National bureau of economic research,
inc., 1942. xix, 362 p.   338.4 43-
6978
    HD9724 .F27 MRR Alc.

Georgetown Economic Data Library.
Compendium of manufacturing
production statistics for the United
States, 1947-1965. Washington [1967]
xxii, 313 p.   338.4/0973 67-9455
    HD9724 .G4 MRR Alc.

McGraw-Hill Publishing Company, inc.
America's manufacturing plants; New
York, [1960] 118 p.   338.476 60-
3420
    HD9724 .M2 MRR Alc.

Shaw, William Howard, Value of
commodity output since 1869. [New
York] National Bureau of Economic
Research, 1947. x, 310 p.   48-566
    HD9724 .S45 MRR Alc.

Trade Relations Council of the United
States. General Counsel. Employment,
output, and foreign trade of U.S.
manufacturing industries.
Washington. 338/.0973 73-30363
    HC101 .T68 MRR Alc Latest edition

United States. Bureau of the Census.
Annual survey of manufacturers.
1949/50- Washington, U.S. Govt.
Print. Off. 338.4 52-60884
    HD9724 .A211 MRR Alc Latest
    edition

United States. Bureau of the Census.
List of materials: consumption items;
[Washington, For sale by the Supt.
of Docs. U.S. Govt. Print. Off.,
1969] 304 p.   339.4 77-601181
    HD9724 .A4 1967b MRR Alc.

United States. Bureau of the Census.
Manufacturers' shipments,
inventories, and orders: 1961-1968.
Washington] U.S. Dept. of Commerce:
[for sale by the Supt. of Docs., U.S.
Govt. Print. Off., 1968] iii, 92 p.
[1.00]   338.4/7/6700973 70-607789
    HD9724 .A4 1961 MRR alc.

UNITED STATES--MANUFACTURES--CATALOGS.
Chemical engineering catalog. 1st-
ed.; 1916- Stamford, Conn. [etc.]
Reinhold Pub. Corp. [etc.] 660.78
16-22887
    TP157 .C4 MRR Alc Latest edition

Fluid power handbook & directory.
Cleveland, Industrial Pub. Corp. 58-
30725
    TJ950 .F5 MRR Alc Latest edition

Municipal index; [1st]- ed.; 1924-
[Pittsfield, Mass., etc.] Buttenheim
Pub. Corp. [etc.] 24-14253
    TD1 .M927 MRR Alc Latest edition

Plant engineering catalog file. New
York, Sweet's Division, McGraw-Hill
Information Systems Co.
338.4/7/67028 72-626783
    TA215 .S8 MRR Alc Latest edition

Romaine, Lawrence B., A guide to
American trade catalogs, 1744-1900.
New York, R. R. Bowker, 1960. xxiii,
422 p.   016.65085 60-16893
    Z7164.C8 R6 MRR Alc.

Sweet's industrial construction and
renovation file. 1974- New York,
Sweet's Division, McGraw-Hill
Information Systems Co.
338.4/7/624102573 74-640340
    TA215 .S85 MRR Alc Latest edition

**UNITED STATES--MANUFACTURES--
DIRECTORIES.**
The American register of exporters
and importers. 1945/46- New York,
American Register of Exporters and
Importers, inc. 382.058 46-15595
    HF3010 .A6 MRR Alc Latest edition

American Society of Heating,
Refrigerating and Air-Conditioning
Engineers. ASHRAE handbook & product
directory. 1973- New York. 697 73-
644272
    TH7011 .A4 MRR Alc Latest edition
    / Sci RR Latest edition

Baudler, Paul G. Directory of
American business in Germany. 4th
ed. Munich, Seibt-Verlag [1971]
xviii, 533 p.   338/.0025/43 72-
178863
    HF3099 .B3 1971 MRR Alc.

Chain drug stores buyers directory of
variety merchandise. 1961- New
York, Directory Division,
Merchandiser Publications.   60-40115

    T12 .C43 MRR Alc Latest edition

Chemical materials catalog mailing
list. [Stamford, Conn.] Reinhold
Pub. Corp. 661/.0025/7 72-620095
    TP12 .R43 Sci RR Latest edition /
    MRR Alc Latest edition

Conover-Mast U.S. industrial
purchasing directory. 1971- [New
York, Cahners Publishing Co., etc.]
338.4/7/6702573 72-623800
    T12 .C769 MRR Alc Latest edition

D-U-N-S code book: New York, Dun &
Bradstreet. 64-5833
    HC102 .D22 MRR Alc Latest edition

Directory of American importers and
exporters. Medina, Wash., World Wide
Trade Service. 63-47591
    HF3010 .D5 MRR Alc Latest edition

Directory of United States employers,
New York, Simon and Schuster [c1970]
823 p.   338/.0025/73 78-24980
    HC102 .K7 MRR Alc.

Dun and Bradstreet, inc. Middle
market directory. 1964- New York.
64-275
    HF5035 .D8 MRR Alc Latest edition

Dun and Bradstreet, inc. Million
dollar directory. 1959- New York.
338.0973 59-3033
    HC102 .D8 MRR Ref Desk Latest
    edition

Dun and Bradstreet, inc. Reference
book of manufacturers. Oct. 1965-
New York. 66-5210
    HF5573 .D72 Sci RR Latest edition
    / MRR Circ Latest edition

Eastern manufacturers' & industrial
directory New York, Bell Directory
Publishers. 54-35021
    Began publication in 1936.
    HC107.A11 E2 MRR Alc Latest
    edition

EITD: electronic industry telephone
directory. [Cleveland, Harris Pub.
Co.] [$10.00]   384.6 74-645053
    HD9696.A3 U513 MRR Alc Latest
    edition

Geyer's "who makes it" directory.
[New York, Geyer-McAllister
Publications] 338.4/7/651202573 74-
647065
    TS1088 .W7 MRR Alc Latest edition

Government Data Publications,
Washington, D.C. Government
production prime contractors
directory. Washington, c1969. 75,
72 p.   338/.0025/73 77-16744
    HD3858 .G625 1969 MRR Alc.

Grocery supermarket non-food buyers
directory. 1961- New York,
Directory Division, Merchandiser
Publications. 60-41591
    T12 .G75 MRR Alc Latest edition

MacRae's blue book. Western Springs,
Ill. [etc.] 56-36154
    T12 .M3 Sci RR Latest edition /
    MRR Alc Latest edition

Manufacturers' Agent Publishing
Company, New York. Verified
directory of manufacturers'
representatives (agents) 1957- New
York. 57-17305
    HD9723 .M33 MRR Alc Latest edition

Marketing economics key plants. 1973-
New York, Marketing Economics
Institute. 338.4/025/73 73-642154
    HC102 .M25 MRR Alc Latest edition

Plant and product directory. 1961-
[New York?] Market Research Dept. of
Fortune. 338.05873 61-12113
    HC102 .P59 MRR Alc Latest edition

Rosenbloom, Joseph. Consumer
complaint guide, 1973. New York, CCM
Information Corp. [1972] iv, 476 p.
338.4/7/602573 73-154774
    T12 .R66 1972 MRR Alc.

Thomas grocery register. 68th-
ed.; 1966- New York, Thomas Publ.
Co. 381/.45/664097 72-623125
    HD9321.3 T5 MRR Alc Latest edition

United States. Office of
International Investment. List of
foreign firms with some
interest/control in American
manufacturing and petroleum companies
in the United States. [Washington]
1972. 61 p.   332.6/73/02573 72-
603415
    HG4909 .A5 1972 MRR Ref Desk.

UNITED STATES--MANUFACTURES-- (Cont.)
Variety department store merchandiser
buyers directory. 1947- New York,
Directory Division, Merchandiser Pub.
Co., [etc.] 338.4/7/670257 48-4264

T12 .S9 MRR Alc Latest edition

UNITED STATES--MANUFACTURES--
DIRECTORIES--BIBLIOGRAPHY.
Klein, Bernard. Guide to American
scientific and technical directories.
1st ed. Rye, N.Y., B. Klein
Publications [1972] v, 324 p.
016.3384/7/6702573 72-91671
Z7914.M3 K53 MRR Ref Desk.

UNITED STATES--MANUFACTURES--
DIRECTORIES--PERIODICALS.
National directory of minority
manufacturers. [Washington] Office
of Minority Business Enterprise.
338/.0025/73 74-645920
HD2346.U5 N33 MRR Alc Latest
edition

UNITED STATES--MANUFACTURES--HISTORY.
Clark, Victor Selden, History of
manufactures in the United States,
1929 ed. New York [etc.] Published
for the Carnegie institution of
Washington by the McGraw-Hill book
company, inc., 1929. 3 v. 29-10065

HD9725 .C52 MRR Alc.

UNITED STATES--MANUFACTURES--STATISTICS.
Lechter, Max. U.S. exports and
imports classified by OBE end-use
commodity categories, 1923-1968;
[Washington] U.S. Office of Business
Economics, Balance of Payments
Division; [for sale by the Supt. of
Docs., U.S. Govt. Print. Off.] 1970
[i.e. 1971] xxii, 411 p. [$4.00]
382.4/0973 75-611180
HF3001 .L43 MRR Alc.

Robert Morris Associates. Annual
statement studies. [Philadelphia]
338/.0973 72-626355
HF5681.B2 R6 MRR Alc Latest
edition

Survey of current business. Business
statistics; 1951- Washington, U.S.
Govt. Print. Off. 330.5 74-643587
HC101.A13122 MRR Alc Latest
edition

Troy, Leo. Almanac of business and
industrial financial ratios. 1972
ed. Englewood Cliffs, N.J., Prentice-
Hall [1971] xxi, 169 p. 338.5/0973
72-181403
HF5681.R25 T68 1971 MRR Alc.

United States. Bureau of Labor
Statistics. Employment and earnings
statistics for the United States.
1909/60- Washington, For sale by the
Superintendent of Documents, U.S.
Govt. Print. Off. l 64-5
HD5723 .A27 MRR Alc MRR Alc Latest
edition

United States. Bureau of the Census.
1963 census of manufactures.
[Washington, For sale by the Supt. of
Docs., U.S. Govt. Print. Off., 1966-
68] 4 v. in 6. 338.4/0973 a 66-
7830
HD9724 .A4 1963 MRR Alc.

United States. Bureau of the Census.
1967 census of manufactures.
[Washington; For sale by the Supt. of
Docs., U.S. Govt. Print. Off.] 1971.
3 v. in 6 v. [$9.00 (varies)]
338.4/7/670973 74-609524
HD9724 .A4445 MRR Alc.

United States. Bureau of the Census.
Annual survey of manufacturers.
1948/50- Washington, U.S. Govt.
Print. Off. 338.4 52-60884
HD9724 .A211 MRR Alc Latest
edition

United States. Bureau of the Census.
Manufacturers' shipments,
inventories, and orders: 1966-1972.
Rev. [Washington] 1972. 84 p.
[$0.70] 338.4/0973 72-602572
HD9724 .A4448 1972 MRR Alc.

UNITED STATES--MANUFACTURES--STATISTICS-
-BIBLIOGRAPHY.
United States. Bureau of the Census.
Numerical list of manufactured
products. [Washington, 1968] 165,
A141, B2 p. 338.4/0973 a 68-7403
HD9724 .A4 1967 MRR Alc.

UNITED STATES--MANUFACTURES--YEARBOOKS.
Moody's industrial manual: 1954-
New York, Moody's Investors Service.
56-14721
HG4961 .M67 MRR Alc Latest edition

UNITED STATES--MAPS.
American heritage. The American
heritage pictorial atlas of United
States history, New York, American
Heritage Pub. Co.; book trade
distribution by McGraw-Hill Book Co.
[1966] 424 p. map66-29
G1201.S1 A4 1966 MRR Alc.

Catchpole, Brian. A map history of
the United States. London, Heinemann
Educational, 1972. vi, 130 p.
[£0.90] 917.3/03 73-330879
E178.2 .C34 MRR Alc.

Oxford University Press. United
States & Canada. Oxford, Clarendon
P., 1967. [12], [35] p. [75/- (35/-
pbk.)] 912.1/3309/73 map68-202
G1201.G1 O9 1967 MRR Alc Atlas.

Rand, McNally and Company. Road
atlas of the United States, Canada
and Mexico. 1926- Chicago. 629.281
map26-19
G1201.P2 R35 MRR Ref Desk Latest
edition / Sci RR Latest edition

The Reader's digest. These United
States; Pleasantville, N.Y.,
Reader's Digest Association [1968]
236 p. 912.73 map68-2
G1200 .R4 1968 MRR Alc Atlas.

United States. Geological Survey.
The national atlas of the United
States of America. Washington, 1970.
xiii, 417 p. [$100.00] 912.73
map79-654043
G1200 .U57 1970 MRR Alc Atlas.

UNITED STATES--MAPS--ADDRESSES, ESSAYS,
LECTURES.
Ristow, Walter William, comp. A la
carte; Washington, Library of
Congress [for sale by the Supt. of
Docs., U.S. Govt. Print. Off.] 1972.
x, 232 p. [$4.00] 912.73 75-
173026
Z663.35 .S42 MRR Alc.

UNITED STATES--MAPS--BIBLIOGRAPHY.
United States. Library of Congress.
Geography and Map Division. Land
ownership maps, a checklist
Washington [For sale by the Supt. of
Docs., U.S. Govt. Print. Off.] 1967.
xxv, 86 g. 016.91273 67-60091
Z663.35 .L37 MRR Alc.

United States. Library of Congress.
Geography and Map Division.
Panoramic maps of Anglo-American
cities; Washington, Library of
Congress; [for sale by the Supt. of
Docs., U.S. Govt. Print. Off.] 1974.
v, 118 p. 016.912/7 73-18312
Z663.35 .P35 MRR Alc.

United States. Library of Congress.
Map Division. A list of maps of
America in the Library of Congress.
New York, B. Franklin [1967?] 2 v.
in 1 (1137 p.) 016.91273 67-7211
Z663.35 .L55 1967 MRR Alc.

United States. Library of Congress.
Map Division. Maps showing
explorers' routes, trails & early
roads in the United States;
Washington, For sale by the
Superintendent of Documents, U.S.
Govt. Print. Off., 1962. vi, 137 p.
62-60066
Z663.35 .M26 MRR Alc.

United States. Library of Congress.
Map Division. Marketing maps of the
United States; [1st]- 1951-
Washington. 016.6588 52-60015
Z663.35 .M3 MRR Alc MRR Alc Full
set

United States. National Archives.
Guide to cartographic records in the
National Archives Washington,
National Archives, National Archives
and Records Service; for sale by the
Supt. of Docs., U.S. Govt. Print.
Off., 1971. xi, 444 p. [$3.25]
016.91273 76-611061
Z6028 .U575 MRR Alc.

Wheat, James Clements. Maps and
charts published in America before
1800; New Haven, Yale University
Press, 1969. xxii, 215 p. [30.00]
016.5268 69-15464
Z6027.A5 W68 MRR Alc.

UNITED STATES--MAPS--BIBLIOGRAPHY--
CATALOGS.
United States. Library of Congress.
Map Division. United States atlases;
Washington, 1950- v. 016.91273
50-62950
Z663.35 .U52 MRR Alc.

UNITED STATES--MILITARY POLICY--
BIBLIOGRAPHY.
Greenwood, John, American defense
policy since 1945; Lawrence,
Published for the National Security
Education Program; by the University
Press of Kansas [1973] xv, 317 p.
016.3554 72-97468
Z1361.D4 G73 MRR Alc.

Larson, Arthur D. National security
affairs; Detroit, Gale Research Co.,
[1973] 411 p. 016.35503/3/ 0973 70-
184013
Z1215 .L37 MRR Alc.

UNITED STATES--MILITARY POLICY--HISTORY.
Bernardo, C. Joseph, American
military policy, its development
since 1775 [2d ed.] Harrisburg,
Pa., Military Service Division,
Stackpole Co. [1961] 548 p. 355
61-15573
UA23 .B43 1961 MRR Alc.

UNITED STATES--NATIONAL GUARD--
OFFICERS' HANDBOOKS.
The Officer's guide. 1st- ed.;
June 1930- Harrisburg, Pa.,
Stackpole Books [etc.] 335 30-21652

U133.A6 O3 MRR Alc Latest edition

UNITED STATES--NATIONAL GUARD--
REGISTERS.
United States. National Guard Bureau.
Official Army National Guard
register. 1922- Washington, U.S.
Govt. Print. Off. 22-26684
UA42 .A16 MRR Biog Latest edition

UNITED STATES--NATIONALITY.
Weinberg, Albert Katz, Manifest
destiny; Baltimore, The Johns
Hopkins press, 1935. xiii, 559 p.
973 35-9403
E179.5 .W45 MRR Alc.

UNITED STATES--NAVY--HISTORY.
Emmons, George Foster, The Navy of
the United States, from the
commencement, 1775 to 1853;
Washington, Printed by Gideon & co.,
1853. 4 p. l., 208 p. 02-7188
E182 .E54 MRR Alc.

UNITED STATES--OCCUPATIONS.
Angel, Juvenal Londono, Employment
opportunities for the handicapped,
New York, World Trade Academy Press;
distributed by Simon & Schuster
[1969] 411 p. 331.5/9 67-22382
HV3018 .A67 MRR Alc.

Angel, Juvenal Londoño, Students'
guide to occupational opportunities
and their lifetime earnings. New
York, World Trade Academy Press;
distributed by Simon & Schuster
[1967] 312 p. 331.702/0973 67-
25270
HF5382 .A57 MRR Alc.

College placement annual.
[Bethlehem, Pa.] College Placement
Council. 371.425 a 58-4606
HF5382.5.U5 C6 MRR Ref Desk Latest
edition

Hutchinson, Edward Prince,
Immigrants and their children, 1850-
1950. New York, Wiley [1956] xiv,
391 p. 331.62 56-6502
HB2595 .H8 MRR Alc.

McKay, Ernest A. The Macmillan job
guide to American corporations for
college graduates, graduate students
and junior executives New York,
Macmillan [c1967] ix, 374 p.
331.115 66-20820
HF5382.5.U5 M3 MRR Alc.

Summer employment directory of the
United States. Cincinnati, National
Directory Service. 54-33991
HF5382.5U5 S76 MRR Alc Latest
edition

United States. Bureau of Employment
Security. Selected characteristics
of occupations (physical demands,
working conditions, training time);
Washington; For sale by the Supt. of
Docs., U.S. Govt. Print. Off., 1966.
xii, 280, 8 p. 331.1/14/0973 70-
601497
HB2595 .A35 1966 MRR Ref Desk.

Whitfield, Edwin A. Guide to careers
through vocational training [1st
ed.] San Diego, Calif., R. R. Knapp
[1968] viii, 312 p. 331.702/0973
68-15874
HF5382.5.U5 W5 MRR Alc.

UNITED STATES--OCCUPATIONS--HANDBOOKS,
MANUALS, ETC.
Occupational outlook handbook. 1949-
[Washington] 371.425 l 49-6
HF5381.A1 O36 MRR Ref Desk MRR Ref
Desk Latest edition

UNITED STATES--OCCUPATIONS--INDEXES.
United States. Bureau of the Census.
1970 census of population.
[Washington, U.S. Bureau of the
Census, Population Division; for sale
by the Supt. of Docs., U.S. Govt.
Print. Off.] 1971. xiv, 165, 201 p.
[$3.00] 331.1/1/0973 74-612012
HA201 1970 .A565 MRR Alc.

UNITED STATES--OFFICIALS AND EMPLOYEES.
Clements, John. Taylor's
encyclopedia of Government officials,
Federal and State. v. 1- 1967/68-
Dallas, Political Research, inc. 67-
22269
    JK6 .T36 Sci RR Latest edition /
    MRR Alc Latest edition

Federal employees' almanac. 1954-
[Washington] 351.1 351.3* 54-18878

    JK671 .F385 MRR Ref Desk Latest
    edition

The Evening star, Washington, D.C.
The New Frontiersmen; Washington,
Public Affairs Press [1961] 254 p.
923.273 61-11685
    E841 .E8 MRR Biog.

United States. Civil Service
Commission. Official register of the
United States. 1907-59. Washington,
U.S. Govt. Print. Off. 08-35096
    JK5 MRR Ref Desk Latest edition

Who's who in American politics. 1st
ed.; 1967/68- New York, Bowker.
320/.0922 67-25024
    E176 .W6424 MRR Biog Latest
    edition

UNITED STATES--OFFICIALS AND EMPLOYEES--
APPOINTMENT, QUALIFICATIONS, TENURE,
ETC.
Delap, Donald J. Civil service
manual, Fond du Lac, Wis., North
Central Consulting Press, 1965. x,
404 p. 353.004 65-18944
    JK716 .D4 MRR Alc.

Harris, Joseph Pratt, The advice and
consent of the Senate; Berkeley,
University of California Press, 1953.
xii, 457 p.   328.735 53-11239
    JK1274 .H3 MRR Alc.

UNITED STATES--OFFICIALS AND EMPLOYEES--
BIOGRAPHY.
American men in government,
[Washington] Public Affairs Press
[1949] xxiii, 472 p.   353 49-11779

    E747 .A68 MRR Biog.

Christmas, Walter, ed. Negroes in
public affairs and government. [1st
ed.] Yonkers [N.Y.] Educational
Heritage [1966-   v.   820.073 67-
31903
    E185.96 .C47 MRR Biog.

Congressional staff directory. [1st]-
ed.; 1959- Washington [etc.]
328.738 59-13987
    JK1012 MRR Ref Desk Latest edition
    / Sci RR Latest edition

Mader, Julius, Who's who in CIA;
Berlin, Julius Mader, 1066 Berlin W
66, Mauerstrasse 69, 1968. 604, [1]
p. [unpriced] 327/.12/0973 70-
389997
    JK468.I6 M323 MRR Biog.

UNITED STATES--OFFICIALS AND EMPLOYEES--
BIOGRAPHY--DICTIONARIES.
Biographical directory of the United
States executive branch, 1774-1971.
Westport, Conn., Greenwood Pub. Co.
[1971] x, 481 p. 973/.099 78-
133495
    E176 .B575 MRR Biog.

UNITED STATES--OFFICIALS AND EMPLOYEES--
DIRECTORIES.
Federal telephone directory. fall
1973- Washington, Consolidated
Directories, inc. [$60.00]
353.002/025 73-88404
    JK6 .F43 MRR Ref Desk Latest
    edition / Sci RR Latest edition

Mosher, Robert Brent, comp.
Executive register of the United
States, 1789-1902; Baltimore, Md.,
The Friedenwald company [1903] 1 p.
l., x, 351 p. 03-10230
    JK661 1902 MRR Alc.

Poore, Benjamin Perley, The
political register and congressional
directory; Boston, Houghton, Osgood
and company, 1878. vi p., 1 l., 716
p. 05-273
    E176 .P82 MRR Alc.

United States. Dept. of state. The
territorial papers of the United
States. Washington, U.S. Govt.
print. off., 1934. xv, 37 p.
973.082 35-26190
    E173 .U57 MRR Alc.

UNITED STATES--OFFICIALS AND EMPLOYEES--
SALARIES, ALLOWANCES, ETC.
Learned, Henry Barrett, The
President's cabinet; New York, B.
Franklin [1972] xii, 471 p.
321.8/043/0973 72-80393
    JK611 .L5 1972 MRR Alc.

United States. Congress. House.
Committee on Post Office and Civil
Service. Current salary schedules of
Federal officers and employees
together with a history of salary and
retirement annuity adjustments; 1945-
72. Washington, U.S. Govt. Print.
Off., 1972. iii, 15 p. [$0.15]
331.2/2 72-600809
    JK775 1972 .A52 MRR Ref Desk.

UNITED STATES--OFFICIALS AND EMPLOYEES--
STATISTICS.
United States. Civil Service
Commission. Minority group
employment in the Federal Government.
May 1970- Washington, For sale by
the Supt. of Docs., U.S Govt. Print.
Off. 331.1/33/0973 72-622550
    JK639 .A42 subser MRR Alc Latest
    edition

UNITED STATES--POLITICS AND GOVERNMENT.
Bain, Richard C. Convention
decisions and voting records 2d ed.
Washington, Brookings Institution
[1973] x, 350, [120] p. [$14.95]
329/.0221 73-1082
    JK2255 .B3 1973 MRR Alc.

Bernhard, Winfred E. A., comp.
Political parties in American
history. New York, Putnam [1974,
c1973-74] 3 v. (xliv, 1324 p.)
[$8.95 per vol.] 329/.02 73-76139

    JK2261 .B47 MRR Alc.

Binkley, Wilfred Ellsworth, American
political parties, 4th ed., enl.
New York, Knopf, 1962. 486 p.   329
62-52807
    JK2261 .B5 1962 MRR Alc.

Bone, Hugh Alvin, American politics
and the party system 3d ed. New
York, McGraw-Hill [1965] x, 684 p.
329 64-7727
    JK2265 .B6 1965 MRR Alc.

Corwin, Edward Samuel, The
President; office and powers, 1787-
1948; [3d ed., rev.] New York, New
York Univ. Press [1948] xvii, 552 p.
353.03 48-7474
    JK516 .C63 1948 MRR Alc.

Ewing, Cortez Arthur Milton, comp.
Documentary source book in American
government and politics, Boston, New
York [etc.] D.C. Heath and company
[c1931] xx, 823 p. 342.738 31-
24918
    JK11 1931 MRR Alc.

Fisher, Louis. President and
Congress; New York, Free Press
[1972] xvi, 347 p. 353.03/72 78-
142362
    JK305 .F55 MRR Alc.

Galloway, George Barnes, History of
the House of Representatives. New
York, Crowell [1962, c1961] xii, 334
p. 328.73 61-17413
    JK1316 .G2 MRR Alc.

Goodman, William, The two-party
system in the United States. 3d ed.
Princeton, N.J., Van Nostrand [1964]
xvi, 672 p. 329 64-17962
    JK2265 .G6 1964 MRR Alc.

Governmental Research Association.
Directory of organizations and
individuals professionally engaged in
governmental research and related
activities. 1935- New York [etc.]
350.6273 35-16469
    JK3 .G627 MRR Alc Latest edition

Harris, Joseph Pratt, The advice and
consent of the Senate; Berkeley,
University of California Press, 1953.
xii, 457 p.   328.735 53-11239
    JK1274 .H3 MRR Alc.

Hatch, Louis Clinton, A history of
the vice-presidency of the United
States, New York, The American
historical society, inc., 1934. viii
p., 2 l., [3]-437 p. 353.03 34-
8999
    E176 .H35 MRR Alc.

Haynes, George Henry, The Senate of
the United States, Boston, Houghton
Mifflin company, 1938. 2 v. 328.73
38-38772
    JK1161 .H28 MRR Alc.

Huszar, George Bernard de, ed. Basic
American documents. Ames, Iowa,
Littlefield, Adams [c1953] 365 p.
973 52-14779
    E173 .H95 MRR Alc.

Jackson, Carlton. Presidential
vetoes, 1792-1945. Athens,
University of Georgia Press [1967]
x, 254 p. 353/.032 67-17405
    JK586 .J3 MRR Alc.

Kent, Frank Richardson, The
Democratic party; a history New
York, London, The Century co. [1928]
xi, 568 p. mrr01-29
    JK2316 .K4 1928a MRR Alc.

Lorant, Stefan, The Presidency; New
York, Macmillan, 1951. 775 p. 973
51-12817
    E183 .L65 MRR Alc.

MacNeil, Neil, Forge of democracy;
the House of Representatives. New
York, D. McKay [1963] 496 p.
328.73 63-11721
    JK1331 .M2 MRR Alc.

Miller, Marion Mills, ed. Great
debates in American history. [The
national ed.] New York, Current
literature publishing company [c1913]
14 v. 13-23912
    E173 .M64 vol. 14 MRR Alc.

Mosher, Robert Brent, comp.
Executive register of the United
States, 1789-1902; Baltimore, Md.,
The Friedenwald company [1903] 1 p.
l., x, 351 p. 03-10230
    JK661 1902 MRR Alc.

Ogg, Frederic Austin, Builders of
the Republic, New Haven, Yale
university press; [etc., etc.] 1927.
3 p. l., 352 p. 27-9284
    E178.5 .P2 vol. 8 MRR Alc.

Parrington, Vernon Louis, Main
currents in American thought; [New
York, Harcourt, Brace and company,
1827-30] 3 v. 27-8440
    PS88 .P3 MRR Alc.

Poore, Benjamin Perley, Perley's
reminiscences of sixty years in the
national metropolis. New York, AMS
Press [1971] 2 v. 917.3/03 74-
158970
    F194 .P824 1971 MRR Alc.

Robinson, Edgar Eugene, The
evolution of American political
parties; New York, Harcourt, Brace
and company [c1924] viii p., 2 l., 3-
382 p. 24-25538
    JK2261 .R6 MRR Alc.

Roseboom, Eugene Holloway, A history
of presidential elections, from
George Washington to Richard M. Nixon
[3d ed. New York] Macmillan [1970]
viii, 639 p. 329/.023 78-101726
    E183 .R68 1970 MRR Alc.

Schlesinger, Arthur Meier, The
coming to power; [1st ed.] New
York, Chelsea House Publishers [1972]
xxi, 550 p. 329/.023/73 70-39588

    E183 .S28114 MRR Alc.

Schlesinger, Arthur Meier, History
of American presidential elections,
1789-1968. New York, Chelsea House
[1971] 4 v. (xxxvii, 3959 p.)
329/.023/73 70-139269
    E183 .S28 MRR Alc.

Smith, William Henry, Speakers of
the House of representatives of the
United States, Baltimore, Md., S. J.
Gaeng, 1928. 4 p. l., [xiii]-xvi,
261 p. 28-9295
    E176 .S69 MRR Biog.

Sorauf, Francis Joseph, Party
politics in America Boston, Little,
Brown [1968] ix, 438 p.
329/.02/0973 68-14138
    JK2265 .S65 MRR Alc.

Stanwood, Edward, A history of the
presidency, New ed.; rev. Boston,
New York, Houghton Mifflin company,
1928. 2 v. 28-26854
    JK511 .S7 1928 MRR Alc.

Stone, Irving, They also ran;
Garden City, N.Y., Doubleday [1966]
xi, 434 p. 973 66-21914
    E176 .S87 1966 MRR Alc.

Theis, Paul A., All about politics;
New York, Bowker, 1972. xii, 228 p.
320 72-8470
    JK1726 .T48 MRR Alc.

Townsend, Malcolm, comp. U.S. An
index to the United States of
America. Boston, D. Lothrop company
[c1890] 6 p. l., 9-482 (i.e. 484) p.
incl. illus., maps (part fold.). 01-
21543
    E174 .T74 MRR Alc.

United States. Congress. American
state papers. Washington, Gales and
Seaton, 1832-61. 38 v. 09-33892
    J33 MRR Alc.

United States. Congress. The debates
and proceedings in the Congress of
the United States; 1834-56.
Washington, Gales and Seaton. 12-
36435
    J11 .A5 MRR Alc (Dk 33) Full set

UNITED STATES--POLITICS AND (Cont.)
United States. Congress. Senate.
Journal of the executive proceedings
of the Senate of the United States.
1828- Washington, Government
Printing Office. 09-23902
    JK1251 .A3 MRR Alc (DK 33) Full
    set

United States. Constitution
sesquicentennial commission. History
of the formation of the union under
the Constitution [Washington, U.S.
Govt. print. off., 1941] x, 885 p.
incl. front., illus. (1 col.: incl.
maps) ports., facsims., tables,
diagrs. 342.73 41-50348
    JK166 1941 MRR Alc.

United States. President. A
compilation of the messages and
papers of the presidents, New York,
Bureau of national literature, inc.
[1917?] 20 v. 353.03 17-7545
    J81 .B97a MRR Alc.

United States. President. Public
papers of the Presidents of the
United States, containing the public
messages, speeches, and statements of
the President. Washington, U.S.
Govt. Print. Off. 353.03 58-61050
    J80 .A283 MRR Alc Full set

United States. Congress. Register of
debates in Congress, comprising the
leading debates and incidents of the
second session of the Eighteenth
Congress: [Dec. 6, 1824, to the first
session of the Twenty-fifth Congress,
Oct. 16, 1837] Washington, Gales &
Seaton, 1825-37. 14 v. in 29. 12-
36436
    J11 .D5 MRR Alc (Dk 33)

Wasby, Stephen L., American
Government and politics New York,
Scribner [1973] xvii, 676 p.
[$14.95] 320.4/73 73-1326
    JK274 .W248 MRR Alc.

Weisbord, Marvin Ross. Campaigning
for president; [Rev. and expanded
ed.] New York, Washington Square
Press [1966] xv, 447 p. 329.023
67-519
    E183 .W4 1966 MRR Alc.

White, William Smith. Citadel, the
story of the U.S. Senate. [1st ed.]
New York, Harper [c1957] 274 p.
328.73 56-11089
    JK1161 .W5 MRR Alc.

Who's who in United States politics
and American political almanac.
Chicago, Capitol House. 923.273 50-
12020
    E747 .W65 MRR Biog Latest edition

UNITED STATES--POLITICS AND GOVERNMENT--
COLONIAL PERIOD, CA. 1600-1775.
Franklin, Benjamin, The writings of
Benjamin Franklin; New York, The
Macmillan company; London, Macmillan
& co., ltd., 1905-07. 10 v. 05-
35396
    E302 .F82 1905 MRR Alc.

Osgood, Herbert Levi, The American
colonies in the eighteenth century,
New York, Columbia university press,
1924. 4 v. 973.2 24-3889
    E195 .082 MRR Alc.

Osgood, Herbert Levi, The American
colonies in the seventeenth century,
New York, The Macmillan company;
London, Macmillan & co., ltd. 1904-
07. 3 v. 04-14597
    E191 .082 MRR Alc.

UNITED STATES--POLITICS AND GOVERNMENT--
COLONIAL PERIOD, CA. 1600-1775--SOURCES.
Kavenagh, W. Keith. Foundations of
colonial America; New York, Chelsea
House, 1973. 3 v. [$95.00]
325/.342/0973 72-80866
    JK49 .K38 MRR Alc.

UNITED STATES--POLITICS AND GOVERNMENT--
REVOLUTION, 1775-1783.
Adams, John, pres. U.S., The works
of John Adams, Boston, Little, Brown
and company [etc.] 1850-56 [v. 1,
'56] 10 v. 08-19755
    E302 .A26 MRR Alc.

Burnett, Edmund Cody, The
Continental Congress. New York, W.
W. Norton [1964, c1941] xii, 757 p.
66-11792
    E303 .B93 1964 MRR Alc.

Franklin, Benjamin, The writings of
Benjamin Franklin; New York, The
Macmillan company; London, Macmillan
& co., ltd., 1905-07. 10 v. 05-
35396
    E302 .F82 1905 MRR Alc.

Hamilton, Alexander, The works of
Alexander Hamilton, [Federal ed.]
New York, London, G. P. Putnam's
sons, 1904. 12 v. 04-19021
    E302 .H24 MRR Alc.

Jefferson, Thomas, Pres. U.S., The
Jeffersonian cyclopedia; New York,
Russell & Russell [1967] 2 v. (1009
p.) 973.46/0924 66-27664
    E332.82 1967 MRR Ref Desk.

Jefferson, Thomas, pres. U.S., The
Jeffersonian cyclopedia, New York,
London, Funk & Wagnalls company
[1900?] 4 p. l., [xiii]-xxii, [2],
1009 p. mrr01-50
    JK113 .J4 1900b MRR Alc.

Jefferson,Thomas, pres. U.S., The
writings of Thomas Jefferson.
Library ed., Washington, D.C.,
Issued under the auspices of the
Thomas Jefferson memorial association
of the United States, 1903-04. 20 v.
353.03 14-3171
    E302 .J469 MRR Alc.

Madison, James, Pres. U.S., Papers.
Chicago] University of Chicago Press
[1962- v. 923.173 62-9114
    E302 .M19 MRR Alc.

Nevins, Allan, The American states
during and after the revolution, 1775-
1789, New York, The Macmillan
company, 1924. xviii p., 1 l., 728
p. 24-23941
    E303 .N52 MRR Alc.

United States. Continental congress.
Journals of the Continental Congress,
1774-1789. Washington, U.S. Govt.
print. off., 1904-37. 34 v. 05-59

    J10 .A5 MRR Alc (Dk 33)

United States. Continental congress.
Secret journals of the acts and
proceedings of Congress, Boston:
Printed and published by Thomas B.
Wait, 1820-21. 4 v. 11-28751
    J10 .A35 MRR Alc (Dk 33)

Wood, Gordon S. The creation of the
American Republic, 1776-1787, Chapel
Hill, Published for the Institute of
Early American History and Culture at
Williamsburg, Va., by the University
of North Carolina Press [1969] xiv,
653 p. [15.00] 320/.0973 71-78861
    JA84.U5 W6 MRR Alc.

UNITED STATES--POLITICS AND GOVERNMENT--
REVOLUTION, 1775-1783--SOURCES.
Paine, Thomas, The complete writings
of Thomas Paine. New York, The
Citadel press [1945] 2 v. 308.1
45-2289
    JC177.A3 1945 MRR Alc.

United States. Continental congress.
Journals of the American congress:
from 1774 to 1788. Washington:
Printed and published by Way and
Gideon, 1823. 4 v. 17-23718
    J10 .A3 MRR Alc.

UNITED STATES--POLITICS AND GOVERNMENT--
1783-1789.
Franklin, Benjamin, The writings of
Benjamin Franklin; New York, The
Macmillan company; London, Macmillan
& co., ltd., 1905-07. 10 v. 05-
35396
    E302 .F82 1905 MRR Alc.

Nevins, Allan, The American states
during and after the revolution, 1775-
1789, New York, The Macmillan
company, 1924. xviii p., 1 l., 728
p. 24-23941
    E303 .N52 MRR Alc.

UNITED STATES--POLITICS AND GOVERNMENT--
1783-1809.
Hamilton, Alexander, The works of
Alexander Hamilton, [Federal ed.]
New York, London, G. P. Putnam's
sons, 1904. 12 v. 04-19021
    E302 .H24 MRR Alc.

UNITED STATES--POLITICS AND GOVERNMENT--
1783-1865.
Adams, John, pres. U.S., The works
of John Adams, Boston, Little, Brown
and company [etc.] 1850-56 [v. 1,
'56] 10 v. 08-19755
    E302 .A26 MRR Alc.

Adams, John Quincy, Pres. U.S.,
Diary, 1794-1845; New York,
Scribner, 1951. xxxv, 586 p.
973.5/5/0924 51-10345
    E377 .A213 MRR Alc.

Adams, John Quincy, pres. U.S.,
Memoirs of John Quincy Adams,
Philadelphia, J. B. Lippincott & co.,
1874-77. 12 v. 04-20138
    E377 .A19 MRR Alc.

Brown, Stuart Gerry, The first
Republicans; [Syracuse] Syracuse
University Press, 1954. 186 p.
329.3 54-9917
    JK2316 .B7 MRR Alc.

Hecht, Marie B. John Quincy Adams;
New York, Macmillan [1972] xiv, 682
p. [$12.95] 973.5/5/0924 B 72-
77279
    E377 .H43 MRR Alc.

Jefferson, Thomas, pres. U.S., The
Jeffersonian cyclopedia, New York,
London, Funk & Wagnalls company
[1900?] 4 p. l., [xiii]-xxii, [2],
1009 p. mrr01-50
    JK113 .J4 1900b MRR Alc.

Jefferson,Thomas, pres. U.S., The
writings of Thomas Jefferson.
Library ed., Washington, D.C.,
Issued under the auspices of the
Thomas Jefferson memorial association
of the United States, 1903-04. 20 v.
353.03 14-3171
    E302 .J469 MRR Alc.

Madison, James, Pres. U.S., The
complete Madison; [1st ed.] New
York, Harper [1953] xi, 361 p.
308.1 53-5445
    E302 .M17 MRR Alc.

Madison, James, pres. U.S., Letters
and other writings of James Madison.
Philadelphia, J. B. Lippincott & co.,
1865. 4 v. 06-24330
    E302 .M18 MRR Alc.

Madison, James, Pres. U.S., Papers.
Chicago] University of Chicago Press
[1962- v. 923.173 62-9114
    E302 .M19 MRR Alc.

Monroe, James, Pres. U.S., The
writings of James Monroe, including a
collection of his public and private
papers and correspondence, now for
the first time printed. New York,
AMS Press [1969] 7 v. 973.5/4 69-
18218
    E302 .M74 1969 MRR Alc.

Tyler, Lyon Gardiner, The letters
and times of the Tylers. New York,
Da Capo Press, 1970 [c1884-86] 3 v.
973.5/8 71-75267
    E397 .T982 MRR Alc.

White, Leonard Dupee, The
Jeffersonians; New York, Macmillan,
1951. xiv, 572 p. 353 51-12490
    JK180 .W5 MRR Alc.

UNITED STATES--POLITICS AND GOVERNMENT--
1789-1797.
United States. 1st Congress, 1789-
1791. Senate. Senate executive
journal and related documents.
Baltimore, Johns Hopkins University
Press [1974] xvii, 574 p.
328.73/01 73-13443
    JK1059 1st .D6 vol. 2 MRR Alc.

UNITED STATES--POLITICS AND GOVERNMENT--
1789-1797--SOURCES.
Documentary history of the First
Federal Congress of the United States
of America. March 4, 1789-March 3,
1791. [Baltimore, Johns Hopkins
University Press, 1972- v.
328.73 s 328.73/01 73-155164
    JK1059 1st .D6 MRR Alc.

UNITED STATES--POLITICS AND GOVERNMENT--
CONSTITUTIONAL PERIOD, 1789-1809.
Cunningham, Noble E., The
Jeffersonian Republicans; Chapel
Hill, Published for the Institute of
Early American History and Culture at
Williamsburg by the University of
North Carolina Press [c1957] x, 279
p. 329.3 58-1263
    JK2316 .C8 MRR Alc.

White, Leonard Dupee, The
Federalists; New York, Macmillan
Co., 1948. xii, 538 p. 973.41 48-
7016
    JK171.A1 W4 MRR Alc.

UNITED STATES--POLITICS AND GOVERNMENT--
CONSTITUTIONAL PERIOD, 1789-1809--
BIBLIOGRAPHY.
Gaines, Pierce Welch. Political
works of concealed authorship in the
United States, 1789-1810, Rev. and
enl. ed. Hamden, Conn., Shoe String
Press, 1965. 190 p. 014.1 65-
17720
    Z1045 .G3 1965 MRR Alc.

UNITED STATES--POLITICS AND GOVERNMENT--
1797-1801.
De Conde, Alexander, The quasi-war;
New York, Scribner [1966] xiv, 498
p. 973.45 66-24492
    E323 .D4 MRR Alc.

UNITED STATES--POLITICS AND GOVERNMENT--
1801-1815.
Fischer, David Hackett, The
revolution of American conservatism;
[1st ed.] New York, Harper & Row
[1965] xx, 455 p. 973.4 65-14680

    E331 .F5 MRR Alc.

UNITED STATES--POLITICS AND GOVERNMENT--1815-1861.
Curtis, George Ticknor, Life of James Buchanan, New York, Harper & brothers, 1883. 2 v.   14-758
   E437 .C98 MRR Alc.

Fillmore, Millard, pres. U.S., Millard Fillmore papers. Buffalo, N.Y., The Buffalo historical society, 1907. 2 v.   08-10420
   E427 .F48 MRR Alc.

Griffis, William Elliot, Millard Fillmore, constructive statesman, defender of the Constitution, president of the United States, Ithaca, N.Y., Andrus & Church [c1915] ix, 159 p.   15-5696
   E427 .G85 MRR Alc.

Nichols, Roy Franklin, Franklin Pierce, [2d ed., completely rev.] Philadelphia, University of Pennsylvania Press [1958] xvii, 625 p.   923.173   58-7750
   E432 .N63 1958 MRR Alc.

Sellers, Charles Grier. James K. Polk, Jacksonian, 1795-1843. Princeton, N.J., Princeton University Press, 1957-   v.   973.610924 B 57-5457
   E417 .S4 MRR Alc.

Van Deusen, Glyndon Garlock, The Jacksonian era, 1828-1848. [1st ed.] New York, Harper [1959] 291 p. 973.56   58-13810
   E338 .V2 MRR Alc.

White, Leonard Dupee, The Jacksonians; New York, Macmillan, 1954. xii, 593 p.   353   54-12436
   JK201 .W45 MRR Alc.

UNITED STATES--POLITICS AND GOVERNMENT--1825-1829.
McCormick, Richard Patrick, The second American party system; Chapel Hill, University of North Carolina Press [1966] x, 389 p.   329/.02   66-10962
   JK2261 .M165 MRR Alc.

UNITED STATES--POLITICS AND GOVERNMENT--1829-1837.
McCormick, Richard Patrick, The second American party system; Chapel Hill, University of North Carolina Press [1966] x, 389 p.   329/.02   66-10962
   JK2261 .M165 MRR Alc.

Schlesinger, Arthur Meier, The age of Jackson, Boston, Little, Brown and company, 1945. xiv, 577 p. 973.56   45-8340
   E381 .S38 MRR Alc.

UNITED STATES--POLITICS AND GOVERNMENT--1857-1861.
Lincoln, Abraham, Pres. U.S., The Illinois political campaign of 1858: [Washington] Library of Congress [1958] 212 p. (p. 25-212, facsim.) 973.68   58-60991
   Z663 .L47 1958 MRR Alc.

UNITED STATES--POLITICS AND GOVERNMENT--CIVIL WAR, 1861-1865.
Welles, Gideon, Diary. New York, W. W. Norton [1960] 3 v.   923.273   60-6275
   E468 .W444 MRR Alc.

UNITED STATES--POLITICS AND GOVERNMENT--1865-1869.
Stryker, Lloyd Paul. Andrew Johnson; a study in courage, New York, The Macmillan company, 1929. xvi p., 1 l., 881 p.   30-6280
   E667 .S823 MRR Alc.

Welles, Gideon, Diary. New York, W. W. Norton [1960] 3 v.   923.273   60-6275
   E468 .W444 MRR Alc.

UNITED STATES--POLITICS AND GOVERNMENT--1865-1877.
McPherson, Edward, The political history of the United States of America during the period of reconstruction, (from April 15, 1865, to July 15, 1870,) 2d ed. Washington, Solomons & Chapman, 1875. v, 6-9, 648 p.   04-7498
   E668 .M17 MRR Alc.

UNITED STATES--POLITICS AND GOVERNMENT--1865-1898.
Nevins, Allan, Grover Cleveland; a study in courage, New York, Dodd, Mead & company, 1933. xiii p., 1 l., 832 p.   923.173   33-23946
   E697 .N465 MRR Alc.

UNITED STATES--POLITICS AND GOVERNMENT--1865-1900.
Faulkner, Harold Underwood, Politics, reform, and expansion, 1890-1900. [1st ed.] New York, Harper [1958] 312 p.   973.8   56-6022
   E661 .F3 MRR Alc.

Leech, Margaret, In the days of McKinley. [1st ed.] New York, Harper [1959] viii, 686 p.   923.173 59-6310
   E711.6 .L4 MRR Alc.

Morgan, Howard Wayne. William McKinley and his America. [Syracuse, N.Y.] Syracuse University Press, 1963. xi, 595 p.   923.173   63-19723
   E711.6 .M7 MRR Alc.

Olcott, Charles Sumner, The life of William McKinley, Boston, New York, Houghton Mifflin company, 1916. 2 v. 16-10505
   E711.6 .O43 MRR Alc.

Tugwell, Rexford Guy, Grover Cleveland New York, Macmillan [1968] xviii, 298 p.   973.8/5/0924 B   68-12399
   E697 .T8 MRR Alc.

White, Leonard Dupee, The Republican era, 1869-1901; New York, Macmillan, 1958. 406 p.   353   58-6209
   JK231 .W5 MRR Alc.

UNITED STATES--POLITICS AND GOVERNMENT--1865-
Bassett, John Spencer, Makers of a new nation, New Haven, Yale university press; [etc., etc.] 1928. 3 p. l., 344 p.   28-24814
   E178.5 .P2 vol. 9 MRR Alc.

UNITED STATES--POLITICS AND GOVERNMENT--1869-1877.
Hesseltine, William Best, Ulysses S. Grant, politician, New York, Dodd, Mead & company, 1935. xiii, 480 p. 923.173   35-17052
   E672 .H46 MRR Alc.

UNITED STATES--POLITICS AND GOVERNMENT--1881-1885.
Howe, George Frederick. Chester A. Arthur; New York, Dodd, Mead & company, 1934. xi, 307 p.   923.173 34-38337
   E692 .H67 MRR Alc.

UNITED STATES--POLITICS AND GOVERNMENT--20TH CENTURY.
Fenno, Richard F., The President's Cabinet; Cambridge, Mass., Harvard University Press, 1959. 327 p. 353.05   59-9272
   JK611 .F4 MRR Alc.

Henry, Laurin L. Presidential transitions. Washington, Brookings Institution [1960] xviii, 755 p. 353.032   60-53252
   E743 .H4 MRR Alc.

Johnson, Walter, 1600 Pennsylvania Avenue; [1st ed.] Boston, Little, Brown [1960] 390 p.   973.91   60-6525
   E743 .J6 MRR Alc.

Martin, Ralph G., Ballots & bandwagons. Chicago, Rand McNally [1964] 480 p.   973.9   64-10021
   E743 .M275 MRR Alc.

Pringle, Henry Fowles, The life and times of William Howard Taft; New York, Toronto, Farrar & Rinehart, inc. [c1939] 2 v.   923.173   39-27878
   E762 .P75 MRR Alc.

Walworth, Arthur Clarence, Woodrow Wilson 2d ed., rev. Boston, Houghton Mifflin Co., 1965. xiv, 436, 439 p.   923.173   64-21740
   E767 .W34 1965 MRR Alc.

UNITED STATES--POLITICS AND GOVERNMENT--20TH CENTURY--ADDRESSES, ESSAYS, LECTURES.
Wrage, Ernest J., ed. Contemporary forum; New York, Harper [1962] 376 p.   815.5082   62-10074
   PS668 .W7 MRR Alc.

UNITED STATES--POLITICS AND GOVERNMENT--1901-1909.
Mowry, George Edwin, The era of Theodore Roosevelt, 1900-1912. [1st ed.] New York, Harper [1958] 330 p. 973.911   58-8835
   E756 .M85 MRR Alc.

UNITED STATES--POLITICS AND GOVERNMENT--1909-1913.
Mowry, George Edwin, The era of Theodore Roosevelt, 1900-1912. [1st ed.] New York, Harper [1958] 330 p. 973.911   58-8835
   E756 .M85 MRR Alc.

UNITED STATES--POLITICS AND GOVERNMENT--1929-1933.
Emerson, Edwin, Hoover and his times; Garden City, N.Y., Garden City publishing company, inc., 1932. xvi p., 1 l., 632 p.   923.173   32-25411
   E801 .E75 MRR Alc.

UNITED STATES--POLITICS AND GOVERNMENT--1929-1933--COLLECTED WORKS.
United States. President, 1929-1933 (Hoover) Herbert Hoover : Washington : U.S. Govt. Print. Off., 1974. 2 v. (iii, 1566 p.) : [$24.55]   353.03/5   74-602466
   J82 .D5 1974 MRR Alc.

UNITED STATES--POLITICS AND GOVERNMENT--1933-1945.
Burns, James MacGregor. Roosevelt: the lion and the fox. [1st ed.] New York, Harcourt, Brace [1956] 553 p. 923.173   56-7920
   E807 .B835 MRR Alc.

Moley, Raymond, The first New Deal [1st ed.] New York, Harcourt, Brace & World [1966] xxiii, 577 p. 973.917   66-22282
   E806 .M68 MRR Alc.

Roosevelt, Franklin Delano, pres. U.S., "Quotations" from Franklin Delano Roosevelt. Washington, D.C., Republican national committee [c1940] 128 p.   973.917   40-32770
   E806 .R7495 1940 MRR Alc.

UNITED STATES--POLITICS AND GOVERNMENT--1945-1953.
Truman, Harry S., Pres. U.S., The Truman administration, New York, New York University Press, 1956. xii, 394 p.   973.918   56-7425
   E813 .T68 MRR Alc.

Truman, Margaret, Harry S. Truman. New York, Morrow, 1973 [c1972] 602 p. [$10.95]   973.918/0924 B   73-170238
   E814 .T8 MRR Alc.

UNITED STATES--POLITICS AND GOVERNMENT--1945-
Barone, Michael. The almanac of American politics. [2d ed.] Boston, Gambit [c1973] xxiii, 1240 p. [$15.00]   328.73   72-96875
   JK271 .B343 1974 MRR Ref Desk.

Burns, James MacGregor. John Kennedy: a political profile. New York, Harcourt, Brace & World [1961] xxiii, 309 p.   923.173   61-65170
   E842 .B8 1961 MRR Alc.

Congressional quarterly almanac. v. 1-   Jan./Mar. 1945- Washington. 328.73   47-41081
   JK1 .C66   Sci RR Latest edition / MRR Alc Full set

Congressional Quarterly Service, Washington, D.C. Congress and the Nation; [1st ed.] Washington [1965-69] 2 v.   320.9/73   65-22351
   KF49 .C653 MRR Ref Desk.

Cronin, Thomas E. comp. The Presidential advisory system. New York, Harper & Row [1969] xx, 375 p. [6.95]   353/.03   69-18487
   JK518 .C7 MRR Alc.

De Toledano, Ralph, One man alone: Richard Nixon. New York, Funk & Wagnalls [1969] 386 p.   [6.95] 973.924/0924 B   71-97942
   E856 .D4 MRR Alc.

First national directory of "rightist" groups, publications, and some individuals in the United States and some foreign countries. 4th ed. Sausalito, Calif., Distributed by the Noontide Press, 1962. 36 p.   62-2510
   E743.5 .F48 1962 MRR Ref Desk.

Forster, Arnold. Danger on the Right, New York, Random House [1964] xviii, 294 p.   320   64-7549
   E743 .F68 MRR Alc.

Johnson, Lyndon Baines, Pres. U.S., A time for action; [1st ed.] New York, Atheneum Publishers, 1964. xv, 183 p.   308.1   64-16425
   E742.5 .J6 MRR Alc.

O'Neill, William L. Coming apart: Chicago, Quadrangle Books, 1971. ix, 442, xxvi p. [$12.50]   973.921   78-152098
   E839 .O5 1971 MRR Alc.

Peirce, Neal R. The megastates of America; [1st ed.] New York, Norton [1972] 745 p. [$12.95]   917.3/03/92   70-163375
   E839.5 .P35 MRR Alc.

Thayer, George, The farther shores of politics; New York, Simon and Schuster [1967] 610 p.   320.9/73 67-16728
   JK2261 .T47 1967 MRR Alc.

United States. Bureau of the Census. 1967 census of governments. [Washington, For sale by the Supt. of Docs., U.S. Govt. Print. Off., 1968-   in   353.000021/2 a   68-7201
   JS3.A257 MRR Alc.

UNITED STATES--POLITICS AND GOVERNMENT--
1945- --BIBLIOGRAPHY.
Kaid, Lynda Lee. Political campaign
communication: a bibliography and
guide to the literature. Metuchen,
N.J., Scarecrow Press, 1974. v, 206
p. 016.329/01/0973 73-22492
   Z7165.U5 K34 MRR Alc.

UNITED STATES--POLITICS AND GOVERNMENT--
1945- --YEARBOOKS.
Historic documents. 1972-
[Washington] Congressional Quarterly,
inc. [$25.00] 917.3/03/9205 72-
97888
   E839.5 .H57 MRR Alc Full set

UNITED STATES--POLITICS AND GOVERNMENT--
1953-1961.
Eisenhower, Dwight David, Pres. U.S.,
The White House years. [1st ed.]
Garden City, N.Y., Doubleday, 1963-
65. 2 v. 973.921 63-18447
   E835 .E47 MRR Alc.

UNITED STATES--POLITICS AND GOVERNMENT--
1961-1963.
Kennedy, John Fitzgerald, Pres. U.S.,
Kennedy and the press; New York,
Crowell [1965] 555 p. 973.922 65-
12271
   E841 .K37 MRR Alc.

Sidey, Hugh. John F. Kennedy,
President. New ed. New York,
Atheneum, 1964. x, 434 p. 973.922
64-772
   E842 .S5 1964 MRR Alc.

The Evening star, Washington, D.C.
The New Frontiersmen; Washington,
Public Affairs Press [1961] 254 p.
923.273 61-11685
   E841 .E8 MRR Biog.

UNITED STATES--POLITICS AND GOVERNMENT--
1963-1969.
Amrine, Michael. This awesome
challenge. New York, Putnam [1964]
283 p. 973.923 64-18001
   E846 .A6 MRR Alc.

Bell, Jack, The Johnson treatment:
[1st ed.] New York, Harper & Row
[1965] 305 p. 923.173 64-25107
   E846 .B4 MRR Alc.

Jacobs, Paul, The new radicals: New
York, Random House [1966] 333 p.
320.973 66-18328
   E839.5 .J3 MRR Alc.

Johnson, Lyndon Baines, Pres. U.S.,
My hope for America, New York,
Random House [1964] 127 p. 329.01
64-8358
   E850 .J6 MRR Alc.

Kluckhohn, Frank L. Lyndon's legacy;
New York, Devin-Adair Co., 1964.
xiv, 335 p. 320.973 64-23751
   E846 .K55 1964a MRR Alc.

Roberts, Charles Wesley, LBJ's inner
circle, New York, Delacorte Press
[1965] 223 p. 973.9230922 65-
21935
   E846 .R56 MRR Alc.

UNITED STATES--POLITICS AND GOVERNMENT--
1963-
Peirce, Neal R. The megastates of
America; [1st ed.] New York, Norton
[1972] 745 p. [$12.95]
917.3/03/92 70-163375
   E839.5 .P35 MRR Alc.

Weekly compilation of Presidential
documents. v. 1- Aug. 2, 1965-
[Washington, Office of the Federal
Register; distributed by Supt. of
Docs., Govt. Print. Off.] 65-9929
   J80 .A284 MRR Alc Partial set

White, Theodore Harold, The making
of the President, 1964 [1st ed.]
New York, Atheneum Publishers, 1965.
xi, 431 p. 973.923 65-18328
   E850 .W5 MRR Alc.

UNITED STATES--POLITICS AND GOVERNMENT--
1969-1974.
Nixon, Richard Milhous, Nixon; the
fourth year of his Presidency.
Washington, Congressional Quarterly
[c1973] 46, 146 p. [$4.00]
320.9/73/0924 72-94077
   E855 .N494 MRR Alc.

Solara, Ferdinand V. Key influences
in the American right, Denver,
Polifax Press [1972] xv, 68 p.
[$4.95] 320.5/12/0973 72-189989
   E839.5 .S64 1972 MRR Ref Desk.

UNITED STATES--POLITICS AND GOVERNMENT--
1969-
see also Watergate Affair, 1972-

Common Cause (U.S.). Campaign Finance
Monitoring Project. 1972 Federal
campaign finances, interest groups,
and political parties. Washington,
Common Cause [1974] 3 v.
329/.025/0973 74-77718
   JK1991 .C655 1974 MRR Alc.

UNITED STATES--POLITICS AND GOVERNMENT--
1969- --PERIODICALS.
National Journal reports. v. 5, no.
30- July 28, 1973- [Washington,
Government Research Corporation]
320.9/73 73-645726
   JK1 .N28 MRR Alc Full set

UNITED STATES--POLITICS AND GOVERNMENT--
ADDRESSES, ESSAYS, LECTURES.
Commager, Henry Steele, ed. Living
ideas in America. New, enl. ed. New
York, Harper & Row [1964] xx, 872 p.
917.3 64-23898
   E173 .C67 1964 MRR Alc.

UNITED STATES--POLITICS AND GOVERNMENT--
ANECDOTES, FACETIAE, SATIRE, ETC.
Gingras, Angele de T. "From bussing
to bugging"; Washington, Acropolis
Books [1973] 168 p. [$6.50]
320.9/73/0207 72-12394
   PN6231.P6 G54 MRR Alc.

Harris, Leon A. The fine art of
political wit; [1st ed.] New York,
Dutton, 1964. 288 p. 827.093 64-
19532
   PN6231.P6 H36 MRR Alc.

UNITED STATES--POLITICS AND GOVERNMENT--
BIBLIOGRAPHY.
Brock, Clifton. The literature of
political science; New York, Bowker,
1969. xii, 232 p. 016.32 79-79426
   Z7161 .B83 MRR Alc.

Larson, Arthur D. National security
affairs: Detroit, Gale Research Co.,
[1973] 411 p. 016.35503/3/0973 70-
184013
   Z1215 .L37 MRR Alc.

Liboiron, Albert A. Federalism and
intergovernmental relations in
Australia, Canada, the United States
and other countries; Kingston, Ont.,
Institute of Intergovernmental
Relations, Queen's University, 1967.
vi, 231 l. [$3.00 Can.] 016.351
68-110060
   Z7165.A8 L5 MRR Alc.

National association of state
libraries. Public document clearing
house committee. Check-list of
legislative journals of states of the
United States of America,
Providence, the Oxford press, 1938.
3 p. l., 274 p. 016.32873 38-38809
   Z1223.5.A1 N27 1938 MRR Ref Desk.

Public Affairs Information Service.
Bulletin ... annual cumulation. 1st-
1915- New York [etc.] 16-920
   Z7163 .P9 MRR Circ Full set

United States. Library of Congress.
Legislative Reference Service.
Intergovernmental relations in the
United States; Washington, 1953. 73
p. 55-60203
   Z663.6 .I6 MRR Alc.

Universal Reference System.
Bibliography of bibliographies in
political science, government, and
public policy; Princeton, N.J.,
Princeton Research Pub. Co. [1968]
xix, 927 p. 016.3 67-29647
   Z7161 .U64 vol. 3 MRR Alc.

Universal Reference System.
Legislative process, representation,
and decision-making; Princeton,
N.J., Princeton Research Pub. Co.
[c1967] xv, 787 p. 016.32 67-
29646
   Z6461 .U64 vol. 2 MRR Alc.

Wynar, Lubomyr Roman, American
political parties; Littleton, Colo.,
Libraries Unlimited, 1969. 427 p.
016.329/02/0973 75-96954
   Z7166.U5 W88 MRR Alc.

UNITED STATES--POLITICS AND GOVERNMENT--
CARICATURES AND CARTOONS.
Lorant, Stefan, The glorious burden:
the American Presidency. New York,
Harper & Row [1968] 959 p. [25.00]
320.9/73 68-15963
   E183 .L64 MRR Alc.

UNITED STATES--POLITICS AND GOVERNMENT--
DICTIONARIES.
Holt, Solomon. Dictionary of
American government Rev. ed. [New
York, Macfadden-Bartell Corp.] 1970.
304 p. [0.95] 353/.003 72-17208
   JK9 .H6 1970 MRR Ref Desk.

McCarthy, Eugene J., The crescent
dictionary of American politics. New
York, Macmillan, 1962. x, 182 p.
320.3 62-10644
   JK9 .M2 MRR Alc.

Mitchell, Edwin Valentine, comp. An
encyclopedia of American politics.
New York, Greenwood Press, 1968
[c1946] 338 p. 320/.0973 69-10135
   JK9 .M55 1968 MRR Alc.

Norton, Charles Ledyard, Political
Americanisms; New York, London,
Longmans, Green & co., 1890. viii,
135 p. 10-31868
   PE2835 .N8 MRR Alc.

Plano, Jack C. The American
political dictionary 3d ed.
Hinsdale, Ill., Dryden Press [1972]
x, 462 p. 320.9/73 72-75601
   JK9 .P55 1972 MRR Alc.

Safire, William L. The new language
of politics: New York, Random House
[1968] xvi, 528 p. 320/.03 68-
14508
   JK9 .S2 MRR Ref Desk.

Smith, Edward Conrad, ed. Dictionary
of American politics 2d ed. New
York, Barnes & Noble [1968] vii, 434
p. 320/.0973 67-28530
   JK9 .S5 1968 MRR Ref Desk

Sperber, Hans, American political
terms; Detroit, Wayne State
University Press, 1962. x, 516 p.
320.3 62-11233
   JK9 .S65 MRR Ref Desk.

UNITED STATES--POLITICS AND GOVERNMENT--
EXAMINATIONS, QUESTIONS, ETC.
Stimpson, George William, A book
about American politics. [1st ed.]
New York, Harper [1952] 554 p.
973.076 52-5472
   E178.25 .S86 MRR Ref Desk.

UNITED STATES--POLITICS AND GOVERNMENT--
HANDBOOKS, MANUALS, ETC.
Blevins, Leon W., The young voter's
manual; Totowa, N.J., Littlefield,
Adams, 1973. xi, 366 p. [$3.95]
320.4/73 73-10377
   JK274 .B623 MRR Alc.

Congressional Quarterly, inc. Guide
to the Congress of the United States;
[1st ed.] Washington, Congressional
Quarterly Service [1971] xxxi, 639,
323a, 21b p. [$35.00] 328.73 78-
167743
   JK1021 .C56 MRR Ref Desk.

Ferguson, John Henry, The American
system of government 11th ed. New
York, McGraw-Hill [1971] ix, 801,
A30, G22, I23 p. 353/.0002/02 78-
158056
   JK274 .F365 1971 MRR Alc.

Ferguson, John Henry, Elements of
American government 7th ed. New
York, McGraw-Hill [1966] 604 p.
353 66-18209
   JK274 .F366 1966 MRR Alc.

Ogg, Frederic Austin, Ogg and Ray's
Introduction to American Government.
13th ed. New York, Appleton-Century-
Crofts [1966] x, 979 p. 353 66-
16282
   JK421 .O5 1966 MRR Alc.

Plano, Jack C. The American
political dictionary 3d ed.
Hinsdale, Ill., Dryden Press [1972]
x, 462 p. 320.9/73 72-75601
   JK9 .P55 1972 MRR Alc.

Public administration organizations,
a directory of unofficial
organizations in the field of public
administration in the United States
and Canada. [1st]- ed.: 1932-
Chicago, Public Administration
Clearing House. 061 33-4186
   AS18 .P8 MRR Alc Latest edition

Townsend, Malcolm, comp. Handbook of
the United States political history
for readers and students; Boston,
Lothrop, Lee & Shepard co. [c1905]
11, 441 p. 05-33512
   JK9 .T7 MRR Alc.

United States Government manual.
1973/74- [Washington] Office of the
Federal Register; [For sale by the
Supt. of Docs., U.S. Govt. Print.
Off.] [$4.00] 353 73-646537
   JK421 .A3 MRR Ref Desk Latest
   edition / MRR Ref Desk Latest
   edition

UNITED STATES--POLITICS AND GOVERNMENT--
PERIODICALS.
C Q weekly report. Washington,
Congressional Quarterly Inc. [etc.]
328.73 52-36903
   JK1 .C15 MRR Ref Desk Partial set

Congressional quarterly almanac. v.
1- Jan./Mar. 1945- Washington.
328.73 47-41081
   JK1 .C66 Sci RR Latest edition /
   MRR Alc Full set

UNITED STATES--POLITICS AND GOVERNMENT--
PERIODICALS--BIBLIOGRAPHY.
Muller, Robert H. From radical left
to extreme right; 2d ed. rev. and
enl. Ann Arbor, Campus Publishers
[c1970- v. 79-126558
   Z7165.U5 M82 MRR Ref Desk.

UNITED STATES--POLITICS AND GOVERNMENT--PERIODICALS--INDEXES.
Smith, Dwight La Vern, The American political process: selected abstracts of periodical literature, 1954-1971. Santa Barbara, Calif., ABC-CLIO [1972] xvi, 630 p. 016.329/00973 72-77549
JK2261 .S73 MRR Alc.

UNITED STATES--POLITICS AND GOVERNMENT--SOURCES.
Dixon, Robert Galloway, comp. American government: basic documents and materials, New York, Van Nostrand, 1950. xx, 420 p. 342.73 50-8523
JK11 1950 .D58 MRR Alc.

Ewing, Cortez Arthur Milton, comp. Documentary source book in American government and politics, Boston, New York [etc.] D.C. Heath and company [c1931] xx, 823 p. 342.738 31-24918
JK11 1931 MRR Alc.

Schlesinger, Arthur Meier, History of U.S. political parties. New York, Chelsea House Publishers, 1973. 4 v. (liv, 3544 p.) 329/.02 72-8682
JK2261 .S35 MRR Alc.

UNITED STATES--POLITICS AND GOVERNMENT--SOURCES--BIBLIOGRAPHY.
United States. Library of Congress. A guide to the microfilm collection of early state records, [Washington] Library of Congress, Photoduplication Service, 1950. 1 v. (various pagings) 016.01573 50-62956
Z663.96 .G8 MRR Alc.

United States. National Archives. Preliminary inventory of the records of the United States House of Representatives, 1789-1946 (Record group 233) Washington, 1959. 2 v. a 59-9361
CD3026 .A32 no. 113 MRR Alc.

UNITED STATES--POLITICS AND GOVERNMENT--YEARBOOKS.
The Book of the States. v. 1- 1935- Lexington, Ky. [etc.], Council of State Governments. 353.9 35-11433
JK2403 .B6 MRR Alc Latest edition / MRR Ref Desk Latest edition

UNITED STATES--POPULATION.
Dublin, Louis Israel, Factbook on man, 2d ed. New York, Macmillan [1965] xiv, 465 p. 312 65-16561
HB3505 .D78 1965 MRR Alc.

Kahn, Ely Jacques, The American people; New York, Weybright and Talley [c1974] viii, 340 p. [$8.95] 301.32/8/73 73-84073
HB3505 .K28 MRR Alc.

Kuznets, Simon Smith, ed. Population redistribution and economic growth: Philadelphia, American Philosophical Society, 1957-64. 3 v. 312.8 301.32* 57-10071
HB1965 .K8 MRR Alc.

Lord, Clifford Lee, Historical atlas of the United States, Rev. ed. New York, Holt [1953] xv, 238 p. 53-10208
G1201.S1 L6 1953 MRR Ref Desk.

Taeuber, Irene Barnes, People of the United States in the 20th century [Washington] U.S. Bureau of the Census; [for sale by the Supt. of Docs., U.S. Govt. Print. Off.] 1971 [i.e. 1972] xxxvii, 1046 p. [$5.75] 301.32/9/73 72-609904
HB3505 .T32 MRR Alc.

Taeuber, Irene Barnes, Population trends in the United States, 1900 to 1960 [Washington] U.S. Dept. of Commerce, Bureau of the Census; [for sale by the Superintendent of Documents, U.S. Govt. Print. Office, 1965] iv, 416 p. a 64-7759
HA205 .T3 MRR Alc.

United States. Bureau of the Census. 1970 census of population. Washington; For sale by the Supt. of Docs., U.S. Govt. Print. Off., 1972- 2 v. in 312/.0973 72-600036
HA201 1970 .A568 MRR Alc.

United States. Bureau of the Census. A century of population growth, Baltimore, Genealogical Pub. Co., 1967. x, 303 p. 312/.0973 67-25405
HA195 .A5 1967 MRR Alc.

United States. Bureau of the Census. Negro population 1790-1915. Washington, Govt. print. off., 1918. 844 p. incl. maps, tables, diagrs. 18-26864
E185 .U56 MRR Alc.

United States. Division of Vital Statistics. Vital statistics of the United States. 1937- [Washington, U.S. Govt. Print. Off.] 40-26272
HA203 .A22 MRR Alc Latest edition

United States. National Archives. Federal population censuses 1790-1890: a price list of microfilm copies of the schedules. Washington, 1969. ix, 186 p. 317.3 70-605086
HA37 .U547 1969 MRR Alc.

Wattenberg, Ben J. This U.S.A.: [1st ed.] Garden City, N.Y., Doubleday, 1965. viii, 520 p. 317.3 65-19858
HA215 .W3 MRR Alc.

UNITED STATES--POPULATION--BIBLIOGRAPHY.
United States. Library of Congress. Census Library Project. Catalog of United States census publications, 1790-1945, Washington, U.S. Govt.Print. Off., 1950. x, 320 p. 016.312 50-60600
Z7554.U5 U62 MRR Alc.

United States. Library of Congress. Census Library Project. State censuses; an annotated bibliography Washington, U.S. Govt. Print. Off., 1948. v, 73 p. 016.312 48-46440
Z7554.U5 U63 1948 MRR Alc.

United States. National Archives. Population schedules, 1800-1870; Washington, 1951. v, 217 p. 016.312 a 51-9540
CD3039 .A53 MRR Alc.

UNITED STATES--POPULATION--STATISTICS.
Greene, Evarts Boutell, American population before the federal census of 1790, New York, Columbia university press, 1932. xxii p., 2 l., [3]-228 p., 1 l. 312.0973 33-718
HB3505 .G7 MRR Alc.

Grove, Robert D. Vital statistics rates in the United States, 1940-1960, Washington, U.S. National Center for Health Statistics; for sale by the Supt. of Docs., U.S. Govt. Print. Off., 1968. ix, 881 p. [$5.25] 312/.0973 75-601797
HA211 .G75 MRR Alc.

United States. Bureau of the Census. 1970 census of population and housing. [Washington; For sale by the Supt. of Docs., U.S. Govt. Print. Off.] 1971- v. [$1.00 (v. 5) varies] 312/.9/0973 73-186611
HA201 1970 .A542 MRR Alc.

United States. Bureau of the Census. Vital statistics rates in the United States, 1900-1940, Washington, U.S. Govt. Print. Off., 1943. vii, 1051 p. 312 43-50838
HA201 1940 .A57 MRR Alc.

Urban Growth Patterns Research Group. Demographic profiles of the United States. Oak Ridge, Tenn., Oak Ridge National Laboratory, 1971-72. 8 v. [$3.00 (v. 1) varies] 312/.0973 76-616120
HA215 .U73 MRR Alc.

UNITED STATES--PROCLAMATIONS.
United States. Federal register. v. 1- March 14, 1936- [Washington, U.S. Govt. Print. off.] 353.005 36-26246
J1 .A2 MRR Alc (Dk 33) Full set

United States. Laws, statutes, etc. United States statutes at large, containing the laws and concurrent resolutions ... and reorganization plan, amendment to the Constitution, and proclamations. v. 1- 1789/1845- Washington, U.S. Govt. Print. Off. 07-35353
LAW MRR Alc (Dk 33) Full set

United States. President, 1929-1933 (Hoover) Herbert Hoover: Washington : U.S. Govt. Print. Off., 1974. 2 v. (iii, 1566 p.) : [$24.55] 353.03/5 74-602466
J82 .D5 1974 MRR Alc.

UNITED STATES--PUBLIC LANDS--HISTORY--SOURCES--INDEXES.
McMullin, Phillip W. Grassroots of America; Salt Lake City, Gendex Corp., 1972. xxvii, 489 p. 333.1/0973 71-186588
J33 .M3 MRR Alc.

UNITED STATES--PUBLIC WORKS.
United States. Work projects administration. Index of research projects ... [Washington, U.S. Govt. print. off., 1938-39. 3 v. 351.80973 38-26877
HD3881 .A56 1938 MRR Alc.

UNITED STATES--PUBLIC WORKS--INDEXES.
United States. Army. Corps of engineers. Analytical and topical index to the reports of the chief of engineers and officers of the Corps of engineers, United States Army,1866-1900 ... Washington, Govt. print. off., 1903. 3 v. 03-27940
TC23 .A3 1866-1900 MRR Alc.

UNITED STATES--RACE QUESTION.
Gossett, Thomas F. Race; the history of an idea in America. Dallas, Southern Methodist University Press, 1963. ix, 512 p. 63-21187
E184.A1 G6 MRR Alc.

Simpson, George Eaton, Racial and cultural minorities; 4th ed. New York, Harper & Row [1972] viii, 775 p. 301.45/1/042 72-76373
HT1521 .S53 1972 MRR Alc.

UNITED STATES--RACE QUESTION--BIBLIOGRAPHY.
Kinton, Jack F. American ethnic groups and the revival of cultural pluralism; 4th ed. [Aurora, Ill., Social Science & Sociological Resources] 1974. 206 p. 016.9173/06 74-171031
Z1361.E4 K55 1974 MRR Alc.

UNITED STATES--RACE QUESTION--COLLECTIONS.
Brown, Francis James, ed. One America; 3d ed. New York, Prentice-Hall, 1952. xvi, 764 p. 325.73 52-1682
E184.A1 B87 1952 MRR Alc.

UNITED STATES--REGISTERS.
Bidwell, Robin Leonard. The major powers and western Europe, 1900-1971; [London] F. Cass, [1973] xi, 297 p. 354/.4/002 72-82958
JN12 .B5 MRR Ref Desk.

Biographical directory of the United States executive branch, 1774-1971. Westport, Conn., Greenwood Pub. Co. [1971] x, 491 p. 973/.099 78-133495
E176 .B575 MRR Biog.

Clements, John. Taylor's encyclopedia of Government officials, Federal and State. v. 1- 1967/68- Dallas, Political Research, inc. 67-22269
JK6 .T36 Sci RR Latest edition / MRR Alc Latest edition

Federal telephone directory. fall 1973- Washington, Consolidated Directories, inc. [$60.00] 353.002/025 73-88404
JK6 .F43 MRR Ref Desk Latest edition / Sci RR Latest edition

Lanman, Charles, Biographical annals of the civil government of the United States. 2d ed. Rev., enl. and completed to date, New York, J. M. Morrison, 1887. iv, [2], 568, cviii p. 05-249
E176 .L292 MRR Biog.

Mosher, Robert Brent, comp. Executive register of the United States, 1789-1902; Baltimore, Md., The Friedenwald company [1903] 1 p. l., x, 351 p. 03-10230
JK661 1902 MRR Alc.

Notable names in American history: 3d ed. of White's conspectus of American biography. [Clifton, N.J.] J. T. White, 1973. 725 p. 920/.073 73-6885
E176 .N89 1973 MRR Biog.

Poore, Benjamin Perley, The political register and congressional directory: Boston, Houghton, Osgood and company, 1878. vi p., 1 l., 716 p. 05-273
E176 .P82 MRR Alc.

Rosenbloom, David L. The political marketplace. [New York] Quadrangle Books [1972] xix, 948 p. [$25.00] 329/.0025/73 72-77926
JK2283 .R64 MRR Ref Desk.

United States. Civil Service Commission. Official register of the United States. 1907-59. Washington, U.S. Govt. Print. Off. 08-35096
JK5 MRR Ref Desk Latest edition

United States. Dept. of state. The territorial papers of the United States. Washington, U.S. Govt. print. off., 1934. xv, 37 p. 873.082 35-26190
E173 .U57 MRR Alc.

United States. Dept. of State. Historical Office. United States Chiefs of Mission, 1778-1973 (complete to 31 March 1973) [Washington] Dept. of State; [for sale by the Supt. of Docs., U.S. Govt. Print. Off.] 1973. v, 229 p. [$2.70] 327/.2/0973 73-602788
JX1706.A59 U54 1973 MRR Ref Desk.

UNITED STATES--REGISTERS. (Cont.)
United States Government manual.
1973/74- [Washington] Office of the
Federal Register; [For sale by the
Supt. of Docs., U.S. Govt. Print.
Off.] [$4.00]   353   73-646537
JK421 .A3   MRR Ref Desk Latest
edition / MRR Ref Desk Latest
edition

Webster's biographical dictionary.
Springfield, Mass., G. & C. Merriam
Co. [1974] xxxvi, 1697 p. [$12.95]
920/.02   73-14908
CT103 .W4 1974 MRR Ref Desk.

UNITED STATES--REGISTERS--PERIODICALS.
National roster of Black elected
officials. Washington, Joint Center
for Political Studies. [$6.00 (per
copy)]   353.002   73-83185
JK1924 .N38 MRR Ref Desk Latest
edition

UNITED STATES--RELATIONS (GENERAL) WITH
FOREIGN COUNTRIES.
Chamber of Commerce of the United
States of America. Foreign Commerce
Dept.   Guide to foreign information
sources. [Rev. Washington] Chamber
of Commerce of the United States
[1960] 26 p.   327.73 61-25832
E744 .C46 1960 MRR Alc.

International Visitors Service
Council. Organizations serving
international visitors in the
National Capital area. [4th ed.]
Washington [1973] vii p., 151 l.,
155-191 p.   917.53/04/4025 72-96925

F191 .I57 1973 MRR Alc.

UNITED STATES--RELATIONS (GENERAL) WITH
LATIN AMERICA.
Sable, Martin Howard. Master
directory for Latin America, Los
Angeles, Latin American Center,
University of California, 1965. xxi,
438 p.   918.03306 66-25
F1406.5 .S3 MRR Alc.

UNITED STATES--RELATIONS (GENERAL) WITH
MEXICO.
Cline, Howard Francis. The United
States and Mexico. Rev. ed., enl.
New York, Atheneum, 1963. 484 p.
63-24587
F1226 .C6 1963 MRR Alc.

UNITED STATES--RELATIONS (GENERAL) WITH
SWITZERLAND--BIBLIOGRAPHY.
Bern. Schweizerische
Landesbibliothek. Die Schweiz und
die Vereinigten Staaten von Amerika;
Bern, 1964. 58 p.   64-6083
Z1361.R4 B45 MRR Alc.

UNITED STATES--RELIGION.
Clark, Elmer Talmage. The small
sects in America. Rev. ed. New
York, Abingdon-Cokesbury Press [1949]
256 p.   280.973 49-10200
BR516 .C57 1949 MRR Alc.

Gaustad, Edwin Scott. Historical
atlas of religion in America. [1st
ed.] New York, Harper & Row, [1962]
179 p.   209.73084 map62-51
G1201.E4 G3 1962 MRR Alc Atlas.

Johnson, Douglas W., Churches &
church membership in the United
States: Washington, Glenmary
Research Center [1974] xiv, 237 p.
[$15.00]   280/.0973 73-94224
BR526 .J64 MRR Alc.

Olmstead, Clifton E. History of
religion in the United States.
Englewood Cliffs, N.J., Prentice-
Hall, 1960. 628 p.   209.73 60-
10355
BR515 .O4 MRR Alc.

Parrington, Vernon Louis, Main
currents in American thought; [New
York, Harcourt, Brace and company,
1927-30] 3 v.   27-8440
PS88 .P3 MRR Alc.

Smith, James Ward, ed. Religion in
American life. Princeton, N.J.,
Princeton University Press, 1961- v.
in   277.3 61-5383
BR515 .S6 MRR Alc.

Weigle, Luther Allan, American
idealism, New Haven, Yale university
press; [etc., etc.] 1928. 3 p. l.,
356 p.   28-25825
E178.5 .P2 vol. 10 MRR Alc.

UNITED STATES--RELIGION--1945-
Hardon, John A. The Protestant
churches of America Rev. ed. Garden
City, N.Y., Image Books [1969] 439
p. [1.45]   280/.4/0973 69-12858
BR516.5 .H3 1969 MRR Alc.

Mathison, Richard R. Faiths, cults,
and sects of America; [1st ed.]
Indianapolis, Bobbs-Merrill [1960]
384 p.   209.73 60-13589
BR516.5 .M29 MRR Alc.

National Council of the Churches of
Christ in the United States of
America. Bureau of Research and
Survey. Churches and church
membership in the United States; New
York, 1956-58. 80 no.   56-12497
BR526 .N3 MRR Alc.

UNITED STATES--RELIGION--BIBLIOGRAPHY.
Burr, Nelson Rollin, Religion in
American life, New York, Appleton-
Century-Crofts [1971] xix, 171 p.
016.2009/73 70-136219
Z7757.U5 B8 MRR Alc.

UNITED STATES--ROAD MAPS.
Leahy's hotel-motel guide & travel
atlas of the United States, Canada
and Mexico. Chicago, American Hotel
Register Co. 647.94 09-20539
TX907 .L5 MRR Alc Latest edition

Rand, McNally and Company. Road
atlas of the United States, Canada
and Mexico. 1926- Chicago. 629.281
map26-19
G1201.P2 R35 MRR Ref Desk Latest
edition / Sci RR Latest edition

UNITED STATES--SEAL.
United States. Dept. of state. The
history of the seal of the United
States. Washington, D.C., Department
of state, 1909. 72 p.   09-35613
CD5610 .A42 MRR Alc.

UNITED STATES--SOCIAL CONDITIONS.
Cavan, Ruth (Shonle) The American
family. 4th ed. New York, Crowell
[1969] xi, 556 p. 301.42/0973 69-
13254
HQ535 .C33 1969 MRR Alc.

Miller, Marion Mills, ed. Great
debates in American history, [The
national ed.] New York, Current
literature publishing company [c1913]
14 v.   13-23912
E173 .M64 vol. 14 MRR Alc.

UNITED STATES--SOCIAL CONDITIONS--1945-
Gendell, Murray, ed. A sociological
almanac for the United States, 2d
ed. [Totowa, N.J.] Bedminster Press
[c1963] xv, 94 p.   309.173 64-2549
HN57 .G4 1963 MRR Alc.

United States. Dept. of Agriculture.
A place to live. Washington [U.S.
Govt. Print. Off., 1963] xxiii, 854
p.   agr63-468
S21.A35 1963 MRR Alc.

UNITED STATES--SOCIAL CONDITIONS--1960-
Acton, Jay. Mug shots; who's who in
the new earth, New York, World Pub.
[1972] 244 p. [$9.95] 920/.073
77-174672
CT220 .A27 1972 MRR Biog.

The Harris survey yearbook of public
opinion. 1970- New York, Louis
Harris and Associates.
301.15/43/309173092 73-184049
HN90.P8 H35 MRR Alc Full set

Jacobs, Paul, The new radicals; New
York, Random House [1966] 333 p.
320.973 66-18328
E839.5 .J3 MRR Alc.

O'Neill, William L. Coming apart;
Chicago, Quadrangle Books, 1971. ix,
442, xxvi p. [$12.50] 973.921 79-
152098
E389 .O5 1971 MRR Alc.

Peirce, Neal R. The megastates of
America; [1st ed.] New York, Norton
[1972] 745 p. [$12.95]
917.3/03/92 70-163375
E839.5 .P35 MRR Alc.

UNITED STATES--SOCIAL CONDITIONS--1960-
--ADDRESSES, ESSAYS, LECTURES.
Teodori, Massimo, comp. The new
left: Indianapolis, Bobbs-Merrill
[1969] xiv, 501 p. [9.95]
301.15/3/0973 70-81291
HN59 .T46 MRR Alc.

UNITED STATES--SOCIAL CONDITIONS--1960-
--BIBLIOGRAPHY.
Index to the contemporary scene. v.
1- 1973- Detroit, Gale Research
Co. [$14.00]   016.3 73-645955
Z7161 .I52 MRR Alc Full set

Miller, Albert Jay. Confrontation,
conflict, and dissent: Metuchen,
N.J., Scarecrow Press, 1972. 567 p.
016.3091/73/092 78-189440
Z7165.U5 M53 MRR Alc.

Tompkins, Dorothy Louise (Campbell)
Culver. Poverty in the United States
during the sixties; [Berkeley]
Institute of Governmental Studies,
University of California, 1970. ix,
542 p. [$10.00] 016.3625/0973 74-
632810
Z7165.U5 T62 MRR Alc.

United States. National Clearinghouse
for Mental Health Information.
Bibliography on the urban crisis;
Chevy Chase, Md., National Institute
of Mental Health [1968] iv, 158 p.
016.3091/73 77-600665
Z7164.S66 U57 MRR Alc.

UNITED STATES--SOCIAL CONDITIONS--
BIBLIOGRAPHY.
Bremner, Robert Hamlett, American
social history since 1860. New York,
Appleton-Century-Crofts [1971] xiv,
126 p.   016.917/03 70-146848
Z1361.C6 B7 MRR Alc.

UNITED STATES--SOCIAL CONDITIONS--
SOCIETIES, ETC.
Youth info digest. 1972-
[Washington] Washington Workshops
Press.   309/.025/73 74-185964
HN55 .Y68 MRR Alc Latest edition

UNITED STATES--SOCIAL LIFE AND CUSTOMS.
Album of American history. New York,
Scribner [1969- v.   973.022/2
74-91746
E178.5 .A482 MRR Alc.

Ross, Ishbel, Taste in America; New
York, Crowell [1967] 343 p.
390/.0973 67-23677
E169.1 .R7773 MRR Alc.

UNITED STATES--SOCIAL LIFE AND CUSTOMS--
COLONIAL PERIOD, CA. 1600-1775.
Davidson, Marshall B. The American
heritage history of colonial
antiques, [New York] American
Heritage Pub. Co.; book trade
distribution by Simon and Schuster
[1967] 384 p.   709/.73 67-23439
NK806 .D38 MRR Alc.

Miller, John Chester, ed. The
colonial image: New York, G.
Braziller, 1962. 500 p.   973.2 62-
9930
E187.O7 M5 MRR Alc.

Phipps, Frances, Colonial kitchens,
their furnishings, and their gardens,
New York, Hawthorn Books [1972]
xxii, 346 p. [$12.95] 643/.3/0974
78-158021
TX653 .P48 1972 MRR Alc.

Wright, Louis Booker, The cultural
life of the American Colonies, 1607-
1763. [1st ed.] New York, Harper
[1957] xiv, 292 p.   973.2 57-250
E162 .W89 MRR Alc.

UNITED STATES--SOCIAL LIFE AND CUSTOMS--
COLONIAL PERIOD, CA. 1600-1775--
BIBLIOGRAPHY.
Leonard, Eugenie (Andruss) The
American woman in Colonial and
Revolutionary times, 1565-1800;
Philadelphia, University of
Pennsylvania Press [1962] 169 p.
016.3090973 61-6949
Z7964.U49 L4 MRR Alc.

UNITED STATES--SOCIAL LIFE AND CUSTOMS--
1783-1865.
Davidson, Marshall B. The American
heritage history of American antiques
from the Revolution to the Civil War,
[New York] American Heritage Pub.
Co.; Distribution by Simon and
Schuster [1968] 416 p. [17.50]
709/.73 68-28301
NK806 .D37 MRR Alc.

UNITED STATES--SOCIAL LIFE AND CUSTOMS--
19TH CENTURY--EXHIBITIONS.
United States. Library of Congress.
Exhibits Office. An American
sampler: Washington, Library of
Congress, 1974. [32] p.   917.3/03
74-16302
Z663.15 .A65 MRR Alc.

UNITED STATES--SOCIAL LIFE AND CUSTOMS--
1865-1918.
Davidson, Marshall B. The American
heritage history of antiques from the
Civil War to World War I, [New York]
American Heritage Pub. Co. [1969]
415 p. [17.50] 745.1/0973 79-
80756
NK806 .D35 MRR Alc.

UNITED STATES--SOCIAL LIFE AND CUSTOMS--
DICTIONARIES.
Phipps, Frances, The collector's
complete dictionary of American
antiques. [1st ed.] Garden City,
N.Y., Doubleday, 1974. xv, 640 p.
[$25.00] 709/.73 72-97257
NK805 .P52 MRR Alc.

UNITED STATES--SOCIAL POLICY.
Nixon, Richard Milhous. Nixon: the
fourth year of his Presidency.
Washington, Congressional Quarterly
[c1973] 46, 146 p. [$4.00]
320.9/73/0924 72-94077
E855 .N494 MRR Alc.

UNITED STATES--SOCIAL REGISTERS.
National social directory. New York.
54-20905
E154.7 .L47 MRR Biog Latest
edition

UNITED STATES--SOCIAL REGISTERS. (Cont.)
Social register locater. v. 1-
1907- New York, Social Register
Association. 07-24776
  E154.7 .A7 MRR Alc Latest edition

UNITED STATES--STATISTICAL SERVICES.
Howell, James M. Dictionary of
economic and statistical terms
Washington] U.S. Dept. of Commerce;
[for sale by the Supt. of Docs., U.S.
Govt. Print. Off., 1969. 73 p.
[1.25] 330/.01/4 70-605347
  HB61 .H68 MRR Alc

United States. Bureau of Labor
Statistics. Guide to area employment
statistics; [Washington] 1960. iii,
227 p. l 60-70
  HD8064 .A52 1960b MRR Alc.

United States. Bureau of the Budget.
Office of Statistical Standards.
Statistical services of the United
States Government. [Washington] 59-
61420
  HA37 .U16 MRR Ref Desk Latest
  edition

United States. Bureau of the Census.
Directory of Federal statistics for
states; Washington, For sale by the
Supt. of Docs, U.S. Govt. Print.
Off., 1967] viii, 372 p. 317.3 a
67-7451
  HA37 .U52 1967 MRR Ref Desk.

United States. Bureau of the Census.
Directory of non-Federal statistics
for State and local areas;
[Washington] For sale by the Supt. of
Docs., U.S. Govt. Print. Off., 1970]
viii, 678 p. [6.25] 317.3 76-
605082
  HA37 .U52 1970 MRR Ref Desk.

United States. Bureau of the Census.
Population and housing inquiries in
U.S. decennial censuses, 1790-1970.
[Washington] U.S. Dept. of Commerce,
Social and Economic Statistics
Administration, Bureau of the Census
[1973] 179 p. [$2.50] 353.008/1
73-600280
  HA37 .U52 1973 MRR Alc.

UNITED STATES--STATISTICS.
Aerospace facts and figures. [1st]-
ed.; 1945- Fallbrook, Calif. [etc.]
Aero Publishers [etc.] 629.13058 46-
25007
  TL501 .A818 Sci RR Latest edition
  / MRR Alc Latest edition

American Gas Association. Dept. of
Statistics. Gas facts. 1967-
Arlington, Va. [etc.]
338.4/7/6657097 72-622849
  TP722 .A59 MRR Alc Latest edition

American Iron and Steel Institute,
New York. Annual Statistical report.
1912- Washington [etc.] 14-3046
  HD9514 .A5 MRR Alc Latest edition

American Library Association. Library
Administration Division. Library
statistics of colleges and
universities, 1965-66] Chicago,
American Library Association, 1967.
viii, 234 p. 027.7/021/2 67-6695
  Z675.U5 A585 MRR Alc.

American Petroleum Institute.
Petroleum facts and figures. [1st]-
ed.; [1928]- New York. 338.2 41-
10749
  HD9561 .A7 MRR Alc Latest edition

Ashby, Lowell De Witt. Growth
patterns in employment by county,
1940-1950 and 1950-1960,
[Washington] U.S. Dept. of Commerce,
Office of Business Economics,
Regional Economics Division; [for
sale by the Superintendent of
Documents, U.S. Govt. Print. Off.,
1965-66] 8 v. 65-61774
  HD5723 .A63 MRR Alc.

Associated Press. The official
Associated Press almanac. 1973- New
York, Almanac Pub. Co. 051 73-
643500
  AY67.N5 T55 MRR Ref Desk Latest
  edition

Automobile facts and figures. 1920-
Detroit, Mich. [etc.] 338.4 36-
19542
  HD9710.U5 A8 MRR Alc Latest
  edition

The Book of the States. v. 1- 1935-
Lexington, Ky. [etc.], Council of
State Governments. 353.9 35-11433
  JK2403 .B6 MRR Alc Latest edition
  / MRR Ref Desk Latest edition

Brewers' almanac. [Washington, etc.]
United States Brewers' Association.
338.476633 45-51432
  Publication began in 1940?
  HD9397.U5 B7 MRR Alc Latest
  edition

Burnham, Walter Dean. Presidential
ballots, 1836-1892. Baltimore, Johns
Hopkins Press [1955] xix, 956 p.
324.73 55-8428
  JK524 .B8 MRR Alc.

The Cadillac modern encyclopedia.
[1st ed.] New York, Cadillac Pub.
Co.; distributed by Derbibooks,
Secaucus, N.J. [1973] xiv, 1954 p.
[$24.95] 031 73-81377
  AG5 .C25 MRR Ref Desk.

Census of the electronic market in
the U.S.A.; Philadelphia, Electronic
engineer, a Chilton Publication
[1968] c1967. 1 v. (unpaged)
338.4/7/6213810973 67-31315
  HD9696.A1 C4 MRR Alc.

Center for Disease Control. Abortion
surveillance. Atlanta. 301 74-
644021
  HQ767.5.U5 C45a MRR Alc Latest
  edition

Commodity year book. 1st- ed.;
1939- New York, Commodity Research
Bureau, inc. 338.0973 39-11418
  HF1041 .C56 MRR Alc Latest edition

Congressional Quarterly, inc. Guide
to the Congress of the United States;
[1st ed.] Washington, Congressional
Quarterly Service [1971] xxxi, 639,
323a, 21b p. [$35.00] 328.73 78-
167743
  JK1021 .C56 MRR Ref Desk.

Congressional Quarterly Service,
Washington, D.C. CQ census analysis:
congressional districts of the United
States: Washington [1964] 1783-1894
p. 312.9 64-7968
  HA217 .C62 MRR Ref Desk.

Congressional Quarterly Service,
Washington, D.C. Federal economic
policy. 4th ed. Washington, 1969.
140 p. [2.95] 338.973 76-79759
  HC106.5 .C67345 1969 MRR Alc.

Cox, Edwin Burk, Basic tables in
business and economics, New York,
McGraw-Hill [1967] xiv, 399 p.
511/.8 66-19284
  HF5699 .C892 MRR Alc.

Deldycke, Tilo. La population active
et sa structure. Bruxelles, Centre
d'economie politique (de l')
Universite libre de Bruxelles,
(1968) viii, 236 p. [360.00]
331.1/12/0212 70-395436
  HD4826 .D34 MRR Alc.

Digest of educational statistics.
1962- ed. [Washington] U.S. Dept.
of Health, Education, and Welfare,
Office of Education; [for sale by the
Superintendent of Documents, U.S.
Govt. Print. Off.] hew62-154
  L111 .A6 MRR Alc Latest edition

Dodd, Donald B. Historical
statistics of the South, 1790-1970;
University, University of Alabama
Press [1973] vi, 85 p. 317.5 73-
1575
  HA218 .D63 MRR Ref Desk.

Douglas, Paul Howard, Real wages in
the United States, 1890-1926,
Boston, New York, Houghton Mifflin
company, 1930. xxviii, 682 p.
331.2973 30-12884
  HD4975 .D6 MRR Alc.

Ebasco Services Incorporated.
Business and economic charts.
Chicago. 59-44534
  HD9685.U7 E3 MRR Alc Latest
  edition

The Economic almanac; 1940- New
York [etc.], Macmillan Co. [etc.]
330.58 40-30704
  HC101 .E38 MRR Ref Desk Latest
  edition

Editor & publisher. Market guide.
v. [1] 1924- New York. 658.8 45-
44873
  HF5905 .E38 MRR Ref Desk Latest
  edition

Employee benefits fact book. [New
York] 331.2/52 76-118375
  HD7125 .E57 MRR Alc Latest edition

The Energy index. [New York,
Environment Information Center,
Energy Reference Dept.] [$50.00]
333.7 73-89098
  HD9502.U5 E525 MRR Alc Full set /
  Sci RR Full set

Evans, George Heberton. Business
incorporations in the United States,
1800-1943. [New York] National
Bureau of Economic Research [1948]
viii, 184 p. 338.7 48-10514
  HD2785 .E85 MRR Alc.

Ferriss, Abbott Lamoyne, Indicators
of trends in the status of American
women New York, Russell Sage
Foundation, 1971. xx, 451 p.
301.41/2/0973 76-153996
  HQ1420 .F4 MRR Alc.

Firestone, John Mitchell, Federal
receipts and expenditures during
business cycles, 1879-1958.
Princeton [N.J.] Princeton University
Press, 1960. xvi, 176 p. 336.73
60-8391
  HJ2051 .F48 MRR Alc.

Folger, John K. Education of the
American population, [Washington]
U.S. Dept. of Commerce, Bureau of the
Census; [for sale by the Supt. of
Docs., U.S. Govt. Print. Off., 1967]
ix, 280 p. [2.25] 370/.973 a 66-
7677
  LA205 .F6 MRR Alc.

Food and Agriculture Organization of
the United Nations. Trade yearbook.
v. 12- 1958- Rome. 338.14058 59-
3598
  HD9000.4 .F58 Sci RR Partial set /
  MRR Alc Latest edition

Franke, David. America's 50 safest
cities. New Rochelle, N.Y.,
Arlington House [1974] 301 p.
[$8.95] 301.36/3/0973 73-21890
  HT123 .F72 MRR Alc.

Friedman, Milton, Monetary
statistics of the United States:
estimates, sources, methods New
York, National Bureau of Economic
Research, 1970. xx, 629 p. [15.00]
332.4/9/73 78-85410
  HG538 .F863 MRR Alc.

Gendell, Murray, ed. A sociological
almanac for the United States, 2d
ed. [Totowa, N.J.] Bedminster Press
[c1963] xv, 94 p. 309.173 64-2549
  HN57 .G4 1963 MRR Alc.

Georgetown Economic Data Library.
Compendium of manufacturing
production statistics for the United
States, 1947-1965. Washington [1967]
xxii, 313 p. 338.4/0973 67-9455
  HD9724 .G4 MRR Alc.

Gertler, Diane (Bochner) Directory:
public elementary and secondary
schools in large school districts
with enrollment and instructional
staff, by race: fall 1967,
[Washington] U.S. National Center for
Educational Statistics; [for sale by
the Supt. of Docs., U.S. Govt. Print.
Off., 1969] v, 840 p. [7.25]
371/.01/02573 72-604076
  L901 .G38 MRR Alc.

Giving USA; a compilation of facts
related to American philanthropy.
New York, American Association of
Fund-Raising Counsel. 361.705873 59-
1874
  HV89 .G5 MRR Ref Desk Latest
  edition

Glenn, Norval D., comp. Blacks in
the United States, San Francisco,
Chandler Pub. Co.; distributed by
Science Research Associates, Chicago
[1969] xiii, 621 p. 301.451/96/073
69-15429
  E185.615 .G55 MRR Alc.

Goeldner, Charles R. Travel trends
in the United States and Canada,
Boulder, Business Research Division,
University of Colorado [1973] vi,
175 l. 338.4/7/9170453 73-166149
  G155.U6 G6 1973 MRR Alc.

Goldenthal, Allan B. The handbook of
U.S. markets and industrial growth
areas. [New York] Regents Pub. Co.
[1969- v. 330.973 71-85525
  HC106.6 .G64 MRR Alc.

Governmental Affairs Institute,
Washington, D.C. Elections Research
Center. America at the polls;
Pittsburgh, University of Pittsburgh
Press, 1965. 521 p. 324.202173 65-
27801
  JK524 .G6 MRR Alc.

Greene, Evarts Boutell, American
population before the federal census
of 1790, New York, Columbia
university press, 1932. xxii p., 2
l., [3]-228 p., 1 l. 312.0973 33-
718
  HB3505 .G7 MRR Alc.

Harris, Seymour Edwin, A statistical
portrait of higher education, New
York, McGraw-Hill [1972] xliv, 978
p. 378.73 72-38334
  LA227.3 .H25 MRR Alc.

UNITED STATES--STATISTICS. (Cont.)
Hauser, Philip Morris, ed.
Government statistics for business
use, 2d ed. New York, Wiley [1956]
xx, 440 p.   311.3973 310.61* 56-
5054
    HA37.U55 H3 1956 MRR Alc.

Henson, Mary F. Trends in the income
of families and persons in the United
States, 1947-1964. [Washington] U.S.
Dept. of Commerce, Bureau of the
Census [1967] v1, 294 p.
339.2/1/0973 a 67-7508
    HC110.I5 H4 MRR Alc.

Institute of Scrap Iron and Steel.
Yearbook. [1st-   ed.; 1939-
Washington [etc.] 338.47672 40-4188

    TS200 .I64 Sci RR Latest edition /
    MRR Alc Latest edition

Inter-University Seminar on Armed
Forces and Society. Handbook of
military institutions. Beverly
Hills, Calif., Sage Publications
[1971] 607 p.   301.5/98 78-127989

    U102 .I65 MRR Alc.

International Labor Office. Year
book of labour statistics. [1st]-
1935/36- Geneva. 1 36-130
    HD4826 .I63 MRR Alc Latest edition

Jacobson, Paul Harold, American
marriage and divorce. New York,
Rinehart [1959] xviii, 188 p.
301.42 59-9748
    HQ535 .J3 MRR Alc.

Jameson, John Franklin, Dictionary
of United States history; Rev. ed.
Detroit, Gale Research Co., 1971.
xi, 874 p.   973/.03 68-30658
    E174 .J32 MRR Alc.

Johnson, Douglas W., Churches &
church membership in the United
States: Washington, Glenmary
Research Center [1974] xiv, 237 p.
[$15.00]   280/.0973 73-94224
    BR526 .J64 MRR Alc.

Keyfitz, Nathan, Population: facts
and methods of demography San
Francisco, W. H. Freeman [1971] x,
613 p. [$13.50] 301.3/2/072 70-
141154
    HB885 .K43 MRR Alc.

Kuznets, Simon Smith, ed. Population
redistribution and economic growth:
Philadelphia, American Philosophical
Society, 1957-64. 3 v.   312.8
301.32* 57-10071
    HB1965 .K8 MRR Alc.

Labor relations yearbook. 1965-
Washington, Bureau of National
Affairs. 331.1973 66-19726
    HD8059 .L33 MRR Alc Latest edition

Lechter, Max. U.S. exports and
imports classified by OBE end-use
commodity categories, 1923-1968;
[Washington] U.S. Office of Business
Economics, Balance of Payments
Division; [for sale by the Supt. of
Docs., U.S. Govt. Print. Off.] 1970
[i.e. 1971] xxii, 411 p. [$4.00]
382.4/0973 75-611180
    HF3001 .L43 MRR Alc.

Lipsey, Robert E. Source book of
statistics relating to construction
New York, National Bureau of Economic
Research; distributed by Columbia
University Press, New York, 1966. x,
307 p.   338.476900973 66-22747
    HD9715.A2 L5 MRR Alc.

The Liquor handbook. New York [etc.]
Gavin-Jobson Associates, inc. [etc.]
338.476635 59-16930
    HD9352 .L5 MRR Alc Latest edition

Livermore, Thomas Leonard, Numbers &
losses in the Civil War in America,
1861-65. Bloomington, Indiana
University Press, 1957. 150 p.
973.74 57-10726
    E491 .L77 1957 MRR Alc.

Long, Clarence Dickinson, Wages and
earnings in the United States, 1860-
1890. Princeton, Princeton
University Press, 1960. xvii, 169 p.
331.2973 60-5756
    HD4975 .L57 MRR Alc.

Lunden, Walter Albin, Facts on
crimes and criminals. Ames, Iowa,
Art Press [1961] iii, 294 p. 62-
1421
    HV6208 .L79 MRR Alc.

McGraw-Hill Publishing Company, inc.
America's manufacturing plants; New
York, [1960] 118 p.   338.476 60-
3420
    HD9724 .M2 MRR Alc.

Military market facts. [Washington]
Army Times Pub. Co. 65-5288
    UC263 .M46 MRR Alc Latest edition

Minerals yearbook. 1932/33-
[Washington, U.S. Govt. Print. Off.]
33-26551
    TN23 .U612 MRR Alc Latest edition
    / Sci RR Partial set

Mueller, Bernard. A statistical
handbook of the North Atlantic area.
New York, Twentieth Century Fund,
1965. 239 p.   301.91821 65-26294
    HA1107 .M8 MRR Alc.

The Municipal year book; 1934-
Washington, D.C. [etc.] International
city manager's association. 34-27121

    JS344.C5 A24 MRR Ref Desk Latest
    edition / MRR Alc Latest edition

National Council of the Churches of
Christ in the United States of
America. Bureau of Research and
Survey. Churches and church
membership in the United States; New
York, 1956-58. 80 no.   56-12497
    BR526 .N3 MRR Alc.

National Industrial Conference Board.
Chartbook of weekly business
indicators. New York. 330.973 58-
24653
    HC106.5 .A2845 MRR Alc Latest
    edition

National Industrial Conference Board.
Graphic guide to consumer markets.
1960- New York. 658.83973 61-4523

    HC101 .N3183 MRR Alc Latest
    edition

Nelson Associates, inc. Public
library systems in the United States;
Chicago, American Library
Association, 1969. xvi, 368 p.
027.4/73 54-54708
    Z731 .N4 MRR Alc.

Organization for Economic Cooperation
and Development. Agricultural and
food statistics, 1952-1963. Paris,
1965. 148 p.   66-33109
    HD1421 .O67 MRR Alc.

Organization for Economic Cooperation
and Development. Basic statistics of
energy, 1950-1964. Paris, O.E.C.D.
[London, H.M.S.O.] 1966. 363 p.
[24/-]   333.8 66-66031
    HD9555.A4 O7 MRR Alc.

Organization for Economic Cooperation
and Development. Foreign trade.
Commerce extérieur. Series C.
Commodity trade. Commerce par
produits. [Paris] 382/.021/2 72-
626755
    HF91 .O67 Latest edition

Organization for Economic Cooperation
and Development. Industrial
production. [Paris,] Organisation
for Economic Co-operation and
Development, 1968. 308 p. [14.00]
338/.09 76-422848
    HC240 .O693 MRR Alc.

Organization for Economic Cooperation
and Development. National accounts
statistics 1950-1968. [Paris, 1970]
415 p. [$7.50 (U.S.)]   339.3 73-
535302
    HC79.I5 O674 MRR Alc.

Organization for Economic Cooperation
and Development. National accounts
statistics, 1960-1971. [Paris, 1973]
471 p. [$7.50 (U.S.)]   339.3 74-
158206
    HC79.I5 O7 1973 MRR Alc.

Organization for Economic Cooperation
and Development. Statistics of
balance of payments, 1950-1961.
[Paris, 1964] 134 p.   65-50190
    HG3881 .O65 MRR Alc.

Organization for Economic Cooperation
and Development. Statistics of
energy, 1953-1967. Paris, 1969. 265
p.   333.8 71-459605
    HD9540.4 .O73 1969 MRR Alc.

Organization for European Economic
Cooperation. Manpower population.
Paris, 1959. vii, 20 p.   331.112
59-65495
    HD5712 .O73 MRR Alc.

Organization for European Economic
Cooperation. Statistics of sources
and uses of finance, 1948-1958.
Paris [1960] 195 p. (chiefly tables)
332.094 60-51684
    HG186 .A1O74 MRR Alc.

Pennsylvania. Dept. of Public
Instruction. Bureau of Statistics.
Rankings of universities in the
United States. Harrisburg, 1966.
iv, 32 p.   378.73 73-628460
    LA226 .P36 MRR Alc.

Petersen, Svend, A statistical
history of the American presidential
elections. New York, Ungar [1963]
xxiii, 247 p.   324.73 62-21786
    JK1967 .P4 1963 MRR Alc.

Pierson, George Wilson, The
education of American leaders; New
York, Praeger [1969] xxxii, 261 p.
331.7/6 68-17173
    LA226 .P5 MRR Alc.

Planned Parenthood-World Population.
Center for Family Planning Program
Development. Need for subsidized
family planning services: United
States, each State and county, 1968.
[New York, 1969] viii, 255 p.
353.008/4 76-604306
    HQ766.5.U5 P56 MRR Alc.

Predicasts, inc. World food supply &
demand / Cleveland : Predicasts,
inc., 1974. v, 90 leaves ;   338.1/9
74-187853
    HD9000.4 .P73 1974 MRR Alc.

Reeves, Vernon H. Your college
degree; Chicago, Science Research
Associates [c1968] 221 p.
373.1/4/20202 77-12816
    LB2381 .R4 MRR Alc.

Resources for the Future. Energy in
the American economy, 1850-1975;
Baltimore, Johns Hopkins Press [1960]
xxii, 774 p.   338.272 60-14304
    HD9545 .R45 MRR Alc.

Robinson, Edgar Eugene, The
presidential vote, 1896-1932,
Stanford University, Calif., Stanford
university press; London, H. Milford,
Oxford university press [c1934] ix,
403 p.   324.73 34-35830
    JK524 .R6 MRR Alc.

Rowland, Howard S. The New York
times Guide to Federal aid for cities
and towns [New York] Quadrangle
Books [1972, c1971] xxxii, 1243 p.
336.1/85 72-78499
    HJ275 .R64 MRR Ref Desk.

Seybert, Adam, Statistical annals,
New York, B. Franklin [1969] xxvii,
803 p.   317.3 68-56774
    HA215 .S5 1969 MRR Alc.

Shaw, William Howard, Value of
commodity output since 1869. [New
York] National Bureau of Economic
Research, 1947. x, 310 p.   48-566
    HD9724 .S45 MRR Alc.

Showers, Victor, The world in
figures. New York, Wiley [1973]
xii, 585 p.   910/.21/2 73-9
    G109 .S52 MRR Ref Desk.

Spencer, Vivian Eberle, Raw
materials in the United States
economy: 1900-1966. [Washington]
U.S. Bureau of the Census [1970] vi,
142 p. [1.50]   338 70-606828
    HF1052 .S6 1970 MRR Alc.

Spencer, Vivian Eberle, Raw
materials in the United States
economy: 1900-1969. [Washington]
U.S. Bureau of the Census [1972] iv,
66 p. [$1.00]   338 72-602741
    HF1052 .S62 MRR Alc.

Standard education almanac. 1968-
Los Angeles, Academic Media. 370/.5
68-3442
    L101 .U6S7 MRR Ref Desk Latest
    edition

Statistical activities of the
American nations, 1940; Washington,
D.C., Inter American statistical
institute, 1941. xxxi, 842 p.
311.397 41-14318
    HA175 .S75 MRR Alc.

Statistical Office of the European
Communities. Basic statistics of the
community; 8th ed. [Brussels, 1967]
218 p. [unpriced]   314 75-386707

    HA1107 .S7 1967 MRR Alc.

Survey of current business. Business
statistics; 1951- Washington, U.S.
Govt. Print. Off. 330.5 74-643587
    HC101.A13122 MRR Alc Latest
    edition

Surveys of consumers. 1971/72- [Ann
Arbor, Mich., Institute for Social
Research, University of Michigan]
658.8/3973 72-619718
    HC110.S3 A3 MRR Alc Latest edition

Taeuber, Irene Barnes, People of the
United States in the 20th century
[Washington] U.S. Bureau of the
Census; [for sale by the Supt. of
Docs., U.S. Govt. Print. Off.] 1971
[i.e. 1972] xxxvii, 1046 p. [$5.75]
301.32/9/73 72-609904
    HB3505 .T32 MRR Alc.

UNITED STATES--STATISTICS. (Cont.)

Taeuber, Irene Barnes. Population trends in the United States, 1900 to 1960 [Washington] U.S. Dept. of Commerce, Bureau of the Census; [for sale by the Superintendent of Documents, U.S. Govt. Print. Office, 1965] iv, 416 p. a 64-7759
HA205 .T3 MRR Alc.

Tax Foundation, New York. Facts and figures on government finance. 1941- New York. 336.73 44-7109
HJ257 .T25 MRR Alc Latest edition / MRR Ref Desk Latest edition

Trade Relations Council of the United States. General Counsel. Employment, output, and foreign trade of U.S. manufacturing industries. Washington. 338/.0973 73-30363
HC101 .T68 MRR Alc Latest edition

Troy, Leo. Almanac of business and industrial financial ratios. 1972 ed. Englewood Cliffs, N.J.: Prentice-Hall [1971] xxi, 169 p. 338.5/0973 72-181403
HF5681.R25 T68 1971 MRR Alc.

Troy, Leo. Manual of performance ratios for business analysis and profit evaluation. Englewood Cliffs, N.J., Prentice-Hall [1966] xvi, 736 p. 658.1513 66-26237
HF5681.R25 T7 MRR Alc.

Twentieth Century Fund. Employment and wages in the United States. New York, 1953. xxxii, 777 p. 331 53-7170
HD8072 .T8 MRR Alc.

U. S. industrial outlook. Washington, Bureau of Competitive Assessment and Business Policy, for sale by the Supt. of Docs., U.S. Govt. Print. Off. 338/.0973 74-644570
HC106.6 .A23 MRR Alc Latest edition

United Nations. Statistical Office. The growth of world industry, 1938-1961: New York, United Nations, 1963. xvi, 849 p. 338.4083 63-25411
HC59 .U46 MRR Alc.

United Nations. Statistical Office. Yearbook of international trade statistics. 1st- issue; 1950- New York. 382.058 51-8987
JX1977 .A2 MRR Ref Desk Latest edition

United States. Agency for International Development. Office of Statistics and Reports. U.S. economic assistance programs administered by the Agency for International Development and predecessor agencies. April 3, 1948- June 30, 1970. [Washington, 1971] iv, 78 p. 338.91/73 70-613871
HC60.U6 I48 1971 MRR Ref Desk.

United States. Board of Governors of the Federal Reserve System. All-bank statistics, [Washington, 1959] vii, 1229 p. 332.10973 58-60050
HG2493 .A517 MRR Alc.

United States. Bureau of Domestic Commerce. Industry profiles. 1958/68- [Washington, For sale by the Supt. of Docs., U.S. Govt. Print. Off.] 338/.0973 72-626646
HC106.5 .A168 MRR Alc Latest edition

United States. Bureau of Labor Standards. State economic and social indicators: wages, and family income, educational attainment, projected growth in labor force, 1970-80 Washington; For sale by the Supt. of Docs., U.S. Govt. Print. Off.] 1970. vii, 96 p. [$1.00] 330/.973 71-610107
HA211 .A48 MRR Alc.

United States. Bureau of Labor Statistics. Characteristics of agreements covering 1,000 workers or more. Washington, For sale by the Supt. of Docs., U.S. Govt. Print. Off. 331/.0973 s 331.89/0973 74-600823
HD8051 .A62 subser HD6501 MRR Alc Latest edition

United States. Bureau of Labor Statistics. Employment and earnings statistics for the United States. 1909/60- Washington, For sale by the Superintendent of Documents, U.S. Govt. Print. Off. l 64-5
HD5723 .A27 MRR Alc MRR Alc Latest edition

United States. Bureau of Labor Statistics. Handbook of labor statistics. 1924/26- Washington, U.S. Govt. Print. Off. l 27-328
HD8064 .A3 MRR Ref Desk MRR Ref Desk Latest edition

United States. Bureau of labor statistics. History of wages in the United States from colonial times to 1928. Washington, U.S. Govt. print. off., 1934. ix, 574 p. incl. tables. 331.2973 l 34-109
HD4975 .A15 1933 MRR Alc.

United States. Bureau of the Census. 1960 census of housing, [Washington, 1961-63] 6 v. in 66 pts. and 1 v. in 420 pts. a 61-8347
HD7293 .A4884 MRR Alc.

United States. Bureau of the Census. 1963 census of business. [Washington, For sale by the Superintendent of Documents, U.S. Govt. Print. Off., 1966] 7 v. in 17. 381.0973 a 66-7302
HF3007 .A5 1963 MRR Alc.

United States. Bureau of the Census. 1963 census of manufactures. [Washington, For sale by the Supt. of Docs., U.S. Govt. Print. Off., 1966-68] 4 v. in 6. 338.4/0973 a 66-7830
HD9724 .A4 1963 MRR Alc.

United States. Bureau of the Census. 1963 census of mineral industries. [Washington, For sale by the Supt. of Docs., U.S. Govt. Print. Off., 1967] 2 v. 338.2/0973 a 66-7829
HD9506.U62 A36 1963 MRR Alc.

United States. Bureau of the Census. 1967 census of business. [Washington: For sale by the Supt. of Docs., U.S. Govt. Print. Off., 1970-71] 5 v. in 9 [$9.50 (v. 1) varies] 338/.0973 72-608032
HF3007 .U55 1970 MRR Alc.

United States. Bureau of the Census. 1967 census of construction industries. [Washington: For sale by the Supt. of Docs., U.S. Govt. Print. Off., 1971. 2 v. [$5.00 (v. 1) $6.50 (v. 2)] 338.4/7/624 79-609528
HD9715.U52 A57352 MRR Alc.

United States. Bureau of the Census. 1967 census of governments. [Washington, For sale by the Supt. of Docs., U.S. Govt. Print. Off., 1968- v. in 353.000021/2 a 68-7201
JS3.A257 MRR Alc.

United States. Bureau of the Census. 1967 census of manufactures. [Washington: For sale by the Supt. of Docs., U.S. Govt. Print. Off.] 1971. 3 v. in 6 v. [$9.00 (varies)] 338.4/7/670973 74-609524
HD9724 .A4445 MRR Alc.

United States. Bureau of the Census. 1967 census of transportation. [Washington: For sale by the Supt. of Docs., U.S. Govt. Print. Off., 1970] 3 v. in 5 [$3.00 (v. 1) varies] 380.5/0973 76-607509
HE18 1967 .A55 MRR Alc.

United States. Bureau of the Census. 1970 census of housing. [Washington; For sale by the Supt. of Docs., U.S. Govt. Print Off., 1972- v. 301.5/4/09791 72-600057
HD7293 .A512 1972 MRR Alc.

United States. Bureau of the Census. 1970 census of population. Washington; For sale by the Supt. of Docs., U.S. Govt. Print. Off., 1972- 2 v. in 312/.0973 72-600036
HA201 1970 .A568 MRR Alc.

United States. Bureau of the Census. 1970 census of population and housing. [Washington; For sale by the Supt. of Docs., U.S. Govt. Print. Off.] 1971- v. [$1.00 (v. 5) varies] 312/.9/0973 73-186611
HA201 1970 .A542 MRR Alc.

United States. Bureau of the Census. 1972 census of governments. [Washington, U.S. Govt. Print. Off.] 1973- v. [$1.25 (v. 2, pt. 1) varies] 317.3 73-600080
JS3 .A244 MRR Alc.

United States. Bureau of the Census. Annual survey of manufacturers. 1949/50- Washington, U.S. Govt. Print. Off. 338.4 52-60884
HD9724 .A211 MRR Alc Latest edition

United States. Bureau of the Census. A century of population growth, Baltimore, Genealogical Pub. Co., 1967. x, 303 p. 312/.0973 67-25405
HA195 .A5 1967 MRR Alc.

United States. Bureau of the Census. Congressional district data book: 93d Congress; [Washington: For sale by the Supt. of Docs., U.S. Govt. Print. Off., 1973] xvii, 550 p. [$8.30] 312/.0973 74-601251
HA205 .B87 1973 MRR Ref Desk.

United States. Bureau of the Census. County and city data book. 1949- [Washington, U.S. Govt. Print. Off.] 317.3 52-4576
HA202 .A36 MRR Desk Latest edition / MRR Desk Latest edition / MRR Alc Latest edition

United States. Bureau of the Census. County business patterns; 1946- [Washington] 49-45747
HC101 .A184 MRR Alc Latest edition

United States. Bureau of the Census. Enterprise statistics, 1963. [Washington, For sale by the Supt. of Docs., U.S. Govt. Print. Off., 1968-70. 3 v. [2.75 (v. 1) varies] 338.4/0973 a 68-7228
HC106.5 .A5393 MRR Alc.

United States. Bureau of the Census. Foreign commerce and navigation of the United States. 1865/66- Washington, U.S. Govt. Print. Off. 07-18228
HF105 .A2 MRR Alc Latest edition

United States. Bureau of the Census. Historical statistics of the United States, [Washington, For sale by the Superintendent of Documents, U.S. Govt. Print. Off., 1960] xi, 789 p. 317.3 a 60-9150
HA202 .A385 1960 MRR Alc.

United States. Bureau of the Census. Housing construction statistics, 1889 to 1964. Washington [For sale by the Superintendent of Documents, U.S. Govt. Print. Off., 1966] v, 805 p. 338.4/7/69080973 a 66-7417
HD7293 .A5 1966d MRR Alc.

United States. Bureau of the Census. Manufacturers' shipments, inventories, and orders: 1961-1968. Washington] U.S. Dept. of Commerce; [for sale by the Supt. of Docs., U.S. Govt. Print. Off., 1968] iii, 82 p. [1.00] 338.4/7/6700973 70-607789
HD9724 .A4 1961 MRR alc.

United States. Bureau of the Census. Manufacturers' shipments, inventories, and orders: 1966-1972. Rev. [Washington] 1972. 84 p. [$0.70] 338.4/0973 72-602572
HD9724 .A4448 1972 MRR Alc.

United States. Bureau of the Census. National survey of court organization. [Washington] U.S. National Criminal Justice Information and Statistics Service; [for sale by the Supt. of Docs., U.S. Govt. Print. Off.] 1973. 257 p. [$2.40] 347./73/1 73-600321
KF8719 .A32 MRR Alc.

United States. Bureau of the Census. Negro population 1790-1915. Washington, Govt. print. off., 1918. 844 p. incl. maps, tables, diagrs. 18-26864
E185 .U56 MRR Alc.

United States. Bureau of the Census. New one-family homes sold and for sale: 1963 to 1967. [Washington] U.S. Dept. of Commerce; [for sale by the Supt. of Docs., U.S. Govt. Print. Off., 1969] iii, 293 p. [4.75] 333.3/33/0973 78-601125
HD7293 .A5 1969c MRR Alc.

United States. Bureau of the Census. Pocket data book U S A. 1967- [Washington, for sale by the Supt. of Docs., U.S. Govt. Print. Off.] 317.3 a 66-7638
HA195 .A54 MRR Ref Desk Latest edition

United States. Bureau of the Census. The social and economic status of the Black population in the United States, 1971. Washington; For sale by the Supt. of Docs. U.S. Govt. Print. Off., 1972] iv, 164 p. [$1.25] 312/.0973 s 301.45/19/6073 72-602571
HA203 .A218 no. 42 MRR Alc.

United States. Bureau of the Census. The statistical history of the United States Stamford, Conn., Fairfield Publishers; distributed by Horizon Press, New York [1965] xxiv, 789 p. 317.3 65-21873
HA202 .A385 1965 MRR Ref Desk.

United States. Bureau of the Census. U.S. exports and imports, 1958-1968; [Washington, For sale by the Supt. of Docs., U.S. Govt. Print. Off., 1969] 175 p. 382/.0973 a 68-7967
HF3002 1969 .A53 MRR Alc.

United States. Bureau of the Census. U.S. foreign trade; exports, commodity groupings by world area. 1970- [Washington, For sale by the Supt. of Docs., U.S. Govt. Print. Off.] 382/.6/0973 70-616577
HF105 .C137152 MRR Alc Latest edition

UNITED STATES--STATISTICS. (Cont.)
United States. Bureau of the Census.
U.S. foreign trade: general imports,
commodity by world area.
[Washington, For sale by the Supt. of
Docs., U.S. Govt. Print. Off.]
382/.5/0973   75-648607
   HF105 .C137182   MRR Alc Latest
      edition

United States. Bureau of the Census.
U.S. foreign trade: general imports,
world area by commodity groupings.
1970- [Washington, For sale by the
Supt. of Docs., U.S. Govt. Print.
Off.] 382/.5/0973   78-649732
   HF105 .C137172   MRR Alc Latest
      edition

United States. Bureau of the Census.
U.S. foreign trade: imports SIC-based
products. [Washington, For sale by
Supt. of Docs., U.S. Govt. Print.
Off.] 382/.5/0973   72-626391
   HF105 .C1371663   MRR Alc Latest
      edition

United States. Bureau of the Census.
U.S. foreign trade: imports, TSUSA
commodity by country. 1970-
[Washington, For sale by the Supt. of
Docs., U.S. Govt. Print. Off.]
382/.5/0973   74-649695
   HF105 .C137232   MRR Alc Latest
      edition

United States. Bureau of the Census.
U.S. foreign trade: exports, SIC-
based products. 1970- [Washington,
For sale by the Supt. of Docs., U.S.
Govt. Print. Off.] 382/.6/0973   71-
648606
   HF105 .C137166   MRR Alc Latest
      edition

United States. Bureau of the Census.
U.S. foreign trade: exports, world
area by commodity groupings. 1970-
[Washington, For sale by the Supt. of
Docs., U.S. Govt. Print. Off.]
382/.6/0973   79-648608
   HF105 .C137132   MRR Alc Latest
      edition

United States. Bureau of the Census.
Economic Statistics and Surveys
Division. Enterprise statistics:
1967. [Washington; For sale by the
Supt. of Docs., U.S. Govt. Print.
Off., Washington, 1971-   [v. 1,
1972]   v.   [$7.75 (v. 1)]
338/.0973   79-186224
   HC106.6 .U55 1972 MRR Alc.

United States. Civil Aeronautics
Board. Handbook of airline
statistics, United States
certificated air carriers. 1938/42-
[Washington, U.S. Govt. Print. Off.]
44-40873
   TL521 .A242   MRR Alc Latest edition

United States. Congress. Senate.
Select Committee on Nutrition and
Human Needs. Poverty, malnutrition,
and Federal food assistance programs:
Washington, U.S. Govt. Print. Off.,
1969. v, 56 p.   338.1/9/73   78-
603619
   HD9006 .A5256 1969 MRR Alc.

United States. Dept. of Agriculture.
Agricultural statistics. 1936-
Washington, U.S. Govt. Print. Off.
338.10973   agr36-465
   HD1751 .A43   MRR Ref Desk Latest
      edition / MRR Alc Latest edition

United States. Dept. of Agriculture.
Economic Research Service. European
Economic Community; agricultural
trade statistics, 1961-67.
[Washington, 1969] 1 v. (unpaged)
382/.41/094   78-601937
   HD9015.A3 U46 MRR Alc.

United States. Dept. of Housing and
Urban Development. Statistical
yearbook. 1966- Washington, For
sale by the Supt. of Docs., U.S.
Govt. Print. Off. 301.5/4/0212 68-
62733
   HD7293.A49H67   MRR Ref Desk Full
      set

United States. Division of Government
Financial Operations. Federal aid to
States. [Washington?] 338.973 72-
618404
   HJ275 .A36   MRR Ref Desk Latest
      edition

United States. Federal Aviation
Administration. F A A statistical
handbook of aviation. Washington,
For sale by the Supt. of Docs., U.S.
Govt. Print. Off. 387.7/0973 73-
609572
   TL521 .A41612   Sci RR Latest
      edition / MRR Alc Latest edition

United States. Interstate Commerce
Commission. Bureau of Accounts.
Transport statistics in the United
States. Washington. 380.5/0973 72-
627360
   HE2708 .I73   MRR Alc Latest edition

United States. Office of Business
Economics. Personal income, by
States, since 1929; New York,
Greenwood Press [1969] iv, 229 p.
339.41/0973   79-92310
   HC110.I5 A55 1969 MRR Alc.

United States. Office of Management
and Budget. The budget of the United
States Government. 1971/72-
[Washington,For sale by the Supt. of
Docs., U.S. Govt. Print. Off.]
353.007/22   70-611049
   HJ2051 .A59   MRR Ref Desk Latest
      edition

United States. Office of Management
and Budget. The Budget of the United
States Government. Appendix. 1971/72-
[Washington, For sale by the Supt.
of Docs., U.S. Govt. Print. Off.]
353.007/22   74-643523
   HJ2051 .A59 Suppl.   MRR Ref Desk
      Latest Edition

United States. President. Manpower
report of the President, and a Report
on manpower requirements, resources,
utilization, and training, by the
U.S. Dept. of Labor. 1963-
[Washington, For sale by the
Superintendent of Documents, U.S.
Govt. Print. Off.] l 63-45
   HD5723 .A43   MRR Alc Latest edition

United States. Treasury Dept. Bureau
of Accounts. Combined statement of
receipts, expenditures and balances
of the United States government.
1871/72- Washington. 10-11510
   HJ10 .A6 MRR Alc Latest edition

Urban Growth Patterns Research Group.
Demographic profiles of the United
States. Oak Ridge, Tenn., Oak Ridge
National Laboratory, 1971-72. 8 v.
[$3.00 (v. 1) varies]   312/.0973 76-
616120
   HA215 .U73 MRR Alc.

Wattenberg, Ben J. This U.S.A.:
[1st ed.] Garden City, N.Y.,
Doubleday, 1965. viii, 520 p.
317.3   65-19858
   HA215 .W3 MRR Alc.

Wolfbein, Seymour Louis, Employment
and unemployment in the United
States; Chicago, Science Research
Associates [1964]   339 p.
331.1120973   64-12588
   HD5724 .W6 MRR Alc.

Woytinsky, Emma (Shadkhan) Profile
of the U.S. economy; New York,
Praeger [1967] xiii, 601 p.
330.973   66-13673
   HC103 .W76 MRR Alc.

UNITED STATES--STATISTICS--ABSTRACTS.
American statistics index. 1973-
Washington, Congressional Information
Service. 016.3173   73-82599
   Z7554.U5 A46 MRR Alc Full set /
      Sci RR Full set

UNITED STATES--STATISTICS--BIBLIOGRAPHY.
American statistics index. 1973-
Washington, Congressional Information
Service. 016.3173   73-82599
   Z7554.U5 A46 MRR Alc Full set /
      Sci RR Full set

Encyclopedia of business information
sources; Detroit, Gale Research Co.,
1970. 2 v. (xxi, 689 p.)   016.33
79-127922
   HF5353 .E52 MRR Ref Desk.

Ferguson, Elizabeth, ed, Sources of
insurance statistics. [New York]
Special Libraries Association, 1965.
v, 191 p.   368.00212   65-25313
   HG8045 .F45 MRR Alc.

Guide to U.S. Government statistics.
1956- [Arlington, Va.] Documents
Index. 016.3173   61-9066
   Z7554.U5 G8 MRR Ref Desk Latest
      edition

Harvey, Joan M. Sources of
statistics [Hamden, Conn.] Archon
Books [1969] 100 p. [4.00] 016.31
74-42258
   Z7554.G7 H3 1969b MRR Alc.

Inter American Statistical Institute.
Bibliography of selected statistical
sources of the American nations. 1st
ed. Washington, 1947. xvi, 689 p.
016.31 48-6568
   Z7554.S75 I4 1947 MRR Alc.

Special Libraries Association.
Business and Finance Division.
Committee on Sources of Commodity
Prices. Sources of commodity prices.
New York, Special Libraries
Association, 1959 [c1960] 170 p.
338.505873 60-8102
   Z7164.P94 S6 MRR Alc.

Special Libraries Association.
Petroleum Section. Committee on U.S.
Sources of Petroleum and Natural Gas
Statistics. U.S. sources of
petroleum and natural gas statistics,
New York, Special Libraries
Association, 1961. vii, 94 p.
016.6655 61-15740
   Z6972 .S65 MRR Alc.

Statistics sources; Rev. 3d ed.
Detroit, Gale Research Co., 1971.
647 p. [$27.50] 016.31 72-127923

   Z7551 .S84 1971 MRR Ref Desk.

Texas. University. Population
Research Center. International
population census bibliography.
Austin, Bureau of Business Research,
University of Texas, 1965-67. 6 v.
016.312 66-63578
   Z7164.D3 T45 MRR Alc.

United States. Bureau of Labor
Statistics. Guide to employment
statistics of BLS; [Washington]
1961. i, 134 p. l 62-75
   HD8064 .A52 1961 MRR Alc.

United States. Bureau of the Budget.
Office of Statistical Standards.
Statistical services of the United
States Government. [Washington] 59-
61420
   HA37 .U16 MRR Ref Desk Latest
      edition

United States. Bureau of the Census.
Bureau of the Census catalog.
[Washington, For sale by the Supt. of
Docs., U.S. Govt. Print. Off.]
016.3173 74-644649
   Z7554.U5 U32 MRR Alc Full set

United States. Bureau of the Census.
Census Bureau programs and
publications; [Washington; For sale
by the Supt. of Docs., U.S. Govt.
Print. Off., 1968] vi, 146 p.
[1.50]   311/.39/73 79-603950
   HA37 .U52 1968 MRR Ref Desk.

United States. Bureau of the Census.
Directory of Federal statistics for
local areas. [Washington, For sale
by the Supt. of Docs., U.S. Govt.
Print. Off.] 1966. vi, 156 p. a
66-7475
   HB2175 .A5 1966 TJ Rm.

United States. Bureau of the Census.
Directory of Federal statistics for
states; Washington, For sale by the
Supt. of Docs, U.S. Govt. Print.
Off., 1967] viii, 372 p.   317.3 a
67-7451
   HA37 .U52 1967 MRR Ref Desk.

United States. Bureau of the Census.
Directory of non-Federal statistics
for States and local areas;
[Washington; For sale by the Supt. of
Docs., U.S. Govt. Print. Off., 1970]
viii, 678 p. [6.25]   317.3 76-
605082
   HA37 .U52 1970 MRR Ref Desk.

United States. Dept. of Commerce.
Library. Price sources: New York,
B. Franklin [1968] iv, 320 p.
016.33852 70-6381
   Z7164.P94 U56 1968 MRR Alc.

United States. Library of Congress.
Census Library Project. Catalog of
United States census publications,
1790-1945, Washington, U.S.
Govt.Print. Off., 1950. x, 320 p.
016.312 50-60600
   Z7554.U5 U62 MRR Alc.

United States. Library of Congress.
Census Library Project. Catalog of
United States census publications,
1790-1945. New York, B. Franklin
[1971] x, 320 p. 016.3173 72-
153029
   Z7554.U5 U62 1971 MRR Ref Desk.

United States. Library of Congress.
Census Library Project. State
censuses; an annotated bibliography
Washington, U.S. Govt. Print. Off.,
1948. v, 73 p. 016.312 48-46440
   Z7554.U5 U63 1948 MRR Alc.

United States. Office of Regional
Development Planning. Guide to
economic projections and forecasts.
[Washington] U.S. Dept. of Commerce,
Economic Development Administration
[1968] iii, 113 p. 016.330973 77-
600326
   Z7165.U5 A48 MRR Alc.

Verwey, Gerlof, The economist's
handbook. Amsterdam, The economist's
handbook, 1934. viii, p., 1 l., 460
p. 016.31 35-4837
   Z7553.E2 V6 MRR Alc.

UNITED STATES--STATISTICS--COLLECTIONS.
U.S. statistical atlas. Elmwood,
Neb. 917.3/03/9240212 78-612817
   HA214 .U57 MRR Ref Desk Latest
      edition

UNITED STATES--STATISTICS, MEDICAL.
Dublin, Louis Israel, Factbook on
man, 2d ed. New York, Macmillan
[1965] xiv, 465 p.   312 65-16561
HB3505 .D78 1965 MRR Alc.

National Health Education Committee.
Facts on the major killing and
crippling diseases in the United
States today. New York. 614.59 55-
3279
RA407.3 .N3 MRR Alc Latest edition

UNITED STATES--STATISTICS, VITAL.
Glick, Paul C. American families,
New York, Wiley [1957] xiv, 240 p.
392 301.42* 57-5910
HQ535 .G6 MRR Alc.

Grove, Robert D. Vital statistics
rates in the United States, 1940-
1960, Washington, U.S. National
Center for Health Statistics; for
sale by the Supt. of Docs., U.S.
Govt. Print. Off., 1968. ix, 881 p.
[5.25] 312/.0973 75-601797
HA211 .G75 MRR Alc.

Preston, Samuel H. Causes of death:
life tables for national population
New York, Seminar Press, 1972. xi,
787 p. 312/.2 72-80305
HB1321 .P73 MRR Alc.

United States. Bureau of the Census.
Vital statistics rates in the United
States, 1900-1940, Washington, U.S.
Govt. Print. Off., 1943. vii, 1051
p. 312 43-50838
HA201 1940 .A57 MRR Alc.

United States. Division of Vital
Statistics. Vital statistics of the
United States. 1937- [Washington,
U.S. Govt. Print. Off.] 40-26272
HA203 .A22 MRR Alc Latest edition

United States. National Center for
Health Statistics. Facts of life and
death. [Rev.] Washington; for sale
by the Supt. of Docs., U.S. Govt.
Print. Off., 1967 [i.e. 1968] iv, 33
p. [$0.30] 312/.0973 74-22508
HA211 .A55 1968 MRR Alc.

United States. Public Health Service.
Where to write for birth and death
records: United States and outlying
areas. [Washington. For sale by the
Supt. of Docs., U.S. Govt. Print.
Off.] 312/.1/072073 77-649981
HA38 .A232 MRR Ref Desk Latest
edition

UNITED STATES--TERRITORIAL EXPANSION.
Billington, Ray Allen, Westward
expansion; 3d ed. New York,
Macmillan [c1967] xvii, 933 p.   973
67-12337
E179.5 .B63 1967 MRR Alc.

Carter, Clarence Edwin, comp. The
territorial papers of the United
States. Washington, U.S. Govt.
Print. Off., 1934- v.   973.082
35-26191
E173 .C3 MRR Alc.

Gabriel, Ralph Henry, The lure of
the frontier; New Haven, Yale
university press; [etc., etc.] 1929.
3 p. l., 327 p.   29-22308
E178.5 .P2 vol. 2 MRR Alc.

Klose, Nelson, A concise study guide
to the American frontier. Lincoln,
University of Nebraska Press, 1964.
xi, 269 p.   973 64-15180
E179.5 .K55 MRR Alc.

Philbrick, Francis Samuel, The rise
of the West, 1754-1830, [1st ed.]
New York, Harper & Row [1965] xvii,
398 p.   973 65-21377
E179.5 .P45 MRR Alc.

United States. Dept. of state. The
territorial papers of the United
States. Washington, U.S. Govt.
print. off., 1934. xv, 37 p.
973.082 35-26190
E173 .U57 MRR Alc.

Weinberg, Albert Katz. Manifest
destiny; Baltimore, The Johns
Hopkins press, 1935. xiii, 559 p.
973 35-9403
E179.5 .W45 MRR Alc.

UNITED STATES--VICE PRESIDENTS
see Vice Presidents--United States

UNITED STATES--GOVERNMENT PUBLICATIONS
(STATE GOVERNMENTS)--BIBLIOGRAPHY.
Parish, David W. State government
reference publications : Littleton,
Colo. : Libraries Unlimited, 1974.
237 p. ; [$11.50] 015/.73 74-
81322
Z1223.5.A1 P37 MRR Alc.

UNITED STATES. 1ST CONGRESS, 1789-1791--
COLLECTIONS.
Documentary history of the First
Federal Congress of the United States
of America, March 4, 1789-March 3,
1791. [Baltimore, Johns Hopkins
University Press, 1972- v.
328.73 s 328.73/01 73-155164
JK1059 1st .D6 MRR Alc.

UNITED STATES. AIR FORCE.
United States. Aerospace Studies
Institute. The United States Air
Force dictionary. [Maxwell Air Force
Base? Ala.] Air University Press; for
sale by the Superintendent of
Documents, U.S. Govt. Print. Off.,
1956. xi, 578 p. 358.403 56-61737
UG630 .U637 1956 MRR Alc.

UNITED STATES. AIR FORCE--BIBLIOGRAPHY.
United States. Library of Congress.
Science and Technology Division. Air
Force scientific research
bibliography, Washington, U.S. Govt.
Print. Off., 1961- v.   016.5 61-
60038
Z663.41 .A36 MRR Alc.

UNITED STATES. AIR FORCE--BIOGRAPHY.
DuPre, Flint O. U.S. Air Force
biographical dictionary, New York,
F. Watts [1965] x, 273 p. 923.573
65-11718
UG633 .D8 MRR Biog.

UNITED STATES. AIR FORCE--FOREIGN
SERVICE.
Air Force bases; [3d ed.]
Harrisburg, Pa., Stackpole Co. [1965]
224 p. 358.417058 65-13381
UG634.5.A1 A7 1965 MRR Alc.

UNITED STATES. AIR FORCE--HANDBOOKS,
MANUALS, ETC.
The Air Force striper's guide.
[Harrisburg, Pa.] Stackpole Books
[1972] 224 p. [$3.95] 358.4/0023
72-169024
UG633 .A657 MRR Alc.

The Airman's guide. 1st- ed.; 1949-
Harrisburg, Pa., Stackpole Books
[etc.] 358.4 49-11403
UG633 .A68 Sci RR Latest edition /
MRR Alc Latest edition

UNITED STATES. AIR FORCE--HISTORY.
Glines, Carroll V., The compact
history of the United States Air
Force New and rev. ed. New York,
Hawthorn Books [1973] 366 p.
358.4/13/0973 72-11218
UG633 .G52 1973 MRR Alc.

UNITED STATES. AIR FORCE--OFFICERS'
HANDBOOKS.
The Air officer's guide. 1st- ed.;
1948- Harrisburg, Pa., Stackpole
Books. 358.41/1/05 48-7046
UG633 .A1A49 MRR Alc Latest
edition

UNITED STATES. AIR FORCE. FAR EAST AIR
FORCES.
Futrell, Robert Frank. The United
States Air Force in Korea, 1950-1953,
[1st ed.] New York, Duell, Sloan
and Pearce [1961] xxi, 774 p.
951.9042 61-16831
DS920.2.U5 F8 MRR Alc.

UNITED STATES. ARMY.
The Army almanac; [2d ed.]
Harrisburg, Pa., Stackpole Co. [1959]
x, 797 p. 355.0973 59-10070
UA25 .A78 1959 MRR Alc.

United States. Dept. of the Army.
Office of Military History. Combat
chronicle, [Washington, 1948?] 109
l. 940.541273 49-45651
D769.29 .A52 MRR Ref Desk.

UNITED STATES. ARMY--BIOGRAPHY.
Billias, George Athan, ed. George
Washington's generals. New York, W.
Morrow, 1964. xvii, 327 p. 973.33
64-12038
E206 .B5 MRR Biog.

Hamersly, Thomas Holdup Stevens,
comp. Complete regular army register
of the United States: for one hundred
years (1779 to 1879) Washington, T.
H. S. Hamersly, 1880. viii, 928,
381, xxxvi p. 07-12444
U11.U5 H3 MRR Biog.

Heitman, Francis Bernard,
Historical register and dictionary of
the United States Army, from its
organization, September 29, 1789, to
March 2, 1903. Urbana, University of
Illinois Press, 1965. 2 v.
355.3/0922 65-15975
U11.U5 H6 1965 MRR Biog.

Powell, William Henry, comp. List of
officers of the army of the United
States from 1779 to 1900, New York,
L. R. Hamersly & co., 1900. 3 p. l.,
863 p. 01-11939
U11.U5 P7 MRR Biog.

UNITED STATES. ARMY--EQUIPMENT.
Lord, Francis Alfred, Civil War
collector's encyclopedia; [1st ed.]
Harrisburg, Pa., Stackpole Co. [1963]
360 p. 355.80973 63-14636
UC23 1861-65 .L6 MRR Alc.

UNITED STATES. ARMY--FIREARMS.
Gluckman, Arcadi, Identifying old
U.S. muskets, rifles & carbines.
Harrisburg, Pa., Stackpole Books
[1965] 487 p. 623.4425 65-20534
UD383 .G5 1965 MRR Alc.

UNITED STATES. ARMY--HISTORY.
Dupuy, Richard Ernest, The compact
history of the United States Army 2d
rev. ed. New York, Hawthorn Books
[1973] 346 p. [$9.95] 973 72-
10984
E181 .D78 1973 MRR Alc.

Ganoe, William Addleman, The history
of the United States Army, Rev. ed.
New York, London, D. Appleton-Century
company, incorporated, 1942. xi, 640
p. 973 42-20792
E181 .G17 1942 MRR Alc.

United States. Dept. of the Army.
Office of Military History. The Army
lineage book. Washington, U.S. Govt.
Print. Off., 1953- v. 355.309
54-61235
UA25 .A516 MRR Alc.

Weigley, Russell Frank. History of
the United States Army, New York,
Macmillan [1967] xiv, 688 p.
355/.000973 67-16051
UA25 .W35 MRR Alc.

UNITED STATES. ARMY--HISTORY--CIVIL
WAR, 1861-1865.
Lord, Francis Alfred, They fought
for the Union. [1st ed.]
Harrisburg, Pa., Stackpole Co. [1960]
375 p. 973.741 60-8813
E491 .L89 MRR Alc.

Shannon, Fred Albert, The
organization and administration of
the Union Army, 1861-1865.
Gloucester, Mass., P. Smith, 1965
[c1928] 2 v. 973.741 65-3210
E491 .S52 1965 MRR Alc.

Wiley, Bell Irvin, The common
soldier in the Civil War. New York,
Grosset & Dunlap [1958] 454, 444 p.
973.74 58-4364
E607 .W48 MRR Alc.

UNITED STATES. ARMY--HISTORY--
BIBLIOGRAPHY.
Dornbusch, Charles Emil, Histories,
personal narratives: United States
Army; Cornwallville, N.Y., Hope Farm
Press, 1967. [15]-399 p. 016.355
67-5273
Z1249.M5 D6 1967 MRR Ref Desk.

United States. Dept. of the Army.
Office of Military History. Unit
histories of World War II,
[Washington, 1950?] iii, 141 p.
016.940541273 51-60137
Z6207.W8 U52 MRR Ref Desk.

UNITED STATES. ARMY--INSIGNIA.
American Society of Military Insignia
Collectors. Catalog of distinctive
insignia of the U.S. Army. [1st ed.
Spokane, c1960- 1 v. (loose-leaf)
61-41520
UC533 .A48 MRR Alc.

Moss, James Alfred, Origin and
significance of military customs,
including military miscellany of
interest to soldiers and civilians,
Menasha, Wis., George Banta
publishing company [c1917] 78 p.
18-509
U766 .M6 MRR Alc.

Wyllie, Robert E., Orders,
decorations and insignia, military
and civil; New York, London, G. P.
Putnam's sons [c1921] 3 p. l., v-xxi
p., 1 l., 269 p. 21-4556
CR4509 .W9 MRR Alc.

UNITED STATES. ARMY--MEDALS, BADGES,
DECORATIONS, ETC.
Wyllie, Robert E., Orders,
decorations and insignia, military
and civil; New York, London, G. P.
Putnam's sons [c1921] 3 p. l., v-xxi
p., 1 l., 269 p. 21-4556
CR4509 .W9 MRR Alc.

UNITED STATES. ARMY--MILITARY LIFE.
Dupuy, Richard Ernest, The compact
history of the United States Army 2d
rev. ed. New York, Hawthorn Books
[1973] 346 p. [$9.95] 973 72-
10984
E181 .D78 1973 MRR Alc.

Wiley, Bell Irvin, The common
soldier in the Civil War. New York,
Grosset & Dunlap [1958] 454, 444 p.
973.74 58-4364
E607 .W48 MRR Alc.

UNITED STATES. ARMY--NON-COMMISSIONED
OFFICERS' HANDBOOKS.
The New noncom's guide. 21st- ed.;
1970- [Harrisburg, Pa.] Stackpole
Books. 355/.005 72-623127
    U123 .N6 MRR Alc Latest edition

UNITED STATES. ARMY--OFFICERS'
HANDBOOKS.
The Officer's guide. 1st- ed.;
June 1930- Harrisburg, Pa.,
Stackpole Books [etc.] 355 30-21652
    U133.A6 O3 MRR Alc Latest edition

UNITED STATES. ARMY--ORDNANCE AND
ORDNANCE STORES.
Hicks, James Ernest, U.S. military
firearms, 1776-1956. La Canada,
Calif., J. E. Hicks [1962] 125, [91]
p.   623.440973 62-10470
    U897.U5 H53 1962 MRR Alc.

Ripley, Warren, Artillery and
ammunition of the Civil War. New
York, Van Nostrand Reinhold Co.
[1970] 384 p.   623.4 75-90331
    UF23 .R56 1970 MRR Alc.

UNITED STATES. ARMY--ORGANIZATION.
Shannon, Fred Albert, The
organization and administration of
the Union Army, 1861-1865.
Gloucester, Mass., P. Smith, 1965
[c1928] 2 v.   973.741 65-3210
    E491 .S52 1965 MRR Alc.

UNITED STATES. ARMY--PICTORIAL WORKS.
Kredel, Fritz, illus. Soldiers of
the American Army, 1775-1954. [Rev.
ed.] Chicago, H. Regnery Co. [1954]
1 v. (unpaged) 355.14 54-13348
    UC483 .K7 1954 MRR Alc.

UNITED STATES. ARMY--REGISTERS.
Amann, William Frayne, ed. Personnel
of the Civil War. New York, T.
Yoseloff [1961] 2 v.   973.74 60-
9890
    E494 .A5 MRR Alc.

Heitman, Francis Bernard,
Historical register and dictionary of
the United States Army, from its
organization, September 29, 1789, to
March 2, 1903. Urbana, University of
Illinois Press, 1965. 2 v.
355.3/0922 65-15975
    U11.U5 H6 1965 MRR Biog.

U.S. Army register. Washington,
Dept. of the Army; for sale by the
Supt. of Docs., U.S. Govt. Print.
Off. 355.3/32/02573 72-627092
    U11 .U4 MRR Biog Latest edition

UNITED STATES. ARMY--SANITARY AFFAIRS.
Beebe, Gilbert Wheeler, Battle
casualties; Springfield, Ill.,
Thomas [1952] xxiii, 277 p.
940.5475 52-11968
    D805.U5 B4 MRR Alc.

UNITED STATES. ARMY--STATISTICS.
Livermore, Thomas Leonard, Numbers &
losses in the Civil War in America,
1861-65. Bloomington, Indiana
University Press, 1957. 150 p.
973.74 57-10726
    E491 .L77 1957 MRR Alc.

United States. Adjutant General's
Office. Army battle casualties and
nonbattle deaths in World War II.
[Washington, Dept. of the Army, 1953]
118 p. (chiefly tables) 940.541273
53-37014
    D797.U6 A52 MRR Alc.

UNITED STATES. ARMY--UNIFORMS--HISTORY.
Kredel, Fritz, illus. Soldiers of
the American Army, 1775-1954. [Rev.
ed.] Chicago, H. Regnery Co. [1954]
1 v. (unpaged) 355.14 54-13348
    UC483 .K7 1954 MRR Alc.

UNITED STATES. ARMY. A.E.F., 1917-1920--
ORGANIZATION.
United States. Army War College.
Historical Section. Order of battle
of the United States land forces in
the World War. Washington, U.S.
Govt. Print. Off., 1931-49. 3 v. in
4.   940.41273 31-27280
    D570 .A353 MRR Alc.

UNITED STATES. ARMY. A.E.F., 1917-1920--
REGIMENTAL HISTORIES.
United States. Army War College.
Historical Section. Order of battle
of the United States land forces in
the World War. Washington, U.S.
Govt. Print. Off., 1931-49. 3 v. in
4.   940.41273 31-27280
    D570 .A353 MRR Alc.

UNITED STATES. ARMY. ARMORED FORCE--
HISTORY.
Stubbs, Mary Lee. Armor-cavalry,
Washington, Office of the Chief of
Military History, U.S. Army; [for
sale by the Supt. of Docs., U.S.
Govt. Print. Off.] 1969- v.
[6.75] 357/.0973 69-60002
    UA30 .S8 MRR Alc.

UNITED STATES. ARMY. CAVALRY--HISTORY.
Stubbs, Mary Lee. Armor-cavalry,
Washington, Office of the Chief of
Military History, U.S. Army; [for
sale by the Supt. of Docs., U.S.
Govt. Print. Off.] 1969- v.
[6.75] 357/.0973 69-60002
    UA30 .S8 MRR Alc.

Wormser, Richard Edward, The
Yellowlegs; [1st ed.] Garden City,
N.Y., Doubleday, 1966. xi, 468 p.
357.10973 64-16226
    UE23 .W6 MRR Alc.

UNITED STATES. ARMY. CONTINENTAL ARMY--
DIRECTORIES.
Berg, Fred Anderson, Encyclopedia of
Continental Army units--battalions,
regiments, and independent corps.
[Harrisburg, Pa.] Stackpole Books
[1972] 160 p. [$6.95] 973.3/4/025
70-38505
    E259 .B47 MRR Alc.

UNITED STATES. ARMY. CONTINENTAL ARMY--
SUPPLIES AND STORES.
Peterson, Harold Leslie, The book of
the Continental soldier; Harrisburg,
Pa., Stackpole Co. [1968] 287 p.
973.3/4 67-27697
    UC263 .P47 MRR Alc.

UNITED STATES. ARMY. SIGNAL CORPS.
Marshall, Max L., ed. The story of
the U.S. Army Signal Corps, New
York, F. Watts [1965] xiv, 305 p.
358.240973 65-11938
    UG573 .M35 MRR Alc.

UNITED STATES. ARMY AIR FORCES.
United States. Air Force. USAF
Historical Division. The Army Air
Forces in World War II. [Chicago]
University of Chicago Press [1948-58]
7 v.   940.544973 48-3657
    D790 .A47 MRR Alc.

UNITED STATES. ARMY AIR FORCES--HISTORY.
Glines, Carroll V., The compact
history of the United States Air
Force New and rev. ed. New York,
Hawthorn Books [1973] 366 p.
358.4/13/0973 72-11218
    UG633 .G52 1973 MRR Alc.

United States. Library of Congress.
The H. H. Arnold collection
Washington, U.S. Govt. Print. Off.,
1952] 11 p.   012 016.3584 52-60060
    Z663.34 .H15 MRR Alc.

UNITED STATES. ATOMIC ENERGY COMMISSION.
Hewlett, Richard G. A history of the
United States Atomic Energy
Commission University Park,
Pennsylvania State University Press,
1962- v.   539.7506173 62-14633
    HD9698.U52 H48 MRR Alc.

UNITED STATES. BUREAU OF LABOR
STATISTICS.
United States. Bureau of Labor
Statistics. Guide to employment
statistics of BLS; [Washington]
1961. i, 134 p. l 62-75
    HD8064 .A52 1961 MRR Alc.

UNITED STATES. BUREAU OF THE CENSUS.
POPULATION. 1970.
Kahn, Ely Jacques, The American
people; New York, Weybright and
Talley [c1974] viii, 340 p. [$8.95]
301.32/9/73 73-84073
    HB3505 .K28 MRR Alc.

UNITED STATES. CENTRAL INTELLIGENCE
AGENCY--OFFICIALS AND EMPLOYEES.
Mader, Julius, Who's who in CIA;
Berlin, Julius Mader, 1066 Berlin W
66, Mauerstrasse 69, 1968. 604, [1]
p. (unpriced) 327/.12/0973 70-
389997
    JK468.I6 M323 MRR Biog.

UNITED STATES. CENTRAL INTELLIGENCE
AGENCY--REGISTERS.
Mader, Julius, Who's who in CIA;
Berlin, Julius Mader, 1066 Berlin W
66, Mauerstrasse 69, 1968. 604, [1]
p. (unpriced) 327/.12/0973 70-
389997
    JK468.I6 M323 MRR Biog.

UNITED STATES. COAST GUARD.
Bloomfield, Howard Van Lieu, The
compact history of the United States
Coast Guard [1st ed.] New York,
Hawthorn Books [1966] ix, 307 p.
359.97 65-12036
    HJ6645 .B6 MRR Alc.

UNITED STATES. COAST GUARD--HANDBOOKS,
MANUALS, ETC.
The Coast guardsman's manual. 1952-
Annapolis, United States Naval
Institute. 351.792 52-61512
    HJ6645 .C66 MRR Alc Latest edition

UNITED STATES. COAST GUARD--HISTORY.
Gurney, Gene. The United States
Coast Guard; New York, Crown
Publishers [1973] ix, 246 p.
[$6.95] 359.9/7/0973 72-84304
    VG53 .G87 1973 MRR Alc.

UNITED STATES. COAST GUARD--REGISTERS.
United States. Coast Guard. Register
of the commissioned and warrant
officers and cadets of the United
States Coast Guard in the order of
precedence. 1915- Washington, U.S.
Govt. Print. Off. 15-26584
    HJ6645 .A31 MRR Biog Latest
    edition

UNITED STATES. CONGRESS. AMERICAN STATE
PAPERS. CLASS IX. CLAIMS--INDEXES.
McMullin, Phillip W. Grassroots of
America; Salt Lake City, Gendex
Corp., 1972. xxvii, 489 p.
333.1/0973 71-186588
    J33 .M3 MRR Alc.

UNITED STATES. CONGRESS. AMERICAN STATE
PAPERS. CLASS VIII. PUBLIC LANDS--
INDEXES.
McMullin, Phillip W. Grassroots of
America; Salt Lake City, Gendex
Corp., 1972. xxvii, 489 p.
333.1/0973 71-186588
    J33 .M3 MRR Alc.

UNITED STATES. CONGRESS.
Bailey, Stephen Kemp. Congress at
work, Hamden, Conn., Archon Books,
1965 [c1952] x, 502 p.   328.73 65-
15011
    JK1061 .B3 1965 MRR Alc.

Berman, Daniel M. In Congress
assembled; New York, Macmillan
[1964] xv, 432 p.   328.73 64-14974
    JK1061 .B44 MRR Alc.

Blair, George S. American
legislatures; New York, Harper & Row
[1967] x, 449 p.   328.73/07 67-
13472
    JK2488 .B55 MRR Alc.

Blanchard, Robert O., comp. Congress
and the news media, New York,
Hastings House [1974] xiv, 506 p.
[$14.95] 323.44/5 74-1091
    PN4738 .B5 MRR Alc.

Bradshaw, Kenneth. Parliament &
Congress Austin, University of Texas
Press [1972] 426 p. [$10.00]
328.42 78-37857
    JN508 .B7 MRR Alc.

Congressional Quarterly, inc. Guide
to the Congress of the United States;
[1st ed.] Washington, Congressional
Quarterly Service [1971] xxxi, 639,
323a, 21b p. [$35.00] 328.73 78-
167743
    JK1021 .C56 MRR Ref Desk.

Evins, Joe Landon, Understanding
Congress. New York, C. N. Potter
[1963] 304 p.   328.73 63-18878
    JK1061 .E85 MRR Alc.

Griffith, Ernest Stacey, Congress:
its contemporary role, 4th ed. New
York, New York University Press,
1967. xiii, 277 p.   328.73 67-
11316
    JK1061 .G7 1967 MRR Alc.

Know your Congress. [Washington,
Capital Publishers, etc.] 1965
"Originally published in 1920."
    JK1051 .K6 MRR Ref Desk Latest
    edition

Twelve studies of the organization of
Congress Washington, 1966. 515 p.
328.73 66-14193
    JK1061 .T9 MRR Alc.

UNITED STATES. CONGRESS--BIBLIOGRAPHY.
United States. Dept. of the Interior.
Division of Documents. Comprehensive
index to the publications of the
United States Government, 1881-1893,
New York, Johnson Reprint Corp.,
[1970] 2 v. (v, 159 p.) 015/.73
75-29071
    Z1223.A 1970 MRR Ref Desk.

United States. Dept. of the Interior.
Division of Documents. Comprehensive
index to the publications of the
United States Government, 1881-1893,
Ann Arbor, J. W. Edwards, 1953. 2 v.
in 1 (v, 1590 p.) 015.73 54-61502
    Z1223.A 1953 MRR Alc.

United States. Superintendent of
Documents. Index to the reports and
documents of the 54th Congress, 1st
session-72d Congress, 2d session,
Dec. 2, 1895-March 4, 1933 with
numerical lists and schedule of
volumes. Being no. [1]-43 of the
"Consolidated index" provided for by
the act of January 12, 1895. 1897-
1933. Washington [Govt. print. off.]
43 v.   06-20448
    Z1223 .A14 Sci RR Full set / MRR
    Alc (Deck 33) Full set

UNITED STATES. CONGRESS-- (Cont.)
United States. Superintendent of
Documents. Numerical lists and
schedule of volumes of the reports
and documents of the 73d- Congress
... 1933/34- Washington [U.S. Govt.
print. off.] 015.73 34-28260
Z1223 .A15 MRR Ref Desk

United States. Superintendent of
documents. Tables of and annotated
index to the congressional series of
United States public documents.
Washington, Govt. print. off., 1902.
769 p. 02-13262
Z1223.A 1902 MRR Ref Desk.

UNITED STATES. CONGRESS--BIOGRAPHY.
Chamberlin, Hope. A minority of
members: women in the U.S. Congress.
New York, Praeger Publishers [1973]
ix, 374 p. 328.73/092/2 B 73-
151950
JK1030.A2 C5 MRR Biog.

Congressional staff directory. [1st]-
ed.; 1859- Washington [etc.]
328.738 59-13987
JK1012 MRR Ref Desk Latest edition
/ Sci RR Latest edition

Engelbarts, Rudolf. Women in the
United States Congress, 1917-1972:
Littleton, Colo., Libraries
Unlimited, 1974. 184 p.
328.73/092/2 73-93278
JK1030.A2 E5 MRR Biog.

Lanman, Charles, Biographical annals
of the civil government of the United
States. 2d ed. Rev., enl. and
completed to date. New York, J. M.
Morrison, 1887. iv, [2], 658, cviii
p. 05-249
E176 .L292 MRR Biog.

Poore, Benjamin Perley, The
political register and congressional
directory: Boston, Houghton, Osgood
and company, 1878. vi p., 1 l., 716
p. 05-273
E176 .P82 MRR Alc.

Ralph Nader Congress Project.
Citizens look at Congress.
Washington, Grossman Publishers,
c1972] 9 v. 328.73/092/2 73-
169366
JK1010 .R35 1972 MRR Ref Desk.

United States. Congress.
Biographical directory of the
American Congress, 1774-1971,
[Washington] U.S. Govt. Print. Off.,
1971. 1972 p. [$15.75]
328.73/0922 B 79-616224
JK1010 .A5 MRR Biog.

United States. Congress. Official
congressional directory, Washington,
U.S. Govt. Print. Off. [etc.] 328.73
06-35330
JK1011 MRR Ref Desk Latest edition
/ MRR Ref Desk Latest edition /
MRR Ref Desk Latest edition / MRR
Alc Partial set / Sci RR Latest
edition

UNITED STATES. CONGRESS--COMMITTEES.
Goodwin, George. The little
legislatures: [Amherst] University
of Massachusetts Press, 1970. xv,
284 p. [8.50] 328.73/07/65 75-
103477
JK1029 .G6 MRR Alc.

Lees, John David. The committee
system of the United States Congress,
London, Routledge & K. Paul; New
York, Humanities P., 1967. xiv, 114
p. [15/- 7/6 (pbk.)] 328.73/07/65
67-22212
JK1029 .L4 MRR Alc.

UNITED STATES. CONGRESS--DIRECTORIES.
Congressional staff directory. [1st]-
ed.; 1959- Washington [etc.]
328.738 59-13987
JK1012 MRR Ref Desk Latest edition
/ Sci RR Latest edition

Poore, Benjamin Perley, The
political register and congressional
directory: Boston, Houghton, Osgood
and company, 1878. vi p., 1 l., 716
p. 05-273
E176 .P82 MRR Alc.

UNITED STATES. CONGRESS--ELECTIONS.
United States. Congress. House.
Statistics of the presidential and
congressional election of November 2,
1920- Showing the highest vote for
presidential electors, and the vote
cast for each nominee for United
states senator, representative,
delegate, and resident commissioner
to the Sixty-seventh- Congress,
together with a recapitulation
thereof, including the electoral
vote. 1921- Washington, U.S. Govt.
Print Off. 324.73 21-26389
JK1967 .A3 MRR Alc Partial set

UNITED STATES. CONGRESS--HISTORY.
Riddick, Floyd Millard,
Congressional procedure, Boston,
Chapman and Grimes [c1941] xvii,
[2], 387 p. incl. illus. (plans)
tables, diagr. 328.735 41-15539
JK1096 .R53 MRR Alc.

UNITED STATES. CONGRESS--PERIODICALS.
Congressional Quarterly, inc.
Congressional roll call. Washington.
328.73/07/75 72-77849
JK1 .C6635 MRR Alc Full set

UNITED STATES. CONGRESS--POWERS AND
DUTIES.
Wallace, Robert Ash, Congressional
control of Federal spending.
Detroit, Wayne State University
Press, 1960. x, 188 p. 328.341 60-
16509
HJ2052 .W3 MRR Alc.

UNITED STATES. CONGRESS--REGISTERS.
Barone, Michael. The almanac of
American politics: [2d ed.] Boston,
Gambit [c1973] xxiii, 1240 p.
[$15.00] 328.73 72-96875
JK271 .B343 1974 MRR Ref Desk.

Congressional pictorial directory.
82d- Cong.; 1951- Washington, U.S.
Govt. Print. Off. 68-61223
JK1011 .A32 MRR Ref Desk Latest
edition

Congressional Quarterly, inc.
Members of Congress, 1789-1970.
Washington, Congressional Quarterly
[1971] 187 p. [$4.00] 328.73/07/3
77-178899
JK1012 .Z5 1971 MRR Ref Desk.

Congressional Quarterly, inc.
Members of Congress, 1945-1970.
Washington, Congressional Quarterly
[1970] 44 p. [2.50] 328.73/07/3
74-120727
JK1012.Z5 1970 MRR Ref Desk.

United States. Congress. Official
congressional directory, Washington,
U.S. Govt. Print. Off. [etc.] 328.73
06-35330
JK1011 MRR Ref Desk Latest edition
/ MRR Ref Desk Latest edition /
MRR Ref Desk Latest edition / MRR
Alc Partial set / Sci RR Latest
edition

United States. Congress. The United
States Congressional Directories,
1789-1840. New York, Columbia
University Press, 1973. 417 p.
[$20.00] 328.73/0025 73-15907
JK1011 .U53 MRR Ref Desk.

UNITED STATES. CONGRESS--RULES AND
PRACTICE.
Froman, Lewis Acrelius, The
congressional process: Boston,
Little, Brown [1967] xvii, 221 p.
328.73/05 67-18261
JK1096 .F7 MRR Alc.

Riddick, Floyd Millard,
Congressional procedure, Boston,
Chapman and Grimes [c1941] xvii,
[2], 387 p. incl. illus. (plans)
tables, diagr. 328.735 41-15539
JK1096 .R53 MRR Alc.

Riddick, Floyd Millard, The United
States Congress; organization and
procedure. Manassas, Va., National
Capitol Publishers [1949] xi, 459 p.
328.735 49-1982
JK1096 .R54 MRR Ref Desk.

Smith, George Howard Edward,
Congress in action; Manassas, Va.,
National Capitol Publishers [1948]
87 p. 328.373 48-782
JK1096 .S55 MRR Alc.

UNITED STATES. CONGRESS--VOTING--
PERIODICALS.
National journal reports. v. 5, no.
30- July 28, 1973- [Washington,
Government Research Corporation]
320.9/73 73-645726
JK1 .N28 MRR Alc Full set

UNITED STATES. CONGRESS BIBLIOGRAPHY.
United States. Superintendent of
Documents. Catalog of the Public
documents of the Congress and of all
departments of the Government of the
United States: the Comprehensive
index provided for the Act of Jan.
12, 1895. no. [1]-25; Mar. 4,
1893/June 30, 1895-Jan. 1, 1939/Dec.
31, 1940. Washington, U.S. Govt.
Print. Off. 06-12151
Z1223 .A13 MRR Gallery Full set /
MRR Alc (Deck 33) Full set

UNITED STATES. CONGRESS. HOUSE.
Carroll, Holbert N. The House of
Representatives and foreign affairs.
Pittsburgh, University of Pittsburgh
[1958] 365 p. 328.73 58-10705
JK1319 .C3 MRR Alc.

Congressional Quarterly Service,
Washington, D.C. Congressional roll
call; a chronology and analysis of
votes in the House and Senate, 91st
Congress, second session. Washington
[1971] 52, 71S, 91R, 4A p. [$8.00]
328.73/077 75-156289
JK1059 91st .C65 MRR Alc.

Galloway, George Barnes, History of
the House of Representatives. New
York, Crowell [1962, c1961] xii, 334
p. 328.73 61-17413
JK1316 .G2 MRR Alc.

MacNeil, Neil, Forge of democracy:
the House of Representatives. New
York, D. McKay [1963] 496 p.
328.73 63-11721
JK1331 .M2 MRR Alc.

Smith, William Henry, Speakers of
the House of representatives of the
United States, Baltimore, Md., S. J.
Gaeng, 1928. 4 p. l., [xiii]-xvi,
261 p. 28-9295
E176 .S69 MRR Biog.

UNITED STATES. CONGRESS. HOUSE--
ARCHIVES.
United States. National Archives.
Preliminary inventory of the records
of the United States House of
Representatives, 1789-1946 (Record
group 233) Washington, 1959. 2 v.
a 59-9361
CD3026 .A32 no. 113 MRR Alc.

UNITED STATES. CONGRESS. HOUSE--
ELECTION DISTRICTS.
Congressional Quarterly, inc.
Congressional districts in the 1970s.
Washington [1973] 236 p. [$10.00]
328.73/07/345 73-2311
JK1341 .C66 MRR Ref Desk.

UNITED STATES. CONGRESS. HOUSE--
ELECTION DISTRICTS--HANDBOOKS, MANUALS,
ETC.
Barone, Michael. The almanac of
American politics: [2d ed.] Boston,
Gambit [c1973] xxiii, 1240 p.
[$15.00] 328.73 72-96875
JK271 .B343 1974 MRR Ref Desk.

UNITED STATES. CONGRESS. HOUSE--
ELECTION DISTRICTS--MAPS.
United States. Bureau of the Census.
Congressional district atlas
(districts of the 93d Congress).
[Washington, For sale by the Supt. of
Docs., U.S. Govt. Print. Off., 1973]
1 v. (unpaged) [$3.70 $3.25 (GPO
bookstore)] 912/.1/3287307345 72-
600344
G1201.F7 U45 1973 MRR Alc.

UNITED STATES. CONGRESS. HOUSE--
ELECTION DISTRICTS--STATISTICS.
Congressional Quarterly Service,
Washington, D.C. CQ census analysis:
congressional districts of the United
States; Washington [1964] 1783-1894
p. 312.9 64-7968
HA217 .C62 MRR Ref Desk.

United States. Bureau of the Census.
Congressional district data book: 93d
Congress; [Washington; For sale by
the Supt. of Docs., U.S. Govt. Print.
off., 1973] xvii, 550 p. [$8.30]
312/.0973 74-601251
HA205 .B87 1973 MRR Ref Desk.

UNITED STATES. CONGRESS. HOUSE--
ELECTIONS--STATISTICS.
Republican Congressional Committee.
1970 congressional vote statistics.
[Washington, 1971] 1 v. (various
pagings) 328.73/077 78-25665
JK1968 1970 .R46 MRR Alc.

Republican Congressional Committee.
1972 congressional vote statistics,
93rd Congress: [Washington, 1973] 1
v. (various pagings) 324/.2 73-
168210
JK1968 1972 .R46 1973 MRR Alc.

UNITED STATES. CONGRESS. HOUSE--HISTORY-
-SOURCES--BIBLIOGRAPHY.
United States. National Archives.
Preliminary inventory of the records
of the United States House of
Representatives, 1789-1946 (Record
group 233) Washington, 1959. 2 v.
a 59-9361
CD3026 .A32 no. 113 MRR Alc.

UNITED STATES. CONGRESS. HOUSE--RULES
AND PRACTICE.
Cannon, Clarence, Cannon's
Precedents of the House of
representatives of the United States
Washington, Govt. print. off., 1935-
41. 6 v. 328.735 41-13680
JK1438 .H62 vol. 6-11 MRR Alc.

Cannon's procedure in the House of
Representatives. 1920- Washington,
U.S. Govt. Print. Off. 20-13113
JK1435 .C35 MRR Ref Desk Latest
edition

UNITED STATES. CONGRESS. HOUSE-- (Cont.)
Hinds, Asher Crosby, Hinds'
Precedents of the House of
representatives of the United States
Washington, Govt. print. off., 1907
[reprinted 1935] 5 v. 328.735 36-
26617
JK1438 .H62 MRR Alc.

United States. Congress. House.
Constitution of the United States,
Jefferson's manual, the rules of the
House of representatives ... and a
digest and manual of the rules and
practice of the House of
representatives. Washington. 06-
17027
JK1304 MRR Ref Desk Latest edition

UNITED STATES. CONGRESS. HOUSE.
COMMITTEE ON THE JUDICIARY.
Congressional Quarterly, inc.
Impeachment and the U.S. Congress.
Washington, 1974. 60 p.
342./73/062 74-5285
KF4985 .C65 MRR Ref Desk.

UNITED STATES. CONGRESS. SENATE.
Congressional Quarterly Service,
Washington, D.C. Congressional roll
call; a chronology and analysis of
votes in the House and Senate, 91st
Congress, second session. Washington
[1971] 52, 71S, 91B, 4A p. [$8.00]
328.73/077 75-156289
JK1059 91st .C65 MRR Alc.

Haynes, George Henry, The Senate of
the United States, Boston, Houghton
Mifflin company, 1938. 2 v. 328.73
38-38772
JK1161 .H28 MRR Alc.

Riddick, Floyd Millard, Majority and
minority leaders of the Senate;
Washington, For sale by the Supt. of
Docs., U.S. Govt. Print. Off., 1969.
19 p. [0.20] 328.73/07 71-602375

JK1161 .R48 MRR Ref Desk.

White, William Smith. Citadel, the
story of the U.S. Senate. [1st ed.]
New York, Harper [c1957] 274 p.
328.73 56-11089
JK1161 .W5 MRR Alc.

UNITED STATES. CONGRESS. SENATE--
ARCHIVES.
United States. National Archives.
Preliminary inventory of the records
of the United States Senate.
Washington, 1950. x, 284 p.
016.32875 a 50-9248
CD3026 .A32 no. 23 MRR Alc.

UNITED STATES. CONGRESS. SENATE--
BIOGRAPHY.
Douth, George. Leaders in profile:
the United States Senate. 1972-
ed. New York, Sperr & Douth. [etc.]
328/.73/0922 [B] 77-188152
JK1154 .D68 MRR Biog Latest
edition

Hatch, Louis Clinton, A history of
the vice-presidency of the United
States, New York, The American
historical society, inc., 1934. viii
p., 2 l., [3]-437 p. 353.03 34-
8999
E176 .B35 MRR Alc.

UNITED STATES. CONGRESS. SENATE--
ELECTIONS.
Pitchell, Robert J., ed. Indiana
votes; Bloomington, Bureau of
Government Research, Indiana
University, 1960. 103 p.
324.209772 62-62552
JK5693 1960 .P5 MRR Alc.

UNITED STATES. CONGRESS. SENATE--RULES
AND PRACTICE.
Harris, Joseph Pratt, The advice and
consent of the Senate; Berkeley,
University of California Press, 1953.
xii, 457 p. 328.735 53-11239
JK1274 .H3 MRR Alc.

United States. Congress. Senate.
Senate manual. Washington. 01-9223

JK1151 MRR Ref Desk Latest edition

UNITED STATES. CONGRESS. SENATE.
COMMITTEE ON FOREIGN RELATIONS.
Farnsworth, David Nelson, The Senate
Committee on Foreign Relations.
Urbana, University of Illinois Press,
1961. vi, 189 p. 327.73 61-62766

JK1240.F6 F3 MRR Alc.

UNITED STATES. CONSTITUTION.
Elliot, Jonathan, ed. The debates in
the several State conventions on the
adoption of the Federal Constitution
as recommended by the general
convention at Philadelphia in 1787
... 2d ed., with considerable
additions. Philadelphia, Lippincott,
1937. 5 v. 342.73/02 mrr01-64
JK141 1937 MRR Alc.

Lieberman, Jethro Koller.
Understanding our Constitution New
York, Walker [1967] 282 p. 342/.73
67-13236
KF4550 .L5 1967 MRR Alc.

McDonald, Forrest. We the people;
Chicago, University of Chicago Press
[1958] x, 436 p. 342.732 58-14905

KF4541 .M24 MRR Alc.

Stearns, Charles Woodward, A
concordance to the Constitution of
the United States of America; New
York, Poole & Maclauchlan, printers,
1872. viii, 153 p. 09-21731
JK246 .S78 MRR Alc.

Thorpe, Francis Newton. comp. The
Federal and State constitutions,
colonial charters, and other organic
laws of the state, territories, and
colonies now or heretofore forming
the United States of America.
Washington, Govt. Print. Off., 1909.
7 v. 09-35371
KF4541 .T48 MRR Alc.

United States. Bureau of rolls and
library. Documentary history of the
Constitution of the United States of
America, 1786-1870. Washington,
Department of state, 1894 [i.e. 1901]-
05. 5 v. 02-10164
JK111 .A52 MRR Alc.

United States. Constitution
sesquicentennial commission. History
of the formation of the union under
the Constitution [Washington, U.S.
Govt. print. off., 1941] x, 885 p.
incl. front., illus. (1 col.; incl.
maps) ports., facsims., tables,
diagrs. 342.73 41-50348
JK166 1941 MRR Alc.

United States. Constitutional
convention, 1787. The records of the
Federal convention of 1787; Rev. ed.
New Haven, Yale university press;
London, H. Milford, Oxford university
press, 1937. 4 v. 342.732 37-
25324
KF4510 .F3 1937 MRR Alc.

United States. Library of Congress.
The Constitution of the United
States, Washington, 1952. 43 p.
342.739 52-60009
Z663 .C6 1952 MRR Alc.

United States. Library of Congress.
Manuscript division. The Declaration
of independence, the Constitution of
the United States, and other historic
material in the Division of
manuscripts of the Library of
Congress. [Washington] The Library
of Congress, Division of manuscripts
[1941] 14, 2 p. 027.5753 091 41-
50007
Z663.34 .D4 MRR Alc.

UNITED STATES. CONSTITUTION--
BIBLIOGRAPHY.
United States. Library of Congress.
Division of bibliography. Select
list of books on the Constitution of
the United States; Washington, Govt.
print. off., 1903. 14 p. 03-16880

Z663.Z8 .S335 MRR Alc.

UNITED STATES. CONSTITUTION--SIGNERS.
McGee, Dorothy Horton. Framers of
the Constitution. New York, Dodd,
Mead [1968] xvii, 394 p.
342.73/0922 67-26154
JK146 .M279 MRR Alc.

UNITED STATES. CONSTITUTION. 1ST-10TH
AMENDMENTS--SOURCES.
Schwartz, Bernard, comp. The Bill of
Rights; a documentary history. New
York, Chelsea House Publishers, 1971.
2 v. (xvii, 1234 p.) 342/.73/029
71-150209
KF4744 1971 MRR Alc.

UNITED STATES. CONSTITUTIONAL
CONVENTION, 1787.
McDonald, Forrest. We the people;
Chicago, University of Chicago Press
[1958] x, 436 p. 342.732 58-14905

KF4541 .M24 MRR Alc.

UNITED STATES. CONTINENTAL CONGRESS.
Burnett, Edmund Cody, The
Continental Congress. New York, W.
W. Norton [1964, c1941] xii, 757 p.
66-11792
E303 .B93 1964 MRR Alc.

Burnett, Edmund Cody, ed. Letters of
members of the Continental Congress.
Gloucester, Mass., P. Smith, 1963. 8
v. 973.31 64-2503
JK1033 .B8 1963 MRR Alc.

UNITED STATES. CONTINENTAL CONGRESS--
BIBLIOGRAPHY.
United States. Continental congress.
Journals of the Continental Congress,
1774-1789. Washington, U.S. Govt.
print. off., 1904-37. 34 v. 05-59

J10 .A5 MRR Alc (Dk 33)

United States. Library of Congress.
Manuscript Division. Bibliographical
notes on the issues of the
Continental Congress, 1774[-1783]
Washington, Govt. Print. Off., 1904-
22. 10 v. in 04-35779
Z663.34 .B5 MRR Alc.

UNITED STATES. CONTINENTAL CONGRESS--
BIOGRAPHY.
United States. Congress.
Biographical directory of the
American Congress, 1774-1971,
[Washington] U.S. Govt. Print. Off.,
1971. 1972 p. [$15.75]
328.73/0922 B 79-616224
JK1010 .A5 MRR Biog.

UNITED STATES. CONTINENTAL CONGRESS--
MANUSCRIPTS.
United States. Library of Congress.
Manuscript division. Calendar of the
correspondence of George Washington,
Washington, Govt. print. off., 1906.
741 p. 06-35011
Z663.34 .C27 MRR Alc.

UNITED STATES. COPYRIGHT OFFICE.
CATALOG OF COPYRIGHT ENTRIES.
Rogers, Joseph William, U.S.
national bibliography and the
copyright law; New York, Bowker,
1960. xii, 115 p. 015.73 60-15545

Z1216 .R6 MRR Alc.

UNITED STATES. COPYRIGHT OFFICE.
United States. Copyright Office. The
Copyright Office of the United States
of America. [1st]- 1952-
[Washington, U.S. Govt. Print. Off.]
655.673 57-60008
Z663.8 .C6 MRR Alc MRR Alc Latest
Edition

UNITED STATES. CUSTOM HOUSE, NEW YORK.
Custom house guide. New York. 99-
1545
HE953.N5 C8 MRR Alc Latest edition

Custom house guide. New York. 99-
1545
HE953.N5 C8 MRR Alc Latest edition

UNITED STATES. DECLARATION OF
INDEPENDENCE.
Boyd, Julian Parks, The Declaration
of independence; Princeton,
Princeton university press, 1945. 2
p. l., 46 p. 973.313 a 45-1832
JK128 .B66 MRR Alc.

Boyd, Julian Parks, The Declaration
of independence; Washington, The
Library of Congress, 1943. 1 p. l.,
5-36 p., 2 l. 973.313 43-52080
Z663 .D38 MRR Alc.

Hawke, David Freeman. A transaction
of free men; New York, Scribner
[1964] 282 p. 973.313 64-13632
E221 .H26 MRR Alc.

Malone, Dumas, The story of the
Declaration of independence. New
York, Oxford University Press, 1954.
282 p. 973.313 54-10002
JK128 .M3 MRR Alc.

United States. Library of Congress.
The Declaration of independence;
Washington, 1950. 20 p. 342.73 50-
62958
Z663 .D4 MRR Alc.

United States. Library of Congress.
Manuscript division. The Declaration
of independence, the Constitution of
the United States, and other historic
material in the Division of
manuscripts of the Library of
Congress. [Washington] The Library
of Congress, Division of manuscripts
[1941] 14, 2 p. 027.5753 091 41-
50007
Z663.34 .D4 MRR Alc.

UNITED STATES. DECLARATION OF
INDEPENDENCE--SIGNERS.
Addis, Raymond E. Re-introducing our
signers of the Declaration of
independence, Holly, Mich., The
Holly herald [c1940] 132 p.
978.313 40-36029
E221 .A45 MRR Alc.

United States. National Park Service.
Signers of the Declaration;
Washington; [For sale by the Supt. of
Docs., U.S. Govt. Print. Off.] 1973
[i.e. 1974] xii, 310 p. [$5.65]
973.3/13/0922 B 73-600028
E221 .U78 1974 MRR Alc.

UNITED STATES. DEPT. OF AGRICULTURE.
Whitlock, Carolyn, Abbreviations
used in the Department of agriculture
for titles of publications,
Washington, D.C. [U.S. Govt. print.
off., 1939] 278 p.   016.05   agr39-
503
    Z6945.A2 W5 MRR Alc.

UNITED STATES. DEPT. OF DEFENSE.
Borklund, Carl W. The Department of
Defense   New York, Praeger [1968] x,
342 p.   353.6   68-16080
    UA23.6 .B58 MRR Alc.

UNITED STATES. DEPT. OF HEALTH,
EDUCATION, AND WELFARE.
United States. Dept. of Health,
Education, and Welfare. Center for
Community Planning. HEW cities
handbook. [Rev. Washington: For
sale by the Supt. of Docs., U.S.
Govt. Print. Off., 1969] 1 v.
(unpaged) [0.50]   353.84   76-604330

    HV85 .A554 1969 MRR Alc.

UNITED STATES. DEPT. OF HOUSING AND
URBAN DEVELOPMENT.
Willmann, John B. The Department of
Housing and Urban Development   New
York, Praeger [1967] xiii, 207 p.
353.85   67-24679
    HT175.U6 W48 MRR Alc.

UNITED STATES. DEPT. OF STATE.
EXECUTIVE AGREEMENT SERIES.
United States. Dept. of state.
Subject index of the Treaty series
and the Executive agreement series.
Washington, U.S. Govt. print. off.,
1932. v, 214 p.   341.273   32-26434

    JX235.9 .A3 Index 1931 MRR Ref
    Desk.

UNITED STATES. DEPT. OF STATE.
Stuart, Graham Henry, The Department
of State; a history of its
organization, procedure, and
personnel; New York, Macmillan Co.,
1949. x, 517 p.   353.1   49-11378
    JK853 .S84 MRR Alc.

UNITED STATES. DEPT. OF STATE--
BIOGRAPHY.
Graebner, Norman A., ed. An
uncertain tradition; American
Secretaries of State in the twentieth
century. New York, McGraw-Hill,
1961. 341 p.   353.1   61-8654
    E744 .G7 MRR Alc.

Patterson, Richard Sharpe, comp. The
Secretaries of State; [Washington,
U.S. Govt. Print. Off., 1956] 124 p.
923.273   sd 57-2
    E183.7 P3 MRR Biog.

UNITED STATES. DIPLOMATIC AND CONSULAR
SERVICE--BIBLIOGRAPHY.
United States. Library of Congress.
Division of bibliography. ... List
of references on the United States
consular service, Washington, Govt.
print. off., 1905. 27 p.   05-3074
    Z663.28 .L583 MRR Alc.

UNITED STATES. EXECUTIVE OFFICE OF THE
PRESIDENT.
Roberts, Charles Wesley, LBJ's inner
circle, New York, Delacorte Press
[1965] 223 p.   973.9230922   65-
21935
    E846 .R56 MRR Alc.

UNITED STATES. GOVERNMENT PUBLICATIONS--
BIBLIOGRAPHY.
United States. Superintendent of
Documents. Numerical lists and
schedule of volumes of the reports
and documents of the 73d-- Congress
... 1933/34- Washington [U.S. Govt.
print. off.]   015.73   34-28260
    Z1223 .A15 MRR Ref Desk

UNITED STATES. INTERNAL REVENUE SERVICE.
Doris, Lillian, ed. The American way
in taxation: Englewood Cliffs, N.J.,
Prentice-Hall [1963] 301 p.
336.206173   63-12128
    HJ5018 .D6 MRR Alc.

UNITED STATES. JOINT PUBLICATIONS
RESEARCH SERVICE--BIBLIOGRAPHY.
White, Thomas N. Guide to United
States-J.P.R.S. research
translations, 1957-1966; Washington,
Research & Microfilm Publications
[1966] 67 p.   017   66-29498
    Z1223.Z7 W55 MRR Alc.

UNITED STATES. JOINT PUBLICATIONS
RESEARCH SERVICE--INDEXES.
Catalog cards in book form for United
States Joint Publications Research
Service translations. v. -8; -
Jan./June 1970. New York [etc.] CCM
Information Corp. [etc.]   75-104064
    Began with vol. for 1957/61.
    Z1223.Z9 K9 Sci RR   Sci RR Partial
    set / MRR Alc Full set

Transdex; v. 9-   July 1970-   New
York, CCM Information Corp. 015/.73
77-612605
    AS36 .U574   Sci RR Full Set / MRR
    Alc Full set

UNITED STATES. LIBRARY OF CONGRESS.
Drake, Alice Hutchins. Mural
decorations in the Library of
Congress, [Washington, D.C., Printed
by J. C. Wood, c1932] 26 p.
027.573   32-17646
    Z733.U58 D85 MRR Ref Desk.

Garfield, James Abram, Pres. U.S.,
James A. Garfield papers.
Washington, Library of Congress,
1970. 177 reels.   016.9738/4/0924
73-9594
    Z663.34 .G34 MRR Alc.

Goodrum, Charles A. The Library of
Congress New York, Praeger [1974]
ix, 292 p.   027.573   72-189909
    Z733.U6 G66 MRR Alc.

Gurney, Gene. The Library of
Congress; New York, Crown Publishers
[1966] 128 p.   027.5753   66-15125
    Z733.U58 G8 MRR Alc.

King, Gilbert William, Automation
and the Library of Congress.
Washington, Library of Congress; [for
sale by the Superintendent of
Documents, U.S. Govt. Print. Off.]
1963 [i.e. 1964] vii, 88 p.   64-
60015
    Z663 .A9 MRR Alc.

L C and you. 1944- Washington.
027.5753   53-60022
    Z663.95 .L5 MRR Alc   MRR Alc Latest
    edition

Lacy, Dan Mabry, The Library of
Congress: Washington, 1950. 157-
179, 235-258 p.   027.5753   50-62998

    Z663 .L445 MRR Alc.

Roberts, Martin Arnold, The Library
of Congress in relation to research,
[Washington] Govt. print. off., 1939.
3 p. l., 54, [1] p.   027.5753   39-
26943
    Z663 .L453 MRR Alc.

[Roberts, Martin Arnold] The annex
of the Library of Congress.
[Washington, U.S. Govt. print. off.,
1938] 1 p. l., 15 p.   027.5753   38-
7454
    Z663 .A85 1938a MRR Alc.

Salamanca, Lucy. Fortress of
freedom: Philadelphia, New York
[etc.] J. B. Lippincott company,
1942. 445 p.   027.5753   42-10055
    Z733.U6 S3 MRR Alc.

Trienens, Roger J. Pioneer imprints
from fifty States, Washington,
Library of Congress; [for sale by the
Supt. of Docs., U.S. Govt. Print.
Off.] 1973. 87 p.   [$4.25]
686.2/0973   72-10069
    Z663 .P5 MRR Alc.

United States. Library of Congress.
English language books by title:
Detroit, Gale Research Co., 1971. 20
v.   018/.1   75-165487
    Z881.A1 C34 MRR Alc (Dk 33)

United States. Library of Congress.
Introduction to the Near East
collections in the Library of
Congress, Washington, 1953. 5 p.
016.956   53-63370
    Z663.387 .I5 MRR Alc.

United States. Library of Congress.
The Library of Congress. 3d ed.
Washington, Govt. print. off.,
Library branch, 1922. 21 p.   22-
26006
    Z663 .L44 1922 MRR Alc.

United States. Library of Congress.
Report of the Librarian of Congress
on the Bryant memorandum,
Washington, 1962. 54 l.   62-64798
    Z663 .R39 MRR Alc.

United States. Library of Congress.
Treasures from the Lessing J.
Rosenwald Collection; Washington,
1973. [57] p.   mrr01-74
    Z663.4 .T74 MRR Alc.

United States. Library of Congress.
Exhibits Office. An American
sampler: Washington, Library of
Congress, 1974. [32] p.   917.3/03
74-16302
    Z663.15 .A65 MRR Alc.

United States. Library of Congress.
Information Systems Office.
Terminals requirements for the
Library of Congress' central
bibliographic system. Washington,
1970. 110 p.   025/.02   71-610454
    Z699.3 .U5 MRR Alc.

United States. Library of Congress.
Manuscript Division. Benjamin
Franklin: a register and index of his
papers in the Library of Congress.
Washington, Library of Congress,
1973. iii, 27 p.   016.9733/2/0924
73-4185
    Z663.34 .F69 MRR Alc.

United States. Library of Congress.
Manuscript Division. Claude Charles
Bloch, Julius Augustus Furer, John
Franklin Shafroth, William Harrison
Standley: a register of their papers
in the Library of Congress.
Washington, Library of Congress,
1973. iii; 6, 10, 4, 11, p.
016.359   73-4374
    Z663.34 .B55 MRR Alc.

United States. Library of Congress.
Planning Committee. Report.
Washington, 1948. 8 p.   027.5753
48-2964
    Z663.18 .R4 1948 MRR Alc.

United States. Library of Congress.
Processing Dept. The role of the
Library of Congress in the
international exchange of official
publications; Washington, 1953. 85
p.   021.852   53-60020
    Z663.7 .R6 MRR Alc.

United States. Library of Congress.
Reference Dept. A guide to special
book collections in the Library of
Congress, Washington, 1949. 2, 66
p.   027.5753   50-60175
    Z663.2 .G78 MRR Alc.

Walter, Emily Loiseau, comp. A
complete collection of the quotations
and inscriptions in the Library of
Congress, 10th rev. ed. Baltimore,
S. J. Gaeng, 1925. 3 p. l., 11-47 p.
25-4054
    Z733.U59 W2 1925 MRR Alc.

Walter, Emily Loiseau, comp. A
complete collection of the quotations
and inscriptions in the Library of
Congress, 6th rev. ed. --
Baltimore, Williams & Wilkins
company, 1907. 3 p. l., 11-45 p.
07-30624
    Z733.U59 W2 1907 MRR Ref Desk.

Wilson, Woodrow, Pres. U.S., Woodrow
Wilson papers. Washington, Library
of Congress [1973] 540 reels.
016.97391/3/0924   73-7658
    Z663.34 .W514 MRR Alc.

Winter, Ezra Augustus, 1886- The
Canterbury pilgrims, Washington
[U.S. Govt. print. off.] 1946.
folder ([6] p.)   751.73   46-27985
    Z663 .C2 MRR Alc.

Winter, Ezra Augustus, The Thomas
Jefferson murals in the Thomas
Jefferson Room, Library of Congress.
Washington [U.S. Govt. Print. Off.]
1946. folder ([4] p.)   751.73   51-
60090
    Z663 .T47 MRR Alc.

UNITED STATES. LIBRARY OF CONGRESS--
APPROPRIATIONS AND EXPENDITURES.
United States. Library of Congress.
Statement of the librarian of
Congress in support of the
supplementary estimates of
appropriations for the fiscal year
1941. [Washington, 1940] 42 p.
027.5753   40-30316
    Z663 .S76 MRR Alc.

UNITED STATES. LIBRARY OF CONGRESS--
BIBLIOGRAPHY.
United States. Library of Congress.
Library of Congress catalogs in book
form and related publications.
[Washington, 1971] [21] p.
015/.753   72-612348
    Z663 .L452 MRR Alc.

United States. Library of Congress.
General Reference and Bibliography
Division. The Library of Congress;
Washington, 1956. vi, 20 p.
016.0275757   56-60082
    Z663.28 .L54 MRR Alc.

UNITED STATES. LIBRARY OF CONGRESS--
CATALOGS.
United States. Library of Congress.
Suggestions for assistants with
reference to catalogues, shelf lists,
uncatalogued books, etc.
[Washington] 1909. 6 l.   53-55565
    Z663.2 .S8 MRR Alc.

United States. Library of Congress.
Processing Dept. The card catalogs
of the Library of Congress;
Washington, 1955. v, 30 p.
027.5753   55-60020
    Z663.7 .C3 MRR Alc.

UNITED STATES. LIBRARY OF CONGRESS--
HANDBOOKS, MANUALS, ETC.
Small, Herbert. Handbook of the new
Library of Congress, Boston, Curtis
& Cameron, 1897. 3 p l., 128 p.
08-32518
Z733.U58 S63 MRR Ref Desk.

United States. Library of Congress.
Departmental & divisional manuals.
Washington, 1946- v. 027.5753
50-60595
Z663 .A3 MRR Alc.

United States. Library of Congress.
Personnel Office. Manual of
personnel policies, Personnel
Division. Washington, 1953- 1 v.
(loose-leaf) 027.5753 53-60001
Z663.85 .M3 MRR Alc.

UNITED STATES. LIBRARY OF CONGRESS--
HISTORY.
Johnston, William Dawson, History of
the Library of Congress. Washington,
Govt. print. off., 1904. 535 p. 04-
33371
Z733.U6 J6 MRR Alc.

Mearns, David Chambers, The story up
to now: Washington [U.S. Govt.
Print. Off.] 1947. iii, 226 p.
027.5753 48-45515
Z733.U6 M45 MRR Alc.

UNITED STATES. LIBRARY OF CONGRESS--
POSITIONS.
United States. Library of Congress.
Representative positions in the
Library of Congress. Washington,
U.S. Govt. Print. Off., 1948. xi,
576 p. 027.5753 48-47298
Z663 .R4 MRR Alc.

UNITED STATES. LIBRARY OF CONGRESS--
REGISTERS.
United States. Library of Congress.
A tribute to those men of the Library
of Congress who gave their lives in
the World War, 1941-1945.
[Washington, 1948] [29] p.
027.5753 49-45538
Z663 .T7 MRR Alc.

UNITED STATES. LIBRARY OF CONGRESS--
VIEWS.
United States. Library of Congress.
The Library of Congress and its work:
Washington, U.S. Govt. Print. Off.]
1950. [63] p. 027.5753 51-60336
Z663 .L45 MRR Alc.

UNITED STATES. LIBRARY OF CONGRESS.
CARD DIVISION.
United States. Library of Congress.
Cooperative cataloging and
classification service. Cooperative
work of Card division, Union catalog,
Cooperative cataloging and
classification service and A.L.A.
Cooperative cataloging committee.
Washington, 1938. v p., 26 numb. l.
cd 38-158
Z663.745.C63 MRR Alc.

UNITED STATES. LIBRARY OF CONGRESS.
CHILDREN'S BOOK SECTION.
Haviland, Virginia. Serving those
who serve children: Washington,
Library of Congress: for sale by the
Supt. of Docs., Govt. Prit. Off.,
1966] 16 p. [0.20] 027.5/753 66-
62960
Z663.292 .H36 MRR Alc.

UNITED STATES. LIBRARY OF CONGRESS.
COOPERATIVE CATALOGING AND
CLASSIFICATION SERVICE.
United States. Library of Congress.
Cooperative cataloging and
classification service. Cooperative
work of Card division, Union catalog,
Cooperative cataloging and
classification service and A.L.A.
Cooperative cataloging committee.
Washington, 1938. v p., 26 numb. l.
cd 38-158
Z663.745.C63 MRR Alc.

UNITED STATES. LIBRARY OF CONGRESS.
GEOGRAPHY AND MAP DIVISION.
United States. Library of Congress.
Geography and Map Division. The
bibliography of cartography. Boston,
G. K. Hall, 1973. 5 v. 016.526 73-
12877
Z6028 .U49 1973 MRR Alc (Dk 33)

United States. Library of Congress.
Geography and Map Division.
Panoramic maps of Anglo-American
cities: Washington, Library of
Congress: [for sale by the Supt. of
Docs., U.S. Govt. Print. Off.] 1974.
v, 118 p. 016.912/7 73-18312
Z663.35 .P35 MRR Alc.

UNITED STATES. LIBRARY OF CONGRESS.
HISPANIC FOUNDATION.
United States. Library of Congress.
The Hispanic activities of the
Library of Congress, Washington,
1946. 36 p. 027.5753 46-26464
Z663.32 .H5 MRR Alc.

UNITED STATES. LIBRARY OF CONGRESS.
LATIN AMERICAN, PORTUGUESE, AND SPANISH
DIVISION.
United States. Library of Congress.
Latin American, Portuguese, and
Spanish Division. The Archive of
Hispanic Literature on Tape:
Washington, Library of Congress: [for
sale by the Supt. of Docs., U.S.
Govt. Print. Off.] 1974. xii, 516 p.
016.86/007/22 73-19812
Z663.32 .A7 MRR Alc.

UNITED STATES. LIBRARY OF CONGRESS.
LEGISLATIVE REFERENCE SERVICE.
United States. Library of Congress.
Legislative Reference Service. The
Legislative Reference Service,
Washington, Library of Congress,
1952. 20 l. 027.5753 54-60561
Z663.6 .L4 MRR Alc.

UNITED STATES. LIBRARY OF CONGRESS.
MANUSCRIPT DIVISION.
United States. Library of Congress.
Manuscript Division. Dudley Wright
Knox: a register of his papers in the
Library of Congress, Washington,
Library of Congress, 1971. 16 p.
016.359/007/22 70-173823
Z663.34 .K66 MRR Alc.

United States. Library of Congress.
Manuscript Division. The Harkness
Collection in the Library of
Congress: Washington, Library of
Congress: [for sale by the Supt. of
Docs., U.S. Govt. Print. Off.] 1974.
xi, 315 p. 016.972/02 73-6747
Z663.34 .H293 MRR Alc.

United States. Library of Congress.
Manuscript Division. William Sowden
Sims: a register of his papers in the
Library of Congress. Washington,
Library of Congress, 1971. 28 p.
016.3593/3/10924 72-600006
Z663.34 .S57 MRR Alc.

UNITED STATES. LIBRARY OF CONGRESS.
MOTION PICTURE DIVISION.
Niver, Kemp R. Motion pictures from
the Library of Congress paper print
collection, 1894-1912, Berkeley,
University of California Press, 1967.
xxii, 402 p. 016.79143 66-28789
Z5784.M9 N58 MRR Alc.

UNITED STATES. LIBRARY OF CONGRESS.
MUSIC DIVISION.
United States. Library of Congress.
The Music Division in the Library of
Congress. Washington, 1960. 25 p.
026.78 60-64676
Z663.37 .M8 MRR Alc.

UNITED STATES. LIBRARY OF CONGRESS.
NATIONAL UNION CATALOG.
United States. Library of Congress.
General Reference and Bibliography
Division. The national union catalog
reference and related services.
Washington, 1973. 33 p. 027.5753
73-602813
Z663.28 .N37 MRR Alc.

UNITED STATES. LIBRARY OF CONGRESS.
ORDER DIVISION.
United States. Library of Congress.
MARC Development Office. Order
Division automated system.
Washington, 1972. 74 p.
025.2/3/02854 72-12530
Z663.757 .O7 MRR Alc.

UNITED STATES. LIBRARY OF CONGRESS.
POETRY OFFICE.
Two lectures: Leftovers: a care
package Washington, Library of
Congress: [for sale by the Supt. of
Docs., U.S. Govt. Print. Off.] 1973.
iii, 31 p. [$0.35] 811/.009 72-
13401
Z663.293 .T9 MRR Alc.

UNITED STATES. LIBRARY OF CONGRESS.
SUBJECT CATALOGING DIVISION. SUBJECT
HEADINGS USED IN THE DICTIONARY
CATALOGS OF THE LIBRARY OF CONGRESS--
INDEXES.
Williams, James G. Classified
Library of Congress subject headings,
New York, M. Dekker, 1972. 2 v.
025.4 72-91323
Z695.U48 W55 MRR Alc.

UNITED STATES. LIBRARY OF CONGRESS.
UNION CATALOG DIVISION.
United States. Library of Congress.
Cooperative cataloging and
classification service. Cooperative
work of Card division, Union catalog,
Cooperative cataloging and
classification service and A.L.A.
Cooperative cataloging committee.
Washington, 1938. v p., 26 numb. l.
cd 38-158
Z663.745.C63 MRR Alc.

UNITED STATES. MARINE CORPS.
Isely, Jeter Allen. The U.S. Marines
and amphibious war: Princeton,
Princeton University Press, 1951.
vii, 636 p. 940.545 51-9463
D769.45 .I7 MRR Alc.

Pierce, Philip N., The compact
history of the United States Marine
Corps New and rev. ed. New York,
Hawthorn Books [1964] 334 p.
359.960973 64-13280
VE23 .P5 1964 MRR Alc.

UNITED STATES. MARINE CORPS--AVIATION.
Swanborough, Frederick Gordon.
United States Navy aircraft since
1911 London, Putnam, 1968. x, 518
p. [84/-] 623.7/46 70-354248
VG93 .S92 MRR Alc.

UNITED STATES. MARINE CORPS--
BIBLIOGRAPHY.
Dollen, Charles. Bibliography of the
United States Marine Corps, New
York, Scarecrow Press, 1963. 115 p.
016.35996 63-7464
Z6725.U5 D6 MRR Alc.

Moran, John B. Creating a legend:
the complete record of writing about
the United States Marine Corps. [1st
ed.] Chicago, Moran/Andrews [1973]
681 p. [$14.95] 016.3599/6/0973
79-139570
Z6725.U5 M67 MRR Alc.

UNITED STATES. MARINE CORPS--BIOGRAPHY.
Schuon, Karl. U.S. Marine Corps
biographical dictionary: New York,
Watts [1963] vii, 278 p. 923.573
63-16821
E182 .S39 MRR Biog.

UNITED STATES. MARINE CORPS--HISTORY.
Blakeney, Jane, Heroes, U.S. Marine
Corps, 1861-1955: [1st ed.
Washington, 1957] xviii, 621 p.
359.96 57-13185
VE23 .B56 MRR Biog.

Heinl, Robert Debs, Soldiers of the
sea: Annapolis, United States Naval
Institute [1962] 692 p. 359.960973
61-18078
VE23 .H4 MRR Alc.

Smith, Stanley E., comp. The United
States Marine Corps in World War II:
New York, Random House [1969] xxi,
965 p. [17.95] 940.542/6 67-22643
D767 .S62 MRR Alc.

United States Naval Institute.
Almanac of naval facts. Annapolis
[1964] 305 p. 973 64-12269
E182 .U587 MRR Alc.

UNITED STATES. MARINE CORPS--HISTORY--
CIVIL WAR, 1861-1865.
Lord, Francis Alfred, They fought
for the Union. [1st ed.]
Harrisburg, Pa., Stackpole Co. [1960]
375 p. 973.741 60-8813
E491 .L89 MRR Alc.

UNITED STATES. MARINE CORPS--MEDALS,
BADGES, DECORATIONS, ETC.
Blakeney, Jane, Heroes, U.S. Marine
Corps, 1861-1955: [1st ed.
Washington, 1957] xviii, 621 p.
359.96 57-13185
VE23 .B56 MRR Biog.

UNITED STATES. MARINE CORPS--OFFICERS'
HANDBOOKS.
Thomas, Gerald Carthrae, The Marine
officer's guide 2d ed., rev.
Annapolis, United States Naval
Institute, 1964. xx, 614 p. 359.96
64-13700
VE153 .T5 1964 MRR Alc.

UNITED STATES. MARINE CORPS--REGISTERS.
Callahan, Edward William, ed. List
of officers of the Navy of the United
States and of the Marine Corps from
1775 to 1900: New York, Haskell
House, 1969. 749 p. 359.3/3/20973
68-31274
V11.U7 C2 1969 MRR Biog.

UNITED STATES. MILITARY ACADEMY, WEST
POINT--REGISTERS.
Register of graduates and former
cadets of the United States Military
Academy. 1972- West Point, N.Y.,
Association of Graduates, USMA.
355/.007/1174731 73-640734
U410 .H35 MRR Biog Latest edition

United States. Military Academy, West
Point. Official register of the
officers and cadets. 1818- New York
[etc.] 07-31770
U410 .H3 MRR Biog Latest edition

UNITED STATES. MINT.
Failor, Kenneth M. Medals of the
United States Mint, [Washington: For
sale by the Supt. of Docs., U.S.
Govt. Print. Off., 1969] v, 274 p.
[3.50] 929.8 74-602460
CJ5805 .F3 MRR Alc.

Taxay, Don. The U.S. Mint and
coinage: New York, Arco Pub. Co.
[1966] xii, 400 p. 332.460973 66-
18413
HG459 .T3 MRR Alc.

UNITED STATES. NATIONAL AERONAUTICS AND
SPACE ADMINISTRATION.
Renetzky, Alvin. NASA factbook:
Orange, N.J., Academic Media [1971]
456 p. 629.4/072/073 70-165274
    TL521.312 .R45 MRR Alc.

UNITED STATES. NATIONAL AGRICULTURAL
LIBRARY.
United States. National Agricultural
Library. Catalog. 1966/70- Totowa,
N.J., Rowman and Littlefield. 016.63
72-84831
    Z5076 .U632b MRR Alc (DK 33) Full
    set / Sci RR Full set

UNITED STATES. NATIONAL ARCHIVES.
Jones, Houston Gwynne, The records
of a nation: [1st ed.] New York,
Atheneum, 1969. xviii, 308 p.
[12.95] 026/.973 69-14373
    CD3023 .J6 1969 MRR Alc.

UNITED STATES. NATIONAL ARCHIVES AND
RECORDS SERVICE.
Jones, Houston Gwynne, The records
of a nation. [1st ed.] New York,
Atheneum, 1969. xviii, 308 p.
[12.95] 026/.973 69-14373
    CD3023 .J6 1969 MRR Alc.

UNITED STATES. NATIONAL SCIENCE
FOUNDATION.
Renetzky, Alvin. NSF factbook:
Orange, N.J., Academic Media [1971]
425 p. 507/.2/073 77-165273
    Q11.U84 R45 MRR Alc.

Schaffter, Dorothy. The National
Science Foundation. New York,
Praeger [1969] xii, 278 p. [7.95]
353.008/5 68-8137
    Q11.U84 S3 MRR Alc.

UNITED STATES. NATIONAL TECHNICAL
INFORMATION SERVICE--BIBLIOGRAPHY.
Government reports index, v. 71-
1971- [Springfield, Va.] National
Technical Information Service.
507/.2073 72-627325
    Z7405.R4 U513 Sci RR Latest
    edition / MRR Alc Full set

UNITED STATES. NAVAL HISTORY DIVISION.
OPERATIONAL ARCHIVES.
United States. Naval History
Division. Operational Archives.
World War II histories and historical
reports in the U.S. Naval History
Division; [Washington] 1973. vi,
226 p. 016.94054/59/73 73-602814
    CD3034 .N38 1973 MRR Alc.

UNITED STATES. NAVAL RESERVE--REGISTERS.
United States. Bureau of Naval
Personnel. Register of commissioned
and warrant officers of the United
States Naval Reserve. Jan. 1, 1921-
Washington, U.S. Govt. Print. Off.
21-26710
    VA80 .A457 MRR Biog Latest edition

UNITED STATES. NAVY.
Ageton, Arthur Ainsley. The naval
officer's guide. [1st]- ed.:1943-
Annapolis [etc.] 359 43-4401
    V133 .A6 MRR Alc Latest edition

Pater, Alan Frederick. United States
battleships: [1st ed.] Beverly
Hills, Calif., Monitor Book Co.
[1968] 279 p. 359.32/52/0973 68-
17423
    VA58 .P3 MRR Alc.

UNITED STATES. NAVY--AVIATION.
Larkins, William T., U.S. Navy
aircraft, 1921-1941. [1st ed.]
Concord, Calif., Aviation History
Publications, c1961. 391 p.
623.746 61-18083
    VG93 .L32 MRR Alc.

Swanborough, Frederick Gordon.
United States Navy aircraft since
1911 London, Putnam, 1968. x, 518
p. [84/-] 623.7/46 70-354248
    VG93 .S92 MRR Alc.

United States. Library of Congress.
Manuscript Division. Washington
Irving Chambers: a register of his
papers in the Library of Congress.
Washington, Library of Congress,
1967. 15 l. 016.3593/32 67-60085
    Z663.34 .C45 MRR Alc.

UNITED STATES. NAVY--BIBLIOGRAPHY.
Smith, Myron J. The American Navy,
1865-1918: Metuchen, N.J., Scarecrow
Press, 1974. xiii, 372 p.
016.359/00973 74-4230
    Z6835.U5 S62 MRR Alc.

UNITED STATES. NAVY--BIOGRAPHY--
DICTIONARIES.
Schuon, Karl. U.S. Navy biographical
dictionary. New York, F. Watts
[1965, c1964] 277 p. 923.573 64-
17396
    E182 .S45 MRR Biog.

UNITED STATES. NAVY--HISTORY.
Bennett, Frank Marion, The steam
navy of the United States. 2d ed.
Pittsburgh, Pa., Warren & company,
1897. 2 v. 08-29480
    VA55 .B49 1897 MRR Alc.

Carrison, Daniel J. The United
States Navy New York, Praeger [1968]
x, 262 p. 359/.00973 68-16081
    VA55 .C3 MRR Alc.

Chapelle, Howard Irving. The history
of the American sailing Navy: [1st
ed.] New York, Norton [1949] xxiii,
558 p. 623.822 49-48709
    VA56 .C5 MRR Alc.

Maclay, Edgar Stanton, A history of
the United States Navy from 1775 to
1901, New and enl. ed. New York, D.
Appleton & company, 1901. 3 v. 973
01-10750
    E182 .M21 MRR Alc.

Pratt, Fletcher, The compact history
of the United States Navy. New and
rev. ed. New York, Hawthorn Books
[1962] 350 p. 973 62-9039
    E182 .P84 1962 MRR Alc.

Pratt, Fletcher, The navy, a
history; Garden City, N.Y., Garden
City publishing co., inc [1941] 4
p. l., xi-xvi, [2], 496 (i.e. 504) p.
359.0973 41-23977
    VA55 .P7 1941 MRR Alc.

Tily, James C., The uniforms of the
United States Navy. New York, T.
Yoseloff [1964] 338 p. 359.140973
63-18235
    VC303 .T5 MRR Alc.

United States. Bureau of Aeronautics
(Navy Dept.) A calendar of
significant events in the growth and
development of United States naval
aviation, 1898-1956. [Washington,
1956] 64 p. 623.74 629.13* 58-
60324
    VG93 .A62 1956 MRR Alc.

United States Naval Institute.
Almanac of naval facts. Annapolis
[1964] 305 p. 973 64-12269
    E182 .U587 MRR Alc.

UNITED STATES. NAVY--HISTORY--
REVOLUTION, 1775-1783--SOURCES.
United States. Library of Congress.
Manuscript Division. Naval records
of the American revolution, 1775-
1788. Washington, Govt. print. off.,
1906. 549 p. 06-35020
    Z1238 .U58 MRR Alc.

United States. Naval History
Division. Naval documents of the
American Revolution. Washington [For
sale by the Supt. of Docs., U.S.
Govt. Print. Off.] 1964- v. 64-
60087
    E271 .U583 MRR Alc.

UNITED STATES. NAVY--HISTORY--CIVIL
WAR, 1861-1865.
Lord, Francis Alfred, They fought
for the Union. [1st ed.]
Harrisburg, Pa., Stackpole Co. [1960]
375 p. 973.741 60-8813
    E491 .L89 MRR Alc.

UNITED STATES. NAVY--HISTORY--
BIBLIOGRAPHY.
United States. Dept. of the Army.
Office of Military History. Unit
histories of World War II,
[Washington, 1950?] iii, 141 p.
016.940541273 51-60137
    Z6207.W8 U52 MRR Ref Desk.

UNITED STATES. NAVY--HISTORY--
CHRONOLOGY.
Cooney, David M. A chronology of the
U.S. Navy, 1775-1965, New York, F.
Watts [1965] 471 p. 359.00973 65-
21636
    E182 .C73 MRR Alc.

UNITED STATES. NAVY--HISTORY--SOURCES--
BIBLIOGRAPHY.
United States. Naval History
Division. Operational Archives.
World War II histories and historical
reports in the U.S. Naval History
Division; [Washington] 1973. vi,
226 p. 016.94054/59/73 73-602814
    CD3034 .N38 1973 MRR Alc.

UNITED STATES. NAVY--LISTS OF VESSELS.
Ships of the United States Navy and
their sponsors. [Norwood, Mass.]
Prov. print. [Plimpton Press, 1913-
v. 359.32 13-24160
    VA61 .S48 MRR Alc.

United States. Naval History
Division. Dictionary of American
naval fighting ships. Washington,
[For sale by the Supt. of Doc., U.S.
Govt. Print. Off.] 1959- v.
623.825 60-60198
    VA61 .A53 MRR Alc.

UNITED STATES. NAVY--MEDALS, BADGES,
DECORATIONS, ETC.
United States. Bureau of Naval
Personnel. Medal of honor, 1861-
1949, the Navy. [Washington, 1950?]
ix, 327 p. 359.134 50-61099
    VB333 .A532 MRR Biog.

Wyllie, Robert E., Orders,
decorations and insignia, military
and civil; New York, London, G. P.
Putnam's sons [c1921] 3 p. l., v-xxi
p., 1 l., 269 p. 21-4556
    CR4509 .W9 MRR Alc.

UNITED STATES. NAVY--OFFICERS'
HANDBOOKS.
Ageton, Arthur Ainsley. The naval
officer's guide. [1st]- ed.:1943-
Annapolis [etc.] 359 43-4401
    V133 .A6 MRR Alc Latest edition

Noel, John Vavasour, Watch officers'
guide. Rev., 9th ed. Annapolis,
U.S. Naval Institute, 1961. 302 p.
359.332 61-1604
    V133 .N63 1961 MRR Alc.

UNITED STATES. NAVY--PETTY OFFICERS'
HANDBOOKS.
Dyer, Frederick Charles, The petty
officer's guide. 6th ed.
[Harrisburg, Pa.] Stackpole Books
[1966] 392 p. 359.338 66-18190
    V123 .D9 1966 MRR Alc.

UNITED STATES. NAVY--REGISTERS.
Callahan, Edward William, ed. List
of officers of the Navy of the United
States and of the Marine Corps from
1775 to 1900: New York, Haskell
House, 1969. 749 p. 359.3/3/20973
68-31274
    V11.U7 C2 1969 MRR Biog.

UNITED STATES. NAVY--SEAMEN'S HANDBOOKS.
The Bluejackets' manual. [1st]-
ed.: 1902- Annapolis [etc.] 359 03-
1595
    V113 .B55 MRR Alc Latest edition

The Coast guardsman's manual. 1952-
Annapolis, United States Naval
Institute. 351.792 52-61512
    HJ6645 .C66 MRR Alc Latest edition

UNITED STATES. NAVY--UNIFORMS.
Tily, James C., The uniforms of the
United States Navy. New York, T.
Yoseloff [1964] 338 p. 359.140973
63-18235
    VC303 .T5 MRR Alc.

UNITED STATES. NAVY--WATCH DUTY.
Noel, John Vavasour, Watch officers'
guide. Rev., 9th ed. Annapolis,
U.S. Naval Institute, 1961. 302 p.
359.332 61-1604
    V133 .N63 1961 MRR Alc.

UNITED STATES. NAVY. CHAPLAIN CORPS.
United States. Bureau of Naval
Personnel. The history of the
Chaplain Corps, United States Navy
[Washington, U.S. Govt. Print. Off.,
1948- v. 3, 1948] v. 359.34 48-
46297
    VG23 .A45 MRR Biog.

UNITED STATES. OFFICE OF EDUCATION--
BIBLIOGRAPHY.
United States. Office of Education.
Bibliography of publications of the
United States Office of Education,
1867-1959. Totowa, N.J., Rowman and
Littlefield, 1971. xiv, 57, x, 158,
v, 157 p. 016.37 73-28324
    Z5815.U5 U5354 MRR Alc.

UNITED STATES. OFFICE OF EDUCATION--
HISTORY.
Kursh, Harry. The United States
Office of Education: [1st ed.]
Philadelphia, Chilton Books [c1965]
xvi, 192 p. 370.6173 65-11513
    LB2807 .K8 MRR Alc.

UNITED STATES. OFFICE OF SCIENTIFIC
RESEARCH AND DEVELOPMENT--BIBLIOGRAPHY.
United States. Library of Congress.
Science and Technology Division. A
catalog of OSRD reports. Washington,
1950- 1 v. (loose-leaf) 016.5072
50-60310
    Z663.41 .C3 MRR Alc.

UNITED STATES. PATENT OFFICE.
Kursh, Harry. Inside the U.S. Patent
Office: [1st ed.] New York, Norton
[1959] 171 p. 608.773 59-11243
    T223.P2 K8 MRR Alc.

UNITED STATES. PEACE CORPS.
Hoopes, Roy. The complete Peace
Corps guide. 4th ed. New York, Dial
Press, 1968. xii, 211 p. [4.95]
309.2/235 67-14997
    HC60.5 .H6 1968 MRR Alc.

UNITED STATES. PUBLICATION BOARD--
BIBLIOGRAPHY.
    Special Libraries Council of
    Philadelphia and Vicinity.
    Correlation index: document series
    and PB reports. New York, Special
    Libraries Association, 1953. x, 271
    p.   016.6   53-10018
        Z7916 .S65 MRR Alc.

UNITED STATES. SECRET SERVICE.
    Bowen, Walter Scott. The United
    States Secret Service [1st ed.]
    Philadelphia, Chilton Co. [1960]   205
    p.   351.742   60-6407
        HV8138 .B6 MRR Alc.

UNITED STATES. SUPERINTENDENT OF
DOCUMENTS. MONTHLY CATALOG OF UNITED
STATES GOVERNMENT PUBLICATIONS.
    Burke, John Gordon. The monthly
    catalog of United States Government
    publications: [Hamden, Conn.] Linnet
    Books, 1973. vi, 113 p.   015/.73
    72-11690
        Z1223 .A184 MRR Ref Desk.

UNITED STATES. SUPREME COURT.
    Warren, Charles. The Supreme court
    in United States history. Rev. ed.
    Boston, Little, Brown, and company,
    1935. 2 v.   347.89 353.5   37-1848
        JK1561 .W3 1935 MRR Alc.

UNITED STATES. SUPREME COURT--BIOGRAPHY.
    Ewing, Cortez Arthur Milton. The
    judges of the Supreme court, 1789-
    1937; Minneapolis, The University of
    Minnesota press [c1938] 3 p. l., 3-
    124 p.   38-28601
        KF8744 .E9 MRR Alc.

    Friedman, Leon, comp. The Justices
    of the United States Supreme Court,
    1789-1969. New York, Chelsea House
    in association with Bowker, 1969. 4
    v. (xxiv, 3373 p.)   347.88/22   69-
    13699
        KF8744 .F75 MRR Alc.

UNITED STATES. SUPREME COURT--
DIRECTORIES.
    Poore, Benjamin Perley. The
    political register and congressional
    directory: Boston, Houghton, Osgood
    and company, 1878. vi p., 1 l., 716
    p.   05-273
        E176 .P82 MRR Alc.

UNITED STATES. TREATIES, ETC. TREATY
SERIES.
    United States. Dept. of state.
    Subject index of the Treaty series
    and the Executive agreement series.
    Washington, U.S. Govt. print. off.,
    1932. v, 214 p.   341.273   32-26434

        JX235.9 .A3 Index 1931 MRR Ref
        Desk.

UNITED STATES. WAR DEPT.--HISTORY.
    Hamersly, Thomas Holdup Stevens,
    comp. Complete regular army register
    of the United States: for one hundred
    years (1779 to 1879) Washington, T.
    H. S. Hamersly, 1880. viii, 928,
    381, xxxvi p.   07-12444
        U11.U5 H3 MRR Biog.

UNITED STATES. WARREN COMMISSION.
INVESTIGATION OF THE ASSASSINATION OF
PRESIDENT JOHN F. KENNEDY; HEARINGS.
    Meagher, Sylvia. Subject index to
    the Warren report and hearings &
    exhibits. New York, Scarecrow Press,
    1966. 150 p.   364.1524   66-13736
        E842.9 .M4 MRR Alc.

UNITED STATES. WARREN COMMISSION.
REPORT OF THE PRESIDENT'S COMMISSION ON
THE ASSASSINATION OF PRESIDENT JOHN F.
KENNEDY.
    Meagher, Sylvia. Subject index to
    the Warren report and hearings &
    exhibits. New York, Scarecrow Press,
    1966. 150 p.   364.1524   66-13736
        E842.9 .M4 MRR Alc.

UNITED STATES. WEATHER BUREAU.
    Whitnah, Donald Robert. A history of
    the United States Weather Bureau.
    Urbana, University of Illinois Press,
    1961. ix, 267 p.   551.591 60-8345

        QC875.U7 W45 MRR Alc.

UNITED STATES. WORK PROJECTS
ADMINISTRATION--BIBLIOGRAPHY.
    Child, Sargent Burrage. Check list
    of Historical Records Survey
    publications; Baltimore,
    Genealogical Pub. Co., 1969. vi, 110
    p.   016.973/08   68-17126
        Z1223.Z7 C52 MRR Alc.

UNITED STATES -BIOGRAPHY--DICTIONARIES.
    Fink, Gary M. Biographical
    dictionary of American labor leaders.
    Westport, Conn., Greenwood Press
    [1974] xiv, 559 p.   331.88/092/2 B
    74-9322
        HD8073.A1 F56 MRR Biog.

UNITED STATES GOVERNMENT RESEARCH
REPORTS. (INDEXES)
    Special Libraries Council of
    Philadelphia and Vicinity.
    Correlation index: document series
    and PB reports, New York, Special
    Libraries Association, 1953. x, 271
    p.   016.6   53-10018
        Z7916 .S65 MRR Alc.

UNITS.
    see also Metric system

UNITS--DICTIONARIES--POLYGLOT.
    Elsevier's lexicon of international
    and national units; Amsterdam, New
    York, Elsevier Pub. Co., 1964. 75 p.
    389.103   63-11366
        QC82 .E37 MRR Alc.

UNIVERSAL HISTORY
    see World history

UNIVERSAL MILITARY TRAINING
    see Military service, Compulsory

UNIVERSITIES AND A COLLEGES--UNITED
STATES--STATISTICS.
    Pennsylvania. Dept. of Public
    Instruction. Bureau of Statistics.
    Rankings of universities in the
    United States. Harrisburg, 1966.
    iv, 32 p.   378.73   73-628460
        LA226 .P36 MRR Alc.

UNIVERSITIES AND COLLEGES.
    see also Education, Higher

    see also Students

    Burn, Barbara B. Higher education in
    nine countries; New York, McGraw-
    Hill [1971] viii, 387 p.   378 79-
    132352
        LB2322 .B85 MRR Alc.

    Chambers, Merritt Madison, ed.
    Universities of the world outside
    U.S.A. 1st ed. Washington, American
    Council on Education, 1950. xvii,
    924 p.   378.058   50-5321
        LA183 .C48 MRR Ref Desk.

    Handbook on international study.
    1955- [New York] Institute of
    International Education.   55-8482
        LB2376 .H3 MRR Ref Desk Latest
        edition

UNIVERSITIES AND COLLEGES--ADMISSION.
    Fine, Benjamin, How to be accepted
    by the college of your choice. 1957-
    ed. New York [etc.] Appleton-
    Century [etc.]   371.214   57-12037
        LB2351 .F513 MRR Alc Latest
        edition

UNIVERSITIES AND COLLEGES--BIBLIOGRAPHY.
    Dressel, Paul Leroy. The world of
    higher education [1st ed.] San
    Francisco, Jossey-Bass, 1971. xv,
    238 p.   016.378 71-158562
        Z5814.U7 D65 MRR Alc.

    Handbook of learned societies and
    institutions: America. Washington,
    D.C., Carnegie institution of
    Washington, 1908. viii, 592 p.   08-
    21011
        Z5055.U39 H2 MRR Alc.

UNIVERSITIES AND COLLEGES--DIRECTORIES.
    American Council on Education.
    Overseas Liaison Committee.
    International directory for
    educational liaison. Washington
    [1972, c1973] xxii, 474 p.
    378/.006/21 72-92152
        L900 .A47 1973 MRR Alc.

    The College blue book. [1st]-   1923-
    New York [etc.] CCM Information
    Corp. [etc.]   378.73   24-223
        LA226 .C685 MRR Ref Desk Latest
        edition

    Garraty, John Arthur. The new guide
    to study abroad: 1974-1975 ed. New
    York, Harper & Row [1974] xiii, 422
    p.   [$10.95]   370.19/6 72-9117
        LB2376 .G33 1974 MRR Ref Desk.

    International handbook of
    universities. 1959- Paris,
    International Association of
    Universities. 378.058 59-4778
        L900 .I58 MRR Ref Desk Latest
        edition

    Liste mondiale. Paris, International
    Association of Universities. a 55-
    6642
    Began in 1952.
        L900 .I57 MRR Alc Latest edition

    World guide to universities. 1st ed.
    New York, R. R. Bowker Co., 1971-72.
    4 v. (xxii, 3609 p.)   378/.0025 73-
    172160
        L900 .W53 MRR Alc.

    The World of learning. [1st]-   1947-
    London, Europa Publications [etc.]
    47-30172
        AS2 .W6 Sci RR Latest edition /
        MRR Ref Desk Latest edition

    Worldwide directory of mineral
    industries education and research.
    Houston, Gulf Pub. Co., 1968. x, 451
    p.   669/.007 68-9304
        TN165 .V66 MRR Alc.

UNIVERSITIES AND COLLEGES--GRADUATE
WORK.
    American Council on Education. A
    guide to graduate study; 1st-   ed.;
    1957- Washington. 65-21729
        LB2371 .A4 MRR Ref Desk Latest
        edition

UNIVERSITIES AND COLLEGES--NAMES.
    Keiser, Albert. College names, their
    origin and significance. New York,
    Bookman Associates [1952] 184 p.
    378 52-11160
        LA225 .K37 MRR Alc.

UNIVERSITIES AND COLLEGES--PERIODICALS--
DIRECTORIES.
    Association des universités
    entièrement ou partiellement de
    langue française. Catalogue des
    publications périodiques
    universitaires de langue française.
    [2. éd. Montréal, 1969] viii, 150
    p.   77-478508
        Z6944.S3 A7 1969 MRR Alc.

UNIVERSITIES AND COLLEGES--SELECTION.
    see also College, Choice of

UNIVERSITIES AND COLLEGES--STUDENTS
    see College students

UNIVERSITIES AND COLLEGES--TERMINOLOGY.
    Current slang; Vermillion,
    University of South Dakota, Dept. of
    English, 1969] xvi, 103 p. [1.25]
    427.09 78-13579
        PE3729.U5 C8 MRR Alc.

    International federation of
    university women. Lexique
    international des termes
    universitaires. [Paris] Fédération
    internationale des femmes diplomées
    des universités, 1939. xvii, 755,
    [1] p.   378.03 40-30813
        LB2331 .I6 MRR Alc.

UNIVERSITIES AND COLLEGES--YEARBOOKS.
    Minerva; 1.- Jahrg.; 1891/92-
    Berlin [etc.] W. de Gruyter [etc.]
    06-13218
        AS2 .M6 MRR Alc Latest edition /
        MRR Ref Desk Latest edition

UNIVERSITIES AND COLLEGES--ASIA,
SOUTHEASTERN--DIRECTORIES.
    Association of Southeast Asian
    Institutions of Higher Learning.
    Handbook. [Bangkok] 68-50481
        L961.A2 A8 MRR Alc Latest edition

UNIVERSITIES AND COLLEGES--AUSTRALIA--
DIRECTORIES.
    Commonwealth universities yearbook.
    1914- London. 378.42 59-24175
        LB2310 .Y5 MRR Ref Desk Latest
        edition

UNIVERSITIES AND COLLEGES--CANADA--
DIRECTORIES.
    Campbell, Gordon, Community colleges
    in Canada. Toronto, New York,
    Ryerson Press [1971] xx, 346 p.
    [$6.00]   378.71 79-26176
        LA417.5 .C35 MRR Alc.

    Commonwealth universities yearbook.
    1914- London. 378.42 59-24175
        LB2310 .Y5 MRR Ref Desk Latest
        edition

    A Complete guide to Canadian
    universities. Toronto, Forum House
    Pub. Co., c1969. 413 p. [4.95]
    378.71 76-494312
        L905 .C64 MRR Alc.

    Ottawa. National Library. Research
    collections in Canadian libraries.
    [Ottawa, Information Canada, 1972-
    v. in   [$1.00 (v. 1) varies]
    027.7/0971 74-159990
        Z735.A1 O88 1972 MRR Alc.

    Universities and colleges of Canada.
    1969- Ottawa, Association of
    Universities and Colleges of Canada.
    378.71 77-219268
        L905 .C452 MRR Alc Latest edition

UNIVERSITIES AND COLLEGES--COMMONWEALTH
OF NATIONS.
    Commonwealth universities yearbook.
    1914- London. 378.42 59-24175
        LB2310 .Y5 MRR Ref Desk Latest
        edition

UNIVERSITIES AND COLLEGES--EUROPE.
    Herman, Shirley Yvonne. Guide to
    study in Europe; New York, Four
    Winds Press [1969] 288 p. [8.50]
    378.4 68-27281
        L914.5 .H4 MRR Alc.

UNIVERSITIES AND COLLEGES-- (Cont.)
International federation of
university women. Lexique
international des termes
universitaires. [Paris] Fédération
internationale des femmes diplomées
des universités, 1939. xvii, 755,
[1] p.   378.03   40-30813
      LB2331 .I6 MRR Alc.

UNIVERSITIES AND COLLEGES--EUROPE--
DIRECTORIES.
European research index; 3d ed.
[St. Peter Port, Guernsey] Francis
Hodgson [1973] 2 v. (2293 p.)
507/.204   70-180255
      Q180.E9 E9 1973 MRR Alc.

UNIVERSITIES AND COLLEGES--FRANCE--
DIRECTORIES.
Dran, Pierre. Le guide pratique de
l'enseignement en France. Verviers,
Gérard et Cie; Paris, l'Inter, 1965.
346 p. [7,30 F.]   370.2544   66-
72289
      L927 .D7 MRR Alc.

UNIVERSITIES AND COLLEGES--GERMANY.
Ueberreiter, Kurt, A statistical
postwar survey on the natural
sciences and German universities.
[Washington] Library of Congress,
European Affairs Division [1950] 31
p.   507.2   50-61523
      Z663.26 .S7 MRR Alc.

UNIVERSITIES AND COLLEGES--GERMANY
(FEDERAL REPUBLIC, 1949-)--DIRECTORIES.
Deutsches Universitäts-Handbuch.
1967-   München, Consultverlag [etc.]
68-84305
      L929 .D42   MRR Alc Latest edition

UNIVERSITIES AND COLLEGES--GREAT
BRITAIN.
Higher education in the United
Kingdom. London, Longmans & Green.
378.42   58-15421
"First published 1936."
      LA637.7 H5   MRR Alc Latest edition

Kitson Clark, George Sidney Roberts,
Guide to research facilities in
history in the universities of Great
Britain and Ireland. 2d ed.,
Cambridge [Eng.] University Press,
1965. 54 p.   65-24953
      D16.4.G7 K5 1965 MRR Alc.

National Union of Teachers.
University & college entrance; 10th
ed. London, [1968] 126 p.   [5/6]
378.1/05/70942   74-458823
      L915 .N39 1968 MRR Alc.

UNIVERSITIES AND COLLEGES--GREAT
BRITAIN--CURRICULA.
Higher education in the United
Kingdom. London, Longmans & Green.
378.42   58-15421
"First published 1936."
      LA637.7 H5   MRR Alc Latest edition

UNIVERSITIES AND COLLEGES--GREAT
BRITAIN--DIRECTORIES.
Commonwealth universities yearbook.
1914-   London. 378.42   59-24175
      LB2310 .Y5 MRR Ref Desk Latest
      edition

Handbook of colleges and departments
of education. 1968- London,
Published for the Association of
Teachers in Colleges and Dept. of
Education by Methuen & Co.
370./73/02542   70-208256
      LB2224 .H35 MRR Alc Latest edition

Industrial research in Britain. 7th
ed. [St. Peter Port, Guernsey] F.
Hodgson [1972] 889 p.   607/.2/42
73-190253
      T177.G7 I52 1972 MRR Alc.

The Year book of technical education
and careers in industry. 1st-   1957-
London, A. and C. Black. 607.42
57-2770
      T61 .Y4   Sci RR Latest edition /
      MRR Alc Latest edition

UNIVERSITIES AND COLLEGES--GREAT
BRITAIN--ENTRANCE REQUIREMENTS.
National Union of Teachers.
University & college entrance; 10th
ed. London, [1968] 126 p.   [5/6]
378.1/05/70942   74-458823
      L915 .N39 1968 MRR Alc.

UNIVERSITIES AND COLLEGES--INDIA--
DIRECTORIES.
Commonwealth universities yearbook.
1914- London. 378.42   59-24175
      LB2310 .Y5 MRR Ref Desk Latest
      edition

Universities handbook; India &
Ceylon. [1st]-   ed.; 1927- New
Delhi [etc.], Inter-university Board
of India & Ceylon [etc.]   e   35-209
      L961.I4 U55 MRR Alc Latest edition

UNIVERSITIES AND COLLEGES--JAPAN.
Japan. Mombusho. Nihon Yunesuko
Kokunai Iinkai. Directory of
researchers and research institutes
on Oriental studies in Japan.
[Tokyo] Japanese National Commission
for UNESCO [1957] 50 p.   068.52 61-
32041
      AS548 .A543 MRR Alc.

Roberts, Dorothy E. A scholar's
guide to Japan. Rev. ed. Boston,
Christopher Pub. House [1969] viii,
125 p.   915.2/04/4   68-58963
      DS811 .R58 1969 MRR Alc.

UNIVERSITIES AND COLLEGES--NEW ENGLAND--
STATISTICS.
Facts about New England colleges and
universities. [Durham, N.H.] [etc.]
67-4398
      LC148 .F3 MRR Alc Latest edition

UNIVERSITIES AND COLLEGES--POLAND.
Wepsiec, Jan. Polish institutions of
higher learning. New York, Polish
Institute of Arts and Sciences in
America, 1959. 110 p.   063.8   59-
37794
      AS258 .W4 MRR Alc.

UNIVERSITIES AND COLLEGES--UNITED
STATES.
American universities and colleges.
[1st]-   ed.; 1928- Washington
[etc.] American Council on Education
[etc.]   378.73   28-5598
      LA226 .A65   MRR Ref Desk Latest
      edition / MRR Alc Latest edition

The College blue book. [1st]-   1923-
New York [etc.] CCM Information
Corp. [etc.]   378.73   24-223
      LA226 .C685 MRR Ref Desk Latest
      edition

Eddy, Edward Danforth. Colleges for
our land and time; [1st ed.] New
York, Harper [1957] xiv, 328 p.
379.123   57-6739
      LA226 .E38 MRR Alc.

Elliott, Edward Charles, ed.
Charters and basic laws of selected
American universities and colleges,
New York city, The Carnegie
foundation for the advancement of
teaching, 1934. 2 p. l., iii-vii p.,
1 l., 640 p.   379.1473 378.73 34-
3109
      LB2525 .E55 MRR Alc.

Gourman, Jack. The Gourman report;
1967-68 ed. Phoenix, Continuing
Education Institute [1967] xxviii,
1187 p.   378.1/001/8   67-6498
      LB2341 .G62 MRR Alc.

Weigle, Luther Allan, American
idealism, New Haven, Yale university
press; [etc., etc.] 1928. 3 p. l.,
356 p.   28-25825
      E178.5 .P2 vol. 10 MRR Alc.

UNIVERSITIES AND COLLEGES--UNITED
STATES--ACCREDITATION.
American Council on Education.
Accredited institutions of higher
education. Sept. 1964- Washington.
64-25852
      L901 .A52   MRR Ref Desk Latest
      edition

UNIVERSITIES AND COLLEGES--UNITED
STATES--ADMISSION.
College admissions data service.
Watertown, Mass., Educational
Research Corp. 378.1/05/60973   74-
646622
      LB2351.A1 C55a MRR Alc Latest
      edition

College Entrance Examination Board.
Admissions and financial aid
requirements and procedures at
College Board member colleges [New
York] 378.1/05/70973 71-617254
      LB2351.A1 C572 MRR Alc Latest
      edition

Mazel, Ella. The New York Times
guide to college selection. New
York, Quadrangle Books. 378.73   72-
178241
      LB2350.5 .M35   MRR Ref Desk Latest
      edition

UNIVERSITIES AND COLLEGES--UNITED
STATES--ALUMNI.
Pierson, George Wilson, The
education of American leaders; New
York, Praeger [1969] xxxii, 261 p.
331.7/6   69-17173
      LA226 .P5 MRR Alc.

UNIVERSITIES AND COLLEGES--UNITED
STATES--BIBLIOGRAPHY.
Willingham, Warren W. The source
book for higher education; New York,
College Entrance Examination Board,
1973. xxii, 481 p. [$15.00]
016.37873   72-97458
      Z5814.U7 S55 MRR Alc.

UNIVERSITIES AND COLLEGES--UNITED
STATES--CURRICULA.
The College blue book. [1st]-   1923-
New York [etc.] CCM Information
Corp. [etc.] 378.73   24-223
      LA226 .C685   MRR Ref Desk Latest
      edition

International Council for Educational
Development. Area studies on U.S.
campuses: a directory. New York,
1971. vi, 71 p.   378.73   71-158546
      D16.25 .I55 MRR Ref Desk.

Lovejoy's college guide. 1940- New
York, Simon and Schuster. 378.73 52-
14368
      LA226 .L6   MRR Ref Desk Latest
      edition

Mazel, Ella. The New York Times
guide to college selection. New
York, Quadrangle Books. 378.73 72-
178241
      LB2350.5 .M35   MRR Ref Desk Latest
      edition

UNIVERSITIES AND COLLEGES--UNITED
STATES--DIRECTORIES.
American Council on Education.
Accredited institutions of higher
education. Sept. 1964- Washington.
64-25852
      L901 .A52   MRR Ref Desk Latest
      edition

American Junior colleges. 1st-
ed.; 1940- [Washington] American
Council on Education. 378.73   40-
33685
      L901 .A53   MRR Ref Desk Latest
      edition

The Annual guide to undergraduate
study. 1971- Princeton, N.J.,
Peterson's Guides, inc. 378.73   73-
642965
      L901 .A55 MRR Alc Latest edition

The Blue book of college athletics.
[1931/32]- Cleveland [etc.] Rohrich
Corp. [etc.] 371.74 ca 31-721
      GV741 .B5   MRR Alc Latest edition

Cass, James. Comparative guide to
American colleges; 6th ed. New
York, Harper & Row [1973] xxxiii,
916 p.   [$5.95]   378.73   73-4068
      L901 .C33 1973 MRR Ref Desk.

Cass, James. Comparative guide to
two-year colleges & four-year
specialized schools and programs,
[1st ed.] New York, Harper & Row
[1969] xxii, 275 p.   [$7.95]   378.73
69-15301
      LB2328 .C36 MRR Ref Desk.

Catholic College Bureau, Chicago. A
guide in the selection of a Catholic
school. 1st-   ed.; 1945- Chicago.
377.82   50-31378
      LC501 .C345   MRR Alc Latest edition

College admissions data service.
Watertown, Mass., Educational
Research Corp. 378.1/05/60973   74-
646622
      LB2351.A1 C55a   MRR Alc Latest
      edition

College Entrance Examination Board.
The College handbook. 1941- [New
York] 371.214   41-12971
      LB2351.A1 C6   MRR Ref Desk Latest
      edition

College Entrance Examination Board.
The New York Times guide to
continuing education in America,
[New York] Quadrangle Books [1972]
811 p.   [$12.50]   374.8/73   74-
183190
      L901 .C74 1972 MRR Ref Desk.

Colleges and specialized schools.
1st-   1952- Boston, P. Sargent. 52-
3398
      L901 .J8   MRR Ref Desk Latest
      edition / MRR Alc Latest edition

Community and junior college
directory. Washington,
Communications Division, American
Association of Community and Junior
Colleges. [$5.00]   378.1/543/02573
73-643804
      LB2328.A1 J8   MRR Alc Latest
      edition

Current financial aids for
undergraduate students. 1969/70-
Moline, Ill., etc., M & L
Enterprises, etc. 378.3/025/73   73-
2076
      LB2338 .C8   MRR Ref Desk Latest
      edition

Fine, Benjamin, Barron's profiles of
American colleges. 1964- Woodbury,
N.Y., Barron's Educational Series,
inc. 68-58041
      L901 .F5   MRR Ref Desk Latest
      edition

UNIVERSITIES AND COLLEGES-- (Cont.)
Handel, Lawrence. College
confidential. New York, Trident
Press [1969] 318 p. [5.95] 378.73
69-13514
L901 .H32 MRR Ref Desk.

Hawes, Gene R. The new American
guide to colleges 4th ed.,
completely rev. and enl. New York,
Columbia University Press, 1972.
xlv, 640 p. 378.73 72-77233
L901 .H37 1972 MRR Ref Desk.

The Insiders' guide to the colleges.
4th ed. [New York] Berkley Pub.
Corp. [1973] 413 p. [$2.25]
378.73 73-161139
L901 .I54 1973 MRR Alc.

Lovejoy's college guide. 1940- New
York, Simon and Schuster. 378.73 52-
14368
LA226 .L6 MRR Ref Desk Latest
edition

Mazel, Ella. The New York Times
guide to college selection. New
York, Quadrangle Books. 378.73 72-
178241
LB2350.5 .M35 MRR Ref Desk Latest
edition

The Official guide to Catholic
educational institutions and
religious communities in the United
States. 1936- New York [etc.]
Catholic Institutional Directory Co.
337.8273 38-4126
LC501 .C35 MRR Alc Latest edition

Plans for Progress. Directory of
Negro colleges and universities,
March, 1967. Washington [1967] ii,
103 p. 378.73 67-61097
LC2801 .P55 1967 MRR Ref Desk.

Proia, Nicholas C. Barron's handbook
of college transfer information,
Rev. ed. Woodbury, N.Y., Barron's
Educational Series [1971] viii, 271
p. [$3.95] 378.169/14/02573 75-
29430
L901 .P73 1971 MRR Alc.

Research centers directory. 1st
ed.; 1960- Detroit, Gale Research
Co. 60-14807
AS25 .D5 Sci RR Latest edition /
MRR Ref Desk Latest edition

United States. Library of Congress.
Education and Public Welfare
Division. Student assistance
handbook; Rev. Washington, U.S.
Govt. Print. Off., 1965. vi, 241 p.
65-62199
L901 .A4 1965 MRR Alc.

Yearbook of higher education. 1969-
Los Angeles, Academic Media. 378.73
69-18308
LB2300 .Y4 MRR Ref Desk Latest
edition

UNIVERSITIES AND COLLEGES--UNITED
STATES--ENTRANCE REQUIREMENTS.
College Entrance Examination Board.
The College handbook. 1941- [New
York] 371.214 41-12971
LB2351.A1 C6 MRR Ref Desk Latest
edition

Proia, Nicholas C. Barron's handbook
of college transfer information,
Rev. ed. Woodbury, N.Y., Barron's
Educational Series [1971] viii, 271
p. [$3.95] 378.169/14/02573 75-
29430
L901 .P73 1971 MRR Alc.

UNIVERSITIES AND COLLEGES--UNITED
STATES--EXAMINATIONS.
Brownstein, Samuel C., How to
prepare for college entrance
examinations 4th rev. ed., enl. and
completely rev. Woodbury, N.Y.,
Barron's Educational Series, inc.
[1969] 538 p. [3.95] 378.1/6/42
68-56405
LB2353 .B75 1969 MRR Alc.

College Entrance Examination Board.
A description of the College Board
achievement tests. 1956-
[Princeton, N.J.] 371.26 59-4353
LB2367 .C6 MRR Alc Latest edition

Turner, David Reuben, Graduate
record examination aptitude test,
[3d ed.] New York, Arco [1972] 440
p. [$4.00] 378.1/6/64 72-190577
LB2367 .T77 1972 MRR Alc.

UNIVERSITIES AND COLLEGES--UNITED
STATES--EXAMINATIONS--PERIODICALS.
College Entrance Examination Board.
Bulletin of information. East-
Midwest-South edition. 1970/71-
[Princeton? N. J.] 378.1/66/4 72-
622333
LB2353 .C582 MRR Alc Latest
edition

UNIVERSITIES AND COLLEGES--UNITED
STATES--FINANCE.
Aid-to-education programs of some
leading business concerns. New York.
378.1 62-4102
LB2342 .C6744 MRR Alc Latest
edition

Harris, Seymour Edwin, Higher
education: resources and finance New
York, McGraw-Hill, 1962. xxxviii,
713 p. 378.1 61-18311
LB2342 .H34 MRR Alc.

UNIVERSITIES AND COLLEGES--UNITED
STATES--GRADUATE WORK.
Roose, Kenneth D. A rating of
graduate programs [Washington]
American Council on Education [c1970]
xi, 115 p. [$4.00] 378.1/553/0973
76-138559
LA227.3 .R65 MRR Ref Desk.

Wasserman, Elga Ruth. The Random
House guide to graduate study in the
arts and sciences New York, Random
House [1967] xv, 361 p.
378.1/553/0973 67-22662
LB2371 .W36 MRR Ref Desk.

UNIVERSITIES AND COLLEGES--UNITED
STATES--GRADUATE WORK--DIRECTORIES.
The Annual guides to graduate study.
1966/67- Princeton, N.J., Peterson's
Guides Inc. 378.73 68-1823
L901 .P46 MRR Alc Latest edition

Graduate & professional school
opportunities for minority students.
Princeton, N.J., Educational Testing
Service. 378.1/553/02573 73-642558

L901 .G717 MRR Ref Desk Latest
edition

Graduate programs and admissions
manual. [Princeton? N.J.] Graduate
Record Examinations Board [1972] 4
v. [$2.50 per vol.] 378.1/553/0973
72-85650
L901 .G72 MRR Ref Desk.

Graduate study in psychology.
Washington, D.C., Educational Affairs
Office, American Psychological
Association. 150/.7/1173 72-626834

Began with v. for 1968/69.
BF77 .G73 MRR Alc Latest edition

Livesey, Herbert B. Guide to
American graduate schools, 2d ed.,
completely rev. and updated. New
York, Viking Press [1970] xxxviii,
410 p. [$5.95] 378.1/553/02573 70-
120742
L901 .L5 1970 MRR Ref Desk.

National Association of Schools of
Public Affairs and Administration.
Graduate school programs in public
affairs and public administration.
Washington. [$5.00] 350/.0007/1173
74-80861
JF1338.A2 N28a MRR Alc Latest
edition

Paynter, Julie. Graduate
opportunities for Black students,
1969-1970. Chicago [1970] xvi, 88
l. [3.00] 378.73 77-11563
LC2801 .P38 MRR Ref Desk.

Searles, Aysel. Guide to financial
aids for students in arts & sciences
for graduate and professional study
Rev. ed. New York, Arco [1974] xii,
107 p. [$3.95] 378.3/025/73 74-
80776
LB2338 .S4 1974 MRR Ref Desk.

UNIVERSITIES AND COLLEGES--UNITED
STATES--HISTORY.
Brubacher, John Seiler, Higher
education in transition; Rev. and
enl. New York, Harper & Row [1968]
vii, 529 p. [$12.00] 378.73 68-
17041
LA226 .B75 1968 MRR Alc.

Hofstadter, Richard, ed. American
higher education, [Chicago]
University of Chicago Press [1961] 2
v. 378.73 61-15935
LA226 .H53 1961 MRR Alc.

Rudolph, Frederick. The American
college and university; a history.
[1st ed.] New York, Knopf, 1962.
516 p. 378.73 62-12991
LA226 .R72 MRR Alc.

UNIVERSITIES AND COLLEGES--UNITED
STATES--HONORS COURSES--DIRECTORIES.
National Collegiate Honors Council.
Index: honors programs in American
colleges and universities. Boulder,
Colo., 1969. 69 p. [1.00]
378.1/7/94202573 76-15405
L901 .N3 MRR Ref Desk.

UNIVERSITIES AND COLLEGES--UNITED
STATES--STATISTICS.
Harris, Seymour Edwin, A statistical
portrait of higher education, New
York, McGraw-Hill [1972] xliv, 978
p. 378.73 72-38334
LA227.3 .H25 MRR Alc.

UNIVERSITY ENVIRONMENT
see College environment

UNIVERSITY PRESSES--DIRECTORIES.
Association of American University
Presses. Directory. [Baltimore] 54-
43046
Z475 .A88 MRR Alc Latest edition

UPHOLSTERY.
see also Furniture

UPHOLSTERY TRADES--DIRECTORIES.
Upholstering industry's directory of
supply sources. [Hoboken, N.J., Hall
Pub. Co.] 381/.45/68412028 72-
627053
TT198 .U55 MRR Alc Latest edition

UPPER HUTT, N.Z.--INDUSTRIES--
DIRECTORIES.
Universal business directory for
Wellington, Hutt [and] Petone.
Auckland, Universal Business
Directories. 53-30822
HC623.W45 U5 MRR Alc Latest
edition

UPPER VOLTA--GAZETTEERS.
United States. Office of Geography.
Upper Volta; official standard names
approved by the United States Board
on Geographic Names. Washington
[U.S. Govt. Print. Off.] 1965. iii,
168 p. 65-61066
DT553.U72 U5 MRR Alc.

URBAN AREAS
see Cities and towns

see Metropolitan areas

URBAN DESIGN
see Cities and towns--Planning

URBAN LIFE
see City and town life

URBAN REDEVELOPMENT
see Cities and towns--Planning

URBAN RENEWAL
see also Cities and towns--Planning

URBAN RENEWAL--UNITED STATES--
BIBLIOGRAPHY.
Housing and planning references. new
ser. no. 1- July/Aug. 1965-
[Washington, U.S. Govt. Print. Off.]
016.3015/4 72-621364
Z7165.U5 A3 MRR Alc Full set

URBAN RENEWAL--UNITED STATES--
DIRECTORIES.
National Association of Housing and
Redevelopment Officials. NAHRO
renewal agency directory. 1969-
Washington. 309.2/62/02573 73-
641791
HD7293.A1 N235 MRR Alc Latest
edition

URBAN RENEWAL--UNITED STATES--HISTORY.
Willmann, John B. The Department of
Housing and Urban Development New
York, Praeger [1967] xiii, 207 p.
353.85 67-24679
HT175.U6 W48 MRR Alc.

URBAN RENEWAL--UNITED STATES--
STATISTICS.
United States. Dept. of Housing and
Urban Development. Statistical
yearbook. 1966- Washington, For
sale by the Supt. of Docs., U.S.
Govt. Print. Off. 301.5/4/0212 68-
62733
HD7293.A49H67 MRR Ref Desk Full
set

URBAN TRAFFIC
see Traffic engineering

URBAN TRANSPORTATION--STATISTICS.
International Union of Public
Transport. Statistiques des
transports publics urbains. (2e
ed.). Bruxelles, Union
internationale des transports
publics, (1968). 211 p. 388/.021/2
76-393796
HE4211 .I56 1968 MRR Alc.

URBAN TRANSPORTATION--NEW YORK (CITY)--
DIRECTORIES.
The Journal of commerce
transportation telephone tickler.
[New York] 53-34476
HE9.U5 N7 MRR Alc Latest edition

URBANIZATION.
Davis, Kingsley, World urbanization,
1950-1970. Berkeley, Institute of
International Studies, University of
California [1969-72] 2 v. [$6.00]
301.36 71-627843
HB2161 .D37 MRR Alc.

URBANIZATION--BIBLIOGRAPHY.
Brode, John. The process of
modernization: Cambridge, Mass.,
Harvard University Press, 1969. x,
378 p. [6.50] 016.3092 69-13765
Z7164.U5 B7 MRR Alc.

Brunn, Stanley D. Urbanization in
developing countries; East Lansing,
Latin American Studies Center,
Michigan State University, 1971.
xviii, 693 p. 016.30136/3/091724
79-172535
Z7164.U7 B7 MRR Alc.

URBANIZATION--DICTIONARIES--POLYGLOT.
Vocabulaire international des termes
d'urbanisme et d'architecture. 1.
ed. Paris, Société de diffusion
des techniques du bâtiment et des
travaux publics, 1970- v.   [133F
(v. 1)] 70-860237
NA31 .V6 MRR Alc.

URBANIZATION--STATISTICS.
Davis, Kingsley, World urbanization,
1950-1970. Berkeley, Institute of
International Studies, University of
California [1969-72] 2 v. [$6.00]
301.36 71-627843
HB2161 .D37 MRR Alc.

URBANIZATION--ATLANTIC STATES.
Gottmann, Jean. Megaloplis; the
urbanized northeastern seaboard of
the United States. New York,
Twentieth Century Fund, 1961. xi,
810 p. 301.36 61-17298
HT123.5.A12 G6 MRR Alc.

URBANIZATION--LATIN AMERICA--
BIBLIOGRAPHY.
Sable, Martin Howard. Latin American
urbanization: Metuchen, N.J.,
Scarecrow Press, 1971. 1077 p.
016.3013/6/098 74-145643
Z7165.L3 S28 MRR Alc.

URDU LANGUAGE--DICTIONARIES--ENGLISH.
The Student's practical dictionary,
12th ed., thoroughly rev. and
improved. Allahabad, R. N. Lal,
1956. 667 p. 73-289068
PK1986 .S7 1956 MRR Alc.

URUGUAY--CIVILIZATION.
Pendle, George. Uruguay. 3d ed.
London, New York, Oxford University
Press, 1963. 127 p. 989.506 63-
3986
F2710 .P4 1963 MRR Alc.

URUGUAY--ECONOMIC CONDITIONS--1918-
Pendle, George. Uruguay. 3d ed.
London, New York, Oxford University
Press, 1963. 127 p. 989.506 63-
3986
F2710 .P4 1963 MRR Alc.

URUGUAY--ECONOMIC CONDITIONS--1945-
Weil, Thomas E. Area handbook for
Uruguay. Washington: For sale by the
Supt. of Docs., U.S. Govt. Print.
Off.] 1971. xiv, 439 p. [$3.25]
309.1/895/06 75-609527
HN353.5 .W45 MRR Alc.

URUGUAY--GAZETTEERS.
United States. Office of Geography.
Uruguay: Washington, U.S. Govt.
Print. Off., 1956. iii, 126 p.
918.91 918.95* 56-61988
F2704 .U5 MRR Alc.

URUGUAY--POLITICS AND GOVERNMENT--1904-
Weil, Thomas E. Area handbook for
Uruguay. Washington: For sale by the
Supt. of Docs., U.S. Govt. Print.
Off.] 1971. xiv, 439 p. [$3.25]
309.1/895/06 75-609527
HN353.5 .W45 MRR Alc.

URUGUAY--SOCIAL CONDITIONS.
Weil, Thomas E. Area handbook for
Uruguay. Washington: For sale by the
Supt. of Docs., U.S. Govt. Print.
Off.] 1971. xiv, 439 p. [$3.25]
309.1/895/06 75-609527
HN353.5 .W45 MRR Alc.

USED CAR TRADE--UNITED STATES.
Red book official used car
valuations. [Chicago] National
Market Reports, inc. 381/.45/628222
72-626398
HD9710.U5 N37 MRR Ref Desk Latest
issue

USEFUL ARTS
see Technology

UTAH--BIBLIOGRAPHY--CATALOGS.
United States. Library of Congress.
Centennial of the settlement of Utah,
exhibition, June 7, 1947-August 31,
1947. Washington, U.S. Govt. Print.
Off., 1947. iii, 72 p. 016.9792
47-46402
Z663.15.A6U8 1947 MRR Alc.

UTAH--CENTENNIAL CELEBRATIONS, ETC.
United States. Library of Congress.
Centennial of the settlement of Utah,
exhibition, June 7, 1947-August 31,
1947. Washington, U.S. Govt. Print.
Off., 1947. iii, 72 p. 016.9792
47-46402
Z663.15.A6U8 1947 MRR Alc.

UTAH--DESCRIPTION AND TRAVEL--1951- --
GUIDE BOOKS.
Mobil travel guide: California and
the west. 1969- [Bloomfield, N.J.]
Simon and Schuster. 917.94/04/5 72-
623503
F859.3 .M6 MRR Alc Latest edition

UTAH--DESCRIPTION AND TRAVEL--GUIDE-
BOOKS.
Writers' Program. Utah. Utah; a
guide to the State. New York,
Hastings House [1954] xxvi, 595 p.
917.92 54-1817
F826 .W75 1954 MRR Ref Desk.

UTAH--EXECUTIVE DEPARTMENTS.
Utah. Secretary of State. Compiled
digest of administrative reports.
1956/57- [Salt Lake City?] 353.9792
59-63353
J87 .U84ac MRR Alc Latest edition

UTAH--POLITICS AND GOVERNMENT.
Utah. Secretary of State. Compiled
digest of administrative reports.
1956/57- [Salt Lake City?] 353.9792
59-63353
J87 .U84ac MRR Alc Latest edition

Utah official roster. [Salt Lake
City, Dept. of Finance] 72-626539
JK8431 date MRR Alc Latest edition

UTAH--REGISTERS.
Directory of Utah municipal
officials. Salt Lake City, Utah
League of Cities and Towns.
352/.005/209792 72-623017
JS451.U87 D53 MRR Alc Latest
edition

UTAH--STATISTICS.
Utah. University. Bureau of Economic
and Business Research. 1969
statistical abstract of Utah. [Salt
Lake City] 1969. xiii, 231 p.
317.92 70-628541
HA664 .U75 MRR Alc.

UTAH. UNIVERSITY. LIBRARY.
Utah. University. Library. Chicano
bibliography. [Salt Lake City, 1973]
295 p. 016.9172/06/68 73-623051
Z1361.M4 U78 1973 MRR Alc.

UTICA--BIBLIOGRAPHY.
Historical records survey. Illinois.
A check list of Utica imprints, 1799-
1830. Chicago, Ill., Illinois
Historical records survey, Illinois
public records project, 1942. viii,
179 p. 015.747 43-5103
Z1215 .H67 no. 36 MRR Alc.

UTOPIAS.
Laidler, Harry Wellington, History
of socialism; [Updated and expanded
ed.] New York, Crowell [1968] xx,
970 p. [12.50] 335/.009 67-29698

HX21 .L37 1968 MRR Alc.

Plato. The Republic, Cambridge,
Mass., Harvard University Press;
London, W. Heinemann, 1935-37. 2 v.
321.07 mrr01-59
PA3612 .P67 1935d MRR Alc.

UTOPIAS--HISTORY.
Berneri, Marie Louise, Journey
through Utopia. London, Routledge &
Paul [1950] xi, 339 p. 321.07 51-
872
HX806 .B4 MRR Alc.

VACATION SCHOOLS--UNITED STATES--
DIRECTORIES.
The Guide to summer camps and summer
schools. 1st- ed.; 1936- Boston,
P. Sargent. 37-4715
GV193 .G8 MRR Alc Latest edition

VACATIONS.
Farm and Ranch Vacations, inc. Farm,
ranch & countryside guide; [25th
anniversary ed.] New York: trade
distributor: Berkshire Traveller
Press, Stockbridge, Mass., 1974. 191
p. [$3.50] 917.3 74-174454
TX907 .F37 1974 MRR Alc.

Reinhold, Meyer, Barron's teen-age
summer guide. 4th rev. ed.
Woodbury, N.Y., Barron's Educational
Series, inc. [1969] iv, 238 p.
[2.95] 910.2 75-4715
LB1047 .R43 1969 MRR Ref Desk.

VACUUM-TUBES.
see also Electronics

VALLEYS.
see also Rivers

VAN BUREN, MARTIN, PRES. U.S., 1782-
1862.
Shepard, Edward Morse, Martin Van
Buren, [Rev. ed.] Boston, New York,
Houghton, Mifflin and company, 1900.
vii p., 1 l., 499, [1] p. 02-854
E387 .S55 MRR Alc.

VAN BUREN, MARTIN, PRES. U.S., 1782-
1862--BIBLIOGRAPHY.
United States. Library of Congress.
Manuscript division. Calendar of the
papers of Martin Van Buren,
Washington, Govt. print. off., 1910.
757 p. 012 10-35006
Z6663.34 .V2 MRR Alc.

VARIATION (BIOLOGY)
see also Genetics

VARIETY STORES--CANADA--DIRECTORIES.
Variety department store merchandiser
buyers directory. 1947- New York,
Directory Division, Merchandiser Pub.
Co., [etc.] 338.4/7/670257 48-4264

T12 .S9 MRR Alc Latest edition

VARIETY STORES--UNITED STATES--
DIRECTORIES.
Directory: General mdse., variety
and Jr. dept. store chains. 36th
ed.; 1970- [New York, Business
Guides, inc.] 381 72-623621
HF5468.A1 C418 MRR Alc Latest
edition

Phelon's retail trade. 1st- ed.;
1960- New York, Phelon-Sheldon
Publications [etc.] 60-2106
HF5465.U4 P5 MRR Alc Latest
edition

Sheldon's retail directory of the
United States and Canada and Phelon's
resident buyers and merchandise
brokers. New York, Phelon, Sheldon &
Marsar. [$50.00] 381 74-644143
HF5429.3 .S52 MRR Alc Latest
edition

Variety department store merchandiser
buyers directory. 1947- New York,
Directory Division, Merchandiser Pub.
Co., [etc.] 338.4/7/670257 48-4264

T12 .S9 MRR Alc Latest edition

VARNISH AND VARNISHING.
Trademark directory. Washington
[etc.] 667.6058 14-18485
TP934.5 .T7 Sci RR Latest edition
/ MRR Alc Latest edition

Trademark directory. Supplement.
Washington [etc.] 667.6058 74-
643570
TP934.5 .T7 Sci RR Latest edition
/ MRR Alc Latest edition

VARNISH AND VARNISHING--DICTIONARIES.
Chatfield, Herbert Walter, Glossary
of terms used in the paint, varnish,
and allied trades. London, Scott,
Greenwood [1951] 200 p. 667.603
51-8149
TP934.3 .C5 MRR Alc.

Martin, John Henry, Guide to
pigments and to varnish and lacquer
constituents, London, L. Hill, 1954.
127 p. 667.603 54-42002
TP934.3 .M3 MRR Alc.

VARNISH AND VARNISHING--DICTIONARIES--
POLYGLOT.
Raaff, J. J. Index vocabulorum
quadrilingius: verf en vernis, [Den
Haag] Vereniging van Vernis- en
Verffabrikanten in Nederland,
Expogroep Verf, 1958. 898 p.
667.603 59-27978
TP934.3 .R2 MRR Alc.

VARNISH PAINTS
see Paint

VASCULAR PLANTS
see Botany

VASES.
see also Glassware

VATICAN CITY.
Gessi, Leone. The Vatican City. 4th
ed. Rome] Istituto Poligrafico dello
Stato [c1954] 136 p. 914.56 55-
3455
DG800 .G36 1954 MRR Alc.

VATICAN COUNCIL. 2D, 1962-1965.
Hastings, Adrian. A concise guide to
the documents of the Second Vatican
Council. London, Darton, Longman &
Todd, 1968- v.   [17/6 (v. 1)]
262/.5 70-381885
BX830 1962 .H37 MRR Alc.

VATICAN COUNCIL. 2D, 1962-1965--
COLLECTIONS.
Lexikon für Theologie und Kirche;
2., völlig neu bearb. Aufl.,
Freiburg, Herder, 1957-65. 10 v.
58-41506
BR95 .L48 MRR Alc.

VAUD--DIRECTORIES.
Annuaire; Livre d'adresses de
Lausanne et du canton de Vaud.
Lausanne, Société de l'annuaire
vaudois. 53-28491
DQ724 .A6 MRR Alc Latest edition

VAUDEVILLE--DISCOGRAPHY.
Rust, Brian A. L., The complete
entertainment discography, from the
mid-1890s to 1942 New Rochelle,
N.Y., Arlington House [1973] 677 p.
[$12.95] 016.7899/12 73-13239
ML156.4.P6 R88 MRR Alc.

VAUDEVILLE--UNITED STATES.
Sobel, Bernard. A pictorial history
of vaudeville. New York, Citadel
Press [1961] 224 p. 782.2 61-
18015
PN1967 .S63 MRR Alc.

**VÁZQUEZ DE CORONADO, FRANCISCO, 1510-
1549.**
Spanish explorers in the southern
United States, 1528-1543: New York,
C. Scribner's sons, 1907. xx, 411 p.
07-10607
E187.C7 S7 MRR Alc.

VEGETABLE JUICES.
Tressler, Donald Kiteley, Fruit and
vegetable juice processing
technology, 2d ed. Westport, Conn.,
Avi Pub. Co., 1971. xi, 486 p.
663/.63 75-138801
TP562 .T72 1971 MRR Alc.

VEGETABLE KINGDOM
see Botany

see Plants

VEGETABLE PATHOLOGY--RESEARCH.
United States. Dept. of Agriculture.
Plant diseases. Washington [U.S.
Govt. Print. Off., 1953] xviii, 940
p. 632 agr55-3
S21 .A35 1953 MRR Alc.

VEGETABLE PATHOLOGY--UNITED STATES.
United States. Dept. of Agriculture.
Plant diseases. Washington [U.S.
Govt. Print. Off., 1953] xviii, 940
p. 632 agr55-3
S21 .A35 1953 MRR Alc.

**VEGETABLE TRADE--GREAT BRITAIN--
DIRECTORIES.**
Castle's guide to the fruit, flower,
vegetable, & allied trades. London,
Castle Pub. Co. 61-26296
HD9251.3 .C3 MRR Alc Latest
edition

VEGETABLES.
see also Cookery (Vegetables)

VEGETABLES--DISEASES AND PESTS.
see also Insects, Injurious and
beneficial

VEHICLES.
see also Automobiles

see also Motor vehicles

see also Space vehicles

VEHICLES, MILITARY.
Vanderveen, Bart Harmannus. The
observer's fighting vehicles
directory, World War II; London, New
York, F. Warne, 1969. 340 p. [25/-]
623.7/4/09044 78-76271
UG680 .V35 MRR Alc.

**VENEREAL DISEASES--BIBLIOGRAPHY--
PERIODICALS.**
Goode, Stephen H., Venereal disease
bibliography. 1966/70- Troy, N.Y.,
Whitston Pub. Co. [$10.00]
016.6169/51 71-189843
Z6664.V45 G66 MRR Alc Full set

VENEZIA GIULIA--DIRECTORIES.
Guida generale di Trieste e della
Venezia Giulia. Trieste, Stab. tip.
nazionale. 53-32897
"Fondata nel 1894."
DB321 .G85 MRR Alc Latest edition

VENEZUELA.
American University, Washington, D.
C. Foreign Areas Studies Division.
Area handbook for Venezuela.
Washington, For sale by the Supt. of
Docs., U.S. Govt. Print. Off., 1964.
xii, 575 p. 67-115017
F2308 .A6 MRR Alc.

Lieuwen, Edwin, Venezuela. London,
New York, Oxford University Press,
1961. 193 p. 918.7 61-66619
F2308 .L54 MRR Alc.

VENEZUELA--BIBLIOGRAPHY.
Anuario bibliográfico venezolano.
1942- Caracas, Editorial Arte [etc.]
015.87 44-9260
Z1911 .A7 Alc Full set

VENEZUELA--BIOGRAPHY.
Quién es quién en Venezuela,
Panamá, Ecuador, Columbia. jun. 30,
1952- [Bogota] O. Perry. 920.086
54-19781
F2205 .Q54 MRR Biog Latest edition

VENEZUELA--BIOGRAPHY--DICTIONARIES.
Diccionario biográfico de Venezuela.
1. ed. Madrid, Blass, 1953. li,
1558 p. pa 54-28
F2305 .D5 MRR Biog.

Rudolph, Donna Keyse, Historical
dictionary of Venezuela, Metuchen,
N.J., Scarecrow Press, 1971. 142 p.
987/.003 70-160283
F2304 .R8 MRR Alc.

VENEZUELA--COMMERCE--DIRECTORIES.
Diccionario biográfico de Venezuela.
1. ed. Madrid, Blass, 1953. li,
1558 p. pa 54-28
F2305 .D5 MRR Biog.

VENEZUELA--GAZETTEERS.
United States. Office of Geography.
Venezuela: official standard names
approved by the United States Board
of Geographic Names. Washington,
U.S. Govt. Print. Off., 1961. v, 245
p. 61-64988
F2304 .U5 MRR Alc.

VENEZUELA--HISTORY.
Morón, Guillermo. A history of
Venezuela. New York, Roy [1964,
c1963] 268 p. 987 64-13612
F2321 .M653 MRR Alc.

VENEZUELA--HISTORY--DICTIONARIES.
Rudolph, Donna Keyse, Historical
dictionary of Venezuela, Metuchen,
N.J., Scarecrow Press, 1971. 142 p.
987/.003 70-160283
F2304 .R8 MRR Alc.

VENEZUELA--STATISTICS.
Venezuela. Dirección General de
Estadística y Censos Nacionales.
Anuario estadístico de Venezuela.
1877- Caracas. 07-25216
HA1091 .A4 MRR Alc Latest edition

Venezuela. Dirección General de
Estadística y Censos Nacionales.
Compendio estadístico de Venezuela.
Caracas, 1968. xxix, 488 p. 318.7
76-391637
HA1091 .A56 1968 MRR Alc.

VENEZUELAN LITERATURE--BIO-BIBLIOGRAPHY.
Anuario bibliográfico venezolano.
1942- Caracas, Editorial Arte [etc.]
015.87 44-9260
Z1911 .A7 MRR Alc Full set

VENEZUELAN PERIODICALS--BIBLIOGRAPHY.
Anuario bibliográfico venezolano.
1942- Caracas, Editorial Arte [etc.]
015.87 44-9260
Z1911 .A7 Alc Full set

VENICE--DESCRIPTION--GUIDE-BOOKS.
Honour, Hugh. The companion guide to
Venice. New York, Harper & Rowe
[1966] 287 p. 914.5310492 64-
12699
DG672 .H6 1966 MRR Alc.

VENTILATION--HANDBOOKS, MANUALS, ETC.
American Society of Heating,
Refrigerating and Air-Conditioning
Engineers. ASHRAE handbook & product
directory. 1973- New York. 697 73-
644272
TH7011 .A4 MRR Alc Latest edition
/ Sci RR Latest edition

**VENTURE CAPITAL--UNITED STATES--
COLLECTIONS.**
Venture capital. v. 1- 1970- [New
York] Technimetrics, inc.]
332.1/025/73 74-20999
HG65 .V4 MRR Alc Latest edition

**VENTURE CAPITAL--UNITED STATES--
DIRECTORIES.**
Rubel, Stanley M. Guide to venture
capital sources, 3d ed. [Chicago]
Capital Pub. Corp. [1974] 334 p.
332.1/025/73 74-75808
HG65 .R8 1974 MRR Alc.

Venture capital. v. 1- 1970- [New
York, Technimetrics, inc.]
332.1/025/73 74-20999
HG65 .V4 MRR Alc Latest edition

**VERGILIUS MARO, PUBLIUS--DICTIONARIES,
INDEXES, ETC.**
Merguet, Hugg, Lexikon zu Vergilius
mit angabe sämtlicher stellen,
Leipzig-R., Kommissionsverlag von R.
Schmidt, 1912. 2 p. l., 786 p. 15-
13878
PA6952 .M4 MRR Alc.

Wetmore, Monroe Nichols, Index
verborum Vergilianus, New Haven,
Yale university press; [etc., etc.]
1911. x, 554 p., 1 l. [$4.00] 11-
2238
PA6952 .W4 MRR Alc.

VERMONT--BIOGRAPHY.
Vermont. Secretary of state. Vermont
legislative directory. 1867-
Montpelier [etc.] 09-34113
JK3031 MRR Alc Latest edition

VERMONT--COMMERCE--DIRECTORIES.
Vermont year book. Chester [etc.]
Vt., National Survey [etc.] 08-14736

Began publication in 1818.
JK3030 .Va MRR Alc Latest edition

**VERMONT--DESCRIPTION AND TRAVEL--GUIDE-
BOOKS.**
Federal Writers' Project. Vermont.
Vermont; a guide to the Green
Mountain State. 3d ed.; rev.
Boston, Houghton Mifflin, 1968. xix,
452 p. 917.43 68-14344
F54 .F45 1968 MRR Ref Desk.

VERMONT--DIRECTORIES.
Vermont year book. Chester [etc.]
Vt., National Survey [etc.] 08-14736

Began publication in 1818.
JK3030 .Va MRR Alc Latest edition

VERMONT--IMPRINTS.
McCorison, Marcus Allen. Vermont
imprints, 1778-1820; Worcester
[Mass.] American Antiquarian Society,
1963. xxiv, 597 p. 015.743 63-
14992
Z1343 .M3 MRR Alc.

VERMONT--MANUFACTURES--DIRECTORIES.
Directory of New England
manufacturers. Boston, Mass., G. D.
Hall, inc. 338.40974 36-5085
HD9723 .D45 Sci RR Latest edition
/ MRR Alc Latest edition

Vermont. Development Commission.
Directory of Vermont manufactured
products. [1st]- ed.; 1942-
Montpelier. 670.58 42-36529
T12 .V45 MRR Alc Latest edition

VERMONT--POLITICS AND GOVERNMENT.
Vermont. Secretary of state. Vermont
legislative directory. 1867-
Montpelier [etc.] 09-34113
JK3031 MRR Alc Latest edition

**VERMONT--POLITICS AND GOVERNMENT--1865-
Nuquist, Andrew Edgerton. Vermont
State Government and administration:
Burlington, Government Research
Center, University of Vermont, 1966.
xiv, 644 p. 353.9743 65-29199
JK3025 1966 .N8 MRR Alc.

VERMONT--REGISTERS.
Vermont. Secretary of State. State
government, Vermont. [Montpelier]
54-62071
JK3030 .A34 MRR Alc Latest edition

Vermont. Secretary of state. Vermont
legislative directory. 1867-
Montpelier [etc.] 09-34113
JK3031 MRR Alc Latest edition

Vermont year book. Chester [etc.]
Vt., National Survey [etc.] 08-14736

Began publication in 1818.
JK3030 .Va MRR Alc Latest edition

**VERMONT. GENERAL ASSEMBLY--RULES AND
PRACTICE.**
Vermont. Secretary of state. Vermont
legislative directory. 1867-
Montpelier [etc.] 09-34113
JK3031 MRR Alc Latest edition

VERSAILLES--DESCRIPTION--GUIDE-BOOKS.
Paris in a week, [English ed.
Paris, Hachette, 1964. 120 p. 64-
47374
DC708 .P2813 1964 MRR Alc.

VERSIFICATION.
Shapiro, Karl Jay, A prosody
handbook New York, Harper & Row
[1965] x, 214 p. 416 64-24535
PN1042 .S57 MRR Alc.

VERTEBRATES.
see also Amphibians

see also Birds

see also Fishes

see also Mammals

see also Reptiles

VERTEBRATES--ANATOMY.
Romer, Alfred Sherwood, The
vertebrate body. 4th ed.
Philadelphia, Saunders, 1970. viii,
601 p. 596/.04 75-92143
QL805 .R65 1970 MRR Alc.

**VERTEBRATES--UNITED STATES--
IDENTIFICATION.**
Blair, W. Frank, Vertebrates of the
United States 2d ed. New York,
McGraw-Hill [1968] ix, 616 p.
596/.09/73 67-18322
QL605 .B58 1968 MRR Alc.

VESSELS (SHIPS)
see Ships

VESTFOLD, NORWAY--DIRECTORIES.
Adressebok for Vestfold fylke og
Drammen med skatteligninger. Oslo,
S. M. Bryde.   53-28837
DL576.V45 A7   MRR Alc Latest
edition

VETERANS.
see also Soldiers

VETERANS--UNITED STATES.
Friedman, I. Edward. Your veterans'
benefits, [1st ed.] Garden City,
N.Y., Doubleday, 1969. x, 161 p.
[1.95]   355.1/15/0973 68-22487
UB357 .F74 MRR Alc.

VETERANS--UNITED STATES--LAWS AND
LEGISLATION.
What every veteran should know.
Moline, Ill. 355.115 45-46768
UB357 .W5   MRR Ref Desk Latest
edition

VETERINARY COLLEGES--UNITED STATES--
DIRECTORIES.
White, Alex Sandri. The new
directory of medical schools, New
1974 ed. Allenhurst, N.J., Aurea
Publications [1973] 143 p. [$5.95]
610/.7/1173 73-175214
R712.A1 W5 1974 MRR Ref Desk.

VETERINARY MATERIA MEDICA AND PHARMACY--
YEARBOOKS.
Veterinarians' blue book. [1st]-
ed.: 1953- [New York, R. H.
Donnelley, etc.] 53-24738
SF915 .V47 Sci RR Latest edition /
MRR Alc Latest edition

VETERINARY MEDICINE.
see also Domestic animals

VETERINARY MEDICINE--BIBLIOGRAPHY.
Bowker's medical books in print.
1972- New York, R.R. Bowker Co.
016.61 78-37613
Z6658 .B65 MRR Alc Latest edition
/ Sci RR Latest edition

VETERINARY MEDICINE--DICTIONARIES.
Miller, William Christopher,
Encyclopedia of animal care. 9th ed.
Baltimore, Williams & Wilkins, 1970.
viii, 1013 p. [$15.50] 636.089/03
75-29859
SF609 .M5 1970b MRR Alc.

VETO--UNITED STATES.
Jackson, Carlton. Presidential
vetoes, 1792-1945. Athens,
University of Georgia Press [1967]
x, 254 p. 353/.032 67-17405
JK586 .J3 MRR Alc.

United States. Congress. Senate.
Library. Presidential vetoes;
Washington, U.S. Govt. Print. Off.,
1969. viii, 252 p. [1.00]
353/.032 70-602991
KF42.2 1969 MRR Ref Desk.

VIBORG, DENMARK (CITY)--DIRECTORIES.
Viborg vejviser. 1.-   arg.; 1960-
Viborg. 64-45532
DL291.V45 V5 MRR Alc Latest
edition

VICE-PRESIDENTS--UNITED STATES.
Harwood, Michael. In the shadow of
Presidents; [1st ed.] Philadelphia,
Lippincott [1966] x, 239 p. 353.03
ac 66-10025
JK609.5 .H3 MRR Alc.

Hatch, Louis Clinton. A history of
the vice-presidency of the United
States. New York, The American
historical society, inc.. 1934. viii
p., 2 l., [3]-437 p. 353.03 34-
8999
E176 .H35 MRR Alc.

Taylor, Tim. The book of presidents.
[1st ed.] New York, Arno Press,
1972. viii, 703 p. [$12.95]
973/.099 B 74-164708
E176.1 .T226 MRR Ref Desk.

Williams, Irving G. The rise of the
Vice Presidency. Washington, Public
Affairs Press [1956] 266 p. 353.03
56-8546
JK609.5 .W56 MRR Alc.

VICE-PRESIDENTS--UNITED STATES--
BIBLIOGRAPHY.
United States. Library of Congress.
General Reference and Bibliography
Division. The Presidents of the
United States, 1789-1962: Washington
[For sale by the Superintendent of
Documents, U.S. Govt. Print. Off.]
1963. xviii, 159 p.   63-61781
Z663.28 .P73 MRR Alc.

VICE-PRESIDENTS--UNITED STATES--
BIOGRAPHY.
Barzman, Sol. Madmen and geniuses :
Chicago : Follett, [1974] xi, 335 p.
: [$8.95] 973/.0992 B 74-78583
E176 .B28 MRR Alc.

VICTORIA, AUSTRALIA.
Victorian year-book. 1874-
Melbourne. ca 05-983
DU200 .V6 MRR Alc Latest edition

VICTORIA, AUSTRALIA--DIRECTORIES.
Sands & McDougall's directory of
Victoria. Melbourne, Sands &
McDougall. 56-52577
DU205 .S3 MRR Alc Latest edition

VIDEO TAPE RECORDS AND RECORDING--
DICTIONARIES.
Levitan, Eli L. An alphabetical
guide to motion picture, television,
and videotape production New York,
McGraw-Hill [1970] xvii, 797 p.
778.5/3/03 69-13610
TR847 .L47 MRR Alc.

VIENNA--COMMERCE--DIRECTORIES.
Handelsregister Österreich. 1960-
Wien, Jupiter-Verlag. 52-24534
HF5167.V5 H3   MRR Alc Latest
edition

Herold Adressbuch von Wien. 1955-
Wien, Herold. 72-622314
HF3550.V5 A45 MRR Alc Latest
edition

Made in Austria. Wien, Jupiter-
Verlag. 380/.025/436 68-77958
HF3543 .M3 MRR Alc Latest edition

VIENNA--DIRECTORIES.
Herold Adressbuch von Wien. 1955-
Wien, Herold. 72-622314
HF3550.V5 A45 MRR Alc Latest
edition

VIETNAM.
American University, Washington, D.C.
Foreign Area Studies Division. Area
handbook for South Vietnam.
Washington, for sale by the Supt. of
Docs., U.S. Govt. Print. Off.; 1967.
xiv, 510 p. 915.97/03/4 67-62089
DS557.A5 A717 MRR Alc.

American University, Washington, D.C.
Foreign Areas Studies Division. Area
handbook for Vietnam. Washington,
For sale by the Supt. of Docs., U.S.
Govt. Print. Off., 1962; reprinted
1964. x, 513 p.   67-115019
DS557.A5 A72 1964 MRR Alc.

VIETNAM--BIBLIOGRAPHY.
Chen, John Hsueh-ming, Vietnam: a
comprehensive bibliography,
Metuchen, N.J., Scarecrow Press,
1973. ix, 314 p.   016.91597 72-
10549
Z3228.V5 C47 MRR Alc.

Trần-thị-KimSa. Bibliography on
Vietnam, 1954-1964. Saigon, National
Institute of Administration [1965]
vii, 255 p.   76-211618
Z3228.V5 T7 MRR Alc.

United States. Library of Congress.
Orientalia Division. Southeast Asia
subject catalog. Boston, G. K. Hall,
1972- v.   016.9159/03 72-5257
Z3221 .U525 MRR Alc (Dk 33)

VIETNAM--BIOGRAPHY.
Who's who in Vietnam. [Saigon]
Vietnam Press Agency. 920/.0597 73-
615807
DS557.A5 A555 MRR Biog Latest
edition

VIETNAM--FOREIGN RELATIONS--UNITED
STATES.
United States. Congress. Senate.
Committee on Foreign Relations.
Background information relating to
Southeast Asia and Vietnam. Jan. 14,
1965- Washington, For sale by the
Supt. of Docs., U.S. Govt. Print.
Off. 327.597/073 72-601275
E183.8.V5 A3 MRR Alc Latest
edition

VIETNAM--GAZETTEERS.
United States. Geographic Names
Division. South Vietnam; [2d ed.]
Washington, 1971. vii, 337 p.
915.97/003 70-613599
DS557.A5 U533 1971 MRR Alc.

VIETNAM--HISTORY.
Buttinger, Joseph. The smaller
dragon; New York, Praeger [1958]
535 p. 959.7 58-7748
DS557.A5 B8 MRR Alc.

Buttinger, Joseph. Vietnam: a dragon
embattled. London, Pall Mall P.,
1967. 2 v. [£6/10/-] 959.7 68-
70118
DS557.A5 B83 1967b MRR Alc.

VIETNAM--HISTORY--1945-
Fall, Bernard B., The two Viet-Nams;
2d rev. ed. New York, Praeger
[1967] xii, 507 p. 959.7 66-14505
DS557.A5 F34 1967 MRR Alc.

VIETNAM--STATISTICS.
Vietnam. Viện Thống-kê và Khảo
Cứu Kinh-tế. Viet-Nam niên-
giam thống-kê. v. 1- 1949/50-
[Saigon] sa 62-148
HA1780.5 .A32 MRR Alc Latest
edition

VIETNAM (DEMOCRATIC REPUBLIC, 1946-)--
GAZETTEERS.
United States. Office of Geography.
Northern Vietnam; official standard
names approved by the United States
Board on Geographic Names.
Washington [U.S. Govt. Print. Off.]
1964. v, 311 p.   64-62408
DS557.A7 U5 MRR Alc.

VIETNAMESE CONFLICT, 1961-
United States. Congress. Senate.
Committee on Foreign Relations.
Background information relating to
Southeast Asia and Vietnam. Jan. 14,
1965- Washington, For sale by the
Supt. of Docs., U.S. Govt. Print.
Off. 327.597/073 72-601275
E183.8.V5 A3 MRR Alc Latest
edition

VIETNAMESE CONFLICT, 1961- --BIOGRAPHY.
Kerrigan, Evans E. The Medal of
Honor in Vietnam, [1st ed.] Noroton
Heights, Conn., Medallic Pub. Co.
[1971- v.   959.7/0434/0922 B 77-
173048
DS557.A6315 K45 MRR Biog.

VIETNAMESE CONFLICT, 1961- --REGIMENTAL
HISTORIES--UNITED STATES.
Stubbs, Mary Lee. Armor-cavalry,
Washington, Office of the Chief of
Military History, U.S. Army; [for
sale by the Supt. of Docs., U.S.
Govt. Print. Off.] 1969- v.
[6.75] 357/.0973 69-60002
UA30 .S8 MRR Alc.

VIETNAMESE CONFLICT, 1961- --UNITED
STATES.
Raskin, Marcus G., ed. The Viet-Nam
reader; New York, Random House
[1965] xv, 415 p.   959.704 65-
26331
DS557.A6 R3 MRR Alc.

VIETNAMESE LANGUAGE--DICTIONARIES--
ENGLISH.
Le-ba-Khanh. Standard pronouncing
Vietnamese-English and English-
Vietnamese dictionary. [New York, F.
Ungar Pub. Co.] 1955] 2 v. in 1.
495.9232 55-12581
PL4376 .L48 MRR Alc.

VIEWS--BIBLIOGRAPHY.
Ellis, Jessie (Croft) Travel through
pictures; Boston, The F. W. Faxon
company 1935. xi, 699 p. 016.91
35-27172
Z6020 .E47 MRR Alc.

VIKINGS.
Arbman, Holger, The Vikings. New
York, Praeger [1961] 212 p. 948.02
61-10520
DL65 .A723 MRR Alc.

VILLAGES.
see also Community development

VIOLENCE--STATISTICS.
Taylor, Charles Lewis. World
handbook of political and social
indicators, 2d ed. New Haven, Yale
University Press, 1972. xiv, 443 p.
[$15.00] 301/.01/8 70-179479
HN15 .T37 1972 MRR Alc.

VIOLENCE--UNITED STATES.
Graham, Hugh Davis. The history of
violence in America: New York, F. A.
Praeger [1969] xxxvi, 822 p.
[11.85] 301.2 70-93570
HN57 .G65 1969c MRR Alc.

Hofstadter, Richard, comp. American
violence; [1st ed.] New York,
Knopf, 1970. xiv, 478, xiii p.
[$10.00] 973 73-111238
E179 .H8 1970 MRR Alc.

Platt, Anthony M., comp. The
politics of riot commissions, 1917-
1970; New York, Macmillan [1971] x,
534 p.   364.14/3 79-150069
HV6477 .P5 MRR Alc.

VIOLENT DEATHS.
Elliot, Gil, Twentieth century book
of the dead. London, Allen Lane,
1972. viii, 242 p. [£2.75]
301.32/2 72-169396
D445 .E555 MRR Alc.

VIOLENT DEATHS--UNITED STATES.
Accident facts. [Chicago, National
Safety Council] 28-14389
HA217 .A4 MRR Ref Desk Latest
edition / MRR Alc Latest edition

VIOLIN.
Bachmann, Alberto Abraham, An
encyclopedia of the violin New York,
Da Capo Press, 1966. vi, 470 p.
787.1 65-23406
ML800 .B13 1966 MRR Alc.

VIOLIN MAKERS.
Bachmann, Alberto Abraham, An
encyclopedia of the violin New York,
Da Capo Press, 1966. vi, 470 p.
787.1 65-23406
ML800 .B13 1966 MRR Alc.

VIOLIN MUSIC--BIBLIOGRAPHY.
Bachmann, Alberto Abraham, An
encyclopedia of the violin New York,
Da Capo Press, 1966. vi, 470 p.
787.1 65-23406
ML800 .B13 1966 MRR Alc.

VIOLINISTS, VIOLONCELLISTS, ETC.--
BIOGRAPHY.
Bachmann, Alberto Abraham, An
encyclopedia of the violin New York,
Da Capo Press, 1966. vi, 470 p.
787.1 65-23406
ML800 .B13 1966 MRR Alc.

VIPERS
see Snakes

VIRGIN ISLANDS OF THE UNITED STATES--
BIOGRAPHY.
Farr, Kenneth R. Historical
dictionary of Puerto Rico and the
U.S. Virgin Islands. Metuchen, N.J.,
Scarecrow Press, 1973. vii, 148 p.
917.29/003 73-7603
F1954 .F37 MRR Alc.

VIRGIN ISLANDS OF THE UNITED STATES--
DESCRIPTION AND TRAVEL--GUIDE-BOOKS.
Marvel, Evalyn. Guide to Puerto Rico
and the Virgin Islands. Rev. ed.
New York, Crown Publishers [1963]
254 p. 917.295 63-24745
F1959 .M3 1963 MRR Alc.

Rand, Abby. Abby Rand's guide to
Puerto Rico and the U.S. Virgin
Islands. New York, Scribner [1973]
ix, 276 p. [$8.95] 917.295/04/53
73-1357
F1959 .R36 1973 MRR Alc.

VIRGIN ISLANDS OF THE UNITED STATES--
DICTIONARIES AND ENCYCLOPEDIAS.
Farr, Kenneth R. Historical
dictionary of Puerto Rico and the
U.S. Virgin Islands. Metuchen, N.J.,
Scarecrow Press, 1973. vii, 148 p.
917.29/003 73-7603
F1954 .F37 MRR Alc.

VIRGIN ISLANDS OF THE UNITED STATES--
HISTORY.
Creque, Darwin D. The U.S. Virgins
and the eastern Caribbean,
Philadelphia, Whitmore Pub. Co.
[1968] vi, 266 p. 972.97/22 67-
31320
F2136 .C7 MRR Alc.

VIRGIN MARY
see Mary, Virgin

VIRGINIA--BIBLIOGRAPHY.
Cappon, Lester Jesse, Bibliography
of Virginia history since 1865,
University, Va., The Institute for
research in the social sciences,
1930. xviii, 900 p. 016.9755 30-
27506
Z1345 .C25 MRR Alc.

Swem, Earl Gregg, A bibliography of
Virginia. Richmond, D. Bottom,
superintendent of public printing,
1916-55. 5 v. 16-4768
Z1345 .S85 MRR Alc.

VIRGINIA--BIOGRAPHY.
Dodson, Edward Griffith, The General
Assembly of the Commonwealth of
Virginia, 1885-1918. Richmond, State
Publication, 1960. 517 p. 328.755
a 61-9339
JK3931 1960 .D6 MRR Alc.

Dodson, Edward Griffith, The General
assembly of the commonwealth of
Virginia 1919-1939. Richmond, State
publication, 1939. 515 p. 328.7558
39-28939
JK3930 .A6 1939 MRR Alc.

Dodson, Edward Griffith, The General
Assembly of the Commonwealth of
Virginia, 1940-1960. Richmond, State
Publication, 1961. 1152 p. a 64-
7405
JK3931 1961 .D6 MRR Alc.

VIRGINIA--BIOGRAPHY--INDEXES.
Swem, Earl Gregg, comp. Virginia
historical index ... Roanoke, Va.,
Designed, printed, and bound by the
Stone printing and manufacturing
company, 1934-36. 2 v. 34-38514
F221 .S93 MRR Ref Desk.

VIRGINIA--CONSTITUTIONAL CONVENTIONS.
Dodson, Edward Griffith, The General
Assembly of the Commonwealth of
Virginia, 1940-1960. Richmond, State
Publication, 1961. 1152 p. a 64-
7405
JK3931 1961 .D6 MRR Alc.

VIRGINIA--DESCRIPTION AND TRAVEL.
Sprouse, Edith Moore. Potomac
sampler; [Alexandria, Va.] c1961.
29 l. 62-27127
F227 .S74 MRR Alc.

VIRGINIA--DESCRIPTION AND TRAVEL--GUIDE-
BOOKS.
Living in Washington; 1st ed.]
Richmond, Westover Pub. Co. [1972]
vii, 259 p. [$3.50] 917.53 72-
188108
F192.3 .L58 MRR Ref Desk.

O'Neal, William Bainter.
Architecture in Virginia; 1st ed.
New York, Published for the Virginia
Museum by Walker, 1968. 192 p.
720.9/755 67-13230
NA730.V8 O5 MRR Alc.

Writers' program. Virginia.
Virginia; a guide to the Old
Dominion, New York, Oxford
university press [1946] xxix, 710
(i.e. 726) p. 917.55 46-5684
F231 .W88 1946 MRR Ref Desk.

VIRGINIA--GENEALOGY--INDEXES.
Swem, Earl Gregg, comp. Virginia
historical index ... Roanoke, Va.,
Designed, printed, and bound by the
Stone printing and manufacturing
company, 1934-36. 2 v. 34-38514
F221 .S93 MRR Ref Desk.

VIRGINIA--GOVERNMENT PUBLICATIONS--
BIBLIOGRAPHY.
Dodson, Edward Griffith, The General
assembly of the commonwealth of
Virginia 1919-1939. Richmond, State
publication, 1939. 515 p. 328.7558
39-28939
JK3930 .A6 1939 MRR Alc.

Swem, Earl Gregg, A bibliography of
Virginia. Richmond, D. Bottom,
superintendent of public printing,
1916-55. 5 v. 16-4768
Z1345 .S85 MRR Alc.

VIRGINIA--GOVERNMENT PUBLICATIONS--
INDEXES.
Dodson, Edward Griffith, The General
Assembly of the Commonwealth of
Virginia, 1885-1918. Richmond, State
Publication, 1960. 517 p. 328.755
a 61-9339
JK3931 1960 .D6 MRR Alc.

Dodson, Edward Griffith, The General
Assembly of the Commonwealth of
Virginia, 1940-1960. Richmond, State
Publication, 1961. 1152 p. a 64-
7405
JK3931 1961 .D6 MRR Alc.

VIRGINIA--HISTORIC HOUSES, ETC.
O'Neal, William Bainter.
Architecture in Virginia; 1st ed.
New York, Published for the Virginia
Museum by Walker, 1968. 192 p.
720.9/755 67-13230
NA730.V8 O5 MRR Alc.

Sprouse, Edith Moore. Potomac
sampler; [Alexandria, Va.] c1961.
29 l. 62-27127
F227 .S74 MRR Alc.

VIRGINIA--HISTORY--COLONIAL PERIOD, CA.
1600-1775--SOURCES.
Tyler, Lyon Gardiner, ed. Narratives
of early Virginia, 1606-1625; New
York, C. Scribner's sons, 1907. xv,
478 p. 07-33220
E187.O7 T9 MRR Alc.

Virginia company of London. The
records of the Virginia company of
London ... Washington, Govt. print.
off., 1906-35. 4 v. 06-35006
Z663 .R38 MRR Alc.

VIRGINIA--HISTORY--INDEXES.
Swem, Earl Gregg, comp. Virginia
historical index ... Roanoke, Va.,
Designed, printed, and bound by the
Stone printing and manufacturing
company, 1934-36. 2 v. 34-38514
F221 .S93 MRR Ref Desk.

VIRGINIA--HISTORY--PERIODICALS--INDEXES.
Swem, Earl Gregg, comp. Virginia
historical index ... Roanoke, Va.,
Designed, printed, and bound by the
Stone printing and manufacturing
company, 1934-36. 2 v. 34-38514
F221 .S93 MRR Ref Desk.

VIRGINIA--IMPRINTS.
Cappon, Lester Jesse, Bibliography
of Virginia history since 1865,
University, Va., The Institute for
research in the social sciences,
1930. xviii, 900 p. 016.9755 30-
27506
Z1345 .C25 MRR Alc.

Swem, Earl Gregg, A bibliography of
Virginia. Richmond, D. Bottom,
superintendent of public printing,
1916-55. 5 v. 16-4768
Z1345 .S85 MRR Alc.

VIRGINIA--INDUSTRIES--DIRECTORIES.
Industrial directory of Virginia.
Richmond, Virginia Chamber of
Commerce. 338/.0025/755 72-621902
HC107.V8 I53 Sci RR Latest edition
/ MRR Alc Latest edition

VIRGINIA--MANUFACTURES--DIRECTORIES.
Directory of Central Atlantic States
manufacturers; 1- 1950-
Baltimore, T. K. Sanderson
Organization. 670.58 50-2706
T12 .D485 Sci RR Latest edition /
MRR Alc Latest edition

VIRGINIA--MAPS.
Salt water sport fishing and boating
in Virginia. Alexandria, Va., 1971.
78 p. [$5.00] 623.89 73-654615
G1291.L1 S2 1971 MRR Alc.

VIRGINIA--MAPS--BIBLIOGRAPHY.
United States. Library of Congress.
Map Division. The Hotchkiss map
collection; Washington, 1951. 67 p.
016.91273 51-60026
Z663.35 .H6 MRR Alc.

VIRGINIA--OFFICIALS AND EMPLOYEES.
Dodson, Edward Griffith, The General
Assembly of the Commonwealth of
Virginia, 1885-1918. Richmond, State
Publication, 1960. 517 p. 328.755
a 61-9339
JK3931 1960 .D6 MRR Alc.

Dodson, Edward Griffith, The General
Assembly of the Commonwealth of
Virginia, 1940-1960. Richmond, State
Publication, 1961. 1152 p. a 64-
7405
JK3931 1961 .D6 MRR Alc.

VIRGINIA--POLITICS AND GOVERNMENT.
League of Women Voters of
Metropolitan Washington.
Metropolitan Washington; District of
Columbia, Maryland, Virginia.
Washington, League of Women Voters
Education Fund [1970] 52 p. [$0.25]
320.4/753 77-27912
JK2725 1970 .L4 MRR Ref Desk.

VIRGINIA--POLITICS & GOVERNMENT
Virginia. Secretary of the
Commonwealth. Report. Richmond. 10-
33120
J87 .V94a MRR Alc Latest edition

VIRGINIA--POLITICS AND GOVERNMENT--
REVOLUTION, 1775-1783.
Madison, James, Pres. U.S., Papers.
Chicago] University of Chicago Press
[1962- v. 923.173 62-9114
E302 .M19 MRR Alc.

VIRGINIA--REGISTERS.
Virginia. Secretary of the
Commonwealth. Report. Richmond. 10-
33120
J87 .V94a MRR Alc Latest edition

VIRGINIA--STATISTICS.
Eisenberg, Ralph. Virginia votes.
[Charlottesville] Governmental and
Administrative Research Division,
University of Virginia, 1971- v.
329/.023/755 72-32113
JK3993 1924 .E57 MRR Alc.

Thomas Jefferson Center for Political
Economy. Statistical abstract of
Virginia, 1966. [Charlottesville,
Va., 1967- v. 317.55 70-606013

HA686 .T43 MRR Alc.

Tayloe Murphy Institute. The
Virginia constituency: election
district data-1970.
[Charlottesville] Tayloe Murphy
Institute and the Institute of
Government, University of Virginia,
1973. v.; 315 p. 328/.755/07345 73-
620026
JK3968 .T39 1973 MRR Alc.

VIRGINIA. GENERAL ASSEMBLY.
Dodson, Edward Griffith, The General
Assembly of the Commonwealth of
Virginia, 1885-1918. Richmond, State
Publication, 1960. 517 p. 328.755
a 61-9339
JK3931 1960 .D6 MRR Alc.

Dodson, Edward Griffith, The General
assembly of the commonwealth of
Virginia 1919-1939. Richmond, State
publication, 1939. 515 p. 328.7558
39-28939
JK3930 .A6 1939 MRR Alc.

VIRGINIA. GENERAL ASSEMBLY--REGISTERS.
Dodson, Edward Griffith, The General
Assembly of the Commonwealth of
Virginia, 1940-1960. Richmond, State
Publication, 1961. 1152 p. a 64-
7405
JK3931 1961 .D6 MRR Alc.

VIRGINIA. UNIVERSITY. LIBRARY.
Virginia. University. Library. The
Jefferson papers of the University of
Virginia. Charlottesville, Published
for the University of Virginia
Library [by] the University Press of
Virginia [1973] xvi, 496 p.
016.9734/6/0924 72-91896
Z6616.J4 V55 1973 MRR Alc.

VIRTUE.
see also Ethics

VIRUS DISEASES.
Microbiology; including immunology
and molecular genetics 2d ed.
Hagerstown, Md., Medical Dept.,
Harper & Row [1973] xv, 1562 p.
576 73-6349
QR41.2 .M49 1973 MRR Alc.

VISIBILITY--BIBLIOGRAPHY.
United States. Library of Congress.
Technical Information Division.
Visibility; a bibliography,
Washington, 1952. vi, 90 p.
016.1521 53-60026
Z663.49 .V5 MRR Alc.

VISIONS.
see also Dreams

VISITORS, FOREIGN--UNITED STATES.
National Council for Community
Services to International Visitors.
National directory of community
organizations serving short-term
international visitors. Washington.
64-55675
Began publication in 1960.
E744.5 .N35 MRR Alc Latest edition

VISITORS, FOREIGN--WASHINGTON, D.C.
International Visitors Service
Council. Organizations serving
international visitors in the
National Capital area. [4th ed.]
Washington [1973] vii, 151 l.,
155-191 p. 917.53/04/4025 72-96925

F191 .I57 1973 MRR Alc.

VISUAL AIDS.
see also Moving-pictures

Taylor, Earl A. A manual of visual
presentation in education and
training, [1st ed.] Oxford, New
York, Pergamon Press [1966] xxi, 300
p. 371.335 66-18389
LB1043.5 .T38 1966 MRR Alc.

VISUAL ARTS
see Art

VISUAL EDUCATION.
see also Audio-visual education

see also Lantern slides

see also Moving-pictures in education

see also Transparencies in education

**VISUALLY HANDICAPPED--UNITED STATES--
DIRECTORIES.**
Directory of agencies serving the
visually handicapped in the United
States. New York, American
Foundation for the Blind.
362.4/1/02573 72-158435
HV1790 .A4 MRR Alc Latest edition

VITAL STATISTICS.
Clark, Colin, Population growth and
land use. London, Melbourne [etc.]
Macmillan; New York, St. Martin's P.,
1967. 406 p. [70/-] 301.3/2 67-
15941
HB871 .C58 1967 MRR Alc.

Keyfitz, Nathan, World population;
Chicago, University of Chicago Press
[1968] xi, 672 p. 312 68-14010
HB881 .K48 TJ Rm.

Preston, Samuel H. Causes of death:
life tables for national population
New York, Seminar Press, 1972. xi,
787 p. 312/.2 72-80305
HB1321 .P73 MRR Alc.

Wolfenden, Hugh Herbert. Population
statistics and their compilation.
Rev. ed.; [Chicago] Published for
the Society of Actuaries by the
University of Chicago Press, 1954.
258 p. 312 54-10735
HB881 .W64 1954 MRR Alc.

VITAL STATISTICS--BIBLIOGRAPHY.
Population index. v. 1- Jan. 20,
1935- [Princeton, N.J., etc.]
016.312 39-10247
Z7164.D3 P83 MRR Alc Partial set

Princeton University. Office of
Population Research. Population
index bibliography. Boston, G. K.
Hall, 1971. 5 v. 016.312 79-30213

Z7164.D3 P852 MRR Alc (Dk 33)

United States. Library of Congress.
Census library project. General
censuses and vital statistics in the
Americas. Washington, U.S. Govt.
print. off., 1943. ix, 151 p.
016.312 44-40643
Z7553.C3 U45 MRR Alc.

VITAL STATISTICS--YEARBOOKS.
Demographic yearbook. 1948- Lake
Success. 312.058 50-641
HA17 .D45 MRR Ref Desk Latest
edition

World health statistics annual. 1962-
Genève, World Health Organization.
312/.2/05 72-624373
RA651.A485 MRR Alc Latest edition
/ Sci RR Latest edition

VITICULTURE.
see also Wine and wine making

The great book of wine. New York,
World Pub. Co. [1970] 459 p.
[50.00] 641 77-124428
TP548 .G6913 MRR Alc.

VITICULTURE--DICTIONARIES.
Simon, Andre Louis, The
International Wine and Food Society's
encyclopedia of wines. [1st American
ed. New York] Quadrangle Books
[1973, c1972] 311 p. [$15.00]
641.2/2/03 72-85052
TP546 .S53 1973 MRR Alc.

VIZCAYA, SPAIN--DIRECTORIES.
Guia-anuario de Aragon, Rioja,
Navarra, Alava, Guipuzcoa y Vizcaya.
Zaragoza, E. Gallegos. 51-22040
DP11 .G78 MRR Alc Latest edition

VOCABULARY.
see also Words, New

Gause, John Taylor. The complete
word hunter. New York, Crowell
[1965] viii, 497 p. 423 55-11106

PE1449 .G345 MRR Alc.

O'Connor, Johnson, English
vocabulary builder. Boston, Human
Engineering Laboratory, 1948-51. 2
v. 423 48-11371
PE1691 .O32 MRR Alc.

Rodale, Jerome Irving, ed. The word
finder; Allentown, Rodale Press,
1947. xxxii, 1317 p. 423 47-11408

PE1680 .R63 1947 MRR Alc.

VOCAL MUSIC.
see also Ballads

see also Music, Popular (Songs, etc.)

VOCAL MUSIC--THEMATIC CATALOGS.
Barlow, Harold. A dictionary of
opera and song themes. New York,
Crown Publishers [1966, c1950] 547
p. 781.97 66-18454
ML128.V7 B3 1950a MRR Alc.

VOCALISTS
see Singers

VOCATION--BIBLIOGRAPHY.
Nicholsen, Margaret E. People in
books; New York, H. W. Wilson Co.,
1969. xviii, 498 p. 016.92 69-
15811
Z5301 .N53 MRR Biog.

VOCATIONAL EDUCATION.
Lederer, Muriel. The guide to career
education. [New York] Quadrangle/New
York Times Book Co. [1974] xiv, 401
p. [$9.95] 370.11/3 73-90169
LC1044 .L42 1974 MRR Alc.

VOCATIONAL EDUCATION--BIBLIOGRAPHY.
Mapp, Edward. Books for occupational
education programs; New York,
Bowker, 1971. xii, 308 p.
016.378/013 70-126013
Z5814.T4 M34 MRR Alc.

Reinhart, Bruce, The vocational-
technical library collection:
Williamsport, Pa., Bro-Dart Pub. Co.;
1970. xiv, 377 p. 016.6 70-122456

Z7911 .R45 MRR Alc.

VOCATIONAL EDUCATION--FILM CATALOGS.
National Information Center for
Educational Media. Index to
vocational and technical education
(multimedia). 1st ed. Los Angeles,
1972. x, 298 p. 016.6 72-190628
T65.5.M6 N28 1972 MRR Alc.

**VOCATIONAL EDUCATION--EUROPE--
DIRECTORIES.**
Organization for Economic Cooperation
and Development. Inventory of
training possibilities in Europe.
[Paris, 1965] 896 p. 65-9050
LC1071.E8 O7 MRR Alc.

**VOCATIONAL EDUCATION--NEW YORK (CITY)--
DIRECTORIES.**
Where to find vocational training in
New York City. New York, Vocational
Advisory Service. 371.4269747 30-
34386
Began publication in 1909.
LC1046.5.N5 W5 MRR Alc Latest
edition

VOCATIONAL EDUCATION--UNITED STATES.
Colleges and specialized schools.
1st- 1952- Boston, P. Sargent. 52-
3398
L901 .J8 MRR Ref Desk Latest
edition / MRR Alc Latest edition

**VOCATIONAL EDUCATION--UNITED STATES--
DIRECTORIES.**
American trade schools directory.
1st- ed.; 1953- Queens Village,
New York, Croner Publications.
607.73 53-8387
T73 .A78 MRR Alc Latest edition

Cass, James. Comparative guide to
junior and two-year community
colleges New York, Harper & Row
[c1972] xix, 396 p. [$10.00]
378.1/543 72-79651
LB2328 .C355 1972 MRR Ref Desk.

The College blue book. [1st]- 1923-
New York [etc.] CCM Information
Corp. [etc.] 378.73 24-223
LA226 .C685 MRR Ref Desk Latest
edition

College Entrance Examination Board.
The New York Times guide to
continuing education in America.
[New York] Quadrangle Books [1972]
811 p. [$12.50] 374.8/73 74-
183180
L901 .C74 1972 MRR Ref Desk.

Colleges and specialized schools.
1st- 1952- Boston, P. Sargent. 52-
3398
L901 .J8 MRR Ref Desk Latest
edition / MRR Alc Latest edition

Edfac Publishing Co. Edfac career
school directory. Colorado Springs
[1973, c1972] xlii, 305 p. [$12.95]
331.7/02 73-169423
L901 .E33 1972 MRR Ref Desk.

Lovejoy, Clarence Earle. Lovejoy's
career and vocational school guide;
4th enl. complete revision. New
York, Simon and Schuster [1973] 184
p. [$3.95 (pbk)] 371.4/25 73-
161263
L901 .L6 1973 MRR Ref Desk.

Miller, Adeline Elizabeth. National
directory of schools and vocations,
2d ed. North Springfield, Pa., State
School Publications, 1963. viii, 703
p. 371.425058 63-19356
L901 .M48 1963 MRR Ref Desk.

Russell, Max M. Occupational
education [New York] CCM Information
Corp. [1972] xi, 897 p. 378.73 73-
157565
L901 .R8 1972 MRR Ref Desk.

VOCATIONAL GUIDANCE.
see also Counseling

see also Occupations

Angel, Juvenal Londoño, Looking for
employment in foreign countries
reference handbook, 6th ed., rev.
and enl. New York, World Trade
Academy Press; distributed by Simon &
Schuster [1972] 727 p. [$25.00]
331.7/02 70-111351
HF5381 .A7847 1972 MRR Alc.

Angel, Juvenal Londoño, Students'
guide to occupational opportunities
and their lifetime earnings, New
York, World Trade Academy Press;
distributed by Simon & Schuster
[1967] 312 p. 331.702/0973 67-
25270
HF5382 .A57 MRR Alc.

College placement annual.
[Bethlehem, Pa.] College Placement
Council. 371.425 a 58-4606
HF5382.5.U5 C6 MRR Ref Desk Latest
edition

The Encyclopedia of careers and
vocational guidance. Rev. ed.
Chicago, J. G. Ferguson Pub. Co.;
distributed to the book trade by
Doubleday [1972] 2 v. 331.7/02 72-
183086
HF5381 .E52 1972 MRR Alc.

Hoppock, Robert, Occupational
information; 3d ed. New York,
McGraw-Hill [1967] xiv, 598 p.
371.42/5 67-14672
HF5381 .H582 1967 MRR Alc.

Lederer, Muriel. The guide to career
education. [New York] Quadrangle/New
York Times Book Co. [1974] xiv, 401
p. [$9.95] 370.11/3 73-90169
LC1044 .L42 1974 MRR Alc.

VOCATIONAL GUIDANCE. (Cont.)
The Year book of technical education
and careers in industry. 1st- 1957-
London, A. and C. Black. 607.42
57-2770
T61 .Y4 Sci RR Latest edition /
MRR Alc Latest edition

VOCATIONAL GUIDANCE--BIBLIOGRAPHY.
Educators guide to free guidance
materials. 1st- ed.: 1962-
Randolph, Wis., Educators Progress
Service. 016.37142 62-18761
HF5381.A1 E3 MRR Alc Latest
edition

United States. Library of Congress.
Division for the Blind. Reading for
profit; Rev. ed. Washington, 1963.
iii, 29 p. 63-60035
Z663.25 .R4 1963 MRR Alc.

VOCATIONAL GUIDANCE--FILM CATALOGS.
Educators guide to free guidance
materials. 1st- ed.: 1962-
Randolph, Wis., Educators Progress
Service. 016.37142 62-18761
HF5381.A1 E3 MRR Alc Latest
edition

VOCATIONAL GUIDANCE--HANDBOOKS,
MANUALS, ETC.
Occupational outlook handbook. 1949-
[Washington] 371.425 l 49-6
HF5381.A1 O36 MRR Ref Desk MRR Ref
Desk Latest edition

VOCATIONAL GUIDANCE--YEARBOOKS.
Modern vocational trends reference
handbook. New York, World Trade
Academy Press. 371.425058 55-3128
HF5381 .M565 MRR Ref Desk Latest
edition

VOCATIONAL GUIDANCE--GREAT BRITAIN.
The Girl's school year book (public
schools) London, Adam & Charles
Black, [etc.] ca 08-3162
LC2055 .A3 MRR Alc Latest edition

VOCATIONAL GUIDANCE--GREAT BRITAIN--
PERIODICALS.
Guide to British employers. London,
Cornmarket Press. 331.702/0942 72-
27261
HF5382.5.G7 G8 MRR Alc Latest
edition

VOCATIONAL GUIDANCE--UNITED STATES.
Angel, Juvenal Londono, Employment
opportunities for the handicapped,
New York, World Trade Academy Press;
distributed by Simon & Schuster
[1969] 411 p. 331.5/9 67-22382
HV3018 .A67 MRR Alc.

Angel, Juvenal Londono, Occupations
for men and women after 45, 3d ed.,
rev. and enl. New York, World Trade
Academy Press; distributed by Regents
Pub. Co. [1964] 200 p. 331.7 64-
55030
HF5381 .A786 1964 MRR Alc.

McKay, Ernest A. The Macmillan Job
guide to American corporations for
college graduates, graduate students
and junior executives New York,
Macmillan [c1967] ix, 374 p.
331.115 66-20820
HF5382.5.U5 M3 MRR Alc.

Reeves, Vernon H. Your college
degree; Chicago, Science Research
Associates [c1968] 221 p.
373.1/4/20202 77-12816
LB2381 .R4 MRR Alc.

VOCATIONAL GUIDANCE--UNITED STATES--
DIRECTORIES.
Directory of counseling services.
1973- [Washington, D.C.]
International Association of
Counseling Services. [$3.00]
362.8/5 73-642742
HF5381.A1 N4273 MRR Alc Latest
edition

VOCATIONAL QUALIFICATIONS.
McKay, Ernest A. The Macmillan Job
guide to American corporations for
college graduates, graduate students
and junior executives New York,
Macmillan [c1967] ix, 374 p.
331.115 66-20820
HF5382.5.U5 M3 MRR Alc.

VOCATIONAL REHABILITATION.
see also Handicapped--Employment

VOCATIONAL REHABILITATION--BIBLIOGRAPHY.
Wright, George Nelson.
Rehabilitation counselor functions:
annotated references Madison,
University of Wisconsin, Regional
Rehabilitation Research Institute,
1968. viii, 451 p. 016.3628/5 68-
63360
HF7256.U6 W56 ser. 1, vol. 1 MRR
Alc.

VOCATIONAL REHABILITATION--UNITED
STATES.
United States. President's Committee
on Employment of the Physically
Handicapped. Employment of the
physically handicapped; [Washington,
U.S. Govt. Print. Off., 1957] vii,
93 p. 331.86 371.91* 57-62036
Z663.28 .E5 MRR Alc.

VOLCANOES.
Lane, Frank Walter. The elements
rage: Newton Abbot (Devon), David &
Charles [1966] xvi, 280 p. [50/-]
551 66-66261
QC866 .L3 1966 MRR Alc.

VOLKSWAGEN AUTOMOBILE.
Fix your Volkswagen. South Holland,
Ill.[etc.] Goodheart-Willcox Co.
629.287 62-9724
TL215.V6 F5 MRR Alc Latest edition

VORARLBERG--COMMERCE--DIRECTORIES.
Herold Adressbuch von Vorarlberg für
Industrie, Handel, Gewerbe. Wien,
Herold. 72-622312
HF3549.V6 A45 MRR Alc Latest
edition

VOTING--TEXAS.
Politics, inc. Texas precinct votes
'66; [Austin, Tex.: 1968, c1967]
ix, 173 p. 324/.24/09764 67-29303
JK4893 1966 .P65 MRR Alc.

VOTING--UNITED STATES.
Michigan. University. Survey Research
Center. The American voter New
York, Wiley [1960] viii, 573 p.
324.73 60-11615
JK1976 .M5 MRR Alc.

Theis, Paul A., All about politics;
New York, Bowker, 1972. xii, 228 p.
320 72-8470
JK1726 .T48 MRR Alc.

VOTING--UNITED STATES--ABSTRACTS.
Smith, Dwight La Vern, The American
political process; selected abstracts
of periodical literature, 1954-1971.
Santa Barbara, Calif., ABC-CLIO
[1972] xvi, 630 p. 016.329/00973
72-77549
JK2261 .S73 MRR Alc.

VOYAGES, SCIENTIFIC
see Scientific expeditions

VOYAGES AND TRAVELS.
Morison, Samuel Eliot, The European
discovery of America. New York,
Oxford University Press, 1971-1974.
2 v. [$15.00 (v. 1) $17.50 (v. 2)]
973.1/3 71-129637
E101 .M85 MRR Alc.

World Association of Travel Agencies.
National tourist information and
general tariff. Geneva. 61-65430
Began in 1953.
G155.A1 G4 MRR Alc Latest edition

VOYAGES AND TRAVELS--1951- --GUIDE-
BOOKS.
Donovan, John. The businessman's
international travel guide. New
York, Stein and Day [1971] ix, 253
p. [$7.95] 910/.202 76-163347
G153 .D6 1971 MRR Alc.

Harian's today's outstanding buys in
freighter travel. 1959- Greenlawn,
N.Y., Harian Publications; trade
distributor: Grosset & Dunlap [etc.,
New York] 910.2 61-1539
HE566.F7 H3 MRR Alc Latest edition

The Jewish travel guide. London,
Jewish Chronicle Publications. 910.2
52-44393
Began publication with 1951 issue.
G153 .J4 MRR Alc Latest edition

New horizons world guide. 1951-
[New York, Simon and Schuster] 54-
5818
G153 .P3 MRR Alc Latest edition

Pan American World Airways, inc. All
you need to know about living abroad;
[3d] fully revised ed. Garden City,
N.Y. Pan American Airways; world-wide
trade distribution by Doubleday
[1968] 832 p. 910/.2/02 68-24158
G150 .P28 1968 MRR Alc.

Pan Am's world guide: [New York,
Random House, 1974] 1012 p.
910/.202 74-176208
G153 .P32 1974b MRR Alc.

VOYAGES AND TRAVELS--1951- --GUIDE-
BOOKS--BIBLIOGRAPHY.
Neal, Jack A., comp. Reference guide
for travellers. New York, Bowker,
1969. xi, 674 p. [17.50] 016.910
69-16399
Z6011 .N4 MRR Alc.

VOYAGES AND TRAVELS--BIBLIOGRAPHY.
Cox, Edward Godfrey, A reference
guide to the literature of travel,
Seattle, The University of
Washington, 1935-49. 3 v. 016.91
36-27679
Z6011 .C87 MRR Alc.

Royal Commonwealth Society. Library.
Subject catalogue of the Library of
the Royal Empire Society, [1st ed.
reprinted] London, Dawsons for the
Royal Commonwealth Society, 1967. 4
v. [60/-/-per set (16/-/- per
vol.)] 016.942 68-70847
Z7164.C7 R82 1967 MRR Alc.

VOYAGES AND TRAVELS--BIBLIOGRAPHY--
CATALOGS.
Royal Commonwealth Society. Library.
Subject catalogue of the Royal
Commonwealth Society, London.
Boston, Mass., G. K. Hall, 1971. 7
v. 017.1 70-180198
Z7164.C7 R83 MRR Alc (Dk 33)

VOYAGES AND TRAVELS--GUIDE-BOOKS.
Encyclopedia of world travel. 2d
rev. ed. Garden City, N.Y.,
Doubleday [1973] 2 v. [$12.95 per
vol.] 910/.202 73-76221
G153 .E5 1973 MRR Alc.

Ford, Norman D., 1921- Harian's
Today's best buys in travel in
Mexico, the West Indies, South
America, Europe, the Orient, Africa,
and around the world [by] Norman D.
Ford and Fredric E. Tyarks, 1960-
Greenlawn, N.Y. Harian Publications;
trade distributor: Crown Publishers
[New York] 910.202 61-836
G153 .F5925 MRR Alc Latest edition

Freed's world travel catalog. 1965-
New York, Freed Publications. 910/.2
66-11940
G153 .F7 MRR Alc Latest edition

Hope, Ronald, ed. The shoregoer's
guide to world ports. London,
Maritime Press [c1963] vi, 340 p.
910.2 64-51355
G140 .H6 MRR Alc.

How to travel without being rich.
Greenlawn, N.Y., Harian Publications;
Trade Distributor: Grosset & Dunlap
[etc., New York] 910.2 60-1057
G153 .H65 MRR Alc Latest edition

OAG travel planner & hotel/motel
guide. [Oak Brook, Ill. R.H.
Donnelley Corp.] [$20.00] 910/.202
73-640442
G153 .018 MRR Ref Desk Latest
edition

Pan Am's world guide: [1st ed.] New
York, Random House [1974, c1973]
1012 p. [$4.95] 910/.202 73-5004
G153 .P32 MRR Alc.

Travel routes around the world.
Greenlawn, N.Y. [etc.] Harian
Publications. 42-44894
G153 .T75 MRR Alc Latest edition

World travel & vacation almanac.
1970- New York, Harper & Row. 910.2
78-111641
G153 .W897 MRR Alc Latest edition

VULCANITE
see Rubber

W.H.O.
see World Health Organization

WAGES.
see also Prices

WAGES--TAXATION.
see also Income tax

WAGES--GREAT BRITAIN--STATISTICS.
Great Britain. Dept. of Employment
and Productivity. British labour
statistics: London, H.M. Stationery
Off., 1971. 436 p. [£7.00]
331/.0942 75-860907
HD8388 .A5 MRR Alc.

WAGES--UNITED STATES.
Douglas, Paul Howard, Real wages in
the United States, 1890-1926,
Boston, New York, Houghton Mifflin
company, 1930. xxviii, 682 p.
331.2973 30-12884
HD4975 .D6 MRR Alc.

Long, Clarence Dickinson, Wages and
earnings in the United States, 1860-
1890. Princeton, Princeton
University Press, 1960. xvii, 169 p.
331.2973 60-5756
HD4975 .L57 MRR Alc.

Twentieth Century Fund. Employment
and wages in the United States, New
York, 1953. xxxii, 777 p. 331 53-
7170
HD8072 .T8 MRR Alc.

WAGES--UNITED STATES. (Cont.)
United States. Bureau of labor statistics. History of wages in the United States from colonial times to 1928. Washington, U.S. Govt. print. off., 1934. ix, 574 p. incl. tables.
331.2973 l 34-109
HD4975 .A15 1933 MRR Alc.

[United States. Library of Congress. Legislative Reference Service] Materials relating to the debate topic: "Resolved, that the Federal government should adopt a permanent program of price and wage control." [Washington, 1951] 40 p. 338.526
52-60020
Z663.6 .M3 MRR Alc.

WAGES--UNITED STATES--STATISTICS.
United States. Bureau of Labor Statistics. Employment and earnings statistics for the United States. 1909/60- Washington, For sale by the Superintendent of Documents, U.S. Govt. Print. Off. l 64-5
HD5723 .A27 MRR Alc MRR Alc Latest edition

WAITE, MORRISON REMICK, 1816-1888-- BIBLIOGRAPHY.
United States. Library of Congress. Manuscript Division. Morrison R. Waite: a register of his papers in the Library of Congress. Washington, 1959. 8 l. 012 59-60069
Z663.34 .W24 MRR Alc.

WALES--BIBLIOGRAPHY.
Bibliotheca celtica, 1909-1927/28; new ser., v. 1- 1929/33- Aberystwyth [National library of Wales] 11-5717
Z2071 .B56 MRR Alc Partial set

Wales. University. Board of Celtic Studies. History and Law Committee. A bibliography of the history of Wales. 2d ed. Cardiff, University of Wales Press, 1962. xviii, 330 p. 63-612
Z2081 .W229 MRR Alc.

WALES--BIOGRAPHY--DICTIONARIES.
The Dictionary of Welsh biography down to 1940. London, 1959. lvii, 1157 p. 920.0429 59-4309
DA710 .A1B913 MRR Biog.

WALES--DESCRIPTION AND TRAVEL.
Hughes, Cledwyn, Royal Wales: the land and its people. London, Phoenix House [1957] 204 p. 942.9 57-39598
DA709 .H8 1957 MRR Alc.

WALES--DESCRIPTION AND TRAVEL--1951-- GUIDE-BOOKS.
Llewellyn, Alun, The Shell guide to Wales; London, [distributed by] Joseph; George Rainbird, 1969. 360 p. [50/-] 914.29/04/85 74-415298
DA735 .L55 MRR Alc.

Rossiter, Stuart. Wales, 5th ed. London, E. Benn; Chicago, Rand McNally, 1969. liii, 300 p. [50/-]
914.29/04/85 73-408442
DA735 .R68 1969 MRR Alc.

WALES--DIRECTORIES--BIBLIOGRAPHY.
Norton, Jane Elizabeth, Guide to the national and provincial directories of England and Wales, London, offices of the Royal Historical Society, 1950. vii, 241 p.
016.9142 51-2465
Z5771 .N6 MRR Alc.

WALES--GAZETTEERS.
Llewellyn, Alun, The Shell guide to Wales; London, [distributed by] Joseph; George Rainbird, 1969. 360 p. [50/-] 914.29/04/85 74-415298
DA735 .L55 MRR Alc.

WALES--HISTORY.
Hughes, Cledwyn, Royal Wales: the land and its people. London, Phoenix House [1957] 204 p. 942.9 57-39598
DA709 .H8 1957 MRR Alc.

WALES--HISTORY--BIBLIOGRAPHY.
Wales. University. Board of Celtic Studies. History and Law Committee. A bibliography of the history of Wales. 2d ed. Cardiff, University of Wales Press, 1962. xviii, 330 p. 63-612
Z2081 .W229 MRR Alc.

WALKER, JOHN GRIMES, 1835-1907-- MANUSCRIPTS.
United States. Library of Congress. Manuscript Division. Charles Goodwin Ridgely, Francis Asbury Roe, John Grimes Walker: a register of their papers in the Library of Congress. Washington, Library of Congress, 1970. 4, 5, 5 l. 359.2/0922 76-607856
Z663.34 .R5 MRR Alc.

WALKING.
see also Hiking

WALL STREET.
Wyckoff, Peter. Wall Street and the stock markets: [1st ed.] Philadelphia, Chilton Book Co. [1972] xiv, 304 p. 332.6/42/0973 72-8277
HG4572 .W87 MRR Alc.

WAR--BIBLIOGRAPHY.
Arms control & disarmament. v. 1- winter 1964/65- [Washington, For sale by the Superintendent of Documents, U.S. Govt. Print. Off.] 64-62746
Z663.28 .A23 MRR Alc MRR Alc Full set

WAR--CASUALTIES (STATISTICS, ETC.)
Bodart, Gaston, Losses of life in modern wars, Austria-Hungary; France, Oxford, The Clarendon press; London, New York [etc.] H. Milford, 1916. x, 207, 6 p. incl. tables. 16-20885
D25.5 .B6 MRR Alc.

Elliot, Gil, Twentieth century book of the dead. London, Allen Lane, 1972. viii, 242 p. [£2.75]
301.32/2 72-169396
D445 .E555 MRR Alc.

Singer, Joel David, The wages of war, 1816-1965: New York, Wiley [1972] xii, 419 p. 301.6/334 75-39120
U21.2 .S57 MRR Alc.

WAR--STATISTICS.
Singer, Joel David, The wages of war, 1816-1965: New York, Wiley [1972] xii, 419 p. 301.6/334 75-39120
U21.2 .S57 MRR Alc.

WAR (INTERNATIONAL LAW)
Friedman, Leon, comp. The law of war, a documentary history. [1st ed.] New York, Random House [1972] 2 v. (xxv, 1764 p.) 341.6/026 72-765
JX4505 .F7 MRR Alc.

Greenspan, Morris. The soldier's guide to the laws of war. Washington, Public Affairs Press [1969] 87 p. [2.00] 341.3 79-75120
JX4521 .G68 MRR Alc.

WAR CRIME TRIALS.
Friedman, Leon, comp. The law of war, a documentary history. [1st ed.] New York, Random House [1972] 2 v. (xxv, 1764 p.) 341.6/026 72-765
JX4505 .F7 MRR Alc.

WAR PROTEST MOVEMENTS (VIETNAMESE CONFLICT, 1961-)
see Vietnamese Conflict, 1961- -- Protest movements

WAREHOUSES--UNITED STATES--DIRECTORIES.
American Warehousemen's Association. A W A membership roster. Chicago. 67-41453
HF5487 .A226 MRR Alc Latest edition

WARSHIPS.
see also Aircraft carriers

Bennett, Frank Marion, The steam navy of the United States. 2d ed. Pittsburgh, Pa., Warren & company, 1897. 2 v. 08-29480
VA55 .B49 1897 MRR Alc.

Blackman, Raymond V. B. The world's warships 4th and completely rev. ed. Garden City, N.Y., Doubleday [1970, c1969] 159 p. [5.95] 623.82/5 70-7563
VA40 .B55 1970 MRR Alc.

Chapelle, Howard Irving. The history of the American sailing Navy [1st ed.] New York, Norton [1949] xxiii, 558 p. 623.822 49-48709
VA56 .C5 MRR Alc.

Les Flottes de combat. Paris, Éditions Maritimes et D'outre-Mer [etc.] 623.825 11-13474
VA40 .F64 MRR Alc Latest edition

Jane's fighting ships. [1st]- 1898- London, S. Low, Marston and Co.[etc.] 07-25192
VA40 .F5 Sci RR Latest edition / MRR Alc Latest edition

Kafka, Roger, ed. Warships of the world. Victory ed. New York, Cornell maritime press [1946] x p., 1 l., 1167 p. 623.825 47-119
VA40 .K3 1946 MRR Alc.

Parkes, Oscar. British battleships, 'Warrior' 1860 to 'Vanguard' 1950: New and revised ed. London, Seeley Service [1966] xv, 701 p. [£8/8/-]
623.82520942 67-72751
VA454 .P28 1966 MRR Alc.

Taylor, John Charles. German warships of World War II Garden City, N.Y., Doubleday [1968, c1966] 168 p. 623.82/5/0943 68-10550
VA513 .T39 1968 MRR Alc.

Watts, Anthony John. Japanese warships of World War II Garden City, N.Y., Doubleday [1967] 400 p. 623.82/5/0952 67-23821
VA653 .W33 1967 MRR Alc.

WARSHIPS--DICTIONARIES.
Quick, John, Dictionary of weapons and military terms. New York, McGraw-Hill [1973] xii, 515 p. 623/.03 73-8757
U24 .Q5 MRR Alc.

WARSHIPS--HANDLING.
Crenshaw, Russell Sydnor, Naval shiphandling, 3d ed. Annapolis, U.S. Naval Institute [1965] xxiii, 533 p. 623.8825 66-3861
VK545 .C7 1965 MRR Alc.

WARSHIPS--NAMES.
Manning, Thomas Davys, British warship names London, Putnam; [label: Cambridge, Md., Cornell Maritime Press, 1959] 498 p. 359.32 59-13450
VA456 .M27 MRR Alc.

United States. Naval History Division. Dictionary of American naval fighting ships. Washington, [For sale by the Supt. of Doc., U.S. Govt. Print. Off.] 1959- v. 623.825 60-60198
VA61 .A53 MRR Alc.

WARSHIPS--RECOGNITION.
Jane's pocket book of major warships. New York, Collier Books [1973] viii, 279 p. [$3.95] 623.82/5 73-9329
V767 .J36 1973b MRR Alc.

WARSHIPS--YEARBOOKS.
Weyer's warships of the world. 1968- Annapolis, United States Naval Institute. 623.82/5/05 67-14517
V10 .W47 Sci RR Latest edition / MRR Alc Latest edition

WARWICK, ENG.--DIRECTORIES.
Kelly's directory of Warwick. Kingston upon Thames, Surrey [etc.] Kelly's Directories Limited. 53-28502
DA670.W3 K45 MRR Alc Latest edition

WARWICKSHIRE, ENG.--DIRECTORIES.
Kelly's directory of Warwick. Kingston upon Thames, Surrey [etc.] Kelly's Directories Limited. 53-28502
DA670.W3 K45 MRR Alc Latest edition

WASHINGTON, BOOKER TALIAFERRO, 1859?-1915--BIBLIOGRAPHY.
United States. Library of Congress. Manuscript Division. Booker T. Washington: a register of his papers in the Library of Congress. Washington, 1958. 105 p. 012 58-60037
Z663.34 .W3 MRR Alc.

WASHINGTON, GEORGE, PRES. U.S., 1732-1799.
Freeman, Douglas Southall, George Washington, a biography. New York, Scribner, 1948-[57] 7 v. 923.173 48-8880
E312 .F82 MRR Alc.

Freidel, Frank Burt. G. Washington: man and monument, Washington, Washington National Monument Association [1965] 69 p. 917.5303 65-25573
E312 .F84 MRR Alc.

United States. George Washington bicentennial commission. History of the George Washington bicentennial celebration ... Washington, D.C., United States George Washington bicentennial commission, 1932. 3 v. 923.173 33-26189
E312.6 .U58 MRR Alc.

WASHINGTON, GEORGE, PRES. U.S., 1732-1799--ANNIVERSARIES, ETC.
United States. George Washington bicentennial commission. History of the George Washington bicentennial celebration ... Washington, D.C., United States George Washington bicentennial commission, 1932. 3 v. 923.173 33-26189
E312.6 .U58 MRR Alc.

WASHINGTON, GEORGE, PRES. U.S., 1732-1799--BIBLIOGRAPHY.
United States. Library of Congress. Manuscript division. List of the Washington manuscripts from the year 1592 to 1775, Washington, Govt. print. off., 1919. iii, 137 p. 19-26005
Z663.34 .W35 MRR Alc.

WASHINGTON, GEORGE, PRES. U.S., 1732-1799--MANUSCRIPTS.
United States. Library of Congress. Manuscript division. Calendar of the correspondence of George Washington, Washington, Govt. print. off., 1906. 741 p.   06-35011
Z663.34 .C27 MRR Alc.

United States. Library of Congress. Manuscript division. Calendar of the correspondence of George Washington, commander in chief of the Continental army, with the officers. Washington, Govt. print. off., 1915. 4 v.   10-35016
Z663.34 .C28 MRR Alc.

WASHINGTON, GEORGE, PRES. U.S., 1732-1799--MANUSCRIPTS--BIBLIOGRAPHY.
United States. Library of Congress. Manuscript Division. A calendar of Washington manuscripts in the Library of Congress. Washington, Govt. Print. Off., 1901. 315 p.   02-10782
Z663.34 .W33 MRR Alc.

WASHINGTON (STATE)--BIBLIOGRAPHY.
Historical records survey. Washington (State) A check list of Washington imprints, 1853-1876. Seattle, Wash., The Washington Historical records survey, 1942. 89 p.   015.797 42-21716
Z1215 .H67 no. 44 MRR Alc.

WASHINGTON (STATE)--COMMERCE--DIRECTORIES.
Washington state international trade directory. Olympia, Office of Foreign Trade. 382/.025/797 73-613364
HF5065.W2 W37 MRR Alc Latest edition

WASHINGTON (STATE)--DESCRIPTION AND TRAVEL--GUIDE-BOOKS.
Writers' Program. Washington. The new Washington; a guide to the Evergreen State. Rev. ed. Portland, Or., Binfords & Mort [1950, c1941] xxx, 687 p.   917.97 51-3893
F891 .W9 1950 MRR Ref Desk.

WASHINGTON (STATE)--HISTORY.
Avery, Mary Williamson, History and government of the State of Washington. Seattle, University of Washington Press, 1961. 583 p.   979.7 61-8211
F891 .A8 MRR Alc.

WASHINGTON (STATE)--HISTORY--ADDRESSES, ESSAYS, LECTURES.
Douglas, William Orville, Washington and manifest destiny; Washington, Library of Congress, 1953. 35 p.   979.7 53-63610
Z663.15.A6W33 MRR Alc.

WASHINGTON (STATE)--IMPRINTS.
Historical records survey. Washington (State) A check list of Washington imprints, 1853-1876. Seattle, Wash., The Washington Historical records survey, 1942. 89 p.   015.797 42-21716
Z1215 .H67 no. 44 MRR Alc.

WASHINGTON (STATE)--OFFICIALS AND EMPLOYEES.
Washington (State). Legislature. Joint rules, rules of the Senate and rules of the House of the state Legislature of Washington. Olympia, Wash. 15-137
JK9271 .A2 MRR Alc Latest edition

WASHINGTON (STATE)--POLITICS AND GOVERNMENT.
Avery, Mary Williamson, History and government of the State of Washington. Seattle, University of Washington Press, 1961. 583 p.   979.7 61-8211
F891 .A8 MRR Alc.

WASHINGTON (STATE)--POLITICS AND GOVERNMENT--HANDBOOKS, MANUALS, ETC.
The Research Council's handbook. 1st-ed.: 1961/62- Seattle, Washington State Research Council. 64-20640
JK9230 .R46 MRR Alc Latest edition

WASHINGTON (STATE)--STATISTICS.
The Research Council's handbook. 1st-ed.: 1961/62- Seattle, Washington State Research Council. 64-20640
JK9230 .R46 MRR Alc Latest edition

Washington (State). Office of Program Planning and Fiscal Management. State of Washington pocket data book. 1970- [Olympia?] 317.97 73-648668
HA693 .A26 MRR Alc Latest edition

WASHINGTON (STATE). LEGISLATURE--RULES AND PRACTICE.
Washington (State). Legislature. Joint rules, rules of the Senate and rules of the House of the state Legislature of Washington. Olympia, Wash. 15-137
JK9271 .A2 MRR Alc Latest edition

WASHINGTON, D.C.--BIBLIOGRAPHY.
Bryan, Wilhelmus Bogart, Bibliography of the District of Columbia. Washington, Govt. print. off., 1900. v, 211 p. 016.9753 33-21026
Z1269 .B92 MRR Alc.

WASHINGTON, D.C.--BIOGRAPHY.
Who's who in the nation's capital. 1921/22-1938/39. Washington, Ransdell Inc.[etc.] 21-14804
F193 .W6 MRR Biog Latest edition

WASHINGTON, D.C.--BIOGRAPHY--DICTIONARIES.
Artists Equity Association. D.C. Chapter. Washington artists; [Washington, 1972] 123 p. 709/.2/2 72-189977
N6535.W3 A68 MRR Biog.

The Gold book of Washington's most distinguished women, 1966. [1st ed.] Washington, R. Moore [c1966] 155 p. 920.09753 66-21176
F193 .G6 MRR Biog.

WASHINGTON, D.C.--BUILDINGS.
A Guide to the architecture of Washington, D.C. [2d ed., rev. and expanded] New York, McGraw-Hill [1974] 246 p. 917.53/04/4 74-1336
NA735.W3 G84 1974 MRR Alc.

WASHINGTON, D.C.--CHURCHES.
Jones, Olga Anna. Churches of the Presidents in Washington; [2d enl. ed.] New York, Exposition Press [1961] 128 p. 277.53 61-66359
F203.2.A1 J63 1961 MRR Alc.

WASHINGTON, D.C.--COMMERCE--DIRECTORIES.
Impact directory. [Washington, Impact Press] 338.7/6/025753 74-645912
HD2346.U52 W355 MRR Alc Latest edition

Manufacturers and distributors directory [of the] Washington, D.C. area. 1st-   ed.; 1954- Washington. 56-1683
HC108.W3 W28 MRR Alc Latest edition / MRR Ref Desk Latest edition

Mintz, Bettie. Top shops & secret services, Washington, D.C. area. [Washington, Manufactured by Plymouth Print. Co., 1971] ix, 213 p. [$3.75] 380.1/025/753 74-151990
HF5429.5.W3 M5 1971 MRR Alc.

WASHINGTON, D.C.--DESCRIPTION.
Caemmerer, Hans Paul, A manual on the origin and development of Washington, Washington, U.S. Govt. print. off., 1939. xi, 365 p. incl. illus., plates, maps, plans, facsim. 917.53 39-29244
F194 .C182 MRR Alc.

Caemmerer, Hans Paul, Washington, the national capital, Washington, U.S. Govt. print. off., 1932. xxv, 736 p. incl. illus., plates, ports., maps, plans, facsims. 917.53 32-26479
F194 .C18 MRR Alc.

WASHINGTON, D.C.--DESCRIPTION--1951---GUIDE-BOOKS.
Living in Washington; 1st ed.] Richmond, Westover Pub. Co. [1972] vii, 259 p. [$3.50] 917.53 72-188108
F192.3 .L58 MRR Ref Desk.

Walker, John Stanley, The Washington guidebook, [Rev. ed. Washington, Metro Publishers Representatives, 1969] 431 p. [1.00] 917.53/04/4 71-7925
F192.3 .W3 1969 MRR Ref Desk.

WASHINGTON, D.C.--DESCRIPTION--GUIDE-BOOKS.
American Institute of Architects. Washington-Metropolitan Chapter. Washington architecture, 1791-1957, New York, Reinhold [1957] 96 p. 720.9753 57-10358
NA735.W3 A6 MRR Alc.

Frome, Michael. Washington; [1st ed.] Garden City, N.Y., Doubleday, 1960. 257 p. 917.53 60-9477
F192.3 .F7 MRR Alc.

Goode, James M. The outdoor sculpture of Washington, D.C. [1st ed.] Washington, Smithsonian Institution Press [distributed by G. Braziller] 1974. 615 p. 917.53 74-5111
NB235.W3 G66 MRR Ref Desk.

A Guide to the architecture of Washington, D.C. [2d ed., rev. and expanded] New York, McGraw-Hill [1974] 246 p. 917.53/04/4 74-1336
NA735.W3 G84 1974 MRR Alc.

Jones, Olga Anna. Churches of the Presidents in Washington; [2d enl. ed.] New York, Exposition Press [1961] 128 p. 277.53 61-66359
F203.2.A1 J63 1961 MRR Alc.

Rider, Fremont, ed. Rider's Washington; New York, The Macmillan company, 1924. 2 p. l., [vii]-xli, 548 p. 26-9259
F199 .R54 1924 MRR Ref Desk.

United States. Congress. Senate. Library. Our Capitol: Washington, U.S. Govt. Print. Off., 1963. iii, 80 p. 917.53 63-62294
F204.A1 U55 1963 MRR Alc.

Washington: the New York times guide to the Nation's Capital. Washington, R. B. Luce [1967] xiii, 348 p. 917.53/04/4 67-24129
F192.3 .W35 MRR Alc.

Writers' Program. District of Columbia. Washington, D.C.; a guide to the Nation's Capital. New rev. ed. New York, Hastings House [1968, c1942] xxxiv, 528 p. 917.53/04/4 67-25608
F199 .P38 1968 MRR Ref Desk.

WASHINGTON, D.C.--DIRECTORIES.
De Bettencourt, Margaret T. The guide to Washington, D.C. foundations, [Washington, Guide Publishers, c1972] viii, 62 p. [$8.00] 001.4/4 72-90810
AS911.A2 D24 MRR Ref Desk.

Howard University, Washington, D.C. Minority Economic Resource Center. The District of Columbia directory of inner city organizations active in the field of minority business-economic development. 3d ed. Washington, 1972. iv, 20 p. 338/.04/025753 73-170762
HD2346.U52 D54 1972 MRR Alc.

International Visitors Service Council. Organizations serving international visitors in the National Capital area. [4th ed.] Washington [1973] vii p., 151 l., 155-191 p. 917.53/04/4025 72-96925
F191 .I57 1973 MRR Alc.

Washington. 1966- Washington, Potomac Books. 917.53/0025 s 66-18579
F192.5 .W3 MRR Ref Desk Latest edition / MRR Ref Desk Latest edition / Sci RR Latest edition

Washington. Supplement. Washington, Potomac Books. 917.53/0025 s 74-643552
F192.5 .W32 MRR Ref Desk Latest edition / MRR Ref Desk Latest edition

WASHINGTON, D.C.--DWELLINGS.
Miller, Hope Ridings. Great houses of Washington, D.C. New York, C. N. Potter; distributed by Crown Publishers [1969] vi, 208 p. [25.00] 975.3 69-13415
F195 .M53 1969 MRR Alc.

WASHINGTON, D.C.--HISTORIC HOUSES, ETC.
Eberlein, Harold Donaldson. Historic houses of George-Town & Washington City, Richmond, Dietz Press [1958] xiv, 480 p. 975.3 58-1398
F195 .E2 MRR Alc.

A Guide to the architecture of Washington, D.C. [2d ed., rev. and expanded] New York, McGraw-Hill [1974] 246 p. 917.53/04/4 74-1336
NA735.W3 G84 1974 MRR Alc.

Maddex, Diane. Historic buildings of Washington, D.C. [1st ed.] Pittsburgh, Ober Park Associates [1973] 191 p. [$17.50] 720/.9753 72-92006
NA735.W3 M32 MRR Alc.

WASHINGTON, D.C.--HISTORY.
Bryan, Wilhelmus Bogart, A history of the national capital. New York, The Macmillan company, 1914-16. 2. v. 14-7093
F194 .B9 MRR Alc.

Caemmerer, Hans Paul, A manual on the origin and development of Washington, Washington, U.S. Govt. print. off., 1939. xi, 365 p. incl. illus., plates, maps, plans, facsim. 917.53 39-29244
F194 .C182 MRR Alc.

Caemmerer, Hans Paul, Washington, the national capital, Washington, U.S. Govt. print. off., 1932. xxv, 736 p. incl. illus., plates, ports., maps, plans, facsims. 917.53 32-26479
F194 .C18 MRR Alc.

WASHINGTON, D.C.--HISTORY. (Cont.)
Green, Constance (McLaughlin)
Washington. Princeton, N.J.,
Princeton University Press, 1962-63.
2 v.   917.53 62-7402
    F194 .G7 MRR Alc.

Poore, Benjamin Perley, Perley's
reminiscences of sixty years in the
national metropolis. New York, AMS
Press [1971] 2 v. 917.3/03 74-
158970
    F194 .P824 1971 MRR Alc.

Proctor, John Clagett, Washington
and environs; [Washington? 1949]
500 p.   975.3 50-494
    F194 .P95 MRR Alc.

Reps, John William. Monumental
Washington; Princeton, N.J.,
Princeton University Press, 1967.
xv, 221 p.   711.4/09753 66-17708
    NA9127.W2 R4 MRR Alc.

Writers' Program. District of
Columbia. Washington, D.C.; a guide
to the Nation's Capital. New rev.
ed. New York, Hastings House [1968,
c1942] xxxiv, 528 p. 917.53/04/4
67-25608
    F199 .F38 1968 MRR Ref Desk.

WASHINGTON, D.C.--HISTORY--ANECDOTES.
Boykin, Edward Carrington, Shrines
of the Republic; Washington, Public
Affairs Press [1953] 76 p.   975.3
52-12863
    F195 .B6 MRR Alc.

WASHINGTON, D.C.--INTELLECTUAL LIFE.
Writers' Program. District of
Columbia. Washington, D.C.; a guide
to the Nation's Capital. New rev.
ed. New York, Hastings House [1968,
c1942] xxxiv, 528 p. 917.53/04/4
67-25608
    F199 .F38 1968 MRR Ref Desk.

WASHINGTON, D.C.--LIBRARIES.
Consortium of Universities of the
Washington Metropolitan Area. Union
list of serials, 3d ed. Washington,
1974. 350 p. [$27.50] 016.05 74-
78294
    Z6945 .C763 1974 MRR Ref Desk.

George Washington University,
Washington, D.C. Biological Sciences
Communication Project. A study of
resources and major subject holdings
available in U.S. Federal libraries
Washington, U.S. Office of Education,
Bureau of Research, 1970. ix, 670 p.
011 79-609579
    Z881.A1 G4 1970b MRR Alc.

United States. Library of Congress.
Division of bibliography. ... A
union list of periodicals,
transactions and allied publications
currently received in the principal
libraries of the District of
Columbia. Washington, Govt. print.
off., 1901. v, 315 p.   01-16622
    Z663.28 .U5 MRR Alc.

WASHINGTON, D.C.--LIBRARIES--
DIRECTORIES.
Library and reference facilities in
the area of the District of Columbia.
[1st]- ed.; 1943- Washington.
021/.0025/753 44-41159
    Z732.D62 U63 Sci RR Latest edition
    / MRR Alc Latest edition

WASHINGTON, D.C.--MANUFACTURES--
DIRECTORIES.
Directory of Central Atlantic States
manufacturers; 1.- ed.; 1950-
Baltimore, T. K. Sanderson
Organization. 670.58 50-2706
    T12 .D485 Sci RR Latest edition /
    MRR Alc Latest edition

WASHINGTON, D.C.--MONUMENTS.
Goode, James M. The outdoor
sculpture of Washington, D.C. [1st
ed.] Washington, Smithsonian
Institution Press [distributed by G.
Braziller] 1974. 615 p.   917.53 74-
5111
    NB235.W3 G66 MRR Ref Desk.

Murdock, Myrtle M. (Cheney) Your
memorials in Washington. Washington,
Monumental Press, 1952. 193 p.
917.53 53-378
    F203.4.A1 M8 MRR Alc.

WASHINGTON, D.C.--PUBLIC BUILDINGS.
Andriot, John L. Guide to the
building inscriptions of the Nation's
Capital. Arlington, Va., Jay-Way
Press, 1955. 57 p.   729 55-4977
    NA4050.I5 A55 MRR Ref Desk.

Sites, Maud Kay. Quotations and
inscriptions in the federal and
public buildings on Capitol hill,
Baltimore, Md., N.T.A. Munder [1934]
22, [2] p. 917.53 35-2954
    F204 .A1S5 MRR Ref Desk.

United States. Congress. Senate.
Library. Our Capitol; Washington,
U.S. Govt. Print. Off., 1963. iii,
80 p. 917.53 63-62294
    F204.A1 U55 1963 MRR Alc.

WASHINGTON, D.C.--RESTAURANTS--
DIRECTORIES.
Barnes, Richard, Capital feasts;
Rev. Washington, Rock Creek Pub.
Co., 1973 [1972] 127 p. [$3.50]
647/.95753 73-152888
    TX907 .B365 1973 MRR Ref Desk.

WASHINGTON, D.C.--SOCIAL LIFE AND
CUSTOMS.
Jensen, Amy (La Follette) The White
House and its thirty-four families.
New enl. ed. New York, McGraw-Hill
[1965] 301, [8] p.   975.3 65-22957
    F204.W5 J4 1965 MRR Alc.

Poore, Benjamin Perley, Perley's
reminiscences of sixty years in the
national metropolis. New York, AMS
Press [1971] 2 v. 917.3/03 74-
158970
    F194 .P824 1971 MRR Alc.

Singleton, Esther, The story of the
White House. New York, The McClure
company, 1907. 2 v.   07-37719
    F204.W5 S6 MRR Ref Desk.

WASHINGTON, D.C.--STREETS--MALL.
United States. Library of Congress.
The grand design; Washington, 1967.
25 p. (chiefly plates (incl. maps,
plans))   711/.5 67-60041
    Z663.15.A6D52 MRR Alc.

WASHINGTON, D.C.--STREETS--PENNSYLVANIA
AVENUE.
United States. Library of Congress.
The grand design; Washington, 1967.
25 p. (chiefly plates (incl. maps,
plans))   711/.5 67-60041
    Z663.15.A6D52 MRR Alc.

WASHINGTON, D.C.--SUBURBS AND ENVIRONS.
Frome, Michael. Washington; [1st
ed.] Garden City, N.Y., Doubleday,
1960. 257 p. 917.53 60-9477
    F192.3 .F7 MRR Alc.

Writers' Program. District of
Columbia. Washington, D.C.; a guide
to the Nation's Capital. New rev.
ed. New York, Hastings House [1968,
c1942] xxxiv, 528 p. 917.53/04/4
67-25608
    F199 .F38 1968 MRR Ref Desk.

WASHINGTON, D.C. CAPITOL.
Aikman, Lonnelle. We, the people;
[9th ed.] Washington, United States
Capitol Historical Society, 1974.
143 p. 917.53 74-174476
    F204.C2 A45 1974 MRR Alc.

Fairman, Charles Edwin, Art and
artists of the Capitol of the United
States of America, Washington, U.S.
Govt. print. off., 1927. xii, 526
p., 1 l. incl. illus., ports., plans,
facsims., tables. 28-26032
    N853 .F4 MRR Ref Desk.

Murdock, Myrtle M. (Cheney) National
Statuary Hall in the Nation's
Capitol. Washington, Monumental
Press, 1955. 128 p. 917.53 55-
1697
    NB235.W3 M8 MRR Ref Desk.

United States. Architect of the
Capitol. Compilation of works of art
and other objects in the United
States Capitol. Washington, U.S.
Govt. Print. Off., 1965. xxiv, 426
p. 708.153 66-60382
    N853 .A52 1965 MRR Alc.

United States. Congress. Senate.
Library. Our Capitol; Washington,
U.S. Govt. Print. Off., 1963. iii,
80 p. 917.53 63-62294
    F204.A1 U55 1963 MRR Alc.

WASHINGTON, D.C. CAPITOL--BIBLIOGRAPHY.
Kerwood, John R., The United States
Capitol; [1st ed.] Norman,
University of Oklahoma Press [1973]
xvii, 448 p. [$25.00] 016.91753
72-870
    Z1270.C2 K43 MRR Alc.

WASHINGTON, D.C. CAPITOL HILL.
Sites, Maud Kay. Quotations and
inscriptions in the federal and
public buildings on Capitol hill,
Baltimore, Md., N.T.A. Munder [1934]
22, [2] p. 917.53 35-2954
    F204 .A1S5 MRR Ref Desk.

WASHINGTON, D.C. WHITE HOUSE.
Hurd, Charles, The White House
story. [1st ed.] New York, Hawthorn
Books [1966] 240 p. 975.3 66-
15233
    F204.W5 H82 MRR Alc.

Jensen, Amy (La Follette) The White
House and its thirty-four families.
New enl. ed. New York, McGraw-Hill
[1965] 301, [8] p.   975.3 65-22957
    F204.W5 J4 1965 MRR Alc.

Singleton, Esther, The story of the
White House. New York, The McClure
company, 1907. 2 v.   07-37719
    F204.W5 S6 MRR Ref Desk.

The White House; [1st]- ed.;1962-
Washington, White House Historical
Association.   62-18058
    F204.W5 W6 MRR Alc Latest edition

The White House library; a short-
title list. Washington, White House
Historical Association, 1967. 219 p.
018/.2 67-5746
    Z988 .W45 MRR Alc.

WASHINGTON, D.C. WHITE HOUSE--
BIBLIOGRAPHY.
United States. Library of Congress.
General Reference and Bibliography
Division. The Presidents of the
United States, 1789-1962; Washington
[For sale by the Superintendent of
Documents, U.S. Govt. Print. Off.]
1963. xviii, 159 p.   63-61781
    Z663.28 .P73 MRR Alc.

United States. Library of Congress.
General Reference and Bibliography
Division. The White House; a
bibliographical list, Washington,
1953. vi, 139 p.   016.91753 53-
60005
    Z663.28 .W5 MRR Alc.

WASHINGTON, D.C., REGION--DESCRIPTION
AND TRAVEL--GUIDE-BOOKS.
Berkovitz, Alan. Greater Washington
area bicycle atlas. Washington,
Potomac Area Council-American Youth
Hostels [1974] 128 p. [$2.00]
917.53/04/4 74-172742
    F192.3 .B43 MRR Alc.

WASHINGTON FAMILY.
United States. George Washington
bicentennial commission. History of
the George Washington bicentennial
celebration ... Washington, D.C.,
United States George Washington
bicentennial commission, 1932. 3 v.
923.173 33-26189
    E312.6 .U58 MRR Alc.

Washington, George, pres. U.S., The
writings of George Washington from
the original manuscript sources, 1745-
1799; Washington, U.S. Govt. print.
off. [1931-44] 39 v. 308 32-11075
    E312.7 1931 MRR Alc.

WASHINGTON METROPOLITAN AREA--
DESCRIPTION--GUIDE-BOOKS.
Shosteck, Robert, Weekender's guide;
places of historic, scenic, and
recreational interest within 200
miles of the Washington-Baltimore
area. Washington, Potomac Books
[c1973] xiii, 400 p. [$2.90]
917.5 74-159051
    F106 .S53 1973 MRR Alc.

WASHINGTON METROPOLITAN AREA--
INDUSTRIES--DIRECTORIES.
Manufacturers and distributors
directory [of the] Washington, D.C.
area. 1st- ed.; 1954- Washington.
56-1683
    HC108.W3 W28 MRR Alc Latest
    edition / MRR Ref Desk Latest
    edition

WASHINGTON METROPOLITAN AREA--POLITICS
AND GOVERNMENT.
League of Women Voters of
Metropolitan Washington.
Metropolitan Washington; District of
Columbia, Maryland, Virginia.
Washington, League of Women Voters
Education Fund [1970] 52 p. [$0.25]
320.4/753 77-27912
    JK2725 1970 .L4 MRR Ref Desk.

WASHINGTON MONUMENT, WASHINGTON, D.C.
Freidel, Frank Burt. G. Washington:
man and monument. Washington,
Washington National Monument
Association [1965] 69 p. 917.5303
65-25573
    E312 .F84 MRR Alc.

WASTE PRODUCTS.
United States. Dept. of Agriculture.
Crops in peace and war. Washington,
U.S. Govt. Print. Off. [1951] 942 p.
630.72 agr55-9
    S21 .A35 1950-1951 MRR Alc.

WATCH MAKING
see Clock and watch making

WATCHES
see Clocks and watches

WATER.
see also Ocean

see also Oceanography

WATER. (Cont.)
see also Rivers

WATER--INFORMATION SERVICES--
DIRECTORIES.
United States. Library of Congress.
National Referral Center for Science
and Technology. A directory of
information resources in the United
States: water. [Washington, For sale
by the Superintendent of Documents,
U.S. Govt. Print. Off.] 1966. v, 248
p.   66-61638
    Z663.379 .D55 MRR Alc.

WATER-BIRDS.
see also Sea birds

WATER-COLORS--CATALOGS.
International auction records. v.
[1]- 1967- [London, etc.]
Editions E. M.--Publisol] 700/.29
78-2167
    N8640 .I5 MRR Alc Full set

WATER GARDENS.
Edwards, Alexander. Rock gardens;
New York, Abelard-Schuman [1958] 255
p.   635.9672 58-3848
    SB421 .E3 1958 MRR Alc.

WATER-MARKS.
Hunter, Dard. Papermaking; 2d ed.,
rev. and enl. New York, A. A. Knopf,
1947. xxiv, 611, xxxvii p.   676 47-
6507
    TS1090 .H816 1947 MRR Alc.

Lister, Raymond. How to identify old
maps and globes. London, G. Bell
[1965] 256 p.   65-3799
    GA201 .L56 1965a MRR Alc.

WATER-POLO.
Amateur Athletic Union of the United
States. Rules for competitive and
synchronized swimming, diving ...
water polo. Indianapolis, Ind.
[etc.] A. A. U. House [etc.]   797.2
46-31932
    Publication began in 1932.
    GV837.A1 A45 MRR Alc Latest
    edition

WATER RESOURCES DEVELOPMENT--
INFORMATION SERVICES--DIRECTORIES.
United States. Library of Congress.
National Referral Center for Science
and Technology. A directory of
information resources in the United
States: water. [Washington, For sale
by the Superintendent of Documents,
U.S. Govt. Print. Off.] 1966. v, 248
p.   66-61638
    Z663.379 .D55 MRR Alc.

WATER SPORTS
see Aquatic sports

WATER-SUPPLY.
see also Forests and forestry

WATER-SUPPLY--EARLY WORKS TO 1800.
Frontinus, Sextus Julius. The
Stratagems. London, W. Heinemann;
New York, G. P. Putnam's sons, 1925.
xl, 483, [1] p.   25-15482
    PA6156.F6 1925 MRR Alc.

WATER-SUPPLY--INFORMATION SERVICES--
DIRECTORIES.
United States. Library of Congress.
National Referral Center for Science
and Technology. A directory of
information resources in the United
States: water. [Washington, For sale
by the Superintendent of Documents,
U.S. Govt. Print. Off.] 1966. v, 248
p.   66-61638
    Z663.379 .D55 MRR Alc.

WATER-SUPPLY--UNITED STATES--
DIRECTORIES.
Public Service Research, inc.,
Plainfield, N.J. American directory
of water utilities. 1968-69.
Plainfield, N.J. [c1968] 10 v. in 1.
[95.00]   363.6/1/02573 68-55746
    HD4461 .P8 MRR Alc.

WATER-SUPPLY--UNITED STATES--YEARBOOKS.
Moody's public utility manual. 1954-
New York, Moody's Investors Service.
56-3827
    HG4961 .M7245 MRR Alc Latest
    edition

WATER TRANSPORTATION
see Shipping

WATER TRANSPORTATION, INLAND
see Inland water transportation

WATERGATE AFFAIR, 1972-
Buschel, Bruce. The Watergate file
New York, Flash Books, [distributed
by Quick Fox, inc., 1973] 158 p.
[$3.95]   364.1/32/0973 73-84001
    E859 .B87 MRR Ref Desk.

Congressional Quarterly, inc.
Impeachment and the U.S. Congress.
Washington, 1974. 60 p.
342/.73/062 74-5285
    KF4985 .C65 MRR Ref Desk.

Sobel, Lester A., comp. Money &
politics : New York : Facts on File,
[1974] 204 p. ;   [$7.95.]
329/.025/0973 74-81147
    JK1994 .S64 MRR Alc.

Watergate and the White House. New
York, Facts on File [1973- v.
[$4.25]   364.1/32/0973 73-83049
    E859 .W37 MRR Ref Desk.

WATERGATE AFFAIR, 1972- --SOURCES.
Nixon, Richard Milhous, The White
House transcripts; New York, Viking
Press [1974] ix, 877 p. [$15.00]
364.1/32/0973 74-8869
    E860 .N57 1974c MRR Alc.

WATERSPOUTS.
Lane, Frank Walter. The elements
rage: Newton Abbot (Devon), David &
Charles [1966] xvi, 280 p. [50/-]
551 66-66261
    QC866 .L3 1966 MRR Alc.

WATFORD, ENG.--DIRECTORIES.
Kelly's directory of Watford.
Kingston upon Thames, Surrey [etc.]
Kelly's Directories Limited.   53-
28498
    DA670.H5 K45 MRR Alc Latest
    edition

WATSON, JOHN CRITTENDEN, 1842-1923--
MANUSCRIPTS.
United States. Library of Congress.
Manuscript Division. John Lansing
Callan; John Crittenden Watson; a
register of their papers in the
Library of Congress. Washington,
Library of Congress, 1968. 6, 8 l.
973 68-67221
    Z663.34 .C29 MRR Alc.

WAX MODELLERS--BIOGRAPHY--DICTIONARIES.
Pyke, E. J. A biographical
dictionary of wax modellers Oxford,
Clarendon Press, 1973. lxvi, 216,
[79] p. [£20.00]   736/.93/0922 '73-
174552
    NK9580 .P94 MRR Biog.

WEALTH.
see also Income tax

see also Money

see also Poverty

see also Saving and investment

WEAPONS
see Arms and armor

see Firearms

WEAPONS SYSTEMS--YEARBOOKS.
Jane's weapon systems. 1st- ed.;
1969/70- New York, McGraw-Hill.
623.4/05 79-12909
    U104 .J35 Sci RR Latest edition /
    MRR Alc Latest edition

WEATHER.
see also Atmospheric pressure

see also Climatology

Forrester, Frank H. 1001 questions
answered about the weather. New
York, Dodd, Mead, 1957. 419 p.
551.5076 57-11396
    QC863 .F72 MRR Alc.

Lane, Frank Walter. The elements
rage: Newton Abbot (Devon), David &
Charles [1966] xvi, 280 p. [50/-]
551 66-66261
    QC866 .L3 1966 MRR Alc.

World weather records. 1921/30-
Washington. 551.59083 59-65360
    QC982 .W6 MRR Alc Latest edition /
    Sci RR Full set

WEATHER CONTROL--RUSSIA--BIBLIOGRAPHY.
Zikeev, Nikolaĭ Tikhonovich,
Weather modification in the Soviet
Union, 1946-1966; Washington,
Library of Congress; [for sale by the
Supt. of Docs., U.S. Govt. Print.
Off.] 1967. x, 78 p.
016.5516/8/0947 67-61609
    Z663.41 Z5 MRR Alc.

WEATHER FORECASTS, LONG-RANGE
see Long-range weather forecasting

WEAVING.
see also Textile industry and fabrics

WEAVING--DICTIONARIES.
Pritchard, Miriam Eleanor. A short
dictionary of weaving. London, Allen
& Unwin [1954] 196 p.   677.02824
55-21897
    TS1490 .P9 MRR Alc.

WEBSTER, DANIEL, 1782-1852.
Fuess, Claude Moore. Daniel Webster.
Hamden, Conn., Archon Books, 1963
[c1958] 2 v.   923.273 63-17434
    E340.W4 F955 MRR Alc.

WEDDING ETIQUETTE.
Bentley, Marguerite, Wedding
etiquette complete, [Rev. ed.]
Philadelphia, Winston [1956] 384 p.
395 56-6323
    BJ2051 .B4 1956 MRR Alc.

Gray, Winifred. Your wedding:
[Atlanta, National Bridal Service,
c1959] 248 p.   395.22 60-16167
    BJ2051 .G7 MRR Alc.

McCall's engagement and wedding
guide, New York, Saturday Review
Press [1972] xvi, 266 p. [$8.95]
395/.22 79-122130
    BJ2051 .M27 MRR Alc.

The Bride's magazine. The bride's
book of etiquette, New York, Grosset
& Dunlap [1967] 184 p. 395/.22 67-
14753
    BJ2051 .B7 1967 MRR Alc.

Vanderbilt, Amy. Etiquette. [New
rev. ed.] Garden City, N.Y.,
Doubleday [1972] xxiii, 929 p.
[$8.95]   395 78-171326
    BJ1853 .V27 1972 MRR Ref Desk.

WEEDS--UNITED STATES.
Spencer, Edwin Rollin, Just weeds.
[New expanded ed.] New York,
Scribner [1957] 333 p.   581.65 57-
9682
    SB612.A2 S6 1957 MRR Alc.

WEEDS--UNITED STATES--IDENTIFICATION.
Jaques, Harry Edwin, How to know the
weeds; Dubuque, Iowa, W. C. Brown
Co. [c1959] 230 p.   632.58 60-2909
    SB612.A2 J3 MRR Alc.

WEEK.
Chases' calendar of annual events.
1958- Flint, Mich., Apple Tree
Press.   57-14540
    GT4803 .C48 MRR Ref Desk Latest
    Edition

WEEVILS
see Beetles

WEIGHT THROWING--STATISTICS.
Batchelor, David A., A handbook of
United States weight events
statistics, [n.p., 1966] xxii, 173
p.   796.4/35/0212 67-2034
    GV1093 .B299 MRR Alc.

WEIGHTS AND MEASURES.
see also Metric system

see also Scales (Weighing instruments)

see also Units

Burns, Arthur Robert, Money and
monetary policy in early times,
London, K. Paul, Trench, Trubner &
co., ltd.; New York, A. A. Knopf,
1927. xiii, 517 p.   27-21334
    HG237 .B86 MRR Alc.

WEIGHTS AND MEASURES--DICTIONARIES.
Doursther, Horace. Dictionnaire
universel des poids et mesures
anciens et modernes, Bruxelles, M.
Hayez, imprimeur de l'Académie
royale, 1840. 2 p. l., iv, 603, [1]
p.   44-44840
    QC82 .D6 MRR Alc.

Zupko, Ronald Edward. A dictionary
of English weights and measures;
Madison, University of Wisconsin
Press, 1968. xvi, 224 p.   389/.1/03
68-14038
    QC82 .Z8 MRR Alc.

WEIGHTS AND MEASURES--DICTIONARIES--
POLYGLOT.
Elsevier's lexicon of international
and national units: Amsterdam, New
York, Elsevier Pub. Co., 1964. 75 p.
389.103 63-11366
    QC82 .E37 MRR Alc.

WEIGHTS AND MEASURES--TABLES, ETC.
Gerolde, Steven. A handbook of
universal conversion factors. Tulsa,
Okla., Petroleum Pub. Co. [1971]
xii, 276 p.   389/.15 71-164900
    HF5714 .G45 MRR Alc.

Le Maraic, A. L., The complete
metric system with the international
system of units (SI). [Rev. and
expanded ed.] Somers, N.Y., Abbey
Books [1973] xiii, 184 p.   389/.152
72-97799
    QC91 .L44 1973 MRR Alc.

Naft, Stephen, International
conversion tables; New York, Duell,
Sloan and Pearce [1961] xii, 372 p.
389 61-10391
    HF5714 .N3 1961 MRR Alc.

Robertson, James, of London.
Dictionary for international
commercial quotations, London, New
York [etc.] H. Milford, Oxford
university press, 1918-19. 2 v.   19-
4807
    HF5715.G7 R6 MRR Alc.

WEIGHTS AND MEASURES--TABLES. (Cont.)
Sprinkle, Leland V. Sprinkle's
conversion formulas, Philadelphia,
P. Blakiston's son & co., inc.
[c1938] xii, 122 p.   510.835 38-
8711
    HF5699 .S75 MRR Ref Desk.

Swiss Bank Corporation. Values and
measures of the world; [London]
1959. 25 p.   332.4083 60-30644
    HF5712 .S8 1959 MRR Alc.

The Economist (London) Guide to
weights and measures, [2d. ed.]
London [1962] 95 p.   65-87714
    HF5712 .E25 1962 MRR Alc.

Zimmerman, Oswald Theodore,
Industrial Research Service's
conversion factors and tables, 3d
ed. Dover, N.H., Industrial Research
Service, 1961. 680 p.   530.83 61-
2586
    QC61 .Z5 1961 MRR Ref Desk.

WEIGHTS AND MEASURES--GREAT BRITAIN--
HISTORY.
Zupko, Ronald Edward. A dictionary
of English weights and measures;
Madison, University of Wisconsin
Press, 1968. xvi, 224 p.   389/.1/03
68-14038
    QC82 .Z8 MRR Alc.

WEIGHTS AND MEASURES--UNITED STATES.
Le Maraic, A. L. The complete
metric system with the international
system of units (SI). [Rev. and
expanded ed.] Somers, N.Y., Abbey
Books [1973] xiii, 184 p.   389/.152
72-97799
    QC91 .L44 1973 MRR Alc.

WELFARE WORK
    see Charities

WELLINGTON, N.Z.--INDUSTRIES--
DIRECTORIES.
Universal business directory for
Wellington, Butt [and] Petone.
Auckland, Universal Business
Directories.   53-30822
    HC623.W45 U5 MRR Alc Latest
    edition

WELLINGTON, N.Z. (PROVINCIAL DISTRICT)--
COMMERCE--DIRECTORIES.
Universal business directory for
Wellington Province (excluding
Wellington City) Auckland, Universal
Business Directories.   53-29068
    HF5299.W4 U62 MRR Alc Latest
    edition

WELLS.
    see also Gas, Natural

    see also Petroleum

WELSH LANGUAGE--BIBLIOGRAPHY.
Bibliotheca celtica, 1909-1927/28;
new ser., v. 1-   1929/33-
Aberystwyth [National library of
Wales] 11-5717
    Z2071 .B56 MRR Alc Partial set

WELSH LANGUAGE--DICTIONARIES--ENGLISH.
Evans, Harold Meurig. Y geiriadur
mawr, the complete Welsh-English,
English-Welsh dictionary [1st ed.]
Llandybïe, Llyfrau'r Dryw [1958]
470, 342 p.   491.6632 59-44325
    PB2191 .E685 MRR Alc.

WELSH LITERATURE--BIBLIOGRAPHY.
Bibliotheca celtica, 1909-1927/28;
new ser., v. 1-   1929/33-
Aberystwyth [National library of
Wales] 11-5717
    Z2071 .B56 MRR Alc Partial set

WELSH LITERATURE--HISTORY AND CRITICISM.
Parry, Thomas, A history of Welsh
literature. Oxford, Clarendon Press,
1955. xii, 534 p.   55-13954
    PB2206 .P33 MRR Alc.

WELSH NEWSPAPERS--BIBLIOGRAPHY.
The Times, London. Tercentenary
handlist of English & Welsh
newspapers, magazines & reviews ...
London, The Times, 1920. 212 p.; 1
l., l. p., 1 l., [215]-324, xxxv p.
21-6520
    Z6956.E5 T5 MRR Alc.

WELSH PERIODICALS--BIBLIOGRAPHY.
The Times, London. Tercentenary
handlist of English & Welsh
newspapers, magazines & reviews ...
London, The Times, 1920. 212 p.; 1
l., l. p., 1 l., [215]-324, xxxv p.
21-6520
    Z6956.E5 T5 MRR Alc.

WEST--BIBLIOGRAPHY.
Adams, Ramon Frederick, Six-guns and
saddle leather; New ed., [Norman]
University of Oklahoma Press, 1969.
xxv, 808 p. [19.95]   016.3641 69-
16729
    Z1251.W5 A3 1969 MRR Alc.

Winther, Oscar Osburn, A classified
bibliography of the periodical
literature of the trans-Mississippi
West, 1811-1957. Bloomington,
Indiana University Press, 1961.
xxvi, 626 p.   016.9178 61-63869
    Z1251.W5 W53 MRR Alc.

WEST--BIBLIOGRAPHY--CATALOGS.
California. University. Santa
Barbara. Library. The William Wyles
collection. Westport, Conn.,
Greenwood Pub. Corp., 1970] 5 v.
016.9173/03 70-19247
    Z1236 .C23 MRR Alc (Dk 33)

Denver. Public Library. Western
History Dept. Catalog. Boston, G.
K. Hall, 1970. 7 v.   016.978 70-
24055
    Z1251.W5 D43 MRR Alc (Dk 33)

Newberry Library, Chicago. A
catalogue of the Everett D. Graff
collection of Western Americana.
Chicago, Published for the Newberry
Library by the University of Chicago
Press, 1968. xxv, 854 p.   016.978
66-20577
    Z1251.W5 N43 MRR Alc.

Soliday, George W., A descriptive
check list, together with short title
index, describing almost 7500 items
of western Americana; [Reprinted
with corrections] New York,
Antiquarian Press, 1960. 1 v.
(various pagings)   016.97 61-45337

    Z1251.W5 S62 MRR Alc.

WEST--BIOGRAPHY--DICTIONARIES.
Dawdy, Doris Ostrander. Artists of
the American West : 1st ed. Chicago
: Sage Books, [1974] viii, 275 p. :
[$12.50]   709/.2/2 72-91919
    N6536 .D38 MRR Biog.

Personalities of the West and
Midwest. Raleigh, N.C., News Pub.
Co.   920.078 68-56857
    CT213 .P4 MRR Biog Latest edition

WEST--BIOGRAPHY--PORTRAITS.
Hunter, John Marvin, The album of
gunfighters. [San Antonio? 1965]
xi, 236 p.   978.020922 66-3801
    F591 .H935 1965 MRR Biog.

WEST--COMMERCE--DIRECTORIES.
Walker's manual of Western
corporations & securities. 65th-
ed.: 1973- San Francisco.
332.6/7/0978 74-640659
    HG5128.C2 W2 MRR Alc Latest
    edition

WEST--DESCRIPTION AND TRAVEL--1951-
National parks of the West. [2d ed.]
Menlo Park, Calif., Lane Magazine &
Book Co. [1970] 286 p.   [11.75]
719/.32/0978 76-108153
    E160 .N36 1970 MRR Alc.

WEST--DESCRIPTION AND TRAVEL--1951- --
GUIDE-BOOKS.
Felsen, W. L. U.S.A. West; the
foreign traveler's sightseeing guide
Stinson Beach, Calif., Peregrination
Press [1967] 269 p.   917.8/04/3 67-
8056
    F595.2 .F4 MRR Alc.

TravelVision. Humble vacation guide
U.S.A.; favorite West Central
recreation regions. Houston, Tex.,
Humble Travel Club [1970] 224 p.
647/.9478 77-17741
    TX907 .T8526 1970 MRR Alc.

WEST--DESCRIPTION AND TRAVEL--
BIBLIOGRAPHY.
Wagner, Henry Raup, The Plains and
the Rockies; 3d ed. Columbus, Ohio,
Long's College Book Co., 1953. 601
p.   016.9178 53-2473
    Z1251.W5 W2 1953 MRR Alc.

WEST--HISTORIC HOUSES, ETC.
United States. National Park Service.
Soldier and brave; [1st ed.] New
York, Harper & Row, 1963. xviii, 279
p.   978 63-10600
    F591 .U59 MRR Alc.

WEST--HISTORY.
Billington, Ray Allen, ed. The
frontier thesis: valid interpretation
of American history? New York, Holt,
Rinehart and Winston [1966] 122 p.
973.01 66-21640
    E179.5 .B625 MRR Alc.

Billington, Ray Allen, Westward
expansion; 3d ed. New York,
Macmillan [c1967] xvii, 933 p.   973
67-12337
    E179.5 .B63 1967 MRR Alc.

Philbrick, Francis Samuel, The rise
of the West, 1754-1830. [1st ed.]
New York, Harper & Row [1965] xvii,
398 p.   973 65-21377
    E179.5 .P45 MRR Alc.

Turner, Frederick Jackson, The
frontier in American history, New
York, H. Holt and company, 1920. 4
p. l., 375 p.   20-18058
    E179.5 .T95 MRR Alc.

United States. National Park Service.
Soldier and brave; [1st ed.] New
York, Harper & Row, 1963. xviii, 279
p.   978 63-10600
    F591 .U59 MRR Alc.

WEST--HISTORY--1848-1950.
Taft, Robert, Artists and
illustrators of the Old West, 1850-
1900. New York, Scribner, 1953.
xvii, 400 p.   709.78 53-7577
    N6510 .T27 MRR Alc.

WEST--HISTORY--BIBLIOGRAPHY.
California. University. Bancroft
Library. Catalog of printed books.
Boston, G. K. Hall, 1964. 22 v.
016.9178 67-52922
    Z881 .C1523 MRR Alc (DK33)

Wallace, William Swilling.
Bibliography of published
bibliographies on the history of the
eleven Western States, 1941-1947;
Albuquerque, N.M., 1953 [i.e. 1954]
224-233 p.   016.016978 55-62545
    Z1251.W5 W25 MRR Alc.

WEST--HISTORY--SOURCES--BIBLIOGRAPHY.
Yale University. Library. A
catalogue of manuscripts in the
collection of western Americana New
Haven, Yale University Press, 1952.
x, 398 p.   016.978 52-5370
    Z1251.W5 Y3 MRR Alc.

WEST--PERIODICALS--INDEXES.
Winther, Oscar Osburn, A classified
bibliography of the periodical
literature of the trans-Mississippi
West, 1811-1957. Bloomington,
Indiana University Press, 1961.
xxvi, 626 p.   016.9178 61-63869
    Z1251.W5 W53 MRR Alc.

WEST INDIES.
The West Indies and Caribbean year
book. 1st- year: 1926/27- London
[etc.] T. Skinner [etc.] 917.29 27-
21166
    F2131 .W47 MRR Alc Latest edition

WEST INDIES--BIBLIOGRAPHY.
Comitas, Lambros. Caribbeana 1900-
1965, a topical bibliography.
Seattle, Published for Research
Institute for the Study of Man [by]
University of Washington Press [1968]
L, 909 p.   016.91729/03/5 68-14239

    Z1501 .C6 MRR Alc.

WEST INDIES--DESCRIPTION AND TRAVEL--
1951-
Clark, Sydney Aylmer, All the best
in the Caribbean, New York, Dodd,
Mead [1969] xii, 461 p. [6.95]
917.29 70-76837
    F2171.2 .C55 1969 MRR Alc.

Slater, Mary. The Caribbean islands.
London, Batsford, 1968. xi, 244 p.
[35/-] 917.29 68-113022
    F1765.2 .S55 MRR Alc.

WEST INDIES--DESCRIPTION AND TRAVEL--
1951- --GUIDE-BOOKS.
Aspinall, Algernon Edward, Sir, The
pocket guide to the West Indies and
British Guiana, British Honduras,
Bermuda, the Spanish Main, Surinam,
the Panama Canal. [10th ed.] rev.
London, Methuen [1960] xx, 474 p.
917.29 61-19408
    F1609 .A84 1960 MRR Alc.

Crocker, John. The Centaur guide to
Bermuda, the Bahamas, Hispaniola,
Puerto Rico and the Virgin Islands.
Arundel, Centaur, 1968. xiv, 226 p.
[30/-] 917.29/04/5 68-86362
    F1609 .C7 MRR Alc.

Deane, Philip, pseud. Caribbean
vacations. Toronto, Longmans Canada
[c1966] 316 p. [$4.50 Can.]
917.29/04/5 67-91414
    F1609 .D4 1966a MRR Alc.

Edson, Wesley. Terry's guide to the
Caribbean. [1st ed.] Garden City,
N.Y., Doubleday, 1970. xvii, 668 p.
[8.95] 917.29/04/5 73-78737
    F1609 .D36 1970 MRR Alc.

Hepburn, Andrew. Complete guide to
the Caribbean & the Bahamas. New
rev. ed. Garden City, N.Y.,
Doubleday, 1962. 159 p.   917.29 62-
7127
    F1612 .H4 1962 MRR Alc.

Pan American World Airways, inc.
Complete reference guide to the
Caribbean and the Bahamas. [1st ed.]
New York, Trade distribution in the
U.S. and Canada by Simon and
Schuster, 1967, c1968] 156 p.
917.29/04/5 67-19411
    F1609 .P3 MRR Alc.

WEST INDIES--DESCRIPTION AND TRAVEL--
GUIDE-BOOKS.
Harman, Jeanne (Perkins) Fielding's
guide to the Caribbean, including the
Bahamas, 1869-70 ed. New York,
Fielding Publications [1968] xxv,
630 p. [7.50] 917.29/04/5 68-
59243
F1609 .H3 MRR Alc.

WEST INDIES--HISTORY.
Nicole, Christopher. The West
Indies. London, Hutchinson [1965]
296 p.   972.9 65-8110
F1621 .N5 MRR Alc.

Williams, Eric Eustace. From
Columbus to Castro: [1st U.S. ed.]
New York, Harper & Row [1971, c1970]
576 p.   [$10.95] 972.9 75-138773
F1621 .W68 1970b MRR Alc.

WEST INDIES--HISTORY--SOURCES.
United States. Library of Congress.
Manuscript division. List of the
Vernon-Wager manuscripts in the
Library of Congress. Washington,
Govt. print. off., 1904. 148 p.   05-
3073
Z663.34 .V4 MRR Alc.

WEST INDIES--POLITICS.
Creque, Darwin D. The U.S. Virgins
and the eastern Caribbean.
Philadelphia, Whitmore Pub. Co.
[1968] vi, 266 p. 972.97/22 67-
31320
F2136 .C7 MRR Alc.

WEST INDIES, BRITISH.
The Caribbean who, what, why. 1st
ed.: 1955/56- [n.p.] L. S. Smith.
972.9 56-4669
F2131 .B85 MRR Biog Latest edition

WEST INDIES, BRITISH--COMMERCE.
The Caribbean who, what, why. 1st
ed.: 1955/56- [n.p.] L. S. Smith.
972.9 56-4669
F2131 .B85 MRR Biog Latest edition

WEST INDIES, BRITISH--GAZETTEERS.
United States. Office of Geography.
British West Indies and Bermuda;
Washington, U.S. Govt. Print. Off.,
1955. v, 157 p.   917.29 55-63708
F2131 .U52 MRR Alc.

WEST INDIES, BRITISH--GOVERNORS.
Burns, Alan Cuthbert, Sir. History
of the British West Indies [Rev. 2d
ed.] London, Allen and Unwin [1965]
849 p.   66-174
F2131 .B96 1965 MRR Alc.

WEST INDIES, BRITISH--HISTORY.
Burns, Alan Cuthbert, Sir. History
of the British West Indies [Rev. 2d
ed.] London, Allen and Unwin [1965]
849 p.   66-174
F2131 .B96 1965 MRR Alc.

WEST INDIES, BRITISH--POLITICS AND
GOVERNMENT.
The Caribbean who, what, why. 1st
ed.: 1955/56- [n.p.] L. S. Smith.
972.9 56-4669
F2131 .B85 MRR Biog Latest edition

WEST INDIES, FRENCH--GAZETTEERS.
United States. Office of Geography.
French West Indies; Washington, U.S.
Govt. Print. Off., 1957. iii, 44 p.
57-61544
F2151 .U5 MRR Alc.

WEST VIRGINIA.
Writers' program. West Virginia.
West Virginia; a guide to the
mountain state, New York, Oxford
university press [1941] xxxi, 559 p.
917.54 41-51884
F241 .W85 MRR Ref Desk.

WEST VIRGINIA--BIBLIOGRAPHY.
Historical records survey. A check
list of West Virginia imprints, 1791-
1830. Chicago, The WPA Historical
records survey project, 1940. 62
numb. l.   015.754 41-50571
Z1215 .H67 no. 14 MRR Alc.

Munn, Robert F. Index to West
Virginiana. Charleston, W.Va.,
Education Foundation [1960] 154 p.
016.9754005 60-50809
Z1349 .M8 MRR Alc.

Norona, Delf, ed. West Virginia
imprints, 1790-1863; Moundsville,
West Virginia Library Association,
1958. 316 p.   015.754 58-1596
Z1349 .N6 MRR Alc.

WEST VIRGINIA--BIBLIOGRAPHY--CATALOGS.
United States. Library of Congress.
West Virginia, the centennial of
statehood, 1863-1963; Washington
[For sale by the Superintendent of
Documents, U.S. Govt. Print. Off.]
1964. 82 p.   64-60068
Z663.15.A6 W4 MRR Alc.

WEST VIRGINIA--CENTENNIAL CELEBRATIONS,
ETC.
United States. Library of Congress.
West Virginia, the centennial of
statehood, 1863-1963; Washington
[For sale by the Superintendent of
Documents, U.S. Govt. Print. Off.]
1964. 82 p.   64-60068
Z663.15.A6 W4 MRR Alc.

WEST VIRGINIA--DESCRIPTION AND TRAVEL--
GUIDE-BOOKS.
Writers' program. West Virginia.
West Virginia; a guide to the
mountain state, New York, Oxford
university press [1941] xxxi, 559 p.
917.54 41-51884
F241 .W85 MRR Ref Desk.

WEST VIRGINIA--EXECUTIVE DEPARTMENTS.
West Virginia blue book. v. [1]-
1916- Charleston. 353.9754 16-
11743
JK4031 date b MRR Alc Latest
edition

WEST VIRGINIA--HISTORY--PERIODICALS--
INDEXES.
Munn, Robert F. Index to West
Virginiana. Charleston, W.Va.,
Education Foundation [1960] 154 p.
016.9754005 60-50809
Z1349 .M8 MRR Alc.

WEST VIRGINIA--IMPRINTS.
Historical records survey. A check
list of West Virginia imprints, 1791-
1830. Chicago, The WPA Historical
records survey project, 1940. 62
numb. l.   015.754 41-50571
Z1215 .H67 no. 14 MRR Alc.

Norona, Delf, ed. West Virginia
imprints, 1790-1863; Moundsville,
West Virginia Library Association,
1958. 316 p.   015.754 58-1596
Z1349 .N6 MRR Alc.

WEST VIRGINIA--MANUFACTURES--
DIRECTORIES.
Directory of Central Atlantic States
manufacturers; 1- ed.; 1950-
Baltimore, T. K. Sanderson
Organization. 670.58 50-2706
T12 .D485 Sci RR Latest edition /
MRR Alc Latest edition

West Virginia manufacturing
directory. 1962- Charleston. 66-
63111
HD9727.W4 W4 MRR Alc Latest
edition / Sci RR Latest edition

WEST VIRGINIA--POLITICS AND GOVERNMENT--
YEARBOOKS.
West Virginia blue book. v. [1]-
1916- Charleston. 353.9754 16-
11743
JK4031 date b MRR Alc Latest
edition

The West Virginia political almanac.
1956- [Charleston] 324.754 57-1342
JK4092 .W4 MRR Alc Latest edition

WEST VIRGINIA--REGISTERS.
West Virginia blue book. v. [1]-
1916- Charleston. 353.9754 16-
11743
JK4031 date b MRR Alc Latest
edition

WEST VIRGINIA--STATISTICS.
Sizer, Leonard Marion. County study
data book; [2d ed.] Morgantown, W.
Va., Agricultural Experiment Station,
1967. 105 p. [1.50] 317.54 68-
64112
HA706 .S5 1967 MRR Alc.

WESTERN AUSTRALIA--STATISTICS.
Western Australian year book. 1st-
13th, 1886-1902/04; new ser. no. 1-
1957-67. [Perth] 319.4/1 59-52412
HA3153 .A45 MRR Alc Latest edition

WESTERN CIVILIZATION
see Civilization, Occidental

WESTERN HEMISPHERE
see America

WESTERN LANGUAGES
see Languages, Modern

WESTLAND, N.Z. (PROVINCIAL DISTRICT)--
COMMERCE--DIRECTORIES.
Universal business directory for
Nelson-Marlborough-west coast.
Auckland, Universal Business
Directories. 52-38722
HF5298 .U55 MRR Alc Latest edition

WHITE, WALLACE HUMPHREY, 1877-1952--
BIBLIOGRAPHY.
United States. Library of Congress.
Manuscript Division. Wallace H.
White; a register of his papers in
the Library of Congress. Washington,
1959. 23 p.   012 59-60024
Z663.34 .W5 MRR Alc.

WHITE RUSSIAN NEWSPAPERS--BIBLIOGRAPHY.
United States. Library of Congress.
Slavic and Central European Division.
Preliminary checklist of Russian,
Ukrainian, and Belorussian newspapers
published since January 1, 1917,
Washington 1952. iv, 97 l.
016.077 52-60042
Z663.47 .P7 MRR Alc.

United States. Library of Congress.
Slavic and Central European Division.
Russian, Ukrainian, and Belorussian
newspapers, 1917-1953; Washington,
1953. xi, 218 p.   016.077 54-60001
Z663.47 .R85 MRR Alc.

WHITMAN, WALT, 1819-1892.
United States. Library of Congress.
Gertrude Clarke Whittall Poetry and
Literature Fund. Walt Whitman: man,
poet, philosopher; Washington,
1955. 53 p. 811.3 55-60021
Z663.293 .W5 MRR Alc.

WHITMAN, WALT, 1819-1892--BIBLIOGRAPHY.
United States. Library of Congress.
Reference Dept. Walt Whitman; a
catalog based upon the collections of
the Library of Congress, Washington,
1955. xviii, 147 p.   012 55-60006
Z663.2 .W3 MRR Alc.

WHITMAN, WALT, 1819-1892--CONCORDANCES.
Eby, Edwin Harold. A concordance of
Walt Whitman's Leaves of grass and
selected prose writings. New York,
Greenwood Press [1969] xiii, 964 p.
811/.3 76-90500
PS3245 .E2 1969 MRR Alc.

WHITMAN, WALT, 1819-1892--MANUSCRIPTS--
BIBLIOGRAPHY.
United States. Library of Congress.
Ten notebooks and a cardboard
butterfly missing from the Walt
Whitman papers. Washington, 1954.
38 p.   54-60375
Z663.34 .T4 MRR Alc.

WHOLESALE TRADE--UNITED STATES.
United States. Bureau of the Census.
1963 census of business.
[Washington, For sale by the
Superintendent of Documents, U.S.
Govt. Print. Off., 1966] 7 v. in 17.
381.0973 a 66-7302
HF3007 .A5 1963 MRR Alc.

WHOLESALE TRADE--UNITED STATES--
DIRECTORIES.
Chain store guide directory: 1973-
[New York, Business Guides] [$49.00]
658.8/6 73-645662
HD9321.3 .D53 MRR Alc Latest
edition

Sheldon's jobbing and wholesale
trade. 87th- ed.; 1960- New York,
Phelon-Sheldon publications [etc.]
381 72-623015
HF5421 .S5 MRR Alc Latest edition

WHOLESALE TRADE--UNITED STATES--
STATISTICS.
Robert Morris Associates. Annual
statement studies. [Philadelphia]
338/.0973 72-626355
HF5681.B2 R6 MRR Alc Latest
edition

United States. Bureau of the Census.
1967 census of business.
[Washington; For sale by the Supt. of
Docs., U.S. Govt. Print. Off., 1970-
71] 5 v. in 9 [$9.50 (v. 1) varies]
338/.0973 72-608032
HF3007 .U55 1970 MRR Alc.

WIESBADEN--DIRECTORIES.
Adressbuch der Landeshauptstadt
Wiesbaden. Wiesbaden, Beleke KG
[etc.] 53-30188
DD901.W58 W48 MRR Alc Latest
edition

WIGS--DICTIONARIES.
Cox, James Stevens. An illustrated
dictionary of hairdressing and
wigmaking; London, Hairdressers'
Technical Council, 1966. xxiii, 359
p. [42/-] 646.72403 67-73133
TT951 .C6 MRR Alc.

WILD FLOWERS--PICTORIAL WORKS--NORTH
AMERICA.
Walcott, Mary Morris (Vaux) Wild
flowers of America. New York, Crown
Publishers [1953] 71 p., 400 col.
plates.   581.97 53-9972
QK112 .W35 MRR Alc.

WILD FLOWERS--NORTH AMERICA.
The New illustrated encyclopedia of
gardening (unabridged). [New and
rev. ed.] New York, Greystone Press
[1972-73] 26 v. (4206 p.) 635/.03
72-192032
SB45 .N424 MRR Alc.

WILD FLOWERS--NORTH AMERICA. (Cont.)
Walcott, Mary Morris (Vaux) Wild
flowers of America. New York, Crown
Publishers [1953] 71 p., 400 col.
plates. 581.97 53-9972
    QK112 .W35 MRR Alc.

**WILD FLOWERS--NORTH AMERICA--
IDENTIFICATION.**
Grimm, William Carey, Recognizing
flowering wild plants. Harrisburg,
Pa., Stackpole Books [1968] 348 p.
[$7.95] 582.13/0973 68-30888
    QK110 .G83 MRR Alc.

**WILD FLOWERS--NORTH AMERICA--PICTORIAL
WORKS.**
Hylander, Clarence John, The
Macmillan wild flower book. New
York, Macmillan [1954] xv, 480 p.
581.873 54-7383
    QK112 .H9 MRR Alc.

WILD FLOWERS--UNITED STATES.
Grimm, William Carey, Home guide to
trees, shrubs, and wild flowers.
[Harrisburg, Pa.] Stackpole Books
[1970] 320 p. [9.95] 582/.09/73
76-100348
    QK482 .G734 MRR Alc.

**WILD FLOWERS--UNITED STATES--
IDENTIFICATION.**
Grimm, William Carey, Recognizing
flowering wild plants. Harrisburg,
Pa., Stackpole Books [1968] 348 p.
[$7.95] 582.13/0973 68-30888
    QK110 .G83 MRR Alc.

**WILD FLOWERS--UNITED STATES--PICTORIAL
WORKS.**
Peterson, Roger Tory, A field guide
to wildflowers of Northeastern and
North-Central North America; Boston,
Houghton Mifflin, 1968. xxviii, 420
p. 582.13/097 67-13042
    QK118 .P5 MRR Alc.

Rickett, Harold William, Wild
flowers of the United States, 1st
ed.] New York, McGraw-Hill [1966-73]
6 v. in 14 pts. 582.130973 66-
17920
    QK115 .F5 MRR Alc.

WILD LIFE, CONSERVATION OF.
see also National parks and reserves

WILDERNESS SURVIVAL.
Explorers Ltd. The Explorers Ltd.
source book. 1st ed. New York,
Harper & Row [c1973] 384 p. [$4.95]
790/.028 72-9115
    GV187 .E95 1973 MRR Alc.

Merrill, William K., The survival
handbook [New York] Winchester Press
[1972] 312 p. [$5.95] 613.6/9 76-
188594
    SK606 .M47 MRR Alc.

WILDLIFE CONSERVATION.
see also Rare animals

WILDLIFE REFUGES.
The World wildlife guide. London
[200 Buckingham Palace Rd, S.W.1),
Threshold Books Ltd, 1971. 416 p.
[£3.50] 639/.95 72-185519
    SB481 .W63 1971 MRR Alc.

WILHELMSHAVEN, GER.--DIRECTORIES.
Stadtadressbuch Wilhelmshaven.
Oldenburg, G. Stalling. 914.3/59 77-
615658
    DD901.W615 A32 MRR Alc Latest
    edition

**WILLIAMSBURG, VA.--DESCRIPTION AND
TRAVEL--GUIDE-BOOKS.**
Colonial Williamsburg, inc. Official
guidebook. [1st]- ed.; 1951-
Williamsburg, Va. 917.554252 56-402

    F234.W7 C745 MRR Alc Latest
    edition

WILLIAMSBURG, VA.--HISTORIC HOUSES, ETC.
Colonial Williamsburg, inc. Official
guidebook. [1st]- ed.; 1951-
Williamsburg, Va. 917.554252 56-402

    F234.W7 C745 MRR Alc Latest
    edition

Kocher, Alfred Lawrence. Colonial
Williamsburg, its buildings and
gardens; Rev. ed. Williamsburg,
Va., Colonial Williamsburg;
distributed by Holt, Rinehart and
Winston, New York [1961] 104 p.
975.54252 61-11479
    F234.W7 K6 1961 MRR Alc.

WILMINGTON, DEL.--LIBRARIES.
Special Libraries Council of
Philadelphia and Vicinity. Directory
of libraries and informational
sources. [1st, 3d]- ed.; 1920,
1923- Philadelphia [etc.] 026.0058
24-5378
    Z732.P6 P5 MRR Alc Latest edition

**WILSON, WOODROW, PRES. U.S., 1856-1924--
MANUSCRIPTS--INDEXES.**
Wilson, Woodrow, Pres. U.S., Woodrow
Wilson papers. Washington, Library
of Congress [1973] 540 reels.
016.97391/3/0924 73-7658
    Z663.34 .W514 MRR Alc.

WILSON, WOODROW, PRES. U.S., 1856-1924.
Baker, Ray Stannard, Woodrow Wilson;
life and letters ... Garden City,
N.Y., Doubleday, Page & co., 1927-39.
8 v. 27-25411
    E767 .B16 MRR Alc.

Link, Arthur Stanley. Wilson.
Princeton, Princeton University
Press, 1947- v. 923.173 47-
3554
    E767 .L65 MRR Alc.

Walworth, Arthur Clarence, Woodrow
Wilson 2d ed., rev. Boston,
Houghton Mifflin Co., 1965. xiv,
436, 439 p. 923.173 64-21740
    E767 .W34 1965 MRR Alc.

Wilson, Woodrow, Pres. U.S., 1856-
1924. The papers of Woodrow Wilson.
Princeton, N.J., Princeton University
Press, 1966- v. [$20.00 per
vol.] 973.91/3/0924 66-10880
    E660 .W717 MRR Alc.

WINCHESTER, ENG.--DIRECTORIES.
Kelly's directory of Winchester and
neighbourhood. Kingston upon Thames.
[-/14/-] 914.22/7 73-642688
    DA690.W67 K4 MRR Alc Latest
    edition

WIND.
see also Tornadoes

WIND INSTRUMENTS--BIBLIOGRAPHY.
United States. Library of Congress.
Music Division. The Dayton C. Miller
flute collection: Washington, 1961.
vi, 115 p. 61-60077
    Z663.37 .D3 MRR Alc.

WINDOW-GARDENING.
see also House plants

WINDS.
see also Storms

WINE AND WINE MAKING.
The great book of wine. New York,
World Pub. Co. [1970] 459 p.
[50.00] 641 77-124428
    TP548 .G6913 MRR Alc.

Johnson, Hugh. The world atlas of
wine; New York, Simon and Schuster
[1971] 272 p. [$25.00]
641.2/2/094 71-163481
    TP548 .J66 MRR Alc.

Ozias, Blake. All about wine. New
York, Crowell [1967, c1966] 144 p.
641.8/72 67-27767
    TP548 .O78 MRR Alc.

Simon, André Louis, comp. Wines of
the world; London, New York [etc.]
McGraw-Hill [1967] 719 p. [5/5/-]
663/.2/009 68-89589
    TP548 .S68 1967 MRR Alc.

WINE AND WINE MAKING--DICTIONARIES.
Lichine, Alexis, Encyclopedia of
wines & spirits. [1st ed.] New
York, Knopf, 1967. xii, 713 p.
663/.2/003 66-18385
    TP546 .L5 1967b MRR Alc.

Schoonmaker, Frank, Encyclopedia of
wine. [4th ed., rev.] New York,
Hastings House [1969] vi, 442 p.
[6.95] 663/.22/03 77-9315
    TP546 .S47 1969 MRR Alc.

Simon, André Louis, The
International Wine and Food Society's
encyclopedia of wines. [1st American
ed. New York] Quadrangle Books
[1973, c1972] 311 p. [$15.00]
641.2/2/03 72-85052
    TP546 .S53 1973 MRR Alc.

WINE AND WINE MAKING--DIRECTORIES.
Harpers directory and manual.
London, Harper Trade Journals.
663/.2/0025 79-3865
    Began in 1914.
    TP500.5 .H37 MRR Alc Latest
    edition

WINE AND WINE MAKING--HISTORY.
Younger, William Antony, Gods, men
and wine London, Wine & Food
Society: Joseph [1966] 526 p. [84/-
] 663.2009 66-74880
    TP549 .Y68 1966a MRR Alc.

WINE AND WINE MAKING--STATISTICS.
Schoonmaker, Frank, Encyclopedia of
wine. [4th ed., rev.] New York,
Hastings House [1969] vi, 442 p.
[6.95] 663/.22/03 77-9315
    TP546 .S47 1969 MRR Alc.

WINE AND WINE MAKING--FRANCE.
Jacquelin, Louis. The wines &
vineyards of France Revised ed.
London, Hamlyn, 1965. 418 p. [63/-]
338.47663220944 66-70303
    TP553 .J313 1965 MRR Alc.

**WINE AND WINE MAKING--UNITED STATES--
DIRECTORIES.**
Red book: encyclopaedic directory of
the wine and liquor industries. New
York, Schwartz Publications, inc.
[$19.50] 338.4/7/663102573 73-
646025
    HD9373 .R43 MRR Alc Latest edition

WINTER SPORTS.
see also Hockey

    see also Skis and skiing

Bass, Howard. International
encyclopedia of winter sports. [1st
American ed.] South Brunswick [N.J.]
Great Albion Books [1972, c1971] 223
p. [$7.95] 796.9/03 79-37616
    GV841 .B32 1972 MRR Alc.

WIRE-TAPPING--UNITED STATES.
United States. Library of Congress.
Legislative Reference Service.
Combating crime in the United States.
Washington, U.S. Govt. Print.Off.,
1967. v, 254 p. 353.007/5 67-
62987
    Z663.6 .C6 MRR Alc.

WISCONSIN--BIBLIOGRAPHY.
Historical Records Survey. Wisconsin.
A check list of Wisconsin imprints,
1833-1849[--1864-1869] Madison,
Wis., The Wisconsin Historical
Records Survey, 1942-53. 5 v.
015.775 42-16157
    Z1215 .H67 no. 23-24, 41-42 MRR
    Alc.

WISCONSIN--BIBLIOGRAPHY--CATALOGS.
United States. Library of Congress.
Wisconsin centennial exhibition, May
29, 1948-August 23, 1948.
Washington, U.S. Govt. Print. Off.,
1948. 64 p. 016.9775 48-46424
    Z663.15.A6 W6 1948 MRR Alc.

WISCONSIN--BIOGRAPHY.
Wisconsin. State Historical Society.
Dictionary of Wisconsin biography.
Madison, 1960. xiv, 385 p.
920.0775 60-63043
    F580 .W825 MRR Biog.

WISCONSIN--CENTENNIAL CELEBRATIONS, ETC.
United States. Library of Congress.
Wisconsin centennial exhibition, May
29, 1948-August 23, 1948.
Washington, U.S. Govt. Print. Off.,
1948. 64 p. 016.9775 48-46424
    Z663.15.A6 W6 1948 MRR Alc.

**WISCONSIN--DESCRIPTION AND TRAVEL--
GUIDE-BOOKS.**
Writers' Program. Wisconsin.
Wisconsin; a guide to the Badger
State. St. Clair Shores, Mich.,
Somerset Publishers, 1973 [c1941]
651 p. 917.75/04/4 72-84517
    F586 .W97 1973 MRR Alc.

Writers' Program. Wisconsin.
Wisconsin; a guide to the Badger
State. New York, Hastings House
[c1954] 651 p. 917.75 55-3162
    F586 .W97 1954 MRR Alc.

WISCONSIN--EXECUTIVE DEPARTMENTS.
Wisconsin. Legislative Reference
Bureau. The organization of
Wisconsin State government.
[Madison] 1972. 146 p. 353.9/775
73-620772
    JK6031 1972 .A54 MRR Alc.

WISCONSIN--HISTORY.
Nesbit, Robert Carrington,
Wisconsin; [Madison] University of
Wisconsin Press [1973] xiv, 573 p.
[$12.50] 977.5 72-7990
    F581 .N47 MRR Alc.

Raney, William Francis. Wisconsin; a
story of progress. Appleton, Wis.,
Perin Press, 1963. xvii, 554 p. '65-
1962
    F581 .R32 1963 MRR Alc.

Smith, Alice Elizabeth, The history
of Wisconsin Madison, State
Historical Society of Wisconsin, 1973-
v. 977.5 72-12941
    F581 .S64 MRR Alc.

WISCONSIN--IMPRINTS.
Historical Records Survey. Wisconsin.
A check list of Wisconsin imprints,
1833-1849[--1864-1869] Madison,
Wis., The Wisconsin Historical
Records Survey, 1942-53. 5 v.
015.775 42-16157
    Z1215 .H67 no. 23-24, 41-42 MRR
    Alc.

WISCONSIN--MANUFACTURES--DIRECTORIES.
Midwest manufacturers and industrial
directory buyers guide. [Detroit,
Industrial Directory Publishers]
338.4/0977 72-626483
    HC107.A15 M5 MRR Alc Latest
    edition

Wisconsin Manufacturers' Association.
Classified directory of Wisconsin
manufacturers. Milwaukee, Wis.
[etc.] 670.58   42-21094
    TS24.W6 W7 Sci RR Latest edition*
    / MRR Alc Latest edition

WISCONSIN--POLITICS AND GOVERNMENT--
HANDBOOKS, MANUALS, ETC.
Wisconsin. Legislative Reference
Bureau. The organization of
Wisconsin State government.
[Madison] 1972. 146 p.   353.9/775
73-620772
    JK6031 1972 .A54 MRR Alc.

WIT AND HUMOR.
Adams, A. K., comp. The home book of
humorous quotations. New York, Dodd,
Mead [1969] xii, 436 p.   [10.00]
808.87 78-95912
    PN6081 .A14 MRR Ref Desk.

Braude, Jacob Morton, ed. Second
encyclopedia of stories, quotations,
and anecdotes. Englewood Cliffs,
N.J., Prentice-Hall, 1957. 468 p.
808.88* 57-5563
    PN6081 .B67 MRR Alc.

Esar, Evan, 20,000 quips and quotes.
[1st ed.] Garden City, N.Y.,
Doubleday, 1968. lxxvi, 908 p.
[7.95] 808.88/2 68-18096
    PN6081 .E8 MRR Alc.

Esar, Evan, ed. The dictionary of
humorous quotations. New York,
Horizon Press, 1853 [c1949] 270 p.
808.87 53-7005
    PN6084.H8 E8 1953 MRR Alc.

Grizer, Leon, Wit and wisdom in
business; [1st ed.] New York,
Exposition Press [c1972] 509 p.
818/.02 75-146907
    HF5391 .G74 MRR Ref Desk.

Prochnow, Herbert Victor, comp. A
dictionary of wit, wisdom & satire,
[1st ed.] New York, Harper [1962]
vi, 243 p.   808.88 62-9814
    PN6081 .P7 MRR Ref Desk.

Prochnow, Herbert Victor, comp. A
treasury of humorous quotations [1st
ed.] New York, Harper & Row [1968,
c1969] viii, 398 p. [6.95]
808.88/2 68-11822
    PN6083 .P7 MRR Ref Desk.

WIT AND HUMOR, PICTORIAL.
see also American wit and humor

WITCHCRAFT.
see also Occult sciences

Burr, George Lincoln, ed. Narratives
of the witchcraft cases, 1648-1706,
New York, C. Scribner's sons, 1914.
xviii, 467 p. [3.00] 14-9773
    E187.07 B8 MRR Alc.

Summers, Montague, The geography of
witchcraft. Evanston [Ill.]
University Books [1958] 623 p.
133.4 58-8303
    BF1566 .S82 1958 MRR Alc.

WITCHCRAFT--DICTIONARIES--ENGLISH.
Robbins, Rossell Hope, The
encyclopedia of witchcraft and
demonology. New York, Crown
Publishers [1959] 571 p.   133.403
59-9155
    BF1503 .R6 MRR Alc.

WITCHCRAFT--HISTORY.
Summers, Montague, The history of
witchcraft and demonology. London,
Routledge & K. Paul [1965] xv, 353
p.   133.409 66-2254
    BF1566 .S8 1965 MRR Alc.

WITCHCRAFT--NEW ENGLAND.
Burr, George Lincoln, ed. Narratives
of the witchcraft cases, 1648-1706,
New York, C. Scribner's sons, 1914.
xviii, 467 p. [3.00] 14-9773
    E187.07 B8 MRR Alc.

WITNESSES--UNITED STATES.
United States. Congress. House.
Committee on Un-American Activities.
Cumulative index to publications of
the Committee on Un-American
Activities. 1939/41- Washington,
U.S. Govt. Print. Off.   42-13283
    E743.5 .A28 MRR Ref Desk Latest
    edition

WOMAN.
see also Family

WOMAN--BIBLIOGRAPHY.
Wheeler, Helen Rippier. Womanhood
media: current resources about women,
Metuchen, N.J.; Scarecrow Press,
1972. 335 p.   016.30141/2 72-7396

    Z7961 .W48 MRR Alc.

WOMAN--BIOGRAPHY.
Deen, Edith. Great women of the
Christian faith. [1st ed.] New
York, Harper [1959] 428 p.   922 59-
12821
    BR1713 .D4 MRR Alc.

Les Femmes célèbres. [Paris] L.
Mazenod [1960-   v.   61-28952
    CT3202 .F4 MRR Biog.

The World who's who of women. v. 1-
1973- Cambridge, Eng., Melrose
Press. [$20.00] 920.72 74-643503
    HQ1123 .W65 MRR Biog Latest
    edition

WOMAN--BIOGRAPHY--INDEXES.
Ireland, Norma (Olin) Index to women
of the world from ancient to modern
times; Westwood, Mass., F. W. Faxon
Co., 1970. xxcviii, 573 p.
016.92072 75-120841
    Z7963.B6 I73 MRR Biog.

WOMAN--DRESS
see Costume

WOMAN--EMPLOYMENT.
see also Labor supply

see also Occupations

WOMAN--EMPLOYMENT--BIBLIOGRAPHY.
Astin, Helen S., Women; Washington,
Human Service Press [1971] v, 243 p.
[$5.95] 016.3314 76-30266
    Z7963.E7 A86 MRR Alc.

WOMAN--EMPLOYMENT--UNITED STATES.
Council on Economic Priorities.
Guide to corporations; [1st ed.]
Chicago, Swallow Press [1974] iii,
393 p. [$4.95] 301.5/5 73-13212
    HD60.5.U5 C7 1974 MRR Alc.

WOMAN--HEALTH AND HYGIENE.
see also Clothing and dress

see also Hygiene

WOMAN--HISTORY AND CONDITION OF WOMEN--
UNITED STATES--BIBLIOGRAPHY.
Krichmar, Albert. The women's rights
movement in the United States, 1848-
1970; Metuchen, N.J., Scarecrow
Press, 1972. ix, 436 p.
016.30141/2/0973 72-4702
    Z7964.U49 K75 MRR Alc.

WOMAN--HISTORY AND CONDITIONS OF WOMEN.
Sochen, June, Movers and shakers;
[New York] Quadrangle [1973] xi, 320
p.   [$8.95]   301.41/2/0973 73-76290

    HQ1426 .S62 1973 MRR Alc.

WOMAN--QUOTATIONS, MAXIMS, ETC.
Bingham, Colin, comp. The affairs of
women; Sydney, Currawong Publishing
Co. [1969] xi, 400 p. [8.95]
808.88/2 77-453352
    PN6084.W6 B5 MRR Alc.

WOMAN--RIGHTS OF WOMEN.
Flexner, Eleanor, Century of
struggle; Cambridge, Belknap Press
of Harvard University Press, 1959.
384 p.   324.30973 59-9273
    HQ1410 .F6 MRR Alc.

Kraditor, Aileen S., comp. Up from
the pedestal; Chicago, Quadrangle
Books [1968] 372 p. [$8.95]
301.41/2/0973 68-26443
    HQ1410 .K7 MRR Alc.

WOMAN--RIGHTS OF WOMEN--BIBLIOGRAPHY.
Krichmar, Albert. The women's rights
movement in the United States, 1848-
1970; Metuchen, N.J., Scarecrow
Press, 1972. ix, 436 p.
016.30141/2/0973 72-4702
    Z7964.U49 K75 MRR Alc.

WOMAN--SOCIAL AND MORAL QUESTIONS.
Kraditor, Aileen S., comp. Up from
the pedestal; Chicago, Quadrangle
Books [1968] 372 p. [$8.95]
301.41/2/0973 68-26443
    HQ1410 .K7 MRR Alc.

WOMAN--SOCIETIES AND CLUBS.
Croly, Jane (Cunningham) The history
of the women's club movement in
America, New York, H. G. Allen & co.
[c1898] 2 p. l. [ix]-xi, [2] p., 1
l., 1184 p.   c 01-313
    HQ1904 .C94 MRR Alc.

McElroy, Edith Wasson. The complete
book for clubwomen, New York, The
Ronald Press Co. [1957] 296 p.
396.062 57-12271
    HQ1885 .M3 MRR Alc.

Monro,Kate M. The clubwoman's manual
New York, Macmillan, 1957. 202 p.
396.062 57-9542
    HQ1885 .M65 MRR Alc.

WOMAN--SOCIETIES AND CLUBS--DIRECTORIES.
National Council of Women of the
United States. International
directory of women's organizations.
[75th anniversary souvenir ed., 1888-
1963. New York, Research and Action
Associates, 1963] 1 v. (various
pagings)   63-25250
    HQ1883 .N3 MRR Alc.

Wheeler, Helen Rippier. Womanhood
media: current resources about women,
Metuchen, N.J.; Scarecrow Press,
1972. 335 p.   016.30141/2 72-7396

    Z7961 .W48 MRR Alc.

Women's organizations & leaders
directory. 1973- Washington, D.C.,
Today Publications & News Service.
301.41/2/06273 72-86473
    HQ1883 .W64 MRR Ref Desk Latest
    edition

WOMAN--SUFFRAGE--UNITED STATES.
Flexner, Eleanor, Century of
struggle; Cambridge, Belknap Press
of Harvard University Press, 1959.
384 p.   324.30973 59-9273
    HQ1410 .F6 MRR Alc.

WOMEN--BIO-BIBLIOGRAPHY.
[Ungherini, Aglauro] Manual de
bibliographie biographique et
d'iconographie des femmes célèbres
... Turin, L. Roux, 1892. xi p.,
896 columns. z 01-207
    Z7963.B6 U5 MRR Biog.

WOMEN--EMPLOYMENT--UNITED STATES.
Directory of special programs for
minority group members: Career
information services, employment
skills banks, financial aid. 1974-
[Garrett Park, Md., Garrett Park
Press] [$6.95]   331.7/02/02573 73-
93533
    HD5724 .D56 MRR Alc Latest edition

Women's rights almanac. 1974-
Bethesda, Md., Elizabeth Cady Stanton
Pub. Co. [$4.95] 301.41/2/0973 74-
77527
    HQ1406 .W65 MRR Ref Desk Latest
    edition

WOMEN--PORTRAITS.
[Ungherini, Aglauro] Manual de
bibliographie biographique et
d'iconographie des femmes célèbres
... Turin, L. Roux, 1892. xi p.,
896 columns. z 01-207
    Z7963.B6 U5 MRR Biog.

WOMEN--PORTRAITS--INDEXES.
Ireland, Norma (Olin) Index to women
of the world from ancient to modern
times; Westwood, Mass., F. W. Faxon
Co., 1970. xxcviii, 573 p.
016.92072 75-120841
    Z7963.B6 I73 MRR Biog.

WOMEN--SOCIETIES AND CLUBS--DIRECTORIES.
Women's rights almanac. 1974-
Bethesda, Md., Elizabeth Cady Stanton
Pub. Co. [$4.95] 301.41/2/0973 74-
77527
    HQ1406 .W65 MRR Ref Desk Latest
    edition

WOMEN--UNITED STATES--YEARBOOKS.
Women's rights almanac. 1974-
Bethesda, Md., Elizabeth Cady Stanton
Pub. Co. [$4.95] 301.41/2/0973 74-
77527
    HQ1406 .W65 MRR Ref Desk Latest
    edition

WOMEN, NEGRO--BIBLIOGRAPHY.
Williams, Ora, American Black women
in the arts and social sciences: a
bibliographic survey. Metuchen,
N.J., Scarecrow Press, 1973. xix,
141 p.   016.3014/12/0922 73-4560
    Z1361.N39 W56 1973 MRR Biog.

WOMEN ARTISTS--UNITED STATES.
Collins, Jimmie Lee, Women artists
in America; [Chattanooga? Tenn.,
1973] 1 v. (unpaged) [$15.00]
709/.2/2 B 73-163882
    N43 .C64 MRR Biog.

WOMEN AS LAWYERS.
Thomas, Dorothy, pseud., ed. Women
lawyers in the United States. [1st
ed.] New York, Scarecrow Press,
1957. xxx, 747 p.   347.058 57-6625

    LAW MRR Biog.

WOMEN AS POETS.
Two lectures: Leftovers: a care
package Washington, Library of
Congress; [for sale by the Supt. of
Docs., U.S. Govt. Print. Off.] 1973.
iii, 31 p. [$0.35] 811/.009 72-
14401
    Z663.293 .T9 MRR Alc.

WOMEN AUTHORS--BIO-BIBLIOGRAPHIES.
[Ungherini, Aglauro] Manual de
bibliographie biographique et
d'iconographie des femmes célèbres
... Turin, L. Roux, 1892. xi p.,
896 columns.   z 01-207
   Z7963.B6 U5 MRR Biog.

WOMEN IN ART.
[Ungherini, Aglauro] Manual de
bibliographie biographique et
d'iconographie des femmes célèbres
... Turin, L. Roux, 1892. xi p.,
896 columns.   z 01-207
   Z7963.B6 U5 MRR Biog.

WOMEN IN GREAT BRITAIN.
National Council of Women of Great
Britain. Yearbook. 1961/62-
London. 301.41/2/06242 72-623463
   HQ1591.N343 MRR Alc Latest edition

WOMEN IN GREAT BRITAIN--BIOGRAPHY--
DICTIONARIES.
The World who's who of women. v. 1-
1973- Cambridge, Eng., Melrose
Press. [$20.00] 920.72 74-643503
   HQ1123 .W65 MRR Biog Latest
   edition

WOMEN IN ITALY--BIOGRAPHY.
Gastaldi, Mario. Dizionario delle
scrittrici italiane contemporanee
Milano, Gastaldi [1957] 247 p.   59-
30423
   CT3450 .G3 1957 MRR Biog.

WOMEN IN LITERATURE.
see also Characters and
characteristics in literature

WOMEN IN POLITICS.
White, William, North American
reference encyclopedia of women's
liberation. Philadelphia, North
American Pub. Co. [c1972] 194 p.
301.41/2/0973 72-84737
   HQ1154 .W47 MRR Alc.

WOMEN IN POLITICS--UNITED STATES.
Engelbarts, Rudolf. Women in the
United States Congress, 1917-1972:
Littleton, Colo., Libraries
Unlimited, 1974. 184 p.
328.73/092/2 73-93278
   JK1030.A2 E5 MRR Biog.

Women's rights almanac. 1974-
Bethesda, Md., Elizabeth Cady Stanton
Pub. Co. [$4.95] 301.41/2/0973 74-
77527
   HQ1406 .W65 MRR Ref Desk Latest
   edition

WOMEN IN POLITICS--UNITED STATES--
HISTORY.
Chamberlin, Hope. A minority of
members: women in the U.S. Congress.
New York, Praeger Publishers [1973]
ix, 374 p. 328.73/092/2 B 73-
151950
   JK1030.A2 C5 MRR Biog.

WOMEN IN THE BIBLE.
Deen, Edith. All of the women of the
Bible. [1st ed.] New York, Harper
[1955] xxii, 410 p. 220.92 55-
8521
   BS575 .D4 MRR Alc.

WOMEN IN THE UNITED STATES.
Engelbarts, Rudolf. Women in the
United States Congress, 1917-1972:
Littleton, Colo., Libraries
Unlimited, 1974. 184 p.
328.73/092/2 73-93278
   JK1030.A2 E5 MRR Biog.

Ferriss, Abbott Lamoyne, Indicators
of trends in the status of American
women New York, Russell Sage
Foundation, 1971. xx, 451 p.
301.41/2/0973 76-153996
   HQ1420 .F4 MRR Alc.

Flexner, Eleanor, Century of
struggle; Cambridge, Belknap Press
of Harvard University Press, 1959.
384 p. 324.30973 59-9273
   HQ1410 .F6 MRR Alc.

Sochen, June, Movers and shakers;
[New York] Quadrangle [1973] xi, 320
p. [$8.95] 301.41/2/0973 73-76290
   HQ1426 .S62 1973 MRR Alc.

United States. President's Commission
on the Status of Women. American
women; New York, Scribner [1965]
xi, 274 p.   301.4120973 65-21367
   HQ1420 .A52 1965 MRR Alc.

WOMEN IN THE UNITED STATES--ADDRESSES,
ESSAYS, LECTURES.
White, William, North American
reference encyclopedia of women's
liberation. Philadelphia, North
American Pub. Co. [c1972] 194 p.
301.41/2/0973 72-84737
   HQ1154 .W47 MRR Alc.

WOMEN IN THE UNITED STATES--
BIBLIOGRAPHY.
Krichmar, Albert. The women's rights
movement in the United States, 1848-
1970; Metuchen, N.J., Scarecrow
Press, 1972. ix, 436 p.
016.30141/2/0973 72-4702
   Z7964.U49 K75 MRR Alc.

Leonard, Eugenie (Andruss) The
American woman in Colonial and
Revolutionary times, 1565-1800;
Philadelphia, University of
Pennsylvania Press [1962] 169 p.
016.3960973 61-6949
   Z7964.U49 L4 MRR Alc.

Wheeler, Helen Rippier. Womanhood
media: current resources about women.
Metuchen, N.J., Scarecrow Press,
1972. 335 p.   016.30141/2 72-7396

   Z7961 .W48 MRR Alc.

WOMEN IN THE UNITED STATES--BIOGRAPHY.
Chamberlin, Hope. A minority of
members: women in the U.S. Congress.
New York, Praeger Publishers [1973]
ix, 374 p. 328.73/092/2 B 73-
151950
   JK1030.A2 C5 MRR Biog.

Dannett, Sylvia G. L., Profiles of
Negro womanhood. [1st ed.] Yonkers,
N.Y., Educational Heritage [1964-66]
2 v. 920.7 64-25013
   E185.96 .D25 MRR Alc.

Foremost women in communications;
New York, Foremost Americans Pub.
Corp. [1970] xvii, 788 p.
001.5/0922 79-125946
   P92.5.A1 F6 MRR Biog.

Ireland, Norma (Olin) Index to women
of the world from ancient to modern
times; Westwood, Mass., F. W. Faxon
Co., 1970. xxcviii, 573 p.
016.92072 75-120841
   Z7963.B6 I73 MRR Biog.

Notable American women, 1607-1950;
Cambridge, Mass., Belknap Press of
Harvard University Press, 1971. 3 v.
920.72/0973 76-152274
   CT3260 .N57 MRR Biog.

Outstanding young women of America.
1965- Washington, D.C., Outstanding
young women of America. 66-3374
   CT3260 .O75 MRR Biog Latest
   edition

Ross, Ishbel, Sons of Adam,
daughters of Eve. [1st ed.] New
York, Harper & Row [1969] viii, 340
p. [7.95] 301.41/2/0922 67-13691

   HQ1412 .R6 MRR Alc.

Willard, Frances Elizabeth, ed. A
woman of the century, Detroit, Gale
Research Co., 1967. 812 p. 920.073
67-21361
   E176 .W691 1967 MRR Biog.

Women's organizations & leaders
directory. 1973- Washington, D.C.,
Today Publications & News Service.
301.41/2/06273 72-86473
   HQ1883 .W64 MRR Ref Desk Latest
   edition

WOMEN IN THE UNITED STATES--BIOGRAPHY--
DICTIONARIES.
Collins, Jimmie Lee, Women artists
in America; [Chattanooga? Tenn.,
1973] 1 v. (unpaged) [$15.00]
709/.2/2 B 73-163882
   N43 .C64 MRR Biog.

Thomas, Dorothy, pseud., ed. Women
lawyers in the United States. [1st
ed.] New York, Scarecrow Press,
1957. xxx, 747 p.   347.058 57-6625

   LAW MRR Biog.

Who's who of American women. 6th
ed.; 1970/71- Chicago, Marquis Who's
Who, Inc. 920.72/0973 72-623128
   E176 .W647 MRR Biog Latest edition

The World who's who of women. v. 1-
1973- Cambridge, Eng., Melrose
Press. [$20.00] 920.72 74-643503
   HQ1123 .W65 MRR Biog Latest
   edition

WOMEN IN THE UNITED STATES--BIOGRAPHY--
INDEXES.
Krichmar, Albert. The women's rights
movement in the United States, 1848-
1970; Metuchen, N.J., Scarecrow
Press, 1972. ix, 436 p.
016.30141/2/0973 72-4702
   Z7964.U49 K75 MRR Alc.

WOMEN IN THE UNITES STATES--HISTORY.
Kraditor, Aileen S., comp. Up from
the pedestal; Chicago, Quadrangle
Books [1968] 372 p. [$8.95]
301.41/2/0973 68-26443
   HQ1410 .K7 MRR Alc.

WOMEN IN WASHINGTON, D.C.--BIOGRAPHY.
The Gold book of Washington's most
distinguished women, 1966. [1st ed.]
Washington, R. Moore [c1966] 155 p.
920.09753 66-21176
   F193 .G6 MRR Biog.

WOMEN'S LIBERATION MOVEMENT.
White, William, North American
reference encyclopedia of women's
liberation. Philadelphia, North
American Pub. Co. [c1972] 194 p.
301.41/2/0973 72-84737
   HQ1154 .W47 MRR Alc.

WOMEN'S LIBERATION MOVEMENT--
DIRECTORIES.
Women's organizations & leaders
directory. 1973- Washington, D.C.,
Today Publications & News Service.
301.41/2/06273 72-86473
   HQ1883 .W64 MRR Ref Desk Latest
   edition

WOMEN'S LIBERATION MOVEMENT--
INFORMATION SERVICES--UNITED STATES.
The New woman's survival catalog.
New York, Coward, McCann & Geoghegan
[1973] 223 p. [$5.00]
016.30141/2/0973 73-85371
   HQ1426 .N48 1973 MRR Alc.

WOMEN'S LIBERATION MOVEMENT--
PERIODICALS--BIBLIOGRAPHY.
Krichmar, Albert. The women's rights
movement in the United States, 1848-
1970; Metuchen, N.J., Scarecrow
Press, 1972. ix, 436 p.
016.30141/2/0973 72-4702
   Z7964.U49 K75 MRR Alc.

WOMEN'S LIBERATION MOVEMENT--UNITED
STATES.
Sochen, June, Movers and shakers;
[New York] Quadrangle [1973] xi, 320
p. [$8.95] 301.41/2/0973 73-76290

   HQ1426 .S62 1973 MRR Alc.

WOMEN'S LIBERATION MOVEMENT--UNITED
STATES--BIBLIOGRAPHY.
The New woman's survival catalog.
New York, Coward, McCann & Geoghegan
[1973] 223 p. [$5.00]
016.30141/2/0973 73-85371
   HQ1426 .N48 1973 MRR Alc.

WOMEN'S RIGHTS--UNITED STATES--
YEARBOOKS.
Women's rights almanac. 1974-
Bethesda, Md., Elizabeth Cady Stanton
Pub. Co. [$4.95] 301.41/2/0973 74-
77527
   HQ1406 .W65 MRR Ref Desk Latest
   edition

WOOD.
see also Forests and forestry

see also Timber

Hough, Romeyn Beck, Hough's
encyclopedia of American woods,
[1st ed.] New York, R. Speller, 1957-
v. 634.98 57-10592
   SD536 .H832 MRR Alc.

Rendle, B. J. World timbers;
London, E. Benn, 1969-70. 3 v.
[£5.25 ($15.25) (v. 1)] 674 74-
398920
   SD536 .R4 MRR Alc.

WOOD--IDENTIFICATION.
Hough, Romeyn Beck, Hough's
encyclopedia of American woods,
[1st ed.] New York, R. Speller, 1957-
v. 634.98 57-10592
   SD536 .H832 MRR Alc.

WOOD-ENGRAVINGS--BELGIUM--CATALOGS.
Polain, Louis, Catalogue des livres
imprimes au quinzieme siecle des
bibliotheques de Belgique.
Bruxelles, Pour la Société des
bibliophiles & iconophiles de
Belgique, 1932. 4 v. 016.083 33-
18424
   Z240 .P76 MRR Alc.

WOOD-ENGRAVINGS--UNITED STATES--
CATALOGS.
Princeton University. Library. Early
American book illustrators and wood
engravers, 1670-1870; Princeton,
N.J., 1958. xlvii, 265 p. 761.2084
58-9784
   Z1023 .P9 1958 MRR Alc.

WOOD FINISHING.
Scharff, Robert. Complete book of
wood finishing. 2d ed. New York,
McGraw-Hill [1974] 370 p.
[$9.95] 684/.084 73-22239
   TT325 .S26 1974 MRR Alc.

WOOD-PULP INDUSTRY.
see also Paper making and trade

WOOD-PULP INDUSTRY--DIRECTORIES.
Post's pulp & paper directory. San
Francisco [etc.] M. Freeman
Publications [etc.] 03-6150
   TS1088 .P85 Sci RR Latest edition
   / MRR Alc Latest edition

WOOD TECHNOLOGY.
United States. Dept. of Agriculture.
Trees. Washington, U.S. Govt. Print.
Off. [1949] xiv, 944 p.   634.90973
agr55-2
  S21 .A35 1949 MRR Alc.

WOOD-USING INDUSTRIES--DICTIONARIES--POLYGLOT.
Elsevier's wood dictionary in seven
languages: Amsterdam, New York,
Elsevier Pub. Co., 1964- v.
634.903 64-14178
  SD431 .E4 MRR Alc.

WOOD-USING INDUSTRIES--FRANCE--DIRECTORIES.
France-bois. [Paris, Éditions A. R.
de Chabassol, 674.058 46-39212
  Fondé en 1822.
  HD9762.3 .F7 MRR Alc Latest
    edition

WOOD-USING INDUSTRIES--UNITED STATES--DIRECTORIES.
Directory of the forest products
industry. San Francisco [etc.] M.
Freeman Publications [etc.] 21-10771
  TS803 .D5 Sci RR Latest edition /
  MRR Alc Latest edition

Dun and Bradstreet, inc. Reference
book: lumber and wood products
industries. [spring] 1968- New
York. 338.7/67/4002573 72-489
  HD9753 .D85 MRR Alc Latest edition

Lumber requirements of factory
consumers in the United States &
Canada. 10th- ed.; 1959- Memphis,
Lumber Requirements Co.
338.1/7/490873 72-622539
  HD9752.L8 MRR Alc Latest edition

WOODWORK.
Adams, Jeannette T. Complete
woodworking handbook, New York, Arco
Pub. Co. [1960] 568 p. 684.8 60-8584
  TT180 .A17 MRR Alc.

WOODWORKERS.
see also Cabinet-workers

WOODWORKING INDUSTRIES--UNITED STATES--DIRECTORIES.
Woodworking directory & handbook.
[Wheaton, Ill., Hitchcock Pub. Co.]
684/.08/02573 72-620600
  TS842 .H5 MRR Alc Latest edition

WOODY PLANTS.
Taylor, Norman, The guide to garden
shrubs and trees (including woody
vines), Boston, Houghton Mifflin,
1965. xxiii, 450 p. 635.97 64-10266
  SB435 .T37 MRR Alc.

WOODY PLANTS--DICTIONARIES--POLYGLOT.
Amelinckx, Frans. Lexicon
dendrologicum Antwerpen, De Sikkel,
1955. xvi, 508 p.   582.1603 56-58034
  SB435 .A6 MRR Alc.

WOODY PLANTS--SOUTHERN STATES.
Dean, Blanche Evans. Trees and
shrubs in the heart of Dixie. Rev.
ed. Birmingham, Ala., Southern
University Press, 1968. xvi, 246 p.
[$7.50] 582/.15/0975 68-57837
  QK484.S88 D4 1968 MRR Alc.

WOODY PLANTS--UNITED STATES.
Grimm, William Carey. Home guide to
trees, shrubs, and wild flowers.
[Harrisburg, Pa.] Stackpole Books
[1970] 320 p. [9.95] 582/.09/73
76-100348
  QK482 .G734 MRR Alc.

WOOL TRADE AND INDUSTRY--DIRECTORIES.
Skinner's wool trade directory of the
world. 1927- Croydon, Eng. [etc.]
T. Skinner. 667.3058 28-14741
  HD9890.3 .S53 MRR Alc Latest
    edition

WOOLLEY, ROBERT WICKLIFF, 1871-1958--BIBLIOGRAPHY.
United States. Library of Congress.
Manuscript Division. Robert W.
Woolley; a register of his papers in
the Library of Congress. Washington,
1960. 21 l.   012 60-60083
  Z663.34 .W6 MRR Alc.

WORD GAMES--GLOSSARIES, VOCABULARIES, ETC.
Elliott, Iris E., Instant word
finder, Philadelphia, Lithographed
by Braceland Bros. [1959] 352 p.
423 59-15222
  PE1680 .E55 MRR Alc.

English word book of over 106,000
words; [Seattle, Pilot Press, 1963]
xx, 829 p.   65-3497
  GV1507.W9 E5 MRR Alc.

WORD PORTRAITS.
Uden, Grant, comp. They looked like
this; New York, Barnes & Noble
[1966] viii, 306 p. 920.042 66-7971
  CT775 .U3 MRR Alc.

WORDS, NEW--ENGLISH.
Hogan, Homer. Dictionary of American
synonyms, New York, Philosophical
Library [1956] ix, 388 p. 424 56-14013
  PE1591 .H6 MRR Alc.

Major, Clarence. Dictionary of Afro-
American slang. [1st ed.] New York,
International Publishers [1970] 127
p. [$5.95] 427.09 79-130863
  PE3727.N4 M3 MRR Alc.

Mueller, Robert Kirk. Buzzwords;
New York, Van Nostrand Reinhold Co.
[1974] xvii, 172 p. 658.4/003 74-1403
  HD19 .M75 MRR Alc.

Pei, Mario Andrew, Double-speak in
America, New York, Hawthorn Books
[1973] 216 p. [$6.95]   422 78-39894
  PE1585 .P38 MRR Alc.

Pei, Mario Andrew, Words in sheep's
clothing [1st ed.] New York,
Hawthorn Books [1969] 248 p. [6.95]
422 69-20348
  PE1585 .P4 1969 MRR Alc.

Versand, Kenneth. Polyglot's
lexicon, 1943-1966. New York, Links
[c1973] 468 p. [$12.50] 423 72-94094
  PE1630 .V4 MRR Alc.

Young, Kenn W. Naz's underground
dictionary; Vancouver, Wash. [Naz
Enterprises, 1973] vi, 67 p.
[$2.00] 427/.9/73 74-156957
  PE3727.N3 Y6 MRR Alc.

WORDS, NEW--ENGLISH--DICTIONARIES.
The Barnhart dictionary of new
English since 1963. [1st ed.]
Bronxville, N.Y., Barnhart/Harper &
Row [1973] 512 p.   423 73-712
  PE1630 .B3 MRR Ref Desk.

WORDS, NEW--FRENCH.
Rheims, Maurice. Dictionnaire des
mots sauvages Paris, Larousse, 1969.
605 p. [45.00]   443 79-413814
  PC2460 .R45 MRR Alc.

WORDS, NEW--HINDI.
Raghu Vira. A comprehensive English-
Hindi dictionary of governmental &
educational words & phrases ...
[Nagpur, Lokesh Chandra,
International Academy of Indian
Culture, 1955] 189, 1579 p.
491.4332 56-19893
  PK1937 .R3 MRR Alc.

WORDS, STOCK OF
see Vocabulary

WORDSWORTH, WILLIAM, 1770-1850--CONCORDANCES.
Cooper, Lane, ed. A concordance to
the poems of William Wordsworth,
London, Smith, Elder & co., 1911.
xiii, 1136 p.   11-28703
  PR5880 .C6 MRR Alc.

WORK.
see also Labor and laboring classes

WORK EXPERIENCE
see Vocational education

WORKERS
see Labor and laboring classes

WORKING-MEN'S ASSOCIATIONS
see Trade-unions

WORKSHOP RECEIPTS.
Swezey, Kenneth M. Formulas,
methods, tips, and data for home and
workshop, New York, Popular Science
Pub. Co. [1969] xvii, 691 p. [7.95]
745.5/02/02 68-54377
  TT153 .S88 MRR Alc.

WORLD HEALTH ORGANIZATION--BIBLIOGRAPHY.
World Health Organization.
Publications; 1947/57- Geneva. 58-4871
  Z6660 .W57 MRR Alc Full set

WORLD HISTORY.
see also Geography

see also History, Modern

Balland, Robert, ed. Histoire
universelle Quillet Paris, A.
Quillet, 1955. 2 v.   55-36261
  D20 .B28 MRR Alc.

Garraty, John Arthur, The Columbia
history of the world. [1st ed.] New
York, Harper & Row [1972] xx, 1237
p. [$14.79 (lib. ed.)]   909 76-181621
  D21 .G28 MRR Alc.

Langer, William Leonard, An
encyclopedia of world history; 5th
ed., rev. and enl. Boston, Houghton
Mifflin 1972. xxxix, 1569 p.
[$17.50] 902/.02 72-186219
  D21 .L27 1972 MRR Ref Desk.

McNeill, William Hardy, A world
history New York, Oxford University
Press, 1967. xii, 478 p. 909 66-22265
  D21 .M32 MRR Alc.

Ploetz, Karl Julius, Ploetz' manual
of universal history, Boston, New
York [etc.] Houghton Mifflin company
[c1933] xvii, [1], 766, lxxxix p.
909 902 35-13687
  D21 .P76 1933 MRR Alc.

Reither, Joseph. World history at a
glance. New rev. ed. New York,
Dolphin Books [1965] xxii,495 p.
909 65-12275
  D21 .R38 1965 MRR Alc.

Wells, Herbert George, The outline
of history, Garden City, N.Y.,
Garden City Books [1961] xvii, 1013
p.   909 61-5985
  D21 .W4 1961 MRR Alc.

WORLD HISTORY--BIBLIOGRAPHY.
List of doctoral dissertations in
history now in progress at
universities in the United States.
Washington [etc.] 016.9 10-12162
  Z5055.U49 L7 MRR Ref Desk Partial
    set

WORLD HISTORY--BIBLIOGRAPHY--CATALOGS.
Foreign Relations Library. Catalog
of the Foreign Relations Library.
Boston, G. K. Hall, 1969. 9 v.
016.327 75-6133
  Z6209 .F656 MRR Alc (Dk 33)

WORLD HISTORY--CHRONOLOGY.
Little, Charles Eugene, Cyclopedia
of classified dates with an
exhaustive index. Detroit, Gale
Research Co., 1967. vii, 1454 p.
902/.02 66-27839
  D9 .L7 1967 MRR Alc.

WORLD HISTORY--OUTLINES, SYLLABI, ETC.
Harper encyclopedia of the modern
world; [1st ed.] New York, Harper &
Row [1970] xxxii, 1271 p. [$17.50]
903 73-81879
  D205 .H35 1970 MRR Ref Desk.

Ploetz, Karl Julius, Ploetz' manual
of universal history, Boston, New
York [etc.] Houghton Mifflin company
[c1933] xvii, [1], 766, lxxxix p.
909 902 35-13687
  D21 .P76 1933 MRR Alc.

WORLD HOCKEY ASSOCIATION.
Hollander, Zander. The complete
encyclopedia of ice hockey : Rev.
ed. Englewood Cliffs, N.J. :
Prentice-Hall, [1974] xi, 702 p. :
[$14.95] 796.9/62/03 73-15019
  GV847.8.N3 H6 1974 MRR Alc.

WORLD LITERATURE
see Literature

WORLD POLITICS.
Documents on international affairs.
1928- London, New York [etc.] Oxford
University Press. 341.08 30-10914
  D442 .S82 MRR Alc Full set

Toscano, Mario. The history of
treaties and international politics.
Baltimore, John Hopkins Press, 1966-
v.   327.209 66-15525
  D217 .T613 MRR Alc.

WORLD POLITICS--20TH CENTURY.
Grenville, John Ashley Soames. The
major international treaties, 1914-
1973; New York, Stein and Day [1974]
xxix, 575 p. [$25.00] 341/.026
75-163352
  JX171 .G74 MRR Alc.

Warren, Sidney, The President as
world leader. [1st ed.]
Philadelphia, Lippincott [1964] xii,
480 p.   327.73 64-22183
  E744 .W295 MRR Alc.

WORLD POLITICS--20TH CENTURY--DICTIONARIES.
Laqueur, Walter Ze'ev, A dictionary
of politics / Rev. ed. New York :
Free Press, 1974, c1973. 565 p. ;
[$14.95] 320.9/04 74-9232
  D419 .L36 1974 MRR Alc.

WORLD POLITICS--1919-1932.
The United States in world affairs.
1931- New York, Simon & Schuster
[etc.] 32-26065
  E744 .U66 MRR Alc Full set

WORLD POLITICS--1933-1945.
Gantenbein, James Watson, ed.
Documentary background of World War
II, 1931-1941. New York, Columbia
Univ. Press, 1948. xxxiii, 1122 p.
940.52 48-11573
  D735 .G25 MRR Alc.

WORLD POLITICS--1933-1945. (Cont.)
United States. Library of Congress.
Legislative reference service.
Events leading up to world war II.
Washington, U.S. Govt. print. off.,
1944. iii, 421 p.   940.5302 44-
41776
   D743.5 .U653 MRR Alc.

WORLD POLITICS--1945-
Crabb, Cecil Van Meter. American
foreign policy in the nuclear age 3d
ed. New York, Harper & Row [1972]
x, 528 p.   327.73 71-168366
   E744 .C793 1972 MRR Alc.

Friedmann, Wolfgang Gaston, An
introduction to world politics, 5th
ed. London, Macmillan; New York, St.
Martin's Press, 1965. xii, 497 p.
327.1 62-17721
   D843 .F75 1965 MRR Alc.

Gross, Franz B., ed. The United
States and the United Nations,
Norman, University of Oklahoma Press
[1964] x, 356 p.   341.13973 64-
20766
   JX1977.2.U5 G7 MRR Alc.

**WORLD POLITICS--1945- --ADDRESSES,
ESSAYS, LECTURES.**
Kertesz, Stephen Denis, ed. American
diplomacy in a new era. Notre Dame,
Ind.] University of Notre Dame Press,
1961. xi, 601 p.   327.73 61-8466
   E744 .K4 MRR Alc.

WORLD POLITICS--1945- --STATISTICS.
Taylor, Charles Lewis. World
handbook of political and social
indicators. 2d ed. New Haven, Yale
University Press, 1972. xiv, 443 p.
[$15.00]   301/.01/8 70-179479
   HN15 .T37 1972 MRR Alc.

WORLD POLITICS--1945- --YEARBOOKS.
Historic documents. 1972-
[Washington] Congressional Quarterly,
inc. [$25.00]   917.3/03/9205 72-
97888
   E839.5 .H57 MRR Alc Full set

WORLD POLITICS--1955-
Johnson, Lyndon Baines, Pres. U.S.,
A time for action; [1st ed.] New
York, Atheneum Publishers, 1964. xv,
183 p.   308.1 64-16425
   E742.5 .J6 MRR Alc.

Kennedy, John Fitzgerald, Pres. U.S.,
Kennedy and the press; New York,
Crowell [1965] 555 p.   973.922 65-
12271
   E841 .K37 MRR Alc.

**WORLD POLITICS--1965- --HANDBOOKS,
MANUALS, ETC.**
The World this year. 1971- New
York, Simon and Schuster. 320.9/046
76-649587
   JF37 .W65 MRR Ref Desk Latest
   edition

WORLD POLITICS--BIBLIOGRAPHY.
Arms control & disarmament. v. 1-
winter 1964/65-   [Washington, For
sale by the Superintendent of
Documents, U.S. Govt. Print. Off.]
64-62746
   Z663.28 .A23 MRR Alc MRR Alc Full
   set

The Foreign affairs 50-year
bibliography; New York, Published
for the Council on Foreign Relations
by R. R. Bowker Co., 1972. xxviii,
936 p.   016.327/09/04 75-163904
   Z6461 .F62 MRR Alc.

Foreign affairs bibliography;
1919/32-1952/62. New York, Published
for the Council on Foreign Relations
by R. R. Bowker [etc.] 016.327
[016.9] 33-7094
   Z6463 .F73 MRR Alc Full set

Larson, Arthur D. National security
affairs: Detroit, Gale Research Co.,
[1973] 411 p.   016.35503/3/0973 70-
184013
   Z1215 .L37 MRR Alc.

Royal Institute of International
Affairs. Library. Index to
periodical articles 1950-1964 in the
Library of the Royal Institute of
International Affairs. Boston, G. K.
Hall, 1964. 2 v.   65-9436
   AI3 .R6 MRR Alc.

Royal Institute of International
Affairs. Library. Index to
periodical articles 1965-1972 in the
Library of the Royal Institute of
International Affairs. Boston, G. K.
Hall, 1973. xxix, 879 p.   016.05
73-166442
   AI3 .R6 1973 MRR Alc.

Universal Reference System.
International affairs; [2d ed.]
Princeton, N.J., Princeton Research
Pub. Co. [1969] xx, 1206 p.
016.327 68-57819
   Z7161 .U64 vol. 1 MRR Alc.

WORLD POLITICS--BIBLIOGRAPHY--CATALOGS.
Foreign Relations Library. Catalog
of the Foreign Relations Library.
Boston, G. K. Hall, 1969. 9 v.
016.327 75-6133
   Z6209 .F656 MRR Alc (Dk 33)

Stuttgart. Bibliothek für
Zeitgeschichte. Bibliothek für
Zeitgeschichte--Weltkriegsbücherei,
Stuttgart; systematischer Katalog.
Boston, G. K. Hall, 1968. 20 v.   74-
225445
   Z6204 .S8 1968 MRR Alc (Dk 33)

WORLD POLITICS--CONGRESSES.
Eubank, Keith. The summit
conferences, 1919-1960. [1st ed.]
Norman, University of Oklahoma Press
[1966] xi, 225 p.   327.1 66-22711
   D455 .E9 MRR Alc.

WORLD POLITICS--DICTIONARIES.
Elliott, Florence. A dictionary of
politics. 6th ed. Harmondsworth,
Penguin, 1971. 480 p. [10/-]
320/.03 72-186214
   D419 .E4 1971 MRR Alc.

Theimer, Walter. An encyclopedia of
modern world politics. New York,
Rinehart [1950] 696 p.   940.5503
50-5768
   D419 .T48 MRR Alc.

White, Wilbur Wallace, White's
Political dictionary, Cleveland,
World Pub. Co. [1947] 378 p.   320.3
47-30518
   D419 .W5 MRR Alc.

WORLD POLITICS--PERIODICALS--INDEXES.
International political science
abstracts. v. 1- 1951- Oxford
[etc.] Basil Blackwell [etc.] 320.82
54-3623
   JA36 .I5 MRR Alc Full set

WORLD POLITICS--YEARBOOKS.
The Book of the world. 1971- New
York, Collier Books [etc.] 910/.5
77-617076
   G1 .B65 MRR Ref Desk Latest
   edition

The Statesman's year-book; [1st]-
1864- London, Macmillan; New York,
St. Martin's Press [etc.] 04-3776
   JA51 .S7 MRR Ref Desk Latest
   edition / MRR Ref Desk Latest
   edition

The Year book of world affairs. v. 1-
1947- London, Stevens.   341.058
47-29156
   JX21 .Y4 MRR Alc Latest edition

WORLD WAR, 1914-1918
see European War, 1914-1918

WORLD WAR, 1939-45--CAMPAIGNS.
United States. Dept. of the Army.
Office of Military History. Combat
chronicle, [Washington, 1948?] 109
l.   940.541273 49-45651
   D769.29 .A52 MRR Ref Desk.

WORLD WAR, 1939-1945.
Benns, Frank Lee, Europe, 1939 to
the present Rev. ed. New York,
Appleton-Century-Crofts [1971] xi,
552 p.   940.55 71-152376
   D1051 .B4 1971 MRR Alc.

Calvocoressi, Peter. Total war;
[1st American ed.] [New York]
Pantheon Books [1972] xiii, 959 p.
[$15.00] 940.53 72-3402
   D743 .C24 1972 MRR Alc.

Churchill, Winston Leonard Spencer,
Sir, The Second World War. Boston,
Published in association with the
Cooperation Pub. Co. [by] Houghton
Mifflin, 1948-53. 6 v. 940.53 48-
2880
   D743 .C47 MRR Alc.

Collier, Basil. A short history of
the Second World War. London,
Collins, 1967. 3-638 p. [63/-]
940.54 67-93912
   D743 .C533 MRR Alc.

Flower, Desmond, ed. The war, 1939-
1945, London, Cassell [1960] 1120
p.   940.53 60-3389
   D743 .F55 MRR Alc.

**WORLD WAR, 1939-1945--AERIAL
OPERATIONS, AMERICAN.**
United States. Air Force. USAF
Historical Division. Air Force
combat units of World War II. New
York, F. Watts [196-] xi, 506 p.
940.544973 63-16919
   D790 .A47 1960z MRR Alc.

United States. Air Force. USAF
Historical Division. The Army Air
Forces in World War II. [Chicago]
University of Chicago Press [1948-58]
7 v.   940.544973 48-3657
   D790 .A47 MRR Alc.

**WORLD WAR, 1939-1945--AMPHIBIOUS
OPERATIONS.**
Isely, Jeter Allen. The U.S. Marines
and amphibious war; Princeton,
Princeton University Press, 1951.
vii, 636 p.   940.545 51-9463
   D769.45 .I7 MRR Alc.

WORLD WAR, 1939-1945--BIBLIOGRAPHY.
The Two world wars; selective
bibliography. Oxford, New York,
Pergamon Press [1965, c1964] 246 p.
016.9403 65-6499
   Z6207.E8 T85 1965 MRR Alc.

Ziegler, Janet, World War II: books
in English, 1945-65. Stanford,
Calif., Hoover Institution Press
[1971] xvii, 223 p.   016.94053 74-
155297
   Z6207.W8 Z5 MRR Alc.

**WORLD WAR, 1939-1945--BIBLIOGRAPHY--
CATALOGS.**
Stuttgart. Bibliothek für
Zeitgeschichte. Bibliothek für
Zeitgeschichte--Weltkriegsbücherei,
Stuttgart:alphabetischer Katalog.
Boston, G. K. Hall, 1968. 11 v.   74-
223844
   Z6209 .S85 1968 MRR Alc (Dk 33)

Stuttgart. Bibliothek für
Zeitgeschichte. Bibliothek für
Zeitgeschichte--Weltkriegsbücherei,
Stuttgart; systematischer Katalog.
Boston, G. K. Hall, 1968. 20 v.   74-
225445
   Z6204 .S8 1968 MRR Alc (Dk 33)

**WORLD WAR, 1939-1945--BIOGRAPHY--
DICTIONARIES.**
Tunney, Christopher, A biographical
dictionary of World War II. London,
Dent, 1972. viii, 216 p. [£3.50]
940.53/092/2 72-193297
   D736 .T78 MRR Biog.

WORLD WAR, 1939-1945--CAMPAIGNS.
Baldwin, Hanson Weightman, Battles
lost and won; [1st ed.] New York,
Harper & Row [1966] xi, 532 p.
940.542 66-20724
   D743 .B34 MRR Alc.

United States. Dept. of the Army.
Office of Military History. Command
decisions. Washington, 1960. viii,
565 p.   940.542 59-60007
   D743 .U44 1960 MRR Alc.

United States. Military Academy, West
Point. Dept. of Military Art and
Engineering. A military history of
World War II; West Point, United
States Military Academy, 1953. 2 v.
and atlas ([3] l., 168 l. of col.
maps, 6 col. diagrs.) 940.542 53-
37497
   D743 .U465 MRR Alc.

**WORLD WAR, 1939-1945--CASUALTIES
(STATISTICS, ETC.)**
Baldwin, Hanson Weightman, Battles
lost and won; [1st ed.] New York,
Harper & Row [1966] xi, 532 p.
940.542 66-20724
   D743 .B34 MRR Alc.

Beebe, Gilbert Wheeler, Battle
casualties: Springfield, Ill.,
Thomas [1952] xxiii, 277 p.
940.5475 52-11968
   D805.U5 B4 MRR Alc.

United States. Adjutant General's
Office. Army battle casualties and
nonbattle deaths in World War II.
[Washington, Dept. of the Army, 1953]
118 p. (chiefly tables) 940.541273
53-37014
   D797.U6 A52 MRR Alc.

WORLD WAR, 1939-1945--CAUSES.
McSherry, James E. Stalin, Hitler,
and Europe, Cleveland, World Pub.
Co. [1968- v.   940.531/12 67-
31018
   D741 .M24 MRR Alc.

Taylor, Alan John Percivale, The
origins of the Second World War.
[1st American ed.] New York,
Atheneum, 1962 [c1961] 296 p.
940.5311 62-7543
   D741 .T34 1962 MRR Alc.

WORLD WAR, 1939-1945--CHRONOLOGY.
United States. Library of Congress.
Legislative reference service.
Events leading up to world war II.
Washington, U.S. Govt. print. off.,
1944. iii, 421 p.   940.5302 44-
41776
   D743.5 .U653 MRR Alc.

United States. Naval History
Division. United States naval
chronology, World War II.
Washington, U.S. Govt. Print. Off.,
1955. vi, 214 p.   940.545973 55-
61999
   D743.5 .U63 MRR Alc.

WORLD WAR, 1939-1945-- (Cont.)
Williams, Mary H., comp. Chronology, 1941-1945. Washington, Office of the Chief of Military History, Dept. of the Army, 1960. 660 p. 940.541273 59-60002
D769 .A533 vol. 8, pt. 5 MRR Alc.

WORLD WAR, 1939-1945--DICTIONARIES.
Greet, William Cabell, World words, 2d ed., rev. and enl. New York, Columbia Univ. Press, 1948. liii, 608 p. 411.5 48-6140
PE1660 .G7 1948 MRR Alc.

WORLD WAR, 1939-1945--FINANCE--UNITED STATES.
Tax Foundation, New York. Facts and figures on government finance. 1941- New York. 336.73 44-7109
HJ257 .T25 MRR Alc Latest edition / MRR Ref Desk Latest edition

WORLD WAR, 1939-1945--LANGUAGE (NEW WORDS, SLANG, ETC.)
Partridge, Eric, A dictionary of Forces' slang, 1939-1945, Freeport, N.Y., Books for Libraries Press [1970] xi, 212 p. 427.09 75-117899
PE3727.S7 P25 1970 MRR Alc.

Ruffner, Frederick G., ed. Code names dictionary; Detroit, Gale Research Co. [1963] 555 p. 423 63-21847
PE1693 .R9 MRR Alc.

Taylor, Anna Marjorie, The language of World War II; Rev. and enl. ed. New York, H. W. Wilson Co., 1948. 265 p. 940.53014 48-8265
PE3727.S7 T3 1948 MRR Alc.

WORLD WAR, 1939-1945--NAVAL OPERATIONS.
Kafka, Roger, ed. Warships of the world. Victory ed. New York, Cornell maritime press [1946] x p., 1 l., 1167 p. 623.825 47-119
VA40 .K3 1846 MRR Alc.

WORLD WAR, 1939-1945--NAVAL OPERATIONS, AMERICAN.
Morison, Samuel Eliot, History of United States naval operations in World War II. [1st ed.] Boston, Little, Brown, 1947-62. 15 v. 940.545973 47-1571
D773 .M6 MRR Alc.

Sawyer, Leonard Arthur. Victory ships and tankers; Cambridge, Md., Cornell Maritime Press [1974] 230 p. 387.2/45/0873 73-22561
VM391 .S39 1974 MRR Alc.

United States. Naval History Division. United States naval chronology, World War II. Washington, U.S. Govt. Print. Off., 1955. v1, 214 p. 940.545973 55-61999
D743.5 .U63 MRR Alc.

WORLD WAR, 1939-1945--NAVAL OPERATIONS, JAPANESE.
Watts, Anthony John. Japanese warships of World War II. Garden City, N.Y., Doubleday [1967] 400 p. 623.82/5/0952 67-23821
VA653 .W33 1967 MRR Alc.

WORLD WAR, 1939-1945--NEGROES.
Lee, Ulysses Grant. The employment of Negro troops, Washington, Office of the Chief of Military History, United States Army; [for sale by the Superintendent of Documents, U.S. Govt. Print. Off.] 1966. xix, 740 p. 940.5403 66-60003
D810.N4 L4 MRR Alc.

WORLD WAR, 1939-1945--PEACE.
Leiss, Amelia Catherine, ed. European peace treaties after World War II; [Boston] World Peace Foundation [1954] xvi, 341 p. 940.53141 54-14902
D814 .L4 MRR Alc.

WORLD WAR, 1939-1945--PERSONAL NARRATIVES.
Flower, Desmond, ed. The war, 1939-1945, London, Cassell [1960] 1120 p. 940.53 60-3389
D743 .F55 MRR Alc.

WORLD WAR, 1939-1945--RECONSTRUCTION
see Reconstruction (1939-1951)

WORLD WAR, 1939-1945--REGIMENTAL HISTORIES--GREAT BRITAIN.
Lewis, Peter M. H. Squadron histories: R.F.C., R.N.A.S. and R.A.F., since 1912 2nd ed. London, Putnam, 1968. 224 p. [50/-] 358.41/3/50942 68-133976
UG635.G7 L47 1968 MRR Alc.

WORLD WAR, 1939-1945--REGIMENTAL HISTORIES--UNITED STATES.
Stubbs, Mary Lee. Armor-cavalry, Washington, Office of the Chief of Military History, U.S. Army; [for sale by the Supt. of Docs., U.S. Govt. Print. Off.] 1969- v. [6.75] 357/.0973 69-60002
UA30 .S8 MRR Alc.

United States. Dept. of the Army. Office of Military History. The Army lineage book. Washington, U.S. Govt. Print. Off., 1953- v. 355.309 54-61235
UA25 .A516 MRR Alc.

United States. Dept. of the Army. Office of Military History. Combat chronicle, [Washington, 1948?] 109 l. 940.541273 49-45651
D769.29 .A52 MRR Ref Desk.

WORLD WAR, 1939-1945--REGIMENTAL HISTORIES--UNITED STATES--BIBLIOGRAPHY.
Dornbusch, Charles Emil, Histories, personal narratives: United States Army; Cornwallville, N.Y., Hope Farm Press, 1967. [15]-399 p. 016.355 67-5273
Z1249.M5 D6 1967 MRR Ref Desk.

United States. Dept. of the Army. Office of Military History. Unit histories of World War II, [Washington, 1950?] iii, 141 p. 016.940541273 51-60137
Z6207.W8 U52 MRR Ref Desk.

United States. Naval History Division. Operational Archives. World War II histories and historical reports in the U.S. Naval History Division; [Washington] 1973. vi, 226 p. 016.94054/59/73 73-602814
CD3034 .N38 1973 MRR Alc.

WORLD WAR, 1939-1945--REGIMENTAL HISTORIES--UNITED STATES--MARINE CORPS.
Smith, Stanley E., comp. The United States Marine Corps in World War II; New York, Random House [1969] xxi, 965 p. [17.95] 940.542/6 67-22643
D767 .S62 MRR Alc.

WORLD WAR, 1939-1945--REGISTERS, LISTS, ETC.
United States. Library of Congress. A tribute to those men of the Library of Congress who gave their lives in the World War. 1941-1945. [Washington, 1948] [29] p. 027.5753 49-45538
Z663 .T7 MRR Alc.

WORLD WAR, 1939-1945--SOURCES.
Eisenhower, Dwight David, Pres. U.S., The papers of Dwight David Eisenhower; the war years. Baltimore, Johns Hopkins Press [1970] 5 v. 940.54/012 65-27672
D735 .E37 MRR Alc.

Gantenbein, James Watson, ed. Documentary background of World War II, 1931-1941. New York, Columbia Univ. Press, 1948. xxxiii, 1122 p. 940.52 48-11573
D735 .G25 MRR Alc.

Langsam, Walter Consuelo, ed. Historic documents of World War II. Princeton, N.J., Van Nostrand [1958] 192 p. 940.53082 58-14435
D735 .L3 MRR Alc.

United States. National Archives. Federal records of World War II. Washington [U.S. Govt. Print. Off.] 1950 [i.e. 1951] 2 v. 940.5373 a 51-9196
D735.A1 U52 1950 MRR Alc.

WORLD WAR, 1939-1945--SOURCES-- BIBLIOGRAPHY.
United States. Naval History Division. Operational Archives. World War II histories and historical reports in the U.S. Naval History Division; [Washington] 1973. vi, 226 p. 016.94054/59/73 73-602814
CD3034 .N38 1973 MRR Alc.

WORLD WAR, 1939-1945--SUPPLIES.
Crow, Duncan. American AFVs of World War II, Windsor (Corburg House, Sheet St., Windsor, Berks.), Profile Publications Ltd., 1972. viii, 240, 63 p. [£6.00] 623.74/75/0873 73-167485
UG446.5 .A694 Vol. 4 MRR Alc.

Kirk, John, Great weapons of World War II. New York, Walker [1961] 347 p. 623.4 61-16984
UF520 .K5 MRR Alc.

WORLD WAR, 1939-1945--TRANSPORTATION.
Vanderveen, Bart Harmannus. The observer's fighting vehicles directory, World War II; London, New York, F. Warne, 1969. 340 p. [25/-] 623.7/4/09044 78-76271
UG680 .V35 MRR Alc.

WORLD WAR, 1939-1945--TREATIES.
Leiss, Amelia Catherine, ed. European peace treaties after World War II; [Boston] World Peace Foundation [1954] xvi, 341 p. 940.53141 54-14902
D814 .L4 MRR Alc.

WORLD WAR, 1939-1945--UNDERGROUND LITERATURE--BIBLIOGRAPHY.
Ulrich's international periodicals directory. [1st]- ed.: [1932]- New York, Bowker. 011 32-16320
Z6941 .U5 Sci RR Latest edition / MRR Ref Desk Latest edition / MRR Ref Desk Latest edition

WORLD WAR, 1939-1945--GREAT BRITAIN.
Churchill, Winston Leonard Spencer, Sir, The Second World War. Boston, Published in association with the Cooperation Pub. Co. [by] Houghton Mifflin, 1948-53. 6 v. 940.53 48-2880
D743 .C47 MRR Alc.

WORLD WAR, 1939-1945--GREECE.
United States. Library of Congress. European Affairs Division. War and postwar Greece; Washington, 1952. xv, 175 p. 949.507 52-60049
Z663.26 .W3 MRR Alc.

WORLD WAR, 1939-1945--PACIFIC OCEAN.
Isely, Jeter Allen. The U.S. Marines and amphibious war; Princeton, Princeton University Press, 1951. vii, 636 p. 940.545 51-9463
D769.45 .I7 MRR Alc.

Smith, Stanley E., comp. The United States Marine Corps in World War II; New York, Random House [1969] xxi, 965 p. [17.95] 940.542/6 67-22643
D767 .S62 MRR Alc.

WORLD WAR, 1939-1945--UNITED STATES.
Buchanan, Albert Russell, The United States and World War II; [1st ed.] New York, Harper & Row [1964] 2 v. (xviii 635 p.) 63-20287
D769 .B8 MRR Alc.

Davis, Kenneth Sydney, Experience of war: [1st ed.] Garden City, N.Y., Doubleday, 1965. ix, 704 p. 940.5373 65-12374
D769 .D3 MRR Alc.

United States. National Archives. Federal records of World War II. Washington [U.S. Govt. Print. Off.] 1950 [i.e. 1951] 2 v. 940.5373 a 51-9196
D735.A1 U52 1950 MRR Alc.

WORSHIP--DICTIONARIES.
Davies, John Gordon, A dictionary of liturgy and worship. [1st American ed.] New York, Macmillan [1972] ix, 385 p. [$10.00] 264/.003 72-90276
BV173 .D28 1972 MRR Alc.

Podhradsky, Gerhard. New dictionary of the liturgy. English ed. Staten Island, N.Y., Alba House [1967, c1966] 208 p. 264/.003 67-5547
BV173 .P613 1967 MRR Alc.

WOUNDED, FIRST AID TO
see First aid in illness and injury

WOUNDS--TREATMENT.
Cole, Warren Henry, ed. First aid, diagnosis and management 5th ed. New York, Appleton-Century-Crofts [1960] 420 p. 614.88 60-5249
RD131 .C62 1960 MRR Alc.

WRESTLING--PICTORIAL WORKS.
Kent, Graeme. A pictorial history of wrestling. London, Spring Books, 1968. 320 p. (chiefly illus.). [25/-] 796.8/12/09 68-109757
GV1195 .K44 MRR Alc.

WRIGHT, ORVILLE, 1871-1948-- BIBLIOGRAPHY.
Renstrom, Arthur George, Wilbur & Orville Wright; Washington, Library of Congress; [for sale by the Supt. of Docs., U.S. Govt. Print. Off.] 1968. vi, 187 p. 016.629133/34/0922 68-60013
Z663.41 .W7 MRR Alc.

WRIGHT, WILBUR, 1867-1912--BIBLIOGRAPHY.
Renstrom, Arthur George, Wilbur & Orville Wright; Washington, Library of Congress; [for sale by the Supt. of Docs., U.S. Govt. Print. Off.] 1968. vi, 187 p. 016.629133/34/0922 68-60013
Z663.41 .W7 MRR Alc.

WRITERS
see Authors

WRITING--DICTIONARIES.
Roman, Klara Goldzieher. Encyclopedia of the written word; New York, F. Ungar Pub. Co. [1968] xviii, 550 p. [$12.50] 155.28/2/03 68-12124
BF889.5 .R6 MRR Alc.

WRITING--HISTORY.
Diringer, David, The alphabet; 3d
ed. New York, Funk & Wagnalls [1968]
2 v. 4!1 68-22369
P211 .D53 1968b MRR Alc

WRITING (AUTHORSHIP)
see Authorship

see Journalism

WRITING OF LETTERS
see Letter-writing

WUPPERTAL--DIRECTORIES.
Adressbuch Wuppertal. Wuppertal-
Elberfeld, Born-Verlag. 53-29087
DD901.W98 A7 MRR Alc Latest
edition

WÜRZBURG--DIRECTORIES.
Adressbuch Stadt Wuzzburg und
Umgebung. 1962- Wurzburg, Verlag
Universitatsdruckerei H. Stürtz.
72-627150
DD901.W92 W9 MRR Alc Latest
edition

WÜRZBURG REGION, GER.--DIRECTORIES.
Adressbuch Stadt Wuzzburg und
Umgebung. 1962- Wurzburg, Verlag
Universitatsdruckerei H. Stürtz.
72-627150
DD901.W92 W9 MRR Alc Latest
edition

WYOMING.
Writers' program. Wyoming. Wyoming;
a guide to its history, highways, and
people, New York, Oxford university
press [c1941] xxvii, 490 p. 917.87
41-52444
F761 .W58 MRR Ref Desk.

WYOMING--BIBLIOGRAPHY.
Historical records survey. Illinois.
A check list of Wyoming imprints,
1866-1890. Chicago, Ill., The
Illinois Historical records survey,
1941. 2 p. l., 3-69 (i.e. 70) numb.
l. 015.787 42-14492
Z1215 .H67 no. 18 MRR Alc.

WYOMING--DESCRIPTION AND TRAVEL--GUIDE-
BOOKS.
Writers' program. Wyoming. Wyoming;
a guide to its history, highways, and
people, New York, Oxford university
press [c1941] xxvii, 490 p. 917.87
41-52444
F761 .W58 MRR Ref Desk.

WYOMING--IMPRINTS.
Historical records survey. Illinois.
A check list of Wyoming imprints,
1866-1890. Chicago, Ill., The
Illinois Historical records survey,
1941. 2 p. l., 3-69 (i.e. 70) numb.
l. 015.787 42-14492
Z1215 .H67 no. 18 MRR Alc.

WYOMING--REGISTERS.
Wyoming. Secretary of State. Wyoming
official directory and election
returns. [Cheyenne, etc.] 10-11585

First published for 1902.
JK7630 .A33 MRR Alc Latest edition

WYOMING--STATISTICS.
Newman, Barbara J. Wyoming data
book. Laramie, Division of Business
and Economic Research, University of
Wyoming, 1967. xi, 215 p. [4.00]
317.87 71-625849
HA726 .N4 MRR Alc.

YACHT RACING.
Bavier, Robert Newton. The new yacht
racing rules, Completely rev. ed.
New York, W. W. Norton, 1965. 160 p.
797.142 65-18771
GV827 .B27 1965 MRR Alc.

YACHTS AND YACHTING.
Phillips-Birt, Douglas Hextall
Chedley, Yachting World handbook
London, Iliffe, New York, St.
Martin's P., 1967. 9, 361 p. [42/-]
797.1/2 67-20507
GV813 .P47 MRR Alc.

YACHTS AND YACHTING--CATALOGS.
Yachting boat owners buyers guide.
[New York, Yachting Pub. Co.] 58-
48197
VM333 .Y3 MRR Alc Latest edition

YACHTS AND YACHTING--DIRECTORIES.
The Yachtsman's guide. New York
[etc.] Motor boating [etc.]
797.1/25/05 01-8330
Began publication in 1877.
GV825 .Y12 MRR Alc Latest edition

YACHTS AND YACHTING--PERIODICALS.
Lloyd's register of American yachts;
New York, Lloyd's register of
shipping. 03-14412
GV825 .L7 MRR Alc Latest edition

YACHTS AND YACHTING--UNITED STATES.
Blanchard, Fessenden Seaver. A
cruising guide to the Chesapeake;
Rev. ed. New York, Dodd, Mead, 1962.
235 p. 917.5 62-12579
F187.C5 B55 1962 MRR Alc.

YACHTS AND YACHTING--UNITED STATES--
DIRECTORIES.
Lloyd's register of American yachts;
New York. Lloyd's register of
shipping. 03-14412
GV825 .L7 MRR Alc Latest edition

YALE UNIVERSITY--REGISTERS.
Yale University. Living graduates
and non-graduates of Yale University.
New Haven, 1968. xv, 1620 p.
378.746 77-3504
LD6322 1968 MRR Alc.

YEAR, CHURCH
see Church year

YEARBOOKS.
see also School yearbooks
Encyclopedia year book; 1947- [New
York] Grolier Society. 909.82 48-
171
D410 .S83 MRR Alc Latest edition

L'Année politique économique,
sociale et diplomatique en France.
1963- Paris, Presses Universitaires
de France. 72-626951
DC398 .A6 MRR Alc Latest edition

YEARBOOKS--BIBLIOGRAPHY.
American reference books annual.
1970- Littleton, Colo., Libraries
Unlimited. 011/.02 75-120328
Z1035.1 .A55 MRR Alc Full set

Österreichs Presse, Werbung,
Graphik; Handbuch. 15.- Jahrg.;
1967- Wien, Verband
Österreichischer
Zeitungsherausgeber. 72-626652
Z6956.A9 H3 MRR Alc Latest edition

Paris. Bibliothèque nationale.
Département des périodiques.
Répertoire national des annuaires
français, 1958-1968, Paris,
Bibliothèque nationale, Éditions
Mercure, 1970. 811 p. 76-501237
Z2174.Y4 P29 MRR Alc.

YEARBOOKS--DIRECTORIES.
Bowker serials bibliography
supplement. 1972- New York, R. R.
Bowker Co. 011 72-2677
Z6941 .U522 MRR Alc Latest edition
/ MRR Ref Desk Latest edition /
Sci RR Latest edition

Irregular serials & annuals; 1st-
ed.; 1967- New York, Bowker. 016.05
67-25026
Z6941 .I78 Sci RR Latest edition /
MRR Ref Desk Latest edition

Willing's press guide. London, J.
Willing, Ltd. [etc.] 53-36485
Began publication with issue for
1874.
Z6956.E5 W5 MRR Alc Latest edition

YEATS, WILLIAM BUTLER, 1865-1939--
CONCORDANCES.
Domville, Eric, A concordance to the
plays of W. B. Yeats. Ithaca [N.Y.]
Cornell University Press [1972] 2 v.
(xix, 1558 p.) [$25.00] 822/.8 71-
162547
PR5906 .A24 MRR Alc.

Parrish, Stephen Maxfield. A
concordance to the poems of W. B.
Yeats. Ithaca, N.Y., Cornell
University Press [1963] xxxvii, 967
p. 821.912 63-11493
PR5907 .P35 MRR Alc.

YELLOWSTONE NATIONAL PARK.
Scharff, Robert, ed. Yellowstone and
Grand Teton National Parks, New
York, D. McKay Co. [1966] xi, 209 p.
917.875 66-17872
F722 .S3 MRR Alc.

YIDDISH LANGUAGE--DICTIONARIES--ENGLISH.
Harkavy, Alexander, [English-
yidisher werterbuch (romanized form)]
22d ed. New York, Hebrew publishing
co. [19--] p. l., vii [1], 759 p.;
v p., 1 l., [vii]-xv, [1], 364 p.
46-39199
PJ5117 .H5 1940z MRR Alc.

Kogos, Fred. A dictionary of Yiddish
slang & idioms, [1st ed.] New York,
Citadel Press [1968, c1967] 167 p.
67-18084
PJ5117 .K58 MRR Alc.

Weinreich, Uriel. Modern English-
Yiddish, Yiddish-English dictionary.
New York, Yivo Institute for Jewish
Research, 1968. xliii, 789, [1], 16
p. 492.49/3/2 67-23848
PJ5117 .W4 MRR Alc.

YIDDISH LANGUAGE--DICTIONARIES--
POLYGLOT.
Britannica world language dictionary,
[Chicago, 1958] 1483-2015 p. 413
58-4491
P361 .B7 1958 MRR Alc.

YIDDISH LANGUAGE--GLOSSARIES,
VOCABULARIES, ETC.
Rosten, Leo Calvin. The joys of
Yiddish; [1st ed.] New York, McGraw-
Hill [1968] xxxix, 533 p.
492.49/3/2 68-28915
PN6231.J5 R67 MRR Alc.

YIDDISH LANGUAGE--IDIOMS, CORRECTIONS,
ERRORS.
Kogos, Fred. A dictionary of Yiddish
slang & idioms. [1st ed.] New York,
Citadel Press [1968, c1967] 167 p.
67-18084
PJ5117 .K58 MRR Alc.

YIDDISH LITERATURE--HISTORY AND
CRITICISM.
Liptzin, Solomon, A history of
Yiddish literature Middle Village,
N.Y., J. David [1972] x, 521 p.
[$10.00] 839/.09/09 79-164519
PJ5120 .L55 MRR Alc.

YIDDISH LITERATURE--TRANSLATIONS INTO
ENGLISH--BIBLIOGRAPHY.
Abramowicz, Dina. Yiddish literature
in English translation; 2d ed., New
York, Yivo Institute for Jewish
Research, 1968 [c1969] 39 p. [2.00]
016.89249/08 71-5971
Z7070 .A2 1969 MRR Alc.

YIDDISH WIT AND HUMOR.
Rosten, Leo Calvin. The joys of
Yiddish; [1st ed.] New York, McGraw-
Hill [1968] xxxix, 533 p.
492.49/3/2 68-28915
PN6231.J5 R67 MRR Alc.

YORK, ENG--DIRECTORIES.
Kelly's directory of York and
neighbourhood. Kingston upon Thames,
Eng., Kelly's Directories.
914.27/4/025 72-623650
DA690.Y6 K4 MRR Alc Latest edition

YOUNG MEN--BIOGRAPHY.
Outstanding young men in America.
1965- Chicago [etc.] 65-3612
E840.6 .O8 MRR Biog Latest edition

YOUNG MEN'S CHRISTIAN ASSOCIATIONS--
YEARBOOKS.
Y M C A year book and official
rosters. New York, Association Press
[etc.] 29-15142
"Published annually since 1875."
BV1005 .A3 MRR Alc Latest edition

YOUTH.
see also Adolescence

see also Conduct of life

YOUTH--EMPLOYMENT.
see also Vocational guidance

YOUTH--EMPLOYMENT--UNITED STATES.
United States. President's Council on
Youth Opportunity. Youth resources
manual for coordinators. Washington;
For sale by the Supt. of Docs., U.S.
Govt. Print. Off., 1971. iii l., 233
p. [$1.75] 301.43/15/0973 74-
612177
HQ796 .U62 MRR Alc.

YOUTH--CANADA--SOCIETIES, ETC.--
DIRECTORIES.
Canada. Dept. of the Secretary of
State. Directory of Canadian youth
organizations. Rev. ed. Ottawa,
[Queen's Printer] 1968. 213, 213 p.
[unpriced] 369.4/025/71 79-384222

HQ799.C2 A5 1968 MRR Alc.

YOUTH--UNITED STATES.
United States. President's Council on
Youth Opportunity. Youth resources
manual for coordinators. Washington;
For sale by the Supt. of Docs., U.S.
Govt. Print. Off., 1971. iii l., 233
p. [$1.75] 301.43/15/0973 74-
612177
HQ796 .U62 MRR Alc.

YOUTH--UNITED STATES--SOCIETIES, ETC.--
DIRECTORIES.
United States. President's Council on
Youth Opportunity. Youth resources
manual for coordinators. Washington;
For sale by the Supt. of Docs., U.S.
Govt. Print. Off., 1971. iii l., 233
p. [$1.75] 301.43/15/0973 74-
612177
HQ796 .U62 MRR Alc.

YOUTH AND DRUGS
see Drugs and youth

YOUTH HOSTELS.
International youth hostel handbook.
Copenhagen, International Youth
Hostel Federation. 55-35966
TX907 .I59 MRR Alc Latest edition

YUGOSLAV PERIODICALS.
Babic, Ivo. Scientific institutions
in Yugoslavia Beograd, Edition
Jugoslavija, 1958. 148 p. 58-43852

AS346 .B25 MRR Alc.

YUGOSLAVIA--BIBLIOGRAPHY.
Horecky, Paul Louis. Southeastern
Europe; Chicago, University of
Chicago Press [1969] xxii, 755 p.
016.91496 73-110336
Z2831 .H67 MRR Alc.

Petrovich, Michael Boro. Yugoslavia;
Washington [Library of Congress for
sale by the Supt. of Docs., U.S.
Govt. Print. Off.] 1974. xiii, 270
p. 016.91497 72-11512
Z2831.47 .Y84 MRR Alc.

YUGOSLAVIA--BIOGRAPHY.
Jugoslovenski savremenici. Beograd,
"Hronometar," 1970. [16], 1208, [66]
p. [240.00Din] 77-977490
DR316 .J84 MRR Biog.

Sedma sila. Novinsko-izdavačko
preduzeće Belgrad. Savezna i
republičke skupstine. Beograd,
1964. 311 p. 65-83351
JN9673 .S45 MRR Alc.

YUGOSLAVIA--COMMERCE--DIRECTORIES.
Privredni adresar S F R J. 1953-
Beograd, Privredni pregled [etc.] 54-
39383
HC407.Y6 P68 MRR Alc Latest
edition

YUGOSLAVIA--DESCRIPTION AND TRAVEL--
BIBLIOGRAPHY.
Milojević, Borivoje Ž., Geography
of Yugoslavia; Washington, Library
of Congress, Reference Dept., Slavic
and East European Division, 1955.
xvii, 78 p. 016.91497 56-60010
Z2663.47 .G4 MRR Alc.

YUGOSLAVIA--DESCRIPTION AND TRAVEL--
GUIDE-BOOKS.
Cuddon, John A. The companion guide
to Jugoslavia London, Collins, 1968.
480 p. [36/-] 914.97/04/2 68-
88033
DR304.5 .C74 MRR Alc.

Fodor's Yugoslavia. 1969- New York,
D. McKay. 914.97/04/2 72-623018
DR304.5 .Y58 MRR Alc Latest
edition

Nickels, Sylvie. Travellers' guide
[to] Yugoslavia. Indianapolis, Bobbs-
Merrill. [1969- v. [5.95]
914.97/04/2 69-20311
DR304.5 .N5 MRR Alc.

Pan American World Airways, inc.
Complete reference guide to Greece,
Turkey, and Yugoslavia. [1st ed.
New York, Trade distribution in the
U.S. and Canada by Simon and
Schuster, 1967] 159 p. 914.9 67-
19409
DF716 .P3 MRR Alc.

Trans-Balkan Highway: Yugoslavia,
Bulgaria, Turkey. Beograd,
Turisticka Stampa; Sofia, Resorts
Magazine [1967] 175 p. [unpriced]
914.96/04 78-391387
GV1025.A2 T7 MRR Alc.

YUGOSLAVIA--DICTIONARIES AND
ENCYCLOPEDIAS.
Enciklopedija Jugoslavije. Zagreb,
Izd. Leksikografskog zavoda FNRJ,
1955- v. 56-29332
DR304 .E5 MRR Alc.

YUGOSLAVIA--EXECUTIVE DEPARTMENTS--
DIRECTORIES.
Directory of Yugoslav officials.
[n.p.] 1970. ix, 216 p.
354.497/002 73-13670
JN9667 .D55 MRR Alc.

YUGOSLAVIA--GAZETTEERS.
United States. Office of Geography.
Yugoslavia; official standard names
approved by the United States Board
on Geographic Names. Washington,
U.S. Govt. Print. Off., 1961. vi,
495 p. 61-64650
DR304 .U6 MRR Alc.

YUGOSLAVIA--HISTORY.
Pavlowitch, Stevan K. Yugoslavia,
New York, Praeger [1971] 416 p.
[$11.00] 320.9/497/02 77-148138
DR317 .P35 1971b MRR Alc.

YUGOSLAVIA--INDUSTRIES--DIRECTORIES.
Privredni adresar S F R J. 1953-
Beograd, Privredni pregled [etc.] 54-
39383
HC407.Y6 P68 MRR Alc Latest
edition

YUGOSLAVIA--LEARNED INSTITUTIONS AND
SOCIETIES.
Babic, Ivo. Scientific institutions
in Yugoslavia Beograd, Edition
Jugoslavija, 1958. 148 p. 58-43852

AS346 .B25 MRR Alc.

YUGOSLAVIA--LEARNED INSTITUTIONS AND
SOCIETIES--DIRECTORIES.
Yugoslav scientific research
directory. 1964- Belgrad [Published
for the National Library of Medicine,
Washington, by the NOLIT Pub. House;
available from the National Technical
Information Service, etc.,
Springfield, Va.] 64-6496
Q180.Y8 Y8 Sci RR Latest edition /
MRR Alc Latest edition

Yugoslav scientific research guide
1970 Belgrade, Nolit Pub. House,
1972. xii, 634 p. 507/.2/0497 73-
159775
Q180.Y8 Y83 MRR Alc.

YUGOSLAVIA--OFFICIALS AND EMPLOYEES--
DIRECTORIES.
Directory of Yugoslav officials.
[n.p.] 1970. ix, 216 p.
354.497/002 73-13670
JN9667 .D55 MRR Alc.

YUGOSLAVIA--POLITICS AND GOVERNMENT--
1918-1945.
Pavlowitch, Stevan K. Yugoslavia,
New York, Praeger [1971] 416 p.
[$11.00] 320.9/497/02 77-148138
DR317 .P35 1971b MRR Alc.

YUGOSLAVIA--POLITICS AND GOVERNMENT--
1945-
Pavlowitch, Stevan K. Yugoslavia,
New York, Praeger [1971] 416 p.
[$11.00] 320.9/497/02 77-148138
DR317 .P35 1971b MRR Alc.

YUGOSLAVIA--POLITICS AND GOVERNMENT--
1945- --ADDRESSES, ESSAYS, LECTURES.
Vucinich, Wayne S. Contemporary
Yugoslavia; Berkeley, University of
California Press, 1969. xiii, 441 p.
[9.50] 320.9/497 69-16512
DR370 .V8 MRR Alc.

YUGOSLAVIA--REGISTERS.
Directory of Yugoslav officials.
[n.p.] 1970. ix, 216 p.
354.497/002 73-13670
JN9667 .D55 MRR Alc.

YUGOSLAVIA--STATISTICS.
Statistical pocket-book of
Yugoslavia. 1955- Beograd. 56-
25947
HA1631 .S8 MRR Alc Latest edition

Statistical yearbook of the Socialist
Federal Republic of Yugoslavia.
[1st]- issue: 1954- Beograd.
314.97 56-41649
HA1631 .A342 MRR Alc Latest
edition

YUGOSLAVIA--STATISTICS--YEARBOOKS.
Statisticki godisnjak S F R J. g.
[1]- 1954- Beograd. 55-30153
HA1631 .A34 MRR Alc Latest edition

YUGOSLAVS IN THE UNITED STATES.
Govorchin, Gerald Gilbert. Americans
from Yugoslavia. Gainesville,
University of Florida Press, 1961.
xii, 352 p. 325.24970973 61-11312

E184.Y7 G6 MRR Alc.

ZAIRE--DICTIONARIES AND ENCYCLOPEDIAS.
Bevel, Maurice Louis. Le
dictionnaire colonial (encyclopédie)
3. ed. Bruxelles, Impr. E. Guyot,
1955. 202 p.; 26 p. 56-39556
DT643 .B45 1955 MRR Alc.

ZAIRE--GAZETTEERS.
United States. Office of Geography.
Republic of the Congo
(Leopoldville); official standard
names approved by the United States
Board on Geographic Names.
Washington [U.S. Govt. Print. Off.]
1964. iv, 426 p. 64-62619
DT643 .U55 MRR Alc.

ZAIRE--GOVERNMENT PUBLICATIONS--
BIBLIOGRAPHY--UNION LISTS.
Witherell, Julian W. French-speaking
central Africa; Washington, General
Reference and Bibliography Division,
Library of Congress; [for sale by the
Supt. of Docs., U.S. Govt. Print.
Off.] 1973. xlv, 314 p. [$3.70]
015/.67 72-5766
Z2663.285 .F7 MRR Alc.

ZAMBIA.
Kaplan, Irving, Area handbook for
Zambia Washington, For sale by the
Supt. of Docs., U.S. Govt. Print.
Off., 1969. xvi, 482 p. [3.75]
916.89/4 79-604730
DT963 .K26 MRR Alc.

ZAMBIA--DIRECTORIES.
The Rhodesia-Zambia-Malawi directory
(including Botswana and Mocambique).
Bulawayo, Publications (Central
Africa) [etc.] 916.89/0025 38-1460

"First published in 1910."
DT947 .R5 MRR Alc Latest edition

ZAMBIA--GAZETTEERS.
United States. Geographic Names
Division. Zambia; official standard
names approved by the United States
Board on Geographic Names.
Washington, 1972. iv, 585 p.
916.89/4/003 72-602626
DT963.2 .U55 MRR Alc.

ZAMBIA--GOVERNMENT PUBLICATIONS--
BIBLIOGRAPHY.
United States. Library of Congress.
African Section. The Rhodesias and
Nyasaland; Washington, General
Reference and Bibliography Division,
Reference Dept., Library of Congress;
[for sale by the Superintendent of
Documents, U.S. Govt. Print. Off.]
1965. xv, 285 p. 65-60089
Z2663.285 .R5 MRR Alc.

ZAMBIA--MANUFACTURES--DIRECTORIES.
The A R N I register of
manufacturers. 1959- Salisbury,
Association of Rhodesian Industries.
[etc.] 66-47368
HD9737.R5 A2 MRR Alc Latest
edition

ZANZIBAR--GOVERNMENT PUBLICATIONS.
United States. Library of Congress.
African Section. Official
publications of British East Africa,
Washington, General Reference and
Bibliography Division, Reference
Dept., Library of Congress, 1960-63.
4 v. 015.676 61-60009
Z2663.285 .O3 MRR Alc.

ZEN BUDDHISM--DICTIONARIES.
Wood, Ernest. Zen dictionary. [1st
British Commonwealth ed.] London, P.
Owen [1963, c1957] 165 p. 294.329
63-24345
BL1403 .W6 1963 MRR Alc.

ZIONISM--DICTIONARIES.
Encyclopedia of Zionism and Israel.
New York, Herzl Press, 1971- v.
956.94/001/03 68-55271
DS149 .E597 MRR Alc.

ZIONISM--YEARBOOKS.
The Zionist year book. 1951/52-
London, Zionist Federation of Great
Britain and Northern Ireland [etc.]
956.94* 52-65547
DS149.A343 MRR Alc Latest edition

ZIP CODE--UNITED STATES.
Directory of post offices (with Zip
codes) 1970- Washington, United
States Postal Service [For sale by
the Supt. of Docs., U.S. Govt. Print.
Off.] 383/.08 s 383/.025/73 73-
644964
HE6311 .A312 subser HD6951 MRR Ref
Desk Latest edition / MRR Ref
Desk Latest edition

ZIP CODE--UNITED STATES--DIRECTORIES.
Directory of post offices (with Zip
codes) 1970- Washington, United
States Postal Service [For sale by
the Supt. of Docs., U.S. Govt. Print.
Off.] 383/.08 s 383/.025/73 73-
644964
HE6311 .A312 subser HD6951 MRR Ref
Desk Latest edition / MRR Ref
Desk Latest edition

ZOOLOGICAL GARDENS.
Kirchshofer, Rosl, comp. The world
of zoos; 1st English language ed.]
New York, Viking Press [1968] 327 p.
590/.744 68-15015
QL76 .K513 MRR Alc.

ZOOLOGICAL GARDENS--DIRECTORIES.
Kirchshofer, Rosl, comp. The world
of zoos; 1st English language ed.]
New York, Viking Press [1968] 327 p.
590/.744 68-15015
QL76 .K513 MRR Alc.

ZOOLOGICAL GARDENS--AMERICA--
DIRECTORIES.
Gersh, Harry. The animals next door;
New York, Fleet Academic Editions
[1971] 170 p. [$6.95] 590/.744/7
71-104745
QL76 .G44 MRR Alc.

ZOOLOGICAL GARDENS--UNITED STATES--
DIRECTORIES.
Gersh, Harry. The animals next door;
New York, Fleet Academic Editions
[1971] 170 p. [$6.95] 590/.744/7
71-104745
QL76 .G44 MRR Alc.

ZOOLOGICAL MYTHOLOGY
see Animals, Legends and stories of

ZOOLOGY.
see also Animals

see also Animals, Habits and behavior
of

see also Birds

see also Domestic animals

see also Marine fauna

see also Paleontology

ZOOLOGY. (Cont.)
Breland, Osmond Philip, Animal facts
and fallacies. London, Faber and
Faber [1950] 245 p.   591.5 50-
12802
    QL50 .B84 1950 MRR Alc.

Larousse encyclopedia of animal life;
London, Hamlyn [1967] 640 p.
[£6/6/-]   591   68-97221
    QL50 .L32 1967 MRR Alc.

ZOOLOGY--BIBLIOGRAPHY.
Smith, Roger Cletus, Guide to the
literature of the zoological
sciences, 7th ed. Minneapolis,
Burgess Pub. Co. [1967] xiv, 238 p.
016.591 66-23383
    Z7991 .S5 1967 MRR Alc.

ZOOLOGY--CLASSIFICATION.
Oppianus. Oppian, Colluthus,
Tryphiodorus, London, W. Heinemann,
ltd.; New York, G. P. Putnam's sons,
1928. lxxx, 635, [1] p.   29-2710
    PA3612 .05 1928 MRR Alc.

ZOOLOGY--COLLECTED WORKS.
Grzimek, Bernhard. Grzimek's animal
life encyclopedia. New York, Van
Nostrand Reinhold Co. [1972- v. 13,
1972] v.   [$29.95 per vol.]   591
79-183178
    QL3 .G7813 MRR Alc.

ZOOLOGY--DICTIONARIES.
Chinery, Michael. A science
dictionary of the animal world: New
York, F. Watts [1969, c1966] 288 p.
[4.95]   591/.03 68-17109
    QL9 .C46 1969 MRR Alc.

Leftwich, A. W. A dictionary of
zoology, 2nd ed. London, Constable;
Princeton (N.J.), Van Nostrand, 1967.
vii, 319 p. [32/6]   591/.03 67-
92630
    QL9 .L4 1967 MRR Alc.

Pennak, Robert William. Collegiate
dictionary of zoology. New York,
Ronald Press Co. [1964] vi, 583 p.
590.3 64-13331
    QL9 .P4 MRR Alc.

ZOOLOGY--PICTORIAL WORKS.
Chinery, Michael. A science
dictionary of the animal world: New
York, F. Watts [1969, c1966] 288 p.
[4.95]   591/.03 68-17109
    QL9 .C46 1969 MRR Alc.

ZOOLOGY--PRE-LINNEAN WORKS.
Ælianus, Claudius. On the
characteristics of animals.
Cambridge, Harvard University Press,
1958-59. 3 v.   888 58-2971
    PA3612 .A18 1958 MRR Alc.

Aristoteles. Generation of animals,
Cambridge, Mass., Harvard University
Press; London, W. Heinemann ltd.,
1943. lxxviii, 607, [1] p.   591.16
888.5   a 44-1496
    PA3612 .A8D28 1943 MRR Alc.

Aristoteles. Historia animalium.
London, Heinemann; Cambridge, Mass.,
Harvard University Press, 1965- v.
591.09014 66-903
    PA3612 .A8H5 MRR Alc.

Aristoteles. Parts of animals,
Cambridge, Mass., Harvard university
press; London, W. Heinemann, ltd.,
1937. v, 555, [1] p.   888.5 38-
4213
    PA3612 .A8D3 1937 MRR Alc.

Oppianus. Oppian, Colluthus,
Tryphiodorus, London, W. Heinemann,
ltd.; New York, G. P. Putnam's sons,
1928. lxxx, 635, [1] p.   29-2710
    PA3612 .05 1928 MRR Alc.

ZOOLOGY--AFRICA, EAST.
Williams, John George, A field guide
to the national parks of East Africa
London, Collins, 1967. 352 p. [45/-
]   591.967 68-76542
    SB484.E3 W54 MRR Alc.

ZOOLOGY--CANADA.
Collins, Henry Hill, Complete field
guide to American wildlife: New
York, Harper [1959] xix, 683 p.
591.973 58-8880
    QL151 .C6 MRR Alc.

ZOOLOGY--CENTRAL AMERICA.
Murie, Olaus Johan, A field guide to
animal tracks. Boston, Houghton
Mifflin, 1954. xxii, 374 p.   591.5
54-9602
    SK282 .M8 MRR Alc.

ZOOLOGY--NORTH AMERICA.
Elman, Robert. The hunter's field
guide to the game birds and animals
of North America. New York, Knopf;
[distributed by Random House] 1974.
655 p.   598.2/97 73-7289
    SK40 .E45 1974 MRR Alc.

Murie, Olaus Johan, A field guide to
animal tracks. Boston, Houghton
Mifflin, 1954. xxii, 374 p.   591.5
54-9602

SK282 .M8 MRR Alc.

The New hunter's encyclopedia.
Updated new print. of 3d. ed. New
York : Galahad Books, [1974?] c1972.
xx, 1054 p. : [$24.95]   799.2/97
73-92819
    SK33 .H945 1974 MRR Alc.

ZOOLOGY--UNITED STATES.
Collins, Henry Hill, Complete field
guide to American wildlife: New
York, Harper [1959] xix, 683 p.
591.973 58-8880
    QL151 .C6 MRR Alc.

ZOOLOGY, ECONOMIC.
see also Insects, Injurious and
beneficial

see also Pest control

ZULU LANGUAGE--DICTIONARIES--ENGLISH.
Doke, Clement Martyn, Zulu-English
dictionary, 2d ed. rev.;
Johannesburg, Witwatersrand
University Press, 1953. xxvi, 918 p.
496.3 55-23865
    PL8843 .D63 1953 MRR Alc.

ZÜRICH--DIRECTORIES.
Adressbuch Stadt Zürich. Zürich,
Orell Füssli. 53-28341
    Began publication in 1875.
    DQ789.2 .A7 MRR Alc Latest edition

ZÜRICH--STATISTICS.
Zürich. Statistisches Amt.
Statistisches Jahrbuch der Stadt
Zürich. 1.- Jahrg.; 1905-
Zürich. 14-19946
    HA1609 .Z65 MRR Alc Latest edition

ZÜRICH (CANTON)--DESCRIPTION AND
TRAVEL--GAZETTEERS.
Adressbuch des Kantons Zürich.
Zürich, Mosse-Annoncen AG. 59-54994

    DQ784.5 .A6 MRR Alc Latest edition

ZÜRICH (CANTON)--INDUSTRIES--
DIRECTORIES.
Firmenverzeichnis des Kantons
Zürich. Zürich, Orell Füssli. 54-
29398
    HC398.Z8 F5 MRR Alc Latest edition